T5-BBO-979

THE

American Catalog

1908-1910

Containing a record under author, title, subject and series of the books published in the United States, recorded from January 1, 1908 *to December* 31, 1910, *together with a directory of publishers.*

NEW YORK
PETER SMITH
1941

PRINTED IN THE UNITED STATES OF AMERICA

CONTENTS

PREFACE

THE present work is the third main volume of the AMERICAN CATALOG series of the twentieth century.

The period of the first main volume covered the five years from January 1, 1900, to January 1, 1905, including only those books of 1905 imprint which were actually published within 1904. The period of the second main volume covered the three years from January 1, 1905, through December 31, 1907, inclusive. It was originally purposed, as stated in the preface to the first volume, to make the second period inclusive of the five years from January 1, 1905, to January 1, 1910, or possibly through the end of 1910, the latter modification with the intent of making five-year periods beginning with the calendar year 1911, and to print an intermediary three-year cumulation, not in permanent binding but to be superseded later. It proved, however, that the cumulative catalog for the three years—1905, 1906, 1907—would be practically of the same bulk as for the five years preceding, and it was therefore decided to make the three-year volume the permanent form of the AMERICAN CATALOG, covering these three calendar years. This is now succeeded by the present volume covering the three calendar years 1908, 1909, 1910. The change of plan is sufficiently justified by the fact that the first five year volume contained 1209 pages in its main alphabet, the second three year volume 1164 pages, and this third three year volume 1540 pages, or a fourth more than either of its predecessors. This change offers a volume of more convenient size and the plan has other advantages.

The present catalog embraces reprints, importations in editions and the law reports of United States and State courts, but it does not attempt to include local directories, periodicals, musical scores, books chiefly blank, unbound maps, tracts and other low-priced pamphlets. Nor does it now cover Government and State publications and publications of societies and institutions (except those publishing through the book trade), for the most part now covered by special bibliographies, with the exception of some works of general rather than of official bearing.

The material of this volume is directly that of *The Publishers' Weekly* monthly and cumulated Reference Lists as preserved by the linotype system, edited into a consistent alphabet and filled out with additional titles not duly recorded in the year of publication. Its typographical scheme embraces: author entries, designated by **Clarendon full-face** type, which type is used also for the first word of anonymous books; title entries in Roman lower case; subject entries, designated by SMALL CAPS; and series entries, designated by *italics*. Thus the advantages of the dictionary catalog, or one-place method, are combined with the advantages of separate alphabets of each class of entry. While the subject entries are thus included in the general alphabet, in place of the second alphabet of the old system, the arrangement of subject entries is, as in the previous system, by specific subjects, not by general classes. Each book is placed under the particular subject of which it treats, and entries under general headings are confined to books of a general rather than of a specific character. As the endeavor has been not to repeat entries, cognate subjects should be looked up in searching for books on a given subject, in which the Index to Subject Headings issued by the American Library Association will be found a useful help. As far as practicable the indications given by words in the title of a book have been followed in the assignment to subject headings.

The Directory of Publishers, whose books have been recorded in the present volume, includes 5184 names as against 3876 names in the 1900–1905 five-year volume, and 3789 in the 1905–1907 three-year volume. It remains true that nine-tenths of American publishing is done by less than one-tenth of this number. The imprint is the name of publisher given on the title-page of the book, changes of firm name or of publisher being indicated, as far as information was obtained in the list of publishers. Of course, many entries of publishers indicate merely printers or designate authors publishing their own books only.

It was intended to continue the system of supplementing this main volume, as in the case of the first and second main volumes, with the full title and descriptive note of each work, as preserved in linotype slugs, and printed in a separate alphabet each year and combined into a supplementary second volume for each period. This plan has been reluctantly abandoned, as the support from libraries and the book trade for this volume did not return its cost and justify its continuance.

R. R. BOWKER.

July, 1911.

DIRECTORY OF PUBLISHERS

Issuing Books from January 1, 1908, *to December* 31, 1910

A DIRECTORY OF PUBLISHERS, PRINTERS & AUTHORS

Issuing Books from January 1, 1908, to December 31, 1910.

A. L. A.	American Library Association Pub. Board..1 Washington St., Chicago.
Abbatt.	Abbatt, William..........................410 E. 22d St., New York.
Abbey Co.	Abbey Co..Hinsdale, Chicago.
Abbey Student.	Abbey Student Press..........St. Benedict's College, Atchison, Kan.
Abbott, A.	Abbott, A.........................Box 808, Sulphur Springs, Okla.
Abbott, C. L.	Abbott, C. L.,.....................................St. Paul, Minn.
Abbott, H.	Abbott, Holker, Tavern Club...................................Chicago.
Abbott, L. A.	Abbott, Lemuel Abijah...........................Williamstown, Vt.
Abbott, T. O.	Abbott, Twyman Osmand.......................................Chicago.
Abel, A. H.	Abel, Annie Heloise..............Woman's College, Baltimore, Md.
Aber, W: W.	Aber, William W...................................Kansas City, Mo.
Aberdeen.	Aberdeen Publishing Co......Masonic Hall, 71 W. 23d St., New York.
Abrams, A.	Abrams, Albert, Philopolis Press.......................San Francisco.
Absolute Press.	Absolute Press.....................P. O. Box 55, Stapleton, N. Y.
Abt, I: A.	Abt, Isaac A.........................4326 Vincennes Ave., Chicago.
Acad. Bk. Room.	Academy Book Room...................................Bryn Athyn, Pa.
Acad. Nat. Sci., Phil.	Academy of Natural Sciences of Philadelphia (E. J. Nolan, Sec'y), 19th and Rose Sts., Philadelphia.
Accountancy.	Accountancy Publishing Co..............32 Waverly Pl., New York.
Acme.	Acme Publishing Co......223-227 Pleasant St., Morgantown, W. Va.
Acme Pub.	Acme Publishing Co..........1413 Williamson Bldg., Cleveland, O.
Acorn Press.	Acorn Press..Mechanicsburg, Pa.
Adams, A. A:	Adams, Albert Augustus..........519 Union St., Council Bluffs, Ia.
Adams, A. M.	Adams, A. M. & M. L...Humboldt, Ia.
Adams, B.	Adams, Brooks.......................................23 Court St., Boston.
Adams, B. S.	Adams, Byron S............512 11th St., N. W., Washington, D. C.
Adams, C: F., jr.	Adams, Charles Francis, Jr...................84 State St., Boston.
Adams, E: D.	Adams, Edward Dean......................71 Broadway, New York.
Adams, E. H.	Adams, Edgar H..................40 Fourth Ave., Brooklyn, N. Y.
Adams, G: M.	Adams, George Matthew................People's Gas Bldg., Chicago.
Adams, J. J.	Adams, Julia J..........................5544 Page Ave., St. Louis.
Adams, J. O.	Adams, J. Orville...Spokane, Wash.
Adams, M. P.	Adams, Matthew Prior...................................New Britain, Ct.
Adams, W. C.	Adams, W. C., & Co...................11 E. 16th St., New York.
Adams, W. F.	Adams, W. F...Springfield, Mass.
Adcock.	Adcock Publishing Co.......................................Hampton, Ky.
Adriaans, J: H:	Adriaans, John Henry...................................Washington, D. C.
Adv. Cyclo.	Advertiser's Cyclopedia Co...............310 Broadway, New York.
Advance.	Advance Printing Co..Liberty, Mo.
Advance Pub. Co. (Chic.)	Advance Publishing Co...........................700 E. 40th St., Chicago.
Advanced Thought Co.	Advanced Thought Publishing Co...........Masonic Temple, Chicago.
Advancement.	Advancement Co...Rutherford, N. J.
Advocate Pub.	Advocate Publishing Co............301 N. 11th St., St. Joseph, Mo.
Aeolian Co.	Aeolian Co., Educational Dept., Music Lovers' Library, 362 Fifth Ave., New York.
Aetna Life.	Ætna Life Insurance Co...Hartford, Ct.
Aetna Pr.	Aetna Printing Co...Indianapolis, Ind.
Agnus, F.	Agnus, Felix, care Baltimore American................Baltimore, Md.
Ainsworth.	Ainsworth & Co.......................378-388 Wabash Ave., Chicago.
Akron Bd. Educ.	Akron Board of Education..Akron, O.
Ala. Chamber of Com.	Alabama Chamber of Commerce..................Birmingham, Ala.
Ala. Supt. Educ.	Alabama Superintendent of Education.............Montgomery, Ala.
Alaskan Yukon.	Alaskan-Yukon-Pacific Exposition Publishing Co......Seattle, Wash.
Albany First Presb. Ch.	Albany First Presbyterian Church.................................Albany, N. Y.
Albrecht, F: C.	Albrecht, Frederick Conrad.....................................Rowayton, Ct.
Albright, J. D.	Albright, Jacob Dissinger, M.D......3228 No. Broad St., Philadelphia.
Alden, F. W.	Alden, Frank Wesley..Delaware, O.
Alden, G: W.	Alden, George W..Brockton, Mass.

Alden Bros.	Alden Bros....Neshantic, N. J.
Alden Pub.	Alden Publishing Co....Chicago.
	Alderbrink Press. *See* Seymour, Ralph Fletcher.
Alderson, J. C.	Alderson, Joseph Coleman....Charleston, W. Va.
Aldine Bk.	Aldine Book Co....32-34 Lafayette St., New York.
Aldine Pr.	Aldine Printing Co....307 Market St., Pittsburgh, Pa.
Alert Pub.	Alert Publishing Co....Chicago.
Alexander Hamilton.	Alexander Hamilton Institute....Astor Pl., New York.
Alexander, J. B.	Alexander, James Bradun....Minneapolis, Minn.
Alexander, J: B. (N. C.)	Alexander, John Brevard....Charlotte, N. C.
Alexandria-Washton.	Alexandria-Washington Lodge, No. 229, F. and A. M..Alexandria, Va.
Allaben.	Allaben, Frank, Genealogical Co....3 W. 42d St., New York.
Allen, A. M.	Allen, Arthur M....454-456 Fulton St., Troy, N. Y.
Allen, C. S.	Allen, Caroline Stetson....432 Waltham St., West Newton, Mass.
Allen, E. W.	Allen, E. W., & Co....Atlanta, Ga.
Allen, F: J.	Allen, Frederick James....2 Park Square, Boston.
Allen, G: H.	Allen, George Hoyt....Clinton, N. Y.
Allen, J: K.	Allen, John Kermott....Chicago.
Allen, L. & S.	Allen, Lane & Scott....1211-1213 Clover St., Philadelphia.
Allen, M. E. L.	Allen, M. E. L....509 Security Bldg., Los Angeles, Cal.
Allen, O. P.	Allen, Orrin Peer....Palmer, Mass.
Allen, W. A.	Allen, W. A....4542 Evans Ave., St. Louis.
Allen, W: F:	Allen, William Frederick....24 Park Place, New York.
Allen, W: H.	Allen, William Harvey..Care of *Atlantic Monthly,* 4 Park St., Boston.
Alliance Press.	Alliance Press Co....Bought by Roger Bros.
Alloway, C: R.	Alloway, Charles Rozell....427 Jackson St., Milwaukee, Wis.
Allyn, A. B.	Allyn, Mrs. Adeline Bartlett, Care of H. C. Wells, Warehouse Point, Ct.
Allyn & B.	Allyn & Bacon....172 Tremont St., Boston.
Alpha Portland.	Alpha Portland Cement Co....Easton, Pa.
Altemus.	Altemus, Henry, Co....507-513 Cherry St., Philadelphia
Altrurians.	Altrurians (The)....12 Mt. Morris Park W., New York.
Altsheler, W: B.	Altsheler, William Brent....Louisville, Ky.
Alvord, S: M.	Alvord, Samuel Morgan....254 Ashley St., Hartford, Ct.
Am. Aberdeen-A.	American Aberdeen-Angus Breeders' Association....Chicago.
Am. Acad. Med.	American Academy of Medicine....52 N. 4th St., Easton, Pa.
Am. Acad. Pol. Sci.	American Acad. of Pol. and Social Science....Station B, Philadelphia.
Am. Adjusters.	American Adjusters Co....Union Trust Bldg., Cincinnati.
Am. Aero. Soc.	American Aeronautical Society....1950 Worth St., Chicago.
Am. Anthropological.	American Anthropological Association, (B. Talbot Hyde, Treas.), 542 Fifth Ave., New York.
Am. Anti-Boycott.	American Anti-Boycott Association....27 William St., New York.
Am. Antiquarian.	American Antiquarian Society....Worcester, Mass.
Am. Art.	American Art Annual, Inc....215 W. 57th St., New York.
Am. Art Assoc.	American Art Association....6 E. 23d St., New York.
Am. Assoc. Freight.	American Assoc. of Local Freight Agents' Assocs. (G. W. Dennison, Sec'y)....Toledo, O.
Am. Assoc. Int. Conciliation.	American Association of International Conciliation, 501 W. 116th St., New York.
Am. Banker.	American Banker....5 Beekman St., New York.
Am. Bankers' Assoc.	American Bankers' Association, Hanover Bank Building, 11 Pine St., New York
Am. Bapt.	American Baptist Publication Society, 1701-03 Chestnut St., Philadelphia.
Am. Bible.	American Bible Society....6 Bible House, New York.
Am. Bd. For. Miss.	American Board of Commissioners for Foreign Missions, 14 Beacon St., Boston.
Am. Bk.	American Book Co....100 Washington Sq., E., New York.
Am. Bk. and Pr.	American Book and Printing Co....Mexico City, Mex.
Am. Burtonizing.	American Burtonizing Co....105 E. 91st St., New York.
Am. Business.	American Business Bureau....29 Broadway, New York.
Am. Business Man.	American Business Man....Chicago.
Am. Cath. Pub.	American Catholic Publication Society....34 Union Sq., New York.
Am. Ceramic.	American Ceramic Society....Columbus, O.
	American Economic Association. *See* Macmillan Co.
Am. Chess.	American Chess Bulletin Co....150 Nassau St., New York.
Am. Chr. Miss.	American Christian Missionary Society....Cincinnati.
Am. Civic League.	American Civic League, John Horace McFarland, Pres., Box 655, Harrisburg, Pa.

Am. Coll. Dressmaking.	American College of Dressmaking, 1330 Chestnut St., Kansas City, Mo.
Am. Coll. Mechano-Therapy.	American College of Mechano-Therapy..................... Chicago.
Am. Corr. Sch. Law.	American Correspondence School of Law.................. Chicago.
Am. Economic Assoc.	American Economic Association.................. Cambridge, Mass.
Am. Educ. Alliance.	American Educational Alliance............18 W. 27th St., New York.
Am. Encyclopedic.	American Encyclopedic Library Association, 22 Thames St., New York.
Am. Entomol.	American Entomological Society...........Logan Sq., Philadelphia.
Am. Esperantist.	American Esperantist Co................700 E. 40th St., Chicago.
Am. Exporter.	American Exporter......................135 William St., New York.
Am. Fashion.	American Fashion Co....................853 Broadway, New York.
Am. Fed. Labor.	American Federation of Labor..801 G St., N. W., Washington, D. C.
Am. Fork.	American Fork & Hoe Company.....................Cleveland, O.
Am. Free Trade.	American Free Trade League............................Boston.
Am. Geog. Soc.	American Geographical Society............15 W. 81st St., New York.
Am. Gymnasia.	American Gymnasia Co................221 Columbus Ave., Boston.
Am. Hist.	American Historical Association, 500 Bond Bldg., Washington, D. C.
Am. Hist. Review.	American Historical Review...............66 Fifth Ave., New York.
Am. Home Economics Assoc.	American Home Economics Association, 525 West 120th St., New York.
Am. Hotel.	American Hotel Register Co......51-53 W. Washington St., Chicago.
Am. Humane.	American Humane Education Society..........45 Milk St., Boston.
Am. Inst. Architects.	American Institute of Architects....The Octagon, Washington, D. C.
Am. Inst. Elec. Eng.	American Institute of Electrical Engineers..25 W. 39th St., New York.
Am. Inst. Law.	American Institute of Law..................60 Wall St., New York.
Am. Inst. Min. Eng.	American Institute of Mining Engineers...25 W. 39th St., New York.
Am. Inst. Social Service.	American Institute of Social Service, Bible House, Astor Pl., New York.
Am. Iron and Steel.	American Iron and Steel Association...261 S. 4th St., Philadelphia.
Am. Jersey.	American Jersey Cattle Club...............8 W. 17th St., New York.
Am. Law Bk.	American Law Book Co......................60 Wall St., New York.
Am. Lumberman.	American Lumberman...................315 Dearborn St., Chicago.
Am. Luth.	American Lutheran Publication Board..1349 Fifth Ave., Pittsburg, Pa.
Am. Math.	American Mathematical Society........501 W. 116th St., New York.
Am. Medical.	American Medical Association, Press of...535 Dearborn St., Chicago.
Am. Museum.	American Museum of Natural History, 77th St. and Columbus Ave., New York.
Am. Negro.	American Negro Academy.........1439 Pierce Pl., Washington, D. C.
Am. News.	American News Co........................9-15 Park Pl., New York.
Am. Nut & Fruit Co.	American Nut & Fruit Co.................Drexel Bldg., Philadelphia.
Am. Peony Soc.	American Peony Society (A. H. Fewkes, Sec.) Cornell University, Ithaca, N. Y.
Am. Philosophical Soc.	American Philosophical Society.........104 S. 5th St., Philadelphia.
Am. Phys. Educ.	American Physical Education Review, 93 Westford Ave., Springfield, Mass.
Am. Pitmanic.	American Pitmanic Shorthand Co.....................Lansing, Mich.
Am. Play.	American Play Co.......................1402 Broadway, New York.
Am. Press.	American Press Co.............................Baltimore, Md.
Am. Press (N. Y.)	American Press...............32 Washington Sq., West, New York.
Am. Protective.	American Protective Tariff League........399 Broadway, New York.
Am. Pub. Assoc.	American Publishers' Association........511 Lakeside Bldg., Chicago.
Am. Pub. Co. (Ga.)	American Publishing Co...............................Atlanta, Ga.
Am. Pub. Co., (Vt.)	American Publishing Co..........................Middlebury, Vt.
Am. Railway.	American Railway Engineering and Maintenance of Way Association, 962 Monadnock Block, Chicago.
Am. Railway Guide.	American Railway Guide Co............................Chicago.
Am. S. S.	American Sunday-School Union......1816 Chestnut St., Philadelphia.
Am. Sabbath Tr. Soc.	American Sabbath Tract Soc. (Seventh Day Baptist)..Plainfield, N. J.
Am. Sch.	American School Board Journal...129 Michigan St., Milwaukee, Wis.
Am. Sch. Art.	American School of Art and Photography.............Scranton, Pa.
Am. Sch. Corr.	American School of Correspondence......Armour Institute, Chicago.
Am. Sch. Deaf.	American School for the Deaf.........................Hartford, Ct.
Am. Sch. Home Economics.	American School of Home Economics....506 West 69th St., Chicago.

Am. Scenic.	American Scenic and Historic Preservation Society, Tribune Bldg., New York.
Am. Seamen's Friend.	American Seamen's Friend Society.........76 Wall St., New York.
Am. Sheep.	American Sheep Breeder Co.............................Chicago.
Am. Soc. Civil Engineers.	American Society of Civil Engineers......220 W. 57th St., New York.
Am. Soc. Mech. Engineers.	American Society of Mechanical Engineers..29 W. 39th St., New York.
Am. Sports.	American Sports Publishing Co........15-21 Warren St., New York.
Am. Steam Gauge.	American Steam Gauge and Valve Mfg. Co..................Boston.
Am. Swedenborg.	American Swedenborg Printing and Publishing Society, 3 W. 29th St., New York.
Am. Text-Bk.	American Text-Book Co............................Philadelphia.
Am. Tr.	American Tract Society.................150 Nassau St., New York.
Am. Unitarian.	American Unitarian Association..............25 Beacon St., Boston.
Americana Germanica.	Americana Germanica Press, Box 10, College Hall, University of Pennsylvania, Philadelphia.
Americus.	Americus Book Co...............................Americus, Ga.
Amerika Pub.	Amerika Publishing Co..........................Madison, Wis.
Ames, E. M. E.	Ames, Mrs. Eleanor Maria Easterbrook...235 W. 75th St., New York.
Analyses.	Analyses Publishing Co..................35 Nassau St., New York.
Anchor.	Anchor Press...................................Waterville, Ct.
Anderson.	Anderson Bros...............................Charlottesville, Va.
Anderson, G: S.	Anderson, George Smith.......................Little Rock, Ark.
Anderson, J. S.	Anderson, Jacob S...........................Minneapolis, Minn.
Anderson, J:	Anderson, John, Publishing Co........183-187 N. Peoria St., Chicago.
Anderson, J: A.	Anderson, John A., & Co.................P. O. box 158, Denver, Colo.
Anderson, J: R.	Anderson, John R., & Co..................76 Fifth Ave., New York.
Anderson, J: W.	Anderson, John Wesley............................Addicks, Tex.
Anderson, L. H.	Anderson, Lewis H...................................Chicago.
Anderson, S. W.	Anderson, Selden W.................................Akron, O.
Anderson, W. H.	Anderson, W. H., Co......................524 Main St., Cincinnati.
Anderson Pub. Co.	Anderson Publishing Co.............................Akron, O.
Andover.	Andover Press..................................Andover, Mass.
Andover, N. H., Com. Hist.	Andover, New Hampshire, Committee on Town History, Andover, N. H.
Andrews, B. A.	Andrews, Mrs. Bessie Ayars......................Vineland, N. J.
Andrews, F. D.	Andrews, Frank D................................Vineland, N. J.
Andrews, H. B.	Andrews, Hiram Bertrand...............166 Devonshire St., Boston.
Andrews, T: S.	Andrews, Thomas Stora, The Evening Wisconsin...Milwaukee, Wis.
Andriessen, H.	Andriessen, Hugo...................................Beaver, Pa.
Andrus.	Andrus & Church....................................Ithaca, N. Y.
Angel Press.	Angel Guardian Press......................92 Ruggles St., Boston.
Angell, F. C.	Angell, Frank Capron..........................Centerdale, R. I.
Angelus Univ.	Angelus University...........................Los Angeles, Cal.
Anglo-Am. Authors.	Anglo-American Authors' Association......225 Fifth Ave., New York.
Anners.	Anners, Henry F., Press....................1229 Arch St., Philadelphia.
Anraku.	Anraku Publishing Co.....Room 1125, 154 Nassau St., New York.
Anstadt.	Anstadt, P., & Sons...................................York, Pa.
Anthony, A. L.	Anthony, Albert L........Room 1, 3 Weybosset St., Providence, R. I.
Antigo.	Antigo Publishing Co..............................Antigo, Wis.
Antiquarian.	Antiquarian Co.............................59 Dearborn St., Chicago.
Antiquarian Soc.	Antiquarian Society.....................Art Institute, Chicago.
Apgar, C: E.	Apgar, Charles E....................5138 Locust St., Philadelphia.
Apostolate.	Apostolate Publishing Co.........................Cleveland, O.
Apothecary.	Apothecary Publishing Co.................145 High St., Boston.
Appeal.	Appeal to Reason............................Box 27, Girard, Kan.
Appleton.	Appleton, D., & Co....................29-35 W. 32d St., New York.
Appleton, R.	Appleton, Robert, & Co...................39 W. 38th St., New York.
Arakelyan.	Arakelyan Press.........................368 Congress St. Boston.
Arcadia.	Arcadia Press...............................310 Broadway, New York.
Arcane.	Arcane Book Concern......................Lock Box 769, Chicago.
Archive.	Archive Publishing Co............P. O. Box 1282, Providence, R. I.
Arden.	Arden Press...............................122 E. 25th St., New York.
Ardrey, R. L.	Ardrey, R. L..................................1116 E. 64th St., Chicago.
Argonaut.	Argonaut Publishing Co...........................San Francisco.
Ariel.	Ariel Press.......................................Westwood, Mass.
Arkansas.	Arkansas, State of..............................Little Rock, Ark.
Arkansas Churchman.	Arkansas Churchman Publishing Co...............Little Rock, Ark.

Arkansas Dept. Pub. Instruct.	Arkansas Department of Public Instruction........Little Rock, Ark.
Arkansas Geol. Survey.	Arkansas Geological Survey (A. H. Purdue, State Geologist), Fayetteville, Ark.
Armes, E.	Armes, Ethel.................1410 St. Charles St., Birmingham, Ala.
Arms and the Man.	Arms and the Man Publishing Co.1502 H St., N. W., Washington, D. C.
Armstrong.	Armstrong, A. C., & Son. *See* Geo. H. Doran Co.
Armstrong, C.	Armstrong, Collin..........................25 Broad St., New York.
Armstrong, J. E.	Armstrong, James E.............Englewood High School, Chicago.
Armstrong, W: C.	Armstrong, William Clinton..................New Brunswick, N. J.
Armstrong Cork.	Armstrong Cork Co...............................Pittsburgh, Pa.
Armstrong-K.	Armstrong-Keyser .... Philadelphia.
Army Service.	Army Service Schools, Book Department.....Fort Leavenworth, Kan.
Arnett, L.	Arnett, Lizzie............................. Lecta, Barren Co., Ky.
Arnold.	Arnold & Co......................418-422 Sansom St., Philadelphia.
Arnold, L. V.	Arnold, Leon Vance.............15 Arnold Ave., Amsterdam, N. Y.
Arnold, T. B.	Arnold, T. B.....................................Glen Ellen, Ill.
Arroyo Guild.	Arroyo Guild Press.................212 Thorne St., Los Angeles, Cal.
Art Assoc. Indianapolis.	Art Association of Indianapolis, John Herron Art Institute, Indianapolis, Ind.
Art. Com. of N. Y.	Art Commission of the City of New York.......City Hall, New York.
Art Inst. of Chic.	Art Institute of Chicago.................................Chicago.
Art Pub.	Art Publishing Co.....................................Scranton, Pa.
Artemesian.	Artemesian Bindery.............................Los Angeles, Cal.
Artil Co.	Artil Co..............................422 Eddy St., Ithaca, N. Y.
Arts and Crafts.	Arts and Crafts Book Shop...............................Chicago.
Aryan.	Aryan Theosophical Press..........................Point Loma, Cal.
Ashburn, J. N.	Ashburn, Joseph Nelson........3859 Cedar Ave., S. E., Cleveland, O.
Ashenfelter, I. G.	Ashenfelter, Ida Goodman.............................Covina, Cal.
Ashley.	Ashley House-Sewage Disposal Co...6515 Normal Boulevard, Chicago.
Ashman, G: C.	Ashman, George Cromwell.............................Peoria, Ill.
Ashmore, D: N.	Ashmore, David Newton.............................Decatur, Ill.
Asiatic Exclusion.	Asiatic Exclusion League.........................San Francisco.
Assoc. Am. Portland Cement.	Association of American Portland Cement Manufacturers, Philadelphia.
Assoc. Architects.	Associated Architects.....................257 Main St., Dallas, Tex.
Assoc. Bk.	Association Book Co. (Now Jas. F. Drake, Inc.), 4 W. 40th St., New York.
Assoc. Charities.	Associated Charities.............................Washington, D. C.
Assoc. Harvard Clubs.	Associated Harvard Clubs....Harvard University, Cambridge, Mass.
Assoc. Imp. Con. Poor.	Association for Improving the Condition of the Poor, 105 E. 22d St., New York.
Assoc. Int. Conciliation.	Association for International Conciliation (Amer. Branch), Sub-Station 84, New York.
Assoc. Life.	Association of Life Insurance Presidents, 1 Madison Ave., R. 4203, New York.
Assoc. Military Surgeons.	Association of Military Surgeons.................Washington, D. C.
	Association Press. *See* Young Men's Christian Association Press.
Assoc. Pub.	Associated Publishers of American Records.........New Haven, Ct.
Assoc. Sch. Dom. Sci.	Associated Schools of Domestic Science..2715 Michigan Ave., Chicago.
Astro Pub.	Astro Publishing Co..................Hodges Bldg., Detroit, Mich.
Astrophysical.	Astrophysical Journal, University of Chicago Press..........Chicago.
Athenia Pub.	Athenia Publishing Co.................................Athenia, N. J.
Athens Pr.	Athens Printery..Athens, O.
Atkins, G. G.	Atkins, Gaius Glenn..............................Providence, R. I.
Atkinson, M., & G.	Atkinson, Mentzer & Grover, 223-225 Washington St., Chicago; 24 W. 39th St., New York.
Atkinson, W.	Atkinson, Wilmer, Co..................1024 Race St., Philadelphia.
Atlantic Deeper Waterways.	Atlantic Deeper Waterways Association................Philadelphia.
Atlantis Press.	Atlantis Press..Boston.
Atlantis Pub.	Atlantis Publishing Co................113 W. 31st St., New York.
Atlanta Univ.	Atlanta University....................................Atlanta, Ga.
Atlas Portland Cement.	Atlas Portland Cement Co................30 Broad St., New York.
Atwater.	Atwater Publishing House..............................Peoria, Ill.
Auburn Pub.	Auburn Publishing Co.................................Auburn, N. Y.
Audel.	Audel, Theodore, & Co....................63 Fifth Ave, New York.
Audit Co.	Audit Co. of New York..................165 Broadway, New York.

Augsburg. Augsburg Publishing House...223-225 Cedar Ave., Minneapolis, Minn.
Augustana. Augustana Book Concern..........Rock Island, Ill.
Augustin, G: Augustin, George..........140 Elk Pl., New Orleans, La.
Augustine, W: A. Augustine, William Azariah..........Box 263, Carey, O.
Auringer, O. C. Auringer, Rev. Obadiah Cyrus..........Forestport, N. Y.
Aurora Grata. Aurora Grata Consistory, Bedford Ave. and Madison St., Brooklyn, N. Y.
Austen, J. I. Austen, J. I., Co..........549 Wabash Ave., Chicago.
Austin. Austin Publishing Co..........10 Arlington St., Rochester, N. Y.
Austin Pr. Austin Printing Co..........Austin, Tex.
Authors' Pub. Authors' Publishing Association..........P. O. Box 1579, Boston.
Auto Review. Auto Review Publishing Co..........312 Chestnut St., St. Louis.
Automobile Blue Book. Automobile Blue Book Pub. Co.:....231-241 W. 39th St., New York.
Automobile Club. So. Cal. Automobile Club of Southern California, 402-6 Laughlin Bldg., Los Angeles, Cal.
Automobile Topics. Automobile Topics..........103 Park Ave., New York.
Ave Maria. Ave Maria Press..........Notre Dame, Ind.
Avenel, P. Avenel, Paul..........Avon-by-the-Sea, N. J.
Averill, A. B. Averill, Anna Boynton..........R. F. D. No. 1, Foxcroft, Me.
Axtell-R. Axtell-Rush Publishing Co..........203 Shady Ave., Pittsburgh, Pa.
Ayer. Ayer, N. W., & Son..........306 Chestnut St., Philadelphia.
Ayres, M. M. Ayres, Mary Morgan..........138 S. Grant St., Wilkes Barre, Pa.
Ayres, R. C. Ayres, Rollin C..........130 Kearny St., San Francisco.
Ayrshire Breeders. Ayrshire Breeders' Association..........Brandon, Vt.
Babcock, W: E. Babcock, William Emerson..........Mishawaka, Ind.
Babsom. Babsom Bros..........Chicago.
Babson, R. W. Babson, Roger Ward..........Wellesley Hills Station, Boston.
Bacharach. Bacharach, S..........224 E. 7th St., Cincinnati.
Bachelor Pub. Bachelor Publishing Co..........25 W. Broadway, New York.
Bacon, A. S. Bacon, Alexander S..........37 Liberty St., New York.
Bacon, D. G. Bacon, Mrs. Daniel G..........Robinson Cottage, Newport, R. I.
Bacon, E. H. Bacon, E. H., & Co..........249 Washington St., Boston.
Bacon, F. E. Bacon, F. E., & Co., Printers..........Boston.
Bacon & B. Bacon & Brown..........47 Langdon St., Cambridge, Mass.
Badger. Badger, Richard G..........194 Boylston St., Boston.
Badger, J: C. Badger, John Cogswell..........191 Sagamore St., Manchester, N. H.
Badgley, N. E. Badgley, Nathan Eddy, M.D..........126 E. 128th St., New York.
Bahnson, F. H. Bahnson, Frederic H..........Box 73-Salem, Winston-Salem, N. C.
Bailey, B. & B. Bailey, Banks & Biddle Co..........Philadelphia.
Bailey-T. Bailey-Tripp Co..........Cambridgeport, Mass.
Bair, J: F. Bair, Rev. John Franklin..........Greensburg, Pa.
Baird. Baird, Henry Carey, & Co..........810 Walnut St., Philadelphia.
Baker, H: M. Baker, Henry M..........1411 F St., N. W., Washington, D. C.
Baker, V. & Co. Baker, Voorhis & Co..........45 John St., New York.
Baker, W. Baker, Walter, & Co., Ltd..........Dorchester, Mass.
Baker, W. H. Baker, Walter H., & Co..........5 Hamilton Pl., Boston.
Baker, W: H:, (Cleveland). Baker, William Henry..........P. O. Box 160, Cleveland, O.
Baker & B. Baker & Bryon Co..........8th and Sycamore Sts., Cincinnati.
Baker & T. Baker & Taylor Co..........33 E. 17th St., New York.
Baker Pr. Baker Printing Co..........251 Market St., Newark, N. J.
Baker Pub. Baker Publishing Co..........St. Louis.
Balance. Balance Publishing Co..........1700 Welton St., Denver, Colo.
Balbach, J. A. Balbach, Julia A.......Hotel Savoy, 5th Ave. and 59th St., New York.
Balch, E. S. Balch, Edwin Swift..........Philadelphia.
Balch, T: W. Balch, Thomas Willing..........Philadelphia.
Baldwin. Baldwin, H. L., Co..........522 Boston Block, Minneapolis, Minn.
Baldwin, F: C. Baldwin, Frederick Clare..........287 Williams St., East Orange, N. J.
Baldwin, G: J. Baldwin, George J..........Savannah, Ga.
Baldwin, T. & B. Baldwin, Tuthill & Bolton..........Grand Rapids, Mich.
Baldwin, T: W. Baldwin, Thomas Williams..........Weston Rd., Wellesley, Mass.
Baldwin, W: J. S. Baldwin, William James St. John..........World Bldg., New York.
Ball, A. Ball, Alwyn, Jr..........395 Broadway, New York.
Ball Pub. Co. Ball Publishing Co..........683 Atlantic Ave., Boston.
Balliett, L. D. Balliett, Mrs. L. Dow, Virginia St. and Atlantic Ave., Atlantic City, N. J.
Ballou, G: D. Ballou, George D'Estin..........707 W. 53d St., Los Angeles, Cal.
Balmer, E. Balmer, Edwin..........1045 Hollywood Ave., Chicago.
Baltimore Bk. Baltimore Book Co..........1369 N. Carey St., Baltimore, Md.
Balto. Pr. Baltimore City Printing and Bindery Co..........Baltimore, Md.

Arkansas Dept. Pub. Instruct.	Arkansas Department of Public Instruction........Little Rock, Ark.
Arkansas Geol. Survey.	Arkansas Geological Survey (A. H. Purdue, State Geologist), Fayetteville, Ark.
Armes, E.	Armes, Ethel..................1410 St. Charles St., Birmingham, Ala.
Arms and the Man.	Arms and the Man Publishing Co.1502 H St., N. W., Washington, D. C.
Armstrong.	Armstrong, A. C., & Son. *See* Geo. H. Doran Co.
Armstrong, C.	Armstrong, Collin..........................25 Broad St., New York.
Armstrong, J. E.	Armstrong, James E.............Englewood High School, Chicago.
Armstrong, W: C.	Armstrong, William Clinton..................New Brunswick, N. J.
Armstrong Cork.	Armstrong Cork Co...............................Pittsburgh, Pa.
Armstrong-K.	Armstrong-Keyser .... Philadelphia.
Army Service.	Army Service Schools, Book Department.....Fort Leavenworth, Kan.
Arnett, L.	Arnett, Lizzie.............................. Lecta, Barren Co., Ky.
Arnold.	Arnold & Co........................418-422 Sansom St., Philadelphia.
Arnold, L. V.	Arnold, Leon Vance.............15 Arnold Ave., Amsterdam, N. Y.
Arnold, T. B.	Arnold, T. B.......................................Glen Ellen, Ill.
Arroyo Guild.	Arroyo Guild Press.................212 Thorne St., Los Angeles, Cal.
Art Assoc. Indianapolis.	Art Association of Indianapolis, John Herron Art Institute, Indianapolis, Ind.
Art. Com. of N. Y.	Art Commission of the City of New York.......City Hall, New York.
Art Inst. of Chic.	Art Institute of Chicago.................................Chicago.
Art Pub.	Art Publishing Co......................................Scranton, Pa.
Artemesian.	Artemesian Bindery.............................Los Angeles, Cal.
Artil Co.	Artil Co..............................422 Eddy St., Ithaca, N. Y.
Arts and Crafts.	Arts and Crafts Book Shop..................................Chicago.
Aryan.	Aryan Theosophical Press..........................Point Loma, Cal.
Ashburn, J. N.	Ashburn, Joseph Nelson........3859 Cedar Ave., S. E., Cleveland, O.
Ashenfelter, I. G.	Ashenfelter, Ida Goodman...............................Covina, Cal.
Ashley.	Ashley House-Sewage Disposal Co...6515 Normal Boulevard, Chicago.
Ashman, G: C.	Ashman, George Cromwell...............................Peoria, Ill.
Ashmore, D: N.	Ashmore, David Newton...............................Decatur, Ill.
Asiatic Exclusion.	Asiatic Exclusion League............................San Francisco.
Assoc. Am. Portland Cement.	Association of American Portland Cement Manufacturers, Philadelphia.
Assoc. Architects.	Associated Architects......................257 Main St., Dallas, Tex.
Assoc. Bk.	Association Book Co. (Now Jas. F. Drake, Inc.), 4 W. 40th St., New York.
Assoc. Charities.	Associated Charities..............................Washington, D. C.
Assoc. Harvard Clubs.	Associated Harvard Clubs....Harvard University, Cambridge, Mass.
Assoc. Imp. Con. Poor.	Association for Improving the Condition of the Poor, 105 E. 22d St., New York.
Assoc. Int. Conciliation.	Association for International Conciliation (Amer. Branch), Sub-Station 84, New York.
Assoc. Life.	Association of Life Insurance Presidents, 1 Madison Ave., R. 4203, New York.
Assoc. Military Surgeons.	Association of Military Surgeons.................Washington, D. C.
	Association Press. *See* Young Men's Christian Association Press.
Assoc. Pub.	Associated Publishers of American Records.........New Haven, Ct.
Assoc. Sch. Dom. Sci.	Associated Schools of Domestic Science..2715 Michigan Ave., Chicago.
Astro Pub.	Astro Publishing Co..................Hodges Bldg., Detroit, Mich.
Astrophysical.	Astrophysical Journal, University of Chicago Press.........Chicago.
Athenia Pub.	Athenia Publishing Co.................................Athenia, N. J.
Athens Pr.	Athens Printery...Athens, O.
Atkins, G. G.	Atkins, Gaius Glenn..............................Providence, R. I.
Atkinson, M., & G.	Atkinson, Mentzer & Grover, 223-225 Washington St., Chicago; 24 W. 39th St., New York.
Atkinson, W.	Atkinson, Wilmer, Co...................1024 Race St., Philadelphia.
Atlantic Deeper Waterways.	Atlantic Deeper Waterways Association.................Philadelphia.
Atlantis Press.	Atlantis Press...Boston.
Atlantis Pub.	Atlantis Publishing Co.................113 W. 31st St., New York.
Atlanta Univ.	Atlanta University..Atlanta, Ga.
Atlas Portland Cement.	Atlas Portland Cement Co.................30 Broad St., New York.
Atwater.	Atwater Publishing House...............................Peoria, Ill.
Auburn Pub.	Auburn Publishing Co..............................Auburn, N. Y.
Audel.	Audel, Theodore, & Co.....................63 Fifth Ave, New York.
Audit Co.	Audit Co. of New York...................165 Broadway, New York.

Augsburg.	Augsburg Publishing House...223-225 Cedar Ave., Minneapolis, Minn.
Augustana.	Augustana Book Concern...Rock Island, Ill.
Augustin, G:	Augustin, George...140 Elk Pl., New Orleans, La.
Augustine, W: A.	Augustine, William Azariah...Box 263, Carey, O.
Auringer, O. C.	Auringer, Rev. Obadiah Cyrus...Forestport, N. Y.
Aurora Grata.	Aurora Grata Consistory, Bedford Ave. and Madison St., Brooklyn, N. Y.
Austen, J. I.	Austen, J. I., Co...549 Wabash Ave., Chicago.
Austin.	Austin Publishing Co...10 Arlington St., Rochester, N. Y.
Austin Pr.	Austin Printing Co...Austin, Tex.
Authors' Pub.	Authors' Publishing Association...P. O. Box 1579, Boston.
Auto Review.	Auto Review Publishing Co...312 Chestnut St., St. Louis.
Automobile Blue Book.	Automobile Blue Book Pub. Co...231-241 W. 39th St., New York.
Automobile Club. So. Cal.	Automobile Club of Southern California, 402-6 Laughlin Bldg., Los Angeles, Cal.
Automobile Topics.	Automobile Topics...103 Park Ave., New York.
Ave Maria.	Ave Maria Press...Notre Dame, Ind.
Avenel, P.	Avenel, Paul...Avon-by-the-Sea, N. J.
Averill, A. B.	Averill, Anna Boynton...R. F. D. No. 1, Foxcroft, Me.
Axtell-R.	Axtell-Rush Publishing Co...203 Shady Ave., Pittsburgh, Pa.
Ayer.	Ayer, N. W., & Son...306 Chestnut St., Philadelphia.
Ayres, M. M.	Ayres, Mary Morgan...138 S. Grant St., Wilkes Barre, Pa.
Ayres, R. C.	Ayres, Rollin C...130 Kearny St., San Francisco.
Ayrshire Breeders.	Ayrshire Breeders' Association...Brandon, Vt.
Babcock, W: E.	Babcock, William Emerson...Mishawaka, Ind.
Babsom.	Babsom Bros...Chicago.
Babson. R. W.	Babson, Roger Ward...Wellesley Hills Station, Boston.
Bacharach.	Bacharach, S...224 E. 7th St., Cincinnati.
Bachelor Pub.	Bachelor Publishing Co...25 W. Broadway, New York.
Bacon, A. S.	Bacon, Alexander S...37 Liberty St., New York.
Bacon, D. G.	Bacon, Mrs. Daniel G...Robinson Cottage, Newport, R. I.
Bacon, E. H.	Bacon, E. H., & Co...249 Washington St., Boston.
Bacon, F. E.	Bacon, F. E., & Co., Printers...Boston.
Bacon & B.	Bacon & Brown...47 Langdon St., Cambridge, Mass.
Badger.	Badger, Richard G...194 Boylston St., Boston.
Badger, J: C.	Badger, John Cogswell...191 Sagamore St., Manchester, N. H.
Badgley, N. E.	Badgley, Nathan Eddy, M.D...126 E. 128th St., New York.
Bahnson, F. H.	Bahnson, Frederic H...Box 73-Salem, Winston-Salem, N. C.
Bailey, B. & B.	Bailey, Banks & Biddle Co...Philadelphia.
Bailey-T.	Bailey-Tripp Co...Cambridgeport, Mass.
Bair, J: F.	Bair, Rev. John Franklin...Greensburg, Pa.
Baird.	Baird, Henry Carey, & Co...810 Walnut St., Philadelphia.
Baker, H: M.	Baker, Henry M...1411 F St., N. W., Washington, D. C.
Baker, V. & Co.	Baker, Voorhis & Co...45 John St., New York.
Baker, W.	Baker, Walter, & Co., Ltd...Dorchester, Mass.
Baker, W. H.	Baker, Walter H., & Co...5 Hamilton Pl., Boston.
Baker, W: H:, (Cleveland).	Baker, William Henry...P. O. Box 160, Cleveland, O.
Baker & B.	Baker & Bryon Co...8th and Sycamore Sts., Cincinnati.
Baker & T.	Baker & Taylor Co...33 E. 17th St., New York.
Baker Pr.	Baker Printing Co...251 Market St., Newark, N. J.
Baker Pub.	Baker Publishing Co...St. Louis.
Balance.	Balance Publishing Co...1700 Welton St., Denver, Colo.
Balbach, J. A.	Balbach, Julia A...Hotel Savoy, 5th Ave. and 59th St., New York.
Balch, E. S.	Balch, Edwin Swift...Philadelphia.
Balch, T: W.	Balch, Thomas Willing...Philadelphia.
Baldwin.	Baldwin, H. L., Co...522 Boston Block, Minneapolis, Minn.
Baldwin. F: C.	Baldwin, Frederick Clare...287 Williams St., East Orange, N. J.
Baldwin, G: J.	Baldwin, George J...Savannah, Ga.
Baldwin, T. & B.	Baldwin, Tuthill & Bolton...Grand Rapids, Mich.
Baldwin, T: W.	Baldwin, Thomas Williams...Weston Rd., Wellesley, Mass.
Baldwin, W: J. S.	Baldwin, William James St. John...World Bldg., New York.
Ball, A.	Ball, Alwyn, Jr...395 Broadway, New York.
Ball Pub. Co.	Ball Publishing Co...683 Atlantic Ave., Boston.
Balliett, L. D.	Balliett, Mrs. L. Dow, Virginia St. and Atlantic Ave., Atlantic City, N. J.
Ballou, G: D.	Ballou, George D'Estin...707 W. 53d St., Los Angeles, Cal.
Balmer, E.	Balmer, Edwin...1045 Hollywood Ave., Chicago.
Baltimore Bk.	Baltimore Book Co...1369 N. Carey St., Baltimore, Md.
Balto. Pr.	Baltimore City Printing and Bindery Co...Baltimore, Md.

Bancroft.	Bancroft Training School for Mentally Subnormal Children, Haddonfield, N. J.
Bancroft, E. A.	Bancroft, Edgar Allison..................184 La Salle St., Chicago.
Bancroft-W.	Bancroft-Whitney Co..........200-214 McAllister St., San Francisco.
Bankers Mag.	Banker's Magazine........................90 William St., New York.
Bankers' Law Pub.	Bankers' Law Publishing Co............................Sedalia, Mo.
Bankers' Pub.	Bankers' Publishing Co...................253 Broadway, New York.
Bankers' Pub. (O.)	Bankers' Publishing Co.................................Toledo, O.
Banking Law.	Banking Law Journal......................27 Thames St., New York.
Banks.	Banks Law Publishing Co. (Supplies books of Banks & Co.), 23 Park Pl., New York.
Banks, E. E.	Banks, Emory E...................................Pembroke, N. Y.
Banks, J. L.	Banks, James Lenox......................27 William St., New York.
Banks & Co.	Banks & Co. (Books supplied by Banks Law Publishing Co.)
Bapt. Bk.	Baptist Book Concern............636-638 Fourth Ave., Louisville, Ky.
Bapt. S. S. Bd.	Baptist Sunday School Board.....710 Church St., Nashville, Tenn.
Bapt. World.	Baptist World Publishing Co......660 So. 4th St., Louisville, Ky.
Barber Asphalt.	Barber Asphalt Co...........................90 West St., New York.
Barbour, S.	Barbour, Sylvester........................863 Main St., Hartford, Ct.
Bardeen.	Bardeen, C. W...............317 E. Washington St., Syracuse, N. Y.
Bardwell, F. L.	Bardwell, Fred Leslie...Massachusetts Institute of Technology, Boston.
Barlow, J: R:	Barlow, John Richard......1726 Whitney Ave., Niagara Falls, N. Y.
Barnes.	Barnes, A. S., & Co..........................381 4th Ave., New York.
Barnes, O. P.	Barnes, Orange Perry....................378 Wabash Ave., Chicago.
Barnes Mfg. Co.	Barnes Manufacturing Co..........................Susquehanna, Pa.
Barnes Pub.	Barnes, Arthur J., Publishing Co...........2201 Locust St., St. Louis.
Barnum, E. M.	Barnum, Edmund Maginness...........204 6th Ave., La Grange, Ill.
Barnum, R. C.	Barnum, R. C., Co.................5712 Carnegie Ave., Cleveland, O.
Barr, J: W:	Barr, John William..............................Sta. G, Cincinnati.
Barrett, C: S.	Barrett, Charles Simon..............................Union City, Ga.
Barrett, H. D.	Barrett, Harrison D..................R. F. D. No. 1, Murphy, Ore.
Barrett, J. A.	Barrett, J. A.........................Box 384, Oklahoma City, Okla.
Barrett Mfg. Co.	Barrett Manufacturing Co......................................Boston.
Barrie.	Barrie, George, & Sons................1313 Walnut St., Philadelphia.
Barry.	Barry, James H., Co.................1124 Mission St., San Francisco.
Barse & H.	Barse & Hopkins (Successors to Brewer, Barse & Co., Chicago), 526 W. 26th St., New York.
Barsuette.	Barsuette, B.......................Williamson Bldg., Cleveland, O.
Bartels.	Bartels, J. M., Co..Boston.
Bartholomew, E. J.	Bartholomew, Elmer Jefferson............134 Mentor Bldg., Chicago.
Bartlett.	Bartlett, C. H., Co..Cuba, Wis.
Bartlett, A.	Bartlett, Alfred...................................69 Cornhill, Boston.
Bartlett, E. J.	Bartlett, Edwin Julius..................................Hanover, N. H.
Bartlett, N. J.	Bartlett, N. J., & Co...........................28 Cornhill, Boston.
Barton, C. J. W.	Barton, Mrs. Catherine Josephine Wigginton, 332 Troost Ave., Kansas City, Mo.
Barton, F. M.	Barton, F. M., Co..................706-712 Caxton Bldg., Cleveland, O.
Barton, S: G.	Barton, Samuel Goodwin..............................Potsdam, N. Y.
Baruch.	Baruch Bros..................................42 Broadway, New York.
Basley, A.	Basley, Mrs. A...Room 626, Chamber of Commerce, Los Angeles, Cal.
Bass, W: W.	Bass, William Wallace..........................Grand Canyon, Ariz.
Bassette.	Bassette, F. A., Co..............Germona Bldg., Springfield, Mass.
Bates.	Bates Publishing Co..................................Rochester, N. Y.
Bates, A. C.	Bates, Albert Carlos..Hartford, Ct.
Bates & G.	Bates & Guild Co............................144 Congress St., Boston.
Batten.	Batten, George, Co..........................11 E. 24th St., New York.
Batten, J: M.	Batten, John Mullin....................................Downingtown, Pa.
Battle, J. M.	Battle, Jesse M...........................2001 Locust St., St. Louis
Baughman.	Baughman, Charles H., & Sons.................Frederick City, Md.
Baughman, N. R. B.	Baughman, Mrs. Nanny R. Ball.....523 Division St., Burlington, Ia.
Baughman Sta. Co.	Baughman Stationery Co...................................Richmond, Va.
Baum, C. L.	Baum, Mrs. C. L..................1325 East Colfax St., Denver, Colo.
Baumgardt.	Baumgardt Publishing Co......116 N. Broadway, Los Angeles, Cal.
Baur.	Baur, R., & Son.......................................Wilkes-Barre, Pa.
Bd. of Educ., Berkeley, (Cal.)	Board of Education..Berkeley, Cal.
Bd. For. Miss.	Board of Foreign Missions of the United Presbyterian Church of N. A.......................921 Witherspoon Bldg., Philadelphia.
Bd. Home Miss.	Board of Home Missions and Church Extension of the M. E. Church, 1026 Arch St., Philadelphia.
Bd. S. S. M. E. Ch.	Board of Sunday Schools of the Methodist Episcopal Church, Chicago.
Beach, E. H:	Beach, Elmer Henry......................................Detroit, Mich.

Beadle, M. L. S.	Beadle, Maude Lenna Streeter....................Marcellus, Mich.
Beal, J. H.	Beal, James Hartley..Scio, O.
Beattys.	Beattys, Frank D., & Co...................225 5th Ave., New York.
Beaver, I. M.	Beaver, I. M.... ....123 N. 6th St., Reading, Pa.
Beaver Pr. (N. Y.)	Beaver Printing Co......................52 E. 59th St., New York.
Beaver Pr. (Pa.).	Beaver Printing Co......................................Greenville, Pa.
Beazley, C: H.	Beazley, Charles Howell..................................Leesburg, Ga.
Becker, W. C.	Becker, W. C..........................688 Cass St., Milwaukee, Wis.
Becktold.	Becktold Printing and Book Mfg. Co..........................St. Louis.
Beede, C: G.	Beede, Mrs. Charles Gould......................................Ames, Ia.
Beers, C. W.	Beers, Clifford Whittingham.......30 Trumbull St., New Haven, Ct.
Beesley, C: N.	Beesley, Charles Norbury.........................Charleston, S. C.
Beggs, W: N.	Beggs, William N., M.D.....14th and Delaware St., Denver. Colo.
Beirly, A.	Beirly, Alfred..............................310 Lakeside Bldg., Chicago.
Belgravia.	Belgravia Press..........................722 Sansom St., Philadelphia.
Belisle Pr.	Belisle Printing & Publishing Co.......112 Front St., Worcester, Mass.
Bell, C: E.	Bell, Charles Erle..................313 Equitable Bldg., Atlanta, Ga.
Bell, C. J.	Bell Claude J..Nashville, Tenn.
Bell, J. D. & F. R.	Bell, J. D. & F. R., Co.......................96 Broadway, New York.
Bell, J. P.	Bell, J. P., Co., Inc...Lynchburg, Va.
Bell Bk.	Bell Book and Stationery Co..........914 E. Main St., Richmond, Va.
Bell Telephone.	Bell Telephone Co. of Pennsylvania..........................Philadelphia.
Bellows, W. C.	Bellows, Walter Clarke..................315 W. 113th St., New York.
Bemidji Pioneer.	Bemidji Pioneer Publishing Co...........................Bemidji, Mich.
Bender, M.	Bender, Matthew, & Co.............511-513 Broadway, Albany, N. Y.
Bender-M.	Bender-Moss Co. (formerly Bender-Chaquette Co.), 54 McAllister St., San Francisco.
Bendure & A.	Bendure & Arthurs............709 Pine St., P. H., Steubenville, O.
Benedictine.	Benedictine Convent..Clyde. Mo.
Benjamin, W: H.	Benjamin, William Howard......457 Western Ave., Albany, N. Y.
Benkendorf, G. H: W:	Benkendorf, Gustavus Henry William.....................Madison, Wis.
Bennett.	Bennett, Dana T., Co......................324 E. 23d St., New York.
Bennett, F. P.	Bennett, F. P., & Co..........................530 Atlantic Ave., Boston.
Bennett Pub.	Bennett Publishing Co.............437 Franklin Ave., Pittsburgh, Pa.
Benton.	Benton Publishing Co..Fowler, Ind.
Benton, H. O.	Benton, Harwood Otis..Oberlin, Kan.
Benton, J. H:	Benton, Josiah Henry..................................Ames Bldg., Boston.
Benton, J: C.	Benton, John Clemens..................................Santa Barbara, Cal.
Benziger.	Benziger Bros ....36 Barclay St., New York.
Berea.	Berea Publishing Co..Berea, Ky.
Berger.	Berger Publishing Co..............265 Norwood Ave., Buffalo, N. Y.
Bergling, J: M.	Bergling, John Mauritz..................3739 Herndon St., Chicago.
Berko, G. D.	Berko, Géza D.................................198 E. 10th St., New York.
Berlage, H. J.	Berlage, Herman Joseph, care of James Coston, 7 Arcade, Hotel Emery, Cincinnati.
Berlinicke & A.	Berlinicke & Adams...........Room 15M, 220 Broadway, New York.
Berry.	Berry, Stephen, Co..............................37 Plum St., Portland, Me.
Bersford, T:	Bersford, Thomas......................70a Sanchez St., San Francisco.
Bertron, G: W.	Bertron, George W., National Publishing Co., 241 S. American St., Philadelphia.
Beshshure.	Beshshure, Beshshure Michael.......P. O. Box 450, West Newton, Pa.
Besse, H: T.	Besse, Henry T...............44 E. Santa Clara St., San Jose, Cal.
Best, J. B.	Best, J. B., & Co...Everett, Wash.
Bethel Pub.	Bethel Publishing Co..Dayton, O.
Betts, C. L.	Betts, Craven Langstroth.......................Hasbrouck Heights, N. J.
Bey, T.	Bey, Theophilus..Williamsport, Pa.
Bexell, J: A.	Bexell, John Andrew..Corvallis, Ore.
Bible Educ.	Bible Educational Society..St. Louis.
Bible House.	Bible House...............................323 Dearborn St., Chicago.
Bible Inst.	Bible Institute Colportage Association....826 La Salle Ave., Chicago
Bible League.	Bible League Book Co.....................86 Bible House, New York.
Bible Study.	Bible Study Publishing Co...............250 Devonshire St., Boston.
Bible Training.	Bible Training School..............................South Lancaster, Mass.
Bibliophile.	Bibliophile Society...Boston.
Bibliotheca Sacra.	Bibliotheca Sacra Co..Oberlin, O.
Bicknell, T: W.	Bicknell, Thomas W...Central Falls, R. I.
Bicycling World.	Bicycling World Co...........................254 Nassau St., New York.
Biddle Press.	Biddle Press.................................1010 Cherry St., Philadelphia.
Bigelow, J:	Bigelow, John..........................21 Gramercy Park, New York.
Bigelow, M. A.	Bigelow, Maurice Alpheus...........Columbia University, New York.
Bigelow, M. E.	Bigelow, Mary Emeline..Parsons, Kan.

Bigelow, S. Bigelow, Smith & Co. .... 11 Cliff St., New York.
Bilhorn. Bilhorn Bros. .... Chicago.
Bill, E. L. Bill, E. L. .... 1 Madison Ave., New York.
Binghamton Bk. Binghamton Book Mfg. Co. .... Binghamton, N. Y.
Bird. Bird, J. A. & W., & Co. .... 34 India St., Boston.
Birkhoff, G: D: Birkhoff, George David .... 1214 W. Johnson St., Chicago.
Bisel. Bisel, George T., Co. .... 724 Sansom St., Philadelphia.
Bishop, I. P. Bishop, Irving Prescott .... 109 Norwood Ave., Buffalo, N. Y.
Bishop Museum. Bishop Museum Press .... Honolulu, H. I.
Bixby, W: K. Bixby, William K. .... St. Louis.
Black Diamond. Black Diamond Co. .... 112 Manhattan Bldg., Chicago.
Black Lion. Black Lion .... Box 1798, Boston.
Blackmer, P. W. Blackmer, Percy W. .... Oak Park, Ill.
Blackwell, H: Blackwell, Henry .... 56 University Pl., New York.
Blair, F. G. Blair, Francis G., Supt. of Public Instruction .... Springfield Ill.
Blaisdell, F. Blaisdell, Frank .... Manchester, N. H.
Blake, G: H. Blake, George Herbert .... P. O. Box 1484, New York.
Blake, J. V. Blake, James Vila .... Chicago.
Blakely. Blakely Printing Co. .... 184-186 Monroe St., Chicago.
Blakely, S. B. Blakely, Stuart Banyar .... 435 W. 59th St., New York.
Blakely-O. Blakely-Oswald Printing Co. .... 126-132 Market St., Chicago.
Blakiston. Blakiston's, P., Sons & Co. .... 1012 Walnut St., Philadelphia.
Blanchard. Blanchard, Isaac H. .... 268-270 Canal St. New York.
Blanchard, F. Q. Blanchard, F. Q. .... 92 Sussex Ave., East Orange, N. J.
Blanchard, F. S. Blanchard, F. S., & Co. .... Worcester, Mass.
Blatter, G: J: Blatter, Rev. George John .... 2940 91st St., Chicago.
Bloch. Bloch Publishing Co. .... 40 E. 14th St., New York
Bloch, S: A. Bloch, Samuel A. .... 681 N. Oakley Ave., Chicago.
Blom, A. Blom, Ada .... 303 E. 71st St., New York.
Blossom Bk. Blossom Book Bourse .... Care of Barrett O'Hara, Chicago.
Blythebourne Pub. Blythebourne Publishing Co. .. Blythebourne Station, Long Island, N. Y.
Boardman, E. L. Boardman, E. L. .... Olympia, Wash.
Bobbitt, J: F. Bobbitt, John Franklin .... Clark University, Worcester, Mass.
Bobbs-M. Bobbs-Merrill Co. .... 9 W. Washington St., Indianapolis, Ind.
Bodmer. Bodmer, R. J., Co. .... 7 W. 22d St., New York.
Boeckmann, P. v. Boeckmann, Paul von .... 103 Park Ave., New York.
Boericke & R. Boericke & Runyon .... 11 W. 42d St., New York.
Boericke & T. Boericke & Tafel .... 1011 Arch St., Philadelphia.
Bogarte. Bogarte. M. E., Book Co. .... Valparaiso, Ind.
Boger. Boger, Frederick, Publishing Co. .... 1 Maiden Lane, New York.
Bohemian Soc. Bohemian Society .... Norfolk, Va.
Boiler Maker. Boiler Maker .... 17 Battery Pl., New York.
Bolton, C: K. Bolton, Mrs. Charles Knowles .... Brookline, Mass.
Bolton, R. P. Bolton, Reginald Pelham .... 527 Fifth Ave., New York.
Bok, E: Bok, Edward .... Merion, Pa.
Boname, L. C. Boname, Louise Catharine .... 1930 Chestnut St., Philadelphia.
Bond. Bond Co. .... Philadelphia.
Bones, H. M. Bones, Mrs. H. M. .... 131 Michigan Ave., Watertown, N. Y.
Bonham, A. N. Bonham, Alfred N. .... 2812 Central Ave., Indianapolis, Ind.
Bonnell. Bonnell, Silver & Co. Books bought by Madison Ave. Bookstore, 587 Madison Ave., New York.
Bonnell, J. D. Bonnell, J. D., & Son .... 152 Purchase St., Boston.
Bonner. Bonner & Co. .... Toledo, O.
Book & Art. Book & Art Exchange .... Room 7, 1 Madison Ave., New York.
Book Pr. Book Print (The) .... Crozer Bldg., Philadelphia.
Book Supply. Book Supply Co. .... 231 W. Monroe St., Chicago.
Booklovers' Assoc. Booklovers' Association .... Chicago.
Bookstore. Bookstore (The) .... East Northfield, Mass.
Boosey. Boosey & Co. .... 9 E. 17th St., New York.
Boot & Shoe. Boot & Shoe Recorder Pub. Co. .... Boston, Mass.
Booth. Booth, Walter S., & Son .. 403-405 Nicolette Ave., Minneapolis, Minn.
Booth, C: E. Booth, Charles Edwin, National Arts Club, 14 Gramercy Park S., New York.
Boss. Boss Publishing Co. .... 87 Madison St., Brooklyn, N. Y.
Boston & Maine. Boston & Maine Railroad .... Boston.
Boston Assoc. Tuberculosis. Boston Association for the Relief and Control of Tuberculosis. 4 Joy St., Boston.
Boston Bk. Boston Book Co. .... 83-91 Francis St., Fenway, Boston.
Boston Law. Boston Law Book Co. .... Boston.
Boston Museum. Boston Museum of Fine Arts .... Copley Sq., Boston.
Boston Music. Boston Music Co. (G. Schirmer, Jr.) .... 26-28 West St., Boston.
Boston Pub. Lib. Boston Public Library .... Boston.

Boston Sch. Com.	Boston School Committee..........Boston.
Boston Soc. of Architects.	Boston Society of Architects..........Boston.
Bottome, W. B.	Bottome, Willard Bodine..........5 Beekman St., New York.
Boulder Pub.	Boulder Publishing Co..........Boulder, Colo.
Boulton.	Boulton Publishing Co..........128 N. Front St., Philadelphia.
Bowdoin, W: G.	Bowdoin, William Goodrich..........430 Fulton St., Brooklyn, N. Y.
Bowdoin College.	Bowdoin College Library..........Brunswick, Me.
Bowen, B. F.	Bowen, B. F., & Co..523-525 Meridian Life Bldg., Indianapolis, Ind.
Bowen, G: O.	Bowen, George Oscar, Institute of Music Pedagogy, Northampton, Mass.
Bowker, W: H.	Bowker, William H..........43 Chatham St., Boston.
Bowles.	Bowles, J. M..........15 E. 34th St., New York.
Bowman.	Bowman, Charles L., & Co..........225 Fifth Ave., New York.
Bowman & C.	Bowman & Crossley..........Care of Iowa State College, Ames, Ia.
Bowron, H: S.	Bowron, Mrs. Henry S..........1925 Seventh Ave., New York.
Boyd, J. S.	Boyd, Rev. James Shields..........Courtenay, N. D.
Brace, G: M.	Brace, George Marshall..........505 Wilson Ave., Menomonie, Wis.
Bradbury, A. R.	Bradbury, Mrs. Anna Rossman..........620 Union St., Hudson, N. Y.
Bradford, G.	Bradford, Gershom, 2d..........Washington, D. C.
Bradford Record.	Bradford Record Publishing Co..........Bradford, Pa.
Bradley, M.	Bradley, Milton, Co..........49 Willow St., Springfield, Mass.
Bradley Polytechnic.	Bradley Polytechnic Institute..........Peoria, Ill.
Bradt.	Bradt Publishing Co..........Jackson, Mich.
Brainard.	Brainard, C. T., Publishing Co..........225 Fifth Ave., New York.
Brainard, L. A.	Brainard, Lucy Abigail..........4 Atwood St., Hartford, Ct.
Branch.	Branch Publishing Co..........Chicago.
Branch, E. W.	Branch, Ernest W.......513 Tremont Bldg., 73 Tremont St., Boston.
Brandeis, L: D.	Brandeis, Louis D..........161 Devonshire St., Boston.
Brandon Pr.	Brandon Printing Co..........Nashville, Tenn.
Brandt, C: E:	Brandt, Charles Edward..........Box 339, Cumberland, Md.
Brandu's.	Brandu's..........767 Lexington Ave., New York.
Branson, I: R.	Branson, Isaac Reichelderfer..........Aurora, Neb.
Brant, S. A.	Brant, Selwyn A..........Madison, Wis.
Brashere, O. M.	Brashere, Ora M..........Salt Lake City, Utah.
Braubach, A. L.	Braubach, Anna Louise..........214 Madison St., San Antonio, Tex.
Brauer, H: J.	Brauer, Henry J., Co., Ltd..........724 Perdido St., New Orleans, La.
Brawley, B: G.	Brawley, Benjamin Griffith..........Atlanta, Ga.
Breeder's Gazette.	Breeder's Gazette..........358 Dearborn St., Chicago.
Brentano, T.	Brentano, Judge Theodore..........Court House, Chicago.
Brentano's.	Brentano's..........Fifth Ave. and 27th St., New York.
Breslow.	Breslow, M. M., Co..........8 Bible House, New York.
Brethren Pub. Ho.	Brethren Publishing House..........16-24 S. State St., Elgin, Ill.
Brewer, B.	Brewer, Barse & Co. *See* Barse & Hopkins.
Brewer, O.	Brewer, Orville, Publishing Co., Auditorium Bldg., Wabash Ave. and Congress St., Chicago.
Brewers Pub.	Brewers Publishing Company of America, 1718 Republic Bldg., Chicago; 426 Mint Arcade, Philadelphia.
Breyfogle, F. H.	Breyfogle, Frank H..........P. O. Box 483, Cincinnati.
Bridge, G.	Bridge, Rev. Gerard..........St. Vincent College, Beatty, Pa.
Briggs, W:	Briggs, William..........29 Richmond St., W., Toronto, Can.
Brigham, F. H.	Brigham, Frank Hartwell.....1356 E. Vernon Ave., Los Angeles, Cal.
Bristol, S. A.	Bristol, S. A., Co..........Cheyenne, Wyo.
	Broadway Publishing Co. *See* B'way Pub.
Brock, C. C.	Brock, Claude Cornelius..........542-544 Ellicott Sq., Buffalo, N. Y.
Brockton Hospital.	Brockton Hospital Ladies' Aid Assoc..........Brockton, Mass.
Bromley, G: W.	Bromley, George W..........34 Pine St., New York.
Bromwell, H. E.	Bromwell, Henrietta E..........Denver, Colo.
Brookline Pub. Lib.	Brookline Public Library..........Brookline, Mass.
Brooklyn Eagle.	Brooklyn Daily Eagle..........Eagle Bldg., Brooklyn, N. Y.
Brooklyn Inst.	Brooklyn Institute of Arts and Sciences..........Brooklyn, N. Y.
Brooklyn Lib.	Brooklyn Public Library..........26 Brevoort Pl., Brooklyn, N. Y.
Brooks, A. P.	Brooks, Asa Passavant..........Comfrey, Minn.
Brooks, E. D.	Brooks, E. D..........89 10th St., Minneapolis, Minn.
Brooks, F. L.	Brooks, Rev. Frank Lester..........Hyannis, Mass.
Brooks Bros.	Brooks Brothers..........946 Broadway, New York.
Broun-G.	Broun-Green Co..........48 John St., New York.
Brown, A.	Brown, Addison..........45 W. 89th St., New York.
Brown, C: G.	Brown, Charles Gardner..........Ithaca, N. Y.
Brown, E. E.	Brown, Elmer Ellsworth.....Bureau of Education, Washington, D. C.
Brown, G.	Brown, Goodwin..........192 Broadway, New York.
Brown, G: G.	Brown, George G..........Louisville, Ky.

Brown, G: W. Brown, George W. ... Youngsville, Pa.
Brown, Glenn. Brown, Glenn ... The Octagon, Washington, D. C.
Brown, H. C. Brown, H. C., Co. ... 156 Fifth Ave., New York.
Brown, H. R. Brown, Hubert R. ... 320 Broadway, New York.
Brown, J. M. Brown, Jennie Marie ... Acton, Ind.
Brown, M. B. Brown, Martin B. ... 49 Park Pl., New York.
Brown, W: B. Brown, William B. ... 1027 Fleming Bldg., Des Moines, Ia.
Brown, W: F. Brown, William Findlay ... Philadelphia.
Brown Alumni. Brown Alumni Magazine Co. ... Providence, R. I.
Brown & Co. Brown & Co. ... Oklahoma City, Okla.
Brown & P. Brown & Page ... 184 Summer St., Boston.
Brown & S. Brown & Sharpe Manufacturing Co. ... Providence, R. I.
Brown Bros. Brown Brothers ... Fifth and Pine Sts., Philadelphia.
Brown Bros. Co. Brown Brothers Co. ... Rochester, N. Y.
Brown Bros. & Co. Brown Bros. & Co. ... 59 Wall St., New York.
Brown Pr. Co. Brown Printing Co. ... 10 N. Lawrence St., Montgomery, Ala.
Brown Press. Brown Press Co. ... Lima, O.
Brown Univ. Brown University ... Providence, R. I.
Browne-Smith, M. A. Browne-Smith, Mary A. ... Richmond, Va.
Browne's Bookstore. Browne's Bookstore ... Fine Arts Bldg., Michigan Blvd., Chicago.
Browne's Business Coll. Browne's Brooklyn Business College, 28 Flatbush Ave., Brooklyn, N. Y.
Browning, E: F. Browning, Edward Franklin ... 18 W. 75th St., New York.
Browning, G: W. Browning, George W. ... Clinton, N. Y.
Browning, O. A. Browning, Otis A., Publishing Co. ... Toledo, O.
Bruce, J: E: Bruce, John Edward ... 228 New Main St., Yonkers, N. Y.
Brumley, O. V. Brumley, Oscar Victor ... 1806 N. High St., Columbus, O.
Bruner, J. D. Bruner, James D. ... Chapelhill, N. C.
Bruner, J. W. Bruner, Jane Woodworth ... 475 Ocean Ave., Long Beach, L. I.
Brunswick. Brunswick-Balke-Collender Co. ... 29 W. 32d St., New York.
Brusie, C. F. Brusie, C. F. ... Ossining, N. Y.
Bryan, R. L. Bryan, R. L., Co. ... 1425 Main St., Columbia, S. C.
Bryan, W: A. Bryan, William Alanson ... Chicago.
Bryant, C. L. Bryant, C. L. ... Buffalo, N. Y.
Bryant, F. A: Bryant, Frank Augustus ... 62 W. 40th St., New York.
Bryant, W. F. Bryant, Wilbur F. ... Hartington, Neb.
Bryant Union. Bryant Union Co. ... 81 Fulton St., New York.
Bu. Information Salt Lake. Bureau of Information ... Temple Block, Salt Lake City, Utah.
Bu. Municipal. Bureau of Municipal Research ... 261 Broadway, New York.
Bu. Public Pr. Bureau of Public Printing ... Manila, P. I.
Bu. Univ. Travel. Bureau of University Travel ... Trinity Pl., Boston.
Bubier. Bubier Publishing Co. ... 130 Market St., Lynn, Mass.
Buchanan. Buchanan, G. H., Co. ... Philadelphia.
Buchanan, F. G. Buchanan, Frances Grant ... Denver, Colo.
Buchanan, J. B. Buchanan, J. Barr ... P. O. Box 521, Los Angeles, Cal.
Buchanan, R. Buchanan, Roberdeau ... 2015 Q St., N. W., Washington, D. C.
Buck, A. H: Buck, Albert Henry, M.D. ... Garden City, Long Island, N. Y.
Buck, B: F. Buck, Benjamin F., & Co. ... 160 Fifth Ave., New York.
Buck, E. C. Buck, Edith Cora ... Cedar Falls, Ia.
Buck, E: N. Buck, Edward N. ... Tonopah, Nev.
Buckenham, J. E. B. Buckenham, J. E. Burnett ... Chestnut Hill, Philadelphia.
Buckey, M. C. Buckey, Mervin Chandos ... Fort Worden, Wash.
Buckham, M. H: Buckham, Rev. Mathew Henry ... Burlington, Vt.
Buckley, M. G. Buckley, M. G. ... Newport, R. I.
Buegeleisen, H. D. Buegeleisen, H. D. ... 489 Fifth Ave., New York.
Buettner. Buettner, T., & Co., Inc. ... Chicago; 465 Broadway, New York.
Buffalo Hist. Soc. Buffalo Historical Society ... Historical Bldg., Buffalo, N. Y.
Buffalo Pub. Lib. Buffalo Public Library ... Buffalo, N. Y.
Buffum, B. C. Buffum, Burt C. ... Worland, Big Horn Co., Wyo.
Bull, C. E. Bull, Clark E. ... 1551 W. Bayaud St., Denver, Colo.
Bull, C. P. Bull, Coates P. ... Minneapolis, Minn.
Bullis & H. Bullis & Holden ... Cleveland, O.
Bullock, A. N. Bullock, A. N. ... Sacramento, Cal.
Bungalowcraft. Bungalowcraft Co. .403 Chamber of Commerce Bldg., Los Angeles, Cal.
Bunn. Bunn Bros. ... Oklahoma City, Okla.
Bunse, F: J. Bunse, Frederick Joseph ... Buffalo, N. Y.
Burbank, A. S. Burbank, Alfred Stevens ... Plymouth, Mass
Burch, A. E. S. Burch, Mrs. Adele E. Shoemaker ... 719 Village St., Kalamazoo, Mich.
Burdick. Burdick & Allen ... Milwaukee, Wis.
Burford. Burford, William B. ... Indianapolis, Ind.

Burgess.	Burgess, Mary Abigail.........Virginia State Library, Richmond, Va.
Burgess, C: F.	Burgess, Charles F..Moosup, Ct.
Burgess, L. & Co.	Burgess, Lang & Co..........................50 State St., Boston.
Burk, A. B.	Burk, Addison B....................815 Crozer Bldg., Philadelphia.
Burk, W: H.	Burk, William Herbert.........All Saints' Rectory, Morristown, Pa.
Burke, J. F.	Burke, James F......................French Bldg, Pittsburgh, Pa.
Burke, J. W.	Burke, J. W., Co..........................508 Cherry St., Macon, Ga.
Burlington Pub. Lib.	Burlington Public Library..............................Burlington, Ia.
Burnham, E.	Burnham, E.......................................70 State St., Chicago.
Burnham, W: H:	Burnham, William Henry........Clark University, Worcester, Mass.
Burns Club.	Burns Club...St. Louis.
Burpee.	Burpee, W. Atlee, & Co....................................Philadelphia.
Burris, M.	Burris, Martin...Hutchinson, Kan.
Burroughs, W. & Co.	Burroughs, Wellcome & Co..............35-39 W. 33d St., New York.
Burrowes, K.	Burrowes, Katharine..Detroit, Mich.
Burrows.	Burrows Brothers Co.............133 Euclid Ave., Cleveland, O.
Burt.	Burt, A. L., Co.............................52 Duane St., New York.
Burt Pub.	Burt, Emerson E., Publishing Co..................Williamsport, Pa.
Burton, A. J.	Burton, Alonzo J...................686 Prospect Pl., Brooklyn, N. Y.
Burton, C: J.	Burton, Charles J.............Iowa Christian College, Oskaloosa, Ia.
Burton, G: W.	Burton, George Ward, Care of Times Mirror Printing and Binding House, Los Angeles, Cal.
Burton, T: W:	Burton, Thomas William.......................................Springfield, O.
Burton Co.	Burton Publishing Co..........709 McGee St., Kansas City, Mo.
Burtscher, W: J:	Burtscher, William John...Ruskin, Tenn.
Bushnell, C. C.	Bushnell, Curtis Clark, Hall of Languages, Syracuse University, Syracuse, N. Y.
Bushnell, J.	Bushnell, Joseph...........................Jackson, Jackson Co., Minn.
Business Aid.	Business Aid Co..Detroit, Mich.
Business Bk.	Business Book Bureau...................13 Astor Pl., New York.
Business Code.	Business Code Co..................929 West End Ave., New York.
Business Law.	Business Law Publishing Co...Room 1022, 320 Broadway, New York.
Business Man's Pub.	Business Man's Publishing Co..........................Detroit, Mich
Business Men's.	Business Men's Association, 5342 E. Washington St., Indianapolis, Ind.
Business Monthly.	Business Monthly Publishing Co..........................Peoria, Ill.
Business Press.	Business Press..........................26 City Hall Pl., New York.
Business Pub.	Business Publishing Co..Peoria, Ill.
Butcher, M. H. M.	Butcher, Madge Hortense Myers.........................Lanham, Md.
Butchers Advocate.	Butchers Advocate Co...................203 Broadway, New York.
Butler Bros.	Butler Bros...............................495 Broadway, New York.
Butt, I. L.	Butt, Israel L...Eastville, Va.
Butterfield, W. A.	Butterfield, W. A...........................59 Bromfield St., Boston.
Butterick.	Butterick Publishing Co., Butterick Bldg., Spring & MacDougal Sts., New York.
Butts, E:	Butts, Edward......................1800 E. 16th St., Kansas City, Mo.
Butts, W: H:	Butts, William Henry..........919 Oakland Ave., Ann Arbor, Mich.
Buyers' Index.	Buyers' Index Co.........................47 Plymouth Pl., Chicago.
Buzzacott, F. H.	Buzzacott, Francis H...........................822 74th St., Chicago.
B'way Pub.	Broadway Publishing Co..................835 Broadway, New York.
Bylsma, R:	Bylsma, Richard..............................Grand Rapids, Mich.
Byrd.	Byrd Printing & Publishing Co...................................Atlanta, Ga.
Byrne.	Byrne, John, & Co.............1322 F St., N. W., Washington, D. C.
Byrne Pub.	Byrne Publishing Co...Tyler, Tex.
Byxbee Pub.	Byxbee Publishing Co....................324 Dearborn St., Chicago.
Cadle, C: F.	Cadle, Mrs. Charles F..Muscatine, Ia.
Cahn, J.	Cahn, Julius.........................Empire Theatre Bldg., New York.
Cain, W: S.	Cain, William Stephen..........1403-1405 Main St., Atkinson, Kan.
Caine, W: R. H.	Caine, William Ralph Hall................................Buffalo, N. Y.
Cal. Assoc. Tuberculosis.	California Association for the Study and Prevention of Tuberculosis. Los Angeles, Cal.
Cal. Dept. Pub. Instruction.	California Department of Public Instruction........Sacramento, Cal.
Cal. L. A.	California Library Association..........................Los Angeles, Cal.
Cal. Promotion.	California Promotion Co.................................San Francisco.
Cal. Sec'y State.	California Secretary of State.......................Sacramento, Cal.
Cal. State Lib.	California State Library..................................Sacramento, Cal.
Cal. State Mining.	California State Mining Bureau........Ferry Bldg., San Francisco.
Caldwell.	Caldwell, H. M., Co......................208-218 Summer St., Boston.
Caldwell, A. B.	Caldwell, A. B..............515-519 Temple Court Bldg., Atlanta, Ga.
Caldwell, W:	Caldwell, Rev. William............605 W. 5th St., Fort Worth, Tex.

Caledonian Press.	Caledonian Press....St. Johnsbury, Vt.
Caledonian Pub.	Caledonian Publishing Co....83 Bible House, New York.
Calkins & Co.	Calkins & Co....formerly 27 E. 22d St., New York.
Callaghan.	Callaghan & Co....401-409 E. Ohio St., Chicago.
Caloric.	Caloric Fireless Cookstove Co....Grand Rapids, Mich.
Camann, H: B.	Camann, Henry Bauer....2341 Racine Ave., Chicago.
Cambria Steel.	Cambria Steel Co....165 Broadway, New York.
Cambridge Pub. Lib.	Cambridge Public Library....Cambridge, Mass.
	Cambridge University Press; books formerly handled by Macmillan, now by Putnam.
Campbell, F.	Campbell, Rev. Frederic....30 First Pl., Brooklyn, N. Y.
Campbell, H. W.	Campbell, Hardy Webster....Lincoln, Neb.
Campbell, J.	Campbell, Jane, care of Civic Club....1615 Walnut St., Philadelphia.
Campbell, W: J.	Campbell, William J....1623 Chestnut St., Philadelphia.
Campbell Co.	Campbell Company....Chicago.
Campion.	Campion & Co....1316 Walnut St., Philadelphia.
Canada, J: W:	Canada, John William....Houston, Tex.
Canada Law.	Canada Law Book Co., Ltd....32-34 Toronto St., Toronto, Can.
Canadian Facts.	Canadian Facts Publishing Co....667 Spadina Ave., Toronto, Can.
Canon City Record.	Canon City Record....Canon City, Colo.
Canterbury Co.	Canterbury Co....328 Wabash Ave., Chicago.
Cantwell, H. J.	Cantwell, Henry James....St. Louis.
Cape, E. P.	Cape, Emily Palmer....410 West End Ave., New York.
Capital City Press.	Capital City Press....Montpelier, Vt.
Carbona.	Carbona Products Co....3-5 Burnet St., Newark, N. J.
Cardashian, V.	Cardashian, Vahan....995 Yale Station, New Haven, Ct.
Carey.	Carey, Thomas J., & Co....63 Fifth Ave., New York.
Carey, B.	Carey, Berlin, Co....Chicago.
Cargill.	Cargill Co....Houston, Tex.
Carleton, W.	Carleton, Will....444 Greene Ave., Brooklyn, N. Y.
Carlisle.	Carlisle, A., & Co....251-253 Bush St., San Francisco.
Carlson, G: L.	Carlson, George L....Norfolk, Neb.
Carnahan.	Carnahan Press....1404 H St., N. W., Washington, D. C.
Carnegie.	Carnegie Institute of Washington....Washington, D. C.
Carnegie Found.	Carnegie Foundation for the Advancement of Teaching, 576 Fifth Ave., New York.
Carnegie H. F. Comm.	Carnegie Hero Fund Commission....Carnegie Bldg., Pittsburgh, Pa.
Carnegie Lib.	Carnegie Library of Pittsburgh....Schenley Park, Pittsburgh, Pa.
Carnegie Museum.	Carnegie Museum....Pittsburgh, Pa.
Carnell.	Carnell & Hoit....Albany, N. Y.
Carpenter, D.	Carpenter, DeWitt....Homer, N. Y.
Carpenter, H. M.	Carpenter, Helen McCowen....Ukiah, Cal.
Carr, H.	Carr, Horace....Cleveland, O.
Carr, S.	Carr, Sadie....Edgar, Neb.
Carrell.	Carrell, Robert R., & Co....Chicago.
Carroll.	Carroll Record Co....Taneytown, Md.
Carroll, C: C.	Carroll, Charles Chauncey....426 E. 4th St., Owensboro, Ky.
Carroll, E:	Carroll, Edward, Jr....64 Church St., New York.
Carroll, J: J.	Carroll, John J....5478 Kimbark Ave., Chicago.
Carroll, W:	Carroll, William....131 Tockwotton St., Providence, R. I.
Carson, D. I.	Carson, Dr. D. I....Atlanta, Ga.
Carson, H. L.	Carson, Hampton Lawrence....Philadelphia.
Carson-H.	Carson-Harper....Denver, Colo.
Carteret.	Carteret Book Club....Newark, N. J.
Cartmell, T: K.	Cartmell, Thomas Kemp....Winchester, Va.
Carver, W.	Carver, Willard....322½ W. Broadway, Oklahoma, Okla.
Cary, C: P.	Cary, Charles Preston....State Superintendent, Madison, Wis.
Cary, S. C.	Cary, Rev. Seth Cooley....Dorchester Centre, Boston.
Cary, T: J.	Cary, Thomas J....103 Park Ave., New York.
Case.	Case, Lockwood & Brainard Co....Hartford, Ct.
Case, C. S.	Case, C. S., Co....Chicago.
Case, G: A.	Case, George A....Joplin, Mo.
Casino.	Casino Publishing Co....116 W. 39th St., New York.
Caspar.	Caspar, C. N., Co....431 E. Water St., Milwaukee, Wis.
Cassell.	Cassell & Co., Ltd....43 E. 19th St., New York.
Castello, B.	Castello, Bernice....566 W. 173d St., New York.
Cataract.	Cataract Printing Co....Niagara Falls, N. Y.
Cates, C. D.	Cates, Cliff Donahue....Decatur, Tex.
Cath. Church Extension.	Catholic Church Extension....738 The Rookery, Chicago.
Cath. Editing.	Catholic Editing Co....1 W. 34th St., New York.

Cath. Educ. Catholic Education Press,
1026 Quincy St., Brookland Station, Washington, D. C.
Cath. Standard and Times. Catholic Standard and Times Pub. Co.....211 S. 6th St., Philadelphia.
Cath. Summer Sch. Catholic Summer School Press...........110 W. 74th St., New York.
Cath. Univ. Catholic University of America..................Washington, D. C.
Cathedral. Cathedral Library.................Mt. St. Alban, Washington, D. C.
Cathedral Lib. Cathedral Library Assoc.......534-536 Amsterdam Ave., New York.
Caulk. Caulk, L. D., Co....................................Milford, Del.
Caxton Club. Caxton Club..Chicago.
Cement & Engineering. Cement & Engineering News...............22 Fifth Ave., Chicago.
Cement Era. Cement Era Publishing Co...........842 Monadnock Bldg., Chicago.
Cen. Me. Central Maine Publishing Co.....................Waterville, Me.
Cen. Pr. Central Printing Co.............................Little Rock, Ark.
Cen. Pr. & Pub. Central Printing & Publishing House................Harrisburg, Pa.
Cen. Real Estate. Central Real Estate Dealers' Association . 625 Jackson St., Topeka, Kan.
Central. Central Publishing House............................Cleveland, O.
Central Pub. Central Publishing House.................519 Main St., Cincinnati.
Central Pub. Co. Central Publishing Co..................80 Wabash Ave., Chicago.
Century Assoc. Century Association......................7 W. 43d St., New York.
Century Co. Century Co..............................33 E. 17th St., New York.
Century Code. Century Code Co...........................2 Stone St., New York.
Century Hist. Century History Co.....................54-56 Dey St., New York.
Century Map. Century Map Co.....................2219 Green St., Philadelphia.
Chadwick, E. L. Chadwick, Earl Leslie...............................Hartford, Ct.
Chaffee. Chaffee Studio............................6 E. 37th St., New York.
Chalmers, C: O. Chalmers, Charles O...............512 Camp St., New Orleans, La.
Chamberlin, M. C. Chamberlin, Mac C., Co............................Dowagiac, Mich.
Chambers, W. L. Chambers, W. Lee.............................Santa Monica, Cal.
Chambon, C. M. Chambon, Celestin M.........St. Louis Cathedral, New Orleans, La.
Champion, D. B. Champion, Dorothy B.,
Todt Hill Road, West New Brighton, Staten Island, N. Y.
Champion Chemical. Champion Chemical Co..............................Springfield, O.
Chandler, A. D. Chandler, Alfred Dupont..........................Brookline, Mass.
Chandler, F. W. Chandler, F. W., & Son............................Brunswick, Me.
Chapin, G. W. Chapin, Gilbert W...................................Hartford, Ct.
Chapin, H. L. Chapin, Harry Lorenzo....................R. D. No. 3, Huron, O.
Chapin News. Chapin News Co.....................................Hartford, Ct.
Chapman, C. Chapman, Clowry....................282 Manhattan Ave., New York.
Chapple Pub. Chapple Publishing Co., Ltd............944 Dorchester Ave, Boston.
Character Development. Character Development League...........31 E. 22d St., New York.
Charities Pub. Charities Publication Committee...........105 E. 22d St., New York.
Charity Organ. Charity Organization Society............105 E. 22d St., New York.
Charnock, S. Charnock, Singleton,
Belcastle Chambers, S. Common St., Lynn, Mass.
Charter Oak. Charter Oak Publishing House....................Marshalltown, Ia.
Chartier, E: M. Chartier, Edward Morris..............................Paris, Tex.
Chase, F. N. Chase, Fessenden N.......................................Bath, Me.
Chase, W. L. Chase, W. L., & Co...................P. O. Box 1384, Boston.
Chatterton. Chatterton, A. L., Co...................81 Duane St., New York.
Chatterton-P. Chatterton Peck Co. Now A. L. Chatterton Co.
Chautauqua Pr. Chautauqua Press............................ Chautauqua, N. Y.
Chavers, P. W: Chavers, Pearl William...............................Columbus, O.
Cheadle, C. M. Cheadle, Clarence McKee...............................Ashton, Ill.
Check, S. Check, Rabbi Sabath......................62 E. 7th St., New York.
Cheek, P. Cheek, Philip...Baraboo, Wis.
Chelston Press. Chelston Press..................P. O. Box 566, Atlantic City, N. J.
Cheltenham Press. Cheltenham Press......................150 Fifth Ave., New York.
Chemical. Chemical Publishing Co...............................Easton, Pa.
Chemical Engineer. Chemical Engineer Publishing Co........355 Dearborn St., Chicago.
Chenoweth, C. V. Chenoweth, Mrs. Caroline Van Dusen.P. O. Box 125, Leicester, Mass.
Chesman. Chesman, Nelson, & Co................1127-1128 Pine St., St. Louis.
Chester & B. Chester & Bergman...................... 124 E. 41st St., Chicago.
Chic. Art. Chicago Art Institute......................................Chicago.
Chic. Assoc. Commerce. Chicago Association of Commerce............................Chicago.
Chic. Automobile. Chicago Automobile Club.................................Chicago.
Chic. City Council. Chicago City Council......................................Chicago.
Chic. Commercial. Pub. Chicago Commercial Publishing Co...........P. O. Box 575, Chicago.

Chic. Daily Journ.	Chicago Daily Journal....Chicago.
Chic. Daily News.	Chicago Daily News....Chicago.
Chic. Directory.	Chicago Directory Co....49 Plymouth Ct., Chicago.
Chic. Harbor Com.	Chicago Harbor Commission....Chicago.
Chic. Hebrew Inst.	Chicago Hebrew Institute....485 W. Taylor St., Chicago.
Chic. Hist.	Chicago Historical Society...Dearborn Ave. and Ontario St., Chicago.
Chic. Legal News.	Chicago Legal News Co....87 Clark St., Chicago.
Chic. Lit. Club.	Chicago Literary Club....Chicago.
Chic. Med. Bk.	Chicago Medical Book Co...Cor. Congress and Honore Sts., Chicago.
Chic., Milwaukee & St. P.	Chicago, Milwaukee & St. Paul Railway....Chicago.
Chic. Pub. Lib.	Chicago Public Library....Chicago.
Chico Record.	Chico Record Press....Chico, Cal.
Chief.	Chief Publishing Co....45 Centre St., New York.
Chilcott, L. S.	Chilcott, Langdon S....116 Hammond St., Bangor, Me.
Childe, H.	Childe, Mrs. Hubert....Wichita, Kan.
Children's Pub.	Children's Publishing Co. Now L. D. Jones, 5413 Woodlawn Ave., Chicago.
Childress, R. J.	Childress, Rufus Jackson....950 N. Clark St., Chicago.
China Inland.	China Inland Mission....235 School Lane, Germantown, Pa.
Chirological Coll.	Chirological College...Inspiration Point, Echo Park, Los Angeles, Cal.
Choate, A.	Choate, Augusta....Baldwin School, Bryn Mawr, Pa.
Chr. Herald.	Christian Herald....Room 92, Bible House, New York.
Chr. Press.	Christian Press Association Publishing Co..26 Barclay St., New York.
Chr. Pub.	Christian Publishing Co. ....Dayton, O.
Chr. Pub. Assoc.	Christian Publishing Association....Dayton, O.
Chr. Pub. Co.	Christian Publishing Co....2712 Pine St., St. Louis.
Chr. Sci.	Christian Science Publishing Co....250 Huntington Ave., Boston.
Chr. Sci. Pub.	Christian Science Publishing Society, Falmouth and St. Paul Sts., Boston.
Chr. Un.	Christian Union Publishing Co....Des Moines, Ia.
Chr. Witness.	Christian Witness Co....151 Washington St., Chicago.
Christ Ch.	Christ Church....Williamsport, Pa.
Christian, J: T.	Christian, John Taylor, D.D....1604 Spring St., Little Rock, Ark.
Christian Liberty.	Christian Liberty Bureau....222 Lawn Ave., Norwood, O.
Christian's Sch.	Christian's School of Applied Food Chemistry, 7 E. 41st St., New York.
Christie.	Christie Publishing Co....171 La Salle St., Chicago.
Chronicle Co.	Chronicle Co., Ltd....90 William St., New York.
Chronicle Pub.	Chronicle Publishing Co....Orange, N. J.
Chrysler, C. B.	Chrysler, Charles Byron....Chicago.
Church.	Church, John, Co....4th and Elm Sts., Cincinnati.
Church Advocate.	Church Advocate Print....1133 Park Ave., New York.
Church Lib.	Church Library Association....Cambridge, Mass.
Church Missions.	Church Missions Publishing Co....211 State St., Hartford, Ct.
Churchill, C. N.	Churchill, Mrs. C. N....834 E. High St., Colorado Springs, Colo.
Cin. Medical.	Cincinnati Medical Book Co....905 Race St., Cincinnati.
Cincinnati & S.	Cincinnati and Springfield Publishing Co....Cincinnati.
Ciocia, V.	Ciocia, Vincent....89 Centre St., New York.
Circle.	Circle Publishing Co....15 W. 26th St., New York.
Circular Adv.	Circular Advertising Co....Cincinnati.
Cisco, J. G.	Cisco, Jay Guy....Vanderbilt Law Bldg., Nashville, Tenn.
Citer-Digest.	Citer-Digest Co....Detroit, Mich.
Citizens Pr.	Citizens Printing Shop....Los Angeles, Cal.
City Club, Chicago.	City Club of Chicago....228 S. Clark Ct., Chicago.
City Hist. Phil.	City History Society of Philadelphia..1623 Chestnut St., Philadelphia.
City Lib. Assoc.	City Library Association....Springfield, Mass.
Civic Forum.	Civic Forum....23 W. 44th St., New York.
Civic League.	Civic League of St. Louis....St. Louis.
Claflin.	Claflin, H. B., Co....224 Church St., New York.
Clairmont, A. de	Clairmont, Adolfo de....10 Gardner Bldg., Toledo, O.
Clapp.	Clapp, David, & Son....Boston.
Clara Vista.	Clara Vista Press....Pasadena, Cal.
Clarion.	Clarion Publishing Co....Swathmore, Pa.
Clarion Democrat.	Clarion Democrat....Clarion, Pa.
Clark, A. H.	Clark, Arthur H., Co....Caxton Bldg., Cleveland, O.
Clark, C: E.	Clark, Charles Eugene....Covington, Ky
Clark, C. M.	Clark, C. M., Publishing Co....211 Tremont St., Boston.
Clark, D. S.	Clark, Daniel S....Pioneer Bldg., Denver, Colo.
Clark, G.	Clark, Galen....Yosemite Valley, Cal.
Clark, H: S.	Clark, Henry Spencer....100 N. 4th St., Paterson, N. J.
Clark, J. E.	Clark, J. E., Supt. of Public Instruction....Santa Fé, N. M.

Clark, M. C.	Clark, Myron C., Publishing Co.......537 So. Dearborn St., Chicago.
Clark, W:	Clark, William.........Carnegie Library, Forbes St., Pittsburgh, Pa.
Clark Pub.	Clark Publishing Co...........................Jacksonville, Ala.
Clark Univ.	Clark University Press..........................Worcester, Mass.
Clarke.	Clarke, Robert, Co.......................Government Sq., Cincinnati.
Clarke, E. C.	Clarke, Mrs. E. C...................................Naples, N. Y.
Clarke, E. H.	Clarke, E. H., & Brother..........................Memphis, Tenn.
Clarke, J: M.	Clarke, John Mason.......................State Hall, Albany, N. Y.
Clarke, W: B.	Clarke, William B., Co...................26 Tremont St., Boston.
Clarkson, D: B.	Clarkson, David B......................338 Wabash Ave., Chicago.
Class Journ.	Class Journal Co.........................Flatiron Bldg., New York.
Classic.	Classic Publishing Co...................................Baxley, Ga.
Clayton & C.	Clayton & Craig...Lynn, Mass.
Clement, E. H:	Clement, Edward Henry..........10 Concord Ave., Cambridge, Mass.
Clements, F: E.	Clements, Frederick E. (State Botanist),.........Minneapolis, Minn.
Clerk Agency.	Clerk Agency...................................Providence, R. I.
Cleveland, R.	Cleveland, Robert.................................San Francisco.
Cleveland Homeopath.	Cleveland Homeopathic Publishing Co., 668 Rose Bldg., Cleveland, O.
Cleveland News.	Cleveland News Co....................1552 W. 3d St., Cleveland, O.
Cleveland Press.	Cleveland Press (Clinical Review Publishing Co.), 346 Ogden Ave., Chicago.
Cleveland Pub. Co.	Cleveland Publishing Co. (now Gardner Printing Co.)......Cleveland.
Cleveland Pub. Lib.	Cleveland Public Library..............................Cleveland, O.
Clews, H:	Clews, Henry.........................15 Broad St., New York.
Clifford & L.	Clifford & Lawton.........................1 E. 28th St., New York.
Cline, G. P.	Cline, George Polk....................................Larned, Kan.
Clinic.	Clinic Publishing Co.................Ravenswood Station, Chicago.
Clinical.	Clinical Review Publishing Co. *See* Cleveland Press.
Clode.	Clode, Edward J.......................156 Fifth Ave., New York.
Cloister.	Cloister Press...Peoria, Ill.
Clough, S. D.	Clough, S. DeWitt.......................................Chicago.
Clover.	Clover Press........................... 48 Cliff St., New York.
Club for Colonial Repr.	Club for Colonial Reprints........................Providence, R. I.
Club Odd Vol.	Club of Odd Volumes.......................................Boston.
Clymer, R. C.	Clymer, Reuben Swinburne............................Allentown, Pa.
Coats, M. C.	Coats, Mack Colvin.............23 Montgomery St., San Francisco.
Cobb, E. L.	Cobb, E. L...................South Branch, N. H. D. V. S., Va.
Cobbey, J. E.	Cobbey, J. E...Beatrice, Neb.
Cobden.	Cobden Publishing Co...........Colorado Bldg., Washington, D. C.
Coburn Press.	Coburn Press...Boston.
Cochran, J: S.	Cochran, Judge John Salesbury.....................St. Clairsville, O.
Cochrane.	Cochrane Publishing Co., Inc...Tribune Bldg., Park Row, New York.
Cockayne, E. O.	Cockayne, E. O.........................211 Tremont St., Boston.
Cocke Co.	Cocke Co...San Antonio, Tex.
Cody, S.	Cody, Sherwin.......................1411 Security Bldg., Chicago.
Coe-M.	Coe-Mortimer Co............................24 Stone St., New York.
Coffin, G. B.	Coffin, Gorham B.......................124 S. Park Ave., Chicago.
Col. Tool Steel.	Columbia Tool Steel Co......................................Chicago.
Coldwater, C: H:	Coldwater, Charles Henry..........1411 Ryan St., Lake Charles, La.
Cole.	Cole, A. I., & Co...Boston.
Cole, A. S.	Cole, Arthur Stanley..............................Manasquan, N. J.
Cole, L. E.	Cole, L. E., Music Publishing Co..............Port Angeles, Wash.
Colegrove.	Colegrove, E. H., Co...................67 Wabash Ave., Chicago.
Coleman, W: M.	Coleman, William Magruder..............52 William St., New York.
Colgrove, C. P:	Colgrove, Chauncey Peter..........2422 Normal St., Cedar Falls, Ia.
College Assoc. Pub.	College Association Publishing Co..................Los Angeles, Cal.
College Pub. Co.	College Publishing Co....................1721 Quincy St., Chicago.
Collier.	Collier, P. F., & Son................416-424 W. 13th St., New York.
Collier, A. L.	Collier, Arthur Luke...................................Beverly, Mass.
Collins, H. C.	Collins, Hilda C....................................San Antonio, Tex.
Collins, H. & Co.	Collins, Hauser & Co..........623 13th St., N. W., Washington, D. C.
Collins, J: M.	Collins, John M...Chicago.
Colo. Manuf.	Colorado Manufacturers' Association........................Denver, Colo.
Colo. Sci. Soc.	Colorado Scientific Society.........................Denver, Colo.
Colo. State Normal.	Colorado State Normal School.......................Greeley, Colo.
Colo. Supt. Sch.	Colorado Superintendent of Schools...................Denver, Colo.
Colonial Press (Ct.)	Colonial Press.....................................Mt. Carmel, Ct.
Colonial Press, (Ind.)	Colonial Press.....................................Fort Wayne, Ind.
Colonial Soc. of Mass.	Colonial Society of Massachusetts..............28 State St., Boston

Columbia Pr.	Columbia Printing Co............Chicago.
Columbia Pub.	Columbia Publishing House............Chicago.
Columbia Sch. Poultry.	Columbia School of Poultry............Waterville, N. Y.
Columbia Univ.	Columbia University Press.........Morningside Heights, New York. Lemcke & Buechner, Agents, 30-32 West 27th St., New York.
Columbus.	Columbus Press............120 W. 60th St., New York.
Columbus Citizens' Tel.	Columbus Citizens' Telephone Co............Columbus, O.
Com. Brazil.	Commission for the Economic Expansion of Brazil, U. S. Organization Office............Room 1781, 50 Church St., New York.
Com. of One Hundred.	Committee of One Hundred on National Health, 69 Church St., New Haven, Ct.
Com. Railway.	Committee on Railway Mail Pay.....Grand Central Station, Chicago.
Com. Town History.	Committee on Town History............Cohasset, Mass.
Combe.	Combe Printing Co............St. Joseph, Mo.
Commercial Pr. Co.	Commercial Printing Co............Raleigh, N. C.
Commercial Pr. Ho.	Commercial Printing House, 388-90 S. Los Angeles St., Los Angeles, Cal.
Commercial Sci.	Commercial Science System............Scranton, Pa.
Commercial World.	Commercial World Publishing Co., 164-172 Griswold St., Detroit, Mich.
Common Sense Pub.	Common Sense Pub. Co............St. Louis.
Commonwealth Pr.	Commonwealth Press............Worcester, Mass.
Commonwealth Pub.	Commonwealth Publishing Co............318 W. 45th St., New York.
Compton.	Compton, F. E., & Co............200 Monroe St., Chicago.
Comstock, W: T.	Comstock, William T., Co............23 Warren St., New York.
Comstock Pub.	Comstock Publishing Co............43 East Ave., Ithaca, N. Y.
Comtelburo.	Comtelburo, Ltd............16 Beaver St., New York.
Concord Comm. Club.	Concord Commercial Club............Concord, N. H.
Concordia Pub.	Concordia Publishing House............St. Louis.
Concrete Engineering.	Concrete Engineering............Cleveland, O.
Concrete Pub.	Concrete Publishing Co............Detroit, Mich.
Confederate Museum.	Confederate Museum............Richmond, Va.
Confederated Southern.	Confederated Southern Memorial Association......New Orleans, La.
Congdon, C. H.	Congdon, C. H............Chicago.
Conger, C. B.	Conger, Clinton Barker...224 So. Prospect St., Grand Rapids, Mich.
Congregation Mikve Israel.	Congregation Mikve Israel.........Broad and York Sts., Philadelphia.
Conjurers Mag.	Conjurers' Magazine Publishing Co.......278 W. 113th St., New York.
Conkey.	Conkey, W. B., Co............Hammond, Ind.
Conklin, A.	Conklin, Arthur............Grant's Pass, Ore.
Conn. Com. Tuberculosis.	Connecticut Commission to Investigate Tuberculosis....Hartford, Ct.
Conn. Hist.	Connecticut Historical Society............Hartford, Ct.
Conn. Lib.	Connecticut State Library............Hartford, Ct.
Conn. Pub. Lib.	Connecticut Public Library Committee............Hartford, Ct.
Connecticut.	Connecticut, State of............Hartford, Ct.
Connelley, W: E.	Connelley, William Elsey............816 Lincoln St., Topeka, Kan.
Connoisseurs' Press.	Connoisseurs' Press............Jersey City, N. J.
Connor, R. D. W.	Connor, Robert Diggs Wimberly............Raleigh, N. C.
Conrad, H: C.	Conrad, Henry C............Wilmington, Del.
Consol. Pub.	Consolidated Publishing Co............St. Louis.
Consolidated Safety.	Consolidated Safety Valve Co............85 Liberty St., New York.
Contant, G: C.	Contant, George C............San Bernardino, Cal.
Contemporary Club.	Contemporary Club............Davenport, Ia.
Contractor Pub	Contractor Publishing Co............318 Security Bldg., Chicago.
Contractors and Dealers.	Contractors' & Dealers' Exchange............New Orleans, La.
Cook.	Cook, David C., Publishing Co............Elgin, Ill.
Cook, C: C.	Cook, Charles Cyrus............R. 926, 150 Nassau St., New York.
Cook, H. M.	Cook, Howard M............Route 2, Concord, N. H.
Cook, S: N.	Cook, Samuel Newton............88 E. Towne St., Columbus, O.
Cooke, P.	Cooke, Patrick............25 Broad St., Room 612, New York.
Cooke, R. G.	Cooke, Robert Grier, Inc............542 Fifth Ave., New York.
Cooke, V. T.	Cooke, V. T........State Director of Dry Farming, Cheyenne, Wyo.
Cooley, J. H.	Cooley, James H............Rogers, O.
Coolidge, A. C.	Coolidge, Asenath Carver....1025 Washington St., Watertown, N. Y.
Coolidge, E. L.	Coolidge, Emelyn Lincoln............7 West 92d St., New York.

Cooney, P. J. Cooney, Patrick Joseph... 142 Frank St., Bridgeport, Ct.
Cooper, W: F. **Cooper, William Funk**... Kreetan, Mich.
Co-operative Pr. Co-operative Printery... 344 Sixth St., Milwaukee, Wis.
Co-operative Pr. Co. Co-operative Printing Co... 5623 Drexel Ave., Chicago.
Co-operative Press. Coöperative Press... Room 303, 203 Broadway, New York.
Co-operative Pub. Co. Co-operative Publishing Co... Columbus, O.
Copeland, L. A. Copeland, Lydia A... Chariton, Ia.
Cornell Univ. Cornell University... Ithaca, N. Y.
Cornish, L. C. Cornish, L. C... Hingham, Mass.
Corona Pub. Corona Publishing Co... 65 West Broadway, New York.
Corp. Manual. Corporation Manual Co... 34 Nassau St., New York.
Corp. Trust Co. Corporation Trust Co... 43 Wall St., New York.
Corporations. Corporations Organization... 100 Broadway, New York.
Corr. Inst. Correspondence Institute of America... Scranton, Pa.
Corwin, R. W. Corwin, R. W... Pueblo, Colo.
Cosmo. Cosmo Studio Co... 437 Fifth Ave., New York.
Cotter, J. S. Cotter, Joseph Seamon... 2306 Magazine St., Louisville, Ky.
Courtright. Courtright, W. H... Denver, Colo.
Countryman, C. C. Countryman, Carl Chapin... 617 Steinway Hall, Chicago.
Courier-Journ. Courier-Journal Job Printing Co... Louisville, Ky.
Courier Press. Courier Press... Winfield, Kan.
Couts, C: O. Couts, Charles O... Newcomerstown, O.
Cowell, A. T. Cowell, Alexander Tyng... Washington, D. C.
Cowing, W. & W. Cowing, White & Wait... 49 Wall St., New York.
Cowles, W: L. Cowles, William Lyman... Amherst, Mass.
Cox, R. L. Cox, Robert Lynn... 1 Madison Ave., R. 2107, New York.
Coxe, M. Coxe, Macgrane... 63 Wall St., New York.
Coyle. Coyle, W. H., & Co... Houston, Tex.
Cozart, W. F. Cozart, Winfield Forrest... Atlantic City, N. J.
Craftsman's Home Study. Craftsman's Home Study Schools... Freeport, Ill.
Cram, G: F. Cram, George F. . 55-61 Market St., Chicago; 130 Fulton St., New York.
Crandall, R. R. N. Crandall, Mrs. Rosa **Ruth Neil**... Jamestown, N. Y.
Crandall, W. D. Crandall, Capt. Warren Daniel... St. Louis.
Crandall Pub. Crandall Publishing Co... 510 Security Bldg., Chicago.
Crane. Crane & Co... 110 E. 8th Ave., Topeka, Kan.
Crane, J. E. Crane, Julia Ettie... 60 Main St., Potsdam, N. Y.
Crane, R. T. Crane, R. T... 1214 So. Canal St., Chicago.
Crane, U. E. Crane, Utley E... 501 Commonwealth Trust Bldg., Philadelphia.
Craven-D. Craven-Dean Co... 140 N. 11th St., Philadelphia.
Crawford, J. S. Crawford, James Shannon... Cherokee, Ia.
Credit Corporation. Credit Corporation of America... St. Louis.
Cree. Cree Publishing Co... 122 S. 6th St., Minneapolis, Minn.
Crescent Pub. Crescent Publishing Association. Care of A. Chittick, 1546 Wieland St., Chicago.
Crist, A. H. Crist, Arthur H., Co... Cooperstown, N. Y.
Critchell, R. S. Critchell, Rob. Siderfin... Chicago.
Critchett, F. E. Critchett, F. E... Watertown, Mass.
Critchfield, N. B. Critchfield, N. B., Sec'y of Agriculture... Harrisburg, Pa.
Criterion. Criterion Publishing Co... Chicago
Critic & G. Critic & Guide Co... 12 Mt. Morris Park W., New York.
Croll, P. C. Croll, Rev. Philip Columbus... Beardstown, Ill.
Crombie & Co. Crombie, Robert J., & Co... Brooklyn, N. Y.
Cromarty. Cromarty Law Book Co... 121 Chestnut St., Philadelphia.
Crosby, J. A. Crosby, J. A... Jamaica Plain, Mass.
Cross, C: R. Cross, Charles Robert... Boston.
Cross Co. Cross Co... Chicago.
Crowell. Crowell, Thomas Y., Co... 426 W. Broadway, New York.
Cullens, F. B. Cullens, F. B... Ozark, Ala.
Cultivator Pub. Cultivator Publishing Co... P. O. Drawer 798, Atlanta, Ga.
Crummer, W. F. Crummer, W. F... 134 S. Kenilworth Ave., Oak Park, Ill.
Cumberland Press. Cumberland Press... Nashville, Tenn.
Cuming, M. A. Cuming, Mari A... 43-49 Bleecker St., New York.
Cummings, W: L. Cummings, William Leon... 803 McBride St., Syracuse, N. Y.
Cuneo. Cuneo, John F. Co... Chicago.
Cunningham, C. & W. Cunningham, Curtiss & Welch... 565-567 Market St., San Francisco.
Cunningham, H: W. Cunningham, Henry Winchester... 89 State St., Boston.
Cupples & L. Cupples & Leon Co... 30th St. and 4th Ave., New York.
Curlander. Curlander, M... 208 N. Calvert St., Baltimore, Md.
Current Lit. Current Literature Publishing Co... 134 W. 29th St., New York.

Currier Pub.	Currier Publishing Co..................107 S. Clinton St., Chicago.
Curry, J.	Curry, Rev. James..................................Newark, Cal.
Curtis, E: S.	Curtis, Edward S..................................Seattle, Wash.
Curtis, H. G:	Curtis, Harris George.............................Appleton, Wis.
Curtis, N. C.	Curtis, Nathaniel Cortlandt..........................Auburn, Ala.
Curtis Adv.	Curtis Advertising Co...............................Detroit, Mich.
Curtis & C.	Curtis & Cameron..........................75 Pierce Bldg., Boston.
Curtiss.	Curtiss Book Co............................Box 607 Denver, Colo.
Curtman, I.	Curtman, Ida.......................3933 Lexington Ave., St. Louis.
Cushing, H. C., jr.	Cushing, Harry C., Jr....................220 Broadway, New York.
Cutter, E.	Cutter, Ephraim.........................251 W. 81st St., New York.
Cycle Press.	Cycle Press...........................421 Atlantic Ave., Boston.
D. A. R., Germantown Chap.	Daughters of the American Revolution...........Germantown, Pa.
D. A. R., Hannah Winthrop Chap.	Daughters of the American Revolution (Hannah Winthrop Chapter), Cambridge, Mass.
D. A. R. Saranac Chap.	Daughters of American Revolution (Saranac Chapter), Plattsburgh, N. Y.
D. C. L. A.	District of Columbia Library Association...........Washington, D. C.
D. D. Pub.	D. D. Publishing Co................4630 Grand Boulevard, Chicago.
Dadant.	Dadant & Sons......................................Hamilton, Ill.
Daggy, M. L.	Daggy, Maynard Lee....Care Democrat Printing Co., Madison, Wis.
Daily Oklahoman.	Daily Oklahoman............................Oklahoma City, Okla.
Daily Record.	Daily Record Co.................................Baltimore, Md.
Dale, J. G.	Dale, James Gary......................................Troy, S. C.
Daly.	Daly & Co.............................P. O. Box 137, Philadelphia.
Damon, F. A.	Damon, Fannie A..............Harris and Chase Sts., Clinton, Mass.
Damon, H: B.	Damon, Henry B...................................Katonah, N. Y.
Dana.	Dana, William B., Co.....................138 Front St., New York.
Dandridge, A. S.	Dandridge, Mrs. A. S.......................Shepherdstown, W. Va.
Daniels, P.	Daniels, Percy..........................R. R. No. 4, Carthage, Mo.
Danner.	Danner Publishing Co...............1508 Polk St., San Francisco.
Danner, T. J.	Danner, Thomas Jefferson.........................Pittsburgh, Pa.
Danziger, G. A.	Danziger, Gustave Adolphe.............30 E. 127th St., New York.
Darling, H. B.	Darling, H. B..................................Washington, D. C.
Darling, J. T.	Darling, Jasper T.........................79 Dearborn St., Chicago.
Dau.	Dau Publishing Co......................40 W. 33d St., New York.
Davenport, A.	Davenport, Allen..........................P. O. Box 1341, Boston.
Davenport, E.	Davenport, Eugene..............College of Agriculture, Urbana, Ill.
Davey, J:	Davey, John..Kent, O.
Davidson, C. W.	Davidson, C. W...............................Cooperstown, N. Y.
Davidson, H. A.	Davidson, Mrs. Hannah Amelia...................Cambridge, Mass.
Davis.	Davis, F. A., Co.................1914-1916 Cherry St., Philadelphia.
Davis, A. McF.	Davis, Andrew McFarland..........................Cambridge, Mass.
Davis, J: A.	Davis, John A...................................Lestershire, N. Y.
Davis, J: M.	Davis, John McCan.................................Springfield, Ill.
Davis, O. P.	Davis, O. P...........................1620 15th St., Denver, Colo.
Davis, R. S.	Davis, R. S., & Co....................441 Wood St., Pittsburgh, Pa.
Davis, S: I.	Davis, Samuel Ishbeyre...........................Nanticoke, Pa.
Davis, W. B.	Davis, Walter B.........................108 Fulton St., New York.
Davis, W: E:	Davis, William Edward, Jr..................1 Nassau St., New York.
Davis & B.	Davis & Banister...................................Worcester, Mass.
Davis Bros.	Davis Bros.......................................Kansas City, Mo.
Davis Press.	Davis Press.......................38-44 Front St., Worcester, Mass.
Davis-G.	Davis-Gibbs Co................350 Dickinson St., Springfield, Mass.
Davison, A.	Davison, Alvin.......................Lafayette College, Easton, Pa.
Davison, A. H.	Davison, A. H......................................Des Moines, Ia.
Davison, A. W.	Davison, Arthur W..............420 Winson St., Jamestown, N. Y.
Davison, E. S.	Davison, Ellen Scott............90 Columbia University, New York.
Dawson, M. T.	Dawson, Minnie Twilight..............622 Rock St., Hannibal, Mo.
Day & K.	Day & Knappen......................Hackney Bldg., St. Paul, Minn.
Dayton Pub. Lib.	Dayton Public Library.......................................Dayton, O.
Dealy.	Dealy, J. V., Co......................................Houston, Tex.
Dearing.	Dearing, Charles T., Printing Co......356 Fourth Ave., Louisville, Ky.
Debar.	Debar, Joseph......................301 Union Bank Bldg., Cincinnati.
De Bower-C.	De Bower-Chapline Co..Chicago.
De Bower-E.	De Bower-Elliott Co.....................315 Dearborn St., Chicago.
Dedham Transcript.	Dedham Transcript Printing and Publishing House...Dedham, Mass.
De La Mare.	De La Mare, A. T., Printing and Publishing Co., 2 Duane St., New York.
De Laurence, S.	De Laurence, Scott & Co............1514 Masonic Temple, Chicago.
Del. College.	Delaware College.......................................Newark, Del.

Delaware Hist. Soc.	Delaware Historical Society	924 Market St., Wilmington, Del.
Delbridge.	Delbridge Co	104 N. 6th St., St. Louis, Mo.
De Long, J: E.	De Long, John Edmund	Kirkland, Ill.
Dell, S.	Dell, Sidney	Los Angeles, Cal.
Delmarter Pub.	Delmarter Publishing Co.	Care of James Elkworth Delmarter, Chicago.
Delp, J. D.	Delp, J. D	Springfield, Mo.
Dement Pub.	Dement Publishing Co	325 Dearborn St., Chicago.
Democracy and Civil Service.	Democracy and Civil Service News	23 Duane St., New York.
Democracy Pr.	Democracy Printing Co	23 Duane St., New York.
Democrat Pr. and Litho.	Democrat Printing and Lithographing Co	Little Rock, Ark.
Democrat Pr. Co.	Democrat Printing Co	Madison, Wis.
Democratic.	Democratic National Committee, Text-book Dept.,	Auditorium Annex, Chicago.
Denholm.	Denholm, McKay Co	Worcester, Mass.
Denison, T: S.	Denison, Thomas Stewart	163 Randolph St., Chicago.
Dennen, E. J.	Dennen, Rev. Ernest Joseph	80 S. Common St., Lynn, Mass.
Denrich.	Denrich Press	Chula Vista, Cal.
Denver & Rio Grande.	Denver & Rio Grande Railroad, Passenger Department,	Denver, Colo.
Denver Int. Corr. Sch.	Denver International Correspondence School of Money.	Care of John A. Anderson & Co., Box 158, Denver, Colo.
De Puy.	De Puy, Clarence C	249 W. Fayette St., Syracuse, N. Y.
Deran-Smith, E.	Deran-Smith, Mrs. Edna	Kalamazoo, Mich.
Deseret News.	Deseret News Co	Salt Lake City, Utah.
Deseret S. S. Un.	Deseret Sunday School Union,	Union Book Store, 44 E. S. Temple St., Salt Lake City, Utah.
Desjardins, A. U.	Desjardins, Arthur Uldéric	321 Hoffman St., Baltimore, Md.
Desmond, H. J.	Desmond, Humphrey Joseph	P. O. Drawer 36, Milwaukee, Wis.
Detroit Bus. Univ.	Detroit Business University	Detroit, Mich.
Dettner-Travers.	Dettner-Travers Press	San Francisco.
Deuther, C: G:	Deuther, Charles George	327 Washington St., Buffalo, N. Y.
De Vinne.	De Vinne Press	395 Lafayette St., New York.
Devney, R. S.	Devney, Raymond Smith	Bowling Green, Ky.
De Waters, L. S.	De Waters, Mrs. Lillian Stephenson	965 E. Main St., Stamford, Ct.
Dewey Pub.	Dewey Publishing Co	San Francisco.
De Witt, C: H.	De Witt, Charles Howard	Valparaiso, Ind.
De Witt & S.	DeWitt & Snelling	9 Telegraph Ave., Oakland, Cal.
De Wolfe.	DeWolfe & Fiske Co	20 Franklin St., Boston.
Dick.	Dick & Fitzgerald	18 Ann St., New York.
Dick, S: M.	Dick, Rev. Samuel Medary	Minneapolis, Minn.
Dickerson, F. B.	Dickerson, F. B., Co	Detroit, Mich.
Dickert, T: W.	Dickert, Rev. Thomas Wilson	Reading, Pa.
Dickey.	Dickey, L. S., & Co	79 Dearborn St., Chicago.
Dickson.	Dickson, J. A., Publishing Co	Chicago.
Didion.	Didion, L., & Co	311 W. 59th St., New York.
Dietz Pr.	Dietz Printing Co	Richmond, Va.
Dietzgen, E.	Dietzgen, Eugene Co.,	214-220 E. 23d St., New York; 181 Monroe St., Chicago.
Dilley.	Dilley, Arthur Urbana, & Co., Inc	5 Park St., Boston.
Dillingham, G: W.	Dillingham, George W., Co	12-16 E. 22d St., New York.
Dinkins, J.	Dinkins, James	2025 Coliseum St., New Orleans, La.
Dilworth, H. P.	Dilworth, Hiram Powers	Chicago.
Dispatch Pub.	Dispatch Publishing Co	Clay Center, Kan.
Dissell.	Dissell Publishing Co	P. O. Box 273, Hartford, Ct.
Distribution League.	Distribution League	21 Union Trust Bldg., Indianapolis, Ind.
Ditmas, C: A.	Ditmas, Charles Andrew	350 Fulton St., Brooklyn, N. Y.
Ditson.	Ditson, Oliver, Co	150 Tremont St., Boston.
Dix, I. S.	Dix, Irving Sidney	Shehawken, Pa.
Dixie.	Dixie Publishing Co	Moravian Falls, N. C.
Dixie Bk.	Dixie Book Shop	41 Liberty St., New York.
Dixie Miller.	Dixie Miller Co	Nashville, Tenn.
Dixon.	Dixon-Hanson Co	315 Dearborn St., Chicago.
Dodd.	Dodd, Mead & Co	443 4th Ave., New York.
Dodge.	Dodge Publishing Co	214-220 E. 23d St., New York.
Dodge, A. J.	Dodge, A. Johnson	20 Wabon St., Boston.
Dodge, B. W.	Dodge, B. W., & Co.	Now Wm. Rickey & Co., 43 W. 27th St., New York.
Dodge, G: M.	Dodge, George M	Valparaiso, Ind.
Dodge City.	Dodge City Kansas Journal	Dodge City, Kan.
Doerflinger, C: H.	Doerflinger, Charles H	254 94th St., Milwaukee, Wis.

Dogdom Pub.	Dogdom Publishing Co....Battle Creek, Mich.
Doherty, J. J.	Doherty, James Joseph....720 Main St., Riverside, Cal.
Doherty Op.	Doherty Operating Co....60 Wall St., New York.
Dolbey.	Dolbey, Edward P., & Co....3607 Woodland Ave., Philadelphia.
Dole, N. H.	Dole, Nathan Haskell....Jamaica Plain, Boston.
Doll, W: F:	Doll, William Frederick....Liberty, N. Y.
Dolphin.	Dolphin Press....1305 Arch St., Philadelphia.
Dom. and For. Mission.	Domestic and Foreign Missionary Society of the Protestant Episcopal Church....281 Fourth Ave., New York.
Domestic Engineering.	Domestic Engineering....49-53 N. Jefferson St., Chicago.
Don Coronado.	Don Coronado Co....Seneca, Kan.
Donlan, T: J.	Donlan, Thomas J....Colonial Bldg., Boston.
Donnelley.	Donnelley, R. R., & Sons Co....Plymouth Court, Chicago.
Donohue.	Donohue, M. A., & Co....407-429 Dearborn St., Chicago.
Donovan, J. M.	Donovan, Joseph Mitchell....121 W. 9th St., Sioux Falls, S. D.
Dony.	Dony, J. H....Washington, D. C.
Doolittle & K.	Doolittle & Kulling, Inc....Philadelphia.
Doran.	Doran, George H., Co. (Supplies books of Life Pub. Co. Purchased books of A. C. Armstrong & Son).35 W. 32d St., New York.
Doremus, P.	Doremus, Philip....Montclair, N. J.
Dorris, C: E. W.	Dorris, Charles Elias Webb....West Nashville, Tenn.
Doscher.	Doscher, C. H., & Co. Books now supplied by J. D. Newton, 156 5th Ave., New York.
Doub.	Doub & Co....717 Market St., San Francisco.
Doubleday, P.	Doubleday, Page & Co. (purchased books of McClure Co.), Garden City, N Y.
Dougherty, C: A.	Dougherty, Charles A....Bristol, Pa.
Douglas Co. Abs.	Douglas County Abstract and Loan Co....Tuscola, Ill.
Douglas Pr.	Douglas Printing Co....Omaha, Neb.
Douglassville.	Douglassville Squab Co....Douglassville, Pa.
Douthat, R. W:	Douthat, Robert William....Morgantown, W. Va.
Dow, G: F.	Dow, George Francis....Essex Institute, Salem, Mass.
Dowler, J. S.	Dowler, J. S., & Co....St. Louis.
Dowling, G:	Dowling, George....280 Dolores St., San Francisco.
Dowling, E. S.	Dowling E. S....Los Angeles, Cal.
Doxey Bk.	Doxey Book Shop Co....formerly Baltimore, Md.
Doyle, J:	Doyle, John....Fayetteville, N. Y.
Downey.	Downey & Co., Inc....Mint Arcade Bldg., Philadelphia.
Downing.	Downing, R. F., & Co....13 William St., New York.
Doyle, G.	Doyle, Gregory....307 W. Genesee St., Syracuse, N. Y.
Doyle, W: S.	Doyle, William S....Asbury Park, N. J.
Drake.	Drake, Frederick J., & Co....1323-1325 Michigan Ave., Chicago.
Drake Law Bk.	Drake Law Book Co....407 Wayne Co., Bank Bldg., Detroit, Mich.
Dramatic.	Dramatic Publishing Co. (C. H. Sergel, Pres.), 358 Dearborn St., Chicago.
Draper, A. S.	Draper, Andrew Sloan....Albany, N. Y.
Draughon's.	Draughon's Practical Business College Co....Nashville, Tenn.
Drew & L.	Drew & Lewis....95 Cliff St., New York.
Dreamers' Press.	Dreamers' Press....132 E. 23d St., New York.
Driggers.	Driggers, James E....Shawnee, Okla.
Druckerman.	Druckerman, S....50 Canal St., New York.
Duffield.	Duffield & Co....36 W. 37th St., New York.
Duggan, F. J.	Duggan, F. J., M.D.... Grand Forks, N. D.
Dulany.	Dulany, William J. C., Co. Now Dulany-Verney Co.
Dulfer Pr.	Dulfer, Alexander, Printing Co....San Francisco.
Dumont, E. R.	Dumont, Earl Royce....18 W. 27th St., New York.
Dumont & H.	Dumont & Hayward....18 W. 27th St., New York.
Dunbar, E. M.	Dunbar, E. M....53 State St., Boston.
Dungan, D: R.	Dungan, David Roberts....1362 26th St., Des Moines, Ia.
Dunlap, C: E.	Dunlap, Charles Eugene....Tower Hill, Ill.
Dunlap Pony Co.	Dunlap Pony Co....Greenfield, O.
Du Pont de Nemours.	Du Pont de Nemours, E. I., Powder Co....Wilmington, Del.
Dupuy, B: H.	Dupuy, Benjamin Hunter....Beverly, W. Va.
Du Puy, H.	Du Puy, Herbert....Pittsburgh, Pa.
Durant, S. H.	Durand, Silas H....Southampton, Pa.
Durkee, J. H.	Durkee, Rev. Jacob Hilton....Rochester, N. Y.
Dutton.	Dutton, E. P., & Co....31 W. 23d St., New York.
Dwight, F:	Dwight, Frederick....52 William St., New York.
Dyke, A. L.	Dyke, Andrew Lee....3947 Washington St., St. Louis.
Dyrsen.	Dyrsen & Pfeiffer. (Books purchased by William R. Jenkins Co.)
E., C. E.	E., C. E....Dewey House, 4th and Hanover Sts., San Francisco.

Eagle.	Eagle Printing and Binding Co........................Pittsfield, Mass.
Eagle Pub.	Eagle Publishing Co...................................Reading, Pa.
Eales, I. J.	Eales, Irving James, M.D.........Main and Spring St., Belleville, Ill.
Earley, G: G.	Earley, George G.......................................Newton, Ia.
Earle.	Earle, James H., & Co.....................125 Summer St., Boston.
Earlham Coll.	Earlham College.....................................Richmond, Ind.
Early.	Early Printing and Publishing Co..................Memphis, Tenn.
Easterday, L. F. M.	Easterday, Levi Fast M..................................Lincoln, Neb.
Eastern Ill. State Normal Sch.	Eastern Illinois State Normal School...............Charleston, Ill.
Eastman Coll.	Eastman College.............................Poughkeepsie, N. Y.
Eastman Kodak.	Eastman Kodak Co.................................Rochester, N. Y.
Easton, F. A.	Easton, F. A............................Box 243, Worcester, Mass.
Eaton, C. & P.	Eaton, Crane & Pike Co...................225 5th Ave., New York.
Eaton & Co.	Eaton & Co.........................623 S. Wabash Ave., Chicago.
Eaton & M.	Eaton & Mains..........................150 Fifth Ave., New York.
Eau Claire Bk.	Eau Claire Book & Stationery Co.................Eau Claire, Wis.
Ebbert & R.	Ebbert & Richardson...Cincinnati.
Eby, H: H.	Eby, Henry Harrison......................................Mendota, Ill.
Eccles, L. F.	Eccles, Lewis Franklin...............................Pullman, Wash.
Echo Press.	Echo Press...............Shortridge High School, Indianapolis, Ind.
Eclipse.	Eclipse Publishing Co...St. Louis.
Eddy County Provost.	Eddy County Provost..........................New Rockford, N. D.
Eddy Press.	Eddy Press Corporation.............................Winchester, Va.
Eden Pub.	Eden Publishing House.............1716-18 Chouteau Ave., St. Louis.
Edes, M. J.	Edes, Marcia Josephine...............................Newport, N. H.
Edgar, J: R.	Edgar, John R., & Co..Manila, P. I.
Edgerley, A. S.	Edgerley, Asa Sanborn.....................................Fresno, Cal.
Editor Co.	Editor Co...Ridgwood, N. J.
Edmonds, F. S.	Edmonds, Franklin S..............614 Franklin Bldg., Philadelphia.
Edmondson, C. H.	Edmondson, Charles Howard........Washburn College, Topeka, Kan.
Edmunds, A. J.	Edmunds, Albert Joseph...............1300 Locust St., Philadelphia.
Educational Aid.	Educational Aid Society......946 First National Bank Bldg., Chicago.
Educ. Co.	Educational Co.....................323 Dearborn St., Chicago.
Educ. Exhibit.	Educational Exhibition Co.........................Providence, R. I.
Educ. Press.	Educational Press, Inc...............17 Wentworth Bldg., Chicago.
Educ. Pub.	Educational Publishing Co..................50 Bromfield St., Boston.
Educ. Review.	Educational Review Publishing Co., W. 116th St., near Amsterdam Ave., New York.
Educator.	Educator School Supply Co..........................Mitchell, S. D.
Edwards.	Edwards & Broughton Printing Co....................Raleigh, N. C.
Edwards, R: H:	Edwards, Richard Henry...........237 Langdon St., Madison, Wis.
Edwards, W. H.	Edwards, Ward Hampton.....................................Liberty, Mo.
Edwards, W. S.	Edwards, W. S., Co.................16 E. Seneca St., Buffalo, N. Y.
Edwards Bk.	Edwards Bookstore.................................Rochester, N. Y.
Egan, J. W:	Egan, James William...Chicago.
Ege, A. H.	Ege, Alexander H...........................Mechanicsburg, Pa.
Eger, A.	Eger, Alexander...........................42 La Salle St., Chicago.
Egerton Press.	Egerton Press...........................934 11th St., Philadelphia.
Eggerth, W.	Eggerth, Werner............1614 Montgomery Ave., Spokane, Wash.
Ehlers, E: M. L.	Ehlers, Edward M. L..Masonic Hall,23d St. and 6th Ave., New York.
Eichelberger.	Eichelberger Book Co.................................Baltimore, Md.
Eickemeyer. C.	Eickemeyer, Carl................Sub-station B, Poughkeepsie, N. Y.
Eickmann, W.	Eickmann, Walter..............................1722 Adams St., New York.
Eiesland, J: A.	Eiesland, John A.......West Virginia University, Morgantown, W. Va.
Elder, P.	Elder, Paul, & Co.....................239 Grant Ave., San Francisco.
Elder, T: L.	Elder, Thomas L...........................32 E. 23d St., New York.
Elec. Journ.	Electric Journal...Pittsburgh, Pa.
Elec. Mag.	Electricity Magazine Corporation..........Monadnock Bldg., Chicago.
Elec. Pub.	Electrical Publishing Co........90 West St., Room 1408, New York.
Electrochemical Pub.	Electrochemical Publishing Co...........239 W. 9th St., New York.
Ellett, F. G.	Ellett, Frank Gates..Mason, Mich.
Elliot, M. M. S.	Elliot, Marietta M. S............................Tufts' College, Mass.
Elliott, J.	Elliott, James...Elliottson, Pa.
Ellis, C: E:	Ellis, Charles Edward.............163 E. Washington St., Chicago.
Ellis, G. H.	Ellis, G. H., Co.............................272 Congress St., Boston.
Ellis Pub.	Ellis Publishing Co..............58 W. Main St., Battle Creek, Mich.
Elm Tree Press.	Elm Tree Press...Woodstock, Vt.
Elmcroft.	Elmcroft Publishing Co...............................Greenwood, Ind.
Elmore, J. B.	Elmore, James Buchanan......................................Alamo, Ind.

Elrod, M. J.	Elrod, Morton J....Missoula, Mont.
Elwell, J. F.	Elwell, J. F., Publishing Co.....247 S. Broadway, Los Angeles, Cal.
Ely, A. D.	Ely, Anson Doner....Birdinhand, Pa.
Elzas, B. A.	Elzas, Barnett Abraham....Charleston, S. C.
Embree Pr.	Embree Printing Co....Belton, Tex.
Emerson, C: W.	Emerson, Mrs. Charles Wesley....Millis, Mass.
Emerson, E.	Emerson, Edwin....30 Church St., New York.
Emerson, G: D.	Emerson, George D....99 West Genesee St., Buffalo, N. Y.
Emerson, G. D. (Phil.)	Emerson, Gilbert D....1200 N. Broad St., Philadelphia.
Empire Bk.	Empire Book Co....68 Murray St., New York.
Empire Pub.	Empire Publishing Co....60 Wall St., New York.
Engberg-H.	Engberg-Holmberg Publishing Co.....358 W. Chicago Ave., Chicago.
Engelhardt, Z.	Engelhardt, Fr. Zephyrin....Watsonville, Cal.
Engelke, G:	Engelke, George....855 N. Clark St., Chicago.
Engineer Sch.	Engineer School, United States Army, Washington Barracks, Washington, D. D.
Engineering Mag.	Engineering Magazine....140 Nassau St., New York.
Engineering News.	Engineering News Publishing Co....220 Broadway, New York.
Englewood Pub.	Englewood Publishing House....Chicago
English Leaflet.	English Leaflet Co....1570 Fulton St., Brooklyn, N. Y.
Enterprise Pr.	Enterprise Printing Co....Milwaukee, Wis.
Enterprise Pub.	Enterprise Publishing Co....Tony, Wis.
Eppendorf, L.	Eppendorf, Lina....Pratt Institute, Brooklyn, N. Y.
Equitable Life.	Equitable Life Assurance Society....120 Broadway, New York.
Equitist.	Equitist Publishing House....Olive, Orange Co., Cal.
Erie Pr.	Erie Printing Co....1314-16 Peach St., Erie, Pa.
Erwood, W: J.	Erwood, William J., Co....717 E. 22d St., Baltimore, Md.
Eshleman, H: F.	Eshleman, Henry F....Lancaster, Pa.
Esoteric.	Esoteric Publishing Co....Applegate, Cal.
Essex Bk.	Essex Book and Print Club....Salem, Mass.
Essex Inst.	Essex Institute....Salem, Mass.
Estabrook, J: D.	Estabrook, John Davis..R. D. Route No. 1, Box 47, Westboro, Mass.
Estes.	Estes, Dana, & Co....208-218 Summer St., Boston.
Esther C. Mack Indust. Sch.	Esther C. Mack Industrial School....Salem, Mass.
Eternal Progress.	Eternal Progress....Fourth National Bank Bldg., Cincinnati.
Etzenhouser, R.	Etzenhouser, Rudolph....Detroit, Mich.
Eureka.	Eureka Publishing Co....Stigler, Okla.
Euwer, J: H.	Euwer, John Hays....New York.
Evangel.	Evangel Publishing House....Chicago.
Evans, C. E.	Evans, C. E....Austin, Tex.
Evans, C:	Evans, Charles....1413 Pratt Ave., Chicago.
Evans, D.	Evans, Mrs. Dudley....Englewood, N. J.
Evans, M. G.	Evans, May Garrettson....Baltimore, Md.
Evans, P.	Evans, Powell....Philadelphia.
Evans Music.	Evans Music Co....26 Cortlandt St., New York.
Evanston Pub. Lib.	Evanston Public Library....Evanston, Ill.
Evarts, L.	Evarts, Mrs. Lulu....Box 333, Capital Hill, Okla.
Evening Capital.	Evening Capital....Annapolis, Md.
Everett.	Everett Press Co....74 India St., Boston.
Evergreen Press.	Evergreen Press....Montrose, Pa.
Everywhere.	Everywhere Publishing Co....150 Nassau St., New York.
Evolution Pub.	Evolution Publishing Co....Park Ridge, Ill.
Ewing, J. G.	Ewing, Joseph Grant....Wilmington, Del.
Excelsior.	Excelsior Publishing House....27 E. 21st St., New York.
Excelsior Pub.	Excelsior Publishing Co....Milwaukee, Wis.
Exeter Bk.	Exeter Book Publishing Co....Exeter, N. H.
Exodus.	Exodus Publishing Co....203 Michigan Ave., Chicago.
Exporters' Enc.	Exporters' Encyclopædia Co....80 Broad St., New York.
Exposé.	Exposé Publishing Co....Roxbury, Mass.
Express.	Express Publishing Co....74 Weybosset St., Providence, R. I.
Expression.	Expression Co....308 Pierce Bldg., Copley Sq., Boston.
Fadner, G: M.	Fadner, George M....3226 Indiana Ave., Chicago.
Fair Pub.	Fair Publication House....Philadelphia.
Fairbanks, T: N.	Fairbanks, Thomas Nast....34 Union Sq., E., New York.
Fairchild Co.	Fairchild Co....42 E. 21st St., New York
Fairfax.	Fairfax Publishing Co....358 Dearborn St., Chicago.
Fairfield.	Fairfield Co....Norwalk, Ct.
Fairfield Hist.	Fairfield Historical Society....Fairfield, Ct.
Fairlie, J: A.	Fairlie, John Archibald....Ann Arbor, Mich.
Falkner, R. P.	Falkner, Roland Post....53 Maltby Bldg., Washington, D. C.

Fallon. Fallon Law Book Co. .... 83 Nassau St., New York.
Faribault Pilot. Faribault Pilot .... Faribault, Minn.
Farlow, A. Farlow, Alfred .... Boston.
Farm Impl. News. Farm Implement News Co .... Chicago.
Farm-Poultry. Farm-Poultry Publishing Co. .... Boston.
Farmer Co. Farmer Co .... Philadelphia.
Farmers' Nat. Farmers' National Congress .... Madison, Wis.
Farmers Trust Co. Farmers Trust Co. of Lancaster .... Lancaster, Pa.
Farquhar, A. B. Farquhar, Arthur B. .... York, Pa.
Farrell. Farrell, Clinton P. .... 117 E. 21st St., New York.
Farwell. Farwell, C. O. .... 134 W. 113th St., New York.
Faulk, J: H. Faulk, Mrs. John H. .... Dover, Mass.
Faurote, F. L. Faurote, Fay Leone .... Lansing, Mich.
Federal Pub. Co. Federal Publishing Co. .... Madison, Wis.
Feldmeyer, C: G. Feldmeyer, Charles G. .... Maryland Ave., Annapolis, Md.
Fell. Fell, William F., & Co .... 1222 Sansom St., Philadelphia
Fellowcraft Shop. Fellowcraft Shop .... Kinderhook, N. Y.
Fellows Gear. Fellows Gear Shaper Co .... Springfield, Vt
Fenno. Fenno, R. F., & Co .... 18 E. 17th St., New York.
Ferguson Pub. Co. Ferguson Publishing Co. .... Sherman, Tex.
Ferguson-A. Ferguson-Allen Co .... Cincinnati.
Ferina, C: Ferina, Rev. Charles .... 325 E. 145th St., New York.
Fernald. Fernald, Frederick Atherton .... 985 Lexington Ave., New York.
Fernald, C: A: Fernald, Charles A., M.D .... 1483 Washington St., Boston.
Fernald, C: H: Fernald, Charles Henry .... Amherst, Mass.
Ferree, J. B. Ferree, James Barr .... 7 Warren St., Room 202, New York.
Ferris. Ferris & Leach .... 27 S. 7th St., Philadelphia
Ferro. Ferro Machine and Foundry Co .... Cleveland, O.
Fewkes, A. H. *See* American Peony Society.
Ffoulke, C: M. Ffoulke, Charles Mathew .... Washington, D. C.
Fidelity & Casualty. Fidelity & Casualty Co .... 97 Cedar St., New York.
Fidlar & C. Fidlar & Chambers .... Davenport, Ia.
Field and Stream. Field and Stream Publishing Co .... 24 E. 21st St., New York.
Field Museum. Field Museum of Natural History (formerly Field Columbian Museum) .... Jackson Park, Chicago.
Financial Calendar. Financial Calendar Co .... 25 W Broadway, New York.
Financial Pub. Financial Publishing Co .... 185 E. State St., Columbus, O.
Fillebrown, C: B. Fillebrown, Charles Bowdoin .... 77 Summer St., Boston.
Finney, F: N. Finney, Frederick Norton .... 216 Oaklawn Ave., South Pasadena, Cal.
First Church of Christ. First Church of Christ .... Hartford, Ct.
First Eng. Evan. Luth. Ch. First English Evangelical Lutheran Church .... Pittsburgh, Pa.
Fischer. Fischer, Carl .... 6 Fourth Ave., New York.
Fischer, J. Fischer, J., & Bro. .... 7 Bible House, New York.
Fish, D. Fish, Daniel .... 2303 3d Ave. S., Minneaoplis, Minn.
Fish, S. Fish, Stuyvesant .... 214 Broadway, New York.
Fisher, F. Fisher, Frank .... Fayette and Liberty Sts., Baltimore, Md.
Fisher, J: I. Fisher, John Irvine, Publishing Co .... Louisville, Ky.
Fishleigh, W. T. Fishleigh, Walter Turner .... Ann Arbor, Mich.
Fiske & Co. Fiske & Co .... Springfield, Ill.
Fiske & Co. (Bost.) Fiske & Co .... 25 Arch St., Boston.
FitzGerald. FitzGerald, Desmond, Inc .... 156 Fifth Ave., New York.
Fitzgerald Bk. Fitzgerald Book Co .... 52 Dearborn St., Chicago.
Flamma, A. Flamma, Ario .... Care of A. L. Gregorio, 781 6th Ave., New York.
Flanagan. Flanagan, A., Co .... 521 S. Wabash Ave., Chicago.
Flanders, E. B. Flanders, Erwin Bixby .... 434 N. 37th St., East St. Louis, Ill.
Flanigan, D: W. Flanigan, David Willis .... Court House, Los Angeles, Cal.
Fleet-M. Fleet-McGinley Co .... Baltimore, Md.
Fleetwood, H: Fleetwood, Henry .... 126 E. 9th St., Los Angeles, Cal.
Fleischmann, M. C: Fleischmann, Maximilian Charles .... Cincinnati.
Fleisher. Fleisher, S. B. & B. W. .... Philadelphia.
Flem Pub. Flem Publishing Co. .... 1507 Forbes St., Pittsburgh, Pa.
Fleming, G: E. Fleming, George Elliott .... 170 Broadway, Room 412, New York.
Fleming, H: S. Fleming, Henry Stuart .... 1 Broadway, New York.
Fleming, W. L. Fleming, Walter Lynwood .... Baton Rouge, La.
Fletcher, H: F. Fletcher, Henry F. .... Hazardville, Ct.
Fletcher, J. W. Fletcher, J. W. .... Parsons, Kan.
Fletorides, N. A. Fletorides, Nicholas A. .... 938 Third Ave., New York.
Fleugel, H. Fleugel, H., & Co. .... 2562 McCulloh St., Baltimore, Md.
Fling, F. M. Fling, Fred. Morrow .... Station A, Lincoln, Neb.
Flom, G: T. Flom, George Tobias .... 611 W. Green St., Urbana, Ill.

Flood.	Flood, T. H., & Co....................201 E. Madison St., Chicago.
Flowers, W: T:	Flowers, William Thomas.............Rt. 2, Box 37, Tolbert, Tex.
Floyd, F: C.	Floyd, Frederick Clark....................P. O. Box 1531, Boston.
Floyd-G.	Floyd-Genther Press.................35 Exchange St., Buffalo, N. Y.
Fluegel, M.	Fluegel, Maurice, Co..................................Baltimore, Md.
Fly, H. K.	Fly, H. K., Co...Pennsylvania Bldg., 5th Ave. and 29th St., New York.
Flynn, P. V.	Flynn, Paul Vincent...................................Newark, N. J.
Flynn, T: J.	Flynn, Thomas J., & Co.....................62-64 Essex St., Boston.
Fogle.	Fogle Publishing Co...................Lock Box 583, Columbus, O.
Fohlin, E. V.	Fohlin, Ernest V...............232 W. 2d St., Salt Lake City, Utah.
Foley, J. W:	Foley, James William................................Bismarck, N. D.
Folk, D: H:	Folk, David Henry.......................................Teague, Tex.
Folsom, C: F.	Folsom, Charles Follen..................15 Marlborough St., Boston.
Fonic.	Fonic Publishing House..................................Ringoz, N. J.
Foote.	Foote, G. H., Publishing Co............................Detroit, Mich.
Foote, A. R.	Foote, Allen Ripley....................................Madison, Wis.
Foote, W. Y.	Foote, W. Y., Co................212 So. Warren St., Syracuse, N. Y.
For. Miss. Soc. of Un. B.	Foreign Missionary Society of United Brethren in Christ..Dayton, O.
Forbes.	Forbes & Co............................325 Dearborn St., Chicago.
Forbes, C: S.	Forbes, Charles S....................................St. Albans, N. Y.
Ford, F. C.	Ford, Francis Chipman....................................Cicero, Ill.
Ford, H:	Ford, Henry..Brownwood, Tex.
Ford, H. M.	Ford, H. M...Syracuse, N. Y.
Fordham Univ.	Fordham University Press...............110 W. 74th St., New York.
Forensic.	Forensic League...Iowa City, Ia.
Forest.	Forest and Stream Publishing Co.........346 Broadway, New York.
Forest Press.	Forest Press.............................15 E. 34th St., New York.
Forestry Quarterly.	Forestry Quarterly.................396 Harvard St., Cambridge, Mass.
Forgan, J. B.	Forgan, James Berwick..............First National Bank, Chicago.
Fornaro, C. de.	Fornaro, Carlo de......................9 W. 45th St., New York.
Fort Hill.	Fort Hill Press...........................176 High St., Boston.
Fort Wayne Sch. Bd.	Fort Wayne School Board......................Fort Wayne, Ind.
Fortnightly Club Anthropology.	Fortnightly Club for the Study of Anthropology, Dr. C. P. G. Scott, Pres...Yonkers, N. Y.
Fortune, W: H:	Fortune, William Henry..................61 Worth St., New York.
Forum of Conscience.	Forum of Conscience and Love........................Concord, N. H.
Foster, C:	Foster, Charles, Publishing Co.........716 Sansom St., Philadelphia.
Foster, L. G.	Foster, Leonard Gurley...........3007 Archwood Ave., Cleveland, O.
Foster, R. O.	Foster, Robert O...Ithaca, N. Y.
Foster & R.	Foster & Reynolds.....1 Madison Ave., New York; St. Augustine, Fla.
Fourtner, S:	Fourtner, Samuel....................P. O. Box 877, Seattle, Wash.
Fowler & W.	Fowler & Wells Co.......................18 E. 22d St., New York.
Fowler-Chumos.	Fowler-Chumos Publishing Co., 312 Fulton St., Station F., Seattle, Wash.
Fox, R: K.	Fox, Richard K..........................340 Pearl St., New York.
Frame, A. J.	Frame, Andrew Jay.....................................Waukesha, Wis.
Franchot, C. P.	Franchot, C. P......................8 College St., New Haven, Ct.
Franciscan Fathers (Ariz.)	Franciscan Fathers..................................St. Michaels, Ariz.
Franciscan Sisters.	Franciscan Sisters of Perpetual Adoration, St. Rose Convent, La Crosse, Wis.
Francisco Ferrer Assoc.	Francisco Ferrer Association...............241 Fifth Ave., New York.
Frank, M. M.	Frank, M. M.......................147 N. Front St., Philadelphia.
Franklin.	Franklin Co...St. Louis.
Franklin, C: G.	Franklin, Charles Goodwin............................Ontario, Cal.
Franklin, J: H.	Franklin, John Henderson............1216 Howard St., Omaha, Neb.
Franklin, M.	Franklin, Moses....................................Grand Junction, Colo.
Franklin Inst.	Franklin Institute.......................15 S. 7th St., Philadelphia.
Franklin Press (Pa.)	Franklin Press......................1310 Sansom St., Philadelphia.
Franklin Press Co.	Franklin Press Co.....................................Petersburg, Va.
Franklin Pr. and Eng.	Franklin Printing and Engraving Co....321 Superior St., Toledo, O.
Franklin Pub. (Neb.)	Franklin Publishing Co............1216 Howard St., Omaha, Neb.
Franklin-T.	Franklin-Turner Co........................65 Ivy St. Atlanta, Ga.
Fraternal Monitor.	Fraternal Monitor....................................Rochester, N. Y.
Free Church.	Free Church Book Concern........322 Cedar Ave., Minneapolis, Minn.

Free Dispensary.	Free Dispensary....................506 S. Warren St., Syracuse, N. Y.
Free Lance-Star.	Free Lance-Star Publishing Co..................Fredericksburg, Va.
Free Meth.	Free Methodist Publishing House............14 N. May St., Chicago.
Free Press.	Free Press Printing Co..............................Burlington, Vt.
Free Sewing.	Free Sewing Machine Co......................................Chicago.
Free Speech.	Free Speech League..................120 Lexington Ave., New York.
Freece, H. P.	Freece, Hans P...................Columbia University, New York.
Freeman, E. L.	Freeman, E. L., Co..................................Providence, R. I.
Freese, N. I.	Freese, Nettie Isabel.................22 Frazee St., Auburn, N. Y.
Freking, H: L.	Freking, Henry L......................................Louisville, Ky.
Fremad.	Fremad Publishing Co.............................Eau Claire, Wis.
French, C: S.	French, Charles Sheldon................35 John St., Dalton, Mass.
French, H. B.	French, Howard Barclay.......4th and Callowhill Sts., Philadelphia.
French, S:	French, Samuel, Ltd..................28-30 W. 38th St., New York.
Fretz, A. J.	Fretz, Rev. Abraham James.......................Oak Ridge, N. J.
Friedenwald, H.	Friedenwald, Harry......................................Philadelphia.
Fritch, G. M.	Fritch, G. M..St. Louis.
Frontier Press.	Frontier Press...............806 Mutual Life Bldg., Buffalo, N. Y.
Frost, H.	Frost, Harwood..........................220 Broadway, New York.
Frost, J. B.	Frost, Jonathan B......................................Atlanta, Ga.
Frost, W. B.	Frost, Walter B., & Co.........48 Custom House St., Providence, R. I.
Fruit-Grower.	Fruit-Grower...St. Joseph, Mo.
Fuller, A. W.	Fuller, Arthur W..............................East Hampden, Me.
Fuller, H. A.	Fuller, Harvey Austin................................Hillsdale, Mich.
Fuller, R.	Fuller, Rufus......................41 Mattoon St., Springfield, Mass.
Fuller, W: H.	Fuller, William Hyslop.................23 School St., Palmer, Mass.
Fuller, W: O.	Fuller, William Oliver...................................Rockland, Me.
Fulton Trust Co.	Fulton Trust Co.........................30 Nassau St., New York.
Funk.	Funk & Wagnalls Co...................44-60 E. 23d St., New York.
Fur News.	Fur News Publishing Co................46 W. 24th St., New York.
Furman Univ.	Furman University.................................Greenville, S. C.
Furst.	Furst, J. H., Co.....................23 S. Hanover St., Baltimore, Md.
Gaines, C. C.	Gaines, Clement Carrington........................Poughkeepsie, N. Y.
Gaines, F. W.	Gaines, Franklin Wilks....................................Medford, Ore.
Gaines, N. S.	Gaines, Mrs. Nettie Stewart...........................Stockton, Cal.
Galbreath, C: B.	Galbreath, Charles B...................................Columbus, O.
Gancel, J.	Gancel, Joseph........................103 W. 64th St., New York.
Gapen, J. K.	Gapen, J. K..............Care of Dr. Strong, Saratoga Springs, N. Y.
Garden Press.	Garden Press...................................16 Arlington St., Boston.
Gardner, F:	Gardner, Frederick................815 N. Cuyler Ave., Oak Park, Ill.
Gardner, M. A.	Gardner, Margaret A...............14 Larch St., Providence, R. I.
Gardner & T.	Gardner & Taplin..Boston.
Gardner Pr.	Gardner Printing Co. (formerly Gardner Publishing Co.), Caxton Bldg., Cleveland, O.
Garnett.	Garnett, Porter.....................Bohemian Club, San Francisco.
Garnett, J. M.	Garnett, James Mercer................................Baltimore, Md.
Garrett, S. B.	Garrett, Samuel Bond.............304½ S. Walnut St., Muncie, Ind.
Garrison, W. C.	Garrison, W. C..................Bureau of Statistics, Trenton, N. J.
Gas. Educ. Fund.	Gas Educational Fund Trustees.................................New York.
Gas Traction.	Gas Traction Co.....................................Minneapolis, Minn.
Gas-Engine.	Gas-Engine Publishing Co...............229 E. 7th St., Cincinnati.
Gathman, H.	Gathman, H., care of C. N. Caspar Co..437 Water St., Milwaukee, Wis.
Gay, J. R.	Gay, Jos. R..............................121 Plymouth Pl., Chicago.
Gay, R: L.	Gay, Richard Lewis..........................6 Beacon St., Boston.
Gazette Co.	Gazette Co..Lawrence, Kan.
Gearhart, L. L.	Gearhart, Lynn L....... ....54 Ketchum Pl., Buffalo, N. Y.
Gebhard, E. L.	Gebhard, Elizabeth Louisa..............................Hudson, N. Y.
Geddes, J.	Geddes, James, Jr.......................Boston University, Boston.
Gemünder, A.	Gemünder, August, & Sons...............42 E. 23d St., New York.
Gen. Council.	General Council Publication House (Lutheran), 1522 Arch St., Philadelphia.
Genealog. and Hist.	Genealogical and Historical Publishing Co...554 Monroe St., Chicago.
Genealog. Assoc.	Genealogical Association...................................New York.
General Electric.	General Electric Co., Testing Dept...............Schenectady, N. Y.
Genesee.	Genesee Press...Rochester, N. Y.
Geographical Soc.	Geographical Society of Philadelphia.....................Philadelphia.
George Jr. Repub.	George Junior Republic..............................Freeville, N. Y.
George Washington Univ.	George Washington University..................Washington, D. C.
Georgetown Univ.	Georgetown University.........................Washington, D. C.
Georgia Lib.	Georgia State Library......................................Atlanta, Ga.
Gerbel, A.	Gerbel, A.........................133 W. 13th St., New York.

Gerhard, W: P.	Gerhard, William Paul....................39 Strong Pl., New York.
Germ. Bapt.	German Baptist Publication Society....3804 Payne Ave., Cleveland, O.
Germ. Kali.	German Kali Works.......................99 Nassau St., New York.
Germ. Lit. Bd.	German Literary Board..............................Burlington, Ia.
Germantown Friends Sch.	Germantown Friends School....Coulter St., Germantown, Philadelphia.
Gernsback, H.	Gernsback, Hugo.........................82 W. Broadway, New York.
Gervaise Press.	Gervaise Press.....................................Rochester, N. Y.
Gessner.	Gessner Co...New Orleans, La.
Gesundheit, M.	Gesundheit, Maurice.................29 Diamond Sq., Pittsburgh, Pa.
Gettner, F. I.	Gettner, Florence I.................................Pittsburgh, Pa.
Gher, A. M.	Gher, Alphonse Moser...............................Carlisle, Pa.
Gibb Bros & M.	Gibb Bros. & Moran........................45 Rose St., New York.
Gibbons, F. C. H.	Gibbons, F. C. H...................................Springfield, Mass.
Gibbons, S.	Gibbons, Stanley, Inc........... Room 803, 198 Broadway, New York.
Gibbs, W. M.	Gibbs, Walter M....................643 Central Ave., Dunkirk, N. Y.
Gibson.	Gibson Brothers.........1238 Pennsylvania Ave., Washington, D. C.
Gibson, C. B.	Gibson, Clarence B.......................................Panora, Ia.
Gibson, C:	Gibson, Charles.........................209 Washington St., Boston.
Gibson, P:	Gibson, Peter.........................320 W. 106th St., New York.
Gibson, T:	Gibson, Thomas............Corn Exchange Bank Bldg., New York.
Gibson Pub.	Gibson Publishing Co....................15 William St., New York.
Gietl, P. A.	Gietl, P. A.......................................Collegeville, Ind.
Gift Bk.	Gift Book Publishing Co...............................Columbus, O.
Gilbert, C. B.	Gilbert, Charles Benajah, & Co..........37 E. 28th St., New York.
Gilbert Bk.	Gilbert Book Co...........................205 N. 4th St., St. Louis.
Gill.	Gill, J. K., Co.........................133-135 3d St., Portland, Ore.
Gillespie & P.	Gillespie & Phillips...................................Lincoln, Neb.
Gilliss Press.	Gilliss Press.............................141 E. 25th St., New York.
Gilmartin.	Gilmartin Co..San Francisco.
Gilliam's.	Gilliam's Sons Co..............Juniper and Cherry Sts., Philadelphia.
Gilman, W: C.	Gilman, William C.............................Norwich Town, Ct.
Gilson.	Gilson, F. H., Co..Boston.
Ginn.	Ginn & Co....................................29 Beacon St., Boston.
Gist, E.	Gist, Elizabeth....................................Albert Lea, Minn.
Givens, R. T.	Givens, Robert T.......................1431 Broadway, New York.
Glad Tidings.	Glad Tidings Publishing Co.............602 Lakeside Bldg., Chicago.
Glass.	Glass, Charles H., & Co...............................Bangor, Me.
Glass, A. W.	Glass, Arthur Wellington............441 Stark Ave., Sycamore, Ill.
Glass, D: R.	Glass, David Rose, San Bernardino Business College, San Bernardino, Cal.
Glasson, W: H:	Glasson, William Henry...............................Durham, N. C.
Gleason, J. T.	Gleason, J. T...........................150 Nassau St., New York.
Glennick.	Glennick Co...Hartford, Ct.
Glens Falls Pub.	Glens Falls Publishing Co......................Glens Falls, N. Y.
Globe Pr. (Wash., D. C.)	Globe Printing Co..................................Washington, D. C.
Globe Sch. Bk.	Globe School Book Co....................148 W. 23d St., New York.
Globe-W.	Globe-Wernicke Co..Cincinnati.
Goddard, H. C.	Goddard, Harold Clarke......Northwestern University, Evanston, Ill.
Goddard, O. E.	Goddard, Oscar Elmo...............................Muskogee, I. T.
Godlover, H. B.	Godlover, Hugh Bliss.................1925 Home St., Berkeley, Cal.
Goerck.	Goerck Art Press.......................925 Sixth Ave., New York.
Goetchius, H: R.	Goetchius, Henry R...................................Columbus, Ga.
Golden, M.	Golden, Rev. Meletios..................................Rutland, Mass.
Golden Press.	Golden Press..................220 N. Hancock St., Los Angeles, Cal.
Golden Rule.	Golden Rule Co...........................Tremont Temple, Boston.
Goldsmith, W: M.	Goldsmith, William M...............................Campbell, Mo.
Goldsmith Bk.	Goldsmith Book and Stationery Co. 122 E. Douglas Ave., Wichita, Kan.
Goldsmith-W.	Goldsmith-Woolard Publishing Co.. 122 E. Douglas Ave., Wichita, Kan.
Good Health.	Good Health Publishing Co. (Successors to Modern Medicine Publishing Co.)..................................Battle Creek, Mich.
Good Thoughts.	Good Thoughts Press......................................Aurora, Ill.
Good Tidings.	Good Tidings Co......................................Pittsburg, Pa.
Good Will.	Good Will Publishing Co.............................Hinckley, Me.
Goodenough & W.	Goodenough & Woglom Co................122 Nassau St., New York.
Goodman, H. M.	Goodman, Herbert Marcus.................4533 Ellis Ave., Chicago.
Goodmann, G.	Goodmann, Gustav.........................345 Broadway, New York.
Goodman's.	Goodman's Sons & Co..................411 Walnut St., Philadelphia.
Goodrich, E. J.	Goodrich, E. J...Oberlin, O.
Goodsell, A. T.	Goodsell, Alfred Taylor..........1143 Iranistan Ave., Bridgeport, Ct.
Goodson, G: A.	Goodson, George Arthur......1030 Andrus Bldg., Minneapolis, Minn.

Goodspeed, C: E. Goodspeed, Charles E. .... 5a Park St., Boston.
Goodspeed, F. L. Goodspeed, Frank Lincoln .... Oakland, Cal.
Goodspeed, W. A. Goodspeed, Weston Arthur .... Chicago.
Goodspeed, W. R. Goodspeed, W. R. .... Hartford, Ct.
Goodwin, I. B. Goodwin, I. B. .... 4041 Jefferson Ave., Sioux City, Ia.
Goodwin, J. H: Goodwin, Joseph Henry .... 1215 Broadway, New York.
Goodwin, W: A. R. Goodwin, Rev. William A. R. .... Williamsburg, Va.
Goodyear, W: H: Goodyear, William Henry..Museum, Eastern Parkway, Brooklyn, N. Y.
Goodyear-M. Goodyear-Marshall Publishing Co. .... Cedar Rapids, Ia.
Gorbach, A. B. Gorbach, August Bernhard .... Cincinnati.
Gordon, J. Gordon, Col. James .... Okolona, Miss.
Gordon, S. S. Gordon, S. S., Co. .... Huntington, N. Y.
Gordon, W: A. Gordon, William A. .... Austin, Tex.
Gorham. Gorham, Edwin S. (Supplies books of the S. P. C. K.),
37 E. 28th St., New York.
Gorham, C. W. Gorham, C. W. .... Olympia, Wash.
Gorrill, T. E. Gorrill, T. E. .... Bel Air, Harford Co., Md.
Gospel Pub. Gospel Publishing House .... 54 W. 22d St., New York.
Gospel Trumpet Co. Gospel Trumpet Co. .... Anderson, Ind.
Gotham Press. Gotham Press .... 129-131 W. 31st St., New York.
Gottschall, A. H. Gottschall, Amos H. .... Harrisburg, Pa.
Gould, J. Gould, Joseph .... Mt. Carmel, Pa.
Gould, J. P. Gould, J. Porter .... P. O. Box 225, Topsfield, Mass.
Gould, W. R. Gould, W. Reid .... 139 Nassau St., New York.
Gourley, S: B. Gourley, Samuel Birch .... 9117 Cottage Grove Ave., Chicago.
Gov. Pr. Off. Government Printing Office .... Washington, D. C.
Grady B: F. Grady, Benjamin Franklin .... Goldsboro, N. C.
Grafton Press. Grafton Press .... 105 W. 40th St., New York.
Grafton Pub. Grafton Publishing Co. .... Los Angeles, Cal.
Graham, A. B. Graham, Albert B. .... Columbus, O.
Graham, H. J. Graham, Harry Jefferson .... 616 W. Chestnut St., Louisville, Ky.
Graham, T: W. Graham, Thomas W. .... Dubuque, Ia.
Gramercy. Gramercy Publishing Co. .... 30-32 E. 20th St., New York.
Grand Army. Grand Army Hall and Memorial Association .... Chicago.
Grand Lodge. Grand Lodge of Minnesota .... St. Paul, Minn.
Grandgent. Grandgent, C. H. .... 107 Walker St., Cambridge, Mass.
Granger, I. P. Granger, I. P. .... Canandaigua, N. Y.
Gratz, H. Gratz, Hermann .... 2420 S. 16th St., Philadelphia.
Graves, H. T. Graves, Mrs. H. T. .... Room 300, Bond Bldg., Washington, D. C.
Graves, W: E. Graves, William E. .... St. Louis.
Gray, A. C. Gray, A. C. .... 110½ Main St., Houston, Tex.
Gray, G A. Gray, George Arthur .... 51 Botolph St., Atlantic, Mass.
Gray, H. W. Gray, H. W., Co. .... 21 E. 17th St., New York.
Grayzell. Grayzell & Co. .... 134 Watkins St., Brooklyn, N. Y.
Great Western Pr. Great Western Printing Co. .... Minneapolis, Minn.
Greaves. Greaves Publishing Co. .... Tribune Bldg., New York.
Green, A. Green, Rev. Andrew .... St. Benedict's College, Atchison, Kan.
Green, H. & A. Green, Hinckley & Allen .... Providence, R. I.
Green, H. L. Green, Hans L. .... Room 210, 170 Summer St., Boston.
Green, J: A. Green, John Albert .... Mobile, Ala.
Green, S: A. Green, Samuel Abbott, ... 1154 Boylston St., Boston.
Green, S: S. Green, Samuel Swett .... Worcester, Mass.
Green Leaf. Green Leaf Publishing Co. .... 450 Monon Bldg., Chicago.
Greendlinger, L. Greendlinger, Leo .... 32 Waverly Pl., New York.
Greene, F. V. Greene, Francis Vinton .... 816 Fidelity Bldg., Buffalo, N. Y.
Greene Co. Home. Greene County Home Coming Association .... Xenia, O.
Greenman, A. A. Greenman, A. A. (University Bookstore) .... Boulder, Colo.
Greenstone, J. H. Greenstone, Julius H. .... Philadelphia.
Greenwood, W. Greenwood, Rev. William .... Des Moines, Ia.
Greer, J. H. Greer, Jos. H. .... Chicago.
Greer Pr. Greer Print, Press of the .... Beaumont, Tex.
Gregg Pub. Gregg Publishing Co.,
151 Wabash Ave., Chicago; 1123 Broadway, New York.
Gregory, A. A. Gregory, Alva Adam .... Oklahoma City, Okla.
Gregory, H. Gregory, H. .... Providence, R. I.
Gregory, J. J. H. Gregory, James J. H., & Son .... Marblehead, Mass.
Gresham, O. Gresham, Otto .... 100 Washington St., Chicago.
Gribben, D: S. Gribben, David Sharpe .... 2328 N. Pennsylvania St., Indianapolis, Ind.
Griffin, C: E. Griffin, Charles E., Care of Van Fleet .... 47 W. 28th St., New York.
Griffin, M. I. J. Griffin, Martin Ignatius Joseph .... 1935 N. 11th St., Philadelphia.
Griffith. Griffith & Rowland Press .... 1701-3 Chestnut St., Philadelphia.
Griffith-S. Griffith-Stillings Press .... 364-372 Congress St., Boston.

Griffiths, T: J.	Griffiths, Thomas J..............Liberty and Hotel Sts., Utica, N. Y.
Grills, M. W.	Grills, Merton W..................................Hagerstown, Md.
Grimes, E. L.	Grimes, E. L., Co..Boston.
Grimes, W. B.	Grimes, Rev. Walter B.......“The Water Wagon,” Moore's Hill, Ind.
Grimke, F. J.	Grimke, Rev. Francis James....1415 Corcoran St., Washington, D. C.
Gritman.	Gritman & Sullivan..Chicago.
Grohusko, J. A.	Grohusko, Jacob Abraham...............204 W. 40th St., New York.
Grolier Club.	Grolier Club..............................29 E. 32d St., New York.
Grose, E: F.	Grose, Edward Fabrique........36 Church Ave., Ballston Spa, N. Y.
Gross, C.	Gross, Rev. Carl..........................Kurtzville, Ontario, Can.
Grosscup, P: S.	Grosscup, Peter S..........................Federal Bldg., Chicago.
Grosset.	Grosset & Dunlap.................518-534 W. 26th St., New York.
Grosvenor Lib.	Grosvenor Library....................................Buffalo, N. Y.
Groszmann.	Groszmann, Maximilian P. E., “Watchung Crest,” Johnston Drive, Plainfield, N. J.
Groton Sch.	Groton School Press...................................Groton, Mass.
Grover & W.	Grover & Wellman........405 Chamber of Commerce Bldg., Boston.
Gruber, C. L.	Gruber, Calvin Luther..................................Kutztown, Pa.
Guarantee.	Guarantee Trust & Safe Deposit Co.....................Philadelphia.
Guarantee Pub.	Guarantee Publishing Co..............99 Madison Ave., New York.
Guest, E. A.	Guest, Edgar A.......................................Detroit, Mich.
Gueth, O.	Gueth, Oswald................5504 Fifteenth Ave., Brooklyn, N. Y.
Guide Pr. and Pub.	Guide Printing and Publishing Co.........15 Spruce St., New York.
Guiding Star.	Guiding Star Publishing House...........................Estero, Fla.
Guilford Battle.	Guilford Battle Ground Co.........................Greensboro, N. C.
Gulf States Med.	Gulf States Medical Journal............................Mobile, Ala.
Gulling, H. M.	Gulling, H. M..Reno, Nev.
Gurley, W. & L. E.	Gurley, W. & L. E...Troy, N. Y.
Guthrie, W: A.	Guthrie, William A.....................................Durham, N. C.
Hackney.	Hackney & Moale Co...............Arden Park, Asheville, N. C.
Hadden, J.	Hadden, James...Uniontown, Pa.
Hadley, L. D.	Hadley, Louis D....................................Los Angeles, Cal.
Haedrich.	Haedrich, William, & Sons..............311 Jay St., Brooklyn, N. Y.
Hagerling, F: J.	Hagerling, Frederick J....................................Belleville, Ill.
Hahn.	Hahn & Harmon Co...................................Minneapolis, Minn.
Hahn, E. E.	Hahn, E. E.................11th and Locust Sts., Kansas City, Mo.
Haight.	Haight, A. V., Co...................................Poughkeepsie, N. Y.
Hailman.	Hailman Printing Co..................................Kansas City, Mo.
Halberstadt, B.	Halberstadt, Baird......................................Pottsville, Pa.
Hale, A.	Hale, Albert .... Boston.
Hale, A. R.	Hale, Mrs. Annie Riley............579 W. 121st St., New York.
Hale, O. F.	Hale, Oscar Fitzalan.................................League City, Tex.
Hale Pub.	Hale Publishing Co....................3550 Vista Ave., St. Louis.
Haley, L: C.	Haley, Louis Coleman..................................Madison, Wis.
Hall, E. E.	Hall, Elmer Edgar...............1501 Le Roy Ave., Berkeley, Cal.
Hall, E. J.	Hall, E. J., Publishing Co..............................Boston, Mass.
Hall, H:	Hall, Henry.................................52 Broadway, New York.
Hall J. A:	Hall, James Augustus................................Watsonville, Cal.
Hall, J. N.	Hall, Mrs. J. N..Fulton, Ky.
Hall, J: M.	Hall, John Manley.................165 Boston Block, Detroit, Mich.
Hall & McC.	Hall & McChesney.......................................Syracuse, N. Y.
Hall & W.	Hall & Williams.......................1942 Stout St., Denver, Colo.
Hallowell, J. M.	Hallowell, James M.......................................Boston.
Halsey, M. D.	Halsey, Mina Deane.......712 W. Hellman Bldg., Los Angeles, Cal.
Haltigan.	Haltigan, Patrick J..........614 Louisiana Ave., Washington, D. C.
Hamburg-American Line.	Hamburg-American Line..................45 Broadway, New York.
Hamersly.	Hamersly, Lewis R., & Co...............1 W. 34th St., New York.
Hamersly & Co.	Hamersly & Co........................1 W. 34th St., New York.
Hamilton, C: H.	Hamilton, Charles H....................................Milwaukee, Wis.
Hamilton, G. P.	Hamilton, Green Polonius.......119 Kimbrough St., Memphis, Tenn.
Hamilton, I.	Hamilton, I...........................201 E. 12th St., New York.
Hamilton, J. G. R.	Hamilton, Joseph Grégoire de Roulhac................Raleigh, N. C.
Hamilton Bk.	Hamilton Book Co.......................44 E. 23d St., New York.
Hamlin, C:	Hamlin, Charles......................P. O. Box 494, Bangor, Me.
Hamlin, C: S.	Hamlin, Charles S..Boston.
Hammerling, L: N.	Hammerling, Louis N.......................World Bldg., New York.
Hammett, J. L.	Hammett, J. L., Co......................116 Summer St., Boston.
Hamming.	Hamming, Andrew..Chicago.
Hammond, C. S.	Hammond, Caleb S., & Co...............142 Fulton St., New York.
Hammond Pr. Co.	Hammond Printing Co...................................Fremont, Neb.
Hammond Pub.	Hammond Publishing Co..............................Lansing, Mich.

Hammond Pub. Co. Hammond Publishing Co. Milwaukee, Wis.
Hampden Pub. Hampden Publishing Co. Springfield, Mass
Hampton, C. E. Hampton, Celwyn Emerson, Capt. 21st Infantry. Fort Bayard, N. M.
Hampton Inst. Hampton Institute Press. Hampton, Va.
Hancock Press. Hancock Press. P. O. Box 2789, Boston.
Hand Made Furniture. Hand Made Furniture Shop. Spokane, Wash.
Hanford & H. Hanford & Horton Co. Middletown, N. Y.
Hanks, A. K. Hanks, Austin Kimball. 961 St. Nicholas Ave., New York.
Hann. Hann & Adair Printing Co. Columbus, O.
Hanna, M. E. Hanna, Matthew Elting. Fort Leavenworth, Kan.
Hannahs, E. H. Hannahs, E. Helen. N. Y. State Normal College, Albany, N. Y.
Hansbrough, L. V. B. Hansbrough, Mrs. Lucinda Victoria Blair. R. F. D. 12, Buechel, Ky.
Hansell. Hansell, F. F., & Brother, Ltd. 537-539 Baronne St., New Orleans, La.
Hansen, H. C. Hansen, H. C., Type Foundry. 43 Centre St., New York.
Hansom & V. Hansom & Van Winkle Co. Newark, N. J.
Hanzsche. Hanzsche & Co. 2936 St. Paul St., Baltimore, Md.
Harbison-W. Harbison-Walker Refractories Co. Pittsburg, Pa.
Harden, E: W. Harden, Edward Walker. 137 Adams St., Chicago.
Hardie, G: R. Hardie, George Robert. Canton, N. Y.
Harding. Harding, Robert, Co. 10-14 S. 11th St., Richmond, Va.
Harding, A. R. Harding, A. R., Publishing Co. 326 E. Broad St., Columbus, O.
Harding Press. Harding Press. Richmond, Va.
Hardman. Hardman Press. St. Joseph, Mo.
Hardwood Record. Hardwood Record Co. 134 Monroe St., Chicago.
Hardy, C. S. Hardy, Carlos S. Chicago.
Hardy, L. P. Hardy, L. P., Co. South Bend, Ind.
Hare, W: H. Hare, Bishop William Hobart. Sioux Falls, S. D.
Harger, C: M. Harger, Charles Moreau. Abilene, Kan.
Harisun. Harisun, Homer, & Co. 37 S. Water St., Chicago.
Harlow, W. E. Harlow, W. E. Springfield, Mo.
Harper. Harper & Bros. Franklin Sq., New York.
Harper, F. P. Harper, Frances P. & Lathrop C. 437 Fifth Ave., New York.
Harper, H: H. Harper, Henry Howard. 100 Boylston St., Boston.
Harper, I. A. H. Harper, Mrs. Ida A. Husted. Everett House, New York.
Harper-Adams. Harper-Adams & Co. Omaha, Neb.
Harriman, A. Harriman, Alice. 542 Fifth Ave., New York.
Harriman, S. F. Harriman, S. F. 1 So. High St., Columbus, O.
Harrington, J: L. Harrington, John Lyle. New Nelson Bldg., Kansas City, Mo.
Harris, C: A: Harris, Charles Augustus. Holliston, Mass.
Harris, G. D. Harris, Gilbert Dennison. Cornell University, Ithaca, N. Y.
Harris, J. Y. Harris, Mrs. Jane Yancey. Breckenridge Street, Henderson, N. C.
Harris, O. T. Harris, Orsamus Turner. 12 W. 32d St., New York.
Harrisburg Pub. Harrisburg Publishing Co. Harrisburg, Pa.
Harrison. Harrison Safety Boiler Works. Philadelphia.
Harrison, H: Harrison, Henry, Co. 70 Linden Ave., Brooklyn, N. Y.
Harrison Co. Harrison Co. 50 E. Hunter St., Atlanta, Ga.
Harrison Pr. Harrison Printing and Advertising Co. Union City, Ind.
Harrison Pub. Harrison Publishing Co. Alaska Bldg., Seattle, Wash.
Hart, C: H: Hart, Charles Henry. 4717 Chester Ave., Philadelphia.
Hart, H: C. Hart, Henry C. 2206 De Lancy Pl., Philadelphia.
Hartford Seminary Press. *See* Scribner.
Hartford, I: J. Hartford, Isaac J. Paxton, Ill.
Hartman Pub. Hartman Publishing House. 100 W. 44th St., New York.
Hartmann, S. Hartmann, Sadakichin. 506 E. 175th St., New York.
Hartranft. Hartranft, F. B. 49 Pearl St., Hartford, Ct.
Hartshorn, W: N. Hartshorn, William Newton. Boston.
Hartung, H. H. Hartung, Harry Hall, M.D. Boston.
Harvard Bk. Harvard Book Co. 164 Lake Ave., Chicago.
Harvard Co-operative. Harvard Co-operative Society. Cambridge, Mass.
Harvard Dramatic. Harvard Dramatic Club. Cambridge, Mass.
Harvard Lampoon. Harvard Lampoon Society. Cambridge, Mass.
Harvard Law. Harvard Law Review Publishing Association. Cambridge, Mass.
Harvard Monthly. Harvard Monthly. Cambridge, Mass.
Harvard Univ. Harvard University. Cambridge, Mass.
Harvey, F. Harvey, Fred. 8th and Delaware Sts., Kansas City, Mo.
Harvey, N. A. Harvey, Nathan A. State Normal College, Ypsilanti, Mich.
Harvey, O. J. Harvey, Oscar J. 20½ Northampton St., Wilkesbarre, Pa.
Harvey, T. L. Harvey, Theodore Lee. P. O. Box 202, Monett, Mo.
Harvey, W. P. Harvey, W. P. Louisville, Ky.

Harvey Pub.	Harvey Publishing Co. (Otto Juettner),....130 Opera Pl., Cincinnati.
Harwood, H: H.	Harwood, Henry H................505 E. Grace St., Richmond, Va.
Haskel, C. A.	Haskel, C. A.....................................Baltimore, Md.
Haskins & S.	Haskins & Sells...........................30 Broad St., New York.
Hastain E.	Hastain, E.......................................Muskogee, Okla.
Hatch.	Hatch Music Co.....................................Philadelphia.
Hatch, W. M.	Hatch, Willis Marion..............................Decatur, Ga.
Hatfield, M. L.	Hatfield, Montraville Lawson......................Oakland, Cal.
Hatfield, R:	Hatfield, Richard........1310 Green Court, N. W., Washington, D. C.
Hathaway, J. T.	Hathaway, James T...............297 Crown St., New Haven, Ct.
Hauenstein, M. F.	Hauenstein, Minnie Ferris.........725 W. Ferry St., Buffalo, N. Y.
Haupt, W: G:	Haupt, William George.....................................Chicago.
Hauser, I. L.	Hauser, I. L., & Co.......................................Chicago.
Hauskins, J. E.	Hauskins, J. E.....................................Tacoma, Wash.
Haven, C.	Haven, Curtis......................1526 W. Ontario St., Philadelphia.
Haverford Coll.	Haverford College..................................Haverford, Pa.
Hawaiian Gazette.	Hawaiian Gazette Co................................Honolulu, H. I.
Hawes, A. F.	Hawes, Austin F....................................Burlington, Vt.
Hawes, C. H.	Hawes, Mrs. C. H...................................Madison, Wis.
Hawk-Eye.	Hawk-Eye Press...................................Mount Vernon, Ia.
Hawks, E. B.	Hawks, Earl Bedford..................................Clinton, Wis.
Hawkins, G: H: E:	Hawkins, George Henry Edward.....care of Fairbanks Co., Chicago.
Hawley, W. A:	Hawley, Walter Augustus.........................Santa Barbara, Cal.
Hawn, W:	Hawn, William...................442 Classon Ave., Brooklyn, N. Y.
Hawthorne, J.	Hawthorne, J..........................234 Fifth Ave., New York.
Hay, H: J.	Hay, Henry J...Meeker, Colo.
Hayden, W. L.	Hayden, Warren Luce...........14 N. Bolton St., Indianapolis, Ind.
Hayen, E.	Hayen, Eberhard.....................................Baltimore, Md.
Hayes, E.	Hayes, Ellen.......................Care of G. H. Ellis Co., Boston.
Hayes, M. D.	Hayes, Milton D., & Co...............439 Sixth Ave., Pittsburgh, Pa.
Hayne, J. E.	Hayne, Jos. Elias.................319 Grand Ave., Brooklyn, N. Y.
Haynes.	Haynes, D. O., & Co...................90 William St., New York.
Haynes, J. B.	Haynes, James B...........630 Brandeis Theatre Bldg., Omaha, Neb.
Haynes, J. E.	Haynes, Jack E.....................................St. Paul Minn.
Hays, G. A.	Hays, Gilbert Adams..................................Sewickley, Pa.
Hayward, W. C.	Hayward, W. C.....................................Des Moines, Ia.
Hazeldine, N. F. W.	Hazeldine, Norton F. W.........967 W. 6th St., Los Angeles, Cal.
Hazzard, L. B.	Hazzard, Linda Burfield......422 Northern Bk. Bldg., Seattle, Wash.
Heacock, W: A.	Heacock, William A..................................Lockport, N. Y.
Head, J. W.	Head, James William..................................Barcroft, Va.
Heald, E: P.	Heald, Edward P...................................San Francisco, Cal.
Health.	Health Publishing Co...................................Dayton, O.
Health-Culture.	Health-Culture Co...................45 Ascension St., Passaic, N. J.
Health-Wealth.	Health-Wealth Publishing Co.......................Lawrence, Mass.
Hearn, E: C.	Hearn, Rev. Edward C....................Merna, McLean Co., Ill.
Heath.	Heath, D. C., & Co.......................120 Bolyston St., Boston.
Hebrew-Chr.	Hebrew-Christian Publishing and Trading Co., 138 Bible House, New York.
Hebrew Pub.	Hebrew Publishing Co.......................85 Canal St., New York.
Hebrew Standard.	Hebrew Standard Press..................87 Nassau St., New York.
Heck, F.	Heck, Frank...Chicago.
Hecox, C. W.	Hecox, Clarence W................................Washington, D. C.
Heer.	Heer, F. J., Printing Co................57 E. Main St., Columbus, O.
Hegyessy, J.	Hegyessy, James.....................................San Francisco.
Heidelberg.	Heidelberg Press..................15th and Race Sts., Philadelphia.
Heidingsfeld, J.	Heidingsfeld, J............................New Brunswick, N. J.
Heilbron, W: C.	Heilbron, W. C.................104 Dispatch Bldg., St. Paul, Minn.
Heilbroner, L:	Heilbroner, Louis.................................Fort Wayne, Ind.
Heindel, J: E.	Heindel, Rev. John Elmer........39 Warner Ave., Jersey City, N. J.
Heindel, M.	Heindel, Max.......................................Seattle, Wash.
Heinemann, H. E. O.	Heinemann, H. E. O.........................145 Lasalle St., Chicago.
Heinrici, M.	Heinrici, Max...Philadelphia.
Heisler, E. F.	Heisler, E. F.....................................Kansas City, Kan.
Heistand, H: O: S.	Heistand, Henry Olcot Sheldon..War Department, Washington, D. C.
Helburn.	Helburn, William ....10 E. 16th St., New York.
Heller, B., & Co.	Heller, B., & Co......................251 S. Jefferson St., Chicago.
Heminway.	Heminway, M., & Sons Silk Co............74 Greene St., New York.
Hemiup.	Hemiup Publishing Co...................................Geneva, N. Y.
Hempstead, F.	Hempstead, Fay..Masonic Temple, Main and 5th St., Little Rock, Ark.
Henderson, H. H.	Henderson, H. H......................................Columbus, O.
Henderson, P:	Henderson, Peter, & Co.................35 Cortlandt St., New York.

Hendler, C. J.	Hendler, C. J. .... 1107 Betz Bldg., Philadelphia.
Hendrix, L. E. G.	Hendrix, Lily Elizabeth Graves .... 1009 Olive St., Mexico, Mo.
Henkels.	Henkels, Stan V., & Co. .... Philadelphia.
Henley.	Henley, Norman W., Publishing Co. ...... 132 Nassau St., New York.
Henneberry.	Henneberry Co. .... 552-556 Wabash Ave., Chicago.
Hennebique.	Hennebique Construction Co. .... 1170 Broadway, New York.
Henry W: A.	Henry, William Arnon .... Madison, Wis.
Henry Phipps Inst.	Henry Phipps Institute .... Philadelphia.
Hensel, H. C.	Hensel, Harry C. .... 327 Dearborn St., Chicago.
Hensel, W: U.	Hensel, William U. .... Lancaster, Pa.
Hentz, J: P.	Hentz, John P. .... Dayton, O.
Herald Pr.	Herald Printing and Publishing Co. .... Beaver Springs, Pa.
Herald Pr. (N. Dak.)	Herald Printing Co. .... Grand Forks, N. D.
Herald Pub. (Md.)	Herald Publishing Co. .... Hagerstown, Md.
Herbert, E.	Herbert, Ewing .... Hiawatha, Kan.
Herder.	Herder, B. .... 17 S. Broadway, St. Louis.
Herman, P.	Herman, Poole & Co. .... Decatur, Ill.
Herr, P. J.	Herr, P. J., Printing Co. .... Columbus, O.
Herr, T. W.	Herr, Theodore Witner .... 49 N. Duke St., Lancaster, Pa.
Herrick.	Herrick Book and Stationery Co .... 934 15th St., Denver, Colo.
Herrick, M. T.	Herrick, Myron T. .... Cleveland, O.
Hertel.	Hertel, Jenkins & Co. Now John A. Hertle Co.
Hertel, J: A.	Hertel, John A., Co. .... 110 W. Jackson Blvd., Chicago.
Herty, C: H.	Herty, Charles H. .... Chapel Hill, N. C.
Hess, H. M.	Hess, Harold Miner .... 125 Monroe St., Chicago.
Hess, T:	Hess, Thomas .... Millville, N. J.
Hesselgren.	Hesselgren, G. C., Publishing Co. .... 146 Worth St., New York.
Hessling.	Hessling, Bruno, Co. .... 64 E. 12th St., New York.
Hewitt, W. P. H.	Hewitt, W. P. H. .... Syracuse, N. Y.
Heydecker, C. D.	Heydecker, Mrs. Catherine Darlington, 137 Franklin Ave., Mount Vernon, N. Y.
Heydecker, C. T.	Heydecker, Christian T. .... Waukegan, Ill.
Heywood, H.	Heywood, Herbert .... Los Angeles, Cal.
Hickman.	Hickman, F. S. .... West Chester, Pa.
Hicks, F: C:	Hicks, Frederick Charles .... U. S. Naval War College, Annapolis, Md.
Hicks, J: S. S.	Hicks, John Solomon Soules .... South Haven, Mich.
Hicks-Chatten.	Hicks-Chatten Engraving Co. .... 671 Schuyler St., Portland, Ore.
Hicks-J.	Hicks-Judd Co. .... San Francisco.
High School Teachers.	High School Teachers' Association of New York, 25 Jefferson Ave., Brooklyn, N. Y.
Higher Life.	Higher Life Publishing Co. .... 709 Maple St., Pasadena, Cal.
Highlands.	Highlands, John .... 1106 Arch St., Philadelphia.
Hightower, J.	Hightower, James .... Colorado Springs, Colo.
Hildreth, C.	Hildreth, Carson .... Franklin, Neb.
Hill, E. B.	Hill, Edwin B. .... Lakeland, Mich.
Hill, E. C.	Hill, Edwin C. .... 1 W. 34th St., New York.
Hill F. C.	Hill, Francis C. .... 150 Nassau St., New York.
Hill, J. J.	Hill, James J. .... Great Northern Ry. Bldg., St. Paul, Minn.
Hill, J. S.	Hill, J. Stacy .... Cincinnati.
Hill, L.	Hill, Lysander .... 1463 Monadnock Block, Chicago.
Hill, W. M.	Hill, Walter M. .... 823 Marshall Field Bldg., Chicago.
Hill-K.-F. Co.	Hill-Kellner-Frost Co. .... Waco, Tex.
Hill Pub.	Hill Publishing Co. *See* McGraw-Hill Book Co.
Hills & H.	Hills & Hafely Co. .... 27 E. 22d St., New York.
Hillside.	Hillside Press .... Englewood, N. J.
Hind, W. D.	Hind, W. D. .... Amherst, Mass.
Hinds.	Hinds, Noble & Eldredge .... 31-35 W. 15th St., New York.
Hine, C: C.	Hine, C. C., Sons Co. .... 100 William St., New York.
Hine, J. S.	Hine, James Stewart .... Ohio State University, Columbus, O.
Hine Bros.	Hine Bros. .... 46 Cedar St., New York.
Hinkle, F: W.	Hinkle, Frederick W. .... Cincinnati.
Hintze, L:	Hintze, Louis .... Ada, Norman Co., Minn.
Hipple.	Hipple Printing Co. .... Pierre, S. D.
Hirshberg.	Hirshberg Art Co. .... 418 N. Howard St., Baltimore, Md.
Hisgen, T: L.	Hisgen, Thomas L., Nomination Club .... Boston.
Hispanic Soc.	Hispanic Society of America .. 156th St., W. of Broadway, New York.
Hist. and Phil. Soc., O.	Historical and Philosophical Society of Ohio .. Station E, Cincinnati.
*Hist. Dept. of I^*	Historical Department of Iowa .... Des Moines, Ia.
Hist Pub. Co. (N. J.)	Historical Publishing Co. .... 3 Boyd Ave., Jersey City, N. J.

Hist. Pub. Co. (Pa.)	Historical Publishing Co............1336 Cherry St., Philadelphia.
Hist. Review.	Historical Review Publishing Co........................Baltimore.
Hist. Soc. Penn.	Historical Society of Pennsylvania......1300 Locust St., Philadelphia.
Hist. Soc. (So. Natick.)	Historical, Natural History and Library Society of South Natick, South Natick, Mass.
Hite, M. H.	Hite, Maxwell H................................Harrisburg, Pa.
Hitlofi, I.	Hitlofi, Iven..Chicago.
Hobart, E. L.	Hobart, Edwin L., 2223 W. 31st Ave., Highland Station P. O., Denver, Colo.
Hockenberry, J: C.	Hockenberry, J: Coulter................515 W. 122d St., New York.
Hocking.	Hocking Publishing Co....................Law Bldg., Norfolk, Va.
Hodgart.	Hodgart, A., Co..Chicago.
Hodges, A. D.	Hodges, Almon Danforth, jr........Union Club, Park St., Boston.
Hodges, G:	Hodges, Rev. George................3 Mason St., Cambridge, Mass.
Hodgman.	Hodgman, Francis Co.................................Climax, Mich.
Hodgson, E. F.	Hodgson, Ernest Franklin...........................Dover, Mass.
Hoe, R.	Hoe, Robert..........................504 Grand St., New York.
Hoeber.	Hoeber, Paul B.....................69 E. 59th St., New York.
Hoenshel, E. U.	Hoenshel, Elmer Ulysses.............................Dayton, Va.
Hoffer, C. M.	Hoffer, Cora M...................................Emporia, Kan.
Hoffert, F. P.	Hoffert, Franklin Pierce...3522 W. Michigan Ave., Indianapolis, Ind.
Hoffman, E: F.	Hoffman, Edward Fenno, 509 Harrison Bldg., Fifteenth and Market Sts., Philadelphia.
Hoffman, J. D:	Hoffman, James David...........Purdue University, Lafayette, Ind.
Hoffman, O. S.	Hoffman, Otto Sichel......21 University Ave., Battle Creek, Mich.
Hofmeister, C. W.	Hofmeister, Christopher W............................Buffalo, Okla.
Hogan, W. F.	Hogan, Wilbur Fisk......1109 Eleventh Ave., N., Birmingham, Ala.
Holden.	Holden Patent Book Cover Co......................Springfield, Mass.
Holeproof.	Holeproof Hosiery Co...........................Milwaukee, Wis.
Holland, J. P.	Holland, Josephine Park......................Box 62, Onset, Mass.
Hollenbeck Press.	Hollenbeck Press..................................Indianapolis, Ind.
Holley, C: D.	Holley, Rev. Charles D...........6112 Carnegie Ave., Cleveland, O.
Hollinger, L. I.	Hollinger, Mrs. L. Israel.........Densmore Hotel, Kansas City, Mo.
Holliswood.	Holliswood Press..........................Hollis, Long Island, N. Y.
Holman.	Holman, A. J., & Co......................1222 Arch St., Philadelphia.
Holman, E. E.	Holman, Emily Elizabeth..........1020 Chestnut St., Philadelphia.
Holmes, E. B.	Holmes, E. B.......................................Philadelphia.
Holst.	Holst Publishing Co...................................Boone, Ia.
Holt.	Holt, Henry, & Co......................34 W. 33d St., New York.
Holt, F.	Holt, Frank, & Co....................739 Broad St., Newark, N. J.
Home Candy.	Home Candy Makers....................................Canton, O.
Home Corr. Sch.	Home Correspondence School....................Springfield, Mass.
Home Educ.	Home Educational Society...........................Philadelphia.
Home Manual.	Home Manual Publishing Co...............................Chicago.
Home Market	Home Market Club...Boston.
Home Pub. Co., (Kan.)	Home Publishing Co..........................Station B, Topeka, Kan.
Homewood.	Homewood Publishing Co..................................Chicago.
Homingwood.	Homingwood Publishing Co.....................South Bend, Ind.
Honeyman.	Honeyman's Publishing House....................Plainfield, N. J.
Hood, G: J.	Hood, G: Jussen...................................Lawrence, Kan.
Hood, H. P.	Hood, H. P., & Sons.....494 Rutherford Ave., Charlestown, Mass.
Hooker, M. H.	Hooker, Margaret Huntington., Care of E. R. Andrews Printing Co., Rochester, N. Y.
Hopewell Press.	Hopewell Press......................150 Michigan Ave., Chicago.
Hopkins, L. W.	Hopkins, Luther W..............833 Calvert Bldg., Baltimore, Md.
Horner, J.	Horner, Dr. Joseph..................524 Penn Ave., Pittsburgh, Pa.
Horseless Age.	Horseless Age Co.......................250 W. 54th St., New York.
Horst.	Horst, E. Clemens, Co............................San Francisco.
Hoskins.	Hoskins, R. D.....................................Bismarck, N. D.
Hosmer, J: G.	Hosmer, John G.............................14 Beacon St., Boston.
Hosterman.	Hosterman Publishing Co..........................Springfield, O.
Hotchkiss, S:	Hotchkiss, Samuel..............................Downsville, N. Y.
Hotel Monthly.	Hotel Monthly........................325 Dearborn St., Chicago.
Hotel Red Book.	Hotel Red Book & Directory Co.......103 Park Ave., New York.
Houdlette E. L.	Houdlette, Edith Laura.....................Melrose Highlands, Mass.
Houghtaling, C: E.	Houghtaling, Charles E...............................Albany, N. Y.
Houghton, H. O.	Houghton, H. O., & Co............................Cambridge, Mass.
Houghton M.	Houghton Mifflin Co.................................4 Park St., Boston.
House of Fun.	House of Fun..........................429 6th Ave., New York.
Housekeeper Corp.	Housekeeper Corporation..........................Minneapolis, Minn.
Houser, W: W.	Houser, William Wesley................................Lincoln, Ill.

Hovey, E. O.	Hovey, Edmund Otis, American Museum of Natural History, New York.
How Pub.	How Publishing Co....Decatur, Ga.
Howard.	Howard Publishing Co....Detroit, Mich.
Howard, D.	Howard, Daniel....Winsor Locks, Ct.
Howard, G: E.	Howard, George E....714 Twelfth St., N. W., Washington, D. C.
Howard Pub. Co.	Howard Publishing Co....714 Twelfth St., N. W., Washington, D. C.
Howard Pub. Co. (N. H.)	Howard Publishing Co....Rochester, N. H.
Howard-S.	Howard-Severance Co....173-175 Fifth Ave., Chicago.
Howe, E. F.	Howe, Edgar F., & Sons....Imperial, Cal.
Howe, J: D.	Howe, John Dicks....1704 Geary St., San Francisco.
Howe & B.	Howe & Barron....Chicago.
Howerton.	Howerton, D. C., Press....Washington, D. C.
Howland, E. H.	Howland, Mrs. Emma H....Acushnet, Mass.
Hubbard, S: F.	Hubbard, Samuel F....20 Parmenter St., Boston.
Hubbell.	Hubbell Publishing Co....309 Broadway, New York.
Huddle, W: P:	Huddle, Rev. William Peter....Madison, Va.
Hudson.	Hudson, Franklin, Publishing Co..22d and Oak Sts., Kansas City, Mo.
Hudson Press.	Hudson Press. (Books supplied by William Rickey & Co.)
Hudson Pub.	Hudson Publishing Co....404 Kasota Bldg., Minneapolis, Minn.
Hudson-Fulton.	Hudson-Fulton Celebration Commission, Tribune Bldg., 154 Nassau St., New York.
Huebsch, B: W.	Huebsch, Benjamin W....225 Fifth Ave., New York.
Hughs, G: S.	Hughs, George Shelley....Chicago.
Hughes, G: W.	Hughes, George Washington....Clinton, Ill.
Hughes, J. E.	Hughes, James E....Lexington, Ky.
Hughes & Co.	Hughes & Co....St. Louis.
Hugo, G: B.	Hugo, George B., Co....147 Shawmut Ave. Boston.
Hugo, T. W.	Hugo, T. W....Duluth, Minn.
Hühner, L.	Hühner, Leon....5 Beekman St., New York.
Huie, W: G.	Huie, William Green....Ringgold, Tex.
Hulburd, E. W.	Hulburd, Ebenezer Wallace....Descanso, Cal.
Hull, J: W.	Hull, John Wellington....Zion City, Ill.
Human Life.	Human Life Publishing Co....530 Atlantic Ave., Boston.
Hume, H. H.	Hume, Harold Hardrada....Glen Saint Mary, Fla.
Humphrey, G: P.	Humphrey, George P....65 Spring St., Rochester, N. Y.
Hungerford-H.	Hungerford-Holbrook Co....Watertown, N. Y.
Hunt, A. W.	Hunt, A. W....48 Abbott Court, Chicago.
Hunt, C. W.	Hunt, C. W., Co....West New Brighton, N. Y.
Hunt, M. A.	Hunt, Mary Amelia....Aurora, Ill.
Hunt, T: F.	Hunt, Thomas F. (President of Soc. for Promotion of Agricultural Science)....State College, Pa.
Hunter & Co.	Hunter & Co., Inc....Richmond, Va.
Hunter, S: J:	Hunter, Samuel John....Lawrence, Kan.
Huntington, A. O.	Huntington, Annie Oakes....31 Glen Road, Jamaica Plain, Mass.
Huntington, A. T.	Huntington, Albert T....1265 Bedford Ave., Brooklyn, N. Y.
Huntting.	Huntting, H. R., Co....317 Main St., Springfield, Mass.
Huntting, T. D.	Huntting, Teunis Dimon....220 Broadway, New York.
Hurd, D. D. S.	Hurd, Mrs. Dena D. Soekland....Collegeport, Tex.
Hurst.	Hurst & Co....395-399 Broadway, New York.
Hurtt, J: M.	Hurtt, John Milton....Pomona, Cal.
Hurwitz, G:	Hurwitz, George....Mason City, Ill.
Husband, A. P.	Husband, A. P....Llanerch, Pa.
Huston, A. J.	Huston, A. J....191 Middle St., Portland, Me.
Hutchinson & B.	Hutchinson & Broadbent....McKeesport, Pa.
Hutt, W: H.	Hutt, William H....1908 Fairmont Ave., Philadelphia.
Hyatt-F.	Hyatt-Fowells School....Pine and Broadway, Seattle, Wash.
Hyde, W: H:	Hyde, William Henry, & Co....Milwaukee, Wis.
Hyland.	Hyland, J. S., & Co....325 Dearborn St., Chicago.
Iles, G:	Iles, George....5 Brunswick St., Montreal, Can.
Ill. Bk.	Illinois Book Exchange....Lakeside Bldg., Chicago.
Ill. Central R. R.	Illinois Central Railroad Co....Chicago.
Ill. Educ. Comm.	Illinois Educational Commission....Springfield, Ill.
Ill. Lab'y Nat. Hist.	Illinois State Laboratory of Natural History, S. A. Forbes, Director, Urbana, Ill.
Ill. Law Review.	Illinois Law Review....37 E. Lake St., Chicago.
Ill. Pr.	Illinois Printing Co....Danville, Ill.
Ill. State Hist. Lib.	Illinois State Historical Library....Springfield, Ill.
Ill. State Journ.	Illinois State Journal Co....Springfield, Ill.
Ill. State Normal.	Illinois State Normal School....Charleston, Ill.

Illuminating Engineering.	Illuminating Engineering Publishing Co....201 E. 16th St., New York.
Imperial Pub.	Imperial Publishing Co....................27 E. 22d St., New York.
Independent.	Independent Publishing Co..........................Indianapolis, Ind.
Independent Pub.	Independent Publishing Co.................................Chicago.
Independent Religious.	Independent Religious Society............140 Dearborn St., Chicago.
India Rubber.	India Rubber Publishing Co.............395 Broadway, New York.
India RubberWorld.	India Rubber World...................15 W. 38th St., New York.
Indian Rights Assoc.	Indian Rights Association........708-9 Provident Bldg., Philadelphia.
Indiana Lib.	Indiana Public Library Commission................Indianapolis, Ind.
Indo-Am. Bk.	Indo-American Book Co..............218 N. Kedzie Ave., Chicago.
Indust.	Industrial Publication Co. (Supply publications of G. Gottsberger Peck.) Now Industrial Book Co.
Indust. Bk.	Industrial Book Co.........................178 Fulton St., New York.
Indust. Educ. Co.	Industrial Education Co.......................................Boston.
Indust. Press.	Industrial Press........................49 Lafayette St.., New York.
Industry.	Industry Publishing Co.....1607 Commonwealth Bldg., Pittsburgh, Pa.
Informant.	Informant Publishing Co...........1730 W. 25th St., Cleveland, O.
Inger, A. J.	Inger, Archie J..Oakland, Cal.
Ingersoll, A. N.	Ingersoll, A. N..............................South Orange, N. J.
Ingersoll, H: H.	Ingersoll, Henry H...................................Knoxville, Tenn.
Ingham, W: A.	Ingham, William Armstrong............333 S. 16th St., Philadelphia.
Ingram, T: D.	Ingram, Thomas Darlington, M.D...P. O. Box 2503, Washington, D. C.
Inland.	Inland Publishing Co...............................Emporium, Kan.
Inland Pr.	Inland Printer Co.......................130 Sherman St., Chicago.
Inland Press.	Inland Press..Asheville, N. C.
Inland Printing Co.	Inland Printing Co..................................Spokane, Wash.
Inland Pub.	Inland Publishing Co..............................Terre Haute, Ind.
Inman, B. R.	Inman, B. R...Middletown, Ind.
Innes.	Innes & Son.......................1311 Sansom St., Philadelphia.
Inquirer.	Inquirer and Mirror Press..........................Nantucket, Mass.
Inst. Colored Youth.	Institute for Colored Youth............................Cheyney, Pa.
Insurance Field.	Insurance Field......................P. O. Box 617, Louisville, Ky.
Insurance Press.	Insurance Press.........................120 Liberty St., New York.
Int. Banking.	International Banking Corporation..........60 Wall St., New York.
Int. Bu. Am. Republics.	International Bureau of the American Republics, 2 Jackson Pl., Washington, D. C.
Int. Cable.	International Cable Directory Co.............17 State St., New York.
Int. Claim.	International Claim Agency..........................Pittsburg, Pa.
	International Committee of Young Men's Christian Association. *See* Y. M. C. A.
Int. Code.	International Code Co................155 W. 61st St., New York.
Int. Correspondence.	International Correspondence Schools.................Scranton, Pa.
Int. Exchange.	International Exchange......................P. O. Box 177, Chicago.
Int. Independent.	International Independent Telephone Associations, 339 Monadnock Block, Chicago.
Int. Law.	International Law and Business Institute, 234 Hennepin Ave., Minneapolis, Minn.
Int. Master Boiler.	International Master Boiler Makers' Association, 95 Liberty St., New York.
Int. Medical.	International Medical Book Co....................Milwaukee, Wis.
Int. Motor.	International Motor Cyclopædia, 313-314 Terminal Bldg., Park Ave. and Forty-first St., New York.
Int. Press.	International Press.....................136 William St., New York.
Int. Pr.	International Printing Co............236 Chestnut St., Philadelphia.
Int. Pub. Co.	International Publishing Co..............394 Atlantic Ave., Boston.
Int. Ref. Bu.	International Reform Bureau, 206 Pennsylvania Ave., Washington, D. C.
Int. Sch. of Peace.	International School of Peace.............29a Beacon St., Boston.
Int. Silver.	International Silver Co...................................Meriden, Ct.
Int. S. S. Assoc.	International Sunday School Association..805 Hartford Bldg., Chicago.
Int. Tax.	International Tax Association..417 Bd. of Trade Bldg., Columbus, O.
Int. Textbk.	International Textbook Co.........................Scranton, Pa.
Int. Union United Brewery.	International Union of United Brewery Workmen of America, Vine and Cahoun St., Cincinnati.
Inter Aid.	Inter Aid Bureau...Streator, Ill.
Intercollegiate Prohibition.	Intercollegiate Prohibition Association.......................Chicago.
Interstate Pr.	Interstate Printing Co...................................St. Louis.

Interstate Prohibition.	Interstate Prohibition Publishing Association, 477 Ellicott Sq., Buffalo, N. Y.
Interstate Sch. Corr.	Interstate School of Correspondence..378-388 Wabash. Ave., Chicago.
Inventors & Investors.	Inventors & Investors Corporation....1114 Chestnut St., Philadelphia.
Iowa Pub.	Iowa Publishing Co..........Des Moines, Ia.
Ipswich Hist.	Ipswich Historical Society..........Ipswich, Mass.
Irish Hand-Woven.	Irish Hand-Woven Linen Damask Co..........Chicago.
Italian Am.	Italian American Printing Co..........17 Chatham Sq., New York.
Italian Sch.	Italian School of Languages..........315 Fifth Ave., New York.
Ithaca Journ.	Ithaca Journal Press..........Ithaca, N. Y.
Ithomites, A.	Ithomites, Apostle..........Raymond, Wash.
Item Pub.	Item Publishing Co..........Sellersville, Pa.
Ivy.	Ivy Press..........Seattle, Wash.
Jackson, A. D.	Jackson, Alma Drayer..........Durham, N. H.
Jackson, E. M.	Jackson, E. M..........Vineland, N. J.
Jackson, F. E.	Jackson, Fred. E..........Jefferson, Mo.
Jackson, G. A.	Jackson, G. A..........8 Pemberton Sq., Boston.
Jackson, G:	Jackson, George..........1005 Bryan St., Dallas, Tex.
Jackson, L.	Jackson, Loulia..........Blackburn, Mo.
Jackson Print.	Jackson Print Shop..........Room 25, 27 E. 22d St., New York.
Jacobs.	Jacobs, George W., & Co..........208 W. Washington Sq., Philadelphia.
Jacobs G. E.	Jacobs, G. E..........1st National Bank Bldg., Gettysburg, Pa.
Jacobs, H:	Jacobs, Henry..........590 Prospect Ave., New York.
Jacobs & Holmes.	Jacobs & Holmes..........167 Adams St., Chicago.
Jager, T. F.	Jager, Theodore F..........Pittsford, N. Y.
James, G.	James, Gorton..........33 Buckminster Rd., Brookline, Mass.
James, G: W., jr.	James, George Watson, Jr..........15 N. 4th St., Richmond, Va.
James M. C.	James, Mrs. M. C..........2608 Regent St., Berkeley, Cal.
James, U. P.	James, U. P..........127 W. 7th St., Cincinnati.
James, W: G.	James, William Grant..........Box 3254, Boston.
Jamison, J. C.	Jamison, James C..........Guthrie, Okla.
Jaros Co.	Jaros Co..........132 Nassau St., New York.
Jeffords, S. G.	Jeffords, Sydney G..........Peoria, Ill.
Jefferson.	Jefferson Publishing Co..........Xenia, Ill.
Jefferson Co. Med. Soc.	Jefferson County Medical Society..........Louisville, Ky.
Jenckes.	Jenckes & Co..........105 Holly St., Cranford, N. J.
Jenison, S. A.	Jenison, Sarah A..........28 Henry St., Grand Rapids, Mich.
Jenkins, L. H.	Jenkins, L. H..........Richmond, Va.
Jenkins, W: R.	Jenkins, William R., Co..........851 Sixth Ave., New York.
Jenner, W: A.	Jenner, William A..........34 Pine St., New York.
Jenness, H. T.	Jenness, Herbert Theodore..........306 Old South Bldg., Boston.
Jennings.	Jennings & Graham..........14 W. Washington St., Cincinnati.
Jennings, J.	Jennings, Janet..........McKinley Pl., Monroe, Wis.
Jensen, G: H.	Jenson, G: H..........Natchitoches, La.
Jensen, J. C.	Jensen, J. C..........405 Charles Bldg., Denver, Colo.
Jepson, G:	Jepson, George..........Roslindale, Mass.
Jersey City Lib.	Jersey City Free Public Library..........Jersey City, N. J.
Jewel Pub.	Jewel Publishing Co..........Springfield, Mo.
Jewett, A. D.	Jewett, Albert Dewey..........1002 Flatiron Bldg., New York.
Jewett, C:	Jewett, Charles, M.D..........300 Clinton Ave., Brooklyn, N. Y.
Jewish Pub.	Jewish Publication Society of America..608 Chestnut St., Philadelphia.
Jewish Theological.	Jewish Theological Seminary of America..531 W. 123d St., New York.
Joab, A. E.	Joab, Albert E., Equitable Bldg., 11th and Pacific Ave., Tacoma, Wash.
Johansen, N:	Johansen, Nicholas, care of Journal of Commerce..........New York.
John Crerar Lib.	John Crerar Library..........Chicago.
Johns Hopkins.	Johns Hopkins Press..........Baltimore, Md.
Johnson, A. L.	Johnson, Mrs. Alta Leonard..408 Second St., N. W., Washington, D. C.
Johnson, B. F.	Johnson, B. F., Publishing Co., Rooms 317-319 Mutual Bldg., Richmond, Va.
Johnson, C: L.	Johnson, Charles L..........P. O. Box 141, Seattle, Wash.
Johnson, D.	Johnson, D..........La Grange, Mo.
Johnson, E. B.	Johnson, E. Bird..........59 Seymour Ave., Minneapolis, Minn.
Johnson, E. C.	Johnson, E. C..........707 Malley Bldg., New Haven, Ct.
Johnson, E. R.	Johnson, Edwin Rossiter..........34 Union Sq., New York.
Johnson, H: H.	Johnson, Henry Herbert..........Macon, Ga.
Johnson, J. M.	Johnson, Jeremiah Monroe..........Frankfort, Ky.
Johnson, K. & Q.	Johnson, Koch & Quin..........427 La Salle St., Chicago.
Johnson, L: D.	Johnson, Louis Diffendorf..........Dos Palos, Cal.
Johnson, M. A.	Johnson, M. Alice..........Casey, Ill.
Johnson, M. W:	Johnson, Martin W., School of Art......1 Madison Ave., New York.

Johnson, T. & J. W.	Johnson, T. & J. W., Co..............535 Chestnut St., Philadelphia.
Johnson, T: M.	Johnson, Thomas M..................................Osceola, Mo.
Johnson, W: M.	Johnson, William Mindred........................Hackensack, N. J.
Johnson & G.	Johnson & Galston........................49 Wall St., New York.
Johnston, C. T.	Johnston, C. T......................................Cheyenne, Wyo.
Johnston, C:	Johnston, Charles......................511 W. 122d St., New York.
Johnston, J. N.	Johnston, James Nicoll........383 Pennsylvania Ave., Buffalo, N. Y.
Johnston, R. W.	Johnston, Ralph W., Studios, Inc....................Pittsburgh, Pa.
Johnston Export.	Johnston Export Publishing Co.........135 William St., New York.
Joline, A. H.	Joline, Adrian Hoffman..................1 W. 72d St., New York.
Jones, A. T.	Jones, Alonzo Trevier..........The Sanitarium, Battle Creek, Mich.
Jones, B: W.	Jones, Benjamin Washington........................Spottsville, Va.
Jones, C. M.	Jones, Clarence Miller..............................Columbus, O.
Jones, C: E.	Jones, Charles Edgeworth............................Augusta, Ga.
Jones, C: H:	Jones, Charles Henry...........Stephen Girard Bldg., Philadelphia.
Jones, E. A.	Jones, Edmund A............Care Heer Printing Co., Columbus, O.
Jones, E: R:	Jones, Edward Richard..............................Madison, Wis.
Jones, F. L.	Jones, F. L..Buffalo, N. Y.
Jones, G: I.	Jones, George I...........................216 Clark St., Chicago.
Jones, G: W.	Jones, George W....................................Jacksonville, Ill.
Jones, H:	Jones, Henry, M.D..................................Preston, Minn.
Jones, Ja.	Jones, James ....Chicago.
Jones, J: C.	Jones, Rev. John Cooper............................Leaf River, Ill.
Jones, L.	Jones, Lynds...Oberlin, O.
Jones, M.	Jones, Marshall, Co......................212 Summer St., Boston.
Jones, M. O.	Jones, Milton Osman..................................Bergenfield, N. J.
Jones, W. B.	Jones, W. B...............................185 Franklin St., Boston.
Jones W. E., Baltimore.	Jones, W. E..Baltimore, Md.
Jones, W. F.	Jones, Mrs. W. F..................202 Mission St., San Rafael, Cal.
Jones, W: B.	Jones, William Boucher...................95 State St., Albany, N. Y.
Jones, W: E.	Jones, William Ellis...................................Richmond, Va.
Jones & Lamson.	Jones & Lamson Machine Co.........................Springfield, Vt.
Jones & Laughlin's.	Jones & Laughlin's Steel Co., American Iron & Steel Works, Pittsburgh, Pa.
Jones' Bk. Store.	Jones' Book Store...................................Los Angeles, Cal.
Jones Bros.	Jones Brothers Publishing Co............................Cincinnati.
Journal Cutaneous.	Journal of Cutaneous Diseases..Room 614, 105 W. 40th St., New York.
Journal Infectious Diseases.	Journal of Infectious Diseases...............................Chicago.
Journal Mental.	Journal of Mental Pathology............P. O. Box 1023, New York.
Journal Nervous Disease.	Journal of Nervous and Mental Disease Publishing Co., 64 W. 56th St., New York.
Journal of Commerce.	Journal of Commerce and Commercial Bulletin...........New York.
Journal of Osteopathy.	Journal of Osteopathy Publishing Co................Kirksville, Mo.
Journal Press. (Ct.)	Journal Press...Lakeville, Ct.
Journal Pr. (Ill.)	Journal Printing Co....................................Freeport, Ill.
Journal U. S. Artillery.	Journal U. S. Artillery............................Fort Monroe, Va.
Joyce, J: A.	Joyce, John A.........226 Maryland Ave., N. E., Washington, D. C.
Judd.	Judd, Orange Co..........................315 4th Ave., New York.
Judd & D.	Judd & Detweiler...................420 11th St., Washington, D. C.
Judge.	Judge Co.....................................225 Fifth Ave., New York.
Judson, F: N.	Judson, Frederick Newton..................Rialto Bldg., St. Louis.
Julien, M. C.	Julien, Matthew C............................New Bedford, Mass.
Juvenile Bk.	Juvenile Book Co...Chicago.
Kagey, C: C.	Kagey, Charles Claudius................................Tuscola, Ill.
Kahlenberg, L:	Kahlenberg, Louis...........University of Wisconsin, Madison, Wis.
Kahn, A. N:	Kahn, Alexander Nicholas................140 Nassau St., New York.
Kaiser.	Kaiser, Ferdmand P......................407 N. Broadway, St. Louis.
Kaiser, H. W.	Kaiser, H. W.......................317 Hennen Bldg., New Orleans.
Kalbfus, J.	Kalbfus, Joseph......................................Harrisburg, Pa.
Kaler, J. O.	Kaler, James Otis, City of South Portland, School Department, South Portland, Me.
Kallmeyer, C:	Kallmeyer, Charles.....................205 E. 45th St., New York.
Kane, F. K.	Kane, F. K..............................129 W. 29th St., New York.
Kansas City Pub. Lib.	Kansas City Public Library........................Kansas City, Mo.
Kansas Prohibitionist.	Kansas Prohibitionist..............................Kansas City, Kan.

Katz, E. Katz, Elizabeth....3 W. 92d St., New York.
Kaufmann, E. Kaufmann, Ernest....22-24 N. William St., New York.
Kaufman, H. Kaufman, Herbert....Chicago.
Kauser. Kauser, A....1402 Broadway, New York.
Kealing, H. T. Kealing, Hightower T....206 Pub. Sq., Nashville, Tenn.
Kearney. Kearney, John E....43 W. 27th St., New York.
Keefe. Keefe Bros....Butte, Mont.
Keefe-D. Keefe-Davidson Law Book Co....St. Paul, Minn.
Keeler, C. O. Keeler, Mrs. Clarissa Olde..715 Rhode Island Ave., Washington, D. C.
Keeler, L. E. Keeler, Lucy Elliot....417 Birchard Ave., Fremont, O.
Keener. Keener, W. T., & Co. (purchased by the Chicago Medical Book Co.).
Keith, M. L. Keith, Max L....Minneapolis, Minn.
Keith & G. Keith & Ginter....Belleville, O.
Kelker, F. Kelker, F....Harrisburg, Pa.
Keller, C: E. Keller, Charles E....Mallet Creek, O.
Keller-C. Keller-Crescent Printing and Engraving Co....Evansville, Ind.
Kellerstrass, E. Kellerstrass, Ernest....Kansas City, Mo.
Kelley, F: Kelley, Frederick....Holton, Mich.
Kellogg, A. H. Kellogg, Andrew H., Co....409-415 Pearl St., New York.
Kellogg, J. Kellogg, J....309 W. 2d St., Little Rock, Ark.
Kellogg-B. Kellogg-Baxter Publishing Co....11 W. 9th St., Kansas City, Mo.
Kelly. Kelly Publishing Co....5 Beekman St., New York.
Kelsey, F. W. Kelsey, Francis Willey....Ann Arbor, Mich.
Kemp & H. Kemp & Hubert....Spokane, Wash.
Kempton. Kempton, George....Sharon, Mass.
Kenedy. Kenedy, P. J., & Sons....5 Barclay St., New York.
Kennan, T: L. Kennan, Thomas L....179 Prospect Ave., Milwaukee, Wis.
Kennebeck. Kennebeck Journal Print....Augusta, Me.
Kennerley, M. Kennerley, Mitchell....2 E. 29th St., New York.
Kent, C. E. Kent, Mrs. C. E....26 T St., N. W., Washington, D. C.
Kent, G: H. Kent, George H....Cambridge, Mass.
Kentucky Dept. Educ. Kentucky Department of Education....Frankfort, Ky.
Kentucky State Lib. Kentucky State Librarian....Frankfort, Ky.
Keogh, A. Keogh, Andrew....Chicago.
Keppel, Pub. Keppel Publishing Co....Tiffin, O.
Keramic. Keramic Studio Publishing Co....Syracuse, N. Y.
Kernodle, P: J. Kernodle, Peter Jefferson....Eton College, N. C.
Kerr. Kerr, Charles H., & Co....118 W. Kinzie St., Chicago.
Kerr, R. Kerr, Robert, Press....2 E. 29th St., New York.
Ketcham, K. P. Ketcham, Rev. Kneeland Platt....337 W. 23d St., New York.
Ketler, H. B. Ketler, Horace B....Camden, N. J.
Keuffel. Keuffel & Esser Co....127 Fulton St., New York.
Keystone Pub. Keystone Publishing Co....809 N. 19th St., Phiadelphia.
Kibler. Kibler & Co....Springfield, Mo.
Kidd, J. H. Kidd, James Harvey....14 N. 2d St., Ionia, Mich.
Kidd, J. N. Kidd, Josiah Nicholas....Winfield, Kan.
Kilbourn. Kilbourn, Dwight C....East Litchfield, Ct.
Kilner. Kilner, H. L., & Co....824 Arch St., Philadelphia.
Kimball Press. Kimball Press....Evanston, Ill.
King. King, Franklin Hiram....1540 University Ave., Madison, Wis.
King, C. F. King, Cardenio F....Journal Bldg., Boston.
King, F: A. King, Frederick Alwin....2 The Romaine, Clifton, Cincinnati.
King, G. G. King, Georgiana G....Bryn Mawr College, Bryn Mawr, Pa.
King, G: W. King, George W., Printing Co....31 S. Howard St., Baltimore, Md.
King, J. L. King, Joseph L....Room 7, 339 Bush St., San Francisco.
King, L. J. King, L. J....1808 Cora Ave., St. Louis.
King, S. J. King, Sidney J....126 Market St., Chicago.
King, W: A. King, William A., Union and Times Press, St. Stephen's Hall, Buffalo, N. Y.
King Bros. King Bros....413 E. Lexington St., Baltimore, Md.
King Pr. King Printing Co....619 Shelby St., Bristol, Tenn.
King-R. King-Richardson Co....137½ State St., Springfield, Mass.
King's Business. King's Business Publishing Co....501 Tremont Temple, Boston.
Kingsley, H: R. Kingsley, Henry Ross....23 James St., Newark, N. J.
Kinnaird, P. Kinnaird, Percy....312½ Third Ave., Nashville, Tenn.
Kinney, A. S. Kinney, Asa Stephen....So. Hadley, Mass.
Kinsey R. B. Kinsey, Robert Baldwin....622 Court St., Reading, Pa.
Kirkpatric, H. Kirkpatric, Howard....University School of Music, Lincoln, Neb.
Kirkpatrick, G: R. Kirkpatrick, George Ross....West La Fayette, O

Kirsch, W:	Kirsch, William....................................Newark, N. J.
Kistler.	Kistler, W. H., Stationery Co.........................Denver, Colo.
Kitchen, J. W.	Kitchen, Mrs. James W..................313 East St., Warren, Pa.
Kitchen, R.	Kitchen, Mrs. R.................341 West Sixth St., Bloomsburg, Pa.
Kittochtinny.	Kittochtinny Press...............................Chambersburg, Pa.
Kittredge, J: H.	Kittredge, John Herbert............................Chillicothe, Mo.
Klaber, W:	Klaber, William...................Columbia University, New York.
Klein, J.	Klein, Jacob.......................36 Fox St., Poughkeepsie, N. Y.
Klopp.	Klopp & Bartlett......................................Omaha, Neb.
Klump	Klump, C. M.......................1208 Chestnut St., Philadelphia.
Knappenberger, J.B.	Knapppenberger, James Buchanan..707 Midland Ave., Syracuse, N. Y.
Knaus, H:	Knaus, Henry...Chicago.
Knega.	Knega Co.....................................Washington, D. C.
Knickerbocker Press.	Knickerbocker Press....................2 W. 45th St., New York.
Knight, L.	Knight, L............................16 Cortlandt St., New York.
Knights King Arthur.	Knights of King Arthur......Taylor and 3d Aves., Detroit, Mich.
Knowlson & M.	Knowlson & Muller............Room 4, Eagle Bldg., Brooklyn, N. Y.
Knox, P. C.	Knox, Philander Chase.............1527 K St., Washington, D. C.
Knox, R. L.	Knox, Robert L...................................Fredericksburg, Va.
Koeckert.	Koeckert, E. C......................702 Rose Bldg., Cleveland, O.
Kohl Technical.	Kohl Technical Publishing Co.............346 Broadway, New York.
Kohlsaat, A. M.	Kohlsaat, Amy M.......................25 E. 73d St., New York.
Kohn & P.	Kohn & Pollock, Inc...............................Baltimore, Md.
Kolb, C: B.	Kolb, Charles B......................................Columbus, O.
Kolesch.	Kolesch & Co........................138 Fulton St., New York.
Kozlay, C: M.	Kozlay, Charles Meeker.............339 Adams St., Brooklyn, N. Y.
Kraft, M. J.	Kraft, Mary Jane, M.D.........313 N. Greenleaf Ave., Whittier, Cal.
Krehbiel.	Krehbiel, C. J., & Co....................................Cincinnati.
Kreider, G: N.	Kreider, George N., M.D.........522 Capitol Ave., Springfield, Ill.
Krohn, J: A.	Krohn, John Albert...........................Newburyport, Mass.
Krull, V. H.	Krull, Rev. Virgilius Herman....................Collegeville, Ind.
Krumreig, E: L.	Krumreig, E: Ludwig.................37 High St., Somerset, Mass.
Kruse, C: H:	Kruse, Charles Henry.............................Petersburg, Va.
Kuehl, G: W.	Kuehl, George W...................................Milwaukee, Wis.
Kullmer, C. J.	Kullmer, C. J....................505 University Pl., Syracuse, N. Y.
Kümmel, H: B.	Kümmel, Henry Barnard........917 Edgewood Ave., Trenton, N. J.
Kuyahora Press.	Kuyahora Press.....................................Newport, N. Y.
La Bree, B:	La Bree, Benjamin, Jr.................................Louisville, Ky.
La. Distrib. Co.	Louisiana Distributing Co. of "Unveiling Tributes," Woodmen of the World.........................P. O. Box 533, Shreveport, La.
La Follia.	La Follia di New York.................190 Grand St., New York.
La. Geol. Survey.	Louisiana Geological Survey.......................Baton Rouge, La.
La. Meadow.	Louisiana Meadow Co.............................New Orleans, La.
La. Pub. Co.	Louisiana Publishing Co......137 Carondalet St., New Orleans, La.
La. State Univ.	Louisiana State University........................Baton Rouge, La.
Laboratory Co.	Laboratory Co...................................Norway Lake, Me.
Lafontaine, J. R.	Lafontaine, J. R.................................San Francisco.
Laing.	Laing, L. I., Co.......................5734 Kimbark Ave., Chicago.
Laird.	Laird & Lee...........................1732 Michigan Ave., Chicago.
Lamb, E. G.	Lamb, Edwin Gifford...................................Norwalk, Ct.
Lamb, H: G.	Lamb, Henry Grant......................................Matawan, N. J.
	Lamb, J. H. *See* Publishing House of the Evangelical Association.
Lamb Pub.	Lamb Publishing Co......................225 Fifth Ave., New York.
Lambert, W: H.	Lambert, William Harrison...........Mutual Life Bldg., Philadelphia.
Lambourne, A.	Lambourne, Alfred............531 6th Ave., Salt Lake City, Utah.
Lamp Pub.	Lamp Publishing Co.......................Graymoor, Garrison, N. Y.
Lanahan.	Lanahan, J........................220 N. Howard St., Baltimore, Md.
Landes, S. W.	Landes, Sarah W..........................Box 504, Stillwater, Okla.
Lane.	Lane, John, Co. (Bodley Head)......110-114 W. 32d St., New York.
Lane, L. P.	Lane, Leasure Porter........................Box 293, Zanesville, O.
Lane, W. D.	Lane, W. D., & Co.........................11 Cliff St., New York.
Langdon, E. F.	Langdon, Mrs. Emma Florence..1395 Lowell Boulevard, Denver, Colo.
Lange.	Lange, Louis, Publishing Co...................................St. Louis.
Lanier, J: J.	Lanier, John Jabez..................................Washington, Ga.
Laning.	Laning Printing Co......................................Norwalk, O.
Lanston.	Lanston Monotype Machine Co...............................Philadelphia.
Lanthorne.	Lanthorne Press...................................Ann Arbor, Mich.
Lanzit, J. J.	Lanzit, Joseph J..Chicago.
Laramie Repub.	Laramie Republican Co.................................Laramie, Wyo.
Larkin.	Larkin Co...Buffalo, N. Y.

Larkin, E:	Larkin, Edward, Sec'y Chicago Chapter, Knights of Columbus, R. A. 12, Great Northern Hotel, Chicago.
Larson, J. H:	Larson, James Henry...Haileybury, Ont.
L'Art de la Mode.	L'Art de la Mode...8 W. 38th St., New York.
La Salle Bureau.	La Salle Bureau of Supplies...50 2d St., New York.
La Salle Extension.	La Salle Extension University...2715-2719 Michigan Ave., Chicago.
Laskowski, P: E.	Laskowski, Peter E...Los Angeles, Cal.
Lathbury, A. A:	Lathbury, Albert Augustus...East Norwich, L. I., N. Y.
Lathrop, L. C.	Lathrop, Lester Cassius...911 Atwood Ave., Madison, Wis.
Laughlin, A.	Laughlin, Annie...Mark West, Cal.
Lavarack, F: C:	Lavarack, Frederick Charles...114 Park St., East Orange, N. J.
Law, E. N.	Law, Mrs. Emma N...Detroit, Mich.
Law, W: H.	Law, William Hainstock...135 Pine St., Detroit, Mich.
Law Acad.	Law Academy of Philadelphia...Philadelphia.
Law Journ.	Law Journal Publishing Co...Plainfield, N. J.
Law Reporting.	Law Reporting Co...67 Wall St., New York.
Law Stamps.	Law Stamps Co...Detroit, Mich.
Lawrence, R: H.	Lawrence, Richard Hoe...15 Wall St., New York.
Lawrence Cement.	Lawrence Cement Co...Room 1, 1 Broadway, New York.
Lawrence Journ.	Lawrence Journal Co...Lawrence, Kan.
Laws, C. R.	Laws, Clarence R...St. Louis.
Lawyers' Co-op.	Lawyers' Co-operative Publishing Co...Rochester, N. Y.
Lay, W: A.	Lay, William August...Cincinnati.
Lea.	Lea & Febiger...706-708 Sansom St., Philadelphia.
Leach J. G.	Leach, Col. Josiah Granville...733 Walnut St., Philadelphia.
Leader Pr.	Leader Printing Co...Guthrie, Okla.
League Am. Municipalities.	League of American Municipalities...95 Dearborn St., Chicago.
League Lib. Com.	League of Library Commissions...The Capitol, St. Paul, Minn.
Leahy, G: V.	Leahy, George V...St. John's Seminary, Brighton, Mass.
Leale, C: A:	Leale, Charles Augustus...604 Madison Ave., New York.
Lee, A.	Lee, Ambrose, Publishing Co...Williamsbridge, N. Y.
Lee, A. S.	Lee, Albert Sherman...Ripley, W. Va.
Lee, E. B.	Lee, Elizabeth Batts...Flushing, N. Y.
Lee, I. L.	Lee, Ivy Ledbetter...20 Broad St., New York.
Lee, J: H.	Lee, John H...Pomona, Cal.
Lee, L. W.	Lee, L. W......1009 Tremont St., Boston.
Lee, R. E.	Lee, R. E., Co...formerly 687 Boylston St., Boston.
Lee & Co.	Lee & Co...Hawthorne, N. J.
Leech, S: V.	Leech, Rev. Samuel Vanderlip...Washington, D. C.
Leffman, H:	Leffman, Henry...1839 N. 17th St., Philadelphia.
Legal.	Legal Advertising Co...Cincinnati.
Legal Adv.	Legal Adviser Publishing Co...92 La Salle St., Chicago.
Legal Aid.	Legal Aid Society...Room 23, 239 Broadway, New York.
Legler, H: E.	Legler, Henry E...Public Library, Chicago.
Lehigh Co. Hist.	Lehigh County Historical Society...Allentown, Pa.
Lehigh Coal.	Lehigh Coal & Navigation Co...108 So. 4th St., Philadelphia.
Lehman, H: H.	Lehman, Henry Harvey...Ashland, O.
Lehmann, J: A.	Lehmann, John Albert...Thompson, O.
Lehmen.	Lehmen Printing Co...Baltimore, Md.
Leiding, H. K.	Leiding, Harriette Kershaw...Charleston, S. C.
Leitch, B. M.	Leitch, B. M...Wawona, Cal.
Leland, S: P.	Leland, Samuel Phelps...Seabreeze, Fla.
Leland Stanford Jr. Univ.	Leland Stanford Jr. University...Stanford University, Cal.
Lemcke.	Lemcke & Buechner...30-32 W. 27th St., New York.
Lenox Coll.	Lenox College...Hopkinton, Ia.
Lenox Pub.	Lenox Publishing Co...New York.
Lent & G.	Lent & Graff Co...137 E. 25th St., New York.
Leoser Bros.	Leoser Bros. & Gilmore...78 Broad St., New York.
Lesan-G.	Lesan-Gould Co...St. Louis.
Leslie-Judge.	Leslie-Judge Co., Brunswick Bldg., Fifth Ave. and 27th St., New York.
Lester Bk.	Lester Book Co...Atlanta, Ga.
Letson, S: B.	Letson, Samuel Brisbin...327 S. Olive St., Los Angeles, Cal.
Levey.	Levey Bros. & Co...Indianapolis, Ind.
Levey, E. J.	Levey, Edgar J...Room 200, 135 Broadway, New York.
Levi, L: E.	Levi, Louis Emanuel...Milwaukee, Wis.
Lewis, G: E:	Lewis, George Edward...Bryantville, Mass.
Lewis, H. A.	Lewis, H. A...Success Co., 29 E. 22d St., New York.
Lewis, J. J:	Lewis, James John...Chicago.
Lewis, Jos. Vance.	Lewis, Joseph Vance...Houston, Tex.

Lewis, S. A.	Lewis, Spenser A., Co............1731 Euclid St., Washington, D C.
Lewis, W: D.	Lewis, William Draper..........34th and Chestnut Sts., Philadelphia.
Lewis & W.	Lewis & White..................................Kosciusko, Miss.
Lewis Pub. Co.	Lewis Publishing Co., 265 Broadway, New York, and 358 Dearborn St., Chicago.
Lewiston Journ.	Lewiston Journal Co., Press of...........................Lewiston, Me.
Lex.	Lex Publishing Co..Jackson, Miss.
Lexington Hist. Soc.	Lexington Historical Society.....................Lexington, Mass.
Libbey, C: T.	Libbey, Charles Thornton.............P. O. Box 465, Portland, Me.
Lib. Bu.	Library Bureau..........................215 Madison St., Chicago.
Lib. Shelf.	Library Shelf.....................850-854 McClurg Bldg., Chicago.
Liberty Pub.	Liberty Publishing Co...............852 Simpson St., New York.
Lichtenstein, G.	Lichtenstein, Gaston...............1419 Grove Ave., Richmond, Va.
Life Pub. Co.	Life Publishing Co.........................17 W. 31st St., New York.
Light and Hope.	Light and Hope Publishing Co......................Birmingham, O.
Liljengren, A.	Liljengren, Adolph...............670 No. High St., Middletown, Ct.
Lilley.	Lilley, M. C., & Co..Columbus, O.
Lincoln.	Lincoln Publishing Co............270 North St., Springfield, Mass.
Lincoln Business.	Lincoln Business College......................................Lincoln, Neb.
Lincoln Fellowship.	Lincoln Fellowship.........................38 W. 21st St., New York.
Lincoln Pub. Co.	Lincoln Publishing Co.......................56 Lincoln St., Boston.
Lincoln Sentinel.	Lincoln Sentinel Print......................................Lincoln, Kan.
Lincoln Temperance.	Lincoln Temperance Press..Chicago.
Lindsay.	Lindsay Publishing Co., 412-414 People's Bank Bldg., Seattle, Wash.
Lindsay, N: V.	Lindsay, Nicholas Vachel.............223 So. 6th St., Springfield, Ill.
Linn, A. D.	Linn, Allen Dawson................32 10th St., Grand Rapids, Mich.
Linn, S:	Linn, Rev. Samuel..Axtell, Neb.
Linnaean.	Linnaean Society of New York..........153 W. 73d St., New York.
Lippincott.	Lippincott, J. B., Co.............E. Washington Sq., Philadelphia.
Liquid Carbonic.	Liquid Carbonic Co...............................440 Wells St., Chicago.
Litchfield, W. J.	Litchfield, Wilford J...................455 Columbus Ave., Boston.
Little, B. & Co.	Little, Brown & Co..............................34 Beacon St., Boston.
Little, W. C.	Little, Weare C., & Co.................525 Broadway, Albany, N. Y.
Little & I.	Little, J. J., & Ives Co................435 E. 24th St., New York.
Little Chronicle.	Little Chronicle Co........................358 Dearborn St., Chicago.
Little Journeys.	Little Journeys Publishing Co............79 Dearborn St., Chicago.
Littlefield.	Littlefield, George Emery..........................67 Cornhill, Boston.
Littlefield, C: W.	Littlefield, Charles Wentworth.....442-3 Central Bldg., Seattle, Wash.
Lively.	Lively, Rev. William Irven..................................Greenville, Ill.
Livingston, J: H:	Livingston, John Henry, Esq..."Clermont," Tivoli P. O., New York.
Lloyd, J. A.	Lloyd, Julius A..Dixon, Ill.
Lloyd, J: W:	Lloyd, John William......................................Westfield, N. J.
Lloyd Bros.	Lloyd Bros.........................Court and Plum Sts., Columbus.
Lloyd Lib.	Lloyd Library of Botany, Pharmacy and Materia Medica, 309 W. Court St., Cincinnati.
Loeser, F:	Loeser, Frederick, & Co...........482 Fulton St., Brooklyn, N. Y.
Loma Linda Coll.	Loma Linda College Press..............................Loma Linda, Cal.
Lomax, E. L.	Lomax, E. L..........G. P. A. Union Pacific R.R. Co., Omaha, Neb.
Lone Star.	Lone Star Publishers..................136 S. Main St., Paris, Tex.
Long, C. E.	Long, Clarence E...Sturgeon, Wis.
Long, G: T.	Long, George Thiell...............400 Manhattan Ave., New York.
Long, J. S.	Long, Joseph Schuyler..............201 Logan St., Council Bluffs, Ia.
Long, J: I. T.	Long, John Ignatius Theodore..........................Fruitland, Md.
Long, M. B.	Long, Maxwell Budd..Gambier, O.
Long, S. P:	Long, Rev. Simon Peter............49 Park Ave., W., Mansfield, O.
Long Branch Press.	Long Branch Press.....................................Long Branch, N. J.
Long Island R. R.	Long Island Railroad Co..................................34th St., New York.
Longanecker.	Longanecker, E. W..Anderson, Ind.
Longest, W: B.	Longest, William Butler.............725-729 S. 3d St., Louisville, Ky.
Longmans.	Longmans, Green & Co...........443-449 Fourth Ave., New York.
L'Ora Queta.	L'Ora Queta Publishing Co..Room 401, 160 Washington St., Chicago.
Lord.	Lord & Thomas...Trude Bldg., Chicago.
Lord, G: W.	Lord, George W., Co...........................2238 N. 9th St., Philadelphia.
Lord Balto. Pr.	Lord Baltimore Press.Greenmount Ave. and Oliver St., Baltimore, Md.
Lord & N.	Lord & Nagel Co...................................144 Congress St., Boston.
Loring S. & H.	Loring, Short & Harmon...........474 Congress St., Portland, Me.
Los Angeles Lib.	Los Angeles Public Library.............................Los Angeles, Cal.
Los Angeles Investment.	Los Angeles Investment Co..............................Los Angeles, Cal.
Los Angeles Liberal.	Los Angeles Liberal Club.........517 S. Broadway, Los Angeles, Cal.
Los Angeles Pr.	Los Angeles Printing Co..................................Los Angeles, Cal.

Los Angeles Pub.	Los Angeles Publishing Co........Los Angeles, Cal.
Lothrop, G: E.	Lothrop, George Edwin........Boston.
Lothrop, L. & S.	Lothrop, Lee & Shepard........93 Federal St., Boston.
Lougee, C. R.	Lougee, C. R........Winterport, Me.
Louisville Pub. Lib.	Louisville Free Public Library........Louisville, Ky.
Love, J: L.	Love, John L........Langston, Okla.
Lovell.	Lovell, Frank, & Co........68 Murray St., New York.
Lowdermilk.	Lowdermilk, W. H., & Co........1424-1426 F St., Washington, D. C.
Lowe, F.	Lowe, Frank........Oklahoma City, Okla.
Lowell, A. W.	Lowell, Abner W........Portland, Me.
Lowell Lib.	Lowell City Library........Lowell, Mass.
Lowman.	Lowman & Hanford Co........616-620 First Ave., Seattle, Wash.
Loveridge, R. T.	Loveridge, Rose Taylor........Marcellus, Mich.
Lowrie, A. W:	Lowrie, Alfred William........7 Pliny St., Hartford, Ct.
Luce, J: W.	Luce, John W., & Co........143 Federal St., Boston.
Lumbermen's Pr.	Lumberman's Printing Co........St. Louis.
Lumbermen's Pub.	Lumbermen's Publishing Co., Bank of Commerce Bldg., 9th floor, Norfolk, Va.
Lunn, A. C.	Lunn, Arthur Constant........5537 Drexel Ave., Chicago.
Luther Press.	Luther Press........P. O. Box 253, Minneapolis, Minn.
Lutheran Bk.	Lutheran Book Concern........505 E. Main St., Columbus, O.
Lutheran Pub.	Lutheran Publication Society........1424 Arch St., Philadelphia.
Lutherans.	Lutherans in all Lands Publishing Co., P. O. Box 253, Minneapolis, Minn.
Lyal Bk.	Lyal Book Concern........Chicago.
Lyceumite.	Lyceumite Press........617 Steinway Hall, Chicago.
Lyman, B: S.	Lyman, Benjamin Smith........708 Locust St., Philadelphia.
Lyman Bros.	Lyman Bros........108 Pearl St., Syracuse, N. Y.
Lynch, H. P.	Lynch, Mrs. Harriet Powe........Cheraw, S. C.
Lyon.	Lyon, James B., Co........30-36 Beaver St., Albany, N. Y.
Lyon & A.	Lyon & Armor........Philadelphia.
Lyon & H.	Lyon & Healy........Cor. Adams St. and Wabash Ave., Chicago.
Lyons, J. A.	Lyons, J. A., & Co........378 Wabash Ave., Chicago.
M. L. & I.	M. L. & I. Co........Lakeport, Cal.
M. O. L. L. (Ill.)	Military Order of the Loyal Legion........320 Ashland Blvd., Chicago.
M. O. L. L. (N. Y.)	Military Order of the Loyal Legion of the United States..New York.
M. O. L. L., (Pa.)	Military Order of the Loyal Legion of the U. S. Commandery of the State of Pennsylvania........Philadelphia.
M. S. Pub.	M. S. Publishing Co........328 Wabash Ave., Chicago.
McAleer, G:	McAleer, George, M.D........155 Main St., Worcester, Mass.
McAllister, J. T.	McAllister, Joseph Thompson........Salem, Va.
McAlpine, J. D.	McAlpine, J. D........Collinwood, O.
McArdle, F.	McArdle, Fred........6432 Ingleside Ave., Chicago.
McArdle & H.	McArdle & Helmholtz........6432 Ingleside Ave., Chicago.
Macaulay.	Macaulay Co........15 W. 38th St., New York.
McBain, H. L.	McBain, Howard Lee........1016 Fourteenth St., Washington, D. C.
McBride.	McBride, John, Co........2 Rector St., New York.
McBride, W.	McBride, Winston Co........6 W. 29th St., New York.
McCabe, R. L.	McCabe, Robert Lorenzo........Dayton, O.
MacCalla.	MacCalla & Co........Philadelphia.
McCallie, S: W.	McCallie, Samuel Washington........Atlanta, Ga.
McCain, C: C.	McCain, Charles C........143 Liberty St., New York.
McCall, N. L.	McCall, Nanetta L........Chicago.
McCann, M. A.	McCann, Sister Mary Agnes........Mt. St. Joseph, Hamilton Co. O.
McCarty.	McCarty, Louis Philippe........3238 Twenty-first St., San Francisco.
McClendon, W: A:	McClendon, William Augustus........R. F. D. No. 4, Abbeville, Ala.
McClintock, G. M.	McClintock, G. M........Brookline, Mass.
McCloskey, F. A.	McCloskey, Francis A........367 Fulton St., Brooklyn, N. Y.
McClure.	McClure Co. *See* Doubleday, Page & Co.
McClure, S. S.	McClure, S. S., Co........44 E. 23d St., New York.
McClure, T. A.	McClure, T. A........Philadelphia.
McClurg.	McClurg, A. C., & Co........330 E. Ohio St., Chicago.
McCollum, A. J.	McCollum, A. J........Atkins, Ark.
McCormic Med.	McCormic Medical Book Co........Chicago.
McCormick, J: N:	McCormick, John Nicholas........Georgetown, Ill.
MacCoun, T.	MacCoun, Townsend........225 Fifth Ave., New York.
McCourt.	McCourt, Robert Shepard........1669 Princeton Ave., St. Paul, Minn.
McCourt, W. E.	McCourt, W. E........Trenton, N. J.
McCune, F. H:	McCune, Frank Henry........2036 Riverside Ave., Spokane, Wash.
McCurdy, D. B.	McCurdy, D. B........Chicago.
McCurry, J. H.	McCurry, J. H........Grubbs, Ark.
McCutcheon, G: B.	McCutcheon, George Barr........1 W. 64th St., New York.
McDaniel, C: F.	McDaniel, Charles Foster........Cedar Rapids, Ia.

MacDonald, A.	MacDonald, Arthur............127 'A" St., N. E., Washington, D. C.
McDonald, D. W:	McDonald, Donald William............Tampa, Fla.
McDonald, K. S.	McDonald, Mrs. Kate S............Berryville, Va.
McDonald, W: J.	McDonald, William Jesse............824 Brozas St., Austin, Tex.
McDonald & Co.	McDonald & Co............Canadian, Tex.
McDonough, J.	McDonough, Joseph............98 State St., Albany, N. Y.
Macdonough, R.	Macdonough, Rodney............5 Bromfield St., Boston.
MacDowell, T. L.	MacDowell, Theodore L............2125 Uber Pl., Philadelphia.
McElroy, J:	McElroy, John............Washington, D. C.
McEvoy, T: J.	McEvoy, Thomas Jefferson............306 Fulton St., Brooklyn, N. Y.
McFadden.	McFadden, Elizabeth A............7 Ware St., Cambridge, Mass.
McGee, G. C.	McGee, Guy C............Caldwell, Id.
MacGerald.	MacGerald, Willis, & Co............Chicago.
McGill, M. R.	McGill, Mary Robson............55 E. Main St., Columbus, O.
McGraw.	McGraw Publishing Co. *See* McGraw-Hill Book Co.
McGraw-H.	McGraw-Hill Book Co. (Successors to Book Depts. of Hill Publishing Co. and McGraw Publishing Co.), 239 W. 39th St., New York.
McGregor Co.	McGregor Co............Athens, Ga.
McIlwaine, H: R.	McIlwaine, Henry Reed, State Librarian, Virginia State Library, Richmond, Va.
McIlwaine, R:	McIlwaine, Rev. Richard............608 W. Grace St., Richmond, Va.
McIntosh.	McIntosh Battery & Optical Co....227-229 Washington St., Chicago.
McIntyre, L. L.	McIntyre, Mrs. Louise Leverenz............Dansville, Ill.
MacIntyre, W: I.	MacIntyre, William Irwin............Thomasville, Ga.
McKay.	McKay, David............604-608 Washington Sq., Philadelphia.
McKeever, W: A.	McKeever, William Archibald, Kansas State Agricultural College, Topeka, Kan.
McKennan.	McKennan Publishing Co............Durley Bldg., Bloomington, Ill.
McKenney, M. M.	McKenney, Mrs. Marie M..Highland Terrace, North St. Paul, Minn.
McKenzie, F. A.	McKenzie, Fayette Avery............83 Sixteenth Ave., Columbus, O.
Mackenzie-K.	Mackenzie-Klink Publishing Co............Chicago.
McKinley Pub.	McKinley Publishing Co............5805 Germantown Ave., Philadelphia.
McKnight, L. A.	McKnight, L. A............Fowler, Ind.
Maclachlan, A. D.	Maclachlan, A. D............502 Boylston St., Boston.
McLaughlin, J. C.	McLaughlin, J. Candor, M.D....308 Junction Bldg., Kansas City, Mo.
McLaughlin, W.	McLaughlin, Wendell............1043 S. Grand Ave., Los Angeles, Cal.
McLean, A. W.	McLean, A. W............Lumberton, N. C.
McLoughlin.	McLoughlin Bros............890 Broadway, New York.
Macmillan.	Macmillan Co............64-66 Fifth Ave., New York.
Macmillan Co.	Macmillan Company of Canada, Ltd............Toronto, Canada.
McMillan, H.	McMillan, Hamilton............Red Springs, N. C.
MacMurray, A.	MacMurray, Arthur............Ames, Ia.
McNair.	McNair Publishing Co............40 Williston Rd., Auburndale, Mass.
MacNeal.	MacNeal Printing Co............Baltimore.
McNeill, G: E.	McNeill, George Edwin............Washington, D. C.
Macoy Pub.	Macoy Publishing and Masonic Supply Co....45 John St., New York.
McPike, E. F.	McPike, Eugene Fairfield, Care of William Abbatt, 141 E. 25th St., New York.
McQuiddy.	McQuiddy Printing Co............Nashville, Tenn.
McVey.	McVey, John Joseph............1229 Arch St., Philadelphia.
Madeira, L.	Madeira, Lucy............1326 Nineteenth St., Washington, D. C.
Madison.	Madison Publishing Co............New York.
Magath, J.	Magath, Julius............Oxford, Ga.
Maglathlin, E. B.	Maglathlin, Rev. E. B............West Bridgewater, Mass.
Magnum Bonum.	Magnum Bonum Co............4665 Lake Ave., Chicago.
Magoun, H. W.	Magoun, Herbert W............70 Kirkland St., Cambridge, Mass.
Mahin Adv.	Mahin Advertising Co............873 American Trust Bldg., Chicago.
Mail Order.	Mail Order News............Fordham, New York.
Main, A. E.	Main, Arthur Elwin.......Alfred Theological Seminary, Alfred, N. Y.
Main, J.	Main, Josiah............University of Tennessee, Knoxville, Tenn.
Maine Farmer.	Maine Farmer Press............Augusta, Me.
Maltbie M. R.	Maltbie, Milo R............154 Nassau St., New York.
Malkan.	Malkan, Henry............42 Broadway, New York.
Mallett.	Mallett, Daniel T............253 Broadway, New York.
Manas Press.	Manas Press............860 Mount Hope Ave., Rochester, N. Y.
Manhattan Bk.	Manhattan Book Co............196 E. Broadway, New York.
Manhattan Trade.	Manhattan Trade School............209 E. 23d St., New York.
Manila Merchants'.	Manila Merchants' Association............Manila, P. I.
Manitou.	Manitou Cliff Dwellers' Ruins Co............Colorado Springs, Colo.
Manns, W. H.	Manns, W. H............Waynesboro, Pa.
Manual Arts.	Manual Arts Press............Peoria, Ill.
Manual of Statistics.	Manual of Statistics Co............20 Vesey St., New York.

Manual Pub.	Manual Publishing Co.......Philadelphia.
Manual Training Sch.	Manual Training School.......Washington University, St. Louis.
Manufacturers' Assoc.	Manufacturers' Association of New York, Manufacturers' Bldg., 198 Montague St., Brooklyn, N. Y.
Manufacturers' Record.	Manufacturers' Record.......Baltimore, Md.
March.	March Brothers.......208-212 Wright Ave., Lebanon, O.
Marigold-F.	Marigold-Foster Printing Co.......Bridgeport, Ct.
Marine Biol.	Marine Biological Association of San Diego.......San Diego, Cal.
Marion Press.	Marion Press.......Jamaica, N. Y.
Markens, I:	Markens, Isaac.......62 Beaver St., New York.
Markoe, R. J.	Markoe, Ralston Joshua.......92 W. Summit Ave., St. Paul, Minn.
Marlborough.	Marlborough, City of.......Massachusetts.
Marley, F. E.	Marley, F. E.......4 Wilson St., Batavia, N. Y.
Marohnic, J.	Marohnic, Josip.......1420 E. Ohio St., Allegheny, Pa.
Marquis.	Marquis, A. N., & Co.......440 S. Dearborn St., Chicago.
Marrs, S. M. N.	Marrs, S. M. N.......401 Johnson St., Terrell, Tex.
Marsh, B: C.	Marsh, Benjamin Clarke.......165 Broadway, N. Y.
Marsh, J: P.	Marsh, John P., & Co.......Chicago.
Marshall.	Marshall & Bruce Co.......Nashville Tenn.
Marshall, P.	Marshall, Park.......Nashville, Tenn.
Marshall Print.	Marshall Print Shop.......Huntington, W. Va.
Marshall, R.	Marshall, Ruth.......Rockford, Ill.
Martin, G:	Martin, George.......State Historical Society, Topeka, Kan.
Martin, G: H.	Martin, George H.......Room 303, Ford Bldg., Boston.
Martin, G: W.	Martin, George Washington.......Topeka, Kan.
Martin, H: D.	Martin, Henry Desires.......Clinton, Mass.
Martin, I. S.	Martin, Mrs. Ida Shaw.......Roxbury Mass.
Martin, J. L.	Martin, James Lee.......Hale, Mo.
Martin, J:	Martin, John.......310 Sansome St., San Francisco.
Martin & A.	Martin & Allardyce.......Fries' Bldg., Frankford, Philadelphia.
Martin & H.	Martin & Hoyt Co.......Atlanta, Ga.
Martindale.	Martindale, G. B.......395 Broadway, New York.
Marvin, T. R.	Marvin, T. R., & Son.......73 Federal St., Boston.
Maryland, Geol.	Maryland Geological Survey.......Baltimore, Md.
Mason, A: L.	Mason, Augustus Lynch.......526 Life Bldg., Indianapolis, Ind.
Mason, C: L.	Mason, Charles L.......North Granville, N. Y.
Mason, E. L.	Mason, Mrs. Eveleen Laura.......4 St. Paul St., Brookline, Mass.
Mason, R. F.	Mason, Rosalind Fay.......673 Lincoln Pk. Blvd., Chicago.
Mason-H.	Mason-Henry Press.......106 So. State St., Syracuse, N. Y.
Masonic Chronicler.	Masonic Chronicler Publishing Co.......315 Dearborn St., Chicago.
Maspeth.	Maspeth Publishing House.......76 Milton St., Maspeth, N. Y.
Mass. Adjutant General.	Massachusetts Adjutant General's Office.......Boston.
Mass. Assoc. Plumbing.	Massachusetts Association of Plumbing Inspectors.......Boston.
Mass. Bd. Educ.	Massachusetts Board of Education.......Ford Bldg., Boston.
Mass. Bd. Health.	Massachusetts State Board of Health..Room 502, State House, Boston.
Mass. Cambridge Bridge.	Massachusetts Cambridge Bridge Commission.......Boston.
Mass. Com. Blind.	Massachusetts Commission for the Blind, Room 309, Ford Bldg., 15 Ashburton Pl., Boston.
Mass. Com. Inland Fisheries.	Massachusetts Commissioners on Inland Fisheries and Game, 158 State House, Boston.
Mass. Gen. Hospital.	Massachusetts General Hospital.......Boston.
Mass. Hist. Soc.	Massachusetts Historical Society.......1154 Boylston St., Boston.
Mass New-Ch. Un.	Massachusetts New-Church Union.......16 Arlington St., Boston.
Masseck, F. L.	Masseck, Frank Lincoln.......Potsdam, N. Y.
Massey.	Massey Business College.......Birmingham, Ala.
Master Sheet Metal.	Master Sheet Metal Workers' Journal, 2213 Chestnut St., Philadelphia.
Maston, R. T.	Maston, Ray Thomas.......4314 Central Ave., Madisonville, O.
Mattatuck Press.	Mattatuck Press, Inc.......Waterbury, Ct.
Matthews, A.	Matthews, Albert.......Hotel Oxford, Boston.
Matthews, S. C.	Matthews, Schuyler Colfax....Room 207, 500 Fifth Ave., New York.
Matthews-N.	Matthews-Northrup Works.......179-183 Washington St., Buffalo.
Matthieu, S. A.	Matthieu, S. A.......Poughkeepsie, N. Y.
Maule, G: E.	Maule, George Edmond.......Ogden, Utah.
Maupin, B: F.	Maupin, Benjamin Franklin, Care of John Lane Co., 110-114 W. 32d St., New York.
Maver.	Maver Publishing Co.......136 Liberty St., New York.

Maw, J. M.	Maw, Jessie Maud....Columbus, Neb.
May, C. E.	May, Clarence Earl....Bloomington, Ind.
Mayer, E.	Mayer, Eli....222 Hamilton Ave., Paterson, N. J.
Mayhew.	Mayhew Publishing Co....92-100 Ruggles St., Boston.
Maynard, C: J.	Maynard, Charles Johnson....447 Crafts St., West Newton, Mass.
Mazda.	Mazda Publishing Co., P. O. Box 83, Merchants' Station, St. Louis.
Mazdaznan.	Mazdaznan Associates of God....Chicago.
Me. Hist.	Maine Historical Society....Portland, Me.
Mead, W. W.	Mead, Willis Waldo....195 Broadway, New York.
Meader's.	Meader's Book Store....Rochester, N. H.
Meakin, J: P.	Meakin, John Phillips....468 First Ave., Salt Lake City, Utah.
Med. Pr.	Medical Printing Co....Danbury, Ct.
Medical Abstract.	Medical Abstract Publishing Co....219 6th St., Pittsburgh, Pa.
Medical Science.	Medical Science Press....St. Louis.
Medico-Dental.	Medico-Dental Publishing Co....Chicago.
Medico-Legal.	Medico-Legal Publishing Co....Room 21, 29 Broadway, New York.
Medico-Legal Pub.	Medico-Legal Publishing Co....201 Market St., St. Louis.
Meehan, M.	Meehan, Michael....Concord, N. H.
Meese, W: A:	Meese, William Augustus....Moline, Ill.
Meier L. W.	Meier, Mrs. Lina Wachtelborn, German Cooking School, Milwaukee, Wis.
Meinert, J: H.	Meinert, John H....Toledo, O.
Melberg, P: L.	Melberg, Peter L....912 N. W. Bldg., Minneapolis, Minn.
Melick, C: W.	Melick, Charles W....College Park, Md.
Mell, C. D.	Mell, Clayton Dissinger....Forest Service, Washington, D. C.
Mellen, E. B.	Mellen, E. B....106 Main St., Brockton, Mass.
Melvin, J. C.	Melvin, James C....88 Clinton St., Boston.
Men of Mark.	Men of Mark Publishing Co....Washington, D. C.
Mendelssohn Club.	Mendelssohn Club....Rockford, Ill.
Mendota.	Mendota Book Co....Madison, Wis.
Mennonite Pub. Ho.	Mennonite Publishing House....Scottdale, Pa.
Mercer, J. K.	Mercer, James Kazerta....55 E. Main St., Columbus, O.
Merchants Assoc.	Merchants' Association of New York....54 Lafayette St., New York.
Merchants' Friend.	Merchants' Friend Stock Calculator, 1122 Grand Ave., Kansas City, Mo.
Merchants' Pub.	Merchants' Publishing Co....Denver, Colo.
Merchants' Record.	Merchants' Record Co....315 Dearborn St., Chicago.
Mercy.	Mercy Hospital....Baltimore, Md.
Meredith, E. T.	Meredith, E. T....209 Tenth St., Des Moines, Ia.
Merriam, G. & C.	Merriam, G. & C., Co....499 Main St., Springfield, Mass.
Merrill, C: E.	Merrill, Charles E., Co....44-60 E. 23d St., New York.
Merrill & W.	Merrill & Webber Co....92 Main St., Auburn, Me.
Merrill-S.	Merrill-Soule Co....Syracuse, N. Y.
Merritt, M. I. L.	Merritt, Mrs. Magdalene Isadora La Grange....Voorheesville, N. Y.
Merrymount.	Merrymount Press (D. P. Updike)....232 Summer St., Boston.
Metallurgical.	Metallurgical and Chemical Engineering..239 W. 39th St., New York.
Metaphysical.	Metaphysical Publishing Co....500 Fifth Ave., New York.
Metcalf, H: H.	Metcalf, Henry Harrison....Concord, N. H.
Metcalf, J. J.	Metcalf, Jeannette J....Hampden, Mass.
Metcalfe, R: L.	Metcalfe, Richard Lee....Box 28, Lincoln, Neb.
	Methodist Book Concern. *See* Eaton & Mains.
Meth. Episcopal.	Methodist Episcopal Book Room....Philadelphia.
Meth. Protestant.	Methodist Protestant Book Concern, 316 N. Charles St., Baltimore, Md.
Metropolitan Adv.	Metropolitan Advertising Co....6 Wall St., New York.
Metropolitan Ch. Assoc.	Metropolitan Church Association, Fountain Spring House, Waukesha, Wis.
Metropolitan Museum.	Metropolitan Museum of Art....Fifth Ave. and 82d St., New York.
Metropolitan Pr.	Metropolitan Printing Co....147 First St., Portland, Ore.
Metropolitan Press (N. Y.)	Metropolitan Press. (Books supplied by William Rickey & Co.)
Metropolitan Press, (Ore.)	Metropolitan Press....Portland, Ore.
Metropolitan Sewerage.	Metropolitan Sewerage Commission of New York, 17 Battery Pl., New York.
Metuchen Bungalow.	Metuchen Bungalow Co....160 Broadway, New York.
Metzgar.	Metzgar Publishing Co....Chicago.
Metzler, R.	Metzler, Reed....Ruggery Bldg., Columbus, O.
Mexican Year Bk.	Mexican Year Book Publishing Co....32 Broadway, New York.

Meyer, M. H.	Meyer, Martin H.........C. Hansen's Laboratory, Little Falls, N. Y.
Meyer & T.	Meyer & Thalheimer...Baltimore, Md.
Miami Pr.	Miami Printing Co...Miami, Fla.
Mich. Agricultural Coll.	Michigan State Agricultural College.................Lansing, Mich.
Mich. Chr. Herald.	Michigan Christian Herald..............83 Park Pl., Detroit, Mich.
Mich. Geol.	Michigan Geological Survey..........P. O. Box 535, Lansing, Mich.
Mich. Law Rev.	Michigan Law Review...................................Ann Arbor, Mich.
Mich. State Normal.	Michigan State Normal College.......................Ypsilanti, Mich.
Mich. Supt. Pub. Instruction.	Michigan Superintendent of Public Instruction........Lansing, Mich.
Michels, J:	Michels, John...West Raleigh, N. C.
Michie.	Michie Co...Charlottesville, Va.
Micou, R: W.	Micou, Richard Wilde, care of Brewer's Printing Co., Louisville, Ky.
Middlebrook, L: F.	Middlebrook, Louis Frank...................................Hartford, Ct.
Middleton, G. M.	Middleton, Gustavus M.............28 Lamboll St., Charleston, S. C.
Middleton, J. C.	Middleton, Mrs. J. C.........400 E. San Salvador St., San José, Cal.
Middleton, T: C.	Middleton, Rev. Thomas C....Villanova College, Delaware Co., Pa.
Midland Pub. Co.	Midland Publishing Co..St. Louis.
Midshipmen's Storekeeper.	Midshipmen's Storekeeper...............................Annapolis, Md.
Mieir, W: O.	Mieir, William O.......................................Westminster, Colo.
Mierow, C: C.	Mierow, Charles C..2 Brick House, Phillips Academy, Andover, Mass.
Milans.	Milans, J. D., & Sons.................................Washington, D. C.
Mildren, N. L.	Mildren, Nan Langdon...Denton, Md.
Milk Com. Assoc.	Milk Commissions Association, Otto P. Geier, Sec'y, 124 Garfield Pl., Cincinnati.
Military Hist. Soc.	Military Historical Society of Massachusetts, Cadet Armory, Ferdinand St., Boston.
Millar, A. V.	Millar, Adam Vause....................222 Charter St., Madison, Wis.
Miller, C. H.	Miller, Clara Huston.......................................Germantown, Pa.
Miller, C. J.	Miller, Celeste J.......Elms Hotel, 53d St. and Cornell Ave., Chicago.
Miller, C:	Miller, Charles...Franklin, Pa.
Miller, C: C.	Miller, Charles C., M.D..............................70 State St., Chicago.
Miller, D. C.	Miller, Dayton Clarence..Cleveland, O.
Miller, E: T.	Miller, Edward T..Columbus, O.
Miller, J. H:	Miller, James Henry..Hinton, W. Va.
Miller, L. W.	Miller, L. W.............................320 So. Broad St., Philadelphia.
Miller, P. F.	Miller, Peyton Farrell......................................Hudson, N. Y.
Miller, T. S.	Miller, T. S..Flat, Tex.
Miller, W: H.	Miller, William Harris.....................................Richmond, Ky.
Miller System.	Miller System Co...Binghamton, N. Y.
Millet.	Millet, J. B., Co................................120 Boylston St., Boston.
Millinery Trade.	Millinery Trade Publishing Co...Room 4, 13 Astor Pl., New York.
Mills, H. E.	Mills, Herbert Elmer...........Vassar College, Poughkeepsie, N. Y.
Mills, M. W.	Mills, Mary Wilda...........................Mary Institute, St. Louis.
Mills & G.	Mills & Gibbs....................Broadway and Grand St., New York.
Mills Pub. Co.	Mills Publishing Co..Denver, Colo.
Milwaukee Pub. Lib.	Milwaukee Public Library.................................Milwaukee, Wis.
Miner, H: C.	Miner, Henry Clay.......................Bowery Theatre, New York.
Miner, W. H.	Miner, W. H..Cedar Rapids, Ia.
Mines Directory.	Mines Directory Co.....D. F. Walker Bldg., Salt Lake City, Utah.
Mining and Scientific.	Mining and Scientific Press..........667 Howard St., San Francisco.
Mining News.	Mining News Co..Joplin, Mo.
Mining Science.	Mining Science Publishing Co..........502 Club Bldg., Denver, Colo.
Minkler, C. R. S.	Minkler, Mrs. Carrie Ruth Stillwell.........................Ashland, Ore.
Minn. Forestry Com.	Minnesota Forestry Commission.........................St. Paul, Minn.
Minn. Hist. Soc.	Minnesota Historical Society.............................St. Paul, Minn.
Minn. Law.	Minnesota Law Book Co..................................Owatonna, Minn.
Minn. Pub. Soc.	Minnesota, Publishing Society of, 1010 Pioneer Press Bldg., St. Paul, Minn.
Minn. State Bd. Immigration.	Minnesota State Board of Immigration.............St. Paul, Minn.
Minn. Tax Commission	Minnesota Tax Commission...............................St. Paul, Minn.
Minter.	Minter Co...Harrisburg, Pa.
Miraglia-Gullotti, P. V.	Miraglia-Gullotti, Paolo Vescovo..........30 Cornelia St., New York.
Mirror.	Mirror Printing Co...Marceline, Mo.
Miss Hills' Sch.	Miss Hills' School for Girls Alumnæ Assoc............Philadelphia.

Miss. Geol. Survey.	Mississippi Geological Survey..........................Jackson, Miss.
Missouri Bapt. San.	Missouri Baptist Sanitarium......919 N. Taylor Ave., St. Louis, Mo.
Missouri Bu. Geol.	Missouri, Bureau of Geology and Mines, H: A. Buehler, Director, Rolla, Mo.
Missouri Dept. Educ.	Missouri Department of Education..............Jefferson City, Mo.
Missouri Hist.	Missouri Historical Society................1600 Locust St., St. Louis.
Missouri Pr.	Missouri Printing and Publishing Co..................Mexico, Mo.
Missouri State Bd.	Missouri State Board of Agriculture..................Columbia, Mo.
Mitchell, J. J.	Mitchell, J. J..........................41 W. 25th St., New York.
Mitchell, S. W.	Mitchell, Silas Weir, M.D..............1524 Walnut St., Philadelphia.
Mitchell & Co.	Mitchell & Co................1504-8 Rockefeller Bldg., Cleveland, O.
Mixer, M. E. K.	Mixer, Mrs. Mary Elizabeth Knowlton, 313 Delaware Ave., Buffalo, N. Y.
Modern Dyer.	Modern Dyer and Cleaner Publishing Co...............Philadelphia.
Modern Electrics.	Modern Electrics........................233 Fulton St., New York.
Modern Lang. Assoc.	Modern Language Association of America, 107 Walker St., Cambridge, Mass.
	Modern Medicine Publishing Co., Ltd. *See* Good-Health Publishing Co.
Modern Mercantile.	Modern Mercantile Co...................................Bucyrus, O.
Modern Methods.	Modern Methods Publishing Co......................Detroit, Mich.
Modern Miller.	Modern Miller Co.....................1032 Pierce Bldg., St. Louis, Mo.
"Modern View."	"Modern View" Publishing Co...............210 Olive St., St. Louis.
Modern Woodmen.	Modern Woodman of America.......................Rock Island, Ill.
Moffat.	Moffat, Yard & Co.......................31 E. 17th St., New York.
Moffat, R. B.	Moffat, Reuben Burnham...................63 Wall St., New York.
Moffett, S: E.	Moffett, Samuel Erasmus..........................Mt. Vernon, N. Y.
Molitor, D: A.	Molitor, David Albert...............Cornell University, Ithaca, N. Y.
Monarch.	Monarch Book Co....................121-127 Plymouth Pl., Chicago.
Monarch Pr.	Monarch Printing Co.......................................Quincy, Ill.
Monetary.	Monetary Publishing Co.................15 William St., New York.
Money and Stamp.	Money and Stamp Brokerage Co...........150 Nassau St., New York.
Monfort.	Monfort & Co. .. ..422 Elm St., Cincinnati.
Moninger, J: C.	Moninger, John C...............111-125 E. Blackhawk St., Chicago.
Monsalvat.	Monsalvat Press..................1501 N. Marshall St., Philadelphia.
Montagu, G.	Montagu, Gordon...St. Louis.
Monterey.	Monterey County Democrat Print.....................Salinas, Cal.
Montgomery, C: A.	Montgomery, Charles Alexander..........P. O. Box 888, New York.
Moods.	Moods Publishing Co..................20 E. 42d St., New York.
Moody Corporation.	Moody Corporation (now Analyses Publishing Co., John Moody, President)...........................35 Nassau St., New York.
Moody's Mag.	Moody's Magazine..........................35 Nassau St., New York.
Moon, J. H.	Moon, J. H...Fallsington, Pa.
Moon, R. C.	Moon, Robert C.............618 Witherspoon Bldg., Philadelphia.
Moore, C. B.	Moore, Clarence B.................1321 Locust St., Philadelphia.
Moore, F. M.	Moore, Francis Marion..............................Hot Springs, S. D.
Moore, J. H.	Moore, Joseph Hampton.............Witherspoon Bldg., Philadelphia.
Moore, J. V.	Moore, James Vernon................................Royal Oak, Md.
Moore, P. E.	Moore, P. E., & Co..................829 Marquette Bldg., Chicago.
Moore, R. L.	Moore, Roy Lewis...Benson, Ill.
Moore, W: W.	Moore, William Walker...Cary, Miss.
Morang.	Morang & Co., Ltd.............90 Wellington St., W., Toronto, Can.
Moras, E. R.	Moras, Edmond Raymond..........................Highland Park, Ill.
Moray, J:	Moray, John...........................Berkeley Springs, W. Va.
Mordecai, S: F.	Mordecai, Samuel Fox....................................Durham, N. C.
Morden, R. O.	Morden, R. O....................20 Palace Bldg., Minneapolis, Minn.
Morehead, J. M.	Morehead, Joseph M.............................Greensboro, N. C.
Moreland, G: M.	Moreland, George Matthew.............................Monterey, Cal.
Morgan, C: C.	Morgan, Charles Carroll...................................Nashua, N. H.
Morgan, J: P.	Morgan, J: Pierpont.......................23 Wall St., New York.
Morgan, W: S.	Morgan, Rev. William S.............150 S. Knox St., Albany, N. Y.
Morgenstern, J.	Morgenstern, Dr. Julius, Sec'y Central Conference, 3450 Highland Pl., Avondale, Cincinnati.
Morning Journ.	Morning Journal, Press of the................Albuquerque, N. M.
Morris, J: D.	Morris, John D., & Co..............1201 Chestnut St., Philadelphia.
Morris, R. P.	Morris, Roy P...........................Carnegie Institute, Pittsburgh, Pa.
Morrison, G. B.	Morrison, Gilbert Burnet.........McKinley High School, St. Louis.
Morrison, J: F.	Morrison, John Frank............................Fort Leavenworth, Kan.
Morrison, M. L.	Morrison, M. L..Peterboro, N. H.
Morrison & M.	Morrison & Martin...Sharon, Pa.
Morse, Art.	Morse Art Co...Quincy, Ill.
Morse, H. H.	Morse, Howard Holdridge..............................Tarrytown, N. Y.

Mortensen, A. C.	Mortensen, Arthon Christian....1326 L St., N. W., Washington, D. C.
Morton.	Morton, John P., & Co., Inc.......440-446 Main St., Louisville, Ky.
Morton Eichman Co.	Morton Eichman Co..............................Lebanon, Ind.
Morton, O. F.	Morton, Oren Frederic..............................Franklin, W. Va.
Morton, P.	Morton, Paul..............................120 Broadway, New York.
Mosby.	Mosby, C. V., Medical Book Co..Grand Ave. and Olive Sts., St. Louis.
Moses, Z.	Moses, Zebina..............................Washington, D. C.
Mosher, T: B.	Mosher, Thomas B..................45 Exchange St., Portland, Me.
Mother Earth.	Mother Earth Publishing Association....210 E. 13th St., New York.
Motley Press.	Motley Press..............................144 Pearl St., New York.
Motor.	Motor..............................2 Duane St., New York.
Motor Boat Pub.	Motor Boat Publishing Co...............1133 Broadway, New York.
Motor Craft.	Motor Craft Encyclopedia Publishing Co...............Cleveland, O.
Moulton, A. W.	Moulton, Arthur Wheelock..............................Lawrence, Mass.
Mt. Tom Press.	Mount Tom Press..............................Northampton, Mass.
Mt. Holyoke Coll.	Mount Holyoke College..............................South Hadley, Mass.
Mount Vernon Ladies' Assoc.	Mount Vernon Ladies' Association of the Union..Mount Vernon, Va.
Mudd, J. A.	Mudd, Joseph Aloysius..............................Hyattsville, Md.
Mudge.	Mudge, Alfred & Son..............................24 Franklin St., Boston.
Mueller, W: C:	Mueller, William Charles.................247 Avenue A, New York.
Mulertt, H.	Mulertt, Hugo..............................Brooklyn, N. Y.
Mulliner, G. S.	Mulliner, Gabrielle Stewart ......Room 808, 320 5th Ave., New York.
Mumper J. I.	Mumper, J. I., and Miller, Robert C..41 Baltimore St., Gettysburg, Pa.
Municipal Art Com. (Los. A.)	Municipal Art Commission..............................Los Angeles, Cal.
Municipal Art Soc.	Municipal Art Society of Hartford...................Hartford, Ct.
Municipal Information.	Municipal Information Bureau.............95 Dearborn St., Chicago.
Municipal Journ.	Municipal Journal and Engineer......231-241 W. 39th St., New York.
Municipal Ownership.	Municipal Ownership Publishing Co......119 Nassau St., New York.
Munk, J. A.	Munk, Joseph Amasa...........819 Security Bldg., Los Angeles, Cal.
Munn.	Munn & Co., Inc..............................361 Broadway, New York.
Munn, C: C.	Munn, Charles Clark..............................Springfield, Mass.
Munroe, J. P.	Munroe, James Phinney....................79 Summer St., Boston.
Munsey.	Munsey, Frank A., Co...................157 Fifth Ave., New York.
Munson, M. E.	Munson, M. E..............................77 Bible House, New York.
Muralo.	Muralo Co..............................New Brighton, N. Y.
Murdoch Law (N. J.)	Murdoch Law Book Co..............................East Orange, N. J.
Murdock, C. A.	Murdock, C. A., & Co...............68 Fremont St., San Francisco.
Murdock, W: G.	Murdock, William G..............................Milton, Pa.
Murdock Press.	Murdock Press..............................San Francisco.
Murphy.	Murphy, John, Co............200 W. Lombard St., Baltimore, Md.
Murphy, G:	Murphy, George, Inc...................57 E. 9th St., New York.
Murphy, Patrick.	Murphy, Rev. Patrick..............................Payette, Id.
Murray, C. H.	Murray, C. H..............................Elgin, Ill.
Murray, L. W.	Murray, Mrs. Louise Welles...........735 S. Main St., Athens, Pa.
Murray, P. H.	Murray, P. H., & Co..............................Joliet, Ill.
Murray, S. V:	Murray, Sara Van Alen................1 Madison Ave., New York.
Murray, T: E:	Murray, Thomas Edward.................55 Duane St., New York.
Murray Bros. Press.	Murray Brothers Press......1733 7th St., N. W., Washington, D. C.
Mushroom Pub.	Mushroom Publishing Co............210 Schutz Bldg., Columbus, O.
Muskogee.	Muskogee Printing Co..............................Muskogee, Okla.
Musgrove.	Musgrove Printing House..............................Bristol, N. H.
Music Teachers' Nat. Assoc.	Music Teachers' National Association, Care of Waldo S. Pratt, 86 Gillett St., Hartford, Ct.
Musselman, D. L.	Musselman, De Lafayette..............................Quincy, Ill.
Mutual.	Mutual Publishing Co..................187 Edgewood Ave., Chicago.
Mutual Bk.	Mutual Book Co..............................70 Franklin St., Boston.
Mutual Pub.	Mutual Publishing Co..............................Raleigh N. C.
Mutual Pub. Co.	Mutual Publishing Co...............67 E. Alabama St., Atlanta, Ga.
Muzzey, D: S.	Muzzey, David Saville...........33 Central Park West, New York.
Myers, M. C.	Myers, Minard C..............................Boston.
Myers, P. M.	Myers, Mrs. Peter M..............................Bedford, O.
Myers, S. E.	Myers, Stella Evelyn..............................Kansas City, Kan.
Myrtle.	Myrtle Publishing Co...................1 W. 34th St., New York.
N. C. Dept. Pub. Instruct.	North Carolina Department of Public Instruction......Raleigh, N. C.
N. C. Geolog. Survey.	North Carolina Geological Survey................Chapel Hill, N. C.

N. C. Hist.	North Carolina Historical Commission................Raleigh, N. C.
N. E. Assoc. Sch. Supts.	New England Association of School Superintendents, Care of R. S. Peck & Co., Hartford, Ct.
N. E. Druggist.	New England Druggist Publishing Co..........145 High St., Boston.
N. E. Hist.	New England Historic Genealogical Soc.....18 Somerset St., Boston.
N. E. Pub. Co.	New England Publishing Co...............................Boston.
N. J. Adj.-Gen.	New Jersey Adjutant-General's Office.................Trenton, N. J.
N. J. Forest.	New Jersey Forest Park Reservation Commission, State House, Trenton, N. J.
N. J. Hist. Soc.	New Jersey Historical Society.........................Newark, N. J.
N. M. Bu. Immigration.	New Mexico Bureau of Immigration............Albuquerque, N. M.
N. M. Cattle.	New Mexico Cattle Sanitary Board............East Las Vegas, N. M.
N. M. Pr.	New Mexican Printing Co..........................Santa Fé, N. M.
N. Y. Age.	New York Age Publishing Co............7 Chatham Sq., New York.
N. Y. Anti-Vivisection.	New York Anti-Vivisection Society......2025 Broadway, New York.
N. Y. Assoc. for Blind.	New York Association for the Blind... ......118 E. 59th St., N. Y.
N. Y. Belting & Packing.	New York Belting & Packing Co...91-93 Chambers St., New York.
N. Y. Botanical.	New York Botanical Garden.................Bronx Park, New York.
N. Y. City.	New York City...............................City Hall, New York.
N. Y. Dept. Agri.	New York State, Department of Agriculture............Albany, N. Y.
N. Y. Dept. Health.	New York Department of Health....6th Ave. and 55th St., New York.
N. Y. Dept. Labor.	New York State, Department of Labor..................Albany, N. Y.
N. Y. Educ. Co.	New York Education Co....................50 State St., New York.
N. Y. Eve. Post.	New York Evening Post Co..............20 Vesey St., New York.
N. Y. Herald.	New York Herald.......................Herald Square, New York.
N. Y. Inst. Deaf and Dumb.	New York Institute for the Instruction of the Deaf and Dumb, Ft. Washington Ave. and 163d St., New York.
N. Y. Inst. Mercantile.	New York Institute of Mercantile Training..36 W. 37th St., New York.
N. Y. Insurance.	New York Insurance School............81 E. 125th St., New York.
N. Y. Labor News.	New York Labor News Co............28 City Hall Pl., New York.
N. Y. Law.	New York Law Book Co......................45 John St., New York.
N. Y. Medical.	New York Medical Book Co.............45 E. 42d St., New York.
N. Y. Pub. Lib.	New York Public Library..............425 Lafayette St., New York.
N. Y. Pub. Service Com.	New York Public Service Commission.................Albany, N. Y.
N. Y. Sch. Automobile Eng.	New York School of Automobile Engineers, 146 W. 56th St., New York.
N. Y. State Educ.	New York State Education Dept....................Albany, N. Y.
N. Y. State Hist.	New York State Historical Association................Albany, N. Y.
N. Y. State Library.	New York State Library..............................Albany, N. Y.
N. Y. State Pharmacy.	New York, State Board of Pharmacy.................Albany, N. Y.
N. Y. State Probation.	New York State Probation Commission................Albany, N. Y.
N. Y. Univ.	New York University..........................New York, N. Y.
N. Y. World.	New York World..........................63 Park Row, New York.
N. Y. Zoological.	New York Zoological Society.......Room 35, 11 Wall St., New York.
Nabuco, J.	Nabuco, Joaquim..............Brazilian Embassy, Washington, D. C.
Nagel, O.	Nagel, Oskar..............................P. O. Box 385, New York.
Nagel, W: J:	Nagel, William J.........................6 Ashburton Pl., Boston.
Nash, C. H. H.	Nash, Clarissa Hosmer Hapgood................West Acton, Mass.
Nashville Bk.	Nashville Book Co...............................Nashville, Tenn.
Nason, A. H.	Nason, Arthur Huntington, 212 Gould Hall, University Heights, New York.
Nason, E. H.	Nason, Mrs. Emma Huntington.......................Augusta, Me.
Nassau Press.	Nassau Press.........................Richmond Hill, L. I., N. Y.
Nat. Am. Woman's Suffrage.	National American Woman Suffrage Association........Warren, O.
Nat. Annot.	National Annotating Co........................Crawfordsville, Ind.
Nat. Art Soc.	National Art Society...Chicago.
Nat. Assoc. Engine and Boat Manf.	National Association of Engine and Boat Manufacturers, 314 Madison Ave., New York.
Nat. Assoc. Lithographers.	National Association of Employing Lithographers...Rochester, N. Y.
Nat. Assoc. Pub. Health.	National Association for the Promotion of Public Health, 50 Church St., New York.
Nat. Assoc. Stationary Engineers.	National Association of Stationary Engineers of America, 315 Dearborn St., Chicago.

Nat. Assoc. Tanners.	National Association of Tanners........................Chicago.
Nat. Assoc. Tuberculosis.	National Association for the Study and Prevention of Tuberculosis, 105 E. 22d St., New York.
Nat. Bapt. Pub.	National Baptist Publishing Board..523 2d Ave., N., Nashville, Tenn.
Nat. Bd. Fire.	National Board of Fire Underwriters.......34 Nassau St., New York.
Nat. Bible.	National Bible Institute..................156 Fifth Ave., New York.
Nat. Bk. Co.	National Book Co..................................Detroit, Mich.
Nat. Bk. (Mo.)	National Book Concern............................St. Louis, Mo.
Nat. Bk. (O.)	National Book Co..................................Collinwood, O.
Nat. Bridge.	National Bridge Co..............................Indianapolis, Ind.
Nat. Business.	National Business League of America, 507 Stock Exchange Bldg., Chicago.
Nat. Child Labor.	National Child Labor Committee, Inc.....105 E. 22d St., New York.
Nat. City Bank.	National City Bank..........................55 Wall St., New York.
Nat. Coll. Electro-Therapeutics.	National College of Electro-Therapeutics, Literary Department, Lima, O.
Nat. Congress Mothers.	National Congress of Mothers, 806 Loan and Trust Bldg., Washington, D. C.
Nat. Corr. Sch. R. R.	National Correspondence School of Railroading.............Chicago.
Nat. Druggist.	National Druggist......................................St. Louis.
Nat. Educ. Assoc.	National Educational Association....................Winona, Minn.
Nat. Elec.	National Electric Light Association........29 W. 39th St., New York.
Nat. Elec. Lamp.	National Electric Lamp Association, 4411 Hough Ave., N. E., Cleveland, O.
Nat. Fed. Rel. Liberals.	National Federation of Religious Liberals....25 Beacon St., Boston.
Nat. Fire Proofing.	National Fire Proofing Co................Flatiron Bldg., New York.
Nat. Game.	National Game Publishing Co..............................St. Louis.
Nat. Geog.	National Geographic Magazine....................Washington, D. C.
Nat. Geographic Soc.	National Geographical Society....................Washington, D. C.
Nat. Guard.	National Guard Magazine............................Columbus, O.
Nat. Hospital.	National Hospital Record Co.........................Detroit, Mich.
Nat. Laundry.	National Laundry Journal....................120 Ann St., Chicago.
Nat. Law.	National Law Book Co...............................Seattle, Wash.
Nat. Lead.	National Lead Co.......................111 Broadway, New York.
Nat. League.	National League for the Civic Education of Women, 222 Madison Ave., New York.
Nat. Lithographers.	National Lithographer..................150 Nassau St., New York.
Nat. Lumber.	National Lumber Exporters' Association..............Baltimore, Md.
Nat. Municipal.	National Municipal League....703 North American Bldg., Philadelphi.a
Nat. Prohibition.	National Prohibtion Press..................92 La Salle St., Chicago.
Nat. Pub.	National Publishing Co.............................Washington, D. C.
Nat. Pub. Co.	National Publishing Co........235-243 American St., So. Philadelphia.
Nat. Soc. of Fine Arts.	National Society of the Fine Arts................Washington, D. C.
Nat. Soc. Promotion Indust. Educ.	National Society for the Promotion of Industrial Education. 18 W. 44th St., New York.
Nat. Tax Assoc.	National Tax Association..............................Columbus, O.
Nat. Text Bk.	National Text Book Co...............2641 Michigan Ave., Chicago.
Nat. Tribune.	National Tribune Co................................Washington, D. C.
Natchitoches Times.	Natchitoches Times Print.............................Natchitoches, La.
Nation.	Nation (The).....................................20 Vesey St., New York.
Navy Blue.	Navy Blue Co.........................Greenlawn, Long Island, N. Y.
Navy Pub.	Navy Publishing Co...........1301 H St., N. W., Washington, D. C.
Nazareth Trade Sch.	Nazareth Trade School Printing Office..........Farmingdale, N. Y.
Neale.	Neale Publishing Co.....................Flatiron Building, New York.
Neall, F. L.	Neall, Frank L..Philadelphia.
Neely, F.	Neely, Flora.........................419 Main St., New Rochelle, N. Y.
Neff, G: O.	Neff, George Oliver.................1881a Sloan Ave., Cleveland, O.
Nelmes, S.	Nelmes, S.......................................23 W. 129th St., New York.
Nelson.	Nelson, Thomas, & Sons.........4th Ave. and 27th St., New York.
Nelson, J: M.	Nelson, John Maurice, care of Columbia University......New York.
Nelson, L. H.	Nelson, L. H., Co....................................Portland, Me.
Nelson, O. B. M.	Nelson, Oscar Battling Matthew......................Hegewisch, Ill.
Nelson, W:	Nelson, William......................................Paterson, N. J.
Nelson Pub.	Nelson Publishing Co.................P. O. Box 185, Savannah, Ga.
Netherland Chamber of Com.	Netherland Chamber of Commerce..........136 Water St., New York.
Neuner.	Neuner Co...Los Angeles, Cal.
Nev. State Educ.	Nevada State Education Department................Carson City, Nev.

New Age.	New Age Publishing Co.................................Westerville, O.
New Church.	New Church Board of Publication...........3 W. 29th St., New York.
New Columbia.	New Columbia Publishing Co...........................Findlay, O.
New Eden.	New Eden Publishing Co...............55 E. Main St., Columbus, O.
New Era Print.	New Era Printing Co...................................Lancaster, Pa.
New Humanity.	New Humanity Publishing Society.....1746 Geneva Ave., Aurora, Col.
New Med.	New Medicine Publishing Co.............72 Madison St., Chicago.
New Reading.	New Reading Publishing Co..............1717 Carroll Ave., Chicago.
New Talmud.	New Talmud Publishing Co..............100 Boylston St., Boston.
New Thought.	New Thought Publishers...............110 W. 34th St., New York.
New Way.	New Way Publishing Co. (Books bought by Roger Bros.)
New York.	New York State.......................................Albany, N. Y.
Newbegin, J: J.	Newbegin, John J......................315 Sutter St., San Francisco.
Newberry, A. S.	Newberry, Arthur St. John.1010-1014 Rockefeller Bldg., Cleveland, O.
Newcomb.	Newcomb & Grauss.....................................Salem, Mass.
Newcomb, G: T:	Newcomb, George Thomas..........................Chattanooga, Tenn.
Newcomb, H. T.	Newcomb, Harry Turner..Metropolitan Bank Bldg., Washington, D. C.
Newman, S. B.	Newman, S. B., & Co...............................Knoxville, Tenn.
Newold.	Newold Publishing Co....................225 Fifth Ave., New York.
Newport Pub.	Newport Publishing Co.................................Ames, Ia.
News-Mail Co.	News-Mail Co......................................Charleston, W. Va.
News Pr. Co. (N. J.)	News Printing Co..................143 Ellison St., Paterson, N. J.
News Pr. Ho.	News Printing House..............................Thomasville, N. C.
News Print.	News Printing Co....................................Aberdeen, S. D.
Newson.	Newson & Co...........................27 W. 23d St., New York.
Newson, J: H:	Newson, John Henry, Co...............................Cleveland, O.
Newton, A. H.	Newton, Alexander Herritage........................Camden, N. J.
Newton, D. W.	Newton, Donald W. (purchased books of C. H. Doscher Co.), 156 Fifth Ave., New York.
Newton, N. B.	Newton, N. B., Co.......................................Toledo, O.
Newton Co.	Newton Co...............................385 Dearborn St., Chicago.
Newton & C.	Newton & Cartwright...................156 Fifth Ave., New York
Ng Poon Chew.	Ng Poon Chew.............809-811 Sacramento St., San Francisco.
Nichols, C. A.	Nichols, C. A., Co....................................Springfield, Mass.
Nichols, J. L.	Nichols, J. L., & Co........Kailer Block, Naperville, Du Page Co., Ill.
Nichols, L. A.	Nichols, Lucy Adda........................Box 102, Nashville, Mich.
Nichols, T: P.	Nichols, Thomas P.......................................Lynn, Mass.
Nichols Print.	Nichols Print, Press of..............................Haverhill, Mass.
Nickerson & C.	Nickerson & Collins......................315 Dearborn St., Chicago.
Nicoletti.	Nicolletti Bros........................242 Lafayette St., New York.
Nida, A.	Nida, August............................182 William St., New York.
Niglutsch.	Niglutsch, Francis R........................29 E. 22d St., New York.
Niles Pub.	Niles Publishing Co.................................Bridgeport, Ct.
Nimmo, D: C.	Nimmo, David Chalmers...................1285 24th St., Detroit, Mich.
Nimsgern, E: G.	Nimsgern, Edward Gray.....................Brown Station, New York.
Ninth Infantry, Tex.	Ninth Infantry..........................Fort Sam Houston, Tex.
Nixon-J.	Nixon-Jones Printing Co...................................St. Louis.
Noble, G: W.	Noble, George W..........Lakeside Bldg., 214-220 Clark St., Chicago.
Noble, I: C.	Noble, Isaac C..............1649 Acushnet Ave., New Bedford, Mass.
Noblest Roman.	Noblest Roman Publishing Co..............................Austin, Tex.
Nolde, J: T.	Nolde, John T., Mfg. Co....................................St. Louis.
Nolen, J:	Nolen, John............Abbot Bldg., Harvard Sq., Cambridge, Mass.
Nonotuck.	Nonotuck Press....................................Northampton, Mass.
Normalist.	Normalist Publishing Co.....................................Elgin, Ill.
North, E. D.	North, Ernest Dressel.........................4 E. 39th St., New York.
North American.	North American Review......................325 Pearl St., New York.
North American, Phil.	North American Co.......................Franklin Sq., Philadelphia.
North Am. Civic.	North American Civil League..................173 State St., Boston.
North-West Mills.	North-West Mills Co...................................Winona, Minn.
Northern Pub.	Northern Publishing Co........1017 Jefferson Ave., Petoskey, Mich.
Northfield Press.	Northfield Press.....................................Northfield, Mass.
Northwest Mining.	Northwest Mining News...............................Spokane, Wash.
Northwest Miller.	Northwestern Miller..............................Minneapolis, Minn.
Northwestern Pub.	Northwestern Publishing House......................Milwaukee, Wis.
Northwestern Sch.	Northwestern School Supply Co., 329 Fourteenth Ave., Minneapolis, Minn.
Northwestern Univ.	Northwestern University.....................................Chicago.
Norton, D. M.	Norton, Dora Miriam..................Pratt Institute, Brooklyn, N. Y.
Norton, O. W.	Norton, Oliver Willcox.......................................Chicago.
Norton, W: H.	Norton, William Harrison............................Fort Valley, Ga.

Novelty.	Novelty Book Concern............................Birmingham, Ala.
Novelty News.	Novelty News Press....................171 Washington St., Chicago.
Noyes, I: P.	Noyes, Isaac Pitman........409 Fourth St., S. E., Washington, D. C.
Nunc Licet.	Nunc Licet Press....................42 W. Coulter St., Philadelphia.
Nuneviller.	Nuneviller, W., Co....................711 Walnut St., Philadelphia.
Nunn.	Nunn & Co.......................535 N. Howard St., Baltimore, Md.
Nutshell.	Nutshell Publishing Co..............................Houston, Tex.
Nweeya, S: K.	Nweeya, Samuel Kasha..............................Philadelphia.
Nye.	Nye Family of American Association (care of George Hyatt Nye), Cleveland, O.
Nyitray.	Nyitray, Emil..............................77 First Ave., New York.
Oak Leaves.	Oak Leaves Co...................105 Warren St., Oak Park, Ill.
Oakleaf, J. B.	Oakleaf, Joseph B..............................Moline, Ill.
Oberlin Coll.	Oberlin College..............................Oberlin, O.
O'Brien, F. G.	O'Brien, Frank George..........................Minneapolis, Minn.
O'Brien, J: E.	O'Brien, John E.................110 Washington Ave., Scranton, Pa.
Observer.	Observer Publishing Co...........................Greensburg, Ind.
Occidental Pub.	Occidental Publishing Co........5810 16th Ave., N. E., Seattle, Wash.
Occult.	Occult Publishing Co......................53 Randolph St., Chicago.
Occult Pub. Co.	Occult Publishing Co.............553 Maple St., Battle Creek, Mich.
Ogilvie, G: W.	Ogilvie, George W., & Co. *See* list of David McKay or Saalfield Pub. Co.
Ogilvie, J. S.	Ogilvie, J. S., Publishing Co..................57 Rose St., New York.
Ogle.	Ogle, George A., & Co..................134 Van Buren St., Chicago.
Ohio Archæolog.	Ohio Archæological and Historical Society..Page Hall, Columbus, O.
Ohio Geolog. Survey.	Ohio Geological Survey..............................Columbus, O.
Ohio Law.	Ohio Law Reporter Co..................806 Main St., Cincinnati.
Ohio Lib. Co.	Ohio Library Co..............................Columbus, O.
Ohio State Acad.	Ohio State Academy of Science......................Columbus, O.
Ohio State Fire Marshal.	Ohio, State Fire Marshal..............................Columbus, O.
Ohio State Univ.	Ohio State University..............................Columbus, O.
Oklahoma Bk.	Oklahoma Book Co..............................Oklahoma City, Okla.
Oklahoma Dept. Educ.	Oklahoma Department of Education..................Guthrie, Okla.
Ohlander, M.	Ohlander, Marcus..........................Box 405, Little Rock, Ark.
Olcott.	Olcott Publishing Co.................. ......Charlestown, W. Va.
Old Corner.	Old Corner Book Store..................27-29 Bromfield St., Boston.
Old Greek Pr.	Old Greek Press......................1411 Security Bldg., Chicago.
Old South Ch.	Old South Church..............................Boston.
Old South Work.	Old South Work, Directors of....Old South Meeting House, Boston.
Old Virginia.	Old Virginia Publishing Co....524 Atlantic Trust Bldg., Norfolk, Va.
Oldach.	Oldach Co..............................51 N. 7th St., Philadelphia.
Oldroyd, O. H.	Oldroyd, Osborn Hamiline..........516 10th St., Washington, D. C.
Oliphant, J. H.	Oliphant, James H., Co......................20 Broad St., New York.
Oliphant, S: G.	Oliphant, Samuel Green..............................Olivet, Mich.
Oliver, F. E.	Oliver, French Earl.............4330 Harrison St., Kansas City, Mo.
Oliver, J:	Oliver, John..............................Palmer, Colo.
Onderdonk, A. J.	Onderdonk, Andrew J.......................71 Wall St., New York.
155th Regimental Assoc.	155th Regimental Association..........................Pittsburgh, Pa.
Oneal, J.	Oneal, James.........................831 N. 3d St., Terre Haute, Ind.
O'Neil, A. B.	O'Neil, A. B..............................Oshkosh, Wis.
O'Neil, R. K.	O'Neil, Robert Kingsley..Care of San José Printing Co., San José, Cal.
O'Neill, F. J.	O'Neill, Rev. Felix J.............. L. B. 42, Stafford Springs, Ct.
Ontario Power.	Ontario Power Co..............................Niagara Falls, N. Y.
Ontario Pub.	Ontario Publishing Co..............................Oswego, N. Y.
Open Court.	Open Court Publishing Co...........378-388 Wabash Ave., Chicago.
Oppenheim, S:	Oppenheim, Samuel..........811 Dawson St., Bronx Borough, N. Y.
Opportunity.	Opportunity Publishing Co...............4 Northampton St., Boston.
Orange Journ.	Orange Journal..............................Orange, N. J.
Oratorio Soc.	Oratorio Society.....................176 W. 86th St., New York.
Order Eastern Star.	Order of the Eastern Star.............25 W. 42d St., New York.
Order of White Rose (Mass.)	Order of the White Rose......24 Strathmore Rd., Brookline, Mass.
Order Transfiguration.	Order of the Transfiguration..........................Cincinnati.
Oriental Esoteric.	Oriental Esoteric Publishing Co..1443 Q St., N. W., Washington, D. C.
Orion Pub.	Orion Publishing Co..............................Nashville, Tenn.
Ormeril.	Ormeril Co..........................Caxton Bldg., Cleveland, O.
Osborn, S. O.	Osborn, Solomon Oliver..........................Kansas City, Mo.
Osgood, C: G., Jr.	Osgood, Charles G., Jr..........................Princeton, N. J.

O'Sheridan, M. G.	O'Sheridan, Mary Grant, care of Henneberry Co., 552 Wabash Ave., Chicago.
Oswald.	Oswald Publishing Co................25 City Hall Pl., New York.
Ottenheimer.	Ottenheimer, I. & M............321 W. Baltimore St., Baltimore, Md.
Otterbein.	Otterbein Press..Dayton, O.
Our Hope.	Our Hope Pub. Co.......................................Mendota, Ill.
Our Hope Office.	Our Hope Office.........................80 Second Ave., New York.
Outing.	Outing Publishing Co....................315 Fifth Ave., New York.
Outing Press.	Outing Press...Deposit, N. Y.
Outlook.	Outlook Co..............................287 Fourth Ave., New York.
Overlock, M. G.	Overlock, Melvin G..................................Worcester, Mass.
Owen, F. A.	Owen, F. A., Publishing Co..........................Dansville, N. Y.
Owen, N. H.	Owen, Mrs. Nellie H.............1210 Park Ave., Richmond, Va.
Owens, C. A.	Owens, Clifford A......................................De Land, Fla.
Oxford Pub.	Oxford Publishing Co...............................Poughkeepsie, N. Y.
Oxford Univ.	Oxford University Press (Am. Branch)....29 W. 32d St., New York.
Pacific Coast.	Pacific Coast Law Publishing Co...................Tacoma, Wash.
Pacific Improvement.	Pacific Improvement Co...........401 Crocker Bldg., San Francisco.
Pacific Press.	Pacific Press Publishing Association...Villa St., Mountain View, Cal.
Pacific Rural.	Pacific Rural Press...............667 Howard St., San Francisco.
Packard, S. S.	Packard, S. S...........................101 E. 23d St., New York.
Pafraets.	Pafraets Book Co......................................Troy, N. Y.
Pagan, W. D.	Pagan, W. D.............................18 Wall St., New York.
Page, H. W.	Page, Howard W.......................................Philadelphia.
Page, L. C.	Page, L. C., & Co...........Hathaway Bldg., 53 Beacon St., Boston.
Page, V. F.	Page, Villa Faulkner..................34 Gramercy Park, New York.
Paine.	Paine Publishing Co.......................................Dayton, O.
Paine Nat. Hist. Assoc.	Paine National Historical Association..120 Lexington Ave, New York.
Painters' Mag.	Painters' Magazine....................100 William St., New York.
Palisades Press.	Palisades Press.......................................Edgewater, N. J.
Palmer, C. A.	Palmer, Clarence A................507 Virginia Ave., St. Paul, Minn.
Palmer, C. F.	Palmer, Clayton F...................................So. Pasadena, Cal.
Palmer, H. K.	Palmer, Harry K.......................................Philadelphia.
Palmer, M. E.	Palmer, Mary E., care of Ruffner Hotel.........Charleston, W. Va.
Palmer, W: C.	Palmer, William C...................................Winona Lake, Ind.
Palmer Co.	Palmer Co................................120 Boylston St., Boston.
Palmer Sch.	Palmer School of Chiropractic.........................Davenport, Ia.
Palmetto Press.	Palmetto Press...................................Roanoke Rapids, N. C.
Pammel, L: H.	Pammel, L: Hermann..Ames, Ia.
Pan. Am. Law.	Pan American Law Book Co., Calumet Bldg., 189 La Salle St., Chicago.
Pan-Pacific.	Pan-Pacific Press....................................Los Angeles, Cal.
Pandex.	Pandex Co.................................30 E. 53d St., Chicago.
Pantagraph.	Pantagraph Printing & Stationery Co..............Bloomington, Ill.
Panunzio, C. M.	Panunzio, C. M..................Wesleyan University, Middletown, Ct.
Panzer, O. L.	Panzer, Otto L......................P. O. Box 186, Brooklyn, N. Y.
Papyrus.	Papyrus Publishing Co...............................East Orange, N. J.
Paragon.	Paragon Press.......................................Montgomery, Ala.
Paramananda.	Paramananda, Swami, Care of Vedanta Society, 135 W. 80th St., New York.
Park.	Park Publishers...Des Moines, Ia.
Parke.	Parke, Vincent, & Co......................32 Union Sq., New York.
Parke, D. & Co.	Parke, Davis & Co...Detroit, Mich
Parker, G: L.	Parker, Rev. George Lawrence........203 Lafayette St., Salem, Mass.
Parker, G: W.	Parker, George Warren..............30 South St., Concord, N. H.
Parker, P. A.	Parker, Prescott Alphonso...............................Volanta, Ala.
Parker, W. P.	Parker, Mrs. W. P........................8 Chestnut St., Salem, Mass.
Parkinson, S. W.	Parkinson, Sarah Woods...................................Carlisle, Pa.
Parks, E. L.	Parks, E. L.............................335 Fourth Ave., New York.
Parks, F. S.	Parks, Frank Sylvester..........2104 H St., N., Washington, D. C.
Parrock, H. P.	Parrock, H. P...Buffalo, N. Y.
Parsons, L. B.	Parsons, Lillian B., "The Buckingham," cor. Mariner and Allen Sts., Buffalo, N. Y.
Parsons, L. L.	Parsons, Lillian L......................."The Castle," Tarrytown, N. Y.
Parsons Pr.	Parsons Printery............................7 Chatham Sq., New York.
Partridge, F. E.	Partridge, F. E..Winsted, Ct.
Patchel, G:	Patchel, George.......................918 Betz Bldg., Philadelphia.
Paterson Hist.	Paterson History Club....................................Paterson, N. J.
Patet, F. J.	Patet, François Joseph....................................Rockford, Ill.
Patriot.	Patriot Publishing Co.................................Springfield, Mass.
Pattee, A. F.	Pattee, Alida Frances..........134 S. 1st Ave., Mount Vernon, N. Y.

Patterson, C: E. Patterson, Charles Edwin....316 Michigan Ave., Grand Rapids, Mich.
Patterson & W. Patterson & White Co.........Philadelphia.
Pattison, E. W. Pattison, Mrs. Everett W..........4254 Olive St., St. Louis.
Patton, J: S. Patton, John Shelton......University of Virginia, Charlottesville, Va.
Pattou, A. A. Pattou, Ange Albert.........Philadelphia.
Paul. Paul, Peter, & Son..........136 N. Pearl St., Buffalo, N. Y.
Paul, H. A. C. Paul, Rev. H. A. C..........1926 South G St., Tacoma, Wash.
Paxton, A. J. Paxton, Amelia J........First Presbyterian Church, Princeton, Ind.
Payne, B. R. Payne, Bruce R........University of Virginia, Charlottesville, Va.
Peabody, C. H. Peabody, Cecil Hobart, care of Mass. Institute of Technology..Boston.
Peabody, F. G. Peabody, Francis Greenwood..Harvard University, Cambridge, Mass.
Peabody Museum. Peabody Museum.........Cambridge, Mass.
Peace Soc. Peace Society..........507 Fifth Ave., New York.
Pearson, J. L. Pearson, James Larkin.........Moravian Falls, N. C.
Pearson, P. Pearson, P.........Ponca City, Okla.
Pearson, P: H: Pearson, Peter Henry.........Lindsborg, Kan.
Pearson Bros. Pearson Brothers..........29 S. 7th St., Philadelphia.
Pearson Pub. Co. Pearson Publishing Co..........435 E. 24th St., New York.
Pease & D. Pease & Denison.........Elgin, Ill.
Peck, J. S. Peck, Mrs. James Sidney..........5 Waverley Pl., Milwaukee, Wis.
Peebles. Peebles Publishing Co.........Battle Creek, Mich.
Peeler, A. J. Peeler, A. J., Standard Blue Book Co. of Texas,
2209 La Branch St., Houston, Tex.
Peffley, D. F. Peffley, D. Frank.........Creston, Wash.
Pegram, H: Pegram, Henry..........4 Hanover St., New York.
Peirce Sch. Peirce School.........Philadelphia.
Peloubet. Peloubet & Hill (formerly S. S. Peloubet)..133 Nassau St., New York.
Pendergast, E. W. Pendergast, Mrs. Ella Worth....374 Broadway, Winter Hill, Boston.
Pendleton. Pendleton Printery.........Pendleton, Ore.
Penfield, F. C. Penfield, Frederic Courtland,
Care of The DeVinne Press, 395 Lafayette St., New York.
Penn. Dept. of Agriculture. Pennsylvania Department of Agriculture..........Harrisburg, Pa.
Penn. Dept. Health. Pennsylvania State Department of Health..........Harrisburg, Pa.
Penn. Inst. Pennsylvania Institution for the Deaf and Dumb,
Mt. Airy, Philadelphia.
Penn. Inst. Blind. Pennsylvania Institution for the Instruction of the Blind,
Overbrook, Philadelphia.
Penn. Mus. and Sch. of Ind. Art. Pennsylvania Museum and School of Industrial Art (Edwin A. Barker, Curator).........Philadelphia.
Penn Pub. Co. Penn Publishing Co..........923 Arch St., Philadelphia.
Penn. Soc., N. Y. Pennsylvania Society of New York (Barr Ferree, Sec'y),
218 Fulton St., New York.
Penn. State Coll. Pennsylvania State College.........State College, Pa.
Pennybacker, P. V. Pennybacker, Mrs. Percy V.........Austin, Tex.
Pennypacker, S: W. Pennypacker, Samuel Whitaker, Historical Society of Pennsylvania.........Philadelphia.
Pentecostal. Pentecostal Publishing Co.........Louisville, Ky.
Pentecostal Union. Pentecostal Union.........Bound Brook, N. J.
Penton. Penton Publishing Co.........Cleveland, O.
People's News. People's News Co.........Lancaster, Pa.
People's Pub. People's Publication Society.........Chicago.
People's Univ. People's University Extension Society....105 E. 17th St., New York.
Pepper Pub. Pepper Publishing and Printing Co.........Gainesville, Fla.
Percy Pub. Percy Publishing Co.,
1905 Termon Ave., North Side, Pittsburgh, Pa.
Perkins, C. B. Perkins, Charlton B., Co..........230½ Yamhill St., Portland, Ore.
Perkins, G: H. Perkins, Prof. George H.........Burlington, Vt.
Perkins Inst. Perkins Institution and Massachusetts School for the Blind....Boston.
Perkiomen Press. Perkiomen Press.........Perkiomen, Pa.
Perley, J. A. Perley, J. A..........614 Diamond Bank Bldg., Pittsburgh, Pa.
Perrin, B. Perrin, B..........191 Yale Station, New Haven, Ct.
Perrine, H. D. Perrine, Howland Delano..........76 William St., New York.
Perry, O. Perry, Adjutant-General Oran.......State House, Indianapolis, Ind.
Personal Help. Personal Help Publishing Co......700 Observer Bldg., Des Moines, Ia
Peters, J: P. Peters, Rev. John Punnett..........227 W. 99th St., New York.
Peters, J. W. S. Peters, James W. S.........Kansas City, Mo.
Petersen, J. C. Petersen, Jens Christian.........Travers City, Mich.
Peterson, E. Peterson, Ephraim.........Independence, Mo.
Pharmaceutical Review. Pharmaceutical Review Publishing Co.........Milwaukee, Wis.
Phelps. Phelps Publishing Co.........Springfield, Mass.

Phelps, E: B.	Phelps, Edward Bunnell....141 Broadway, N. Y.
Phila. Bk.	Philadelphia Book Co....17 S. 9th St., Philadelphia.
Phila. Free Lib.	Philadelphia, Free Library of....Philadelphia.
Phila. Pr.	Philadelphia Printing & Publishing Co....Philadelphia.
Phil. Trades Sch.	Philadelphia Trades School....Philadelphia.
Philbrook, H: B.	Philbrook, Henry B....23 Park Row, New York.
Philippine Educ.	Philippine Education (care of Frank R. Lutz)....Manila, P. I.
Philipps, M.	Philipps, Martin....1107 Main St., Buffalo, N. Y.
Phillips, C.	Phillips, Cropley, Co. (Successors to World Railway Publishing Co.), 1412 Tribune Bldg., Chicago.
Phillips, F. F.	Phillips, Mrs. Fannie Frank....122 Stedman St., Brookline, Mass.
Phillips, I: N.	Phillips, Isaac Newton....Springfield, Ill.
Phillips, J: B.	Phillips, John B....Boulder, Colo.
Phillips, W: H.	Phillips, William H....Amherst, Mass.
Phillips & E.	Phillips & Erickson....Cameron, Wis.
Phillips Bros.	Phillips Bros....Springfield, Ill.
Phillips Pr.	Phillips Printing and Publishing Co....Los Angeles, Cal.
Philopolis Press.	Philopolis Press....San Francisco.
Philosophical.	Philosophical Publishing Co....Box 64, Allentown, Pa.
Philosophical Soc.	Philosophical Society of Washington....Washington, D. C.
Phoenix.	Phoenix Publishing Co....823 Lexington Ave., New York.
Phonograph.	Phonographic Institute Co....224 W. 4th St., Cincinnati.
Physical Culture.	Physical Culture Extension Society....57 Washington St., Chicago.
Physical Therapy.	Physical Therapy Library Publishing Co....59 Market St., Chicago.
Physicians' Drug.	Physicians' Drug News Co....Newark, N. J.
Pickens, W:	Pickens, William....Talladega, Ala.
Pickering, E: C:	Pickering, Prof. Edward Charles....Cambridge, Mass.
Pickett, C. A.	Pickett, Cora A....Talcott Hall, Oberlin, O.
Pierce.	Pierce, Norman, Co....1129 Broadway, New York.
Pierce, D: R.	Pierce, David Rand....Fitchburg, Mass.
Pierce, G. H.	Pierce, Grace Howard....Salem, Mass.
Pierce, J: A.	Pierce, J: Alfred....Yellville, Ark.
Pierce, W. H.	Pierce, Mrs. Willard H....Bernardston, Mass.
Piggott, C: H:	Piggott, Charles Henry....4-6 Mulkey Bldg., Portland, Ore.
Pilger.	Pilger Publishing House....Reading, Pa.
Pilgrim Press.	Pilgrim Press....14 Beacon St., Boston.
Pillar of Fire.	Pillar of Fire....1845 Champa St., Denver, Colo.
Pillot, T.	Pillot, T....Houston, Tex.
Pilot Co.	Pilot Co....Marquette, Mich.
Pimbley, A. F.	Pimbley, Arthur Francis....Baltimore, Md.
Pioneer Pub. Co.	Pioneer Publishing Co....358 Dearborn St., Chicago.
Pioneers Farmers' Repub.	Pioneers of the Farmers' Republic....Somerville, N. J.
Pipes-R.	Pipes-Reed Book Co....725 Wyandotte St., Kansas City, Mo.
Pitblado.	Pitblado, Rev. Edwy Guthrie....2459 Lawrence Ave., Toledo, O.
Pitkin.	Pitkin, J. M., & Co....Newark, N. Y.
Pitman.	Pitman, Isaac, & Son....2-6 W. 45th St., New York.
Pitt, S. W.	Pitt, Sammie Wall....Clarksville, Tenn.
Pittman, R. H.	Pittman, Reden Herbert....Luray, Va.
Pittsburgh.	Pittsburgh Printing Co....Pittsburgh, Pa.
Pittsburgh Chamber of Com.	Pittsburgh Chamber of Commerce....Pittsburgh, Pa.
Pittsburgh Civic.	Pittsburgh Civic Commission....Pittsburgh, Pa.
Pittsburgh-W.	Pittsburgh-Westmoreland Coal Co....Pittsburgh, Pa.
Platt & P.	Platt & Peck....395 Broadway, New York.
Plimpton.	Plimpton Press....Norwood, Mass.
Plymouth Rock.	Plymouth Rock Squab Co....287 Atlantic Ave., Boston.
Poe. E. A., Memorial.	Poe, Edgar Allan, Memorial Association....Baltimore, Md.
	Poet Lore Co. *See* Badger.
Point of View.	Point of View....Nyack, N. Y.
Police Chronicle.	Police Chronicle and Civil Service Journal..33 Park Row, New York.
Polk.	Polk, R. L., & Co....Detroit, Mich.
Polley.	Polley, George H., & Co....61 Court St., Boston.
Pomfret.	Pomfret Press....Pomfret Center, Ct.
Pomroy, G:	Pomroy, George....National Military Home, Danville, Ill.
Pond, F. J.	Pond, Francis Jones....Stevens Institute, Hoboken, N. J.
Pool.	Pool Publishing Co....Mason City, Ia.
Pool, B. F.	Pool, Bettie Freshwater....207 Dyer St., Elizabeth City, N. C.
Poole, A.	Poole, Arthur, & Co....129 Confederation Life Bldg., Toronto, Can.
Pooley, P:	Pooley, Peter....Chicago.
Poor's.	Poor's Railway Manual Co....68 William St., New York.

Pope, C: H:	Pope, Charles Henry............................Pope Bldg., Boston.
Popham, W: L.	Popham, William Lee..................................Louisville, Ky.
Popp.	Popp & Hogan...San Jose, Cal.
Popper.	Popper, William C., & Co.............Pearl and Elm Sts., New York.
Popular.	Popular Publishing Co....................194 Broadway, New York.
Popular Astronomy.	Popular Astronomy...............................Northfield, Minn.
Popular Electricity.	Popular Electricity Publishing Co..............................Chicago.
Popular Mechanics.	Popular Mechanics' Co..................225 Washington St., Chicago.
Porter, G: F.	Porter, George F........................143 Dearborn St., Chicago.
Porter, I. W.	Porter, Ira W.....................403 W. O. W. Bldg., Omaha, Neb.
Porter, W. J.	Porter, W. J.................210 Blanchard Bldg., Los Angeles, Cal.
Portland.	Portland Printing House..............388 Taylor St., Portland, Ore.
Portland (Ore.) L. A.	Portland Library Association............................Portland, Ore.
Portland (Ore.) Sch. Astrology.	Portland School of Astrology..........................Portland, Ore.
Porter, D.	Porter, Dwight.......Massachusetts Institute of Technology, Boston.
Post, C. W.	Post, C. W...Battle Creek, Mich.
Post, L. D.	Post, Lyman D..............................154 Nassau St., New York.
Post, L: F.	Post, Louis F...............................357 Dearborn St., Chicago.
Potomac Press.	Potomac Press........................Munsey Bldg., Washington, D. C.
Pott.	Pott, James, & Co........................214-220 E. 23d St., New York.
Potter, A.	Potter, Alexander..........................116 Liberty St., New York.
Potter, S: L.	Potter, Samuel L.......................................Shelby, Mont.
Potter, T. F.	Potter, T. F., & Co...............................Downers Grove, Ill.
Potterdon, C. M.	Potterdon, C. M.....................................Hawthorne, N. J.
Poultry Culture.	Poultry Culture Publishing Co..........................Topeka, Kan.
Poultry Monthly.	Poultry Monthly Publishing Co........................Syracuse, N. Y.
Poultry Review.	Poultry Review..Elmira, N. Y.
Poultry Trib.	Poultry Tribune.......................................Mount Morris, Ill.
Powell, L. D.	Powell, L. D., Co...................................Los Angeles, Cal.
Powell Pub.	Powell Publishing Co...............................Los Angeles, Cal.
Power-Bk.	Power-Book Library..............304 Central St., Auburndale, Mass.
Power Pub.	Power Publishing Co......................730 17th Ave., Denver, Colo.
Powers.	Powers & Lyons..............................337 Wabash Ave., Chicago.
Powers, J. C.	Powers, J. C. & W. E........................65 Duane St., New York.
Powers, L., Sch.	Powers, Leland, School of the Spoken Word, 177 Huntington Ave., Boston.
Powers, W. F.	Powers, W. F., Co...........................30 Ferry St., New York.
Practical Text-book Co.	Practical Text-Book Co...................................Cleveland, O.
Practitioners' Pub.	Practitioners' Publishing Co..............55 W. 126th St., New York.
Praise Pub.	Praise Publishing Co...............1530 Chestnut St., Philadelphia.
Prang.	Prang Co..............................113 University Pl., New York.
Pratt, A. S.	Pratt, A. S., & Sons., National Bank Agents........Washington, D. C.
Pratt, J. R.	Pratt, James Randall...Ilion, N. Y.
Pratt, J. W.	Pratt, J. W., Co...............................52 Duane St., New York.
Pratt Inst.	Pratt Institute Free Library............Ryerson St., Brooklyn, N. Y.
Preetorius, C.	Preetorius, Carl........................P. O. Box 168, Evanston, Ill.
Prentis, C.	Prentis, C...Topeka, Kan.
Presb. Bd.	Presbyterian Board of Publication....1319 Walnut St., Philadelphia.
Presb. Bk.	Presbyterian Bookstore......712 Pennsylvania Ave., Pittsburgh, Pa.
Presb. Pub.	Presbyterian Committee of Publication, 212-216 N. 6th St., Richmond, Va.
Presbrey.	Presbrey, F., Co..............................3 W. 29th St., New York.
Prescott.	Prescott Co...Menominee, Mich.
President's Home Com.	President's Home Commission........................Washington, D. C.
Press Pub.	Press Publishing Co....New York World, Pulitzer Bldg., New York.
Presser, T.	Presser, Theodore, Co...............1708 Chestnut St., Philadelphia.
Preston.	Preston & Rounds..............98 Westminster St., Providence, R. I.
Price, B: L.	Price, Benjamin Lincoln..................................Valparaiso, Ind.
Price, W: T.	Price, William T..........................144 Broadway, New York.
Prince Soc.	Prince Society..Boston.
Princeton Univ.	Princeton University Library............................Princeton, N. J.
Priscilla.	Priscilla Publishing Co..................................85 Broad St., Boston.
Prison Reform.	Prison Reform League.............443 S. Main St., Los Angeles, Cal.
Professional.	Professional Publishing Co..........923-925 Spruce St., Philadelphia.
"Professional Memoirs."	"Professional Memoirs"....................Washington Barracks, D. C.
Progress Club.	Progress Club..................................50 Bromfield St., Boston.
Progress Co.	Progress Co....................515-519 Rand-McNally Bldg., Chicago.

Progressive Lit.	Progressive Literature Co. (Bought by Roger Bros.)
Progressive Thinker.	Progressive Thinker Publishing House.....106 Loomis St., Chicago.
Progressive Woman.	Progressive Woman Publishing Co.......................Girard, Kan.
Prophet Pub.	Prophet Publishing Co.................................Philadelphia.
Prosch, T: W.	Prosch, Thomas Wickham..............................Seattle, Wash.
Prude, A. M.	Prude, Alfred Marion...............................Birmingham, Ala.
Prudential.	Prudential Insurance Co........................Newark, N. J.
Psychic World.	Psychic World Publishing Co...1119 Washington St., Kansas City, Mo.
Psychological Clinic.	Psychological Clinic Press..36th St. and Woodland Ave., Philadelphia.
Psychological Review.	Psychological Review......Johns Hopkins University, Baltimore, Md.
Pub. Assoc. Friends.	Publishing Association of Friends....................Plainfield, Ind.
Pub. Ed. Assoc.	Public Education Assoc.................281 Fourth Ave., New York.
Pub. Ho. of Evangelical Assoc.	Publishing House of the Evangelical Association (C. Hauser, Agt.), 1903-1923 Woodland Ave., S. E., Cleveland, O.
Pub. Ho. of M. E. Ch., So.	Publishing House of the Methodist Episcopal Church, South (Smith & Lamar, Agts.)..................................Nashville, Tenn.
Pub. Pr.	Publishers Printing Co....................................Enid, Okla.
Pub. Pr. Co.	Publishers Printing Co.............419-421 Lafayette St., New York.
Pub. Sch. Pub.	Public School Publishing Co.......................Bloomington, Ill.
Pub. Syndicate.	Publishers' Syndicate....................................Cincinnati.
Pub. Weekly.	Publishers' Weekly......................298 Broadway, New York.
Public.	Public, The...............Ellsworth Bldg., 357 Dearborn St., Chicago.
Public Pub.	Public Publishing Co............First National Bank Bldg., Chicago.
Public Sch. Pub.	Public School Publishing Co......................Bloomington, Ill.
Publicity.	Publicity Publishing Co.................88-90 Wabash Ave., Chicago.
Pueblo Pub.	Pueblo Publishing Co............................Los Angeles, Cal.
Pugsley, R: M.	Pugsley, Richard Marriotte..................................New York.
Puritan Press.	Puritan Press...Oak Park, Ill.
Puritan Pub.	Puritan Publishing Co...................................Philadelphia.
Purity Pub.	Purity Publishing Co.......................367 Atlantic Ave., Boston.
Pustet.	Pustet, Frederick, & Co..................52 Barclay St., New York.
Puterbaugh, L. P.	Puterbaugh, Lewis Prather.......................N. Yakima, Wash.
Putnam.	Putnam, G. P., & Sons...............2-6 W. 45th St., New York.
Putnam, E.	Putnam, Eber...............................26 Broad St., Boston.
Quaker Hill.	Quaker Hill Conference Association............Quaker Hill, N. Y.
Queen's Shop.	Queen's Shop........7 Devon Road, Chestnut Hill, Brookline, Mass.
Quick News.	Quick News Publishing Co....Room 1803, 27 William St., New York.
Quikrite Pub.	Quikrite Publishing Co., 124 Erie Co. Savings Bank Bldg., Buffalo, N. Y.
Quinn, D.	Quinn, Daniel.....................................Yellow Springs, O.
R. & S. Pub.	R. & S. Publishing Co...................................Superior, Wis.
R. I. Coll.	Rhode Island College of Agriculture and Mechanic Arts., Kingston, R. I.
R. I. Dept. Educ.	Rhode Island Department of Education...............Providence, R. I.
R. I. Hist.	Rhode Island Citizens' Historical Association........Providence, R. I.
R. I. Normal.	Rhode Island Normal School..........................Providence, R. I.
R. I. State Lib.	Rhode Island State Library..........................Providence, R. I.
Radford Architectural.	Radford Architectural Co.................Medinah Bldg., Chicago.
Raible, M.	Raible, Marie..St. Louis.
Raidabaugh-V.	Raidabaugh-Voorhees Co...........................Plainfield, Ind.
Railroad Gazette.	Railroad Gazette..........................81 Fulton St., New York.
Railway Age Gazette.	Railway Age Gazette.......................81 Fulton St., New York.
Railway Educ.	Railway Educational Association......227 Monroe St., Brooklyn, N. Y.
Railway World.	Railway World Publishing Co........Witherspoon Bldg., Philadelphia.
Rainier Pr.	Rainier Printing Co., Inc.........116 Third Ave., So., Seattle, Wash.
Ralston Health.	Ralston Health Club............................Washington, D. C.
Ralston Univ.	Ralston University Publishing Co., 1307-1329 15th St., Washington, D. C.
Ramsay, J. P.	Ramsay, James P.......................................Lowell, Mass.
Ramsay, R. L.	Ramsay, Robert Lee...................................Columbia, Mo.
Rand, McN. & Co.	Rand, McNally & Co., 42 E. 22d St., New York; 160-174 Adams St., Chicago.
Randall, J. A.	Randall, James A., N. E. cor. Grand Boulevard and Brush St., Detroit, Mich.
Randall, T. A.	Randall, T. A., & Co................................Indianapolis, Ind.
Randolph, C. F.	Randolph, Corliss F.....................................Newark, N. J.
Randolph, H. S. F.	Randolph, Howard Stelle Fitz............1730 Broadway, New York.

Randolph, V. C.	Randolph, Vern Curtis.................8 Perry St., Salamanca, N. Y.
Rane, F. W.	Rane, Frank William..........................6 Beacon St., Boston.
Ranger, W. E.	Ranger, Walter Eugene..........................Providence, R. I.
Ransom, J. H.	Ransom, J. H..W. Lafayette, Ind.
Ratcliffe, F. A.	Ratcliffe, Rev. Francis Asbury..........................Pelham, Ga.
Rational Cult.	Rational Cult Co..........................Box 323, Freeport, Ill.
Ratner, H: W.	Ratner, Henry Wolf..Chicago.
Raub, A. D.	Raub, Adams Danforth..................................Lafayette, Ind.
Raudabaugh, I. F.	Raudabaugh, Israel Franklin..................................Celina, O.
Raum, H. A.	Raum, Harry Angle............1500 Pacific Ave., Atlantic City, N. J.
Rawie, H:	Rawie, Henry..........................Harrison Bldg., Columbus, O.
Rawley, J. P.	Rawley, Joseph P..................................57 Broadway, N. Y.
Rawlins, J: A., Post.	Rawlins, John A., Post 43..........................Marlboro, Mass.
Raymer, C. D.	Raymer, C. D., & Co...............1522 First Ave., Seattle, Wash.
Read, H. P.	Read, Harmon Pumpelly..............................Albany, N. Y.
Read & W.	Read & White..Bloomington, Ill.
Reade, P.	Reade, Philip......................871 Lake View Ave., Lowell, Mass.
Reade, W.	Reade, Willoughby......................Drawer 148, Alexandria, Va.
Reber, T:	Reber, Thomas..Natchez, Miss.
Rebman.	Rebman Co......................................1123 Broadway, New York.
Record Co.	Record Co..St. Augustine, Fla.
Record Pr. (*Mich.*)	Record Printing Co......................................Detroit, Mich.
Rector.	Rector, J. Logan..........................Pleasant Hill, Maine Co., O.
Red Diamond.	Red Diamond Press........................137 E. 25th St., New York.
Redfield.	Redfield Bros......................311-319 W. 43d St., New York.
Reed, C: K.	Reed, Charles K....................75 Thomas St., Worcester, Mass.
Reed, F. A.	Reed, Mrs. Frank A......................................Detroit, Mich.
Reed, G: M.	Reed, George Matthew..................................Columbia, Mo.
Reed, W. B.	Reed, W. B..White Cloud, Mich.
Reed, W: B.	Reed, William B....................79 Thames St., Newport, R. I.
Reed Press.	Reed Press..Lewiston, Me.
Reedy, W: M.	Reedy, William Marion..................10th and Pine Sts., St. Louis.
Rees, H.	Rees, Herman, Press of..................................Syracuse, N. Y.
Reeve, B.	Reeve, Budd..Buxton, N. D.
Reeve, J. S.	Reeve, J. Stanley..Philadelphia.
Ref. Ch. Pub.	Reformed Church Publication Bd..15th and Race Sts., Philadelphia.
Ref. Ch., S. S. Bd.	Reformed Church, S. S. Board..Fifteenth and Race Sts., Philadelphia.
Reform Club.	Reform Club......................................42 Broadway, New York.
Reformed.	Reformed (Dutch) Church in America, Board of Pub., 25 E. 22d St., New York.
Regan.	Regan Printing House..Chicago.
Regan, T.	Regan, T..Boise, Idaho.
Reid, D: C.	Reid, Rev. David C..................................Stockbridge, Mass.
Reid Pub.	Reid Publishing Co......................30 Huntington Ave., Boston.
Reilly & B.	Reilly & Britton Co....................319 S. Wabash Ave., Chicago.
Reilly, P:	Reilly, Peter..........................133 N. 13th St., Philadelphia.
Reinhardt, V.	Reinhardt, Victor..Terrell, Tex.
Rel. Educ.	Religious Education Association......332 S. Michigan Ave., Chicago.
Rel. Pub.	Religious Publishing Co..................192 Michigan Ave., Chicago.
Reliable Incubator.	Reliable Incubator and Brooder Co..........................Quincy, Ill.
Reliable Poultry Journ.	Reliable Poultry Journal Publishing Co....................Quincy, Ill.
Reliance.	Reliance Trading Co....................120 W. 14th St., New York.
Remick.	Remick, Schilling & Co..........................32 Warren St., New York.
Remick, J. H.	Remick, Jerome H., & Co....................131 W. 41st St., New York.
Remington, C: H.	Remington, Charles H..................................Providence, R. I.
Renn, G: B.	Renn, George B..................................1341 Dakin St., Chicago.
Renshaw, R. R.	Renshaw, Raemer Rex..........Wesleyan University, Middletown, Ct.
Rep. Bank Note.	Republic Bank Note Co..................................Pittsburgh, Pa.
Rep.-Courier.	Republican-Courier Print..................................Bozeman, Mont.
Rep. Pr. Co.	Republican Printing Co..................................Dowagiac, Mich.
Rep. Pub.	Republican Publishing Co..................................Hamilton, O.
Reporter-Journal.	Reporter-Journal Press..................................Gardiner, Me.
Reser, A. O.	Reser, Alva O..Lafayette, Ind.
Restitution.	Restitution Publishing House..................................Ashland, O.
Revell.	Revell, Fleming H., & Co....................158 Fifth Ave., New York.
Revell, A. H.	Revell, Alexander Hamilton..............198 Wabash Ave., Chicago.
Review and Herald Pub.	Review and Herald Publishing Association........Washington, D. C.
Review of Reviews.	Review of Reviews Co..........................13 Astor Pl., New York.
Review Press (*Ill.*)	Review Press..Decatur, Ill.
Review Pub.	Review Publishing Co..........................31 E. 17th St., New York.

Review Pub. Co.	Review Publishing Co. . . . . Minneapolis, Minn.
Reyburn, S: W.	Reyburn, Samuel W. . . . . . . Union Trust Co., Little Rock, Ark.
Reymershoffer, C:	Reymershoffer, Charles. . . . . Galveston, Tex.
Reynolds, J: P.	Reynolds, John Phillips. . . . . 50 State St., Boston.
Reynolds, P. R.	Reynolds, Paul R. . . . . 70 Fifth Ave., New York.
Reynolds, R. G.	Reynolds, R. G. . . . . Hanover, N. H.
Reynolds Lib.	Reynolds Library. . . . . Rochester, N. Y.
Rhoades, S: N.	Rhoades, Samuel N. . . . . 920 Walnut St., Philadelphia.
Rhodes, E. S.	Rhodes, Edwin S. . . . . 118 So. 5th St., New Philadelphia, O.
Rhodes, J: C.	Rhodes, John C. . . . . Valley Junction, Ia.
Rhodes, L. R.	Rhodes, Ledru Rollin. . . . . Fort Collins, Colo.
Rhodes & M.	Rhodes & McClure Publishing Co. . . . . Chicago.
Rice, F. P.	Rice, Franklin P. . . . . 17 Abbott St., Worcester, Mass.
Rice, G.	Rice, Grantland. . . . . Nashville, Tenn.
Richards, E. G.	Richards, Edwin Gilmore, Co. . . . . Sharon, Mass.
Richards, R. C.	Richards, Ralph Coffin. . . . . Geneva, Ill.
Richardson, H. H.	Richardson, Hugh Hudson. . . . . Jacksonville, Fla
Richardson, M. T.	Richardson, M. T., Co. . . . . 27 Park Pl., New York.
Richmond, E.	Richmond, E. . . . . 219 Mint Arcade, Philadelphia.
Richmond-A.	Richmond-Arnold Publishing Co. . . . . . 1411 Masonic Temple, Chicago.
Richmond Dept. of Health.	Richmond Department of Health. . . . . Richmond, Va.
Richmond Press.	Richmond Press. . . . . Richmond, Va.
Rickey, W: & Co.	Rickey, William, & Co. . . . . 43 W. 27th St., New York.
Ricks, J.	Ricks, Joel. . . . . 193 E. 2d St., Logan, Utah.
Riddell-Huston, E. H.	Riddell-Huston, Mrs. Evelyn H. . . . . Clintondale, Pa.
Riddell Pub.	Riddell Publishing Co. . . . . 5240 Indiana Ave., Chicago.
Rider & D.	Rider and Driver Publishing Co. . . . . 1123 Broadway, New York.
Ridgway.	Ridgway Co. . . . . Spring and Macdougal Sts., New York.
Riedinger, L. R.	Riedinger, Mrs. Laura Rhodes. . . . . R. F. D. No. 2, Alliance, O.
Ries, W. F.	Ries, W. F. . . . . Toledo, O.
Rigby, W. O.	Rigby, Will O. . . . . Topeka, Kan.
Riggs, J: F.	Riggs, John Franklin. . . . . Des Moines, Ia.
Riley, B: F.	Riley, Benjamin F. . . . . Birmingham, Ala.
Riley, F. T.	Riley, Frank T., Publishing Co. . . . . Kansas City, Mo.
Riley, W: B.	Riley, William B. . . . . 1006 Harmon Pl., Minneapolis, Minn.
Riley & C.	Riley & Chandler. . . . . Richmond, Va.
Rinaldo, J.	Rinaldo, Joel. . . . . 206 W. 41st St., New York.
Ritchie.	Ritchie & Co. . . . . 37 E. Randolph St., Chicago.
Ritzmann, B., & Co.	Ritzmann, Brooks & Co. . . . . Wells and Illinois Sts., Chicago.
Riverdale Press.	Riverdale Press. . . . . Brookline, Mass.
Riverside Press.	Riverside Press. . . . . Cambridge, Mass.
Ro Co.	Ro Co. . . . . 15 E. 7th St., Cincinnati.
Roadtown.	Roadtown Press. . . . . 150 Nassau St., New York.
Robarts, H.	Robarts, Heber, M.D. . . . . 5899 Cater Ave., St. Louis.
Robb, D: B.	Robb, David B. . . . . Rose Farm, O.
Robbins, R. C.	Robbins, Reginald Chauncey. . . . . Boston.
Roberts, C. M.	Roberts, Mrs. C. M. . . . . 109 S. 38th St., Philadelphia.
Roberts, J: G.	Roberts, John Gray. . . . . 418½ E. Adams St., Springfield, Ill.
Roberts, P.	Roberts, Philip. . . . . Box 32, Yale Station, New Haven, Ct.
Roberts, W. F.	Roberts, W. F., Co., Inc. . . . . 1413 New York Ave., Washington D. C.
Roberts, W: W.	Roberts, Willliam W., Co. . . . . Portland, Me.
Roberts & R.	Roberts & Roberts. . . . . 512 Abington Bldg., Portland, Ore.
Roberts Bros.	Roberts Bros. Co. . . . . Lockport, N. Y.
Robertson, A. M.	Robertson, A. M. . . . . 222 Stockton St., San Francisco.
Robertson, G.	Robertson, Georgia. . . . . 74 The Kensesaw, Washington, D. C.
Robertson, S: L.	Robertson, Samuel L. . . . . 1324 Ina St., Birmingham, Ala.
Robinson, A. J.	Robinson, Arthur J. . . . . Spokane, Wash.
Robinson, C: A.	Robinson, Charles Asbury. . . . . Greenfield, Ind.
Robinson, E.	Robinson, E., & Co. . . . . 49 Liberty St., New York.
Robinson, H.	Robinson, Humphrey. . . . . Louisville, Ky.
Robinson, J. W.	Robinson, James Watts. . . . . Brookline, Mass.
Robinson, Leigh.	Robinson, Leigh. . . . . Washington, D. C.
Robson.	Robson & Adee. . . . . 309 State St., Schenectady, N. Y.
Robson, F. H.	Robson, Frank H. . . . . 79 William St., Worcester, Mass.
Rockefeller Inst.	Rockefeller Institute for Medical Research, 66th St. and Ave. A, New York.
Rodeffer, J: D:	Rodeffer, John David. . . . . Salem, Va.
Roger & S.	Roger & Smith Co. . . . . Chicago.
Roger Bros.	Roger Bros. . . . . 429 Sixth Ave., New York.
Rogers, A. E.	Rogers, Allen E. . . . . Orono, Me.
Rogers, C. E.	Rogers, Corydon Eugene. . . . . 382 Second Ave., New York.

Rogers & M.	Rogers & Manson..Boston.
Rohlfing.	Rohlfing Sons Music Co..........90 Wisconsin St., Milwaukee, Wis.
Rollins, M.	Rollins, Montgomery........................6 Hancock Ave., Boston.
Rohrer, C. W. G.	Rohrer, Caleb Wyand Geeting........................Lauraville, Md.
Rokker, H. W.	Rokker, H. W...Springfield, Ill.
Rolling Stone.	Rolling Stone Club........................Bell Bldg., Medina, N. Y.
Rollins, M.	Rollins, Montgomery........................6 Hancock Ave., Boston.
Romance.	Romance Press..............................156 Fifth Ave., New York.
Rominger, C. A.	Rominger, Cornelius A....................................Zion City, Ill.
Ronald Press.	Ronald Press Co..........................229 Broadway, New York.
Rooks Press.	Rooks Press....................................196 Clark St., Chicago.
Roose, T: W.	Roose, Thomas Walter...........28 Green St., Charlestown, Mass.
Root, A. I.	Root, A. I., Co..Medina, O.
Root, E: T.	Root, Rev. Edward Tallmadge.....141 Chester Ave., Providence, R. I.
Rorke, T. S.	Rorke, T. Scott..................223 A St., N. E., Washington, D. C.
Rosary (Ill.)	Rosary Publishing Co..Chicago, Ill.
Rosary (O.)	Rosary Press Co..Somerset, O.
Rose.	Rose Publishing Co..Cleveland, O.
Rose, J. A.	Rose, James A..Springfield, Ill.
Rose, W: B.	Rose, William B..............................14 N. May St., Chicago.
Rosemary.	Rosemary Press...Needham, Mass.
Rosenbloom, J.	Rosenbloom, Jacob.........................437 W. 59th St., New York.
Rosengarten, J. G:	Rosengarten, Joseph George, 411 Real Estate Trust Bldg., Philadelphia.
Rosewater, V.	Rosewater, Victor..Omaha, Neb.
Rosicrucian.	Rosicrucian Fellowship.....................................Seattle, Wash.
Ross, C.	Ross, Clinton...Binghamton, N. Y.
Ross, R. R.	Ross, Riley R...............235 N. Fulton Ave., Mt. Vernon, N. Y.
Ross, W. M.	Ross, Will Monroe.....................................Stevens Point, Wis.
Rotch, A. L.	Rotch, Abbott Lawrence....Blue Hill Observatory, Hyde Park, Mass.
Roth, E:	Roth, Edward...............................1135 Pine St., Philadelphia.
Rough Notes.	Rough Notes Co................220 E. Ohio St., Indianapolis, Ind.
Row, P. & Co.	Row, Peterson & Co.....................625 S. Wabash Ave., Chicago.
Row, S. B.	Row, S. B...Philipsburg, Pa.
Rowe, F: L:	Rowe, Frederick Louis.........................422 Elm St., Cincinnati.
Rowe, S: M.	Rowe, Samuel McMath........................364 Monadnock, Chicago.
Rowe, W: H.	Rowe, William H., Jr..Hartford, N. Y.
Rowell, B: W.	Rowell, Benjamin Winslow...Boston.
Roxburgh.	Roxburgh Publishing Co., Inc........................61 Court St., Boston.
Royal Baking.	Royal Baking Powder Co......................................New York.
Royce, C. H. B.	Royce, Mrs. Caroline Halstead Barton......Astor Library, New York.
Roycrofters.	Roycrofters (The)..East Aurora, N. Y.
Roys, C. D.	Roys, Cyrus D...Elkhart, Ind.
Rudder.	Rudder Publishing Co.............................1 Hudson St. New York.
Rude, A. D.	Rude, A. D., & Son..................1133-1135 Broadway, New York.
Rudolph, J. F. S.	Rudolph, Johannes F. S..............606 Garden St., Hoboken, N. J.
Ruebush-E.	Ruebush-Elkins Co..Dayton, Va.
Ruggles, F. A.	Ruggles, Frank A.................................53 State St., Boston.
Ruledge.	Rulege Playing Card Co..............................Port Huron, Mich.
Rumford Press.	Rumford Press...Concord, N. H.
Runyon & H.	Runyon & Harris, Press of.....................................Cincinnati.
Rural.	Rural Publishing Co...........................409 Pearl St., New York.
Rural Pub.	Rural Publishing Co...Columbus, O.
Russell, E.	Russell, Edgar.......................................Fort Leavenworth, Kan.
Russell, H. L.	Russell, Harry L...Madison, Wis.
Russell, M. C.	Russell, M. C...Lake City, Minn.
Russell Pr.	Russell Printing Co.......................................Buffalo, N. Y.
Rust-Craft.	Rust-Craft Shop......................410 E. 11th St., Kansas City, Mo.
Ruther, F:	Ruther, Frederick...Hickville, L. I.
Rutherford, F. E.	Rutherford, Frank Emory......................................Dallas, Tex.
Ruxton	Ruxton, Philip, Inc...............................290 Broadway, New York.
Ryan, J: B.	Ryan, John Barry...............................18 W. 10th St., New York.
Ryder Bros.	Ryder Bros...Baker City, Ore.
S. A. R., Me. Soc.	Sons of the American Revolution, Maine Society......Portland, Me.
S. A. R., N. J. Soc.	Sons of the American Revolution, New Jersey Society of, 312 Belleville Ave., Newark, N. J.
S. C. Hist.	South Carolina Historical Commission..................Columbia, S. C.
S. S. Bd. So. Bapt.	Sunday School Board of the Southern Baptist Convention, 167 N. Cherry St., Nashville, Tenn.
S. S. Times.	Sunday School Times Co..............1031 Walnut St., Philadelphia.
Saalfield.	Saalfield Publishing Co..Akron, O.
Sachse, J. F.	Sachse, Julius F.........................Masonic Temple, Philadelphia.

Sadler-R.	Sadler-Rowe Co....................12 N. Charles St., Baltimore, Md.
Saginaw.	Saginaw Printing and Publishing Co., 216 N. Franklin St., Saginaw, E. S., Mich.
Salem Co. Hist. Soc.	Salem County Historical Society........................Salem, N. J.
Salem Press.	Salem Press Co...Salem, Mass.
Salem Pub. Lib.	Salem Public Library...................................Salem, Mass.
Salesmanship.	Salesmanship Co............................200 Monroe St., Chicago.
Sames, C: M.	Sames, Charles MacCaughey...542 Bramhall Ave., Jersey City, N. J.
Salt Lake Trib.	Salt Lake Tribune............................Salt Lake City, Utah.
Salter.	Salter, Nelson L..............................Yosemite Valley, Cal.
Sametz.	Sametz, William F., & Co................540 Pearl St., New York.
Sampson.	Sampson Publishing Co.....................6 Beacon St., Boston.
San. F. Lib.	San Francisco Public Library.......................San Francisco.
San F. Motor.	San Francisco Motor Club...568 Golden Gate Ave., San Francisco.
San F. St. Normal.	San Francisco State Normal School, Buchanan and Waller Sts., San Francisco.
Sanborn, B: H.	Sanborn, Benjamin H., & Co...............120 Boylston St., Boston.
Sanders. H. F.	Sanders, Helen Fitzgerald...........514 N. Henry Ave., Butte, Mont.
Sanders, P: J.	Sanders, Peter James..............................Murray City, Utah.
Sanders Pub.	Sanders Publishing Co....................358 Dearborn St., Chicago.
Sandison, H.	Sandison, Howard..............404 N. Center St., Terre Haute, Ind.
Sanford, J: I.	Sanford, John Ithiel.............444 Bergen Ave., Jersey City, N. J.
Sargent, C. S.	Sargent, C. S..............Arnold Arboretum, Jamaica Plains, Mass.
Sangster, U. N.	Sangster, Urania N......................97 Bird Ave., Buffalo, N. Y.
Saratogian.	Saratogian Co............................Saratoga Springs, N. Y.
Saturday News.	Saturday News.....................................Watertown, S. D.
Sault.	Sault News Printing Co.....................Sault Ste. Marie, Mich.
Saumenig, J: H.	Saumenig, John H., & Co.............229 Park Ave., Baltimore, Md.
Saunders.	Saunders, W. B., Co....................925 Walnut St., Philadelphia
Saurusaitis, P:	Saurusaitis, Rev. Peter................36 James St., Waterbury, Ct.
Sauter, E.	Sauter, Edwin..St. Louis.
Sauveur, A.	Sauveur, Albert......................Retch Bldg., Cambridge, Mass.
Saward, F: E:	Saward, Frederick Edward.................20 Vesey St., New York.
Sawyer, C: W.	Sawyer, Charles W.......................41 Humphreys St., Boston.
Saxton, E.	Saxton, Edmund..........41 Bladensburg Rd., Washington, D. C.
Scaife.	Scaife, William B., & Sons, Co......................Pittsburgh, Pa.
Scenic America.	Scenic America Publishing Co......................Los Angeles, Cal.
Sch. Liberal Arts.	School of Liberal Arts and Sciences......156 Fifth Ave., New York.
Sch. Methods.	School Methods Co.......................380 Wabash Ave., Chicago.
Sch. of Eng.	School of English.......................1411 Security Bldg., Chicago.
Sch. of R. R. Signaling.	School of Railway Signaling.................................Utica, N. Y.
Sch. Pedagogy.	School of Pedagogy, N. Y. University..Washington Sq., E., New York.
Schaad, J. A.	Schaad, Rev. Julius A.............415 W. 13th St., Kansas City, Mo.
Schaefer & K.	Schaefer & Koradi...............4th and Wood Sts., Philadelphia.
Schaffner, J: H:	Schaffner, John..Columbus, O.
Schapiro, B. A. M.	Schapiro, B. A. M.........................138 Bible House, New York.
Schaus, W:	Schaus, William...........................415 5th Ave., New York.
Schechter, S.	Schechter, Solomon.....................535 W. 123d St., New York.
Scheiman, W: H.	Scheiman, William H.....................................Fort Wayne, Ind.
Schenck, C. A.	Schenck, Carl Alvin...................................Pisgah Forest, N. C.
Schenck, F. J.	Schenck, Frank Joseph................75 State St., Rochester, N. Y.
Schilling, H. K.	Schilling, Hugo K...............2316 Le Conte Ave., Berkeley, Cal.
Schilling, W: P.	Schilling, William Paul.......................131 W. 23d St., New York.
Schirmer.	Schirmer, G...................................35 Union Sq., W., New York.
Schirmer, R: C.	Schirmer, Richard C.................822 N. Broad St., Philadelphia.
Schleif, O.	Schleif, Oscar...Philadelphia.
Schleppey, B. B.	Schleppey, Mrs. Blanche Bloor 634 E. 11th St., Indianapolis, Ind.
Schmalz.	Schmalz Publication Co.......................31 Ames Bldg., Boston.
Schmidt, A. P.	Schmidt, Arthur P..........................120 Boylston St., Boston.
Schnell, A. F.	Schnell, Albert Frederick.................................Ridgefield, N. J.
Schoenhof.	Schoenhof Book Co.........................128 Tremont St., Boston.
Scholes, T:	Scholes, Thomas, & Co......................333 Wabash Ave., Chicago.
Schomer, A. S.	Schomer, Abraham S......................5 Beekman St., New York.
Schott, C: J.	Schott, Charles Joseph..Seattle, Wash.
Schuberth.	Schuberth, Edward, & Co...................11 E. 22d St., New York.
Schuette, H. G:	Schuette, H. G..............................Box 19, Manitowoc, Wis.
Schulte.	Schulte, Theodore E.........................132 E. 23d St., New York.
Schultz, F: W.	Schultz, Frederick Walter...........P. O. Box 515, Baltimore, Md.
Schumaker, E:	Schumaker, Edward, & Son................................Hibert, Wis.
Schwartz, J: R.	Schwartz, John Robley..................................Camp Hill, Pa.

Schwartz, K. & F.	Schwartz, Kirwin & Fauss..............42 Barclay St., New York.
Sci. Authors'.	Scientific Authors' Publishing Co.......329 W. 57th St., New York.
Science Pr., (N. Y.)	Science Press..............................Sub-Station 84, New York.
Scientific American.	Scientific American.........................361 Broadway, New York.
Scientific Press.	Scientific Press....................135 Johnson St., Brooklyn, N. Y.
Scofield, W: J.	Scofield, William J............436 Murphy Ave., San Antonio, Tex.
Scott, E.	Scott, Elwood...Marion, Ind.
Scott, F. & Co.	Scott, Foresman & Co...............623 S. Wabash Ave., Chicago.
Scott, Jennie.	Scott, Jennie..Armour, S. Dak.
Scott, W. L.	Scott, Walter L...Tivoli, N. Y.
Scott-M.	Scott-Miller Co.......................................Indianapolis, Ind.
Scranton.	Scranton, S. S., & Co..................281 Asylum St., Hartford, Ct.
Scribner.	Scribner, Charles, Sons.............153-157 Fifth Ave., New York.
Scriven, G: P.	Scriven, George P..................................Governor's Island, N. Y.
Scruby, J. J.	Scruby, J. J...Dayton, O.
Scudder.	Scudder, Bros. Co..................................630 W. 6th St., Cincinnati.
Scullin, P. H.	Scullin, P. H.......................761 Fillmore St., San Francisco.
Searcy.	Searcy Publishing Co...Griffin, Ga.
Seares, F: H.	Seares, Frederick Hanley, Mount Wilson Solar Observatory, Pasadena, Cal.
Sears Invest.	Sears Investment Co..Boston.
Sears Roebuck.	Sears Roebuck & Co...Chicago.
Seattle Pub. Lib.	Seattle Public Library...Seattle, Wash.
Seaver, J. W.	Seaver, Jay W.....................25 Lynwood Pl., New Haven, Ct.
Secord, L. M.	Secord, L. M.......................1303 Clark Ave., Cleveland, O.
Sedlasky, F. J.	Sedlasky, Ferdinand James..................................Fort Dodge, Ia.
Seeds, R. S.	Seeds, Robert S...Birmingham, Pa.
Seeman.	Seeman Printery...Durham, N. C.
Seewir.	Seewir, Charles C....................917 Mass. St., Lawrence, Kan.
Segal, J.	Segal, Josephine. Majestic Hotel, Second and Broad Sts., Philadelphia.
Seide, J. N.	Seide, Joseph N...San Antonio, Tex.
Seiler.	Seiler, Adolph G.................1224 Amsterdam Ave., New York.
Self Mastery.	Self Mastery Press...Corry, Pa.
Seligman, E. R. A.	Seligman, Edwin Robert Anderson......324 W. 86th St., New York.
Sellers, E. J.	Sellers. Edwin Jaquett.................800 Betz Bldg., Philadelphia.
Sells, E. W.	Sells, Elijah W.............Haskins & Sells, 30 Broad St., New York.
Sellstedt, L. G.	Sellstedt, Lars Gustaf.............78 W. Mohawk St., Buffalo, N. Y.
Semsch, O. F.	Semsch, Otto Francis..........................35 Wall St., New York.
Senour, C. S.	Senour, Mrs. Caro Smith......................................Hollywood, Cal.
Sentinel.	Sentinel Co...North St. Paul, Minn.
Sentinel (N. H.)	Sentinel Printing Co..Keene, N. H.
Sentinel Pr.	Sentinel Printing Co......123-125 W. Market St., Indianapolis, Ind.
Sentinel Pub.	Sentinel Publishing Co..Pontiac, Ill.
Sentinel Pub. (Cal.)	Sentinel Publishing Co...Santa Cruz, Cal.
Sentinel Pub. Co.	Sentinel Publishing Co...Indianapolis, Ind.
Sergel.	Sergel, Charles H., & Co.........................358 Dearborn St., Chicago.
Servants Immaculate Heart.	Servants of the Immaculate Heart of Mary.............Scranton, Pa.
Severance, H. S.	Severance, Howard S...Novi, Mich.
Severn River.	Severn River Press...Annapolis, Md.
Sexton, M. B.	Sexton, Marian B...Monmouth, Ill.
Seymour.	Seymour, Ralph Fletcher.........................Fine Arts Bldg., Chicago.
Shakespeare Press.	Shakespeare Press...Westfield, N. J.
Shallcross.	Shallcross Printing Co................................419 N. 4th St., St. Louis.
Shamburger, R. L.	Shamburger, Mrs. R. L.......................................Pittsburgh, Tex.
Shanley.	Shanley, Hobart J., Co...Burlington, Vt.
Shannon, W. W.	Shannon, W. W. (State Superintendent of Printing). Sacramento, Cal.
Sharman, J: T:	Sharman, John Thomas..Reedsburg, Wis.
Sharon Hist. Soc.	Sharon Historical Society......................................Sharon, Mass.
Sharp, A. G.	Sharp, Mrs. Abigail Gardner......Arnold's Park, Lakes Okoboji, Ia.
Sharp, J. R.	Sharp, James Robert...Nashville, Tenn.
Sharp, R. W.	Sharp, Robert W.....................207 Market St., Newark, N. J.
Sharp & A.	Sharp & Alleman Co.............................100 S. 9th St., Philadelphia.
Sharpe, W: C.	Sharpe, William C..Seymour, Ct.
Shaw, C. B.	Shaw, Clement B....................74 Auditorium Bldg., Chicago.
Shaw, C: E.	Shaw, Charles Edgar, Jr..Chicago.
Shaw, L.	Shaw, Luella...Hotchkiss, Colo.
Shaw, R. H.	Shaw, Ralph H.....................................69 Burtt St., Lowell, Mass.
Shaw Bros.	Shaw Bros...........................Bond Bldg., Washington, D. C.
Shaw Pub.	Shaw Publishing Co.......................................Grand Rapids, Mich.
Shayler, E. V.	Shayler, Rev. Ernest Vincent.....................................Oak Park, Ill.
Sheehy, J.	Sheehy, Jerry.........................447 Minna St., San Francisco.

Sheer.	Sheer, H. M., Co.	Quincy, Ill.
Sheffey, J: P.	Sheffey, John P.	Marion, Va.
Shelby Co. Leader.	Shelby County Leader	Shelbyville, Ill.
Sheldon, A. E.	Sheldon, Addison Erwin	State University, Lincoln, Neb.
Sheldon Univ.	Sheldon University Press	Libertyville, Ill.
Shepard, F.	Shepard, Frank, Co.	190-194 W. Broadway, New York.
Shepherd, J. W.	Shepherd, J. W.	317-319 5th Ave., No., Nashville, Tenn.
Sheppard, M.	Sheppard, Morris	Texarkana, Tex.
Shepperson, A. B.	Shepperson, Alfred B.	65 Cotton Exchange Bldg., New York.
Sherman.	Sherman & Co.	7 Cherry St., Philadelphia.
Sherman, E. E.	Sherman, E. E., & Co.	Boston.
Sherman, E. J.	Sherman, Edgar Jay	Boston.
Sherman, F.	Sherman, French & Co.	6 Beacon St., Boston.
Sherman, F. F.	Sherman, Frederic Fairchild	42 W. 39th St., New York.
Sherman, J: D.	Sherman, Mrs. John D.	73 E. 47th St., Chicago.
Sherman, M. J. M.	Sherman, Mrs. Margaret Jane McMurphy	Brodhead, Wis.
Sherrill, C. O.	Sherrill, Clarence Osborne	Fort Leavenworth, Kan.
Sherwin-W.	Sherwin-Williams Co.	Cleveland, O.
Shiel, R. R.	Shiel, Roger R.	Shiel Apartment House, Indianapolis, Ind.
Shippers' Freight.	Shippers' Freight Service	First National Bank Bldg., Chicago.
Shockley Bros.	Shockley Brothers & Cook	Oskaloosa, Ia.
Shoenfeld, G.	Schoenfeld, Mrs. Gabrielle	New Orleans, La.
Shoop, M. P.	Shoop, Max Pardoe	Amherst College, Amherst, Mass.
Shores, R. J.	Shores, Robert J.	East Orange, N. J.
Shorter, R. G.	Shorter, Robert Graves	Nashville, Tenn.
Showalter, L. P.	Showalter, Lewis Pendleton	Eaton, O.
Showalter-P.	Showalter-Patton Co.	Dallas, Tex.
Shreve, W: P.	Shreve, William P.	Boston.
Shriver, C. H.	Shriver, C. H.	84 State St., Boston.
Shuman.	Shuman, G. L., & Co.	Chicago.
Sibley.	Sibley & Co.	120 Boylston St., Boston.
Sickles, D. E.	Sickles, General D. E.	23 Fifth Ave., New York.
Sieger, P. G:	Sieger, Rev. P. George	Lancaster, Pa.
Sigma.	Sigma Publishing Co.	210 Pine St., St. Louis.
Silk, R. A.	Silk, Reeve A.	1 Madison Ave., New York.
Silver.	Silver, Burdett & Co.	239 W. 39th St., New York.
Silver Lotus.	Silver Lotus Shop	Pittsfield, Mass.
Silver Manufacturing.	Silver Manufacturing Co.	Salem, O.
Simmons.	Simmons, Parker P.	3 E. 14th St., New York.
Simmons, H. A.	Simmons, H. A., & Co.	20 Broad St., New York.
Simmons, M. & D.	Simmons, Manning & Dawson	74 Lafayette St., New York.
Simmons, R. J. H.	Simmons, Robert Jasper Hogue	Hartford, Ala.
Simon, A.	Simon, Abram	2802 Cathedral Ave., Washington, D. C.
Simon, F. P:	Simon, Ferdinand Peter	132 Hill St., New Haven, Ct.
Simon, L. C.	Simon, Lemuel C.	Philadelphia.
Simplified Spell. Bd.	Simplified Spelling Board	1 Madison Ave., New York.
Simpson.	Simpson Bros.' Corporation	Boston.
Simpson, J.	Simpson, Mrs. Jerry	Wichita, Kan.
Simpson, T: J.	Simpson, Thomas Jefferson	Clarksburg, Mo.
Sims, M. H.	Sims, Mrs. Mamie Hunt	216 E. 53d St., Chicago.
Sinclair, A.	Sinclair, Angus Co.	116 Liberty St., New York.
Singer.	Singer Co.	55 E. 20th St., New York.
Singer, J.	Singer, Jacob	Philadelphia.
Singleton, T. W.	Singleton, Terrell Wingfield	Cincinnati.
Sinnett, C: N.	Sinnett, Charles Nelson	Carthage, Miner Co., S. D.
Sinnickson.	Sinnickson, Clew & Sons	Camden, N. J.
Sisters of Charity.	Sisters of Charity	Cincinnati.
Sisters of St. Joseph.	Sisters of St. Joseph	Wichita, Kan.
Site and Relic.	Site and Relic Society of Germantown	Germantown, Pa.
Skal, G. von.	Skal, Georg von	5 Beekman St., New York.
Skelton.	Skelton Publishing Co.	235 Edison St., Salt Lake City, Utah.
Skelton, E. O.	Skelton, Edward Oliver	Boston.
Sketch Bk.	Sketch Book Press	Little Rock, Ark.
Skrainka, P.	Skrainka, Philip	St. Louis.
Skinner & K.	Skinner & Kennedy	St. Louis.
Slaught, H. E.	Slaught, H. E.	American Mathematical Society, Chicago.
Sloan, E. E.	Sloan, Emily Eva	Belle Fourche, S. Dak.
Sloane, J. R.	Sloane, James Robinson	2715 Bryant Ave. So., Minneapolis, Minn.
Slocum, G: E.	Slocum, George Engs	Scottsville, N. Y.
Slocum Pub.	Slocum Publishing Co.	218 13th St., Toledo, O.
Slovak Press.	Slovak Press	188 Ave A, New York.

Small.	Small, Maynard & Co.......................15 Beacon St., Boston.
Small, C: W.	Small, Charles Wilder..................105 Summer St., Boston.
Smallwood, W: M.	Smallwood, William Martin.......................Syracuse, N. Y.
Smeltzer, J. R.	Smeltzer, Jeannie Ringland.......................Fort Dodge, Ia.
Smiley, A. J.	Smiley, Amanda Jane..........................W. Lafayette, Ind.
Smiley, A. W.	Smiley, Alfred Wilson...............................Foxburg, Pa.
Smiley, F. T.	Smiley, Frank T., Printing and Publishing Co.; 5 Beekman St., New York.
Smiley, J. L.	Smiley, Rev. James Lawrenson.......................Annapolis, Md.
Smith.	Smith Printing Co...................................Pine Bluff, Ark.
Smith, A. H.	Smith, Albert Herman...............................Lowville, N. Y.
Smith, B. D.	Smith, B. D., & Bro.......................................Pulaski, Va.
Smith, C: A.	Smith, Charles Alphonso.........................Chapel Hill, N. C.
Smith, C: H.	Smith, Charles H..................5701 Euclid Ave., Cleveland, O.
Smith, C. S.	Smith, Caroline Sprague, Care of Cheltenham Press, 150 Fifth Ave., New York.
Smith, D: E.	Smith, Prof. David Eugene............525 W. 120th St., New York.
Smith, E. A. F.	Smith, Emma A. F., Washington Headquarters Soc., Morris Mansion, New York.
Smith, E. B.	Smith, Egbert Bull.............................Port Jefferson, N. Y.
Smith, E. B. (Pa.)	Smith, Earl B..Philadelphia.
Smith, E. R.	Smith, Elsie Rhea...................................Marshall, Tex.
Smith, F.	Smith, Frank..Dover, Mass.
Smith, F. J.	Smith, Frank J.................................Pleasanton, Kan.
Smith, G: K.	Smith, George K.................606 S. Saliwa Ave., Syracuse, N. Y.
Smith, J. A.	Smith, J. Augustine (Ideal Concrete Manufacturing Co) South Bend, Ind.
Smith, J: P., Pr.	Smith, John P., Printing Co.......................Rochester, N. Y.
Smith, J. W.	Smith James Washington..............................Decatur, Miss.
Smith, L. K.	Smith, Leonard Kingsley.............417 Kansas St., Huron, S. D.
Smith, L: P.	Smith, Louis P...Toledo, O.
Smith, O. C.	Smith, Oliver Cromwell..............................Dodgeville, Wis.
Smith, P.	Smith, Payson (State Superintendent of Public Schools), Augusta, Me.
Smith, R.	Smith, Robert, Printing Co..................................Lansing, Mich.
Smith, W: C.	Smith, William Cadid..Delphi. Ind.
Smith, W: C. (Mass.)	Smith, William Christopher..............................Chatham, Mass.
Smith, W. E.	Smith, W. E..Corvallis, Ore.
Smith, W. R. C.	Smith, W. R. C., Publishing Co...........Grant Bldg., Atlanta, Ga.
Smith & B.	Smith & Butterfield...................................Evansville, Ind.
Smith & L.	Smith & Lamar..Nashville, Tenn.
	See also Publishing House of the Methodist Episcopal Church, South.
Smith & McC.	Smith & McCance...................................38 Bromfield St., Boston.
Smith & S.	Smith & Sale..........................45 Exchange St., Portland, Me.
Smith Bros.	Smith Bros...................816 Fourth St., N. W., Washington, D. C.
Smith. Inst.	Smithsonian Institution..............................Washington, D. C.
Smith-B.	Smith-Brooks Printing Co...................................Denver, Colo.
Smith-L.	Smith-Linsley Co...Hartford, Ct.
Smyth, P. G.	Smyth, P. G..............................Merchants' Building, Chicago.
Smyth, S: G.	Smyth, Samuel Gordon..........................West Conshohocken, Pa.
Smythe, A. H.	Smythe, A. H..................................41 S. High St., Columbus, O.
Snead & Co.	Snead & Co.......................Foot of Pine St., Jersey City, N. J.
Snow, J. E.	Snow, Jane Elliott..........................4201 Clinton Ave., Cleveland, O.
Snow & F.	Snow & Farnham............15 Custom House St., Providence, R. I.
Snyder, S. P.	Snyder, Sherwood Percy..................................Box 58, Dayton, O.
So. Clinic Pr.	Southern Clinic Print...................4 E. Clay St., Richmond, Va.
So. Sch. Bk.	Southern School Book Co..Dallas, Tex.
Soc. Americana.	Society Americana.......................................6 Beacon St., Boston.
	Society for the Promotion of Agricultural Science. *See* Hunt, T: F.
Soc. Cal. Pioneers.	Society of California Pioneers of Washington, D. C..Washington, D. C.
Soc. Colon. Wars, D. C.	Society of Colonial Wars, District of Columbia....Washington, D. C.
Soc. Colon. Wars (O.)	Society of Colonial Wars, Ohio.......................................Cincinnati.
Soc. Divine Word.	Society of the Divine Word...Techny, Ill.
Soc. Dofobs.	Society of Dofobs...........................Care of Roswell Field, Chicago.
Soc. for Propagation of Faith.	Society for the Propagation of the Faith, 462 Madison Ave., New York.
Social Index.	Social Index Publishing Co..Newport, R. I.
Social Justice.	Social Justice Publishing Co...2630 Fifth Ave., S., Minneapolis, Minn.
Social Register.	Social Register Association...............................29 Broadway, New York.
Socialist.	Socialist Party, National Headquarters..180 Washington St., Chicago.

Socialist Lit. Co.	Socialist Literature Co....................15 Spruce St., New York.
Solar Lit.	Solar Literary and Musical Bureau, Care of Arthur Franklin Fuller, Fort Worth, Tex.
Somerville.	Somerville, Ivan, & Co..............225 Fourth Ave., New York.
Soney.	Soney & Sage.........................42 Clinton St., Newark, N. J.
Sonneck, O. G: T.	Sonneck, Oscar George Theodore....1732 20th St., Washington, D. C.
Soper, G: A.	Soper, George Albert..........29 Broadway, Room 259, New York.
Sorley, L. S.	Sorley, Lewis Stone, Capt. 14th Infantry, U. S.A...Baton Rouge, La.
South-West Pub.	South-West Publishing Co....Box F, University Station, Austin, Tex.
Southern California Pr.	Southern California Printing Co..................Los Angeles, Cal.
Southern Churchman.	Southern Churchman Co............................Richmond, Va.
Southern Engineer.	Southern Engineer...................................Atlanta, Ga.
Southern Hist. Pub.	Southern Historical Publication Society..............Richmond, Va.
Southern Med.	Southern Medical Publishing Co..3026 W. Worth Ave., Baltimore, Md.
Southern Missionary.	Southern Missionary Society.........................Nashville, Tenn.
Southern Planter.	Southern Planter Publishing Co.....................Richmond, Va.
Southern Pub.	Southern Publishing Assoc., 24th Ave., N., and Hyde St., Nashville, Tenn.
Southern Pub. (Ala.)	Southern Publishing Co..................................Mobile, Ala.
Southern Pub. (Tex.)	Southern Publishing Co..................................Dallas, Tex.
Southern Ruralist.	Southern Ruralist Co...................................Atlanta, Ga.
Southern Sch. R'way Sci.	Southern Schools of Railway Science........................Chicago.
Southern Sch. Supply.	Southern School Supply Company.................Knoxville, Tenn.
Southwest Pub.	Southwest Publishing Co...............................Pulaski, Va.
Southwestern Co. (Nashville.)	Southwestern Publishing Co.......150 Fourth Ave., Nashville, Tenn.
Southwick, J. E.	Southwick, Mrs. Jessie Eldridge, Emerson College of Oratory, Chickering Hall, Boston.
Sower.	Sower, Christopher, Co...............124 N. 18th St., Philadelphia.
Sower, J. W.	Sower, John William....................................Atlanta, Ga.
Spalding.	Spalding, A. G., & Bros.................126 Nassau St., New York.
Spalding, J. A.	Spalding, James Alfred..............627 Congress St., Portland, Me.
Spaulding, W.	Spaulding, Rev. Wayland...............411 W. 115th St., New York.
Spear, W: E.	Spear, William E..........................Kimball Bldg., Boston.
Spectator.	Spectator Co..............................135 William St., New York.
Spenceley.	Spenceley, Frederick.....................56 W. 39th St., New York.
Spencer, E.	Spencer, Enos.........Spencerian Commercial School, Louisville, Ky.
Spencer, K. S.	Spencer, Mrs. Katherine Smith.........1530 Main St., Racine, Wis.
Sperle, C: H.	Sperle, Charles H..............................Somerville, N. J.
Spice Mill.	Spice Mill Publishing Co...................97 Water St., New York.
Spiegel, M., S., Co.	Spiegel, May, Stern Co......................................Chicago.
Spon.	Spon & Chamberlain....................123 Liberty St., New York.
Spooner, J: C.	Spooner, John Coit.......................32 Liberty St., New York.
Sprague.	Sprague Publishing Co.................................Detroit, Mich.
Sprague, C: E.	Sprague, Charles Ezra......................701 Sixth Ave., New York.
Spring, L. W.	Spring, Leverett W...........Williams College, Williamstown, Mass.
Springborn, W: J:	Springborn, William John...............................Cleveland, O.
Springfield Lib. Assoc.	Springfield City Library Association................Springfield, Mass.
Springfield Lib. Pub.	Springfield Library Publishing Co.....................Springfield, Ill.
Springfield Mu. Nat. Hist.	Springfield Museum of Natural History...........Springfield, Mass.
Sproul.	Sproul, George D................Room 408, 150 5th Ave., New York.
Squire, E.	Squire, Edwin..Claremont, Cal.
Squire-C.	Squire-Cooley Co..Toledo, O.
Srygley, F. B.	Srygley, F. B...Nashville, Tenn.
St. Andrew's Soc.	St. Andrew's Society.....................................Philadelphia.
St. Boniface's.	St. Boniface's Industrial School.......................Banning, Cal.
St. Hubert's Guild.	St. Hubert's Guild of Art Craftsmen.......................Akron, O.
St. John, T: M.	St. John, Thomas M....................848 Ninth Ave., New York.
St. Johnsbury Repub.	St. Johnsbury Republican Co.......................St. Johnsbury, Vt.
St. Joseph's Pr.	St. Joseph's Printing Office.......................Collegeville, Ind.
St. L. Centennial.	St. Louis Centennial Association.............................St. Louis.
St. L. Com. Tuberculosis.	St. Louis Municipal Commission on Tuberculosis............St. Louis.

St. L. Lumberman.	St. Louis Lumberman........St. Louis.
St. L. Republic.	St. Louis Republic........St. Louis.
St. L. Univ.	St. Louis University........St. Louis.
St. Louis & San Francisco R. R.	St. Louis & San Francisco Railroad Co........71 Broadway, N. Y.
St. Mary's Coll.	St. Mary's College........St. Marys, Kan.
St. Mary's Indust.	St. Mary's Industrial School........Odanah, Wis.
St. Paul Pub. Lib.	St. Paul Public Library........St. Paul, Minn.
St. Thomas Church.	St. Thomas Church........New York.
Stackpole, E. S.	Stackpole, Everett Schermerhorn........Bradford, Mass.
Staff Coll.	Staff College Press........Fort Leavensworth, Kan.
Stafford.	Stafford Publishing Co........110 E. Main St., Marion, Ill.
Stafford Engraving.	Stafford Engraving Co........Indianapolis, Ind.
Standard Cotton.	Standard Cotton Grading School........Dallas, Tex.
Standard Diary.	Standard Diary Co........26 Blackstone St., Cambridge, Mass.
Standard Pr. Co.	Standard Printing Co........Providence, R. I.
Standard Pub.	Standard Publishing Co........16 E. 9th St., Cincinnati.
Standard Pub. Co.	Standard Publishing Co........Boston.
Standard Sanitary	Standard Sanitary Manufacturing Co..Bessemer Bldg., Pittsburgh, Pa.
Stanford Univ.	Stanford, Leland, Junior University Press...Stanford University, Cal.
Stanford Univ. Bkstore.	Stanford University Bookstore........Stanford University, Cal.
Stanley & W.	Stanley & Wagner........Room 703, 45 W. 34th St., New York.
Stanley Inst.	Stanley Institute........Philadelphia.
Stanley-T.	Stanley-Taylor Co........San Francisco.
Stanton, H. L.	Stanton, H. L., Co........Los Angeles, Cal.
Stanyan, E: M.	Stanyan, Edward M........Milford, N. H.
Stapleton, A.	Stapleton, Rev. Ammon........York, Pa.
Star-Gazette.	Star-Gazette Co........Elmira, New York.
Starbuck, R. M.	Starbuck, Robert Macy, & Sons........284 Asylum St., Hartford, Ct.
Starkey, L. C.	Starkey, L. Cheston........Philadelphia.
Starrett, D. W.	Starrett, D. W........4325 View St., Oakland, Cal.
State Cap.	State Capital Printing Co........Guthrie, Okla.
State Co.	State Co........Columbia, S. C.
State Consol.	State Consolidated Publishing Co........Tucson, Ariz.
State Gazette.	State Gazette........Point Pleasant, W. Va.
State Hist., Ia.	State Historical Society of Iowa........Iowa City, Ia.
State Hist., Ill.	State Historical Society of Illinois........Springfield, Ill.
State Hist., Kan.	State Historical Society of Kansas........Topeka, Kan.
State Hist., N. D.	State Historical Society of North Dakota........Bismarck, N. D.
State Hist., Wis.	State Historical Society of Wisconsin........Madison, Wis.
State Horticultural.	State Horticultural Commission........Sacramento, Cal
State Hospital Insane.	State Hospital for the Insane........Norristown, Pa.
State Journ. Co.	State Journal Co........Lincoln, Neb.
State Pr. (Kan.)	State Printing Office........Topeka, Kan.
State Register.	State Register Co........Springfield, Ill.
State St. Trust Co.	State Street Trust Co........Boston.
State Temperance.	State Temperance Union........Topeka, Kan.
States Pub.	States Publishing Co........17 Van Buren St., Chicago.
Staton Bros.	Staton Bros........5402 Germantown Ave., Philadelphia.
Stearns, I: N.	Stearns, Isaac N........115 E. Illinois St., Kirksville, Mo.
Stearns, L. M.	Stearns, Lyman Marshall........1333 Elm St., Manchester, N. H.
Stebbins.	Stebbins & Co........1427 Union St., Brooklyn, N. Y.
Stebbins, C. A.	Stebbins, C. A........2004 Delaware St., Berkeley, Cal.
Stechert.	Stechert, G. E., & Co........151-155 W. 25th St., New York.
Steel, E. T.	Steel, Estelle Thomas........Ashland, Pa.
Steiger.	Steiger, E., & Co........49 Murray St., New York.
Stein, B.	Stein Block Co........Rochester, N. Y.
Stein Pub.	Stein Publishing Co........Philadelphia.
Steiner & Co.	Steiner & Co........Box 269, Toledo, O.
Steinbiss, H. W.	Steinbiss, H. W........Room 307, Panama Bldg., St. Louis.
Steinman & F.	Steinman & Foltz........Lancaster, Pa.
Stepanek, W. H.	Stepanek, W. H........Cedar Rapids, Ia.
Stephens.	Stephens, E. W........Columbia, Mo.
Stephens, J: R.	Stephens, John Rittenhouse..Keith and Perry Bldgs., Kansas City, Mo.
Stephens Coll.	Stephens College Press........Columbia, Mo.
Steppes, J: P.	Steppes, John P........662 Quincy St., Brooklyn, N. Y.
Sterling.	Sterling Publishers, The........3634 Michigan Ave., Chicago.
Stern.	Stern, Edward, & Co. (books now supplied by Barse & Hopkins).
Stern, D.	Stern, Daniel........355 Dearborn St., Chicago.

Stetson, A. E.	Stetson, Augusta Emma....................7 W. 96th St., New York.
Stettiner.	Stettiner Bros........................52-58 Duane St., New York.
Stevens, A. L.	Stevens, Agnes L.................343½ Yamhill St., Portland, Ore.
Stevens, F.	Stevens, Frank..............55 Montgomery St., Jersey City, N. J.
Stevens, H. J.	Stevens, Horace Jared............................Houghton, Mich.
Stevens, J.	Stevens, J., Arms and Tool Co................Chicopee Falls, Mass.
Stevens, J: F.	Stevens, John Frank....N. Y. & N. H. H. R.R. Co., New Haven, Ct.
Stevens, M. B.	Stevens, Milo B., & Co..........................Washington, D. C.
Stevens, N. E.	Stevens, N. E., & Son..................................Paxton, Ill.
Stevens, W. L.	Stevens, Walter Le Conte.........................Lexington, Va.
Stewart, A. V.	Stewart, A. V...Boston.
Stewart, J.	Stewart, Judd..............................165 Broadway, New York.
Stewart, J. S.	Stewart, Joseph Spencer.................................Athens, Ga.
Stewart, R. A.	Stewart, Robert Armistead.......320 E. Franklin St., Richmond, Va.
Stewart, W. K.	Stewart, W. K., Co................................Indianapolis, Ind.
Stickley, G.	Stickley, Gustav.........................29 W. 34th St., New York.
Still, A. T.	Still, Andrew Taylor...............................Kirksville, Mo.
Stillman.	Stillman Publishing Co...........313 Forty-first St., Brooklyn, N. Y.
Stilwell & R.	Stilwell & Ross.......................................Dryden, N. Y.
Stinson, J. C.	Stinson, James Cyrus...............................Greenville, Tex.
Stoddard, E. J.	Stoddard, Eliot Joseph...........28 Warren Ave., W., Detroit, Mich.
Stokes.	Stokes, Frederick A., Co...............443 Fourth Ave., New York.
Stollnitz, H: S.	Stollnitz, Henry Sande....................................Tampa, Fla.
Stone, C: J:	Stone, Charles J.........................Security Bldg., Chicago.
Stone, G: H.	Stone, George H...........................Colorado Springs, Colo.
Stone, J. J.	Stone, J. J., & Co...................................Greensboro, N. C.
Stone, W: J.	Stone, William Jasper...............................Tecumseh, Okla.
Stone & B.	Stone & Barringer..................22 S. Tryon St., Charlotte, N. C.
Stone & W.	Stone & Webster...............................147 Milk St., Boston.
Stone Pr.	Stone Printing & Manufacturing Co...................Roanoke, Va.
Stoneman.	Stoneman Press Co.......................................Columbus, O.
Storey, M.	Storey, Morfield.........Care of Storey, Thorndike, Palmer & Thayer. 735 Exchange Bldg., Boston.
Storey, T: A.	Storey, Thomas Andrew, M.D., College of the City of New York, New York.
Storrs, E. P.	Storrs, E. P. (Dartmouth College Bookstore).........Hanover, N. H.
Stott, W: T.	Stott, William Taylor..............................Knightstown, Ind.
Stoutenburgh, H: A.	Stoutenburgh, Henry A...................23 Broad St., New York.
Stow, M. C.	Stow, Marion Cook..............710 Washington St., Portland, Ore.
Stradling.	Stradling, J. M., & Co................................Beverley, N. J.
Strange.	Strange Co...San Francisco.
Street, C: S.	Street, Charles Stuart...................240 E. 51st St., New York.
Strawbridge & C.	Strawbridge & Clothier........Market and Eighth Sts., Philadelphia.
Strohecker, C.	Strohecker, Clifford...................................Zelienople, Pa.
Stromberg, A. & Co.	Stromberg, Allen & Co...................................Chicago.
Stromberg-C.	Stromberg-Carlson Telephone Mfg. Co.............Rochester, N. Y.
Strout, C: H:	Strout, Charles Henry...............St. Luke's School, Wayne, Pa.
Student Vol.	Student Volunteer Movement for Foreign Missions, 125 E. 27th St., New York.
Students Bk.	Students Book Store...................................Baltimore, Md.
Stumpf, A.	Stumpf, Anthony, Publishing Co............22 Pine St., New York.
Sturgis & W.	Sturgis & Walton Co..................31-33 E. 27th St., New York.
Sturmer, J. W:	Sturmer, Prof. Julius William........107 Fowler Ave., Lafayette, Ind.
Sturtevant.	Sturtevant, John L., & Co..................................Albany, N. Y.
Stutzman, L. W.	Stutzman, Mrs. Luella Walden......................McPherson, Kan.
Stuyvesant Press.	Stuyvesant Press. (Books supplied by William Rickey & Co.)
Sub-Target.	Sub-Target Gun Co...Boston.
Success Co.	Success Co...............................29 E. 22d St., New York.
Sudwarth Co.	Sudwarth Printing Co.....510 Twelfth St., N. W., Washington, D. C.
Suggestion.	Suggestion Publishing House.........1511 Marquette Bldg., Chicago.
Sugranes, E.	Sugranes, Eugene.....................................San Gabriel, Cal.
Sullivan, J. W:	Sullivan, James William.........1937 Stillwell Ave., Brooklyn, N. Y.
Summerhayes, M.	Summerhayes, Mrs. Martha........................Nantucket, Mass.
Summy, C. F., Co.	Summy, Clayton F., Co......................220 Wabash Ave., Chicago.
Sun.	Sun Publishing Co.......................................Paducah, Ky.
Sun Dial.	Sun Dial Classics Co....................201 E. 12th St., New York.
Sun Pr.	Sun Printing Office....................................Baltimore, Md.
Sun Press.	Sun Press...Spring Valley, Wis.
Surdus.	Surdus Publishing Co.....................156 Fifth Ave., New York.
Surgery.	Surgery Publishing Co......................92 William St., New York.
Sutcliffe, A. C.	Sutcliffe, Mrs. Alice C.................177 Lexington Ave., New York.

Sutherland, D. F. Sutherland, Daniel Francis........Quitman, Tex.
Sutliff, S: M. Sutliff, Samuel Milton........1515 Masonic Temple, Chicago.
Sutton. Sutton, A. D., & Co........Fort Smith, Ark.
Svovoda. Svovoda's Print........Youngstown, O.
Swadener, E. E. Swadener, E. E........131 Wabash Ave., Chicago.
Swan, L. P. Swan, Mrs. Laura Prentice........1011 Beacon St., Brookline, Mass.
Swank, J. M. Swank, James Moore........261 S. 4th St., Philadelphia.
Swanson, C. A. Swanson, Governor Claude A........Richmond, Va.
Sweet. Sweet, J. S., Publishing Co........Santa Rosa, Cal.
Sweet, L. Sweet, Lacroix, Co........429 Sixth Ave., New York.
Sweet, M. P. Sweet, M. P........Unadilla, N. Y.
Swenk, M. H. Swenk, Myron Harmon........318 N. 27th St., Lincoln, Neb.
Sweny, H. R. Sweny, Harry Roy........Albany, N. Y.
Swetland. Swetland Publishing Co........239 W. 39th St., New York.
Swift, E. G. Swift, E. G........P. O. Box 478, Detroit, Mich.
Swing, P: F. Swing, Peter F........Cincinnati.
Swinnerton, H: U. Swinnerton, Henry U........Cherry Valley, New York.
Sylvan Press. Sylvan Press........934 Hornbeck Ct., Kalamazoo, Mich.
Sylvester, H. M. Sylvester, Herbert Milton........Harrison, Me.
Syms-York. Syms-York Co........Boise, Idaho.
Syndicate Pub. Syndicate Publishing Co........12-14 W. 32d St., New York.
Syracuse Chamber of Commerce. Syracuse Chamber of Commerce........Syracuse, N. Y.
System. System Co........151-153 Wabash Ave., Chicago.
Szymanowski, S. K. Szymanowski, Stephen Korwin...849 W. 34th St., Los Angeles, Cal.
Taber, C: A. M. Taber, Charles Austin Mendell........Wakefield, Mass.
Taber, S. R. Taber, S. R........532 Monadnock Block, Chicago.
Taft, W. H. Taft, William Howard........Washington, D. C.
Tagliapietra, M. T. Tagliapietra, Mrs. Margaret Townsend....343 W. 34th St., New York.
Taintor, C: W. Taintor, Charles W........8 Congress St., Boston.
Takahira, K. Takahira, Baron Kogoro,
Japanese Legation, 1310 N St., Washington, D. C.
Talbert, D. H. Talbert, Daniel H....616 Traction Terminal Bldg., Indianapolis, Ind.
Talley, J. M. Talley, Jos. M........512 Westminster St., Providence, R. I.
Tallman, M. C. Tallman, Myrtle C........Genoa, Neb.
Tandy, F. D. Tandy, Francis D., Co. *See* Tandy-Thomas Co.
Tandy-T. Tandy-Thomas Co. (now Tandy Publishing Co.), 31 E. 27th St.,
New York.
Tanner, H: S: Tanner, Henry Samuel, M.D........Long Beach, Cal.
Tax Reform. Tax Reform Association........56 Pine St., New York.
Taylor, B. F. Taylor, B. F........Columbia, S. C.
Taylor, C. W. Taylor, Carr White........Hutchinson, Kan.
Taylor, H. Taylor, Hannis........1415 H St., N. W., Washington, D. C.
Taylor, H. L. Taylor, Herbert L........1936 University Ave., St. Paul, Minn.
Taylor, H., & Co. Taylor, H., & Co........Chicago.
Taylor, J: E. Taylor, John Edwin........Skawhegan, Me.
Taylor, W: J. Taylor, William J........59 Broad St., New York.
Taylor & C. Taylor & Carpenter........Ithaca, N. Y.
Taylor Instrument. Taylor Instrument Companies........Rochester, N. Y.
Taylor-H. Taylor-Holden Co........Springfield, Mass.
Taylor-T. Taylor-Trotwood Publishing Co........Nashville, Tenn.
Teachers' Coll. Teachers' College (L. F. Snow Publication Bureau),
525 W. 120th St., New York.
Teachers Co-op. Teachers Co-operative Co......1112 Stahlman Bldg., Nashville, Tenn.
Teachers' Supply. Teachers' Supply Co........Grayson, Ky.
Teagar, M. M. Teagar, Michael Moores........Flemingsburg, Ky.
Technical High Sch. Technical High School Printshop........Cleveland, O.
Technical Lit. Technical Literature Co........220 Broadway, New York.
Technical Press. Technical Press........Brattleboro, Vt.
Technical Pub. Technical Publishing Co........Caxton Bldg., Cleveland, O.
Technical Pub. Co. Technical Publishing Co........San Francisco.
Technical Supply. Technical Supply Co........Scranton, Pa.
Temple Seminary. Temple Seminary Press........537 N. Fulton Ave., Baltimore, Md.
Templeton, F. Templeton, Frank........847 Spitzer Bldg., Toledo, O.
Tenafly Presb. Ch. Tenafly Presbyterian Church........Tenafly, N. J.
Tengg. Tengg, Nicholas........220 W. Commerce St., San Antonio, Tex.
Tennant. Tennant & Ward........122 E. 25th St., New York.
Tenney, E: P. Tenney, Edward P........Box R, Nahant, Mass.
Tenny Press. Tenny Press........1193 Broadway, New York.
Terrell, E. H. Terrell, Edwin Holland........San Antonio, Tex.
Terry. Terry, Stewart Bruce, & Co........Kansas City, Kan.

Terry, E: S.	Terry, Edward S. .... 309 Broadway, New York.
Texarkanian.	Texarkanian, The .... Texarkana, Ark.
Texas.	Texas, State of .... Austin, Tex.
Theo. Pub. Co.	Theosophical Publishing Co. .... 253 W. 72d St., New York.
Theosophical Bk.	Theosophical Book Co. .... Ridgewood, N. J.
Theosophical Soc.	Theosophical Society, American Section .... 103 State St., Chicago.
Therapeutic.	Therapeutic Publishing Co., 703 Washington St., Dorchester Center, Boston.
Thomas, F. H.	Thomas, F. H., Law Book Co. .... 14 S. Broadway, St. Louis.
Thomas, G: C.	Thomas, George Clifford .... Philadelphia.
Thomas, J. D.	Thomas, Joseph D. .... Pawhuska, Okla.
Thomas, J. M.	Thomas, J. Morriston .... 169 Tenth St., Newark, O.
Thomas, T. G:	Thomas, Theodore George .... Houston, Tex.
Thomas, W: H.	Thomas, William Holcombe, ... Montgomery, Ala.
Thomas-W.	Thomas-Wilson Publishing Co. .... Houston, Tex.
Thompson.	Thompson Reporting Co. .... 10 Tremont St., Boston.
Thompson, A.	Thompson, Alonzo .... 307 Commonwealth Bldg., Denver, Colo.
Thompson B.	Thompson Brown Co. (now Johnson, Blagden & McTurnan), 1 Madison Ave., New York.
Thompson, C. C.	Thompson, Charles C., Co. .... 1226 S. Wabash Ave., Chicago.
Thompson, C. W.	Thompson, C. W., & Co. .... A. and B. Park St., Boston.
Thompson, E. F.	Thompson, E. F. .... Worcester, Mass.
Thompson, E:	Thompson, Edward, & Co. .... Northport, L. I.
Thompson, G. A.	Thompson, G. A. .... White Plains, N. Y.
Thompson, J. W.	Thompson, J. Walter, Co. .... 44 E. 23d St., New York.
Thompson, J:	Thompson, John .... Glasgow Junction, Ky.
Thompson, N. D.	Thompson, N. D., Publishing Co. .... 2d and Olive Sts., St. Louis.
Thompson, P. J.	Thompson, Priscilla Jane .... Rossmoyne, O.
Thompson, S.	Thompson, Slason, Bu. of Railway News and Statistics .... Chicago.
Thompson, W: A.	Thompson, William Alexander .... Pontiac, Mich.
Thompson, W: B.	Thompson, William B. .... 808 Perido St., New Orleans, La.
Thompson & Co.	Thompson & Co. .... Chicago.
Thompson & T.	Thompson & Thomas. *See* Charles C. Thompson Co.
Thompson Pub.	Thompson Publishing Co. .... Thompson Bldg., St. Louis.
Thompson Pub. Co.	Thompson Publishing Co. .... Philadelphia.
Thompson Pub. Co. (Chic.)	Thompson Publishing Co., Chicago (N. Y. Agts., J. F. Taylor & Co., 18 E. 17th St.).
Thorburn, J. M.	Thorburn, J. M., & Co. .... 33 Barclay St., New York.
Thornton, A: W.	Thornton, Augustus Willoughby .... Ferndale, Wash.
Thorpe, D.	Thorpe, Durrant .... 332 Washington St., Boston.
Thrall, W. R.	Thrall, W. R. .... Cincinnati.
Throop Poly. Inst.	Throop Polytechnic Institute .... Pasadena, Cal.
Thrum.	Thrum, Thomas G. .... Honolulu, H. I.
Thurber, O. E.	Thurber, Orray E. .... 90 West St., New York.
Tice & L.	Tice & Lynch .... 16 Beaver St., New York.
Tichenor, H: D.	Tichenor, Henry Dodge .... Washington, D. C.
Ticker Pub.	Ticker Publishing Co. .... 2 Rector St., New York.
Tiffany Studios.	Tiffany Studios .... Madison Ave. and 45th St., New York.
Tillinghast, J: A.	Tillinghast, John A. .... 1039 Banigan Bldg., Providence, R. I.
Tilyou, G: C.	Tilyou, George C. .... Steeplechase Park, Coney Island, Brooklyn, N. Y.
Timayenis, T. T:	Timayenis, Telemachus Thomas .... 77 Bedford St., Boston.
Timby.	Timby, H. H. .... Ashtabula, O.
Times-News.	Times-News Co. .... Connersville, Ind.
Times Pub. Co.	Times Publishing Co. .... New Brunswick, N. J.
Times Pub. Co., (Pa.)	Times Publishing Co. .... Bethlehem, Pa.
Times Pub. Co., (Wis.)	Times Publishing Co. .... De Forest, Wis
Tinkham, E. A.	Tinkham, E. A. .... Duluth, Minn.
Tinus-H.	Tinus-Harmon Publishing Co. .... Chicago.
Titus Pub. Co.	Titus Publishing Co. .... Cor. 3d and Pine Sts., Jamestown, N. Y.
Tobacco Leaf.	Tobacco Leaf Publishing Co. .... 82 Beaver St., New York.
Tocci, F.	Tocci, Francesco .... 520 Broadway, New York.
Toch.	Toch Brothers .... 320 Fifth Ave., New York.
Todd, D:	Todd, Mrs. David .... Amherst, Mass.
Todd, M. I.	Todd, Mary Ives .... 2656 Eighth Ave., New York.
Tombo, R.	Tombo, Rudolf, Jr., Germanistic Society of America, Columbia University, New York.
Tome Sch.	Tome School for Boys .... Port Deposit, Md.
Toof, M. D.	Toof, M. D. .... Red Oak, Ia.
Topsfield Hist. Soc.	Topsfield Historical Society .... Topsfield, Mass.
Torch Press.	Torch Press .... 1424-1426 F St., Cedar Rapids, Ia.

Torrey.	Torrey Botanical Club...N. Y. Botanical Garden, Bronx Park, N. Y.
Torrey, D: C.	Torrey, David Clarence......Bedford, Mass.
Totten, M. B.	Totten, Mrs. Martha Barr......Crawfordsville, Ind.
Tourgée, E. K.	Tourgée, Emma K......Mayville, N. Y.
Tousey, S.	Tousey, Sinclair......59 W. 46th St., New York.
Tower.	Tower (The)......Hagerstown, Md.
Tower, F. W.	Tower, Frank Warren......8 Municipal Bldg., Springfield, Mass.
Tower Press.	Tower Press......First National Bank Bldg., Cincinnati.
Towle Mfg.	Towle Manufacturing Co......Newburyport, Mass.
Towne, E: C.	Towne, Rev. Edward Cornelius..124 West Main St., Westboro, Mass.
Towne, E. J.	Towne, Mrs. Elizabeth J......Holyoke, Mass.
Towne, S. D.	Towne, Rev. Salem D......203 Sudbury Bldg., Boston.
Towne, W: E.	Towne, William E......Holyoke, Mass.
Townsend, F. H.	Townsend, F. H......Providence, R. I.
Townsend, L. T.	Townsend, Luther Tracy......Brookline, Mass.
Tracy, G. & Co.	Tracy, Gibbs & Co......Madison, Wis.
Tracy, S.	Tracy, Suzanne......1922 Sacramento St., San Francisco.
Trade Journ.	Trade Journal Advertiser......315 Dearborn St., Chicago.
Trade Periodical.	Trade Periodical Co......355 Dearborn St., Chicago.
Trades Unionists.	Trades Unionists' Publishing Co......Washington, D. C.
Tradesman.	Tradesman Co......Grand Rapids, Mich.
Train Dispatchers'.	Train Dispatchers' Bulletin......Toledo, O.
Transcript.	Transcript Publishing Co......Holyoke, Mass.
Transylvania.	Transylvania Printing Co......Lexington, Ky.
Trauger.	Trauger, J. L., Printing Co......Columbus, O.
Travis, J: C.	Travis, John Coleridge......171 W. 76th St., New York.
Treadwell, A:	Treadwell, Augustus......204 Montagu St., Brooklyn, N. Y.
Treat.	Treat, E. B., & Co......241 W. 23d St., New York.
Trenton Lib.	Trenton Free Public Library......Trenton, N. J.
Trenton Iron Co.	Trenton Iron Co......Trenton, N. J.
Trevor, J. E.	Trevor, Joseph Ellis..Care of Day & Heaton, 80 Broadway, New York.
Trezise, F. J.	Trezise, F. J......Chicago.
Tribune Assoc.	Tribune Association......Tribune Bldg., New York.
Tribune Pr. Co., (Fla.)	Tribune Printing Co......Tampa, Fla.
Tribune Pr. Co., (N. Dak.)	Tribune Printing Co......Bismarck, N. D.
Tribune Pr. Co. (W. Va.)	Tribune Printing Co......Charleston, W. Va.
Tricoche, G: N.	Tricoche, George Nestler......U. S. Hotel, Morristown, N. J.
Tridon, A.	Tridon, André......301 W. 106th St., New York.
Trigger, T. C.	Trigger, Theodore Clark..580 Talbot St., St. Thomas, Ontario, Can.
Trinity Coll.	Trinity College, Dept. of Education......Dunham, N. C.
Triune Order.	Triune Order......138 Spring St., New York.
Trolley Press.	Trolley Press......Hartford, Ct.
Trouvillon, H. W.	Trouvillon, H. W......Herrin, Ill.
Trow Press.	Trow Press......201-213 E. 12th St., New York.
Trowbridge, F. B.	Trowbridge, Francis Bacon......New Haven, Ct.
Trueblood, B: F.	Trueblood, Benjamin Franklin......31 Beacon St., Boston.
Truedson, N. P.	Truedson, Nils Peter......Grandy, Minn.
Truro.	Truro Publishing Co......Care of Henry Truro Brady, Chicago.
Trussed Concrete.	Trussed Concrete Steel Co......Detroit, Mich.
Trust, E:	Trust, Edward......1422 Master St., Philadelphia.
Trustee.	Trustee Printing Co......Seattle, Wash.
Truth Seeker.	Truth Seeker Publishing Co......62 Vesey St., New York.
Tubby, G. O.	Tubby, Gertrude O......7 W. 42d St., New York.
Tubercle Press.	Tubercle Press Bureau......Chicago.
Tuck.	Tuck, Raphael, & Sons Co......122-124 Fifth Ave., New York.
Tucker, B: R.	Tucker, Benjamin R......502 Sixth Ave., New York.
Tucker, G. B.	Tucker, Guy B......Little, Rock, Ark.
Tucker, G. M.	Tucker, Gilbert Milligan......304 State St., Albany, N. Y.
Tucker, H: H., Jr.	Tucker, Henry Harrison, Jr. (Post Office refuses to deliver mail). Kansas City, Kan.
Tucker, J: A.	Tucker, John Atherton......954 Canton Ave., Mattapan, Mass.
Tucker, W. G.	Tucker, Willis G., M.D.....Albany Medical College, Albany, N. Y.
Tucker & V.	Tucker & Vinton......Park Ave. and 41st St., New York.
Tucker-V.	Tucker-Vernon Co......Larned, Kan.
Tudor Press.	Tudor Press......120 E. 14th St., New York.
Tufts, J. H.	Tufts, James Hayden......University of Chicago, Chicago.
Tufts' Coll.	Tufts' College Press......Tufts' College, Mass.
Turberg.	Turberg, Philip......116 Walker St., New York.
Turner, C. A. P.	Turner, Claude Allen Porter....816 Phœnix Bldg., Minneapolis, Minn.

Tutt, R. G.	Tutt, R. G. ....Box 1076, St. Louis.
Tuttle, C: R:	Tuttle, Charles Richard............358 Arcade Annex, Seattle, Wash.
Tuttle, M. & T.	Tuttle, Morehouse & Taylor Co......125 Temple St., New Haven, Ct.
Tuttle & P.	Tuttle & Pike...............Shubert Theatre Bldg., Kansas City, Mo.
Tuttle Co.	Tuttle Co..Rutland, Vt.
Tuttle Pub.	Tuttle Publishing Co...........................Berlin Heights, O.
Tweedy, J:	Tweedy, John..Danbury, Ct.
Twentieth Century.	Twentieth Century Club.........................5 Park Sq., Boston.
Twentieth Century Pub.	Twentieth Century Publishing Co..........2 W. 16th St., New York.
Twining, H. L.	Twining, Harry Le Verne.......1308 Calumet St.. Los Angeles, Cal.
Twitchell, R. E.	Twitchell, Ralph Emerson..................East Las Vegas, N. M.
Tyler, L. G.	Tyler, Lyon Gardner..............................Williamsburg, Va.
Tyler Pub.	Tyler Publishing Co..............................Ann Arbor, Mich.
Tyrell's Hygiene Inst.	Tyrrell's Hygienic Institute...............321 Fifth Ave., New York.
U. P. & S. P. R. R.	Union Pacific and Southern Pacific Railroads, 120 Broadway, New York.
U. S. Brewers' Assoc.	United States Brewers' Association..109-111 E. 15th St., New York.
U. S. Cath.	United States Catholic Historical Society....29 Reade St., New York.
U. S. Cavalry.	United States Cavalry Association..........Fort Leavenworth, Kan.
U. S. Fidelity.	United States Fidelity and Guaranty Co..............Baltimore, Md.
U. S. Infantry.	United States Infantry Association..............Washington, D. C.
U. S. Military Pub.	United States Military Publishing Co..............Washington, D. C.
U. S. Mortgage.	United States Mortgage & Trust Co.........55 Cedar St., New York.
U. S. Mushroom.	U. S. Mushroom & Spawn Co....550 Dayton Ave., St. Paul, Minn.
U. S. Naval Inst.	United States Naval Institute........................Annapolis, Md.
U. S. Playing Card.	United States Playing Card Co...............................Cincinnati.
U. S. Revolver.	United States Revolver Association, Room 1901, Flatiron Bldg., New York.
U. S., Supt. of Docs.	United States, Office of the Superintendent of Documents, Washington, D. C.
Ulbrich.	Ulbrich, Otto, & Co.....................386 Main St., Buffalo, N. Y.
Ullman, B. L:	Ullman, Berthold Louis.............University of Chicago, Chicago.
Umbendenstock-F.-P.	Umbendenstock-Frisky-Porter Co...........................Chicago.
Un. B. Pub.	United Brethren Publishing House..Fourth and Main Sts., Dayton, O.
Un. Editors.	United Editors' Association...............225 Fifth Ave., New York.
Un. Evangelical.	United Evangelical Publishing House.................Harrisburg, Pa.
Un. Pacific R. R.	Union Pacific Railroad Co..................................Omaha, Neb.
Un. Presb. Bd.	United Presbyterian Board of Publication..207 9th St., Pittsburgh, Pa.
Un. Press.	United Press Syndicate...............................San Francisco.
Un. Pub. Assoc.	United Publishers' Association..5 Beekman St., Room 314, New York.
Un. Soc. C. E.	United Society of Christian Endeavor....600 Tremont Temple, Boston.
Underhill, J. E.	Underhill, Mrs. Jennie E...............................New London, Ct.
Underwood.	Underwood & Underwood....5 W. 19th St., cor. 5th Ave., New York.
Underwood Typewriter.	Underwood Typewriter Co................241 Broadway, New York.
Union Bk.	Union Book and Publishing Co.............356 Dearborn St., Chicago.
Union Press.	Union Press...........................1816 Chestnut St., Philadelphia.
Union Pub. Co., (Nashville.)	Union Publishing Co..............832 Meridian St., Nashville, Tenn.
Union Times.	Union Times Print....................................Netcong, N. J.
Union Trust Co.	Union Trust Company...............................Pittsburgh, Pa.
Unitarian Club.	Unitarian Club....................................Washington, D. C.
Unitarian S. S.	Unitarian Sunday School Society...............25 Beacon St., Boston.
United R. R. of S. F.	United Railroads of San Francisco, Wells Fargo Bldg., San Francisco.
Unity.	Unity Publishing Co....................209 Oakwood Blvd., Chicago.
Unity Tr.	Unity Tract Society..................................Kansas City, Mo.
Univ. Alliance.	University Alliance, Inc...................43 W. 27th St., New York.
Univ. Bk. Store.	University Book Store................................Seattle, Wash.
Univ. Co-op.	University Co-operative Co..........................Madison, Wis.
Univ. Extension.	University Extension Association..............................Chicago.
Univ. Extension Dept.	University Extension Dept., University of the South..Sewanee, Tenn.
Univ. of Ariz.	University of Arizona.....................................Tucson, Ariz.
Univ. of Ark.	University of Arkansas..............................Fayetteville, Ark.
Univ. of Cal.	University of California Press.......................Berkeley, Cal.
Univ. of Chic.	University of Chicago Press........58th St. and Ellis Ave., Chicago.

Univ. of Cin.	University of Cincinnati Press........................Cincinnati.
Univ. of Col.	University of Colorado............................Boulder, Colo.
Univ. of Ia.	University of Iowa............................Iowa City, Ia.
Univ. of Ill.	University of Illinois............................Urbana, Ill.
Univ. of Kan.	University of Kansas............................Lawrence, Kan.
Univ. of Mich.	University of Michigan............................Ann Arbor, Mich.
Univ. of Minn.	University of Minnesota............................Minneapolis, Minn.
Univ. of Mo.	University of Missouri............................Columbia, Mo.
Univ. of Mont.	University of Montana............................Missoula, Mont.
Univ. of N. C.	University of North Carolina........................Chapel Hill, N. C.
Univ. of Neb.	University of Nebraska............................Lincoln, Neb.
Univ. of Nev.	University of Nevada............................Reno, Nev.
Univ. of O.	University of Ohio............................Columbus, O.
Univ. of Ore.	University of Oregon............................Eugene, Ore.
Univ. of Penn.	University of Pennsylvania.....34th and Chestnut Sts., Philadelphia.
Univ. of Penn. [Appleton.]	University of Pennsylvania......Care of D. Appleton Co., New York.
Univ. of Tex.	University of Texas............................Austin, Tex.
Univ. of Toronto.	University of Toronto Library........................Toronto, Can.
Univ. of Va.	University of Virginia............................Charlottesville, Va.
Univ. of W. Va.	University of West Virginia........................Morgantown, W. Va.
Univ. of Wash.	University of Washington............................Seattle, Wash.
Univ. of Wis.	University of Wisconsin............................Madison, Wis.
Univ. Press.	University Press............................Cambridge, Mass.
Univ. Press (Notre Dame.)	University Press............................Notre Dame, Ind.
Univ. Press (Sewanee.)	University Press, University of the South...........Sewanee, Tenn.
Univ. Pub.	University Publishing Co.........134 N. Eleventh St., Lincoln, Neb.
Univ. Pub. Co.	University Publishing Co............................Chicago.
Univ. Soc.	University Society, Inc................44-60 E. 23d St., New York.
Universal Business.	Universal Business Institute, Inc...........27 E. 22d St., New York.
Universal-Good.	Universal-Good Publishing Society, Inc..1 Madison Ave., New York.
Universal Portland Cement.	Universal Portland Cement Co............................Chicago.
Universalist.	Universalist Publishing House............359 Boylston St., Boston.
University Med.	University Medical Society.............45 W. 34th St., New York.
	Updike, D. B. *See* Merrymount Press.
Uplift.	Uplift Publishing Co............................Philadelphia.
Uplook Pub.	Uplook Publishing Co............1204 Sharp Ave., Spokane, Wash.
Upson Memorial.	Upson Memorial Committee........118 S. 6th St., Minneapolis, Minn.
Upton, C: E.	Upton, Charles Elmer............................Placerville, Cal.
Urbana Univ.	Urbana University............................Urbana, O.
Urquhart, W. W.	Urquhart, W. W.........................142 Hicks St., Brooklyn, N. Y.
Ursenbach, O. F.	Ursenbach, Octave F...........562 Driggs Ave., Salt Lake City, Utah.
Usher, E: P.	Usher, Edward Preston............................Grafton, Mass.
Usher, S.	Usher, S............................Boston.
Usona.	Usona Book Co............................Chicago.
Utica Lib.	Utica Public Library............................Utica, N. Y.
Uzzell.	Uzzell, E. M., & Co............................Raleigh, N. C.
Vail, M. H.	Vail, Morrison Huggins............................Dixon, Ill.
Vail, W. H.	Vail, W. H.........................141 Second Ave., Newark, N. J.
Vallette, J. C.	Vallette, J. C............................N. Franklin, Ct.
Van-American.	Van-American Press........................522 Kimball Hall, Chicago.
Vance.	Vance, Wilson J.........................164 Market St., Newark, N. J.
Vancouver.	Vancouver Columbian Print.............Vancouver, B. C., Canada.
Vandegrift.	Vandegrift, F. B., & Co...................15-25 Whitehall St., New York.
Van Deusen & E.	Van Deusen & Elms..........833 So. Figueroa St., Los Angeles, Cal.
Vanderhoof-G.	Vanderhoof-Gunn Co................1502 Marquette Bldg., Chicago.
Van Deventer, H. R.	Van Deventer, H. R............................Sumter, S. C.
Van Dyke, J. S.	Van Dyke, Joseph Smith............................Hightstown, N. J.
Van Kirk, J. W:	Van Kirk, James William...........1314 Shely St., Youngstown, O.
Van Loan, I. A.	Van Loan, Ida A.........................75 John St., New York.
Van Meter, H. F.	Van Meter, Harriet F............121 West Broadway, Salem, N. J.
Van Noppen.	Van Noppen, Charles L............................Greensboro, N. C.
Van Nostrand.	Van Nostrand, D., Co.....23 Murray and 27 Warren Sts., New York.
Vansant.	Vansant, William R., & Co..............121 Plymouth Pl., Chicago.
Van Voorhis, J: S.	Van Voorhis, John S.................319 N. 6th St., Reading, Pa.
Varsity Supply.	Varsity Supply Co............................Columbus, O.
Vassar Bros.	Vassar Brothers Institute........................Poughkeepsie, N. Y.
Vaughan Pub.	Vaughan Publishing Co.................315 Dearborn St., Chicago.
Vedanta.	Vedanta Society.......................135 W. 80th St., New York.

Velasco, S. F. de Velasco, S. Fabiar de....................128 Water St., New York.
Vermont Lib. Vermont State Library....................Montpelier, Vt.
Vernon Law Bk. Vernon Law Book Co....................Kansas City, Mo.
Verplanck, W: E. Verplanck, William E............16 Central Park West, New York.
Viavi. Viavi Co., Inc....................San Francisco.
Village Press. Village Press (Frederic W. and Bertha M. Goudy), 225 Fourth Ave., New York.
Vinson. Vinson, M. A....................Caxton Bldg., Cleveland, O.
Vir. Vir Publishing Co....................200 N. 15th St., Philadelphia.
Virginia State Lib. Virginia State Library....................Richmond, Va.
Visscher, W: L. Visscher, William Lightfoot, Care of Atwell Printing & Binding Co., Chicago.
Volkening, R. Volkening, Rudolph....................St. Louis.
Volland. Volland, P. F., & Co....................24 Adams St., Chicago.
Volsfreund Press. Volksfreund Press....................Buffalo, N. Y.
Volta. Volta Bureau....................1525 35th St., Washington, D. C.
Volunteer. Volunteer Press Print....................38 Cooper Sq., New York.
Von Boeckmann-J. Von Boeckmann-Jones Co....................Austin, Tex.
Vorbeck, J. C. Vorbeck, Joseph Chester........102A Main St., Cape Girardeau, Mo.
Vreeland. Vreeland Publishing Co....................113-117 31st St., New York.
Waddell, C: W. Waddell, Charles Wesley....................Rogers, Ark.
Waddell, W: Waddell, William....................2711½ Armand Pl., St. Louis.
Waddy. Waddy, Everett, Co....................1105 Main St., Richmond, Va.
Wadsworth, J. W. Wadsworth, James Wolcott, Jr....................Geneseo, N. Y.
Wagner. Wagner, Joseph F....................9-11 Barclay St., New York.
Wagner, C: P. Wagner, Charles Philip.....1021 E. University Ave., Ann Arbor, Mich.
Wagner, J. B. Wagner, Joseph Bernard....................Yonkers, N. Y.
Wagner, P. M. Wagner, Philip Matthew....................Canal Dover, O.
Wagner, W: H: Wagner, William Henry....................Los Angeles, Cal.
Wagner & H. Wagner & Hanson Co....................170 South Clinton St., Chicago.
Wagoner. Wagoner Printing Co....................Galesburg, Ill.
Wahl-Henius. Wahl-Henius Institute....................327 Fullerton Ave., Chicago.
Wahr. Wahr, George................103-5 N. Main St., Ann Arbor, Mich.
Waite. Waite, C. V., & Co....................479 Jackson Blvd., Chicago.
Wakeham, R. Wakeham, Robert....................Lagrange, O.
Walden. Walden Press....................64 Fulton St., New York.
Walden & M. Walden & Mowry....................P. O. Box 43, Madison, Wis.
Waldin, W. Waldin, Walter....................Miami, Fla.
Walker, A. H: Walker, Albert Henry....................Park Row Bldg., New York.
Walker, C. I. Walker, Gen. Cornelius Ivins....................Charleston, S. C.
Walker, E. C. Walker, Edwin C....................244 W. 143d St., New York.
Walker, E. & C. Walker, Evans, & Cogswell, 3-5 Broad and 117 East Bay Sts., Charleston, S. C.
Walker, H. D. Walker, H. D................454 Montgomery St., San Francisco.
Walker, J. G. Walker, Rev. James Garfield, St. James' Presbyterian Church, Greensboro, N. C.
Walker, S. G. Walker, Rev. S. G....................Burlington, N. C.
Walker, T. M. Walker, T. M...................."The Builder," Pittsburgh, Pa.
Wall, J: P. Wall, John Patrick....................New Brunswick, N. J.
Wall, W. C. Wall, W. C....................Stockton, Cal.
Wall, W: E. Wall, William Edmund....................Somerville, Mass.
Wallace, C: W: Wallace, Charles William..............1539 S. 21st St., Lincoln, Neb.
Waller, E. Waller, Elbert....................Viola, Ill.
Walsh, J: Walsh, Rev. John....................Troy, N. Y.
Walsh, R. Walsh, Ralph, M.D....................1807 H St., Washington, D. C.
Walter. Walter, L. W., Co....................121-127 Plymouth St., Chicago.
Walter, W: W. Walter, William Wilfrid..............326 New York St., Aurora, Ill.
Walters, C. L. Walters, Clarence Lambert....................Bedford, Ind.
Walton, M. A. Walton, Mary Alice....................Baltimore Md.
Walton, S. Walton, Stokes....................Montgomery, Ala.
Wanamaker. Wanamaker, John....................Philadelphia.
Ward, A. S. Ward, Agnes Snow.........Dept.. of Public Charities, New York.
Warden-E. Warden-Ebright....................Oklahoma City, Okla.
Ware. Ware Bros. Co....................1010 Arch St., Philadelphia.
Ware, E. F. Ware, Eugene Fitch....................Kansas City, Kan.
Ware, H. E. Ware, Horace Everett....................110 Summer St., Boston.
Ware & Co. Ware & Co....................Box 158, Denver, Colo.
Warfield, E. D. Warfield, Ethelbert Dudley............Lafayette College, Easton, Pa.
Waring, J. W. Waring, J. W....................27 W. 30th St., New York.
Waring, L. H. Waring, Luther Hess.......1503 30th St., N. W., Washington, D. C.
Waring, R. L. Waring, Robert L..............609 F St., N. W., Washington, D. C.
Warlick, C. W. Warlick, Rev. C. W....................Martinsburg, Pa.

Warne. Warne, Frederick, & Co....................12 E. 33d St., New York.
Warren, E: H: Warren, Edward Henry....................84 State St., Boston.
Warren, W. Warren, Winslow....................Boston.
Warwick-Y. Warwick-York, Inc....................Baltimore, Md.
Washburn. Washburn Publishing Co............1103 N. 18th St., Omaha, Neb.
Washburn, H. E. Washburn, Howard E....................Ann Arbor, Mich.
Wash. Bk. Washington Book and Art Shop, 819 Colorado Bldg., Washington, D. C.
Wash. Civil Service. Washington Civil Service School....................Washington, D. C.
Wash. Co. Hist. Soc. Washington County Historical Society............Washington, Pa.
Wash. Pub. Lib. Washington Public Library....................Washington, D. C.
Wash. R. R. Com. Washington Railroad Commission....................Olympia, Wash.
Wash. State Lib. Washington State Library....................Olympia, Wash.
Wash. Supt. Sch. Washington Superintendent of Schools............Olympia, Wash.
Washington, L. Washington Lee, 604 Colorado Bldg., Fourteenth and G Sts., Washington, D. C.
Washington, W: D. Washington, William D'Hertburn........1 Madison Ave., New York.
Waterloo. Waterloo Systems Co....................Waterloo, Ia.
Waters, J. K., Co. Waters, J. K., Co....................311 Atlantic Ave., Boston.
Watkins, J. L. Watkins, J. L., & Sons....................New York.
Watkins, L. B. Watkins, Lucian B....................Fort D. A. Russell, Wyo.
Watkins, R. L. Watkins, Robert Lincoln............20 W. 34th St., New York.
Watkins, S. G. Watkins, Solomon Glen....................Topeka, Kan.
Watson, A. W. R. Watson, Mrs. Annah Walker Robinson, 132 Montgomery St., Memphis, Tenn.
Watson, C. B. Watson, Chandler Bruer....................Ashland, Ore.
Watson, D. Watson, Donald....................Watervliet, N. Y.
Watson, T: E: Watson, Thomas Edward....................Thomson, Ga.
Watson, W. J. Watson, Wilbur Jay............1328 Citizens' Bldg., Cleveland, O.
Watt, W. J. Watt, W. J., & Co....................43 W. 27th St., New York.
Watters, H: E. Watters, Henry E....................Martin, Tenn.
Watts, R. J. Watts, R. J....................Amherst, Mass.
Watts, T: T. Watts, Thomas T....................Highlands, N. J.
Wayland, J: W. Wayland, John Walter....................Charlottsville, Va.
Wayland-Smith. Wayland-Smith, Francis....................Kenwood, N. Y.
Weaver, A. Weaver, Anderson....................Rutherford College, N. C.
Webb. Webb Publishing Co............47-51 E. 47th St., St. Paul, Minn.
Webb, E. G: Webb, Eugene George............318 Main St., Springfield, Mass.
Webb, J. M. Webb, James Morris....................Seattle, Wash.
Webb, M. P. Webb, Mabelle Philips....................Warrensburg, Mo.
Webber, H. E. Webber, Harry Endicott............3 Ocean Ave., Salem, Mass.
Webber, J. P. Webber, James Plaisted....................Exeter, N. H.
Weber, F. C: Weber, Fred Charles..........2217 Budlong Ave., Los Angeles, Cal.
Webster, H: S. Webster, Henry Sewall....................Gardiner, Me.
Webster, W: F. Webster, William Franklin....................Minneapolis, Minn.
Wedel, C. H. Wedel, Cornelius H....................Newton, Kan.
Weed-Parsons. Weed-Parsons Printing Co....................Albany, N. Y.
Weekly Bulletin. Weekly Bulletin Publishing Co....................Boston.
Weeks, F. E. Weeks, Frank Edgar....................Clarksfield, O.
Wegelin, O. Wegelin, Oscar....................29 W. 42d St., New York.
Wegman. Wegman Press....................Rochester, N. Y.
Weidel. Weidel & Webster....................3838 Olive St., St. Louis.
Weimar. Weimar Press............3015 S. Main St., Los Angeles, Cal.
Weiss. Weiss, Louis, & Co............116 Fulton St., New York.
Weitzel, L. A. Weitzel, Louise A....................Lilitz, Pa.
Welch, C: H. Welch, Charles H....................Mount Union, Pa.
Welles. Welles Brothers & Co..........421 Kasota Bldg., Minneapolis, Minn.
Wells, E. M. Wells, Ebenezer Miller....................Dallas, Tex.
Wells, F: H. Wells, Frederick Howard..........228 Partridge St., Albany, N. Y.
Welsh. Welsh, Rees, & Co....................901 Sansom St., Philadelphia.
Welsh, L. Welsh, Lilian, M.D....................Baltimore, Md.
Weltmer. Weltmer Institute of Suggestive Therapeutics, 206 S. Ash St., Nevada, Mo.
Weltz Press. Weltz Press....................9 Clinton St., New York.
Wendel, J: A. Wendel, Dr. John Adolph....672 Twenty-sixth St., Milwaukee, Wis.
Wenzlick, W: Wenzlick, William....................1206 Lawrence Ave., Chicago.
Werner. Werner, Edgar S., & Co....................43 E. 19th St., New York.
Werner Co. Werner Co....................Akron, O.
Wertenbaker. Wertenbaker, Thomas J....................Charlottesville, Va.
Wescott, M. E. Westcott, Morgan Ebenezer....................Mora, Minn.
Wesleyan Univ. Wesleyan University....................Middletown, Ct.

Wessels.	Wessels, A. (Publications sold by Wessels & Bissell.)
Wessels, E. J.	Wessels, Edwin J....................2 Rector St., New York.
Wessels & B.	Wessels & Bissell....................225 Fifth Ave., New York.
West, A. C.	West, Andrew Cassius....................Boston.
West, J. H.	West, James H., Co....................93 Milton Ave., Boston.
West Point.	West Point Military Academy....................West Point, N. Y.
West Pub.	West Publishing Co..............52-58 W. 3d St., St. Paul, Minn.
Westchester Press.	Westchester Press....................Rye, N. Y.
Westermann.	Westerman, L. A., Co....................41 Union Sq., New York.
Western Corr. Sch.	Western Correspondence School of Mining Engineering, Des Moines, Ia.
Western Hist.	Western Historical Publishing Co. 311 Jamieson Bldg., Spokane, Wash.
	Western Methodist Book Concern. *See* Jennings & Graham.
Western Press.	Western Press....................1323 Commerce St., Dallas, Tex.
Westinghouse.	Westinghouse Air Brake Co....................Pittsburgh, Pa.
Westinghouse, G:	Westinghouse, George....................Pittsburgh, Pa.
Westminster.	Westminster Press. *See also* Presb. Bd. of Publication. 1319 Walnut St., Philadelphia.
Westminster (Chic.)	Westminster Press....................Chicago.
Weston, S. B.	Weston, S. B....................1415 Locust St., Philadelphia.
Whaples, E: S.	Whaples, Edward S....................West Haven, Ct.
Wheat, W. V.	Wheat, W. V., Co....................315 Dearborn St., Chicago.
Wheeler, G.	Wheeler, Giles....................Concord, N. H.
Wheeler, M. P.	Wheeler, Marcus Pratt....................De Forest, Wis.
Wheelock, I. S.	Wheelock, Mrs. Ida S....................St. Paul, Minn.
Whelan, N. J.	Whelan, Nicholas Joseph....................Holland, Mich.
Whipple, J. R.	Whipple, J. R., Co....................Boston.
Whist Club.	Whist Club....................13 W. 36th St., New York
Whitaker & R.	Whitaker & Ray-Wiggin Co.....770-776 Mission St., San Francisco.
Whitcher, W: F:	Whitcher, William Frederick....................Woodsville, N. H.
Whitcomb.	Whitcomb & Barrows....................Huntington Chambers, Boston.
White, A. L.	White, Almira L....................73 Broadway, Haverhill, Mass.
White, C: F.	White, Charles Fred....................Box 1006, Easthampton, Mass.
White, E:	White, Edward............1607 Commonwealth Ave., Pittsburgh, Pa.
White, G: R.	White, George Ransom....................Nashville, Tenn.
White, H.	White, Hervey....................Woodstock, N. Y.
White, J: B.	White, John Barber....................Kansas City, Mo.
White, J. T., & Co.	White, James T., & Co....................29 E. 22d St., New York.
White Dental.	White, S. S., Dental Mfg. Co....Chestnut St. cor. 12th, Philadelphia.
White Peril.	White Peril Co....................Danbury, Ct.
White Rats.	White Rats of America....................1553 Broadway, New York.
White-S.	White-Smith Music Publishing Co....................Boston.
Whitehead, J. B.	Whitehead, Prof. J. B......Johns Hopkins University, Baltimore, Md.
Whiteley, L. C.	Whiteley, Lillian C....................Philadelphia.
Whiteside, G. K.	Whiteside, Guy Kenneth....................White Hall, Ill.
Whitfield, E. W.	Whitfield, Erle W....................220 Broadway, New York.
Whitlock, C. E. H.	Whitlock, C. E. H....................154 Elm St., New Haven, Ct.
Whitman, W:	Whitman, William, & Co....................78 Chauncey St., Boston.
Whitney, F.	Whitney, Fred....................262 Kingsley Ave., Palo Alto, Cal.
Whitney, J. R.	Whitney, J. R., State Printer....................Salem, Ore.
Whitson, A. R.	Whitson, Andrew R....................Madison, Wis.
Whittaker.	Whittaker, Thomas, Inc....................2 Bible House, New York.
Whittet.	Whittet & Shepperson....................1001 Main St., Richmond, Va.
Whittier, C. C.	Whittier, Charles Collyer........374 Blue Hills Ave., Roxbury, Mass.
Whittle, W: C.	Whittle, William C....................Norfolk, Va.
Wichelman, F. A.	Wichelman, Frederick Augustus............202 West St., New York.
Wichita.	Wichita Publishing Co....................Wichita, Kan.
Wickersham.	Wickersham Co....................Lancaster, Pa.
Wickliffe, E. L.	Wickliffe, Elizabeth Lockhart....................Wickliffe, Ky.
Wickwire, A. M.	Wickwire, Arthur Manley.......Room 1412, 5 Nassau St., New York.
Widney, R. M.	Widney, Robert M....................Los Angeles, Cal.
Wiers, C: R.	Wiers, Charles Robert....................Buffalo, N. Y.
Wight, C: A.	Wight, Rev. Charles Albert.......128 Court St., Chicopee Falls, Mass.
Wilbur Pub.	Wilbur Publishing Co....................Pasadena, Cal.
Wilcox, M. B.	Wilcox, M. B....................28 Spruce St., New York.
Wilcox Bks.	Wilcox Books Concern....................163 Randolph St., Chicago.
Wilcoxon, M. H.	Wilcoxon, M. H....................Hot Springs, Ark.
Wilde.	Wilde, W. A., Co....................120 Boylston St., Boston.
Wilde, A. G.	Wilde, Ada Godfrey....................Vicksburg, Miss.
Wiles, F. L.	Wiles, F. L....................8 Pemberton Sq., Boston.
Wiley.	Wiley, John, & Sons....................41-45 E. 19th St., New York.

Wiley, R: T.	Wiley, Richard Taylor	Elizabeth, Pa.
Wiley & W.	Wiley & Wright	Guymon, Okla.
Wilgus, W: J:	Wilgus, William John	165 Broadway, New York.
Wilkie & C.	Wilkie & Coan	924 Real Estate Trust Bldg., Philadelphia.
Wilkins, T.	Wilkins, Dr. T.	40 Loomis St., Chicago.
Wilkinson, E. H.	Wilkinson, Elizabeth Hays	526 N. Negley Ave., Pittsburgh, Pa.
Wilkinson, H. S.	Wilkinson, Herbert Swan	Mitchell, S. D.
Willers, M. A.	Willers, Mrs. M. A.	Romulus, N. Y.
Willett Press.	Willett Press	5 W. 20th St., New York.
Williams, A.	Williams, Alfred, & Co	Raleigh, N. C.
Williams, C. S.	Williams, C. S.	Room 34, 206 Broadway, New York.
Williams, D:	Williams, David	239 W. 29th St., New York.
Williams, J. M.	Williams, J. M., & Son	Waunakee, Wis.
Williams, J: H.	Williams, John Harvey	Tacoma, Wash.
Williams, L. M.	Williams, Lewis Milton	Oskaloosa, Ia.
Williams, T. A.	Williams, Tom A.	1758 K St., Washington, D. C.
Williams W. L.	Williams, Walter Long	115 Valentine Pl., Ithaca, N. Y.
Williams, W.: C.	Williams, William Carlos	131 Passaic Ave., Rutherford, N. J.
Williams & W.	Williams & Wilkins Co	2427-29 York Road, Baltimore, Md.
Williams Pr.	Williams Printing Co	Richmond, Va.
Williams Pr. (N. Y.)	Williams Printing Co	437 Eleventh Ave., New York.
Williamson Law Bk.	Williamson Law Book Co	41 State St., Rochester, N. Y.
Willis, J. L. M.	Willis J. L. M.	Eliot, Me.
Willis, W. H.	Willis, W. H., Co	Cincinnati; Chicago.
Willis Music.	Willis Music Co	Cincinnati.
Willows Shop.	Willows Shop	Clintonville, Mich.
Willwerscheid.	Willwerscheid & Raith	St. Paul, Minn.
Wilshire Bk.	Wilshire Book Co	200 William St., New York.
Wilson, E: L.	Wilson, Edward L.	122 E. 25th St., New York.
Wilson, E: S.	Wilson, Edward Stansbury	1043 Franklin Ave., Columbus, O.
Wilson, F. E.	Wilson, Frazer Ells	Greenville, O.
Wilson, G: R.	Wilson, George Robert	Jasper, Ind.
Wilson, H: L.	Wilson, Henry Lawrence	Los Angeles, Cal.
Wilson, H. W.	Wilson, H. W., Co.,	1401-1405 University Ave., S. E., Minneapolis, Minn.
Wilson, J., & Son.	Wilson, J., & Son	Cambridge, Mass.
Wilson, J. F.	Wilson, J. F.	Knoxville, Tenn.
Wilson, J. L.	Wilson, J. L., & Son	Collinsville, Tex.
Wilson, J. R.	Wilson, Joseph Robert	606-607 Commonwealth Bldg., Philadelphia.
Wilson, T: W.	Wilson, Thomas W.	Eureka, Cal.
Wilson, V. T.	Wilson, Victor Tyson	Lansing, Mich.
Wilson & M.	Wilson & McMaster	East Lansing, Mich.
Wilson Pub. Co.	Wilson Publishing Co	710 Trinity Bldg., 111 Broadway, New York.
Wilt, A. D.	Wilt, Abraham Darst	Dayton, O.
Wilt, D. W.	Wilt, Dorah W.	Bradshaw, Neb.
Wiltzius.	Wiltzius, M. H., Co. (now Diederich-Shafer Co.),	413-417 Broadway, Milwaukee, Wis.
Winkelman.	Winkelman, G. W.	Rochester, N. Y.
Winn & H.	Winn & Hammond	Detroit, Mich.
Winona.	Winona Publishing Co. (assigned Jan., 1910),	24-26 Adams St., Chicago.
Winsett, R. E.	Winsett, Robert Emmet	Doxey, Okla.
Winship, M. G.	Winship, Mary Gray	2720 Church Ave., Flatbush, Brooklyn, N. Y.
Winslow, A. J.	Winslow, Mrs. Anna J. Frazer	Moderno, Cal.
Winslow, H.	Winslow, Horatio	Madison, Wis.
Winsor.	Winsor, Thomas	Seattle, Wash.
Winston.	Winston, John C., Co	1006 Arch St., Philadelphia.
Wisconsin Dept. Pub. Instruction.	Wisconsin, Dept. of Public Instruction	Madison, Wis.
Wisconsin Free Lib.	Wisconsin Free Library Commission	Madison, Wis.
Wisconsin Hist.	Wisconsin History Commission	Madison, Wis.
Wis. State Barbers' Bd.	Wisconsin State Barbers' Board of Examiners	Milwaukee, Wis.
	Wisconsin State Historical Society. *See* State Hist., Wis.	
Wise, W. H.	Wise, W. H., & Co	161 State St., Chicago.
Wise Pub.	Wise Publishing House	Newport News, Va.
Wishard, S: E.	Wishard, Samuel Ellis, D.D.	135 E. Ave. 53, Los Angeles. Cal.
Wistar.	Wistar Institute	36th St. and Woodland Ave., Philadelphia.
Withers, Z.	Withers, Zachary	Baker Ave., P. O. Box 323 Elmhurst, Cal.
Witter, C: A.	Witter, Charles A.	Redlands. Cal.
Witter & K.	Witter & Kintner	503 Fifth Ave., New York.

Woerner, W: F.	Woerner, William F....St. Louis.
Wolf, B.	Wolf, Blair....Winterset, Ia.
Wolfe, A. J:	Wolfe, Archibald John....170 Broadway, New York.
Wolfe, J. M.	Wolfe, J. M., Co....Omaha, Neb.
Wolfe & M.	Wolfe & McKenzie....San Jose, Cal.
Wolverine.	Wolverine Book Publishing Co....Grand Rapids, Mich.
Woman's For. Miss.	Woman's Foreign Missionary Society of the Methodist Episcopal Church in America....150 Fifth Ave., New York.
Woman's Nat. Prog. League.	Woman's National Progressive League....200 William St., New York.
Women's Educ.	Women's Educational and Industrial Union....Boston.
Wood.	Wood, William, & Co....51 Fifth Ave., New York.
Wood, A. A.	Wood, Arthur A....Slocum, R. I.
Wood, F. A.	Wood, Frances A....Vassar College, Poughkeepsie, N. Y.
Wood, H.	Wood, H....Kansas City Star, Kansas City, Mo.
Wood, H. A.	Wood, Howard Athons....Burlington, Wis.
Wood, H. G.	Wood, Rev. Hermon Gaylord....6 Lyndhurst St., Dorchester, Mass.
Wood, J. G.	Wood, Joshua Gibson....U. S. Land Office, Topeka, Kan.
Wood, R. M.	Wood, R. M....127 Montgomery St., San Francisco.
Wood, S. G.	Wood, Sumner Gilbert....Blandford, Mass.
Wood-B.	Wood-Brownlee Printing Co....San Antonio, Tex.
Woodbury, S. E.	Woodbury, Sarah Eliza....2931 Kansas Ave., Los Angeles, Cal.
Woodman, H. R.	Woodman, Hannah Rea....1 Franklin St., Poughkeepsie, N. Y.
Woodruff Pub.	Woodruff Publishing Co....Boston.
Woodruff-C.	Woodruff-Collins Co....217 N. 11th St., Lincoln, Neb.
Woods.	Woods Publishing Co....27 E. 22d St., New York.
Woods, C. E.	Woods, Clinton E., & Co....Brooklyn, N. Y.
Woods, E.	Woods, Dr. E., Jr....Charlottesville, Va.
Woods, H: E.	Woods, Henry E....P. O. Box 3372, Boston.
Woods, P. T.	Woods, Prince T....Middleton, Mass.
Woodward, J. T.	Woodward, Joseph T....Augusta, Me.
Woodward & L.	Woodward & Lothrop....1013 F St., Washington, D. C.
Woolbridge, C. R.	Woolbridge, Clifton Rodman....3031 Michigan Ave., Chicago.
Woolsey, C. M.	Woolsey, C. M....Milton, N. Y.
Woolsey, J: M.	Woolsey, John Martin....40 S. 13th Ave., Mt. Vernon, N. Y.
Worcester.	Worcester, City of, W. Henry Towne, City Clerk..Worcester, Mass.
Worcester Bd. Trade.	Worcester Board of Trade....Worcester, Mass.
Worcester Nat. Hist.	Worcester Natural History Society....Worcester, Mass.
Worcester Press.	Worcester Press....Old South Bldg., Boston.
Worcester Pub. Lib.	Worcester Public Library....Worcester, Mass.
Worcester Sch. Com.	Worcester School Committee....Worcester, Mass.
Worcester Soc. Antiquity.	Worcester Society of Antiquity....Worcester, Mass.
Word Sign.	Word Sign Publishing Co....627 Bartlett Bldg., Atlantic City, N. J.
Workman, F.	Workman, Florence....Mansfield, O.
Workman, H. C.	Workman, Mrs. Helen Chaffee....Detroit, Mich.
World Bk.	World Book Co....Park Hill, Yonkers, N. Y.
World Corporation.	World Corporation....6 Beacon St., Boston.
World R'way.	World Railway Pub. Co. *See* Phillips, Cropley, Co.
World Supply.	World Supply Co....Louisville, Ky.
World To-day.	World To-day Co....Chicago.
World's Dispensary.	World's Dispensary Medical Assoc....Buffalo, N. Y.
World's Events Co.	World's Events Co....La Salle Ave. and Ohio St., Chicago.
Worrall, T. W.	Worrall, Mrs. T. Worcester, Flag House Chapel, D. A. R., Tacony St., Frankford, Philadelphia.
Worth, P. W.	Worth, Pauline Wilson....1539A Cambria St., Los Angeles, Cal.
Wright, B: C.	Wright, Benjamin C....San Francisco.
Wright, C: W.	Wright, Capt. Charles W., U. S. Steamboat Inspection Service, Baltimore, Md.
Wright, L. L.	Wright, L. L.,....State Supt. of Public Instruction, Lansing, Mich.
Wright, T. A.	Wright, Tobias A....150 Bleecker St., N. Y.
Wright & P.	Wright & Potter Printing Co....Boston.
Wy. Co. Public Lands.	Wyoming Commissioner of Public Lands....Cheyenne, Wyo.
Wy. Dept. of Immigration.	Wyoming Dept. of Immigration....Cheyenne, Wyo.
Wy. State Dry Farming.	Wyoming State Dry Farming Commission....Cheyenne, Wyo.
Wyand, E. C.	Wyand, E. Clayton....1242 Morton St., Mattapan, Mass.

Wyatt, F: F.	Wyatt, Frederick Fuller........................San Angelo, Tex.
Wycil.	Wycil & Co..............................83 Nassau St., New York.
Wyeth, M. S.	Wyeth, Marion Sims, & Co...........244 Lexington Ave., New York.
Wyllys-Overland.	Wyllys-Overland Co....................................Toledo, O.
Wyman, L.	Wyman, Mrs. Lloyd...............418 Walnut Ave., Painesville, O.
Wynkoop, H.	Wynkoop, Hallenbeck, Crawford Co.....497 Pearl St., New York.
X-ray.	X-ray Publishing Co...............................Butte, Montana.
Y. M. C. A.	Young Men's Christian Association, International Committee of, 124 E. 28th St., New York.
Y. W. C. A.	Young Women's Christian Association National Board, 125 E. 27th St., New York.
Yale, R. H.	Yale, Rodney Horace...............................Beatrice, Neb.
Yale Co-op.	Yale Co-operative Corporation.......................New Haven, Ct.
Yale Courant.	Yale Courant.......................................New Haven, Ct.
Yale Pub.	Yale Publishing Association, Inc.........135 Elm St., New Haven, Ct.
Yale Univ.	Yale University Press...............................New Haven, Ct.
Yale Univ. Lib.	Yale University Library.............................New Haven, Ct.
Yates, K. M.	Yates, Katherine Meriette, Co.............5340 Cornell Ave., Chicago.
Ye Planry.	Ye Planry Publishing Co..........................Los Angeles, Cal.
Year Bk.	Year Book Publishers.....................40 Dearborn St., Chicago.
Yellow Jacket.	Yellow Jacket Press.........................Moravian Falls, N. C.
Yellowstone.	Yellowstone Park Publishing Co..............................Chicago.
Yergin, H. A.	Yergin, H. A., M.D.....................446 Garfield Ave., Chicago.
Yogi Pub.	Yogi Publication Society.............1408 Masonic Temple, Chicago.
Yonkers Pub.	Yonkers Publishing Co..................13 Main St., Yonkers, N. Y.
Yordy.	Yordy, E. B., Co..................41 W. Market St., Wilkesbarre, Pa.
Youmans, H. M.	Youmans, H. M...Waukesha, Wis.
Young, F: R.	Young, Frederick R..................................Metropolis, Ill.
Young, G. A.	Young, Gilbert Amos...........................West Lafayette, Ind.
Young Churchman.	Young Churchman Co............484 Milwaukee St., Milwaukee, Wis.
Young Israels.	Young Israels........................224-226 E. 7th St., Cincinnati.
Young Lady Across the Way.	Young Lady Across the Way Co.......................Columbus, O.
Young People's Miss.	Young People's Missionary Movement....156 Fifth Ave., New York.
Youth's Companion.	Youth's Companion..Boston.
Yuma County.	Yuma County Commercial Club.........................Yuma, Ariz.
Yungbluth, A. J.	Yungbluth, A. J.....................................Ishpening, Mich.
Zartmann, P. E.	Zartmann, Parley E.............................Winona Lake, Ind.
Zeagler, J: W.	Zeagler, John Wesley............558 Pennsylvania St., Denver, Colo.
Ziegler.	Ziegler, P. W., Co.........................267 S. 4th St., Philadelphia.
Zigzag.	Zigzag Publishing Co..........................Colorado Springs, Colo.
Zimmerman, L. M.	Zimmerman, L. M., D.D.............421 Hanover St., Baltimore, Md.
Ziv, R. L.	Ziv, R. L..............................35 W. 139th St., New York.
Zuriel.	Zuriel Publishing Co.............250 Colonial Arcade, Cleveland, O.

THE AMERICAN CATALOG

1908-1910

By Author, Title, Subject and Series

NOTE

In this catalog the books are recorded under (1) *author, in* **Clarendon** *type; anonymous books having* **Clarendon** *type for the first word;* (2) *title in* Roman; (3) *subject-heading in* SMALL CAPS; (4) *name of series in Italics. The figures in parentheses are not the imprint date, but refer to the date of "The Publishers' Weekly" in which full title entry will be found and not to the day of publication, for which information should be sought in the full title entry thus indicated. When month only is given in parentheses this is the original entry and title will not be found in Weekly Record. Where not specified, the binding is cloth.*

Up to April 16th, 1910, *the prices of net books published under the rules of the American Publishers' Association are preceded in this list by a double asterisk* **, *and the word net follows the price. The prices of fiction* (*not net*) *published under the rules are preceded by a dagger* †. *The prices of net books not covered by the rules, whether published by members of the American Publishers' Association or not, are preceded by a single asterisk, and the word net follows the price. Since April 16th,* 1910, *all net books are so indicated, but no further distinction has been made.*

The abbreviations are usually self-explanatory. A colon after initial designates the most usual given name, as: A: Augustus; B: Benjamin; C: Charles; D: David; E: Edward; F: Frederick; G: George; H: Henry; I: Isaac; J: John; L: Louis; N: Nicholas; P: Peter; R: Richard; S: Samuel; T: Thomas; W: William.

Sizes are designated as follows: F. (*folio: over* 30 *centimeters high*); *Q.* (4*to: under* 30 *cm.*); *O.* (8*vo:* 25 *cm.*); *D.* (12*mo:* 20 *cm.*); *S.* (16*mo:* 17½ *cm.*); *T.* (24*mo:* 15 *cm.*); *Tt.* (32*mo:* 12½ *cm.*); *Ff.* (48*mo:* 10 *cm.*). *Sq., obl., nar., designate square, oblong, narrow books of these heights. In cases where the record is not made directly from the books, the designations* 4*to,* 8*vo,* 12*mo, etc., are used.*

Prices are added except when not supplied by publisher or obtainable only on specific request.

Months are abbreviated as follows: Ja January; F February; Mr March; Ap April; My May; Je June; Jl July; Ag August; S September; O October; N November; D December.

The full name of publisher and address will be found in the Directory of American Publishers, pp. vii–lxxxvi.

THE AMERICAN CATALOG

CUMULATED, 1908–1910

Of books recorded January 1, 1908, *to December* 31, 1910, *by* **Author**, Title, SUBJECT, *and Series entry.*

A B C about collecting. Yoxall, J. H: $2 net. Jacobs.
A B C and X Y Z of bee culture. Root, A. I. $1.50-$2.50. A. I. Root.
A B C book for good boys and girls. Lewin, F. G. $1.50. Stokes.
A B C des Skat in Deutsch und English. Liedtke, F. W. 50 c. Schaefer & K.
A B C guide to sensible horseshoeing. Magner, D. $1. Saalfield.
A B C of bookkeeping. Dicksee, L. R. 80 c. Longmans.
A B C of collecting old English pottery. $2 net. Jacobs.
A B C of five-figure logarithms. Woodward, C. J. $1.25. Spon.
A B C of good hearing. Barrett, J. A. 25 c. J. A. Barrett.
A B C of philosophy. Landsberg, G. F. 75 c. Fenno.
A B C of railroad signaling. Elliott, W. H. $1. Mackenzie-K.
A B C of taxation. Fillebrown, C: B. $1.20. Doubleday, P.
A B C of the motor cycle. Jackman, W. J. $1; $1.50. C: C. Thompson.
A B C of the steam engine. Lisk, J. P. 50 c. Spon.
A B C of the steel square and its uses. Hodgson, F: T: 50 c. Drake.
A B C of vocalization. Panseron, A. M. $1. Ditson.
A. L. A. Library handbooks. *See* American Library Association.
A-roving he would go. Reed, M. *$1.25 net. Sherman, F.
A to Z horoscope delineator. George, L. $2. Portland (Ore.) Sch. Astrology.
A vol d' oiseau. Jallade, E. J. $1. W: R. Jenkins.

Aaron, Eug. Murray-.
See Murray-Aaron, Eug.

Aaron Burr. O'Brien, W: L. (Add. pubs. for price.) Review Pub. Co.

Aarons, S. Jervois, M.D.
Gynæcological therapeutics. '10(D) 12°, $2 net. Wood.

Aaronsohn, Aaron.
Agricultural and botanical explorations in Palestine. '10(S) 64 p. il. 8°, (U. S., Dept. of Agriculture; Bu. of Plant Industry, bull.)

Ab vrbe condita. *See* Livy.
Abaft the funnel. Kipling, R. †$1.50. B. W. Dodge.
Abandoned. *See* Verne, Jules.

Abarbanell, Jacob Ralph.
Heart of the people. '08(D12) il. 12°, $1.50. C. M. Clark.

ABATTOIRS.
Ayling, R. S. Public abattoirs. $3.50. Spon.

Abba, Father. Hyde, W: DeW. *50 c. net. Revell.
Abba, Father. Lowrie, W. *$1 net. Longmans.
Abbatial crosier. Sue, M. J. E. 50 c. N. Y. Labor News.

Abbe, Cleveland.
Mechanics of the earth's atmosphere; collection of translations; 3d collection. '10 (Je) 4+617 p. figs. O. pap. Smith. Inst.

—, and Nichols, Mrs. Josephine Genung.
Townsend genealogy: record of the descendants of John Townsend, 1743-1821, and of his wife, Jemima Travis, 1746-1832. '09(Ap17) c. 12°, (Allaben genealogical ser.) $2. Allaben.

Abbey, Edn. Austin.
Quest of the Holy Grail: portfolio of paintings. '09(Mr27) 4°, $5; subjects sold separately, ea., 50 c. Curtis & C.

Abbey, G:
Balance of nature and modern conditions of cultivation. '09(Ap17) 8°, *$2 net. Dutton.

Abbey, H:
Dream of love: a mystery: [poems.] '10 (Ja1) c. D. 75 c. Riverside Press.

Abbey, Myron Jay.
Normal school instruction in agriculture. '10(Mr5) 8°, (U. S., Dept. of Agriculture, Office of Experiment Stations, circular.)

Abbey classics. 16°, pap., 25 c.; bds., 50 c.; leath., $1. Abbey Co.
—Burns. Cotter's Saturday night.
—Longfellow. Building of the ship.
—Lowell. Vision of Sir Launfal.
—Milton. Ode on the morning of Christ's nativity.
—Whittier. Snow-bound.

Abbey ser. 2 v. '10(D) 12°, ea., leath., $1; pap., 50 c. Dodge.

ABBEYS.
Dixon, C. Abbeys of Great Britain. *$1.50 net. Scribner.
Gasquet, F. A. Greater abbeys of England. **$3.50 net. Dodd.
Lang, E. M. Some old English abbeys. 60 c.; $1. Stokes.
See also Cathedrals;—France;—*also* names of abbeys.

Abbot, Allan.
See Baker, Franklin T:

Abbot, C: Greeley, and Fowle, F. E., jr.
Annals of the Astrophysical Observatory of the Smithsonian Inst. v. 2. '08 (Ag22) tables, figs. Q. gratis. U. S., Supt. of Docs.

Abbot, H: Larcom.
Regulation of rivers in the interest of navigation, and modes of gauging the flow of water. '09, [1910.] (F) 2 p. 8°, $1.25. "Professional Memoirs."

Abbot, Willis J:
Story of our navy for young Americans, from colonial days to the present time. '10(O15) c. il. O. $2. Dodd.

Abbott, A. J., rep.
See New Mexico Territory. *Sup. ct.* Repts.

Abbott, Arth. J.
Individual singing exercises; 4th grade. '10(My21); 5th grade (S); 6th grade (O); 7th grade, 8th grade (N) c. O. pap., ea., 10 c. Am. Bk.
Music manual for teachers of rural schools, to accompany Short course in music by Frederic H. Ripley and T: Tapper. '10 (O22) c. D. pap., 15 c. Am. Bk.

Abbott, Alex. Crever, M.D.
Principles of bacteriology. 8th ed., rev. '09 (Ag) 631 p. il. 12°, *$2.75 net. Lea.

Abbott, C. L.
Common sense Bible teacher. '09(N) c. 64 p. il. 25 c. C. L. Abbott.

Abbott, C: Conrad.
Archæologia nova Cæsarea: [New Jersey.] '07, '08(Je) 2 v., il. 8°. (Add. author for price.) C: C. Abbott.

Abbott, D: Phelps.
History of a strange case: study in occultism. '08(Ag22) 8°, pap. (Add. pubs. for price.) Open Court.
Marvelous creations of Joseffy. '08(D5) c. il. O. pap., 15 c. Open Court.

Abbott, Edith.
Women in industry; study in American economic hist.; with an introd. note by Sophonisba P. Breckenridge. '09(D11) c. D. **$2 net. Appleton.

Abbott, Rev. Edn. Abbott.
Indices to Diatessarica: [harmony of the four Gospels;] with a specimen of research. '08(Ap11) 8°, *$1.25 net. Macmillan.
Message of the Son of Man. '09(Ag7) 8°, *$1.75 net. Macmillan.

Abbott, Eleanor Hallowell.
Molly Make-Believe. '10(O1) c. il. S. $1 net. Century Co.

Abbott, Ernest Hamlin.
On the training of parents. '08(Ap18) c. D. **$1 net. Houghton, M. & Co.
What they did with themselves. '09(S18) c. D. (What is worth while ser.) leatherette, **30 c. net. Crowell.

Abbott, Frances Matilda.
The simple single. '09, [1910.] (Ap) c. 48 p. 16°, 50 c. Rumford Press.

Abbott, Fk. Frost.
Society and politics in ancient Rome. '09 (S11) c. D. **$1.25 net. Scribner.

Abbott, G: F:
Turkey in transition. '09(N20) il. pors. O. *$4.25 net. Longmans.
—, ed. Greece in evolution; studies prep. under the auspices of the French League for the Defence of the Rights of Hellenism. '10(Je11) O. $1.50 net. Wessels & B.

Abbott, G: Knapp, M.D., comp.
Technique of hydrotherapy and Swedish massage as employed at the Loma Linda Sanitarium. [2d ed.] '09, [1910.] (F) c. 40 p. 8°, 25 c. Loma Linda Coll.

Abbott, Herbert Vaughan.
See Baker, Franklin T:

Abbott, Holker.
Silver wedding of the Bear; memorial of the celebration of the 25th anniversary of the Tavern Club, 15 Jan., 1909. '10 (Je) c. 53 p. front. 8°. (Priv. pr.) H. Abbott.

Abbott, Howard Strickland.
Summary of the law of public corporations. '08(N) c. 24+786 p. O. (Add. pubs. for price.) Keefe-D.

Abbott, J. H. M.
Letters from Queer Street: some of the correspondence of the late John Mason. '08(Je6) 8°, *$1.75 net. Macmillan.
South seas, (Melanesia. '08(S19) il. map, 12°, (Peeps at many lands ser.) *75 c. net. Macmillan.

Abbott, Jacob.
Rollo at work, and Rollo at play: introd. by Lucy Crump. '08(F22) 16°, (Everyman's lib.) *35 c. net; leath., *70 c. net. Dutton.

ABBOTT, Lawrence.
Green, S: A. Memoir of Abbott Lawrence. 35 c. S: A. Green.

Abbott, Lemuel Abijah.
Personal recollections and Civil War diary, 1864. '08, [1909.] (Mr) 10+296 p. por. 8°, (Add. author for price.) L. A. Abbott.

Abbott, Leonard Daldon.
Ernest Howard Crosby, the Puritan anarchist: a valuation and a tribute. '08(F) pors. 12°, 50 c.; pap., 25 c. Ariel.

Abbott, Luther Jewett.
Hist. and civics of Oklahoma. '10(N) 8+220 p. il. fold. map, $1 net. Ginn.

Abbott, Lyman, D.D.
Home builder. '08(N14) c. D. **75 c. net. Houghton M.
Seeking after God. '10(Ag6) c. D. $1. Crowell.
Spirit of democracy. '10(D3) c. D. $1.25 net. Houghton M.
The temple. '09(N13) c. D. **$1.25 net. Macmillan.
—, and McFadyen, J: Edg.
Interpreter's commentary on the New Tesment. v. 1-6. '09(Ap17) ea., $1.50. Barnes.
See also King, H: Churchill.

Abbott, Nat Thurston.
Cases on the law of equity jurisprudence and trusts; sel. from Am. and Eng. decisions. '09(D) c. O. (Add. pubs. for price.) Flood.

Abbott, Stanley Warde.
That same old lover. '09(Jl) 12 p. front. 8°, 50 c. B. Castello.

Abbott, Twyman Osmand.
Automobile law for motorists. '09(Jl10) c. D. flex. leath., $2.50. Reilly & B.
Primer of the law of negligence for conductors and motormen, and rules for their guidance in their relations with the public. [New ed.] '09(Jl) c. 42 p. Tt. pap. (Add. author for price.) T. O. Abbott.
Road rights of motorists; cont. rules of the road and automobile laws of all states. '10(Jl2) c. D. $1.50 net. Outing.

ABBREVIATIONS.
Weaver, A. B. Abbreviated longhand. $2. Quickrite Pub.

ABD AL-RAHMAN KHAN, *Amir.*
See Afghanistan.

Abderhalden, Emil.
Text-book of physiological chemistry. In 30 lectures. '08(Ag29) c. 8°, **$5 net. Wiley.

ABDOMEN.
Barnard, H. L. Contributions to abdominal surgery. $4.20 net. Longmans.
Douglas, R: Surgical diseases of the abdomen. *$6 net. Blakiston.
Kelly, H. A., *and* Noble, C: P., *eds.* Gynecology and abdominal surgery. v. 2. *$8 net; *$9.50 net. Saunders.
Sawyer, J. E. H. Physical signs of diseases of thorax and abdomen. *$2 net. Wood.
See also Digestion;—Hernia;—Intestines;—Stomach;—Tuberculosis.

Abdominal tuberculosis. Maylard, A. E. *$4 net. Blakiston.

Abdu'l-Baha.
Some answered questions: [doctrines of Bahaism:] collected and tr. from the Persian by Laura Clifford Barney. '08 (O17) O. *$1.50 net. Lippincott.

Abel, Annie Heloise.
Indians in the Civil War; [repr. from the *American Historical Review,* Jan., 1910.] [1910.] (Je) 281-296 p. 4°. (Not for sale.) Am. Hist. Review.
Proposals for an Indian state, 1778-1878. '09, [1910.] (Jl) 89-104 p. 8°. Gov. Pr. Off.

—, and Lord, Eleanor Louisa, comps.
Brief guide to points of historical interest in Baltimore city. '08(Ap.) c. 12 p. il. 8°, 20 c. A. H. Abel.

Abel, Mrs. Mary W. Hinman.
Care of food in the home. '09, [1910.] (F) 46 p. il. 8°, (U. S., Dept. of Agriculture: farmers' bull.) pap.

Aber, W: W.
Dawn of another life. '10(Ag20) c. por. 8°, $1.50. W: W. Aber.

Abercrombie, Lascelles.
Interludes and poems. '08(Ap25) D. *$1.25 net. Lane.

Abercrombie-Miller, Edith.
See Miller, Edith Abercrombie-.

Aberdeen, Ishbel Maria, Countess of.
Edward Marjoribanks, Lord Tweedmouth, 1849-1909. '10(Jl9) il. pors. 8°, $2 net. Dutton.
Our Lady of the Sunshine and her international visitors; [acct. of visit of International Council of Women to Canada.] '10(Je4) 8°, bds., 50 c. net. Dutton.

ABERDEEN-ANGUS CATTLE.
See Cattle.

Abernethy, Arth. Talmage.
The Jew a negro: study of the Jewish ancestry. '10(Ap9) 12°, 50 c. Dixie.

Abernethy, Larkin S:
Shorthand. Rev. ed. '08(Ja11) 12°, bds., $1.50. Driggers.

ABINGDON, Eng.
Townsend, J. A. Hist. of Abingdon. $3 net. Oxford Univ.

ABNORMAL CHILDREN.
See Children.

Abnormal psychology. Coriat, I. $2 net. Moffat.

Abolished rites. Gottschall, A. H., *comp.* 7 c. A. H. Gottschall.

ABOLITIONISTS.
See Slavery.

ABORTION.
Taussig, F: J. Prevention and treatment of abortion. $2. Mosby.

About, Edmond François Valentin.
La mère de la marquise; with explanatory notes in English by Prof. C. Fontaine. '10(Mr26) c. 16°, (Contes choisis.) 25 c. W: R. Jenkins.
Les jumeaux de l'Hotel Corneille; ed. by S. Tindall. '09(O16) S. (Shorter French texts.) *25 c. net. Crowell.

About Dickens, Leffman, H: *50 c. net. H: Leffman.

About panics. Kohler, J. P. 15 c. Outing.

About the farm; il. description of the New Boston dairy and other industries at Valley View, Muzzey, and Hutchinson farms, which are a part of the supply department of Young's Hotel, Parker House, and Hotel Touraine. [1910.] (N) c. 62 p. il. 8°, bds., boxed, gratis. J. R. Whipple.

Above life's turmoil. Allen, J. $1. Putnam.

Abraham, Ashley Perry.
Rock-climbing in Skye. '08(Je13) il. map, O. *$7 net. Longmans.

Abraham, G: D.
Complete mountaineer. '08(Mr21) il. O. (Geographical lib.) *$4.80 net. Doubleday, P.
Mountain adventures. '10(O8) il. O. $3.80 net. Doubleday, P.

Abrahams, Israel.
Judaism. '07, [1909.] (Ap) 8°, (Religions ancient and modern.) *40 c. net. Open Court.

Abram, Annie.
Social England in the xvth century; study of the effects of economic conditions. '09 (D18) 12°, (Research lib.) *$1 net. Dutton.

Abrams, Albert.
Diagnostic therapeutics; guide for practitioners in diagnosis by aid of drugs and methods other than drug giving. '10(F) c. 18+1039 p. il. 8°, $5. Rebman.
Bibliography (9 p.).

Abrams, Albert.—*Continued.*
Spondylotherapy; spinal concussion and the application of other methods to the spine in the treatment of disease. '10(F) c. 17+400 p. il. 8°, $3.50. A. Abrams.
Bibliography (3 p.).
Abrams, Duff And.
See Talbot, Arth. Newell.
ABRUZZI MOUNTAINS.
See Italy.
Absente reo; by the author of "Pro Christo et ecclesia." '10(Jl16) 12°, $1.60 net. Macmillan.
Absentee (The). *See* Edgeworth, Maria. Castle Rackrent.
Absolute idealism and immortality. Ball, J. W. (Add. pubs. for price.) Woodruff-C.
Absolute necessity of baptism. Johnson, S: L. *10 c. net. Revell.
ABSOLUTION.
See Confession.
Absolution. Viebig, C. †$1.50. Lane.
ABSOLUTISM.
See Philosophy.
ABSORPTION.
See Spectrum.
Abstracters and title insurance, 1908. Niblack, W: C. *$2 net. Callaghan.
Abstracters of title. Niblack, W: C. *$2 net. Callaghan.
ABSTRACTION.
See Psychology.
Abt, I: Arth.
Inquiry into the status of the kindergarten. '09, [1910.] (My) c. 23 p. 8°, 50 c. I: A. Abt.
—, and Ridlon, J:, eds.
Pediatrics; [and] Orthopedic surgery; with the collaboration of A. Steindler. '08, [1909.] (F) 239 p. il. (Practical medicine ser. of year books.) $1.25. Year Bk.
Abû 'l-Mahâsin Jamâl ad-Dîn Yûsuf ibn Taghrî Birdî.
See Yúsuf ibn Taghri Birdi.
ABUNDANCE, Jean d'.
Carnahan, D: H. Jean d'Abundance. $1. Univ. of Ill.
Abuse of the singing and speaking voice. Moure, J. G. E. $1 net. Scribner.
ABYSSINIA, Africa.
Stigand, C. H. To Abyssinia through an unknown land. $3.50 net. Lippincott.
Academic algebra. Bradbury, W: F. $1.08. Thompson B.
Academic and industrial efficiency. Cooke, M. L. Carnegie.
Academic dictionary. Worcester, J. E. $1.50. Lippincott.
Academy of Pacific Coast History pubs. 8°. Univ. of Cal.
—Breen. Diary of Patrick Breen, one of the Donner party. 15 c.
—Costanso. Narrative of the Portola expedition. 50 c.
—Kelsey. United States consulate in California. (Free to Fellows of the Academy.)
—Plehn. San Francisco clearing house certificates of 1907-1908. 10 c.
—San Francisco Committee of Vigilance of 1851. Papers. 50 c.
—Smith *and* Teggart. Diary of Gaspar de Portola. 50 c.
—Teggart. Official account of the Portola expedition.

Academy ser. of English classics. 12°. 40 c. Allyn & B.
—Macaulay. Essay on Warren Hastings.
ACARINA.
See Mites.
ACCENT.
Fitzhugh, T: Prolegomena to history of Italico-Romanic rhythm. 25 c. Anderson.
See also Prosody.
ACCIDENTS.
Crawford, M. M., *and* Welton, T. S. Before the doctor comes. $1. Chr. Herald.
Dulles, C: W. Accidents and emergencies. *$1 net. Blakiston.
Eastman, C. Work-accidents and the law. $1.50. Charities Pub.
Fidelity and Casualty Co., New York. The prevention of industrial accidents. '09 (D) il. 12°, 25 c. Fidelity & Casualty.
Hall, C. Coal-mine accidents: their causes and preventions. 15 c. U. S., Supt. of Docs.
Hartung, H. H. First aid to the injured. 50 c. H. H. Hartung.
Gulick, *Mrs.* C. E. V. Emergencies. 40 c. Ginn.
Lawrence, J. B. Accidents and emergencies. *75 c. net. W: R. Jenkins.
Lynch, C: American Red Cross abrgd. text book on first aid. General ed. 30 c. Blakiston.
Lynch, C:, *and* Shields, M. J. American Red Cross abridged text-book. 30 c. net. Blakiston.
Magruder, W: E: Claims arising from results of personal injuries. $2.50. Spectator.
Quick helps to the injured; [chart.] 25 c. W: R. Jenkins.
Richards, R. C. Conservation of men. 50 c. R. C. Richards.
Van Schaack, D:, *ed.* Safeguards for the prevention of industrial accidents. 50 c. Ætna Life.
Warwick, F. J., *and* Tunstall, A. C. First aid to the injured and sick. $1 net. W: R. Jenkins.
See also Damages; — Drowning; — Insurance; — Negligence; — Railroads; — Street railways; — Surgery;—*also* names of states.
ACCIDENTS INSURANCE.
See Insurance.
Accidents of an antiquary's life. Hogarth, D: G: $2.50 net. Macmillan.
Accomplished through sacrifice. Everett, B. N. 50 c. Review Press, (Ill.)
According to Maria. Lane, *Mrs.* J: $1.50. Lane.
Account of the departure which the most serene Prince of Wales made from this city of Madrid, on the 9th of Sept. of the present year of 1623, accompanied by our lord the King, and by the infant Charles and the Cardinal his brother, to San Lorezo el Real of the Escurial, where His Highness took leave of his Majesty [facsim.] '02, [1909.] (N) 4°, $3. Hispanic Soc.
Account of the manners and customs of the modern Egyptians. Lane, E: W: *35 c. net; *70 c. net. Dutton.
ACCOUNTING.
See Bookkeeping.

Accounting ser. 8°. Powers.
—Lyons. Modern corporation accounting. $1.25.
Accurate tool work. Goodrich, C. L. *$2 net. Hill Pub.
Accusative with infinitive and some kindred constructions in English. Zeitlen, J. **$1 net. Lemcke.
ACETYLENE.
Leeds, F. H:, *and* Butterfield, W. J. A. Acetylene. $2.75 net. Lippincott.
ACETYLENE LIGHT.
See Lighting.
Acharnians (The). *See* Aristophanes.
Achievements of Luther Trant. Balmer, E. $1.50. Small.
Achorn, J: Warren, M.D.
Nature's help to happiness. '09(Ap3) c. D. **50 c. net. Moffat.
Some physical disorders having mental origin. '08(D12) c. 12°, (Religion and medicine publications.) pap., *25 c. net. Moffat.
Ackermann, Alfr. Seabold Eli.
Popular fallacies. '08(Mr7) il. O. *$1.50 net. Lippincott.
Acolyte's companion; ceremonial and prayer-book combined. 4th ed., rev. [1910] (My) 13+360 p. 24°, 35 c. net. Herder.
Acorn ser. 29 v. '09(Ag28) 16°, ea., 50 c. Dodge.
Acquisition of speed in shorthand. Cope, E: A. 20 c. Pitman.
Acquisitions of Oregon territory. Schafer, J. pt. 1. gratis. Univ. of Ore.
ACROBATS AND ACROBATISM.
Gwathmey, J. T. Tumbling for amateurs. 10 c. Am. Sports.
Worth, H: W. Ground tumbling. 10 c. Am. Sports.
Acropolis of Athens. D'Ooge, M. L. *$4 net. Macmillan.
Across Europe in a motor boat. Rowland, H: C. **$2 net. Appleton.
Across Panama and around the Caribbean. Nicholas, F. C. $1.50. Caldwell.
Across Papua. Mackay, J. A. K. *$2.50 net. Scribner.
Across the arid zone. Cramp, W. S. C. M. Clark.
Across the Sahara. Vischer, H. $3.50 net. Longmans.
ACTING.
See Actors and actresses;—Drama and dramatists;—Plays;—Theatre
Actions and reactions. *See* Kipling, Rudyard.
ACTIONS AT LAW.
Armstrong, T: Procedure in justice cases. Lord Balto. Press.
Bates, C. L. Federal procedure at law. 2 v. $12. Flood.
New York [State.] Code of civil procedure by Amasa J. Parker, jr. $3.50. Banks & Co.
New York [State.] Code of civil procedure prep. by J: C. Thomson. $4. M. Bender.
See also Equity;—Evidence;—Forms (*in law*);—Jury;—Pleading and practice;—Trials.
Active footsteps. Churchill, *Mrs.* C. N. $1.25. C. N. Churchill.
Acton, E. Hamilton.
See Darwin, Fs.
Acton, J: Emerich E: Dalberg-Acton, [Lord Acton.]
Cambridge modern history; ed. by Adolphus W: Ward, G: Wa. Prothero and Stanley Mordaunt Leathes. In 12 v. v. 5, The age of Louis XIV. '08(F29); v. 6, The eighteenth century. '09(D25); v. 11, The growth of nationalities. '09(Ja23); v. 12, The latest age. '10(D31) c. 8°, ea., **$4 net. Macmillan.
Historical essays and studies. '08(Ja11) 8°, *$3 net. Macmillan.
History of freedom and other essays; ed., with an introd., by J: Neville Figgis and Reginald Vere Laurence. '08(Ja11) por. 8°, *$3 net. Macmillan.
Lectures on the French Revolution ed. by J: Neville Figgis and Reginald Vere Lawrence. '10(D24) 8°, $3.25 net. Macmillan.
Acton, Martin W:, ["Nocta W. Nitram."]
Secret Bible hist. of Adamic innocence. '09(N6) c. D. $2. New Age.
Actor's story. Williams, B. *$2 net. Scribner.
ACTORS AND ACTRESSES
American stage of to-day; biographies and photographs of one hundred leading actors and actresses. $2.50. Collier.
Briscoe, J. Actors' birthday book. **$2 net.—Third ser. $2 net. Moffat.
Catalogue of the American Play Co., with original casts. 50 c. Am. Play.
Diary of a Daly débutante; being passages from the journal of a member of Augustin Daly's famous company of players. $1.25 net. Duffield.
Fyvie, J: Tragedy queens of the Georgian era. *$4 net. Dutton.
Golden, G: F. My Lady Vaudeville and her White Rats. $1. White Rats.
Mantzius, K. History of theatrical art in ancient and modern times. In 5 v. v. 4, 5. ea., *$3.50 net. Lippincott.
O'Conner, J. B. Chapters in the history of actors and acting in ancient Greece. $1. Univ. of Chic.
Rennert, H. A. Spanish stage in the time of Lope de Vega. *$3 net. Hispanic Soc.
Who's who on the stage, 1908. *$3 net; *$3.50 net. B. W. Dodge.
Winter, W: Other days: memoirs of the stage. **$3 net. Moffat.
See also Theatre;—*also* Jefferson, Joseph;—Mansfield, Richard;—Siddons, *Mrs.* Sarah Kemble.
Actress (The). Hale, *Mrs.* L. C. †$1.50. Harper.
ACTS OF THE APOSTLES.
See Bible.
Acts of the apostles of the sea. American Seamen's Friend Society. gratis. Am. Seamen's Friend.
Actual government as applied under American conditions. Hart, A. B. $2.25. Longmans.
ACUSHNET, Mass.
Howland, F. Hist. of the town of Acushnet, Bristol County, Mass. $5. E. H. Howland.
Acworth, W: Mitchell.
Relation of railroads to the state: an address del. as president of Economic Science and Statistics, at the annual meeting of the British Assoc. for the Advance-

ment of Science, at Dublin, Ireland, Sept. 2, 1908. '08(N) 14 p. O. pap., gratis. Allen, L. & S.

Ad Miriam. Law, F: H. **$1 net. Putnam.

Adair, W. W.
Wrecks and heroes: [lessons on New Testament heroes.] '09(Mr13) pap., 10 c. Y. M. C. A.

Adam, Fk.
Clans, septs and regiments of the Scottish Highlands. '09(Jl3) il. fold. map, O. *$6 net. Scribner.

Adam, Ja.
Religious teachers of Greece: Gifford lectures; ed. with a memoir by his wife, Adela Marion Adam. '08(Je20) 8°, *$4 net. Scribner

Adam Bede. *See* Eliot, G:

Adami, J: G:, M.D.
Inflammation; introd. to the study of pathology; being the repr. (rev. and enl.) of an article in Prof. Allbutt's "System of medicine." '10(F) 18+254 p. il. 12°, *$1.50 net. Macmillan.
Bibliography.
Principles of pathology. In 2 v. v. 1, General pathology. '08(Ag22); v. 2, Systemic (incl. special) pathology, by J: G: Adami, M.D., and Albert G. Nicholls. M.D. '09(N); 2d ed. 2 v. '10(N) il. 8°, per v., *$6 net. Lea.

ADAMNAN, *St.*
Boswell, C. S. An Irish precursor of Dante. [St. Adamnan.] *$3.50 net. Scribner.

Adam's dream. Corbin, A. 75 c. Scribner.

Adams, Albert A:
True love. '09(O) c. 3-95 p. 16°, 75 c. A. A: Adams.

Adams, Alice Dana.
Neglected period of anti-slavery in America, (1808-1831.) '09(Jl31) c. 8°, (Radcliffe College monographs.) **$1.50 net. Ginn.

Adams, Arth. H.
Galahad Jones. '10(F12) D. $1.50. Lane.

Adams, Braman B., and Hitt, Rodney, comps.
Railroad signal dictionary. '08(O) 472 p. il. 4°, $6. Railroad Gazette.

Adams, C: Christopher.
Ecological survey of Isle Royale, Lake Superior; prep. under the direction of C: C. Adams; rept. from the University of Michigan Museum, pub. by the State Biological Survey, as a part of the rept. of the Board of the Geological Survey for 1908. '09, [1910.] (Mr) 14+468 p. il. maps, 8°, 85 c. Mich. Geol.
Includes "References" and "Bibliography."

Adams, C: Collard.
Middletown Upper Houses: history of the north society of Middletown, Conn., from 1650 to 1800, with genealogical and biographical chapters on early families and a full genealogy of the Ranney family. '08(Ag1) c. il. pors. facsims., 8°, **$10 net. Grafton Press.

Adams, C: Follen.
Yacob Strauss, and other poems. '10 (Ag20) c. il. por. D. $1. Lothrop, L. & S.

Adams, C: Fs.
Physical laboratory manual for secondary schools. Rev. ed. '09(Ag7) c. il. tabs., D. 60 c. Am. Bk.
Physics for secondary schools. '08(O3) c. il. D. $1.20. Am. Bk.
Teacher's manual to accompany Physics for secondary schools. '09(S11) c. D. pap., 25 c. Am. Bk.

Adams, C: Fs., jr.
"The Solid South" and the Afro-American race problem; speech at the Academy of Music, Richmond, Va., Oct. 24, 1908. '09 (My) 8°, pap. (Priv. pr.) C: F. Adams.

Adams, C: Kendall, and Trent, W: Peterfield.
History of the United States. Rev. ed. '09 (Je5) c. il. por. maps, 12°, (Allyn & Bacon's ser. of school histories.) $1.50. Allyn & B.

Adams, Cyrus Cornelius.
Elem. commercial geography. '09(Ja23) c. il. maps, 12°, $1.10. Appleton.
Text-book of commercial geography. '08 (D12) c. il. maps, 12°, (Twentieth century text-books.) **$1.30 net. Appleton.

Adams, D. E., comp.
See Missouri. Index.

Adams, E. J.
See Washington. Adams' briefs.

Adams, Edg. Holmes.
Official premium list of United States private and territorial gold coins. '09(D4) c. il. D. $2; leath., $2.50, boxed. E. H. Adams.

Adams, E: Dean.
Hudson-Fulton medal; designed under direction of the American Numismatic Society; adopted as its one official medal by the Hudson-Fulton Celebration Commission, and issued under the seals of both organizations. '09, [1910.] (Ap.) 8 p. front. 4°. (Add. author for price.) E: D. Adams.

Adams, Ephriam Douglass.
British interests and activities in Texas, 1838-1846; Albert Shaw lectures on diplomatic hist., 1909. '10(My21) c. D. $1.50. Johns Hopkins.

Adams, Ernest Owen.
Diseases of the digestive system. '10(Jl) c. 349 p. 12°, $2. Cleveland Homœopath.

Adams, Fs.
Songs of the army of the night, and The mass of Christ. New and rev. ed. '10 (D3) 12°, $1 net. M. Kennerley.

Adams, Fk. R.
See Harding, J: W.

Adams, F: Upham, comp.
Waters Pierce case in Texas. '08(D) por. O. 25 c. Skinner & K.

Adams, G: Plimpton.
The mystical element in Hegel's early theological writings. '10(O) 67-102 p. O. (Univ. of Cal. pubs.; Philosophy.) pap., 35 c. Univ. of Cal.

Adams, H. Travers.
Physical development in relation to perfect voice production. '09(N) 79 p. 8°, pap., *75 c. net. Scribner.

Adams, H:
Building construction; notes on materials, processes, principles and practice. '08 (N21) il. 8°, *$3 net. Cassell.

Adams, Mrs. Hugh, and Browne, Edith A., eds.
Social calendar, 1910. '10(My14) 12°, $1.25. Macmillan.

Adams, Ja. Orville.
Cruiser; romance of the Idaho timber land frauds. '10(Ja2) c. il. D. J. O. Adams.

Adams, Ja. Truslow.
Some notes on the currency problem. '08, [1909.] (F) c. 35 p. 8°, gratis. Broun-G.

Adams, Rev. J:
Israel's ideal; or, studies in Old Testament theology. '10(Je4) 12°, $1.50 net. Scribner.
Sermons in accents; or, studies in the Hebrew text. '08(Je20) D. *$1.50 net. Scribner

Adams, J:
Exposition and illustration in teaching. '10 (Ja22) c. D. **$1.25 net. Macmillan.

Adams, Jos. H:
Harper's indoor book for boys. '08(Ap18) c. il. O. (Harper's practical books for boys.) $1.75. Harper.
Harper's machinery book for boys. '09 (Ap24) c. il. D. (Harper's practical books for boys.) $1.75. Harper.

Adams, Josephine L.
Character book [record book]. '10(S) 12°, 75 c.; ooze, $1.25. Barse & H.

Adams, Julia J.
Jimmy. '10(D) 100 p. il. 75 c. J. J. Adams.

Adams, Matthew Prior.
Simple physics in every-day life. '07, [1908.] (Jl) c. 197+12 p. 4°. (Add. author for price.) M. P. Adams.

Adams, Oscar Fay.
Motley jest: Shapespearean diversions. '09 (Mr6) c. D. *$1 net. Sherman, F.

Adams, S:
Writings of Samuel Adams; collected and ed. by Harry Alonzo Cushing. Limited ed. In 4 v. v. 4, 1778-1802. '08(Ag8) c. 8°, hf. leath., subs., **$5 net. Putnam.

Adams, S: Hopkins.
Flying death. '08(F8) c. il. D. †$1.50. McClure.

Adams, T:
Sermons; ed. by J: Brown. '09(Ag21) 16°, 45 c. Putnam.

Adams, W. Poynter.
Motor car mechanism and management. pt. 2, Electric and petrol electric vehicles. '08(D19) il. 12°, *$2 net. Lippincott.

Adams, Wa. Sydney.
Investigation of the displacements of the spectrum lines at the sun's limb. '10(Je) 32 p. il. tabs., 4°, (Contributions from the Mount Wilson Solar Observatory.) (Not for sale.) Carnegie.
Spectroscopic investigations of the rotation of the sun during the year 1908. '09 (My) 36 p. il. 8°. (Contributions from the Mount Wilson Solar Observatory.) pap. (Not for sale.) Carnegie.
Summary of the results of a study of the Mount Wilson photographs of sun-spot spectra. '09(D11) tabs., 4°, (Contribs. from the Mount Wilson Solar Observatory.) pap. (Add. Institution for price.) Carnegie.
See also Hale, G: Ellery.

Adams, Washington Irving Lincoln.
Photographing in old England; with some snap shots in Scotland and Wales. '10 (S24) c. il. Q. $2.50 net, boxed. Baker & T.

Adams, W: Ja.
Hints on amalgamation and the general care of gold mills. 2d ed., rev. and enl. '08 (Jl11); 3d ed., rev. and enl. '10(Ja29) c. il. S. leath., ea., $2. Mining and Scientific.

Adams, W: Taylor, ["Oliver Optic."]
Brave old salt. '08(Jl4) 12°, (Young America lib.) 50 c. Hurst.
Building himself up; or, the cruise of the "Fish Hawk." '10(Je4) il. 12°, $1. Lothrop, L. & S.
Fighting Joe. '08(Jl11) 12°, (Young America lib.) 50 c. Hurst.
Louis Chiswick's mission. '10(O) il 12°, $1. Lothrop, L. & S.
Lyon Hart's heroism. '10(O) il. 12°, $1. Lothrop, L. & S.
Professor's son. '10(O) il. 12°, $1. Lothrop, L. & S.
Royal Tarr's pluck. '10(O) il. 12°, $1. Lothrop, L. & S.
Striving for his own. '10(O) il. 12°, $1. Lothrop, L. & S.
Yankee middy. '08(Je27) 12°, (Young America lib.) 50 c. Hurst
Young lieutenant. '08(Je6) 12°, (Young America lib.) 50 c. Hurst.
Work and win. '08(Jl18) 12°, (Young America lib.) 50 c. Hurst.

Adams prize essay. *See* Brown, Ernest W.

Adaptation of the schools to industry and efficiency. Draper, A. S. gratis. A. S. Draper.

Adcock, Ja. Pringle.
Wooing in rusticity. '09(O) 288 p. 12°, $1.50. Adcock.

Addams, Jane.
Spirit of youth in our city streets. '09 (N6) c. D. **$1.25 net. Macmillan.
Twenty years in Hull House; with autobiographical notes. '10(D3) c. il. pors. O. $2.50 net. Macmillan.
See also Stelzle, C:

Added interest tables, 1909. Fisher, J: I. $5. J: I. Fisher.

Addingley, Amy, comp.
In friendship's meditation. '10(O1) c. S. 75 c., boxed; ooze, $1.50, boxed. Platt & P.

Addington, Keene H., ed. and rep.
See Illinois. *Appellate cts.* Repts.—Notes on the repts.

Addison, Jos., and Steele, R:
Coverley papers from the *Spectator;* ed., with introd. and notes, by O. M. Myers. '08(D12) facsim., D. 50 c. Oxford Univ.
Selections from *The Spectator;* ed. by J. H. Lobban. '10(Ag13) 12°, 40 c. net. Putnam.

Addison, Jos., and Steele, R:—*Continued.*
Sir Roger de Coverley; ed. by T: Cartwright. '08(Ag15) 16°, (Every child's lib.) 50 c. Dutton.
Sir Roger de Coverley papers, from the *Spectator;* ed., with introd. and notes, by J: Calvin Metcalf. [1910.] (Je) c. 28+208 p. pors. map, 16°, (Johnson ser. of English classics.) 25 c. B. F. Johnson.
The Spectator. 4 v. '08(O17) 16°, (Best books ser.) leath., *$1 net. Dutton.
The Spectator; ed. by G: Atherton Aitken. In 8 v. vs. 1-6. '08(Je6) 12°, (New Universal lib.) 50 c.; leath., 75 c. Dutton.
The Spectator; essays 1-50; with an introd. and notes J: Morrison. '08(N21) 16°, *50 c. net. Macmillan.
—, Steele, Sir R:, and Budgell, Eustace.
Sir Roger de Coverley papers in the *Spectator;* ed., with notes, outline study and examination questions, by Maud Elma Kingsley and Fk. Herbert Palmer. '10 (My7) c. 16°, (Kingsley English texts.) 40 c. Palmer Co.
ADDISON, Joseph.
Macaulay, T: B. Life and writings of Addison; Samuel Johnson. **25 c. net. Scribner.
See also Spectator (The).
Addison, Mrs. Julia De Wolf Gibbs.
Arts and crafts in the Middle Ages; with some account of special artisans in the early Renaissance. '08(O3) c. il. O. $3, boxed. L. C. Page.
Boston Museum of Fine Arts; giving a descriptive and critical acct. of its treasures, which represent the arts and crafts from remote antiquity to the present time. '10 (Jl16) il. pors. plans, 12°, boxed, $3. L. C. Page.
Mrs. John Vernon: a study of a social situation. '08(D12) c. front. D. $1.50. Badger.
Addleshaw, W: Percy.
Sir Philip Sidney. '09(D11) il. O. *$3.50 net. Putnam.
Addresses and letters of travel. Nye, S. G. (Add. pubs. for price.) Stanley-T.
Addresses from a Glasgow pulpit. Morrison, G. H. *$1.50 net. Armstrong.
Addresses on notable occasions. Fowler, C: H: *$1.50 net. Jennings.
Addresses to teachers. Beale, D. 50 c. Longmans.
ADELAIDE, Eugénie Louisa, *Princess* d'Orleans.
Arnaud, R. Louis-Philippe and his sister. [Adelaide of Orleans.] *$4.20 net. Scribner.
Adelborg, Ottilia.
Clean Peter and the children of Grubbylea; tr. by Ada Wallas. [New ed.] '10(S24) il. in col. obl. D. $1.25. Longmans.
"Adeler, Max," pseud.
See Clark, C: Heber.
Adeney, Wa. F:, D.D.
Greek and Eastern Churches. '09(Ja9) O. (International theological lib.) *$2.50 net. Scribner.
ADENOMYOMA.
See Tumors.
Adiassewich, A.
English prices with Russian equivalents, calculated at fourteen rates of exchange in roubles per pood; giving rate per lb. and equivalents per ton. '09(Ap3) 32°, 50 c. Spon.
ADIRONDACK MOUNTAINS, N. Y.
Hardie, G: R. Where to go in the Adirondacks. 25 c. G: R. Hardie.
See also Fire.
Adjusting and repairing violins. Broadley, A. 40 c. Scribner.
Adler, Cyrus, and Casanowicz, Immanuel Moses.
Collection of Jewish ceremonial objects in the United States National Museum. '08 (O10) il. O. pap. (Add. Supt. for price.) U. S., Supt. of Docs.
Adler, Elkan Nathan.
Auto de fé and Jew; [bound with a pamphlet on the Inquisition in Peru published in Baltimore.] '08(N21) tabs., facsims., O. bds., $1.75. Oxford Univ.
Adler, Felix.
See Dewey, J:
Adler, Herbert M., and Davis, Arth., eds.
Service of the synagogue; new ed. of the festival prayers with an English tr. in prose and verse. 6 v. '09(N) 8°, $15. H. D. Buegeleisen.
Adler, Hermann, D.D.
Anglo-Jewish memories, and other sermons. '09(Ag21) 8°, *$1.50 net. Bloch.
Administration of estates in Texas. Simkins, W: S. $5.25. Von Boeckmann-J.
Administration of justice in the United States. American Academy of Political and Social Science. $1. Am. Acad. Pol. Sci.
Administration of public education in the United States. Dutton, S: T. *$1.75 net. Macmillan.
Administrative and industrial organization. Griffith, J. B. 50 c. Am. Sch. Corr.
ADMINISTRATIVE LAW.
See Law.
Administrative problems of British India. Chailley-Bert, J. $3.25 net. Macmillan.
ADMINISTRATORS.
See Executors and administrators.
Admirable Bashville. *See* Shaw, G: Bernard.
Admiral's little housekeeper. Gould, E. L. $1. Penn Pub. Co.
Admiral's log. Evans, R. D. **$2 net. Appleton.
ADMIRALTY.
Ashburner, W. Rhodian sea-law. $5.75. Oxford Univ.
Benedict, E. C. American admiralty, its jurisdiction and practice. $6.30. Banks & Co.
Admiralty of the Atlantic. Hislam, P. A. *$2 net. Longmans.
Admission of Chinese students to American colleges. Fryer, J. (Add. Superintendent for price.) U. S., Supt. of Docs.
Adonis, Attis, Osiris. Frazer, J. G: *$3.25 net. Macmillan.
Adopting of Rosa Marie. Rankin, *Mrs.* C. W. †$1.50. Holt.
Adoption. Chapin, H. L. $1.25. H. L. Chapin.
Adoption of the fourteenth amendment. Flack, H. E. $2. Johns Hopkins.

Adriaans, J: H:
Has a negro the right to vote?; or, the validity of the 14th amendment to the U. S. Constitution denied. '08(D12) c. 8°. (Add. author for price.) J: H: Adriaans.

ADRIATIC SEA.
See Austria-Hungary.

Adrift on an ice-pan. Grenfell, *Sir* W. T. **75 c. net. Houghton M.

Adrift on the Pacific. Rockwood, R. 60 c. Grosset.

Adult Bible class. Pearce, W: C. 25 c. Westminster.

Adult male alto. Stubbs, G: E: 75 c. H. W. Gray.

ADULTERATION.
See Food adulteration.

Advance agent. McCarthy, M. 75 c. Excelsior.

ADVENT.
See Second advent.

Advent, Christmas, New Year, Easter, and other sermons. MacArthur, R. S. $1. Am. Bapt.

Advent of Arthur. Hunt, E. L. $2. Lippincott.

Adventure in exile. Duffy, R: $1.50. B. W. Dodge.

Adventure of Lady Ursula. Hawkins, A. H. 50 c. S: French.

Adventure ser. il. D. *$1.50 net. Lippincott
—Cody. On trail and rapid. $1 net.
—Hyrst. Adventures among wild beasts.—Adventures in the Arctic regions.
—Stead. Adventures on the high seas.

Adventurers in America. Moncrieff, A. R. H. $1.75. Macmillan.

Adventures among red Indians. Wright, S. H. $1.50 net. Lippincott.

Adventures among the Arabs. Forder, A. $1. Gospel Pub.

Adventures among wild beasts. Wright, S. H. *$1.50 net. Lippincott.

Adventures at sea; by F. H. Converse, J: R. Coryell, Rear-Admiral T. H. Stevens, Maria Louise Pool, and others. '08(N14) c. il. D. (Young people ser.) †60 c. Harper.

Adventures every child should know. *See* Lorenzini, Carlo.

Adventures in field and forest; by Fk. H. Spearman, Harold Martin, F. S. Palmer, W: Drysdale, and others. '09(Mr20) c. il. D. (Harper's young people ser.) 60 c. Harper.

Adventures in friendship. Grayson, D:, *pseud.* $1.20, fixed. Doubleday, P.

Adventures in home making. Shackleton, R. $1.75. Lane.

Adventures in London. Douglas, J. **$1.75 net. Cassell.

Adventures in socialism. Cullen, A. $2 net. Macmillan.

Adventures in the Arctic regions. Hyrst, H. W. G. *$1.50 net. Lippincott.

Adventures of a brownie. *See* Craik, *Mrs.* Dinah Maria Mulock.

Adventures of a dodo. Farrow, G: E: $1.25. Wessels.

Adventures of a green dragon. Osborne, T: M. (Priv. pr.) Auburn Pub.

Adventures of a nice young man. Aix, *pseud.* †$1.50. Duffield.

Adventures of an A. D. C. Bradley, S. $1.50. Lane.

Adventures of Borbee and the Wisp. Upton, F. K. *$1.50 net. Longmans.

Adventures of Charles Edward. Rhodes, H. G. †$1.50. Little, B. & Co.

Adventures of Dumpy Dimple and his dog! Byron, M. 50 c. Stokes.

Adventures of Gil Blas. *See* Le Sage, Alain René.

Adventures of "Jack" Cribbs. Cribbs, J: W: 3 v. ea., 50 c. Clarion Democrat.

Adventures of John Johns. Carrel, F. $1.50. M. Kennerley.

Adventures of Lady Susan. Brady, C. T. †$1.50. Moffat.

Adventures of Little Knight Brave. Rees, F. B. †$1.50. Appleton.

Adventures of Louis Blake. Becke, G: L: $1.50. Lippincott.

Adventures of Pathfinder. Haight, M. N., *comp.* 35 c. Am. Bk.

Adventures of pirates and sea-rovers; by Howard Pyle, Rear-Admiral J. H. Upshur, Paul Hull, Reginald Gourley, and others. '08(Je20) c. il. D. (Harper's young people ser.) 60 c. Harper.

Adventures of Princess Sylvia. Williamson, *Mrs.* A. M. L. Metropolitan Press, (N. Y.)

Adventures of Robinson Crusoe. *See* Defoe, Dan.

Adventures of the North. Parker, *Sir* G. $1.25. Harper.

Adventures of the world's greatest detectives. Barton, G: 75 c. Winston.

Adventures of Tom Sawyer. *See* Clemens, S: Langhorne.

Adventures of Tommy Postoffice. Jackson, *Mrs.* G. E. $1.25. Dutton.

Adventures of two ants. Hammerström, N. $1. Stokes.

Adventures on the high seas. Stead, R: *$1.50 net. Lippincott.

Adventures with four-footed friends. Brain, B. M. *$1.25 net. Revell.

Adventures with Indians; by Philip V. Mighels, W. O. Stoddard, Major G. B. Davis, Frances McElrath and others. '08(F1) c. il. D. (Harper's young people ser.) 60 c. Harper.

Advertisements of *The Spectator.* Lewis, L. $2. Houghton M.

Advertiser's hdbk.; book of reference dealing with plans, copy, typography, illustration, mediums, management, and other details of advertising practice. '10(D3) c. T. $1.25; leath., $1.50. Int. Textbk.

ADVERTISING.
Ayer, N. W., & Son. 1869-1909: forty years of advertising. (Add. pubs. for price.) Ayer.
Balmer, E. Science of advertising. 25 c. E. Balmer.
Balmer, E. *and* T. Science of advertising. 50 c. net. Duffield.
Bellamy, F., *ed.* Effective magazine advertising. *$5 net. M. Kennerley.
Borsodi, W:, *ed.* Advertisers cyclopedia of selling phrases. $15.—Financial advertising. $2. Adv. Cyclo.

ADVERTISING.—*Continued.*
Bridgewater, H. Advertising. 50 c. Pitman.
Bunting, H: S. Specialty advertising. Novelty News.
Chapman, C. Law of advertising and sales. 2 v. $10. C. Chapman.
De Weese, T. A. Principles of practical publicity. **$2 net. Jacobs.
Edgar, A. E. How to advertise a retail store. $3.50. Outing Press.
Egan, J. W: Five practical chapters on retail advertising. (Add. pubs. for price.) J. W: Egan.
Farrington, F. Retail advertising. $1. Byxbee Pub.
French, G: Art and science of advertising. **$2 net.. Sherman, F.
Griffith, J. B. Advertising and sales organization. 50 c. Am. Sch. Corr.
Hawkins, G: H: E: Poster advertising. $3. G: H: E: Hawkins.
Holeproof Hosiery Co., Milwaukee, Wis. New ideas in merchandising, for the retailers of America. [1910.] (F) c. '09. 91 p. il. 12°, $1. Holeproof.
Lewis, E. S. Financial advertising. $5. Levey.
Lewis, H: H., *and* Duff, O. S., *comp.* How fortunes are made in advertising. $1. Publicity.
Lewis, L. Advertisements of *The Spectator.* $2. Houghton M.
MacGregor, T. D. Pushing your business; text-book of advertising. $1. Bankers Pub.
Mahin advertising data book. $2. Mahin Adv.
Murdoch, G: H. Building a law business; how to advertise. $10. Murdoch Law, (N. J.)
Pratt, W: K. Advertising manual. $3.50. D. Stern.
Scott, W. D. Psychology of advertising. **$2 net. Small.
Starch, D. Principles of advertising. $1. Univ. Co-op.
Stryker, A. M. Advertiser's hdbk. written and comp according to the latest advertising knowledge. $1. Trade Journ.
Thompson, J. Walter, Co. J. W. T. book: series of talks on advertising. '09(N) c. 63 p. il. 12°. (Add. pubs. for price.) J. W. Thompson.
Thompson, W: A. Druggists' and dispensers practical show card. $1. W: A. Thompson.
Westermann, L. A., Company. Drawings made for commercial use. gratis. Westermann.
See also Banks and banking;—Church (The);—Lettering;—Window dressing.

Advice to consumptives. Bardswell, N. D. 75 c. net. Macmillan.
Advisability of electing United States senators by popular ballot. Mohn, E. J: (Priv. pr.) Georgetown Univ.

ADVOCACY.
See Pleading and practice.

Ady, Mrs. H:
See Cartwright, Julia.

Aechte deutsche kochkunst. Meier, *Mrs.* L. W. $2.50. L. W. Meier.
Aegean echoes. Crew, H. C. $1.50. Badger.
Æneid. *See* **Virgil, Maro Publius.**
Æneid for boys and girls. Church, A. J: †$1.50. Macmillan.

AERIAL NAVIGATION.
Alexander, J. H. Model balloons and flying machines. $1.50. Henley.
Berget, T: C. X. A. Conquest of the air. **$3.50 net. Putnam.
Brackett, P. Bibliography of aeronautics. $2.25; $2. Smith. Inst.
Brewer, R. W. A. Art of aviation. $3.50. McGraw-H.
Brooklyn Public Library. Aeronautics; list of books and references to periodicals in the Library. gratis. Brooklyn Lib.
Chatley, H. How to design an aeroplane. 50 c. Van Nostrand.
Collins, F. A. Boy's book of model aeroplanes. $1.20 net. Century Co.
Delacombe, H. Boys' book of air-ships. $2. Stokes.
Epitome of the *Aeronautical Annual.* $1. W: B. Clarke.
Ferris, R: How it flies. $1.20 net. Nelson.
Hatch, D. S. Aërial navigation. $1. Am. Sch. Corr.
Hearne, R. P. Airships in peace and war. *$3.50 net. Lane.
Hildebrandt, A. Airships past and present. *$3 net. Van Nostrand.
Jackman, W. J., *and* Russell, T: H. Flying machines, construction and operation. $1; $1.50. C: C. Thompson.
Johnson, V. E. Theory and practice of model aeroplanning. $1.50. Spon.
Kasmar, M. K. First lessons in aeronautics. $2. Am. Aero. Soc.
Kennedy, D. R. Aeroplane portfolio. 50 c. net. Spon.
Lanchester, F. W. Aerial flight. 2 v. *$6 net. Van Nostrand.
Langley, S: P. Researches and experiments in aerial navigation. (Add. pubs. for price.) U. S., Supt. of Docs.
Lougheed, V. Vehicles of the air. *$2.50 net. Reilly & B.
Maxim, *Sir* H. S. Artificial and natural flight. *$1.75 net. Macmillan.
Morgan, A. P. How to build a 20 ft. biplane glider. 50 c. Spon.
Mowbray, J. H: Conquest of the air by airships and other flying machines. $1.50. Nat. Pub. Co.
Petit, R. How to build an aeroplane. $1.50 net. Van Nostrand.
Pierce, P. Monoplane-drawing with descriptive matter. 15 c. Spon.
Rotch, A. L. Benjamin Franklin and the first balloons. (Not for sale.) A. L. Rotch.
Rotch, A. L. Conquest of the air. **$1 net. Moffat.
Squier, G: O. Present status of military aeronautics. 80 c. Am. Soc. Mech. Engineers.
Turner, C: C. Aerial navigation of today. *$1.50 net. Lippincott.

AERIAL NAVIGATION.—*Continued.*
Twining, E. W. Model aeroplanes.—Model gliders, birds, butterflies and aeroplanes. ea., 50 c. Spon.
See also Air;—Kites;—War;—Wind.

AERIAL TRAMWAYS.
See Wire rope transportation.

Aerial warfare. Hearne, R. P. *$2.50 net. Lane.

AERONAUTICS.
See Aërial navigation.

Aeroplane boys ser. See Lamar, Ashton.

Aeroplane express. Lamar, A. 60 c. Reilly & B.

Aeschylus.
Eumenides of Æschylus; with an introd., commentary and translation by Arth. Woollgar Verrall. '08(My16) 8°, *$3 net. Macmillan.
Plays; tr. by Wa. Headlam and C. E. S. Headlam. '09(D25) 12°, (Bohn's libraries.) *$1 net. Macmillan.
Seven against Thebes; with introd., critical notes, commentary, translation and a recension of the Medicean Scholia by T. G. Tucker. '08(N7) 8°, *$3 net. Putnam.
Suppliant maidens; The Persians; The seven against Thebes; The Prometheus bound; tr. in Eng. verse by Edmund Doidge Anderson Morshead. '08(My9) 16°, (Golden treasury ser.) $1. Macmillan.

ÆSCHYLUS.
Harry, J. E: Problems in the Prometheus. 50 c. Univ. of Cin.

Aesop.
Fables. '10(D10) col. il. 4°, vel., $20 net. (500 copies.) Doran.
Fables. '08(S5) il. O. bds., 50 c. Stokes.
Fables. '08(O3) il. Q. (Dandelion classics for children.) †$1.50. Stokes.
Fables, told to children by Lena Dalkeith. '08(Je6) il. 16°, (Told to the children ser.) 50 c. Dutton.

Æsopic fables in the Mireoir Historical of Jehan de Vignay. Snavely, G. E. gratis. Johns Hopkins.

ÆSTHETICS.
Balfour, A. J. Questionings on criticism and beauty. 70 c. Oxford Univ.
Croce, B. Æsthetic as science of expression and general linguistic. *$3 net. Macmillan.
Furry, W: D. Æsthetic experience: its nature and function. $1.60. Johns Hopkins.
Gordon, K. Esthetics. $1.50. Holt.
Hogarth, W: Analysis of beauty. *$1.50 net. Silver Lotus.
Howard, W: G., *ed.* Laokoon. $1.50. Holt.
See also Criticism;—Fine arts;—Music.

ÆTHER.
See Ether.

Affair of dishonor. De Morgan, W: F. $1.75. Holt.

Affinities who never meet. Verland, F. 25 c. Homingwood.

Affinity. Raum, H. A. $1.50. H. A. Raum.

AFGHANISTAN.
Bouillane de Lacoste, E. A. H. de. Around Afghanistan. $3 special net. Appleton.

AFGHANISTAN.—*Continued.*
Martin, F: A. Under the absolute Amir. *$2.25 net. Harper.
Pennell, T. L. Among the wild tribes of the Afghan frontier. *$3.50 net. Lippincott.

Aflalo, F: G:
Sunset playgrounds: fishing days and others in California and Canada. '09 (My15) il. O. *$2.25 net. Scribner.

Afloat and ashore. Cooper, J. F. 50 c. Hurst.

Afloat in freedom's cause. Kaler, J. O. †$1. Burt.

Afloat in the forest. *See* Reid, *Captain* Mayne.

AFRICA.
Baird, J. B. Children of Africa. 60 c. net. Revell.
Brodhead, *Mrs.* C. A. S., *ed.* Our free Methodist missions in Africa. $1. Aldine Pr.
Bronson, E. B. In closed territory. *$1.75 net. McClurg.
Burton, R: F. First footsteps in East Africa. 35 c. net; 70 c. net. Dutton.
Camphor, A. P. Missionary story sketches, folk-lore from Africa. *$1.50 net. Jennings.
Chapman, A. On safari: big game hunting in British East Africa. *$4.50 net. Longmans.
Churchill, W. S. My African journey. *$1.50 net. Doran.
Dearborn, N. Catalogue of a collection of birds from British East Africa. 50 c. Field Museum.
Dickinson, F. A. Lake Victoria to Khartoum. *$4 net. Lane.
Donaldson, S. A. Church life and thought in North Africa. *$1.25 net. Putnam.
Dugmore, A. R. Camera adventures in the African wilds. **$6 net. Doubleday, P.
Forbes, E. A. Land of the white helmet. $1.50 net. Revell.
Guggisberg, *Mrs.* L. D. M. *and* F: G. We two in West Africa. *$3.50 net. Scribner.
Heller, E. Five new rodents from British East Africa. Smith. Inst.
Kirkland, C. Some African highways. $1.50. Estes.
Knox, T: W. In wild Africa: [fiction.] †$1.50. Wilde.
Lambert, J: C. Missionary heroes in Africa. *75 c. net. Lippincott.
Lang, J: Land of the golden trade (West Africa). $2 net. Stokes.
Lowe, F. J. Around Africa and across the Andes. 50 c. F. J. Lowe.
Lundeberg, A., *and* Seymour, F: Great Roosevelt African hunt and the wild animals of Africa. $1.75. D. B. McCurdy.
McCutcheon, J: T. In Africa. $3. Bobbs-M.
MacQueen, P: In wildest Africa. $3. L. C. Page.
Mecklenburg-Strelitz, A. F., *Duke* of. In the heart of Africa. $5 net. Cassell.

AFRICA.—*Continued.*
Miller, G. S. New rodent of the genus Saccestomus from British East Africa. Smith. Inst.
Miller, J. M. Hunting big game in the wilds of Africa; cont. thrilling adventures of the famous Roosevelt expedition. $1.50. Nat. Pub. Co.
Milligan, R. H. Jungle folk of Africa. *$1.50 net. Revell.
Mowbray, J. H: Roosevelt's marvelous exploits in the wilds of Africa. $1. G: W. Bertron.
Neil, H: Roosevelt's thrilling experiences in the wilds of Africa. $2. Bible House.
Patterson, J: H: In the grip of the Nyika. **$2 net.—Man-eaters of Tsavo. *$2 net. Macmillan.
Rainsford, W: S. Land of the lion. **$3.80 net. Doubleday, P.
Roosevelt, T. African game trails. $4 net. Scribner.
Selous, F: C. African nature notes and reminiscences. *$2 net. Macmillan.
Seymour, F: Roosevelt in Africa. $2; $2.75. Educ. Co.
Shoemaker, M. M. Islam lands. $2.50 net. Putnam.
Springer, J: M. Heart of Central Africa; mineral wealth and missionary opportunity. *$1 net. Jennings.
Springer, *Mrs.* J: M. Snap shots from sunny Africa. *$1 net. Revell.
Stratton, C. R. Picturesque Asia and Africa. $1. Nat. Pub. Co.
Swann, A. J. Fighting the slave-hunters in Central Africa. *$3.50 net. Lippincott.
Tjader, R: Big game of Africa. $3 net. Appleton.
Vischer, H. Across the Sahara from Tripoli to Bornu. $3.50 net. Longmans.
Weule, J. K. K. Native life in East Africa. *$4.50 special net. Appleton.
Wollaston, A. F. R-. From Ruwenzori to the Congo. *$5 net. Dutton.
See also Abyssinia;—Algeria;—Bedouins;—Congo Free State;—Egypt;—Mammalia; — Morocco;— Nandi; — Negroes; — Niger river; — Nubia;— Orangia; — Rhodesia; — Ruwenzori; — Sahara desert;—Sierra Leone; — Soudan;—Slavery; — South Africa;—Tripoli; — Tunis;—Uganda; — Yoruba.
African and European addresses. Roosevelt, T. $1.50 net. Putnam.
AFRICAN METHODIST EPISCOPAL CHURCH.
Butt, I. L. History of African Methodism in Virginia. $1. I. L. Butt.
African mimetic butterflies. Eltringham, H. $15. Oxford Univ.
African nature notes. Selous, F: C. *$3 net. Macmillan.
AFRO-AMERICANS.
See Negroes.
After big game in Arctic and tropic. Fleischmann, M. C: (Priv. pr.) M. C: Fleischmann.
After care (The) of the insane. Beers, C. W. gratis. C. W. Beers.
After death—what? Lombroso, C. **$2.50 net. Small.
After-dinner sleights and pocket tricks. Neil, C. L. 50 c. Lippincott.
After hour idyls. Steele, F: M. $3. Smith & S.
After prison—what? Booth, *Mrs.* M. B. C. *$1.25 net. Revell.
After sunrise. Wagner, P. M. $1. P. M. Wagner.
After the cataclysm. Blanchard, H: P. $1.25. Cochrane.
After the confession. Danziger, G. A. (Add. author for price.) G. A. Danziger.
After the pardon. Serao, M. $1.50. Stuyvesant Press.
After Waterloo. Frye, W: E: (Add. pubs. for price.) P. R. Reynolds.
Afternoons. Snow, *Mrs.* J. F. $1.20; $1.25. Ulbrich.
Against the current. Steiner, E: A. $1.25 net. Revell.
Agar, T: Leyden-.
Homerica: emendations and elucidations of the Odyssey. '08(O24) O. $4.75. Oxford Univ.
AGASSIZ MUSEUM, Cambridge, Mass.
See Harvard University.
AGATHOCLES.
Tillyard, H: J. W. Agathocles. *$1.50 net. Putnam.
Agathos. Wilberforce, S: *45 c. net. Putnam.
Age (L') d'or de la litterature française. 90 c. Heath.
Age of fable. *See* Bulfinch, T:
Age of gold. Campbell, L. E. *$1.25 net. Whitaker & R.
Age of Louis XIV. *See* Acton, J: E. E: D.-A., *Lord.*
Age of mammals. Osborn, H: F. $4.50 net. Macmillan.
Age of mental virility. Borland, W: A. N. **$1 net. Century Co.
Age of quickened conscience. Angell, J. B. Univ. of Mich.
Age of Shakespeare. Swinburne, A. C: **$2 net. Harper.
Age of the earth. Becker, G: F. 5 c. Smith. Inst.
Age of truth and right Stearns, I: N. $1.50. I: N. Stearns.
Age to come. **Lay, W: A.** 25 c. W: A. **Lay.**
AGENTS.
See Business;—Insurance;—Principal and agent.
Ager, Waldemar Theodor.
Hverdagsfolk. '08(Jl) c. 96 p. 12°, 25 c. Fremad.
Agnes Grey. *See* Brontë, Anne.
Agnetti, Mary Prichard.
Vincenza: the home of "The Saint"; with a preface by Antonio Fogazzaro. '10 (O1) il. [in col.] 8°, $3.50 net. Doran.
Agnew, Paul G.
Approximate experimental method for the analysis of E. M. F. waves, [April 5, 1909.] '09, [1910.] (Mr) 95-106 p. il. 4°, pap. (Add. Superintendent for price.) U. S., Supt. of Docs.
Agnostic in medicine. Ward, J. W: Murdock Press.
AGNOSTICISM.
Fitchett, W: H: Beliefs of unbelief. *$1.25 net. Eaton & M.
Ingersoll, R. G. The ghosts.—The gods. ea., 25 c. Farrell.

Agnus, Felix.
Woman of war, and other stories. '08(My.) c. 209 p. il. 12°. (Add. author for price.) F. Agnus.

Agnus, Orme.
Sarah Tuldon. '08(My.) c. 12°, (Popular ed. of recent fiction.) †75 c. Little, B. & Co.

Agricola (The). *See* Tacitus, Caius Cornelius.

Agricultural bacteriology. Russell, H. L. $1.25. H. L. Russell.

Agricultural Blue Book and the Live Stock Breeders' directory of the United States. '10(Ja22) c. 8°, $1. Hale Pub.

AGRICULTURAL CHEMISTRY.
Hatch, K. L. Simple exercises illustrating some applications of chemistry to agriculture. 15 c. U. S., Supt. of Docs.
Ingle, H. Elem. agricultural chemistry. *$1.50 net. Lippincott.
Jensen, C: A. Seasonal nitrification as influenced by crops and tillage. Gov. Pr. Off.
Lincoln, A. T:, *and* Walton, J. H., *jr.* Exercises in elem. quantitative analysis for students of agriculture. *$1.50 net. Macmillan.
United States. *Dept. of Agriculture. Bu. of Soils.* Reference list on the electric fixation of atmospheric nitrogen and the use of calcium cyanamid and calcium nitrate on soils.
Wiley, H. W. Principles and practice of agricultural analysis. v. 2. $4.50. Chemical.
See also Bacteria;—Fertilizers;—Paris green;—Soils.

AGRICULTURAL MACHINERY.
Casson, H. N. Romance of the reaper. **$1 net. Doubleday, P.
Davidson, J. B., *and* Chase, L. W. Farm machinery and farm motors. $2. Judd.
Gas Traction Co., Minneapolis. Modern farming; the passing of the horse. gratis. Gas Traction.
Thwaites, R. G. Cyrus Hall McCormick and the reaper. 50 c. State Hist., Wis.
United States. *Dept. of Commerce and Labor.* American agricultural implements in Europe, Asia, and Africa, by Roland R. Dennis. '09(Je) 88 p. il. 8°, pap. (Add. Superintendent for price.)

AGRICULTURE.
Aaronsohn, A. Agricultural and botanical explorations in Palestine. Gov. Pr. Off.
Abbey, G: Balance of nature and modern conditions of cultivation. *$2 net. Dutton.
Abbey, M. J. Normal school instruction in agriculture. (Add. Superintendent for price.) U. S., Supt. of Docs.
Agricultural Blue Book and the Live Stock Breeders' Directory of the United States of America. $1. Hale Pub.
American agriculturist handbook. 50 c. Judd.
Bailey, L. H. College of agriculture and the state. gratis. L. H. Bailey.
Bailey, L. H. On the training of persons to teach agriculture in the public schools. pap., 15 c. U. S., Supt. of Docs.

AGRICULTURE.—*Continued.*
Bailey, L. H. Principles of agriculture. **$1.25 net. Macmillan.
Bailey, L. H., *ed.* Cyclopedia of American agriculture. In 4 v. v. 3, 4. ea., **$5 net; per set, **$20 net; **$32 net. Macmillan.
Barto, D. O. Manual of agriculture for secondary schools. 50 c. Heath.
Batten's agricultural directory. $1. Batten.
Buckham, M. H: Agriculture in the high school. gratis. M. H. Buckham.
Bull, C. P. Rural school agriculture. 60 c. C. P. Bull.
Burkett, C: W: Farm crops. $1.50. Judd.
Burritt, M. C. Agricultural conditions in southern New York. Gov. Pr. Off.
Chilcott, E. C. Study of cultivation methods and crop rotations for the Great Plains area. Gov. Pr. Off.
Collins, T. B. New agriculture. $2. Munn.
Cook, O. F. Vegetation affected by agriculture in Central America. (Add. Superintendent for price.) U. S., Supt. of Docs.
Copeland, E. B. Elements of Philippine agriculture. 96 c. World Bk.
Coulter, J: L. Organization among the farmers of the United States. 10 c. Yale Pub.
Coulter, J: M., *and others.* Pract. nature study and elem. agriculture. $1.35. Appleton.
Crosby, D. J. School exercises in plant production. Gov. Pr. Off.
Curtler, W. H. R. Short history of English agriculture. $2.15. Oxford Univ.
Davenport, E. Next step in agricultural education. gratis. E. Davenport.
Draper, A. S. Agriculture and its educational needs. 50 c. Bardeen.
Duggar, J: F: Agriculture for southern schools. *75 c. net.—Virginia supplement to Agriculture for southern schools *12 c. net. Macmillan.
Earle, F. S. Southern agriculture. **$1.25 net. Macmillan.
Ferguson, A. M., *and* Lewis, L. L. Elementary principles of agriculture. $1. Ferguson Pub. Co.
Fisher, M. L., *and* Cotton, F. A. Agriculture for common schools. $1. Scribner.
Flowers, W: T: Farmer and his relation to the country. 50 c. W: T: Flowers.
Hamilton, J: Address on better agriculture and how to get it. (Add. pubs. for price.) N. B. Critchfield.
Hamilton, J: Progress in agricultural education extension. Gov. Pr. Off.
Hatch, K. L., *and others.* Elem. agriculture. 40 c. Row, P. & Co.
Hays, W. M. Agriculture, industries, and home economics in our public schools. gratis. Nat. Educ. Assoc.
Hays, W. M. Co-operation in agriculture. U. S., Supt. of Docs.
Hays, W. M. Farm development. $1.50. Judd.
Hilgard, E. W., *and* Osterhout, W. J. V. Agriculture for schools of the Pacific slope. **$1 net. Macmillan.

AGRICULTURE.—*Continued.*

Hill, J. J. Address del. before the Farmers' National Congress, Madison, Wis., Sept. 24, 1908. gratis. Farmers' Nat.

Institutions in the United States giving instruction in agriculture. '10(Jl) 15 p. 8°, (U. S., Dept. of Agri., Office of Experiment Stations, cir.) Gov. Pr. Off.

International Institute of Agriculture. International crop-reporting service. (Add. Superintendent for price.) U. S., Supt. of Docs.

Ivins, L. S. Agriculture in the public schools. 35 c. March.

Jackson, C. R., and Daugherty, A. C. Agriculture through the laboratory and school garden. *$1.50 net. Judd.

Jewell, J. R. Agricultural education. U. S., Supt. of Docs.

Knapp, S. A. Demonstration work on southern farms. Gov. Pr. Off.

List of periodicals currently received in the library of the U. S. Dept. of Agriculture; arr. by title and by subject. '09, [1910.] (Mr) 72 p. 8°, (U. S., Dept. of Agriculture, Library, bull.) pap. (Add. Superintendent for price.)

Long, H. C., *and* Percival, J: Common weeds of the farm and garden. $2 net. Stokes.

Macmillan standard agricultural library. 9 v. per set, $10 net. Macmillan.

Main, J. Manual for high schools; with special reference to science and agriculture. gratis. J. Main.

Massachusetts Agricultural College, Amherst. Short Course Dept. List of books on agriculture. gratis. W. D. Hind.

Nolan, A. W. One hundred lessons in elementary agriculture. 65 c. Acme.

Organization, work and publications of the Agricultural Education Service. (Add. Superintendent for price.) U. S., Supt. of Docs.

Perry, S. P. Tariff and the farmer. 50 c. F. S. Blanchard.

Portland (Ore.) Library Association. List of books on agriculture, gratis. Portland (Ore.) L. A.

Public school agriculture, 1909. gratis. R. J. Watts.

Smith, M. Agricultural graphics. Gov. Pr. Off.

Snyder, J. L. Agriculture and democracy Mich. Agricultural Coll.

Soule, A. M., *and* Turpin, E. H. L. Agriculture. 75 c. B. F. Johnson.

Stockbridge, H. E: Land teaching; hdbk. of soils, plants, gardens and grounds. $1. Southern Ruralist.

Taylor, C: M. Touring Alaska and the Yellowstone. *$1.25 net. Jacobs.

Thomas, T. G: Modern guide for fruit and truck shippers and poultry raisers in the southern states. $2. Thomas-W.

True, A. C: Notes on the history of agricultural pedagogy in U. S. gratis. T: F. Hunt.

AGRICULTURE.—*Continued.*

True, A. C: Secondary education in agriculture in the United States. (Add. Superintendent for price.) U. S., Supt. of Docs.

True, A. C:, *and* Crosby, D. J. American system of agricultural education. (Add. Superintendent for price.) U. S., Supt. of Docs.

Tucker, G. M. American agricultural periodicals. (Priv. pr.) G. M. Tucker.

United States. *Dept. of Agriculture.* Agriculture: list of publications of the United States Agriculture Department. gratis.

United States. *Dept. of Agriculture.* Boys' and girls' agricultural clubs.

United States. *Dept. of Agriculture.* Experiment Station Office: bulletins, circulars, Experiment Station record, and reports of colonial experiment stations; Agriculture Dept., U. S. A.; for sale by Superintendent of Documents. '09(N) 32 p. 8°, gratis. U. S., Supt. of Docs.

United States. *Dept. of Agriculture.* Federal legislation, regulations, and rulings affecting agricultural colleges and experiment stations. (Add. Superintendent for price.) U. S., Supt. of Docs.

United States. *Dept. of Agriculture. Forest Service.* Classified list of publications available for distribution, April 1, 1909. '09(Ag) 4 p. 12°, pap., gratis.

United States. *Dept. of Agriculture.* Public documents issued by the secretary's office. Gov. Pr. Off.

United States. *Superintendent of Documents.* Agriculture; Public documents issued from the Office of the Secretary of Agriculture, U. S. A.; for sale by the Superintendent of Documents. '09(O) 33 p. 8°. gratis. U. S., Supt. of Docs.

United States. *Superintendent of Documents.* Bulletins, circulars, etc. gratis.

United States. *Superintendent of Documents.* Plant Industry Bureau; bulletins, circulars and misc. publications rel. to plants. gratis.

United States. *Superintendent of Documents.* Plant Industry Bureau publications. gratis.

United States. *Superintendent of Documents.* Public documents issued by the Agriculture Dept. gratis.

United States. *Superintendent of Documents.* Statistics Bureau; bulletins, circulars, foreign markets, separates from yearbook and crop reporter. gratis.

Upham, A. A. Introd. to agriculture. 75 c. Appleton.

Warren, G: F: Elements of agriculture. **$1.10 net.—Teacher's manual. *12 c. net. Macmillan.

Welborn, W. C. Elements of agriculture, southern and western. *75 c. net. Macmillan.

Wilkinson, J: W. Practical agriculture. $1. Am. Bk.

Wilkinson, J: W. Institute hdbk. on agriculture and domestic science; for teachers. 30 c. Oklahoma Bk.

AGRICULTURE.—*Continued.*
Willers, D. New York state agricultural college at Ovid, and higher agricultural education. gratis. M. A. Willers.
Willis, J: C. Agriculture in the tropics. $2.75. Putnam.
Wyoming. *State Board of Immigration.* Agriculture in Wyoming. (Add. pubs. for price.) S. A. Bristol.
See also Agricultural chemistry;—Agricultural machinery;—Alfalfa;—Bacteria; — Barley;—Botany; —Butter; — California;—Cereals;—Clover; —Co-operation;—Corn;—Country life;—Dairy; —Domestic animals;—Domestic economy;—Ensilage;—Farms and farming;—Fertilizers;—Forests and forestry;—Fruit;—Fungi;—Gardens and gardening;—Grain;—Insects;—International Institute of Agriculture; — Irrigation; — Milk; — Milo;—Onions;—Plowing;—Potatoes;—Poultry; —Rye;—Seed; — Sheep; — Soils;—Tobacco; — Trees;—Wheat;—Zoology;—*also* Columbia River Valley;—Long Island.

Aguilar, Grace.
Days of Bruce. '08(O10) il. D. (Bowman's illustrated lib. of world-favorite books.) $1. Bowman.
Tales from British history. In 2 v. v. 1, Edmund the exiled prince; Wallace, the dauntless chief; v. 2, MacIntosh, the Highland chief. '08(N21) 12°, ea., $1.50. Dutton.

Ah Moy. Wheat, *Mrs.* L. **$1.50 net. Grafton Press.

Aicard, Jean François Victor.
Diverting adventures of Maurin; tr. from the French by Alfr. Allinson. '09(N20) D. $1.50. Lane.
Maurin, the Illustrious; tr. from the Fr. by Alfr. Allison. '10(Ap9) D. $1.50. Lane.

Aid to Kansas history. Benton, H. O. 25 c. H. O. Benton.

Aid to materia medica. Dawborn, R. H. M. **$1.75 net. Macmillan.

Aids in book selection. Kroeger, A. B. 15 c. A. L. A.

Aids to medicine. Hudson, B. *$1.25 net Wood.

Aids to obstetrics. Nall, S: *$1 net. Wood.

Aids to ophthalmology. Harman, N. B. *$1 net. Wood.

Aids to osteology. Turner, P. *$1.25 net. Wood.

Aids to surgery. Cunning, J. *$1.25 net. Wood.

Aids to tropical medicine. Brooke, G. E. *$1 net. Wood.

Aiken, Wa. H.
Melody studies for primary grades. '10 (Mr26) c. O. (Standard musical lib.) pap., 15 c. Am. Bk.
Music course; in one book. '08(O3) c. O. 50 c. Am. Bk.
—, **comp. and ed.** For high schools; part songs for mixed voices. '08(My2) c. O. 65 c. Am. Bk.

Aikens, Charlotte Albina.
Clinical studies for nurses; text-book for second and third year pupil nurses and a hand-book for all who are engaged in caring for the sick. '09(N) c. 510 p. il. 8°, $2. Saunders.
Hospital housekeeping. 2d ed. '10(O) 162 p. il. plan, 12°, $1.25. Nat. Hospital.

Aikens, Charlotte Albina.—*Continued.*
Primary studies for nurses; cont. courses of studies in anatomy, physiology, hygiene, bacteriology, therapeutics and materia medica, dietetics, and invalid cookery. '09(Ap) c. 5-428 p. il. 8°, *$1.75 net. Saunders.

Aikin, W. A., M.D.
The voice; introd. to pract. phonology. [2d ed.] '10(D10) fold. tab., O. $2.25 net. Longmans.

Ailsa Paige. Chambers, P. W: $1.50. Appleton.

Ailshie, Ja. F., comp.
See Idaho. *Sup. ct.* Digest.

Aimard, Gustave.
Indian scout. '09(Ap2) 16°, (Everyman's lib.) 35 c. net; leath., 70 c. net. Dutton.

Ainge, T: Styles.
Sanitary sewerage of buildings. '09(Ap24) c. il. tabs., 12°, $1.50. Domestic Engineering.

Ainslee, Rev. P:
Among the Gospels and the Acts: being notes and comments covering the life of Christ in the flesh, and the first thirty years' history of His church. '08(O17) O. $1.50. Temple Seminary.
God and me: brief manual of the principles that make for a closer relationship of the believer with God. '08(Je) c. 48 p. 12°, 45 c. Temple Seminary.

Ainslie, Kathleen.
Votes for Catherine, Susan and me. '10 (D) col. il. bds., 25 c. Stokes.

Ainslie, P:
Introd. to the study of the Bible; being the outline of a full course of Bible study, incl. system of marking the Bible. '10(D3) c. 12°, 50 c. Temple Seminary.

Ainslie booklets. il. S. 50 c. Stokes.
—Handler. Sea-scamps.

Ainsworth, J: H., and Gansey, R. Johnston.
Discussion of Telephone competition; with preface by Fk. L. Beam. '08(Je) c. 37 p. 8°. (Add. pubs. for price.) Columbus Citizens' Tel.

Ainsworth, Percy C.
Heart of happiness. '10(Jl16) c. 12°, $1 net. Revell.
Pilgrim church, and other sermons. '10 (My7) 12°, $1.25 net. Revell.

Ainsworth, W: Harrison.
Crichton. '08(Jl11) 16°, (New universal lib.) 50 c.; leath., 75 c. Dutton.
Flitch of bacon. '08(Jl11) 16°, (New universal lib.) 50 c.; leath., 75 c. Dutton.
Guy Fawkes. '08(Je20) 16°, (New universal lib.) 50 c.; leath., 75 c. Dutton.
Miser's daughter. '08(Je20) 16°, (New universal lib.) 50 c.; leath., 75 c. Dutton.
The spendthrift. '08(Je20) 16°, (New universal lib.) 50 c.; leath., 75 c. Dutton.
Tower of London. '10(Ap2) 16°, (Everyman's lib.) 35 c. net; leath., 70 c. net. Dutton.

AINSWORTH, William Harrison.
Ellis, S. M. William Harrison Ainsworth and his friends. $10 net. Lane.

Ain't it awful. Lewis, E. C., *comp.* 50 c. Caldwell.

AIR.
Abbe, C. Mechanics of the earth's atmosphere. Smith. Inst.
Barus, C. Condensation of vapor as induced by *nuclei* and by *ions.* Report III. $1.25. Carnegie.
Clayton, H: H., *and* Ferguson, S. P. Exploration of the upper air with balonsondes. $1. Harvard Univ.
Cordeiro, F: J. B. The atmosphere. $2.50. Spon.
Richards, E. H. S., *and* Woodman, A. G. Air, water, and food from a sanitary standpoint. $2. Wiley.
Woodbridge, S: H. Pure air as an investment. 15 c. A. D. Maclachlan
See also Atmosphere;—Chemistry;—Compressed air;—Hygiene; — Liquid air; — Meteorology;—Ventilation.

Air and health. MacFie, R. $2.50 net. Dutton.
Air and the hospital. Woodbridge, S: H. 20 c. Maclachlan.

AIR BRAKE.
Blackall, R: H. Air brake catechism. $2. Henley.
Conger, C. B. Air brake catechism. $1. C. B. Conger.
Denehie, G: R. Motorman's practical air brake instructor. $1.50. Drake.
Dukesmith, F. H. Modern air-brake practice. $1.50. Drake.
Kirkman, M. M. Air brake. $6.—Air brake portfolio. $5. C. Phillips.
McArdle, F., *and* Helmholtz, H:, *eds.* Westinghouse diagramatic and sectional views; air brake and air signal instruction charts. $2. McArdle & H.
National Correspondence School of Railroading. Air brake text for engineers and firemen. Nat. Corr. Sch. R. R.
Randolph, V. C. Air brake catechism and instruction book. $1. V. C. Randolph.
Turner, W. V. Brake operation and manipulation. 50 c. Westinghouse.
Wood, W: W., *and* Westinghouse, E. T. An air brake instruction pocket book. $2. Henley.

AIR MACHINERY.
See Fans;—Ventilation.

AIR-SIGNAL.
See Air-brake.

Air valves for steam heating systems. Wakeman, W: H: 25 c. Domestic Engineering.
Airship almanac. Allen, L. 75 c. J: W. Luce.
Airship boys ser. *See* Sayler, H. L.

AIRSHIPS.
See Aërial navigation.

Airships in animal land. Bingham, C. $1.50. Dutton.
Airy fairy Lilian. Hungerford, *Mrs.* M. H. 50 c. Hurst.
Airy way. Dewar, G: A. B. $1.75 net. Macmillan.

AITAREYA ARANYAKA.
See Manuscripts.

Aitken, Robert, ["Hudson Douglas."]
Beyond the skyline: [short stories.] '09 (My1) D. $1.50. B: W. Huebsch.
Lantern of luck. '09(D4) c. il. D. $1.50. W. J. Watt.
The man in the mirror. '10(O) c. il. 12°, $1.50. W. J. Watt.
Million a minute. '08(N21) c. il. 8°, $1.50. W. J. Watt.

Aiton's encyclop.; pract. work of reference for the home, school and library. In 5 v. '10(Ag20) c. il. (partly col.) maps, 4°, $20. Welles.
Aix, pseud.
Adventures of a nice young man: a novel. '08(O10) c. 12°, †$1.50. Duffield.
Ajax ser. 12°. †$1.25. Dodd.
—Roe. Day of fate.

AKBAR, *Emperor of India.*
Garbe, R. Akbar, Emperor of India. *50 c. net. Open Court.

Aked, C: Frederic, D.D.
Lord's prayer; its meaning and message for to-day. '10(Ap23) c. 12°, $1. Revell.
Old events and modern meanings, and other sermons. '08(O24) c. 12°, *$1.25 net. Revell.
Wells and palm trees: cool water and abundant rest on life's rough way. '08(N14) c. por. 16°, $1; leath., $2. Dodge.
—, **comp.** One hundred responsive readings from the Scriptures. '08(Ja18) 12°, *75 c. net. Revell.
Aker, J. W.
Curse of Ham. '09(S) c. 190 p. 12°, $1.25. B'way Pub.
Akers, Floyd.
Boy fortune hunters in China. '09(D18) c. front. 12°, 60 c. Reilly & B.
Boy fortune hunters in Egypt. '08(O17) c. il. D. (Boy fortune hunters ser.) 60 c. Reilly & B.
Boy fortune hunters in Yucatan. '10(D) il. 12°, (Boy fortune hunter ser.) 60 c. Reilly & B.
Akron, O. *Board of Education.* Rules governing medical inspection in Akron public schools. '09(D) 7 p. 8°. (Add. pubs. for price.) Akron Bd. Educ.
Alabama. Chancery pleading and practice, with forms for pleading; being an examination of the procedure in chancery formerly in use in England as affected by statutes and supreme decisions of the state of Alabama; by H: Upson Sims. '09(Ag) c. 68+576 p. O. shp., $7.50. Callaghan.
Alabama. Code adopted by act of legislature approved July 27, 1907, [etc.] In 3 v. v. 1, Political; v. 2, Civil; v. 3, Criminal: prepared by Ja. J. Mayfield. '08(Ap.) c. O. buckram, $8. Marshall.
Alabama. *Dept. of Education.* Alabama library day; program and selections for the observance of library day, Nov. 4th, by the schools of Alabama. '09(D) 22 p. 8°. (Not for sale.) Ala. Supt. Educ.
Alabama. *Supreme ct.* Repts.: (Lawrence H. Lee.) v. 147. '08(Ja4); v. 148 (Je); v. 149-151. '08, [1909.] (Ja); v. 152 (Ap); v. 153 (Je); c. O. shp., ea., $3.75; v. 154 (Ag) $2.50; v. 155, 156 (N); v. 157 (D); v. 158. '10(Mr); v. 159 (Ap); v. 160 (Je); v. 161 (Jl); v. 162-164 (D) c. O. shp., ea., $2.50. Brown Pr. Co.
Alabama. *Supreme ct.* Repts. of cases. 2d ed., unabr. Bk. 19; containing a verbatim repr. of v. 19, 20 of the Ala. repts. '08 (Ja4); Bks. 18-17; repr. of v. 15, 16, 17, 18. '07. '08(F); Bks. 16-15; repr. of v. 11, 12, 13, 14. '08(Ap); Bk. 14; repr. of v. 9, 10. '08(My) Bk. 13; repr. of vs. 7 and 8

(N); Bk. 12; repr. of vs. 5 and 6 (D); Bk. 11, cont. a verbatim repr. of v. 3, 4 of the Ala. repts. '09(Jl); Bk. 10. '09(N); Bk. 9. '10(F); Bk. 8 (Mr); Bk. 7-4 (D); O. shp., ea., $6. (Sold only in sets.) (Repr. backwards.) West Pub.

ALABAMA.

Armes, E. Story of coal and iron in Alabama. $5. Ala. Chamber of Com.

Du Bose, J. C. Alabama history. 75 c. B. F. Johnson.

McBain, H. L., *and* Hill, I: W: How we are governed in Alabama and the nation. 65 c. Bell Bk.

Thomas, W: H: Some educational hist. of Alabama methodism. (Add. author for price.) W: H. Thomas.

United States. *Dept. of the Interior. U. S. Geolog. Survey.* Iron ores, fuels and fluxes of the Birmingham district, Ala.

See also Baptist church;—Cahaba;—Mobile.

Alabama student. Osler, W: *$2 net. Oxford Univ.

Alabaster box. Wilkinson, H. S. 50 c. H. S. Wilkinson.

Alain de Lille, [Alanus de Insulis.]

Complaint of nature tr. from the Latin by Douglas Maxwell Moffat. '09(Ap17) 8°, (Yale studies in English.) pap., 75 c. Holt.

Alanus de Insulis.

See Alain de Lille.

Alarm talks. Read, H. E. 30 c. Business Monthly.

ALASKA.

Altsheler, W: B., *comp.* Maladministration through the Alaska syndicate. 10 c. Altsheler.

Birds and mammals of the 1907 Alexander Expedition to Southwestern Alaska. 75 c. Univ. of Cal.

Brooks, A. H., *and others.* Mineral resources of Alaska. (Add. Superintendent for price.) U. S., Supt. of Docs.

Callahan, J. M. Alaskan purchase and Americo-Canadian relations. 50 c. Univ. of W. Va.

Covert, C. C., *and* Ellsworth, C. E. Water-supply investigations in the Yukon-Tanana region, Alaska, 1907-'08. (Add. Superintendent for price.) U. S., Supt. of Docs.

Edwards, W: S. Into the Yukon. Jennings.

Everman, B. W. Fishes of Alaska. $1. U. S., Supt. of Docs.

Gilmore, C: W: Smithsonian exploration in Alaska in 1907 in search of *Pleistocene* fossil vertebrates. (Add. Institution for price.) Smith. Inst.

Government of Alaska; statements before the Committee on Territories, United States Senate, on the bill S. 5436, to create a legislative council in the district of Alaska, to confer legislative powers thereon, and for other purposes. [Jan. 20 and 22, 1910.] '10(Mr) 72 p. 8°. U. S., Supt. of Docs.

Gunnison, R. A. Condition of natives of Alaska. 10 c. U. S., Supt. of Docs.

Greely, A. W. Hdbk. of Alaska. **$2 net. Scribner.

ALASKA.—*Continued.*

Hallock, C: Peerless Alaska. $1.25. B'way Pub.

Herbert, A., *and* A Shikâri, *pseud.* Two Dianas in Alaska. *$4 net. Lane.

Higginson, *Mrs.* E. R. Alaska, the great country. $2.50. Macmillan.

Kellogg, R. S. Forests of Alaska. Gov. Pr. Off.

Knopf, A. Geology of the Seward Peninsula tin deposits. (Add. Superintendent for price.) U. S., Supt. of Docs.

Moffit, F. H. Mineral resources of the Kotsina-Chitina region, Alaska. (Add. Superintendent for price.) U. S., Supt. of Docs.

Moffit, F. H., *and others.* Mineral resources of the Nabesna-White River district, Alaska. Gov. Pr. Off.

Osgood. W. H. Biological investigations in Alaska and Yukon territory. (Add. Superintendent for price.) U. S., Supt. of Docs.

Our northern domain. $2. Estes.

Powell, A. M. Trailing and camping in Alaska. *$2 net. Wessels.

Prindle, S. M. Forty mile quadrangle, Yukon-Tanana region. (Add. Superintendent for price.) U. S., Supt. of Docs.

Rickard, T: A. Through the Yukon and Alaska. $2.50. Mining and Scientific.

Schmitter, F. Upper Yukon native customs and folk-lore. 12 c. Smith. Inst.

Sullivan, M. K. Trail of a sourdough. $1.50. Badger.

Tarr, R. S., *and* Butler, B. S. Yakutat Bay region, Alaska; physiography and glacial geography; areal geology. (Add. Superintendent for price.) U. S., Supt. of Docs.

United States. *Adjutant-General's Office. Military Information Division.* Explorations in Alaska, 1899. pap., 20 c.

United States. *Dept. of the Interior. U. S. Geolog. Survey.* Innoko gold-placer district, Alaska, with accounts of the central Kuskokwim Valley and the Ruby Creek and Gold Hill placers. (Add. Superintendent for price.)

Wright, F. E. *and* C: W. Ketchikan and Wrangell mining districts, Alaska. (Add. Superintendent for price.) U. S. Supt. of Docs.

See also Bear;—Coal;—Klondike;—Mammals;—Mt. McKinley;—Yukon.

Alaska repts. v. 3; cont. the decisions Jan. 1, 1906, to Jan. 1, 1910; ed., arr. and digested by Ja. Wickersham. '10(N) c. O. $10. West Pub.

Alaska-Yukon-Pacific Exposition, 1909. Official guide. '09(S11) c. il. pors. plan, O. pap., 25 c. Alaskan-Yukon.

ALASKA-YUKON-PACIFIC EXPOSITION, Seattle, Wash.

Craig, D. B., *comp.* Catalogue of educational exhibits in the Washington Educational Building, A.-Y.-P. Exposition. Wash. Supt. Sch.

Glimpses of the Alaska-Yukon-Pacific Exposition, Seattle, Wash. 75 c.; 25 c. Laird.

ALASKA-YUKON-PACIFIC EXPOSITION.—*Cont.*
Smithsonian Institute. Exhibits of the Smithsonian Institution and United States National Museum at the Alaska-Yukon-Pacific Exposition. 50 c. Smith. Inst.
United States. *Congress. House. Committee on Industrial Arts and Expositions.* Alaska-Yukon-Pacific Exposition, 1908. gratis. U. S., Supt. of Docs.
Washington. *Dept. of Education.* A.-Y.-P. exposition as an educator. gratis. Wash. Supt. Sch.
See also Education;—Roads.

Albanesi, Mrs. Effie Adelaide Maria.
Forbidden road. '08(Ap4) c. D. 75 c. Cupples & L.
Laughter of life. '08(D5) c. 12°, 75 c. Cupples & L.

ALBANIA, Turkey.
Durham, M. E. High Albania. *$4 net. Longmans.

ALBANY, Louisa von Stolberg, *Countess* of.
Lee, V., *pseud.* Countess of Albany. *$1.50 net. Lane.

ALBANY, N. Y.
See First Presbyterian Church.

ALBANY COUNTY, N. Y.
Judd, W. W. Birds of Albany County. $2.50. A. M. Allen.

Albe, Edmund Edward Fournier d'.
Electron theory; popular introd. to the new theory of electricity and magnetism; with preface by G. Johnstone Stoney. 3d ed. '10(Je4) il. D. $1.25 net. Longmans.
New light on immortality. '08(N7) il. D. *$1.75 net. Longmans.
Wonders of physical science. '10(D) 12+204 p. maps, 12°, (Readable books in natural knowledge.) 50 c. net. Macmillan.

Albee, Fred Houdlett.
See Taylor, H: Ling.

Albee, Mrs. Helen Rickey.
Hardy plants for cottage gardens. '10 (Je25) c. il. plan, D. (American nature ser.; group IV., Working with nature.) $1.60 net. Holt.

Albee, J:
Confessions of boyhood. '10(Je18) c. D. $1.50 net. Badger.

ALBEMARLE COUNTY, Va.
Woods, E. History of Albemarle County, Va. $2. E. Woods.

Albert, Allen D., jr.
Customs frauds in New York; article in the *Washington Times* of Sunday evening, May 23, 1909, entitled The chase of the sugar smugglers. '09(Ag) 13 p. diagr., 8°. (Add. Superintendent for price.) U. S., Supt. of Docs.

Albert, J: C.
Roosevelt and the money power: responsibility of dishonest high finance for the panic of 1907. '08(F22) c. nar. S. pap., 10 c. Sudwarth Co.

Alberta, pseud.
See Robertson, Elbertine.

ALBERTA, Canada.
See Rocky Mountains.

Albertson, C: Carroll.
College sermons. '10(J29) c. por. 12°, 75 c. Westminster.

Albertson, Ralph, comp.
Fellowship songs: [poems.] '08(Ag22) c. pap., 25 c. Public Pub.

Albion ser. of Anglo-Saxon and Middle English poetry. 8°. Ginn.
—Riddles of the Exeter book. $2.50.

Albrecht, F: Conrad.
"World movement"; extract from Mr. Thdr. Roosevelt's address del. at Berlin, May 12, 1910; criticism and the "world movement' from another point of view. '10(D3) c. 24°, 50 c. F: C. Albrecht.

Albrecht, Johann Friedrich Ernst.
Primer of eye diseases and their treatment; fr. the German of the 5th ed.; tr. and notes by Otto G. Haussmann. '09(Je) c. 78 p. il. 8°, 25 c. Ware.

Albright, E:
Early hist. of Middle Tennessee. '09. [1910.] (N) 207 p. il. 12°. Brandon Pr.
Starke, J. Alcohol, the sanction for its use scientifically established. $1.50 net. Putnam.
Wente, A. O., *and* Tolman, L. M. Potato culls as a source of industrial alcohol. Gov. Pr. Off.

Albright, Jacob Dissinger, M.D.
Practical treatise on rectal diseases, their diagnosis and treatment by ambulant methods. '09(Ag) 11+17-455 p. il. 8°, $4. J. D. Albright.

Albright, Victor Eight.
Shakespearian stage. '09(N6) il. 8°, (Columbia Univ. studies in English.) *$1.50 net. Macmillan.
Typical Shakespearean stage: the inner stage; Third Chapter study of the Shakespearean stage. '08(Ap4) c. 8°. (privately pr.) Putnam.

Albright ser. 12°. Pub. Ho. of Evangelical Assoc.
—Boroman. Great salvation. 50 c.
—Gamertsfelder. Bible study on prayer. 40 c.

Alcestis. Montenegro, C. M. $1.25. Badger.
Alchemist's secret. Williams, I. C. 85 c. Kenedy.
Alchemy of happiness. Al Ghazzali, A. H. M. 60 c. net. Dutton.

Alcock, Deborah.
Romance of Protestantism. [1910] (My) 8°, $1.25 net. Eaton & M.

Alcock, N. H., and Ellison, F. O'B.
Text-book of experimental physiology; with preface by E. H. Starling, M.D. '09(D18) il. 8°, *$1.50 net. Blakiston.

ALCOHOL.
American Association for the Study of Alcohol and other Narcotics. Some scientific conclusions concerning the alcoholic problem and its practical relations to life. U. S., Supt. of Docs.
Horsley, *Sir* V. A. H., *and* Sturge, M. D. Alcohol and the human body. *$1.50 net. Macmillan.
Rivers, W. H. R. Influence of alcohol and other drugs on fatigue. *$1.70 net. Longmans.
Starke, J. Alcohol; the sanction for its use scientifically established. $1.50 net. Putnam.

ALCOHOL.—*Continued.*
United States. *Treasury Dept. Office of Internal Revenue.* Denatured alcohol at at home and abroad. 10 c.
Wente, A. O., *and* Tolman, L. M. Potato culls as a source of industrial alcohol. Gov. Pr. Off.
Wiley, H. W., *and others.* Manufacture of denatured alcohol. (Add. Superintendent for price.) U. S., Supt. of Docs.
Williams, H: S. Alcohol: how it affects the individual, the community and the race. **50 c. net. Century Co.
See also Fuel.

ALCOHOLISM.
See Alcohol;—Temperance.

Alcono cook book. Neil, M. H., *comp* 50 c. Pitkin.

Alcorn, Edg. Greenville.
Duties and liabilities of bank directors. '09(Ap3) c. 12°, $1.50. Financial Pub.

ALCOTT, Amos Bronson.
Sanborn, F. B: Bronson Alcott at Alcott House, England, and Fruitlands, New England. *$3 net. Torch Press.

Alcott, Louisa May.
Flower fables. '09(N13) il. Q. $1. McLoughlin.
Garland for girls. '08(S19) c. il. D. (Spinning-wheel ser.) †$1.50. Little, B. & Co.
Little women; or, Meg, Jo, Beth, and Amy. '08(Jl18) c. il. Q. price to the trade only, **63 c. net. Little, B. & Co.
Louisa Alcott reader. '08(F22) c. il. 12°, *50 c. net. Little, B. & Co.
Louisa Alcott story book; ed. for schools by Fanny E. Coe; with biographical sketch of Miss Alcott. '10(S10) c. front. S. 50 c. net. Little, B. & Co.
Modern Cinderella. '08(Ag1) 12°, (Home ser.) 50 c. Hurst.
Proverb stories. '08(S19) c. il. D. (Spinning-wheel ser.) †$1.50. Little, B. & Co.
Silver pitchers and independence. '08(S19) c. il. D. (Spinning-wheel ser.) †$1.50. Little, B. & Co.
Spinning-wheel stories. '08(S19) c. il. D. (Spinning-wheel ser.) †$1.50. Little, B. & Co.

ALCOTT, Louisa May.
Gowing, C. Alcotts as I knew them. $1.25. C. M. Clark.
Moses, B. Louisa May Alcott, dreamer and worker. **$1.25 net. Appleton.

Alcotts as I knew them. Gowing, C. $1.25. C. M. Clark.

ALCUIN.
Page, R. B. Letters of Alcuin. $1; 50 c. Forest Press.

Alcuin Club collections. Q. Longmans.
—Atchley. Hist. of the use of incense in divine worship. *$17.50 net. Longmans.
—Dearmer. Fifty pictures of Gothic altars. $6 net.
—Eeles. Traditional ceremonial and customs connected with the Scottish liturgy. $6 net.
—Kennedy. "Interpretations" of the bishops and their influence on Elizabethan episcopal policy. 50 c.
—Pontifical services. 4 v. ea., *$6 net.

Alden, Fk. Wesley, comp.
John Alden of Ashfield, Mass., and Chautauqua County, New York, his Alden ancestors and his descendants. '09, [1910.] (Je) 84 p. il. por. 8°, $1.50. F. W. Alden.

Alden, Mrs. G. R.
See Alden, *Mrs.* Isabella Macdonald.

Alden, G: W.
Fifteen reasons why no-license is better than license; by a Brocton man. '08(D) c. 23 p. O. pap., 10 c. G: W. Alden.

Alden, H: Mills.
Magazine writing and the new literature. '08(O10) c. por. O. **$2 net. Harper.
—, ed. *See* Howells, W: Dean.

Alden, Mrs. Isabella Macdonald, [Mrs. G. R. Alden; "Pansy," pseud.]
Browns at Mt. Hermon. '08(O17) c. D. (Pansy books.) †$1.50. Lothrop, L. & S.

Alden, Lucy Chaffee.
Songs of hope; il. by J. Jeannette Metcalf. '09 [1910.] (F) c. 60 p. il. por. 8°, $1. J. J. Metcalf.

Alden, Percy, ed.
Hungary of to-day by members of the Hungarian government, etc. '09(Jl) il. pors. 8°, *$3 net. Brentano's.

Alden, Raymond MacDonald.
Introduction to poetry, for students of English literature. '09(Ap17) c. D. $1.25. Holt.
Palace made by music. '10(D31) c. S. 50 c. Bobbs-M.
Why the chimes rang. New ed. of "The knights of the silver shield." '08(O3) il. 8°, †$1.25; '10(Ja22) c. S. 50 c.; leath., $1. Bobbs-M.

Alden among the Indians. Ellis, E: S. $1; per set, $2. Winston.

ALDEN FAMILY.
See Genealogies.

Alden, the pony express rider. Ellis, E: S. $1; per set, $2. Winston.

Alderman, Edn. Anderson.
Classics old and new: ser. of school readers: 1st reader. [Rev. ed.] '08(F1) c. il. D. 25 c.—5th reader. '08(Ja11) 40 c. Am. Bk.
Growing South: address del. before the Civic Forum, New York City, March 22, 1908. '08(D5) por. 12°, (Civic Forum addresses.) pap., 10 c. Civic Forum.
—, Harris, Joel Chandler, ["Uncle Remus,"] Kent, C: W:, and others, eds.
Library of southern literature. In 15 v. vs. 1-7. '09(Je5) il. 8°, per set, $80-$200. Martin & H.

Alderson, Jos. Coleman.
Hand book of southern West Virginia: the Kanawha or middle measures of coal; the Coal River basin; Alderson Land & Development Company's survey. '08 (Jl18) il. 4°, pap., 25 c. J. C. Alderson.

Alderson, W: A., comp.
Here's to you: [toasts.] '08(Je20) il. D. $1.25; leath., $2, boxed. Dodge.

Aldin, Cecil C: Windsor.
Black puppy book. '09(D) bds., 75 c. Doran.

Aldin, Cecil C: Windsor.—*Continued.*
Farm babies: day in the life of a venturesome duckling. '10(D10) col. il. 4°, bds., $1.25. Doran.
Pickles: a day in the life of a naughty puppy. '09(D) il. in col. *$2 net. Doran.
The twins: the adventures of two troublesome puppies. '10(D10) col. il. 4°, bds., $2 net. Doran.
White kitten book. '10(D) il. (partly col.) 4°, bds., 75 c. Doran.
White puppy book. '09(D) bds., 75 c. Doran.
See also Emanuel, Walter, *pseud.*

Aldine readers. See Spaulding, Fk. Ellsworth, *and* Bryce, Catherine T.

Aldrich, Mrs. Flora L. S., M.D.
The one man. '10(O22) c. D. $1.25. Roxburgh.

Aldrich, Mrs. Marg. Chanler.
Sonnets for choice. '10(Je4) c. D. bds., $1 net. Moffat.

Aldrich, Nelson Wilmarth.
Address before the Economic Club of New York, Nov. 29, 1909, on the work of the National Monetary Commission. '10(Jl) 29 p. 8°. Gov. Pr. Off.

Aldrich, T: Bailey.
Little violinist, and other prose sketches; in the amanuensis style of phonography, by Benn Pitman and Jerome B. Howard. '08(D19) S. pap., 25 c. Phonograph.
Marjorie Daw. '08(O24) c. il. O. †$2, boxed. Houghton M
Poems. Astor ed. of poets. '08(S5) c. por. D. 60 c. Crowell.

ALDRICH, Thomas Bailey.
Greenslet, F. Life of Thomas Bailey Aldrich. **$3 net; **$5 net. Houghton M.

Alembic Club reprints. por. pls. 12°. Univ. of Chic.
—Mayow. Medico-physical works. *$1.25 net.

Aleramo, Sibilla, pseud.
Woman at bay, (Una donna:) authorized tr. from the Italian by Maria H. Lansdale. '08(O24) c. front. D. †$1.50. Putnam.

Alexander, Alex. S.
Horse secrets. '09(D) c. 64 p. 8°, 25 c. W. Atkinson.

Alexander, Archibald Browning Drysdale.
Ethics of St. Paul. '10(Je11) O. $2 net. Macmillan.
Short hist. of philosophy. 2d ed., rev. and enl. '10(Ap9) 8°, $2.75 net. Macmillan.

ALEXANDER, Charles McCallon.
Davis, G: T. B. Twice around the world with Alexander. $1. Chr. Herald.

Alexander, C: McCallon, comp.
Gospel songs. '08(O3) c. *30 c. net; pap., *15 c. net. Revell.

Alexander, De Alva Stanwood.
Political hist. of the state of New York. v. 3, 1861-1882. '09(O9) c. O. **$2.50 net. Holt.

Alexander, E. W.
Writings on practical bee culture; ed. and comp. by H. H. Root. '09(Jl3) O. pap., 50 c. A. I. Root.

Alexander, F., pseud.
See Chandler, F. Alex.

Alexander, Georgia and Grace.
Child classics. Primer; 1st-5th readers. '09(Ag21) c. il. (partly col.) 12°, primer, 30 c.; 1st reader, 35 c.; 2d reader, 40 c.; 3d reader, 50 c.; 4th reader, 55 c.; 5th reader, 60 c. Bobbs-M.
Spelling book. New and enl. ed., syllabicated. '08(Jl18) c. D. 25 c.; also in 2 pts., pt. 1, 14 c.; pt. 2, 18 c. Longmans.

Alexander, Grace.
See Alexander, Georgia.

Alexander, Rev. Gross, ed.
Doctrines and discipline of the Methodist Episcopal Church, South, 1910. '10(D3) c. S. 40 c. net. Pub. Ho. M. E. Ch., So.

Alexander, Hartley Burr.
Odes on the generations of man. '10(F19) c. D. **$1 net. Baker & T.
Religious spirits of the American Indian as shown in the development of his religious rites and customs. '10(S3) c. il. O. pap., 30 c. Open Court.

Alexander, H: Aaron.
Mechanics' and materialmen's lien laws of the southeastern states. '09(S) c. 7+767 p. 8°, *$6 net. Harrison Co.

Alexander, J. H.
Model balloons and flying machines; with short acct. of the progress of aviation. '10(D17) il. $1.50. Henley.

Alexander, Ja.
Prisoner in holy orders; or, the ill fate of Stephen Helwyn. '09, [1910.] (Ja) (Add. pubs. for price.) Dutton.

Alexander, Ja. Bradun.
Dynamic theory of life and mind. 2d ed. '09(N) c. 1067 p. il. 8°, $2.75. J. B. Alexander.
Foot prints on the sands of time, and other pieces. '10(O) c. 125 p. 8°, 50 c. J. B. Alexander.
Lunarian professor. '09(My8) c. D. $1. J. B. Alexander.
Soul and its bearings. '09(Ap3) c. D. *$1 J. B. Alexander.

Alexander, Ja. M.
Islands of the Pacific. 2d ed., rev. and enl. '08(D5) c. il. pors. maps, 8°, $1.50. Am. Tr.

Alexander, J: Brevard.
Reminiscences of the past sixty years. '08, [1909.] (Jl) c. 513 p. por. 8°, $2. J: B. Alexander, (N. C.)

Alexander, J: L.
Sex instruction for boys. '10(Je) 8 p. S. pap., 5 c. Westminster.

Alexander, Lucien Hugh, ed.
James Wilson, (1742-1798,) signer of the Declaration of Independence; ed. by Lucien Hugh Alexander; with an introd. by James Bryce; issued under the auspices of the St. Andrew's Society of Philadelphia, the Historical Society of Pennsylvania, and the North Carolina Historical Association. Ed. de luxe. '08(Mr7) il. 8°, hf. mor. or parchment, subs. (Add. Society for price.) St. Andrew's Soc.

Alexander, Rev. R: W., pseud.
See Gallagher, Antonia Mercedes.

Alexander, S:
Locke. '09(Jl31) 12°, (Philosophies ancient and modern from Pythagoras to Spencer.) *50 c. net. Dodge.

Alexander, Taylor.
Itoma; forest romance. '09, [1910.] (Ap) c. 13-193 p. 12°, $1. Kuyahora Press.

Alexander, W: Hardy.
Some textual criticisms on the eighth book of the De vita Cæsarum of Suetonius. '08(D12) Q. (Univ. of Col. pubs., Classical philology.) pap., 30 c. Univ. of Cal.

ALEXANDER, *Sir* William, *called Lord* Stirling.
Armstrong, W: C. Lord Stirling at the telescope. 50 c. W: C. Armstrong.

ALEXANDER *the Great.*
Kirkman, M. M. Romance of Alexander and Roxana.—Romance of Alexander the king.—Romance of Alexander the prince [fiction.] ea., $1.50. C. Phillips.

ALEXANDER III., *Czar of Russia.*
Lothrop, A. S. Court of Alexander III. $1.50 net. Winston.

ALEXANDER EXPEDITION.
See Alaska.

ALEXANDER FAMILY.
See Genealogies: Boggs, M. A., *ed.*

Alexandre, Arsène.
See Utrillo, *Don* Miguel.

Alexandrian romances. See Kirkman, Marshall Monroe.

Alexandrian series. 10 v. '09(O2) S. ea., $1, boxed; limp leath., $1.50. Caldwell.

Alexandrian ser. of famous poems. Fraternity ed. 10 v. '10(D) 16°, ea., $1.50. Caldwell.

ALFALFA.
Brand, C: J:, *and* Waldron, L. R. Cold resistance of alfalfa and some factors influencing it. Gov. Pr. Off.
Brand, C: J:, *and* Westgate, J: M. Alfalfa in cultivated rows for seed production in semi-arid regions. pap., 5 c. U. S., Supt. of Docs.
Fortier, S: Irrigation of alfalfa. (Add. Superintendent for price.) U. S., Supt. of Docs.
Hansen, N. E. Wild alfalfas and clovers of Siberia. pap., 10 c. U. S., Supt. of Docs.
Myers, A. O. Alfalfa, "the grass," in Ohio. $1. Heer.
United States. *Dept. of Agriculture. Bu. of Plant Industry.* Westgate, J. M. Variegated alfalfa. U. S., Supt. of Docs.
Westgate, J: M. Alfalfa. 5 c. U. S., Supt. of Docs.
Wing, J. E. Alfalfa farming in America. $2. Sanders Pub.
See also Seed.

Alford, Rev. Bradley Hurt.
Old Testament hist. and literature. '10 (F26) D. *$1.50 net. Longmans.

Alford, Fremont, comp.
Wit of Lincoln, the wisdom of Franklin, and other bits of wit. '08(Ja4) 12°, 25 c. Scott-M.

ALGAE.
See Seaweed.

ALGEBRA.
Barnard, S., *and* Child, J. M. New Algebra. v. 1, containing pts. 1, 2 and 3; without answers, *60 c. net. Macmillan.

ALGEBRA.—*Continued.*
Bôcher, M. Introduction to higher algebra. *$1.90 net. Macmillan.
Bradbury, W: F., *and* Emery, G. C. Academic algebra. $1.08. Thompson B.
Brenke, W: C: Text-book on advanced algebra and trigonometry. $2 net. Century Co.
Brooks, E: Normal standard algebra. $1.22. C. Sower.
Collins, J. V. Pract. algebra. 85 c.—Pract. elem. algebra. $1; Answers. 10 c. Am. Bk.
Davison, C: Algebra for secondary schools. *$2 net. Putnam.
Davisson, S. C. College algebra. *$1.50 net. Macmillan.
Eiesland, J: A. Advanced algebra for technical schools and colleges. $2. J. A. Eiesland.
French, C. H., *and* Osborn, G. Elem. algebra. *$1.50 net. Putnam.
Gorse, F. School algebra. In 3 pts. ea., *25 c. net. Putnam.
Hawkes, H. E., Luby, W: A., *and* Touton, F. C. First course in algebra. $1. Ginn.
Hedrick, E. R. Algebra for secondary schools. $1. Am. Bk.
Keller, S: S. Mathematics for engineering students: algebra and trigonometry. *$1.75 net. Van Nostrand.
Lubarsky, L: H:, *ed.* Elem. algebra. $1.50. Engineering News.
Metzler, W: H:, *and others.* College algebra. $1.50. Longmans.
Milne, W: J. Key to Standard algebra. —Standard algebra. ea., $1. Am. Bk.
Nicholson, J. W. School algebra. $1. Am. Bk.
Paterson, W. E. School algebra. In 2 pts. ea., 60 c.; complete, $1; [with answers.] In 2 pts. ea., 75 c.; complete, $1.25. Oxford Univ.
Reid, L. W. Elements of the theory of algebraic numbers. $3.50 net. Macmillan.
Rietz, H: L., *and* Crathorne, A. R. College algebra. **$1.40 net. Holt.
Schultze, A. Elem. of algebra. 85 c. net.—Graphic algebra. *80 c. net. Macmillan.
Schultze, A., *and* Manguse, W: P., *comps.* Answers to Elements of algebra. 20 c. net. Macmillan.
Scoones, P., *and* Todd, L. Eton algebra. pt. 1. *50 c. net. Macmillan.
Shaw, J. B. Synopsis of linear associative algebra. $1.50. Carnegie.
Slaught, H. E. Suggestions on the teaching of algebra with special reference to Slaughter and Lennes's high school algebra. gratis. Allyn & B.
Slaught, H. E., *and* Lennes, N. J. High school algebra. 65 c.; $1.20.—Key to High school algebra, elementary course, [teachers only.] 75 c. Allyn & B.
Somerville, F: H. Elementary algebra. $1. —Answers. 10 c. Am. Bk.
Tanner, J: H: Key to high school algebra. 75 c. Am. Bk.

ALGEBRA.—*Continued.*
Wells, W. First course in algebra. $1.—Key to Wells' first course in algebra. $2. —Second course in algebra. $1. Heath.
Young, J: W: A. Elem. algebra. **$1.12 net. Appleton.
Young, J. W: A., *and* Jackson, L. L. First course in elem. algebra. 95 c. net.—Second course in elem. algebra. 70 c. net. Appleton.
See also Equations.

Alger, Ellice Murdoch.
Refraction and motility of the eye, with chapters on color blindness and the field of vision, designed for students and practitioners. '10(Jl) c. 11+380 p. il. 8°, $1.50. Davis.

Alger, Horatio, jr.
Ben Logan's triumph; or, the boys of Boxwood academy. '08(Ag1) c. il. 12°, 60 c. Cupples & L.
Bertha's Christmas vision. '08(Je13) 12°, (Home ser.) 50 c. Hurst.
Paul Prescott's charge. '08(Jl4) 12°, (Alger ser.) 50 c. Hurst.
Telegraph boy. '08(Jl18) 12°, (Alger ser.) 50 c. Hurst.
Wait and win: story of Jack Drummond's pluck. '08(Ap4) c. 12°, †$1. Burt.
Young miner. '08(Ag1) 12°, (Alger ser.) 50 c. Hurst.

ALGERIA, Africa.
Miltoun, F., *pseud.* In the land of the mosques and minarets: [Algeria and Tunis.] $3; $7. L. C. Page.
Phillipps, L. M. In the desert; the hinterland of Algiers. $2. Longmans.
Rivot, C. G. Souvenirs d' Algérie et nouveaux pastels, prose et poésie. [in French.] *$1 net. Neale.
See also Biskra.

Al Ghazzali, Abu Hamid Mohammed.
Alchemy of happiness; tr. from the Hindustanée by Claud Field. '10(O8) 16°, (Wisdom of the East ser.) 60 c. net. Dutton.
Confessions of Al Ghazali: tr. by Claud Field. '09(F13) 16°, (Wisdom of the East ser.) *40 c. net. Dutton.

Algodón. su cultivo. Burkett, C: W: $1.50. S. F de Velasco.
Alhambra (The). *See* Irving, Washington.

Ali, Syred Ameer.
Islam. '07, [1909.] (Ap) 8°, (Religions ancient and modern.) *40 c. net. Open Court.

Alice Brenton. Gale, M. J. $1.50. C. M. Clark.
Alice in Sunderland. Torrey, J. A. $1. Cochrane.
Alice in Wonderland. *See* Dodgson, C: Lutwidge.
Alice Mansfield's sin. Thompson, J. W. $1. Thompson Pub. Co.
Alice's adventures in Wonderland [in words of one syllable]. Maybank, T: 50 c. Dutton.
Alice's adventures in Wonderland. *See* Dodgson, C: Lutwidge.
Aline of the Grand Woods. Henshaw, N. G. $1.50. Outing.

ALKALI.
Lunge, G: Manufacture of sulphuric acid and alkali. v. 2. *$15 net. Van Nostrand.

ALKALOIDS.
See Medicine.

Al-Kindi, Abu' Umar Muhammad Ibn Yusuf ibn Ya' qub.
History of the governors of Egypt; ed. from a unique manuscript in the British Museum, by Nicholas Koenig. pt. 1. '08 (D12) 8°, (Columbia Univ. contrib. to Oriental history and philology.) pap., **$1 net. Lemcke.
—, comp. History of the Egyptian eadis; together with additions by Abu Al-Hasan Ahmad ibn 'Abd Al-Ramman ibn Burd; ed. from the unique ms. in the British Museum by R: J. H. Gottheil. '09(Je5) Q. hf. leath., *$3.50 net. Stechert.

All about poultry. Postell, J. G. 50 c. J. W. Burke.
All about salads. Lucas, P. E.-S. 75 c. Cathedral Lib.
All about the baby. Tooker, R. N. *$1.50 net. Rand, McN. & Co.
All about the primary. Sudlow, *Mrs.* E. W. 50 c. Hammond Pub. Co.
All among the loggers. Burleigh, C. B. †$1.50. Lothrop, L. & S.
All around Asia. Redway, J. W. 60 c. Scribner.
All-around athletics. White, E. C. 10 c. Am. Sports.
All-around recitations. West, E. E., *comp.* 35 c. Werner
All around the Civil War. Hawn, W: 75 c. W: Hawn.
All change here. '09(D) col. il. 32°, bds., 25 c. Doran.
"All His benefits." Ostrom, H: 30 c. Praise Pub.
All in the same boat. Flagg, J. M. bds., 75 c. Life Pub. Co.
All is well. Pennington, J. G., *ed.* 50 c. Dodge.
All kinds of gems of prose and verse. Housley, W. H. B'way Pub.
All-of-a-sudden Peggy. Donny, E. 50 c. S: French.
All on the Irish shore. Somerville, E. A. O. $1 net. Longmans.
All that man should be unto woman. Clark, S. C. $1.50. C. M. Clark.
All things considered. Chesterton, G. K. *$1.50 net. Lane.

Allaben, Fk.
Ancestry of Leander Howard Crall; monographs on the Crall, Haff, Beatty, Ashfordby, Billesby, Heneage, Langton, Quadring, Sandon, Fulnetby, Newcomen, Wolley, Cracroft, Gascoigne, Skipwith, Plantagenet, Meet, Van Ysselsteyn, Middagh, Bergen, and De Rapalje families, with coat armor, pedigree, charts, and documentary appendices. '08(Ap18) c. il. pors. facsims., 8°, **$50 net. Grafton Press.
John Watts de Peyster. '08(Ag1) In 2 v. il. pors. D. (Allaben biographical ser.) per set, *$2.50 net. Allaben.

Allaben biographical ser. D. Allaben.
—Allaben. John Watts de Peyster. 2 v. *$2.50 net.

Allaben genealogical ser. il. 12°. Allaben.
—Abbe *and* Nichols. Townsend genealogy. $2.
—Colver. Colver-Culver genealogy.
—Smith. Jesse Smith, his ancestors and descendants. $4; $6.
—Stevens. Stephens-Stevens genealogy. $5.

Allan, H. Warner.
See Wesseley, J. E.

Allan, son of a gunmaker. Rowell, H. $1.50. Cochrane.

Allan, Sidney, pseud.
See Hartmann, Sadakichi.

Allan, Rev. W: Temple.
Council sermon preached in the Church of the Advent, Birmingham, Alabama, 1909. '09, [1910.] (Ja) c. 33 p. 24°, 5 c. Clark Pub.

Allbutt, Sir T: Clifford, M.D., and Rolleston, Humphry Davy, M.D., eds.
System of medicine, by many writers. Rev. ed. in 12 v. v. 4, pt. 1. '08(N7); v. 4, pt. 2 (D26); v. 5. '09(S); v. 6 (D); v. 7 (S); v. 8. '10(D) il. 8°, ea., $6 net; shp., $7 net; hf. mor., $8 net. (Sold in sets by subscription only.) Macmillan.

Alldridge, T: Joshua.
Transformed colony; Sierra Leone. '10 (Mr26) il. map, O. $3.50 net. Lippincott.

Alle fünf! Stökl, *Mrs.* H. B. 30 c. Heath.

Alleged structural defects in battleships of United States navy. United States. *Navy Department.* 15 c. U. S., Supt. of Docs.

ALLEGHENY CITY, Pa.
See Pittsburgh.

ALLEGORIES.
Traver, H. Four daughters of God: study of the versions of this allegory. $1. Winston.

Alleman, Herbert Christian, and Dunbar, W. H.
Book and the message. pt. 1, by Herbert C. Alleman, D.D.; pt. 2, by W. H. Dunbar, D.D. '09(N) c. 4+158 p. il. 8°, (Lutheran teacher-training ser. for the sunday-school.) 50 c. Lutheran Pub.

Allen, A. M.
Hist. of Verona; ed. by E: Armstrong. '10(O1) il. maps, O. (Historic states of Italy.) $3.50. Putnam.

Allen, Alfr. H:, M.D.
Commercial organic analysis; treatise on the properties, modes of assaying, and proximate analyt. examination of the various organic chemicals and products employed in the arts, manufactures, medicine, etc.; with concise methods for the detection and estimation of their impurities, adulterations, and products of decomposition. 4th ed., entirely rewritten; ed. by H: Leffmann and W: A. Davis. v. 1. '09, [1910.] (F); v. 2 (Je); v. 3 (Jl); v. 4 (S) il. 8°, ea., $5 net. Blakiston.

Allen, Bernard Melzar, and Phillips, J: Lewis.
Latin composition. '09(My) c. 10+230 p. 12°, $1. Allyn & B.

Allen, Caroline Stetson.
Little old-time Sunday, and other stories. '08(Ap4) il. O. 75 c. C. S. Allen.

Allen, "Cedarine," pseud.
See Allen, G: Hoyt.

Allen, E: Ellis.
Impressions of institutions for the blind in Germany and Austria. '10(N) 20 p. il. 8°, gratis. Perkins Inst.

Allen, E: Heron-.
See Heron-Allen, E:

Allen, Eldreth Gordon.
Manual training for common schools; organized course in wood-working; ed. by Fassett A. Cotton. '10(Je4) c. il. 8°, $1. Scribner.

Allen, Emory Adams.
Gems of immortality; book of consolation and help. '09(Jl) c. 400 p. il. 8°, $2.25; hf. mor., $2.75; mor., $3.75. Central Pub.
Hist. of civilization. 8 v. '10(Ap9) il. pors. maps, 4°, $21. Ferguson-A.

Allen, Florence Ellinwood.
Paris: [poems.] '08(Je6) c. nar. D. bds., $1 H. Carr.

Allen, Fs. H:
Bibliography of Henry David Thoreau. '08 (D26) c. por. facsim., O. **$5 net, boxed. Houghton M.

Allen, Fk. Waller.
Golden road. '10(D17) c. il. O. $1.50 net, boxed. Wessels & B.

Allen, Franklin W.
Insurance enactments of 1909, [etc.] '10 (Ap) c. 1496 p. Q. $10. Law Reporting.

Allen, Frederic Sturges.
Noah Webster's place among English lexicographers: address del. before the Modern Language Club of Yale University, at the commemoration of the 150th anniversary of the birth of Noah Webster, October 16th, 1758. '09(Je12) c. O. pap., 25 c. G. & C. Merriam.

Allen, F: Ja.
In crystal hills, North Conway, N. H.: [poems.] '08(Ag) c. 56 p. il. sq. S. pap., 50 c. F: J. Allen.

Allen, Gardner Weld, M.D.
Our naval war with France. '09(My15) c. il. pors. map, D. **$1.50 net. Houghton M.

Allen, G:
Science of accounts made clear and simple; text-book for use in the public schools; embracing single entry and double entry bookkeeping. High school ed. '09(N) c. 136 p. 8°, $1; Graded sch. ed., 60 c. Edwards.

Allen, G: Hoyt, ["Cedarine" Allen.]
"I am reminded." '09(N) c. 31 p. il. 16°, pap., 5 c. G: H. Allen.

Allen, Glover Morrill.
See Tozzer, Alfr. Marston.

Allen, Grant.
Evolution in Italian art. '08(O10) il. O. *$3.50 net. Wessels.

Allen, H: C., 1836-1909.
Materia medica of the nosodes with provings of the X-ray. '10(Mr) c. 8+583 p. por. 8°, $4. Boericke & T.

Allen, H: Covert.
See Colorado justice manual.

Allen, Horace.
Modern power gas producer: treatise dealing with the gasification of various classes of fuels by the pressure and suction system of producer. '09(Ja16) 8°, *$2.50 net. Van Nostrand.

Allen, Horace Newton, M.D.
Things Korean: sketches missionary and diplomatic. '08(D5) c. 12°, *$1.25 net. Revell.

Allen, J. C.
Heroes of Indian hist., and stories of their times. '10(D10) il. maps, D. bds., 50 c. Longmans.
Narrative of Indian history for high schools. '09(Jl3) il. pors. maps, D. 90 c. Longmans.

Allen, J. W.
Wheel magic: [cycling in England.] S. (Jl31) *$1.25 net. Lane.

Allen, Ja.
Above life's turmoil. '10(Je18) c. S. $1. Putnam.
As a man thinketh. '09(Mr20) 32°, (Ariel booklets.) leath., 75 c., boxed. Putnam.
As a man thinketh. 4th ed. '08, [1909.] (My) 61 p. 16°, 50 c.; pap., 15 c. Sheldon Univ.
Entering the kingdom. '08(D) 82 p. 12°, pap., 15 c. Fenno.
From passion to peace. '10(Ag13) c. D. 50 c. net. Crowell.
Heavenly life. '08(Je27) D. 50 c.; pap., 15 c. Fenno.
Mastery of destiny. '09(N6) c. S. bds., **$1 net. Putnam.

Allen, Ja. Lane.
Bride of the mistletoe. '09(Jl3) c. D. †$1.25. Macmillan.
Doctor's Christmas Eve. '10(D17) c. D. $1.50. Macmillan.

Allen, J: Kermott.
George Morton of Plymouth Colony and some of his descendants. '08(Je) 2+43+3. 8°. [privately pr.] J: K. Allen.
—, **ed.** Hot water for domestic use; complete guide to the methods of supplying and heating water for domestic purposes, giving each step to be taken and explaining why it is done. '10(D) 7-122 p. il. 16°, 50 c. Domestic Engineering.
Roughing-in house drains: a complete guide from the digging of the sewer to finishing length of the house drain. '08 (Ag15) c. il. diagrs., S. 50 c. Domestic Engineering.
Sizes of flow and return steam mains. 2d ed. '09(Je19) c. il. tabs., 16°, 50 c. Domestic Engineering.

Allen, J: Robins, and Bursley, Jos. Aldrich.
Heat engines: steam, gas, steam turbines, and their auxiliaries. '10(N12) c. il. 8°, $3. McGraw-H.

Allen, J: Romilly.
Celtic art in Pagan and Christian times. '08(D19) 8°, *$3 net. Jacobs.

Allen, Lewis.
Airship almanac; little light literature on high life, telling how to get off the earth and how to get on again. '09(D18) c. D. bds., 75 c. J: W. Luce.

Allen, Lyman Whitney.
Abraham Lincoln: a poem. Centennial (4th) ed. '09(F13) c. D. **$1.25 net. Putnam.
Parable of the rose, and other poems. '08 (D5) c. D. **$1.25 net. Putnam.
Triumph of love; poem. '10(F19) c. 12°, **$1.25 net. Putnam.

Allen, Mrs. Mary Wood-.
Making the best of our children; 1st ser., 1 to 8 years; 2d ser., 8 to 16 years of age; ed. by Rose Wood-Allen Chapman. '09(N6) c. D. ea., *$1 net. McClurg.

Allen, Nellie Burnham.
Industrial studies. '10(D31) c. il. D. 65 c. Ginn.

Allen, Orrin Peer.
Allen memorial, second series: descendants of Samuel Allen of Windsor, Conn., 1640-1907. '07, [1908.] (Ap.) 303 p. il. pors. 8°, $3.75. O. P. Allen.
Descendants of Nicholas Cady of Watertown, Mass., 1645-1910. '10(Ag) 546 p. pl. 8°, $5. O. P. Allen.

Allen, Philip Schuyler, ed.
Herein! first German readings. '10(Mr26) c. map, D. 70 c. Holt.

Allen, R: W., M.D.
Opsonic method of treatment and vaccine therapy. 3d ed., enl. '10(S) 10+277 p. $2. Blakiston.
Vaccine therapy and the opsonic method of treatment. '09(Ja23) c. 8°, *$2 net. Blakiston.

Allen, Rob. Cameron.
Bible in our public schools. '09(My) c. 60 p. 12°, pap., 25 c. Jennings.

Allen, T: Newton.
Chronicles of Oldfields. '09(D11) c. por. O. *$1.50 net. A. Harriman.

Allen, Cardinal W:
Briefe historie of the glorious martyrdom of twelve reverend priests: Father Edmund Campion and his companions; with contemporary verses by the venerable H: Walpole; repr. from the (probably unique) copy in the British Museum, and ed. by the Rev. J. H. Pollen. '08 (D5) 8°, *$1.25 net. Herder.

Allen, W: Alex.
Unclaimed millions in England; cont. much of value and interest to persons interested in chancery cases or lost estates. '10 (Je11) c. T. pap., $1. W. A. Allen.

Allen, W: F:
Railway operating associations; addresses del. before the Graduate School of Business Administration of Harvard University, Jan. 11, 1909. '09(Jl) 28 p. 8°. (Priv. pr.) W: F: Allen.

Allen, W: Harvey.
Broader motive for school hygiene. '08, [1909.] (Mr) 16 p. 24°. (Priv. pr.) W: H. Allen.
Civics and health: with an introd. by W: T. Sedgwick. '09(Ap3) c. il. D. (Efficient citizen ser.) $1.25. Ginn.
See also Snedden, D: S.

Allen, Willis Boyd, comp.
Violet book. '09(O2) front. O. **$1.80 net. Jacobs.

ALLEN FAMILY.
See Genealogies.

Allerton, Mark, and Browning, R.
Golf made easy. '10(S) il. 8°, 35 c. net. Cassell.

Allgemeine bücherkunde zur neueren deutschen literaturgeschichte. Arnold, R. S. $2.25. Stechert.

ALLIGATOR.
Reese, A. M. Development of the American alligator. 50 c.—Development of the brain of the American alligator. 10 c. Smith. Inst.

Allinson, Alfr.
Days of the Directoire. '09(N20) il. O. *$5 net. Lane.

Allinson, Anne Crosby Emery.
See Allinson, Fs. Greenleaf.

Allinson, Fs. Greenleaf and Anne Crosby Emery.
Greek lands and letters. '09(D11) c. il. O. **$2.50 net. Houghton M.

ALLIONIACEAE.
See Botany.

Allison, S: Buell, and Perdue, H. Avis, comps.
Sixteen stories: supplementary reader for adv. first and second grades. '08(Ag1) c. il. D. 25 c. Flanagan.

Allison, T: Jefferson.
Della Dorn; or, struggles of the Boers: [in verse.] '08(D) 266 p. il. por. 12°, $1.25. Hyland.

Allison, Young Ewing.
Delicious vice, [novel reading;] pipe dreams and fond adventures of an habitual novel-reader among some great books and their people. '08(F29); Second ser. '09(Ap17) c. S. (Bookish books.) ea., *55 c. net. Burrows.

Allison's lad. Dix, B. M. **$1.35 net. Holt.

Alloway, C: Rozell.
Ode to the memory of our country's Father. '08(Je27) c. il. pors. S. 25 c. C: R. Alloway.

ALLOYS.
Law, E: F. Alloys and their industrial application. *$4 net. Lippincott.

All's lost by lust. *See* Middleton, T: Spanish gipsie.

Allsop, F: C:
Telephones, their construction and fitting. 8th ed., with addenda. '09(Je19) il. 12°, $1.25. Spon.

Alltägliches. Lambert, M. B. 75 c. Heath.

Allyn, Adeline Bartlett, comp.
Black Hall traditions and reminiscences [Griswold family.] '09(F13) c. map. D. bds., $1. A. B. Allyn.

Allyn, Eunice Gibbs.
Cats' convention. '09, [1910.] (F) c. 225 p. il. 8°, $1.50. Cochrane.

Allyn & Bacon's college Latin ser. 16°. Allyn & B.
—Cicero. Tusculan disputations. I., II., V. $1.50.

Allyn & Bacon's ser. of German texts. 12°. *50 c. net. Allyn & B.
—Zschokke. Der zerbrochene krug; Das wirtshaus zu Cransac.

Allyn & Bacon's ser. of school histories. il. 12°. Allyn & B.
—Adams *and* Trent. History of the United States. $1.50.

Alma mater ser. 44 v. '10(N) il. ea., $1, boxed. Caldwell.

Almack, E:
Bookplates. '08(O17) il. S. (Little books on art.) *$1 net. McClurg.

Almanach de Gotha, 1909. '09(Ja16) 8°; 1910. '09(D25) pors. T. ea., $2.70. Lemcke.

ALMANACS AND ANNUALS.
Annual register: review of public events at home and abroad, 1907; 1908; 1909. ea., $6. Longmans.
Bo-Peep: treasury for the little ones. 75 c. Cassell.
Brooklyn Daily Eagle almanac, 1908; 1909; 1910. ea., 50 c. Brooklyn Eagle.
Cassell's annual for boys and girls. $1.75; $1.25. Cassell.
Catholic home annual for 1909. 25 c. Benziger.
Father Tuck's annual. $2.50; $1.75. Tuck.
Happenings of future years foretold in the Welsh almanacs. 25 c. H: Blackwell.
Hazell's annual for 1910. *$1.50 net. Scribner.
Hinkende (Der) bote am Mississippi-volkskalender, 1909. 5 c.; per doz., 30 c.; per gross, $3. Herder.
Laird & Lee's diary and time-saver, 1909; 1910; 1911. ea., 25 c. Laird.
Langland, J., *ed.* *Chicago Daily News* almanac and year book, 1909. 40 c. Chic. Daily News.
Living Church annual and Whittaker's Churchman's almanac: church cyclopedia and almanac, 1910; 1911. ea., 75 c.; 50 c. Young Churchman.
McKinney, I. S. T. Year book of English authors. $1.50; $3. Caldwell.
New international year-book, 1907; 1908; 1909. ea., $5-$12.50. Dodd.
Oklahoma almanac industrial record. 50 c. Daily Oklahoman.
Standard every man's memo-book. 50 c.; 25 c. Laird.
Statesman's year-book, 1908; 1909; 1910. ea., *$3 net. Macmillan.
Tribune almanac and political register, 1908; 1909; 1910. ea., 25 c. Tribune Assoc.
Whitaker's almanack, 1909; 1910. ea., *$1.25 net. Scribner.
World almanac and encyclopedia, 1908; 1909; 1910. ea., 25 c. Press Pub.
See also Calendars and year-books;—*also* under special subjects.

Almost fairy children. Lewis, C. $1.25. Bobbs-M.

Al-moveth. Koplowitz, I. 75 c. Bloch.

Along the Old Trail. Vernon, J. S. $1. Tucker-V.

Along the rivieras of France and Italy. Home, G. C. *$3 net. Macmillan.

Along the trail of the friendly years. Hatcher, W: E. $1.50 net. Revell.

Along the way. Canfield, W: W. $1.50. Fenno.

Along the way. Hoople, C. M. *$1.50 net. Grafton Press.
Along the western Brandywine. MacElree, W. W. $5. Hickman.
Alongshore. Reynolds, S. $1.50. Macmillan
Alpens, Marquesa d'.
See Savallo, Teresa de.
Alpha. Grills, M. W. 25 c. M. W. Grills.
Alpha and Omega. Hull, J: W. 50 c. J: W. Hull.
Alpha Portland cement for eternity. '10 (My) c. 48 p. il. 4°, gratis. Alpha Portland.
Alphabetical oddities. Krull, V. H. V. H. Krull.
ALPHABETS.
Binion, S: A: Phyllanthography: [pictorial alphabet of flowers and leaves.] $3. Fenno.
Dulac, E. Lyrics, pathetic and humorous, from A to Z. **$2 net. Warne.
Holbrook, F. Hiawatha alphabet. 75 c. Rand, McN. & Co.
Irwin, W. A. Bird cage: [alphabet book in verse.] $1.50. B. W. Dodge.
Shaylor, H. W. Book of alphabets for use in schools. 10 c.; per doz., $1. Ginn.
Stevens, W: O. Another Annapolis alphabet. 50 c. Lord Balto. Pr.
See also Inscriptions;—Lettering;—Penmanship.
Alpines and bog plants. Farrer, R. J. $4. Longmans.
ALPS (The).
Baedeker, K. Eastern Alps. *$3 net. Scribner.
Conway, *Sir* W: M. The Alps. $1.50 net. Macmillan.
Coolidge, W: A: B. Alps in nature and in history. *$2.50 net. Dutton.
Freeston, C: L. High roads of the Alps; motoring guide. $3. Scribner.
Harrison, F. My Alpine jubilee. *$1.25 net. Dutton.
McMurry, C: A. The Alps. 10 c. Flanagan.
Stephen, *Sir* L. Playground of Europe. *$1.75 net. Putnam.
See also Flowers;—Switzerland.
Al-Raschid, Mme. Bey.
See Böhlau, Helene.
ALSACE, France.
Kaeppelin, C: E. R. Alsace throughout the ages. $1.50. C: Miller.
Alston, Rev. E. A., and Turton, Rev. Z. H.
Origines eucharisticæ. '08 (O3) 12°, pap., *35 c. net. Whittaker.
Alston, Leonard.
Education and citizenship in India. '10 (My21) D. $1.25 net. Longmans.
Modern constitutions in outline; introd. study in political science. Rev. ed. '10 (F5) D. 90 c. Longmans.
ALSTON, *Mrs.* Theodosia Burr.
Pidgin, C: F. Theodosia, the first gentlewoman of her time. *$2.50 net: *$3 net. C. M. Clark.
Altar devotions. Smith, C: E., *comp.* **25 c. net; **50 c. net. Longmans.
Altar stairs. Lancaster, G. B. †$1.50. Doubleday, P.
ALTARS.
See Church furniture.

Altars of sacrifice. Teagar, M. M. $1.25. M. M. Teagar.
Altars to mammon. Neff, E. †$1.50. Stokes.
Altemus' classic ser. 24°, $1, boxed. Altemus.
—Hale. Man without a country.
Altemus handbooks for animal owners. D. $1. Altemus.
—Barton. Dog.—Horse.
—Williams. Cat.
Altemus' mother stories ser. il. 8°, 50 c. Altemus.
—Mother animal stories.
—O'Donnell. Mother Santa Claus stories.
Altemus one syllable ser. il. 12°, 50 c. Altemus.
—Child's story of the New Testament.
—Remy. Bible stories for little children.—Story of Jesus.
Altemus' popular manuals. S. bds., 50 c. Altemus.
—Collins. Human nature in selling goods.
Alten, Georg Karl Friedrich Viktor von.
Studies in applied tactics; authorized tr., (with substitution of American army organization,) by Major C. H. Barth. '08 (N) c. 261 p. fold. maps, 8°, $2. Hudson.
Altera colloquia Latina. Erasmus, D. *40 c. net. Putnam.
ALTERNATING CURRENTS.
Avery, A. H. Auto-transformer designs. $1.50. Spon.
Bedell, F:, *and* Pierce, C. A. Direct and alternating currents. *$2 net. Van Nostrand.
Cramp, W:, *and* Smith, C: F: Vectors and vector diagrams applied to alternating current circuit with examples of their use in the theory of transformers. *$2.50 net. Longmans.
Crocker, F. B., *and* Torda, T. Direct and alternating-current machine design. *$5 net. McGraw.
Drysdale, C. V. Foundations of alternating current theory. $2.50 net. Longmans.
Esty, W: Alternating-current machinery. $3. Am. Sch. Corr.
Franklin, W: S. Electric waves; advanced treatise. on alternating-current theory **$3 net. Macmillan.
Goldschmidt, R. Alternating current commutator motor, and The leakage of induction motors. *$3 net. Van Nostrand.
Kapp, G. Transformers for single and multiphase currents. *$3 net. Macmillan.
McAllister, A. S. Alternating current motors. *$3 net. McGraw-H.
Marshall, A. W. Alternating currents simply explained. 25 c. Spon.
Sheldon, S., Mason, H. *and* Housman. Alternating-current machines; being the 2d v. of Dynamo electric machinery. **$2.50 net. Van Nostrand.
Steinmetz, C: P. Theory and calculation of alternating current phenomena. *$5 net. McGraw.
Taylor, W: T. Stationary transformers. *$1.50 net. McGraw.
See also Dynamos and motors;—Electric wires;—Electricity.
Alternative (The). McCutcheon, G: B. †$1.25. Dodd.

Althea. Lee, V. $1.50 net. Lane.
Althea. Nirdlinger, D. E. 60 c. Benziger.
ALTITUDES.
Hayford, J: F., *and* Pike, L. Hypsometry: precise leveling in the U. S., 1903-07. pap., 45 c. U. S., Supt. of Docs.
United States. *Dept. of the Interior. U. S. Geolog. Survey.* Results of spirit leveling in Illinois, 1896 to 1908. (Add. Superintendent for price.)
Alton Locke. *See* Kingsley, *Rev.* C:
ALTRUISM.
See Ethics.
Altsheler, Jos. Alex.
Forest runners: story of the great war trail in early Kentucky. '08(S26) c. il. D. †$1.50. Appleton.
Free Rangers: story of early days along the Mississippi. '09(O9) c. col. il. D. †$1.50. Appleton.
Horsemen of the plains. '10(O22) il. D. $1.50. Macmillan.
Last of the chiefs: story of the great Sioux war. '09(O9) c. col. il. D. $1.50. Appleton.
The recovery: story of Kentucky. '09 (Ap10) c. D. $1.50. Lovell.
Riflemen of the Ohio. '10(O1) c. il. D. $1.50. Appleton.
Altsheler, W: Brent, comp.
Maladministration through the Alaska syndicate; extract from the official record; five years "Conservation" as set forth in the congressional investigation of the Interior Department and Forestry Service; the Ballinger-Pinchot controversy. '10 (S17) c. 12°, pap., 10 c. W: B. Altsheler.
Alvarez de Aillón, Pedro, and Hurtado de Toledo, Luis.
Comedia Tibalda; ahora por primera vez publicada según la forma original por Adolfo Bonilla y San Martín. '03 [1909.] (N) 77 p. (Bibliotheca hispanica.) $1. Hispanic Soc.
"Alvidas," pseud.
See Hodges, H: Clay.
Alvord, C: H.
Dairy industry in Texas. '09, [1910.] (N) 105 p. il. 8°, (Texas, Dept. of Agriculture, bull.) Von Boeckmann-J.
Alvord, Clarence Walworth.
British ministry and the treaty of Fort Stanwix. '09(Ap17) O. pap., 25 c. State Hist., Wis.
—, ed. *See* Illinois State Historical Library.
Alvord, S: Morgan, comp.
Genealogy of the descendants of Alexander Alvord, an early settler of Winsor, Conn., and Northampton, Mass. '08, 1909.] (S) 9-823 p. il. pors. 8°, *$5 net. S: M. Alvord.
ALVORD FAMILY.
See Genealogies.
Alwood, W: Bradford.
Enological studies. I, Experiments in cider making applicable to farm conditions; II, Notes on the use of pure yeasts in wine making. '09, [1910.] (Mr) 32 p il. tabs., 8°, (U. S., Dept. of Agriculture, Bu. of Chemistry, bull.) pap. (Add. Superintendent for price.) U. S., Supt. of Docs.
Alwood, W: Bradford.—*Continued.*
Fermenting power of pure yeasts and some associated fungi. '08(Ap18.) il. 8°, (U. S. Dept. of Agriculture, Bureau of Chemistry, bull.) pap., 15 c.
Alymer-Small, Sidney.
See Small, Sidney Alymer-.
Am anfang. Tuckerman, J. 50 c. Holt.
AM HA-ARETZ.
See Jews.
Am I my brother's keeper? Deran-Smith, *Mrs.* E. $1.10. E. Deran-Smith.
Amabel Channice. Sedgwick, A. D. †$1.50. Century Co.
AMADE, *General* Albert Gérard Léo d'.
Rankin, J. R. L. In Morocco with General d' Amade. *$2.50 net. Longmans.
AMADIS, *of Gaul.*
Davidson, N. J., *ed.* Knight errant and his doughty deeds. $1.50. Lippincott.
AMALGAMATION (of metals).
See Gold.
AMANA COMMUNITY.
Shambaugh, B. M. H. Amana: the community of true inspiration. $3. State Hist., Ia.
Amateur Angler, pseud.
See Marston, E:
Amateur art. Cosgrove, *Mrs.* H. C. J. $1. Donnelley.
Amateur astronomer. Riegler, G. $1.25 net. Dodd.
Amateur Athletic Union of the United States.
Official hdbk.; constitution, by-laws, general and athletic rules. '09(D25) c. 12 p. front. 12°, (Spalding athletic lib.) pap., 10 c. Am. Sports.
Amateur electrician's workshop. Bottone, S. R. 75 c. McKay.
AMATEUR JOURNALISM.
See Journalism.
Amateur motorist. Pemberton, M. **$3.75 net. McClurg.
Amateur performance. Evinson, E. $1. B'way Pub.
Amazing adventures of an inventor. Jones, A. G. †$1.50. Winston.
Amazing marriage. *See* Meredith, G:
AMAZON RIVER.
Bates, H. W. Naturalist on the Amazon. 35 c. net; 70 c. net. Dutton.
Ambard, Eug. M.
Tourist guide to the West Indies, Venezuela and Isthmus of Panama. '09(My) c. 97 p. il. map, 16°, pap., (gratis to passengers). Hamburg-American Line.
AMBASSADORS.
Turkish diplomatic life in Washington under the old regime, by the wife of a diplomat. $1. Cochrane.
Ambler, C: H:
Sectionalism in Virginia from 1776 to 1861. '10(Je18) c. D. $1.50 net. Univ. of Chic.
AMBLYSTOMA.
See Amphibia.
Amédée's son. Smith, H. J. †$1.50. Houghton M.
Amen. Ryno, W. $1. B'way Pub.
AMERICA.
See Alaska; — Canada; — Central America;—Explorers;—Maps; — Mexico;—North America;—Panama; — South America;—Spanish America; —Spanish colonies;—Spanish dependencies;—United States.

America across the seas; our colonial empire, described by Hamilton Wright, C. H. Forbes-Lindsay, [and others.] '09(Je5) c. il. maps, Q. $1. C. S. Hammond.

America and the Far Eastern question. Millard, T: F. F. **$4 net. Moffat.

America at home. Low, A. M. *$1.75 net. Scribner.

America ser. f°, pap. Union Bk.
—Baxter. America. $12.50.

American Aberdeen-Angus Breeders' Association. Supremacy of Aberdeen-Angus Cattle; results of leading fat stock shows during past decades in Great Britain and America; classification of special premiums and American Aberdeen-Angus Breeders' Association sales for the year 1909; ed. by C: Gray. '09(D) 3-105 p. il. fold. tab., 8°. (Add. pubs. for price.) Am. Aberdeen-A.

American Academy of Medicine. Prevention of infant mortality; papers and discussions at the conference at New Haven, Ct., Nov. 11-12, 1909. '10(Jl) 347 p. 8°, $5. Am. Acad. Med.

AMERICAN ACADEMY OF MEDICINE.
See **Barker, Jeremiah.**

American Academy of Political and Social Science. Administration of justice in the United States. '10(Jl9) F. (Annals.) pap., $1. Am. Acad. Pol. Sci.

American Academy of Political and Social Science. American business conditions. '09 (D18) Q. (Annals of the American Academy of Political and Social Science.) $1.50; pap., $1. Am. Acad. Pol. Sci.

American Academy of Political and Social Science. American waterways. '08(F15) Q. (Annals of the Am. Acad of Pol. and Social Science.) pap., $1. Am. Acad. Pol. Sci.

American Academy of Political and Social Science. Banking problems. '10(D24) F. (Annals.) pap., $1. Am. Acad. Pol. Sci.

American Academy of Political and Social Science. Child employing industries; proceedings of the 6th annual meeting of the National Child Labor Committee. '10 (Ap9) O. (Annals of the Academy.) $1.50; pap., $1. Am. Acad. Pol. Sci.

American Academy of Political and Social Science. Child labor and social progress; proceedings of the fourth annual meeting of the National Child Labor Committee. '08(Jl18) c. Q. (Annals of the Am. Acad. of Pol. and Social science, Supplement.) pap., $1. Am. Acad. Pol. Sci.

American Academy of Political and Social Science. Child labor legislation: schedules of existing statutes and the standard child labor law; comp. by Jospehine C. Goldmark. Handbook, 1908. '08(Je6) Q. (Annals of the Am. Acad. of Pol. and Soc. Science.) 50 c. Am. Acad. Pol. Sci.

American Academy of Political and Social Science. Child workers of the nation: proceedings of fifth annual meeting of the National Child Labor Committee. '09(Ap3) Q. (Annals of the Am. Acad. of Pol, and Social Science.) pap., $1. Am. Acad. Pol. Sci.

American Academy of Political and Social Science. Chinese and Japanese in America. (O2) Q. (Annals of the American Academy of Political and Social Science.) pap., $1. Am. Acad. Pol. Sci.

American Academy of Political and Social Science. Commercial relations bet. the United States and Japan; [and] The significance of the awakening of China. '10 (Jl9) c. F. (Supp. to the Annals.) pap. Am. Acad. Pol. Sci.

American Academy of Political and Social Science. Conservation of natural resources. '09(Je19) 4°, (Annals of the Am. Acad. of Pol. and Soc. Science.) pap., $1; $1.50. Am. Acad. Pol. Sci.

American Academy of Political and Social Science. Consumer's control of production: the work of the National Consumers' League. '09(Ag14) c. Q. (Supplement to Annals of American Academy of Political and Social Science.) pap., 75 c. Am. Acad. Pol. Sci.

American Academy of Political and Social Science. Control of municipal public service corporations. '08(Je6) Q. (Annals of the Am. Acad. of Pol. and Soc. Science.) pap., $1. Am. Acad. of Pol. Sci.

American Academy of Political and Social Science. Development of Germany as a world power; introd. address, by Hon. Charlemagne Tower; address, by Count J. H. von Bernstorff. '10(Ap16) 4°, (Supplement to the Annals of the Academy.) 50 c. Am. Acad. Pol. Sci.

American Academy of Political and Social Science. Federal regulation of industry. '08(Jl18) c. Q. (Annals of the Am. Acad. of Pol. and Social Science.) pap., $1. Am. Acad. Pol. Sci.

American Academy of Political and Social Science. Industrial education. '09(Ja9) Q. (Annals of the Am. Acad. of Pol. and Soc. Science.) pap., $1. Am. Acad. Pol. Sci.

American Academy of Political and Social Science. Labor and wages. '09(Ap3) Q. (Annals of the Am. Acad. of Pol. and Social Science.) pap., $1. Am. Acad. Pol. Sci.

American Academy of Political and Social Science. Lessons of the financial crisis. '08(Ap4) c. Q. (Annals of the Am. Acad. of Pol. and Social Science.) pap., $1. Am. Acad. Pol. Sci.

American Academy of Political and Social Science. New South; Supplement; development of Germany as a world power; introd. address by Hon. Charlemagne Tower; address by Count J. H. von Bernstoff, 1910. '10(Ja1) Q. (Annals of the Am. Acad. of Political and Social Science.) pap., $1. Am. Acad. Pol. Sci.

American Academy of Political and Social Science. Public recreation facilities. '10 (Ap9) Q. (Annals of the Academy.) $1.50. pap., $1. Am. Acad. Pol. Sci.

American Academy of Political and Social Science. Race improvement in the United States. '09(Ag7) Q. (Annals of the American Academy of Political and Social Science.) pap., $1. Am. Acad. Pol. Sci.

American Academy of Political and Social Science. Regulation of the liquor traffic. '08(D5) Q. (Annals of the Am. Acad. of Pol. and Social Science.) pap., $1. Am. Acad. Pol. Sci.

American Academy of Political and Social Science. Settlement of labor disputes. '10 (O1) Q. (Annals.) pap., $1. Am. Acad. Pol. Sci.

American Academy of Political and Social Science. Significance of the woman suffrage movement. '10(Je18) c. Q. (Supp. to Annals.) pap., 50 c. Am. Acad. Pol. Sci.

American Academy of Political and Social Science. Stocks and the stock market. '10(Je11) Q. (Annals.) pap., $1. Am. Acad. Pol. Sci.

American Academy of Political and Social Science. Tariff revision. '08(O3) Q. (Annals of the Am. Acad. of Pol. and Social Science.) pap., $1. Am. Acad.

American Academy of Political and Social Science. Work of the Consumers' League during the year ending March 1, 1910. '10 (O1) Q. (Supt. to annals.) pap. Am. Acad. Pol. Sci.

American Academy of Political and Social Science publications. 8°, pap. Am. Acad. Pol. Sci.

—Fouse. Recent developments in the life insurance business. 15 c.

—Haney. Vocational training and trade teaching in the public schools. 15 c.

—Huebner. Five years of railroad regulation. 25 c.

—Johnson. Trend of governmental regulation of railroads. 15 c.

—Koler. Un-American character of race legislation. 25 c.

—Schaffner. Effect of the recent boycott decisions. 25 c.

American accountants' lib. *See* American School of Correspondence.

American addresses at the Second Hague Peace Conference. Choate, J. H. $1.50. Ginn.

American Adjusters Co. Directory of reliable lawyers and banks in the United States and Canada, [etc.;] June, 1908. '09 (Je19); June, 1910. [1910.] (Je) c. O. ea., $5.50. Am. Adjusters.

American admiralty. Benedict, E. C. $6.30. Banks & Co.

American agricultural periodicals. Tucker, G. M. (Priv. pr.) G. M. Tucker.

American agriculturist hand book. '09(Ap10) c. il. 8°, 50 c. Judd.

American and English annot cases; sel. from the current Am., Canadian and Eng. repts.; (W: M. McKinney, D: S. Garland and H. Noyes Greene.) v. 8. '08(Mr); v. 9 (Je); v. 10 (O); v. 11. '09(Mr); v. 12 (Je); v. 13-14. '09, [1910.] (F); v. 15 (My); v. 16 (S) c. O. shp., ea., $5.—Digest. vs. 1-10, with tab. of cases. '09(Mr) c. 679 p. O. gratis to subs. of Am. and Eng. Annot. cases. E: Thompson.

American and English banking contrasted. Baird, H: C. (Add. pub. for price.) Baird.

American and English encyclopædia of law and practice. *See* McKinney, W: M., *ed.*

American and English encyclopædia of law. (2d ed.) Supp.; ed. by D: Garland and C: Porterfield under the supervision of Ja. Cockcroft. v. 5. '08(N) c. O. shp., $7.50. E: Thompson.

American and English genealogies in the Library of Congress. $1.05. Gov. Pr. Off.

American (The) annual of photography; ed. by J: A. Tennant, 1908. v. 22. '08(Ja18); 1909. v. 23. '08(D5); 1910. v. 24 '10 (Ja15); 1911. v. 25 (D24) c. il. O. ea., $1.25; pap., 75 c. G: Murphy.

American Anthropological Association memoirs. 8°, pap. Am. Anthropological.

—Churchill. Weather words of Polynesia. 80 c.

—Pepper *and* Wilson. Hidatsa shrine. 50 c.

—Spinden. Nez Percé Indians. 95 c.

American Antiquarian Society. Manuscript records of the French and Indian War in the library of the Society; prep. from the origs. under direction of the library committee, by C: H: Lincoln. '10(Jl16) facsims., 4°, (Transactions and collections.) $2.50. Am. Antiquarian.

American apple orchard. Waugh, F. A. $1. Judd.

American Archæological Expedition to Syria, pubs. il. f°. Century Co.

—Prentice. Greek and Latin inscriptions. **$10 net.

AMERICAN ART.
See Painters and paintings.

American art annual. Levy, F. v. 7. $1.50. Am. Art.

American artisan manuals. il. 12°. D. Stern.

—Pratt. Advertising manual. $3.50.

American as he is. Butler, N: M. **$1 net. Macmillan.

American Association for Labor Legislation. Review of labor legislation of 1909. '10 (F5) 8°, (Am. Assoc. for Labor Legislation; Legislative review.) gratis. Parsons Pr.

American Association for the Study of Alcohol and other Narcotics. Some scientific conclusions concerning the alcoholic problem and its practical relations to life; papers read at the semi-annual meeting at Washington. D. C., March 17, 18 and 19, 1909. '09(S) 179 p. 8°. (Add. Superintendent for price.) U. S., Supt. of Docs.

American Association of Foreign Language Newspapers. The unreached millions. '09, [1910.] (Ap) 58 p. por. 8°, pap. (Add. pubs. for price.) L: N. Hammerling.
Contains list of foreign newspapers published in U. S.

American Association of International Conciliation pubs. 12°. Am. International Conciliation.

—Kelly. American public school as a factor in international conciliation. gratis.

American Association of Local Freight Agents' Associations. Compilation of convention topics: comp. by order of the association by H. M. Waring, under direction and supervision of J. J. Sherlock, J. L. Harrington and I. R. Van Tuyl. '09, [1910.] (My) c. 3-670 p. 8°. $1.50. Am. Assoc. Freight.

American Association of Medical Milk Commissions. Manual of working methods and standards for the use of the Medical Milk Commission. '09, [1910.] (S) 24 p. 8°, gratis. Milk Com. Assoc.

AMERICAN AUTHORS.
See Authors.

American Automobile Association. Automobile book, 1910 ed. In 4 v. v. 1, New York state; v. 2, New England; v. 3, New Jersey, Pennsylvania, and South; v. 4, Middle West. '10(Je4) 8°, leath., ea., $2.50. Automobile Blue Book.

American baby abroad. Crewdson, *Mrs.* L. C. $1.50. Little, B. & Co.

American Bankers' Association. Forms for trust companies; sel. and arr. by a committee of the Trust Company Section, American Bankers' Association, from forms in use by trust companies of the United States. '10(Jl2) c. forms, 4°, $20. Am. Bankers' Assoc.

American Bankers' Association. Rept. of the Currency Commission to the American Bankers' Association: and remarks by Hon. Alonzo Barton Hepburn, chairman. '08 (Je6) 8°. (Add. Association for price.) Am. Bankers' Assoc.

American Bankers' Association. Savings Bank Section. Proceedings of the 7th annual meeting, held in Denver, Colo., Sept. 28, 1908; ed. by W: Hanhart. '09(S11) pors. O. ¾ leath. (Add. Assoc. for price.) Am. Bankers' Assoc.

American bankruptcy repts.; annot.; ed. by J: T. Cook. v. 19. '08(Jl); v. 20. '08, [1909.] (Ja); v. 21 (Jl); v. 22. '10(F); v. 23 (Jl) O. shp., ea., $5.—Digest of v. 15 to 20, incl., (1906-1909,) [etc.,] by Melvin T. Bender and Harold J. Hinman. v. 2. '09(Je) c. O. per set of 2 v., $8.50. M. Bender.

American Baptist year-book, 1908; ed. by J. G. Walker. '08(My23); 1909. '09(My8) il. pors. O. pap., ea., *50 c. net. Am. Bapt.

American bastiles. Keeler, *Mrs.* C. O. 25 c. C. O. Keeler.

American battleship and life in the navy. Beyer, T: $1.25. Laird

American beauties. Fisher, H. $3. Bobbs-M.

AMERICAN BIBLE SOCIETY.
Fox, J: Round the world for the American Bible Society. gratis. Am. Bible.

American bibliography. Evans, C: In 6 v. v. 5. $15. C: Evans; [Blakely Press.]

American biographical directories. 8°. Potomac Press.
—District of Columbia: concise biographies of contemporary citizens. $6; $7.50.

AMERICAN BOARD OF COMMISSIONERS FOR FOREIGN MISSIONS.
Strong, W: E. Story of the American Board. $1.75 net. Pilgrim Press.

American book prices current. *See* Livingston, Luther S:, *comp.*

American boy at Henley. Cannon, F. E. $1.50. Little, B. & Co.

American business and accounting encyclopedia; ed. by W. W. Thorne. In 6 v. v. 1, 2. New ed., (3d.) '08(D) c. il. forms, f°, ea., $3. Business Man's Pub.

American business conditions. American Academy of Political and Social Science. $1. Am. Acad. Pol. Sci.

American business law. Sullivan, J: J. **$1.50 net. Appleton.

American business methods, (down to the minute.) '08, [1909.] (S) c. 376 p. il. 4°, $2. Business Man's Pub.

American business woman. Cromwell, J: H. $2 net. Putnam.

American campaigns. Steele, M. F. (Add. Superintendent for price.) U. S., Supt. of Docs.

American case book ser.; ed. by Ja. Brown Scott. O. West Pub.
—Costigan. Cases on wills, descent and administration. $4.50.
—Gilmore. Cases on the law of partnership. $3.75.
—Green. Cases of the law of carriers. $4.
—Lorenzen. Cases on the conflict of laws. $4.50.
—Mechem *and* Gilbert. Cases on damages.
—Mikell. Cases on criminal law. $4.
—Smith *and* Moore. Cases on the law of bills and notes. $4.50.

American catalog, 1905-1907. In 2 v. v. 1, Record, under author, title, subject and series of the books published in the U. S. recorded in *The Publishers' Weekly*, "Weekly Record," from Jan., 1905-Dec., 1907, together with a directory of publishers. '08 (Je27) c. Q. hf. mor., *$7.50 net; v. 2, Full title entries with annotations. '08(Je18) c. Q. hf. mor., *$6 net; per set, *$13.50 net. Pub. Weekly.

American citizen. Brooks, J: G. $1.50 net. Houghton M.

American citizen in Pennsylvania. Maltby, A. E. $1. Am. Bk.

American citizen ser.; ed. by Albert Bushnell Hart. 12°. Longmans.
—Dewey. Financial history of the United States. **$2 net.
—Hart. Actual government as applied under American conditions. $2.25.
—McClain. Constitutional law in the United States. $2.25.
—Seligman. Principles of economics. $2.50.
—Wright. Outline of practical sociology. $2.

American Civic Association pubs. 8°, pap. Am. Civic League.
—White house conference on the conservation of natural resources. (Add. pub. for price.)

American Civic Association pubs. Department of Nuisances: il. 12°, gratis. Am. Civic League.
—Olmstead, *and others.* Smoke nuisance.
—Woodruff. Billboard nuisance.

American civics. Clancy, J. $1. Democracy Pr.

American civil government; outline study for secondary schools; prep. by the Committee of the New England History Teachers' Association. '10(O8) 12°, bds., 50 c. net; teachers' ed., 60 c. net. Macmillan.

AMERICAN CIVIL WAR.
See Civil War (United States).

American classics for seventh and eighth grade reading. Webster, H. H., *ed.* **80 c. net. Houghton M.

American college. Flexner, A. **$1 net. Century Co.

AMERICAN COLLEGE, Rome.
Brann, H: A. Hist. of the American College of the Roman Catholic Church of the United States. $2. Benziger.

American college and private school directory; [comp. and ed. by Harry J. Myers.] 2d ed. '09(Mr) 204 p. 8°, $2. Educational Aid.

American college education and life. Tufts, J. H. (Add. author for price.) J. H. Tufts.

American College of Mechano-Therapy, Chicago, Ill. Text-book of chiropractic. '10 (S) c. 94 p. il. 12°, $2. Am. Coll. Mechano-Therapy.

American College of Mechano-Therapy, Chicago, Ill. Text book of osteopathy. '10 (Jl) c. 96 p. il. 12°, $2. Am. Coll. Mechano-Therapy.

American commentary on the Old Testament. Book of Genesis, by Prof. Calvin Goodspeed and Prof. D. M. Welton. [1910.] (Jl) c. '08, '09. 37+39-253 p. 8°. $2 net. Am. Bapt.

American commonwealth. *See* Bryce, Ja.

American commonwealths ser.; ed. by Horace E. Scudder. D. Houghton M.
—Folwell. Minnesota. **$1.25 net.
—Thwaites. Wisconsin. **$1.25 net.

American communities. Hinds, W: A. $1.50. Kerr.

American corporations. Sullivan, J: J. $2 net. Appleton.

American cotton system. Miller, T: S. $1.50. T. S. Miller.

American criminal repts.; cases determined in the federal and state cts. in the U. S., [etc.] v. 14; (J: F. and H: C. Geeting.) '08, [1909.] (Mr); v. 15 (O) c. O. shp., ea., *$5 net.—Digest of cases and notes cont. in Amer. crim. repts. v. 1-15; together with a table of cases alphabetically examined. '10(Ag) c. O. shp., $6. Callaghan.

American crisis biographies; ed. by Ellis Paxson Oberholtzer. por. D. **$1.25 net. Jacobs.
—Dodd. Jefferson Davis.
—Du Bois. John Brown.
—Hale, *jr.* William H. Seward.
—Haynes. Charles Sumner.
—Hunt. John C. Calhoun.
—Pendleton. Alexander H. Stephens.
—White. Stonewall Jackson.

American cyclopedia of the automobile, by T: H. Russell and C: P. Root, assisted by a corps of experts. 6 v. '09(My22) c. il. 8°, $18.50. Thompson & T.

American decisions and American repts.; digest of decisions cont. in the 160 vs.; by Stewart Rapalje. 3 v. '10(Mr) c. O. $15. Bancroft-W.; Lawyers' Co-op.

American decisions; comp. and annot. by J: Proffatt and A. C. Freeman. Extra annotated v. 1-20. '10(Mr) c. O. $55; vs. 21-40. '01(Ag) c. O. ea., $2.75; per set, $55; '10 (D) In 10 v. ea., $5. Bancroft-W.; Lawyers' Co-op.

American decisions; notes showing how each case in these repts. has been applied, developed, strengthened, limited, [etc.] v. 1, incl. 1-7 Am. dec. '09(N); v. 2, incl. 8-14 (D); v. 3, incl. 15-22 Am. dec. '10(F); v. 4 (My); v. 5, incl. 31-37 Am. dec. (Jl); v. 6, incl. 38-45 Am. dec.; v. 7, incl. 46-53 Am. dec. (N); c. O. ea., $6.50. Bancroft-W.; Lawyers' Co-op.

American digest, annot., 1907B, [etc.] '08 (Ap); 1908 A. '08(O); 1908 B. '09(Ap) c. O. (Am. digest system.) ea., $6. West Pub.

American digest. Decennial ed. 1906; complete digest of all reported cases from 1897 to 1906. v. 1. '08(Je); v. 2, 3 (Ag); v. 4 (N); v. 5 (D); v. 6. '08, [1909.] (F); v. 7 (Ap); v. 8 (Je); v. 9 (Jl); v. 10 (S); v. 11 (N); v. 12 (D); v. 13. '10(Mr); v. 14 (Ap); v. 15 (My); v. 16 (Je); v. 17 (Jl); v. 18 (S); v. 19, 20 (D) c. O. (Am. digest system.) ea., $6. (Sold only in complete sets.) West Pub.

American digest system, State ser. O. West Pub.
—Kansas digest. In 5 v. v. 1-5. ea., $6.
—Michigan digest. 5 v. ea., $7.50.
—Oklahoma and Indian Territory. Digest. 2 v. $15.

American Economic Association. Handbook, 1908. '08(Mr7) O. (Pub. of the Am. Economic Assoc.) pap., 25 c. Macmillan.

American Economic Association pubs. O. pap. Macmillan.
—Watkins. Growth of large fortunes. $1.

American Economic Association quarterly. O. pap. Am. Economic Assoc.
—Barnett. The Printers. $2; pap., $1.
—Price. Life insurance reform in New York. 75 c.
—Seligman. Progressive taxation. $1.75; $1.25.

American education. Draper, A. S. **$2 net. Houghton M.

American educational list, 1908; 1909; 1910. *See* Publishers' Weekly.

American Egypt. Arnold, C. *$3.80 net. Doubleday, P.

American Episcopal church in China. Richmond, A. B. 75 c.; 50 c. Dom. and For. Mission; Sadler-R.

American examination and review book. Pollock, H. M. $1.50. N. Y. Educ. Co.

American executive. Finley, J: H. **$1.25 net. Century Co.

American fairy tales. Baum, L. F. †$1.25. Bobbs-M.

American farmer's figurer. Atwater, J. 50 c.; 75 c.; $1. Atwater.

American Federation of Labor, Wash., D. C. Buck's Stove and Range Co. injunction suit and contempt proceedings. '10(Mr.) c. O. pap., 25 c. Trades Unionists.
Bibliography (1 p.).

American Federation of Labor, Wash., D. C. Industrial education; consisting of an investigation and rept. by a competent special committee; rept. of officers and committees; action of A. F. of L. convention; the attitude of organized labor and others toward the problem. '10(Ap16) c. 8°, 25 c. Am. Fed. Labor

AMERICAN FEDERATION OF LABOR.
Trant, W: Trade unions, their origin and objects, influence and efficacy; with an appendix showing hist. and aims of the American Federation of Labor. 10 c. Am. Fed. Labor.

American Federation of Labor, Eight hour ser. 12°. G: E. McNeill.
—McNeill. Eight hour primer. (Add. author for price.)

American fertilizer handbook: directory of the fertilizer industry and allied trades, 1908. '08(Mr); 1909. '09(My); 1910. '10 (Ag) c. il. tabs., 4°, ea., $3. Ware.

American fights and fighters ser. See Brady, Cyrus Townsend.

American flower garden. *See* Blanchan, Neltje.

American foreign policy; by a diplomatist. '09(N6) c. D. **$1.25 net. Houghton M.

American Fork & Hoe Company, Cleveland, O. Gardening for health and recreation; booklet of information about gardening for busy men and women. [1910.] (N) c. 28 p. il. 8°. Am. Fork.
Bibliography (3 p.).

American garment cutter. Ardleigh, H. $15. Am. Fashion.

American girl. Fisher, H. *$3.50 net. Scribner.

American government. Ashley, R. L. *$1.25 net. Macmillan.

American grain computator. Atwater, J. $3.50. Atwater.

American handy book of brewing. Wahl, R. 2 v. $12. Wahl-Henius.

American hero stories. Tappan, E. M. $1.50. Houghton M.

American high school. Brown, J: F. **$1.40 net. Macmillan.

American highways and byways ser. il. O. **$2 net. Macmillan.
—Johnson. Highways and byways of the Pacific coast.

American Historical Association. Study of history in the elementary schools; rept. by the Committee of Eight. '09(N20) c. 12°, pap., 50 c. Scribner.

American Historical Association prize essays. 12°. Am. Hist.
—Carter. Great Britain and the Illinois country. $1.50.
—Krehbiel. The interdict. $1.50.

American historical ser. il. O. Holt.
—Hazen. Europe since 1815. $3.

AMERICAN HISTORY.
See United States.

American history and encyclopedia of music. Hubbard, W: L., *ed.* In 10 v. ea., $3.50; $4.50; $6. Squire-C.

American history leaflets; ed. by A. B. Hart and E. Channing. 12°. Simmons.
—Hart, *ed.* Extracts from official papers relating to the Isthmian canal, 1512-1909. 10 c.

American hope. Cole, W: M. $1.50 net. Appleton.

American house building in Messina. Belknap. $2 net. Putnam.

American Hoyle. Dick, W: B. $1.50; 75 c.; 50 c. Dick.

American illustrated medical dictionary. Dorlan, W: A. N. *$4.50 net; *$5 net. Saunders.

American in Paris. Savidge, E. C. $1.50. Lippincott.

American in Spain. Cid, P. 50 c. McKay.

American insects. Kellogg, V. L. **$5 net. Holt.

American Institute of Architects. Matters rel. to competitions; extracts from the repts. of 1905-8. '08, [1909.] (My) 33 p. 8°, 50 c. Am. Institute Architects.

American Institute of Architects. Relations of railways to city development; papers read before the American Institute of Architects, Dec. 16, 1909, New Willard Hotel, Washington, D. C.; Glenn Brown, ed. '10(Ag20) il. plans, (1 fold.,) 8°, $1. Glenn Brown.

American Institute of Electrical Engineers, Library. Catalogue of the Wheeler gift of books, pamphlets and periodicals; ed. by W: D. Weaver; with introd., descriptive and critical notes by Brother Potamian. 2 v. '09(My) il. pors. 8°, $8. Am. Inst. Elec. Eng.

American Institute of Mining Engineers. General alphabetical and analytical index: Transactions; v. 1-35, (1871-1904.) '08(F1) O. $5; hf. mor., $6. Am. Inst. Min. Eng.

American Institute of Sacred Literature ser. New ed. 10 v. '09(Jl) Univ. of Chic.
Contents: Burton, Ernest D., Founding of the Christian church, 54 c.; Four letters of Paul, 27 c.; Life of Christ, 54 c.; Chamberlin, Georgia L., Origin and religious teaching of the Old Testament books, 54 c.; Harper, W: R., Book of Job, or the problem of human suffering, 27 c.; Foreshadowings of the Christ, 54 c.; Work of the Old Testament priests, 54 c.; Work of the Old Testament sages, 54 c.; Mathews, Shailer, Social and ethical teachings of Jesus, 54 c.; Smith, J: M. P., *and* Chamberlin, Georgia L., Universal element in the psalter, 50 c.

American institutions for the education of the deaf. Ferreri, G. (Add. Institute for price.) Penn. Inst.

American Iron and Steel Association. Canadian supp. to the Directory to the iron and steel works of the United States; cont. a complete list of the blast furnaces, rolling mills, and steel works in Canada, corr. to Dec. 1, 1908. '08, [1909.] (My) 19 p. 8°. (Add. pubs. for price.) Am. Iron and Steel.

American Iron and Steel Association. Directory to the iron and steel works of the U. S. 17th ed., corrected to March 1, 1908. c. 8°, $12. Am. Iron and Steel.

American Jersey Cattle Club. Jersey sires with their tested daughters, also a complete alphabetical list of tested cows; all tests accepted by the American Jersey Cattle Club to March 31, 1909. '09(D) 16+294 p. il. 8°, $2. Am. Jersey.

American Jersey Cattle Club. Register of merit of Jersey cattle, established by the American Jersey Cattle Club, May 6, 1903; individual excellence and dairy performance. '09, [1910.] (Mr.) 7+3-211 p. il. 8°, gratis. Am. Jersey.

American Jewish year book, 5669, September 26, 1908, to September 15, 1909; ed. by Herbert Friedenwald. '08(O3); 5670, Sept. 16, 1909, to Oct. 3, 1910; '09(S18); 5671;

Oct. 4, 1910, to Sept. 22, 1911; ed. by Herbert Friedenwald. '10(O1) c. D. ea., 75 c. Jewish Pub.

American law. Andrews, J. D. 2 v. *$12 net. Callaghan.

American law and procedure. In 14 v.; prep. under the editorial supervision of Ja. Parker Hall and Ja. DeWitt Andrews. '10 (Jl) c. O. hf. shp. La Salle Extension.

American law digest and legal directory, [etc.,] 1908-09; ed. by W: F. Wernse. '08 (D) c. 820+51 p. O. (Add. pubs. for price.) Bankers' Pub. Co.

American law directory. *See* Martindale, Ja. Boyd.

American leaders and heroes. Gordy, W. F. 60 c. Scribner.

American lectures on the history of religions. O. **$1.50 net. Putnam.

—Bloomfield. Religion of the Veda.

American Library Association catalog, [1908.] pap., $1. U. S., Supt. of Docs.

Formerly published in 2 pts. *See notice* American catalog, 1900-1904, [1904.]

American Library Association. *Committee on Bookbinding.* Binding for small libraries: suggestions prep. by the A. L. A. committee on bookbinding. '10(F26) 12°, (A. L. A., Library hdbk.) 15 c. A. L. A.

American Library Association Publishing Board foreign book list. 12°, pap. A. L. A.

—Campbell, *comp.* Selected list of Hungarian books. 15 c.

—Gattiker, *comp.* Selected list of German books. 50 c.

—Kildal, *comp.* Selected list of Norwegian and Danish books. 25 c.

American Library Association Publishing Board library-hdbks. 12°. A. L. A.

—A. L. A. *Committee on Bookbinding.* Binding for small libraries. 15 c.

—Kroeger *and* Cattell. Aids in book selection. 15 c.

American Library Association Publishing Board, library tracts. 12°. A. L. A.

—Brown, *comp.* Mending and repair of books. 15 c.

—Hadley. Why do we need a public library? 5 c.

—Wyer. U. S. government documents in small libraries. 15 c.

AMERICAN LITERATURE.

Alderman, E. A., *and others, eds.* Library of southern literature. In 15 v. v. 1-7. per set, $80-200. Martin & H.

Bowen, E. W. Makers of American literature. *$2.50 net. Neale.

Brevard, C. M. Literature of the South. $1.50. B'way Pub.

Cairns, W: B., *ed.* Selections from early American writers, 1607-1800. **$1.25 net. Macmillan.

Hanscom, E. D., *ed.* Friendly craft: collection of American letters. **$1.25 net. Macmillan.

Heydrick, B: A. One year course in English and American literature. $1. Hinds.

Howes, A. W. Primer of American literature. **50 c. net. Heath.

Pattee, F. L. Hist. of American literature. $1.20 net. Silver.

AMERICAN LITERATURE.—*Continued.*

Pearson, P: H: Questions for interpretive and literary study. 16 v. ea., 7 c. P: H: Pearson.

Raub, A. N. Studies in Eng. and Am. literature from Chaucer to present time. $1.50. Stradling.

Short stories and poems by American authors. $1. Cochrane.

Simonds, W: E: Student's history of American literature. $1.10. Houghton M.

Stanton, T., *ed.* Manual of American literature. **$1.75 net. Putnam.

Webster, H. H., *ed.* American classics for seventh and eighth grade reading. **80 c. net. Houghton M.

See also Authors;—Bibliographies;—English literature;—Essays;—Fiction; — Poets;—Poetry;—Quotations;—South (The);—Wit and humor.

American lithography. '10(Ja22) 16° o. p. Nat. Assoc. Lithographers.

American machinist gear book. Logue, C: H. $2.50 net. McGraw-H.

American machinists' handbook. Colvin, F. H., *comp.* $3. Hill Pub.

American madonna. Todd, *Mrs.* M. Van L. I. $1.25. Binghamton Bk.

American Mathematical Society, New York. Catalogue of the library, January, 1910. '10(Ap) 35 p. 8°, pap., gratis. Am. Math.

American meat. Leffingwell, A. $1.25 net. Schulte.

American Medical Association. Laws (abstract) regulating the practice of medicine in the United States and elsewhere; rev. to July 15, 1909. 15th ed. '09, [1910.] (F) c. 160 p. fold. tab., 12°, pap., 30 c. Am. Medical.

American Medical Association. New and non-official remedies; cont. descriptions of the articles which have been accepted by the Council on Pharmacy and Chemistry of the American Medical Association. '09 (Je) 168 p. 12°, *50 c. net. Am. Medical.

American Medical Association. Papers to be presented before the Section on Laryngology and Otology, Chicago, June 2-5, 1908. '08(Je27) il. 8°, $1.50. Am. Medical.

American Medical Association. Papers to be presented before the Section on Laryngology and Otology of the American Medical Association, Atlantic City, June 8-11, 1909. '09(Je) c. 214 p. il. 8°. (Add. pubs. for price.) Am. Medical.

American Medical Association. Papers to be presented before the Section on Ophthalmology, Chicago, June 2-5, 1908. '08(Je27) c. il. 8°, pap., $1.50. Am. Medical.

American Medical Association. Papers to be presented before the Section on Ophthalmology of the American Medical Association, Atlantic City, June 8-11, 1909. '09 Je) c. 13-336 p. il. 8°. (Add. pubs. for price.) Am. Medical.

AMERICAN MEDICAL ASSOCIATION.

Strong, H: R. Machinations of the American Medical Association. 25 c. Nat. Druggist.

American medicinal barks. Henkel, A. (Add. Superintendent for price.) U. S., Supt. of Docs.

AMERICAN MISSIONARY ASSOCIATION.
Beard, A: F. Crusade of brotherhood: hist. of the American Missionary Association. *$1.25 net. Pilgrim Press.
American Museum of Natural History bull. il. 8°. Am. Museum.
—Gregory. Orders of mammals. $5.
American Museum of Natural History, Memoirs. il. f°. Am. Museum.
—Brown. Conard fissure. $2.50.
—Emmons. Chilkat blanket. $2.
American nation. *See* Hart, A. B., *ed.*
American National Red Cross text-book. Lynch, C: *$1 net. Blakiston.
American nature ser.; group I, Natural history. il. Q. Holt.
—Knowlton. Birds of the world. **$7 net.
American nature ser.; group II., Classification of nature. il. Q. Holt.
—Britton *and* Shafer. North American trees. **$7 net.
—Kellogg. American insects. **$5 net.
American nature ser.; group IV., Working with nature. pls. D. Holt.
—Albee. Hardy plants for cottage gardens. $1.60 net.
—Doane. Insects and disease. $1.50 net.
—Eggeling *and* Ehrenberg. Aquarium and its inhabitants. **$2 net.
—Fernow. Care of trees in lawn, street and park. $2 net.
—Kellogg. Shell-fish industries. **$1.75 net.
—Sternberg. Life of a fossil hunter. **$1.60 net.
American nature ser.; group V., Diversions from nature. il. Q. Holt.
—Holder *and* Jordan. Fish stories. **$1.75 net.
—Kellogg. Insect stories. **$1.50 net.
American negligence digest, from 1897 to 1907, [etc.;] by Wa. J. Eagle. '09(D) c. 2+1695 p. O. $8.50. Remick.
American Negro Academy occasional papers. 8°, pap. Am. Negro Acad.
—Grimké. Modern industrialism and the negroes of the United States. 15 c.
—Moorland. Demand and the supply of increased efficiency in the negro ministry. 15 c.
American newspaper. Rogers, J. E: *$1 net. Univ. of Chic.
American newspaper annual, 1908. [28th year.] '08(Ap18); 1909. [29th year.] '09 (Mr20) maps, 4°, *$5 net. Ayer.
American normal readers. Harvey, M. L. Bk. 3. 50 c. Silver.
American notes. Dickens, C: *35 c. net; *70 c. net. Dutton.
American of the future. Matthews, J. B. **$1.25 net. Scribner.
American oratory. Shurter, E. Du B., *ed.* $1.65. South-West Pub.
American Osteopathic Association. Osteopathic directory and year book of the A. O. A. '08(My.) c. il. por. 8°, $1. Journal of Osteopathy.
AMERICAN PAINTING.
See Painters and painting.
American patrician. Lewis, A. H. **$2 net. Appleton.
American Patty. Thompson, A. E. †$1.25. Lothrop, L. & S.
American pearl. Washburn, H. E. 50 c. H. E. Washburn.
American people. Low, A. M. **$2.25 net. Houghton M.
American Philosophical Society. Calendar of the papers of Benjamin Franklin in the library of the American Philosophical Society; ed. by I. Minis Hays. '07 [1909.] (N) (Not for sale.) Am. Philosophical Soc.
AMERICAN PHILOSOPHICAL SOCIETY, Philadelphia.
Rosengarten, J. G: American Philosophical Society. 25 c. Am. Philosophical Soc.
American phonography. Anderson, W: L. $1.20. Ginn.
American pilgrim's way in England. Huish, M. B. $6; $15. W. E. Jones, Baltimore.
American Pitmanic shorthand. Gardner, E. E. $1.25. Am. Pitmanic.
American playgrounds; pioneer book on public recreation; ed. by Everett B. Mero, with contrib. from 25 authorities. 2d ed., rev. and enl. '10(My14); 3d ed. (D17) c. il. plans, O. ea., $2 net. Baker & T.
American playgrounds: their construction, equipment, maintenance and utility; ed. by Everett B. Mero. '08(N21) c. il. O. *$1.50 net. Am. Gymnasia.
American pocket medical dictionary. Dorland, W: A. N., *ed.* *$1 net; with thumb index, *$1.25 net. Saunders.
AMERICAN POETRY.
See Poetry.
American Pomological Society. Fruits recommended by the American Pomological Society for cultivation in the various sections of U. S. and Canada; rev. by a committee. '09(Ag) 69 p. tabs., map, 8°, (U. S., Dept. of Agriculture, Bu. of Plant Industry bull.) pap., 15 c.
American poultry culture. Sando, R. B. *$1.50 net. McClurg.
American practice of gas piping. Gerhard, W: P. *$3 net. McGraw.
American practice of surgery. *See* Bryant, Jos. Decatur.
American primitive music. Burton, F: R. **$5 net. Moffat.
American princess. Eldridge, W: T. $1.50. Sturgis & W.
American problems from the point of view of a psychologist. Münsterberg, H. $1.60 net. Moffat.
American producer gas practice and industrial gas engineering. Latta, M. N-. *$6 net. Van Nostrand.
American prohibition year book for 1910; eds. C: R. Jones, Alonzo E. Wilson, Fred D. L. Squires. '10(My14) c. il. pors. D. 50 c.; pap., 25 c. Nat. Prohibition.
American prose masters. Brownell, W: C. **$1.50 net. Scribner.
American Psychological Association. *Committee on the Teaching of Psychology.* Report on the teaching of psychology; presented to the Association Dec. 29, 1909. [1910.] (Ag) 93 p. 4°, (Psychological monographs.) $1. Psychological Review.

American public addresses. De Barrios, A. $1. Aberdeen.
American public library. Bostwick, A. E. $1.50 net. Appleton.
American public problems; ed. by Ralph Curtis Ringwalt. D. Holt.
—Coolidge. Chinese immigration. **$1.75 net.
American Railway Engineering and Maintenance of Way Association. Manual of recommended practice for railway engineering and maintenance of way. '08(O10) il. tabs., 8°, $3; hf. mor., $3.50. Am. Railway.
American Railway Master Mechanics' Association. Locomotive dictionary. 1909 ed. '09(D25) c. il. f°, $6. Railroad Age.
American railway transportation. Johnson, E. R. **$1.50 net. Appleton.
American ready reckoner. Ayres, E. (Add. pubs. for price.) Popular.
American Red Cross abridged text-book on first aid. Lynch, C: 30 c. net. Blakiston.
AMERICAN REVOLUTION.
Andrews, F. D. Tea-burners of Cumberland County, [N. J.,] who showed their resistance to British tyranny by burning a cargo of East India tea. 30 c. F. D. Andrews.
Banks, J. L. David Sproat and naval prisoners in the War of the Revolution; with mention of William Lenox of Charleston. (Priv. pr.) J. L. Banks.
Burke, E. Speech on conciliation with the colonies. **25 c. net. Scribner.
Chase, E. Beginnings of the American Revolution. 3 v. $7.50 net; $15 net. Baker & T.
Connecticut Historical Society, Hartford. Lists and returns of Connecticut men in the Revolution. $3. Conn. Hist.
Fisher, S. G: Struggle for American independence. 2 v. **$4 net. Lippincott.
Gardner, F. A. Glover's Marblehead regiment in the war of the Revolution. 50 c. Salem Press.
Griffin, M. I. J. Catholics and the American Revolution. In 2 v. v. 2. $3. M. I. J. Griffin.
Haltigan, J. Irish in the American Revolution. $2. Haltigan.
Jenks, T. When America won liberty. $1.25. Crowell.
Johnston, A. Myths and facts of the American Revolution. $1.50 net. W: B. Clarke.
Leffmann, H: Notes on the secret service of the Revolutionary Army operating around Philadelphia. 25 c. City Hist., Phil.
New York [State.] Commissioners for Detecting and Defeating Conspiracies. Minutes of the Commissioners in the State of New York. In 2 v. v. 1, 1778-1779; v. 2, 1780-1781. (Distributed officially and by exchange.) New York.
Stark, J. H: Loyalists of Massachusetts and the other side of the American Revolution. $5. W: B. Clarke.
Thwaites, R. G., *and* Kellogg, L. P., *eds.* Revolution on the upper Ohio, 1775-1777. $1.50. State Hist., Wis.

AMERICAN REVOLUTION.—*Continued.*
Wall, J: P. New Brunswick [N. J.] in the critical period of the Revolution. (Priv. pr.) J: P. Wall.
See also Brandywine (Battle of);—Bunker Hill (Battle of);—Claverack, N. Y.;—Fredericksburg, N. Y.;—Georgia;—Guilford Court House (Battle of);—Indians;—Lexington;—Long Island (Battle of);—Lynn;—Mecklenburg declaration of independence;—Philadelphia;—Presbyterian church;—South Carolina;—Valley Forge, Pa.;—*also* Connolly, John;—Dodge, John;—Pulaski, Kazimierz.
American rural school. Foght, H. W. $1.25 net. Macmillan.
American School of Correspondence. Architectural drawing and lettering. pt. 1, Architectural drawing, by Fk. A. Bourne and H. V. von Holst; pt. 2, Architectural lettering, by Fk. Chouteau Brown. '10(F19) c. il. plan, 4°, $1. Am. Sch. Corr.
American School of Correspondence. Bank bookkeeping; by C: A: Sweetland. '10 (Jl30) c. il. 8°, (American accountants' lib.) $1.50. Am. Sch. Corr.
American School of Correspondence. Business management; by Ja. Bray Griffith. 2 v. '10(Jl30) c. il. 8°, (American accountants' lib.) $4. Am. Sch. Corr.
American School of Correspondence. Commercial law; by J: Aldrich Chamberlain. '10(Jl30) c. il. 8°, (American accountants' lib.) $3. Am. Sch. Corr.
American School of Correspondence. Corporation accounts and voucher system; by Ja. Bray Griffith. Pt. 1, Corporation accounts. Pt. II, Voucher system-accounting charts. '10(Jl30) c. il. 8°, (American accountants' lib.) $1. Am. Sch. Corr.
American School of Correspondence. Cyclopedia of applied electricity: general reference work on dynamo-electric machinery, generators, motors, storage batteries, electric wiring, electrical measurements, [etc.] 6 v. '08(O10) c. il. pors. 8°, hf. mor., $36. Am. Sch. Corr.
American School of Correspondence. Cyclop. of automobile engineering. '09(Ag7) c. 4 v., il. 8°, $12. Am. Sch. Corr.
American School of Correspondence. Cyclop. of carpentry and contracting; prepared by a corps of architects, carpenters, contractors, and building experts of the highest professional standing. In 4 v. '10(Ap16) c. plans, 8°, $12. Am. Sch. Corr.
American School of Correspondence. Cyclopedia of civil engineering; editor-in-chief, F: E. Turneaure. 8 v. '09(Ja16) c. il. maps, charts, 8°, $18.60. Am. Sch. Corr.
American School of Correspondence. Cyclopedia of commerce, accountancy, business administration. 10 v. '10(Ja29) c. il. forms, 8°, $24. Am. Sch. Corr.
American School of Correspondence. Cyclop. of heating, plumbing and sanitation. 4 v. '09(Ag28) il. tabs., 8°, $12. Am. Sch. Corr.
American School of Correspondence. Cyclopedia of mechanical engineering; editor-in-chief, Howard Monroe Raymond. 7 v. '09 (F20) c. il. 8°, $18.60. Am. Sch. Corr.
American School of Correspondence. Department store accounts; by C: A: Sweetland. Pt. 1, Department store accounts; Pt. II,

Retailers' accounts. '10(Jl30) c. il. 8°, (American accountants' lib.) $1.50. Am. Sch. Corr.

American School of Correspondence. Factory accounts. '10(Jl30) c. il. 8°, (American accountants' lib.) $1.50. Am. Sch. Corr.

American School of Correspondence. Gas producers; instruction paper prepared by S: S. Wyer. '09(Ja16) c. il. 8°, $1. Am. Sch. Corr.

American School of Correspondence. Heating and ventilation. pt. 1; instruction paper, prep. by C: L. Hubbard. '09(Ag7) c. il. 8°, $1.50. Am. Sch. Corr.

American School of Correspondence. Insurance and real estate accounts; by C: A: Sweetland. Pt. 1, Insurance accounts; Pt. II, Real estate accounting. '10(Jl30) c. 8°, (American accountants' lib.) $1.50. Am. Sch. Corr.

American School of Correspondence. Pract. bookkeeping; by Ja. Bray Griffith. '10 (Jl30) c. il. 8°, (American accountants' lib.) $2. Am. Sch. Corr.

American School of Correspondence. Stairbuilding and the steel square. pt. 1, Stairbuilding, by Fred. T. Hodgson and Morris Williams; pt. 2, The steel square, by Morris Williams. '09(F26) c. il. 8°, $1. Am. Sch. Corr.

American School of Correspondence pubs. il. 8°. Am. Sch. Corr.
—Bacon. Forging. $1.
—Byrne *and* Phillips. Highway construction. $1.
—Chamberlain. Commercial law. pt. 1. 50 c.
—Collins. Woolen and worsted spinning. $3.
—Crocker. Dynamo-electric machinery. $1.50.
—Dickerman *and* Boyer. Refrigeration. $1.
—Dickinson. Accounting practice. 50 c.
—Diemer. Automobiles. $1.50.
—Dufour. Bridge engineering. $3.
—Esty. Alternating current machinery. $3.
—Everett *and* Lawrence. Freehand and perspective drawing. $1.
—Gray *and* Ball. Plumbing. $1.50.
—Griffin. Machine design. $1.50.
—Griffith. Administrative and industrial organization.—Advertising and sales organization.—Corporation accounts.—Credit organization.—Purchasing and stores department.—Records of labor and manufacturing orders.—Shipping department. (Priv. pr.) —Single entry bookkeeping.—Single proprietors' and partners' accounts.—Voucher system accounting charts.—Wholesale, commissioner, and storage account. ea., 50 c.
—Griffith *and* Sweetland. Trustees', executor's, and stock broker's accounts. 50 c.
—Gunsaulus. Modern engineering practice. 12 v. $29.80.
—Hathaway *and* Griffith. General expense and cost summaries. 50 c.
—Hedrick. Cotton spinning. $3.
—Hubbard. Heating and ventilation. $1.50.
—Kenison. Mechanical drawing. 50 c.
—Knox *and* Shadd. Electric wiring and lighting. $1.
—Leland. Boiler accessories. $1.—Steam turbines. $1.50.

American School of Correspondence pubs.—Continued.
—Lybrand, *and others*. Accounting for modern corporations. 50 c.
—Marston. Sewers and drains. $1.
—Metcalf. Knitting. $3.
—Metcalf, *comp.* Knit goods finishing. 50 c.
—Montgomery. Auditing. 3 v. ea., 50 c.
—Nelson. Weaving. $3.
—Nelson, *comp.* Jacquard machines. 50 c.
—Neubecker. Sheet-metal work. $3.
—Newell *and* Dow. Steam boilers. $1.
—Nichols. Building superintendence. $1.50. —Estimating. $1.
—Olney. Textile chemistry and dyeing. $3.
—Phillips. Surveying. $1.50.
—Plant. Contracts and specifications. $1.
—Plant *and* Zapf. Contracts and specifications. $1.
—Stimpson. Foundry work. $1.
—Sweetland. Bank bookkeeping.—Brewers' accounts.—Publishers' and printers' accounts. ea., 50 c.
—Thom *and* Collins. Electric telegraph. $1.
—Timmermann. Woolen and worsted finishing. $3.
—Timmerman, *comp.* Felt. 50 c.
—Tucker. Steel construction. $1.50.
—Turneaure. Water supply. $1.50.
—Turneaure *and* Black. Hydraulic engineering. $1.
—Umpleby. Textile design. $3.
—Webb *and* Gibson. Masonry and reinforced concrete. $3.
—Wightman, *comp.* Compressed air. $1.
—Wright. Contractors' accounts. 50 c.

American School of Home Economics, Chicago. Food values: pract. methods in diet calculations. '09, [1910.] (Mr.) 31 p. il. 12°, (American Sch. of Home Economics, bull.) pap., 10 c. Am. Sch. Home Economics.

American science ser., Advanced course. il. 8°. Holt.
—Bessey. Botany for high schools. $2.20.
—Chamberlin *and* Salisbury. College text-book of geology. **$3.50 net.
—Dewey *and* Tufts. Ethics. $2.
—Martin. Human body. **$2.50 net.
—Remsen. College text-book of chemistry. $2.25.

American science ser., Briefer course. D. Holt.
—Remsen. Introd. to the study of chemistry. $1.25.
—Salisbury. Physiography for high schools. $1.50.

American science ser., elem. course. il. maps, D. Holt.
—Salisbury. Elem. physiography. $3.50.

American Seamen's Friend Society. Acts of the apostles of the sea; an eighty years' record of the work of the American Seamen's Friend Society. '09(N) 118 p. il. pors. 8°, gratis. Am. Seamen's Friend.

American shotgun. Askins, C: $2 net. Outing.

American shrines in England. Story, A. T: *$2 net. Macmillan.

American singer in Paris. Workman, M. C. S. $1.20. F. Workman.

American soaps. Gathman, H. $15. H. Gathman.

American social progress ser.; ed. by S: McCune Lindsay. D. Macmillan.
—Devine. Misery and its causes. **$1.25 net.
—Jenks. Governmental action for social welfare. $1 net.
—Seager. Social insurance. $1 net.

American Society of Mechanical Engineers. Transactions; v. 29, Indianapolis and New York meetings, 1907. '09(F6) c. il. 8°, hf. mor., *$11 net. Am. Soc. Mech. Engineers.

American Sociological Society. Papers and proceedings. v. 1, 1st annual meeting, held at Providence, R. I., Dec. 27-29, 1906; v. 2, 2d annual meeting, Dec. 28-31, 1907; v. 3, 3d annual meeting, held at Atlantic City, N. J., Dec. 28-30, 1908; v. 4, 4th annual meeting, held at New York City, Dec. 27-31, 1909. '10(Je11) Q. pap., ea., $1.50 net. Univ. of Chic.

American sovereign. Merrill, J. M. $1.50. C. M. Clark.

American stage. Eaton, W. P. **$1.50 net. Small.

American stage of to-day; biographies and photographs of 100 leading actors and actresses; with introd. by W: Winter. '10 (My7) il. pors. 8°. $2.50. Collier.

American stallion register. Battell, J. $5. Am. Pub. Co., (Vt.)

American state repts.; (A. C. Freeman.) v. 117, 118. '08(Ap); v. 119 (Jl); v. 120 (S); v. 121 (N); v. 122 (D); v. 123. '09(Mr); v. 124 (Je); v. 125 (Jl); v. 126 (S); v. 127 (N); v. 128 (D); v. 129. '10(Mr); v. 130 (My); v. 131 (Je); v. 132-133 (N); v. 134 (D) c. O. shp., ea., $4 net.—Digest. v. 4, by E. S. Green. '09(My) c. Q. shp., $6. Bancroft-W.

American state ser.; ed. by W. W. Willoughby. D. **$1.25 net. Century Co.
—Finley *and* Sanderson. American executive.

American statesmen: second ser.; large pap. ed. pors. 8°. Houghton M.
—Stanwood. James Gillespie Blaine. (Add. pubs. for price.)

American stationary engineering. Crane, W: E: $2. Henley.

American street railway investments. 16th annual. '09, [1910.] 495 p. f°. $5. McGraw-H.

American student in France. Klein, F. *$2.50 net. McClurg.

American Sugar Refining Co.
The sugar trust: articles from the *New York World* of June 9, 1909, showing the settlement out of court of the case brought against the American Sugar Refining Company by the Pennsylvania Sugar Refining Company for $30,000,000. '09(Jl) 2 p. 8°. (Add. Superintendent for price.) U. S., Supt. of Docs.

American supremacy. Critchfield, G: W. 2 v. **$6 net. Brentano's.

American system of agricultural education. True, A. C. (Add. Superintendent for price.) U. S., Supt. of Docs.

American system of dressmaking. Merwin. P. $20. Am. Coll. Dressmaking.

American system of shorthand. S. Phonograph.
—Pitman *and* Howard. Business letters. no. 4, Insurance correspondence. 25 c.—Legal forms. (Add. pubs. for price.)

American teachers' ser.; ed. by Ja. Earl-Russel. D. Longmans.
—Lloyd *and* Bigelow. Teaching of biology in the secondary schools. $1.50.

American telegraphy. Maver, W:, *jr.* $5. Maver.

American transportation conditions. Peyton, J: H. 50 c. Courier-Journ.

American transportation system. Rankin, G: A. **$1.50 net. Putnam.

American tropics. Corlett, W: T. $1.50. Burrows.

American verse, 1625-1807. Otis, W: B. **$1.75 net. Moffat.

American waiter. Goins, J: B. $1. Hotel Monthly.

American waterways. American Academy of Political and Social Science. $1. Am. Acad. Pol. Sci.

American waterways. il. O. **$3.50 net, boxed. Putnam.
—Chambers. Mississippi river and its wonderful valley.
—Curwood. Great Lakes.
—Lyman. Columbia river.
—Quick. American inland waterways.

American woman's cook book. Blackstone, E. M. $1.50. Laird.

American writers of to-day. Vedder, H: C. $1.50. Silver.

Americana (The): universal reference library; comprising the arts and sciences, literature, history, biography, geography, commerce, etc., of the world. Editor-in-chief, F: Converse Beach; managing editor, G: Edn. Rines. '08(My23) c. 16 v., il. pors. maps, plans, charts, 8°. (Add. pubs. for price.) Scientific American.

Americana Germanica. O. Univ. of Penn.
—MacLean. "Uncle Tom's cabin" in Germany. $1.50.

Americana Germanica new ser.; ed. by Marion Dexter Learned. Q. Univ. of Penn.
—Seipt. Schwenkfelder hymnology. $2.

Americanism in religion. Roosevelt, T. 35 c. E. E. Swadener.

Americanisms.
Clapin, S. New dictionary of Americanisms. $1. Weiss.

Americanization of Canada. Moffett, S. E. [priv. pr.] S: E. Moffett.

Americans. Francis, A. *$1.50 net. Appleton.

Americans of to-day and to-morrow. Beveridge, A. J. 50 c. Altemus.

Ames, C: Gordon.
Book of prayers. '08(D12) 12°, *$1.50 net; leath., *$2.50 net. Am. Unitarian.

Ames, E: Scribner.
Psychology of religious experience. '10 (O8) c. O. $2.50 net. Houghton M.

Ames, Mrs. Eleanor Maria Easterbrook, ["Eleanor Kirk."]
The Christ of the red planet. '09(D) c. 18+138 p. 12°, $1. E. M. E. Ames.

Ames, Mrs. Ernest.
Little red fox. '09, [1910.] (F) il. sq. 4°, †60 c. Estes.

Ames, F. W., rep.
See North Dakota. *Sup. ct.* Repts.

Ames, Fisher, jr.
By reef and trail: Bob Leach's adventures in Florida. '09(N13) c. il. D. $1.50. Brown & P.
By reef and trail; Bob Leach's adventures in Florida. '10(S10) c. il. D. $1.50. Scribner.

Ames, Herman Vandenburg.
Outlines of lectures on American political and institutional history during the colonial and revolutionary periods; with references for collateral reading. 3d ed. '08 (N7) c. Q. pap., $1. Longmans.

Ames, Ja. Barr, and Smith, Jeremiah.
Selection of cases on the law of torts. 3d ed. v. 1, pt. 1, 2, by Ja. Barr Ames; v. 2, by Jeremiah Smith. '09(N) 619 p. O. ea., $6. Harvard Law.
See also Negotiable instruments law.

Ames, Jos. Bushnell.
Pete, cow-puncher. '08(N14) c. il. D. †$1.50. Holt.

AMES, Joseph Sweetman.
Benton, J: R. Problems in physics to accompany Ames's Text-bk. of general physics. Am. Bk.

Ames, Mrs. Mary Lesley, ed.
Life and letters of Peter and Susan Lesley. 2 v. '10(F12) c. pors. 8°, $5. Putnam.

Ames, Percy W., ed.
Milton memorial lectures, 1908; read before the Royal Society of Literature; ed., with an introd. '09(Je19) il. O. $2. Oxford Univ.

Amethyst cross. Hume, F. W. $1.50. Cassell.

AMHARICA LANGUAGE.
See Semitic languages.

AMHERST COLLEGE, Amherst, Mass.
Shoop, M. P. Sabrina, the class goddess of Amherst College. $1.25. M. P. Shoop.

AMINOPHTHALIC ACID.
See Ammonia.

Ammerman, Ada.
Pro patria; il. patriotic recitation with lesson talk. '09(Jl) c. 24 p. il. D. pap., 35 c. Werner.

AMMONIA.
Lunge, G: Coal. tar and ammonia. 2 v. *$15 net. Van Nostrand.
Renshaw, R. R. 4-aminophthalic acid and some of its derivatives. (Add. author for price.) R. R. Renshaw.

Ammons, E. M.
Forest reservations; address del. before the joint session of the Colorado legislature, March, 1909. '10(Ag) 18 p. 8°. Gov. Pr. Off.

AMMUNITION.
See Gunpowder.

Among friends. Crothers, S: M. $1.25 net. Houghton M.
Among many witnesses. Williams, M. B. 80 c. Revell.
Among school gardens. Greene, M. L. $1.25. Charities Pub.
Among the Danes. Butlin, F. M. *$2.50 net. Pott.
Among the giants. Neher, B. M. 40 c. Flanagan.
Among the Gospels and the Acts. Ainslee, P: $1.50. Temple Seminary.
Among the humorists. Patten, W:, *comp.* $2.25. Collier.
Among the lighthouses of the Great Lakes. Law, W: H. 10 c. W. H. Law.
Among the maples. Jackson, S: A. *90 c. net. Un. Presb. Bd.
Among the meadow people. Pierson, C. D. 40 c. Dutton.
Among the Sioux ser. O. McClurg.
—Hanson. With Sully into the Sioux land. $1.50.
Among the wild tribes of the Afghan frontier. Pennell, T. L. *$3.50 net. Lippincott.
Amortization. Sprague, C: E. 50 c. C: E. Sprague.

AMORY, Augustine Heard.
Moulton, A. W. Memoir of Augustine Heard Amory. $1.25. A. W. Moulton.

Amours of Henri de Navarre and of Marguerite de Valois. Haggard, A. C: P. $4.50 net. Brentano's.

AMPHIBIA.
Powers, J. H. Morphological variation and its causes in *Amblystoma tigrinum*. $1. Univ. of Neb.
See also Alligators;—Frogs.

AMPHIPODA.
See Crustaceans.

Ampler sky. Fallow, L. *$1 net. Macmillan.

Amram, D: Werner.
Makers of Hebrew books in Italy; being chapters in the hist. of the Hebrew printing press. '10(F19) c. il. pors. facsims.. 8°, *$3 net. (500 copies.) J. H. Greenstone.

Amrine, T: Hamer.
Comparative tests of carbon, metallized carbon and tantalum filament lamps. '07, [1909.] (Ap) 44 p. il. 8°, (Univ. of Ill. bull.; Engineering experiment station.) pap. (Add. Univ. for price.) Univ. of Ill.
Lighting country homes by private electric plants. '09(Ja16) il. plans, 8°, (Univ. of Ill. Engineering Experiment Station bull.) gratis. Univ. of Ill.

—, and Guell, Antonio.
Tests of tungsten lamps. '10(My) 33 p. il. O. (Univ. of Ill., Engineering Experiment Station bull.) pap., gratis. Univ. of Ill.

Amsbary, Wallace Bruce.
French-Canadian in prose and verse. [1910.] (N) c. 24 p. 8°, 25 c. La Salle Extension.
"Books recommended to be consulted and read" (2 p.).

Amstutz, N. S.
Hand-book of photo-engraving: enlargement and revision of Jenkins' Manual of photo-engraving; with supp. chapters on the theory and practice of half-tone color work by F: E. Ives and Stephen H. Horgan. 3d ed. '08(Ja4) il. por. D. $3. Inland Pr.

Amundsen, Roald Engelbregt Gravning.
Northwest Passage: being the record of a voyage of exploration of the ship "Gjoa" in the years 1903-07; [with a supplement by Lieut. Hansen.] 2 v. '08(Ag15) il. maps, O. *$8 net. Dutton.

Amurru, the home of the northern Semites. Clay, A. T. $1.25. S. S. Times.

Amusement situation in the city of Boston; based on a study of the theatres for ten weeks, from Nov. 28, 1909, to Feb. 5, 1910; rept. prep. by the Drama Committee of the Twentieth Century Club. '10(Je18) 12°, pap., 10 c. Twentieth Century Club

AMUSEMENTS.
- Beard, L. *and* A. B. Little folks' handy book. 75 c. Scribner.
- Biederwolf, W: E: Christian and amusements. 15 c. Glad Tidings.
- Fowler, M. Morality of social pleasures. $1.25 net. Longmans.
- Glover, E. H. "Dame Curtsey's" book of guessing contests. *50 c. net. McClurg.
- Hamilton, W: W. Worldly amusements. **10 c. net. Am. Bapt.
- Hartt, R. L. People at play. **$1.50 net. Houghton M.
- Johnston, B. Home occupation for boys and girls. 50 c. Jacobs.
- Palm, *Baroness* L. von. Rainy day pastimes for children. $1. Estes.
- Reisner, C. F. Social plans for the young people. *75 c. net. Jennings.
- Wells, C. Pleasant day diversions. **$1 net. Moffat.

See also Athletics;—Cards;—Charades;—Children;—Circus;—Conjuring; — Dancing; — Drills; — Entertainments;—Games; — Music;—Opera; — Palmistry;—Playgrounds;—Plays; —Puzzles;—Recitations;—Sports.

Amy, the stolen wife. McCormick, C: N. $2. McCormick Med.

Anabasis. *See* Xenophon.

ANAESTHETICS.
See Anesthetics.

ANALYSIS.
See Assaying;—Chemistry;—Food;—Metals and metallurgy;—Spectrum;—*also* names of substances analyzed.

Analysis of beauty. Hogarth, W: *$1.50 net. Silver Lotus.

Analysis of play construction. Price, W: T. $5. W: T. Price.

Analysis of the evolution of musical form. Glyn, M. H. *$3.50 net. Longmans.

Analysis of the Gettysburg address. Oakleaf, J. B., *comp.* gratis. J. B. Oakleaf.

Analyzed Bible. *See* Morgan, G: Campbell, *D.D.*

Anarchist woman. Hapgood, H. *$1.25 net. Duffield.

ANARCHY.
- Eltzbacher, P. Anarchism. $1.50. B: R. Tucker.
- Goldman, E. Anarchism. $1 net. Mother Earth.
- Hebberd, S. S. Impending anarchy. (Add. pubs. for price.) Maspeth.

See also Socialism.

Anastatic reprints. various sizes. Stechert.
—Beesly. Catiline, Clodius, and Tiberius. *$3 net.
—Dragondorff. Plant analysis. *$3.50 net.

Anathema. Andreyev, L. N. $1.25 net. Macmillan.

ANATOMY.
- Campbell, W: F. Text-book of surgical anatomy. *$5 net; *$6.50 net. Saunders.
- Cunningham, D. J: Manual of pract. anatomy. 2 v. ea., $2.50 net. Wood.

ANATOMY.—*Continued.*
- Cunningham, D. J., *ed.* Text-book of anatomy. *$6 net; *$7.50 net. Wood.
- Davis, G. G: Applied anatomy. $6. Lippincott.
- Eddy, W. H. Text-book in general physiology and anatomy. $1.20. Am. Bk.
- Eecles, W: M. Elem. anatomy and surgery for nurses.. $1. W: R. Jenkins.
- Ford, F. C. Hdbk. of regional anatomy. $1.50. F. C. Ford.
- Gray, H: Anatomy, descriptive and surgical. *$6 net; *$7 net. Lea.
- Kimber, D. C. Text book of anatomy and physiology for nurses. *$2.50 net. Macmillan.
- Lewis, L. Anatomy and physiology for nurses. *$1.75 net. Saunders.
- Macewen, J: A. Surgical anatomy. *$3 net. Wood.
- McLachlan, J: Applied anatomy: surgical, medical and operative. In 2 v. *$6 net. Wood.
- Piersol, G: A., *ed.* Human anatomy. 2 v. $15. Lippincott.
- Quain, J. *and Sir* R: Elements of anatomy. In 4 v. v. 1, $3; v. 2, pt. 1, $3.50; v. 2, pt. 2, $4.50; v. 3, pt. 1, $4.50; pt. 2, $4.50. Longmans.
- Skillern, P.-G. Descriptive anatomy. $2. Dolbey.
- Sobotta, J. Atlas and text-book of human anatomy. In 3 v. vs. 2 and 3. ea., *$6 net; *$7.50 net. Saunders.
- Streeter, G: L. Lab'y guide in anatomy. 50 c. Wahr.
- Wiedersheim, R. Comparative anatomy of vertebrates. *$3.75 net. Macmillan.
- Wilder, H. H. Hist. of the human body. $3. Holt.
- Witkowski's atlas of the human body. *$2 net. W: R. Jenkins.
- Woolsey, G: Applied surgical anatomy, regionally presented. *$4.50 net. Lea.
- Young, J. K. Hdbk. of anatomy. $1.75. Davis.

See also Abdomen;—Anatomy for artists;—Animals;—Anthropometry;—Arm;—Blood;—Bones;—Brain;—Domestic animals; — Ear; — Eye; — Foot;—Generative organs;—Head; — Heart; — Histology;—Intestines; —Mammalia;—Muscles;—Neck;—Nervous system;—Nose;—Nurses and nursing;—Pathology; — Physiology;—Rabbit;—Spine; — Surgery; — Teeth; — Thorax; — *also* Vesalius, Andreas.

Anatomy and some of the biological aspects of the "American mistletoe." York, H. H. 50 c. Univ. of Tex.

ANATOMY FOR ARTISTS.
- Fripp, *Sir* A. D. Human anatomy for the art student. $1.75 net. Lippincott.

Anatomy of the automobile. Dyke, A. L. $2. A. L. Dyke.

Anatomy of the central nervous system. Skillern, P., *jr.* *$1 net. Dolbey.

ANCESTRY.
See Genealogies;—Heredity.

Ancestry of Abraham Lincoln. Lea, J. H: $10. Houghton M.

Ancient accepted Scottish rites. Brockaway, C: A. $1. Aurora Gratia.

Ancient and modern imperialism. Cromer, *Earl* of. 90 c. net. Longmans.

Ancient and modern Sunday-school methods. Boyd, R. H. 25 c. Nat. Baptist Pub.

Ancient Arabic Order of the Nobles of the Mystic Shrine, Montpelier, Vt. Mt. Sinai Temple. Mt. Sinai Temple nobles of the mystic shrine; its pioneers, organizers, officers and nobles, Montpelier, Vt., 1876-1910. [Ed. de luxe.] [1910.] (N) c. 388 p. il. pors. 4°, $12.50. E. J. Hall.

Ancient China simplified. Parker, E: H. *$3 net. Dutton.

Ancient cities ser. See Dutton's.

Ancient English Christmas carols. Rickert, M. E., *comp.* $3.25 net. Duffield.

Ancient Greek historians. Bury, J: B. $2.25. Macmillan.

Ancient Hawaiian house. Brigham, W: T. $3. Bishop Museum.

ANCIENT HISTORY.
See History.

Ancient law. Glasgow, E. A. G. †$1.50. Doubleday, P.

Ancient mariner. *See* Coleridge, S: Taylor.

Ancient mysteries and modern masonry. Vail, C: H. $1. Macoy Pub.

Ancient mysteries and modern revelation. Colville, W: W. J. $1 net. Fenno.

Ancient myths and modern poets. Clarke, H. A. $2 net. Baker & T.

Ancient Persian lexicon. Tolman, H. C. $1.25. Am. Bk.

Ancient plants. Stopes, M. C. $2 net. Van Nostrand.

Ancient ruins in the Southwest. Hewett, E. L. Denver & Rio Grande.

Ancient science of numbers. Clement, L. $1. Roger Bros.

Ancient tales and folk lore of Japan. Smith, R: G. *$6 net. Macmillan.

And so they were married. Kingsley, A. M. †$1. Dodd.

And this is war. Dudley, C. H. $1. Cochrane.

Andean land. Osborn, C. S. In 2 v. *$5 net. McClurg.

Anders, Ja. Meschter.
Text-book of the practice of medicine. 9th ed., thoroughly rev. '09(O) c. 1326 p. il. partly col., 8°, $5.50. Saunders.

Andersen, Hans Christian.
Fairy tales. '09(Ag28) il. 8°, *$1.50 net. Dodge.
Fairy tales. '08(N7) il. D. $1.50. Lippincott.
Fairy tales and stories. '08(O10) il. D. (Bowman's illustrated lib. of world favorite books.) $1. Bowman.
Fairy tales; told in easy French by Kathleen Fitzgerald. '09, [1910.] (Ja) il. (Children's favorites.) *50 c. net. Jacobs.
Fairy tales told to the children by Mary Macgregor. '08(Je6) il. 16°, (Told to the children ser.) 50 c. Dutton.
Fairy tales; tr. by W. Angeldorff; ed. by Wa. Jerrold. '10(D) 12°, (Children's classics.) $1.25. Dutton.
Fairy tales; tr. by Mrs. Edg. Lucas. '10 (N12) il. 8°, $3. Dutton.
Three tales of Hans Andersen. '10(D31) il. 8°, $1.50. Macmillan.

Andersen, Hans Christian.—*Continued.*
Ugly duckling, and other stories: in the amanuensis style of phonography by Benn Pitman and Jerome B. Howard. '08 (Ap4) 16°, 25 c. Phonograph.

Anderson, A. J.
Romance of a friar and a nun; being the romance of Fra Lippo Lippi. '09(D25) il. 8°, *$2.50 net. Dodd.

Anderson, Mrs. Ada Woodruff.
Heart of the red firs. '08(Ap11) c. il. D. †$1.50. Little, B. & Co.
Strain of white. '09(My8) c. il. D. †$1.50. Little, B. & Co.

Anderson, And.
Game of draughts. 7th ed., rev. and extended, by Rob. M'Culloch. '10(Jl30) O. $1. McKay.

Anderson, Archibald.
Course of study in history and hdbk. to the State ser. advanced text. '09(Mr) 4°, (San Francisco State Normal School bulls.; new ser.) pap., 30 c. San. F. St. Normal.

Anderson, Asher, D.D.
Congregational faith and practice. '10(D) 29 p. pap., 5 c. Pilgrim Press.

Anderson, Bp. C: Palmerston.
Confirmation or the laying on of hands. '09(Jl10) c. 16°, pap, 10 c. McClurg.

Anderson, E: Lowell.
Horses and riding. '09(N) c. 68 p. il. 8°, $1. U. S. Cavalry.

Anderson, Fk. Maloy, comp.
Constitutions and other select documents illustrative of the history of France, 1789-1907. Rev. ed. '08(D) 693 p. 12°, *$2.50 net. H. W. Wilson.

Anderson, Rev. Galusha.
Hitherto untold. '10(F19) c. D. $1. Cochrane.
Story of a border city [St. Louis] during the Civil War. '08(O3) c. il. pors. O. **$1.50 net. Little, B. & Co.

Anderson, G: G.
Some aspects of irrigation development in Colorado [from proceedings of the Colorado Scientific Society.] '09, [1910.] (Ap) 273-314 p. 8°, 50 c. Colo. Sci. Pub.

Anderson, G: Smith.
Adner Ward, the boy Christian; the Christ-life in childhood. [1910.] (Je) c. 65 p. por. 12°, 25 c. G: S. Anderson.

Anderson, H: S., and Schell, Stanley.
Artistic work and gymnastic games. Rev. and enl. ed. '09(Je19) c. il. S. 75 c. Werner.

Anderson, Ida Frances.
In love's garden, and other verses. [1910.] (F) c. '09. 95 p. 12°, $1. Arroyo Guild.

Anderson, Isabel, [Mrs. Larz Anderson.]
Great sea horse. '09(D18) c. col. il. O. **$2 net; vellum, **$15 net. Little, B.

Anderson, J. Wemyss.
Refrigeration. '08(Ap25) il. O. *$2.25 net. Longmans.

Anderson, Jacob Severt.
Simple creamery computator. '08(Je6) c. 8°, leath., $5 J. S. Anderson.

Anderson, J: A:
See Jones, Harry Clary.

Anderson, J: Wesley.
From the plains to the pulpit. '08(F1) c. il. pors. D. $1. J: W. Anderson.
Refrigeration. '08(Ap25) il. O. *$2.25 net. Longmans.

Anderson, Jos. Ferguson.
Methodist dictionary; brief work on Methodist terminology; prep. in the interest of ministers, members, and friends of the Methodist Episcopal church. '10 (My14) c. 16°, 25 c. net. Eaton & M.

Anderson, Mrs. Larz.
See Anderson, Isabel.

Anderson, Lewis F.
History of common school education. '09 (My1) c D. $1.25. Holt.

Anderson, Lewis H.
Mystery of love scientifically and philosophically considered. 3d ed., rev. and enl. '10(Mr5) c. il. por. 8°, $2. L. H. Anderson.

Anderson, Melville Best.
Happy teacher. '10(D24) c. O. bds., 60 c. net. B: W. Huebsch.

Anderson, Rob. A.
Fighting the Mill Creeks: being personal acct. of campaigns against Indians of the northern Sierras. '10(F19) c. pors. D. pap., 50 c. Chico Record.

Anderson, W:
Japanese wood engravings. '08(O17) 24°, *75 c. net; leath., *$1 net. Dutton.

Anderson, W: B., and Watson, C: R.
Far north in India: survey of the mission field and work of the United Presbyterian church in the Punjab. '09(My) c. 9+17-312 p. il. pors. map, 12°, 50 c. Bd. For. Miss.
Bibliography (3 p).

Anderson, W: J.
Architecture of the Renaissance in Italy. 4th ed., rev. and enl. '09(Ag21) il. 8°, *$5 net. Scribner.

—, and Spiers, R. Phené.
Architecture of Greece and Rome. 2d ed., rev. and enl. by R. Phené Spiers. '08 (My9) il. 8°, *$7.50 net. Scribner.

Anderson, W: Lincoln.
American phonography. Rev. ed. '08(D19) 12°, $1.20; Graded exercises in phonography to accompany "American phonography." O. pap., 50 c. Ginn.

Anderson & Goodwin Company. Standard historical atlas of Sioux County, Iowa; cont. maps of villages, cities and townships of the county; maps of state, United States and world. '08(Je13) c. f°, $15. I. B. Goodwin.

ANDERSONVILLE PRISON, Georgia.
Bullard, K. C., *comp.* Over the dead-line; or, who killed "Poll Parrot": [incident in Andersonville prison.] *$1 net. Neale.
Connecticut. Andersonville Monument Commission. Dedication of the monument at Andersonville, Ga. (Add. pubs. for price.) Connecticut.
Page, J. M., *and* Haley, M. J. True story of Andersonville prison. $2. Neale.

Andés, L: Edgar.
Treatment of paper for special purposes; tr. from the German by C: Salter. '08 (D12) il. 12°. (Add. pubs. for price.) Van Nostrand.

Andes and the Amazon. Enock, C. R. $1.50 net. Scribner.

Andom, R.
Enchanted ship: a story. '08(My16) D. $1.25. Cassell.

ANDOVER, Mass.
Perrin, L. J. My three years at Andover. $1. Mahew.
Robbins, *Mrs.* S. S. Old Andover days. *$1 net. Pilgrim Press.

ANDOVER, N. H.
Eastman, J: R. Hist. of the town of Andover, New Hampshire, 1751-1906. $3; $3.75. Andover, N. H., Com. Hist.

Andreini, Jos. Manuel.
J. Winfred Spenceley: his etchings and engravings in the form of book plates. '10(Je11) 8°, $4. Assoc. Bk.

Andreiyeff, Leonidas.
See Andreyev, Leonid Nikolaevich.

Andrew, Abram Piatt.
Substitute for cash in the panic of 1907. '08. 497-516 p. il. fold. tab., 8°. (Add. pub. for price.) Ellis.
—, comp. Financial diagrams. '10(O) 24 col. fold. diagrs., f°. Gov. Pr. Off.

Andrewes, Amy G., ed.
Story of Bayard; [founded on the "Histoire du bon Chevalier Bayard," by the "Loyal Serviteur."] '10(My21) il. D. $1.50 net. Lane.

Andrews, Alb. H:, ed.
See Wood, Casey Alb., *ed.*

Andrews, Alice Ebba.
See Newcomer, Alphonso Gerald.

Andrews, Annulet, [Mrs. J. Kingsley Ohl.]
Wife of Narcissus. '08(F15) c. D. †$1.25. Moffat.

Andrews, B: R:
Museums of education; their history and use. '08, [1909.] (S) 98 p. (Teachers' College record.) pap., 30 c. Teachers' Coll.

Andrews, Mrs. Bessie Ayars.
Colonial and old houses, of Greenwich. '08 (Ap11) il. D. $1; pap., 50 c. B. A. Andrews.

Andrews, C. D., pseud.
New standard speller; word-book of progressive lessons in spelling, pronunciation and word building; for use in primary, intermediate and grammar grades. '08, [1909.] (Ap) 218 p. front. 12°, bds., 25 c. Laird.

Andrews, Rev. C. F.
Christ in India; study in indigenous Christian development. '10(D) 12°, $1.50 net. Doran.

Andrews, C: McLean.
British committees, commissions, and councils of trade and plantations, 1622-1675. '08(Je13) c. O. (Johns Hopkins Univ. studies in hist. and pol. science.) pap., 75 c. Johns Hopkins.

Andrews, C: McLean, and Davenport, Frances Gardiner.
Guide to the manuscript materials for the history of the United States to 1783, in the British Museum, in minor London archives, and in the libraries of Oxford and Cambridge. '08(F13) Q. (Carnegie Institution of Washington pubs.) pap., $2. Carnegie.

—, Gambrill, J: Montgomery, and Tall, Lida Lee.
Bibliography of history for schools and libraries, with descriptive and critical annotations; pub. under the auspices of the Association of History Teachers of the Middle States and Maryland. '10(Jl9) c. D. 60 c. net. Longmans.

ANDREWS, *Bp.* Edward Gayer.
McConnell, F. J. Edward Gayer Andrews, [Methodist bishop.] *$1.50 net. Eaton & M.

Andrews, E: Lewis.
Napoleon and America: outline of the relations of the United States to the career and downfall of Napoleon Bonaparte. '09 (Mr20) 4°, *$2 net. M. Kennerley.
Stock Exchange and the public; reprinted from *The Bankers' Magazine.* '09(Jl3) O. pap., 25 c. Bankers' Magazine.

Andrews, Eliza Frances.
War-time journal of a Georgia girl, 1864-1865. '08(S26) c. il. pors. O. **$2.50 net. Appleton.

Andrews, Fk. D.
Tea-burners of Cumberland County, [N. J.,] who showed their resistance to British tyranny and unjust taxation by burning a cargo of East India tea. '08, [1909.] (Mr) 5-41 p. il. 8°, 30 c. F. D. Andrews.
—, comp. Inscriptions on the grave stones in the old "New England Town" burying ground Fairton, New Jersey; with historical sketch, list of the signers of the Cohansey Compact, 1697, and the names of some of the early settlers of Fairfield. '09, [1910.] (Ag13) 12°, 25 c. F. D. Andrews.
—, ed. Business men of the city of Hartford (Ct.) in the year 1799, printed from the orig. manuscript with notes. '09, [1910.] (D) 24 p. 12°, 35 c. F. D. Andrews.

Andrews, G: Arth.
What is essential? '10(Ag13) c. D. $1 net. Crowell.

Andrews, Rev. H. T.
Acts of the Apostles. '08(Ag15) 16°, (Westminster N. T.) *75 c. net. Revell.

Andrews, H: Russell.
Midwifery for nurses. 2d ed. '09, [1910.] (F) 11+310 p. il. D. *$1.25 net. Longmans.

Andrews, Hiram Bertrand.
Design of reinforced concrete slabs, beams and columns, conforming to the recommendations of the Joint Committee on Concrete and Reinforced Concrete composed of committees of the American Society of Civil Engineers, American Society for Testing Materials, [etc.] '10(Ap16) c. tabs., 8°, $1. H. B. Andrews.

Andrews, Hiram Bertrand.—*Continued.*
Practical reinforced concrete standards. '08(Ag15) c. il. 4°, $2. Simpson.

Andrews, Ja. De Witt.
American law: a commentary on the jurisprudence, Constitution and laws of U. S. 2d ed. 2 v. '08(Mr.) c. 2100 p. 8°, *$12 net. Callaghan.

Andrews, Ja. P.
See Conn. *Sup. ct. of errors.* Repts.

Andrews, L: Robins.
White peril; or, how I cured myself of consumption at home. Rev. ed., ed. and comp. by Athole Burnett Reader. '09 (S4) c. por. D. $1. White Peril.

Andrews, Mrs. Mary Raymond Shipman, [Mrs. W: Shankland Andrews.]
Better treasure. '08(N7) il. O. $1.25. Bobbs-M.
Enchanted forest. '09(O23) il. 12°, $1.50. Dutton.
Lifted bandage. '10(Mr19) c. D. bds., **50 c. net. Scribner.
Perfect tribute. [Centenary ed.] '08(D12) c. 8°, †$1. Scribner.

Andrews, P. J., rep.
See Connecticut. *Supreme ct. of errors.* Repts.

ANDREWS, Richard Snowden.
Smith, T., *ed.* Richard Snowden Andrews, lieutenant-colonel commanding the First Maryland Artillery, Confederate States Army. $1.50 net. Eichelberger.

Andrews, Rob. W.
Japan mission of the American church. '08(Jl) c. 12+159 p. il. pors. map, 8°, (Soldier and servant ser.) $1; pap., 50 c. Church Missions.

Andrews, T: Stora, comp.
World's sporting annual record book, 1908. '08(F22); 1909. '08(D) c. pors. T. ea., pap., 10 c. T: S. Andrews.

Andrews, W:
Old English towns. '09(D18) il. O. *$2 net. Pott.

Andrews, W: Loring.
Jacob Steendam, Nochvaster: a memoir of the first poet in New Netherlands, with translations of his poems descriptive of the colony. '08(Je27) c. il. 12°, **$7.50 net. Dodd.

Andrews, Mrs. W: Shankland.
See Andrews, *Mrs.* Mary Raymond Shipman.

Andrews, W: Symes.
Magic squares and cubes; with chapters by Paul Carus, L. S. Frierson and C. A. Browne, jr., and introd. by Paul Carus. '08(Ag1) il. 8°, *$1.50 net. Open Court.

Andreyev, Leonid Nikolaevich.
A dilemma; tr. from the Russian by J: Cournos. '09(N20) $1. Brown Bros.
Anathema; tragedy; auth. tr. by Herman Bernstein. '10(O29) c. D. $1.25 net. Macmillan.
Seven who were hanged: a story; author. tr. from the Russian by Herman Bernstein. '09(My1) c. D. $1. J. S. Ogilvie.
Silence. '08(S) 32 p. (Modern authors' ser.) bds., 25 c. Brown Bros.

Andriessen, Hugo.
Poetische auslese. '10(O) 12°, pap., 50 c. H. Andriessen.
Andromaque. *See* Racine, Jean Baptiste.
ANDROS, *Sir* Edmund.
Davis, A. McF. Was it Andros? [priv. pr.] A. McF. Davis.
Andújar, Manuel.
Spain of to-day from within. '09(Ap17) c. il. D. *$1.25 net. Revell.
Anecdota Oxoniensia, classical ser. O pap. Oxford Univ.
—Clark. Inventa Italorum. $3.
—Keith, *ed.* Aitareya Aranyaka. $7.75.
Anecdota Oxoniensia; Mediaeval and modern ser. 8°. Oxford Univ.
—John, *of Worcester.* Chronicle. *$1.90 net.
Anecdotes sur Napoléon. *See* Saint-Hilaire, Marco de.
ANEMIA.
Hunter, W: Severest anæmias. v. 1. *$3.25 net. Macmillan.
ANEMONES.
See Marine zoology.
Aneroid barometer. Plympton, G: W. 50 c. Van Nostrand.
ANESTHETICS.
Collum, R. W., *and* Gray, H. M. M. Practice of anæsthetics, and General surgical technique. *$3 net. Wood.
De Ford, W: H. Lectures on general anæsthetics in dentistry. $3. J. T. Nolde.
Eliot, C: W: Fruits of medical research with the aid or anæsthesia and asepticism. (Not for sale.) Mass. Gen. Hospital.
Gardner, H. B. Surgical anæsthesia. *$2.25 net. Wood.
Nee, F. E. Practical points in anesthesia. 60 c.; $1.50. Surgery.
Probyn-Williams, R. J. Pract. guide to the administration of anesthetics. *$1.60 net. Longmans.
Anet, Claude.
Through Persia in a motor-car, by Russia and the Caucasus; tr. by M. Beresford Ryley. '08(O10) il. O. *$4.50 special net. Appleton.
Anfang und ende. Heyse, P. J. L. 35 c. Ginn.
Anfang und ende. Heyse, P. J. L. 40 c. Holt.
Angel, Myron.
La piedra pintada; the painted rock of California; legend. '10(D10) c. il. 8°, $1.25. Grafton Pub.
Angel (The). Thorne, G. †$1.50. G: W. Dillingham.
Angel and the star. *See* Gordon, C: W:
Angel Esquire. Wallace, E. †$1.50. Holt.
Angel of Lonesome Hill. Landis, F: 50 c. net. Scribner.
Angel of thought. Murphy, E. A. $1. Badger.
Angela's quest. Bell, L. L. $1.50. Duffield.
Angelic Angelina. Paddock, M. 60 c. Cupples & L.
Angelico, Fra, [Frate Giovanni da Fiesole.]
Masterpieces. '09(Jl31) il. 24°, (Painters' ser.) pap., *25 c. net; leath., *75 c. net. Stokes.
ANGELICO, *Fra* (Frate Giovanni da Fiesole).
Mason, J. Fra Angelico. *65 c. net. Stokes.
Angell, Emmett Dunn.
Play; comprising games for the kindergarten, playground, schoolroom, and college; how to coach and play girls' basket-ball, etc. '10(My14) c. il. D. $1.50 net. Little, B. & Co.
Angell, Fk. Capron.
Annals of Centerdale in the town of North Providence, Rhode Island, its past and present, 1636-1909. '09(N) c. 15+196 p. il. map, 8°, $2.50. F. C. Angell.
Angell, Ja. Burrill.
Age of quickened conscience; baccalaureate address. '09(N) 10 p. O. pap. (Add. University for price.) Univ. of Mich.
Angell, Ja. Rowland.
Psychology: an introd. study of the structure and function of human consciousness. 4th ed., rev. '08(O10) c. il. 8°, $1.60. Holt.
Angellier, Auguste.
Pages choisies: prose et vers; ed. by Émile Legoius; seule édition antorisée. '09 (Mr6) por. S. (Oxford higher French ser.) $1.15. Oxford Univ.
Angels of Savonarola. Baird, E. S. 50 c. Am. Tr.
Angelus (The) and the Regina Cæli; with a few short notes, explanatory and historical. '10(Mr5) S. pap., 25 c. Longmans.
Angelus University text-books, course in the history of the world's greatest nations. il. 8°. Angelus Univ.
—Morris. Historical tales. 15 v. (Sold by subs. only.)
Angers, F.
See Conan, Laure, *pseud.*
Angier, A. Gordon.
Far East revisited; with a preface by Sir Rob. Hart. '08(D19) il. 8°, *$4.20 net. Scribner.
Angler's guide. Bradford, C: B. $1; 50 c. Nassau Press.
Angler's guide. Held, R. J., *ed.* 50 c. Field and Stream.
Angler's guide. Randall, W., *ed.* 60 c.; 50 c. Field and Stream.
Angler's secret. Bradford, C: *$1 net. Nassau Press.
Angler's workshop. il. S. $1. Forest.
—Frazer. Rodmaking for beginners.
ANGLICAN CHURCH.
See Church of England;—Protestant Episcopal church.
Anglican Church hdbks.; ed. by W. H. Griffith Thomas, D.D. D. 40 c. net. Longmans.
—Carter. English Church in the 17th century.—English church in the 18th century.
—Chadwick. Social work.
—D'Arcy. Christianity and the supernatural.
—Girdlestone. Old Testament theology and modern ideas.
—Joynt. Pastoral work.
—Lees. Joy of Bible study.
—Spencer. Old Testament history.
—Stock. English church in the nineteenth century.
—Thomas. Christianity is Christ.
—Tisdall. Comparative religion.
—Warman. New Testament theology.

Anglican liberalism; by twelve churchmen. '08(D12) D. (Crown theological lib.) *$1.50 net. Putnam.

ANGLICAN ORDERS.
Lowndes, A. Vindication of Anglican orders. *$3.50 net. Gorham.

ANGLICANISM.
See Church of England.

ANGLING.
See Fish and fishing.

Anglo-American legal hist. *See* Select essays.

ANGLO-BOER WAR.
See South Africa.

Anglo-Jewish memories. Adler, H. *$1.50 net. Bloch.

Anglo-Saxon chronicle; tr. by E. E. C. Gomme. '09(Jl17) 12°, *$2 net. Macmillan.

Anglo-Saxon Congregationalism in the South. Jenkins, F. E. (Add. pubs. for price.) Franklin-T.

ANGLO-SAXON LANGUAGE.
Bale, C. E. Syntax of the genitive case in the Lindisfarne Gospels. 50 c. Univ. of Ia.
Peloubet, S. S. Students' law dict. of words and phrases in law Latin, law French and Anglo-Saxon. $1.50; $2. Peloubet.

ANGLO-SAXON LITERATURE.
Ayres, H. M. Bibliographical sketch of Anglo-Saxon literature. 25 c. net. Lemcke.
Riddles of the Exeter book. $2.50. Ginn.

ANGORA GOATS.
See Goats.

ANGOULÊME, Marie Thérèse Charlotte, *Duchess* d'.
Gosselin, L. L. T. G. Daughter of Louis XVI., Marie-Thérèse-Charlotte de France. *$4 net. Lane.
Turquan, J. Madame Royale, the last Dauphine; Marie Thérèse Charlotte de France, Duchesse d'Angouleme. $3.75 net. Brentano's.

Angus, D. C.
Japan: the eastern wonderland. New and enl. ed. '10(O1) il. 8°, $1 net. Cassell.

Anharmonic co-ordinates. Hime, H: W. L. $3 net. Longmans.

ANILINE.
Blanck, F. C. Nitration of aniline and certain of its derivatives. 40 c. Johns Hopkins.

Animal analogues. Wood, R. W. **50 c. net. P. Elder.

Animal autobiographies ser. *See* Macmillan's.

Animal behavior ser. *See* Macmillan's.

Animal castration. Liautard, A. $2. W: R. Jenkins.

Animal figures in the Maya codices. Tozzer, A. M. $1. Peabody Museum.

Animal life. Gamble, F. W. *$2 net. Dutton.

Animal parasites. Kaupp, B: F. $2.25. A. Eger.

ANIMAL PSYCHOLOGY.
Coupin, H. E. V., *and* Lea, J: Wonders of animal ingenuity. 75 c. Lippincott.

Animal trainer. Guigou, P. $1.25. Duffield.

ANIMALS.
Beard, D. C. Animal book and camp-fire stories. $1.75 net. Moffat.

ANIMALS.—*Continued.*
Bourne, G. C. Comparative anatomy of animals. v. 1. *$1.40 net. Macmillan.
Brain, B. M., *comp.* Adventures with four-footed friends. *$1.25 net. Revell.
Bralliar, F. Elo, the eagle, and other stories. $1. Pacific Press.
Breck, E: Wilderness pets at Camp Buckshaw. $1.50 net. Houghton M.
Cesaresco, *Countess* E. M. Place of animals in human thought. *$3 net. Scribner.
Dale, J: T: Heroes and greathearts and their animal friends. $1. Fairfax.
Daniel, J. F. Animal life of Malaysia. **$1.20 net. Bobbs-M.
Darton, F. J. H. Wonder book of birds and beasts. $1.50. Stokes.
Dugmore, A. R. Camera adventures in the African wilds. **$6 net. Doubleday, P.
Dumas, A. My pets. *$1.75 net. Macmillan.
English, D. "Wee tim'rous beasties": studies in animal life. $1.50. Cassell.
Farrow, G: E: Zoo babies. $1.25. Stokes.
Finn, F. Wild beasts of the world. 2 v. $8 net. Dodge.
Golding, H., *ed.* Book of animals; for boys and girls. $1.50. Stokes.
Grimm, J. L. K. *and* W. K. Animal stories. $1.50. Duffield.
Guizou, A. Animals in the Ark. $1.25. Duffield.
Hagenbeck, C. Beasts and men; being Carl Hagenbeck's experiences for half a century among wild animals. *$3.50 net. Longmans.
Haviland, M. D. Lives of the fur folk. $1.35 net. Longmans.
Hawkes, C. Black Bruin: [fiction.] †$1.50. Jacobs.
Kellner, O. Scientific feeding of animals. $1.90 net. Macmillan.
Knight, C: R. Animals of the world for young people. **$2 net. Stokes.
Knobel, E: Wild animals of North America. $2.50. Lovell.
Long, W: J. Northern trails: [animal life in the far north.] Bks. 1, 2. ea., 45 c. Ginn.
McCrea, R. C. Humane movement. $2 net. Lemcke.
Macleod, M., *ed.* Tiny true tales of animals. 50 c. Stokes.
Meier, W: H. D. Animal study. 75 c. Ginn.
Miller, G. S., *jr.* New carnivore from China. Gov. Pr. Off.
Mitton, G: E., *ed.* Animal autobiography ser. 7 v. ea., $1.40 net. Macmillan.
Morgan, C. L. Animal behaviour. $2.50. Longmans.
Mother animal stories. †50 c. Altemus.
Pycraft, W. P. Animal why book. $2. Stokes.
Roberts, C: G: D. Kings in exile. $1.50. Macmillan.
Seton, E. T. Life histories of northern animals. In 2 v. *$18 net. Scribner.
Thayer, G. H. Concealing-coloration in the animal kingdom. $7. Macmillan.

ANIMALS.—*Continued.*
Thomson, M. R. *and* J. A. Threads in the web of life. 50 c. net. Macmillan.
Washburn, M. F. Animal mind. *$1.60 net. Macmillan.
White, F. E., *comp.* Animal lover's birthday book. 50 c. Macmillan.
Wilson, P. Nature round the house: [animals.] $1. Longmans.
See also Amphibia;—Cattle;—Domestic animals;—Embryology;—Evolution;—Game preserving;—Hunting; — Mammals; — Natural history; — Parasites;—Protozoa;—Sports and sportsmen;—Taxidermy; — Theosophy; —Vertebrates;—Veterinary medicine and surgery;—Vivisection;—Zoology;—*also* names of animals.
Ann Veronica. Wells, H. G: †$1.50. Harper.
ANNA MONICA PIA, *Duchess of Saxony.*
Kremer, *Mrs.* I. Struggle for a royal child, Anna Monica Pia, Duchess of Saxony. $1.50. M. Kennerley.
Annals of a parish. *See* Galt, J:
Annals of Ann. Sharber, K. T. $1.50. Bobbs-M.
Annals of Cæsar. Sihler, E. G. $1.75 net. Stechert.
Annals of Fairyland; reign of King Cole; [ed. by J. M. Gibbon.] '09(Mr27) 16°, (Everyman's lib.) *35 c. net; leath., *70 c. net. Dutton.
Annals of Fairyland; reign of King Oberon; [ed. by Wa. Copeland Jerrold.] '09(Mr27) 16°, (Everyman's lib.) *35 c. net; leath., *70 c. net. Dutton.
Annals of the Astronomical Observatory of Harvard College. il. 4°. Harvard Univ.
—Sampson. Discussion of the eclipse of Jupiter's satellites. $1.
ANNAND, James.
Hodgson, G: B. From smithy to senate; the life story of James Annand. *$1.75 net. Cassell.
Annandale, Nelson.
Fresh-water sponges collected in the Philippines by the Albatross expedition. '09 (N) 131-132 p. 8°, pap. (Add. Superintendent for price.) U. S., Supt. of Docs.
ANNANDALE, N. Y.
See St. Stephen's College.
ANNAPOLIS, Md.
Evening Capital, Annapolis, Md. Historical and industrial ed., portraying the glorious past and future posibilities of Annapolis. 25 c. Evening Capital.
Annapolis first classman. Beach, E: L. $1.25. Penn Pub. Co.
Annapolis second classman. Beach, E: L. †$1.25. Penn Pub. Co.
Annapolis youngster. Beach, E: L. †$1.25. Penn Pub. Co.
ANNE, *Queen of England.*
Ryan, P. F. W: Queen Anne and her court. 2 v. *$6 net. Dutton.
Anne Kempburn. Bryant, M. $1.30 net. Duffield.
Anne Nelson. Curtis, A. T. $1.25. Fenno.
Anne of Avonlea. Montgomery, L. M. $1.50. L. C. Page.
Anne of Green Gables. Montgomery, L. M. †$1.50. L. C. Page.
Anne of Tréboul. Goetchius, *Mrs.* M. L. $1 net. Century Co.
Anne Page. Syrett, N. $1.50. Lane.
Anneau (L') d'argent. *See* Bernard, Charles de.
Année (Une) de collège à Paris. Laurie, A. 35 c. net. Macmillan.
Anne's terrible good nature. Lucas, E: V. $1.75. Macmillan.
Annesley, C:, [pseud. of C: and Anna Tittmann.]
Standard opera glass; detailed plots of one hundred and fifty-five celebrated operas. New ed., rev., with additions and portraits. '10(D31) c. pors. 12°, $1.50 net; leath., $2.50 net. Brentano's.
Standard opera glass: hand-book for operagoers, giving the details of the plots and characters of 120 operas. New special ed. '08(Ap18) c. 12°, $1.50; hf. mor., $3. Brentano's.
Annesley, Mrs. Maude.
Door of darkness. '08(Je20) D. †$1.50. Lane.
Wind along the waste. '10(D17) 12°, $1.50. Lane.
Anniversaries and holidays. Hazeltine, M. E., *ed.* 25 c. Wisconsin Free Lib.
Annual American catalog, 1908; record, under author, title, subject and series; also the full titles, with descriptive notes, of all books recorded in *The Publishers' Weekly;* directory of publishers, etc.; (first supplement to the American Catalog, 1905-1907.) '09(Ap17) c. Q. $3. Pub. Weekly.
Annual American catalog, 1909; cont. record under author, title, subject, and series of all books recorded in *The Publishers' Weekly,* 1909; with directory of publishers, authors, and printers issuing books during the year; and directory of booksellers in the principal towns of the U. S. and Canada; [second supplement to the American catalog, 1905-1907.] '10(Ap16) c. Q. $3 net. Pub. Weekly.
Annual library index. *See* Fletcher, W: I:, *ed.*
Annual magazine subject-index for 1908: a subject index to 120 Am. and Eng. periodicals and society publications, by F: Winthrop Faxon. '09(My8) 8°, $3. Boston Bk.
Annual magazine subject-index, 1909; subject-index to a selected list of American and English periodicals and society transactions not elsewhere indexed; the Dramatic Index for 1909 is incl. as part 2. v. 3. '10(Je4) 8°, $5.50 net. Boston Bk.
Annual register: review of public events at home and abroad for the year 1907. '08 (Je13); 1908. '09(Je19); 1909. '10(Je18) O. ea., $6. Longmans.
ANNUALS.
See Almanacs and annuals;—Calendars and yearbooks.
ANNUITIES.
See Insurance.
ANNULMENT.
See Marriage.
Another Annapolis alphabet. Stevens, W: O. 50 c. Lord Balto. Pr.
Another fairy reader. Baldwin, J. 35 c. Am. Bk.
Another mile. Chapman, J. W. *25 c. net; *75 c. net. Revell.

Another three weeks. Metcalfe, J. S. 25 c. Life Pub.

Anschütz, E:
Gott und sein volk; das Alte Testament in predigten dargelegt; ein schlüssel zum selbständigen forschen der einzelnen schriften. '10(Ag) c. 304 p. por. 8°. (Gottes botschaft an die menschleit; die Bibel in predigten dargelegt.) $1.50. Germ. Bapt.

Ansell, Florence Jean, and Fraprie, Fk. Roy.
Art of the Munich galleries; being a hist. of the progress of the art of painting, illuminated and demonstrated by critical descriptions of the great paintings in the Old Pinakothek, the New Pinakothek, and the Schack Gallery in Munich. '10 (D3) c. il. D. (Art galleries of Europe ser.) il. $2 net, boxed; ¾ leath., $5 net, boxed. L. C. Page.

ANSELM, *St.*
Foley, G: C. Anselm's theory of the atonement. **$1.50 net. Longmans.

Anshutz, E: Pollock.
Guide to the twelve tissue remedies of biochemistry, the cell-salts, biochemic or Schuessler remedies. '09(Je) c. 91 p. 16°, 75 c. Boericke & T.
Sexual ills and diseases; popular manual based on the best homœopathic practice and text-bks. 2d ed., rev. and enl. '10 (N) 170 p. $1 net. Boericke & T.

Anson, Sir W: Reynell.
Law and custom of the constitution. In 3 v. v. 1, Parliament. 4th ed. '09(D); v. 2, The crown. pt. 1. '08(Ja18) ea., $3.40 net; pt. 2. '08(D19) O. $2.90. Oxford Univ.
Principles of the English law of contract and of its agency in its relation to contract. 12th ed., rev. by M. L. Gwyer. '10(S) $3.25 net. Oxford Univ.

Anson, W. S. W., ed.
Christmas book of carols and song. '10 (D31) col. il. 8°, lambskin, $3, boxed; velvet cf., $4, boxed. Barse & H.

Ansonia classics. 16°, 50 c. Hurst.
—Field. Sister's cake, and other stories.
—Gellibrand. J. Cole.

Anstadt, P:
Recognition of our friends in heaven. 4th ed. '07. [1908.] (Mr.) c. 256 p. il. 12°, $1; leath., $1.50. Anstadt.

"Anstey, F.," pseud.
See Guthrie, T: Anstey.

Answer to the charge of railroad robbery. Washington, W: D'H. (Priv. pr.) W: D. Washington.

Answer to "Three years in Arkansas." Hughes, *Mrs.* M. E. 25 c. Wiley & W.

Answers to questions prescribed by medical state boards. Ludy, R. B., *ed.* $1.50. McVey.

ANTARCTIC REGIONS.
Shackleton, *Sir* E. H. Heart of the Antarctic. **$10 net. Lippincott.

Antcliffe, H:
Schubert. '10(O8) il. 16°, (Bell's miniature ser. of musicians.) 50 c. net; $1 net. Macmillan.

ANTELOPES.
Ewing, H: E. Oribatoidea of Illinois. 50 c. Ill. Lab'y Nat. Hist.

Anthologie du théatre français contemporain (prose et verse). Pellissier, G. J. M., *comp.* $1.25. Lemcke.

ANTHOLOGIES.
See Ballads; — Christmas; — French literature; — French poetry; — Friendship; — German literature;—Greek literature;—Irish poetry;—Italy;—Latin literature;—Latin poetry;—London;—Music;—Nature;—New York City;—Ocean;—Poetry;—Treasury ser.;—United States.

ANTHONY, *St.*
Flaubert, G. Temptation of St. Anthony. $1.25. A. Harriman.

Anthony, Albert L.
Hist. of Cavalry Commandery for fifty years, ending with Nov. 13, 1909. [1910.] (Mr) 650 p. il. $5. (300 copies.) A. L. Anthony.

Anthony, Gardner Chace.
Machine drawing. '10(D24) c. il. tabs., 12°, (Technical drawing ser.) $1.50. Heath.

—, and Ashley, G. Fs.
Descriptive geometry. '09(My15) c. diagrs., obl. 16°, (Technical drawing ser.) $2. Heath.

ANTHONY, Susan Brownell.
Harper, *Mrs.* I. A. H. Life and work of Susan B. Anthony. In 3 v. v. 3. Nat. Am. Woman Suffrage.

Anthony, W: Arnold.
Lecture-notes on the theory of electrical measurements; prepared for the third-year classes of the Cooper Union night-school of science. 3d ed., rev. by Albert Ball. '08(O3) c. figs. 12°, $1. Wiley.

Anthony Cuthbert. Bagot, R: *$1.50 net. Brentano's.

ANTHRACITE.
See Coal.

ANTHROPOLOGY.
See Archæology;—Ethnology;—Man;—Secret societies.

ANTHROPOMETRY.
Seaver, J. W. Anthropometry and physical examination. $1.50. J. W. Seaver.
United States. *Immigration Commission.* Changes in bodily form of descendants of immigrants. '10(Jl) 2+113 p. il. 8°.

ANTIETAM (Battle of).
Spear, W: E. North and the South at Antietam and Gettysburg. $1. W: E. Spear.

ANTIETAM RIVER.
Hays, H. A. Antietam and its bridges. $3.50. Putnam.

ANTILLES.
See West Indies.

Anti-matrimony. Mackaye, P. W. $1.25 net. Stokes.

Anti mias. Walker, R. J. $6.50 net. Macmillan.

ANTIMONY.
Wang, C. Y. Antimony. *$4 net. Lippincott.

ANTI-PEDO BAPTISTS.
See Baptist church.

Anti-pragmatism. Schinz, A. $1.50. Small.

Antiquary's books. il. O. Scribner.
—Unwin. Gilds and companies of London. *$2 net.

ANTIQUES.
See Ceramics;—Collecting;—Furniture.

ANTIQUITIES.
See Archæology;—*also* names of countries and places.

Antiquities of central and south-eastern Missouri. Fowke, G. 40 c. Smith Inst.

Antiquities of the Ouachita Valley. Moore, C. B. $3.75. C. B. Moore.

ANTISELL FAMILY.
See Genealogies: Wyman, *Mrs.* M. E. T.

ANTISEMITISM.
See Jews.

ANTISEPSIS.
Eliot, C: W: Fruits of medical research with the aid of anæsthesia and asepticism. (Not for sale.) Mass. Gen. Hospital.

ANTITOXINS.
See Serum;—Tetanus.

Anton, the man who saw. Brownson, E. L. $1. Mayhew.

Antoninus, Marcus Aurelius.
Imperator ad se ipsvm; recognovit breviqve adnotaticne critica instrvxit I. H. Leopold. '08(O24) D. (Scriptorum classicorum Bibliotheca Oxoniensis.) 75 c. Oxford Univ.
Meditations of Marcus Aurelius. '08(O10) 12°, ("Best books" ser.) leath., *$1 net. Dutton.
Thoughts; ed. by Dana Estes. '08(D19) c. pors. 12°, (Noble thought ser.) bds., $1.50, boxed; parchment, $5, boxed. Estes.

ANTONINUS, Marcus Aurelius.
Bussell, F. W. Marcus Aurelius. $1.25. Scribner.

Antonio. Oldmeadow, E. **$1.30 net. Century Co.

Antony and Hero. Simon, F. P: $1. F. P: Simon.

Antremer, Jos. D'.
See D'Antremer, Jos.

Antrim, Eug. Marion.
Greatest things in religion; being studies in some of the Christian fundamentals with sidelights on the "new theologies." '10 (D17) c. 8°, 75 c. Jennings.

Antrim, Mrs. Minna Thomas.
Don'ts for bachelors and old maids. '08 (Ag29) c. T. 50 c.; ooze cf., $1. Altemus.
Jester Life and his marionettes. '08, [1909.] (Mr) c. il. 24°, ooze cf., $1. Altemus.

ANTS.
Hammarström, N. Adventures of two ants. $1. Stokes.
Bertelli, L. Prince and his ants. $1.35 net. Holt.
McCook, H: C. Ant communities and how they are governed. **$2 net. Harper.
Wheeler, W: M. Ants; the structure, development and behavior of ants. $5. Lemcke.

ANUS AND RECTUM.
Albright, J. D. Practical treatise on rectal diseases. $4. J. D. Albright.
Hirschman, L: J. Hdbk. of diseases of the rectum. $4. Mosby.
Mason, R. D. Office treatment of rectal diseases explained and simplified. $2.50. Burton Co.
Mummery, P. L. Diseases of the colon and their surgical treatment. $3.25 net. Wood.

ANUS AND RECTUM.—*Continued.*
Richardson, D. D. Treatise on diseases of the rectum, prostate and associate organs. (Add. pubs. for price.) Campbell Co.

Anwyl, E:
Celtic religion. '07, [1909.] (Ap) 8°, (Religions ancient and modern.) *40 c. net. Open Court.

Anyam gila. Mason, O. T. (Add. Superintendent for price.) U. S., Supt. of Docs.

AORTA.
See Heart.

AOSTA VALLEY, Italy.
Ferrero, F. Valley of Aosta. $2. net. Putnam.

Apartment houses of the metropolis (New York City). '08(Ag15) c. il. plans, $16; leath., $18. Hesselgren.

APARTMENTS.
George, W: Law of apartments, flats and tenements. $4. Fallon.
See also Architecture;—Tenement house.

APENNINES, Italy.
See Italy.

Apgar, Austin Craig.
Ornamental shrubs of the United States (hardy, cultivated). '10(Ag20) c. il. D. $1.50. Am. Bk.

APHIDS.
See Flies.

APHORISMS.
Fleckenstein, N. T. Widow's wisdom. 75 c. Caldwell.
Friend, J: W. Legal aphorisms. (Add. pubs. for price.) Whittet.
Glyn, *Mrs.* E. S. Sayings of grandmamma. $1.25. Duffield.
Hunter, W: C. Brass tacks; "capsule optimism." 50 c. net. Reilly & B.
Huxley, T: H: Aphorisms and reflections. $1. Macmillan.
Joyce, J: A. Truth: [axioms, proverbs, etc.] $1. J: A. Joyce.
Macy, A. W: Short-cut philosophy. 75 c. Sturgis & W.
Rowland, H. Reflections of a bachelor girl. 75 c. Dodge.
Sampter, J. E. Great adventurer: [apotheosis of life and death.] 75 c. Kerr Press.
See also Epigrams;—Maxims;—Mottoes.

APIARIES.
See Bees.

APICULTURE.
See Bees.

Apocalypse (The). *See* Bible. N. T. Revelation.

APOCRYPHA.
See Bible.

Apogamy in the maize plant. Collins, G. M. U. S., Supt. of Docs.

APOLLO (*god*).
See Greek literature.

Apollo and the seaman. Trench, H. *$1.50 net. Holt.

Apollo song book. Chapman, F: E. $1. Ginn.

Apollonius of Rhodes.
Apollonii Rhodii Argonavtica; recognovit breviqve adnotatione critica instrvxit R. C. Seaton. '10(Mr26) D. (Scriptorum classicorum bibliotheca Oxoniensis.) $1. Oxford Univ.

APOLLONIUS *of Tyana.*
Campbell, F. W. G. Appolonius of Tyana. *$1 net. M. Kennerley.
Apologetic of modern missions. Murray, J. L. 15 c. Student Volunteer.
Apologetic of the New Testament. Scott, E. F. *$1.50 net. Putnam.
APOLOGETICS.
See Christianity.
Apologia. *See* Apuleius, Lucius.
Apologia diffidentis. Leith, W. C. *$2.50 net. Lane.
Apologie for poetrie. *See* Sidney, *Sir* Philip.
Apologies for love. Myers, F. A. †$1.50. Badger.
Apology of Socrates. *See* Plato.
Apostle of Alaska. Arctander, K. J. L. W. A. *$1.50 net. Revell.
Apostle of the North. Cody, H. A. *$2.50 net. Dutton.
APOSTLES.
Jones, J: D. Glorious company of the apostles. *75 c. net. Doran.
Stafford, E: R. Shop talks; ser. of addresses on Jesus Christ and His disciples. 75 c. Jennings.
Thompson, R. E. Apostles as every day men. 50 c. net. S. S. Times.
Travel studies on the apostolic heroes. 20 c. Underwood.
APOSTLES' CREED.
Foster, J: M. To know and believe: studies in the Apostles' creed. **90 c. net. Longmans.
See also Creeds.
Apostolic age. Von Dobschutz. $1. Am. Unit.
APOSTOLIC CHURCH.
See Church history.
APOSTOLIC SUCCESSION.
Hall, A. C. A. Apostolic ministry. 25 c. Longmans.
Thompson, R. E. Historic episcopate. $1.50. Westminster.
See also Infallibility;—Popes.
Apostrophe to the skylark. Stoddard, C: W. $1. Arroyo Guild.
Apostrophes. Kreymborg, A. 50 c. Grafton Press.
Appeal to common sense. Hathaway, S., *comp.* 50 c. Common Sense Pub.
Appeal to Pharaoh. McKinley, C. E. $1. State Co.
Appeal to the boy. Peters, W: H. 10 c.; per 100, $5. Archive.
Appearance and reality. Bradley, F. H. *$3 net. Macmillan.
Appearances of our Lord after the Passion. Swete, H: B. *80 c. net. Macmillan.
APPENDICITIS.
Kelly, H. A. Appendicitis and other diseases of the vermiform appendix. $6. Lippincott.
Tilden, J: H: Etiology of cholera infantum, typhoid fever and appendicitis. $5. Merchants' Pub.
Vale, F. P. Has surgical treatment lessened the mortality from appendicitis? 50 c. Snow & F.
Apperley, C: Ja., ["Nimrod."]
Condition of hunters: their choice and management; the veterinary portions brought up to date by Fk. Townsend Barton. '08 (My23) O. *$4 net. Lane.

Appleborne, L:
See Jacobs, Jos.
Appler, A: C.
Christian science exposed. '08(Jl) c. 239 p. D. pap., $1. Eclipse.
APPLES.
Waugh, F. A. American apple orchard. $1. Judd.
See also San José scale.
Appleton, Lilla Estelle.
Comparative study of the play activities of adult savages and civilized children; investigation of the scientific basis of education. '10(Je25) c. O. pap., 54 c. Univ. of Chic.
Appleton arithmetics. *See* Young, Jacob W: Albert.
APPLETON FAMILY.
See Genealogies: Waters, T: F.
Appleton's business ser. il. 12°, **$1.50 net. Appleton.
—Johnson. American railway transportation.
—Meade. Corporation finance. $2 net.
Appleton's international scientific ser. D. $1.75 net. Appleton.
—Combarieu. Music.
—Depéret. Transformation of the animal world.
—Garrett. Periodic law.
—Le Bon. Evolution of forces.
—Macnamara. Evolution and function of living purposive matter—Human speech.
—Makower. Radioactive substances.
—Poincaré. New physics.
Appleton's lib. of useful stories. il. D Appleton.
—Smith. Story of iron and steel. **75 c. net.
—Tower. Story of oil. **$1 net.
Appleton's modern clinical medicine ser. il. 8°. Appleton.
—Cabot, *ed.* Diseases of metabolism of the blood. $5.
—Church, *ed.* Diseases of the nervous system. $7 net; $8 net.
—Jacobi. Diseases of children. $6.
—Wilson, *ed.* Infectious diseases. $6. Appleton.
Appleton's new pract. cyclopedia; new work of reference based upon the best authorities, and systematically arranged for use in home and school; ed. by Marcus Benjamin [and others;] with introd. by Elmer Ellsworth Brown. 6 v. '10(O15) c. il. (partly col.) maps, 8°, $18; hf. mor., $24. Appleton.
Appleton's railway ser. 8°. Appleton.
—Morris. Railroad administration. $2 net.
Appleton's science lib. 20 v. [1910.] (D) il. 3 v., ea., 40 c.; 11 v., ea., 30 c.; ¾ mor., 3 v., ea., 75 c.; 2 v., ea., 60 c.; 15 v., ea., 60 c. Lamb.
Formerly published by Appleton.
Appleton's scientific primers; ed. by Reynolds Green. il. 16°, 50 c. net. Appleton.
—Dyson. Astronomy.
—Gibson. Biology.
—Green. Botany.
—Gregory. Geology.
—Sherrington. Physiology.
—Tilden. Chemistry.
Appletree Cottage. Lane, *Mrs.* E. M. 50 c. net. Harper.

Application of highly superheated steam locomotives. Garbe, R: *$2.50 net. Henley.

Application of statistical methods to the problems of psychophysics. Urban, F. M. $2.50. Psychological Clinic.

Applied bronze work. Hessling, E. $8. Hessling.

Applied business English. Hagar, H. A. $1.25. Gregg Pub.

Applied business punctuation and business forms. Hagar, H. A. 40 c. Gregg Pub.

Applied ideals in work with boys, [by] C. Ward Crampton, Winfield S. Hall, [and others.] '10(O22) c. 12°, $1. Y. M. C. A.

Applied mechanics for engineers. Hancock, E: L. **$2 net. Macmillan.

Applied surgical anatomy. Woolsey, G: *$4.50 net. Lea.

Applied vocalization. Kirkpatrick, H. 50 c. H. Kirkpatrick.

Appreciation of music. Surette, T: W., *and* Mason, D. G. **$1.50 net. Baker & T.

Appreciation series. 6 v. New ed. '09 (Ap17) c. il. 12°, ea., *$1.50 net. Baker & T.

Appreciation ser. il. O. **$1.50 net. Baker & T.

—Caffin. Appreciation of the drama.

—Surette *and* Mason. Appreciation of music.

Appreciations with an essay on style. *See* Pater, Wa.

Apprentice to truth. Huntington, *Mrs.* H. M. G. $1.50. Putnam.

Apprentices' course in experimental physics. Maxim, J. L. 50 c. Longmans.

APPRENTICESHIP.
See Useful arts.

Apprenticeship in American trade unions. Motley, J. M. 50 c. Johns Hopkins.

Apprenticeship of Washington. Hodges, G: **$1.25 net. Moffat.

Approach to the social question. Peabody, F. G. **$1.25 net. Macmillan.

Approach to Walt Whitman. Noyes, C. E. $1.25. Houghton M.

April fool doll. Gates, *Mrs.* J. S. †$1.25. Bobbs-M.

April-fool twins. Timlow, E. W. †$1.25. Dutton.

Apt and meet. Nichols, W: F. *$1 net. Whittaker.

Apuleius, Lucius.
Apologia and Florida; tr. by H. E. Butler. '09(D4) D. $1. Oxford Univ.
Metamorphoses; or, the golden ass; tr. by H. E. Butler. In 2 v. '10(Mr26) D. $2. Oxford Univ.

Aquarian gospel of Jesus the Christ. "Levi," *pseud., comp.* $2. E. S. Dowling.

Aquarian philosophy. "Levi," *pseud.* $1. E. S. Dowling.

AQUARIUM.
Eggeling, O., *and* Ehrenberg, F: Fresh-water aquarium and its inhabitants. **$2 net. Holt.

ARAB HORSE.
See Horse.

ARABIA.
Doughty, C: M. Wanderings in Arabia. 2 v. $4.50. Scribner.

ARABIA.—*Continued.*
Forder, A. Adventures among the Arabs in desert, tent, and town. $1. Gospel Pub.
Hume-Griffith, *Mrs.* M. E. *and* A. Behind the veil in Persia and Turkish Arabia. *$3.50 net. Lippincott.
Young, J: C. Children of Arabia. 60 c. net. Revell.
See also Arabic literature;—Mohammed and Mohammedanism.

Arabian and Chinese classics; with biographical and critical sketches by Epiphanius Wilson. '08(Je27) c. 8°, $1.75; hf. mor., $3.50. Lamb Pub.

Arabian nights; ed. by Anna Tweed. '10 (D3) c. D. (Golden books for children.) $1. Baker & T.

Arabian nights; their best-known tales; ed. by Kate Douglas Wiggin and Nora A. Smith; il. in color by Maxfield Parrish. '09 (N20) c. O. †$2.50. Scribner.

Arabian nights' entertainments; tr. from the Arabic by E: W: Lane. '08(O10) il. (Bowman's illustrated lib. of world-favorite books.) $1. Bowman.

Arabian nights' entertainments. [Expurgated ed.] '09(Ag21) il. 12°, $1.50. Dodge.

Arabian nights' entertainments; told in easy French by Kathleen Fitzgerald. '09, [1910.] (Ja) il. (Children's favorites.) *50 c. net. Jacobs.

ARABIAN NIGHTS.
See Blanchaud, R. de, *ed.*

ARABIAN POETRY.
Baerlein, H: Singing caravan. 60 c. net. Dutton.

Arabian wisdom; tr. by Dr. J: Wortabet. '08(Je6) 16°, (Wisdom of the East.) *40 c. net. Dutton.

ARABIC LANGUAGE.
English - Arabic conversation dictionary. $1.50. Lemcke.
Green, A. O., *comp.* Pract. Arabic grammar. 2 v. v. 1, $2.15; v. 2, $3. Oxford Univ.
Nicholson, R. A. Elem. Arabic second reading-book. $2. Putnam.
Weir, T. H. Arabic prose composition. $2 net. Putnam.
See also Semitic languages.

ARABIC LITERATURE.
Green, A. O., *comp.* Modern Arabic stories. In 2 pts. pt. 1, $1.75; pt. 2, $1.50. Oxford Univ.
Nathaniel ibn al-Fayyumi. Bustan al-ukul: [account of the Jews of southern Arabia in the Middle Ages.] *$2.50 net. Lemcke.

Araby. Hutten, *Baroness* B. v. 50 c. B. W. Dodge.

Arai, S.
See Canada, J: W.

ARAMAIC LANGUAGE.
Margolis, M. L. Manual of the Aramaic language of the Babylonian Talmud. $3 net. Stechert.

ARAMAIC LITERATURE.
See Hebrew literature.

Araminta. Snaith, J: C. †$1.50. Moffat.

Arber's English reprints. 16°. Macmillan.
—Sidney. Apologie for poetrie. *35 c. net.

Arbib-Costa Alfonso, ["L. Arno."]
Italian lessons. '09(F) $1. Tocci.
Manuale di corrispondenza commerciale e familiare italiana-inglese; contenente un gran numero di modelli di lettere in italiano e in inglese, i regolamenti postali in uso agli Stati Uniti, ed utili informazioni per chi vuol scrivere lettere in italiano e in inglese. '09, [1910.] (O) 7-173 p. 8°, 50 c. F. Tocci.

ARBITRATION (*International*).
Balch, T: W. L'Evolution de l'arbitrage international. $2. Allen, L. & S.
Griffin, A. P. C., *comp.* List of references on international arbitration. 20 c. U. S., Supt. of Docs.
Hale, E: E., *and* Brewer, D: J. Mohonk addresses. $1. Int. Sch. of Peace.
Ralston, J. H. International arbitral law and procedure. $2. Ginn.
Rodeffer, J: D: Pioneer in international arbitration. 40 c. J: D: Rodeffer.
Trueblood, B: F. International arbitration at the opening of the twentieth century. 5 c. B: F. Trueblood.
United States. Convention bet. the U. S. and other powers for the pacific settlement of international disputes. '10(Jl) 50 p. 8°. Gov. Pr. Off.
See also Fish and fishing;—Hague Peace Conferences;—Peace;—Reciprocity;—War.

Arblay, Mme. Frances Burney d', [Fanny Burney.]
Evelina; hist. of a young lady's entrance into the world. '10(F19) il. 12°, $1.25. Macmillan.
Evelina; introd. by R. B. Johnson. '09 (Mr27) 16°, (Everyman's lib.) *35 c. net; leath., *70 c. net. Dutton.

ARBOR DAY.
Ranger, W. E., *comp.* Nineteenth annual program for the observation of Arbor Day in the schools of Rhode Island. 1910. gratis. W. E. Ranger.
Revell, E. I., *comp.* Arbor day exercises. 25 c. Educ. Pub.
Schauffler, R. H., *ed.* Arbor Day. **$1 net. Moffat.
See also Natural resources.

ARBORICULTURE.
See Forests and forestry.

Arbuthnot, Mrs. P. Stewart-Mackenzie.
See Mary, *Queen of Scots.*

Arcadian calendar. Hill, V. **$1.50 net. Lane.
Arcana coelestia. *See* Swedenborg, Emanuel.
Arcana of nature. Tuttle, H. *$1.50 net. Stillman.
Arcane teaching. Atkinson, W: W. $1. Arcane.
Arch-satirist. Fenwick, F. de W. $1.50. Lothrop, L. & S.
Archæologia nova Cæsarea. Abbott, C: C. 2 v. (Add. author for price.) C: C. Abbott.

ARCHAEOLOGY.
Astley, H. J: D. Pre-historic archæology and the Old Testament. *$2 net. Scribner.
Darius I., *King of Persia.* Behistan inscription: translation. 50 c. Lemcke.

ARCHAEOLOGY.—*Continued.*
Fairbanks, A. Athenian lekythoi: [vases for wine or oil.] $4. Macmillan.
Johnson, W. Folk-memory; or, the continuity of British archæology. $4.15. Oxford Univ.
Michaelis, A. Century of archæological discoveries. $4. Dutton.
Wheeler, J. R. Archæology: [lecture.] (Add. pubs. for price.) Columbia Univ.
See also Asia Minor;—Babylonia;—Bible;—Brasses;—Cliff dwellers;—Coins and medals;—Crete;—Cuneiform writing;—Egypt;—Epitaphs;—Ethnology;—Folk-lore;—Hawaiian Islands;—Herculaneum;—History;—Indians;—Inscriptions;—Italy;—Jerusalem;—Man; —Manabi;—Manners and customs;—Middle Ages;—Monuments;—Mound builders;—Music;—Orangia;—Palestine;—Papyri;—Pseira, Crete;—Sculpture;—Seals;—Semitic literature; — Sicily; — South Africa;—Totemism.

Archer, F. M.
Dog in health and disease. '10(O) 12°, 50 c. Fenno.

Archer, Gleason Leonard.
Ethical obligations of the lawyer. '10(D17) c. 8°, $3 net. Little, B. & Co.
Law office and court procedure. '10(F) c. O. *$3 net. Little, B. & Co.

Archer, R: Lawrence, Lewis, W. J., and Chapman, A. E.
Teaching of geography in elem. schools. '10(Je4) D. $1.10 net. Macmillan.

Archer, W:
Through Afro-America; an English reading of the race problem. '10(My14) 8°, $3 net. Dutton.

—, and Barker, H. Granville.
Scheme and estimates for a national theatre. '08(F15) c. Q. $2.50. Duffield.

ARCHERY.
Maxson, L: W., *comp.* Official archery guide. 10 c. Am. Sports.

ARCHES.
Balet, J. W. Analysis of elastic arches. *$3 net. Engineering News.
Cam, W: Theory of solid and braced elastic arches. 50 c. Van Nostrand.
Reuterdahl, A. Theory and design of reinforced concrete arches. $2. M. C. Clark.

Archibald, And. Webster, D.D.
Easter hope. '09(Je12) c. por. O. $1. S. D. Towne.

Archibald, Raymond Clare.
Carlyle's first love, Margaret Gordon, Lady Bannerman; an account of her life, ancestry and homes; her family and friends. '09(N6) il. facsim., tab., O. *$3.50 net. Lane.

Archimedes.
Geometrical solutions derived from mechanics; tr. from the Greek by Dr. J. L. Heiberg; with an introd. by D: Eugene Smith; English version tr. from the German by Lydia G. Robinson. '09(O23) pap., 50 c. Open Court.

ARCHITECTS.
Chancellor, E. B. Lives of the British architects from William of Wykeham to Sir William Chambers. $2 net. Scribner.

Architects' and builders' pocket book. Kidder, F. E. $5. Wiley.

Architects' directory and specification index for 1909; containing a complete list of the architects in the United States, Canada, Cuba and Porto Rico, classified by states and towns. 9th ed. '09(O2) c. Q. *$3 net. W: T. Comstock.

Architects' lib.; ed. by F. M. Simpson. O. Longmans.

—Pite. Building construction. In 2 v. v. 1. $5 net.

ARCHITECTURAL DRAWING.

American School of Correspondence. Architectural drawing and lettering. $1. Am. Sch. Corr.

Curtis, N. C. Elements of graphics, orthographic projections, shades, shadows and perspective. $1.50. N. C. Curtis.

Dana, W: S. B. Primer of architectural drawing for young students. $1.25. W: T. Comstock.

Edminster, C. F. Structural drawing. $2.50. D: Williams.

Hicks, I: P. Building plans and how to draw them. 50 c. Indust.

Lawrence, W: H: Principles of architectural perspective. (Add. pubs. for price.) W: B. Clarke.

Peker, C: G. How to read plans. 50 c. Indust.

See also Perspective.

Architectural history of the Christian church. Hill, A. G: *60 c. net. Young Churchman.

Architectural lib. il. pls. plans, O. Int. Textbk.

—International library of technology. In 10 v. ea., $5.

Architectural New Orleans. '08(Ap.) 92 p. il. pls. F. pap. (Add. pubs. for price.) Contractors and Dealers.

ARCHITECTURE.

American Institute of Architects. Matters rel. to competition. 50 c. Am. Inst. Architects.

Anderson, W: J. Architecture of the Renaissance in Italy. *$5 net. Scribner.

Anderson, W: J., *and* Spiers, R. P. Architecture of Greece and Rome. *$7.50 net. Scribner.

Architects' directory and specification index for 1909. *$3 net. W: T. Comstock

Ball, J. T. Detailed working drawings of the five orders of architecture. $6.50; $7.50; $4. W: T. Comstock

Bloomfield, R. Mistress art: [architecture.] *$1.40 net. Longmans.

Bragdon, C. Beautiful necessity; seven essays on theosophy and architecture. $2. Manas Press.

Browne, E. A. Greek architecture.—**Romanesque** architecture. ea., $1.75 net. Macmillan.

Bruce, W: G:, *and others, comps.* School architecture. 75 c. Am. Sch.

Bungalows and cottages. 50 c. M. L. Keith.

Bungalows, camps and mountain houses $2. W: T. Comstock.

ARCHITECTURE.—*Continued.*

Bungalow plans. $1. Metuchen Bungalow.

Chancellor, E. B. Private palaces of London—past and present. *$5 net. Lippincott.

Clay Products Assoc. of America. House of brick; plea for the greater use of brick in our domestic architecture. 50 c. Rogers & M.

Construction of Association buildings. 15 c. Y. M. C. A.

Crane, E. A., *and* Soderholtz, E. E. Examples of colonial architecture in South Carolina and Georgia. $16. Hessling.

Dan, H., *and* Wilmott, E. C. M. English shop-fronts old and new. $6. Helburn.

Davison, T. R. Modern homes. *$5.25 net. Macmillan.

Delineator prize $3000 house. $1. B. W. Dodge.

Desmond, H: W., *and* Frohne, H. W. Building a home. **$1.80 net. Baker & T.

Detached dwellings; country and suburban. $5. Swetland.

Dictionary of terms used in architecture and building. 50 c. Indust. Bk.

Ditchfield, P. H. Manor houses of England. $3 net. Scribner.

Du Cerceau, J. A. French chateaux and gardens in the XVII century. *$10 net. Scribner.

Embury, A., 2d. One hundred country houses. **$3 net. Century Co.

Fifty house plans designed for home builders in the Southwest. 50 c. Assoc. Architects.

Fletcher, B. F. *and* H. P. English home. $4 net. Scribner.

Garner, T:, *and* Stratton, A. Domestic architecture of England during the Tudor period. In 3 pts. $48 net. Scribner.

Gotch, J: A. Growth of the English house. *$3 net. Scribner.

Gourlay, C: Construction of a house. $2.75 net. Lane.

Green, W. C. Old cottages and farmhouses in Surrey. *$2.50 net. Macmillan.

Hawlin, A. D. F. Text-book of the history of architecture. $2. Longmans.

Hayward, J. W. Essentials in a convenient, comfortable and healthy house $4. Spon.

Hodgson, E. F. Wigwam portable houses. (Add. author for price.) E. F. Hodgson.

Hodgson, F: T:, *ed.* Treatise on the five orders of architecture. $2. Drake.

Holman, E. E. Picturesque camps, cabins and shacks. — Picturesque suburban houses. ea., $2. E. E. Holman.

House of brick of moderate cost. 50 c. Rogers & M.

Kemp, O. Wilderness homes; book of the log cabin. *$1.25 net. Outing.

Lethaby, W: R: Greek buildings represented by fragments in the British Museum. *$4.20 net. Scribner.

Low cost suburban homes: [designs and pictures.] 25 c. Winston.

ARCHITECTURE.—*Continued.*

Macartney, M. E. English houses and gardens in the 17th and 18th centuries. *$6 net.—Recent English domestic architecture. *$3.50 net. Scribner.

Marquand, A. Greek architecture. **$2.25 net. Macmillan.

Masterpieces of Moorish architecture.—Masterpieces of Spanish architecture. ea., 25 c. Stokes.

Mencken, H:, *ed.* Bungalowcraft; book on bungalow and cottage building. $1.—California bungalow homes. $1 net. Bungalowcraft.

Nason, E. H. Old Colonial houses in Maine. (Add. author for price.) E. H. Nason.

Newson, J: H: Homes of character. $1. J: H: Newson.

Old houses of Rouen of the 17th and 18th century. $15. Hessling.

Osborne, C: F., *ed.* Historic houses and their gardens. $6. Winston.

Petersen, J. C. "Cream of a thousand plans." 25 c. J. C. Petersen.

Polk's architects', engineers', builders' and contractors' directory. 2 v. $5. Polk.

Polley, G: H:, *comp.* Gothic architecture, furniture and ornament of England from the 11th to the 16th century. 2 v. in 1. $40. Polley.

Porter, A. K. Medieval architecture: its origins and development. 2 v. $15. Baker & T.

Pract. bungalows of southern California built at moderate cost; designed and erected by the Los Angeles Investment Co. [1910.] (Je) c. 128 p. il. 12°, 50 c. Los Angeles Investment.

Radford, W: A. Artistic bungalows. $1.—Artistic homes.—Combined house and barn plan book. $1.—Modern homes. $1.—Portfolio plans. $2. Radford Architectural.

Richardson, C: J. Fragments and details of architecture, decoration and furniture of the Elizabethan period. $12; $15. Helbrun.

Rivoira, G. T. Lombardic architecture, its origin and derivation. $20. Helburn.

Roberts' home builder. $1. Roberts & R.

Robinson, J: B. Architectural composition. *$2.50 net. Van Nostrand.

Rogers, A. D. House of brick for ten thousand dollars. 25 c. Rogers & M.

Ruskin, J: Seven lamps of architecture. *$1 net.—Stones of Venice. 3 v. ea., **$1 net. Dutton.

Sale, E. T. Manors of Virginia in Colonial times. *$5 net. Lippincott.

Salvatore, S. Italian architecture. $25. Polley

Saylor, H: H., *ed.* Distinctive homes of moderate cost. $2 net. McBride, W.

Shackleton, R. *and* E. Adventures in home making. $1.75. Lane.

Simpson, F. M. History of architectural development. In 3 v. v. 2. *$6 net. Longmans.

Smith, T. R., *and* Slater, J: Architecture: classic and early Christian.—Architecture: Gothic and Renaissance. ea., $1.25. Gorham.

Spanish colonial architecture. $30. Polley.

Sparrow, W. S. English house; how to judge its periods and styles. *$2.50 net. Lane.

Sternberg, G: M. Report of committee on model houses. (Add. Superintendent for price.) U. S., Supt. of Docs.

Stickley, G. Craftsman homes. $2. G. Stickley.

Strack, H. Brick architecture of the middle ages and the renaissance in Italy. $11; $8. Helburn.

Sturgis, R. Hist. of architecture. In 3 v. v. 2, **$5 net; **$7.50 net. Baker & T.

Sturgis, R. Short history of architecture: Europe. **$2.50 net. Macmillan.

Two family and twin houses. $2. W: T. Comstock.

Uhde, C. Architectural forms of the classic ages. $20. Hessling.

Vallance, A., *and* Salaman, M. C: Art in England during Elizabethan and Stuart periods. *$2.50 net; *$3 net. Lane.

Wallis, F. E. How to know architecture. $2 net. Harper.

Wilson, H: L. Bungalow book. $1. H: L. Wilson.

Wolfe & McKenzie. Book of designs. $2. Wolfe & M.

Ye Planry Building Co. Bungalows. $1. Ye Planry.

Young, C., *and* Brooks, S. M. Spon's architects' and builders' pocket price-book. $1.50. Spon.

See also Abattoirs;—Abbeys;—Æsthetics;—Apartments;—Archæology; — Arches;—Architects;—Architectural drawing; — Barns; — Bridges; — Building;—Building laws;—Building materials;—Carpentry; — Cathedrals; — Cement;—Chimneys;—Church architecture; — Church decoration;—Churches;—Columns;—Concrete;—Earthwork;—Elevators;—Fine arts;—Garage;—Heating;—House decoration; — Lead; — Librarians and libraries;—Lighting;—Mantels;—Masonry; — Mills;—Plumbing; — Roofs;—Sanitary engineering;—Schools; — Stair-building;—Steel; — Strength of materials;—Trusses;—Ventilation;—Woodwork; — *also* Architectural lib.; — New York City.

Archives of philosophy; ed. by F: J. E. Woodbridge. Q. pap. Science Pr., (N. Y.)

—Elkus. Concept of control. 40 c.

—Stettheimer. Will to believe. $1.

Archives of psychology; ed. by R. S. Woodworth. il. O. pap. Science Pr., (N. Y.)

—Brown. Time in Eng. verse rhythm. 70 c.

—Bruner. Hearing of primitive peoples. $1.

—Froeberg. Relation between the magnitude of stimulus and the time of reaction. 35 c.

—Hamilton. Perceptual factors in reading. 50 c.

—Hollingworth. Inaccuracy of movement. 80 c.

—Jones. Influence of bodily posture on mental activities. 50 c.

—Kirkpatrick. Studies in development and learning. $1.

—Norsworthy. Psychology of mentally deficent children. $1.

—Poincairé. Value of science. $1.25.

—Ruger. Psychology of efficiency.

—Wells. Statistical study of literary merit. 30 c.

—Woodrow. Quantitative study of rhythm. 60 c.

Arctander, Karl Johan Ludwig Wilhelm August.
Apostle of Alaska: story of William Duncan of Metlakahtla. '09(My22) c. il. pors. map, O. *$1.50 net. Revell.
Guilty? '10(My14) c. il. 12°, $1.25. Cochrane.

ARCTIC REGIONS.
Bellot, J. R. Journal d'un voyage aux mers polaires. 60 c. Oxford Univ.
Brooklyn Public Library. Polar regions; list of books in library. gratis. Brooklyn Lib.
Edwards, D. M. Toll of the Arctic seas. $2.50 net. Holt.
Franklin, *Sir* J: Narrative of a journey to the shore of the Polar Sea in the years 1819, 20, 21, 22. 35 c. net; 70 c. net. Dutton.
Greely, A. W. Hdbk. of polar discoveries. $1.50 net. Little, B. & Co.
Harrison, A. H. In search of a polar continent. *$3.50 net. Longmans.
Hobbs, W: H. Characteristics of the inland-ice of the Arctic regions. $2. Am. Philosophical.
Holmes, *Mrs.* B. F. Log of the "Laura" in polar seas. (Add. pubs. for price.) Univ. Press, (Camb.)
Maclean, J. K. Heroes of the polar seas. $1.50. Lippincott.
Mikkelsen, E. Conquering the arctic ice. *$3.50 net. Jacobs.
Mowbray, J. H. Discovery of North Pole by Cook and Peary. $1.50. G: W. Bertron.
Neil, H: True story of the Cook and Peary discovery of the North Pole; incl. account of all other polar expeditions. $1.50. Educ. Co.
Peary, R. E. North Pole; its discovery in 1909. $4.80; $5 net; Autographed ed., $15 net. Stokes.
Rasmussen, K. People of the polar north. *$5 net. Lippincott.
Whitney, H. Hunting with the Eskimos. $3.50 net. Century Co.
Wright, *Mrs.* H. S. Great White North; story of polar exploration. $2.50 net. Macmillan.
Wright, S. H. Adventures in the Arctic regions. *$1.50 net. Lippincott.
See also Antarctic regions;—Northwest passage;—Wit and humor;—*also* Cook, Frederick Albert;—Peary, Robert Edwin.

Ardagh, W. M.
The Magada. '10(Ap9) D. $1.50. Lane.

ARDENNES (The), Belgium.
See Liège.

Ardleigh, Hugh.
Am. garment cutter: treatise on cutting of men's garments. 2d ed. '08(Ag15) c. il. diagrs., 4°, $15. Am. Fashion.

Ardrey, R. L.
Railway capitalization: a review of the corporate history of ten leading western railroads. '09(O2) c. 8°, $10. R. L. Ardrey.

Are bees reflex machines? Buttel-Reepen, H. v. 50 c. A. I. Root.
Are our prayers heard? Egger, J. S. J. 15 c. Herder.
Are the dead alive? Rider, A. F. $1.75, fixed. B. W. Dodge.
Are you my wife? Marcin, M. $1.25 net. Moffat.

Arendt, Morton.
See Crocker, Fs. Bacon.

ARGENTINE REPUBLIC.
Hirst, W: A. Argentina. $3 net. Scribner.
International Bureau of American Republics. Argentine Republic; general descriptive data. (Add. pubs. for price.) Int. Bu. Am. Republics.
Pennington, A. S. Argentine Republic. $3 net. Stokes.

Argles, Mrs.
See Hungerford, *Mrs.* Marg. Hamilton.

Argonovitica. *See* Apollonius *of Rhodes.*

ARGUMENTATION.
See Debating.

Argyll, J:, Douglas Sutherland Campbell, Duke of.
Intimate society letters of the eighteenth century. '10(D3) il. por. facsims., O. $10. Lane.
Life of Queen Victoria. New ed. '09(D4) il. 12°, (Bohn's libraries.) *$1 net. Macmillan.
Passages from the past. '08(Ag8) 2 v., il. 8°, *$6.50 net. Dodd.

Arid agriculture. Buffum, B. C. $1.50. B. C. Buffum.

Ariel booklets. 32°, leath., 75 c., boxed. Putnam.
—Allen. As a man thinketh.
—Arnold. Light of Asia.
—Balzac. Maxims.—Passion in the desert.
—Browning. Shorter poems.
—De Quincy. Confessions of an English opium eater.
—Dickens. The chimes.
—Emerson. Essays.
—Goethe. Hermann and Dorothea.
—Heine. Songs and lyrics.
—Henton. Mystery of pain.
—Keats. Lyrics.
—Landor. Imaginary conversations.
—Longfellow. Courtship of Miles Standish.
—Lowell. Vision of Sir Launfal.
—Mérimée. Carmen
—Mill. On liberty.
—Storm. Immensée.
—Story. Roman lawyer in Jerusalem.
—Tennyson. Enoch Arden and Maud.—Idylls of the king. 2 v.
—Thackeray. Ballads.
—Thoreau. Friendship.
—Wilde. Happy prince.

ARIKARE INDIANS.
See Indians.

Ariston-dilettante series. 21 v. '09(O2) O. ea., bds., $1.50, boxed. Caldwell.

Aristophanes.
The Acharnians, the knights and the birds; Frere's translation. '09(Mr27) 16°, (Everyman's lib.) *35 c. net; leath., *70 c. net. Dutton.
The Acharnians; with introd., critical notes and commentary by W. Rennie. '09 (My8) D. *$1.70 net. Longmans.
Acharnians; with introd., English prose tr., critical notes and commentary by W. J. M. Starkie. '10(Ja15) 8°, *$3 net. Macmillan.

Aristophanes—*Continued.*
Comedies; tr. by B: Bickley Rogers. pt. 1, The knights; pt. 2, The Acharnians. 2 pts. in 1 v. '10(Jl16) 8°, $5 net. Macmillan.
The plays: a metrical version; with notes and an essay on Aristophanic comedy by J: Hookham Frere. '08(S19) 12°, (New universal lib.) 50 c.; leath., 75 c. Dutton.

ARISTOPHANES.
Croiset, M. Aristophanes and the political parties at Athens. *$2 net. Macmillan.

Aristotle.
Works; tr. into English under the editorship of J. A. Smith and W. D. Ross. v. 1, Parva naturalia, by J. I. Beare and G. T. R. Ross. '08(Ap11) $1.15; v. 2, De Lineus insecabilibus, by H. H. Joachim. '08(Ap11) 85 c.; v. 3, Metaphysica (v. 8), by W. D. Ross. '08(Ap11) $2.50; v. 4, De mirabilibus auscultationibus, by L. C. Dowdall. '10(Mr26) 70 c.; v. 5, Historia animalium (v. 6), by D'Arcy Wentworth Thompson. '10(D) $3.40; v. 6, De generatione animalium, by Arth. Platt. (D24) 12°, $2.50. Oxford Univ.
Aristotle on his predecessors; tr. by A. E. Taylor. '10(Je) 12°, (Religion of science lib.) pap., 40 c. Open Court.
Aristotle on the art of poetry; a rev. text, with critical introd., translation and commentary by Ingram Bywater. '09(S11) O. $5.25. Oxford Univ.
De anima; with translation, introd. and notes by R. D. Hicks. '08(F29) 8°, *$5.50 net. Putnam.
Nicomachean ethics, bk. 6; with essays, notes and tr. by L. H. G. Greenwood. '09(Mr) 7+214 p. 8°, *$1.75 net. Putnam.
Politics of Aristotle. *See* Plato. Dialogues.
Rhetoric: tr. by Sir R: Claverhouse Jebb; ed., with an introd. and supplementary notes, by J. Edn. Sandys. '09(Mr) 27+207 p. 8°, *$1.75 net. Putnam.

ARISTOTLE.
Watson, J. M. Aristotle's criticisms of Plato. $1 Oxford Univ.

ARITHMETIC.
Arnold, L. V. Supplemental problems in arithmetic. 25 c. L. V. Arnold.
Ayres, E. American ready reckoner. (Add. pubs. for price.) Popular.
Bailey, M. A., *and* Germann, G: B. Number primer. 30 c. Am. Bk.
Bendure & Arthur's practical and complete guide for the use of auditors, agents and railroad men generally: [ready reckoner.] $3. Bendure & A.
Byrnes, J. C., *and others.* Pupils' arithmetic primary book. In 2 pts. pt. 1, *26 c. net; pt. 2, *30 c. net; complete in 1 v., 45 c. net. Macmillan.
Calmerton, G. Primary arithmetic. (Not for sale.) Fort Wayne Sch. Bd.
Chancellor, W: E. Elem. school mathematics by grades. bk. 6, rev. and adapt. to grades 6A and 6B in the N. Y. City schools. *28 c. net. Globe Sch. Bk.
Colaw, J: M., *and others.* School arithmetic. 35 c. B. F. Johnson.

ARITHMETIC.—*Continued.*
Colvin, F. H. Machine shop arithmetic. 50 c. Henley.
Crelle, A. L. Calculating tables. $5. Lemcke.
Curtis, U. Modern business arithmetic. (Add. pubs. for price.) Bobbs-M.
Eby, E. G. Handy tables by which over 500,000 problems of the busy man are already solved: [ready-reckoner.] $2.50. J. F. Smith.
Ellis Publishing Co. Model arithmetic for commercial colleges and department schools. '09(N) c. 8+250 p. il. 8°, 69 c. Ellis Pub.
Gleason, C. H., *and* Gilbert, C: B. Gilbert arithmetics. 3 v. bk. 1, 36 c. net; bk. 2, 40 c. net; bk. 3, 45 c. net. Macmillan.
Gray, J: C. Number by development; method of number instruction. **$1 net. Lippincott.
Gribben, D: S. Mathematics made easy. v. 1. $1. D: S. Gribben.
Hamilton, S. Complete arithmetic. 60 c.—Elementary arithmetic. 35 c.—Key to arithmetic. 80 c. Am. Bk.
Harvey, L. D. Practical arithmetic. In 2 bks. bk. 1, 35 c.; bk. 2, 50 c. Am. Bk.
Hopkins, J: W., *and* Underwood, P. H. New arithmetics: Advanced book. *50 c. net. Macmillan.
International Correspondence Schools. Tratado de aritmética mercantil. Int. Text-bk.
Jones, D: R. Course of study in primary arithmetic. 30 c. San F. St. Normal.
Jones, W. S. Pract. arithmetic. 50 c. Am. Bk.
Kent, E. Manual of arithmetic: outline of work in number for use in schools for the deaf. 65 c. Atkinson, M. & G.
Lee, A. S. Ten weeks in arithmetic. $1. A. S. Lee.
Low, F. F. Hampton arithmetic. $1. Hampton Inst.
Luman, J: A., *ed.* Comprehensive arithmetic. $1.50. Peirce Sch.
Lusby, J. W. Stocks and bonds made easy. 50 c. Teachers' Supply.
McClymonds, J. W., *and* Jones, D. R. Essentials of arithmetic. 60 c. Am. Bk.
Mercer, G: E., *and* Bonsall, M. Complete arithmetic. pt. 1. 54 c. World Bk.
Myers, G: W: Arithmetic, grammar school. 60 c. Scott, F. & Co.
Nicholson, J. W. Elem. arithmetic. 34 c. —Grammar school arithmetic. 45 c. Am. Bk.
Nihart, B: F., *and* Stryker, W: New century arithmetics. 2 v. (Add. pubs. for price.) Silver.
Patchel, G: Eureka rate tables, calculated for any given number of pounds at any given gross tonnage rate. $50. G: Patchel.
Payne, E. L. Pract. arithmetic for advanced grades. 65 c. Inland.
Preston, D. F. A., *and* Stevens, E: L. Series of arithmetics. bk. 1, 35 c. net; bk. 2, 50 c. net. Macmillan.
Sadler, W. H. New essentials of business arithmetic. 90 c. Sadler-R.

ARITHMETIC.—*Continued.*

Smith, D: E. Rara arithmetica. *$5.50 net.—Rara arithmetica: catalogue of the arithmetics written before the year MDCI, with description of those in library of G: Arth. Plimpton. 2 v. $20. Ginn.

Smith, D: E. Teaching of arithmetic. 75 c.; 30 c. Teachers' Coll.

Southworth, G. A:, *and* Stone, J: C: Arithmetic. In 3 bks. bk. 1, 42 c.; bk. 2, 45 c.; bk. 3, 50 c. B: H. Sanborn.

Stevens, F. L., *and others.* Practical arithmetic. **65 c. net. Scribner.

Stone, C. W. Arithmetical abilities and some factors determining them. $1. Teachers' Coll.

Stone, J: C., *and* Millis, J. F. Secondary arithmetic, commercial and industrial. *75 c. net. B: H. Sanborn.

Sweet, J. S. Modern business arithmetic. $1.25. Sweet.

Walsh, J: H: Arithmetic for upper grades. 50 c.; with appendix, 55 c.—Graded mental arithmetic. *50 c. net. Heath.

Walton, G: A:, *and* Holmes, S. H. Arithmetics; 2d bk. 40 c.; 3d bk. 45 c.; 4th bk. 50 c. Am. Bk.

Watson, B. M., *and* White, C: E. Grammar school arithmetic. 60 c. Heath.

Wentworth, G: A. New elementary arithmetic. 35 c. Ginn.

Wentworth, G: A., *and* Smith, D: E. Complete arithmetic. 60 c.—Oral arithmetic. 35 c. Ginn.

Young, J. W: A., *and* Jackson, L. L. Appleton arithmetics; grammar-school book. 55 c.—Primary books. 35 c. Appleton.

See also Bookkeeping;—Engineering;—Graphics;—Interest; — Mensuration;—Numerals;—Percentage.

Arithmetic of electricity. Sloane, T: O. $1. Henley.

Arithmetical abilities and some factors determining them. Stone, C. W. $1. Teachers' Coll.

Arizona ser. See Ellis, E: Sylvester.

Arizona Territory. *Supreme ct.* Repts.; (E. R. Lewis.) v. 9. '08(My); v. 10. '09(S); (Ja. R. Dunseath.) v. 11. '10(N) c. O. shp., ea., $4.25. Bancroft-W.

ARIZONA TERRITORY.

Brewer, I: W. Treatment of tuberculosis in Arizona. gratis. Wood.

Grey, Z. Last of the plainsmen: [record of a hunting trip across the Arizona desert with "Buffalo" Jones.] *$1.50 net. Outing.

Griffiths, D: Protected stock range in Arizona. U. S., Supt. of Docs.

Hornaday, W: T. Camp-fires on desert and lava. **$3 net. Scribner.

Macdougal, D. T. Across Papaguerio. 50 c. Am. Geog. Soc.

Munk, J. A. Arizona bibliography. gratis. J. A. Munk.

Summerhayes, *Mrs.* M. Vanished Arizona. $1.60. M. Summerhayes.

Swath, H. S. Two new owls from Arizona. 10 c. Univ. of Cal.

See also Grand Canyon;—Yuma.

Ark that glue built. Williams, C. A. $1. Stokes.

Arkansas. *Bureau of Mines, Manufacture and Agriculture.* Descriptive catalogue of the diamond bearing rock, by Philip F. Schneider; to accompany the exhibit of periodic rock. '07, [1909.] (Mr) 4 p. 8°, pap., gratis. G. B. Tucker.

Arkansas. *Dept. of Public Instruction.* Suggestive program for the schools of Arkansas for use in celebration of Robert E. Lee day, Jan. 19. [1910] (My) 19 p. il. 8°, gratis. Arkansas Dept. Pub. Instruct.

Arkansas. *Supreme ct.* Repts., v. 84; (T. D. Crawford.) '08(Ap); v. 85 (Jl); v. 86. '09(Ap); v. 87 (Je); v. 88 (Ag); v. 89 (N); v. 90. '10(F); v. 91, 92 (S) c. O. shp., ea., $1.50. Arkansas.

ARKANSAS.

Branner, J: C. Clays of Arkansas. (Add. Supt. for price.) U. S., Supt. of Docs.

Brown, B. Conard fissue, a Pleistocene bone deposit in northern Arkansas. $2.50. Am. Museum.

Hinemon, J: H. Geography of Arkansas. 50 c. Rand, McN. & Co.

Hughes, *Mrs.* M. E. Answer to "Three years in Arkansas." 25 c. Wiley & W.

McCollum, A. J. New Arkansas form book: pleadings and practice. $3.50. A. J. McCollum.

McQuillin, E., *and* Campbell, W: S. Forms of code pleading for Missouri and Arkansas. $7.50. F. H. Thomas.

Purdue, A. H., *and* Branner, J: C. Slates of Arkansas. gratis. Arkansas Geol. Survey.

Schneider, P. F. Preliminary rept. on the Arkansas diamond field. (Add. pubs. for price.) Cen. Pr.

Shinn, J. H. Pioneers and makers of Arkansas. (Add. pubs. for price.) Genealog. and Hist.

United Confederate Veterans, Arkansas Division. Confederate women of Arkansas in the Civil War. $1. J. Kellogg.

United States. *Dept. of Agriculture. Forest Service.* National forests of Arkansas.

See also Little Rock;—St. Francis Valley;—University of Arkansas.

Arkansas Diamond Co. Brief account of the discovery and investigation and the official repts. of geologist and mining engineer on the occurrence of diamonds in Pike Co., Arkansas. '08, [1909.] (My) c. 37 p. il. map, 8°, pap. (Not for sale.) S: W. Reyburn.

Arkansas Geological Survey pubs. il. 8°. Arkansas Geol. Survey.

—Purdue *and* Branner. Slates of Arkansas. gratis.

Arkansas overruled cases, [etc.] 1st ed., 1909; comp. by H. H. Booth. '09(N) c. 65 p. S. $1.50. F. H. Thomas.

Arkansas sharpshooter. Galloway, G: W. 50 c. Smith.

Arkinsaw cousins. Ellis, J: B. †$1.50. Holt.

ARM.

Ashhurst, A. P. C. Anatomical and surgical study of fractures of the lower end of the humerus. $2.75 net. Lea.

Armagnat, H.
Theory, design and construction of induction coils; tr. and ed. by Otis Allen Kenyon. '08(Je13) c. figs. O. *$2 net. McGraw.

ARMATURES.
Horstman, H: C:, *and* Tousley, V. H. Practical armature. $1.50. Drake.

Armbruster, C. H.
Initia Amharica; introd. to spoken Amharic. pt. 1, grammar; pt. 2, English-Amharic vocab., with phrases. '10(O8) O. pt. 1, $3.50 net; pt. 2, $5 net. Putnam.

ARME BLANCHE.
See War.

ARMENIA.
Basmajian, K. H. Life in the Orient. $1 net. Am. Tr.

ARMENIAN CHURCH.
Arpee, L. Armenian awakening. *$1.25 net. Univ. of Chic.

ARMENIAN LITERATURE.
Babylonian and Assyrian literature. [Also] Armenian literature. $1.75; $3.50. Lamb Pub.

Armes, Ethel.
Midsummer in Whittier's country; a little study of Sandwich Center. '10(Ap) 73 p. il. 12°, 75 c. E. Armes.
Story of coal and iron in Alabama. '10 (My21) c. il. pors. O. $5. Ala. Chamber of Com.

Armfield, Constance.
Flower book. '10(D31) col. il. 8°, $2 net. Warne.

Arminel of the West. Trevena, J: $1.50. Moffat.

Armington, M. A.
See Telford, Emma Paddock.

Armistead, Wilson H.
Trout waters: management and angling. '08(O17) 12°, *$1.75 net. Macmillan.

Armitage, W. J.
Church year: studies for the Sundays, sacred seasons and saints' days; with introductory note by Bp. W: Boyd Carpenter. '08(D26) 8°, $1. Oxford Univ.

Armor and ships; revision, Armor and ships, *Journal U. S. Artillery*, July-August, 1906. '10(O) 135 p. il. tab., diagrs., O. pap., 50 c. Journ. U. S. Artillery.

Armour, Frances J.
Brotherhood of wisdom. '08(S5) D. †$1.50. Lane.

Armour, G. Denholm.
British sport past and present. '09(D) 500 p. col. il. 4°, *$6 net. Doran.

Arms, Mary W.
Italian vignettes. '09(O23) c. il. D. *$1.25 net. M. Kennerley.

ARMS (*Coats of*).
See Heraldry.

ARMS AND ARMOR.
Ashdown, C: H: Arms and armour. $4. Dodge.
ffoulkes, C: Armour and weapons. $2.15. Oxford Univ.
See also Heraldry.

Arms and the maid. Sabatini, R. $1.25 net. Putnam.

Armsby, H: Prentiss.
Feeding for meat production. '09(Mr6) 8°, (U. S., Supt. of Agriculture, Bu. of Animal Industry, bull.) pap., 10 c.
Principles of animal nutrition; with special reference to the nutrition of farm animals. 3d ed., rev. '09(F6) c. tabs., 8°, $4. Wiley.

—, and Fries, J. August.
Available energy of red clover hay: investigations with the respiration calorimeter. '08(Ap18) il. tabs., 8°, (U. S. Dept. of Agriculture, Bureau of Animal Industry, bull.) pap., 10 c. U. S., Supt. of Docs.

Armstrong, C: Wicksteed.
Mystery of existence in the light of an optimistic philosophy. '09(Je12) D. *90 c. net. Longmans.

Armstrong, Collin.
Relation of speculation to business. '08 (Je13) c. O. pap., gratis. C. Armstrong.

Armstrong, E. Frankland.
Simple carbohydrates and the glucosides. '10(Mr26) O. (Monographs on biochemistry.) *$1.20 net. Longmans.

Armstrong, E: Cooke.
Syntax of the French verb; with exercises by De La Warr B. Easter. '09(Je12) c. D. 90 c. Holt.

Armstrong, Emma Kate.
Chateaubriand's America. '07, [1909.] (Ja) 345-370 p. 8°, $1. Grandgent.

Armstrong, H: E:
Teaching of scientific method, and other papers on education. 2d ed. '10(Ag13) 12°, $1.75 net. Macmillan.

Armstrong, H: Herbert.
Autobiographic elements in Latin inscriptions. '10(O8) 8°, (Univ. of Michigan studies, Humanistic ser.) pap., 40 c. Macmillan.

Armstrong, Ja. E.
Advantages of limited sex segregation in the high school. '10(Ag) 339-350 p. diagrs., 8°, pap., 15 c. J. E. Armstrong.

Armstrong, Maurice McNeill.
In the shadow of San Juan. '10(Jl16) c. il. 8°, $1. Pueblo Pub.

Armstrong, Rob. Allen.
Historical and literary outlines of the Old Testament; with introd. in which are presented discussions of materials, manuscripts, versions, etc. '08(Ag1) c. 12°, $1. Acme.

Armstrong, S: Chapman.
Ideas on education. '08, [1909.] (My) 37 p. 8°. (Add. pubs. for price.) Hampton Inst.

Armstrong, Sir Wa.
Art in Great Britain and Ireland. '09 (O2) c. il. D. (Ars una: species mille; general history of art.) **$1.50 net. Scribner.

Armstrong, W: Clinton.
Lord Stirling at the telescope. '08(Je6) 8 p. diagrs., 4°, 50 c. W: C. Armstrong.
—, ed. Patriotic poems of New Jersey. '08 (Je6) il. $1.50. A. R., N. J. Soc.

Armstrong Cork Co., Pittsburg. Nonpareil corkboard insulation for cold storage warehouses, abattoirs, breweries, ice plants, fur storage vaults, dairies, creameries, candy factories, bakeries, fish freezers, canneries, refrigerators, freezing tanks, and generally wherever refrigeration is employed. [1910.] (Ja) c. '09. 7-118 p. il. 8°, gratis. Armstrong Cork.

ARMY.
See Military art and science;—*also* names of countries.

Army horses. Wolcott, E. F., *comp.* $1. U. S., Supt. of Docs.

Army letters from an officer's wife. Roe, *Mrs.* F. M. A. M. **$2 net. Appleton.

Army mule. Thompson, C: M. $1 net. Houghton M.

Army rifles. Hinkle, F: W. (Not for sale.) F: W. Hinkle.

Arnaud, Raoul.
Louis-Philippe and his sister; Adelaide of Orleans, (1777-1847;) tr. by E. L. Sharlwood. '08(D19) pors. 8°, *$4.50 net. Scribner.

Arndt, Ernst Moritz.
Deutsche patrioten in Ruszland zur zeit Napoleons; ed., with introd., notes, and vocab., by W: Arnold Colwell. '09(N6) c. map, S. (Heath's modern language ser.) 30 c. Heath.

Arner, Ezra Emerson.
Truth: [government; politics; trusts; prosperity; panics.] '08(Je27) c. 12°, pap., 25 c. Faribault Pilot.

Arner, G: Byron L:
Consanguineous marriages in the American population. '08(Jl11) c. O. (Columbia Univ. studies in hist., economics and public law.) pap., 75 c. Longmans.

Arnett, Lizzie.
'Mongst the hills of Kentucky. '09(Ap) c. 258 p. 8°, $1; pap., 50 c. L. Arnett.

Arnim, Mary Annette Beauchamp Gräfin von.
The caravaners. '10(O8) c. il. D. $1.50. Doubleday, P.

Arnold, Bion Jos., Freeman, J: Ripley, and Olmsted, F: Law.
City planning for Pittsburgh; outline and procedure; rept.; adopted by the Commission December, 1909. '10(N19) c. 8°, gratis. Pittsburg Civic.

Arnold, Channing, and Frost, F: J.
American Egypt; record of travel in Yucatan. '09(O16) il. maps, plans, Q. *$3.80 net. Doubleday, P.

Arnold, E: Vernon.
Cothvrnvlvs: three short Latin historical plays for beginners, with vocab. '08(F22) 12°, *35 c. net. Macmillan.

Arnold, Sir Edn.
Light of Asia. '09(Ap10) front. 32°, (Ariel booklets.) leath., 75 c., boxed. Putnam.
Light of the world; or, the great consummation. Pocket ed. '09(O2) front. S. (Longmans' pocket lib.) *75 c. net. Longmans.

Arnold, Felix.
Attention and interest; study in psychology and education. '10(Mr12) c. figs. D. **$1 net. Macmillan.
Text-book of school and class management. In 2 v. v. 1, Theory and practice. '08(D5); *$1.25 net; v. 2, Administration and hygiene. '10(Jl30) c. il. D. $1 net. Macmillan.

Arnold, Mrs. Gertrude Weld, comp.
Mother's list of books for children. '09 (O30) c. S. $1. McClurg.

Arnold, Hans, [pseud. for Frau Babette Eberty von Bülow.]
Fritz auf ferien; ed., with notes and vocab., by Mary Thomas. '08(O3) c. S. 25 c. Am. Bk.

Arnold, Jesse Oglevee.
See Galley, Henrietta.

Arnold, Jos. Alfr.
Guide for business corporations in the state of New York; with notes and forms. 2d ed., rev. and enl. '08(Ja4) O. $1.50; pap., $1.25. Baker, V. & Co.
See also New York [State.] Business corporations.

Arnold, Leon Vance.
Supplemental problems in arithmetic. [2d ed.] '09(Ja16) c. S. pap., 25 c. L. V. Arnold.

Arnold, Lucy Edith, ed.
Graded memory work for schools. '07, [1908.] (Je.) c. '03. 2 v., 16°. (Add. pub. for price.) T. Pillot.

Arnold, Marie.
Handbook of German construction and complete verb scheme. '09(Ja23) c. D. 60 c. Flanagan.

Arnold, Matthew.
Essays in criticism; 3d series; with an introd. by E. J. O'Brien. '10(O1) c. D. $1.25 net. Ball Pub.
On the study of Celtic literature and other critical essays; with introd. by Ernest Rhys and supp. by Lord Strangford, and reprints from Nash's Taliesin. '10(D10) 16°, (Everyman's lib.) 35 c. net; leath., 70 c. net. Dutton.
Poems, 1840-1866. '08(S19) 16°, (Everyman's lib.) *35 c. net; leath., *70 c. net. Dutton.
Select poems; ed., with introd. and notes, by E: Everett Hale, jr. '08(N21) c. 16°, (Belles-lettres ser.; Section VI., Nineteenth century poets.) 60 c. Heath.
Selected poems; ed., with introd. and notes, by Hereford B. George and A. M. Leigh. '09(Ap3) map, D. 50 c. Oxford Univ.
Sohrab and Rustum, and other poems; ed., with notes and an introd., by Ashley H. Thorndike. '10(My21) D. (Longmans' English classics.) 25 c. Longmans.
Thyrsis and The scholar gipsy. '10(D) 16°, (Golden text ser.) pap., 40 c.; bds., 60 c.; Japan vel., $1, boxed. T: B. Mosher.
See also Macaulay, T: Babington, *Lord.* Lays of ancient Rome.

Arnold, Paul, and Steele, Marshall, comps.
Nursery rhymes. Bks. 1 and 2. '08(My16) il. obl. S. pap., 20 c. Cassell.

Arnold, Ralph, and Anderson, Rob.
Preliminary report on the Coalinga oil district, Fresno and Kings counties, California. '09(F6) il. fold. maps, O. (U. S. Dept. of the Interior, U. S. Geol. Survey bull.) pap., 20 c. U. S., Supt. of Docs.

Arnold, Rob. S.
Allegemeine bücherkunde zur neueren deutschen literaturgeschichte. '10(N12) O. $2.25. Stechert.

Arnold, Sarah Louise, and Kittredge, G: Lyman.
Mother tongue. Rev. ed. 2 bks. '08(S19) c. il. D. bk. 1, 45 c.; bk. 2, 60 c.; with composition, 70 c. Ginn.

Arnold, Mrs. T. B., ed.
Pract. Sabbath-school commentary on the International lessons; ed. by Rev. D: B. Warner. '10(N12) c. 12°, 50 c. net. Revell.

Arnold Arboretum pubs. il. f°. C. S. Sargent.
—Shaw. Pines of Mexico. *$25 net.

Arnold-Forster, Hugh Oakeley.
English Socialism of to-day. '08(Ap18) 12°, *$1.25 net. Dutton.
Hist. of England. New ed. 2 v. '10(S) il. per set, $2 net. Cassell.

ARNOLD-FORSTER, Hugh Oakeley.
Arnold-Forster, M. S.-M. Right Honourable Hugh Oakeley Arnold-Forster. $4.20 net. Longmans.

Arnold-Forster, Mrs. Hugh Oakeley.
See Arnold-Forster, Mary Story-Maskelyne.

Arnold-Forster, Mary Story-Maskelyne, [Mrs. Hugh Oakeley Arnold-Forster.]
Right Honourable Hugh Oakeley Arnold-Forster; memoir by his wife. '10(D10) pors. O. $4.20 net. Longmans.

ARNOLD *of Brescia.*
See Church history.

Arnold's geological ser.; ed. by J. E. Marr. il. D. Longmans.
—Gibson. Geology of coal and coal-mining. $2.50.
—Lake *and* Rastall. Text-book of geology. $4.50 net.
—Thomas *and* MacAlister. Geology of ore deposits. $2.50.
—Woodward. Geology of water-supply $2.50.

Arnold's practical Sabbath-school commentary. *See* Olmstead, *Rev.* W: B., *and* Warner, *Rev.* D. S., *eds.*

Arnold's tempter. Comfort, B: F. $1.50. C. M. Clark.

Arnott, Ja. A., and Wilson, J:
Petit-Trianon—Versailles: il. by a ser. of measured drawings and photographs of the entire building, exterior and interior. In 3 pts. pt. 2. '08(My9) f°, in portfolios, per set, *$27.50 net. Scribner.

Arnott, S.
Gardening in the north; with chapters on the cultivation of fruits and vegetables and plants under glass by R. P. Thurston. '09(Jl3) il. D. *$1 net. Cassell.

Arnoul, the Englishman. Aveling, F. $1.50. Herder.

Arny, H: Vinecome.
Principles of pharmacy. '09(O) c. 9-1179 p. il. 8°, *$5 net. Saunders.

Around Afghanstan. Bouillane de Lacoste, E. A. H. de. $3 special net. Appleton.

Around Africa and across the Andes. Lowe, F. J. International Press.

Around the Emerald Isle. O'Donnell, W: C:, *jr.* $1. Roxburgh.

Around the farm. '09(O2) (Playtime ser. of toy books.) bds., 40 c.; pap., 25 c. Warne.

Around the world. Stephens, E. W: $5. Stephens.

Around the world. *See* Tolman, *Mrs.* S. W. C.

Around the world in a year. Carlisle, G: L. **$2 net. Baker & T.

Around the world in seven days. Strang, H. $1.25 net. Doran.

Around the world readers. *See* Tolman, *Mrs.* Stella Webster Carroll.

Around the world with a business man. Bigger, L. A. 4 v. $12. Winston.

Around the world with the battleships. Miller, R. J: $1.25. McClurg.

Around town boys. Oeland, P: J. $1.50. Walker, E. & C.

A-roving he would go. Reed, M. *$1.25 net. Sherman, F.

Arpee, Leon.
Armenian awakening; hist. of the Armenian church, 1820-1860. '09(O9) c. por. D. *$1.25 net. Univ. of Chic.

Arrangement of finger points indentification. Brayley, F. A: $2. Worcester Press.

Arrhenius, Svante August.
Worlds in the making: evolution of the universe; tr. by H. Borns. '08(Mr21) c. il. O. **$1.60 net. Harper.
Life of the universe as conceived by man from the earliest ages to the present time; tr. by Dr. H. Borns. '10(Ja29) 2 v., 12°, (Harper's lib. of living thought.) ea., *75 c. net. Harper.

"Arrima, Jehn," pseud.
See Harriman, J: Emery, *jr.*

Arrom de Ayala, Cecilia Francisca Josefa Böhl von Faber y Larrea, ["Fernan Caballero."]
Un serviton y un liberalito ō tres almas de dios; ed., with introd., notes and vocab., by Carlos Bransby. '09(O2) c. S. (Heath's modern language ser.) 50 c. Heath.

Ars moriendi; [facsim.] '02 [1909.] (N) il. 4°, $5. (100 copies.) Hispanic Soc.

Ars una: species mille; general history of art. il. 12°. Scribner.
—Armstrong. Art in Great Britain and Ireland. **$1.50 net.
—Ricci. Art of northern Italy. $1.50 net.

Arsène Lupin. Jepson, E. †$1.50. Doubleday, P.

Arsène Lupin, gentleman burglar. *See* Leblanc, Maurice.

Arsène Lupin versus Sherlock Holmes. *See* Leblanc, Maurice.

ARSENIC.
Headden, W: P. Occurrence of arsenic in soils, plants, fruits and animals. 50 c. Colo. Sci. Soc.

ART.
See Æsthetics;—Fine arts;—Painters and painting;—Useful arts.

Art and craft of the author. Hirsch, C. E. **$1.50 net. Grafton Press.

Art and curio collector's guide to London. Jerningham, C: E: W. 35 c. net. Cassell.

Art and economy in home decoration. Priestman, M. T. **$1.50 net. Lane.

Art and letters lib. il. 8°, *$3 net. Duffield.
—Davies *and* Hunt. Stories of English artists.
—Francis *of Assisi, St.* Little flowers.

Art and letters lib.—Continued.
—Reynolds. Stories from the Flemish and Dutch artists.
—Seeley. Artists of the Italian Renaissance.
—Stories of the Italian artists from Vasari.
—Stirling-Maxwell. Stories of the Spanish artists.
—Turner *and* Baker, *eds.* Stories of the French artists.
Art and practice of typography. Gress, E. G. $5. Oswald.
Art and science of advertising. French, G: **$2 net. Sherman, F.
Art and the human spirit. Griggs, E: H. *50 c. net; *25 c. net. B: W. Huebsch.
Art Association of Indianapolis. John Herron Art Institute. Catalogue of sculptured works of Augustus Saint-Gaudens, with biographical sketch; memorial exhibition opening Dec., 1909, and extending through Jan. and Feb., 1910. [1910.] (N) 95 p. il. por. 8°. Art Assoc. Indianapolis.
Bibliography (3 p.).
Art collections of Europe ser. 16°. Dutton.
—Cruttwell. Guide to the paintings in the churches and minor museums of Florence. *$1.25 net.
Art crafting in metal for amateurs. Chandler, F. A. $1.50. Fort Hill.
Art-crafts booklets. il. O. pap., 25 c. Hirshberg.
—Hopkins, *ed.* Decorating fabrics by stenciling.
Art craftsman ser. il. 12°. Spon.
—Jewelry enamelling. 25 c.
ART CRITICISM.
See Fine arts.
ART EDUCATION.
See Fine arts.
Art galleries of Europe. il. D. $2 net; ¾ mor., $5 net. L. C. Page.
—Ansell *and* Fraprie. Art of the Munich galleries.
—Preyer. Art of the Netherland galleries.
Art in Buffalo. Sellstedt, L. G. $1.50. L. G. Sellstedt.
Art in England during the Elizabethan and Stuart periods. Vallance, A. *$2.50 net; *$3 net. Lane.
Art in Great Britain and Ireland. Armstrong, *Sir* W. **$1.50 net. Scribner.
Art in needlework. Day, L. F. *$2 net. Scribner.
Art monograms and lettering. Bergling, J: M. 3 v. ea., $1.50; v. 1, 2, $3; 3 vs. in same cover, $4.25. J: M. Bergling.
Art needlework ser. See Heminway's.
Art of accompanying plain chant. Springer, M. $1.50. J. Fischer.
Art of aviation. Brewer, R. W. A. $3.50. McGraw-H.
Art of baking. Laskowski, P: E. $1. P: E. Laskowski.
Art of business college soliciting. Haupt, W: G: $2. W: G: Haupt.
Art of chess. Mason, J. $1.25. McKay.
Art of decorating show windows. Tracy, C: A., *comp.* $3.50. Merchants' Record.
Art of expression. Atkinson, W: W. $1. Progress Co.
Art of handling men. Collins, J. H. 50 c. Altemus.
Art of home candy making. Home Candy Makers, Canton, O. Home Candy.
Art of lecturing. Lewis, A. M. 25 c. Kerr.
Art of life ser.; ed. by E: Howard Griggs. D. *50 c. net. B: W. Huebsch.
—Griggs. Human equipment.
—Higginson. Things worth while.
—Hyde. Self-measurement.
—Patten. Product and climax.
—Ross. Latter day sinners and saints.
Art of living. Creighton, *Mrs.* L. *50 c. net. Longmans.
Art of logical thinking. Atkinson, W: W. $1. Progress Co.
Art of magic. Downs, T: N. $5. W. S. Edwards.
Art of massage. Hale, A. C. $2. W: R. Jenkins.
Art of millinery. Ben Yûsuf, *Mme.* A. $2. Millinery Trade.
Art of modern bookkeeping. Spencer, E. $3. E. Spencer.
Art of modern conjuring and drawing room entertainment; by a modern magician. '10 (D24) il. D. $1.25. Reilly & B.
Art of natural sleep. Powell, L. P. **90 c. net. Putnam.
Art of northern Italy. Ricci, C. $1.50 net. Scribner.
Art of painting in the nineteenth century. Mach, E. R. O. v. *$1.25 net. Ginn.
Art of paper-making. Watt, A. $3. Van Nostrand.
Art of retail selling. Hirschler, D. $1. N. Y. Inst. Mercantile.
Art of roadmaking. Frost, H. $3. H. Frost.
Art of securing better teaching positions. Lincoln, E. B. 60 c. Progress Club.
Art of self-control. Ingalese, R: $1. Occult.
Art of sermon illustration. Jeffs, A. *$1 net. Revell.
Art of short story writing. Chester, G: R. $3.50. Pub. Syndicate.
Art of singing. Lieber, F. 50 c. Ditson.
Art of singing. Santley, *Sir* C: **$1.25 net. Macmillan.
Art of singing. Shakespeare, W: $2. Ditson.
Art of skating. Brokaw, I. $5 net. Scribner.
Art of speech and deportment. Morgan, A. *$1.50 net. McClurg.
Art of sympathy. Knowlson, T: S. $1. Warne.
Art of tatting. Hoare, *Lady* K. L. $7 net. Longmans.
Art of the Belgian galleries. Singleton, E. **$2 net. L. C. Page.
Art of the Netherland galleries. Preyer, D: C. *$2 net; *$5 net. L. C. Page.
Art of the plasterer. Bankart, G: P. *$10 net. Scribner.
Art of the short story. Gerwig, G: W: *75 c. net. Percy Pub.
Art of theatrical make-up. Morton, C. *$2.50 net. Macmillan.
Art of vocalization. *See* Marzo, Eduardo.
Art of voice production. Pattou, A. A. 50 c. A. A. Pattou.
Art of writing and speaking the English language. Cody, S. 50 c. Old Greek Pr.

Art prices current, 1908-9; record of sale prices at Christie's during the season, with an index to artists' and engravers' names. [1910.] (Jl) 414 p. $3.25 net. Dodd.
Art songs for high schools. Earhart, W. 80 c. Am. Bk.
Art talks with young folks. Collmann, S. M. $1.50. Young Israels.
ARTAXERXES III., OCHUS, *King of Persia.*
Hirschy, N. C. Artaxerxes III. Ochus and his reign. *75 c. net. Univ. of Chic.
Arte of rhetorique. Wilson, *Sir* T: $1.75. Oxford Univ.
Arteaga y Pereira, F. de, comp.
Nine Spanish poems. '09(My15) pap., *40 c. net. Oxford Univ.
Artemis to Actæon. Wharton, *Mrs.* E. N. J. **$1 net. Scribner.
Artemision. Hewlett, M. H: *$1 net. Scribner.
ARTERIES.
Warfield, L. M. Arterio-sclerosis, etiology, diagnosis, prognosis, prophylaxis and treatment. $2. Mosby.
ARTHRITIS.
Jones, R. L. Arthritis deformans; comprising rhumatoid arthritis, osteo-arthritis, and spondylitus deformans. *$4 net. Wood.
Arthrosteopedic surgery. McCurdy, S. L. $1. Medical Abstract.
ARTHUR, *Duke of Brittany.*
Jeanrenaud, H. Duke of Brittany. *60 c. net. McClurg.
ARTHUR, *King.*
Baldwin, J. Stories of the king. 50 c. Am. Bk.
Children's King Arthur. 75 c. Doran.
Cox, J: H. Knighthood in germ and flower; Anglo-Saxon epic, Beowulf, and Arthurian tale, Sir Gawein and the Green Knight. $1.25. Little, B. & Co.
Haydon, A. L. Stories of King Arthur. 50 c. Cassell.
Lang, A., *comp.* Tales of King Arthur and the round table. 30 c. Longmans.
Malory, *Sir* T: Boy's King Arthur. $2. Scribner.
Malory, *Sir* T: King Arthur stories. **40 c. net. Houghton M
Malory, *Sir* T: Le morte d'Arthur. *$7.50 net.—Le morte d'Arthur. 2 v. ea., *$1 net. Dutton.
Malory, *Sir* T: Selections from Le Morte d'Arthur. **25 c. net. Macmillan.
Morris, C: King Arthur and the Knights of the Round Table. $1.25. Lippincott.
Pyle, H. Story of the Grail and The passing of Arthur. $2.50 net. Scribner.
Senior, D. King who never died. $1.50. Macmillan.
Sommer, H. O., *ed.* Vulgate version of the Arthurian romances. v. 1, 2. ea., $5; v. 3, pt. 1, $5. Carnegie.
Arthur, Ja.
Time and its measurement; [repr. from *Popular Mechanics Magazine.*] '10(Ja15) c. il. por. 4°, $1.50. Popular Mechanics.
Arthur, W:
New building estimator; guide to estimating the cost of labor and material in building construction, from excavation to finish. '09(My1) c. il. tabs., 16°, $2.50. D: Williams.
New building estimator; pract. guide to estimating the cost of labor and material in building construction, from excavation to finish. 3d ed., rev. and enl. '10(Je18) il. tabs., 16°, $2.50. D: Williams.
Arthur's. Lyons, A. N. $1.50. Lane.
Article in Theocritus. Leutner, W. G: gratis. Johns Hopkins.
Artificial and natural flight. Maxim, *Sir* H. S. *$1.75 net. Macmillan.
Artificial manures. Ville, G. *$3 net. Longmans.
Artificial water-ways. Hepburn, A. B. **$1 net. Macmillan.
ARTILLERY.
Hines, F. T:, *and* Ward, F. W. Service of coast artillery. $3.50 net. Goodenough & W.
Spaulding, O. L., *jr.* Notes on field artillery. $1; with maps, $1.25. U. S. Cavalry.
See also Explosives;—Firearms.
Artillery of Nathan Bedford Forrest's cavalry. Morton, J: W. $2.50. Pub. Ho. of M. E. Ch., So.
Artist songs. Richardson, E. *$1.15 net. Wessels.
Artistic crafts ser. of technical hdbks.; ed. by W. R. Lethaby. D. Macmillan.
—Hooper. Hand-loom weaving. $2.25 net.
Artistic entertainments. Jackson, M. M. 25 c. Flanagan.
Artistic homes. Priestman, *Mrs.* M. T: $2 net. McClurg.
Artistic tone production. Brouillet, G. A. $2. F. E. Bacon.
Artistic work and gymnastic games. Anderson, H: S. 75 c. Werner.
Artist's way of working. Sturgis, R. $5 net. Dodd.
ARTISTS.
Brinton, C. Modern artists. $6. Baker & T.
Cary, E. L. Artists past and present. **$2.50 net. Moffat.
Collmann, S. M. Jews in art. $1.50. Bacharach.
Cyr, *Mrs.* E. M. Story of three great artists: Raphael, Michael Angelo, Leonardo da Vinci. 50 c. Ginn.
Davies, R., *and* Hunt, C. Stories of English artists from Vandyck to Turner. *$3 net. Duffield.
Huneker, J. G. Promenades of an impressionist. $1.50 net. Scribner.
Knight, W: A. Six lectures on some nineteenth century artists, English and French. $2. Art. Inst. of Chic.
Reynolds, V. Stories of the Flemish and Dutch artists from the Van Eycks to the end of the XVIIth century. *$3 net. Duffield.
Seeley, E. L., *comp.* Artists of the Italian Renaissance.—Stories of the Italian artists from Vasari. ea., *$3 net. Duffield.
Turner, P. M., *and* Baker, C. H. C., *eds.* Stories of the French artists. *$3 net. Duffield.
See also **Anatomy for artists;—Architects;—Engravers and engravings;—Musicians;—Painters and painting.**

Artman, S: R.
Legalized outlaw: [liquor traffic.] '08(Jl4) c. D. $1. Business Men's.
Arts and crafts in the Middle Ages. Addison, *Mrs.* J. DeW. G. $3. L. C. Page.
Arts and crafts of older Spain. Williams, L. 3 v. *$4.50 net. McClurg.
Arts connected with building. Schultz, R. W. *$2 net. Scribner.
Arts course at medieval universities. Paetow, L: J: $1. Univ. of Ill.
Arts of Japan. Dillon, E. *$1 net. McClurg.
ARTZ COLLECTION.
See Boston Public Library.
Arundell, J: Fs., Baron Arundell of Wardour.
Some papers of Lord Arundell of Wardour, 12th Baron, Count of the Holy Roman Empire, etc., with a preface by the dowager Lady Arundell of Wardour. '09 (Jl3) por. O. *$3 net. Longmans.
Arvat. Myers, L. H. *$1.25 net. Longmans.
ARYAN LANGUAGES.
Denison, T: S. Mexican-Aryan comparative vocab. $2. T: S. Denison.
Holbrooke, G: O. Aryan word-building. $2. Knickerbocker Press.
See also Language.
ARYANS.
Denison, T: S. Primitive Aryans of America. $3.25; $2.50. T: S. Denison.
As a man lives. Oppenheim, E. P. †$1.50. Little, B. & Co.
As a man thinketh. *See* Allen, Ja
As far as the East is from the West. Bidwell, D. D. $1.50; $2.25. Scranton.
As gold in a furnace. Copus, J: E. 85 c. Benziger.
As it happened. Hilliers, A. *$1.35 net. Putnam.
As old as the moon. Stoddard, F. J. **$1 net. Doubleday, P.
As others see us. Brooks, J: G. **$1.75 net. Macmillan.
As others see us. Hill, J: L. 75 c. Standard Pub.
As the gods decree. Morris, D. H: B'way Pub.
As they came to me. Elliot, M. M. S. $1. M. M. S. Elliot.
As we see it. Waring, R. L. $1.50. R. L. Waring.
"As ye will." Leavitt, S. $1.50. Magnum Bonum.
As you like it. *See* Shakespeare, W:
ASBURY, *Bp.* Francis.
Du Bose, H. M. Francis Asbury. $1. Pub. Ho. M. E. Ch., So.
Mains, G: P. Francis Asbury. *25 c. net. Eaton & M.
Ascanio. *See* Dumas, Alexandre.
Ascending effort. Bourne, G: $1.50 net. Dutton.
"Ascott, Rob. Hope," pseud.
See Moncrieff, Ascott Rob. Hope.
Asendi. Strouse, *Mrs.* G: H. $1.50. Chemical.
Asfordby family. *See* Genealogies. Turk, W. A. C.
Ash, E:, M.D.
Mind and health; the mental factor and suggestion in treatment, with special reference to neurasthenia and other common nervous disorders. [1910.] (Je) 12°, $1.50 net. Wood.
Ash, Fenton.
Trip to Mars. '10(Ja1) il. 12°, $1.50. Lippincott.
Ash, Mark and W:, eds.
See New York [City.] Greater N. Y. City charter.
Ashburn, Jos. Nelson.
Hist. of the Eighty-sixth Regiment, Ohio Volunteer Infantry. '09, [1910.] 149 p. il. pors. 8°, $1.50. J. N. Ashburn.
Ashburn, Percy Moreau.
Elements of military hygiene, especially arranged for officers and men of the line. '09(Ag14) c. D. **$2 net. Houghton M.
Ashburner, Wa.
Rhodian sea-law; ed. from the manuscripts. '09(S11) O. $5.75. Oxford Univ.
ASHBURNHAM, Mass.
Vital records of Ashburnham, Mass., to the end of the year 1849. $2.70. F. P. Rice.
Ashby, H:
Notes on physiology. 8th ed.; rev. by Hugh T. Ashby. '10(O15) il. D. $1.50. Longmans.
ASHBY CAVALRY.
McDonald, W: N. Hist. of the Laurel brigade, originally Ashby cavalry of the Army of No. Va. and Chew's battery. $3. K. S. McDonald.
Ashcroft, Edg. A.
Study of electrothermal and electrolytic industries; statistics by I. J. Moltkehansen. In 3 pts. pt. 1, Introductory. '09(My22) c. figs. fold. fig. O. *$2 net. McGraw.
Ashdown, C: H:
Arms and armour. '09(Je19) il. O. $4. Dodge.
Ashdown, Mrs. C: H:
British costume during 19 centuries (civil and ecclesiastical). '10(O29) il. O. $1.50 net. Stokes.
Ashe, S: A'Court.
History of North Carolina. In 2 v. v. 1, From 1584 to 1783. '08(D5) c. il. pors. maps, O. $5; ¾ mor., $6. Van Noppen.
Ashe, Sydney Whitmore.
Electricity experimentally and practically applied. '10(Ag13) il. $2 net. Van Nostrand.
Ashe, W: Willard.
Shade trees for North Carolina. '08(D) 74 p. il. 4°, (N. C. Geological and economic survey bull.) 8 c. Uzzell.
Terracing of farm lands. '08(D) 38 p. diagrs. 4°, (N. C. geological and economic survey bull.) 6 c. Uzzell.
Ashenfelter, Ida Goodman.
The truth. '08(Ag) c. 134 p. 16°, $1. I. G. Ashenfelter.
Ashenhurst, Rev. Ja. Oliver.
Day of the country church. '10(O8) c. D. $1 net. Funk.
Ashes. Deledda, G. †$1.50. Lane.
Ashes of love. Garvice, C: 25 c. J. S. Ogilvie.
ASHEVILLE, N. C.
See Methodist Episcopal church.

Ashford, C. E., and Kempson, E. W. E.
Elem. theory of direct current dynamo electric machinery. '08(D5) 8°, *$1 net. Putnam.

Ashhurst, Astley Paston Cooper, M.D.
Anatomical and surgical study of fractures of the lower end of the humerus; Samuel D. Gross prize essay of the Philadelphia Academy of Surgery, 1910. '10(D) c. 17-163 p. il. 4°, $2.75 net. Lea.
See also Deaver, J: Blair.

Ashleman, Lorley Ada.
Dramatic French reader: 12 historical French plays designed for high school use; resumé of French grammar required in first year high school course. '08(F1) c. front. D. 75 c. Flanagan

Ashley, Burton J:
Cesspool and its dangers. [1910.] (F) c. '09. 12 p. O. pap., gratis. Ashley.
Principles of decay as applied to biologic sewage purification. 2d ed. [1910.] (F) c. '09. 15 p. O. pap., gratis. Ashley.

Ashley, G: Fs.
See Anthony, Gardner Chace.

Ashley, G: Hall, and Fisher, Cassius Asa.
Valuation of public coal lands; the value of coal land, by G: H. Ashley; Depth and minimum thickness of beds as limiting factors in valuation, by Cassius A. Fisher. '10(Mr12) 8°, (U. S., Geolog. Survey bull.) (Add. Superintendent for price.) U. S., Supt. of Docs.

Ashley, Roscoe Lewis.
American government: a text-book for secondary schools; [also] Hendricks, Eldo Lewis. Hist. and civil government of Indiana. '08(Ag22) c. 12°, *$1.25 net.—Rev. and rewritten. '10(Ap9) c. il. map, D. $1 net. Macmillan.

Ashley, W: Ja., ed.
British industries: series of general reviews for business men and students. 2d ed. '08(F15) D. *$1.80 net. Longmans.

Ashman, G: Cromwell.
Studies in radio-activity. '08, [1910.] (Ap) 24 p. il. 8°. G: C. Ashman.

Ashmead-Bartlett, Ellis.
Passing of the Shereefian Empire. '10 (N12) c. il. maps, 8°, $4 net. Dodd.

Ashmore, D: Newton.
This, that and the other. '09(N) c. 124 p. por. 12°, $1; pap., 75 c. D: N. Ashmore.

Ashmun, Marg.
Composition in the high school. '09(Ap17) 12°, (Univ. of Wis. bulletin.) pap., 10 c. Univ. of Wis.
—, **ed.** Prose literature for secondary schools, with some suggestions for correlation and composition; with introd. by Willard G. Bleyer. '10(N5) c. D. 80 c. Houghton M.

ASHOKAN RESERVOIR, Brown Station, N. Y.
Nimsgern, E: G. Illustrated and descriptive account of the main dams and dikes of the Ashokan reservoir, Brown Station, N. Y. 50 c. E: G. Nimsgern.

Ashton, W: Easterly.
Text-book on the practice of gynecology, for practitioners and students. 4th ed., rev. and enl. '09(N) c. 11-1099 p. il. 8°, $6.50. Saunders.

Ashton-Kirk, investigator. McIntyre, J: T: $1.20 net. Penn Pub. Co.

ASIA.
Bates, L. W., *jr.* Russian road to China. $3 net. Houghton M.
Benn, *Mrs.* E. A. F. P. Overland trek from India by side-saddle, camel and rail. *$5 net. Longmans.
De Lesdain, *Count.* From Pekin to Sikkim, through the Ordos, the Gobi Desert and Thibet. *$4 net. Dutton.
Fraser, D: Short cut to India: journey along the route of the Baghdad railway. *$5 net. Scribner.
Grant, P. S. Observations in Asia. **$1.25 net. Brentano's.
Hedin, S. A. Overland to India. 2 v. $7.50 net. Macmillan.
Johnston, R. F. From Peking to Mandalay: journey from north China to Burma. *$5 net. Dutton.
Lambert, J: C. Missionary heroes in Asia. *75 c. net. Lippincott.
Redway, J. W. All around Asia. 60 c. Scribner.
Stratton, C. R. Picturesque Asia and Africa. $1. Nat. Pub. Co.
Williams, A. Wonders of Asiatic exploration. 75 c. Lippincott.
See also Afghanistan;—Arabia;—Armenia;—Assyria;—Babylonia; — Baluchistan; — Burma;—China;—Far East;—Geology;—Himalaya Mts.;—India;—Japan;—Mongolia;—Mustagh Range;—Persia;—Siberia;—Tibet;—Turkestan.

ASIA MINOR.
Garstang, J: The land of the Hittites; account of the recent explorations and discoveries in Asia Minor. $4 net. Dutton.
Ramsay, *Sir* W: M. Cities of St. Paul. *$3 net. Armstrong.
Ramsay, *Sir* W: M., *and* Bell, G. L. The thousand and one churches. $5 net. Doran.

ASILUS.
See **Flies.**

Askew, Mrs. Alice J. de C. Leake, and Claude, Arth. Cary.
Plains of silence. '08(Ap18) front. T. †$1.50. Cassell.
Rod of justice. '10(Jl16) D. $1.50. Brentano's.
Tempting of Paul Chester. '10(F12) D. $1.50. Fenno.
Testimony. '09(N20) D. $1.50. Lane.

Askew, Claude Arth. Cary.
See Askew, Alice J. de C. Leake.

Askins, C:
American shotgun. '10(D31) il. 8°, $2 net. Outing.

Askwith, E: Harrison, D.D.
Analytical geometry of the conic sections. '08(O3) il. 12°, *$2.60 net. Macmillan.

Asoka, or Piyadasi, Emperor of India.
Edicts of Asoka; ed. in English, with an introd. and commentary by Vincent A. Smith. '09(My15) front. Q. bds., $6.75. Oxford Univ.

ASOKA, *or* PIYADASI, *Emperor of India.*
Smith, V. A. Asoka: Buddhist emperor of India. $1.15. Oxford Univ.

ASPARAGUS.
Herrman, H. French method of intensive cultivation and asparagus forcing. $1. H: L. Freking.
Aspects of Anglicanism. Moyes, J. *$1 net. Longmans.
Aspects of Christ. Selbie, W: B. $1.50 net. Doran.
Aspects of George Meredith. Curle, R: H. P. *$1.75 net. Dutton.
Aspects of modern opera. Gilman, L. **$1.25 net. Lane.
Aspects of recent Russian literature. Wolfe, A. J: (Not for sale.) A. J: Wolfe.
Aspects of the Hebrew genius. Simon, L., *ed.* $1. Bloch.
Aspects of the speech in the later Roman epic. Lipscomb, H. C. $1. Furst.
Aspects of the spiritual. Brierley, J. *$1.40 net. Whittaker.
ASPHALT.
Boorman, T: H. Asphalts: their sources and utilizations. $3. W: T. Comstock.
Peckham, S. F: Solid bitumens. $5. M. C. Clark.
See also Pavements;—*also* Venezuela.
ASPIDIOTUS PERNICIOSUS.
See San José scale.
Aspinwall, Mrs. Alicia.
Can you believe me stories. '09(N) 8+374 p. il. 8°, $1.50. Dutton.
Listen to me stories. '10(N12) il. 8°, $1.50. Dutton.
Assassination of Abraham Lincoln. Dewitt, D: M. $2.25. Macmillan.
ASSAYING.
Furman, H. Van F. Manual of practical assaying. $3. Wiley.
Seamon, W: H: Manual for assayers and chemists. $2.50 net. Wiley.
Smith, J. R. Modern assaying. $1.50 net. Lippincott.
See also Metals and metallurgy;—Mineralogy.
Assembly song book. Rix, F. R. *50 c. net. Barnes.
Assertio septum sacramentorum. Henry VIII. *$2 net. Benziger.
ASSESSMENTS.
See Taxation.
Assessor's manual for Iowa. Toof, M. D. 25 c. M. D. Toof.
Assessors' land valuations. Chandler, F. R., *ed.* $5. Donnelley.
ASSIMILATION.
See Digestion;—Metabolism.
ASSISI, Italy.
Goff, *Mrs.* R. Assisi of St. Francis. *$6 net. Dodd.
Assisting the boy in the choice of a vocation. McKeever, W: A. gratis. W: A. McKeever.
ASSOCIATION.
See Psychology.
Association for Improving the Condition of the Poor. *New York Milk Committee.* Infants' milk depots and their relation to infant mortality. '09(Ja16) il. tabs., maps, 50 c. Assoc. Imp. Con. Poor.
Association of American Portland Cement Manufacturers. Plans for suburban concrete dwellings; prize competition. '09(F6) il. plans, 4°, $1. Assoc. Am. Portland Cement.
Association of Collegiate Alumnæ. *Washington Branch, comp.* List of poems chosen from standard Eng. poets, suitable to be learned by children between the ages of five and fourteen. '08(Ag22) c. 8°, pap., 25 c. L. Madeira.
ASSYRIA.
King, L. W: Hist. of Babylonia and Assyria. In 3 v. v. 1. $4.80 net. Stokes.
Rogers, R. W: Religion of Babylonia and Assyria, especially in its relation to Israel. *$2 net. Eaton & M.
Toffteen, O. A. Researches in Assyrian and Babylonian geography. pt. 1. *$1 net. Univ. of Chic.
See also Babylonia;—Semitic language;—*also* Sargon.
ASSYRIAN CHURCH.
See Oriental religions.
ASSYRIAN LANGUAGE.
Harper, R. F. Assyrian and Babylonian letters belonging to the Kouyunjik collections of the British Museum. v. 9. $6 net. Univ. of Chic.
Prince, J: D. Assyrian primer. $1 net. Lemcke.
ASSYRIAN LITERATURE.
Babylonian and Assyrian literature. $1.75; $3.50. Lamb Pub.
Astir. Thayer, J: A. $1.20 net. Small.
Astley, Rev. Hugh J: Dukinfield.
Pre-historic archæology and the Old Testament: Donellan lectures, 1906-1907. '08 (Je20) O. *$2 net. Scribner.
Astolat classics. 8 v. [1910.] (D) sq. 16°, ea., leath., 75 c. net; cf., $1.25 net. Jacobs.
Aston, W: G:
Shinto: ancient religion of Japan. '07, [1909.] (Ap) 8°, (Religions ancient and modern.) *40 c. net. Open Court.
Astor ed. of poets. 98 v. '08(D) ea., 60 c. Crowell.
Astor prose ser. D. Crowell.
—Lincoln. Abraham Lincoln. 60 c.
Astounding revelations. Buzzacott, F. H. $2. F. H. Buzzacott.
Astral world. Tiffany, J. $2. De Laurence, S.
ASTROLOGY.
Dalton, J. G. Spherical basis of astrology. $2.50. Spenceley.
George, L. The A to Z horoscope delineator. $2. Portland (Ore.) Sch. Astrology.
Hodges, H: C. Science and key of life. In 6 v. v. 4-6. ea., $2. Astro Pub.
Merton, H. W. Heliocentric astrology. $1.50. McKay.
Phelps, J. R. Birthday horoscopes, character readings. 50 c. Brewer, B.
Ruyl, B. B. Zodiac birthday book. $1 net. Baker & T.
Sepharial, *pseud.* Astrology—how to make your own horoscope. 50 c. Fenno.
Towne, *Mrs.* E. J., *and* Twing, C. S., *comps.* Character delineation and inspiration for those born under the sign of Capricorn. 75 c. E. J. Towne.
Astronomer's wife. Hall, A. $1. Nunn.

ASTRONOMY.
Armstrong, W. C: Lord Stirling at the telescope: [transit of Venus, 1769.] 50 c. W: C. Armstrong.
Ball, *Sir* R. S. Treatise on spherical astronomy. *$3.75 net. Putnam.
Barton, S: G. Halley's comet. gratis. S: G. Barton.
Borgmeyer, C: J. Halley's comet. (Priv. pr.) St. Louis Univ.
Burton, C: J. Astronomy and the Bible. $1. C: J. Burton.
Chambers, G: F: Halley's comet. 25 c.—Story of the comets simply told. $2. Oxford Univ.
Clarke, E. C. Astronomy from a dipper. **60 c. net. Houghton M.
Clerke, A. M. Popular history of astronomy. *$2.60 net. Macmillan.
Comstock, G. C. Text book of field astronomy for engineers. $2.50. Wiley.
Dolmage, C. G. Astronomy of to-day. *$1.50 net. Lippincott.
Dyson, F. W. Astronomy. 50 c. net. Appleton.
Elson, H: W: Comets, their origin, nature and history.—Star-gazer's hdbk. ea., *50 c. net. Sturgis & W.
Emerson, E. Comet lore; Halley's comet in hist. and astronomy. 25 c. E. Emerson.
Forbes, G: Hist. of astronomy. **75 c. net. Putnam.
Hale, G: E. Study of stellar evolution. *$4 net. Univ. of Chic.
Hollis, H. P. Chats about astronomy. *$1.25 net. Lippincott.
Hosmer, G: L. Text-book on pract. astronomy. $2 net. Wiley.
Howe, H. A. Elements of descriptive astronomy. $1.25. Silver.
Jacoby, H. Astronomy: [lecture.] 25 c. Macmillan.
Kullmer, C. J. Star maps and star facts. 15 c. net. C. J. Kullmer.
Leahy, G: V. Astronomical essays. $1. G: V. Leahy.
Lowell, P. Evolution of worlds. **$2.50 net. Macmillan.
MacPherson, H., *jr.* Romance of modern astronomy. $1.50 net. Lippincott.
Maunder, E: W. Astronomy of the Bible. *$2 net. M. Kennerley.
Olcott, W. T. In Starland with a three-inch telescope. **$1 net. Putnam.
Perrine, C: D., *and others.* Determination of the solar parallax from photographs of Eros made with the Crossley reflector of the Lick Observatory, University of California. Carnegie.
Philippine Islands. *Weather Bu.* Return of Halley's comet and popular apprehensions; by G: M. Zwack. Bu. Public Pr.
Pickering, E: C: Future of astronomy. E: C: Pickering.
Pickering, W: H: Researches of the Boyden department.—Search for a planet beyond Neptune. ea., $1. Harvard Univ.
Richards, L. A. Comets. Eddy Press.
Riegler, G. Amateur astronomer. $1.25 net. Dodd.

ASTRONOMY.—*Continued.*
Rogers, J. E. Earth and sky every child should know. $1.20 net. Doubleday, P.
Rudaux, L. How to study the stars. *$2 net. Stokes.
Schnell, A. F: Astronomy. $1.50. A. F: Schnell.
Schurig, R: Tabulae caelestes continentes stellas caeli borealis. $1. Lemcke
Seares, F: H. Pract. astronomy for engineers. *$2.25 net. F: H. Seares.
See, T: J. J. Researches on the evolution of the steller systems. v. 2. $10. T: P. Nichols.
Serviss, G. P. Astronomy with the naked eye.—Curiosities of the sky. ea., **$1.40 net.—Round the year with the stars. $1 net. Harper.
Todd, D: P. Halley's comet. gratis. Am. Bk.
Turner, H. H. Halley's comet. 35 c. Oxford Univ.
Wilde, W. Celestial ejectamenta. $10. Oxford Univ.
See also Almanacs and annuals; — Astrology; — Bible;—Indexes;—Jupiter;—Longitude; —Mars; Mt. Wilson;—Moon;—Navigation;—Smithsonian Institution;—Solar system;—Stars;—Sun;—Tide;—Time;—Universe.
"ASTRONOMY AND ASTRO-PHYSICS."
See Indexes.
ASTROPHYSICAL OBSERVATORY.
See Smithsonian Institution.
ASTROPHYSICS.
See Astronomy.
Asymptotic properties of the solutions of ordinary linear differential equations. Birkhoff, G: D: (Add. author for price.) G: D: Birkhoff.
At Cloudy Pass. Hurlburt. R. P. $1.50. C. M. Clark.
At Cornell. Engein, O. D. v. $1.50. Artil Co.
At Flower Farm. Holloway, J. $1. Stern.
At home in the water. Corsan, G: H. 75 c.; 50 c. Y. M. C. A.
At home with God. Russell, M. $1.25 net. Longmans.
At large. Benson, A. C. **$1.50 net. Putnam.
At last. Kingsley, C: 50 c. net. Macmillan.
At Molokai. Shores, R. J. 50 c. R. J. Shores.
At school in the Cannibal Islands. Houston, E. J. †$1.25. Griffith.
At sound of the gavel. Cuming, M. A. 25 c. M. A. Cuming.
At sunset. Howe, *Mrs.* J. W. $1.25 net. Houghton M.
At the back of the North Wind. Macdonald, G: $1.50. Lippincott.
At the feet of Jesus. Gretchen, *pseud., comp.* *25 c. net. Hills & H.
At the foot of the rainbow. Porter, G. S. $1.50. Doubleday, P.
At the home plate. Dudley, A. T. $1.25. Lothrop, L. & S.
At the library table. Joline, A. H. $1.50. Badger.
At the New Theatre. Eaton, W. P. $1.50 net. Small.
At the root of socialism. Power, M. *10 c. net. Herder.

At the shrine of song. Bashford, H. *$1.25 net. Whitaker & R.

At the sign of the Blue Anchor. Osgood, G. R. $1.50. C. M. Clark.

At the sign of the burning bush. Little, M. $1.50. Holt.

At the Sign of the Hobby Horse. Bisland, E. $1.25 net. Houghton M.

At the Villa Rose. Mason, A. E: W. $1.50. Scribner.

Atchison, Clyde Shepherd.
Curves with a diretrix. '08, [1909.] (S) 25 p. diagrs., 4°. (Add. pubs. for price.) Johns Hopkins.

Atchley, E: Godfrey Cuthbert Frederic.
Hist. of the use of incense in divine worship. '10(F5) il. Q. (Alcuin Club collections.) *$17.50 net. Longmans.

ATHANASIAN CREED.
Legg, J. W. Popular use of the Athanasian creed. *60 c. net; *40 c. net. Longmans.
See also Creeds.

Athenian lekythoi. Fairbanks, A. $4. Macmillan.

ATHENS, Greece.
D'Ooge, M. L. Acropolis of Athens. *$4 net. Macmillan.
Savage, C: A. Athenian family: sociological and legal study. *$1.50 net; *$1.25 net. Lord Balto. Pr.
See also Aristophanes.

ATHENS, Pa.
Murray, *Mrs.* L. W. Hist. of old Tioga Point and early Athens, Pa. *$5 net. L. W. Murray.

Atherton, Mrs. Gertrude Franklin Horn.
The Californians. New ed. '08(Mr21) c. 12°, †$1.50. Macmillan.
Gorgeous isle: a romance; scene, Nevis, B. W. I., 1842. '08(O24) c. D. **90 c. special net. Doubleday, P.
Patience Sparhawk and her times. '08 (My9) c. '05, '07, '08. D. †$1.50. Macmillan.
Tower of ivory. '10(Mr5) c. D. †$1.50. Macmillan.

Athletic boys' lib. 2 v. '10(D) il. 12°, ea., $1.25. Estes.
Contents: Ellis, Our Jim; Eustace, Substitute quarter-back, or, the quality of mercy.

ATHLETICS.
Amateur Athletic Union of the United States. Official hdbk. 10 c. Am. Sports.
Dudley, G., *and* Kellor, F. A. Athletic games in the education of women. **$1.25 net. Holt.
Gardiner, E. N. Greek athletic sports and festivals. $2.50 net. Macmillan.
Graham, J:, *and* Clark, E. H. Pract. track and field athletics. $1. Duffield.
Inter-Collegiate Association of Amateur Athletes of America. Constitution, by-laws and laws of athletics. 10 c. Am. Sports.
Inter-Scholastic Athletic Association of the Middle Atlantic States. Official hdbk. [1910.] gratis. Am. Sports.
Larned, C: W: Athletics from a historical and educational standpoint. (Add. pubs. for price.) Am. Phys. Educ.
Mitchel, J. S. Weight throwing. 10 c. Am. Sports.

ATHLETICS.—*Continued.*
Official athletic rules and official hdbk. of the Amateur Athletic Union of the United States. 10 c. Am. Sports.
On track and on diamond: [fiction.] 60 c. Harper.
Orton, G: W., *ed.* Athletic training for school boys. 10 c. Am. Sports.
Public Schools Athletic League. Official handbook. 10 c. Am. Sports.
Ruhl, A. B. Athletics in accounting: being an account of the organization and exploits of the Haskins & Sells Athletic Association. (Not for sale.) Haskins & S.
Spalding's official athletic almanac, 1908-1910. ea., 10 c. Am. Sports.
Sullivan, J. E. Athletes' guide.—School-yard athletics. ea., 10 c. Am. Sports.
White, E. C., *and* Clark, E. H. All-around athletics. 10 c. Am. Sports.
See also Acrobats and acrobatism;—Archery;—Baseball; — Bowling; — Boxing; — Cricket; — Dumb-bells; —Football;—Games;—Golf;—Gymnastics and physical culture;—Hockey;—Indian clubs:—Jiu-jitsu; — Lacrosse; — Quoits;—Rowing;—Running;—Skating; — Swimming;—Tennis;—Wrestling.

ATHOL, Mass.
Vital records of Athol. $3. F. P. Rice.

Athonia. Schuette, H. G: $1.50. H. G: Schuette.

Atkey, Bertram.
Easy money. '09(Je19) il. D. †$1.50. Estes.

Atkins, Arth.
Extracts from the letters of Arth. Atkins, with notes on painting and landscape written during the period of his work as a painter in the last two years of his life, 1896-98. '09(F20) c. 12°, bds., *$1.25 net. A. M. Robertson.

Atkins, Evan A.
Practical sheet and plate metal work. '08 (D26) 12°, *$2 net. Macmillan.

Atkins, Gaius Glenn, D.D.
Things that remain; some sermons given in the First Congregational Church in Detroit. '10(My) c. 127 p. por. 8°, $1.25. G. G. Atkins.

Atkins, G: Sargent.
Business getters; series of commercial, social and pract. letters. '10(O15) c. 12°, 75 c. Cochrane.

Atkins, Smith Dykins.
Abraham Lincoln; [an address] at the Opera House, Streator, Illinois, Feb. 12, 1909, at invitation of G. A. R., Woman's Relief Corps, Spanish-American Veterans, and the Daughters of the American Revolution. '10(Ap23) O. pap., gratis. Journal Pr., (Ill.)

Atkinson, Christopher T:
Hist. of Germany, 1715-1815. '10(F26) map, plans, 8°, *$4 net. Jacobs.

Atkinson, E:
Views on the occupations in their relation to the tariff published in the *Quarterly Journal of Economics* for Feb., 1903. '09 (Jl) 10 p. 8°, pap. (Add. Superintendent for price.) U. S., Supt. of Docs.

Atkinson, Eleanor.
Boyhood of Lincoln. '08(N7) c. il. D. **50 c. net. McClure.

Atkinson, Eleanor.—*Continued.*
Lincoln's love story. '09(F6) c. il. D. **50 c. net. Doubleday, P.
Story of Chicago and national development, 1534-1910; ed. and extended by the editorial staff of the Little Chronicle Co. [1910.] (Ja) c. '09. 5-6+122 p. il. 8°, 85 c. Little Chronicle.

Atkinson, Mrs. Frances Antoinette Bridges.
Frances Bridges Atkinson; a record of her life prepared by her friends; foreword by Marg. E. Sangster. '08, [1909.] (F) c. 148 p. pors. 12°, 90 c. Y. W. C. A.

Atkinson, Fk. H.
Atkinson sign painting up to now; complete manual of the art of sign painting. '09(D25) c. il. 8°, $3. Drake.

Atkinson, G: Fs.
Botany for high schools. '10(O1) c. il. D. $1.25. Holt.

Atkinson, H: A.
See Jenkins, Fk. E.

Atkinson, Louise Warren.
Story of Paul of Tarsus; home work book. '10(Ja29) c. D. (Constructive Bible studies.) pap., *25 c. net. Note book for pupils, with maps and pictures to be pasted in. Q. 50 c. net.—Manual for teachers. *$1 net. Univ. of Chic.

Atkinson, Mary Josephine.
Château in Brittany. '10(N12) c. il. 8°, $2.50. Pott.

Atkinson, T: G.
Functional diagnosis: application of physiology to diagnosis. '09(D) 213 p. 8°, $1.50. Chic. Med. Bk.

Atkinson, Timothy R.
Irrigation in North Dakota. '09(D) 39 p. fold. map, 8°, (U. S. Dept. of Agriculture; Office of Experimental Stations; bull.) pap. (Add. Superintendent for price.) U. S., Supt. of Docs.

Atkinson, W: Walker, ["Yogi Ramacharaka."]
Arcane teaching; or, secret doctrine of the ancient Atlantis, Egypt, Chaldea and Greece. 2d ed. '09(Ag) c. 336 p. 12°, $1. Arcane.
Art of expression and the principles of discourse. '10(Ap) 9-199 p. 8°, $1. Progress Co.
Art of logical thinking; or, the laws of reasoning. '10(Ap16) c. 12°, $1. Progress Co.
Hindu-Yogi science of breath; complete manual of the Oriental breathing philosophy of physical, mental, psychic and spiritual development. '10(F12) 12°, 75 c.; pap., 50 c. Yogi Pub.
Human nature, its inner states and outer forms. '10(N12) c. il. 12°, $1. Progress Co.
Inner consciousness: course of lessons on the inner planes of the mind, intuition, instinct, automatic mentation and other wonderful phases of mental phenomena. '08(O10) c. 12°, 50 c. Advanced Thought.
Inner teachings of the philosophies and religions of India. '09(Ap3) c. 8°, *$1 net. Yogi Pub.

Atkinson, W: Walker.—*Continued.*
Memory; how to develop, train and use it. '09(My1) (New psychology ser) $1. Progress Co.
Mind and body; or, mental states and physical conditions. '10(S3) c. 12°, $1. Progress Co.
Mind-power; or, the law of dynamic mentation. '09(F13) c. O. $2. Progress Co.
Mystic Christianity; or, the inner teachings of the Master. '08(N) c. 269 p. 12°, $1. Yogi Pub.
New psychology. '09(My1) (New psychology ser.) $1. Progress Co.
Practical mental influence: lessons on mental vibrations, psychic influence, [etc.] '08(Je27) c. 12°, (Lyal ser.) 50 c. Lyal Bk.
Practical psychomancy and crystal gazing. '08(Je27) c. 12°, (Lyal ser.) 50 c. Lyal Bk.
Psychology of salesmanship. '10(Ap) 9-246 p. 8°, $1. Progress Co.
Psychology of success; or, mental paths to power. '10(S3) c. 12°, $1. Progress Co.
Reincarnation and the law of Karma. '08 (O10) $1.10. Advanced Thought.
Science of psychic healing; sequel to "Hatha Yoga." '09, [1910.] (Jl) 190 p. 12°, $1. Yogi Pub.
Secret of success. '08(O10) c. 12°, 50 c. Advanced Thought.
Subconscious and the superconscious planes of mind. '10(Ap16) c. 12°, $1. Progress Co.
Suggestion and auto-suggestion. '09(My1) (New psychology ser.) $1. Progress Co.
Thought-culture; or, pract. mental training. '10(Ap16) 12°, $1. Progress Co.
The will: its nature, power and development. '09(D) c. 205 p. 12°, $1. Progress Co.

Atlanta University pubs. 8°, pap. Atlanta Univ.
—Du Bois. Economic co-operation among negro Americans. $1.
—Du Bois, *ed.* Efforts for social betterment among negro Americans. 75 c.

ATLANTIC CITY, N. J.
Lichtenstein, G. Visit to Young's Pier at Atlantic City, N. J. (Add. author for price.) G. Lichtenstein.

ATLANTIC COAST.
See Yachts and yachting.

Atlantic Deeper Waterways Association. Conference held at Philadelphia Nov. 18, 19, 20, 1907; rept. of the proceedings; comp. by Addison B. Burk. '08(Ap18) pors. map, O. pap., gratis. Book Pr.

Atlantic Deeper Waterways Association. 1st annual convention, held at Baltimore, Nov. 17, 18, 19, 1908; report of the proceedings; comp. and ed. by Addison B. Burk. '09 (Mr20) front. O. pap., gratis. Atlantic Deeper Waterways.

ATLANTIC MONTHLY.
Perry, B. Park-Street papers. **$1.25 net. Houghton M.

Atlantic reporter, v. 67, 68. Permanent ed. '08(Je); v. 69 (O); v. 70. '08, [1909.] (F); v. 71 (Je); v. 72 (N); v. 73. '09, [1910.]

(F); v. 74 (My); v. 75 (Ag); v. 76 (N) c. O. (National reporter system, state ser.) ea., $4. West Pub.

Atlas of absorption spectra. Mees, C. E. K. *$2 net. Longmans.

Atlas of clinical surgery. Bockenheimer, P. 3 v. $24. Lippincott.

Atlas of external diseases of the eye. Greeff, R: $10. Rebman.

Atlas of literary and historical geography. v. 1, Europe. '10(D10) c. il. maps, 16°, (Everyman's lib.) 35 c. net; leath., 70 c. net. Dutton.

Atlas Portland Cement Co., New York. Concrete houses and cottages. 2 v. '10(Ja22) v. '09. il. plans, f°, ea., $1. Atlas Portland Cement.

Atlas Portland Cement Co., New York. Concrete in railroad construction; treatise on concrete for railroad engineers and contractors. '09(N6) c. il. 8°, $1. Atlas Portland Cement.

ATLASES.
Bartholemew, J: G: Handy reference atlas of the world. *$2.50 net. Dutton.
Bartholomew, J: G: School economic atlas. 85 c. Oxford Univ.
Cassell's atlas. **$4 net. Cassell.
Cram, G: F. Atlas of the world, ancient and modern. $12.50; $15; $17.50.—Standard American railway system atlas of the world. $10.50-$20.—Superior reference atlas of North and South Dakota and the world. (Add. pubs. for price.) G: F. Cram.
Hammond's handy atlas of the world. $1; $1.50; 50 c.—Pictorial atlas of the world. $5. C. S. Hammond.
Patten, W:, *and* Homans, J. E., *eds.* New encyclopedic atlas and gazetteer of the world. 50 c. Collier.
Rand, McNally & Co. Enlarged business atlas and shipper's guide. $10.50; $12.50. Rand, McN. & Co.
Reich, E. Atlas antiquus. *$3 net. Macmillan.
Stieler, A. Atlas of modern geography. *$15 net. Lemcke.
United States. *Library of Congress.* List of geographical atlases in the Library of Congress. 2 v. (Add. Superintendent for price.) U. S., Supt. of Docs.
See also Gazetteers;—Geography;—*also* names of countries and places;—*also* special subjects.

Atlay, J. B.
Victorian chancellors. In 2 v. v. 2, Lord St. Leonards, Lord Cranworth, Lord Chelmsford, Lord Campbell, Lord Westbury, Lord Cairns, Lord Hatherly, Lord Selborne, Lord Halsbury, and Lord Herschell. '08(Jl18) il. 8°, *$4 net. Little, B. & Co.

ATMOSPHERE.
Houston, E. J. Wonder book of the atmosphere. **$1.50 net. Stokes.
See also Air;—Meteorology.

ATOMIC WEIGHTS.
See Chemistry;—Weights and measures.

Atoned, adpt. from the German by the Rev. L. A. Rendter, [and] The two Christmas eves. '10(Mr26) S. 50 c. Soc. Divine Word.

ATONEMENT.
Burton, E. D., *and others.* Biblical ideas of atonement. $1. Univ. of Chic.
Champion, J: B: Living atonement. $1.25. Griffith & R.
Foley, G: C. Anselm's theory of the atonement. **$1.50 net. Longmans.
Forsythe, P: T. Cruciality of the cross. *$1.50 net. Doran.
Mabie, H: C. How does the death of Christ save us? **50 c. net. Am. Bapt.
Morgan, C: C. Lawyer's brief on the atonement. 75 c. C: C. Morgan.
Nash, H: S. Atoning life. **$1 net. Macmillan.
Randolph, B. W: Precious blood of Christ: being thoughts on the doctrine of the atonement. *75 c. net. Longmans.
Stalker, J. The atonement. *$1 net. Armstrong.
Walker, W: L. Gospel of reconciliation or at-one-ment. *$2 net. Scribner.
See also Jesus Christ.

Atonement. Young, F. E. M. $1.50. Lane.

Atoning life. Nash, H: S. **$1 net. Macmillan.

ATRIUM OF THE VESTALS, Rome.
Van Deman, E. B. Atrium Vestæ. (Add. Institution for price.) Carnegie.

ATTACHMENT.
See Names of states.

Attack upon Cartagena by the French in 1697. Hart, F. R. 50 c. Assoc. Pub.

Attacks upon the Spain Main by Admiral Vernon. Hart, F. R. 50 c. Assoc. Pub.

Attainment of efficiency. Latson, W. R. C. $1. Health-Culture.

Attention. Pillsbury, W. B. *$2.75 net. Macmillan.

Attention and interest. Arnold, F. **$1 net. Macmillan.

Atteridge, And. Hilliard.
Napoleon's brothers. '09(Jl31) il. 8°, *$5 net. Brentano's.

Attic and Elizabethan tragedy. Watt, L. M. *$2 net. Dutton.

Attic boarders. Jacberns, R. $1.50. Lippincott.

Attic guest. Knowles, R. E: *$1.20 net. Revell.

Attic orators from Antiphon to Isaeus. Jebb, *Sir* R: C. 2 v. *$5.50 net. Macmillan.

Attica (The). *See* Pausanias.

Attitudes and avowals. Le Gallienne, R: $1.50 net. Lane.

Atton, H:, and Holland, H: Hurst.
King's customs: account of maritime revenue and contraband traffic in England, Scotland and Ireland, from the earliest times to the year 1800; with a preface by F. S. Parry. '08(Jl11) por. 8°, *$3.50 net. Dutton.

ATTORNEYS.
See Lawyers.

Attwood, E: Lewis.
Text-book of theoretical naval architecture. 5th ed., rev. and enl. '09(S11) figs. tabs., D. $2.50. Longmans.
War-ships: text-book on the construction, protection, stability, turning, etc., of war vessels. 3d ed. '08(My2); 4th ed. '10 (Jl9) il. O. ea., *$3 net. Longmans.

Atwater, Helen Woodard.
Bread and bread making. '10(Je) 47 p. il. 8°, (U. S., Dept. of Agriculture, farmers' bull.) U. S., Supt. of Docs.

Atwater, Joshua.
American farmer's figurer, enl. '10(Mr26) c. por. 12°, 50 c.; hf. leath., 75 c.; leath., $1. Atwater.
American grain computator. '09(N) c. 151 p. 8°, $3.50. Atwater.

Atwater, Wallace Wa.
See Salisbury, Rollin D.

Atwood, Alice Cary, comp.
Catalogue of the botanical lib. of J: Donnell Smith presented to the Smithsonian Institution. '08(Ag15) 8°, (Smithsonian Inst., U. S. National Museum.) pap., 25 c. U. S., Supt. of Docs.

Atwood, F: Julius.
Kansas rhymes and other lyrics. '02, [1909.] (Ap) 96 p. 8°, $1. Crane.

Atys, a Grecian idyl. Wagstaff, *Mrs.* B. S. $1.25. M. Kennerley.

Aubury, Lewis E.
Copper resources of California. '09(Je5) il. fold. maps, 8°, (Cal. State Mining Bureau bull.) pap., *$1 net. Cal. State Mining.

Aucassin and Nicolette: the lovers of Provence; ms. song-story of the twelfth century rendered into modern French by Alexandre Bida; tr. into English verse and prose by A. Rodney MacDonough. '09 (O2) c. il. 75 c.; limp. leath., $1.25. Caldwell.

Aucassin and Nicolette, and 15 other mediæval romances and legends; sel. and newly tr. by Eug. Mason. '10(D10) 16°, (Everyman's lib.) 35 c. net; leath., 70 c. net. Dutton.

Auchincloss, W: Stuart.
Chronology of the Holy Bible; introd. by A. H. Sayce. '08(D5); 3d ed., enl. '10 (Je4) c. fold. map, fold. tab., 8°, ea., $1. Van Nostrand.

AUCTION BRIDGE *(card game).*
See Bridge *(card game).*

Audel's gas engine manual: treatise rel. to the theory and management of gas, gasoline and oil engines, including chapters on producer gas plants, marine motors and automobile engines. '08(Ap18) c. il. 12°. $2. Audel.

Audenried, W: Grattan, jr.
Irrigation. '08(Je6) c. il. 8°. (Add. pubs. for price.) Rep. Bank Note.

Audit Company of New York, *comp.* Trust companies of the U. S., 1907. '08(Ja18) il. O. bds. (Not for sale.) U. S. Mortgage.

AUDITING.
See Bookkeeping.

Auerbach, Berthold.
Brigitta: erzählung; with introd., notes, exercises and vocab. by J. Howard Gore. '08(S19) c. S. (Internat. modern lang. ser.) 40 c. Ginn.

Auerbach, Matilda.
Elementary course in graphic mathematics. '10(S) c. 54 p. diagrs., 12°, 35 c. Allyn & B.

Auerbacher, L: J:
Electrical contracting; shop system, estimating, wiring, construction methods, and hints on getting business. '08(Ag1); 2d ed., corr. and slightly rev. '10(My7) c. il. 8°, ea., $2 net. McGraw-H.

Auf der universitat. Storm, T. 35 c. Holt.

AUGUSTA VICTORIA, *Empress.*
See William II., *of Germany.*

Augustana library pubs. 4°, pap. Augustana.
—Rydberg. Scandinavians who have contributed to the knowledge of the flora of North America. $1.
—Udden. Report on a geological survey of the lands belonging to the New York and Texas Co., Ltd. 50 c.

Augustana synod; brief review of its hist., 1860-1910. [1910.] (Jl) c. 267 p. il. pors. 8°, $1.50; in Swedish, $2.50. Augustana.

Augustin, G:
Hist. of yellow fever. '09, [1910.] (Mr) c. 14+1194 p. por. plan, charts, 8°, $6. G: Augustin.
Contains bibliographies.

Augustine, St.
Confessions; tr. and arr. by E. B. Pusey. '08(O24) front. 12°, *$2 net. Dutton.
Confessions; tr. by E. B. Pusey. '08(O17) 16°, (Best books ser.) leath., *$1 net. Dutton.
Confessions; tr. by E: Bouverie Pusey; ed. by Temple Scott; with introd. by Alice Meynell. '10(S10) il. O. $2 net. Stokes.
Soliloquies of St. Augustine; tr. into English by Rose Eliz. Cleveland; with notes and introd. by the translator. '10(O22) c. D. $1.50 net. Little, B. & Co.

AUGUSTINE, *St.*
Simpson, W: J: S. St. Augustine and African church divisions. $1.25 net. Longmans.

Augustine, W: Azariah, ["Azariah Frejolity."]
Itinerary of Azariah Frejolity; or, what becomes of old barbers. '08, [1909.] (F) c. 232 p. 12°. (Add. author for price.) W: A. Augustine.

Augustus. Jersey, M. E. L. V., *Countess* of. 50 c. Stokes.

Aulard, François Victor Alphonse.
The French Revolution; political hist., 1789-1804; tr. from the French of the 3d ed.; with preface, notes and historical summary by Bernard Miall. In 4 v. v. 1, The revolution under the monarchy, 1789-1792; v. 2, The democratic republic, 1792-1795; v. 3, The revolutionary government, 1793-1797; v. 4, The bourgeois republic and the consulate, 1797-1804. '10 (S17) O. per set, $8 net, boxed. Scribner.

Aumerle, R:
Between friends. '09(Ap3) c. D. 85 c. Benziger.
Brownie and I. '10(My7) c. D. 85 c. Benziger.

Aunt Amity's silver wedding. Stuart, *Mrs.* R. N. †$1. Century Co.

Aunt Carrie's poems. Post, *Mrs.* C. L. $1. C. W. Post.

Aunt Jane's nieces at Millvill. Van Dyne, *Mrs.* E. 60 c. Reilly & B.

Aunt Jane's nieces at work. Van Dyne, *Mrs.* E. 60 c. Reilly & B.

Aunt Jane's nieces in society. Van Dyne, E. 60 c. Reilly & B.

Aunt Maud. Oldmeadow, E. †$1.50. McClure.
"Aunt Naomi," pseud.
Jewish fairy tales and fables. '08(D5) il. 8°, *$1 net. Bloch.
Aunt Tirzah. Van Steinburg, D. F. B'way Pub.
AURAL SURGERY.
See Ear.
Auringer, Rev. Obadiah Cyrus.
Death of Maid McCrea. '10(Mr5) c. D. $1. Badger.
Twin poems of the Revolution: The death of Maid McCrea, and The lover's tragedy. '09(Ja16) $1. O. C. Auringer.
AURORA BOREALIS.
Birkeland, K. Norwegian Aurora Polaris Expedition, 1902-1903. v. 1, On the cause of magnetic storms and the origin of terrestrial magnetism. 1st section. $1. Longmans.
Aurora of Poverty Hill. Walton, E. 50 c. B'way Pub.
AURORA POLARIS.
See Aurora borealis.
Aus Amerika. Fritsch, W. A. 40 c. Lemcke.
Ausgewählte märchen und gedichte. Baumbach, R. 45 c. Ginn.
Ausmus, Irvin.
Poems. '09, [1910.] (D) c. 72 p. por. 8°, $1. D. Johnson.
Austen, Jane.
Works. St. Martin's ed.; text revised and with summary, bibliographical and biographical notes by R. Brimley Johnson. In 10 v. vs. 1, 2, Pride and prejudice; vs. 3, 4, Sense and sensibility. '08(N21); v. 5, Northanger Abbey; v. 6, Persuasion; vs. 7, 8, Emma; vs. 9, 10, Mansfield Park. '08(D5) 8°, ea., *$1.25 net; per set, *$12 net. Duffield.
Works. De luxe ed. 2 v. '10(D) 16°, ea., mor., $1.50 net. (Sets only.) Nelson.
Novels and letters. In 12 v.: ed. by R. Brimley Johnson; with introd. by Prof. W: Lyon Phelps. Chawton ed. '08 (Je27) c. il. $21. Lamb Pub.
Emma. '08(O17) 16°, (Best books ser.) leath., *$1 net. Dutton.
Emma. '09(O23) il. 12°, $2. Dutton.
Emma; with an introd. by E. V. Lucas. Pocket ed. '09(Mr6) por. S. (World's classics.) 35 c. Oxford Univ.
Mansfield Park. '08(O17) 16°, (Best books ser.) leath., *$1 net. Dutton.
Mansfield Park. '08(N21) il. 12°, (English idylls ser.) $2. Dutton.
Northanger Abbey, and Persuasion. '08 (O17) 16°, (Best books ser.) leath., *$1 net. Dutton.
Persuasion. '09(O23) il. 12°, $2. Dutton.
Pride and prejudice. '08(O10) 12°, (Best books ser.) leath., *$1 net. Dutton.
Pride and prejudice; ed. by Josephine Woodbury Heermans. '08(N21) 24°, (Pocket Am. and Eng. classics.) *25 c. net. Macmillan.
Pride and prejudice. '10(Je4) 12°, 40 c. Putnam.
Sense and sensibility. '08(O17) 16°, (Best books ser.) leath., *$1 net. Dutton.
Sense and sensibility. '08(N21) il. 12°, (English idylls ser.) $2. Dutton.

AUSTEN, Jane.
Helm, W: H: Jane Austen and her country-house comedy. *$3.50 net. Lane.
Austen, Sir W: Chandler Roberts-.
See Roberts-Austen, *Sir* W: Chandler.
Austin, Alfr.
Bridling of Pegasus; prose papers on poetry. '10(Ap16) O. $2.40 net. Macmillan.
Haunts of ancient peace. '07(O24) il. 8°, (Color books.) *$2 net. Macmillan.
Sacred and profane love, and other poems. '08(Je6) 12°, *$1.40 net. Macmillan.
Austin, B: Fish, ["Benjamin Nitsua."]
Mystery of Ashton Hall. '10(D3) plan, 8°, $1.25. Austin.
Austin, Herb. H:
Scamper through the Far East; incl. visit to Manchurian battlefields. '09(N6) il. maps, O. $5. Longmans.
Austin, Leonard Strong.
Metallurgy of common metals, gold, silver, iron, copper, lead, and zinc. 2d ed., rev. and enl. '09(N20) c. il. O. $4. Mining and Scientific.
Austin, Mrs. Mary Hunter.
The basket woman; book of Indian tales for children. School ed. [1910.] (S) c. 11+222 p. il. 12°, 60 c. Houghton M.
Lost borders. '09(N6) c. il. D. †$1.25. Harper.
Santa Lucia. '08(Ap11) c. D. †$1.50. Harper.
Austin, Stanley Elston.
History of engraving from its inception to the time of Thomas Bewick. '09(F13) il. pors. D. *$1.50 net. Scribner.
AUSTRALIA.
Fraser, J: F. Australia. $1.75. Cassell.
Glasson, W: H: Australian voting system. 20 c. W: H: Glasson.
Lang, W. H. Australia. *$2 net. Stokes.
Mathews, C. H. S. Parson in the Australian bush. $2. Longmans.
Nixon-Roulet, M. F. Our little Australian cousin. 60 c. L. C. Page.
St. Ledger, A. Australian socialism. *$1.50 net. Macmillan.
Thomas, N. W. Kinship organizations and group marriage in Australia. *$2 net. Putnam.
Wise, B. R. Commonwealth of Australia. *$3 net. Little, B. & Co.
See also New South Wales;—Papua;—Queensland;—Tasmania.
AUSTRIA-HUNGARY.
Bartlett, F. Christmas in Austria. 50 c. Estes.
Drage, G. Austria-Hungary. $6. Dutton.
Jackson, F: H. Shores of the Adriatic: the Austrian side. *$6 net. Dutton.
See also Blind (The);—Bohemia;—Bosnia;—Croatian language; — Dalmatia; — Dolomite Mountains; — Franco-Austrian campaign; — Herzegovina;—Hungary;—Tyrol; — Vienna;—*also* Elizabeth, *Empress*;—Elizabeth Stuart, *Queen of Bohemia*; — Francis Joseph I.; — Grillparzer, Franz.
Austrian diplomatist in the fifties. Satow, *Sir* E. M. 50 c. Putnam.
Auswahl deutscher prosa der gegenwart. Hein, G. 70 c. Oxford Univ.
AUTHORITY.
See Liberty.

Authority and person of our Lord. Hutton, J: A. 50 c. net. Revell.
Authority and the light within. Grubb, E: *80 c. net. Winston.
Authority in religion. Leckie, J. H. *$2 net. Scribner.
Authority of law in language. Krapp, G: P. 50 c. Univ. of Cin.

AUTHORS.

Brownell, W: C. American prose masters; Cooper, Hawthorne, Emerson, Poe, Lowell, Henry James. **$1.50 net. Scribner.
Burton, R: Masters of the English novel. $1.25. Holt.
Chubb, E. W. Stories of authors. $1.25 net. Sturgis & W.
Darmesteter, *Mme.* A. M. F. French procession; pageant of great writers. **$3.50 net. Duffield.
Dawson, W: J. *and* Coningsby W:, *eds.* Great English novelists. $1 net. Harper.
Erskine, J: Leading American novelists. $1.75 net. Holt.
Graham, H: G. Scottish men of letters of the eighteenth century. *$2 net. Macmillan.
Gribble, F. H: Passions of the French Romantics. $3.75 net. Scribner.
Hazlitt, W: Comic writers of Great Britain. 35 c. net; 70 c. net. Dutton.
Hinchman, W. S., *and* Gummere, F. B. Lives of great English writers, from Chaucer to Browning. **$1.50 net. Houghton, M. & Co.
Jackson, H. Great English novelists. **$1.50 net. Jacobs.
Johnson, E. R., *ed.* Author's digest; the world's great stories in brief. (Add. author for price.) E. R. Johnson.
Moore, F. F. Georgian pageant: [stories of XVIII. century writers.] $3.50. Dutton.
Orgain, K. A. Southern authors in poetry and prose. *$2 net. Neale.
Payne, W: M. Leading American essayists. $1.75 net. Holt.
Phelps, W: L. Essays on modern novelists. **$1.50 net. Macmillan.
Phillips, M. E. Laureled leaders for little folk. $2. Lothrop, L. & S.
Rowbotham, F. J. Story-lives of great authors. $1.50. Stokes.
Scott, *Sir* W. Lives of the novelists. 35 c. net; 70 c. net. Dutton.
Shelley, H: C: Literary by-paths in old England. **$1.50 net. Little, B. & Co.
Strachey, L., *ed.* Love letters of famous poets and novelists. *$2 net. McBride.
Thorold, A. L. Six masters in disillusion: [Fontenelle, Prosper Mérimée, Ferdinand Fabre, Huysmans, Maeterlinck and Anatole France.] *$1.50 net. Dutton.
Vedder, H: C. American writers of today. $1.50. Silver.
Visscher, W: L. Ten wise men, and some more; [writers.] (Not for sale.) W: L. Visscher.
Wauchope, G: A., *comp.* Writers of South Carolina. $2. State Co.
Winchester, C. T: Group of English essayists of the early nineteenth century. **$1.50 net. Macmillan.

AUTHORS.—*Continued.*

Winter, W: Old friends; being literary recollections of other days. **$3 net. Moffat.

See also Almanacs and annuals;—Authorship;—Bibliographies;—Copyright;—Drama and dramatists;—Fiction;—Historians; —Literature;—*also* Days with great writers;—names of literatures.

Authors' and printers' dictionary. Collins. F: H. 35 c. Oxford Univ.

AUTHORSHIP.

Cochrane, C: H. How and where to sell mss. 50 c. Cochrane.
Davies, F. Pract. story writing. Walden.
Esenwein, J. B. Writing the short-story. $1.25. Hinds.
Gerwig, G: W: Art of the short story. *75 c. net. Percy Pub.
Hadlock, E. H. Profitable authorship. $3. Un. Press.
Hirsch, C. E. Art and craft of the author. **$1.50 net. Grafton Press.
Reeve, J. K. Pract. authorship. $1.50. Editor Co.
Rickard, T: A. Guide to technical writing. $1. Mining and Scientific.
Writer's book. $2.50. Editor Co.
Young, D. F. Fiction writer's workshop. 50 c. Editor Co.

See also Poetry;—Rhetoric;—Songs;—Versification.

Authorship of Timon of Athens. Wright, E. H. $1.25 net. Lemcke.
Auto boys. Braden, J. A. $1. Saalfield.
Auto boys' outing. Braden, J. A. $1. Saalfield.
Auto boys' quest. Braden, J. A. $1. Saalfield.
Auto de fé and Jew. Adler, E. N. $1.75. Oxford Univ.
Autobiographic elements in Latin inscriptions. Armstrong. H: H. 40 c. Macmillan.

AUTOBIOGRAPHY.

Burr, *Mrs.* A. R. B. The autobiography; critical and comparative study. **$2 net. Houghton M.
Trenton, N. J. Free Public Library. List of entertaining autobiographies. gratis. Trenton Lib.

Autobiography of a clown. Turnour, J. **$1 net. Moffat.
Autobiography of a disembodied soul. Carleton, G. M. $1.50 Vreeland.
Autobiography of a neurasthene. Cleaves, M. A. $1.50. Badger.
Autobiography of an electron. Gibson, C: R. $1.50 net. Lippincott.
Autobiography of Ithuriel. Ware, E. F. (Not for sale.) E. F. Ware.
Autobiography of Jeremy L., the actor dog. Whitcomb, C. G. N. 50 c. net. Bassette.
Autobiography of Methuselah. Bangs, J: K. $1. B. W. Dodge.
Autocrat of the breakfast table. *See* Holmes, Oliver Wendell.
Autogenous welding of metals. Bernier, L: L. $1. Boiler Maker.
Autograph letters and autographs of the signers of the Declaration of Independence. Thomas, G: C. [privately pr.] G: C. Thomas.

Autograph poets. 12°, $1; hf. leath., $1.50. Houghton M.
—Emerson. Poems.
—Harte. Poems.
—Holmes. Poems.
—Longfellow. Poems.
—Lowell. Poems.
—Tennyson. Poems.
—Whittier. Poems.

AUTOGRAPHS.
Broadley, A. M. Chats on autographs. $2 net. Stokes.
Fetherston, *Sir* G: R. Secret signatures of my friends. [Autograph book.] 50 c. net. Stokes.
Williams, H. My chums in caricature. *50 c. net. McClurg.
Your hidden skeleton; novel autograph book. 30 c. Winston.

AUTO-INTOXICATION.
Combe, A. Intestinal auto-intoxication. *$4 net. Rebman.
See also Milk.

Autology (study thyself) and autopathy (cure thyself). Moras, E. R. $2. E. R. Moras.
Automatic block signals and signal circuits. Scott, R. *$2.50 net. McGraw.
Automatic capitalists. Payne, W. †$1. Badger
Automatic screw machines. Goodrich, C. L. *$2 net. Hill Pub.
Automatic system. Clark, I. C. $1; 50 c. D. S. Clark.
Automatic telegraphy. Hitchcock, R. (Add. Superintendent for price.) U. S., Supt. of Docs.
Automobile blue book of Wisconsin. 2d ed. '10(F19) c. 12°, *$2 net. Caspar.
Automobile boys of Lakeport. Stratemeyer, E: $1.25. Lothrop, L. & S.
Automobile Club of Southern California Tour Book. '09(Ap3) c. il. maps, 8°, pap., $1.50; leath., $2.50. Automobile Club So. Cal.
Automobile girls ser. See Crane, Laura Dent.
Automobile (The) in *Munsey's Magazine;* series of special articles that trace the growth of the motor car industry in America. '10(N) 96 p. 16°, pap. (Priv. pr.) Munsey.
Automobile laws of the New England states, New York, New Jersey and Pennsylvania; comp. by Arth. Crawford Wyman. '08 (Je13) O. (Rhode Island State Library, Legislative reference bull.) pap. (Add. pub. for price.) R. I. State Lib.
Automobile official 1908 blue book: touring guide to the best and most popular routes. In 4 v. '08(Jl4) c. maps, 8°, leath., ea., $2.50. Class Journ.

AUTOMOBILES.
Abbott, T. O. Automobile law for motorists. $2.50. Reilly & B.
Abbott, T. O. Road rights of motorists. $1.50 net. Outing.
Adams, W. P. Motor car mechanism and management. *$2 net. Lippincott.
American Automobile Association. Automobile book, 1910 ed. In 4 v. ea., $2.50. Automobile Blue Book.

AUTOMOBILES.—*Continued.*
American cyclopedia of the automobile. 6 v. $18.50. Thomson & T.
American School of Correspondence. Cyclopedia of automobile engineering. 4 v. $12. Am. Sch. Corr.
Batey, J: Motor car and its engine. *$1.50 net. Jacobs.
Becker, N. D. Road rules and the law of automobiles. $1. E. W. Whitfield.
Berry, C. P. Treatise on the law rel. to automobiles. *$3 net. Callaghan.
Bottone, S. R. Magnetos for automobiles. *$1 net. Van Nostrand.
Boyance, J. Chauffeur hdbk. 50 c. Beaver Pr.
Brewer, R. W. A. Motor car. **$2 net. Van Nostrand.
Caspar's automobile road maps of Wisconsin. $1.25. Caspar.
Chase, J. C. Motor car operation. $1. Motor.
Chauffeur question and the answer. (Add. pubs. for price.) N. Y. Sch. Automobile Eng.
Chicago Automobile Club. Official motor guide. $1.50; $2. Chic. Automobile.
Clough, A. L., *ed.* Operation, care and repair of automobiles. $1. Horseless Age.
Craig, A. E. S. Motor driving for a living. 50 c. Spon.
Diemer, H. Automobiles. $1.50. Am. Sch. Corr.
Dutton, A. I., *ed.* How to sell an Overland; selling points for the benefit of dealers selling Overland automobiles. $2. Willys-Overland.
Dyke, A. L. Anatomy of the automobile. $2.—Automobile and gasoline engine encyclop. $3.—Course of automobile engineering. $10.—Troubles, remedies and repairs of the automobile and gasoline engine. $2. A. L. Dyke.
Dyke, A. L., *and* Dorris, G. P. Diseases of of a gasolene automobile. $1. A. L. Dyke.
Fitch, G: The automobile. 35 c. Collier.
Freeston, C: L. High roads of the Alps; a motoring guide. $3. Scribner.
Gunn, J. Pract. design of motor cars. $3 net. Longmans.
Hamilton, C: H. Chart of the law of automobiles. $1. C: H. Hamilton.
Hearne, R. P. Motoring. 50 c. Dutton.
Homans, J: E: Self-propelled vehicles. $2. Audel.
Home, G. C. Motor routes of France. $2 net; $2.25 net. Chr. Press.
Huddy, X. P. Law of automobiles. $3.50. M. Bender.
International motor cyclopædia: year book. $10. Int. Motor.
Irwin, S: P. Auto roads from Chicago to points in central Ill. and St. Louis. $1.50. Pantagraph.
King, S. J., *comp.* Official route guide. $2. S. J. King.
Knight, J. H. Motor repairing for amateurs. *$1 net. Spon.
Kuehl, G: W. Automobile blue book of Wisconsin. *$2 net. G: W. Kuehl.
Kuehl, G: W. Automobile guide book of Illinois. $2 net. Caspar.

AUTOMOBILES.—*Continued.*
Leechman, D. Making of a motor car. 50 c. Spon.
Levitt, D. Woman and the car. *$1 net. Lane.
Longest, W: B. Whys and wherefores of the modern motor car. 50 c. W: B. Longest.
Machines, tools and methods of automobile manufacture. 25 c. Indust. Press.
Marshall's handy automobile record. $1 net. Winston.
Massachusetts. New motor vehicle law; arr. for the use of owners, dealers, garages, operators and chauffeurs by C: J. Babbitt. **$1 net. Little, B. & Co.
Metropolitan automobile guide. $2.50. Automobile Blue Book.
Michales, H. S. Principal automobile routes of the United States and Canada, 1910. $2. Henneberry.
Missouri state automobile blue book. $3. Auto Review.
Montagu, *Lord.* Motor cars and how to drive them. $1.50. Spon.
New York Herald. National highway route book; N. Y. City to Atlanta. (Add. pubs. for price.) N. Y. Herald.
New York [State.] Automobile law. $1. Sturtevant.
New York State. New York automobile law. Banks & Co.
Nichols, C. G., *comp.* Automobilists' ready legal adviser. 50 c. Glennick
1909 year book. $6. Automobile Topics.
Official year book and directory of golf and automobiling, 1909. $5. Stettiner.
Paris, B. J. Care of automobiles. $1. Doubleday, P.
Pedley, G. F. Motor car mechanics. 50 c. Spon.
Pemberton, M. Amateur motorist. **$3.75 net. McClurg.
Penn-Jersey automobile road guide and route list. $1. Nuneviller.
Pulitzer, W: My auto book. $1. Outing.
Rand-McNally photo-auto guide. (Add. pubs. for price.) Rand, McN. & Co.
"Red book" interstate automobile guide, 1908.—1909. ea., $2.50. F. S. Blanchard.
Root, C: P. Automobile troubles and how to remedy them. $1; $1.50. C: C. Thompson.
Russell, T: H. Automobile driving self taught.—Ignition, timing and valve setting. ea., $1; $1.50.—Automobile motors and mechanism. $1.50. C: C. Thompson.
St. John, T: M. Study of electric motors by experiment. 25 c. T: M. St. John.
San Francisco motor club tour book. $1.50. San F. Motor.
Scarfoglio, A. Round the world in a motor car. *$5 net. M. Kennerley.
Schmidt, O. C., *ed.* Pract. treatise on automobiles. $12. Am. Text-Bk.
Sloss, R: T. The automobile. $1.25 net. Outing.
Standard road-book of New York state. $1.50. W. L. Chase.
Street, J. L. My enemy the motor: [fiction.] †$1. Lane.

AUTOMOBILES.—*Continued.*
Ward, H. Girl and the motor: [story.] $1. Gas Engine.
Welsh, C:, *ed.* Chauffeur chaff: anecdotes, [etc.] 50 c. Caldwell.
White, T. H. Petrol motors and motor cars. $1.40 net. Longmans.
Whitman, R. B. Motor car principles: the gasoline automobile. **$1.50 net. Appleton.
Wyman, A. C., *comp.* Automobile laws of the New England states, New York, New Jersey and Pennsylvania. (Add. pubs. for price.) R. I. State Lib.
See also Air-brake;—Bicycles;—Boats;—Garage;—Rand-McNally photo-auto guides.

AUTO-SUGGESTION.
See Suggestion (Mental).

Autumn leaves. Ellis, *Mrs.* O. $1. Times Pub. Co.
Autumn leaves. Winship, M. G. 50 c. M. G. Winship.
Autumnal sprays. Princeton University. H: W. Swinnerton.

Auvergne, Edm. B. d'.
Castles of England. '08(O10) il. 8°, *$2 net; ¾ levant, *$4 net. Pott.
Lola Montez. '09(Jl3) O. *$4 net. Lane.
A queen at bay; the story of Cristina and Don Carlos. '10(O8) pors. O. $5 net. Lane.

Auxiliarium. Gross, C. 45 c. C. Gross.
Auxilium. Greenwood, W: *40 c. net; *30 c. net. W: Greenwood.
Auxilium infirmorum. Eaton, R. *45 c. net. Herder.

Auzas, A., ed.
Poemes Napoléoniens. '09(O16) S. (Shorter Fr. texts.) *25 c. net. Crowell.

Available energy of red clover hay. Armsby, H: P. 10 c. U. S., Supt. of Docs.
Avare (L'). *See* Molière, J. B. P. de.
Ave atque vale. Jones, T: S., *jr.* 25 c. G: W: Browning.

Avebury, Lord.
See Lubbock, *Sir* J:

Aveling, Fs., D.D.
Arnoul, the Englishman. '08(D5) 8°, $1.50. Herder.
See also Sharpe, *Rev.* Alfr. Bowyer.

Avellanus, Arcadius.
Palaestra: being the primer of the Tusculan system of learning, and of teaching Latin to speak, for class use and for self instruction. 3d, newly written, ed. In 3 pts., in about 35 nos. '08(D) c. Q. pap., ea., 25 c. A. Avellanus.

Avenger (The). Oppenheim, E: P. †$1.50. Little, B. & Co.
Avengers (The). Grainger, F. E. 50 c. B. W. Dodge.

Averill, Anna Boynton.
Birch stream, and other poems. '08(Jl) c. 13+297 p. il. por. 12°, $1.50. A. B. Averill

Avery, Alfr. H.
Auto-transformer design: pract. hdbk. for manufacturers and contractors and wiremen. '09(D18) 8°, $1.50. Spon.

Avery, Elroy McKendree.
Hist. of the United States and its people. In 15 v. v. 4. '08(My16); v. 5. '09 (Mr20); v. 6. '10(Ja15); v. 7 (Jl2) c.

il. pors. maps, subs., per v., *$6.25 net; hf. lev., *$12.50 net; lev., *$17.50 net. Burrows.

Avery, Mabel Allen.
Mother Goose on bridge. '09(Jl3) c. il. D. $1. Lyman Bros.

Avery-Stuttle, Mrs. Lilla Dale, Mann, Mina, and Robinson, Ella M., comps. and eds.
Selections for our little folks, especially adapted as a reciter for use in church schools, missionary societies, temperance societies, etc. '09(Je) c. 12+13-260 p. 12°, 60 c. Pacific Press.

Avesta.
Index verborum of the fragments of the Avesta, by Montgomery Schuyler. '09 (F6) 8°, (Columbia Univ. Indo-Iranian ser.) price reduced from $2 to $1.50. Lemcke.

AVILA, Spain.
See Spain.

AVOCADOS.
See Fruit.

Avocat (L') Patelin. Brueys, D. A. de. *25 c. net. Crowell.

AVON RIVER, England.
Bradley, A. G. The Avon and Shakespeare's country. $3.50 net. Dutton.

AVRAMVILLEA.
See Seaweeds.

Awakening of China. Wu Ting Fang. 10 c. Civic Forum.

Awakening of Helena Richie. Deland, *Mrs.* M. W. C. †$1.50. Harper.

Awakening of Helena Ritchie: a play. Thompson, C. (Add. pub. for price.) Kauser.

Awakening of spring. Wedekind, F. *$1.25 net. Brown Bros.

Awakening of the soul; tr. fr. the Arabic by Dr. Paul Bronnle. '08(Je6) 16°, (Wisdom of the East.) *40 c. net. Dutton.

Awakening of Turkey. Knight, E: F: *$3 net. Lippincott.

Awakening of Zojas. Michelson, M. $1, fixed. Doubleday, P.

A-wearying for you. Stevens, E., *comp.* 75 c.; $1.50. Platt & P.

Axel. Tegnér, E. $1. Cochrane.

Axenfeld, Theodor.
Bacteriology of the eye; tr. by Angus Macnab. '08(N21) il. 8°, *$6 net. Wood.

Axioms of religion. Mullins, E. Y. **$1 net. Am. Bapt.

Axtell, E:
Boston terrier and all about it: breeding of the American dog. '10(Ap16) c. il. pors. 12°. $1.50. Dogdom Pub.

Axtell, Ja. Wickleff.
Superintendent's hdbk. for 1909. '08(O); 1910; cont. the lesson text, golden text, review suggestions, [etc.,] outline program and statistical blanks for every Sunday in the year; also list of lessons for 1911. '09(Ag) T. leath., ea., 35 c. Cumberland Press.
Teacher's hdbk. for 1909. '08(O); 1910; cont. lesson text, golden text, definitions, [etc.,] for every Sunday in the year; with teaching suggestions, and the list of lessons for 1911. '09(Ag) T. leath., ea., 35 c. Cumberland Press.

Ayars, J: E.
People's hand-book of the Bible: introd. to the study of the Holy Scriptures, on the plan of J. Angus. 7th ed., rev. '08 (O17) c. por. map, S. 85 c. Meth. Episcopal.

Aye, Olive, and Spangler, Martha.
Freddie and Santa Claus in circus land. '08(O3) c. il. Q. pap., 30 c. Laird & L.

Ayer, Mary Allette, ed.
Keep up your courage; key-notes to success; with introd. by Rev. J. R. Miller. '08(N14) c. D. **$1 net, boxed; ed. de luxe, mor., **$2 net, boxed. Lothrop, L. & S.

Ayer, Mary Farwell.
Early days on Boston Common. '10(Je4) il. $4 net. (250 copies.) C: E. Goodspeed.
—, comp. Check-list of Boston newspapers, 1704-1780; with bibliographical notes by Albert Matthews. '08(Je13) 8°, (Pubs. of the Colonial Soc. of Mass., Collections.) $3.50. Colonial Soc. of Mass.

Ayer, N. W., & Son.
1869-1909; forty years of advertising; a collection of somewhat intimate talks on certain phases of advertising by the largest and leading agency. '09(S) c. 9-60 p. 12°, leath. (Add. pubs. for price.) Ayer.

Ayers, S: H:, and Johnson, W: Trimble, jr.
Bacteriology of commercially pasteurized and raw market milk. '10(D) 98 p. il. tabs., 8°, (U. S., Dept. of Agriculture, Bu. of Animal Industry bull.)
"References to literature" (2 p.).

Ayling, R. Stephen.
Public abattoirs: their planning, design and equipment. '09(Mr13) il. 4°, $3.50. Spon.

Aylmer-Small, C: Sidney.
See Small, C: Sidney Aylmer.

Aylwin's friends. Smith, *Mrs.* E. T. $1.50. Dutton.

Ayres, E.
American ready reckoner. '08(Mr.) c. 160 p. 24°. (Add. pubs. for price.) Popular.

Ayres, Harry Morgan.
Bibliographical sketch of Anglo-Saxon literature. '10(D10) O. pap., 25 c. net. Lemcke.

Ayres, Leonard Porter.
Laggards in our schools: study of retardation and elimination in city school systems. '09(Je12) c. O. (Russell Sage Foundation pubs.) $1.50. Charities Pub.
Open air schools. '10(Jl30) c. il. D. $1.20 net. Doubleday, P.
Some factors affecting grade distribution. '09(F20) 8°, pap., 10 c. Psychological Clinic.

Ayres, Mary Morgan.
Four Christmases. '08(Ja4) D. pap., 50 c. M. M. Ayres
Playing house in kindergarten. [1910.] (F) c. '09. 8 p. il. obl. 8°, pap., 50 c. M. M. Ayres.

Ayres, Philip Wheelock.
Commercial importance of the White Mountain forests. '09(D) 32 p. fold.

map, tabs., 8°, (U. S., Dept. of Agriculture; Forest Service; circular.) pap. U. S., Supt. of Docs.

Ayres, Stephen Cooper.
Sketch of the life and services of Vice Admiral Stephen C. Rowan, U. S. Navy; read before the Ohio Commandery of the Loyal Legion, April 6, 1910. '10(Jl16) il. por. 8°, gratis. W. R. Thrall.

Ayres, Steven B.
Bridge. '09(Mr20) c. D. (Dunwoodie books of games.) *$1 net. Brentano's.

AYRSHIRE COW.
See Cow.

Ayrton, W: E:
Pract. electricity. New ed. '10(D) il. $2.50 net. Cassell.

Ayscough, J:, pseud.
Dromina. '09(Ap10) c. D. †$1.50. Putnam.
Marotz. '08(Ag15) D. †$1.50. Putnam.
San Celestino. '09(D4) c. D. †$1.50. Putnam.

Az Amerikai magyar népszava jubileumi díszalbuma. Berko, G. D. $5. G. D. Berko.

AZIMUTH.
See Navigation.

AZTECS.
Diven, T: J. Aztecs and Mayas. In 2 v. v. 1. $1. Antiquarian.
See also Aryans.

B., A.
Travels of a lady's maid. '08(O17) c. D. $1.50. L. C. Page.

B., C. S.
Modernism: what it is and why it was condemned. '08(F22) 8°, pap., *10 c. net. Herder.

B., E. V.
The peacock's pleasaunce; 8 full-page il. '08(Ag8) D. *$1.50 net. Lane.

"B., J.," pseud.
See Brierley, *Rev.* J:

B., T., pseud.
See Benson, Arth. Christopher.

Baar, Gustav.
Modern view of syphilis and its treatment. '10(D) c. 12+285 p. il. 8°, $2. Appleton.
Bibliography (8 p.).

Babbitt, Irving.
Literature and the American college: essays in defense of the humanities. '08 (Mr28) c. D. **$1.25 net. Houghton, M. & Co.
New Laokoon; essay on the confusion of the arts. '10(Je11) c. D. $1.25 net. Houghton M.

Babbitt, Ja. Bradford.
Physical history of the earth in outline. '09 (Ja23); Rev. ed.; with appendix. '09 (S18) c. il. O. ea., $1.50. E. E. Sherman.

Babcock, Blandine S.
Children's daily service. '08(D12) c. 16°, *50 c. net. Whittaker.

Babcock, Rev. C: Edn.
Persecution of Stephen Strong. '08, [1909.] (F) c. 12+145 p. front. 12°, $1. B'way Pub.

Babcock, Ernest B.
Suggestions for garden work in Califoruia schools. [1910.] (S) 48 p. il. O. (Univ. of California Agricultural Experiment Station, circular.) pap. Univ. of Cal.
Bibliography (2 p.).

Babcock, Ja. Woods.
See Lavinder, Claude H.

Babcock, Maltbie Davenport, D.D.
Joy of work; repr. chapters from "Fragments that remain"; comp. by Jessie B. Goetchius. '10(S17) c. 16°, (Right living ser.) bds., 35 c. net. Revell.

BABCOCK, Maltbie Davenport.
Stone, J: T. Footsteps in a parish: appreciation of Maltbie Davenport Babcock. **75 c. net. Scribner.

Babcock, Philip S., comp.
See United States. Compilation of laws rel to trust companies.

Babcock, W: Emerson, comp.
Hess-Higbee genealogy. '09, [1910.] (F) c. 175 p. il. 8°, $2.60. W: E. Babcock.

Babcock, Mrs. Winnifred Eaton.
See Watanna, Onoto.

Babe of Bethlehem. Price, C. F. per 100, $2.50. Eaton & M.

Babees' book: mediæval manners for the young; done into modern English from Dr. Furnivall's texts by Edith Rickert. '08 (O24) il. 12°, (New mediæval lib.) pigskin, *$2 net. Duffield.

Babes and birds. Pope, J. 75 c. Caldwell.

Babes and blossoms. Jerrold, W. C. 75 c. Caldwell.

Babes in the wood. Mord, W. 35 c. Stokes.

BABIES.
See Children.

Babies of other countries. '09(D) col. il. bds., $1. Doran.

BABISM.
Abdu'l-Baha. Some answered questions: [doctrines of Babism.] *$1.50 net. Lippincott.
Hammond, E., *comp.* Splendor of God: extracts from the sacred writings of the Bahais. **60 c. net. Dutton.
Stenstrand, A. J. Call of attention to the Behaists or Babists of America. (Add. author for price.) A. J. Stenstrand.

Babson, Roger Ward.
Business barometers used in the accumulation of money: a text-book on fundamental statistics for investors and merchants. '09(Ag14); [2d ed.] '10(Jl16) c. il. S. ea., $2; leath., $3. R. W. Babson.
Investments: what and when to buy; the use of statistics in accumulating a fortune. '07. [1908.] (Mr.) c. 18-108 p. forms, 12°, flexible leath., $2. R. W. Babson.
Miscellaneous stocks and how to find their market. [1908.] (Mr.) flexible leath., $5. R. W. Babson.
Printed bankers' directory for England. $7.50.—For Germany. $5.—For Holland. $3.50. [1908.] (Mr.) R. W. Babson.
Special bond circulars: [issued every six months.] [1908.] (Mr.) hf. leath., $10. R. W. Babson.
Stock brokers and bond dealers of London, with names especially interested in American securities capitalized. [1908.] (Mr.) $5. R. W. Babson.

Baby. Nesbit, W. D., ***comp. and ed.*** **50 c. Volland.**

Baby (The). Brown, D. R. *$1 net. Whitcomb.

Baby Bob. Whitaker, E. $1.50. Lippincott.

Baby Bunting & Co. **Payne, I. 50 c Jacobs.**

Baby days. Corbett, B. L. $1.50. **Rand, McN. & Co.**

Baby Goose book. Ostrander, F. E. 3 v. ea., 50 c. Laird.

Baby ser. See Howie, H. M. Stokes.

BABYLONIA.

Harper, R. F. Assyrian and Babylonian letters belonging to the Kouyunjik collections of the British Museum. v. 9. $6 net. Univ. of Chic.

Hilprecht, H. V. **Earliest version of the Babylonian deluge story, and The temple** library at Nippur.—So-called Peters-Hilprecht controversy [over Babylonian excavations.] ea., *75 c. net. Holman.

Hinke, W: J: **New boundary stone of** Nebuchadrezzar I. **from Nippur. $3.50. Univ. of Penn.**

King, L. W: Hist. of Babylonia and Assyria. In 3 v. v. 1. $4.80 net Stokes.

Langdon, S., ***ed.*** **Sumerian and Baby**lonian psalms. $6. Stechert.

Myhrman, D: W. Sumerian administrative documents, dated in the reigns of the kings of the second dynasty of Ur, from the archives of Nippur preserved in Philadelphia. $6. Univ. of Penn.

Poeble, A. Babylonian legal and business documents from the time of the 1st dynasty. $6. Univ. of Penn.

Radau, H., *ed. and tr.* Letters to Cassite kings from the Temple archives of Nippur. $6. Univ. of Penn.

Rogers, R. W: Religion of Babylonia and Assyria, especially in its relation to Israel. *$2 net. Eaton & M.

Toffteen, O. A. Researches in Assyrian and Babylonian geography. pt. 1. *$1 net. Univ. of Chic.

See also Aramaic language;—Bel (*god*);—Bible;—Sargon, *King of Assyria;*—Sumerian language.

Babylonian and Assyrian literature: comprising the Epic of Izdubar, Hymns, Tablets and Cuneiform inscriptions; with introd. by Epiphanius Wilson; [Also] Armenian literature, comprising poetry, drama, folklore and classic traditions; tr. into English. '08(Je27) c. 8°, $1.75; hf. mor., $3.50. Lamb Pub.

Babylonian Expedition of the University of Pennsylvania, series A, Cuneiform texts; ed. by H. V. Hilprecht. Univ. of Penn.

—Myhrman. Sumerian administrative documents. $6.

—Poebel. Babylonian legal and business documents. $6.

—Radau, *ed. and tr.* Letters to Cassite kings. $6.

Babylonian Talmud; complete in 10 v.; tr. from the original text into Eng. by Dr. Michael L. Rodkinson. '08(My23) royal 8°, $50; hf. mor., $75; mor., $100. New Talmud.

Baby's book. Weyburn, C. M. $1.50; $3; $4. Barse & H.

Baby's childhood days: [book for the record of the events in a baby's life.] '08(O17) c. D. bds., 20 c.; ed. de luxe, 50 c. boxed; Persian ooze, $1, boxed. Reilly & B.

Baby's day. Wiederseim, G. G. 60 c. Stokes.

Baby's grandmother. Walford, *Mrs.* L. B. 50 c. Hurst.

Baby's history. Fritch, G. M., ***ed.*** **60 c. G. M. Fritch.**

Baby's history. Runyon, S. D. $3; $4; $7.50; $2. Stokes.

Baby's own book. '10(D24) c. Q. $1.50; gift ed., $3, boxed; Ed. de luxe, $6, boxed. Reilly & B.

Baccalaureate sermon. Hodges, G: gratis. G: Hodges.

Bacchæ (The). See Euripides.

BACCIOCCHI, Elisa Bonaparte, *Princess of Piombino.*

See Bonaparte family.

Bach, Johann Sebastian.

Piano composition; ed. by Ebenezer Prout. v. 2, Larger compositions. '08(D5) c. por. 4°, (Musician's lib.) $2.50; pap., $1.50. Ditson.

BACH, Johann Sebastian.

Parry, *Sir* C: H. H. Johann Sebastian Bach. **$3.50 net. Putnam.

Bachellé, Cecil von, ed.

See Dudley, Emilius Clark.

Bacheller, Dora, comp.

Housekeeper pudding book. '09(Ja23) c. D. pap., 50 c. Housekeeper Corp.

Bacheller, Irving Addison.

Hand-made gentleman. '09(Ap24) c. D. †$1.50. Harper.

In various moods; poems and verses. '10 (O8) c. front. D. $1 net. Harper.

The master; being in part copied from the minutes of the school for novelists; a round table of good fellows who, long since, dined every Saturday at the Sign o' the Lanthorne, on Golden Hill, in New York City. '09(N6) c. D. **$1.20, fixed. Doubleday, P.

"Bachelor, Billy," pseud.

See Shea, Christopher Ambrose.

Bachelor and the baby. Cameron, M. †50 c. Harper.

Bachelor belles; with il. by Harrison Fisher; decorations by Thdr. B. Hapgood. '08(O24) c. Q. **$3 net, boxed. Dodd.

Bachelors. *See* Irving, Washington.

Bacher, Otto H:

With Whistler in Venice. '08(O3) c. il. Q. bds., **$4 net, boxed. Century Co.

Bachman, Nathan, D.D.

Light in dark places; or, lectures on the Epistle to the Philippians. '10(Ap9) c. por. D. 60 c. net. Presb. Pub.

Bachmann, Philipp.

New message in the teaching of Jesus. '08 (Mr14) c. S. (Foreign religious ser.) *40 c. net. Eaton & M.

Bachye, Rabbi.

Duties of the heart; tr. by Edn. Collins. '08 (Je6) 16°, (Wisdom of the East.) *40 c. net. Dutton.

BAGILLI.

See Tuberculosis.

Back in the harness. Farrington, F. 50 c. Merchants' Helps.

Back to Hampton Roads. Matthews, A. F. $1.50. B: W. Huebsch.
Back to Holy Church. Von Ruville, A. $1.20 net. Longmans.
Back to slavery. Teitsworth, G: W., *ed.* 75 c. Craven-D.
Back to the land. "C," *pseud.* $1.50 net. Longmans.
Background of the Gospels. Fairweather, W: *$3 net. Scribner.
Backhouse, E.
See Bland, J: Otway Percy.
Backward children. Cornell, W. S. 25 c. Davis.
Backwoods surgery. Moody, C: S. 75 c. net. Outing.
Backwoodsmen. Roberts, C: G: D. †$1.50. Macmillan.
Bacon, Alex. S:
Illegal trial of Christ. 2d ed. '09(Ap24) por. O. pap., 25 c. A. S. Bacon.
Woolly horse: [papers on timely topics.] '09(Ap24) por. O. pap., $1. A. S. Bacon.
Bacon, Mrs. Anna Tilden.
See Sandwick, R: Lanning.
Bacon, A: Octavius.
The Democrats and the tariff; article from the *Saturday Evening Post* of Dec. 25, 1909, regarding the attitude of the Democratic senators to the present tariff law. '10(Mr12) 8°. (Add. Superintendent for price.) U. S., Supt. of Docs.
Bacon, B: Wisner, D.D.
Founding of the church. '09(N13) c. S. (Modern religious problems.) 50 c. Houghton M.
Fourth Gospel in research and debate: series of essays on problems concerning the origin and value of anonymous writings attributed to the apostle John. '01(F12) c. O. **$4 net. Moffat.
Introduction to the New Testament. '09 (Ap3) 12°, (New Testament handbooks.) Price raised from *75 c. net to *$1 net. Macmillan.
Modern commentary; the beginnings of Gospel story: historico-critical inquiry into the sources and structure of the Gospel according to Mark; with expository notes upon the text. '09(Mr20) c. O. *$2.25 net. Yale Univ.
Bacon, Mrs. Dolores Marbourg, [pseud. for Mrs. Mary Schell Hoke Bacon.]
Pictures that every child should know. '08 (S12) c. D. ("Every child should know" ser.) **$1.20 net. Doubleday, P.
Bacon, E:
Last hurdle. '09(Jl) c. 272 p. 12°. (Not for sale.) D. G. Bacon.
Bacon, Edn. Munroe.
Boy's Hakluyt: English voyages of adventure and discovery. '10(Je4) c. il. pors. maps, facsims., 8°, $1.50. Scribner.
Boys' Drake. '10(O22) c. il. pors. facsims., O. $1.50 net. Scribner.
English voyages of adventure and discovery retold from Hakluyt. '08(S26) c. il. pors. map, facsim., O. $1.50. Scribner.
—, comp. *See* Weeks, Lyman Horace.
Bacon, Mrs. Eugenia Jones.
Red moon. '10(Je4) c. 8°, $1.25. Neale.

Bacon, Fs., Lord.
Advancement of learning; and Novum organum; with introd. by Ja. E: Creighton. '08(Je27) c. il. 8°, $1.75; hf. mor., $3.50. Lamb Pub.
Essays. '08(O10) 12°, (Best books ser.) leath., *$1 net. Dutton.
Essays; or, counsels civil and moral; ed. by Fred Allison Howe. '08, [1909.] (Ja) c. 37+250 p. 16°, (English classics.) *35 c. net. Heath.
Essays; ed., with introd. and notes, by Clark Sutherland Northrup. '08(Mr7) c. por. D. (Riverside literature ser.) *40 c. net; pap., *30 c. net. Houghton, M. & Co.
Essays; ed., with introd. and notes, by Mary Augusta Scott. '08(F15) c. D. **$1.25 net. Scribner.
Essays and Wisdom of the ancients. '09, [1910.] (F) 12°, *40 c. net. Little, B. & Co.

BACON, Francis, *Lord.*
Booth, W: S. Hidden signatures of Francesco Colonna and Francis Bacon. $1.50 net. W. A. Butterfield.
Gallup, *Mrs.* E. W. Bi-literal cypher of Sir Francis Bacon discovered in his works. $2.—Concerning the bi-literal cypher of Francis Bacon. 75 c. Howard.
Bacon, Gorham, M.D.
Manual of otology; with an introd. chapter by Clarence J: Blake, M.D. 5th ed., thoroughly rev. '09(O) 500 p. il. 12°, *$2.25 net. Lea.
Bacon, J: Lord.
Elem. forge practice. '08(N14) c. figs. 12°, $1.50. Wiley.
Forging. '09(F20) c. il. 8°, (American School of Correspondence pubs.) $1. Am. Sch. Corr.
Bacon, Mrs. Josephine Dodge Daskam, ["Ingraham Lovell."]
Biography of a boy. '10(Ja22) c. il. D. †$1.50. Harper.
Idyll of All fools' day. '08(N14) c. il. D. †$1.25. Dodd.
In the border country. '09(O23) c. il. D. **$1, fixed. Doubleday, P.
Margarita's soul. '09(O16) c. il. D. †$1.50. Lane.
Ten to seventeen: a boarding-school diary. '08(F1) c. il. D. †$1.50. Harper.
Bacon, Mrs. Mary Schell Hoke.
See Bacon, *Mrs.* Dolores Marbourg, *pseud.*
Bacon, Paul Valentine.
Im vaterland. '10(Mr5) c. il. por. map, 12°, $1.25. Allyn & B.
Bacon, Roger.
Liber primus communium naturalium Fratris Rogeri; partes prima et secunda; edidit Robert Steele. '09(D25) O. (Opera hactenus inedita Rogeri Baconi fasc. II.) pap., $3.40. Oxford Univ.
Metaphysica Fratris Rogeri ordinis fratrum minorum de viciis contractis in studio theologie; omnia quae supersunt nunc primum; edidit Robert Steele. '09(D25) O. (Opera hactenus inedita Rogeri Baconi fasc. I.) pap., $1.75. Oxford Univ.

Bacon, Victor V., and Booth, F:
Refraction: essentials of systematized, condensed and elucidated. '09(Ag) 61 p. il. 24°, leatherette, $1; pap., 75 c. Chic. Med. Bk.

BACTERIA.
Abbott, A. C. Principles of bacteriology. *$2.75 net. Lea.
Axenfeld, T. Bacteriology of the eye. *$6 net. Wood.
Ball, M. V. Essentials of bacteriology. *$1 net. Saunders.
Burnet, E. Campaigns against microbes. *$2.50 net. Wood.
Conn, H. W: Agricultural bacteriology. $2. Blakiston.
Dieudonné, A. Bacterial food poisoning: ptomaine poisoning. *$1 net. Treat.
Elliott, S. M. Household bacteriology. $1.50. Am. Sch. Home Economics.
Ellis, D: Outlines of bacteriology. *$2.50 net. Longmans.
Frost, W: D., *and* McCampbell, E. F. Textbk. of general bacteriology. $1.60 net. Macmillan.
Herzog, M. J. Text-bk. on disease producing microörganisms, especially intended for the use of veterinary students and practitioners. $4.75. Lea.
Hiss, P. H., *jr.*, *and* Zinsser, H. Textbook of bacteriology. $3.75. Appleton.
Iowa University, College of Medicine. Contributions from the Dept. of Pathology and Bacteriology. v. 1. 25 c. Univ. of Ia.
Jordan, E. O. Text-book of general bacteriology. $3. Saunders.
Lafar, F. Technical mycology. v. 2, pt. 2. $4 net. Lippincott.
Lipman, J. G. Bacteria and country life. *$1.50 net. Macmillan.
McFarland, J. Text-book upon the pathogenic bacteria. $3.50. Saunders.
McIsaac, I. Bacteriology for nurses. **$1.25 net. Macmillan.
Palmer, W: C. Farm bacteriology. 15 c. W: C. Palmer.
Park, W: H., *and* Williams, A. W. Pathogenic micro-organisms, incl. bacteria and protozoa. $3.75 net. Lea.
Prudden, T. M. Dust and its dangers.—Story of the bacteria and their relation to health and disease. ea., 75 c. Putnam.
Russell, H. L., *and* Hastings, E. G: Agricultural bacteriology. $1.25.—Outlines of dairy bacteriology. $1. H. L. Russell.
Stitt, E: R. Pract. bacteriology, blood work and animal parisitology. *$1.50 net. Blakiston.
Stoney, E. M. A. Bacteriology and surgical technic for nurses. $1.50. Saunders.
Williams, H. U. Manual of bacteriology. *$2 net. Blakiston.
Winslow, C: E: A. Systematic relationship of the *coccaceæ;* with discussion of principles of bacterial classification. $2.50. Wiley.

See also Auto-intoxication;—Dairy;—Diagnosis; Digestion;—Diphtheria;—Fermentation;—Food;—Fumigation;—Infectious diseases;—Kissing;—Milk;—Parasites;—Tuberculosis;—Water;—**Water-supply.**

BACTERIOLOGY.
See **Bacteria.**

Bacuez, Nicolas Louis.
Priestly vocations and tonsure; tr. from the French. '08(S5) *$1 net. Cathedral Lib.

Baddeley, J: F.
Russian conquest of the Caucasus. '08 (D5) Q. *$5 net. Longmans.

BADEN.
See **Brucksales, Castle of.**

Baden-Powell, Lieutenant General Sir Rob. Stephenson Smyth.
See Seton, Ernest Thompson.

Badger, J: Cogswell.
Giles Badger and his descendants, first four generations and a portion of the fifth, sixth, and seventh generations, by a descendant. '09, [1910.] (My) 64 p. por. O. pap., $1. J: C. Badger.

BADGER FAMILY.
See **Genealogies.**

Badgley, Nathan Eddy, M.D.
Equitable Union: life and its duties briefly explained. pt. 1, Spiritual, religious and ethical conclusions; pt. 2, Political, economic and philosophic conclusions. '08 (My2) c. por. D. $1.50. N. E. Badgley.

"Badsworth," pseud.
See Lister, A. Lindsay.

Baedeker, Karl.
Belgium and Holland. '10(Je4) il. maps, plans, 16°, $1.80 net. Scribner.
Berlin and its environs. 3d ed. '08(D5); 4th ed. '10(D3) maps, plans, 16°, ea., 90 c. net. Scribner.
Central Italy and Rome. 15th ed. '09 (My22) il. maps, plans, 16°, $2.25. Scribner.
Eastern Alps, including the Bavarian Highlands, Tyrol, Salzburg, Upper and Lower Austria, Styria, Carinthia, and Carniola. 11th ed., rev. and augmented. '08(D5) il. maps, plans, 16°, *$3 net. Scribner.
Egypt and the Sudân. 6th remodelled ed. '08(D5) il. maps, plans, 16°, *$4.50 net. Scribner.
Greece. New ed. '08(D19) il. maps, 16°, *$2.40 net. Scribner.
Hdbk. of Great Britain. 7th ed., rev. and enl. '10(Je4) maps, plans, 16°, $3 net. Scribner.
Italy from the Alps to Naples. 2d ed. '09 (F13) il. maps, plans, S. *$2.40 net. Scribner.
London and its environs. 15th ed., rev. '08(D5) maps, plans, 16°, *$1.80 net. Scribner.
Northern France, from Belgium and the English Channel to the Loire, excluding Paris and its environs. 5th ed. '09 (Je26) plans, fold. maps, S. *$2.25 net. Scribner.
Northern Germany as far as the Bavarian and Austrian frontiers; hdbk. for travellers. 15th rev. ed. 38+430 p. il. maps, *$2.40 net. Scribner.
Norway, Sweden and Denmark, with excursions to Iceland and Spitzbergen. 9th ed., rev. and enl. '09(Jl31) maps, plans, 16°, $2.40. Scribner.

Baedeker, Karl.—*Continued.*
Paris and its environs, with routes from London to Paris. 17th rev. ed. '10(D3) maps, plans, 16°, $1.80 net. Scribner.
The Rhine. '10(Je4) il. maps, plans, 16°, $2.10 net. Scribner.
Southern Germany. '10(Je4) il. maps, plans, 16°, $1.80 net. Scribner.
Southern Italy and Sicily; with excursions to Malta, Sardinia, Tunis and Corfu. New and rev. ed., (15th.) '08(D5) maps, plans, 12°, *$1.80 net. Scribner.
Spain and Portugal. 3d ed. '08(Je20) maps, plans, S. *$4.80 net. Scribner.
United States; with excursions to Mexico, Cuba, Porto Rico and Alaska. 4th rev. ed. '09(My22) maps, plans, 16°, *$4.50 net. Scribner.

BAER FAMILY.
See Genealogies: Bare, D. M.

Baerlein, H:
The singing caravan; some echoes of Arabian poetry. '10(O8) 16°, (Wisdom of the East ser.) 60 c. net. Dutton.

Bagby, Alfr., D.D.
King and Queen County, Virginia. '08(Jl4) c. il. pors. map, O. *$3.50 net. Neale.

Bagby, G: W:
Old Virginia gentleman and other sketches; ed., with introd. by T: Nelson Page. '10(O1) c. por. D. $1.50 net. Scribner.

Bagehot, Wa.
Lombard Street; description of the money market. New ed.; with introd. and corrections by Hartley Withers. '10(D10) 12°, $1.25 net. Dutton.

Bagg, Helen F.
His model wife: a comedy. '08(N7) c. D. pap., 15 c. Penn Pub. Co.
Untangling Tony: a comedy. '08(N7) c. D. pap., 25 c. Penn Pub. Co.

BAGHDAD RAILWAY.
See Asia.

Bagley, W: Chandler.
Education and utility. '09, [1910.] (S) 20 p. 8°, (Normal School bull.) pap., gratis. Eastern Ill. State Normal.

Bagot, Josceline Fitz Roy.
George Canning and his friends. '09(Ap17) 2 v., il. 8°, *$9 net. Dutton.

Bagot, R:
Anthony Cuthbert. '09(Je26) D. *$1.50 net. Brentano's.

Bagwell, R:
Ireland under the Stuarts and during the interregnum. In 2 v. '09(Mr6) maps, O. $10.50. Longmans.

BAHAISM.
See Babism.

Bahama Bill. Hains, T. J. $1.50. L. C. Page

BAHAMA ISLANDS.
Millspaugh, C: F: Prænunciæ Bahamenses. pt. 2. 50 c. Field Museum
Northrop, J: I. Naturalist in the Bahamas. $2.50 net. Lemcke.

Bähr, H. A., comp.
See Putzel, C:

Baikie, Rev. Ja.
Sea-kings of Crete. '10(D10) il. fold. plan, O. $2 net. Macmillan.
Story of the Pharaohs. '08(O17) il. maps, 8°, $2 net. Macmillan.

Bailes, G: Mitcheson.
Modern mining practice. 5 v. '09(My) il. 8°, ea., $3. Van Nostrand.

Bailey, Mrs. A. G.
See Bailey, *Mrs.* Alice Ward.

Bailey, Mrs. Alice Ward, [Mrs. A. G. Bailey, "A. B. Ward."]
Sage brush parson. '08(Ap4) c. D. (Popular eds. of recent fiction.) †75 c. Little, B. & Co.
See also Morgan, Anna.

Bailey, Carolyn Sherwin.
Stories and rhymes for a child. '09(N20) il. 12°, $1. M. Bradley.

Bailey, Cyril.
Religion of ancient Rome. '07, [1909.] (Ap) 8°, (Religions ancient and modern.) *40 c. net. Open Court.

Bailey, Edg. H: Summerfield, and Cady, Hamilton Perkins.
Lab'y guide to the study of qualitative analysis, based upon the application of the theory of electrolytic dissociation and the law of mass action. 6th ed., enl. '10(O8) c. il. fold. tabs., 8°, $1.25. Blakiston.

Bailey, Eliza R., and Manly, J: Matthews.
Spelling book. '08(F1) c. D. *30 c. net. Houghton, M. & Co.

"Bailey, Fk.," pseud.
See Millard, Fk. Bailey.

Bailey, F: Randolph, M.D.
Text-book of histology. 3d rev. ed. '10 (N) c. 18+589 p. il. tab., fold. diagr., 8°, $3.50 net. Wood.
"General references for further study" at end of most of the chapters.

—, and Miller, Adam Marion, M.D.
Text-Book of embryology. '09(Ap) 686 p. il 8°, *$4.50 net; leath., *$5.50 net. Wood.

Bailey, H: Christopher.
Colonel Greatheart. '08(O17) c. il. D. †$1.50. Bobbs-M.
God of clay. '08(N14) c. il. D. †$1.50. Brentano's.
Storm and treasure. '10(Ag13) D. $1.50. Brentano's.

Bailey, H: Turner.
When little souls awake. '10(N5) c. D. pap., 25 c. net., in envelope. Pilgrim Press.
—, ed. Nature drawing from various points of view. '10(Je11) c. il. in col. O. $1.50. Davis Press.

Bailey, Hollis Russell.
Attorneys and their admission to the bar of Massachusetts. '08(F) c. 167 p. O. $2.50. W: J. Nagel.

Bailey, J: Cann.
Claims of French poetry; nine studies in the greater French poets: [studies of the work of Marot, Ronsard, Le Fontaine, André Chénier, Victor Hugo, Leconte de Lisle, and Heredia.] '09(Jl31) 8°, $2.50. M. Kennerley.

Bailey, J: Read.
Mackinac, formerly Michilimackinac; hist. and guide book. Tourists' ed. 6th rev., '09. '09, [1910.] (Ja) c. 248 p. il. pors. map, 8°, $1. Tradesman.

BAILEY, Joseph Weldon.
Cocke, W: A. Bailey controversy in Texas. $3.90; $4.90. Cocke Co.

Bailey, Jos. Whitman.
First impressions of Europe. '08(Je20) c. il. D. **$1.25 net. Grafton Press.

Bailey, Liberty Hyde.
Beginners' botany. '09(Mr13) c. il. D. **60 c. net. Macmillan.
College of agriculture and the state: address del. on the occasion of Farmers' Week at Cornell University, Feb. 26, '09(My22) O. pap., gratis. L. H. Bailey.
Forcing book: manual of the cultivation of vegetables in glass houses. 7th ed. '08 (My9) c. il. 12°, (Rural science ser.) **$1.25 net. Macmillan.
Garden making. 12th ed. '08(My2) c. il. 12°, (Rural science ser.) **$1.50 net. Macmillan.
Horticulturist's rule-book. New and rev. ed. '09(Je19) 12°, (Garden-craft ser.) 75 c. Macmillan.
Manual of gardening; pract. guide to the making of home grounds and the growing of flowers, fruits and vegetables for home use. '10(Mr26) c. D. **$2 net. Macmillan
Nature-study idea. 3d ed., rev. '09(O30) *$1.25 net. Macmillan.
On the training of persons to teach agriculture in the public schools. '08(Je6) (U. S. Bureau of Education bull.) pap., 15 c.
Practical garden book. '08(F) il. 12°, 75 c. Grosset.
Principles of agriculture. [Rev. ed.] '09 (O2) c. il. 12°, (Rural science ser.) *$1.25 net. Macmillan.
Principles of fruit-growing. 10th ed. '08 (F8) il. 12°, (Rural science ser.) **$1.50 net. Macmillan.
Principles of vegetable gardening. 6th ed. '08(F22) c. il. 12°, (Rural science ser.) **$1.50 net. Macmillan.
State and the farmer. '08(Ag15) c. 12°, **$1.25 net. Macmillan.
Training of farmers. '09(O9) c. D. **$1 net. Century Co.

— and Coleman, Wa.
First course in biology. pt. 1, Plant biology, by L. H. Bailey; pt. 2, Animal biology; pt. 3, Human biology, by Wa. M. Coleman. '08(Ag1) c. il. 12°, *$1.25 net. Macmillan.

—, ed. Cyclopedia of American agriculture. In 4 v. v. 3, Animals. '08(Jl11); v. 4, Farm and the community. '09(Ap3) c. Q. subs., **$5 net, boxed; per set, **$20 net; hf. mor., **$32 net. Macmillan.

Bailey, Middlesex Alfr., and Germann, G: B.
Number primer. '09, [1910.] (Ja22) 176 p 30 c. Am. Bk

Bailey, Pearce.
Diseases of the nervous system resulting from accident and injury. 2d ed. '08 (Ap25) c il. 8°, $5: hf. leath., $6. Appleton.

Bailey, S: E.
See Ritter, W: Emerson.

Bailey, S: Willson, and Osborne, Harold Allen.
Wrinkles; few suggestions and innovations. '10(Je4) c. il. 8°. 50 c. Bailey-T.

Bailey, Solon Irving.
Peruvian meteorology. '08(My23) 4°. (Annals of Astronomical Observatory of Harvard University.) pap., $1.50. Harvard Univ.

Bailey, Vernon.
Key to animals on which wolf and coyote bounties are often paid. '09(Jl) 3 p. il. 8°, (U. S. Dept. of Agriculture, Bu. of Biological Survey circular.) (Add. Superintendent for price.)

Bailey, W: Whitman.
Poems. '10(F12) c. O. *$1.25 net. Preston & R.

Baillie, D: Gemmell.
Swiftsure phonetic shorthand system; introd. by Ervin Wardman; note by G: Harvey. '08(Ja18) 8°, $1. Phillips Pr.

Baillie-Grohman, W: Adolphe.
Tyrol. '08(Jl11) il. 12°, (Color books.) *$2 net. Macmillan.

Bailly, Auguste.
Divine minstrels; narrative of the life of Saint Francis of Assisi with his companions; tr. by Ernest Barnes. '10 (Mr26) front. D. *$1.25 net. Scribner.

Baily, Ja. T:, and Pollitt, S.
Woodwork for schools on scientific lines. '09(D18) 75 c. Manual Arts.

Baily, W: L.
Trees, plants and flowers; where and how they grow; a familiar hist. of the vegetable kingdom. '10(Ap2) il. D. 60 c. Lippincott.

Bain, Fs. W:
Incarnation of the snow; tr. from the original manuscript. '08(S26) c. front. O. †$1.25. Putnam.
Mine of faults; tr. from the orig. ms. by F. W. Bain. '10(F19) c. O. **$1.25 net. Putnam.

Bain, Harry Foster, ed.
More recent cyanide practice. '10(O15) c. il. figs. O. $2. Mining and Scientific.

Bain, Rob. Nisbet.
Last king of Poland and his contemporaries. '09(O2) O. *$3 net. Putnam.
Slavonic Europe: political hist. of Poland and Russia, 1447 to 1796. '08(Mr21) 8°, (Cambridge historical ser.) *$2 net. Putnam.

Bainbridge, Oliver.
Devil's note book. '08(N7) c. il. D. $1. Cochrane.

Bainbridge, W: Seaman, M.D.
Life's day: guide-posts and danger-signals in health. '09(Ap17) c. D. **$1.35 net. Stokes.

Bainbridge mystery. Pratt, G. T. $1.20 net. Sherman, F.

Baines, C. E.
Short hist. of English literature. '10(F19) D. *$1 net. Longmans.

Bair, Rev. J: Franklin.
Complete poetical works. '08(F1) c. il. pors. 8°, $1.50; $1.75. J: F. Bair.

Baird, Annie L. A.
Daybreak in Korea. '09(Ap10) c. 12°, *60 c. net. Revell.

Baird, Eliza Strang.
Angels of Savonarola. '10(N12) c. il. pors. 12°, 50 c. Am. Tr

Baird, H: Carey.
American and English banking contrasted: an issue for Mr. Carnegie; together with an attempt to explain the very simple cause of the New York City bank crisis of 1907. '08(O10) 8°, pap. (Add. pub. for price.) Baird.
"Fiat": the sign and token of real money; Mexico's fatal blunder; the gold standard; economic law governing prices of raw materials and finished commodities. '08(D) 8°, pap. (Priv. pr.) Baird.
John Sherman: critical examination of his claims to statesmanship, in a letter addressed to Theod. E. Burton. '08(D) 8°, pap. (priv. pr.) Baird.
Practical dry cleaner, scourer, and garment dyer; comprising dry, chemical, or French cleaning; purification of benzine; removal of stains or spotting; wet cleaning; finishing cleaned fabrics; cleaning and dyeing furs, skin rugs and mats; cleaning and dyeing feathers, [etc.;] ed. by W: T. Brannt. 3d ed., rev. and enl. '09(Mr27) c. il. 12°, *$2.50 net. Baird.
The South: shall it ever become so far civilized as to be fit for a Republican form of government? or shall we for another seventy-five years be subject to its vicious legislation, its turbulence and its wars? Answer: the Dingley tariff, causing the development of the vast mineral and other resources of the southern states, through work and wages, nearer and greater markets, wealth and power, is solving this supreme national problem; addressed in criticism of his economic views and recommendations to President Roosevelt. '08(D5) O. pap., gratis. Baird.

Baird, Ja. B.
Children of Africa. '10(N12) 12°, 60 c. net. Revell.

Baird, Jean Katherine.
Boy next door. '10(N12) c. il. 12°, 50 c. net. Am. Tr.
Coming of Hester. '09(S11) c. D. (Hester ser.) †$1.25. Lothrop, L. & S.
Hester's counterpart. '10(Ag20) c. il. D. (Hester books.) $1.25. Lothrop, L. & S.
Sixty-five on time. '09(N13) c. O. $1.25. Saalfield.

Baird, J: Cranmer.
Traveler and the grapes. '08(F29) c. il. D. $1.50. B'way Pub.

Baird, Lewis C.
Hist. of Clark County, Ind., by Captain Lewis C. Baird, assisted by well known local talent. '09, [1910.] (Jl) 17-919 p. il. pors. maps, 4°, $15. B. F. Bowen.

Baker, Alfr.
Life of Sir Isaac Pitman, (inventor of phonography.) '08(D19) il. tabs., pors. O. *$2 net. Pitman.

Baker, Mrs. Amelia Louisa Svenson.
See Svenson, Emily.

Baker, Arth.
Introd. to Esperanto; with a short story and vocabulary. '09(Ja23) c. 16°, pap., 10 c. Am. Esperantist.

Baker, Austin H.
Theory and practice of veterinary medicine. 2d ed. '09(F) c. 265 p. 8°, $3.50. A. Eger.

Baker, B. Granville.
Walls of Constantinople. '10(D) 262 p. il. 8°, $4 net. Pott.

Baker, C. H. Collins, ed.
See Turner, Percy M., *ed.*

Baker, C. S.
What Sheila did; the adventures of an only child. '09(O9) il. S. 50 c. Stokes.

Baker, C: McCoy, and Inglis, Alex. Ja.
High school course in Latin composition. '09(F6) c. D. $1.—In 2 v. and 3 pts. [New ed.] '09(O9) 12°, v. 1, pts. 1, 2, *60 c. net; v. 2, pt. 3, **55 c. net. Macmillan.

Baker, Charlotte Alice.
Books as tools for children. '09(N) 7 p. 16° o. p. Carson-H.

Baker, Mrs. Cornelia McGhee.
Magic image from India. '09(N6) c. col. il. Q. $1.25, boxed. Stern.

Baker, D: C:
Lincoln vs. liquor. '08(D) c. 35 p. por. 12°. (Add. pubs. for price.) Baker Pub.

Baker, Elwood T:, comp.
Genealogy of Eber and Lydia Smith Baker of Marion, Ohio, and their descendants; rev. to Oct., 1909. '09, [1910.] (Ja) c. 3-87 p. pors. forms, 8°, 50 c. L. A. Copeland.

Baker, Ernest Albert.
Voices of nature: a sequel to "Praise of a simple life." '08(D) 12+292 p. 16°, (Wayfaring books.) *$1 net. Dutton.
—, ed. Praise of a simple life: [an anthology.] '08(F8) 16°, (Wayfaring books.) *$1 net. Dutton.

Baker, Mrs. Etta Anthony.
Frolics at Fairmount. '10(O1) c. il. D. (Fairmount girls ser.) $1.50. Little, B. & Co.
Girls of Fairmount. '09(O9) c. il. D. (Fairmount girls ser.) †$1.50. Little, B. & Co.

Baker, Fk. Collins.
Ecology of the Skokie Marsh area, with special reference to the mollusca. '10 (Je) 58 p. il. figs. 4°, (Ill. State Lab'y of Natural Hist. bull.) pap., 60 c. Ill. Lab'y Nat. Hist.

Baker, Franklin T:, comp.
Bibliography of children's reading: [also] The use of the school library, by Allan Abbot. '08(Ag29) 8°, pap., 60 c. Teachers' Coll.
—, and Abbott, Herbert Vaughan.
English composition. '08(O10) c. D. 80 c. Holt.
—, Carpenter, G: Rice, and Dulon, Julie T.
Primer. '09(Jl17) c. il. D. (Language reader ser.) **25 c. net. Macmillan.

Baker, Fred Abbott.
Duration of municipal street grants. '10 (Ap) c. $2.50. Record Pr., (Mich.)

Baker, G: H:
Brakeman's preparatory instruction. 3 v. '10(F12) c. il. por. 8°, $20. R'way Educ.
Fireman's preparatory instruction. 3 v. '10 (F12) c. il. por. 8°, $20. R'way Educ.

Baker, G: H:—*Continued.*
Locomotive fuel economy; economical firing, economical boiler feeding, economical use of steam. 09(Ag7) c. il. D. $1. R'way Educ.

Baker, G: Melville, ed.
Pieces people ask for; serious, humorous, pathetic, patriotic, and dramatic selections in prose and poetry for readings and recitations. '09(Mr) c. '08. 127 p. 12°, 25 c. W. H. Baker.

Baker, G: Merrick, comp. and ed.
German stories; ed., with notes and vocabulary. '09(Ap3) c. S. 40 c. Holt.

Baker, H: F:
Introduction to the theory of multiply periodic functions. '08(F1) 8°, *$3.75 net. Putnam.

Baker, H: Moore.
First siege of Louisburg, 1745: address del. before the New Hampshire Society of Colonial Wars, Sept. 2, 1909. '10(Ap2) O. pap. (Priv. pr.) H: M. Baker.

Baker, Ira Osborn.
Treatise on masonry construction. 10th ed., entirely rewritten and enl. '09(S18) c. il. tabs., 8°, $5. Wiley.
Voids, settlement and weight of crushed stone. '08(N) 29 p. 8°, (Univ. of Ill. engineering experiment station, bull.) gratis. Univ. of Ill.
See also Rolfe, C: Wesley.

Baker, Ja. Heaton.
Lives of the governors of Minnesota. '08, [1909.] (Ap) c. 12+480 p. por. 8°, (Collections of the Minnesota Historical Society.) $2.50. Minn. Hist. Soc.

Baker, Ja. Hutchins.
Educational aims and civic needs. '08(D) 31 p. 12°, (Univ. of Colorado bull.) (Add. pubs. for price.) Univ. of Col.

Baker, Ja. W:
Reference book; 20th century bookkeeping and office practice; designed for use in all schools that teach bookkeeping. 7th ed., rev. '09(N6) il. form, 4°, $1. Southwestern Co., (Nashville.)

Baker, Jos. Black.
See Onken, W: H:, *jr.*

Baker, Julia Wetherill.
Wandering joy. '10(O) $1. B'way Pub.

Baker, Ray Stannard.
Following the color line; account of negro citizenship in the American democracy. '08(D19) c. il. pors. O. **$2 net. Doubleday, P.
New ideals in healing: [Emmanuel Movement.] '09(Mr20) c. il. pors. 12°, **85 c. net. Stokes.
Spiritual unrest. '10(Ap16) c. D. $1.35 net. Stokes.

Baker, Smith, D.D.
See Jenkins, Fk. E.
—, **and Jenkins, Fk. E., D.D.**
Master profession: challenge to the young men of the twentieth century. '08(S12) c. 12°, 50 c. Franklin-T.

Baker, T. Thorne.
The spetroscope: its uses in general analytical chemistry. '08(F1) il. 8°, *$1.75 net. Wood.
Telegraphic transmission of photographs. '10(Ag13) il. 12°, $1.25 net. Van Nostrand.

Baker, Tarkington.
Yard and garden: pract. information for the amateur gardener. '08(My9) c. D. **$2 net. Bobbs-M.

Baker, T: R.
New physics. '09(Mr) $1. Stradling.

Baker, T: Stockham.
Preparatory school question. '10(O) 10 p. O. (Tome School for Boys bull.) pap. Tome Sch.

Baker, W: H:
Dictionary of engraving. '08(N14) c. il. tabs., T. bds., 75 c. W: H. Baker, (Cleveland.)
Dictionary of men's wear. '08(Ag15) 8°, $2 hf. mor., $3. W. H. Baker (Cleveland).

BAKER FAMILY.
See Genealogies.

Bakewell, C: Montague.
Source book in ancient philosophy. '08 (Mr28) c. 8°, **$1 net. Scribner.

BAKING.
See Cake;—Cookery.

BAKING-POWDER.
Foot, F: N. Baking powder and other leavening agents. $1.50. Spice Mill.

Balance of nature. Abbey, G: *$2 net. Dutton.

BALATA.
See India rubber.

Balbach, Mrs. E:
See Balbach, Julia A. Nenninger.

Balbach, Julia A. Nenninger, [Mrs. E: Balbach.]
Cupid intelligent. '10(My7) c. il. D. $1. J. A. Balbach.

Balcarres, Lord.
Evolution of Italian sculpture. '10(F19) 8°, *$6 net. Dutton.

Balch, Edn. Swift.
Art in America before the Revolution: address del. before the Society of Colonial Wars in the commonwealth of Pennsylvania, March 12, 1908. '08(Je) c. 22 p. 8°. (Add. author for price.) E. S. Balch.

Balch, Emily Greene.
Our Slavic fellow citizens. '10(Je4) c. il. pors. maps, O. $2.50. Charities Pub.

Balch, Lewis.
Manual for boards of health and health officers; also the public health law, constituting chap. 25 of the general law, with all amendatory and supplemental statutes, incl. those of 1908. '08(O) c. 3-242 p. D. *$1.50 net. Banks & Co.
See also New York [State.] Public health law.

Balch, T:
Calvinism and American independence, 1876. '09(D) 18 p. 4°, $1. Allen, L. & S.

BALCH, Thomas.
Edmonds, F. S. Thomas Balch and the Geneva tribunal. (Add. author for price.) F. S. Edmonds.

Balch, T: Willing.
Free coinage and a self-adjusting ratio: paper read before the Philadelphia Social Science Association, February 23, 1877. '08(Ag1) 4°,. (Not for sale.) T: W. Balch.
La question des pêcheries de l'Atlantique; un différend entre les Etats-Unis et l'Empire Britannique. '10(F19) 8°, $1.25. (50 copies.) Allen, L. & S.
Law of Oresme, Copernicus, and Gresham: paper read before the American Philosophical Society, April 23, 1908. '08 (O24) 4°, $1. Allen, L. & S.
L'Evolution de l'arbitrage international. '09(Ja16) 8°, $2. Allen, L. & S.
Bald knobbers. Tuck, C. E. $1. B. F. Bowen.
Balderston, Caleb Canby.
See Sharpless, I: Philips.
Balderston, Lloyd.
Elem. physics: a text-book. '08(O) c. 8+9-352 p. il. pors. 12°, $1.22. Sower.
Baldness and grayness. Robinson, T. *$1 net. W: R. Jenkins.
Baldry, Alfr. Lys.
Burnes-Jones. '09(Ap17) il. O. (Masterpieces in colour.) bds., *65 c. net. Stokes.
Sir Joshua Reynolds. '09(D) various paging, il. Q. (Great artist ser.) *$2 net. Doran.
Leighton. '08(D19) il. O. (Masterpieces in colour.) bds., *65 c. net. Stokes.
Millais. '08(D19) il. O. (Masterpieces in colour.) bds., *65 c. net. Stokes.
Baldur, the beautiful. Litchfield, G. D. $1 net. Putnam.
Baldwin, A. Le S.
See Hayford, J: F.
Baldwin, C: Sears.
Composition, oral and written. '09(N13) c. D. $1.20. Longmans.
Summary of punctuation. '08(F8) D. pap., 5 c. Longmans.
Writing and speaking: text-book of rhetoric. '09(Je5) c. D. $1.20. Longmans.
Baldwin, C: W.
Geography of the Hawaiian Islands. '08 (S12) il. maps, O. 60 c. Am. Bk.
Baldwin, E: Chauncey, and Paul, Harry G., eds.
English poems. '08(My23) c. D. $1. Am. Bk.
Baldwin, F: Clare.
Life melodious: [poems.] '10(F19) c. por. D. $1.25. F. C. Baldwin.
Baldwin, Ja.
Another fairy reader. '08(F1) c. il. D. (Eclectic readings.) 35 c. Am. Bk.
Stories of the king. '10(My14) c. il. D. (Eclectic readings.) 50 c. Am. Bk.
—, **comp.** Stories of Don Quixote written anew for young people. '10(N19) c. il. D. (Eclectic readings.) 50 c. Am. Bk.
Baldwin, Ja. Mark.
Darwin and the humanities. '10(F19) 12°, (Lib. of genetic science and philosophy.) $1.50. Psychological Review.
Thought and things: study of the development and meaning of thought or genetic logic. v. 2, Experimental logic, or genetic theory of thought. '08(Mr21) 8°, *$2.75 net. Macmillan.

Baldwin, Josephine L.
Record of credits; prep. for use in the junior department of the Sunday school. '10(S) 100 p. 16°, 35 c. net. Eaton & M.
Baldwin, May.
Barbara Bellamy, a public-school girl. '10 (Ap2) il. 8°, $1.50. Dutton.
Golden Square High School. '08(D26) D. $1.25. Lippincott.
Holly House and Ridges Row. '08(N7) il. D. $1.50. Lippincott.
Muriel and her Aunt Lee; or, school and art life in Paris. '10(Ja1) 12°, $1.50. Lippincott.
Sarah's school friend. '10(D31) il. 12°, $1.50. Lippincott.
Two school-girls of Florence. '10(O8) col. il. 12°, $1.50. Dutton.
Baldwin, Ralph L.
Progressive melodies for sight singing. '10 (My21) c. O. 35 c. Ginn.
Baldwin, T: Williams.
Patten genealogy; William Patten of Cambridge, 1635, and his descendants. '08 (N) c. 290 p. map, fold. facsim., 8°, $5. T: W. Baldwin.
—, **comp.** Vital records of Wrentham, Mass., to the year 1850. In 2 v. '10(Jl16) 8°, $5.50. Gilson.
Baldwin, W: Alpheus.
High school: its weaknesses and suggested modifications. '10(My7) 12°, 5 c. N. E. Pub. Co.
—, **Mrs. W: Alpheus, and others.**
Industrial-social education. '08(Ap18) il. 8°, $1.50. M. Bradley.
BALDWIN, William Henry, *jr.*
Brooks, J: G. An American citizen; the life of William Henry Baldwin, jr. $1.50 net. Houghton M.
Baldwin, W: Ja. St. John.
Hot water heating and fitting; modern hot water apparatus, the methods of their construction and the principles involved. 4th ed., rev. and enl. '08, [1909.] c. 15+306 p. il. tabs., 8°, *$4 net. McGraw.
On heating; or, steam heating for buildings, revised. 16th ed., rev. and enl. '08 (Je20) il. figs. 12°, $2.50. Wiley.
Ventilation of our court rooms and halls of justice. [1910.] (Je) c. 22 p. S. pap., gratis. W: J. S. Baldwin.
Baldwin, Willis.
See Michigan. Law of taxation.
—, **ed.** *See* Michigan. Law of personal injuries.
Baldwin lectures. *See* Wenley, Rob. Mark.
Bale, Christian Emil.
Syntax of the genitive case in the Lindisfarne Gospels. 1907, [1908.] (O) 51 p. 8°, (Univ. of Ia. bull.; studies in language and literature.) 50 c. Univ. of Ia.
BALEARIC ISLANDS.
Calvert, A. F: Catalonia, and Balearic Isles. $1.50 net. Lane.
BALER (Siege of).
Cerezo, S. M. Under the red and gold; being notes and recollections of the siege of Baler. $1.25. Hudson.
Balestier, C: Wolcott.
See Kipling, Rudyard.

Balet, Jos. W.
Analysis of elastic arches; two-hinged, three-hinged and hingeless, of steel, masonry and concrete. '08(Ja4) il. tabs., 8°, *$3 net. Engineering News.

Balfour, Arth. Ja.
Decadence: Henry Sidgwick memorial lecture. '08(Ag29) D. *50 c. net. Putnam.
Questionings on criticism and beauty. '10 (Ja22) O. pap., 70 c. Oxford Univ.

Baliff's maid. John, E. 50 c. Hurst.

BALKANS (The).
Cowen, J. Speeches on the Near Eastern question. $1. Longmans.
Henderson, P. E. British officer in the Balkans. *$3.50 net. Lippincott.
Hutchinson, F. K. Motoring in the Balkans. *$2.75 net. McClurg.
Jaekel, F. B. Lands of the tamed Turk. $2.50. L. C. Page.
Miller, W: The Balkans: Roumania, Bulgaria, Servia and Montenegro. $1.50; $1.75. Putnam.
Murray, W: S. Making of the Balkan states. $1.50. Longmans.
Singleton, E., *comp. and ed.* Turkey and the Balkan states, as described by great writers. **$1.60 net. Dodd.
See also Bosnia;—Herzegovina;—Servia;—Turkey.

Ball, Carleton Roy.
Three much-misrepresented sorghums. '10 (My) 14 p. il. 8°, (U. S. Dept. of Agriculture, Bu. of Plant Industry, circular.)

—, and Leidigh, Arth. H.
Milo as a dry-land grain crop. '09(F20) 8°, (U. S., Dept. of Agriculture; farmers' bulletin.) pap., 5 c.

Ball, C: Backus.
See Gray, W: Beall.

—, and Sherriff, H. T.
Plumbing catechism. 2d ed. 08(Jl11) c. 12°, $1. Domestic Engineering.

Ball, C: E.
Brokerage questions and problems. '10 (Ag) c. 5-55 p. 8°, (with course) $20. Universal Business.

Ball, Eustace Alfr. Reynolds-.
See Reynolds-Ball, Eustace Alfr.

Ball, Mrs. Eva Blanche Allen, comp.
See Porter, *Mrs.* Arina Louelah Abbott.

Ball, Ja. Moores, M.D.
Andreas Vesalius, the reformer of anatomy. '10(D3) c. il. por. F. pap., $5. Medical Science.
Modern ophthalmology: anatomy, physiology, and diseases of the eye. 2d ed. '08(My23) c. 4°, *$7 net; *$8.50 net. Davis.

Ball, Ja. Turner.
Detailed working drawings of the five orders of architecture: [5 charts.] '08 (Ap4) mounted on muslin, $6.50; on cardboard, $7.50; *also* Portfolio ed., containing 17 pls., $4. W: T. Comstock.

Ball, Jessie Winecoffe.
Absolute idealism and immortality. '08 (D) 12+76 p. 8°. (Add. pubs. for price.) Woodruff-C.

Ball, Marg.
Principles of outlining, for colleges and advanced classes in secondary schools. '10 (Jl30) c. 12°, 65 c. B: H. Sanborn.

Ball, Marg.—*Continued.*
Sir Walter Scott as a critic of literature. '08(F22) 8°, (Columbia Univ. studies in English.) pap., *$1 net. Lemcke.

Ball, Michael Valentine.
Essentials of bacteriology; being a concise and systematic introd. to the study of bacteria and allied microörganisms. 6th ed., thoroughly rev. '08(D) c. 290 p. il. 12°, (Saunders' question-compends.) *$1 net. Saunders.

Ball, Sir Rob. Stawell.
Treatise on spherical astronomy. '08(D19) 8°, *$3.75 net. Putnam.

Ball, Rob. Steele.
Natural sources of power. '08(D5) il. 8°, (Westminster ser.) *$2 net. Van Nostrand.

Ball, W. V.
Law affecting engineers. '09, [1910.] (F) 300 p. 8°, (Westminster ser.) *$2 net. Van Nostrand.

BALL.
See Baseball;—Basket ball;—Bat-ball;—Cricket;—Drills (*fancy*);—Football;—Gymnastics and physical culture;—Lacrosse.

Ball and the cross. Chesterton, G. K. †$1.50. Lane.

BALL FAMILY.
See Genealogies, Deas, A. S.

Ballad of Reading Gaol. *See* Wilde, Oscar.

BALLADS.
Cameron, C. Stories of the ballads 50 c. Dutton.
Couch, *Sir* A. T: Quiller-, *comp. and ed.* Oxford book of ballads. $1.90. Oxford Univ.
Ker, W: P. On the hist. of the ballads, 1100-1500. v. 4. 60 c. Oxford Univ.
Lothrop, G: E. Historical, dramatic and romantic ballads. (Add. author for price.) G: E. Lothrop.
Macgregor, M. Stories from the ballads. 50 c. Dutton.
Sidgwick, F., *ed.* Ballads and lyrics of love.—Legendary ballads. ea., *$2 net. Stokes.
Sidgwick, F., *ed.* Old ballads. *50 c. net. Putnam.
Skotlands rimur: Icelandic ballads on the Gowrie conspiracy. $1.15. Oxford Univ.
Tappan, E. M. Old ballads in prose. 40 c. net. Houghton M.
Tileston, *Mrs.* M. W. F., *comp.* Children's book of ballads. $1.50. Little, B. & Co.
Witham, R. A., *comp.* English and Scottish popular ballads. 40 c. Houghton M.
See also Poetry;—Songs;—Spanish poetry.

Ballads and barrack room ballads. Kipling, R. **$1.50 net. Doubleday, P.

Ballads of a Cheechako. Service, R. W: $1. Stern.

Ballads of Irish chivalry. Joyce, R. D. 90 c. Longmans.

Ballads of the plains. Sloan, E. E. $1. E. E. Sloan.

Ballads of the season. Johnson, G: S. $1.50. Aberdeen.

Ballads of the western mines. Fitch, A. 75 c. Cochrane.

Ballance, C: Alfr.
Some points in the surgery of the brain and its membranes. 2d ed. '08(My2) il. 8°, *$5 net. Macmillan.

Ballantyne, J. W., M.D., ed.
See Encyclopedia and dictionary of medicine.

Ballantyne, Rob. Michael.
Dog Crusoe and his master. '08(O10) il. D. (Bowman's illustrated lib. of world-favorite books.) $1. Bowman.
Ungava; introd. by Ernest Rhys. '08(F22) 16°, (Everyman's lib.) *35 c. net; leath., *70 c. net. Dutton.

Ballard, Addison, D.D.
From text to talk. '10(Ag6) c. O. $1.20 net. Sherman, F.

Ballard, Emerson Etheridge.
Complete index to Ballard's Law of real property. v. 1-12; rev. and repr. with each new v. of the ser., [etc.] '09(Ap) c. 231 p. O. $6.50. Flood.
Law of real property. v. 12; ed. by Arth. W. Blackmore. '09(Ap) c. O. shp., $6.50 Flood.
—, ed. Index-digest of Ballard's Law of real property. vs. 1-12. '10(Mr) c. O. $4. Flood.

Ballard, Fk., D.D.
Christian essentials. '08(Ap11) O. *$1.50 net. Eaton & M.
The true God: a modern summary of the relations of theism to naturalism, monism, pluralism, and pantheism. '08(Ag15) D. *$1 net. Eaton & M.

Ballard, Rev. J: Hudson.
Spirit, soul and body. '10(S17) c. 12°, $1. Alliance Press.

Balleine, G: Reginald.
History of the Evangelical party in the Church of England. '08(Je20) il. D. *$1 net. Longmans.

Ballenger, Edg. Garrison.
Genito-urinary diseases and syphilis. '08 (D) 12+276 p. il. 8°, *$3 net. E. W. Allen.

Ballenger, W: Lincoln, M.D.
Treatise on medical and surgical diseases of the nose, throat and ear. '08(My2); 2d ed. '09(N) il. 8°, ea., *$5.50 net. Lea.

Ballentine, Ja. A.
See California. *Sup. ct. and district cts. of appeals.* Complete supp. digest.

Ballet, Gilbert.
Neurasthenia; tr. from the 3d French ed. by P. Campbell Smith, M.D. '09(Ag) 436 p. figs. 8°, $2.50 net. Hoeber.

Balliet, M. R.
Some of nature's antics. '10(Je11) c. D. $1. Roxburgh.

Balliett, Sarah Joanna Dennis, [Mrs. L. D. Balliett.]
Philosophy of numbers. '08(F) c. 8°. $1.50. L. D. Balliett.

Ballinger, R: Achilles.
See Washington. Remington & Ballinger's annot. codes.

Ballinger, Wa. F., and Perrot, Emile G:
Inspector's hdbk. of reinforced concrete. '10(F5) c. il. 12°, $1. Engineering News.

BALLISTICS.
See Rifles.

BALLOONS.
See Aerial navigation.

Ballou, Mrs. Aurelia Anna, and Cooper, W: Funk.
The Dobyns-Cooper and allied families of Ballou, Bramble, Coulter, Credit, Duval, Henry, Kemp, Larew, Lyon, Norwood, Perry, Pierce and Taylor. '08, [1910.] (Mr) 31 p. 8°, 50 c. W: F. Cooper.

Ballou, G: D'Estin.
Seven essentials to life and health; pract. primary treatise on hygiene. '10(Ap2) il. por. D. $1.50 net. G: D. Ballou.

BALLSTON SPA, N. Y.
Grose, E: F. Centennial history of the village of Ballston Spa, including towns of Ballston and Milton. $2. E: F. Grose.

Balmer, Edn.
Science of advertising. '09(Ag14) S. 25 c. E. Balmer.
Waylaid by wireless. '09(Je19) c. il. D. †$1.50. Small.
—, and Balmer, T:
Science of advertising; force of advertising as a business influence, its place in the national development, and the public result of its pract. operation. '10(Ag27) c. S. 50 c. net. Duffield.
—, and MacHarg, W:
Achievements of Luther Trant. '10(Ap16) c. il. D. $1.50. Small.

BALSAMO, Giuseppe.
See Cagliostro, *Count* Alessandro di.

Baltasar. Gomez de Avellaneda, G. 65 c. Am. Bk.

Balthasar. *See* France, Anatole.

Baltimore, Md. Public service corporations of the city; a compilation of the public and private grants of rights, franchises, easements, privileges and immunities to the various public service corporations engaged in the public utilities of Baltimore city; comp. by C: Fielert. '08, [1909.] (Ja) c. shp., $8. G: W. King.

BALTIMORE, Md.
Abel, A. H., *and* Lord, E. L., *comps.* Brief guide to points of hist. interest in Baltimore city. pap., 20 c. A. H. Abel.
Fassig, O. L. Climate and weather of Baltimore. *$2.50 net. Maryland Geol.
Polk's vest pocket street directory and car line guide of Baltimore. 25 c. Polk.
See also Jews.

BALUCHISTAN.
Tate, G. P. Frontiers of Baluchistan. *$5 net. Scribner.

Balzac, Honoré de.
Works. De luxe ed. 18 v. '10(N) il. levant, $54. Crowell.
Works. 18 v. New imperial lib. ed. '10 (D) il. 8°, ea., $1.25; hf. cf., $2.25; New il. sterling ed., ea., $1. (Sets only.) Estes.
[Works.] Comédie humaine. Centenary ed.; tr. by Katharine Prescott Wormeley. '09(D25) 12°, ea., $1.50. Little, B. & Co.
Contents: v. 34, Letters to Mme. Hanska; v. 35, A woman of thirty and other studies; tr. by G: Burnham Ives; v. 36, The muse of the department and other stories, tr. by G. Burnham Ives.
Cat and Racket, etc.; introd. by G: Saintsbury. '09(Mr27) 16°, (Everyman's lib.) **35 c. net; leath., *70 c. net. Dutton.

Balzac, Honoré de.—*Continued.*
Catherine de Medici; with introd. by G. Saintsbury. '10(Ap2) 16°, (Everyman's lib.) 35 c. net; leath., 70 c. net. Dutton.
Cesar Birotteau; ed. by Wilhelmine E. Delp. '09(My15) D. (Oxford modern French ser.) 60 c. Oxford Univ.
Les Chouans ou Le Bretagne en 1799; préface de Gustave Lanson. '08(Ag1) il. 12°, (Les classiques Français illustrés.) *$1.40 net. Macmillan.
The Chouans; introd. by G: Saintsbury. '08(F22) 16°, (Everyman's lib.) *35 c. net; leath., *70 c. net. Dutton.
Christ in Flanders, and other stories; in trod. by G: Saintsbury. '08(F22) 16°, (Everyman's lib.) *35 c. net; leath., *70 c. net. Dutton.
Cousin Pons; with introd. by G: Saintsbury. '10(D10) c. 16°, (Everyman's lib.) 35 c. net; leath., 70 c. net. Dutton.
Eugénie Grandet; ed. by H. E. Berthon. '09(Mr6) il. por. S. (Oxford higher French ser.) 85 c. Oxford Univ.
Le médecin de campagne; ed., with introd. and notes, by de Payen-Payne. '09(Mr) 20+310 p. 16°, (Pitt Press ser.) *90 c. net. Putnam.
Maxims. '09(Ap10) front. 32°, (Ariel booklets.) leath., 75 c. net. Putnam.
Passion in the desert and other stories. '10 (D) front. 32°, (Ariel booklets.) 75 c. boxed. Putnam.
Quest of the absolute; introd. by G: Saintsbury. '08(F22) 16°, (Everyman's lib.) *35 c. net; leath., *70 c. net. Dutton.
Stories by Balzac. '09(Jl17) 12°, (World's story tellers ser.) *40 c. net. Dutton.
Tales. '09(D4) c. S. (Wayside lib.) leath., $1. Brentano's.
Une ténébreuse affaire; ed. by Marie A. Péchinet. '09(Mr6) S. (Oxford modern French ser.) 60 c. Oxford Univ.

BALZAC, Honoré de.
Gillette, F. B., *comp.* Title index to the works of Honoré de Balzac. 25 c. Boston Bk.
Lawton, F: Balzac. $4 net. Wessels & B.

Bamford, Harry.
Moving loads on railway underbridges. '08 (Ja25) il. 8°, *$1.25 net. Macmillan.

Bampton lectures. *See* Liddon, H: Parry.

Bancroft, Edg. Addison.
Destruction or regulation!; address [on trusts.] '07, [1908.] (S) 20 p. 4°. (priv. pr.) E. A. Bancroft.

Bancroft, G:
Abraham Lincoln: a tribute. '08(O17) c. D. **60 c. net. Wessels.

BANCROFT, George.
Howe, M. A. DeW. Life and letters of George Bancroft. In 2 v. **$4 net. Scribner.

Bancroft, Jessie Hubbell.
Games for the playground, home, school and gymnasium. '09(D18) c. il. O. **$1.50 net. Macmillan.

Bancroft, Marg., and Farington, E. A., comps.
Manual of the course of study, Bancroft Training School for Mentally Subnormal Children, Haddonfield, N. J. '09(My) 120 p. 12°. (Not for sale.) Bancroft.

Bancroft, Marie Effie Wilton, Lady and Sir Squire Bancroft.
The Bancrofts: recollections of sixty years. '09(Je12) il. 8°, $5. Dutton.

Bancroft, Sir Squire Bancroft.
See Bancroft, Marie Effie Wilton, *Lady.*

BANDAGES.
See Surgery.

Bandana days. Cook, J. M. 60 c. B'way Pub.

Bandelier, Adolph Fs. Alphonse.
Islands of Titicaca and Koati '10(Mr5) c. il. fold. maps, 8°, $5. Hispanic Soc.

Bandelier, —, and Roepke, Otto.
Tuberculin in diathesis and treatment: text book of the specific diagnosis and therapy of tuberculosis; tr. from the 2d German ed. by Egbert C. Morland. '09(Jl) il. fold. charts, 8°, *$3 net. Wood.

Banderet, P., and Reinhard, Ph.
First lessons in French: adpt. by Grace Sandwith. '09(Je19) D. (Modern lang. ser.) *50 c. net. Crowell.

Bandini, Helen Elliott.
History of California. '08(S12) c. map, D. 75 c. Am. Bk.

Bandler, S: Wyllis, M.D.
Medical gynecology; 135 original il. '08 (Ag8) c. 8°, *$5 net; hf. mor., *$6.50 net. Saunders.

Banerjea, S. B.
Tales of Bengal; ed. by Fs. H: Skrine. '10(Ap23) D. $1 net. Longmans.

Banfield, E. J.
Confessions of a beachcomber; scenes and incidents in the career of an unprofessional beachcomber in tropical Queensland. '10(My14) c. il. map, O. $4 special net. Appleton.

Bang, Ole, ed.
Good-luck book: extracts from famous American, English, German and Scandinavian poets. '10(D17) 16°, $1. Brandu's

Bangs, Ella Matthews.
The king's mark: story of early Portland. '08(N14) c. il. D. $1.50. C. M. Clark.

Bangs, Hal Crumpton, ed.
See Illinois. *Courts.* Repts.

Bangs, J: Kendrick.
Autobiography of Methuselah; ed. by J: Kendrick Bangs. '09(D25) c. il. 12°, $1. B. W. Dodge.
Genial idiot: his views and reviews. '08 (O17) c. D. †$1.25. Harper.
Mollie and the Unwiseman abroad. '10(O1) c. col. il. O. $1.50. Lippincott.
Potted fiction being a series of extracts from the world's best sellers, put up in thin slices for hurried consumers; The United States Literary Canning Co. '08 (S19) c. D. †50 c.; pap., †25 c. Doubleday, P.
Real thing, and three other farces. '09 (O16) c. il. S. †$1. Harper.
Songs of cheer. '10(Je4) c. D. $1 net. Sherman, F.
See also Briscoe, Marg. Sutton.

Bangs, Mary Rogers.
Jeanne D'Arc; the Maid of France. '10 (N5) c. D. $1.25 net. Houghton M.

BANGS, Nathan, *D.D.*
Tuttle, A. H. Nathan Bangs. *25 c. net. Eaton & M.

BANK OF ENGLAND.
See Banks and banking.

Bankart, G: P.
Art of the plasterer: account of the decorative development of the craft chiefly in England from the XVIIth to the XVIIIth century; with chapters on the stucco of the classic period and of the Italian Renaissance; also on sgraffito, pargetting, Scottish, Irish, and modern plaster work. '09(Ap3) il. Q. *$10 net. Scribner.

Banker's encyclopedia for 1909. [1910.] (Mr) c. 1686 p. $6. A. Stumpf.

Banker's green book: directory of financial institutions. '08(Jl) c. 12°, $1. Banker.

Banker's views on religious and other important subjects. Harris, T. (Add. pub. for price.) W. P. Harvey.

Bankers and merchants perpetual maturity guide for the purpose of quickly determining the accurate number of days between any two given dates—both inclusive. '10(N19) c. 8°, $5. Bankers Pub.

Bankers' handy ser. 24°, 50 c. Bankers' Pub.
—Crawford. Bank directors and their powers.
—Gardner. Moneys of the world.
—Herrick. How to increase the business of a trust company.
—Roberts *and* Sprague. Central bank of issue. 50 c.

Bankers' telegraph and cable code. '09(D) c. 4+328 p. 16°, $3.50. Business Code.

BANKING.
See Banks and banking.

BANKING LAW.
See Banks and banking.

BANKRUPTCY.
American bankruptcy repts., annot. v. 19-23. ea., $5.—Digest. v. 15-20. per set of 2 v., $8.50. M. Bender.
Collier, W: M. Law and practice of bankruptcy. $7.50. M. Bender.
Hagar, M. S., *and* A. T: Forms, rules and general orders in bankruptcy. $6.50. M. Bender.
New York [State.] Court rules and bankruptcy rules and orders. $4.50. Banks.
Remington, H. Treatise on the bankruptcy law of the United States. v. 1-3. ea., *$6 net. Michie.
Staples, A. Suit in bankruptcy (Add. pubs. for price.) Michie.
Woodman, A. S. Treatise on the law of trustees in bankruptcy. $6.50. Little, B. & Co.
See also Receivers;—Sale;—*also* names of states.

Bankruptcy of Bryan Kane. Vane, V. $1.20. Bates.

Banks, Emory E.
Twentieth century poultry buildings and how to build them. '10(O1) c. il. plans, O. pap., 50 c. E. E. Banks.

Banks, Ja. Lenox.
David Sproat and naval prisoners in the war of the Revolution, with mention of William Lenox, of Charlestown. '09, [1910.] (F) 127 p. 12°. (Priv. pr.) J. L. Banks.

Banks, L: Albert, D.D.
Problems of youth; series of discourses for young people on themes from the book of Proverbs. '09(N20) c. D. **$1.30 net. Funk.
Sermons which have won souls. '08(Je27) c. D. **$1.40 net. Funk.
World's childhood; sermons from the first three chapters of Genesis. '10(O22) c. D. $1.30 net. Funk.

Banks, Nathan.
Catalogue of the nearctic *Hemiptera-Heteroptera.* '10(N) 103+8 p. 8°, $1. Am. Entomol.
Directions for collecting and preserving insects; by Nathan Banks in collaboration with various members of the Bureau of Entomology, Dept. of Agriculture. '09(O23) il. O. (Smithsonian Institution, U. S. National Museum bull.) pap. (Add. Superintendent for price.) U. S., Supt. of Docs.
List of works on North American entomology; compiled for use of students and other workers. '10(Mr5) 8°, (U. S., Dept. of Agriculture, Bu. of Entomology, bull.)

Banks, Col. Rob. Webb.
Battle of Franklin, Nov. 30, 1864. '08(O24) c. D. $1.25. Neale.

BANKS AND BANKING.
Alcorn, E. G. Duties and liabilities of bank directors. $1.50. Financial Pub.
Aldrich, N. W. Address before the Economic Club of New York, Nov. 29, 1909, on the work of the National Monetary Commission. Gov. Pr. Off.
American Academy of Political and Social Science. Banking problems. $1. Am. Acad. Pol. Sci.
American Adjusters Co. Directory of reliable lawyers and banks in the U. S. and Canada. $5.50. Am. Adjusters.
American Bankers' Association. Forms for trust companies. $20.—Savings Bank Section. Proceedings of the 7th annual meeting, Denver, Colo., 1908. (Add. Assoc. for price.) Am. Bankers' Assoc.
American School of Correspondence. Bank bookkeeping $1.50. Am. Sch. Corr.
Audit Company of New York, *comp.* Trust companies of the United States. 1907 ed. (Not for sale.) U. S. Mortgage.
Babson, R. W. Printed bankers' directory for England. $7.50.—For Germany. $5. —For Holland. $3.50. R. W. Babson.
Baird, H: C. American and English banking contrasted. (Add. pub. for price.) Baird.
Bankers' encyclopedia for 1909. $6. A. Stumpf.
Bankers' green book: directory of financial institutions. $1. Banker.
Breckinridge, R. M. Hist. of banking in Canada. (Add. Superintendent for price.) U. S., Supt. of Docs.
Brigham, J. Banker in literature. $2. Bankers Pub.

BANKS AND BANKING.—*Continued.*

California and Nevada. Attorneys and bankers directory, 1908-09. $2. C. A. Murdock.

Cannon, Ja. Graham. Clearing houses. '01 (Jl) 8+335 p. facsims., tabs., 8°. Gov. Pr. Off.

Caswell, L. B. Postal savings bank: paper entitled "Do we want the postal savings bank." (Add. Superintendent for price.) U. S., Supt. of Docs.

Clearing-house systems of the world. $1. Banking Law.

Cleveland, F: A. Bank and the treasury. **$2 net. Longmans.

Clews, H: No government guarantee of bank deposits and no ownership of railroads by the government. (Add. author for price.) H: Clews.

Conant, C: A. Banking system of Mexico. —National bank of Belgium. Gov. Pr. Off.

Conant, C: A. History of modern banks of issue. **$3.50 net. Putnam.

Conant, C: A. Principles of banking. **$1.75 net. Harper.

Crawford, J: J. Bank directors, their powers, duties and liabilities. 50 c. Bankers' Pub.

Credit corporation of America. Law and bank list. $2. Credit Corporation.

Davis, A. M. Origin of the national banking system. Gov. Pr. Off.

Davis, J. F. Bank organization, management and accounts. $2. Pitman.

Devine, H: C. Peoples' co-operative banks. *35 c. net. Cassell.

Dewey, D. R., *and* Chaddock, R. E. State banking before the Civil War, and The safety fund banking system in New York. Gov. Pr. Off.

Evening Post book of bank reports at the close of business, February 14, 1908. 15 c. N. Y. Eve. Post.

Flux, A. W: Swedish banking system. Gov. Pr. Off.

Forgan, J. B. Should national bank deposits be guaranteed by the government. (Add. pubs. for price.) J. B. Forgan.

Frame, A. J. Insuring bank deposits is purely theoretical, unpractical, revolutionary and fatal to conservatism. 15 c. A. J. Frame.

Gandy, J. P. Elements of banking. 50 c. Pitman.

Germany. *Benkenquete-kommission.* German bank inquiry of 1908: stenographic reports. '10(Je) 1162 p. fold. tab., 8°. U. S., Supt. of Docs.

Gookin, F: W: Our defective American banking system. (Priv. pr.) Chic. Lit. Club.

Griffin, A. P. C., *comp.* Library of Congress list of works rel. to the first and second banks of the U. S. 25 c.—Library of Congress sel. list of books rel. to currency and banking. 25 c.—Library of Congress list of books rel. to postal savings banks. 15 c. Gov. Pr. Off.

Hague, G: Banking and commerce.—Practical treatise on banking and commerce. ea., $3. Bankers Pub.

BANKS AND BANKING.—*Continued.*

Hale, A. Savings bank investments. $1.50. A. Hale.

Herrick, C. How to increase the business of a trust company. 50 c.—Trust companies; their organization, growth and management. *$4 net. Bankers' Pub.

Herrick, M. T. Guarantee of bank deposits. gratis. M. T. Herrick.

Holdsworth, J: T., *and* Dewey, D. R. First and second banks of the United States. Gov. Pr. Off.

Holland, R. W., *and* Nixon, A. Banking law. $1.75. Longmans.

How to increase a bank's deposits; tried out plans that attract commercial accounts and saving deposits—advertising campaigns and ideas that pull—soliciting schemes and follow-up systems that produce results—selling talks that create business, as used and proved successful in twenty-six banks. 5th rev. ed. '09, [1910.] (N) c. 128 p. il. 12°, (System "how-books.") System.

Ireton, R. E. Central bank. $1.60. A. Stumpf.

Jacobs, L. M. Bank acceptances. Gov. Pr. Off.

Johnson, J. F. Canadian banking system. Gov. Pr. Off.

Kniffin, W. H., *jr., comp.* New York Savings Bank cases. $5. Haedrich.

Koch, R: German imperial banking laws. Gov. Pr. Off.

Landmann, J. Swiss banking law. U. S., Supt. of Docs.

Laughlin, J. L. Guaranty of bank deposits. Johnson, K. & Q.

McCabe, R. L. Central bank of issue in the United States. 10 c. R. L. McCabe.

MacGregor, T. D. Pushing your business: advice on advertising for banks, trust companies, [etc.] *$1 net. Bankers Pub.

Manley, W. D., *comp. and ed.* Georgia country banker. $1.25. Mutual Pub. Co.

Margraff, A. W. International exchange. $5. Int. Exchange.

Morawetz, V. Banking and currency problem in the United States. *$1 net. North American.

Morgan, A. T., *and* Ridpath, J: C. Bank of the beast. 25 c. Ware & Co.

Muhleman, M. L: Monetary and banking systems, 1908. *$2 net. Monetary.

Murray, L. O. Co-operation as a factor in effective bank supervision. (Priv. pr.) Nat. City Bank.

New York [State.] Banking law; with notes, [etc.,] by Amasa J. Parker. $3. Banks.

New York [State.] Banking law; with annots., [etc.,] by C: J. Hailes. $2.50. Banks & Co.

New York [State.] Laws of the state rel. to banks, banking, trust companies, etc., by W. S. Paine. $6. M. Bender.

Patron, M., *and* Neymarck, A. Bank of France in its relation to national and international credit. Gov. Pr. Off.

Perine, E: T. American trust companies. gratis. Am. Bankers' Assoc.

BANKS AND BANKING.—*Continued.*
Pitman's banking phrase book. 25 c. Pitman.
Postal savings banks. gratis. Univ. of Wis.
Pratt's digest; laws rel. to banks. $2. A. S. Pratt.
Reichsbank, 1876-1900. U. S., Supt. of Docs.
Revell, A. H. Guaranty of bank deposits. (Add. author for price.) A. H. Revell.
Robbins, E. A., *comp.* Sel. articles on a central bank of the United States. $1 net. H. W. Wilson.
Roberts, G: E., *and* Sprague, O. M. W. Central bank of issue. Bankers' Pub.
Robinson, H. Simple explanation of modern banking customs. (Add. author for price.) H. Robinson.
Robinson, H. Simple explanation of modern banking customs. 25 c. net. Small.
Scott, W: A. Money and banking. $2. Holt.
Sharp & Alleman Co.'s lawyers' and bankers' directory for 1908, 1909, 1910, 1911. Jan. ed.—July ed. ea., $5. Sharp & A.
Sherwood, G. M., *comp.* Summary of the general banking laws of the commercial states. gratis. R. I. State Lib.
Sweetland, C: A: Bank book keeping. 50 c. Am. Sch. Corr.
Taylor, W: G: L. Financial legislation in principle and history. $1. Univ. of Neb.
Thomas, F. W. Cost accounting in a bank. $2. Bankers' Pub., (O.)
Trust companies of the United States. gratis. U. S. Mortgage.
Tulane University of Louisiana. Triangular debate bet. Tulane Univ. of La., Univ. of N. C., and Univ. of Va.: resolved, that postal savings banks should be established. $1. H. W. Kaiser.
United States. Compilation of laws rel. to trust companies. (Add. pubs. for price.) Am. Bankers' Assoc.
United States. *Comptroller of the Currency.* Digest of national bank decisions. $1. U. S., Supt. of Docs.
United States. *Congress. Senate. Committee on Finance.* Statistics on banking and currency in the U. S. and other countries. 25 c. U. S., Supt. of Docs.
United States. Instructions and suggestions of the Comptroller of the Currency relative to the organization, etc., of national banks, 1909. '09, [1910.] (Je) 47 p. 8°.
United States. *National Monetary Commission.* Interviews on the banking and currency systems of England, Scotland, France, Germany, Switzerland, and Italy, under the direction of Hon. Nelson W. Aldrich. (Jl) 541 p. fold. tabs., 8°.
United States. *National Monetary Commission.* Miscellaneous articles on German banking. '10(Ag) 478 p. 8°.
United States. *National Monetary Commission.* Publications in course of preparation for the National Monetary Commission, Nov. 1, 1909. '09, [1910.] (Mr) 19 p. 8°.
United States. *National Monetary Commission.* Publications issued by and in preparation for the National Monetary Commission.
United States. *National Monetary Commission.* Replies to circular letter of inquiry of Sept. 26, 1909, on suggested changes in administrative features of the national banking laws. '08, [1909.] (O) c. 8°.
United States. *National Monetary Commission.* Special rept. from the banks of the United States, April 28, 1909. '09, [1910.] (Je) 65 p. tabs., f°.
United States. *Treasury Dept. Comptroller of Currency.* Instructions and suggestions of the comptroller of the currency relative to the organization, etc., of national banks. '09(Je) 47 p. 8°, pap.
United States. *Treasury Dept.* Information concerning national banks; letter from the Sec'y of the Treasury, transmitting a response to the resolution of the House making inquiry as to numbers, capital, circulation, deposits, etc., of the national banks. '08, [1909.] (My) 238 p. 8°.
Warburg, Paul M. Discount system in Europe. '10(Jl) 43 p. 8°. Gov. Pr. Off.
Weitzel, F. W: Law of deposits. $1. Milans.
Welldon, S: A., *comp.* Digest of state banking statutes. U. S., Supt. of Docs.
White, H. Money and banking, illustrated by American history. *$1.80 net; *$1.50 net. Ginn.
Widney, R. M. National currency and banks. (Add. author for price.) R. M. Widney.
Wilt, A. D. Banking and the currency problem. (Add. author for price.) A. D. Wilt.
Withers, H., *and others.* English banking system. Gov. Pr. Off.
Wright, B: C. Banking in California. $2. B: C. Wright.
See also Advertising;—Codes;—Credit;—Exchange;—Farmers' Trust Company of Lancaster;—Finance;—Gold (*as money*);—Interest;—Money;—Negotiable instruments;—Panics;—Political economy;—Stock brokers;—Stocks;—*also* Andrios, *Sir* Edmund;—Brown Bros. & Co.;—National Bank of the Northern Liberties of Phil.;—*also* names of countries and states.

Banks' New York state lawyers' diary, 1908. '08(Ja4); 1909. '09(D); 1910. '10(F) c. O. hf. roan, ea., $2. Banks & Co.

Banner, G. A.
Practical engraving on metal. 2d ed. '09 (Ap24) il. 16°, $1.25. Van Nostrand.

Bannerman, Helen.
Story of Little Black Bobtail. '10(D17) c. il. in col. T. bds., 50 c. Stokes.
Story of Little Black Quasha. '08(S5) c. il. T. (Dumpy books for children.) bds., 50 c. Stokes.
See also Potter, Beatrix.

BANNERMAN, Margaret Gordon, *Lady.*
Archibald, R. C. Carlyle's first love, Margaret Gordon, Lady Bannerman. *$3.50 net. Lane.

Banners of the coast. Rutledge, A. H. $1. State Co., (S. C.)

Bannon, Alice.
Letter writing and model letters. '08(My9) c. 16°, 50 c. Bardeen.

BANQUE DE FRANCE, Paris.
See **Banks and banking.**

BANQUE NATIONALE DE BELGIQUE, Brussels.
See **Banks and banking.**

Banquet (The). *See* Plato.

Banquet songs and ballads. '09(Je19) 12°, bds., 25 c., in envelope. Reilly & B.

BANTAMS.
See **Poultry.**

Banzai!. Grautoff, F. H. †$1.50. Baker & T.

BAPTISM.
Boston, S. L. Baptism. 5 c. Presb. Bd.
Christian, J: T. Form of baptism in sculpture and art. $1. J: T. Christian.
Dayton, A. C. Theodosia Ernest: [conversation between two children and their mother on the subject of baptism.] *75 c. net. Baptist Bk.
Grime, J. H. Hist. of alien immersion and valid baptism. *15 c. net. Baptist Bk.
Johnson, J. M. Hdbk. on infant baptism. 25 c. J. M. Johnson.
Johnson, S: L. Absolute necessity of baptism. *10 c. net. Revell.
Mozley, J. B. Review of the baptismal controversy. $1.25. Longmans.
Ratcliffe, F. A., *and* Smith, H. T. Baptism. 30 c. F. A. Ratcliffe.
See also **Friends (*Society of*).**

BAPTIST CHURCH.
American Baptist year-book, 1908, 1909. ea., *50 c. net. Am. Bapt.
Baptist Congress. Proceedings of the 27th annual session of the Baptist Congress held in the Madison Ave. Baptist Church, New York City, Nov. 9, 10 and 11, 1909. [1910.] (Ap) 224 p. 8°, pap., 50 c. net. Univ. of Chic.
Centennial celebration of the Baptists of Alabama, by the Alabama Baptist State Convention and the Baptist Woman's Missionary Union. '08, [1909.] (S) 20 p. 8°, pap., gratis. Paragon.
Church clerk; hdbk. for clerks of Baptist churches. 25 c. Am. Bapt.
Collinsworth, J. R. Pseudo church doctrine of anti-Pedo-Baptists defined and refuted. $2.50. Hudson.
Daniel, J. C. Hist. of the Baptists of Hill Co., Texas. $1. Hill-K-F. Co.
Flory, J: S: Literary activity of the German Baptist Brethren in the eighteenth century. $1.25. Brethren Pub. Ho.
Folk, E. E. Baptist principles. $1. S. S. Bd., So. Bapt.
Frost, J. M. Our church life; serving God on God's plan. 90 c. S. S. Bd. So. Bapt.
Griffith, E. C. Epochs in Baptist history. (Add. pubs. for price.) Advance.
Jones, P. L. Restatement of Baptist principles. **50 c. net. Am. Bapt.
Mullins, E. Y. Axioms of religion: interpretation of Baptist faith. **$1 net. Am. Bapt.
Pittman, R. H., *ed.* Biographical hist. of primitive or old school Baptist ministers of the United States. $2. R. H. Pittman.

BAPTIST CHURCH.—*Continued.*
Riley, B: F. Hist. of Baptists of Texas. **$1.50 net. Am. Bapt.
Seventh Day Baptists in Europe and America. 2 v. $5. Am. Sabbath Tr. Soc.
Stott, W: T. Indiana Baptist history. $2. W: L. Stott.
Van Ness, I: J., *ed.* Training in church membership: text book in study courses with the individual, with the church B. Y. P. U., [etc.] 50 c.; 30 c. S. S. Bd. So. Bapt.
See also **Sunday-school;—*also* Craig, Lewis.**

Baptist handbook for 1909. '09(Mr) 85 p. T. pap., 10 c. Am. Bapt.

Baptist Young People's Union of America, Christian culture courses. D. Am. Bapt.
—Conley. Young Christian and the early church. **50 c. net.

BAR.
See **Lawyers.**

Bar B. boys. Sabin, E. L. †$1.50. Crowell.

Bar—20. Mulford, C. E: $1.50. McClurg.

Barahona, Diego.
Glosa a la obra de Don Jorge Manrrique; hecha por Diego Barahona dirigida al muy yllu stre Señor Dom Gaspar destuñiga de auellaneda abad de Castro. [facsim.] '02, [1909.] (N) front 4°, $4. Hispanic Soc.

Barahona de Soto, Luis.
Primera parte de la Angelica de Lvys; al excelentissimo Señor Duque de Offuna. [facsim.] '03, [1909.] (N) 251 p. 8°, $8.50. (100 copies.) Hispanic Soc.

Bárány, Robert.
Physiology and pathology of the semicircular canals; being an excerpt of the clinical studies of Dr. Robert Barany with notes and addenda gathered from the Vienna clinics; by Adolph E. Ibershoff, M.D., and a foreword by Royal S. Copeland. '10(Je) 64 p. il. 12°. $1. Hoeber.

BARBADOS, West Indies.
Davis, N. D. Notes on the hist. of the Jews in Barbados. $1. Bloch.

Barbara. *See* **Root, E: T. Redemption of Paradise Pond.**

"Barbara," pseud.
See Wright, *Mrs.* Mabel Osgood.

Barbara, a woman of the West. Whitson, J: H. †75 c. Little, B. & Co.

Barbara and the five little Purrs. Gould, E. L. 75 c. Caldwell.

Barbara Bellamy. Baldwin, M. $1.50. Dutton.

Barbara Rebell. Belloc-Lowndes, *Mrs.* M. A. 50 c. B. W. Dodge.

Barbarelli, Giorgio.
See Carpaccio, Vittore *and* Giorgione.

Barbarians of Morocco. Sternberg, *Count* **$2 net. Duffield.

Barbarous Mexico. Turner, J: K. $1.50. Kerr.

BARBARY.
See **Rodgers, John.**

Barbe, Waitman.
Famous poems explained; with biographical notes of the authors represented; with an introd. by R: G. Boone. '09 (My8) c. 12°, $1. Hinds.

Barber, Amzi Lorenzi.
Best road and the right way to make it. '09(Mr13) c. il. O. pap. (Not for sale.) Barber Asphalt.

Barber, Edn. Atlee.
Lead glazed pottery. pt. 1, (common clays:) plain glazed, sgraffito and slip-decorated wares. '08(Mr14) c. il. O. (Primers of art.) bds., **90 c. net. Doubleday, P.
Maiolica of Mexico. '08, [1909.] (F) c. 115 p. il. 8°, (Art hdbks. of the Pa. Museum and School of Industrial Art.) $2.10. Penn. Mus. and Sch. of Ind. Art.
Pottery and porcelain of the United States, to which is appended a chapter on the pottery of Mexico. 3d ed., rev. and enl. '09(Je26) c. il. O. **$5 net. Putnam.

Barber, Eli.
Home memories. '08(F29) c. D. $1.50. Badger.

Barber, Marcin.
Britz, of headquarters. '10(Je4) D. $1.50. Moffat.

Barber, Marion Louise, comp.
The mother-heart. '10(D3) c. il. D. pap., 50 c., boxed. G: W. Parker.

BARBER FAMILY.
See Genealogies: Wilson, L. M., *ed.*

BARBERS.
Drexel, A. Progressive barber; a book for the apprentice and for barbers. $1. Wis. State Barbers' Bd.

Barbery bushes and wheat. Davis, A. McF. (Not for sale.) A. McF. Davis.

BARBIZON SCHOOL.
Faulkner, H. W. Homes of the men of 1830; [paintings.] (Priv. pr.) W: Schaus.
La Farge, J: Higher life in art. [Barbizon school.] **$2.50 net. Doubleday, P.

Barbour, Mrs. Fannie Cooley Williams.
Spelman genealogy; English ancestry and American descendants of Richard Spelman of Middletown, Connecticut, 1700. [1910.] (N) c. 559 p. il. pors. map, plans, facsims., 8°, $5. Allaben.

Barbour, J:
The Bruce; ed. by W. M. Mackenzie. '09 (S4) 12°, *$1.90 net. Macmillan.

Barbour, Levi L.
Peter White as man and citizen: address at joint session of the Classical and Historical Conferences at Ann Arbor, Mich., Mar. 31, 1909. '09(N) 22 p. 8°. (Add. Univ. for price.) Univ. of Mich.

Barbour, Ralph H:
Captain Chub. '09(O2) c. il. D. †$1.50. Century Co.
Double play: story of school and baseball. '09(O9) col. il. D. †$1.50. Appleton.
Forward pass: story of the "new football." '08(O3) c. il. D. †$1.50. Appleton.
Golden Heart. '10(N12) c. col. il. O. $2, boxed. Lippincott.
Harry's Island. '08(O3) c. il. D. †$1.50. Century Co.
Kingsford, quarter. '10(O1) c. il. D. $1.50. Century Co.

Barbour, Ralph H:—*Continued.*
Lilac girl. '09(N6) c. col. il. O. $2, boxed. Lippincott.
My lady of the fog. '08(N7) c. il. O. †$2, boxed. Lippincott.
New boy at Hilltop, and other stories. '10(O8) c. il. D. $1.50. Appleton.
Winning his "Y." '10(O1) c. il. D. $1.50. Appleton.

Barbour, Sylvester.
Reminiscences, by Sylvester Barbour, a native of Canton, Conn. '08(O) c. 11-166 p. il. pors. 8°, $1. S. Barbour.

BARBOUR FAMILY.
See Genealogies.

Barca, Mme. Calderon de la.
Life in Mexico during a residence of two years in that country; with preface by W. H. Prescott. 3d ed. '10(Jl30) O. $2.25. Am. News.

Barchester Towers. *See* Trollope, Anthony.

Barclay, Cornelia Barclay.
Our American Barclays. '08(Ap18) c. 12°. [privately pr.] Grafton Press.

Barclay, Mrs. Florence Louisa Charlesworth.
Mistress of Shenstone. '10(O22) c. D. $1.35 net. Putnam.
The rosary. '09(D4) c. D. **$1.35 net.—Holiday ed. '10(D17) il. 8°, $2.50 net. Putnam.
Wheels of time. '08(O3) c. D. (What is worth while ser.) leatherette, *30 c. net. Crowell.
Wheels of time. '10(S17) c. il. D. 50 c. net. Crowell.

Barclay, Sir T:
Problems of international practice and diplomacy, with special reference to the Hague conferences and conventions. '08 (F1) 8°, $6.50. Boston Bk.

Barclay, W. C.
See Eiselen, F: C.

BARCLAY FAMILY.
Barclay, C. B. Our American Barclays. [privately pr.] Grafton Press.

Barclay of the guides. Strang, H. *$1.25 net. Doran.

Bard, Harry Erwin.
The city school district; statutory provisions for organization and fiscal affairs. '09 (D25) c. 8°, (Teachers' College, Columbia University; Contribs. to education.) $1. Teachers' Coll.

BARD FAMILY.
Seilhamer, G: O. Bard family. $10. Kittochtinny.

Bard of Mary Redcliffe. Lacy, E. $5. Sherman.

Bardeen, C: W:
John Brody's astral body, and other stories about schools. '09(Ja23) c. D. $1. Bardeen.
Little fifer's war diary; with introd. by N: Murray Butler. '10(D25) c. il. pors. maps, O. $3 net. Bardeen.
New York school officers' hdbk.; manual of common school law. 9th ed. '10 (Ja22) c. O. *$1.50 net. Bardeen.
—, comp. Fifty fables for teachers. '10 (My21) c. il. D. $1. Bardeen.
—, ed. Fundamental facts of elementary physics: consisting of full answers to all

the examinations in that subject given by the regents of the University of the State of New York, 1896-1905. '09(Ja23) c. il. figs. D. $1. Bardeen.

Bardenhewer, Otto.
Patrology: the lives and works of the fathers of the church; tr. from the 2d ed. by T: J. Shahan. '08(D5) 8°, *$3.75 net. Herder.

Bardswell, Noel Dean, M.D.
Advice to consumptives. '10(Ag13) 12°, 75 c. net. Macmillan.
Expectation of life of the consumptive after sanatorium treatment. '10(D) 5+130 p. tabs., 8°, (Oxford medical pubs.) $1.50 net. Oxford Univ.

Bardwell, Fred Leslie, and Speer, Elwood B., comps.
Lab'y experiments in inorganic chemistry; comp. from various sources for the use of students of the Massachusetts Institute of Technology. '09, [1910.] (F) c. 80 p. 8°, 75 c. F. L. Bardwell.

Bare, Dan. Mathias and Rob. Bruce, comps.
Genealogy of Johannes Baer, 1749-1910. '10 (N) 288 p. pors. map, 8°, $2 net. Cen. Pr. & Pub.

Barefoot days. Williams, B. $1.50. Conkey.

Barfield, T. C.
Longmans' historical illustrations. In 6 portfolios. no. 1, The XI century; no. 2, The XII century; no. 3, The XIII century; no. 4, The XVI century. '10(Je11); no. 5, England in the Middle Ages; no. 6, England in the Middle Ages. '10(D3) F. ea., 90 c. net. Longmans.

Bargain book. Jerningham, C: E: W. $3.50 net. Warne.

Barine, Arvede, pseud.
See Vincens, Cécile.

Baring, Evelyn.
See Cromer, *Earl* of.

Baring, Maurice.
Dead letters. '10(Je4) D. $1.25 net. Houghton M.
Landmarks in Russian literature. '10(Je11) D. $1.75 net. Macmillan.

Baring-Gould, Rev. Sabine.
Cornish characters and strange events. '08 (D5) il. 8°, *$5 net. Lane.
Family names and their story. '10(Ja1) 8°, *$3 net. Lippincott.
Life of Napoleon Bonaparte. New and cheaper ed. '08(O3) il. pors. O. *$3.50 net, boxed. Stokes.

Bark, Don Hurdman.
Irrigation in Kansas. '09(Jl) 28 p. maps, 8°, (U. S. Dept. of Agriculture, Office of Experiment Stations bull.) pap. (Add. Superintendent for price.)

Barker, Adrian.
Pocket hand-book of checkers. '10(S) 12°, 60 c. net. Ball Pub. Co.

Barker, E: Harrison.
France of the French. '09(F13) il. pors. D. *$1.50 net. Scribner.

Barker, Elsa.
Frozen grail and other poems. '10(My7) c. D. $1.25 net. Duffield.
Son of Mary Bethel. '09(S4) c. 12°, $1.50. Duffield.

Barker, Ethel Ross.
Buried Herculaneum. '08(N21) il. plans, 8°. *$3 net. Macmillan.

Barker, H. Granville.
See Archer, W:

Barker, J. Ellis.
British socialism: examination of its doctrines, policy, aims, and practical proposals. '08(D5) 8°, *$3 net. Scribner.
Great and greater Britain. '10(F19) 12°, *$3 net. Dutton.
Modern Germany: her political and economic problems, her foreign and domestic policy. 2d and enl. ed., completely rev. and brought up to date. '08(F22) 8°, *$3 net. Dutton.
101 points against free trade; article by J. Ellis Barker, with letters by Jos. Chamberlain and others. '09, [1910.] (Mr) 67 p. 8°. Gov. Pr. Off.

Barker, J. S.
Games for the playground; with preface by Dr. Alfr. A. Mumford. '10(O1) il. D. 60 c. net. Longmans.

BARKER, Jeremiah.
Spalding, J. A. Jeremiah Barker, M.D. (Add. author for price.) J. A. Spalding.

Barker, Perry.
See Parr, S: Wilson.

Barker, W. M., and Hall, Lillian J. Smith, [Mrs. J. N. Hall.]
Memoirs of Elder J. N. Hall, the peerless defender of the Baptist faith. '08(O) 4+7-349 p. pors. 8°, $1.50. J. N. Hall.

BARLEY.
Carleton, M. A. Barley culture in the northern great plains. 15 c. U. S., Supt. of Docs.
Clark, C. C., *comp.* Barley crops of the United States, 1866-1906. 5 c. U. S., Supt. of Docs.
Le Clerc, J. A., *and* Wahl, R. Chemical studies of American barleys and malts. U. S., Supt. of Docs.

Barlow, Jane.
Irish idylls; il. by photographs taken from life by Clifton Johnson. [New ed.] '10 (D) 8°, $2 net. Dodd.

Barlow, J: R:
Maiden of the mist: Indian legend of Niagara; origin of the great paintings, the red man's fact and the white man's fancy. '09(Ja2) c. O. pap., 25 c. J: R: Barlow.

Barlow, Madge.
Cairn of the badger: [a novel.] '08(D12) front. D. $1.50. Cassell.

Barnaby, Horace T:
The decade: a story. '08(D5) c. front. D. $1.25. Wolverine.

Barnaby, Sydney W.
Marine propellers. 5th ed., rev. '09 (Mr13) 8°, $4.50 net. Spon.

Barnaby Bright. 2 v. Bearne, D: *80 c. net. Benziger.

Barnard, Annie E.
My first cousin or myself. '09(D) c. 86 p. 12°, 75 c. Cochrane.

Barnard, Clive H.
British Empire in pictures. '10(D31) col. il. 8°, (World in pictures ser.) bds., 75 c. net. Macmillan.

Barnard, Clive H.—*Continued.*
British Isles in pictures. '10(D31). col. il. maps, 8°, (World in picture ser.) bds., 75 c. net. Macmillan.

Barnard, Ella Kent.
Early Maltby with some Roades history and that of the Maulsby family in America, descendants of William and Mary Maltby, emigrants from Nottinghamshire, England, to Pennsylvania. '09(Je12) c. il. por. facsims., 8°, $6.25. S: N. Rhoades.

Barnard, Harold Leslie.
Contributions to abdominal surgery; ed. by Ja. Sherren. '10(Ap) 19+391 p. il. O. $4.20 net. Longmans.

Barnard, Ja. Underwood.
Missouri. '08(Ap4) il. map, sq. 8°, (Tarr and McMurry geographies, supplementary v.) pap., *20 c. net. Macmillan.

Barnard, Melville Clemens.
Mystery of the sandal-wood box: being an adventure of Harlan Nims, the amateur American detective. '07, [1908.] (My.) c. 6+116 p. il. 12°, $1. Mayhew.

Barnard, S., and Child, J. M.
New algebra. v. 1, cont. pts. 1, 2 and 3; without answers. '08(O24) 12°, *60 c. net. Macmillan.

Barnes, Annie Maria.
Little lady at the fall of Quebec. '09(N13) c. il. D. †$1.25. Penn Pub. Co.

Barnes, Mrs. Arth. J.
See Barnes, Louisa Ellen.

Barnes, Burt.
Scissors book. '10(D24) il. 4°, 75 c. Dodd.
Scissors Mother Goose. '10(D24) il. 4°, 75 c. Dodd.

Barnes, C. L.
Lessons in elementary practical physics. v. 3. pt. 1, Practical acoustics. '09(Ap3) il. 12°, (Stewart and Gee ser.) *$1.10 net. Macmillan.

Barnes, Rev. C: Randall, ed.
People's Bible encyclop.; biographical, geographical, historical, and doctrinal. 2 v. '10(N19) c. il. 8°. $9. People's Pub.

Barnes, C: Reid.
See Coulter, J: Merle.

Barnes, Earl.
Child study in relation to elementary art education. '08, [1909.] (F) c. 20 p. 8°. (Add. pubs. for price.) Am. Art.

Barnes, Everett
Short American history for intermediate grades: navigators and explorers, early inhabitants of North America, the colonies to the close of the French and Indian War. 2 v. '08, [1909.] (F) c. il. fold. map, 12°, v. 1, 70 c.; v. 2, 75 c.; complete, $1. Heath.

Barnes, Fred Asa.
See Crandall. C: Lee.

Barnes, G: Owen.
Beraysheeth, or, in the beginning: ed. by Mary B. Craig. [1910.] (S) c. 5-142 p. 12°, $1. J. J. Scruby.

Barnes, Harold Edg., and Milner, Byron Alb.
Sel. cases on constitutional law. '10(D) c. O. pap., $1.50. Lyon & A.

Barnes, Harry Cleveland.
Interstate transportation; treatise on the federal regulation of interstate transportation and common carriers; revised to date. '10(D) c. 39+1378 p. O. $6. Bobbs-M.

Barnes, Ja.
Clutch of circumstance. '08(Ap11) il. D. †$1.50. Appleton.
See also Boys on the railroad.

Barnes, Louisa Ellen, [Mrs. Arth. J. Barnes.]
Barnes' business letters in shorthand; with explanatory notes, designed especially for students of Benn Pitman phonography. '10(Ag20) 12°, $1. A. J. Barnes.
Heald's Pitman-Graham shorthand. '10 (F) c. 172 p. 12°, $1.25. E: P. Heald.
Modern Graham shorthand. '10(Ag20) c. 12°, $1.25. A. J. Barnes.
Practical course in shorthand. '09(N) c. 172 p. 12°, $1.25. A. J. Barnes.
Shorthand dict. and phrase book: Barnes-Pitmanic shorthand; cont. 18,000 words and 3,500 phrases; easy words omitted. '10(Mr5) c. nar. D. $1.25; leath., $1.40; indexed, 15 c. extra. A. J. Barnes.
Shorthand lessons by the sentence method; American Pitman phonography. '08(N) c. 4+151 p. 12°, $1.25. A. J. Barnes.

Barnes, Orange Perry, ["Klahowya."]
Fly fishing in wonderland. '10(Jl30) c. il. (partly col.) obl. 16°, $1. O. P. Barnes.

Barnes, Parker T.
House plants and how to grow them. '10 (Ja22) c. il. D. (Garden lib.) $1.10. Doubleday, P.

Barnes, Stephen Goodyear.
Voices of faith and love: [poems.] '08 (My.) c. 103 p. por. 12°, $1. Caledonian Press.

Barnes, W. Emory, D.D.
Lex in corde (the law in the heart); studies in the psalter. '10(O1) D. $1.50 net. Longmans.

Barnes, W:
Selected poems; chosen and ed. by T: Hardy, with a preface and glossarial notes. '09(Je19) 16°, (Oxford lib. of prose and poetry.) 90 c. Oxford Univ.

BARNES COUNTY, N. D.
Alden Publishing Co. Standard atlas of Barnes County, N. D., incl. a plat book of the villages, cities and townships of the county; map of the state, United States and world; patrons directory, reference business directory and departments devoted to general information; analysis of the system of U. S. land surveys, digest of the system of civil government. '10(Mr) 7-143 p. il. maps, f°, $15. Alden Pub.

Barnes-Grundy, Mrs. Mabel Sarah.
Gwenda. '10(Ap9) c. front. D. $1.50. Baker & T.
Hilary on her own. '08(S19) c. D. †$1.50. Baker & T.

Barnes' first year book. Kahn, A. 30 c. net. Barnes.

Barnesby, Norman, M.D.
Medical chaos and crime. '10(D17) 12°, $1.50 net. M. Kennerley.

Barnett, Evelyn Snead.
The dragnet. '09(N20) c. D. $1.50. B: W. Huebsch.

Barnett, G: Ernest.
The printers; a study in American trade unionism. '09(N) c. 7+387 p. O. (American Economic Association quarterly.) $2; pap., $1. Am. Economic Assoc.

Barnett, Mrs. Henrietta Octavia Rowland.
See Barnett, *Canon* S: A:

Barnett, Ja. Duff.
Indirect central administration of Wisconsin. '08, [1909.] (D) 111 p. 8°, (Univ. of Wis. bull.; Economics and political science series.) pap., 25 c. Univ. of Wis.

Barnett, J: Morrison.
Annals of the early Protestant churches at Superior. '08(Ag) 217-243 p. por. 8°, 35 c. State Hist., Wis.

Barnett, L. D.
Heart of India: sketches in the hist. of Hindu religion and morals. '08(O24) 16°, (Wisdom of the East ser.) *60 c. net. Dutton.
Hinduism. '07, [1909.] (Ap) 8°, (Religions ancient and modern.) *40 c. net. Open Court.
—, comp. Golden town, and other tales from Soma Deva's Ocean of romance rivers. '09 (Jl17) 12°, (Romance of the East ser.) *$1 net. Dutton.

Barnett, Mrs. Percy Arth., and another.
Drifting thistledown. '10(Je11) D. 90 c. net. Longmans.

Barnett, Canon S: A: and Mrs. Henrietta Octavia Rowland.
Towards social reform. '09(F20) 12°, *$1.50 net. Macmillan.

Barney, Laura Clifford.
God's heroes: drama in five acts. '10(D3) c. 8°, $3 net. Lippincott.

Barnham Beach: poem. Young, *Mrs.* J. E. D. $1.50. Floyd-G.

BARNS.
Radford, W: A., *ed.* Combined house and barn plan book.—Pract. barn plans. ea., $1. Radford Architectural.

Barnum, Edm. Maginness.
Weasels, trapping, raising and preparing skins for market. '10(Je) c. 16 p. 16°, 25 c. E. M. Barnum.

Barnum, Madelene D.
See Maxwell, W: H:

Barnyard ballads for children. Terhune, A. $1.25 net. Schirmer.

Barnyard manure. Minns, E: R. gratis. Sears Roebuck.

Baroggio, Alex., comp.
Two hundred seating furniture in historical styles, photographic reproductions from rare and characteristic specimens of chiefly English, French, Italian, Flemish, Spanish, and partly Oriental origin, from original photographs. '09(O) il. f°, $12. A. Gerbel.

BAROMETER.
Marvin, C: F: Barometers and the measurement of atmospheric pressure. U. S., Supt. of Docs.
Plympton, G: W. Aneroid barometer. 50 c. Van Nostrand.

Baron (The), pseud.
See Ronzone, B: Anthony.

Baron, E: D:
Inscrutable woman, an autobiography, 1896-1910. '10(Ag) c. 339 p. D. $1; $1.50. B'way Pub.

Barr, Mrs. Amelia Edith Huddleston.
Hands of compulsion. '09(Ap10) c. front. D. †$1.50. Dodd.
House on Cherry Street. '09(D4) c. front. D. †$1.50. Dodd.
Reconstructed marriage. '10(O15) c. front. D. $1.25 net. Dodd.
Strawberry handkerchief: romance of the Stamp Act. '08(O10) c. D. †$1.50. Dodd.

Barr, J. Stoddart.
See Barr, T:

Barr, Ja. A.
Testing for metallurgical processes. '10 (D31) c. il. 12°, $2. Mining and Scientific.

Barr, Ja. R.
Principles of direct current electrical engineering. '08(Je6) 8°, *$3.25 net. Macmillan.

Barr, J: H:
Kinematics of machinery. 2d ed. '10(N) 8°, $2.50. Wiley.
See Kimball, Dexter Simpson.

Barr, J: W:
Inductive method of learning stonework; simplified system for acquiring the art of preparing forms for letter-press printing, based on the folded signature as an elementary and infallible guide for imposition. '09(N) c. 16 p. 8°, $3.50. J: W: Barr.

Barr, Rob., ["Luke Sharpe."]
Cardillac. '09(O9) c. col. front. D. †$1.50. Stokes.
Measure of the rule. '08(Mr7) D. †$1.50. Appleton.
The sword maker. '10(S24) c. D. $1.25. Stokes.
Young Lord Stranleigh. '08(My23) c. il. D. †$1.50. Appleton.

Barr, T:, M.D., and J. Stoddart.
Manual of diseases of the ear; incl. those of the nose and throat in relation to the ear. 4th ed., entirely rev. and largely rewritten. '09(Ap) 40+477 p. il. 8°, *$4.50 net. Macmillan.
Bibliography.

Barr, W: Miller.
Pumping machinery. 2d ed. '08(Je20) c. il. diagrs., 8°, $5. Lippincott.

Barraca (La) Blasco. Ibáñez, V. 90 c. Holt.

Barradall, E:
See Virginia Colony. *General ct.*

Barranco, Mariano.
See Carrión, Miguel Ramos.

Barratt, Norris S., and Sachse, Julius Friedrich, comps.
Freemasonry in Pennsylvania, 1727-1907. '08(D) c. 23+477 p. il. 8°, *$5 net. J. F. Sachse.

Barré, Rev. François Théophile.
English accentuation. '10(F) c. '09. 16+78 p. 8°, 60 c. Kenedy.

Barrett, Byron Simeon.
Book of homonyms; with copious exercises on homogeneous and homophonous words, and chapters on compound and hyphenated words, use of the apostrophe, use of figures, rules for spelling, the formation of plurals and contractions, with extended exercises. '09(Mr6) c. D. *75 c. net. Pitman.

Barrett, C: J.
Poems and addresses. '08, [1909.] (F) c. 227 p. por. 8°. (Add. pubs. for price.) Orange Journ.

Barrett, C: Simon.
Mission, hist. and times of the Farmers' Union: narrative of the greatest industrial-agricultural organization in history, and its makers. '09(Je) 419 p. pors. 8°. (Add. author for price.) C: S. Barrett.

Barrett, Eaton Stannard.
The heroine; with an introd. by Wa. Raleigh. '09(My15) S. (Oxford lib. of prose and poetry.) 90 c. Oxford Univ.

Barrett, Edm.
Family doctor; dict. of domestic medicine and surgery especially adapted for family use. '10(D) 4+330 p. il. 12°, $1.25 net. Dutton.

Barrett, Fk. W: Zelotes.
Mourning for Lincoln. '09(My22) c. D. **$1 net. Winston.

Barrett, Harrison D.
Pantheistic idealism. '10(Je) c. 54 p. por. 16°, $1. H. D. Barrett.

Barrett, J. A.
A-B-C of good hearing. '09, [1910.] (Ap) 16 p. il. nar. 16°, 25 c. J. A. Barrett.

Barrett, J:
Latin America, the land of opportunity; a reprint of official reports and special articles. '09(S18) il. 8°, pap., gratis. Int. Bu. Am. Republics.
United States and Latin America. '08(F22) 8°, pap., gratis. Int. Bu. Am. Republics.

Barrett, S: Alfr.
Ethno-geography of the Pomo and neighboring Indians. '08(Mr7) maps, O. (Univ. of Cal. pub., Am. archæology and ethnology.) pap., $3.25. Univ. of Cal.
Material culture of the Klamath Lake and Modoc Indians of northwestern California and southern Oregon. '10(Jl16) Q. (Univ. of Cal. pubs., Archæology and ethnology.) pap., 75 c. Univ. of Cal.
Pomo Indian basketry. '09(Ja9) il. figs. Q. (Univ. of Cal. pubs.; American archæology and ethnology.) pap., $1.75. Univ. of Cal.

—, and Kroeber, Alfr. L:
Geography and dialects of the Miwok Indians, by S: Alfred Barrett. [Also] On the evidences of the occupation of certain regions by the Miwok Indians, by A. L. Kroeber. '08(Mr7) map, Q. (Univ. of Cal. pub., Am. archæology and ethnology.) pap., 50 c. Univ. of Cal.

Barrett, Stephen Melvil.
Practical pedagogy. '08, [1909.] (Ja) c. 137 p. 12°, $1. Heath.

Barrett Manufacturing Co. Tarvia and pitch filler; digest of the proceedings of the tarvia meeting, held in Chicago, Dec. 8th and 9th, 1908. '09(Ap) c. 20 p. il. 8°. (Not for sale.) Barrett Mfg. Co.

Barri, Odoardo.
The Flower Queen: cantata for unchanged voices; ed. by Wa. H. Aiken. '10(Ap9) c. O. (Standard musical lib.) pap., 20 c. Am. Bk.

Barrie, G:, jr.
See Barrie, Rob.

Barrie, Ja. Matthew.
Neither Dorking nor the Abbey. '10(Ap23) S. pap., 50 c. Browne's Bookstore.
Peter Pan in Kensington Gardens; with drawings by Arth. Rackham. '10(N5) c. O. $1.50 net. Scribner.

Barrie, Rob. and G:, jr.
Cruises, mainly in the Bay of the Chesapeake. '10(Ja8) c. il. map, O. bds., $2. Franklin Press, (Pa.)

Barrier (The). Beach, R. E. †$1.50. Harper.

Barrier (The). *See* Bazin, René.

Barron, E:
Lost goddess. '08(F29) c. D. †$1.50. Holt.

Barron, S: Benton.
Lone Star defenders: chronicle of the third Texas cavalry, Ross' brigade. '09(Ja23) c. O. *$2 net. Neale.

Barrows, B: H.
Columbia river; issued by Passenger Dept., Union Pacific Railroad Co. [1910.] (Je) c. 3-94 p. il. maps, 12°. pap., gratis. E. L. Lomax.

Barrows, C: H:
Hist. of Springfield in Mass.; for the young; being also in some part the hist. of other towns and cities in the county of Hampden. '09(My) c. 166 p. il. 12°, 80 c. W. F. Adams.

Barrows, D: P.
History of the Philippines. '08(Ap11) c. il. maps, D. $1. Bobbs-M.

Barrows, Harlan H.
Geography of the middle Illinois Valley. '10(N) 12+128 p. il. map. diagrs., 8°, (Illinois State Geological Survey bull.) 10 c. Univ. of Ill.

Barrows, Mary Minerva, ed.
Value of happiness: introd. by Marg. E. Sangster. '09(O9) c. O. (Value ser.) $1.50; $2; chamois, $2.50; leath., $4; cf., $5. Caldwell.

Barrows, Wayne Groves.
Law of the range. '09(N20) c. il. D. $1.50. C. M. Clark.

Barrows, W: E:
Electrical illuminating engineering. '08 (N21) c. figs. O. *$2 net. McGraw.

Barrows lectures. *See* Hall, C: Cuthbert.

Barrus, Clara, M.D.
Nursing the insane. '08(My9) c. 8°. **$2 net. Macmillan.

Barry, C: E.
Lake and rail transportation. '10(N5) c. 8°, 25 c. La Salle Extension.

Barry, J. C.
Ideals and principles of church reform. '10(Ag27) 12°, $1.25 net. Scribner.

Barry, Rev. J. G. H.
Christian's day book. '10(D) c. 12°, $1.50 net. Gorham.

BARRY, John.
Griffin, M. I. J. Story of Commodore John Barry. $1; 50 c. M. I. J. Griffin.

Barry, J: Dan.
Julia Marlowe. New ed. '08(Ja11) il. pors. D. (Sock and buskin biographies.) $1. E. H. Bacon.

Barry, Jos. Gayle Hurd.
Meditations on the office and work of the Holy Spirit. '08(D12) c. D. *$1.50 net. Young Churchman.

Barry, W: D.D.
Tradition of scripture: its origin, authority and interpretation. 2d ed., rev. '08 (Ag22) D. (Westminster lib.) **$1.20 net. Longmans.

Barry, W: Fs.
Hygiene of the schoolroom. Rev. ed. '09 (O16) c. 12°, $1.50. Silver.

Barry Gordon. Payson, W: F. †$1.50. McClure.

Barse, Mrs. Mary Emma Salisbury, ["Mary E. Blain."]
Games for all occasions. '09(Jl) c. 11-208 p. 8°, 60 c. Barse & H.

Barselma's kiss. Lee, M. B. $1.50. C. M. Clark.

Barss, J: Edm.
Writing Latin. Bk. 1.; rev. ed., based on Lodge's vocab. of high school Latin. '10(D24) c. 12°, (Gildersleeve-Lodge Latin ser.) 50 c. net. Heath.

Barstow, Mrs. Montague.
See Orczy, Emma Magdalena Rosalia Maria Josefa Barbara, *Baroness.*

Bartels, J: Murray, comp.
See Randall, W. W.

Barth, Fritz.
Gospel of St. John and the synoptic gospels. '08(Ja4) S. (Foreign religious ser.) *40 c. net. Eaton & M.

Barthel, Christopher, M.D.
Methods used in the examination of milk and dairy products; tr. by W. Goodwin. '10(Je11) il. tabs., O. $1.90 net. Macmillan.

Bartholomew, Elmer Jefferson.
Man, woman, know thyself!: illustrated treatise on practical psychology. '09 (Ja2) c. il. charts, por. 8°, $2. E. J. Bartholomew.

Bartholomew, Ethel.
House book to the hostess. '10(D24) 8°, $1.50 net; ooze, $2.50 net. Dodge.

Bartholemew, J: G:
Handy reference atlas of the world. New ed.; with general index and geographic statistics. '08(D12) il. 12°, leath., *$2.50 net. Dutton.
School economic atlas; with introd. by L. W. Lyde. '10(My14) maps, Q. 85 c. Oxford Univ.

Bartlett, Clarence.
Text-book of clinical medicine: treatment. '08(Ap18) c. il. 4°, $8; hf. mor., $10. Boericke & T.

Bartlett, Edn. Julius.
Calculations of the quantitative chemical laboratory with problems. '09(N) c. 47 p. 12°, 75 c. E. J. Bartlett.

Bartlett, Ellis Ashmead-.
See Ashmead-Bartlett, Ellis.

Bartlett, Frances
Christmas in Austria; or, Fritzl's friends. New ed. '10(Ag20) c. il. D. (Christmas in many lands ser.) 50 c. Estes.

Bartlett, Fk. W., and Johnson, Thdr. W.
Engineering descriptive geometry. '10(S) 6+159 p. figs. 8°, $1.50 net. Wiley.

Bartlett, F: Orin.
Prodigal pro tem. '10(N5) c. il. D. $1.50. Small.
Seventh noon. '10(F5) c. il. D. †$1.50. Small.
Web of the Golden Spider. '09(F27) c. il. D. †$1.50. Small.

Bartlett, Ja. L.
Frosts in Wisconsin: occurrence, prediction, and methods of prevention. '09 (Jl3) O. (Univ. of Wis. bull.; University extension ser.) pap., 25 c. Univ. of Wis.

Bartlett, W: H.
Handy book of American government. '08 (D19) c. pl. 12°, (Handy information ser.) 50 c. Crowell.

Bartley, Elias Hudson.
Text-book of medical and pharmaceutical chemistry. 7th rev. ed. '09, [1910.] (F) c. 15+734 p. il. 8°, $3. Blakiston.

Barto, D. O.
Manual of agriculture for secondary schools; studies in soils and crop production; with introd. by E. Davenport. '10 (Je4) c. 16°, 50 c. net. Heath.

Bartoli, Giorgio.
Primitive church and the primacy of Rome. [1910.] (My) 8°, $1.50 net. Doran.

Barton, Mrs. Catherine Josephine Wigginton.
An interlude. '08(N) pap., 50 c.; silk velvet, $1.50. C. J. W. Barton.
Mother of the living. '08(N) c. 79 p. 8°, $1.50; pap., 50 c. C. J. W. Barton.

Barton, Edn. H:
Text-book on sound. '08(Jl11) il. 8°, *$3 net. Macmillan.

Barton, Fk. Townend.
Dog in health, accident, and disease. '08 (Je27) c. D. (Altemus' handbooks for animal owners.) $1. Altemus.
Non-sporting dogs. '10(D31) $1.75. W: R. Jenkins.
Sporting dogs. '10(D31) 12°, $2.50. W: R. Jenkins.
Terriers: their points and management. '08 (Ja18) il. 8°, *$1.60 net. M. Kennerley.
The cat; its points and management. '10 (D31) 12°, $1. W: R. Jenkins.
The horse: ailments and accidents. '08 (Je27) c. D. (Altemus' handbooks for animal owners.) $1. Altemus.
The horse: its selection and purchase; together with the law of warranty, sale, etc. '08(Mr28) il. 8°, *$2.50 net. Chic. Med. Bk.
Toy dogs. '10(D31) 12°, $1. W: R. Jenkins.
Vet book: account of the ailments of and accidents to domestic animals. '08(O10) il. S. (Country handbook ser.) *$1 net. Lane.

Barton, G:
Adventures of the world's greatest detectives. '09(Ap3) c. il. D. 75 c. Winston.

Barton, G:, Guilday, P: K., Taggart, Marion Ames, and others.
Lady of the tower, and other stories. '09 (My8) c. D. $1.25 Benziger.

Barton, G: Aaron.
See International critical commentary.
—, **ed.** Haverford [College] Library collection of cuneiform tablets, or documents from the temple archives of Telloh. In 2 pts. pt. 2. [1910.] (D) il. f°, ea., $5 net. Winston.

Barton, Ja. Levi, D.D.
Daybreak in Turkey. '09(Ja16) c. O. bds., *$1.50 net. Pilgrim Press.
Unfinished task of the Christian church: studies in the problem of the world's evangelization. '08(Ap18) c. D. 50 c.; pap., 35 c. Student Vol.

Barton, Llewellyn, comp.
Maine official index and court directory. '09(Je) c. 160 p. O. $1. Smith & S.

Barton, S: Goodwin.
Halley's comet. [1910.] (N) 5-23 p. il. 8°, gratis. S: G. Barton.

Barton, Rev. W: Eleazar.
Congregational manual; theory and practice, for the use of ministers, churches and deliberative assemblies governed by Congregational usage. '10(Je18) c. 16°, $1. Puritan Press.

Bartow, E:
Chemical and biological survey of the waters of Illinois; rept. for year ending Aug. 31, 1906. '08(Ja25) il. tabs., O. (Univ. of Ill. bull., Water survey ser.) pap., gratis. Univ. of Ill.
Municipal water supplies of Illinois. '07, [1909.] (Ap) 123 p. map, 8°, (Univ. of Ill. bull.; water survey ser.) pap. (Add.. University for price.) Univ. of Ill.
—, **Udden, Johan August, and others.**
The mineral content of Illinois waters. '09 (D) 8+192 p. il. 8°, (Illinois, State Geological Survey; bull.) pap., gratis. Univ. of Ill.

Bartram, J. W.
Longmans' illustrated first conversational German reader. '09(O30) D. 80 c. Longmans.

Bartsch, Paul.
See Dall, W: Healey.

Barty Crusoe and his man Saturday. Burnett, *Mrs.* F. H. **$1 net. Moffat.

Baruch, Simon, M.D.
Principles and practice of hydrotherapy: application of water in disease. 3d ed., rev. and enl. '08(Ap25) il. 8°, *$4 net. Wood.

Barus, Carl.
Condensations of vapor as induced by *nuclei* and by *ions*. 3d rept. '08(D12) $1.25; 4th rept. '10(Je18) c. figs tabs., O. pap., 75 c. Carnegie.

Barwell, J. W.
Science, the mind, revelation, the heart, of God; outcome of all the creeds. '09 (Je12) S. pap., 25 c. Jacobs & H.

Barwell, Noel.
Someone pays. '09(Ap17) D. $1.50. Lane.

Barwick, Allen J.
Manual of physiology and hygiene in primary grades, suggested outlines of oral instruction to be given by public school teachers. '09, [1910.] (My) 38 p. il. 8°, (North Carolina, Dept. of Public Instruction; educational bull.) gratis. N. C., Dept. of Pub. Instruct.
Opening exercises for public schools in North Carolina. '09, [1910.] (Ap) 32 p. 8°, (North Carolina, Dept. of Public Instruction; educational bull.) gratis. N. C., Dept. of Pub. Instruct.

Bascom, Elva Lucile.
Selected books on nature study for schools and libraries. '10(Jl16) 8°, (N. Y. State Educ. Dept. bull.) gratis. N. Y. State Educ.

BASEBALL.
Chadwick, H:, *ed.* Spalding's official base ball guide, 1908. 10 c. Am. Sports.
Evers, J: J., *and* Fullerton, H. S. Touching second. $1.25. Reilly & B.
Foster, J: B., *ed.* Spalding's official base ball guide.—Spalding's official baseball record, 1909. ea., 10 c. Am. Sports.
Heilbroner, L:, *comp.* Baseball blue book. $1. L: Heilbroner.
Howe baseball scoring record. 10 c. Howe & B.
McGillicuddy, C. How to play base-ball. pap., 25 c. Barse & H.
McGraw, J: J. Scientific baseball. 10 c. R: K. Fox.
Murnane, T. H. How to play base ball. 10 c. Am. Sports.
National Amateur Playground Ball Association of the United States. Official handbook. 10 c. Am. Sports.
Spalding's official metropolitan baseball book. 10 c. Spalding.
Spink, A. H: National game. $1.50. Nat. Game.
Sullivan, J. E: How to catch. 10 c. Am. Sports.
Who's who and what's what in baseball. 25 c. Klump.
Wray, J. E:, *ed.* How to play first base. 10 c.—How to play shortstop. 10 c.—How to play third base. 10 c. Am. Sports.

Base-ball ballads. Rice, G. $1. G. Rice.
Baseball boys of Lakeport. Stratemeyer, E: †$1.25. Lothrop, L. & S.

Basel, Edm.
Poems. '08(Je13) T. 75 c. Nazareth Trade Sch.
Songs and ballads; Walter and Lilian. '09 (Ag28) S. pap. (Add. pubs. for price.) Nazareth Trade Sch.

Bashford, H: Howarth.
Pilgrim's march. '09(Mr6) c. D. †$1.50. Holt.

Bashford, Herbert.
At the shrine of song; with introd. by G: Wharton James. '09(Jl) c. 128 p. por. 12°, *$1.25 net. Whitaker & R.

Bashford, Bp. Ja. Whitford.
China centennial documents. v. 1, The awakening of China; v. 2, The healing art in China. '08(D19) v. 1, D.; v. 2, O. (Not for sale.) Bd. For. Miss. M. E. Ch.

Bashore, Harvey Brown, M.D.
Sanitation of recreation camps and parks. '08(Je20) c. il. 12°, $1. Wiley.
Basil, the page. Whitham, G. F. †$1.25. Dodge.
Basily-Callimaki, Mme. de.
J.-B. Isabey, sa vie—son temps, 1767-1855; suivi du catalogue de l'œuvre gravée par et d'apres Isabey. '09(D18) il. pors. facsims., F. pap., *$80 net. Lemcke.
Basis of ascendancy. Murphy, E. G. **$1.50 net. Longmans.
Basis of musical pleasure. Gehring, A. $1.50. Putnam.
Baskerville, C:
General inorganic chemistry. '09(D18) 12°, $1.50. Heath.
—, and Curtis, Rob. W.
Lab'y exercises to be used in conjunction with General inorganic chemistry. '09 (D18) c. il. 12°, 40 c. Heath.
—, and Curtman, L: J.
Course in qualitative chemical analysis. '10 (D31) 8°, $1.40 net. Macmillan.
—, and Estabrooke, W: Ludlow.
Progressive problems in general chemistry. '10(D3) c. 12°, 90 c. Heath.
BASKET BALL.
Berensen, S., *ed.* Spaulding's official women's basket ball guide. 10 c. Am. Sports.
Clapp, A. B. Collegiate basket ball rules. 15 c. Univ. Pub.
Smith, T: H. Official basket ball guide and Protective Association rules for 1908-'09. 10 c. R: K. Fox.
Basket willow culture. Mell, C. D. 25 c. C. D. Mell.
Basket woman. Austin, *Mrs.* M. H. 60 c. Houghton M.
BASKETRY.
Barrett, S: A. Pomo Indian basketry. $1.75. Univ. of Cal.
Mason, O. T. Anyam gila (mad weave): Malaysian type of basket work.—Vocab. of Malaysian basket-work. (Add. Superintendent for price.) U. S., Supt. of Docs.
Turner, L. W. Basket maker. 75 c. Davis Press.
Baskett, G: T.
See Bedichek, Una.
Basley, Mrs. A.
Poultry book; tells you what to do and how to do it. '08, [1909.] (F) 192 p. il. por. 8°, $1. A. Basley.
Western poultry book. '10(Je4) c. il. por. 8°, $1. A. Basley.
Basmajian, Krikor Hagop.
Life in the Orient. '10(Je18) c. il. pors. 8°, $1 net. Am. Tr.
Basore, J: W:
Scholia on hypokrisis in the Commentary of Donatus. '08(S5) 8°, pap., gratis. Johns Hopkins.
BASQUE LANGUAGE.
See Language.
Bass, C: Cassedy.
See Dock, G:
Bass, E: Cary.
Miss Marshall's boys. '10(Mr5) c. D. $1. Badger.
Bass, F. H.
Outlines of the hist. of medicine. [1910.] (Mr) *$6 net. W: R. Jenkins.
Formerly published by E. R. Pelton.
Bass, W: L:
Dutch standard in the U. S. tariff law, 1909, H. R. 1438; to the Hon. Sen. Reed Smoot, from W. C. Bass, July 1, 1909. '09(O) 16 p. 8°, pap. (Add. Superintendent for price.) U. S., Supt. of Docs.
Bass, W: Wallace.
Rhymes and jingles. '09, [1910.] (Ap) c. 48 p. 8°, 50 c. W: W. Bass.
BASS.
Harris, W: C., *and* Bean, T. H. The basses, fresh-water and marine. $3 net. Stokes.
Jordan, D: S., *and* Richardson, R. E. Review of the surranidæ. Gov. Pr. Off.
Bassler, Anthony.
Diseases of the stomach and upper alimentary tract. '10(O) c. 18+3-836 p. il. 8°, $6. Davis.
References at end of chapters.
Bassler, Ray Smith.
Cement resources of Virginia, west of the Blue Ridge; with an introd. chapter on the materials and manufacture of hydraulic cements, by Edn. C. Eckel. '09, [1910.] (Ap) 12+309 p. il. map, 4°, (Virginia, Geological Survey, bull.) (Add. pubs. for price.) Univ. of Va.
Bibliography (3 p.).
Basswood (*tilia Americana*). '09(Je) 3 p. 8°, (U. S., Dept. of Agriculture, forest service, forest planting leaflet.) pap. (Add. Superintendent for price.)
Bastiat, Frederic.
Fallacies of protection; being the Sophismes economiques of Frederic Bastiat; tr. from the 5th ed. of the French by Patrick Ja. Stirling; with introd. note by H. H. Asquith. '09(Ag21) 8°, *$1 net. Putnam.
Bastile ser. D. Lippincott.
—Stevenson. Path of honor. $1.50.
Bastin, Edson Sunderland, and Davis, C: Albert.
Peat deposits of Maine, prep. in co-operation with the Maine State Survey Commission. '09(My) 127 p. figs. il. O. pap. U. S., Supt. of Docs.
BASUTOLAND, South Africa.
Lagden, *Sir* G. Y. The Basutos. In 2 v. $6 special net. Appleton.
BAT-BALL.
Pertuch, R. German schlagball (German bat-ball). 15 c. McVey.
Bataille de dames. Scribe, A. E. 30 c. Am. Bk.
Bataille (La) de Waterloo. *See* Hugo, Victor.
Batailles de terre et de mer. Bouët-Willaumez, *Comte* L. E. 60 c. Oxford Univ.
Batchelder, Ernest Allen.
Design in theory and practice. '10(S17) c. il. O. $1.75 net. Macmillan.
Principles of design. 3d ed. '08(Ag1) c. il. O. $3. Inland Pr.
Batchelor, D: Oren.
Unstrung bow; story of conquest. '10 (O22) c. 286 p. $1.20 net. Sherman, F.

Batdorf, J: W.
Why pay tribute? The limitation of income, remedy for watered capitalization, progressive income tax, with tabulation. '08(Ag) c. 112 p. 8°, 25 c. Volunteer.

Bate, Herbert N.
Healthful spirit; with introd. by the Bp. of London. '10(F19) D. *90 c. net. Longmans.

BATE, William Brimage.
Marshall, P. Life of William B. Bate, citizen, soldier and statesman. $1.25. P. Marshall.

Bateman, Matilda Eugenie Shea.
Light that never fails. '10(My14) c. 12°, 60 c. Cochrane.

Baterden, J. R.
Timber. '09(Je19) il. 8°, (Westminster ser.) *$2 net. Van Nostrand.

Bates, Arlo.
Intoxicated ghost, and other stories. '08 (My2) c. D. †$1.50. Houghton, M. & Co.

Bates, C. L.
Federal procedure at law: a treatise on the procedure in suits at common law in the circuit courts of the United States. 2 v. '08(O) c. O. shp., $12. Flood.

Bates, Clement.
Pleading, practice parties and forms under the code; with full authorities from all states using a code, together with decisions from the common law practice. 3 v. '08(F) c. 8°, per set, $18. W. H. Anderson.

Bates, Emily Katharine.
Do the dead depart?, and other questions. '09(My1) c. D. $1.50. Dodge.
Psychical science and Christianity. '10 (Ja8) c. 12°, $1.50. Dodge.

Bates, Ernest Sutherland.
Study of Shelley's drama, "The Cenci." '08 (Ap11) 8°, (Columbia Univ. studies in English.) pap., *$1 net. Lemcke.

Bates, Esther W.
Engaging Janet: a farce. '08(N7) D. pap., 15 c. Penn Pub. Co.

Bates, Fk. Amasa, ["Matasiso."]
Camping and cooking. '09(My8) c. il. S. *75 c. net. Ball Pub.

Bates, H. W.
Naturalist on the Amazon. '10(Ap2) il. 16°, (Everyman's lib.) 35 c. net; leath., 70 c. net. Dutton.

Bates, Ja. H:
Miller's guide book. '10(Jl) c. 64 p. 8°, $1. Dixie Miller.

BATES, Lewis Benton.
Harvey, *Mrs.* E. M. B. My wonder book; pages from the life of Lewis Benton Bates. $1. Chapple Pub.

Bates, Lindon Wallace.
Retrieval at Panama: [Panama canal.] '08 (Mr.) 554 p. il. maps, 8°, $5. Technical Lit.

Bates, Lindon Wallace, jr.
Russian road to China. '10(Je4) c. il. fold. map, O. $3 net. Houghton M.

Bates, Lois.
Fairy tale of a dog and an old dame by the sea. '08(Jl11) S. (Longmans' infant fairy-readers.) 15 c. Longmans.

Bates, Mrs. Marg. Holmes Ernsperger.
Paying the piper. '10(D31) c. front. D. $1.50. B'way Pub.
Silas Kirkendown's sons. '08(D12) il. 12°, $1.50. C. M. Clark.

Bates, Putnam A.
Equipment of country houses with electricity repr.; from the *Journal of the Franklin Institute.* '09(Jl17) il. 8°, pap., 25 c. Franklin Inst.

Bates, Ralph Orr.
Billy and Dick from Andersonville prison to the White House. '10(Jl) c. 99+3 p. il. pors. 12°, pap., 50 c. Sentinel Pub., (Cal.)

Bates, Mrs. Virginia Breckinridge.
How may I know the voice of God in my soul? '08(F1) c. D. 35 c. Presb. Bd.

Bateson, W:
Mendel's principles of heredity. '09(My15) il. pors. figs. 8°, *$3.50 net. Putnam.
Methods and scope of genetics: inaugural lecture del. Oct. 23, 1908. '09(My) 12°, 50 c. Putnam.

Batey, J:
Motor car and its engine; pract. treatise for motor engineers, incl. owners and chauffeurs. '10(Mr26) 16°, *$1.50 net. Jacobs.

BATH COUNTY, Va.
See Virginia.

BATHS.
Gerhard, W: P. Modern baths and bath houses. *$3 net. Wiley.

Batiffol, Louis.
Marie de Médicis and the French court in the XVIIth century; tr. from the French by Mary King; ed. by H. W. Carless Davis Ball. '08(Je20) por. O. *$2 net. Scribner.

BATRACHIA.
See Frogs.

BATS.
Grinnell, J. Two heretofore unnamed wrens; Savannah sparrow; second record of the spotted bat (*Euderma maculatum.*) 15 c. Univ. of Cal.

Batson, Henrietta M., [Mrs. Stephen Batson.]
Summer garden of pleasure. '09(Ap10) il. O. $3.50. McClurg.

Batson, Mrs. Stephen.
See Batson, Henrietta M.

Battell, Jos.
Ellen; or, the whisperings of an old pine: [talks about science.] v. 2. 2d ed., rev. and enl. '08(My16) c. il. 8°, $3; mor., $4. Am. Pub. Co., (Vt.)
New physics; sound. '09(O2) c. figs. O. $1.25. Am. Pub. Co. (Vt.)
—, comp. American stallion register, incl. all stallions prominent in the breeding of the American roadster, trotter and pacer from the earliest records to 1902; and this includes nearly all imported English thoroughbreds, and their more distinguished get; together with many of the English stallions from which they are descended. '09(My) c. il. 4°, $5. Am. Pub. Co., (Vt.)

Batten, J: Mullin.
Over the waters to Edinburgh town. '10 (D) c. 246 p. por. 12°, $2. J: M. Batten.

Batten, S: Zane, D.D.
Christian state; the state, democracy and Christianity. '09(Jl17) c. D. *$1.50 net. Am. Bapt.
Working temperance programme; published for the Social Service Commission of the Northern Baptist Convention. '10 (Mr5) c. 12°, (Social service ser.) 15 c. Am. Bapt.

Batten's agricultural directory: directory of the agricultural press of the U. S. and Canada, together with detailed repts. of farm products and values by states and provinces. '08(N) c. 5-271 p. 8°, $1. Batten.

BATTERIES.
See Electric batteries.

Battershall, Fletcher Williams.
See New York. Law of domestic relations.

Battle, Herbert B., and Gascoyne, W: J:
Chemical conversion tables for use in the analysis of commercial fertilizers, cotton seed, iron and food products, etc. '09 (D) c. 78 p. 12°, $2.50. Williams & W.

Battle, Jesse M.
Why I am not a Roman Catholic, an answer to a letter received from the Rev. Father —— —. ———, S.J. '09(D) c. 294 p. 12°, $1.50. J. M. Battle.

Battle, Mrs. Laura Eliz. Lee.
Forget-me-nots of the Civil War; romance containing reminiscences and original letters of two Confederate soldiers. '09(O) c. il. por.. 8°, $1.50. J. M. Battle.

Battle (The). Moffett, C. †$1.50. G: W. Dillingham.

Battle Creek Sanitarium diet list. Kellogg, J: H. 25 c. Modern Medicine.

Battle for the Pacific. Stevens, R. †$1.25. Harper.

Battle of the microbes: nature's fight for pure water; clear description of the methods of sewage disposal. '08(D19) il. O. pap., gratis. Merchants' Assoc.

Battle of the strong. Parker, *Sir* G. $1.50. Harper.

BATTLE OF THE WILDERNESS.
See Wilderness, Battle of the.

Battle ship's order book. Ho, A. B. $1. U. S. Naval Inst.

BATTLES.
Creasy, *Sir* E: S. Decisive battles of the world. $1.75; $3.50. Lamb Pub.
Creasy, *Sir* E: S. Fifteen decisive battles of the world. 35 c. net; 70 c. net. Dutton.
Dawson, L. H. Book of battles and sieges. 50 c. Dutton.
Hart, A. B., *and others.* Decisive battles of America. $1.50. Harper.
Steele, M. F. American campaigns. (Add. Superintendent for price.) U. S., Supt. of Docs.
See also Antietam;—Brandywine;—Bull Run;—Bunker Hill; — Gettysburg; — Guilford Court House;—Leipzig campaign;—Long Island (Battle of);—Louisburg (Siege of);—Point Pleasant (Battle of);—Waterloo;—Wilderness, Battle of the.

Baty, T:
International law. '09(O30) O. *$2.75 net. Longmans.

BATZ, *Baron* de.
Gosselin, L. L. T. Gascon royalist in revolutionary Paris. 3.50 net. Dodd.

Baudelaire, Charles.
Poems in prose; tr. by Arth. Symons. '09 (D) 32°, (Ideal ser. of little masterpieces.) *50 c. net; *$1 net. T: B. Mosher.

Baudot, Jules.
Lectionary, its sources and history; tr. from the French by Ambrose Cator. '10 (D) 8+214 p. 8°, $1 net. Herder.
Roman breviary, its sources and history; tr. from the French by a priest of the diocese of Westminster. '09(A7) 8°, *$1 net. Herder.

Baugh, F: H:, and Schmeisser, W: Christian.
Theory and practice of estate accounting for accountants, lawyers, [etc.] '10(Mr) O. $4. Curlander.

Baughman, Mrs. Nanny Randolph Ball.
True way of life: [talks on true marriage.] '07, '08(Je) c. 108 p. pors. $1. N. R. B. Baughman.

Baum, Lyman Fk.
American fairy tales. '08(O24) c. O. †$1.25. Bobbs-M.
Dorothy and the wizard in Oz. '08(S19) c. O. $1.25. Reilly & B.
Emerald city of Oz. '10(D31) c. il. 8°, bds., $1.25. Reilly & B.
Juvenile speaker. '10(D10) il. 8°, $1.25. Reilly & B.
Road to Oz. '09(Ag7) c. il. D. $1.25. Reilly & B.

Baum, Mary Eliza Davis, [Mrs. C. L. Baum.]
Studies in divine science. '09(O2) c. D. *$1 net. C. L. Baum.

Baum, Millicent.
Little helper: supplementary primer to accompany "The rational method in reading." '08(Ap11) c. il. D. 28 c.—Bk. 2 (Ag1) 32 c. Silver.

Baum, W: L., M.D., and Moyer, Harold N:, M.D., eds.
Skin and venereal diseases; miscellaneous topics. '08, [1909.] (Mr) 248. p. il. 12°, (Pract. medicine ser.) $1.25. Year Bk.

Baumann, F:, M.D.
Gonorrhea, its diagnosis and treatment. '08 (F1); 2d ed., rev. '10(Mr) c. il. 8°, ea., $1.50. Appleton.

Baumbach, Rudolph.
Ausgewählte märchen und gedichte; ed., with introd., notes, exercises and vocab., by Edn. Manley. '10(Ag20) c. por. S. 45 c. Ginn.
Das Habichtsfräulein: dorfgeschichte aus dem Thüringer wald; with introd., notes, vocab. and composition exercises, by Dr. Morton C. Stewart. '09(Je12) c. front. S. 40 c. Holt.
Der schwiegersohn: eine schneidergeschichte; with notes, vocab., and illustrative exercises, by Otto Heller. '08(Jl11) c. S. 40 c. Holt.
Der schwiegersohn; nouvelle; with introd., notes, exercises, and vocab. by Hedwig Hulme. '09(O23) c. por. (International modern language ser.) 40 c. Ginn.

Baumgarten, Paul Maria.
Henry Charles Lea's historical writings: critical inquiry into their method and merit. '09(Ja16) c. D. *90 c. net. Wagner.

Bavinck, Herman.
Philosophy of revelation: the Stone lectures for 1908-1909, Princeton Theological Seminary. '09(F20) c. O. **$2 net. Longmans.

Bawden, H: Heath.
Principles of pragmatism. '10(Mr19) c. **$1.50 net. Houghton M.

Bawr, Sophie de Champgrand, Baroness de.
Michel Perrin; ed. by F. G. Harriman. '09 (O16) S. (Shorter French texts.) *25 c. net. Crowell.

Bax, Ernest Belfort.
Roots of reality: being suggestions for a philosophical reconstruction. '08(Mr14) O. *$2 net. B. W. Dodge.
See also Morris, W:

Baxter, Gregory Paul, and others.
Researches upon the atomic weights of cadmium, manganese, bromine, lead, arsenic, iodine, silver, chromium, and phosphorus. '10(D17) il. O. (Carnegie Inst. of Washington pubs.) pap., $2. Carnegie.

Baxter, J. S.
America: her grandeur and her beauty. 25th ed. '08, [1909.] (Ja) c. 420 p. il. f°, (America ser.) pap., $12.50. Union Bk.

Baxter, R:
Excerpt from Reliquiæ Baxterianæ; or, Mr. Richard Baxter's narrative of the most memorable passages of his life and times, also an essay by Sir Ja. Stephen on Richard Baxter; ed., with preface, notes and appendices, by Fs. John, Bishop of Chester. '10(D10) pors. O. $1.75 net. Longmans.
Saints' everlasting rest. New ed., ed. by W: Young. '09(Mr13) por. O. *$2.50 net. Lippincott.

Baxter, W:, jr.
Hydraulic elevators; their design, construction, operation, care and management. '10(Je4) c. il. O. $2.50 net. McGraw-H.
Switchboards for power, light and railway service, direct and alternating currents, high and low tension. '10(Je4) c. il. 8°, $1.50. Henley.

BAYARD, *Chevalier de,* (Pierre de Terrail.)
Andrews, A. G., *ed.* Story of Bayard. $1.50 net. Lane.

Bayard of India. Trotter, L. *35 c. net; **70 c. net. Dutton.

Baylee, J: Tyrrell.
Gazetteer of the world. '08(F8) 32°, (Dutton's miniature reference lib.) leath., 50 c. Dutton.

Bayley, Fk. Tappan, D.D.
Can the modern man pray? '09(Mr13) pap., 10 c. Y. M. C. A.
"Little ten-minutes"; or, a pastor's talks with his children. 2d ed., rev. and enl. '09(D11) c. por. D. *$1 net. Revell.

Bayley, Harold.
New light on the Renaissance; displayed in contemporary emblems. '09(My22) il. 8°, *$4 net. Dutton.

Baylies, E:
See New York [State.] Bender's justices' manual of civil and criminal law.

Baylies, Edn.
Test questions for law students on law, equity, practice, pleadings, and evidence, with answers and references; also, rules for admission of attorneys in the state of New York. '08(O) c. 6+444 p. O. (Add. pubs. for price.) M. Bender.

Bayliss, Mrs. Clara Kern.
Little cliff dweller. '09(Ag7) il. 16°, 35 c. Pub. Sch. Pub.
Old man Coyote. '08(O10) c. il. D. †$1. Crowell.
Two little Algonkin lads. '07, [1909.] (O) c. il. fold map, 12°, 50 c. Educ. Pub.

Bayliss, W: Maddock.
Nature of enzyme action: [treatise on the chemical compounds that cause fermentation.] '08(N21) figs. O. (Monographs on biochemistry.) bds., *$1 net. Longmans.

Bayne, Mrs. Mary Addams.
Bluegrass and wattle; or, the man from Australia. '09(D18) c. il. 12°, $1.25. Standard Pub.

Bayne, S: Gamble.
Fantasy of Mediterranean travel. '09(O23) c. il. por. O. **$1.25 net. Harper.
Quicksteps through Scandinavia; with a retreat from Moscow. '08(Je20) c. il. sq. O. **$1.25 net. Harper.

BAYOU LACOMB, La.
See Indians.

Bazancourt, Baron de.
Secrets of the sword; tr. from the orig. French by C. F. Clay. '08(D12) il. 12°, *$1.25 net. Macmillan.

Bazin, René.
Coming harvest, (Le blé qui lève;) tr. by Edna K. Hoyt. '08(S19) D. †$1.25. Scribner.
Contes choisis; sel. and ed., with notes and vocab., by Victor E. François. '08(Ja18) S. (Modern lang. ser.) 35 c. Heath.
Italians of to-day; tr. by W: Marchant. '08(N21) c. D. **$1.25 net. Holt.
La barrière. '10(Jl30) 12°, pap., $1. Brentano's.
The barrier (La barrière); tr. by Mary D. Frost. '10(S17) c. D. $1 net. Scribner.
The nun, (*L'isolée;*) from the French. '08 (My16) O. $1. Scribner.
Redemption, ("De toute son âme;") tr. by A. S. Rappaport. '08(Ag8) D. †$1.50. Scribner.
"This, my son," (Les Noellets;) tr. by Dr. A. S. Rappoport. '09(Mr6) c. D. †$1.25. Scribner.

Be good to yourself. Marden, O. S. $1 net. Crowell.

"Be of good cheer." Van Dyke, J. S. $1. J. S. Van Dyke.

Be strong. Pennington, J. G., *ed.* 50 c. Dodge.

Beach, Chandler B.
See Cornyn, Juan Humberto.

—, and McMurry, Fk. Morton, eds.
New student's reference work for teachers, students and families. '09(N) c. 4 v., il. (partly col.) pors. maps, 8°, subs., $16.50. Compton.

Beach, Rev. C: Fisk.
Individual evangelism, Christian witnessing and work, the call of Christ to the laity. '08(My23) por. 8°, *$1 net. Allen, L. & S.

Beach, C: Worth, and Preston, P. J.
Irrigation in Colorado. '10(S) 48 p. fold. map, 8°, (U. S., Dept. of Agriculture, Office of Experiment Stations, bull.)

Beach, E: Latimer.
Annapolis first classman. '10(D3) c. il. D. $1.25. Penn Pub. C.o
Annapolis second classman. '09(N13) c. il. D. †$1.25. Penn Pub. Co.
Annapolis youngster; il. by Fk. T. Merrill. '08(Ag8) c. 12°, †$1.25. Penn Pub. Co.
Midshipman Ralph Osborn at sea; story of the U. S. navy. '10(N5) c. il. D. $1.50. Wilde.
Ralph O'sborn—midshipman at Annapolis; story of life at the U. S. Naval Academy. '09(O9) c. il. D. †$1.50. Wilde.

Beach, Rex Ellingwood.
Going some; romance of strenuous affection suggested by the play by Rex Beach and Paul Armstrong. '10(My14) c. il. D. $1.25. Harper.
Silver horde. '09(S25) c. il. D. †$1.50. Harper.
The barrier. '08(Mr28) c. il. D. †$1.50. Harper.

Beach, Elmer H:, and Thorne, W. W., eds.
International business encyclop.; up-to-date, down-to-the-minute business dictionary. '10(Jl30) c. il. pors. $4. E. H: Beach.

Beach patrol. Drysdale, W: †$1.50. Wilde.

Beacon biographies; ed. by M. A. DeWolfe Howe. T. 50 c. net. Small.
—Ford. George Washington.
—Macy. Edgar Allan Poe.
—Swift. Benjamin Franklin.
—Whitlock. Abraham Lincoln.

Beacon ser.; a graded course of study for the Sunday-School. 8°. Unitarian S. S.
—Billings. Movements and men of Christian history. 45 c.; 35 c.; 65 c.
—Fairfield. Stories from the New Testament. 35 c.; 25 c.; 65 c.
—Lane. First book of religion. 35 c.; 25 c.; 60 c.
—Park. Jesus of Nazareth. 40 c.; 30 c.; 65 c.
—Parker. Stories from the Old Testament. 35 c.; 25 c.; 65 c.
—Secrist. Comparative studies in religion. 45 c.; 35 c.; 65 c.
—Sunderland. Bible and the Bible country. 60 c.
—Wilson. Bible as literature. 45 c.; 35 c.

Beaconsfield, Earl of.
See Disraeli, B:

Beadle, Maude Lenna Streeter, [Mrs. W. M. Beadle.]
Frogville wheelman. '09, [1910.] (Ap) 39 p. il. 8°, $1. M. L. S. Beadle.

Beadle, Mrs. W. M.
See Beadle, Maude Lenna Streeter.

Beadnell, H. J. Llewellyn.
Egyptian oasis: an account of the oasis of Kharga, in the Lybian Desert, with special reference to its history, physical geography, and water supply. '09(Ag21) il. maps, 8°, $3.50. Dutton.

Beadnell, Maria.
See Winter, *Mrs.* Maria Beadnell.

Beahan, Willard.
Field practice of railway location. [2d ed.] '10(Ap9) c. il. plans, 8°, $3. Engineering News.

Beak, G. B.
Indexing and précis writing. '08(Ag8) 16°, *50 c. net; [also] A key to indexing and précis writing. *50 c. net. Macmillan.

Beal, Ja. Hartley.
Prescription practice and general dispensing. '08(Mr14) c. il. O. $1.50. J. H. Beal; Harper.

Beal, Leonard Hathaway.
Poems, by L. H. Beal, with a few choice selections by other authors. '09, [1910.] c. 225 p. por. 12°, $1. Merrill & W.

Bealby, J: T.
Canada. '09(D4) il. in col. 12°, (Peeps at many lands ser.) 75 c. Macmillan.
Fruit ranching in British Columbia. '09 (D4) il. 12°, *$1.50 net. Macmillan.

Beale, Dorothea.
Addresses to teachers. '10(F19) D. 50 c. Longmans.

Beale, J. Fk.
Abraham Lincoln; a brief biography. '09 (S) 48 p. il. por. 16°, $1. Strawbridge & C.

Beale, Jos. H:
Collection of cases on the measure of damages. 2d ed. '09(O) c. O. $3.50. Little, B. & Co.
Selection of cases on carriers and other bailment and quasi-bailment services. '09 (N) c. 8+634 p. 8°, hf. shp., $4. Harvard Law.

Beale-Demy, S. Sophia, ed.
Recollections of a spinster aunt. '09(Jl31) 8°. (Add. pubs. for price.) P. R. Reynolds.

Beall, Dorothy Landers.
Poems. '10(Je) 131 p. 8°, $1.50 net. M. Kennerley.

Beall, Mrs. Mary Stevens.
Story of the Washington coachee and of the Powel coach which is now at Mount Vernon. '08, [1909.] (Mr) c. 74 p. il. 8°. (Priv. pr.) Neale.

Beall, Col. Ninian.
See Moses, Zebina.

Beam, Ella.
A family history [Hyder family.] '09(D) c. 44 p. 8°, 50 c. Carroll Record Co.

BEAMS.
See **Strength of materials.**

Bean, Burt Clifford, [C. A. Burt.]
Making the business pay. '09(Je19) c. 12°, $1. Domestic Engineering.

Bean, C. E. W.
On the wool track. '10(N19) il. D. $1.50 net. Lane.

Bean, Rob. Bennett, M.D.
Racial anatomy of the Philippine Islanders. '10(D31) c. il. 8°, $2 net. Lippincott.

Bean, Tarleton H.
See Harris, W: C.

Bean, W: Jos.
Royal Botanic Gardens, Kew; with introd. by Sir W: Thiselton Dyer. '08(D5) il. *$7.50 net. Cassell.

BEANS.
Wait, C: E. Studies on the digestibility and nutritive value of legumes. 25 c. U. S., Supt. of Docs.

BEAR.
Osgood, W. H. Peculiar bear from Alaska. 50 c. Field Museum.
Wright, W: H: The black bear. $1 net.—Grizzly bear; narrative of a hunter-naturalist. **$1.50 net. Scribner.

BEAR FAMILY.
See Genealogies: Bare, D. M.

Beard, Adelia Belle.
See Beard, Lina.

Beard, A: Field.
Crusade of brotherhood; hist. of the American Missionary Association. '09(N6) c. pors. O. *$1.25 net. Pilgrim Press.
Story of John Frederic Oberlin. '09(N13) c. por. O. *$1.25 net. Pilgrim Press.

Beard, C: Austin.
American government and politics. '10 (Jl2) c. D. $2.10 net. Macmillan.
Politics: [a lecture.] '08(N21) c. 8°, pap. (Add. pubs. for price.) Columbia Univ.
See also Robinson, Ja. Harvey.
—, comp. Readings in American government and politics. '09(O2) c. O. **$1.90 net. Macmillan.

Beard, C: Heady.
Ophthalmic surgery; treatise on surgical operations pertaining to the eye and its appendages, with chapters on para-operative technic and management of instruments. '10(F) c. 9+674 p. il. 8°, $5. Blakiston.

Beard, Dan. Carter.
Animal book and camp-fire stories; il. by the author. New and enl. ed. '10(Jl30) 8°, $1.75 net. Moffat.
Boy pioneers; sons of Daniel Boone. '09 (O23) c. O. **$2 net. Scribner.
—, ed. *See* Browne, Bellmore H.

Beard, Ja. Carter.
Billy Possum. '09(O30) c. il. O. bds., †$1. Stokes.

Beard, Ja. Thom.
Mine gases and explosions. '08(Ja11) il. 12°, **$3 net. Wiley.

Beard, Lina and Adelia Belle.
Little folks' handy book. '10(Je4) c. il. 8°, 75 c. Scribner.

Beard, T: Fs.
Biblische symbole; oder, die Bibel in bildern für jung und alt; aus dem englischen übersetzt von Rev. W. A. Schutte; vorwort von J. L. Nuelsen. '09 (Jl) c. 182 p. il. 8°, $1.75; $2.25; $2.50. J. A. Hertel.

BEARDSLEY, Aubrey.
Ross, R. Aubrey Beardsley. *$1.25 net. Lane.

Beardsley, E: J: Gillespie.
See Hare, Hobart Amory.

Bearings. '08(My23) c. il. 8°, (Machinery's reference ser.) pap., 25 c. Indust. Press.

Bearne, Mrs. Catherine Mary Charlton.
Four fascinating French women; the Comtesse de Flahaut, the Duchesse de Duras, the Duchesse de Berry, the Princess Bonaparte. '10(D10) il. 8°, $3.50 net. Brentano's.

Bearne, Mrs. Catherine Mary Charlton.—*Cont.*
Royal quartette. '09(Jl3) pors. 8°, *$3 net. Brentano's.

Bearne, Rev. D:
Barnaby Bright. 2 v. '08, [1909.] (S) il. ea., *80 c. net. Benziger.
Claud Denvil, artist: [12 short novels.] '09 (Ja16) 12°, *$1 net. Herder.
Jack South and some other Jacks. '09 (Mr27) 8°, $1. Herder.
Our Lady's lutenist, and other stories. '10(O22) c. D. 65 c. Benziger.
Romance of the silver shoon; story of the sixteenth century. '09(D11) c. D. 85 c. Benziger.
Sheer pluck, and other stories of the bright ages. '08(F8) c. D. 85 c. Benziger.

Beary, Harriet Rebecca.
Individual development of man: discussion of the influence of labor on the evolution of the individual. '09(Ag7) 12°, $1. Hartman Pub.

Beasley, H:
Book of prescriptions; with an index of diseases and remedies; with an introd. by Arth. Latham. 9th ed., rewritten by E. W. Latham. '08, [1909.] (Mr) 16+366 p. 16°, *$2 net. Blakiston.

Beasley's Christmas party. Tarkington, N. B. †$1.25. Harper.

Beast (The). Lindsey, B: B. $1.50 net. Doubleday, P.

Beasts and men. Hagenbeck, C. *$3.50 net. Longmans.

Beasts of business. Moncrieff, A. R. H. $1.50. Macmillan.

BEATITUDES.
See **Sermon on the Mount.**

Beatrice. Gordon, G: A. 50 c. Pilgrim Press.

Beatrice. Stellwagen, C. F. (Priv. pr.) W. F. Roberts Co.

Beatrice; legend of our Lady; written in the Netherlands in the fourteenth century; tr. by Harold De Wolf Fuller. '10(F12) c. T. bds., *50 c. net. Harvard Co-op.

Beatrice Sumpter. Cheatham, C. V. $1.50. C. M. Clark.

Beatrice the Sixteenth. Clyde, I. $1.50. Macmillan.

Beattie, Ja. Martin, M.D., and Dickson, W. E. Carnegie, M. D.
Text-book of pathology. v. 1, General pathology. '08, [1909.] (Mr); v. 2, Special pathology. '09(Je) il. 8°, ea., *$5 net. Blakiston.

Beattie, W: Renwick.
Onion culture. '09(Je) 36 p. il. 8°, (U. S., Dept. of Agriculture, farmers' bull.) pap.
Peanuts. '09(Je) 40 p. il. 8°, (U. S., Dept. of Agriculture, farmers' bull.) pap. (Add. Superintendent for price.)
Sweet potatoes. '09(F20) il. 8°, (U. S., Dept. of Agriculture; farmers' bulletin.) pap., 5 c. U. S., Supt. of Docs.

BEATTY FAMILY.
See Genealogies (Turk, W. A. C.).

Beau Brummel. Fitch, W: C. **$1.50 net. Lane.

Beau Sabreur. Trowbridge, W: R. H. *$4.50 net. Brentano's.

Beauchamp, Harvey.
Graded Sunday school; text book on Sunday school organization and management. [1910.] (D) c. 222 p. il. plans, 12°, 75 c. S. S. Bd. So. Bapt.

Beaulieu, Paul Leroy-.
Collectivism; tr. and abr. by Sir Arth. Clay. '08(D19) 8°, *$3 net. Dutton.

Beaumont, Fs.
Knight of the burning pestle, and A king and no king; ed. by Raymond M. Alden. '10(Jl9) c. por. 16°, (Belles-lettres ser., Section 3.) 60 c. Heath.

—, and Fletcher, J:
Works; the text ed. by A. R. Waller. In 10 v. v. 5. '08(Ja11); v. 6. '09(F27); v. 7. '10(Ja29); v. 8 (Jl8); v. 9 (D17) c. D. (Cambridge Eng. classics.) ea., $1.50 net. Putnam.
Works. Variorum ed. 12 v. v. 2. '08 (D); v. 3, The faithful shepherdess, The mad lover, The loyal subject, Rule a wife and have a wife, The laws of Candy. '09 (Ja) il. 8°, ea., *$3.50 net. Macmillan.
Knight of the burning pestle; ed., with introd., notes and glossary, by Herbert S. Murch. '08(Jl4) O. (Yale studies in English.) $2.50; pap., $2. Holt.

BEAUMONT, Tex.
Standard blue book of Texas, 1908-09. Ed. de luxe of Beaumont. $5. A. J. Peeler.

Beauties of friendship. Woolard, S. F., *ed.* *50 c. net; *$1.25 net. Goldsmith-W.

Beauties of the gloaming. Fuller, H. A. $1; 30 c. H. A. Fuller.

Beautiful Bermuda. Bell, *Mrs.* E. Y. $1; 50 c. J. D. & F. R. Bell.

Beautiful children. McFall, C. H. **$5 net. Dodd.

Beautiful England ser. il. O. $1.25. Estes.
—Bradley. English lakes.
—Danks. Canterbury
—How. Oxford
—Jerrold. Shakespeareland.
—Mitton. The Thames.
—Thomas. Windsor Castle.

Beautiful flowers and how to grow them. Wright, H. J. $8 net. Dodge.

Beautiful necessity. Bragdon, C. $2. Manas Press.

Beautiful queen. Steele, F. M. F. $3.50 net. Dodd.

Beautiful rebel. Campbell, W: W. $1.50. Doran.

Beautiful thoughts from John Ruskin. Ruskin, J: $1. Pott.

BEAUTY (*in art*).
See Æsthetics.

BEAUTY (*personal*).
Burnham, E. Colored charts of the E. Burnham system of beauty culture. $1.50. E. Burnham.
Henrich, H. C. Types of California beauties. $50. H. Heywood.
Hubbard, *Mrs.* S. A. Duty of being beautiful. 50 c. McClurg.
Max, J. Hdbk. of cosmetics. $1 net. Treat.

BEAUTY (*personal*).—*Continued.*
Mixter, M. Health and beauty hints. $1. Cupples & L.
Potter, *Mrs.* C. U. Secrets of beauty and mysteries of health. **$1.75 net. P. Elder.
Saalfeld, E. Lectures on cosmetic treatment. $1.75 net. Hoeber.
See also Costume;—Girls;—Gymnastics and physical culture;—Hygiene.

Beauty (The). Woodrow, N. M. W. $1.50. Bobbs-M.

Beauty and the barge. Jacobs, W: W. 50 c. S: French.

Beauty and the Beast. *See* Lang, Andrew, *ed.*

Beauty of every day. Miller, J. R. 65 c. net. Crowell.

Beauty of God. Hood, J: *$1.25 net. Lanahan.

Beaux and the dandies. Jerrold, C. $5 net. Lane.

BEAVER.
Roberts, C: G: D. House in the water: [story of the beaver.] $1.50. Doubleday, P.

Beavers, Ja. Claudius.
Farm practice in the use of commercial fertilizers in the south Atlantic states. '10 (Jl) 24 p. tabs., 8°, (U. S., Dept. of Agriculture; farmers' bull.) Gov. Pr. Off.

Beazeley, C: Howell.
Crackerlings and caramels. '10(Mr26) c. por. S. $1; pap., 50 c. C. H. Beazley.

Bebbly. Walker, T: H. B. 60 c. Pepper Pub.

Bechdolt, F: Ritchie.
Hard rock man. '10(S3) c. D. $1 net. Moffat.
See also Hopper, Ja. Marie.

Beck, Amanda Kathryn.
Reference hand-book for nurses. 2d ed., rev. '08(D) c. 7-199 p. il. 16°, flex. leath., *$1.25 net. Saunders.

Beck, Carl R:
Nature of ore deposits; tr. and rev. by Wa. Harvey Weed. '09(Je5) il. 8°, $6. Hill Pub.

Beck, Christopher.
Strong-hand Saxon. '10(D31) il. 12°, $1. Lippincott.

Beck, Emil G., M.D.
Bismuth paste in chromic suppurations; its diagnostic importance and therapeutic value; with introd. by Carl Beck, M.D., and a chapter on its application in sinuses and diseases of the nose, by Jos. C. Beck, M.D. '10(O) 200 p. il. 8°, $2. Mosby.

Becke, G: L:
Adventures of Louis Blake. '08(N7) D. $1.50. Lippincott.
Call of the south. '08(Mr7) D. †$1.50. Lippincott.
'Neath Austral skies. '09(Je19) D. $1.50. Lippincott.

Becker, Carl Heinrich.
Christianity and Islam. '10(Ja29) 12°, (Harper's lib. of living thought.) *75 c. net. Harper.

Becker, Carl Lotus.
Hist. of political parties in the province of New York, 1760-1776. '10(My14) 8°, (Univ. of Wis., bull.; Hist. ser.) 75 c. Univ. of Wis.

Becker, Felix, ed.
See Thieme, Ulrich.

Becker, Fk. S.
Bender's code citations analyzed, 1907. '08 (Ja4) obl. Tt. pap., $1. M. Bender.
—, ed. *See* New York [State.] Village laws.

Becker, G: Ferdinand.
Age of the earth. '10(Jl) 28 p. O. (Smithsonian miscellaneous collections.) pap., 5 c. Smith. Inst.
Relations between local magnetic disturbances and the genesis of petroleum. '09 (N) 24 p. map, 8°, (U S. Geolog. Survey; bull.) (Add. Superintendent for price.)
—, and Van Orstrand, C. E., comps.
Hyperbolic functions. '09(Jl17) il. O. (Smithsonian mathematical tables.) $4. Smith. Inst.

Becker, Henrietta Katherine, and Rhoades, Lewis Addison.
Becker-Rhoades elements of German; pract. course for beginners in German. Rev. ed. '09(D11); [Rev. ed.] '09(O16) c. D. (Lake German ser.) ea., $1. Scott, F. & Co.

Becker, Neal Dow.
Road rules and the law of automobiles, with special reference to the laws of N. Y., N. J., Conn. and Mass. '10(D) c. 5+81 p. S. $1. E. W. Whitfield.

Becker, Otto Matthew.
High-speed steel; development, nature, treatment, and use of high-speed steels, together with some suggestions as to the problems involved in their use. '10(O8) c. il. 8°, $4. McGraw-H.

Becker, Tracy Chatfield, M.D.
See Witthaus, Rudolph August, *M.D.*

Becker, W: C.
Der Nietzschekultus. '09(S) 75 c. W. C. Becker.

BECKFORD, William.
Melville, L. Life and letters of William Beckford. $3.50 net. Duffield.

Beckingsale, Jennie.
Pomegranate: story of a Chinese school girl. '09, [1910.] (F) 192 p. 12°, $1. Northfield Press.

Beckoning heights. Lecky, P. F. $1.50. Neale.

Beckoning of the wand. Dease, A. $1. Herder.

Beckwith, Carmelita.
See Shaw, Adele Marie.

Beckwith, Mary Helen.
Story telling with the scissors. '08(Je13) il. obl. 12°, 50 c. M. Bradley.

Becky Compton. Jacberns, R. $1.50. Lippincott.

Becquer, Gustavo Adolfo Dominguez.
Legends, tales and poems; ed., with introd., notes, and vocab., by Everett Ward Olmsted. '08(F1) c. por. D. (Internat. modern lang. ser.) $1. Ginn.
The "rimas"; tr. [from the Spanish] by Jules Renard. '08(F29) c. D. bds., $1.25. Badger.

Becquer, Gustavo Adolfo Dominguez.—*Cont.*
Romantic legends of Spain; tr. by Cornelia Frances Bates and Katherine Lee Bates. '09(S11) c. il. O. **$1.50 net. Crowell.

Bed-time ser. 3 v. '10(D) ea., bds., 25 c. Cassell.

Bed-time stories. See Garis, Howard Roger.

Beddard, Arth. Philip, M.D., Edkins, J. S., Hill, Leonard, and others.
Pract. physiology; ed. by M. S. Pembrey. 3d ed. '10(D10) il. O. $4 net. Longmans.

Bede, The Venerable.
Ecclesiastical hist. of the English nation, and the lives of the Holy Abbots of Weremouth and Jarrow; with introd. by Vida D. Scudder and notes to the history. '10(D10) 16°, (Everyman's lib.) 35 c. net; leath., 70 c. net. Dutton.

Bedell, Edn. A., rep.
See New York [State.] *Ct. of appeals.* Repts.

Bedell, F:, and Pierce, Clarence A.
Direct and alternating current testing. '09 [1910.] (F) 275 p. il. 8°, *$2 net. Van Nostrand.

Bedell, W: Lyon D:
Practical electro-plating. '09(Ap3) c. 12°, $2. Hansom & V.

Bedford, E: J.
Introductory mechanics. '08(O10) il. S. 50 c. Longmans.

Bedford, Jessie.
See Godfrey, Eliz., *pseud.*

Bedichek, Una, and Baskett, G: Terrell.
Consolidation of rural schools with and without transportation. 2d ed., rev. by A. Caswell Ellis. '08(F1) il. O. (Univ. of Tex. bull.) pap., 25 c. Univ. of Tex.

Bédier, Joseph.
Romance of Tristram and Iseult; tr. from the French by Florence Simmonds. '10 (D3) col. il. 4°, $3.75 net, boxed. Lippincott.

BEDINGER, George Michael.
Dandridge, *Mrs.* D. B. George Michael Bedinger: a Kentucky pioneer. $2. A. S. Dandridge.

BEDOUINS.
Lees, G: R. Witness of the wilderness, the Bedawin of the desert. $1.25. Longmans.

Bee Martin, king of the birds. Lang, O. 30 c. Flanagan.

Beebe, C: W:
See Beebe, Mary Blair.

Beebe, Ella M.
Picture primer; with an introd. by C: L. Spain. '10(Ja29) c. il. D. 25 c. Am. Bk.

Beebe, Mary Blair Rice and C: W:
Our search for a wilderness; acct. of two ornithological expeditions to Venezuela and to British Guiana. '10(My14) c. il. O. $2.75 net. Holt.

Beebe, W. L.
See Reynolds, M. H.

Beech, Merwyn Worcester Howard.
Tidong dialects of Borneo; with preface and notes by Abraham Anthony Fokker. '09(Ja23) il. S. $1.75. Oxford Univ.

BEECH.
Maury, *Mrs.* S. W. The beech. 25 c. net. Lane.
Beecher, Franklin A.
Law of contracts in Michigan; exhaustively treating of internal structure, with forms. '10(S) 446 p. O. Drake Law Bk.
Beecher, Willis Judson, D.D.
Dated events of the Old Testament: presentation of Old Testament chronology. '08(F8) c. O. *$1.50 net. S. S. Times.
Beecher (Lyman) lectures. *See* Faunce, W: Herbert Perry.
Beecher-Kummer, Clare.
See Kummer, Clare Beecher-.
Beeching, Canon H: C:
William Shakespeare: player, playmaker, and poet; reply to Mr. George Greenwood, M.P. '09(My8) facsims., D. *$1 net. Lane.
Beechy. Hutten, *Baroness* B. v. †$1.50. Stokes.
Beeckman, Ross.
Last woman. '09(D4) c. il D. $1.50. W. J. Watt.
Princess Zara. '09(Ap10) c. il. D. $1.50. W. J. Watt.
Beecroft, Willey Ingraham, comp.
Who's who among the ferns. '10(Mr26) c. il. D. *$1 net. Moffat.
Who's who among the wild flowers. '10 (Ja22) c. il. D. **$1.20 net. Moffat.
Beede, C: Gould.
Reincarnated: [poem.] '09(Ja) $1.25. Newport Pub.
Soul shadows: [poems.] '08(F) c. 54 p., O. 75 c. C: G. Beede.
BEEF TRUST.
Russell, C: E: Greatest trust in the world: [beef trust.] 50 c. B. W. Dodge.
Shiel, R. R. Twenty years in hell with the beef trust. 60 c.; 50 c. R. R. Shiel.
Beeman versus Jackman. Spooner, J: C. (Add. author for price.) J: C. Spooner.
Beer, G: L:
Origins of the British Colonial system, 1578-1660. '08(O24) c. O. **$3 net. Macmillan.
BEER.
Thomann, G. American beer; glimpses of its hist. and description of its manufacture. 50 c. U. S. Brewers' Assoc.
See also Liquors.
Beerbohm, Max.
Yet again. '10(F19) D. *$1.50 net. Lane.
Beers, Clifford Whittingham.
The after care of the insane: hist. of its development and a discussion of its nature and value as an agency in the prevention of mental disorders, together with a plan for its pract. application in Connecticut and other chosen fields. '09, [1910.] (Mr) c. 45 p. 8°, pap., gratis. C. W. Beers.
Bibliography (2 p.).
Mind that found itself; autobiography. '08 (Mr28); 2d ed. '10(Jl30) c. O. ea., $1.50 net. Longmans.
Beers, H: Augustin.
Milton's tercentenary; address del. before the Modern Language Club of Yale University on Milton's three hundredth birthday. '10(Jl9) D. bds., 50 c. Yale Univ.

Beers, H: Augustin.—*Continued.*
Ways of Yale in the consulship of Plancus. New and further enl. ed. '10(Jl2) c. il. S. $1.20 net. Holt.
BEES.
Alexander, E. W. Writings on practical bee culture. 50 c. A. I. Root.
Buttel-Reepen, H. v. Are bees reflex machines? 50 c. A. I. Root.
Doolittle, G. M. Year's work in an out-apiary. 50 c. A. I. Root.
Edwardes, T. Lore of the honey bee. *$2.40 net. Scribner.
Gates, B. N. Miscellaneous papers on apiculture; bee keeping in Massachusetts. 5 c. U. S., Supt. of Docs.
Jones, H: Radical cure for the swarming of bees. 25 c. H: Jones.
Langstroth, L. L. On the hive and honey bee. $1.20. Dadant.
Lockard, J: R. Bee hunting. 25 c. A. R. Harding.
Lyon, D. E. How to keep bees for profit. $1 net. Macmillan.
Potter, T. C. Bee-keeping for sedentary folk. gratis. A. I. Root.
Root, A. I. *and* E. R. A B C and X Y Z of bee culture. $1.50; $2.25; $2.50. A. I. Root.
Swenk, M. H. Specific characters in the bee genus *colletes.* 50 c. M. H. Swenk.
Beesley, C: Norbury.
Illustrated guide to St. Michael's church, Charleston, S. C. '08(D19) c. il. obl. T. pap., 50 c. C. N. Beesley.
Beesly, E: Spencer.
Catiline, Clodius, and Tiberius. '08(Ja18) O. (Anastatic reprint.) *$3 net. Stechert.
Beeson, C: H:
See Hale, W: Gardner.
BEET SUGAR.
See Sugar.
Beethoven, Ludwig v.
Letters. Critical ed.; with explanatory notes by Dr. Alfr. C. Kalischer; tr. with preface by J. S. Shedlock. 2 v. '08(D5) 8°, *$7.50 net. Dutton.
Piano compositions; ed., [with introd.,] by Eugen d'Albert. In 2 v. v. 1. '09(D4) por. 4°, (Musicians' lib.) $2.50; pap., $1.50. Ditson.
BEETHOVEN, Ludwig v.
Diehl, A. M. Life of Beethoven. $3. Clode.
Diehl, A. M. Life of Beethoven. *$3 net. Doran.
Rau, H. Beethoven: a biographical romance. $1.50. Ditson.
Beetle (The). Marsh, R: $1.50. Brentano's.
BEETLES.
Pierce, W: D. On the biologies of the *phynchophora* of North America. (Not for sale.) Univ. of Neb.
Wolcott, A. B. Notes on some *cleridae* of Middle and North America. 50 c. Field Museum.
See also Insects.
Before and after Waterloo. Stanley, E: *$3.75 special net. Appleton.
Before marriage. Homan, *Mrs.* A. L. R. **35 c. net. Vir Pub.

Before the doctor comes. Crawford, M. M. $1. Chr. Herald.
Before the war. Neall, W. H. 15 c. Penn Pub. Co.

Begbie, Harold.
Tables of stone. '08(S19) D. †$1.50. Doubleday, P.
Twice-born men; clinic in regeneration; footnote in narrative to Prof. W: James's "The varieties of religious experience." '10((F12) c. 12°, *$1.25 net. Revell.
Published in England with title "Broken earthenware."
The Vigil. '08(Ap11) c. D. †$1.50. Dodd.

Beggar in evening dress. Fleming, G: E. (Add. author for price.) G: E. Fleming.
Beggar in the heart. Rickert, M. E. †$1.50. Moffat.
Beggar or a king. Read, H. E. 30 c. Business Pub.
Beginner's botany. Bailey, L. H. **60 c. net. Macmillan.
Beginner's (The) primer. '08(F1) c. il. D. *25 c. net. Houghton, M. & Co.
Beginnings at Jerusalem. Lacey, T: J. 60 c. Gorham.
Beginnings in industrial education. Hanus, P. H. **$1 net. Houghton M.
Beginnings of English America. Connor, R. D. W. gratis. N. C. Hist.
Beginnings of independent life. Clarke, J: M. 50 c. J: M. Clarke.
Beginnings of New York. Forsythe, M. I. 25 c. Badger.
Beginnings of Texas. Clark, R. C. 75 c. Univ. of Tex.

BEHAISTS.
See **Babism.**

Behind the veil in Persia and Turkish Arabia. Hume-Griffith, *Mrs.* M. E. *$3.50 net. Lippincott.
Behind the world and beyond. Stimson, H: A. $1.25 net. Eaton & M.

BEHISTAN INSCRIPTION.
See **Archæology.**

Behm, Blanche.
Hist. of some French kings. '10(D31) 8°, $2 net. Macmillan.

Behnke, Kate Emil, and Henslowe, E. Colin.
Broadlands cookery book; comprehensive guide to the principles and practice of food reform. '10(Jl16) 12°, $1 net. Macmillan.

Behold the Lamb of God: Lententide sermons by eminent servants of God; tr. from the German by Fk. Carroll Longaker and Rob. Neumann. '08(Mr) c. 100 p. 12°, 85 c. Germ. Lit. Bd.

Behrens, C.
Louis XVI. painting; designs in a modern treatment after old original designs of the second half of the 18th century, text by Bruno Hessling. '09(Ag21) il. portfolio, $8. Hessling.

Beibitz, Rev. J. H.
Gloria crucis: addresses del. in Lichfield Cathedral Holy Week and Good Friday, 1907. '08(Ja25) D. $1. Longmans.

Beiden (Die) freunde. Moltke, *Count* H. K. B. v. *35 c. net. Holt.

Beirly, Alfr.
New harbor for Chicago: plans and suggestions; paper written at the request of the Harbor Commission appointed by His Honor Frederic A. Busse. '08(Jl4) c. plan, 8°, pap., gratis. A. Beirly.

Beissel, Stephan.
Lord's prayer and the Hail Mary; points for meditation. '08, [1909.] (Mr) c. 6+227 p. 12°, *90 c. net. Herder.

Beith, Ian Hay.
See Hay, Ian, *pseud.*

BEL (*god*).
Radau, H. Bel, the Christ of ancient times. *75 c. net. Open Court.

Belabre, Baron de.
Rhodes of the knights; [description of the existing monuments of the Knights of St. John of Jerusalem.] '09(Ja23) il. figs. $9.75. Oxford Univ.

Belasco, D:
See Klein, C:—O'Higgins, Harvey Jerrold.

Belasco, Rev. G: S.
God of our fathers, and other sermons. '08(Ag8) 8°, *$1.20 net. Bloch.

Belden, A. W., Delamater, G. R., and Groves, J. W.
Washing and coking tests of coal, at the fuel-testing plant, Denver, Colo., July 1, 1907, to June 30, 1908. '09(My) 54 p. il. figs. tabs., O. pap. 10 c. U. S., Supt. of Docs.

BELGIUM.
Baedeker, K. Belgium and Holland. $1.80 net. Scribner.
Bumpus, T: F. Cathedrals and churches of Belgium. $2 net. Pott.
Conant, C: A. National bank of Belgium. U. S., Supt. of Docs.
Guide to Belgium. $1. Pratt & P.
Higinbotham, J: U. Three weeks in Holland and Belgium. $1.50. Reilly & B.
Omond, G: W: T. Belgium. *$6 net. Macmillan.
Omond, G: W: T. Belgium. *75 c. net. Macmillan.
Rowntree, B. S. Land and labor; lessons from Belgium. $3.50 net. Macmillan.
Singleton, E. Art of the Belgian galleries. **$2 net. L. C. Page.
See also Machinery;—*also* Liege;—Waterloo.

Belgravia art monographs. $1.50 net; $1.75 net. Caldwell.
—Muther, R: Rembrandt.
—Schaeffer. Sandro Botticelli.

BELIEF.
See Faith.

Belief in a personal God. Huizinga, A. v. C. P. *50 c. net. Sherman, F.
Beliefs of unbelief. Fitchett, W: H: *$1.25 net. Eaton & M.

Belknap, Reginald Rowan.
American house building in Messina and Reggio; acct. of the American Naval and Red Cross combined expedition, to provide shelter for the survivors of the great earthquake of Dec. 28, 1908. '10 (N12) c. il. O. $2 net. Putnam.

Bell, Acton, pseud.
See Brontë, Anne.

Bell, Adelaide Fuller.
The vassalage. '09, [1910.] (F) c. 318 p. il. 12°, $1.50. C. M. Clark.
Bell, Alex. Graham.
Few thoughts concerning eugenics. '08 (My.) c. 119-123 p. tab., 8°, 25 c. Nat. Geog.
Mechanism of speech. 2d ed. '08(F29) c. O. **$1.20 net. Funk.
BELL, Alexander Melville.
Curry, S: S. Alexander Melville Bell; some memories, with fragments from a pupil's note book. $1. Expression.
Bell, Archie.
The Clyde Fitch I knew. '09(D) $1. B'way Pub.
Bell, Rev. C. C.
Children's round of fast and festival. '09 (Ap10) il. bds., *40 c. net. Young Churchman.
Story of the promise; being simple readings on the Old Testament. '09(Ap10) il. bds. *60 c. net. Young Churchman.
Bell, C: Erle, comp.
Everyday freight rules and tariff manual applicable to interstate traffic. '10(Jl2) c. 4°, $1. C: E. Bell.
"Bell, Currer," pseud.
See Brontë, Charlotte
Bell, Ellis, pseud.
See Brontë, Emily Jane.
Bell, Ernest Albert, ed.
War on the white slave trade. '10(Ja29) c. il. pors. 12°, $1.50. C: C. Thompson.
Also issued under title "Fighting the traffic in young girls."
Bell, Mrs. Euphemia Young.
Beautiful Bermuda, from different viewpoints. [3d ed., rev. and enl.] '09(Je5) c. il. fold. maps, fold. plans, 12°, $1: pap., 50 c. J. D. & F. R. Bell.
Bell, Lady Florence Eveleen Olliffe, [Mrs. Hugh Bell.]
Fairy tale plays and how to act them. '09 (Jl31) il. $1.50. Longmans.
Bell, Rev. G: Milner, ed.
Social service; hdbk. for workers and visitors in London and other large towns; with appendix of local charitable agencies; with a preface by the Bishop of Stepney. '08(D12) D. 60 c. Longmans.
Bell, Gertrude Lowthian.
Desert and the sown: [travel in Syria.] New cheaper ed. '08(Ja18) il. map, 12°, *$3 net. Dutton.
See also Ramsay, *Sir* W. M.
Bell, Mrs. Hugh.
See Bell, *Lady* Florence Eveleen Olliffe.
Bell, Ja., comp.
"The Teacher" guide to the certificate exams. of the Bd. of Educ. (England), 1908-9; with questions set in 1907 and solutions to papers in math. '08(Ag) il. diagrs. 12°, *50 c. net. Pitman.
Bell, Ja. Mackintosh.
See Brown, Abbie Farwell.
Bell, Ja. Munro, comp.
Furniture designs of Thomas Chippendale; with an introd. and critical estimate by Arth. Hayden. '10(D24) il. 4, $6 net. Scribner.

Bell, Ja. Munro, comp.—*Continued.*
Furniture designs of George Hepplewhite; with an introd. and critical estimate by Arth. Hayden. '10(D24) il. 4°, $6 net. Scribner.
Bell, J: Joy.
Oh! Christina! '09(Ap24) c. il. D. *60 c. net. Revell.
Thou fool! '08(Ag29) c. il. D. †$1.50. Baker & T.
Whither thou goest: a romance of the Clyde. '09(F27) c. D. *$1.20 net. Revell.
Wullie McWattie's master. '10(Je11) c. D. 60 c. net. Revell.
Bell, Lettice.
Go-to-bed stories. '09(Ag14) c. il. plan, 8°, $1. Gospel Pub.
Lost garden: stories of familiar Old Testament characters. '10(D) il. 12°, (Never-old stories ser.) $1.25 net. Doran.
Never-old stories: some stories of Old Testament kings. '10(D) il. 12°, (Never-old stories ser.) $1.25 net. Doran.
Bell, Lilian Lida, [Mrs. Arth. Hoyt Bogue.]
Angela's quest. '10(D10) c. il. D. $1.50. Duffield.
Concentrations of Bee. '09(N6) c. front. D. $1.50. L. C. Page.
Bell, Lucia Chase.
Obil, keeper of camels; being the parable of the man whom the disciple saw casting out devils. '10(Ap23) c. 12°, 50 c. P. Elder.
—, **and James, Rita Bell.**
Slumber Sea chanteys; music by Carrie Stone Freeman. '10(O15) F. pap., $1. P. Elder.
Bell, Malcolm.
Drawings of Rembrandt. '08(D5) il. 4°, (Drawings by the great masters.) *$2.50 net. Scribner.
Sir Edward Burne-Jones. '09(D) various paging, il. Q. (Great artist ser.) *$2 net. Doran.
Bell, Mowry.
Weeds and wild flowers: [poems.] '08 (F1) c. D. bds., $1.25. Badger.
Bell, Ralcy Husted.
Changing values of English speech. '09 (Mr6) 12°, $1.25. Hinds.
Bell, Rob., ed.
Songs of the great dramatists. Cabinet ed. '08(D19) 12°, (British poets ser.) $1.50. Estes.
Bell, W. Blair.
Principles of gynæcology. '10(S) 27+551 p. col. il. O. $6 net. Longmans.
Bell, Warren.
Jim Mortimer. '08(N21) il. 12°, $1.50. Macmillan.
Bell, Bp. W: Melvin.
Social message of Our Lord. '09(O) c. 181 p. por. 12°, *60 c. net. Otterbein.
Bell, W: Temple.
Various verses. '09(Jl3) c. D. $1. Cochrane Pub.
Bell cow. Sherman, B. E. $1.50. C. M. Clark.

Bell Telephone Company of Pennsylvania. Specifications no. 3300; general specifications for aerial cable construction; the Bell Telephone Company of Pennsylvania and controlled companies; Engineering Department. '09, [1910.] (Ap) c. 103 p. il. 16°. (Add. pubs. for price.) Bell Telephone.

Bella Donna. Hichens, R. S. †$1.50. Lippincott.

Bellamy, Fs., ed.
Effective magazine advertising; ed., with an introd., The science of advertising copy. '09(Mr13) c. il. 4°, *$5 net. M. Kennerley.

Bellamy, W:
More charades. '09(O2) c. D. **$1 net. Houghton M.

Bellamy, W: Woolsey.
Shorthand construction. '10(D31) c. 16°, 25 c. W: W. Bellamy.

Bellcroft Priory. Cooke, W. B. $1.50. Lane.

Belle (La) au bois dormant. *See* Fisher, Emma.

Belle (La) San Antone. Bennett, J. $1.50. Neale.

Belle Islers. Newman, R: B. †$1.50. Lothrop, L. & S.

"BELLEROPHON," The.
Fraser, E: "Bellerophon," "the bravest of the brave." $2. Stokes.

Belles, beaux and brains of the 60's. De Leon, T: C. *$3 net. G: W. Dillingham.

Belles-lettres ser. Section 1, English literature. 16°. Heath.
—Caedmon. Exodus and Daniel. *60 c. net.

Belles-lettres ser.; Section 3, English drama; ed. by G. P. Baker. il. 16°, 60 c. Heath.
—Beaumont. Knight of the burning pestle and A king and no king.
—D'Avenant. Love and honour, and The siege of Rhodes.
—Middleton *and* Rowley. Spanish gipsie, and All's lost by lust.
—Otway. The orphan, and Venice preserved.
—Shelley. Cenci.

Belles-lettres ser.: Section 6, Nineteenth century poets; ed. by R: Burton. 16°, 60 c. Heath.
—Arnold. Select poems.
—Shelley. Select poems.
—Tennyson. Select poems.

Bellet, Louise Pecquet du.
Some prominent Virginia families: [Edward Jaquelin—Martha Carey.] '08(Ja4) 4 v., il. pors. tabs., 8°, $10. J. P. Bell.

BELLINI, Giovanni.
Hay, G: Bellini. *65 c. net. Stokes.

Belloc, Jos. Hilaire Pierre.
Marie Antoinette. '09(N20) c. il. facsims., O. **$2.75 net. Doubleday, P.
On anything. '10(D10) 12°, $1.25 net. Dutton.
On everything: [essays.] '10(Ap23) 12°, $1.25 net. Dutton.
On nothing, and kindred subjects. '08(D) 20+262 p. 16°, *$1.25 net. Dutton.

Belloc-Lowndes, Mrs. Marie Adelaide.
Barbara Rebell. '08(Ap11) c. il. 12°, (Popular priced copyrights.) 50 c. B. W. Dodge.
Pulse of life: a story. '09(F13) c. D. †$1.50. Dodd.
Studies in wives. '10(Je4) c. 12°, $1.50. M. Kennerley.
Uttermost farthing. '09(O23) c. 8°, $1.25. M. Kennerley.

Bellot, Lieut. Jos. René.
Journal d'un voyage aux mers polaires; ed. by H. J. Chaytor. '08(Ja18) map, D. (Oxford mod. French ser.) 60 c. Oxford Univ.

Bellows, Wa. Clarke.
Campeche: some notes on the most remarkable postage stamp ever issued [Mexican.] '09(Jl) 8°, $3.50. W. C. Bellows.

Bell's cathedral ser.; ed. by G: White and E: F. Strange. il. 12°, 60 c. Macmillan.
—Woodhouse. Churches of Coventry.
—Worley. Priory church of St. Bartholomew-the-Great.

Bell's miniature ser. of great writers. il. 16°, *50 c net. Macmillan.
—Buckland. Oliver Goldsmith.

Bell's miniature ser. of musicians. il. 16°, *50 c. net; limp leath., *$1 net. Macmillan.
—Antcliffe. Schubert.
—Lee. Grieg.
—Runciman. Haydn.—Purcell.

Bell's miniature ser. of painters. il. 16°, 50 c.; limp leath., $1. Macmillan.
—Cust. Botticelli.—Leonardo Da Vinci.
—Konody. Brothers Van Eyck.

Bells across the snow. Havergal, F. R. 25 c. Stokes.

Bells and pomegranates. Farrar, F: W: $1.50 net. Whittaker.

Bells of Atchison. Green, A. 75 c. A. Green.

Bellum Catilinae. *See* Sallustius Crispus, C.

Belote, Thdr. T:
Scioto speculation and the French settlement at Gallipolis. '08(Je6) maps, O. (University studies.) pap., 75 c. Univ. of Cin.

BELVOIR CASTLE, Grantham, Eng.
See Gardens and gardening.

Belz, Jacob Otto.
See Briggs, Lyman Ja.

BEMIDJI, Minn.
Bemidji Pioneer. Bemidji the acknowledged "hub" of the Great Northwest; idealistic pleasure and health resort of the Great Northwest; bread basket of the Great Northwest and center of the picturesque lakes of the Great Northwest. [1910.] (Mr) 104 p. il. pors. f°, pap., 50 c. Bemidji Pioneer.

Ben Logan's triumph. Alger, H., *jr.* 60 c. Cupples & L.

Ben Yûsuf, Mme. Anna.
Art of millinery; complete ser. of pract. lessons. '10(Ap16) c. il. 12°, $2. Millinery Trade.

BENARES, India.
Cape, C. B. Benares; stronghold of Hinduism. $2 net. Badger.
Havell, E. B. Benares, the sacred city. $3. Caldwell.

Bench and bar of Litchfield County, Conn. Kilbourn, D. C. $5. Kilbourn.

Bender, C. W.
Electric train lighting hdbk. for railway electrical engineers; by Engineering Dept. of the National Electric Lamp Assoc. '10(Jl) 342 p. il. tabs., 12°. (Not for sale.) Nat. Elec. Lamp.

Bender, Ida C.
See Emerson, H: Pendexter.

Bender, Melvin T.
See American bankruptcy repts. Digest.—Street railway repts.

Bender, Wilbur H.
Iowa. '08(S19) c. il. 4°, (Tarr and McMurry geographies, supplementary v.) pap., *20 c. net. Macmillan.

Bender's code citations analyzed. Becker, F. S. $1. M. Bender.

Bender's Lawyers' diary and directory for the state of New York. '10(F) c. O. hf. leath., $2. M. Bender.

Bender's Lawyers' reference book and diary, 1910. '09, [1910.] c. O. $2. M. Bender.

Bender's national lawyers' diary and directory for the state of New York, 1908. '08(Ja4); *Same,* 1909. 6th year. '08(D) c. O. hf. roan, ea., $2. M. Bender.

Bender's practice time-table; consisting of the times required for each step in the practice of law in the state of N. Y.; ed. by A. B. Griffin. '10(S) c. O. $2. M. Bender.

Bender's selected statutes. *See* New York.

Bendure & Arthurs' practical and correct guide for the use of auditors, agents, and railroad men generally. '09(Jl) c. 43 p. 12°, $3. Bendure & A.

Beneath the Star of Bethlehem. Wells, E. H. $1. Neale.

Benedict, A. L.
Golden rules of dietetics; general principles and empiric knowledge of human nutrition; analytic tables of foodstuffs; diet lists and rules for infant feeding and for feeding in various diseases. '08, [1909.] (Je) 5-407 p. tabs., 8°, (Medical guide and monograph ser.) $3. Mosby.

Benedict, Clare.
A resemblance, and other stories. '09 (Mr6) c. D. †$1.50. Putnam.

Benedict, Erastus Cornelius.
American admiralty; its jurisdiction and practice, [etc.] 4th ed., rev. by E: Grenville Benedict. '10(Je) c. O. $6.30. Banks & Co.

Benedict, Fs. Gano, and Carpenter, Thorne M.
Influence of muscular and mental work on metabolism and the efficiency of the human body as a machine. '09(Je) 100 p. il. 8°, (U. S., Dept. of Agriculture, Office of Experiment Stations bull.) 15 c.

Metabolism and energy transformations of healthy man during rest. '10(Ag) Q. pap., $1.75. Carnegie.

Respiration calorimeters for studying the respiratory exchange and energy transformations of man. '10(My7) il. Q. pap., 75 c. Carnegie.

Benedict, Fs. Gano, and Joslin, Elliott Proctor.
Metabolism in diabetes mellitus. '10(D) 6+234 p. il. fold. chart, O. (Carnegie Institution of Washington pub.) pap., $2. Carnegie.

Benedict, Rob. Russell.
Mystery of Hamlet, Prince of Denmark. '10(Ap2) c. D. $1 net. Lippincott.

Benedict, Roswell Alphonzo.
Malefactors of great wealth! '08(F29) c. por. O. $2. Am. Business.

Benediction (The). Dolbeer, W: H. 75 c. Lutheran Pub.

Benedix, Roderich J.
Eigensinn: [a play.] '09(N13) S. pap., 15 c. Oxford Univ.

Beneficiary features of American trade unions. Kennedy, J. B. 50 c. Johns Hopkins.

Benefit of the Hepburn law. Hanks, C: S. 50 c. Authors' Pub.

BENEFIT SOCIETIES.
Fraternalism and the church. $1. M. C. Chamberlin.
Hardy, C. S. Fraternal society law. $10. R. Smith.
Hardy, C. S., *comp.* Fraternal society law: digest of the laws concerning fraternal beneficiary societies. 12°; *$10 net. C. S. Hardy.
See also Freemasonry;—Trade-unions;—Woodmen of the world.

Benett, W.
Ethical aspects of evolution regarded as the parallel growth of opposite tendencies. '08(N21) O. $2. Oxford Univ.

BENGAL, India.
Banerjea, S. B. Tales of Bengal. $1 net. Longmans.

Bengough, J: Wilson.
Whole hog book: being [Henry] George's thoro' going work "Protection or free trade?" rendered into words of one syllable, and il. with pictures. '08(Ag15) c. il. 16°, pap., 25 c. Free Trade.

Benham, Allen, Rogers, ed.
See Padelford, F: Morgan.

Benjamin, C: T:
Fall of David's tabernacle, rebuilt by Christ. '08(Ag) c. 160 p. por. 12°, 75 c. Reliance.

Benjamin, Marcus.
John Bidwell, pioneer: address del. before the Society of California Pioneers of Washington, D. C. '08(Ap11) il. 12°, pap., gratis. Soc. Cal. Pioneers.

Benjamin, Ruthella.
Echoes from Oak Street. '08(D) 162 p. 16°, 50 c. Donohue.

Benjamin, W: Howard.
Biographies of celebrated organists of America. '08(D) c. 155 p. il. 8°. subs., $25. W: H. Benjamin.

Benkendorf, Gustavus H: W:, and Hatch, Kirk Lester.
Profitable dairying; a manual for farmers and dairymen. '08(Ag) c. 64 p. il. 12°, gratis. Babsom.

—, **comp. and ed.** Catalogue of the postal dairy library. '10(My) c. 64 p. obl. 24°, gratis. G. H: W: Benkendorf.

Benn, Alfr. W:
Early Greek philosophy. '09(Jl31) 12°, (Philosophies ancient and modern from Pythagoras to Spencer.) *50 c. net. Dodge.

Benn, Mrs. Edith Annie Fraser Parker.
Overland trek from India by side-saddle, camel, and rail; the record of a journey from Beluchistan to Europe. '09(N13) il. map, O. *$5 net. Longmans.

Benn, H. P., and Bolwock, W. C.
Characteristics of old furniture style in England, 1600-1800. '08(D19) 4°, pap., *$1 net. Scribner.

Bennet, Rob. Ames.
Into the primitive. '08(Ap11) c. il. $1.50. McClurg.
The Shogun's daughter. '10(O15) c. O. col. il. $1.35 net. McClurg.
Volunteer with Pike; the true narrative of one Dr. John Robinson and his love for the fair Señorita Vallois. '09(O9) c. il. in col. O. $1.50. McClurg.

Bennett, C: Alpheus.
Problems in mechanical drawing. '08(D5) c. obl. S. pap., $1; bds., $1.20. Manual Arts.

Bennett, C: Edn.
First year Latin. '09, [1910.] (F) c. 288 p. il. 12°, $1. Allyn & B.
Latin grammar. Rev. ed. '08(Je27) c. 12°, (Bennett's Latin ser.) 80 c. Allyn & B.

Bennett, C: J. C.
Formal discipline. '08(F8) figs. tabs., O. pap., 50 c. Teachers' Coll.

Bennett, E: T.
Psychic phenomena; with a foreword by Sir Oliver Lodge. '09(Jl3) 12°, *75 c. net. Brentano's.

Bennett, Enoch Arnold.
Buried alive: tale of these days. '10(Je25) S. $1. Brentano's.
Clayhanger. '10(O15) c. D. $1.50 net. Dutton.
The glimpse: adventures of the soul. '09(O23) c. D. †$1.50. Appleton.
Helen with the high hand; an idyllic diversion. '10(O15) D. $1.20 net. Doran.
How to live on 24 hours a day. '10(D24) c. D. bds., 50 c. net. Doran.
Human machine: ser. of studies. '10(D) 75 c. net. Doran.
Literary taste: how to form it. '10(D) 75 c. net.. Doran.
Old wives' tale. '09(Je26) D. *$1.50 net. Doran.
The reasonable life; essays. '10(D) bds., 50 c. net. Doran.
What the public wants: a play. '10(D) $1 net. Doran.
See also Phillpotts, Eden.

Bennett, F.
Story of W. J. E. Bennett, founder of St. Barnabas', Pimlico and vicar of Froome-Selwood, and of his part in the Oxford Church movement of the nineteenth century. '09(N13) por. O. *$2.25 net. Longmans.

Bennett, Homer Clark, M.D.
Electro-therapeutic guide. 8th ed., rev. and condensed. '08(Ja11) il. por. O. $2. Nat. Coll. Electro-Therapeutics.

Bennett, Hugh Garner.
Manufacture of leather. '10(My15) il. 8°, $4.50 net. Van Nostrand.

Bennett, Ida D.
Vegetable garden. '08(Jl4) c. O. (Country home lib.) **$1.50 net. McClure.

Bennett, Ja. O'Donnell, ed.
When good fellows get together: [verse and prose selections.] '08(S19) c. O. bds., $1. Reilly & B.

Bennett, Ja. Rob. Sterndale.
Life of William Sterndale Bennett. '08 (F1) 8°, *$3.50 net. Putnam.

Bennett, Johannas.
La belle San Antone. '09(N13) c. D. $1.50. Neale.

Bennett, J: W:
Roosevelt and the republic. '08(Je20) c. D. $1.50. B'way Pub.

Bennett, Maurice Eug.
Method in teaching writing. '08(O) c. 129 p. 8°, $1.25. Bennett Pub.

Bennett, Rob. Jos., comp.
See Michigan. Law of negotiable paper.

Bennett, Virginia.
Old farm story box. 4 v. '08, [1909.] (Jl) il. 12°, per set, $1. Dutton.

Bennett, W: Harper.
Catholic footsteps in old New York, from 1524 to 1808. '09(Ap3) c. O. $2.50. Schwartz, K. & F.

Bennett, Sir W: H:
Injuries and diseases of the knee-joint, considered from the clinical aspect. '09 (Mr27) il. 12°, *$2 net. Wood.
Lectures on the use of massage and early movements in recent fractures, and other common surgical injuries, sprains and their consequences, rigidity of the spine, and the management of stiff joints generally. 4th ed. '09(Je5) il. O. *$1.75 net. Longmans.

Bennett, W: H:, ed.
Religion of the post-exilic prophets, 586-300 B.C. '08(My16) 12°, (Literature and religion of Israel.) *$2 net. Scribner.

BENNETT, William James Early.
Bennett, F. Story of W. J. E. Bennett. *$2.25 net. Longmans.

BENNETT, *Sir* William Sterndale.
Bennett, J. R. S. Life of William Sterndale Bennett. *$3.50 net. Putnam.

Bensley, B: Arth.
Pract. anatomy of the rabbit. '10(Mr) 6+203 p. il. 8°, *$2 net. Blakiston.

Benson, Allan L:
What help can any workingman expect from Taft or Bryan? '08(D19) D. pap., 5 c. Socialist.

Benson, Arth. Christopher, ["J. T;" "T. B."]
Poems. '09(F6) 12°, *$1.50 net. Lane.
At large: [essays.] '08(O10) c. D. **$1.50 net. Putnam.
The schoolmaster: commentary upon the aims and methods of an assistant-master in a public school; with an introd. to the American ed. '08(My16) D. *$1.25 net. Putnam.

Benson, Arth. Christopher.—*Continued.*
Silent isle. '10(N19) c. D. $1.50 net. Putnam.

Until the evening. '09(S18) c. D. (What is worth while ser.) leatherette, **30 c. net. Crowell.

Benson, Blackwood Ketcham.
Who goes there?; the story of a spy in the Civil War. '10(O1) c. D. $1.50. Macmillan.

Benson, E: Frederic.
A reaping. '09(S11) D. $1.25, fixed. Doubleday, P.

Blotting book. '08(Ag29) c. '07, '08. D. †$1. Doubleday, P.

The climber. '09(F6) c. front. D. **$1.40 net. Doubleday, P.

English figure skating '09(Ja9) il. 12°, *$2.50 net. Macmillan.

Fascinating Mrs. Halton. '10(Mr26) c. il. D. $1.20, fixed. Doubleday, P.

Margery. '10(D17) c. 12°, $1.20. Doubleday, P.

The Osbornes. '10(S10) c. D. $1.20. Doubleday, P.

Benson, Harrison T.
Compendium on mines, mining, minerals, ores, rocks, weights of metals and rocks, effect of heat on various substances, water measure, tanks and piping; atomic weights explained, chemical symbols, etc. '10(Jl30) c. il. D. limp leath., $2. Hall & W.

Benson, Irene Elliott.
Yellow princess. '08, [1909.] (Ap) c. 8°, 25 c. McLoughlin.

Benson, Marg.
Venture of rational faith. '09(Ja23) 8°, *$2 net. Macmillan.

Benson, Percival Ramsey.
Lord of lands. '08(S12) c. D. $1.50. Holt.
Melchisedec. '09(S25) c. D. †$1.50. Holt.

Benson, Reuel Allen.
Nursery manual; the care and feeding of children in health and disease. '08(D) c. 184 p. 12°, *$1 net. Boericke & T.

Benson, Father Rob. Hugh.
A winnowing. '10(Jl9) c. 12°, $1.50. Herder.

The conventionalists. '09(Mr6) c. D. $1.50. Herder.

Cost of a crown; story of Douay and Durham; sacred drama in 3 acts. '10 (N5) D. bds., $1 net. Longmans.

Lord of the world. '08(Ap25) c. D. †$1.50. Dodd.

Mystery play in honour of the nativity of our Lord. '08(D19) il. D. 90 c.; New ed., (text only.) '09(D25) S. pap., 20 c. Longmans.

The necromancers. '09(N20) 12°, $1.50. Herder.

Non-Catholic denominations. '10(D24) D. (Westminster lib.) $1.20 net. Longmans.

Bensusan, S: Levy.
Holbein. '08(Ap17) il. O. (Masterpieces in colour.) bds., *65 c. net. Stokes.

Bensusan, S: Levy.—*Continued.*
Home life in Spain. '10(D10) il. D. $1.75 net. Macmillan.
Lawrence. '10(Jl30) il. D. (Masterpieces in color.) bds., 65 c. net; leath., $1.50 net. Stokes.
Murillo. '10(D17) col. il. O. (Masterpieces in colour.) bds., 65 c. net. Stokes.
Rubens. '09(Ap17) il. O. (Masterpieces in colour.) bds., *65 c. net. Stokes.
Tintoretto. '08(O3) O. (Masterpieces in colour.) bds., *65 c. net. Stokes.
Titian. '08(Jl4) il. O. (Masterpieces in colour.) bds., *65 c. net. Stokes.

Bentalou, Paul.
See Clarke, J:

Bentley, Alys E.
Song series: book one. '08(My2) c. il. O. 35 c.; Bk. 2. '10(My21) c. il. 8°, 40 c. net. Barnes.

—, and Johnston, Geneva R.
Child's world primer. '08(My2) c. il. D. 30 c. Barnes.

Bentley, Arth. Fisher.
Process of government. '08(Ap11) c. O. *$3 net. Univ. of Chic.

Bentley, Harry Clark, and Conyngton, T:.
Corporate finance and accounting. '08 (Mr21) c. 8°, $4. Ronald Press.

Benton, Arth. Burnett.
The Mission inn; sketches by W: Alex. Sharp. '08(Ag) c. 4°, pap., $2; leath., $4. M. E. L. Allen.

Benton, Caroline French, [pseud. for Caroline Benedict Burrell.]
Living on a little. '08(S5) c. D. $1.25. Estes.

Benton, C: W:
Pract. bookkeeping; designed for use of high schools, normal schools, business colleges and private study. '10(F) c. 6+7-222 p. 4°, $1.50. Bogarte.

Benton, Elbert Jay.
International law and diplomacy of the Spanish-American war. '08(Mr14) c. O. (Albert Shaw lectures on diplomatic history.) $1.50. Johns Hopkins.

Benton, Guy Potter.
Real college. '09(Je19) c. D. *75 c. net. Jennings.

Benton, Harwood Otis, and Bertram, J:, comps. and eds.
Aid to Kansas history, to be used in connection with Noble L. Prentis' "History of Kansas." '08(Ag22) c. D. pap., 25 c. H. O. Benton.

Benton, Joel.
Memories of the Twilight Club. '09(D) $1; leath., $1.50. B'way Pub.

Benton, J: Clemens.
Legal aspect of prohibition. '09(N) c. 45 p. 8°, 50 c. J: C. Benton.

Benton, J: Rob.
Problems in physics to accompany Ames's Text-bk. of general physics. '09, [1910.] (D) c. 2+46 p. il. 8°. Am. Bk.

Benton, Josiah H:
Book of common prayer: its origin and growth. '10(O) 3-68 p. 8°. (Priv. pr.) J: H: Benton.

Benton, Josiah H:—*Continued.*
Lawyer's official oath and office. '09, [1910.] (F) c. 133 p. 8°, $1.50. Boston Bk.
Bibliography (6 p.).
Story of the old Boston town house, 1658-1711. '09(F6) c. il. pors. plan, facsim., 4°. (Priv. pr.) Merrymount.
Working of the Boston Public Library: address before the Beacon Society of Boston, Jan. 2, 1909. '09(Mr13) O. (Not for sale.) J. H: Benton.

Bentwich, Norman De Mattos.
Philo-Judæus of Alexandria. '10(Ap2) c. D. $1.25. Jewish Pub.

Bentztown Bard, pseud.
See McKinsey, Folger.

Benziger's ecclesiatical diary and note-book for the special use of the reverend clergy in the United States, 1909. '09(F6) c. S. leath., *75 c. net. Benziger.

Benziger's elementary geography for Catholic schools. '09(N) c. 133 p. il. 4°, 54 c. Benziger.

BEOWULF.
Cox, J: H. Knighthood, in germ and in flower; Anglo-Saxon epic, Beowulf, and the Arthurian tale, Sir Gawein and the Green Knight. $1.25. Little, B. & Co.
Deeds of Beowulf. $1. Oxford Univ.
Marshall, H. E. Stories of Beowulf. 50 c. Dutton.

Beppo. Cramp, W: H. 75 c. Small.

Béranger, Pierre Jean de.
Chansons choisies; ed. by Jean Edmond Mansion. '08(N14) por. S. (Oxford higher French ser.) $1.15. Oxford Univ.

Beraysheeth. Barnes, G: O. $1. J. J. Scruby.

Berean ser.; ed. by J. T. McFarland. nar. T. Eaton & M.
—International S. S. lessons. Lesson handbook, 1909. *20 c. net; *25 c. net.
—Meyer. Lesson hdbk., 1910, 1911. ea., *25 c. net.

Berenson, Bernhard.
Florentine painters of the Renaissance. 3d ed., rev. and enl. '09(Ap17) c. front. 12°, **$1.50 net. Putnam.
Sienese painter of the Franciscan legend. '10(Ja15) O. *$2 net. Lane.

Berenson, Senda, ed.
Spalding's official women's basket ball guide. '08(D12) c. il. pors. 16°, (Spalding's athletic lib. pap., 10 c. Am. Sports.

Berg, Ernst Julius.
Electrical energy, its generation, transmission, and utilization. '08(F29) c. il. O. *$2.50 net. McGraw.

Berge, Mme.
Every woman her own dressmaker. '09(D) il. *$1.25 net. Doran.

Bergen, Jos. Young.
Essentials of botany. '09(Ja23) c. il. D. $1.20. Ginn.

Berger, Christian L:
Hand-book and illustrated catalogue of the engineers' and surveyors' instruments of precision made by C. L. Berger & Sons. '08(Ap.) c. 212 p. il. 8°, 60 c. C. L. Berger.

Berget, Thomas Claude Xavier Alphonse.
Conquest of the air; aeronautics, aviation; hist., theory and practice. '10(F12) c. il. 8°, **$3.50 net. Putnam.

Bergey, D: Hendricks.
Principles of hygiene; pract. manual for students, physicians, and health-officers. 3d ed., thoroughly rev. and enl. '09, [1910.] (Ja) c. 7-555 p. il. 8°, $3. Saunders.

Bergh, L: de Coppet.
Safe building construction. New ed., thoroughly rev. '08(Ap18) c. il. tabs., 12°, **$5 net. Macmillan.

Bergin, Rev. Alfr.
Swedish settlements in central Kansas; address del. before the Kansas State Historical Society at its thirty-fourth annual meeting, December 7, 1909. [1910.] (D) 28 p. il. pors. fold. map, 8°, gratis. State Hist., Kan.

Bergling, J: Mauritz.
Art monograms and lettering; for the use of engravers, artists, designers and art workmen. In 3 v. v. 1, Lettering; v. 2, Monograms and other designs; v. 3, Colored monograms, arts and craft. etc. '10 (Jl16) c. il. f°, in portfolio, ea., $1.50; v. 1, 2, in cl. bound portfolio, $3; 3 vs. in same cover, $4.25. J: M. Bergling.

Bergold, Lilian Clara.
Abraham Lincoln centennial; collection of authentic stories, with poems, songs, and programs. '09(Mr6) c. il. por. 12°, 40 c. Educ. Pub.

Bergquist, Nils W.
Swedish folk dances. '10(My14) 4°, $1.50. Barnes.

Bergson, Henri Louis.
Time and free will; essay on the immediate data of consciousness; tr. by F. L. Pogson. '10(O8) 8°, (Lib. of philosophy.) $2.75 net. Macmillan.

BERING SEA.
Niedieck, P. Cruises in Bering Sea. *$5 net. Scribner.

Berington, Jos., and Kirk, J:, comps.
Faith of Catholics, confirmed by Scripture and attested by the fathers of the first five centuries of the church; rev. and recast by Rev. Ja. Waterworth; with preface, corrections and additions by Rt. Rev. Mgr. T. J. Capel. 4th rev. and enl. ed. 3 v. '10(Jl16) c. fronts. 8°, $6 net. Pustet.

Berkeley, Frances Campbell, ed.
College course in writing from models; arranged, with introd. and notes. '10 (Mr26) c. D. $1.25. Holt.

Berkeley, G:, Bp. of Cloyne.
George Berkeley on several queries proposed to the public, 1735-37. '10(N) c. 116 p. 8°, $1. Lord Balto. Pr.
New theory of vision and other select philosophical writings; (The principles of human knowledge and Three dialogues between Hylas and Philonous;) with introd. by A. D. Lindsay. '10(D10) c. 16°, (Everyman's lib.) 35 c. net; leath., 70 c. net. Dutton.

Berkeley, G:—*Continued.*
The querist; containing several queries proposed to the consideration of the public. pts. 1-3, Dublin, 1735-37. '08(F22) 8°, (Reprints of economic tracts.) subs., per set of 4 tracts, pap., *$2 net. Johns Hopkins.

BERKELEY, George, *Bishop of Cloyne.*
Fraser, A. C. Berkeley. *50 c. net. Dodge.
Mead, H. R., *comp.* Bibliography of George Berkeley, Bishop of Cloyne. Univ. of Cal.

Berkeley, H.
Mysticism in modern mathematics. '10 (Ag27) c. O. $3.20. Oxford Univ.

Berkeley, J:, pseud.
Modern revolt from Rome. '10(D24) 8°, $1.25 net. Jennings.

Berko, Géza D.
Az Amerikai magyar népszava jubileumi diszalbuma, 1899-1909. '10(Ap) 404 p. il. pors. 4°, $5. G. D. Berko.

BERKSHIRE, Eng.
Lamborn, E. A. G. School history of Berkshire. 50 c.—Stories from the history of Berkshire. 25 c. Oxford Univ.

BERKSHIRE HILLS, Mass.
Phillips, W: H. Pathfinder to Greylock Mountain, the Berkshire Hills, and historic Bennington. $1. W: H. Phillips.
Smith, J. E. A. Taghconic: romance and beauty of the Berkshire Hills. $1.15. Eagle.

Berkwitz, W: Leonard.
Encyclopædia of the mail order business. '08, [1909.] (Je) c. 270 p. il. 8°, $5. Mail Order.
The $500.000 course in mixing; a course in mixing, preparing, originating and putting up preparations and specialties of all kinds suitable for mail order business. '08, [1909.] (S) c. 103 p. 8°. (Add. pubs. for price.) Mail Order.
Reminiscences; composed of actual mail order experiences. '08, [1909.] (Je) 50 p. 8°, $1. Mail Order.
Ups and downs of a mail order aspirant, described in a series of ten letters, written by Andrew Morton, a young mail order aspirant, to his father on the old farm. '08, [1909.] (Je) 44 p. 8°, $1. Mail Order.

Berlage, Herman Jos.
Incognito: Greek tragedy in four acts. '08(Jl18) S. pap. (Add. author for price.) H. J. Berlage.

BERLIN, Germany.
Baedeker, K. Berlin and its environs. *90 c. net. Scribner.
Dickie, J. F. In the Kaiser's capital. $2 net. Dodd.

Berlin discussion of the problem of evolution. Wasmann, E. *$1.60 net. Herder.

Berlinicke, Harry R.
Legal information. '10(Jl) c. O. pap., 25 c. Berlinicke & A.

Berman, H:
Tyrant in white. '09(N) c. 320 p. 12°, $1.50. Lovell.

BERMUDA.
Bell, *Mrs.* E. Y. Beautiful Bermuda. $1; 50 c. J. D. & F. R. Bell.
Hayward, W. B. Bermuda, past and present. $1.25 net. Dodd.
Ober, F: A. Guide to the West Indies and Bermudas. **$2.25 net. Dodd.
Shilling Bermuda guide and history. 25 c. S. Nelmes.
See also Moore, Thomas.

Bermuda verse. Chittenden, W: L. **$1.50 net. Putnam.

Bernard, Auguste Joseph.
Geofroy Tory; tr. by G: B. Ives. '09 (Ap10) il. 4°, bds., *$37.50 net. Houghton M.

Bernard, Charles de.
L'anneau d'argent; ed. by L: Sers. '10 (D24) c. 16°, (Macmillan's new ser. of French texts.) 35 c. net. Macmillan.

Bernard de Clairvaux, St.
On consideration; tr. by G: Lewis. '08 (N21) D. $1. Oxford Univ.

Bernard of Cluny.
Source of "Jerusalem the golden": together with other pieces attributed to Bernard of Cluny; in English tr. by H: Preble; introd., notes and annotated bibliog. by S: Macaulay Jackson. '10(Ap9) facsims., O. $1.25 net. Univ. of Chic.

Bernays, Hermann Uhde-.
See Uhde-Bernays, Hermann.

Berner, Gottfried.
Der pfarrherr von Silberburg. '08(F1) c. D. *$1.50 net. Ulbrich.

Bernhardt, Christian.
Indian raids in Lincoln County, Kansas, 1864 and 1869. '10(N5) il. pors. fold. map, 8°, 50 c. Lincoln Sentinel.

Bernhardt, Wilhelm, ed.
Der weg zum glück: zwei erzählungen für die jugend; sel. and ed., with exercises, notes and vocab., by Dr. Wilhelm Bernhardt. '08(Ap11) c. il. map, S. (Modern lang. ser.) 40 c. Heath.

Bernier, L: Leon.
Autogenous welding of metals; tr. from reports of the National School of Arts and Trades of France. '08(Jl18) c. il. 16°, $1. Boiler Maker.

Bernstein, E:
Evolutionary socialism: criticism and affirmation; tr. by Edith C. Harvey. '09 (D4) (Socialist lib.) *$1 net. B: W. Huebsch.

BERNSTORFF, *Count* Albrecht von.
Ringhoffer, K. Bernstorff papers. *$6 net. Longmans.

BERRIES.
Card, F: W. Bush-fruits. **$1.50 net. Macmillan.

Berry, Abbé L. Claude.
Favorite and favors of the Sacred Heart of Jesus; tr. by a Sister of Mercy. '08 (Ap.) c. 243 p. 12°, *75 c. net. Chr. Press.

Berry, C: W:
Temperature-entrophy diagram. 2d ed., rev. and enl. '08(N14) c. figs. 12°, $2. Wiley.

Berry, Claude Perrin.
Treatise on the law rel. to automobiles. '09 (Je) c. 15+305 p. O. *$3 net. Callaghan.

Berry, G: Ricker, D.D.
Old Testament among the Semitic religions. '10(Mr12) c. O. *$1 net. Griffiths & R.

Berry, J: Benton Nathaniel.
Some assurances of immortality. '09 (Ap17) c. nar. D. $1. Fenno.

Berry, Mary Anne.
Woman of uncertain age. '09(Je) 293 p. front. 12°, $1.50. Stuyvesant Press.

Berry, Rob.
Germany of the Germans. '10(Je4) 12°, $1.50 net. Scribner.

Berry, W. Grinton.
Bishop Hannington and the story of the Uganda mission. '08(O10) 12°, *$1 net. Revell.
France since Waterloo. '09(Ap3) il. maps, D. *$1.50 net. Scribner.

Berryman, J. R., ed.
See Camp, Edg. W.

Bersford, T:
Theories and facts for students of longevity and health. '08(S19) c. 12°, $1. T: Bersford.

Bertelli, Luigi, ["Vamba."]
Prince and his ants (Ciondolino); tr. from the 4th Italian ed. by S. F. Woodruff, and ed. by Vernon L. Kellogg. '10(Je4) c. il. D. $1.35 net. Holt.

Bertha's Christmas vision. Alger, H., *jr.* 50 c. Hurst.

Berthet, Elie.
Le douanier de mer; ed. by Rob. J. E. Bué. '09(Ap3) D. (Oxford modern French ser.) 60 c. Oxford Univ.

Bertholet, Alfr.
Transmigration of souls; tr. by Rev. H. J. Chaytor. '10(Ja29) 12°, (Harper's lib. of living thought.) *75 c. net. Harper.

Berthon, H. E., and Starkey, V. G.
Tables synoptiques de phonologie de l'ancien français. '09(Ap3) sq. F. pap., 85 c. Oxford Univ.

Bertillon, Jacques.
International classification of causes of sickness and death; rev. by the International Commission at the session of Paris, July 1 to 3, 1909, for use beginning Jan. 1, 1910, and until Dec. 31, 1919. '10(Jl) 146 p. 4°. Gov. Pr. Off.

Bertram, J:
See Benton, Harwood Otis.

Bertrand of Brittany. Deeping, G: W. †$1.50. Cassell.

Beruete y Moret, A. de.
School of Madrid: [art and artists.] '09 (Je26) D. (Library of art.) *$2 net. Scribner.

Berwick, Mary Hasell.
Escapades of an American youngster. '10 (My14) 12°, $1. Brentano's.

BERYLLIUM.
Parsons, C: L. Chemistry and literature of beryllium. $2. Chemical.

Besant, Mme. Annie Wood.
Karma, once more. '10(Mr12) D. pap., 15 c. Manas Press.

BESANT, *Mme.* Annie Wood.
Bragdon, C. Brief life of Annie Besant. 15 c. Manas Press.

Besant, Sir Wa.
Early London: prehistoric, Roman, Saxon and Norman. '08(Je6) il. 4°, *$7.50 net. Macmillan.
London city. '10(D24) il. maps, 12°, $7.50 net. Macmillan.
London in the nineteenth century. '09 (D25) map, 4°, *$7.50 net. Macmillan.

—, and others.
Shortditch and the East End. '08(N21) il. map, 16°, (Fascination of London ser.) *90 c. net. Macmillan.

Beshshure, Beshshure Michael.
Rosaline. '08(Ag) c. 47 p. il. por. 12°, 26 c. P. O. Box 450, West Newton, Pa. Beshshure.

Besier, Rudolf.
Don; comedy in three acts. '10(Ag20) por. D. (Plays of to-day and to-morrow.) $1 net. Duffield.

Bess of Hardwick. *See* Shrewsbury, Elizabeth Hardwick, *Countess of.*

Besse, Rev. H: True.
Church history. '08(Je6) c. il. pors. 8°, $2. H: T. Besse.

Bessey, C: Edn.
Botany for high schools and colleges. 7th ed., rev. '08(O10) c. il. 8°, (American science ser., Advanced course.) $2.20. Holt.

Bessier, Fernand.
Miss Peackle: a French comedy. '08(N7) c. D. pap., 15 c. Penn Pub. Co.

Best, Fk. E.
See Nye, G: Hyatt.

Best, Lyman Austin.
Teachers' retirement fund; address given at Washington Jan. 16, 1909, before the College Women's Club. '10(Jl) 9 p. 8°. Gov. Pr. Off.

Best, Nolan Rice.
Beyond the natural order: essays on prayer miracles and the incarnation. 2d ed. '08 (D26) c. D. *75 c. net. Revell.

Best, W: Mawdesley.
Principles of the law of evidence; with elem. rules for conducting the examination and cross-examination of witnesses. 8th Eng. ed., by J. M. Lely; 3d Am. ed., by C: F. Chamberlayne. '08(Jl) c. 82+703 p. O. $3.50. Boston Bk.

Best American essays. Howard, J: R., *comp.* 35 c. Crowell.

Best American orations. Howard, J: R., *comp. and ed.* 35 c. net. Crowell.

Best book ser. *See* Dutton's.

Best books for Old and New Testament study. McFadyen, J: E. 20 c. Pub. Ho. of M. E. Ch., So.

Best road and the right way to make it. Barber, A. L. (Not for sale.) Barber Asphalt.

Best stories by the foremost Catholic authors; with introd. by Maurice Francis Egan. In 10 v. '10(Ap30) c. S. (given with one $2 sub. to *Benziger's Magazine* and $1 extra, or free with 2 subs.) Benziger.

Best type of canal for Panama. '09(Je5) il. 8°, pap. (Add. Superintendent for price.) U. S., Supt. of Docs.
Besuch (Der) im karzer. Eckstein, E. 50 c. Ginn.
Betelguese. Esque, J. L: de. $1.25. Connoisseurs' Press.
Beth, Karl.
Miracles of Jesus. '08(Ja4) S. (Foreign religious ser.) *40 c. net. Eaton & M.
Betham-Edwards, Matilda Barbara.
French vignettes: series of dramatic episodes, 1787-1871. '09(O23) pors. 8°, *$3 net. Brentano's.
Unfrequented France. '10(D17) il. O. $3 net. Stokes.
BETHANY, Ct.
Sharpe, W: C., *comp.* Bethany sketches and records. $1.50. W: C. Sharpe.
BETHLEHEM, Palestine.
Burrell, D: J. In David's town. 50 c. Am. Tr.
Bethlehem to Olivet. Miller, J. R. **$1.50 net. Crowell.
Bethlehem's star. Ebright, W. H., *comp.* *$2 net per 100. Eaton & M.
Béthune, Maximilien de, Baron de Rosny.
See Sully, *Duc* de.
Betrayal (The). Neale, W. $1.50. Neale.
Betrothal of Ronald and Thusnelda. Cook, N. P. 60 c. Weimer.
Betten, Rev. Fs. Sales.
Roman index of forbidden books. '09 (Mr20) 12°, *35 c. net. Herder.
Better crop of boys and girls. McKeever, W: A. gratis. W: A. McKeever.
Better man. Brady, C. T. $1.50. Dodd.
Better part. Leavitt, S. $2.50. Magnum Bonum.
Better times. Lloyd-George, D: $1 net. Doran.
Better treasure. Andrews, *Mrs.* M. R. S. $1.25. Bobbs-M.
Betterment briefs. Jacobs, H: W: $3.50. Wiley.
Bettex, Frédéric.
First page of the Bible; tr. from the 2d German ed., with the former tr. compared and rev. by the Rev. F. C. Longaker. '08(F1) O. pap., 25 c. Germ. Lit. Bd.
BETTING.
See Gambling.
Betts, Anson Gardner.
Lead refining by electrolysis. '08(Mr7) il. figs. 8°, $4. Wiley.
Betts, G: Herbert.
Distribution and functions of mental imagery. '09(N) 99 p. 8°, (Columbia Univ. Teachers' College, contributions to education.) $1; pap., 75 c. Teachers' Coll.
Betts, Harold Scofield.
Properties and uses of the southern pines. '09(O) c. 30 p. il. 8°, (U.. S., Dept. of Agriculture. Forest Service; circular.) pap. (Add. Superintendent for price.)
Betty, pseud.
See Garity, Mary E.
Betty Baird ser. *See* Weikel, Anna Hamlin.
Betty Baird's golden year. Weikel, A. H. †$1.50. Little, B. & Co.
Betty Gaston. Taggart, M. A. $1.50. Wilde.
Betty in Canada. McDonald, *Mrs.* E. G. B. 60 c. Little, B. & Co.
Betty of the rectory. Smith, *Mrs.* E. T. $1. Grosset.
Betty Vivian. *See* Smith, *Mrs.* E. T.
Betty Wales, B.A. Warde, M. †$1.25. Penn Pub. Co.
Betty Wales & Co. Warde, M. $1.25. Penn Pub. Co.
Betty Wales on the campus. Warde, M., *pseud.* $1.25. Penn Pub. Co.
Betty's happy days. Wells, C. $1.50. Century Co.
Between friends. Aumerle, R: 85 c. Benziger.
Between the Testaments. Grant, C. M. *75 c. net. Revell.
Between-time poems. Davies, O. *$1.25 net. Lane.
Between two rebellions. Coolidge, A. C. $1. A. C. Coolidge.
Betz, F:, ed.
Die Schildbürger, ihre weisheit und grosze torheit; sel. and ed., with notes, exercises and vocab. '10(O8) c. S. (Heath's modern language ser.) 35 c. Heath.
Beuve, Charles Augustin, Sainte-.
See Sainte-Beuve, Charles Augustin.
Bevan, E: J:
See Cross, C. F.
Bevan, T:
Stories from British history. '10(Jl16) 12°, 50 c. net. Little, B. & Co.
Bevel gear tables. Engstrom, D. A. $1. Henley.
Bevel gearing. Flanders, R. E. 25 c. Indust. Press.
BEVERAGES.
Emerson, E: R. Beverages, past and present. 2 v. **$5 net. Putnam.
Rigby, W. O. Reliable candy teacher, [and summer drinks.] $2. W. O. Rigby.
See also Liquors;—Soda water.
Beveridge, Albert Jeremiah.
Americans of to-day and to-morrow. '08 (O17) c. S. 50 c. Altemus.
Meaning of the times, and other speeches. '08(Jl11) c. por. O. **$1.50 net. Bobbs-M.
Work and habit. '08(Jl4) c. S. 50 c.; ooze cf., $1. Altemus.
Beveridge, Wilfred W: Ogilvie.
See Wanhill, C. F.
Beveridge, W: H:
Unemployment; problem in industry. 2d ed. '10(Mr12) O. *$2.40 net. Longmans.
Bevier, Isabel, and Usher, Susannah.
Food and nutrition. Rev. ed. '08(O24) c. D. *$1 net. Whitcomb.
—, and Van Meter, Anna R.
Selection and preparation of food, lab'y guide. Rev. ed. '10(N5) c. 12°, 75 c. Whitcomb.
Bewer, Julius A., ed.
See Bible.
Bexell, J: Andrew.
The business side of farming: text-book for students in agriculture and a manual for home-study. '09(D) c. forms, 8°, 50 c. J: A. Bexell.

Bey, Theophilus.
Williamsport illustrated. '10(Ag) 150 p. il. pors. f°, $1.50. T. Bey.

Beyer, T:
American battleship and life in the navy; also humorous yarns as told by a blue-jacket: (American battleship in commission;) pub. by special authority of U. S. Navy Department; endorsed by Admiral Dewey and Rear-Admiral Evans. '08 (Ap4) c. por. tabs., map, D. $1.25. Laird.
Life in the navy, (the American battleship;) also humorous yarns. '09(F13) c. il. facsims., tabs., D. pap., 25 c. Laird.

Beyerle, Lincoln Hamlin.
The quitters. '10(S24) c. il. D. $1.50. Conkey.

Beygrau, F. R.
See Hammond, H. W.

Beynon, R:
Drapery and drapers' accounts. '09(Ag28) tabs., D. (Pitman's traders' hdbks.) $1. Pitman.

Beyond the blue grass. Gill, G: C. $1.50. Neale.

Beyond the border. Rogers, L. W. 10 c. Theosophical Bk.

Beyond the borderline of life. Myers, G. *$1 net. Ball Pub.

Beyond the marshes. Gordon, C: W: *25 c. net. Revell.

Beyond the Mexican Sierras. Wallace, D. $2 net. McClurg.

Beyond the natural order. Best, N. R. *75 c. net. Revell.

Beyond the rocks. Glyn, *Mrs.* E. S. †$1.50. Duffield.

Beyond the skyline. Aitken, R. $1.50. B: W. Huebsch.

Beyond the sunset. Dorr, *Mrs.* J. C. R. $1.25. Scribner.

Beyond these voices. O'Leary, A. M. $1.25. B'way Pub.

Beyond this ignorant present. D., L. S. T. $1.25. Cassell.

Beza, Thdr.
Life of John Calvin; tr. by H: Beveridge. '09(Je12) D. 50 c. Westminster Press.

Bezold, Friedrich, and Siebenmann, Friedrich.
Text-book of otology for physicians and students, in 32 lectures. '08(Mr.) c. 314 p. il. 8°, *$3.50 net. Colegrove.

Bhagavad gita. *See* Mahabharata.

BHUTAN, India.
White, J. C. Sikhim and Bhutan. *$6 net. Longmans.

Biagi, Guido.
Men and manners of old Florence. '09 (O16) il. O. *$3.50 net; hf. cf. or hf, mor., *$6.50 net. McClurg..

Bianca's daughter. Forman, J. M. $1.50. Harper.

Bianchi, Mrs. Alex.
See Bianchi. *Mrs.* Martha Gilbert Dickinson.

Bianchi, Mrs. Martha Gilbert Dickinson, [Mrs. Alex. Bianchi.]
Cuckoo's nest. '09(Je19) 12°, $1.50. Duffield.
Modern Prometheus. '08(Mr4) c. front. D. †$1.50. Duffield.

Bianchi, Mrs. Martha Gilbert Dickinson, comp.
Russian lyrics, songs of Cossack, lover, patriot and peasant done into English verse. '10(My7) c. D. $1.25 net. Duffield.

Biart, Lucien.
Monsieur Pinson; ed. by Otto Siepmann. '10(D24) 16°, (Macmillan's new ser. of French texts.) 35 c. net. Macmillan.

Bibelns gudomlighet. Truedson, N. P. $1. N. P. Truedson.

Bible. Authorized version of the English Bible 1611; ed. by W: Aldis Wright. 5 v. '09. 23+495; 617; 775; 425; 575 p. 8°, (Cambridge English classics.) ea., *$1.50 net; per set, *$6.50 net. Putnam.

Bible. Bible and its story; ed. by Prof. C: F. Horne and Rev. Julius A. Bewer. '08 (D) c. il. map, 4°. (Add. pub. for price.) Niglutsch.

Bible. Bible for home and school; ed. by Shailer Mathews. Acts: the second volume of Luke's work on the beginnings of Christianity; with interpretative comment, by G: Holley Gilbert. '09(Ja9) 16°, 75 c.—Epistle of Paul to the Galatians, by B: W. Bacon. '09(O23) c. S. **50 c. net.—Epistles to the Colossians and Ephesians; ed. by Gross Alexander. '10(Ja22) c. S. **50 c. net.—Isaiah, by J: Edg. McFadyen. '10(D3) c. map, S. 90 c. net.—Hebrews; ed. by Edg. Johnson Goodspeed. '08(D12) c. S. *50 c. net.—Genesis, by Hinckley G. Mitchell. '09 (N13) c. S. **90 c. net. Macmillan.

Bible. Cambridge Bible for schools and colleges: the Wisdom of Solomon, ed. by J. A. F. Gregg. '09(My15) 16°, 50 c. Putnam.

Bible. Cambridge Bible; revised version. Epistle of Paul the apostle to the Ephesians, Philippians, Colossians, and to Philemon; ed. by W. K. Lowther Clarke. '09 (My) 8+98 p. 16°, *50 c. net. Putnam.

Bible. Christian worker's Holy Bible; indexed and marked in red on all subjects connected with the theme of salvation; with introd. by Rev. Jesse Lyman Hurlbut, D.D. Authorized version. '10(Ja1) c. il. O. limp leath., $2.50. Winston.

Bible. Companion Bible; being the authorized version of 1611; with the structures and notes, critical, explanatory, and suggestive. pt. 1, Genesis to Joshua; pt. 2, Joshua to Job; with 10 appendices. '10 (D24) O. ea., $1.50; leath., $2.50. Oxford Univ.

Bible. Happy Sunday hours. [Bible stories.] '09, [1910.] (F) 312 p. il. 4°, $2. Nelson.

Bible. Helping hand: suggestions for winners of souls; arr. by W: Wistar Hamilton. '08(Ap25) c. 12°, leath., 25 c.; pap., 15 c. Am. Bapt.

Bible. Holy Bible; marked on temporal blessings; auth. version marked on all subjects connected with the theme of temporal blessings; marked by J. G. Lawson; clear type, self-pronouncing ed. '10(Ag27) c. il. O. (International ser.) limp leath., $3.30, boxed; $7.50, boxed. Winston.

Bible. Ideal Holy Bible, self-pronouncing, self-interpreting, self-explanatory; ed. and arr. by Arth. Roberts; 100 p. of half-tone il. '08(Ag15) c. pls. forms, 4°, $5; hf. leath., $7.50; leath., $10. Spiegel, M., S. Co.
Issued in 1906 under title "The analytical Holy Bible," by The Egyptian Publishing Co., Carbondale, Ill. *See* "American catalog," 1905-07, [1906.]

Bible. Key to the Bible: an encyclopedia of the persons, places and things of the Bible. '08(Mr.) c. 447 p. il. 4°. (Add. pub. for price.) Mutual.

Bible. Marginal chain-reference Bible; containing Thompson's original and exhaustive system of topical chain references in which topics printed on the margins are so connected in series of chains as to enable the reader to trace with ease through the entire Scriptures any important subject selected; self-pronouncing text; comp. and ed. by Fk. C: Thompson. '08(D) c. maps, 8°. (Add. pubs. for price.) Eaton & M.

Bible. Narrative Bible; ed. by Clifton Johnson. '10(D3) c. il. D. $1.50 net. Baker & T.

Bible. New indexed Bible; alphabetically indexes and combines the studies of Biblical biography, geography, history, theology, the cardinal virtues, moral philosophy and character building; rev. and enl. from the orig. ed. '10(Ja15) c. 3 pts. in 1 v., il. maps, forms, 4°, $8.75; Teachers' ed., $7.75. J. A. Dickson.

Bible. Red letter holy Bible; prophetic types and prophecies in the Old Testament referring to Christ, also references to portions of the Old Testament quoted and referred to by Jesus [and] words spoken by Jesus printed in red; tr. out of the orig. tongues. Author. version, self-pronouncing text. '10(Ja1) maps, O. limp leath., $2.50. Winston.

Bible. Scofield reference Bible; authorized version, with a new system of connected topical references to all the greater themes of Scripture, with annotations, revised marginal renderings, summaries, definitions, and index; ed. by Rev. Cyrus Ingerson Scofield. '09(My8) c. maps, 8°, *$2 net; French mor., *$3.50 net; *$4 net; Alaska seal, *$5 net; Oxford India pap. ed., Alaska seal, *$6.50 net; *$7 net; mor., *$8 net; sealskin, *$10 net. Oxford Univ.

Bible. [Selections.] Blessings; being Bible mosaics of blessings, promises, commands, admonitions and answers; comp. by Agness Greene Foster. '09(D18) c. il. 16°, Reliance ed., flex. Florentine, *75 c. net; Fabriano ed., *$1.25 net, boxed. P. Elder.

Bible. [Selections.] Father and child; [comp.] by M. E. B., [Mrs. J: Crosby Brown.] '10(Ja1) c. S. 50 c. Am. Tract.

Bible. [Selections.] Railway through the Word; or, the holy Bible analyzed; being an arrangement of the topics, persons, places, and things mentioned and discussed in the Old and New Testaments; by Montgomery Ford Essig. '08(O) c. 776 p. il. 4°, $5.75. Southwestern Co., (Nashville.)

Bible. Self-interpreting Bible, with commentaries, references, harmony of the Gospels and the helps needed to understand and teach the text; introd. by Bp. J: H. Vincent; references, explanatory notes and tabulated statistics, ed. and rev. by Rev. Ja. W. Lee; geographical, historical and explanatory comments by Josiah L. Porter; expository notes, dissertations and side lights by H: Cooke; references, reflections, tabulated statistics and comments by J: Brown. 4 v. '09(Je12) c. il. maps, f°, $26. Bible Educ.

Bible. Textual concordance of the Holy Scriptures; arr. especially for use in preaching. '08(O17) c. 8°, *$3.50 net. Benziger.

Bible. O. T. Coptic (Sahidic) version of certain books of the Old Testament from a papyrus in the British Museum; ed. by Sir Herbert Thompson. '09(Ja23) facsim., O. $5. Oxford Univ.

Bible. O. T. Golden thoughts from the Hebrew prophets; ed., with a preface, by F. G. Montefiore. '08(D5) 16°, (Golden thoughts lib.) *50 c. net; leath., *75 c. net. Lane.

Bible. O. T. Hebrew prophets for English readers in the language of the Revised Version of the English Bible, printed in their poetical form, with headings and brief annotation; ed. by Fs. H. Woods and Fs. E. Powell. In 4 v. v. 1, Amos, Hosea, Isaiah (1-39) and Micah. '09(Ap3) D. 85 c. Oxford Univ.

Bible. O. T.: Hebrew prophets for English readers in the language of the revised version of the English Bible; printed in their poetical form, with headings and brief annotation; ed. by Francis H. Woods and Francis E. Powell. In 4 v. v. 2, Zephaniah, Nahum, Habakkuk and Jeremiah. '10 (Mr26) D. 85 c. Oxford Univ.

Bible. O. T. Heroes of Israel; with notes and questions for young students, by Thdr. Gerald Soares. '09(Ja23) c. il. maps, Teacher's manual, D. (Constructive Bible studies; Elementary ser.) ea., $1. Univ. of Chic.

Bible. O. T. Interlinear Psalms: authorized version and the revised version with the marginal notes of the revised version. '08 (Je6) T. *45 c. net. Putnam.

Bible. O. T. Literary man's Bible: selection of passages from the Old Testament, historic, poetic and philosophic, illustrating Hebrew literature; arranged with introd. essays and annotations by W. L. Courtney. [4th ed.] '09(My15) O. *$1.25 net. Crowell.

Bible. O. T. Narrative episodes from the Old Testament; ed., with introd., notes and outline study, by Maud Elma Kingsley and Fk. Herb. Palmer. '10(D10) c. 16°, (Kingsley English texts.) 40 c. Palmer Co.

Bible. Old Testament. 4 v. v. 1 and 2, Law and history; v. 3, Prophecy and poetry; v. 4, Homiletic, wisdom and apocalyptic. '08 (O10) 12°, ("Best books" ser.) leath., ea., *$1 net. Dutton.

Bible. Old-Testament history; narrated for the most part in words of the Bible; sel. and arr. by G: Carter. '08(O24) maps, D. 50 c. Oxford Press.

Bible. O. T. Old Testament in Greek, according to the text of Codex Vaticanus, supplemented frcm other uncial manuscripts, with a critical apparatus containing the variants of the chief ancient authorities for the text of the Septuagint; ed. by Alan England Brooke and Norman McLean. v. 1, part 1, Genesis; pt. 2, Exodus and Leviticus. '09(My22) 4°, bds., ea., *$4 net. Putnam.

Bible. O. T. Old Testament narratives, sel. and ed. by E: Chauncey Baldwin. '10(N5) c. S. (Eclectic English classics.) 20 c. Am. Bk.

Bible. O. T. Old Testament narratives; sel. and ed. by G: H: Nettleton. '09(Je12) c. S. (English readings.) 60 c. Holt.

Bible. O. T. Old Testament narrative separated out, set in connected order and ed. by Alfr. Dwight Sheffield. '10(D17) c. D. $1.50 net. Houghton M.

Bible. O. T. Selections; ed., with introd. and notes, by Fred. Newton Scott. '10 (O8) 24°, (Amer. and Eng. pocket classics.) 25 c. net. Macmillan.

Bible. O. T. Book of Esther; critical edition of the Hebrew text, with notes by Paul Haupt. '08(Je20) 8°, pap., *$1 net. Univ. of Chic.

Bible. O. T. Deuteronomy. The Washington manuscript of Deuteronomy and Joshua, by H: A. Sanders. '10(O8) c. facsim. 4°, (Univ. of Michigan studies; Humanistic ser.) pap., $1. Macmillan.

Bible. O. T First book of Kings; rev. version by H. C. O. Lanchester. '10(Jl9) c. 12°, 50 c. net. Putnam.

Bible. O. T. Isaiah; tr. from a text rev. in accordance with the results of recent criticism; with introds., critical notes and explanations; together with a prefatory note by S. R. Driver, D.D.; tr. by G: Herbert Box. '09(S18) maps, 8°, *$2.25 net. Macmillan.

Bible. O. T. Job: Book of Job; introd. by G. K. Chesterton. '09(Ap28) il. 16°, ooze, *$2 net. Dodge.

Bible. O. T. Micah, by Max L. Margolis. '09(F20) c. D. (Holy Scriptures, with commentary.) cl., 75 c. Jewish Pub.

Bible. O. T. Psalms. Commentary on the Psalms; comp. from the theological works of Emanuel Swedenborg by the Rev. Rob. S. Fischer. '10(S) c. 7+520 p. 12°, $1.25. Mass. New Ch. Un.

Bible. O. T. Psalms. Ninety-first psalm. '10(D24) 16°, ooze, 75 c.; pap., 50 c. Dodge.

Bible. O. T. Psalms. Rhythmic psalter; ed. by F. H. Wales. '10(D24) D. $1.40. Oxford Univ.

Bible. New Testament. '08(O17) 16°, ("Best books" ser.) leath., *$1 net. Dutton.

Bible. N. T.: Bible in modern English; or, the modern English Bible (New Testament); rendering from the origs. by an American making use of the best scholarship and latest researches at home and abroad. '10(Ap23) c. D. $1.10 net. Perkiomen Press.

Bible. N. T. Compilation of the healings of Christ and his apostles as recorded in the New Testament; comp. by Madge Hortense Myers Butcher. '08(O) 13-71 p. 12°, 50 c. M. H. M. Butcher.

Bible. N. T. Epitomē tēs Kaines Diathēkēs: an epitome of the New Testament; by the Rev. N. J. Stoffel; rev. by Michael Fs. Oswald. [2d ed.] '08(N7) c. 12°, $1. Univ. Press, (Notre Dame.)

Bible. N. T. Four Gospels and the Acts of the Apostles of the New Testament of Our Lord and Savior Jesus Christ and the Psalms; tr. [into Chamorro] out of the original tongues. '08, [1909.] (O) 462 p. 12°, pap., 30 c. Am. Bible.

Bible. N. T. Gospel according to St. Luke; introd. and notes by A. S. Walpole. '10 (Ag20) c. O. 40 c. Oxford Univ.

Bible. N. T. Gospel, according to St. Mark; with introd. and notes by Rev. A. S. Walpole. '09(Ap3) S. 40 c. Oxford Univ.

Bible. N. T. Life of Christ, told in words of the gospels; arranged by Mary Lape Fogg. '09, [1910.] (Ja) c. 195 p. il. 8°, 50 c. Angel Press.

Bible. N. T. Life of our Lord; chronologically arr. by the Rev. J: F. Lawis. '08 (F22) 16°, *30 c. net; leath., *60 c. net. Dutton.

Bible. N. T.: Modern speech New Testament; idiomatic tr. into English from the resultant Greek Testament, by R: Fs. Weymouth; ed. and rev. by E. Hampden-Cook. '10(My14) 12°, $1.25 net; leath., $2.25 net. Baker & T.

Bible. N. T. New Testament in Greek; according to the authorized version, together with the variations adopted in the revised version; ed. by F. H. A. Scrivener. '08(Je6) D. *90 c. net; *$1.10 net; India pap., *$1.40 net; *$1.50 net. Putnam.

Bible. N. T. New Testament in the revised version of 1881, with fuller references; ed. by A. W. Greenup and J. H. Moulton. '10 (D17) 8°, $3; limp mor., $4.50; Oxford India pap. ed., $7.50. Oxford Univ.

Bible. N. T. The pictorial New Testament; with pictures and engravings from drawings made in Bible lands by J. Clark and the late H. A. Harper for the Scripture Gift Mission. '08(Ag22) T. 65 c.; smooth sheepskin, $1.25. Am. S. S.

Bible. N. T.: [Selections.]: What Jesus said; topical arrangement and analysis of all His words in the New Testament; separated from the context. '10(Ap9) c. 12°, $1.25 net. Revell.

Bible. N. T. Students' comprenensive topical Bible commentary; embracing the 27 books of the New Testaments in both the authorized and revised versions, arranged in alternating verses, elucidated with critical and explanatory notes; together with a complete hist. and biog. dict.; the words and works of Jesus. [Standard comparative ed.] '09(N) c. il. pors. maps, 4°, $4.25; mor., $5.25. O. A. Browning.

Bible. N. T. University New Testament in modern historical and literary form; for the church, the school, and the home; embracing the life of Jesus Christ in the words of Mark, Matthew, Luke and John, and the church of the apostles according to Acts, the Epistles and Revelation historically harmonized by the Rev. S. Townsend Weaver. '09(D) c. 26+496 p. 12°, $3.25. Winston.

Bible. N. T. Works of Jesus; being the Bible narrative of His acts of healing and other deeds, in chronological order; with the Sermon on the Mount as His own summary of His teachings; arranged by Edna S. Little. '09(D18) il. 8°, Bethlehem ed., flex. fabriano, *75 c. net; Olivet ed., fabriano bds., *$1.25 net, boxed. P. Elder.

Bible. N. T. Apocalypse of St. John I-III: the Greek text; with introd., commentary, and additional notes by F. J. A. Hort. '08(Je13) 8°, **$1 net. Macmillan.

Bible. N. T. Apocryphal books. Paralipomena: remains of gospels and sayings of Christ, by Rev. Bernhard Pick. '08(Ag1) c. 11+158 p. facsim., 12°, (Christianity of to-day ser.) bds., *75 c. net. Open Court.

Bible. N. T. The four gospels, (American standard version.) '08(Mr21) 4 v., Tt. pap., ea., 5 c. Nelson.

Bible. N. T. Galatians: Der brief Pauli an die Galater, ausgelegt von Joh. Ph. Köhler. '10(Ap) 143 p. 8°, 75 c. Northwestern Pub.

Bible. N. T. Galatians; ed. by A. L. Williams. '10(Jl9) c. 8°, (Cambridge Greek Testament ser.) $1 net. Putnam.

Bible. N. T. Gospels: Synoptic Gospels; ed., with introd. and commentary, by C. G. Montefiore, together with a series of additional notes by I. Abrahams. In 3 v. v. 1, 2. '10(Ap9) 8°, ea., $2.50 net. Macmillan.

Bible. N. T.: Gospels. Synoptic Gospels arranged in parallel columns by J. M. Thompson. '10(Mr26) O. $2.50. Oxford Univ.

Bible. N. T. Gospels: Walks and words of Jesus; paragraph harmony of the four Gospels, originally comp. by Rev. M. N. Olmsted. Rev. ed., to which is added "New sayings of Jesus." '10(D17) 12°, $1.50. G. M. McClintock.

Bible. N. T. James, Epistle of; the Greek text; with introd., notes and comments, by Jos. Bickesteth Mayor. 3d ed. '10(Jl16) 8°, $4.50 net. Macmillan.

Bible. N. T. John. Magical message according to Iōannēs, (To kata Iōannēn Euangelion,) commonly called the Gospel according to [St.] John; verbatim tr. from the Greek done in modern English, with introd. essays and notes by Ja. M. Pryse. '09, [1910] (F5) c. 8°, $2. Theo. Pub. Co.

Bible. N. T. Mark. Pronaunsing Baibl; Gospel acôrding tu Mârc; transliterated by permission from the American standard ed. of the rev. Bible, into a fonetic pronouncing print; by O. C. Blackmer. '09, [1910.] (N) 14+5-49+12 p. 12°, 10 c. P. W. Blackmer.

Bible. N. T. Matthew. Gospel of Matthew: from the Twentieth Century New Testament. '10(O) 16°, pap., 5 c. net. Revell.

Bible. N. T. St. Luke. Rev. ed., by E. Wilton Smith; with introd., notes and map. School ed. '08(D19) 8°, *50 c. net. Putnam.

Bible. N. T. St. Paul's epistles to Colossae and Laodicea; the epistle to the Colossians viewed in relation to the epistle to the Ephesians; with introd. and notes by J: Rutherfurd. '08(D12) O. *$2.25 net. Scribner.

Bible. N. T. St. Paul's epistles to the Thessalonians and to the Corinthians: new translation by the late W. G. Rutherford; with a prefatory note by Spenser Wilkinson. '08(Ag1) 8°, *$1.10 net. Macmillan.

Bible. N. T. Sermon on the Mount. '08 (F29) c. nar. D. (Rubric ser.) **60 c. net. Duffield.

BIBLE.

Abbott, C. L. Common sense Bible teacher. 25 c. C. L. Abbott.

Acton, M. W: Secret Bible hist. of Adamic innocence. $2. New Age.

Ainslie, P: Introd. to the study of the Bible. 50 c. Temple Seminary.

Aked, C: F., *comp.* One hundred responsive readings from the Scriptures. *75 c. net. Revell.

Allen, R. C. Bible in our public schools. 25 c. Jennings.

Auchincloss, W: S. Chronology of the Holy Bible. $1. Van Nostrand.

Ayars, J: E. People's hand-book of the Bible. 85 c. Meth. Episcopal.

Barnes, C: R., *ed.* People's Bible encyclopedia. 2 v. $9. People's Pub.

Barry, W: Tradition of scripture: its origin, authority and interpretation. **$1.20 net. Longmans.

Beard, T: F. Biblische symbole. $1.75; $2.25; $2.50. J: A. Hertle.

Bosch, *Mrs.* H. Bible stories told to "Toddles." 80 c. net. Longmans.

Boughton, L. G. Plain man and his Bible. **60 c. net. Am. Bapt.

Bowman, E. S. Bible doctrine of devotion. *20 c. net. Un. B. Pub.

Brown, G: G., *comp.* Holy Bible repudiates "prohibition." $1; 25 c. G: G. Brown.

Burton, C: J. Astronomy and the Bible. $1. C: J. Burton.

Child, T: Bible: its rational principle of interpretation 50 c. Warne.

Church pulpit commentary. In 12 v. v. 1-8. ea., *$2 net. Gorham.

Clarke, W: N. Sixty years with the Bible. **$1.25 net. Scribner.

Conley, J: W. Educative value of the Bible. 5 c.; per 100, $2.50. Am. Bapt.

Cook, A. S. Authorized version of the Bible and its influence. $1 net. Putnam.

De Laurence, L. W: God, the Bible, truth and Christian theology. $3.50. De Laurence, S.

Dolin, S. Evolution of the spiritual world; new discovery which reveals mysteries of the Bible. 15 c. C. D. Raymer.

Donaldson, O. F. Workingman's view of the Bible. *$1.20 net. Sherman, F.

BIBLE.—*Continued.*

Driver, S: R. Modern research as illustrating the Bible. $1.20. Oxford Univ.

Dummelow, J: R., *ed.* Commentary on the Holy Bible. **$2.50 net. Macmillan.

Egypt Exploration Fund, Græco-Roman Branch. Fragments of an uncanonical gospel from Oxyrhynchus. 40 c. Oxford Univ.

Ellicott, *Bp.* C: J: Bible commentary for English readers. In 12 v. ea., 75 c. net; $1.25 net. Cassell.

Errett, I: Querists' drawer; discussion of difficult subjects and passages of the Scriptures. $1.50. Standard Pub.

Ewing, W., *and* Thompson, J. E. H. Temple dict. of the Bible. $4 net. Dutton.

Faunce, D. W. Mature man's difficulties with his Bible. **75 c. net. Am. Bapt.

Figgis, J: N. Gospel and human needs. *$1.25 net. Longmans.

Foster, C: Story of the Bible from Genesis to Revelation, told in simple language. $1.50. C: Foster.

Foster, *Mrs.* M. J. C. Mother the child's first Bible teacher. *25 c. net. Jennings.

Gaffney, T: C., *comp. and ed.* Bible symbols. $2. J: A. Hertel.

Gilbert, G: H. Interpretation of the Bible. **$1.25 net. Macmillan.

Godbey, S: M. Bible and problem of poverty. *$1 net. Revell.

Gray, C. E. Experimental object lessons; Bible truths simply taught. 75 c. net. Revell.

Grover, N. W. Catechetical Bible lessons. 10 c. Winona.

Haldeman, I: M. Thinking above what is written. 10 c. C: C. Cook.

Hale, H. G., *and* Hall, N. M., *comps.* Biblical dramas for use especially in young people's meetings and the evening services of the church. 12 v. ea., 15 c. Pilgrim Press.

Harvey, E. L. Sermons on Bible characters. 50 c. Metropolitan Ch. Assoc.

Hastings, J., *ed.* Dictionary of the Bible. **$5 net. Scribner.

Hentz, J: P. Hist. of the Lutheran version of the Bible. $1.25. J: P. Hentz.

Hicks, W: Bible thoughts; with questions and answers. 25 c. Nat. Bapt. Pub.

Houghton, *Mrs.* L. S. Telling Bible stories to children. **$1.25 net. Scribner.

Huntington, G: Charms of the old Book. *90 c. net. Am. S. S.

Hurlburt, J. L. Bible atlas. $2.75. Rand, McN. & Co.

Hurlbut, J. L., *ed.* Handy Bible encyclopedia. $1.50; $2; $3. Winston.

Jackson, S: T. Lincoln's use of the Bible. *25 c. net. Eaton & M.

Jacobus, M. W., *ed.* Roman Catholic and Protestant Bibles compared. **$1.25 net. Scribner.

Jacobus, M. W., *and others, eds.* Standard Bible dictionary. $6; $10; $12; indexed, 50 c. extra. Funk.

Jefferson Bible (The). 25 c.; 50 c. McKay.

BIBLE.—*Continued.*

Jordan, W. G. Biblical criticism and modern thought. *$3 net. Scribner.

Kecht, *Bp.* F. J. Child's Bible hist. 25 c.—Pract. commentary on Holy Scripture, for the use of those who teach Bible hist. $4.20 net. Herder.

Keeble, S: E., *ed.* Social teaching of the Bible. *$1 net. Eaton & M.

Keeler, B. C. Short history of the Bible. 75 c.; 50 c. Farrell.

Kemble, D. Teachings of the holy Scriptures. *40 c. net. Am. S. S.

Kennedy, *Mrs.* M. G. Our boys and girls; how to interest and instruct them in Bible study. 75 c. Wilde.

Keyser, L. S. Rational test; Bible doctrine in the light of reason. 75 c.; 60 c. Lutheran Pub.

Knight, C: R., *and* Hardcastle, E. Birds of the Bible for young people. $2. Stokes.

Lastinger, C. Key to the Bible. Tribune Pr. Co., (Fla.)

Leavitt, J: M. Bible League essays in Bible defence and exposition. $1. Bible League.

Lee, F. T. Sidelights on the Bible. **$1 net. Winston.

Lees, H. C. Joy of Bible study. *40 c. net. Longmans.

Lewis, T: H. Divine credentials of the Bible. $1.25. Meth. Protestant.

Limerick, D. T., *ed.* How to know the holy Bible. 20 c. Praise Pub.

Lofthouse, W. F. Bible, its origin and authority. *50 c. net. Eaton & M.

McComb, S: Making of the English Bible. **$1 net. Moffat.

McCormick, J: N. Bible holiness. 50 c. Pub. Assoc. Friends.

McFadyen, J: E., *and* Votaw, C. W., *comps.* Best books for Old and New Testament study. 20 c. Pub. Ho. of M. E. Ch., So.

McFarland, J: T: The Book and the child. *5 c. net. Eaton & M.

Maclaren, A. Expositions of the Holy Scriptures. In 30 v. 3d and 4th ser., in 6 v. ea., per set, *$7.50 net. Armstrong.

MacPhail, M. L. Magnetism of the Bible. *75 c. net. Am. S. S.

Magnus, *Lady.* Picture stories from the Bible. $2; $1.75. Tuck.

Mamreov, A. F. Day with the Good Shepherd; [interpretation of texts referring to shepherds.] 50 c. net. Eaton & M.

Maunder, E: W. Astronomy of the Bible. *$1.25 net. Doran.

Maunder, E: W. Astronomy of the Bible. *$2 net. M. Kennerley.

Mauro, P. Life in the Word. *50 c. net. Revell.

Médaille, P. Meditations on the Gospels for every day in the year. *$1.50 net. Herder.

Messmer, S. G. Outlines of Bible knowledge. $1.80 net. Herder.

Miller, J. R. Devotional hours with the Bible. In 8 v. vs. 1, 2, 3, 4. ea., *$1.25 net. Doran.

BIBLE.—*Continued.*

Mills, L. H. Avesta eschatology compared with the books of Daniel and Revelations. 50 c.; 75 c. Open Court.

Moninger, H. H. Standard commentary on the International Sunday-school lessons. 75 c. Standard Pub.

Montefiore, C. G. Bible for home reading. pt. 2. $1.50 net. Macmillan.

Moody, D. L. Fulness of the gospel. *50 c. net. Revell.

Moore, W. W: Indispensable book. 75 c. net. Revell.

Mord, W. Friends from the Book of books: twelve Bible stories. $1.50. Stokes.

Morgan, G: C. Analyzed Bible. v. 2, O. T., Job to Malachi; v. 3, The New Testament introduction, Matthew to Revelation; v. 4, The Gospel according to John; v. 5, Book of Job; v. 6, Romans; v. 7, Prophecy of Isaiah, v. 1; v. 8, Prophecy of Isaiah, v. 2. ea., $1 net.—Bible and the cross. *50 c. net.—Study and teaching of the English Bible. 50 c. net. Revell.

Mortimer, *Mrs.* M. New peep of day: Bible lessons for children.] 50 c. Doran.

Mullany, J: F. Bible studies. $1.25. Mason-H.

Murray, W: D. Bible stories to tell children. $1 net. Revell.

Nash, L. L. Early morning scenes in the Bible. $1 net. Revell.

Newman, A. Writing on the clouds. 90 c. net. Sherman, F.

Norvell, P. A. Studies in Old Testament history.—Studies in the apostolic age.—Studies in the life of Christ. ea., *20 c. net. Am. Bapt.

Orr, J. Revelation and inspiration. *75 c. net. Scribner.

Peake, A. S: Bible in the twentieth century. $1.25 net. Doran.

Picton, J. A. Man and the Bible. **$2 net. Holt.

Piercy, W: C., *ed.* Illustrated Bible dictionary. *$5 net. Dutton.

Pierson, A. T. Bible and spiritual life. $1.50. Gospel Pub.

Porter, *Mrs.* G. S-. Birds of the Bible. $2. Jennings.

Potter, S: L. Bible stories as they are recorded in the Bible. $1.50. S: L. Potter.

Ragg, L. Book of Books; story of the Bible. $1.40 net. Longmans.

Rand, J. L. Systematic supplementary Bible studies. In 3 pts. pt. 1, **5 c. net; pts. 2 and 3, ea., **10 c. net. Am. Bapt.

Reimensyder, J: M. Ancient history and the Bible. 35 c. 20 c. Lutheran Pub.

Remy, J. S. Bible stories for little children in words of one syllable. 50 c. Altemus.

Rice, E. W. Orientalisms in Bible lands. $1 net. Am. S. S.

Robertson, F: W: Sermons on Bible subjects. *$1 net. Dutton.

Schenck, F. S. Sociology of the Bible. *$1.50 net. Reformed.

BIBLE.—*Continued.*

Scott, T. Pleasure of reading the Bible. 50 c.; $1. M. Kennerley.

Seeberg, R. Revelation and inspiration. *75 c. net. Harper.

Seymour, R. G. Fresh water from old wells: being the wells of the Bible with their spiritual and moral lessons. **80 c. net. Am. Bapt.

Shearer, J. B. Scriptures, fundamental fact and features. 60 c. Presb. Pub.

Sheldon, W. L. Story of the Bible from the standpoint of modern scholarship. $1. S. B. Weston.

Smith, S: G. Religion in the making; study in Biblical sociology. **$1.25 net. Macmillan.

Soulsby, L. H. M. Suggestions on Bible reading. 35 c. Longmans.

Soulsby, L. H. M., *comp.* Year's Bible readings. 35 c. Longmans.

Standard biblical atlas. 75 c. Funk.

Stewart, M., *ed.* "Tell me a true story": tales of Bible heroes. *$1.25 net. Revell.

Sunday stories for a year. 75 c. Nelson.

Sunderland, J. T: Bible and the Bible country. 60 c. Unitarian S. S.

Sunderland, J. T: Origin and character of the Bible, and its place among the sacred books. *$1.20 net. Am. Unitarian.

Swete, H: B., *ed.* Essays on some Biblical questions of the day. *$3.75 net. Macmillan.

Temple treasury; a Biblical diary. $1.50. Am. Tr.

Tilly, F: E., *ed.* God bless you; collection of Bible stories. 25 c. E. Kaufmann.

Todd, J. Looking forward; or, Bible studies into the future. 50 c. Highlands.

Toffteen, O. A. Researches in Biblical archæology. v. 1, Ancient chronology; v. 2, The historic Exodus. ea., *$2.50 net. Univ. of Chic.

Townsend, L. T. Bible inspiration. 10 c. L. T. Townsend.

Watters, H: E. The Bible of superhuman origin. 50 c.; 25 c. H: E. Watters.

Weaver, A. Lesson book for Bible study. $1. A. Weaver.

Wells, A. R. Bible miniatures: character sketches of one hundred and fifty heroes and heroines of Holy Writ. *$1.25 net. Revell.

Wells, A. R. Introd. to Bible study. 30 c. Presb. Bd.

Wells, A. R. Living Bible: course of Bible-reading. 75 c.—Why we believe the Bible. $1. Un. Soc. C. E.

Wiener, H. M. Origin of the Pentateuch. 35 c. Bibliotheca Sacra.

Williams, M. B. Among many witnesses; book for Bible students. 80 c. Revell.

Williams, T. R. Shall we understand the Bible? *40 c. net. Macmillan.

Wilson, J: M. Bible as literature. 45 c.; 35 c. Unitarian S. S.

World's Bible auxiliary and beautiful teachings of the Bible. $8; $10; $12. J. R. Gay.

Young, J. B. Charms of the Bible. $1 net. Eaton & M.

BIBLE.—*Continued.*

Zorn, C. M. Hdbk. for the beginner's home study in the word of God. $1.25. Concordia Pub.

O. T. Acton, M. W: Secret Bible hist. of Adamic innocence. $2. New Age.

O. T.: Adams, J: Israel's ideal; or, studies in Old Testament theology. $1.50 net. Scribner.

O. T.: Alford, B. H. Old Testament hist. and literature. *$1.50 net. Longmans.

O. T.: Anschütz, E: Gott und sein volk; das Alte Testament in predigten dargelegt. $1.50. Germ. Bapt.

O. T.: Armstrong, R. A. Historical and literary outlines of the Old Testament. $1. Acme.

O. T. Beecher, W. J. Dated events of the Old Testament. *$1.50 net. S. S. Times.

O. T. Bell, C. C. Story of the promise: simple readings on the Old Testament. *60 c. net. Young Churchman.

O. T.: Bell, L. Lost garden: stories of familiar Old Testament characters.—Never-old stories: some stories of Old Testament kings. ea., $1.25 net. Doran.

O. T.: Berry, G: R. Old Testament among the Semitic religions. *$1 net. Griffith.

O. T. Brown, C: Birth of a nation: studies in Old Testament stories. *$1 net. Revell.

O. T.: Cantrell, E: A. Bible and modern literature. 50 c. Los Angeles Liberal.

O. T. Codex Taurinensis (Y): [earliest known manuscript of the "Dodekapropheton" in the Lucianic recension of the Septuagint.] $1.60. Oxford Univ.

O. T. Coppens, C: Choice morsels of the bread of life; or, select readings from the Old Testament. *60 c. net. Herder.

O. T. Cornill, C. H. Music in the Old Testament. 50 c. Open Court.

O. T.: Cragin, L. E. Old Testament stories for little children. $1.25 net. Revell.

O. T.: Driver, S: R. An introd. to the literature of the Old Testament. *$2.50 net. Scribner.

O. T. Duff, A. Hints on Old Testament theology. *$1 net. Macmillan.

O. T. Duncan, J. G. Exploration of Egypt and the Old Testament. *$1.50 net. Revell.

O. T.: Fluegel, M. Exodus, Moses and the Decalogue legislation. $2. Fluegel.

O. T. Geden, A. S. Outlines of introduction to the Hebrew Bible. *$3.50 net. Scribner.

O. T. Girdlestone, R. B. Old Testament theology and modern ideas. *40 c. net. Longmans.

O. T. Goodrich, A. S. Normal class manual of Old Testament history. *50 c. net. Revell.

O. T. Harper, R. F., *and others, eds.* Old Testament and Semitic studies in memory of William Rainey Harper. 2 v. *$10 net. Univ. of Chic.

O. T. Hodges, G: Garden of Eden; stories from the first nine books of the Old Testament. $1.50. Houghton M.

BIBLE.—*Continued.*

O. T. Hoyt, W. Some of the reasons why I cannot accept the results of the destructive criticism of the Old Testament. 10 c. Am. Bapt.

O. T. Huffman, J. A. Old Testament messages of the Christ. 75 c. Bethel Pub.

O. T.: Kennett, R. H. Church's gain from modern thought as shown in Old Testament study. 20 c. net. Longmans.

O. T.: Kent, C: F. Founders and rulers of united Israel from the death of Moses to the division of the Hebrew kingdom.—Heroes and crises of early Hebrew history from the creation to the death of Moses.—Kings and prophets of Israel and Judah. ea., **$1 net.—Sermons, epistles and apocalypses of Israel's prophets. $2.75 net. Scribner.

O. T. Knudson, A. C. Old Testament problem. *35 c. net. Jennings.

O. T.: Macy, S. B. From slavery to freedom. $1.25 net. Longmans.

O. T.: Mayer, E. Joshua to Ruth: a Sabbath-school book. 30 c. E. Mayer.

O. T.: Medbury, C: S. From the Jordan to the throne of Saul. 25 c. Standard Pub.

O. T. Miller, M. F. Lure of the Book. $1. Winona.

O. T. Mozley, J. B. Ruling ideas in early ages and their relation to Old Testament faith. *$1.25 net. Longmans.

O. T.: Parker, C. H. S. Stories from the Old Testament. 35 c.; 25 c.; 65 c. Unitarian S. S.

O. T. Platt, S., *comp.* Stories from the Old Testament; retold. $1.50. Dodge.

O. T. Robinson, C: H: Human nature a revelation of the divine: argument for the Old Testament. 25 c. Longmans.

O. T.. Rule, U. Z. Old Testament institutions. $2 net. Gorham.

O. T.: Sampey, J: R: Heart of the Old Testament. 50 c. S. S. Bd., So. Bapt.

O. T.: Shearer, J: B. Selected Old Testament studies. 60 c. net. Presb. Bd.

O. T. Smith, J: M. P. Books for Old Testament study. *50 c. net. Univ. of Chic.

O. T.: Spencer, F. E. Old Testament history. *40 c. net. Longmans.

O. T.: Stebbins, E. W. H., *and* Saunderson, H: H. Old Testament narratives. In 2 pts. ea., 40 c.; 30 c. Unitarian S. S.

O. T. Tappan, E. M. An old, old storybook. $1.50. Houghton M.

O. T.: Thackeray, H: St. J. Grammar of the Old Testament in Greek according to the Septuagint. v. 1. *$2.75 net. Putnam.

O. T. Thomas, J. E. Old Testament in the light of the religion of Babylonia and Assyria. *$1.40 net. Macmillan.

O. T. Thomas, J: M. Christian faith and the Old Testament. **$1 net. Crowell.

O. T. Trumbull, C: G. Men who dared: studies in Old Testament manhood. (Add. pubs. for price.) Y. M. C. A.

BIBLE.—*Continued.*

O. T.: Walker, R. H., *and* Miller, R. B: Studies in the prophets of Israel. 25 c. Eaton & M.

O. T., Pentateuch: Fleugel, M. Humanity, benevolence and charity legislation of the Pentateuch and Talmud. *$2 net. H. Fleugel.

O. T. Pentateuch: Midbury, C: S. From Eden to the Jordan: [lessons in the Pentateuch.] 50 c.; 30 c. Standard Pub.

O. T. Pentateuch: Wiener, H. M. Essays in Pentateuchal criticism. $1.50. Bibliotheca Sacra.

O. T. Daniel: Haskell, S. N. Story of Daniel the prophet. $1-$1.75. Bible Training.

O. T. Daniel: Hicks, J: S. S. Divine time table. 50 c.; 30 c. J: S. S. Hicks.

O. T. Daniel: Pettingill, W: L. Simple studies in Daniel. (Not for sale.) F. Kelker.

O. T. Exodus: Caedmon. Exodus and Daniel: two old English poems. *60 c. net. Heath.

O. T. Exodus: Gearhart, A. F. Story of Moses adapted for primary grades. 10 c. Flanagan.

O. T. Exodus: Knox, E. M. Bible lessons for schools: Exodus. *40 c. net. Macmillan.

O. T. Ezra: Torrey, C: C. Ezra studies. *$1.50 net. Univ. of Chic.

O. T. Genesis: American commentary on the Old Testament. Book of Genesis. $2 net. Am. Bapt.

O. T. Genesis: Bettex, F. First page of the Bible. 25 c. Germ. Lit. Bd.

O. T. Genesis: Goggin, T. E. Man's great charter: exposition of the first chapter of Genesis. *$1.75 net. Gorham.

O. T., Genesis: Gordon, A. R. Early traditions of Genesis. *$2.25 net. Scribner.

O. T. Genesis: Gray, J. M. Great epochs of sacred hist. and the shadows they cast. 50 c. Revell.

O. T. Genesis: Macy, S. B. In the beginning; being the book of Genesis told to children. $1.25 net. Longmans.

O. T. Genesis: Stinson, J. C. The searchlight; a scientific review of Genesis. 25 c. J. C. Stinson.

O. T. Genesis: Williams, H: R. Blighted life of Methuselah. $1. Nat. Bapt. Pub.

O. T. Genesis: Williams, L. M. Jacob the heel-grasper: [sermons.] $1. L. M. Williams.

O. T. Isaiah: Exell, J. S. Biblical illustrator. *$2 net. Revell.

O. T., Isaiah: Glazebrook, M. G: Studies in the book of Isaiah. $1.90. Oxford Univ.

O. T., Isaiah: Lazell, F: J: Isaiah as a nature-lover. 60 c. Torch Press.

O. T., Isaiah: Robinson, G: L. Book of Isaiah. 75 c. Y. M. C. A.

O. T. Isaiah: Rogers, A. Prophecy and poetry: studies in Isaiah and Browning. **$1.25 net. Longmans.

BIBLE.—*Continued.*

O. T., Job: Brown, C: R. Strange ways of God: study in the Book of Job. *75 c. net. Pilgrim Press.

O. T. Job: Villiers, H: M. Perfect through suffering; being thoughts on the Book of Job. *$1.50 net. Longmans.

O. T. Joel: Gaebelein, A. C. Prophet Joel. 75 c. Our Hope Office.

O. T. Jonah: Boyd, J. S. Story of Jonah: the truant prophet. *75 c. net. J. S. Boyd.

O. T. Obadiah: Peckham, G: A. Introd. to the study of Obadiah. 25 c. net. Univ. of Chic.

O. T. Proverbs: Banks, L: A. Problems of youth; series of discourses for young people on themes from the book of Proverbs. **$1.30 net. Funk.

O. T. Proverbs: Kosmos; poem from the proverbs of Solomon. 50 c. MacCalla.

O. T. Psalms: Barnes, W. E. Lex in corde (the law in the heart); studies in the psalter. $1.50 net. Longmans.

O. T. Psalms: Bonner, D: F. Psalmody question: an examination of the alleged divine appointment of the book of Psalms as the exclusive manual of praise. *50 c. net. Hanford & H.

O. T., Psalms: Boyd, F. L. Law and love: a study of "quomodo dilexi," (Psalm cxix, 97-104.) *90 c. net. Longmans.

O. T., Psalms: Crane, F. Song of the Infinite. *50 c. net. Pilgrim Press.

O. T., Psalms: Elliott, J: H: Brook in the pasture: [lesson drawn from twenty-third psalm.] 25 c. Un. Soc. Chr. E.

O. T. Psalms: Gasquet, F. A., *and* Bishop, E. Bosworth psalter. *$4.50 net. Macmillan.

O. T. Psalms: Prothero, R. E. Psalms in human life. *35 c. net; *70 c. net. Dutton.

O. T. Psalms: Ruutz-Rees, J. E. Reflections on the Psalms. 50 c. Newson.

O. T. Psalms: Steps unto heaven; meditations and prayers on the Psalms. $1.50. Northfield Press.

O. T. Psalms: Voices of prayer; or, thoughts on Psalm eighty-six. $1. Longmans.

O. T. Ruth: Quayle, W: A. Book of Ruth. *$1.50 net; *$2.50 net. Dodge.

O. T. Samuel: Spaulding, A. W. Man of valor: a story of the life of Jonathan, son of Saul. 75 c. Review and Herald Pub.

O. T. Samuel: Willett, H. L. Studies in the first book of Samuel. $1.50. Univ. of Chic.

O. T.: Song of Solomon: Brett, J. Garden of God; some characteristics of the spiritual life mainly from the Song of Solomon. *$1.20 net. Longmans.

O. T.: Song of Solomon: Quayle, W: A. Song of songs. 35 c. net. Eaton & M.

O. T. Zephaniah: Zandstra, S. Witness of of the Vulgate, Peshitta and Septuagint to the text of Zephaniah. *$1 net. Macmillan.

Apocrypha: Wisdom of the Apocrypha. 60 c. net. Dutton.

BIBLE.—*Continued.*

N. T. Abbott, L., *and* McFadyen, J: E. Interpreter's commentary on the New Testament. v. 1-6. ea., $1.50. Barnes.

N. T. Adair, W. W. Wrecks and heroes: [lessons on New Testament heroes.] 10 c. Y. M. C. A.

N. T. Ainslie, P: Among the Gospels and the Acts. $1.50. Temple Seminary.

N. T. Bacon, B: W. Introd. to the New Testament. *$1 net. Macmillan.

N. T. Bullinger, E. W: Critical lexicon and concordance to the English and Greek New Testament. $5.25. Longmans.

N. T.: Butler, A. A: How to understand the words of Christ. *90 c. net. Whittaker.

N. T. Child's story of the New Testament in words of one syllable. 50 c. Altemus.

N. T.: Clark, G. W. People's commentary. In 9 v. v. 9, I, II and III John, Jude and Revelation. $1.25. Am. Bapt.

N. T.: Craigin, L. E. Kindergarten stories for the Sunday-school and home. *$1.20 net. Doran.

N. T.: Deissmann, G. A. Light from the ancient East. $4 net. Doran.

N. T.: Fairfield, O. J. Stories from the New Testament. 35 c.; 25 c.; 65 c. Unitarian S. S.

N. T. Gould, E. P. Biblical theology of the New Testament. *$1 net. Macmillan.

N. T. Greene, J. N. Gospel in literature. 75 c. Jennings.

N. T. Gregory, C. R. Griechischen handschriften des Neuen Testaments. $3.30. Lemcke.

N. T. Harnack, C. G. A. New Testament studies: II., sayings of Jesus. *$1.75 net. Putnam.

N. T. Historical and linguistic studies in literature related to the New Testament. Second ser. v. 1, *$3 net; v. 2, pt. 1, *50 c. net. Univ. of Chic.

N. T. Hodge, R: M. New Testament authors and their works. *30 c. net. Seiler.

N. T. MacDonald, H. L. *and* G. W. New Testament alphabet in rhyme for little people. $1 net. Pott.

N. T. Maclaren, A. Expositions of Holy Scripture. In 30 v. 5th ser. in 8 v. $10. (Sold in series only.) A. C. Armstrong.

N. T.: Mathews, S. Gospel and the modern man. $1.50 net. Macmillan.

N. T.: Mathews, S. Social gospel. **50 c. net. Griffith & R.

N. T. Moninger, H. H. New Testament church, for advanced teacher-training classes. 50 c.; 30 c.—Studies in the Gospels and Acts. (Add. pubs. for price.) Standard Pub.

N. T.: Moorehead, W: G. Outline studies in the New Testament: Catholic epistles. 75 c. net. Un. Presb. Bd.

N. T. Nicoll, *Sir* W: R., *ed.* Expositor's Greek Testament. v. 4, 5. ea., $7.50. Dodd.

N. T.: Norton, F: O. Hexicographical and historical study of Diatheke. *75 c. net. Univ. of Chic.

N. T.: Park, J: E. Wonder of His gracious works. *$1 net. Pilgrim Press.

N. T.: Peake, A. S: Critical introd. to the New Testament. *75 c. net. Scribner.

N. T.: Philbrook, H: B. The Bible: interpretation of its parables. 20 c. H: B. Philbrook.

N. T. Pick, B. Apocryphal acts. $1.25. Open Court.

N. T. Pullan, L. New Testament criticism during the past century. *30 c. net. Longmans.

N. T. Ramsay, A. Revelation and the Johannine epistles. 75 c. net. Revell.

N. T. Riddle, M. B. Story of the Revised New Testament. *75 c. net. S. S. Times.

N. T.: Robertson, A. T: Short grammar of the Greek New Testament. $1.50. Armstrong.

N. T. Scott, E. F. Apologetic of the New Testament. *$1.50 net Putnam.

N. T.: Sewell, E. G. Gospel lessons and life history. *$1.15 net. McQuiddy.

N. T.: Strachan, J. Captivity and pastoral epistles. 75 c. net. Revell.

N. T. Taylor, W. B. Studies in the Epistles and Revelation. 75 c. Standard Pub.

N. T. Vedder, H: C. Our New Testament: how did we get it? **$1 net. Am. Bapt.

N. T. Vincent, J: M. History of the textual criticism of the New Testament. *$1 net. Macmillan.

N. T. Von Hase, K. New Testament parallels in Buddhistic literature. *40 c. net. Eaton & M.

N. T. Warman, F. S. G. New Testament theology. 40 c. net. Longmans.

N. T.: Whitaker, R. Gospel at work in modern life. 50 c. net. Griffith & R.

N. T. Winstanley, E: W: Spirit in the New Testament. *$1.10 net. Putnam.

N. T.: Wrede, W: Origin of the New Testament. *75 c. net. Harper.

N. T.: Wright, J. Grammar of the Gothic language, and the Gospel of St. Mark; selections from the Second Epistle to Timothy. $1.75. Oxford Univ.

N. T.: Zahn, T. Introd. to the New Testament. In 3 v. *$12 net. Scribner.

N. T., Acts: Andrews, H. T. Acts of the Apostles. *75 c. net. Revell.

N. T. Acts: Bosworth, E: I. New studies in Acts. 75 c.; 50 c. Y. M. C. A.

N. T., Acts: Cecelia, *Madame*. Acts of the Apostles: Catholic Scripture manual. bks. 1, 2. $1.25. Benziger.

N. T. Acts: Harnack, C. G. A. New Testament studies. III., Acts of the Apostles. *$1.75 net. Putnam.

N. T. Acts: Rice, E. W. Commentary on the Acts. *$1.25 net. Am. S. S.

N. T. Acts: Williams, C: B. Participle in the Book of Acts. *50 c. net. Univ. of Chic.

N. T. Corinthians: Mackintosh, R. Thessalonians and Corinthians. *75 c. net. Revell.

BIBLE.—*Continued.*

N. T. Corinthians: Rendall, G. H: Epistle of St. Paul to the Corinthians. *$1 net. Macmillan.

N. T. Gospels: Abbott, E. A. Indices to Diatessarica: [harmony of the four Gospels.] *$1.25 net. Macmillan.

N. T., Gospels: Barth, F. Gospel of St. John and the synoptic gospels. *40 c. net. Eaton & M.

N. T. Gospels: Chapman, D. J. Notes on the early history of the Vulgate gospels. $5.25. Oxford Univ.

N. T. Gospels: Charles, R. H., *ed.* Testaments of the twelve patriarchs. *$5.25 net. Macmillan.

N. T., Gospels: Edmunds, A. J. Buddhist and Christian gospels now first compared from the originals. In 2 v. ea., *$2 net. A. J. Edmunds.

N. T. Gospels: Foster, C: Story of the Gospel. 75 c. C: Foster.

N. T. Gospels: Hawkins, *Sir* J: C. Horae synopticae. $3.40. Oxford Univ.

N. T., Gospels: Hodges, G:, *comp.* When the King came: stories from the four Gospels. **$1.25 net. Houghton M.

N. T., Gospels: Horner, J. Gospels of Matthew and Luke. *60 c. net; *40 c. net. —Supp. to "The Gospels of Matthew and Luke." 10 c. J. Horner.

N. T., Gospels. Petrie, W: M. F. Growth of the Gospels as shown by structural criticism. 90 c. net. Baker & T.

N. T., Gospels: Schmiedel, P. W. Johannine writings. *$1.50 net. Macmillan.

N. T. Gospels: Stalker, J. Ethic of Jesus according to the synoptic Gospels. *$1.75 net. Armstrong.

N. T. Gospels: Stanton, V. H: Gospels as historical documents. In 4 pts. pt. 1, *$2.50 net; pt. 2, *$3.25 net. Putnam.

N. T. Hebrews: Du Bose, W: P. High priest and sacrifice: exposition of the epistle to the Hebrews.

N. T., Hebrews: Moule, H. C. G. Messages from the epistle to the Hebrews. *60 c. net. Doran.

N. T., Hebrews. Peake, A. S. Heroes and martyrs of faith: exposition of the 11th chapter of the Epistles to the Hebrews. $1.50 net. Doran.

N. T., James. Cook, S. A. Meaning of life: study in the Epistle of James. 35 c. Jennings.

N. T. James: Hort, F. J: A. Epistle of St. James. *$1.10 net. Macmillan.

N. T. John: Bacon, B: W. Fourth Gospel in research and debate. **$4 net. Moffat.

N. T. John: Clark, H: W. Gospel of St. John. *75 c. net. Revell.

N. T. John: Eckman, G: P. Studies in the gospel of John. *$1 net. Jennings.

N. T., John: Lewis, F. G. Irenæus testimony to the fourth Gospel. *50 c. net. Univ. of Chic.

N. T. John: Ridgway, W: H. Ridgway's religion for folks who don't have any: notes on John. **50 c. net. Griffith.

BIBLE.—*Continued.*

N. T. John: Robinson, J. A. Historical character of St. John's gospel. 25 c. Longmans.

N. T., John: Scott, E. F. Historical and religious value of the fourth Gospel. 50 c. Houghton M.

N. T. John: Seekings, H. S. For joy's sake: studies in the teaching of St. John. *50 c. net. Jennings.

N. T., John: Swedenborg, E. Commentary on the Gospel of John. $1.25. Mass. New-Ch. Un.

N. T. John: Worsley, F. W. Fourth Gospel. **$1.25 net. Scribner.

N. T., John, Epistles of: Findlay, G: G. Fellowship in the life eternal; exposition of Epistles of St. John. *$2.50 net. Doran.

N. T., John, First epistle of: Law, R. Tests of life: study of the first epistle of St. John. *$3 net. Scribner.

N. T. Luke: MacDermott, G. M. Gospel according to St. Luke. 35 c. net. Young Churchman.

N. T. Mark: Bacon, B: W. Modern commentary: beginnings of Gospel story, Mark. *$2.25 net. Yale Univ.

N. T., Mark: Green, S: G. Gospel of St. Mark: [commentary.] *75 c. net. Revell.

N. T. Mark: MacDermott, G. M. Gospel according to St. Mark. 35 c. Young Churchman.

N. T. Matthew: Horton, R. F. Devotional commentary on the gospel of St. Matthew. *$1 net. Revell.

N. T. Matthew: MacDermott, G. M. Gospel according to St. Matthew. 35 c. Young Churchman.

N. T. Matthew: McLaughlin, G: A. Commentary on the Gospel according to St. Matthew. $1.50. Chr. Witness.

N. T. Matthew: Plummer, A. Exegetical commentary on the Gospel according to St. Matthew. *$3 net. Scribner.

N. T. Matthew: Rice, E. W. Commentary on the Gospel according to Matthew. $1.25. Am. S. S.

N. T. Matthew: Robinson, L. Gates and keys to Matthew. 50 c. Pentecostal.

N. T. Matthew: Smith, D: Gospel of St. Matthew. *75 c. net. Revell.

N. T. Paul, Epistles of: Scott, R. Pauline Epistles. *$2 net. Scribner.

N. T., Philippians: Bachman, N. Light in dark places; or, lectures on the Epistle to the Philippians. 60 c. net. Presb. Pub.

N. T. Philippians: Jowett, J. H. High calling: meditations on St. Paul's letter to the Philippians. *$1.25 net. Revell.

N. T. Philippians. Norton, S. A. Call of the heights; echoes from the Letter to the Philippians. 50 c. net. Pilgrim Press.

N. T. Revelation: Downey, W: Thoughts on themes from Patmos. v. 1. $1.25. Downey.

BIBLE.—*Continued.*
N. T. Revelation: Gowen, H. H: Revelation of "the things that are": an exposition of Revelation IV. and V. *50 c. net. Whittaker.
N. T. Revelation: Inger, A. J. Revealed translation of John's Revelation. 50 c. A. J. Inger.
N. T., Revelation. Jowett, G: T: Apocalypse of St. John. 40 c. Oxford Univ.
N. T. Revelation: Knappenberger, J. B. Exposition of the Book of Revelation. $1. J. B. Knappenberger.
N. T. Revelation: Mead, W. W. Apocalypse of Jesus Christ: an exposition. **$1 net. W. W. Mead.
N. T. Revelation: Moorehead, W: G. Studies in the Book of Revelation. *75 c. net. Un. Presb. Bd.
N. T. Revelation. Nowell, W: C. Lectures on the book of Revelation. $1. Edwards.
N. T., Revelation: Smith, F: G: Revelation explained. $1. Gospel Trumpet Co.
N. T. Revelation: Swete, H. B. Apocalypse of St. John. *$3.75 net. Macmillan.
N. T., Romans: Broughton, L. G. Salvation and the old theology: pivot points in Romans. *75 c. net. Revell.
N. T. Thessalonians: Buckland, A. R. First Epistle to the Thessalonians.—St. Paul's second Epistle to the Thessalonians. ea., *$1 net. Am. S. S.
N. T. Thessalonians: Mackintosh, R. Thessalonians and Corinthians. *75 c. net. Revell.
N. T. Thessalonians. Milligan, G: St. Paul's Epistle to the Thessalonians. *$2.60 net. Macmillan.
See also Apostles;—Apostolic succession;—Atonement;—Bedouins;—Catechisms; — Christian science;—Christianity; — Church history; — Commandments;—Congregational church;—Conversion; — Creation; — Deluge; —Devotional exercises and meditations;—God;—Hebrew literature;—Higher criticism;—Holy Spirit;—Holy week;—Illustrations (*religious*);—International critical commentary;—Jesus Christ;—Jews;—Law;—Lord's prayer;—Miracles;—Palestine;—Parables—Paul, *St.*;—Prophecies;—Prophets;—Religion;—Religion and science;—Revivals;—Saints;—Sermon on the Mount;—Sermons;—Sunday school; — Temple; — Theology; — *also* author entries under Bible; — Century Bible hdbks;—*also* Texts and studies; ed. by J. A. Robinson.

Bible and labor. Hitchens, E. L. 25 c. Baker & B.
Bible application of Freemasonry. Huie, W: G. $1.50. W: G. Huie.
BIBLE CLASS.
See Sunday-school.
Bible in Shakespeare. Burgess, W: *$1.50 net. Revell.
Bible nature series. Cady, M. E. no. 1. $1.25. Pacific Press.
Bible of nature. Thomson, J: A. **$1 net. Scribner.
Bible on instrumental music. Wyatt, F: F. 25 c. F: F. Wyatt.
Bible readings and hymns for school use; prepared at the request of the Board of Education, Ann Arbor, Michigan. '09 (My1) c. O. 50 c. Wahr.
Bible rhymes for the not too young. Kummer, C. B. 75 c. net. Dodge.
Bible-school vision. Welshimer, P. H. 50 c.; 30 c. Standard Pub.
Bible studies for adult classes. See Norvell, Philip A.
Bible studies in missions. D. Revell.
—Carver. Missions in the plan of the ages. *$1.25 net.
Bible study on prayer. Gamertsfelder, S. J. 40 c. Pub. Ho. of Evangelical Assoc.
Bible study union (Blakeslee) graded lessons. il. 12°. Bible Study.
—Gates. Heroes of the faith. 50 c.
Bible study union lessons; senior grade. il. 12°. Bible Study.
—Boone. Conquering Christ. 50 c.
BIBLEOPATHY.
See Hygiene.
Biblical account of the creation. Sabiston, M. $1.50. Knickerbocker Press.
Biblical criticism. Jordan, W. G. *$3 net. Scribner.
Biblical ideas of atonement. Burton, E. D. $1. Univ. of Chic.
Biblical stories retold for children. See Harrison, Edith Ogden.
Bibliographical contributions of the Library of Harvard University. 8°. Harvard Univ.
—Morgan. Bibliography of Persius. 75 c.
Bibliographical puzzle. Davis, A. M. (Priv. pr.) J. Wilson.
BIBLIOGRAPHIES.
Accidents: Lynch, C. American National Red Cross text-book on first aid and relief columns. *$1 net. Blakiston.
Advertising: Lewis, E. S. Financial advertising. $5. Levey.
Advertising: Scott, W. D. Psychology of advertising. **$2 net. Small.
Advertising: Starch, D. Principles of advertising. $1. Univ. Co-op.
Advertising: Stryker, A. M. Advertiser's hdbk. [Trade journals and class publications: advertising information.] $1. Trade Journ.
Aerial navigation: Brockett, P. Bibliog. of aeronautics. $2.25; $2. Smith. Inst.
Aerial navigation: Brooklyn Public Library. Aeronautics; list of books and references to periodicals in the Library. gratis. Brooklyn Lib.
Aerial navigation: Turner, C: C. Aerial navigation of to-day. *$1.50 net. Lippincott.
Æsthetics: Gordon, K. Esthetics. $1.50. Holt.
Æsthetics: Howard, W: G., *ed.* Laokoon. $1.50. Holt.
Agricultural chemistry: United States. *Dept. of Agriculture. Bu. of Soils.* Reference list on electric fixation of atmospheric nitrogen and the use of calcium cyanamid and calcium nitrate on soils. (Add. Superintendent for price.)
Agricultural education: United States. *Dept. of Agriculture.* Boys' and girls' agricultural clubs. (Add. Superintendent for price.) U. S., Supt. of Docs.
Agricultural machinery: Davidson, J. B., *and* Chase, L. W. Farm machinery and farm motors. $2. Judd.

BIBLIOGRAPHIES.—*Continued.*

Agricultural periodicals: Tucker, G. M. American agricultural periodicals. (Priv. pr.) G. M. Tucker.

Agriculture: Bailey, L. H. On the training of persons to teach agriculture in the schools. 15 c. U. S., Supt. of Docs.

Agriculture: Bull, C. P. Rural school agriculture. 60 c. C. P. Bull.

Agriculture: Fisher, M. L., *and* Cotton, F. A. Agriculture for common schools. $1. Scribner.

Agriculture: List of periodicals currently received in the library of the U. S. Department of Agriculture. (Add. Superintendent for price.)

Agriculture: Main, J. Manual for high schools, with special reference to science and agriculture. gratis. J. Main.

Agriculture: Massachusetts Agricultural College, Amherst. Short Course Dept. List of books on agriculture. gratis. W. D. Hind.

Agriculture: Organization, work and publications of the Agricultural Education Service. (Add. Superintendent for price.) U. S., Supt. of Docs.

Agriculture: Portland, Ore. Library Association. List of books on agriculture. gratis. Portland (Ore.) L. A.

Agriculture: Public school agriculture, 1909. gratis. R. J. Watts.

Agriculture: United States. *Dept. of Agriculture.* Agriculture; list of publications of the United States Agriculture Department. gratis. U. S., Supt. of Docs.

Agriculture: United States. *Dept. of Agriculture.* Agriculture. Public documents issued from the office of the Superintendent of Documents. gratis.

Agriculture: U. S., *Dept. of Agriculture.* Classified list of publications available for distribution April 1, 1909. gratis.

Agriculture: United States. *Dept. of Agriculture.* Experiment Stations Office: bulletins, circulars, Experiment Station record, and reports of colonial experiment stations. gratis.

Agriculture: United States. *Dept. of Agriculture.* Public documents issued by the secretary's office. gratis. Gov. Pr. Off.

Agriculture: United States. *Dept. of Agriculture.* Publications, and how they are distributed. gratis.

Agriculture: United States. *Superintendent of Documents.* Bulletins, circulars, etc. gratis.

Agriculture: United States. *Superintendent of Documents.* Plant Industry Bureau; bulletins, circulars and misc. publications rel. to plants. gratis.

Agriculture: United States. *Superintendent of Documents.* Public documents issued by the Agriculture Dept. gratis.

Agriculture: United States. *Superintendent of Documents.* Statistics Bureau; bulletins, circulars, foreign markets, separates from yearbook, and crop reporter. gratis. U. S., Supt. of Docs.

Agriculture: Upham, A. A. Introd. to agriculture. 75 c. Appleton.

Agriculture: Warren, G: F: Elements of agriculture. **$1.10 net. Macmillan.

Agriculture: Wilkinson, J: W. Practical agriculture. $1. Am. Bk.

Ainsworth, William Harrison: Ellis, S. M. William Harrison Ainsworth and his friends. $10 net. Lane.

Alaska: Greely, A. W. Hdbk. of Alaska. **$2 net. Scribner.

Alaska survey publications: Wright, F. E. *and* C: W. Ketchikan and Wrangell mining districts, Alaska. (Add. Superintendent for price.) U. S. Supt. of Docs.

Alcohol: Stark, J. Alcohol. $1.50 net. Putnam.

Alcott, Louisa May: The Louisa Alcott story book, with biographical sketch. 50 c. net. Little, B. & Co.

Alcuin: Page, R. B. Letters of Alcuin. $1; 50 c. Forest Press.

Aldrich, T: B.: Greenslet, F. Life of Thomas Bailey Aldrich. **$3 net; **$5 net. Houghton M.

Alston, *Mrs.* Theodosia Burr: Pidgin, C: F. Theodosia, the first gentlewoman of her time. *$2.50 net; *$3 net. C. M. Clark.

American literature: Bowen, E. W. Makers of American literature. *$2.50 net. Neale.

American literature: Pattee, F. L. Hist. of American literature. $1.20 net. Silver.

American literature: Simonds, W: E: Student's history of American literature. $1.10. Houghton M.

American literature: Stanton, T., *ed.* Manual of American literature. **$1.75 net. Putnam.

American poetry: Otis, W: B. American verse, 1625-1807. **$1.75 net. Moffat.

Ammonia: Renshaw, R. R. 4-aminophthalic acid and some of its derivatives. (Add. author for price.) R. R. Renshaw.

Anarchy and anarchism: Eltzbacher, P. Anarchism. $1.50. B: R. Tucker.

Anatomy: Wiedersheim, R. Comparative anatomy of vertebrates. *$3.75 net. Macmillan.

Anemia: Hunter, W: Severest anæmias. v. 1. *$3.25 net. Macmillan.

Angellier, A.: Page choisies. $1.15. Oxford Univ.

Anglo-Saxon language: Bale, C. E. Syntax of the genitive case in the Lindisfarne Gospels. 50 c. Univ. of Ia.

Anglo-Saxon literature: Ayres, H. M. Bibliographical sketch of Anglo-Saxon literature. 25 c. net. Lemcke.

Anglo Saxon literature: Riddles of the Exeter book. $2.50. Ginn.

Anthropometry: Seaver, J. W. Anthropometry and physical examination. $1.50. J. W. Seaver.

Appendicitis: Vale, F. P. Has surgical treatment lessened the mortality from appendicitis. 50 c. Snow & F.

Arbitration: Griffin, A. P. C., *comp.* List of references on international arbitration. 20 c. U. S., Supt. of Docs.

BIBLIOGRAPHIES.—*Continued.*

Arches: Reuterdahl, A. Theory and design of reinforced concrete arches. $2. M. C. Clark.

Architects: Chancellor, E. B. Lives of the British architects. $2 net. Scribner.

Architecture: Gotch, J. A. Growth of the English house. *$3 net. Scribner.

Arctic regions: Brooklyn Public Library. Polar regions; list of books in the Library. gratis. Brooklyn Lib.

Arctic regions: Greely, A. W. Hdbk. of polar discoveries. $1.50 net. Little, B. & Co.

Argentine Republic: Hirst, W: A. Argentina. $3 net. Scribner.

Aristophanes. Acharnians. $3 net. Macmillan.

Arithmetic: Smith, D: E. Rara arithmetica. *$5.50 net. Ginn.

Arithmetic: Smith, D: E. Rara arithmetica: catalogue of the arithmetics written before MDCI. $20. Ginn.

Arizona: Munk, J. A. Arizona bibliography. gratis. J. A. Munk.

Arkansas: Purdue, A. H., *and* Branner, J: C. Slates of Arkansas, with bibliog. of geology of Arkansas. gratis. Arkansas Geol. Survey.

Armenian church: Arpee, L. Armenian awakening. *$1.25 net. Univ. of Chic.

Arnold-Forster, Hugh Oakeley: Arnold-Forster, M. S.-M. The Right Honourable Hugh Oakeley Arnold-Forster. $4.50 net. Longmans.

Aryan language: Denison, T: S. Mexican-Aryan comparative vocab. $2. T: S. Denison.

Asoka: Smith, V. A. Asoka: Buddhist emperor of India. $1.15. Oxford Univ.

Astronomy: Forbes, G: Hist. of astronomy. **75 c. net. Putnam.

Athens, Greece: D'Ooge, M. L. Acropolis of Athens. *$4 net. Macmillan.

Athens, Greece: Savage, C: A. Athenian family: sociological and legal study. *$1.50 net; *$1.25 net. Lord Balto. Pr.

Athens, Pa.: Murray, *Mrs.* L. W. History of old Tioga Point and early Athens, Pa. *$5 net. L. W. Murray.

Atlases: United States. *Library of Congress.* List of geographical atlases in the Library of Congress. 2 v. (Add. Superintendent for price.)

Augustine, *St.:* Simpson, W. J. S. St. Augustine and African church divisions. $1.25 net. Longmans.

Austen, J. Works. St. Martin's ed. In 10 v. ea., **$1.25 net; per set, **$12 net. Duffield.

Austen, J.: Helm, W. H: Jane Austen and her country-house comedy. *$3.50 net. Lane.

Authors: Phelps, W: L. Essays on modern novelists. **$1.50 net. Macmillan.

Authorship: Gerwig, G: W: Art of the short story. *75 c. net. Percy Pub.

Autobiography: Burr, *Mrs.* A. R. The autobiography. **$2 net. Houghton M.

Autobiography: Griggs, E: H. Great autobiographies. *50 c. net; *25 c. net. B: W. Huebsch.

BIBLIOGRAPHIES.—*Continued.*

Autobiography: Trenton, N. J. Free Public Library. List of entertaining autobiographies. gratis. Trenton Lib.

Aztecs: Diven, T: J. Aztecs and Mayas. In 2 v. v. 1. $1. Antiquarian.

Babylonian inscriptions: Hinke, W: J: New boundry stone of Nebuchadrezzar I. from Nippur. $3.50. Univ. of Penn.

Bacon, F., *Lord.* Essays. *35 c. net. Heath.

Bacteria: Elliott, S. M. Household bacteriology. $1.50. Am. Sch. Home Economics.

Bacteria: Hiss, P. H., *jr.* Text-book of bacteriology. $3.75. Appleton.

Bacteria: Park, W: H., *and* Williams, A. W. Pathogenic micro-organisms. $3.75. Lea.

Balkans (The): Murray, W: S. Making of the Balkan states. $1.50. Longmans.

Balzac, Honoré de: Gillette, F. B., *comp.* Title index to the works of Honoré de Balzac. 25 c. Boston Bk.

Bancroft, George: Howe, M. A. DeW. Life and letters of George Bancroft. In 2 v. **$4 net. Scribner.

Banks and banking: Griffin, A. P. C., *comp.* Library of Congress list of books rel. to postal savings banks. 15 c.—List of works rel. to the first and second banks of the U. S.—Sel. list of books rel. to currency and banking. ea., 25 c. U. S., Supt. of Docs.

Banks and banking: Ireton, R. E. Central bank. $1.60. A. Stumpf.

Banks and banking: Johnson, J. F. Canadian banking system. Gov. Pr. Off.

Banks and banking: Robbins, E. C., *comp.* Sel. articles on a central bank of the United States. $1 net. H. W. Wilson.

Banks and banking: Scott, W: A. Money and banking. $2. Holt.

Banks and banking: Taylor, W: G: L. Financial legislation in principle and in history. $1. Univ. of Neb.

Banks and banking: United States. *National Monetary Commission.* Publications in course of preparation for the National Monetary Commission. (Add. Superintendent for price.)

Banks and banking: United States. *National Monetary Commission.* Publications issued by and in preparation for the National Monetary Commission.

Bannerman, Margaret Gordon, *Lady:* Archibald, R. C. Carlyle's first love. *$3.50 net. Lane.

Baptism: Christian, J: T. Form of baptism in sculpture and art. $1. J: T. Christian.

Baxter, R: An excerpt from Reliquiæ Baxterianæ, with essay by Sir Ja. Stephen on Richard Baxter. $1.75 net. Longmans.

Beaumont, F. Knight of the burning pestle. 60 c. Heath.

BIBLIOGRAPHIES.—*Continued.*

Beet-sugar: United States. *Dept. of Agriculture.* Beet-sugar industry in the United States. 15 c.

Beetles: Pierce, W: D. On the biologies of the *phynchophora:* [beetles.] (Not for sale.) Univ. of Neb.

Berkeley, G.: Mead, H. R., *comp.* Bibliography of George Berkeley, Bishop of Cloyne. Univ. of Cal.

Bernard *of Cluny.* Source of "Jerusalem the golden"; together with other pieces. $1.25 net. Univ. of Chic.

Beryllium: Parsons, C: L. Chemistry and literature of beryllium. $2. Chemical.

Bible: Auchincloss, W: S. Chronology of the Holy Bible. $1. Van Nostrand.

Bible: Barnes, C: R., *ed.* People's Bible encyclopedia. 2 v. $9. People's Pub.

Bible: Houghton, *Mrs.* L. S. Telling Bible stories. **$1.25 net. Scribner.

Bible: Jacobus, M. W., *ed.* Roman Catholic and Protestant Bibles compared. **$1.25 net. Scribner.

Bible: McFadyen, J: E., *and* Votaw, C. W., *comps.* Best books for Old and New Testament study. 20 c. Pub. Ho. of M. E. Ch., So.

Bible: MacPhail, M. L. Magnetism of the Bible. *75 c. net. Am. S. S.

Bible: Moninger, H. H. Standard commentary on the International Sunday-school lessons. 75 c. Standard Pub.

Bible: Orr, J. Revelation and inspiration. *75 c. net. Scribner.

Bible: Sheldon, W. L. Story of the Bible from the standpoint of modern scholarship. $1. S. B. Weston.

Bible, O. T.: Alford, B. H. Old Testament hist. and literature. *$1.50 net. Longmans.

Bible. O. T.: Berry, G: R. Old Testament and Semitic religions. *$1 net. Griffith.

Bible. O. T.: Bible for home and school; Isaiah. 90 c. net. Macmillan.

Bible. N. T.: Hodge, R: M. New Testament authors and their works. *30 c. net. Seiler.

Bible. O. T.: Kent, C: F. Sermons, epistles and apocalypses of Israel's prophets. $2.75 net. Scribner.

Bible, O. T.: Smith, J: M. P. Books for Old Testament study. *50 c. net. Univ. of Chic.

Bible, O. T.: Thackeray, H: S. Grammar of the Old Testament in Greek according to the Septuagint. v. 1. *$2.75 net. Putnam.

Bible. O. T. Isaiah: Robinson, G: L. Book of Isaiah. 75 c. Y. M. C. A.

Bible. O. T. Obadiah: Peckham, G: A. Introd. to study of Obadiah. 25 c. net. Univ. of Chic.

Bible Apocrypha: Pick, B. Apocryphal acts. $1.25. Open Court.

Bible. Apocryphal books. Paralipomena. *75 c. net. Open Court.

Bible, N. T.: Mathews, S. Social gospel. **50 c. net. Griffith & R.

BIBLIOGRAPHIES.—*Continued.*

Bible, N. T.: Peake, A. S: Critical introd. to the New Testament. *75 c. net. Scribner.

Bible, N. T., Gospels: Synoptic gospels. In 3 v. v. 1, 2. $3 net. Macmillan.

Bible. N. T. Matthew: Plummer, A. Exegetical commentary on the Gospel according to St. Matthew. *$3 net. Scribner.

Bible, N. T., Revelation: Jowett, G: T: Apocalypse of St. John. 40 c. Oxford Univ.

Biography: Carnegie Library, Pittsburgh. Lives and letters. 10 c. Carnegie Lib.

Biography: Faris, J: T. Winning their way; [short biographical sketches.] $1.50. Stokes.

Biography: McTurnan, L. Personal equation. $1.25 net. Moffat.

Biography: Thackeray, W: M. English humorists. **25 c. net. Macmillan.

Biology: Johnstone, J. Conditions of life in sea. $3. Putnam.

Biology: Lloyd, F. E., *and* Bigelow, M. A. Teaching of biology in the secondary schools. $1.50. Longmans.

Biology: Locy, W: A. Biology and its makers. *$2.75 net. Holt.

Biology: McFarland, J. Biology. $1.75. Saunders.

Biology: Pennsylvania University. Wistar Institute of Anatomy and Biology. List of biological serials, exclusive of botany, in the libraries of Philadelphia. gratis. Wistar.

Biology: Rinaldo, J. Polygeneric theory. $1.50. J. Rinaldo.

Biology: United States. *Dept. of Agriculture. Bu. of Biological Survey.* Bulletins. gratis. U. S., Supt. of Docs.

Biology: United States. *Dept. of Agriculture. Bu. of Biological Survey.* List of publications of the Biological Survey. gratis. U. S., Supt. of Docs.

Birds: Cory, C: B. Birds of the Seeward Islands, Caribbean Sea. 50 c. Field Museum.

Birds: Dearborn, N. Catalogue of a collection of birds from British East Africa. 50 c. Field Museum.

Birds: Grinnell, J. Bibliography of California ornithology. $1.50. W. L. Chambers.

Birds: Grosvenor Library, Buffalo, N. Y. Reading list on birds and bird study. gratis. Grosvenor Lib.

Birds: Seattle, Wash. Public Library. List of books about birds in the Seattle Public Library. gratis. Seattle Pub. Lib.

Björnson, B.: Payne, W: M. Björnstjerne Björnson. 50 c. net. McClurg.

Blake, William Phipps: Published writings. 50 c. net. Univ. of Ariz.

Blasco Ibáñez, V. La barraca, novela. 90 c. Holt.

Blind (The): Perkins Institution and Massachusetts School for the Blind. Circulating library. Perkins Inst.

BIBLIOGRAPHIES.—*Continued.*

Blind: Perkins Institutions and Massachusetts School for the Blind. List of embossed books, maps, appliances and tangible apparatus for the use of the blind. gratis. Perkins Inst.

Blood: Crawley, H. Studies on blood and blood parasites. (Add. Superintendent for price.) U. S., Supt. of Docs.

Blood: Meyer, W., *and* Schmieden, V. Bier's hyperemia treatment. *$3 net. Saunders.

Boccaccio, G.: Jones, F. N. Boccaccio and his imitators. 50 c. Univ. of Chic.

Bolivar, S.: Petre, F. L. Simon Bolivar. $4 net. Lane.

Bologna, Italy: James, E. E. C. Bologna, its hist., antiquity, and art. $4.80. Oxford Univ.

Bonaparte, N.: Frêmeaux, P. Drama of Saint Helena. $3 net. Appleton.

Bones: Dickson, W. E. C. Bone marrow. *$12 net. Longmans.

Book of common prayer: Dimock, N. Hist. of the Book of common prayer. 75 c. net. Longmans.

Book-plates: Almack, E: Bookplates. *$1 net. McClurg.

Bookbinders and bookbinding: Davenport, C. J. H. The book. *$2 net. Van Nostrand.

Books: A. L. A. catalog. $1. U. S., Supt. of Docs.

Books: American catalog, 1905-07; with directory of publishers. $7.50; v. 2 with notices, *$6 net. Pub. Weekly.

Books: Annual American catalog. 1908, 1909. ea., $3 net. Pub. Weekly.

Books: Betten, F. S. Roman index of forbidden books. *35 c. net. Herder.

Books: Carnegie Library of Pittsburgh. Classified catalogue, 1902-1906. In 2 v. $5. Carnegie Lib.

Books: Cole, G: W., *comp.* Catalogue of books consisting of English literature and miscellanea. 2 v. $75. Dodd.

Books: English catalogue of books for 1907, 1908, 1909; directory of publishers, ea., $1.50 net. Pub. Weekly.

Books: Evans, C: American bibliography, 1639-1820. In 6 v. ea., $15. C: Evans.

Books: Fletcher, W: I:, *ed.* Annual library index, 1907-1909. ea., $5 net. Pub. Weekly.

Books: Forbush, W: B. Broadening Path. 2 v. $5; $8. B. F. Bowen.

Books: James, M. R. Descriptive catalogue of the manuscript in the library of Gonville and Caius College. 2 v. *$3.50 net. Putnam.

Books: Laneham, R. Letter: [Captain Cox's library.] *$1.75 net. Duffield.

Books: List of books for college and high school libraries. (Add. pubs. for price.) Eau Claire Bk.

Books: List. of publications of the University of Texas. gratis. Univ. of Tex.

Books: New York State Library. Catalogue of Duncan Campbell collection. gratis. N. Y. State Library.

BIBLIOGRAPHIES.—*Continued.*

Books: Nolhac, A. M. P. G. de. Petrarch and the ancient world, [with special account of his library.] $6. Merrymount.

Books: North Carolina. *Dept. of Public Instruction.* Approved list of books for rural libraries. N. C., Dept. Pub. Instruct.

Books: Philadelphia. Free Library. Bulletin no. 8: a list of serials in principal libraries of Philadelphia and its vicinity. $2. Phila. Free Lib.

Books: Publishers' trade list annual, 1908, 1909, 1910. ea., $2. Pub. Weekly.

Books: Publishers' Weekly. Am. educational list, 1908, 1909, 1910. ea., 50 c. Pub. Weekly.

Books: Rutherford, H. W., *comp.* Catalogue of the library of C: Darwin. *30 c. net. Putnam.

Books: Shorter, C. K. Immortal memories. $1.50. Harper.

Books: Sonnenschein, W: S. Best books; reader's guide. In 3 pts. pt. 1. $3.50 net. Putnam.

Books: Soulsby, L. H. M., *comp.* Record of a year's reading. 30 c. Longmans.

Books: United States. *War Department.* Index-catalogue of the lib. of the Surgeon-General's Office. v. 13. $2. U. S., Supt. of Docs.

Books: Virginia. *Board of Education.* List of books for rural school libraries in Virginia. gratis. W: E. Jones.

Books. Whitaker's reference catalogue of current literature. 3 v. $6 net. Pub. Weekly.

Books: World's best books: suggestions for selection of a home library. 50c. Globe-W.

Books: Young Men's Christian Associations. *Educational Dept.* Outlines of courses of study. 50 c.; 35 c. Y. M. C. A.

See also Children's reading; — Fiction; — U. S. Dept. of Agriculture pubs.;—U. S. Dept. of Commerce and Labor pubs;—U. S. Pub. Health and Marine Hospital pubs.

Boston: Benton, J. H: Story of the old Boston town house, 1658-1711. (Priv. pr.) Merrymount.

Boston: Boston Public Library. Helps in the public library to the study of the hist. of Boston in the public schools. gratis. Boston Pub. Lib.

Botany: Adams, C: C. Ecological survey of Isle Royale, Lake Superior. 85 c. Mich. Geol.

Botany: Atwood, A. C., *comp.* Catalogue of botanical lib. of J: Donnell Smith presented to Smithsonian Institution. 25 c. U. S., Supt. of Docs.

Botany: Coulter, J: M., *and* Chamberlain, C: J. Morphology of gymnosperms. $4 net. Univ. of Chic.

Botany: Elliot, G: F. S. Botany of to-day. *$1.50 net. Lippincott.

Botany: Gardner, N. L. Variations in nuclear extrusion among the fucaceæ. 15 c. Univ. of Cal.

Botany: Graves, C: B., *and others.* Catalogue of the flowering plants and ferns of Connecticut. 75 c. Conn. Lib.

BIBLIOGRAPHIES.—*Continued.*

Botany: Stevens, F. L. Diseases of economic plants. $2 net. Macmillan.

Botany: Strasburger, E., *and others.* Text-book of botany. *$5 net. Macmillan.

Botany: United States. *Dept. of Agriculture. Bu. of Plant Industry.* Publications of the Bu. of Plant Industry. (Add. Superintendent for price.)

Boys: Jenks, J. W. Life questions of high school boys. (Add. pubs. for price.) Y. M. C. A.

Boys: Society for the Promotion of Social Service. Juvenile delinquent and the Young Men's Christian Association. 50 c. Y. M. C. A.

Brahms, Johannes: Colles, H. C. Brahms. $1. Brentano's.

Breathing: Benedict, F. G., *and* Carpenter, T. M. Respiration calorimeters, for studying the respiratory exchange and energy transformations of man. 75 c. Carnegie.

Brewing: Wahl, R., *and* Henius, M. American handy book of brewing. 2 v. $12. Wahl-Henius.

Bridges: Grimm, C. R. Secondary stresses in bridge trusses. $2.50. Wiley.

Briquets: Wright, C: L. Briquetting tests at the United States fuel testing plant, Norfolk, Va., 1907-8. 10 c. U. S., Supt. of Docs.

Brown, John: Villard, O. G. John Brown, 1800-1859. $5 net. Houghton M.

Browning, R. Selection from poems and plays. 40 c. Scott, F. & Co.

Browning, R. Shorter poems. **25 c. net. Scribner.

Building (construction): Jacoby, H: S. Structural details. $2.25. Wiley.

Building (construction): Radford's cyclopedia of construction. 12 v. ea., $2. Radford Architectural Co.

Bulwer-Lytton, *Sir* E: G: E. L. Last days of Pompeii. *25 c. net. Macmillan.

Burgundy, *Duchess* of: Williams, H. N. Rose of Savoy. *$3.50 net. Scribner.

Burke, E. Speech on conciliation with the colonies. **25 c. net. Scribner.

Burnet, *Bp.* Gilbert: Clarke, T. E. S., *and* Foxcroft, H. C. Life of Gilbert Burnet. *$4.50 net. Putnam.

Burns, Robert: Carlyle, T: Essay on Burns. 25 c. C: E. Merrill.

Business: Brookline, Mass. Public Library. Selected list of books on business and related subjects in the Public Library, Dec., 1909. gratis to public libraries. Riverdale Press.

Butterflies: Eltringham, H. African mimetic butterflies. $15. Oxford Univ.

Cæsar, Caius Julius: Sihler, E. G. Annals of Cæsar. $1.75 net. Stechert.

Calcium-lighting: Pond, G: G. Calcium carbide and acetylene. gratis. Penn. State Coll.

California: Engelhardt, Z. Missions and missionaries of California. v. 1. *$2.50 net. Barry.

California, James, G: W. Heroes of California. $2 net. Little, B. & Co.

BIBLIOGRAPHIES.—*Continued.*

Campbell, Alexander: Egbert, J: Alexander Campbell and Christian liberty. $1.50. Chr. Pub. Co.

Campion, T: Works. $3.40. Oxford Univ.

Canada: Amsbary, W. B. French-Canadian in prose and verse. 25 c. La Salle Extension.

Canada: Griffin, G. G., *comp.* Writings on American history. [U. S. and Canada:] bibliography, 1907, 1908. ea., *$2.50 net. Macmillan.

Canada: Wrong, G: M., *and* Langton, H. H., *eds.* Review of historical publications relating to Canada. v. 12, 13. ea., $1.50; $1. Morang.

Capital punishment: Fanning, C. E., *comp.* Select articles on capital punishment. $1. H. W. Wilson.

Carlyle, T: Essay on Burns. **25 c. net. Scribner.

Carnegie Institution of Washington. Year book no. 7, 1908. $1.25; $1. Carnegie.

Carnegie Library, Pittsburg. Index to subject catalogue of the Technology Dept. Carnegie Lib.

Carver, J.: Lee, J: T: Bibliography of Carver's travels. 35 c. State Hist., Wis.

Cathedrals: Pratt, H. M. Cathedral churches of England. $2.50 net. Duffield.

Cathedrals: Rose, E. W. Cathedrals and cloisters of the Isle de France. In 2 v. $5 net. Putnam.

Catherine of Siena, St.: Gardner, E. G. St. Catherine of Siena. *$4 net. Dutton.

Catholic Church: Bennett, W: H. Catholic footsteps in old New York. $2.50. Schwartz, K. & F.

Catholic Church: Complete catalogue of Catholic literature. 15 c. T: J. Flynn.

Catholic Church: Martin, C: A. Catholic religion. $1. Apostolate.

Catholic Church: Plummer, C: Vitae sanctorum Hiberniae. In 2 v. $9.75. Oxford Univ.

Catholic Church: Wolferstan, B. Catholic church in China. $1.30 net. Herder.

Catholic literature: Chicago Public Library. Catholic reading list. [Catholic authors.] 25 c. E: Larkin.

Catholic periodicals: Middleton, T: C. Catholic periodicals published in the United States, [1809-1892.] (Priv. pr.) T: C. Middleton.

Catholic schools: Burns, J. A. Catholic school system in the U. S. $1.25. Benziger.

Catholic theology: Scannell, T: B. Priest's studies. $1.20 net. Longmans.

Cellini, Benvenuto: Life of Benvenuto Cellini. 2 v. per set, $9 net. Macmillan.

Cells: Hertwig, O., *and* Campbell, H: J. The cell. *$2.25 net. Macmillan.

Cement: Bassler, R. S. Cement resources of Virginia. (Add. pubs. for price.) Univ. of Va.

Census. United States. *Dept. of Commerce and Labor.* Publications, 10th, 11th and 12th censuses. gratis.

BIBLIOGRAPHIES.—*Continued.*

Central America: Palmer, F. Central America and its problems. **$2.50 net. Moffat.

Ceramics: Branner, J: C. Bibliog. of clays and the ceramic arts. $2. Am. Ceramic.

Ceramics: Burton, W: *and* H. Hdbk. marks on pottery and porcelain. *$2.25 net. Macmillan.

Ceramics: Hayden, A. Chats on old earthenware. $5. Stokes.

Ceramics: Solon, L. M. E. Ceramic literture. $15 net. Lippincott.

Cereals: Reed, G: M. Mildews of the cereals. (Not for sale.) G: M. Reed.

Cervantes, S. M. de. Don Quixote. *35 c. net; *70 c. net. Dutton.

Challoner, *Bp.* Richard: Burton, E. H. Life and times of Bishop Challoner. In 2 v. *$7 net. Longmans.

Chambers, John: Parish, J: C. John Chambers. $2. State Hist. Ia.

Chancellorsville (Campaign of): Bigelow, J:, *jr.* Campaign of Chancellorsville. $10 net. Yale Univ.

Character: Sisson, E: O. Essentials of character. $1 net. Macmillan.

Chaucer, Geoffrey: Canterbury tales. 35 c. net; 70 c. net. Dutton.

Chaucer, Geoffrey: Hammond, E. P. Chaucer. *$3 net. Macmillan.

Chaucer, Geoffrey: Hinckley, H: B. Notes on Chaucer. $3. Nonotuck.

Chaucer, Geoffrey. The prologue, and The knight's tale. *75 c. net. Putnam.

Checkers: Call, W: T. Literature of checkers. $1. C. M. Potterdon.

Cheese: Thom, C: Camembert cheese problems in the U. S. (Add. Superintendent for price.) U. S., Supt. of Docs.

Cheese: Van Slyke, L. L., *and* Publo, C: A. Science and practice of cheese-making. *$1.75 net. Judd.

Chemistry: Armstrong, E. F. Simple carbohydrates and glucosides. *$1.20 net. Longmans.

Chemistry: Emery, F. B. Elementary chemistry. $1.50. Chemical.

Chemistry: Hawk, P. B. Pract. physiological chemistry. $2.50. Blakiston.

Chemistry: Lee, E. Textbook of experimental chemistry. *$1.50 net. Blakiston.

Chemistry: Lincoln, A. T:, *and* Walton, J. H., *jr.* Exercises in elem. quantitative chemical analysis. *$1.50 net. Macmillan.

Chemistry: Meade, R: K. Chemists' pocket manual. $3. Chemical

Chemistry: Nelson, J: M. Some compounds derived from the ethyl *p*-duminosuc-cinylosuccinate. (Add. author for price.) J. M. Nelson.

Chemistry: Philip, J. C. Physical chemistry. $2.10 net. Longmans.

Chemistry: Rogers, A. Laboratory guide of industrial chemistry. $1.50. Van Nostrand.

Chemistry: Smiles, S: Relations bet. chemical constitution and some physical properties. $4 net. Longmans.

BIBLIOGRAPHIES.—*Continued.*

Chemistry: Stewart, A. W. Recent advances in organic chemistry. *$2.50 net. Longmans.

Chemistry: Thorpe, *Sir* E: Hist. of chemistry. In 2 v. v. 1, 2. ea., **75 c. net. Putnam.

Chemistry: United States. *Superintendent of Documents.* Chemistry Bureau. Bulletins, circulars, etc. gratis.

Children: Appleton, L. E. Comparative study of the play activities of adult savages and civilized children. 54 c. Univ. of Chic.

Children: Mangold, G: B: Child problems. $1.25 net. Macmillan.

Children: Partridge, G. E. Outline of individual study. $1.25 net. Sturgis & W.

Children: Willard De F. Surgery of childhood, including orthopædic surgery. $7. Lippincott.

Children: Wilson, L: N., *comp.* Bibliography of child study for the year 1907. 25 c. Clark Univ.

Children's reading: Arnold, *Mrs.* G. W., *comp.* Mother's list of books for children. $1. McClurg.

Children's reading: Baker, F. T: Bibliog. of children's reading. 60 c. Teachers' Coll.

Children's reading: Boston Public Library. Brief list of books for home reading for boys and girls in the Public Library. gratis. Boston Pub. Lib.

Children's reading: Brookline, Mass. Public Library. Something to read for boys and girls. o. p. Brookline Pub. Lib.

Children's reading: Buffalo Public Library. Class-room libraries for public schools. 25 c. Buffalo Pub. Lib.

Children's reading: Carnegie Library, Pittsburgh. Catalogue of books, annot. and arr. for the use of the first eight grades. 35 c. Carnegie Lib.

Children's reading: Carnegie Library, Pittsburgh. Catalog of books in the children's department. *$1 net. Carnegie Lib.

Children's reading: Cary, C: P., *ed.* List of books for free high school libraries in the state of Wisconsin. gratis. C: P. Cary.

Children's reading: Church Library Association. Catalogue of books recommended by the Church Library Association for Sunday-school and parish libraries. 25 c. Church Lib.

Children's reading: Connecticut Public Library. Helps in library work with children. gratis. Conn. Pub. Lib.

Children's reading: Hassler, H. E., *comp.* Graded list of stories for reading aloud. gratis. Indiana Lib.

Children's reading: Illinois State Normal School, Charleston. List of books in the schoolroom libraries of the first six grades in the Eastern Illinois State Normal School. Ill. State Normal.

BIBLIOGRAPHIES.—*Continued.*

Children's reading: Kirkpatrick, E. A. Fundamentals of child study. *$1.25 net. Macmillan.

Children's reading: Mabie, H. W., *ed.* Young folks' treasury. 12 v. Univ. Soc.

Children's reading: Missouri. *Dept. of Educ.* State course of study for the rural and graded schools and for approved high schools in the State of Missouri, 1909; [with] list of library books from which school libraries must be selected. (Add. pubs. for price.) Missouri, Dept. Educ.

Children's reading: Potter, M. E., *and others, comps.* Children's catalog; guide to the best reading for young people. $6 net. H. W. Wilson.

Children's reading: Poucher, Mrs. F. H. Boy and the books. 75 c. Kimball Press.

Children's reading: Power, E. L., *comp.* Selected list of children's books for school libraries, Mich. gratis. L. L. Wright.

Children's reading: Public school libraries: 500 books and how to buy them. gratis. Mich. State Normal Coll.

Children's reading: South Carolina State Board of Education. South Carolina list of library books. gratis. R. L. Bryan.

Children's reading: Summer reading for boys and girls. 15 c. net. Germantown Friends Sch.

Children's reading: Wisconsin. *Dept. of Education.* List of books for free high school libraries in the state of Wisconsin. gratis. C: P. Cary.

China: Cecil, *Lord* R. W: E. G- *and Lady* F. M. B.-W. Changing China. $3 special net. Appleton.

China: Morse, H. B. International relations of the Chinese Empire. $6 net. Longmans.

Chinese question: Cowan, R. E., *and* Dunlap, B., *comps.* Bibliog. of the Chinese question. *$1.40 net. A. M. Robertson.

Chopin, F. F.: Greater Chopin. $2.50; $1.50. Ditson.

Christian unity: Dimock, N. Christian unity. 50 c. net. Longmans.

Christianity: Hall, T: C. Hist. of ethics within organized Christianity. $3 net. Scribner.

Christianity: Hall, T: C. Social solution in the light of Christian ethics. *$1.50 net. Eaton & M.

Christianity: Schaff, P. Hist. of the Christian church. v. 2, pt. 2. $3.25 net. Scribner.

Christianity: Thomas, W. H. G. Christianity is Christ. *40 c. net. Longmans.

Christmas: Pratt Institution, Brooklyn. Free Library. Books for Christmas for the children. gratis. Pratt Inst.

Church (The): Dulles, A. M. True church *$1.25 net. Revell.

Church (The): Foster, E. C. Boy and the church. 75 c. S. S. Times.

Church (The): Thompson, C. B. Churches and the wage earners. **$1 net. Scribner.

BIBLIOGRAPHIES.—*Continued.*

Church architecture: Bond, F. Screens and galleries in English churches. $2. Oxford Univ.

Church history: Davison, E. S. Some forerunners of St. Francis of Assisi. (Add. author for price.) E. S. Davison.

Church history: Flick, A. C. Rise of the mediæval church. **$3.50 net. Putnam.

Church history: Glover, T. R. Conflict of religions in the early Roman Empire. *$2.50 net. Scribner.

Church history: Gulick, S. L. *and* E: L. Outline studies of the growth of the kingdom of God. 50 c. net. Pilgrim Press.

Church history: Gwatkin, H: M. Early church hist. *$5.25 net. Macmillan.

Church history: Hutton, W: H. Age of revolution: being an outline of the church from 1648-1815. *$1.50 net. Macmillan.

Church history: Moncrief, J: W. Short history of the Christian church. *$1.50 net. Revell.

Church history: Weber, N. A. History of simony in the Christian church. *$1.50 net. Furst.

Church music: Lutkin, P: C. Music in the church. $1 net. Young Churchman.

Church of England: Balleine, G. R. Hist. of the evangelical party in the Church of England. *$1 net. Longmans.

Church of England: Dearmer, P. Everyman's history of the English church. *75 c. net; *$1 net; *50 c. net. Warne.

Church of England: Hole, C: Manual of English church hist. $1.25 net. Longmans.

Church of England: Lacey, T. A. Roman diary and other documents rel. to the papal inquiry into English ordinations. $3.50 net. Longmans.

Church of England: Nelson, W: Controversy over the proposition for an American episcopate. $2.50. Paterson Hist.

Cicero, M. T. Cato Maior de senectvte.—Laelivs de amicitia. ea., 75 c. Heath.

Cities: Marsh, B: C., *and* Ford, G: B. Introduction to city planning. $1. B: C. Marsh.

Cities: Seattle, Wash. Public Library. Municipal plans; a list of books and references to periodicals in the Seattle Public Library. gratis. Seattle Pub. Lib.

Cities: Strong, J. Challenge of the city. *$1 net. Young People's Miss.

Civil War: Morton, J: W. Artillery of Nathan Bedford Forrest's cavalry. $2.50. Pub. Ho. of M. E. Ch., So.

Civilization: Seignobos, M. J. C. History of contemporary civilization. v. 3. **$1.25 net. Scribner.

Clay, Henry: Clay, T: H: Henry Clay. **$1.25 net. Jacobs.

Clay: United States. *Dept. of the Interior. U. S. Geolog. Survey.* Colloid matter of clay. 10 c.

Clemens, Samuel Langhorne: Bibliog. of the work of Mark Twain, Samuel Langhorne Clemens. $5. Harper.

BIBLIOGRAPHIES.—*Continued.*

Cleopatra, Queen of Egypt: Sergeant, P. W. Cleopatra of Egypt. $4 net. Dodd.

Coal: Burrows, J: S. Mine sampling and chemical analysis of coals. (Add. Superintendent for price.) U. S., Supt. of Docs.

Coal: Goss, W: F. M. Comparative tests of run-of-mine and briquetted coal on locomotives. 15 c. U. S., Supt. of Docs.

Coal: Parr, S: W., *and* Barker, P. Occluded gases in coal. gratis. Univ. of Ill.

Coins: Rawlins, G. B. Coins and how to know them. *$1.50 net. Stokes.

Coleridge, S: T. Ancient mariner. **25 c. net. Scribner.

Colleges and universities: Paetow, L: J. Arts course at medieval universities. $1. Univ. of Ill.

Collins, W: Poems. 90 c. Oxford Univ.

Colonial government: Keller, A. G. Colonization. $3. Ginn.

Columbia River Valley: Hunter, B., *and* Jayne, S. O. Suggestions to settlers on the sandy soils of the Columbia River Valley. Gov. Pr. Off.

Columbia University. University bibliog. Columbia Univ.

Commerce: United States. *Superintendent of Documents.* Transportation; list of publications rel. to interstate commerce, [etc.] gratis. Gov. Pr. Off.

Composition: Sykes, F: H. English composition. *65 c. net. Scribner.

Concrete: Moisseiff, L. S. Review of the literature of reinforced concrete. 5 c. Engineering News.

Conduct of life: Jenks, J. W. Life questions of high school boys. 40 c. Y. M. C. A.

Conduct of life: Wright, H: B. Will of God and a man's lifework. 90 c. Y. M. C. A.

Confederate publications: Freeman, D. S. Calendar of Confederate papers. $2.50. Confederate Museum.

Congo languages: Starr, F: Bibliography of Congo languages. *$1 net. Univ. of Chic.

Congress: United States. *Superintendent of Documents.* Proceedings of Congress. gratis. U. S., Supt. of Docs.

Connecticut: Pond, E. L. Tories of Chippeny Hill, Connecticut. **$1 net. Grafton Press.

Consciousness: Bergson, H. L. Time and free will; essay on the immediate data of consciousness. $2.75 net. Macmillan.

Consolatio: Sage, E. T. Pseudo-Ciceronian Consolatio. 50 c. Univ. of Chic.

Constitution: Elliott, E: G. Biographical story of the Constitution (American). **$2 net. Putnam.

Cookery: Landes, S. W. Elem. domestic science. pt. 1, Food and cookery. 50 c. S. W. Landes.

Co-operation: Fay, C: R. Co-operation at home and abroad. *$3 net. Macmillan.

Corea: Gale, J. S. Korea in transition. 50 c.; 35 c. Young People's Miss.

BIBLIOGRAPHIES.—*Continued.*

Corn: Bowman, M. L., *and* Crossley, B. W: Corn: growing, judging, breeding, feeding, marketing. $2.50. Bowman & C.

Cost: Meyer, H. H: B., *comp.* Select list of references on the cost of living and prices. 15 c. Gov. Pr. Off.

Costume: Brooklyn Public Library. Reading and reference list on costume. gratis. Brooklyn Lib.

Costume: Saunders, C. Costume in Roman comedy. **$1 net. Macmillan.

Cotton: Bowman, F. H. Structure of the cotton fibre. *$2.75 net. Macmillan.

Cotton: Watkins, J. L. King Cotton: historical and statistical review. $1.50. J. L. Watkins.

Courts-martial: Davis, G: B. Treatise on the military law of the United States; together with the practice and procedure of courts-martial. $7 net. Wiley.

Cox, T: Reid, H. Thomas Cox. State Hist. Ia.

Creation: Caldwell, W: Idea of creation: its origin and value. 50 c. Caldwell.

Crete (*Island of*): Baikie, J. Sea-kings of Crete. $2 net. Macmillan.

Crime and criminals: MacDonald, A. Juvenile crime and reformation. 50 c. U. S., Supt. of Docs.

Crime and criminals: Potts, C: S. Crime and the treatment of the criminal. gratis. Univ. of Texas.

Criminal law: Wigmore, J: H: Preliminary bibliog. of modern criminal law and criminology. 65 c. Northwestern Univ.

Cripple Creek, Col.: Rastall, B: M. Labor history of the Cripple Creek district. 50 c. Univ. of Wis.

Criticism: Spingarn, J. E. History of literary criticism in the renaissance. *$1.50 net. Columbia Univ.

Crystallography: Wadsworth, M. E: Crystallography. *$3 net. McVey.

Cuba: Perez, L. M. Bibliografia de la Revolucion de Yara. In 3 pts. pt. 1. $1.25. Stechert.

Cyclops: Byrnes, E. F. Fresh water *Cyclops* of Long Island. 80 c. Brooklyn Inst.

Cyprus: Cobham, C. D., *ed.* Excerpta Cypria. *$6.30 net. Putnam.

Dairy: Benkendorf, G. H: W:, *comp. and ed.* Catalogue of the postal dairy library. gratis. G. H: W: Benkendorf.

Dairy: United States. *Dept. of Agriculture. Bu. of Animal Industry.* Publications of interest to dairymen. gratis.

Dairy: U. S. public documents rel. to the American dairy industry. gratis. U. S., Supt. of Docs.

Dana, R: H:, *jr.* Richard Henry Dana, jr., speeches in stirring times and letters to a son. $3 net. Houghton M.

Dana, R: H:, *jr.* Two years before the mast. *25 c. net. Macmillan.

Dancing: Gulick, L. H. Healthful art of dancing. $1.40 net. Doubleday, P.

BIBLIOGRAPHIES.—*Continued.*

Danish books: Kildal, A., *comp.* Selected list of Norwegian and Danish books. 25 c. A. L. A.

Dante Alighieri: Flamini, F. Introd. to the study of the Divine comedy. $1.25. Ginn.

Dante Alighieri. La divina commedia. v. 7, Inferno. $1.25. Heath.

Dante Alighieri. Readings on the Paradiso of Dante. $4 net. Macmillan.

Davis, Jefferson: Dodd, W: E: Jefferson Davis. **$1.25 net. Jacobs.

Debating: Iowa State University. Constructive and rebuttal speeches. 2 v. ea., $1. Forensic.

Debating: Phelps, E. M., *comp.* Selected articles on the initiative and referendum. $1. H. W. Wilson.

Debussy, Claude Achille: Liebich, L. Claude-Achille Debussy. *$1 net. Lane.

Dewey, D. R., *and* Chaddock, R. E. State banking before the Civil War and The safety fund banking system in New York. Gov. Pr. Off.

Diagnosis: Abrams, A. D. Diagnostic therapeutics. $5. Rebman.

Dickens, C: Christmas carol. 25 c.; 15 c. Crane.

Dickens, C: Posthumous papers of the Pickwick Club. 35 c. net; 70 c. net. Dutton.

Digestion: Billings, F., *ed.* Diseases of the digestive system. $6. Appleton.

Diphtheria: Goodman, H. M. Experimental studies on diphtheric immunity. 25 c. H. M. Goodman.

Diphtheria: Nuttall, G: H:, *and* Graham-Smith, G: S., *eds.* Bacteriology of diphtheria. *$7 net. Putnam.

Dissertations: Carnegie Institution of Washington. *Dept. of Historical Research.* List of doctoral dissertations in progress, Dec., 1909. Carnegie.

District of Columbia: Dodd, W. F. Government of the District of Columbia. $1.50. Byrne.

Divorce: Wilkins, H. J. Hist. of divorce and re-marriage for English churchmen. $1.25 net. Longmans.

Domestic animals: United States. *Superintendent of Documents.* Animal Industry Bureau; repts., bulletins and circulars rel. to animal industry. gratis.

Domestic economy: Dodd, M. E. Chemistry of the household. $1.25. Am. Sch. Home Economics.

Domestic economy: Langworthy, C: F. U. S. government publications as sources of information for students of home economics. (Add. Assoc. for price.) Home Economics Assoc.

Don Pedro *of Castile:* Storer, E: Peter the Cruel; the life of the notorious Don Pedro of Castile. $4 net. Lane.

Drainage: United States. Dept. of Agriculture. Organization work, and publications of drainage investigations. gratis. U. S., Supt. of Docs.

Drake, Daniel: Juettner, O. Daniel Drake and his followers. $5. Harvey Pub.

BIBLIOGRAPHIES.—*Continued.*

Drama and dramatists: Crowley, T. J. Character-treatment in the mediæval drama. $1; 75 c. Univ. Press, (Notre Dame.)

Drama and dramatists: Faxon, F: W., *ed.* Dramatic index for 1909. $3.50 net. Boston Bk.

Drama and dramatists: Evanston, Ill. Public Library. The drama; catalogue of books on dramatic literature contained in the Evanston Public Library. Evanston Pub. Lib.

Drama and dramatists: Marks, J. English pastoral drama, [1660-1798.] *$1.50 net. Stechert.

Drama and dramatists: Mulliken, C. A. Reading list on modern dramatists. 20 c. Boston Bk.

Drama and dramatists: Murray, J: T. English dramatic companies, 1558-1642. 2 v. $7.50 net. Houghton M.

Drama and dramatists: Ristine, F. H. English tragicomedy. $1.50. Columbia Univ.

Drama and dramatists: Schelling, F. E. Elizabethan drama, 1558-1642. 2 v. **$7.50 net. Houghton, M. & Co.

Drama and dramatists: Wright, H: B. Recovery of a lost Roman tragedy. $1.50. Yale Univ.

Dutch art: Preyer, D: C. Art of the Netherland galleries. *$2 net; *$5 net. L. C. Page.

Dyeing: Farrell, F. J. Dyeing and cleaning. (Add. pubs. for price.) Lippincott.

Dyspepsia: Fenwick, W. S. Dyspepsia. $3. Saunders.

Ear: Barr, T: *and* J. S. Manual of diseases of the ear. *$4.50 net. Macmillan.

Ear: Knight, C: H., *and* Bryant, W: S. Diseases of the nose, throat and ear. $4.50. Blakiston.

Ear: Kopetzky, S: J. Surgery of the ear. $4. Rebman.

Earthquakes: Brooklyn Public Library. Earthquakes and volcanoes: list of books with reference to periodicals in the Library. gratis. Brooklyn Lib.

Ecuador: Saville, M. H. Antiquities of Manabi, Ecuador. $25. F. P. Harper.

Education: Andrews, B: R: Museums of education. pap., 30 c. Teachers' Coll.

Education: Buffum, H. S: Federal and state aid to education in Iowa. $1. Univ. of Ia.

Education: Burnham, W: H:, *and* Suzzalo, H: History of education as a professional subject. 50 c. Teachers' Coll.

Education: Carlton, F. T. Economic influences upon educational progress in the United States, 1820-1850. (Add. pubs. for price.) Univ. of Wis.

Education: Edson, A. W. Bibliography of a course on school administration, summer session. 10 c. Teachers' Coll.

Education: Ellis, C: C. Lancasterian schools in Philadelphia. (Not for sale.) Univ. of Penn.

Education: Graves, F. P. Hist. of education during the Middle Ages and the transition to modern times. $1.10 net. Macmillan.

BIBLIOGRAPHIES.—*Continued.*

Education: Haney, J: D. Registration of city school children. $1.50. Teachers' Coll.

Education: Heck, W. H. Mental discipline and educational values. **$1 net. Lane.

Education: Henderson, E. N. Text-book in the principles of education. $1.75 net. Macmillan.

Education: Hoyt, C: O. Studies in the history of modern education. $1.50. Silver.

Education: Jones, A. J. Syllabus for the study of the hist. of education. 25 c. R. I. Normal.

Education: Kansas. *Committee of Course of Study.* Course of study for common schools of Kansas. 18 c. Crane.

Education: Maennel, B. Auxiliary education, the training of backward children. $1.50. Doubleday, P.

Education: Munroe, J. P. Educational ideal. $1. Heath.

Education: New York State. *Education Dept.* Course of study and syllabus for elem. schools. N. Y. State Educ.

Education: Norton, A. O. Readings in the history of education. 85 c. Harvard Univ.

Education: O'Shea, M. V. Social development and education. $2. Houghton M.

Education: Publishers' Weekly. American educational list, 1909. 50 c. Pub. Weekly

Education: Ruediger, W: C. Principles of education. **$1.25 net. Houghton M.

Education: Scott, C. A. Social education. $1.25. Ginn.

Education: United States. *Bureau of Education.* Bibliography of education for 1908-9.

Education: United States. *Bu. of Education.* List of publications, 1867-1910.

Education: United States. *Bureau of Education.* List of pubs. of the U. S. Bureau of Education, 1867-1907. (Add. Supt. for price.) U. S., Supt. of Docs.

Education: United States. *Bureau of Education.* Teacher's professional library: classified list of one hundred titles. (Add. Superintendent for price.)

Education: United States. *Library of Congress. Smithsonian Division.* Want list of publications of educational institutions. (Add. Superintendent for price.) U. S., Supt. of Docs.

Education: United States. *Superintendent of Documents.* Education: list of government publications. gratis.

Education: Wyer, J. I., *and* Phelps, M. L., *comps.* Bibliography of education for 1907. (Add. Superintendent for price.) U. S., Supt. of Docs.

Egypt: Al Kindi. History of the governors of Egypt. **$1 net. Macmillan.

Egypt: Baedeker, K. Egypt and the Sudan. *$4.50 net. Scribner.

Elections: Griffin, A. P. C., *comp.* Library of Congress list of references on corrupt practices in elections. (Add. Supt. for price.) U. S., Supt. of Docs.

Elections: Merriman, C: E: Primary elections. *$1.25 net. Univ. of Chic.

BIBLIOGRAPHIES.—*Continued.*

Elections: Schaffner, M. A. The recall. 5 c. Wisconsin Free Lib.

Electric light: Huels, F: W: Comparison of the effects of frequency on the light of incandescent and Nernst lamps. 25 c. Univ. of Wis.

Electric railroads: Fowle, F. F. Protection of railroads from overhead transmission line crossings. $1.50. Van Nostrand.

Electric railroads: Modern electric railway practice. 4 v. $22.50. W. V. Wheat.

Electrical engineering: Stone and Webster. Current literature references, [electrical engineering,] 1907. (Add. pubs. for price.) Stone & W.

Electricity: Albe, E. E. F. d'. Electron theory. $1.25 net. Longmans.

Electricity: American Institute of Electrical Engineers, Library. Catalogue of the Wheeler gift of books, pamphlets and periodicals. $8. Am. Inst. Elec. Eng.

Electricity: Karapetoff, V. Electric circuit. $1.30. Andrus.

Electricity: Munro, J: Story of electricity. 92 c. S. S. McClure.

Electricity: Whittaker, E. T. Hist. of the theories of æther and electricity. $4.50 net. Longmans.

Eliot, George. Silas Marner. **40 c. net. C: E. Merrill.

Elizabeth, *Queen of England:* Mumby, F. A., *comp.* Girlhood of Queen Elizabeth. **$3 net. Houghton M.

Elizabethan drama: Gildersleeve, V. C. Government regulation of the Elizabethan drama. *$1.25 net. Lemcke.

Embryology: Bryce, T: H., *and others.* Contributions to the study of the early development and imbedding of the human ovum. *$4 net. Macmillan.

Embryology: Lillie, F. R. Development of the chick; introd. to embryology. **$4 net. Holt.

Emerson, R. W.: Cooke, G: W., *comp.* Bibliography of Ralph Waldo Emerson. **$5 net. Houghton, M. & Co.

Emerson, R. W.: Harrison, J: S. Teachers of Emerson. $1.50 net. Sturgis & W.

Empedocles: Fragments of Empedocles; tr. into English verse by W: Ellery Leonard. $1. Open Court.

Employment agencies: Devine, E: T: Report on the desirability of establishing an employment bureau in the city of New York. (Priv. pr.) Charities Pub.

Enamel: Dawson, *Mrs.* N. Enamels. *$1 net. McClurg.

Engineering: Burlington, Ia. Public Library. Pract. books in the library on electricity, engineering, railroading and other subjects. Burlington Pub. Lib.

Engineering: Derr, L:, *ed.* Cyclopedia of engineering. 6 v. (Add. pubs. for price.) Am. Sch. Corr.

Engineering: Reynolds Library, Rochester, N. Y. Catalogue of works on engineering and allied subjects in Library. (Add. Lib. for price.) Reynolds Lib.

BIBLIOGRAPHIES.—*Continued.*

Engineering: United States. *Superintendent of Documents.* Engineering; mechanics; Government documents. gratis.

England: Cannon, H: L. Reading references for English hist. $2.50. Ginn.

England: Firth, C: H. Last years of the Protectorate. 2 v. *$7 net. Longmans.

England: Gwyther, G. M. English history in the class-room. 80 c. Longmans.

England: Maxwell, *Sir* H. E. Century of empire, 1801-1900. In 3 v. v. 1, 1801-1832. *$4 net. Longmans.

England: Reynolds, K. B. Outline lessons in English history. 75 c. Putnam.

England: Trenholme, N. M. Outline of English hist. for use in high schools and colleges. 50 c. Ginn.

England: Welsford, J. W. W. Strength of England. *$1.75 net. Longmans.

England: White, A. B. Making of the English constitution, 449-1485. **$2 net. Putnam.

English language: Edwards, W. H. Parts of speech, suggested definitions for a logical grammar of the English language. 25 c. W. H. Edwards.

English language: Jonson, B. English grammar. *75 c. net. Sturgis & W.

English language: Krapp, G: P. Modern English. **$1.25 net. Scribner.

English literature: Goldsmith, O., *and* Gray, T: Goldsmith's The traveller and The deserted village, and Gray's Elegy in a country churchyard. 25 c. Heath.

English literature: Hooker, E. R. Study book in English literature from Chaucer to the close of the romantic period. $1. Heath.

English literature: Long, W: J. English literature. *$1.35 net. Ginn.

English literature: Marshall, H. E. Child's English literature. *$2.50 net. Stokes.

English literature: Pancoast, H: S., *and* Shelly, P. V. First book in English literature. $1.25. Holt.

English literature: Schelling, F. E. English literature during the lifetime of Shakespeare. $2.50. Holt.

English literature: Ward, A. W., *and* Waller, A. R., *eds.* Cambridge hist. of English literature. In 14 v. v. 4-6. ea., **$2.50 net. Putnam.

English poetry: Bronson, W. C., *comp. and ed.* English poems. v. 3. *$1 net. Univ. of Chic.

English universities: Vaugn, E. V. Origin and early development of the English universities. $1. Univ. of Mo.

Engraving: Hind, A. M. Short history of engraving and etching. *$5 net. Houghton M.

Entomology: Colcord, M., *comp.* List of publications of the Bureau of Entomology. gratis. U. S., Supt. of Docs.

Ether: May, C. E. Oxygen ethers of the type—N: C. (O R), derived from certain nitrogen heterocycles. (Add. author for price.) C. E. May.

Ethics: Hayden, E. A. Social will. $1. Psychological Review.

BIBLIOGRAPHIES.—*Continued.*

Ethics: Nicholson, A. M. Concept standard; historical survey of what men have conceived as constituting or determining life values. $1.50. Teachers' Coll.

Ethics: Sadler, M. E., *ed.* Moral instruction and training in schools. 2 v. ea., *$1.50 net. Longmans.

Ethics: Westermark, E: Origin and development of the moral ideas. In 2 v. v. 2. *$3.50 net. Macmillan.

Ethnology: Dieserud, J. Scope and content of the science of anthropology. *$2 net. Open Court.

Ethonology: Haddon, A. C. Races of man and their distribution. *50 c. net. Stokes.

Ethnology: McCabe, J. Prehistoric man. 50 c. net. Stokes.

Ethnology: Thomas, W: I: Source book for social origins. *$4.50 net. Univ. of Chic.

Ethnology: United States. *Superintendent of Documents.* Ethnology: titles and prices of those published documents of the U. S. Bu. of American Ethnology which are now available for distribution. gratis. U. S., Supt. of Docs.

Eugenics: Saleeby, C. W. Parenthood and race culture. **$2.50 net. Moffat.

Europe: Frazar, *Mrs.* M. D. Practical European guide. $1.50. Small.

Europe: Hazen, C: D. Europe since 1815. $3. Holt.

Europe: Nichol, J: Tables of European history, literature, science and art; and of American history, literature and art. *$2 25 net. Macmillan.

Europe: Robinson, J. H., *and* Beard, C. A. Readings in modern European history. v. 1. $1.40. Ginn.

Everyman. *35 c. net; leath., *70 c. net. Dutton.

Everyman: a morality play. *$1 net. M. Kennerley.

Eye: Fernald, G. M. Effect of achromatic conditions on the color of phenomena of peripheral vision. $1. Psychological Review.

Factories: Diemer, H. Factory organization and administration. $3. McGraw-H.

Fairfield, Ct.: Child, F. S: Fairfield, ancient and modern. 50 c. Fairfield Hist.

Fairy tales: Boston Public Library. Finding lists of fairy tales and folk stories in books at the branches of the Public Library. 5 c. Boston Pub. Lib.

Faith: Inge, W: R. Faith and its psychology. *75 c. net. Scribner.

Fatigue: Yoakum, C. S. Experimental study of fatigue. $1.35. Psychological Review.

Feathers: Jones, L. Development of nestling feathers. 50 c. L. Jones.

Fermentation: Bayliss, W: M. Nature of enzyme action. *$1 net. Longmans.

Fiction: English prose fiction. 15 c. H. W. Wilson.

Fiction: Fiction catalog. 25 c.; 20 c.; 15 c.; 5 c. H. W. Wilson.

BIBLIOGRAPHIES.—*Continued.*

Fiction: Jeffers, Le R. List of editions selected for economy in book buying. 25 c. A. L. A.

Fiction: Jeffers, Le R., *comp.* Reference list of titles suggested for a special library binding. (Add. Library for price.) N. Y. Pub. Lib.

Fiction: Johnson, J. G. Southern fiction prior to 1860: attempt at a first-hand bibliography. $2. Michie.

Fiction: Utica, N. Y., Public Library. Selected list of historical fiction. gratis. Utica Lib.

Figs: Van Velzer, A. C. Fig culture. $1.50. Dealy.

Finance: Davies, A. E. Money and the stock and share markets. 50 c. Pitman.

Finance: Plehn, C. C. Introduction to public finance. **$1.75 net. Macmillan.

Finance: United States. *Superintendent of Documents.* Finance; public documents now available. gratis.

Fine arts: Addison, *Mrs.* J. De G. Arts and crafts in the Middle Ages. $3. L. C. Page.

Fine arts: Armstrong, *Sir* W. Art in Great Britain and Ireland. *$1.50 net. Scribner.

Fine arts: Garesché, M. R. Art of the ages. $1.25. Prang.

Fine arts: Weiss, A. Introd. to the philosophy of art. 50 c. Univ. of Cal.

Fish and fishing: Borchardt, E. M., *comp.* North Atlantic coast fisheries arbitration. Gov. Pr. Off.

Fish and fishing: United States. *Dept. of Commerce and Labor. Bureau of Fisheries.* List of publications of the Bureau of Fisheries available for distribution. gratis.

Fish and fishing: United States. *Dept. of Commerce and Labor. Bureau of Fisheries.* List of publications. gratis.

Fish and fishing: United States. *Superintendent of Documents.* Fishes; in the U. S. public documents great attention is given to fish and fisheries; documents cont. information on these subjects are sold at cost of pap., etc. gratis. U. S., Supt. of Docs.

Flags: Horner, H. H., *ed.* American flag. gratis. N. Y. State Educ.

Flies: Merchants' Association of New York. House-fly at the bar. gratis. Merchants' Assoc.

Floods: Carnegie Library, Pittsburgh. Floods and flood protection. 15 c. Carnegie Lib.

Florence, Italy: Staley, E. Famous women of Florence. $3.50. Scribner.

Florence, Italy: Vernon, M. In and out of Florence. $2.50 net. Holt.

Fonts: Bond, F. Fonts and font covers. $4.80. Oxford Univ.

Food: Food and nutrition investigations of the Office of Experiment Stations. Gov. Pr. Off.

Food: Hunt, C. L. Daily meals of children. U. S., Supt. of Docs.

Food: Leach, A. E. Food inspection and analysis. $7.50. Wiley.

Food: Norton, *Mrs.* A. P. Food and dietetics. $1.25. Am. Sch. Home Economics.

Food: Organization, work, and publications of food and nutrition investigations. gratis. U. S., Supt. of Docs.

Food: Priced list of public documents rel. to food. gratis. U. S., Supt. of Docs.

Food: Snyder, H. Human foods and their nutritive value. *$1.25 net. Macmillan.

Food: United States. *Dept of Agriculture. Bu. of Chemistry.* Bulletins, circulars and food inspection decisions of the bureau. gratis. U. S., Supt. of Docs.

Food: United States. *Superintendent of Documents.* Food and diet; price list. gratis.

Food preservatives: Food preservation: statement of facts in the case, together with references to the authorities. 50 c. Nat. Assoc. Pub. Health.

Food preservatives: United States. *Dept. of Agriculture.* Influence of sodium benzoate on the nutrition and health of man. $1. U. S., Supt. of Docs.

Forests and forestry: United States. Forest service. Bulletins, circulars, maps and silvical leaflets rel. to forests. gratis.

Forests and forestry: United States. *Superintendent of Documents.* Forest Service. Bulletins, circulars, etc. gratis.

Forgery: Osborn, A. S. Questioned documents. $5.25. Lawyers' Co-op.

France: Bracq, J. C. France under the Republic. $1.50 net. Scribner.

France: Cousin, V. La société française en XVIIe siècle. $1.15. Oxford Univ.

France: Hall, J: R. Bourbon restoration. *$4 net. Houghton M.

Francis *of Assisi, St.:* Muzzey, D: S. Spiritual Franciscans. gratis. D: S. Muzzey.

Franck, C.: D'Indy, V. César Franck. *$2.50 net. Lane.

Franklin, B: Autobiography. 30 c. Scott, F. & Co.

Frankpledge system: Morris, W: A. Frank pledge system. $1.75. Longmans.

Freedom of the press: Schroeder, T., *comp.* Free press anthology. $2. Truth Seeker.

French language: Voltaire, F. M. A. de. Zaïre; tragedy in verse. 30 c. Heath.

French literature: Konta, *Mrs.* A. L. History of French literature. **$2.50 net. Appleton.

French literature: Stephens, W. French novelists of to-day. $1.50. Lane.

French Revolution: Christophelsmeier, C. H. First revolutionary step [in France.] $1. Univ. of Neb.

Friends (*Society of*): Edmunds, A. J. Quaker literature in the libraries of Philadelphia. (Add. author for price.) A. J. Edmunds.

Fruit: Hume, H. H. Citrous fruits and their culture. $2.50 net. Judd.

BIBLIOGRAPHIES.—*Continued.*

Fruit. Los Angeles. Public Library. California, United States and experiment station documents of interest to California horticulturists. (Add. Library for price.) Los Angeles Lib.

Fuel: Lewes, V. B. Liquid and gaseous fuels. *$2 net. Van Nostrand.

Fuel: Randall, D. T. Tests of coal and briquets as fuel for house-heating boilers. 10 c. U. S., Supt. of Docs.

Fulton, Robert: Brooklyn Public Library. List of books and magazine articles on Henry Hudson and the Hudson River, Robert Fulton and early steam navigation. gratis. Brooklyn Lib.

Fulton, Robert: Homer, H. H., *comp. and ed.* Hudson-Fulton celebration. (Add. pubs. for price.) N. Y. State Educ.

Gardens and gardening: American Fork & Hoe Company, Cleveland, O. Gardening for health and recreation. Am. Fork.

Gardens and gardening: Babcock, E. B. Suggestions for garden work in California schools. Univ. of Cal.

Gardens and gardening: Bailey, L. H. Horticulturists' rule-book. 75 c. Macmillan.

Gardens and gardening: Lowell, Mass. City Library. Gardens and gardening: list of books in Lowell City Library. gratis. Lowell Lib.

Gardens and gardening: Weed, C. M., *and* Emerson, P.. School garden book. $1.25. Scribner.

Garrett, E.: Cook, E: T. Edmund Garrett. *$3 net. Longmans.

Gaskell, *Mrs.* E. C. S. Cranford. 25 c. Scribner.

Gaskell, *Mrs.* E. C. S. Sylvia's lovers; [incl. a chronology of Mrs. Gaskell's life and works.] 35 c. net; 65 c. net. Oxford Univ.

"Gaspee" (The): Knox, H. B. Destruction of the "Gaspee"; [British schooner destroyed by people of Rhode Island, 1772.] gratis. R. I. Dept. Educ.

Gautier, T. Trois grotesques. 70 c. Oxford Univ.

Genealogies: Watson, *Mrs.* A. W. R. "Of sceptered race." $10. Early.

Generative organs: Ballenger, E. G. Genito-urinary diseases and syphilis. *$3 net. E. W. Allen.

Generative organs: Watson, F. S., *and* Cunningham, J: H:, *jr.* Diseases and surgery of the genito-urinary system. 2 v. $12; $17. Lea.

Geography: Calmerton, G. Geography—history. (Not for sale.) Fort Wayne Sch. Bd.

Geography: Sutherland, W: J. Teaching of geography. $1.25. Scott, F. & Co.

Geography: Tarr, R. S., *and* McMurry, F. M. New geographies. In 2 bks. Bk. 1. complete, 65 c. net; bk. 2, complete, $1.10 net. Macmillan.

Geology: Clarke, J: M., *and others.* Geologic map and descriptions of the Portage and Nunda quadrangles. 20 c. N. Y. State Educ.

BIBLIOGRAPHIES.—*Continued.*

Geology: Emmons, W: H. Reconnaissance of some mining camps in Elko, Lander and Eureka counties, Nev. U. S., Supt. of Docs.

Geology: Kemp, J. F., *and* Ruedemann, R. Geology of the Elizabethtown and Port Henry quadrangles. 40 c. N. Y. State Educ.

Geology: Nickles, J: M. Bibliography of North American geology for 1908. (Add. Superintendent for price.) U. S., Supt. of Docs.

Geology: Phalen, W: C. Economic geology of the Kenova quadrangle: Kentucky, Ohio and West Virginia. 25 c. U. S., Supt. of Docs.

Geology: Ries, H. Economic geology; with special reference to the United States. $3.50 net. Macmillan.

Geology: United States. *Geological Survey.* Publications, (not incl. topographic maps.) gratis. U. S., Supt. of Docs.

Geology: United States. *Geological Survey.* Publications of the United States Geological Survey.

Geology: United States. *Geological Survey.* Technologic publications of the United States Geological Survey. gratis.

Geology: Weeks, F. B., *and* Nickles, J. M. Bibliography of North American geology for 1906-'07. 30 c. U. S., Supt. of Docs.

Geometry: Stamper, A. W. Hist. of the teaching of elem. geometry. $1.50; $1.15. Teachers' Coll.

George I. *of England:* Melville, L. First George, in Hanover and England. *$6 net. Scribner.

German-Americans: Helbig, R: E. German-American researches: collection in N. Y. Public Library, 1906-07. gratis. N. Y. Pub. Lib.

German art: Metropolitan Museum of Art. Exhibition of contemporary German art; list of books and periodicals relating to modern German art in the library of the Museum. gratis. Metropolitan Museum.

German books: Brooklyn Public Library. German books in the Brooklyn Public Library. 5 c. Brooklyn Lib.

German books: Gattiker, E., *comp.* Sel. list of German books. 50 c. A. L. A.

German language: Evans, M. B. High school course in German. (Add. University for price.) Univ. of Wis.

German language: Hillern, *Frau* W. B. v. Höher als die kirche. 50 c. C: E. Merrill.

German literature: Arnold, R. S. Allgemeine bücherkunde zur neueren deutschen literaturgeschichte. $2.25. Stechert.

German literature: Buffalo Public Library. Books in German printed by the German Young Men's Association. gratis. Buffalo Pub. Lib.

German literature: Collitz, K. H., *comp.* Selections from early German literature. $1. Am. Bk.

German literature: Flory, J: S: Literary activity of the German Baptist Brethren in the eighteenth century. $1.25. Brethren Pub. Ho.

BIBLIOGRAPHIES.—*Continued.*

German literature: Phillips, M. E. Hdbk. of German literature. *$1 net. Macmillan.

German literature: Weinhold, K. List of first editions and other rare books in the Weinhold library. (Add. pub. for price.) Univ. of Cal.

German literature: Wernaer, R. M. Romanticism and the romantic school in Germany. **$2 net. Appleton.

German poetry: Bithell, J. The Minnesingers. v. 1. $2. Longmans.

Germans in the United States: Faust, A. B. German element in the United States. 2 v. **$7.50 net. Houghton M.

Germany: Barker, J. E. Modern Germany. *$3 net. Dutton.

Ghosts: Hawkins, J., *comp.* Ghost stories and tales of the supernatural. 20 c. Boston Bk.

Glaciers: Fairchild, H. L. Glacial waters in central New York. 40 c. N. Y. State Educ.

Gladstone, W. E.: Brooklyn Public Library. William Ewart Gladstone, 1809-1898; list of books and of references to periodicals in the Brooklyn Public Library. gratis. Brooklyn Lib.

Glands: Ochsner, A. J., *and* Thompson, R. L. Surgery and pathology of the thyroid and parathyroid glands. $6 net. Mosby.

Goethe, J. W. v.: Hermann und Dorothea. 60 c. Am. Bk.

Goethe, J. W. v.: Torquato Tasso. 80 c. Ginn.

Gold: Laney, F. B. Gold Hill mining district of North Carolina. N. C. Geolog. Survey.

Goldsmith, Oliver: Buckland, E. S. L. Oliver Goldsmith. *50 c. net. Macmillan.

Goldsmith, Oliver. The traveller and The deserted village. **30 c. net. Appleton.

Gordon, Leon: Rhine, A. B. Leon Gordon. 75 c. Jewish Pub.

Gordon, W: F: Gordon, A. C. William Fitzhugh Gordon, a Virginian of the old school. *$3 net. Neale.

Gothic language: Wright, J. Grammar of the Gothic language, and the Gospel of St. Mark; selections from the Second Epistle to Timothy. $1.75. Oxford Univ.

Gould, George Milbry, *M.D.* Bibliog. of the contributions of G: M. Gould to ophthalmology, general medicine, literature, etc. gratis. Andrus.

Government publications: United States. *Superintendent of Documents.* Proceedings of Congress; being a complete list of the volumes of the Annals of the Congress, Register of Debates in Congress, etc. (Add. Superintendent for price.)

Granite: Dale, T: N. Chief commercial granites of Massachusetts, New Hampshire and Rhode Island. (Add. Superintendent for price.) U. S., Supt. of Docs.

Great Britain: Frazar, *Mrs.* M. D. Pract. guide to Great Britain and Ireland. In 2 v. **$1 net. Small.

BIBLIOGRAPHIES.—*Continued.*

Great Britain: Herbertson, A. J., *and* Jowett, L., *eds.* British Isles; descriptive geography. *75 c. net. Macmillan.

Great Britain: Johnson, W. Folk-memory. $4.15. Oxford Univ.

Greece: Farnell, L. R: Cults of the Greek states. In 5 v. v. 5. $6. Oxford Univ.

Greece: Fowler, H. N., *and others.* Hdbk. of Greek archæology. $2. Am. Bk.

Greece: Gardiner, E. N. Greek athletic sports and festivals. $2.50 net. Macmillan.

Greece. Guide to Greece. *$2.75 net. Macmillan.

Greece: Walden, J: W. H. Universities of ancient Greece. **$1.50 net. Scribner.

Greek historians: Bury, J: B. Ancient Greek historians. $2.25. Macmillan.

Greek language: Buck, C. D. Introd. to the study of Greek dialects. $2.75. Ginn.

Greek poetry: Ogden, C: J. De infinitive finalis vel consecutive constructione apud priscos poetas Græcos. **$1.25 net. Macmillan.

Grey, *Lady* Jane: Davey, R: Nine days' queen. *$3.50 net. Putnam.

Grieg, E. H. Fifty songs.—Larger piano compositions. ea., $2.50; $1.50. Ditson.

Grieg, E. H.: Finck, H: T. Grieg and his music. **$2.50 net. Lane.

Grillparzer, F. König Ottokars glück und ende. 60 c. Holt.

Grillparzer, F.: De Walsh, F. C: Grillparzer as a poet of nature. $1 net. Lemcke.

Grolier, Jean: Le Roux de Lincy, A. J. V. Researches concerning Jean Grolier; with a partial cat. of his books: [Checklist of libraries containing Grolier books.] (Add. Grolier Club for price.) Grolier Club.

Guatemala: Winter, N. O. Guatemala and her people of to-day. $3. L. C. Page.

Guilds: Unwin, G: Gilds and companies of London. *$2 net. Scribner.

Gutzkow, K. F. Uriel Acosta. 35 c. Holt.

Gymnastics: Bowen, W. P. Teaching of elem. school gymnastics. $1. Bassette.

Gymnastics: Skarstrom, W: Gymnastic kinesiology. *$1.25 net. Bassette.

Harnett, C.: Connor, R. D. W. Cornelius Harnett. $1.50. R. D. W. Connor.

Hawthorne, N.: House of the seven gables. 40 c. C: E. Merrill.

Haydn, F. J.: Runciman, J: F. Haydn. *50 c. net; *$1 net. Macmillan.

Hearn, Lafcadio: Gould, G: M. Concerning Lafcadio Hearn. **$1.50 net. Jacobs.

Heart: Hirschfelder, A. D. Diseases of the heart and aorta. $6 net. Lippincott.

Heat: Young, G. A. Elem. notes on thermodynamics. $1. G. A. Young.

Heating: American School of Correspondence. Cyclopedia of heating, plumbing and sanitation. $12. Am. Sch. Corr.

Hebrew literature: Cantrell, E: A. Bible and modern literature. 50 c. Los Angeles Liberal.

BIBLIOGRAPHIES.—*Continued.*

Herculaneum: Waldstein, C:, *and* Shoobridge, L. Herculaneum. *$5 net. Macmillan.

Hercules: Winter, J: G. Myth of Hercules at Rome. 50 c. net. Macmillan.

Heredity: Bateson, W: Mendel's principles of heredity. *$3.50 net. Putnam.

Heredity: Guyer, M. F. Deficiencies of the chromosome theory of heredity. Univ. of Cin.

Heredity: Thomson, J: A. Heredity. *$3.50 net. Putnam.

Heredity: Walker, C: E: Hereditary characters and their modes of transmission. $2.40 net. Longmans.

Higher criticism (*of the Bible*): Duff, A. Hist. of Old Testament criticism. 75 c. net. Putnam.

Hildreth family: Reade, P. H., *comp.* First generation of the name of Hildreth in Middlesex Co. in Mass. $1.25. P. Reade.

Histology: Bailey, F: R. Text-book of histology. $3.50 net. Wood.

Historical novels: Burdick, J. E., *ed.* General index [to The history of nations.] $2.75; $3.75; $5. J: D. Morris.

History: Acton, J: E. E: D.-A. Cambridge modern history. In 12 v. v. 12. $4 net. Macmillan.

History: American Historical Association. Study of hist. in the elementary schools. 50 c. Scribner.

History: Andrews, C: M., *and others.* Bibliography of history for schools and libraries. 60 c. net. Longmans.

History: Calmerton, G. Geography—history. (Not for sale.) Fort Wayne Sch. Bd.

History: Chamberlain, H. S. Foundations of the nineteenth century. 2 v. $10 net. Lane.

History: Johnson, H: Problem of adapting history to children in the elementary school. 30 c. Teachers' Coll.

History: Kemp, E. W. Outline of history for the grades. $1.25. Ginn.

Holidays: Hazeltine, M. E., *ed.* Anniversaries and holidays. 25 c. Wisconsin Free Lib.

Holmes, Oliver Wendell: Brooklyn Public Library. Oliver Wendell Holmes, 1809-1894; a list of books and references to periodicals in the Library. gratis. Brooklyn Lib.

House decoration: Lenygon, F. Decoration and furniture of English mansions during the seventeenth and eighteenth centuries. *$1 net. Scribner.

Hudson, Henry: Brooklyn Public Library. List of books and magazine articles on Henry Hudson and the Hudson River, Robert Fulton and early steam navigation. gratis. Brooklyn Lib.

Hudson, Henry: Horner, H. H., *comp. and ed.* Hudson-Fulton celebration. (Add. pubs. for price.) N. Y. State Educ.

Hughes, T: Tom Brown's school days. *25 c. net. Macmillan.

BIBLIOGRAPHIES.—*Continued.*

Hugo, V. Notre-Dame de Paris. $1.15. Oxford Univ.

Hungarian books: Campbell, J. M., *comp.* Sel. list of Hungarian books. 15 c. A. L. A.

Hunt, L.: Miller, B. Leigh Hunt's relations with Byron, Shelley and Keats. $1.25 net. Lemcke.

Hydraulic engineering: Harza, L. F. Investigation of the hydraulic ram. 25 c. Univ. of Wis.

Hydraulic engineering: Mead, D. W: Relations of experimental results to the theory of the tangential water wheel. 40 c. Univ. of Wis.

Hydraulic engineering: Mead, D. W. Water power engineering. *$6 net. McGraw.

Hygiene: Brooklyn Public Library. Personal hygiene and physical development. gratis. Brooklyn Lib.

Hygiene: Ditman, N. E. Education and its economic value in the field of preventive medicine. (Add. pubs. for price.) Columbia Univ.

Hygiene: Elliott, S. M. Household hygiene. $1.25. Am. Sch. Home Economics.

Hygiene: Godfrey, H. Health of the city. $1.25 net. Houghton M.

Hygiene: New England Assoc. of School Supts. Rept. on the physical welfare of the public school child. gratis. N. E. Assoc. Sch. Supts.

Hygiene: Peabody, S. W. Historical study of legislation regarding public health in the states of New York and Massachusetts. $1. Journal Infectious Diseases.

Hygiene: Porter, C: Sanitary law. 90 c. net. Longmans.

Hygiene: Powell, T: Fundamentals and requirements of health and disease. $5. Powell Pub.

Hygiene: Richards, E. H. S., *and* Woodman, A. G. Air, water, and food from a sanitary standpoint. $1. Wiley.

Hygiene: Sadler, W: S. Science of living. $1.50 net. McClurg.

Hygiene: Smith, A. W., *comp.* Selected bibliography of sanitary science and allied subjects. *50 c. net. Stechert.

Hygiene: Whipple, G. M. Questions in school hygiene. 60 c. Bardeen.

Hymns and hymn writers: Seipt, A. A. Schwenkfelder hymnology. $2. Univ. of Penn.

Hypnotism: Moll, A. Hypnotism. $1.50. Scribner.

Iberville, Pierre Le Moyne, *Sieur* d': Reed, C: B. First great Canadian. $2 net. McClurg.

Ibsen, Henrik: Ibsen, H. Brand, et dramatisk digt. $1.50. J: Anderson.

Ibsen, Henrik: Moses, M. J. Henrik Ibsen. *$1.50 net. M. Kennerley.

Icelandic literature: Islandica: an annual rel. to Iceland. $1. Cornell Univ.

Ichthyosauria: Merriam, J: C. Triassic ichthyosauria. $3. Univ. of Cal.

Idealism: Horne, H. H. Idealism in education. $1.25 net. Macmillan.

BIBLIOGRAPHIES.—*Continued.*

Idiocy: Seguin, E: Idiocy; and its treatment by the physiological method. $2. Teachers' Coll.

Illinois: Bogges, A. C. Settlement of Illinois, 1778-1830. $3. Chic. Hist.

Illinois: Jones, L. E. Decisive dates in Illinois hist. $2. Ill. Pr.

Illinois: Olson, E. W., *ed.* History of the Swedes of Illinois. In 2 v. *$20 net; *$25 net. Engberg-H.

Illinois: Robinson, L. E., *and* Moore, I. Hist. of Illinois. 60 c. Am. Bk.

Illinois: Schuyler, R. L. Transition in Illinois from British to American government. *$1.25 net. Columbia Univ.

Immigration: Edwards, R: H:, *ed.* Immigration. 10 c. R: H: Edwards.

Immigration: Immigrant and the community. 75 c. Y. M. C. A.

Immigration: Ray, M. K. Immigration problem. 25 c. Wis. Free Lib.

Immigration: United States. *Dept. of Commerce and Labor. Bureau of Immigration and Naturalization.* Catalogue of books and blanks used by the immigration service. (Add. Superintendent for price.) U. S., Supt. of Docs.

Incarnation: Streatfeild, G: S. The Incarnation. *40 c. net. Longmans.

India: Anderson, W: B., *and* Watson, C: R. Far north in India. 50 c. Bd. For. Miss.

India: Macaulay, T: B., *Lord.* Essays on Lord Clive and Warren Hastings. 40 c. C: E. Merrill.

Indian names: Douglas-Lithgow, R. A. Dict. of American-Indian place and proper names in New England, $7. Salem Press.

Indiana: Lindley, H. Government of Indiana. 50 c. Ginn.

Indians: Barrett, S: A. Ethno-geography of the Pomo and neighboring Indians. $3.25. Univ. of Cal.

Indians: Eastman, C: A. Smoky Day's wigwam evenings. 60 c. Little, B. & Co.

Indians: Lumpkin, W. Removal of Cherokee Indians from Georgia. 2 v. Dodd.

Indians: McKenzie, F. A. Indian in relation to the white population of the U. S. $1; 50 c. F. A. McKenzie.

Indians: Merriam, C. H., *ed.* Dawn of the world: [Mewan Indian myths.] $3.50. A. H. Clark.

Indians: United States. *Superintendent of Documents.* Indians; price list. gratis.

Induction coils: Armagnat, H. Theory, design and construction of induction coils. *$2 net. McGraw.

Infallibility: Simpson, W: J: S. Roman Catholic opposition to papal infallibility. $2 net. Young Churchman.

Infantry: Lloyd, E. M. Review of the history of infantry. *$2 net. Longmans.

Inflammation: Adami, J: G: Inflammation. *$1.50 net. Macmillan.

Injunctions: American Federation of Labor. Buck's Stove and Range Co. injunction suit. 25 c. Trades Unionists.

BIBLIOGRAPHIES.—*Continued.*

Inland navigation: Griffin, A. P. C., *comp.* Library of Congress list of works rel. to deep waterways from the Great Lakes to the Atlantic. 25 c. U. S., Supt. of Docs.

Inland navigation: List. of works relating to deep waterways from the Great Lakes to the Atlantic Ocean. gratis. U. S., Supt. of Docs.

Inland navigation: Meyer, H. H: B., *comp.* Select list of references on inland waterways in Europe. Engineer Sch.

Inquisition: Vacandard, E. The Inquisition. *$1.50 net. Longmans.

Insanity: Beers, C. W. The after care of the insane. gratis. C. W. Beers.

Insanity: Storring, G. Mental pathology in its relation to normal psychology. *$2.75 net. Macmillan.

Inscriptions: Pier, G. C. Inscriptions of the Nile monuments. **$5 net. Putnam.

Insects: Banks, N. List of works on North American entomology. (Add. Superintendent for price.) U. S., Supt. of Docs.

Insects: Doane, R. W. Insects and disease. $1.50 net. Holt.

Insects: Pierce, W: D. Monographic revision of the twisted winged insects comprising the order *Strepsiptera* Kirby. U. S., Supt. of Docs.

Insects: Some insects injurious to truck crops. Gov. Pr. Off.

Insects: Stebbins, F. A. Insect galls of Springfield, Massachusetts. $1.50. Springfield Mu. Nat. Hist.

Insects: United States. Entomology Bureau; bulletins, circulars and technical ser. rel. to insects. gratis. U. S., Supt. of Docs.

Insects: United States. *Superintendent of Documents.* Entomology Bureau; bulls., circulars, [etc.]

Insects: Weed, C. M. Farm friends and farm foes. 90 c. Heath.

Insurance: Eke, A. J. Elements of insurance. 50 c. Pitman.

Insurance: Frankel, L. K. Workingmen's insurance in Europe. $2.50. Charities Pub.

Insurance: Gow, W: Marine insurance. $1.10 net. Macmillan.

Insurance: Griffin, A. P. C. Library of Congress select list of references on workingmen's insurance. (Add. Supt. for price.) U. S., Supt. of Docs.

Insurance: Griffin, A. P. C., *comp.* Library of Congress list of works rel. to government regulations of insurance, U. S. and foreign countries. (Add. Supt. for price.) U. S., Supt. of Docs.

Interdict: Krehbiel, E: B. The interdict, its history and its operation, with especial attention to the time of Pope Innocent III. $1.50. Am. Hist.

Intestines: Schmidt, A. Examination of the function of the intestines by means of the test diet. *$1.50 net. Davis.

Investments: Rollins, M. Money and investments. $2 net. Estes.

BIBLIOGRAPHIES.—*Continued.*

Iowa: Downey, E. H. Hist. of labor legislation in Iowa. $2. State Hist., Ia.

Ireland: Brown, S. J. Reader's guide to Irish fiction. $1.25 net. Longmans.

Iron: Cushman, A. S., *and* Gardner, H: A. Corrosion and preservation of iron and steel. $4 net. McGraw-H.

Iron: Sang, A. Corrosion of iron and steel. $1. McGraw-H.

Iron and steel: Stansbie, J. H. Iron and steel. *$2 net. Van Nostrand.

Irrigation: United States. *Dept. of Agriculture.* Organization, work, and publications of irrigation investigations. gratis.

Irving, Henry: Brereton, A. Life of Henry Irving. 2 v. *$6.50 net. Longmans.

Italian art: Powers, H. H., *and others.* Outlines for the study of art. 2 v. ea., $1.50. Bu. Univ. Travel.

Italian cathedrals: Bumpus, T: F. Cathedrals and churches of northern Italy. $2.50. L. C. Page.

Italian paintings: Jewett, L. R. History of Italian painting, outlines and references. 60 c. Mt. Holyoke Coll.

Italy: Jordan, L: H:, *and* Labanca, B. Study of religion in Italian universities. $2.40. Oxford Univ.

Italy: Macdonell, A. In the Abruzzi. *$2 net. Stokes.

Italy: Peet, T. E. Stone and bronze ages in Italy and Sicily. $5.25. Oxford Univ.

Jackson, *Gen.* Thomas Jonathan, ["Stonewall."]: White, H: A. Stonewall Jackson. **$1.25 net. Jacobs.

Japan: Dillon, E. Arts of Japan. *$1 net. McClurg.

Japan: Longford, J. H. Story of old Japan. $1.75 net. Longmans.

Jefferies, John Richard: Thomas, E: Richard Jefferies, his life and work. *$3 net. Little, B. & Co.

Jesus Christ: Bond, A. R. Master preacher. $1 net. Am. Tr.

Jesus Christ: Burkitt, F. C. Earliest sources for the life of Jesus. **50 c. net. Houghton M.

Jesus Christ: Chandler, W. M. Trial of Jesus from a lawyer's standpoint. 2 v. *$5 net. Empire Pub.

Jesus Christ: Granbery, J: C: Outline of New Testament Christology. 50 c. Univ. of Chic.

Jesus Christ: King, H: C. Ethics of Jesus. **$1.50 net. Macmillan.

Jesus Christ: Lepin, M. Christ and the Gospel. $2. McVey.

Jesus Christ: Schweitzer, A. Quest of the historical Jesus. $3.50 net. Macmillan.

Jesus Christ: Stalker, J. Ethic of Jesus. *$1.75 net. Armstrong.

Jewelry: Davenport, C. Jewellery. *$1 net. McClurg.

Jews: Calisch, E: N. Jew in English literature. *$2 net. Bell Bk.

Jews: Harris, M. H: Modern Jewish hist. from the Renaissance to the Russian exodus. 30 c. net.—Thousand years of Jewish hist. $1. Bloch.

BIBLIOGRAPHIES.—*Continued.*

Jews: Jenks, O. R. Last prophets of Israel. 35 c. Our Hope.

Jews: Oesterley, W: O. E., *and* Box, G: H. Religion and worship of the Synagogue. *$3 net. Scribner.

Jews: Schomer, A. S. Primary cause of antisemitism. $1. A. S. Schomer.

Johnson, S:: Brooklyn Public Library. Samuel Johnson, 1709-1784; list of books with references to periodicals in the library. gratis. Brooklyn Lib.

Johnson, S.: Yale Univ. Library. Catalogue of an exhibition of mss., first eds., early engravings and various literature rel. to Samuel Johnson. 25 c. Yale Univ. Lib.

Johnson, S.: Yale Univ. Library. List of books and articles rel. to Samuel Johnson. 25 c. Yale Univ. Lib.

Juvenile courts: Hornbeck, S. K. Juvenile courts. 25 c. Wisconsin Free Lib.

Juvenile courts: Travis, T. Young malefactor. **$1.50 net. Crowell.

Kansas: Prentis, N. L. Hist. of Kansas. 60 c. C. Prentis.

Kelvin, William Thomson, *Lord:* Thompson, S. P. Life of William Thomson. $7.50 net. Macmillan.

Kentucky: McElroy, R. M. Kentucky in the nation's history. **$5 net. Moffat.

Kentucky: Phillips, P. L. First map of Kentucky by J: Filson. $2.50 net. Torch Press.

Kings Co., N. Y.: Ditmars, C: A. Historic homesteads of Kings County. $5. C: A. Ditmars.

Knowledge: Coursault, J. H. Learning process. *$1 net. Teachers' Coll.

Labor and laboring classes: Chapin, R. C. Standard of living among workingmen's families in New York City. $2. Charities Pub.

Labor and laboring classes: Edwards, R: H:, *ed.* Labor problem. 10 c. R: H: Edwards.

Labor and laboring classes: Griffin, A. P. C., *comp.* Library of Congress list of books rel. to the eight-hour working day. 15 c. U. S., Supt. of Docs.

Labor and laboring classes: Putnam, B. H. Enforcement of the statutes of labourers during the first decade after the Black Death. pap., $4. Longmans.

Labor and laboring classes: Stelzle, C: The church and labor. **50 c. net. Houghton M.

Labor and laboring classes: True, E. I. Labor problem. 25 c. Wis. Free Lib.

Labor and laboring classes: U. S. public documents rel. to the wage-workers. gratis. U. S., Supt. of Docs.

Lace: Old lace manual. $1. A. M. Kohlsaat.

Lady-beetle: Johnson, R. H. Determinate evolution in the color-pattern of the lady-beetles. $1. Carnegie.

Lamartine, A. M. L. Jocelyn. $1. Oxford Univ.

Lamb, C: Essays of Elia. 40 c. Heath.

BIBLIOGRAPHIES.—*Continued.*

Lamb, C: Essays of Elia. 50 c. C: E. Merrill.

Land: Johnson, A. H. Disappearance of the small land owner. $1.75. Oxford Univ.

Land: Treat, P. J. National land system. $2.50.. Treat.

Land: U. S. *Superintendent of Documents.* Land; U. S. public documents rel. to lands. gratis.

Larkin, T. O: Kelsey, R. W. United States consulate in California. Univ. of Cal.

Latin language: Mood, J. R. Some figurative usages of *venire* and *ire.* gratis. Johns Hopkins.

Latin language: Reiley, K. C. Studies in the philosophical terminology of Lucretius and Cicero. *$1.25 net. Columbia Univ.

Latin literature: Clark, A. C., *comp.* Fontes prosae nvmerosae. $1.50. Oxford Univ.

Law: Lobingier, C: S. People's law. **$4 net. Macmillan.

Law: Shive, R. J. Handy digest (civil) to the books that contain the law. $4.75. State Cap.

Law: Townes, J: C: Law books and how to use them. $2.50. Austin Pr.

Law: United States. *Superintendent of Documents.* Laws of the U. S. for sale by Superintendent of Documents. gratis.

Lawyers: Benton, J. H: Lawyer's official oath and office. $1.50. Boston Bk.

Leadwork: Weaver, L. English leadwork. $10 net. Scribner.

Lebanon County, Pa.: Croll, C. P. Lebanon County imprints. 25 c. C. P. Croll.

Legal education: Wilgus, H. L. Legal education in the United States. (Not for sale.) Mich. Law Rev.

Leibnitz, G. W. v. Philosophical works. $2.50. Tuttle, M. & T.

Leicester, Mass.: Chenoweth, *Mrs.* C. Van D. History of the Second Congregational church. $1.50. C. V. Chenoweth.

Leipzig campaign: Maude, *Col.* F. N. Leipzig campaign. *$1.60 net. Macmillan.

Lettering: French, T: E. Essentials of lettering. $1. Varsity Supply.

Liberty of the press: Schroeder, T., *comp.* Free press anthology. $2. Free Speech.

Librarians and libraries: Brown, Z. M., *comp.* Buying list of books for small libraries. gratis. N. Y. State Educ.

Light: Rentschler, H. C. New method for measuring the index of refraction of a gas for different light-waves and the results obtained for several gases. 20 c. Johns Hopkins.

Lincoln, Abraham: Boston Public Library. Abraham Lincoln: short list of books, for school use. gratis. Boston Pub. Lib.

Lincoln, Abraham: Brooklyn Public Library. Abraham Lincoln: list of Lincoln's works relating to Lincoln in the Library. gratis. Brooklyn Lib.

BIBLIOGRAPHIES.—*Continued.*

Lincoln, Abraham: Chicago. Public Library. List of books and magazine articles on Abrahah Lincoln. gratis. Chic. Pub. Lib.

Lincoln, Abraham: Grand Army flag day, Rhode Island, February twelfth, 1909. (Add. pub. for price.) R. I. Dept. Educ.

Lincoln, Abraham: Illinois State Historical Library. Collections, v. 3; Lincoln ser., v. 1, Lincoln-Douglas debates. (Not for sale.) Int. State Hist. Lib.

Lincoln, Abraham: Lowell [Mass.] City Library. List of Lincoln's writings and works rel. to Lincoln in the library. gratis. Lowell Lib.

Lincoln, Abraham: Miller, F. T. Portrait life of Lincoln. $2. Patriot.

Lincoln, Abraham: Mitchell, W. B. Abraham Lincoln. 50 c. Smith & S.

Lincoln, Abraham: Russell, L. E. Abraham Lincoln; contribution toward a bibliography. 50 c. Torch Press.

Lincoln-Douglas debates: Sparks, E. E., *and others, eds.* Semi-centennial of Lincoln-Douglas debates. 35 c. Phillips Bros.

Liquor: Edwards, R: H:, *ed.* Liquor problem. 10 c. R: H: Edwards.

Literature: Welch, J: S. Literature in the school. $1.25. Silver.

Lodge, T: Rosalynde; or, Euphue's golden legacy. 35 c. Ginn.

London, Eng.: Foord, A. S. Springs, streams and spas of London—hist. and associations. $3.50 net. Stokes.

Longfellow, H: W.: Livingston, L. S., *comp.* Bibliography of the first editions in book form of the writings of Henry Wadsworth Longfellow. *$3 net; *$10 net. Dodd.

Longfellow, H: W: Narrative poems. 40 c. Scott, F. & Co.

Lord's supper: Stone, D. History of the doctrine of the holy eucharist. 2 v. *$8.50 net. Longmans.

Louisiana: Ficklen, J: R. Hist. of Reconstruction in Louisiana. $1.50; $1. John Hopkins.

Louisiana: Morris, A. Studies in the civil government of the state of Louisiana and the Constitution of the United States. 50 c. Natchitoches Times.

Lower California: North, A. W. Mother of California. **$2 net. P. Elder.

Luther, Martin: Waring, L. H. Political theories of Martin Luther. $1.50. Putnam.

Lyon, M.: Gilchrist, B. B. Life of Mary Lyon. $1.50 net. Houghton M.

Macaulay, T: B., *Lord.* Essay on Lord Clive.—Essay on Warren Hastings. ea., 25 c. net. Longmans.

Macaulay, T: B., *Lord.* Essay on Warren Hastings. 40 c. Allyn & B.

Macaulay, T: B., *Lord:* Essays on Clive and Hastings. 35 c. Scott, F. & Co.

Macaulay, T: B., *Lord.* Hist. of England. 3 v. ea., 35 c. net; 70 c. net. Dutton.

BIBLIOGRAPHIES.—*Continued.*

Machinery: Portland (Ore.) Library Association. List of practical books on machine shop practice, foundry work and electricity. gratis. Portland (Ore.) L. A.

Magendie, François: Dawson, P. M. Biography of François Magendie. *$1.25 net. A. T. Huntington.

Magnesite: Hess, F. L. Magnesite deposits of California. (Add. Superintendent for price.) U. S., Supt. of Docs.

Maintenon, Francoise d'Aubigné, *Marquise* de.: Dyson, C. C. Madame de Maintenon. *$4 net. Lane.

Maitland, F: W: : Smith, A. L. Frederic William Maitland. *85 c. net. Oxford Univ.

Malaysia: Daniel, J. F. Animal life of Malaysia. **$1.20 net. Bobbs-M.

Mammalia: Gregory, W: K. Orders of mammals. $5. Am. Museum.

Mammalia: Osborn, H: F.. Age of mammals in Europe, Asia and North America. $4.50 net. Macmillan.

Manganese: Harder, E. C. Manganese deposits of the United States. Gov. Pr. Off.

Mansfield, Richard: Wilstach, P. Richard Mansfield. **$3.50 net. Scribner.

Manual training: Hammock, C. S. *and* A. G. Teachers' manual to accompany The manual arts for elem. schools. gratis. Heath.

Manuscripts: Bradley, J: W. Illuminated manuscripts. *$1 net. McClurg.

Manuscripts: Keidel, G: C: Hist. of French fable manuscripts. $1. Modern Lang. Assoc.

Marie Amélie *of France:* Dyson, C. C. Life of Marie Amélie, last queen of the French, 1782-1866. $3.50 special net. Appleton.

Marine engineering: Linch, C· S. Marine engine indicating. $2. Am. Steam Gauge.

Marsh, *Captain* Grant Prince: Hanson, J. M. Conquest of the Missouri. *$2 net. McClurg.

Mary, *Virgin.* Jenner, *Mrs.* H: Our Lady in art. $1 net. McClurg.

Maryland: Russell, W: T. Maryland. $1.75. Furst.

Massachusetts: Hilkey, C: J. Legal development in colonial Massachusetts, 1630-1686. $1.25. Longmans.

Massachusetts Bay: Ford, W. C., *and* Mathews, A. Bibliography of the laws of the Massachusetts Bay, 1641-1776. (Priv. pr.) Univ. Press, (Camb.)

Mathematics: American Mathematical Society, New York. Catalogue of the library, Jan., 1910. gratis. Am. Math.

Mathematics: Phillips, E: C: On the pentacardoid. 35 c. Johns Hopkins.

Mathematics: White, W: F. Scrap-book of elem. mathematics. $1. Open Court.

Mayas (The): Bowditch, C: P. Numeration, calendar systems and astronomical knowledge of the Mayas. (Priv. pr.) Univ. Press.

BIBLIOGRAPHIES.—*Continued.*

Mechanics: United States. *Superintendent of Documents.* Engineering: mechanics; government documents.

Medical jurisprudence: Ewell, M. D. Manual of medical jurisprudence. $2.50. Little, B. & Co.

Medici (The): Ross, *Mrs.* J. A. D- G., *ed. and tr.* Lives of the early Medici. $4 net. Badger.

Medici (The): Vaughan, H. M. Medici popes. *$4 net. Putnam.

Medici (The): Young, G: F: The Medici. 2 v. *$8 net. Dutton.

Medicine: Allbutt, *Sir* T: C., *and* Rolleston, H. D., *eds.* System of medicine. $6; $7; $8. Macmillan.

Medicine: John Crerar Library, Chic. List of current medical periodicals and allied serials. 10 c. John Crerar Lib.

Medicine: Josephson, A. G. S. Incunabula [medical] in the Senn collection at the John Crerar Library. (Priv. pr.) Am. Medical.

Medicine: New York State Library, Albany. Medical serials with bibliography. 25 c. N. Y. State Educ.

Medicine: Straub, P. F: Medical service in campaign. $1.50. Blakiston.

Menander, *of Athens.* Four plays. $2.50. Ginn.

Mennonites: Smith, C. H: Mennonites of America. $2. Mennonite Pub. Ho.

Mental science: Bruce, H: A. B. Riddle of personality. **$1.50 net. Moffat.

Metals and metallurgy: Barr, J. A. Testing for metallurgical processes. $2. Mining and Scientific.

Meteorology. United States. *Dept. of Agriculture Weather Bu. Lib.* Brief list of meteorological text-books and reference books. gratis.

Meteorology: United States. *Dept. of Agriculture. Weather Bu.* Bulletins, circulars, maps, and monthly weather review. gratis.

Mexican language: Denison, T: S. Mexican-Aryan comparative vocab. $2. T: S. Denison.

Micronesia: Bliss, *Mrs.* E. T. C. Micronesia. 30 c. J: G. Hosmer.

Microscopes: Gage, S. H. Microscopes. $1.50. Comstock Pub.

Middle Ages: Munro, D. C., *and* Carleton, G: C. Syllabus of medieval history. $1. Longmans.

Middles Ages: Walsh, J. J. Thirteenth, greatest of centuries. $2.50. Cath. Summer Sch.

Middleton, T:, *and* Rowley, W: Spanish gipsie, and All's lost by lust. 60 c. Heath.

Military art and science: Sayre, F. Map maneuvers. 60 c.; 75 c. Staff Coll.

Military art and science: Willcox, C. De W. French-English military technical dict. U. S., Supt. of Docs.

Milk: Ayers, S: H., *and* Johnson, W: T., *jr.* Bacteriology of commercially pasteurized and raw market milk. Gov. Pr. Off.

BIBLIOGRAPHIES.—*Continued.*

Milk: Herschell, G: A. Soured milk and pure cultures of lactic acid bacilli in the treatment of disease. 50 c. Chic. Med. Bk.

Millais, *Sir* J. E.: Reid, J. E. Sir J. E. Millais. $1.25. Scribner.

Milton, John: Beers, H: A. Milton's tercentenary. 50 c. Yale Univ.

Milton, John: Catalogue of an exhibition commemorative of the tercentenary of the birth of John Milton; held at the Grolier Club. (Priv. pr.) Grolier Club.

Milton, John: Comus, L'allegro, Il penseroso, and Lycidas, with other of Milton's shorter poems. 25 c. Scribner.

Mineralogy: Dana, E: S., *and* Ford, W: E. Second appendix to Dana's system of mineralogy. $1.50. Wiley.

Mineralogy: Dana, J. D. System of mineralogy. $12.50. Wiley.

Mines and mining: Emmons, W: H. Some ore deposits in Maine and the Milan mine. Gov. Pr. Off.

Mines and mining: Halse, E: Dict. of Spanish and Spanish-American mining, metallurgical and allied terms. *$3.50 net. Lippincott.

Mines and mining: Hancock, E. T. Notes accompanying the lectures on geology applied to mining. $1. New Era Print.

Mines and mining: Ransome, F: L. Notes on some mining districts in Humboldt County, Nevada. U. S., Supt. of Docs.

Mines and mining: Rice, G: S. Explosibility of coal dust. Gov. Pr. Off.

Mines and mining: Trumbull, L. W. Manual of underground surveying. $3. McGraw-H.

Miniatures: Davenport, C. Miniatures. *$1 net. McClurg.

Miniatures: Foster, J. J. Chats on old miniatures. $2. Stokes.

Miniatures: Heath, D. Miniatures. *$7.50 net. Putnam.

Mirabeau, Honoré Gabriel Riquetti, *Comte* de: Trowbridge, W: R. H. Mirabeau, the demi-god. *$3.75 net. Scribner.

Missions and missionaries: Brown, A. J. Why and how of foreign missions. *50 c. net. Young People's Miss.

Missions and missionaries: Helm, M. Upward path. 50 c.; 35 c. Young People's Miss.

Missions and missionaries: Malden, R. H. Foreign missions. $1.25 net. Longmans.

Missions and missionaries: Mills, J. S., *and others.* Our foreign missionary enterprise. *50 c. net; *35 c. net. Un. B. Pub.

Missions and missionaries: Montgomery, H. B. Western women in eastern lands. $1.50 net. Macmillan.

Missions and missionaries. Murray, J. L. Apologetic of modern missions. 15 c. Student Vol.

Missions and missionaries: Pfeiffer, E: Mission studies. *75 c. net. Lutheran Bk.

Missions and missionaries: Platt, W. The frontier. 50 c.; 35 c. Am. Bapt.

BIBLIOGRAPHIES.—*Continued.*

Missions and missionaries: Ray, T. B., *and others.* Southern Baptist foreign missions. 50 c. S. S. Bd. So. Bapt.

Missions and missionaries: Students and the present missionary crisis. $1.50. Student Vol.

Modernism: Lilley, A. L. Modernism. *$1.75 net. Scribner.

Mohawk Valley, N. Y.: Diefendorf, M. R. Historic Mohawk. $2 net. Putnam.

Mollusks: MacFarland, F. M. Opisthobranchiate *Mollusca* of the Branner-Agassiz expedition to Brazil. $1. Stanford Univ.

Money: Adams, J. T. Some notes on the currency problem. (Add. author for price.) Broun-G.

Money: Davies, A. E. Money and the stock and share markets. 50 c. Pitman.

Money: White, H. Money and banking illustrated by American history. *$1.80 net; *$1.50 net. Ginn.

Monkeys: Peterson, O. A. Revision of the Entelodontidæ. $2.50. Carnegie Museum.

Monopolies: Jenckes, A. L. Origin, the organization and the location of the staple of England. (Add. pubs. for price.) Univ. of Penn.

Montaigne, Michel Eyquemde: Compayrè, J. G. Montaigne, and education of the judgment. **90 c. net. Crowell.

Montana: Fisher, C. A. Geology of the Great Falls coal field, Mont. (Add. Superintendent for price.) U. S.. Supt. of Docs.

Montreux: Gribble, F. Montreux. *$2.50 net. Macmillan.

Mortgages: Campbell, R. A. Mortgage taxation. 25 c. Wisconsin Free Lib.

Mosses: Evans, A. W:, *and* Nichols, G: E. Bryophytes of Connecticut: [mosses.] 30 c. Conn. Lib.

Mt. Athos: Lake, K. Early days of monasticism on Mount Athos. $2.90. Oxford Univ.

Municipal betterment: Municipal betterment bibliog. gratis. Kansas City Pub. Lib.

Municipal government: Munroe, W: B. Government of European cities. **$2.50 net. Macmillan.

Municipal government: Schaffner, M. A. Municipal home rule charters. 25 c. Wisconsin Free Lib.

Mushrooms: Hard, M. E. Mushroom, edible and otherwise. $4.75; $6; $7.50. Mushroom Pub.

Music: Boston. Public Library. Catalogue of the Allen A. Brown collection of music. v. 1, pt. 1, A-Boosey. $1. Boston Pub. Lib.

Music: Dickinson, E: Study of the history of music. **$2.50 net. Scribner.

Music: Grosvenor Lib., Buffalo, N. Y. Catalogue of the books rel. to music in the Library. gratis. Grosvenor Lib.

Music: Hamilton, C. G. Outlines of music history. $1.50. Ditson.

BIBLIOGRAPHIES.—*Continued.*

Music: Hooper, L. M. Selected list of music and books about music for public libraries. 25 c. A. L. A.

Music: Lucas, C. Story of musical form. *$1.25 net. Scribner.

Music: New York Public Library. Selected list of works rel. to the hist. of music. gratis. N. Y. Pub. Lib.

Music: Princeton Univ. Library. Finding list for the music library, 1909. $1.25 net. Princeton Univ.

Music: San Francisco. Public Library. Music catalogue. gratis. San Francisco Lib.

Music: Winn, E. L. Child violinist. $1.25. Fischer.

Napoleon I: Gonnard, P. Exile of St. Helena. *$3.50 net. Lippincott.

Napoleon I: Hathaway, E. V. Little Corsican, Napoleon Bonaparte. $1. Rand, McN. & Co.

Napoleon I: Sloane, W: M. Life of Napoleon Bonaparte. 4 v. $10 net. Century Co.

Napoleon III.: Simpson, F. A. Rise of Louis Napoleon. *$3.50 net. Putnam.

Natural gas: Arnold, R., *and* Anderson, R. Preliminary report on the Coalinga oil district, [Cal.] 20 c. U. S., Supt. of Docs.

Natural history: United States. *Dept. of Agriculture. Bu. of Biolog. Survey.* Biolog. Survey; bulletins, circulars, [etc.] gratis.

Nature: Bascom, E. L. Selected books on nature study for schools and libraries. gratis. N. Y. State Educ.

Nature: Holtz, F: L. Nature-study. **$1.50 net. Scribner.

Nature: St. Paul Public Library. Select list of books on birds, insects and nature study. gratis. St. Paul Pub. Lib.

Nature: Schmucker, S: C. Study of nature. $1.25. Lippincott.

Navies: United States. *Office of Naval Intelligence.* Information concerning the principal navies of the world. (Add. Superintendent for price.)

"Ne temere": Creagh, J: T: Commentary on the decree "Ne temere." $1.25. Furst.

Needlework: Lowes, *Mrs.* E. L. Chats on old lace. $2. Stokes.

Negroes: Brawley, B: G. Negro in literature and art. 50 c. B: G. Brawley.

Negroes: Edwards, R: H:, *ed.* Negro problem. 10 c. R: H: Edwards.

Negroes: Sieg, V., *comp.* Negro problem: bibliography. 25 c. Wisconsin Free Lib.

Negroes: Stephenson, G. T: Race distinctions in American law. $1.50 net. Appleton.

Negroes: Weatherford, W. D. Negro life in the South. 75 c. Y. M. C. A.

Nervous system: Bailey, P. Diseases of the nervous system. $5; $6. Appleton.

Nervous system: Church, A. Diseases of the nervous system. subs., $7 net; $8 net. Appleton.

New Jersey: Ellis, E: S., *and* Snyder, H: Brief hist. of New Jersey. 60 c. Am. Bk.

BIBLIOGRAPHIES.—*Continued.*

New York City: Kelley, F. B., *comp.* Historical guide to the city of New York. **$1.50 net. Stokes.

New York City: Van Rensselaer, M. G. History of the city of New York. In 2 v. **$5 net. Macmillan.

New York Society Library: Keep, A. B. Hist. of New York Society Library. $7.50. Scribner.

New York State: Alexander, De A. S. Political history of the state of New York. v. 3, 1861-1882. *$2.50 net. Holt.

New York State: Becker, C. L. Hist. of political parties in the province of New York, 1760-1776. 75 c. Univ. of Wis.

Newport News, Va.: Green, B. W. How Newport's News got its name. gratis. W. E. Jones.

Newspapers: American Assoc. of Foreign-Language Newpapers. Unreached millions. (Add. pubs. for price.) L: N. Hammerling.

Newspapers: Ayer, M. F., *comp.* Check-list of Boston newspapers, 1704-1780. $3.50. Colonial Soc. of Mass.

Newspapers: Thwaites, R. G. Ohio Valley press before the war of 1812-15. (Not for sale.) Davis Press.

Newspapers: United States. *Library of Congress.* Want list of American 18th century newspapers.

Nietzsche, Friedrich Wilhelm: Mencken, H: L: Philosophy of Friedrich Nietzsche. *$2 net. Luce & Co.

Nitroquinazolones: Klaber, W: On certain 7-nitro-4-quinazolones. (Add. author for price.) W: Klaber.

North Carolina: Laney, F. B. Bibliography of North Carolina geology, mineralogy and geography, with a list of maps. 25 c. N. C. Geolog. Survey.

North Dakota: Boyle, J. E. Government of North Dakota. $1. Am. Bk.

Norway: Monroe, W. S. Norway. $3. L. C. Page.

Norwegian books: Kildal, A., *comp.* Selected list of Norwegian and Danish books. 25 c. A. L. A.

Norwegians in U. S.: Flom, G: T. H. Hist. of Norwegian immigration to the U. S. (Priv. pr.) G: T. Flom.

Nose: Burnham, W: H: Hygiene of the nose. (Add. author for price.) W: H. Burnham.

Novels: Wigmore, J: H: List of legal novels. 40 c. Ill. Law Review.

Numbers: Goudy, H: Trichotomy in Roman law. $1.35. Oxford Univ.

Oberammergau passion play: Day, E. H. Ober-Ammergau and the Passion Play. 45 c. net. Young Churchman.

Oberammergau passion play: Passion play of Oberammergau. $1.50. Duffield.

Ohio poets: Venable, E., *ed.* Poets of Ohio. **$1.50 net. Clarke.

Oils and fats: Leathes, J: B. The fats. $1.25 net. Longmans.

Opera: Lee, E. M. Story of opera. $1.25 net. Scribner.

BIBLIOGRAPHIES.—*Continued.*

Opera: Sonneck, O. G: T., *comp.* Library of Congress dramatic music: catalogue of scores. 40 c. U. S., Supt. of Docs.

Orangia, South Africa: Johnson, J. P. Geological and archæological notes on Orangia. $3 net. Longmans.

Oratory: Pearson, P. M., *ed.* Intercollegiate debates. $1.50. Hinds.

Oregon: Parkman, F. Oregon trail. 25 c. net. Longmans.

Oriental literature: Conant, M. P. Oriental tale in England in the eighteenth century. **$2 net. Lemcke.

Otsego, N. Y.: Blakely, S. B. Hist. of Otsego. (Add. author for price.) S. B. Blakely.

Otway, T: The orphan, and Venice preserved. *60 c. net. Heath.

Paganini, Nicolo: Stratton, S. S: Nicolo Paganini. *$2 net. Scribner.

Painters and painting: De Groot, C. H. Catalogue raisonné of the works of the most eminent Dutch painters of the seventeenth century. In 10 v. v. 3. $7.50 net. Macmillan.

Painters and painting: Mach, E. R. O. v. Art of painting in the nineteenth century. *$1.25 net. Ginn.

Painters and painting: Stirling-Maxwell, *Sir* W: Stories of the Spanish artists until Goya. $3 net. Duffield.

Paleontology: Eastman, C: R. Devonic fishes of the New York formations. $1.25. N. Y. State Educ.

Paleontology: Kofoid, C: A. Revision of the genus *ceratocorys,* based on skeletal morphology. 10 c. Univ. of Cal.

Palestine: Masterman, E. W: G. Studies in Galilee. *$1 net. Univ. of Chic.

Panics: American Academy of Political and Social Science. Lessons of the financial crisis. $1. Am. Acad. Pol. Sci.

Paradiso (*by Dante*): Vernon, W: N. Readings on the Paradiso. 2 v. *$4 net. Macmillan.

Parliament (*English*): McIlvain, C: H. High Court of Parliament and its supremacy. $2.50 net. Yale Univ.

Patents: United States. Patent Office. Price list of publications. gratis. Gov. Pr. Off.

Pathology: Coplin, W: M. L. Manual of pathology, incl. bacteriology. $4. Blakiston.

Paul, *St.*: Alexander, A. B. D. Ethics of St. Paul. $2 net. Macmillan.

Paul, *St.*: Moffatt, J. Paul and Paulism. **50 c. net. Houghton M.

Pausanias. The Attica. $1.65. Ginn.

Peace: Brooklyn Public Library. International peace: list of books, with references to periodicals, in the Brooklyn Public Library. (Add. Library for price.) Brooklyn Lib.

Peace: Mead, E. D. Literature of the peace movement. gratis. Int. Sch. of Peace.

Pecan: Hume, H. H. Pecan and its culture. $1.50. H. H. Hume.

BIBLIOGRAPHIES.—*Continued.*

Pellagra: Lavinder, C. H., *and others.* Prevalence of pellagra in the U. S. (Add. Superintendent for price.) U. S., Supt. of Docs.

Pennsylvania: Bishop, A. L. State works of Pennsylvania. $1.50. Yale Univ.

Pepperrell, *Sir* W: Journal kept during the expedition against Louisbourg. $1. Am. Antiquarian.

Pereda, J. M. de. Pedro Sanchez. $1. Ginn.

Periodicals: Brief manual of leading periodicals in the United States and Canada. gratis. Chesman.

Periodicals: Catholic University of America Library. Periodicals and serials in the library of the Catholic University of America, 1910. (Priv. pr.) Cath. Univ.

Periodicals: Goodnight, Scott Holland. German literature in American magazines prior to 1846. 50 c. Univ. of Wis.

Periodicals: MacDonald, K. I. Magazines for the small library. (Add. pubs. for price.) League Lib. Com.

Periodicals: United States. *Library of Congress.* Want list of periodicals.

Periodicals: United States. *Superintendent of Documents.* Periodicals issued by United States government with foreign and domestic subscription prices. gratis. Gov. Pr. Off.

Persius Flaccus, Aulus: Morgan, M. H. Bibliography of Persius. 75 c. Harvard Univ.

Personality: Ribot, T. A. Diseases of the personality. $1. Boericke & T.

Perugia: Heywood, W: Hist. of Perugia. $3.50 net. Putnam.

Peruvian literature: Brown University. Books printed in Lima and elsewhere in South America after 1800. 50 c. Brown Univ.

Peruvian newspapers: Winship, G: P. Early South American newspapers. $1. Am. Antiquarian.

Pestalozzi: Holman, H. Pestalozzi: an account of his life and work. *$1.10 net. Longmans.

Petrarch, Francesco: Petrarch's letters to classical authors. **$1 net. Univ. of Chic.

Petroleum: Arnold, R., *and* Anderson, R. Preliminary report on the Coalinga oil district, [Cal.] 20 c. U. S., Supt. of Docs.

Pharmacy: Arny, H. V. Principles of pharmacy. *$5 net. Saunders.

Pharmacy: Cushny, A. R. Textbook of pharmacology and therapeutics. $3.75. Lea.

Philippine Islands. *Bureau of Printing.* Price list of public documents for sale by the Bureau of Printing, Manila, P. I. Bu. Public. Pr.

Philippine Islands: Robertson, J. A. Bibliography of the Philippine Islands. *$10 net. A. H. Clark.

Philo-Judæus: Benturch, N. Philo-Judæus of Alexandria. $1.25. Jewish Pub.

BIBLIOGRAPHIES.—*Continued.*

Songs: Sonneck, O. G: T., *comp.* Report on "The Star Spangled Banner," "Hail Columbia," "America," "Yankee Doodle." U. S., Supt. of Docs.

South (The): Moses, M. J. Literature of the South. $2.50 net. Crowell.

South (The): South in the building of the nation. full mor., $90. Southern Hist. Pub.

South America: Mozans, H. J. Up the Orinoco and down the Magdalena following the conquistadores. $3 net. Appleton.

South America: Neely, T: B: South America: its missionary problems. 50 c.; 35 c. Young People's Miss.

South Dakota: Robinson, J. L. D. Hist. of South Dakota. 75 c. Educator.

Spain: Williams, L. Arts and crafts of older Spain. 3 v. *$4.50 net. McClurg.

Spanish America: Hale, A. B. Practical guide to Latin America. **$1 net. Small.

Spanish-America: International Bureau of American Republics. List of Latin American hist. and description in the Columbus Memorial Library. gratis. Int. Bu. Am. Republics.

Spanish America: International Bureau of the American Republic, Washington, D. C. List of publications published or distributed by the International Bureau of American Republics. (Add. pub. for price.) Int. Bu. Am. Republics.

Spanish literature: Foulché-Delbosc, R. Bibliographie hispanique, 1905, 1906. ea., $1.25. Hispanic Soc.

Speculation: Fayant, F. Some thoughts on speculation. (Priv. pr.) Baruch.

Spine: Abrams, A. Spondylotherapy. $3.50. A. Abrams.

Spiritism: Tanner, A. E. Studies in spiritism. $2.50 net. Appleton.

Sponges: Cotte, J. Sponge culture. U. S., Supt. of Docs.

Sponges: Moore, H. F. Commercial sponges and the sponge fisheries. U. S., Supt. of Docs.

Stäel-Holstein, A. L. G. N., *Baronne* de. De l'Allemagne. 85 c. Oxford Univ.

Stanley, *Sir* H: M. Autobiography. $5. Houghton M.

State publications: Bowker, R: R., *ed.* State publications. pt. 4. $10 for complete work. Pub. Weekly.

Statistics: United States. *Dept. of Agriculture. Bu. of Statistics.* Statistics Bureau: bulletins, circulars, foreign markets, separates from year book, and crop reporter. gratis.

Stedman, Edmund Clarence: Stedman, L., *and* Gould, G: M. Life and letters of Edmund Clarence Stedman. $6.50 net. Moffat.

Stenography: Gregg, J: R. Gregg reporter. $1.50. Gregg Pub.

Sterne, L.: Sichel, W. S. Sterne; a study. $2.50. Lippincott.

BIBLIOGRAPHIES.—*Continued.*

Stomach: Bassler, A. Diseases of the stomach and upper alimentary tract. $6. Davis.

Story-telling: Lyman, E. Story telling. 75 c. net. McClurg.

Story-telling: St. John, E: P. Stories and story-telling in moral and religious education. *60 c. net. Pilgrim Press.

Story-telling: Wyche, R: T: Some great stories and how to tell them. $1. Newson.

Stowe, H. B. Uncle Tom's cabin. *35 c. net; *70 c. net. Dutton.

Strength of materials: Derleth, C:, *jr.* Moment diagrams and typical live loads. 10 c. Univ. of Cal.

Stuart, Henry: Shield, A. Henry Stuart, Cardinal of York. *$3.50 net. Longmans.

Suffrage: Phelps, E. M., *comp.* Selected articles on woman suffrage. $1 net. H. W. Wilson.

Sugar: Meyer, H. H: B., *comp.* Library of Congress select list of references on sugar, chiefly in its economic aspects. 25 c. U. S., Supt. of Docs.

Sugar: Nikaido, Y. Beet-sugar making and its chemical control. $3. Chemical.

Sugar: Tayler, A. J. W. Sugar machinery. $2 net. Van Nostrand.

Suggestion (Mental): Winbigler, C: F. Suggestion. $2.50. S. A. Lewis.

Sunday-school: Oliver, C. A. Preparation for teaching, [Sunday-schools.] 25 c. Westminster Press.

Sunday-school: Sloan, P. J. Sunday-school teacher's guide to success. *75 c. net. Benziger.

Superstitions: Stewart, C. T. Origin of the werewolf superstition. 50 c. Univ. of Mo.

Surgery: Kolle, F: S. Subcutaneous hydrocarbon protheses. **$2.50 net. Grafton Press.

Surgery: Lexer, E. General surgery. $6. Appleton.

Surveying: Johnson, J: B. Theory and practice of surveying. $3.50 net. Wiley.

Swedenborg, Emanuel: Hyde, J. Bibliog. of the works of Emanuel Swedenborg. $10. New Church.

Sweet pea: Crane, D. B. Book of the sweet pea. *$1.50 net. Lane.

Swift, J. Prose works. v. 12. *$1 net. Macmillan.

Swinburne, A. C: List of the original manuscripts of Algernon C: Swinburne. W. M. Hill.

Symbols: Jenner, *Mrs.* H. Christian symbolism. $1 net. McClurg.

Syphilis: Barr, G. Modern view of syphilis and its treatment. $2. Appleton.

Syphilis: Malsbary, G: E. Diagnosis of syphilis. $5. Harvey Pub.

Syphilis: Noguchi, H. Serum diagnosis of syphilis. **$2 net. Lippincott.

Tacitus, C. C. Histories. bks. 1 and 2. 60 c. net. Macmillan.

Tariff: Giesecke, A. A. American commercial legislation before 1789. $1.50. Appleton.

BIBLIOGRAPHIES.—*Continued.*

Tariff: United States. *Superintendent of Documents.* Tariff, list of United States public documents rel. to the various tariff laws.

Taxation: Kennan, K. K. Income taxation. $3.50. Burdick.

Taxation: Phelps, E. M., *comp.* Selected articles on the income tax. $1 net. H. W. Wilson.

Taxation: Seligman, E. R. A. Shifting and incidence of taxation. $3. E. R. A. Seligman.

Teachers and teaching: Arnold, F. Text-book of school and class management. In 2 v. v. 2. $1 net. Macmillan.

Teachers and teaching: Black, J. E. New primary methods. 2 v. $7. Interstate Sch. Corr.

Teachers and teaching. Boyer, C: C. Modern methods for teachers. $1.50. Lippincott.

Teachers and teaching: Burritt, E. G. Pupil and how to teach him. 60 c. W. B. Rose.

Teachers and teaching: Hess, *Mrs.* G. F., *comp.* List of books for teachers in the Seattle Public Library. gratis. Seattle Pub. Lib.

Teachers and teaching: Kandel, I: L. Training of elem. school teachers in Germany. $1.50. Teachers' Coll.

Teachers and teaching: Lomer, G. R: Concept of method. $1. Teachers' Coll.

Teachers and teaching: Neet, G: W. Pract. methodology. $1.25. Bogarte.

Teachers and teaching: Pattee, F. L. Elements of religious pedagogy. *75 c. net. Eaton & M.

Teachers and teaching: Rowe, S. H: Habit-formation and the science of teaching. **$1.50 net. Longmans.

Teachers and teaching: Sandiford, P: Training of teachers in England and Wales. $1.50. Columbia Univ.

Teachers and teaching: Thorndike, E: L. Teaching staff of secondary schools in the United States. (Add. Superintendent for price.) U. S., Supt. of Docs.

Technical education: Chamberlain, A. H: Conditions and tendencies of technical education in Germany. 50 c. Bardeen.

Technical education: Dean, A. D. Worker and the state; study of education for industrial workers. $1.20 net. Century Co.

Telephone: Scott, L. Telephones; interchange of service. 25 c. Wisconsin Free Lib.

Tellurites: Wolesensky, E. Study of the metallic tellurites. 25 c. Univ. of Wis.

Temperance: Hammell, G: M., *ed.* Passing of the saloon. $2; $2.75; $3.50. Tower Press.

Temperance: Warner, H. S. Social welfare and the liquor question. $1; 35 c. Intercollegiate Prohibition.

Temple (The): Osgood, P. E. Temple of Solomon. 30 c. Open Court.

BIBLIOGRAPHIES.—*Continued.*

Tennyson, Alfred, *Lord:* Brooklyn Public Library. Alfred Tennyson, 1809-1892; list of books with references to periodicals in the Brooklyn Public Library. gratis. Brooklyn Lib.

Terence, Afer P. Phormio. 60 c. Scott, F. & Co.

Texas: Ramsdell, C: W: Reconstruction in Texas. $2.50; $4 net. Longmans.

Textile fabrics: Lowell, Mass., City Library. Textiles. gratis. Lowell Lib.

Textile fabrics: Watson, K. H. Textiles and clothing. $1.25. Am. Sch. Home Economics.

Theocritus: Kerlin, R. T: Theocritus in English literature. $1.50. J. P. Bell.

Theocritus: Leutner, W. J: The article in Theocritus. gratis. Johns Hopkins.

Theology: Davies, E. O. Prolegomena to systematic theology. *$1.25 net. Doran.

Thomas à Kempis. Imitation of Christ. 25 c. net. Macmillan.

Thoreau, Henry David: Allen, F. H: Bibliography of Henry David Thoreau. **$5 net. Houghton M.

Thoreau, H: D: Walden. 50 c. Houghton M.

Tobacco: Gilbert, W: W. Root-rot of tobacco. (Add. Superintendent for price.) U. S., Supt. of Docs.

Tolstoy, *Count* Lyoff Nicholaievich: Maude, A. Life of Tolstoy. 2 v. $6 net. Dodd.

Tory, Geofroy: Bernard, A. J. Geofroy Tory. *$37.50 net. Houghton M.

Toys: Jackson, E. Toys of other days. *$7.50 net. Scribner.

Trees: Fernow, B. E. Care of trees in lawn, street and park. $2 net. Holt.

Trenton, N. J.: Trenton Public Library. City of Trenton. gratis. Trenton Pub. Lib.

Tuberculosis: Keyes, T: B. Renewal of life. Tubercle Press.

Tuberculosis: Massachusetts. *Committee of International Congress on Tuberculosis 6th, Washington.* Tuberculosis in Massachusetts. (Add. pubs. for price.) Wright & P.

"Uncle Tom's cabin": MacLean, G. E. "Uncle Tom's cabin" in Germany. $1.50. Univ. of Penn.

United States: American civil government. 50 c. net; 60 c. net. Macmillan.

United States: Ames, H. V. Outline of lectures on American political and institutional hist. during the colonial and revolutionary periods. $1. Longmans.

United States: Andrews, C: M., *and* Davenport, F. G. Guide to the manuscript materials for the hist. of the U. S. to 1783, in the British Museum, in minor London archives, and in the libraries of Oxford and Cambridge. $2. Carnegie.

United States: Ashley, R. L. American government. $1 net. Macmillan.

United States: Beard, C: A. American government and politics. $2.10 net. Macmillan.

BIBLIOGRAPHIES.—*Continued.*

United States: Bradford, T: L. Bibliographer's manual of American hist. In 5 v. v. 2, 3, 4, 5. per v., $3.50 net; per set, $17.50. Henkels.

United States: Brooks, J: G. As others see us: progress in the U. S. **$1.75 net. Macmillan.

United States: Brooks, R. C. Corruption in American politics and life. $1.25 net. Dodd.

United States: Bruce, H: A. B. Romance of American expansion. **$1.75 net. Moffat.

United States: Caldwell, H. W., *and* Clark, E. P. Source hist. of the United States. $1.25. Ainsworth.

United States: Coman, K. Industrial hist. of the United States. $1.50 net. Macmillan.

United States: Ellis, E: S., *ed.* Hist. of our country from the discovery of America to the present time. 8 v. $48. Jones Bros.

United States: Evans, L. B. Essential facts of American history. $1. B: H. Sanborn.

United States: Everhart, E. Hdbk. of United States public documents. $2.50 net. H. W. Wilson.

United States: Fanning, C. E., *comp.* Selected articles on the election of United States senators. $1. H. W. Wilson.

United States: Fischer, H: Landeskunde des Vereinigten Staaten. 2 v. 40 c. Stechert.

United States: Follett, M. P. Speaker of the House of Representatives. $1.75 net. Longmans.

United States: Foote, A. E., *and* Skinner, A. W. Makers and defenders of America. 60 c. Am. Bk.

United States: Forman, S: E. Hist. of the United States for schools. $1 net. Century Co.

United States: Griffin, A. P. C., *comp.* Bibliography of American historical societies. $1. U. S., Supt. of Docs.

United States: Griffin, G. G., *comp.* Writings on American hist., 1906, 1907, 1908; bibliography. ea., $2.50 net. Macmillan.

United States: Grosvenor Library. Index-catalogue of books in the dept. of local history and genealogy. 25 v. Grosvenor Lib.

Unitel States: Hasse, A. R. Materials for a bibliography of the public archives of the thirteen original states. (Add. Supt. for price.) U. S. Supt. of Docs.

United States: Howard, G: E. Biography of American statesmanship; analyt. reference syllabus. 50 c. Univ. of Neb.

United States: Jenks, T. When America became a nation. $1.25. Crowell.

United States: Johnston, A. Hist. of American politics. 90 c. Holt.

United States: Low, A. M. American people. **$2.25 net. Houghton M.

United States: Miyakawa, M. Powers of the American people. **$2.50 net. Baker & T.

BIBLIOGRAPHIES.—*Continued.*

United States: Montgomery, D: H: Leading facts of American history. $1. Ginn.

United States: Nichol, J: Tables of European hist., literature, science and art; and of Am. hist., literature and art. *$2.25 net. Macmillan.

United States: Outline for the study of American civil government. 50 c. net. Macmillan.

United States: Redway, J. W. School hist. $1 net. Silver.

United States: Riley, F. L., *and others.* Our republic; hist. of the United States for grammar grades. 65 c. Riley & C.

United States: Robertson, J. A. List of documents in Spanish archives rel. to the hist. of the United States. $2.25. Carnegie.

United States: Shepherd, W: R. Guide to the materials for the history of U. S. in Spanish archives. 50 c. Carnegie.

United States: Thwaites, R. G. The colonies, 1492-1750. $1.25. Longmans.

United States: Want list of American historical serials. (Add. Superintendent for price.) U. S., Supt. of Docs.

United States: Wyer, J. I. United States government documents in small libraries. 15 c. A. L. A.

United States Colonial Possessions. United States: United States public documents rel. to non-contiguous territory and to Cuba. gratis.

U. S. Congress: United States proceedings of Congress. (Add. Superintendent for price.) U. S., Supt. of Docs.

United States. *Dept. of Commerce and Labor.* List of publications available for distribution.

United States Navy: Fanning, C. E., *comp.* Selected articles on the enlargement of the United States navy. $1. H. W. Wilson.

United States Public Health and Marine Hospital Service. Publications.

United States. *Superintendent of Documents.* Library of Congress publications sold by the Superintendent of Documents. gratis.

U. S. Supreme court: Meyer, H. H: B., *comp.* Library of Congress list of works rel. to the Sup. Ct. of the United States. 20 c. U. S., Supt. of Docs.

University of California, Berkeley, Cal. Publications. (Add. University for price.) Univ. of Cal.

University of Michigan: Koch, T. W. Hdbk. of the libraries of the University of Michigan. 10 c. Wahr.

Useful arts: Ashley, W: J., *ed.* British industries. *$1.80 net. Longmans.

Useful arts: Dayton, O., Public Library. List of books in the Dayton Public Library of practical interest to men in shops, machinists, electricians, molders, plumbers, woodworkers. 5 c. Dayton Pub. Lib.

Useful arts: International Congress of Arts and Science. International University lectures. In 12 v. per set, $49.50. Univ. Alliance.

BIBLIOGRAPHIES.—*Continued.*

Useful art: Louisville, Ky. Free Public Library. List of practical books in the library on electricity, machine shop practice, foundry practice, plumbing and woodwork. (Add. pubs. for price.) Louisville Pub. Lib.

Utah: Widtsoe, J: A., *and* Peterson, W: Dodge's geography of Utah. *35 c. net. Rand, McN. & Co.

Valera, J. Pepita Jiménez. 90 c. Heath.

Van Schurman, A. M.: Birch, U. Anna Van Schurman. *$2 net. Longmans.

Venereal diseases: Vecki, V. G. Prevention of sexual diseases. $1.50 net. J: J. Newbegin.

Venice, Italy: Monnier, P. Venice in the eighteenth century. $3 net. Badger.

Verona, Italy: Allen, A. M. Hist. of Verona. $3.50. Putnam.

Vertebrates: Gaskell, W. H. Origin of vertebrates. *$6 net. Longmans.

Villiers, George, *First Duke of Buckingham:* Gibbs, P. Romance of George Villiers. *$3.50 net. Putnam.

Vinci, Leonardo da: Cust, R. H. H. Leonardo Da Vinci. 50 c.; $1. Macmillan.

Virgil, M. P. Æneid. 25 c. Macmillan.

Virginia: Ambler, C: H: Sectionalism in Virginia. $1.50 net. Univ. of Chic.

Virginia: Bruce, P. A. Institutional hist. of Virginia in the seventeenth century. $6 net. Putnam.

Virginia: Lingley, C: R. Transition in Virginia from colony to commonwealth. $1.50 net. Longmans.

Virginia: Virginia State Library, Richmond. Trial bibliog. of colonial Virginia. $1. Virginia State Lib.

Virginia: Watson, T: L. Mineral resources of Virginia. gratis. C. A. Swanson.

Virginia: Wertenbaker, T: J. Patrician and plebeian in Virginia. $1.50. Wertenbaker.

Vocations: Choosing a career: circular of information for boys; for girls. ea., 10 c. High School Teachers.

Voyages and travels: Grosvenor, G. H., *ed.* Scenes from every land. $1; $2.50.—Second ser. $2. Nat. Geographic Soc.

War: Bordwell, W. P. Law of war between belligerents. $3.50. Callaghan.

War: Kirkpatrick, G: R. War—what for? $1.20. G: R. Kirkpatrick.

Washington, G:, *and* Webster, D. Washington's farewell address, and Webster's first Bunker Hill oration. **25 c. net. Appleton; Scribner.

Water: Richards, E. H. S. Laboratory notes on industrial water analysis. 50 c. Wiley.

Water: United States. *Superintendent of Documents.* Water pollution; water purification: priced list of documents. gratis.

Water cure: Kellogg, J: H. Rational hydrotherapy. $6 net; $7.50 net. Davis.

Water-supply: United States. *Dept. of the Interior, U. S. Geological Survey.* Publications of the United States Geological Survey rel. to water resources. gratis.

BIBLIOGRAPHIES.—*Continued.*

Wealth: Edwards, R: H:, *ed.* Concentrated wealth. 10 c. R: H: Edwards.

Wealth: Watkins, G. P. Growth of large fortunes. $1. Macmillan.

Weevil: Pierce, W: D. Studies of parasites of the [Mexican] cotton boll weevil. 25 c. U. S., Supt. of Docs.

West (The): Gephart, W: F. Transportation and industrial development in the Middle West. $2. Longmans.

West (The): McCarty, D. G. Territorial government of the Old Northwest. $2. State Hist., Ia.

West (The): Smith, C: W. Check-list of books and pamphlets rel. to the hist. of the Pacific northwest to be found in representative libraries of that region. Washington State Lib.

Westminster Abbey: Bond, F. Westminster Abbey. $4. Oxford Univ.

Wexford: Wheeler, H. F. B., *and* Broadley, A. M. War in Wexford. $4 net. Lane.

Whales and whaling: Peabody Academy of Science. Whaling industry. gratis. Salem Pub. Lib.

Wheat: Dondlinger, P: T. Book of wheat. *$2 net. Judd.

Whistler, J. A. M.: Hartmann, S. Whistler book. $2.50. L. C. Page.

Whitman, Marcus: Smith, C: W. Contribution toward a bibliography of Marcus Whitman. (Add University for price.) Univ. of Wash.

Whitney, Josiah Dwight: Brewster, E. T. Life and letters of Josiah Dwight Whitney. **$2 net. Houghton M.

Whittier, John Greenleaf: Woodman, *Mrs.* A. J. Reminiscences of John Greenleaf Whittier. *$1 net. Essex Inst.

Wilson, Richard: Fletcher, B. Richard Wilson, R. A. *$1.25 net. Scribner.

Wireless telegraphy: Collins, A. F: Manual of wireless telegraphy and telephony. **$1.50 net. Wiley.

Wisconsin: Wisconsin State Historical Society. Check-list of publications of the Society. 15 c. State Hist. Wis.

Woman: Abbott, E. Women in industry. **$2 net. Appleton.

Woman: Butler, E. B. Women and the trades. *$1.50 net. Charities Pub.

Woman: Chapman, A. B. W. *and* M. W. Status of women under the English law. *75 c. net. Dutton.

Woman: MacLean, A. M. Wage-earning women. $1.25 net. Macmillan.

Woman: Talbot, M. Education of woman. $1.25 net. Univ. of Chic.

Woman: Talmey, B. S. Woman: treatise on normal and pathological emotions of feminine love. $3. Practitioners' Pub.

Wood distilling: Harper, W. B: Utilization of wood waste by distillation. $3. St. L. Lumberman.

Woodruff family: Woodruff, F. E. Woodruffs of New Jersey. **$5 net. Grafton Press.

Wool: Bowman, F. H. Structure of the wool fibre. *$2.60 net. Macmillan.

BIBLIOGRAPHIES.—*Continued.*
Words: Taylor, J. S. Word study in the elem. school. $1. Educ. Pub.
Words: Trendelenburg, A. Contribution to the hist. of the word person. 40 c. Open Court.
Wulfstan: Dodd, L. H. Glossary of Wulfstan's homilies. **$1 net. Holt.
Yale University: Burns, W: S., *comp.* Bibliog. of the writings of members of the class of 1887 in Yale College. (Add. pubs. for price.) Marigold-F.
Yellow fever: Augustin, G: Hist. of yellow fever. $6. G: Augustin.
Yellowstone National Park: Haynes, J. E. Official guide, Yellowstone. 25 c. J. E. Haynes.
Young Men's Christian Association: Murray, W: D. Principles and organization of the Young Men's Christian Association. 60 c. net. Y. M. C. A.
Zoology: Hegner, R. W. Introd. to zoology. $1.90 net. Macmillan.
Zoroaster: Dhalla, M. N. Nyaishes or Zoroastrian litanies. **$2 net. Lemcke.
See also Cataloguing;—Indexes;—Librarians and libraries.

Bibliography of economics for 1909; cumulation of bibliography appearing in the *Journal of Political Economy* from February, 1909, to January, 1910, inclusive; ed. by the Faculty of the Department of Political Economy of the University of Chicago. '10(Ag27) O. $2.50 net. Univ. of Chic.

Bibliophiles' lib. 16°, *50 c. net; leath., *75 c. net. Lane.
—Rhoades. Training of the imagination.

Biblioteca popolare "Gerolamo Savonarola." 12°. P. V. Miraglia-Gullotti.
—Miraglia-Gullotti. Vera scienza e vera religione.

Bibliotheca ascetica mystica. 12°, *$1.10 net. Herder.
—Ponte. Meditationes de praecipiis fidei nostrae mysteriis.

Bibliothekar, Der. Moses, G. v. 40 c. Holt.

Biblische symbole. Beard, T: F. $1.75; $2.25; $2.50. J: A. Hertel.

Bickel, Milton Valentine.
Poultry packers' guide; compendium of useful information for poultry dressers. '09, [1910.] (F) c. 51 p. il. 8°, $2. Pool.

Bickham, Warren Stone.
Text-book of operative surgery, covering the surgical anatomy and operative technic involved in the operations of general surgery. 3d ed., greatly enl. '08(D) c. 1206 p. il. 8°, *$6.50 net. Saunders.

Bickley, Fs. Lawrence.
Kings' favorites. '10(N19) il. O. $3.50. Lane.

Bicknell, Jos. D.
The Wissahickon. '09(D) 24 p. il. (City Hist. Society of Philadelphia pub.) $1. (Sold to members only.) City Hist., Phil.

Bicknell, T: Williams.
Sowams; with ancient records of Sowams and parts adjacent; il. by T: W. Bicknell. '08(Ag1) c. pors. maps, facsims., 4°, $3. Assoc. Pub.
—, ed. Addresses and poem in commemoration of the Captain Michael Pierce fight, Mar. 26, 1676. '08(O) 41 p. por. 8°. (Add. pub. for price.) T: W. Bicknell.

BICYCLES AND BICYCLING.
Allen, J. W. Wheel magic; [cycling in England.] *$1.25 net. Lane.
Jackman, W. J. A B C of the motor cycle. $1; $1.50. C: C. Thompson.

Bicycling World Company. Care and repair of motorcycles. '08(Mr.) c. 56 p. il. 12°, pap. 25 c. Bicycling World.

BIDPAI.
Wollaston, *Sir* A. N., *comp.* Tales within tales; adpt. from Fables of Pilpai. $1 net. Dutton.

Biddle, Clarence Simons.
Principles, pleading and practice obtaining in the court of chancery of New Jersey in divorce and other causes matrimonial; with forms. '08(Ja4) O. $3. Soney.

Bidwell, Dan. Doane.
As far as the east is from the west; tales of a traveller. '10(D24) c. il. maps, O. $1.50; leath., $2.25. Scranton.

BIDWELL, John.
Benjamin, M. John Bidwell, pioneer. gratis. Soc. Cal. Pioneers.

Biederwolf, W: E:
Christian and amusements; is dancing sinful?; is card-playing wrong?; is theater-going harmful? '09, [1910.] (S) 53 p. 12°, pap., 15 c. Glad Tidings.
Christian Science tested by philosophy, medicine and revelation. '10(Jl16) c. pap., 10 c. net. Revell.
How can God answer prayer? '10(F12) c. 12°, *75 c. net. Revell.
White life. '10(Jl16) c. pap., 10 c. net. Revell.

Bielschowsky, Albert.
Life of Goethe: authorized tr. from the German by W: A. Cooper. In 3 v. v. 3. '08(Ap18) c. il. por. O. **$3.50 net. Putnam.

Bierce, Ambrose.
Collected works. 10 v. '09(Mr27) c. pors. 8°, cl., $25 per set; leath., ea., $10. Neale.
Shadow on the dial, and other essays. '09 (Ag7) c. O. *$2 net. A. M. Robertson.
Write it right; little blacklist of literary faults. '09(N13) c. T. *50 c. net. Neale.

Bierly, Willis Reed.
Juries and jury trials, state and federal; common law and statutory; the grand jury, petit jury, rights and duties of the district attorney, [etc.] '08(N) c. 17+464 p. O. (Add. pubs. for price.) Welsh.

Biermann, Ernest H., ed.
See Osthaus, Carl Wilhelm Ferdinand.

Bier's hyperemic treatment in surgery, medicine and specialties. Meyer, W. *$3 net. Saunders.

Bierwirth, Heinrich Conrad.
Beginning German; a series of lessons with an abstract of grammar. 2d ed., rev. and enl. '09(S) c. 8+300 p. 12°, 90 c. Holt.
German inflections, arranged in parallels. '08(O10) c. 12°, 40 c. Holt.

Biffel. Hyatt, S. P. $1.50 net. Dodge.
Big brother of Sabin Street. Thurston, *Mrs.* I. T. *$1 net. Revell.
Big cinch. Landau, L. A. $1.50. Franklin.
Big fellow. Palmer, F: †$1.50. Moffat.
Big game at sea. Holder, C: F: *$2 net. Outing.
Big game of Africa. Tjader, R: $3 net. Appleton.
Big John Baldwin. Vance, W. J. †$1.50. Holt.
Big shellbark: king-nut hickory (*hicoria laciniosa*). '09(N) 4 p. 8°, (U. S., Dept. of Agriculture, forest service, silvical leaflet.) pap. (Add. Superintendent for price.) U. S., Supt. of Docs.
Big Stick and the Golf Stick. Sweny, H. R. 50 c. Lyon.
Big strike at Siwash. Fitch, G: †50 c. Doubleday, P.
Big trees of California. Clark, G. $1; 50 c. G. Clark.

Bigelow, Mrs. Ella A. Fisher.
Historical reminiscences of the early times in Marlborough, Mass. '10(N19) c. il. pors. 8°, $3. Marlborough.

Bigelow, Fk. Hagar.
Daily normal temperature and the daily normal precipitation of the United States. '09(Mr6) tabs., 4°, (U. S., Dept. of Agriculture, Weather Bureau, bull.) $1.75.
Manual for observers in climatology and evaporation. '09(Ag) 106 p. tabs., 8°, pap. (Add. Superintendent for price.) U. S., Supt. of Docs.
Rept. on the temperatures and vapor tensions of the United States reduced to a homogeneous system of 24 hourly observations for the 33-year interval, 1873-1905. '09(Je) 302 p. tabs., f°, (U. S., Dept. of Agriculture, Weather Bureau bull.) $1.15; pap., 75 c.

Bigelow, Herbert Seely.
Mission of a liberal church. '09(S) 13 p. S. pap., 5 c. Public.

Bigelow, J:
Folly of building temples of peace with untempered mortar; The necessity of building temples of peace with tempered mortar. '10(N19) O. $1 net. B: W. Huebsch.
Panama Canal and the Daughters of Danaus. '08(F15) plan, O. *50 c. net. Baker & T.
Reply of J: Bigelow in answer to an invitation by the Civic Forum of New York City to attend its annual municipal dinner. '09, [1910.] (Mr) 4 p. 8°, pap. U. S., Supt. of Docs.
Retrospection of an active life. In 3 v. v. 1, 1817-1863; v. 2, 1863-1865; v. 3, 1865-1866. '09(D4) c. il. pors. Q. **$12 net, boxed. Baker & T.

Bigelow, J:—*Continued.*
Substitute for the tariff upon imports and a provision for an equitable distribution of the wealth of nations; suggested in a letter addressed to His Excellency C: E. Hughes. '09(Ja23) O. pap. (Priv. pr.) J: Bigelow.
See also Howells, W: Dean.
—, ed. *See* Tilden, S: Jones.

Bigelow, J:, jr.
Campaign of Chancellorsville; strategic and tactical study. '10(O1) c. maps, plans, Q. $10 net, boxed. Yale Univ.

Bigelow, Mary Emeline.
New way to write music. '07, [1908.] (Mr.) c. 5 p. 8°. (Add. author for price.) M. E. Bigelow.

Bigelow, Maurice Alpheus.
Relation of nature-study and science teaching. '08, [1909.] (Mr) 33-40 p. 8°, pap. M. A. Bigelow.
See also Lloyd, Fs. Ernest.

Bigelow, Melville Madison.
Law of torts. 3d ed. '08(N7) 8°, *$4 net. Putnam.

Bigelow, Willard Dell.
Food legislation during the year ended June 30, 1907. '08(Ag1) 2 pts., 8°, (U. S. Dept. of Agriculture, Bureau of Chemistry, bull.) pap. (Add. Superintendent of Docs. for price.) U. S., Supt. of Docs.

—, and Cook, Fk. Cummings.
Meat extracts and similar preparations. '09(F20) tabs., 8°, (U. S., Dept. of Agriculture, Bureau of Chemistry, bull.) pap., 10 c. U. S., Supt. of Docs.

Bigelow, W: Sturgis.
Buddhism and immortality; the Ingersoll lecture, 1908. '08(N7) c. D. **75 c. net. Houghton M.

Bigg, C:, D.D.
Origins of Christianity; ed. by T. B. Strong. '09(Je19) O. $4.15. Oxford Univ.
Spirit of Christ in common life: addresses and sermons; sel. and ed. by the Dean of Christ Church; with an introd. by the Bishop of Oxford. '09(Mr13) O. *$2 net. Longmans.

Bigger, E: Clarence.
See Bishop, W: G:

Bigger, Leander Adams.
Around the world with a business man. In 4 v. '10(Je4) c il. por. O. $12. Winston.

Biggle, Jacob.
Biggle poultry book; concise and pract. treatise on the management of farm poultry. '10, [1910.] D. 162 p. il. (partly in col.) 16°, (Biggle farm lib.) 50 c. W. Atkinson.
Garden book; vegetables, small fruits and flowers for pleasure and profit. '09 (Ja23) c. il. 24°, (Biggle farm lib.) 50 c. W. Atkinson.
Horse book: a concise and practical treatise on the horse. '08(N14) c. il. T. (Biggle farm lib.) 50 c. W. Atkinson.

Bigham, F. T. R.
See King, Jos.

Bigham, Madge A.
Overheard in Fairyland. '09(O23) c. col. il. D. †$1.50. Little, B. & Co.

Bigot, Marie Healy, [Mme Charles Bigot, "Jeanne Mairet."]
La petite princesse; ed. by Edith Healy. '10(Ja22) c. S. 35 c. Am. Bk.
Bildad Akers: his book. Ivey, T: N. $1. Mutual Pub.
Biles, J: Harvard.
Design and construction of ships. v. 1, Calculation and strength, complete in itself. '08(D19) il. 8°, *$7.50 net. Lippincott.
"Bilger, Billy," pseud.
See Pendleton, And. L., *jr.*
Bilhorn, P: Philip, and others, eds.
Hymns of His grace; no. 1, for the evangelist, church, Sunday school, and young people's society. '07, [1909.] (Ja) 192 p. 8°, 30 c.; per 100, $25. Bilhorn.
Bi-literal cypher of Sir Francis Bacon. Gallup, *Mrs.* E. W. $2. Howard.
Bill, E: Lyman.
Sword of the pyramids; story of many wars. [1910.] (D) 6+363 p. 12°, 50 c. Fenno.
Bill, a cheerful dog. White, F: **$1 net. Moffat.
Bill Bruce of Harvard. Standish, B. L., *pseud.* $1.25. Dodd.
Bill Possum: his book. Whiteside, M. B. $1. Byrd.
Bill-toppers (The). Castaigne, A. †$1.50. Bobbs-M.
Bill Truetell. Brennan, G: H. $1.50. McClurg.
Billard, Max.
Marriage ventures of Marie Louise; English version by Evelyn, Duchess of Wellington. '10(D24) il. 8°, $3.50 net. Pott.
Billboard advertising. Civic League of St. Louis. gratis. Civic League.
BILLBOARDS.
See Nuisance.
BILLIARDS.
Brunswick-Balke-Collender Co. Complete hdbk. of standard rules of all the prominent games of billiards and pool as practiced by the great professionals and other leading players in all parts of the world. Rev. ed. '10(Ap) c. 129 p. il. 12°, gratis. Brunswick.
Complete hand book of standard rules of all the prominent games of billiards and pool. gratis. Brunswick.
Garno, B: Modern billiards. $1. Brunswick.
Modern billiards: with diagrams showing various shots. $1. Brunswick.
See also Games.
Billings, C: T.
Movement and men of Christian history. '09(N) c. 6+72+15 p. 8°, (Beacon ser.) 45 c.; pap., 35 c.; Teacher's ed., 65 c. Unitarian S. S.
Billings, Fk., M.D., ed.
Diseases of the digestive system. 2d ed. '09(Mr) c. 16+824 p. il. 8°, (Modern clinical medicine.) $6. Appleton.
—, and Salisbury, Jerome H:, M.D., eds.
General medicine. '08(Je6); '09(My); '10 (O) c. il. 12°, (Pract. medicine ser.) ea., $1.25. Year Bk.
Billings, J: D.
Hist. of the 10th Mass. Battery of Light Artillery in the War of the Rebellion; fromerly of the Third Corps, and afterwards of Hancock's Second Corps, Army of the Potomac, 1862-1865. '09(Ap) 496 p. il. pors. maps, 8°, $2. Arakelyan.
Billings, Josh, pseud.
See Shaw, H: Wheeler.
Billionaire phrase code. '09(Ap17) c. O. leath., $1.50. Business Code.
Billopp, C: Farmar, comp.
History of Thomas and Anne Billopp Farmar, and some of their descendants in America; comp. from authentic documents. '08(My9) il. pors. 8°. (Add. pubs. for price.) Grafton Press.
BILLS.
See Negotiable instruments.
BILLS OF LADING.
Millner, W. D. Bill of lading. 50 c. Stone Pr.
Billy and Dick from Andersonville prison to the White House. Bates, R. O. 50 c. Sentinel Pub., (Cal.)
Billy Possum. Beard, J. C. †$1. Stokes.
Billy To-morrow. Carr, *Mrs.* S. P. $1.25. McClurg.
Billy To-morrow in camp. Carr, *Mrs.* S. P. $1.25. McClurg.
Billy Topsail and Company. Duncan, N. $1.50. Revell.
Billy Whiskers at the circus. Wheeler, F. G. $1. Saalfield.
Billy Whiskers at the fair. Wheeler, F. G. †$1. Saalfield.
Billy Whiskers kidnaped. Montgomery, *Mrs.* F. T. $1. Saalfield.
Billy Whiskers ser. il. O. Saalfield.
—Naylor. Dicky Delightful in Rainbow land. $1.
Billy Whiskers' grandchildren. Montgomery, F. T. $1. Barse & H.
Billy Whiskers' vacation. Montgomery, F. T. bds., $1. Barse & H.
Billy Wise. Johnson, L: D. $1.50. L: D. Johnson.
Biltz, Heinrich.
Introd. to experimental inorganic chemistry; author. tr. from the German by W: T: Hall and Jos. W. Phelan. '09(D) 16+185 p. 12°, $1.25. Wiley.
—, and Wilhelm.
Laboratory methods of inorganic chemistry. '09(Je26) c. figs. 8°, $3. Wiley.
Biltz, Wilhelm.
See Biltz, Heinrich.
Bimbi. *See* De la Ramée, Louise.
Bimbi ser. il. D. bds., **40 c. net. Crowell.
—Butterworth. Little sky high.
—Clark. How Dexter paid his way.
—Douglas. In the poverty year.
—Harbour. Marcia and the major.
—La Ramée. Dog of Flanders.—Little earl.—Nürnberg stove.
—MacDonald. Light princess.
—Pratt. Little cave-dwellers.
—Spofford. Children of the valley.
—Wells. Little Dick's son.
BIMETALLISM.
See Finance;—Money.

Binder, Rudolph M., ed.
See Bliss, W: Dwight Porter.

BINDING.
See Bookbinders and bookbinding.

Binding of the strong. Mason, C. A. $1.50. Revell.

Bindloss, Harold.
Boy ranchers of Puget Sound. '10(S10) c. il. D. $1.50. Stokes.
By right of purchase. '08(S5) c. front. D. †$1.50. Stokes.
Damaged reputation. '08(O24) c. D. $1. Fenno.
Delilah of the snows. '08(My23) c. D. †$1.50. Stokes.
For Jacinta. '08(Ja18) il. D. †$1.50. Stokes.
Gold trail. '10(My7) c. col. front. D. $1.30 net. Stokes.
Greater power. '09(S11) c. front. D. **$1.30 net. Stokes.
Long odds. '08(O10) c. il. D. †$1.50. Small.
Lorimer of the northwest. '09(Ja30) c. il. D. †$1.50. Stokes.
Masters of the wheatlands. '10(N19) c. D. $1.30 net. Stokes.
Thrice armed. '09(Je26) c. D. †$1.50. Stokes.
Thurston of Orchard Valley. '10(F26) c. col. front. D. **$1.30 net. Stokes.

BINDWEED.
Cox, H. R. Eradication of bindweed, or wild morning-glory. (Add. Superintendent for price.) U. S., Supt. of Docs.

Bingham, Clifton.
Airship in Animal Land. '10(D) 28 p. il. 8°, bds., $1.50. Dutton.
Come and go; verses for children; [cont. colored pictures which move with strings.] '10(Ja22) 4°, $2. Dutton.

BINGHAM, Harry.
Metcalf, H: H. Memorial of Hon. Harry Bingham. (Not for sale.) H: H. Metcalf.

Bingham, Hiram, D.D.
Gilbertese-English dictionary. '08(D19) O. $1.50. Am. Bd. For. Miss.
Journal of an expedition across Venezuela and Colombia, 1906-1907. '09(Je5) c. il. fold. map in pocket, O. *$2.25 net. Yale Pub.

Bingham, W: Van Dyke.
Studies in melody. '10(O) 6+88 p. il. diagrs., 8°, (Psychological Review monograph supplements.) $1. Psychological Review.

Binion, S: A:
Phyllanthography of leaf and flower writing; and a "Basket of choice roses": [pictorial alphabet of flowers and leaves.] '09(Mr27) c. il. por. 4°, $3. Fenno.

BINNEY, Horace.
Carson, H. L. Sketch of Horace Binney. (Not for sale.) H. L. Carson.

Binnie, J: Fairbain, M.D.
Operative surgery. v. 1. 4th ed., rev. and enl. '09(Mr) 815 p. il. 12°, *$3.50 net. Blakiston.

Binnie-Clark, Georgina.
Summer on the Canadian prairies. '10 (Ap9) il. D. $1.75 net. Longmans.

Binns, C: Fergus.
Potter's craft; pract. guide for the studio and workshop. '10(My14) il. 8°, $2 net. Van Nostrand.

Binns, C: Laurence, and Marsden, Rufus E.
Principles of education woodwork; hdbk. for teachers and others interested in education. '09, [1910.] (F) 8+310 p. il. 12°, *$1.50 net. Dutton.

Binns, H: Bryan.
Botticelli. '08(F22) O. (Masterpieces in colour.) il. bds., *65 c. net. Stokes.
Life of Abraham Lincoln. '08(Ja18) 8°, *$1.50 net. Dutton.

Binstead, Herbert Ernest.
Furniture styles; with chapters on modern mission and craftsman furniture by J: Newton Nind and Gustav Stickley. '09(My) c. 8+212 p. 8°, $2. Trade Periodical.

Binyon, Laurence.
Painting in the Far East: an introd. to the history of pictorial art in Asia, especially China and Japan. '08(N21) il. Q. watered silk, *$6 net. Longmans.

Biochemical conception of dominance. Moore, A. R. Univ. of Cal.

Biochemical treatment of domestic animals. Meinert, F. $2. J: H. Meinert.

BIO-CHEMISTRY.
See Chemistry.

Biographic clinics. Gould, G: M. v. 6. *$1 net. Blakiston.

Biographical story of the Constitution Elliott, E: G. **$2 net. Putnam.

Biographies of leading Americans; ed. by W. P. Trent. il. O. Holt.
—Erskine. Leading American novelists. $1.75 net.
—Jordan, *ed.* Leading American men of science. $1.75 net.
—Payne. Leading American essayists. $1.75 net.

BIOGRAPHY.
Almanach de Gotha; annuaire généalogique, diplomatique et statistique, 1910. $2.70. Lemcke.
Anderson, G. Hitherto untold; [incl. reminiscences of Beecher, Leland Stanford, Grant, Lee, etc.] $1. Cochrane.
Baker, J. H. Lives of the governors of Minnesota. $2.50. Minn. Hist. Soc.
Bearne, *Mrs.* C. M. C. Four fascinating French women. $3.50 net. Brentano's.
Behm, B.. Hist. of some French kings. $2 net. Macmillan.
Bickley, F. Kings' favorites. $3.50. Lane.
Bleackley, H. W: Ladies fair and frail. *$5 net. Lane.
Butler, H: M. Ten great and good men. $2. Longmans.
Buttles, J. R. Queens of Egypt. *$3 net. Appleton.
Capes, B. Historical vignettes. $2.50 net. Stokes.
Carnegie Library, Pittsburgh. Lives and letters. 10 c. Carnegie Lib.
Carr, J. W: C. Some eminent Victorians. *$3.50 net. Scribner.
Catholic who's who and year book, 1909. *$1.50 net. Benziger.

BIOGRAPHY.—*Continued.*

Chadwick, E. L. Conservative advocate; book of biographies of Connecticut's successful men. $5. E. L. Chadwick.

Chi è; annuario bigrafico italiano. $1. Stechert.

Classic memoirs. 3 v. $5.25; $10.50. Lamb Pub.

Copeland, C: T., *and* Hersey, F. W. C., *comps and eds.* Representative biographies of English men of letters. **$1.25 net. Macmillan.

Cousin, J: W. Short biographical dict. of English literature. 35 c. net; 70 c. net. Dutton.

Cust, *Mrs.* H: Gentlemen errant: journeys and adventures of four noblemen in Europe during the xv. and xvi. centuries. *$4 net. Dutton.

De Leon, T: C. Belles, beaux and brains of the 60's. $3 net. G: W. Dillingham.

District of Columbia: concise biographies of its prominent and representative contemporary citizens. $6; $7.50. Potomac Press.

Dreier, T: Heroes of insurgency. 50 c. Human Life.

Emerson, R. W. Representative men. *35 c. net; *70 c. net. Dutton.

Faris, J: T. Winning their way: [short biographical sketches.] $1.50. Stokes.

Fyvie, J: Wits, beaux and beauties of the Georgian era. *$4 net. Lane.

Gilliat, E: Heroes of modern crusades.—Heroes of modern India. ea., *$1.50 net. Lippincott.

Griggs, E: H. Great autobiographies. *50 c. net; *25 c. net. B: W. Huebsch.

Haaren, J: H:, *and* Poland, A. B. Famous men of modern times. 50 c. Am. Bk.

Hale, E: E., *ed.* Lights of two centuries. $1.50. Little, B. & Co.

Hale, E: E., *ed.* Modern achievement; or, making of the modern world. 10 v. $9. Westminster, (Chic.)

Hall, T. Love intrigues of royal courts. $3.50 net. Dodd.

Hamel, F. Famous French salons. *$3.50 net. Brentano's.

Hancock, M. S. Children of history. In 2 v. v. 1. ea., **50 c. net. Little, B. & Co.

Harrison, F., *ed.* New calendar of great men: 558 worthies in positivist calendar of A. Comte. *$2.50 net. Macmillan.

Hayler, G. Famous fanatics, historical and religious. 60 c. Funk.

Hemphill, J. C., *ed.* Men of mark in South Carolina. v. 1. $10. Men of Mark.

Hensman, H., *and* Webb, C. When and where of famous men and women. 50 c. Dutton.

Herringshaw, T: W., *and others, eds.* National lib. of American biography. 5 v. ea., $10. Am. Pub. Assoc.

Higginson, T: W. Carlyle's laugh and other surprises. **$2 net. Houghton M.

Hodges, G: Apprenticeship of Washington and other sketches of significant colonial personages. **$1.25 net. Moffat.

BIOGRAPHY.—*Continued.*

Holland, R. S. Builders of united Italy. **$2 net. Holt.

Holland, R. S. Historic boyhoods.—Historic girlhoods. ea., *$1.50 net. Jacobs.

Howard, G: E. Biography of American statesmanship; analyt. reference syllabus. 50 c. Univ. of Neb.

Hubbard, *Mrs.* A. M. Life lessons; truths concerning people who have lived. $3. Roycrofters.

Hubbard, E. Little journeys to the homes of good men and great. (Add. pubs. for price.) Roycrofters.

Huneker, J. G. Egoists: book of supermen: Stendhal, Baudelaire, Flaubert, Anatole France, Huysmans, Barrés, Nietzsche, Blake, Ibsen, Stirner and Hello. **$1.50 net. Scribner.

Hurlbut, J. L., *ed.* Stories of great Americans. 75 c. Winston.

Iles, G:, *ed.* Little masterpieces of autobiography. 6 v. ea., **75 c. net; per set, **$4.50 net. Doubleday, P.

Ingersoll, R. G. The great infidels. 25 c. Farrell.

Jerrold, C. Beaux and the dandies: Nash, Brummell and D'Orsay. $5 net. Lane.

Johnston, C: H. L. Famous scouts. $1.50. L. C. Page.

Kirk, J: Biographies of English Catholics in the 18th century. *$2.75 net. Benziger.

Lang, L. B. Book of princes and princesses. **$1.60 net. Longmans.

Leonard, J: W. Who's who in Pennsylvania. $5. Hamersly.

Lewis, A. M. Ten blind leaders of the blind: [Benjamin Kidd, Henry George, Immanuel Kant, Prof. Richard T. Ely, Cesare Lombroso, Max Sterner, Thomas Carlyle, Albert Shäffle, Auguste Comte, Bp. Spalding.] 50 c. Kerr.

Locy, W: A. Biology and its makers. **$2.75 net. Holt.

Loliée, F. Gilded beauties of the Second Empire. $4 net. Brentano's.

Mabie, H. W., *and* Stephens, K., *eds.* Heroines that every child should know. **90 c. net; **$1.50 net. Doubleday, P.

MacCunn, J: Six radical thinkers. $1 net. Longmans.

McKilliam, A. E. Makers of history. 60 c. net. Cassell.

McTurnan, L. Personal equation. $1.25 net. Moffat.

Makers of America. 3 v. per set, $50. A: B. Caldwell.

Marvellous year, [1909.] *$1.25 net. B: W. Huebsch.

Men and women of America; biograph. dict. of contemporaries. $10. Hamersly.

Men of America: biographical dict. of contemporaries. $10. Hamersly.

Mercer, J. K. Representative men of Ohio. $25. J. K. Mercer.

Northen, W: J., *ed.* Men of mark in Georgia. In 6 v. v. 2. '09. per set, $50; $100. A. B. Caldwell.

BIOGRAPHY.—*Continued.*

Osborn, N. G., *ed.* Men of mark in Connecticut. 4 v. $30; $50; $60. W. R. Goodspeed.

Plutarch, Lives. 2 v. $2.50. Crowell.

Powell, L. P. Heavenly heretics. **$1.25 net. Putnam.

Qui etes-vous?, [Who are you?] Annuaire des contemporains, 1908. *$2 net. Lemcke.

Qui-etes-vous? [Who are you?] Annuaire des contemporains, 1909. $2. Stechert.

Ramsay, *Sir* W: Essays, biographical and chemical. *$2.50 net. Dutton.

Rappoport, A. S. Mad majesties; or, raving rulers and submissive subjects.—Royal lovers and their favorites. ea., *$4 net. Brentano's.

Redall, H: F. Climbing the ladder of fame. 75 c. Educ. Pub.

Romantic stories of famous families: account of certain noted English families. 40 c. Scribner.

Ruoff, H: W., *ed.* Masters of achievement. $5.50; $6.25; $7.50. Frontier Press.

Russell, *Lady* C. Rose Goddess and other sketches. $7 net. Longmans.

Russell, G: W: E. Sketches and snapshots. $2.50 net. Duffield.

Sage, A. C. Boys and girls of the White House. $1.50. Stokes.

Slicer, T: R. From poet to premier; the centennial cycle, 1809-1909; Poe, Lincoln, Holmes, Darwin, Tennyson, Gladstone. *$3 net. Grolier Club.

Smith, C: F. Reminiscences and sketches. *$1.25 net. Pub. Ho. of M. E. Ch., So.

Sons of the Puritans: group of brief biographies. *$1.50 net. Am. Unitarian.

Speer, E. Lincoln, Lee, Grant, and other biog. addresses. *$2 net. Neale.

Speer, R. E. Servants of the King: [missionaries.] 50 c.; 35 c. Young People's Miss.

Steffens, J. L. Upbuilders: [five biographies.] **$1.20 net. Doubleday, P.

Stephen, *Sir* L., *and* Lee, S. L., *eds.* Dict. of national biography. In 22 v. ea., *$4.25 net. (Sold in sets only.) Macmillan.

Stevens, E. R., Keyes, E. W:, Holand, H. R., *and* Burr, W. J. John B. Cassoday; Julius Taylor Clark; Nils Otto Tank; William Freeman Vilas. 20 c. State Hist., Wis.

Stevenson, A. E. Something of men I have known. *$2.75 net. McClurg.

Stevenson, B. E. Child's guide to biography; American men of action.—Guide to biography; American men of mind. ea., **$1.25 net. Baker & T.

Stoker, B. Famous impostors. $2 net. Sturgis & W.

Thackeray, W: M. English humorists. **25 c. net. Macmillan.

Thursfield, J. R. Nelson and other naval studies. $4. Dutton.

Trowbridge, W. R. H. Seven splendid sinners. *$4.50 net. Brentano's.

BIOGRAPHY.—*Continued.*

Trumbull, C: G. Men who dared: studies in Old Testament manhood. (Add. pubs. for price.) Y. M. C. A.

Ward, W. P. Ten personal studies. *$3 net. Longmans.

Watkins, *Mrs.* C. L. Young life of famous folk. 75 c. Pub. Ho. of M. E. Ch., So.

Wer ist's? zeitgenossen-lexikon, 1908. *$3.50 net. Stechert.

White, J. T. Character lessons in American biography for public schools and home instruction. 50 c. Character Development.

Who's who, (Catholic.) *See* Catholic.

Who's who, (German.) *See* Wer ists.

Who's who along the north shore of Massachusetts. $2.50. Salem Press.

Who's who in America. 1908-1909. *$4 net.—1910-1911. $5 net. Marquis.

Who's who in New England. $5. Marquis.

Who's who in New York City and state. $5. Hamersly.

Who's who, 1909, 1910, 1911. ea., *$2.50 net. Macmillan.

Who's who in Pennsylvania. $5. Hamersly.

Who's who year-book for 1908. *35 c. net. Macmillan.

Wyzewa, T. de. Some women, loving or luckless. *$2.50 net. Lane.

See also Actors and actresses;—Architects;—Artists;—Authors;—Bible;—Birthday books;—Bishops;—Booksellers;—Botanists; — Boys;—Business;—Character;—Children;—Christian biography;—Epitaphs; — Explorers; — Fathers of the church;—Genealogy;—Girls; — Heroes;—Historians;—Insurance;—Judges; — Lawyers;—Martyrs;—Ministers (*of the Gospel*);—Missions and missionaries; — Musicians; — Names; — Napoleonic wars;—Negroes;—Orators and oratory;—Orders of knighthood and chivalry;—Organ and organists;—Painters and painting;—Peerage;—Physicians; — Poets; — Popes; — Sailors; — Saints;—Scientists;—Sculptors; — Socialism;—Statesmen;—Teachers and teaching;—Unitarian church; — Woman;—*also* Cushing family; — India;—*also* names of countries, individuals and classes.

Biography of a boy. Bacon, *Mrs.* J. D. D. †$1.50. Harper.

Biography of a New York hotel scrub. Blom, A. 25 c. A. Blom.

Biography of a silver fox. Seton, E. T. †$1.50. Century Co.

Biography of youthful Willie and Wall Street Bill. Norton, B: 60 c. Cupples & L.

Biological studies and addresses. *See* Macmillan's.

BIOLOGY.

Alexander, J. B. Dynamic theory of life and mind. $2.75. J. B. Alexander.

Bailey, L. H., *and* Coleman, W. M. First course in biology. In 3 pts. *$1.25 net. Macmillan.

Clarke, J: M. Beginning of independent life. 50 c. J: M. Clarke.

De Vries, H. Mutation theory. In 2 v. ea., $4 net. Open Court.

Dietrich, G. Biology of sex. 50 c. Educ. Press.

Driesch, H. Science and philosophy of the organism. In 2 v. ea., *$3 net. Macmillan.

Gibson, H. Biology. 50 c. net. Appleton.

Johnstone, J. Conditions of life in the sea. $3. Putnam.

BIOLOGY.—*Continued.*
Kirkaldy, J. W., *and* Drummond, I. M. Introd. to the study of biology. $1.60. Oxford Univ.
Laboratory directions in general biology: (zoological half,) first semster. 50 c. Wahr.
Lloyd, F. E., *and* Bigelow, M. A. Teaching of biology in the secondary schools. $1.50. Longmans.
Locy, W: A. Biology and its makers. **$2.75 net. Holt.
McFarland, J. Biology. $1.75. Saunders.
Macnamara, N. C. Evolution and function of living purposive matter. $1.75 net. Appleton.
Metchnikoff, E. Prolongation of life. *$2.50 net. Putnam.
Minot, C: S. Problem of age, growth and death. **$2.50 net. Putnam.
Needham, J. G. General biology. $2 net. Comstock Pub.
Pennsylvania University. Wistar Institute of Anatomy and Biology. List of biological serials, exclusive of botany, in the libraries of Philadelphia. gratis. Wistar.
Pollock, J. B., *ed.* Lab'y directions for general biology; botanical pt. 40 c. Wahr.
Rinaldo, J. Polygeneric theory. $1.50. J. Rinaldo.
Roosevelt, T. Biological analogies in hist. 60 c.; 35 c. Oxford Univ.
Smallwood, W: M. Syllabus of lectures on animal biology. $1.35. W: M. Smallwood.
Thomson, W: H. Some wonders of biology. **$1.20 net. Dodd.
United States. Biological Survey. Bulletins, circulars and North American fauna of this bureau; Agriculture Department. gratis. U. S., Supt. of Docs.
United States. *Dept. of Agriculture. Bu. of Biological Survey.* List of publications of the Biological Survey. gratis.
Wilson, E. B. Biology: [a lecture.] (Add. pubs. for price.) Columbia Univ.
See also Anatomy; — Botany; — Cells;—Death;—Embryology;—Eugenics; —Evolution;—Fermentation; — Frog;—Future life;—Heredity;—Histology;—Longevity;—Man;—Medical electricity;—Medicine;—Morphology; — Poisons;—Sex; —Teeth;—*also* Marine Biological Assoc.

Biometrical study of egg production in the domestic fowl. Pearl, R. (Add. Superintendent for price.) U. S., Supt. of Docs.

BIOTA.
See Zoology.

Birch, Una.
Anna Van Schurman; artist, scholar, saint; with portraits. '09(D4) O. *$2 net. Longmans.

Birch, Wa. de Gray.
Seals. '08(Ja25) il. Q. (Connoisseurs' lib.) *$7.50 net, boxed. Putnam.

Birch-rod days. Jones, W: C. $1. Cuneo.

Birch stream. Averill, A. B. $1.50. A. B. Averill.

Birchall, Sara Hamilton.
Songs of Saint Bartholomew. '09(Jl) 71 p. 18°, *$1 net. A. Bartlett.

BIRD, Isabella.
See Bishop, *Mrs.* Isabella Bird.

Bird, Mary Herrick.
How the Indian suit ran away. '08(O24) c. S. (Toyland ser. of Juvenile gift-books.) 40 c. Stern.
Snow-man's Christmas. '08(O24) c. S. (Toyland ser. of juvenile gift books.) 40 c. Stern.
Wreck of the nursery flyer. '08(O24) c. (Toyland ser. of juvenile gift books.) 40 c. Stern.
Three above volumes in Christmas box, $1.25.

Bird, T: Alex., comp. and ed.
Hardware window dressing; a complete manual of window display for the hardware man, with full instructions for showing all classes of merchandise carried by a hardware store. '08(N) c. 256 p. il. 8°, $2.50. Merchants Record.

Bird book. '10(D) col. il. $1 net. Doran.

Bird cage. Irwin, W. A. $1.50. B. W. Dodge.

Bird in the box. Mears, M. M. $1.20 net. Stokes.

Bird lyrics. Jackson, C: E. $1. Smith & S.

BIRDS.
Beebe, *Mrs.* M. B. R. *and* C: W: Our search for a wilderness. $2.75 net. Holt.
Bonhote, J. L. Birds of Britain. *$6 net. Macmillan.
Braislin, W: C. List of the birds of Long Island. 75 c. Linnaean.
Burba, G: F. Our bird friends. $1. Outing.
Chapman, F. M. Camps and cruises of an ornithologist. **$3 net. Appleton.
Clark, A. H. Birds collected and observed during the cruise of the U. S. fisheries steamer "Albatross" in the North Pacific Ocean, [etc.] U. S., Supt. of Docs.
Cooke, W. W. Distribution and migration of North American shore birds. Gov. Pr. Off.
Cory, C: B. Birds of Illinois and Wisconsin. $4.—Birds of the Leeward Islands. 50 c. Field Museum.
Darton, F. J. H. Wonder book of birds and beasts. $1.50. Stokes.
Dawson, W: L., *and* Bowles, J: H. Birds of Washington [state.] 2 v. $12; $15; $20; $25. Occidental Pub.
Dearborn, N. Catalogue of a collection of birds from British East Africa.—Guatemala. ea., 50 c. Field Museum.
Dewar, D. Birds of the plains: [India.] *$4 net.—Indian birds. $2 net. Lane.
Eaton, E. H. Birds of New York. In 2 v. v. 1. $3. N. Y. State Educ.
Ferry, J: F. Catalogue of a collection of birds from Costa Rica. 50 c. Field Museum.
Gilmore, A. F. Birds through the year. 50 c. Am. Bk.
Grinnell, J. Bibliog. of California ornithology. $1.50. W. L. Chambers.
Grosvenor Library, Buffalo, N. Y. Reading list on birds and bird study. gratis. Grosvenor Lib.
Hammond, S. T. My friend the partridge. $1. Forest.

BIRDS.—*Continued.*

Heywood, E. E. Fifty common birds around the capital, [Topeka, Kan.] 25 c. Crane.

Job, H. K. How to study birds. $1.50 net.
—Sport of bird study. *$2 net. Outing.

Johns, C: A. Birds in their haunts. *$3 net. Dutton.

Jones, L. Development of nestling feathers. 50 c. L. Jones.

Judd, W. W. Birds of Albany County, [N. Y.] $2.50. A. M. Allen.

Keyser, L. S. Our bird comrades. $1.25; $1.75. Rand, McN. & Co.

Knight, C: R., *and* Hardcastle, E. Birds of the Bible for young people. $2 net. Stokes.

Knight, O. W. Birds of Maine. subs., $3.50. Glass.

Knowlton, F. H. Birds of the world. **$7 net. Holt.

Lea, J: Romance of bird life. *$1.50 net. Lippincott.

Lodge, R. B. Bird-hunting through wild Europe. $2.50 special net. Appleton.

McGregor, R: C. Manual of Philippine birds. $4. Macmillan.

Marks, J. A., *and* Moody, J. Holiday with the birds. 75 c. Harper.

Massachusetts. *State Bd. of Agriculture.* Special rept. on the decrease of certain birds and its causes, with suggestions for bird protection; by E: Howe Forbush. 2d ed. rev. June, 1908. '08, [1909.] (My) 118 p. il. 8°. (Add. pubs. for price.) Wright & P.

Maynard, C: J. Directory to the birds of eastern North America. $2; $2.50; $6. C: J. Maynard.

Millais, J: G. Natural hist. of British game birds. *$60 net. Longmans.

Miller, *Mrs.* H. M. Bird our brother. **$1.25 net. Houghton, M. & Co.

Miller, L. H. Wading birds from the quaternary asphalt beds of Rancho la Brea. 10 c. Univ. of Cal.

Pennsylvania. *Game Commissioners.* Save our birds and game; methods whereby game and wild birds can best be protected and cared for; recommendations as to the trapping and care of quail. '10(Ag) 18 p. il. O. pap., gratis. J. Kalbfus.

Porter, *Mrs.* G. S. Birds of the Bible. $2.
—Music of the wild. $2.50. Jennings.

Reed, C. A. Bird guide. 2 pts. ea., $1 net; pts. 1 and 2 in 1 v., $2.25 net. Doubleday, P.

Rhode Island. Check list of Rhode Island nesting birds. (Not for sale.) C: H. Remington.

Ridgway, R. Manual of North American birds. $5 net. Lippincott.

Saunders, M. M. My pets; real happenings in my aviary. $1.25. Am. Bapt.

Seattle, Wash. Public Library. List of books about birds in Seattle Public Library. gratis. Seattle Pub. Lib.

Shaw, W: T. China or Denny pheasant in Oregon; with notes on the native grouse. **$1.50 net. Lippincott.

Shufeldt, R. W. Osteology of birds. (Add. pubs. for price.) N. Y. State Educ.

Stebbins, C. A. Guide to the birds of the Pacific coast. 25 c. C. A. Stebbins.

Thomas, E: Some British birds. *$2 net. Doran.

Thomson, A. L. Britain's birds and their eggs. $6.50 net. Lippincott.

Thoreau, H: D: Notes on New England birds. $1.75 net. Houghton M.

Trafton, G. H. Methods of attracting birds. $1.25 net. Houghton M.

Walker, M. C. Bird legend and life **$1.25 net. Baker & T.

Walter, H. E. *and* A. H. Wild birds in city parks. 35 c. St. Johnsbury Repub.

Wright, H. W. Birds of the Boston Public Garden. **$1 net. Houghton M.

Wymper, C: Egyptian birds. *$6 net. Macmillan.

See also Bats;—Canaries; — Cowbird; — Ducks;—Flying;—Geese;—Grouse;—House martin;—Nature;—Owl;—Peacock; — Pheasants;—Pigeons;—Poultry;—Quail; — Sparrows; — Turkeys;—Vultures;—Woodcock;—Wrens.

Birds and mammals of the 1907 Alexander Expedition to Southeastern Alaska. '09 (Ap3) il. map, Q. (Univ. of Cal. pubs.; Zoology.) pap., 75 c. Univ. of Cal.

Birds of the cross [poems]. Lockhart, A. J. $1. C. R. Lougee.

Birdsall, Katharine Newbold, ed.
See Burnett, *Mrs.* Frances Hodgson, *ed.*

Birdseye, Clarence Fk.
Reorganization of our colleges. '09(Mr6) c. O. **$1.75 net. Baker & T.
—, **ed.** *See* New York [State.] Annot. consolidated laws.

Birge, E: Bailey.
Choruses and part songs for high schools. '08(O3) c. O. 65 c. Am. Bk.

Birkeland, Kr.
Norwegian Aurora Polaris Expedition, 1902-1903. v. 1, On the cause of magnetic storms and the origin of terrestrial magnetism. 1st section. '09(F20) figs. O. pap., $7. Longmans.

Birkhead, Alice.
The master-knot. '08(Ap25) D. †$1.50. Lane.

BIRKHEAD, Henry.
Mackail, J: W: Henry Birkhead and the foundation of the Oxford chair of poetry. 35 c. Oxford Univ.

Birkhoff, G: D:
Asymptotic properties of the solutions of ordinary linear differential equations containing a parameter with application to boundary value and expansion problems. '08, [1909.] (Jl) c. 219-231; 373-395 p. 4°. (Add. pubs. for price.) G: D: Birkhoff.

BIRMINGHAM, Ala.
See Alabama.

BIRMINGHAM, Eng.
See Newman Memorial Church.

BIRMINGHAM, Pa.
See Genealogies, Cope, G.

Birt, F. B. Bradley-.
See Bradley-Birt, F. B.

Birth of a nation. Brown, C: *$1 net. Revell.

Birth of humility. Marett, R. R. 35 c. Oxford Univ.

Birth of liberty. Lane, J: H. *$1 net. Bell Bk.

Birth of modern Italy. Mario, *Mme.* J. W. *$3.50 net. Scribner.

BIRTHDAY BOOKS.
Ghesiri, *Mme.* Fortune telling birthday book. $1; $2. Platt & P.
Kipling, R. Birthday book. **$1.50 net. Doubleday, P.
Ruyl, B. B. Zodiac birthday book. $1 net. Baker & T.
White, F. E., *comp.* Animal lover's birthday book. 50 c. Macmillan.

Birthday books. New ed. 6 v. '10(D) ea., ooze, $1.25. Dodge.
Contents: Emerson; Longfellow; Shakespeare; Dickens; Whittier; American poets.

Birthday horoscopes. Phelps, J. R. 50 c. Brewer, B.

Birthday of hope. Jones, J: D. *25 c. net. Revell.

BISCUIT.
See Cake.

Bisgood, Mary.
Powder and Jam. '09(O9) il. in col., obl. T. $1. Stokes.

Bishop, Avard Longley.
State works of Pennsylvania. '08(Ja4) maps, O. (Pubs. of Yale Univ.) pap., $1.50. Yale Univ.
See Gregory, Herbert Ernest.

BISHOP, *Mrs.* Bernice Pauahi.
Krout, M. H. Memoirs of the Hon. Bernice Pauahi Bishop. (Not for sale.) Putnam.

Bishop, C: McTyeire.
Jesus the worker; Cale lectures, 1909. '10 (S17) c. 12°, $1.25 net. Revell.

Bishop, E. Stanmore.
Lectures on surgical nursing. '10(Ag) 193 p. il. 16°, $1 net. Wood.

Bishop, Edm.
See Gasquet, Fs. Aidan.

Bishop, Mrs. Emily M.
Daily ways to health. '10(Ag27) c. D. $1.50 net. B: W. Huebsch.

Bishop, G: Sayles.
Doctrines of grace; and kindred themes. '10(S) c. 3-509 p. 8°, $1.50. Gospel Pub.

Bishop, Hudson D.
Motherhood; manual on the management of pregnancy and the principles and methods of infant feeding up to the third year of the child's life; prep. especially for mothers, nurses and students of medicine. '10(Jl) c. 24°. $1.50. Rose.

Bishop, Irving Prescott.
Methods and outlines for teaching physiology. Rev. and enl. '10(F) c. 78 p. diagrs., 8°, 50 c. I. P. Bishop.
Bibliography (2 p.).

BISHOP, *Mrs.* Isabella Bird.
Stoddart, A. M. Life of Mrs. Isabella Bird Bishop. *$2 net. Dutton.

Bishop, L: Faugeres.
Heart disease, blood-pressure, and the Nauheim-Schott treatment. 3d ed. '09 (N) c. 284 p. il. 8°, $3. Treat.

BISHOP, Sarah.
Enright, M. Ridgefield tavern: a romance of Sarah Enright. $1.25; 75 c. Brooklyn Eagle.

Bishop, Seth Scott.
Diseases of the nose, throat and ear and their accessory cavities. 4th rev. ed. '08, [1909.] (Je) c. 23+564 p. il. 8°, $4.50; hf. leath., $6. Davis.

Bishop, W. Chatterley.
Rubrical revision; an appeal to principle. '10(D3) O. pap., 36 c. net. Longmans.

Bishop, W: G:
Short course in business training, for normal schools, high schools, common schools, teachers, and independent students. '09(My) c. 7+9-85 p. 8°, 65 c. Univ. Pub.

—, and Bigger, E: Clarence.
Introductory bookkeeping and business practice. [3d ed., rev.] '10(O) c. 168 p. 8°, $1.20. Lincoln Business.

Bishop, W: S:, D.D.
Development of trinitarian doctrine in the Nicene and Athanasian creeds; study in theological definition. '10(D3) c. D. 75 c. net. Longmans.

Bishop and the boogerman. Harris, J. C. **$1 net. Doubleday, P.

Bishop in the rough. Duthie, D. W., *ed.* *$2 net. Dutton.

Bishop (Bernice Pauahi) Museum memoirs. il. f°. Bishop Museum.
—Brigham. Ancient Hawaiian house. $3.—Volcanoes of Kilauea and Mauna Loa. $4.50.

"Bishop Sunbeams." Metcalfe, R: L. $1. R: L. Metcalfe.

Bishop's emeralds. Townley, H. $1.50. W. J. Watt.

Bishop's letters. Lacey, T. A., *ed.* *50 c. net. Young Churchman.

Bishop's scapegoat. Clegg, T: B. †$1.50. Lane.

BISHOPS.
Haywood, M. D. Lives of the bishops of North Carolina. $1.50. A. Williams.

BISKRA, Algeria.
Leeder, S. H. Desert gateway: Biskra and thereabouts. $1.75 net. Cassell.

Bisland, Eliz., [now Mrs. C: W. Wetmore.]
At the Sign of the Hobby Horse. '10 (My21) c. O. $1.25 net. Houghton M.

—, and Hoyt, Anne.
Seekers in Sicily; being a quest for Persephone by Jane and Peripatetica, done into the vernacular. '09(Ag21) il. D. *$1.50 net. Lane.

BISMUTH PASTE.
See Medicine.

Bispham, G: Tucker.
Principles of equity; treatise on the system of justice administered in courts of chancery; expanded, [etc.,] by Sharswood Brinton. 8th ed. '09(N) c. 159+862 p. O. $6. Banks.

Biss, Gerald.
Fated five; tale of a tontine. '10(Ap30) D. $1.50. Brentano's.
The dupe. '09(O23) D. †$1.50. Brentano's.

Bisseker, H.
Problems of discipleship. '09(Ap10) D. *50 c. net. Eaton & M.

Bissell, C: Humphrey.
See Graves, C: Burr.

Bit of old ivory. Nixon-Roulet, M. F. $1.25. Benziger.

Biter (The). Cramp, W. S: $1.50. C. M. Clark.

Bithell, Jethro.
Hdbk. of German commercial correspondence. '08(D12) D. (Longmans' commercial ser.) $1.25. Longmans.
The Minnesingers. v. 1, Translations. '09 (Ap17) O. $2. Longmans.

Bitting, Arvill Wayne.
Canning of peas, based on factory inspection and experimental data. '09(Ag) 32 p. il. 8°, (U. S., Dept. of Agriculture, Bu. of Chemistry bull.) (Add. Superintendent for price.)

BITUMEN.
See Pavements.

BITUMINOUS COAL.
See Coal.

Bjerknes, Vilhelm Friman Koren, and others.
Dynamic meteorology and hydrography. '10 (D31) figs. diagrs., Q. pap. Carnegie.

Bjerregaard, Carl Henrik Andreas.
Inner life; lecture before the Theosophical Society, New York, at their hall, 244 Lenox Ave. '09, [1910..] (D) 16 p. 8°, $2. Theo. Pub. Co.

Björklund, Johan Gustaf.
Death and resurrection from the point of view of the cell-theory; tr. from the Swedish by J. E. Fries. '10(Jl2) c. por. 12°, $1 net. Open Court.

Bjorling, Philip R.
Pipes and tubes: their construction and joining. 2d ed. '08(O10) il. 12°, (Whittaker's lib. of arts, sciences and industries.) *$1.25 net. Macmillan.

Björnson, Björnstjerne.
Lesson in marriage: play. '10(D31) S. bds,. 50 c. net. Brandu's.
Mary; tr. from the Norwegian by Mary Morison. '09(S4) 12°, $1.25. Macmillan.
Novels. New ed.; ed. by Edm. Gosse. v. 9, 10. In God's way: a novel; tr. from the Norwegian by Elizabeth Carmichael. '08(F8); vs. 11 and 12, The heritage of the Kurts; tr. from the Norwegian by Cecil Fairfax. '08(Ap18) 16°, per v., $1.25. Macmillan.
Sigurd Slembe; dramatic trilogy; tr. from the Norwegian by W: Morton Payne. [New ed.] '10(D17) c. O. $1.50 net. Sergel.
Wise-Knut; from the Norwegian by Bernard Stahl. '10(Ja22) c. '09. por. D. *$1 net. Brandu's.

BJÖRNSON, Björnstjerne.
Payne, W: M. Björnstjerne Björnson. 50 c. net. McClurg.

Black, Adolph.
See Turneaure, F: Eug.

Black, Greene Vardiman.
Work on operative dentistry. '08(O10) c. 2 v., il. 4°, $10. Medico-Dental.

Black, H: Campbell.
Hdbk. of American constitutional law. 3d ed. '10(Je) c. O. (Hornbook ser.) $3.75. West Pub.

Black, Hugh, D.D.
Comfort. '10(S17) c. 8°, $1.50 net. Revell.
Friendship booklets. 6 v. '10(S17) 16°, ea., bds., 35 c. net. Revell.
Gift of influence. '08(D5) c. 8°, (University sermons.) *$1.25 net. Revell.

Black, Mrs. J. D.
See Potter, Marg. Horton.

Black, Jessie Eliz.
New primary methods; ser. of pract. home studies in pedagogy. 2 v. '10(Ja15) c. il. 8°, $7. Interstate Sch. Corr.

Black, M. Wesley.
Reminiscences and travels of Capt. M. Wesley Black, with comical jokes, personal matters, politics and events, with reminiscences of the campaigns of Lincoln and McClellan, Grant and Seymour, Grant and Greeley, Taft and Bryan. '09, [1910.] (F) c. 63 p. por. 8°, pap., 25 c. Case.

Black, S: C:, D.D.
Plain answers to religious questions modern men are asking; with introd. by Howard Agnew Johnston. '10(D17) c. por. D. 75 c. Presb. Bd.

Black, S: L., comp.
See Kinkead, Edg. B., *comp.*

Black, W: Harmon.
Real Wall Street: an understandable description of a purchase, a sale, a "short sale." '08(My16) c. D. $1.25; pap., $1. Corporations.

Black bag. Vance, L: J. †$1.50. Bobbs-M.

BLACK BASS.
See Fish and fishing.

Black bear. Wright, W: H: $1 net. Scribner.

Black Beauty. *See* Sewell, Anna.

Black bishop. Page, J. *$2 net. Revell.

Black Bruin. Hawkes, C. †$1.50. Jacobs.

Black cross. Briggs, O. M. †$1.50. Moffat.

Black cross clove. Luby, J. P. K. $1.20 net. B: W. Huebsch.

Black death of 1348 and 1349. Gasquet, F. A. *$2 net. Macmillan.

Black Diamond's directory of coal mine operators. '09(My) c. 8°, $5. Black Diamond.

Black dwarf. *See* Scott, *Sir* Wa.

Black elephant of Reading. Walker, A. H. gratis. A. H: Walker.

Black flier. Macvane, E. †$1.50. Moffat.

BLACK FOREST, Germany.
Hughes, C: E. Book of the Black Forest. $3 net. Dutton.

Black Hall traditions. Allyn, A. B., *comp.* $1. A. B. Allyn.

Black hand. Blakeman, W. C. $1.50. B'way Pub.

BLACK HAWK WAR.
Middling, T. Lincoln in the Black Hawk War. $1.25. Sigma.
Wakefield, J: A. Hist. of the Black Hawk War. (Add. pubs. for price.) Caxton Club.

Black man, the father of civilization. Webb, J. M. 75 c. J. M. Webb.

Black plague of the American continent. Sutherland, D. F. 50 c. D. F. Sutherland.

BLACK PRINCE.
See Edward, Prince of Wales.

Black puppy book. Aldin, C. C: W. 75 c. Doran.

Black Rock. *See* Gordon, C: W:

Black sheep. Sharts, J. W: $1.50. Duffield.

Black smiles. Bryant, F. H: 25 c. Southern Missionary.

Black walnut (*juglans nigra*). '09(N) 5 p. 8°, (U. S., Dept. of Agriculture, forest service, forest planting leaflet.) pap. (Add. Superintendent for price.)

Black Watch. Burton, St. G. E: W: $1.25 net. Cassell.

Blackall, Rob. H:
An air brake catechism. 23d rev. and enl. ed. '09(D) c. 380 p. il. 12°, $2. Henley.

Blackburne, S. S.
Terms and themes of chess problems: being a new and enl. ed. of Problem terms and characteristics; with preface by A. F. Mackenzie. '08(Jl11) il. 12°, *$1 net. Dutton.

Blacker, G:, M.D.
See Galabin, Alfr. Lewis, *M.D.*

Blacker, J. F.
A B C of collecting old English pottery. '10(Je11) 8°, $2 net. Jacobs.
Chats on oriental china. '08(N7) il. O. ("Chats" ser.) *$2 net; ¾ levant, *$5 net. Stokes.

Blackest Reading. Walker, A. H: gratis. A. H: Walker.

Blackford, C: Minor, jr.
Smithsonian Institution; repr. from the *North American Review* for Jan., 1909, with revisions by the author. '09(My) 11 p. 8°, pap. (Add. Superintendent for price.) U. S., Supt. of Docs.

BLACKFRIAR'S THEATRE, London.
Wallace, C: W: Children of the Chapel at Blackfriar's, 1597-1603. *$2.50 net. C: W: Wallace.

Blackie, J: Stuart.
On self-culture. [New ed.] '08(Ap25) D. 75 c. Funk.

Blackmar, Fk. Wilson.
Playgrounds and parks. '10(My) c. 12 p. 12°, (Univ. of Kansas, Social betterment ser.) gratis. Univ. of Kan.
Bibliography (2 p.).

Blackmore, Arth. W., ed.
See Ballard, Emerson Etheridge.

Blackmore, R: Doddridge.
Lorna Doone. Dulverton ed. '10(D) il. 8°, $7.50, boxed; India pap. ed., 16°, limp lambskin, $1.75; cf., $2.50. Barse & H.
Lorna Doone. 2 v. '10(D) il. $2.50, boxed. Crowell.
Lorna Doone. '08(O17) 16°, (Best books ser.) leath., *$1 net. *Same.* '08(Mr7) 16°, (Everyman's lib.) *35 c. net; leath., *70 c. net. Dutton.
Lorna Doone; with introd. and notes by H. Snowden Ward. Dooneland ed. '09 (Ja23) il. maps, 8°, $2.50. Harper.
Lorna Doone, a romance of Exmore; abridged and ed. by Harry C. Davis. '08, [1909.] (Mr) c. 288 p. il. pors. 16°. 60 c. Hinds.

Blackmore, R: Doddridge.—*Continued.*
Lorna Doone. '09(My1) 2 v., il. S. (Winston's ideal classics.) flex. leath., $2.50, boxed. Winston.
Springhaven. '09(Mr27) 16°, (Everyman's lib.) *35 c. net; leath., *70 c. net. Dutton.

Black's [A. & C.] guide to Ireland. 24th ed. '08(Ja25) il. maps, 16°, $1.75. Macmillan.

Black's medical dictionary; ed. by J: D. Comrie. 4th ed. '10(D) c. 10+856 p. il. in col. 12°, $2.25 net. Macmillan.

BLACKSMITHING.
Cran, J. Machine blacksmithing. 25 c. Indust. Press.
See also Horseshoeing.

Blacksmith's hammer. *See* Sue, M. J. E.

Blackstick papers. Ritchie, A. I., *Lady.* **$1.75 net. Putnam.

Blackstone, Ella M.
American woman's cook book; approved household recipes, incl. many excellent dishes never before presented in a cook book: thorough alphabetical index. '10 (Mr19) c. front. O. washable oil-cloth, $1.50. Laird.

Blackstone, Sir William.
See Mordecai, S: F.

Blackstone, W: E.
Jesus is coming. (Re-rev. ed.) '09(F6) c. 8°, *50 c. net; pap., *25 c. net. Revell.

Blackwood, Alex. Leslie.
Contagious, constitutional and blood diseases. '10(O) c. 7+367 p. 12°, $1.75. Boericke & T.
Food tract, its ailments and disease of the peritoneum. '09(N) c. 8+359 p. 12°, $1.50. Boericke & T.

Blackwood, Algernon.
Education of Uncle Paul. '10(Ap16) c. D. $1.50. Holt.
Jimbo: a fantasy. '09(Mr13) c. D. †$1.25. Macmillan.
John Silence, physician extraordinary. '09 (Mr20) D. $1.50. J: W. Luce.

BLADDER.
Folen, C. Clinical diagnosis of disorders of the bladder. $2. Treat.
Rumple, O. Cystoscopy as adjuvant in surgery. $8.50 net. Rebman.

Blaikie, W: Garden.
Steps unto heaven; meditations and prayers on the Psalms. '10(Ja1) c. 8°, $1.50. Northfield Press.

Blain, Herbert E., ed.
Pitman's secretary's hdbk.: guide to the work and duties in connection with the position of secretary to a joint-stock company, public institution, member of parliament, etc. '08(Ap4) O. $2. Pitman.

Blain, Mary E.
See Barse, *Mrs.* Mary Emma Salisbury.

Blaine, Harriet Bailey Stanwood, [Mrs. Ja. Gillespie Blaine.]
Letters; ed. by Harriet S. Blaine Beale, [1875-1890.] '08(O17) c. 2 v., 8°, *$4 net. Duffield.

BLAINE, James Gillespie.
Stanwood, E: James Gillespie Blaine. (Add. pubs. for price.) Houghton M.

Blaine, Mrs. Ja. Gillespie.
See Blaine, Harriet Bailey Stanwood.

Blaine, Rob. Gordon.
Calculus and its applications; pract. treatise for beginners, especially engineering students. '10(F19) il. 16°, *$1.50 net. Van Nostrand.

Some quick and easy methods of calculating; simple explanation of the theory and use of the slide-rule, logarithms, etc.; with numerous examples. 3d ed., rev. '07, [1910.] (Mr) 12+152 p. front. il. tabs., 16°, $1. Spon.

Blair, And. Alex.
Chemical analysis of iron. 7th ed. '08 (D19) c. il. tabs., 8°, **$4 net. Lippincott.

Blair, Emma Helen, and Robertson, Ja. Alex., eds. and trs.
Philippine Islands, 1493-1898. In 55 v. v. 53, 54, 55, Analytical index. '09(S11) c. pors. facsims., O. per v., *$4 net. A. H. Clark.

Blair, Matilda.
Bunnie Cottontail: a rabbit's own story. '08(O17) c. il. F. bds., 75 c. McLoughlin.

—, comp. Our holidays: recitations and exercises for New Year, Lincoln's and Washington's birthdays, Memorial, Flag, Independence, Labor, Thanksgiving, and Christmas days. '08(Ap4) c. il. pors. D. 50 c. McLoughlin.

BLAIR, *Rev.* Robert Downey.
Hansbrough, *Mrs.* L. V. B. Life of Rev. Downey Blair. $1.50. L. V. B. Hansbrough.

Blaisdell, Alb. Franklin.
How to keep well; text-book of physiology and hygiene for the lower grades of schools. Rev. ed. '10(Je11) c. il. 12°, 45 c. Ginn.

Blaisdell, Fk.
One hundred years of New Hampshire surgery. '07, [1908.] (Mr.) 40 p. 8°, pap. (Add. author for price.) F. Blaisdell.

Blaisdell, Mary Frances.
Polly and Dolly. '09(N13) c. il. D. 60 c. Little, B. & Co.

Blake, C. F.
Mathematics of machine design, with special reference to shafting and efficiency of hoisting machinery. '08(Je6) c. diagrs., 8°, (Machinery's reference ser.) pap., 25 c. Indust. Press.

Blake, Emily Calvin.
Engaged girl sketches. '10(Jl9) c. front. D. $1. Forbes.

Great moments in a woman's life. '10 (D17) c. D. 75 c. Forbes.

Blake, Forest.
Saint Josephine. '09(N6) c. D. *$1.25 net. Jennings.

Blake, G: Herbert.
United States paper money: a reference list of paper money, incl. fractional currency, issued since 1861, also a list of United States coins. '08(D5) c. tabs., Q. pap., $1. G: H. Blake.

Blake, Sir H: Arth.
China by Mortimer Menpes. '09(O2) il. Q. (Menpes crown ser.) *$1.50 net. Macmillan.

Blake, Ja. Vila.
The months. '08(Ja18) S. *75 c. net. J. H. West.

So like her father; drama, in prelude and three acts. '09, [1910.] (F) c. 83 p. 8°. (Not for sale.) J. V. Blake.

Blake, Katharine Evans.
Stuff of a man. '08(Mr21) c. front. D. †$1.50. Bobbs-M.

BLAKE, Martin.
Chanter, J: F: Life and times of Martin Blake. *$3.50 net. Lane.

Blake, Mrs. Warrenne, ed.
Memoirs of a vanished generation, 1813-1855; with an introd. by the Lady St. Helier. '08(D12) il. O. *$5 net. Lane.

BLAKE, William.
De Selincourt, B. William Blake. *$2 net. Scribner.

BLAKE, William Phipps.
Published writings of William Phipps Blake, D.Sc., LL.D., territorial geologist of Arizona, professor of geology, emeritus, University of Arizona; with introd. by Kendric C: Babcock. '10(N) 17 p. 12°, 50 c. net.. Univ. of Ariz.

Blake-Hedges, Florence Edythe.
Story of the catacombs. '09(Ap24) c. D. *$1 net. Jennings.

Blakely, Gilbert Sykes.
Teachers' outlines for studies in English; based on the requirements for admission to college. '08(Jl4) c. S. 50 c. Am. Bk.

Blakely, Stuart Banyar.
History of Otsego, N. Y. '08(Ag22) map, 12°. (Add. author for price.) S. B. Blakely.

Blakeman, Wilbert C.
Black hand. '08(D) c. 1+316 p. 12°, $1.50. B'way Pub.

Blaker, Ernest, and Fisher, Willard Ja.
Experiments in physics, for students of science; printed expressly for students in a first year laboratory course in general physics in Cornell University. 2d ed. '09(S) c. 213 p. il. tabs., 8°, *$1.25 net. Taylor & C.

Blakeslee, C. G.
See Mason, Herbert Delevan.

Blakeslee, G: Hubbard, ed.
China and the Far East; Clark University lectures. '10(Mr26) c. O. **$2 net. Crowell.

Blakiston's quiz-compend ser. il. 12°, *$1 net; *$1.25 net. Blakiston.
—Radasch. Compend of histology.
—Stewart. Compend of pharmacy.

Blakiston's science ser. il. O. Blakiston.
—Duff. Physical measurements. $1.50 net.
—Duff, *ed.* Text-book of physics. *$2.75 net.
—Duff *and* Guthe. Mechanics and the properties of matter. $1.60.
—McClung. Conduction of electricity through gases and radio-activity. *$1.50 net.

Blanchan, Neltje, [pseud. for Mrs. Nellie B. Doubleday.]
American flower garden; planting lists by Leonard Barron. '09(Je19) c. il. f°, $10, boxed.—New ed. '10(D) c. '09. il. f°, $5. Doubleday, P.

Blanchard, Amy Ella.
Dear little girl at school. '10(S3) c. il. D. $1.25. Jacobs.
Four Corners abroad. '09(S4) c. il. D. (Corner ser.) †$1.50. Jacobs.
Four Corners in camp. '10(S10) c. il. D. (Corner ser.) $1.50. Jacobs.
Four Corners at school. '08(Ag8) c. il. D. (Corner ser.) †$1.50. Jacobs.
Glad lady. '10(Ag20) c. il. O. $1.50. Estes.
Journey of joy. '08(O3) c. il. O. †$1.50. Estes.
Little maid Marian. '08(Ag8) c. il. D. †$1. Jacobs.
Playmate Polly. '09(Jl10) c. il. D. $1. Jacobs.
Wit's End. '09(S25) c. O. †$1.50. Estes.

—, and Waugh, Ida.
When mother was a little girl. '10(Ap23) il. in col. 4°, $2. Dutton.

Blanchard, Arth. Alphonzo.
Synthetic inorganic chemistry. 2d ed., rev. and enl. '10(O22) 12°, $1 net. Wiley.
Synthetic inorganic chemistry. '08(Je20) 12°, *$1 net. Wiley.

Blanchard, Ferdinand Quincy.
For the King's sake. '09(O) 28 p. 8°, 35 c. F. Q. Blanchard.

Blanchard, Grace.
Phil's happy girlhood. '10(N5) D. $1.50. Wilde.

Blanchard, H: Percy.
After the cataclysm; romance of the age to come. '09(D) c. 136 p. 12°, $1.25. Cochrane.

Blanchaud, R. de, ed.
One thousand common French words. '09 (Ag28) S. (Modern language ser.) *25 c. net. Crowell.
Progressive French idioms. '10(Ap2) D. (Heath's modern language ser.) 60 c. Heath.
Quatre contes des Mille et une nuits. '10 (Ja29) S. (Crowell's shorter French texts.) *25 c. net. Crowell.

Blanck, F: Conrad.
Nitration of aniline and certain of its derivatives. '08, [1910.] (Ap) 37 p. 8°, pap., 40 c. Johns Hopkins.

Bland, Mrs. Edith Nesbit, [Mrs. Hubert N. Bland.]
Daphne in Fitzroy street. '09(O16) c. col. front. D. †$1.50. Doubleday, P.
Enchanted castle. '08(My16) c. il. D. †$1.25. Harper.
Harding's luck. '10(S10) c. il. D. $1.50. Stokes.
House of Arden. '09(D18) il. 12°, $1.50. Dutton.
House with no address. '09(Mr13) c. D. †$1.50. Doubleday, P.

Bland, Hubert N.
Happy moralist: [essays.] '08(Ag8) 8°, buckram, *$1.25 net. M. Kennerley.
See also Bland, *Mrs.* Edith Nesbit.

Bland, Mrs. Hubert N.
See Bland, *Mrs.* Edith Nesbit.

Bland, J: Otway Percy.
Houseboat days in China. '09(N20) il. fold. map, O. $5. Longmans.

—, and Backhouse, E.
China under the Empress Dowager; being the hist. of the life and times of Tzu Hsi, comp. from the state papers and the private diary of the controller of her household. '10(D17) il. map, Q. $4 net. Lippincott.

Bland-Sutton, J:, M.D.
Tumors, innocent and malignant; their clinical characters and appropriate treatment. 4th ed. [1910.] (My) 556 p. il. $5 net. Funk.

BLANDFORD, Mass.
Wood, S. G. Taverns and turnpikes of Blandford. *$2 net. S. G. Wood.

Blandin, Mrs. Isabella Marg. Eliz. John.
History of higher education of women in the South prior to 1860. '09(Ja23) c. O. *$3 net. Neale.
Hist. of Shearn Church, 1837-1907. '08 (O) c. 229 p. il. por. 8°, $1. Dealy.

Blaney, C: E:
Girl and the detective. '09(Ja2) il. 12°, pap., 25 c. J. S. Ogilvie.
Girl from Texas. '09(O23) il. 12°, pap., 25 c. J. S. Ogilvie.
Little terror. '09(O23) 12°, pap., 25 c. J. S. Ogilvie.
Sheriff of Angel Gulch. '08(D) 120 p. 12°, pap., 25 c. J. S. Ogilvie.
Sporting deacon. '09(O30) il. 12°, pap., 25 c. J. S. Ogilvie.
Tennessee Tess. '09(J2) il. 12°, pap., 25 c. J. S. Ogilvie.
Young Buffalo in N. Y. '09(O30) il. 12°, pap., 25 c. J. S. Ogilvie.

Blanking dies. '08(Je6) c. il. 8°, (Machinery's reference ser.) pap., 25 c. Indust. Press.

Blasco Ibáñez, Vicente.
La barraca, novela; ed., with introd., notes and vocab., by Hayward Keniston. '10 (O1) c. por. S. 90 c. Holt.
Shadow of the cathedral; tr. by Mrs. W. A. Gillespie. '09(Ag21) front. O. *$1.35 net. Dutton.

Blashfield, De Witt C., ed.
See Mack, W:

BLAST FURNACES.
See Furnaces.

BLASTING.
Maurice, W: Electric blasting apparatus and explosives. $3.50. Van Nostrand.

Blatchford, Ambrose N.
Church councils and their decrees. '09 (N20) *80 c. net. Am. Unitarian.

BLATCHFORD, Robert.
Lyons, A. N. Robert Blatchford. 75 c. net. Lane.

Blatter, G: J:, ["Fiscar Marison."]
O'er oceans and continents with the setting sun. 3d ser. Jerusalem, Palestine in Bedouin garb, Syria and the islands of the Mediterranean, Smyrna, Constantinople, Athens, Corfu. '09(Mr) c. 11-227 p. il. 12°, $1.29; per set of 4 v., $5.16. G: J: Blatter.

Blätter and blüten. Hubel, H. $1. Brentano's.

BLAVATSKY, *Mme.* Helena Petrovna Hahn-Hahn.
Bragdon, C. Episodes from an unwritten history. 15 c. Manas Press.

Blaxine. Cobb, M. S. $1.50. Neale.

Blaze Derringer. Lyle, E. P., *jr.* $1.20, fixed. Doubleday, P.

Blazing the way. Denny, E. I. $2.50. Rainier Pr.

Blé (Le) qui lève. *See* Bazin, René.

Bleackley, Horace W:, ["Tivoli."]
Ladies fair and frail: sketches of the demi-monde during the eighteenth century. '09(Mr27) il. 8°, *$5 net. Lane.
Story of a beautiful duchess: account of the life and times of Elizabeth Gunning, Duchess of Hamilton and of Argyll. '08 (F22) pors. 8°, *$5 net. Dutton.

Blech, Gustavus M.
Pract. suggestions in borderland surgery for the use of students and practitioners. '10(Jl) c. 7-219 p. 12°, $1.50. Professional.

Bledsoe, Anthony Jennings.
Business law for business men; for use in state of New York. '10(Ap) v. O. shp., $4.50. Business Law.

Bledsoe, S. T.
Indian land laws, being a treatise on the law of acquiring title to, and the alienation of, allotted Indian lands, [etc.] '09 (N) c. 27+686 p. O. $6. Pipes-R.

BLEDSOE FAMILY.
See Sumner Co., Tenn.

Blei, Franz.
Powder-puff; ladies' breviary; from the German of Franz Blei. '10(F5) c. S. *$1.25 net. Duffield.

Bleichert system of aerial tramways. Hewitt, W: gratis. Trenton Iron Co.

Blessed Joan of Arc. Ford, E. A. $1 net. Chr. Press.

Bligh, S. M.
Direction of desire; suggestions for the application of psychology to everyday life. '10(Ag20) c. D. 70 c. net; leath., $1. Oxford Univ.

Bligh, W: G:
Practical design of irrigation works. '08 (F8) il. 8°, *$6 net. Van Nostrand.

Blighted life of Methuselah. Williams, H: R. $1. Nat. Bapt. Pub.

BLIND (The).
Allen, E: E. Impressions of institutions for the blind in Germany and Austria. gratis. Perkins Inst.
Jones, G: W. Braille or New York point? gratis. G: W. Jones.
Keller, H. A. World I live in. $1.20. Century Co.
Kunz, M. Physiology of the blind. 50 c. Volta.
Massachusetts. *Commission for the Blind.* Bulletin no. 1, Needlessly blind for life. gratis; per 1000, $30. Mass. Com. Blind.
New York Association for the Blind. First rept., from its foundation Nov. 25, 1905-Nov. 1, 1907. gratis. N. Y. Assoc. for Blind.

BLIND.—*Continued.*
New York Association for the Blind. *Special Committee on Prevention of Blindness.* Prevention of blindness. gratis. N. Y. Assoc. for Blind.
Pennsylvania Institution for the Instruction of the Blind, Overbrook, Philadelphia. About a school for children and youth who have bad eyesight. gratis. Penn. Inst. Blind.
Perkins Institution and Massachusetts School for the Blind, Boston. Brief summary of the history of the Institution. gratis. Perkins Inst.
Perkins Institution and Massachusetts School for the Blind. Circulating library. Perkins Inst.
Perkins Institution and Massachusetts School for the Blind. List of embossed books, maps, appliances and tangible apparatus for the use of the blind. gratis. Perkins Inst.
See also Eye.

Blind hopes. Wallace, H. $1.50. Cassell.

Blindness of Dr. Grey. Sheehan, P. A. $1.50. Longmans.

Blindness of virtue. Hamilton, C. $1.50. Brentano's.

Bliss, Edn. Munsell, D.D.
Missionary enterprise. '08(Ag1) c. 12°, *$1.25 net. Revell.

Bliss, Mrs. Ella Theodora Crosby.
Micronesia: fifty years in the island world: history of the mission of the American Board. '07, [1908.] (My.) 8+167 p. il. map, 12°, pap., 30 c. J: G. Hosmer.

Bliss, W: Dwight Porter, Binder, Rudolph M., and others, eds.
New encyclopedia of social reform. New ed. '08(Je6) c. tabs., O. **$7.50 net; shp., **$9.50 net; hf. mor., **$12 net; mor., **$14 net. Funk.

Bloch, Jean de.
Future of war. [1910.] (My) 12°, (International lib.) 50 c. net. Ginn.

Block, L: Ja.
World's triumph: a play. '09(Ap24) c. D. **$1.25 net. Lippincott.

Block, Rudolph Edgar, ["Bruno Lessing."]
Jake—or Sam. '09(D4) c. il. D. bds., 50 c. FitzGerald.

BLOCK SIGNALS.
See Signals and signalling.

Blocking and hitting. McFadden, G: 10 c. R: K. Fox.

Blodgett, Andrew Burr.
See Blodgett, Frances Eggleston.

Blodgett, Frances Eggleston and Andrew Burr.
Blodgett readers by grades. Bks. 1, 2, 3. '10(Ag27); Bk. 4. '08(N14); Bk. 5 (Ap30); c. il. D. Bk. 1, 30 c.; Bk. 2, 35 c.; Bk. 3, 40 c.; Bk. 4, 65 c.; Bk. 5, 75 c. Ginn.

Blodgett, Harry Thornton.
Shorthand speed book. In 2 pts. '08(Ja4) O. pap., ea., $1. Long Branch Press.

Blom, Ada.
Biography of a New York hotel scrub. '09 (Je26) D. pap., 25 c. A. Blom.

Blomfield, C. H.
See Jones, A. Clement.

Blomfield, Reginald.
Mistress art: [architecture.] '08(N7) D. *$1.40 net. Longmans.

Blond lady. Leblanc, M. 50 c. Doubleday, P.

Blood, C: W.
See United States. Federal penal code.

Blood, Percy Erford.
See Siisbee, Wa. Everett.

BLOOD.
Bishop, L: F. Heart disease, blood pressure, and the Nauheim-Schott treatment. $3. Treat.
Brunton, *Sir* L. Therapeutics of the circulation. *$1.50 net. Blakiston.
Burnett, S: H. Clinical pathology of the blood of domesticated animals. *$2.50 net. Taylor & C.
Cabot, R: C., *ed.* Diseases of metabolism and of the blood. $5. Appleton.
Craig, C: F. Malarial fevers, hæmoglobinuric fever and blood protozoa of man. *$4.50 net. Wood.
Crawley, H. Studies on blood and blood parasites. (Add. Superintendent for price.) U. S., Supt. of Docs.
Crile, G: W. Hemorrhage and transfusion. $5; $6. Appleton.
Harvey, W: Anatomical disquisition on the motion of the heart and blood in animals. *35 c. net; *70 c. net. Dutton.
Meyer, W., *and* Schmieden, V. Bier's hyperemic treatment in surgery, medicine and all specialties. *$3 net. Saunders.
Neusser, E. V. Clinical treatises on the symptomatology and diagnosis of disorders of respiration and circulation. pt. 1, $1.50; pt. 2, *$1.25 net. Treat.
Reichert, E: T., *and* Brown, A. P. Differentiation and specificity of corresponding proteins and other vital substances in relation to biological classification and organic evolution. $9. Carnegie.
Schleip, K. F. W. Hematological atlas, with description of the technic of blood examination. $10. Rebman.
Watkins, R. L. Catechism of hæmatology: [examination of the blood.] $2. R. L. Watkins.
Wile, I. S. Blood examination in surgical diagnosis. $2. Surgery.
See also Anemia;—Arteries;—Bacteria;—Bones;—Diagnosis; —Heart; — Inflammation;—Malaria; —Parasites;—Serum;—Tuberculosis.

Bloom, Solomon.
Treatise on the law of mechanics' liens and building contracts, with annotated forms. '10(Je) c. O. shp., $7.50. Bender-M.

Bloomer, Howard B.
See McGregor, Malcolm.—Michigan corporation law.

Bloomfield, Dan.
Important events in musical history from A.D. 300 to 1908; arranged in chronological form. '08(N21) c. 12°, 25 c. Presser.

Bloomfield, J. K.
The Oneidas. '07. [1908.] (Mr.) c. 395 p. pors. pls. 8°, *$2.25 net. Alden Bros.

Bloomfield, Maurice.
Religion of the Veda, the ancient religion of India. '08(F29) c. O. (American lectures on the history of religions.) **$1.50 net. Putnam.

BLOOMINGDALE.
See New York City.

Blossoming of the waste. Ellison, *Mrs.* E. N. $1.50. Calkins & Co.

Blossoms of nature. Foster, L. G. $1. L. G. Foster.

Blotting book. Benson, E: F. †$1. Doubleday, P.

Blount, Ralph E.
See Everly, Lu Lester.

Blow, B. E.
Revenue law and the retail liquor dealer. '10(O) c. 72 p. O. $1. R. M. Wood.

Blow, Susan Eliz.
Educational issues in the kindergarten. '08 (D5) c. 12°, (International education ser.) **$1.50 net. Appleton.

Blowing away of Mr. Bushy Tail. Davidson, E. B. 50 c. Duffield.

BLOWPIPE.
Butler, G. M. Pocket hdbk. of blowpipe analysis. 75 c. net. Wiley.
Moses, A. J. Elements of mineralogy, crystallography and blowpipe analysis. $2.50 net. Van Nostrand.

Blue and gray. Lancaster, W: J. C. $1.25. Cassell.

Blue and the gray. Finch, F. M. **$1.30 net. Holt.

Blue arch. Miller, *Mrs.* A. D. $1.20 net. Scribner.

Blue bird. Maeterlinck, M. **$1.20 net; $2 net. Dodd.

Blue calf. Fairman, L. 75 c. Griffith-S.

Blue goops and red. Burgess, F. G. **$1.35 net. Stokes.

Blue lagoon. Stacpoole, H. D. †$1.50. Lippincott.

Blue lawn. Kolle, *Mrs.* L. E. D. $1 net. Fenno.

"Blue Peter": sea yarns. Roberts, M. $1.50. L. C. Page.

Blue waters and green. Smith, F. D. $1.50. Crane.

Blueberry pasture. Whittemore, H: W. 75 c. Tufts Coll.

Bluegrass and wattle. Bayne, *Mrs.* M. A. $1.25. Standard Pub.

Bluejacket's manual. McLean, R. $1.25. U. S. Naval Inst.

Bluestocking in India. Heston, W. $1 net. Revell.

Blum, Edg. C.
Robert Emmet's wooing. '10(My14) c. il. por. 12°, $1. Cochrane.

Blum, Isidor.
Jews of Baltimore; historical summary of their progress and status as citizens of Baltimore. '10(Jl30) il. pors. 8°, $3. Hist. Review.

Blumenthal (George) lectures. See Columbia Univ. George Blumenthal foundation.

Blümner, Hugo.
Home life of the ancient Greeks; tr. from the German by Alice Zimmern. 3d ed. [1910.] (Ap) il. $2 net. Cassell.

Blundell, Mrs. Fs. Nicholson.
See Blundell, Mary E. Sweetman.

Blundell, Mary E. Sweetman, [Mrs. Fs. Nicholson Blundell; "M E. Francis."]
Madge-make-the-best-of-it. '09(Je19) il. 12°, (St. Nicholas ser. of beautiful books.) *80 c. net. Benziger.

Blundell, Odo.
Catholic Highlands of Scotland. v. 1, Central Highlands. '09(O) 13+229 p. il. 8°. *$1.10 net. Herder.

Blunt, Mrs. Eliz. Lee.
When folks was folks. '10(Jl30) 12°, $1.50. Cochrane.

Blushful South and Hippocrene. Loveman, R. **$1 net. Lippincott.

Blythe, S: G:
We have with us to-night; what happens at that great American institution, the banquet. '09(Je5) c. S. bds., 50 c. Altemus.

Boardman, Edn. A:
Small yacht: its management and handling for racing and sailing; with chapters on construction. '09(Je26) c. il. O. **$2 net. Little, B. & Co.

Boardman, G: Nye.
Shakespeare; five lectures. '09(F13) c. 12°, *$1 net. Revell.

Boas, Franz.
Anthropology. '08(F29) c. 8°, pap., 25 c. Macmillan.

Boas, F: S:, ed.
Taming of a shrew: being the old play used by Shakespeare in "The taming of the shrew." '08(D5) facsim., 16°, (Shakespeare lib.: Shakespeare classics.) bds., *$1 net; Persian, *$1.60 net; Lib. ed., hf. parchment, 12°, *$1.70 net. Duffield.

Boat club boys of Lakeport. Stratemeyer, E: †$1.25. Lothrop, L. & S.

BOATS.
Elliott, B. E., *and* Ward, P. R. Motor craft encyclopedia. $1. Encyclopedia.
Ferro Machine and Foundry Co., Cleveland, O. Marine gasoline engines and equipment: design, construction, installation and operation of power boats. 25 c. Ferro.
How to design and construct a power boat. $1. Rudder.
Life preservers on motor vessels. (Add. Superintendent for price.) U. S., Supt. of Docs.
Motorboat handbook. *$1 net. Motor Boat Pub.
National Association of Engine and Boat Manufacturers. Foreign trade and yacht club directory. (Not for sale.) Nat. Assoc. Engine and Boat Manufact.
Nine motorboats and how to build them. $1. Motor Boat Pub.
Rudder (The). How to build an 18-foot racing cat [boat.] $1. Rudder.
Russell, T: H. Motor boats; construction and operation. $1; $1.50. C: C. Thompson.
See also Canoeing;—Naval art and science;—Navigation;—Rowing;—Ships and shipbuilding;—Submarines;—Yachts and yachting.

Bob Carleton. Taine, H. G. $1.50. C. M. Clark.

Bob Knight's diary with the circus. Smith, C. C. †$1.50. Dutton.

Bob Lindsay and his school, by one of his old pupils. '08(D) 45 p. il. 12°, bds., 75 c. Dodge.

Bob O'Link, pseud.
Outwitted: society sketch for girls, in one act. '08(S19) c. 12°, pap., 15 c. Dick.

Bob the castaway. Webster, F. V. 35 c. Cupples & L.

Bobbitt, J: Franklin.
Growth of Philippine children. '09(O9) il. O. pap. (Add. author for price.) J: F. Bobbitt.

Bobby Blake. Weiderseim, G. G. 50 c. Stokes.

Bobo's adventures. Howie, H. M. 35 c. Stokes.

Bob's Cave boys. Burton, C: P. †$1.50. Holt.

Bob's Hill braves. Burton, C: P. $1.50. Holt.

Bobtail Dixie. Smith, A. N. 60 c. Educ. Pub.

Boccaccio, Giovanni.
The Decameron "La commedia umana," now for the first time completely tr. by J: Payne; with introd. by Hugo Albert Rennert; il. by Jacquez Wagrez. [10 sections.] [1910.] (Jl) c. f°, $300. Barrie.

BOCCACCIO, Giovanni.
Hutton, E: Giovanni Boccaccio. *$5 net. Lane.
Jones, F. N. Boccaccio and his imitators; "The Decameron." 50 c. Univ. of Chic.

Boccaccio. Zell, F. $2. Ditson.

Bôcher, Maxime.
Introduction to higher algebra; prep. with the co-operation of E. P. R. Duval. '08 (Ja11) 8°, *$1.90 net. Macmillan.
Introduction to the study of integral equations. '09(Mr) 2+72 p. 8°, (Cambridge tracts in mathematics and mathematical physics.) pap., *75 c. net. Putnam.

Bockenheimer, Philipp.
Atlas of clinical surgery, with special reference to diagnosis and treatment for practitioners and students; English adaptation by C. F. Marshall. 3 v. '08(N) c. il. 4°, $24. Rebman.

Böckmann, Friedrich.
Celluloid; its raw material, manufacture, properties and uses; tr. from the 3d rev. German ed. by Chas. Salter. '08(Ap25) il. 12°, $2.50. Van Nostrand.

Bode, Boyd H:
Outline of logic. '10(Mr26) D. $1. Holt.

Bode, Wilhelm.
Florentine sculptors of the Renaissance. '09(Ap3) il. Q. *$4 net. Scribner.
Great masters of Dutch and Flemish painting; tr. by Marg. L. Clarke. '09(Ap3) il. pors. D. *$2 net. Scribner.

Bodger, J.
A toy party. '10(N12) col. il. obl. S. bds., 50 c. Warne.

Bodkin, McDonnell.
Quests of Paul Beck. '10(S10) il. D. $1.50. Little, B. & Co.

BODLEIAN LIBRARY, Oxford, Eng.
Padelford, F: M., *and* Benham, A. R., *eds.* Songs of Rawlinson ms. C813, [in Bodleian Library.] (Add. University for price.) Univ. of Wash.

Body, Canon G:
The Good Shepherd. '10(Mr5) 12°, *80 c. net. Whittaker.

BODY (*Human*).
See Anatomy;—Anthropometry;—Athletics;—Gymnastics and physical culture;—Hygiene;—Mind and body;—Physiology;—Psychotherapy.

Body and its defenses. Jewett, *Mrs.* F. G. 65 c. Ginn.

Body and soul. Dearmer, P. *$1.50 net. Dutton.

Body at work. Hill, A. *$4.50 net. Longmans.

Body at work. Jewett, *Mrs.* F. G. 50 c. Ginn.

Boeckmann, Paul v.
Physique; treatise on deep breathing and the care and development of the lungs and muscular system. '10(My14) c. il. por. 12°, $1. P. v. Boeckmann.

Boehm, Theobald.
Flute and flute playing in acoustical, technical, and artistic aspects; tr. and annot. by Dayton Clarence Miller. '09(F) c. 9+100 p. il. pors. 12°, $1.50. D. C. Miller.

Boehn, Max von.
See Von Boehn, Max.

Boenninghausen, C. M. F. von, M.D.
Lesser writings; comp. by T: Lindsay Bradford, M.D. '08(Ag22) c. 8°, $1.50. Boericke & T.

Boer boy of the Transvaal. Rabb, K. M. $1.25. Penn Pub. Co.

BOER WAR.
See South Africa.

Bogert, H: Lawrence.
Year book of the Holland Society of New York, 1906. '08(Ag) il. pors. 4°, vellum and cl. or silk, $5. Knickerbocker Press.

Boggess, Arth. Clinton.
Settlement of Illinois, 1778-1830. '09(My8) c. maps, 8°, (Chicago Historical Society collections.) $3. Chic. Hist.

Boggs, Marion Alexander, ed.
Alexander letters, 1787-1900. '10(Jl) 387 p. front. pors. fold. geneal. tab., 4°. (Priv. pr.) G: J. Baldwin.

Boggy solitudes of Nantucket. Wilson, A. $1.25. Neale.

Bogle, Artemas Melvin.
Teacher's manual to accompany "Comprehensive bookkeeping." '08(Ap18) 12°, *$1 net. Macmillan.

Bogue, Mrs. Arth. Hoyt.
See Bell, Lilian Lida.

Bogue, Virgilia.
Strength to yield; the psychology of a great temptation. '09(O23) c. col. front. 8°, $1.50. Cunningham, C. & W.

Bohan, Eliz. Baker.
The drag-net; prison story of the present day. '09(D) c. 332 p. il. 12°, $1.50. C. M. Clark.

Bohannan, W: J. H.
Nephilim: [shows the truth of the Bible and the error of science.] '08(F22) c. 12°, $1.50. R. A. Silk.

Bohannon, Hattie Donovan.
Light of stars. '09(My1) c. D. *$1 net. Fenno.

BOHEMIA, Austria-Hungary.
Lützow, F. H. H. V., *Graf* v. Bohemia. 35 c. net; 70 c. net. Dutton.
Monroe, W. S. Bohemia and the Czechs. $3. L. C. Page.
See also Elizabeth Stuart, *Queen of Bohemia.*

Bohemian jinks. Garnett, P. *$1.50 net. Garnett.

Böhlau, Helene, [Mme. Al-Raschid, Bey.]
Ratsmädelgeschichten; ed., with notes and vocab., by Emma Haevernick. '08(My9) c. S. (Modern lang. ser.) 40 c. Heath.

Bohlen lectures. *See* Foley, G: Cadwalader.

Böhme, Margarete, ed.
Diary of a lost one. '08(Ag) c. 5-319 p. D. $1.50. Hudson Press.

Bohn's classical lib. 12°. Macmillan.
—Lucretius. On the nature of things. *$1.50 net.
—Swift. Prose works. v. 12. *$1 net.

Bohn's libraries. 12°. Macmillan.
—Æschylus. Plays. *$1 net.
—Argyll. Life of Queen Victoria. *$1 net.
—Homer. Iliad. v. 1, bks. I.-XII. *$1 net.

Boigne, [Charlotte Louise Elénore Adelaide d' Osmond,] Comtesse de.
Memoirs, 1820-1830; ed. from the original ms. by M. C: Nicoullaud. v. 3. '08 (Mr7) c. por. O. **$2.50 net. Scribner.

Boileau-Despreaux, Nicholas.
Satires épitres et l' art poëtique; preface d'Augustin Filon. '08(N7) por. nar. S. (Les classiques français.) limp leath., *$1 net. Putnam.
Selections from Boileau; ed., with an introd. and notes, by Oscar Kuhns. '08 (Ap25) c. S. (Modern lang. ser.) 50 c. Heath.

BOILERS.
Christie, S. Boiler; boiler rules and tables used in the construction, testing and operation of steam boilers. $1.75. Christie.
Collins, H. E. Boilers. $1. Hill Pub.
Darling, P. G. Safety valve capacity. gratis. Consolidated Safety.
Leland, W. S. Boiler accessories. $1. Am. Sch. Corr.
Lord, G: W. Boiler troubles and their treatment. gratis. G: W. Lord.
Newell, W: S., *and* Dow, C. S. Steam boilers. $1. Am. Sch. Corr.
Peabody, C. H. Steam boilers. $4. Wiley.
Rules and formulæ with suggestions pertaining to good practice, indorsed and adopted by the International Master Boiler Makers' Association. '10(D) 7-65 p. 16°, $1. Int. Master Boiler.
Snodgrass, J. M. Tests of two types of tile-roof furnaces under a water-tube boiler. gratis. Univ. of Ill.
Walker, S. F. Steam boilers, engines and turbines. *$3.50 net. Van Nostrand.
Stromeyer, C: E. Marine boiler management and construction. *$4 net. Longmans.
See also Coal;—Engines;—Fuel;—Heating;—Locomotives;—Marine engineering;—Metal work;—Steam engines.

"Bois, Victor du," pseud.
See Butterfield, Cornelia du Bois.

Boissarie, Prosper Gustave.
Heaven's recent wonders; or, the work of Lourdes; author. tr. by Rev. C. Van der Donckt. '10(Ja22) il. pors. 8°, $1.50. Pustet.

Bojer, Johan.
Power of a lie; tr. from the Norwegian by Jessie Muir; with an introd. by Hall Caine. '09(Mr13) c. D. $1.25. M. Kennerley.

Bojus, Gustav Herrman.
Dumb bell exercises. '10(Je25) c. il. por. 12°, (Spalding athletic lib.) pap., 10 c. Am. Sports.

Bolax. Culpeper, *Mrs.* J. *$1 net. Murphy.

Bolduan, C: F:
Immune sera: concise exposition of our present knowledge concerning the constitution and mode of action of antitoxins, agglutinins, hæmolysins, bacteriolysins, precipitins, cytoxins and opsonins. 3d ed., enl. '08(Ag29) c. 12°, $1.50. Wiley.

BOLIVAR, Simon.
Petre, F. L. Simon Bolivar. $4 net. Lane.

BOLIVIA.
Calderon, I. Economic conditions of Bolivia. W. F. Roberts.
International Bureau of American Republics. Bolivia, general descriptive data. Int. Bu. Am. Republics.
See also Koati Island;—Titicaca Island.

Bolles, Albert Sidney.
Every man's lawyer. 3 v. New ed. of "Home library of law." '08(O) c. S. $3. Doubleday, P.

BOLOGNA, Italy.
James, E. E. C. Bologna, its hist., antiquity and art. $4.80. Oxford Univ.

Bolognese, Stefano.
Economical interpreter, for Italians to learn English: easy dialogues printed in 3 parallel columns. '08(Ag29) obl. 18°, pap., 50 c. Caspar.

Bolster, Roy Hale.
See Hall, Maxcy Reddick.

Bolster book. Graham, H. $1.50 net. Duffield.

Bolton, C: Knowles.
Scotch Irish pioneers in Ulster and America. '10(Jl16) c. il. maps, 8°, $2 net. Bacon & B.

Bolton, Mrs. C: Knowles.
See Bolton, Ethel Stanwood.

Bolton, Ethel Stanwood, [Mrs. C: Knowles Bolton.]
Farm life a century ago. '09(Ap3) O. pap. (Priv. pr.) C: K. Bolton.

Bolton, F: Elmer.
Principles of education. '10(D24) c. il. 8°, $3. Scribner.

Bolton, Reginald Pelham.
Elevator service. '08(Ap.) c. 70 p. diagrs., 4°, *$5 net. R. P. Bolton.

BOLTON, Ct.
Vital records of Bolton to 1854 and Vernon to 1852. $3. Conn. Hist.

BOLTON, Mass.
Vital records of Bolton. $3. F. P. Rice.

Bolwock, W. C.
See Benn, H. P.

Bom-tu floor work for lodge staffs. Carpenter, H. M. $1. H. M. Carpenter.

Bomb (The). Harris, F. $1.50. M. Kennerley

Bomberger, J: Huston, comp.
Three thousand practical illustrations in religion and morals, a classified collection of anecdotes, incidents and thought-germs for preachers, platform speakers, Sunday-school superintendents and teachers, Christian workers and Bible readers, with copious indexes: homiletic, topical, textual, Biblical, biographical, junior congregation and Sunday-school lesson. '09(N) c. 5+450 p. 8°, $2. Central.

Bomberger, Maude Ada.
Colonial recipes from old Virginia and Maryland manors. '08(Ja4) D. $1.25. Neale.

BOMPAS, *Bp.* William Carpenter.
Cody, H. A. Apostle of the north: life and memoirs of William Carpenter Bompas, DD. *$2.50 net. Dutton.

Boname, Louise Catherine.
Study and practice of French in school for beginners. pt. 1; natural method on a new plan with thorough drill in pronunciation. 4th ed. '10(D24) c. D. 60 c.—pt. 2, Essentials of grammar, conversation, composition (French text.) 5th ed., rev. '08, [1910.] (D) c. 24+270 p. D. 90 c. L. C. Boname.

BONAPARTE, Napoleon.
See Napoleon I.

BONAPARTE FAMILY.
Atteridge, A. H. Napoleon's brothers. *$5 net. Brentano's.
Turquan, J. Sisters of Napoleon: Elisa, Pauline and Caroline Bonaparte. *$3.75 net. Scribner.
Williams, H. N. The women Bonapartes: mother and three sisters of Napoleon I. $6. Scribner.

Bonapartism. Fisher, H. A. L. *$1.15 net. Oxford Univ.

Bonar, Ja.
Philosophy and political economy in some of their historical relations. [New ed.] '09(S18) 8°, *$2.75 net. Macmillan.

Bonaventura, St., [Bp. of Albany.]
See Francis of Assisi, *St.*

Bonbons: [poems.] Savinien, F. P. (Add. pubs. for price.) B'way Pub.

Bond, Alb. Richmond.
Master preacher; study of the homiletics of Jesus; introd. by Edn. C: Dargan. '10(D24) c. front. 8°, $1 net. Am. Tr.

Bond, Alex. Russell, comp. and ed.
Handy man's workshop and laboratory. '09(D4) c. O. $2. Munn.
Scientific American boy at school. '09 (D4) c. il. O. $2. Munn.

Bond, Fs.
Fonts and font covers. '09(My15) il. O. $4.80. Oxford Univ.
Screens and galleries in English churches. '08(O24) il. O. $2. Oxford Univ.

Bond, Fs.—*Continued.*
Visitor's guide to Westminster Abbey. '09 (N13) il. plans. S, 40 c. Oxford Univ.
Westminster Abbey. '10(Ja1) il. O. $4. Oxford Univ.
Wood carvings in English churches. v. 1, Misericords. '10(Ag27) il. O. (Church art in England.) $2.50. Oxford Univ.

Bond, W: Sidney.
His struggle magnificent. '10(O8) c. 12°, $1.50. Cochrane.

Bond (The). Boyce, N., *pseud.* †$1.50. Duffield.

Bond of music. MacDougall, D., *ed.* $1.25; $2. Stokes.

BONDS.
Babson, R. W. Special bond circulars. $10. R. W. Babson.
Davis, W: E., *jr.* I have a little money: what shall I do with it? $1. W: E. Davis.
Lownhaupt, F: Investment bonds. **$1.75 net. Putnam.
Lownhaupt, F: Series on bonds. 6 v. ea., 10 c. Moody's Mag.
Robinson, J. W. Robinsonian bond and investment tables. $5. J. W. Robinson.
Rollins, M. Municipal and corporation bonds. 60 c. Estes.
Rollins, M. Table showing the net return from serial and installment bonds. $5. M. Rollins.
Walker, M. B. Treatise on the law of fidelity bonds with special reference to corporate fidelity bonds. $3. King Bros.
See also Finance;—Investments;—Speculation;—Stock brokers;—Stocks.

Bone, Florence.
Brownie's box. '10(Ja22) il. 12°, $1. Am. Tr.
Other side of the rainbow; being the adventures of Old-fashioned Jane. '10 (O15) c. D. 85 c. net. Eaton & M.

"Bonehill, Captain Ralph," pseud.
See Stratemeyer, E:

BONES.
Cornell, W. S. Hdbk. of osteology and syndesmology. 75 c. Davis.
Dickson, W: E. C. Bone marrow: cytological study. *$12 net. Longmans.
Goldthwait, J. E., *and others.* Diseases of the bones and joints. $6. Heath.
Sutton, H. A., *and* Drinker, C. K. Osteology and syndesmology. $1.50. Blakiston.
Turner, P. Aids to osteology. *$1.25 net. Wood.
See also Arm; — Arthritis; — Foot;—Fracture;—Hand;—Knee;—Osteopathy;—Spine.

Bonfort's wine and spirit trade directory; being a complete list of the licensed wholesale dealers, licensed rectifiers and leading registered distillers in the United States; also, new tariff rates and list of "wet and dry" counties in the United States. [1910.] (Ja) 24°, $3. Leoser Bros.

Bonham, Alfr. N.
Misconceptions of life insurance policy holders; anaylsis and explanation of each popular form of legal reserve life insurance policy; instructions for correcting adverse policies without reduction of insurance and how to buy and what to pay for life insurance. '09(My) c. 10+229 p. 12°, $3. A. N. Bonham.

BONHEUR, Rosa.
Stanton, T., *ed.* Reminiscences of Rosa Bonheur. $3 net. Appleton.

Bonhote, J. Lewis.
Birds of Britain. '08(Ja25) il. 8°, (Color books.) *$6 net. Macmillan.

Bonner, D: Findley, D.D.
Psalmody question: examination of the alleged divine appointment of the book of Psalms as exclusive manual of praise. '08(My2) c. D. *50 c. net. Hanford & H.

Bonner, Geraldine.
Emigrant trail. '10(My7) c. front. D. $1.50 Duffield.

Bonner, Jos. C.
Plans and methods used under Bonner farm cost system. '08(Je6) il. por Q. pap. (Add. pub. for price.) Bonner.

Bonnett, P. P.
Compact rhyming dict. '10(D10) 32°, im. mor., 50 c. Dutton.

Bonney, Sherman Grant, M.D.
Pulmonary tuberculosis and its complications, with special reference to diagnosis and treatment for general practitioners and students. pt. 1. '08(Ag8); 2d ed., thoroughly rev. '10(Je) c. il. 8°, ea., $7 net; hf. mor., $8.50 net. Saunders.

Bonnie Belmont. Cochran, J: S. $1.50. J: S. Cochran.

Bonnier, C:, comp.
La lignée des poètes au XIXe siècle: being an anthology of modern French poetry. '08, [1909.] (My) 12°, $1. Oxford Univ.

Bonomelli, Bp. Jeremias.
New series of homilies for the whole year; tr. by Right Rev. T: Sebastian Byrne. In 4 v. '09(D25) c. O. $5, boxed. Benziger.

Bonsall, Mabel.
See Mercer, G: E.

Bonsall, Marian.
Tragedy of the Mormon woman. '09(Ja23) c. il. pors. O. pap., 35 c. Housekeeper Corp.

Bonser, E. A.
Buccaneers. '09, [1910.] (F) 12°, 75 c. Estes.

BONTOC IGOROT LANGUAGE.
See Philippine Islands.

Bonum Meritum, pseud.
War of words between President Roosevelt and J. Pierpont Morgan concerning railroad, tariff and trust questions and the panic of 1907; supposed arguments between President Roosevelt and J. Pierpont Morgan. '08(Mr21) c. il. D. $1; pap., 25 c. Donohue.

Book, F: W:
Psychology of skill with special reference to its acquisition in typewriting. '09 (Je12) il. O. (Univ. of Montana pubs.; Psychology.) pap., $1. Univ. of Mont.

Book, W: H:
Columbus Tabernacle sermons; stenographically reported by Wa. C. Galbraith, 1909. [1910.] (F) c. '09. 231 p. por. 12°. $1. Standard Pub.

Book (The). Davenport, C. J. H. *$2 net. Van Nostrand.

Book about Yorkshire. Fletcher, J. S. *$2 net. Doubleday, P.

Book (The) and the child. McFarland, J: T. *5 c. net. Eaton & M.

Book and the message. Alleman, H. C. 50 c. Lutheran Pub.

BOOK COLLECTING.

Hunnewell, J. F. Collectors: [book collecting.] [priv. pr.] Club Odd Vol.

Savage, E. A. Story of libraries and book-collecting. *75 c. net. Dutton.

BOOK ILLUSTRATION.

Penrose's process yearbook. 1908-9. $2.50. Tennant.

Swisher, C: C., *ed.* Twenty lessons in illustrating. $5. Art Pub.

See also Dickens, C:

Book of a hundred bears. Smith, F. D. 75 c. Rand, McN. & Co.

Book of American municipalities. League of American Municipalities. $3.50. Municipal Information.

Book of animals. Golding, H., *ed.* $1.50. Stokes.

Book of anniversaries. Tucker, H. B. 50 c. Dutton.

Book of battles and sieges. Dawson, L. H. 50 c. Dutton.

Book of books. Ragg, L. $1.40 net. Longmans.

Book of Ceylon. Cave, H: W: *$4.50 net. Cassell.

Book of Christmas; with an introd. by Hamilton W. Mabie. '09(O23) c. il. S. **$1.25; Large paper ed. '10(D24) c. il. 8°, $2 net. Macmillan.

Book of common praise. Reformed Episcopal Church. 90 c. Armstrong-K.

BOOK OF COMMON PRAYER.

Benton, J. H: Book of common prayer; its origin and growth. (Priv. pr.) J. H: Benton.

Dimock, N. Hist. of the book of common prayer in its bearing on eucharistic controversies. 75 c. net. Longmans.

Eeles, F. C. Traditional ceremonial and customs connected with the Scottish liturgy. $6 net. Longmans.

First and second prayer books of King Edward VI. 35 c. net; 70 c. net. Dutton.

Gurney, T: A. Nunc dimittis. *60 c. net. Longmans.

Hart, S: Book of common prayer. $1.50. Univ. Press, (Sewanee.)

Prayer book of the Protestant Episcopal church simplified and arranged. 30 c. Ritzmann B.

Book of Cupid; being an anthology from the English poets; with introd. by H: Newbolt. '10(D17) il. D. $1 net. Stokes.

Book of Daniel Drew. White, B., *ed.* $1.50 net. Doubleday, P.

Book of Days. Gordon, W. *60 c. net. Dutton.

Book of days; collection from the best authors of appropriate quotations for each day in the year. '10(D) 16°, lambskin, $1.25; cf., $2. Barse & H.

Book of designs. Wolfe & McKenzie. $2. Wolfe & M.

Book (The) of Easter; with introd. by the Rt. Rev. W: C. Doane. '10(Mr12) c. il. S. **$1.50 net, boxed. Macmillan.

Book of facts, truths and reason. Simpson, T: J. $1. T: J. Simpson.

Book of Fate; now tr. into English from the German of an ancient Egyptian manuscript; formerly in the possession of Napoleon. '10(Ja22) c. map, $1; pap., 50 c. Anglo-Am. Authors'.

Book of fern culture. Hemsley, A. *$1 net. Lane.

Book of filial duty. Hsaio Ching. *40 c. net. Dutton.

Book of fish and fishing. Rhead, L. J. **$1.50 net. Scribner.

Book of friendship. Kauffman, R. W. 75 c. Altemus.

Book of friendship. Ransome, A., *comp.* $2.50 net. Stokes.

Book of friendship. Warren, I. R., *comp.* $1.50 net. Jacobs.

Book of friendship; with introd. by S: McChord Crothers. '10(N5) c. il. S. (Friendly lib.) $1.25 net, boxed; leath., $1.75 net, boxed. Macmillan.

Book of garden pests. Pearson, R. H. *$1 net. Lane.

Book of Georgian verse. Braithwaite, W: S., *comp.* **$2 net; **$3.50 net. Brentano's.

Book of glame. Edgerly, W. $4. Ralston Univ.

Book of golden deeds. Yonge, C. M. *35 c. net; *70 c. net. Dutton.

Book of good cheer. Grover, E. O., *ed.* $1. Volland.

Book of good fellowship. Grover, E. O., *ed.* $1. Volland.

Book of gratitude. Kauffman, R. W. 75 c. Altemus.

Book of Greek verse. Headlam, W. G: *$1.75 net. Putnam.

Book of guessing contests. Glover, E. H. **50 c. net. McClurg.

Book of happy days. Boult, E. M. $3. Pomfret.

Book of homonyms. Barrett, B. S. *75 c. net. Pitman.

Book of hospitalities and record of guests; with foreword on old house mottoes by Arth. Guiterman. '10(D10) c. Q. hf. leath., $1.50 net, boxed. P. Elder.

Book of hours. Thompson, E. $1.50. Forest Press.

Book of Latin prose composition. Elmore, J. $1. B: H. Sanborn.

Book of limericks. Lear, E: $1.50. Little, B. & Co.

Book of living poets. Jerrold, W. C., *ed.* *$2.50 net. Lane.

Book of love. Kauffman, R. W., *comp.* 75 c. Altemus.

Book of lullabies. Hix, M., *comp.* 40 c. Educ. Pub.

Book of lumbershed construction. Saley, M. L. $1.50. Am. Lumberman.
Book of my heart. Weil, A. M. $1. Lib. Shelf.
Book of nature. Jones, J., *pseud.* *25 c. net; *50 c. net. P. Elder.
Book of operas. Krehbiel, H: E: **$1.75 net. Macmillan.
Book of porcelain. Rackham, B. $4 net. Macmillan.
Book of precious stones. Wodiska, J. **$2.50 net. Putnam.
Book of princes and princesses. Lang, L. B. **$1.60 net. Longmans.
Book of quatrains. Marvin, F. R. $1. Sherman-F.
Book of Radcliffe College songs. '09(Jl17) c. Q. pap., $1. Boston Music.
Book of Restoration verse. Braithwaite, W: S., *ed.* *$2 net; *$3 net. Brentano's.
Book of satyrs. Spare, A. O. *$6 net. Lane.
Book of studies in plant form. Lilley, A. E. V. *$2 net. Scribner.
Book of sweethearts: pictures by famous artists. '08(O24) c. Q. $2.50, boxed. Bobbs-M.
Book of the animal kingdom. Westell, W: P. $4 net. Dutton.
Book of the Black Forest. Hughes, C: E. $3 net. Dutton.
Book of the Christ child. Broadus, E. H. $1.75. Appleton.
Book of the cottage garden. Thonger, C: *$1 net. Lane.
Book of the divine consolation of Saint Angela Da Foligno. '08(D5) il. 12°, (New mediæval lib.) pigskin, *$2.50 net. Duffield.
Book of the dry fly. Dewar, G: A. B. $2.50 net. Macmillan.
Book of the Duke of True Lovers. Christine *de Pisan.* *$2.50 net. Duffield.
Book of the flower show. Curtis, C: H. $1 net. Lane.
Book of the little past. Peabody, J. P. $1.50. Houghton M.
Book of the pansy, viola and violet. Crane, H. H. *$1 net. Lane.
Book of the pearl. Kunz, G: F: **$12.50 net. Century Co.
Book of the Poe centenary. Kent, C: W:, *ed.* $1. J: S. Patton.
Book of the Psychic Society. Edgerly, W. $2. Ralston Univ.
Book of the railway. Mitton, G. E. *$2 net. Macmillan.
Book of the rose. Melliar, A. F. $2 net. Macmillan.
Book of the saints. Dawson, L. H. 50 c. Dutton.
Book of the simple way. Lâo-Tsze. *$1.25 net. Badger.
Book of the supervisors of Dutchess County, N. Y., A.D. 1718-1722. '08(D26) Q. pap. (Add. pubs. for price.) Vassar Bros.
Book of the sweet pea. Crane, D. B. *$1.50 net. Lane.
Book of veterinary posology. Brumley, O. V. $1.25. O. V. Brumley.
Book of wheat. Dondlinger, P: T. *$2 net. Judd.
Book of winter sports. Syers, E., *ed.* *$4.20 net. Longmans.
Book of witches. Hueffer, O. M. *$2.50 net. J: McBride.

BOOK-PLATES.
Almack, E: Book plates. *$1 net. McClurg.
Andreini, J. M. J. Winfred Spenceley; his etchings and engravings in the form of book plates. $4. Assoc. Bk.
Hapgood, T. B. Bookplates. set of 12 brochures, per set, $18; $30. Goodspeed.
Spenceley, J. W. Check-list [chronologically arranged] J. Winifred Spenceley's book-plates. 35 c. Assoc. Bk.
See also French, Edwin Davis.

BOOK-PRICES.
Livingston, L. S. American book prices current. v. 14, 15. ea., **$6 net; **$15 net. Dodd.

BOOKBINDERS AND BOOKBINDING.
American Library Association. *Committee on Bookbinding.* Binding for small libraries. 15 c. A. L. A.
Dana, J: C. Notes on bookbinding for libraries. $1. Lib. Bu.
Emerson, G. D. Book binding for libraries. gratis. G. D. Emerson, (Phil.)
Freeman, S. J. Syllabus of a course on elementary bookmaking and bookbinding. 30 c. Teachers' Coll.
Jeffers, Le R., *comp.* Reference list of titles suggested for a special library binding. (Add. Library for price.) N. Y. Pub. Lib.
Linton, C. B. Hints on forwarding, finishing and ruling. $2. Burt Pub.

Book stack and shelving. Green, B. R. gratis. Snead & Co.
Booke of hunting, 1576. Turberville, G: $2.50. Oxford Univ.
Bookhunter. Burton, J: H. *$1 net. Dutton.
Bookish books. 16°, *55 c. net. Burrows.
—Allison. Delicious vice. (1st ser.; 2d ser.)
—My favorite novelists.
Bookkeeper's hdbk.; convenient reference book for bookkeepers and business men. '10(D3) c. T. $1.25; leath., $1.50. Int. Correspondence.

BOOKKEEPING.
Allen, G: Science of accounts made clear and simple. $1. Edwards.
American business and accounting encyclopedia. In 6 v. v. 1, 2. ea., $3. Business Man's Pub.
American School of Correspondence. Department store accounts. $1.50.—Pract. bookkeeping. $2. Am. Sch. Corr.
Baker, J. W. Reference book: 20th century bookkeeping and office practice. $1. Southwestern Co. (Nashville.)
Benton, C: W: Pract. bookkeeping designed for use of high schools, normal schools, business colleges and private study. $1.50. Bogarte.
Beynon, R: Drapery and drapers' accounts. $1. Pitman.
Bishop, W: G:, *and* Bigger, E: C. Introd. bookkeeping and business practice. $1.20. Lincoln Business.

BOOKKEEPING.—*Continued.*

Bogle, A. M. Teacher's manual to accompany "Comprehensive bookkeeping." *$1 net. Macmillan.

Bookkeeping outlines. '09(S) c. 56 p. 4°. (Priv. pr.) Ellis Pub.

Brown, J. S. Typewriter bookkeeping. gratis. Underwood Typewriter.

Cole, W: M. Accounting and auditing. $4.80. Cree.

Cole, W: M. Accounts. $2. Houghton M.

Davenport, C. J. H. The book: its history and development. *$2 net. Van Nostrand.

Day, C. M. Accounting practice. **$6 net. Appleton.

Delp, J. D. Comprehensive modernized rapid calculator 75 c. J. D. Delp.

Dewhirst, J: M. Elements of bookkeeping. $1. Wagoner.

Dickinson, A. L. Accounting practice and procedure. 50 c. Am. Sch. Corr.

Dicksee, L. R. A. B. C. of bookkeeping. 80 c. Longmans.

Dicksee, L. R. Auditing. $5. Ronald Press.

Ellis, C. B. Practical bookkeeping. $1.35.—Reference book for use with Ellis's Practical bookkeeping. 75 c. Allyn & B.

Ellis Publishing Co. Students' guide to accompany the Ellis cabinet system of teaching bookkeeping and business practice. $1.50.—Students' guide to accompany the Ellis tablet method of teaching bookkeeping and business practice. $1. Ellis Pub.

Forse, W: H., *jr.* Electric railway auditing and accounting. *$2 net. McGraw.

Garrison, E. E. Accounting every business man should know. **$1.20 net. Doubleday, P.

Goodwin, J. H: Improved book-keeping. $3. J. H: Goodwin.

Goodyear, L. E. Progressive business accounting. $2. Waterloo.

Goodyear, S: H. Advanced accounting with business practice by office and tablet methods. $1. Goodyear-M.

Goodyear, S: H. *and* L. E. Higher accounting. 90 c.—Modern inductive bookkeeping. 2 v. $3.75.—Railway accounting. 30 c.—Wholesale accounting. 30 c. Goodyear-M.

Greendlinger, L. Accountancy problems, with solutions. $5. Business Bk.

Griffith, J. B. Purchasing and stores department.—Records of labor and manufacturing orders.—Single entry bookkeeping.—Single proprietors' and partners' accounts.—Voucher system accounting charts.—Wholesale, commission, and storage accounts. ea., 50 c. Am. Sch. Corr.

Griffith, J. B., *and* Sweetland, C: A: Trustees', executors', and stock brokers' accounts. 50 c. Am. Sch. Corr.

Hatfield, H: R. Modern accounting. **$1.75 net. Appleton.

Heitmann, H: Course in the theory and practice of higher accounting prep. for students of Eastman College. $2. Eastman College.

BOOKKEEPING.—*Continued.*

Hirsch, A. Science of commercial bookkeeping. $2. J. S. Ogilvie.

Hyans, E: M. Theory of accounts for accountant students. $5. Universal Business.

International accountants' manual. $3. Business Man's Pub.

Kaib, D. J. Bookkeeping for parish priests. $1.25. Wiltzius.

Lamb, H: G. Farm bookkeeping. $1. H: G. Lamb.

Lyons, J. A. Modern corporation accounting. $1.25. Powers.

Moffett, L: B. Manual of bookkeeping and accounting. $1.25. Pierce Sch.

Montgomery, R. H. Auditing. 3 v. ea., 50 c. Am. Sch. Corr.

Moull, J: Auditing for accountant students. (Add. pubs. for price.) Universal Business.

Musselman, D. L. Bookkeeping for business colleges, schools, and private instructions. $2. D. L. Musselman.

Neal, E. V., *and* Craigin, C. T. Modern illustrative bookkeeping. $1. Am. Bk.

Neff, G: O. The check-figure: [new system of checking accounts.] 60 c. G: O. Neff.

Nelson, R: J. New bookkeeping. $3. Cincinnati & S.

New complete accountant. $1.10. Powers.

New York University. School of Commerce, Accounts and Finance. Graded accounting problems. 3 v. $2. L. Greendlinger.

Pearce, W. B. Practical bookbinding. 50 c. Spon.

Pixley, F. W. Accountancy. $2. Pitman.

Porritt, H. W., *and* Nicklin, W: Bookkeeping for retailers. 50 c. Pitman.

Renn, G: B. Practical auditing. $3. G: B. Renn.

Rowe, H. M. Bookkeeping and accountancy. $1.50. Sadler-R.

Spear, R. H., *and others, eds.* Commercial World encyclopedia of accounting. In 2 v. v. 1. per set, $15. Commercial World.

Spencer, E. Art of modern bookkeeping and accounting. $3. E. Spencer.

Sprague, C: E. Philosophy accounts. $3. C: E. Sprague.

Stephens, J: R. Principles of accounting. $1.25. J: R. Stephens.

Student's guide to accompany the Ellis tablet method of teaching bookkeeping and business practice. 55 c. Ellis Pub.

Sweetland, C: A: Brewer's accounts. 50 c. Am. Sch. Corr.

Tutt, R. G. Telephone accounting. $1. R. T. Tutt.

Wallace, D: Simple mine accounting. $1. Hill. Pub.

Weber, F. C: Introductory bookkeeping. 50 c. F. C. Weber.

Whigham, W. H., *and* Frederick, O. D. Bookkeeping and business practice. $1. Heath.

Wightman, W: W., *comp.* Students' guide to the principles of bookkeeping. $1—Students' guide to the principles of bookkeeping in chart-form. 50 c. Ellis Pub.

BOOKKEEPING.—*Continued.*

Wildman, J: R. Cost accounting problem. $3. Accountancy.

Williams, L: L., *and* Rogers, F. E. Supplementary exercises in bookkeeping. 20 c. Am. Bk.

Witter, C: A. Business and accounts, for public schools and home use. 75 c. C: A. Witter.

Wolff, A. Practical accounting. (Not for sale.) Universal Business.

Woods, C. E. Practical cost accounting. $2.50. Universal Business.

Woods, C. E. Repts. on industrial organization, systematization and accounting. In 12 pts. pts. 1 and 2. per set, $15. C. E. Woods.

Wright, H. Contractor's accounts. 50 c. Am. Sch. Corr.

See also Agriculture;—Arithmetic;—Banks and banking;—Bills of lading; — Business; — Commerce;—Commercial law;—Corporations;—Engineering;—Factories;—Farms and farming;—Insurance;—Interest;—Investments; — Plumbing; — Railroads;—Real property; — Stocks; — *also* New York City.

BOOKS AND READING.

Arnold, G. W., *comp.* Mother's list of books for children. $1. McClurg.

Baker, C. A. Books as tools for children. o. p. Carson-H.

Brown, M. W., *comp.* Mending and repair of books. 15 c. A. L. A.

Carey, A. P. Reader's basis. $1. Echo Press.

Cary, C: P., *ed.* List of books for free high school libraries in the state of Wisconsin. gratis. C: P. Cary.

Dobson, H: A. De libris. $1.50. Macmillan.

Doyle, *Sir* A. C. Through the magic door: [essays about books.] **$1.25 net. McClure.

Gaige, R. C., *and* Harcourt, A., *comps.* Books and reading. **$1.50 net. Baker & T.

Hix, M., *comp.* Brief outline of the books I have read. 25 c. Hinds.

Illinois State Normal School, Charleston. List of books in the schoolroom libraries of the first six grades in the Eastern Illinois State Normal School. Ill. State Normal.

Kroeger, A. B. Guide to the study and use of reference books. *$1.25 net. A. L. A.

Kroeger, A. B., *and* Cattell, S. W. Aids in book selection. 15 c. A. L. A.

Kuhns, L. O. Love of books and reading. $1 net. Holt.

List of books for college and high school libraries. (Add. pubs. for price.) Eau Claire Bk.

Mabie, H. W., *ed.* Young folks' treasury. Univ. Soc.

Macy, J: Child's guide to reading. **$1.25 net. Baker & T.

Marvin, F. R. Excursions of a booklover. $1.50 net. Sherman, F.

North Carolina. *Dept. of Public Instruction.* Approved list of books for rural libraries. N. C. Dept. Pub. Instruct.

BOOKS AND READING.—*Continued.*

Potter, M. E., *and others, comps.* Children's catalogue; a guide to the best reading for young people. $6 net. H. W. Wilson.

Public school libraries; 500 books and how to buy them. gratis. Mich. State Normal Coll.

Scott, T. Pleasure of reading. *$1.25 net. M. Kennerley.

Smith, L: P. Wanderings of a literary pilgrim. 25 c. L: P. Smith.

Sonnenschein, W: S. Best books; reader's guide. In 3 pts. pt. 1. $3.50 net. Putnam.

Soulsby, L. H. M., *comp.* Record of a year's reading. 30 c. Longmans.

Summer reading for boys and girls; lists of books sel. and arr. by classes. 15 c. net. Germantown Friends Sch.

Swan, H. In praise of books. 50 c. Dutton.

Sylvester, C: H. Journeys through Bookland. 10 v. $22.50; $29.50. Thompson Pub. Co., (Chic.)

Virginia. *Board of Education.* List of books for rural school libraries in Virginia. gratis. W: E. Jones.

Wisconsin. *Dept. of Education.* List of books for free high school libraries in the state of Wisconsin. gratis. C: P. Cary.

World's best books. 50 c. Globe-W.

See also Bibliographies;—Book collecting;—Book illustration; — Book-plates; — Book-prices; — Bookbinders and bookbinding;—Cataloging;—Christmas; — Copyright; —Criticism;—Fiction;—Incunabula;—Librarians and libraries;—Literature;—Printers and printing;—Publishers and publishing.

Books for the people. Legler, H: E. gratis. H: E. Legler.

Books for the young. il. T. 50 c. Stokes.
—Kingsley. Heroes.
—Seven champions of Christendom.

BOOKSELLERS.

Directory of booksellers, newsdealers and stationers in the U. S. and Canada. $5. H. W. Wilson.

International directory of booksellers and bibliophile's manual. $2. Dodd.

Knight, C. Shadows of the old booksellers. 50 c.; 75 c. Dutton.

BOOM (The).

See Gymnastics and physical culture.

BOONE, Daniel.

Bruce, H: A. B. Daniel Boone and the wilderness road. $1.50. Macmillan.

Lindsay, C: H. A. F-. Daniel Boone, backwoodsman. $1.50. Lippincott.

Boone, Ilsley.

Conquering Christ. '10(N19) c. il. 12°, (Bible study union lessons; senior grade.) 50 c. Bible Study.

Boorman, T: Hugh.

Asphalts: their sources and utilizations; asphalts for dustless roads. '09(Ja16) 8°, $3. W: T. Comstock.

Booth, C: Edn.

One branch of the Booth family; showing the lines of connection with 100 Massachusetts Bay colonists. '10(D) 11+259 p. il. por. O. $5. C: E. Booth.

Booth, E: C.
Doctor's lass. '10(Ag20) c. front. D. $1.30 net. Century Co.
The post-girl. '08(Je27) c. front. D. †$1.50. Century Co.

Booth, Eva Gore-.
Sorrowful princess: [a play.] '08(Ja25) D. $1. Longmans.

Booth, Evangeline.
Love is all. '08(Ap18) c. por. 12°, 30 c. Reliance.

Booth, F:
See Bacon, Victor V.

Booth, H. H., comp.
See Arkansas overruled cases.

Booth, Mary Hannah.
How to read character in handwriting. '10 (Ag6) il. S. bds., 50 c. Winston.

Booth, Mrs. Maud Ballington Charlesworth.
After prison—what? New ed. '08(Mr21) c. 12°, *$1.25 net. Revell.

Booth, Wa. S., comp.
See Minnesota. Justice's manual.—Township manual.—Village manual.

Booth, W: H., and Kershaw, J: Baker Cannington.
Smoke prevention and fuel economy. '09 (D) c. 194 p. il. 8°, $2.50. Henley.

Booth, W: Stone.
Hidden signatures of Francesco Colonna and Francis Bacon; comparison of their methods, with the evidence of Marston and Hall that Bacon was the author of Venus and Adonis. '10(My14) $1.50 net. W. A. Butterfield.
Some acrostic signatures of Francis Bacon, Baron Verulam of Verulam, Viscount St. Alban, together with some others, all of which are now for the first time deciphered. '09(Je19) c. il. 4°, **$6 net. Houghton M.

BOOTH FAMILY.
See Genealogies.

Bo-peep: treasury for the little ones. '08 (D5); '09(N6); '10(D) col. il. 8°, ea., $1; bds., 75 c. Cassell.

Bo-peep ser. 6 v. '10(D) ea., bds., 20 c. Cassell.

Borchardt, Edn. Montefiore, comp.
North Atlantic coast fisheries arbitration; coastal waters; English translations of extracts from works of French, German, Austrian, Argentinian, Spanish, Swiss, Russian, Italian and Belgian publicists; comp. by Edn. M. Borchardt, for use before the Permanent Court of Arbitration at the Hague, assembled under the provisions of the special agreement between the United States of America and Great Britain, concluded January 27, 1909. '10 (D) 4+362 p. 8°. Gov. Pr. Off.
Short biographical notices.

Borchers, Johannes Albert Wilhelm.
Electric furnaces: production of heat from electrical energy, and the construction of electric furnaces; tr. by H: G. Solomon. '08(O3) il. O. *$2.50 net. Longmans.

Borden, G: Rome.
Physical training for the school and class room (suitable for between desks.) '09 (D25) c. il. por. 12°, (Spalding's athletic lib.) pap., 10 c. Am. Sports.

BORDER (The).
See Scotland.

Border of the lake. Lee, *Mrs.* A. $1 net. Sherman, F.

Borderland and the blue beyond. Day, L. C. $2.50. Saalfield.

Borderland studies. v. 2. Gould, G: M. $2. Blakiston.

Bordet, Jules.
Studies in immunity; collected and tr. by F: P. Gay. '09(O30) c. 8°, $6. Wiley.

Bordwell, Wa. Percy.
Law of war between belligerents. '08 (D) c. 24+374 p. 8°, $3.50. Callaghan.

BORGHESE, Pauline Bonaparte, *Princess of Guastalla.*
See Bonaparte family.

Borgmeyer, C: J.
Halley's comet; lecture del. at St. Louis, Mo., Jan. 25, 1910. [1910.] (O) 43 p. il. diagrs., 8°, (St. Louis Univ. bull.) (Priv. pr.) St. Louis Univ.

Boris in Russia. McDonald, *Mrs.* E. A. B. 60 c. Little, B. & Co.

Bornemann, Friedrich Wilhelm Bernhard, and others.
Jesus as a problem, teacher, personality and force; author. tr. by G: W: Gilmore. '10(O22) c. D. $1 net. Funk.

BORNEO.
Walker, H. W. Wanderings among South Sea savages and in Borneo and the Philippines. $2.50 net. Scribner.
See also Tidong language.

Bornier, Vicomte Henri de.
La fille de Roland; ed., with introd. and notes, by C. A. Nelson. '09(Ja16) c. S. 30 c. Heath.

Borrow, G: H:
Works. Uniform ed. In 5 v. '08(Je27) 24°, *$2.50 net, boxed; flex. leath., *$3.50 net, boxed. Lane.

BORROW, George Henry.
Walling, R. A. J: George Borrow, the man and his works. *$1.75 net. Cassell.

Borrowed baby. Brock, L. 75 c. Badger.

"Borrowings" ser. 12°. Dodge.
—Brooks, *comp.* Old friends are best. $1.25; $2.

Borsodi, W:, ed.
Advertisers cyclopedia of selling phrases. '09(Je12) c. il. 4°, $15. Adv. Cyclo.
Financial advertising. '09(Je12) $2. Adv. Cyclo.

BORTON FAMILY.
See Genealogies: Mason, F. C.

Bosanketh, E:
Pharisee and the publican. '10(D31) c. O. B'way Pub.

Bosanquet, W: Cecil, M.D.
Serums, vaccines and toxins, in treatment and diagnosis. [1910.] (My) 344 p. 8°, $2 net. Funk.

—, and Clogg, Herbert Sherwell.
Stomach, intestines and pancreas; ed. by Ja. Cantlie. '10(F) 673 p. il. 12°, (Medico-Chirurgical ser.) *$4 net. Wood.

Bosch, Mrs. Hermann.
Bible stories told to "Toddles." '10(Ap2) c. front. D. 80 c. net. Longmans.
Bridget. '08(My9) c. il. D. $1.50. B. W. Dodge.

Bosher, Mrs. Kate Lee Langley.
Mary Cary, "frequently Martha." '10(F19) c. front. D. **$1 net. Harper.

BOSNIA, Austria Hungary.
Holbach, *Mrs.* M. M. Bosnia and Herzegovina. *$1.50 net. Lane.

Boss, Lewis.
Preliminary general catalogue of 6188 stars for the epoch 1900, including those visible to the naked eye and other well-determined stars; prep. at the Dudley Observatory, Albany, N. Y. '10(My7) Q. pap., $7. Carnegie.

Boss, W: Leslie.
Hist. of the panic of 1907, its origin and mainspring. '09(S) $1. Boss.

Bosse, G: von.
Das deutsche element in den Vereinigten Staaten unter besonderer berücksichtigung seines politischen, ethischen, sozialen und erzieherischen einflusses. Preisgekröte schrift. '08(D5) c. il. O. $3. Lemcke.

Bossuet, Rev. Jacques Benigne.
Oraisons funèbres. '08(D12) 12°, (Les classiques français illustrés.) limp leath., *$1 net. Putnam.

"Boston," pseud.
See Lindsay, Forbes.

Boston, Ben, pseud.
See Magill, Harry Byron.

Boston, Rev. S. L.
Baptism: its significance and mode. '08 (F8) c. T. pap., 5 c. Presb. bd.

Boston. First Church. John Cotton, 1582-1633-1652; exercises at the unveiling of the John Cotton memorial in the Berkeley street edifice of the First Church in Boston, Thursday, Oct. 10, 1907. '08, [1909.] (Mr) 64 p. front. il. 8°. $1. C. H. Shriver.

Boston. Public Library. Catalogue of the Allen A. Brown collection of music in the Public Library. v. 1, pt. 1, A-Boosey. '08 (Jl11) f°, pap., $1. Boston Pub. Lib.

Boston. Public Library. Helps in the public library to the study of the hist. of Boston in the public schools. '10(Ja15) 8°, gratis. Boston Pub. Lib.

BOSTON, Mass.
Ayer, M. F. Early days on Boston Common. $4 net. C: E. Goodspeed.
Ayer, M. F., *comp.* Check-list of Boston newspapers, 1704-1780. $3.50. Colonial Soc. of Mass.
Benton, J. H: Story of the old Boston town house, 1658-1711. (Priv. pr.) Merrymount.
Boston. Public Library. Helps in the public library to the study of the hist. of Boston in the public schools. gratis. Boston Pub. Lib.
Cashin's Theatre Ticket Office. Boston theatres and halls with hist. notes. 25 c. W. B. Jones.
Chamberlain, M. Documentary hist. of Chelsea, incl. the Boston precincts of Winnisimmet, Rumney Marsh, and Pullen Point, 1624-1824. 2 v. $5. Mass. Hist. Soc.
Conrad, A. Z., *ed.* Boston's awakening: acct. of great Boston revival. 50 c. King's Business.

BOSTON, Mass.—*Continued.*
Crawford, M. C. Old Boston days and ways.—Romantic days in old Boston. ea., $2.50 net. Little, B. & Co.
Crawford, M. C. St. Botolph's Town: account of old Boston in colonial days. $2.50; $6. L. C. Page.
Cutter, W: R., *ed.* Genealogical and personal memoirs rel. to the families of Boston and eastern Mass. Lewis Pub.
Drake, S: A. Old Boston taverns and tavern clubs. 50 c. W. A. Butterfield.
Getchell, E. L. Field trips in the Boston Basin. 60 c. net. Little, B. & Co.
Howe, M. A. D. W. Boston common. $6 net. Houghton M.
Lovett, J. De W. Old Boston boys and the games they played. **$1.50 net. Little, B. & Co.
Murdock, H., *ed.* 1872: letters written by a gentleman in Boston to his friend in Paris describing the great fire. *$5 net. Houghton M.
Pinanski, A. E. Street railway system of metropolitan Boston. *$1 net. McGraw.
Pratt, W. M. Burning of Chelsea. $1.50. Sampson.
State Street Trust Co. Collection of interesting and historic prints. gratis. State St. Trust Co.
See also Checkley, Samuel;—Emanuel Church;—Leland Powers School;—Tavern Club.

Boston & Maine Railroad. Outdoors in New England. '09, [1910.] (Ja) c. 92 p. il. 8°. (Add. pubs. for price.) Boston & Maine.

Boston Association for the Relief and Control of Tuberculosis. Narrative of the work done in a year; fifth annual report, Nov. 1, 1907, to Oct. 31, 1908. '09(My8) il. O. pap., 15 c. Boston Assoc Tuberculosis.

BOSTON MUSEUM OF FINE ARTS, Boston.
Addison, *Mrs.* J. de W. G. Boston Museum of Fine Arts; giving a descriptive and critical account of its treasures. $3. L. C. Page.
Okabe-Kakuya. Museum of Fine Arts: Japanese sword guards. $1.25. Boston Museum.

BOSTON OPERA HOUSE, Boston.
Jackson, F. H. Monograph of the Boston Opera House. (Add. pub. for price.) W. A. Butterfield.

Boston Public Library. Abraham Lincoln, Feb. 12, 1809-Apr. 15, 1865; a short list of books for school use cont. in the Public Library of the city of Boston. '09(Mr) no paging, D. pap., gratis. Boston Pub. Lib.

Boston Public Library. Brief list of books for home reading for boys and girls in the Public Library; comp. by a committee of the Boston Home and School Association. '09(Mr13) D. pap., gratis. Boston Pub. Lib.

Boston. Public Library. Finding lists of fairy tales and folk stories in books at the branches of the Public Library. '09(Ja23) 8°, pap., 5 c. Boston Pub. Lib.

Boston. Public Library. List of the books forming the gift of Louise Chandler Moulton to the Public Library of the city of Boston. '09(D) 26 p. 4°. (Not for sale.) Boston Pub. Lib.

BOSTON PUBLIC LIBRARY.
Benton, J. H: Working of the Boston Public Library. (Not for sale.) J. H: Benton.

Boston School Committee. Rept. of the Commission appointed by the School Committee of the city of Boston to investigate the problem of tuberculosis among school children. '09(N) 11 p. il. 8°. (Not for sale.) Bost. Sch. Com.

BOSTON TERRIER.
See Dogs.

BOSTON THEATRE, Boston, Mass.
Tompkins, E., *and* Kilby, I., *comps.* Hist. of the Boston Theatre, 1854-1901. **$5 net; $15. Houghton M.

Bostwick, Arth. Elmore.
American public library. '10(Je25) il. D. $1.50 net, Appleton.

Bostwick, Mrs. Lizzie E.
See O'Brien, Fk. G:

Bosville, Godfrey.
Horses, horsemen and stable management. '08(O24) il. 8°, hf. leath., *$2 net. Dutton.

Boswell, C. S.
Irish precursor of Dante: study on the vision of heaven and hell ascribed to the eighth century Irish Saint Adamnan; with tr. of the Irish text. '08(D19) 12°, (Grimm lib.) *$3.50 net. Scribner.

Boswell, Ja.
Life of Johnson. In 2 v. '08(D19) front. 12°, (Crowell's thin paper sets.) $2.50; hf. mor., $3. boxed. Crowell.
Life of Johnson; ed. by Augustine Birrell. In 6 v. '09(Je19) fronts. por. D. $5. Dodge.
Life of Johnson. 2 v. '08(O10) 12°, (Best books ser.) leath., ea., *$1 net. Dutton.
Life of Samuel Johnson; newly ed., with notes, by Roger Ingpen. In 2 v. '09 (O16) Q. *$6 net. Sturgis & W.
Tour in the Hebrides with Dr. Johnson. '09(Mr27) 16°, (Everyman's lib.) *35 c. net; leath., *70 c. net. Dutton.

Bosworth, E: Increase, D.D.
Christ in everyday life. '10(Je4) c. 16°, 75 c. Y. M. C. A.
Modern interpretation of the call to the ministry. '09(Mr) c. 21 p. 12°, (Claims and opportunities of the Christian ministry.) 10 c. Y. M. C. A.
New studies in Acts. '09(Ja23) c. 8°, 75 c.; pap., 50 c. Y. M. C. A.
Weak church and the strong man. '09(Mr) c. 11 p. 12°, (Claims and opportunities of the Christian ministry.) 5 c. Y. M. C. A.

—, and Hutchinson, Reno.
Working together: the [Y. M. C. A.] Association and the church; introd. by Fred. B. Smith. '08(Ag22) c. 12°, 40 c. Y. M. C. A.

Bosworth, G: F.
Essex. [1910.] (My) 8+168 p. 8°, (Cambridge county geographies.) 45 c. Putnam.
Kent. [1910.] (My) 8+146 p. 8°, (Cambridge county geographies.) 45 c. Putnam.

Bosworth, G: F.—*Continued.*
Surrey. [1910.] (My) 8+152 p. 8°, (Cambridge county geographies.) 45 c. Putnam.
Sussex. [1910.] (My) 8+144 p. 8°, (Cambridge county geographies.) 45 c. Putnam.

Bosworth psalter. Gasquet, F. A. *$4.50 net. Macmillan.

BOTANISTS.
Rydberg, P. A. Scandinavians who have contributed to the knowledge of the flora of North America. $1. Augustana.

BOTANY.
Aaronsohn, A. Agricultural and botanical explorations in Palestine. Gov. Pr. Off.
Adams, C: C. Ecological survey of Isle Royale, Lake Superior. 85 c. Mich. Geol.
Atkinson, G: F. Botany for high schools. $1.25. Holt.
Atwood, A. C., *comp.* Catalogue of botanical lib. of J: Donnell Smith presented to Smithsonian Institution. 25 c. U. S., Supt. of Docs.
Bailey, L. H. Beginner's botany. **60 c. net. Macmillan.
Baily, W. L. Trees, plants and flowers. 60 c. Lippincott.
Bergen, J. Y. Essentials of botany. $1.20. Ginn.
Bessey, C: E. Botany for high schools and colleges. $2.20. Holt.
Bower, F: O. Origin of a land flora. *$5.50 net. Macmillan.
Brandegee, T. S. Plantae Mexicanae purpusianae. 15 c.—Plantae Mexicanae purpusianae, II. 10 c. Univ. of Cal.
Britton, N. L. Genus *Ernodea:* study of species and races.—Taxonomic aspect of the species question. ea., 25 c. N. Y. Botanical.
Caldwell, O. W: High school course in botany. gratis. C. P. Cary.
Cannon, W: A., *and* Knox, A. A. Topography of the *chlorophyll* apparatus in desert plants; [also] Induction, development, and heritability of fascinations. 75 c. Carnegie.
Chase, A. Plant babies and their cradles. 40 c. Educ. Pub.
Clute, W. N. Lab'y botany for the high school. 75 c. Ginn.
Coulter, J: M. New manual of botany of the central Rocky Mountains (vascular plants). $2.50. Am. Bk.
Coulter, J: M., *and* Chamberlain, C: J. Morphology of gymnosperms. $4 net. Univ. of Chic.
Coulter, J. M., *and others.* Textbook of botany for colleges and universities. $2. Am. Bk.
Darbishire, O. V. Plant book for schools. *$1 net. Macmillan.
Darwin, F., *and* Acton, E. H. Practical physiology of plants. *$1.25 net. Putnam.
Davenport, E. Domesticated animals and plants. $1.25.—Principles of breeding. $2.50 Ginn.

BOTANY.—*Continued.*

Densmore, H. D. Origin, structure and function of the polar caps in *smilacina amplexicaulis, Nutt.* 35 c. Univ. of Cal.

De Vries, H. Mutation theory. In 2 v. v. 1, $4 net; v. 2, $3 net. Open Court.

Dragendorff, J. G. N. Plant analysis, qualitative and quantitative. *$3.50 net. Stechert.

Druce, G: C., *comp.* List of British plants containing the *Spermophytes, Pteridophytes* and *Charads.* 85 c. Oxford Univ.

Elliott, G: F. S. Botany of to-day. *$1.50 net.—Wonders of the plant world. 75 c. Lippincott.

Farrer, R. J. Alpines and bog plants. $4. Longmans.

Furneaux, W: S. Field and woodland plants. *$1.50 net. Longmans.

Ganong, W: F. Laboratory course in plant physiology. $1.75. Holt.

Ganong, W: F Teaching botanist. $1.25 net. Macmillan.

Gardner, N. L. Leuvenia, a new genus of flagellates. 10 c. Univ. of Cal.

Graves, C: B., *and others.* Catalogue of the flowering plants and ferns of Connecticut. 75 c. Conn. Lib.

Gray, A. New manual of botany. $2.50; $3. Am. Bk.

Green, J. R. Botany. 50 c. net. Appleton.

Green, J. R. Hist. of botany, 1860-1900. $3.15. Oxford Univ.

Greene, E: L. Landmarks of botanical history. 65 c. Smith Inst.

Greenman, J. M. New or noteworthy spermatophytes from Mexico, Central America and the West Indies. 50 c. Field Museum.

Haig, H. A. Plant cell; its modifications and vital processes. $2 net. Lippincott.

Hall, H. M. Compositæ of southern California. $3. Univ. of Cal.

Harding, A. R. Ginseng and other medicinal plants. $1. A. R. Harding.

House, H. D. North American species of the genus *Ipomœa.* 35 c. Columbia Univ.

House, H. D. Studies in North American *Convolvulacae.* IV., Genus *Exogonium.* 25 c. N. Y. Botanical.

Jackson, J. Catalogue of the flowering plants and ferns of Worcester Co., Mass. $1. Worcester Nat. Hist.

Jepson, W. L. Flora of California. In about 15 pts. pt. 1, 90 c.; pt. 2, 80 c. Cunningham, C. & W.

Jepson, W. L. Synopsis of the North American godetias. 40 c. Univ. of Cal.

Jordan, D: S., *and* Kellogg, V. L. Scientific aspects of Luther Burbank's work. *$1.75 net. A. M. Robertson.

Kent, G: H. Ware collection of Blaschka glass flower models; [in the Agassiz Museum, Cambridge, Mass.] 35 c. G: H. Kent.

Knuth, P. Hdbk. of flower pollination. 3 v. v. 1, $6.75; v. 2, $10.75; v. 3, $9.75. Oxford Univ.

Kraemer, H: Text-book of botany and pharmacognosy. **$5 net. Lippincott.

BOTANY.—*Continued.*

Lloyd, F. E. Physiology of stomata. $1.50. Carnegie.

MacDougal, D. T. Botanical features of North American deserts. $1.75. Carnegie.

Massee, G: Diseases of cultivated plants and trees. $2.25 net. Macmillan.

Meier, W. H. D. Plant study and plant description. 75 c. Ginn.

Millspaugh, C: F: Prænunciæ Bahamenses-2; contribs. to a flora of the Bahamian Archipelago. 50 c. Field Museum.

Osterhout, W. J. V. Value of sodium to plants by reason of its protective action; [also] On the effects of certain poisonous gases of plants. 10 c. Univ. of Cal.

Pammel, L: H. Manual of poisonous plants. $2.50. Torch Press.

Pammel, L: H. Talk on weeds. 50 c. L. H. Pammel.

Pond, R. H. Further studies of solution, tension and toxicity in lipolysis: [effect of chemicals on plants.] 25 c. N. Y. Botanical.

Richards, H. M. Botany: [lecture.] 25 c. Macmillan.

Robinson, C: B. *Alabastra philippinensia.* 25 c. N. Y. Botanical.

Schaffner, J: H: Lab'y outlines for general botany. 75 c. J: H. Schaffner.

Scott, D. H: Introduction to structural botany. 2 pts. pt. 1, Flowering plants; pt. 2, Flowerless plants. ea., *$1 net. Macmillan.

Shallow, E: B., *and* Cullen, W. T. Nature study made easy. *40 c. net. Macmillan.

Shull, G: H. Bursa bursa-pastoris and bursa heegeri biotypes and hybrids. (Add. Institution for price.) Carnegie.

Solreder, H. Systematic anatomy of the dicotyledons: hdbk. for laboratories of pure and applied botany. In 2 v. $8.75. Oxford Univ.

Spalding, V. M. Distribution and movements of desert plants. $2. Carnegie.

Spruce, R: Notes of a botanist on the Amazon and Andes. 2 v. $6.50. Macmillan.

Standley, P. C. Allioniaceae of the United States with notes on the Mexican species. U. S., Supt. of Docs.

Stevens, F. L., *and* Hall, J: G. Diseases of economic plants. $2 net. Macmillan.

Stevens, G: T: Illustrated guide to flowering plants. $2.50 net. Dodd.

Stevens, W: C. Plant anatomy from the standpoint of the development and functions of the tissues and hdbk. of microtechnic. $2 net. Blakiston.

Stopes, M. C. Ancient plants. $2 net. Van Nostrand.

Strasburger, E. Hdbk. of practical botany. *$2.50 net. Macmillan.

Strasburger, E., *and others.* Text-book of botany. *$5 net. Macmillan.

Tilden, J. E. Minnesota *Algæ.* $1. F: E. Clements.

BOTANY.—*Continued.*
United States. *Dept. of Agriculture. Bu. of Plant Industry.* New methods of plant breeding. (Add. Superintendent for price.) U. S., Supt. of Docs.
Walcon, G: L. Practical guide to the wild flowers and fruits. **$1.50 net. Lippincott.
Ward, J: J. Life histories of familiar plants. *$1.75 net. Cassell.
Warming, J. E. B. Oecology of plants. $2.90. Oxford Univ.
Weed, C. M. Wild flower families. **$1 net. Lippincott.
White, J. H. On polystely in roots of *Orchidaceae.* 50 c. Univ. of Toronto.
Willis, J: C. Manual and dict. of the flowering plants and ferns. *$2.75 net. Putnam.
See also Agriculture; — Bacteria; — Biology; — Clover; — Evergreens; — Evolution;—Ferns;—Flowers;—Forests and forestry;—Fruit;—Fungi;—Gardens and gardening;—Grafting;—Heredity;—Histology; — Lichens; — Mistletoe; — Mosses;—Mushrooms; — Nature; — Orchids; — Paleontology;—Seaweeds; —Sumach;—Trees;—Willows;—*also* names of countries and places.

BOTANY SCHOOL, Cambridge, Eng.
See Cambridge University.

Both sides of the veil. Robbins, A. M. *$1.25 net. Sherman, F.

Botsford, G: Willis.
Roman assemblies, from their origin to the end of the Republic. '09(O2) c. O. **$4 net. Macmillan.

Böttcher, Anton.
Cranes; tr. and supplemented with foreign practice by A. Tolhausen. '09(My) 577 p. il. 4°, *$10 net. Van Nostrand.

Botticelli, Sandro.
Masterpieces. '08(D19) T. (Painters' ser.) pap., *25 c. net; leath., *75 c. net. Stokes.

BOTTICELLI, Sandro.
Binns, H: B. Botticelli. *65 c. net. Stokes.
Cust, R. H. H. Botticelli. 50 c.; $1. Macmillan.
Davey, R: Botticelli. *$2 net. Doran.
Schaeffer, E. Sandro Botticelli. $1.50 net; $1.75 net. Caldwell.

Bottle in the smoke. Carlos, *Mrs.* L. C. D-. $1.50. Fenno.

Bottome, Mrs. Marg.
Heart to heart letters; extracts from letters of Marg. Bottome to a son. '10 (Ja8) c. 12°, $1. Doran.

Bottome, Willard Bodine.
Stenographic expert. '10(D31) c. 8°, $2. W. B. Bottome.

Bottomley, Gordon.
Riding to Lithend. '10(D) 16°, (Lyric garland.) pap., 50 c. net; Japan vel., $1 net, boxed. T: B. Mosher.
Vision of Giorgione; three variations on Venetian themes. '10(Je18) c. 12°, $1.50. T: B. Mosher.

Bottone, Selino Romeo.
Amateur electrician's workshop; hdbk. of pract. instruction. New and enl. ed. '10 (Jl30) il. D. 75 c. McKay.
Electrical engineering for students. In 2 v. v. 1, pt. 1, Magnetism and magnetic apparatus; pt. 2, Static electrical instruments; v. 2, Modern dynamos and batteries for amateurs and students. '10 (Ag6) il. D. ea., 75 c. McKay.
Ignition devices for motors. New ed., thoroughly rev. and enl. '10(Jl30) D. 75 c. McKay.
Magnetos for automobiles; how made and how used. '09(My) 88 p. il. 12°, *$1 net. Van Nostrand.

Boucher, J: Newton, ed.
Century and a half of Pittsburg and her people. 4 v. '08. c. il. pors. 4°, ea., 25 c. Lewis Pub.

Boucicault, Dion.
London assurance; comedy in five acts; acting version of Yale Dramatic Assoc. '10(Ja22) pors. O. 50 c.; pap., 25 c. P. Roberts.

Bouët-Willaumez, Comte Louis Edouard.
Batailles de terre et de mer jusques et y compris la bataille de L'Alma; ed. by A. H. Smith. '08(N21) D. (Oxford modern French ser.) 60 c. Oxford Univ.

Bouffons (Les). *See* Zamacoïs, Miguel.

Bougaud, Abbé L: Victor Emile.
History of St. Vincent de Paul, founder of the Congregation of the Mission (Vincentians), and of the Sisters of Charity; tr. from the 2d French ed. by the Rev. Jos. Brady; with an introd. by the Cardinal Archbishop of Westminster. 2 v. in 1. '08(Mr21) D. *$1.50 net. Longmans.

Bouillane de Lacoste, Emile Antoine Henri de.
Around Afghanistan; with preface by Georges Leygues; tr. from the French by J. G. Anderson. '10(My14) il. pors. maps. 8°, $3 special net. Appleton.

Boulger, Demetrius C: de Kavanagh.
Life of Sir Halliday Macartney, commander of Li Hung Chang's trained force in the Taeping Rebellion. '08(Je27) 8°, *$6 net. Lane.

Boulger, G: Simonds.
Wood: manual of the natural history and industrial applications of the timbers of commerce. 2d ed., rev. and enl. '08 (Mr28) O. $4.20. Longmans.

Boult, Ella M., and Stevens, Beatrice.
Book of happy days. '10(O8) c. f°, bds., $3. Pomfret.

Boulting, T:
Woman in Italy; from the introduction of the chivalrous service of love to the appearance of the professional actress. '10 (D3) il. 8°, $4 net. Brentano's.

Boulton, W: B.
In the days of the Georges. '10(My7) il. 8°, $4. Pott.

BOUNTIES.
Bailey, V. Key to animals on which wolf and coyote bounties are often paid. (Add. Superintendent for price.) U. S., Supt. of Docs.

Bouquet of rhymes. Randolph, A. *$1.50 net. Bonnell.

BOURBON, Charles, *Duc de.*
Hare, C. Charles de Bourbon, High Constable of France. $4 net. Lane.

Bourbon restoration. Hall, J: R. *$4 net. Houghton M.

Bourgeois (Le) gentilhomme. *See* Molière, J. B. P.

Bourgeois (The). Stacpoole, H: De V. $1. Brentano's.

Bourget, Paul Charles Joseph.
Un saint; ed. by Cloudesley Brereton. '10 (D24) 16°, (Macmillan's new ser. of French texts.) 35 c. net. Macmillan.
Weight of the name [*L'émigré*]; tr. from the French by G: Burnham Ives. '08 (Mr28) c. D. †$1.50. Little, B. & Co.
See also My favorite novelist.

Bourhill, Mrs. E. J., and Drake, Mrs. J. B., comps.
Fairy tales from South Africa. '08(O17) il. 12°, (Golden ser. of il. juvenile books.) $1.50. Macmillan.

BOURIGNON, Antoinette.
Macewen, A. R. Antoinette Bourignon, quietist. $1.25 net. Doran.

BOURIGNONISTS.
See Bourignon, Antoinette.

Bourne, Fk. A., Holst, H. V. v., and Brown, Fk. Chouteau.
Architectural drawing and lettering. *See* American School of Correspondence.

Bourne, G:
Ascending effort. '10(Jl16) 12°, $1.50 net. Dutton.

Bourne, Gilbert C.
Comparative anatomy of animals. v. 1. 2d ed. '09(S4) price raised from *$1.10 net to *$1.40 net. Macmillan.
Herbert Spencer and animal evolution; Herbert Spencer lecture del. at the Museum on the 2d December, 1909. '10 (Mr26) O. pap., 50 c. Oxford Univ.

Bourne, Jonathan, jr.
Popular v. delegated government; speech in the Senate of the United States, Thursday, May 5, 1910. '10(O) 16 p. 8°. Gov. Pr. Off.

Bourrienne, Louis Antoine Fauvelet de.
Memoirs of Napoleon. 2 v. '10(D) il. $2.50, boxed. Crowell.

Bousset, Wilhelm.
Faith of a modern Protestant; tr. by F. B. Low. '09(F6) c. D. **75 c. net. Scribner.

BOUTWELL, George Sewall.
Thayer, W: R., *and* Warren, W. Commemorative exercises in connection with the erection of a memorial tablet to George Sewall Boutwell. gratis. W. Warren.

Bouvet, Marie Marguerite.
Clotilde. '08(O10) c. il. D. $1.25. McClurg.

Bouyer, Achille, jr.
See Moure, Jean Gabriel Emile.

Bovill, W. B. Forster.
Hungary and the Hungarians. '08(D5) il. O. *$2 net. McClure.

Bowden-Smith, Alice Georgette.
English student's wander-year in America. '10(Ap2) D. $1.50 net. Longmans.

Bowditch, C: Pickering.
The numeration, calendar systems and astronomical knowledge of the Mayas. '10 (Jl) 16+346 p. il. tabs., (partly fold.,) 4°. (Priv. pr.) Univ. Press.
Bibliography (4 p.).

Bowditch, Nathaniel.
Extracts from American pract. navigator; epitome of navigation and nautical astronomy. '10(N) 92 p. 4°. Gov. Pr. Off.

Bowdoin, W: Goodrich.
The bunch of violets. '07, [1908.] (Mr.) c. 20 p. front. D. pap., $1. W: G. Bowdoin.

Bowen, Edn. Winfield.
Makers of American literature. '08(F15) c. O. *$2.50 net. Neale.
Questions at issue in our English speech. '09(Ap3) c. 12°, $1. B'way Pub.

Bowen, G: Oscar.
Teacher's manual of music for elem. schools; the aims, course of study, lesson plans, studies in written work and definitions. [1910.] (F) 51 p. O. pap., 25 c. G: O. Bowen.

Bowen, Marjorie, [**pseud. for Gabriella Vere Campbell.**]
Leopard and the lily. '09(S11) c. D. $1.25. fixed. Doubleday, P.
Sword decides. '08(Ap25) c. D. †$1.50. McClure.

Bowen, Wilbur Pardon.
Teaching of elem. school gymnastics. '10 (F5) c. il. 8°, $1. Bassette.

Bower, B. M., [pseud. for B. M. Sinclair.]
Happy Family. '10(Ap30) c. front. D. $1.25. G: W. Dillingham.
Lonesome trail. '09(Mr20) c. front. D. †$1.25. G: W. Dillingham.
Long shadow. '09(O30) c. il. D. †$1.25. G: W. Dillingham.

Bower, F.
Dictionary of economic terms. '08(D19) 32°, (Miniature reference lib.) leath., 50 c. Dutton.

Bower, F: Orpen.
Origin of a land flora. '08(Mr7) il. 8°, *$5.50 net. Macmillan.

Bowers, Mary Berry.
Dorothy and her wardrobe; just how to make the things a good doll should have. '09(O2) c. il. 12°, (School arts booklets.) pap., 35 c. Davis Press.

BOWERY.
See New York City.

Bowes, Alpin Marshall.
Time to strike; or, our nation's curse '08 (D) c. 151 p. 12°, 50 c. Pentecostal.

Bowie, A: Jesse, jr.
Practical irrigation: its value and cost. '08 (Jl11) c. il. O. *$3 net. McGraw.

Bowker, R: Rogers, ed.
State publications. In 4 pts. pt. 4, Southern states. '09(F27) c. O. pap., $10, for complete work. Pub. Weekly.

Bowker, W: H.
Plant food; its sources, conservation, preparation and application. 2d ed. '10 (Mr26) c. O. 25 c.; pap., gratis. W: H. Bowker.

Bowker, W: Rushton.
Dynamo, motor and switchboard circuits. 2d ed., greatly enl. '09(My) 180 p. il. 8°, *$2.50 net. Van Nostrand.

Bowles, Emily.
Auriel Selwode. '08(D12) 8°, *$1.60 net. Herder.

Bowles, J. D.
Acteylene for lighting country houses. '10 (D) 34 p. il. plans, 8°, (Univ. of Missouri, Engineering Experiment Station. bull.) Univ. of Mo.

Bowles, Ja. Ten Broeck.
See Davis, G: Jacob, *jr.*

Bowles, J: Hooper.
See Dawson, W: Leon.

Bowles, Oliver.
Tables for the determination of common rocks. '10(S17) c. 16°, (Van Nostrand's science ser.) 50 c. Van Nostrand.

BOWLING.
Greig, J. W. Game of bowling on the green or lawn bowls. 10 c. Am. Sports.
See also Games.

Bowman, E: S.
Bible doctrine of devotion. '09(O) 16°, (Devotional ser.) *20 c. net. Un. B. Pub.

Bowman, Frederic Hungerford.
Structure of the cotton fibre in its relation to technical applications. '08(My9) il. 12°. *$2.75 net. Macmillan.
Structure of the wool fibre, and its relation to the use of wool for technical purposes. '08(N21) il. 12°, *$2.60 net. Macmillan.

Bowman, G: T:
Our military rifle and how to use it. '09 (S) c. 22 p. il. 24°, pap., 10 c. Arms and the Man.

Bowman, Isaiah, and Reeds, Chester Albert.
Water resources of the East St. Louis district. '07, [1908.] (Jl) 10+130 p. il. map, 8°, (Ill. State Geolog. Survey bull.) pap. (Add. pub. for price.) Univ. of Ill.

Bowman, Melville Le Roy, and Crossley, Bruce W:
Corn: growing, judging, breeding, feeding, marketing. '09(Jl31) c. il. fold. map, fold. tab., 8°, price reduced from $2.50 to $2. Bowman & C.

Bowman, Bp. T:
Great salvation. '09(Ap) c. 127 p. 12°, (Albright ser.) 50 c. Pub. Ho. of Evangelical Assoc.

Bowman's illustrated lib. of world-favorite books. il. D. $1. Bowman.
—Aguilar. Days of Bruce.
—Andersen. Fairy tales.
—Arabian nights' entertainment.
—Ballantyne. Dog Crusoe.
—Bunyan. Pilgrim's progress.
—Cervantes. Life and adventures of Don Quixote.
—Craik. John Halifax.
—Defoe. Life and adventures of Robinson Crusoe.
—Grimm. Fairy tales.
—Hughes. Tom Brown's schooldays.
—Lamb. Tales from Shakespeare.
—Marryat. Masterman Ready.
—Poe. Tales of mystery and imagination.
—Reid. Scalp-hunters.

Bowman's il. lib. world-favorite books.—Cont.
—Stowe. Uncle Tom's cabin.
—Swift. Gulliver's travels.
—Thackeray. Henry Esmond.
—Warner. Wide, wide world.
—Wyss *and* Montolieu. Swiss family Robinson.

Bowne, Borden Parker.
Essence of religion. '10(D3) c. D. $1.50 net. Houghton M.
Personalism. '08(Mr7) c. O. (N. W. Harris lectures for 1907, Northwestern Univ.) **$1.50 net. Houghton, M. & Co.
Philosophy of Christian Science. '08(O17) c. S. pap., *10 c. net. Eaton & M.
Studies in Christianity. '09(Mr20) c. D. **$1.50 net. Houghton M.

BOWNE, Borden Parker.
Pyle, C: P. Philosophy of Borden Parker Bowne, and its application to the religious problem. $1 net. S. F. Harriman.

Bownocker, J: Adams, Lord, Nathaniel Wright, and Somermeier, E. E.
Coal: pt. 1, Coals of the Monongahela formation or upper productive coal measures; pt. 2, Chemical tests of the Clarion, lower Kittanning, middle Kittanning and upper Freeport coals. '08, [1909.] (Ap) 12+342 p. il. fold. maps, 8°, (Ohio; Geological Survey; 4th ser., bull.) pap., 50 c. Ohio Geol.

Bowron, Eliz. Moore, [Mrs. H: S. Bowron.]
Our flag: its history and what it stands for. '08(Je13) c. D. pap., 50 c. H: S. Bowron.

Bowron, Mrs. H: S.
See Bowron, *Mrs.* Eliz. Moore.

Box, G: Herbert.
See Oesterley, W: Oscar Emil.

BOX.
See Evergreens.

Box furniture. Brigham, L. **$1.60 net. Century Co.

Box of oil. *See* Eccles, L. F. Trumpet voice from the throne.

Box of treasure. Carradine, B. $1. Chr. Witness.

Boxelder (*acer negundo*). '09(Je) 3 p. 8°, (U. S., Dept. of Agriculture, Forest Service, forest planting leaflet.) pap. (Add. Superintendent for price.)

BOXING.
McFadden, G: Blocking and hitting. 10 c. R: K. Fox.
O'Hara, B. From Figg to Johnson; complete hist. of the heavy-weight championship. $1. Blossom Bk.
See also Johnson, Jack;—Roosevelt, Theodore.

Boy aeronaut's club. Lamar, A. 60 c. Reilly & B.

Boy and a secret. Jacberns, R. $1.25. Lippincott.

Boy and the books. Poucher, *Mrs.* F. H. 75 c. Kimball Press.

Boy aviators ser. *See* Lawton, Wilbur.

Boy chum ser. il. 12°. Burt
—Ely. Young plume hunters. $1.

Boy explorer ser. il. D. †$1.50. Stokes.
—Dimock. Dick in the Everglades.

Boy fortune hunter ser. *See* Akers, Floyd.

Boy forty-niners. McNeil, E. †$1.50. McClure.

Boy from the ranch. Webster, F. V. 35 c. Cupples & L.

Boy geologist at school. Houston, E. J. †$1. Altemus.

Boy hunters ser. il. 12°. Cupples & L.
—Stratemeyer. Out with gun and camera. 60 c.

Boy Jesus. Myers, C. **60 c. net. Am. Bapt.

Boy life. Howells, W: D. 50 c. Harper.

Boy next door. Baird, J. K. 50 c. net. Am. Tr.

Boy pickets. Chipman, W: P. $1. Burt.

Boy pilot of the lakes. Webster, F. V. 35 c. Cupples & L.

Boy pioneers. Beard, D. C. **$2 net. Scribner.

Boy ranchers of Puget Sound. Bindloss, H. $1.50. Stokes.

Boy-savers' guide. Quin, G: E: *$1.35 net. Benziger.

Boy scouts. Chipman, W: P. †$1. Burt.

BOY SCOUTS OF AMERICA.
Payson, H. Boy scouts. 60 c. Hurst.
Seton, E. T., *and* Baden-Powell, *Sir* R. S. S. Boy scouts of America: hdbk. of woodcraft, scouting and life-craft; [manual for the association.] 25 c. Doubleday, P.
United States. Incorporation of the Boy Scouts of America; hearing before the Committee on Education, House of Representatives. '10(Jl) 25 p. 8°. Gov. Pr. Off.

Boy trappers. *See* Castlemon, Harry.

Boy who won. Ostrander, F. E. $1.25. L. C. Page.

Boy with the U. S. foresters. Rolt-Wheeler, F. $1.50. Lothrop, L. & S.

Boy with the U. S. Survey. Rolt-Wheeler, F. †$1.50. Lothrop, L. & S.

Boyance, Jos.
Chauffeur hdbk.; requirements for chaffeur's examination, how to drive airship, etc. '10(Ag) 78 p. 16°, 50 c. Beaver Pr.

Boyce, Sir Herbert.
Mosquito or man. '09(D) 16+268 p. 8°, *$3.50 net. Dutton.

Boyce, Neith, [pseud. for Mrs. Hutchins Hapgood.]
The bond. '08(Ap11) c. D. †$1.50. Duffield.

Boyce, Sir Rubert W:
Health, progress and administration in the West Indies. '10(Ap23) il. 8°, $3.50 net. Dutton.

Boycott, G. W. M.
Compressed air work and diving: hdbk. for engineers. '09(Ag14) il. 8°. **$4 net. Van Nostrand.

BOYCOTTING.
Schaffner, M. A. Effect of the recent boycott decisions. 25 c. Am. Acad. Pol. Sci.
See also Injunctions.

Boyd, D: French.
General W. T. Sherman as a college president; repr. from *The American College,* April, 1910. '10(D) 8 p. 8°, (La. State Univ. bull.) pap., gratis. La. State Univ.

Boyd, Rev. Fs. Leith.
Law and love: a study of "quomodo dilexi" (Psalm cxix., 97-104); with an introd. by the Bishop of London. '09(F20) D. *90 c. net. Longmans.

Boyd, Rev. Ja. Shields.
Story of Jonah, the truant prophet; told for its practical lessons by Rev. Ja. Shields Boyd; with a large part of one chapter by Rev. H: Clay Trumbull. '09 (My) c. 178 p. il. 12°, *75 c. net. J. S. Boyd.

Boyd, L., comp.
Irvines and their kin; also short sketches of their kindred, the Carlisles, McDowells, Johnstons, Maxwell, McElroys, etc.; from A.D. 373 to the present time. '08 (O3) 8°, $5; hf. mor., $10; leath., $25. Donnelly.

Boyd, Marg. A.
Wanderings; collection of beautiful thoughts comp from the poets, and of observations made by the children of the city schools under the direction of Margaret A Boyd '10(Jl) c. 143 p. col. il. 4°, 75 c. Times-News.

Boyd, R: H:, D.D.
Ancient and modern Sunday-school methods. '10(Ja22) c. bds., 25 c. Nat. Bapt.
Separate, or "Jim crow" car laws, or legislative enactments of fourteen southern states; together with the report and order of the Interstate Commerce Commission to segregate negro or "colored" passengers on railroad trains and in railroad stations. '09(Je5) S. limp bds., 25 c. Nat. Bapt. Pub.

—, and Ellington, Rev. W. S., eds.
National Baptist Sunday school lesson commentary of the International lessons for 1908. '08(F1); for 1909. '08(D26); for 1910. '10(F5) c. il. maps, O. ea., 75 c.; hf. mor., $1. Nat. Bapt. Pub.

Boyd, T: Parker.
How and why of the Emmanuel movement; hdbk. on psycho-therapeutics. '09(Jl3) c. 12°, *$1 net. Whitaker & R.

Boyden, Edna.
Odd moments: [essays.] '08(D12) 12°, 75 c.; pap., 50 c. Cochrane.

Boyer, C: Clinton.
Modern methods for teachers. '09(Ja23) c. O. $1.50. Lippincott.

Boyer, Fs. Howard.
See Dickerman, C:

Boyer, Rev. Matthew G.
Wonderful story of life and death, as written in the books of nature and revelation. '08, [1909.] (Mr) c. 8+9-390 p. 12°, $1.50. Lutheran Pub.

Boyer, Michael K.
$100,000 per year from poultry; Curtiss poultry book. '10(D31) c. il. 8°, 25 c. W. Atkinson.
Poultry secrets, gathered, tested and now disclosed. [7th ed.] '09(My) 56 p.; [8th ed.] '10(D) 64 p. c. il. 8°, ea., 25 c. W. Atkinson.

Boyer, Michael K., ed.
$6.41 per hen per year; the Corning egg book, illustrating the poultry methods originated by the late Prof. G. M. Gowell and perfected by Edward and Gardner Corning. [10th ed.] '10(D) 64 p. il. plans, 8°, 25 c. W. Atkinson.

Boyhood of Christ. *See* Wallace, Lew.

Boyhood of Lincoln. Atkinson, E. **50 c. net. McClure.

Boylan, Mrs. Grace Duffie.
Steps to Nowhere. '10(D3) c. col. il. O. $1.50. Baker & T.
Yama Yama Land, where everything is different. '09(O30) col. il. O. (Yama Yama ser.) †$1.50. Reilly & B.

—, and Morgan, Ike.
Kids of many colors. [1910.] (F) c. '09. 5-156 p. il. 8°, $1. Hurst.

Boyle, Ja.
King Edward VII. as a man and a monarch: memorial address del. at Trinity Episcopal Church, Columbus, O., evening of Sunday, May 15, 1910. '10(Je11) c. pors. O. bds., 60 c.; pap., 25 c. A. H. Smythe.

Boyle, Ja. Ernest.
Financial history of Kansas. '09(F6) O. (Univ. of Wis. bulletin; Economics and political science ser.) pap., 50 c. Univ. of Wis.
Government of North Dakota. '10(Jl9) c. il. maps, D. $1. Am. Bk.
Methods of assessment as applied to different classes of subjects. '07, [1909.] (Mr) c. pap., 7 c.; per 100, $5. Nat. Tax. Assoc.

Boyle, Mrs. Maizie Madeleine Ryan.
Quest of the Christ in New York City, and Cosmic corals. [1910.] (My) c. '09. 93 p. il. por. 8°, $1.25. B'way Pub.

Boyles, Kate and Virgil Dillin.
Homesteaders. '09(O2) c. il. O. $1.50. McClurg.
Spirit trail. '10(D3) c. col. il. O. $1.50. McClurg.

Boylston, Herbert Melville.
See Sauveur, Albert.

Boynton, C. W.
Portland cement sidewalk construction. 2d ed. '09(O16) c. il. tabs., O. pap. (Add. pubs. for price.) Universal Portland Cement.

Boynton, Percy H.
See Moody, W: Vaughn.

Boynton, Wa. Channing, and Marshall, Roy, comps.
How to use concrete. '10(Mr12) il. 8°, $1. Concrete Pub.

Boy's book of railways. Howden, J. R. $2. Stokes.

Boy's book of warships. Howden, J. R. $2. Stokes.

Boy's-eye view of the Sunday-school. Rogers, W: O. *60 c. net. S. S. Times.

Boy's Hakluyt. Bacon, E. M. $1.50. Scribner.

Boy's King Arthur. Malory, *Sir* T: $2. Scribner.

Boy's life of General Grant. Knox, T: W. $1.25. Saalfield.

Boy's Napoleon. Wheeler, H. F. B. $1.50. Crowell.

Boy's ride. Zollinger, G., *pseud.* $1.50. McClurg.

Boy's text book on gas engines. Faurote, F. L. (Add. author for price.) F. L. Faurote.

Boys.
Applied ideals in work with boys. $1. Y. M. C. A.
Boston Public Library. Brief list of books for home reading for boys and girls in the Public Library. gratis. Boston Pub. Lib.
Dickinson, G: A. Your boy, his nature and nurture. *$1 net. Doran.
Edwards, E. Personal information for boys. 50 c. Fenno.
Fiske, G: W. Boy life and self-government. $1. Y. M. C. A.
Forbush, W: B. Church work with boys. 50 c. net. Pilgrim Press.
Foster, E. C. Boy and the church. *75 c. net. S. S. Times.
Gelston, W. L. Organizations for boys. 10 c. Presb. Bd.
Green, P: How to deal with lads. 80 c. net. Longmans.
Hall, W. S. From youth into manhood. 50 c. Y. M. C. A.
Holland, R. S. Historic boyhoods. *$1.50 net. Jacobs.
Horton, C. B., *ed.* Reaching the boys of an entire community. $1. Y. M. C. A.
Jenks, J. W. Life questions of high school boys. (Add. pubs. for price.) Y. M. C. A.
Keeler, L. H. If I were a boy. *$1 net. Revell.
McKenney, A. H. Our big boys in the Sunday-school. 50 c. net. Revell.
McKeever, W: A. Better crop of boys and girls.—Teaching the boys to save. ea., gratis. W: A. McKeever.
Merrill, L. Winning the boy. *75 c. net. Revell.
Moon, E. L. Contents of the boy. $1. Jennings.
Mowry, W: A: Talks with my boys. $1. Silver.
Pell, E: L: My boy. 10 c. Harding.
Peters, W: H. Appeal to the boy. 10 c.; per 100, $5. Archive.
Quin, G: E: Boy-saver's guide: society work for boys in their teens. *$1.35 net. Benziger.
Religious work for boys. 15 c. Y. M. C. A.
Russell, C: E: B., *and* Rigby, C. M. Working lads clubs. *$1.50 net. Macmillan.
Society for the Promotion of Social Service. Juvenile delinquent and the Young Men's Christian Association. 50 c. Y. M. C. A.
Stall, S. What a young boy ought to know. $1. Vir.
Sweet, F. H. Illustrious boys of many lands. 50 c. McLoughlin.
Sweetser, K. D. Ten boys from history. $2. Duffield.
Taylor, C: K. Real letters to real boys. *50 c. net. Revell.

Boys.—*Continued.*
Trades for London boys. *25 c. net. Longmans.
"Uncle Ned," *pseud.* Little letters to boys grown tall. 80 c.; 50 c. Abbey.
Wayne, K. H. Building your boy. 50 c. net. McClurg
Willson, R. N. Nobility of boyhood. 50 c. Winston.
See also Agriculture;—Athletics;—Boy Scouts;—Camping;—Children;—Cigarettes; — Conduct of life; — Gymnastics and physical culture; — Hygiene;—Sex;—Useful arts;—Vocations;—Young men;—Young people.

Boys and girls at home. 2d year of issue. '09, [1910.] (F) 4°, $1.75, bds., $1.25. Caldwell.

Boys and girls from Dickens. Dickens, C: $2. Macaulay.

Boys and girls of seventy-seven. Smith, *Mrs.* M. P. W. †$1.25. Little, B. & Co.

Boys and girls of the White House. Sage, A. C. $1.50. Stokes.

Boys of Bellwood School. Webster, F. V. 40 c. Cupples & L.

Boys of Brookfield Academy. Eldred, W. L. $1.50. Lothrop, L. & S.

Boys of business ser. See Chapman, A.

Boys of liberty library. 30 v. '10(Je4) c. il. D. ea., 50 c. McKay.
Contents: De Morgan, J:, Cruise of the "Lively Bee"; Fighting Hal; First shot for liberty; Fooling the enemy; The hero of Ticonderoga; Into the jaws of death; Marion and his men; On to Quebec; Paul Revere; The young ambassador; The young guardsman; Hancock, Harrie Irving, Captain of the Minute Men; Harbaugh, C. T., In buff and blue; The Tory plot; Under Greene's banner; Washington's young spy; Lounsberry, Lieut., By order of the colonel; A call to duty; Fighting for freedom; In glory's van; The Quaker spy; Ralph, *Capt.* Frank, The king's messenger; Sheridan, Frank, The cruise of the "Essex": Dashing Paul Jones; From midshipman to commodore; Harbaugh, C. T., For freedom's cause; or, on to Saratoga; Lounsberry, Lionel, The trader's captive; or, the young guardsman and the French spies; The young patriot; or, the young guardsman of Fort William Henry; Ober, F: Albion, Old Put the patriot; or, fighting for home and country; Post, *Commander,* The league of five; or, Washington's boy scouts.

Boys of the army ser. See Hancock, Harrie Irving.

Boys of the old glee club. Riley, J. W. **$1.50 net. Bobbs-M.

Boys of the service ser. il. O. Scribner.
—Brady. On the old 'Kearsage." **$1.35 net.

Boys on the railroad; by Molly Elliot Seawell, James Barnes, Ellen Douglas Deland, John R. Coryell, E. Carruth, and others. '09(S18) c. il. D. (Harper's athletic ser.) 60 c. Harper.

Boys' and girls' ser. 7 v. '10(D) col. fronts. 16°, ea., 25 c. Doran.
Contents: Defoe, Robinson Crusoe; Hughes, Tom Brown's school days; Tales from Shakespeare; Tales from Hans Andersen; Mungo Park's travels; Ballantyne, Coral island; Kingston, True blue.

Boys' and girls' travel lib. 6 v. '10(N) il. 8°, $1. Estes.
Volumes: Butterworth, Hezekiah, Travel tales of South Africa; Travel tales of China; Travel tales of Central America; Browne, G: Waldo, Travel tales of Hawaiian Island; Travel tales of Philippine Islands.

Boys' annual, 1910. '10(D) $1.50. Cassell.

Boys' book of air-ships. Delacombe, H. $2. Stokes.

Boys' book of locomotives. Howden, J. R. $2. Stokes.

Boys' book of model aeroplanes. Collins, F. A. $1.20 net. Century Co.

Boys' book of steamships. Houden, J. R. $2. McClure.

Boys' corn growing contest. Missouri. *State Board of Agriculture.* gratis. Mo. State Bd.

Boys' Cuchulain. Hull, E. $1.50 net. Crowell.

Boys' Drake. Bacon, E. M. $1.50 net. Scribner.

Boys' Iliad. Perry, W. C. $1.50. Macmillan.

Boys' lib. of legend and chivalry. il. 8°, $2. Scribner.
—Malory. Boy's King Arthur.

Boys' life of Ulysses S. Grant. Nicolay, H. $1.50. Century Co.

Boys' Odyssey. Perry, W. C. $1.50. Macmillan.

Boys' own authors series. v. 27-30. '08 (D19); v. 31-41. '10(N) il. 12°, ea., †$1. Estes.
Contents: Lord of Lowedale, R. D. Chetwode; Afloat on the Dogger Bank, H. C. Moore; The crystal city, Andre Laurie; Tommy Joyce and Tommy Joy, Harriet A. Cheever; Young express agent, Kellogg; Play away, Allen; Six boys, Champney; Adventures of a boy reporter in the Philippines, Morrison; Four boys on the Mississippi, Kellogg; Messenger no. 48, Kaler; Teddy, Kaler; Down the slope, Kaler; Struggle for a fortune, Castlemon; First capture, Castlemon; Open air boy, Hewett.

Boys' own lib. il. D. †75 c. McKay.
—Standish. Frank Merriwell's champion.—Frank Merriwell's courage.—Frank Merriwell's daring.—Frank Merriwell's faith.—Frank Merriwell's loyalty.—Frank Merriwell's reward.—Frank Merriwell's return to Yale.—Frank Merriwell's secret.—Frank Merriwell's skill.—Frank Merriwell's victory.

Boys' round table. *See* Forbush, W: B.

Boys' stories of the army ser. il. O. $1.50. L. C. Page.
—Russel. In West Point gray.

Boys' story of the railroad ser. il. O. †$1.50. L. C. Page.
—Stevenson. Young train master.

Boyton, Mrs. Paul, comp.
Heroic priest; memoirs of Joseph Francis Brophy, apostle of Coney Island. '10 (Jl9) il. pors. T. $1. G: C. Tilyou.

Bracco, Roberto.
Il trionfo. '08(Mr.) c. 78 p. 16°. (Add. pub. for price.) V. Ciocia.

Brace, G: Marshall.
Wood finishing and cabinet work at Stout Institute. '10(Jl16) c. 8°, 50 c. G: M. Brace.

Brace, Harrison H.
Gold production and future prices. '10 (Ag20) c. 8°, $1.50. Bankers' Pub.

Bracebridge Hall. *See* Irving, Washington.

Brackett, E: A.
Materialized apparitions: if not beings from another life what are they? '09(Je19) c. D. $1.25. Badger.
World we live in. '09(Je19) c. D. $1. Badger.

Bracq, Jean Charlemagne.
France under the Republic. '10(O22) c. O. $1.50 net. Scribner.

Bradbury, Mrs. Anna Rossman.
Hist. of the city of Hudson, New York, with biographical sketches of Henry Hudson and Robert Fulton. '08, [1909.] (Mr) c. 9-13+223 p. 12°, $1.50. A. R. Bradbury.

Bradbury, H. B.
Forms of pleading in legal and equitable actions adapted to codes of procedure. In 2 v. '08(N) c. 41+1000; 1001-2272 p. O. $13. Banks.

Bradbury, W: Frothingham, and Emery, Grenville C.
Academic algebra. '09(N) c. 6+448 p. il. 12°, (Bradbury's mathematical ser.) $1.08. Thompson B.

BRADDOCK, *General* Edward.
Society of Colonial Wars. *District of Columbia.* Hist. address of Marcus Benjamin, with other papers rel. to the dedication of the Braddock boulder in the cathedral grounds, Mount St. Albans, Washington, D. C. gratis. Soc. Colon. Wars, D. C.

Braden, Ja. Andrew.
Auto boys. '08(O17) il. D. (Auto boys ser.) $1. Saalfield.
Auto boys' outing. '10(Ja22) il. 16°, (Auto boys' ser.) $1. Saalfield.
Auto boys' quest. '10(Ag13) il. 12°, (Auto boys' ser.) $1. Saalfield.

Bradford, Amory Howe.
My brother. '10(D10) c. D. $1.25 net. Pilgrim Press.

Bradford, C: Barker.
Angler's guide. '08(O3) c. nar. D. $1; pap., 50 c. Nassau Press.
Angler's secret. '09(My) il. 16°, *$1 net. Nassau Press.
Determined angler. '09(My) il. 16°, 60 c. Nassau Press.
Wild-fowlers; or, duck shooting in the great lagoon. '09(My) il. 16°, *$1 net. Nassau Press.

Bradford, Ernest Smith.
Commission government in American cities; address before the National Municipal League at Cincinnati, Ohio, Nov. 20, 1909. '10(Je4) 8°, $4. Nat. Municipal.

Bradford, Gamaliel, jr.
Matthew Porter: a story. '08(Ap11) c. front. D. $1.50. L. C. Page.

Bradford, J: Ewing, ed.
James McBride manuscripts; selections rel. to Miami University. '09(Jl) 8°, (Historical and Philosophical Soc. of Ohio pubs.) (Not for sale.) Hist. and Phil. Soc., O.

Bradford, Laurence.
Historic Duxbury in Plymouth County, Massachusetts. 3d ed. '10(D) 160 p. il. 8°, $1. G. Bradford.

Bradford, Morgan, jr., and Wells, A. Wade.
How to become a detective. '10(Jl2) c. 8°, $2. Globe Pr., (Wash., D. C.)

Bradford, T: Lindsley, M.D., comp.
Bibliographer's manual of American history; cont. an account of all state, territory, town and county histories rel. U. S., with verbatim copies of their titles, and useful bibliograph. notes, together with the prices at which they have been sold for the last 40 years, with index by titles, and by states; ed. and rev. by Stan V. Henkels. In 5 v. v. 2, F. to L. Nos. 1601 to 3103. '08(F22); v. 3, M to Q. Nos. 3104 to 4527. '09(F13); v. 4. '10 (Mr5); v. 5 (O22); Q. buckram, subs., per v., $3.50. Henkels.

Bradford, W:
History of Plymouth plantation, 1606-1646; ed. by W: T. Davis. '08(Mr28) c. map, facsims., 8°, (Original narratives of early American history.) **$3 net. Scribner.
History of the Plymouth Settlement, 1608-1650; rendered into modern English by Valerian Paget. '09(N20) c. D. *$1.50 net. McBride.

Bradley, And. Cecil.
Oxford lectures on poetry. '09(Je19) O. *$3 net. Macmillan.
—, comp. Essays and studies by members of the English Association. '10(D3) O. $1.75. Oxford Univ.

Bradley, Arth. Granville.
Avon and Shakespeare's country. '10(Jl30) il. 4°, $3.50 net. Dutton.
English Lakes. '10(Jl30) il. O. (Beautiful England ser.) bds., $1.25, boxed. Estes.
Making of Canada, 1763-1814. '08(D12) maps, 8°, *$3 net. Dutton.
Rivers and streams of England; painted by Sutton Palmer. '10(F12) map, O. (Color books ser.) *$6 net. Macmillan.
Romance of Northumberland. '09(O2) il. map, O. *$2.75 net. McClurg.
Wiltshire. [1910.] (My) 12+156 p. 8°, (Cambridge county geographies.) 45 c. Putnam.
Worcestershire. '09(Jl17) il. map, 8°, (Color books.) *$3 net. Macmillan.
The Wye. '10(Je4) col. il maps, 8°, (Macmillan's color book ser.) $3 net. Macmillan.

Bradley, Catherine, and Cooper, Edith, ["Michael Field."]
Wild honey from various thyme: [poems.] '08(Je6) D. *$1.65 net. Wessels.

Bradley, Cuthbert, ["Whipster."]
Good sport with famous packs, 1885. '10 (D10) il. (partly in col.) 4°, $5 net. Dutton.

Bradley, Fs. Herbert.
Appearance and reality. 2d ed., rev. '09 (F13) 8°, (Library of philosophy.) *$3 net. Macmillan.

Bradley, I: S:, comp.
See Wisconsin State Historical Society.

Bradley, J. Chester.
Notes on two amphipods of the genus *Corophium* from the Pacific coast. '08 (Je20) il. Q. (Univ. of Cal. pubs., Zoology.) pap., 30 c. Univ. of Cal.

Bradley, J: W.
Illuminated manuscripts. '09(O9) S. (Little books on art.) *$1 net. McClurg.

Bradley, Kenneth McPherson.
Harmony and analysis. '08(N) c. 160 p. 8°, $1.50. C. F. Summy Co.

Bradley, S: Carlyle.
Jesus of Nazareth: a life. '08(N14) c. O. *$2 net. Sherman, F.

Bradley, Shelland.
Adventures of an A. D. C. '10(Ap2) D. $1.50. Lane.

Bradley, W: Aspenwall, comp. and ed.
Garden muse; poems for garden lovers; with introd. '10(Je4) c. front. D. $1.25 net. Sturgis & W.

Bradley Polytechnic Institute, Peoria, Ill.
Bradley Polytechnic Institute; the first decade, 1897-1907. '08(N) 180 p. il. pors. 8°, $1.50. Bradley Polytechnic.

Bradley-Birt, Fs. Bradley.
Through Persia from the Gulf to the Caspian. '09(D18) il. 8°, *$3.50 net. Dutton.

Bradt, H. Ja.
Lightning estimator. 6th ed. '10(N12) c. il. 12°, $1. Bradt.

Brady, Cyrus Townsend, D.D.
Adventures of Lady Susan. '08(D12) c. front. D. †$1.50. Moffat.
The better man. '10(O15) c. D. $1.50. Dodd.
Island of Regeneration. '09(O23) c. col. il. D. †$1.50. Dodd.
Love test, and other sermons long and short. '08(Ap11) c. por. D. *$1.25 net. Young Churchman.
On the old "Kearsarge": story of the Civil War. '09(O23) c. il. O. (Boys of the Service ser.) $1.50 net. Scribner.
Ring and the man. '09(Mr13) c. il. D. †$1.50. Moffat.
South American fights and fighters, and other tales of adventure. '10(My7) c. il. O. (American fights and fighters ser.) $1.50. Doubleday, P.

Brady, J:
Mrs. Featherweight's musical moments. '08 (Je6) c. 8°, 75 c. Goerck.
Mrs. Featherweight's musical moments. '10 (D17) c. D. bds., 75 c. net. A. Harriman.

Brady, Nayd Churton.
Modern marriage and how to bear it. '09 (Ja2) 12°, $1.25. M. Kennerley.

BRADY FAMILY.
See **Genealogies: Murdock, W: G.**

Bragdon, Claude.
Beautiful necessity; essays on theosophy and architecture. '10(D31) c. il. 8°, $2. Manas Press.
A brief life of Annie Besant, president of the Theosophical Society. '09(D) c. 20 p. 12°, 15 c. Manas Press.
Episodes from an unwritten history. '10 (S3) c. D. pap., 15 c. Manas Press.
Theosophy and the Theosophical Society. '09(Ag14) c. D. pap., 25 c. Manas Press.

—, and Fiske, J. Parker B.
Tapestry brick work. '09(D4) c. il. Q. pap., 20 c. Fiske & Co., (Bost.)

Bragg, G: F., D.D.
First negro priest on southern soil. '10 (Ja8) c. il. pors. 12°, 75 c. Church Advocate.

Bragdon, Guy F., and Postance, W:
Governor and the boss. '08(D) 120 p. 12°, pap., 25 c. J. S. Ogilvie.

Brahma knowledge: an outline of the philosophy of the Vedanta, as set forth by the Upanishads and by Sánkara; tr. by L. D. Barnett. '08(Je6) 12°, (Wisdom of the East.) *60 c. net. Dutton.

Brahms, Johannes.
Hungarian dances; for piano, four hands. [Standard ed.] Bk. 1. (nos. 1-5); Bk. 2 (nos. 6-10). '10(D) 29; 29 p. pap., ea., $1.50. Ditson.
Selected piano compositions; ed. by Rafael Joseffy; with preface by Ja. Huneker. '10(N19) por. O. (Musicians' lib.) $2.50; pap., $1.50. Ditson.
[Songs;] collection of fifty songs with piano accompaniment; ed. by Max Spicker; preceded by a biograph. and critical essay by H. E. Krehbiel; English tr. by H: G. Chapman; published in 2 eds., one for high voice and one for low voice. '10(Jl30) c. por. F. (Golden treasury of music.) $2 net. Schirmer.

—, Herzogenberg, Heinrich v. and Elisabet v.
Johannes Brahms: the Herzogenberg correspondence; ed. by Max Kalbeck; tr. by Hannah Bryant. '09(F13) 8°, *$3.50 net. Dutton.

BRAHMS, Johannes.
Colles, H: C. Brahms. $1. Brentano's.

Braid, Ja.
Advanced golf. '08(Ag1) il. pors. 8°, *$3 net. Jacobs.
Ladies' field golf book. '08(Je20) il. D. pap., *40 c. net. Scribner.

BRAILLE SYSTEM.
See **Blind.**

Brailsford, E: J.
Spiritual sense in sacred legends: 40th Fernley lecture. '10(N12) 12°, $1.25 net. Eaton & M.

Brain, Belle Marvel, comp.
Adventures with four-footed folk and other creatures of the animal world. '08(O17) c. il. pors. 8°, *$1.25 net. Revell.

BRAIN.
Ballance, C: A. Some points in the surgery of the brain and its membranes. *$5 net. Macmillan.
Krause, F. Surgery of the brain and spinal cord. $6. Rebman.
Spear, R. O. Cerebration; is the science of the psychic mental and physiological functions of the brain in the brain and body. $2. Rational Cult.
Witkowski's atlas of the brain. *$2 net. W: R. Jenkins.
See also **Hysteria; — Hypnotism; — Insanity; — Mind; — Mind and body; — Nervous system; — Psychology; — Telepathy; — Touch.**

Brain and brawn ser. *See* Drysdale, W:

Brain and the voice in speech and song. Mott, F: W. 75 c. net. Harper.

Brain roofs and porticos. Fowler, J. A. $1. Fowler & W.

Brainard, Addison.
Study of God, man and destiny as disclosed by love and fidelity of truth and by the evil reverse of such love and fidelity. '10(Je) c. 123 p. 12°, $1. Cochrane.

Brainard, Lucy Abigale.
Genealogy of the Brainerd-Brainard family in America, 1649-1908; descendants of Daniel, the emigrant ancestor. '08(N) 3 v., il. pors. facsims., 8°, $15. L. A. Brainard.

BRAINARD FAMILY.
See Genealogies.

Brainerd, Mrs. Eleanor Hoyt.
Personal conduct of Belinda. '10(Mr26) c. il. D. $1.20, fixed. Doubleday, P.

Brainerd, Eveline Warner, comp.
Great hymns of the Middle Ages. '09(O9) c. T. (Thumb-nail ser.) leath., $1, boxed. Century Co.

Brainerd, Ira Hutchinson, ed.
Edwin Davis French [American artist bookplates, 1851-1906]. '08(Je6) c. il. pors. 8°. (privately pr.) De Vinne.

Brainerd, Norman, [pseud. for S: R: Fuller.]
Winning his shoulder-straps; or, Bob Anderson at Chatham Military School. '09 (S11) c. il. D. †$1.25. Lothrop, L. & S.
Winning the Eagle prize; or, the pluck of Billy Hazen. '10(Ag20) c. il. D. (Five chums ser.) $1.25. Lothrop, L. & S.

Braislin, W: C.
List of the birds of Long Island. '08(D) 75 c. Linnaean.

Braithwaite, J. Bevan.
A "Friend" of the nineteenth century; life and letters by his children. '10(D) il. pors. 8°, $2.50 net. Doran.

Braithwaite, W: Stanley.
House of falling leaves; with other poems. '08(Ag8) c. D. *$1 net. J: W. Luce.
—, comp. Book of Georgian verse; with notes. '08(D26) c. S. **$2 net; flex. mor., **$3.50 net. Brentano's.
—, ed. Book of Restoration verse. '09(Jl31) 16°, *$2 net; flex. mor., *$3 net. Brentano's.

Brakeman's preparatory instruction. Baker, G: H: 3 v. $20. Railway Educ.

BRAKEMEN.
See Railroads.

Bralliar, Floyd.
Elo, the eagle, and other stories. '08(D26) c. il. O. $1. Pacific Press.

Brambles and twigs of song. Keane, J: A. $1.50. B'way Pub.

Bramwell, J: Milne.
Hypnotism and treatment by suggestion. [1910.] (My) 216 p. 12°, $1.75 net. Funk.

Branch, Anna Hempstead.
Rose of the wind, and other poems. '10 (D10) c. D. $1.25 net. Houghton M.

Branch, Ernest W., comp.
Atlas of the city of Quincy, Norfolk Co., Mass. '07, [1908.] (D) c. 30 p. f°. $15. E. W. Branch.

Branch, Rev. Ja. Orson.
Sermons. '09(D) c. 9-323 p. 12°. $1.25. J. Magath.

Branch, Jos. Gerald.
Conversations on electricity. '08(My.) c. 282 p. il. 8°, $2. Rand, McN. & Co.
Electric wiring. '10(S17) il. tabs., 12°, $2. Branch.
Engineers' descriptive charts, with full explanatory text. '08(Je20) c. il. obl. 16°, $1. Rand, McN. & Co.
Stationary engineering. '08(Je20) c. 3 v., il. tabs., 12°, per v., $2.50. Rand, McN. & Co.

Branch of may. Reese, L. *$1 net; *50 c. net. T: B. Mosher.

Branches of the cross. Scott, A. B. *$1.50 net. Doran.

Brand, Alex. Thdr., M.D., and Keith, J: Rob., M.D.
Clinical memoranda for general practitioners. '09(N) 12°, *$1.50 net. Wood.

Brand, C: J:, and Waldron, Lawrence Root.
Cold resistance of alfalfa and some factors influencing it. '10(O) 80 p. il. plan, tabs., 8°, (U. S., Dept. of Agriculture, Bureau of Plant Industry; Bull.)
—, **and Westgate, J: Minton.**
Alfalfa in cultivated rows for seed production in semi-arid regions. '09(Jl) 23 p. il. 8°, (U. S. Dept. of Agriculture, Bu. of Plant Industry circular.) pap. (Add. Superintendent for price.)

Brand, Capt. Jack.
By wild waves tossed. '08(My9) c. il. D. †$1.50. McClure.

Brand, Rob. H:
Union of South Africa. '10(Ja1) O. $2. Oxford Univ.

Brand, et dramatisk digt. Ibsen, H. $1.50. J: Anderson.

Brand (The) H. W. Broderick, T. *$1.50 net. A. Harriman.

Brand new doctor. Devney, R. S. $1.25. R. S. Devney.

Brandegee, Townshend Stith.
Plantae Mexicanae purpusianae. '09(Jl10) Q. (Univ. of Cal. pubs.; Botany.) pap., 15 c.—Plantae Mexicanae purpusianae. II. '10(Je) 85-95 p. Q. (Univ. of Cal. pubs.; Botany.) pap., 10 c. Univ. of Cal.

Brandeis, L: Dembitz, and Goldmark, Josephine.
Women in industry: decision of the U. S. supreme court in Curt Muller vs. State of Oregon, upholding the constitutionality of the Oregon ten hour law for women and brief for the State of Oregon. '08(S) 113+8 p. O. pap., gratis. L: D. Brandeis.

Brandes, G:
Anatole France. '08(O10) front. facsim., D. (Contemporary men of letters ser.) *75 c. net. McClure.
William Shakespeare: critical study. New ed. '08(F1) 8°, *$2.60 net. Macmillan.

BRANDING.
See Cattle

Branding needle. Sue, M. J. E. 50 c. N. Y. Labor News.

Brandreth, Paulina.
Plays and poems. '10(D31) c. D. $1. B'way Pub.

Brandt, C: E:
Road locating and building simplified. '08 (Ag) c. 5+106 p. il. pls. por. 12°, $1. C. E. Brandt.

BRANDY.
United States. *Office of Internal Revenue.* Regulations and instruction concerning the distillation of brandy from apples, peaches, grapes, pears, pineapples, oranges, apricots, berries, prunes, figs, or cherries exclusively, Sept. 16, 1908. '09(O) 25 p. 8°. (Add. Superintendent for price.)

BRANDYWINE, Battle of.
MacElree, W. W. Along the western Brandywine. $5. Hickman.

Branford, Benchara.
Study of mathematical education; incl. the teaching of arithmetic. '08(S26) 8°, $1.10. Oxford Univ.

Branham, Grace Bagnall, and Mason, Rosalind Fay, eds.
Dulci fistula; book of nonsense verse, (Bryn Mawr, 1910.) [1910.] (Jl) c. 9-99 p. il. 16°, 75 c. R. F. Mason.

Branigan, Rev. W: H:
Abraham Lincoln. '09(Je19) O. pap. (Add. pubs. for price.) M. L. Morrison.

Brann, H: Athanasius, D.D.
Hist. of the American college of the Roman Catholic Church of the United States. '10(Je11) c. il. pors. O. $2. Benziger.

Brannan, Jos. Doddridge, ed.
See Negotiable instruments law.

Branner, J: Casper.
Bibliography of clays and the ceramic arts. '08(Ag1) 8°, $2. Am. Ceramics.
Brief grammar of the Portuguese language, with exercises and vocabularies. '10 (D3) c. D. $1.25. Holt.
Clays of Arkansas. '08(D26) figs. O. (Dept. of the Interior, U. S. Geolog. Survey.) pap. (Add. Superintendent for price.)
See also Purdue, Albert Homer.

Brannt, W: Thdr., ed.
Metallic alloys: pract. guide for the manufacture of all kinds of alloys, amalgams, and solders, used by metal-workers. 3d ed., thoroughly rev. and enl. '08(My2) c. 8°, *$5 net. Baird.

Branson, I: Reichelderfer.
Yosemite against corporation greed; shall half of Yosemite national park be destroyed by San Francisco?: thesis against it. '09(O9) c. front. D. pap., gratis. I: R. Branson.

Branston, J: W:, ["R. B. Brown."]
Girders for electric overhead cranes. '09 (D25) c. il. 8°, (Machinery's references ser.) pap., 25 c. Indust. Press.

Brant, J: Ira.
New regime, A.D. 2202. '09(Jl31) c. D. $1. Cochrane.

Brantly, W: T., rep.
See Maryland. *Ct. of appeals.* Repts.

Brashere, Ora M.
Science and suffrage; an inquiry into the causes of sex differences. '09, [1910.] (Ap) c. 15 p. 8°, 25 c. O. M. Brashere.

Brass tacks. Hunter, W: C. 50 c. net. Reilly & B.

BRASSES.
Suffling, E. R. English church brasses; from the 13th to the 17th centuries. $4.20. Scribner.

Brassey, T: Allnutt, ed.
Naval Annual, 1909. '09(S4) il. tabs., O. *$6 net. Scribner.

Brasted, Fred.
The gang; story of the middle west. '10 (Ap9) c. il. D. $1.25. Griffith.

Bratten, Arno.
Redemption of Arthur True; a rural school story; with an introd. by E. G. Lentz. '09(S) c. 139 p. por. 12°, 75 c. Stafford.

Braubach, Anna Louise.
Taquigrafia fonetica, Sloan-Duployan. '08 (Ag) c. 72 p. 12°, $1.50. A. L. Braubach.

Brauereibetrieb in den Vereinigten Staaten. Wahl, R. $3. Wahl-Henius.

Braun, Maximilien Gustav, M.D., and Lühe, M.
Hdbk. of pract. parasitology; tr. by Linda Forster. [1910.] (Je) il. 8°, $3.50 net. Wood.

Braune (Die) Erica. Jensen, W. 35 c. Heath.

Brauns, Reinhard.
Mineral kingdom; tr. with additions by L. J. Spencer. '10(S) 440 p. il. 4°, hf. leath., $16.50 net. Lippincott.

Brave Beowulf. Cartwright, T: 50 c. Dutton.

Brave heart ser. *See* Thompson, Adele Eugenia.

Brave little Peggy. Rhoades, N. †$1. Lothrop, L. & S.

Brave old salt. Adams, W: T. 50 c. Hurst.

BRAVERY.
See Heroes.

Bravo, Bob! Home, A. $1.50. Lippincott.

Brawley, B: Griffith.
Negro in literature and art. '10(Jl2) c. 12°, 50 c. B: G. Brawley.

Bray, Blanche A.
Robin's love story. '08(O24) 12°, pap., 50 c. Cochrane.

Bray, H: Truro.
Living universe. '10(Je25) c. 8°, $3.50. Truro.

Bray, Mrs. Mary Matthews.
My grandmother's garden, and An orchard ancestral. '10(D3) c. 16°, leath., $1. Badger.
Romance of Barnstable. '09(Je19) c. D. $1.50. Badger.

Bray, Reginald A.
The town child; study of the life of a child in the large cities. '10(Mr26) 12°, *$2 net. Jacobs.

Brayley, Frederic A:
Arrangement of finger points identification and their uses, for police departments, prisons, lawyers, banks, homes, trust companies, and in every branch of business where an infallible system of identification is necessary. '10(Jl30) c. il. por. 8°, $2. Worcester Press.

BRAZIL.
Cook, W: A. By horse, canoe and float through the wilderness of Brazil. $2. Werner Co.
Cook, W: A. Through the wilderness of Brazil. $1.50. Am. Tr.
Gammon, S: R. Evangelical invasion of Brazil. 75 c. Presb. Pub.
International Bureau of American Republics. Brazil. (Add. pubs. for price.) Int. Bu. Am. Republics.
Nabuco, J. Spirit of nationality in the history of Brazil. (Not for sale.) J. Nabuco.
Oakenfull, J. C. Brazil in 1910. gratis. Com. Brazil.

BRAZIL.—*Continued.*
Winter, N. O. Brazil and her people of to-day. $3. L. C. Page.
Wright, *Mrs.* M. R. New Brazil. *$10 net Barrie.

BRAZILIAN NATIONAL EXPOSITION.
Wright, *Mrs.* M. R. Brazilian National Exposition of 1908; [held at Rio de Janeiro.] $2.50. Barrie.

BREAD.
Atwater, H. W. Bread and bread making. U. S., Supt. of Docs.
See also Cookery.

Breakfast foods. Frear, W: (Add. pubs. for price.) Harrisburg Pub.
Breaking dawn. Patterson, J: A. $1. Chronicle Pub.
Breaking down Chinese walls. Osgood, E. I. *$1 net. Revell.
Breaking in of a yachtsman's wife. Vorse, *Mrs.* M. M. H. †$1.50. Houghton, M. & Co.
Breaking of bonds. Ficke, A. D. $1 net. Sherman, F.

BREAST.
Rodman, W: L: Diseases of the breast, with special reference to cancer. *$4 net. Blakiston.

Breasted, Ja. H.
History of Egypt from the earliest times to the Persian conquest. 2d ed., fully rev. '09(Jl31) c. il. maps, 8°, **$5 net. Scribner.
History of the ancient Egyptians. '08(Je6) c. D. (Historical ser. for Bible students.) maps, plans, **$1.25 net. Scribner.
Monuments of Sudanese Nubia. '08(Ag29) c. 8°, pap., *50 c. net. Univ. of Chic.

Breath of the mountains. Doran, B. $1. Badger.
Breath of the world. Nichols, S. H. **$1.50 net. Putnam.

BREATHING.
Benedict, F. G., *and* Carpenter, T. M. Respiration calorimeters for studying the respiratory exchange and energy transformations of man. 75 c. Carnegie.
Fletcher, A. E. Law of the rhythmic breath. *$1 net. Fenno.
Foringer, W. S. How to breathe and how to be well. $1. B'way Pub.
Neusser, E. v. Clinical treatises on the symptomatology and diagnosis of disorders of respiration and circulation. pt. 1, $1.50; pt. 2, *$1.25 net. Treat.
See also Gymnastics and physical culture;—Hygiene;—Nose;—Throat;—Voice.

Breazeale, Ja. Fk.
Canning vegetables in the home. '09(Jl) 16 p. il. 8°, (U. S. Dept. of Agriculture: Farmers' bull.) pap. (Add. Superintendent for price.) U. S., Supt. of Docs.

Brebner, Percy J:, ["Christian Lys."]
Gentleman of Virginia. '10(O8) 12°, $1.50. Macmillan.
Royal ward. '09(My15) c. il. D. †$1.50. Little, B. & Co.
Testing of Olive Vaughan. '09(Mr20) c. D. $1.50. Doscher.
Vayenne. '08(Ap4) c. D. $1.50. J: McBride.

Breck, E:, M.D.
Way of the woods: manual for sportsmen in northeastern United States and Canada. '08(Ap4) c. D. **$1.75 net. Putnam.
Wilderness pets at Camp Buckshaw. '10 (My14) c. il. O. $1.50 net. Houghton M.

Breckenridge, Lester Paige, and Diserens, Paul.
Fuel tests with Illinois coal; (comp. from tests made by the technologic branch of the United States Geological Survey, at the St. Louis fuel testing plant, 1904-June 30, 1907.) '08, [1910.] (F) 54 p. il. tabs., diagrs., 8°, (University of Illinois, Engineering Experiment Station.) pap., gratis. Univ. of Ill.

Breckenridge, Roeliff Morton.
Hist. of banking in Canada. '10(Ap) 6+3-308 p. tabs., 8°. (Add. Superintendent for price.) U. S., Supt. of Docs.

Breckenridge, W: Edn., Mersereau, S: Foster, and Moore, C: Forrest.
Shop problems in mathematics. '10(Ag20) c. D. $1. Ginn.

Bredon, Juliet.
Sir Robert Hart: romance of a great career. '09(O2) il. 12°, *$1.75 net. Dutton.

BREECHES.
See Tailoring.

Breed, C: Blaney, and Hosmer, G: Leonard.
Principles and practice of surveying. v. 2, Higher surveying. '08(S12) c. il. 8°, $3. Wiley.

Breed and the pasture. Chambers, J. L. $1. Stone & B.

BREEDING.
See Botany;—Domestic animals.

Breeding and the Mendelian discovery. Darbishire, A. D. $1.75 net. Cassell.
Breeding minks in Louisiana for their fur. Elfer, W: A. 75 c. Gessner.

Breen, Patrick.
Diary of Patrick Breen, one of the Donner Party; ed. by F: J. Teggart. '10(S) 16 p. facsim., O. (Academy of Pacific Coast history pubs.) pap., 15 c. Univ. of Cal.

Breen villagers. Garretson, B. C. $1. B'way Pub.
Breezes from the Southland. Mayes, J. S. $1. B'way Pub.

Bremner, O. E.
Destructive insects and their control. '10 (Jl2) il. O. pap., gratis. State Horticultural.

Brenan, Gerald, and Statham, E: Phillips.
House of Howard. In 2 v. '08(O10) il. O. *$6 special net. Appleton.

Brenke, W: C:
Text-bk. on advanced algebra and trigonometry; with tables; [protractor in pocket.] '10(D24) c. O. $2 net. Century Co.

Brennan, B. A.
Compendium of useful legal information for business men. '08(N14) c. 16°, mor., *$5 net. Wiley.

Brennan, G: Hugh.
Bill Truetell: story of theatrical life. '09 (F27) c. O. $1.50. McClurg.

Brent, Bp. C: H:
Leadership: William Belden Noble lectures. '08(O10) c. D. **$1.25 net. Longmans.
Mind of Christ Jesus in the church of the living God. '08(F15) c. O. **50 c. net. Longmans.

Brent, J:
Empire of the West (a compilation). '10 (S) 303 p. il. map, D. pap. Un. Pacific R. R.
What every school boy and school girl should known (a compilation). [1910.] (S) c. 116 p. il. map. Un. Pacific R. R.

Brentano's cable code. '10(D) 18°, $1 net. Brentano's.

Brentano's international art ser. 8 v. [1910.] (D) il. ea., $1.50. Brentano's.
Contents: Stahl, Fritz, Great English masters; Hutton, E:, Hogarth; Mauclair, Camille, Delacroix; Klein, Rudolph, Fritz Boehle; Crappe, Georges, Dugas; Symons, Arth., D. G. Rossetti; Binyon, Lawrence, Japanese art; Klein, Rudolph, Louis Corinth.

Brereton, Austin.
Life of Henry Irving. '08(O3) 2 v., il. pors. O. *$6.50 net, boxed. Longmans.
Literary hist. of the Adelphi and its neighborhood; with a new introd. '09(D18) 8°, $3.50. Duffield.

Brereton, Captain F: Sadlier.
Great aeroplane; thrilling tale of adventure. '10(S24) il. D. $1.25. Caldwell.
Hero of Sedan. '09, [1910.] (Ja) 12°, $1.25. Caldwell.
How Canada was won. '08(N7) c. il. D. $1.25. Caldwell.
Indian and scout; tale of the gold rush to California. '10(O1) il. D. $1.25. Caldwell.
John Bargreave's gold. '09, [1910.] (Ja) 12°, $1.25. Caldwell.
Roughriders of the Pampas. '08(D26) c. il. D. $1.25. Caldwell.

Brereton, Rob. Maitland.
Question: did Sir Francis Drake land on any part of the Oregon coast? '09(Mr) 24 p. map, 8°, pap., *25 c. net. Gill.

Bresson, Mme. Cartier-.
See Cartier-Bresson, *Mme.*

BRETHREN.
See Plymouth Brethren.

Bretons at home. Gostling, *Mrs.* F. M. P. *$2.50 net. McClurg.

Brett, Allen, ed.
Reinforced concrete. '09(Mr27) c. il. tabs. 24°, $1. Technical Pub

BRETT, *Mme.* Catheryna.
Sutcliffe, *Mrs.* A. C. Homestead of a colonial dame. 50 c. A. C. Sutcliffe.

Brett, G. S.
Philosophy of Gassendi. '08(O24) 8°, *$3 net. Macmillan.
—, **comp.** Representative English poems; sel. and ed., with introd. and notes, by G. S. Brett. '09(F6) 16°, *75 c. net. Macmillan.

Brett, Rev. Jesse.
Divine friendship. '09(Mr13) D. *$1 net. Longmans.
Garden of God; some characteristics of the spiritual life mainly from the Song of songs. '10(F19) D. *$1.20 net. Longmans.

Brett, Rev. Jesse.—*Continued.*
Holy Mount: meditations on the transfiguration of our Lord as revealing the life of prayer. '09(Ap10) *60 c. net. Young Churchman.
Incarnate love: meditations on the love of Jesus. '08(Mr21) S. 75 c. Longmans.

Brevard, Caroline Mays.
Literature of the South. '08(D12) c. D. $1.50. B'way Pub.

BREVIARY.
See Catholic church.

Brewer, D: Josiah.
Mission of the United States in the cause of peace. '10(Ap2) O. (International School of Peace pamphlet ser.) pap., gratis. Int. Sch. Peace.
See also Hale, E: Everett.

Brewer, D: Josiah, [and others,] eds.
Crowned masterpieces of eloquence that have advanced civilization, as presented by the world's best orations, from the earliest period to the present time. Lyceum ed. 10 v. '08(D) c. il. pors. 8°. (Add. pubs. for price.) Kaiser.
See also Hughes, C: Evans.

Brewer, G: Emerson, M.D.
Text-book of surgery; for students and practitioners. 2d ed., thoroughly rev. and much enl. '09(N) c. 9+17-915 p. il. 8°, *$5 net; leath., *$6 net. Lea.

Brewer, I: Williams, M.D.
Observations on the treatment of tuberculosis in Arizona. '08(Je27) 12°, gratis. Wood.
Personal hygiene in tropical and semitropical countries. '08(Ap4) c. 16°, *$1 net. Davis.
Rural hygiene: hdbk. of sanitation designed for the use of students in agricultural schools and colleges. '09(N20) c. il. figs. D. **$1.25 net. Lippincott.

Brewer, Rob. W. A.
Art of aviation. '10(Ag20) c. il. 16°, $3.50. McGraw-H.
Motor car: pract. manual. '09(Ag14) il. 12°, **$2 net. Van Nostrand.

Brewer, Willis.
Egypt and Israel; inquiry into the influence of the more ancient people upon Hebrew history and Jewish religion; and some investigation into the facts and statements made as to Jesus of Nazareth. '10 (N12) il. O. $2 net. Torch Press.

Brewer's accounts. Sweetland, C: A: 50 c. Am. Sch. Corr.

Brewers and bottlers universal encyclop.; complete reference book and guide. '10 (Jl) c. 640 p. il. f°, $25. Brewers Pub.

Brewerton, Alfr. West.
Drawing for newspapers, cartooning, "comics," news illustrating, etc. '10(S17) c. il. 8°, $1.50. Am. Pub. Co., (Ga.)

BREWING.
Brewing water, its defects and their remedy. '09, [1910.] (Ap) c. 46 p. O. pap., gratis. Am. Burtonizing.
Schlüter, H. Brewing industry and the brewery workers' movement in America. $1; $1.50. Int. Union United Brewery.

BREWING.—*Continued.*
Wahl, R., *and* Henius, M. American handy book of the brewing, malting and auxiliary trades. 2 v. $12.—Brauereibetrich in den Vereinigten Staaten von Nord Amerika. $3. Wahl-Henius.

BREWING INDUSTRIES.
Wright, H. E. Handy book for brewers. *$5 net. Van Nostrand.
See also Beer;—Beverages;—Hops.

Brewster, Edith Gilman.
Cheer-up book: [verses for children.] '08 (N21) c. il. obl. D. pap., 50 c. Rust-Craft.
To the zoo: [verses for children.] '08 (N21) c. il. obl. D. pap., 50 c. Rust-Craft.

Brewster, Edn. Tenney.
Life and letters of Josiah Dwight Whitney. '09(D4) c. por. D. **$2 net. Houghton M.
Swimming. '10(Mr26) c. il. D. **$1 net. Houghton M.

Brewster, L. D., comp.
See Negotiable instruments law.

Brewster, Mary K.
Tasman [dog story.] '07, [1910.] (O) 39 p. D. bds., 75 c. Everett Press.

Brewster, W: N.
Cost of Christian conquest. '08(Mr14) c. S. *35 c. net. Jennings.

BREWSTER FAMILY.
See Genealogies, Jones, E. C. P.

Brick architecture. Strack, H. $11; $8. Helburn.

Brick House books. D. †$1. Lothrop, L. & S.
—Rhoades. Brave little Peggy.—Other Sylvia.

BRICK HOUSES.
See Architecture.

BRICK PRESBYTERIAN CHURCH, New York City.
Knapp, S. History of the Brick Presbyterian Church in the city of New York. 2 v. $5. Scribner.

BRICK WORK.
See Masonry.

Brickdale, J. M. Fortescue-.
See Fortescue-Brickdale, J. M.

BRICKLAYING.
Gilbreth, F. B. Bricklaying system. *$3 net. M. C. Clark.
Hodgson, F: T: Practical bricklaying self-taught. $1. Drake.
See also Masonry.

BRICKS.
National Brick Manufacturers' Assoc. of U. S. Study of the chemical status of the carbon, iron and sulphur in clays during the various stages of burning. $1. Randall.
Rolfe, C: W., *and others.* Paving brick and paving brick clays of Illinois. (Add. pubs. for price.) Univ. of Ill.
Wheeler, H. A. Vitrified paving brick. $2. T. A. Randall.
See also Architecture;—Columns;—Masonry.

Brickwood, Albert W.
Sackett on instructions to juries; cont. a treatise on jury trials and appeals, with forms of approved instructions and charges annotated; also erroneous instructions with comment of the court in condemning them. 3 v. '08(O) c. O. $19.50. Callaghan.
See also Illinois supplement.

Bride and the pennant. Chance, F. L. 60 c.; 25 c. Laird.
Bride of Christ. Carus, P. *75 c. net. Open Court.
Bride of Lammermoor. *See* Scott, *Sir* Wa.
Bride of the mistletoe. Allen, J. L. †$1.25. Macmillan.
Bride of the violin. James, G: W. 50 c. G: W. James, jr.
Bride on trust. Curties, H: $1.50. Estes.
Bride's cook book. Davenport, *Mrs.* L., *comp.* $2; $4; $6. Reilly & B.

Bridge, Sir F:
See Meredith, G:

Bridge, Rev. Gerard, comp.
See Shakespeare, W:

Bridge, J. F:
Counterpoint. '08(D) 75 c. Ditson.

Bridge, Ja. Howard.
Purification of public water supplies: comparison in methods, costs and results. '08 (Ag15) 8°, pap. (Add. pubs. for price.) Aldine Bk.

Bridge, Norman, M.D., ed.
See Butler, G: F., *ed.*

BRIDGE (*card game*).
Avery, M. A. Mother Goose on bridge. $1. Lyman Bros.
Ayres, S. B. Bridge. *$1 net. Brentano's.
Browning, H. S. Auction bridge and how to play it. *75 c. net. Dutton.
Camp, W. C. Condensed bridge for the busy man. 35 c. Collier.
Crowninshield, F. W. Bridge-fiend. $1. Moffat.
Dalton, W: Auction bridge up-to-date. $1. Wycil.
Dalton, W: Bridge and auction bridge. $1.20 net. Stokes.
Dalton, W: Interferences at bridge. *40 c. net. Lippincott.
Elwell, J. B. Practical bridge. **$1.50 net. —Principles, rules and laws of auction bridge. $1.25 net. Scribner.
Emery, *Mrs.* B. B. Don'ts in bridge. 50 c. net. W: R. Jenkins.
Fitch, G: Bridge whist. 35 c. Collier.
Foster, R. F: Auction bridge. **$1 net.—Auction bridge up to date. $1 net. Stokes.
Foster, R. F: Bridge manual. $1.25. Brentano's.
"Hellespont," *pseud.* Complete auction bridge. $1.25 net. Lippincott.
Hingley, S. H. Hints on advanced bridge. 75 c. net. Macmillan.
Laws of auction bridge. 50 c. Whist Club.
Lindsay, C: H. A. F-. Bridge, and how to play it. 50 c. Penn Pub. Co.
Lister, A. L. Principles of auction bridge. $1.25 net. Putnam.
Meyer, V. M. K. Enlarged small talks on bridge. 50 c. Ruledge.

BRIDGE (*card game*).—*Continued.*
Meyer, V. M. K. Small talks on auction bridge. 50 c.; Score book to accompany above, 25 c. P. Elder.
Pennell, V. Auction bridge. *$1 net. Lippincott.
Reading, A. S., *comp.* My bridge scores. $1. Daly.
Street, C: S. Outlines of auction bridge. 75 c. C: S. Street.
Tinkham, E. A. How to play bridge. $1. E. A. Tinkham.
Wells, C. Rubaiyat of bridge: [humorous verses.] $1. Harper.
See also Cards.

Bridge builders. Ray, A. C. †$1.50. Little, B. & Co.

BRIDGES.
Bamford, H. Moving loads on railway underbridges. *$1.25 net. Macmillan.
Burr, W: Hubert, *and* Falk, M. S. Design and construction of metallic bridges. $5. —Graphic method by influence lines for bridge and roof computations. $3. Wiley.
Dufour, F. Bridge engineering. $3. Am. Sch. Corr.
Grimm, C. R. Secondary stresses in bridge trusses. $2.50. Wiley.
Ketchum, M. S. Design of highway bridges. *$4 net. Engineering News.
Morris, C. T. Designing and detailing of simple steel structures. $2.25. Hann.
National Bridge Company, Indianapolis. Luten bridges. '09(N) c. 5-86 p. il. 8°, gratis. Nat. Bridge.
National Bridge Co. Reinforced concrete bridges, Luten patents. gratis. Nat. Bridge.
Sherrill, C. O. Examination and repair of simple highway bridges. 25 c. Staff Coll.
Thomson, W: C. Bridge and structural design. $2.—Design of typical steel railway bridges. *$2 net. Engineering News.
Tyrrell, H: G. Concrete bridges and culverts. $3. M. C. Clark.
Watson, W. J. General specifications for concrete bridges. $1. Vinson.
See also Arches; — Building; — Strength of materials;—*also* Cambridge Bridge.

Bridget. Bosch, *Mrs.* H. $1.50. B. W. Dodge.

Bridgetstow. Pearse, M. G. *$1 net. Jennings.

Bridgewater, Howard.
Advertising; or, the art of making known; simple exposition. '10(Je11) D. (Pract. primers of business.) 50 c. Pitman.

Bridgewater, Mass. Proceedings of the 250th anniversary of old Bridgewater at West Bridgewater, Mass., June 13, 1906. '07, [1908.] (D) 149 p. il. pors. 8°, 75 c. E. B. Maglathlin.

Bridgman, Howard Allen.
Real religion; friendly talks to the average man on clean and useful living. '10(N5) c. D. 75 c. net. Pilgrim Press.

Bridgman, Lewis Jesse.
My high school days. Alma Mater ed. [1910.] (My) 8°, $2.50, boxed. Caldwell.
My high school days: [memory-book.] '08 (Je6) c. O. $1.50; hf. mor., $3; limp mor., $5, boxed. Caldwell.

Bridgman, Raymond Landon.
Passing of the tariff. '09(F20) c. D. **$1.20 net. Sherman, F.
World organization. [1910.] (My) 12°, (International lib.) 50 c. net. Ginn.

Bridling of Pegasus. Austin, A. $2.40 net. Macmillan.

Brief analysis of the United States Steel Corporation. Taintor, C: W. $3. C: W. Taintor.

Brief history of German literature. Priest, G: M. **$1.50 net. Scribner.

Brief history of the campaign against tuberculosis. New York [City.] *Dept. of Health.* gratis. N. Y., Dept. of Health.

Brief making. Cooley, R. W., *cd.* $2. West Pub.

Brief manual of leading periodicals in the United States and Canada. '09(N20) pors. D. pap., gratis. Chesman.

Brief outline of the books I have read. Hix, M., *comp.* 25 c. Hinds.

Brief pilgrimage in the Holy Land. Hazard, C. **$1.25 net. Houghton M.

Brief survey of equity jurisdiction. Langdell, C. C. (Add. pub. for price.) Harvard Law.

Briefe historie of the glorious martyrdom of twelve reverend priests. Allen, W: *$1.25 net. Herder.

Brierley, Rev. Jonathan, ["J. B."]
Aspects of the spiritual. '10(Ja8) 12°, *$1.40 net. Whittaker.
Life and the ideal. '10(D10) D. $1.25 net. Pilgrim Press.
Side lights on religion. '08(D5) D. *$1.40 net. Whittaker.

Brieux, Eugène.
Maternity: play in three acts; tr. from the French by Mrs. Bernard Shaw. '07, [1908.] (Jl) c. 78 p. 12°. (Add. pub. for price.) B: R. Tucker.

Briggs, C: A:, D.D.
Church unity: studies of its most important problems. '09(O2) c. O. **$2.50 net. Scribner.
Virgin birth of Our Lord; with introd. by Wilford L. Robbins. '09(Mr6) 12°, pap., *25 c. net. Whittaker.

Briggs, Edg.
Profits in poultry keeping solved; Briggs' system and secrets of successful poultry raising; ed. and rev. by H: Trafford. 4th ed. '10(F26) c. il. 8°, $1. Hosterman.

Briggs, Ernest E:
Angling and art in Scotland. '08(O10) il. O. *$4 net. Longmans.

Briggs, Job Sweet.
"Express": hdbk. cont. reliable information for shippers regarding the methods governing express shipments, etc. '08(F) c. 212 p. il. D. bds., $2. Express.
Published for Expressmen's Beneficial and Sick Benefit Association.

Briggs, Lyman Ja., and Belz, Jacob Otto.
Dry farming in relation to rainfall and evaporationn. '10(D) 71 p. il. front., fold. map, 8°, (U. S., Dept. of Agriculture, Bu. of Plant Industry; bull.)

Briggs, Olive Mary.
Black cross. '09(F20) c. D. †$1.50. Moffat
Fir and the palm. '10(Mr19) c. D. †$1.50. Scribner.

Briggs, T: H:, and Coffman, Lotus D.
Reading in public schools. '08(N) c. 274 p. 12°, $1.25. Row, P. & Co.

Brigham, Albert Perry.
See Gilbert, Grove Karl.

Brigham, Arth. Amber.
Progressive poultry culture. '08(F15) c. por. D. $1.50. Torch Press.

Brigham, Clarence Saunders, comp.
List of books upon Rhode Island history. '09(Ap3) O. (R. I. educational circulars; historical ser.) pap., gratis. R. I. Dept. Educ.

—, **ed.** *See* Brown, Rob. Perkins.

Brigham, Fk. Hartwell, ed.
Conjugation of Spanish verbs, complete. '09(Ag) 54 p. 12°, 60 c. F. H. Brigham.

Brigham, Johnson.
Banker in literature. '10(D17) c. pors. 8°, $2. Bankers Pub.

Brigham, Louise.
Box furniture. '09(Je5) c. il. D. **$1.60 net. Century Co.

Brigham, W: Tufts.
Ancient Hawaiian house. '08, [1910.] (Ap) 4+194 p. il. f°, (Memoirs of the Bernice Pauahi Bishop Museum.) $3. Bishop Museum.
Volcanoes of Kilauea and Mauna Loa on the Island of Hawaii; their variously recorded hist. to the present time. '10 (Ap2) il. F. (Memoirs of the Bernice Pauahi Bishop Museum.) pap., $3.50; $4.50. Bishop Museum.

Bright, C:
Life story of Sir Charles Bright, civil engineer; with which is incorporated the story of the Atlantic cable and the first telegraph to India and the colonies. 2d ed. '09(Ag14) il. 8°, *$4.50 net. Van Nostrand.

BRIGHT, *Sir* Charles Tilston.
Bright, C: Life story of Sir Charles Bright, civil engineer. *$4.50 net. Van Nostrand.

Bright, Ja. Wilson, and Miller, Raymond Durbin.
Elements of English versification. '10(Ap9) c. D. 80 c. Ginn.

Bright and Strong papers. O. pap. Home Market.
—Clarke. Tariff made plain. 10 c.

Bright eyes story book; volume of stories and pictures by many well-known writers. '10 (Ap23) 8°, bds., $1.50. Dutton.

Bright side. Skinner, C: R., *comp. and ed.* 50 c. Beattys.

Bright-wits, Prince of Mogadore. Loughlin, B. 75 c. Caldwell.

Brightmore, A. W.
Structural engineering. '08, [1909.] (Mr) 296 p. il. 8°, *$3.75 net. Cassell.

BRIGHT'S DISEASE.
Benedict, F. G., *and* Joslin, E. P. Metabolism in diabetes mellitus. $2. Carnegie.

BRIGHT'S DISEASE.—*Continued.*
Noorden, C. H. v., *ed.* Clinical treatises on the pathology and therapy of disorders of metabolism and nutrition. pt. 7, Diabetes mellitus. $1.50. Treat.

Brigitta. Auerbach, B. 40 c. Ginn.

Brill, G: Reiter.
Rhymes of the golden age. '08(O24) c. il. 8°, $1.50. Stern.

BRIMFIELD, Mass.
Tarbell, M. A. Stage days in Brimfield, $1. Bassette.

Brinkerhoff, J. H. G.
Hist. of Marion County, Ill. '09, [1910.] (N) 17-862 p. il. pors. 4°. B. F. Bowen.

Brinton, Christian.
Modern artists. '08(Ap11) c. il. pors. O. $6. Baker & T.

Brinton, Selwyn.
Renaissance in Italian art. 9 v. 2d ed. '09 (My) il. 12°, ea., $1. Scribner.

BRIQUETS.
See Coal.

Brisbane, Arth.
Mary Baker G. Eddy. '08(Je20) c. il. por. D. bds., *$1 net. Ball Pub. Co.

Briscoe, Johnson.
Actors' birthday book; 2d series. '08(D12); 3d series; authoritative insight into the lives of the men and women of the stage born between Jan. 1 and Dec. 31. '09, [1910.] (My) c. 13-296 p. pors. 8°, ea., $2 net. Moffat.

Briscoe, Marg. Sutton, [Mrs. A. J. Hopkins.]
Image of Eve. '09(N13) c. front. D. †$1.25. Harper.

—, **Bangs, J: Kendrick, Creevey, Caroline A., and others.**
Harper's book of little plays; sel. for home and school entertainments, with an introd. by Madalene D. Barnum. '10(O1) c. il. D. $1. Harper.

Bristol, Fk. Milton, D.D.
Life of Chaplain McCabe. '08(S12) c. 8°, *$1.50 net. Revell.

BRITAIN.
See England.

Britain at bay. Wilkinson, H: S. *$1.50 net. Putnam.

Britain's birds and their eggs. Thomson, A. L. $6.50 net. Lippincott.

BRITISH ARMY.
See England.

BRITISH ARTS.
See Fine arts;—Painters and painting.

BRITISH COLONIES.
See British Empire;—*also* names of colonies.

BRITISH COLUMBIA, Canada.
Bealby, J: T. Fruit ranching in British Columbia. *$1.50 net. Macmillan.

British committees, commissions, and councils of trade. Andrews, C: McL. 75 c. Johns Hopkins.

British costume during 19 centuries. Ashdown, *Mrs.* C: H: $4.50 net. Stokes.

British country life in autumn and winter. Thomas, E: *$3.75 net. Doran.

British country life in spring and summer. Thomas, E: *$3.75 net. Doran.

BRITISH EAST AFRICA.
See Africa;—Mammalia.

BRITISH EMPIRE.
Barnard, C. H. British Empire in pictures. 75 c. net. Macmillan.
Beer, G: L: Origins of the British colonial system, 1578-1660. **$3 net. Macmillan.
Curzon, G: N., *Baron.* Frontiers. 50 c. Oxford Univ.
Denison, G: T. Struggle for imperial unity. *$2.25 net. Macmillan.
Fraser, J: F. Quaint subjects of the king: [account of little-known races who live in King Edward's dominions.] *$1.25 net. Cassell.
Harrison, F. National and social problems. **$1.75 net. Macmillan.
Lucas, C: P. Historical geography of the British colonies. v. 1, $1.25; v. 2, $1.90; v. 3, $2; v. 4, pt. 1, $2.40; v. 5, pt. 1, $1.50; v. 6, $1.90. Oxford Univ.
Marshall, H. E. Empire story; stories of India and the greater colonies. *$2.50 net. Stokes.
Silburn, P. A. B. Colonies and imperial defense. $2. Longmans.
Stokes, R. S. G. Mines and minerals of the British Empire. *$4.20 net. Longmans.
See also Australia;—Canada;—Ceylon;—Colonial government;—Egypt; — England;—Gibraltar;—Great Britain;—India; — Ireland; — New Zealand;—Scotland;—Wales;—West Indies.
British floral decoration. Felton, R. F. $2.50 net. Macmillan.
BRITISH GUIANA.
Beebe, *Mrs.* M. B. R. *and* C: W: Our search for a wilderness. $2.75 net. Holt.
British highways and byways from a motor car. Murphy, T: D. $3; $7. L. C. Page.
British historical portraits: [v. 1,] Richard II. to Henry Wriothesley, 1400-1600; the lives by C: Rob. Leslie Fletcher, the portraits chosen by Emery Walker; with an introd. on the history of portraiture in England by C. F. Bell. '09(My1) pors. Q. $2.90. Oxford Univ.
British hunting. Coaten, A. W., *ed.* $65 net. Little, B. & Co.
British industries. Ashley, W: J., *ed.* *$1.80 net. Longmans.
BRITISH INSTITUTION, London, Eng.
Graves, A. British Institution, 1806-1867. *$18 net. Macmillan.
British interests and activities in Texas, 1838-1846. Adams, E. D. $1.50. Johns Hopkins.
BRITISH ISLES.
See Great Britain.
British Journal. *See* Brown, G: E., *ed.*
British (The) Journal photographic almanac and photographer's daily companion for 1908. '08(Ja18); for 1909, with which is incorporated the "Year book of photography" and "Amateurs' guide for 1909"; ed. by G: E. Brown. '09(D25) D. ea., $1; pap., 50 c. G: Murphy.
British ministry and the treaty of Fort Stanwix. Alvord, C. W. 25 c. State Hist. Wis.
BRITISH MUSEUM, London.
Hulbert, A. B., *comp. and ed.* Crown collection of American maps [in the British Museum.] In 5 v. v. 4, 5. ea., $100. A. H. Clark.

BRITISH MUSEUM.—*Continued.*
Lethaby, W: R: Greek buildings represented by fragments in the British Museum. *$4.20 net. Scribner.
BRITISH NAVY.
See England.
British officer in the Balkans. Henderson, P. E. *$3.50 net. Lippincott.
British place-names in their historical setting. McClure, E. $2. Gorham.
British poets ser. 12°, $1.50. Estes.
—Bell, *ed.* Songs of the great dramatists.
—Burns. Poetical works.
—Gray. Poetical works.
—Keats. Poetical works.
—Shelley. Poetical works.
British socialism. Barker, J. E. *$3 net. Scribner.
British sports past and present. Armour, G. D. *$6 net. Doran.
British tar in fact and fiction. Robinson, C: N. *$4 net. Harper.
Brito, Bernardo de.
Silvia de Lysardo; recopilada por Lourenço Craesbéck. [facsim.] '03. [1909.] (N) 54 p. 8°, $3. (200 copies.) Hispanic Soc.
Brittain, Carlo B., comp.
Elements of naval warfare; treatise prep. for use as a text-book at the U. S. Naval Academy. '09, [1910.] (F) c. 124 p. 12°. (Add. pubs. for price.) U. S. Naval Inst.
Brittannicus. *See* Racine, Jean Baptiste.
BRITTANY, France.
Atkinson, M. J. Chateau in Brittany. $2.50 net; $5 net. Pott.
Edwards, G: W. Brittany and the Bretons. $6 net. Moffat.
Gostling, *Mrs.* F. M. P.. Bretons at home. *$2.50 net. McClurg.
Britton, Frederic H.
Teddie; simple, little out-of-door story about a child. '10(Ag20) c. D. $1. F. B. Dickerson.
Britton, Nathaniel Lord.
Genus *Ernodea:* study of species and races. '08, [1909.] (Mr) 203-208 p. 8°, (Contributions from the New York Botanical Garden.) pap., 25 c. N. Y. Botanical.
Taxonomic aspect of the species question. '08, [1909.] (Mr) 225-242 p. 4°, (Contributions from the New York Botanical Garden.) pap., 25 c. N. Y. Botanical.
—, and Shafer, J: Adolph.
North American trees. '08(My16) il. Q. (American nature ser.; group II., Classification of nature.) **$7 net. Holt.
Britton, Wiley.
Civil war on the border. 2 v. '09(Ag) 8°, $4. Hudson.
White slavery: study of the present trades-union system. '09(N20) c. D. $1.50. Werner Co.
Britz of headquarters. Barber, M. $1.50. Moffat.
Broad lines in science teaching. Hodson, F., *ed.* *$1.25 net. Macmillan.
Broad stone of empire. Bruce, *Sir* C: 2 v. $9. Macmillan.

Broadbent, Fk.
Chats on electricity told in plain language for the non-technical. '10(Je4) il. D. $1.25 net. Lippincott.

Broadening path. Forbush, W: B. 2 v. $5; $8. B. F. Bowen.

Broadening the field of the marine steam turbine. Westinghouse, G:, *comp.* (Priv. pr.) G: Westinghouse.

Broader motive for school hygiene. Allen, W: H. (Priv. pr.) W: H. Allen.

Broadhurst, Cyrus Napoleon.
Wireless messages: possibilities through prayer. '10(Ag20) c. 12°, $1 net. Revell.

Broadhurst, G:
See Terhune, Albert Payson.

Broadlands cookery book. Behnke, K. E. $1 net. Macmillan.

Broadley, Alex. Meyrick.
Chats on autographs. '10(O29) il. facsims., O. ("Chats" ser.) $2 net; leath., $5 net. Stokes.
Doctor Johnson and Mrs. Thrale; with an introd. essay by T: Seccombe. '10(Ja15) map, facsim., O. *$5 net. Lane.
Napoleon in caricature, 1785-1821; with introd. essay on pictorial satire as a factor in Napoleonic hist. 2 v. '10(D10) il. (partly in col.) O. $12.50 net; Ed. de luxe, $50 net. Lane.
See also Wheeler, H. F. B.

Broadley, Arth.
Adjusting and repairing violins, 'cellos, etc. '09(Jl3) por. figs. D. pap., 40 c. Scribner.

Broadus, Eleanor Hammond.
Book of the Christ child. '10(N12) c. col. il. O. $1.75. Appleton.

Brock, A. Clutton-.
See Clutton-Brock, A.

Brock, Claude Cornelius, comp.
Solitaire: the great European game of "Patience"; for one or more players; how to play forty games. '09(My8) c. il. O. pap., 25 c. C. C. Brock.

BROCK, *Sir* Isaac.
Nursey, W. R. Story of Isaac Brock; hero, defender, and savior of upper Canada. *$1.50 net. McClurg.

Brock, Lilian.
Borrowed baby. '08(F1) c. il D. 75 c. Badger.

Brockaway, C: A.
Ancient accepted Scottish rites; one hundred years of Aurora Grata, 1808-1908. '08(O) c. 11+115 p. il. pors. facsims., 8°, $1. Aurora Grata.

Brockelmann, Carl..
Kurzegefasste vergleichende grammatik der semitischen sprachen: elemente der laut- und formenlehre. '08(S5) D. (Porta linguarum orientalium.) $3. Lemcke.

Brockett, Paul.
Bibliography of aeronautics; Hodgkins fund. '10(Je18) O. (Smithsonian miscellaneous collections.) $2.25; pap., $2. Smith. Inst.

Brockton Hospital Ladies' Aid Association.
Brockton Hospital cook book. 1910 ed. '10(Ja) c. 239 p. 8°, 50 c. Brockton Hospital.

Brockwell, Maurice W.
Leonardo da Vinci. '09(Mr13) il. O. (Masterpieces in colour.) bds., *65 c. net; leath., *$1.50 net. Stokes.
—, ed. *See* National Gallery.

Brodé, Julien L.
Oil-seed products and feed stuffs; transmitted to Congress in compliance with the act of March 4, 1909, authorizing investigations of trade conditions abroad. '10(O) 32 p. 8°. Gov. Pr. Off.

Broderick, M.
Trial and crucifixion of Jesus Christ of Nazareth. '08(Je13) D. *$1.25 net. Longmans.

Broderick, Therese, ["Tin Schreiner."]
The brand H. W.; tale of the Flathead Reservation. '09(D18) c. front. D. *$1.50 net. A. Harriman.

Brodhead, Mrs. Chloe Anna Sanford, ed.
Our free Methodist missions in Africa, to April, 1907. '08(Ag8) c. 77 p. il. f°, $1. Aldine Pr.

Brodie, Ethel Mary.
Rose-colored world, and other fantasies. '10(N12) c. il. D. $1.25 net. Metropolitan Press, (N. Y.)

Brodie, Orrin Lawrence.
See Morrison, C: E:

Brodie, Rob. Donald.
Changing voices, and other poems. '09 (D4) c. D. $1. Badger.

Brokaw, Mrs. Estella Bachman.
Soul of the world: [story advocating balanced land tenure.] '09(Mr) 370 p. $1. Equitist.

Brokaw, Irving.
Art of skating; its hist. and development with pract. directions; with contributions by eminent skaters. '10(Je4) il. 4°, $5 net. Scribner.

Broken earthenware. *See* Begbie, Harold.

Broken law. Burland, J: B. H-. 75 c. Cupples & L.

Broken links. Taylor, J. $1.50. C. M. Clark.

Broken snare. Lewisohn, L. $1.50. B. W. Dodge.

Broken statue de Fontange. Gammans, H. W. 60 c.; 40 c. Ruebush-E.

Broken wheel. May, F. L. $1.50. C. M. Clark.

BROKERS.
See Stock Brokers.

Bromhall, Marshall, ed.
Chinese Empire: general and missionary survey; pref. by Sir Ernest Satow. '08 (F) il. pors. map. 8°, $2. China Inland.

Bromley, G: W. and Wa. S.
Owners' names of the city of New York, Borough of Manhattan. '08(Je27); '10 (Je4) c. obl. 4°, ea., $30. G: W. Bromley.

Bromley, Wa. S.
See Bromley, G: W.

Bromwell, H: Pelham Holmes.
Song of the Wahbeek: a poem. '09(Je5) por. D. $1; leath., $2. H. E. Bromwell.

Bromwich, T. J. I'anson.
Introduction to the theory of infinite series. '08(Ap4) diagrs., 8°, *$4.50 net. Macmillan.

Bronchain, C: L: Laurent.
Meditations for every day in the year according to the doctrine and spirit of St. Alphonsus Mary de Liguori, doctor of the church, for the use of all who aspire to perfection: priests, religious and laymen; tr. from the 12th Belgian ed.; ed. by Rev. Ferreol Girardy. 2 v. '10 (D17) c. 8°, $5 net. **Herder.**

Broncho book. Crawford, J: W. $2. Roycrofters.

Bronk, Isabelle, tr.
See Furetière, Antoine.

Bronner, Milton.
Maurice Hewlett; critical review of his prose and poetry. '10(Je11) por. D. $1.25 net. J: W. Luce.

Bronson, Edg. Beecher.
In closed territory. '10(Mr12) c. il. O. *$1.75 net. McClurg.
The red-blooded. '10(S24) il. c. O. $1.50. McClurg.
Reminiscences of a ranchman. '08(N7) c. D. †$1.50. McClure.
Reminiscences of a ranchman. New rev ed. '10(S24) c. il. O. $1.50. McClurg.

Bronson, Wa. Cochrane, comp. and ed.
English poems; sel. and ed., with illustrative and explanatory notes and bibliographies. In 4 v. v. 1, Old English and Middle English periods (1450-1550). '10 (Jl2); v. 2, Elizabethan age and the Puritan period (1550-1650). '09(S4); v. 3, The Restoration and the eighteenth century (1660-1800). '08(Je27) c. O. ea., library ed., *$1.50 net; school ed., *$1 net. Univ. of Chic.

Bronson of the rabble. Hancock, A. E. †$1.50. Lippincott.

Brontë, Anne, ["Acton Bell."]
Agnes Grey. Pocket ed. '09(Mr6) por. S. (World's classics.) 35 c. Oxford Univ.
Tenant of Wildfell Hall. Pocket ed. '09 (Mr6) por. S. (World's classics.) 35 c. Oxford Univ.

—, Charlotte, [Mrs. Nicholls: "Currer Bell"], and Emily Jane, ["Ellis Bell."]
Complete Brontë; édition de luxe in 7 v.; with introds. by Mrs. Humphry Ward. v. 1, Jane Eyre; v. 2, Shirley; v. 3, Villette; v. 4, The professor; v. 5, Wuthering Heights and Agnes Gray; v. 6, The tenant of Wildfell Hall; v. 7, The life of Charlotte Brontë, by Mrs. Gaskell; with an introd. and notes by Clement K. Shorter. '09(Jl3) il. pors. facsims., hf. vel., subs., $35. Harper.

Brontë, Charlotte, [Mrs. Nicholls; "Currer Bell."]
Works. De luxe ed. 6 v. '10(D) $18. Crowell.
Works. De luxe ed. 5 v. '10(D) 16°, ea., mor., $1.50 net. (Sets only.) Nelson.
Jane Eyre; introd. by May Sinclair. '08 (F22) 16°, (Everyman's lib.) *35 c. net; leath., *70 c. net. Dutton.
Jane Eyre. '08(F22) 16°, (York lib.) 80 c.; leath., $1.25. Macmillan.
The professor. '10(Ap23) 16°, (Everyman's lib.) 35 c. net; leath., 70 c. net. **Dutton.**

Brontë, Charlotte.—*Continued.*
Shirley; introd. by May Sinclair. '08 (F22) 16°, (Everyman's lib.) *35 c. net; leath., *70 c. net. Dutton.
Villette; introd. by May Sinclair. '09 (Mr27) 16°, (Everyman's lib.) *35 c. net; leath., *70 c. net. Dutton.
See also Brontë, Anne.

BRONTË, Charlotte.
Gaskell, *Mrs.* E. C. S. Life of Charlotte Brontë. *35 c. net; *70 c. net. Dutton.

BRONTË FAMILY.
Shorter, C. K., *comp.* The Brontës; life and letters. **$6 net. Scribner.

BRONZE AGE.
See Italy.

Bronze bell. *See* Vance, L: Jos.

BRONZES.
Hessling, E. *and* W. Applied bronze work in the style of Louis XVI. $8. Hessling.
Johns, C. H. W. Ur-Engur, a bronze of the fourth millenium. [priv. pr.] F. F. Sherman.
See also Metal work.

Bronzino, Angioli di Cosimo, called.
Masterpieces. '08(O10) il. T. (Painters' ser.) leath., *75 c. net; pap., *25 c. net. Stokes.

Brood house. McCutcheon, G: B. $5. G: B. McCutcheon.

BROOK CLIFF COAL FIELD.
See Coal.

Brook in the pasture. Elliott, J: H: 25 c. Un. Soc. C. E.

Brooke, Arth.
"Romeus and Juliet": being the original of Shakespeare's "Romeo and Juliet"; newly ed. by J. J. Munro. '08(Mr28) facsim., S. (Shakespeare lib.: Shakespeare classics.) bds., *$1 net; Persian, *$1.60 net; Lib. ed., hf. parchment, 12°, *$1.70 net. Duffield.

Brooke, C. F. Tucker, ed.
Shakespeare apocrypha: being a collection of fourteen plays which have been ascribed to Shakespeare; ed., with introd., notes and bibliography. '08(Je27) D. *$1.75 net; India pap., *$2.50 net. Oxford Univ.

Brooke, Gilbert E.
Aids to tropical medicine. '08(Ag22) c. il. charts, 16°, *$1 net. Wood.

Brooke, H:
Fool of quality; introd. by Fs. Coutts. In 2 v. '09(F6) T. *$1 net. Lane.

Brooke, Leonard Leslie.
Johnny Crow's party; another picture book drawn by L. Leslie Brooke. [1910.] (Mr) 48 p. il. 8°, $1 net. Warne.

Brooke, Rev. Stopford A:
Four Victorian poets: study of Clough, Arnold, Rossetti, Morris; with an introd. on the course of poetry from 1822 to 1852. '08(My2) c. O. **$1.75 net. Putnam.
Theology in the English poets: Cowper, Coleridge, Wordsworth, Burns; with introd. note by Ernest Rhys. '10(D10) 16°, (Everyman's lib.) 35 c. net; leath., 70 c. net. Dutton.

Brookes, Leonard Elliott.
Automobile handbook. new 1910 ed.; rev. and enl. by Calvin F. Swingle and other experts. '10(D31) c. il. fold. pls. tabs., diagrs., 16°, $2. Drake.

Brookfield, Frances M.
Friar observant. '09(Ap24) 8°, $1.50. Herder.

BROOKFIELD, Mass.
Vital records of Brookfield, Mass. (Add. pub. for price.) F. P. Rice.

Brookline, Mass. Public Library. Selected list of books on business and related subjects in the Public Library, Dec., 1909. '10 (Je4) 12°, gratis to public libraries. Riverdale Press.

Brookline, Mass. Public Library. Something to read, for boys and girls. '08, [1909.] (F) 31 p. 12°, o. p. Brookline Pub. Lib.

BROOKLYN, N. Y.
See Long Island (Battle of);—New York City.

Brooklyn Daily Eagle almanac, 1908. '08 (Ja25); 1909. '09(Ja30); 1910. '10(F12) c. (fold. map in pocket,) O. (Eagle lib.) ea., 50 c. Brooklyn Eagle.

Brooklyn Institute of Arts and Sciences; Cold Spring Harbor monographs. O. Brooklyn Inst.
—Byrnes. Fresh water *cyclops* of Long Island. 80 c.

Brooklyn Public Library. Abraham Lincoln: list of Lincoln's writings and works rel. to Lincoln in the Brooklyn Public Library. '09(Mr) 24 p. S. pap., gratis. Brooklyn Lib.

Brooklyn Public Library. Aeronautics or aerial navigation; list of books and references to periodicals in the Brooklyn Public Library. '10(Ap9) 16°, pap., gratis. Brooklyn Lib.

Brooklyn Public Library. Alfred Tennyson, 1809-1892: list of books with references to periodicals in the library. '09(Ag7) S. pap. gratis. Brooklyn Lib.

Brooklyn Public Library. Earthquakes and volcanoes: list of books with reference to periodicals in the library. 2d ed., enl. '09 (Mr13) S. pap., gratis. Brooklyn Lib.

Brooklyn Public Library. German books in the Brooklyn Pub. Library. '08(F22) 8°, pap., 5 c. Brooklyn Lib.

Brooklyn Public Library. International peace: list of books, with references to periodicals, in the Library; comp. by Alys M. Gordon. '09(Mr6) 16°. (Add. Library for price.) Brooklyn Pub.

Brooklyn Public Library. List of books and magazine articles on Henry Hudson and the Hudson River, Robert Fulton and early steam navigation. '09(Jl31) S. pap., gratis. Brooklyn Lib.

Brooklyn Public Library. Oliver Wendell Holmes, 1809-1894; list of books with references to periodicals in the Brooklyn Public Library. '09(O2) S. pap., gratis. Brooklyn Lib.

Brooklyn Public Library. Personal hygiene and physical development; list of books in the Brooklyn Public Library. '10 (D) 28 p. 16°, gratis. Brooklyn Lib.

Brooklyn Public Library. Polar regions; list of books in the Library. '10(Ja8) 16°, pap., gratis. Brooklyn Lib.

Brooklyn Public Library. Reading and reference list of books on building and building trades. '10(N) 29 p. 12°, pap., gratis. Brooklyn Lib.

Brooklyn Public Library. Reading and reference list on costume. '09(D25) O. pap., gratis. Brooklyn Lib.

Brooklyn Public Library. Samuel Johnson, 1709-1784; list of books with references to periodicals in the Brooklyn Public Library. '09(O2) S. pap., gratis. Brooklyn Lib.

Brooklyn Public Library. William Ewart Gladstone, 1809-1898; list of books and of references to periodicals in the Brooklyn Public Library. '09, [1910.] (Ap) 30 p. 16°, pap., gratis. Brooklyn Lib.

Brooks, A. M., comp.
Unwritten hist. of old St. Augustine; copied from the Spanish archives in Seville, Spain, by A. M. Brooks and tr. by Mrs. Annie Averette. '09(Ag) 15+233 p. il. 12°, 75 c. Record Co.

Brooks, Alfr. Hulse, and others.
Mineral resources of Alaska; rept. on progress in investigations in 1907. '08(O10); rept. on progress of investigations in 1908. '09(Ag7) fold. maps, O. (U. S., Dept. of the Interior, U. S. Geol. Survey bull.) ea., pap.

Brooks, Alfr. Mansfield.
Somes House. '09(Jl17) 12°, *$1.25 net. Dutton.

Brooks, Amy.
Dorothy Dainty in the country. '09(S11) c. il. 12°, (Dorothy Dainty ser.) †$1. Lothrop, L. & S.
Dorothy Dainty's gay times. '08(N14) c. il. D. (Dorothy Dainty ser.) †$1. Lothrop, L. & S.
Dorothy Dainty's winter. '10(Ag20) c. il. D. (Dorothy Dainty ser.) $1. Lothrop, L. & S.
Little sister Prue. '08(S5) c. il. D. (Prue books.) †$1. Lothrop, L. & S.
Princess Polly. '10(O1) c. il. D. (Princess Polly ser.) $1. Platt & P.
Prue at school. '09(S11) c. il. 12°, (Prue books.) †$1. Lothrop, L. & S.
Prue's playmates. '10(Ag20) c. il. D. (Prue books.) $1. Lothrop, L. & S.

Brooks, Asa Passavant.
The reservation: romance of the pioneer days of Minnesota. '08(Ja4) D. pap., 50 c. A. P. Brooks.

Brooks, Dorothy.
Stories of the red children; with il. by Louise E. Norris. Rev. ed. '08(Ag29) c. 12°, (Choice lit. lib.) 40 c.; bds., 30 c. Educ. Pub.

Brooks, E:
Normal standard algebra; designed for public and private schools, normal schools, academies. '09(D18) c. il. 12°, $1.22. Sower.
Wonder stories from the Mabinogion. '08 (O3) c. il. D. †$1.25. Penn Pub.

Brooks, Eug. Clyde.
Comparison of school systems. [1910.] (N) 23 p. 8°, (Trinity College (Durham, N. C.) Dept. of Education; bull.) Trinity Coll.

Brooks, Eva Cannon.
Francisco, our little Argentine cousin. '10 (D3) c. il. 12°, (Little cousin ser.) 60 c. L. C. Page.

Brooks, Rev. Fk. Lester.
Prevailing prayer: sermons. '09(Jl31) c. por. 12°, 60 c. F. L. Brooks.

Brooks, Harlow.
See Greene, Rob. Holmes.

BROOKS, John Cotton.
Sharp, J. C. John Cotton Brooks. $1.50. Burgess, L. & Co.

Brooks, J: Graham.
American citizen; life of William Henry Baldwin, jr. '10(Jl9) c. pors. D. $1.50 net. Houghton M.
As others see us: a study of progress in the United States. '08(N7) c. il. pors. O. **$1.75 net. Macmillan.
Conflict between private monopoly and good citizenship. '09(D25) c. S. **50 c. net. Houghton M.

Brooks, Bp. Phillips.
Sermons. 10 v. '10(D31) 12°, per set, $6 net; (formerly ea., $1.50.) Dutton.

Brooks, Ralph O.
Federal spice standards, interpretation and possibilities of. '09, [1910.] (Ja) c. 60 p. 16°, 50 c. Spice Mill.

Brooks, R:, comp.
Old friends are best. '10(D17) 12°, ("Borrowings" ser.) $1.25; ooze, $2. Dodge.

Brooks, Rob. Clarkson.
Corruption in American politics and life. '10(D3) c. D. $1.25 net. Dodd.
Odd prices and bargains in retail trade. '09(My8) O. (Univ. of Cin. studies.) pap., 50 c. Univ. of Cin.

Brooks, Sarah Warner.
Garden with house attached. [New ed.] '10(D31) c. '04-'10. il. O. $1.50 net, boxed. Badger.

Brooks, Standford M.
See Young, Clyde.

Brooks, T. J.
March of intellect; review of man's achievements that make for the advancement of civilization and a glimpse of the future. [1910.] (D) c. '09. 164 p D. $1. B'way Pub.

Brooks, Ulysses Rob.
Butler and his cavalry in the War of Secession, 1861-1865. '09(O23) c. il. pors. 8°, $2.50. State Co.
South Carolina bench and bar. v. 1. '08 (O) c. pors. 8°, *$1.50 net. State Co.

Brooks, Van Wyck.
Wine of the Puritans; study of the present day in America. '09(N20) c. 8°, *$1 net. M. Kennerley.

BROOM, Jacob.
Campbell, W: W. Life and character of Jacob Broom. 50 c. Delaware Hist. Soc.

Broomell, A. W., M.D.
See Frear, W:

Broomell, I: Norman, and Fischelis, Philipp.
Anatomy and histology of the mouth and teeth. 3d ed., rev. '09(D) c. 13+454 p. il. 8°, $3. Blakiston.
—, **comp. and ed.** Practical dentistry. '08, [1909.] (F) c. 7+496 p. 8°, $2.50. Caulk.

Broomhall, Marshall.
Present-day conditions in China. '08(N7) 16°, *50 c. net. Revell.
—, **ed.** Chinese empire. '08. 24+472 p. il. map, $2.50. China Inland.

BROPHY, Joseph Francis.
Boyton, *Mrs.* P., *comp.* A heroic priest. $1. G: C. Tilyou.

Bross lectures. *See* Thomson, J: Arth.

Bross lib. 8°. T. R. Marvin.
—Hopkins. Evidences of Christianity. $1.25.

Brother and the brotherhood. Dodd, I. S. **$1.50 net. Dodd.

Brother Jonathan ser. T. pap. Fruit Grower.
—Farmers' shipping associations. gratis.

Brother Luke. Smith, E. R. 50 c. E. R. Smith.

Brother of girls. Crittenton, C: N. $1. World's Events.

Brotherhood. Van Kirk, J. W: $1. J. W: Van Kirk.

Brotherhood of wisdom. Armour, F. J. †$1.50. Lane.

Brother's sacrifice. Jüngst, A. 50 c. Soc. Divine Word.

Brothers all. Schwartz, J. M. W. Van der P. †$1.50. Appleton.

Brothers in fur. White, E. O. $1. Houghton M.

Broughton, J: Cam Hobhouse, Lord.
Recollections of a long life, by Lord Broughton; with additional extracts from his private diaries; ed. by his daughter, Lady Dorchester. In 2 v. '09(D11) pors. O. *$6 net. Scribner.

Broughton, Leonard Gaston, D.D.
The kingdom parables and their teaching. '10(D10) 12°, 75 c. net. Revell.
Plain man and his Bible. '09(Je19) c. D. **60 c. net. Am. Bapt.
Religion and health. '09(Ap10) c. 16°, bds., *25 c. net. Revell.
Salvation and the old theology: pivot points in Romans. '08(Mr21) c. 12°, *75 c. net. Revell.

Brouillet, Georges Antoine.
Artistic tone production through natural breathing; Brouillet-method. '10(F5) c. il. 16°, $2. F. E. Bacon.

Brower, Ja. Hattan.
The mills of Mammon. '09, [1910.] (Ja) c. 491 p. il. D. $1.50. P. H. Murray.

Brower, Josephine, ed.
Morris dance; descriptions of eleven dances as performed by the Morris-men of England. '10(Ap) 38 p. il. 4°, $1. H. W. Gray.

Brown, —, and Martin, —.
French and English dictionary; additions by Duhamel. '08(Je20) 48°, (Miniature reference lib.) leath., 50 c. Dutton.

Brown, A. C. B., ed.
Selections from the Latin literature of the Early Empire. Pt. A: the inner life. '10(D3) D. $1.10. Oxford Univ.

Brown, Abbie Farwell.
The Christmas angel. '10(O15) c. il. D. bds., 60 c. net. Houghton M.
Fresh posies: rhymes to read and pieces to speak. '08(O17) c. il. O. $1.50. Houghton M.
John of the woods. '09(N6) c. il. D. †$1. Houghton M.

—, and Bell, Ja. Mackintosh.
Tales of the Red Children. '09(O9) c. D. †$1. Appleton.

Brown, Addison.
Elgin Botanic Garden, its later history and relation to Columbia College, the New Hampshire grants and the treaty with Vermont in 1790. '08(Je6) c. 8°, $1. A. Brown.

Brown, Alice.
Country neighbors. '10(Ap16) c. D. $1.20 net. Houghton M.
John Winterbourne's family. '10(O1) c. O. $1.35 net. Houghton M.
Rose MacLeod. '08(My2) c. front. D. †$1.50. Houghton M.
Story of Thyrza. '09(Mr20) c. front. O. **$1.35 net Houghton M.

Brown, Allen A.
See Boston Public Library.

Brown, Amos Peaslee.
See Frazer, Persifor;—Reichert, E: Tyson.

Brown, Arth. Judson, D.D.
Why and how of foreign missions. [Churchman's ed.] '09(Ap) 12+275 p. 12°, 50 c.; pap., 35 c.; Leaders' helps, 10 c. Dom. and For. Mission.
Why and how of foreign missions. 3d ed. '08, [1909.] (F) c. 12+286 p. il. 12°, (Forward mission study courses.) *50 c. net. Young People's Miss.
See also Zwemer, S: Marinus.

Brown, Barnum.
Conard fissue, a Pleistocene bone deposit in northern Arkansas; with descriptions of two new genera and twenty new species of mammals. '08(D) 155-208 p. il. 4°, (Memoirs of the Am. Museum of Natural History.) $2.50. Am. Museum.

Brown, C. W.
Petrol engine: troubles and remedies. '08 (Ag1) il. 12°, 50 c. Spon.

Brown, Calvin Smith.
Lignite of Mississippi. '07. [1908.] (Ag) 71 p. il. 8°, (Mississippi State Geological Survey, bull.) pap. (Add. pub. for price.) Brandon Pr.

Brown, C:
Birth of a nation: studies in Old Testament stories. '09(My1) 12°, *$1 net. Revell.
See also Greenhough, J. G.

—, Darlow, T. H., Greenhough, J. G., and others.
God's garden; sermons for harvest and flower festivals. '09(N20) D. *$1 net. Eaton & M.

Brown, C: Campbell.
China in legend and story. '08(Ap4) il. pors. D. *$1.25 net. Revell.

Brown, C: Franklin.
Drainage of irrigated lands. '09(D) 52 p. il. plans, 8°, (U. S., Dept. of Agriculture, farmers' bull.) pap. (Add. Superintendent for price.) U. S., Supt. of Docs.

Brown, C: Gardner.
Good, the beautiful, the true; poems. '09 (Ap10) c. il. S. $1. C: G. Brown.

Brown, C: Reynolds, D.D.
Cap and gown. '10(N5) c. D. $1 net. Pilgrim Press.
Faith and health. '10(Ja29) c. D. **$1 net. Crowell.
Gospel of good health. '10(F26) c. 12°, ooze leath., *75 c. net; pap., *35 c. net. Pilgrim Press.
Strange ways of God: study in the book of Job. '08(S12) c. D. bds., *75 c. net. Pilgrim Press.
Young man's affairs. '09(Ag21) c. D. **$1 net. Crowell.

Brown, Colin Campbell.
Children of China. '10(N12) 12°, 60 c. net. Revell.

Brown, Dan. Rollins, M.D.
The baby: a book for mothers and nurses. '08(D26) c. D. *$1 net. Whitcomb.

Brown, D: Wa.
Commercial power of Congress, considered in the light of its origin; the origin, development, and contemporary interpretation of the commerce clause of the Federal Constitution, from the New Jersey representations, of 1778, to the embargo laws of Jefferson's second administration, in 1809. '10(D17) c. 12°, $2. Putnam.

Brown, D: Wolfe.
Factors of shorthand speed; or, how to become a stenographic expert; book of pract. aids and suggestions to the student, the teacher, and the young reporter. '10(O) c. 194 p. 12°, 75 c. Gregg Pub.

Brown, Demetra Vaka, [Mrs. Kenneth Brown.]
Finella in Fairyland. '10(O1) c. il. S. bds., 50 c. net. Houghton M.
Haremlik; some pages from the life of Turkish women. '09(My22) c. **$1.25 net. Houghton M.

—, and Kenneth.
Duke's price. '10(Mr5) c. il. D. **$1.20 net. Houghton M.

Brown, Mrs. Eliz. Deborah Jewett.
Nell Beverly, farmer; story of farm life. '09(Ap) c. '08. 190 p. 12°, pap., 50 c. Rural.

Brown, Elmer Ellsworth.
Distinctive functions of university, college and normal school in the preparation of teachers. '09(Mr) 6 p. 8°. (Add. author for price.) E. E. Brown.
Government by influence and other addresses. '10(Ap2) O. $1.25 net. Longmans.

Brown, Ernest W:
Inequalities in the motion of the moon due to the direct action of the planets; Adams prize essay, University of Cambridge. (Eng.,) 1907. '08(N7) 4°, *$2 net. Putnam.

Brown, Fs., D.D., ed.
See Harper, Rob. Fs.

Brown, Fred Radford.
Hist. of the Ninth U. S. Infantry, 1799-1909. '09, [1910.] (F) c. 842 p. il. pors. maps, 8°, $4.75; hf. mor., $5.25; ¾ mor., $5.50. Ninth Infantry, Tex.

Brown, G:, D.D.
George Brown, D.D.: pioneer, missionary and explorer: autobiography. '09(Je19) 8°, *$3.50. Revell.

Brown, G:
Melanesians and Polynesians. '10(N19) il. 8°, $3 net. Macmillan.

Brown, G: E., ed.
British Journal, Photographic Almanac, and Photographer's Daily Companion, with which is incorporated the "Year Book of Photography and Amateurs' Guide," 1909. '09(Ja9) il. D. $1; pap., 50 c. G: Murphy.

Brown, G: G., comp.
Holy Bible repudiates "prohibition"; compilation of all verses cont. the words "wine" or "strong drink," proving that the Scriptures commend and command the temperate use of alcoholic beverages. '10(O1) c. por. O. $1; pap., 35 c. G: G. Brown.

Brown, G: Pliny.
Physiology and psychology of education. '08(F) c. 56 p. 12°, 25 c. Public Sch. Pub.

Brown, G: Washington.
Old times in oildom; the writer's experiences during fifty years in the oil regions. '10(Ap2) por. O. $1. G: W. Brown.

Brown, Gertrude L., comp.
See Evanston (Ill.) Public Library.

Brown, Goodwin.
Scientific nutrition simplified: condensed statement and explanation for every one of the discoveries of Chittenden, Fletcher, Fisher and others. '08(Ap18) c. D. *75 c. net. Stokes.

Brown, Goold.
Institutes of English grammar; rev. and rearranged by J: W. Davis. '07, [1909.] (Je) 8+344 p. 8°, (Brown's grammar ser.) 80 c. Wood.

Brown, Haydn, M.D.
The wife: her book. Rev. Am. ed. '08 (Jl4) c. 12°, **$1 net. Jacobs.

Brown, Herbert D.
Civil-service retirement in Great Britain and in New Zealand; prep. under the direction of C: P. Neill. '10(Mr) 203 p. 8°, pap. (Add. Superintendent for price.) U. S., Supt. of Docs.

Brown, Herbert Hillier.
Little girl I used to love, and other poems. '07, [1908.] (My.) c. 67 p. por. 12°, $1. Brown Press.

Brown, Ira Smith.
Typewriter bookkeeping as applied to the "unit order," "retail bill and charge" and "condensed billing" systems on the Underwood. '09(S) c. 36 p. il. 4°, gratis. Underwood Typewriter.

Brown, Ja. Newton.
Estimates and agents' companion. Rev. ed.; clear exposition of the cubic foot rule for estimating the approximate value of buildings, with data as to cost of materials and sugggestions for building. '08, [1909.] (Mr) c. '07. 103 p. 16°, $1; leath., $1.50. Rough Notes.

Brown, J:, M.D., 1810-1882.
Horae subsecivae; with an introd. by Austin Dobson. Pocket ed. '09(Mr6) por. S. (World's classics.) 35 c. Oxford Univ.
Our dogs. '09(D) 64 p. 24°. 50 c. Altemus.
Rab and his friends. '09(O16) c. por. S. 50 c. Altemus.
Rab and his friends. '10(D17) por. Ff. (Oxford moment ser.) silk or limp leath., 40 c. Oxford Univ.
Rab and his friends; with biographical sketch. [1910.] (Ap) c. '09. 9-84 p. il. por. 12°, (Golden classics.) 50 c. Rand, McN. & Co.

BROWN, John, 1800-1859.
Du Bois, W: E: B. John Brown. **$1.25 net. Jacobs.
Huhner, L. Some Jewish associates of John Brown. o. p. L. Hühner.
Leech, S: V. Raid of John Brown at Harper's Ferry. 40 c. S: V. Leech.
Sanborn, F. B: John Brown; life and letters. $1.50 net. Torch Press.
Villard, O. G. John Brown, 1800-1859; biography fifty years after. $5 net. Houghton M.

BROWN, JOHN, BELL.
See **Marlborough, Mass.**

Brown, J: Crosby.
Hundred years of merchant banking; hist. of Brown Brothers & Co., Brown, Shipley & Co., and the allied firms, Alexander Brown & Sons, Baltimore; William and James Brown & Co., Liverpool; John A. Brown & Co., Browns & Bowen, Brown Brothers & Co., Phila.; Brown Brothers & Co., Boston. '09, [1910.] (F) c. 33+374 p. il. pors. facsims., 8°. (Priv. pr.) Brown Bros. & Co.

Brown, Mrs. J: Crosby, comp.
See Bible. Selections. Father and child.

Brown, J: Franklin.
American high school. '09(Je5) c. tabs., D. **$1.40 net. Macmillan.

Brown, J: G.
Reinforced concrete construction for factories and warehouses. '08, [1909.] (F) c. 24 p. il. 8°. (Add. pubs. for price.) Doolittle & K.

Brown, J: Mason.
Lectures on the statutory provisions rel. to government contracts; rel. before the Engineer School, U. S. A., Washington Barracks, D. C., Mar., 1908. '08(O) c. O. pap. (Add. pub. for price.) J: M. Brown.

Brown, Katharine Holland.
The messenger. '10(Mr19) c. front. D. bds., **50 c. net. Scribner.
Philippa at Halcyon. '10(Je4) c. il. D. $1.50. Scribner.
White roses. '10(N5) c. il. D. $1.20 net. Duffield.

Brown, Mrs. Kenneth.
See Brown, Demetra Vaka.

Brown, Mrs. Laura Nettleton.
Scientific living for prolonging the term of human life; new domestic science; cooking to simplify living and retain the life elements in food. '10(F19) D. $1. Health-Culture.

Brown, Leonard.
Our own Columbia that is to be. '08(Je) c. 608 p. por. 8°, $2. E. T. Meredith.

Brown, Marg. Wright, comp.
Mending and repair of books. '10(Jl16) 12°, (A. L. A. Publishing Board, library hdbk.) 15 c. A. L. A.

Brown, Martin Shepherd.
"Sleepin' at the foot," and other poems. Memorial ed.; collected by Mrs. Jennie Marie Brown. '09(S) c. 72 p. il. por. 12°, $1. J. M. Brown.

Brown, Mrs. Mary Alice Abbott, comp.
Dainty dining; a few simple luncheons and a few not so simple; but with tried receipts for each and all; with a post-script for dinners. '09(Mr13) c. 4°, $1.50. Reed Press.

Brown, Nellie Clarke, and Locke, Elma Iona, eds.
Priscilla Hardanger book; collection of beautiful designs in Hardanger embroidery, with lessons and stitches. '09, [1910.] (F) c. 48 p. il. 4°, 25 c. Priscilla.

Brown, P: Hume.
Hist. of Scotland. In 3 v. v. 3, From the revolution of 1689 to the disruption, 1843. '09(O30) D. $1.50. Putnam.

"Brown, R. B.," pseud.
See Branston, J: W:

Brown, R. Grant.
Half the battle in Burmese; manual of the spoken language. '10(Mr26) S. $2. Oxford Univ.

Brown, Rob. Perkins, Palmer, H: Robinson, Koopman, Harry Lyman, and Brigham, Clarence Saunders, eds.
Memories of Brown: traditions and recollections gathered from many sources. '09 (Ap3) c. il. pors. 8°, $2.50; mor., $5. Brown Alumni.

Brown, Stephen J.
Reader's guide to Irish fiction. '10(D3) $1.25 net. Longmans.

Brown, Stimson Jos.
Trigonometry and stereographic projections; prepared for the use of the midshipmen at the U. S. Naval Academy. '09(Mr) c. 9+111 p. diagrs., 12°. (Not for sale.) Lord Balto. Pr.

Brown, Rev. Theron.
Under the mulberry trees. '09(N6) c. front. D. $1.50. Badger.

Brown, T: E:
Poems; sel. and arr. with an introd. and notes by H. F. B. and H. G. D. '08 (Je13) por. 16°, (Golden treasury ser.) $1. Macmillan.

Brown, Vincent.
Glory and the abyss. '10(Ag6) D. $1.25 net. Dutton.
The screen. '10(Ap2) 12°, $1.25 net. Dutton.

Brown, W. Carnegie.
Sprue and its treatment. '08(D) 273 p. il. 4°, *$2.50 net. Wood.

Brown, W. Langdon, M.D.
Physiological principles in treatment. '08 (D26) 12°, *$2 net. Wood.

Brown, Wa. F. A., ed.
See Yendes, Lucy A., *ed.*

Brown, Warner.
Judgment of difference with special reference to the doctrine of the threshold, in the case of lifted weights. '10(O) 71 p. O. (Univ. of Cal.. pubs.; Psychology.) pap., 50 c. Univ. of Cal.
Time in English verse rhythm: empirical study of typical verses by the graphic method. '08(S5) tabs., O. (Archives of psychology.) pap., 70 c. Science Pr., (N. Y.)

Brown, W: Adams, D.D.
Morris Ketchum Jesup. '10(D24) c. por. O. $2.50 net. Scribner.

Brown, W: Bartholomew.
Family hist. of Jeremiah Fenton (1764-1841) of Adams County, Ohio, and his descendants. '10(Je) 13+199 p. il. facsim., 8°, $3.50. W: B. Brown.

Brown, W: C.
See Hoile, Ja. T.

Brown, W: Findlay.
See Philadelphia. Supp. to digest.

Brown, Bp. W: Montgomery.
Crucial race question; or, when and how shall the color line be drawn. 2d ed. '08(Mr.) c. '07. 36+323 p. 12°. (Add. pub. for price.) Arkansas Churchman.
Level plan for church union; with introd. on the Origin and development of the historic episcopate by the Rev. G: Williamson Smith; with appendix on The chief barrier to Christian unity by "Anglican Presbyter." '10(N12) $1.50 net. Whittaker.

Brown, Zaidee M., comp.
Buying list of books for small libraries. '10(Je4) 8°, gratis. N. Y. State Educ.

BROWN BROS & Co.
Brown, J: C. Hundred years of merchant banking. (Priv. pr.) Brown Bros. & Co.

BROWN FAMILY.
See Genealogies: Miller, W: H.

Brown rat in the U. S. Lantz, D: E. (Add. Superintendent for price.) U. S., Supt. of Docs.

BROWN STATION, N. Y.
See Ashokan Reservoir.

Brown University. Books printed in Lima and elsewhere in South America after 1800 [John Carter Brown Library.] '09 (My22). 4°, 50 c. Brown Univ.

Brown University. Facsimile of the first issue of the *Gazeta de Lima*, with a description of a file for the years 1744-1763, [John Carter Brown Library.] '09(Jl31) 12°, $2. Brown Univ.

Brown University. Three proclamations concerning the lottery for Virginia, 1613-1621. '08(O10) facsims., f°, (John Carter Brown Library.) pap. (Add. pub. for price.) Brown Univ.

BROWN UNIVERSITY, Providence, R. I.
Brown, R. P., *and others, eds.* Memories of Brown. $2.50; $5. Brown Alumni.
General information concerning Brown University, Providence, R. I. [1910.] 14 p. il. 8°. Brown Univ.
Growth of Brown University in recent years, 1899-1909. '09, [1910.] (N) 14 p. 8°. Brown Univ.

Browne, Bellmore H.
Guns and gunning; ed. by Dan. Carter Beard. '08(Jl) c. 106 p. il. 8°, 30 c.; pap., 20 c. J. Stevens.

Browne, Edith A.
Greek architecture. '09(Jl3) il. 8°, (Great buildings and how to enjoy them.) *$1.75 net. Macmillan.
Greece. '09(D25) il. map, 12°, (Peeps at many lands.) *75 c. net. Macmillan.
Romanesque architecture. '10(Jl30) il. O. (Great buildings and how to enjoy them.) $1.75 net. Macmillan.
Spain. '10(N19) col. il. map, 12°, (Peeps at many lands ser.) 75 c. net. Macmillan.
—, ed. *See* Adams, *Mrs.* Hugh, *ed.*

Browne, Edmond Cornelius.
See Browne, T: Rob.

Browne, G: H:
Vest-pocket memory-test Latin word-list for secondary schools: vocab. of Cæsar's complete works and of Cicero's orations grouped according to frequency of occurrence. '08(F1) c. T. mor., 75 c.; also, A memory-test note-book, pap., 15 c. Ginn.

Browne, G: Waldo, ["Victor St. Clair."]
Ruel Durkee, master of men. '10(S3) c. front. D. $1.50. Badger.

—, and Dole, Nathan Haskell.
New America and the Far East; with general introd. by E: S. Ellis. 9 v. '10 (Je4) c. il. fold. maps, 4°, $36.25; hf. leath., $40.75. M. Jones.

Browne, Harriet Augusta.
Dewdrop on ocean wave: [poems.] '08 (O) c. 3-144 p. por. 16°, $1. J. M. Williams.

Browne, Horace B., comp.
Short plays from Dickens, for the use of amateur and school dramatic societies. '09(My15) il. D. *$1 net. Scribner.

Browne, Sir Ja. Crichton-.
Parcimony in nutrition. '09(Mr6) D. **75 c. net. Funk.

Browne, J: Hutton Balfour.
Some further letters to an elector and some political fables. '10(Ap9) O. pap., 25 c. Longmans.

Browne, Leda Gano.
Eva's choice and other poems. '10(O) c. 58 p. por. 12°, 60 c. Cochrane.

Browne, Lewis Allen, ["Paul R. Dash."]
Cook-ed-up Peary-odd-ical dictionary and who's hoot in the best Arctic circles. '10(F26) c. D. bds., *60 c. net. J: W. Luce.

Browne, Marion J., ["Marion J. Brunowe."]
New scholar at St. Anne's. '09(F20) c. D. 85 c. Benziger.

Browne, Rev. Patrick W:
Where the fishers go: the story of Labrador. '09(Jl3) c. il. fold. map, O. $1.75. Cochrane.

Browne, Porter Emerson.
A fool there was. '09(Ja8) c. il. D. $1.50. H. K. Fly.
The spendthrift; novelized from the play by E: Marshall. '10(N5) c. il. D. $1.50. G: W: Dillingham.

Browne, Rob. H:
Abraham Lincoln and the men of his time. Rev. 2d ed. '08(My16) c. 2 v., il. pors. 12°, $3. Blakely-O.

Browne, Sir T:, and Digby, Sir Kenelm.
Browne's Religio medici, and Digby's Observations. '10(Ja1) D. $1.75. Oxford Univ.

Browne, T: Rob. and Edmond Cornelius, comps. and eds.
Miscellaneous correspondence, commercial and legal forms. pt. 1. '09(Ja9) c. O. 50 c. Browne's Business Coll.

BROWNE, Tom.
Johnson, A. E. Tom Browne, R.I. *$1.50 net. Macmillan.

Browne, Warren C.
Metal plate printing; treatise on printing in the lithographic manner from zinc and aluminum plates; comp., ed. and elucidated in the office of the *National Lithographer.* '10(F19) il. 12°, $2. Nat. Lithographer.

BROWNE, William Washington.
Davis, D. W. Life and public services of Rev. Wm. Washington Browne. $1. M. A. Browne-Smith.

Brownell, Eliz. B.
Really babies. '08(D19) il. 4°, $1.25. Rand, McN. & Co.

Brownell, Myron G:
Information from *Mining Science;* reproduction of certain notes and articles appearing in *Mining Science* during the year 1909. v. 1. '10(My) c. il. 16°, $1. Mining Science.

Brownell, W: Crary.
American prose masters—Cooper, Hawthorne, Emerson, Poe, Lowell, Henry James. '09(N6) c. O. **$1.50 net. Scribner.

Brownie and I. Aumerle, R: 85 c. Benziger.
Brownie Clown of Brownie Town. Cox, P. $1. Century Co.
Brownie's box. Bone, F. $1. Am. Tr.
Brownies (The). Ewing, *Mrs.* J. H. G. $1. Macmillan.
Brownies' latest adventures. Cox, P. $1.50. Century Co.

Browning, Carl Hamilton.
See Muir, Rob.

Browning, E: Franklin.
Genealogy of the Brownings in America from 1621-1908. '09(My8) il. 4°, $7.50. E: F. Browning.

Browning, Eliza Gordon.
Lockerbie's assessment list of Indianapolis, 1835. '09, [1910.] (F) 399-434 p. 8°, (Indiana Historical Society pubs.) 25 c. W. K. Stewart.

Browning, Mrs. Eliz. Barrett.
Lady Geraldine's courtship. '09(N6) c. 4°, 50 c. Altemus.
Letters; ed. by Frederic G. Kenyon, with biographical additions. '10(D24) c. 12°, $1.50 net. Macmillan.

Browning, Mrs. Eliz. Barrett.—*Continued.*
Sonnets from the Portuguese. '10(D) il. bds., 50 c. net. Doran.
Sonnets from the Portuguese. '09(S11) c. 12°, (Rubric ser.) **60 c. net. Duffield.
Sonnets from the Portuguese. '08(Ag15) 16°, (Eng. masterpieces ser.) 50 c.; pap., 25 c. Dutton.
Sonnets from the Portuguese; with lyric interludes; ed., with preface, notes and appendix, introducing Robert Browning's related poems by Arth. Guiterman. '10 (N5) c. por. D. bds., $1.75. P. Elder.
Sonnets from the Portuguese. '09, [1910.] (F) col. il. $2; leath., $3; antique cf., $4. Putnam.

Browning, H. S.
Auction bridge and how to play it. '09 (Je19) 24°, *75 c. net. Dutton.

Browning, Oscar.
Memories of sixty years at Eton, Cambridge, and elsewhere. '10(Ap30) il. O. $5 net. Lane.

Browning, Philip Embury.
Introduction to the rarer elements. 2d ed., rev. '08(D12) 8°, *$1.50 net. Wiley.
See also Gooch, Fk. Austin.

Browning, R.
See Allerton, Mark.

Browning, Rob.
Works. De luxe ed. 12 v. '10(N) il. levant, $36. Crowell.
Complete poetical works. '08(D19) front. 12°, (Crowell's thin paper poets.) ooze leath., $1.75, boxed. Crowell.
Browning day by day; ed. by C. M. Spender. '10(D) 12°, (Day by day ser.) 60 c.; ooze, $1. Crowell.
Dramatis personæ and Dramatic romances and Lyrics. '09(D11) il. in col. 8°, *$2 net. Lippincott.
Italy, my Italy: IV. lyrics. '10(D) 16°, (Venetian ser.) pap., 50 c. net; Japan vel., $1 net. T: B. Mosher.
Lyric love. '10(Jl16) 16°, (Vest pocket ser.) 50 c.; leath., 75 c.; Japan vellum, $1; pap., 25 c. T: B. Mosher.
Lyrical poems; sel. and arr. by A. T. Quiller-Couch. '08(D19) S. (Select English classics.) 10 c. Oxford Univ.
Men and women. New ed. '10(Jl) 312 p. 16°, (Oxford lib. of prose and poetry.) $1 net. Oxford Univ.
Pied piper of Hamelin; child's story. '10 (N12) c. col. il. Q. $1.25. Rand, McN. & Co.
Pied piper of Hamelin; il. [in color] by Kate Greenaway. '10(N12) Q. bds., $1.50 net. Warne.
Pippa passes. '09(N6) c. 12°, (Rubric ser.) **60 c. net. Duffield.
Pippa passes and Men and women. '10 (S17) il. S. leath., $1.25 net. Houghton M.
Pippa passes and Men and women. '09 (D11) il. in col. 8°, *$2 net. Lippincott.
Poems and plays, 1833-1844; 1844-1864. '08 (O17) 16°, (Best books ser.) ea., leath., *$1 net. Dutton.

Browning, Rob.—*Continued.*
Rabbi Ben Ezra. '09(Ap24) c. sq. T. vellum, *$1 net, boxed; bds., *60 c. net, boxed. T: B. Mosher.
Selections from the poems and plays of Robert Browning; ed. for school use by Myra Reynolds. '09(D11) c. S. (Lake English classics.) 40 c. Scott, F. & Co.
Shorter poems; [with introd. by Augustine Birrell.] '08(D12) 32°, (Ariel booklets.) leath., 75 c. Putnam.
Shorter poems; selected and ed., with introd. and notes, by J: W: Cunliffe. '09 (Ap17) c. por. 16°, (Scribner English classics.) **25 c. net. Scribner.

—and Eliz. Barrett.
Love poems from the works of Rob. Browning and Elizabeth Barrett Browning; selected and arranged by Ethel Harris; il. with reproductions from the works of master painters. '09(D) c. 127 p. il. por. 8°, $1.25; leath., $1.75, boxed. Rand, McN. & Co.

—, and Hunt, Leigh.
Love poems. '09(Je26) c. D. padded silk, $1.50; leath., $2, boxed. Dodge.

BROWNING, Robert.
Clarke, H. A. Browning's England. **$2 net. Baker & T.
Curry, S: S. Browning and the dramatic monologue. $1.25. Expression.
Griffin, W. H. Life of Robert Browning. $3.50 net. Macmillan.
Hodell, C: W. Old yellow book: source of Browning's "The ring and the book." $7. Carnegie.
Hornbrooke, F. B. Ring and the book; an interpretation. **$1.50 net. Little, B. & Co.
Nettleship, J: T. Robert Browning: essays and thoughts. *$2.25 net. Scribner.
Omar and the Rabbi; Fitzgerald's translation of the Rubáiyát of Omar Khayyám and Browning's Rabbi Ben Ezra arranged in dramatic form. *25 c. net. Harvard Co-op.
Orr, A. L. Life and letters of Robert Browning. *$2 net. Houghton M.
Rogers, A. Prophecy and poetry: studies in Isaiah and Browning. **$1.25 net. Longmans.

Browning, W: Dale.
Dimensions of pipe, fittings, and valves, comp. and arr. for engineers, architects and draftsmen; also cont. some information on steam heating, bath room fixtures, etc. 3d ed. [1910.] (D) c. 87 p. il. diagrs., 8°, 75 c. Nat. Bk.

BROWNING FAMILY.
See Genealogies.

Brownlee, Jane.
Moral training in the public schools. '08, [1909.] (Mr) c. 29 p. il. 12°, 10 c. Holden Pat. Bk.

Brownlee, Roy Hutchison.
On precipitated sulphur. '07, [1908.] (Jl) 1032-1050 p. diagrs., 8°, pap. (Add. pub. for price.) Chemical.

Brown's grammar ser. *See* Brown, Goold.

Browns at Mt. Hermon. Alden *Mrs.* I. M. †$1.50. Lothrop, L. & S.

Brownscombe, Fred J.
State control of courses of study; with appendices on religious instruction and the grading of school systems. '08(D26) c. D. $1. Silver.

Brownson, Earl Leo.
Anton, the man who saw. '08, [1909.] (F) 75 p. il. 12°, $1. Mayhew.

Brownson, Ja. Irwin.
Life and times of Senator James Ross. '10 (Ag13) il. por. O. pap., gratis. Wash. Co. Hist. Soc.

Brownson, Rev. Orestes Augustine.
Watchwords from Dr. Brownson; chosen and ed. by D. J. Scannell O'Neill. '10 (D24) c. por. D. 50 c. Soc. Divine Word.

BROWNSVILLE AFFRAY.
See **United States Army.**

Brownyboo. Lapen, F. $1.25. Saalfield.

Broyles, Lester Everret, ["Retsel Terreve."]
Man without principle: [a novel.] '09 (Ja16) c. il. D. $1.50. Hocking.

Brubacher, Abraham Royer, and Snyder, Dorothy Ermina.
High school English. '10(D3) il. 12°, $1. C: E. Merrill.

Brubaker, Albert P.
Text-book of human physiology; incl. a section on physiologic apparatus. 3d ed., rev. and enl. '08(D) c. 12+752 p. il. 8°, *$3 net; leath., *$4 net. Blakiston.

Bruce, Arth. Loring, pseud.
See Crowninshield, Fs. Welsh.

Bruce, Sir C:
Broad stone of empire; problems of crown colony administration, with records of personal experience. In 2 v. '10(D24) por. maps, 8°, $9. Macmillan.

Bruce, C: Granville.
Twenty years in the Himalaya. '10(D10) il. map, O. $4.20 net. Longmans.

Bruce, Fk. M., comp.
See Bruce, W: G:, *comp.*

Bruce, H:
Letters from Malabar, and on the way; 33 il. and map. '09(D) 34+142 p. 8°, *$2 net. Dutton.

Bruce, H: Addington Bayley.
Daniel Boone and the wilderness road. '10 (Je4) c. il. pors. D. (Stories from Amer. hist.) $1.50. Macmillan.
Historic ghosts and ghost hunters. '08 (S26) c. D. **$1.25 net. Moffat.
Riddle of personality. '08(Mr14) c. D. **$1.50 net. Moffat.
Romance of American expansion. '09 (Ap3) c. il. pors. O. **$1.75 net. Moffat.

Bruce, J: E:, comp.
Short biographical sketches of eminent negro men and women in Europe and the United States, with brief extracts from their writings and public utterances. In 4 v. v. 1. '10(Ap) c. 8°, $1. J: E: Bruce.

Bruce, J: Mitchell, M.D.
Materia medica and therapeutics; introd. to the rational treatment of disease. Rev. ed. [1910.] (My) 8°, $2 net. Funk.

Bruce, Kenneth, ["Diedrich Crayon, jr."]
Return of the "Half Moon." '09(N20) c. il. 12°, $1. B'way Pub.

Bruce, Mary Stone.
Lectures faciles. '08(My23) c. D. (Modern lang. ser.) 60 c. Heath.

Bruce, Philip Alex.
Institutional hist. of Virginia in the seventeenth century. 2 v. '10(Je4) O. $6 net, boxed. Putnam.

Bruce, Wallace.
[Poetical works.] In 3 v. Leaves of gold; Scottish poems; Wanderers. '08(Ja4) D. ea., $1.25; per set, $3. Bryant Union.

Bruce, W: C., comp.
See Bruce, W: G:, *comp.*

Bruce, W: G:, W: C. and Fk. M., comps.
School architecture; handy manual for the use of architects and school authorities. '10(Ap23) c. il. T. 75 c. Am. Sch.

Bruce, W: Herschel, and Cody, C. C.
Elements of plane geometry. '10(N19) c. il. 12°, 75 c. Southern Pub., (Tex.)

Bruce (The). Barbour, J: *$1.90 net. Macmillan.

Bruce Douglas. Gunn, R. A. $1.50. Mayhew.

Bruck, Alfr.
Diseases of the nose, mouth, pharynx and larynx; textbook for students and practicians of medicine; ed. and tr. by F. W. Forbes Ross, assisted by Friedrich Gans. '10(Ap) c. 24+615 p. il. 4°, $5. Rebman.

Brückner, Alex.
Literary history of Russia; ed. by Ellis H. Minns; tr. by H. Havelock. '08(D12) O. (Library of literary history.) $4. Scribner.

BRUCKSALES, Castle of.
Hirsch, F. Castle of Brucksales-das Brucksaler schloss-aus anlass der renovation, (1900-1909.) $25. Hessling.

Brudno, Ezra Selig.
The tether. '08(S26) c. D. †$1.50. Lippincott.

Brueys, David Auguste de, and Palaprat, Jean.
L'avocat Patelin; abrdg. and ed., with introd., notes and exercises, by Marc Ceppi. '09(O16) S. (Shorter French texts.) *25 c. net. Crowell.

Brumbaugh, H: Boyer.
Onesimus, the runaway slave. '10(Jl16) 12°, 75 c. Brethren Pub. Ho.

Brumbaugh, Martin Grove.
Philanthropy and public education. '10 (Jl9) 8°, gratis. Phil. Trades School.
See also Schauffler, Adolphus F.

Brumley, Oscar Victor.
Book of veterinary posology and prescriptions. '09(O) 190 p. 12°, $1.25. O. V. Brumley.

BRUMMELL, George Bryan, (*called* Beau Brummell.)
De Monvel, R. B. Beau Brummell and his times. *$2.50 net. Lippincott.

Brummitt, Dan. Brearley, ed.
Notes on the Epworth League devotional meeting topics. 2d ser., 1908, July-December. '08(Je13); 1st ser., 1909, January-June. '09(Ja2); 2d ser., 1909, July-December. '09(Je19); 1st ser., 1910, January-June. '09(D18); 2d ser., 1910, July-December. '10(Je18) c. D. pap., ea., *15 c. net; per doz., *$1.20 net. Eaton & M.

Brundage, Albert Harrison.
Manual of toxicology: concise presentation of the principal facts rel. to poisons, with detailed directions for the treatment of poisoning; also a table of doses of the principal and many new remedies. 6th ed., rev. '08(N); 7th ed., rev. '09, [1910.] (F) c. 16°, ea., $1.50; Illustrated ed., $2. H: Harrison.

Bruner, Fk. G.
Hearing of primitive peoples: experimental study of the auditory acuity and the upper limit of hearing of Whites, Indians, Filipinos, Ainu and African Pigmies. '08 (S5) tabs., O. (Archives of psychology.) pap., $1. Science Pr., (N. Y.)

Bruner, Ja. Dowden.
Compression in the French classical drama; repr. from the *Sewanee Review.* '08(D) 12 p. O. pap., 10 c. J. D. Bruner.
Studies in Victor Hugo's dramatic characters; with an introd. by R: Green Moulton. '08(Ap25) c. D. $1. Ginn.

Bruner, Jane Woodworth.
Question of Romanism; historical review of the system of Romanism from its organization to the present. '08, [1909.] (Ap) c. 9-307 p. 8°, $1.50. J. W. Bruner.

Brunhilda of Orr's Island. Nicolls, W: J. †$1.50. Jacobs.

Brunner, Josef.
Tracks and tracking. '09(D4) c. il. D. *$1.25 net. Outing.

Bruno. Dewey, *Mrs.* B. S. †50 c. Little, B. & Co.

Brunowe, Marion J., pseud.
See Browne, Marion J.

Brunton, Sir Lander.
Therapeutics of the circulation. '08(N) c. 11+280 p. 8°, *$1.50 net. Blakiston.

Brush, pen and pencil ser. il. O. Macmillan.
—Johnson. Lawson Wood. $1.75 net.—Tom Browne, R.I. *$1.50 net.

BRUSSELS (BELGIUM) UNIVERSAL AND INTERNATIONAL EXHIBITION.
United States. *Dept. of State.* Universal and International Exhibition, Brussels. gratis. U. S., Supt. of Docs.

BRUTON PARISH CHURCH, Williamsburg, Va.
Goodwin, W: A. R. Bruton Parish Church restored. $2.61. W: A. R. Goodwin.

Bryan, Albert Hughes.
Methods for the analysis of maple products and the detection of adulterants. '09 (F20) 8°, (U. S., Dept. of Agriculture, Bureau of Chemistry, circular.) pap., 5 c.

Bryan, C: Wa.
See Johnson, J: Butler.

Bryan, Ja. Wallace.
Development of the English law of conspiracy. '09(My8) O. (Johns Hopkins Univ. studies in historical and pol. science.) pap., 75 c. Johns Hopkins.

Bryan, Jos. Harris.
Organized adult Bible class. '09(Ap) c. 163 p. il. 16°, 50 c. Chr. Pub. Co.

Bryan, W: Jennings.
Fruits of the tree. '10(D10) 16°, bds., 35 c. net. Revell.
Pacific Scientific Institution [Honolulu]: an address. '08(O10) 8°, (Pacific Institution pubs., Special ser.) pap., gratis. W: A. Bryan.
Prince of peace. '09(N13) c. 12°, pap., in envelope, 35 c. Reilly & B.
The real Bryan: being extracts from the speeches and writings of "a well-rounded man"; comp. by R: J. Metcalfe. '08 (Jl18) c. pors. D. $1.25. Personal Help.
Speeches; rev. and arranged by himself; with a biographical introd. by Mary Baird Bryan, his wife. In 2 v. '09(D11) c. pors. S. *$2 net, boxed. Funk.
Thou shalt not steal: [political ethics.;] address del. before the Civic Forum. '08 (D5) por. 12°, (Civic Forum addresses.) pap., 10 c. Civic Forum.

BRYAN, William Jennings.
Gale, A. L., *and* Kline, G: W. Bryan the man. $1. Thompson Pub.
Mangasarian, M. M. Bryan on religion. 10 c. Independent Religions.
Morgan, A: T. On our way to the Orient; or, Mr. Bryan don't you know. 25 c. Denver Int. Corr. Sch.

Bryant, Edn. Eustace.
Treatise on the civil and criminal jurisdiction of justices of the peace, and the powers and duties of constables in executing process in the state of Wisconsin. 8th ed. by W: Ryan. '08(O) c. 14+1465 p. O. *$6.50 net. Callaghan.

Bryant, Ernest A.
New self-help. '08(D5) il. $1.50. Cassell.

Bryant, Fk. A:, M.D.
George Watson, the trials and triumph of a stammerer. '09(Je) c. 39 p. 12°, pap., 10 c. F. A: Bryant.

Bryant, Franklin H:
Black smiles; or, the sunny side of sable life. '10(Ap9) c. il. por. 8°, 25 c. Southern Missionary.

Bryant, J: C.
Business man's commercial law and business forms combined; a vade-mecum for the counting-house; ed. by G: W. Clinton. 16th ed., rev. '10, [1909.] (N) 240+57 p. por. 8°, $1.50. C. L. Bryant.

Bryant, Jos. Decatur, M.D., and Buck, Albert H:, M.D., eds.
American practice of surgery. In 8 v. v. 4. '08(Mr28); v. 5. '09(Ja16); v. 6 (Ag); v. 7. '10(Je) c. il. 8°, subs., ea., $7; leath., $8; hf. mor., $9. Wood.

Bryant, Laura.
Institute song book. '10(D) 64 p. bds., 30 c. Barnes.

Bryant, Mrs. Lorinda Munson.
Pictures and their painters. New ed. '10 (D24) c. il. pors. 8°, $2.50 net. Lane.
What pictures to see in Europe in one summer. '10(Je4) c. il. D. $1.50 net. Lane.

Bryant, Marguerite.
Anne Kempburn: truth-seeker. '10(O15) c. D. $1.30 net. Duffield.
Christopher Hibbault, roadmaker. '09 (F13) 12°, †$1.50. Duffield.

Bryant, Ober Wilson.
Progress rept. on experiments in supplemental irrigation with small water supplies at Cheyenne and Newcastle, Wyoming, 1905-1908. '10(Mr) 51 p. il. tabs., 8°, (U. S., Dept. of Agriculture, Office of Experiment Stations, circular.) pap.

Bryant, Wilbur Franklin.
Historical Man of Nazareth. '08(Ag1) c. por. 12°, 75 c. W. F. Bryant.

Bryant, W: Cullen.
Thanatopsis; [30 full-page etchings by Walworth Stilson.] 09(O16) 4°, hf. parchment, *$10 net. Tandy-T.

Bryant, W: Sohier.
See Knight, C: Huntoon.

Bryce, Alex., M.D.
Laws of health. '10(Je4) il. O. $2 net. Lippincott.

Bryce, Catharine Turner.
See Spaulding, Fk. Ellsworth.
—, comp. Child-lore dramatic reader. '08 (D19) c. il. D. (Add. pubs. for price.) Scribner.

Bryce, Clarence Archibald, M.D.
The gentleman's dog, his rearing, training and treatment. '09(D25) front. D. $1. So. Clinic Pr.

Bryce, G:
Romantic settlement of Lord Selkirk's colonists [the pioneers of Manitoba]. '10 (S) 328 p. il. pors. 8°, $1.50 net. Barse & H.

Bryce, Ja.
American commonwealth; chapter on the Tweed ring in New York by Rufus Rockwell Wilson. In 2 v.; from the 2d ed., rev. '08, [1910.] (F) 1700 p. 12°, $4. Commonwealth Pub.
American commonwealth. In 2 v. v. 1, The national government; the state governments; v. 2, The party system; public opinion; illustrations and reflections; social institutions. New ed., completely rev. throughout, with additional chapters. '10(D3) c. O. $4, boxed. Macmillan.
Hindrances to good citizenship. '09(D11) c. D. (Yale lectures on the responsibilities of citizenship.) *$1.15 net. Yale Univ.

Bryce, T: Hastie, Teacher, J: H., and Kerr, J: M. Munro.
Contributions to the study of the early development and imbedding of the human ovum. '08(O24) il. 4°, *$4 net. Macmillan.
—, ed. *See* Quain, Jones.

Bryn Mawr College monographs. 8°, pap., $1. Winston.
—Traver. Four daughters of God.

Bryn Mawr spelling book. King, G. G. 25 c. G. G. King.

Bryophytes.
See Mosses.

Bryozoa.
Robertson, A. Incrusting *Chilostomatus bryozoa* of the west coast of North America. $1. Univ. of Cal.

Bryson, C: Lee.
Tan and Teckle. '08(S12) c. 12°, *$1.25 net. Revell.

Bryson, Ernest.
See Pollitt, Arth. W.

Bubier, E: Trevert, ["E: Trevert."]
How to make electric batteries. 3d ed., rev. and enl. '10(Mr) c. 5-59 p. il. 12°, 50 c.; pap., 25 c. Bubier.

Buccaneers.
Adventures of pirates and sea-rovers. 60 c. Harper.
Esquemeling, J. Buccaneers of America. $4 net. Dutton.
Haring, C. H. Buccaneers in the West Indies in the xviith century. $3.50 net. Dutton.

Buccaneers. Bonser, E. A. 75 c. Estes.

Buchanan, Frances Grant, and Grant, Mary Leonard.
In Cupid's realm, and other poems; consisting of an operetta and a number of poems here published collectively for the first time. '09(N) c. 7+70 p. 12°, $1.15. F. G. Buchanan.

Buchanan, J. Barr.
Carbon print; treatise for portrait operators and printers, and miniature painters; modern methods and formulae. '10 (Je) c. 23 p. 12°, 50 c. J. B. Buchanan.

Buchanan, Ja.
Works of James Buchanan, [President of U. S. 1856-1860;] comprising his speeches, state papers, and private correspondence; collected and ed. by J: Bassett Moore. In 12 v. v. 1. '08(My9); v. 2 (Je13); v. 3 (Jl18); v. 4 (S5); v. 5 (D12); v. 6. '09(Ja30); v. 7 (Je19); v. 8, 9 (Ag21); v. 10, 11. '10(Je4) c. por. O. per v., *$5 net, boxed. Lippincott.

Buchanan, Roberdeau.
Occasional verses; written during leisure hours. '10(Jl16) c. 12°, $1. R. Buchanan.

Buchanan, Uriel.
Ideals and conduct. '10(Je4) c. 12°, $1. Cochrane.

Buchheim, E. S.
Der ungebetene gast: [a play.] '09(N13) S. pap., 15 c. Oxford Univ.

Buchholz, Heinrich Ewald.
Governors of Maryland from the Revolution to the year 1908. 2d ed. '09(Ja16) c. pors. O. $2.50. Williams & W.

Buck, Albert H:, M.D.
Bucks of Wethersfield, Connecticut, and the families with which they are connected by marriage; biographical and genealogical sketch. '09, [1910.] (Ap) 152 p. 4°. (Priv. pr.) A. H: Buck.
—, ed. *See* Bryant, Jos. Decatur, *M.D., ed.*

Buck, Carl Darling.
Introd. to the study of Greek dialects; grammar, selected inscriptions, glossary. '10(Je4) c. map, charts, 12°, (College ser. of Greek authors.) $2.75. Ginn.

Buck, C: Neville.
Key to yesterday. '10(S24) c. il. D. $1.50. W. J. Watt.

Buck, Edith Cora.
Guide to the teacher's mastery of texts, and aids in elementary instruction. [2d ed. rev.] '08, [1909.] (Ap) c. 266 p. 12°, 85 c. E. C. Buck.

Buck, E: Nelson.
Some fugitive verse. '10(Ag20) 4°, $1.75. E: N. Buck.

Buck, Gertrude.
"Make-believe grammar;" repr. from the *School Review.* '09(My) 21-23 p. 8°. (Priv. pr.) Univ. of Chic.

Buck, Irving Ashby.
Cleburne and his command. '09(Mr13) c. por. map, O. *$3 net. Neale.

Buck, Jirah Dewey.
Constructive psychology; or, the building of character by personal effort. '08(S12) c. D. (Supplemental harmonic ser.) $1. Indo-Am. Bk.
Lost word found in the great work, (magnum opus:) [freemasonry.] '08(D26) c. S. (Harmonic booklet ser.) 50 c. Indo-Am. Bk.

BUCK FAMILY.
See Genealogies.

Bucket brigade to flying squadron. Jenness, H. T. $1.50. H. T. Jenness.

Buckey, Captain Mervyn Chandos.
Manual for the instruction of gunners of mine companies. '08(My.) c. 3+53 p. O. 50 c. M. C. Buckey.

Buckham, J: Wright, D.D.
Personality and the Christian ideal: discussion of personality in the light of Christianity. '09(D25) c. O. *$1.50 net. Pilgrim Press.

Buckham, Rev. Mathew H:
Agriculture in the high school; address to the students of the winter course in the University of Vermont, Jan. 5, 1910. '10(My) 7 p. 8°, gratis. M. H: Buckham.
Culture of the imagination; lecture in the teachers' course, University of Vermont. '09(Jl) 11 p. 8°. (Add. author for price.) M. H: Buckham.
Moral conditions in intellectual attainment; closing lecture of the teachers' course in the University of Vermont, June 8, 1909. '09, [1910.] (My) 18 p. 8°, gratis. M. H: Buckham.

Buckingham, Edg.
On the definition of the ideal gas. '10(Je) 409-429 p. 8°. U. S., Supt. of Docs.

BUCKINGHAM, George Villiers, *First Duke of.*
See Villiers, George.

BUCKINGHAMSHIRE, Eng.
Edwardian inventories for Buckinghamshire. *$6 net. Longmans.
Shorter, C. K. Highways and byways in Buckinghamshire. $2 net. Macmillan.

Buckland, Rev. A: Rob.
First epistle to the Thessalonians. '08, [1909.] (My) 12°, (Devotional commentaries.) *$1 net. Am. S. S.
St. Paul's Second Epistle to the Thessalonians: devotional commentary. '09 (My1) D. (Devotional commentaries.) *$1 net. Am. S. S.

Buckland, E. S. Lang.
Oliver Goldsmith. '09(Ap3) il. 16°, (Bell's miniature ser. of great writers.) *50 c. net. Macmillan.

Buckland, Fk. Merton.
Rhymes of the stream and forest. '09(Je) 12°, $1.25. Forest.

Buckland, W: Warwick.
Roman law of slavery; condition of the slave in private law from Augustus to Justinian. '08(D5) 8°, *$5.75 net. Putnam.

Buckle, Mary.
See Day, Lewis Foreman.

Buckle my shoe picture book. Crane, W., il. $1.25 net. Lane.

Buckley, Edith E.
Snare of circumstance. '10(Mr5) c. il. D. †$1.50. Little, B. & Co.

Buckley, Edm., Hoppin, Ja. Mason, and Churchill, Alfr. Vance, eds.
Fine arts: course in sculpture, painting, architecture, [etc.] '07, [1908.] (Jl) 11-800 p. il. f°. (Add. pub. for price.) Nat. Art Soc.

Buckley, Elsie Finnimore.
Children of the dawn: old tales of Greece; introd. by Arth. Sidgwick. '09(My15) il. 8°, $1.50. Stokes.

Buckley, Ernest Robertson.
Geology of the disseminated lead deposits of St. François and Washington counties, [Mo.] '09(Jl) c. 16+259 p. il. maps, tab., 4°, (Missouri Bu. of Geology and Mines rept.) (Add. pubs. for price.) Missouri Bu. Geol.
Public roads, their improvement and maintenance. '08(Ja4) il. Q. (Missouri Bu. of Geology and Mines, repts.) (Add. pub. for price.) Missouri Bu. Geol.

Buckley, J. P.
Modern dental materia medica, pharmacology and therapeutics. '09(N); 2d ed. '10(My) il. 8°, ea., *$2.50 net. Blakiston.

Buckley, Rev. Ja. Monroe.
Wrong and peril of woman suffrage. '09 (D) c. 128 p. 12°, *75 c. net. Revell.
—, ed. *See* Goodsell, Dan. Ayres.

Buckley, R: Wallace.
Last of the Houghtons. '08(Ja4) D. $1.50. Neale.

Buckley, Rob. Burton.
Facts, figures and formulas for irrigation engineers. '08(Jl4) 8°, $4.25. Spon.

Buckner, Franklin Fernando.
Wreath of song. '08, [1909.] (Mr) c. 9-98 p. 16°, 75 c. Roberts Bros.

Buckwalter, Geoffrey.
Fourth reader. pt. 1. '09(F) 42 c. Simmons.

BUCKWHEAT.
Clark, C: C., *comp.* Buckwheat crops of the United States, 1866-1906. 5 c. U. S., Supt. of Docs.

Bucky O'Connor. Raine, W. M. $1.50. G: W. Dillingham.

Bucyrus, the railroad wrecker. Lorimer, J. M. 25 c. Muskogee.

Buddecke, Albert.
Tactical decisions and orders: study in troop-leading, (based on the operations of an independent division,) for individual instruction. 3d rev. ed.; tr. from the German by Capt. A. L. Conger. '08(N) c. 9-231 p. fold. maps, 8°, No. 1, $1.25; No. 2, $1.50. Hudson.

Buddha.
Sayings of Buddha; the Iti Vuttaka: a Pali work of the Buddhist Canon; tr. with introd. and notes by Justin Hartly Moore. '09(F27) 8°, (Columbia Univ. Indo-Iranian ser.) **$1.50 net. Lemcke.

Buddha: Way of the Buhhda; tr. by Herbert Baynes. '08(Je6) 16°, (Wisdom of the East.) *60 c. net. Dutton.

BUDDHA AND BUDDHISM.
Bigelow, W: S. Buddhism and immortality. **75 c. net. **Houghton M.**
Buddhaghosha. The Jataka: stories of Buddha's former births. v. 6. *$4 net. Putnam.
Copleston, R. S. Buddhism: primitive and present; in Magadha and in Ceylon. *$3 net. Longmans.
Creed of Buddha. $1.50. Lane.
Dahlke, P. Buddhist essays. *$3 net. Macmillan.
Davids, *Mrs.* C. A., *tr. and ed.* Psalms of the early Buddhists. $2. Oxford Univ.
Edmunds, A. J. Buddhist and Christian gospels now first compared from the originals. 2 v. ea., *$2 net. A. J. Edmunds.
Hall, H. F. Inward light. **$1.75 net. Macmillan.
Lloyd, A. Wheat among the tares: studies of Buddhism in Japan. *$1.10 net. Macmillan.
Suzuki, D. T. Outlines of Mahayana Buddhism. *$2.50 net. Open Court.
Von Hase, K. New Testament parallels in Buddhistic lit. *40 c. net. Eaton & M.
See also Hinduism;—Miracles.

Buddhaghosha.
The Jataka; or, stories of the Buddha's former births; tr. from the Pali by various hands under the editorship of E. B. Cowell. v. 6, by E. B. Cowell and W. H. D. Rouse. '08(F8) 8°, *$4 net. Putnam.

Buddhism and immortality. Bigelow, W: S. **75 c. net. Houghton M.

Budge, Ernest Alfr. Thompson Wallis, ed.
Paradise or garden of the holy fathers; being histories of the anchorites, recluses, monks, Coenobites and ascetic fathers of the deserts of Egypt between about A.D. 250 and A.D. 400; comp. by Athanasius, Archbishop of Alexandria, Palladius, Bishop of Helenopolis, Saint Jerome, and others; now tr. out of the Syriac, with notes and introd. 2 v. '09(Je12) 8°, *$4 net. Duffield.

Budge and Toddie. Habberton, J: $1. Grosset.

Budgell, Eustace.
See Addison, J.

BUDGET.
See Finance.

Budgett, J: S:
Work of John Samuel Budgett: being a collection of his zoological papers, together with a biographical sketch by A. E. Shipley, and contributions by R: Assheton, E: J. Bliss, E: T. Browne, J. Hubert Budgett and J. Graham Kerr; ed. by J. Graham Kerr. '08(D19) por. F. *$7 net. Putnam.

Budgett, Sidney Payne.
Essentials of physiology; prepared especially for students of medicine. 3d ed., thoroughly rev. by Haven Emerson. '09(N) c. 250 p. il. 12°, (Saunders' question-compends.) $1. Saunders.

Budgett, Mrs. Sidney Payne.
See Dejeans, Eliz.

Budington, Rob. Allyn.
See Conn, Herbert W:

Buds and blossoms. Colton, C: H: $1.25. Benziger.

BUECHELER, —.
Tolman, J. A., *jr.* Study of the sepulchral inscriptions in Buecheler's "Carmina Epigraphica Latina." 80 c. Univ. of Chic.

Buehler, H: And.
Lime and cement resources of Missouri. '07, [1909.] (Mr) 16+255 p. il. fold. map, 4°, (Missouri; Bureau of Geology and Mines, repts.) pap., 25 c. Missouri Bu. Geol.

Buell, Jennie.
One woman's work for farm women; the story of Mary A. Mayo's part in rural social movements. '08, [1909.] (F) c. 6+78 p. por. 12°, 50 c.; pap., 25 c. Whitcomb.

BUENOS AIRES.
See International Bureau of American Republics, Washington, D. C. Municipal organizations.

BUFALO, Gaspare del.
Sardi, V. Leben des seligen Kaspar del Bufalo. *75 c. net. P. A. Gietl.

Buffalo Public Library. Books in German; printed by the German Young Men's Association for the encouragement of the reading of the German language. '08, [1909.] (Mr) 7-155 p. 4°, pap., gratis. Buffalo Pub. Lib.

Buffalo. Public Library. Class-room libraries for public schools, listed by grades. 3d ed.; to which is added a list of books suggested for school reference libraries. '09(Je26) O. pap., 25 c. Buffalo Pub. Lib.

Buffalo Public Library. Means of education and self-culture offered day-workers by the city of Buffalo. '09(Jl17) D. pap., gratis. Buffalo Pub. Lib.

BUFFALO, N. Y.
Fernald, F. A. Index guide to Buffalo and Niagara Falls. 25 c. Fernald.
Sellstedt, L. G. Art in Buffalo. $1.50. L. G. Sellstedt.
Snow, J. F. Early recollections of Buffalo. $1. Ulbrich.

"Buffalo Bill," pseud.
See Cody, W: F:

Buffalo Historical Society pubs.; ed. by **Fk.** H. Severance. il. 8°. Buffalo Hist. Soc.
—Canal enlargement in New York state. $5.
—Fillmore. Addresses, private correspondence and miscellaneous writings. 2 v. *$7 net.
—Hill. Historical review of waterways and canal construction in New York State. $5; $4. Buffalo Hist. Soc.

"BUFFALO JONES."
See Arizona.

Buffington, Bertha Elinor, Weimer, Theresa, and Jones, A. R.
Circus book for children. '09(N13) c. il. D. 50 c. B: H. Sanborn.

Buffington, F. C.
Physical training for Filipinos. '09(My22) c. il. 12°, $1. Heath.

Buffum, Burt C.
Arid agriculture; handbook for the western farmer and stockman. '09(My) c. 443 p. il. 12°, $1.50. B. C. Buffum.

Buffum, Hugh Straight.
Federal and state aid to education in Iowa. '07, [1909.] (Mr) 6+152 p. 4°, $1. Univ. of Ia.
References (2 p.).

Bugbee, E. Holmes, comp.
See Gray, G: Arth.

Bugbee, Willis N.
Christmas medley; for boys and girls. '08 (S19) c. 12°, pap., 25 c. Dick.
Easter tidings: entertainments for girls. '08 (S19) c. 12°, pap., 25 c. Dick.
Jolly bachelors: motion song or recitation. '08(S19) c. 12°, pap., 25 c. Dick.
Merry old maids: motion song or recitation. '08(S19) c. 12°, pap., 25 c. Dick.

Builders of Spain. Perkins, C. C. 2 v. $5. Holt.

Builders of united Italy. Holland, R. S. **$2 net. Holt.

Builders' guide. Hicks, I: P. $1. D: Williams.

BUILDING (*construction*).
Adams, H. Building construction. *$3 net. Cassell.
Arthur, W: New building estimator. $2.50. D: Williams.
Bergh, L: de C. Safe building construction. **$5 net. Macmillan.
Bradt, H. J. Lightning estimator; simple, reliable guide for estimating the cost of frame buildings. $1. Bradt.
Brooklyn Public Library. Reading and reference list of books on building and building trades. gratis. Brooklyn Lib.
Dictionary of terms used in architecture and building. Indust. Bk.
Dustman, W. M. Book of plans and building construction for general contractors and home builders. $2. C. C. Thompson.
Gillette, H. P. Hdbk. of cost data for contractors and engineers. $5. M. C. Clark.
Gourlay, C: Construction of a house. $2.75 net. Lane.
Hicks, I: P. Builders' guide. $1.—Estimator's price book and pocket companion. $1. D: Williams.
Hodgson, F: T: Estimating frame and brick houses, barns, stables, factories and outbuildings. $1. D: Williams.
Hodgson, F: T: Light and heavy timber framing made easy. $2.—Pract. steel construction. $1. Drake.
International library of technology. In 10 v. ea., $5. Int. Textbk.
Jacoby, H. S. Structural details; or elements of design in heavy framing. **$2.25 net. Wiley.

BUILDING (*construction*).—*Continued.*
Johnson, J: B., *and others.* Theory and practice of modern framed structure. pt. 1, Stresses in simple structure. $3 net. Wiley.
Joslin, A. W. Estimating the cost of buildings. $1. D: Williams.
Kidder, F. E. Architects' and builders' pocket-book. $5. Wiley.
Kidder, F. E. Building construction and superintendence. $6. W: T. Comstock.
Morris, C. T. Designing and detailing of simple steel structure. $2.25. Hann.
National Board of Fire Underwriters. Building code. (Add. pubs. for price.) Nat. Bd. Fire.
Newman, J: Scamping tricks and odd knowledge; occasionally practiced on public works. $1. Spon.
Nichols, E: Building superintendence. 2 v. $1.50.—Estimating: guide to systematic methods in taking off quantities and making up estimates. $1. Am. Sch. Corr.
Peker, C: G. Practical house framing. 50 c. Indust. Bk.
Pite, A. B., *and others.* Building construction. In 2 v. v. 1. $5 net. Longmans.
Plant, J: C., *and* Zapf, A. E., *eds.* Contracts and specifications: manual of correct forms covering relations of architect, contractor, and owner. In 2 pts. $1. Am. Sch. Corr.
Radford, W: A., *and others.* Framing; practical manual of approved up-to-date methods of house framing and construction. $1. Radford Architectural.
Radford's cyclopedia of construction. 12 v. ea., $2. Radford Architectural.
Rexford, E. A. Tables and diagrams for obtaining the resisting moments of eccentric riveted connections. *$1 net. Engineering News.
Richey, H. G. Building mechanics' ready reference; The building foreman's pocket-book and ready reference. $5. Wiley.
Schneider, C: C. General specifications for structural work of buildings. 75 c. Engineering News.
Schultz, R. W., *and others.* Arts connected with building. *$2 net. Scribner.
Thomson, W: C. Bridge and structural design. $2. Engineering News.
Young, C., *and* Brooks, S. M. Spon's architects' and builders' pocket price-book. $1.50. Spon.
See also Arches;—Architectural drawing;—Architecture; — Bridges; —Building materials;—Carpentry;—Chimneys;—Columns; — Concrete; — Earthwork;—Engineering; — Lumber;—Masonry;—Retaining walls;—Roofs;—Saws;—Steel;—Stone-cutting;—Strength of materials;—Tuberculosis.

BUILDING (*inspection*).
See Sanitary engineering.

Building a home. Desmond, H: W. **$1.80 net. Baker & T.

Building a law business. Murdock, G: H. $10. Murdoch Law, (N. J.)

Building and care of the body. Millard, C. N. 40 c. net. Macmillan.

BUILDING AND LOAN ASSOCIATIONS.
Clark, C: E. Local building association: a cornerstone of the commonweal. 10 c. C: E. Clark.
See also Interest (on money).
Building himself up. Adams, W: T. $1. Lothrop, L. & S.
BUILDING LAWS.
New York City. Bureau of Municipal Research. Tenement house administration. (Add. pubs. for price.) Bu. Municipal.
Veiller, L. Model tenement house law. $1.25. Charities Pub.
See also Apartments.
BUILDING MATERIALS.
Fireproof construction. gratis. Nat. Fire Proofing.
Hughes, C. H. Terra cotta hollow tiles for walls of houses. gratis. Nat. Fire Proofing.
Humphry, R: L. Fire-resistance properties of various building materials. 30 c. U. S., Supt. of Docs.
Miller, C. H. New hollow tile construction. gratis. Nat. Fire Proofing.
Munby, A. E. Introduction to the chemistry and physics of building materials. *$2 net. Van Nostrand.
Waterproofing of structures. Bird.
See also Architecture;—Bricks;—Cement;—Concrete;—Marble; — Masonry;—Steel;—Strength of materials.
Building mechanics' ready reference. *See* Richey, Harry Grant.
Building of the church. Jefferson, C: E: $1.25 net. Macmillan.
Building of the ship. *See* Longfellow, H: Wadsworth.
Building plans. Hicks, I: P. 50 c. Indust.
Building the walls; book of prayer and thanksgiving for family and private use; with an introd. by the Archbp. of Canterbury. '10(F19) 16°, *65 c. net. Macmillan.
Building your boy. Wayne, K. H. 50 c. net. McClurg.
BULBS.
See Gardens and gardening.
Bulfinch, T:
Age of fable. '10(N12) 16°, (Everyman's lib.) 35 c. net; leath., 70 c. net. Dutton.
Bull, Clark E.
Philosophy of life, mortal and immortal; with a rich collection of communications from the spirit side of life pertaining to philosophy; subjects of antiquity and religious thought. '09(Ag28) D. $1.60. C. E. Bull.
Bull, Coates P.
Rural school agriculture. '07, [1908.] (My.) 116 p. il. 8°, 60 c. C. P. Bull.
Bull, Percival G:
Simple experiments in static electricity. '08 (Je20) c. il. 12°, pap., 25 c. Spon.
Bull of the Kraal and heavenly maidens. Kidd, D. *$2 net. Macmillan.
BULL RUN (1st battle of).
Clement, E: H: Bull-Run rout. (Add. author for price.) E. H. Clement.
Bullard, K. C., comp.
Over the dead-line; or, who killed "Poll Parrot." '09(Jl17) c. D. *$1 net. Neale.
Bullard, Warren Gardner.
See Metzler, W: H.
Bullard, W: Hannum Grubb.
Naval electricians' text book. '08(D5) c. il. 8°, $6.50. U. S. Naval Inst.
BULLDOG.
See dog.
Bullen, Fk. T:
Call of the deep: being some further adventures of Frank Brown. '08(Ja18) 12°, $1.50. Dutton.
Cruise of "The Cachalot." '08(Jl11) 12°, (Young America lib.) 50 c. Hurst.
Seed of the righteous. '08(N7) c. il. D. $1.25. Eaton & M.
Young Nemesis. '09(Mr13) il. 12°, $1.50. Dutton.
Buller, Arth. H: Reginald.
Researches on fungi; an account of the production, liberation, and dispersion of the spores of *hymenomycetes* treated botanically and physically; also some observations upon the discharge and dispersion of the spores of *ascomycetes* and of *pilobolus*. '09(S11) il. figs. O. *$4 net. Longmans.
Bulletin of Bibliography pamphlets. 12°, pap. Boston Bk.
—Hawkins. Ghost stories. 20 c.
—Mulliken. Reading list on modern dramatists. 20 c.
Bullet's flight from powder to target. Mann, F. W. $4. Munn.
Bullinger, Ethelbert W:, D.D.
Critical lexicon and concordance to the English and Greek New Testament, together with an index of Greek words and several appendices. 5th ed., rev. '08 (Ag1) Q. $5.25. Longmans.
Bullock, C: Jesse.
Introd. to the study of economics. 3d ed., rev. and enl. '08(S19) c. D. $1.28. Silver.
Bülow, Frau Babette Eberty von.
See Arnold, Hans, *pseud.*
Bulwer-Lytton, Sir E G: Earle Lytton, [Lord Lytton.]
Works. De luxe ed. 4 v. '10(D) 16°, ea., mor., $1.50 net. (Sets only.) Nelson.
[Works.] Edinburgh ed. In 12 v. '09 (D18) il. 8°, per set, *$25 net. Dutton.
Works. 15 v. New imperial lib. ed. '10 (D) il. 8°, ea., $1.25; hf. cf., $2.25. New il. sterling ed., ea., $1. (Sets only.) Estes.
Works. [Edinburgh ed.] In 12 v. '08 (Ag22) il. 8°, $24; ¾ Persian cf., $36. L. Knight.
Last days of Pompeii. '08(O17) 16°, (Best books ser.) leath., *$1 net. Dutton.
Last days of Pompeii; ed., with introd. and notes, by J. H. Castleman. '08(Je6) 12°, (Pocket Am. and Eng. classics.) *25 c. net. Macmillan.
Lost tales of Miletus. '09(My8) D. *$1.25 net. Sturgis & W.
Pilgrims of the Rhine. '09(Mr27) 16°, (Everyman's lib.) *35 c. net; leath., *70 c. net. Dutton.
Rienzi: the last of the Roman tribunes. '08 (Ap4) 12°, (New universal lib.) 50 c.; leath., 75 c. Dutton.

BULWER-LYTTON, *Sir* Edward George Earle Lytton, [*Lord* Lytton.]
Escott, T: H. S. Edward Bulwer, first Baron of Knebworth. $2.50 net. Dutton.
Bumbletoes. Sowerby, M. 75 c. Duffield.
Bumpus, J: T.
Short history of English cathedral music. 2 v. '08(O10) il. *$4 net. Pott.
Bumpus, T: Fs.
Canterbury cathedral. '09, [1910.] (Ja) il. plan, **90 c. net. Jacobs.
Cathedrals and churches of Belgium. '10 (My14) il. 12°, $2 net. Pott.
Cathedrals and churches of northern Italy, their history and their architecture; together with much of interest concerning the bishops, rulers, and other personages identified with them. '08(O3) c. il. D. (Cathedral ser.) $2.50, boxed. L. C. Page.
Cathedrals and churches of Norway, Sweden and Denmark. '08(O10) il. 8°, *$4 net; ¾ levant, *$7.50 net. Pott.
Cathedrals of northern France. '10(D24) il. 12°, $2. Pott.
London churches, ancient and modern. 2 v. '08(O10) il. *$4 net; ¾ levant, *$8 net. Pott.
BUNCE JONES **PROTEIN.**
See **Proteids.**
Bunch of violets. Bowdoin, W: G. $1. W: G. Bowdoin.
Bundle of myrrh. Neihardt, J: G. *$1 net. Outing.
Bungalow plans, as designed and built exclusively by the Bungalow Colony of Neighborly Metuchen, New York. '09(Jl3) c. il. plans, f°, $1. Metuchen Bungalow.
BUNGALOWS.
See **Architecture.**
Bungalows and cottages: choice collection of 100 designs for bungalows and inexpensive cottages costing to build from $400 to $3000. '08, [1909.] (My) 96 p. il. plans, 4°, 50 c. M. L. Keith.
Bungalows, camps and mountain houses. '08 (Ap4) il. plans, Q. bds., $2. W: T. Comstock.
Bunker, Alonzo, D.D.
Sketches from the Karen Hills. '10(S17) D. $1 net. Revell.
Bunker, Rob. Emmet, ed.
Cases on suretyship. [1910.] (N) c. 13+464 p. O. $3.50. Wahr.
BUNKER HILL (Battle of).
Clarke, J:, *and* Bentalou, P. Impartial and authentic narrative of the battle fought on the 17th of June, 1775, between His Britannic Majesty's troops and the American provincial army on Bunker's Hill [and] Pulaski vindicated. To subscribers, $1.65. Abbatt.
See also **Prescott, William.**
Bunker Hill oration. *See* Washington, G:—Webster, D.
Bunn, Clinton Orrin.
See Okla. Codes of civil procedure;—*also* Evans, C:
—, comp. *See* Oklahoma. Constitution.
Bunn, W: C., comp.
See Oklahoma. Constitution.

Bunner, H: C.
Seven old ladies of Lavender Town; operetta in two acts; music by Oscar Weil. '10(N12) c. obl. D. 75 c. Harper.
Bunnie Cottontail. Blair, M. 75 c. McLoughlin.
Bunnikin Brown ser. 3 v. '10(D) 32; 32; 32 p. col. il. 12°, ea., 50 c. net. Doran.
Bunnikins-bunnies in camp. Davidson, E. B. **50 c. net. Houghton M.
Bunnikins-bunnies in Europe. Davidson, E. B. 50 c. net. Houghton M.
"Bunny," pseud.
See Schultz, Carl Emil.
Bunny book. Pope, J. 60 c. Dodge.
Bunse, F: Jos.
Latin grammar. 2d ed. '08(S) c. 316+32 p. 8°. (Not for sale.) Bunse.
Bunsen, Mme. Charles de.
See Bunsen, M. I. W. von.
Bunsen, Mary Isabella Waddington von, [Mme. Charles de Bunsen.]
In three legations. '10(Ja29) il. 8°, $3.50. Scribner.
Bunston, Anna.
Mingled wine: [poems.] '10(F5) D. *$1.20 net. Longmans.
Bunting, H: Stanhope.
Specialty advertising. '10(O22) c. nar. O. Novelty News.
Bunyan, J:
Grace abounding to the chief of sinners; ed., with introd., by E: Chauncey Baldwin. '10(Ap9) c. S. (Standard English classics.) 35 c. Ginn.
Pilgrim's progress; with a memoir of the author condensed from his Grace abounding and the Life of Bunyan, by Canon Edmunds Venables. [New ed.] '09(Je26) c. il. O. *50 c. net. Am. Tract.
Pilgrim's progress. '08(O10) il. D. (Bowman's illustrated lib. of world-favorite books.) $1. Bowman.
Pilgrim's progress; told to the children by Mary Macgregor. '10(Ap23) col. il. 16°, (Told to the children ser.) 50 c. net. Dutton.
Pilgrim's progress. '09(D18) il. 8°, *$3 net. Dutton.
Pilgrim's progress; with an introd. and notes by Marg. A. Eaton. '09(Jl10) c. por. S. (Classic lib.) pap., 15 c. Educ. Pub.
Pilgrim's progress from this world to that which is to come. '09(N6) col. il. O. $2, boxed. Fenno.
Pilgrim's progress; with notes explanatory and practical, by Rev. Jos. Ivimey; also, Life of John Bunyan, by himself. '08 (O24) il. O. *$1 net. Jennings.
Pilgrim's progress. pt. 1; ed., with introd. and notes, by Ernest C. Noyes. '10 (Ap9) c. por. 16°, (Merrill's English texts.) 40 c. C: E. Merrill.
Pilgrim's progress every child can read; ed. by Rev. Jesse Lyman Hurlbut, D.D. '10(Ja1) c. il. D. (Winston's every child's lib.) 75 c. Winston.
BUNYAN, John.
Willey, J: H. Midsummer nights with the great dreamer: [address on Pilgrim's progress.] *$2 net. Eaton & M.

Buonarotti, Michelangelo.
Masterpieces of Michaelangelo. '09(D25) il. 24°, (Painters' ser.) leath., *75 c. net; pap., *25 c. net. Stokes.
Work of Michelangelo; with a biographical introd. abr from Fritz Knapp. '08(D19) c. Q. (Classics in art ser.) **$2.50 net, boxed. Brentano's.

Bur, Lawrence J.
See Pennsylvania. Index.

Burba, G: Fs.
Our bird friends. '08(Jl18) c. il. O. $1. Outing.

Burbank, Alfr. Stevens.
Guide to historic Plymouth, localities and objects of interest. [New ed.] [1910.] (N) c. 96 p. il. 12°, 10 c. A. S. Burbank.

BURBANK, Luther.
Jordan, D: S., *and* Kellogg, V. L. Scientific aspects of Luther Burbank's work. *$1.75 net. A. M. Robertson.

Burch, Mrs. Adelle E. Shoemaker.
Know thyself, and other poems. '09, [1910.] (Ja) c. 182 p. por. 16°, $1. A. E. S. Burch.

Burch, R. M.
Color printing and color printers. '10 (D31) 8°, $3 net. Baker & T.

Burchard, H: H., M.D.
Text-book of dental pathology and therapeutics. 3d ed., rewritten by Otto E. Inglis. '08(Ag29) 567 eng., 8°, *$5 net. Lea.

Burchell, H: Philip, ed.
Spalding's roller skating guide. '10(S) c. 101 p. il. 16°, (Spalding's athletic lib.) pap., 10 c. Am. Sports.

Burchenal, Eliz., ed.
Folk-dances and singing games; twenty-six folk-dances of Norway, Sweden, Denmark, Russia, Bohemia, Hungary, Italy, England, Scotland and Ireland; with music, full directions for performance, and numerous illustrations. '10 (Ja8) c. f°, $2.50; pap., $1.50. Schirmer.

Burchill, Georgine, Ettinger, W: L., and Shimer, Edg. Dubs.
Progressive road to reading. bks. 1, 2. '09 (My) c. bk. 1, 32 c.; bk. 2, 40.—Bk. 3. (N13) c. il. D. 48 c. Silver.

Burckhardt, Jakob Christoph.
The cicerone: an art guide to painting in Italy; tr. from the German by Mrs. A. H. Clough; a new and il. impression, with a preface by P. G. Konody. '08(My16) il 12°, (Handbook of art in Italy.) $1.50. Scribner.

Burden bearer. Williams, F. H. **$2.50 net. Jacobs.

Burden of Isis. Dennis, J. T. 60 c. net. Dutton.

Burdette, Mrs. Clara Bradley.
Rainbow and the pot of gold; [story of life of Temple Baptist Church, Los Angeles.] '08, [1909.] (Ap) c. 11+147 p. il. pors. 8°, $1. Clara Vista.

Burdick, Esther E., comp.
Hudson-Fulton celebration; catalogue of an historical exhibition held by the Free Public Library of Jersey City, September-December, 1909. '09, [1910.] (O) 37 p. il. O. pap. Jersey City Pub. Lib.

Burdick, Fs. Marion.
Essentials of business law. '08(O) c. 20+309 p. D. (Twentieth century text-bks.) **$1.10 net. Appleton.
Law of torts. 2d ed., rev. and enl. '08(O) c. 89+550 p. O. $3. Banks & Co.
See also Massachusetts. Uniform sales act.

Burdick, Gordon Granger, M.D.
X-ray and high frequency in medicine. '10 (Ag) 7+318-10 p. il. 8°, $2.75. Physical Therapy.

Burdick, J. Ellis, ed.
General index [to The history of nations.] '08, [1909.] (Ja) c. 1080 p. 8°, (History of nations.) $2.75; ¾ mor., $3.75; full mor., $5. J: D. Morris.

Bureau of Social Research, New York. Chattel loan business: rept. prepared under the direction of the Bureau of Social Research, New York School of Philanthropy, by Arth. H. Ham. '09(Mr) c. 58 p. 8°, (Russell Sage Foundation pubs.) 25 c. Charities Pub.

Bureau of University Travel, Boston. Cruises of the "Athena" in Greece and the eastern Mediterranean, 1910. [1910.] (Jl) 28 p. il. 16°, pap., gratis. Bu. Univ. Travel.

Burgess, Albert Franklin.
Requirements to be complied with by nurserymen or others who make interstate shipments of nursery stock. '08, [1909.] (O) 7 p. 8°, (U. S., Dept. of Agriculture, Bureau of Entomology; circular.) pap.

Burgess, C: F., ed.
Historic Groton; comprising historic and descriptive sketches pertaining to Groton Heights, Center Groton, Poquonnoc Bridge, Noank, Mystic and Old Mystic, Conn., by local writers. '09(S) c. 101 p. il. 4°, $1.50; gilt edge, $2. C: F. Burgess.

Burgess, Fs.
Rudiments of Gregorian music. '09(S18) D. pap., *20 c. net. Scribner.

Burgess, Fk. Gelett.
Blue goops and red; manual of polite deportment for children who would be good; showing how and how not to behave everywhere. '09(N13) c. il. Q. **$1.35 net. Stokes.
Lady Mechante; or, life as it should be. '09(N13) c. il. O. **$1.50 net. Stokes.

Burgess, I: Bronson, ed.
Life of Christ, for use of classes in secondary schools and in the secondary division of the Sunday-school; adapt. from the life of Christ by Ernest D. Burton and Shailer Mathews. '08(O17) c. il. maps, O. (Constructive Bible studies; secondary ser.) $1. Univ. of Chic.

Burgess, J: W:
German Emperor and the German government: address del. before the Germanistic Society of America, January 5, 1909. '09 (F13) O. pap. (Add. pubs. for price.) Columbia Univ.

Burgess, Mary Abigail.
Richmond guide book; sketches and views of Richmond, Virginia, supplemented by sketches of Williamsburg, Jamestown, Yorktown; description and map, historic battlefields; location given of all pictures in book. '09, [1910.] (My) 87 p. il. map, S. pap., 25 c. Burgess.

Burgess, Thornton Waldo.
Old Mother West Wind. '10(O1) c. il. S. $1. Little, B. & Co.

Burgess, W:
Bible in Shakespeare. '09(D) c. '03. 288 p. 8°, *$1.50 net. Revell.
Formerly published by Winona Publishing Co.
Religion of Ruskin. '09(D) c. '03. 448 p. 8°, *$2 net. Revell.

Burgin, G: Brown.
Shutters of silence. '08(Ap11) c. 12°, (Popular priced copyrights.) 50 c. B. W. Dodge.

BURGOS, Spain.
Calvert, A. F: Leon, Burgos and Salamanca. *$1.25 net. Lane.

BURGUNDY, France.
Miltoun, F., *pseud.* Castles and chateaux of old Burgundy. $3. L. C. Page.

BURGUNDY, Marie Adelaide, *Duchess* of.
Williams, H. N. Rose of Savoy. *$3.50 net. Scribner.

Burhans, Viola.
Cave-woman; novel of to-day. '10(Je18) c. D. $1.50. Holt.

BURIAL.
Nevin, W. S., *comp.* Manual for undertakers. $1. Manual Pub.
Scanlan, C: M. Law of church and grave. $1.35. Benziger.
See also Cremation;—Embalming;—Epitaphs.

Buried alive. Bennett, E. A. $1. Brentano's.
Buried city of Kenfig. Gray, T: $3.50 net. Appleton.
Buried Herculaneum. Barker, E. R. *$3 net. Macmillan.

Burk, Addison B., comp.
See Atlantic Deeper Waterways Association.

—, and Schoff, Wilfred Harvey, comps.
Project of the Atlantic Deeper Waterway Association; summary of papers on the subject with statistics of coastwise commerce. '10(Jl16) il. pors. maps, 8°, gratis. A. B. Burk.

Burk, Frederic, and McFadden, Effie B.
Course of study in grammar, and hdbk. to the state ser. text. '09(Mr) 4°, (San Francisco State Normal School bulls.; new ser.) pap., 30 c. San F. St. Normal.

Burk, W: Herb.
Historical and topographical guide to Valley Forge. '10(Jl) c. 142 p. il. fold. map, 12°, 50 c. W: H. Burk.

Burke, Ashworth P:
See Burke, *Sir* J: Bernard.

Burke, C. E.
Child study and education. '08, [1909.] (Mr) 184 p. 75 c. Benziger.

Burke, Edm.
Reflections on the French Revolution and contingent essays; with introd. by A. J. Grieve. '10(D10) 16°, (Everyman's lib.) 35 c. net; leath., 70 c. net. Dutton.

Burke, Edm.—*Continued.*
Speech of Edmund Burke, on moving his resolutions for conciliation with the colonies, March 22, 1775; ed., with introd. and notes, by T: Arkle Clark. '08(Je20) c. por. S. (Scribner English classics.) **25 c. net. Scribner.
Speeches and letters on American affairs. '08(S19) 16°, (Everyman's lib.) *35 c. net; leath., *70 c. net. Dutton.

Burke, Ja. Fs.
Some of the public services of Hon. Philander Chase Knox: speech before the Pennsylvania delegation in Congress, Dec. 4, 1907. '08(F) O. pap. (Add. author for price.) J. F. Burke.

Burke, Sir J: Bernard and Ashworth P:
Genealogical and heraldic history of the peerage and baronetage, the privy council, knightage and companionage. 70th ed. '08(F8) il. (coats of arms) 8°, *$12 net. Putnam.

Burke, Rev. J: Ja.
Great problem; sermon for every Sunday and feast day in the year. '09(Ag7) c. 12°, *$1 net. Herder.
Reasonableness of Catholic ceremonies and practices. 3d ed. '09(Mr13) c. T. *25 c. net; pap., 13 c. Benziger.

Burke, Mary C.
School room echoes; book 1. '09(D25) c. por. D. $1.50. Badger.

Burke, Mrs. May Morse-.
Key to the laws of the occult psyche science; or, glimpse of Beulah land as viewed from earth through the psyche commune, of May Morse-Burke. '10 (Ag20) c. front. por. 8°, $1. Titus Pub. Co.

Burke, R: Maurice.
Cosmic consciousness: a study in the evolution of the human mind. '08(D) 318 p. 4°, $4.25. Progress Co.

Burkett, C: W:
Algodón, su cultivo elaboración y mercadería, del inglés original de C: W: Burkett y Clarence Hamilton Poe; [tr. by] S. Fabián de Velasco. '08(D) c. 222 p. il. tabs., 8°, $2; pap., $1.50. S. F. de Velasco.
Farm crops; pract. treatise on the growing of American field crops. '10(N19) c. il. 12°, $1.50. Judd.
Farm stock: practical treatise on horses, cattle, sheep and swine. '09(Mr27) c. il. 12°, *$1.50 net. Judd.
Farmers' veterinarian; pract. treatise on the diseases of farm stock. '09(D11) il. 12°, *$1.50 net. O. Judd.
—, ed. Domestic animals. '09(Ja23) il. 4°, *$3.50 net. Ginn.

Burkitt, Fs. Crawford.
Earliest sources for the life of Jesus. '10 (F26) c. S. (Modern religious problems.) **50 c. net. Houghton M.

Burland, J: Burland Harris-.
Broken law. '08(D12) c. il. 12°, 75 c. Cupples & L.
Love the criminal. '08(D5) c. 12°, 75 c. Cupples & L.

Burleigh, Clarence Blendon.
All among the loggers. '08(O17) c. il. O. (Norman Carver ser.) †$1.50. Lothrop, L. & S.
With pickpole and peavey; or, two live boys on the East Branch drive. '09 (S11) c. il. O. (Norman Carver ser.) †$1.50. Lothrop, L. & S.
Young guide; or, two live boys in the Maine woods. '10(D17) c. il. 12°, (Norman Carver ser.) $1.50. Lothrop, L. & S.

BURLINGAME, Elmer.
Cleveland, R. What Burlingame did. (Add. author for price.) R. Cleveland.

Burlingham, Gertrude Simmons.
Study of the *Lactariae* of the United States: [mushrooms.] '08(O) 109 p. il. 8°, (Torrey Botanical Club memoirs.) $1.25. Torrey.

Burlington (Ia.) Public Library. Pract. books in the library on electricity, engineering, railroading and other subjects for workers in the various trades and professions. '10(O) 30 p. 16°. Burlington Pub. Lib.

BURLINGTON, Wis.
Wood, H. A. Burlington; its early hist., growth and progress. 35 c. H. A. Wood.

BURMA.
Bunker, A. Sketches from the Karen Hills. $1 net. Revell.
Burn-Murdoch, W. G. From Edinburgh to India and Burmah. *$3.50 net. Dutton.
Hall, H. F. Inward light: [Buddhism in Burma.] **$1.75 net. Macmillan.
Kelly, R. T. Burma. *75 c. net. Macmillan.
O'Connor, V. C. S. Mandalay, and other cities of the past in Burma. *$5 special net. Appleton.
Yoe, S. The Burman; his life and notions. $3.25 net. Macmillan.
See also Burmese language;—Far East.

BURMESE LANGUAGE.
Brown, R: G. Half the battle in Burmese. $2. Oxford Univ.

Burn-Murdoch, W. G.
From Edinburgh to India and Burmah. '08 (O17) 8°, *$3.50 net. Dutton.

Burnand, Sir Fs. Cowley, ed.
Poems from *Punch*. '08(N7) c. por. T. (Remarque ser. of literary masterpieces.) 40 c.; limp leath., 75 c.; chamois, $1.25, boxed. Caldwell.

BURNE-JONES, *Sir* Edward.
Baldry, A. L. Burne-Jones. *65 c. net. Stokes.
Bell, M. Sir Edward Burne-Jones. *$2 net. Doran.

Burnet, Etienne, M.D.
Campaign against microbes. '09(O) 259 p. 8°, *$2.50 net. Wood.

BURNET, *Bp.* Gilbert.
Clarke, T. E. S., *and* Foxcroft, H. C. Life of Gilbert Burnet, bishop of Salisbury. *$4.50 net. Putnam.

Burnet, J:
Early Greek philosophy. 2d ed. '08(Ag1) 8°, *$3 net. Macmillan.

Burnet, Margaretta.
Laboratory manual of zoölogy. '08(F8) c. D. 50 c. Am. Bk.

Burnett, Mrs. Frances Hodgson, [now Mrs. Stephen Townesend.]
Barty Crusoe and his man Saturday. '09 (D4) c. il. O. **$1 net. Moffat.
Emily Fox-Seton; being "The making of a marchioness" and "The methods of Lady Walderhurst. '09(O30) c. D. †$1.50. Stokes.
Good wolf. '08(N7) c. il. O. **$1 net. Moffat.
Land of the Blue Flower. '09(O16) c. col. front. D. **75 c net. Moffat.
Spring cleaning; as told by Queen Crosspatch. '08(O17) c. il. S. †60 c. Century Co.

—, Birdsall, Katharine Newbold, and Burnett, Vivian, eds.
Children's book. '09(D4) c. il. O. †$1.50. Moffat.

Burnett, P: Hardeman.
Path which led a Protestant lawyer to the Catholic church; ed. and abridged by Rev. Ja. Sullivan. '09(Je5) c. 8°, *$1.50 net. Herder.

Burnett, S: Howard.
Clinical pathology of the blood of domesticated animals. '08(Ag22) c. il. 8°. *$2.50 net. Taylor & C.

Burnett, Thdr. Creti.
On the rise of temperature in rabbits, caused by the injection of salt solutions. '10(O) 5-7 p. O. (Univ. of Cal. pubs.: Physiology.) pap. Univ. of Cal.

Burnett, Vivian, ed.
See Burnett, *Mrs.* Frances Hodgson, *ed.*

Burney, Rev. C: Fox.
Israel's hope of immortality: four lectures. '09(My15) O. bds., $1. Oxford Univ.

Burney, Fanny.
See Arblay, *Mme.* Frances Burney d'.

Burnham, Mrs. Clara Louise Root.
Clever Betsy; a novel. '10(S17) c. il. D. $1.25 net. Houghton M.
Flutterfly. '10(Mr5) c. il. in col. D. †75 c. Houghton M.
Leaven of love. '08(S12) c. front. D. †$1.50. Houghton M.
Quest flower. '08(O17) c. il. D. †$1. Houghton M.

Burnham, E.
Colored charts of the E. Burnham system of beauty culture. '09(S18) c. il. Q. $1.50. E. Burnham.

Burnham, Frederic L.
Supervision and teaching of the manual arts in the high school; repr. from the 72d rept. of the Mass. Bd. of Educ. '09 (D) 30 p. O. pap., gratis. G: H. Martin.

Burnham, Maud.
Descriptive stories for all the year: for home, kindergarten and primary school. '08(Je27) c. 12°, 50 c. M. Bradley.

Burnham, W: H:
Hygiene of the nose. '08, [1909.] (Mr) 155-169 p. 8°. (Add. author for price.) W: H: Burnham.
One session a day, or two in the public schools. '09(Ap24) O. (Hygiene and physical education ser.) pap., 10 c. Bassette.

Burnham, W: H:, and Suzzallo, H:
History of education as a professional subject. '09(Ap24) 8°, 50 c. Teachers' Coll.

Burning Daylight. London, J. $1.50. Macmillan.

Burning gauze. Croudace, L. $1. J. R. Lafontaine.

Burning issue, and what co-operation will do. Callahan, J. Y. 25 c. Pub. Pr.

Burning of Chelsea. Pratt, W. M. $1.50. Sampson.

Burns, Cecil Laurence, and Marsden, Rufus E.
Principles of educational woodwork; hdbk. for teachers and others. '09(O2) il. 12°, *$1.50 net. Dutton.

Burns, E: Fs.
Songs of cloud and star. '09(F6) c. D. *$1.25 net. Ball Pub.

Burns, Elmer Ellsworth.
Story of great inventions. '10(D3) c. il. O. $1.25. Harper.

Burns, Harrison, comp.
See Indiana. Burns' annot. statutes.—Corporation law.—General index.

Burns, Rev. Ja.
Revivals, their laws and leaders. '09(D) 12+312 p. O. *$1.50 net. Doran.

Burns, Rev. Ja. Aloysius.
Catholic school system in the U. S. '08 (Je13) c. D. $1.25. Benziger.

Burns, Judson Doctor, M.D.
What is man?; or, creationism vs. evolutionism. '08(Ag1) c. il. por. D. $2. Cochrane.

Burns, Rob.
Complete poetical works. '08(D19) 12°, (Crowell's thin paper poets.) ooze leath., $1.75, boxed. Crowell.
Cotter's Saturday night and other poems. '10(D) 16°, (Abbey classics.) pap., 25 c., boxed; bds., $1, boxed. Abbey Co.
Formerly published by Paul Elder.
The Geddes Burns. '09(Ap10) por. facsims., 8°. (Add. Society for price.) Bibliophile.
Poems and letters in the hand-writing of Robert Burns reproduced in facsimile through the courtesy of W: K. Bixby and F: W. Lehmann by the Burns Club of St. Louis; with an introd. and explanatory notes by Wa. B. Stevens. '08(Jl18) c. il. pors. f°. (Not for sale.) Burns Club.
Poems and songs. '08(O17) 16°, (Best books ser.) leath., *$1 net. Dutton.
Poetical works. Cabinet ed. In 2 v. '08 (D19) 12°, (British poets ser.) ea., $1.50. Estes.
Sel. poems and songs; ed., with notes and an introd., by Philo Melvin Buck, jr. '08 (F8) por. 24°, (Macmillan's pocket Am. and Eng. classics.) *25 c. net. Macmillan.
Tam O'Shanter. '08(O24) c. il. O. $1, boxed. Saalfield.

BURNS, Robert.
Carlyle, T: Essay on Burns. 25 c. C: E. Merrill.
Carlyle, T: Essay on Burns. **25 c. net. Scribner.

BURNS, Robert.—*Continued.*
Carlyle, T:, *and* Macaulay, T: B., *Lord*. Robert Burns, by T: Carlyle; Samuel Johnson, by Lord Macaulay. 30 c.; 20 c. Newson.
Jean Armour Burns Club, Washington, D. C. Speeches and essays with poems on Burns. gratis. Gibson.
Joab, A. E. Robert Burns. 50 c. A. E. Joab.
Joyce, J: A. Robert Burns. $1. J: A. Joyce.

Burns, W: Savage, comp.
Bibliography of the writings of members of the class of 1887 in Yale College; repr. from the Vicennial record of the class. '09, [1910.] (Ja) 28 p. 8°, pap. (Add. pubs. for price.) Marigold-F.

Burnt offering. Cotes, *Mrs.* S. J. D. $1.50. Lane.

Burnt offering. Ellison, *Mrs.* E. N. $1.25. B'way Pub.

Burpee, Lawrence Johnstone.
Search for the western sea: story of the exploration of north-western America. '08(O10) il. maps, O. *$5 special net. Appleton.

BURR, Aaron.
Lewis, A. H: An American patrician, or, the story of Aaron Burr. **$2 net. Appleton.
Wood, W. Tragedy of the deserted isle. $1.50. C. M. Clark.

Burr, Amelia Josephine.
Plays in the market-place. '10(D3) c. 8°, $3. Hillside.

Burr, Mrs. Anna Robeson Brown.
The autobiography; critical and comparative study. '09(O30) c. O. **$2 net. Houghton M.

Burr, Jane, [pseud. for Punch, Rosalind Mae Guggenheim.]
Letters of a Dakota divorcee. '09(N) c. 148 p. D. $1. Roxburgh.

BURR, Theodosia.
See Alston, *Mrs.* Theodosia Burr.

Burr, W: Hubert, and Falk, Myron S:
Design and construction of metallic bridges. 2d ed., rev. '08(N14) il. figs. 8°, $5. Wiley.
Graphic method by influence lines for bridge and roof computations. 2d ed. '08 (Je6) c. diagrs., 8°, $3. Wiley.

Burrage, Champlin.
New facts concerning John Robinson; pastor of the Pilgrim Fathers. '10(D3) facsim. O. pap., 60 c. Oxford Univ.

Burrage, Wa. Lincoln.
Gynecological diagnosis. '10(Ag) 16+656 p. il. 8°, $6. Appleton.

Burrell, Caroline Benedict.
See Benton, Caroline French. *pseud.*
—, ed. Mother's book; suggestions regarding the mental and moral development of children; incl. articles by Mrs. Annie Winsor Allen, Mrs. Marg. E. Sangster, Ida Prentice Whitcomb, [and others.] [1910.] (N) c. 7+277 p. 8°. Univ. Soc.

Burrell, D: Ja., D.D.
Cloister book, for shut-in worshippers and pastorless congregations. '09(D) 340 p. 12°, $1. Am. Tr.

Burrell, D: Ja.—*Continued.*
In David's town. '10(N12) c. il. 12°, 50 c. Am. Tr.
Lure of the city: book for young men. '08 (O10) c. D. **$1 net. Funk.

Burris, Martin.
True sketches of the life and travels of Martin Burris on the western plains, the Rocky Mountains and the Pacific coast, U. S. A. '10(S3) c. por. 12°, 50 c. M. Burris.

Burritt, Eldon Grant.
The pupil and how to teach him; introd. by John La Due. '10(Ap9) c. 12°, 60 c. W. B. Rose.

Burritt, Maurice Chase.
Agricultural conditions in southern New York. '10(O) 19 p. il. 8°, (U. S., Dept. of Agriculture; Bureau of Plant Industry; circular.)

Burroughs, J:
Complete writings. Riverby ed. In 15 v. '08(D26) ea., $1.75; hf. mor., $3.50; per set, $26.25; hf. mor., $52.50. Houghton M.
In the Catskills; selections from the writings of John Burroughs. '10(S17) c. il. O. $1.50 net. Houghton M.
Leaf and tendril: [essays.] '08(Ap18) por. D. **$1.10 net. Houghton M.
See also In American fields and forests.

Burroughs, W: Dwight.
Wonderland of stamps. '10(S10) c. il. D. $1.50. Stokes.

Burrow, N: Trigant.
Determination of the position of a momentary impression in the temporal course of a moving visual impression; [repr. from *Psychological Review.*] '10 (My7) il. 4°, (Johns Hopkins studies in philosophy and psychology.) 65 c. Psychological Review.

Burrowes, Katharine.
Burrowes course of music study; teachers' manual. 3 v. 3d ed. '10(N19) c. 8°, $3. K. Burrowes.

Burrows, C: W:
Best method of demagnetizing iron in magnetic testing. '09(My) 205-274 p. il. tabs., 8°, pap. (Add. Superintendent for price.)

Burrows, J: Shober.
Mine sampling and chemical analyses of coals tested at the United States fuel-testing plant, Norfolk, Va., in 1907. '09 (Mr6) 8°, (U. S., Geol. Survey, bull.)
Results of purchasing coal under government specifications, with a paper on burning the small sizes of anthracite for heat and power purposes by Dwight T. Randall. '09(My) 44 p. tabs., O. pap. (Add. Superintendent for price.)

Burrows, Julius Caesar.
Marine Corps; hist. of the Marine Corps. '09(My) 6 p. 8°, pap. (Add. Superintendent for price.) U. S., Supt. of Docs.

Burrows, Montagu.
Autobiography; ed. by his son, Stephen Montagu Burrows; with a supplementary note by Professor Oman. '08(Je13) il. 8°, *$2.60 net. Macmillan.

BURRUSS, Harry William.
Burruss, *Mrs.* M. S. Harry William Burruss. *$1.25 net. Revell.

Burruss, Mrs. Mary Schey.
Harry William Burruss. '10(F12) c. 12°, *$1.25 net. Revell.

BURSA BURSA-PASTORIS.
See Botany.

BURSA HEEGERI.
See Botany.

Bursley, Jos. Aldrich.
See Allen, J: Robins.

Burstall, Sara A.
Impressions of American education in 1908. '09(F6) D. *$1.25 net. Longmans.

Burt, C. A., pseud.
See Bean, Burt Clifford.

Burt, Mary Eliz., ed.
Poems that every child should know. 3 v. School ed. '09(Jl31) c. 12°, $1.50. Doubleday, P.
Prose that every child should know: selection of the best prose of all times. '08 (Ap18) c. front. D. (Every child should know ser.) **90 c. net; leath., **$1.50 net. Doubleday, P.

Burt, Bp. W:
Europe and Methodism. '09(D11) c. 16°, (Little books on missions.) 35 c. Jennings.

Burton, Alonzo J.
Eastern Star; a collection of historic papers, reminiscences, poems, essays, etc., etc., rel. to the Eastern Star. '09(S) c. 94 p. il. pors. 12°, pap., 75 c. A. J. Burton.

Burton, C: J.
Astronomy and the Bible. '08(S) c. 176 p. il. por. 12°, $1. C: J. Burton.

Burton, C: Pierce.
Bob's Cave boys: sequel to "The boys of Bob's Hill. '09(Mr27) c. il. D. †$1.50. Holt.
Bob's Hill braves. '10(S24) c. il. D. $1.50. Holt.

Burton, Clarence Monroe.
Ephraim Douglass and his times; fragment of hist., with the journal of George McCully (hitherto unpublished), and various letters of the period. [*Magazine of History;* extra number.] '10(N19) por. 12°, $1.85, (to magazine subscribers.) Abbatt.
John Connolly, a Tory of the Revolution; [repr. from the Proceedings of the American Antiquarian Society for Oct., 1909.] '09, [1910.] (Jl) 38 p. 8°, 50 c. Am. Antiquarian.

Burton, Edn. Hubert, D.D.
Life and times of Bishop Challoner, (1691-1781.) In 2 v. '09(O30) il. pors. O. *$7 net. Longmans.

Burton, Ernest Dewitt, and Mathews, Shailer.
Life of Christ, for the use of classes in secondary schools and in the secondary division of the Sunday-school; adapted by I: Bronson Burgess. '08, [1909.] (Mr) c. 307 p. il. plan, 8°, (Constructive Bible studies; ed. by E. D. Burton; secondary ser.) $1. Univ. of Chic.

—, Smith, J: Merlin Powis and Gerald Birney.
Biblical ideas of atonement. '09(N13) c. D. $1. Univ. of Chic.

Burton, F: Russell.
American primitive music; with especial attention to the songs of the Ojibways. '09(N20) c. front. O. **$5 net. Moffat.
Redcloud of the lakes. '09(Jl31) c. il. D. $1.50. G: W. Dillingham.
Strongheart: novel founded on W: C. de Mille's play. '08(S19) c. D. †$1.50. G: W. Dillingham.

Burton, G: Ward.
Book on California and its sunlit skies of glory; also, letters from Europe and miscellaneous essays in literature, ethics and politics. '09(N) il. 4°, $2.50. G: W. Burton.

Burton, Hobson.
See Burton, W:

Burton, J: Hill.
Book hunter; ed. by J. Herbert Slater. '08 (Ag15) 12°, (London lib.) *$1 net. Dutton.

Burton, Rev. Marion Le Roy.
Problem of evil; criticism of the Augustinian point of view. '09(N6) c. D. $1.25. Open Court.

Burton, R:
From the book of life: poems. '09(O2) c. D. **$1.25 net. Little, B. & Co.
Masters of the English novel; study of principles and personalities. '09(D18) c. D. $1.25. Holt.
Midsummer memory: elegy on the death of Arth. Upson. '10(D31) O. bds., $1.25. (500 copies.) E. D. Brooks.
Three of a kind: story of an old musician, a newsboy and a cocker dog. '08(O3) c. il. D. †$1.50. Little, B. & Co.

Burton, Sir R: F.
First footsteps in East Africa; with introd. by H. W. Nevinson. '10(D10) 16°, (Everyman's lib.) 35 c. net; leath., 70 c. net. Dutton.

Burton, St. George E: W:
Black Watch; record of an historical regiment. New rev. ed. '10(D) $1.25 net. Cassell.

Burton, T: W:
What experience has taught me; autobiography. '10(Jl16) c. il. pors. 8°, $1.50. T: W: Burton.

Burton, W: and Hobson.
Hdbk. of marks on pottery and porcelain. '09(O30) figs. D. *$2.25 net. Macmillan.

Burton-Fanning, F. W.
Open air treatment of pulmonary tuberculosis. '09(Ag); 2d ed. '10(Jl) figs. ea., *$1.50 net. Hoeber.

Burtscher, W: J:
Yellow Creek humor. '09(Je5) c. D. $1. W: J: Burtscher.

Burwick, Ja. Monroe.
Conductor Jim, his story in his own words: ed. by Paul J. Gilbert; introd. by J. Wilbur Chapman; poem by Fanny J. Crosby. '08(Jl4) c. il. pors. D. $1. Y. M. C. A.

Bury, Lady Charlotte Susan Maria Campbell.
Diary of a lady-in-waiting; being the diary illustrative of the times of George the Fourth, interspersed with original letters from the late Queen Caroline; ed. with an introd. by A. Fs. Steuart. '08(O10) 2 v., il. O. *$7.50 net. Lane.

Bury, J: Bagnell.
Ancient Greek historians; (Harvard lectures.) '09(Ja30) c. O. $2.25. Macmillan.
Constitution of the later Roman Empire. '10(Je4) 8°, 50 c. net. Putnam.

Busbey, Katharine Graves.
Home life in America. '10(D17) il. D. $2 net. Macmillan.

Busch, Wilhelm.
Edward's dream: the philosophy of a humorist; tr. and ed. by Dr. Paul Carus from the German. '09(Jl31) c. por. S. *$1 net. Open Court.

BUSCH, Wilhelm.
Winther, F. William Busch als dichter kunstler, psychologe und philosoph. 75 c. Univ. of Cal.

Bush, Bertha E.
Prairie Rose. '10(O15) c. il. D. $1.50. Little, B. & Co.

Bush, Harold Montfort.
Diary of an enlisted man. '09(Ag28) D. 50 c.; pap., 25 c. E: T. Miller.

Bush, Wa. Nelson, and Clarke, J: Bernard.
Elements of geometry. '09(O16) c. il. 12°, $1.25. Silver.

Bush-fruits. Card, F: W. **$1.50 net. Macmillan.

BUSHEY CAVERN, Md.
Peabody, C:, *and* Moorhead, W. K. Exploration of Bushey cavern near Cavetown, Md., pt. 1; Fort Ancient, pt. 2. 75 c. Andover.

Bushman paintings copied [in color] by M. Helen Tongue; with a preface by H: Balfour. '09(N13) il. Q. pap., $19.25, boxed. Oxford Univ.

Bushnell, Mrs. Belle Johnston.
John Arrowsmith—planter. '09(D4) c. il. D. $1.50. Torch Press.

Bushnell, Curtis Clark.
Christmas day and other poems. '10(D31) 8°, 50 c.; pap., 40 c. C. C. Bushnell.
Readings from Latin verse; with notes. '09 (Ja9) c. 12°, 75 c. Allyn & B.

Bushnell, D: I., jr.
The Choctaw of Bayou Lacomb, St. Tammany Parish, Louisiana. '09, [1910.] (Je) 8+35 p. pls. map, 8°, (Smithsonian Inst., Bu. of American Ethnology, bull.) U. S., Supt. of Docs.

Bushnell, Jos.
Voices of the past, present and future: [poems.] '09(N6) c. D. 50 c. J. Bushnell.

Bushnell, Jos. P., comp.
What to do and how to do it: manual, treating of the home and its interests, the culinary art, health, the farm, [etc.] '09(Je12) c. 8°, $2. Home Manual.

BUSINESS.
American Academy of Political and Social Science. American business conditions. $1.50; $1. Am. Acad. Pol. Sci.
American business methods (down-to-the-minute); comp. by the Board of Experts of the *Business Man's Magazine.* $2. Business Man's Pub.
American School of Correspondence. Business management. $4.—Cyclopedia of commerce, accountancy, business administration. 10 v. $24. Am. Sch. Corr.

BUSINESS.—*Continued.*

Atkinson, W: W. Psychology of salesmanship. $1. Progress Co.

Babson, R. W. Business barometers used in the accumulation of money. $2. R. W. Babson.

Beach, E. H:, *and* Thorne, W. W., *eds.* International business encyclop. $4. E. H: Beach.

Berkwitz, W: L. Encyclopædia of the mail order business. $5.—Reminiscences, composed of actual mail order experiences. $1.—Ups and downs of the mail order business. $1. Mail Order.

Bishop, W: G. Short course in business training. 65 c. Univ. Pub.

Blain, H. E., *ed.* Pitman's secretary's handbook. $2. Pitman.

Brookline, Mass. Public Library. Selected list of books on business and rel. subjects in the Public Library, Dec., 1909. gratis to public libraries. Riverdale Press.

Butterfield, C. d'B. Suggestion as applied to business. $1. Colonial Press, (Ct.)

Collins, J. H. Human nature in selling goods. 50 c. Altemus.

Comtelburo business calendar, 1909; 1910. ea., $1. Comtelburo.

Cooper, F. Financing an enterprise. 2 v. $4. Ronald Press.

Corbion, W: A., *and* Grimsdale, G. E. Salesmanship. $1. Pitman.

Cottingham, W. H. Business success. *75 c. net; *$1.25 net. Dodge.

Cromwell, J: H. American business woman. $2 net. Putnam.

Cronk, V. D. Selection of business forms, incl. local precedents and official forms under the laws of Wisconsin and Minnesota. (Add. pubs. for price.) Flood.

Davis, L. B. Our pract. method for raising capital. $7. Business Aid.

Dean, E: P., *comp.* Merchant's friend stock calculator tables. $5. Merchant's Friend.

Deland, L. F. Imagination in business. **50 c. net. Harper.

Dicksee, L. R. Business organization. $1.50. Longmans.

Directory of directors in the city of New York, [1909.] *$5 net. Audit Co.

Douglas, G. How to make money. 50 c. net. Dutton.

Edwards, R: H:, *ed.* Business morals. 10 c. R: H: Edwards.

Emerson, H. Efficiency as a basis for operation and wages. $2. Engineering Mag.

Farrington, F. Back in the harness: [talks on retail trade.] 50 c. Merchants' Helps.

Fox, P. One thousand ways to make money. 50 c. B'way Pub.

Frank, R. J: Commentary on the science of organization and business development. $2.75; $3. S: A. Bloch; Chic. Commercial.

Garrison, C: L. How to conduct a successful shoe-store. $1. Boot & Shoe.

BUSINESS.—*Continued.*

Grant, J: W: D. How to market ability. 50 c. Advancement.

Griffith, J. B. Administrative and industrial organization. 50 c.—Shipping department. (Priv. pr.) Am. Sch. Corr.

Haddock, F. C. Business power. $3. Power-Bk.

Hall, S: R. How to get a position and how to keep it. **50 c. net. Funk.

Haupt, W: G: Art of business college soliciting. $2. W: G: Haupt.

Heacock, W: A. Best way to start a mail order business. $3. W: A. Heacock.

Hirschler, D. Art of retail selling; textbk. for salespeople. $1. N. Y. Inst. Mercantile.

Holman, W. C. Talking points and selling arguments. 2 v. $5 Salesmanship.

How to increase your sales. $2. System.

Hubbard, E. Helpful hints as business helpers. 10 c.—Little journeys to the homes of great business men. $2; $3; $5; $10. Roycrofters.

International accountants' manual; or, twentieth century bookkeeping and business practice. $3. Business Man's Pub.

Kallmeyer, C: Pract. legal and business manual. 75 c. C: Kallmeyer.

Knowlson, T: S. Business!; pract. hints for master and man. *40 c. net. Warne.

Lawrence, H: C. Making him buy. $2. Consol. Pub.

Lenington, N. G. Seven principles of successful salesmanship. $1. Commercial Sci.

Lennen, P. W. How to double the day's work. $2. System.

Letters to salesmen. $1. Col. Tool Steel.

Lewson, J: Monopoly and trade restraint cases, incl. conspiracy, injunction, [etc.] 2 v. (Add. pubs. for price.) Flood.

Lindgren, C: New salesmanship and how to do business by mail. $1.50; $2. Laird.

Marden, O. S. Not the salary but the opportunity. **10 c. net. Crowell.

Mason, F. R. Business principles and organization., $4.80. Cree.

Menace to business of Sherman anti-trust act. 20 c. Am. Banker.

Mercantile speller. $2.50 net. Franklin Press.

Messenger, F. M. Catacombs of worldly success. 50 c. Metropolitan Ch. Assoc.

Modern business ser. 12 v. $78, with course. Alexander Hamilton.

Morals in modern business. *$1.25 net. Yale Univ.

New business code. $7.50. Business Code.

Nichols, J. L., *and* Goodrich, H. H. Robinson's business points: a compendium of legal and business forms. $1. J. L. Nichols.

Parson, C. C. Business administration. $3. System.

Parsons, T. Law of business. $4. Scranton.

Parsons, W: F. Hdbk. of forms. $4. Nashville Bk.

BUSINESS.—*Continued.*

Putzel, C:, *and* Bähr, H. H., *comps.* Commercial precedents sel. from the column of Replies and decisions of the N. Y. *Journal of Commerce and Commercial Bulletin.* (Add. pubs. for price.) Am. Pub.

Quinn, F. O. How to be a good salesman. 50 c. Harper-Adams.

Read, H. E. Alarm talks. 30 c. Business Monthly.

Read, H. E. Lessons in salesmanship. 85 c. J. A. Lyons.

Reddall, H: F. Wit and humor of business. **50 c. net; **80 c. net. Jacobs.

Roe, E: T: 700 lessons in business. $1. J: A. Hertel.

Russell, T: H., *and others., eds.* International business lib. 5 v. Int. Law.

Saunders, F. W. Letters to a business girl. $1.25. Laird.

Selecman, E. H. Specialty salesman. $1. Progress Co.

Slater, J: A. Pitman's business man's guide. $1.25. Pitman.

Stepanek, W. H. Business methods in a hardware store. $1.50. W. H. Stepanek.

Stoll, A., *jr., comp.* Clever business sketches. $1. Business Man's Pub.

Success in retailing, the variety business; hdbk. for earnest beginners in merchandising. Butler Bros.

Sullivan, J: J. American business law. $1.50. Appleton.

United Publishers' Association "blue book." $30, (with service.) Un. Pub. Assoc.

Van Dyke, J: C: Money god: chapters of heresy and dissent concerning business methods. **$1 net. Scribner.

Walker, H: C. How to get a better situation. $2. Opportunity.

Warren, W. P. Thoughts on business. 2d ser. $1.25. Forbes.

Wilbur, M. A. Every-day business for women. $1.25 net. Houghton M.

Wood, H: A. W. Money hunger. **$1 net. Putnam.

Woodbury, M. H. Pract. business hints. Newcomb.

Woods, C. E. Industrial organization, systematization and accounting. 3 v. $24. Woods.

Woods, C. E. Repts. on industrial organization, systemization and accounting. In 12 pts. pts. 1 and 2. per set, $15. C. E. Woods.

See also Advertising;—Automobiles;—Banks and banking; — Bookkeeping; — Clothing trade; — Codes;—Coffee;—Commerce; — Commercial correspondence;—Commercial law;—Corporations; —Credit; — Debt; — Education; — English language;—Farms and farming;—Finance;—Hardware; —Insurance;—Investments; — Lettering; —Letter writing;—Money;—National Business League of America;—Prices;—Real property;—Stocks;—Success;—Tariff;—Telephone;—Trusts (*industrial*);—Window-dressing;—Woman.

Business administration; Hon. Robt. M. La Follette, supervising editor; Wm. M. Handy and C: Higgins, managing editors; University extension course, La Salle University, Chicago. 12 v. '09(Ap3) c. il. map, 4°, per set, $72. Du Mont & H.

BUSINESS ARITHMETIC.
See Arithmetic.

Business barometers. Babson, R: W. $2; $3. R. W. Babson.

Business boy. Chapman, A. 60 c. Cupples & L.

Business, commerce and finance. il. 8°. Cree.
—McVey. Railroad transportation. $5.
—Putney. Foreign laws. $5.
—Putney, *and others.* Manufactures, mining; irrigation, real estate.
—Skinner *and* Putney. Government revenue, taxation, tariffs, public utilities. $4.80.

BUSINESS CORRESPONDENCE.
See Commercial correspondence.

Business correspondence in shorthand, no. 7; being a portion of the letters contained in "Pitman's 20th century dictation book and legal forms"; with printed key, and the matter for speed practice in either shorthand or typewriting; in the reporting style of phonography. 20th century ed. '09 (Je26) D. pap, 25 c. Pitman.

BUSINESS LAW.
See Commercial law.

Business man in the amusement world. Grau, R. $5. B'way Pub.

Business man's quiz book. '09(Jl) gratis. Am. Inst. Law.

Business of dairying. Lane, C. B. *$1.25 net. Judd.

Business side of farming. Bexell, J: A. 50 c. J: A. Bexell.

Business side of religion. Roche, J. T: *15 c. net. Wiltzius.

Business speller. Marshall, C. C. 90 c. Goodyear-M.

Business venture ser. il. O. †$1.50. Estes.
—Kaler. Cruise of the "Phœbe."—"Sarah Jane."

Bussell, F: W:, D.D.

Marcus Aurelius, and the later Stoics. '10 (Je4) 12°, (World's epoch makers' ser.) $1.25. Scribner.

Roman Empire; essays on the constitutional hist. from the accession of Domitian, 81 A.D., to the retirement of Nicephorus III., 1081 A.D. 2 v. '10(D10) O. $9 net. Longmans.

Bustan al-ukul. Nathaniel ibn al-Fayyumi. *$2.50 net. Lemcke.

Buster, Mary Jane and Tige. Outcault, R: F. 60 c. Stokes.

Buster Brown on his travels. '10(D) col. il. obl. 4°, bds., 60 c. Cupples & L.

Buster Brown, the busybody. Outcault, R: F. 60 c. Cupples & L.

Buster Brown up to date. Outcault, R: F. 60 c. Stokes.

But still a man. Knapp, M. L. †$1.50. Little, B. & Co.

Butcher, Madge Hortense Myers.
See Bible. N. T.

Butler, Alford A:, D.D.

How to understand the words of Christ; pract. hdbk. for teachers and Bible students. '10(Ja8) c. D. *90 c. net. Whittaker.

Butler, Arth.

Dictionary (miniature) of philosophical terms. '09(Mr13) 32°, (Miniature reference lib.) leath., 50 c. Dutton.

Butler, Arth. J:, ed.
Forerunners of Dante; selection from Italian poetry before 1300. '10(O1) D. $2. Oxford Univ.

Butler, Bert S.
See Tarr, Ralph Stockman.

Butler, C: H:
Review of decisions of the federal and state courts in cases involving the relative effect of stipulations in treaties between the United States and foreign powers. '07, [1908.] (My.) 62 p. 8°, (Add. pubs. for price.) Banks.
—, rep. *See* United States. *Sup. ct.* Repts.

Butler, E:
Carburettors, vaporizers, and distributing valves used in internal combustion engines. '09(O9) il. 8°, *$2 net. Lippincott.

Butler, Elinor Brotherton.
Diamond spider and other stories. '10 (D17) c. il. D. $1.25 net. A. Harriman.

Butler, Lady Eliz.
From sketch-book and diary. '09(D25) il. O. (Color books ser., Miscellaneous.) *$2.50 net. Macmillan.

Butler, Eliz. Beardsley.
Women and the trades; Pittsburgh, 1907-1908. '09(D25) c. il. O. (Russell Sage foundation pubs.: Pittsburgh Survey findings.) *$1.50 net. Charities Pub.

Butler, Ellis Parker.
Cheerful smugglers. '08(Ap18) c. il. D. †$1. Century Co.
Mike Flannery on duty and off. '09(Je12) c. il. D. 50 c. Doubleday, P.
That pup. '08(N14) c. il. D. †50 c. McClure.
Thin Santa Claus; the chicken yard that was a Christmas stocking. '09(O16) c. il. D. (Little comic masterpieces.) †50 c. Doubleday, P.
Water goats and other troubles. '10(Je25) c. il. D. 50 c. Doubleday, P.

Butler, G: Fk., M.D.
Exploits of a physician detective. '08(N) c. 322 p. il. 12°, $1. Clinic.
Text-book of materia medica, pharmacology and therapeutics. 6th ed., thoroughly rev. and enl. and adapt. to the eighth revision of the U. S. pharmacopœia. '08 (D) 9-708 p. 8°, *$4 net; hf. mor., *$5.50 net. Saunders.
Treasures of truth. [1910.] (F) c. '09. 82 p. 12°, 75 c. S. D. Clough.
—, Favill, H: Baird, M.D., and Bridge, Norman, M.D.
Materia medica and therapeutics; preventive medicine; climatology. '08, [1909.] (F) c. 360 p. il. 12°, (Practical medicine ser. of year books.) $1.50. Year Bk.

Butler, Glentworth Reeve, M.D.
Diagnostics of internal medicine. 3d rev. ed. '09(N) c. 34+1193 p. col. il. 8°, $6. Appleton.

Butler, Gurdon Montague.
Pocket hdbk. of blowpipe analysis; designed for the use of students and prospectors with the idea of making oral instruction unnecessary. '10(D17) c. 16°, 75 c. net. Wiley.
Pocket handbook of minerals. '08(Ap25) c. figs. 16°, leath., $3. Wiley.

Butler, Harold Edgeworth.
Post-Augustan poetry from Seneca to Juvenal. '09(Ap3) O. $2.90. Oxford Univ.

Butler, H: Montagu, D.D.
Ten great and good men; lectures. '09 (N13) D. $2. Longmans.

Butler, Hiram Erastus.
Goal of life; or, science and revelation. '08 (Ap4) c. il. por. 12°, $2. Esoteric.

Butler, J: Cromwell.
See Butler, W: D:

Butler, Jos. Marion.
See Butler, W: D:

Butler, Lewell Colbert.
Unveiling tributes; [Woodmen of the World.] '09, [1910.] (F) c. 113 p. il. por. O. $1. La. Distrib. Co.

BUTLER, *General* M. C.
Brooks, W. R. Butler and his cavalry in the War of Secession. $2.50. State Co.

Butler, N: Murray.
American as he is. '08(D5) c. D. **$1 net. Macmillan.
Education in the United States; series of monographs. '10(S17) c. O. $2.50. Am. Bk.
Philosophy: [a lecture.] '08(N21) c. 8°, pap. (Add. pubs. for price.) Columbia Univ.

Butler, Orma Fitch.
Studies in the life of Heliogabalus. '08 (O17) 8°, (Univ. of Mich., Humanistic ser.) pap., $1.25. Macmillan.

Butler, S:
Erewhon; or, over the range. '10(Je4) 8°, $1.25 net. Dutton.
Erewhon revisited twenty years later. '10 (Je4) 8°, $1.25 net. Dutton.
Way of all flesh. '10(Je4) O. $1.50 net. Dutton.

Butler, Bp. S:
Characters and passages from note-books; ed. by A. R. Waller. '08(N21) 8°, (Cambridge English classics.) *$1.50 net. Putnam.

BUTLER, *Bp.* Samuel.
Holland, H: S. Optimism of Butler's "Analogy." 70 c. Oxford Univ.

Butler, Tait.
See Stevens, Fk. Lincoln.

Butler, W: D:, J: Cromwell and Jos. Marion, comps.
Butler family in America. [1910.] (Ap) 296 p. il. pors. facsims., 8°, $2.50; seal. $5. Shallcross.

BUTLER FAMILY.
See Genealogies.

Butler's story. Train, A. C. †$1.25. Scribner.

Butlin, F. M.
Among the Danes. '09(O23) col. il. 8°, *$2.50 net. Pott.

Butt, Rev. Israel La Fayette.
History of African Methodism in Virginia; introd. by Rev. B: F. Lee. '08(Je6) c. il. pors. 8°, $1. I. L. Butt.

Butt Chanler, freshman. Hamilton, J. S. †$1.50. Appleton.

Buttel-Reepen, H. v.
Are bees reflex machines? '08(Mr7) O. pap., 50 c. A. I. Root.

BUTTER.
McKay, G: L., *and* Larsen, C. Principles and practice of butter-making. **$1.50 net. Wiley.
Meyer, M. H. Treatise on commercial starters in butter and cheese making. gratis. M. H. Meyer.
Michels, J: Creamery butter-making. $1.50. J: Michels.
Publow, C: A. Questions and answers on butter-making. 50 c. Judd.
Rogers, L. A. Paraffining butter tubs. 5 c. U. S., Supt. of Docs.
Rogers, L. A., *and* Gray, C. E. Influence of acidity of cream on the flavor of butter. 10 c. U. S., Supt. of Docs.
Schroeder, E. C:, *and* Cotton, W. E. Tubercle bacilli in butter. 15 c. U. S., Supt. of Docs.
See also Milk.

Buttercups and daisies ser. 3 v. '10(D) 56; 56; 56 p. col. il. 4°, ea., 50 c. net. Doran.

Butterfield, Cornelia du Bois, ["Victor du Bois."]
Suggestion as applied to business. Pocket ed. '10(S3) c. 16°, $1. Colonial Press, (Ct.)

Butterfield, Kenyon Leech.
Chapters in rural progress. '08(F8) c. D. *$1 net. Univ. of Chic.

Butterfield, W. J. Atkinson.
See Leeds, Fk. H:

BUTTERFLIES.
Eltringham, H. African mimetic butterflies. $15. Oxford Univ.
Thomas, E: Some British butterflies and insects. *$2 net. Doran.
See also Moths.

Butterfly man. McCutcheon, G: B. $1.25. Dodd.

Butterworth, Hezekiah.
Little sky high. '08(S19) c. front. D. (Bimbi ser.) bds., **40 c. net. Crowell.

Buttles, Janet R.
Queens of Egypt; with a preface by Professor G. Maspero. '08(O10) il. O. *$3 net. Appleton.

BUTTMAN FAMILY.
See Genealogies: Wyand, E. C.

Buttner, Jacques Louis, M.D.
Fleshless diet; vegetarianism as a rational dietary. '10(S10) c. D. $1.35 net. Stokes.

Button's Inn. Tourgée, A. W. $1. E. K. Tourgée.

Butts, E:
Statement no. 1: the swastika. '08, [1910.] (F) 9-42 p. il. 4°, $1; pap., 25 c. E: Butts.

Butts, W: H:
Elliptic cylinder function of class K, synthetic treatment and computation of tables. '08, [1909.] (D) 29 p. il. f°, 50 c. Lord Balto. Pr.

Buxton, C: Roden.
Turkey in revolution. '09(My15) il. map, O. *$2.50 net. Scribner.

Buxton, Ethel M. Wilmot-.
See Wilmot-Buxton, Ethel M.

Buxton, Rev. Harry J: Wilmot.
Notes on sermons for a year. pt. 1. '09 (O16); pt. 2. '10(Mr5) 12°, ea., *$1 net. Whittaker.

Buxton, Rev. Harry J: Wilmot.—*Continued.*
Old road; thirty plain sermons. '09(O16) 12°, *$2 net. Whittaker.

—, and Koehler, S. R.
Painting: English and American. '10(D) 12°, (Hdbks. of art hist.) hf. leath., $1.25. Gorham.

— and Poynter, Sir E: J:
Painting: German, Flemish and Dutch. '10 (D) 12°, (Hdbks. of art hist.) hf. leath., $1.25. Gorham.

Buyers' reference directory. '08(My.) c. 12°, pap., gratis. Puritan Pub. Co.

Buying list of books for small libraries. Brown, Z. M., *comp.* gratis. N. Y. State Educ.

Buzzacott, Fs. H.
Astounding revelations; or, light in dark places; missing links, by "Buzzacott." [1910.] (Je) c. '09. 613 p. il. por. maps, 8°, $2. F. H. Buzzacott.

Buzzard, E. Farquhar.
See Yeo, I. Burney.

By force of circumstances. Holmes, G. $1.50. Clode.

By grandsire's well. Letts, *Mrs.* A. M. B. $1. Kellogg-B.

By horse, canoe and float through the wildernesses of Brazil. Cook, W: A. Werner Co.

By inheritance. Thanet, O. $1.50. Bobbs-M.

By law of might. Ridgely, A. N. $1.50. H. A. Simmons.

By reef and trail. *See* Ames, F., *jr.*

By right of conquest. Hornblow, A. †$1.50. G: W. Dillingham.

By right of purchase. Bindloss, H. †$1.50. Stokes.

By the bay. Smith, *Mrs.* L. E. L. *$1 net. P. Elder.

By the Christmas fire. Crothers, S: M. **$1.25 net. Houghton M.

By the good Sainte Anne. Ray, A. C. †75 c. Little, B. & Co.

By the Great Wall. Williams, *Mrs.* I. B. R. *$1.50 net. Revell.

By the grey sea. Spring, H. $1. Herder.

By the shores of Arcady. Eaton, I. G. $1.25. Outing.

By the waters of Egypt. Lorimer, N. *$4 net. Pott.

By the way. Foster, A. G. $1.50 net. P. Elder.

By the wayside. Yates, K. M. 50 c. K. M. Yates.

By their fruits. Praed, R. C. M. $1.50. Cassell.

By wild waves tossed. Brand, J. †$1.50. McClure.

Byers, Morton Lewis.
Economics of railway operation. '08(Ja18) il. *$5 net. Engineering News.

Byfield, Shadrach.
Narrative of a light company soldier's service in the Forty-first regiment of foot, (1807-1814). [*Magazine of History;* extra number.] '10(N19) c. 4°, $2.75, (to magazine subscribers.) Abbatt.

Byford, H: Turman, M.D.
To Panama and back. '08(Ap25) c. il. map, 12°. (Add. pubs. for price.) Conkey.

Byington, Edn. Hallock.
Children's pulpit. '10(Ag) c. 104 p. 12°, 75 c. Pilgrim Press.
Byng, L. Cranmer.
See Cranmer-Byng, L.
Byrne, Austin T., and Phillips, Alfr. E.
Highway construction: guide to modern methods of roadbuilding. '08(Ap11) c. il. 8°, (American School of Correspondence pubs.) $1. Am. Sch. Corr.
Byrne, H: E:
Simplified shorthand. 6th ed. '08(Je6) c. 16°, $5. Byrne Pub.
See also Glenn, Fk. A.
Byrne (J:) & Co.'s quiz books. S. pap., 50 c. Byrne.
—Tyler, *comp.* Questions and answers on contracts.—Questions and answers on real property.
Byrne, Lee, ed.
Syntax of high school Latin; statistics and selected examples arranged under grammatical headings and in order of occurrence by fifty collaborators. '09(S11) c. O. *75 c. net. Univ. of Chic.
Byrne, Mary Agnes.
Peggy-Alone. '09(Jl3) c. 8°, $1.25. Saalfield.
See also Mosher, M. B.
Byrne duplex English. Guthrie, J. D. $1. Byrne Pub.
Byrnes, Esther Fussell.
Fresh water *Cyclops* of Long Island. '09 (Je12) O. (Brooklyn Inst. of Arts and Sciences; Cold Spring Harbor monographs.) bds., 90 c.; pap., 80 c. Brooklyn Inst.
Byrnes, Ja. C., Richman, Julia, and Roberts, J: S.
Pupils' arithmetic; primary book. '09 (My1) 12°, *45 c. net. In 2 pts. pt. 1. (O23) c. figs. D. **26 c. net; pt. 2 (D11) D. *30 c. net. Macmillan.
Byrnes, W.
See New York [State.] Civil procedure repts.
Byrom, T. H., and Christopher, J. E.
Modern cooking practice, incl. the analysis of materials and products. '09(D) c. 156 p. il. 8°, *$3.50 net. Henley.
Byron, G: Gordon Noel, Lord.
Complete poetical and dramatic works; with introd. by W. P. Trent. 3 v. '10 (D10) 16°, (Everyman's lib.) ea., 35 c. net; leath., 70 c. net. Dutton.
Poetical works; ed., with a memoir, by Hartley Coleridge. '10(D24) por. 12°, $1.75 net. Scribner.
Childe Harold, canto the fourth; The prisoner of Chillon and Mazeppa; ed., with introd. and notes, by C: Swain Thomas. '09(D18) c. 12°, (Riverside literature ser.) 25 c. Houghton M.
Childe Harold; ed., with introd. and notes, by H. F. Tozer. 3d ed. '10(D3) 50 c. Oxford Univ.
BYRON, George Gordon Noel, *Lord.*
Edgcumbe, R: Byron, the last phase. *$3 net. Scribner.
Gribble, F. H: Love affairs of Lord Byron. $3.75 net. Scribner.
BYRON, George Gordon Noel.—*Continued.*
Leonard, W: E. Byron and Byronism in America. *$1 net. Lemcke.
See also **Hunt, James Henry Leigh.**
Byron, H:
Day-dreamer's harvest: volume of meditations on life and the art of living. '08 (My16) c. 12°, *$1.25 net. F. F. Sherman.
Byron, May.
Adventures of Dumpy Dimple and his dog. '08(S5) il. O. bds., 50 c. Stokes.
Cat's cradle. '09(Ag) 48 p. il. in col. 4°, 60 c. Dodge.
Friday and Saturday: adventures of two little pickles. '08(S5) il. obl. D. bds., 50 c. Stokes.
Just for a change. '08(S5) Tt. (Quaint ser.) bds., 25 c. Stokes.
Little Robin Hood. '09(D) il. *50 c. net. Doran.
Little wee bear and Golden Hair. '08(S5) Tt. (Quaint ser.) bds., 25 c. Stokes.
Topsy-Turvy Land. '08(S5) Tt. (Quaint ser.) bds., 25 c. Stokes.
Bywater, Ingram.
Erasmian pronunciation of Greek and its precursors; Jerome Aleander, Aldus Manutius, Antonio y Lebrixa: a lecture. '09(Mr6) pap., 35 c. Oxford Univ.
Byways of collecting. Deane, E. *$2.50 net. Cassell.
"C²," pseud.
Back to the land; medley. '10(Je11) D. $1.50 net. Longmans.
C., D. R.
Chums; or, an experiment in economics. '08(D26) c. O. $1.25. G. O. Tubby.
C., M. A., comp.
See Rowe, F: L:
Cab and caboose. Munroe, K. $1.25. Putnam.
Cab no. 44. Foster, R. F: †$1.25. Stokes.
Caballero, Fernan, pseud.
See Arrom de Ayala Cecilia Francisca Josefa Böhl von Faber.
CABBAGE.
Gregory, J. J. H. Cabbages and cauliflowers: how to grow them. 30 c. J. J. H. Gregory.
Cabeen, Fs. von Albede.
Colonel and the Quaker. '10(Ja15) c. 8°, $3.50 (985 copies.) Goodman's.
Cabell, Ja. Branch.
Chivalry. '09(N6) c. il. in col. O. **$2 net. boxed. Harper.
Cords of vanity. '09(Mr27) c. front. 12°, †$1.50. Doubleday, P.
CABIN JOHN BRIDGE, Washington, D. C.
Robinson, *Mrs.* J. E., *ed.* Restoration of the name of Jefferson Davis to the Cabin John Bridge, Washington, D. C. 75 c. Confederated Southern.
CABINETWORK
Brace, G: M. Wood finishing and cabinet work at Stout Institute. 50 c. G: M. Brace.
Hasluck, P. N., *ed.* Cabinetwork and joinery. $3. McKay.
Hodgson, F: T: Pract. cabinet maker. $2. Drake.

CABINETWORK.—*Continued.*
Selden, F. H. Elem. cabinetwork for manual training classes. $1.25. Rand, McN. & Co.
Wells, P. A., *and* Hooper, J: Modern cabinet work. $5 net. Lane.
See also Furniture.

CABINS.
See Architecture.

Cable, G: Washington.
Kincaid's battery. '08(N21) c. il. D. †$1.50. Scribner.
"Posson Jone" and Père Raphael; with a new word setting forth how and why the two tales are one. '09(N6) c. il D. †$1.50. Scribner.

Cable, Lucy Leffingwell, ["Lucy Dunton."]
School children the world over. '09(S11) c. Q. $1.50. Stokes.

Cable code. *See* Brentano's.

CABLES.
See Electric wires;—Telegraphy;—Telephone.

Cabot, Mrs. Ella Lyman.
Ethics for children. '10(Ag13) c. D. $1.25. Houghton M.

Cabot, Follen.
Clinical diagnosis and treatment of disorders of the bladder with technique of cystoscopy. '09(Mr) 225 p. il. 12°, *$2 net. Treat.

CABOT, John and Sebastian.
Ober, F: A. John and Sebastian Cabot. **$1 net. Harper.

Cabot, Oliver C.
Man without a shadow. '09(Ap24) c. il. D. †$1.50. Appleton.

Cabot, R: Clarke, M.D.
Physical diagnosis. 4th rev. ed. '09(Ag) 601 p. il. figs. sq. 12°, *$3 net. Wood.
Psychotherapy in its relation to religion. '08(D12) c. 12°, (Religion and medicine publications.) pap., **25 c. net. Moffat.
Social service and the art of healing. '09 (O16) c. D. **$1 net. Moffat.
—, ed. Diseases of metabolism and of the blood, animal parasites, toxicology; authorized tr. from "Die deutsche klinik" under the general editorial supervision of Julius L. Salinger, M.D. '09(D) 14+649 p. il. 8°, (Modern clinical medicine.) $5. Appleton.

Cactus and pine. Hall, S. M. $1.50 net. Sherman, F.

Cadet of the Black Star Line. Paine, R. D. $1.25. Scribner.

Cadle, Mrs. C: Fs., comp.
List of one hundred and fifteen colonial ancestors of Cornelius Cadle, Muscatine, Iowa; Member, Missouri Society of Colonial Wars. [1910.] (F) 12 p. 4°. (Priv. pr.) C: F. Cadle.

CADLE, Cornelius.
Cadle, *Mrs.* C: F., *comp.* List of one hundred and fifteen colonial ancestors of Cornelius Cadle, Muscatine, Iowa. (Priv. pr.) C: F. Cadle.

Cadwallader, Rawlins.
Handbook of obstetrics. '08(N) c. 12+370 p. il. 8°, *$2 net. Davis.

CADY, Edward Everett.
Hubbard, E. Little journey to a great dentist. 25 c. Roycrofters.

Cady, Rev. H. Emilie.
Finding the Christ in ourselves. '08(N7) obl. Tt. pap., 15 c. Roger Bros.
God a present help. '08(O3) c. D. $1. Roger Bros.
God's hand, and Loose him and let him go. '08(N7) nar. S. pap., 10 c. Roger Bros.
Lessons in truth: course of twelve lessons in practical Christianity. '08(S) 160 p. D. cl., $1; pap., 50 c. Unity Tr.
Oneness with God, and Neither do I condemn thee. '08(N7) obl. Tt. pap., 15 c. Roger Bros.
Trusting and resting, and In his name. '08 (N7) S. pap., 10 c. Roger Bros.

Cady, Hamilton Perkins.
See Bailey, Edg. H: Summerfield.

Cady, Jay.
Moving of the waters. '09(N13) c. il. D. $1.50. J: McBride.

Cady, Marion Ernest.
Bible nature series, no. 1; a natural development of geography, physiology, and the other elementary sciences, with the Bible and nature as a basis of study. '09(F20) c. il. maps, D. $1.20. Pacific Press.

CADY FAMILY.
See Genealogies: Allen, O. P.

Caedmon.
Exodus and Daniel: two old English poems preserved in ms. Junius 11 in the Bodleian Library of the Univ. of Oxford, England; ed. by Fs. A. Blackburn. '08(Je13) c. 16°, (Belles-lettres ser., Section 1, Eng. literature.) *60 c. net. Heath.

Caesar, Caius Julius.
Cæsar in Britain; selections from the fourth and fifth books of Cæsar's Gallic war; ed., with historical introd., notes, vocabs. and English exercises. '10(My14) por. S. 25 c. Oxford Univ.
Cæsar's Gallic war; books I-II and selections from V-VII; with introd., notes, and vocab., by J: C. Rolfe and Arth. W. Roberts. '10(D24) c. il map, 12°, (Roberts and Rolfe Latin ser.) $1.25. Scribner.
Commentaries on the Gallic war: tr. into Eng. by T: Rice E: Holmes. '09(Ja23) maps, D. *$1.40 net. Macmillan.
Expeditions to Britain; De bello Gallico, IV. 20-36; V. 1-23, by W: A. Edward. '09(My22) il. D. 50 c. Longmans.
Four books of Cæsar's Gallic war; by W: Rainey Harper and Herbert Cushing Tolman. '08(S12) c. il. D. hf. leath., $1. Am. Bk.
[Gallic war:] Preparatory Cæsar: De bello Gallico, book II.; [ed.] by Frank Ritchie. '08(Ap18) il. maps, D. *40 c. net: Bks. 2 and 3 [in 1 v.] '09(Ap17) D. 50 c. Longmans.
Gallic war; bks. I.-VII.; ed. by Archibald Livingston Hodges. '09(O16) il. maps, D. (Macmillan's Latin ser.) **$1.25 net; Text ed. '10(My7) 35 c. net. Macmillan.

CAESAR, Caius Julius.
Holmes, T: R. E: Ancient Britain and the invasions of Julius Cæsar. $6.75. Oxford Univ.

CAESAR, Caius Julius.—*Continued.*
Jenner, W. A., *and* Wilson, H: E. Cæsar's first campaign. $1 net. Appleton.
Sihler, E. G. Annals of Cæsar; critical biography. $1.75 net. Stechert.
Café cackle. "Clivette, the Man in Black," *pseud.* 50 c. Laird.
Caffin, C: H:
Appreciation of the drama. '08(N21) c. il. O. (Appreciation ser.) **$1 net. Baker & T.
Child's guide to pictures. '08(Ag8) c. il. O. **$1.25 net. Baker & T.
Story of Dutch painting. '09(D4) c. il. O. **$1.20 net. Century Co.
Story of Spanish painting. '10(N12) c. il. O. $1.20 net. Century Co.
CAGE FAMILY.
See Sumner Co., Tenn.
CAGLIOSTRO, *Count* Alessandro di, *assumed name of* Giuseppe Balsamo.
Trowbridge, W: R. H. Cagliostro; splendor and misery of a master of magic. $3.50. Dutton.
CAHABA, Ala.
Fry, *Mrs.* A. M. G. Memories of old Cahaba. $1. Pub. Ho. of M. E. Ch., So.
Cahn, Julius.
Official theatrical guide; cont. authentic information of the theatre and attractions in the U. S., Canada, Mexico and Cuba. '09(N) 838 p. il. 8°, $1. J. Cahn.
Cahokia records. *See* Virginia.
CAHUILLA INDIANS.
See Indians.
Caico, Mrs. Louise.
Sicilian ways and days. '10(O1) il. O. $3.50 special net. Appleton.
Cain, G: M. A.
See Taggart, Marion Ames.
Cain, Georges.
Walks in Paris; tr. by Alfr. Allinson. '09 (My8) il. plans, D. $2. Macmillan.
Cain, J: Cannell.
Chemistry of the diazo-compounds. '08 (Ap25) O. *$3 net Longmans.
Cain, W:
Pract. designing of retaining walls; with appendices on stresses in masonry dams. 6th ed., rev. and enl. '10(My7) c. il. 24°, (Van Nostrand's science ser.) 50 c. Van Nostrand.
Theory of solid and braced elastic arches. 2d ed., rev. and enl. '09(Ap24) c. il. 24°, (Van Nostrand's science ser.) 50 c. Van Nostrand.
Cain, W: Stephen.
Autobiography of Captain W. S. Cain; biographical sketches of relatives, reminiscences of 1861-1865. '08(D) 126 p. il. 12°. (Priv. pr.) W: S. Cain.
Cain. Snyder, J. U. 75 c. Missouri Pr.
CAIN FAMILY.
Cain, W: S. Autobiography of Captain W. S. Cain; biographical sketches of relatives. (Priv. pr.) W: S. Cain.

Caine, T: H: Hall.
Cobwebs of criticism. '08(F8) 12°, (New universal lib.) 50 c.; leath.. 75 c. Dutton.
My story. '09(F27) c. il. pors. facsims., O. **$2 net. Appleton.
White prophet: a novel. '09(S4) c. il. D. †$1.50. Appleton.
Caine, W: Ralph Hall.
The cruise of the "Port Kingston." '07, [1908.] (Mr.) c. 28 p. 8°. (Add. author for price.) W: R. H. Caine.
Cain's wife. Oliver, F. E. $1.50. F. E. Oliver.
Caird, E:
Critical philosophy of Immanuel Kant. 2d ed. '08(N21) 2 v., 8°, *$6.25 net. Macmillan.
Essays on literature. '09(O30) O. $1.75. Macmillan.
Cairn of the badger. Barlow, M. $1.50. Cassell.
Cairns, W: B.
Forms of discourse; with an introd. chapter on style. Rev. ed. '09(Jl31) c. D. $1.15. Ginn.
—, ed. Selections from early American writers, 1607-1800. '09(Je12) c. D. **$1.25 net. Macmillan.
Caius.
See Gaius.
CAIUS COLLEGE, Cambridge, Eng.
See Gonville and Caius College.
Cajori, Florian.
History of the logarithmic slide rule and allied instruments. '09(O16) c. il. 12°, $1. Engineering News.
CAKE.
Douglas, E. Cake and biscuit book. 50 c. McKay.
New York cake book. 50 c. Stokes.
Southworth, M. E., *comp.* One hundred and one layer cakes. **$1 net; **$2 net; **50 c. net. P. Elder.
See also Cookery.
Cake shop. Jerrold, W. C. 25 c. Dutton.
CALAVERAS GROVE, California.
United States. *Congress. House. Committee on Public Lands.* To create the Calaveras big tree national forest. 5 c.
CALCIMINING.
See Painting (*mechanical*).
CALCIUM.
St. John, C: E: Absolute wave-lengths of the H and K lines of calcium in some terrestrial sources. gratis. Carnegie.
See also Spectrum.
CALCIUM CYANAMID.
See Agricultural chemistry.
CALCIUM LIGHT.
See Lighting.
CALCIUM NITRATE.
See Agricultural chemistry.
Calculation of change wheels for screw-cutting on lathes. De Vries, D. $1.25. Spon.
Calculations of elements of machine design. '08(S12) c. diagrs., 8°, (Machinery's reference ser.) pap., 25 c. Indust. Press.
Calculations of general chemistry. Hale, W: J. $1. Van Nostrand.
Calculations of the quantitative chemical laboratory with problems. Bartlett, E. J. 75 c. E. J. Bartlett.

CALCULUS.
Baker, H: F: Introduction to the theory of multiply periodic functions. *$3.75 net. Putnam.
Blaine, R. G. Calculus and its applications. *$1.50 net. Van Nostrand.
Bromwich, T. J. I. Introduction to the theory of infinite series. *$4.50 net. Macmillan.
De Morgan, A: Elem. illustrations of the differential and integral calculus. *$1 net. Open Court.
Hancock, H. Lectures on the theory of elliptic functions. v. 1. $5 net. Wiley.
Hedrick, E. R., *and* Kellogg, O. D. Applications of the calculus to mechanics. $1.25. Ginn.
Johnson, W: W. Differential and integral calculus. $2.50.—Elem. treatise on differential calculus. $1.50. Wiley.
Keller, S: S. Mathematics for engineering students: analytical geometry and calculus. $2. Van Nostrand.
Lester, O. C. Integrals of mechanics. 80 c. Ginn.
Mercer, J. W. Calculus for beginners. $2 net. Putnam.
Murray, D. A. Differential and integral calculus. $2. Longmans.
Osgood, W: F: Differential and integral calculus. *$2 net. Macmillan.
Percival, A. S. Practical integration. *80 c. net. Macmillan.
Smith, P. F., *and* Granville, W: A. Elem. analysis. $1.50. Ginn.
Townsend, E. J., *and* Goodenough, G: A. Essentials of calculus. $2.—First course in calculus, [with answers.] $2.50. Holt.
Wright, E. J. Invariants of quadratic differential forms. *75 c. net. Putnam.
Young, W: H: Fundamental theorems of the differential calculus. 75 c. net. Putnam.
See also Mechanics.

Caldecott, Watson.
Exercises on Edward's The story of the kings of Rome. '10(O29) S. pap., 15 c. net. Putnam.

Calderon, Ignacio.
Economic conditions of Bolivia; lecture del. before the special class in commerce at Harvard University, March 17, 1910. '10(Jl16) fold. map, 8°. (Priv. pr.) W. F. Roberts.

Calderon de la Barca, Pedro.
La vida es sveño; comedia famosa de D. Pedro Calderon de la Barca, 1639; ed. by Milton A. Buchanan. v. 1. '09(O2) Q. Univ. of Toronto.

Calderwood, W: Leadbetter.
Salmon rivers and lochs of Scotland. '09 (D4) il. maps, O. *$6 net. Longmans.

Caldwell, C: Tufts, M.D.
William Coaldwell, Caldwell or Coldwell of England, Massachusetts, Connecticut and Nova Scotia; historical sketch of the family and name and record of his descendants. '10(Jl9) O. pap. Judd & D.

Caldwell, Fk.
Wolf, the storm leader. '10(O15) c. il. front. O. $1.60 net. Dodd.

Caldwell, Howard Wa.
Outlines of American hist., 1785-1861; with references and questions, for use in colleges, normal schools and advanced classes in high schools. '10(D3) c. 12°, $1.25. Univ. Pub.

—, and Clark, Edm. Persinger.
Source hist. of the United States, from discovery (1492) to end of reconstruction (1877), for use in high schools, normal schools, and colleges. '09(N) c. 16+484 p. 12°, *$1.25 net. Ainsworth.

Caldwell, Jos. Stuart.
See Ritchie, J: Woodside.

Caldwell, Joshua W:
Joshua William Caldwell; memorial volume, containing his biography, writings and addresses; prep. and ed. by a committee of the Irving Club of Knoxville, Tenn. [1910.] (Mr) 338 p. por. 8°, $2.50. H: H. Ingersoll.

Caldwell, Otis W:
High school course in botany; part of a paper read at Wisconsin State Teachers' Association, Milwaukee, Nov. 13, 1908. '09, [1910.] (F) 8 p. 8°, pap., gratis. C. P. Cary.

Caldwell, W:
Idea of creation; its origin and its value. '09(O) 42 p. 8°, 50 c. W: Caldwell.

CALDWELL FAMILY.
See **Genealogies.**

Caldwell's boys and girls at home. '08(D12) il. 4°, $1.75; bds., $1.25. Caldwell.

Caldwell's character and wisdom ser. 16°, 50 c.; $1. Caldwell.
—Norton. Woman's cause.
—Stocking. Dearest spot on earth.

Caldwell's remarque ser. of literary masterpieces. por. T. 40 c.; limp leath., 75 c.; chamois, $1.25, boxed. Caldwell.
—Burnand, *ed.* Poems from *Punch.*
—Ruskin. Sesame and lilies.

Caldwell's stories old and new. 14 v. '10 (S3) il. [in col.] D. ea., 60 c. Caldwell.

Caleb Cobweb's comparisons. Wells, A. R. 50 c. McNair.

Caleb Koons. Carter, R. K. $1.50. C. M. Clark.

Caleb Trench. Taylor, M. I. †$1.50. Little, B. & Co.

Calef, J:
Siege of Penobscot by the rebels: cont. a Journal of the proceedings of His Majesty's forces detached from the 74th and 82d regiments, consisting of about 700 rank and file, under the command of Captain Brigadier-General Fs. M'Lean and of three of His Majesty's sloops of war, of 16 guns each, under the command of Captain H: Mowat, senior officer; to which is annexed a Proclamation issued June 15, 1779, by General M'Lean and Captain Barclay to the inhabitants; also Brigadier-General Lovell's Proclamation to the inhabitants; and his letter to Commodore Saltonstall, found on board the rebel ship "Hunter"; together with the names, force, and commanders, of the rebel ships destroyed in Penobscot Bay and River, August 14 and 15, 1779; with a chart of the Peninsula of Maja-

bigwaduce, and of Penobscot River; to which is subjoined a Postscript wherein a short account of the country of Penobscot is given; by J. C., esq., a volunteer. '10(N) 55 p. map, 4°, (*Magazine of History*, with Notes and Queries, extra Number, v. 1.) $2.75. Abbatt.

Calendar of Confederate papers. Freeman, D. S. $2.50. Confederate Museum.

Calendar of the papers of Benjamin Franklin. *See* American Philosophical Society.—Pennsylvania University Library.

Calendared isles. Holt, H. J. $1.50. Badger.

CALENDARS AND YEAR BOOKS.

Barry, J. G. H. Christian's day book. $1.50 net. Gorham.

Book of days; collection from the best authors of appropriate quotations. $2. Barse & H.

Carnegie Institution of Washington. Year book, 1907; 1908; 1909. Carnegie.

Chesney, E., *comp.* Life and the great forever. *$1.50 net. Lane.

Du Bois, M. R. J., *comp.* Pleasant thought year book. **$1 net. Holt.

Fite, *Mrs.* E. M. S., *ed.* Lover's yearbook. 60 c.; $1. Crowell.

Giles, C. Chauncey Giles year book. $1.25. Lippincott.

Greenough, *Mrs.* J. A. B., *comp.* Year of beautiful thoughts. $1. Crowell.

Hardy, L. A. Fort Dearborn year book. 50 c. net. McClurg.

Herford, O., *and* Collins, S. Smoker's year book. **$1 net. Moffat.

Hill, V. Arcadian calendar. **$1.50 net. Lane.

Kilburn, H. M., *comp. and ed.* Calendar of the fellowship, 1910. *75 c. net. Bacon & B.

Knowles, F. L., *comp.* Year book of famous lyrics. $1.50; $3. Caldwell.

Lander, M. J., *comp.* Friendship through the year. $1; $1.50. Dodge.

Methodist year book, 1910. *25 c. net. Eaton & M.

Mumford, E., Mizner, A., *and* Herford, O. Perfectly good cynic's calendar, [1909.] **75 c. net. P. Elder.

Perin, F. P., *comp.* Optimist's good night. $1 net. Little, B. & Co.

Porter, *Mrs.* D. L., *comp.* Year of ideals for every-day living. *75 c. net. Pilgrim Press.

Ruskin, J: Ruskin calendar. **50 c. net. Crowell.

Shakespeare, W: Shakespeare calendar. **50 c. net. Crowell.

Sheldon, C: M. A Charles M. Sheldon year book. $1. Crane.

Stevenson, R. L. Stevenson calendar. 60 c.; $1. Crowell.

Thoreau, H: D: Thoreau calendar. 60 c.; $1. Crowell.

Vincent, J: H. Calendar for 1909; 1910; 1911. ea., *10 c. net. Eaton & M.

Washington, G: Year book. *$1 net. McClurg.

Wells, C. Year book of old favorites and new fancies. $1.25. Holt.

CALENDARS AND YEAR BOOKS.—*Continued.*

Words and phrases calendar, 1909-10. (Not for sale.) West Pub.

Wordsworth, W: Wordsworth calendar. 60 c.; $1. Crowell.

See also **Almanacs and annuals;—Birthday books;—Day by day ser.;—*also* under special subjects.**

Calhoun, Frances Boyd.

Miss Minerva and William Green Hill. '09 (Mr13) c. il. D. $1. Reilly & B.

Calhoun, Guy K.

Products of arcs and sines of 15-degree rhumbs; computed for use in analysis of deviations when 15-degree rhumbs are used. '10(Jl) 8 p. 4°. Gov. Pr. Off.

CALHOUN, John Caldwell.

Hunt, G. John C. Calhoun. $1.25. Jacobs.

Calhoun, Patrick.

Some facts regarding Francis J. Heney, Esq., acting as assistant district attorney of the city and county of San Francisco. '10(F19) fold. tab., O. pap., gratis. United R. R. of S. F.

Calhoun Strout: psychic. Holland, J. P. 50 c. J. P. Holland.

Calico cat. Thompson, C: M. †$1.25. Houghton M.

California. *Alaska-Yukon Exposition Commission.* California: its products, resources, industries and attractions; what it offers the immigrant, homeseeker, investor and tourist; ed. by T. G. Daniells. '09(O) 174 p. il. 8°. (Add. pubs. for price.) W. W. Shannon.

California. Code of civil procedure, adopted Mar. 11, 1872; with amendments, [etc.;] ed. by Ja. H. Deering, Legislative history by C: H. Fairall. '09(Jl) c. 7+1169 p. S. shp., $5. Bancroft-W.

California. Codes; as amended and in force at the close of the 38th session of the legislature, 1909. In 8 v. v. 1, 2, Civil code; v. 3, 4, Civil procedure; v. 5, Penal code; v. 6, Political code; v. 7, General laws; v. 8, 1909 annot. supp. [1910.] (My) 8°, v. 1, 2, $20; v. 3, 4, $25; v. 5, $10; v. 6, $7.50; v. 7, $7.50; v. 8, $10; Pocket ed., annot. by Ja. M. Kerr. 5 v. '09(D) 16°, ea., leath., $6; per set, $27.50. Bender-M.

California. Codes; biennial supplement to Kerr's cyclopedic, and Henning's general laws; fully annot. by Ja. M. Kerr. '10 (Ap) c. O. shp., $10. Bender-M.

California. *District cts. of appeals.* Repts.; (C. P. Pomeroy and H. L. Gear.) v. 4. '08(Ap); v. 5 (Je); v. 6 (O) ea., $2.30; v. 7. '09(Ap) $2.30; v. 8, (Ag) $3; v. 9 (N) *$3 net; v. 10. '10(F); v. 11 (Je); v. 12 (O) O. shp., ea., $3. Bancroft-W.

California. General laws, as amended up to the end of the session of 1909; ed. by Ja. H. Deering. '10(F) c. S. shp., $5. Bancroft-W.

California. General laws of the state, as amended to 1909. '10(Mr) c. 2174 p. S. leath., $6. Bender-M.

California. General street laws, text of statute law, with synopsis of decided law and invaluable foot notes and forms (up-to-date) by Sidney Dell. '09(Jl) c. 174 p. O. pap., $2. S. Dell.

California. Index to the laws of California, 1850-1907, incl. the statutes, the codes, and the constitution of 1879, together with amendments thereto; code commissioner's notes, sessions of 1905 and 1907; prepared in accordance with acts of the legislature approved Mar. 15, 1907, and Mar. 18, 1907, under the supervision of J: F. Davis. '08 (D) 1057 p. 8°. (Add. pubs. for price.) Bancroft-W.

California. Penal code of state, with amendments to 1909; ed. by Ja. H. Dearing; legislative history by C: H. Fairall. '09(N) c. 20+1204 p. S. shp., $5. Bancroft-W.

California. Political code of the state; ed. by Ja. H. Deering. '09, [1910.] c. 1878 p. S. shp., $5. Bancroft-W.

California. Shepard's California citations. 3d ed. '08(Je) c. 369+135 p. 8°, flex. mor., $10. F. Shepard.

California. State Library, Sacramento. Information comp. for the use of members of the legislature under the supervision of Ja. L. Gillis, state librarian. '09(D) 30 p. 16°, gratis. Cal. State Lib.

California. Statutes and amendments to the codes passed at the extra session of the 37th legislature, 1907. '09(S) 1391 p. 8°, shp., $4.75. Bancroft-W.

California. *Supreme ct.* Repts.; (C. P. Pomeroy.) v. 150. '08(F); v. 151, 152 (N); v. 153. '08, [1909.] (F); v. 154 (O); v. 155. '10(Mr); v. 156 (Jl) c. O. shp., ea., $3. Bancroft-W.

California. *Supreme ct. and district cts. of appeal.* Complete supp. digest; covering cases officially reported in v. 148-154 of the sup. ct. repts.; vs. 2-9 dist. cts. of appeals repts.; and v. 1-5 Coffey's prob. decis., by Ja. A. Ballentine. In 7 v. v. 7. '10(Ag) c. O. $8.50. Bancroft-W.

CALIFORNIA.

Arnold, R., *and* Anderson, R. Preliminary report on the Coalinga oil district, Fresno and Kings counties, California. 20 c. U. S., Supt. of Docs.

Aubury, L. E. Copper resources of California. $1 net. Cal. State Mining.

Automobile Club of Southern California. Tour book. $1.50; $2.50. Automobile Club So. Cal.

Bandini, H. E. Hist. of California. 75 c. Am. Bk.

Barrett, S: A. Ethno-geography of Pomo and neighboring Indians. $3.25. Univ. of Cal.

Barrett, S: A., *and* Kroeber, A. L: Geography and dialects; [also] On the evidences of the occupation of certain regions by Miwok Indians. 50 c. Univ. of Cal

Burton, G: W. Book on California. $2.50. G: W. Burton.

Clark, G. Big trees of Cal. $1; 50 c. G. Clark.

Coats, M. C. California products and how to grow them. 50 c. M. C. Coats.

Craig, G. W: Selected cases on water-rights and irrigation law in California and western states. $3. Bancroft-W.

CALIFORNIA.—*Continued.*

Curry, F. E., *comp.* National flag; Magna Charta; act admitting Cal. to the Union; constitution of Cal., [etc.] gratis. Cal. Sec'y State.

Derleth, C: Destructive extent of the California earthquake. *$1.25 net. A. M. Robertson.

Diller, J. S. Geology of the Taylorsville region, California. (Add. Superintendent for price.) U. S., Supt. of Docs.

Eakle, A. S. Notes on some California minerals. 15 c. Univ. of Cal.

Eaves, L. Hist. of California labor legislation. $4. Univ. of Cal.

Engelhardt, Z. Missions and missionaries of California. v. 1. *$2.50 net. Engelhardt.

Forbes, H. R. P. S. Missions tales in the days of the dons; [stories of California.] $1.50. McClurg.

Gardner, N. L. New *chlorophyceae* from California. 10 c. Univ. of Cal.

Green, E. S., *comp.* Complete index to California codes and laws. $640. Bancroft-W.

Grinnell, F., *jr.* Quaternary myriopods and insects of California. 10 c. Univ. of Cal.

Grinnell, J. Bibliog. of California ornithology. $1.50. W. L. Chambers.

Grinnell, J. Three new song sparrows from California. 5 c. Univ. of Cal.

Hall, H. M. Compositæ of southern California. $3. Univ. of Cal.

Halsey, M. D. Tenderfoot in southern California. $1. M. D. Halsey.

Hasse, A. R. Index of economic material in documents of the states of the U. S.: California, 1849-1904. $2.25. Carnegie.

Hayford, J: F., *and* Baldwin, A. Le S. Earth movements in California earthquake of 1906. pap., 15 c. U. S., Supt. of Docs.

Henrich, H. C. Types of California beauties. $50. H. Heywood.

Hess, F. L. Magnesite deposits of California. (Add. Superintendent for price.) U. S., Supt. of Docs.

Hichborn, F. Story of the session of the California legislature of 1909. $1.25. Barry.

Isaman, S. W. Tourist tales of California. *$1 net. Reilly & B.

James, G: W. Heroes of California.—Through Ramona's country. ea., **$2 net. Little, B. & Co.

Jepson, W. L. Flora of California, in about 15 pts. pt. 1, 90 c.; pt. 2, 80 c.—Trees of California. *$2.50 net. Cunningham, C. & W.

Jones, T: W., *comp.* Scenic treasures of California. 50 c. F. Harvey.

Jordan, D: S., *ed.* California earthquake of 1906. *$3.50 net. A. M. Robertson.

Kroeber, A. L: Mission record of the California Indians, from a manuscript in the Bancroft library. 25 c. Univ. of Cal.

Leitch, B. M. Mariposa grove of big trees, Cal. 50 c. B. M. Leitch.

McClendon, J. F. *Ophiurans* of the San Diego region. 30 c. Univ. of Cal.

CALIFORNIA.—*Continued.*
McIlhany, E: W. Recollections of a 49er. $1. Hailman.
McLaren, J: Gardening in California. *$3.75 net. A. M. Robertson.
Martin, J: **Public benefits derived from water power developments in California.** gratis. J: Martin.
Mendenhall, W. C. Ground waters and irrigation enterprises in the foot-hill belt, southern California. 50 c.—Ground waters of the Indo region, Cal.; with sketch of the Colorado desert.—Some desert watering places in southeastern California and southwestern Nevada. (Add. Superintendent for prices.) U. S., Supt. of Docs.
Menken, H:, *ed.* **California bungalow homes.** $1 net. Bungalowcraft.
Mission record of the California Indians. Univ. of Cal.
North, A. W. Camp and camino in lower California. $3 net. Baker & T.
Pack, R. W. Notes on *echinoids* from the tertiary of California. 10 c. Univ. of Cal.
Peixotto, E. C. **Romantic California.** $2.50 net. Scribner.
Rand, McNally & Co. Guide to California via the Santa Fé. (Add. pubs. for price.) Rand, McN. & Co.
Rodman, W. Hist. of the bench and bar of southern California. $17.50. W. J. Porter.
Torrey, H. B. *Leptomedusae* of the San Diego region. 20 c. Univ. of Cal.
Van Winkle, W., *and* Eaton, F: M. Quality of surface waters of California. Gov. Pr. Off.
Walker, H. D., *comp.* Manual of California securities and directory of directors. $3. H. D. Walker.
Weaver, C: E. New *echinoids* from the Tertiary of California. 5 c.—Stratigraphy and palæontology of the San Pablo formation in middle California. 25 c. Univ. of Cal.
Wickson, E: J. California fruits and how to grow them. $3. Pacific Rural.
See also Architecture; — Banks and banking; — Channel Islands;—Earthquakes;—Ellis Landing; —Fox;—Fruit;—Gardens and gardening;—Hydrography;—Imperial Valley;—Indians; — Insects; — Los Angeles; — Lower California; — Mount Wilson;—Pacific coast; — Riverside; — San Antonio Canyon;—San Bernadino mountains;—San Diego;—San Francisco;—San Francisco disaster;—San Joaquin Valley;—San Luis Obispo Co.;—Santa Barbara:—Trinity County; —Vegetables;—Yosemite Valley;—*also* Bidwell, John;—Portola, Gaspare de;—Sutter, *Gen.* J: A:

CALIFORNIA, Pa.
See **Southwestern State Normal School.**

California and Nevada. Attorneys and bankers' directory, 1908-09. '08(Ag) c. O. cl., $2. C. A. Murdock.
California and other sonnets. Palmer, F. P. *$1.50 net. P. Elder.
California Association for the Study and Prevention of Tuberculosis. Warfare against tuberculosis and the relation of teachers thereto. '09(Jl) 8 p. 12°. (Add. pubs. for price.) Cal. Assoc. Tuberculosis.
California Association of Teachers of German. Four years' course in German for secondary schools. '08. 15 p. O. pap., 25 c. H. K. Schilling.
California classics ser. 16°. Arroyo Guild.
—Stoddard. **Apostrophe to the skylark. $1.**
California earthquake of April 18, 1906; rept. of the State Earthquake Investigation Commission. In 2 v. and atlas. v. 1, pts. 1, 2. '08(O10) il. plans, Q. pap., $17; v. 2, The mechanics of the earthquake, by Harry Fielding Reid. **'10(Je11) figs. fold. chart, Q. pap., $2. Carnegie.**
California songs. Wade, R. A. S. 75 c. B'way Pub.
California State Mining Bureau bull. il. 8°, pap. Cal. State Mining.
—Aubury. Copper resources of California. **(Add. pubs. for price.)**
California state ser. il. maps, 12°. Cal. Dept. Pub. Instruct.
—Dunn. Civics, the community and the citizen. 50 c.
—McMaster. Brief hist. of the U. S.
—Tarr *and* McMurry. Advanced geography. $1.
California story book. [1910.] c. '09. 195 p. il. 12°, $1.25. Univ. of Cal.
Californians (The). Atherton, *Mrs.* G. F. H. †$1.50. Macmillan.
Calisch, Rabbi E: Nathaniel.
Jew in English literature, as author and as subject. '09(Je12) 12°, *$2 net. Bell Bk.
CALISTHENICS.
See Drills (*fancy*);—Gymnastics and physical culture.
Calisto. *See* Allen, H. Warner, *ed.* Celestina.
Calkins, Gary Nathan.
Text-book of protozoölogy. '09(Ag) 349 p. il. 8°, *$3.25 net. Lea.
Calkins, Mary Whiton.
First book in psychology. '10(Jl2) c. D. $1.90 net. Macmillan.
Persistent problems of philosophy. 2d rev. ed. '08(Ap18) 12°, *$2.50 net. Macmillan.
Calkins, Wolcott, D.D.
Parables for our times; study of present-day questions in the light of Christ's illustrations. 2d ed., rev. '10(F19) c. 16°, 50 c. Pilgrim Press.
Call, Annie Payson.
Nerves and common sense. '09(D25) c. 12°, **$1.25 net. Little, B. & Co.
Call, W: Timothy.
Literature of checkers. '08(Ag8) c. D. $1. C. M. Potterdon.
Vocabulary of checkers. '09(D25) c. figs. D. $2. C. M. Potterdon.
Call of attention to the Behaists. Stenstrand, A. J. (Add. author for price.) A. J. Stenstrand.
Call of Kansas. Clark, E. M. 25 c. Seewir.
Call of Korea. Underwood, H. G. *75 c. net; *35 c. net. Revell.
Call of the city. Robinson, C: M. **$1.25 net. P. Elder.
Call of the country church. Hoyt, A. S. 5 c.; per 100, $4. Y. M. C. A.
Call of the deep. Bullen, F. T: $1.50. Dutton.

Call of the drum. Wyndham, H. C. $1.50. Cassell.

Call of the heart. Way, L. N. †$1.50. G: W. Dillingham.

Call of the heights. Norton, S. A. 50 c. net. Pilgrim Press.

Call of the nation. Jordan, D: S. $1. Am. Unitarian.

Call of the South. Becke, G: L: †$1.50. Lippincott.

Call of the South. Durham, R. L. $1.50. Page.

Call of the waters. Crowell, K. R. *50 c. net; *30 c. net. Revell

Call to confirmation. Smith, C: E. 20 c. Longmans.

Callahan, C: H.
Memorial to Washington the Mason, to be erected at Alexandria, Virginia, the home town of George Washington, by the Masons of America. '10(O) c. 32 p. il. (partly col.) 8°, $1. Alexandria-Washington.

Callahan, Ja. Morton.
Alaska purchase and Americo-Canadian relations. '08(Je13) c. O. (West Virginia Univ. studies in American history, Diplomatic history.) pap., 50 c. Univ. of W. Va.
Evolution of Seward's Mexican policy. '09 (Je5) O. (W. Va. Univ. studies in American History; ser. 1, Diplomatic history.) pap., 75 c. Univ. of W. Va.
Introduction to American expansion policy. '08(Ag) c. 36 p. 8°, 50 c. Univ. of W. Va.
Russo-American relations during the American Civil War. '08(My23) c. D. (West Virginia Univ. studies in American history.) pap., 30 c. Univ. of W. Va.

Callahan, Ja. Yancy.
Burning issue, and what co-operation will do: [co-operative agriculture.] '08, [1909.] (F) c. 59 p. 12°, pap., 25 c. Pub. Pr.

Callahan, Maud Fulcher.
Evolution of the constitution of West Virginia. '09(S4) c. O. (West Va. Univ. studies in West Va. hist.; Constitutional hist.) pap., 50 c. Univ. of W. Va

Callaway, Emilie H.
Widow's wiles: comedy in three acts. '08 (S19) c. 12°, pap., 25 c. Dick.

Callaway, Morgan, jr.
Incidental teaching of English. '09(D) 13 p. 8°, (Univ. of Texas, bull.) pap., 15 c. Univ. of Tex.

Callender, Geoffrey Arth. Romaine.
Sea kings of Britain. [v. 1,] Hawkins to Blake. '08(F15) maps, plans, D. 75 c.; [v. 2,] Albemarle to Hawke. '09(Je5) maps, plans, D. $1. Longmans.

Callender, Guy Stevens.
Selections from the economic hist. of the United States, 1765-1860; with introd. essays. '09(N13) c. O. $2.75. Ginn.

Calling of Dan Matthews. Wright, H. B. $1.50. Book Supply.

Calls of the Conqueror. Larrabee, E: A. *60 c. net. Young Churchman.

Calmerton, Gail.
English; language; literature; ethics; reference. '09(D) 11-96 p. 8°. (Not for sale.) Fort Wayne Sch. Bd.
Geography—history. '09(D) 158 p. 8°. (Not for sale.) Fort Wayne Sch. Bd.
Primary arithmetic. '09(D) 5-30 p. 8°. (Not for sale.) Fort Wayne Sch. Bd.
Programs; public library; kindergarten; occupations; reference list; teachers' books. '09(D) 76 p. 8°. (Not for sale.) Fort Wayne Sch. Bd.
Reading; phonics; spelling; penmanship. '09 (D) 84 p. 8°. (Not for sale.) Fort Wayne Sch. Bd.

Calmette, A., M.D.
Venoms: venomous animals and antivenomous serum-therapeutics; tr. by Ernest E. Austin. '08(S19) il. 4°, *$5 net. Wood.

Calmour, Alfr. C.
Rumbo-rhymes; or, the great combine. '10 (N12) col. il. O. $2 net. Harper.

Caloric Fireless Cookstove Company. Book of recipes. '08(Jl) c. 9-156 p. il. 12°, 50 c. Caloric.

CALORIMETER.
Fries, J. A. Methods and standards in bomb calorimetry. Gov. Pr. Off.
See also Breathing.

Calthrop, Dion Clayton.
Charm of gardens. '10(N19) col. il. 8°, (Color books.) $2.50 net. Macmillan.
Everybody's secret. '09(S4) c. D. †$1.50. G: W. Dillingham.
Tinsel and gold. '10(Ap23) c. il. D. $1.50. G: W. Dillingham.

Calvary Church, Pittsburgh, Pa. Calvary Church, Pittsburgh, Pennsylvania. '08(Jl) c. 50+8 p. il. 4°, $1. Badger.

Calvary Commandery. *See* Freemasonry.

Calvert, Albert F:
Catalonia, and the Balearic Isles; historical and descriptive acct. '10(N19) D. (Spanish ser.) $1.50 net. Lane.
Goya: an account of his life and works. '08(Mr28) 12°, (Spanish ser.) *$1.25 net. Lane.
Granada: present and bygone. '08(Je13) 8°, *$2.50 net. Dutton.
Leon, Burgos and Salamanca. '08(F1) il. D. (Spanish ser.) *$1.25 net. Lane.
Madrid. '09(Ap10) il. D. (Spanish ser.) *$1.50 net. Lane.
Royal palaces of Spain. '09(My1) il. D. (Spanish ser.) *$1.50 net. Lane.
Southern Spain. '08(N21) il. 8°, (Color books.) *$6 net. Macmillan.
Valladolid, Oviedo, Segovia, Zamora, Avila, and Zaragoza. '08(S19) il. D. (Spanish ser.) *$1.25 net. Lane.

—, and Hartley, C. Gasquoine.
El Greco: account of his life and works. '09(Ap10) il. D. (Spanish ser.) *$1.50 net. Lane.
Velasquez: account of his life and works. '08(F1) il. D. (Spanish ser.) *$1.25 net. Lane.

Calvert, Alfr.
Shipping office organization, management and accounts. '10(Mr26) forms, facsims., O. $2. Pitman.

Calvert of Maryland. Kaler, J. O. 35 c. Am. Bk.

CALVIN, John.
Beza, T. Life of John Calvin. 50 c. Westminster.
Richards, G: W., *and* Good, J. I: Life pictures of Calvin for young and old. 25 c. Heidelberg.
Vollmer, P. John Calvin. 75 c. Heidelberg.

Calvin and the Reformation: a symposium. '09(Jl31) 8°, *$1.25 net. Revell.

Calvin memorial addresses; del. before the General Assembly of the Presbyterian Church in the United States, at Savannah, Ga., May, 1909. '09(N6) c. il. pors. O. $1.50. Presb. Pub.

CALVINISM.
Balch, T: W. Calvinism and American independence. $1. Allen, L. & S.
Strong, J. S. Essential Calvinism. *75 c. net. Pilgrim Press.
See also Congregational church; — Presbyterian church.

Calwell, W:, M.D.
Text-book of medical treatment, (alphabetically arranged.) '10, [1909.] (D) 4+630 p. O. *$4.50 net. Longmans.

Camac, C: Nicoll Bancker, comp.
Epoch-making contributions to medicine, surgery and the allied sciences. '09(Mr) 435 p. por. 8°, *$4 net. Saunders.

Camann, H: Bauer.
Indian club exercises and exhibition drills; arr. for the use of teachers and pupils in high school classes, academies, private schools, colleges, gymnasiums, normal schools. '10(Jl16) c. il. 8°, 75 c. H: B. Camann.

Cambria Steel Co. Cambria steel; hdbk. of information rel. to structural steel manuf. by the Cambria Steel Co., cont. useful tables, rules, data and formulæ for the use of engineers, architects, builders and mechanics; prepared and comp. by George E. Thackray. [9th ed.] '09, [1910.] (F) c. 10+474 p. tabs., diagrs., fold. front., 16°, $1. Cambria Steel.

Cambrian geology and paleontology. Walcott, C: D. nos. 1-5. (Add. Institution for price.) Smith. Inst.

CAMBRIDGE, Eng.
Conybeare, J: W: E: Highways and byways in Cambridge and Ely. $2 net. Macmillan.

CAMBRIDGE, Mass.
Daughters of the American Revolution, Mass. Hannah Winthrop Chapter, Cambridge. Historic guide to Cambridge. $1.25. D. A. R., Hannah Winthrop Chapter.
See also Radcliffe College;—Harvard University Law School.

Cambridge biological ser.; ed. by Arth. Everett Shipley. il. 8°. Putnam.
—Johnstone. Conditions of life in the sea. $3.
—Ward. Trees. v. 4-5. ea., *$1.50 net.
—Willis. Agriculture in the tropics.—Manual and dictionary of the flowering plants and ferns. ea., *$2.75 net.

CAMBRIDGE BRIDGE, Mass.
Massachusetts. Cambridge Bridge Commission. Rept. of the Cambridge Bridge Commission and rept. of the chief engineer upon the construction of Cambridge Bridge. '09, [1910.] (Ap) 8+353 p. il. plans (partly fold.) fold. tabs., 8°. Mass. Cambridge Bridge.

Cambridge classics. D. †$1. Houghton M.
—Cooper. Pathfinder.—Pioneers.—Prairie.

Cambridge county geographies; ed. by F. H. H. Guillemard. 8°, 45 c. Putnam.
—Bosworth. Essex.—Kent.—Surrey.—Sussex.
—Bradley. Wiltshire.
—Dutt. Norfolk.—Suffolk.
—Knight. Somerset.
—Knight *and* Dutton. Devonshire.
—Lydekker. Hertfordshire.
—Marr. Westmoreland.
—Salmon. Dorset.

Cambridge devotional ser. 16°, *45 c. net; *60 c. net; leath., *75 c. net. Putnam.
—Pascal. Thoughts.
—Smith. Sermons.

Cambridge ed. of the poets; ed. by Bliss Perry. por. O. Houghton M.
—Spenser. Complete poetical works. $3-$7.50.

Cambridge engineering tracts. 8°, pap. Putnam.
—Hopkinson. Vibrations of systems having one degree of freedom. 75 c. net.

Cambridge English classics. D. *$1.50 net. Putnam.
—Beaumont *and* Fletcher. Works. In 10 v. v. 5-8. ea., *$1.50 net.
—Bible. Authorized version, 1611. 5 v.
—Butler. Characters and passages from note-books.
—Fletcher. Poetical works. v. 1. *$1.50 net.

Cambridge English literature for schools. 16°, *40 c. net. Putnam.
—Cobbett. Rural rides.
—Defoe. Memoirs of a cavalier.
—Hazlitt. Characters of Shakespeare's plays.
—Scott. Tales of a grandfather.
—Smith. True travels.

Cambridge geological ser. il. 12°. Putnam.
—Harker. Petrology. *$2 net.

Cambridge Greek Testament ser. 8° Putnam.
—Bible. Epistle of Paul the Apostle to the Galatians. $1 net.

Cambridge historical essays. 8°. Putnam.
—Cree. Claudian as an historical authority. *$1.50 net.
—Tillyard. Agathocles. *$1.50 net.

Cambridge historical ser.; ed. by G: W. Prothero. 16° and 8°. Putnam.
—Bain. Slavonic Europe. *$2 net.
—Sands. Client princes of the Roman Empire under the Republic. *$1.50 net.
—Vernon. Italy from 1494 to 1790. *$1.75 net.

Cambridge history of English literature. *See* Ward, A. W:, *and* Waller, A. R., *eds.*

Cambridge modern history. *See* Acton, J: Emerich E: Dalberg-Acton, *Lord.*

Cambridge natural history. *See* Harmer, Sidney F:

Cambridge patristic texts. 12°. Putnam.
—Novitian. De Trinitate liber. *$2 net.

Cambridge physical ser.; ed. by F. H. Neville and W. C. D. Whetham. il. O. Putnam.
—Pickford. Elementary projective geometry. $1.25 net.
—Searle. Experimental elasticity. $1.50.

CAMBRIDGE (Mass.) PUBLIC LIBRARY.
Rolfe, W. J., *comp.* Hist. of the Cambridge Public Library, 1858-1908. (Not for sale.) Cambridge Pub. Lib.

Cambridge tracts on mathematics and mathematical physics. 8°. Putnam.
—Bôcher. Introduction to the study of integral equations. *75 c. net.
—Leatham. Elementary theory of the symmetrical optical instrument. *75 c. net.
—Wright. Invariants of quadratic differential forms. *75 c. net.
—Young. Fundamental theorems of the differential calculus. 75 c. net.

CAMBRIDGE UNIVERSITY, England.
Clark, J: W., *ed.* Letters patent of Elizabeth and James the First, addressed to the University [of Cambridge.] Putnam.
Hist. of the Cavendish Laboratory. $2.60 net. Longmans.
Johnson, R. B. Cambridge colleges. **90 c. net. Jacobs.
Oxford and Cambridge. $6 net. Wessels & B.
Rutherford, H. W. Catalogue of the library of C. Darwin, now in the Botany School, Cambridge. *30 c. net. Putnam.
Searle, W: G:, *ed.* Grace book; cont. records of the University of Cambridge, 1501-1542. *$6 net. Putnam.
Vaughn, E. V. Origin and early development of the English universities to the close of the XIIIth century. $1. Univ. of Mo.
See also Gonville and Caius College.

CAMDEN, N. J.
Cooper, H. M. Historical sketch of Camden, N. J. $1. H. B. Ketler.

Camelot ser. 113 v. [1910.] (Jl) ea., 40 c. Simmons.

CAMEMBERT CHEESE.
See Cheese.

CAMERA.
See Photography.

Camera adventures in the African wilds. Dugmore, A. R. **$6 net. Doubleday, P.

Cameralists (The). Small, A. W. *$3 net. Univ. of Chic.

Cameron, Agnes Deans.
New north; being some account of a woman's journey through Canada to the Arctic. '09(D4) c. il. O. **$3 net. Appleton.

Cameron, Catherine.
Stories of the ballads. '09(F13) 24°. (Told to the children ser.) 50 c. Dutton.

Cameron, Fk. Kenneth, and Gallagher, Fş. E.
Moisture content and physical condition of soils. '08(Je6) pap., 15 c. U. S. Supt. of Docs.

Cameron, Mabel Ward.
See Conway, Katherine Eleanor.

Cameron, Marg., [Mrs. H. C. Lewis.]
Bachelor, and the baby. '08(O10) c. il. D. †50 c. Harper.
Cat and the canary. '08(F22) c. il. D. †$1. Harper.
Involuntary chaperon. '09(O23) c. il. D. †$1.50. Harper.

Cameron, W. J.
Poems. '10(F19) S. *$1.40 net. Longmans.

Camoens, Luis de.
Os lvsiadas de lvys de Camoes; co todas as liceças necessarias em Lisboa [facsim.] '03 [1909.] (N) 141 p. 8°, $6 (200 copies). Hispanic Soc.

CAMOENS, Luiz de.
Nabuco, J. Place of Camoens in literature. (Add. author for price.) J. Nabuco.

Camp, Edg. Whittlesey, ed.
Encyclop. of evidence. v. 4. '09, [1910.] (F) c. O. shp., $6. L. D. Powell.

—, Berryman, J: R., and Tuttle, E: W., eds.
1st biennial supplement to the encyclopedia of evidence; bringing down to Sept., 1908, by means of annots., citations and additions, all articles contained in the first 11 vs. of the work. '08(D) c. O. shp., $6. L. D. Powell.

—, and Crowe, J: F., eds.
Encyclopædia of evidence. v. 12. '08(Ag); v. 13. '09(Jl) c. O. shp., ea., $6. L. D. Powell.

Camp, S: Granger.
Fishing kits and equipment. '10(Ap2) c. il. D. $1 net. Outing.

Camp, Wa. Chauncey.
Book of foot-ball. '10(N5) c. il. pors. O. (Walter Camp's lib. of sport.) $2 net. Century Co.
Condensed bridge for the busy man. '09 (D4) c. 12°, 35 c. Collier.
Jack Hall at Yale: football story. '09 (O9) c. col. il. D. †$1.50. Appleton.
The substitute: football story. '08(O3) c. il. D. †$1.50. Appleton.
—, ed. Spalding's how to play foot ball. New ed., rev. for 1909. '09(O); rev. for 1910. [1910.] (S) c. il. por. 16°, (Spalding's athletic lib.) pap., ea., 10 c. Am. Sports.
—, ed. Spalding's official foot ball guide, 1908. '08(Ag15); for 1909. '09(Ap28) c. il. pors. S. (Spalding's athletic lib.) pap., ea., 10 c. Am. Sports.

Camp and camino in lower California. North, A. W. $3 net. Baker & T.

Camp and trail. White, S. E: *$1.25 net. Doubleday, P.

Camp-fires on desert and lava. Hornaday, W: T. **$3 net. Scribner.

Campaign against tuberculosis in the United States. Jacobs, P. P., *comp.* $1. Charities Pub.

Campaign of 1844. Ford, W. C. 50 c. Davis Press.

Campan, Madame Jeanne Louise Henriette Genest.
Mémoires, 1785-1792; ed. by H. C. Bradby. '09(Mr6) por. S. (Oxford higher French ser.) 85 c. Oxford Univ.

Campbell, A. M., and Mord, W.
Fairy flights in Cloudland. '09(S) col. il. Q. (Fairy flights ser.) bds., $1. Stokes.
Fairy flights to Moonland. '09(S) col. il. Q. (Fairy flights ser.) bds., 35 c. Stokes.
Fairy flights to the Zodiac Zoo. '09(S) col. il. Q. (Fairy flights ser.) bds., 35 c. Stokes.

CAMPBELL, Alexander.
Egbert, J. Alexander Campbell and Christian liberty. $1.50. Chr. Pub. Co.
Johnston, R. W. To-day's pictorial story of Alexander Campbell and the Christian churches. 75 c. R. W. Johnston.
McLean, A. Alexander Campbell as a preacher. *30 c. net. Revell.
See also Disciples of Christ.

Campbell, Mrs. Amarita Bernice James.
The sacrifice. '10(Mr19) c. il. D. $1.25. Badger.

Campbell, D: Newton Emanuel.
Searchlight on the Panama canal; or, America's greatest enterprise. '10(F26) c. il. pors. 8°, $1.25. Baltimore Bk.

Campbell, Delwin Morton, and Lacroix, J. V.
Essentials of parasitology, including a brief discourse on zoology. '07, [1908.] (Mr.) c. 96 p. tab., 8°, flexible leath., $1.25. E. Herbert.

Campbell, Douglas.
Law rel. to securities carried on margin. Rev. ed. '10(D) c. 47 p. T. pap., 50 c. Dixie Bk.

Campbell, Duncan.
See New York State Library.

Campbell, Emma F. R.
Hymn "Jesus of Nazareth passeth by," its hist., and other verses. '10(F5) c. 12°, $1.25. M. E. Munson.

Campbell, F. W. Groves.
Apollonius of Tyana: study of his life and times; with an introd. by Ernest Oldmeadow. '09(My22) 8°, *$1 net. M. Kennerley.

Campbell, Rev. Frederic.
Robert Campbell genealogy; record of the descendants of Robert Campbell of County Tyrone, Ulster, Ireland. '09, [1910.] 175 p. il. pors. 12°, $3.25. F. Campbell

Campbell, Gabriella Vere.
See Bowen, Marjory, *pseud.*

Campbell, Hardy Webster.
Campbell's 1907 soil culture manual. '08 (Ja25) il. por. D. $2.50. H. W. Campbell.

Campbell, Harry Clay.
Leucocytes in milk: methods of determination and the effect of heat upon their number, by H. C. Campbell, (in co-operation with the Pennsylvania State Live-stock Sanitary Board.) '09(D) 19 p. tabs., 8°, (U. S., Dept. of Agriculture, Bureau of Animal Industry, bull.)

Campbell, Helen M.
Life of Abraham Lincoln. '09(Mr) 64 p. 12°, *25 c. net. Educ. Pub.

Campbell, Helen Y.
Pract. motherhood. '10(D10) il. O. $2.50. Longmans.

Campbell, H: Johnstone.
See Hertwig, Oscar.

Campbell, Ja. H., comp.
Magistrate's manual: practical guide for magistrates who are not lawyers. '07, [1908.] (Mr.) c. 80 p. S. pap., $1. Popp & H.

Campbell, Ja. Mann, D.D.
Paul the mystic. '08(Je6) D. (Crown theological lib.) *$1.50 net. Putnam.

Campbell, Jane.
Sixteen excursions to places of historic interest in Philadelphia. '08(Jl) c. 44 p. map, 16°, pap., 25 c. J. Campbell.

Campbell, Jane Maud, comp.
Sel. list of Hungarian books; adopt. for use by the League of Library Commissions. '08(F1) D. (A. L. A. Publishing Board foreign book list.) pap., 15 c. A. L. A.

Campbell, J: Douglas Sutherland, Duke of Argyll, ed.
See Argyll, *Duke* of, *ed.*

Campbell, Leon.
Comparison stars for 252 variables of long period prepared for publication under the direction of E: C. Pickering. '08, [1909.] (Je) 211-288 p. tabs., 4°, (Astronomical Observatory of Harvard College annals.) Harvard Univ.

Campbell, Luther Eug.
Age of gold; being a collection of northland tales, song, sketch and narrative, miner-legend and camp-fire reflections, all gleaned at first hand and done in doubtful metre by an eager listener. '09 (O) 8+115 p. 12°, *$1.25 net. Whitaker & R.

Campbell, Norman Rob.
Modern electrical theory. '08(Mr21) 8°, *$2.25 net. Putnam.

Campbell, Reau.
New rev. complete guide and descriptive book of Mexico. '09(Mr) c. '08. 6+352 p. il. fold. map, 12°, $1.50. Rogers & S.

Campbell, Rev. Reginald J:
Thursday mornings at the City Temple: [sermons.] '08(S26) 12°, *$1.50 net. Macmillan.
See also Lodge, *Sir* Oliver Jos.

Campbell, Rob., ed.
Ruling cases; with Am. notes by Ja. T. Keen. v. 27. '08(Je) c. 43+708 p. O. $5.50. Boston Bk.

Campbell, Rob. Argyll.
Mortgage taxation. '09(Mr6) D. (Comparative legislation bull.) pap., 25 c. Wisconsin Free Lib.

Campbell, Rob. Granville.
Neutral rights and obligations in the Anglo-Boer war. '08(Je6) c. O. (Johns Hopkins Univ. studies in hist. and pol. science.) pap., 75 c. Johns Hopkins.

Campbell, Rev. T: Jos.
Pioneer priests of North America, 1642-1710. v. 1, [Tribes of the northwest.] '08(Je) c. 16+33 p. il. 8°, $1.60 net. Fordham Univ.
Pioneer priests of North America, 1642-1710. v. 2, Among the Hurons. '10 (Ap16) il. 8°, $2. Am. Press, (N. Y.)

Campbell, W. B., comp.
Hdbk. of modern treatment and medical formulary; condensed and comprehensive manual of practical formulæ and general remedial measures. '08, [1909.] (Mr); 2d rev. ed. '10(Ap) c. 8°, ea., *$2.50 net. Davis.

Campbell, W. S.
"Passerby" in London. '08(Je20) il. map, O. *$1.75 net. Scribner.

Campbell, W: Fs., M.D.
Text-book of surgical anatomy. '08(Ap4) c. il. 8°, *$5 net; hf. mor., *$6.50 net. Saunders.

Campbell, W: H.
Illinois hist. stories for use in elementary schools. '10(My14) c. il. maps, 12°, 55 c. Appleton.

Campbell, W: S.
See McQuillin, Eug.

Campbell, W: W.
Life and character of Jacob Broom. '09 (My) 37 p. 8°, (Papers of the Historical Soc. of Del.) pap, 50 c. Delaware Hist. Soc.

Campbell, W: Wilfred.
Beautiful rebel; romance of Upper Canada. '09(N13) c. 12°, $1.50. Doran.

CAMPBELL FAMILY.
See **Genealogies.**

Campbell-Thomson, H:, M.D.
Diseases of the nervous system. [1910.] (My) 480 p. il. 8°, $2.75 net. Funk.

CAMPBELLITES.
See **Disciples of Christ.**

Campeche. Bellows, W. C. $3.50. W. C. Bellows.

Camphor, Alex. Priestly.
Missionary story sketches, folk-lore from Africa; with introd. by M. C. B. Mason, D.D. '09(Je19) c. il. D. *$1.50 net. Jennings.

CAMPING.
Bates, F. A. Camping and cooking. *75 c. net. Ball Pub. Co.
Kephart, H. Camp cookery. $1 net. Outing.
Kreps, E. H. Camp and trail methods. 60 c. A. R. Harding.
Robinson Crusoe Library. 3 v. $4 net. Outing.
Shelford, F. Pioneering for engineers; incl. most suitable camp equipment, rations, medicines, clothing, etc. $1.25. Spon.
Wallace, A. F. Land cruising and prospecting. 60 c. A. R. Harding.
See also Alaska;—Nova Scotia;—Sports and sportsmen.

Camping in the forest. Clayton, M. *$1 net. Warne.

CAMPION, *Father* Edmund.
See Martyrs.

Campion, T:
Works; ed. by Percival Vivian. '10(Ja1) facsims., map, O. (Oxford English texts.) $3.40. Oxford Univ.

CAMPS.
See **Architecture.**

Camps and cruises of an ornithologist. Chapman, F. M. **$3 net. Appleton.

CAMS.
Designing and cutting cams. 25 c. Indust. Press.

Can it be defended?; by a lay member of the recent general conference. '10(D) 41 p. pap., 10 c. Pub. Ho. of M. E. Ch., So.

Can the modern man pray? Bayley, F. T. 10 c. Y. M. C. A.

Can the world be won for Christ? Maclean, M. $1.25 net. Doran.

Can you believe me stories. Aspinall *Mrs.* A. $1.50. Dutton.

CANAAN.
See **Palestine.**

Canada, J: W:, and Arai, S.
How to plant and cultivate an orange orchard; summary of the main points. '09 (My) c. 16 p. 8°, 50 c. J: W: Canada.

Canada. Criminal law digest, 1892-1907. '07, [1908.] (My.) 401 p. 8°, $6. Canada Law.

Canada. Digest of Canadian criminal case law; by G: E. McCrossan, S: D. Schultz and Andrew M. Harper. '08(My.) 53+1151 p. 8°, $8. A. Poole.

Canada. *Supreme ct.* Rules, promulgated June 19th, 1907; with notes, forms, and precedents, by E: Rob. Cameron. '09(Ja23) O. ¾ leath., $6. A. Poole.

CANADA.
Aberdeen, I. M., *Countess* of. Our lady of the sunshine and her international visitors; [acct. of visit of International Council of Women to Canada.] 50 c. net. Dutton.
American Iron and Steel Association. Canadian supp. to the Directory to the iron and steel works of the United States. Am. Iron and Steel.
Amsbary, W. B. French-Canadian in prose and verse. 25 c. La Salle Extension.
Bealby, J: T. Canada. 75 c. Macmillan.
Binnie-Clarke, G. Summer on the Canadian prairie. $1.75 net. Longmans.
Bradley, A: G. Making of Canada. *$3 net. Dutton.
Breckenridge, R. M. Hist. of banking in Canada. (Add. Superintendent for price.) U. S., Supt. of Docs.
Callahan, Ja. M. Alaska purchase and Americo-Canadian relations. 50 c. Univ. of W. Va.
Cameron, A. D. New north. **$3 net. Appleton.
Chase, E. B. Trans-continental sketches. $1.50. Winston.
Colby, C: W. Canadian types of the old régime, 1608-1698. **$2.75 net. Holt.
Commercial convention bet. France and Canada. (Add. Superintendent for price.) U. S., Supt. of Docs.
Cost of living in Canada; letter from the Consul-General at Ottawa, Canada, in response to instructions by telegram dated Feb. 22, 1910, asking him to forward such data as he might be able to obtain in regard to the cost of living in Canada. '10 (Ap) 96 p. tabs., 8°. U. S., Supt. of Docs.
Cran, *Mrs.* G: A woman in Canada. $3 net. Lippincott.

CANADA.—*Continued.*
Dionne, N. E., *ed.* Le parler populaire des Canadiens français. *$3.50 net. Stechert.
Elkington, E. W. Canada. $1.75 net. Macmillan.
Ewart, J: S. The kingdom of Canada. $2.50. Morang.
Gibb's travellers' route and reference book of the United States and Canada. $3. Gibbs Bros. & M.
Griffin, G. G., *comp.* Writings on American history: bibliography of books and articles on U. S. and Canadian hist. pub. during 1906; 1907. ea., **$2.50 net. Macmillan.
Hill, J. J. Highways of progress. $1.50 net. Doubleday, P.
Hough, E. The sowing: [fiction.] $1.25. Vanderhoof-G.
Koch, F. J: Little journey to northern wilds. 50 c. Flanagan.
Laut, A. C. Canada. **$1.75 net. Ginn.
Laut, A. C. Conquest of the great Northwest. $5. Moffat.
Lucas, *Sir* C: P. History of Canada, 1763-1812. $4.15. Oxford Univ.
Mason, W. S. Frozen Northland. $1. Jennings.
Michaels, H. S. Principal automobile routes of the United States and Canada, 1910. $2. Henneberry.
Moffett, S. E. Americanization of Canada. [priv. pr.] S: E. Moffett.
Music trade directory in U. S. and Canada. $5. Thompson.
Parker, W: R. P., *and* Clark, G: M. Canadian company law. $6.50. Cromarty.
Plummer, M. W. Roy and Ray in Canada. **$1.75 net. Holt.
Porritt, E: Sixty years of protection in Canada. *$1.50 net. Macmillan.
Steel, E. T: Land of fortune. 75 c. E. T: Steel.
Tracy, F. B. Tercentenary history of Canada, from Champlain to Laurier, 1608-1908. (Add. pub. for price.) Collier.
Willson, B. Canada. *$2 net. Stokes.
Wrong, G: M. Canadian manor and its seigneurs: [Malbaie, now Murray Bay.] *$3 net. Macmillan.
Wrong, G: M., *and* Langton, H. H., *eds.* Review of historical publications rel. to Canada. v. 14. $1.50; $1. Univ. of Toronto Press.
Wrong, G: M., *and* Langton, H. H., *eds.* Review of historical publications relating to Canada. v. 12, 13. ea., $1.50; $1. Morang.
Yeigh, F., *comp.* 5000 facts about Canada. 25 c. Canadian Facts.
See also Banks and banking;—British Columbia;—Hudson Bay Co.;—Irrigation;—Lawyers;—Manitoba;—Medicine;—Nova Scotia;—Periodicals;—Railroads;—Rocky Mountains;—Royal Canadian Mounted Police;—St. Lawrence river;—War of 1812;—*also* Brock, *Sir* Isaac;—Iberville, Pierre Le Moyne, *Sieur* d';—Machray, *Archbp.* Robert.

CANADA BLUEGRASS.
Oakley, R. A. Canada blue grass. Gov. Pr. Off.

Canadian heroes ser. il. D. McClurg.
—Nursey. Story of Isaac Brock. *$1.50 net.

Canadian manor and its seigneurs. Wrong, G: M. *$3 net. Macmillan.

Canadian repts.; appeal cases, appeals allowed or refused by the Judicial Committee of the Privy Council on appeal from the Dominion of Canada; arr., annot. and ed. by Wa. Edn. Lear. v. 1, 1908. '09(N) 8°, hf. cf., $7.50; continued each year in parts, $6.50. A. Poole.

Canadian types of the old régime. Colby, C: W. **$2.75 net. Holt.

CANALS.
Canal enlargement in New York state; papers on the barge canal campaign and related topics. '09, [1910.] (Mr) 17+446 p. il. pors. 8°, (Buffalo Historical Society pubs.; ed. by Fk. H. Severance.) $5. Buffalo Hist. Soc.
Jones, C. L. Economic hist. of anthracite tide water canals. $1.50. Univ. of Penn.; [Appleton.]
See also Inland navigation;—Roads.

Canaway and Lustigs. Leiser, J. $1. Young Israels.

Canby, G:
Evolution of the American flag; from materials collected by the late George Canby, by Lloyd Balderston. '09(N20) il. pors. facsims., D. $1. Ferris.

Canby, H: Seidel.
Short story in English. '09(O30) c. D. $1.60. Holt.

—, Pierce, F: Erastus, MacCracken, H: Noble, and others.
English composition in theory and practice. '09(O30) c. D. **$1.25 net. Macmillan.

CANCER.
Keith, S. *and* G: E. Cancer: relief of pain and possible cure. **$1.25 net. Macmillan.
Massey, G: B. Ionic surgery in the treatment of cancer. $3. Chatterton.
Rodman, W: L: Diseases of the breast, with special reference to cancer. *$4 net. Blakiston.
Williams, W. R. Natural history of cancer. *$5 net. Wood.

Cancioneira, General.
Cancioneiro, geral: cum preuilegio [facsim.] '04 [1909.] (N) 227 p. 8°, $55 (200 copies). Hispanic Soc.
Cancionero general nueuamete añadido Otra vez ympresso con adicon de muchas y esgocidas obras: las quales quien mas presto querra ver: vaya ala tabla: y todas aquellas que ternan esta señal son las nueuamente añadidas [facsim.] '04 [1909.] (N) 203 p. 8°, $55 (200 copies). Hispanic Soc.

Cancionero llamado dança de galanes, en el qual se contienen inumerables para cantar, y baylar, con sus respuestas y para desposorios y otros plazeres [facsim.] '03 [1909.] (N) no paging 8°, $4.50 (200 copies.) Hispanic Soc.

Cancionero llamdo Vergel de amores recopilado delos mas excelentes poetas Castellanos assi antiguos como modernos: y con diligecio corregido [facsim.] '03 [1909.] (N) 2+36 p. 4°, $4 (200 copies). Hispanic Soc.

Candidates and the issues. Salt, M. H., *ed.* $1.50. Vansant.

Candle as a symbol and sacramental in the Catholic church. Theiler, H: 50 c. Pustet.

Candlelight tea. Dunlap, L. $1. Transylvania.

Candler, Allen D., comp.
Revolutionary records of the state of Georgia; comp. and pub. under authority of the Legislature. 3 v. '08(O) 4°, $1.50. Franklin-T.

Candler, G: H:, M.D.
Everyday diseases of children and their rational treatment. '07, [1908.] (N) c. 10+386 p. 12°, $1. Clinic.

Candler, Bp. Warren A.
Dangerous donations and degrading doles; or, a vast scheme for capturing and controlling the colleges and universities of the country. '09(Jl3) 16°, pap., 10 c. Lester Bk.

Candles in the wind. Diver, M. $1.50. Lane.

CANDLEWOOD.
See Ipswich, Mass.

Candole, H. L. C. V. de.
Confirmation, authority, confession: three sermons preached in Holy Trinity Church, Cambridge. '09(F6) D. *36 c. net. Longmans.

Candy, Albert Luther.
Elements of plane and solid analytic geometry; with supplement. '09(My) c. 12+368 p. il. 12°, *$2 net. Heath.

CANDY.
Davison, A. W. Little candy maker. $1. A. W. Davison.
Home Candy Makers, Canton, O. Art of home candy making. $2. Home Candy.
Metzgar, C: M. Home-made ice cream and candy. $1; 50 c. Metzgar.
Parloa, M., *and* Hill, *Mrs.* J. M. Chocolate and cocoa recipes and home made candy recipes. gratis. W. Baker.
Pease, M. A. Candy making secrets. $3. Pease & D.
Rigby, W. O. Reliable candy teacher. $2. W. O. Rigby.

Cane, W. Ralph Hall.
Isle of Man. '09(D25) col. il. sq. 8°, (Color books ser.) *$2 net. Macmillan.

Canerio, Nicolò de.
Opus Nicolay de Caneiro Ianuensis [facsim.] '07 [1909.] (N) map, $20. Hispanic Soc.
See also Stevenson, E: Luther.

Canevin, Bp. J. F. Regis.
Inquirer's guide: an easy way to learn what the Catholic church is, and what the Catholic church teaches. '08, [1909.] (Mr) c. 80 p. 16°, 10 c.; per 100, $5. Cath. Church Extension.

Canfield, Chauncey L.
The City of Six. '10(Ap9) c. il. O. $1.50. McClurg.

Canfield, Mrs. Flavia A. C., [Mrs. James H. Canfield.]
Kidnapped campers. '08(O10) c. il. D. †$1.25. Harper.

Canfield, Mrs. Ja. H.
See Canfield, *Mrs.* Flavia A. C.

Canfield, W: Walker.
Along the way. '09(Ag28) c. il. D. $1.50. Fenno.

—, and Clark, J. E.
Things worth knowing about Oneida County, [New York.] '09(Ap10) c. il. O. *$1 net. T: J. Griffiths.

Cann, G: Turner.
Requests to charge in civil and criminal cases; with citations of authorities and forms for instructions to petit juries, incl. the requisites of charges to the grand jury. '09(F13) c. O. $6.25. Harrison Co.

Cannan, Gilbert.
Devious ways. '10(Ag20) c. D. $1.50. Duffield.
"Peter Homunculus": novel. '09(N6) D. †$1.50. Duffield.

Canning, Alb. Stratford G:
Sir Walter Scott studied in eight novels. '10(Jl30) O. $2.50 net. Wessels & B.

CANNING, George.
Bagot, J. F. George Canning and his friends. *$9 net. Dutton.

CANNING.
See Preserving.

Cannon, Annie Jump.
Maxima and minima of variable stars of long period, by Annie J. Cannon, under the direction of E: C. Pickering; printed from funds resulting from the will of Josiah Quincy, jr. '09, [1910.] (D) 95-291 p. 4°, (Annals of the Astronomical Observatory of Harvard College.) $1. Harvard Univ.

Cannon, H: Lewin.
Reading references for English hist. '10 (N5) c. D. $2.50. Ginn.

Cannon, Jos. Gurney.
Speech before the Middlesex Club, Boston, Mass., Sat., April 30, 1910, on "Ulysses S. Grant, the modest, courageous man, the normal American." '10(Ag) 15 p. 8°. Gov. Pr. Off.

CANNON, Joseph Gurney.
Moore, J. H. With Speaker Cannon through the tropics. $2. Book Pr.

Cannon, W: Austin.
Studies in heredity as illustrated by the trichomes of species and by the trichomes of species and hybrids of juglans, oenothera, papava, and solanum. '09 (N13) il. Q. (Carnegie Inst. of Washington pubs.) pap., 75 c. Carnegie.

—, and Knox, Alice Adelaide.
Topography of the *chlorophyll* apparatus in desert plants, by W. A. Cannon; [also] Induction, development, and heritability of fasciations by Alice A. Knox. '08 (D12) 8°, pap., 75 c. Carnegie.

CANOEING.
Canoes and canoeing. 10 c. Am. Sports.

Canoes and canoeing; paddling, sailing, cruising and racing canoes. '08(D19); '10(Jl2) c. il. por. 16°, (Spalding's athletic lib.) pap., ea., 10 c. Am. Sports.

CANTATAS.
Barri, O. The Flower Queen; cantata for unchanged voices. 20 c. Am. Bk.
Stanford, C: V. Resurrection: short cantata for Eastertide. 30 c. Ditson.

CANTERBURY, Eng.
Danks, W: Canterbury. $1.25. Estes.
Stanley, A. P. Memorials of Canterbury. *$1 net. Dutton.
CANTERBURY CATHEDRAL, Canterbury, Eng.
Bumpus, T: F. Canterbury Cathedral. **90 c. net. Jacobs.
Canterbury classics. 16°. Rand, McN. & Co.
—Chaucer. Story of Chaucer's Canterbury pilgrims. 40 c.
—Scott. Lady of the lake. 45 c.
Canterbury poets. 12°. Hurst.
—Trowbridge. The vagabonds. 75 c.
Canterbury poets. 98 v. [1910.] (Jl) ea., 40 c. Simmons.
Canterbury puzzles. Dudeney, H: E. *$1.25 net. Dutton.
Canterbury tales. *See* Chaucer, Geoffrey.
Canticles of Niagara. Deuther, C: G: $2.50. C: G: Deuther.
Cantor lectures. *See* Guttmann, Oscar.
Cantrell, E: Adams.
Bible and modern literature; comparing literature of to-day with ancient Jewish scriptures. '10(Mr5) c. 8°, 50 c. Los Angeles Liberal.
CANTRELL FAMILY.
See **Cantrill family.**
CANTRILL FAMILY.
Christie, *Mrs.* S. C. Cantrill-Cantrell genealogy. **$5 net. Grafton Press.
Cantwell, Harry Ja.
Importance of the mining industry to the industrial and commercial life of a nation: an address del. before the American Mining Congress at Joplin, Missouri. '08(My16) 8°, pap., gratis. H. J. Cantwell.
Canvas door. Sanborn, *Mrs.* M. F. S. $1.50. B. W. Dodge.
CANVASSING.
See **Business.**
Canyon voyage. Dellenbaugh, F: S: **$3.50 net. Putnam.
Cap and gown. Brown, C: R. $1 net. Pilgrim Press.
Capart, Jean.
Une rue de tombeaux à Saggarah: réproduction et description de trôis monuments funéraires de l'ancien empire égyptien. In 2 v. '08(Mr14) il. f°, special leath., $15. Stechert.
Cape, C. P.
Benares: stronghold of Hinduism. '10 (D31) il. 8°, $2 net, boxed. Badger.
Cape, Emily Palmer.
Fairy surprises for little folks. '08(Mr14) c. il. S. *75 c. net. E. P. Cape.
Cape Cod. *See* Thoreau, H: D:
CAPE COLONY, Africa.
Rogers, A. W., *and* Du Toit, A. L. Introd. to the geolcgy of Cape Colony. *$3.50 net. Longmans.
Capecelatro, Cardinal Alphonsus.
Christ, the church and man: essay on new methods in ecclesiastical studies and worship; with some remarks on a new apologia for Christianity in relation to the social question. '09(Jl) 78 p. 8°, *55 c. net. Herder.
Capers, J: G.
See United States. **Federal laws.**

Capes, Bernard.
Historical vignettes. '10(D17) O. $2.50 net. Stokes.
Why did he do it? '10(My14) 12°, $1.50. Brentano's.
Capes, H. M.
Footsteps in the ward, and other stories. '10(O) 4+164 p. il. 12°, 50 c. net. Herder.
Poets' May and other stories. '10(O) 127 p. il. 12°, 50 c. net. Herder.
Capital. *See* Marx, Karl.
CAPITAL AND LABOR.
Beveridge, A. J. Work and habit. 50 c.; $1. Altemus.
Daniels, P. Swollen fortunes and the problem of the unemployed. 15 c. P. Daniels.
Eliot, C: W: Future of trades unionism and capitalism in a democracy. $1 net. Putnam.
Franklin, M. Reward of capital. 25 c. M. Franklin.
George, W. L. Labor and capital at Port Sunlight: [account of an experiment in the conduct of a manufacturing enterprise.] *$1.40 net. Scribner.
Lincoln, J. T. City of the Dinner-pail. **$1.25 net. Houghton M.
Ries, W. F. Monkeys and monkeyettes: a reply to ex-President Roosevelt. 10 c. W. F. Ries.
Taft, W: H. Labor and capital. gratis. W: H. Taft.
Toynbee, A. Lectures on the industrial revolution of the eighteenth century in England. $1. Longmans.
See also Injunctions;—Interest;—Labor and laboring classes;—Money; — Monopolies; — Poor;—Railroads;—Trade-unions;—Trusts;—Wages; —Wealth.
CAPITAL PUNISHMENT.
Fanning, C. E., *comp.* Selected articles on capital punishment. $1. H. W. Wilson.
Fogle, H. M. Palace of death; or, the Ohio Penitentiary Annex. $1. Fogle.
Capps, S. R.
See Moffit, Fred Howard.
Capps-Oliver, Martha, comp.
Round the year with the poets: compilation of nature poems. '09(O9) c. il. D. $1.50; limp leath., $3. Caldwell.
Caprice: her book. Senior, D. $1.50 net. Macmillan.
Captain Chub. Barbour, R. H: †$1.50. Century Co.
Captain Desmond, V.C. Diver, M. †$1.50. Lane.
Captain Ferrercourt's widow. Hutchinson, M. F. $1.50. Longmans.
Captain Jack. Roys, C. D. $1.50. C. D. Roys.
Captain Jinks. White, F. H. $1. L. C. Page.
Captain Kidd and other charades. Sahler, F. S. $1. Stokes.
Captain Kidd, jr., and Sinbad the sailor. Senour, *Mrs.* C. S. $1. C. S. Senour.
Captain Love. Roberts, T. †$1.50. L. C. Page.
Captain Margaret. Masefield, J: *$1.50 net. Lippincott.
Captain of industry. Johnson, E. $1.50. C. M. Clark.

Captain of the Amaryllis. Cooley, S. $1.50. C. M. Clark.
Captain of the camp. Ellis, E: S. $1. Winston.
Captain of the eleven. Knipe, A. A. $1.25. **Harper.**
Captain of the school team. Earl, J: P. $1.25. Penn Pub. Co.
Captain **Pete of Alaska.** Wheeler, J. C. $1.50. **Dutton.**
Captain Pete of Cortesana. Wheeler, J. C. $1.50. Dutton.
Captain Pete of Puget Sound. Wheeler, J. C. $1.50. Dutton.
Captain Phil. Thomas, M. M. $1.50. Holt.
Captain Polly of Annapolis. Jackson, *Mrs.* G. E. S. $1.25. Dutton.
Captain Spink. Roberts, M. †$1.50. Lippincott.
Captain Ted. Waggaman, M. T. 60 c. Benziger.
Captain's wife. Lloyd, J: $1.50. M. Kennerley.
Captives of Israel. Mord, W. 35 c. Stokes.
Captivity and pastoral epistles. Strachan, J. 75 c. net. Revell.
Captivity of Mrs. Johnson; with an introd. by Horace W. Bailey, Esq. '08(Ag22) c. (Indian captivities ser. reprints.) ant. bds., $3; $5. Huntting.
Capture and escape. Kellogg, J: A. $1. Wisconsin Hist.
Car and the lady. Megargel, P. F. †$1.50. Baker & T.
Car builders' dictionary. Master Car Builders' Association. $6. Railway Age Gazette.
Car interchange manual; abridged ed., 1908; useful information for master car builders and car inspectors. '08(D19) c. 24°, pap., 25 c. J. D. McAlpine.
Caracciolo, Jos. Fs., comp.
Guida dell' operaio italiano in America; raccolta di notizie importantissime intorno alla, cittadinanza americana, servizio militare, uffici governativi italiani negli Stati Uniti e loro protezione agli immigranti, ecc., con aggiunta la Dichiarazione dell' independenza, Costituzione degli Stati Uniti ed ammendamenti tr. in italiano; comp. da Jos. F. Caracciolo. [1910.] (Ag) c. 96 p. 8°, 50 c. Italian Am.
Caravaners (The). Arnim, M. A. B. *Gräfin* v. $1.50. Doubleday, P.
CARBOHYDRATES.
See Chemistry.
CARBON.
Meyer, H. Determination of radicles in carbon compounds. **$1.25 net. Wiley.
Remsen, I. Introd. to the study of compounds of carbon. $1.20. Heath.
Weston, F. E. Scheme for the detection of the more common classes of carbon compounds. 90 c. Longmans.
CARBON MONOXIDE.
See Gas and gas-fitting.
Carbon print. Buchanan, J. B. 50 c. J. B. Buchanan
CARBURETTORS.
See Engines.
Carcassonne. Nadaud, G. (Priv. pr.) T: N. Fairbanks.
Card, Ernest M.
See Washington [State] laws.
Card, F: Wallace.
Bush-fruits: horticultural monograph of raspberries, blackberries, dewberries, currants, gooseberries, and other shrub-like fruits. 4th ed. '08(F1) il. 12°, (Rural science ser.) **$1.50 net. Macmillan.
Card club record. '08(N14) c. O. $1; full leath., $2, boxed. Brewer, B.
Cardashian, Vahan.
Ottoman empire of the twentieth century. '08(Je13) c. il. pors. D. $1. V. Cardashian.
Carden, Godfrey L.
Machine-tool trade in Belgium; transmitted to Congress in compliance with the act of March 4, 1909, authorizing investigations of trade conditions abroad. '09 (N) 93 p. il. 8°. (Add. Superintendent for price.) U. S., Supt. of Docs.
Carden, Rob. W.
City of Genoa. '08(O10) il. *$2.50 net; ¾ levant, *$5 net. Pott.
Cardigan and Lancastre, Adeline Louise Maria de Horsey, Countess of.
My recollections. '09(D25) pors. O. *$3.50 net. Lane.
Cardillac. Barr, R. †$1.50. Stokes.
Cardinal Democrat: Henry Edward Manning. Taylor, I. A. *$1.25 net. Herder.
Cardinal's pawn. Montgomery, K. L. 75 c. McClurg.
CARDIOID.
See Mathematics.
Cardiphonia. Witte, G: R. 75 c. Bookstore.
Cardozo, B: Nathan.
Jurisdiction of the court of claims of the state of New York. 2d ed. '09(Ap) c. 16+331 p. D. $3. Banks & Co.
CARDS.
Hoyle, E. Games modernized. *75 c. net. Dutton.
Hoyle, E. Standard games and bridge whist, 500, fan tan, solo hearts and card tricks. 75 c.; 25 c. Laird.
Hoyle's games of cards. 25 c. Ottenheimer.
Lowe, P. E., *comp.* Hoyle's card games. 15 c. Ottenheimer.
Schmalz, J: B. Nuggets from King Solomon's Mine. $2. Schmalz.
United States Playing Card Co. Official rules of card games; Hoyle up-to-date. Publishers' 14th ed. of rules of popular games. [1910.] (Mr) c. '09. 205 p. il. 12°, 25 c. U. S. Playing Card.
See also Bridge;—Euchre;—Fortune tellers;—Skat;—Solitaire.
Carducci, Giosuè.
Poems; with an introd. and tr. by Maud Holland. '08(Mr14) 12°, *$1.25 net. Scribner.
Care and culture of men. Jordan, D: S. $1.25. Whitaker & R.
Care and feeding of children. Holt, L. E. 75 c. Appleton.
Care and repair of dynamos and motors. '09 (Ap24) c. il. 8°, (Machinery's reference ser.) pap., 25 c. Indust. Press.
Care and repair of motorcycles. Bicycling World Co. 25 c. Bicycling World.

Care and training of children. Kerr, L. 75 c. net. Funk.
Care of automobiles. Paris, B. J. $1. Doubleday, P.
Care of babies. Cradock, *Mrs.* H. C. *35 c. net. Macmillan.
Care of books. Clark, J: W. *$2.50 net. Putnam.
Care of mother and child. Cheadle, C. M. $2; $2.50. C. M. Cheadle.
Care of natural monuments. Conwentz, H. *$1 net. Putnam.
Care of the child. Chance, *Mrs.* B. *$1 net. Penn Pub. Co.
Care of the patient. Hawes, A. T. $1 net. Blakiston.
Care of trees. Fernow, B. E: $2 net. Holt.
CAREER.
See Vocations.
Career of a journalist. Salisbury, W: *$1.50 net. B. W. Dodge.
Career of Joy. Towndrow, G. E. $1.25. C. M. Clark.

Carew, Mrs. Ja.
See Terry, Ellen.

Carey, Angeline Parmenter.
Reader's basis. '08(N) c. 13+200 p. 12°. $1. Echo Press.

Carey, C:, pseud.
See Waddell, *Mrs.* C: Carey.

Carey, Ja. F.
See Hugo, G: B.

Carey, Rosa Nouchette.
For Lilias. '08(Jl11) 12°, (Home ser.) 50 c. Hurst.
Key of the unknown. '09(O9) c. D. †$1.50. Lippincott.
Mistress of Brae farm. '10(D) 75 c. Burt.
Nellie's memories. '08(Jl4) 12°, (Home ser.) 50 c. Hurst.
Search for Basil Lyndhurst. '08(Ag1) 12°, (Home ser.) 50 c. Hurst.
Sunny side of the hill. '08(N14) c. D. †$1.50. Lippincott.

Carey, T: J., ["F. M. Payne."]
Real estate educator. '09(Jl31) c. 16°, *$2 net. Carey.

CAREY, William.
Smith, G: Life of William Carey. *35 c. net; *70 c. net. Dutton.

Carey, Wymond.
Love, the judge. '10(Mr26) c. front. D. †$1.50. Dodd.

Carhart, H: Smith.
Physics for college students. '10(N19) c. il. 8°, $2.25. Allyn & B.

CARIBBEAN SEA.
Nicholas, F. C. Across Panama and around the Caribbean. $1.50. Caldwell.
United States. *Hydrographic Office.* Navigation of the Gulf of Mexico and Caribbean Sea. 2 v. (Add. Superintendent for price.) U. S., Supt. of Docs.

CARICATURE.
Caruso, E. Caricatures: text in English and Italian. In 4 pts. $3; $5. La Follia.
Brewerton, A. W. Drawing for newspapers, cartooning, "comics," newspaper illustrating, etc. Am. Pub. Co., (Ga.)

CARICATURE.—*Continued.*
Zimmerman, E. Cartoons and Caricatures. $5. Corr. Inst.
See also Cartoons;—Wit and humor;—*also* Napoleon.

Caricature: wit and humor of a nation in picture, song and story. 7th ed. '08(Je27) c. il. obl. 4°, $1.12; 11th ed. '10(Ap23) c. il. 4°, $3. Leslie-Judge.

Carità.
Lacis: practical instructions in filet brodé or darning on net. '09(O9) il. 4°, *$3.50 net. Lippincott.

Carless, Albert.
See Rose, W:

Carleton, Mark Alfr.
Barley culture in the northern great plains. '08(Ag1) 8°, (U. S., Dept. of Agriculture, Bureau of Plant Industry, circular.) pap., 15 c. U. S., Supt. of Docs.

Carleton, Monroe Guy.
Autobiography of a disembodied soul. '10 (O1) c. il. D. $1.50. Vreeland.

Carleton, Will.
Drifted in. '08(D5) c. il. O. $1.50. Moffat.
Farm festivals. New ed. '09(My) c. 10+151 p. il. 12°, $1.25. Harper.
Thousand thoughts from Will Carleton. '08(D) c. 159 p. S. 50 c. Everywhere.
Carleton case. Clark, E. H. $1.50. Bobbs-M.

Carling, J: R.
The doomed city. '10(S24) c. il. D. $1.50. Clode.
Shadow of the czar. '08(My.) c. 12°, (Popular ed. of recent fiction.) †75 c. Little, B. & Co.
Viking's skull. '08(My.) c. 12°, (Popular ed. of recent fiction.) †75 c. Little, B. & Co.

Carlisle, G: Lister.
Around the world in a year. '08(Ag15) c. il. **$2 net. Baker & T.

Carlisle, Ja. H:
Addresses of J. H. Carlisle, 1825-1909, Wofford College, Spartanburg, S. C.; ed. by his son, J. H. Carlisle, jr. '10(Ag) 252 p. pors. 8°, $1.50. State Co.

Carlisle, R. H:
Fox hunting past and present. '08(Je27) il. 8°, *$1.50 net. Lane.

CARLISLE FAMILY.
See Irvine family.

Carlos, Mrs. Louisa Cooke Don-.
Bottle in the smoke. '08(Je6) c. front. D. $1.50. Fenno.
Carlota. Fox, F. M. $1. L. C. Page.
Carlota of the rancho. Raymond, *Mrs.* E. H. †60 c. Penn Pub. Co.
Carlotta's intended. Stuart, *Mrs.* R. M. †$1.25. Harper.
Carlovingian coins. *See* Sue, Marie Joseph Eugène.

Carlson, G: Lloyd.
Studies in horse breeding; il. treatise on the science and practice of horse breeding. [2d ed.] '10(D) 321 p. pl. 8°, $2. G: L. Carlson.

Carlton, Fk. Tracy.
Economic influences upon educational progress in the United States, 1820-1850. '08(D) 135 p. 8°, (Univ. of Wis. bull., Economics and political science ser.) 50 c. Wisconsin Hist.
Education and industrial evolution. '08 (O10) 12°, (Citizens' lib. of economics, politics and sociology.) *$1.25 net. Macmillan.

Bibliography (3 p.).

Carlyle, Alex. Ja.
See Carlyle, Rob. Warrand.

Carlyle, Mrs. Jane Welsh.
See Carlyle, T:

Carlyle, Rob. Warrand and Alex. Ja.
Hist. of mediæval political theory in the West. In 3 v. v. 1, Second century to the ninth; v. 2, Political theory of the Roman lawyers and economists in the Middle Ages up to 1250. '10(F) 8°, ea., *$3.50 net. Putnam.

Carlyle, T:
Works. De luxe ed. 10 v. '10(D) $30. Crowell.
Works. 10 v. New imperial lib. ed. '10 (D) il. 8°, ea., $1.25; hf. cf., $2.25; New il. sterling ed., ea., $1. (Sets only.) Estes.
Carlyle: [selections;] ed. by A. W. Evans. '09(N20) por. D. (Masters of literature.) *$1.10 net. Macmillan.
Essay on Burns: with selected poems by Burns; ed., with introd. and notes, by Julian W. Abernethy. '10(D3) c. pors. 16°, (Merrill's English texts.) 25 c. C: E. Merrill.
Essay on Burns; ed., with introd. and notes, by Archibald MacMechan. '08(Je20) c. S. (Scribner English classics.) **25 c. net. Scribner.
French Revolution. 2 v. '10(D) il. $2.50, boxed. Crowell.
French Revolution. In 2 v. '08(D19) front. 12°, (Crowell's thin paper sets.) hf. mor., $3, boxed. Crowell.
French Revolution. '08(O10) 2 v., 12°, Best books ser.) leath., ea., *$1 net. Dutton.
French Revolution; with introd. by Julian Hawthorne. '08(Je27) c. 2 v., il. 8°, $3.50; hf. mor., $7. Lamb Pub.
French Revolution. 3 v. '09(Ag28) il. pors. S. (Ideal classics.) leath., ea., $1.25, boxed. Winston.
Lectures on heroes, hero-worship, and the heroic in history; ed. by P. C. Parr. '10 (N19) D. 50 c. Oxford Univ.
Letters and speeches of Cromwell; introd. by W. A. Shaw. '08(F22) 3 v., 16°, (Everyman's lib.) ea., *35 c. net; leath., *70 c. net. Dutton.
Life of Frederick the Great; abdg. and ed. by Edg. Sanderson: with an introd. by Roger Ingpen. '09(O2) pors. map, D. *$1.50 net. McClurg.
Life of John Sterling; with an introd. by W. Hale White. Pocket ed. '09(Mr6) S. (World's classics.) 35 c. Oxford Univ.

Carlyle, T:—*Continued.*
Past and present; with introd. by G. K. Chesterton. '09, [1910.] (F) 331 p. 16°, (World's classics.) 35 c.; 65 c. **Oxford Univ.**
Pocket Carlyle; ed. by Rose Gardner. '08 (Je6) 16°, (Wayfaring books.) *$1 net. Dutton.
Sartor resartus; Heroes and hero worship, etc. '08(O10) (Best books ser.) leath., *$1 net. Dutton.
Sartor resartus, and Heroes and hero worship; introd. by Prof. Hudson. '08(F22) 16°, (Everyman's lib.) *35 c. net; leath., *70 c. net. Dutton.
Wisdom of Carlyle; selected and introd. by E: Clark Marsh. '09(D4) c. T. (Wisdom ser.) leath., **$1 net. Brentano's.

—, and Jane Welsh.
Love letters; ed. by Alex. Carlyle '09 (My1) c. 2 v., il. O. **$8 net. Lane.

—, and Macaulay, T: Babington, Lord.
Robert Burns, by T: Carlyle; Samuel Johnson, by Lord Macaulay; ed., with introd. and notes, by E: Everett Hale, jr. '09 (Ja30) c. pors. 12, (Standard literature ser.) 30 c.; pap., 20 c. Newson.

CARLYLE, Thomas.
Archibald, R. C. Carlyle's first love. *$3.50 net. Lane.
Conway. M. D. Thomas Carlyle. $1. Harper.
Craig, R. S. Making of Carlyle. *$4 net. **Lane.**
Higginson, T: W. Carlyle's laugh **and** other surprises. **$2 net. Houghton **M.**
Roe, F: W: Thomas Carlyle as a **critic** of literature. $1.25 net. Lemcke.

Carmack, E: Ward.
Character; or, the making of the man. '09, [1910.] (Ja) 66 p. por. 8°, $1. **McQuiddy.**

Carman, J. Ernest.
Mississippi Valley between Savanna and Davenport. '09, [1910.] (Jl) 11+96 p. il. pls. maps, 8°, (Ill. State Geological Survey, bull.) 8 c. Univ. of Ill.

Carman, W: Bliss.
Gate of peace: [poem.] '08(Ja18) long 4°, subs., *$5 net. Village Press.
Making of personality. '08(Ap4) c. front. D. $1.50; levant mor., $3.50. L. C. Page.
Rough rider, and other poems. '10(Ja8) c. 16°, $1. M. Kennerley.

Carmel, J: Prosper.
Nature's message. '09(Ag28) il. f°, $1. Dodge.

Carmen. *See* Mérimée, Prosper.

Carmichael, Amy Wilson-.
See Wilson-Carmichael, Amy.

Carmichael, Jos.
'Mid pines and heather and the true and the counterfeit. '10(Ag) 4+184 p. 8°. 60 c. net. Herder.

Carmichael, Montgomery.
Francia's masterpiece: essay on the beginnings of the immaculate conception in art. '09(D18) il. 12°, *$2 net. Dutton.

Carmichael, Philip.
Man from the moon. '09(O9) il. O. †$1.50. Stokes.

Carmina. Daly, T: A. **$1.50 net. Lane.

CARMINA EPIGRAPHICA LATINA.
See Buechler. —.

Carnacki. Hodgson, W: H. 25 c. P. R. Reynolds.

Carnahan, D: Hobart.
Jean d' Abundance; study of his life and three of his works. '10(Mr12) c. O. (Univ. of Ill. bull.; University studies.) pap., $1. Univ. of Ill.

Carnegie, And.
Path to peace; repr. from the London *Times* of June 19, 1909, (slightly rev.) '09(Ag21) D.; Supplement to The path of peace; repr. from the London *Times* and *Westminster Gazette.* pap. (Add. pubs. for price.) Peace Soc.
Problems of to-day: wealth—labor—socialism. '08(D19) c. O. $1.40. Doubleday, P.

Carnegie, Canon W: Hartley.
Churchmanship and character. '10(F) 36+236 p. 8°, *$1.25 net. Dutton.

Carnegie Foundation for the Advancement of Teaching. Financial status of the professor in America and in Germany. '08(Jl11) tabs., O. pap., gratis. Carnegie Found.

Carnegie Foundation for the Advancement of Teaching. Papers rel. to the admission of state institutions to the system of retiring allowances of the Carnegie Foundation. '08(Ag15) 4°, (Bull. of Carnegie Foundation.) pap., gratis. Carnegie Found.

Carnegie Foundation for the Advancement of Teaching. Plan for an exchange of teachers between Prussia and the United States. '08(Je6) Q. pap., gratis. Carnegie Found.

Carnegie Foundation for the Advancement of Teaching. Rules for the admission of institutions for the granting of retiring allowances. '09(My8) 4°, pap., gratis. Carnegie Found.

Carnegie Foundation for the Advancement of Teaching. Second annual rept. of the president and treasurer. '08(F1) Q. pap., gratis. Carnegie Found.

Carnegie Foundation for the Advancement of Teaching. Standard forms for financial reports of colleges, universities, and technical schools. '10(Jl9) il. F. (Bulletin.) pap., gratis. Carnegie Found.

Carnegie Foundation for the Advancement of Teaching. Third annual report of the president and treasurer. '09(F27) Q. pap., gratis. Carnegie Found.

Carnegie Foundation for the Advancement of Teaching bull. tabs., O. Carnegie Found.
—Cooke. Academic and industrial efficiency.

Carnegie Hero Fund Commission. Carnegie Hero Fund Commission created by Andrew Carnegie. '09(S) 68 p. front. 8°, gratis. Carnegie H. F. Comm.

Carnegie Institution of Washington. *Dept. of Historical Research.* List of doctoral dissertations in progress, Dec., 1909. [1910.] (Jl) 24 p. 8°. Carnegie.

Carnegie Institution of Washington; founded by Andrew Carnegie; scope and organization; issued on the occasion of the dedication of the Aministration Building at Washington, Dec. 13, 1909. '10(Mr5) il. Q. pap. Carnegie.

Carnegie Institution of Washington. Papers from the Tortugas Laboratory. v. 1. '09 (F13) $2; v. 2. '09(Mr13) $3; v. 4. '10 (D31) $4. il. figs. Q. (Carnegie Inst. of Wash. pubs.) Carnegie.

Carnegie Institution of Washington. Year book, no. 6, 1907. '08(F1); no. 7, 1908. '09 (Mr6); no. 8, 1909. '10(Mr12) il. plans, map, Q. ea., $1.25; pap., $1. Carnegie.

Carnegie Institution of Washington pubs. il. O and Q. pap. Carnegie.
—Andrews *and* Davenport. Guide to the manuscript materials for the history of the United States to 1783, in the British Museum, [etc.] $2.
—Baxter, *and others.* Researches upon the atomic weights of cadmium, manganese, [etc.] $2.
—Benedict, *and* Joslin. Metabolism in diabetes mellitus. $2.
—Cannon. Studies in heredity. 75 c.
—Castle, *and others.* Studies of inheritance in rabbits. 75 c.
—Conard. Structure and life history of the hay-scented fern. 50 c.
—Davenport. Inheritance in canaries. 80 c.
—Inheritance of characteristics in domestic fowl. $4.50.
—Durand. Researches on the performance of the screw propeller. 75 c.
—Eigenmann. Cave vertebrates of America. $5.
—Goss. High steam pressures in locomotive service. $1.25.
—Handbook of learned societies and institutions: America. $4.
—Hasse. Index of economic material in the documents of the states of U. S.: Massachusetts. $2.25.—New York. $3.75.—Rhode Island. 75 c.
—Hay. Fossil turtles of North America. $9.
—Hodell. Old yellow book. $7.
—Lloyd. Physiology of stomata. $1.50.
—Lutz. Variation and correlation of certain taxonomic characters of *Gryllus.* 40 c.
—Noguchi. Snake venoms. $10.
—Perrine, *and others* Determination of the solar parallax from photographs of Eros. $2.50.
—Peters. Heliographic positions of sunspots. $2.50.
—Shaw. Synopsis of linear associative algebra. $1.50.
—Shepherd. Guide to the materials for the history of U. S. in Spanish archives. 50 c.
—Sommer. Vulgate version of the Arthurian romances. $5.
—Spalding. Distribution and movements of desert plants. $2.
—Van Deman. Atrium Vestæ. $1.50.
—Van Tyne *and* Leland. Guide to the archives of the government of the U. S. $1.25.
—Willis. Research in China. v. 2. $2.

Carnegie Library, Pittsburgh. Catalogue of books; annot. and arr., and provided by the Carnegie Library of Pittsburgh for the use of the first eight grades in the Pittsburgh schools. '08(Ap4) O. pap., 35 c. Carnegie Lib.

Carnegie Library, Pittsburgh. Catalogue of books in the children's department. '09 (F27) O. pap., *$1 net. Carnegie Lib.

Carnegie Library, Pittsburgh. Classified catalogue. In 2 v. v. 1. '08(S5); v. 2 (D) O. ea., $5. Carnegie Lib.

Carnegie Library, Pittsburgh. Floods and flood protection; references to books and magazine articles. '08(D) 48 p. 8°, pap., 15 c. Carnegie Lib.

Carnegie Library. Pittsburg. Index to subject catalogue of the Technology Dept. '10 (D) 50 p. 8°, 10 c. Carnegie Lib.
Publications of the library now in print (3 p.).

Carnegie Library, Pittsburg. Lives and letters; sel. and annot. list; rev. and enl. ed. of "List of one hundred entertaining biographies." '10(D) 36 p. 8°, 10 c. Carnegie Lib.

Carnegie Technical School text bks. 8°. Van Nostrand.
—Gibbs. Textbook of physics. pt. 1. $1.50.
—Keller. Mathematics for engineering students: algebra and trigonometry. *$1.75 net.—Plane and solid geometry. *$1.25 net.
—*and* Knox. Mathematics for engineering students: analytical geometry and calculus. $2.
—Leeds. Mechanical drawing for trade schools. **$1.25 net; *$2 net.

Carney, W: Austen.
Promoter's assistant and improved secretary's manual: compendium of forms, instructions and legal information for promoters, secretaries of corporations and others. 2d ed. '09(A9) c. 9+5-329 p. 8°, $3. Carlisle.

CARNIVORE.
See Animals.

Carnot, Rev. Maurus.
Pilgrim from Ireland; tr. by Mary E. Mannix. '08(F8) front. S. 45 c. Benziger.

Caro, M. T., M.D.
Restricted diet made palatable; with a preface by Alb. Abrams. '10(S) 12°, $1 net. Ball Pub.

Carol Carew. Green, E. E. 75 c. McKay.

Carolina: [state song.] Pool, B. F. 50 c. B. F. Pool.

CAROLINE, *Queen of England.*
See George IV., *King of England.*

CAROLS.
Anson, W. S. W., *ed.* Christmas book of carols and song. $3; $4. Barse & H.
Dann, H., *comp. and ed.* Christmas carols and hymns for school and choir. 45 c. Am. Bk.
Rickert, M. E., *comp.* Ancient English Christmas carols MCCCC to MDCC. $3.25 net. Duffield.
Terhune, A. Colonial carols for children. $1.25 net. Schirmer.

Carotti, G.
History of art. v. 1, Ancient art, rev. by Mrs. Arth. Strong. '08(Je6); v. 2, Early Christian and Neo-Oriental art; European art (north of the Alps); tr. by Beryl de Zoete. '09(My22) 8°, ea., leath., *$1.50 net. Dutton.

Carov posol. Verne, J. $1 Slovak Press.

Carpaccio, Vittore, and Giorgione (Giorgio Barbarelli).
Masterpieces of Carpaccio (active 1478-1522) and Giorgione (1478-1510). '10 (S10) il. T. (Painters' ser.) leath., 75 c. net; pap., 25 c. net. Stokes.

Carpenter, C: U.
Profit making in shop and factory management. '08(My9) c. 8°, (Works management lib.) $2. Engineering Mag.

Carpenter, DeWitt.
Facts for farmers; to the farmer, by a farmer, for the farmer. '09(D) 20 p. 8°, 10 c. D. Carpenter.

Carpenter, Edm. Janes.
Roger Williams; study of the life, times and character of a political pioneer. '09 (D4) c. por. D. (Grafton historical ser.) **$2 net. Grafton Press.

Carpenter, E:
Sketches from life in town and country, and some verses. '08(My2) por. 12°, $1.50. Macmillan.

CARPENTER, Edward.
Ellis, E. M. O. L. Three modern seers—James Hinton, Nietzsche, Edward Carpenter. $1.25 net. M. Kennerley.

Carpenter, Fk. G:
How the world is clothed. '08(O24) il. D. (Readers on commerce and industry.) 60 c. Am. Bk.

Carpenter, G: Rice.
Walt Whitman. '09(Ap10) c. D. (English men of letters ser.) **75 c. net. Macmillan.

See also Baker, Franklin T:

Carpenter, Helen McCowen.
Bom-tu floor work (Grapevine-Poma Indian) for lodge staffs. '09(O) c. 65 p. il. 12°, $1. H. M. Carpenter.

Carpenter, Mrs. Kate E. Rushmore.
Story of Frederick the Great for boys and girls. '08(S5) c. por. O. $1. Lothrop, L. & S.

Carpenter, Mary L.
See Pope, Amy Eliz.

Carpenter, Rolla Clinton.
Heating and ventilating buildings: manual for heating engineers and architects. 5th ed., rev. and enl. '09(D) 16+562 p. figs. 8°, $4. Wiley.

—, and Diedrichs, Herman.
Internal combustion engines. '08(D5); 2d ed. '10(N) c. il. tabs., 8°, ea., *$5 net. Van Nostrand.

Carpenter, Seymour D:
Genealogical notes of the Carpenter family; ed. by Edn. Sawyer Walker. '07, [1908.] (Mr.) c. 242 p. pors. facsims., map, 8°, $5. G: N. Kreider.

Carpenter, Thorne M.
See Benedict, Fs. Gano.

Carpenter, W: Boyd, D.D.
Popular history of the Church of England. '09(N) 16+518 p. il. 8°, *$1.50 net. Dutton.

CARPENTER FAMILY.
See Genealogies.

CARPENTRY.
American School of Correspondence. Cyclopedia of carpentry and contracting. In 4 v. $12. Am. Sch. Corr.
Craftsman's Home Study Schools. First lessons in manual training and carpentry. Craftsman's Home Study.
Ellis, G: Modern practical joinery. *$6 net. Scribner.
Hodgson, F: T: Carpenters' and joiners' pocket companion. 50 c. Indust. Bk.
Peker, C: G. Hints for carpenters.—Short cuts in carpentery ea., 50 c. Indust.
Sylvester, W. A. Modern carpentry and building. $1.50. D: Williams.
See also Barns; — Cabinetwork; — Coopers and cooperage;—Furniture;—Planers;—Repairing;—Squares;—Stair building;—Tools;—Turning; —Wood-carving;—Woodwork.

CARPETS.
Claflin, H. B., Co. Rugs and carpets from the Orient. gratis. Claflin.
Humphries, S. Oriental carpets, runners and rugs, and some Jacquard reproductions. $10.50 net. Macmillan.
See also Rugs.

Carr, C. T.
Collective ownership otherwise than by corporations or by means of the trust. '08 (F29) 8°, *$1.50 net. Putnam.

Carr, Clark Ezra.
My day and generation. '08(Ap11) c. il. pors. O. *$3 net. McClurg.
Railway mail service; its origin and development. '09, [1910.] (F) 6+48 p. il. pors. bds., *50 c. net. McClurg.
Stephens A. Douglas; his life, public services, speeches and patriotism. '09(N20) c. il. pors. O. *$2 net. McClurg.

Carr, Mrs. Comyns.
North Italian folk. New ed. '10(D24) il. 16°, 50 c. net. Macmillan.

Carr, J: Foster.
Guida degli Stati Uniti per l'immigrante italiano. '10(Ag20) c. il. pors. fold. map, forms, D. pap., 10 c. Doubleday, P.

Carr, Jos. W: Comyns.
Some eminent Victorians: personal recollections in the world of art and letters. '09(F13) il. pors. facsim., O. *$3.50 net. Scribner.
See also Phillips, Stephen.

Carr, Kent.
Rivals and chums. '08(N7) il. D. $1.25. Lippincott.

Carr, Maggie Blauvelt.
Abraham Lincoln; a tribute. [1910.] (D) c. 7 p. 16°, 25 c. Williams Pr., (N. Y.)

Carr, Manley Earl.
Preliminary rept. on the Volusia soils, their problems and management. '09(D) 22 p. il. map, 8°, (U. S., Dept. of Agriculture, Bureau of Soils, bull.) pap. (Add. Superintendent for price.)

Carr, Rob. Van.
Cowboy lyrics. '08(My16) c. 16° (Add. pubs. for price.) Conkey.

Carr, Sadie.
Goldenrod: poems. '09(Je5) c. por. D. $1. S. Carr.

Carr, Mrs. Sarah Pratt.
Billy To-morrow. '09(S18) c. il. D. (Billy To-morrow ser.) $1.25. McClurg.
Billy To-morrow in camp. '10(N5) c. il. D. (Billy To-morrow ser.) $1.25. McClurg.

Carr, Wilbert Lester.
See Hale, W: Gardner.

Carradine, Beverly.
Box of treasure. '10(S17) c. 12°, $1. Chr. Witness.
Living illustrations. '08, [1909.] (F) c. 290 p. 12°, $1. Chr. Witness.
People I have met. '10(S3) c. 12°, $1. Chr. Witness.

Carrel, Frederic.
Adventures of John Johns. '08(Mr28) 8°, $1.50. M. Kennerley.
Methods of Mr. Ames: [a novel.] '08 (Ag22) c. 12°, $1.50. M. Kennerley.

Carrell, Rob. R.
Carrell's carols; sonnets of sunshine and other poems. [1910.] (Je) c. il. f°, 50 c. Carrell.

CARRIAGE PAINTING.
See Painting (*mechanical*).

Carrick, Hartley.
Muse in motley: [humorous verse.] '08 (Ja25) 16°, *$1.10 net. Macmillan.

Carrick, Rev. J: C:
Wycliffe and the Lollards. '08(Je20) D. (World's epoch-makers.) *$1.25 net. Scribner.

CARRIERS.
Beale, J. H. Selection of cases on carriers. $4. Harvard Law.
Green, F: Cases of the law of carriers. $4. West Pub.
New York [State.] Public service commissions law, 1907. $1. Banks & Co.
Smith, J. R. Ocean carrier: history and analysis of the service and a discussion of the rates of ocean transportation. **$1.50 net. Putnam.
Stephens, J. E. R. Law of carriage. $2. Pitman.
Watkins, E. Shippers and carriers of interstate freight. $6. Flood.
See also Commerce;—Railroads.

Carrington, Mrs. Frances Courtney.
My army life and the Fort Phil. Kearney massacre; with acct. of the celebration of "Wyoming opened." '10(Jl30) c. il. maps, D. $2 net. Lippincott.

Carrington, General H: Beebee.
Dream and story. In 2 pts. pt. 1, The voyage of life; pt. 2, Saint Christopher. '08(My.) c. 20 p. il. 12°, *75 c. net. Pilgrim Press.
Indian question; address before the geographical and biological sections of the British Association for the Advancement of Science, at their forty-fifth meeting, at Bristol. 1875. '09(O16) fold. maps, 8°, *60 c. net; pap., *30 c. net. De Wolfe & F.

Carrington, Hereward.
Coming science; with an introd. by Ja. H. Hyslop. '08(D12) c. D. **$1.50 net. Small.
Eusapia Palladino and her phenomena. '09 (D11) c. il. por. O. *$2 net. B. W. Dodge.

Carrington, Hereward.—*Continued.*
Vitality, fasting and nutrition: physiological study of the curative power of fasting; with an introd. by A. Rabagliati. '08 (Mr7) c. il. O. $5. Rebman.

Carrión, Miguel Ramos, Criado, Luis Cocat y Heliodoro, and Barranco, Mariano.
Tres comedias modernas et un acto y en prosa; La muela del judicio, por Miguel Ramos Carrión; Las solteronas, por Luis Cocat y Heliodoro Criado; Los pantalones, por Mariano Barranco; ed., with notes and vocab., by Frederic W: Morrison. '09(D18) c. S. 60 c. Holt.

Carroll, C: Chauncey.
Synthesis and analysis of the poetry of Sidney Lanier. '10(Je11) c. D. pap., 25 c. C: C. Carroll.

Carroll, E:, jr., comp.
Law printing laws; laws and rules of courts and judicial bodies of the U. S. and the state of N. Y. '09(D) c. O. pap., $1. E: Carroll.

Carroll, J: D.
See Kentucky statutes.

Carroll, Lewis, pseud.
See Dodgson, C: Lutwidge.

Carruth, E. *See* Boys on the railroad.

Carruth, W: Herbert.
Each in his own tongue, and other poems. '08(D26) c. S. **$1 net. Putnam.

Carse, Roland.
Monarchs of merry England, (William I. to Richard III.;) humorous rhymes of historical times. '08(D19) il. Q. bds., $1.50. Stokes.

Carslaw, Horatio Scott.
Plane trigonometry. '09(D4) 12°, *$1.10 net. Macmillan.

Carson, And. Carlisle.
Cluster of buckeyes: [poems.] '08(D) c. 9-51 p. il. 12°. (Add. pubs. for price.) Smith-B.

Carson, Blanche Mabury.
From Cairo to the Cataract. '09(Ap17) c. il. map, D. $2.50, boxed. L. C. Page.

Carson, Hampton Lawrence.
Sketch of Horace Binney. '07, [1908.] (N) 94 p. front. 8°. (Not for sale.) H. L. Carson.

Carson, Jos. Dickson.
In nature's temple. '10(My14) c. il. por. O. $1.25. Oldach.

Carson, Mrs. Norma Bright.
From Irish castles to French châteaux. '10(Jl9) c. il. D. $1.50 net. Small.

Carson, Rose M.
Through the valley of the shadow and beyond. '08(D12) c. il. O. $3. Hudson.

Carson, W: English.
Mexico, the wonderland of the south. '09 (N6) c. il. D. **$2.25 net. Macmillan.

CARTAGENA, Colombia.
Hart, F. R. Attack upon Cartagena by the French in 1697.—Attacks upon the Spanish Main by Admiral Vernon: [siege of Cartagena.] ea., 50 c. Assoc. Pub.

Carter, Ada.
Seamless robe. '09(N6) c. D. †$1.50. Wessels.

Carter, B: Franklin.
French word-lists. '09(Ja23) c. D. 25 c. Holt.

Carter, Rev. C. Sydney.
English Church in the 17th century. '09 (N13) D. (Anglican Church hdbks.) *40 c. net. Longmans.
English Church in the 18th century. '10 (O1) D. (Anglican Church hdbks.) *40 c. net. Longmans.

Carter, C: F:
When railroads were new; with introd. note by Logan G. McPherson. '09(Ap10) c. il. O. **$2 net. Holt.

Carter, C: Milton.
Art; outline of study, elementary schools, Denver. '09, [1910.] (Ap) c. 53 p. 8°. pap., gratis. Colo. Supt. Sch.

Carter, Clarence E:
Great Britain and the Illinois country. '10 (N19) 12°, (Prize essays of the Amer. Historical Assoc.), $1.50. Am. Hist.

Carter, Mrs. Cornelia Miranda Redington.
John Redington of Topsfield, Mass., and some of his descendants, with notes on the Wales family; ed. by Josiah Granville Leach. '09(Ap) c. 4+3-86 p. il. pors. 8°. (Add. pub. for price.) J. G. Leach.

Carter, E: E.
Methods of increasing forest productivity. '10(F19) 8°, (U. S., Dept. of Agriculture; Forest Service, circular.) pap.

Carter, Dean F. E.
Preaching. '09(O16) D. (Handbooks for the clergy.) *90 c. net. Longmans.

Carter, Herbert Pering
First exercises in Latin. '08, [1909.] (Mr) 94 p. 12°, 60 c. B. S. Adams.

Carter, Herbert R.
Modern flax, hemp, and jute, spinning and twisting. '08(Ag1) il. 12°, *$3 net. Van Nostrand.

Carter, J: F., jr.
The destroyers. '08(Ja11) D. $1.50. Neale.

Carter, Lilian.
Modelling from nature. '10(S) il. 8°, pap., 35 c. net. Cassell.

Carter, Nick, pseud.
See Coryell, J: Russell.

Carter, Russel Kelso.
Caleb Koons. '10(D3) il. 12°, $1.50. C. M. Clark.

Carter, S: Thomson, D.D.
Wanted—a theology. '08(Je6) c. D. **75 c. net. Funk.

Carter, T: Thellusson.
Stories from Shakespeare retold. '10(S17) il. O. $1.50 net. Crowell.

Carter, W: Giles Harding.
Giles Carter of Virginia: genealogical memoir. '09(Je19) pors. 8°, *$2.50 net. Lord Balto. Pr.
West Point in literature. '10(F5) 8°, *$2.50 net. Lord Balto. Pr.

CARTER FAMILY.
See **Genealogies.**

CARTHAGE, Africa.
See **Tunis.**

Cartier-Bresson, Mme.
How to make baby Irish crochet. '10(Ap) 25 c. Mills & G.
How to make Irish crochet lace. '10(Ap) 25 c. Mills & G.
How to work embroidery stitches; pract. method. '09, [1910.] (Ap) c. 47 p. il. 8°, 25 c. Mills & G.

Cartilla para enseñar aler a los ninos; con la doctrina Christiana que se canta, Amador hernanos [facsim.] '02 [1909.] (N) 22 p. 4°, $3.50 (200 copies). Hispanic Soc.

Cartmell, Fannie Sydnor, [Mrs. D. W. Shanks.]
Two demands. '09, [1910.] (N) c. 151 p. pors. 12°. Roycrofters.

Cartmell, T: Kemp.
Shenandoah Valley pioneers and their descendants; hist. of Frederick County, Virginia (illustrated), from its formation in 1738 to 1908; comp. mainly from original records of old Frederick County, now Hampshire, Berkeley, Shenandoah, Jefferson, Hardy, Clarke, Warren, Morgan and Frederick. '09(D) 7+587 p. il. 4°, $5. T: K. Cartmell.

CARTOONS.
Fisher, H. C. Mutt and Jeff cartoons. 50 c. net. Ball Pub.
Flagg, J. M. City people. *$3.50 net. Scribner.
Hogarth, W: Marriage à la mode. (Add. pubs. for price.) Dutton.
Zimmerman, E. Cartoons and caricatures. $5. Corr. Inst.
See also Caricature; — Punch; — *also* Roosevelt, Theodore.

Cartwright, Julia, [Mrs. H: Ady.]
Baldassare Castiglione: the perfect courtier. '08(O10) 2 v., il. pors. 8°, *$7.50 net. Dutton.

CARTWRIGHT, Peter.
Watters, P. M. Peter Cartwright. *25 c. net. Eaton & M.

Cartwright, T:
Brave Beowulf. '08(O10) 16°, (Every child's lib.) 50 c. Dutton.
One for Wod and one for Lok; or, Asgard, Midgard and Utgard. '08(Ag22) col. il. S. (Every child's lib.) 50 c. Dutton.

Carus, Paul.
Bride of Christ: a study in Christian legend lore. '08(D26) c. il. O. *75 c. net. Open Court.
Foundations of mathematics: contribution to the philosophy of geometry. '08(D5) c. D. *75 c. net. Open Court.
God: inquiry into the nature of man's highest ideal, and a solution of the problem from the standpoint of science. '08 (Ag1) *$1 net. Open Court.
Philosopher's martyrdom: a satire. '08 (Ag1) il. bds., *$1 net. Open Court.
Philosophy as a science; synopsis of the writings of Dr. Paul Carus, cont. introd. written by himself, summaries of his books, and list of articles to date. '10 (Ap2) c. D. 50 c. Open Court.
The pleroma; essay on the origin of Christianity. '09(D4) c. D. $1. Open Court.

Carus, Paul, ed.
Nestorian monument: ancient record of Christianity in China; with special reference to the expedition of Fritz V. Holm, containing Mr. Holm's account of how the replica was procured, the original Chinese text of the inscription, A. Wylie's English tr., and historical notes on the Nestorians; repr. from *The Open Court* of January, 1909, with numerous additions. '09(Jl31) c. il. O. pap., 40 c. Open Court.

Carus-Wilson, Mrs. C: Ashley.
See Wilson, Mary L. G. P.

Carus-Wilson, Mary L G. Petrie, [Mrs. C: Ashley Carus-Wilson.]
Expansion of Christendom: study in religious history. '10(D) 12°, $1.50 net. Doran.

Caruso, Enrico.
Caricatures; text in English and Italian. In 4 pts. '08(My16) c. il. por. f°, $3; ed. de luxe, $5. La Follia.

Caruthers, W: A.
Knights of the horseshoe. '09(Ap10) il. 12°, (Standard fiction) $1. Burt.

CARVER, Jonathan.
Lee, J: T: Bibliography of Carver's travels. 35 c. State Hist., Wis.

Carver, Willard.
Chiropractic analysis as applied to anatomy, physiology, chiropractic principles, symptomatology and diagnosis. [1910.] (Mr) c. '09. 15+3-486 p. 8°, $7.50. W. Carver.

Carver, Rev. W: Owen.
Missions and modern thought. '10(D24) c. D. $1.50 net. Macmillan.
Missions in the plan of the ages. '09(D18) c. D. (Bible studies in missions.) *$1.25 net. Revell.

CARVER, Mass.
See Plymouth County, Mass.

Cary, Austin.
Manual for northern woodsmen. '09(F13) il. map, O. *$2 net. Harvard Univ.

Cary, C: Preston.
Superintendent and superintendence: [school supervision.] '08(D) 57 p. 12°. (Add. author for price.) C: P. Cary.
—, **ed.** List of books for free high school libraries in the state of Wisconsin, with instructions for cataloging. '09(Ap3) O. pap., gratis. C: P. Cary.

Cary, Claude Arth.
See Askew, *Mrs.* Alice J. de C. Leake.

Cary, Elisabeth Luther.
Artists past and present: random studies. '09(O16) c. il. pors. O. **$2.50 net. Moffat.

Cary, Otis, D.D.
Hist. of Christianity in Japan. In 2 v. v. 1, Roman Catholic and Greek Orthodox missions; v. 2, Protestant missions. '09 (S11) c. 8°, ea., *$2.50 net. Revell.
Later Cary poems. 3d ed. '08(Je27) il. pors. O. pap., 50 c. S. C. Carey.

Cary, Rev. Seth Cooley, comp.
John Ainsworth Dunn, Gardner, Mass. '08 (Je) 11-76 p. il. pors. 8°, pap. (Not for sale.) S. C. Cary.

Casanowicz, Immanuel Moses.
Collection of rosaries in the United States National Museum. '09(My15) il. O. pap. U. S., Supt. of Docs.

See also Adler, Cyrus.

CASAS, Bartolomé de las.
MacNutt, F. A: Bartholomew de Las Casas. **$3.50 net. Putnam.

Case, Calvin S.
Practical treatise on the technics and principles of dental orthopedia, incl. drawings and working details of appliances and apparatus for all forms of irregularities of the teeth. '08(Je27) c. 4°, $10. C. S. Case.

Case, Carl Delos.
Incarnation and modern thought. '08(Je20) c. 8°, pap., *50 c. net. Univ. of Chic.

Case, Mrs. Eliz. York.
There is no unbelief: a poem. '08(Ja18) 16°, (New Amphion classics.) pap., 50 c. Somerville.

Case, Fes. Powell, ["Frances Powell."]
Old Mr. Davenant's money. '08(Je20) c. D. †$1.50. Scribner.

Case, G: A.
Giant American causeway: outline of plan for industrial development. '08(D26) c. il. O. pap., 15 c. G: A. Case.

Case against Christian Science. Paget, S. 10 c. Cassell.

Case against protection. Cooke, E. C. 10 c. Cassell.

Case against socialism. London Municipal Society. *$1.50 net. Macmillan.

Case for the goat. Robertson-Scott, J. W. *$1.25 net. Dutton.

Case of Lady Broadstone. Marchmont, A. W. $1.50. Empire Bk.

Case of rebellious Susan. Jones, H: A. 75 c.; 50 c. S: French.

CASEROLE RECEIPTS.
See Cookery.

Casey, Kellogg Kennon Venable.
See Wilson, H. C.

Cash, panics and industrial depressions. Libby, C: T. gratis. C: T. Libby.

Cash intrigue. Chester, G: R. †$1.50. Bobbs-M.

Cashin's Theatre Ticket Office.
Boston theatres and halls; with historical notes, past and present. '07, [1908.] (Ap.) c. 32 p. il. 4°, pap., 25 c. W. B. Jones.

CASHMERE.
See Kashmir.

Caskey, W: G:, ed.
See Trueblood, T: Clarkson, *ed.*

"Caskoden, Edn.," pseud.
See Major, C:

Caspar, Leopold, M.D.
Text-book of genito-urinary diseases. 2d ed.; tr. by C: W. Bonney. '09(Ja23) c. 8°, *$5 net. Blakiston.

Caspari, C:, jr.
Treatise on pharmacy for students and pharmacists. 4th ed., enl. and rev. '10 (N) 11+17-913 p. il. 8°, $4.25 net. Lea.

Caspar's automobile road maps of Wisconsin; comp. with aid of prominent members of Milwaukee Automobile Club and the Automobile Club of Wisconsin. [5 maps.] [1910.] (My) maps 1 and 2, 75 c.; maps 3, 4 and 5, ea., 35 c.; per set, $1.25. Caspar.

Caspar's guide and map of the city of Milwaukee. 8th ed. '09(F6) c. 12°, pap., 25 c. Caspar.

Casque's lark. *See* Sue, Marie Joseph Eugène.

Cassell's A B C of gardening. Wright, W. P. *$1.25 net. Cassell.

Cassell's annual for boys and girls, 1909; comp. by the editor of *Little Folks.* '09 (N6); 1910. '10(D) col. il. Q. ea., $1.75; bds., $1.25. Cassell.

Cassell's atlas [88 maps]. '09, [1910.] (Ja) **$4 net. Cassell.

Cassell's cyclopedia of mechanics. Hasluck, P. N., *ed.* 5 v. ea., *$2.50 net. Cassell.

Cassell's famous juvenile classics. 18 v. '10 (N) il. ea., 75 c. Cassell.
Contents: Captain Cook's voyages; Fairy tales, stories and legends; Grimm's fairy tales; Gulliver's travels; Ivanhoe; Life of Nelson; Mr. Midshipman Easy; Oliver Twist; Peter the whaler; Pilgrim's progress; Robinson Crusoe; The sketch book; Swiss family Robinson; The three midshipmen; Tom Brown's school days; Uncle Tom's cabin; Vicar of Wakefield; Westward ho!

Cassell's guide to London. New ed. '10 (O1) il. 25 c. Cassell.

Cassell's house decoration. Hasluck, P. N., *ed.* *$3 net. Cassell.

Cassell's household cookery. Heritage, L. $1.50. Cassell.

Cassell's little classics; introds. by G. K. Chesterton, Austin Dobson, A. T. Quiller-Couch and J. A. Hobson. 25 v. '10(S) 16°, ea., 25 c. net. Cassell.

Cassell's people's library. [Masterpieces of biography, fiction, poetry, science, essays, etc.] v. 1-100. '09(My22); v. 100-120. '09, [1910.] (F) ea., 35 c.; leath., 75 c. Cassell.

Cassell's picture books. 2 v. '10(D) col. il. bds., 75 c. Cassell.

Cassell's story books. 6 v. '10(D) ea., bds., 40 c. Cassell.

Cassell's story juveniles. 11 v. '10(D) il. (partly col.) ea., $1.25. Cassell.

Casson, Herbert Newton.
Cyrus Hall McCormick, his life and work. '09(N13) c. por. O. $1.50. McClurg.
Hist. of the telephone. '10(S17) c. il. pors. O. $1.50 net. McClurg.
Romance of the reaper. '08(Je6) c. D. **$1 net. Doubleday, P.

CAST IRON.
See Iron.

Castaigne, André.
The bill-toppers. '09(S18) c. il. D. †$1.50. Bobbs-M.

CASTE.
See India.

Caste: a novel. Hauser, I. L. (Add. author for price.) I. L. Hauser.

Castellani, Aldo, M.D., and Chalmers, Alb. J., M. D.
Manual of tropical medicine. [1910.] (Je) 1270 p. il. 8°, $6 net. Wood.

CASTIGLIONE, Baldassare, *Count.*
Cartwright, J. Baldassare Castiglione. 2 v. *$7.50 net. Dutton.
Hare, C. Courts and camps of the Italian renaissance: being a mirror of the life and times of Baldassare Castiglione. *$2.50 net. Scribner.
Castle, Mrs. Agnes Sweetman and Egerton.
Diamonds cut paste. '09(O23) c. D. †$1.50. Dodd.
Flower o' the Orange, and other tales. '08 (F29) c. front. D. †$1.50. Macmillan.
Wroth. '08(S26) 12°, †$1.50. Macmillan.
Castle, Egerton.
See Castle, *Mrs.* Agnes Sweetman.
Castle, Fk.
Logarithmic and other tables for schools. '08(Je6) 12°, pap., *20 c. net. Macmillan.
Castle, W: Ernest, and others.
Studies of inheritance in rabbits. '09(Ag14) il. tabs., O. (Carnegie Institution of Washington pubs.) 75 c. Carnegie.
Castle builders. Munn, C: C. $1.50. Lothrop, L., & S.
Castle by the sea. Watson, H: B. †$1.50. Little, B. & Co.
Castle gates. Pearson, J. L. $1. J. L. Pearson.
CASTLE OF BRUCKSALES.
See **Brucksales, Castle of.**
Castle of Dawn. Kramer, H. M. †$1.50. Lothrop, L. & S.
Castle of dreams. Syrett, N. $1.25. McClurg.
Castle of four towers. Syrett, N. $1.50. Fenno.
Castle of Grumpy Grouch. Donahey, M. D. $1.25. Stern.
Castle of the shadows. Williamson, *Mrs.* A. M. L. $1.50. Hudson Press.
Castle Rackrent. *See* Edgeworth, Maria.
Castle stories, by Castle girls. '08(O) c. 3+13 p. il. 8°, $1.20. L. L. Parsons.
Castlemon, Harry, [pseud. for C: Austin Fosdick.]
Boy trappers. '08(Je27) 12°, (Young America lib.) 50 c. Hurst.
Frank in the woods. '08(Je6) 12°, (Young America lib.) 50 c. Hurst.
Frank on the prairie. '08(Jl18) 12°, (Young America lib.) 50 c. Hurst.
Castles and chateaux of old Burgundy. Miltoun, F., *pseud.* $3. L. C. Page.
Castles of England. Auvergne, E. B. d'. *$2 net; *$4 net. Pott.
CASTOR FAMILY.
See **Genealogies, Martin, R. A.**
CASTRATION.
Liautard, A. Animal castration. $2. W: R. Jenkins.
Castro, Miguel de.
Vida del soldado español Miguel de Castro (1593-1611) escrita por el mismo y publicada por A. Paz y Mélia. '00 [1909.] (N) 5-9+232 p. 4°, (Bibliotheca hispanica.) $3. Hispanic Soc.
Caswell, Lucien B.
Postal savings banks: paper entitled "Do we want the postal savings bank?" '09 (My) 4 p. 8°, pap. (Add. Superintendent for price.) U. S., Supt. of Docs.

CAT.
Allyn, E. G. Cat's convention. $1.50. Cochrane.
Barton, F. T. The cat. $1. W: R. Jenkins.
Champion, D. B. Everybody's cat book. $2. D. B. Champion.
Davison, A. Mammalian anatomy, with special reference to the cat. *$1.50 net. Blakiston.
Hill, J. W. Diseases of the cat. $1.25. W: R. Jenkins.
Merriam, J: C. S. Skull and dentition of an extinct cat closely allied to *felix atrox* Leidy. 15 c. Univ. of Cal.
Simpson, F. New book of the cat. *$5 net. Cassell.
Williams, *Mrs.* L. The cat. $1. Altemus.
Cat and Racket. *See* Balzac, Honoré de.
Cat and the canary. Cameron, M. †$1. Harper.
Cat school. Marshall, F. *30 c. net. Educ. Pub.
CATACOMBS, Rome.
Blake-Hedges, F. E. Story of the catacombs. *$1 net. Jennings.
Catacombs of worldly success. Messenger, F. M. 50 c. Metropolitan Ch. Assoc.
CATALLA, *Fr.* Magin.
Engelhardt, Z. Holy man of Santa Clara; or, life, virtues and miracles of Fr. Magin Catala. 75 c. Barry.
Catalog rules: author and title entries; comp. by committees of the A. L. A. and the (British) Library Assoc. '08(O) 16+88 p. 4°, 60 c. A. L. A.
Catalogi librorum reprobatorum & prælegendoru ex indicio Academiæ Louaniensis [facsim.] '96 [1909.] (N) no paging 4°, $5 (100 copies). Hispanic Soc.
Catalogue of the American Play Co., with original casts. '09(F6) c. O. pap., 50 c. Am. Play.
CATALOGUES.
See **Bibliographies.**
CATALOGUING.
Carnegie Library, Pittsburgh. Index to subject catalogue of the Technology Dept. 10 c. Carnegie Lib.
Catalog rules: author and entry titles; comp. by committees of the A. L. A. and the (British) Library Assoc. 60 c. A. L. A.
Graydon, S: Some notes on catalog making. $1. Trow Press.
Hanson, J. C. M. Subject catalogs of the Library of Congress. H. W. Wilson.
John Crerar Library, Chicago, Ill. Catalogue rules. (Not for sale.) John Crerar Lib.
United States. *Library of Congress* Preliminary list of subject subdivisions. Gov. Pr. Off.
See also **Classification.**
Catalogus librorum reprobatorum ex ivdicio Academiæ Lovaiensis cvm edicto Cæsareæ maiestatis evvlgatus [facsim.] '96 [1909.] (N) no paging, $5 (100 copies). Hispanic Soc.
CATALONIA, Spain.
Calvert, A. F: Catalonia, and the Balearic Isles. $1.50 net. Lane.
Catamount Camp. Ellis, E: S. $1. Winston.

CATARACT.
See Eye.
Catchwords of friendship: collection of two hundred sentiments in verse and prose. '08(O10) c. front. S. bds., *50 c. net. McClurg.
Catchwords of patriotism. Rice, W. de G. C., *comp.* *$1 net. McClurg.
Catchwords of worldly wisdom. Inglehart, M., *comp.* *75 c. net; *$1.25 net; *$1 net. McClurg.
Catechism of hæmatology. Watkins, R. L. $2. R. L. Watkins.
Catechism of harmony. Schwartz, G: F. 50 c. White-S.
Catechism of manual of guard duty, United States Army. Selkirk, W. O. 50 c. net. Wiley.
CATECHISMS.
Catecismo primario de la Iglesia Metodista Episcopal y de la Iglesia Metodista Episcopal Del Sur. per 100, $5; per doz., 60 c. Eaton & M.
Dalton, M. L. Church catechisms in anecdote. *$1 net. Whittaker.
Faerber, F. W. Catechism for the Catholic parochial schools of the United States. 40 c. Svovoda.
Gerberding, G: H: Lutheran catechist. $1.50. Lutheran Pub.
Horine, J: W. The catechist's hdbk. 90 c. Gen. Council.
Luther, M. Small catechism, with Hints and helps to the way of salvation. 25 c. P. G: Sieger.
Luther, M. Small catechisms.—Two catechisms. ea., 50 c. Luther Press.
Mangasarian, M. M. New catechism. $1. Independent Religious.
Stumpf, J. Explanation of Luther's small catechism. 35 c.; 50 c. Gen. Council.
Urban, A. Easy catechetics for the first school year. 60 c.—Sunday-school teacher's explanation of the Baltimore catechism. $1. Wagner.
See also Creeds.
Catecismo primario de la Iglesia Metodista Episcopal y de la Iglesia Metodista Episcopal Del Sur [a translation of the Junior Catechism into Spanish.] '10(Ap) 28 p. 12°, pap., 5 c.; per doz., 60 c.; per 100, $5. Eaton & M.
Catering for two. James, A. $2; $5. Putnam.
Cates, C: T., jr., rep.
See Tennessee. *Sup. ct.* Repts.
Cates, Cliff Donahue.
Pioneer history of Wise County, [Texas.] '07, [1908.] (D) c. 471 p. il. 8°, $2. C. D. Cates.
Cathalogus libroru qui prohibetur mandato Illustrissimi Reverend D. D. Ferdinandi de Valdes Hispaleñ [facsim.] '96, [1909.] (N) 27 p. 4°, $5.50. (100 copies.) Hispanic Soc.
CATHARI.
See **Church history.**
CATHEDRAL MUSIC.
See Church music.
CATHEDRAL OF ST. PETER AND ST. PAUL.
See Washington (D. C.) Cathedral.
Cathedral ser. il. D. $2.50 boxed. L. C. Page.
—Bumpus. Cathedrals and churches of northern Italy.

CATHEDRALS.
Bumpus, T: F. Cathedrals and churches of Belgium. $2 net.—Cathedrals and churches of Norway, Sweden, and Denmark. *$4 net; *$7.50 net.—Cathedrals of northern France. $2. Pott.
Bumpus, T: F. Cathedrals and churches of northern Italy. $2.50. L. C. Page.
Collins, W. W. Cathedral cities of Spain. **$3.50 net. Dodd.
Grierson, *Mrs.* E. W. Children's tales of English minsters. *$2 net.—Tales of English minsters. 7 v. ea., 50 c. net. Macmillan.
James, J. L., *comp.* Twenty English cathedrals. $1. M. C. James.
Perkins, C. C. French cathedrals and chateaux. 2 v. *$5 net. Holt.
Pratt, H. M. Cathedral churches of England. $2.50 net. Duffield.
Rose, E. W. Cathedrals and cloisters of the Isle de France. In 2 v. $5 net. Putnam.
Singleton, E., *comp. and ed.* Famous cathedrals, as seen and described by great writers. **$1.60 net. Dodd.
See also Abbeys;—France;—Stained glass;—*also* Canterbury Cathedral;—Washington Cathedral; —*also* names of abbeys.
Cathedrals of England and Wales; with short notes by Nugent M. Clougher. In 2 v. '09 (Mr13) T. pap., ea., *25 c. net. Stokes.
CATHERINE DE MEDICI, *Queen of France.*
Sichel, E. Later years of Catherine de Medici. *$3 net. Dutton.
CATHERINE *of Braganza, Queen of England.*
Davidson, L. C. Catherine of Braganza: [wife of Charles II.] *$5 net. Dutton.
CATHERINE *of Genoa, St.*
Hügle, *Baron* F. v. Mystical element in religion as studied in St. Catherine of Genoa and her friends. 2 v. *$6 net. Dutton.
CATHERINE *of Siena, St.*
Gardner, E. G. St. Catherine of Siena. *$4 net. Dutton.
Catherine's child. De la Pasture, *Mrs.* E. B. **$1.20 net. Dutton.
Catholic atlas. Grafton, C: C. **$2.50 net. Longmans.
Catholic centenary, 1808-1908. McNally, A. F. **$1.25 net. Moffat.
Catholic Church. Office of the Blessed Virgin Mary and office of the dead: Latin and English. '08(Ag8) 45 c.; leath., 75 c. Herder.
CATHOLIC CHURCH.
Acolyte's companion; ceremonial and prayer-book combined. 35 c. net. Herder.
Battle, J. M. Why I am not a Roman Catholic. $1.50. J. M. Battle.
Baudot, J. Lectionary: its sources and history.—Roman breviary, its sources and history. ea., *$1 net. Herder.
Bennett, W: H. Catholic footsteps in Old New York. $2.50. Schwartz, K. & F.
Benziger's ecclesiastical diary and notebook, 1909. *75 c. net. Benziger.
Berington, J., *and* Kirk, J., *comps.* The faith of Catholics, confirmed by Scripture and attested by the fathers of the first five centuries of the church. $6 net. Pustet.

CATHOLIC CHURCH.—*Continued.*

Bruner, J. W. Question of Romanism. $1.50. J. W. Bruner.

Burke, J. J. Reasonableness of Catholic ceremonies and practices. *25 c. net; *13 c. net. Benziger.

Burnett, P: H. Path which led a Protestant lawyer to the Catholic church. *$1.50 net. Herder.

Canevin, J. F. R. Inquirer's guide: easy way to learn what the Catholic church is. 10 c.; per 100, $5. Cath. Church Extension.

Cecilia, *Madame*. More short spiritual readings for Mary's children. $1.25. Benziger.

Champagnat, J. B. Qualities of a good superior. *$1.25 net. Herder.

Clarke, C: C. Hdbk. of the divine liturgy. 90 c. Herder.

Complete catalogue of Catholic literature. 15 c. T: J. Flynn.

Constantinus, *Brother*. Young Christian teacher encouraged. $1.25 net. Herder.

Conway, J. P. Question of the hour. *$1.25 net. J: McBride.

Cooney, P. J. Roman Catholicism and socialism. 10 c. P. J. Cooney.

Coyle, H:, Mayhew, T., *and* Hickey, F. S., *comps*. Our church, her children and institutions. 3 v. $8. Angel Press.

Cox, W: J. E: Errors of Romanism. $1. Dearing.

Curtis, G. P., *ed*. Some roads to Rome in America: conversions to the Catholic church. *$1.75 net. Herder.

Devas, C: S. Key to the world's progress: account of the historical significance of the Catholic church. 20 c. Longmans.

De Zulueta, F. M. Early steps in the fold. $1. Kenedy.

Dolan, T: S. Papacy and the first councils of the church. *75 c. net. Putnam.

Dolan, T: S. See of Peter and the voice of antiquity. *60 c. net. Herder.

Drake, F. W. Way of fellowship. $1 net. Longmans.

Dunn, L: V. Catholic church in Clinton County, Iowa. $2. Torch Press.

Ferina, C:, *comp*. Saint Rita's prayer books. (Add. pub. for price.) C: Ferina.

Fogarty, J. H: Priest and parson; or, let us be one. *$1.25 net. Chr. Press.

Fradryssa, G. V. Roman Catholicism capitulating before Protestantism. $1.50. Southern Pub. (Ala.)

Francis, P. J., *and* Jones, S. Prince of the apostles: [argument favoring the union of the Catholic church and the Church of England.] *75 c. net. Lamp Pub.

Geirmann, P: Mission remembrance of the Redemptorist fathers. 50 c. Benziger.

Gerrard, T: J. Cords of Adam. *$1.50 net. Longmans.

Hilgers, J. Roman index and its latest historian. *10 c. net. Herder.

Kirk, J: Biographies of English Catholics in the 18th century. *$2.75 net. Benziger.

Kirlin, J. L. J. Catholicity in Philadelphia from the earliest missionaries down to the present time. $3.50. McVey.

CATHOLIC CHURCH.—*Continued.*

Krehbiel, E: B. The interdict, its hist. and its operation, with especial attention to the time of Pope Innocent III. $1.50. Am. Hist.

Krull, V. H. Alphabetical oddities. V. H. Krull.

Lasance, F. X. Young man's guide. 75 c.; $1; $1.50. Benziger.

Leith, W: F. Memoirs of Scottish Catholics during the XVIIth and XVIIIth centuries. In 2 v. *$7 net. Longmans.

Leonard, A. W. Roman Catholic church at the fountain head, in the light of the Fairbanks - Roosevelt - Vatican incidents. 15 c. Jennings.

Liguori, *St.* A. On retreat. pap., *6 c. net. Herder.

Lynch, J. S. M. Essentials of the Five Scapulars. 25 c. Cathedral Lib.

McCabe, J. Decay of the Church of Rome. *$2.50 net. Dutton.

McGavick, J. E: Catholic belief and practice. 25 c. Wiltzius.

McNicholas, J: T. New legislation on engagements and marriage [in Catholic church:] commentary on the decree "Ne temere." 10 c. Dolphin.

Martin, C: A. Catholic religion. $1. Apostolate.

Martique, L. F. Scarlet mother on the Tiber. [Anti-catholicism.] $1. L. J. King.

Meschler, M. Sublimity of the holy eucharist, also A visit to the seven churches in Rome on the occasion of the jubilee. 75 c. net. Herder.

Middleton, T: C. Catholic periodicals published in the United States, [1809-1892.] (Priv. pr.) T: C. Middleton.

Morton, F. T. Roman Catholic church and its relation to federal government. $2. Badger.

Murphy, E: J. Latin pronounced for altar boys. *50 c. net. Chr. Press.

Nainfa, J: A. F. P. Costume of prelates of the Catholic church. *$1.50 net. Murphy.

Navaho-English catechism of Christian doctrine for the use of Navaho children. $1. Franciscan Fathers.

Newman, J: H: Church of the fathers. *75 c. net. Longmans.

O'Dwyer, E: T: Cardinal Newman and the Encyclical *Pascendi Dominici Gregis*. *36 c. net. Longmans.

Official Catholic directory and clergy list for 1908; 1909; 1910. ea., $1.75-$3. Wiltzius.

Pace, E: A., *and* Shields, T: E: Religion; first book. *40 c. net. Cath. Educ.

Petre, M. D. Catholicism and independence. *$1.20 net. Longmans.

Plummer, C: Vitae sanctorum Hiberniae. 2 v. $9.75. Oxford Univ.

Pontifical services. 3 v. *$6 net. Longmans.

Pulpit commentary on Catholic teaching. v. 1. $2. Wagner.

CATHOLIC CHURCH.—*Continued.*

Roche, J. T: Business side of religion. *15 c. net; per 100, *$10 net.—Die geschæftliche seite der religion. *10 c. net; per 100, $6.50.—Obligation of hearing mass on Sundays and holy days. 10 c. net; per doz., 75 c. net; per 100, $5 net. Wiltzius.

Sabatier, P. Open letter to His Eminence, Cardinal Gibbons, apropos of his interview on the separation of church and state in France. *60 c. net. Sherman, F.

Scannell, T: B. Priest's studies. *$1.20 net. Longmans.

Schiffini, S. De vera religione seu de Christi ecclesia ejusque munere doctrinali. *$2.75 net. Herder.

Smyth, N. Passing Protestantism and coming Catholicism. **$1 net. Scribner.

Sumichrast, F: C. J: M. S: R. de. Church and state in France. 25 c. F. H. Robson.

Theiler, H: Candle as a symbol and sacramental in the Catholic church.—Holy water and its significance for Catholics. ea., 50 c. Pustet.

United States. *Congress. Senate. Committee on the Philippines.* Catholic church claims in Philippine Islands.

Von Ruville, A. Back to Holy Church. $1.20 net. Longmans.

Walsh, J: Mass and vestments of the Catholic church. *$2 net. J: Walsh.

Ward, B. Dawn of the Catholic revival in England. 2 v. *$7 net. Longmans.

Wolferstan, B. Catholic church in China from 1860 to 1907. $1.30 net. Herder.

See also American College, Rome;—Apostolic succession;—Bishops;—Catechisms; — Celibacy; — Church history;—Church of England;—Confirmation;—Confession;—Creeds;—Cross; —Devotional exercises and meditations;—Fathers of the church;—Fiction;—Holy week; — Hymns;—Index expurgatorius;—Infallibility; — Inquisition; —Italy;—Jesus (*Society of*);—Jesus Christ;—Knights of Columbus; — Latin language; — Legends; — Lent; — Lord's supper; — Martyrs;— —Mary, *Virgin*;—Miracles;—Missions and missionaries;—Modernism; — Monasticism; —Nunneries;—Penance; — Popes;—Port Royalists;—Priests;—Rationalism;—Readers;—Reformation; —Religious education;—Religious orders;—Rosary;—Sacraments;—Saints; — Scientists;—Sermons;—Sunday-school; —Syracuse;—Theology; —Vatican;—*also* Loyola, Ignatius de:—Perraud, *Abbé* C. A.;—Peter, *St.*;—Pius x.

Catholic church in the United States of America; ed. by Ernesto Begni, [and others.] In 6 v. v. 1. '08(S19); v. 2. '09(D18) c. il. pors. f°, subs., Popular ed., hf. leath., $90; Ed. de luxe, mor., $180. Cath. Editing.

Catholic churchmen in science; second ser. Walsh, J. J. $1. Dolphin.

Catholic encyclopedia; ed. by C: G. Herbermann, E: A. Pace, [etc.] In 15 v. v. 3. '08(Je6); v. 4 (D5); v. 5. '09(Je5); v. 6 (N13); v. 7. '10(Mr19); v. 8 (Jl30); v. 9 (D3) c. il. pors. maps, Q. ea., $6; ¾ mor., $8; full mor., $15. R. Appleton.

Catholic Highlands of Scotland. v. 1. *$1.10 net. Herder.

Catholic home annual for 1909. '08(O10); 1910. '09(D25) il. sq. O. pap., ea., 25 c. Benziger.

CATHOLIC LITERATURE.
See **Catholic church.**

Catholic reading list. Chicago Public Library. 25 c. E. Larkin.

Catholic school system in the United States. Burns, J. A. $1.25. Benziger.

Catholic socialism. Nitti, F. S. *$2.75 net. Macmillan.

Catholic University of America. Library. Periodicals and serials in the Library of the Catholic University of America, 1910. '10 (Ag) 113 p. 8°. (Priv. pr.) Cath. Univ.

Catholic who's who and year book, 1909; ed. by Sir Fs. Cowley Burnand. '09(Ap3) D. *$1.50 net. Benziger.

CATHOLICITY.
See **Catholic church.**

Catholics and the American Revolution. Griffin, M. I. J. In 2 v. v. 2. $3. M. I. J. Griffin.

"Catholicus," pseud.
See Leahy, *Rev.* G: Vincent.

CATILINE, Lucius Sergius.

Beesly, E: S. Catiline, Clodius and Tiberius. *$3 net. Stechert.

Catlin, G:

Boy's Catlin; my life among the Indians; ed., with a biographical sketch, by Mary Gay Humphreys. '09(O2) c. il. O. **$1.50 net. Scribner.

Cato Maior de senectvte. *See* Cicero, M. T.

Catrevas, Christina.

That freshman. '10(O1) c. il. D. $1.50. Appleton.

Cat's cradle. Byron, M. 60 c. Dodge.

CATS.

Gardner, A. P. Mews and musings. 75 c. Cochrane.

Jackson, *Mrs.* G. E. S. Adventures of Tommy Postoffice. $1.25. Dutton.

Cats and kitts. Montgomery, F. T. 50 c. Brewer, B.

CATSKILL MOUNTAINS, N. Y.

Burroughs, J: In the Catskills. $1.50 net. Houghton M.

Cattell, H: Ware, M.D., ed.

Lippincott's new medical dictionary: vocab. of terms used in medicine and allied sciences, with their pronunciation, etymology, and signification. '10(D) 18+1108 p. il. flex. leath., $5 net. Lippincott.

Cattell, Ja. McKeen, ed.

American men of science; biographical dictionary. 2d ed. '10(D31) 4°, $5. Science Press.

Cattell, Sarah Ware.
See Kroeger, Alice Bertha.

CATTLE.

Agricultural Blue Book and the Live Stock Breeders' Directory of the United States of America. $1. Hale Pub.

American Aberdeen-Angus Breeders' Association. Supremacy of Aberdeen-Angus cattle. (Add. pubs. for price.) Am. Aberdeen-A.

American Jersey Cattle Club. Jersey sires with their tested daughters. $2.—Register of merit of Jersey cattle. gratis. Am. Jersey.

CATTLE.—*Continued.*
Holstein-Friesian Association of America. Outlines of the advanced registry system of the Holstein-Friesian Association of America. (Add. pubs. for price.) Transcript.
Murray, A. J. Diseases of the stomach and bowels of cattle. (Add. Superintendent for price.) U. S., Supt. of Docs.
New Mexico [Territory.] Cattle Sanitary Board. $1.50. N. M. Cattle.
Shaw, T: Management and feeding of cattle. *$2 net. Judd.
Special rept. on diseases of cattle. Rev. ed., 1908. '09(My) 551 p. il. 8°, pap., $1. U. S., Supt. of Docs.
See also Abattoirs;—Butter;—Clover;—Cow;—Dairy—Domestic animals;—Ensilage;—Milk;—Tuberculosis;—Veterinary medicine and surgery.

CATTLE TICK.
Hunter, W. D: Practical demonstration of a method for controlling the cattle tick. U. S., Supt. of Docs.

Catullus.
Catulli carmina; [Poems of Catullus;] ed. by C: Stuttaford, with introd. and notes. '09(My15) 16°, *$1.50 net. Macmillan.

CATULLUS.
Ullman, B. L: Identification of the manuscripts of Catullus cited in Statius' edition of 1566. 75 c. B. L: Ullman.

CAUCASIC LANGUAGES.
See Language.

CAUCASUS (The).
Baddeley, J: F. Russian conquest of the Caucasus. *$5 net. Longmans.
Graham, S. Vagabond in the Caucasus. $4 net. Lane.

Caught on the fly. Newberry, A. St. J. (Priv. pr.) A. S. Newberry.

Caught with the goods. Dumont, F. 15 c. Penn Pub. Co.

CAULIFLOWER.
See Cabbage.

Caunt, G: W:
See Jessop, C: M.

Causal geology. Schwarz, E. H. L. $2.50. Van Nostrand.

Cause and cure of colds. Sadler, W. S: $1 net. McClurg.

Cause of geologic periods. Taber, C: A. M. 75 c. Ellis.

Cause of our financial panics. Fourtner, S: 50 c. S: Fourtner.

Causeries du lundi. *See* Sainte-Beuve, Charles Augustin.

Causes and consequences. Chapman, J: J. $1.25. Moffat.

Causes and cure of unbelief. Laforet, N: J. 60 c.; 30 c. Kilner.

Causes of disability as applied under accident and health insurance policies. Harbaugh, C: H. $6. Spectator.

Causes of present discontent in India. O'Donnell, C: J. **85 c. net. Wessels.

Cavalcaselle, Giovanni Battista.
See Crowe, *Sir* Jos. Archer.

Cavalier of Virginia. Roberts, G: E: T. $1.50. L. C. Page.

CAVALRY.
Gray, A. Cavalry tactics as illustrated by the war of the rebellion. pt. 1. $1.50. U. S. Cavalry.

Cavanagh. Garland, H. $1.50. Harper.

Cave, H: W:
Book of Ceylon: guide to its railway system and an account of its varied attractions. '08(My23) maps, O. *$4.50 net. Cassell.

Cave of the Bottomless Pool. Hunting, H: G. †$1.50. Holt.

Cave vertebrates of America. Eigenmann, C. H. $5. Carnegie.

Cave-woman. Burhans, V. $1.50. Holt.

Cavenagh, Fs. A.
Ethical end of Plato's theory of ideas: thesis. '09(N13) O. pap., 50 c. Oxford Univ.

CAVENDISH, William.
See Newcastle, William Cavendish, *Duke* of.

CAVENDISH LABORATORY.
See Cambridge University.

Caverns of dawn. Voorhees, J. P. $1.25. Raidabaugh-V.

Caw, Ja. Lewis.
Raeburn. '10(Jl2) col. il. 8°, (Masterpieces in colour.) bds., 65 c. net; leath., $1.50 net. Stokes.
Scottish painting, past and present, 1620-1908. '09(O2) il. Q. *$8 net. Stokes.

Cawein, Madison Julius.
An ode; read August 15, 1907, at the dedication of the monument erected at Gloucester, Mass., in commemoration of the founding of the Massachusetts Bay Colony in the year 1623. '08(Ap11) D. bds., 25 c. Morton.
Giant and the star; little annals in rhyme. '09(O2) c. D. **$1 net. Small.
Poems. 5 v. '08(D12) il. ed. de luxe, **$15 net, boxed. Small.
Shadow garden (a phantasy), and other plays. '10(My7) c. D. $1.50 net. Putnam.

Caxton thin paper classics. 16°, limp lambskin, *$1.25 net. Scribner.
—Poe. Tales of the grotesque and arabesque.

Cebes.
Greek Pilgrim's progress, generally known as The picture, by Kebes, a disciple of Sokrates?; tr. from the Greek text pub. by B. G. Tuebner, of Leipzig; set in type, il. and ornamented by Kenneth Sylvan Guthrie. [1910.] (D) c. 51 p. 12°, (Wisdom of the ancients lib.) $1. Monsalvat.

Cecil, Alicia Marg. Tyssen Amherst, [Mrs. Evelyn Cecil.]
Hist. of gardening in England. '10(Ap23) il. 4°, $3.50 net. Dutton.

Cecil, Mrs. Evelyn.
See Cecil, Alicia Marg. Tyssen Amherst.

Cecil, Lady Florence Mary Bootle-Wilbraham.
See Cecil, Lord R. W: E. G-.

Cecil, Lord Hugh R: Heathcote.
Liberty and authority. '10(F19) D. $1. Longmans.

Cecil, Rev. Lord Rupert W: Ernest Gascoyne- and Lady Florence Mary Bootle-Wilbraham.
Changing China. '10(My21) il. map, O. $3 special net. Appleton.

Cecilia, Madame.
Acts of the apostles: Catholic Scripture manual. bks. 1, 2. '08(Ag8) 12°, $1.25. Benziger.
More short spiritual readings for Mary's children. '10(N12) c. D. $1.25. Benziger.
Celebrated crimes. *See* Dumas, Alexandre.
Celebrated criminal cases of America. Duke, T: S: $3 net. Barry.
Celestial ejectamenta. Wilde, W. $10. Oxford Univ.
Celestina (The). *See* Rojas, F. de.
CELIBACY.
Scharnagl, A. Das feierliche gelübde als ehehindernis in seiner geschichtlichen entwicklung dargestellt. *$1.50 net. Herder.
See also Perraud, *Abbé* C. A.
Cell (The) of self-knowledge: seven early English mystical treatises printed by H: Pepwell in 1521; ed., with an introd. and notes, by Edm. G. Gardner. '10(S10) front. S. (New medieval lib.) pigskin, $2 net, boxed. Duffield.
Cellini, Benvenuto.
Life of Benvenuto Cellini; new version by Rob. H. Hobart Cust. 2 v. '10(D10) il. pors. fold. tab., O. $9 net, boxed. Macmillan.
'CELLO.
See Violoncello.
CELLS.
Hertwig, O., *and* Campbell, H: J. The cell: outlines of general anatomy and physiology. *$2.25 net. Macmillan.
McFadyen, A. Cell as the unit of life, and other lectures. *$3 net. Blakiston.
See also Biology;—Botany;—Histology.
CELLULOID.
Bockman, F. Celluloid: its raw material, manufacture, [etc.] $2.50. Van Nostrand
Celt and Saxon. Meredith, G: $1.50. Scribner.
CELTIC ART.
See Fine arts.
CELTIC LITERATURE
Arnold, M. On the study of Celtic literature. 35 c. net; 70 c. net. Dutton.
CEMENT.
Alpha Portland cement for eternity. gratis. Alpha Portland.
Bassler, R. S. Cement resources of Virginia. Univ. of Va.
Boynton, C. W. Portland cement sidewalk construction. (Add. pubs. for price.) Universal Portland Cement.
Buehler, H: A. Lime and cement resources of Missouri. 25 c. Missouri Bu. Geol.
Crider, A. F. Cement and Portland cement materials of Mississippi. (Add. pub. for price.) Brandon Pr.
Dragon Portland cement. Lawrence Cement.
Eckel, E. C. Portland cement from a financial standpoint. $2. Moody's Mag.
Gatehouse, F. B. Hdbk. for cement workers. *$1.75 net. Lippincott.
Glasenapp, M. Plaster, overburnt gypsum and hydraulic gypsum. 50 c. Cement & Engineering
Hansen, E: S. Cement pipe and tile. $1. Cement Era.

CEMENT.—*Continued.*
Lewis, M. H: Popular hdbk. for cement and concrete users. $2.50. Henley.
Palliser, C: Modern cement sidewalk construction. 50 c. Indust.
Portland cement industry in the United States; directory. (Add. pub. for price.) Assoc. Am. Portland Cement.
Radford, W: A. Cement houses and how to build them. 50 c. Radford Architectural.
Radford, W: A., *ed.* Cement and how to use it. $1. Radford Architectural.
Richey, H. G. Building mechanics' ready reference. Cement workers' and plasterers' ed. **$1.50 net. Wiley.
Representative cement houses. 50 c. Universal Portland Cement.
Smith, J. A. Present and future of the cement block. 25 c. J. A. Smith.
Waterbury, L. A. Cement laboratory manual. $1. Wiley.
See also Concrete;—Pavements;—Railroads.
Cena, Giovanni.
The forewarners: a novel; tr. from the Italian by Olivia Agresti Rossetti; with a preface by Mrs. Humphry Ward. '08 (D26) D. $1.50. Doubleday, P.
Cenci (The). *See* Shelley, Percy Bysshe.
Ceneres. *See* Deledda, Grazia.
CENSUS.
United States. *Dept. of Commerce and Labor. Bureau of Census.* Century of population growth, from the first census of the U. S. to the twelfth, 1790-1900.
United States. *Dept. of Commerce and Labor. Bureau of Census.* Heads of families at the first census, 1790. $1.
United States. *Dept. of Commerce and Labor. Bureau of Census.* Publications, 10th, 11th, and 12th censuses and permanent bureau. '09(My) 13 p. 8°, pap. $1.10.
See also Churches;—Statistics;—*also* Newington, Ct.
Censvra generalis contra errores, quib recentes hæretici sacram scripturam asperserunt, edita a supremo senatu Inquisitionis aduersus hereticam prauitatem & apostasiam in Hispania, & aliis regnis, & dominiis, Cesareæ Magestatis constituto. [facsim.] '96, [1909.] (N) no paging, 4°, $5. (100 copies.) Hispanic Soc.
CENT.
See Money.
Centenary Missionary Conference records: report of the great Shanghai Conference, held April 25 to May 7, 1907. '08(My9) c. 8°, *$2.50 net. Am. Tr.
Centenary of Tennyson. Warren, T: H. 35 c. Oxford Univ.
Centenary of the Geological Society of London, celebrated Sept. 26 to Oct. 3, 1907; recorded by Prof. W. W. Watts. '09(Jl3) por. O. pap., *75 c. net. Longmans.
CENTERDALE, R. I.
Angell, F. C. Annals of Centerdale in the town of North Providence, Rhode Island. $2.50. F. C. Angell.
CENTRAL AFRICA.
See Africa.

CENTRAL AMERICA.
Cook, O. F. Vegetation affected by agriculture in Central America. (Add. Superintendent for price.) U. S., Supt. of Docs.
Corlett, W: T. American tropics. [West Indies, Central America, Venezuela.] $1.50. Burrows.
Meek, S. E. Notes on fresh-water fishes from Mexico and Central America. 50 c. Field Museum.
Palmer, F: Central America and its problems. **$2.50 net. Moffat.
Pittier de Fábrega, H. F. New or noteworthy plants of Colombia and Central America. (Add. Superintendent for price.) U. S., Supt. of Docs.
See also Costa Rica;—Guatemala;—Honduras;—Monroe doctrine;—Nicaragua;—Salvador.
Central bank. Ireton, R. E. $1.60. Stumpf.
Central bank of issue. Roberts, G: E. 50 c. Bankers' Pub.
Central bank of issue for the United States. McCabe, R. L. 10 c. R. L. McCabe.
Central (The) real estate directory of Iowa, Kansas and Texas. '08(Ap.) c. por. 16°, $5. Cen. Real Estate.
Central topics in geography. S. pap., 10 c. Flanagan.
—McMurry. The Alps.—The Rhine.
Centralized schools in Ohio. Graham, A. B. gratis. A. B. Graham.
CENTRIFUGAL PUMPS.
See Pumps.
Centurion (The). Routhier, A. B. $1.50. Herder.
Centurion's story. Macfarlane, P: C. *25 c. net. Revell.
Century Bible handbooks; ed. by Wa. F. Adeney. v. 1-8. '09(D); v. 9, 10. '10(D) 24°, bds., ea., *40 c. net. Doran.
Contents: Andrews, H. T., Apocryphal books; Bennett, W. H., Old Testament history; Franke, R. S., Man, sin and salvation; Horton, Robert F., The early church; Mackintosh, Rob., Christian ethics; Martin, G. Currie, Books of the New Testament; Peake, A. S., Religion of Israel; Selbie, W. B., Life and teachings of Jesus Christ; Adeney, New Testament doctrine of Christ; Garvie, Life and teaching of Paul.
Century Club of American Newspapers. '09, [1910.] (F) c. 33 p. il. pors. F. pap. (Not for sale.) St. L. Republic.
Century Code Co. Century standard telegraphic code, by J. S. Kornicker. '08 (Ja18) 4°, limp leath., $10. Century Code.
Century cook book. Ronald, M. $2. Century Co.
Century Map Company. New century atlas, Oneida county, N. Y. '07, [1908.] (Jl) c. 180 p. maps, f°, $16.50; $25. Century Map.
Century of achievement. Lowndes, A. 2 v. $5. Gorham.
Century of archæological discoveries. Michaelis, A. $4. Dutton.
Century of empire. Maxwell, *Sir* H. E. In 3 v. v. 1, 2. ea., *$4 net. Longmans.
Century of French poets. Eccles, F. Y. $3 net. Dutton.
Century of the child. Key, E. K. **$1.50 net. Putnam.
Century outlines for a course in English literature. Pyre, J. F. A. 75 c. net. Century Co.
Century Shakespeare. il. 16°. Cassell.
—Furnivall *and* Munro. Shakespeare. *35 c. net; *65 c. net.
Century students' manual. Knowlson, T: S. **$1 net. Warne.
CERAMICS.
Barber, E. A. Lead glazed pottery. pt. 1. **90 c. net. Doubleday, P.
Barber, E. A. Maiolica of Mexico. $2.10. Penn. Mus. and Sch. of Ind. Art.
Barber, E. A. Pottery and porcelain of the United States. **$5 net. Putnam.
Binns, C: F. Potter's craft. $2. Van Nostrand.
Blacker, J. F. A B C of collecting old English pottery. $2 net. Jacobs.
Blacker, J. F. Chats on Oriental china. *$2 net; *$5 net. Stokes.
Branner, J: C. Bibliography of clays and the ceramic arts. $2. Am. Ceramic.
Burton, W: *and* H. Hdbk. of marks on pottery and porcelain. *$2.25 net. Macmillan.
Chaffers, W: Collector's hdbk. to keramics of the Renaissance and modern periods. *$1.50 net. Scribner.
Chu Yen. Description of Chinese pottery and porcelain. $4.75. Oxford Univ.
Clarke, J. M. English gold lustres.—Swiss influence on the early Pennsylvania slip decorated majolica. (Add. author for price.) J: M. Clarke.
Davison, R. C. Concrete pottery and garden furniture. $1.50. Munn.
Dillon, E: Porcelain and how to collect it. $2 net. Dutton.
Dyer, W. A. Lure of the antique. $2.40 net. Century Co.
Getz, J: Catalogue of the Macomber collection of Chinese pottery. $1.25. Boston Museum.
Hainbach, R. Pottery decorating. *$3 net. Van Nostrand.
Hayden, A. Chats on old earthenware. $5. Stokes.
Hobson, R. L. Porcelain. $2.15 net. Stokes.
Hsiang Yuan-P'ien. Chinese porcelain. $34, boxed. Oxford Univ.
Loeb, J. Loeb collection of Arrentine pottery catalogued. $10. Harvard Co-op.
Masterpieces of handicraft; ed. by T. Leman Hare. 6 v. ea., *75 c. net. Dodd.
More, *Mrs.* N. H. Delftware, Dutch and English. **$1 net. Stokes.
Pier, G. C. Pottery of the Near East. **$3.50 net. Putnam.
Pottier, E. Douris and the painters of Greek vases. $2.50. Dutton.
Rackham, B. Book of porcelain. $4 net. Macmillan.
Rum Bellow, H: A. Factory glazes for ceramic engineers. *$10 net. Spon.
Solon, L. M. E. Ceramic literature. $15 net. Lippincott.
Wylde, C. H. How to collect continental china. $2. Macmillan.
See also China painting;—Glass;—*also* Harbison-Walker Refractories Co.;—Wedgewood, J.
CERATIUM.
See Zoölogy.
CERATOCORY.
See Paleontology.

CEREALS.
Chamberlain, J. S. Feeding value of cereals. 10 c. U. S., Supt. of Docs.
Farrell, F. D: Dry-land grains in the Great Basin. Gov. Pr. Off.
Reed, G: M. Mildews of the cereals. (Not for sale.) G: M. Reed.
McLaughlin, W. W. Irrigation of grain. Gov. Pr. Off.
See also **Grain;—Wheat.**

CEREBRATION.
See Brain.

Ceres' runaway. Meynell, A. C. T. *$1.25 net. Lane.

Cerezo, Saturnino Martin.
Under the red and gold; being notes and recollections of the siege of Baler; tr. and ed. by F. L. Dodds. '09(Ag21) c. il. por. map, plan, 8°, $1.25. Hudson.

CERIANTHUS.
See Marine Zoology.

Certain rich man. White, W: A. †$1.50; †$2. Macmillan.

Cervantes Saavedra, Miguel de.
Don Quixote. 2 v. '10(D) il. $2.50, boxed. Crowell.
Don Quixote; Motteux's translation. 2 v. '09(Mr27) 16°, (Everyman's lib.) ea., *35 c. net; leath., *70 c. net. Dutton.
Don Quixote de la Mancha; tr. into English by Robinson Smith. '10(D10) 8°, $3.50 net. Dutton.
Don Quixote de la Mancha. Tercentenary issue. Critical ed. In 7 v. v. 1, Facsimile reproductions of first Madrid ed. of the 1st pt. (1605); v. 2, Facsimile reproductions of the first ed. of the 2d pt. (Madrid, 1615); v. 3, Facsimile reproduction of 4th Madrid ed. (1605); v. 4, 5, 6, 7, Critical text of 1st and 2d pts., prep. by M. Raymond Foulché-Delbosc; with an introd. by Ja. Fitzmaurice Kelly. '07 [1909.] (N) 8°, First impression, ea., $20 (100 copies); Second impression, ea., $10 (200 copies); Third impression, ea., $5 (500 copies). Hispanic Soc.
Don Quixote of the Mancha; retold by Judge Parry; il. by Wa. Crane. '09, [1910.] (Je) 12+245 p. il. 8°, $1.50. Lane.
Don Quixote; tr. by C: Jervas; ed., with notes and an introd. by Ja. Fitzmaurice-Kelly. '08(Ap11) 2 v., 16°, (World's classics.) ea., 50 c.; leath., 75 c. Oxford Univ.
Life and adventures of Don Quixote de la Mancha; tr. from the Spanish. '08(O10) il. D. (Bowman's illustrated lib. of world-favorite books.) $1. Bowman.
Selections from Don Quixote; ed., with notes and vocab., by J. D. M. Ford. '08 (O17) c. D. (Modern lang. ser.) 80 c. Heath.
Stories by Cervantes. '09(S11) front. 12°, (World story-teller ser.) *40 c. net. Dutton.

CERVANTES SAAVEDRA, Miguel de.
Baldwin, J., *comp.* Stories of Don Quixote written anew for young people. 50 c. Am. Bk.
Havell, H. L., *comp.* Stories from Don Quixote; retold. $1.50. Dodge.

César Birotteau. *See* Balzac, Honoré de.

Cesaresco, Countess Evelyn Lilian Hazeldine Carrington Martinengo-.
Place of animals in human thought. '09 (D11) il. O. *$3 net. Scribner.

Cesspool and its dangers. Ashley, B. J: gratis. **Ashley.**

CEYLON.
Cave, H: W: Book of Ceylon. *$4.50 net. Cassell.
Clark, A. Ceylon. 75 c. net. Macmillan.
Corner, *Mrs.* C. Ceylon, the paradise of Adam. *$4 net. Lane.
Farrer, R. J. In old Ceylon. $4. Longmans.

Chace, E: Mackay.
See Powell, G: H.

Chaddock, Rob. Emmet.
Ohio before 1850: study of the early influence of Pennsylvania and southern populations in Ohio. '08(Jl11) c. O. (Columbia Univ. studies in hist., economics and public law.) pap., $1.50. Longmans.
See also Dewey, Davis Rich.

Chadman, C: Erehart.
Concise legal directory adapted to the use of law students and all persons studying the fundamentals of Eng. and Amer. law. '09(S) c. 4+625 p. O. hf. shp., $6. Am. Corr. Sch. Law.
—, ed. Cyclopedia of law. '08(Ap25) c. 12 v., pors. 8°, hf. shp., $60. Am. Corr. Sch. Law.

Chadwick, Earl Leslie.
Conservative advocate; book of biographies of Connecticut's successful men; with essays on conservatism by well known writers. '10(F19) c. pors. 8°, $5. E. L. Chadwick.

Chadwick, French Ensor.
Relations of the United States and Spain; diplomacy. '09(D25) c. O. **$4 net. Scribner.

Chadwick, H:, ed.
Spalding's official base ball guide, 1908. 32d year. '08(Ap4) c. il. pors. S. (Spalding's athletic lib.) pap., 10 c. Am. Sports.

Chadwick, Lester.
Quarter-back's pluck; story of college football. '10(N5) c. il. D. (College sports ser.) $1. Cupples & L.
The rival pitchers: story of college baseball. '10(My14) c. il. 12°, $1. Cupples & L.

Chadwick, Mrs. Mara Louise Pratt-, ["Francesca Marshall."]
The cat school. '08, [1909.] (Mr) 96 p. il. 12°, (Folk lore books; Folleti linchetti ser.) 30 c. Educ. Pub.
Nixie well; The goat and the troll: northern Europe folk lore tales. '08, [1909.] (Mr) 88 p. il. 12°, (Folk lore ser.) *30 c. net. Educ. Pub.
Stories of colonial children. Rev. ed. '08, [1909.] (Je) 7-223 p. il. 12°, (Choice literature lib.) 60 c.; bds., 40 c. Educ. Pub.

Chadwick, Mary Alice, ed.
See Rowe, F: L:

Chadwick, W. E:, D.D.
Pastoral teaching of St. Paul: his ministerial ideals. '08(Mr7) O. $2.50. Scribner.
Social relationships in the light of Christianity; (Hulsean lectures for 1909-1910.) '10(F26) D. *$1.50 net. Longmans.
Social work. '09(F27) D. (Anglican Church handbooks.) *40 c. net. Longmans.

Chafer, Lewis Sperry.
Satan. '09(Ag14) 75 c. Gospel Pub.

Chaffee, Adeliza Brainerd.
Cupid and Psyche in sculpture and painting. '09, [1910.] (Ja) c. 70 p. 12°, $1.50. Chaffee.

Chaffee, W: H:
Chaffee genealogy. '09(My22) il. 8°, *$15 net. Grafton Press.

CHAFFEE FAMILY.
See Genealogies.

Chaffers, W:
Collector's hdbk. to keramics of the Renaissance and modern periods; selected from his larger work, entitled "The keramic gallery." '10(Mr26) il. D. *$1.50 net. Scribner.

Chaffin, W: Ladd.
Biographical hist. of Robert Randall and his descendants, 1608-1909. '09, [1910.] 20+247 p. 8°, *$5 net. Grafton Press.

Chafin, Eugene W.
Lincoln, the man of sorrow. '08(Ag29) c. D. 50 c. Lincoln Temperance.

Chailley-Bert, Jos.
Administrative problems of British India; tr. by Sir W: Meyer. '10(My7) map, 8°, $3.25. Macmillan.

Chaimovitch, I:
Tables for calculating sizes of steam pipes for low pressure heating. '08(D12) c. il. tabs., 12°, $2. Domestic Engineering.

CHAINS.
Goodenough, G: A., *and* Moore, L. E. Strength of chain links. (Add. Univ. for price.) Univ. of Ill.

Challenge of the city. Strong, J. 35 c.; 50 c.; *$1 net. Young People's Miss.

Challice, Rachel.
Secret hist. of the court of Spain, 1802-1906. '09(D11) il. 8°, *$4 special net. Appleton.

CHALLONER, *Bp.* Richard.
Burton, E. H. Life and time of Bishop Challoner. In 2 v. *$7 net. Longmans.

Chalmers, Alb. J., M.D.
See Castellani, Aldo, *M.D.*

Chalmers, Stephen.
Vanishing smuggler. '09(O23) c. col. il. D. $1.50. Clode.
When love calls men to arms; autobiography of love and adventure, truthfully set down by Rorie Maclean, Laird of Kilellen, in the XVII century, and here rewritten from the original mss. into clearer English. '10(Jl9) c. il. D. $1.50. Small.

Chalmers, W. P., comp. and ed.
Deutsche gedichte zum auswendiglernen. '09(Je19) D. (Modern lang. ser.) *40 c. net. Crowell.

Chaloner, J. A.
Scorpio: sonnets: [satires.] '07, [1908.] c. 142 p. 12°, cl., $1.50. Palmetto Press.

CHAMARRO LANGUAGE.
See Guam.

Chamberlain, Arth. Bensley.
George Romney. '10(Je4) 8°, (Scribner's classics in art ser.) $5. Scribner.

Chamberlain, Arth. H:
Conditions and tendencies of technical education in Germany. '08(Ap25) c. D. 50 c. Bardeen.
Standards in education, with some consideration of their relation to industrial training. '09(Ja9) c. D. $1. Am. Bk.

Chamberlain, C: Jos.
See Coulter, J: Merle.

CHAMBERLAIN, Daniel Henry.
Green, J. Personal recollections of Daniel Henry Chamberlain, once governor of South Carolina. 25 c. Davis & B.

Chamberlain, Esther and Lucia.
Coast of chance. '08(My9) c. †$1.50. Bobbs-M.

Chamberlain, Fk.
Hudson tercentenary; an historical retrospect regarding the object and quest of an all-water route from Europe to India; also Hudson's voyage to America in 1609. '09(S25) c. O. (Add. pubs. for price.) Lyon.

Chamberlain, Houston Stewart.
Foundations of the nineteenth century; from the German by J: Lees; with introd. by Lord Redesdale. 2 v. '10(D3) O. $10 net. Lane.

Chamberlain, Jacob, D.D.
Kingdom in India: [condition of the Church in India.] '08(Je13) c. 12°, *$1.50 net. Revell.

Chamberlain, Ja. Franklin.
How we travel: geographical reader. '08 (Jl11) il. 16°, *40 c. net. Macmillan.

Chamberlain, J: Aldrich.
Commercial law; instruction paper. pt. 1. '09(N20) c. forms, 8°, (American School of Correspondence pubs.) 50 c. Am. Sch. Corr.
Principles of business law covering the fundamental principles of law rel. to ordinary business transactions. '08(O) c. 16+430 p. O. $2.50. W. H. Anderson.
See also Am. Sch. of Correspondence.

Chamberlain, Jos. Scudder.
Feeding value of cereals, as calculated from chemical analyses. '09(My) 64 p. tabs., 8°, (U. S., Dept. of Agriculture; Bureau of Chemistry, bull.) pap., 10 c.

Chamberlain, Lucia.
Other side of the door. '09(My8) c. il. D. †$1.50. Bobbs-M.
Son of the wind. '10(N12) c. il. D. $1.50. Bobbs-M.
See also Chamberlain, Esther.

Chamberlain, Mellen.
Documentary history of Chelsea, incl. the Boston precincts of Winnisimmet, Rumney Marsh, and Pullen Point, 1624-1824; coll. and arr., with notes, by Mellen Chamberlain. '08(Ag22) 2 v., il. pors. maps, 8°, $5. Mass. Hist. Soc.

Chamberlain bibliographies. O. Dodd. —Livingston. Bibliog. of the first editions in book form of the writings of Henry Wadsworth Longfellow. *$3 net; *$10 net.

CHAMBERLAIN FAMILY.
Fretz, A. J. Genealogical record of the descendants of Benjamin Chamberlain of Sussex Co., N. J. $1.25; pap., 75 c. A. J. Fretz.
Harding, W: J. Ancestry in the line of her fathers of Adelia Chamberlain Harding, daughter of Rev. Hiram Chamberlain, and Anna Adelia Griswold. $1. E. Putnam.

Chamberlayne, C: F., ed.
See Best, W. M.

Chamberlin, Georgia Louise, and Kern, Mary Root.
Child religion in song and story. [v. 2,] Walks with Jesus in His home country. '09(N6) c. O. (Constructive Bible studies, elementary ser.) $1.38. Univ. of Chic.
Reminders of Walks with Jesus in His home country. '09(N13) il. D. pap., 45 c. Univ. of Chic.

Chamberlin, Jos. Edgar.
Ifs of history. '08(F8) c. D. $1. Altemus.

Chamberlin, Rollin T:
Gases in rocks. '08(D5) Q. (Contributions to cosmogony and the fundamental problems of geology.) pap., 50 c. Carnegie.
Notes on explosive mine gases and dusts, with special reference to explosions in the Monongah, Darr, and Naomi coal mines. '09(O) 67 p. diagr., 8°, (U. S. Dept. of the Interior, U. S. Geological Survey bull.) pap., 10 c.

Chamberlin, T: Chrowder, and Salisbury, Rollin D.
College text-book of geology. '09(O30) c. il. maps, figs. D. (American science ser., advanced course.) **$3.50 net. Holt.

—, Moulton, Forest Ray, Slichter, C: Sumner, and others.
Tidal and other problems. '09(Ap24) figs. fold. chart, Q. (Contributions to cosmogony and the fundamental problems of geology.) pap., $1.50. Carnegie.

Chambers, A. M.
Constitutional history of England. '09 (O2) *$1.40 net. Macmillan.

Chambers, Rev. Arth.
Problems of the spiritual. '08(Ag1) c. 12°, **$1 net. Jacobs.

Chambers, C: Haddon.
Sir Anthony; comedy of the outskirts in three acts. '09, [1910.] (Je) c. 5-118 p. 12°, 50 c. S: French.

Chambers, G: F:
Halley's comet: with brief notes on comets in general. '10(Ag27) il. O. pap., 25 c. Oxford Univ.
Story of the comets, simply told for general readers. '09(N13); 2d ed. '10(O1) il. O. ea., $2. Oxford Univ.

Chambers, J:
Autobiography; ed. by J: Carl Parish. '08 (D5) c. front. pors. *$4 net. State Hist., Ia.

CHAMBERS, John.
Parish, J: C. John Chambers. $2. State Hist., Ia.

Chambers, Jos. Lenoir.
The breed and the pasture. '10(F) c. 125 p. 12°, $1. Stone & B.

Chambers, Julius.
Mississippi River and its wonderful valley; twenty-seven hundred and seventy-five miles from source to sea. '10(O1) il. maps, O. (American waterways ser.) $3.50 net, boxed. Putnam.
On a margin: a novel. '08(My9) c. 12°, $1.50. M. Kennerley.

Chambers, Rob. W:
Ailsa Paige; a novel. '10(S10) c. il. D. $1.50. Appleton.
Danger mark. '09(O9) c. il. D. **$1.50 net. Appleton.
Firing line. '08(Ag22) c. il. D. †$1.50. Appleton.
Green mouse. '10(Ap23) c. col. il. D. $1.50. Appleton.
Hide and seek in Forestland. '09(D11) c. il. 12°, **40 c. net. Appleton.
Some ladies in haste. '08(Ap25) il. D. †$1.50. Appleton.
Special messenger. '09(Ap3) c. il. D. †$1.50. Appleton.

Chambless, Edg.
Roadtown. '10(O8) c. D. $1.25 net; with cover picture hand colored, $1.35 net. Roadtown.

Chambon, Rev. Celestin M.
In and around the old St. Louis Cathedral of New Orleans. '08(D) c. 181 p. il. pors. 12°, 50 c. C. M. Chambon.

Chamisso, Adelbert von.
Shadowless man (Peter Schlemihl); tr. by Sir J: Bowring. '10(D31) il. (col. front.) 8°, $1 net. Warne.

Champagnat, Jos. Benoit Marcellin.
Qualities of a good superior; comp. chiefly from the instructions of the Venerable Father Champagnat, founder of the Little Brothers of Mary; ed. by Rev. Ferreol Girardley. '08, [1909.] (Mr) 17+295 p. 8°, *$1.25 net. Herder.

Champion, Dorothy Bevill.
Everybody's cat book. '10(F19) c. il. 8°, $2. D. B. Champion.

"Champion, Mrs. H."
See Champion, Sarah Eliz. Booth.

Champion, J: B.
The living atonement. '10(Ag20) c. O. $1.25. Griffith.

Champion, Sarah Eliz. Booth, ["Mrs. H. Champion."]
Our flag; its history and changes from 1607 to 1910. 4th ed. '10(D3) c. col. il. obl. 24°, $1. Tuttle, M. & T.

Champion spelling book. Hicks, W. E. 25 c.; in 2 pts., ea., 18 c. Am. Bk.
Champion text-book on embalming. Myers, E. $5; $5.50; $6. Champion Chemical.
Champlain. Harper, J: M. *$1.75 net. Lane.

CHAMPLAIN, LAKE.
See **Lake Champlain.**

CHAMPLAIN VALLEY, N. Y.
Tuttle, M. J. B., *comp and ed.* Three centuries in Champlain valley. $1.50 net. D. A. R. Saranac Chap.

Champlin, J: Denison.
Young folks' cyclopædia of persons and places. 5th ed., rev. '09(Je19) c. il. 8°, **$3 net. Holt.

Champney, Mrs. Eliz. Williams.
Romance of Imperial Rome. '10(D3) c. il. fold. plan, O. $3.50, boxed. Putnam.
Romance of Roman villas: (the Renaissance.) '08(S12) c. il. O. **$3.50 net, boxed. Putnam.

Champneys, Arth. C.
Irish ecclesiastical architecture. '10(D24) il. 8°, $7.50 net. Macmillan.

Champol, F.
For my name's sake; tr. fr. the French of Champol's "Soeur Alexandrine." '08 (Ag8) il. 8°, $1.10. Herder.

Chance, Mrs. Burton.
See Chance, Maria Scott Beale.

Chance, Maria Scott Beale, [**Mrs. Burton Chance.**]
Care of the child. '09(N13) c. D. front. (Family books.) *$1 net. Penn Pub. Co.
Mother and daughter; book of ideals for girls. '10(O29) c. S. $1 net. Century Co.

Chance, Fk. Leroy.
Bride and the pennant; with preface by C: A. Comisky. '10(My21) il. por. D. 60 c.; pap., 25 c. Laird.

Chancellor, Edn. Beresford.
Lives of the British architects from William of Wykeham to Sir William Chambers. '10(Je4) il. pors. plans, 12°, $2 net. Scribner.
Private palaces of London—past and present. '09(O9) 4°, *$5 net. Lippincott.
Wanderings in London—Piccadilly, Mayfair and Pall Mall. '09(O23) il. in col. *75 c. net. Pott.

Chancellor, Mrs. Louise Isabel Beecher.
Players o' London: tale of the Elizabethan smart set. '09(N6) c. O. *$1.75 net, boxed. B. W. Dodge.
Transitus in lucem, and other verses in memory of or by Louise Beecher Chancellor; [by W: Estabrook Chancellor.] '10(Mr12) c. por. O. pap., 60 c. Fairfield.

Chancellor, W: Estabrook.
Class teaching and management. '10(O15) c. il. D. $1. Harper.
Elem. school mathematics by grades: Chancellor arithmetic, bk. 6, rev. and adapt. to grades 6A and 6B in the N. Y. City schools. '08(O24) c. 12°, (Globe ser.) *28 c. net. Globe Sch. Bk.
Our city schools; their direction and management. '08(D) 338 p. 12°, *$1.25 net. Heath.

—, and others.
Graded spelling lists. '10(D31) 12°, 16 c. net. Macmillan.

CHANCELLORS.
See England.

CHANCELLORSVILLE (Campaign of).
Bigelow, J:, *jr.* Campaign of Chancellorsville: strategic and tactical study. $10 net. Yale Univ.

CHANCERY.
Allen, W: A. Unclaimed millions in England; book cont. much of value and interest to persons interested in chancery cases or lost estates. $1. W. A. Allen.
Stace, F. A. Chancery forms and precedents. (Add. pubs. for price.) Drake Law Bk.
See also Equity.

Chandler, Alfr. Dupont.
Local self government, elective town meetings for large towns; with a general legislative bill therefor, and the recent charter of the city of Newport, R. I., based thereon. '08(Je.) 5-68 p. 4°, (privately pr.) A. D. Chandler.

Chandler, F. Alex., [**"F. Alexander."**]
Art crafting in metal for amateurs. '09 (Ap24) il. D. $1.50. Fort Hill.

Chandler, F. R., ed.
Assessors' land valuations, city of Chicago, from the quadrennial assessment of 1907; with systems of valuing real estate, tables showing increase of population and of values; with map of Chicago. '08(Je) c. 3+370 p. il. 4°, $5. Donnelley.

Chandler, G:
Textbook of civics for the state of Washington. '10(Je25) c. il. D. $1. Am. Bk.

Chandler, Izora Cecilia.
Little comrade.. '10(D17) c. il. D. $1.25 net. Berger.

CHANDLER, John.
Chase, C: A: John Chandler of Worcester, his will. 50 c. Worcester Soc. Antiquity.

Chandler, Julian Alvin Carroll.
See Riley, Franklin Lafayette.

Chandler, Wa. M.
Trial of Jesus, from a lawyer's standpoint. v. 1, The Hebrew trial; v. 2, The Roman trial. '08(D5) c. il. O. ¾ leath., *$5 net, boxed. Empire Pub.

Chandler, W: H:, ed.
New complete condensed encyclopedia. New ed. '09(Jl) c. 8+1703 p. il. maps, 4°, $3.75; leath., $5. Collier.

Chaney's stratagem. Pinnix, *Mrs.* H. C. $1.50. C. M. Clark.

CHANGE.
See Philosophy.

Change gear devices. Perrigo, C: O. E. $1. Henley.
Changes in the theory and tactics of the (German) social-democracy. Kampffmeyer, P. 50 c. Kerr.
Changing China. Cecil, *Lord* R. W: E. G.- $3 special net. Appleton.
Changing conceptions in education. Cubberley, E. P. **35 c. net. Houghton M.
Changing values of English speech. Bell, R. H. $1.25. Hinds.
Changing voices. Brodie, R. D. $1. Badger.

CHANNEL ISLANDS, Cal.
Holder, C: F: Channel Islands of California. $2 net. McClurg.

Channing, E:
Elements of United States hist.; [written] in consultation with Susan J. Ginn. '10 (Jl30) c. il. maps, D. 90 c. net. Macmillan.

Channing, E:—*Continued.*
History of the United States. In 8 v. v. 2, A century of colonial history, 1660-1760. '08(O3) maps, 8°, *$2.50 net. Macmillan.
Short hist. of the United States; rev. in consultation with Susan J. Ginn. '09 (S18) il. 12°, *$1 net. Macmillan.

—, and Lansing, Marion Florence.
Story of the Great Lakes. '09(Ap10) c. il. maps, D. **$1.50 net. Macmillan.

Channon, Fk. Ernest.
American boy at Henley. '10(N5) c. D. (Henley schoolboy ser.) $1.50. Little, B. & Co.

Chansons choisies. Béranger, P. J. de. $1.15. Oxford Univ.

Chantecler. *See* Rostand, E.

Chanter, J: F:
Life and times of Martin Blake, B.D., (1593-1673;) vicar of Barnstable and prebendary of Exeter Cathedral; with some acct. of his conflicts with the Puritan lecturers and persecutions. '10(Mr19) il. O. *$3.50 net. Lane.

CHANTS.
See Church music.

Chapel in every home. Wilson, J. R. (Priv. pr.) J. R. Wilson.

Chapel talks. Knowles, D. C. *$1 net. Eaton & M.

CHAPELS.
See Church architecture.

CHAPIN, Calvin, *D.D.*
Parker, E. P. Appreciation of Calvin Chapin. (Priv. pr.) G. W. Chapin.

Chapin, C: Value.
Sources and modes of infection. '10(O) 9+399 p. 8°, $3 net. Wiley.

Chapin, Fanny.
See Johnston, Bertha.

Chapin, Frederic.
Toodles of Treasure Town and her snow man. '08(O24) c. il. O. $1.50. Saalfield.

Chapin, Harry Lorenzo, M.D.
Adoption, and other sketches, poems and plays. '09(N) c. 196 p. por. D. $1.25. H. L. Chapin.

Chapin, H: Dwight.
Theory and practice of infant feeding; with notes on development. 3d rev. ed. '09 (Mr6) il. 8°, *$2.25 net. Wood.

—, and Pisek, Godfrey Roger.
Diseases of infants and children. '09(S) c. 628 p. il. in col. 8°, *$4.50 net. Wood.

Chapin, Howard Millar.
Life of Deacon Samuel Chapin of Springfield. '08(D19) il. facsims., O. (Chapin Family Association pubs.) pap. (Add. pubs. for price.) G. W. Chapin.

Chapin, Louella.
Round about Chicago. '08(F1) c. il. 8°, *$1.50 net. Unity.

Chapin, Rob. Coit.
Standard of living among workingmen's families in New York City. '09(Ap3) c. figs. O. (Russell Sage Foundation pubs.) $2. Charities Pub.

CHAPIN, Samuel.
Chapin, H. M. Life of Deacon Samuel Chapin of Springfield. (Add. pubs. for price.) G. W. Chapin.

Chapin Family Association pubs. il. 8°. (Priv. pr.) G. W. Chapin.
—Chapin. Life of Deacon Samuel Chapin.
—Parker. Appreciation of Calvin Chapin, D.D.

Chapman, A. B. Wallis-.
See Wallis-Chapman, A. B.

Chapman, A. E.
See Archer, R: Lawrence.

Chapman, Abel.
On safari: big game hunting in British East Africa; with studies in bird life. '08(N14) il. maps, O. *$4.50 net. Longmans.

Chapman, Allen.
Business boy. '08(D5) c. il. 12°, (Boys of business ser.) 60 c. Cupples & L.
Darewell chums on a cruise; or, Fenn Masterson's odd discovery. '09(D18) c. il. 12°, (Darewell chums ser.) 60 c. Cupples & L.
Darewell chums; or, the heroes of the school. '08(D5) c. il. 12°, (Darewell chums ser.) 60 c. Cupples & L.
Darewell chums in the city. '08(D5) c. il. 12°, (Darewell chums ser.) 60 c. Cupples & L.
Darewell chums in the woods. '08(D5) c. il. 12°, (Darewell chums ser.) 60 c. Cupples & L.
Ralph on the engine; or, the young fireman of the limited mail. '09(S) c. 4+250 p. il. 12°, (Railroad ser.) 60 c. Grosset.

Chapman, Annie Beatrice Wallis-.
See Wallis-Chapman, Annie Beatrice.

Chapman, C: Hiram.
Story of Oregon and its people. '09(N13) c. il. maps, pors. D. 60 c. O. P. Barnes.
Law of advertising and sales; and related general business law; with which is combined Advertising and sales that develop good will. In 2 v. '09(N6) c. il. O. bds., $10, boxed. C. Chapman.

Chapman, E: Mortimer.
English literature in account with religion, 1800-1900. '10(Mr26) c. O. **$2 net. Houghton M.

Chapman, Ervin S., D.D.
Particeps criminis; story of the California rabbit drive. '10(N12) c. 12°, 75 c. net. Revell.

Chapman, Fs., comp.
See Pennsylvania. Mechanics' liens.

Chapman, Fk. Michler.
Camps and cruises of an ornithologist. '08 (D12) c. il. O. **$3 net, boxed. Appleton.

Chapman, F: E., and Whiting, C: E., comps. and eds.
Apollo song book for male voices. '10 (Je18) c. O. $1. Ginn.

Chapman, G:
Tragedies; ed., with notes and introd., by T: Marc Parrot. '10(D10) 12°, $2 net. Dutton.
See also Marlowe, Christopher.

Chapman, G: E., ed.
See Illinois cases.

CHAPMAN, Henry Cadwalader.
Nolan, E: J. Biography of Dr. Henry Cadwalader Chapman. **Acad. Nat. Sci. Phil.**

Chapman, J. Wilbur, D.D.
Another mile, and other addresses. '08 (Ap18) c. 12°, *75 c. net; pap., *25 c. net. Revell.

Chapman, J: H.
Notes on the early history of the Vulgate Gospels. '08(N21) O. $5.25. Oxford Univ.

Chapman, J: Jay.
Causes and consequences. New ed. '09 (Je19) 12°, $1.25. Moffat.
Emerson, and other essays. New and rev. ed. '09(Jl17) c. D. **$1.25 net. Moffat.
Four plays for children. '08(Je27) c. D. **$1 net. Moffat.
Maid's forgiveness: a play. '08(D5) c. D. **75 c. net. Moffat.
Practical agitation. New ed. '09(Je19) 12°, $1.25. Moffat.
Sausage from Bologna: a comedy. '09 (Jl3) c. D. **75 c. net. Moffat.

Chapman, Mary Wallis-.
See Wallis-Chapman, M.—Wallis-Chapman, Annie Beatrice.

Chapman, Sydney J:
Work and wages; in continuation of Lord Brassey's "Work and wages," and "Foreign work and English wages." pt. 2, Wages and employment; with an introd. by Lord Brassey. '08(Mr7) O. $4. Longmans.

Chapman, Wa.
See Parkinson, Ethel.

Chapple, Jos. Mitchell.
Happy habit. '08(Je6) c. D. $1.50. Chapple Pub.

Chapters in rural progress. Butterfield, K. L. *$1 net. Univ. of Chic.
Chapters of opera. Krehbiel, H: E: **$3.50 net. Holt.
Chapters on municipal administration and accounting. Cleveland, F: A. **$2 net. Longmans.
Chapters on Spanish literature. Fitzmaurice-Kelly, J. $1.75. Hispanic Soc.

CHARACTER.
Buck, J. D. Constructive psychology or, the building of character by personal effort. $1. Indo-Am. Bk.
Carmack, E: W. Character; or the making of the man. $1. McQuiddy.
Carnegie, W: H. Churchmanship and character. *$1.25. Dutton.
Clark, H: W: Studies in the making of character. 75 c. net. Revell.
Doyle, J: World's great character builder and practical thoughts for every day living. 50 c. J: Doyle.
George, M. M. Character building. In 2 v. ea., $1.25. Flanagan.
Hubbard, E. Divine in man. 10 c. Roycrofters.
Hull, E. R. Formation of character. 15 c. net. Herder.
Kellogg, *Mrs.* E. E. Studies in character building. $1. Modern Medicine.
Kenyon-Warner, *Mrs.* E. E. Character building readers. 8 v. 1st reader, pts. 1 and 2, ea., 25 c.; 35 c.; 2d reader, pt. 1, 30 c.; pt. 2, 35 c.; 3d and 4th years, ea., 45 c.; 5th, 6th and 7th years, ea., 50 c. Hinds.

CHARACTER.—*Continued.*
Kirtley, J. S:, *ed.* Half-hour talks on character building by self-made men and women. $2. Hamming.
Kleiser, G. How to develop self-confidence in speech and manner. $1.25 net. Funk.
Lindsay, A. A. Mind the builder: [character building.] $1. Lindsay Pub. Co.
Melegari, D. Makers of sorrow and makers of joy. $1.25 net. Funk.
Mitchell, J. C. Character: some talks to young men. **75 c. net. Jacobs.
Rawley, J. P. Character reading dict. gleaned from the books of all ages. $1. J. P. Rawley.
Segno, A. V. Cours scientifique de l'analyse du caractère. $5.75. Chirological Coll.
Sisson, E: O. Essentials of character. $1 net. Macmillan.
White, J. T. Character lessons in American biography. 50 c. Character Development.
Wiggins, *Mrs.* L. K Know thy neighbor; or, character reading. $1.25. J. L. Nichols.
See also **Christian life;—Conduct of life;—Ethics;—Handwriting;—Phrenology.**

Character book. Adams, J. L. 75 c.; $1.25. Barse & H.
Character delineation and inspiration for those born under the sign of Capricorn. Towne, *Mrs.* E. J., *comp.* 75 c. E. J. Towne. E. J. Towne.
Character of Jesus. Jefferson, C: E: **$1.50 net. Crowell.
Characteres. *See* Theophrastus.
Characteristic passages from the hundred best English prose writers. Gowans, A. L., *comp.* 35 c. Crowell.
Characteristics and the religion of modern socialism. Ming, J: J. $1.50. Benziger.
Characteristics of old furniture styles in England. Benn, H. P. *$1 net. Scribner.
Characteristics of the inland-ice of the Arctic regions. $2. Philosophical.
Characteristics of the Southern negro. Randle, E. H. $1 net. Neale.
Characters and events of Roman history from Cæsar to Nero. Ferrero, G. **$2.50 net Putnam.
Characters and passages from note-books. Butler, S: *$1.50 net. Putnam.
Characters of Shakespeare's plays. *See* Hazlitt, W:
Characters of Theophrastus. Jebb, *Sir* R: C. *$2.25 net. Macmillan.

CHARADES.
Bellamy, W: More charades. **$1 net. Houghton M.
Forman, E. S. Guess work: 101 charades. $1. Badger.
Harnwell, *Mrs.* A. J. W. Locks to pick. $1. Badger.
Hosmer, S. H. C. Folded meanings: a book of charades. $1. Badger.
Sahler, F. S. Captain Kidd and other charades. $1. Stokes.
See also **Puzzles.**

Chardenal, C. A.
Complete French course. New ed., rev. and rewritten by Maro S. Brooks. '08 (Mr14) c. 12°, $1. Allyn & B.

CHARDIN, Jean Baptiste Simeon.
Konody, P. G. Chardin. *65 c. net; *$1.50 net. Stokes.
Chariot of fire. Phelps, *Mrs.* E. S. 50 c. net. Harper.
Chariot race. *See* Wallace, Lew.
Chariots of the Lord. Hocking, J. $1.50. Eaton & M.
CHARITIES.
Conyngton, M. How to help. $1.50. Macmillan.
Kaneko, J. C. Little sister of the poor. 25 c. Progressive Woman.
Loch, C: S. Charity and social life. $2 net. Macmillan.
New York [City] charities directory, 1909. $1. Charity Organ.
Warner, A. G. American charities. **$2 net. Crowell.
See also Christian work;—Education;—Jews;—Milk.
Charity of Christ. Schuyler, H: C. 50 c. net. P: Reilly.
CHARLATANS.
See Quacks and quackery.
CHARLEMAGNE.
Schmidt, F. Charlemagne. 50 c. net. McClurg.
CHARLES II., *King of England.*
Crawfurd, R. Last days of Charles II. $1.75. Oxford Univ.
See also Catherine of Braganza.
CHARLES V. *of Spain.*
Haggard, A. C: P. Two great rivals (François I. and Charles V.) and the women who influenced them. $4 special net Appleton.
CHARLES IX. *of Sweden.*
Mérimée, P. La chronique du regne de Charles IX. $1. Oxford Univ.
CHARLES XII., *King of Sweden.*
Voltaire, F. M. A. de. Life of Charles XII. *35 c. net; *70 c. net. Dutton.
CHARLES, *Archduke of Austria.*
Petre, F. L. Napoleon and the Archduke Charles: hist. of the Franco-Austrian campaign. *$4 net. Lane.
CHARLES *the Bold, Duke of Burgundy.*
Putnam, R. Charles the Bold, last Duke of Burgundy. **$1.35 net; **$1.60 net. Putnam.
Charles, Frances.
In the country God forgot. '08(My.) c. 12°, (Popular ed. of recent fiction.) †75 c. Little, B. & Co.
Siege of youth. '08(My.) c. 12°, (Popular ed. of recent fiction.) †75 c. Little, B. & Co.
Charles, R. H., D.D., ed.
Testaments of the twelve patriarchs; tr. from the editor's Greek text and ed. with introd., notes and indices. '08(Ap11) 8°, *$5.25 net. Macmillan.
Charles, Vera Katharine.
See Patterson, *Mrs.* Flora Wambaugh.
Charles di Tocca. Rice, C. Y. (Add. pubs. for price.) Doubleday, P.
CHARLESTON, S. C.
Leiding, H. K. "Street cries of an old Southern city." 25 c. H. K. Leiding.
See also St. Michael's Church.
Charlewood, Mrs. E. P., comp.
See Chesney, E., *comp.*

CHARLOTTESVILLE, Va.
See University of Virginia.
Charlton, Rev. Emanuel C.
Puritan captain. '08(S5) c. D. $1. Chr. Pub.
Charlton, Randal.
Virgin widow. '08(Mr28) c. D. †$1.50. G: W. Dillingham.
Charm of gardens. Cathrop, D. C. $2.50 net. Macmillan.
Charm of the English village. Ditchfield, P: H. *$3 net. Scribner.
Charm of the road. Hissey, J. J: $3 net. Macmillan.
Charming humbug. Clark, I. *$1.20 net. Dutton.
Charms of the Bible. Young, J. B. $1 net. Eaton & M.
Charms of the old Book. Huntington, G: *90 c. net. Am. S. S.
Charnock, Singleton.
Injunctions in labor disputes and the remedy. [1910.] c. (Je) 20 p. por. 8°, 10 c. S. Charnock.
Chart of the law of automobiles. Hamilton, C: H. $1. C: H. Hamilton.
Charter of liberties. Penn, W: 50 c. Henkels.
Charters, Werrett Wallace.
Methods of teaching, developed from a functional standpoint. '09(D18) c. 12°, $1.10. Row, P. & Co.
Chartier, E: Morris.
Dictation to reporting shorthand. '08(S) c. 208 p. 12°, $1.50. E: M. Chartier.
Chartres, Anita Vivanti, [Mrs. J: Chartres.]
The devourers. '10(Je18) c. D. $1.25. Putnam.
Chartres, Mrs. J:
See Chartres, Anita Vivanti.
Chase, Annie.
Plant babies and their cradles; for first year pupils. '09(Ag21) c. il. 12°, (Field and forest ser.) 40 c. Educ. Pub.
Chase, C: A:
John Chandler of Worcester, his will. '07, [1908.] (Je.) 15 p. O. pap., 50 c. Worcester Soc. Antiquity.
Chase, C: W.
See Devens, R: Miller.
Chase, Eliza Brown.
Transcontinental sketches; gleaned on tours in northeastern and middle Canada and the Pacific states. '10(Ja1) c. il. D. $1.50. Winston.
Chase, Ellen.
Beginnings of the American Revolution. 3 v. '10(D31) il. O. $7.50 net; ed. de luxe, bds., $15 net. Baker & T.
Chase, Fannie Dickerson.
Speaker's manual of pronunciation. '08 (D19) c. T. 25 c. Review and Herald.
Chase, Fessenden N.
Government employ; exhaustive information concerning applications for positions in the government service, incl. sample examination questions, marking of papers, appointments and salaries. '09(O16) c. por. O. pap., 15 c. F. N. Chase.
Punctuation and paragraphing; with practical word lists. '09(O16) c. por. O. pap., 15 c. F. N. Chase.

Chase, Fessenden N.—*Continued.*
Stenographer and employer; daily desk reference for stenographers, printers, lawyers, and employers. '09(N) c. 85 p. il. O. pap., $1. F. N. Chase.
Stenographers' guide for daily desk reference. '09(O16) c. por. O. pap., 15 c. F. N. Chase.
Women stenographers; a little "risk" and roboreous but "pigs is pigs" and facts is facts. '09(O) c. 26 p. il. O. pap., 40 c. F. N. Chase.

Chase, Fk. Eug., comp.
Club and lodge-room entertainments. '08 (O) c. 159 p. il. 12°, 25 c. W. H. Baker.

Chase, F: H:, D.D.
Confirmation in the Apostolic Age. '09 (D25) 12°, *80 c. net. Macmillan.

Chase, G:, ed.
See New York [State.] Code of civil procedure.

Chase, Mrs. Jessie Anderson.
Daughter of the Revolution. '10(O29) c. il. D. $1. Badger.

Chase, Julian Clement.
Motor car operation. '10(Je4) c. il. 12°, $1. Motor.

Chase, Leon Wilson.
See Davidson, Jay Brownlee.

Chase, Leslie.
Rooseveltiana: [articles antagonistic to Mr. Roosevelt's policies reprinted from newspapers.] '09(Mr6) 12°, 50 c. Grafton Pr.

Chase, Mary Wood.
Natural laws in piano technic. '10(N19) c. il. O. (Music students lib.) $1.25. Ditson.

Chateau and country life in France. Waddington, *Mrs.* M. A. K. $2.50 net. Scribner.

Chateau (Le) de la vie. *See* **Laboulaye, Edouard R. L.**

Chateau d'Or. Holmes, *Mrs.* M. J. H. †$1. G: W. Dillingham.

Chateau in Brittany. Atkinson, M. J. $2.50 net; $5 net. Pott.

Chateau of Haar.
See **Haar, Chateau of.**

Chateaubriand, François René Auguste Vicomte de.
Stories by Chateaubriand. '09(Jl17) 12°, (World's story tellers ser.) *40 c. net. Dutton.

Chateaubriand, François René Auguste, *Vicomte* de.
Armstrong, E. K. Chateaubriand's America. $1. Grandgent.
Gribble, F. H: Chateaubriand and his court of women. *$3.75 net. Scribner.

Chatelaine of Vergi: a romance of the XIIIth century; tr. by Alice Kemp-Welch; French text from the edition Raynault; introd. by L. Brandin. '08(O17) il. 16°, (New mediæval lib.) pigskin, with clasps, *$2 net. Duffield.

Chater, Melville.
The eternal rose. '10(S17) c. D. $1 net. Revell.

Chatfield, Mary A.
Light on dark places at Panama, by An Isthmian stenographer. '08(My9) c. D. $1.50. B'way Pub.

Chatfield-Taylor, Hobart Chatfield.
See Taylor, Hobart Chatfield Chatfield-

Chatham, *Earl* of.
See **Pitt, William.**

Chatley, Herbert.
Force of the wind [in aeronautics.] '09 (Ap17) figs. D. (Griffin's scientific textbooks.) *$1.25 net. Lippincott.
How to design an aeroplane. '10(D) 90 p. il. 16°, (Van Nostrand science ser.) bds., 50 c. Van Nostrand.
How to use water power. '08(Ag1) il. 12°, *$1 net. Van Nostrand.
Stresses in masonry. '10(Ja1) il. 12°, *$1.25 net. Lippincott.

Chatrian, Alexandre.
See Erckmann, Emile.—Wilson-Green, A.

Chats about astronomy. Hollis, H. P. *$1.25 net. Lippincott.

Chats on autographs. Broadley, A. M. $5. Stokes.

Chats on electricity. Broadbent, F. $1.25 net. Lippincott.

Chats on old earthenware. Hayden, A. *$2 net; *$5 net. Stokes.

Chats on old lace. Lowes, *Mrs.* E. L. $2. Stokes.

Chats on old miniatures. Foster, J. J. $2. Stokes.

Chats on old silver. Lowes, *Mrs.* E. L. *$2 net; *$5 net. Stokes.

Chats on photography. Wallington, W. $1.25 net. Lippincott.

Chats on Oriental china. Blacker, J. F. *$2 net; *$5 net. Stokes.

Chats on violoncellos. Racster, O. *$1.25 net. Lippincott.

"Chats" ser. il. O. $2 net; ¾ levant, $5 net. Stokes.
—Blacker. Chats on Oriental china.
—Broadley. Chats on autographs.
—Foster. Chats on old miniatures.
—Hayden. Chats on old earthenware.
—Lowes. Chats on old lace and needlework.
—Chats on old silver.

Chattel loans.
See Loans.

Chatterbox book of birds; ed. by Anna Robinson. [1910.] (F) c. '09. 205 p. il. 4°, $1. Estes.

Chatterbox book of cats and dogs; ed. by Anna Robinson. [1910.] (F) c. '09. 207 p. il. 4°, $1. Estes.

Chatterbox book of pictures. '09, [1910.] (F) 4°, bds., $1. Estes.

Chatterbox book of wild animals. '09, [1910.] (F) 4°, bds., $1. Estes.

Chatterbox for 1908; founded by J. Erskine Clarke. '08(O24); for 1909. '09(O2); for 1910. '10(S10) c. il. O. ea., $1.75; bds., $1.25. Estes.

Chatterbox (New) picture book ser. 2 v. '10(D) il. 8°, ea., $1. Estes.
Contents: Chatterbox book of soldiers and sailors; Chatterbox book of horses.

Chatterton. *See* Vigny, Alfred Victor, *Comte* de.

Chatterton, E: Keble.
Romance of the ship. '10(D31) 12°, (Romance ser.) $1.50 net. Lippincott.
Sailing ships and their story. '10(Ja1) 8°, *$3.75 net. Lippincott.
Steamships and their story. '10(O1) il. col. front. 8°, $5 net. Cassell.

CHATTERTON, Thomas.
Ingram, J: H. True Chatterton. $3 net. Scribner.
Russell, C: E: Thomas Chatterton, the marvelous boy. **$2.50 net. Moffat.

Chaucer, Geoffrey.
Canterbury tales. '08(O17) 16°, (Best books ser.) leath., *$1 net. Dutton.
Canterbury tales; ed. by Principal Burrell: [18 tales.] '08(Mr7) 16°, (Everyman's lib.) *35 c. net; leath., *70 c. net. Dutton.
Canterbury tales for the modern reader; prep. and ed. by Arth. Burrell. '10 (Ap23) il. 16°, (Everyman's lib.) 35 c. net; leath., 70 c. net. Dutton.
Canterbury tales: the nun's priest's tale; ed., with introd. and notes, by Alfr. W. Pollard. '08(Ja11) 16°, (Eng. classics.) *40 c. net. Macmillan.
Clerkes tale, and The squieres tale; ed. by Lilian Winstanley. '08(D19) S. (Pitt Press ser.) *75 c. net. Putnam.
Prologue, and The knight's tale. '08(D19) S. (Pitt Press ser.) *75 c. net. Putnam.
Selections; ed., with an introd., notes and glossary, by Edn. A. Greenlaw. '08(F1) c. S. (Lake Eng. classics.) 40 c. Scott, F. & Co.
Story of Chaucer's Canterbury pilgrims; retold for children, by Katharine Lee Bates. '09(Ap3) c. il. 12°, (Canterbury classics.) 40 c. Rand, McN. & Co.

CHAUCER, Geoffrey.
Coulton, G. G. Chaucer and his England. *$3.50 net. Putnam.
Darton, F. J. H., *comp.* Pilgrim's tales from Tales of the Canterbury pilgrims. 60 c. Dodge.
Darton, F. J. H., *comp.* Tales of the Canterbury pilgrims. $1.50. Stokes.
Goddard, H. C. Chaucer's Legend of good women. (Add. author for price.) H. C. Goddard.
Hammond, E. P. Chaucer: a bibliographical manual. *$3 net. Macmillan.
Hinckley, H: B. Notes on Chaucer. $3. Nonotuck.
Tappan, E. M., *comp.* Chaucer story book. $1.50. Houghton M.

Chauffeur and the chaperone. Williamson, C: N. †$1.50. McClure.
Chauffeur chaff. Welsh, C:, *ed.* 50 c. Caldwell.
Chauffeur hdbk. Boyance, J. 50 c. Beaver Pr.
Chauffeur question and the answer. '09(Jl3) 4°, pap. (Add. pubs. for price.) N. Y. Sch. Automobile Eng.
Chautauqua home reading ser. 12°. Chautauqua Pr.
—Chautauqua Literary and Scientific Circle. Studies in European literature. $1.50.
—Smith, *ed.* Studies in Dickens. $1.25.
Chautauqua Literary and Scientific Circle. Studies in European literature. '08(N) c. 3-302 p. 12°, (Chautauqua home reading ser.) $1.50. Chautauqua Pr.

Chavers, Pearl W:
Conditions that confront the colored race. '08(D) c. 24 p. il. 8°. (Add. author for price.) P. W: Chavers.

Chaytor, Alfr. H:
Letters to a salmon fisher's sons. '10(Ag20) il. O. $3 net. Houghton M.

Chaytor, H. J.
First Spanish book. '10(Ap23) D. 80 c. Longmans.

Cheadle, Clarence McKee.
Care of mother and child; with an introd. by C: Edwin Ruth. '09(Ap) 20+354 p. 12°, $2; leath., $2.50. C. M. Cheadle.

Cheatham, Carrie Vandiver.
Beatrice Sumpter. '09(Ap3) c. il. D. $1.50. C. M. Clark.

Check, Rabbi Sabbath.
See Jews. Newly improved prayer book.

Check-figure (The). Neff, G: O. 60 c. G: O. Neff.
Checkerberry. Macdonald, L. S. $1.50. Cochrane.

CHECKERS.
Anderson, A. Game of draughts. $1. McKay.
Barker, A. Pocket hand-book of checkers. 60 c. net. Ball Pub. Co.
Call, W: T. Literature of checkers. $1.—Vocabulary of checkers. $2. C. M. Potterdon.
Hill, J. Synopsis of draughts openings. 50 c. Warne.
Lees, J. Complete guide to the game of draughts. 50 c Warne.
Richmond, J. L. Game of draughts. 50 c. Warne.
Stearns, L. M., *ed.* Draughts marvel and twentieth century checker compendium. $4. L. M. Stearns.

Checkley, Edn.
Natural method of physical training. New rev. ed. '09(S) 174 p. il. **$1.25 net. Baker & T.

Checkley, S:
Diary of the Rev. S: Checkley, 1735; ed. by H: Winchester Cunningham. '09 (N) 271-306 p. facsim. 8°. (Priv. pr.) H: W. Cunningham.

CHECKS.
See Banks and banking;—Negotiable instruments.

Cheek, Philip, comp.
Hist. of the Sauk County riflemen, known as Company "A," Sixth Wisconsin Veteran Volunteer Infantry, 1861-1865. '09, [1910.] (F) c. 220 p. pl., pors., 8°, $1.50. P. Cheek.

Cheer up. Raymond, C: F. 75 c.; $1.25. Dodge.
Cheer-up book. Brewster, E. G. 50 c. Rust-Craft.
Cheerful life ser. 16°. Dodge.
—Rutherford. Cheeriness. 75 c.; leath., $1.25.
—Look on the brighter side. 75 c.; leath., $1.25.
Cheerful smugglers. Butler, E. P. †$1. Century Co.

CHEERFULNESS.
Chapple, J. M. Happy habit. $1.50. Chapple Pub.
Desmond, H. J. Little uplifts. 40 c. H. J. Desmond.
Jordan, D: S. Philosophy of hope. *75 c. net. Am. Unitarian.
Loomis, C: B. Knack of it: essays in optimism. *75 c. net. Revell.

CHEERFULNESS.—*Continued.*
Raymond, C: F. Cheer up. $1.25. Dodge.
Robinson, S. C., *ed.* Royal messages of cheer and comfort. *$1 net; *$2 net. Treat.
Rutherford, W. R. Cheeriness.—Look on the brighter side. ea., 75 c.; $1.25. Dodge.
Cheeriness. Rutherford, W. R. 75 c.; $1.25. Dodge.
Cheery and the chum. Yates, K. M. 60 c. K. M. Yates.
CHEESE.
Decker, J: W. Cheese making. $1.75. Mendota.
Meyer, M. H. Treatise on commercial starters in butter and cheese making. gratis. M. H. Meyer.
Publow, C: A. Fancy cheese in America from the milk of cows, sheep and goats. 75 c. Am. Sheep.
Thom, C: Camembert cheese problems in the United States. (Add. Superintendent for price.) U. S., Supt. of Docs.
Van Slyke, L. L., *and* Publo, C: A Science and practice of cheesemaking. *$1.75 net. Judd.
Cheetham, F. H.
Louis Napoleon and the genesis of the Second Empire. '08(N21) il. pors. O. *$5 net. Lane.
Cheetham, S:, D.D.
Hist. of the Christian church since the Reformation. '08(F15) 12°, *$2.60 net. Macmillan.
Cheever, Mrs. Harriet A.
Animal stories for little folks. 8 v. '10 (N) il. 12°, ea., 50 c. Estes.
Contents: The rock frog; Lady Spider; Lord Dolphin; Mother Bunny; Doctor Robin; Madame Angora; Ted's little dear; The strange adventures of Bill Trill.
CHEIROGNOMY.
See Palmistry.
CHEIROMANCY.
See Palmistry.
Chekhov, Anton Pavlovich.
Cherry garden: a comedy; tr. from the original Russian by Max S. Mandell, with an introd. by the translator. '08(Jl4) facsim., O. 75 c.; pap., 40 c. Yale Courant.
CHELSEA, Mass.
See Boston.
Chemical analysis of iron. Blair, A. A. **$4 net. Lippincott.
Chemical and biological survey of the waters of Illinois. Bartow, E: gratis. Univ. of Ill.
Chemical basis of pharmacology. Francis, F. *$4 net. Longmans.
CHEMICAL DENUDATION.
See Chemistry.
Chemical determinative mineralogy. Erni, H: (Add. pubs. for price.) Baird.
CHEMICAL ENGINEERING.
See Engineering.
CHEMICAL GEOLOGY.
See Geology.
CHEMICAL PHYSIOLOGY.
See Physiology.
Chemical technology and analysis of oils, fats and waxes. 3 v. Lewkowitsch, J. I. *$15 net. Macmillan.

CHEMISTRY.
Abderhalden, E. Text-book of physiological chemistry. **$5 net. Wiley.
Allen, A. H: Commercial organic analysis. v. 1-4. ea., *$5 net. Blakiston.
Armstrong, E. F. Simple carbohydrates and the glucosides. *$1.20 net. Longmans.
Bailey, E. H: S., *and* Cady, H. P. Lab'y guide to the study of qualitative analysis, based upon the application of the theory of electrolytic dissociation and the law of mass action. $1.25. Blakiston.
Baker, T. T. Spectroscope: its uses in general analytical chemistry. *$1.75 net. Wood.
Bardwell, F. L., *and* Speer, E. B., *comps.* Lab'y experiments in inorganic chemistry. 75 c. F. L. Bardwell.
Bartlett, E. J. Calculations of the quantitative chemical laboratory with problems. 75 c. E. J. Bartlett.
Bartley, E. H. Text-book of medical and pharmaceutical chemistry. $3. Blakiston.
Baskerville, C: General inorganic chemistry. $1.50. Heath.
Baskerville, C:, *and* Curtis, R. W. Lab'y exercises to be used in conjunction with General inorganic chemistry. 40 c. Heath.
Baskerville, C:, *and* Curtman, L: J. Course in qualitative chemical analysis. $1.40 net. Macmillan.
Baskerville, C:, *and* Estabrooke, W: L. Progressive problems in general chemistry. 90 c. Heath.
Baxter, G. P., *and others.* Researches upon the atomic weights of cadmium, manganese, bromine, lead, arsenic, iodine, silver, chromium, and phosphorus. $2. Carnegie.
Biltz, H. Introd. to experimental chemistry. $1.25. Wiley.
Biltz, H. *and* W. Laboratory methods of inorganic chemistry. $3. Wiley.
Blanchard, A. A. Synthetic inorganic chemistry. $1 net. Wiley.
Browning, P. E. Introd. to the rarer elements. *$1.50 net. Wiley.
Cain, J: C. Chemistry of the diazo-compounds. *$3 net. Longmans.
Chesneau, G. Theoretical principles of the methods of analyt. chemistry based upon chemical reactions. $1.75 net. Macmillan.
Clarke, F. W. Preliminary study of chemical denudation. 5 c. Smith. Inst.
Clowes, F., *and* Coleman, I. B. Quantitative chemical analysis. *$3.50 net. Blakiston.
Coblentz, V. Manual of volumetric analysis. *$1.75 net. Blakiston.
Cummings, W: L. Modern formulary: text book of chemistry as applied to the manufacture of proprietary specialties. $2.50. W: L. Cummings.
Daggett, C. H. Theory of pharmaceutical chemistry. $2.75 net. Lea.
Dannerth, F: Methods of textile chemistry. $2. Wiley.

CHEMISTRY.—*Continued.*

Dictionary of chemical and metallurgical machinery, appliances and material manufactured or sold by advertisers in *Electro-Chemical and Metallurgical Industry.* 50 c. Electrochemical Pub.

Durkee, F. W: Experiments in general inorganic chemistry. 50 c. Tufts Coll.

Emery, F. B. Elementary chemistry. $1.50. Chemical.

Ewell, A. W. Text-book of physical chemistry. *$2.25 net. Blakiston.

Fenton, H: J: H. Outlines of chemistry. pt. 1. *$3 net. Putnam.

Fischer, E. Introd. to the preparation of organic compounds. $1.25 net. Van Nostrand.

Foulk, C: W: Introd. notes on quantitative chemical analysis. $2.50. Heer.

Friend, J. A. N. Theory of valency: [theories of chemical combination.] $1.60. Longmans.

Garrett, A. E. Periodic law. *$1.75 net. Appleton.

Getman, F: H. Laboratory exercises in physical chemistry. **$2 net. Wiley.

Gilman, A. F. Laboratory outline for determinations in quantitative chemical analysis. *90 c. net. Chemical.

Godfrey, H. Elem. chemistry. $1.10.—Lab'y manual to accompany Godfrey's "Elem. chemistry." 36 c. Longmans.

Gooch, F. A., *and* Browning, P. E. Outlines of qualitative chemical analysis. **$1.25 net. Wiley.

Gore, H. C: Apparatus for use in the determination of volatile acids in wines and vinegars. (Add. Superintendent for price.) U. S., Supt. of Docs.

Gorsline, E. E. Study of the Claisen condensation. 55 c. Johns Hopkins.

Greene, W: H. Lessons in chemistry. $1. Lippincott.

Hale, W: J. Calculations of general chemistry. $1. Van Nostrand.

Hammarsten, O. Text-book of physiological chemistry. $4. Wiley.

Hanson, E: K., *and* Dodgson, J: W. Intermediate course of laboratory work in chemistry. *$1.20 net. Longmans.

Hawk, P. B. Pract. physiological chemistry. $2.50. Blakiston.

Hinds, J: I. D. Qualitative chemical analysis from the standpoint of solubilities, ionization, and mass action. $2. Chemical.

Holland, J. W: Text-book of medical chemistry and toxicology. *$3 net. Saunders.

Holleman, A. F. Text-book of inorganic chemistry.—Text-book of organic chemistry. ea., $2.50. Wiley.

International library of technology. 11 v. (Chemistry lib.) ea., $5. Int. Text-Bk.

Jenks, T. Chemistry for young people. **$1.50 net. Stokes.

Jones, H. C. Introd. to physical chemistry. $1.60 net. Macmillan.

Jones, H. C., *and* Strong, W: W. Study of absorption spectra of solution of certain salts, as affected by chemical agents and by temperature. $5. Carnegie.

CHEMISTRY.—*Continued.*

Kahlenberg, L: Lab'y exercises in general chemistry. 90 c. L: Kahlenberg.

Kahlenberg, L: Outlines of chemistry. **$2.60 net. Macmillan.

Keane, C: A. Modern organic chemistry. *$1.50 net. Scribner.

Klaber, W: On certain 7-nitro-4 quinazolones. (Add. author for price.) W: Klaber.

Knecht, E., *and* Hibbert, E. New reduction methods in volumetric analysis. $1 net. Longmans.

Lassar-Cohn, —. Chemistry in daily life. *$1.75 net. Lippincott.

Lee, E. Text-book of experimental chemistry. *$1.50 net. Blakiston.

Levi, L: E., *and* Manuel, E. V. Tanners' and chemists' hdbk. $5. L: E. Levi.

Lewis, E. I. Inorganic chemistry. *$1.25 net. Putnam.

Long, J: H. Text-book of physiological chemistry. $2.50. Blakiston.

Lunge, G: General methods used in technical analysis. In 3 v. v. 1 in 2 pts. *$15 net.—Technical chemist's handbook. *$3.50 net. Van Nostrand.

McGregory, J. F. Manual of qualitative chemical analysis. $1. Ginn.

Mason, W: P. Notes on qualitative analysis. 80 c. Chemical.

Mathewson, C. H. First principles of chemical theory. $1. Wiley.

Matthews, J. M. Laboratory manual of dyeing and textile chemistry. $3.50. Wiley.

Meade, R: K. Chemist's pocket manual. $3. Chemical.

Meade, R: K. Design and equipment of small chemical laboratories. *$2 net. Chemical Engineer.

Mears, B. Osmotic pressure of cane sugar solutions at 15° centigrade. 40 c. Johns Hopkins.

Miller, E. H. Calculations of analyt. chemistry. $1.50 net. Macmillan.

Moore, F. J. Outlines of organic chemistry. $1.50 net. Wiley.

Morgan, J: L. R. Elements of physical chemistry. $3.—Physical chemistry for electrical engineers. **$1.50 net. Wiley.

Morse, H. V. Osmotic pressure of cane sugar solutions at 10°. 40 c. Johns Hopkins.

Mulliken, S: P. Method for the identification of pure organic compounds. v. 3. $5. Wiley.

Nagel, O. Mechanical appliances of the chemical and metallurgical industries. *$2

Nelson, J: M. Some compounds derived from the ethyl *p*-düminosuc-cinylosuccinate. (Add. author for price.) J: M. Nelson.

Nernst, W. Theoretical chemistry. *$4.50 net. Macmillan.

net. O. Nagel.

Newell, L. C. Course in inorganic chemistry, for colleges. *$2 net.—Descriptive chemistry. $1.20. Heath.

Olsen, J: C: Text-book of quantitative chemical analysis. $4. Van Nostrand.

CHEMISTRY.—*Continued.*

Ostwald, W. Fundamental principles of chemistry. $2.25. Longmans.

Ostwald, W. Principles of inorganic chemistry. *$6 net.—Scientific foundations of analytical chemistry. *$2 net. Macmillan.

Ostwald, W., *and* Morse, H. W. Elem. modern chemistry. $1. Ginn.

Peters, F. N. Key to Modern chemistry. 60 c. C: E. Merrill.

Philip, J. C. Physical chemistry. $2.10 net. Longmans.

Philip, J. C. Romance of modern chemistry. *$1.50 net. Lippincott.

Plimmer, R. H. A. Pract. physiological chemistry. $1.80 net. Longmans.

Pond, F. J. Notes on non-metals. $1.50. F. J. Pond.

Ramsay, *Sir* W: Essays, biographical and chemical. *$2.50 net. Dutton.

Ransom, J. H. Experimental general chemistry. 60 c. J. H. Ransom.

Redgrove, H. S. On the calculation of thermo-chemical constants. *$1.70 net. Longmans.

Remsen, I. College text-book of chemistry. $2.25.—Introd. study of chemistry. $1.25. Holt.

Richards, T. W:, *and* Willard, H. H. Determination of atomic weights; further investigation concerning the atomic weights of silver, lithium and chlorine; methods used in precise chemical investigation. Carnegie.

Rockwood, E. W: Introd. to chemical analysis. *$1.50 net. Blakiston.

Rogers, A. Laboratory guide of industrial chemistry. *$1.50 net. Van Nostrand.

Roscoe, *Sir* H: E., *and* Schorlemmer, C. Treatise on chemistry. In 2 v. v. 2. *$7.50 net. Macmillan.

Roth, W. A. Exercises in physical chemistry. *$2 net. Van Nostrand.

Schimpf, H: W: Manual of volumetric analysis for the use of pharmacists, sanitary and food chemists. $5. Wiley.

Seamon, W: H: Manual for assayers and chemists. $2.50 net. Wiley.

Segerblom, W. First year chemistry. $1.50.—Tables of properties of over fifteen hundred common inorganic substances. $3. Exeter Bk.

Segerblom, W. Laboratory manual of qualitative analysis. $1.25. Longmans.

Sellers, J. F. Elem. treatise on qualitative chemical analysis. $1. Ginn.

Simon, W: Manual of chemistry. *$3 net. Lea.

Smiles, S: Relations between chemical constitution and some physical properties. $4 net. Longmans.

Smith, A. General chemistry for colleges. **$2.15 net. Century Co.

Stanislaus, I. V. S., *and* Kimberly, C. H. Pharmaceutical chemistry. *$2.50 net. Blakiston.

Stillman, T: B. Engineering chemistry. $5. Chemical.

CHEMISTRY.—*Continued.*

Stewart, A. W. Recent advances in organic chemistry.—Recent advances in physical and inorganic chemistry. ea., *$2.50 net. Longmans.

Stoddard, J: T. Introd. to general chemistry. $1.60 net. Macmillan.

Stoddard, J: T. Quantitative experiments in general chemistry. $1. Longmans.

Strong, W: W. Ionization in closed vessels. 25 c. Johns Hopkins.

Sudborough, J: J., *and* James, T. C. Pract. organic chemistry. *$2 net. Van Nostrand.

Talbot, H. P. Introd. course of quantitative chemical analysis. *$1.50 net. Macmillan.

Thomsen, H. P. J. Thermo-chemistry. $2.50. Longmans.

Thorpe, *Sir* T: E: Hist. of chemistry. In 2 v. ea., **75 c. net. Putnam.

Tilden, *Sir* W: A: Chemistry. 50 c. net. Appleton.

Tilden, *Sir* W: A: The elements; speculations as to their nature. 75 c. net. Harper.

Tillman, S: E. Descriptive general chemistry. **$3 net. Wiley.

Tower, O. F. Quantitative chemical analysis of inorganic substances. *$1 net. Blakiston.

Treadwell, F: P. Analytical chemistry. v. 2. $4. Wiley.

United States. Chemistry Bureau; bulletins, circulars and food inspection decisions.; Agriculture Department, U. S. A.; for sale by the Superintendent of Documents. '09(O) 8°. U. S., Supt. of Docs.

United States. *Superintendent of Documents. Chemistry Bureau.* Bulletins, circulars, etc. gratis.

Van Nostrand's chemical annual. *$2.50 net. Van Nostrand.

Vulte, H. T., *and* Goodell, G: A. Lab'y notes in household chemistry. $1.25. Chemical.

Walker, P. H. Some technical methods of testing misc. supplies, incl. paints and paint materials, inks, lubricating oils, soaps, etc. U. S., Supt. of Docs.

Williams, R. P. Essentials of chemistry. $1.25. Ginn.

Young, S. Stoichiometry. $2. Longmans.

Zsigmondy, R. A. Colloids and the ultramicroscope. $3. Wiley.

See also Acetylene;—Agricultural chemistry;—Air;—Ammonia; —Aniline; — Assaying;—Bacteria;—Barley;—Beryllium; — Blowpipe;—Botany;—Carbon;—Coal;—Cookery;—Cyanide process;—Dairy; — Diagnosis; — Distillation; — Electro-chemistry;—Explosives;—Fertilizers; —Fermentation;—Fuel;—Gases; — Heat;—Hydrogen; —Iron; —Leather;—Machinery; — Malt;—Mathematics; —Medical chemistry;—Medicine;—Metals and metallurgy;—Microscope;—Mineral waters;—Mineralogy;—Nitrogen;—Oils and fats;—Paint;—Paper;—Pharmacy;—Photography; —Physics;—Physiology; — Poisons;—Proteids;—Radio-activity; — Radium; — Rocks; —Smelter wastes;—Spectrum;—Sulphur;—Sulphuric acid;—Tellurides;—Useful arts.

Chemistry for launderers. Townsend, C: F. $1. Nat. Laundry.

Chemistry of gas manufacture. Royle, H. M. $4.50. Henley.

Chemists' pocket manual. Meade, R: K. $3. Chemical.

Cheney, Bp. C: E:
The second Norman conquest of England. '07, [1908.] (Je.) c. 50 p. map, 12°, (Club papers.) pap. (Not for sale.) Chic. Lit. Club.

Cheney, J: Vance.
Time of roses. '08(N21) c. 24°, *75 c. net; Japan vellum, *$1.50 net. T: B. Mosher.
—, **comp. and ed.** Memorable American speeches. v. 1, The colonial period. '08 (O17) por. S. (Patriotic classics.) *$1.50 net, boxed. Reilly & B.

Cheney, Mrs. J: Vance.
What it is that heals. '08(F8) c. D. bds., $1. R. G. Cooke.

Chenoweth, Mrs. Caroline Van Dusen.
History of the Second Congregational church and society in Leicester, Mass. '08(Jl) c. 7+199 p. il. pors. 8°, $1.50. C. V. Chenoweth.

CHEROKEE INDIANS.
See Indians.

Cherry feasts for barbarous Fourths. Coolidge, A. C. 25 c. Hungerford-H.

Cherry garden. Chekhov, A. P. 40 c. Yale Courant.

Cherub Devine. *See* Ford, Sewell.

CHESAPEAKE BAY.
See Yachts and yachting.

Chesneau, Gabriel.
Theoretical principles of the methods of analyt. chemistry based upon chemical reactions; auth. tr. by Azariah T: Lincoln and D: Hobart Carnahan. '10 (Ap16) c. il. O. $1.75 net. Macmillan.

Chesney, E., [Mrs. E. P. Charlewood,] comp.
Life and the great forever; daily readings in prose and verse. '09(D25) S. *$1.50 net. Lane.

Chesney, Sir G:
The dilemma: a tale of the mutiny. New ed. '08(Jl18) D. $1.50. Abbatt.

CHESS.
Blackburne, S. S. Terms and themes of chess problems. *$1 net. Dutton.
Keidanz, H., *comp. and ed.* Rice gambit: [chess.] 17 c. Am. Chess
Mason, J. Art of chess.—Principles of chess in theory and practice. ea., $1.25. McKay.
Young, F. K. Chess generalship. v. 1. $1.75 net. Int. Pub. Co.

Chesson, W. H.
Cruikshank. '08(O10) 24°, (Popular lib. of art.) *75 c. net; leath., *$1 net. Dutton.

Chester, Chandler Bell.
Science of diamonds; self educational book on diamonds, the only one of its kind in the world. [1910.] (O) c. 7-56 p. il. 12°, 50 c. Chester & B.

Chester, Clarence L.
See Hall, Alfr. Bates.

Chester, Eliza, pseud.
See Paine, Harriet Eliza.

Chester, G: Randolph.
Art of short story writing. '10(F19) c. 8°, $3.50. Pub. Syndicate.
Cash intrigue. '09(O30) c. il. D. †$1.50. Bobbs-M.

Chester, G: Randolph.—*Continued.*
Early bird; business man's love story. '10 (Je4) c. il. D. $1.50. Bobbs-M.
Get-rich-quick Wallingford. '08(Ap25) c. il. D. †$1.50. Altemus.
Making of Bobby Burnit. '09(Je19) c. il. D. †$1.50. Bobbs-M.
Young Wallingford. '10(O22) c. il. D. $1.50. Bobbs-M.

Chester, Lillian Gimblin.
Taming a vaquero. '09(N) c. 87 p. 16°, $1. Whitaker & R.

Chester, Lord, pseud.
Great red dragon; or, the flaming devil of the Orient. '09(N) 148 p. 8°, 75 c.; pap., 35 c. Guiding Star.

CHESTER Co., Pa.
MacElree, W. W. Along the western Brandywine. $5. Hickman.

Chesterton, Gilbert Keith.
All things considered: [essays.] '08(O17) D. *$1.50 net. Lane.
Ball and the cross. '09(D11) c. D. †$1.50. Lane.
George Bernard Shaw. '09(O2) c. D. **$1.50 net. Lane.
Gilbert K. Chesterton: a criticism. [Anonymous.] '09(Ja16) por. D. *$1.50 net. Lane.
Man who was Thursday: a nightmare. '08 (Ap11) c. D. †$1.50. Dodd.
Orthodoxy. '08(N7) c. D. **$1.50 net. Lane.
Tremendous trifles. '09(D4) c. D. *$1.20 net. Dodd.
What's wrong with the world. '10(S24) c. O. $1.50. Dodd.

Chesterton, Rupert.
Phantom battleship. '10(D31) il. 12°, $1.50. Lippincott.

CHESTNUT TREE.
Metcalf, H. Immunity of the Japanese chestnut to the bark disease. 5 c. U. S., Supt. of Docs.
Weiss, H. F. Progress in chestnut pole preservation. 10 c. U. S., Supt. of Docs.

"Chet." Yates, K. M. $1.25. McClurg.

Chetwood, Edith, and Thompson, E: P.
Hearts atour; a novel. '10(S17) c. il. D. $1.50. Evening Post.

Chevalerie Vivien; facsimile phototypes of the Sancti Bertini manuscript of the Bibliothèque Municipale of Boulogne-sur-mer; with introd. and notes by Raymond Weeks. '10(Jl9) c. il. F. (Univ. of Mo. studies; literary and linguistic ser.) pap., $1.25. Univ. of Mo.

CHEW'S BATTERY.
See Virginia.

CHEYENNE.
See Wyoming.

Cheyney, E: Potts.
Readings in English history drawn from the original sources, intended to illustrate "A short history of England." '08(D19) c. D. $1.80. Ginn.

Chi è: annuario biografico italiano; compilato a cura di Guido Biagi. '09(Jl10) D. hf. mor., $1. Stechert.

Chicago. *City Council. Committee on Local Transportation.* Electrification of railway terminals as a cure for the locomotive smoke evil in Chicago, with special consideration of the Illinois Central Railroad. '08, [1909.] (Mr) 7-353 p. il. 8°. (Add. pubs. for price.) Donnelley.

Chicago. *City Council. Committee on Local Transportation.* Rept. on the transportation subway systems of Boston, New York, Philadelphia, Paris, London. '09, [1910.] (F) 151 p. 8°. (Add. Council for price.) Chic. City Council.

Chicago. *Harbor Commission.* Rept. to the mayor and aldermen of the city of Chicago by the Chicago Harbor Commission. '09 (Jl) 8+383 p. il. 8°. (Add. pubs. for price.) Chic. Harbor Com.

Chicago. Municipal court, with marginal notes; by Stephen A. Foster. '08(Ja4) O. $2.50. Callaghan.

Chicago. Public Library. Catholic reading list; catalogue of books (in English) by Catholic authors in the Chicago Public Library; comp. by a committee of the Catholic Writers' Guild. '08, [1909.] (Mr) c. 8+55 p. 8°, 25 c. E: Larkin.

Chicago. Public Library. List of books and magazine articles on Abraham Lincoln. '09 (Ja30) O. pap., gratis. Chic. Pub. Lib.

CHICAGO, Ill.

Atkinson, E. Story of Chicago and natural development, 1534-1910. 85 c. Little Chronicle.

Beirly, A. New harbor for Chicago: plans and suggestions. gratis. A. Beirly.

Chandler, F. R., *ed.* Assessors' land valuations, Chicago. $5. Donnelley.

Chapin, L. Round about Chicago. *$1.50 net. Unity.

Cook, F: F. Bygone days in Chicago. $2.75 net. McClurg.

McDonald, J. N., *comp.* Chicago as a medical center. $2. Stromberg, A., & Co.

Notable men of Chicago and their city. Chicago Daily News.

Plumbe, G: E: Chicago; its natural advantages as an industrial and commercial center and market. 15 c. Chic. Assoc. Commerce.

Porter, H: H. How to provide for Chicago's growth. (Priv. pr.) G: F. Porter.

Winchell, S: R., *comp. and ed.* Civic manual for Chicago, Cook County and Illinois. 50 c. Flanagan.

Wooldridge, C. R. Twenty years a detective in the wickedest city in the world. $2; 75 c. C. R. Wooldridge.

See also Docks;—Fish and fishing;—Hull House;—Lawyers;—Prostitution.

CHICAGO AND NORTHWESTERN RAILWAY.
See Railroads.

Chicago Art Institute. Catalogue of sculptured works of Augustus Saint-Gaudens, with biographical sketch, August, September, 1909. '10(F) 99 p. por. il. 4°. o. p. Chic. Art.

Chicago Automobile Club. Official motor guide. '10(Mr5) c. il. maps, 12°, $1.50; limp leath., $2. Chicago Automobile.

Chicago Daily News almanac and year book, 1909. Langland, J., *ed.* 40 c. Chic. Daily News.

Chicago Directory Co. Plan of re-numbering city of Chicago; complete table showing new and old numbers affected by ordinance passed by the City council of the city of Chicago, June 22, 1908, and as amended by ordinance passed June 21, 1909. '09, [1910.] (Ja) c. 176 p. map, 4°, pap., $1.25. Chic. Directory.

Chicago Hebrew Institute. Program of celebrations during Lincoln week; [Abraham Lincoln and the Jewish spirit: address.] '09(S) 8 p. il. 12°, pap., 5 c. Chic. Hebrew Inst.

Chicago Historical Society collections. 8°. Chic. Hist.

—Boggess. Settlement of Illinois. $3.

Chicago law directory, 1909; by C: Gritman. '09(Je); 1910. '10(Je) c. O. ea., $1. Gritman.

Chicago Literary Club papers. 12°. (Not for sale.) Chic. Lit. Club.

—Cheney. Second Norman conquest.

—Gookin. Our defective American banking system.

—Little. John Milton.

—Payne. Quarter-century of English literature.

Chicago literary papyri. Goodspeed, E. J. *50 c. net. Univ. of Chic.

Chicago, Milwaukee & St. Paul Railway. North Pacific coast country. '09, [1910.] (Ja) c. 63 p. il. maps, 8°. (Add. pubs. for price.) Chic., Milwaukee.

Chichester intrigue. Cobb, T: †$1.50. Lane.

CHICKASAW INDIANS.
See Indians.

Chicken world. Smith, E. B. $2. Putnam.

CHICKENS.
See Poultry.

Chicot the jester. *See* Dumas, Alexandre.

Chief sources of sin. McDonough, M. V. 75 c. Murphy.

Chien (Le) du capitaine. Enault, L. 45 c. net. Putnam.

CHIHUAHUA, Mexico.

Hovey, E. O. Geological reconnaissance in the western Sierra Madre of Chihuahua. 45 c. E. O. Hovey.

Chilcott, Ellery Channing.

Study of cultivation methods and crop rotations for the Great Plains area. '10 (D) 78 p. map, front, 8°, (U. S., Dept. of Agriculture, Bu. of Plant Industry, bull.)

Chilcott, Langdon S.

Templar tactics and manual. '08(Jl4) il. D. leath., $1.50. L. S. Chilcott.

Child, C: G., jr., M.D.

Epitome of gynecology. '09(N) 210 p. il. sq. 12°, (Lea's ser. of medical epitomes.) *$1 net. Lea.

Child, Clarence Griffin, ed.

Second shepherds' play, Everyman, and other early plays; tr., with introd. and notes, by Clarence Griffin Child. '10 (Ag13) D. (Riverside literature ser.) 40 c. Houghton M.

Child, Fk. S:
Fairfield [Ct.], ancient and modern. '09 (My8) c. il. O. pap., 50 c. Fairfield Hist.
Old New England church, established religion in Connecticut; being an historical sketch of the first Church of Christ and the Prime Ancient Society, Fairfield, commemorating the 170th anniversary of public worship in the town. '10(Ap) c. 20+165 p. il. 8°, $1. Fairfield Hist.

Child, J. M.
See Barnard, S.

Child, R: Washburn.
Jim Hands. '10(D3) c. front. D. $1.50. Macmillan.

Child, T:
Bible: its rational principle of interpretation. '08(Ja11) por. 12°, 50 c. Warne.

Child and his religion. Dawson, G: E. *75 c. net. Univ. of Chic.

Child and the dream. Cook, M. 50 c. Metropolitan Pr.

Child classics. *See* Alexander; Georgia.

Child Conference for Research and Welfare. Proceeding, 1909. '10(Ja29) c. O. *$2 net; pap., *$1.50 net. Stechert.

Child countess. Maude, S. 75 c. Benziger.

Child employing industries. American Academy of Political and Social Science. $1.50; $1. Am. Acad. Pol. Sci.

Child in our midst. Wright, E. D. 50 c. Cochrane.

Child in the house. *See* Pater, Wa.

Child in the midst. Paul, N. $1. Longmans.

Child in the normal home. McCrimmon, A. L. 15 c. Am. Bapt.

CHILD LABOR.
See Children.

Child-life in prose. *See* Whittier, J: Greenleaf.

Child life in town and country. *See* France, Anatole, *pseud.*

Child of chance. Formont, M. †$1.50. Lane.

Child problems. Mangold, G: B: $1.25 net. Macmillan.

Child religion in song and story. *See* Chamberlin, Georgia Louise.

Child slaves and other poems. Long, S. L. $1.25. Courier Press.

CHILD STUDY.
See Children.

Child violinist. Winn, E. L. $1.25. Fischer.

Child wife. Reid, M. †$1. Dutton.

Child workers of the nation; Proceedings of the fifth annual conference, Chicago, Ill., Jan. 21-23, 1909. '09(My15) O. $1.25; pap., $1. Nat. Child Labor.

Child you used to be. Pease, L. $1.50. McClurg.

Childe, C: Plumley.
Operative nursing and technique: book for nurses, dressers, house surgeons, etc. '09 (Jl) 238 p. il., *$2 net. Wood.

Childe, Mrs. Hubert.
See Childe, Nellie Stice.

Childe, Nellie Stice, [Mrs. Hubert Childe,] comp.
Life and song: [poems.] '08(Je20) c. 8°, 50 c. H. Childe.

"Childe Harold," pseud.
See Field, E: Salisbury.

Childe Harold. *See* Byron, G: Gordon Noel, *Lord.*

Childers, Erskine.
War and the arme blanche; with introd. by Rt. Hon. Field-Marshal Earl Roberts. '10(Je25) O. $2.10 net. Longmans.

Childhood. Sowerby, M. $1.50. Duffield.

Childhood, and other verses. Earl, I. P. 50 c. Cochrane.

Childhood and ponyhood blended. White, O. A. 35 c. Dunlap Pony Co.

Childhood of Jesus Christ. Durand, A. $1.50 net. McVey.

Childhood of man. Frobenius, L. *$3 net. Lippincott.

Childhood of our blessed Lord Jesus Christ. Twining, A. G. *60 c. net. Young Churchman.

Childlore dramatic reader. Bryce, C. T., *comp.* (Add. pubs. for price.) Scribner.

CHILDREN.
Allen, *Mrs.* M. W.- Making the best of our children. 1st and 2d ser. ea., *$1 net. McClurg.
American Academy of Medicine. Prevention of infant mortality. $5. Am. Acad. Med.
American Academy of Political and Social Science. Child employing industries. $1.50; $1.—Child labor and social progress. $1.—Child labor legislation: schedules of existing statutes and the standard child labor law. 50 c.—Child workers of the nation. $1. Am. Acad. Pol. Sci.
Appleton, L. E. Comparative study of the play activities of adult savages and civilized children. 54 c. Univ. of Chic.
Arnold, *Mrs.* G. W., *comp.* Mother's list of books for children. $1. McClurg.
Association for Improving the Condition of the Poor. *New York Milk Committee.* Infants' milk depots and their relation to infant mortality. 50 c. Assoc. Imp. Con. Poor.
Ayres, L. P. Laggards in our schools. $1.50. Charities Pub.
Babees' book: mediæval manners for the young. *$2 net. Duffield.
Baby's childhood days: [book in which to make a record of a baby's life.] 20 c.; 50 c.; $1. Reilly & B.
Baby's own book. $1.50; $3; $6. Reilly & B.
Bailey, H: T. When little souls awake. 25 c. net. Pilgrim Press.
Baker, F. T: Bibliog. of children's reading. 60 c. Teachers' Coll.
Bancroft, M., *and* Farrington, E. A., *comps.* Manual of the course of study, Bancroft Training Sch. for Mentally Subnormal Children. (Not for sale.) Bancroft
Bayley, F. T. Little ten minutes; or, a pastor's talks with his children. *$1 net. Revell.
Benson, R. A. Nursery manual; the care and feeding of children in health and disease. *$1 net. Boericke & T.
Bobbitt, J: F. Growth of Philippine children. (Add. author for price.) J: F. Bobbitt.

CHILDREN.—*Continued.*

Boston Public Library. Brief list of books for home reading for boys and girls in the Library. gratis. Boston Pub. Lib.

Bray, R. A. Town child. *$2 net. Jacobs.

Brown, D. R. Baby: a book for mother and nurses. *$1 net. Whitcomb.

Brookline, Mass. Public Library. Something to read, for boys and girls. o. p. Brookline Pub. Lib.

Burke, C. E. Child study and education. 75 c. Benziger.

Burrell, C. B., *ed.* Mother's book. Univ. Soc.

Cabot, *Mrs.* E. L. Ethics for children. $1.25. Houghton M.

Candler, G: H: Every-day diseases of children and their rational treatment. $1. Clinic.

Chance, *Mrs.* B. Care of the child. *$1 net. Penn Pub. Co.

Chapin, H: D. Theory and practice of infant feeding. *$2.25 net. Wood.

Chapin, H: D., *and* Pisek, G. R. Diseases of infants and children. *$4.50 net. Wood.

Child Conference for Research and Welfare. Proceedings of the Child Conference for Research and Welfare, 1909. *$2 net; *$1.50 net. Stechert.

Child workers of the nation. $1.25; $1. Nat. Child Labor.

Clark, J: K. Systematic moral education. $1 net. Barnes.

Cleveland Public Library. Work of the Cleveland Public Library with the children. (Add. Library for price.) Cleveland Pub. Lib.

Clopper, E: N: Child labor in Indiana. gratis. Nat. Child Labor.

Coolidge, E. L. First aid in nursery ailments. $1. E. L. Coolidge.

Corbett, B. L. Baby days. $1.50. Rand, McN. & Co.

Cornell, W. S. Backward children in the public schools. 25 c. Davis.

Cradock, *Mrs.* H. C. Care of babies. *$1.25 net.—Training of children. *60 c. net. Macmillan.

Dickens, C: Dickens' stories about children every child can read. 75 c. Winston.

Diseases of children. 4 v. $20. Holt.

Duns, M. A. Pract. care and feeding of children. $1.50. Chic. Med. Bk.

Edwards, W. S. Christian view of childhood. *25 c. net. Jennings.

Evans, *Mrs.* F. Purity, birth and sexual problems for mothers. (Add. pubs. for price.) Purity Pub.

Falkner, R. P. Retardation: its significance and its measurement. (Add. pubs. for price.) Educ. Review.

First International Congress in America for the welfare of the child, held under the auspices of the National Congress of Mothers at Washington, D. C., Mar. 10 to 17, 1908. '08, [1909.] (My) 3-350 p. il. pors. 8°, pap., $1. Nat. Congress Mothers.

Fischer, L: Diseases of infancy and childhood. *$6.50 net; *$8 net. Davis.

CHILDREN.—*Continued.*

Fiske, J: Meaning of infancy. **35 c. net. Houghton M.

Fordyce, D. Hygiene of infancy and childhood. $2.50 net. Wood.

Forsyth, D: Children in health and disease. *$3 net. Blakiston.

Fritch, G. M., *ed.* Baby's history. 60 c. G. M. Fritch.

Godfrey, E., *pseud.* English children in the olden time. *$3 net. Dutton.

Goodhart, J. F., *and* Still, G: F. Diseases of children. $5. Blakiston.

Gould, F. J. Conduct stories; for the moral instruction of children. $1. Macmillan.

Groszmann, M. P. E. Classification of exceptional children as a guide in determining segregation—Groszmann School for Nervous and Atypical Children. Groszmann.

Hale, P. L. Great portraits: children. $1.50. Bates & G.

Hall, F: S. Scholarships for working children. (Add. pubs. for price.) Nat. Child Labor.

Hancock, M. S. Children of history. In 2 v. ea., **50 c. net. Little, B. & Co.

Harrison, *Mrs.* E. Misunderstood children. $1. Central Pub. Co.

Hart, H. H. Cottage and congregate institutions for children. $1; 50 c. Charities Pub.

Harvey, N. A. Mental ontogeny. 50 c. N. A. Harvey.

Herter, C. A. On infantilism from chronic intestinal infection. *90 c. net. Macmillan.

Hewitt, *Mrs* E. C. How to train children. 50 c Jacobs.

Hirshberg, L. K., *ed.* What you ought to know about your baby. 25 c. Butterick.

Hogan, L. E. S. How to feed children. **$1 net. Lippincott.

Holt, L. E. Care and feeding of children. 75 c.—Diseases of infancy and childhood. $6. Appleton.

Howard, W: L. Start your child right. 75 c. net. Revell.

Hutchinson, R. Lectures on diseases of children. *$2.40 net. Longmans.

Jacobi, A., *ed.* Diseases of children. $6. Appleton.

Kaplan, A. O. New baby's biography. $2.50. Brentano's.

Kelley, S: W. Surgical diseases of children. *$5 net. Treat.

Kennedy, *Mrs.* M. G. Our boys and girls; how to interest and instruct them in Bible study. 75 c. Wilde.

Kerley, C: G. Short talks with young mothers on the management of infants. *$1 net. Putnam.

Kerley, C: G. Treatment of the diseases of children. $5. Saunders.

Kerr, L. Care and training of children. 75 c. net. Funk.

Kerr, L. The baby, its care and development. *$1 net. A. T. Huntington.

Key, E. K. S. Century of the child. **$1.50 net.—Education of the child. **75 c. net. Putnam

CHILDREN.—*Continued.*

Kirkpatrick, E. A. Fundamentals of child study. *$1.25 net. Macmillan.

Kirkpatrick, E. A., *ed.* Studies in development and learning. $1. Science Pr. (N. Y.)

Klykken, O. Our homes and our children. 75 c. Lutheran Pub.

Koplik, H: On diseases of children. $5 net. Lea.

Lamoreaux, *Mrs.* A. A. Unfolding life: study of development with reference to religious training. 75 c. Rel. Pub.

Learmount, J. In God's orchard; being courses of talks to the young folks. *$1 net. Eaton & M.

Lodge, *Sir* O. J. Parent and child. 50 c. net. Funk.

Lord, E. W. Child labor and the public schools. (Add. pubs. for price.)—Topics and suggestions for debates on child labor. gratis. Nat. Child Labor.

Lovejoy, O. R. Children in the glass industry in Pennsylvania. (Add. pubs. for price.) Nat. Child Labor.

MacCarthy, F. H. Hygiene for mother and child. $1.25 net. Harper.

McCrea, R. C. Humane movement. $2 net. Lemcke.

McCrimmon, A. L. Child in the normal home. 15 c. Am. Bapt.

MacDonald, A. Studies of juvenile criminals. (Add. pubs. for price.) A. MacDonald.

McFall, C. H. Beautiful children. **$5 net. Dodd.

McKelway, A. J. Child labor in the Carolinas. gratis. Nat. Child Labor.

Maennel, B. Auxiliary education, the training of backward children. $1.50. Doubleday, P.

Mangold, G: B: Child problems. $1.25 net. Macmillan.

Marriott, L. M. Mother and child; being letters from an old nurse to a young mother. 40 c. Simmons.

Martin, E: S. Luxury of children. $1.50. Harper.

Mumford, E. E. R. Dawn of character; study of child life. $1.20 net. Longmans.

Mundy, W: N., *M.D.* Eclectic practice in diseases of children. $3. Scudder.

Musselman, H. T:, *ed.* National Teachers' Training Institute text books. Bk. 5, Child study for Sunday school teachers. **40 c. net; **25 c. net. Am. Bapt.

Nesbit, W. D., *comp. and ed.* Baby. 50 c. Volland.

New York [City.] Board of Health. Bureau of child hygiene. 35 c. Bu. Municipal.

Norsworthy, M. Psychology of mentally deficient children. $1. Science Pr. (N. Y.)

Partridge, G. E. Outline of individual study. $1.25 net. Sturgis & W.

Partsch, H. Messages to mothers: simple, practical and natural scheme for the right diet, care and treatment of mother and child. **$1.50 net. P. Elder.

Patch, K. W. Sensitive child. **75 c. net. Moffat.

Phelps, E: B. Statistical study of infant mortality. (Add. author for price.) E: B. Phelps.

Poucher, *Mrs.* F. H. Boy and the books: [bibliography.] 75 c. Kimball Press.

Power, E. L., *comp.* Selected list of children's books for school libraries of Michigan. gratis. L. L. Wright.

Preble, G: H., *comp.* Did your child say this? 50 c. J: W. Luce.

Ruhräh, J: Manual of the diseases of infants and children. *$2 net. Saunders.

Runyon, S. D. Baby's history. $3; $4; $7.50; $2. Stokes.

Sadlier, S. H. Infant feeding by artificial means. *$1.25 net. Dutton.

Sage (Russell) Foundation. Dept. of Child Hygiene. Pamphlets. 37 v. $2 per 100. Charities Pub.

Sands, B. Weepers in playtime: [fiction.] †$1.50. Lane.

Scantlebury, E. E. World babies. *35 c. net. Educ. Pub.

Shields, T: E: Making and unmaking of a dullard. *$1 net. Cath. Educ.

Shinn, M. W. Notes on the development of a child. $2.50. Univ. of Cal.

Shuttleworth, G. E., *and* Potts, W. A. Mentally deficient children. $2. Blakiston.

Smith, S. K., *and* Perrett, L., *comps.* Our baby's record. $1; $2; $2.50. Dodge.

Stories of royal children. **65 c. net. Century Co.

Tappan, E. M. Letters from Colonial children. $1.50. Houghton M.

Tooker, R. N. All about the baby. *$1.50 net. Rand, McN. & Co.

Tracy, F., *and* Stimpfl, J. Psychology of children. $1.20. Heath.

Tuley, H: E. Diseases of children. $5. Southern Med.

United States. *Dept. of Commerce and Labor. Bureau of Labor.* Woman and child wage-earners in Great Britain.

United States. Establishment of a children's bureau; Committee on Expenditures in the Department of Commerce and Labor [Hearing] Apr. 13, 1910. [1910.] (Jl) 40 p. 8. Gov. Pr. Off.

Van Vorst, *Mrs.* J: Cry of the children. **$1.25 net. Moffat.

Washburne, *Mrs.* M. F. Mother's yearbook: application of the results of scientific child-study to the problems of the first year of childhood. **$1.25 net. Macmillan.

Wells, C. Seven ages of childhood. **$2 net. Moffat.

West, C: How to nurse sick children. *40 c. net. Longmans.

Weyburn, C. M. Baby's book. $1.50; $3; $4. Barse & H.

Wheeler, M. The baby, his care and training. *$1 net. Harper.

Whipple, G. M. Manual of mental and physical tests. $2.50 net. Warwick-Y.

Whittier, J: G., *ed.* Child-life in prose. $1.50. Houghton M.

Wilcox, S. F. Surgery of childhood. $3.50. Boericke & R.

CHILDREN.—*Continued.*

Willard, De F. Surgery of childhood, incl. orthopædic surgery. $7. Lippincott.

Wilson, L: N., *comp.* Bibliography of child study for the year 1907. 25 c. Clark Univ.

Wilson-Carmichael, A. Lotus buds; [children of India.] *$5 net. Armstrong.

Young, D. H. First aid to the child. $1.25. Dutton.

See also Amusements;—Arabia;—Africa;—Books and reading; — Boys; — China; — Christmas;— Crime and criminals;— Diarrhœa;—Domestic economy; — Education; —Emergencies;—Entertainments; — Eugenics;—Family;—Fine arts;— Food; — Games; — Gardens and gardening; — George Junior Republic;—Girls;—Heredity;— India;—Juvenile courts;—Kindergarten;—Manual training; — Missions and missionaries; — Mothers; — Music; —Needlework;—Nurses and nursing;—Orphans;—Painters and painting;— Parks;—Playgrounds;—Plays;—Portraits;—Probation system;—Race suicide;—Recitations;— Reform schools;—Roentgen rays;—Schools;— Sermons; — Sex; — Songs; — Story-telling; — Sunday-school;—Teachers and teaching;—Tuberculosis;—Voice.

Children and gardens. Jekyll, G. *$2 net. Scribner.

Children of destiny. Rosenfeld, S. 50 c. G: W: Dillingham.

CHILDREN OF HER MAJESTY'S REVELS.
See Blackfriar's Theatre, London.

Children of Israel. Mord, W. $1.50. Stokes.

CHILDREN OF THE CHAPEL.
See Blackfriar's Theatre, London.

Children of the dawn. Buckley, E. F. $1.50. Stokes.

Children of the summer. Howells, W: D. *$1.35 net. Harper.

Children of the valley. Spofford, *Mrs.* H. E. P. **40 c. net. Crowell.

Children's action songs. Steele, M. *35 c. net. Cassell.

Children's book. Burnett, *Mrs.* F. H., *ed.* †$1.50. Moffat.

Children's book. Scudder, H. E., *ed.* $2.50. Houghton M.

Children's book of art. Conway, A. E. *$2 net. Macmillan.

Children's book of Celtic stories. Grierson, *Mrs.* E. W. *$2 net. Macmillan.

Children's book of gardening. Sidgwick, *Mrs.* C. U. *$2 net. Macmillan.

Children's bookcase; ed. by E. Nesbit. v. 1-4. '09(D); v. 5. '10(D) il. ea., *50 c. net. Doran.

Contents: Nesbitt, E., *ed.*, Old nursery stories; Herbertson, A. F., Cap o' Yellow; Browne, F., Granny's wonderful chair; Kingsley, C:, Water babies. Yonge, C. M., Little duke.

Children's bookshelf. 16°. Dodge.
—Darton, *comp.* Old English stories. 50 c. —Pilgrim's tales. 60 c.
—Macleod, *comp.* Red Cross knight and Sir Guyon. 60 c.—Robin Hood and his merry men. 50 c.—Story of King Arthur. 60 c.

Children's catalog. *See* Potter, Marion E., *comp.*

Children's classic booklets. 24 v. in 4 sets. '09(Je19) il. 12°, ea., bds., 20 c. Reilly & B.

Contents: Peter Rabbit set: The story of Peter Rabbit, Uncle Tom's cabin—Topsy, The story of Little Black Sambo, The night before Christmas, Mother Goose rhymes and jingles, J. Cole; Black Beauty set: Black Beauty, Rab and his friends, The adventures of a brownie, The little lame prince, Rip Van Winkle, Snow White and Rose Red; Red Riding Hood set: Little Red Riding Hood, Sleeping Beauty, Cinderella, or the little glass slipper, Dick Whittington and his cat, Jack and the bean stalk, The three bears; Alice's adventures set: Alice's adventures in Wonderland, Through the looking glass—Humpty Dumpty, Robinson Crusoe—his man Friday, Andersen's fairy tales—the ugly duckling, Grimm's fairy tales—Hansel and Gretel, The Swiss family Robinson.

Children's classics. 10 v. '08(O3) c. il. D. flex. linen, ea., 15 c.; pap., 10 c. Penn Pub. Co.

Contents: Æsop's fables; Aladdin and the wonderful lamp; Pilgrim's progress, Bunyan; Stories from Chaucer; Little Snow-white and other Grimm fairy tales; Wonder tales, Hawthorne; King Arthur and the knights of the Round Table, Malory; Tales from the travels of Baron Munchausen, Raspe; Lady of the lake, Scott; Gulliver's travels, Swift.

Children's classics; ed. by Wa. Jerrold. il. 12°, $1.25. Dutton.
—Andersen. Fairy tales.
—Defoe. Robinson Crusoe.
—Grimm. Fairy tales.
—Mother Goose nursery tales.
—Mother Goose. Old Mother Goose nursery rhymes.
—Wyss *and* Montolieu. Swiss Family Robinson.

Children's classics in dramatic form. Stevenson, A. Bk. 1, **40 c. net; Bk. 2, **35 c. net. Houghton M.

CHILDREN'S COURTS.
See Juvenile courts.

Children's creed. Twinning, A. G. *60 c. net. Young Churchman.

Children's crimson classics; formerly McClure's library of children's classics. *See* Wiggin, Kate Douglas Smith.

Children's daily service. Babcock, B. S. *50 c. net. Whittaker.

Children's dialogues and entertainments. '08 (O3) c. bds., ea., 40 c.; pap., 25 c. Penn Pub. Co.

Children's Dickens. *See* Dickens, C:;—Jackson, Alice F., *ed.*

Children's favorites; [told in easy French.] il. *50 c. net. Jacobs.
—Andersen. Fairy tales.
—Arabian nights' entertainments.
—Defoe. Robinson Crusoe.
—Grimm. Fairy tales.
—La Fontaine. Fables.
—Perrault. Fairy tales.

Children's heroes ser. *See* Dutton's.

Children's King Arthur: stories from Tennyson and Malory. '10(D) col. il. 4°, bds., 75 c. Doran.

Children's Paul. Stevenson, J. G. 85 c. net. Eaton & M.

CHILDREN'S POETRY.

Arnold, P., *and* Steele, M., *comps.* Nursery rhymes. 20 c. Cassell.

Brill, G: R. Rhymes of the golden age. $1.50. Stern.

Chisholm, L., *comp.* Golden staircase. *$1 net. Putnam.

Chisholm, L., *ed.* Nursery rhymes. 50 c. Dutton.

Coussens, P. W., *ed. and comp.* Poems children love. $1.25; $2. Dodge.

Curly-locks and other nursery rhymes. 50 c. Stokes.

Edgar, M. G., *comp.* Treasury of verse for little children. $2.50. Crowell.

Esmond, D. W:, *comp.* Poetry of childhood. $1.50. B'way Pub.

CHILDREN'S POETRY.—*Continued.*
Familiar nursery jingles. $1.25. Stokes.
Field, E. Cradle lullabies. 50 c. Canterbury Co.
Fillebrown, *Mrs.* R. H. M. Rhymes of happy childhood. **$2 net. Winston.
Good Shepherd; narrative and poems for young people. 25 c. E. Kaufmann.
Harrison, F. Rhyme of a run. $2. Caldwell.
Ivimey, J: W: Complete version of ye three blind mice. *50 c. net. Warne.
Longfellow, H: W. Children's Longfellow. $3. Houghton M.
Mayhew, E: Lyrics of childhood. **$1 net. Grafton Press.
Mother's verses and home songs. 75 c. Caldwell.
Old rhymes pictured by Mabel Lucie Attwell. $1.50. Tuck.
Peabody, J. P. Book of the little past. $1.50. Houghton M.
Riley, J. W. Orphant Annie book. **$1.50 net. Bobbs-M.
Rossetti, C. G. Sing-song: nursery rhyme book. 80 c.; $1.25. Macmillan.
Seven little women. Twelvetrees, R. C. 75 c. Stokes.
Sivern, L., *and* Sherwood, R. Primer of nursery rhymes. 30 c. Houghton M.
Smith, J. W., *comp.* Child's book of old verses. $2.50. Duffield.
Song of sixpence picture book. $1.25. Lane.
Tileston, *Mrs.* M. W. F., *comp.* Child's harvest of verse.—Children's book of ballads. ea., $1.50. Little, B. & Co.
Wee Willie Winkie: a little book of nursery rhymes. 50 c. Stokes.
See also Alphabets;—Mother Goose;—Songs.

Children's pulpit. Byington, E. H. 75 c. net. Pilgrim Press.

CHILDREN'S READING.
See Books and reading.

Children's red books. 12 v. '09(Je19) il. 12°, ea., bds., 25 c. Reilly & B.
Contents: Peter Rabbit and Dick Whittington; Little Black Sambo and Uncle Tom's Cabin; The night before Christmas and Mother Goose rhymes and jingles; Black Beauty, and The little lame prince; Rab and his friends, and J. Cole; The adventures of a brownie, and The Swiss family Robinson; Little Red Riding Hood, and Sleeping Beauty; Cinderella, and The three bears; Jack and the beanstalk, and Robinson Crusoe; Alice's adventures in Wonderland, and Through the looking-glass; Andersen's fairy tales, and Rip Van Winkle; Grimm's fairy tales, and Snow White and Rose Red.

Children's round of fact and festival. Bell, C. C. *40 c. net. Young Churchman.

Children's Scott. *See* Jackson, Alice F., *ed.*

Children's services. Grossman, R. 10 c. Bloch.

Children's Shakespeare. *See* Shakespeare, W:

Children's speakers. '08(O3) c. il. D. bds., ea., 25 c.; pap., 15 c. Penn Pub. Co.

Children's store. Williams, C. A. 75 c. Stokes.

Children's stories that never grow old. Stone, M., *comp.* $1. Reilly & B.

Children's story of Westminster Abbey. Troutbeck, G. E. $1.35. Stokes.

Children's tales of English minsters. Grierson, E. *$2 net. Macmillan.

Children's theatre. Williams, C. A. $1. Stokes.

Children's treasure trove of pearls. Tileston, *Mrs.* M. W. F., *ed.* †$1.50. Little, B. & Co

Childress, Rufus Jackson.
Oaten reeds; poems; his second book. '10 (S) 120 p. il. por. 8°, 60 c. R. J. Childress.

Child's Bible history. Kecht, *Bp.* F. J. 25 c. Herder.

Child's book of old verses. Smith, J. W., *comp.* $2.50. Duffield.

Child's Christmas. Sharp, E. $2. Caldwell.

Child's English literature. Marshall, H. E. *$2.50 net. Stokes.

Child's garden of verses. *See* Stevenson, Rob. L:

Child's guide to American history. Elson, H: W: **$1.25 net. Baker & T.

Child's guide to biography. Stevenson, B. E. **$1.25 net. Baker & T.

Child's guide to music. Mason, D. G. **$1.25 net. Baker & T.

Child's guide to mythology. Clarke, H. A. **$1.25 net. Baker & T.

Child's guide to pictures. Caffin, C: H. **$1.25 net. Baker & T.

Child's guide to reading. Macy, J: A. **$1.25 net. Baker & T.

Child's harvest of verse. Tileston, *Mrs.* M. W. F., *comp.* $1.50. Little, B. & Co.

Child's history of England. Dickens, C *30 c. net; *70 c. net. Dutton.

Child's history of Westminster Abbey. Twining, A. C. *$1.50 net. Young Churchman.

Child's Rip Van Winkle. Irving, W. $1.50. Stokes.

Child's song treasury. Ehrmann, M. B. $2. W. H. Willis.

Child's story of the New Testament in words of one syllable. '09(S) c. 9-112 p. il. 12°, (Altemus' one syllable ser.) 50 c. Altemus.

Child's world in pictures. Wyss, C. v. 75 c. net. Macmillan.

Child's world primer. Bentley, A. E. 30 c. Barnes.

Childs, Mrs. Eleanor Stuart.
The postscript. '08(My2) c. D. †$1.25. McClure.

Childs, Mrs. Jessie Dow Hopkins.
Sea of matrimony. '10(Ja15) c. 12°, $1.50. B'way Pub.

Childs, Mrs. Mary Fairfax.
De namin' ob de twins. '08(Je20) c. O. *$1 net. B. W. Dodge.

CHILE.
International Bureau of American Republics, *comp.* Chile: a handbook. $1. Int. Bu. Am. Republics.

Chilkat blanket. Emmons, G: T. $2. Am. Museum.

Chillacoe Charlie. Macdonald, R. M $1.50. Brentano's.

CHIMARIKO INDIANS.
See Indians.
Chimes (The). *See* Dickens, C:
Chimes of cheer. O'Brien, F. G: $2. F. G: O'Brien.
Chimes of childhood. McCullough, A. W. $1. Ditson.
Chimes of Swathmore. Reynolds, W. D. 45 c. Clarion.
CHIMNEYS.
House chimneys. 25 c. D: Williams.
CHINA.
American Acad. of Polit. and Social Science. Commercial relations bet. the U. S. and Japan; [and] The significance of the awakening of China. Am. Acad. Pol. Sci.
Bashford, J. W. China centennial documents. In 2 v. (Not for sale.) Bd. For. Miss. M. E. Ch.
Bates, L. W., *jr.* Russian road to China. $3 net. Houghton M.
Blake, *Sir* H: A. China. $1.50 net. Macmillan.
Blakeslee, G: H., *ed.* China and the Far East. **$2 net. Crowell.
Bland, J: O. P. Houseboat days in China. $5. Longmans.
Bland, J: O. P., *and* Backhouse, E. China under the Empress Dowager. $4 net. Lippincott.
Boulger, D. C: de K. Life of Sir Halliday Macartney, commander of Li Hung Chang's force in the Taeping Rebellion. *$6 net. Lane.
Broomhall, M. Present-day conditions in China. *50 c. net. Revell.
Broomhall, M., *ed.* Chinese Empire. $2.50. China Inland.
Brown, C: C. Children of China. 60 c. net. —China in legend and story. *$1.25 net. Revell.
Carus, P., *ed.* Nestorian monument: ancient record of Christianity in China. 40 c. Open Court.
Cecil, *Lord* R. W: E. G.- *and Lady* F. M. B.-W. Changing China. $3 special net. Appleton.
Centenary Missionary Conference records: report of the great Shanghai conference, 1907. *$2.50 net. Am. Tr.
Chitty, J. R. Things seen in China. *75 c. net; *$1 net. Dutton.
Conger, S. P. Letters from China. *$2.75 net. McClurg.
Convention between the U. S. and China; arbitration. (Add. Superintendent for price.) U. S., Supt. of Docs.
Davis, M. H., *and* Chow-Leung. Chinese fables and folk stories. 40 c. Am. Bk.
Degroot, J. J. M. Religion of the Chinese. **$1.25 net. Macmillan.
Dobson, W: H. Modern medicine in China. (Not for sale.) George Washington Univ.
Geil, W: E. Great wall of China. $5. Sturgis & W.
Getz, J: Catalogue of the Macomber collection of Chinese pottery. $1.25. Boston Museum.
Hardy, E. J. John Chinaman at home. *$1.50 net. Scribner.

CHINA.—*Continued.*
Headland, I: T. Court life in China. *$1.50 net. Revell.
Hirth, F. Ancient history of China to the end of the Chóu dynasty. **$2.50 net. Lemcke.
Holcombe, C. Real Chinaman. *$2 net. Dodd.
Jeffreys, W. H., *and* Maxwell, J. L. Diseases of China, incl. Formosa and Korea. $6. Blakiston.
Johnston, L. E. China. *75 c. net. Macmillan.
Johnston, R. F. Lion and dragon in northern China. $5. Dutton.
Kemp, E. G. Face of China. *$6 net. Duffield.
Lesdain, *Count* de. From Pekin to Sikkim through the Ordos, the Gobi desert, and Tibet. $4. Dutton.
Liddell, T. H. China, its marvel and mystery. $6.50 net. Lane.
Little, A. B. In the land of the blue gown. $2.50 net. Appleton.
Macgowan, J. Sidelights on Chinese life. *$3.75 net. Lippincott.
Merwin, S: Drugging a nation: story of China and the opium curse. *$1 net. Revell.
Morse, H. B. Gilds of China. *$1.20 net. —International relations of the Chinese Empire. $6 net.—Trade and administration of the Chinese Empire. *$2.50 net. Longmans.
Mott, J: R. Chinese student migration to Tokyo. 5 c. Y. M. C. A.
Osgood, E. I. Breaking down Chinese walls. *$1 net. Revell.
Parker, E: H. Ancient China simplified. *$3 net.—John Chinaman and a few others. *$1.25 net.—Studies in Chinese religion. $3 net. Dutton.
Pontius, A. W., *comp.* Protection extended to patents, designs, trade-marks and copyrights in China, Japan and Korea. (Add. Superintendent for price.) U. S., Supt. of Docs.
Richmond, A. B. American Episcopl church in China. 75 c.; 50 c. Dom. and For. Mission.
Robbins, *Mrs.* H. H. M., *ed.* George, Earl of Macartney, first British ambassador to China. *$5 net D[illegible]-ton.
Roe, A. S. China as I saw it. $3 net. Macmillan.
Ross, J: Orig. religion of China. *$1.25 net. Eaton & M.
Stanford, E: Atlas of the Chinese Empire. $4. China Inland.
Stratton, C. R. Picturesque China. $1. Nat. Pub. Co.
Thomson, J. S. The Chinese. $2.50. Bobbs-M.
Williams, *Mrs.* I. B. R. By the Great Wall; (letters from China.) *$1.50 net. Revell.
Willis, B. Research in China. v. 2. $2. Carnegie.
Wolferstan, B. Catholic Church in China from 1860 to 1907. $1.30 net. Herder.
Wu T'ing Fang. Awakening of China. 10 c. Civic Forum.

CHINA.—*Continued.*
Yung Wing. My life in China and America. **$2 net. Holt.
See also Animals;—Chinese in the United States;—Corn;—Mongolia;—Mongols; — Painters and painting;—Russo-Japanese war;—Yellow peril;—Yunnan.

CHINA (*porcelain*).
See Ceramics.

China or Denny pheasant in Oregon. Shaw, W: T. **$1.50 net. Lippincott.

CHINA PAINTING.
Class room. [Instructions and designs for pupils in china-painting.] $3. Keramic.
Monachesi, *Mrs.* H. D. Manual for china painters. $1.25, boxed. Lothrop, L. & S.

CHINATOWN.
See San Francisco.

Chinatown trunk mystery. Harper, O. 25c. J. S. Ogilvie.

Chinese child's day. Terhune, A. *$1.25 net. Schirmer.

Chinese fables and folk stories. Davis, M. H. 40 c. Am. Bk.

Chinese fairy stories. Pitman, N. H. $1. Crowell.

CHINESE IN THE UNITED STATES.
American Academy of Political and Social Science. Chinese and Japanese in America. $1. Am. Acad. Pol. Sci.
Coolidge, M. E. B. R. S. Chinese immigration. **$1.75 net. Holt.
Cowan, R. E., *and* Dunlap, B., *comps.* Bibliography of the Chinese question. *$1.40 net. A. M. Robertson.
Fryer, J: Admission of Chinese students to American colleges. (Add. Superintendent for price.) U. S., Supt. of Docs.
Ng Poon Chew. Treatment of the exempt classes of Chinese in the United States. 5 c. Ng Poon Chew.
United States. *Dept. of Commerce and Labor. Bu. of Immigration.* Treaty, laws and regulations governing the admission of Chinese; regulations approved Oct. 30, 1909. U. S., Supt. of Docs.
United States. *Dept. of Commerce and Labor. Bu. of Immigration and Naturalization.* Treaty, laws, and regulations governing the admission of Chinese; regulations approved Dec. 15, 1909; ed. of Dec., 1909. '09, [1910.] (Mr) 70 p. 8°. U. S., Supt. of Docs.

Chinese lantern. Housman, L. (Priv. pr.) Brentano's.

CHINESE LITERATURE.
Arabian and Chinese classics. $1.75; $3.50. Lamb Pub.
Cranmer-Byng, L. A., *comp.* Lute of jade. *60 c. net. Dutton.

Chinese porcelain. Hsiang Yuan-P'ien. $34, boxed. Oxford Univ.

CHINESE POTTERY.
See Ceramics.

Chinese student migration to Tokyo. Mott, J: R. 5 c. Y. M. C. A.

Chiniqui, —.
Priest, the woman and the confessional: [anti-Catholic work by a former priest.] '08(N) 296 p. $1. L. J. King.

CHINOOK JARGON.
See Indians.

Chip. Young, F. E. M. $1.50. Lane.

Chip of the old block. Houston, E. J. $1.25. Griffith.

Chipman, C: Phillips.
Page and the prince; or, a fight for a throne. '09(O9) c. il. D. †$1.25. Ball Pub.

Chipman, G: E., ed.
Illinois cases, common law pleading. 2d ed. '09(S) 241 p. 8°, $2. Callaghan.

Chipman, W: Pendleton.
Boy pickets; boy's story of the battle of New Orleans. '10(O1) c. il. 12°, $1. Burt.
Boy scouts: story of Burgoyne's defeat in 1777. '09(My) 284 p. il. 12°, †$1. Burt.
In defense of liberty: story of the burning of the British schooner "Gaspee" in 1772. '08(Ap4) c. il. 12°, †$1. Burt.
In ship and prison: story of five years in the continental navy with Captain Samuel Tucker. '08(Ag1) c. D. $1.50. Saalfield.

CHIPPENDALE FURNITURE.
See Furniture.

Chippendales (The). Grant, R. $1.50. Scribner.

CHIPPENY HILL, Ct.
See East Plymouth, Ct.

Chippewa music. Densmore, F. 45 c. Smith. Inst.

CHIROPODY.
Hughes, M. L. Manual of chiropody. *25 c. net. W: R. Jenkins.

CHIROPRACTIC.
American College of Mechano-Therapy, Chicago, Ill. Text-book of chiropractic. $2. Am. Coll. Mechano-Therapy.
Bartlett, J. Science of chiropractic. v. 3, $8; v. 4, $2; v. 5, $2; per set, $15. Palmer Sch.
Carver, W. Chiropractic analysis as applied to anatomy, physiology, chiropractic principles, symptomatology and diagnosis. $7.50. W. Carver.

Chirpings of Dusty Mike. Walsh, J. J. (Add. pubs. for price.) Dietz Pr.

Chisholm, G: Goudie.
Hdbk. of commercial geography. 7th ed., with additional chapter on trade routes. '09(My22) maps, tabs., fold. maps, 8°, *$4 80 net. Longmans.

Chisholm, Louey.
Simple Susan. '08(Ag15) 24°, (Told to the children ser.) 50 c. Dutton.
Stories from Shakespeare. 2d ser. '10 (D) 10+118 p. il. 16°, (Told to the children ser.; ed. by Louey Chisholm.) 50 c. net. Dutton.
—, comp. Golden staircase: poems and verses for children. New ed. '09(N) col. il. O. *$1.50 net; School ed., *$1 net. Putnam.
—, ed. Nursery rhymes. '08(Je6) il. 16°, (Told to the children ser.) 50 c. Dutton.

Chiswick calendars. 12°, 60 c.; $1. Crowell.
—Stevenson. Calendar.
—Thoreau. Calendar.
—Wordsworth. Calendar.

Chiswick classics. il. D. **50 c. net. Crowell.
—Miller. Glimpses of the heavenly life.
—Ruskin. Calendar.
—Shakespeare. Calendar.

Chittenden, Fk. Hurlbut.
Control of the Mediterranean flour moth by hydrocyanic-acid gas fumigation. '09 (D) 22 p. il. 8°, (U. S., Dept. of Agriculture, Bureau of Entomology, circular.) pap. (Add. Superintendent for price.)

Chittenden, Hiram Martin.
Forests and reservoirs in their relation to stream flow, with particular reference to navigable rivers; with discussion by F. Collingwood, T: P. Roberts, etc. '10 (My7) il. map, 8°, $1.50. Am. Soc. Civil Engineers.

"Chittenden, Larry," pseud.
See Chittenden, W: Lawrence.

Chittenden, Lucius Eug.
Lincoln and the sleeping sentinel. '09 (Ja30) c. por. D. *50 c. net. Harper.

Chittenden, W: Lawrence, ["Larry Chittenden."]
Bermuda verses. '09(My15) c. il. O. **$1.50 net. Putnam.

Chittick, Alex., comp.
Medicine; 1000 questions and answers for state board examinations. '10(Je) c. 259 p. 12°, $2. Crescent Pub.

Chitty, J. R.
Things seen in China. '08(O10) 16°, ("Things seen" ser.) *75 c. net; leath., *$1 net. Dutton.

CHIVALRY.
Cornish, F. W. Chivalry. *$1.25 net. Macmillan.
Lansing, M. F., *comp.* Page, esquire and knight; tales of chivalry. 35 c. Ginn.
Stories of chivalry. **65 c. net. Century Co.

Chivalry. Cabell, J. B. **$2 net. Harper.

Chlapowski, Countess Bozenta.
See Modjeska, Helena.

CHLOROPHYCEAE.
See Seaweeds.

CHLOROPHYL.
See Botany.

Choate, Augusta, and Hartman, Gertrude.
Exercises for parsing and analysis. '09 (D4) c. tabs., D. $1. A. Choate.

Choate, G: A.
See Florida. *Sup. ct.* Digest.

Choate, Jos. Hodges.
Abraham Lincoln and other addresses in England. '10(O15) c. por. O. $2 net. Century Co.

—, **Porter, General Horace, and Scott, Ja. Brown.**
American addresses at the Second Hague Peace Conference; ed., with introd. notes, by Ja. Scott Brown. '10(F5) c. O. $1.50. Ginn.

CHOCOLATE.
Parloa, M., *and* Hill, *Mrs.* J. M. Chocolate and cocoa recipes. gratis. W. Baker.

CHOCTAW INDIANS.
***See* Indians.**

Choice dishes at small cost. Payne, A. G. $1.25 net. Cassell.

Choice literature lib. il. 12°. Educ. Pub.
—Brooks. Stories of the red children. 40 c.; 30 c.
—Chadwick. Stories of colonial children. 60 c.; 40 c.

Choice morsels of the bread of life. Coppens, C: *60 c. net. Herder.

Choir-boy's manual. Clare, H. N. *25 c. net. Schirmer.

Choirmaster's manual. Clare, H. N. *75 c. net. Schirmer.

Choix de contes. Daudet, A. 30 c. Heath.

Choix de contes populaires de la Haute-Bretagne. Sébillot, P. *25 c. net. Crowell.

Choix de poésies faciles. Daniels, W. M., *comp. and ed.* *25 c. net. Crowell.

CHOLERA.
***See* Hog.**

CHOLERA INFANTUM.
Tilden, J: H: Etiology of cholera infantum, typhoid fever and appendicitis. $5. Merchants Pub.

Cholmondeley, Mary.
Hand on the latch. '09(Ap10) c. front. D. †$1.25. Dodd.

Choosing a career; a circular of information for boys. '09(S18) c. O. pap., 10 c. High School Teachers'.

Choosing a career; a circular of information for girls. '09(S18) c. O. pap., 10 c. High School Teachers'.

Choosing a vocation. Parsons, F. **$1 net. Houghton M.

Chopin, Frédéric François.
Greater Chopin; ed. by Ja. Huneker. '09 (Ja16) c. por. F. (Musicians' lib.) $2.50; pap., $1.50. Ditson.

CHOPIN, Frédéric François.
Dickinson, E: New musical education; popular course on Chopin. $1. Aeolian Co.
Jonson, G. C. A. Hdbk. to Chopin's works. $2 net. Scribner.

Chords and discords. Hawkins, W. E. $1.25. Murray Bros. Press.

Chords of the zither. Scollard, C. $1.25. G: W. Browning.

Chorister's Christmas eve. Earls, M. 25 c. Herder.

Chorus lady. Harding, J. W: †$1.50. G: W. Dillingham.

CHORUSES.
***See* Songs.**

Chosen people. Mord, W. $1. Stokes.

Chouans (Les). *See* Balzac, Honoré de.

Chouville, L.
Histoires courtes et longues pour lecture expliquée et reproduction. '10(Mr26) D. (Cours de français et d'allemand.) 60 c. Oxford Univ.

Chow-Leung.
See Davis, Mary Hayes.

Chrestomathie française. Passy, J. *$1.25 net. Stechert.

CHRIST.
***See* Jesus Christ.**

Christ among the cattle. Marvin, F: R. 50 c. Pafraets.

Christ and the eastern soul. Hall, C: C. **$1.25 net. Univ. of Chic.

CHRIST CHURCH, Williamsport, Pa.
Eckel, E: H: Chronicles of Christ church parish, Williamsport, Pa., 1840-1896. $2. Christ Ch.

Christ in everyday life. Bosworth, E: I. 75 c. Y. M. C. A.

Christ in Flanders. Balzac, H. de. *35 c. net; *70 c. net. Dutton.
Christ in Flanders. Seymour, R. F. $1.25; $5. Seymour.
Christ in song. New ed., rev. and enl. '08 (N) 576 p. 60 c.; flex., 40 c.; hf. mor., $1. Review and Herald Pub.
Christ legends. Lagerlöf, S. O. L., *comp.* **$1.25 net. Holt.
Christ of the red planet. Ames, *Mrs.* E. M. E. $1. E. M. E. Ames.
Christ way. Doc, *pseud.* 75 c. Good Thoughts.

CHRISTABEL.
See **Coleridge, Samuel Taylor.**

Christen, Mrs. Rodolphe.
See Christen, Sydney Mary Thompson.

CHRISTEN, Rodolphe.
Christen, S. M. T. Rodolphe Christen; story of an artist's life. $7 net. Longmans.

Christen, Sydney Mary Thompson, [Mrs. Rodolphe Christen.]
Rodolphe Christen; story of an artist's life, by his wife. '10(D17) col. il. pors. O. $7 net. Longmans.

Christian, Eug.
Suncooked food; treatise on how to get the highest form of human energy from food. 6th ed., retitled and rewritten to keep pace with progress. '09(D) c. 365 p. por. 12°, $1. Christian's Sch.

Christian, G: L.
See McGuire, Hunter Holmes.

Christian, J: Taylor, D.D.
Form of baptism in sculpture and art. '08 (F1) c. il. D. $1. J: T. Christian.

CHRISTIAN (*sect*).
Dorris, C: E. W. Interesting correspondence; discussion bet. C. E. W. Dorris and Miss Nora Yount (Christians), and A. E. Clement, W. H. Lowell, [etc.,] (Methodists.) $1. C: E. W. Dorris.
See also Creeds.

Christian and amusements. Biederwolf, W: E: 15 c. Glad Tidings.
Christian and Catholic. Grafton, C: C. **$1.50 net. Longmans.
Christian art. Cram, R. A., *ed.* 3 v. *$15 net. Badger.

CHRISTIAN BIOGRAPHY.
Walker, W. Greatest men of the Christian church. $1.50. Univ. of Chic.

CHRISTIAN CHURCH.
See **Christianity.**

Christian church and education. Gailor, T: F. $1 net. Whittaker.

CHRISTIAN DOCTRINE.
See Theology.

Christian doctrine of God. Clarke, W: N. **$2.50 net. Scribner.
Christian doctrine of sacerdotium. Dimock, N. 75 c. Longmans.

CHRISTIAN EDUCATION.
See **Religious education.**

Christian educational ser. O. Luther Press.
—Luther. [Sermons.] 3 v. v. 1, 50 c.; v. 2, 3, ea., $1.65.—Small catechism.—Two catechisms explained by himself. ea., 50 c.

Christian epoch-makers. Vedder, H: C. **$1.20 net. Am. Bapt.
Christian essentials. Ballard, F. *$1.50 net. Eaton & M.

CHRISTIAN ETHICS.
See **Christianity.**

Christian evangelism. Coombs, J. V. 75 c.; 25 c. Standard Pub.
Christian evidence. Schenck, F. S. 75 c. Y. M. C. A.

CHRISTIAN EVIDENCES.
See **Christianity.**

Christian faith and the Old Testament. Thomas, J: D. **$1 net. Crowell.

CHRISTIAN FESTIVALS.
See Fasts and feasts.

Christian festivals ser. 12°. Jennings.
—Eckman. Passion week sermons. $1.
—Hughes. Thanksgiving sermons. *$1 net.
—McConnell. Christmas sermon. *$1 net.
—Spencer. Easter reflections. $1.

Christian Greece and living Greek. Rose, A. $1. Stechert.
Christian ideas and ideals. Ottley, R. L. $2.50. Longmans.

CHRISTIAN LIFE.
Allen, J. Entering the kingdom. 15 c. Fenno.
Andrews, G: A. What is essential? $1 net. Crowell.
Ballard, A. From text to talk. $1.20 net. Sherman, F.
Bate, H. N. Healthful spirit. *90 c. net. Longmans.
Bates, *Mrs.* V. B. How may I know the voice of God in my soul? 35 c. Presb. Pub.
Bigg, C: Spirit of Christ in common life. *$2 net. Longmans.
Bisseker, H. Problems of discipleship. *50 c. net. Eaton & M.
Bosworth, E: I. Christ in everyday life. 75 c. Y. M. C. A.
Brent, C: H: Leadership. **$1.25 net. Longmans.
Chambers, A. Problems of the spiritual. **$1 net. Jacobs.
Clow, W. M. Cross in Christian experience. *$1.50 net. Jennings.
De Waters, *Mrs.* L. S. Thinking heavenward. 50 c. L. De Waters.
Doak, A. M. How to be rich. $1. Jennings.
Du Bose, H. M. Life at its best. *50 c. net. Pub. Ho. of M. E. Ch., So.
Gibbons, J. True manhood. 50 c. McClurg.
Gilbert, P. J. The King's greatest business. *75 c. net. Revell.
Gordon, S: D. Quiet talks with world winners. **75 c. net. Armstrong.
Grenfell, *Sir* W. T. A man's helpers. 50 c. net.—What life means to me. *35 c. net. Pilgrim Press.
Haering, T. v. Ethics of Christian life. *$3 net. Putnam.
Hamilton, W. W. How to grow in the Christian life. *25 c. net; *10 c. net. Am. Bapt.
Harvey-Jellie, *Mrs.* Into the sunshine. $1. Northeld Press.
Higley, E. E. Homespun religion. **30 c. net. Crowell.
Holden, J. S. Price of power. *50 c. net. Revell.

CHRISTIAN LIFE.—*Continued.*
Houtz, A. Ties that bind. 50 c. I. M. Beaver.
Jenness, J. F. Our rich inheritance. **30 c. net. Crowell.
Lawrence, H. Light beyond the shadows. **50 c. net. Moffat.
Leighton, R. Rules and instructions for a holy life. *60 c. net. Longmans.
McIntyre, D: M. Life in His name. $1.25. Armstrong.
McLeod, M. J. Comfortable faith. *$1 net. Revell.
Mahan, A. T. Harvest within. **$1.25 net. Little, B. & Co.
Mahood, J: W. Make Jesus king. *25 c. net. Eaton & M.
Meyer, R. J. World in which we live. *$1.50 net. Herder.
Miller, J. R. Go forward. **50 c. net. Crowell.
Moore, T: V. Honoring God with our substance. *5 c. net. Presb. Bd.
Morgan, G: C. Christian principles. *50 c. net. Revell.
Mudge, J. Riches of His grace. *$1 net. Eaton & M.
Norton, W: H. Ideal Christian life. $1. W: H. Norton.
Orr, C: E. Hidden life; or, walks with God. 60 c. Gospel Trumpet Co.
Ostrom, H: "All His benefits." 30 c.—Rich in yesterdays; message to the aged. 75 c. Praise Pub.
Ridgeway, C: J: Social life: [duties of the Christian in social life.] *60 c. net. Cassell.
Robinson, A. W. Co-operation with God. *60 c. net. Cassell.
Schofield, A. T. Divine in man. *75 c. net. Armstrong.
Scott, A. B. Branches of the cross. *$1.50 net. Doran.
Shettle, G. T. Pathway of the cross. 40 c. Whittaker.
Silkwood, B. Steps in the Christian life. 50 c. Jennings.
Slattery, M. Seed, the soil and the sower. 35 c. net. F. M. Barton.
Smith, R. Lost Christ. *25 c. net. Doran.
Steele, D. Love enthroned: essays on evangelical perfection. $1.20. Eaton & M.
Swift, A. First principles of Christian citizenship. *75 c. net. Revell.
Telford, J: Man's partnership with Divine Providence. *$1.25 net. Eaton & M.
Tomkins, F. W. Helps toward nobler living. **50 c. net: **75 c. net. Jacobs.
Watkinson, W: L. Mistaken signs: addresses on Christian experience. *50 c. net. Revell.
Watson, F. Christian life here and hereafter. *$2 net. Whittaker.
White, E. G. H. Steps to Christ. 60 c.; $1.25. Pacific Press.
Whitney, W. Epochs and phases of Christian experience. $1. Observer.
See also Christian work;—Conduct of life;—Conscience;—Conversion;—Devotional exercises and meditations; — Faith; — Love;—Monasticism;—Religious education;—Repentance;—Revivals;—Saints; -- Temperance; — Temptation; —Young men;—Young people.

Christian life ser.; ed. by Rev. H: C: Beeching. D. *60 c. net. Cassell.
—Diggle. Home life.
—Ridgeway. Social life.
Christian martyrs. Foxe, J. $1.50. C: Foster.
Christian method of ethics. Clarke, H: W. *$1.25 net. Revell.
Christian ministry. Warlick, C. W. $1. C. W. Warlick.
Christian ministry and the social order. Macfarland, C: S., *ed.* *$1.25 net. Yale Univ.
Christian pastor in the new age. Lyman, A. J. **$1 net. Crowell.
Christian pedagogy. Halpin, P. A. $1.50. J. F. Wagner.
Christian race. Smith, H. L. 20 c.; 75 c. Y. M. C. A.
Christian reconstruction. Douglass, H. P. *$1.50 net. Pilgrim Press.
Christian religion as a healing power. Worcester, E. **$1 net. Moffat.
Christian sanity. Schofield, A. T. *$1 net. Armstrong.

CHRISTIAN SCIENCE.
Appler, A: C. Christian science exposed. $1. Eclipse.
Biederwolf, W: E: Christian Science tested by philosophy, medicine and revelation.—White life. ea., 10 c. net. Revell.
Conant, A. F., *comp.* Complete concordance to "Science and health." (Add. pubs. for price.) A. V. Stewart.
De Barrios, A. Shepherdess of to-day: [fiction.] $1. Aberdeen.
De Waters, *Mrs.* L. S. Glad tidings. $1.25. L. S. De Waters.
Doc, *pseud.* Christ way. 75 c. Good Thoughts.
Downe, B. P. Philosophy of Christian Science. *10 c. net. Eaton & M.
Eddy, *Mrs.* M. M. B. G. Christian science vs. pantheism and other messages to the Mother church. 25 c.—Manual of the mother church. $1.—No and yes.—Unity of good. A. V. Stewart.
Eddy, *Mrs.* M. M. B. G. Personal contagion; also, What our leader says. 10 c. Chr. Sci.
Farlow, A. Relation of government to the practice of Christian Science. ea., 3 c.; per 100, $3. A. Farlow.
Farnsworth, E: C. Sophistries of Christion science. $1.25. Smith & S.
Greenbarry, H. The sermon. 50 c. Good Thoughts.
Haldeman, I: M. Christian science in the light of Holy Scripture. *$1.50 net. Revell.
Haldeman, I: M. Mental assassination; or, Christian Science a physical, intellectual, moral and spiritual peril. 10 c. C: C. Cook.
Hanna, S. J. Christian science. 6 c Chr. Sci.
Harker, R. C. Christian Science. *50 c. net. Jennings.
Horn, *Mrs.* D. H. Timely aid: [analysis of Christian science and spiritualism in form of fiction.] $1.25. Austin.
Josselyn, A. A. Thoughts of a thinker. *75 c. net. Fowler & W.

CHRISTIAN SCIENCE.—*Continued.*

Kimball, E: A. Christian science. pap., 6 c.; per doz., 60 c.; per 25, $1.15; per 50, $2.25.—Christian science, (La science chrétienne;) le pouvoir de l'homme sur mal.—Christian science, (La science chrétienne;) ses bienfaits pour l'humanité. ea., 6 c. Chr. Sci.

Krull, V. H. Common sense view of Christian science. 25 c. V. H. Krull.

Lambert, L: A. Christian science before the bar of reason. *$1 net. Chr. Press.

Leonard, F. H. Christian science; demonstrable religion. 6 c. Chr. Sci.

Letson, S: B. Christian Science as it is. 25 c.; 50 c. S: B. Letson.

McCrackan, W: D. Christian science. 6 c. Chr. Sci. Pub.

McKenzie, W: P. Christian science, (La science chrétienne;) ou, la délivrance du mal. 6 c. Chr. Sci.

Mars, G. C. Interpretation of life; relation of modern culture to Christian Science. **$3 net. Appleton.

Marsten, F. E: Mask of Christian Science. $1. Am. Tr.

Meehan, M. Mrs. Eddy and the late suit in equity. $2.50; $3.50. M. Meehan.

Miller, *Mrs.* A. A. Little old outlaws; [verses for children presenting lessons of Christian Science.] 75 c. net. McClurg.

Milmine, G. Life of Mary Baker G. Eddy and the hist. of Christian science. **$2 net. Doubleday, P.

Mind over body. [Christian science.] $1. J. H. West.

Murray, S. V. Christian science *versus* personal opinion.—Flesh and matter: the Scriptures *vs.* Christian Science. ea., 50 c. S. V. Murray.

Paget, S. Case against Christian Science. 10 c. Cassell.

Paget, S. Faith and works of Christian Science. *$1.25 net. Macmillan.

Parker, G: A: Out of the depths: [fiction.] $1.25. Reid Pub.

Peabody, F: W: Religio-medical masquerade; complete exposure of Christian Science. $1. Hancock Press.

Podmore, F. Mesmerism and Christian science. *$1.50 net. Jacobs.

Pope, F. Stranger's visit: [Christian science.] 60 c. Zuriel.

Schaad, J. A. Only a mask? comparison of the teachings of the Christ and of Christian science. 25 c. J. A. Schaad.

Sindell, M. Satisfied at last: [fiction.] $1.50. Reid Pub.

Sturge, M. C. Truth and error of Christian Science. *$1 net. Dutton.

Tomlinson, I. C. Christian science: both Christian and scientific. 6 c. Chr. Sci.

Whitehead, J: Illusions of Christian science. $1. Garden Press.

Wood, J. G. Fallacies of Christian Science. $1. J. G. Wood.

Young, B. Christian science. 6 c. Chr. Sci.

See also **Divine healing;—Faith cure;—Mental science;—Mind and body;—New thought;—Suggestion (Mental).**

Christian science hymnal; selection of spiritual songs. '10(F26) c. 8°, $1.15; hf. mor., $1.40; full mor., $2.50; levant, $3.50; pocket ed., full mor., $3. Chr. Sci. Pub.

Christian secret of a happy life. Smith, *Mrs.* H. W. *$1 net. Revell.

CHRISTIAN SOCIOLOGY.

See **Social science.**

Christian state. Batten, S: Z. *$1.50 net. Am. Bapt.

Christian symbolism. Jenner, *Mrs.* H: $1 net. McClurg.

CHRISTIAN UNITY.

Briggs, C: A: Church unity. **$2.50 net. Scribner.

Brown, W: M. Level plan for church union. $1.50 net. Whittaker.

Dimock, N. Christian unity. 50 c. net. Longmans.

Firth, F. J. Christian unity in effort. **$1.50 net. Lippincott.

Gore, C: Orders and unity. *$1.35 net. Dutton.

Grafton, C: C. Christian and Catholic. **$1.50 net. Longmans.

Jones, A. T. Church federation and the kingdom of God. 25 c. A. T. Jones.

Overman, N. Public discussion on the question: Does the church of Christ offer a Scriptural basis for the union of all Christians. (Add. pubs. for price.) Donohue.

Slattery, C: L. Historic ministry and the present Christ. **50 c. net. Longmans.

Spence, F. Christian reunion; or, a plea for the restoration of "The ecclesia of God." *$1.50 net. Doran.

"That all may be one": a plea for the reunion of all Christians. *$1 net. Franklin Press Co.

Thompson, R. E. Historic episcopate. $1.50 Westminster.

Christian view of childhood. Edwards, W. S. *25 c. net. Jennings.

CHRISTIAN WORK.

Keogh, A. Institutional church and the public library. (Add. author for price.) A. Keogh.

See also Social science.

Christian worship. Richard, J. W. $1.50. Lutheran Pub.

CHRISTIANITY.

Ballard, F. Christian essentials. *$1.50 net. Eaton & M.

Batten, S: Z. Christian state; the state, democracy and Christianity. *$1.50 net. Am. Bapt.

Becker, C. H. Christianity and Islam. *75 c. net. Harper.

Bigg, C: Origins of Christianity. $4.15. Oxford Univ.

Billings, C: T. Movements and men of Christian history. 45 c.; 35 c.; 65 c. Unitarian S. S.

Bowne, B. P. Studies in Christianity. **$1.50 net. Houghton M.

Cady, H. E. Lessons in truth: practical Christianity. $1; 50 c. Unity Tr.

Carus, P. The pleroma; essay on the origin of Christianity. $1. Open Court.

Carus-Wilson, M. L. G. P. Expansion of Christendom. $1.50 net. Doran.

CHRISTIANITY.—*Continued.*

Chadwick, W. E: Social relationships in the light of Christianity. *$1.50 net. Longmans.

Chesterton, G. K. Orthodoxy: [essays on religion.] **$1.50 net. Lane.

Clark, H: W. Laws of the inner kingdom. *$1.25 net. Revell.

Congreve, G: Christian progress. $1.50 net. Longmans.

Cunningham, W. Christianity and social questions. 75 c. net. Scribner.

Cutten, G: B. Psychological phenomena of Christianity. **$2.50 net. Scribner.

D'Arcy, C: F: Christianity and the supernatural. *40 c. net. Longmans.

Delk, E. H. Three vital problems. 50 c. Lutheran Pub.

Driver, S: R., *and* Sanday, W: Christianity and other religions: three short sermons. 50 c. Longmans.

Drummond, R. J. Faith's certainties. *$1.50 net. Doran.

Elsee, C: Neoplatonism in relation to Christianity. *75 c. net. Putnam.

Eucken, R. C. Christianity and the new idealism. *75 c. net. Harper.

Everett, C: C. Theism and the Christian faith. *$3.50 net. Macmillan.

Flower, B: O. Christian science as a religious belief and a therapeutic agent. $1. Twentieth Century Pub.

Foster, G: B. Finality of the Christian religion. pt. 1. *$2.50 net. Univ. of Chic.

Garvie, A. E. Christian certainty and modern perplexity. $2 net.—Gospel for to-day. $1.50 net. Doran.

Golden, M., *ed.* Conversion of a high priest into a Christian worker. $1. M. Golden.

Gordon, G: A. Sure and living faith. **30 c. net. Crowell.

Goucher. J: F. Christianity and the United States. *50 c. net. Eaton & M.

Gulick, S. L. *and* E: L. Outline studies of the growth of the kingdom of God. *50 c. net. Pilgrim Press.

Haldeman, I: M. New religion; or, Athenian culture and Christianity. 10 c. C: C. Cook.

Hall, T: C. Hist. of ethics within organized Christianity. $3 net. Scribner.

Hall, T: C. Social solutions in the light of Christian ethics. *$1.50 net. Eaton & M.

Harnack, C. G. A. Mission and expansion of Christianity in the first three centuries. *$7 net. Putnam.

Hartman, E: R. Socialism versus Christianity. $1.50. Cochrane.

Headlam, A. C. History, authority, and theology. $2 net. Young Churchman.

Hill, D: R. Philosophy of Christianity and the philosophy of government, together with a criticism of God's word, history and reason applied to false teachers. $1.50. Tribune Pr. Co., (W. Va.)

Holmgren, C: J: A: Story of twentieth century Christianity. (Add. pubs. for price.) Forum of Conscience.

Hopkins, M. Evidences of Christianity. $1.25. T. R. Marvin.

CHRISTIANITY.—*Continued.*

Hubbard, E., *and* Albertson, C: C. Joint debate Hubbard-Albertson; question: resolved That Christianity is declining. 25 c. Roycrofters.

Jefferson, C: E: Essentials: address on the fundamentals of Christian faith and service. 35 c. Y. M. C. A.

Jenner, *Mrs.* H: Christian symbolism. $1 net. McClurg.

Kern, J: A. Study of Christianity as organized. $2.50. Pub. Ho. of M. E. Ch., So.

Ketcham, K. P. Organized Christianity. 75 c. K. P. Ketcham.

King, H: C. Letters on the greatness and simplicity of the Christian faith. *75 c. net. Pilgrim Press.

Leighton, G. Scientific Christianity. $1.25 net. Moffat.

Lipscomb, D: Queries and answers. $1.50. J. W. Shepherd.

Lloyd, A. S. Christianity and religions. **75 c. net. Dutton.

Love, J. F. Unique message and the universal mission of Christianity. $1.25 net. Revell.

Lyon, M. H. For the life that now is; the present worth of Christian faith. 75 c. Revell.

Mabie, H: C. Divine right of missions: Christianity the world-religion. **50 c. net. Am. Bapt.

McComb, S: Christianity and the modern mind. $1.50 net. Dodd.

Mackenzie, W: D. Final faith, statement of the nature and authority of Christianity as the religion of the world. $1.75 net. Macmillan.

Maclean, N. Can the world be won for Christ? $1.25 net. Doran.

Marshall, E: A. Christianity and non-Christian religions compared. 50 c. Bible Inst.

Mauro, P. Number of man. *$1.25 net. Revell.

Matthews, S. Social gospel. 50 c. net. Pilgrim Press.

Meyer, A. Jesus or Paul. *75 c. net. Harper.

Montgomery, G: R. Unexplored self. $1.25. Putnam.

Moore, W: W. Christianity in the light of reason and revelation. $1.50. W: W. Moore.

Muir, P. M. Modern substitutes for Christianity. $1.50 net. Doran.

Orr, J. Faith of a modern Christian. $1.50 net. Doran.

Otten, B. J. Old Christianity vs. new paganism. 25 c. Herder.

Ottley, R. L. Christian ideas and ideals. $2.50. Longmans.

Parker, T. Transient and permanent in Christianity. *$1 net. Am. Unitarian.

Paton, L. B., *ed.* Recent Christian progress. **$3 net. Macmillan.

Peake, A. S: Christianity, its nature and truth. *$1.25 net. Crowell.

Peile, J. H. F. Ecclesia discens: the church's lesson from the ages. *$1.60 net. Longmans.

CHRISTIANITY.—*Continued.*

Pesch, T. Christian philosophy of life; reflections on the truths of religion. *$4.50 net. Herder.

Peters, J: P. Modern Christianity. **$1.50 net. Putnam.

Pfleiderer, O. Development of Christianity. $1.50 net. B: W. Huebsch.

Pfleiderer, O. Primitive Christianity; its writings and teachings. In 4 v. v. 2, 3. ea., *$3 net. Putnam.

Quackenbos, J: D. Enemies and evidences of Christianity. $1.50. Eaton & M.

Raupert, J: G. F. Supreme problem; examination of historical Christianity. $1.50. Paul.

Roads, C: Rural christendom; or, the problem of Christianizing country communities. *90 c. net. Am. S. S.

Robertson, F: W: Sermons on Christian doctrine. *$1 net. Dutton.

Robinson, C: H: Human nature a revelation of the Divine. 40 c. net. Longmans.

St. John, C: E. Religion of the dawn. 60 c. net. Am. Unitarian.

Schaff, P. Hist. of the Christian Church. v. 2, pt. 2. $3.25 net. Scribner.

Schenck, F. S. Christian evidences and ethics. 75 c. Y. M. C. A.

Seeberg, R. Fundamental truths of the Christian religion. *$1.50 net. Putnam.

Sharman, J: T: Confirming the faith. $1.25. J: T: Sharman.

Slack, S. B. Early Christianity. *40 c. net. Open Court.

Speer, R. E. Christianity and the nations. $2 net. Revell.

Strong, J., *ed.* Studies in the gospel of the kingdom. 75 c.; 60 c. Am. Inst. Social Service.

Temple, W: The faith and modern thought. $1 net. Macmillan.

Thomas, W. H. G. Christianity is Christ. *40 c. net. Longmans.

Thomas, W: H. Contemporaneous pagan views of the early Christian. 25 c. W: H. Thomas.

Tomkins, F: W. Faith and life of a Christian. *75 c. net. Am. S. S.

Turton, W. H., *comp.* Truth of Christianity. $1.25. Putnam.

Usher, E: P. Greek gospel: an interpretation of the coming faith. $1. E: P. Usher.

Waite, C: H. B. History of the Christian religion to the year 200. $2.50. Waite.

Wayland-Smith, F. Materialism and Christianity. 25 c. Wayland-Smith.

Williams, C: D: Valid Christianity for to-day. **$1.50 net. Macmillan.

Wilmshurst, W. L. Christianity and science. *$1 net. Badger.

See also Agnosticism; — Apostolic succession; — Bible; — Catholic church; — Church history;—Conversion; — God; — History; — Holy Spirit; — Hymns; — Jesus Christ;—Legends;—Ministers;—Miracles;—Missions and missionaries;—Monotheism;—Mysticism; — Personality;—Protestantism;—Psychical research;—Religion;—Religion and science;—Religious orders;—Skepticism;—Social science;—Theology;—Worship;—*also* Century Bible handbooks;—Little books on religion;—*also* subjects beginning with Christian and Church;—*also* names of churches.

Christianity at the crossroads. Tyrrell, G: *$1.50 net. Longmans.

Christianity in Japan. Harris, M. C. *35 c. net. Jennings.

Christianity to-day ser. 12°. Open Court.
—Bible. N. T. Apocryphal books: Paralipomena. *75 c. net.

Christian's day book. Barry, J. G. H. $1.50 net. Gorham.

Christic reign. MacArthur, R. S. $1.25. Am. Bapt.

Christie, Archibald H.

Traditional methods of pattern designing; introd. to the study of decorative art. '10(My14) il. O. $2. Oxford Univ.

Christie, Emerson B.

Mindanao the Subanuns of Sindangan Bay. '10(Jl2) il. $1.25. Bu. Public Pr.

Christie, Stephen.

The boiler; boiler rules and tables. '09 (F6) c. il. tabs., O. price reduced from $2.50 to $1.75. Christie.

Christie, Mrs. Susan Cantrill.

Cantrill-Cantrell genealogy: record of the descendants of Richard Cantrill, who was a resident of Philadelphia prior to 1689, and of earlier Cantrills in England and America. '08(Ag1) c. front. 8°, **$5 net. Grafton Press.

Christie Johnson. *See* Reade, C: Peg Woffington.

CHRISTINA, *Queen of Sweden.*

Taylor, I. A. Christina of Sweden. *$4 special net. Appleton.

CHRISTINA, *Queen Regent of Spain.*
See **Maria Christina.**

Christine de Pisan.

Book of the Duke of True Lovers; with notes and introd. by Alice Kemp Welch; [original MS. now in the Bibliothèque Royale, Brussels.] '08(O17) il. 16°, (New medieval lib.) il. pigskin, with clasps, *$2.50 net. Duffield.

Christman (The). Marvin, D. E. $1.50. B'way Pub.

CHRISTMAS.

Anson, W. S. W., *ed.* Christmas book of carols and song. $3; $4. Barse & H.
Book of Christmas. **$1.25 net; $2 net. Macmillan.

Bugbee, W. N. Christmas medley. 25 c. Dick.

Coolidge, A. C. Christmas vs. Fourth of July. 25 c. A. C. Coolidge.

Dickens, C: Christmas carol. $1 net. Oxford Univ.

Duncan, N. Christmas eve at Topmast Tickle. 25 c. Revell.

Earls, M. Choristers Christmas eve; little play for the Christmas days, with a modern legend and the old Christmas carols. 25 c. Herder.

Ebright, W. H., *comp.* Bethlehem's star: a service for Christmas. per 100, *$2 net. Eaton & M.

Irving, W. Christmas, Christmas eve, Christmas day. 35 c. Macmillan.

Irving, W. Old English Christmas. $1.25 net. Jacobs.

Irving, W. Old fashioned Christmas day. —Old fashioned Christmas eve. ea., 50 c. net. Doran.

CHRISTMAS.—*Continued.*
Jefferson, C: E: Christmas builders. **50 c. net. Crowell.
Keppel, F: Christmas in art. *$2.50 net. Duffield.
Knight, W: A. Signs in the Christmas fire. *50 c. net; *35 c. net. Pilgrim Press.
Knight, W: A., *ed.* Poets on Christmas. *$1 net. Gorham.
Koogle, E. L., *comp.* Christmas collation: [recitations, songs, etc.] 25 c. March.
Mabie, H. W. Christmas to-day. **75 c. net. Dodd.
McConnell, F. J. Christmas sermons. *$1 net. Eaton & M.; Jennings.
McCutcheon, J: T., *and* Jones, J. L. What does Christmas really mean? 50 c. Forbes.
Page, V. F. Christmas message to you [and] with the new year. 50 c. V. F. Page.
Pratt Institute, Brooklyn. Free Library. Books for Christmas for the children. gratis. Pratt Inst.
Price, C. F. Babe of Bethlehem; Christmas service. per 100, $2.50. Eaton & M.
Scott, T., *comp.* Christmas treasury of song and verse. $1.25 net. Baker & T.
Seidel, H. German Christmas Eve. 50 c.; 25 c. Abbey Co.
Sindelar, J. C:, *ed.* New Christmas book: recitations, plays, tableaux, etc. 30 c. Flanagan.
Stewart, J. A. Christmas book. *75 c. net. Am. Bapt.
Willard, E. M. Yuletide entertainments. 25 c. T: S. Denison.
See also Austria;—Carols;—Hymns;—Santa Claus;—Spain.

Christmas angel. Brown, A. F. 60 c. net. Houghton M.
Christmas bells. '10(D) col. il. 16°, bds., 50 c. net. Doran.
Christmas book. Henland, C. *50 c. net. Jacobs.
Christmas books. Dickens, C: In 5 v. per set, $5. Dutton.
Christmas books. *See* Thackeray, W. Makepiece.
Christmas carol. *See* Dickens, C:
Christmas every day. Howells, W: D. †$1.75. Harper.
Christmas in many lands ser. il. D. 50 c. Estes.
—Bartlett. Christmas in Austria.
—Hoxie. Hilda's wish, Christmas in Denmark.
—Pomeroy. Christmas in Spain.
Christmas in the heart; book of gladness and devotion. '09(N13) il. in col. S. bds., *50 c. net. Doran.
Christmas letter. Lefferts, S. T. 60 c. Cupples & L.
Christmas Makers' Club. Sawyer, E. A. $1.50. L. C. Page.
Christmas mystery. Locke, W: J: 75 c. net. Lane.
Christmas stories. *See* Dickens, C:
Christmas tree. *See* Dickens, C: Holly Tree Inn.
Christologies ancient and modern. Sanday, W: $1.75. Oxford Univ.

Christopheismeier, Carl Heinrich.
First revolutionary step [in France,] (June 17, 1789.) '09(Je12) 8°, (University studies.) $1. Univ. of Neb.
Christopher, J. E:
See Byrom, T. H.
Christopher Hibbault, roadmaker. Bryant, M. †$1.50. Duffield.
Christ's second coming. Fairbanks, A. D. $1. Roxburgh.
Christ's table talk. Hendrix, E. R. *$1 net. Pub. Ho. of M. E. Ch., So.
Christ's way of winning souls. Sligh, J: C. 60 c. Pub. Ho. of M. E. Ch., So.
Christus centuriarum. Dingwell, J. D. $1. Badger.
Christus crucifixus. Simpson, J. G. $1.50 net. Doran.
Christy, Howard Chandler, il.
Christy book of drawings. '08(D5) c. il. obl. F. **$3.50 net, boxed. Moffat.
CHROMOSOME THEORY.
See Heredity.
Chronic constipation. MacMillan, J. A. $2. Burton Co.
Chronicle history of the London stage. Fleay, F: G. *$6 net. Stechert.
Chronicle of friendships, 1873-1900. Low, W. H. **$3 net. Scribner.
Chronicle of the Cid; cronica del famoso cauallero Cid Ruy Diez Campeador. [facsim.] '03, [1909.] (N) 116 p. 8°, $25. (200 copies.) Hispanic Soc.
Chronicle of the Cid; coronica del muy efforcado y inuencible cauallero el Cid Ruy Diaz Campeador delas Españas. [facsim.] '03, [1909.] (N) no paging, 4°, $12. (200 copies.) Hispanic Soc.
Chronicle of the conquest of Grenada. *See* Irving, Washington.
Chronicle of Thomas of Eccleston. Cuthbert, *Father.* *75 c. net. Herder.
Chronicles of England, France and Spain. *See* Froissart, *Sir* J:
Chronicles of Manuel Alanus. Wyneken, L. E. $2. Cochrane.
Chronicles of Oldfields. Allen, T: N. *$1.50 net. A. Harriman.
Chronicles of pharmacy. Wooton, A. C. In 2 v. $6.50. Macmillan.
Chronicles of Rhoda. Cox, F. T. †$1.25. Small.
Chronicles of service life in Malta. Stuart, N. $2. Longmans.
Chronicles of the crusades. Villehardouin, G. de. *35 c. net; *70 c. net. Dutton.
Chronique (La) du règne de Charles IX. Mérimée, P. $1. Oxford Univ.
CHRONOLOGY.
Auchinloss, W: S. Chronology of the Holy Bible. $1. Van Nostrand.
Toffteen, O. A. Researches in Biblical archæology. v. 1, Ancient chronology. pt. 1; v. 2, The historic Exodus: [Biblical chronology.] ea., *$2.50 net. Univ. of Chic.
See also Bible.
Chronology of municipal history and election statistics. Waterville, Maine. Given, C. M. $1.50. Maine Farmer.
CHRONOPHOTOGRAPHY.
See Cinematograph;—Photography;—Stereopticon.

Chrysalis (The). Kramer, H. M. †$1.50. Lothrop, L. & S.

Chrysler, C: Byron.
White slavery. [1910] (F) c. '09. 251 p. 12°, $1. C. B. Chrysler.

Chrysostom John, Brother, originally Jos. J: Conlan, ed.
Manual of Christian doctrine; comprising dogma, moral, and worship, by a seminary professor; authorized English version. 10th ed. '09(N) c. 9+14+588 p. 12°, (Course of religious instruction, Institute of the Brothers of the Christian Schools.) $1. McVey.

Chu Yen.
Description of Chinese pottery and porcelain; being a tr. of the T'ao Shuo; with introd., notes and bibliography by Stephen W. Bushnell. '10(Ag27) O. $4.75. Oxford Univ.

Chuang Tzu.
Musings of a Chinese mystic; selections from the philosophy of Chuang Tzu; tr. by Lionel Giles. '08(Je6) 16°, (Wisdom of the East.) *60 c. net. Dutton.

Chubb, Edn. Watts, comp.
Stories of authors, British and American. '10(Mr12) c. pors. D. *$1.25 net. Sturgis & W.

Chubb, Percival, ed.
See Lincoln, Abraham.

CHUMASH LANGUAGE.
See Indians.

Chumos, Mrs. O. S. Fowler-.
See Fowler-Chumos, *Mrs.* O. S.

Chums. Cole, *Mrs.* D. R. B. $1.25. G. O. Tubby.

Church, Alex. Hamilton.
Production factors in cost accounting and works management. '10(D17) c. forms, 12°, (Works management lib.) $2. Engineering Mag.
Proper distribution of expense burden. '08 (D5) c. 12°, (Works management lib.) $1. Engineering Mag.

Church, Rev. Alfr. J:
Æneid for boys and girls; told from Virgil in simple language. '08(O3) c. il. D. †$1.50. Macmillan.
Faery Queen and her knights; stories retold from Edmund Spenser. '09(O30) c. col. il. D. $1.50. Macmillan.

Church, Archibald, M.D., ed.
Diseases of the nervous system; auth. tr. from "Die deutsche klinik" under the general editorial supervision of Julius L. Salinger, M.D. '10(My) 21+1205 p. il. 8°, (Modern clinical medicine.) $7 net; hf. leath., $8 net. Appleton.
"Literature" at end of some of the chapters.

—, and Peterson, F:
Nervous and mental diseases. 6th ed., thoroughly rev. '08(D) c. 11-945 p. il. 8°, *$5 net; hf. mor., *$6.50 net. Saunders.

Church, Calvin Grant.
See Straughn, M. N.

Church, Dan. Webster.
An interview. '10(My14) c. D. $1. B. Carey.

Church, Irving Porter.
Mechanics of engineering; comprising statics and kinetics of solids the mechanics of the materials of construction, or strength and elasticity of beams, columns, shafts, arches, etc. Rev. ed., partly rewritten. '08(S12) il. figs. 8°, $6. Wiley.
Mechanics of internal work (or work of deformation) in elastic bodies and systems in equilibrium, incl. the method of least work. '10(D17) c. figs. 8°, $1.50 net. Wiley.

Church, J. W.
Crucible; southerner's impression of Hampton. '10(N) 14 p. il. 12°, gratis. Hampton Inst.
Deep in piney woods. '10(S3) c. il. O. $1.20 net. Crowell.

Church, S: Harden.
Religious progress in America; address del. before centennial convention of the Christian Church at Carnegie Music Hall, Pittsburgh, Pa., Oct. 16, 1909. '10(Ja8) O. pap., 25 c. Carnegie.
Short history of Pittsburgh, 1758-1908. '08 (N7) c. il. pors. O. *$1.25 net. De Vinne.

Church, Mrs. Virginia.
Commencement days; novel. '10(My14) c. il. D. $1.50. L. C. Page.

Church, W. S.
New probate law and practice, with annots. and forms for use in Alaska, Ariz., Cal., Colo., Id., Kan., Mont., Nev., N. M., N. D., Okla., Ore., S. D., Utah, Wash. and Wyo. In 2 v. v. 1. '09(Mr); v. 2 (Ap) c. O. per set, $13. Bender-M.

CHURCH (The).
Ashenhurst, J. O. Day of the country church. $1 net. Funk.
Barry, J. C. Ideals and principles of church reform. $1.25 net. Scribner.
Bigelow, H. S. Mission of a liberal church. 5 c. Public.
Crooker, J. H: Church of to-day. *75 c. net. Am. Unitarian; Pilgrim Press.
Crowell, K. R. Call of the waters: study of the frontier. *50 c. net; *30 c. net. Revell.
Danner, T: J. Plea for the old faith of the old church. 25 c. T. J. Danner.
Denney, J. The church and the kingdom. 50 c. net. Doran.
Dulles, A. M. True church. *$1.25 net. Revell.
Earp, E. L. Social aspects of religious institutions. *75 c. net. Eaton & M.
Fairbairn, A. M. Studies in religion and theology. *$3.50 net. Macmillan.
Fraternalism and the church. $1. M. C. Chamberlin.
Gladden, W. Church and modern life. **$1.25 net. Houghton-M. Co.
Gladstone, W: E. Correspondence on church and religion. 2 v. $5. Macmillan.
Hobhouse, W. The church and the world in idea and in history. $3.25 net. Macmillan.
Hough, S: S., *ed.* Church in earnest. 25 c. For. Miss. Soc. of Un. B.

CHURCH (The).—*Continued.*
Ireland, J: Church and modern society. 2 v. *$3 net. Herder.
Jefferson, C: E: Building of the church. $1.25 net. Macmillan.
Jowett, J. H. Transfigured church. $1.25 net. Revell.
McAfee, C. B. Growing church. *50 c. net. Northfield Press.
Marvin, D. E. Church and her prophets. 50 c. B'way Pub.
Masterman, J: H. B. Rights and responsibilities of national churches. *75 c. net. Putnam.
Medley, D. J. Church and the Empire. $1.40 net. Macmillan.
O'Neill, F. J. Does Christ say go to church? 5 c. F. J. O'Neill.
Paradise, F. I. Church and the individual. $1.50 net. Moffat.
Powell, L. P. Credentials of the church. 25 c. net. Whittaker.
Smith, W: H: Church and men. $1.50. B'way Pub.
Smyth, N. Passing Protestanism and coming Catholicism. **$1 net. Scribner.
Stelzle, C: Church and the labor movement. 10 c. Am. Bapt.
Stelzle, C: The church and labor. **50 c. net. Houghton M.
Stelzle, C: Principles of successful church advertising. *$1.25 net. Revell.
Tippy, W. M., *ed.* Socialized church: address. *$1 net. Eaton & M.
Walker, C:, *ed.* Ritual "reason why." *$1 net. Young Churchman.
Warlick, C. W. Christian ministry; or, the problem of the church. $1. C. W. Warlick.
Wishart, A. W. Social mission of the church. 20 c. Am. Bapt.
Wright, J: C: Thoughts on modern church life and work. *$1 net. Longmans.
Zueblin, C: Religion of a democrat: [relation of the church to the state.] *$1 net. B: W. Huebsch.
See also Boys;—*also* names of churches and subjects under Church in entries following.

Church (The) and life of to-day: attitude of the church toward the great questions of to-day. '10(D) 12°, $1.50 net. Doran.
Church and missionary education. Young People's Missionary Movement. $1.25. Young People's Miss.
Church and modern men. Palmer, W: S. *$1.20 net. Longmans.
Church and social evils ser. D. pap. H. Gregory.
—Deans. Suicide. 15 c.
Church and state in France. Sumichrast, F: C. J: M. S: R. de. 25 c. F. H. Robson.
Church and the slum. Crawford, W: H: 75 c. Eaton & M.

CHURCH ANTIQUITIES.
See Brasses.

CHURCH ARCHITECTURE.
Bond, F. Screens and galleries in English churches. $2. Oxford Univ.
Champneys, A. C. Irish ecclesiastical architecture. $7.50 net. Macmillan.

CHURCH ARCHITECTURE.—*Continued.*
Euster, W: T. Philosophy of church building. $3.50. Pendleton.
Hill, A. G: Architectural history of the Christian church. *60 c. net. Young Churchman.
Kidder, F. E. Churches and chapels. $3. W: T. Comstock.
Vail, M. H. Church plans and designs. (Add. author for price.) M. H. Vail.
Wright, J: Some notable altars in the Church of England, and the American Episcopal Church. *$6 net. Macmillan.
See also Abbeys; — Cathedrals;—Church decoration and ornament.

Church art in England. il. O. Oxford Univ.
—Bond. Wood carvings in English churches. v. 1. $2.50.
Church catechisms in anecdotes. Dalton, M. L. *$1 net. Whittaker.
Church cook book; published for the benefit of church work and charity. '08, [1909.] (Jl) 180 p. il. 12°, oil cl., 75 c. Williams & W.

CHURCH DECORATION AND ORNAMENT.
Bond, F. Fonts and font covers. $4.80. Oxford Univ.
Duthie, A. L: Practical church decoration. $1.25. Painters' Mag.

CHURCH FATHERS.
See Fathers of the church.

Church federation. Jones, A. T. 25 c. A. T. Jones.

CHURCH FINANCE.
See Bookkeeping.

CHURCH FURNITURE.
Dearmer, P. Fifty pictures of Gothic altars. $6 net. Longmans.
Hartel, A., *comp. and ed.* Altars and pulpits; examples taken mostly from famous German cathedrals. $10.70. Hessling.
See also Brasses.

CHURCH HISTORY.
Adeney, W. F. Greek and Eastern churches. *$2.50 net. Scribner.
Bacon, B: W. Founding of the church. 50 c. Houghton M.
Bartoli, G. Primitive church and the primacy of Rome. $1.50 net. Doran.
Bede, *The Venerable.* Ecclesiastical hist. of the English nation. 35 c. net; 70 c. net. Dutton.
Besse, H: T. Church history. $2. H: T. Besse.
Burns, J. Revivals, their laws and leaders. *$1.50 net. Doran.
Cheetham, S: History of the Christian church since the reformation. *$2.60 net. Macmillan.
Conley, J: W. Young Christian and the early church. **50 c. net. Am. Bapt.
Davison, E. S. Some forerunners of St. Francis of Assisi. (Add. author for price.) E. S. Davison.
Duchesne, L. M. O. Churches separated from Rome. *$2 net. Benziger.
Duchesne, L. M. O. Early history of the Christian church. *$2.50 net. Longmans.
Duchesne, L. M. O. Roman church before Constantine. 10 c. Cathedral Lib.
Edghill, E. A. Spirit of power as seen in the Christian church of the second century. $1.40 net. Longmans.

CHURCH HISTORY.—*Continued.*
Flick, A. C. Rise of the mediæval church. **$3.50 net. Putnam.
Funk, F. X. Manual of church hist. v. 1. $2.75 net. Herder.
Glover, T. R. Conflict of religions in the early Roman Empire. *$2.50 net. Scribner.
Gray, J. Great epochs of sacred hist., and the shadows they cast. 50 c. net. Revell.
Gulick, S. L., *and* E: L. Outline studies of the growth of the kingdom of God. 50 c. net. Pilgrim Press.
Gwatkin, H: M. Early church hist. to A.D. 313. *$5.25 net. Macmillan.
Harnack, C. G. A. Constitution and law of the church in the first two centuries. $1.75 net. Putnam.
Hutton, W: H. Age of revolution: being an outline of the church from 1648-1815. *$1.50 net. Macmillan.
Klingman, G: A. Church hist. for busy people. $1. F: L: Rowe.
McGlothlin, W: J. Guide to the study of church history. *$1.50 net. Bapt. World.
Moncrief, J: W. Short history of the Christian church. *$1.50 net. Revell.
Morgan, C: H., Taylor, T: E. *and* S. E. Studies in the early church. 75 c. Jennings.
Musselman, H. T:, *ed.* National Teacher-training Institute text books. bk. 6, Early church-history and doctrine, by J: Wesley Conley. **50 c. net. Am. Bapt.
Ragg, L. Church of the Apostles. *$1.40 net. Macmillan.
Ramsay, *Sir* W: M. Pictures of the Apostolic church. $1.50 net. S. S. Times.
Remensnyder, J. B: Post-apostolic age and current religious problems. $1.25. Lutheran Pub.
Schaff, P. Hist. of the Christian church. v. 5, pt. 2. $3.25 net. Scribner.
Schubert, H. v. Outlines of church history. *$3 net. Putnam.
Srygley F. D. New Testament church. $1. F. B. Srygley.
Summerbell, J. J. Outline of church hist. of the first six centuries. 75 c. Chr. Pub. Assoc.
Vedder, H: C. Church history handbooks. Bks. 1, 2, 3, 4. ea., **40 c. net. Am. Bapt.
Von Dobschutz. Apostolic age. $1. Am. Unitarian.
Weber, N. A. History of simony in the Christian church. *$1.50 net. Furst.
Westcott, B. F. Two empires; the church and the world. *$1.75 net. Macmillan.
See also Apostles;—Apostolic succession;—Bible;—Catholic church;—Celibacy;—Christianity;—Church polity; — Confession; — Creeds; — Crusades; — Fasts and feasts; — Fathers of the church;—Inquisition;—Jesus (*Society of*);—Jews;—Martyrs;—Miracles;—Missions and missionaries;—Monasticism;—Priests; —Protestantism; —Reformation;—Religious orders;—Sacraments; — Saints; — Sunday; —Theology;—*also* names of churches;—*also* Texts and studies, ed. by J. A. Robinson.

Church Library Association. Catalogue of books recommended by the Church Lib. Assoc. for Sunday-school and parish libraries. '10(Ja8) S. pap., 25 c. Church Lib.

CHURCH MUSIC.
Bumpus, J: T. Short history of English cathedral music. 2 v. *$4 net. Potts.
Burgess, F. Rudiments of Gregorian music. *20 c. net. Scribner.
Lloyd, F. E. J., *comp.* Church musicians' directory, 1910. $3.50. Ritzmann, B. & Co.
Lorenz, E. S. Practical church music. *$1.50 net. Revell.
Lutkin P: C. Music in the church. $1 net. Young Churchman.
Morse, C: H., *and* Vernon, A. W., *eds.* Songs for the chapel. **$1.50 net. Scribner.
Pollitt, A. W., *and* Bryson, E. Unison chant choir-book. $1. Oxford Univ.
Springer, M. Art of accompanying plain chant. $1.50. J. Fischer.
Wyatt, F: F. Bible on instrumental music. 25 c. F: F. Wyatt.
See also Hymns and hymn writers;—Singing.

CHURCH OF ENGLAND.
Anglican liberalism. *$1.50 net. Putnam.
Armitage, W. J. Church year. $1. Oxford Univ.
Balleine, G: R. History of the evangelical party in the Church of England. *$1 net. Longmans.
Bishop, W. C. Rubrical revision. 36 c. net. Longmans.
Carpenter, W: B. Popular hist. of the Church of England. *$1.50 net. Dutton.
Carter, C. S. English church in the 17th century.—English church in the 18th century. ea., *40 c. net. Longmans.
Chadwick, W. E. Social work. *40 c. net. Longmans.
Clayton, H. J. Church defence. 90 c. net. Longmans.
Day-hours of the Church of England. *$1.25 net. Longmans.
Dearmer, P. Everyman's history of the English church. *75 c. net; *$1 net; *50 c. net. Warne.
English Church manuals. v. 1-19. ea., *4 c. net; per doz., *36 c. net; per 100, *$3 net. Longmans.
Francis, P. J., *and* Jones, S. Prince of the apostles: [argument favoring the union of the Catholic church and the Church of England.] *75 c. net. Lamp Pub.
Handbooks of English Church expansion. 6 v. ea., 80 c. Young Churchman.
Henson, H. H. National church: essays on its history and constitution and criticisms of present administration. *$1.50 net. Macmillan.
Hole, C: Manual of English church hist. $1.25 net. Longmans.
Holmes, E. E: The church; her books and her sacraments. $1 net. Longmans.
Kempson, F. C. Church in modern England. *$1.25 net. Dutton.
Kennedy, W. M. "Interpretations" of the bishops and their influence on Elizabethan Episcopal policy. 50 c. Longmans.
Kinsman, F: J. Principles of Anglicanism. $1 net. Longmans.

CHURCH OF ENGLAND.—*Continued.*
Lacey, T. A. Roman diary and other documents rel. to the papal inquiry into English ordinations, 1896. $3.50 net. Longmans.
Mallock, W: H. Doctrine and doctrinal disruption: examination of the intellectual position of the Church of England. *$1.50 net. Macmillan.
Meyrick, F. Doctrine of the Church of England on the holy communion. $1.—Scriptural and Catholic truth and worship; or, faith and worship of primitive, mediæval and reformed Anglican churches. $1. Longmans.
Moule, H. C. G., Drury, T: W., *and* Girdlestone, R. B. English church teaching on faith, life and order. *40 c. net. Longmans.
Moyes, J. Aspects of Anglicanism. *$1 net. Longmans.
Nelson, W: Controversy over the proposition for an American episcopate, 1767-1774. $2.50. Paterson Hist.
Palmer, W: S. Church and modern men. *$1.20 net. Longmans.
Patterson, M. W. History of the Church of England. *$2 net. Longmans.
Sanders, H: M. Message of the church in collect, epistle and gospel. v. 1, 2. ea., *$1.20 net. Longmans.
Simpson, W: J: S. Use of vestments in the English church. *20 c. net. Longmans.
Stephens, W: R: W., *and* Hunt, W:, *eds.* New hist. of the English church. In 8 v. v. 8. $2 net. Macmillan.
Stock, E. English church in the nineteenth century. 40 c. net. Longmans.
Stone, D. Episcopacy and valid orders in the primitive church.—Invocation of saints. ea., *40 c. net Longmans.
Usher, R. G. Reconstruction of the English church. 2 v. $6 net. Appleton.
Ware, S. L. Elizabethan parish. 50 c. Johns Hopkins.
See also Anglican orders;—Apostles' creed;—Apostolic succession;—Athanasian creed;—Baptism;—Book of common prayer;—Cathedrals;—Church history;—Church polity;—Church unity;—Confession;—Confirmation;—Creeds;—Cross;—Devotional exercises;—Easter;—Incarnation;—Marriage;—Ministers (*of the Gospel*);—Protestant Episcopal church;—Reformation;—Sacraments;—Sermons;—Worship.

CHURCH OF ROME.
See Catholic church.

Church of Sweden. Williams, G. M. 50 c. Young Churchman.

Church of the Apostles. Ragg, L. *$1.40 net. Macmillan.

Church of the Brethren. Two centuries of the Church of the Brethren; or, the beginnings of the Brotherhood; bicentennial addresses at the annual conference held at Des Moines, Ia., June 3, 1908. '08, [1909.] (Mr) c. 398 p. pors. 8°, $1.50; hf. leath., $2.50. Brethren Pub. Ho.

Church of the fathers. Newman, J: H: *75 c. net. Longmans.

CHURCH OF THE REDEEMER, Jersey City, N. J.
Heindel, J: E. Short hist. of the English Evangelical Lutheran Church of the Redeemer. 50 c. J: E. Heindel.

Church on wheels. Rust, C: H. 50 c. Am. Bapt.

CHURCH POLITY.
Blatchford, A N. Church councils and their decrees. *80 c. net. Am. Unitarian.

Church pulpit commentary. In 12 v. v. 1, Genesis-Deuteronomy; v. 2, Joshua-2 Chronicles; v. 3, Ezra-Isaiah; v. 4, Jeremiah-Malachi; v. 5, St. Matthew; v. 6, St. Mark-St. Luke VII.; v. 7, St. Luke VIII-St. John V.; v. 8, St. John VI-Acts X. '09 (Mr27) ea., *$2 net. Gorham.

CHURCH SINGING.
See Church music.

CHURCH UNITY.
See Christian unity.

Church universal; ed. by W. H. Hutton. 12°. Macmillan.
—Hutton. Age of revolution. *$1.50 net.
—Medley. Church and the Empire. $1.40 net.

CHURCH WORK.
Ostrom, H: Crisis in church work. *50 c. net. Jennings.
See also Christian work.

Church work with boys. Forbush, W: B. 50 c. net. Pilgrim Press.

Church year. Armitage, W. J. $1. Oxford Univ.

CHURCHES.
Donaldson, S. A. Church life and thought in North Africa. *$1.25 net. Putnam.
New York church and musical directory of New York and Brooklyn and other adjacent suburbs. 50 c. W: G. James.
Ramsay, *Sir* W. M., *and* Bell, G. L. The thousand and one churches. $5 net. Doran.
Stabb, J: Some old Devon churches. *$3 net. Scribner.
Thompson, C. B. Churches and the wage earners. **$1 net. Scribner.
United States. *Dept. of Commerce and Labor. Bu. of the Census.* Religious bodies, 1906. '09(O) 91 p. diagrs., f°. (Add. Superintendent for price.)
Woodhouse, F: W. Churches of Coventry. *60 c. net. Macmillan.
See also Abbeys;—Cathedrals;—Church architecture;—Church decoration and ornament;—*also* names of churches;—*also* London;—New York City.

Churches outside the church. Coleman, G: W: 15 c. Am. Bapt.

Churchill, Alfr. Vance, ed.
See Buckley, Edm.

Churchill, Mrs. Caroline Nichols.
Active footsteps. '09(S11) c. por. D. $1.25. C. N. Churchill.

Churchill, Lady Randolph Spencer.
See Cornwallis-West, Jennie Jerome.

Churchill, W:
Weather words of Polynesia. '08(My16) 8°, (Memoirs of the American Anthropological Assoc.) pap., 80 c. Am. Anthropological.

Churchill, Winston.
Mr. Crewe's career. '08(My16) c. il. D. †$1.50. Macmillan.
Modern chronicle. '10(Ap9) c. il. D. $1.50. Macmillan.

Churchill, Winston Leonard Spencer.
Liberalism and the social problem. '10 (F5) D. *$1.50 net. Doran.
My African journey. '09(Ap17) il. maps, D. *$1.50 net. Doran.
Churchman's ready reference. Haverstick, A. C. $1. Young Churchman.
Churchmanship and character. Carnegie, W: H. *$1.25 net. Dutton.
Church's gain from modern thought. Kennett, R. H. 20 c. net. Longmans.
Church's mission to the mountaineers of the South. Hughson, W., *comp.* 75 c.; 50 c. Church Missions.
Churchward, Alb., M.D.
Signs and symbols of primordial man: explanation of the evolution of religious doctrines from the eschatology of the ancient Egyptians. '10(Jl16) il. 4°, $8 net. Dutton.
Cicero, Marcus Tullius.
Cato Maior de senectvte; ed., with introd. and commentary, by Edn. W. Bowen. '10(Je4) c. 12°, (Gildersleeve-Lodge Latin ser.) 75 c. Heath.
Cicero's letters sel. and ed. by Ernest Riess. '10(D10) c. D. 60 c. net. Macmillan.
De finibus bonorum et malorum; libri quinque; with introd. and commentary by W. M. L. Hutchinson. '09(My22) O. *$2.40 net. Longmans.
Essay on friendship (Lælius de amicitia); tr. from the Latin with notes by Alex. J. Inglis. '09(Mr) c. '08. 83 p. por. 12°, 50 c. Newton & C.
Laelivs de amicitia: ed., with introd. and commentary, by Edn. W. Bowen. '10 (Je4) c. 12°, (Gildersleeve-Lodge Latin ser.) 75 c. net. Heath.
Letters; sel. and ed. by Ernst Riess. '10 (N19) 12°, (Macmillan's Latin classics.) 60 c. net. Macmillan.
Orationes; pro. P. Quinctio, [etc.;] recognovit brevique adnotatione critica instruxit, Albertus Curtis Clark. '09(Je10) D. 75 c. Oxford Univ.
Orations; tr. by C: Duke Yonge; with introd. by C: Hermann Ohly. '08(Je27) c. il. 8°, $1.75; hf. mor., $3.50. Lamb Pub.
Philippic orations, 1, 2, 3, 5, 7; ed. by J: R. King. 2d ed.; rev. by A. C. Clark. '08 (S26) 8°, 90 c. Oxford Univ.
Select letters and orations; introd. by J: Milne. '09(Mr27) 16°, (Everyman's lib.) *35 c. net; leath., *70 c. net. Dutton.
Six orations (Allen and Greenough's edition); rev. by Ja. G. Greenough and G: L. Kittredge, with a special vocab. by Ja. B. Greenough. '09(Ap10) c. oil. maps, fold. plan, D. hf. leath., $1. Ginn.
Tusculan disputations I, II, V; with introd. and notes by H. C. Nutting. '10(Ja22) 16°, (Allyn & Bacon's college Latin ser.) $1.50. Allyn & B.
—, and Emerson, Ralph Waldo.
On friendship by Marcus Tullius Cicero; Friendship by Ralph Waldo Emerson. '09 (N6) c. D. **$2.50 net, boxed. Putnam.
—, and Sallust [Lat. Sallustius] Crispus, C.
Selected orations and letters of Cicero, to which is added The Catiline of Sallust; with historical introd., outline of the Roman constitution, notes, vocabulary and index, by Harold Whetstone Johnston; rev. by Hugh MacMaster Kingery. '10 (S10) il. plans, D. (Lake classical ser.) Six oration ed., $1; Ten oration ed., $1.25; class-room text, gratis. Scott, F. & Co.
CICERO, Marcus Tullius.
Clark, A. C. Inventa Italorum; being a contrib. to the textual criticism of Cicero. $3. Oxford Univ.
Merrill, W: A. Cicero's knowledge of Lucretius's poem. 10 c. Univ. of Cal.
Sage, E. T. Pseudo-Ciceronian Consolatio. 50 c. Univ. of Chic.
Cicerone (The). Burckhardt, J. C. $1.50. Scribner.
Ciceronianus. Erasmus, D. $1. Teachers' Coll.
Cid, Pío.
The American in Spain; being a pocket interpreter and guide to Spain and its language. '10(O15) il. D. 50 c. McKay.
Cid (Le). *See* Corneille, Pierre.
CID COMPEADOR.
Chronicle of the Cid; cronica del famoso Cavellero Cid Ruy Diez Campeador. [facsim.] $25. Hispanic Soc.
Chronicle of the Cid; coronica del muy esforçado y invencible cavellero el Cid Ruy Diaz Campeador delas Españas. [facsim.] $12. Hispanic Soc.
Plumer, M. W., *comp.* Stories from the chronicles of the Cid. 90 c. net. Holt.
CIDER.
Alwood, W: B. Enological studies: 1, Experiments in cider making applicable to farm conditions; 2, Notes on the use of pure yeast in wine making. U. S., Supt. of Docs.
Ciechanowski, S.
Prostate hypertrophy. [1910.] (Mr) *$2 net. W: R. Jenkins.
Formerly published by E. R. Pelton.
CIGARETTES.
Hubbard, E. Cigarettist; being a preachment. 10 c. Roycrofters.
McKeever, W: A. Cigarette smoking boy. gratis. W: A. McKeever.
Cimon and Pericles. *See* Plutarch.
CINCINNATI, Ohio.
Drake, D. Notices concerning Cincinnati. 2 v. in 1. (Not for sale.) Hist. and Phil. Soc., O.
Social register, Cincinnati and Dayton. $2.50. Social Register.
Cinderella. Eickemeyer, C. 25 c. C. Eickemeyer.
Cinderella. *See* Moore, C. C. Night before Christmas.
Cinderella owl book. Gordon, M. L. 50 c. Jacobs.
Cinderella ser. 12 v. '09(D) il. in col. ea., bds., 25 c. Doran.
Contents: Cinderella; Dick Whittington; Red Ridinghood; Please tell me a story; My very first book; My pretty reading book; Doggie and his ways; Pussy and her ways; Farmyard folk and their ways; Story of Jesus; Words of Jesus; Work of Jesus.

CINEMATOGRAPH.
Hite, M. H. Lessons how to become a successful moving picture machine operator. $5. M. H. Hite.
CINTRA, Portugal.
See Portugal.
CIPHER CODES.
See Codes.
Cipperly, J: Alb., comp.
See New York [State.] Labor laws.
Circle and square. Fuller, R. R. Fuller.
Circuit rider's wife. Harris, C. M. W. $1.50. Altemus.
Circular staircase. Rinehart, M. R. †$1.50. Bobbs-M.
CIRCULATION (of the blood).
See Blood.
Circumstantial evidence. Rhodes, L. R. 75 c. L. R. Rhodes.
CIRCUS.
Buffington, B. E., *and others*. Circus book for children: [a reader.] 50 c. B: H. Sanborn.
Greenwood, I: J: The circus; its origin and growth prior to 1835. *$5 net. Abbatt.
Turnour, J. Autobiography of a clown. **$1 net. Moffat.
Circus and all about it. Smith, E. B. $2. Stokes.
Circus book. Buffington, B. E. 50 c. B: H. Sanborn.
Circus boys ser. *See* Darlington, Edg. B. P.
Cisco, Jay Guy.
Historic Sumner County, Tennessee, with genealogies of the Bledsoe, Cage and Douglass families, and genealogical notes of other Sumner County families. '09 (My15) c. il. pors. 12°, $2. J. G. Cisco.
CITIES.
American Institute of Architects. Relation of railways to city development. $1. Glenn Brown.
League of American Municipalities. Book of American municipalities. [1908.] $2; 1909. $3.50. League Am. Municipalities.
League of American Municipalities. Book of American municipalities, [1910.] $3.50. Municipal Information.
Marsh, B: C., *and* Ford, G. B. Introduction to city planning. $1. B: C. Marsh.
Robinson, C: M. Call of the city. **$1.25 net. P. Elder.
Seattle, Wash. Public Library. Municipal plans; list of books and references to periodicals in the Seattle Public Library. gratis. Seattle Pub. Lib.
Singleton, E. Guide to great cities; Northwestern Europe. $1.25 net. Baker & T.
Strong, J. Challenge of the city. 50 c.; 35 c.; *$1 net. Young People's Miss.
Warner, A. D. The modern city. 25 c. Baumgardt.
Woodruff, C. R. The city: as it is and is to be. 20 c. Am. Bapt.
See also Children;—Great cities of the world ser.;—Local government;—Municipal government;—Municipal law;—Municipal ownership;—Parks;—Taxation;—Towns.
Cities of St. Paul. Ramsay, W: M. *$3 net. Armstrong.
Citizens of no mean city. Dower, H. T. (Add. pubs. for price.) Lutheran Pub.
Citizens' lib. of economics, politics and sociology; ed. by R: T. Ely. D. *$1.25 net. Macmillan.
—Carlton. Education and industrial evolution.
—MacLean. Wage-earning women.
—Mangold. Child problems.
—Parmelee. Principles of anthropology and sociology in their relation to criminal procedure.
—Wilcox. Great cities in America.
CITIZENSHIP.
Brooks, J: G. Conflict between private monopoly and good citizenship. **50 c. net. Houghton M.
Bryce, J. Hindrances to good citizenship. *$1.15 net. Yale Univ.
Cleveland, S. G. Good citizenship. 50 c. Altemus.
Hughes, C: E. Conditions of progress in democratic government. $1.15 net. Yale Univ.
Hughes, E. H. Teaching of citizenship. $1.25. Wilde.
Pam, M. Place of religion in good government. 50 c. Univ. Press, (Notre Dame.)
Richman, J., *and* Wallach, I. R. Good Citizenship. 45 c. Am. Bk.
Roeder, A. Practical citizenship. *$1.50 net. Blanchard.
Tucker, W: J. Public mindedness. $2. Rumford Press.
See also Education;—Naturalization;—Patriotism.
CITROUS FRUIT.
See Fruit;—Lemons;—Oranges.
City (The). Woodruff, C. R. 20 c. Am. Bapt.
City beautiful. Robinson, C: M. $1. Municipal Art Com., (Los A.)
City Club bull. pap. City Club, Chicago.
—Public Utility Commission of New York City. o. p.
City garden. Stillman, L. (Add. pubs. for price.) Ulbrich.
CITY GOVERNMENT.
See Municipal government.
CITY HALL PARK.
See New York City.
City History Society of Philadelphia pubs. 8°. (Sold to members only.) City Hist. Phil.
—Bicknell. The Wissahickon. $1.
—Garber. Settlements on the Delaware prior to the coming of William Penn.
—Heyl. Battle of Germantown. 25 c.
—Leffmann. Consolidation.—Notes on the secret service of the Revolutionary Army operating around Philadelphia.—Philadelphia celebrations. ea., 25 c.
—Lynch. Southwark. 50 c.
City of Beautiful Nonsense. Thurston, E. T. †$1.50. Dodd.
City of delight. Miller, E. J. †$1.50. Bobbs-M.
City of dreams, (Guanajuato.) Myers, C. B. G. 50 c. P. M. Myers.
City of encounters. Hazeltine, H. $1.50. M. Kennerley.
City of Penn. Gummere, A. M. 20 c. Biddle Press.
City of Six. Canfield, C. L. $1.50. McClurg.

City of splendid night. Harding, J: W: †$1.50. G: W. Dillingham.

City of the Dinner-pail. Lincoln, J. T. **$1.25 net. Houghton M.

City of the Golden Gate. Green, E. E. $1.25. Dodge.

City people. Flagg, J. M. **$3.50 net. Scribner.

CITY PLANNING.
See Town-planning.

City roads and pavements. Judson, W: P. *$2 net. Engineering News.

City school district. Bard, H. E. $1. Teachers' Coll.

City that is. Steel, R. *$1 net. A. M. Robertson.

City with foundations. M'Fadyen, J: E. *$1.25 net. Armstrong.

Civic Forum addresses. 12°, pap., 10 c. Civic Forum.
—Alderman. Growing South.
—Bryan. Thou shalt not steal.
—Eiden. Practical communism.
—Eliot. Lawlessness.
—Folk. Era of conscience.
—Hughes *and* Brewer. Idea of public office.
—Knox. People, the railroads and the national authority.
—Langdon *and* Markham. Struggle between graft and democracy.
—Miliukov. Constitutional government of Russia.
—Taft. Delays and defects in the enforcement of law in this country.
—Wu T'ing Fang. Awakening of China.

Civic League of St. Louis. *Housing Committee.* Housing conditions in St. Louis; text by Charlotte Rumbold. '08(Ap.) 84 p. il. O. pap. (Add. pubs. for price.) Civic League.

Civic League of St. Louis. Merit system in appointment to office; rept. of the Civil Service Committee of the Civic League to the Board of Freeholders of St. Louis, 1909. '10(Ja15) 8°, gratis. Civic League.

Civic League of St. Louis. *Signs and Billboards Committee.* Billboard advertising in St. Louis; rept. '10(Ap) 40 p. il. 8°, pap., gratis. Civic League.

Civic reader for new Americans. '08(Ap18) c. D. 38 c. Am. Bk.

CIVICS.
See Political science.

Civics and health. Allen, W: H. $1.25. Ginn.

CIVIL ENGINEERING.
See Engineering.

Civil engineering ser. *See* Longman's.

CIVIL GOVERNMENT.
See Political science;—*also* names of countries and states.

CIVIL LAW.

Jenks, E:, *ed.* Digest of English civil law. Bk. 2. pts. 1, 2, 3. ea., $1.25. Boston Bk.

Justinian I. Digest of Justinian. v. 2. *$4 net. Macmillan.

North Carolina. Notes on the code of civil procedure. (Priv. pr.) Seeman.

See also Cases;—Law, and references under that subject;—*also* names of states.

CIVIL SERVICE.

Brown, H. D. Civil-service retirement in Great Britain and in New Zealand. U. S., Supt. of Docs.

Chase, F. N. Government employ. 15 c. F. N. Chase.

Civic League of St. Louis. Merit system in appointment to office. gratis. Civic League.

Ewart, J. A., *and others.* Civil service manual. In 3 v. $2.50. Home Corr. Sch.

Foltz, E. B. K. Federal civil service as a career. **$1.50 net. Putnam.

Goff, R. R. Preparation for United States civil service examinations. $3. Clark Agency.

Goodwin, E. H. Merit system; letter in defense of the Civic League's detailed provision for a new city charter. 25 c. Civic League.

Graham, H. J. Civil service self-instructor. $2.50. H. J. Graham.

Hopkins, E. P. Government positions and how to secure them. 25 c. Wash. Civil Service.

Lachaussée, C: A. Custom house and internal revenue services, how to enter them. 25 c. Chief.

Rorke, T. S. Government positions. $1.25. Rorke.

Seely, W. *and* F: How to become an inspector on public works. (Add. pubs. for price.) M. C. Clark.

United States. *Civil Service Commission.* Information for boards of examiners concerning applications, examinations, and appointments, June 1, 1909. (Add. Superintendent for price.)

See also Examinations;—Police;—Post-Office;—*also* Philippine Islands.

CIVIL WAR (United States).

Abbott, L. A. Personal recollections and Civil War diary. (Add. pubs. for price.) L. A. Abbott.

Andrews, E. F. War time journal of a Georgia girl, 1864-1865. **$2.50 net. Appleton.

Ashburn, J. N. Hist. of 86th regiment, Ohio volunteer infantry. $1.50. J. N. Ashburn.

Bardeen, C: W: Little fifer's war diary. $3 net. Bardeen.

Barron, S: B. Lone Star defenders: a chronicle of the third Texas cavalry, Ross' brigade. *$2 net. Neale.

Battle, *Mrs.* L. E. L. Forget-me-nots of the Civil War. $1.50. J. M. Battle.

Billings, J: D. Hist. of the 10th Mass. Battery of Light Artillery in the War of the Rebellion. $2. Arakelyan.

Britton, W. Civil war on the border. 2 v. $4. Hudson.

Check, P. Hist. of Sauk Co. riflemen, 1861-1865. $1.50. P. Cheek.

Clark, W:, *comp.* Hist. of Hampton battery F, independent Pennsylvania light artillery. $2. W: Clark.

De Leon, P. M. Navies in war and the Confederate Navy in the war between the states. 25 c. H. T. Graves.

CIVIL WAR.—*Continued.*

Dougherty, M. Prison diary of Michael Dougherty. (Not for sale.) C: A. Dougherty.

Dyer, F: H., *comp.* Compendium of the war of the Rebellion. *$10 net. Torch Press.

Eby, H: H. Observations of an Illinois boy in battle, camp and prison, 1861 to 1865. $1. H: H. Eby.

Eggleston, G: C. Hist. of the Confederate War. $4 net. Sturgis & W.

Favill, J. M. Diary of a young officer serving with the armies of the United States during the war of the rebellion. *$1.50 net. Donnelley.

Fearn, F. H., *ed.* Diary of a refugee. $1.25 net. Moffat.

Fite, E. D: Social and industrial conditions in the North during the Civil War. **$2 net. Macmillan.

Fletcher, W: A. Rebel private, front and rear: experiences through the Civil War. $1. Greer Pr.

Floyd, F: C. History of the Fortieth (Mozart) Regiment, New York Volunteers: [from Bull Run to Appomattox.] $3. F: C. Floyd.

Formby, J: American Civil War. With book of maps, $4.50 net. Scribner.

Fox, S. M. Early hist. of the Seventh Kansas Cavalry. State Hist., Kan.

Freeman, D. S. Calendar of Confederate papers. $2.50. Confederate Museum.

Gause, I: Four years with five armies. *$2 net. Neale.

Gilpin, E. N. Last campaign: cavalryman's journal, [account of Gen. James H. Wilson's Cavalry Campaign in Alabama and Georgia.] 50 c. U. S. Cavalry.

Gould, J. Story of the 48th: a record of the campaigns of the 48th Regiment of Pennsylvania Veteran Volunteers Infantry during the four eventful years of its service in the war for the preservation of the Union. $4. J. Gould.

Hagood, J. Memoirs of the war of secession. $3. State Co.

Hall, H. A. History of the Sixth New York Cavalry, Army of the Potomac, 1861-1865. $5. F. A. Easton.

Hawn, W: All around the Civil War. 75 c. W: Hawn.

Hays, G. A., *comp.* Under the red patch; story of 63d Regiment Pa. Volunteers, 1861-1864; with personal narrative by W: H. Morrow, Company A. $2. G. A. Hays.

Hobart, E. L. Semi-hist. of a boy-veteran of the 28th Regiment Illinois Infantry Volunteers. $1.25. E. L. Hobart.

Hopkins, L. W. From Bull Run to Appomattox. $1.50. L. W. Hopkins.

Hubbard, J: M. Notes of a private. $1. E. H. Clarke.

Jacobs, M. Notes on the Rebel invasion of Maryland and Pennsylvania, and the battle of Gettysburg. $1; 25 c. G. E. Jacobs.

Johnson, E. R. Hist. of the War of the Secession, 1861-1865. $2 net. Wessels & B.

CIVIL WAR.—*Continued.*

Jones, B: W. Under the stars and bars. $1. B: W. Jones.

Kellogg, J: A. Capture and escape: narrative of army and prison life. $1. Wisconsin Hist.

Kidd, J. H. Personal recollections of a cavalryman with Custer's Michigan cavalry brigade in the Civil War. $2. J. H. Kidd.

Ledford, P. L. Reminiscences of the Civil War, 1861-1865. 25 c. News Pr. Ho.

McClendon, W: A: Recollections of war times, by an old veteran, while under Stonewall Jackson and Lieut.-Gen. James A. Longstreet. $1.25. W: A: McClendon.

McDonald, W: N. Hist. of the Laurel brigade, originally Ashby cavalry of the Army of North Virginia and Chew's battery. $3. K. S. McDonald.

McGuire, H. H., *and* Christian, G: L. Confederate cause and conduct in the war between the states. (Add. pub. for price.) L. H. Jenkins.

McKim, R. H. Soldier's recollections. $2 net. Longmans.

Military Historical Society of Massachusetts. v. 3, Campaigns in Virginia, Maryland, Pennsylvania, 1862-63. (Add. pubs. for price.)—v. 7, [Kentucky and Tennessee campaigns and their battles.] $2.50. Military Hist. Soc.

Mixson, F. M. Reminiscences of a private. $1. State Co.

Morton, J: W. Artillery of Nathan Bedford Forrest's cavalry. $2.50. Pub. Ho. of M. E. Ch., So.

Munford, B. B. Virginia's attitude toward slavery and secession. $2 net. Longmans.

O'Brien, J: E. Telegraphing in battle; reminiscences of the Civil War. $2 net. J: E. O'Brien.

Pennsylvania Cavalry. 18*th Reg't*, 1862-1865. History of the Eighteenth regiment of cavalry, Pennsylvania volunteers. $1. Wynkoop, H.

Polk, J. M. Confederate soldier. 35 c. J. Von Boeckmann.

Polley, J. B: Hood's Texas Brigade. $3.50 net.—Soldier's letters to charming Nellie. *$2 net. Neale.

Powe, J. H. Reminiscences and sketches of Confederate times by one who lived through them. H. P. Lynch.

Ragan, R. A. Escape from East Tennessee to the federal lines. $1. Dony.

Redway, G: W: War of the Secession, 1861-1862. $1.60. Macmillan.

Reed, J: A. Hist. of the 101st Regiment, Pennsylvania Veteran Volunteer Infantry, 1861-1865. $5. Dickey.

Robinson, A. J. Memorandum and anecdotes of the Civil War, 1862-1865. 25 c. A. J. Robinson.

Sawyer, G: H: V. Grant's campaign in Virginia, 1864, (the Wilderness campaign.) *$1.60 net. Macmillan.

Scofield, L. T. Retreat from Pulaski to Nashville, Tenn. (Add. pubs. for price.) Burrows.

CIVIL WAR.—*Continued.*
Sherrill, S: W: Heroes in gray. 30 c. C. J. Bell.
Shreve, W: P., *comp.* Story of the Third Army Corps Union. $1.50. W: P. Shreve.
Smith, C: H. Hist. of Fuller's Ohio brigade, 1861-1865. $3. C. H. Smith.
Smith, R. G. Brief acct. of the services rendered by the Second Regiment Delaware Volunteers in the war of the Rebellion. 50 c. Delaware Hist. Soc.
Stearns, A. A. Lady nurse of ward E. **$1.20 net. Baker & T.
Stevens, W: B. History of the 50th Reg. of Infantry, Mass. vol. militia. $2. Griffith-S.
Under the Maltese cross; Antietam to Appomattox. $5. 155th Regimental Assoc.
Union army: hist. of military affairs. 8 v. $48. Federal Pub. Co.
United States. Federal and state military organizations; history of certain federal troops which, by reason of short or disputed service, has no pensionable status, and state militias which were actively engaged in the Civil War for different periods of time, but which were never mustered into the service, and which, therefore, have no pensionable status. '10 (Ap) 52 p. 8°, pap. Gov. Pr. Off.
Van Alstyne, L. Diary of an enlisted man. $2. Tuttle, M. & T.
Walker, C. I. Women of the southern Confederacy during 1861-5. In 2 v. ea., $25. C. I. Walker.
Westcott, M. E. Civil war letters. 25 c. M. E. Westcott.
Whittle, W: C. Cruises of the Confederate States steamers "Shenandoah" and "Nashville." 50 c. W: C. Whittle.
Wright, M. J., *comp.* Tennessee in the war, 1861-1865. $1.50. A. Lee.
See also Andersonville prison;—Antietam;—Ashby cavalry;—Bull Run;—Cahaba, Ala.;—Cavalry;—Chancellorsville;—Cleburne, P. R.;—Dred Scott case;—Franklin (Battle of);—Georgia;—Gettysburg;—Grant, *General* U. S.;—Habeas corpus;—Indians;—Insurance;—Iowa;—Louisburg (Siege of);—Maine;—Military Order of the Loyal Legion;—Massachusetts;—Mississippi marine brigade;—Missouri;—Mosby's Rangers;—New Brunswick, N. J.;—North Carolina;—St. Louis, Mo.;—Shiloh;—South (The);—Vicksburg campaign;—Virginia;—West Point;—Wilderness (Battle of);—*also* Andrews, *Col.* R. S.;—Butler, *General* M. C.;—Davis, Jefferson;—Douglas, Stephen Arnold;—King, Richard;—Lee, Robert Edward;—Lusk, W: T.;—Porter, Joseph C.;—Quantrell, W. C.

Civil war and rebellion in the Roman empire. Henderson, B. W: *$2.60 net. Macmillan.

CIVILIZATION.
Albrecht, F: C. "World movement." 50 c. F: C. Albrecht.
Allen, E. A. Hist. of civilization. 8 v. $21. Ferguson-A.
Brooks, T. J. March of the intellect; review of man's achievements that make for the advancement of civilization. $1. B'way Pub.
Mahaffy, J: P. What have the Greeks done for modern civilization? **$2.50 net. Putnam.

CIVILIZATION.—*Continued.*
Mauro, P. Number of man; climax of civilization. *$1.25 net. Revell.
Seignobos, M. J. C. History of contemporary civilization. v. 3, [Modern civilization.] **$1.25 net. Scribner.
See also Education;—Ethics;—History;—Man;—Social science;—Superstition.

Claassen, H.
Beet sugar manufacture; auth. tr. from the 3d German ed. by W: T. Hall. '10(D17) c. 8°, $3 net. Wiley.

Claflin, H. B., Co.
Rugs and carpets from the Orient. '07, [1909.] c. 111 p. il. 8°, gratis. Claflin.

Claiborne, J. Herbert.
Cataract extraction: a ser. of papers read before the ophthalmological section N. Y. Academy of Medicine. '08(Ag22) il. 8°, *$2 net. Wood.

CLAIMS.
International Claim Agency, Pittsburgh, Pa. Next of kin, heirs at law, legatees, etc., etc., etc. $1. Int. Claim.

Claims and opportunities of the Christian ministry; ed. by J. R. Mott. 12°. Y. M. C. A.
—Bosworth. Modern interpretation of the call to the ministry. 10 c.—Weak church and strong man. 5 c.
—Gordon. Claims of the ministry on strong men. 10 c.
—Hodges. Independence of the ministry. 10 c.
—Hoyt. Call of the country church. 5 c.; per 100, $4.
—Jefferson. Minister as preacher. 5 c.; per 100, $4.
—McDowell. Right sort of men for the ministry. 10 c.; per 100, $8.
—Moore. Preparation of the modern minister. 10 c.; per 100, $8.
—Wilson. Minister and the community. 10 c.; per 100, $8.

Claims arising from results of personal injuries. Magruder, W: E: $2.50. Spectator.
Claims of French poetry. Bailey, J: C. $2.50. M. Kennerley.
Claims of the ministry on strong men. Gordon, G: A. 10 c. Y. M. C. A.

Clairmont, Adolfo de, M.D.
Guide to modern Peru. '08(Mr21) c. il. pors. O. pap. (Add. pub. for price.) A. de Clairmont.

Clairmont, Ralph de.
Reform: essay on the political, financial, and social condition of the United States. 4th ed. '09(F13) c. por. $1. Roxburgh.

CLAISEN CONDENSATION.
See Chemistry.

Clancy, Ja.
American civics, descriptive of the government of New York City, the states of New York and New Jersey, of the United States, and of political methods in nation and state; ed. by Hugh Hastings. '09 (D4) c. bds., $1. Democracy Pr.

Clans, septs and regiments of the Scottish Highlands. Adam, F. *$6 net. Scribner.

Clapin, Sylva.
New dictionary of Americanisms. '08(D) 581 p. 8°, $1. Weiss.

Clapp, Anne Barr, and Pound, Louise, eds.
Collegiate basket ball rules for women. '08(Jl4) c. il. 16°, pap., 15 c. Univ. Pub.

Clapp, F: Gardner.
Underground waters of southern Maine; with records of deep wells by W: Shirley Bayley. '09(Jl) 268 p. il. maps, 8°, (U. S. Dept. of the Interior; U. S. Geol. Survey bull., Water-supply paper.) pap., 55 c.

Clapperton, G:
Practical paper-making. 2d ed., rev. and enl. '08(Ap25) il. tabs., 12°, $2.50. Van Nostrand.

CLARE, *St.*
Life of Saint Clare. $1. Dolphin.
Du Puis, *Brother* F. Life and legend of the lady Saint Clare. $1.25 net. Longmans.

Clare, Harold Newton.
Choir-boy's manual; containing daily exercises in breathing and vocalizing. '08 (O17) c. O. pap., *25 c. net. Schirmer.
Choirmaster's manual. '08(O17) c. O. *75 c. net. Schirmer.

Clare, Israel Smith.
Illustrated hist. of all nations; cont. a record of the human race from the earliest historical period to the present time; embracing a general survey of the progress of mankind in national and social life, civil government, religion, literature, science and art. 15 v. '09(N) c. il. maps, facsims., 8°. (Add. pubs. for price.) Chr. Herald.

Clare, J:
Poems; ed., with an introd., by Arth. Symons. '09(My15) S. (Oxford lib. of prose and poetry.) 90 c. Oxford Univ.

Clare Loraine. "Lee," *pseud.* 85 c. Benziger.

Claretie, Arnaud Arsène, known as Jules.
Pierrille; ed., with introd., notes and vocab., by Hugh A. Smith and Casimir Zdanowicz. '10(Mr26) c. S. 40 c. Holt.

Claretie, Jules.
See Claretie, Arnaud Arsène.

Clarise, Henri, pseud.
See Cosgrove, *Mrs.* Henrietta Clarissa Jackson.

Clark, Lady.
Cookery book of Lady Clark of Tillypronie; ed. by C. F. Frere. '10(Je4) 4°, $2 net. Dutton.

Clark, Albert Curtis.
Cursus in mediæval and vulgar Latin; (paper read to the Oxford Philological Society on Feb. 18, 1910.) '10(My21) O. pap., 70 c. Oxford Univ.
Inventa Italorum; being a contribution to the textual criticism of Cicero; Pro Qvinctio, Pro Roscio Comoedo, Pro Caecina, De lege agraria contra Rvllvm, Pro Rabiro perdvellionis reo, Pro Flacco, In Pisonem, Pro Rabirio postvmo. '90(D25) facsims., O. (Anecdota Oxoniensia, classical ser.) pap., $3.40. Oxford Univ.
—, **comp.** Fontes prosae nvmerosae. '09(D25) O. bds., $1.50. Oxford Univ.

Clark, Albert Willistine.
Public school penmanship: hdbk. for teachers. '09(Je5) c. figs. D. 75 c. Ginn.

Clark, Alfr.
Ceylon. '10(D24) col. il. 12°, (Peeps at many lands ser.) 75 c. net. Macmillan.

CLARK, ARTHUR H., Co.
See **Printers and printing.**

Clark, Arth. Hamilton.
Clipper ship era, 1843-1869; epitome of famous American and British clipper ships, their owners, builders, commanders, and crews. '10(D31) il. 8°, $2 net. Putnam.

Clark, Austin Hobart.
Birds collected and observed during the cruise of the United States fisheries steamer "Albatross" in the North Pacific Ocean, and in the Bering, Okhotsk, Japan and eastern seas, from April to Dec., 1906. '10(My) 74 p. O. pap. U. S., Supt. of Docs.
On a collection of feather stars, or comatulids, from Japan. '08(Ag8) O. (Smithsonian Institution bulletin.) pap., 15 c. U. S., Supt. of Docs.

Clark, B. W.
See Hopkins, T: Cramer.

CLARK, Billy James.
Durkee, J. H. Hist. of World's Temperance Centennial Congress and memorial of Dr. Billy J. Clark, held at Saratoga Springs, N. Y., June 14-23, 1908. $1. J. H. Durkee.

Clark, C: C., comp.
Barley crops of the United States, 1866-1906. '08(Jl) 8°, (U. S. Dept. of Agriculture, Bureau of statistics, bull.) pap., 5 c. U. S., Supt. of Docs.
Buckwheat crops of the United States. 1866-1906. '08(Jl) 8°, (U. S. Dept. of Agriculture, Bureau of Statistics, bull.) pap., 5 c. U. S., Supt. of Docs.
Corn crops of the United States, 1866-1906. '08(Jl) 8°, (U. S. Dept. of Agriculture, Bureau of Statistics, bull.) pap., 5 c. U. S., Supt. of Docs.
Hay crops of the United States, 1866-1906. O. (U. S. Dept. of Agriculture, Bureau of Statistics, bull.) pap., 15 c. U. S., Supt. of Docs.
Oat crops of the United States, 1866-1906. '08(Jl) 8°, (U. S. Dept. of Agriculture, Bureau of Statistics, bull.) pap., 5 c. U. S., Supt. of Docs.
Potato crops of the United States, 1866-1906 '08(Jl) 8°, (U. S. Dept. of Agriculture, Bureau of Statistics, bull.) pap., 5 c. U. S., Supt. of Docs.
Rye crops of the United States, 1866-1906. '08(Jl) 8°, (U. S. Dept. of Agriculture, Bureau of Statistics, bull.) pap., 5 c. U. S., Supt. of Docs.
Wheat crops of the United States, 1866-1906. '08(Jl) 8°, (U. S. Dept. of Agriculture. Bureau of Statistics, bull.) pap., 5 c. U. S., Supt. of Docs.

Clark, C: Eug.
Local building association: a cornerstone of the commonweal; an address. '09 (S) 10 p. 12°, pap., 10 c. C: E. Clark.

Clark, C: Heber, ["Max Adeler."]
Great natural healer. '10(My14) c. il. S. bds., 50 c. Jacobs.

Clark, C: Sumner.
Tyranny of power; romance of two notable wars of the United States before the Rebellion. '10(My14) c. il. 12°, $1.50. C. M. Clark.
Clark, Edm. Persinger.
See Caldwell, Howard Wa.
Clark, Eleanor Jane.
Outlines of civil government, with suggestions for civic training by orig. work. '10(N19) c. 12°, 75 c. Palmer Co.
Clark, Ellery Harding.
Carleton case. '10(Ap16) c. il. D. $1.50. Bobbs-M.
Dick Randall, the young athlete. '10(D31) c. il. D. $1.50. Bobbs-M.
Loaded dice. '09(Mr13) c. il. D. †$1.50. Bobbs-M.
See also Graham, J:—White, Ernest Cleveland.
Clark, Esther Mary.
Call of Kansas, and other verses. [1910.] (S) c. 16 p. Tt. bds., 25 c. Seewir.
Clark, F. A.
Jack the Giant Killer; a juvenile operetta. '09(S) 40 c. Ditson.
Clark, Felicia Buttz.
The Jesuit. '08(D5) c. D. $1.25. Eaton & M.
Clark, Fs. E:, D.D., and Harriet Eliz. Abbott.
Gospel in Latin lands: outline studies of Protestant work in the Latin countries of Europe and America. '09(My22) c. maps, D. **50 c. net. Macmillan.
Clark, Galen.
Big trees of California. '08(My16) c. il. por. D. $1; pap., 50 c. G. Clark.
Indians of the Yosemite Valley and vicinity. 3d ed. '08(My16) c. il. por. D. $1; pap., 50 c. G. Clark.
Yosemite Valley; its history, characteristic features, and theories regarding its origin. '10(Jl16) D. $1; 50 c. Salter.
Clark, Rev. G: L.
Notions of a Yankee parson. '10(Ag6) c. D. $1 net. Sherman, F.
Clark, G: M.
See Parker, W: Ruston Percival.
Clark, G: Ramsey, Stevens, W: Oliver, and others.
The navy, 1775 to 1909. v. 1. '10(Ap) c. 482 p. por. 12°, $3. Midshipmen's Storekeeper.
Clark, Rev. G: Whitfield.
People's commentary; popular commentary upon a critical basis, especially designed for pastors and Sunday schools. In 9 v. v. 9, I, II, and III John, Jude and Revelation, by O. P. Eaches. '10 (O15) c. D. $1.25. Am. Bapt.
Clark, Georgina Binnie-.
See Binnie-Clark, Georgina.
Clark, H. H., D.D.
Sword of the nation, and other sermons. '10(Ap2) D. $1. Severn River.
Clark, Harriet Eliz. Abbott.
See Clark, Fs. E:
Clark, Harry Willard, and Gage, Stephen De Meritte.
Review of twenty-one years' experiments upon the purification of sewage at the Lawrence Experiment Station; [repr. from the 40th annual rept. of the State Board of Health.] '09, [1910.] (D) 291 p. tabs., 8°. (Priv. pr.) Mass. Bd. Health.
Clark, H: Spencer, comp. and ed.
Record of the lands and past descendants of Henry and Anne Clark, who settled on the head-branches of Whippany River, Roxiticus, Old Hunterdon County, N. J., 1728. '09(Ag28) por. O. pap., 50 c. H: S. Clark.
Clark, H: W:
Christ from without and within; a study of the Gospel by St. John. 2d ed. '09 (Ag14) 12°, *$1.25 net. Revell.
Christian method of ethics. '08(O3) 12°, *$1.25 net. Revell.
Gospel of St. John. '08(Ap25) 16°, (Westminster New Testament.) *75 c. net. Revell.
Laws of the inner kingdom. '10(F12) 12°, *$1.25 net. Revell.
Studies in the making of character. '10 (Jl16) 16°, 75 c. net. Revell.
Clark, Imogen.
Charming humbug. '09(Jl17) 12°, *$1.20 net. Dutton.
We four and two more. '09(S11) c. front. in col. D. †$1.25. Crowell.
Clark, Ira Crane.
Automatic system: treating of the doctrine of the triple tax. '08(Mr7) c. por. O. $1; pap., 50 c. D. S. Clark.
Clark, J. E.
See Canfield, W. W.
Clark, Jean Wilde.
Desk book on the etiquette of social stationery. '10(Ap23) c. il. 12°, $1. Eaton, C. & P.
—, ed. Weddings and wedding anniversaries; book of good form in the conduct of marriage ceremonies; with added chapters about the various anniversaries. '10(Je18) c. 8°, 25 c. Butterick.
Clark, J: Calvin Lawrence.
Tom Moore in Bermuda. 2d ed. '09(D4) c. il. O. bds., *$2 net. Smith & McC.
Clark, J: Jesse.
Slide rule; elem. treatise. [1910.] (F) c. '09. 62 p. fold. pl., 12°, 60 c. Technical Supply.
Clark, J: King.
Systematic moral education; with daily lessons in ethics. '10(N12) c. D. $1 net. Barnes.
Clark, J: Maurice.
Standards of reasonableness in local freight discriminations. '10(Jl9) c. O. (Columbia Univ. studies in history, economics and public law.) pap., $1.25 net. Longmans.
Clark, J: Willis.
Care of books: essay on the development of libraries and their fittings. 2d and cheaper ed. '09(My1) il. 4°, *$2.50 net. Putnam.
—, ed. Letters patent of Elizabeth and James the First, addressed to the University [of Cambridge,] with other docs.; (with a translation of the letters of Elizabeth.) '08 (F8) 8°, 75 c. Putnam.

Clark, Julia Gilman.
Ways of Eleanor, told by her mother. '08, [1909.] (Mr) 50 p. il. por. 8°. (Priv. pr.) Case.

Clark, Mrs. Kate Upson.
How Dexter paid his way. '08(S19) c. front. D. (Bimbi ser.) bds., **40 c. net. Crowell.

Clark, L. Pierce, M.D., and Diefendorf, Allen Ross, M.D.
Neurological and mental diagnosis. '08 (S19) il. *$1.25 net. Macmillan.

Clark, Rob. Carlton.
Beginnings of Texas, 1684-1718. '08(D19) map, O. (Univ. of Tex. bulletin; humanistic ser.) pap., 75 c. Univ. of Tex.

Clark, S: N.
Delegates from Denver: farcical comedy. '08(S19) c. 12°, pap., 25 c. Dick.

Clark, Solomon H:
How to teach reading in the public schools. '08(Ap25) 12°, $1. Scott, F. & Co.

Clark, Mrs. Susanna Rebecca Graham.
Janet Vardoff. '10(N12) c. il. O. $1.50. Griffith.

Clark, Susie Champney.
All that man should be unto woman; psychic story. '10(O15) c. 12°, $1.50. C. M. Clark.

Clark, W:, comp.
Hist. of Hampton battery F, independent Pennsylvania light artillery, organized at Pittsburgh, Pa., Oct. 8, 1861, mustered out in Pittsburgh, June 26, 1865. [1910.] (F) c. '09. 11-179 p. il. pors. double map, 4°, $2. W: Clark.

Clark, W: Lawrence.
Quiz book on Clark's elementary law; introductory course in the American Institute of Law. '09(S) c. 68 p. O. pap. (Add. pubs. for price.) Am. Law Bk.
—, **and Marshall, W: L.**
Supplement to Private corporations, bringing the law of each section of the original work down to the present time; with forms; by Arth. L. Helliwell; being v. 4 of the set. '08 (S) c. 8°, shp., $6.50. Keefe-D.
—, **comp.** Elementary law. '09(Je) c. 14+490 p. O. $5. Am. Law Bk.
—, **ed.** *See* Probate repts. annot.

Clark, Rev. W: Meade, ed.
Colonial churches in the original colony of Virginia. 2d ed., rev. and improved. '08 (O) c. 317 p. il. pors. $1.25. Southern Churchman.

CLARK COUNTY, Ind.
Baird, L. C. Hist. of Clark County, Ind. $15. B. F. Bowen.

CLARK FAMILY.
See Genealogies.

Clark University, Worcester, Mass. Twentieth anniversary, 1909.. [1910.] (F) 28 p. 12°. (Add. Univ. for price.) Clark Univ.

Clarke, Albert.
Tariff made plain. '08(Ja11) O. (Bright and Strong papers.) pap., 10 c. Home Market.

Clarke, C: Cameron, jr.
Common difficulties in reading French. '10 (F19) c. D. $1. W: R. Jenkins.

Clarke, C: Cowley.
Hdbk. of the divine liturgy; brief study of the historical development of the mass; with introd. by Rt. Rev. G. A. Burton, D.D. '10(My) 16+180 p. 12°, 90 c. Herder.

Clarke, Dan. Allen.
Commercial forest trees of Massachusetts; how you may know them. [2d ed.] '08, [1909.] (Mr) 66 p. il. 8°. (Add. pubs. for price.) Wright & P.

Clarke, Eliot Channing.
Astronomy from a dipper. '09(N6) c. charts, obl. Tt. **60 c. net. Houghton M.

Clarke, F.
School hist. of Hampshire. '10(Ja1) maps, D. 50 c. Oxford Univ.
—, **ed.** Short hist. of Southampton. In 2 pts. pt. 1, The story of Southampton in relation to the hist. of England, by F. J. C. Hearnshaw; pt. 2, Some aspects of town-life, by members of the Southampton Historical Association and others; ed. by F. Clarke. '10(O8) il. D. 70 c. Oxford Univ.

Clarke, Fk. Wigglesworth.
Analyses of rocks and minerals from the lab'y of the U. S. Geolog. Survey, 1880 to 1908. '10(My) 12+323 p. 8°. (U. S. Geolog. Survey, bull.)
Preliminary study of chemical denudation. '10(S) 19 p. 8°, (Smithsonian misc. collections.) pap., 5 c. Smith. Inst.
Recalculation of the atomic weights. 3d ed., rev. and enl. '10(Jl) 4+ 548 p. 8°, (Smithsonian misc. coll.) Smith. Inst.

Clarke, Helen Archibald.
Ancient myths and modern poets. '10(O8) c. il. O. $2 net. Baker & T.
Browning's England: a study of English influences in Browning. '08(N21) c. il. pors. O. **$2 net. Baker & T.
Child's guide to mythology. '08(D5) c. il. O. **$1.25 net. Baker & T.
Hawthorne's country. '10(D3) c. il. por. O. $2.50 net, boxed. Baker & T.
Longfellow's country. '09(N6) il. pors. O. **$2 net, boxed. Baker & T.

Clarke, Hugh Archibald.
Harmony on the inductive method. '08 (D) c. 144 p. 12°, $1. Ditson.

Clarke, J. Jackson, M.D.
Protozoa and disease. pt. 2, Comprising sections on the causation of smallpox, syphilis and cancer. '08(F15) il. figs. sq. 8°, *$2.50 net. Wood.

Clarke, Ja. Freeman.
Transfiguration of life. '09(N20) D. *$1 net. Am. Unitarian.

Clarke, J:, and Bentalou, Paul.
Impartial and authentic narrative of the battle fought on the 17th of June, 1775, between His Britannic Majesty's troops and the American provincial army on Bunker's Hill. 2d ed.; by J: Clarke; [and] Pulaski vindicated from unsupported charge inconsiderately or malignantly introduced in Judge Johnson's Sketches of the life and correspondence of Major Gen. Nathaniel Greene; by Paul Bentalou; (*Magazine of History with Notes and Queries;* extra no.) '10 (My21) 4°, to subscribers, $1.65. Abbatt.

Clarke, J: Bernard.
See Bush, Wa. Nelson.

Clarke, J: H., M.D.
Vital economy; or, how to conserve your strength. '09(D11) c. D. 50 c.; pap., *30 c. net. Wessels.

Clarke, J: Mason.
Beginnings of independent life. '08(Je.) 50 c. J: M. Clarke.
Early Devonic hist. of New York and eastern North America. pt. 1. '08(D) il. pls. 4°, (N. Y. State Museum memoirs.) pap., $2.50. N. Y. State Educ.
English gold lustres. '08(Je6) il. O. pap. (Add. author for price.) J: M. Clarke.
Swiss influence on the early Pennsylvania slip decorated majolica. '08(Je6) il. O. pap. (Add. author for price.) J: M. Clarke.

—, Luther, D. Dana, and Fairchild, Herman Le Roy.
Geologic map and descriptions of the Portage and Nunda quadrangles, incl. a map of Letchworth Park, by J: M. Clarke and D. Dana Luther; accompanied by a report on the Pleistocene history of the Genesee Valley, by Herman L. Fairchild. '08(Ag1) il. maps, 8°, (N. Y. State Museum bull., Paleontology.) pap., 20 c. N. Y. State Educ.

Clarke, Jos. Ignatius Constantine, and Hubbard, Elbert.
Manhattan, an ode by Jos. I. C. Clarke; Henry Hudson, an essay by Elbert Hubbard. '10(O) 9-62 p. 8°, $2. Roycrofters.

Clarke, Rebecca Sophia, ["Sophie May."]
Little Prudy ser. 3 v. '09(O2) c. D. per set, $2, boxed. (Sold in sets only.) Caldwell.
Little Prudy's Dotty Dimple. '08(Jl18) 12°, (Home ser.) 50 c. Hurst.
Little Prudy's story book. '08(Je13) 12°, (Home ser.) 50 c. Hurst.

Clarke, T. E. S., and Foxcroft, Helen Charlotte.
Life of Gilbert Burnet, bishop of Salisbury; with bibliographical appendixes: with an introd. by C. H. Firth. '08(F1) 8°, *$4.50 net. Putnam.

Clarke, W: Ja. Patmore, ["W: J. Patmore."]
Happy night. '08(N) c. 208 p. 12°, $1.50. Cochrane.

Clarke, W: Newton.
Christian doctrine of God. '09(Mr20) c. O. (International theological lib.) **$2.50 net. Scribner.
Sixty years with the Bible: a record of experience. '09(O9) c. D. **$1.25 net. Scribner.

Clarke, W: Packer.
Official history of the militia and the National guard of the state of Pennsylvania, from the earliest period of record to the present time. 3 v. [1910.] (Jl) pors. f°, $50. C. J. Hendler.
"Tables of authorities" (1 p.).

CLARKSFIELD, Ohio.
Weeks, F. E. Pioneer hist. of Clarksfield. *$1 net. F. E. Weeks.

Clarkson's standard American dict. of the English language; prepared under the ed. supervision of T: H. Russell, Albert C. Bean, L. B. Vaughan, [and others.] '08(O) c. 24+1956 p. il. maps, 4°, $7.75. D: B. Clarkson.

Class notes in music history. Pratt, W. S. *30 c. net. Schirmer.

Class room (The). No. 1, The art of teaching, a color palette and its use, ground laying, lustres; No. 2, Flower painting on porcelain. '09(O2) il. F. pap., ea., $3, boxed. Keramic.

Class-room libraries for public schools. Buffalo Public Library. 25 c. Buffalo Pub. Lib.

Class struggle. Kautsky, K. 50 c.; 25 c. Kerr.

Class teaching and management. Chancellor, W: E. $1. Harper.

Classic drama: plays by Greek, Spanish, French, German and English dramatists; with introd. by Albert Ellery Bergh. '08 (Je27) c. 2 v., il. 8°, $3.50; hf. mor., $7. Lamb Pub.

Classic lib. S. 25 c.; pap., 15 c. Educ. Pub.
—Bunyan. Pilgrim's progress.
—Longfellow. Tales of a wayside inn.
—Shakespeare. Antony and Cleopatra.—Merchant of Venice.—Taming of the shrew.
—Whittier. Snowbound.

Classic memoirs. In 3 v. '08(Je27) c. il. 8°, $5.25; hf. mor., $10.50. Lamb Pub.

Classic stories for boys and girls. D. Penn Pub. Co.
—Edmison. Stories from the Norseland. †$1.25.

Classical Conference, Ann Arbor, Mich., 1908. Value of humanistic, particularly classical, studies as a preparation for the study of theology, from the point of view of the profession; a symposium from the Proceedings of the Classical Conference held at Ann Arbor, Michigan, April 1, 1908. [1910.] (Ap) 47 p. 4°. (Add. pubs. for price.) Univ. of Mich.

CLASSICAL EDUCATION.
See Education.

CLASSICAL LITERATURE.
Smith, *Sir* W: Smaller classical dict. 35 c. net; 70 c. net. Dutton.
Zielinski, F. F. Our debt to antiquity; [reasons advanced for maintenance of the classics as groundwork for education.] *75 c. net. Dutton.

Classical moralists. Rand, B:, *comp.* **$3 net. Houghton M.

CLASSICAL PHILOLOGY.
Jones, H. L. Poetic plural of Greek tragedy in the light of Homeric usage. 80 c. Longmans.
Morgan, M. H. Addresses and essays. $1.50. Am. Bk.
Postgate, J: P. Flaws in classical research. *$1.40 net. Oxford Univ.

Classical scholarship. *See* Sandys, J: Edn.

Classical ser. *See* Macmillan's.

Classics in art ser. il. Q. Brentano's.
—Buonarotti. Work of Michelangelo. **$2.50 net.
—Correggio. [Work of] Correggio. *$3 net.

Classics of the bar. Sellers, A. V. $2. Classic.

Classics old and new. Alderman, E. A. 1st reader. 25 c.—5th reader. 40 c. Am. Bk.

CLASSIFICATION.
Carnegie Library, Pittsburgh. Index to subject catalogue of the Technology Dept. 10 c. Carnegie Lib.
Goodyear, W: H: Desirable projection of art museums as suggested by the desirable classification of art libraries. (Priv. pr.) W: H: Goodyear.

Classification of religions. Ward, D. J. H. 75 c. Open Court.

Classiques (Les) français; ed. by M. H. Warner Allen and D. S. O'Connor. 12°, *$1 net. Putnam.
—Boileau-Despréaux. Satires épitres.
—Bossuet. Oraisons funèbres.
—Hugo. Poèmes choisis, 1822-1860.
—Rousseau. Julie.

Classiques (Les) français illustrées. il. 12°, *$1.40 net. Macmillan.
—Balzac. Les chouans.
—Sand, *pseud.* François le Champi.—La mare au diable.—Les maîtres sonneurs.

Claud Denvil, artist. Bearne, D: *$1 net. Herder.

CLAUDINUS, Claudius.
Crees, J. H. E: Claudian as an historical authority. *$1.50 net. Putnam.

CLAVERACK, N. Y.
Gebhard, E. L. Parsonage between two manors. $1.50. E. L. Gebhard.

Clavis universalis. Collier, A. $1.50. Open Court.

Clawson, W: Hall.
Gest of Robin Hood. '09(Ag14) O. (Univ. of Toronto studies, Philological ser.) pap., $1. Univ. of Toronto.

Clay, Albert Tobias.
Amurru, the home of the northern Semites; study showing that the religion and culture of Israel are not of Babylonian origin. '10(Ja15) c. map, 8°, $1.25. S. S. Times.
Legal and commercial transactions dated in the Assyrian, Neo-Babylonian and Persian periods, chiefly from Nippur. 08, [1909.] (Ja) 9+85 p. il. facsims., f°, (Babylonian expedition of the Univ. of Penn.) $6. Univ. of Penn.

CLAY, Henry.
Clay, T: H. Henry Clay. **$1.25 net. Jacobs.

Clay, J: Cecil, comp.
See Herford, Oliver, *comp.*

Clay, T: Hart.
Henry Clay; by his grandson; completed by Ellis Paxon Oberholtzer. '10(F26) c. por. D. (American crisis biographies.) **$1.25 net. Jacobs.

CLAY.
Branner, J: C. Bibliography of clays and ceramic arts. $2. Am. Ceramics.
Branner, J: C. Clays of Arkansas. (Add. Supt. for price.) U. S., Supt. of Docs.
Lester, K. M. Clay work: hdbk. for teachers. $1.25. Manual Arts.
Logan, W: N. Clays of Mississippi. pt. 1. (Add. pubs. for price.) Brandon Pr.

CLAY.—*Continued.*
Ries, H. Clays of Texas. $2. Univ. of Tex.
Ries, H. Clays, their occurrences, properties and uses. **$5 net.—Hist. of the clay-working industry in the United States. **$2.50 net. Wiley.
United States. *Dept. of the Interior. U. S. Geolog. Survey.* Colloid matter of clay. 10 c. U. S., Supt. of Docs.
Veatch, O. Second rept. on the clay deposits of Georgia. gratis. S: W. McCallie.
See also Bricks;—Mississippi;—Modelling.

Clay Products Association of America, New York. House of brick; plea for the greater use of brick in our domestic architecture. '10(Mr5) c. il. plans, 4°, 50 c. Rogers & M.

Clayhanger. Bennett, A. $1.50 net. Dutton.

CLAYPOOL, *Mrs.* Elizabeth Griscom Ross Ashburn [Betsy Ross].
Parry, O. R. Betsy Ross and the United States flag. 20 c.; 10 c. T. W. Worrall.

Clayton, Edwy Godwin, comp.
Compendium of food microscopy; with sections on drugs, water and tobacco; comp. with additions and revisions from the late Dr. A. H. Hassall's works on food. '09(N) 471 p. il. 8°, *$4 net. Wood.

Clayton, Rev. H. J.
Church defense. '10(D3) S. (Hdbks. for the clergy.) 90 c. net. Longmans.

Clayton, H: Helm, and Fergusson, Stirling Price.
Exploration of the air with ballon-sondes, at St. Louis, and with kites at Blue Hill. '09(Jl3) il. tabs., 4°, (Annals of the Astronomical Observatory of Harvard Univ.) pap., $1. Harvard Univ.

Clayton, Jos. Culbertson.
True constitution. '08(Je6) c. pors. O. *$3 net. Assoc. Pub.

Clayton, Marg.
Camping in the forest; the adventures of five children. '09(O2) il. O. *$1 net. Warne.

Clayton, W: Brasher, and Craig, Ja. Watt.
Questions and answers about electrical apparatus: summary of a two-years' course in the testing department of the General Electric Company. '08(Je27) c. O. 50 c.; pap., 35 c. Clayton & C.; T: P. Nichols.

Clean and strong. King, E. A. $1. Un. Soc. C. E.

Clean milk. Coit, H: L. (Add. pubs. for price.) Jefferson Co. Med. Soc

Clean Peter and the children of Grubbylea. Adelborg, O. $1.25. Longmans.

CLEANING.
—— "from cellar to garret; textbook on household science. 10 c. Carbona.
Baird, H: C. Pract. dry cleaner, scourer and garment dyer. *$2.50 net. Baird.
Courvoisier, C. T. Spots; or, 202 cleansers. $2; $3 net. P. Elder.
Farrell, F. J. Dyeing and cleaning. (Add. pubs. for price.) Lippincott.
Osman, E. G. Cleaning and renovating at home. 75 c. net. McClurg.

CLEANING.—*Continued.*
Owen, F. A., *and* Standage, H. C. Dyeing and cleaning of textile fabrics. $2. Wiley.
Pawlie, E: Pract. hdbk. of garment dyeing and cleaning. $3.75. M. M. Frank.
Cleanliness versus corruption. Sutherland-Gower, R., *Lord.* 25 c. Longmans.
"Clear, Claudius," pseud.
See Nicoll, *Sir* W: Robertson.
CLEARING HOUSE.
See **Banks and banking.**
Clearing-house systems of the world; review of the methods used in clearing checks in the principal countries; also the origin and development of banker's clearing houses; American Bankers' Convention yearbook, 1910. '10(D10) c. il. tabs., forms, 4°, $1. Banking Law.
Cleary, J: M.
See Missouri. St. Louis, the Kansas City and the Springfield *Cts. of appeals.* Cases.
Cleaves, Marg. Abigail, M.D.
Autobiography of a neurasthene, as told by one of them and recorded by Marg. A. Cleaves. '09(N6) c. D. $1.50. Badger.
CLEBURNE. *General* Patrick Ronayne.
Buck, I. A. Cleburne and his command. *$3 net. Neale.
Cleft grafting. Couts, C: O. 50 c. C: O. Couts.
Clegg, Ja., ed.
See International directory of booksellers.
Clegg, T: Bailey.
Bishop's scapegoat. '08(My2) D. †$1.50. Lane.
Joan of the hills. '09(Je12) D. $1.50. Lane.
Clemens, G. C.
Township officers' guide; manual of the laws concerning townships and township officers in Kansas. 13th ed.; rev. 1909 by W. L. Harvey. '09(S) c. 116 p. O. pap., 50 c. Crane.
—, comp. *See* Kansas General election laws.
Clemens, S: Langhorne, ["Mark Twain."]
Complete works. Hillcrest ed. v. 24, 25. '08(Ap11) c. il. 12°, subs. (Add. pubs. for price.) Am. Pub.
Writings of Mark Twain. Author's national ed. 25 v. [1910.] (D) il. pors. 12°. (Subs. only.) Harper.
Adventures of Tom Sawyer. '10(O22) c. il. O. $2 net, boxed. Harper.
Extract from Captain Stormfield's visit to Heaven. '09(O23) c. front. O. †$1. Harper.
Is Shakespeare dead?; from my autobiography. '09(Ap17) c. O. **$1.25 net. Harper.
Mark Twain's (burlesque) autobiography. '10(S17) D. pap., 25 c. Ormeril.
Mark Twain's speeches; with introd. by W: Dean Howells. '10(Jl2) c. front. por. D. $2 net. Harper.
Travels at home; sel. from the works of Mark Twain by Percival Chubb and arr. for home supplementary reading in the sixth, seventh, and eighth grades. '10 (Ap30) c. il. por. D. (Harper's modern ser. of supp. readers for the elem. schools.) 50 c. Harper.
Travels in history; sel. from the works of Mark Twain by C. N. Kendall, and arr. for home and supp. reading in the sixth, seventh and eighth grades. '10(Ag27) c. il. D. (Harper's modern ser. of supp. readers for the elem. schools.) 50 c. Harper.
See also Stories of humor.
CLEMENS, Samuel Langhorne.
Cooke, P. Our misunderstanding concerning the Jews: being a criticism principally of an article—"Concerning the Jews"—by Mark Twain. (Add. author for price.) P. Cooke.
Howells, W: D. My Mark Twain. $1.40 net. Harper.
Johnson, M., *comp.* Bibliography of the work of Mark Twain, Samuel Langhorne Clemens, $5. Harper.
Clement, E: H:
Bull-Run rout; scenes attending the first clash of volunteers in the civil war. '09, [1910.] (F) 13 p. 8°, pap. (Add. author for price.) E: H: Clement.
Clement, J. K.
On the rate of formation of carbon monoxide in gas producers. '09(Ag21) il. tabs., O. (Univ. of Ill. bull.; Engineering experiment station.) pap. (Add. Univ. for price.) Univ. of Ill.
—, and Egy, Willard Leo.
Thermal conductivity of fire-clay at high temperatures. [1910.] (Ag) 31 p. il. 8°, (Univ. of Ill., Engineering Experiment Station bull.) pap., gratis. Univ. of Ill.
—, and Garland, Claude Mallory.
Study in heat transmission; (the transmission of heat to water in tubes as affected by the velocity of the water.) '09, [1910.] 17 p. figs. tabs., O. (Univ. of Ill.; Engineering Experiment Station, bull.) pap. Univ. of Ill.
Clement, Luo.
Ancient science of numbers: practical application of its principles in the attainment of health, success, and happiness. '08(My23) c. D. $1. Roger Bros.
Clements, Frederic E:
Genera of *fungi.* '09(D) 227 p. 8°, $2. H. W. Wilson.
Clements, Jos., M.D.
Metaphysics of the nature and in the conception of the soul: its habitat? '10 (Mr12) c. 12°. $1. Roxburgh.
Clendening, Lura Kelsey.
Ropes of sand: [poems.] '08(F22) c. D. $1.50. Badger.
Clennell, J: E:
Chemistry of cyanide solutions resulting from the treatment of ores. 2d ed., corrected and enl. '10(Mr5) c. tabs., O. *$2.50 net. McGraw-H.
Cyanide hdbk. '10(My14) c. O. $5 net. McGraw-H.
CLEOPATRA, *Queen of Egypt.*
Sergeant, P. W. Cleopatra of Egypt. $4 net. Dodd.
CLERGY.
See Ministers (*of the Gospel*);—Priests.

CLERGYMEN.
See Ministers (*of the Gospel*)

Clerical humour of olden time. How, F: D. $2. Pitman.

CLERIDAE.
See Beetles.

Clerk, Dugald.
Gas, petrol and oil engine. v. 1, General principles of the internal combustion engine, together with historical sketch. New ed., rev. and enl. '09(Ag14) figs. 8°, *$4 net. Wiley.

Clerke, Agnes Mary.
Popular history of astronomy during the nineteenth century. '08(My2) il. 8°, price reduced from *$4 net to *$2.75 net; now *$2.60 net. Macmillan.

Clerkes tale. *See* Chaucer, Geoffrey.

Cléry, Jean Baptiste Cant-Hanet.
Royal family in the Temple Prison; (journal of the imprisonment;) with a supplementary chapter on the last hours of Louis XVI. by his confessor, l'Abbe Edgeworth de Firmont; tr. from the French by E. Jules Meras. '09(N6) c. front. D. (Court ser. of French memoirs.) $1.50. Sturgis & W.

Cleveland, F: Albert.
Bank and the treasury: bank capitalization and the problem of elasticity. New ed., rev '08. c. il. O. **$2 net. Longmans.
Chapters on municipal administration and accounting. '09(Je5) c. O. **$2 net. Longmans.

—, and Powell, Fred. Wilbur.
Railroad promotion and capitalization in the United States. '09(My22) c. O. **$2 net. Longmans.

CLEVELAND, Grover.
Gilder, R: W. Grover Cleveland; record of friendship. $1.80 net. Century Co.

Cleveland, Rob.
What Burlingame did: true story of a young electrician. '08(D) c. 11-90 p. il. por. 24°. (Add. author for price.) R. Cleveland.

Cleveland, Stephen Grover.
Addresses, state papers and letters; ed. by Albert Ellery Bergh. '09(Je) c. 499 p. por. 12°. (Add. pubs. for price.) Sun Dial.
Good citizenship. '08(Jl11) c. S. 50 c. Altemus.

CLEVELAND, Stephen Grover.
Parker, G: F. Recollections of Grover Cleveland. **$3 net. Century Co.
Williams, J. L. Mr. Cleveland. **50 c. net. Dodd.

Cleveland, Treadwell, jr.
Status of forestry in the United States. '09(D18) 8°, (U. S., Dept. of Agriculture, Forest Service, circular.) pap.

CLEVELAND, Ohio.
Springborn, W: J: Cleveland garbage disposal plant. gratis. W: J: Springborn.

Cleveland Public Library. Work of the Cleveland Public Library with the children, and the means used to reach them: pub. for the information of the citizens of Cleveland and the members of the National Educational Association. '08, [1909.] (Mr) 48 p. il. 8°. Cleveland Pub. Lib.

Clevenger, Shobal Vail, M.D.
Fun in a doctor's life: numerous short stories and essays. '08(O3) $1. Evolution Pub.

Clever Betsy. Burnham, *Mrs.* C. L. R. $1.25 net. Houghton M.

Clever business sketches. Stoll, A., *jr., comp.* $1. Business Man's Pub.

Clews, H:
Fifty years in Wall Street: "Twenty-eight years in Wall Street;" revised and enlarged by a resumé of the past twenty-two years. '08(Je20) c. il. pors. map, O. *$3 net. H: Clews.
Financial and trade situation, past, present and future; reviewing the crisis of 1907, with causes and remedies; an address del. at the annual meeting of the Pittsburgh Chapter, American Inst. of Banking, Feb. 25, 1908. '08(D) (Add. pubs. for price.) H: Clews.
Individualism versus socialism: address at the Columbia Theatre, Brooklyn, on Sunday afternoon, May 12. '07, [1908.] (Mr.) 2+12 p. 12°. Add. author for price.) H: Clews.
No government guarantee of bank deposits, and no ownership of railroads by the government; address del. at the annual meeting of the American Institute of Banking, Baltimore Chapter, Baltimore, Md., Oct. 13, 1908. '08(D) 14 p. 8°, pap. (Add. author for price.) H: Clews.

Cliartho Philanders. Dounce, H. E. 25 c. G: W. Browning.

Client princes of the Roman Empire. Sands, P. C. *$1.50 net. Putnam.

Clif Stirling ser. *See* Standish, B. L., *pseud.*

CLIFF DWELLERS.
Fewkes, J. W. Antiquities of the Mesa Verde National Park; Spruse Tree House. (Add. Superintendent for price.) U. S., Supt. of Docs.
Manitou cliff dwellers' ruins. 25 c. Manitou.

Clifford, Lady.
See De la Pasture, *Mrs.* Eliz. Bonham.

Clifford, Clifford Robbins.
Color value. '08(My16) c. il. map, 8°, *$1 net. Clifford & L.

Clifford, H: B.
Rocks in the road to fortune; or, the unsound side of mining. '08(My16) c. il. por. 12°, $1.50. Gotham Press.

Clifford, Mrs. Lucy Lane, [Mrs. W: Kingdon Clifford.]
Plays: Hamilton's second marriage; Thomas and the princess; The modern way. '10(My14) c. 12°, $1.50. M. Kennerley.
Proposals to Kathleen. '08(Mr7) c. front. D. †$1.50. Barnes.
Three plays: Hamilton's second marriage; Thomas and the princess; Modern way. '10(Je4) 12°, $1.50. M. Kennerley.

Clifford, Mrs. W: Kingdon.
See Clifford, *Mrs.* Lucy Lane.

Clifton, R:
Miller and the toad. '08(D5) c. D. *$1.20 net. Sherman, F.

Clifton, W.
Notes on colour; showing how laws that regulate monochrome can in most cases be applied to colour when painting. '08 (Ap18) oblong 8°, bds., 50 c. Warne.

CLIMATE.
United States. *Weather Bureau.* Rept. on "The influence of forests on climate and on floods," by Willis L. Moore. '10 (Ap) 38 p. charts, 8°.
Ward, R. De C. Climate considered especially in relation to man. **$2 net. Putnam.
Yeo, I. B. Therapeutics of mineral springs and climates. $3.50 net. Funk.
See also Meteorology.

Climate and weather of Baltimore. Fassig, O. L. *$2.50 net. Maryland Geol.

Climax (The). *See* Jenks, G: C.

Climber (The). Benson, E: F. **$1.40 net. Doubleday, P.

Climbing Courvatels. Townsend, E: W. †$1.50. Stokes.

Climbing doom. Young, L. D. †$1.50. G: W. Dillingham.

Climbing the ladder of fame. Reddall, H: F. 75 c. Educ. Pub.

Climbing up to nature. Lewis, F. J. $1.50. C. M. Clark.

Clinch, G:
English costume from prehistoric times to the end of the eighteenth century. '10 (O1) il. O. $2.50 net. McClurg.

Cline, G: Polk.
Polk Cline's book, by the old sage of the Arkansaw. '10(S) c. 414 p. 8°, $2. G: P. Cline.

Clinic repertory. Shedd, P. W: $1.50. Boericke & T.

CLINICAL CHEMISTRY.
See Medical chemistry.

CLINICAL DIAGNOSIS.
See Diagnosis.

Clinical lectures on the surgical diseases of the urinary organs. Freyer, P. J. *$4 net. Wood.

Clinical manual for the study of diseases of the throat. Downie, J. W. *$3.25 net. Macmillan.

Clinical materia medica. Farrington, E. A. $6; $7. Boericke & T.

Clinical memoranda. Brand, A. T. *$1.50 net. Wood.

Clinical methods. Hutchison, R. $2.50 net. Funk.

Clinical obstetrics. Jardine, R. *$6.50 net; *$7.50 net. Wood.

CLINICAL PATHOLOGY.
See Pathology.

Clinical pathology of the blood of domesticated animals. Burnett, S: H. *$2.50 net. Taylor & C.

Clinical studies for nurses. Aikens, C. A. $2. Saunders.

CLINICAL THERAPEUTICS.
See Medicine.

Clinical treatises on the pathology and therapy of disorders of metabolism and nutrition. Noorden, C. H. v., *ed.* pts. 7-8. ea., $1.50. Treat.

Clinical treatises on the symptomatology and diagnosis of disorders of respiration and circulation. Neusser, E. v. pt. 3, $1. Treat.

CLINTON COUNTY, Iowa.
Dunn, L: V. Catholic church in Clinton County, Iowa. $2. Torch Press.

Clipper ship era. Clark, A. H. $2 net. Putnam.

CLIVE, Robert, *Lord.*
Macaulay, T: B., *Lord.* Essay on Lord Clive. 25 c. net. Longmans.
Macaulay, T: B., *Lord.* Essays on Clive and Hastings. 35 c. Ginn.
Macaulay, T: B., *Lord.* Essays on Lord Clive and Warren Hastings. 40 c. Houghton M.
Macaulay, T: B., *Lord.* Essays on Lord Clive and Warren Hastings. 40 c. C: E. Merrill.

Clivette, the Man in Black, pseud.
Café cackle, from dumps to Delmonico's. '09(O2) c. il. por., S. 50 c. Laird.
Confessions of a palmist. '09(F20) c. il. D. pap., 25 c. Laird.
The rubber-neck: [poem.] '08(Je) c. 5-79 p. il. S. pap., 15 c. L. Sweet.

CLOCKS AND WATCHES.
Arthur, J. Time and its measurement. $1.50. Popular Mechanics.

Clodd, E:
Animism. '07, [1909.] (Ap) 8°, (Religions ancient and modern.) *40 c. net. Open Court.

CLODIUS, *Roman demagogue.*
Beesly, E: C. Catiline, Clodius, and Tiberius. *$3 net. Stechert.

Clogg, Herbert Sherwell.
See Bosanquet, W. C.

Cloister and the hearth. *See* Reade, C:

Cloister book. Burrell, D. J. $1. Am. Tr.

Cloister to court. Cotton-Walker, F. M. $1.40. Longmans.

Cloke, Harold E:
Gunners' examiner. 3d ed., rev. and enl. '08(Ag29) c. il. 8°, $1.50. Wiley.
—, comp. Enlisted specialists' examiner. '08 (N21) c. figs. 8°, *$2 net. Wiley.

Clopper, E: N:
Child labor in Indiana. '09(Je19) il. 8°, (National Child Labor Committee pubs.) pap., gratis. Nat. Child Labor.

Closed book. Everett, L. L. $1.25 net. Wessels.

Closed book. **Le Queux, W: 50 c. B. W. Dodge.**

Closed or open shop? Hubbard, E. 10 c. Roycrofters.

Closet and altar. Rankin, I: O. 25 c. net. Pilgrim Press.

CLOTHING.
See Hygiene.

CLOTHING-TRADE.
Tate, W: R. Criminal commercialism; the true story of the systematic frauds of a big corporation of interest to all and especially the clothing trade. Nicoletti.

Clotilde. Bouvet, M. M. $1.25. McClurg.

Cloud rifts. Lively, *Rev.* W: I. $1. Lively.

Clough, Alb. L., ed.
Operation, care and repair of automobiles; ed. from the files of the *Horseless Age.* Rev. ed. '10(Jl16) c. il. 8°, $1. Horseless Age.

Clough-Leighter, H:
Youth and spring: [songs with music.] '08 (O3) F. pap., *$1.25 net. Schirmer.

Clouston, J. Storer.
Prodigal father. '09(O30) c. D. †$1.50. Century Co.

Clouston, R. S.
Sir Thomas Lawrence. '08(Ap18) il. 8°, (Newnes' art lib.) bds., *$1.25 net. Warne.

CLOVER.
Armsby, H: P., *and* Fries, J. A. Available energy of red clover hay: investigations with the respiration calorimeter. 10 c. U. S., Supt. of Docs.
Hansen, N. E. Wild alfalfas and clovers of Siberia. 10 c. U. S., Supt. of Docs.
Hunter, B. Clover seed production in the Willamette Valley, Oregon. (Add. Superintendent for price.) U. S., Supt. of Docs.
McDermott, L. F. Illustrated key to the North American species of trifolium. $4. Cunningham, C. & W.

Clow, Rev. W. M.
Cross in Christian experience. '09(Ag) 12°, *$1.50 net. Jennings.
Day of the cross; course of sermons '09 (N13) O. *$1.50 net. Doran.
Secret of the Lord. '10(D) 12°, $1.50 net. Doran.

Clowes, Fk., and Coleman, I. Bernard.
Quantitative chemical analysis. 8th ed., rev. '09(N) 24+565 p. il. 8°, *$3.50 net. Blakiston.

CLOWNS.
See Circus.

Club and lodge-room entertainments. Chase, F. E. 25 c. W. H. Baker.

CLUB SWINGING.
See Gymnastics and physical culture; — Indian clubs.

Club woman's friend. Strong-Tracy, *Mrs.* E. $1. Dealy.

Clue (The). Wells, C. †$1.50. Lippincott.

Cluster of buckeye. Carson, A. C. (Add. pubs. for price.) Smith-B.

Clutch of circumstance. Barnes, J. †$1.50. Appleton.

Clutch of circumstance. Hardy, A. L. $1. Mayhew.

Clutch of circumstance. Senior, D. $1.50. Macmillan.

Clute, Willard Nelson.
Laboratory botany for the high school. '09 (N20) c. D. 75 c. Ginn.

Clutton-Brock, Arth.
Shelley, the man and the poet. '09(N20) il. O. *$3.50 net. Putnam.

Clyde, Irene.
Beatrice the Sixteenth. '09(N6) 12°, $1.50. Macmillan.

CLYDE RIVER, Scotland.
Munro, N. The Clyde. *$6 net. Macmillan.

Clymer, Reuben Swinburne, D.D., ["Pythagoras 38."]
Imperial ritual of magic; incl. full instruction in the genuine kaballa, the making of talismans and amulets, and other secret matter concerning the Imperialistic Council and Venerable Order of Magicians. '09(N) 7-208 p. il. 8°, leath., $1. Philosophical.
International system of magnetic (alchemic) therapeutics. '09(Mr) c. 9-152 p. il. 12°, gratis. R. C. Clymer.
Mystery of Osiris; or, Egyptian initiation: work setting forth the Egyptian mythology in all its beauty and giving the inner and more sacred teachings of the Egyptian initiation; notes by F. Oscar Biberstein. '09(Je12) c. 8°, $5. Philosophical.
The Rosicrucians, their teachings and mysteries. 2d ed. '10(Jl16) c. il. 8°, $3. Philosophical.

COACHING.
Beall, *Mrs.* M. S. Story of the Washington coachee and of the Powel coach which is now at Mount Vernon. (Priv. pr.) Neale.
See also Brimfield, Mass.

Coakley, Cornelius Godfrey.
Laryngology: manual of diseases of the nose and throat. 4th ed. '08(Ag29) il. 8°, $2.75. Lea.

COAL.
Altsheler, W: B., *comp.* Maladministration through the Alaska syndicate. 10 c. W: B. Altsheler.
Armes, E. Story of coal and iron in Alabama. $5. E. Armes.
Ashley, G: H., *and* Fisher, C. A. Valuation of public coal lands. U. S., Supt. of Docs.
Belden, A. W., *and others.* Washing and coking tests of coal. 10 c. U. S., Supt. of Docs.
Black Diamond's directory of coal mine operators. $5. Black Diamond.
Bownocker, J: A., *and others.* Coal [in Ohio.] 50 c. Ohio Geol.
Breckenridge, L. P., *and* Diserens, P. Fuel tests with Illinois. gratis. Univ. of Ill.
Burrows, J: S. Mine sampling and chemical analysis of coals tested at the United States fuel-testing plant, Norfolk, Va., 1907. 5 c.—Results of purchasing coal under government specifications. (Add. Superintendent for price.) U. S., Supt. of Docs.
Fleming, H: S. Report on the present and future of the bituminous coal trade. $5. H: S. Fleming.
Gibson, W. Geology of coal and coal-mining. $2.50. Longmans.
Goss, W: F. M. Comparative tests of run-of-mine and briquetted coal on locomotives. 15 c. U. S., Supt. of Docs.
Halberstadt, B. General map of the bituminous coal fields of Pennsylvania. $6. B. Halberstadt.
Hall, C. Coal-mine accidents: their causes and preventions. 5 c. U. S., Supt. of Docs.

COAL.—*Continued.*

Hancock, E. T: Notes accompanying the lectures on geology applied to mining. $1. New Era Print.

Kuhn, H. A. Substantial prosperity: coal production and exhaustion of coal. $2. Pittsburgh-W.

Lunge, G: Coal, tar, and ammonia. 2 v. *$15 net. Van Nostrand.

Mauchline, R. Mine foreman's hdbk. of pract. and theoretical instruction on the opening, ventilating and working of collieries. $3.75. Baird.

Parr, S: W., *and* Barker, P. Occluded gases in coal. gratis. Univ. of Ill.

Parr, S: W., *and* Francis, C: K. Modification of Illinois coal by low temperature distillation. gratis. Univ. of Ill.

Parr, S: W., *and* Hamilton, N: D. Weathering of coal. gratis. Univ. of Ill.

Parr, S: W., *and* Wheeler, W. F. Unit coal and the composition of coal ash. —Weathering of coal. ea., gratis. Univ. of Ill.

Porter, H. C., *and* Ovitz, F. K. Volatile matter of coal. Gov. Pr. Off.

Randall, D. T. Purchase of coal under government and commercial specifications. 15 c.—Tests of coal and briquets as fuel for house-heating boilers. (Add. Superintendent for price.) U. S., Supt. of Docs.

Randall, D. T., *and* Weeks, H. W. Smokeless combustion of coal in boiler plants. 20 c. U. S., Supt. of Docs.

Ray, W. T., *and* Kreisinger, H: Comparative tests of run-of-mine and briquetted coal on the torpedo boat "Biddle." (Add. Superintendent for price.) U. S., Supt. of Docs.

Rice, G: S. Explosibility of coal dust. Gov. Pr. Off.

Richardson, G. B. Reconnaissance of the Brook Cliffs Coal Field, bet. Grand River, Colo., and Sunnyside, Utah. 20 c. U. S., Supt. of Docs.

Roy, A. History of the coal miners of U. S. $1.75. Trauger.

Saward, F: E:, *comp.* Large coal consumers of New England. $10. F: E: Saward.

Tonge, J. Coal. *$2 net. Van Nostrand.

United States. *Dept. of Agriculture. Forest Service.* Papers received by the Bureau of Forestry from Louis R. Glavis rel. to Alaska coal claims. '10(Jl) 7 p. 8°. Gov. Pr. Off.

United States. *Dept of Commerce and Labor. Bu. of Manufactures.* Coal trade in Latin America. '10(Jl) 32 p. 8°.

United States. *Dept. of the Interior.* Coal lands in Oklahoma; message from the President of the United States, transmitting repts. rendered in connection with the investigation to determine the extent and value of the coal deposits in and under the segregated coal lands of the Choctaw and Chickasaw nations in Oklahoma. '10(Jl) 374 p. maps, 8°.

COAL.—*Continued.*

Walker, A. H: Black elephant of Reading. —Blackest Reading. ea., gratis. A. H: Walker.

White, D: Effect of oxygen in coal. 25 c. U. S., Supt. of Docs.

Wright, C: L. Briqueting tests at the United States fuel testing plant, Norfolk, Va. 10 c. U. S., Supt. of Docs.

See also Carbon; — Coke; — Explosives;—Inland navigation;—Machinery;—Mines and mining; —Peat;—*also* West Virginia.

COAL DUST.
See Coal.

COAL TAR COLORS.

Zerr, G., *and* Mayer, C. Tests of coal colors in aniline lakes. $5.50 net. Lippincott.

COALINGA OIL DISTRICT, Cal.
See California.

Coan, Maris Blair.

Coming peril: [socialism.] '09(My8) c. D. 50 c. Wilkie & C.

COAST DEFENSE.
See Military art and science.

Coast of chance. Chamberlain, E. †$1.50. Bobbs-M.

Coaten, Arth. W., ed.

British hunting; complete hist. of the national sport of Great Britain and Ireland from the earliest records. '10(Jl16) il. 4°, hf. mor., $65 net. Little, B. & Co.

Coates, Mrs. E: H.
See Coates, Florence Earle.

Coates, Florence Earle, [Mrs. E: H. Coates.]

Lyrics of life. '09(D18) c. D. $1.25. Houghton M.

Coates, H: Troth, comp.

Fireside encyclop. of poetry; comprising the best poems of the most famous writers, English and American. '10(O8) 8°, Memorial ed., il. $5, boxed; ¾ mor., $7.50, boxed; Popular ed., $2; leath., $3. Winston.

Coats, Mack Colvin.

California products and how to grow them. '09(O23) c. 12°, pap., 50 c. M. C. Coats.

COATS.
See Tailoring.

Cobb, Margaret Smith.

Blaxine, halfbreed girl. '10(Ap2) c. D. $1.50. Neale.

Cobb, T:

Chichester intrigue. '08(Mr7) c. D. †$1.50. Lane.

Cobbett, W:

Rural rides; sel. and ed. by J. H. Lobban. '09(My) 20+231 p. 16°, (Cambridge English literature for schools.) *40 c. net. Putnam.

Cobbey, J. E.

See Nebraska. Cobbey's comp. statutes.—Cobbey's annot. statutes.

Cobbey's annot. statutes. *See* Nebraska.

Cobbler (The). Travis, E. A. $1.25. Outing.

COBDEN, Richard.

Morley, J: Life of Richard Cobden. 2 v. $3. Macmillan.

Cobham, Claude Delaval, ed.

Excerpta Cypria; materials for a history of Cyprus: tr. and transcribed by Claude Delaval Cobham; with an appendix on the bibliography of Cyprus. '08(N7) 4°, *$6.30 net. Putnam.

Cobleigh, Rolfe.
Handy farm devices and how to make them. '09(D11) il. 12°, *$1.50 net. O. Judd.

Coblentz, Virgil.
Manual of volumetric analysis. 2d ed., rev., completely reconstructed and enl., by Anton Vorisek. '09(O) c. 8+234 p. il. 8°, *$1.75 net. Blakiston.
Newer remedies, incl. their synonyms, sources, tests, solubilities, incompatibles, medicinal properties and doses as far as known, together with such proprietaries as have similar titles. 4th ed., rev. and enl. '08(N) c. 133 p. 4°, $1. Apothecary.
See also Sadtler, S: Philip.

Coblentz, W: Weber.
Investigations of infra-red spectra. pt. 5, Infra-red reflection spectra; pt. 6, Infra-red transmission spectra; pt. 7, Infra-red emission spectra. '08(D12) figs. Q. pap. (Add. pubs. for price.) Carnegie.
Note on the thermoelectric properties of tantalum and tungsten. '09, [1910.] (Mr) 107-110 p. il. 4°, pap. Gov. Pr. Off.
Radiation constants of metals. '09(Je) 339-379 p. diagrs., 4°, pap. (Add. Superintendent for price.) U. S., Supt. of Docs.
Selective radiation from various solids, II. '10(Jl) 301-319 p. il. 8°. Gov. Pr. Off.
See also Ives, Herb. Eug.

Coburn, Alvin Langdon.
London; with introd. by Hilaire Belloc. '09 (D4) il. F. bds., $6. Brentano's.

Coburn, Foster Dwight.
Swine in America; text-book for the breeder, feeder and student. '09(My8) il. 8°, *$2.50 net. Judd.

Cobwebs of criticism. Caine, T: H: H. 50 c.; 75 c. Dutton.

COCCACEAE.
See Bacteria.

Cochran, Judge J: Salisbury.
Bonnie Belmont. '08(Ja4) pors. O. $1.50. J: S. Cochran.

Cochran, W: Cox.
Charles Grandison Finney; memorial address del. at the dedication of the Finney Memorial Chapel, Oberlin, June 21, 1908. '09(Mr) c. '08. 94 p. il. 8°. (Priv. pr.) Lippincott.

Cochrane, C: H.
How and where to sell mss. '09(D) 50 c. Cochrane.

Cock-a-doodle Hill. Haines, A. C. †$1.50. Holt.

Cockcroft, Ja., ed.
See American and Eng. ency. of law.

Cocke, W: Alex.
Bailey controversy in Texas. 2 v. '08(O) 1100 p. il. pors. 4°, silk, $3.90; hf. mor., $4.90. Cocke Co.

Cockle doodle doo. '10(D) col. il. 50 c. Saalfield.

Cockshott, Winnifred.
Pilgrim fathers. '09(D11) il. map, O. *$2.50 net. Putnam.

Coco Bolo. Hamp, S. F: $1. Badger.

COCOA.
See Chocolate.

Cocroft, Susanna.
Growth in silence. '08(Ja4) por. O. (Know thyself ser.) pap., 60 c. Physical Culture Ex.

Codd, Marg. Jane.
With Evans to the Pacific: a story of the battle fleet. '09(S11) c. il. por. D. 60 c. Flanagan.

CODES.
Bankers' telegraph and cable code. $3.50. Business Code.
Billionaire phrase code. $1.50. Business Code.
Brentano's cable code. $1 net. Brentano's.
Century Code Co. Century standard telegraphic code. $10. Century Code.
Green, H. L. Waste merchants standard code. $5. H. L. Green.
Master code. $12. Business Code.
Miners' and smelters' code. $1. Business Code.
Sellers, D: F. Unofficial telegraph and cable code. $2.50. Navy Pub.

Codex Taurinensis (Y): [earliest known mss. of the "Dodekapropheton" in the Lucian recension of the Septuagint;] tr. and collated by Rev. W. O. Oesterley, D.D. '08 (D19) O. $1.60. Oxford Univ.

CODLING MOTH.
See Moths.

Cody, C. C.
See Bruce, W: Herschel.

Cody, Grace Ethelwyn.
Jacquette: a sorority girl. '08(F8) c. il. S. †$1.25. Dutton.

Cody, Hiram Alfred.
Apostle of the north: the life and memoirs of William Carpenter Bompas, D.D., first bishop of Athabasca, 1874-1884, bishop of of Mackenzie River, 1884-1891, bishop of Selkirk, 1891-1896; with introd. by the Most Rev. S. P. Mattheson. '08(Mr21) il. pors. 8°, *$2.50 net. Dutton.
The frontiersman; tale of the Yukon. '10 (O8) c. D. $1.20 net. Doran.
On trail and rapid, by dog-sled and canoe. '10(D31) il. 12°, $1 net. Lippincott.

Cody, Sherwin.
Art of writing and speaking the English language. 6 v. '08(Je13) c. 16°, ea., 50 c. Old Greek Pr.
Geographical reference list and commercial map of the United States. '10(F5) c. fold. map, 16°, $1. S. Cody.
How to do business by letter. '08(F29) c. D. $1. Sch. of Eng.

Cody, W: F:, ["Buffalo Bill."]
True tales of the plains. '08(D5) c. il. pors. 12°, $1; pap., 50 c. Cupples & L.

CODY, William Frederick.
Griffin, C: E. Four years in Europe with Buffalo Bill. $1. C: E. Griffin.

Coe, Alice Rollit.
Lyrics of fir and foam. '09(Ja2) c. il. D. bds., $2, boxed. A. Harriman.

Coe, Edn. Delos.
Reminiscences of a pioneer in the Rock River country. '08(Ag) 189-203 p. 8°, 35c. State Hist., Wis.

Coe, Fanny E.
First book of stories for the story-teller. [1910.] (O) c. 13+222 p. 12°, 80 c. Houghton M.
School reader. Third grade; Fourth grade. '09(F20) c. il. D. Third grade, 40 c.; Fourth grade, 50 c. Am. Bk.

Coe, G: Albert.
Progress in religious and moral education; annual survey of the Religious Education Association. '09(Ag) 16 p. 8°, pap., 25 c. Rel. Educ.

CO-EDUCATION.
See Woman.

COENOBIC PLANTS.
See Seaweeds.

Coerne, L: Adolphe.
Evolution of modern orchestration. '08 (S26) 8°, *$3 net. Macmillan.

COEUR D'ALENE INDIAN RESERVATION, Idaho.
See Indians.

COFFEE.
Dowler, J. S., & Co. Coffee calculator. (Add. pub. for price.) J. S. Dowler.
Keable, B. B. Coffee, from grower to consumer. 75 c. Pitman.

Coffee and a love affair. Sheldon, M. B. †$1.50. Stokes.

Coffey, W: Harrison.
Sis; Missouri Valley story. '10(Mr5) c. front. 16°, 50 c. Burton Co.
Tim, a Kentucky mountain story. '08, [1909.] (Mr) c. 93 p. il. 16°, 50 c. Burton Co.

Coffin, C: Carleton.
Following the flag. '08(Je6) 12°, (Young America lib.) 50 c. Hurst.
My days and nights on the battlefield. '08 (Jl18) 12°, (Young America lib.) 50 c. Hurst.
Winning his way. '08(Jl11) 12°, (Young America lib.) 50 c. Hurst.

Coffin, Captain G:
Pioneer voyage to California and round the world, 1849 to 1852. '08(O10) c. il. por. plan, O. $1.50. G. B. Coffin.

Coffin, Rev. H: Sloan, and Vernon, Ambrose White, eds.
Hymns of the Kingdom of God, with tunes. '10(Ag20) 8°, $1.50 net. Barnes.

Coffin, Jos. G:
Vector analysis: introduction to vector methods and their various applications to physics and mathematics. '09(My22) figs. 12°, *$2.50 net. Wiley.

Coffin nails. Hastings, *Mrs.* R. B. 50 c. Dispatch Pub.

Coffman, Lotus D.
See Briggs, T: H:

Coggins, Herbert Leonard, comp.
Stories worth telling. '09(N13) c. il. S. 50 c. Penn Pub. Co.

Coggins, Paschal Heston.
Parliamentary law; for quick use in public meetings of all sorts. '09(N13) c. S. 50 c. Penn Pub. Co.

COHASSET, Mass.
Davenport, G: L., *and* Osgood, E. Genealogies of the families of Cohasset, Massachusetts. $5. Com. Town History.

Cohen, Alfr. J.
See Dale, Alan, *pseud.*

Cohen, Emily Solis-, jr.
David, the giant killer, and other tales of grandma Lopez. '08(Je6) c. D. $1.25. Jewish Pub.

Cohen, Jos. E.
Socialism for students. '09(D25) c. S. 50 c. Kerr.

Cohen, Myer Solis-.
See Solis-Cohen, Myer.

Cohn, Rev. J. B.
Sermon on the Mount as viewed from the modern standpoint: [sermons.] '08(Jl) 179 p. 12°, $1.40. Whittaker.

Cohn, Lassar-, Dr.
See Lassar-Cohn, *Dr.*

Cohnheim, Paul.
Diseases of the digestive canal: esophagus, stomach, intestine; from the 2d German ed.; ed. and tr. by Dudley Fulton. '09 (F) c. 375 p. 8°, **$4 net. Lippincott.

Coign of vantage. Herridge, W: T: *$1 net. Revell.

Coin of sacrifice. Tiernan, *Mrs.* F. C. F. 15 c. Ave Maria.

COINS AND MEDALS.
Adams, E. H. Official premium list of United States private and territorial gold coins. $2; $2.50. E. H. Adams.
Mehl, B. M. Star coin book. 50 c. net. Caspar.
Money and Stamp Brokerage Co. Money and stamp manual. $1. Money and Stamp.
Rawlings, G. B. Coins and how to know them. *$1.50 net. Stokes.
White, A. F., *comp.* Coins of the world. $1. Banking Law.
See also Gold (*as money*);—Hudson-Fulton celebration;—Money.

COIT, Daniel Wadsworth.
Gilman, W: C. Memoir of Daniel Wadsworth Coit, of Norwich, Connecticut. $1.25. W: C. Gilman.

Coit, H: A:
School sermons. '09(Ap3) c. D. **$1.50 net. Moffat.

Coit, H: L.
Clean milk in its economic and medical relations with special reference to certified milk. '09(Jl31) 8°. (Add. pubs. for price.) Jefferson Co. Med. Soc.

Coit, J: Eliot.
Peony check-list, including the leading varieties. '07, [1908.] (My.) 232 p. il. 8°, $5. Am. Peony Soc.

Coke, H: J:
Domain of belief. '10(N19) 8°, $2.50 net. Macmillan.

COKE, Thomas.
Upham, F. B. Thomas Coke. *25 c. net. Eaton & M.

COKE.
Byrom, T. H., *and* Christopher, J. E. Modern coking practice. *$3.50 net. Henley.

Coker, Fs. W:
Organismic theories of the state; nineteenth century interpretations of the state as organism or as person. '10(S10) c. O. (Columbia Univ. studies in history, economics and public law.) pap., $1.50. Longmans.

Coker, Rob. Ervin.
Experiments in oyster culture in Pamlico Sound, North Carolina. '07, [1908] (S) 10+74 p. il. map, 4°, (North Carolina Geological and Economic Survey.) (Add. pubs. for price.) Uzzell.

Colaw, J: Marvin, Duke, Fk. Williamson, and Powers, Ja. Knox.
School arithmetic; [with answers.] '08 (F29) c. il. D. (Johnson ser.) 35 c. B. F. Johnson.

Colborn, E: Fenton.
Glimpse of Utah, its resources, attractions and natural wonders. '09(Je19) il. 4°, pap., gratis. Denver & Rio Grande.

Colby, Albert Ladd.
Reinforced concrete in Europe, including its applications, economies, and endurance. '09(S4) c. 8°, $3.50. Chemical.

Colby, C: W.
Canadian types of the old régime, 1608-1698. '08(S12) c. il. pors. O. **$2.75 net. Holt.

Colby, Fk. Moore.
Constrained attitudes. '10(D10) c. D. $1.20 net. Dodd.

Colby, Lou Eleanor.
Talks on drawing, painting, making, decorating, for primary teachers. '09(N20) c. il. (partly col.) 4°, $1.50. Scott, F. & Co.

Colcock, C: Jones.
History of the progenitors and some South Carolina descendants of Colonel Ann Hawkes Hay. '08(Je.) 14+202 p. pl. 8°. (privately pr.) Genealog. Assoc.

Colcord, Mrs. Anna L.
Friend in the kitchen: [vegetarian cook book.] 16th ed. '08(O17) il. D. 50 c.; pap., 25 c. Review and Herald.

Colcord, Mabel, comp.
List of publications of the Bureau of Entomology. '09(Ag) 29 p. 8°, (U. S., Dept. of Agriculture, Bu. of Entomology, circular.) gratis. U. S., Supt. of Docs.

Cold facts. Darling, J. T. $1.50 per 100 copies. J. T. Darling.

COLD STORAGE.
See **Refrigeration.**

Cold-storage baby. O'Sullivan, D. 25 c. Ontario Pub.

COLDS.
Sadler, W: S: Cause and cure of colds. $1 net. McClurg.

Coldwater, C: H:
Helping hand for every day's want: recipes for the kitchen, bath, toilet, laundry, household, sick room, garden, and farm; with etiquette. '09(Ja16) c. por. 12°, $1.50. C: H: Coldwater.

Cole, Arth. Stanley, comp.
Scott family of Shrewsbury, N. J.; being the descendants of W: Scott and Abigale Tilton Warner. '08(N) 72 p. pors. facsims., 4°, $2. A. S. Cole.

Cole, Cornelius.
Memoirs of Cornelius Cole, ex-Senator of the U. S. from California. '08(Ag8) por. sq. 8°, $2.50. McLoughlin.

Cole, Mrs. Donna Rieta Bramhall.
Chums; or, an experiment in economics. '08(D26) c. O. $1.25. G. O. Tubby.
Faith-Hope, child of the slums; ed. by G. O. Tubby. '10(Ap16) c. O. $1. G. O. Tubby.

Cole, Edn. Tuttle, and Stuart, Edn. R.
Individual and combined military sketching. 2d ed., rev. '08(Je6) c. il. 8°, $1. U. S. Cavalry.

Cole, Emma Taylor.
Guide to the mushrooms. '10(D17) c. il. S. $1.50 net, boxed. Doubleday, P.

Cole, Ernest Byron.
Descendants of James Cole of Plymouth, 1633; also a record of the families of Lieutenant Thomas Burnham, of Ipswich, 1635, Lieutenant Edward Winship, of Cambridge, 1635, and Simon Huntington, of Norwich, England, 1635. with a complete record of the Cole, Coole, and Cowle families of America in the Revolution. '08(Je20) c. il. pors. maps, 8°, *$7 net. Grafton Press.

Cole, G: Watson, comp.
Catalogue of books consisting of English literature and miscellanea, including many original editions of Shakespeare, forming a part of the library of E. Dwight Church. '09(My15) 2 v., il. facsims., 4°, subs., $75. Dodd.

Cole, Lindon Albertia.
See Kahl, J: Corliss

Cole, Lou E.
Voices of the West: poems of Washington. '09(Jl) c. 37 p. por. il. 8°, 50 c. L. E. Cole.

Cole, M.
Tempering steel; annealing and case hardening iron. '09(Mr) 23 p. 32°, (Handbook ser.) pap., 10 c. Sampson.

Cole, Mary Eliza Gully.
Essays. '09(D) c. 9-213 p. front. 12°, $1. B'way Pub.

Cole, Percival R:, comp.
Later Roman education in Ausonius, Capella and the Theodosian code; with translations and commentary. '09(S18) c. O. (Columbia Univ., Teachers' College, Contributions to education.) pap., 25 c. Teachers' Coll.

Cole, Rob. Jermain, ["The Kurnel."]
Photography in a nutshell. '09(D) c. 64 p. 12°, 25 c. Tennant.

Cole, S. W. R., D.D.
Sermons outlined. 5th ed.; [also national Baptist pastor's guide.] '10(Ja22) S. 50 c. Nat. Baptist.

Cole, S: Winkley, and Lewis, Leo Rich.
Melodia; a course in sight-singing. '09 (Ag14) $1.50. Ditson.
—, ed. Exercises in sight singing (Solfeggio), by Cherubini, Catel, Mehul, Gossec, Sanglé. '08(F22) c. Q. pap., *60 c. net. Boston Music.

Cole, Sylvester.
De oddilo: the seed. '08(Ag8) c. 12°, $1.50. Connoisseurs' Press.
Don vascaeno: the fruit. '08(Ag8) c. 12°, $1.50. Connoisseurs' Press.
La vermix: the harvest. '08(Ag8) c. 12°, $1.50. Connoisseurs' Press.

Cole, W: I.
Motives and results of the social settlement movement; notes on exhibit installed in the Social Museum of Harvard University. '08(D) 36 p. 8°, (Harvard Univ. pubs., Dept. of Social Ethics.) (Add. pubs. for price.) Harvard Univ.

Cole, W: Morse.
Accounting and auditing. '10(O15) c. 8°, $4.80. Cree.
Accounts. '08(D5) c. O. $2. Houghton M.
American hope. '10(My21) c. D. $1.50 net. Appleton.

Cole, Willis Vernon.
Our leader, and other poems; [dedicated to Mary Baker G. Eddy.] '08(F) 12°, bds., $1; limp mor., $2. Anglo-Am. Authors.
Poems that heal the sick. '09(N) c. '08. 48 p. il. 8°, pap., 75 c.; ooze, $2. Universal-Good.

COLE FAMILY.
Cole, E. B. Descendants of James Cole of Plymouth, 1633. *$7 net. Grafton Press.

Coleman, G: W:
Churches outside the church; pub. for the Social Service Commission of the Northern Baptist Convention. '10(Jl30) c. 12°, (Social service ser.) 15 c. Am. Bapt.
Searchlights. '10(Ap) c. 12°, 75 c. Golden Rule.

Coleman, I. Bernard.
See Clowes, Fk.

Coleman, Nannie McCormick.
Constitution and its framers. [2d ed.] '10 (Mr12) c. pors. O. $3; leath., $5. Progress Co.

Coleman, Silas Ellsworth.
New laboratory manual of physics. '09 (Ja23) c. figs. D. 80 c. Am. Bk.

Coleman, T: Everit.
Retaining walls in theory and practice. '09 (Ap3) il. 12°, $2. Spon.

Coleman, Wa. Moore.
Lessons in hygienic physiology. New ed., rev. and enl. '08(F1) il. 12°, *60 c. net. Macmillan.
Physiology for beginners; with an appendix on nature study. New ed., rev. and enl. '08(F1) il. 12°, *40 c. net. Macmillan.
See also Bailey, Liberty Hyde.

Coleman, W: Magruder.
Pressure of Asia and the unification of the English-speaking people: address del. at a dinner of the Canadian Club of New York at the Hotel Flanders, January 14, 1908. '08(Ap11) O. pap. (Add. author for price.) W: M. Coleman.

COLEOPTERA.
See Insects.

Coleridge, Christabel R.
Story of English literature. Rev. ed. [1910.] (D) $1.25 net. Cassell.

Coleridge, Hartley.
Complete poetical works; ed. by Ramsay Colles. '08(Jl11) 16°, (New universal lib.) 50 c.; leath., 75 c. Dutton.

Coleridge, Mary Eliz.
Gathered leaves from the prose of Mary E. Coleridge; with a memoir by Edith Sichel. '10(Jl30) por. O. $2 net. Dutton.

Coleridge, Mary Eliz.—*Continued.*
Holman Hunt. '08(Jl4) il. O. (Masterpieces in colour.) bds., *65 c. net. Stokes.

Coleridge, S: Taylor.
Ancient mariner, and select poems; with introd. and notes, by H: Marvin Belden. '08(D5) c. por. 16°, (English classics.) **25 c. net. Scribner.
Cristabel. '10(D) il. 30 c.; cf., $1. Barse & H.
Lectures and notes on Shakespeare, and other dramatists. '08(F22) 12°, (New universal lib.) 50 c.; leath., 75 c. Dutton.
Literary criticism; with an introd. by J: W: Mackail. '09(My15) S. (Oxford lib. of prose and poetry.) 90 c. Oxford Univ.
Poems; introd. by A. T. Quiller-Couch. '09 (My15) 16°, (World's classics.) 40 c.; leath., 75 c. Oxford Univ.
Poems of nature and romance, 1794-1807; ed. by M. A. Keeling. '10(Ag20) c. 8°, 90 c. Univ. Press.
Rime of the ancient mariner. '10(O22) col. il. F. $5 net, boxed. Crowell.
Rime of the ancient mariner; with notes and regents' questions collected by R: Saunders. '08(D5) c. por. S. (Manhattan classics.) 25 c.; pap., 10 c. Manhattan Bk.
Rime of the ancient mariner; ed., with introd., notes, outline study and examination questions, by Maud Elma Kingsley and Fk. Herbert Palmer. '10(S3) c. 16°, (Kingsley English texts.) 25 c. Palmer Co.

—, Poe, Edg. Allan, and Rossetti, Dante Gabriel.
Poetical works of Coleridge, Poe and Rossetti; cont. only those poems which time has proven immortal. '10(N12) c. 8°, $1.50. Clover.

COLERIDGE, Samuel Taylor.
Helmholtz, A. A. Indebtedness of Samuel Talyor Coleridge to August Wilhelm von Schlegel. 40 c. Univ. of Wis.
Wahlert, E. Completion of Coleridge's Christabel. 50 c. Cochrane.

Coles, Arth.
Pitman's guide for the company secretary; with introd. by Herbert E. Blain. '10 (Ja22) O. $2. Pitman.

Coles, R: T:
Events and reflections. '08(O17) c. 12°, pap., 50 c. Mayhew.

Coles-Finch, W:
Water, its origin and use. '10(Jl2) il. 8°, $5 net. Van Nostrand.

COLET, John.
Lupton, J. H. Life of John Colet, D.D., Dean of St. Paul's. *$2.75 net. Macmillan.

Colgrove, Chauncey P:
Making of a teacher. '08(Ag1) c. 12°, 75 c. C. P: Colgrove.
The teacher and the school. '10(O1) c. 12°, $1.25 net. Scribner.

COLIGNY CALENDAR.
See Ireland.

COLIN, *Father.*
Colin, life of the venerable Father Colin; founder and First Superior-General of the Society of Mary; tr. from the French by a religious of same Society [Guay, Marcellin]. '09(O) 8°, 9+366 p., *$1.25 net. Herder.
Colin, Henriette Louise Thérèse, and Sérafon, Amélie.
Pract. lessons in French grammar. '10 (O15) c. 12°, $1.12. B: H. Sanborn.
Collaboration of Webster and Dekker. Pierce, F: E. $1. Holt.
Collectanea. 24°, pap., 10 c. E. B. Hill.
—Hill. Henry Thoreau's mother.
—Thoreau. Emerson's obituary.
COLLECTING.
Deane, E. Byways of collecting. *$2.50 net. Cassell.
Yoxall, J. H: A B C about collecting. $2 net. Jacobs.
See also Book collecting;—Ceramics;—Coins and medals;—Fan;—Fine arts;—Furniture; — Pewter;—Postage stamps.
COLLECTING OF ACCOUNTS.
See Commercial correspondence.
Collection and disposal of municipal waste. Morse, W: F. $5. Municipal Journ.
Collection of easy hymns. Hahn, B. F. 35 c. St. Boniface's.
COLLECTIVISM.
Beaulieu, P. L-. Collectivism. *$3 net. Dutton.
Carr, C. T. Collective ownership otherwise than by corporations or by means of the trust. *$1.50 net. Putnam.
See also Municipal ownership.
Collector's hdbk. to keramics of the Renaissance and modern periods. Chaffers, W: $1.50 net. Scribner.
Collector's handbooks. il. O. **$1 net. Stokes.
—Moore. Delftware.
Collectors. Hunnewell, J. F. [priv. pr.] Club Odd Vol.
College algebra. Davisson, S. C. *$1.50 net. Macmillan.
College algebra. Rietz, H: L. **$1.40 net. Holt.
College athletic ser. il. D. †$1.25. Penn Pub. Co.
—Hare. Sophomore half-back.
College course in writing from models. Berkeley, F. C., *ed.* $1.25. Holt.
College days essays. Gibson, R. A. $1. Nixon-J.
College Entrance Examination Board. Questions set at the examinations held June 15-20, 1908. '08(D19) c. O. 60 c. Ginn.
College entrance requirements in English, 1909-1915, (for study and practice;) Shakespeare's Macbeth, Milton's minor poems; Burke's Conciliation with colonies; Washington's Farewell address, and Webster's First Bunker Hill oration; Macaulay's Life of Johnson; Carlyle's Burns. '10 (Je4) D. (Eclectic English classics.) 90 c. Am. Bk.
College freshman's don't book. Evans, G: F. 75 c. P. Elder.
College histories of art; ed. by J: C. Van Dyke. il. D. Longmans.
—Hamlin. Text-book of the history of architecture. $2.

COLLEGE JOURNALISM.
See Journalism.
COLLEGE OF THE CITY OF NEW YORK, N. Y.
See Gymnastics and physical culture.
College ser. of Greek authors; ed. by J: Williams White, T: Day Seymour and C: Burton Gulick. O. Ginn.
—Buck. Introd. to the study of Greek dialects. $2.75 net.
—Menander, *of Athens.* Four plays. $2.50.
—Pausanias. The Attica. $1.65.
—Plato. Apology of Socrates. $1.40.
College ser. of Latin authors. D. Ginn.
—Martial. Selected epigrams. $1.50.
College sermons. Albertson, C: C. 75 c. Westminster.
College sports ser. *See* Chadwick, Lester.
College taxation. Eliot, C: W: gratis. Harvard Univ.
College years. Paine, R. D. †$1.50. Scribner.
COLLEGES AND UNIVERSITIES.
American college and private school directory. $2. Educational Aid.
Babbitt, I. Literature and the American college. **$1.25 net. Houghton M.
Benton, G. P. Real college. *75 c. net. Jennings.
Birdseye, C. F. Reorganization of our colleges. **$1.75 net. Baker & T.
Bowden-Smith, A. G. English student's wander-year in America. $1.50 net. Longmans.
Brown, C: R. Cap and gown. $1 net. Pilgrim Press.
Candler, W. A. Dangerous donations and degrading doles; [gifts to colleges and universities.] 10 c. Lester Bk.
Carnegie Foundation for the Advancement of Teaching. Standard forms for financial repts. of colleges, universities, and technical schools. gratis. Carnegie Found.
Corbin, J: Which college for the boy? **$1.50 net. Houghton M.
Curzon, G: N., *Baron.* Principles and methods of university reform. 50 c.; 85 c. Oxford Univ.
Dabney, C: W: Unity of the University. (Not for sale.) Univ. of Cin.
Eliot, C: W: University administration. **$1.50 net. Houghton M.
Flexner, A. American college: a criticism. **$1 net. Century Co.
Flom, G: T. Hist. of Scandinavian studies in Am. universities. 50 c. Univ. of Ia.
Fryer, J: Admission of Chinese students to American colleges. U. S., Supt. of Docs.
Hayes, E. Letters to a college girl. 60 c. E. Hayes.
Hazard, C. College year; vesper addresses. $1.25 net. Houghton M.
Jordan, L: H:, *and* Labanca, B. Study of religion in the Italian universities. $2.40. Oxford Univ.
McAndrew, W: College influence on public high schools. 30 c. Bardeen.
National Business League of America. American universities, American foreign service and an adequate consular law. (Add. pubs. for price.) Nat. Business.

COLLEGES AND UNIVERSITIES.—*Continued.*
Olin, *Mrs.* H. M. R. Women of a state university. **$1.50 net. Putnam.
Ordahl, G: College curricula. gratis. Univ. of Nev.
Paetow, L: J: Arts course at medieval universities. $1. Univ. of Ill.
Pritchett, H: S. Relations of Christian denominations to colleges. gratis. Carnegie Found.
Reed, E. E. Mission of the Christian college. gratis. Lenox Coll.
Slosson, E. E. Great American universities. $2.50 net. Macmillan.
Stevens, W. L. College standardization. (Not for sale.) W. L. Stevens.
Tucker, W: J. Personal power; counsels to college men. **$1.50 net. Houghton M.
Tufts, J. H. American college education and life. (Add. author for price.) J. H. Tufts.
United States. *Library of Congress. Smithsonian Division.* Want list of publications of educational institutions. '09 (My) 14 p. 8°. (Add. Superintendent for price.) U. S., Supt. of Docs.
Walden, J: W: H: Universities of ancient Greece. **$1.50 net. Scribner.
See also Agriculture;—Debating;—Dissertations;—Education;—Medicine;—Orators and oratory;—Religious education;—Teachers and teaching;—Young men;—Young Men's Christian Association; — *also* Amherst Coll.; — Brown Univ.; — Cambridge Univ.;—Clark Univ.;—Eton Coll.; — Georgetown Univ.; — Gonville and Caius Univ.;—Harvard Univ.;—Haverford Coll.;—Knox Coll.; — Miami Univ.; — Mt. Holyoke Coll.:—Ohio Wesleyan Univ.;—Oxford Univ.;—St. Stephen's Coll.;—Trinity Coll., Dublin;—Univ. of Arkansas;—Univ. of Colorado;—Univ. of Leipzig;—Univ. of Virginia;—Vassar Coll.;—Yale Univ.

Collegiate basket ball rules. Clapp, A. B. 15 c. Univ. Pub.

Collegiate course for home study. Skinner, H. M., *ed.* $29.95; $39 95; $57. Cree.

Colles, H: Cope.
Brahms. '08(F1) por. D. (Music of the masters.) $1. Brentano's.

Collet, Harold.
Water softening and purification of hard and dirty waters. 2d ed., rev. '08(Ag1) il. 12°, $2. Spon.

COLLETES.
See Bees.

Colleton, Arth. Stanley.
Isle of temptation. '09(Je) c. 6+292 p. D. $1.50. Stuyvesant Press.

Collier, Arth.
Clavis universalis; ed., with an introd. and notes, by Ethel Bowman. '09(O23) $1.50. Open Court.

Collier, Arth. Luke.
Steel. '10(N12) il. 12°, 35 c. A. L. Collier.

Collier, Horace Stansfield, ed.
See Hutchison, Rob.

Collier, Price.
England and the English from an American point of view. '09(Ap3) c. O. **$1.50 net. Scribner.

Collier, W:
Book of etiquette entitled "Don't do that." v. 1. '09(My) c. 59 p. il. 16°, 50 c. Bennett.

Collier, W: Miller.
Law and practice in bankruptcy under the national bankruptcy act of 1898. 4th ed., by W: H. Hotchkiss. 7th ed., rev. and enl. by Fk. B. Gilbert. '09(Je); 8th ed. '10(N) c. O. ea., $7.50 net. M. Bender.

COLLIERIES.
See Coal.

Collings, Jesse.
Land reform: occupying ownership, peasant proprietary and rural education. New and popular ed. '08(Je13) por. O. $1. Longmans.

Collingwood, G: Elmer, ed.
Standard train rule examination. 7th ed. '10(F12) c. nar. S. $1.50; leath., $2. Train Dispatcher's.

Collingwood, Harry, pseud.
See Lancaster, W: Jos. Cosens.

Collins, Archie F:
Design and construction of induction coils. '09(My15) c. figs. O. *$3 net. Munn.
Manual of wireless telegraphy and telephony. 2d ed., enl. '09(Ag28) c. figs. 12°, **$1.50 net. Wiley.
See also Thom, C:

Collins, F. Howard.
Authors' and printers' dictionary. '09 (Ag14) S. 35 c. Oxford Univ.

Collins, Fs. Arnold.
Boys' book of model aeroplanes; how to build and fly them; with the story of the evolution of the flying machine. '10 (O15) c. il. D. $1.20 net. Century Co.

Collins, Guy N.
Apogamy in the maize plant. '09(O) 453-455 p. 8°, (Smithsonian Inst. U. S. National Museum; contribs. from U. S. National Herbarium.) pap. (Add. Superintendent for price.) U. S., Supt. of Docs.
A new type of Indian corn from China. '09, [1910.] (F) 30 p. il. 8°, (U. S., Dept. of Agriculture, Bureau of Plant Industry, bull.) pap.

Collins, Hilda C.
Nadia Grey; novel. '09, [1910.] (Ap) c. 211 p. 8°, $1.50. H. C. Collins.

Collins, Hubert Edwin.
Boilers. '09(F13) c. il. tabs., 12°, (Power handbooks.) $1. Hill Pub.
Erecting work. '08(N21) il. 12°, (Power handbooks.) $1. Hill Pub.
Knocks and kinks. '08(N21) il. 12°, (Power handbooks.) $1. Hill Pub.
Pipes and piping. '08(N21) il. 12°, (Power handbooks.) $1. Hill Pub.
Pumps. '08(N21) il. (Power handbooks.) $1. Hill Pub.
Shaft governors. '08(N21) il. (Power handbooks.) $1. Hill Pub.
Shafting, pulleys, belting and rope transmission. '09(F13) c. il. 12°, (Power handbooks.) $1. Hill Pub.
Steam turbines. '09(Je19) c. il. 12°, (Power handbooks.) $1. Hill Pub.
Valve setting: simple methods of setting the plain slide valve, Meyer cut-off, Corliss and Poppet types. '08(N21) il. 8°, $2. Hill Pub.

Collins, Ja. Franklin, and Preston, Howard Willis.
Key to New England trees, wild and commonly cultivated. '09(Je12) c. T. pap., 40 c. Preston.

Collins, Ja. H.
Art of handling men. '10(D3) c. 16°, 50 c. Altemus.
Human nature in selling goods. '09(My8) S. (Altemus' popular manuals.) bds., 50 c. Altemus.

Collins, J: M.
Power and weakness of trade unions; the reason of the unemployed. '10(Ap9) c. il. por. 12°, 10 c. J: M. Collins.

Collins, Jos., M.D.
Letters to a neurologist, to which are appended brief replies purporting to set forth concisely the nature of the ailments therein described, with remarks on their appropriate treatment. '08(D19) 12°, *$1 net. Wood.

Collins, Jos. Victor.
Pract. algebra, first year course. '10 (27) c. por. S. 85 c. Am. Bk.
Pract. elem. algebra. '08(S12) c. D. hf. leath., $1; Answers to above. S. pap., 10 c. Am. Bk.

Collins, Miles.
Woolen and worsted spinning. '09(My8) c. il. diagrs., 8°, (American School of Correspondence pubs.) $3. Am. Sch. Corr.

COLLINS, Nathaniel.
Mather, C. Elegy on the much-to-be-deplored death of that never-to-be-forgotten person, the Reverend Nathaniel Collins. $3. Baumgardt.

Collins, Sewell.
See Hereford, Oliver.

Collins, T. Byard.
New agriculture. '08(My16) c. il. 12°, $2. Munn.

Collins, Varnum Lansing.
Continental Congress at Princeton [1783]. '08(Ap11) c. il. pors. facsim. O. *$3 net. Princeton Univ.

Collins, W. W.
Cathedral cities of Spain. '09(D4) c. col. il. O. **$3.50 net. Dodd.

Collins, Wilkie.
Moonstone. '08(Jl11) 12°, (Magnolia lib.) 50 c. Hurst.
Woman in white; with introd. by Ernest Rhys. '10(D10) 16°, (Everyman's lib.) 35 c. net; leath., 70 c. net. Dutton.

Collins, W:
Poems; ed. by Christopher Stone. '08 (O24) il. por. S. 90 c. Oxford Univ.

Collinsworth, Ja. Ragan.
Pseudo church doctrine of anti-Pedo-Baptists defined and refuted; rev. by Rev. W. T. Dale, D.D. '09(O) 647+17 p. il. por. 8°, $2.50. Hudson.

Collitz, Frau Klara Hechtenberg, comp.
Selections from early German literature. '10(Mr12) c. D. $1. Am. Bk.

Collmann, Sophie Marie.
Art talks with young folks. '09(D25) c. il. O. $1.50. Young Israel.
Jews in art. '10(F26) il. pors. 8°, $1.50. Bacharach.

"Collodi, C.," pseud.
See Lorenzini, Carlo.

Colloid matter of clay. United States. *Dept. of the Interior. U. S. Geolog. Survey.* 10 c.

COLLOIDS.
See Chemistry.

Colloquy (A). Gourley, S: B. (Add. author for price.) S: B. Gourley.

Collot, A. S.
French-English and English-French dict.; cont. definitions of technical, scientific and abstract terms. Rev. ed. '10(Ap16) c. 8°, $2.75 net. W: R. Jenkins.

Collum, Rowland W., and Gray, H. M. W.
Practice of anæsthetics by Rowland W. Collum; and General surgical technique by H. M. W. Gray; ed. by Ja. Cantlie. '09(Jl) 392 p. il. 12°, *$3 net. Wood.

Collyer, Moses Wakeman.
See Verplanck, W: E:

Collyer, Rev. Rob.
Some memories. '08(N14) por. D. *$1.25 net. Am. Unitarian.
Where the light dwelleth; with a memoir by C: Hargrave. '08(N14) por. D. *$1.40 net. Am. Unitarian.

Colmore, G., pseud.
See Weaver, Gertrude Renton.

Colomba. *See* Mérimée. Prosper.

COLOMBIA (Republic of).
Bingham, H. Journal of an expedition across Venezuela and Colombia, 1906-1907. *$2.25 net. Yale Pub.
International Bureau of American Republics. Colombia; general descriptive data. Int. Bu. Am. Republics.
Pittier de Fábrega, H. F. New or noteworthy plants from Colombia and Central America. (Add. Superintendent for price.) U. S., Supt. of Docs.
United States. *Dept. of Commerce and Labor.* Rept. on trade conditions in Colombia. 10 c. U. S., Supt. of Docs.
United States. *Dept. of Commerce and Labor.* Rept. on trade conditions in Colombia, by G. C: M. Pepper; repr. and distributed by the International Bureau of American Republics. '09(D) 53 p. 8°. Int. Bu. Am. Republics.
See also Cartagena.

COLON.
See Anus and rectum.

Colonel and the Quaker. Cabeen, F. A. $3.50. Goodman's.

Colonel Greatheart. Bailey, H: C. †$1.50. Bobbs-M.

Colonel Wilton's daughters. Finklea, *Mrs.* A. B. $1.25. B'way Pub.

Colonial and old houses of Greenwich, N. J. $1; 50 c. B. A. Andrews.

Colonial carols for children. Terhune, A. $1.25 net. Schirmer.

Colonial churches. Clark, W: M., *ed.* $1.25. Southern Churchman.

Colonial days. Gordy, W. F. *50 c. net. Scribner.

Colonial families of America. Smith, F. M. $2. Allaben.

COLONIAL GOVERNMENT.
Alvord, C. W:. British ministry and the treaty of Fort Stanwix. 25 c. State Hist., Wis.

COLONIAL GOVERNMENT.—*Continued.*
Andrews, C: McL. British committees, commissions, and councils of trade and plantations, 1622-1675. 75 c. Johns Hopkins.
Bruce, *Sir* C: Broad stone of empire. 2 v. $9. Macmillan.
Keller, A. G. Colonization: study of the founding of new societies. $3. Ginn.
Morris, H: C. History of colonization. 2 v. *$4 net. Macmillan.
Silburn, P. A. B. Governance of empire. $3 net. Longmans.
See also Philippine Islands;—United States colonial possessions;—Yellow peril.

Colonial holidays. Tittle, W., *comp.* $2.50 net. Doubleday, P.

Colonial recipes. Bomberger, M. A. $1.25. Neale.

Colonial Society of Massachusetts, collections. 8°. Colonial Soc. of Mass.
—Ayer, *comp.* Check-list of Boston newspapers, 1704-1780. $3.50.

Colonial war services of Colonel Ninian Beall, etc. Moses, Z. (Add. author for price.) Z. Moses.

COLONIES (The).
See United States.

Colonies (The) alert; selections from the *Youth's Companion.* '09(O) c. 64 p. il. 12°, (Companion lib.) pap., 10 c. Youth's Companion.

Colonies and imperial defense. Silburn, P. A. B. $2. Longmans.

COLONNA, Francesco.
Booth, W: S. Hidden signatures of Francesco Colonna and Francis Bacon. $1.50 net. W. A. Butterfield.

COLOR.
Clifford, C. R. Color value. *$1 net. Clifford & L.
Clifton, W. Notes on colour. 50 c. Warne.
Fernald, G. M. Effect of achromatic conditions on the color phenomena of peripheral vision. $1. Psychological Review.
Hatt, J. A. H: The colorist. $1.50. Van Nostrand.
Maire, F: Colors. 60 c. Drake.
Nutting, P. G. Method for constructing the natural scale of pure color. U. S., Supt. of Docs.
Sanford, J: I. Manual of color. 50 c. J: I. Sanford.
See also Coal tar colors;—Paint.

Color book ser. See Macmillan's.

Color books for boys and girls. See Macmillan's.

COLOR IN ANIMALS.
See Animals.

Color in the flower garden. Jekyll, G. *$3.75 net. Scribner.

Color of Paris. Descaves, L., *ed.* *$6 net. Dodd.

COLOR PHOTOGRAPHY.
See Photography.

COLOR-PRINTING.
See Engravers and engravings; — Printers and printing.

COLOR PRINTS.
See Engravers and engravings.

Colorado. Revised statutes, 1908; cont. the Declaration of Independence, the Constitution of the U. S., the enabling act, the Constitution of the state of Colorado, the code of civil procedure, and all general laws. '08(D) c. 1831 p. O. shp., $7.50. Smith-B.

Colorado. *Supreme ct.* Repts.; (Irving B. Melville.) v. 36, 37. '08(Ja4); v. 38. '08 (F); v. 39 (Ap); v. 40 (Ag8) c. O. shp., ea., *$5 net. Mills Pub. Co.

COLORADO.
Anderson, G: G. Some aspects of irrigation development in Colorado. 50 c. Colo. Sci. Soc.
Beach, C: W., *and* Preston, P. J. Irrigation in Colorado. Gov. Pr. Off.
Hatch, D. R. Civil government of Colorado. 60 c. Herrick.
Magill, H. B. Little journeys to ancient sanctuaries [in Colorado.] *$1 net. Little Journeys.
Mendenhall, W. C. Ground waters of the Indo region, Cal.; with sketch of the Colorado desert. (Add. Superintendent for price.) U. S., Supt. of Docs.
Momyer, G: R. Normal institute manual of Colorado school law, Dec., 1909. 25 c. Herrick.
Morrison, R. S., *and* De Soto, E. D. Corporation manual of the statute laws of Colo. $3. W. H. Courtright.
Parsons, E. Making of Colorado. 60 c. Flanagan.
Phillips, J: B. Freight rates and manufactures in Colorado; chapter in economic history. 75 c.; 50 c. J: B. Phillips.
Ramaley, F. Wild flowers and trees of Colorado. $1.25; $1. A. A. Greenman.
Shaw, L. True hist. of some of the pioneers of Colorado. $1. L. Shaw.
United States. *Congress. House. Committee on the Judiciary.* Establishing boundary line between Colorado and New Mexico and Oklahoma. 5 c. U. S., Supt. of Docs.
Warren, E: R. Mammals of Colorado. $3.50 net. Putnam.
See also Cliff dwellers;—Cripple Creek;—Denver; — Leadville; — San Juan Mts.; — Suffrage; — Univ. of Colo.

Colorado code, annot.; with all amendments up to and incl. the 1909 session of the legislature; by R. S. Morrison and Emilio D. De Soto. '10(D) c. S. $6. Courtright.

Colorado justice manual; by H: C. Allen. '10(D) c. T. $5. Courtright.

Colorado Manufacturers' Association, *comp.* Pocket ed. of 25,000 freight and express rates, covering Colo., Idaho, Kan., Mont., Neb., N. M., Utah. Wyo., and misc. rates from the principal cities in the U. S. '09 (D) c. 127 p. 16°, $3. Colo. Manuf.

Colorado poems. Hay, H: J. 75 c. H: J. Hay.

COLORADO RIVER.
Dellenbaugh, F: S: Canyon voyage: second Powell expedition down the Green-Colorado River. **$3.50 net. Putnam.
Jones, T: W., *comp.* Scenic treasures of California, incl. Grand Canyon of Arizona. 50 c. F. Harvey.

COLORADO SPRINGS, Col.
Floy, H: Compilation of the records of the Colorado Springs lighting controversy. $4. Illuminating Engineering.
Colorado State Normal School bull. D. pap. Colo. State Normal.
—Hugh. Bulletin concerning rural schools.
Colorado State Organization of the International Congress on Tuberculosis. Colorado souvenir book for the International Congress on Tuberculosis; ed. by W: N. Beggs, '08, [1909.] (Mr) 200 p. il. maps, tab., 8°. (Add. pub. for price.) W: N. Beggs.
Coloratura album for soprano. Marzo, E., *comp and ed.* $1. Ditson.
COLORED PEOPLE.
See Negroes.
Colorist (The). Hatt, J. A. H: $1.50. Van Nostrand.
COLORS.
See Color.
Colour of Rome. Potter, O. M. *$5 net. Jacobs.
Colour photography. Holme, C., *ed.* *$3 net. Lane.
Colton, Bp. C: H:
Buds and blossoms. '10(My14) c. D. $1.25. Benziger.
COLUMBIA COUNTY, N. Y.
See Claverack.
Columbia elementary geography. Schmucker, S: C. 60 c. Hinds.
Columbia encyclopedia of useful knowledge. Neil, H: $2.50. Columbia Pub.
COLUMBIA RIVER.
Barrows, B: H. Columbia River. gratis. E. L. Lomax.
Lyman, W: D. Columbia River. **$3.50 net. Putnam.
COLUMBIA RIVER VALLEY.
Hunter, B., *and* Jayne, S. O. Suggestions to settlers on the sandy soils of the Columbia River Valley. Gov. Pr. Off.
Columbia School of Poultry Culture textbooks. Course A. In 12 sections. '09 (D18) c. O. pap., per set, $2. Columbia Sch. Poultry.
Columbia University. Currency problem and the present financial situation: addresses del. at Columbia University. '08(Mr21) 8°, *$1.50 net; pap., *$1.25 net. Macmillan.
Columbia University. University bibliography, 1910. '10(Jl9) 35 p. pap. Columbia Univ.
COLUMBIA UNIVERSITY.
See Elgin Botanic Garden.
Columbia University biological ser. il. 8°. Lemcke.
—Wheeler. Ants. $5 net.
Columbia University contributions from the Dept. of Botany. 8°, pap. Columbia Univ.
—House. North American species of the genus *Ipomoea.* 35 c.
Columbia University contributions to Oriental history and philology. 8°, pap.., $1 net. Lemcke.
—Al-Kindi. History of the governors of Egypt.
—Sumerian hymns.
—Zandstra. Witness of the Vulgate, Peshitta and Septuagint to the text of Zekhama.

Columbia Univ., Extension syllabi, Ser. A. 8°, pap. Teachers' Coll.
—Monroe. Syllabus of a course of study on the history and principles of education. 20 c.
Columbia University Germanic studies. 8°. Lemcke.
—De Walsh. Grillparzer as a poet of nature. $1 net.
—Hauhart. Reception of Goethe's Faust in England in the first half of the nineteenth century. *$1 net.
—Kind. Edward Young in Germany. *$1.25 net.
Columbia University Indo-Iranian ser. 8°. Lemcke.
—Avesta. Index verborum. $1.50 net.
—Buddha. Sayings of Buddha. **$1.50 net.
—Dhalla. Nyaishes or Zoroastrian litanies. **$2 net.
—Gray. Indo-Iranian phonology. $2 net.
Columbia Univ. lectures, George Blumenthal foundation. 12°, $1.50 net. Lemcke.
—Ford. Cost of our national government.
—Gray. Nature and sources of the law.
—Jenks. Principles of politics.
—Wilson. Constitutional government.
Columbia University lectures; Jesup lectures. il. 8°. Lemcke.
—Maclaurin. Light. **$1.50 net.
Columbia University lectures on science, philosophy and art, 1907-1908. '09(Mr13) O. *$5 net. Lemcke.
COLUMBIA UNIVERSITY LIBRARY, New York City.
Poe, E. A. Material by and about Edgar Allan Poe to be found in the Library (Add. Univ. for price.) Columbia Univ.
Columbia Univ., Oriental studies. 8°. Lemcke.
—Nathaniel ibn al-Fayyumi. Bustan al-ukul. *$2.50 net.
Columbia Univ. studies in classical philology. 12°. Lemcke.
—Ogden. De infinitivi finalis vel consecutivi constructione apud priscos poetas Græcos. $1 net.
—Reiley. Studies in the philosophical terminology of Lucretius and Cicero. $1.25 net.
—Saunders. Costume in Roman comedy. $1.25 net.
Columbia Univ. studies in comparative literature. 12°. Lemcke.
—Conant. Oriental tale in England in the eighteenth century. **$2 net.
—Spingarn. History of literary criticism in the Renaissance. *$1.50 net.
—Upham. French influence in English literature. $2 net.
Columbia Univ. studies in English, 2d ser. il. 8°. Lemcke.
—Albright. Shakespeare stage. *$1.50 net.
—Ball. Sir Walter Scott as a critic of literature. *$1 net.
—Bates. Study of Shelley's drama, "The Cenci." *$1 net.
—Gildersleeve. Government regulation of the Elizabethan drama. $1.25 net.
—Goddard. Studies in New England transcendentalism. *$1 net.

Columbia Univ. studies in English.—Cont.
—Jackson. Outlines of the literary history of colonial Pennsylvania. *$1.25 net.
—Leonard. Byron and Byronism in America. *$1 net.
—Loshe. Early American novel. *$1 net.
—Miller. Leigh Hunt's relations with Byron, Shelley and Keats. $1.25 net.
—Ristine. English tragicomedy. $1.50.
—Tucker. Verse satire in England before the Renaissance. *$1 net.
—Wood, A. I. P. Stage history of Shakespeare's King Richard the Third. *$1.25 net.
—Wright. Authorship of Timon of Athens. 25 c. net.
—Zeitlen. Accusative with infinitive. **$1 net.

Columbia Univ. studies in history, economics and public law; ed. by the Faculty of Political Science. O. Longmans.
—Arner. Consanguineous marriages in the American population. 75 c.
—Chaddock. Ohio before 1850. $1.50.
—Clark. Standards of reasonableness in local freight discriminations. $1.25 net.
—Coker. Organismic theories of the state. $1.50.
—Davis. Psychological interpretations of society. $2.
—Fry. New Hampshire as a royal province. $3.
—Gephart. Transportation and industrial development in the Middle West. $2.
—Hains. Conflict over judicial powers in the United States. $1.50.
—Hankins. Adolphe Quetlet as statistician. *$1.25 net.
—Hayes. Introduction to the sources relating to the Germanic invasions. $1.50.
—Hilkey. Legal development in colonial Mass. $1.25.
—Hill. Public domain and democracy. $2.
—Lichtenberger. Divorce. **$1.50 net.
—Lingley. Transition in Virginia from colony to commonwealth. $1.50 net.
—MacLear. Early New England towns. *$1.50 net.
—Miller. Legislature of the province of Virginia. *$2 net; *$1.50 net.
—Murray. Making of the Balkan states. $1.50.
—Odum. Social and mental traits of the negro. $2 net.
—Parsons. Responsibility for crime. $1.50.
—Putnam. Enforcement of the statutes of laboures during the first decade after the Black Death. $4.
—Ramsdell. Reconstruction in Texas. $4 net.
—Shapiro. Social reform and the Reformation. $1.25.
—Tanner. Province of New Jersey, 1664-1738. $4.50; $4.
—Underwood. Distribution of ownership. *$2 net; *$1.50 net.
—Weld. Private freight cars and American railways. *$1.50 net.
—West. Inheritance tax. *$2.50 net; *$2 net.
—Whiton. Factory legislation in Maine. $1.
—Woolston. Study of the population of Manhattanville. $1.25.

Columbia Univ. studies in romance, philology and literature. 12°. Lemcke.
—Cushing. Pierre Le Tourneur. **$1.50 net.
—Stuart. Stage decoration in France in the Middle Ages. $1.50 net.

Columbia University Teachers' College. Educational Museum. Exhibition of material illustrating the historical development of mathematics from the collection of David Eugene Smith. '09(Mr) 8 p. 8°, pap., gratis. D. E. Smith.

Columbia Univ. Teachers' College, contributions to education. O. pap. Teachers' Coll.
—Bard. City school district. $1.
—Betts. Distribution and functions of mental imagery. $1; 75 c.
—Cole, *comp.* Later Roman education. 25 c.
—Coursault. Learning process. *$1 net.
—Earhart. Systematic study in the elementary schools. $1.
—Erasmus. Ciceronianus. (Historical ser.) $1.
—Goodsell. Conflict of naturalism and humanism. $1.50.
—Haney. Registration of city school children. $1.50.
—Jackson. Development of school support in colonial Massachusetts. $1; 75 c.
—Kandel. Training of elem. school teachers in Germany. $1.50.
—Lodge. Vocabulary of high school Latin. *$1.50 net.
—Lomer. Concept of method. $1.
—Nicholson. Concept standard. $1.50.
—Sandiford. Training of teachers in England and Wales. $1.50.
—Snyder. Legal status of rural high schools in the U. S. $1.50.
—Stamper. Hist. of the teaching of elem. geometry. $1.50; $1.15.
—Stone. Arithmetical abilities. $1.
—Updegraff. Origin of the moving school in Massachusetts. $1.50.

Columbia University, Teachers' College, education reprints. O. Teachers' Coll.
—Seguin. Idiocy. $2.

Columbia Univ., Teachers' College, extension syllabi. 8°. Teachers' Coll.
—Sachs. Syllabus of general course on theory and practice of teaching. 20 c.

Columbia Univ., Teachers' College record. il. 8°. Columbia Univ.; Teachers' Coll.
—Education of nurses. 30 c.
—Kinne. Equipment for teaching of domestic science. 30 c.
—Johnson. Problem of adapting history to children in the elementary school. 30 c.
—Sachs, *ed.* Studies in secondary education. 30 c.
—Smith. Teaching of arithmetic. 30 c.
—Thorndike. Educational psychology. $1.50.
—Handwriting. 30 c.

Columbia Univ., Teachers' College ser. 8°. Teachers' Coll.
—Andrews. Museums of education. 30 c.
—Stowe. English grammar schools in the reign of Queen Elizabeth. *$1.50 net.

Columbia Univ., Teachers' College, syllabi. 8°. Teachers' Coll.
—Edson. Bibliography of a course on school administration, summer session, Teachers' College, 1910.
—Freeman. Syllabus of course on elem. bookmaking. 30 c.

COLUMBUS, Christopher.
Helps, *Sir* Arth. Life of Columbus. 35 c. net; 70 c. net. Dutton.
Kerr, A. C. Short life of Christopher Columbus. *$1 net. Herder.
Kitchen, M. L. K. Essay on the life of our patriotic admiral, Christopher Columbus. 50 c. R. Kitchen.

Columbus, Ferdinand.
Catalogue of Ferdinand Columbus Library reproduced in facsimile from the unique ms. in the Columbine Library of Seville. [facsim.] '05, [1909.] (N) no paging, 4°, $70. Hispanic Soc.

COLUMBUS MEMORIAL LIBRARY, Washington, D. C.
International Bureau of American Republics. List of Latin American hist. and description in the Columbus Memorial Library. gratis. Int. Bu. Am. Republics.

Columbus Tabernacle sermons. Book, W: H: $1. Standard Pub.

Column and line in the Peninsula War. Oman, C: W: 40 c. Oxford Univ.

COLUMNS.
Talbot, A. N. Tests of brick columns and terra cotta block columns. gratis. Univ. of Ill.
See also Strength of materials.

Colver, Frederic Lathrop.
Colver-Culver genealogy; descendants of Edward Colver of Boston, Dedham, and Roxbury, Massachusetts, and New London, and Mystic, Ct. [1910.] (Je) c. 271 p. 12°, (Allaben genealogical ser.) $5. Allaben.

COLVER-CULVER FAMILY.
See Genealogies.

Colvill, Mary H.
Saint Teresa of Spain. '09(N) 16+344 p. il. 8°, *$2.50 net. Dutton.

Colville, Helen Hester.
Lady Julia's emerald. '08(Je27) D. †$1.50. Lane.

Colville, W: Wilberforce Juvenal.
Ancient mysteries and modern revelation. '10(Ag20) c. por. D. $1 net. Fenno.
Glints of wisdom; or, helpful sayings for busy moments. '10(Jl2) c. 12°, 40 c. Macoy.
Health from knowledge; or, the law of correspondences as related to psychotherapy, in seven lectures. '09(D) c. 143 p. 12°, 50 c. Macoy.
Life and power from within. '10(O) 12°, $1 net. Fenno.

Colvin, Fred Herbert.
Engine lathe work. '09(Je26) il. $1. Hill Pub.
Link motions, valves and valve setting. 2d ed. '09(D) c. 82 p. 24°, 50 c. Henley.
Machine shop arithmetic. 5th ed. '10(Je4) c. 50 c. Henley.
Machine shop calculations. '08(N21) il. $1. Hill Pub.

Colvin, Fred Herbert.—*Continued.*
Machine shop drawings, reading drawings, making shop sketches, laying out work. '09(O16) c. il. 12°, $1. McGraw-H.
Pocket-railroad dict. and vade mecum. '10 (My21) $1. Henley.
See also Richards, Jos. W:

—, and Cheney, —.
Engineer's arithmetic. 2d ed. '09(D) 122 p. 16°, bds., 50 c. Henley.

—, and Stanley, Fk. Arthur, comps.
American machinists' handbook and dictionary of shop terms. '08(D3) c. il. tabs., 16°, $3. Hill Pub.
Hill kink books. '08(Mr7) 10 v., il. 16°, ea., 50 c. Hill Pub.

Colvin, Ian D.
South Africa. '09(O9) il. in col. map, O. (Romance of history ser.) *$2 net. Stokes.

Colvin, Stephen Sheldon.
Some facts in partial justification of the so-called dogma of discipline. [1910.] (Ap) 29 p. il. 8°, (Univ. of Ill., School of Education, bull.) pap., gratis. Univ. of Ill.

Colwell, Eliz.
Songs and sonnets. '09(D18) c. O. pap., *$2.50 net, boxed. F. F. Sherman.

Colwell, Nathan Porter.
Need, methods and value of medical college inspection. '09(N) 11 p. 8°, pap., gratis. Am. Medical.

Colyer, J. F.
Dental surgery and pathology; being the 3d ed. of Diseases and injuries of the teeth, by Morton Smale and J. F. Colyer. '10(N) 16+1000 p. il. O. $7 net. Longmans.

Coman, Katharine.
Industrial hist. of the United States. New and rev. ed. '10(O8) c. il. maps, D. $1.50 net. Macmillan.

COMATULIDS.
See Echinoderms.

Combarieu, Jules Léon Jean.
Music; its laws and evolution; auth. tr. '10(Ap2) D. (International scientific ser.) $1.75 net. Appleton.

Combat with ignorance. Rosewater, V. (Priv. pr.) V. Rosewater.

Combe, Adolphe.
Intestinal auto-intoxication; together with an appendix on the lactic ferments with particular reference to their application in intestinal therapeutics, by Albert Fournier; only author. Eng. adapt. by W: Gaynor States. '08(D) c. 18+461 p. il. 8°, *$4 net. Rebman.

COMBINATIONS.
See Trusts.

Combined Spanish method. Tornos, A. de. $1.50. Appleton.

Combined tonics and other related auditory phenomena. Peterson, J. $1.50. Psychological Review.

COMBUSTION ENGINES.
See Engines.

Come and find me. Robins, E. †$1.50. Century Co.

Come and go. Bingham, C. $2. Dutton.

Comédie (La) classique en France. 50 c. Am. Bk.
Comédie humaine. *See* Balzac, Honoré de.
Comedie of errors. *See* Shakespeare, W:
COMEDY.
See Plays.
Comedy of Mammon. Garvey, I. †$1.50. Estes.
Comedy of petty conflicts. Wall, I. B. F. $1.50. B'way Pub.
Comet (The). Dix, I. S. 15 c. I. S. Dix.
Comet (The). Doyle, E: $1.25. Badger.
COMETS.
See Astronomy.
Comfort, B: Franklin.
Arnold's tempter. '08(N14) c. il. D. $1.50. C. M. Clark.
Comfort, Will Levington.
Routledge rides alone. '10(Ap9) c. front. D. $1.50. Lippincott.
Comfort, W: Wistar.
Exercises in French prose composition. '08 (Ja4) S. (Modern lang. ser.) 25 c. Heath.
—, **comp. and ed.** Les maîtres de la critique littéraire au XIXme siècle. '09(N6) c. S. (Modern language ser.) 50 c. Heath.
COMFORT.
See Consolation.
Comfort of the hills. *See* Mitchell, S. W.
Comfortable faith. McLeod, M. J. *$1 net. Revell.
Comic dialogues. Dennis, J: R. 50 c.; 30 c. Penn Pub. Co.
Comic juveniles. *See* Stokes'.
COMIC OPERAS.
See Operas.
Comic writers of Great Britain. Hazlitt, W: 35 c. net; 70 c. net. Dutton.
Coming conflict of nations. Fitzpatrick, E. H. $2. H. W. Rokker.
Coming harvest. Bazin, R. †$1.25. Scribner.
Coming kingdom. Rominger, C. A. $1. C. A. Rominger.
Coming motherhood. Spaeth, L: A. *$1 net. P: Reilly.
Coming of Hester. Baird, J. K. †$1.25. Lothrop, L. & S.
Coming of the king. Synan, A. 35 c. net. Herder.
Coming people. Dole, C: F. 75 c. Crowell.
Coming peril. Coan, M. B. 50 c. Wilkie & C.
Coming religion. Dole, C: F. $1 net. Small.
Coming science. Carrington, H. **$1.50 net. Small.
Coming struggle in eastern Asia. Weale, B. L. P., *pseud.* *$3.50 net. Macmillan.
COMMANDMENTS.
Hornyold, J: J. Commandments and sacraments. 75 c. Chr. Press.
Laws of the King. 60 c. Benziger.
Walker, S. G. Household catechism on the Decalogue. 25 c.; 40 c. S. G. Walker.
Commemoration of the faithful. Thompson, W. (Priv. pr.) Gorham.
Commencement days. Church, *Mrs.* V. $1.50. L. C. Page
COMMENTARIES.
See under special subjects.
Commentary (A). Galsworthy, J: $1.50. Putnam.
Commentary on the science of organization and business development. *See* Frank, R. J:
Comments of Bagshot. Spender, J: A. **$1.25 net. Holt.
COMMERCE.
Adams, C. C. Elem. commercial geography. $1.10.—Text-book of commercial geography. **$1.30 net. Appleton.
American Academy of Political and Social Science. Commercial relation between the United States and Japan. Am. Acad. Pol. Sci.
American School of Correspondence. Cyclopedia of commerce, accountancy, business administration. 10 v. $24. Am. Sch. Corr.
Briggs, J. S. "Express"; information for shippers regarding express shipments. $2. Express.
Buyers' reference directory. gratis. Puritan Pub. Co.
Calvert, A. Shipping office organization. $2. Pitman.
Chisholm, G: G. Hdbk. of commercial geography. *$4.80 net. Longmans.
Cody, S. Geographical reference list and commercial map of the United States. $1. S. Cody.
Cooke, F: H. Commerce clause of the federal constitution. $4.50. Baker, V. & Co.
Cunningham, W. English industry and commerce in modern times. In 2 pts. *$5.25 net. Putnam.
Daish, J: B. Procedure in interstate commerce cases. *$5 net. Lowdermilk.
Drinker, H: S., *jr.* Treatise on the interstate commerce act. 2 v. $10. Bisel.
Export commission houses, New York City. Directory. $2. Am. Exporter.
Foreign trade of the United States in forest products. Gov. Pr. Off.
Graham, J., *and* Oliver, G: A. S. French commercial practice connected with the export and import trade to and from France, and the French colonies, pt. 2. *$1 net. Macmillan.
Gregory, H E., *and others.* Physical and commercial geography. $3. Ginn.
Hague, G: Pract. treatise on banking and commerce. $3. Bankers' Pub.
Hall, A., *and* Heywood, F. Shipping: guide to the routine in connection with the shipment of goods. 50 c. Pitman.
Hanks, C: S. Benefit of the Hepburn law to the banker, broker, shipper and the public. 50 c. Authors' Pub.
Heywood, J: W. Hints on exporting; suggestions for guidance of millers. (Not for sale.) Northwestern Miller.
Hooper, F:, *and* Graham, J. Import and export trade. *$1 net. Macmillan.
Hough, B: O. Elem. lessons in exporting. $3. Johnston Export.
Knox, P. C. Future of commerce. (Add. author for price.) P. C. Knox.
Motley, J. Importers' ready reference tables. $1.25. Motley Press.

COMMERCE.—*Continued.*

National Business League of America. Pract. suggestions for the development of American export trade, with directories of the chief cities of Brazil, South America, Chile, Panama, southeast Africa.—European and Asiatic Turkey, by E: F. Ozmun; Russia, by W: Dawson; Argentina, S. A., by Allan G. Snyder.—Switzerland, by Silas C. McFarland; Haiti, W. I., by J: B. Terres; Ecuador, S. A., by Herman R. Dietrict. (Add. pubs. for price.) Nat. Business.

Pigott, C:, *ed.* Exporters' encyclopædia, 1909; 1910, ea., $5. Exporters' Enc.

Rea, R. Imports and employment. 10 c. Cassell.

Rocheleau, W: F. Geography of commerce and industry. $1. Educ. Pub.

Selling foreign manufactures in United States at prices lower than the domestic prices. '09(Je) 126 p. 8°, pap. (Add. Superintendent for price.) U. S., Supt. of Docs.

Shipping and tariffs; extracts from the London *Fairplay* of March 17 and March 24, 1910. '10(Jl) 6 p. 8°, pap., 5 c. Gov. Pr. Off.

Thompson, R. J., *comp.* Suggestions for the development of American export trade to Germany. gratis. Nat. Business.

United States. *Dept. of Agriculture. Bu. of Statistics.* Exports of farm and forest products, 1906-1908. 10 c.

United States. *Dept. of Agriculture. Bu. of Statistics.* Exports of farm products from the United States, 1851-1908. 15 c.

United States. *Dept. of Agriculture. Bu. of Statistics.* Imports of farm products into the United States, 1851-1908. 15 c.

United States. *Dept. of Commerce and Labor. Bureau of Statistics.* Commercial America. (Add. Superintendent for price.) U. S., Supt. of Docs.

United States. *Dept. of Commerce and Labor. Bureau of Statistics.* Exports of domestic merchandise from the U. S. during the year ending June 30, 1908. '09 (Ag) 711-778 p. 4°, pap. (Add. Superintendent for price.)

United States. *Dept. of Commerce and Labor. Bureau of Statistics.* Foreign commerce and navigation of the United States for the year ending June 30, 1907. $2.50; for the year ending June 30, 1908, $2; for the year ending June 30, 1909.

United States. *Dept. of Commerce and Labor. Bureau of Statistics.* Imports and exports of gold and silver and imports and exports of merchandise into and from the U. S. by countries and customs districts and by customs districts and countries during the year ending June 30, 1908. '08, [1909.] (My) 71-155 p. 4°. (Add. Superintendent for price.)

United States. *Dept. of Commerce and Labor. Bureau of Statistics.* Imports and exports of merchandise into and from the U. S. by countries and principal articles during the years ending June 30, 1904-1908. '09(My) 975-1063 p. tabs., 4°, pap. (Add. Superintendent for price.)

COMMERCE.—*Continued.*

United States. *Dept. of Commerce and Labor. Bureau of Statistics.* Internal commerce of the U. S. for Jan.-Dec., 1906, 1907 and 1908, by Morris Jacobson. '09 (Ag) 630 p. tabs., 4°, pap. (Add. Superintendent for price.)

United States. *Dept. of Commerce and Labor. Bureau of Statistics.* Tonnage movement of American and foreign vessels in the foreign trade of the United States during the year ending June 30, 1908. '09(My) 1065-1134 p. tabs., 4°, pap.

United States. *Dept. of Commerce and Labor.* Manufactured products sold in foreign markets at lower rates than in American; letter from the Acting Secretary of Commerce and Labor, transmitting in response to Senate resolution of Apr. 5 information respecting manufactured products. '09(Je) 8 p. 8°, pap.

United States. *Dept. of State.* Foreign trade and treaty relations; letter from the secretary of state, transmitting a request for an appropriation of $100,000 to enable the Department of State to defray the necessary expenses incurred in connection with foreign trade and treaty relations. '09(O) 9 p. 8°. (Add. Superintendent for price.) U. S., Supt. of Docs.

United States. *Dept. of State.* Steamship communication to South America: repts. from consular officers of the U. S. rel. to steamship communication between the U. S. and South America. '10(Jl) 68 p. 8°.

United States. *Superintendent of Documents.* Transportation: list of publications rel. to interstate commerce, roads, inland waterways, merchant marine, etc., for sale by the Superintendent of Documents. '10(Jl) 75 p. 8°, gratis.

See also Advertising;—Atlases;—Bankruptcy;—Banks and banking;—Bookkeeping;—Business;—Carriers;—Commercial correspondence;—Commercial law;—Contracts;—Co-operation;—Corporations;—Cotton;—Credit;—Erie canal;—Exchange;—Express;—Finance;—Great Lakes;—Inland navigation;—Interest;—Loans;—Money;—Monopolies;—Panics;—Political economy;—Railroads;—Sale;—Ship subsidies;—Statistics;—Stocks;—Tariff;—Trade unions;—Transportation;—Trusts;—Warehouses;—Weights and measures;—*also* names of countries.

Commercial and technical terms in the English and Spanish languages. Monteverde, R. D. *70 c. net. Macmillan.

COMMERCIAL ARITHMETIC.
See Arithmetic.

COMMERCIAL BOOKKEEPING.
See **Bookkeeping.**

COMMERCIAL COLLEGE.
See **Business.**

COMMERCIAL CORRESPONDENCE.

Arbib-Costa, A. Manuale di corrispondenza commerciale e familiare italiana-inglese. 50 c. F. Tocci.

Bithell, J. Handbook of German commercial correspondence. $1.25. Longmans.

Browne, T: R. *and* E. C. Miscellaneous correspondence, commercial and legal forms. pt. 1. 50 c. Brown's Business Coll.

COMMERCIAL CORRESPONDENCE.—*Continued.*
Cody, S. How to do business by letter. $1. Sch. of Eng.
Crissey, F. Hand-book of modern business correspondence. $1. Thompson & T.
Hagar, H. A. Applied business punctuation and business forms. 40 c. Gregg Pub.
Hammond, H. W. Style-book of business English. 85 c. Pitman.
Hickox, W: E. Correspondents' manual for stenographers. 50 c. Lothrop, L. & S.
How to write letters that win. $2. System.
Letters that collect; or, how to get money by mail. $1. Modern Mercantile.
Pitman, B., *and* Howard, J. B. Business letters. no. 4, Insurance correspondence. 25 c. Phonograph.
Pitman, *Sir* I: International mercantile letters: English-French. 85 c.—English-Italian. $1.—[English-German.] 85 c.—English-Portuguese. $1.25. Pitman.
Smith, W: N. Pract. correspondence. 75 c. Massey.
Wiers, C: R. How to write a business letter. $1. C: R. Wiers.
Witter, C: A. Business and accounts for public schools and home use. 75 c. C: A. Witter.
See also Stenography.

COMMERCIAL EDUCATION.
See Business.

Commercial feeding stuffs of the United States. Haywood, J: K. 25 c. U. S., Supt. of Docs.

Commercial forest trees of Massachusetts. Clarke, D. A. (Add. pubs. for price.) Wright & P.

COMMERCIAL GEOGRAPHY.
See Commerce.

Commercial grinding by the use of plain grinding machines; hand book for the shop. '10(Je) c. 104 p. il. 8°, 25 c. Brown & S.

COMMERCIAL LAW.
American School of Correspondence. Commercial law. $3. Am. Sch. Corr.
Barnes, H. C. Interstate transportation. $6. Bobbs-M.
Brennan, B. A. Compendium of useful legal information for business men. *$5 net. Wiley.
Bryant, J: C. Business man's commercial law. $1.50. C. L. Bryant.
Burdick, F. M. Essentials of business law. **$1.10 net. Appleton.
Chamberlain, J: A. Commercial law. pt. 1. 50 c. Am. Sch. Corr.
Chamberlain, J: A. Principles of business law. $2.50. W. H. Anderson.
Crane, W. E. Commercial law for business men. $1.75. W. E. Crane.
Cushner, M. B. Commercial law for accountant students. (Add. pubs. for price.) Universal Business.
Davis, H. G. Interstate Commerce Commission. 10 c. La Salle Extension.
Douglas, A. H. Elements of commercial law. 50 c. Pitman.

COMMERCIAL LAW.—*Continued.*
Drinker, H: S., *jr.* Supp. to a treatise on the interestate commerce act and digest of decisions construing the same. v. 3. $5. Bisel.
Fitch, A. N. New commercial law. $1.05. Am. Bk.
Ford, H: 600 business law points for the business man. $3.50. H: Ford.
Frank, R. J. Commentary on the science of organization and business development. (Add. pub. for price.) Chic. Legal News.
Hills, A. T. Commercial law. (Add. pubs. for price.) Practical Text-book Co.
Ketchum, E. S. Interstate commerce law. 25 c. La Salle Extension.
McMaster, J. S. Commercial digest and business forms. $6. Weed-Parsons.
Mannierre, L: Business law. (Not for sale.) Am. Business Man.
Moore, W: V. Legal secretary: series of articles on commercial law. $3. Boger.
Nelson, J: H. Law rel. to the Interstate Commerce Commission, the Sherman anti-trust act, and the Bureau of Corporations. $5. Banks.
Nims, H. D. Law of unfair business competition. $6.50. Baker, V. & Co.
Osgood, W: T. Law points for business men. (Add. pubs. for price.) Tudor Press.
Parsons, T. Laws for business for all the states and territories. $4. Scranton.
Pierce, E: B. Digest of the decisions of the courts and Interstate Commerce Commission under the act to regulate commerce from 1887 to 1908. *$6 net. Callaghan.
Putney, A. H. Commercial law. $4.80. Cree.
Roe, E: T:, *and* Loomis, E. G. Business law. $2.75-$3.50. Hertel.
Ryer, J. C. Principles of commercial law. (Add. pubs. for price.) Cross Co.
Simons, C: C. Commercial law simplified. $5. Business Man's Pub.
Slater, J: A. Pitman's mercantile law. $2. Pitman.
Sullivan, J. J. American business law. **$1.50 net. Appleton.
United States. *Interstate Commerce Commission.* Index digest of the repts., rulings and decisions. $5. Edwards.
United States. Interstate commerce laws. 50 c. Railway Age Gazette.
United States. Law of interstate commerce and federal regulation thereof. $7.50. M. Bender.
Van Buren, A. B. Supp. no. 1 to index-digest of the repts. and rulings of the Interstate Commerce Commission. 35 c. Edwards.
Virginia. Business man's code of laws. $5. B. D. Smith.
See also Bankruptcy;—Carriers;—Consuls;—Contracts;—Corporations; —Exchange;—Insurance; — Negotiable instruments; — Patents; — Railroads;—Sale;—Trusts;—*also* names of states.

Commercial organic analysis. *See* Allen, A. H.

COMMERCIAL PAPER.
See Negotiable instruments.
Commercial peat. Gissing, F: T. *$2 net. Lippincott.
COMMERCIAL POLICIES.
See Tariff.
Commercial precedents. Putzel, C:, *comp.* (Add. pubs. for price.) Am. Pub.
Commercial products of India. Watt, *Sir* G: *$5 net. Dutton.
Commercial science ser. S. $1. Commercial Sci.
—Lenington. Seven principles of successful salesmanship.
Commercial World encyclopedia of accounting.. Spear, R. H., *ed.* In 2 v. v. 1. per set, $15. Commercial World.
Commercialism and journalism. Holt, H. **$1 net. Houghton M.
COMMISSION GOVERNMENT.
See Municipal government.
COMMISSIONERS.
See Notaries.
Committee on Railway Mail Pay. Railway mail pay primer. '10(Ap30) S. pap. (Add. pubs. for price.) Com. Railway.
Common, T:
Nietzsche as philosopher, critic, poet, prophet. '08(D19) il. 12°, *$2 net. Dutton.
Common affections of the liver. White, W. H. *$2 net. Wood.
Common difficulties in reading French. Clarke, C: C. $1. W: R. Jenkins.
Common honesty. Donaldson, O. M. 50 c. Van-American.
COMMON LAW.
See names of states.
Common lot (The). Herrick, R. $1.50. Macmillan.
COMMON SCHOOLS.
See Schools.
Common sense Bible teacher. Abbott, C. L. 25 c. C. L. Abbott.
Common sense in politics. Hedges, J. E. $1.25. Moffat.
Common-sense in religion. Smith, M. R. $1. Longmans.
Common sense of socialism. Spargo, J: $1; 25 c. Kerr.
Common sense of political economy. Wicksteed, P. H: $4.25 net. Macmillan.
Common sense of the milk question. Spargo, J: **$1.50 net. Macmillan.
Common-sense poultry doctor. Robinson, J: H. 50 c. Farm-Poultry.
Common sense recipes. Robertson, G., *comp.* 25 c. G. Robertson.
Common-sense view of Christian science. Krull, V. H. 25 c. V. H. Krull.
Common sense view of the mind-cure. Westall, *Mrs.* L. M. H. **75 c. net. Funk.
COMMON SERVICE.
See Evangelical Lutheran church.
Common weeds of the farm and garden. Long, H. C. $2 net. Stokes.
Common words commonly misspelled. Payne, B. R. B. F. Johnson.
Commons, J: R., Phillips, Ulrichs B., Gilmore, Eugene A., and others, eds.
Documentary hist. of American industrial society; prepared under the auspices of the American Bureau of Industrial Research, with the co-operation of the Carnegie Institution of Washington; with a preface by R: T. Ely and introd. by J: B. Clark. In 10 v. v. 1, 2, Plantation and frontier, by Ulrich B. Phillips; v. 3, 4, Labor conspiracy cases, 1806-1842, by J: R. Commons and Eugene A. Gilmore; v. 5, 6, Labor movement, 1820-1840, by J: R. Commons and Helen L. Sumner; v. 7, 8, Labor movement, 1840-1860, by J: R. Commons; v. 9, 10, Labor movement, 1860-1880, by J: R. Commons and J: B. Andrews, analytical index. '09(O9) c. il. pors. 4°, per set, *$50 net. Issued two volumes bi-monthly, beginning Sept. 1. A. H. Clark.
Commonweal (The). Hillier, A. P: *$1.50 net. Longmans.
Commonwealth of Australia. Wise, B. R. *$3 net. Little, B. & Co.
Commonwealth of man. Holland, R. A. *$1 net. Young Churchman.
COMMUNION.
See Lord's supper.
COMMUNISM.
Eeden, F: van. Practical communism. 10 c. Civic Forum.
Marx, K., *and* Engels, F: Manifests of the communist party. 50 c. Kerr.
More, *Sir* T: Utopia. *50 c. net. Macmillan.
See also Individualism;—Socialism.
COMMUNITIES.
Hinds, W: A. American communities and co-operative colonies. $1.50. Kerr.
Pressy, E. P. Vision of new Clairvaux; [introducing experiences of Montague, Mass., colony of idealists]. *$1.25 net. Sherman, F.
See also Community of true inspiration.
Communium naturalium. *See* Bacon, Roger.
Compact (The). Cullum, R. *$1.20 net. Doran.
Compact rhyming dictionary. Bennett, P. P. 50 c. Dutton.
Companion library. il. 12°. Youth's Companion.
—Colonies alert. 10 c.
Companion life ser. 8°. C: W. Littlefield.
—Littlefield. Twelve vitalized tissue remedies for private and domestic use. $2.50.
Companion ser. il. 12°. Youth's Companion.
—Under the crown. 50 c.
Companionship. Elshemus, L: M. *$1.25 net. Dreamer's Press.
COMPANY LAW.
See Corporations.
Comparative legislation bulletin. *See* Wisconsin Free Library Commission.
Comparative mythology. Muller, M. 50 c.; 75 c. Dutton.
COMPARATIVE RELIGION.
See Religion.
Comparative reserve tables. Dawson, M. M. $25. Chronicle Co.
Comparative studies in religion. Secrist, H: T. 45 c.; 35 c.; 65 c. Unitarian S. S.
Comparetti, Domenico.
Vergil in the Middle Ages; tr. by E. F. M. Benecke; with an introd. by Robinson Ellis. '08(O17) 12°, *$1.75 net. Macmillan.

Comparison of the effects of frequency on the light of incandescent and Nernst lamps. Huels, F: W: 25 c. Univ. of Wis.

Comparisons simplified. Webb, E. G., *comp.* $3. Bassette.

COMPASS.

Calhoun, G. K. Products of arcs and sines of 15-degree rhumbs, computed for use in analysis of deviations when 15-degree rhumbs are used. Gov. Pr. Off.

Guthrie, W: A. McDuffie's discovery of the natural causes for the variations of the magnetic needle of the compass. 50 c. W: A. Guthrie.

Compayré, Jules Gabriel.

Yvan Gall, le pupille de la marine; ed., with notes and vocab., by O. B. Super. '09(Ja23) c. il. S. 35 c. Holt.

Montaigne, and education of the judgment. '08(Ap25) por. D. (Pioneers in education ser.) **90 c. net. Crowell.

Compendium of every day wants. Minter, L. $1.90; $2.75. Minter.

Compendium of food microscopy. Clayton, E. G., *comp.* *$4 net. Wood.

Compendium of history. Kerney, M. J. *$1.25 net. Murphy.

Compendium of the war of the rebellion. Dyer, F: H., *comp.* *$10 net. Torch Press.

COMPETITION.

See Commercial law.

Compilations of the healings of Christ. *See* Bible. N. T.

Complaint of nature. Alain de Lille. 75 c. Holt.

Complete angler. *See* Walton, Izaak.

Complete catalogue of Catholic literature; cont. all Catholic books published in the United States, together with a selection from the catalogues of the Catholic publishers of England and Ireland. '10(Jl16) c. 8°, 15 c. T: J. Flynn.

Complete cynic. Herford, O., *and others.* 75 c. Elder.

Complete farmer ser. *See* McConnell, Primrose.

Complete guide to the game of draughts. Lees, J. 50 c. Warne.

Complete (A) hand-book of standard rules of all the prominent games of billiards and pool as practiced by the great professionals and other leading players. Rev. ed. '08 (Ap11) c. il. 12°, gratis. Brunswick.

Complete hockey player. White, E. E. **$2 net. Jacobs.

Complete Mother Goose. *See* Mother Goose.

Complete mountaineer. Abraham, G: D. *$4.80 net. Doubleday, P.

Complete oarsman. Lehmann, R. C. *$3 net. Jacobs.

Complete pocket guide to Europe. Stedman, E. C., *ed.* $1.25 net. W: R. Jenkins.

Complete self-instructing library of practical photography. Schriever, J. B. 8 v. $32; $40; $48. Am. Sch. Art.

Complete version of ye three blind mice. Ivimey, J: W: *50 c. net. Warne.

COMPOSERS.

See Musicians.

Compositae of southern California. Hall, H. M. $3. Univ. of Cal.

COMPOSITION.

See English language;—Painters and paintings;—Rhetoric;—*also* names of languages.

Comprehensive standard dict. of the English language; designed to give the orthography, pronunciation, meaning, and etymology of about 38,000 words and phrases in the speech and literature of the English-speaking peoples; abgd. from the Funk and Wagnalls Standard dictionary of the English language, by Ja. C. Fernald. '01, [1909.] (D) c. 5-8-533 p. il. 8°, $1.50. Funk.

COMPRESSED AIR.

Boycott, G. W. M. Compressed air. **$4 net. Van Nostrand.

Harris, E. G. Compressed air. $1.50 net. McGraw-H.

Hiscox, G. D. Compressed air, its production, uses and applications. $5. Henley.

Peele, R. Compressed air plant. $3.50 net. —Compressed air plant for mines. $3. Wiley.

Wightman, L. I., *comp.* Compressed air. $1. Am. Sch. Corr.

See also Machinery.

Compression in the French classical drama. Bruner, J. D. 10 c. J. D. Bruner.

Compton, Alwne T.

Essentials of surgery. '08(Ag8) il. 12°, *$1.50 net. Keener.

Compton, C. G.

Princess of Hackney. '08(D5) D. $1.50. Lane.

Compulsory education in the South. Milton, G: F. gratis. Nat. Child Labor.

COMPUTATION.

See Arithmetic.

Computations for marine engines. Peabody, C. H. (For private distribution.) C. H. Peabody.

Comrade Kropotkin. Robinson, V. $1. Altrurians.

Comrades. Dixon, T:, *jr.* †$1.50. Doubleday, P.

Comrades courageous ser. il. 12°. Badger. —Whitcomb. Skimming the skies. $1.25.

Comrades of the saddle. Webster, F.. V. 40 c. Cupples & L.

Comrades of the trails. Roberts, G: E: T. $1.50. L. C. Page.

Comrades on river and lake. Victor, R. 60 c. Chatterton.

Comrades on the farm. Victor, R. 60 c. Chatterton-P.

Comrades ser. for boys. *See* Victor, Ralph.

Comstock, G: Comstock.

Text-book of field astronomy for engineers. 2d ed., rev. and enl. '08(N7) il. figs. 8°, $2.50. Wiley.

Comstock, Mrs. Hattie Theresa.

Janet of the dunes. '08(Ja18) D. †$1.50. Little, B. & Co.

Comstock, Warren Ennis.

Days of long ago, and Immortality, (antithesis of The Rubáiyát:) [two poems.] '08(D26) il. O. pap., 50 c. Badger.

COMTE, Auguste.

Mill, J: S. Auguste Comte and positivism. 75 c. Dutton.

Whittaker, T: W. Comte and Mill. *50 c. net. Dodge.

Comte, Isidore Auguste.
General view of positivism; with an introd. by F: Harrison. '08(O10) 24°, (New universal lib.) 50 c.; leath., 75 c. Dutton.

Comte (Le) de Monte Cristo. Dumas, A. 40 c. Am. Bk.

Comtelburo business calendar, 1909; containing information of business holidays throughout the world and a supply of business maxims for every day of the year. '09(Mr6); 1910. '10(Ap) c. tabs., O. ea., $1. Comtelburo.

Comus. *See* Milton, J:

Comyn, D: C: E: ffrench.
Service and sport in the Sudan; record of administration in the Anglo-Egyptian Sudan; with some intervals of sport and travel. '10(O29) il. pors. map, O. $4 net. Lane.

Conan, Laure, [pseud. for F. Angers.]
Master motive: tale of the days of Champlain; tr. from the French by Theresa A. Gethin. '09(Mr) 2+254 p. 8°, $1. Herder.

Conant, Albert Fs., comp.
Complete concordance to "Science and health"; with key to the Scriptures, together with an index to the marginal headings and a list of the Scriptural quotations cont. therein; rev. from the 1908 ed. of "Science and health" as rev. by its author, Mary Baker G. Eddy. 13th thousand. '08(My23) c. 8°. (Add. pub. for price.) A. V. Stewart.

Conant, C: Arthur.
Banking system of Mexico. '10(Jl) 284 p. tabs., 8°. Gov. Pr. Off.
History of modern banks of issue; with account of the economic crises of the nineteenth century. 3d ed., with chapter on the crisis of 1907. '08(Ag29) D. $3; 4th ed., rev. and enl. '09(Ap10) c. tabs., O. **$3.50 net. Putnam.
National bank of Belgium. '10(Ap) 238 p. 8°. U. S., Supt. of Docs.
Principles of banking: second part separately issued of The principles of money and banking. '08(My16) c. D. **$1.75 net. Harper.
—, **comp.** *See* United States. New banking law.

Conant, Levi Leonard, ed.
Five-place logarithmic and trigonometric tables based on the tables of F. G. Gauss. '09(N20) c. O. 50 c. Am. Bk.
Plane and spherical trigonometry. '09 (N13) c. il. O. 85 c.; with Five-place logarithmic and trigonometric tables, $1.20. Am. Bk.
Plane trigonometry. '09(N20) c. O. 60 c.; bound with Five-place logarithmic and trigonometric tables, 90 c. Am. Bk.

Conant, Martha Pike.
Oriental tale in England in the eighteenth century. '08(F22) c. 12°, (Columbia Univ. studies in comparative literature.) **$2 net. Lemcke.

Conard, H: Shoemaker.
Structure and life-history of the hay-scented fern. '08(Jl18) il. tabs., O. (Carnegie Institution of Washington pub.) pap., 50 c. Carnegie.

Conard, Howard L:
Reconstructing Eden: [satire on some current tendencies.] '09(Mr) c. 66 p. il. 16°, 50 c.; pap., 25 c. New Eden.

Conard fissure. Brown, B. $2.50. Am. Museum.

Concealing-coloration in the animal kingdom. Thayer, G. H. $7. Macmillan.

Conceited puppy. Emanuel, W. 50 c. Dutton.

Concentrated wealth. Edwards, R: H:, *ed.* 10 c. R: H: Edwards.

Concentrations of Bee. Bell, L. L. $1.50. L. C. Page.

Concept of control. Elkus, S. A. 40 c. Science Pr., (N. Y.)

Concept of method. Lomer, G. R: $1. Teachers' Coll.

Concept standard. Nicholson, A. M. $1.50. Teachers' Coll.

Concerning Lafcadio Hearn. Gould, G: N. **$1.50 net. Jacobs.

Concerning the Christ. Freeman, J: D. *$1 net. Armstrong.

CONCERTS.
See Music.

Concise Standard Dictionary of the English language; abr. from the Funk & Wagnalls Standard dictionary of the English language by Ja. C. Fernald. '10(Je4) c. il. 12°, 60 c. Funk.

CONCORD, N. H.
Concord, the city beautiful; its attractions and advantages; issued by the Concord Commercial Club. '09, [1910.] (N) 64 p. il. 12°. Concord Comm. Club.
Cook, H. M. Wayside jottings. $1.50. H. M. Cook.

Concord of sweet notes. Linden, L. M. $1. Hyland.

CONCORDANCES.
See Bible;—*also* names of authors of whom concordances are made.

CONCRETE.
Andrews, H. B. Design of reinforced concrete slabs, beams and columns, conforming to the recommendations of the Joint Committee on Concrete and Reinforced Concrete. $1. H. B. Andrews.
Andrews, H. B. Practical reinforced concrete standards. $2. Simpson.
Association of American Portland Cement Manufacturers. Plans for suburban concrete dwellings. $1. Assoc. Am. Portland Cement.
Atlas Portland Cement Co., N. Y. Concrete construction about the home and on the farm. 7th rev. ed., 1909. '09(S) c. '05. 160 p. il. 8°, pap., gratis.—Concrete houses and cottages. In 2 v. ea., $1.—Concrete in railroad construction. $1. Atlas Portland Cement.
Ballinger, W. F., *and* Perrot, E. G. Inspectors' hdbk. of reinforced concrete. $1. Engineering News.
Boynton, W. C., *and* Marshall, R., *comps.* How to use concrete. $1. Concrete Pub.
Brett, A., *ed.* Reinforced concrete field handbook. $1. Technical Pub.

CONCRETE.—*Continued.*
Brown, J: G. Reinforced concrete construction for factories and warehouses. (Add. pubs. for price.) Doolittle & K.
Colby, A. L. Reinforced concrete in Europe. $3.50. Chemical.
Construction of concrete fence posts; prep. by the Office of Public Roads. '10(Jl) 31 p. il. 8°, (U. S., Dept. of Agriculture; farmers' bull.)
Davison, R. C. Concrete pottery and garden furniture. $1.50. Munn.
Dodge, G. F. Diagrams for designing reinforced concrete structures. $4 net. M. C. Clark.
Douglas, W. J. Practical hints for concrete constructors. 25 c. Engineering News.
Gilbreth, F. B. Concrete system. *$5 net. Engineering News.
Gillette, H. P., *and* Hill, C: S. Concrete construction. *$5 net. M. C. Clark.
Godfrey, E: Structural engineering. bk. 2, Concrete. $2.50. E: Godfrey.
Heidenrich, E. L. Engineers' pocket book of reinforced concrete. $3. M. C. Clark.
Hennebique Construction Co. Hennebique armored concrete system. 50 c. Hennebique.
Hill, C: S. Concrete inspection. *$1 net. M. C. Clark.
Houghton, A. A. Concrete floors and sidewalks.—Concrete wall forms. ea., 50 c. —Concrete from sand molds.—Ornamental concrete without molds. ea., $2. Henley.
Humphrey, R: S. Strength of concrete beams. (Add. Supt. for price.) U. S., Supt. of Docs.
Johnson, L. J. Reinforced concrete. $1 net. Moffat.
Kahn system standards. 50 c.—Hdbk. of practical calculation and application of reinforced concrete. $1.50. Trussed Concrete.
Lewis, M. H: Popular hdbk. for cement and concrete users. $2.50. Henley.
McCullough, E. Reinforced concrete. *$1.50 net. M. C. Clark.
McCullough, F. M. Tests on the permeability of concrete. 25 c. Univ. of Wis.
Marsh, C: F. Concise treatise on reinforced concrete. $2.50 net. Van Nostrand.
Marsh, C: F., *and* Dunn, W: Manual of reinforced concrete. $2.50 net. Van Nostrand.
Mensch, L. J. Reinforced concrete pocket book. $4. M. C. Clark.
Mensch, L. J. Reinforced concrete pocket book. $10. Engineering News.
Middleton, G: A. T: Elements of reinforced concrete building. $1.50. Spon.
Moisseiff, L. S. Review of the literature of reinforced concrete. 5 c. Engineering News.
Mörsch, E. Concrete steel construction. *$5 net. Engineering News.
Palliser, C: Pract. concrete block making. 50 c. Indust.
Porter, H. F. Concrete, its composition and use. $2. Concrete Engineering.

CONCRETE.—*Continued.*
Potter, T: Concrete: its use in building from foundations to finish. *$3 net. Van Nostrand.
Rings, F: Reinforced concrete. $2.50 net. Van Nostrand.
Talbot, A. N. Tests of cast-iron and reinforced concrete culvert pipe.—Tests of reinforced concrete beams.—Tests of three large reinforced concrete beams. ea., gratis. Univ. of Ill.
Taylor, F: W., *and* Thompson, S. E. Concrete, plain and reinforced. $5.—Extracts on reinforced concrete design. $2 net. Wiley.
Thompson, S. E. Concrete in highway construction. $1. Atlas Portland Cement.
Trautwine, J: C., *jr. and* J: C., *3d.* Concrete, plain and reinforced. *$2 net. Wiley.
Trussed Concrete Steel Co., Detroit, *comp.* Kahn system standards. $1.50. Trussed Concrete.
Tucker *and* Vinton. Reproductions from photographs of representative concrete structures. (Add. pubs. for price.) Tucker & V.
Turneaure, F: E., *and* Maurer, E: R. Principles of reinforced concrete construction. $3.50. Wiley.
Turner, C. A. P. Concrete steel construction. pt. 1, Buildings. $20. C. A. P. Turner.
Twelvetrees, W. N. Simplified methods of calculating reinforced concrete beams. 20 c. Macmillan.
Tyrrell, H: G. Concrete bridges and culverts. $3. M. C. Clark.
Watson, W. J. General specifications for concrete work. 50 c. W. J. Watson.
Webb, W. L., *and* Gibson, W. H. Masonry and reinforced concrete. $3. Am. Sch. Corr.
Withey, M. O. Tests on bond between concrete and steel in reinforced concrete beams.—Tests on plain and reinforced concrete. ea., 25 c. Univ. of Wis.
See also Arches;—Bridges;—Building;—Cement.
Concrete construction: form work, estimating, superintendence, inspection-cost, etc. '08(Je13) c. il. 8°, pap. (Add. pub. for price.) Technical Pub.
Concrete workers' reference book. 12°. Henley.
—Houghton. Concrete floors and sidewalks. 50 c.
CONDE, Louise Adélaide de Bourbon, *Princesse* de.
Piépape, *General* de. Princess of strategy; life of Anne Louise Bénédicte de Bourbon-Condé, Duchess du Maine. $4 net. Lane.
Condensation of vapor. *See* Barus, C.
Condensed bridge for the busy man. Camp, W. C. 35 c. Collier.
Conder, Claude Reignier.
City of Jerusalem. '09(Je5) il. 8°, *$4 net. Dutton.
Rise of man. '08(Je13) 8°, *$3 net. Dutton.
Condition of hunters. Apperley, C: J. *$4 net. Lane.

Condition of natives of Alaska. Gunnison, R. A. 10 c. U. S., Supt. of Docs.

Conditions and future of the Philippines. Winslow, E. (Add. Superintendent for price.) U. S., Supt. of Docs.

Conditions and tendencies of technical education in Germany. Chamberlain, A. H: 50 c. Bardeen.

Conditions of life in the sea. Johnstone, J. $3. Putnam.

Conditions of progress in democratic government. Hughes, C: E. $1.15 net. Yale Univ.

Conditions that confront the colored race. Chavers, P. W: (Add. author for price.) P. W: Chavers.

Condor-like vultures of Rancho La Brea. Miller, L. H. 15 c. Univ. of Cal.

CONDUCT OF LIFE.

Abbott, L. The temple. **$1.25 net. Macmillan.

Allen, J. Above life's turmoil. $1. Putnam.

Allen, J. From passion to peace. 50 c. net. Crowell.

Allen, J. Heavenly life. 50 c.; 15 c. Fenno.

Babcock, M. D. Joy of work. 35 c. net. Revell.

Badgley, N. E. Equitable Union: life and its duties briefly explained. $1.50. N. E. Badgley.

Bryant, E. A. New self-help. $1.50. Cassell.

Buchanan, U. Ideals and conduct. $1. Cochrane.

Burrell, D: J. Lure of the city. **$1 net. Funk.

Byron, H: Day-dreamer's harvest: meditations on life and the art of living. *$1.25 net. F. F. Sherman.

Cocroft, S. Growth in silence. 60 c. Physical Culture Ex.

Confucius. Conduct of life. *40 c. net. Dutton.

Confucius. Sayings of Confucius. *$1.25 net. Longmans.

Cope, H: F: Levels of living: essays on everyday ideals. *$1 net. Revell.

Del Mar, E. Living ideals. $1. Progressive Lit.

Diggle, J: W: Home life. *60 c. net. Cassell.

Dods, M. Footsteps in the path of life. $1.25 net. Doran.

Dodsley, R. Economy of human life. $1.50. C. A. Owens.

Emerson, R. W. Nature, and The conduct of life. *35 c. net; *70 c. net. Dutton.

Emery, C. Way that He willeth for me. 25 c. Reid Pub.

Fénelon, F. de S. de La Mothe-Fénelon. Spiritual counsels. 45 c. net. Herder.

Fisher, H. W Making life worth while. $1.20 net. Doubleday, P.

Fosdick, H. E. Second mile: [reflections upon the conduct of life.] *40 c. net. Y. M. C. A.

Gaut, H. L. Trails to peace. 50 c. H. L. Stanton.

CONDUCT OF LIFE.—*Continued.*

Gordon, S: D. Crowding out the Christ-child. 25 c. net.—The quietest talk; a foot-note to Quiet talks on home ideals. 10 c. net. Revell.

Gordon, S. D. *and* M. K. Quiet talks on home ideals. *75 c. net. Revell.

Graham, W: Duty; twelve conferences to young men. 75 c. Wagner.

Hammond, E. V., *comp.* Looking upward day by day. *$1 net. Dutton.

Higginson, T: W. Things worth while. *50 c. net. B: W. Huebsch.

Hobart, A. S. Tillage of the heart. 50 c. Am. Bapt.

Holland, R. A. Commonwealth of man. *$1 net. Young Churchman.

Horton, R. F. Making the best of both worlds. 25 c. net. Union Press.

Horton, R. F. Triumphant life. 50 c. Revell.

Hovis, W: F. Quality folks: practical meditations. *$1 net. Jennings.

Hsaio Ching. Book of filial duty. *40 c. net. Dutton.

Hubbard, E. So here cometh White hyacinths: an attempt to body forth ideas and ideals. $2. Roycrofters.

Huebschmann, J. S. Boys, youths, men. 50 c. Central.

Hyde, W: D. Self-measurement: a scale of human values with directions for personal application. *50 c. net. B: W. Huebsch.

Ingalese, R: Art of self-control. $1. Occult.

Jefferson, C: E: An original year. 50 c. net. Pilgrim Press.

Jenks, J. W. Life questions of high school boys. 40 c. Y. M. C. A.

Jordan, D: S. Higher sacrifice. *80 c. net. Am. Unitarian.

Jordan, W: G. Power of purpose. 35 c. net. Revell.

Kirkham, S. D. Resources; an interpretation of the well-rounded life. **$1.25 net. Putnam.

Knight, G. H. Full allegiance. *$1 net. Armstrong.

Lamoreaux, *Mrs.* A. A. Unfolding life: study of development with reference to religious training. 75 c. Rel. Pub.

Lorentz, A. M. Individual sovereignty. $1. Mayhew.

Loyola, *Mother* M. Heavenwards. $1.25 net. Kenedy.

Lubbock, *Sir* J: The value of time. 40 c.; 75 c. Caldwell.

Ludlow, J. M. Discovery of self. 35 c. net. Revell.

Lyman, *Mrs.* E. H. If I were you. $1.12. Miss Hills' Sch.

McGavick, A. J. Some incentives to right living. *$1 net. Wiltzius.

M'Intyre, D: M. Life in His name. *$1.25 net. Armstrong.

Mackey, W. M. Man in the street. $1.50 net. Doran.

McSorley, J. Sacrament of duty, and other essays. $1. Columbus.

CONDUCT OF LIFE.—*Continued.*
Marden, O. S. Be good to yourself.—Peace, power and plenty. ea., **$1 net. Crowell.
Marden, O. S., *and* Connolly, M. Do it to a finish. **30 c. net. Crowell.
Miller, J. R. Beauty of every day. 65 c. net.—Turning northward. **30 c. net. Crowell.
Moore, A. Heir of the ages and his inheritances. 75 c. Doran.
Nelson, T: Home, health and success. $1. Gospel Trumpet Co.
Newcomb, *Mrs.* K. H. Steps along the path. **$1.40 net. Lothrop, L. & S.
Pennington, J. G., *ed.* Be strong. 50 c. Dodge.
Peters, M. C. How to make things go. 25 c. Laird.
Pierson, A. T. Godly self-control. *50 c. net. Armstrong.
Remensnyder, J. B: Heavenward: a guide for youth. 50 c. Lutheran Pub.
Rickaby, J. Four-square; or, the cardinal virtues. *60 c. net. Wagner.
Rogers, L. W. Life sublime: lectures on the application of the higher principles to the conduct of daily life. 10 c. Theosophical Bk.
Scudder, D. Passion for reality. 50 c. net. Revell.
Shepherd, A. Men in the making. *$1.25 net. Jennings.
Smith, J. W. Controversy between truth and falsehood. 75 c. J. W. Smith.
Speer, R. E. Master of the heart. *$1 net. Revell.
Stanton, S. B. Essential life.—Soul and circumstance. ea., $1 net. Scribner.
Sunderland, J. T: Oh to be rich and young. $1. Am. Unitarian.
Thomas à Kempis. Imitation of Christ. 25 c. net. Macmillan.
Tomkins, F. W. Faith and life of a Christian. *75 c. net. Am. S. S.
Trine, R. W. On the open road. **50 c. net. Crowell.
Tuttle, C: R: New idea: continuous course of study for self-life unfoldment. $5. C: R: Tuttle.
Vance, J. I: Tendency. $1.25 net. Revell.
Vaubert, T. F. How to walk before God. 40 c. Herder.
Waite, R: A., *jr.* Gospel in athletic phrases. 25 c. Y. M. C. A.
Watkinson, W: L. Frugality in the spiritual life. *$1 net.—Lessons of prosperity, and other addresses on personal conduct.—Noon day addresses: on themes affecting life. ea., *50 c. net. Revell.
Wilson, C. D. Making the most of ourselves. *$1 net. McClurg.
Wilson, W. Free life. **75 c. net. Crowell.
Wright, H: B. Will of God and a man's life work. 90 c. Y. M. C. A.
Young, D. T. Messages for home and life. *$1.25 net. Jennings.
See also Boys;—Catholic church;—Character;—Cheerfulness;—Christian life;—Culture;—Ethics;—Etiquette;—Family;—Girls;—Happiness;—Success;—Temptation;—Vocations;—Young men;—Young people.

Conduct stories. Gould, F. J. $1. Macmillan.
Conduction of electricity through gases. McClung, R. K. *$1.50 net. Blakiston.
Conductor Jim. Burwick, J. M. $1. Y. M. C. A.
CONDUCTORS.
See Railroads;—Street railroads.
Cone, Helen Gray.
Soldiers of the light; [poems.] '10(D31) c. D. $1 net. Badger.
Cone, R: Wood.
Speaking voice; its scientific basis in music. '09(Mr) c. 150 p. por. 8°, $1. Evans Music.
Cone, Trenmor, comp.
See Nebraska. Liquor Laws.
Cone, Victor M.
See Fortier, S:
Conerly, Luke Ward.
Pike County, Mississippi, 1798-1876; pioneer families and Confederate soldiers, reconstruction and redemption. '09, [1910.] (Ja) c. 368 p. il. pors. 8°, $2. Brandon Pr.
CONFECTIONERY.
See Candy;—Cookery.
CONFEDERACY.
See Civil War:—United States;—*also* Davis, Jefferson;—Douglas, Stephen Arnold.
Confederate soldier. Polk, J. M. 35 c. Von Boeckmann-J.
CONFEDERATE WAR.
See Civil War (United States).
Confederate women of Arkansas in the Civil War. United Confederate Veterans, Arkansas Division. $1. J. Kellogg.
Conference for the Study of the Problems of Rural Life. 2d., Charlottesville, Va., 1909. Address del. at the Univ. of Va. summer school in connection with the Conference for the Study of the Problems of Rural Life, July 13 to 16, 1909. '09. [1910.] (F) 98 p. 8°, pap. (Add. pub. for price.) B. R. Payne.
Confessio medici. Paget, S. **$1.25 net. Macmillan.
CONFESSION.
Hoare, E. Shall I go to confession? *20 c. net. Am. S. S.
Confession, and other verses. Low, M. A. *80 c. net. Sherman, F.
Confession of a rebellious wife. '10(N5) c. D. 50 c. net. Small.
Confession of Seymour Vane. Snow, E. 50 c. Fenno.
Confessional hist. of the Lutheran church. Richard, J. W: $3. Lutheran Pub.
Confessions. *See* Augustine, *St.*
Confessions and autobiography. Orchard, H. **$1 net. McClure.
Confessions of a barbarian. Viereck, G: S. $1.25 net. Moffat.
Confessions of a beach-comber. Banfield, E. J. $4 special net. Appleton.
Confessions of a clergyman. '10(Ap9) D. 90 c. net. Macmillan.
Confessions of a con man. Irwin, W: H: *$1 net. B: W. Huebsch.
Confessions of a Macedonian bandit. Sonnichsen, A. $1.50. Duffield.
Confessions of a neurasthenic. Marrs, W: T. *$1 net. Davis.

Confessions of a newspaper. North American, Philadelphia. gratis.
North American, Phil.
Confessions of a palmist. "Clivette, the Man in Black," *pseud.* 25 c. Laird.
Confessions of a princess. '08(Je13) c. D. $1.50. Doscher.
Confessions of a railroad signalman. Fagan, J. O. $1. Houghton M.
Confessions of Al Ghazzali. Al-Gazali, A. H. M. *40 c. net. Dutton.
Confessions of an English opium eater. *See* De Quincey, T:
Confessions of boyhood. Albee, J: $1.50 net. Badger.
Confessions of Linda Poindexter. Ruley, C. N. $1. B'way Pub.
Confessions of Saint Augustine. *See* Augustine, *St.*
Confidantes of a king. Goncourt, E. L. A. H. de. In 2 v. *$4 special net. Appleton.
Confidence, or national suicide. Stilwell, A. E: $1. Bankers' Pub.
Confidences. Lowry, E. B. 50 c. net. Forbes.

CONFIRMATION.
Anderson, C: P. Confirmation or the laying on of hands. 10 c. McClurg.
Candole, H. L. C. V. de. Confirmation, authority, confession. *36 c. net. Longmans.
Chase, F: H: Confirmation in the apostolic age. *80 c. net. Macmillan.
Richter, A. Order of salvation. 20 c. E. Kaufmann.
Smith, C: E. Call to confirmation. 20 c. Longmans.
See also Lord's supper.

Confirming the faith. Sharman, J: T: $1.25. J: T: Sharman.
Conflict between individualism and collectivism in a democracy. Elliot, C: W: 90 c. net. Scribner.
Conflict between private monopoly and good citizenship. Brooks, J: G. **50 c. net. Houghton M.
Conflict of colour. Weale, B. L. P., *pseud.* $2 net. Macmillan.
Conflict of naturalism and humanism. Goodsell, W. $1.50. Teachers' Coll.
Conflict of religions in the early Roman Empire. Glover, T. R. *$2.50 net. Scribner.
Conflict over judicial powers in the United States. Hains, C: G. $1.50. Longmans.

Confucius.
Classics of Confucius: Book of history; tr. by W. Gorn Old. '08(Je6) 16°, (Wisdom of the East.) *40 c. net. Dutton.
Classics of Confucius: Book of odes; tr. by L. Cranmer-Bying. '08(Je6) 16°, (Wisdom of the East.) *40 c. net. Dutton.
Conduct of life: the Universal Order of Confucius; tr. by Ku Hung Ming. '08 (Je6) 16°, (Wisdom of the East.) *40 c. net. Dutton.
Sayings of Confucius; tr. by Lionel Giles. '08(Je6) 16°, (Wisdom of the East.) *60 c. net. Dutton.
Sayings of Confucius; tr. by Leonard A. Lyall. '09(O2) O. *$1.25 net. Longmans.

Conger, Clinton Barker.
Air brake catechism and instruction book on the construction and operation of the Westinghouse and the New York air brakes, with a list of examination questions for enginemen and trainmen. 24th ed. '10(Ap) c. 269 p. il. 16°, $1. C. B. Conger.

Conger, Mrs. Edn. Hurd.
See Conger, Sarah Pike.

Conger, Sarah Pike, [Mrs. Edn. Hurd Conger.]
Letters from China, with particular reference to the Empress Dowager and the women of China. '09(My1) c. il. map, O. *$2.75 net. McClurg.

CONGO FREE STATE, Africa.
Doyle, *Sir* A. C. Crime of the Congo. 25 c. Doubleday, P.
Johnston, *Sir* H. H. George Grenfell and the Congo. 2 v. $7.50 special net. Appleton.
Starr, F: Bibliography of Congo languages. *$1 net. Univ. of Chic.
United States. *Dept. of State.* Affairs in the Kongo. U. S., Supt. of Docs.
Ward, H: **Voice from the Congo. $2.50 net. Scribner.**

Congregation Mikve Israel, Philadelphia. Dedication of the new synagogue of the Congregation Mikve Israel at Broad and York streets on Sept. 14, 1909 Elul 29, 5669. '09, [1910.] (F) 29 p. il. pors. fold. facsims., 8°, 75 c. Congregation Mikve Israel.

CONGREGATIONAL CHURCH.
Anderson, A. Congregational faith and practice. 5 c. Pilgrim Press.
Barton, W: E. Congregational manual. $1. Puritan Press.
Jefferson, C: E. Congregationalism. 25 c. net. Pilgrim Press.
Jenkins, F. E., *and others.* Anglo-Saxon Congegationalism in the South. (Add. pubs. for price.) Franklin-T.
Nash, C: S. Congregational administration. *75 c. net. Pilgrim Press.
Peace, D. Have Congregationalists abandoned the Bible? $1; 50 c. S. D. Towne.

Congregational Church, Topsfield, Mass. Historical manual, 1663-1907. '07, [1908.] 5-60 p. il. pors. plan, 8°, 50 c. J. P. Gould.

CONGRESS.
See United States.

Congressional history of railways in the United States. Haney, L. H: 50 c. Univ. of Wis.

Congreve, G:
Christian progress; with other papers and addresses. '10(O1) D. $1.50 net. Longmans.

CONIC SECTIONS.
See Geometry.

CONIFEROUS TREES.
See Trees.

Conigsby, W:, ed.
See Dawson, W: Ja.

Conjugation of Spanish verbs. Brigham, F. H. 60 c. F. H. Brigham.

CONJURING.
Art of modern conjuring. $1.25. Reilly & B.
Bailey, S: W., *and* Osborne, H. A. Wrinkles. 50 c. Bailey-T.

CONJURING.—*Continued.*
Devant, D: Tricks for every one. 50 c. Lippincott.
Downs, T: N. Art of magic. $5. W. S. Edwards.
Goldston, W. More tricks and illusions without mechanical apparatus. 50 c.—Tricks and illusions for amateurs and professional conjurors. *$1.25 net. Dutton.
Haley, L: C. Dramatic art of magic. $1.15. L: C. Haley.
Hatton, H:, *and* Plate, A. Magician's tricks. $1.60 net. Century Co.
Neil, C. L. After-dinner sleights and pocket tricks.—Modern card manipulation. ea., 50 c. Lippincott.
See also Magic and magicians.
Conjuror's house. White, S. E: 75 c. Grosset.

Conklin, G: W.
Vest-pocket argument settler. New ed., rev. and enl. and brought down to date by Paul E. Lowe. '10(N19) c. nar. T. 25 c.; leath., 50 c. McKay.
See also Vest pocket reference book ser.

CONKLING FAMILY.
See Genealogies, Prosch, T: W.

Conlan, Jos. J:
See Chrysostom John, *Brother.*

Conley, J: Wesley, D.D.
Educative value of Bible study, and The Bible and the schools, from The Bible in modern light. '09(Jl) 163-193 p. 16°, pap., 5 c.; per 100, $2.50. Am. Bapt.
Young Christian and the early church. '08 (Jl18) c. D. (Christian culture courses, Baptist Young People's Union of America.) bds., **50 c. net. Am. Bapt.
See also Musselman, Hugh T:

Conley, W: G., rep.
See West Virginia. *Sup.ct. of appeals.* Repts.

Conly, Mrs. Ella Madge Smith.
Lady of France. '09(Ja16) c. il. 12°, $1.50. Homewood.

Conn, Herbert W:
Agricultural bacteriology; a study of the relation of germ life to the farm with laboratory experiments for students. 2d ed., rev. and enl. '09(S) c. 10+331 p. il. 8°, $2. Blakiston.
Elementary physiology and hygiene, for use in upper grammar grades; rev. and enl. ed. '09(O) c. 334 p. il. 12°, *60 c. net. Silver.
Introductory physiology and hygiene. Rev. and enl. ed. '08(Ap25) il. 12°, (Conn ser. of physiologies.) 36 c. Silver.

—, and Budington, Rob. Allyn.
Advanced physiology and hygiene, for use in secondary schools. '09(N6) c. il. D. (Conn ser. of physiologies.) $1.10. Silver.

—, and Webster, Lucia Washburn Hazen.
Preliminary report on the algae of the fresh waters of Connecticut. '08, [1909.] (Mr) 5-75 p. il. 8°, (Conn. state geol. and natural hist. survey bull.) 35 c. Conn. Lib.

Conn ser. of physiologies. il. D. Silver.
—Conn *and* Budington. Advanced physiology and hygiene. $1.10.

Connan, J: C.
Switchboard measuring instruments for continuous and polyphase systems. '09 (Mr13) il. 8°, $2. Spon.

Connecticut. Andersonville Monument Commission. Dedication of the monument at Andersonville, Ga., Oct. 23, 1907, in memory of the men of Connecticut who suffered in southern military prisons, 1861-1865. '08 (D) 73 p. il. pors. 4°. (Add. pubs. for price.) Connecticut.

Connecticut. Commission to Investigate Tuberculosis. Rept. of factory conditions in Connecticut as related to tuberculosis; prepared by Horace B. Cheney and Omar La Rue, M.D. '08(D) 8 p. 8°. (Add. pubs. for price.) Conn. Com. Tuberculosis.

Connecticut. Public Library. Helps in library work with children. '09((D) 6 p. 8°, (Conn. Public Library document.) pap., gratis. Conn. Pub. Lib.

Connecticut. Sales act (public acts, 1907, ch. 212); complete text of statute as enacted, supplemented by the conditional sales act and the sales in bulk act, with notes; by J: Elliott. '09(Jl) c. 10+933 p. O. $6. Dissell.

Connecticut. *Supreme ct. of errors.* Cases; (Ja. P. Andrews.) v. 80, 81. '09(O); v. 82. '10(Ag) c. O. shp., ea., $2.30. Banks.

CONNECTICUT.
Chadwick, E. L. Conservative advocate; book of biographies of Connecticut's successful men. $5. E. L. Chadwick.
Conn, H. W:, *and* Webster, L. W. H. Preliminary report on the algae of the fresh waters of Connecticut. 35 c. Conn. Lib.
Evans, A. W:, *and* Nichols, G: E. Bryophytes of Connecticut: [mosses.] 30 c. Conn. Lib.
Genthe, M. K. Valley towns in Connecticut. 50 c. Am. Geog. Soc.
Gregory, H. E., *and* Ellis, E. E. Underground water resources of Connecticut. U. S., Supt. of Docs.
Gregory, H. E., *and* Robinson, H: H. Preliminary geological map of Connecticut. (Add. pubs. for price.) Conn. Lib.
Newton, A. H. Out of the briars; autobiography and sketch of the 29th regiment, Connecticut volunteers. $1.25. A. H. Newton.
Osborn, N. G., *ed.* Men of mark in Connecticut. 4 v. $30; $50; $60. W. R. Goodspeed.
Taylor, J: M. Witchcraft delusion in colonial Connecticut. **$1.50 net. Grafton Press.
Vaill, D. L. County regiment; sketch of 2d regiment of Connecticut volunteer heavy artillery. $1.50. F. E. Partridge.
See also Bethany;—Bolton;—East Granby;—East Plymouth;—Fairfield County; — Groton;—Hartford;—Litchfield Co.;—Middletown; — Newington;—Sherman;—Tuberculosis;—Vernon.

Connecticut Academy of Arts and Sciences. Transactions, v. 15. July, 1909. To the University of Leipzig on the occasion of the 500th anniversary of its foundation, from Yale University and the Connecticut Academy of Arts and Sciences. '09(S11) $3.50. **Yale Univ.**

Connecticut Historical Society, **Hartford.** Lists and returns of Connecticut men in the Revolution, 1775-1783. '09, [1910.] (Ap) 11+489 p. 8°, (Collections of the society.) $3. Conn. Hist.

Connecticut State Geological and Natural History Survey bull. 8°. Conn. Lib.
—Conn *and* Webster. Preliminary report on the algae of the fresh waters of Connecticut. 35 c.
—Evans *and* Nichols. Bryophytes of Connecticut. 30 c.
—Graves, *and others.* Catalogue of the flowering plants and ferns of Connecticut. 75 c.
—Gregory *and* Robinson. Preliminary geological map of Connecticut. (Add. pubs. for price.)
—White. Second rept. on the hymeniales of Conn. 35 c.

Connell, A. C.
Pitman's companies and company law; together with the Companies (Consolidation) Act, 1908. '09(Mr) 12+332 p. O. cl., $2. Pitman.

Connelley, W: Elsey.
Eastern Kentucky papers; founding of Harman's Station, with acct. of the Indian captivity of Mrs. Jennie Wiley to which is affixed a brief acct. of the Connelley family and some of its collateral and related families. '10(D31) c. il. pors. maps, 8°, $2. W: E. Connelley.
Ingalls of Kansas; character study. '10 (Ja29) c. por. 8°, $2. W: E. Connelley.
Quantrill and the border wars.. '09(D18) 8°, $3.50. Torch Press.

CONNEMARA, Ireland.
Gwynn, S. L. Holiday in Connemara. *$2 net. Macmillan.

Conner, C: Chambers.
From nature to man: [essays.] '10(F12) c. D. 75 c. Hampden Pub.

Connoisseur's library; ed. by Cyril Davenport. il. Q. *$7.50 net. Putnam.
—Birch. Seals. *$7.50 net.
—Heath. Miniatures. *$7.50 net.
—Smith. Jewellery.

Connolly, Ja.
Socialism made easy; in two sections; section 1, Workshop talks; section 2, Political action of labor. '09(Ap3) D. pap., 10 c. Kerr.

Connolly, Ja. Brendan.
Olympic victor: story of the modern games. '08(S5) c. il. O. †$1.25. Scribner.
Open water. '10(O8) c. il. D. $1.20 net Scribner.

CONNOLLY, John.
Burton, C. M. John Connolly, a Tory of the Revolution. 50 c. Am. Antiquarian.

Connolly, Marg.
See Marden, Orison Swett.
—, ed. Friendship year book. '10(O1) c. D. (Day by day ser.) 60 c., boxed; leath., $1, boxed. Crowell.

Connor, Jean.
So as by fire. '10(Ja1) c. D. $1.25. Benziger.

"Connor, Ralph," pseud.
See Gordon, C: W:

Connor, Rob. Diggs Wimberly.
Beginnings of English America: Sir Walter Raleigh's settlements on Roanoke Island, 1584-1587. '08(Ap11) il. map, O. pap., gratis. N. C. Hist.
Cornelius Harnett; essay in North Carolina history. '10(Ja22) c. D. $1.50. R. D. W. Connor.
North Carolina's priority in the demand for a Declaration of Independence; the resolution of the Congress at Halifax, April 12, 1776, and its influence on the sentiment for independence in the United Colonies. '09, [1910.] (F) 23 p. 8°, pap., 50 c. R. D. W. Connor.

Connor, Selden.
Address [delivered] May 5, 1909, at a meeting of the Maine Commandery of the Military Order of the Loyal Legion of the United States at Riverton Park Casino, Portland, Me., to commemorate the 100th anniversary of the birth of Hannibal Hamlin, in Paris, Me., Aug. 27, 1809. '09(Ag21) por. O. pap. (Not for sale.) C: Hamlin.

Conover, F: K., rep.
See Wisconsin. *Sup. ct.* Repts.

Conover, J.
See On the gridiron.

Conover, Ja. F.
Mental mouth wash. '09, [1910.] (Mr) 7 p. 8°, 25 c. Roycrofters.

Conover, Ja. Potter.
Personality in education. '08(N14) c. D. **$1.25 net. Moffat.

Conquering Christ. Boone, I. 50 c. Bible Study.

Conquering the arctic ice. Mikkelsen, E. *$3.50 net. Jacobs.

Conquest of consumption. Hutchinson, W. **$1 net. Houghton M.

Conquest of disease through animal experimentation. Warbasse, J. P: $1. Appleton.

Conquest of Granada. *See* Irving, Washington.

Conquest of Mexico. **Prescott, W: H. 2 v. ea., *35 c. net; *70 c. net. Dutton.**

Conquest of Peru. Prescott, W: H. *35 c. net; *70 c. net. Dutton.

Conquest of the air. Berget, T: C. X. A. **$3.50 net. Putnam.

Conquest of **the air. Rotch, A. L. **$1 net. Moffat.**

Conquest of the air by airships and other flying machines. Mowbray, J. H: $1.50. Nat. Pub. Co.

Conquest of the great Northwest. Laut, A. O. $5. Moffat.

Conquest of the Isthmus. Weir, H. C. **$2 net. Putnam.

Conquest of the Missouri, Hanson, J. M. *$2 net. McClurg.

Conquest of the North. Ingersoll, E. 10 c. C. S. Hammond.

Conrad, Arcturus Z., ed.
Boston's awakening; complete acct. of the great Boston revival under the leadership of J. Wilbur Chapman and Charles M. Alexander, Jan. 26th to Feb. 21st, 1909. [1910.] (F) c. '09. 290 p. pors. 12°, 50 c. King's Business.

Conrad, H: Clay.
History of the state of Delaware. '08, [1909.] (F) c. 3 v., il. 4°, $12. H: C. Conrad.

Conrad, Jos.
Point of honor: military tale. '08(O10) c. il. D. †$1.25. McClure.

Consanguineous marriages. Arner, G: B. L: 75 c. Longmans.

CONSCIENCE.
Angell, J. B. Age of quickened conscience. (Add. author for price.) Univ. of Mich.
Lipscomb, T. H. Conscience and its culture. $1. Pub. Ho. M. E. Ch., So.

CONSCIOUSNESS.
Atkinson, W: W. The subconscious and the superconscious planes of mind. $1. Progress Co.
Bergson, H. L. Time and free will. $2.75 net. Macmillan.

Consciousness. Marshall, H: R. *$4 net. Macmillan.

CONSCRIPT.
See Soldiers.

Conscript. *See* Erckmann, Emile.

CONSERVATION.
See Natural resources.

Conservation of men. Richards, R. C. 50 c. R. C. Richards.

Conservation of water. Mathews, J: L. $2 net. Small.

Conservation primers. D. Doubleday, P. —Pinchot. Fight for conservation. 60 c. net.

Conservative advocate. Chadwick, E. L. $5. E. L. Chadwick.

Conservative gynecology. Massey, G: B. *$4 net. Davis.

CONSERVATORIES.
See Greenhouses.

Consideration. *See* Bernard de Clairvaux, *St.*

Consideration of Macaulay's comparison of Dante and Milton. Courthope, W: J: 40 c. Oxford Univ.

Considerations on music. Whitmer, T. C. 50 c. Stephens Coll.

"Consistency," pseud.
See Foley, J: Thaddeus.

CONSOLATIO.
See Cicero, Marcus Tullius.

CONSOLATION.
Allen, E. A. Gems of immortality; book of consolation and helps. $2.25; $2.75; $3.75. Central Pub.
Black, H. Comfort. $1.50 net. Revell.
Eaton, R. Night thoughts for the sick and desolate. *45 c. net. Herder.
Gleams of sunshine for hearts in shadow. 35 c. Good Tidings.
Jones, J: C. Words of consolation and encouragement for the sorrowing. $2.75. J: C. Jones.
Knight, G. H. In the dark and cloudy day. $1.25 net. Doran.
MacArthur, R. S., *and others.* Royal messages of cheer and comfort. *$2 net. Treat.
Micou, *Mrs.* M. D., *comp.* Reflected light from Paradise: comfort-thoughts. *50 c. net. Young Churchman.
Piercy, W. D. Death and its sorrow. $1. Neale.

CONSOLATION.—*Continued.*
Sloane, J. R., *comp.* Golden gleanings to comfort the afflicted. $1. J. R. Sloane.
Van Dyke, J. S. "Be of good cheer." $1. J. S. Van Dyke.
Villiers, H: M. Perfect thoughts suffering. *$1.50 net. Longmans.
Wright, Fannie J. Golden curves; simple thoughts of comfort. 25 c. net. Hills & H.
See also Hymns;—Sympathy.

Consolidation of Philadelphia. Leffmann, H: 25 c. City Hist. Phil.

Consolidation of rural schools. Bedichek, U. 25 c. Univ. of Tex.

CONSPIRACY.
Bryan, J. W. Development of the English law of conspiracy. 75 c. Johns Hopkins.
New York [State.] *Commissioners for Detecting and Defeating Conspiracies.* Minutes of the commissioners, Albany County sessions, 1778-1781. In 3 v. (Distributed officially and by exchange.) New York.

Conspiracy at Rome in 66-65 B.C. Nutting, H. C. 10 c. Univ. of Cal.

Conspiracy of Pontiac. Parkman, F. 2 v., ea., *35 c. net; *70 c. net. Dutton.

Constable, J:
Masterpieces of Constable. '10(D17) il. 24°, (Painters' ser.) leath., 75 c. net; pap., 25 c. net. Stokes.

CONSTABLE, John.
Hind, C: L. Constable. *65 c. net; *$1.50 net. Stokes.

CONSTABLE BOURBON.
See Bourbon, Charles, *Duc* de.

CONSTABLES.
Pennsylvania. Constables' guide. (Add. pubs. for price.) T. & J. W. Johnson.
See also Justices of the peace.

Constance Sherwood. Fullerton, *Lady* G. L. G. 40 c. Connoisseurs' Press.

Constant, Alphonse L:, ["Eliphas Lévi."]
Transcendental magic, its doctrine and ritual; complete tr. of "Dogme et rituel de la haute magie," with a biograph. preface by Arth. E: Waite. '10(S3) c. il. por. 8°, $3.75. De Laurence, S.

CONSTANTINE *the Great.*
Pfättisch, J. M. Die rede Konstantins des Grossen an die versammlung der heiligen auf ihre echtheit untersucht. *$1 net. Herder.

Constantineau, Alb.
Treatise on de facto doctrine in its relation to public officers, [etc.] '10(Je) c. O. shp., $6. Lawyers' Co-op.

CONSTANTINOPLE, Turkey.
Baker, B. G. Walls of Constantinople. $4 net. Pott.
Coufopoulus, D. Guide to Constantinople. *$1.25 net. Macmillan.
Ramsay, *Sir* W. M. Revolution in Constantinople and Turkey in 1909. $3.75 net. Doran.
See also Robert College.

Constantinus, Brother.
Young Christian teacher encouraged; or, objections to teaching answered; with introd. by the Rt. Rev. J: L. Spalding. 2d ed. '10(Ag) 24+381 p. 8°, $1.25 net. Herder.

CONSTIPATION.
Gant, S: G. Constipation and intestinal obstruction. *$6 net. Saunders.
MacMillan, J. A. Chronic constipation. $2. Burton Co.
Constitution of the late Roman Empire. Bury, J: B. 50 c. net. Putnam.
CONSTITUTIONAL CONVENTION.
See United States.
Constitutional history of England. Chambers, A. M. *$1.40 net. Macmillan.
Constitutional history of England. Maitland, F: W: **$3.50 net. Putnam.
CONSTITUTIONAL LAW.
Barnes, H. E., *and* Milner, B. A. Sel. cases in constitutional law. $1.50. Lyon & A.
Black, H: C. Hdbk. of American constitutional law. $3.75. West Pub.
Davis, E. G. Text book of constitutional law. (Add. pubs. for price.) Franklin-H.
Dicey, A. C. Introd. to the study of the law of the Constitution. *$3.50 net. Macmillan.
McClain, E. Constitutional law in the United States. $2.25. Longmans.
McClain, E. Selection of cases on constitutional law. $5. Little, B. & Co.
North Carolina. Notes on the code of civil procedure; notes on constitutional law. (Priv. pr.) Seeman.
Willoughby, W. W. Constitutional law of the U. S. v. 1, 2. $12. Baker, V. & Co.
See also Parliament;—Railroads;—*also* names of states and countries.
CONSTITUTIONS.
Alston, L. Modern constitutions in outline. 90 c. Longmans.
Anson, *Sir* W. R. Law and custom of the constitution. In 3 v. v. 1. *$3.40 net. Oxford Univ.
Dodd, W. F. Revision and amendment of state constitutions. $2. Johns Hopkins.
Dodd, W. F., *comp.* Modern constitutions. *$5 net. Univ. of Chic.
Thorpe, F. N., *comp.* Federal and state constitutions. (Add. Superintendent for price.) U. S., Supt. of Docs.
See also Political science;—*also* names of countries and states.
Constrained attitudes. Colby, F. M. $1.20 net. Dodd.
CONSTRUCTION.
See also Building (*construction*);—Building materials;—Engineering;—Machinery.
Construction and flying of kites. Miller, C: M. 20 c. Manual Arts.
Construction and maintenance of railway roadbed and track. Prior, F: J: $2. Drake.
Construction of Association buildings. '09 (Mr13) pap., 15 c. Y. M. C. A.
Construction of classifications and tariffs. Ketchum, E. S. 25 c. La Salle Extension.
Construction, tuning and care of the pianoforte. Norton, E: Q. $1. Ditson.
Construction work. McGaw, V. 60 c. Flanagan.
Constructive and rebuttal speeches. Iowa State University. 2 v. ea., $1. Forensic.
Constructive Bible studies. See University of Chicago.
Constructive drawing. Hanstein, H. $1. Keuffel.
Constructive exercises in English. Frank, M. M. 50 c. Longmans.
Constructive interests of children. Kent, E. B. 50 c. Teachers' Coll.
Constructive psychology. Buck, J. D. $1. Indo-Am. Bk.
CONSULS.
Harlan, R: D. Two pre-requisites for the permanent improvement of the Am. consular service: a new law and a special training school. (Add. pub. for price.) Nat. Business.
National Business League of America. American universities, American foreign service and an adequate consular law. (Add. pubs. for price.) Nat. Business.
Stowell, E. C. **Consular cases and opinions from the decisions of the Eng. and** Am. courts. $5. Byrne.
Consumer's control of production. American Academy of Political and Social Science. 75 c. Am. Acad. Pol. Sci.
CONSUMERS' LEAGUE.
American Academy of Political and Social Science. Work of the Consumers' League during the year ending March 1, 1910. Am. Acad. Pol. Sci.
CONSUMPTION.
See Lungs;—Tuberculosis.
CONTAGION.
Chapin, C: V. Sources and modes of infection. $3. Wiley.
See also Bacteria;—Infectious diseases.
Contagious, constitutional and blood diseases. Blackwood, A. L. $1.75. Boericke & T.
Contant, G: C.
Pardoned lifer; life of George Sontag, former member notorious Evans-Sontag gang, train robbers; written by Opie L. Warner. '09(N) c. 211 p. por. 12°, $1.25. G: C. Constant.
Contemporaneous pagan views of the early Christians. Thomas, W: H. 25 c. W: H. Thomas.
Contemporary France. *See* Hanotaux, Gabriel.
Contemporary Ireland. Paul-Dubois, L. F. A. *$2 net. Baker & T.
Contemporary men of letters ser.; ed. by W: A. Bradley. S. *75 c. net. McClure.
—Brandes. Anatole France.
Contemporary science ser. See Scribner's.
Contented rivals. MacArthur, J. 75 c. Mich. Chr. Herald.
Contents of the boy. Moon, E. L. $1. Jennings.
Contes à ma sœur. Moreau, H. *25 c. net. Crowell.
Contes choisis. Bazin, R. 35 c. Heath.
Contes choisis. 16°. W: R. Jenkins.
—About. La mère de la marquise. 25 c.
Contes des marins de la Haute-Bretagne. Sébillot, P. 25 c. Crowell.
Contes du petit château. *See* Macé, Jean.
Contes et nouvelles. Mérimée, P. 70 c. Oxford Univ.
Contes extraits de Myrrha. Lemaître, J. 30 c. Heath.

Contet, F., ed.
Examples of old iron work of the second half of the 18th century; [portfolio.] '09 (Je19) il. $13.40. Hessling.

CONTINENTAL CONGRESS.
See United States.

Continuous current machine design. Cramp, W: $2.50. Van Nostrand.

CONTRA COSTA CO., California.
See Squirrels.

CONTRACTING.
See Carpentry.

Contractor's accounts. Wright, H. 50 c. Am. Sch. Corr.

CONTRACTS.
Anson, *Sir* W: R. Principles of the English law of contract and of its agency in its relation to contract. $3.25 net. Oxford Univ.
Beecher, F. A. Law of contracts in Michigan. Drake Law Bk.
Brown, J: M. Lectures on the statutory provisions rel. to government contracts. (Add. pub. for price.) J: M. Brown.
Gilbreth, F. B., Worden, C. A., *and others.* Pract. talks on contracting. $1.50. Contractor Pub.
McIntosh, A. C. Selected cases on the law of contracts. (Add. pubs. for price.) Edwards.
Moll, T. J. Treatise on the law of independent contractors and their liability. $3.75. W. H. Anderson.
Simpkins, W: S. Contracts and sales. $6.50. Von Boeckmann-J.
Tyler, F: S., *comp.* Questions and answers on contracts. 50 c. Byrne.
Willis, H. E. Principles of the law of contracts. $3. Keefe-D.
See also Engineering;—Mortgages;—Principal and agent;—Sale.

Contracts and specifications. Plant, J: C. In 2 pts. $1. Am. Sch. Corr.

Contrasts in social progress. Tenney, E: P. 85 c. E: P. Tenney.

Contributions from the Mount Wilson solar observatory. il. 4°. Carnegie.
—Adams. Investigation of the displacements of the spectrum lines at the sun's limb. (Not for sale.)—Spectroscopic investigations of the rotation of the sun. (Not for sale.)—Summary of the results of a study of the Mount Wilson photographs of sun-spot spectra.
—Hale. Tower telescope of the Mount Wilson solar observatory. (Not for sale.)
—Hale *and* Adams. Photography of the "flash" spectrum with an eclipse.
—Julius. Anomalous refraction phenomena. (Not for sale.)
—Kapteyn. On certain statistical data which may be valuable in the classification of the stars. gratis.—On the absorption of light in space. (Not for sale.)
—King. Correspondence between Zeeman effect and pressure displacement for the spectra of iron, chromium, and titanium.—Further study of the H and K lines of calcium.—On the separation in the magnetic field of some lines occurring as doublets and triplets in sun-spot spectra. (Not for sale.)—Relative intensities of the yellow, orange and red lines of calcium. (Not for sale.)
—Ritchey. 60-inch reflector of the Mt. Wilson solar observatory. (Not for sale.)
—St. John. Absolute wave-lengths of the H and K lines of calcium. gratis.

Contributions to abdominal surgery. Barnard, H. L. $4.20 net. Longmans.

Contributions to cosmogony and the fundamental problems of geology. Q. pap. Carnegie.
—Chamberlin. Gases in rocks. 50 c.
—Chamberlin, *and others.* Tidal and other problems. $1.50.

Contributions to South American archæology. il. F. P. Harper.
—Saville. Antiquities of Manabi, Ecuador. $25.

Contributions to the knowledge of the California species of *crustaceous corallines.* Nichols, M. B. 10 c.—II., 15 c. Univ. of Cal.

Contributions to the life histories of fishes. Gill, T. N: (Add. pubs. for price.) Smith. Inst.

CONTROL.
See Psychology.

Control of body and mind. Jewett, *Mrs.* F. G. 50 c. Ginn.

Control of flies and other household insects. Felt, E: P. 15 c. N. Y. State Educ.

Control of household insects. Felt, E. P. gratis. N. Y. State Educ.

Control of municipal public service corporations. American Acad. of Political and Social Science. $1. Am. Acad. Pol. Sci.

Control processes in modified handwriting. Downey, J. E. $1.50. Psychological Review.

Controversy between truth and falsehood. Smith, J. W. 75 c. J. W. Smith.

Controversy over the proposition for an American episcopate, 1767-1774. Nelson, W: $2.50. Paterson Hist.

Convent (The) horror; story of Barbara Ubryk: [story of a convent life.] '08(N) c. 25 c. L. J. King.

Convention normal manual for Sunday-school workers; Baptist first standard course in three divisions. '09(Jl) c. 224 p. il. maps, 12°, 50 c.; pap., 35 c. Bapt. S. S. Bd.

Conventionalists (The). Benson, R. H. $1.50. Herder.

Conventions and how to care for them. Foster, E. C. *25 c. net. S. S. Times.

CONVENTS.
See Port Royalists.

CONVERSATION.
Krans, H. S., *ed.* Lost art of conversation. $1.50 net. Sturgis & W.

Conversationaliste français. Roth, E: $1. E: Roth.

Conversations on electricity. Branch, J. G. $2. Rand, McN. & Co.

Converse, Florence.
House of prayer; [for children.] '08(N21) 12°, *$1.50 net. Dutton.
Long Will. '08(S19) 16°, (Everyman's lib.) *35 c. net; leath., *70 c. net. Dutton.

Converse, Florence.—*Continued.*
Long Will; romance of the days of Piers Plowman. '10(N12) il. 8°, $1.50 net. Dutton.
Masque of sibyls. '10(My21) D. $1 net. Houghton M.

Converse, Mrs. Harriet Maxwell Clarke.
Myths and legends of the New York State Iroquois. '08, [1909.] (Mr) 195 p. il. pors. 8°, (N. Y. State Museum bull.) 75 c.; pap., 50 c. N. Y. State Educ.

Converse, (John H.,) lectures. *See* Dennis, Ja. Shepard.

CONVERSION.
Beach, C: F. Individual evangelism. *$1 net. Allen, L. & S.
Bible. Helping hand: suggestions for winning souls. 25 c.; 15 c. Am. Bapt.
Coombs, J. V. Christian evangelism. 75 c.; 25 c. Standard Pub.
Evans, W: Personal soul-winning. $1. Bible Inst.
Goodman, F. S. Evangelism through Bible study. *25 c. net. S. S. Times.
Green, O. O. Normal evangelism. $1 net. Revell.
Hallenbeck, E. F. Passion for men. 40 c. net. Revell.
Hamilton, W: W. Helping hand: suggestions for winners of souls. **25 c. net; **15 c. net.—Sane evangelism. **75 c. net. Am. Bapt.
Hudson, M. A. How to reach men. *50 c. net. S. S. Times.
Jackson, G: Fact of conversion. *$1.25 net. Revell.
Jefferson, C: E. Next step; [to be used in following up results of evangelistic campaigns.] 35 c.; condensed, 5 c. Y. M. C. A.
Krumreig, E: L. Shadowing wing; [acct. of author's experience.] $1.50. E: L. Krumreig.
Leete, F: D. Every-day evangelism. *$1 net. Jennings.
McAfee, J. E. Missions striking home. 75 c. Revell.
Nichols, J: H. Golden candlestick. 10 c.; per doz., $1. Smith & L.
Rust, C: H. Church on wheels. 50 c. Am. Bapt.
Sligh, J: C. Christ's way of winning souls. 60 c. Pub. Ho. of M. E. Ch., So.
Stapleton, *Rev.* A. Flashlights on evangelical history. $1. A. Stapleton.
Stone, J: T. Recruiting for Christ. $1 net. Revell.
Trumbull, C: Gallaudet. Taking men alive. *60 c. net; *40 c. net. Y. M. C. A.
Wood, H. W. Winning men one by one. *50 c. net. S. S. Times.
See also Christian life;—Missions;—Repentance;—Revivals;—Salvation.

Convert (The). Hudgins, C: B. $1.50. Neale.

Convertible securities. Rollins, M. $3. M. Rollins.

CONVEYANCING.
Moore, D. C. Treatise on fraudulent conveyances and creditors remedies at law and in equity. 2 v. $12. M. Bender.

Convict life at the Minnesota State Prison, Stillwater, Minnesota. Heilbron, W: C. 25 c. H. L. Taylor.

Convict's sweetheart. Harper, O. 25 c. J. S. Ogilvie.

CONVICTS.
See Crime and criminals;—Prisons.

Convivio. *See* Dante Alighieri.

CONVOLVULUS FAMILY.
See Botany.

Conway, Agnes Ethel and Sir W: Martin.
Children's book of art. '09(O23) col. il. O. *$2 net. Macmillan.

Conway, Emma Ellis.
To ports beyond; [poems.] '10(D24) c. por. D. 90 c. Editor Co.

Conway, Jos. P.
The question of the hour; survey of the position and influence of the Catholic church in the United States. '09(D11) c. D. *$1.25 net. J: McBride.

Conway, Katherine Eleanor, and Cameron, Mabel Ward.
Charles Francis Donnelly; memoir, with an acct. of the hearings on a bill for the inspection of private schools in Mass. in 1888-1889. '09, [1910.] (F) c. 265 p. il. pors. facsim., 8°. (Priv. pr.) J. T. White & Co.

—, **comp.** Story of a beautiful childhood; comp. from the journals of Joseph Astley Gallagher. '09(D) c. 107 p. por. 12°, $1. C. M. Clark.
The woman who never did wrong, and other stories. '09(D11) c. 12°, 75 c. T: J. Flynn.

Conway, Moncure Dan.
Moncure D. Conway; addresses and reprints, 1850-1907; published and unpublished work representing the literary and philosophical life of the author. '09(Jl10) c. O. $3. Houghton M.
Thomas Carlyle. '09(My) c. 7+13-255 p. il. pors. facsim., $1. Harper.

CONWAY, Moncure Daniel.
Walker, E. C. Sketch and appreciation of Moncure Daniel Conway. 15 c. E. C. Walker.

Conway, T:, jr.
Traffic problems of interurban electric railroads; repr. from the *Journal of Accountancy,* Mar. 6, 1909. '09(N) 31 p. 8°, gratis. Univ. of Penn.

Conway, Sir W: Martin.
The Alps. '10(Je18) il. 8°, (Color books.) $1.50 net. Macmillan.

Conwell, Russell Herman.
He goeth before you. '10(Ja22) c. il. D. bds., 50 c. F. M. Barton.

Conwentz, Hugo Wilhelm.
Care of natural monuments, with special reference to Great Britain and Germany. '09(Mr) 11+185 p. il. 12°, *$1 net. Putnam.

Conybeare, F: Cornwallis.
Myth, magic and morals. '10(D31) 8°, $2.50 net. Am. Unitarian.

CONYBEARE, Frederick Cornwallis.
Sanday, W. New Marcion; being a criticism of Mr. F. C. Conybeare's "Myth, magic and morals." *36 c. net. Longmans.

Conybeare, Rev. J: W: E:
Highways and byways in Cambridge and Ely. '10(D10) il. fold. maps, O. $2 net. Macmillan.

Conyers, Dorothea.
Three girls and a hermit. '08(O24) 12°, $1.50. Dutton.

Conyngton, Mary.
How to help. '09(My1) 12°, *$1.50 net. Macmillan.

Conyngton, T:
Manual of corporate management; cont. forms, directions and information for the use of lawyers and corporation officials. 3d ed. '09, [1908.] (D) c. 422 p. 8°, $3. [After Apr. 5, '09, $3.50.] Ronald Press.
Manual of corporate organization. Enl. ed. '08(My2) c. 8°, $3. Ronald Press.
Modern corporation, its mechanism, methods, formation and management. 3d ed. '08(O); 4th ed. '10(My7) c. 8°, ea., $2. Ronald Press.
See also Bentley, Harry Clark.

"Coo-ee." Leighton, R. $1. Lippincott.

Cook, Alb. Stanburrough.
Authorized version of the Bible, and its influence. '10(D3) c. D. $1 net. Putnam.
—, **ed.** Concordance to the English poems of Thomas Gray. '08(D5) c. O. **$2.50 net. Houghton M.
—, **and Tinker, Chauncey Brewster, eds.**
Select translations from Old English prose. '08(F22) c. D. $1.25. Ginn.

Cook, C: A:
Stewardship and missions. '09(Ja2) c. D. **50 c. net; pap., **35 c. net. Am. Bapt.

Cook, C: Cyrus.
Truth about grace, by a Berean. '09(Ja9) c. S. pap., 25 c. C: C. Cook.

Cook, E: Tyas.
Edmund Garrett: memoir. '09(N13) por. O. *$3 net. Longmans.
Gardens of England. '08(Ag1) il. 8°, (Color books.) *$2.50 net. Macmillan.

Cook, Fk. Atwood.
Subsistence guide for the national guard (the organized militia). '09, [1910.] (Jl) 58 p. il. tabs., 8°, $1. U. S. Military Pub.

Cook, Fk. Cummings.
Comparison of beef and yeast extracts of known origin. '10(D) 7 p. 8°, (U. S., Dept. of Agriculture, Bu. of Chemistry; cir.)
See also Bigelow, Willard Dell.

Cook, F: Albert, M.D.
To the top of the continent: discovery, exploration and adventure in sub-arctic Alaska; first ascent of Mt. McKinley, 1903-1906. '08(Mr7) c. il. por. maps, O. (Geographical lib.) **$2.50 net. Doubleday, P.

COOK, Frederick Albert, *M.D.*
Ingersoll, E. Conquest of the North; authentic account of the finding of the North Pole by Dr. Frederick A. Cook, Com. R. E. Peary, U. S. N., together with biographies of the explorers and a brief hist. of Arctic discovery. 10 c. C. S. Hammond.
See also **Arctic regions.**

Cook, F: Fs.
Bygone days in Chicago; recollections of the "Garden City" of the sixties. '10 (Ap30) c. il. O. $2.75 net. McClurg.

Cook, H. O.
How to make improvement thinnings in Massachusetts woodlands; by H. O. Cook under the direction of F. W. Rane. '10(My) 21 p. il. O. pap. F. W. Rane.

Cook, Howard M.
Wayside jottings; or, rambles around Concord, N. H. '09, [1910.] (F) 13+201 p. il. por. 12°, $1.50. H. M. Cook.

Cook, Joel.
Mediterranean and its borderlands. In 2 v v. 1, Western countries; v. 2, Eastern countries. '10(D17) c. il. O. $5, boxed; leath., $10, boxed. Winston.

Cook, J: T., ed.
See American bankruptcy repts.—New York [State.] *Cts. of appeals.* Repts.—Code of criminal procedure.

Cook, Jos. Merwin.
Bandana days: [verses.] '08(D) c. 21 p. 12°, 60 c. B'way Pub.

Cook, Rev. Joshua Floore.
Old Kentucky. '08(Ag8) c. por. O. *$3 net. Neale.

Cook, Marion.
Child and the dream: Christmas story. '08, [1909.] (Mr) c. 22 p. front. 8°, 50 c. Metropolitan Pr.
Where flows Hood River: [poems.] '08 (Ap4) c. sq. 12°, bds., $1. Hicks-Chatten.

Cook, Metta Horton.
Yennycott folks. '10(Ag27) il. 12°. $1 J. S. Ogilvie.

Cook, Neander P.
Betrothal of Ronald and Thusnelda: dramatic poem. [2d ed.] '08, [1909.] (My) 5-61 p. il. 12°, 60 c. Weimar.

Cook, Orator Fuller.
Local adjustment of cotton varieties. '09 (D) 75 p. 8°, (U. S., Dept. of Agriculture, Bureau of Plant Industry, bull.) pap. (Add. Superintendent for price.)
Mutative reversions in cotton. '10(My) 18 p. 8°, (U. S., Dept. of Agriculture, Bureau of Plant Industry, circular.)
Origin of the Hindi cotton. '09, [1910.] (F) 12 p. 8°, (U. S., Dept. of Agriculture, Bureau of Plant Industry, circular.) pap.
Vegetation affected by agriculture in Central America. '09(Je) 30 p. il. 8°, (U. S., Dept. of Agriculture; Bureau of Plant Industry bull.) pap. (Add. Superintendent for price.) U. S., Supt. of Docs.

Cook, S: Newton.
Norma Lane, the daughter of an "absent brother." '10(F5) 12°, $1.25. S: N. Cook.
Also published under title "Norma Lane, the daughter of an Elk."

Cook, Silas Arth.
Meaning of life; study in the Epistle of James. '10(D17) c. 16°, 35 c. Jennings.

Cook, Stanley A.
Religion of ancient Palestine. '09(Ap24) 8°, (Religions ancient and modern.) *40 c. net. Open Court.

Cook, W: Azel.
By horse, canoe and float through the wildernesses of Brazil. '10(Ja15) c. il. pors. 8°, $2. Werner Co.
Through the wilderness of Brazil, by horse, canoe and float. '10(N5) c. il. O. $1.50. Am. Tr.

Cook, W: Wallace.
Quarter to four. '09(My1) c. il. D. †$1.50. G: W. Dillingham.

Cook, W: Wilson.
Treatise on the law of corporations having a capital stock. 4 v. 6th ed., rev. and enl. '08(D) 4300 p. O. *$26 net. Callaghan.

COOK-BOOKS.
See Cookery.

COOK COUNTY.
See Illinois.

Cooke, E. Cozens.
Case against protection; summary of the proceedings of the International Free Trade Congress. '09(Ap24) D. pap., 10 c. Cassell.

Cooke, Edm. Vance.
The high chair [poems about children]. '10(D) $1 Dodge.
"I rule the house." '10(D17) 12°, $1 net. Dodge.
Little songs for two. '09(Ag) 73 p. il. 12°, *$1 net; ooze, *$1.50 net. Dodge.

Cooke, Frances.
"My Lady Beatrice." '08(F15) D. $1.25. Benziger.
Unbidden guest. '09(D4) c. D. $1.25. Benziger.

Cooke, F: Hale.
Commerce clause of the federal constitution. '08(My.) c. 92+302 p. O. $4.50. Baker, V. & Co.
Law of combinations, monopolies and labor unions. 2d ed. '09(O) c. O. $6. Callaghan.

Cooke, G: Willis, comp.
Bibliography of Ralph Waldo Emerson. '08(Je20) c. por. 8°, **$5 net. Houghton M.

Cooke, Mrs. Grace MacGowan.
Power and the glory. '10(Ag6) c. il. D. $1.20, fixed. Doubleday, P.

Cooke, Ja. Fs.
Standard hist. of music; first hist. for students of all ages; 40 illustrated story lessons in the development of musical art, adapted for beginners, musical clubs, private teaching, classwork and general reading, incl. an appendix upon club organization and management, together with a map of musical Europe. '10(D17) O. $1.25. T. Presser.

Cooke, J:, ed.
Dublin book of Irish verse, 1728-1909. '10 (Ja1) D. $1.75; India cl., $2.50; leath., $3.50, boxed. Oxford Univ.

Cooke, Rev. J: Hunt.
Johann Gerhard Oncken: his life and work. '09(Mr) (Light and truth ser.) **50 c. net. Am. Bapt.

Cooke, Jos. Brown, M.D.
Nurse's handbook of obstetrics, for use in training-schools. 4th ed., rev. '09(N) c. 403 p. il. 8°, $2. Lippincott.
Obstetrical technique as applied to private practice. 6th ed., enl. and fully rev. '08 (N) c. '00, '02. 258 p. 12°, **$1.50 net. Lippincott.

Cooke, Marjorie Benton.
Girl who lived in the woods. '10(O8) c. col. il. O. $1.50. McClurg.
More modern monologues. '08(F8) c. D. $1.25. Dramatic.

Cooke, Morris Llewellyn.
Academic and industrial efficiency. '10 (D24) tabs., O. (Bulletin.) pap. Carnegie.

Cooke, Patrick.
Our misunderstanding concerning the Jews: an article on the political aspect of the Jewish question in the United States: being a criticism principally of an article—"Concerning the Jews"—by Mark Twain. '08(O) c. 63 p. 16°. (Add. author for price.) P. Cooke.

Cooke, R: Jos.
Questions for High-Churchmen; with historical and explanatory note. '10(F19) c. S. **25 c. net. Eaton & M.

Cooke, V. T.
Dry farming in Wyoming; pub. under the supervision of the State Dry Farming Commission, Cheyenne, Wyoming. '09, [1910.] (Ja) c. 16 p. il. 8°, gratis. V. T. Cooke.
Dry farming in Wyoming. '07, [1908.] (O) 5-13 p. pl. O. (Wyoming, Dry Farming Commission bull.) pap., gratis. Wy. State Dry Farming.

Cooke, W. Bourne.
Bellcroft Priory. '10(O22) D. $1.50. Lane.
Her faithful knight. '08(My16) D. $1.50. Cassell.

Cooke, Wells Woodbridge.
Distribution and migration of North American shore birds. '10(N) 100 p. il. 8°, (U. S., Dept. of Agriculture, Biological Survey bull.)

Cook-ed up and Peary oddical dict. and who's hoot in the best Arctic circles. Browne, L. A. *60 c. net. J: R. Luce.

COOKERY.
Bacheller, D., *comp.* Housekeeper pudding book. 50 c. Housekeeper Corp.
Bates, F. A. Camping and cooking. *75 c. net. Ball Pub. Co.
Behnke, K. E., *and* Henslowe, E. C. Broadlands cookery book. $1 net. Macmillan.
Bevier, I., *and* Van Meter, A. R. Selection and preparation of food, lab'y guide. 75 c. Whitcomb.
Blackstone, E. M. American woman's cook book. $1.50. Laird.
Bomberger, M. A. Colonial recipes from old Virginia and Maryland manors. $1.25. Neale.
Book of recipes for Acme automatic fireless cooker. '10(Ag) c. 80 p. il. 8°, $2. Sheer.

COOKERY.—*Continued.*

Brockton Hospital Ladies' Aid Association. Brockton hospital cook book. 50 c. Brockton Hospital.

Brown, *Mrs.* M. A. A., *comp.* Dainty dining. $1.50. Reed Press.

Caloric Fireless Cookstove Co. Book of Recipes. 50 c. Caloric.

Caro, M. T. Restricted diet made palatable. $1 net. Ball Pub.

Church cook book. 75 c. Williams & W.

Clark, *Lady.* Cookery book of Lady Clark of Tillypronie. $2 net. Dutton.

Colcord, *Mrs.* A. L. Friend in the kitchen: [vegetarianism.] 50 c.; 25 c. Review and Herald.

Curtis, *Mrs.* I. G., *comp.* Good housekeeping woman's home cook book. 60 c. Reilly & B.

Cutter, *Mrs.* S. G. R. Practical recipes. **$1.25 net. Duffield.

Daughters of the American Revolution, Penn.: Germantown chapter. Germantown D. A. R. cook-book. 25 c. D. A. R., Germantown Chap.

Davenport, *Mrs.* L., *comp.* Bride's cook book. $2; $4; $6.—Small family cook book. $1.25. Reilly & B.

Doherty, J. J. Household baker. $1.50. J. J. Doherty

Douglas, E. Cake and biscuit book.—Pudding and pastry book.—Soup and sauce book. ea., 50 c. McKay.

Dudley, G. M., *Countess of, comp.* Dudley book of cookery. *$2 net. Longmans.

Dunlap, L. Candlelight tea [beverages, salads, sandwiches].—Heart of the wheat [bread, cakes, pies].—Out of the blue grass [soups, meats, vegetables]. ea., $1. Transylvania.

Economy cook book. 50 c. Inter Aid.

Ewart, N. E. Daily living: pract. cook book. *$1.84 net. H. P. Hood.

Fellows, C: Selection of dishes and the Chef's reminder. $1. Hotel Monthly.

Foster, O. H. Cookery for little girls. 75 c. net. Duffield.

Fuller, E. G., *comp.* Up-to-date sandwich book. *$1 net. McClurg.

Gancel, J. Ready reference of menu terms. $1. J. Gancel.

Glover, E. H. "Dame Curtsey's" book of recipes. *$1 net. McClurg.

Good things to eat and how to prepare them. 15 c. Larkin.

Goold, M. New England cook book. 75 c. M. G. Buckley.

Government cook book. 10 c. Brooklyn Eagle.

Green, O. How to cook fish. **90 c. net.—How to cook meat and poultry. **$1 net. Putnam.

Heritage, L. Cassell's household cookery. $1.50. Cassell.

Hill, *Mrs.* J. M. Cooking and serving en-casserole and things we relish. 10 c. Int. Silver.

Hill, *Mrs.* J. M. Cooking for two. **$1.50 net. Little, B. & Co.

Hiller, *Mrs.* E. O., *comp.* Pract. cook book. $1. Doherty Op.

COOKERY.—*Continued.*

Howland, M. R. Woman's world cook book. 10 c. Currier Pub.

Hulse, O. M. Two hundred recipes for making salads, with thirty recipes for dressings and sauces. $1. Hopewell Press.

Huntington, E. A. Fireless cooker. 25 c. Univ. of Wis.

Institute for Colored Youth, Cheney, Pa. Applied domestic science: daily menu for the school year. 50 c. Inst. Colored Youth.

Jenkinson, E. L. Ocklye cookery book. 60 c. net. Cassell.

Johnson, C. When mother lets us cook. **75 c. net. Moffat.

Johnson, F. K. Large meals for little money. 10 c. People's Univ.

Jones, M. M. W., *ed.* San Rafael cook book. $1. W. F. Jones.

Kander, *Mrs.* S. "Settlement" (Jewish) cook book. $1. Caspar.

Kaufman, N. M., *comp.* Our sisters' recipes. $1. J. A. Perley.

Keen, A., *comp.* With a saucepan over the sea. $1.50 net. Little, B. & Co.

Kephart, H. Camp cookery. $1 net. Outing.

Keyser, *Mrs.* F. French household cooking. *60 c. net. Scribner.

Kirk, *Mrs.* A. G. People's home recipe book. $3. R. C. Barnum.

Landes, S. W. Elem. domestic science. pt. 1, Food and cookery. 54 c. S. W. Landes.

Laskowski, P: E. Art of baking. $1. P: E. Laskowski.

Laughlin, A., *ed.* The reappear: book of recipes. 60 c. A. Laughlin.

Lee, W: H:, *and* Hansey, J. A., *comps.* Standard domestic science cook book. $2.50; $1.75; $1.70. Laird.

Lloyd, *Mrs.* E. B. Grandma's cook book. $1.25. Jennings.

Lovewell, *Mrs.* C. F. B., *and others.* Fireless cooker: how to use it. $1. Home Pub. Co., (Kan.)

Lucas, P. E.-S. All about salads. 75 c. Cathedral Lib.

Macon cook book. $1. J. W. Burke.

Maddocks, M., *ed.* *Good Housekeeping* family cook book. 50 c. Phelps.

Malone cook book. $1.25. Tuttle Co.

Malzbender, M. Praktischer ratgeber für conditoren cakebäcker und brot bäcker. $2. Volksfreund Press.

Mario, A. Easy French cookery. **60 c. net. Cassell.

Marvin, *Mrs.* A. I., *comp.* Cook book. 50 c. Cochrane.

Meier, *Mrs.* L. W. Aechte deutsche kochkunst: German cooking. $2.50. L. W. Meier.

Mendelssohn Club, Rockford, Ill. Mendelssohn Club cook book. $1.50. Mendelssohn Club.

Menu book. $1.25. Reilly & B.

Middleton, M., *comp.* Recipes from old Mexico. 25 c. J. C. Middleton.

Missouri Baptist Sanitarium. Saint Louis cook book. $1. Missouri Bapt. San.

COOKERY.—*Continued.*

Mitchell, M. J. Fireless cook book. $1.25. Doubleday, P.

Muckenstrum, L: J. Louis' every woman's cook book. $1.50. Caldwell.

Neely, F. Hdbk. for the kitchen and housekeeper's guide. $1.50. F. Neely.

Neil, M. H., *comp.* Alcono cook book. 50 c. Pitkin.

Otterbein cook book. 50 c. R. R. Inman.

Palisades cook book. Tenafly Presb. Ch.

Parloa, M. New cook book and marketing guide. $1.50. Estes.

Payne, A. G. Choice dishes at small cost. $1.25 net. Cassell.

People's home library; people's home medical book, people's home recipe book, people's home stock book. $4.50. R. C. Barnum.

Phillips, *Mrs.* F. F., *and* Levy, R. H., *comps.* Universal cook book. $1; 50 c. F. F. Phillips.

Pierce, E. A. Hartley House cook book and household economist. 60 c. net. Wessels & B.

Poindexter, *Mrs.* C. M., *comp.* Jane Hamilton's recipes. $1. McClurg.

Porter, *Mrs.* A. L. A., *and* Ball, *Mrs.* E. B. A., *comps.* Crumbs from everybody's table. $1. Monterey.

Pratz, C. de. French dishes for English tables. $1. McKay.

Princeton, Ind. First Presbyterian Church. Princeton cook book. $1. A. J. Paxton.

Reed, M. How to cook vegetables.—One thousand salads. ea., **$1 net. Putnam.

Retail Grocers' Association of Richmond. Old Virginia cooking. gratis. Richmond Press.

Riedinger, *Mrs.* L. R. Fireless cookery with the hay box. 10 c. L. D. Riedinger.

Robertson, G., *comp.* Common sense recipes. 25 c. G. Robertson.

Ronald, M. Century cook book. $2. Century Co.

Royal Baking Powder Co. My favorite recipe. 50 c. Royal Baking.

Sachse, H. V. How to cook for the sick and convalescent. $1.25. Lippincott.

Seely, *Mrs.* F. Fireless cookery. 25 c. Assoc. Schs. Dom. Sci.

Sexton, M. B., *comp.* Monmouth Baptist ladies' cook book. 60 c.; 85 c.. M. B. Sexton.

Smith, *Mrs.* J. H., comp. Famous old recipes. **$2 net. Winston.

Snyder, S. P., *comp.* Treatise on foods; also complete list of recipes. $1. Health.

Southworth, M. E., *comp.* One hundred and one entrees. **$1 net; **$2 net; **50 c. net. P. Elder.

Spring, H. M. Individual recipes in use at Drexel Institute. 50 c. Winston.

Standard domestic science cook book. $1.75; $1.25. Laird.

Swain, R. Cooking for health. $1. Health-Culture.

Tatum, J. W., *comp.* Information of great value to newly married people. gratis. H. K. Palmer.

Telford, E. P., *and* Armington, M. A. Evening Telegram cook book. 75 c.; 35 c. Cupples & L.

365 foreign dishes. **50 c. net; **40 c. net. Jacobs.

365 orange recipes. 50 c. Jacobs.

365 vegetable dishes. 50 c. net. Jacobs.

Tracy, S. Practical cook book. $1. S. Tracy.

Underhill, *Mrs.* J. E., *comp.* Sunshine cook book. 50 c. J. E. Underhill.

Van Buren, S. Good living: practical cookery-book for town and country. $2.50. Putnam.

Warren cook book. $1. J. W. Kitchen.

What Salem dames cooked. $1. Esther C. Mack Indust. Sch.

Wheelock, I. S. Salads. 50 c. I. S. Wheelock.

Wilkinson, *Mrs.* M. E. M. Cook book for the poor, the rich, the sick, the well. $1. Conkey.

Williams, J. C. Us two cook book. $1. Barse & H.

Wilson, E. L. Good things to eat. $3. Pub. Ho. of M. E. Ch., So.

See also Baking powder;—Beverages;—Bread;—Cake;—Candy;—Dining;—Domestic economy;—Food;—Hygiene;—Ice cream;—Luncheon;—Meat;—Oysters;—Preserving;—Spices;—Vegetarianism.

Cooking for health. Swain, R. $1. Health-Culture.

Cool, C: Dean, comp.
See Giese, W: Frederic, *comp.*

Cooley, Mrs. Alice Woodworth.
See Webster, W: Franklin.

Cooley, C: Horton.
Social organization: study of the larger mind. '09(Ap10) c. O. **$1.50 net. Scribner.

Cooley, Ja. H.
Welfare of the church, Rev. John Hiland and Uniontown: [fiction.] '10(Jl2) c. D. 75 c. J. H. Cooley.

Cooley, Roger W., ed.
Brief making and the use of law books, by W: M. Lile, H: D. Redfield, and others. 2d ed. '09(N) c. 12+574 p. O. $2. West Pub.

Cooley, Stoughton.
Captain of the Amaryllis. '10(D31) il. 12°. $1.50. C. M. Clark.

Coolidge, Archibald Cary.
United States as a world power. '08(S26) 12°, *$2 net. Macmillan.

Coolidge, Asenath Carver.
Between two rebellions. '09(Mr6) il. por. D. $1. A. C. Coolidge.
Cherry feasts for barbarous Fourths. '09 (Jl31) c. por. D. bds., 25 c. Hungerford-H.
Christmas vs. Fourth of July. '08(Ag) c. 39 p. 12°, pap., 25 c. A. C. Coolidge.
Human beings *vs.* things. '10(Ap9) c. il. pors. D. $1. Hungerford-H.
Our nation's altar. '10(Ag13) c. por. D. bds., 25 c. A. C. Coolidge.
Prophet of peace. '08(Ap11) c. il. D. $1. Hungerford-H.

Coolidge, Dane.
Hidden water. '10(D3) c. O. $1.35 net. McClurg.

Coolidge, Emelyn Lincoln.
First aid in nursery ailments. '10(O) c. 76 p. 24°, $1. E. L. Coolidge.

Coolidge, Helen Eliz.
Poems. '09(Mr) 102 p. 12°, $1.25. Badger.

Coolidge, Julian Lowell.
Elements of non-Euclidean geometry. '09 (S11) O. *$5 net. Oxford Univ.

Coolidge, L: Arth.
Old-fashioned senator, Orville H. Platt of Connecticut; story of a life unselfishly devoted to the public service. '10(Ap30) c. il. pors. O. $3 net. Putnam.

Coolidge, Mrs. Mary Eliz. Burroughs Roberts Smith.
Chinese immigration. '09(S11) c. D. (American public problems.) **$1.75 net. Holt.

Coolidge, W: A: Brevoort.
Alps in nature and in history. '08(Ag15) 8°, *$2.50 net. Dutton.

Coombs, Fs. Lovell.
Young railroaders; tales of adventure and ingenuity. '10(O1) c. il. D. $1.50. Century Co.

Coombs, Ja. Vincent.
Christian evangelism. '08(Ap4) c. 12°, 75 c.; flex., 25 c. Standard Pub.

Coombs, Zelotes Wood.
Samuel Swett Green, Worcester Free Public Library, Worcester, Mass.: director, 1867-1871, librarian, 1871-1909. '09, [1910.] (F) 18 p. por. 8°. (Add. Lib. for price.) Worcester Pub. Lib.

Coon, C: Lee.
How to teach reading; manual for teachers. '09, [1910.] (My) 41 p. 8°, (North Carolina; Dept. of Public Instruction; Educational bull.) gratis. N. C. Dept. Pub. Instruct.
Significant educational progress in North Carolina, 1900-1906. '07 [1908.] (N) 23 p. il. 8°, (N. C. Dept. of Public Instruction; educational bull.) (Not for sale.) N. C. Dept. Pub. Instruct.

Coon, Fred Lewis.
Cœur de'Alene Indian Reservation, situated in Kootenai Co., Idaho. '08(N) c. 32 p. il. fold. map, 8°, pap., 25 c. Inland Pr. Co.

Coon, Rev. J. M.
Self pronouncing lesson commentary on the International Sunday school lessons, 1909. '09(Mr) 125 p. 32°, leath., 35 c.; interleaved, 50 c. G: W. Noble.

Coone, H: Herbert.
Draughon's pract. speller and dict. for use in commercial colleges and high schools. [1910.] (N) c. 103 p. 8°, 60 c. Draughon's.

Cooney, Patrick Jos.
Roman Catholicism and socialism; appreciation of the one and a plea for the other. '08, [1909.] (Je) c. 32 p. 12°, pap., 10 c. P. J. Cooney.

Coons, Jos. D., ed.
See Pennsylvania. Luzerne [Co.] legal register repts.

Cooper, Arth.
Sexual disabilities of man and their treatment. '09(Ag) 184 p. il. *$1 net. **Hoeber.**

Cooper, C: H., ed.
Responsive readings for schools. '09(D) (Add. pubs. for price.) Barnes.

Cooper, C. S., and Westell, W. Percival.
Trees and shrubs of the British Isles; native and acclimatised. 2 v. '09(D18) il. f°, *$7 net. Dutton.

Cooper, Edith.
See Bradley, Catherine.

Cooper, E: Herbert.
Marquis and Pamela. '08(Mr21) c. D. †$1.50. Duffield.
My brother the king; tale of James Darcy (King James I. of Yalmal) and his sister, Wyemarke Darcy. '10(S17) D. $1.50. Lane.

Cooper, Fs.
Financing an enterprise: manual of information and suggestion for promoters, investors, and business men generally. 3d ed. In 2 v. '09(N6) O. $4. Ronald Press.

Cooper, Howard M.
Historical sketch of Camden, N. J.; with introd. by Hon. C: Van Dyke Joline. '09 (O) c. 74 p. il. pors. 8°, $1. H. B. Ketler.

Cooper, Ja. Fenimore.
Works. De luxe ed. 12 v. '10(N) il. levant, $36. Crowell.
Works. 16 v. New imperial lib. ed. '10 (D) il. 8°, ea., $1.25; hf. cf., $2.25. New il. sterling ed. ea., $1. (Sets only.) **Estes.**
Afloat and ashore. '08(Jl4) 12°, (**Young** America lib.) 50 c. **Hurst.**
Last of the Mohicans. '10(N5) c. col. il. O. $1.35 net. Holt.
Leatherstocking tales from Cooper every child can read; ed. by Rev. Jesse Lyman Hurlbut. '08(N14) c. il. D. (Every child's lib.) †75 c. Winston.
The pathfinder; with an introd. by Susan Fenimore Cooper. '08(O3) c. D. (Cambridge classics.) †$1. Houghton M.
The pioneers; with an introd. by Susan Fenimore Cooper. '08(O3) c. D. (Cambridge classics.) †$1. Houghton M.
The prairie; with an introd. by Susan Fenimore Cooper. '08(O3) D. (Cambridge classics.) †$1. Houghton M.
The spy; ed., with introd. and notes, by S: Thurber, jr. '09(F20) por. T. (Macmillan's pocket American and English classics.) 25 c. Macmillan.

COOPER, James Fenimore.
Haight, M. N., *comp.* Adventures of Pathfinder adapted.—Last of the Mohicans; adapted. ea., 35 c. Am. Bk.

Cooper, W: Funk.
See Ballou, *Mrs.* Aurelia Anna Pierce.

Cooper Ornithological Club of California pubs. 4°. W. L. Chambers.
—Grinnell. Bibliog. of California ornithology. (Pacific coast avifauna.) $1.50.

CO-OPERATION.
Callahan, J. Y. Burning issue, and what co-operation will do: [agricultural co-operation.] 25 c. Pub. Pr.
Crafts, W. F. Internationalism: [co-operation among nations.] 40 c.; 25 c. Int. Ref. Bu.

CO-OPERATION.—*Continued.*
Fay, C: R. Co-operation at home and abroad. *$3 net. Macmillan.
Fowlkes, B: P. Co-operation the solution of the so-called negro problem. (Add. pubs. for price.) Novelty.
Kirwan, T: Reciprocity (social and economic) in the thirtieth century, the coming co-operative age: [fiction.] *$1 net. Cochrane.
See also Socialism;—Trade-unions.

Co-operation as a factor in effective bank supervision. Murray, L. O. (Priv. pr.) Nat. City Bank.

Co-operation with God. Robinson, A. W. *60 c. net. Cassell.

COOPERS AND COOPERAGE.
Wagner, J. B. Cooperage. $5. J. B. Wagner.

Cooperstown, N. Y. To commemorate the foundation of the village of Cooperstown and its corporate existence of one hundred years, this memorial celebration was held Aug. 4-10, 1907. '07, [1908.] (D) 180 p. por. pls. 8°, $1.25. C. W. Davidson.

Co-ordinate geometry. Fine, H: B. *$1.60 net. Macmillan.

Copa: the hostess of the inn; neglected classic; ed. by C: Loomis and J: Cotton Dana. '10(Ja15) c. il. pors. 12°, bds., $1. Elm Tree Press.

Cope, E: A.
Acquisition of speed in shorthand; with facsimile notes of famous fast writers of Pitman's shorthand. Rev. and enl. ed. '10(Jl9) D. pap., 20 c. Pitman.

—, and Robins, Herbert W. H.
Solicitor's office organisation, management and accounts. '10(Ap16) il. O. $2. Pitman.

Cope, F: J.
Tarry. '09(N) c. 235 p. por. 12°, $1.. Pentecostal.

Cope, Gilbert, comp. and ed.
Genealogy of the Darlington family; record of the descendants of Abraham Darlington of Birmingham, Chester Co., Pa., and of some other families of the name. '00 [1909.] (N) 579 p. 8°, *$4 net. C. D. Heydecker.

Cope, H: F:
Friendly life. '09(S4) c. 16°, (Right living ser.) bds., *35 c. net. Revell.
Home as the school for social living; pub. for the Social Service Commission of the Northern Baptist Convention. '10 (Jl30) c. 12°, (Social service ser.) 15 c. Am. Bapt.
Levels of living: essays on everyday ideals. '08(My23) c. D. *$1 net. Revell.

Copeland, C: Finney.
Poems of inspiration. De luxe ed. '08(D) c. 101 p. il. 8°, $1.50. Union Bk.

Copeland, C: Townsend, and Hersey, Fk. Wilson Cheney, comps. and eds.
Representative biographies of English men of letters. '09(O16) c. D. **$1.25 net. Macmillan.

—, and Rideout, H: Milner, eds.
Selections from Byron, Wordsworth, Shelley, Keats and Browning. '09(S4) c. S. (Gateway ser.) 40 c. Am. Bk.

Copeland, Edn. Bingham.
Elements of Philippine agriculture. '08 [1909.] (Mr) c. 15+192 p. il. 8°, (Philippine education ser.) 96 c. World Bk.

Copeland, Wa., pseud.
See Jerrold, Wa. Copeland.

—, and Robinson, C:
The cakeshop. '08(Ag15) 48°, bds., 25 c. Dutton.
The sweetshop. '08(Ag15) 48°, bds., 25 c. Dutton.
The toyshop. '08(Ag15) 48°, bds., 25 c. Dutton.

COPERNICUS.
See Money.

Coping saw work. Johnson, B. W. 20 c. Manual Arts.

Copleston, Bp. Reginald Stephen.
Buddhism: primitive and present; in Magadha and in Ceylon. 2d ed. '08(Jl11) O. *$3 net. Longmans.

Copley prints: reproductions of notable paintings publicly and privately owned in America; also of the mural decorations in the new Library of Congress, the Boston Public Library. '08(Ja18) 12°, pap., ea., 25 c. Curtis & C.

Coplin, W: Michael Late.
Manual of pathology, incl. bacteriology, the technic of postmortems, and methods of pathologic research. 4th ed., rewritten and enl., reprinted with corrections. '10 (O) c. 27+994 p. il. 8°, $4. Blakiston.
Bibliographical foot-notes.

Coppée, François.
Contes choisis; ed. by Marg. F. Skeat. '10 (D24) 16°, (Macmillan's new ser. of French texts.) 35 c. net.. Macmillan.
Pour la couronne; with introd. by Richmond Laurin Hawkins. '10(D31) c. 12°, 35 c. Holt.

Coppens, Rev. C:
Brief hist. of philosophy. '09(N) c. 10+144 p. 12°, $1. Schwartz, K. & F.
Choice morsels of the bread of life; or, select readings from the Old Testament. '09(My) 9+672 p. 16°, *60 c. net. Herder.

COPPER.
Aubury, L. E. Copper resources of California. *$1 net. Cal. State Mining.
Hixon, H. W. Notes on lead and copper smelting. $3. Hill Pub.
Stevens, H. J. Copper hand-book. v. 7, 1907; v. 8, 1908; v. 9, 1909. ea., $5; $7.50. H. J. Stevens.

Copping, Arth. E.
Gotty and the gov'ner. '08(Ja18) 8°, $1.50. M. Kennerley.
Gotty in furrin parts. '09(Jl10) il. D. $1.50. M. Kennerley.
Jolly in Germany. '10(D) il. 12°, $1.25 net. Doran.

Copus, Rev. J: Edn., ["Cuthbert."]
"As gold in a furnace": college story (sequel to "Shadows lifted"). '10(D3) c. il. D. 85 c. Benziger.
Making of Mortlake; story of a Rockland friendship. '09(O16) c. D. 85 c. Benziger.
Son of Siro: a story of Lazarus. '08(D26) c. front. D. *$1.50 net. Benziger.

COPYRIGHT.
Jenner, W: A. The octopus: reaching for books: considerations upon the pending copyright bills.—Publisher against the people. ea., gratis. W: A. Jenner.
Steiger, E. Urheberrecht und nachdruck in Nord-Amerika. gratis. Steiger.
United States. *Congress. Senate. Committee on Patents.* Revision of copyright laws. $1. U. S., Supt. of Docs.
United States. Copyright law of the U. S. of America in force July 1, 1909; together with rules for practice and procedure under section 25, by the Sup. ct. of the U. S. '09(Ag) 3+43 p. 8°, (Copyright Office bull.) pap. 10 c.
See also Trade-marks.

CORALLINES.
See Seaweeds.

Corbett, Bertha L.
Baby days; sunbonnet record. '10(N12) c. il. in col. Q. $1.50, boxed. Rand, McN.. & Co.

Corbett, Rev. F: St. John.
Thousand thoughts for pract. preachers. '10(D24) 12°, $2 net. Whittaker.

Corbett, Julian Stafford.
Campaign of Trafalgar. '10(Jl2) il. O. $4.50 net. Longmans.

Corbin, Alice.
Adam's dream, and two other miracle plays for children. '09(O30) c. il. 12°, 75 c. Scribner.

Corbin, J:
Husband and The forbidden guests; two plays. '10(N12) c. D. $1.25 net. Houghton M.
Which college for the boy?: leading types in American education. '08(My2) c. il. D. **$1.50 net. Houghton M.

Corbin, T: W.
Engineering of to-day. '10(D31) il. 8°, $1.50 net. Lippincott.
"How does it work" of electricity. '10 (Ag13) il. 12°, (How does it work ser.) 75 c. Fenno.
"How does it work" of modern engines. '10 (Ag13) il. 12°, (How does it work ser.) 75 c. Fenno.

Corbin, W: H., ed.
See New Jersey. Act concerning corporation.

Corbion, W: Amelius, and Grimsdale, G. E.
Salesmanship. '08(D19) D. $1. Pitman.

CORDAGE.
See Ropes.

Cordeiro, F: Joaquin Barbosa.
The atmosphere; its characteristics and dynamics. '10(Ap23) c. il. 8°, $2.50. Spon.
Gonorrhea. [1910.] (Mr) *25 c. net. W: R. Jenkins.
Formerly published by E. R. Pelton.

Corder, G: A.
Miner's geology and prospector's guide. '08 (F8) c. il. 12°, $2. Spon.

CORDIALS.
See Liquors.

Cords of Adam. Gerrard, T: J. *$1.50 net. Longmans.
Cords of vanity. Cabell, J. B. †$1.50. Doubleday, P.
Corduroy road. Dunham, A. C. $1.25. Werner Co.

COREA.
Allen, H. N. Things Korean. *$1.25 net. Revell.
Baird, A. L. Daybreak in Korea. *60 c. net. Revell.
Coulson, C. J. D. Korea. 75 c. net. Macmillan.
Davis, G: T. B. Korea for Christ. 25 c. net. Revell.
Gale, J. S. Korea in transition. 50 c.; 35 c. Young People's Miss.
Ladd, G: T. In Korea with Marquis Ito. **$2.50 net. Scribner.
McKenzie, F. A. Tragedy of Korea. *$2 net. Dutton.
Pontius, A. W., *comp.* Protection extended to patents, designs, trade-marks and copyrights in China, Japan and Korea. (Add. Superintendent for price.) U. S., Supt. of Docs.
Underwood, H. G. Call of Korea. *75 c. net; *35 c. net. Revell.
Underwood, *Mrs.* L. H. Fifteen years among the top-knots; or, life in Korea. $1.50. Am. Tr.
Wagner, E. C. Kim Su Bang, and other stories of Korea. 50 c. Pub. Ho. M. E. Ch., So.
See also Far East.

Corelli, Marie.
Devil's motor; fantasy. '10(D3) col. il. Q. $3 net. Doran.
Holy orders. '08(S19) c. D. †$1.50. Stokes.

Coriat, Isador H., M.D.
Abnormal psychology. '10(Ap30) c. O. $2 net. Moffat.
New psychology in medicine. '10(Jl30) 8°, $2 net. Moffat.
Some familiar forms of nervousness. '08 (D12) c. D. (Religion and medicine publications.) pap., **25 c. net. Moffat.
See also Worcester, Elwood.

CORINTHIANS, Epistles to.
See Bible.

CORIZUS.
See Insects.

Corkey, Alex.
Truth about Ireland; or, through the Emerald Isle with an aeroplane; with an introd. chapter showing the bright future of Ireland by Hon. W: Jennings Bryan. '10(Ap23) c. il. por. 8°, 75 c. Shockley Bros.
Victory of Allan Rutledge. '10(D24) il. 12°, $1.50. H. K. Fly.

Corlett, W: T:
American tropics: [West Indies, Central America, Venezuela;] notes from the log of a midwinter cruise. '09(Ja23) c. il. 12°, $1.50. Burrows.

CORLISS VALVE-GEAR.
See Valves.

Cormack, G:
Egypt in Asia: plain account of the pre-Biblical Syria and Palestine. '08(D5) il. maps, 8°, *$3 net. Macmillan.

CORN.
Bowman, M. L., *and* Crosley, B. W: Corn: growing, judging, breeding, feeding, marketing. $2. Bowman & C.
Clark, C: C., *comp.* Corn crops of the United States. 5 c. U. S., Supt. of Docs.

CORN.—*Continued.*
Collins, G. N. New type of Indian corn from China. U. S., Supt. of Docs.
Missouri. *State Board of Agriculture.* Boys' corn growing contest. gratis. Missouri State Bd.
Shoesmith, V. M. Study of corn. 50 c. Judd.
Smith, W: C. How to grow one hundred bushels of corn per acre on worn soils. $1. W. C. Smith.
Straughn, M. N., *and* Church, C. G. Influence of environment on the composition of sweet corn, 1905-1908. U. S., Supt. of Docs.

Corneille, Pierre.
Le Cid; with introd., notes and vocab. by Ja. D. Bruner. '08(D5) c. S. 45 c. Am. Bk.
Nicomède: tragédie; ed. by G. H. Clark. '10(D24) 16°, (Macmillan's new ser. of French texts.) 35 c. net. Macmillan.

Cornell, Hughes.
Dotty Seaweed; verses. [1910.] (S) c. '08. 35 p. il. obl. 4°, $2. Philopolis Press.

Cornell, Rev. J:
See Duyckinck, Whitehead Cornell.

Cornell, Wa. Stewart.
Backward children in the public schools. '08(Je13) c. il. 12°, pap., 25 c. Davis.
Hdbk. of osteology and syndesmology. [1910.] ((D) 101 p. il. 8°, 75 c. Davis.

Cornell studies in classical philology; ed. by C: Edn. Bennet, J: Rob. Sitlington Sterrett, and G: Prentice Bristol. O. Longmans.
Formerly published by Macmillan.
—Jones. Poetic plural of Greek tragedy in the light of Homeric usage. 80 c.
—Lane. Index to the fragments of the Greek Elegiac and Iambic poets. 80 c.

Cornell studies in history and political science. 8°. Holt.
—Olmstead. Western Asia in the days of Sargon. **$1.25 net.

Cornell studies in philosophy. O. 8°. Longmans.
—Cunningham. Thought and reality in Hegel's system. $1.25.

Cornell study bulletins for teachers; ed. by C: De Garmo. il. Q. Bardeen.
—De Garmo. Laboratory exercises in art. 40 c.
—Whipple. Guide to high school observation. 40 c.—Questions in general and educational psychology. 75 c.—Questions in school hygiene. 60 c.

CORNELL UNIVERSITY, Ithaca, N. Y.
Engeln, O. D. v. At Cornell. $1.50. Artil Co.
See also Fiske Icelandic collection.

Corner, Mrs. Caroline.
Ceylon, the paradise of Adam. '08(F29) il. O. *$4 net. Lane.

Corner in Spain. Wood, W. $2 net. Pott.

Corner ser.. See Blanchard, Amy Ella.

Cornill, Carl Heinrich.
Music in the Old Testament. '09(O23) il. 50 c. Open Court.

Cornish, Fs. Warre.
Chivalry. New ed. '08(O17) il. 12°, *$1.25 net. Macmillan.

Cornish, Vaughan.
Panama Canal and its makers. '09(Je19) il. maps, plans, 8°, *$1.50 net. Little, B. & Co.

Cornish characters and strange events. Baring-Gould, S. *$5 net. Lane.

Cornwall, W. W., rep.
See Iowa. *Sup. ct.* Repts.

CORNWALL, England.
Baring-Gould, S. Cornish characters and strange events. *$5 net. Lane.
Hudson, W: H: Land's End: a naturalist's impression in West Cornwall. *$3 special net. Appleton.
Salmon, A. L. Cornwall coast. $2.25 net. Stokes.

Cornwallis-West, Jennie Jerome, [Mrs. G: Cornwallis-West, formerly Lady Randolph Spencer Churchill.]
Reminiscences of Lady Randolph Churchill. '08(N7) c. il. pors. O. **$3.50 net. Century Co.

Cornyn, Juan Humberto.
Mexican topics prep. for The new student's reference work [by Chandler B. Beach and others.] '10(Ap) c. 2245-2292 p. il. 8°, sold only with New student's reference work, $25. Compton.

COROT, Louis Jacques.
Meynell, E. Corot and his friends. **$3.25 net. Wessels.

Corpier, Lula Belle.
Dreams and realities. 2d ed. '09(S) c. 244 p. por. 12°. (Priv. pr.) Pub. Ho. of M. E. Ch., So.

Corporation legal manual. v. 15, 1907; ed. by J. S. Parker. '08(F) O. *$6.50 net.—Corporation manual supplement, 1908-09. '08 (D) 384 p. 8°, *$3.50 net; per set, *$10 net. Callaghan.

CORPORATIONS.
Abbott, H. S. Summary of the law of public corporations. (Add. pubs. for price.) Keefe-D.
American School of Correspondence Corporation accounts and voucher system. $1. Am. Sch. Corr.
Arnold, J. A. Guide for business corporations in the state of New York. $1.50; $1.25. Baker, V. & Co.
Bentley, H. C., *and* Conyngton, T: Corporate finance and accounting. $4. Ronald Press.
Carney, W: A. Promoter's assistant and improved secretary's manual. $3. Carlisle.
Clark, W: L., *jr., and* Marshall, W: L. Supplement to Private corporations; by Arth. L. Helliwell; being v. 4 of the set. $6.50. Keefe-D.
Coles, A. Pitman's guide for the company secretary. $2. Pitman.
Connell, C. Pitman's companies and company law; together with the Companies (Consolidated) Act, 1908. $2. Pitman.
Conyngton, T: Manual of corporate management. $3.50.—Manual of corporate organization. $3.—Modern corporation. $2. Ronald Press.

CORPORATIONS.—*Continued.*

Cook, W: W. Treatise on the law of corporations having a capital stock. In 4 v. *$26 net. Callaghan.

District of Columbia. Corporation law. 75 c. Byrne.

Eastman, F. M. Supp. to 2d ed. of Eastman on private corporations, [Pennsylvania.] $1.50.—Treatise on the law rel. to private corporations [in Pennsylvania.] 2 v. (Add. pubs. for price.) Bisel.

Elliott, C: B. Principles of the law of public corporations. $4. Callaghan.

Foote, A. R. Speech del. before Wis. legislature: [public utilities bills of Wis. and N. Y.] (Add. author for price.) A. R. Foote.

Frost, T: G. Treatise on the incorporation and organization of corporations, created under the "business corporation acts" of all the states and territories. **$5 net. Little, B. & Co.

Gordon, W: A. Texas corporation manual. W: A. Gordon.

Griffith, J. B. Corporation accounts. 50 c. Am. Sch. Corr.

Hallowell, J. M. Taxation of domestic manufacturing corporations in Massachusetts. gratis. J. M. Hallowell.

Hanks, C: S. Growth of corporate wealth and its effect upon us as individuals. 50 c. Authors' Pub.

Illinois. Law of corporations. $5. Flood.

Illinois. Treatise on the incorporation and management of corporations. $7.50. Callaghan.

Indiana corporation law. $7.50. Bobbs-M.

Joline, A. H. Method and conduct of the reorganization of corporations. (Priv. pr.) A. H. Joline.

Jones, S. W. Treatise on the law of insolvent and failing corporations. $6.50. Vernon Law Bk.

Lybrand, W: M., *and others.* Accounting for modern corporations. 50 c. Am. Sch. Corr.

Lyons, J. A. Modern corporation accounting. $1.25. Powers.

Machen, A. W. Treatise on the federal corporation tax law of 1909. $1.50.—Treatise on the modern law of corporations. 2 v. **$12 net. Little, B. & Co.

Mason, A: L. Corporations and social changes. (Priv. pr.) A: L. Mason.

Meade, E: S. Corporation finance. $2 net. Appleton.

Michigan. Modern law of general business corporations. $4. Drake Law Bk.

Missouri. Law governing manufacturing and business corporations. $4.50. Nixon-J.

Moody's manual of railroads and corporation securities, 1908. $10; $12. Moody Corporation.

Morrison, R. S., *and* De Soto, E. D. Corporation manual of statute laws of Colorado. $3. Courtright.

New Mexico. Kanen's corporation laws. $7. Morning Journ.

CORPORATIONS.—*Continued.*

New York. Manual of corporation law. $3.50. Ronald Press.

Noyes, W. C. Treatise on the law of intercorporate relations. $6. Little, B. & Co.

Overland, M. U. Manual of the statutory corporation law: classified corporation laws of all the states. $4, incl. 1909 supplement. Ronald Press.

Parker, J: S. Draft of by-laws for a New Jersey corporation.—Draft of by-laws for a New York corporation. ea., 50 c.—Where and how; corporation hdbk. $1; 50 c. Broun-G.

Parker, J: S., *ed.* Corporation manual. $6.50. Corp. Manual.

Parker, W: R. P., *and* Clark, G: M. Canadian company law. $6.50. Cromarty.

Putney, A. H. Corporations. $4.80. Cree.

Rumsey, J. S. On corporations. $6.30. Banks & Co.

Sells, E. W. Corporate management compared with government control. gratis. Haskins & S.

Sullivan, J: J. American corporations. $2 net. Appleton.

Thompson, S. D. Commentaries on the law of private corporations. In 7 v. ea., $6. Bobbs-M.

Tompkins, L. J. Selection of cases on the law of private corporations. $6. Baker, V. & Co.

United States. *Dept. of Commerce and Labor. Bu. of Corporations.* Taxation of corporations. '09(Ag) 8°, pap., 20 c.

United States. *Office of Internal Revenue.* Law and regulations relative to excise tax on corporations, joint stock companies, associations and insurance companies; imposed by authority of section 38, act of Aug. 5, 1909; Dec. 3, 1909. '09, [1910.] (Mr) 16 p. 8°, pap.

Warren, E. H., *ed.* Select cases and other authorities on the law of private corporations. $5. E: H: Warren.

Warren, E: H., *and* Hildebrand, I. P. Select cases and other authorities on the law of private corporations. Texas supp. $4. E: H: Warren.

White, F. Corporations; cont. the laws as amended to Jan. 1, 1910. $7. Baker, V. & Co.

See also Bankruptcy;—Bonds;—Commercial law; —Investments; — Monopolies;—Municipal government;—Municipal ownership;—Railroads; —Stocks; — Taxation; — Trusts;—*also* names of countries and states.

Corpus Schwenckfeldianorum. Schwenckfeld von Ossig, C. v. 1. *$7.50 net. Lemcke.

Correct chicken culture. Sperle, C: H. gratis. C: H. Sperle.

Correct social usage; course of instruction in good form, style and deportment, by eighteen distinguished authors. 11th rev. ed. 2 v. '09(Ap) c. il. 8°, $1.95; per set, $2.95; hf. leath., $3.95. H. A. Lewis.

Correction and prevention. Henderson, C: R., *ed.* 4 v. ea., $2.50; per set, $10. Charities' Pub.

Corrector of destinies. Post, M. D. $1.50. Clode.

Correggio, Antonio Allegri da.
Correggio. '09(Jl3) il. 8°, (Classics in art ser.) *$3 net, boxed. Brentano's.
Masterpieces; 60 reproductions from the original paintings. '08(O24) T. (Painters' ser.) leath., *75 c. net; paper, *25 c. net. Stokes.

Correlation of efficiency in mathematics and efficiency in other subjects. Rietz, H. L. 35 c. Univ. of Ill.

Correlation of the physician and the layman. Drewry, W: F. (Priv. pr.) Williams Pr.

CORRESPONDENCE.
See Commercial correspondence;—Letter-writing;—Letters (Correspondence);—Stenography.

Corrie who? Foster, M. †$1.50. Small.

CORROSION.
See Iron;—Steel.

Corruption in American politics and life. Brooks, R. C. $1.25 net. Dodd.

CORSAIRS.
See Buccaneers.

Corsan, G: Hebden.
At home in the water; swimming, diving, life saving, water sports, natatoriums. '10 (Ag13) c. il. D. 75 c.; pap., 50 c. Y. M. C. A.

CORSICA (*Island of*).
Renwick, G: Romantic Corsica. *$3 net. Scribner.
Young, E. Corsica. *75 c. net. Macmillan.

Corsican (The). *See* Napoleon I.

Cort, Howard R.
Donakin circus; from Don's book of Donakins. '09(D25) c. il. in col. obl. O. bds., $1. Stokes.

Cortes, Fernando.
Letters of Cortes: the five letters of relation from Fernando Cortes to the Emperor Charles V.; tr. and ed., with a biograph. introd. and notes comp. from orig. sources, by Fs. A: MacNutt. '08 (My2) c. 2 v., il. pors. maps, plans, O. hf. cl., **$10 net. Putnam.

CORTES, Fernando.
MacNutt, F. A: Fernando Cortes and the conquest of Mexico. **$1.35 net. Putnam.

Corthurnulus. Arnold, E: V. *35 c. net. Macmillan.

Corwin, Minnie Lahr.
Ethel Wright; or, only a music teacher. '09(N20) c. 12°, $1. Cochrane.

Corwin, R: Warren, M.D.
Modern model school house on the unit plan. '08(S) 32 p. il. plans, 8°, pap., 10c. R. W. Corwin.

Cory, C: Barney.
Birds of Illinois and Wisconsin. '09(O) 764 p. il. (Field Museum of Natural History pubs.; Zoölogical ser.) pap., $4. Field Museum.
Birds of the Leeward Islands, Caribbean Sea. '09, [1910.] (F) 193+255 p. map, 8°, (Field Museum of Natural History pub., Ornithological ser.) 50 c. Field Museum.
Bibliography (2 p.).

Cory, G: E:
Rise of South Africa; hist. of the origin of South African colonization and of its development toward the east from the earliest times to 1857. In 4 v. v. 1, From the earliest times to the year 1820. '10 (Mr12) il. map, plans, O. $5. Longmans.

Cory, Vivian, ["Victoria Cross."]
Eternal fires. '10(Ap30) c. D. $1.50. M. Kennerley.
Five nights. '08(Je) $1.50. M. Kennerley.
Paula; a sketch from life. '08(O) c. 223 p. 12°, 75 c. Fenno.
Religion of Evelyn Hastings. '08(D) 9-291 p. 12°, $1.50. M. Kennerley.

Coryell, J: Russell, ["Nick Carter."]
Old homestead; novelized from Denman Thompson's great play. Authorized ed. '08(Ap25) c. il. 12°, 75 c. G: W. Dillingham.
See also Adventures at sea.—Boys on the railroad.

Cosby, Arth. Fortunatus, comp.
See New York [City.] Code of ordinances.

Cosen, Jos. E.
Socialism for students. '09(D25) c. S. 50 c. Kerr.

Cosgrove, Mrs. Henrietta Clarissa Jackson, ["Henri Clarise."]
Amateur art: oil and water color painting, painting on China, modeling in clay and ware painting, pyrography or burnt wood etching. [22d ed. rev.] '09(Ag14) c. il. 8°, $1. Donnelley.

Cosgrove, J: Jos.
History of sanitation. '09(My15) c. il. O. $1.50. Standard Sanitary Mfg.
Plumbing estimates and contracts. '10 (Ag6) c. tabs., 8°, $3. Standard Sanitary Mfg.
Plumbing plans and specifications. '10 (Ag6) c. il. plans, 8°, $3. Standard Sanitary Mfg.
Sewage purification and disposal. '09(Je5) c. figs. O. $3. Standard Sanitary Mfg.
Wrought-pipe drainage systems. '10 (My7) c. il. tabs., O. $2. Standard Sanitary Mfg.

Cosimo, Angelo di.
See Bronzino.

COSMETICS.
See Beauty (*personal*).

Cosmic consciousness. Burke, R: M. $4.25. Progress Co.

Cosmic corals. *See* Boyle, Mrs. M. M. R. Quest of the Christ.

Cosmo collection; consisting of duotone and hand-colored reproductions of the most famous paintings and sculpture from all schools of the world; editor-in chief, G: Hall Baker; art editors, Harry W. Watrous, Will H. Low. Complete in 10 v. '09(Ap17) c. Q. ea., $3.75; full vellum, $5; full mor., $10. Cosmo.

Cosmographiæ introductio. Waldseemüller, M. $5. U. S. Cath.

COSMOLOGY.
See Universe.

Cosmos (The). Zaring, P. A. $1.50 net. Badger.

Cosmos and dia-cosmos. Snider, D. J. $1.50. Sigma.

Cossio, Aluigi.
Sulla "Vita nuova" di Dante; studio critico-letterario. '08(D12) il. O. $3. Stechert.

COST.
Church, A. H. Production factors in cost accounting and works management. $2. Engineering Mag.
Gillette, H. P. Hdbk. of cost data for contractors and engineers. $5 net. M. C. Clark.
Gillette, H. P., *and* Dana, R: T. Cost keeping and management engineering. $3.50. M. C. Clark.
Goodwin, F. E. Cost accounting pathfinder. 50 c. Midland Pub. Co.
Hathaway, C: E., *and* Griffith, J. B. General expense and cost summaries. 50 c. Am. Sch. Corr.
Nichols, W: G. Cost finding. 50 c. Am. Sch. Corr.
Unckless, L. How to find manufacturing costs and selling costs. $1.50. Modern Methods.
Wildman, J: R. Cost accounting problems. $3. Accountancy.
See also Building (*construction*); — Knitting; — Prices;—Wages.

Cost accounting in a bank. Thomas, F. W. $2. Bankers' Pub., (O.)
Cost, capitalization and estimated value of American railways. Thompson, S. 50 c. S. Thompson.
Cost of a crown. Benson, R. H. $1 net. Longmans.
Cost of Christian conquest. Brewster, W: N. *35 c. net. Jennings.
Cost of cleanness. Richards, *Mrs.* E. H. S. $1. Wiley.
Cost of food. Richards, *Mrs.* E. H. S. $1. Wiley.

COST OF LIVING.
Massachusetts. *Commission on the Cost of Living.* Rept. of the Commission on the Cost of Living. gratis. Wright & P.
Massachusetts. *Commission on High Cost of Living.* Wages and prices of commodities. Gov. Pr. Off.
Meyer, H. H: B., *comp.* Select list of references on the cost of living and prices. 15 c. U. S., Supt. of Docs.
United States. *Bu. of Statistics. Dept. of Agriculture.* Wages and prices of commodities; letter from the Secretary of Agriculture transmitting results of the inquiry into the prices paid by consumers and prices paid by retail dealers to wholesale dealers or producers for eggs, butter, milk and chickens in the last week in January, 1910, in representative cities of the United States. '10(Ag) 14 p. 8°
United States. *Dept. of Commerce and Labor. Bu. of Labor.* Wages and prices of commodities; cost of living of the working classes in the principal industrial towns of Great Britain, the German empire, France and Belgium. '10(Ag) 87 p. tabs., 8°.
United States. *Dept. of Commerce and Labor. Bu. of Labor.* Wages and prices of commodities; digest of recent statistical publications relative to prices and wages and hours of labor in Austria, Belgium, Bulgaria, Finland, France, Italy, Norway, Sweden, and the United Kingdom. '10(Ag) 135 p. tabs. 8°.
United States. *Dept. of Commerce and Labor. Bu. of Labor.* Wages and prices of commodities; wages and hours of labor of union carpenters in the United States and in English-speaking foreign countries during the first quarter of 1910. '10(Ag) 18 p. tabs., 8°.
United States. *Dept. of State.* Wages and prices abroad; repts. from consular officers of the U. S., giving present retail and wholesale prices of certain commodities and prices obtaining in 1900; together with salaries paid various classes of government employees. 4 v. '10(Ag) tabs., 8°.
United States. Investigation relative to wages and prices of commodities.
United States. Rept. of the Select Committee on Wages and Prices of Commodities. '10(Ag) tabs., 8°. Gov. Pr. Off.
See also Prices.

Cost of living to railways. Harden, E: W. E: W. Harden.
Cost of mining. Finlay, J. R. *$5 net. McGraw-H.
Cost of our national government. Ford, H. J. $1.60 net. Lemcke.
Cost reduction. Gesundheit, M. [Not for sale.] M. Gesundheit.

Costa, Alfonso Arbib-.
See Arbib-Costa, Alfonso.

COSTA RICA, Central America.
International Bureau of American Republics. Costa Rica. (Add. pubs. for price.) Int. Bu. Am. Republics.
See also Birds.

COSTANOAN LANGUAGE.
See Indians.

Costanso, Mighuel.
Narrative of the Portola expedition, 1769-1770; ed. by Adolph van Hemert-Engert and F: J. Teggart. '10(Ap) c. 69 p. O. (Publications of the Academy of Pacific Coast History.) pap., 50 c. Univ. of Cal.

Costantini, Mme. Anna.
Ragna; novel. '10(Ap30) c. D. $1.50. Sturgis & W.

Costello, F: Hankerson.
Sure-dart: a story of strange hunters and stranger game in the days of monsters. '09(O9) c. il. D. $1.25. McClurg.

Costello, Mary.
Peggy the millionaire. '10(Jl) 4+144 p. front. 35 c. net. Herder.

Costigan, G: Purcell, jr.
Cases on wills, descent, and administration; sel. from decis. of Eng. and Am. courts. '10(S) c. 781 p. (Amer. case-book ser.) $4.50. West Pub.
Hdbk. on American mining law. '08(D) c. 14+765 p. O. (Hornbook ser.) $3.75. West Pub.

Costin, W: Wilberforce.
Introduction to the genetic treatment of the faith-consciousness in the individual. '09 (Mr27) 8°, *65 c. net. Williams & W.

COSTUME.
Ashdown, *Mrs.* C: H: British costume during 19 centuries. $4.50 net. Stokes.
Baker, W: H: Dict. of men's wear. $2; $3. W: H: Baker, (Cleveland.)
Brooklyn Public Library. Reading and reference list on costume. gratis. Brooklyn Lib.
Clinch, G: English costume from prehistoric times to the end of the eighteenth century. $2.50 net. McClurg.
Earle, *Mrs.* A. M. Two centuries of costume in America, 1620-1820. $2.50 net. Macmillan.
Lee, E. B. Talks on successful gowning. $1.50. E. B. Lee.
McClellan, E. Historic dress in America, 1800-1870. $6 net. Jacobs.
Saunders, C. Costume in Roman comedy. **$1 net. Lemcke.
See also Dressmaking;—Hygiene.

Costume of prelates of the Catholic church. Nainfa, J: A. F. P. *$1.50 net. Murphy.

Cotes, Mrs. Everard.
See Cotes, *Mrs.* Sara Jeannette Duncan.

Cotes, Hornor.
The counterpart. '09(N) c. 324 p. col. front. 12°, $1.50. Macaulay.

Cotes, Mrs. Sara Jeannette Duncan, [Mrs. Everard Cotes.]
The burnt offering. '10(Je18) D. $1.50. Lane.
Cousin Cinderella: [a Canadian girl in London.] '08(S12) c. D. †$1.50. Macmillan.

Cotonio, Thdr., comp.
See Louisiana. Annotations.

COTSWOLDS (The), England.
Duckworth, F. R. G. The Cotswolds. *$2.50 net. Macmillan.

Cottage and congregate institutions for children. Hart, H. H. $1; 50 c. Charities Pub.

Cottage homes of England. Dick, S. *$7 net. Longmans.

Cottage pie. Lyons, A. N. $1.50. Lane.

COTTAGES.
See Architecture.

Cotte, Jules.
Sponge culture. '10(Je) 587-614 p. 8°. U. S., Supt. of Docs.
Bibliography (2 p.).

Cotter, Jos. Seamon.
White song and a black one. '09(O9) c. por. D. 50 c. J. S. Cotter.

Cotter's Saturday night. *See* Burns, Rob.

Cottingham, Wa. Horace.
Business success. '08(N14) c. D. bds., *75 c. net; leath., *$1.25 net. Dodge.

Cotton, C:
See Walton, Izaak.

Cotton, Fassett Allen.
See Fisher, Martin L.

Cotton, Frederic Jay.
Dislocations and joint-fractures. '10(Ag) 654 p. il. 8°, $6. Saunders.

Cotton, Howard Preble.
We three. '10(D31) il. 12°, $1.50. C. M. Clark.

COTTON, John.
Boston. First Church. Exercises at the unveiling of the John Cotton memorial in the Berkley St. edifice of the First church in Boston. $1. C. H. Schriver.

Cotton, J: Storrs.
Improvement of pastures in eastern New York and the New England states. '10 (My) 10 p. pls. 8°, (U. S., Dept. of Agriculture, Bu. of Plant Industry, circular.) U. S., Supt. of Docs.

Cotton, W: Edn.
See Schroeder, Ernest C:

COTTON.
Bowman, F. H. Structure of the cotton fibre in its relation to technical application. *$2.75 net. Macmillan.
Burkett, C: W: Algodón, su cultivo, elaboración y mercadería: [cotton.] $1.50. S. F. de Velasco.
Cook, O. F. Local adjustment of cotton varieties.—Mutative reversions in cotton. —Origin of Hindi cotton. U. S., Supt. of Docs.
Delbridge, C: L. Cotton calculator, by 16ths and 5 points, 300 to 699 pounds. $3.50. Delbridge.
Fortune, W: H: Costs in currency of British, German, French and Austrian cotton goods. $4. W: H: Fortune.
Goodrich, C: L. Profitable cotton farm. U. S., Supt. of Docs.
Hedrick, C: C. Cotton spinning. $3. Am. Sch. Corr.
Heylin, H: B. Cotton weaver's handbook: pract. guide to the construction and casting of cotton fabrics, with studies of designs. *$2.50 net. Lippincott.
International Bu. of Am. Repubs. Cotton. U. S., Supt. of Docs.
Knapp, S. A. Cotton; greatest of cash crops. U. S., Supt. of Docs.
McArthur, N. J. Pen pictures of standard cotton grades. $1. Mutual Pub. Co.
McCrary & Johnson's rules and instructions for grading cotton. (Add. pubs. for price.) Standard Cotton.
Martin, H: D. Progress and profit for mill men [cotton manufacture]. $1. H: D. Martin.
Miller, T: S. American cotton system historically treated. $1.50. T. S. Miller.
Noble, I: C. Cotton spinners' companion. $1. I: C. Noble.
Peake, R. J. Cotton from the raw material to the finished product. 50 c. Pitman.
Rept. of special committee of the New Orleans Cotton Exchange on discrimination in transportation rates and other burdens upon the cotton commerce of the city of New Orleans. '09, [1910.] (Je) 31 p. O. pap. W: B. Thompson.
Shepperson, A. B. Cotton facts. $1. A. B. Shepperson.
Taylor, J: T. Cotton weaving and designing. $2.50. Longmans.
Textile World Record. Kinks for cotton superintendents. (Sold to subscribers of *Textile World Record* only.) Lord & N.

COTTON.—*Continued.*

Thompson, W: B. American distributing markets for American cotton.—Analysis and exposition of the Scott Anti-Cotton Future Bill.—Narrowing of the cotton market. gratis. W: B. Thompson.

United States. *Dept. of Commerce and Labor. Bureau of Census.* Cotton production, 1908.—Instructions to special agents; cotton statistics. '09, [1910.] (Mr) 21 p. 16°.—Supply and distribution of cotton for the year ending August 31, 1909.

Watkins, J. L. King Cotton: historical and statistical review. $1.50. * J. L. Watkins.

See also Fertilizers;—New Orleans Cotton Exchange;—Stocks;—Warehouses.

COTTON-SEED PRODUCTS.

Herty, C: H. Per cent. tables for oil in cottonseed products, with method of analysis. $2. C: H. Herty.

Singleton, T. W. Cotton-seed-buyer's book. $3.50. T. W. Singleton.

Soule, A. M. Feeding of cotton seed meal and hulls. (Add. pub. for price.) B. F. Taylor.

Cotton shippers' book; comprising a directory in the American South of cotton buyers, cotton shippers, cotton f. o. b. shippers, cotton exporters and cotton merchants; also cotton selling agents in New England. '08, [1909.] (F) c. 8°. (Add. pubs. for price.) Nelson Pub.

Cotton-Walker, Frances M.

Cloister to court: scenes from the life of Charlotte of Bourbon, Abbess of Jouarre, Princess of Orange. '09(My22) front. D. $1.40. Longmans.

Cottrell, Marie, pseud.

See Harlan, *Mrs.* M. R.

Couch, Sir Arth. T: Quiller-, ["Q."]

Lady Good-for-nothing. '10(O8) c. D. $1.20 net. Scribner.

Oxford book of ballads. '10(D24) D. $1.90. Oxford Univ.

Sleeping beauty and other fairy tales from the old French retold; il. in col. by Edm. Dulac. '10(D10) 4°, $5 net; ed. de luxe, vel., $20 net. Doran.

True Tilda. '09(Ag28) c. D. $1.50. Scribner.

Couch, Stata B.

In the shadow of the peaks. '09(D) 319 p. 12°, $1.50. Cochrane.

Coufopoulos, Demetrius.

Guide to Constantinople. 3d ed. '08(Je27) il. maps, 16°, *$1.25 net. Macmillan.

COUGHS.

See Tuberculosis.

ulevain, Pierre de.

See Favre de Coulvain, *Mlle.*

Coulson, Constance J. D.

Korea. '10(D24) col. il. 12°, (Peeps at many lands ser.) 75 c. net. Macmillan.

Coulter, J: G.

See Coulter, J: Merle.

Coulter, J: Lee.

Organization among the farmers of the United States; pap. '09, [1910.] (Mr) 28 p. 8°, (Yale Review reprints.) 10 c. Yale Pub.

Coulter, J: Merle.

New manual of botany of the central Rocky Mountains (vascular plants); rev. by Aven Nelson. '10(Ja8) c. O. $2.50. Am. Bk.

—, Barnes, C: Reid, and Cowles, H: Chandler.

Textbook of botany for colleges and universities. v. 1, Morphology and physiology. '10(O8) c. il. O. $2.. Am. Bk.

—, and Chamberlain, C: Jos.

Morphology of gymnosperms. '10(O22) c. il. O. $4 net. Univ. of Chic.

— and J: G., and Patterson, Alice Jean.

Pract. nature study and elem. agriculture. '09(My22) c. D. $1.35. Appleton.

Coulton, G: Gordon.

Chaucer and his England. '08(S26) il. por. O. *$3.50 net. Putnam.

Council sermon. Allan, W: T. 5 c. Clark Pub.

Councilman, W: T:

Methods and the object of state examinations. '09, [1910.] (Ja) 15 p. 8°, pap., gratis. Am. Medical.

Counsels by the way. Van Dyke, H: J. **$1. Crowell.

Count and the congressman. Harrison, *Mrs.* C. C. 75 c. Cupples & L.

Count of Monte Cristo. *See* Dumas, Alexandre.

Counterfeit citizen. Scudder, S. $1.50. B'way Pub.

Counterpart (The). Cotes, H. $1.50. Macaulay.

COUNTERPOINT.

Bridge, J. F: Counterpoint. 75 c. Ditson.

Goetschius, P. Exercises in elem. counterpoint. $1.50 net. Schirmer.

York, F. L. Text-book in simple strict counterpoint. $1.25. Ditson.

See also Harmony;—Music.

Countersign (The). Jones, C. P. $1.50. Badger.

Countess Diane. Rowland, H: C. †$1.25. Dodd.

Country band. Shute, H: A: $1. Badger.

Country boy. Davenport, H. C. $1.25 net. G: W: Dillingham.

Country Contributor, pseud.

See Strauss, Juliet Virginia.

Country handbooks; ed. by Harry Roberts. il. S. *$1 net. Lane.

—Boston. Vet book.

—Green. Small holding.

—Harrison *and* Douglas. Photographer's hdbk.

Country home lib. il. O. **$1.50 net. McClure.

—Bennett. Vegetable garden.

COUNTRY LIFE.

"C[2]," *pseud.* Back to the land; [search for country home in England.] $1.50 net. Longmans.

Hays, W. M. Education for country life. U. S., Supt. of Docs.

Plunkett, *Sir* H. C. Rural life problem of the United States. $1.25 net. Macmillan.

Rawnsley, *Mrs.* W. Country sketches for city dwellers. *$3 net. Macmillan.

COUNTRY LIFE.—*Continued.*
Standish, B. H. Country life and agricultural education. In 3 v. $2.25; [also] set of charts of colored il. to accompany above, $10. Caspar.
Thomas, E: British country life in autumn and winter.—British country life in spring and summer. ea., *$3.75 net. Doran.
Ver Beck, H: R. Garden in the wilderness. **$1.50 net. Baker & T.
Williams, M. M. Landlover and his land. (Priv. pr.) E. W. Sells.
See also Education;—Gardens and gardening;—Nature;—Outdoor life;—Schools.

Country life education ser. il. 8°. Ginn.
—Davenport. Principles of breeding. $2.50.
—Duggar. Fungous diseases of plants. $2.
—Hopkins. Soil fertility and permanent agriculture. $2.75.

Country life lib. il. 8°. Scribner.
—English vegetable garden. *$3 net.
—Jackson. Toys of other days. *$7.50 net.
—Jekyll. Children and gardens. *$2 net.
—Keyser. French household cooking. *60 c. net.
—Meyer. Rock and water gardens. $2.

Country neighbors. Brown, A. $1.20 net. Houghton M.
Country sketches. Pollock, M. I. 50 c. Cochrane.
Country sketches for city dwellers. Rawnsley, *Mrs.* W. *$3 net. Macmillan.
Country sweetheart. Russell, D. 75 c. Rand, McN. & Co.
Country (The) to which you go. '10(My) 12 p. il. pors. map, S. pap., gratis. Y. M. C. A.
Country walks about Florence. Hutton, E: $1.50. Scribner.

Countryman, Carl Chapin.
Three senses; a few poems. '08, [1909.] (Mr) c. 11-95 p. 24°, 50 c.; leath., 75 c.; pap., 25 c. C. C. Countryman.

County coast ser. O. Stokes.
—Dutt. Norfolk and Suffolk coast. $2.25 net.
—Heath. South Devon and Dorset coast. $2.25 net.
—Salmon. Cornwall coast. $2.25 net.

County examiner. Lusby, J. W: bds., $1. Teachers' Supply.
County lieutenancies and the army, 1803-1804. Fortescue, J: W: *$3 net. Macmillan.
COUNTY PALATINE of Durham, Eng.
See England.

Coupin, Henri Eugène Victor, and Lea, J:
Wonders of animal ingenuity. '10(Ja1) 12°, 75 c. Lippincott.
Coupon bonds. Trowbridge, J: T. 50 c. Hurst.

COURAGE.
Green, T: E. In praise of valor. $3; $5. Torch Press.
Haddock, F. C. Culture of courage. $3. Power-Bk.

Courage of Captain Plum. Curwood, J. O. †$1.50. Bobbs-M.
Courage of Christ. Schuyler, H: C. *50 c. net. P: Reilly.

Courlander, Alphonse.
Henry in search of a wife. '09(O23) D. $1.50. Brentano's.
Uncle Polperro. '10(D31) 12°, $1.35 net. Brentano's.

Cours de français et d'allmand; ed. by D. L. Savory. D. Oxford Univ.
—Chouville. Histoires courtes et longues. 60 c.
—Dumas. Alexandre Dumas (père). 50 c.

Cours scientifique de l'analyse du caractère. Segno, A. V. $5.75. Chirological Coll.

Coursault, Jesse Harliaman.
Learning process; or, educational theory implied in theory of knowledge. '08 (Mr21) 8°, (Columbia Univ., Teachers' Coll. contribs. to education.) *$1 net. Teachers' Coll.

Course in dyeing for garment dyers. Prag. E: $5. Modern Dyer.
Course of religious instruction, Institute of the Brothers of the Christian Schools. 12°. McVey.
—Chrysostom John. Manual of Christian doctrine. $1.

Course of study and teachers' hdbk. in the common literature of life. Ware, A. 40 c. San F. St. Normal.
Course of study in language. McFadden, E. B. 55 c.; 30 c. San F. St. Normal.
Court-Harmon girls. Smith, *Mrs.* E. T. $1.50. Dutton.

COURT-HOUSES.
See Ventilation.

Court life in China. Headland, I: T. *$1.50 net. Revell.
Court of Alexander III. Lothrop, A. S. $1.50 net. Winston.
Court of boyville. White, W: A. $2. Macmillan.
Court of inquiry. Richmond. *Mrs.* G. L. S. *$1, fixed. Doubleday, P.
Court of Louis XIII. Patmore, K. A. *$3.50 net. Brentano's
Court of Lucifer. Gallizier, N. $1.50. L. C. Page.
Court of Russia. Hodgetts, E: A. B. 2 v. *$6 net. Scribner.

Court ser. of French memoirs; ed. by E. Jules Méras. il. D. Sturgis & W.
—Cléry. Royal family in the Temple Prison. $1.50.
—Elliott. During the Reign of Terror. $1.50 net.
—Léonard. Recollections. *$1.50 net.

COURT TENNIS.
See Tennis.

Courthope, W: J:
Consideration of Macaulay's comparison of Dante and Milton; from the proceedings of the British Academy. v. 3. '09(Ja23) O. pap., 40 c. Oxford Univ.
Hist. of English poetry. In 6 v. v. 5, The constitutional compromise of the 18th century; v. 6, The romantic movement in English poetry. '10(Ap9) 12°, ea., $3.25 net. Macmillan.

Courtin'. *See* Lowell, Ja. Russell.

COURTS.
Jessup, H: W. Law and practice in the surrogates' courts in the state of New York. $10. Banks.

COURTS.—*Continued.*
Long, J. R. Outline of the jurisdiction and procedure of the federal courts. $1.50. Michie.
New York [State.] Court rules. $4.50. Banks.
Owen, R. L. Establishment of the probation system in United States courts. U. S., Supt. of Docs.
Smith, F. C. Court to court procedure with forms. $5.50; $5.75. Fiske & Co.
See also **Chancery;—Family;—Juvenile courts;—Law;—Pleading and practice;—*also* Pennsylvania;—United States Supreme Court;—*also* names of states.**
Courts and camps of the Italian renaissance. Hare, C. *$2.50 net. Scribner.
COURTS-MARTIAL.
Davis, G: B. Treatise on the military law of the United States; together with the practice and procedure of courts-martial. $7 net. Wiley.
Dudley, E. S. Military law and the procedure of courts-martial. $2.50 net. Wiley.
Courts of the temple. Kelman, J. 35 c. net. Revell.
Courtship of Miles Standish. *See* Longfellow, H: Wadsworth.—Poe, Edg. Allan. The raven.
Courtship under contract. Eagar, J. H. L. $1.20 net. Health-Culture.
Courvoisier Clarice Town.
Spots; or, 202 cleansers. '10(D31) 25 c. net; Tomove ed., $2; Craftsman ed., $3 net. P. Elder.
Cousin, J: W.
Short biographical dict. of English literature. '10(Ap23) 16°, (Everyman's lib.) 35 c. net; leath., 70 c. net. Dutton.
Cousin, Victor.
La société française au XVIIe siècle; ed. by Leon Delbos. '09(D4) por. S. (Oxford higher French ser.) $1.15. Oxford Univ.
Cousin Cinderella. Cotes, *Mrs.* S. J. D. †$1.50. Macmillan.
Cousin Kate. Davies, H. H: 50 c. W. H. Baker.
Cousin Phillis. *See* Gaskell, *Mrs.* Eliz. Cleghorn Stevenson.
Cousin Pons. *See* Balzac, Honoré de.
Cousin Tom. Meyers, R. C. P. *25 c. net. Penn Pub. Co.
Coussens, Penrhyn Wingfield, ed. and comp.
Poems children love. '08(N14) c. D. $1.25: leath., $2. Dodge.
Couts, C: Orie.
Cleft grafting. '10(Je18) c. il. 16°, 50 c. C: O. Couts.
Covenant Vivien. *See* Chevalerie Vivien.
COVENTRY, Eng.
Woodhouse, F: W. Churches of Coventry. *60 c. net. Macmillan.
Coverley papers. *See* Addison, Jos.
Covert, Clermont Calvert, and Ellsworth, C. E.
Water-supply investigations in the Yukon-Tanana region, Alaska, 1907 and 1908; Fairbanks, Circle and Rampart districts. '09(Jl) 108 p. il. maps, 8°, (U. S. Geological Survey, Water-supply paper.) pap. (Add. Superintendent for price.)
Covert-side courtship. Reeve, K. R. $1.50. Lippincott.

COW.
Ayrshire Breeders' Association. Ayrshire cow. [1910] (F) c. '09. 19 p. il. 16°, gratis. Ayrshire Breeders.
Maynall, G. Cows, cowhouses and milk. $1. A. Eger.
See also **Milk;—Tuberculosis;—Veterinary medicine and surgery.**
Cowan, Rob. Ernest, and Dunlap, Boutwell, comps.
Bibliography of the Chinese question in the United States. '09(Ag7) c. Q. bds., *$1.40. A. M. Robertson.
COWBIRD.
Grinnell, J. New cowbird of the genus *molothrus.* 5 c. Univ. of Cal.
Cowboy cavalier. Morse, H. C. $1.50. C. M. Clark.
Cowboy lyrics. Carr, R. V. (Add. author for price.) Conkey.
Cowboy songs. Lomax, J: A., *comp.* $1.50 net. Sturgis & W.
Cowell, Alex. Tyng.
Tactics at Gettysburg as descrbed by participants in the battle. '10(Ag) c. 81 p. il. 12°, 25 c. A. T. Cowell.
Cowen, B: Rush.
Abraham Lincoln; by one who knew him. '09(F13) bds., *$1 net. Clarke.
Cowen, Jos.
Speeches on the Near Eastern question; foreign and imperial affairs, and on the British Empire; rev. by his daughter. '09(Mr13) por. O. $1. Longmans.
Cowing, Rufus Billings.
Speculative transactions as affected by recent New York legislation. '08(D) c. 22 p. 8°, gratis. Cowing, W. & W.
Cowles, H: Chandler.
See Coulter, J: Merle.
Cowles, W: Lyman, ed.
Selections from Ennius, Catullus, Tibullus, and Propertius, with parallel passages from Horace, Ovid and Martial. '09 (My22) c. il. D. 60 c. W: L. Cowles.
Cowley, Arth. Ernest, ed.
Samaritan liturgy. In 2 v. '10(My14) O. $19.25. Oxford Univ.
Cowley, Eliz. Buchanan.
Plane curves of the eighth order with two real four fold points having distinct tangents and with no other point singularities. '08, [1909.] (Mr) 23 p. il. 8°. (Not for sale.) New Era Print.
Cowley, Matthias Foss, ed.
Wilford Woodruff, fourth president of the Church of Jesus Christ of Latter-day Saints; hist. of his life and labors as recorded in his daily journals. '09(D4) c. il. por. 8°, $3.50. Deseret News.
Cowper, W:
Letters: a selection; ed. by E: Verrall Lucas. '08(D) 38+511 p. 16°, (World's classics.) 40 c.; leath., 75 c. Oxford Univ.
See also Gray, T:
Cowperthwaite, Allen Corson.
Text-book of materia medica and therapeutics, characteristic, analytical and comparative. 10th ed., with an appendix, enl., incl. new remedies. '09(N) c. 17+864 p. 8°, $5. Boericke & T.

Cox, F. G. Snead-.
See Snead-Cox, F. G.

Cox, Florence Tinsley.
Chronicles of Rhoda. '09(O2) c. il. D. †$1.25. Small.

Cox, Herbert Randolph.
Eradication of bindweed, or wild morning-glory. '09(O) 19 p. il. 8°, (U. S., Dept. of Agriculture, Farmers' bull.) pap.

Cox, J: Harrington.
Knighthood, in germ and in flower; the Anglo-Saxon epic, Beowulf, and the Arthurian tale, Sir Gawein and the Green Knight; tr. from orig. sources and adptd. for use in the home, the school, and pupils' reading circles. '10(O1) c. il. D. $1.25. Little, B. & Co.
Literature in the common schools. New ed. '08(S19) c. 12°, **90 c. net. Little, B. & Co.

Cox, Mrs. Marian Metcalf.
Crowds and the veiled woman. '10(Ap2) c. D. $1.50. Funk.

Cox, Palmer.
Brownie Clown of Brownie Town. '08(D5) c. il. obl. S. bds., $1. Century Co.
Brownies' latest adventures. '10(O15) c. il. Q. bds., $1.50. Century Co.

Cox, Rob. Lynn.
Geographical distribution of the investments of life insurance companies; address del. at the bi-monthly meeting of the Association of Life Insurance Presidents at New York, April 2, 1909. '09(O9) fold. map, O. pap., gratis. Assoc. Life.
Impropriety of taxing returns to life insurance policy-holders: address del. at the 26th annual banquet of the Boston Life Underwriters' Assoc. at Boston, Mass., Feb. 16, 1909. '09(Jl) 6 p. 8°, pap., gratis. R. L. Cox.
Life insurance and legislation in 1909; rept. June 4, 1909. '09(S) 8 p. O. pap., gratis. Assoc. Life.
Taxation of life insurance in the U. S. 16 p. O. pap., gratis. Assoc. Life.

Cox, Thomas.
Reid, H. Thomas Cox. State Hist. Ia.

Cox, Rev. W: Ja. E:
Errors of Romanism. '08(Ja11) 12°, $1. Dearing.

Cox, W: T.
See Price, Overton Westfeldt.

Coxe, Macgrane.
Chancellor Kent at Yale, 1777-1781; a paper written for the *Yale Law Journal.* '09 (S) c. 3-53 p. il. por. 8°. (Priv. pr.) M. Coxe.

Coxe, Rob. Davison.
Legal Philadelphia; comments and memories. '08(My.) c. 253 p. D. (Add. pub. for price.) W: J. Campbell.

Coxhead, Marg. Duncan.
Mexico. '09(D25) col. il. map, O. (Romance of history ser.) **$2 net. Stokes.

Coyle, Dan., and Howe, F. J. O.
Electric cables, their construction and cost. '09(D18) il. 12°, limp leath., *$5 net. Spon.

Coyle, H., Mayhew, Thdr., and Hickey, Fk. S., comps.
Our church, her children and institutions: terse and timely articles by Cardinal Gibbons, E: P. Allen and many other writers of note. 3 v. '08(D) c. D. 4°, $8. Angel Press.

Coyle, Rob. McCurdy.
Fenceless France: the story of an automobile ride. '08(Ag8) c. il. 12°. [priv. pr.] Buchanan.

Coyote.
See Wolf.

Coyote-proof pasture experiment. Jardine, J. T. (Add. Superintendent for price.) U. S., Supt. of Docs.

Cozart, Winfield Forrest.
Mannaseh; story of mixed marriages. '09, [1910.] (Je) c. 8°, 25 c. W. F. Cozart.

Crabbe, G:
Poems: selection; arranged and ed. by Bernard H: Holland. New ed. '09 (N13) por. D. *$1 net. Longmans.
Poetical works; ed. by A. J. Carlyle and R. M. Carlyle. '09(Je19) por. (Oxford poets.) $1.25; Oxford India pap. ed., $1.75. Oxford Univ.

Crabtree, Harold.
Elem. treatment of the theory of spinning tops and gyroscopic motion. '09(Je5) il. figs. O. *$1.50 net. Longmans.

Crackerlings and caramels. Beazley, C: H. $1; 50 c. C: H. Beazley.

Craddock, C: Egbert, pseud.
See Murfree, Mary Noailles.

Cradle days of New York. MacAtamey, H. E., *comp.* 50 c. Drew & L.

Cradle lullabies. Field, E. 50 c. Canterbury Co.

Cradle of a poet. Godfrey, E., *pseud.* $1.50. Lane.

Cradle of the deep. Treves, *Sir* F: $2.50 net; *$4 net. Dutton.

Cradle of the rose. Owen, M. C. **$1.50 net. Harper.

Cradock, Mrs. H. C.
Care of babies. '08(Je27) il. 12°, *35 c. net. Macmillan.
Training of children; from cradle to school: guide for young mothers, teachers and nurses. '09(N6) il. D. *60 c. net. Macmillan.

Crafts, Sara Jane Timanus.
See Crafts, Wilbur Fisk.

Crafts, Rev. Wilbur Fisk.
Internationalism: [co-operation among nations.] 2d ed., rev. '08(D) 96 p. 12°, 40 c.; pap., 25 c. Int. Ref. Bu.
National perils and hopes; study based on current statistics and observations of a cheerful reformer. '10(S3) c. D. 50 c. net. F. M. Barton.

—, and others.
Intoxicating drinks and drugs in all lands and times. '10(Ja22) il. pors. facsim., D. 75 c. Int. Ref. Bu.

—, and Sara Jane Timanus, [Mrs. W. F. Crafts.]
World book of temperance. [Abridged ed.] '08(D) c. 128 p. il. 8°, 75 c.; pap., 35 c. Int. Ref. Bu.

Crafts.
See Fine arts.

Craftsman homes. Stickley, G. $2. G. Stickley.

Craftsman's Home Study Schools. First lessons in manual training and carpentry. '07, [1908.] (Mr.) c. 32 p. il. 8°. (Add. pubs. for price.) Craftsman's Home Study.

Craftsman's plant-book. Hatton, R: G. $7.50 net. Dutton.

Crag-nest. De Leon, T: C. $1.25. G: W. Dillingham.

Cragin, Edn. Bradford.
Essentials of gynecology, arranged in the form of questions and answers, prepared especially for students of medicine. 7th ed., thoroughly rev. by Fk. S. Mathews. '09, [1910.] (F) c. 9-232 p. il. 12°, (Saunders' question-compends.) $1. Saunders.

Cragin, Laura Ella.
Kindergarten stories for the Sunday school and home; New Testament ser. '10(S) il. 12°, $1.25 net. Doran.
Old Testament stories for little children. '10(N5) c. il. D. $1.25 net. Revell.

Craig, A. E. S.
Motor driving for a living. '08(Jl4) 12°, bds., 50 c. Spon.

CRAIG, Austin.
Harwood, W: S. Life and letters of Austin Craig. *$1.50 net. Revell.

Craig, C: Franklin, M.D.
Importance to the army of diseases transmitted by mosquitoes and methods for their prevention. '10(Ag) 17 p. 8°, gratis. Assoc. Military Surgeons.
Malarial fevers, hæmoglobinuric fever and blood protozoa of man. '09(S) c. 489 p. il. charts, 8°, *$4.50 net. Wood.

Craig, Clara E.
See Eaton, Amasa Mason.

Craig, Dora Belle, comp.
Catalogue of educational exhibits in the Washington Educational Building A. Y. P. Exposition. '10(Ja) 36 p. D. pap. Wash. Supt. Sch.

Craig, Gavin W:
Selected cases on water rights and irrigation law in California and western states. '10(F) c. O. $3. Bancroft-W.

Craig, Ja. Watt.
See Clayton, W: Brasher.

CRAIG, Lewis.
Thompson, L. N. Lewis Craig, the pioneer Baptist preacher. 35 c. Bapt. World.

Craig, Rob. S.
Making of Carlyle. '09(Ap10) por. O. *$4 net. Lane.

Craig Cameron. Sweet, F. H. 75 c. Standard Pub.

Craigie, W: A.
Scandinavian religion. '07, [1909.] (Ap) 8°, (Religions ancient and modern.) *40 c. net. Open Court.

Craigin, C. T.
See Neal, E. Virgil.

Craigin, Laura E.
Kindergarten stories for the Sunday-school and home. New ed. '09(D) il. 12°, (New Testament ser.) *$1.25 net. Doran.

Craik, Mrs. Dinah Maria Mulock, [Miss Mulock.]
Adventures of a brownie as told to my child. '08, [1909.] (Ap) c. 128 p. il. 8°, 50 c. McLoughlin.
John Halifax, gentleman. '08(O10) il. D. (Bowman's illustrated lib. of world-favorite books.) $1. Bowman.
John Halifax, gentleman. '08(O10) 12°, (Best books ser.) leath., *$1 net. Dutton.
Little lame prince and his travelling cloak. '08(Mr21) il. 12°, (Every boy's and every girl's ser.) *75 c. net. Macmillan.
Little lame prince and his travelling cloak. '09(O16) c. O. †$1.25. Rand, McN. & Co.

Craik, G: Lillie.
Manual of English literature. '09(Mr27) 16°, (Everyman's lib.) *35 c. net; leath., *70 c. net. Dutton.

Craik, Sir H:
Impressions of India. '08(Ag1) 12°, *90 c. net. Macmillan.

Crain, Arth. H.
Creation: a poem founded on the book of Genesis. 50 c. Hughes & Co.

CRALL FAMILY.
Allaben, F. Ancestry of Leander Howard Crall: monographs on the Crall, Haff, Beatty, [etc.] families. **$50 net. Grafton Press.

Cram, G: F.
Atlas of the world, ancient and modern; thoroughly rev., rewritten, and newly illustrated ed. by G: F. Cram, editorially assisted by Dr. Eugene Murray-Aaron. '08(Je13) c. il. maps, 4°, $12.50; hf. leath., $15; leath., $17.50. G: F. Cram.
Standard American railway system atlas of the world; accompanied by concise and orig. ready reference index. '10(Ap9) col. maps, f°, Business ed., $10.50 net; hf. mor., $12.50 net; leath., $15 net; World ed., $12.50 net; hf. mor., $15 net; leath., $20 net. G: F. Cram.
Superior reference atlas of North and South Dakota and the world. '08(N21) c. f°, (Add. pub. for price.) G: F. Cram.

Cram, Rev. Jacob.
Journal of a missionary tour through the new settlements of northern New Hampshire and Vermont; from the orig. manuscript. '09(Ap10) 8°, bds., $1.50. G: P. Humphrey.

Cram, Marshall Perley.
Fractionation of crude petroleum by capillary filtration. '08, [1910.] (Ap) 50 p. il. 8°, pap., 50 c. Johns Hopkins.
See also Gilpin, Jos. Elliott.

Cram, Ralph Adams.
Excalibur, an Arthurian drama. '09(Mr) c. 160 p. 8°, bds., $2; leath. $10. Badger.
—, ed. Christian art. 3 v. '09(D) il. 4°, *$15 net. Badger.

Cramp, Wa. S:
Across the arid zone. '10(D3) il. 12°, $1.50. C. M. Clark.
Beppo. '08(D26) il. 16°, 75 c. Small.
The biter. '09(N20) c. D. $1.50. C. M. Clark.
Heart of silence. '09(D) 7-325 p. 12°, $1.50. C. M. Clark.

Cramp, W:
Continuous current machine design. '10 (D) 8°, $2.50. Van Nostrand.

—, and Smith, C: F.
Vectors and vector diagrams, applied to the alternating current circuit. '09(F6) il. O. *$2.50 net. Longmans.

Crampton, C: Ward, M.D., comp.
Folk dance book for elementary schools, class room, playground, and gymnasium. '09(My22) c. Q. $1.50. Barnes.

Crampton, H: E:
Zoology. '08(F29) c. 8°, pap., 25 c. Macmillan.

Cran, Mrs. G:
A woman in Canada. '10(Ap2) il. por. O. $3 net. Lippincott.

Cran, Ja.
Machine blacksmithing. '09(S18) c. il. 8°, (Machinery's reference ser.) pap., 25 c. Indust. Press.

Cranbrook, Gathorne Hardy, Earl of.
Gathorne Hardy, first Earl of Cranbrook; memoir, with extracts from his diary and correspondence; ed. by the Hon. Alfr. E. Gathorne-Hardy. In 2 v. '10(Ap9) il. pors. O. $7 net. Longmans.

Crandall, C: H:
Songs from sky meadows: poems. '09 (My8) c. D. *$1 net. Outing.

Crandall, C: Lee.
The transition curve, by offsets and by deflection angles; [with this is bound his "Field book for railroad surveying."] 2d ed., rev. and enl. '09(D11) tabs., 12°, $2. Wiley.

—, and Barnes, Fred Asa.
Field book for railroad surveying. '10 (O22) c. il. 16°, mor., $2. Wiley.

Crandall, Harriet Eve.
First year English book. '08(Ag15) c. il. 16°, $1. Atkinson, M. & G.

Crandall, Mrs. Rosa Ruth Neil.
Neil family, Sweden-America, 1718-1908. '08, [1909.] (Je) 73 p. il. pors. 8°. (Add. author for price.) R. R. N. Crandall.

Crandall, Capt. Warren Dan.
Hist. of the ram fleet and the Mississippi marine brigade in the war of the Union on the Mississippi and its tributaries: story of the Ellets and their men; written and pub. under the auspices of their society of survivors. '08(Ap11) il. pors. 12°. $2.50. W. D. Crandall.

Crandon, Le Roy Goddard, M.D.
Surgical after-treatment. '10(Je) 803 p. il. $6 net; hf. mor., $7.50 net. Saunders.

Crane, Aaron Martin.
Search after ultimate truth; divine perfection inherent in man and in all creation. '10(Ap30) c. D. $1.50 net. Lothrop, L. & S.

Crane, D. B.
Book of the sweet pea. '09(N20) il. D. (Hdbks. of practical gardening.) *$1.50 net. Lane.

Crane, E: A., and Soderholtz, E. E.
Examples of colonial architecture in South Carolina and Georgia. New ed. '08 (Je6) il. f°, pap., $16. Hessling.

Crane, Eleanor Maud.
Rainbow kimona: comedy in two acts for girls. '08(Mr14) c. D. pap., 25 c. Dick.

Crane, Fk.
Song of the Infinite; monograph on the one hundred and third psalm. '09(N13) c. D. bds., *50 c. net. Pilgrim Press.

Crane, Herbert Stanley, comp.
Lawyers' guide, cont. complete table of Missouri cases; overruled, reversed, modified and distinguished by the U. S. ct., the sup. ct. of Mo. and the Mo. cts. of appeals. 1st ed. '09(Ap) c. 25 p. D. pap., $1. F. T. Riley.

Crane, Howard H.
Book of the pansy, viola and violet. '08 (O10) il. D. (Handbooks of practical gardening.) *$1 net. Lane.

Crane, Julia Ettie.
Music teacher's manual. 6th ed. '09, [1910.] (F) c. 140 p. 8°, pap., 75 c. J. E. Crane.

Crane, Laura Dent.
Automobile girls along the Hudson; or, fighting fire in Sleepy Hollow. '10(D) il. 12°, (Automobile girls ser.) $1. Altemus.
Automobile girls at Newport; or, watching the summer parade. '10(D) il. 12°, (Automobile girls ser.) $1. Altemus.
Automobile girls in the Berkshires; or, the ghost of lost man's trail. '10(D) il. 12°, (Automobile girls ser.) $1. Altemus.

Crane, P: Bela.
Quack grass eradication; prepared especially for farmers desirous of destroying this dangerous pest. '10(S) c. 114 p. il. por. 12°, $1. Webb Pub. Co.

Crane, R: Teller.
Utility of all kinds of higher schooling; an investigation. '10(F19) O. $1.—Crane's reply to criticisms on his book. '10 (My21) D. pap., gratis. R: T. Crane.

Crane, Utley Edn.
Commercial law for business men. '08(S) c. 331 p. O. bds., $1.75. U. E. Crane.

Crane, Wa., il.
The buckle my shoe picture book; containing One, two, buckle my shoe, A gaping-wide-mouth-waddling frog, My mother. '10(O15) O. $1.25 net. Lane.
See also Song of sixpence picture book.

Crane, Wa. R:
Gold and silver; economic history of mining in the United States. '08(Jl11) c. il. 8°, **$5 net. Wiley.
Index of mining engineering literature. '09 (Jl31) c. 8°, **$4 net; mor., **$5 net. Wiley.
Ore mining methods. '10(Jl30) c. il. (incl. plans) 8°, $3 net. Wiley.

Crane, W: E:
American stationary engineering; pract. work which begins at the boiler room and takes in the whole power plant; contains complete examination for a license. 2d ed. '10(Je4) c. il. 8°, $2. Henley.

Crane, W: Howe.
A scientific currency. '10(Ag20) c. por. 12°, $1. B'way Pub.

Crane classics. 12°, 25 c.; pap., 15 c. Crane.
—Dickens. Christmas carol.
—Irving. Legend of Sleepy Hollow.
—Longfellow. Tales of a wayside inn. 3 v.
—Shakespeare. Othello.

CRANES.
See Hoisting machinery;—Machinery.

Cranford. *See* Gaskell, *Mrs.* Eliz. Cleghorn Stevenson.

Cranke, J. P.
In the land of to-morrow. '10(O8) c. 12°, $1.50. B'way Pub.

Cranmer-Byng, Lancelot Alfr., comp.
Lute of jade; selections from the classical poets of China. '09(Ap17) 16°, (Wisdom of the East ser.) *60 c. net. Dutton.

Cranston, Leslie Atwood.
On instructions to juries. In 3 v. '09, [1910.] (F) c. O. $22.50. Flood.

Crapsey, Algernon Sidney, D.D.
See Mangasarian, Mangasar M.

Crary, Lottie Elva.
Textbook of field zoology; insects and their near relatives and birds. '10(Je) 12+364 p. il. 12°, $1.25 net. Blakiston.

Crashaw brothers. Pier, A. S. $1.50. Houghton M.

Crathorne, Arth. Rob.
See Rietz, H: Lewis.

Craveison, Ollis.
Fun on the farm: in old Kentucky. '10 (Mr12) c. il. D. $1.25. Kuyahora Press.

Craven, Priscilla, pseud.
See Shore, *Mrs.* Teignmouth.

Craven, Roger Carey.
In the twilight zone. '09(D) 327 p. il. 12°, $1.50. C. M. Clark.

Craven's Choyce. Sharpe, E: S. 10 c. Salem Co. Hist. Soc.

Craw, G: Rockhill.
Roxana; social drama in three acts. '09, [1910.] (F) c. 123 p. 16°, 75 c. Sterling.

Crawford, Annie Maria.
Roses and rue: [poems.] '10(Mr26) c. D. $1.50. Badger.

Crawford, C. M.
See Franklin, W: Suddards.

Crawford, Caroline.
Folk dances and games. '08(Je27) c. front. Q. $1.50. Barnes.

Crawford, F. D.
See Arkansas. *Sup. ct.* Repts.

Crawford, Floretta Newbury.
Dreaming back. '09(D) c. 7-61 p. 12°, $1. B'way Pub.

Crawford, Fs. Marion.
Diva's ruby: a sequel to "Primadonna" and "Fair Margaret." '08(O17) c. il. 12°, †$1.50. Macmillan.
The primadonna: sequel to "Fair Margaret." '08(My2) c. front. D. †$1.50. Macmillan.
Stradella. '09(O9) c. il. D. †$1.50. Macmillan.
Undesirable governess. '10(Ap30) c. il. D. $1.50. Macmillan.
Venice, the place and the people; salve Venetia; gleanings from Venetian history. '09(Je19) c. 2 v., il. 8°, *$5 net. Macmillan.

Crawford, Fs. Marion.—*Continued.*
White sister. '09(My8) c. il. D. †$1.50. Macmillan.
Zoroaster; and Marzio's crucifix. '08 (Ap11) 12°, †$1.50. Macmillan.

"Crawford, Captain Jack."
See Crawford, J: Wallace.

Crawford, Ja. Pyle Wickersham.
Spanish composition. '10(O1) c. S. 75 c. Holt.

Crawford, Ja. Shannon.
Political Socialism, would it fail in success?; book for busy men. '10(Ag) 105 p. 12°, 25 c. J. S. Crawford.

Crawford, J: Jay.
Bank directors, their powers, duties and liabilities. '09(Je) c. 36 p. 24°, (Bankers handy ser.) 50 c. Bankers' Pub.
Negotiable instruments law. 3d ed. '08 (Ag) c. O. $2.50. Baker, V. & Co.

Crawford, J: Wallace, ["Captain Jack Crawford."]
Broncho book; being buckjumps in verse. '08(S5) c. por. 12°, $2. Roycrofters.

Crawford, Mary Caroline.
Old Boston days and ways; from the dawn of the Revolution until the town became a city. '09(O23) c. il. O. **$2.50 net. Little, B. & Co.
Romantic days in old Boston; story of the city and of its people during the nineteenth century. '10(N5) c. il. pors. $2.50 net, boxed. Little, B. & Co.
St. Botolph's Town; account of old Boston in Colonial days. '08(O17) c. il. map, D. (Little pilgrimages ser.) $2.50, boxed; ¾ levant mor., $6, boxed. L. C. Page.

Crawford, Mary Merritt, M.D., and Welton, Thurston, S., M.D.
Before the doctor comes; ready reference book, giving the symptoms of common diseases, and indicating proper emergency treatment in case of sudden illness or accident pending the physician's arrival. '09(D) c. 376 p. il. 8°, $1. Chr. Herald.

Crawford, Raymond.
See Yeo, I. Burney.

Crawford, Rebekah, and Tousey, Eliz.
Great musicians' art and glory told in picture and in story. '10(Je4) c. il. pors. 4°, $2.50 net. D. W. Newton.

Crawford, T. D., rep.
See Arkansas. *Sup. ct.* Repts.

Crawford, Mrs. Virginia M.
Ideals of charity. '08(D5) 8°, *75 c. net. Herder.

CRAWFORD, William Harris.
Shipp, J. E. D. Giant days; or, the life and times of William H. Crawford. $3 Americus.

Crawford, W: H:
Church and the slum: study of English Wesleyan mission halls. '08(D26) c. il. pors. O. 75 c. Eaton & M.
—, ed. Thoburn and India; semi-centennial sermon and addresses delivered at the Thoburn jubilee, celebrating the fiftieth anniversary of Bishop James M. Thoburn's sailing for India. '09(O23) c. por. D. *$1 net. Eaton & M.

Crawfurd, Raymond.
Last days of Charles II. '09(S11) pors. O. $1.75. Oxford Univ.

Crawley, Rev. Alfr. Ernest.
Idea of the soul. '10(Ja8) 8°, *$2.25 net. Macmillan.

Crawley, Howard.
Studies on blood and blood parasites. '09 (D) 31 p. il. 8°, (U. S., Dept. of Agriculture, Bureau of Animal Industry, bull.) pap. (Add. Superintendent for price.) U. S., Supt. of Docs.

Crawshaw, Fred Duane.
Metal spinning. '09(N20) il. 16°, (Popular mechanics 25 cent hdbk. ser.) 25 c. Popular Mechanics.
Problems in wood-turning. '09(D18) c. il. obl. S. pap., 80 c. Manual Arts.
See also Willard, G. H.

"Crayon, Diedrich, jr.," pseud.
See Bruce, Kenneth.

Creagh, J: T:
Commentary on the decree "Ne temere." '08(Je27) c. 8°, $1.25. Furst.

Creagmile, W: B.
See Rowland, Arth. J:

"Cream of a thousand plans." Petersen, J. C. 25 c. J. C. Petersen.

Creamer, E: S.
An epic of heaven and other poems. '10 (Jl2) 12°, $1. B'way Pub.

Creamery butter making. Michels, J: $1.50. J: Michels.

Crean, Mildred Corning.
Daughter of to-day. '10(N12) c. il. 12°, $1. C. M. Clark.

Creasy, Sir E: Shepherd.
Decisive battles of the world; with introd. and supplementary chapters on the battles of Gettysburg, Sedan, Santiago and Manila, by J: Gilmer Speed. '08(Je27) c. il. 8°, $1.75; hf. mor., $3.50. Lamb Pub.
Fifteen decisive battles of the world; introd. by Ernest Rhys. '08(Mr7) 16°, (Everyman's lib.) *35 c. net; leath., *70 c. net. Dutton.

CREATION.
Caldwell, W: Idea of creation; its origin and value. 50 c. W: Caldwell.
Holbrook, D: L. Panorama of creation, as presented in Genesis. *50 c. net. S. S. Times.
Kavanagh, M. A. Proof of design in creation. 10 c. Flanagan.
Sabiston, M. Biblical account of the creation; shown to be in accordance with the discoveries of science. $1.50. Knickerbocker Press.
See also Bible;—Evolution;—Universe.

Creation: a poem. Crain, A. H. 50 c. Hughes & Co.

Creators (The). Sinclair, M. $1.30 net. Century.

Credentials of the church. Powell, L. P. 20 c. Whittaker.

CREDIT.
Griffith, J. B. Credit organization. 50 c. Am. Sch. Corr.
See also Banks and banking;—Money.

Credit corporation of America. Law and bank list: a commercial law list published for the use of credit men and large forwarders of commercial business. '08(Ag) c. 79 p. 8°, $2. Credit Corporation.

CREDIT GUIDES.
See Business.

CREDITORS.
See Conveyancing;—Debt.

Creed of Buddha; by the author of "The creed of Christ." '08(My23) c. D. $1.50. Lane.

CREEDS.
Drawbridge, C. L. Old beliefs and new knowledge. 25 c. Longmans.
Gibson, E. C. S. Three creeds. *$1.40 net. Longmans.
Russell, C: T., *and* White, L. S. Debate: public discussion [of creeds of Millennial Dawn and Christian sects.] $1.10; 60 c. F: L: Rowe.
Twining, A. G. Children's creed. *60 c. net. Young Churchman.
See also Apostles' creed; — Athanasian creed; — Catechism;—Nicene creed;—*also* names of denominations.

CREEK INDIANS.
See Indians.

Creel, G:
Quatrains of Christ; preface by Julian Hawthorne. '08(O3) c. front. S. bds., **75 c. net; Galilee ed. '10(D) 53 p. front. 50 c. net. P. Elder.

Creelman, Ja.
Why we love Lincoln. '09(Mr13) c. pors. facsim., O. *$1.25 net. Outing.

Crees, Ja. Harold E:
Claudian as an historical authority. '08 (D19) 8°, (Cambridge historical essays.) *$1.50 net. Putnam.

Creevy, Caroline A.
See Priscoe, Marg. Sutton.

Creighton, Ja. Edn.
Introductory logic. 3d ed., rev. and enl.; with the addition of new problems and examples. '09(O9) 12°, *$1.40 net. Macmillan.

Creighton, Mrs. Louise von Glehn, [Mrs. Mandell Creighton.]
Art of living and other addresses to girls. '09(O2) D. *50 c. net. Longmans.
Some famous women. '09(O16) il. pors. D. 50 c. Longmans.

Creighton, Mrs. Mandell.
See Creighton, *Mrs.* Louise von Glehn.

Creighton, W: H: Paul.
Steam-engines and other heat-motors. 2d ed., rev. and enl. '09(O30) c. figs. 8°, $5. Wiley.

Crelle, A. L.
Calculating tables; giving the products of every two numbers from one to one thousand and their application to the multiplication and division of all numbers above one thousand. New ed., by O. Seeliger; with tables of the square-numbers and cube-numbers from 1-1000. '08(Ag1) F. $5. Lemcke.

CREMATION.
Sutherland-Gower, R., *Lord.* Cleanliness versus corruption. 25 c. Longmans.

CREMER, *Sir* William Randal.
Evans, H. Sir Randal Cremer. $1.40 net. Ginn.
Creole's slave's revenge. Harper, O. 25 c. J. S. Ogilvie.
Cresson, W: Penn.
Persia: the awakening east. '08(Je13) c. O. **$3.50 net. Lippincott.
Cressy. Perry, F: A. $1.25. Hammond Pub.
Creswick, Paul.
Honesty's garden. '10(Je18) D. $1.25. Putnam.
CRETE (*Island of*).
Baikie, J. Sea-kings of Crete. $2 net. Macmillan.
Evans, A. J: Scripta Minoa; the written documents of Minoan Crete. v. 1. $12.75. Oxford Univ.
Hall, E. H. Decorative art of Crete in the bronze age. (Add. pubs. for price.) Winston.
Hawes, C: H: *and* H. B. Crete, the forerunner of Greece. *75 c. net. Harper.
Hawes, *Mrs.* H. A. B., *and others.* Gournia, Vasilike and other prehistoric sites on the Isthmus of Hierapetra, Crete. $26; $25. C. H. Hawes.
Mosso, A. Palaces of Crete and their builders. *$5.25 net. Putnam.
See also Persia.
Crew, Helen Coale.
Aegean echoes and other verses. '10(D31) c. D. $1.50. Badger.
Crew, H:
Elements of physics, for use in high schools; rev. by Franklin T. Jones. '09 (N6) c. D. **$1.10 net. Macmillan.
General physics. '08(Je13) c. il. 8°, *$2.75 net. Macmillan.
Principles of mechanics. '08(Je13) c. il. O. $1.50. Longmans.
—, and Jones, Franklin Turner.
Elements of physics: rev. by Franklin T. Jones. '09(O16) il. 12°, *$1.10 net. Macmillan.
Crewdson, Mrs. C: N.
See Crewdson, Lula Cox.
Crewdson, Lula Cox, [Mrs. C. N. Crewdson.]
American baby abroad: how he played Cupid to a Kentucky beauty. '10(My14) c. il. D. $1.50. Little, B. & Co.
Creyton, Paul, pseud.
See Trowbridge, J: Townsend.
Criado, Luis Cocat y Heliodoro.
See Carrión, Miguel Ramos.
Cribbs, J: W:
Adventures of "Jack" Cribbs. 3 v. '10 (Je) c. pors. 12°, ea., 50 c. Clarion Democrat.
Crichfield, G: W.
American supremacy: rise and progress of the Latin American republics and their relations to the United States under the Monroe doctrine. In 2 v. '08(D29) c. O. **$6 net, boxed. Brentano's.
Crichton, Mrs. F. E.
Little wizard of White Cloud Hill. '10 (O29) il. D. $1.25. Longmans.
Peep-in-the-world. '08(N7) il. D. $1.25. Longmans.
Crichton-Browne, Sir Ja.
See Browne, *Sir* Ja. Crichton-.

Crichton. Ainsworth, W: H. 50 c.; 75 c. Dutton.
CRICKET (*game*).
Lucas, E: V., *ed.* Hambledon men: [cricket.] 90 c. Oxford Univ.
Patterson, W: S. Sixty years of Uppingham cricket. *$2 net. Longmans.
CRICKETS.
Lutz, F: E. Variation and correlations of certain taxonomic characters of *Gryllus.* 40 c. Carnegie.
Crider, Albert Foster
Cement and Portland cement materials of Mississippi. '07, [1908.] (Ag) 73 p. il. 8°, (Mississippi State Geol. Survey, bull.) pap. (Add. pub. for price.) Brandon Pr.
Crile, G: W.
Hemorrhage and transfusion: experimental and clinical research. '09(My) c. 13+560 p. il. tabs., 8°, subs., $5; hf. leath., $6. Appleton.
CRIME AND CRIMINALS.
Booth, *Mrs.* M. B. C. After prison—what? *$1.25 net. Revell.
Deran-Smith, *Mrs.* E. Am I my brother's keeper? $1.10. E. Deran-Smith.
Drummond, A. L. True detective stories. $1.50. G: W. Dillingham.
Duke, T: S: Celebrated criminal cases of America. $3 net. Barry.
Ellis, H: H. The criminal. $1.50. Scribner.
Folsom, C: F. Studies of criminal responsibility. (Priv. pr.) C: F. Folsom.
Henderson, C: R., *ed.* Correction and prevention; prison reform. In 4 v. ea., $2.50; per set, $10. Charities Pub.
Holmes, T: Known to the police. *$3 net. Longmans.
MacDonald, A. Criminal statistics in Germany, France and England. 25 c. A. MacDonald.
MacDonald, A. Juvenile crime and reformation. 50 c.—Study of the criminal, pauper, and defective classes. 25 c. U. S., Supt. of Docs.
Morrison, W: D. Crime and its causes. $1. Scribner.
Munsterberg, H. On the witness stand: essays on psychology and crime. **$2.50. McClure.
Parmelee, M. Principles of anthropology and sociology in their relation to criminal procedure. *$1.25 net. Macmillan.
Parsons, P. A. Responsibility for crime. $1.50. Longmans.
Philippine Islands. *Bureau of Justice.* Criminality in the Philippine Islands, 1903-1908. Bu. Public Pr.
Potts, C: S. Crime and the treatment of the criminal. gratis. Univ. of Tex.
Quinton, R: F. Crime and criminals, 1876-1910. $1.50 net. Longmans.
Society for the Promotion of Social Service. Juvenile delinquent and the Young Men's Christian Association. 50 c. Y. M. C. A.
Train, A. C. True stories of crime. †$1.50. Scribner.

CRIME AND CRIMINALS.—*Continued.*
United States. *Dept. of Justice.* Memoranda relative to the extraditio nof fugitives from the United States in foreign jurisdiction, 1909. '09(D) 6 p. 8°. (Add. Superintendent for price.)
See also Capital punishment;—Children;—Criminal law; — Detectives; — Highwaymen; — Indictments;—Juvenile courts;—Prisons;—Probation system; — Prostitution; — Reform schools; — Tramps;—*also* Chicago.

Crime and criminals. '10(Mr26) c. por. S. $1. Prison Reform.

Crime Club. Holt-White, W: E: B. $1.50. Macaulay.

Crime of Sylvestre Bonnard. *See* France, Anatole.

Crime of the Congo. Doyle, *Sir* A. C. 25 c. Doubleday, P.

Crime on canvas. White, F. M. $1.50. Fenno.

Criminal commercialism. Tate, W: R. 50 c. Nicoletti.

CRIMINAL LAW.
American criminal repts.; digest. v. 1-15. $6. Callaghan.
Canada. Criminal law digest. $6. Canada Law.
Canada. Digest of Canadian criminal case law. $8. A. Poole.
May, J: W. Law of crimes. $3.50. Little. B. & Co.
Mickell, W: E. Cases on criminal law sel. from decisions of Eng. and Am. cts. $4. West Pub.
New York [State.] Code of criminal procedure. $3. Banks.
New York [State.] Criminal repts. v. 22. $5; v. 23, $5.50. W. C. Little.
New York [State.] Penal law. $3. Banks.
New York [State.] Penal law. $2.50. Banks & Co.
New York [State.] Penal law. $1.50. Chief.
New York [State.] Penal law and code of criminal procedure. $7.50; [Bender's ed.] $4. M. Bender.
Oklahoma. Codes of civil and criminal procedure. $3.50. Bunn.
Oklahoma. *Criminal ct. of appeals.* Repts. v. 3. $1.50. State Cap.
Sibley, M. W. Criminal appeal and evidence. *$5 net. Wessels.
Stoner, G. Students' quiz book, on the law of criminal proceedings. 50 c. Callaghan.
Train, A. C. Prisoner at the bar; sidelights on the administration of criminal justice. $1.50. Scribner.
Underhill, H. C. Treatise on the law of criminal evidence. $7.50. Bobbs-M.
United States. Federal penal code. $3 net. Little, B. & Co.
United States commissioner's record of proceedings in criminal cases. $3.75. W. H. Anderson.
Van Voorhis, J: S. Pocket digest of criminal law. 30 c. Eagle Pub.
Welch, N. H. Cases on criminal law. $1.50. Thompson & Co.

CRIMINAL LAW.—*Continued.*
Wigmore, J: H: Preliminary bibliography of modern criminal law and criminology. 65 c. Northwestern Univ.
See also Conspiracies;—Crime and criminals;—Evidence;—Jury;—Law, and references under that subject; — Prisons; — Tramps; — Trials; — *also* names of states.

Criminal slang. Sullivan, J. M., *comp.* 15 c. Worcester Press.

CRIMINOLOGY.
See Crime and criminals.

Crimson azaleas. Stackpole, H: D. †$1.50. Duffield.

Crimson ramblers. Eldred, W. L. $1.50. Lothrop, L. & S.

CRINOIDS.
See Echinoderms.

CRIPPLE CREEK, Col.
Rastall, B: M. Labor history of the Cripple Creek district. 50 c. Univ. of Wis.

Crisis in church work. Ostrom, H: *50 c. net. Jennings.

Crisis (The): the unions and the courts. Hunter, W. R. 10 c. S: A. Bloch.

Crispe, T: E:
Reminiscences of a K. C. '10(Jl2) c. 8°, $3.50 net. Little, B. & Co.

Crissey, Forrest.
Hand-book of modern business correspondence. '09(F6) c. 12°, $1. Thompson & T.

Cristabel. *See* Coleridge, S: Taylor.

Critchell, Rob. Siderfin.
Recollections of a fire insurance man, incl. his experience in U. S. Navy (Mississippi squadron) during the Civil War. '09(D18) c. il. pors. facsim., 12°, $1.25. R. S. Critchell.

Critic (The). *See* Sheridan, R: Brinsley.

Critical introduction to the New Testament. Peake, A. S: *75 c. net. Scribner.

Critical miscellanies. Morley, J: V. v. 4. **$1.50 net. Macmillan.

Critical philosophy of Imanuel Kant. Caird, E. *$6.25 net. Macmillan.

Critical study of current theories of moral education. Hart, J. K. 50 c. net. Univ. of Chic.

CRITICISM.
Arnold, M. Essays in criticism. $1.25 net. Ball Pub.
Balfour, A. J. Questionings on criticism and beauty. 70 c. Oxford Univ.
Bennett, E. A. Literary taste: how to form it. 75 c. net. Doran.
Caine, T: H: H. Cobwebs of criticism. 50 c.; 75 c. Dutton.
Coleridge, S: T. Literary criticism. 90 c. Oxford Univ.
De Quincey, T: Literary criticism. 50 c. Oxford Univ.
Dickinson, T: H., *and* Roe, F: W., *eds.* Nineteenth century English prose: [critical essays.] $1. Am. Bk.
Dionysius *of Halicarnassus.* On literary criticism. $3 net. Macmillan.
Frye, P. H. Literary reviews and criticisms. **$1.25 net. Putnam.
Klein, D: Literary criticism from the Elizabethan dramatists. $1.50 net. Sturgis & W.

CRITICISM.—*Continued.*
Le Gallienne, R: Retrospective reviews: literary log. 2 v. $3.50 net. Lane.
Maxim, H. Science of poetry and philosophy of language. $2.50 net. Funk.
Moulton, C: W., *ed.* Library of literary criticism. 8 v. $40. Malkan.
Poe, E. A. Selections from critical writings. **75 c. net. Holt.
Pollard, P. Their day in court; [criticism of modern fiction.] *$3 net. Neale.
Pope, A. Essay on criticism. 50 c. Oxford Univ.
Raymond, G: L. Fundamentals in education, art and criticism. $1.40 net. Funk.
Scott-James, R. A. Modernism and romance. *$2.50 net. Lane.
Sedgwick, H: D. New American type: essays. **$1.50 net. Houghton M.
Shelley, P. B. Literary and philosophical criticism. 90 c. Oxford Univ.
Shuman, E. L. How to judge a book; handy method of criticism. $1.25 net. Houghton M.
Smith, D: N. Function of criticism. 35 c. Oxford Univ.
Spingarn, J. E. History of literary criticism in the renaissance. *$1.50 net. Columbia Univ.
Spingarn, J. E., *ed.* Critical essays of the seventeenth century. 2 v. ea., $1.75. Oxford Univ.
Wells, F. L. Statistical study of literary merit, with remarks on new phases of the method. 30 c. Science Pr., (N. Y.)
See also Æsthetics; — Literature; — Rhetoric; — *also* names of arts and literatures.

CRITICISM (*of the Bible*).
See Higher criticism.

Critique of practical reason. *See* Kant, Immanuel.

Critique of pure reason. *See* Kant, Immanuel.

Crito. *See* Plato. Apology of Socrates.

Crittenton, Celia Louise, ["Lambkin Sprinx."]
Wisdom for the foolish. '08(D19) c. D. 75 c. Badger.

Crittenton, C: Nelson.
Brother of girls; life story of Charles N. Crittenton as told by himself. '10(Je4) c. il. pors. 8°, $1. World's Events.

CROATIAN LANGUAGE.
Marohnic, J. English-Croatian letter-writer. $1. J. Marohnic.
See also English language;—Lochmer, A.

Croce, Benedetto.
Æsthetic as science of expression and general linguistic; tr. from the Italian by Douglas Ainslie. '09(N20) O. *$3 net. Macmillan.

CROCHETING.
Fleisher's knitting and crocheting manual. 25 c. Fleisher.
Hettich, L. B., *ed.* Priscilla crochet book. 25 c. Priscilla.

Crocker, Fs. Bacon.
Dynamo-electric machinery. '08(O17) c. il. por. diagrs., O. (American School of Correspondence pubs.) $1.50. Am. Sch. of Corr.

Crocker, Fs. Bacon, and Arendt, Morton.
Electric motors; their action, control and application. '10(Jl30) il. $2.50 net. Van Nostrand.

—, and Torda, Thdr.
Direct- and alternating-current machine design: being instructions for the design of motors and generators. '09(Mr27) c. il. 8°, *$5 net.. McGraw.

—, Sager, Lawrence K., Cushing, H: Cooke, jr., and Trow, Harris C.
Practical lessons in electricity; working guide to the fundamental principles of electrical science and approved American practice in the construction and use of storage batteries and the installation of conductors for power, lighting, and other purposes. '09(N) il. tabs., 8°, (American School of Correspondence pubs.) $1.50. Am. Sch. Corr.

Crocker, G: Glover.
Principles of procedure in deliberative bodies. 4th ed., rev. and enl. '10(Ap30) c. S. 75 c. net. Putnam.

Crocker, H: Graham.
Situation in southeastern Europe: address del. at the seventh annual meeting of the Society of American Wars, Commandery of the District of Columbia. '09(Je19) O. pap. (Add. pubs. for price.) B. S. Adams.

Crockett, C: Winthrop.
Methods for earthwork computations. '08 (Mr28) figs. 8°, *$1.50 net. Wiley.

Crockett, S: Rutherford.
Deep Moat Grange. '08(Mr21) c. D. †$1.50. Appleton.
Footsteps of Scott: story of the writer as revealed in his country. '08(D19) il. 12°, *$1.25 net. Jacobs.
The iron lord. '08(F15) c. il. D. 75 c. Cupples & L.
Love's young dream. '10(S24) c. D. $1.50. Macmillan.
Men of the mountain. '09(Ag28) c. il. D. †$1.50. Harper.
Red Cap adventures: being the second series of "Red Cap tales." '08(S12) c. il. O. †$1.75. Macmillan.
Red Cap tales from Sir Walter Scott. v. 5-7. '10(D24) c. il. in col. 12°, ea., 75 c. net. Macmillan.
Contents: Antiquary; Guy Mannering; Rob Roy.

Crockett, Wa. Hill.
History of Lake Champlain. '09(Jl10) c. il. por. D. pap., 75 c. Shanley.

Croftan, Alfr. Careño.
Clinical therapeutics; hdbk. on the special treatment of internal disease. 3d ed., rev. '10(Mr) c. 16+626 p. 4°, $5. Cleveland Press.

Crofton, Rev. W. J.
See Ross, G: Alex. Johnston.

Croiset, Maurice.
Aristophanes and the political parties at Athens; tr. by Ja. Loeb. '10(Ja1) O. *$2 net. Macmillan.

Croisilles. *See* **Musset, L. C. A. de.**

Croisset, Fs. de.
See **Jepson, Edg.**

Croll, Rev. Philip Columbus.
Lebanon County imprints and bibliography; paper read before the Lebanon County Historical Society, Feb. 21, 1908. '08, [1909.] (Mr) 153-199 p. 8°, (Lebanon County Historical Society papers.) pap., 25 c. P. C. Croll.

Croly, Herbert.
Promise of American life. '09(N13) c. O. **$2 net. Macmillan.

Cromer, Earl of, [Evelyn Baring.]
Ancient and modern imperialism; published by permission of the Classical Association. '10(Ap16) D. 90 c. net. Longmans.
Modern Egypt. In 2 v. '08(Mr14) c. por. map, O. per set, **$6 net. Macmillan.

Cromie, W: Ja.
Parallel bar exercises. '09(D25) c. il. por. 12°, (Spalding's athletic lib.) pap., 10 c. Am. Sports.
Pyramid building. '09(D25) c. 2 v., il. pors. 12°, (Spalding's athletic lib.) pap., 10 c. Am. Sports.

Cromwell, J: Howard.
American business woman; guide for the investment, preservation, and accumulation of property. 2d rev. ed. '10(N12) c. O. $2 net. Putnam.

CROMWELL, Oliver.
Carlyle, T: Letters and speeches of Cromwell. 3 v. *35 c. net; *70 c. net. Dutton.
Marshall, H. E. Story of Cromwell. 50 c. Dutton.

Cronau, Rudolf.
Our wasteful nation: story of American prodigality and the abuse of our national resources. '08(D19) c. il. D. bds., $1. M. Kennerley.

Cronica Rimada; reproduced in facsimile from the ms. in the Bibliothèque Nationale by Archer M. Huntington. '04, [1909.] (N) 188-201 p. 4°, $12. (300 copies.) Hispanic Soc.

Cronin, Rev. Michael.
Science of ethics. '09(D) 662 p. 8°, *$4.50 net. Benziger.

Cronk, Victor D.
Selection of business forms, incl. local precedents and official forms under the laws of Wisconsin and Minnesota, [etc.] '09, [1910.] (F) c. O. Flood.

Crook, Herbert Evelyn, M.D.
High frequency currents: their production, physical properties, physiological effects and therapeutical uses. 2d ed. '09(D) 244 p. il. 8°, *$2 net. Wood.

Crook, I:, D.D.
Great five: the first faculty of the Ohio Wesleyan University. '08(D26) c. S. bds., *25 c. net. Jennings.

Crook, W: H:
Through five administrations; reminiscences; ed. by Margarita Spalding Gerry. '10(N5) c. pors. O. $1.80 net. Harper.

Crooked trail. Miller, L. B. 50 c.; 25 c. Axtell-R.

Crooker, Jos. H:, D.D.
Church of to-day. '08(My2) c. D. *75 c. net. Am. Unitarian; Pilgrim Press.
Jesus brought back. [New ed.] '09(Ap17) 12°, *75 c. net. Sherman, F.

Crookes, Sir W:
Diamonds. '10(F19) il. 16°, (Harper's lib. of living thought.) *75 c. net. Harper.

Croonian lectures. *See* Rivers, W. H. R.

CROPS.
See Farms and farming;—Hay;— *also* names of crops.

Crops that pay. Dygert, H. A. 10 c. Am. Nut & Fruit Co.

CROQUET.
Jacobus, C:, *ed.* Croquet and its rules. 10 c. Am. Sports.
Roque guide and official rules governing the game, as adopted by the National Roque Association of America; only authorized ed., rev. and corr. by the National Association up to August, 1910. '10(Ag) c. 68 p. il. pors. 16°, (Spalding's athletic lib.) pap., 10 c. Am. Sports.

Crosbee, M. Florence.
The message. [1910.] c. 48 p. 12°, 50 c. Tudor Press.

Crosby, Arth. F., comp.
See New York City. Code of ordinances.

Crosby, Dick Jay.
School exercises in plant production. '10 (O) 48 p. il. 8°, (U. S., Dept. of Agriculture, farmers' bull.) Gov. Pr. Off.
See also True, Alfr. C.

Crosby, Ernest Howard.
Labor and neighbor: an appeal to first principles. '08(O) 155 p. por. 12°, pap., 25 c. L: F. Post.

CROSBY, Ernest Howard.
Abbott, L. D. Ernest Howard Crosby, the Puritan anarchist. 50 c.; 25 c. Ariel.

Crosby, Everett U., and Fiske, H: A.
Crosby-Fiske hdbk. of fire protection. 4th ed. '09(Ag) 495 p. il. tabs., 16°, $4. Insurance Field.

Crosby, J: F.
Advisability of inserting the word sex before the word race in the fifteenth amendment of the constitution of the United States. Mallory prize essay. '10(D) 16 p. O. pap., gratis. Georgetown Univ.

Crosby, Kingsland.
Strange case of Eleanor Cuyler. '10(O15) c. col. front. D. $1.20 net. Dodd.

Crosby, Oscar Terry.
Strikes; when to strike, how to strike; book of suggestion for the buyers and sellers of labour. '10(Je4) c. D. (Questions of the day ser.) $1.25. Putnam.

Crosland, T: W: Hodgson.
Little stings. '08(Ag8) c. 12°, *75 c. net. J: W. Luce.

Cross, C: F:, and Bevan, E: J:
Text-book on paper making. 3d ed., partly rewritten with new matter. '08(F8) c. 12°, $5. Spon.

Cross, C: Rob.
Notes on mechanics; printed for the use of students in the Massachusetts Institute of Technology. '08(O10) c. diagrs., 8°. (Not for sale.) C: R. Cross.

Cross, Mrs. J: W.
See Eliot, George, *pseud.*

Cross, R.
Voyage of the "Oregon" from San Francisco to Santiago in 1898; [with introd. by John Adams Aiken.] '08(S12) 4°. (Priv. pr.) Merrymount.

Cross, Tabitha Ann.
See Dunham, *Mrs.* Anna Cross.

Cross, Victoria, pseud.
See Cory, Vivian.

Cross, Wilbur Lucius.
Life and times of Laurence Sterne. '09 (Je5) c. il. pors. O. *$2.50 net. Macmillan.

CROSS.
Message of the cross: notes for the use of clergy taking the three hours' service and for private devotion. *60 c. net. Young Churchman.
Morgan, G: C. Bible and the cross. *50 c. net. Revell.
Mortimer, A. G. In the light of the cross. *80 c. net. Whittaker.
Simpson, A. B. Cross of Christ. 75 c. Alliance Press.
Watson, F: Seven words from the cross. 81 c. Whittaker.
Way of the cross. 4 v. ea., 15 c. Benziger.
See also Atonement;—Good Friday.

Cross and dagger. Durrant, W: S. $1.50. Lane.

Cross in Christian experience. Clow, W. M. *$1.50 net. Jennings.

CROSS-TIES.
Sherfesse, W: F. Seasoning and preservative treatment of hemlock and tamarack cross-ties. 15 c. U. S., Supt. of Docs.

Crossing familiar paths. Fellers, J: E. 80 c. Booklovers' Assoc.

Crossing the bar. Gordon, G: A. *50 c. net. Pilgrim Press.

Crossing the Connecticut. Wright, G: E: $5. Smith-L.

Crossley, Bruce W:
See Bowman, Melville Le Roy.

Crossley, Ruth, comp.
Old sweethearts; poems you ought to know. '10(S24) c. D. $1, boxed; full leath., $2, boxed. Platt & P.

Crossways (The). Martin, *Mrs.* H. R. †$1.50. Century Co.

Crotch, Arth.
Elements of telephony. '10(D31) 12°, 60 c. Spon.
Telegraphic systems and other notes. '08 (My23) D. *$2 net. Lippincott.

Crothers, S: McChord, D.D.
Among friends. '10(N19) c. D. $1.25 net. Houghton M.
By the Christmas fire: [essays.] '08(D12) c. il. D. **$1.25 net. Houghton M.
Making of religion. '09(Ap10) 16°, *40 c. net. Am. Unitarian.
Oliver Wendell Holmes, the autocrat, and his fellow boarders; with selected poems. '09(S25) c. por. D. **75 c. net. Houghton M.

CROTON VALLEY.
See Reservoirs.

Crouch, Jos.
Puritanism and art; an inquiry into a popular fallacy, with introd. by the Rev. C. Silvester Horne. '10(O1) il. por. 8°, $3.75 net. Cassell.

Croudace, Lenore.
Burning gauze, and other poems. [1910.] (O) c. 233 p. 12°. $1. J. R. Lafontaine.

Crow-Step. Fraser, G. $1.50. Witter & K.

Crowd (The). Le Bon, G. $1.50 net. Macmillan.

Crowding out the Christ-child. Gordon, S: D. 25 c. net. Revell.

Crowds and the veiled woman. Cox, M. M. $1.50. Funk.

Crowe, J: F., ed.
See Camp, Edg. Whittlesey.

Crowe, Sir Jos. Archer, and Cavalcaselle, Giovanni Battista.
History of painting in Italy; Umbria, Florence and Siena, from the 2d to the 16th century; ed. by Langdon Douglas. In 6 v. '09(F13) il. O. ea., *$6 net. Scribner.
New history of painting in Italy from the second to the sixteenth century; ed. by E: Hutton. In 3 v. v. 1. '08(D12); v. 2. '09(Jl17); v. 3. '10(F19) il. 8°, ea., *$5 net. Dutton.

Crowell, Joshua Freeman.
Frogs O'Poolo. '09(N) 178 p. il. 4°, $1.50. Dutton.

Crowell, Kath. Roney.
Call of the waters: study of the frontier. '08(Ag1) c. 12°, (Home mission ser.) *50 c. net; pap., *30 c. net. Revell.
Fair America. '10(Jl2) c. il. maps, F. $2 net. Doran.
Pioneers. '08 (Jl) c. 89+7 p. maps, 12°, 40 c.; pap., 25 c. Willets Press.

Crowell's handy information ser. 12°, 50 c. Crowell.
—Bartlett. Handy book of American government.
—Mead. How words grow.
—Walker, *comp.* Handy book of proverbs.

Crowell's handy volume classics. 41 v. New ed. '10(D) il. 16°, Missal ed., ea., vel., 75 c., boxed; "Fleur de lis" ed., silk, ea., 75 c.; Tuxedo ed., ea., ooze, $1.25. Crowell.

Crowell's handy volume classics, pocket ed. por. S. 35 c. Crowell.
—Gowans, *comp.* Characteristic passages from the hundred best English prose writers.
—Howard, *comp.* Best American essays.—Best American orations.

Crowell's lib. of economics and politics; ed. by R: T. Ely. D. Crowell.
—Wines. Punishment and reformation. *$1.75 net.

Crowell's modern language ser. D. Crowell.
—Banderet *and* Reinhard. First lessons in French. *50 c. net.
—Blanchaud. One thousand common French words. *25 c. net.
—Chalmers. Deutsche gedichte zum auswendiglernen. *40 c. net.
—Fisher. Dornröschen. *25 c. net.
—Hein. Exercises in French conversation. *40 c. net.
—Levi. Easy German stories. *40 c. net.
—Reichenbach. Das Rothkäppchen. *25 c. net.

Crowell's poets. Premier ed. 30 v. '10(N) leath., ea., $2; thin paper ed., 14 v., mor., ea., $2.50; il. ed., 5 v., mor., ea., $3.50. Crowell.

Crowell's shorter course texts; ed. by J. E. Mansion. S. *25 c. net. Crowell.
—About. Les jumeaux de l'Hotel Corneille.
—Auzas, *ed.* Poemes Napoléoniens.
—Bawr. Michel Perrin.
—Blanchaud. Quatre contes des Mille et une nuits.
—Brueys *and* Palaprat. L'avocat Patelin.
—Daniels, *comp.* Choix de poesies faciles.
—Dumas. L'evasion épisode tiré de Vingt ans aprés.—Récits tirés des Impressions de voyage.
—Erckmann *and* Chatrian. Le trésor du vieux seigneur.
—Fisher. La belle au bois dormant.
—Hugo. Bataille de Waterloo.
—Laboulaye. Le château de la vie.
—Lailavoix. La farce de Paquin fils.
—Macé. Contes du petit château.
—Molière. L'avare.—Le bourgeois gentilhomme.—Le médecin malgré lui.
—Moreau. Contes à ma sœur.
—Musset. Croisilles.
—Reichenbach. Deux comédies enfantines.
—Rozan. Les petites ignorances de la conversation.
—Saint-Hilaire. Anecdotes sur Napoléon.
—Scribe. Mon étoile.
—Sébillot. Choix de contes populaires.—Contes des marins de la Haute-Bretagne.

Crowell's thin paper poets ser. D. limp leath., $1.25, boxed; ooze leath., $1.75. Crowell.
—Browning. Complete poetical works.
—Burns. Complete poetical works.
—Keats. Complete poetical works.
—Longfellow. Complete poetical works.
—Lowell. Poems.
—Scott. Complete poetical works.
—Shelley. Complete poetical works.
—Tennyson. Complete poetical works.
—Ward, *comp.* Dictionary of quotations.
—Whittier. Complete poetical works.
—Wordsworth. Complete poetical works.

Crowell's thin paper sets. front. 12°, flex. leath., $1.25; mor., $3. Crowell.
—Boswell. Life of Johnson. 2 v.
—Carlyle. French revolution. 2 v.
—Elliott, *pseud.* Works. 8 v.
—Sue. Wandering Jew. 2 v.

Crowell's young people ser. il. D. †75 c. Crowell.
—Fitzhugh. Galleon treasure.
—Kaler, Two stowaways aboard the "Ellen Maria."

Crowley, Mary Catherine.
Daughter of New France. '08(My.) c. 12°, (Popular ed. of recent fiction.) †75 c. Little, B. & Co.
Heroine of the strait. '08(My.) c. 12°, (Popular ed. of recent fiction.) †75 c. Little, B. & Co.
In treaty with honor. [Popular ed.] '09 (N) front 12°, 75 c. Little, B. & Co.
Love thrives in war. '08(My.) c. 12°, (Popular ed. of recent fiction.) †75 c. Little, B. & Co.

Crowley, Rev. Timothy J.
Character-treatment in the mediæval drama. '07, [1909.] (Mr) 16+17-181 p. 8°, $1; pap., 75 c. Univ. Press, (Notre Dame.)

Crown-imperial. Kawai, W. 2 v. McClurg.

Crown of individuality. Jordan, W: G: *$1 net. Revell.

Crown of toil. Stine, W. M. $1.50. Acorn Press.

Crown of wild olive. *See* Ruskin, J:

Crown theological library. D. Putnam.
—Anglican liberalism. *$1.50 net.
—Campbell. Paul the mystic. *$1.50 net.
—Eucken. Life of the spirit. *$1.50 net.
—Gardner. Modernity and the churches. $1.50 net.
—Harnack. Constitution and law of the church in the first two centuries. $1.75 net. —Monasticism. $1.50 net.—New Testament studies: II., Sayings of Jesus. *$1.75 net.—New Testament studies: III., Acts of the Apostles. **$1.75 net.
—Kruger. Papacy. $1.50 net.
—Loisy. Religion of Israel. $1.50 net.
—Neville. Old Egyptian faith. $1.50 net.
—Peters. Modern Christianity. $1.50 net.
—Programme of modernism. *$1.50 net.
—Scott. Apologetic of the New Testament. *$1.50 net.
—Seeberg. Fundamental truths of the Christian religion. *$1.50 net.

Crowned masterpieces of eloquence. Brewer, D: J., *ed.* 10 v. (Add. pubs. for price.) Kaiser.

Crowninshield, Fs. Welsh, ["Arth. Loring Bruce."]
Bridge-fiend; cheerful book for bridge-whisters. '09(N20) col. front. D. $1. Moffat.
Manners for the metropolis: an entrance key to the fantastic life of the 400. '08(N14) c. il. D. bds., **$1 net. Appleton.

Crowstep. Fraser, G. $1.50. Witter & K.

Crowther, Cornelia Sisson, comp,
Pensées et réflexions de La Bruyère et autres auteurs français. '09(Ja16) c. S. $1. W: R. Jenkins.

CROWTHER, *Bp.* Samuel Adjar.
. Page, J. Black bishop: Samuel Adjar Crowther. *$2 net. Revell.

Crozier, Alfr. Owen.
The magnet: romance of the battles of modern giants. '08(F8) c. il. D. †$1.50. Funk.

Crozier, J: Beattie.
My inner life. Reissue in 2 v. '08(D5) O. *$2.50 net. Longmans.

Crozier, W: Armstrong, ed.
Virginia heraldica: registry of Virginia gentry entitled to coat armor: with genealogical notes of the families. '09 (Ja9) 8°, (Virginia County record ser.) $3. Genealog. Assoc.

Crucé, Emeric.
Le novveav Cynée; the new Cyneas of Émeric Crucé; the French text; repr. from the orig. ed. of 1623; together with an English tr. and introd. by T: Willing Balch. '09(D25) 8°, $2. Allen, L. & S.

Crucial race question. Brown, W: M. (Add. pub. for price.) Arkansas Churchman.

Cruciality of the cross. Forsythe, P: T. *$1.50 net. Doran.

Crucifixion (The), by an eye-witness: letter, written seven years after the crucifixion, by a personal friend of Jesus in Jerusalem, to an Esseer brother in Alexandria. '08(F1) c. front. D. (Supplemental harmonic ser.) $1. Indo-Am. Bk.
Crude rubber. Pearson, H: C. $10. India Rubber.
CRUIKSHANK, George.
Chesson, W. H. Cruikshank. *$1 net; *75 c. net. Dutton.
Cruise of "The Cachalot." Bullen, F. T: 50 c. Hurst.
Cruise of the "Golden Eagle." Reynolds, J: P. (Not for sale.) J: P. Reynolds.
Cruise of the "Phœbe." Kaler, J. O. †$1.50. Estes.
Cruise of the "Pickering." Kaler, J. O. †$1. Burt.
Cruise of the "Port Kingston." Caine, W: R. H. (Add. author for price.) W: R. H. Caine.
Cruise of the "Sally D." Kaler, J. O. 60 c. Penn Pub. Co.
Cruiser (The). Adams, J. O. J. O. Adams.
Cruises in Bering Sea. Niedieck, P. *$5 net. Scribner.
Cruises, mainly in the Bay of the Chesapeake. Barrie, R. *and* G: $2. Franklin Press, (Pa.)
Cruises of the Confederate States steamers "Shenandoah" and "Nashville." Whittle, W: C: 50 c. W: C: Whittle.
Crum, Mrs. Eliza Tilden.
Nature, and other verse. '09(Jl) c. 7-115 p. 12°, $1; pap., 50 c. E. J. Goodrich.
Crumbs from everybody's table. Porter, *Mrs.* A. L. A., *comp.* $1. Monterey.
Crummer, Mrs. Emma C. Cushman.
Mig Robin, his story. '09(Jl) 5-120 p. il. $1. W. F. Crummer.
Crusade of brotherhood. Beard, A: F. *$1.25 net. Pilgrim Press.
CRUSADES.
Kelman, J. H. Stories from the Crusades. 50 c. Dutton.
Villehardouin, G. de, *and* Joinville, J. de. Chronicle of the crusades. *35 c. net; *70 c. net. Dutton.
CRUSTACEANS.
Bradley, J. C. Notes on two amphipods of the genus *Corophium*. 30 c. Univ. of Cal.
Byrnes, E. F. Fresh water *Cyclops* of Long Island. 80 c. Brooklyn Inst.
Cruttwell, Maud.
Guide to the paintings in the churches and minor museums of Florence. '08(Je13) il. 16°, (Art collections of Europe ser.) *$1.25 net. Dutton.
Cry of the children. Van Vorst, *Mrs.* J: **$1.25 net. Moffat.
Cryer, Matthew H:
See Cunningham, Dan. J:
CRYSTAL GAZING.
Atkinson, W: W. Practical psychomancy and crystal gazing. 50 c. Lyal Bk.
See also Hinduism.
Crystal palace. Frary, M. H. 60 c.. Stebbins.
Crystalline structure and chemical constitution. Tutton, A. E: H. *$1.60 net. Macmillan.
CRYSTALLIZATION.
See Blood.
CRYSTALLOGRAPHY.
Moses, A. J. Elements of mineralogy, crystallography and blowpipe analysis. $2.50 net. Van Nostrand.
Reeks, M. Hints for crystal drawing. *$1.10 net. Longmans.
Ruskin, J: Ethics of the dust. 50 c.; 75 c.; $1. Dutton.
Tutton, A. E: H. Crystalline structure and chemical constitution. *$1.60 net. Macmillan.
Wadsworth, M. E: Crystallography. *$3 net. McVey.
See also Mineralogy.
CUBA.
Cuba: population, history and resources, 1907; comp. by Victor H. Olmsted, director, and H: Gannett, assistant director; census of Cuba, taken in the year 1907. '09(My) 275 p. por. il. 8°, pap. U. S., Supt. of Docs.
Draper, A. S. Rescue of Cuba. $1. Silver.
International Bureau of American Republics. Cuba. (Add. pubs. for price.) Int. Bu. Am. Republics.
Military Historical Society of Massachusetts. Naval actions and operations against Cuba and Porto Rico. v. 11. $2.50. Military Hist. Soc.
Perez, L. M. Bibliografia de la Revolucion de Yara. $1.25. Stechert.
Reynolds, C: B. Standard guide to Cuba. 50 c. Foster & R.
United States. *Dept. of Commerce and Labor.* Rept. on trade conditions in Cuba by C: M. Pepper, special agent of the Department of Commerce and Labor. '09, [1910.] (Jl) 45 p. 8°.
United States. U. S. public documents rel. to non-contiguous territory and to Cuba. gratis.
Whelan, N. J. Ten days in Cuba. 35 c. N. J. Whelan.
Wilson, J. H. Free trade with Cuba. U. S., Supt. of Docs.
Wright, I. A. Cuba. $2.50 net. Macmillan.
See also Legends;—Spanish-American war.
Cubberley, Ellwood Patterson.
Changing conceptions of education. '09 (O23) c. D. (Riverside educational monographs.) **35 c. net. Houghton M.
Cuckoo's nest. Bianchi, M. G. D. $1.50. Duffield.
Cuddy. McCarter, *Mrs.* M. H. 50 c. Crane.
Cuddy's baby. McCarter, M. H. 50 c. Crane.
Cuénot, G.
Deformations of railroad tracks and the means for remedying them; author. tr. by W. C. Cushing. '07, [1908.] (F) c. 142 p. il. 8°, $2. Railroad Gazette.
Cuentos modernos; ed., with introd., notes and vocab., by Albert Bushnell Johnson. '08(Ag1) c. S. 60 c. Am. Bk.

Culbreth, D: Marvel Reynolds, M.D.
Manual of materia medica and pharmacology; comprising all organic and inorganic drugs which are or have been official in the United States pharmacopœia, together with important allied species and useful synthetics. 5th ed., enl. and thoroughly rev. '10(O) 7-986 p. il. 8°, $4.75. Lea.
University of Virginia: memories of her student life and professors. '08(D5) c. il. pors. O. *$5 net. Neale.

Cullen, Alex.
Adventures in socialism; new Lanark Establishment and Orbiston Community. '10 (Ap9) il. pors. O. $2 net. Macmillan.

Cullen, Clarence L:
The eddy. '10(Ap2) c. il. D. $1.50. G: W. Dillingham.

Cullen, J:, D.D., comp.
Hundred best hymns in the English language. '08(O17) c. 24°, (Golden anthologies.) 50 c.; leath., 75 c. Dutton.

Cullen, Rev. P: J.
Socialism and the Christian religion; appeal to right reason. '08. [1909.] (My) c. '08. 101 p. 16°, 35 c. Mirror.

Cullen, T: Stephen.
Adenomyoma of the uterus. '08(D) c. 13+270 p. il. 4°, *$6.50 net. Saunders.
See also Kelly, Howard Atwood.

Cullen, Winifred T.
See Shallow, E: Byrne.

Cullens, F. B.
Serpent's trail; or, memoirs of Harold Bagote, physician; tale of the South and of Cuba. '10(My) c. 168 p. 12°, $1. F. B. Cullens.

Culler, D: D.
Problems of pulpit and platform. '08(Ja11) 12°, 75 c. Brethren Pub. Ho.

Culler, Jos. Albertus.
Text-book of general physics for colleges; mechanics and heat. '09(O9) c. il. 8°, $1.80. Lippincott.

Cullings of forty years. Hackney, *Mrs.* A. J. H., *comp.* $1. Bapt. Bk.

Cullum, Ridgwell.
The compact: the story of an unrecorded conspiracy in South Africa. '09(Ag21) D. *$1.20 net. Doran.
Sheriff of Dyke Hole; story of a Montana mining camp. '10(My14) c. O. $1.50. Jacobs.
Watchers of the plains. '09(Ap3) c. front. O. †$1.50. Jacobs.

Culpeper, Mrs. Josephine.
Bolax: imp or angel—which? '09(S4) c. front. D. *$1 net. Murphy.

Culter, Mrs. Mary Nantz McCrae.
Jolly half dozen. '10(D24) il. 12°, $1 net. Jennings.
Prodigal daughter. '08(D) c. 7-184 p. 12°, 50 c. Monfort.

Cults, customs and superstitions of India. Oman, J: C. **$3.50 net. Jacobs.

Cults of the Greek states. *See* Farnell, L. R:

CULTURE.
Blackie, J: S. On self-culture. 75 c. Funk.
Waters, R. Culture by self-help; in a literary, an academic or an oratorical career. **$1.20 net. Dodd.

CULTURE.—*Continued.*
Young, J. B. To-day: an age of opportunity. *$1.25 net. Jennings.
See also Conduct of life;—Education;—Etiquette.

Culture of courage. Haddock, F. C. $3. Power-Bk.

Culture of the imagination. Buckham, M. H: (Add. author for price.) M. H: Buckham.

Culture of the Luiseño Indians. Sparkman, P. S. 50 c. Univ. of Cal.

CULVERTS.
Tyrrell, H: G. Concrete bridges and culverts. $3. M. C. Clark.

CUMBERLAND COUNTY, Pa.
Schwarz, J: R. Cumberland blue book. $1. J: R. Schwarz.

Cuming, E: W: Dirom.
The three jovial puppies; rhymes by E. D. Cuming; [pictures] by J. A. Shepherd. '09(O2) F. bds., $2. Caldwell.
See also Gilbey, *Sir* Wa.

Cuming, Mari A.
At sound of the gavel: [poetry;] published in behalf of the Brooklyn Masonic Temple. '07, [1908.] (Ap.) c. por. O. pap., 25 c. M. A. Cuming.
Drummer boy: [poems.] '08(Ap.) c. 32 p. il. D. $1. M. A. Cuming.

Cumming, Rob. Cushing, ed.
See New York [State.] Annot. consolidated laws.—Court rules.—Tax law.

Cummings, Mrs. Ella Sterling.
See Mighels, Ella Sterling.

Cummings, G: Willis.
Electricity and magnetism in telephone maintenance. '09(F6) c. diagrs., 8°, $1.50. McGraw.

Cummings, Horace Hall.
Nature study by grades. '09(Ja9) c. il. D. $1.—Text-book for lower grammar grades. '10(Ja22) c. D. 60 c.; for higher grammar grades. '10(S17) c. D. 75 c. Am. Bk.

Cummings, T: Harrison, ed.
Schriever, Ja. Boniface.

Cummings, W: Leon.
Modern formulary: text book of chemistry as applied to the manufacture of proprietary specialties. '09(Ap24) c. D. $2.50. W: L. Cummings.

Cummins, Eleanor A.
See Keith, Henrietta P.

Cumner's son. Parker, *Sir* H. G. $1.20 net. Harper.

Cumulative index for current law. v. 1-9. '08(D) 336 p. 4°. (Add. pubs. for price.) Keefe-D.

Cundall, Herbert Minton.
History of British water-color painting; with a chronological list of the painters, with dates of birth and death. '08(D12) il. 8°, *$6 net. Dutton.

CUNEIFORM WRITING.
Barton, G: A., *ed.* Haverford [College] Library; collection of cuneiform tablets. 2 pts. pt. 2. $5 net. Winston.
Clay, A. T. Legal and commercial transactions dated in the Assyrian, Neo-Babylonian and Persian periods. $6. Univ. of Penn.

CUNEIFORM WRITING.—*Continued.*
Radau, H., *ed. and tr.* Letters to Cassite kings from the Temple archives of Nippur. $6. Univ. of Penn.
Tolman, H. C. Cuneiform supplement (autographed) to the author's Ancient Persian lexicon and texts. $1.25. Am. Bk.

Cunliffe, J: W:, Pyre, Ja. Fs. Augustine, and Young, Karl, eds.
Century readings for a course in English literature. '10(D17) c. 8°, $2.50. Century Co.

Cunliffe, R: J:
New Shakespearean dictionary. '10(Jl2) 8°, $2.50 net. Scribner.

Cunning, Jos., M.D.
Aids to surgery. 2d ed. '08(Ap4) 16°, (Students' aids ser.) *$1.25 net. Wood.

Cunningham, Brysson.
Treatise on the principles and practice of harbour engineering. '08(Ap11) il. O. *$5 net, boxed. Lippincott.

Cunningham, Dan. J:, M.D.
Manual of pract. anatomy. 2 v. 4th rev. ed. '10(S) 641; 616 p. il. ea., $2.50 net. Wood.

—, Waterston, D:, and Cryer, Matthew H:
Imperial sterescopic anatomy of the head and neck; adapted to the use of the specialist on diseases of the brain and nervous system, the head surgeon, the ear, nose and throat specialist, the dentist, etc. [102 cards in 3 cases.] '09, (N) c. il. 12°, $10 section. Imperial Pub.

—, ed. Text-book of anatomy. 3d ed. '09 (Ag) 1467 p. il. 8°, *$6 net; hf. mor., *$7.50 net. Wood.

Cunningham, Elmer Tiling.
See Haller, G: Fs.

Cunningham, Frances Berkeley.
Priest or pretender. '09(Ap3) c. il. D. $1.50. C. M. Clark.

Cunningham, Gustavus Watts.
Thought and reality in Hegel's system. '10 (D31) O. (Cornell studies in philosophy.) pap., $1.25. Longmans.

Cunningham, J: H:, jr.
See Watson, Fs. Sedgwick.

Cunningham, Mary Moffat.
Verses. '08(Je6) c. D. *$1 net. Bonnell.

Cunningham, W., D.D.
Christianity and social questions. '10(O1) D. (International theological lib.) 75 c. net. Scribner.
Cure of souls: lectures on pastoral theology. '08(N7) 8°, *$1.10 net. Putnam.
English industry and commerce in modern times. In 2 pts. '08(Mr21) 8°, *$5.25 net. Putnam.

Cunnington, Susan.
Stories from Dante. '10(S17) il. O. $1.50 net. Crowell.

Cup of Elijah. Steiner, E: A. *25 c. net. Revell.

Cupa revisited. Mannix, M. E. 45 c. Benziger.

CUPID AND PSYCHE.
Book of Cupid: [anthology from the English poets.] $1 net. Stokes.
Chaffee, A. B. Cupid and Psyche in sculpture and painting. $1.50. Chaffee.

Cupid intelligent. Balbach, J. A. N. $1. J. A. Balbach.

Cupid the surgeon. Meader, H. L. †$1. Altemus.

Cupid's almanac and guide to hearticulture. Hereford, O., *comp.* **90 c. net. Houghton M.

Cupid's cyclopedia. Herford, O. $1 net. Scribner.

Cupid's pack of cards. Pulitzer, W. $1. J: W. Luce.

Cupid's understudy. Field, E: S. $1.25. W. J. Watt.

Cupola furnace. Kirk, E: $3.50. Baird.

Cupper, Percy A.
See Lewis, J: H.

Cuppy, Will Jacob.
Maroon tales. '09(D18) 12°, $1.25. Forbes.

Curb to predatory wealth. Marshall, W: V. $1. Fenno.

Cure for care. Miller, J. R. **30 c. net. Crowell.

Cure of consumption, coughs and colds. Kaessman, F. G. 10 c. Health-Wealth.

Cure of rupture by paraffin injections. Miller, C: C. $1. C: C. Miller.

Cure of souls. Cunningham, W: *$1.10 net. Putnam.

Cure of souls. Milton, W: H. *$1 net. Whittaker.

Cure of souls. Webb, W: W. $1.50 net. Young Churchman.

Curiosities of music. Elson, L: C: $1. Ditson.

Curiosities of the skies. Serviss, G. P. **$1.40 net. Harper.

Curiosity land for young people. '08(D5) il. $1; bds., 75 c. Cassell.

Curious case of Lady Purbeck. Longueville, T: $2. Longmans.

Curle, R: H. P.
Aspects of George Meredith. '08(Ap4) 8°, *$1.75 net. Dutton.

Curlewis, Mrs. H. R.
See Turner, Ethel.

Curly-Locks, and other nursery rhymes. '08 (S5) il. S. (Mother Goose's nursery rhymes.) bds., 50 c. Stokes.

Curr, Rob.
Lake ship yard methods of steel ship construction. '08(Ag29) c. il. por. 8°, $2. Penton Pub.

CURRANT RUST.
See Pine trees.

CURRENCY.
See Banks and banking;—Coins and medals;—Finance;—Gold (*as money*);—Money.

Current (The) cyclopedia of reference; ed. by C: Leonard-Stuart and C: Smith Morris. 8 v. '09(S) c. il. maps, 8°, $24; hf. leath., $36. Syndicate Pub.

Current events index: cumulative guide to material in newspapers; [quarterly,] 1908. '09(Jl10) 4°, subs., per year, $3. Wis. Free Lib.

Current issues. Shaw, L. M. **$2 net. Appleton.

Current practice in steam engineering design. Trovien, O. N. 25 c. Univ. of Wis.

Currente calamo. Du Pont de Nemours, P. F. $1.50. Patterson & W.

CURRENTS.
See Alternating currents:—Electricity.

Curriculum of the elementary school; repr. from *Teachers' College Record*, v. 7, nos. 1 and 4; v. 8, nos. 1, 3 and 4. '08(F8) il. O. $2. Teachers' Coll.

Currie, Donald H.
Second International Conference on Leprosy, held in Bergen, Norway, Aug. 16 to 19, 1909. '09(D) 10 p. 8°. (Add. Superintendent for price.) U. S., Supt. of Docs.

Currier, C: Gilman.
Outlines of pract. hygiene. 6th ed. '10 (D) 498 p. il. 8°, $2 net. Treat.

Curry, C: Madison.
New reading note-book; comprising explanatory notes, questions and suggestions for study, biographical notes and reading lists, pronouncing list, and other material, designed for use in connection with the Howe readers. '09, [1910.] (Mr) c. 15+248 p. 12°, $1. Inland Pub.

Curry, F. E., comp.
National flag; Magna Charta; Declaration of Rights of American colonies, 1765 and 1774; Declaration of Independence; articles of Confederation; Constitution of the United States; treaty with Mexico; General Riley's proclamations, 1849; act admitting California into the Union; constitution of California, 1849; constitution of California, 1879; proposed amendments to the constitution to be voted upon in November, 1910. '10(My14) S. gratis. Cal. Sec'y State.

Curry, Ja., D.D.
History of the San Francisco Theological Seminary of the Presbyterian church in the U. S. A., and its alumni association. '07, [1908.] (Ap.) 206 p. il. pors. 12°, $1.50. J. Curry.

Curry, Ja. S:
Euclid shorthand manual: Graham-Pitmanic. '08(N7) c. D. $1.50. Burrows.

Curry, S: Silas.
Alexander Melville Bell; some memories, with fragments from a pupil's note-book. '09(Ag) c. 84 p. por. 12°, $1. Expression.
Browning and the dramatic monologue. '08 (Ap11) c. D. $1.25. Expression.
Mind and voice; principles and methods in vocal training. '10(O8) c. D. $1.50. Expression.

Curse of Carnes' Hold. Henty, G: A. 50 c. Hurst.

Curse of Ham. Aker, J. W. $1.25. B'way Pub.

CURSUS.
Clark, A. C. Cursus in mediæval and vulgar Latin. 70 c. Oxford Univ.
Frick, C. Cursus philosophicus in usum scholarum. *$1.10 net. Herder.

Curties, Captain H:
Bride on trust. '09(My1) D. $1.50. Estes.
Queen's Gate mystery. '08(N14) c. D. †$1.50. Estes.

Curtin, Jeremiah.
Journey in southern Siberia. '09(N13) c. il. map, O. **$3 net. Little, B. & Co.
Mongols in Russia. '08(O24) c. front. map, O. **$3 net. Little, B. & Co.

Curtis, Albert C:
Good sword Belgarde. '08(N14) c. il. †$1.50. Dodd.

Curtis, Alice Turner.
Anne Nelson, little maid of Province Town. '10(S3) c. il. D. $1.25. Fenno.
Grandpa's little girls and their friends. '09 (N13) c. il. D. †$1. Penn Pub. Co.
Grandpa's little girls at school. '08(O3) c. il. D. (Sunbeam ser. for young people.) †$1. Penn Pub. Co.
Grandpa's little girls' house-boat party. '10 (D3) c. il. D. $1. Penn Pub. Co.
Little heroine at school. '09(S11) c. il. D. (Little heroine ser.) $1.25. Lothrop, L. & S.
Little heroine of Illinois: young girl's patriotism and daring. '08(S5) c. il. D. (Little heroine ser.) †$1.25. Lothrop, L. & S.

Curtis, C: H.
Book of the flower show. '10(Jl30) il. D. (Lane's hdbks. of pract. gardening.) $1 net. Lane.
Orchids for every-one. '10(D10) col. il. 4°, $6 net. Dutton.

Curtis, C: Newman.
Epoch in the spiritual life. '08(My9) c. D. *$1.25 net. Eaton & M.

Curtis, E: S.
North American Indian: ser. of vols. rel. to Indians of U. S. and Alaska; ed. by F: Webb Hodge; foreword by Thdr. Roosevelt; field research conducted under patronage of J. Pierpont Morgan. '07, [1908.] (Mr.) c. il. f°. (Add. author for price per v. or set.) E: S. Curtis.

Curtis, G: W:
Prue and I and Lotos eating. '10(Ap23) 16°, (Everyman's lib.) 35 c. net; leath., 70 c. net. Dutton.

Curtis, Georgina Pell.
Trammelings and other stories. '10(Ja22) 8°, $1.50. Herder.
—, **ed.** Some roads to Rome in America; being personal records of conversions to the Catholic church. '09(Ap) c. 9+532 p. 8°, *$1.75 net. Herder.

Curtis, Harris G:
Threads of gold: [poems.] '10(O) c. 211 p. por. 8°, $1. H. G: Curtis.

Curtis, H: Ellsworth.
Elizabeth Crane; a novel. '10(D31) c. D. B'way Pub.

Curtis, H: Holbrook.
Voice building and tone placing. 3d ed. '09 (Ap3) c. il. 12°, $2. Appleton.

Curtis, Mrs. Isabel Gordon, comp.
Good housekeeping woman's home cook book. '09(Je19) 8°, 60 c. Reilly & B.
Also issued under title Good housekeeping every day cook book.
See also Morse, Sidney Levi.

Curtis, Nathaniel Cortlandt.
Elements of graphics, orthographic projections, shades, shadows, and perspective. '09(D) c. 34 p. il. 4°, $1.50. N. C. Curtis.

Curtis, Rob. W.
See Baskerville, C:

Curtis, Roy Emerson.
Proportional representation. '09(Mr6) D. (Comparative legislation bull.) pap., 25 c. Wisconsin Free Lib.

Curtis, Uriah.
Modern business arithmetic. '08(D12) c. diagrs., 12°. (Add. pubs. for price.) Bobbs-M.

Curtis, W: Eleroy.
One Irish summer. '09(My8) c. il. 8°, **$3.50 net. Duffield.

Curtiss, Fk. Homer, ed.
Letters from the teacher (of the Order of the 15), transmitted by Rahmea, priestess of the flame. v. 1. '10(Je11) c. D. $1.10. Curtiss.

Curtler, W. H. R.
Short history of English agriculture. '09 (S11) D. $2.15. Oxford Univ.

Curtman, L: J.
See Baskerville, C:

Curtman, Wilhelm Jacob Georg.
Short stories for children; tr. from the German by Ida Curtman. '10(F12) c. O. 75 c. Curtman.

CURVES.
Atchison, C. S. Curves with a diretrix. (Add. pubs. for price.) Johns Hopkins.
Cowley, E. B. Plane curves of the eighth order. (Not for sale.) New Era Print.
Crandall, C: L. Transition curve, by offsets and by deflection angles. $2. Wiley.
Diamant, S. Curves for calculating beams, channels and reactions. $2. McGraw.
Duncan, R. H. Pract. curve tracing. $1.60 net. Longmans.
Frere, F. H. Permanent way diagrams, giving the spread of crossings for turnouts. $1.25. Spon.
Sullivan, J: G. Spiral tables; prep. for the Canadian Pacific Railroad. $1.50 net. McGraw-H.
Williamson, H. Metric tables for setting out curves in metres. 80 c. Spon.
***See also* Geometry.**

Curves for calculating beams, channels and reactions. Diamant, S. $2. McGraw.

Curwood, Ja. Oliver.
Courage of Captain Plum. '08(O24) c. il. D. †$1.50. Bobbs-M.
The danger trail. '10(Mr19) c. il. D. †$1.50. Bobbs-M.
Gold hunters. '10(F5) c. il. 12°, †$1.50. Bobbs-M.
Great Lakes; the vessels that plough them; their owners, their sailors, and their cargoes. '09(My1) c. il. map, O. (American waterways.) **$3.50 net, boxed. Putnam.
Wolf hunters: tale of adventure in the wilderness. '08(D12) c. il. D. †$1.50. Bobbs-M.

Curzon, G: Nathaniel, [1st Baron Curzon of Keddleston, formerly Viceroy and Governor-General of India.]
Frontiers; the Romanes lecture, 1907. '08 (Ja18) O. pap., 50 c. Oxford Univ.
Principles and methods of university reform. '09(My15) O. 50 c. Oxford Univ.

Cushing, C: Cyprian Strong.
Nathan Hale of '73: a drama. '08(D26) il. nar. O. pap., *$1 net. Yale Pub.

Cushing, Harry Alonzo, ed.
See Adams, S:

Cushing, Harry Cooke, jr.
Standard wiring for electric light and power as adopted by the fire underwriters of the United States. [1910. 16th ed.] '10(F19) c. il. tabs., 16°, $1. H. C. Cushing.
See also Crocker, Fs. B:—Radcliffe, W: Hiram.

Cushing, J: J.
Law of success: for agents and tradesmen. '08(O3) c. 12°, $1. Jenckes.

Cushing, Mary Gertrude.
Pierre Le Tourneur. '08(N21) 12°, (Columbia Univ. studies in romance, philology and literature.) **$1.50 net. Lemcke.

CUSHING FAMILY.
Haight, T. W. Three Wisconsin Cushings; Howard B., Alonzo H. and William B. Cushing. $1. Wisconsin Hist.

Cushman, Allerton Seward.
Preservation of iron and steel. '09(Jl3) il. fold. fig. O. (U. S., Dept. of Agriculture, Office of Public Roads bull.) pap. 10 c. U. S., Supt. of Docs.

—, and Gardner, H: Alfr.
Corrosion and preservation of iron and steel. '10(My14) c. il. O. $4 net. McGraw-H.

Cushman, Herb. Ernest.
Beginner's history of philosophy. In 2 v. v. 1, Ancient and mediæval philosophy. '10(D17) c. front. D. $1.60 net. Houghton M.

Cushner, Meyer Barnard.
Commercial law for accountant students. '08, [1909.] (Ja) c. O. 372 p. hf. leath. Universal Business.

Cushny, Arth. Robertson.
Textbook of pharmacology and therapeutics; or, the action of drugs in health and disease. 5th ed., thoroughly rev. '10 (S) c. 744 p. il. 4°, $3.75 net. Lea.
Contains bibliographies.

Cust, Mrs. H.
See Cust, Nina.

Cust, Nina, [Mrs. H. Cust.]
Gentlemen errant: being the journeys and adventures of four noblemen in Europe during the XV. and XVI. centuries. '09 (Ap17) pors. maps, 8°, *$4 net. Dutton.

Cust, Rob. H: Hobart.
Botticelli. '08(F15) il. 24°, (Bell's miniature ser. of painters.) 50 c.; leath., $1. Macmillan.
Leonardo Da Vinci. '08(My9) il. 16°, (Bell's miniature ser. of painters.) 50 c.; leath., $1. Macmillan.

CUSTOM HOUSE.
***See* Civil service.**

CUSTOMS.
See Tariff.
CUTANEOUS DISEASES.
See Skin.
"Cuthbert," pseud.
See Copus, *Rev.* J: Edn.
Cuthbert, Father.
Chronicle of Thomas of Eccleston. '09(O) 39+168 p. 8°, *75 c. net. Herder.
Cuthbertson, W:
Pansies, violas and violets. '10(Jl30) col. il. O. (Garden flowers in color.) bds., 65 c. net. Stokes.
Cutler, Ida McLenan, and So Relle, Rupert P.
Rational typewriting; new idea in teaching touch typewriting; thoroughly rev., 1910, by Rupert P. So Relle. '10(O) c. 104 p. il. 12°, $1. Gregg Pub.
Cutten, G: Barton.
Psychological phenomena of Christianity. '08(N14) c. O. **$2.50 net. Scribner.
Cutter, Mrs. B. B.
See Cutter, Sophia Genevieve Robinson.
Cutter, Sophia Genevieve Robinson, [Mrs. B. B. Cutter.]
Practical recipes. '09(O16) D. *$1.25 net. Duffield.
Cutter, W: R:, ed.
Genealogical and family history of northern New York; record of the achievements of her people in the making of a commonwealth and the founding of a nation. 3 v. '10(D) il. pors. 4°, $25. Lewis Pub.
Genealogical and personal memoirs rel. to the families of Boston and eastern Mass. 4 v. '08, [1910.] (N) il. pors. 4°. Lewis Pub.
Genealogical and personal memoirs rel. to the families of the state of Massachusetts; prep. under the ed. supervision of W: R: Cutter, assisted by W: F: Adams. 4 v. '10(Je) il. pors. 4°, $25. Lewis Pub.
Historic homes and places and genealogical and personal memoirs relating to the families of Middlesex Co., Mass. '08, [1909.] (Ja) c. 4 v., il. pors. 4°. (Add. pubs. for price.) Lewis Pub.
Cutting, Mrs. Mary Stewart Doubleday.
Just for two. '09(O16) c. il. D. *$1 net, fixed. Doubleday, P.
The unforeseen. '10(O29) c. il. D. $1.20, fixed. Doubleday, P.
The wayfarers. '08(Jl4) c. il. D. †$1.50. McClure.
Cuypers, B. J. H.
Chateau of Haar; le Chateau de Haar à Haarzuylens; 75 plates, with descriptive il. text. in French. '10(Ap23) $40. Hessling.
Cy Hains's sermo-phone. Taylor, J: E. 50 c. J: E. Taylor.
Cy Whittaker's place. Lincoln, J. C. †$1.50 Appleton.
CYANIDE PROCESS.
Bain, H. F., *ed.* More recent cyanide practice. $2. Mining and Scientific.
Clennell, J: E: Chemistry of cyanide solutions resulting from the treatment of ores. *$2.50 net.—Cyanide hdbk. $5 net. McGraw-H.

CYANIDE PROCESS.—*Continued.*
Megraw, H. A. Pract. data for the cyanide plant. $2. McGraw-H.
Wilson, E. B: Cyanide processes. $1.50. Wilson.
Cycle of sunsets. Todd, *Mrs.* M. L. $1.25 net. Small.
Cycles of speculation. Gibson, T: $1.50. Moody's Mag.
CYCLING.
See Bicycles and bicycling.
Cyclopedia of engineering; editor-in-chief, L: Derr. '10(Ja22) 7 v., il. pors. tabs., 8°, ea., $2.60. Am. Sch. Corr.
Cyclopedia of modern shop practice; Howard Monroe Raymond, ed.-in-chief, assisted by a corps of mechanical engineers, designers and specialists in shop methods and management. 4 v. '09(O) c. il. 8°, $12.80. Am. Sch. Corr.
CYCLOPEDIAS.
See Encyclopædias.
CYCLOPS.
See Crustaceans.
CYLINDERS.
See Engines.
Cylinders and other ancient oriental seals in the library of J: Pierpont Morgan. Morgan, J: P. (Priv. pr.) J: P. Morgan.
Cynewulf.
Poems of Cynewulf; tr. into English prose with an introd. by C. W. Kennedy. '10(Jl30) 8°, $2 net. Dutton.
Cynical kids. Newkirk, C. 75 c. Caldwell.
Cynthia in the wilderness. Wales, H., *pseud.* $1.50. Stuyvesant Press.
Cynthia's chauffeur. Tracy, L. $1.50. Clode.
CYPRUS (*Island of*).
Cobhan, C. D., *ed.* Excerpta Cypria; material for a history of Cyprus. *$6.30 net. Putnam.
Haggard, H: R. Winter pilgrimage: travels through Palestine, Italy, and the island of Cyprus. $1.50. Longmans.
Mariti, G. Travels in the Island of Cyprus. *$1.25 net. Putnam.
Stewart, B. My experiences in Cyprus. *$2 net. Dutton.
Cyr, Mrs. Ellen M., [now Mrs. Ruel Perley Smith.]
Story of three great artists: Raphael, Michael Angelo, Leonardo da Vinci. '09 (Je5) c. il. D. (Graded art readers.) 50 c. Ginn.
Cystoscopy as adjuvant in surgery. Rumple, O. $8.50 net. Rebman.
CYTOMORPHOSIS.
See Biology.
D., L. S. T.
Beyond this ignorant present. '10(S) 8°, $1.25. Cassell.
Dabney, C: W:
Unity of the university. '09(O) 6 p. 8°, pap. (Not for sale.) Univ. of Cin.
Da Costa, J: Chalmers, jr., M.D.
Modern surgery, general and operative. 6th ed., thoroughly rev. and enl. '10 (Mr) c. 9-1502 p. il. 8°, *$5.50 net. Saunders.
Principles and practice of physical diagnosis. '08(D) c. 548 p. il. 8°, *$3.50 net. Saunders.

Daffan, Katie.
Texas hero stories: hist. reader. '08(Mr7) c. il. pors. 12°, 50 c. B: H. Sanborn.
Woman in history. '09(Ja23) c. O. *$2 net. Neale.

DAFFODILS.
Jacob, J. Daffodils. 65 c. net. Stokes.

Daggett, C: H.
Theory of pharmaceutical chemistry. '10 (O) c. 7+540 p. il. 8°, $2.75 net. Lea.

Daggett, Mabel Potter.
In Lockerbie Street; little appreciation of James Whitcomb Riley. '09(D25) c. il. por. 8°, 50 c. B. W. Dodge.

Daggett, Stuart.
Railroad reorganization. '08(My23) c. O. (Harvard economic studies.) **$2 net. Houghton M.

Daggy, Maynard Lee.
Principles of public speaking; pract. text book for colleges. '10(Ja22) 8°, $1.50. M. L. Daggy.

Dahlgren, Ulric, and Kepner, W: Allison.
Text-book of the principles of animal histology. '08(Jl11) il. 8°, *$3.75 net. Macmillan.

Dahlke, Paul.
Buddhist essays; tr. from the German by Bhikkhu Silacara. '08(O24) 8°, *$3 net. Macmillan.

Daily food. New ed. '10(D) 50 c., boxed; limp leath., $1. Barse & H.

Daily living. Ewart, N. E. *$1.84 net. H. P. Hood.

Daily meals of children. Hunt, C. L. (Add. Superintendent for price.) U. S., Supt. of Docs.

Daily normal temperature and the daily normal precipitation of the United States. Bigelow, F. H. $1.75. U. S., Supt. of Docs.

Daily ways to health. Bishop, *Mrs.* E. M. $1.50 net. B: W. Huebsch.

Daingerfield, Mrs. Nettie Gray.
Frescati: a page from Virginia history. '09(My1) c. D. *$1 net. Neale.

Dainty dining. Brown, *Mrs.* M. A. A., *comp.* $1.50. Reed Press.

DAIRY.
Anderson, J. S. Simple creamery computation. $5. J. S. Anderson.
Barthel, C. Methods used in the examination of milk and dairy products. $1.90 net. Macmillan.
Benkendorf, G. H: W:, *and* Hatch, K. L. Profitable dairying. gratis. Babsom.
Benkendorf, G. H: W:, *comp. and ed.* Catalogue of the postal dairy library. gratis. G. H: W: Benkendorf.
Dissemination of disease by dairy products. Gov. Pr. Off.
Douglas, L. M. Refrigeration in the dairy. $1. Nickerson & C.
Grotenfelt, G. Principles of modern dairy practice from a bacteriological point of view. $2. Wiley.

DAIRY.—*Continued.*
Gurler, H: B: Farm dairy. $1. Breeders' Gazette.
Jamestown Exposition. Eleventh annual convention of the Association of State and National Food and Dairy Departments, held at Jamestown Tercentennial Exposition. $3. Wiley.
Lane, C. B. Business of dairying. *$1.25 net. Judd.
Maynall, G. Cows, cowhouses and milk. $1. A. Eger.
Michels, J: Market dairying. $1. J: Michels.
Rawl, B. H., *and others.* Dairy industry in the South. (Add. Superintendent for price.) U. S., Supt. of Docs.
Ross, H. E. Dairy lab'y guide. 50 c. Judd.
Russell, H. L., *and* Hastings, E. G: Experimental dairy bacteriology. $1. Ginn.
Russell, H. L., *and* Hastings, E. G: Outlines of dairy bacteriology. $1. H. L. Russell.
Sheldon, J. P. Farm and the dairy. *$1 net. Macmillan.
Spillman, W: J. Successful poultry and dairy farm. (Add. Superintendent for price.) U. S., Supt. of Docs.
United States. *Dept. of Agriculture. Bu. of Animal Industry.* Publications of interest to dairymen. '09(My) 5 p. 8°, pap. gratis. U. S., Supt. of Docs.
United States public documents rel. to the American dairy industry. '09(My) 37 p. 12°, pap., gratis. U. S., Supt. of Docs.
Van Norman, H. E. First lessons in dairying. *50 c. net. Judd.
Woll, F. W., *and others.* Hdbk. for farmers and dairymen. $1.50. Wiley.
See also **Butter; — Cow; — Domestic animals; — Milk;—*also* Texas.**

Daish, J: Broughton.
Procedure in interstate commerce cases, with illustrative precedents and forms. '09(Mr) c. 14+494 p. O. *$5 net. Lowdermilk.

Daisy chain ser. 8 v. '09(D) c. ea. 44 p. il. in col. 8°, ea., 15 c. Doran.
Contents: The daisy chain; Dolly's picture book; Blind man's buff; Puss in the corner; For doggie and me, Baby's own picture book; Oranges and lemons; Hide and seek.

Daisy (The); or, cautionary stories in verse, adapted to the ideas of children from four to eight years old. '10(Ag20) col. il. Q. bds., $1.25. Caldwell.

DAKOTA INDIANS.
See **Sioux Indians.**

Dalbiac, Philip Hugh.
See Harbottle, T: Benfield.

Dale, Alan, [pseud. for Alfr. J. Cohen.]
Great wet way. '09(Ap3) c. il. D. **$1.50 net. Dodd.

Dale, Darley, pseud.
See Steele, F. M. F.

Dale, Ja. Gary.
Mexico and our mission (Associate reformed Presbyterian). '10(D31) c. il. pors. fold. map, 8°, $1. J. G. Dale.

Dale, J: T:
Flashlights from real life. '10(D31) c. 12°, $1. Fairfax.
—, comp. Heroes and greathearts and their animal friends. '08(S12) c. il. pors. D. $1. Fairfax.

Dale, Mrs. Lucy.
Landmarks of British hist. '10(My21) il. (4 in col.) D. 90 c. Longmans.
Stories from European hist. '10(My21) il. (4 in col.) D. 50 c. net. Longmans.

Dale, Mary, [pseud. for Mayone Dawson.]
Miss Eagle: the suffragette. '09(Je) 12°, 50 c. Aberdeen.

Dale, T: Nelson.
Chief commercial granites of Massachusetts, New Hampshire and Rhode Island. '09(Mr6) il. maps, 8°, (U. S. Geol. Survey, bull.) 30 c. U. S., Supt. of Docs.
Granites of Vermont. '09, [1910.] (Je) 138 p. il. 8°, (U. S., Dept. of the Interior, Geological Survey bull.)
Bibliography of economic geology of granite (3 p.).

Dale memorial lectures in Mansfield College, Oxford. il. O. Armstrong.
—Ramsay. Cities of St. Paul. *$3 net.

Daley, Myra.
Jerd Cless. '09(D25) c. 12°, $1.50. Cochrane.

Dalhousie, Earl of.
See Ramsay, Fox Maule, Baron Panmure, *Earl* of Dalhousie.

Dalkeith, Lena.
Little plays. '08(D19) il. 16°, (Told to the children ser.) 50 c. Dutton.
Stories from French history. '09(N6) col. il. 24°, *50 c. net. Dutton.
Stories from Roman history. '08(Ag1) il. 24°, (Stories from history.) 50 c. Dutton.

Dall, W: Healey.
Contributions to the Tertiary paleontology of the Pacific coast; 1, Miocene of Astoria and Coos Bay, Ore. '09(My) 278 p. il. map, 4°, (U. S., Dept. of the Interior; U. S. Geol. Survey; Professional papers.) pap., 50 c. U. S., Supt. of Docs.
Description of two new pulmonate mollusks, with a list of other species from the Solomon Islands, collected by Dr. George A. Dorsey. '10(Ap) 215-221 p. il. 8°, (Field Museum of Natural History pubs.; Zoölogical ser.) 50 c. Field Museum.

—, and Bartsch, Paul.
Monograph of West American pyramidellid mollusks. '09, [1910.] (Ap) 12+258 p. il. 8°, (Smithsonian Institution, U. S. National Museum, bull.) pap., 35 c. U. S., Supt. of Docs.

DALLAS, Tex.
Lindsley, P. History of greater Dallas and vicinity. v. 1. per set, $20. Lewis Pub.

Dallıba, Gerda.
Earth poem, and other poems; with an introd. by Edn. Markham. '08(D12) c. por. 8°, **$2 net. Putnam.

Dallimore, W.
Holly, yew and box; with notes on other evergreens; descriptions of the varieties of the common holly are based on the monograph by T: Moore. '08(O10) il. O. $2.50. Lane.

DALMATIA, Austria-Hungary.
Frothingham, A. L. Roman cities in Italy and Dalmatia. $1.75 net. Sturgis & W.
See also Austria-Hungary.

Dalrymple, C. Leona.
Mrs. Forrester's crusade: farce. '08(My16) c. 16°, pap., 15 c. Dick.
Surprises: a farce. '08(Mr14) c. D. pap., 15 c. Dick.

Dalrymple, Julia.
Make-believe boys. '08(N7) c. il. D. †$1. Little, B. & Co.
See also McDonald, *Mrs.* Etta Blaisdell.

Dalton, Jos. Grinnell.
Spherical basis of astrology; being a comprehensive table of houses for latitudes 22° to 56°. 3d ed. '08(N) c. 6+67 p. 4°, $2.50. Spenceley.

Dalton, Rev. L. M.
Sermon outlines. '10(D24) 12°, 80 c. net. Whittaker.

Dalton, Rev. M. L.
Church catechism in anecdote. '09(O16) 12°, *$1 net. Whittaker.

Dalton, W:
Auction bridge up-to-date. '10(Ag6) S. $1. Wycil.
Bridge and auction bridge. '10(N12) c. il. D. $1.20 net. Stokes.
Inferences at bridge. '09(Je5) S. *40 c. net. Lippincott.

Daly, T: Augustine.
Carmina. '09(Ap10) c. D. **$1.50 net. Lane.

Damaged reputation. Bindloss, H. $1. Fenno.

DAMAGES.
Beale, J. H: Collection of cases on the measure of damages. $3.50. Little, B. & Co.
Farmer, J. A. Trial manual of personal injury laws; Illinois. $4. Fiske & Co.
Mechem, F. R., *and* Gilbert, B. Cases on damages. $4. West Pub.
Russell, I. F., *comp.* Cases on measure of damages. $4. Callaghan.
Sedgwick, A. G: Elements of the law of damages. $3; $3.50. Little, B. & Co.
Wilkinson, J. D. Personal injuries. $7. Hansell.
Willis, H. E. Principles of the law of damages. $3. Keefe-D.
See also names of states.

DAMASCUS, Syria.
See Syria.

Da Masserano, Giuseppe Maria.
Life of St. Leonard of Port Maurice, missionary apostolic of the Order of the Reformed Friars, minor of the Retreat of St. Bonaventure, Rome; tr. from the Italian by Rev. Antonio Isoleri. '09(Ap) 370 p. il. 8°, $1.50. Kilner.

Dame, Arth. K.
Nebraska. Supp. to the law of probate.

"Dame Curtsey," pseud.
See Glover, Ellye Howell.

Dame Wiggins and her seven wonderful cats. *See* Ruskin, J:

Damon, Fannie A.
In the shadow of the pines: [poems.] '07, [1908.] (Mr.) c. 13-76 p. il. D. $1. F. A. Damon.

Damon, H: B., comp.
Gems of thought. '07, [1909.] (Mr) (Priv. pr.) H: B. Damon.

Damphool in the Kentucky legislature. Kennedy, H: C. $1. Conkey.

DAMS.
Gatun Dam and earth dams in general; article from the *Engineering News* of Apr. 1, 1909. '09(Je) 10 p. il. 8°, pap. (Add. Superintendent for price.) U. S., Supt. of Docs.
Morrison, C: E:, *and* Brodie, O. L. High masonry dam design. $1.50. Wiley.
Prelini, C: Graphical determination of earth slopes, retaining walls, and dams. **$2 net. Van Nostrand.
Schuyler, J. D. Reservoirs: for irrigation, water-power, and domestic water supply; with account of various types of dams. $6. Wiley.
See also Panama canal;—Reservoirs.

Damsel and the sage. Glyn, *Mrs.* E. S. †$1.25. Duffield.

Dan, Horace, and Willmott, E. C. Morgan.
English shop-fronts old and new: examples by leading architects. '08(F22) il. 8°, $6. Helburn.

Dan Merrithew. Perry, L. $1.50. McClurg.

Dana, C: Loomis, M.D.
Text-book of nervous diseases and psychiatry. 7th ed., completely revised. '08 (O3) il. 8°, *$5 net; leath., *$6 net. Wood.
—, **ed.** *See* Horace, [Quintus Horatius Flaccus.]

Dana, E: Salisbury, and Ford, W: Ebenezer.
Second appendix to the 6th ed. of Dana's System of mineralogy; completing the work to 1909. '09(S18) c. il. 4°, $1.50. Wiley.

Dana, Ja. Dwight.
System of mineralogy, 1837-1868; descriptive mineralogy. 6th ed., by E: Salisbury Dana; entirely rewritten and much enl.; with appendix 1, completing the work to 1899. '09(Je19) il. 4°, hf. mor., $12.50. Wiley.

Dana, J: Cotton.
Library primer. 5th rev. ed. '10(My21) c. il. 12°, $1. Lib. Bu.
Modern American library economy, as illustrated by the Newark, N. J., Free Public Library. pt. 1, The lending department; section 1, The work of the registration desk, by Sara C. Van de Carr. '09(Ja16) il. pap., 25 c.;—pt. v., The school department; section 2, Course of study for normal school pupils on the use of a library, by Marjary L. Gilson. '09(Je12) c. O. pap., 75 c. Elm Tree Press.
Notes on bookbinding for libraries. Rev. and enl. ed. '10(Jl30) il. 12°, $1. Lib. Bu.
—, **ed.** *See* Horace, [Quintus Horatius Flaccus.]

Dana, R: H:, jr.
Richard Henry Dana, jr. (author of "Two years before the mast"); speeches in stirring times and letters to a son; ed., with introd. sketch and notes by R: H: Dana, 3d. '10(D3) c. pors. O. $3 net. Houghton M.
Two years before the mast. '09(Mr27) 24°, (Pocket Am. and Eng. classics.) *25 c. net. Macmillan.

Dana, R: T.
See Gillette, Halbert Powers.

Dana, W: Sumner Barton.
Primer of architectural drawing for young students; being a progressive series of drawing board problems. '10(Ag27) c. il. D. $1.25. W: T. Comstock.

Dana kids. Whiteley, L. C. 50 c. L. C. Whiteley.

Danaher, Albert J., rep.
See New York State. Repts.

Danaher, Franklin Martin.
Bar examinations (New York) and courses of law study, cont. the statutes and rules of court regulating admission to the bar in N. Y. State and forms and instructions, [etc.] 4th ed. '09(My) c. 12+447 p. O. $4. Lyon.

Danbury Rodd. Palmer, F: $1.50. Scribner.

Danby, Fk., [pseud. for Mrs. Julia Frankau.]
Heart of a child: being passages from the early life of Sally Snape, Lady Kidderminster. '08(Mr14) c. D. †$1.50. Macmillan.
Let the roof fall in. '10(N5) c. il. D. $1.50. Appleton.
Sebastian. '09(Ap24) c. D. †$1.50. Macmillan.

DANCING.
Bergquist, N. W. Swedish folk dances. $1.50. A. S. Barnes.
Brower, J., *ed.* Morris dance; descriptions of eleven dances as performed by the Morris-men of England. $1. H. W. Gray.
Burchenal, E., *ed.* Folk-dances and singing games. $2.50; $1.50. Schirmer.
Crampton, C: W., *comp.* Folk dance book for elem. schools. $1.50. Barnes.
Crawford, C. Folk dances and games. $1.50. Barnes.
Davison, W: J. Gymnastic dancing. $1. Y. M. C. A.
Duncan, I. The dance. $1. Forest Press.
Gulick, L. H. Healthful art of dancing. $1.40 net. Doubleday, P.
Lamb, W: How and what to dance. 50 c. Fenno.
Satori, J. A. Modern dances. 25 c.; 15 c. V. H. Krull.
Scott, E: New dancing as it should be. 50 c. Dutton.
Seton, E. T. War dance and the fire-fly dance. 10 c. Doubleday, P.
Swedish folk dance, "Vafva Vadmal." 25 c. Bassette.

Dandelion classics for children; ed. by Lucy Fitch Perkins. il. Q. †$1.50. Stokes.
—Æsop. Fables.
—Hawthorne. Wonderbook.

Dandelion ser. *See* Rankin, Carroll Watson.

Dandridge, Mrs. Danske Bedinger.
George Michael Bedinger; a Kentucky pioneer. '09(Ag) 4+232 p. por. 8°, $2. A. S. Dandridge.
Historic Shepherdstown. '10(O) c. 6+362 p. map, 8°, $2. Michie.
Bibliography (3 p.).

Danger mark. Chambers, R. W. **$1.50 net. Appleton.

Danger trail. Curwood, J. O. †$1.50. Bobbs-M.

Dangerous currency system of the United States. Wichelman, F: A: 10 c. F: A: Wichelman.

Dangerous donations and degrading doles. Candler, W. A. 10 c. Lester Bk.

Dangers and chemistry of fire. Maris, C. (Add. pubs. for price.) Ohio State Fire Marshal

Dangers of the day. Vaughan, J: S. $1. Ave Maria.

Daniel, J. C.
History of the Baptists of Hill County, Texas. '07, [1908.] (O) 9-132 p. pors. 12°, $1. Hill-K.-F. Co.

Daniel, J. Fk.
Animal life of Malaysia. [2d ed.] '09 (Ap3) c. il. O. **$1.20 net. Bobbs-M.

Daniel, J: Warwick.
Lumber schedule; paper entitled Data on the lumber schedule; also a sworn statement of the difference in the wage scale of the U. S. and Canada, etc. '09(Ag) 8 p. 8°, pap. (Add. Superintendent for price.) U. S., Supt. of Docs.

DANIEL (Book of).
See Bible. O. T.

Daniels, C: Wilberforce, and Wilkinson, E.
Tropical medicine and hygiene. In 3 pts. pt. 1, Diseases due to protozoa. '10(F) il. 8°, **$3 net. Wood.

Daniels, Fred Hamilton.
Furnishing of a modest home. '08(Jl4) c. il. plans, O. $1. Davis Press.
School drawing. '10(F5) c. il. 8°, $1.26. M. Bradley.

Daniels, J:
Outline of economics. '08(N21) c. O. 40 c. Ginn.

Daniels, Percy.
Swollen fortunes and the problem of the unemployed. '08, [1909.] (My) c. 74 p. 8°, pap., 15 c. P. Daniels.

Daniels, W. M., comp. and ed.
Choix de poésies faciles. '09(O16) S. (Crowell's shorter French texts.) *25 c. net. Crowell.

DANISH LANGUAGE.
See Norwegian language.

DANISH LITERATURE.
Kildal, A., *comp.* Selected Norwegian and Danish books. 25 c. A. L. A.

Danks, Canon W:
Canterbury. '10(Jl30) col. il. O. (Beautiful England ser.) bds., $1.25, boxed. Estes.

Dann, Hollis.
School hymnal; collection of hymns and chants; incl. sacred, patriotic, and occasional songs, for use in normal, high and private schools. '10(O8) c. O. 50 c. Am. Bk.

Dann, Hollis, comp. and ed.
Christmas carols and hymns for school and choir. '10(O22) c. Q. 45 c. Am. Bk.

Danner, T: Jefferson.
Plea for the old faith of the old church. '09, [1910.] (Ja) c. 66 p. 8°, 25 c. T: J. Danner.

Dannerth, Frederic.
Methods of textile chemistry: being the syllabus of a lecture course. '08(O14) c. 12°, $2. Wiley.

Dante. Raymond, G: L. **$1.25 net. Putnam.

Dante Alighieri.
Cary's Divine comedy of Dante. '08(O10) 12°, (Best books ser.) leath., *$1 net. Dutton.
Convivio; tr. into English by W: Walrond Jackson. '09(Ag14) 8°, (Oxford lib. of translations.) *$1 net. Oxford Univ.
Divine comedy. pt. 1, The inferno; with introd. and notes, arranged for high schools, colleges, and literary societies. '08, [1909.] (Ja16) c. por. charts, 12°, (Lakeside classics.) *50 c. net. Ainsworth.
Divine comedy, (Cary's translation;) ed. by Edmund Gardner. '08(Mr7) 16°, (Everyman's lib.) *35 c. net; leath., *70 c. net. Dutton.
Divine comedy; tr. by H: Fs. Cary, with special introd. by C: Eliot Norton. '08 (Je27) c. il. 8°, $1.75; hf. mor., $3.50. Lamb Pub.
Divine comedy; tr. by H: Wadsworth Longfellow; ed. by C: Welsh. 4 v. '09 (N) c. il. 8°, $6. W. D. Lane.
La divina commedia; ed. and annot. by C. H. Grandgent. v. 1, Inferno. '09(Ap3) c. D. (Modern lang. ser.) $1.25. Heath.
Quaestio de aqua et terra; ed. and tr. by C: Lancelot Shadwell. '10(F19) D. $1.50. Oxford Univ.
Readings on the Paradiso of Dante, chiefly based on the commentary of Benvenuto da Imola, by the Hon. William Warren Vernon; with introd. by the Bp. of Ripon. 2d ed., rev. 2 v. '09, [1910.] (My) il. 12°, $4 net. Macmillan.
List of authors and of editions quoted (23 p.).
Stories from Dante told to the children, by Mary Macgregor. '10(My21) c. il. 24°, (Told to the children ser.) 50 c. Dutton.

DANTE ALIGHIERI.
Cassio, A. Sulla "Vita nuova" di Dante. $3. Stechert.
Cunnington, S. Stories from Dante. $1.50 net. Crowell.
Flamini, F. Introd. to the study of the Divine comedy. $1.25. Ginn.
Henderson, H: F. With Dante on the mountain. 75 c. Jennings.
Reade, W: H: V. Moral system of Dante's Inferno. $4.15. Oxford Univ.
Rose, *Mrs.* H. D. Dante; dramatic poem. $2 net. M. Kennerley.
Rossetti, D. G. Dante at Verona. 50 c. net; $1 net. T: B. Mosher.
Santayana, G: Three philosophical poets; Lucretius, Dante, and Goethe. $2.25. Harvard Univ.
Snell, F: J: Hdbk. to the works of Dante. *$1.50 net. Macmillan.

DANTE ALIGHIERI.—*Continued.*
Toynbee, P. J. Dante Alighieri, his life and works. $1.50.—Dante in English literature. 2 v. *$5 net. Macmillan.
See also Paradiso.
Dante and Beatrice. Drummond, *Mrs.* S. K. W. **$1.25 net. Macmillan.
DANTON, Georges Jacques
Warwick, C: F. Danton and the French Revolution. **$2.50 net. Jacobs.
Danvers, Mass. Celebration of the one hundred and fiftieth anniversary of the establishment of the town of Danvers, Mass., as a separate municipality, June 15, 16, 17, 1902. '07, [1908.] (Mr.) 222 p. pors. pls. 8°. (Add. pub. for price.) S. Usher.
DANVERS, Mass.
Vital records of Danvers, Mass., to the end of the year 1849. *$4.45 net. Essex Inst.
Danziger, Gustave Adolphe.
After the confession, and other verses. '08 (O) c. 48 p. 16°. (Add. author for price.) G. A. Danziger.
Daphne in Fitzroy street. Bland, *Mrs.* E. N. †$1.50. Doubleday, P.
Darbishire, A. D.
Breeding and the Mendelian discovery. '10 (D10) $1.75 net. Cassell.
Darbishire, Otto V.
Plant book for schools. '08(My9) il. 8°, *$1 net. Macmillan.
Darby, Mrs. Sarah.
That affair in Philadelphia. '09(My8) c. D. $1. B'way Pub.
D'Arcy, Bp. C: F:
Christianity and the supernatural. '09 (F27) D. (Anglican Church handbooks.) *40 c. net. Longmans.
Darewell chums ser. *See* Chapman, Allen.
Dargan, Edn. Preston.
Hylas and other poems. '10(F12) c. D. bds., $1. Badger.
Dargan, Olive Tilford.
Lords and lovers and other dramas. 2d ed. '09. [1910.] (F) **$1.50 net. Scribner.
Semiramis, and other plays. [2d ed.] '09 (My22) *$1 net. Scribner.
Darier, Armand, M.D.
Therapeutics; tr. by Sydney Stephenson. '10(Ag) 14+444 p. il. 8°, (International system of ophthalmic practice; ed. by W. L. Pyle.) $4. Blakiston.
"Daring, Hope," pseud.
See Johnson, Anna.
Darius I., King of Persia.
Behistan inscription; translation and critical notes to the Persian text with special reference to recent re-examinations of the rock, by Herbert Cushing Tolman. '08(My16) O. (Vanderbilt Univ. studies.) pap., 50 c. Lemcke.
Darius Green and his flying machine. Trowbridge, J: T. 50 c. net. Houghton M.
Dark corner. McGhee, Z. $1. Grafton Press.
Darley, G:
Complete poetical works; introd. by Ramsay Colles. '08(F22) 12°, (Muses' lib.) 50 c.; leath., 75 c. Dutton.
Darling, C: Rob.
Heat for engineers. '09(Mr13) il. 8°, (Finsbury technical manuals.) $5. Spon.
Darling, Jasper T.
Cold facts; the pen of Col. Lee writes the indictment against the sword of General Lee; address del. at Freeport, Ill., May 30, 1910. [1910.] (S) c. 15 p. por. 12°, pap., $1.50 per 100 copies. J. T. Darling.
Heart of hope. '09(Je12) c. il. por. O. pap. (Not for sale.) J. T. Darling.
Darling, Philip Grenville.
Safety valve capacity. [2d ed.] '09 (My22) c. il. O. pap., gratis. Consolidated Safety.
Darling, S: T., M.D.
Studies in relation to malaria. '10(Ag) 38 p. O. pap. Gov. Pr. Off.
Darlington, Edg. B. P.
Circus boys on the flying rings; or, making the start in the sawdust life. '10 (N12) c. il. 12°, (Circus boys ser.) $1. Altemus.
DARLINGTON FAMILY.
See Genealogies: Cope, G.
Darlow, T. H.
See Brown, C:
Darmesteter, Mme. Agnes Mary Frances Robinson, [now Mme. Duclaux.]
French procession; pageant of great writers. '09(D4) pors. O. **$3.50 net. Duffield.
Darrieus, Pierre Jos. Gabriel Georges.
War on the sea: strategy and tactics; basic principles. '08(Ag22) c. il. 8°, $2. U. S. Naval Inst.
Darrow, Clarence S.
"The open shop": [argument in favor of trade-unions.] '09(Ap3) c. S. pap., 10 c. S: A. Bloch.
Darrow, R: Putnam, comp.
See Jenkins, Floyd, *comp.*
DARTMOUTH COLLEGE, Hanover, N. H.
Grover, E. O., *and* Wellman, H. R., *comp.* Songs of Dartmouth College. *$1.20 net. Grover & W.
White, J: Z. Dartmouth College case decision. 5 c. Timby.
Darton, F. J. Harvey.
Merry tales of the wise men of Gotham. '08(S5) il. sq. D. $1. Stokes.
Wonder book of birds and beasts. '09, [1910.] 403 p. il. 8°, (Fine art juveniles.) $1.50. Stokes.
—, **comp.** Old English stories. '10(O17) col. il. 16°, (Children's bookshelf.) bds., 50 c. Dodge.
Pilgrim's tales, from Tales of the Canterbury pilgrims. '09(Ag) 120 p. il. 16°, (Children's bookshelf.) 60 c. Dodge.
Tales of the Canterbury pilgrims; introd. by F: Ja. Furnivall. '08(D19) il. 8°, $1.50. Stokes.
Darton, Nelson Horatio.
Geology and underground waters of South Dakota. '09, [1910.] (F) 156 p. O. (U. S., Dept. of the Interior; U. S. Geolog. Survey bull.) pap.
Darwin, C: Rob.
Foundations of the origin of species; two essays written in 1842 and 1844; ed. by Fs. Darwin. '09, [1910.] (F) 8°, *$2.50 net. Putnam.

DARWIN, Charles Robert.
Baldwin, J. M. Darwin and the humanities. $1.50. Psychological Review.
Dewey, J: Influence of Darwin on philosophy, and other essays. $1.40 net. Holt.
Fifty years of Darwinism: centennial address in honor of Charles Darwin. **$2 net. Holt.
Geikie, *Sir* A. Charles Darwin as geologist. 75 c. Putnam.
Order of the proceedings at the Darwin celebration held at Cambridge, June 22 to 24, 1909; with sketch of Darwin's life. '09, [1910.] (F) il. pors. (Add. pubs. for price.) Putnam.
Poulton, E: B. Charles Darwin and The origin of species. $3. Longmans.
Seward, A. C:, *ed.* Darwin and modern science. *$5 net. Putnam.
Thomson, J: A. Darwinism and human life. $1.50 net. Holt.

Darwin, Fs., and Acton, E. Hamilton.
Practical physiology of plants. New ed. '08(F15) 12°, *$1.25 net. Putnam.

Darwin, Sir G: Howard.
Scientific papers. v. 1, Oceanic tides and lunar disturbance of gravity. '08(F1); v. 2, Tidal friction and cosmogony. '09 (Je26); v. 3, Figures of equilibrium of rotating liquid and geophysical investigations. '10(Ap23) 8°, ea., *$4.50 net. Putnam.

Darwin, Major Leonard.
Municipal ownership. '08(F22) 12°, *$1.25 net. Dutton.

DARWINISM.
See Evolution.

Dasent, Arth. Irwin.
Life and correspondence of John Thadeus Delane, editor of the London *Times*, 1840-1877. '08(My23) 2 v., il. *$7.50 net. Scribner.

Dasent, Sir G: Webbe, ed.
Norse fairy tales; from the tr. by Sir G: Webbe Dasent. '10(D31) il. 8°, $1.75. Lippincott.

Dash, Paul R., pseud.
See Browne, Lewis Allen.

Dash at the pole. Phelps, W: L. 75 c. Ball Pub. Co.

Daskam, Josephine Dodge.
See Bacon, *Mrs.* J. D. D.

Dassler, C. F. W., rep.
See Kansas. General statutes.

Dated events of the Old Testament. Beecher, W. J. *$1.50 net. S. S. Times.

Daudet, Alphonse.
Choix de contes; selected and ed., with notes and vocab., by C. Fontaine. Special ed., with vocab. '08(Mr14) c. por. S. (Modern lang. ser.) 40 c.; without vocab., 30 c. Heath.
Jack. pt. 1, Le Gymnase Moronval, etc.; ed. by E: L. Goldberg. '10(D24) c. 16°, (Macmillan's new ser. of French texts.) 35 c. net. Macmillan.
Lettres de mon moulin; ed. by G. H. Clarke. '10(D24) 16°, (Macmillan's new ser. of French texts.) 35 c. net. Macmillan.

Daudet, Alphonse.—*Continued.*
Lettres de mon moulin; selected and ed. by G. H. Clarke. '09(D25) map, 12°, (Siepmann's advanced French ser.) *60 c. net. Macmillan.
Sappho; tr. by G: Burnham Ives; with an introd. by Ja. L. Ford. '08(Ap4) c. front. D. (Popular eds. of recent fiction.) †75 c. Little, B. & Co.
Tartarin of Tarascon [and] Tartarin on the Alps. '10(Ap2) 16°, (Everyman's lib.) 35 c. net; leath., 70 c. net. Dutton.

Daudet, Louis Marie Ernest.
La Tour des Maures; ed. by A. H. Wall. '10(D24) 16°, (Macmillan's new ser. of French texts.) 35 c. net. Macmillan.

Daugherty, Amelia Crum.
See Jackson, Caroline Ruth.

Daughter (The). Smedley, A. C. †$1.50. Moffat.

Daughter of France. Maud, C. E. $1.50. Lane.

Daughter of Louis XVI. Gosselin, L. L. T. *$4 net. Lane.

Daughter of New France. Crowley, M. C. †75 c. Little, B. & Co.

Daughter of the Highlanders. Melton, F. J. $1.50. Roxburgh.

Daughter of the hills. Marmon, *Mrs.* W. F. $1.50. Neale.

Daughter of the manse. Taylor, S. C. $1.50. Winston.

Daughter of the Marionis. Oppenheim, E: P. $1.50. Little, B. & Co.

Daughter of the Revolution. Chase, *Mrs.* J. A $1. Badger.

Daughter of the storm. Shaw, F. H. $1.50. Cassell.

Daughter of to-day. Crean, M. C. $1. C. M. Clark.

Daughter of Virginia Dare. Wall, M. V. $1.50. Neale.

Daughters of the American Revolution, Massachusetts. Hannah Winthrop Chapter, Cambridge. Historic guide to Cambridge. 2d ed., rev. '09(O23) c. il. maps, O. $1.25. D. A. R., Hannah Winthrop Chap.

Daughters of the American Revolution, Penn.: Germantown chapter. Germantown D. A. R. cook-book: favorite receipts. '07, [1908.] (Mr.) c. 48 p. 8°, 25 c. D. A. R., Germantown Chap.

Daughters of Suffolk. Nicolls, W: J. $1.50. Lippincott.

Daughters of the rich. Saltus, E. E. $1.25. M. Kennerley.

Daulton, Mrs. Agnes McClelland.
Fritzi, or, the Princess Perhaps. '08(Mr28) c. D. †$1.50. Century Co.
From Sioux to Susan. '09(O2) c. il. D. †$1.50. Century Co.

Daulton, G:
Helter Skelters. '09(O16) c. col. il. D. †$1.25. Stokes.

Dauphines of France. Hamel, F. $4 net. Pott.

D'Autremer, Jos.
Japanese Empire and its economic condition. '10(D24) 8°, $3 net. Scribner.

Dave Porter and his classmates. Stratemeyer, E: †$1.25. Lothrop, L. & S.

Dave Porter at Star Ranch. Stratemeyer, E: $1.25. Lothrop, L. & S.

D'Avenant, Sir W:
Love and honour and The siege of Rhodes; ed. by Ja. W. Tupper. '09(N6) c. por. 16°, (Belles-lettres ser.: Section III., The English drama.) 60 c. Heath.

Davenport, Allen.
Leadership of Shakespeare. '08(F22) c. D. (Miscellaneous pamphlet ser.) pap., 10 c. A. Davenport.

Davenport, B: Rush, ed.
Digest of literature; ed., with suggestions from the Rt. Hon. W: E. Gladstone, the assistance of the fellowship of Christ Church, Oxford, England, and also the faculties of the leading American universities. 3 v. '09(Je5) c. front. pors. 4°. (Add. pubs. for price.) Hist. Pub.

Davenport, C: Benedict.
Eugenics; the science of human improvement by better breeding. '10(Je4) c. il. 16°, 50 c. net. Holt.
Experimental morphology. [New ed.] '08 (Ap18) il. 8°, *$3.50 net. Macmillan.
Inheritance in canaries. '08(Jl18) il. Q. (Carnegie Institution of Washington pub.) pap., 80 c. Carnegie.
Inheritance of characteristics in domestic fowl. '10(Mr12) col. il. tabs., Q. (Carnegie Inst. of Washington pubs.; Papers of the Station for Experimental Evolution.) pap., $4.50. Carnegie.

Davenport, Cyril Ja. H.
The book: its history and development. '08(S19) il. O. (Westminster ser.) *$2 net. Van Nostrand.
Jewellery. '08(O17) il. S. (Little books on art.) *$1 net. McClurg.
Miniatures, ancient and modern. '08(O17) il. S. (Little books on art.) *$1 net. McClurg.

Davenport, Eug.
Domesticated animals and plants; brief treatise upon the origin and development of domesticated races, with special reference to the methods of improvement. '10 (D3) c. il. D. $1.25. Ginn.
Education for efficiency; a discussion of certain phases of our experiment in universal education with particular reference to academic ideals and methods. '08(N) 24 p. 8°, gratis. E. Davenport.
Education for efficiency; discussion of certain phases of the problem of universal education, with special reference to academic ideals and methods. '09(N6) c. 184 p. 12°, $1. Heath.
Industrial education with special reference to the high school; address read at the High School Conference, Univ. of Ill., Nov. 20, 1908. '09(My) 20 p. 8°, pap., gratis. E. Davenport.
Next step in agricultural education. '08 (Ap) 22 p. 8°, pap., gratis. E. Davenport.
Principles of breeding: principles and practices involved in the economic improvement of domesticated animals and plants; with appendix by H. L. Rietz. '08(F1) c. il. O. (Country life education ser.) $2.50. Ginn.

Davenport, Frances Gardiner.
See Andrews, C: McLean.

Davenport, G: Lyman and Eliz. Osgood.
Genealogies of the families of Cohasset, Mass.; comp. under the direction of the Committee on Town History. '09(D18) il. pors. 8°, $5. Com. Town History.

Davenport, Herbert Jos.
Value and distribution. '08(Mr7) c. O. *$3.50 net. Univ. of Chic.

Davenport, Homer Calvin.
The country boy; the story of his own early life by Homer Davenport. '10(O8) c. il. D. $1.25 net. G: W: Dillingham.
My quest of the Arab horse. '09(N6) c. il. O. **$2 net. B. W. Dodge.

Davenport, Mrs. Laura, comp.
Bride's cook book. '08(My16) c. il. O. $2; ed. de luxe, mor., $4: bridal ed., leath., $6. Reilly & B.
Small family cook book. '10(D24) c. il. D. $1.25. Reilly & B.

Davenport, Warren G.
Butte and Montana beneath the X-ray; being a collection of editorials from the files of the Butte X-ray during the years 1907-08. '09(D) c. 381 p. 12°, pap., 75 c. X-ray.

Davey, J:
Gloryville or Hellburg, which?: showing America, past, present, future. '08 (My16) c. S. J: Davey.

Davey, R:
Botticelli. '09(D) various paging, il. Q. (Great artist ser.) *$2 net. Doran.
Nine days' queen; Lady Jane Grey and her times; ed., with an introd., by Martin Hume. '09(N20) il. O. (Romantic history.) *$3.50 net. Putnam.
Tower of London. '10(N12) il. 8°, $3 net. Dutton.

David, Jules.
Le serment; ed. by Cécile Hugon. '09 (Mr6) S. (Oxford modern French ser.) 40 c. Oxford Univ.

DAVID, *King.*
Cohen, E. S-, *jr.* David the giant killer. $1.25. Jewish Pub.

David. Rice, C. Y. **$1.25 net. Doubleday, P.

David Bran. Roberts, M. $1.50. L. C. Page.

David Copperfield. *See* Dickens, C:

Davids, Mrs. Caroline Augusta, [Mrs. T: W: Rhys Davids,] tr. and ed.
Psalms of the early Buddhists. v. 1, Psalms of the sisters; published for the Pali Text Society. '10(D24) O. $2. Oxford Univ.

Davids, T: W: Rhys.
Early Buddhism. '08, [1909.] (Ap) 8°, (Religions ancient and modern.) *40 c. net. Open Court.

Davids, Mrs. T: W: Rhys.
See Davids, *Mrs.* Caroline Augusta.

Davidson, Augusta M. Campbell.
Present-day Japan. '08(Je20) il. 12°, *$1.50 net. Scribner.

Davidson, Edith B.
Blowing away of Mr. Bushy Tail. '10 (D24) c. il. S. bds., 50 c. Duffield.
Bunnikins-bunnies in camp. '09(O9) il. in col. bds., **50 c. net. Houghton M.
Bunnikins-bunnies in Europe. '10(N5) c. col. il. S. bds., 50 c. net. Houghton M.

Davidson, Gladys.
Stories from the operas; with short biographies of the composers. 3d ser. '10 (F19) pors. 12°, (Music lover's lib.) *$1.25 net. Lippincott.

Davidson, Mrs. Hannah Amelia Noyes, [H. A. Davidson.]
Study of King Henry Fourth. pts. 1-2. '08 (D) c. 66 p. 12°, (Studies of the historical plays of Shakespeare.) pap., 25 c. H. A. Davidson.
Study of King Henry Fifth. '08(D) c. 47 p. 12°, (Studies of the historical plays of Shakespeare.) pap., 25 c. H. A. Davidson.
Study of Romola; with critical notes, references and topics for study. '08(F15) sq. 16°, (Study-guide ser.) 50 c. H. A. Davidson.
Study of Shakepeare's King John. '08(D) c. 47 p. 12°, (Studies of the historical plays of Shakespeare.) pap., 25 c. H. A. Davidson.
Study of Shakespeare's King Richard the Second. '08(D) c. 43 p. 12°, (Studies of the historical plays of Shakespeare.) pap., 25 c. H. A. Davidson.

Davidson, Jay Brownlee, and Chase, Leon Wilson.
Farm machinery and farm motors. '08 (Mr28) c. il. 12°, $2. Judd.

Davidson, J:, (1857-1909.)
Fleet Street, and other poems. '09(Jl17) c. D. *$1 net. M. Kennerley.
Man forbid, and other essays; with introd. by E: J. O'Brien. '10(Je11) c. S. $1.25 net. Ball Pub.
Selected poems. '10(D24) 16°, $1.25 net; leath., $1.50 net. Lane.

Davidson, J:, (1869-1905,) and Gray, Alex.
Scottish staple at Veere: study in the economic history of Scotland. '09(F27) il. O. *$4.50 net. Longmans.

Davidson, Mrs. K. L.
Gardens past and present. '09(F13) il. D. *$1.50 net. Scribner.

Davidson, Lilias Campbell.
Catherine of Bragança: Infanta of Portugal and Queen Consort of England. '08 (My9) il. pors. 8°, *$5 net. Dutton.
Lost millionaire. '08(My16) front. D. $1.50. Cassell.

Davidson, Norman J., ed.
Knight errant and his doughty deeds; story of Amadis of Gaul. '10(D3) il. 8°, $1.50. Lippincott.

Davie and Elizabeth. Dyar, M. C. †$1. Harper.

Davies, Albert Emil.
Money, and the stock and share markets. '09(Ag7) tabs., D. (Practical primers of business.) 50 c. Pitman.

Davies, Arth. C: Fox-.
See Fox-Davies, Arth. C:

Davies, Arth. Ernest.
Moral life; study in genetic ethics. '10 (F12) 8°, *$2 net. Psychological Review.

Davies, E. O.
Prolegomena to systematic theology; study of authority. '09(N13) O. *$1.25 net. Doran.

Davies, Emily.
Thoughts on some questions rel. to women, 1860-1908; with prefatory note by E. E. Constance Jones. '10(O8) pors. 12°, $1.25 net. Macmillan.

Davies, F. H.
Electric power and traction. '08(Mr7) il. O. (Westminster ser.) *$2 net. Van Nostrand.

Davies, Franklin.
Pract. story writing. '10(O1) c. 16°, 50 c. Walden.

Davies, Gerald Stanley.
Ghirlandaio. '09(My22) il. 4°, *$4 net. Scribner.

Davies, H: Rodolph.
Yün-nan; the link between India and the Yangtze. '09(Mr) 12+431 p. il. maps, 8°, *$5 net. Putnam.

Davies, Hubert H:
Cousin Kate; comedy in three acts. '10 (Mr5) c. D. pap., 50 c. W. H. Baker.

Davies, Morgan W.
Theory and practice of bridge construction in timber, iron and steel. '08(D26) il. 12°, *$3.75 net. Macmillan.

Davies, Oliver.
Between-time poems. '09(N6) D. *$1.25 net. Lane.

Davies, Randall, and Hunt, Cecil.
Stories of the English artists from Vandyck to Turner, 1600-1851. '08(N7) 8°, (Art and letters lib.) *$3 net. Duffield.

Daviess, Maria Thompson.
Miss Selina Lue and the soap-box babies. '09(O9) c. il. D. †$1. Bobbs-M.
Road to Providence. '10(N5) c. il. D. $1.50. Bobbs-M.

Davis, A., ed.
See Adler, H. M., *ed.*

Davis, Allan.
Promised land: a drama. '09(Ap3) 8°, $1. Harvard Dramatic.

Davis, Alvin.
Human body and health. '08(O10) c. il. D. 80 c. Am. Bk.

Davis, Andrew Jackson.
Harmonial philosophy. 35th ed. 27 v. '09(D) 8°, $30. Austin.
Principles of nature: her divine revelations. 35th ed. '09(D) 8°, $3.50. Austin.

Davis, Andrew McFarland.
Barbery bushes and wheat. '08(Je6) 8°, pap. (Not for sale.) A. McF. Davis.
A bibliographical puzzle; [repr. from the publications of the Colonial Society of Mass.] '10(S) 15 p. 8°. (Priv. pr.) J. Wilson & Son.
Relates to the "News from the moon," issued in Boston in 1721, and attributed by Evans in his American bibliography, 2281 to the press of J. Franklin.
Hints of contemporary life in the writings of Thomas Shepard. '08, [1909.] (N) 137-162 p. 8°. (Priv. pr.) A. McF. Davis.
John Harvard's life in America. '08(S12) 8°, pap. (Not for sale.) A. McF. Davis.
Origin of the national banking system. '10 (N) 213 p. 8°. Gov. Pr. Off.

Davis, Andrew McFarland.—*Continued.*
Two forgotten pamphleteers in the Massachusetts currency controversy, 1720-1740. '10(Ag) 22 p. 8°. (Priv. pr.) A. McF. Davis.
Was it Andros? '08(O) 16 p. 8° [priv. pr.] A. McF. Davis.

Davis, Andrew P.
Neuropathy; the new science of drugless healing amply illustrated and explained, embracing ophthalmology, osteopathy, chiropractic science, suggestive therapeutics, magnetism, instructions on diet, deep breathing, bathing, etc.; advice to mothers—how to care for children—physical manipulations to cure chronic and acute diseases; many invaluable recipes for home use—instructions how to cure diseases without medicine, and some conditions where certain domestic remedies are useful. '09(N) c. 55+175 p. il. por. 8°, $5. F: L: Rowe.

Davis, Anna Chase.
Stories of the United States for youngest readers. Rev. ed. '09(My) c. 256 p. il. pors. fold. map, 12°, 40 c.; bds., 30 c. Educ. Pub.

Davis, C: Albert.
Peat, essays on its origin, uses and distribution in Michigan. '07, [1908.] (Ap) 95-395 p. il. pls. diagrs., maps, 8°, $1. Mich. Geol. Survey.
Bibliography (10 p.).
See also Bastin, Edson Sunderland.

Davis, C: Belmont.
Lodger overhead and others. '09(Ap24) c. il. D. †$1.50. Scribner.
Stage door. '08(My16) c. il. D. †$1.50. Scribner.

Davis, C: Gilbert, M.D.
Philosophy of life. New ed. '09(Jl) 12°, 75 c.; pap., 25 c.; 5th ed. '10(D3) c. por. D. $1.25. D. D. Pub.
Why not now? '09(D11) c. D. $1. Badger.

Davis, C: H: Stanley, M.D.
Consumption: its prevention and cure without medicine; with chapters on sanitation and prevention of other diseases. 2d ed. '08(Jl4) 12°, $1. Treat.

Davis, C: Thornton, comp.
See Massachusetts land court decisions.

Davis, Dan. Webster.
Life and public services of Rev. Wm. Washington Browne, founder of the Grand fountain u. o. of true reformers; with an introd. by Rt. Rev. B: F. Lee. [1910.] (D) c. 10+11-192 p. il. pors. 8°, $1. M. A. Browne-Smith.

Davis, Edm. Walstein.
Woodcock shooting. '08(D19) c. il. 8°. (Priv. pr.) De Vinne.

Davis, E: Parker.
Obstetric and gynecologic nursing. 3d ed., thoroughly rev. '08(D) c. 436 p. il. 8°, *$1.75 net. Saunders.

Davis, Edn. G.
Text-book of constitutional law; act. of Mar. 3, 1875. ['06, 1908.] (D) c. 283 p. D. (Add. pubs. for price.) Franklin-H.

Davis, Floyd.
Mine investors' guide. '09(My22) c. il. D. $1.50. Western Corr. Sch.

Davis, Foxcroft.
The whirl: a romance. '09(Je5) c. il. D. †$1.50. Dodd.

Davis, G. Howlett.
One hundred years of masonry in the Oranges, 1809-1909. [1910] (F) c. '09 139 p. 8°, $2. Chronicle Pub.

Davis, G: Breckenridge.
Elements of international law. 3d ed., rev. to date. '08(Ag29) c. O. $3. Harper.
Treatise on the military law of the United States; together with the practice and procedure of courts-martial and other military tribunals. 2d ed., rev. '09, [1910.] (Je) 8+772 p. 8°, $7 net. Wiley.
"List of authorities cited" (4 p.).
See also Adventures with Indians.

Davis, G: Jacob, jr., and Bowles, Ja. Ten Broeck.
Sewage purification with special reference to Wisconsin conditions. '09, [1910.] (O) 87 p. il. map, tabs., 8°, (Univ. of Wis. bull.; Engineering ser.) 30 c. Univ. of Wis.

Davis, G: Thompson Brown.
Korea for Christ. '10(N12) c. 12°, 25 c. net. Revell.
Twice around the world with Alexander. '08(Ja18) il. pors. 12°, $1. Chr. Herald.

Davis, Gwilym G:
Applied anatomy; construction of the human body considered in relation to its functions, diseases, and injuries. [1910.] (N) c. 10+630 p. il., partly col., 4°, $6. Lippincott.

Davis, Harry Garfield.
Interstate Commerce Commission. '10 (Ap) c. 93 p. 8°, 10 c. La Salle Extension.
Bibliography (1 p.).

Davis, Harvey Nathaniel.
See Marks, Lionel Simeon.

Davis, H: Edg.
Development of the District of Columbia; paper from the proceedings of the Washington Academy of Science. '09(Jl) 20 p. 8°. (Add. Superintendent for price.) U. S., Supt. of Docs.

Davis, Hubert H:
Mrs. Gorringe's necklace; play in four acts. '10(Mr5) c. D. pap., 50 c. W. H. Baker.

Davis, J. F.
Bank organization, management and accounts. '10(My21) O. $2. Pitman.

Davis, J. L.
Mountain preacher; being some experiences told in the language of the people among whom he so successfully labored. '09 (Ap) c. 75 p. il. 12°, 50 c. F: L. Rowe.

DAVIS, Jefferson.
Dodd, W: E: Jefferson Davis. **$1.25 net. Jacobs.
Fleming, W. L. Jefferson Davis, the negroes and the negro problem. gratis. W. L. Fleming.
Fleming, W. L. Jefferson Davis at West Point.—Religious life of Jefferson Davis. La. State Univ.
See also Cabin John Bridge.

Davis, J:
Travels of four years and a half in the United States of America during 1798, 1799, 1800, 1801, and 1802; with an introd. and notes by A. J. Morrison. '09(O30) O. *$2.50 net. Holt.

DAVIS, *Rev.* John A.
Harrington, C: H: A God enthused man: life story of Evangelist Rev. John A. Davis. 75 c. J: A. Davis.

Davis, J: McCan.
How Abraham Lincoln became president. Centennial ed. '09(F13) c. il. pors. D. *75 c. net. J. M. Davis.

Davis, J: Wa., and Julien, Fanny.
Finger play reader. pts 1 and 2, for first year classes. '09(Jl10) c. il. (partly col.) D. (Davis-Julien ser. of readers.) ea., 35 c.; Teachers' ed., ea., 50 c. Heath
—, **ed.** Young America's manual: the child's guide to patriotism. Rev. ed. '08(Mr28) c. il. 12°, 25 c. Educ. Pub.

Davis, Jos. Baker.
Surveying for beginners. '10(My14) figs. D. 90 c. Wahr.
—, **and Merrick, H. B.**
Direction of a line. '10(Je18) c. figs. fold. charts in envelope, D. 75 c. Wahr.

Davis, Katherine Wallace.
The punchinellos: a story of southern Italy. '08(Ag8) c. il. S. 40 c. Flanagan.

Davis, Leslie Barron.
Our pract. method for raising capital. '10 (N19) c. 8°, $7. Business Aid.

Davis, Lilian E., comp.
See McFadden, Eliz. Apthorp.

Davis, Lyman Edwyn.
Jonathan Twigg. '09(Jl) 389 p. 8°, $1. O. P. Davis

Davis, Madison.
Old cannon foundry above Georgetown, D. C., and its first owner, Henry Foxall; repr. from the records of the Columbia Hist. Society, v. 2, 1908. '09(F6) il. por. facsim., O. pap. (Add. pubs. for price.) New Era Print.

Davis, Mrs. Mary Evalyn Clay.
Revelations of the life beautiful. '08(D) c. 7+222 p. por. 8°, $1. Baumgardt.

Davis, Mrs. Mary Evelyn Moore.
Moons of Balbanca. '08(O3) c. il. D. †$1. Houghton M.

Davis, Mary Hayes, and Chow-Leung.
Chinese fables and folk stories; with an introd. by Yin-Chwang Wang Tsen-Zan. '08(Jl18) c. il. D. (Eclectic readings.) 40 c. Am. Bk.

Davis, Michael Marks.
Psychological interpretations of society. '09 (Je5) O. (Columbia Univ. studies in history, economics and public law.) pap., $2. Longmans.

Davis, Nathan Smith, jr.
Consumption: how to prevent it and how to live with it; its nature, its causes, its prevention, and the mode of life, climate, exercise, food, clothing necessary for its cure. 2d ed., rev. '08(Ag29) c. 8°, *$1 net. Davis.

Davis, Nathaniel Newnham-.
See Newnham-Davis, Nathaniel.

Davis, N: Darnell.
Notes on the hist. of the Jews in Barbados. '10(F5) 8°, $1. Bloch.

Davis, Norah.
Wallace Rhodes. '09(Ap10) c. D. †$1.50. Harper.

Davis, Oscar King.
William Howard Taft, the man of the hour; with the platform of the Republican party, and a sketch of the nominee for vice-president, incl. a chapter by Thdr. Roosevelt. '08(D19) c. il. pors. O. $1. Ziegler.
See also Davis, Schroeder, *pseud.*

Davis, Mrs. Ozora S.
Hero tales. '10(D) 237 p. 8°, bds., $1.25 net. Pilgrim Press.

Davis, R: Harding.
Once upon a time. '10(S24) c. il. D. $1.50. Scribner.
Vera, the medium. '08(Je13) c. D. †$1.50. Scribner.
White Mice. '09(Je5) c. il. D. †$1.50. Scribner.

Davis, Rob. Courtney.
See Stewart, Merch Bradt.

Davis, S: Ishbeyre.
Lyrics of the fields. '09, [1910.] (F) 206 p. por. 12°, $1. S: I. Davis.

Davis, Schroeder, [pseud. of Oscar King Davis and Reginald Schroeder.]
Storm birds. '10(Je4) c. D. $1.50. Moffat.

Davis, Thdr. M.
Excavations: Biban el Moluk; the funeral papyrus of Iouiya. '08(Jl18) f°, *$12.50 net. Dutton.
—, **Maspero, Gaston Camille Charles, and Newberry, Percy E:**
Tomb of Iouiya and Touiyou; The finding of the tomb, by Thdr. M. Davis; Notes on Iouiya and Touiyou, by Gaston Maspero; Description of the objects found in the tomb, by Percy E. Newberry. '08 (F8) il. f°, *$12.50 net. Dutton.

Davis, Wa. B.
Specimen faces, linotype composition; borders, rules and dashes. '09, [1910.] (Ja.) c. 12°. pap., gratis. W. B. Davis.

Davis, W: Eduard, jr.
I have a little money: what shall I do with it? '07, [1908.] (D) 76 p. 12°, $1. W: E. Davis.

Davis, W: Hawley.
Training for debate. '10(O) 48 p. O. (Univ. of Kansas bull.: Debating ser.) pap. Univ. of Kan.

Davis, W: Morris.
Geographical essays; ed. by Douglas Wilson Johnson. '10(F5) c. O. $2.75. Ginn.
Practical exercises in physical geography. '08(O31) c. D. 50 c.; Atlas to accompany Practical exercises in physical geography, 30 c. Ginn.

Davis, W: Stearns.
Influence of wealth in imperial Rome. '10 (O29) c. O. $2 net. Macmillan.
Outline hist. of the Roman Empire. '09 (S18) map, 12°, *65 c. net. Macmillan.

Davis, Yorke, pseud.
Green cloak. '10(Je25) c. il. D. $1.50. Sturgis & W.

DAVIS FAMILY.
See Genealogies, Estabrook, J: D.

Davison Alvin.
Dust as a carrier of disease in the schoolroom. '09(N) c. 15 p. il. 16°, pap., 10 c. A. Davison.
Health lessons. [In 2 bks.] '10(Ag6) il. D. bk. 1, 35 c.; bk. 2, 60 c. Am. Bk.
Human body and health: an intermediate text-book of essential physiology, applied hygiene, and practical sanitation for schools. '09(S11) c. il. pors. D. 50 c.; Elementary. '10(Mr26) c. il. por. D. 40 c. Am. Bk.
Mammalian anatomy, with special reference to the cat. 2d ed., rev., with 114 il. '10 (F) 13+246 p. il. 8°, *$1.50 net. Blakiston.

Davison, Arth. H., comp.
See Iowa. Statistical abstract.

Davison, Arth. W.
Little candy maker: [recipes.] '08(Je27) c. il. O. pap., $1. A. W. Davison.

Davison, C:
Algebra for secondary schools. '08(N7) 8°, *$2 net. Putnam.
Class book of trigonometry. '10(O22) D. $1 net. Putnam.

—, and Richards, C. H.
Plane geometry. '08(F29) 8°, *$1 net. Putnam.

Davison, Ellen Scott.
Some forerunners of St. Francis of Assisi: [Apostolic sects allied to the Cathari, Arnold of Brescia and the Humiliati.] '07, [1908.] (Mr.) 75 p. 8°. (Add. author for price.) E. S. Davison.

Davison, L. A.
Percentage and its applications. '10(D17) D. bds., 30 c. Bardeen.

Davison, Ralph C.
Concrete pottery and garden furniture. '09 (D4) c. il. D. $1.50. Munn.

Davison. T. Raffles.
Modern homes; with a foreword by Sir Aston Webb. '09(Jl17) il. 4°, *$5.25 net. Macmillan.

Davison, W: J.
Gymnastic dancing. '09(S18) il. 12°, bds., $1. Y. M. C. A.

Davison, Rev. W: Theophilus.
Life spiritual: studies of the life of the spirit. '10(D) 12°, $1.50 net. Doran.

Davisson, Ralph Boardman.
Yoke fellow. '08, [1909.] (Mr) c. 311 p. il. 12°, $1.50. C. M. Clark.

Davisson, Schuyler C.
College algebra. '10(O1) D. hf. leath., $1.50 net. Macmillan.

Davy Jones's yarns. Ybarra, T: R. **$1.25 net. Holt.

Dawbarn, Climenson Yelverton C:
Liberty and progress. '09(O23) O. *$3 net. Longmans.
Social contract, more particularly in relation to taxation. '10(Je25) O. $1.25 net. Longmans.

Dawbarn, Rob. H. M., M.D.
Aid to materia medica. 4th ed., rev. and enl. by Eden V. Delphey, M.D. '08 (Ap18) c. D. **$1.75 net. Macmillan.

Dawber, E. Guy.
See Schultz, Rob. W.

Dawe, W. Carlton.
The woman, the man and the monster. '09 (Je) c. 345 p. front. D. $1.50. Stuyvesant Press.

Dawn-builder. Neihardt, J: G. $1.50. M. Kennerley.

Dawn by Galilee. Gordon, C: W: 35 c. Doran.

Dawn of another life. Aber, W: W. $1.50. W: W. Aber.

Dawn of character. Mumford, E. E. R. $1.20 net. Longmans.

Dawn of modern England. Lumsden, C. B. $3 net. Longmans.

Dawn of the Catholic revival in England. Ward, B. 2 v. *$7 net. Longmans.

Dawn of the constitution. Ramsay, *Sir* J. H: *$2.75 net. Macmillan.

Dawn of the world. Merriam, C. H., *ed.* $3.50. A. H. Clark.

Dawn of womanhood. Jackson, *Mrs.* G. E. S. *$1.25 net. Revell.

Dawson, A. J.
Finn the wolfhound. '10(Ja1) il. 8°, $1.50. Lippincott.

Dawson, Mrs. Belvidere Pauline Casey.
Evalena. '09, [1910.] (F) c. 35 p. il. por. 8°, 60 c. Cochrane.

Dawson, Coningsby W:
Murder Point. '10(Ap2) c. D. $1.50. Doran.
See also Dawson, W: Ja.

—, comp. *See* Dawson, W: Ja., *comp.*

—, ed. *See* Dawson, W: Ja., *ed.*

Dawson, E. Rumley.
Secret of sex; discovery of a new law of nature: how sex is caused. '09(D) c. 64 p. pors. 12°, 50 c. Cochrane.

Dawson, Rev. Edn. Collas.
Heroines of missionary adventure. '08(N7) D. (Heroes ser.) *$1.50 net. Lippincott.

Dawson, Fs. Warrington.
The scar. '10(Ap2) c. D. $1.50. Small.

Dawson, G: E.
Child and his religion. '09(O30) c. D. *75 c. net. Univ. of Chic.

Dawson, Lawrence H.
Book of battles and sieges. '09(Ap17) 32°, leath., 50 c. Dutton.
Book of the saints. '08(F22) 32°, (Miniature reference lib.) leath., 50 c. Dutton.
Nicknames and pseudonyms. '08(Je20) 32°, (Miniature ref. lib.) leath., 50 c. Dutton.

Dawson, Mayone.
See Dale, Mary, *pseud.*

Dawson, Miles Menander.
Comparative reserve tables. 2d ed., rev. and enl. '08(My16) c. 8°, $25. Chronicle Co.
Survivorship annuity tables; net single, net annual, and one-year term premiums, mean and terminal reserves, 3½ per cent., American experience table, for life of nominator; Danish government survivorship annuity table, for life of annuitant. '10(Ag20) $25. Chronicle Co.
See also Frankel, L. K.

Dawson, Minnie Twilight.
Stillwell murder; or, a society crime. '07, [1908.] (D) c. 154 p. il. 8°, $2. M. T. Dawson.

Dawson, Mrs. Nelson.
Enamels. '08(O17) il. S. (Little books on art.) *$1 net. McClurg.

Dawson, Percy Millard, M.D.
Biography of François Magendie. '08 (My2) c. pors. 8°, *$1.25 net. A. T. Huntington.

Dawson, Philip.
Electric traction on railways. '10(Ag13) il. tabs., $9 net. Van Nostrand.

Dawson, Warrington.
The scourge. '10(N12) c. D. $1.50. Small.

Dawson, W: Harbutt.
Evolution of modern Germany. '08(D19) 8°, *$4 net. Scribner.

Dawson, W: H:
Sunshine of hope, and other poems. '10 (S) c. 93 p. il. por. 8°, $1. Modern Woodmen.

Dawson, W: Ja., D.D.
Divine challenge. '10(Jl30) c. 12°, 50 c. Doran.
Masterman and Son. '09(O23) c. D. *$1.20 net. Revell.
One night in Bethlehem; Christmas story. [1910.] (D) c. 54 p. col. il. 8°, 75 c. Doran.
Quest of the simple life: [essays.] '08 (Jl11) 12°, $1.50. Dutton.
Soldier of the future. '08(S12) c. 12°, $1.50. Revell.
Threshold of manhood. '09(O2) 12°, *$1.25 net. Revell.

—, and Coningsby W:
Great English letter writers. 2 v. '08(S12) c. 16°, (Readers' lib.) ea., *$1 net. Revell.

—, and Coningsby W:, comps. and eds.
Great English novelists; with introd. essays and notes. '10(D10) c. 12°, (Readers' lib.) ea., $1 net. Harper.
Great English short-story writers; with introd. essays. In 2 v. '10(F19) c. D. (Reader's lib.) ea., **$1 net. Harper.

—, and Coningsby W:, eds.
Great English essayists, with introd. essays and notes. '09(N13) c. D. (Readers' lib.) *$1 net. Harper.
Great English letter-writers; with introd. essays and notes. '09(Jl31) c. 2 v., D. (Readers' lib.) ea., **$1 net. Harper.

Dawson, W: Leon, and Bowles, J: Hooper.
Birds of Washington; a complete, scientific and popular account of the 372 species of birds found in the state. '09(Ag7) c. 2 v., il. 8°, subs. only, $12; hf. mor., $15; mor., $20; large paper ed., $25. Occidental Pub.

Dawson-Scott, Catharine Amy.
Treasure trove; story of unusual situations on the text of "Finding is keeping!" '09 (O2) $1.50. Duffield.

Day, Clarence Munro.
Accounting practice. '08(S26) c. il. tabs., O. **$6 net. Appleton.

Day, Edm.
See Murray, J:

Day, Ernest Hermitage, D.D.
Ober-Ammergau and the Passion Play; pract. and historical hdbk. for visitors. '10(Je11) S. pap., 45 c. net. Young Churchman.

Day, Fk. A., and Knappen, Thdr. M.
Life of John Albert Johnson, three times governor of Minnesota. '10(Je11) il. pors. O. $2; ¾ leath., $3.50; leath., $5. Forbes.

Day, Holman Fs.
Eagle badge. '08(O17) c. il. D. †$1.25. Harper.
King Spruce: a novel. '08(Ap11) il. D. †$1.50. Harper.
The ramrodders. '10(Ap30) c. D. $1.50. Harper.

Day, Leigh Cross.
Borderland and the blue beyond: [poems.] '08(O3) c. obl. Q. bds., $2.50. Saalfield.

Day, Lewis Foreman.
Enamelling: comparative account of the development and practice of the art. '08 (Mr14) il. 8°, *$3 net. Scribner.
Nature and ornament; nature the raw material of design, ornament its finished product. '10(Mr26) il. O. *$5 net.—In 2 v. v. 1. '09(My15); v. 2. '09, [1910.] (Mr) il. 8°, v. 1, *$2 net; v. 2, *$3 net. Scribner.
Windows; book about stained and painted glass. 3d ed., rev. and enl. '10(Mr26) il. O. *$7.50 net. Scribner.

—, and Buckle, Mary.
Art in needlework: book about embroidery. 3d ed., rev. and enlarged. '08(Je20) il. D. *$2 net. Scribner.

Day, R: Edn.
New poems. '10(Ap9) c. 12°, $1. Grafton Press.

Day, Sarah J.
Fresh fields and legends old and new: [poems.] '09(My15) c. front. O. **$1.25 net. Putnam.
Mayflowers to mistletoe: [poems.] 2d ed. '09(Je26) c. il. O. **$1.25 net. Putnam.

Day, T: Fleming.
Four and the fire; or, five nights in a yacht club. '08(Mr14) c. il. 8°, $1. Rudder.

Day, T: Franklin.
New Bible-country. '10(O15) c. D. leatherette, 30 c. Crowell.

Day, W: A.
Address of Vice-President W: A. Day at the 50th anniversary of the founding of the Equitable Life Assurance Society of the United States, New York, July 28, 1909. [1910.] (My) 19 p. O. pap. Equitable Life.

Day (A) at the menagerie. '10(D) col. il. bds., $1.25. Saalfield.

Day by day ser. D. 60 c.; leath., $1. Crowell.
—Browning. Browning day by day.
—Connolly, *ed.* Friendship year book.
—Emerson. Emerson day by day.
—Fite, *ed.* Lovers' year book.
—Johnson, *ed.* Year book of humor.
—Keats. Keats day by day.
—Longfellow. Longfellow day by day.
—Lowell. Lowell day by day.

Day by day ser.—Continued.
—Matson, *ed.* Nature year book.
—Ruskin. Ruskin day by day.
—Shakespeare. Shakespeare day by day.
—Shelley. Shelley day by day.
—Stevenson. Stevenson day by day.
—Tennyson. Tennyson day by day.
—Thoreau. Thoreau day by day.
—Whittier. Whittier day by day.
—Wordsworth. Wordsworth day by day.
Day-dreamer's harvest. Byron, H: *$1.25 net. F. F. Sherman.
Day dreams. Minkler, *Mrs.* C. R. S. $1. C. R. S. Minkler.
Day dreams of Greece. Stork, C: W. *75 c. net. Lippincott.
Day-hours of the Church of England. Rev. ed. '09(My22) D. *$1.25 net. Longmans.
Day in court. Wellman, F. L. **$2 net. Macmillan.
Day in the temple. Maas, *Rev.* A. J. *50 c. net. Herder.
Day of fate. Roe, E: P. †$1.25. Dodd.
Day of souls. Jackson, C: T. †$1.50. Bobbs-M.
Day of the country church. Ashenhurst, J. O. $1 net. Funk.
Day of the cross. Clow, W. M. *$1.50 net. Doran.
Day unto day. Matheson, G: *50 c. net. Revell.
Day with the Good Shepherd. Mamreov, A. F.. 50 c. net. Eaton & M.
Daybreak in Korea. Baird, A. L. A. *60 c. net. Revell.
Daybreak in Turkey. Barton, J. L. *$1.50 net. Pilgrim Press.
Dayrell, Eliphinstone.
Folk stories from Southern Nigeria, West Africa; with an introd. by And. Lang. '10(Je4) front. D. $1.50. Longmans.
Day's work. Kipling, R. **$1.50 net. Doubleday, P.
Days before history. Hall, H. R. $1.50. Crowell.
Days in Hellas. Moore, M. **$2 net. Jacobs.
Days of Bruce. Aguilar, G. $1. Bowman.
Days of His flesh. Smith, D: $2 net. Doran.
Days of June. White, M. C. *50 c. net. Revell.
Days of long ago. Comstock, W. E. 50 c. Badger.
Days of the Directoire. Allinson, A. *$5 net. Lane.
Days spent on a Doge's farm. Symonds, M. *$2.50 net. Century Co.
Days with great musicians. v. 1-3. '10(D) col. il. 12°, ea., 50 c. net. Doran.
Contents: Beethoven; Schubert; Mendelssohn.
Days with great writers. v. 1-3. '10(D) col. il. 12°, ea., 50 c. net. Doran.
Contents: Dickens; Thackeray; Stevenson.
Days with the poets. v. 1-6. '09(D); v. 7-9. '10(D) col. il. 12°, ea., 50 c. net. Doran.
Contents: Tennyson; Browning; Burns; Keats; Longfellow; Wordsworth; Shelley; Byron; Scott.
Daysman (The). '10(F19) c. D. $1.50. Cochrane.
Dayton, A. C.
Theodosia Ernest. '09(S18) D. *75 c. net. Bapt. Bk.

DAYTON, O.
Social register, Cincinnati and Dayton. $2.50. Social Register.
Dayton, Ohio, Public Library. List of books in the Dayton Public Library of practical interest to men in the shops, machinists, electricians, molders, plumbers, woodworkers. '07, [1908.] (Ap.) 23 p. 24°, pap., 5 c. Dayton Pub. Lib.
Dazey, C: Turner.
See Marshall, Davis E:
Dazzling Miss Davison. James, *Mrs.* F. A. P. $1.50. H. K. Fly.
De anima. Aristotle. *$5.50 net. Putnam.
De bello Gallico. *See* Cæsar, Caius Julius.
De compositione verborum. *See* Dionysius *of Halicarnassus.*
De facto doctrine. *See* Law.
De finibus bonorum et malorum. *See* Cicero, Marcus Tullius.
De infinitivi finalis vel consecutivi constructione apud priscos poetas Græcos. Ogden, C: J. $1 net. Lemcke.
De l'Allemagne. *See* Stäel-Holstein, Anne Louise Germaine Necker, *Baronne* de.
De libris. Dobson, H: A. $1.50. Macmillan.
De namin' ob de twins. Childs, *Mrs.* M. F. *$1 net. B. W. Dodge.
De oddilo: the seed. Cole, S. $1.50. Connoisseurs' Press.
De profundis. *See* Wilde, Oscar.
De profundis clamavi. Hunter, J: *$1.50 net. Macmillan.
De quibus. Taylor, W: H: $1.50. Bell Bk.
De rerum natura. *See* Lucretius, C. T.
De Trinitate liber. *See* Novitian
De vera religione. Schiffini, S. *$2.75 net. Herder.
Deacon, Renée M.
Bernard Shaw as artist-philosopher: an exposition of Shavianism. '10(S17) c. D. $1 net. Lane.
DEAD (The).
See Death.
Dead letters. Baring, M. $1.25 net. Houghton M.
Dead man's love. Gallon, T. $1.50. Brentano's.
Deaderick, W: Heiskell.
Pract. study of malaria. '09(D) c. 11-402 p. il. pors. 8°, $4.50. Saunders.
DEAF AND DUMB.
Bell, A. G. Mechanism of speech. **$1.20 net. Funk.
De Land, F. Dumb no longer. $1.50. Volta.
Ferreri, G. American institutions for the education of the deaf. (Add. pubs. for price.) Penn. Inst.
Kent, E. Manual of arithmetic: being an outline of work in number for use in schools for the deaf. 65 c. Atkinson, M. & G.
Long, J. S. Sign language. $2. J. S. Long.
New York Institution for the Instruction of the Deaf and Dumb. 100th anniversary of the birth of Abraham Lincoln; commemorative exercises. (Add. pubs. for price.) N. Y. Inst. Deaf and Dumb.

DEAF AND DUMB.—*Continued.*
Sparrow, R. E., *comp.* Stories and rhymes in Melville Bell symbols; comp. and ed. at the Rochester School for the Deaf. $1. Volta.
See also Lip-reading.

DEAFNESS.
See Deaf and dumb;—Ear.

Dealey, Ja. Quayle.
Development of the state: its governmental organization and its activities. '09(Ap24) c. D. $1.50. Silver.
Ethical and religious significance of the state. '09(Jl) c. 8°, (Social service ser.) pap., **10 c. net. Am. Bapt.
Sociology; its simpler teachings and applications. '09(O9) c. D. $1.50. Silver.

Dean, Arth. Davis.
Education of workers in the shoe industry. '09(Ap3) map, 8°, (Nat. Soc. for the Promotion of Industrial Education, bulletin.) pap., 10 c. Nat. Soc. Promotion Indust. Educ.
Industrial education and a state policy; address before the National Society for the Promotion of Industrial Education, Milwaukee, Dec. 3, 1908. '10(Je) 16 p. 8°, o. p. N. Y. State Educ.
Industrial education considered in its relation to the high school problem. '10(D17) D. bds., 30 c. Bardeen.
Worker and the state; study of education for industrial workers. '10(O29) c. D. $1.20 net. Century Co.

Dean, E: P., comp.
Merchant's friend stock calculator tables. 2d ed., enl. '09(N) c. 143 p. il. 4°, $5. Merchant's Friend.

Dean, Eva.
In peanut land; verses. '08(O24) c. il. Q. $1.75; bds., $1.25. Fenno.

Dean, Mark.
System of green house heating for steam or hot water. '09(Ja23) c. 12°, $2. Domestic Engineering.
Steam fitters' computation and price book. '09(Ja23) c. 12°, flex. leath., $3. Domestic Engineering.

Dean, Olin Sandeford.
Quest of the ages; or, a search for the poles of truth. '10(O15) 16°, 50 c. Cochrane.

Dean, Sara.
Disciple of chance. '10(Mr19) c. D. $1.50. Stokes.
Travers: a story of the San Francisco earthquake. '08(Ja18) il. D. †$1.50. Stokes.

Deane, Ethel.
Byways of collecting. '08(My23) O. *$2.50 net. Cassell.
"None so blind." '10(Jl16) c. il. 12°, $1.50. Reid Pub.

Deans, Rev. J:
Suicide; foreword by Rev. E: S. Ninde, D.D. '08(Ja11) D. (Church and social evils.) pap., 15 c. H. Gregory.

Deans, R: Storry.
Trials of five queens: [Katherine of Aragon, Anne Boleyn, Mary, Queen of Scots, Marie Antoinette, and Caroline of Brunswick.] '09(Jl31) pors. 8°, *$3.50 net. Brentano's.

Dear friend. Nirdlinger, D. E. 60 c. Benziger.
Dear little girl at school. Blanchard, A. E. $1.25. Jacobs.
Dear old father. Woolard, S: F., *comp.* 50 c. Goldsmith-W.

Dearborn, G: Van Ness.
Text-book of physiology, for students and practitioners. '08(S5) c. il. 8°, *$3.75 net. Lea.

Dearborn, Ned.
Catalogue of a collection of birds from British East Africa. '09(Ag) 141-190 p. map, 8°, (Field Museum of Natural History pubs.; Ornithological ser.) 50 c. Field Museum.
Catalogue of a collection of birds from Guatemala. '08(Ap18) il. maps, 8°, (Field Museum of Natural History pub., Ornithological ser.) pap., 50 c. Field Museum.

Dearest spot on earth. Stocking, J. T. 50 c.; $1. Caldwell.

Dearmer, Mabel White, [Mrs. Percy Dearmer.]
The sisters. '08(Mr21) c. D. †$1.50. McClure.

Dearmer, Rev. Percy.
Body and soul: enquiry into the effect of religion upon health; with a description of Christian works of healing from the New Testament to the present day. '09 (Jl17) 12°, *$1.50 net. Dutton.
Everyman's hist. of the English church. '09 (O9) D. *75 c. net; cl. gilt, *$1 net; pap., *50 c. net. Warne.
Fifty pictures of Gothic altars. '10(D24) il. 4°, (Alcuin Club collections.) bds., $6 net. Longmans.

Deas, Anne Simons.
Recollections of the Ball family of South Carolina and the Comingtee plantation. [Private ed.] '09(N) c. 189 p. il. pors. facsims., plan, 8°, $5. A. Ball.

Dease, Alice.
Beckoning of the wand: sketches of a lesser-known Ireland. '08(Ag8) 8°, $1. Herder.
Marrying of Brian, and other stories. [1910.] (My) 6+83 p. il. 12°, 50 c. net. Herder.

DEATH.
Björklund, J. G. Death and resurrection from the point of view of the cell-theory. $1 net. Open Court.
Catholic Church. Office of the Blessed Virgin Mary and office of the dead: Latin and English. 45 c.; 75 c. Herder.
Hague, W. Death ends all. 75 c.; 40 c. Timby.
Jowett, J. H: Our blessed dead. 25 c. net. Revell.
Klarmann, A. F. Life in the shadow of death. $1 net. Pustet.
Robinovitch, L. G. Resuscitation of subjects in a condition of apparent death, caused by chloroform, electrocution, etc. $1. Journal Mental.
See also Burial;—Capital punishment;—Embalming;—Epitaphs;—Future life; — Immortality;—Philosophy.

Death and its sorrow. Piercy, W. D. $1. Neale.

Death in the kiss: treatise on innocent infection, by a New York physician. '08(Jl4) c. D. pap., 25 c. B'way Pub.
Death of Gracchus. Sauter, E. (Not for sale.) E. Sauter.
Death of Lincoln. Laughlin, C. E. **$1.50 net. Doubleday, P.
Death of Maid McCrea. *See* Auringer, Obadiah Cyrus. Twin poems of the Revolution.
Death Valley Slim. Worth, P. W. 75 c. P. W. Worth.
Deaver, J: Blair, M.D., and Ashhurst, Astley Paston Cooper, M.D.
Surgery of the upper abdomen: stomach and duodenum. v. 1. '09(Ja23) c. 8°, *$5 net. Blakiston.
De Barrios, Adelaide.
Shepherdess of to-day. '10(My21) c. O. $1. Aberdeen.
De Bary, R:, ["Brother Angelo."]
Franciscan days of vigil: narrative of personal views and developments. '10(S10) D. $1.50 net. Longmans.
Land of promise: account of the material and spiritual unity of America. '08(N7) map, D. *$1.50 net. Longmans.
Debaters' handbook ser. 12°, $1 net. H. W. Wilson.
—Fanning, *comp.* Selected articles on capital punishment.—Selected articles on the enlargement of the United States navy.
—Phelps, *comp.* Selected articles on the income tax.—Selected articles on the initiative and referendum.—Selected articles on woman suffrage.
—Robbins, *comp.* Sel. articles on a central bank of the United States.—Selected articles on the commission plan of municipal government.
DEBATING.
Conklin, G: W. Vest-pocket argument settler. 25 c.; 50 c. McKay.
Davis, W: H. Training for debate. Univ. of Kan.
Denney, J. V., *and others.* Argumentation and debate. $1.25. Am. Bk.
Foster, W: T. Argumentation and debating. **$1.25 net. Houghton M.
Iowa State University. Constructive and rebuttal speeches of the representatives of the State University of Iowa in the intercollegiate debates. 2 v. ea., $1. Forensic.
Kleiser, G. How to argue and win. $1.25 net. Funk.
Kline, R. E. P. Argumentation and debate. 25 c. La Salle Extension.
Lyman, R. L. V. Principles of effective debating. 15 c. Univ. of Wis.
Pattee, G. K. Practical argumentation. **$1.10 net. Century Co.
Pearson, P. M., *ed.* Intercollegiate debate. $1.50. Hinds.
Percival, M., *and* Jeliffe, R. A., *comps.* Specimens of exposition and argument. *90 c. net. Macmillan.
Phelps, E. M., *comp.* Selected articles on the initiative and referendum. $1. H. W. Wilson.
Shurter, E. D. Science and art of debate. *$1.25 net. Neale.

DEBATING.—*Continued.*
Thomas, R. W. Manual of debate. 80 c. Am. Bk.
Tulane University of Louisiana. Triangular debate bet. Tulane Univ. of La., Univ. of N. C. and Univ. of Va. $1. H. W. Kaiser.
See also Elocution;—Orators and oratory;—Parliamentary law;—*also* special topics.
DE BATZ, *Baron.*
See Batz, *Baron* de.
De Becker, J. E.
Nightless city; or, the hist. of the Yoshiwara Yukwaku. '10(Ja15) il. 8°, *$10 net. Wessels.
De Bekker, Leander Jan.
Stokes' encyclopedia of music and musicians. '08(D5) c. O.; Rev. and enl. ed. '10(F) 6+753 p. 8°, ea., **$3 net. Stokes.
De Bercy affair. Holmes, G. $1.50. Clode.
Debit and credit. *See* Freytag, Gustav.
"Deborah." *See* Leavitt, Ezekiel. Songs of grief.
Deborah's diary. *See* Manning, Anne Mary Powell.
Debs, Eug. Victor.
Debs: his life, writings and speeches; with a department of appreciations; authorized ed. '08(O31) c. por. O. $2. Appeal.
Debs: his life, writings and speeches. New library ed. '10(S) $1. Kerr.
DEBT.
Dooling, J: C. Equitable remedies of creditors in Michigan. $4. Drake Law Co.
Lawrence, H: C. Making him pay: [collecting of accounts.] (Add. pubs. for price.) Consol. Pub.
See also Taxation.
De Bunsen, Mary Isabella Waddington.
See Bunsen, M. I. W. von.
De Bunsen, Victoria.
Soul of a Turk. '09(N6) il. O. *$3.50 net. Lane.
DEBUSSY, Claude Achille.
Liebich, L. Claude-Achille Debussy. *$1 net. Lane.
Debutante (The); record book. [1910.] (My) 8°, Popular ed., $2; Gift ed., $3.50; De luxe ed., $6. Reilly & B.
Decade (The). Barnaby, H. T: $1.25. Wolverine.
Decadence. Balfour, A. J. *50 c. net. Putnam.
Decameron (The). *See* Boccaccio, Giovanni.
De Camp, E. J.
Nature's law of health and disease and the ladies' toilet; concise up-to-date family medical work and ladies' companion. [1910.] (Jl) c. 177 p. il. 12°, $1. Winkelman.
DE CARPENTIER FAMILY.
See Genealogies, Sellers, E. J.
Decay of the Church of Rome. McCabe, J. *$2.50 net. Dutton.
De Cerkez, Florence Euphemia.
Driftwood, and other poems. '10(D31) c. 12°, $1.50. Badger.
De Cesare, Raffaele.
Last days of Papal Rome, 1850-1870; abr. and tr. by Helen Zimmern; with an introd. chapter by G. M. Trevelyan. '09 (S25) il. pors. O. *$3.50 net. Houghton M.

Decisive battles of America. *See* Hart, Albert Bushnell.

Decisive battles of the world. *See* Creasy, *Sir* E: Shepherd.

Decisive hour of Christian missions. Mott, J: R. $1. Student Vol.

Deck and field. Hackett, F. W. *$1.25 net. Lowdermilk.

Decker, Ida Smith.
Patience and her garden. '10(O15) D. pap., 35 c., in envelope. P. Elder.

Decker, J: Wright.
Cheese making. 5th rev. ed. by F. W. Woll. '09(F13) c. il. figs. O. $1.75. Mendota.

Decker, Ward.
Complete condensed electricity: a practical and simplified course of study for beginners. In 3 pts. pt. 1. '09(O2) il. D. pap., ea., $4; per set, $12. Barnes.

DECLAMATION.
See Elocution;—Orators and oratory;—Readers;—Recitations.

DECLARATION OF INDEPENDENCE.
Connor, R: D. W. North Carolina's priority in the demand for a Declaration of Independence. 50 c. R. D. W. Connor.
Thomas, G: C. Autograph letters and autographs of the signers of the Declaration of Independence. (Priv. pr.) G: C. Thomas.
United States. Constitution of the United States of America and Declaration of Independence. *25 c. net. G. A. Jackson.

Decline and fall of the Roman Empire. *See* Gibbon, E:

Decoration and furniture of English mansions. Lenygon, F. *$1 net. Scribner.

DECORATION AND ORNAMENT.
Batchelder, E. A. Design in theory and practice. $1.75 net. Macmillan.
Batchelder, E. A. Principles of design. $3. Inland Pr.
Christie, A. H. Traditional methods of pattern designing. $2. Oxford Univ.
Contet, F., *ed.* Examples of old iron work. $13.40. Hessling.
Day, L. F. Nature and ornament. In 1 v. *$5 net; In 2 v. v. 1. *$2 net; v. 2, *$3 net. Scribner.
Ganz, H: F. W. Pract. hints on modelling, design and mural decoration. *$1 net. Lippincott.
Haebler, O. Stil-lehre; study of style for colored surface decoration, including textiles, wall-paper, etc. $8. Hessling.
Hall, E. H. Decorative art in Crete in the bronze age. (Add. pubs. for price.) Winston.
Hatton, R: G. Craftsman's plant-book: figures of plants sel. from the XVI century herbals. $7.50 net. Dutton.
Hopkins, J. F:, *comp. and ed.* Decorating fabrics by stenciling. 25 c. Hirshberg.
Lilley, A. E. V., *and* Midgley, W. Book of studies in plant form; with suggestions for their application to design. *$2 net. Scribner.
Priestman, *Mrs.* M. T. Handicrafts in the home. $2 net. McClurg.

DECORATION AND ORNAMENT.—*Continued.*
Richardson, C: J. Fragments and details of architecture, decoration and furniture of the Elizabethan period. $12; $15. Helburn.
Speltz, A. Styles of ornament. $6.70. Hessling.
Standage, H. C., *ed.* Decoration of metal, wood, glass, etc. $2. Wiley.
Studio year book of decorative art. 1908. *$5 net; 1909. *$3 net; *$2.50 net. Lane.
White, G. Practical designing. *$1.25 net. Macmillan.
See also Alphabets;—Book illustration;—Ceramics; — China painting; — Church decoration and ornament:—Embroidery; — Enamel;—Fine arts; — Furniture; — Heraldry;—House decoration;—Lettering;—Needlework; — Painters and painting;—Sculpture;—Textile fabrics;—Upholstery;—Wall decoration;—Woodcarving.

Decorative art in Crete in the bronze age. Hall, E. H. (Add. pubs. for price.) Winston.

Decorative glass processes. Duthie, A. L: **$2 net. Van Nostrand.

Decorative heraldry. Eve, G: W. *$2 net. Macmillan.

Decorator ser. of practical books; ed. by A. S. Jennings. il. 12°, $1.25. Painters' Mag.
—Duthie. Practical church decoration.

Decree on daily communion. Ferreres, J. B. *$1.50 net. Herder.

DEDHAM, Mass.
Rudd, E: H. Dedham's ancient landmarks and their national significance. $1. Dedham Transcript.
See also Dover, Mass.

Deeds of Beowulf; done into modern prose by J. Earle. '10(Ag20) c. O. (Oxford translations.) $1. Oxford Univ.

Deep hole drilling. '09(F13) c. il. 8°, (Machinery's reference ser.) pap., 25 c. Indust. Press.

Deep in piney woods. Church, J. W. $1.20 net. Crowell.

Deep Moat Grange. Crockett, S: R. †$1.50. Appleton.

Deep sea ser. 12°, 60 c. Grosset.
—Rockwood. Adrift on the Pacific.

Deep sea warriors. Lubbock, A. B. †$1.50. Dodd.

Deep-water ser.: popular tales of the sea. D. $1.25. Sturgis & W.
—Russell. Wreck of the "Grosvenor."

Deeper stain. Hird, F. †$1.50. Appleton.

Deeping, G: Warwick.
Bertrand of Brittany. '08(Ap25) c. D. †$1.50. Cassell
Mad Barbara. '09(F13) c. front. D. †$1.50. Cassell.
Red Saint. '09(O23) col. front. D. $1.50. Cassell.
Rust of Rome. '10(Je4) front. D. $1.20 net. Cassell.
Seven streams. '09(N6) D. $1.50. Cassell.

Deering, Ja. H., ed.
See California. Code of civil procedure.—General laws.—Political code.

DEFECTIVE CHILDREN.
See Children.

Defence of Duffer's drift. *See* Summer night's dream.

Defence of poesie. *See* Sidney, *Sir* Philip.

Defence of the Mecklenburg declaration of independence. Moore, J. H. *$1.50 net. Stone & B.

Defence of the truth. Sedlasky, F. J. $1.25. F. J. Sedlasky.

Defense of the faith and the saints. Roberts, B. H. v. 1. $1.50. Deseret News.

Defense of the government of Guatemala before the Central-American Court of Justice at Cartago, in the case of Honduras. '09 (Mr13) O. pap. (Add. pubs. for price.) Int. Bu. Am. Republics.

Definitions in navigation and nautical astronomy. Groves-Showell, P. *$1.25 net. Lippincott.

Defoe, Dan.

Works. 8 v. New imperial lib. ed. '10 (D) il. 8°, ea., $1.25; hf. cf., $2.25; New il. sterling ed., ea., $1. (Sets only.) Estes.

Adventures of Robinson Crusoe; with introd. and notes by T. W. Silverdale. '08 (Ap4) il. D. *75 c. net.—*Same,* (Ap18) front. D. (Class-books of English literature.) *50 c. net. Longmans.

Defoe: [selections;] ed. by J: Masefield. '09(D25) 12°, (Masters of literature.) *$1.10 net. Macmillan.

Journal of the plague year; introd. by G. A. Aitken. '08(F22) 16°, (Everyman's lib.) *35 c. net; leath., *70 c. net. Dutton.

Life and adventures of Robinson Crusoe. '08(O10) il. D. (Bowman's illustrated lib. of world-favorite books.) $1. Bowman.

Life and adventures of Robinson Crusoe. '08(D5) D. (Thin paper ser. of popular classics.) limp leath., $1.25. Lippincott.

Life and adventures of Robinson Crusoe. pt. 1; with introd. and notes by C: Rob. Gaston. '09(O23) c. T. (Pocket Am. and Eng. classics.) 25 c. Macmillan.

Life and adventures of Robinson Crusoe; ed., with introd. and notes, by A. C. Liddell. [Pt. 1.] '10(N19) il. map, D. 50 c. Oxford Univ.

Life and strange surprising adventures of Robinson Crusoe. '09(S25) il. in col. O. *$1.50 net; '08(D5) 2 v., il. *$5 net; Large pap. ed., in 4 v., **$18 net. Houghton M.

Memoirs of a cavalier; introd. by G. A. Aitken. '08(F22) 16°, (Everyman's lib.) *35 c. net; leath., *70 c. net. Dutton.

Memoirs of a cavalier; or, a military journal of the wars in Germany and the wars in England from the year 1632 to the year 1648; ed., with introd. and notes, by Eliz. O'Neill. '09(My) 11+292 p. 16°, (Cambridge English literature for school.) *40 c. net. Putnam.

Robinson Crusoe. '10(D10) col. il. 8°, $2 net, boxed. Doran.

Robinson Crusoe. '10(O) il. 8°, $1.50. Fenno.

Robinson Crusoe. '10(F5) il. in col. 12°, *$2 net. Macmillan.

Robinson Crusoe;; ed. by Wa. Jerrold. '10 (D) 12°, (Children's classics.) $1.25. Dutton.

Robinson Crusoe, told to the children by J: Lang. '08(Je6) il. 16°, (Told to the children ser.) 50 c. Dutton.

Defoe, Dan.—*Continued.*

Robinson Crusoe; told in easy French by Kathleen Fitzgerald. '09, [1910.] (Ja) sq. 16°, (Children's favorites.) *50 c. net. Jacobs.

Robinsono Kruso: lia vivo kaj strangaj, mirindegaj aventuroj de Danielo Defo; kun multaj illustrajoj. [Esperanto ed.] '08(N21) c. S. bds., 50 c. Altemus.

Teacher's Robinson Crusoe; manual for primary teachers; the story rewritten, modernized and adptd., with additional incidents for use in the later primary grades as a center and material for oral and written language, nature study, social and industrial hist., ethics, drawing and the manual arts; the adaptation, with additional incidents, introduction and suggestive treatments of the text by S: B. Allison. [1910.] (N) c. 199 p. il. 12°, 50 c. Educ. Pub.

DEFOE, Daniel.

Davis, A. M. Bibliographical puzzle. [Relates to "News from the moon," issued in Boston in 1721 and attributed by Evans to press of J. Franklin.] (Priv. pr.) J. Wilson & Son.

De Ford, W: H.

Lectures on general anæsthetics in dentistry. '08(Je6) c. il. por. O. $3. J: T. Nolde.

Deformations of railroad tracks. Cuénot, G. $2. Railroad Gazette.

Defrauding the government. Theobald, W: H: $1.50. Myrtle.

De Garmo, C:

Laboratory exercises in art appreciation. '09(Ja23) il. Q. (Cornell study bulletins for teachers.) 40 c. Bardeen.

Principles of secondary education. v. 2, Processes of instruction. '08(D12); v. 3, Ethical training. '10(O8) 12°, ea., *$1 net. Macmillan.

De Geer.

See Dubois.

De Goesbriand, Bp. L:

Young converts; or, memoirs of the three sisters—Debbie, Helen and Anna Barlow. '08, [1909.] (Mr) 304 p. 12°, *75 c. net. Chr. Press.

Degrais, —.

See Wickham, Louis.

De Groot, C. Hofstede.

Catalogue raisonné of the works of the most eminent Dutch painters of the seventeenth century; based on the work of J: Smith, by C. Hofstede de Groot, (with the assistance of Dr. W. R. Valentiner and others;) tr. and ed. by E: G. Hawke. In 10 v. v. 1. '08(F15); v. 2. '09(Je5); v. 3. '10(O8) 8°, ea., *$7.50 net. Macmillan.

Degroot, Jan Jakob Maria.

Religion of the Chinese. '10(Ja29) c. D. **$1.25 net. Macmillan.

Dehan, R:

One braver thing. '10(Jl30) c. D. $1.40. Duffield.

De Hart, R: P., ed.

Past and present of Tippecanoe County, Ind. 2 v. '09, [1910.] (N) pors. 4°. B. F. Bowen.

Deissmann, Gustav Adolf.
Light from the ancient East. (Light from Anatolia): the New Testament and the new and recently discovered manuscripts of the Græco-Roman world. '10(Jl30) il. 8°, $4 net. Doran.

Deitch, Guilford A.
Digest of insurance cases. v. 20. '08 (My) $3; v. 21. '09(S) $3; v. 22. '10(Je) c. O. hf. shp., $3.50.—General index, embracing all decisions in any manner affecting insurance companies or their contracts, [etc.] v. 1-20. In 6 v. '09(D) c. 973+515 p. O. $36. Rough Notes.

Deity of Christ. Speer, R. E. *25 c. net. Revell.

Deity of Jesus Christ. Pratt, S: W. *50 c. net. S. S. Times.

DEITZ, John F.
Phillips, T: W. Story of John F. Deitz, the defender of Cameron Dam, (Thornapple River.) 27 c. Phillips & E.

Dejeans, Eliz., [now Mrs Sidney Budgett.]
Heart of desire. '10(Ap9) c. il. D. $1.50. Lippincott.
Winning chance. '09(My22) c. front. D. †$1.50. Lippincott.

DEKKER, Thomas.
Pierce, F: E. Collaboration of Webster and Dekker. $1. Holt.

Delacombe, Harry.
Boys' book of airships. '10(Ja1) c. il. O. $2. Stokes.

Delafield affair. Kelly, *Mrs.* F. F. $1.50. McClurg.

Delamater, G. R.
See Belden, A. W.

De Lancey, Fk. W.
A to Z of pigeons and bantams. '10(S) 97 p. il. 8°, 50 c. Item Pub.

Deland, Ellen Douglas.
Miss Betty of New York. '08(N14) c. il. D. †$1.25. Harper.
See also Boys on the railroad.

De Land, Fred.
Dumb no longer; romance of the telephone. '09(Je5) c. il. pors. O. $1.50. Volta.

Deland, Lorin Fuller.
Imagination in business; rev. and enl. '09 (N6) D. **50 c. net. Harper.

Deland, Mrs. Lorin Fuller.
See Deland, *Mrs.* Marg. Wade Campbell.

Deland, Mrs. Marg. Wade Campbell, [Mrs. Lorin Fuller Deland.]
Awakening of Helena Richie. [Margaret Anglin ed.] '09(N20) c. il. O. †$1.50. Harper.
R. J.'s mother and some other people. '08 (My16) c. il. D. †$1.50. Harper.
The way to peace. '10(O8) c. il. O. $1.50, boxed. Harper.
Where the laborers are few. '09(O23) c. il. O. †$1.50, boxed. Harper.

DELANE, John Thaddeus.
Dasent, A. I. Life and correspondence of John Thaddeus Delane, editor of the London *Times.* *$7.50 net. Scribner.

Delannoy, Burford.
Prince Charlie. '08(Ap4) D. *$1 net. Fenno.

Delany, Selden Peabody.
Ideal of Christian worship. '09(Ap10) c. S. *50 c. net. Young Churchman.

De la Pasture, Mrs. Eliz. Bonham, [Mrs. H: De la Pasture, now Lady Clifford.]
Catherine's child. '09(Ja30) c. D. **$1.20 net. Dutton.
Grey knight. '08(My9) D. †$1.50. Dutton.
The tyrant. '09(D) 8+382 p. 12°, *$1.25 net. Dutton.
Unlucky family. '08(Mr28) c. il. D. †$1.50. Dutton.

De la Ramée, Louise, ["Ouida."]
Bimbi; stories for children. '10(N12) c. col. il. O. $1.50. Lippincott.

De La Rochelle, Philippe.
Guide to French pronunciation and practical phonetics. '09(Ap24) c. D. *50 c. net. Stechert.
New and progressive study of French verbs, with idiomatic expressions in French and English. 2d ed. '10(N12) c. 12°, $1.50. F. K. Kane.
New study of French verbs. '10(Ja15) c. D. *$1.50 net. Stechert.

De Laurence, Lauron W:
God, the Bible, truth and Christian theology. '09(Jl) c. 14+542 p. il. por. 12°, $3.50. De Laurence, S.
"Immanence of God"; "Know thyself"; "God (the soul) and the man"; "The book of self" (God); "Faith" (the primary will) as taught by "Jesus the master." '08, [1909.] (F) c. various paging, 12°, $3.25. De Laurence, S.
Mystic test book of "The Hindu occult chambers;" The magic and occultism of India; Hindu and Egyptian crystal gazing; The Hindu magic mirror. '09(Jl) c. 177 p. por. il. 12°, $2. De Laurence, S.

DELAWARE.
Conrad, H: C. History of the state of Delaware. $12. H: C. Conrad.
Hasse, A. R. Index of economic material in the documents of the United States; Delaware. $1.50. Carnegie.
Messersmith, G: S. Government of Delaware. $1. Am. Bk.
Smith, R. G. Brief acct. of the services rendered by the Second Regiment Delaware Volunteers in the War of the Rebellion. 50 c. Delaware Hist. Soc.
See also Drawyers Presbyterian Church;—Sussex County.

DELAWARE, Ohio.
See Ohio Wesleyan University.

Delaware College bull.; new ser. 8°. Del. College.
—Sypherd *and* Messersmith. High school course in English. gratis.

Delaware Historical Society papers. 8°, pap. Delaware Hist. Soc.
—Campbell. Life and character of Jacob Broom. 50 c.
—Higgins. Historical address delivered before the "Friends of old Drawyers." (Add. pubs. for price.)
—Pennewill *and* Macdonough. Addresses at the unveiling of a memorial tablet to Commodore Thomas Macdonough. 50 c.

DELAWARE INDIANS.
See Indians.

DELAWARE RIVER.
Garber, J: P. Settlements on the Delaware prior to the coming of William Penn. (Sold to members only.) City Hist. Phil.

Delays and defects in the enforcement of the law in this country. Taft, W: H. 10 c. Civic Forum.

Delbosc, R. Foulché-.
See Foulché-Delbosc, R.

Delbridge, C: Lomax.
Delbridge cotton calculator, by 16ths and 5 points, 300 to 699 pounds. '10(N19) c. 12°, $3.50. Delbridge.

Deledda, Grazia.
Ashes, (Ceneres;) tr. from the Italian by Helen Hester Colvill. '08(Ap25) D. †$1.50. Lane.

De Lee, Jos. Bolivar, M.D.
Obstetrics for nurses. 3d ed., thoroughly rev. and enl. '08(D) c. 512 p. il. fold. chart, 8°, *$2.50 net. Saunders.

—, and Stowe, Herbert M., eds.
Obstetrics. '09(S) c. 236 p. il. 12°, (Practical medicine ser.) $1.25. Year Bk.

Delegates from Denver. Clark, S: N. 25 c. Dick.

De Leon, Edn. Warren, comp.
Manual of liability insurance cont. the rules, instructions, rates and classifications adopted by the Conference of Liability Companies and amended to Jan. 1, 1905; together with the latest policy forms of liability insurance; also, various liability and automobile policies of individual companies. '09(S) 127 p. 8°, $2. Spectator.

De Leon, Perry M.
Navies in war and the Confederate Navy in the war between the states; address del. before Camp 171, United Confederate Veterans of Washington, D. C. '10 (Ag20) c. il. por. 8°, 25 c. H. T. Graves.

De Leon, T: Cooper.
Belles, beaux and brains of the 60's. '09 (Je5) c. pors. O. *$3 net. G: W. Dillingham.
Crag-nest; romance of the days of Sheridan's ride. '10(Mr5) c. il. D. $1.25. G: W. Dillingham.
John Holden, unionist; romance of the days of Forrest's ride with Emma Sanson. '10(Ap23) c. il. D. $1.50. G: W. Dillingham.

De Lesdain, Count.
From Pekin to Sikkim, through the Ordos, the Gobi Desert and Thibet; with preface by J: Murray. '08(My9) il. map, 8°, *$4 net. Dutton.

DELFTWARE.
See Ceramics.

Delicious vice. *See* Allison, Young Ewing.

Delight. Smith, G. 50 c. Altemus.

Delights of wisdom. Swedenborg, E. $1.25. Am. Swedenborg.

Delilah of the snows. Bindloss, H. †$1.50. Stokes.

Delineator prize $3,000 houses. '09(D11) il. plans, F. $1. B. W. Dodge.

Delitzsch, Friedrich.
Whose son is Christ?: two lectures on progress in religion; tr. by F. L. Pogson. '09(Je19) D. *80 c. net. Am. Unitarian.

Delk, Edn. Heyl.
Three vital problems: the higher and the highest criticism; the modern church and the social crisis; the centrality of Christian fellowship. '09(N) c. 83 p. 12°, 50 c. Lutheran Pub.

Dell, Sidney.
See California. General street laws.

Della Dorn. Allison, T: J. $1.25. Hyland.

Dellenbaugh, F: S:
Canyon voyage: the narrative of the second Powell expedition down the Green-Colorado River from Wyoming. '08(O24) c. il. O. **$3.50 net, boxed. Putnam.

Del Lungo, Isidore.
Women of Florence; tr. by Mary C. Steegman; with preface by Dr. Guido Biagi. '08(O3) il. O. *$2.25 net. Doubleday, P.

Del Mar, Eug.
Living ideals. '08(F1) c. 16°, $1. Progressive Lit.

Del Mar, W: Arth.
Electric power conductors. '09(S11) il. 12°, *$2 net. Van Nostrand.

Delmarree. Martin, J. L. (Add. author for price.) J. L. Martin.

Delmarter, Ja. Ellsworth.
Elements of vocal music; self-instructor in the theory of notation and sight-reading, incl. a brief dict. of musical terms. '09 (N) c. 54 p. 12°, 35 c. Delmarter Pub.

De Long, Allen Percy.
When the lilacs bloom. '08, [1909.] (Je) c. 412 p. il. 12°, $1.25. Benton.

De Long, Arth. Hamilton.
Pastor's ideal funeral book; Scripture selections, topics, texts and outlines, suggestive themes and prayers, quotations and illustrations, forms of services, etc.; with introd. by Bp. W: A. Quayle. '10(D17) c. 16°, $1. Jennings.

DeLong, J: Edm.
The joys that live. [1910.] (D) c. 101 p. 16°, 75 c. J: E. DeLong.

De Lorme, M. F., M.D.
Manual of pharmacy for physicians. 2d ed., rev. and enl. '10(D) 8+199 p. il. 12°, $1.25 net. Blakiston.

Delp, Jos. Dan.
Comprehensive modernized rapid calculator. '10(N12) il. por. D. 75 c. J. D. Delp.

Delpit, Louise.
L'age d'or de la litterature française. '09 (N20) c. tabs., D. (Modern language ser.) 90 c. Heath.

DELUGE (The).
Magoun, H. W. Glacial epoch and the Noachian deluge. 25 c. H. W. Magoun.
See also Babylonia.

Demagog (The). Hereford, W: R: †$1.50. Holt.

Demand and the increased supply of increased efficiency in the negro ministry. 15 c. Am. Negro.

Demarest, Clifford.
Hints on organ accompaniment. '10(N19) c. 12°, 50 c. H. W. Gray.

Demarest, Virginia, pseud.
Fruit of desire; a novel. '10(Jl30) D. $1.20 net. Harper.

De Menil, Alex. Nicolas.
Forest and town: poems. '10(D17) S. $1.25 net. Torch Press.

Dement, I: Strange.
Dement's Pitmanic shorthand. 4th ed., rev. and re-engraved throughout. '09, [1910.] (Je) 17+263 p. 12°, $2. Dement Pub.

DEMENTIA.
See Insanity.

De Mill, R: Mead.
Foundation and the superstructure; or, the faith of Christ and the works of man. '08(D19) c. O. **$3 net. Putnam.

De Mille, W: C.
See Burton, F: R.

De Milt, Aida Rodman.
Ways and days out of London. '10(N19) c. il. O. $2.50 net, boxed. Baker & T.

Deming, Horace E:
Government of American cities: program of democracy; study of municipal organization and of the relation of the city to the state; also a reprint of the municipal program of the National Municipal League. '09(Mr27) c. O. **$1.50 net. Putnam.

DEMOCRACY.
Abbott, L. Spirit of democracy. $1.25 net. Houghton M.
De Tocqueville, A. Democracy in America. 2 v. $3.50; $7. Lamb Pub.
Flack, A. G. Democracy. 50 c. Cochrane Pub.
Hill, R. T. Public domain and democracy. $2. Longmans.
Howe, F. C. Privilege and democracy in America. **$1.50 net. Scribner.
Ostrogorski, M. I. Democracy and the party system in the United States. $1.75 net. Macmillan.
Snyder, J. L. Agriculture and democracy. (Add. pubs. for price.) Mich. Agricultural Coll.
Thum, W: Step forward for the democracy of to-morrow. $1. Twentieth Century.
Zueblin, C: Democracy and the overman. $1 net. B: W. Huebsch.
See also Money;—Political science;—Suffrage;—United States.

Democratic foundations. Ulrich, J: 10 c. Co-operative Pr.

Democratic Party. National Committee. Campaign text book of the Democratic party of the United States, 1908, '08(D) 312 p. front. 8°, 25 c. Democratic.

DEMOCRATIC PARTY.
See Parties (*political*).

DEMOLITIONS.
See Military art and science.

Demons and tongues. White, *Mrs.* A. 30 c. Pentecostal Union.

De Monvel, Roger Boutet.
Beau Brummell and his times; with a chapter on dress and the dandies by Mary Craven. '08(O3) il. pors. O. *$2.50 net. Lippincott.

De Morgan, A:
Elem. illustrations of the differential and integral calculus. New ed. '09(Mr) 8+144 p. *$1 net. Open Court.
On the study and difficulties of mathematics. 2d ed. '09(Mr) 8+288 p. *$1.25 net. Open Court.

De Morgan, J:
Old Ironsides. '08(N14) c. il. O. (Our old ships and their commanders.) 75 c. McLoughlin
Taming the Barbary pirates. '08(O17) c. il. O. (Our old ships and their commanders.) 75 c. McLoughlin.
Yankee ship and a Yankee crew in the good ship "United States." '08(O17) c. il. O. (Our old ships and their commanders.) 75 c. McLoughlin.

De Morgan, W: Frend.
An affair of dishonor. '10(S24) c. D. $1.75. Holt.
It never can happen again. '09(D4) c. D. †$1.75. Holt.
Somehow good. '08(F8) c. D. †$1.75. Holt.

Demosthenes.
Orations pronounced to excite the Athenians against Philip, King of Macedon; and on occasions of public deliberation; with introd. by the translator, T: Leland, and special introd. by Epiphanius Wilson. '08(Je27) c. il. 8°, $1.75; hf. mor., $3.50. Lamb Pub.
Philippics, 1, 2, 3; with introd. and notes by Gilbert A. Davies. '09(My) 35+126 p 16°, *60 c. net. Putnam.

De Musset, Alfr.
Tales. '09(D4) c. S. (Wayside lib.) leath., $1, boxed. Brentano's.

Demy, S. Sophia Beale-, ed.
See Beale-Demy, S. Sophia.

DENATURED ALCOHOL.
See Alcohol.

Dench, E: Bradford.
Diseases of the ear; a text-book for practitioners and students of medicine. 4th ed., rev. and enl. '09(O) 25+718 p. il. 8°, $5. Appleton.

Denehie, G: R.
Motorman's practical air brake instructor; concise up-to-date treatise on the construction and operation of the different air brake equipments used in modern electric transportation. '09(S) c. 280 p. il. 16°, leath., $1.50. Drake.

Denifle, Rev. H:
Humanity; its destiny and the means to attain it; tr. from the German by Very Rev. Ferdinand Brossart. '09(O30) c. por. D. *$1.25 net. Pustet.

Denison, G: Taylor.
Struggle for imperial unity; recollections and experiences. '09(Ap24) por. O. **$2.25 net. Macmillan.

Denison, T: Stewart.
Mexican-Aryan comparative vocab.; radicals of Mexican or Nautl language with their cognates in the Aryan languages of the old world, chiefly Sanskrit, Greek, Latin and Germanic. '10(Ja8) c. O. pap., $2. T: S. Denison.

Denison, T: Stewart.—*Continued.*
Morphology of the Mexican verb compared with the Sanskrit, Greek, and Latin verb; also morphology of Mexican abstract nouns, with an appendix discussing numerals, phonology of labials, etc. [1910.] (O) c. 31 p. Q. pap., 75 c. T: S. Denison.
Primitive Aryans of America; origin of the Aztecs and kindred tribes, showing their relationship to the Indo-Iranians and the place of the Nauatl or Mexican in the Aryan group of languages. '09(Ja16) c. O. $3.25; pap., $2.50. T: S. Denison.

Denizens of the deep. Duncan, F. M. *$1.75 net. Cassell.

DENMARK.
Baedeker, K. Norway, Sweden and Denmark, with excursions to Iceland and Spitzbergen. $2.40. Scribner.
Bumpus, T. F. Cathedrals and churches of Norway, Sweden, and Denmark. *$4 net; *$7.50 net. Pott.
Butlin, F. M. Among the Danes. *$2.50 net. Pott.
Convention between the U. S. and Denmark. (Add. Superintendent for price.) U. S., Supt. of Docs.
Thomson, M. P. Denmark. 75 c. net. Macmillan.
See also **Ribe.**

Dennen, Rev. Ernest Jos.
Knights of King Arthur, Dept. of the Order of Sir Galahad; club for boys and young men, especially for boys and young men of the Episcopal church; founded and developed with adaptations from the Knights of King Arthur. [1910.] (D) c. 53 p. il. 12°, 25 c. E. J. Dennen.

Dennett, R. E.
Nigerian studies. '10(D24) il. map, 8°, $2.75 net. Macmillan.

Denney, Ja., D.D.
Church and the kingdom. '10(Je4) 16°, 50 c. net. Doran.
Jesus and the Gospel: Christianity justified in the mind of Christ. '09(F20) c. O. **$2 net. Armstrong.

Denney, Jos. Villiers.
See Scott, Fred Newton.

—, Duncan, Carson S., and McKinney, Fk. C.
Argumentation and debate. '10(N19) c. D. $1.25. Am. Bk.

—, ed. American public addresses. '10(My21) c. D. $1. Scott, F. & Co.

Dennis, Ja. Shepard, D.D.
New horoscope of missions: [John H. Converse lectures on missions.] '08(My16) c. D. *$1 net. Revell.

Dennis, Ja. Teackle.
Burden of Isis: being the lament of Isis and Nephthys. '10(Ap23) 12°, (Wisdom of the East ser.) 60 c. net. Dutton.

Dennis, J: R., and others.
Comic dialogues. '08(O3) c. D. 50 c.; pap., 30 c. Penn Pub. Co.

Dennis, Oregon Milton.
Some reasons for failure of fish protective legislation, and some suggested remedies; address before the Fourth International Fishery Congress, Washington, Sept. 22 to 26, 1908. '10(Mr26) 8°, (U. S., Bu. of Fisheries, bull.)

DENNISON, Eliphalet Whorf.
Dennison, H: S. E. W. Dennison; memorial. Merrymount.

Dennison, H: Sturgis.
E. W. Dennison; memorial. '09, [1910.] (N) 102 p. il. pors. facsims, 8°. Merrymount.

Dennistoun, Ja.
Memoirs of the Dukes of Urbino; illustrating the arms, arts and literature of Italy, 1440-1630. New ed., with notes by E: Hutton. '08(D5) 3 v., il. tabs., O. *$12 net, boxed. Lane.

Denny, Arth. A.
Pioneer days on Puget Sound; ed. by Alice Harriman. '08(Ap18) c. D. (Puget Sound historical ser.) subs., *$2 net; *60 c. net. A. Harriman.

Denny, Emily Inez.
Blazing the way; or. true stories, songs and sketches of Puget Sound and other pioneers. '09(O) 503 p. il. pors. 8°, $2.50. Rainier Pr.

Denny, Ernest.
All-of-a-sudden Peggy; light comedy in three acts. '10(D17) c. plans, 12°, 50 c. S: French.

Denominational mission study course. 8°, 50 c.; pap., 35 c. Un. B. Pub.
—Weekley *and* Fout. Our heroes.

DENOMINATIONS.
See **Sects.**

Denslow, W: Wallace.
When I grow up. '09(O9) il. (partly in col.) Q. **$1 net. Century Co.

Densmore, Frances.
Chippewa music. '10(D17) il. pors. O. (Smithsonian Institution, Bu. of Am. Ethnology, bull.) 45 c. Smith Inst.

Densmore, Hiram D.
Origin, structure and function of the polar caps in *smilacina amplexicaulis,* Nutt. '08 (D19) il. O. (Univ. of Cal. pubs., Botany.) pap., 35 c. Univ. of Cal.

DENTAL METALLURGY.
See **Teeth.**

DENTISTRY.
See **Teeth.**

Denton, Clara J.
See Irish, Marie.

—, comp. Program book; collection of new recitations, dialogues, drills and choruses for boys and girls of all ages. '10(Ap9) c. 12°, 40 c. J. Fischer.

DENVER, Col.
Who's who in Denver society. $1. Kistler.

Denver International Correspondence School of Money. Catalogue and curriculum. '09 (Mr) c. '08. 23 p. D. pap., 25 c. Denver Int. Corr. Sch.

De Packh, Baroness M.
Twenty years in Siberia. '09(Mr27) 12°, $1.25. Guarantee Pub.

Department store accounts. American School of Correspondence. $1.50. Am. Sch. Corr.

Departmental ditties, *and* Ballads, and barrack room ballads. *See* Kipling, Rudyard.

Departmental teaching in elementary schools. Kilpatrick, V. *60 c. net. Macmillan.

DEPENDENCIES.
See **Colonial government.**

Depéret, Charles.
Transformation of the animal world. '09 (Ap17) fold. tabs. D. (International scientific ser.) *$1.75 net. Appleton.

Depew, Chauncey Mitchell.
Orations, addresses and speeches; ed. by J: Denison Champlin. In 8 v. [Ed. de luxe.] '10(D31) c. pors. 8°, ea., $6.25. C. M. Depew.

DE PEYSTER, John Watts.
Allaben, F. John Watts de Peyster. 2 v. *$2.50 net. Allaben.

Deportmental ditties. Graham, H. $1. Duffield.

DEPOSITS.
See Banks and banking.

Depot master. Lincoln, J. C. $1.50. Appleton.

De Pratz, Claire.
Education of Jacqueline. '10(My21) c. D. $1.50. Duffield.
Elizabeth Davenay. '09, [1910.] (F) $1.50. M. Kennerley.

Depreciated currency and diminished railway rates. '09(Jl10) O. pap. (Add. pubs. for price.) Railway World.

Depreciation of factories. Matheson, E. $4. Spon.

Depue, Oscar B.
See Jenkins, C: Fs.

De Quincey, T:
Confessions of an English opium-eater. '09 (Ap10) front. 32°, (Ariel booklets.) leath., 75 c., boxed. Putnam.
Literary criticism; ed. by Helen Darbishire. '09, [1910.] (F) 16°, (Oxford lib. of prose and poetry.) 90 c. Oxford Univ.
Selections: incl. Joan of Arc, The English coach, Levana and our ladies of sorrow, and Savannah la mar; ed. for school use by W: Vaughn Moody. '09(Jl31) c. 16°, (Lake English classics.) 25 c. Scott, F. & Co.
Spanish military nun and Revolt of the Tartars; ed., with introd. and notes, by V. H. Collins. '09(D4) map, S. 50 c. Oxford Univ.

Deran-Smith, Mrs. Edna.
Am I my brother's keeper? '10(N19) c. por. D. $1.10. E. Deran-Smith.

Derby day in the Yukon. Yukon Bill, *pseud.* $1 net. Doran.

DERBY FAMILY.
See Genealogies: Peabody, R. E.

DERBYSHIRE, Eng.
Moncrieff, A. R. H. Peak country: [Derbyshire.] *$2.50 net. Macmillan.

Derleth, C:
Destructive extent of the California earthquake. '09(Jl10) il. 12°, *$1.25 net. A. M. Robertson.

Derleth, C:, jr.
Moment diagrams and typical live loads. '08(Ja4) tab., O. (Univ. of Cal. pubs., Engineering.) pap., 10 c. Univ. of Cal.

DERMATOLOGY.
See Skin.

DERMOCHROMES.
See Skin.

Derr, L:, ed.
Cyclopedia of engineering. '08(Ja18) 6 v., il. pors. tabs., 8°. (Add. pubs. for price.) Am. Sch. Corr.

De Saix, Tyler.
Man without a head. '08(Ag29) c. D. **$1.50 net. Moffat.

De Saussure, Mrs. Nancy Bostick.
Old plantation days. '10(Ja29) c. front. 8°, $1. Duffield.

Desborough, Arth.
See Watteyne, Victor.

Descaves, Lucien, ed.
Color of Paris. '09(D25) il. 8°, *$6 net, boxed. Dodd.

Descendants of John Mowry. Mowry, W: A: $3. Preston.

Desch, Cecil H:
Metallography. '10(My14) D. (Textbooks of physical chemistry.) $3 net. Longmans.

De Schweinitz, G: Edm., M.D.
See Schweinitz, G. Edm. de, *M.D.*

Descriptive anatomy. Skillern, P.-G. $2. Dolbey.

Descriptive chemistry. Newell, L. C. $1.20. Heath.

DESCRIPTIVE GEOMETRY.
See Geometry.

Descriptive meteorology. Moore, W. L. $3 net. Appleton.

Descriptive stories for all the year. Burnham, M. 50 c. M. Bradley.

De Selincourt, Basil.
William Blake. '09(Je26) il. D. (Library of art ser.) *$2 net. Scribner.

De Sêlincourt, Hugh.
High adventure. '08(S19) D. †$1.50. Lane.
The way things happen. '09(S18) D. $1.50. Lane.

Desert and the sown. Bell, G. L. *$3 net. Dutton.

Desert gateway. Leeder, S. H. $1.75 net. Cassell.

Desert home. Reid, M. †$1. Dutton.

Deserted farm house. Lincoln, V. $1. Gilson.

Deserted village. *See* Goldsmith, Oliver. The traveller.

DESERTS.
MacDougal, D. T. Botanical features of North American deserts. $1.75. Carnegie.
See also Botany;—Sahara desert.

Deshong, Maurice W.
Quoits; game of skill, courage and endurance. '10(Jl2) c. il. 12°, (Spalding's athletic lib.) pap., 10 c. Am. Sports.

DESIGN.
See Architecture;—Decoration and ornament;—Textile fabrics.

Design and color in printing. Trezise, F: J. $1. Inland Pr.

Design and construction of induction coils. Collins, A. F. *$3 net. Munn.

Design and construction of metallic bridges. Burr, W: H. $5. Wiley.

Design and construction of oil engines. Goldingham, A. H. $2.50. Spon.

Design and construction of ships. Biles, J: H. v. 1. *$7.50 net. Lippincott.

Design and equipment of small chemical laboratories. Meade, R: K. *$2 net. Chemical Engineer.

Design in nature. Pettigrew, J. B. 3 v. *$16 net. Longmans.

Design of electric and overhead cranes. '09(O16) c. il. 8°, (Machinery's reference ser.) pap., 25 c. Indust. Press

Design of reinforced concrete slabs. Andrews, H. B. $1. H. B. Andrews.

Design of steel mill buildings. Ketchum, M. S. $3. Engineering News.

Design of typical steel railway bridges. Thomson, W: C. *$2 net. Engineering News.

Designing and cutting cams. '08(My23) c. il. 8°, (Machinery's reference ser.) pap., 25 c. Indust. Press.

Desire. Silberrad, U. L. $1.50. Doubleday, P.

DESIRE.
See Psychology.

Desjardins, Arth. Uldéric.
Manual of materia medica for students and state board candidates; prep. from lectures by William Caspari, jr., and other reliable sources (Potter, Wilcox, Simon). [1910.] (Ap) c. '09. 135 p. 12°, pap., $1.50. A. U. Desjardins.

DesJardins, B: Myrrick.
Wild flower poems. '09(F6) c. il. pors. T. 50 c.; 75 c.; pap., 25 c. Chapin News.

Desk book of facts for physicians and pharmacists. Walsh, R. $1.50. R. Walsh.

Desk book on the etiquette of social stationery. Clark, J. W. $1. Eton, C. & P.

Desmond, H: W:, and Frohne, H. W.
Building a home. '08(Ap18) c. il. plans drawn to scale, O. **$1.80 net. Baker & T.

Desmond, Humphrey Jos.
Little uplifts; paragraphs which may cheer or inspire as they catch the mood. '09 (D) c. 77 p. 16°, 40 c. H. J. Desmond.

Desnoyers, Louis Claude Joseph Florence.
Les mésaventures de Jean-Paul Choppart; ed., with notes, vocab. and exercises, by C. Fontaine. '09(My15) c. S. (Modern lang. ser.) 40 c. Heath.

De Soto, Emilio Dominquez.
See Colorado code.—Morrison, Rob. Stewart.

Desperate remedies. *See* Hardy, T:

DES PLAINES VALLEY, Ill.
Goldthwait, J. W. Physical features of the Des Plaines Valley. Univ. of Ill.

Destiny and desire. Watson, M. (Add. pubs. for price.) Casino.

Destroyer (The). Knott, H. 75 c. Vansant.

Destroyers (The). Carter, J. F., *jr.* †$1.50. Neale.

Destruction of the "Gaspee." Knox, H. B. gratis. R. I. Dept. Educ.

Destruction or regulation? Bancroft, E. A. [priv. pr.] E. A. Bancroft.

Destructive extent of the California earthquake. Derleth, C: *$1.25 net. A. M. Robertson.

Detached dwellings; country and suburban; [portfolio of plates and plans.] '09(Ap3) f°, $5. Swetland.

Detached pirate. Milecete, H. †75 c. Little, B. & Co.

Detailed working drawings of the five orders of architecture. Ball, J. T. $6.50; $7.50; $4. W: T. Comstock.

Details of machine tool design. '08(Jl4) c. il. 8°, (Machinery's reference ser.) pap., 25 c. Indust. Press.

DETECTIVES.
Barton, G: Adventures of the world's greatest detectives. 75 c. Winston.
Bradford, M., *jr., and* Wells, A. W. How to become a detective. $2. Globe Pr. (Wash., D. C.)

Deterioration of lead sheaths of aerial and underground telephone cables. Spencer, T: G. gratis. Stromberg-C.

Determinate evolution in the color-pattern of the lady-beetles. Johnson, R. M. $1. Carnegie.

Determination of radicals in carbon. Meyer, H. **$1.25 net. Wiley.

Determination of rock-forming minerals. Johannsen, A. $4. Wiley.

Determination of the position of a momentary impression. Burrow, N. T. 65 c. Psychological Review.

Determined angler. Bradford, C: 60 c. Nassau Press.

Dethronement of the city boss. Hamilton, J: J. $1.20 net. Funk.

De Tocqueville, Alexis.
Democracy in America; with introd. by J: T. Morgan and J: J. Ingalls. '08 (Je27) c. 2 v., il. 8°, $3.50; hf. mor., $7. Lamb Pub.

Detonation of gun cotton. Munroe, C: E: (Priv. pr.) Am. Philosophical.

DETROIT, Mich.
Marquis, A. N., *ed.* Book of Detroiters. $10. Marquis.

Dettmann, F: O.
Complete text-book of phono-stenography; for self-instruction and use in public and private schools. pt. 1, Corresponding style. 3d ed., rev. and enl. '09(S11) D. *$1 net. Stechert.

Deutches reformlesebuch. Savay, D. L., *comp.* 60 c. Oxford Univ.

Deuther, C: G:
Canticles of Niagara, and other poems. '09(My) c. 86 p. por. 16°, $2.50. C: G: Deuther.

Deutsch, Emanuel.
See Rapaport, S:

Deutsch, Gotthard.
Hist. of the Jews. '10(O15) c. D. 60 c. Bloch.
Israel Bruna: historical tragedy. '08(O24) c. D. $1.25. Badger.

Deutsch, Solomon.
Medical German. [1910.] (Mr) *$2 net. W: R. Jenkins.
Formerly published by E. R. Pelton.

Deutsch-America. Raible, M. $1. M. Raible.

Deutsch-englischer lesebücher für katholische schulen; German-English readers for Catholic schools. [In 3 v.] '09(D25) c. il. D. v. 1, 13½ c.; v. 2, 16⅔ c.; v. 3, 25 c. Benziger.

Deutsche (Das) element in den Vereinigten Staaten. Bosse, G. v. $3. Lemcke.

Deutsche gedichte zum auswendiglernen. Chalmers, W. P., *comp. and ed.* *40 c. net. Crowell.

Deutsche (Das) lied. Kaun, H., *comp.* $1. Rohlfing.

Deutsche patrioten in Ruszland zur zeit Napoleons. Arndt, E. M. 30 c. Heath.

Deutscher literaturatlas. Könnecke, G. *$1.50 net. Stechert.

Devant, D:
Magic made easy. Rev. ed. '10(D) il. 50 c. net. Cassell.
Tricks for every one. '10(Ja1) 12°, bds., 50 c. Lippincott.

Devas, C: Stanton.
Key to the world's progress; being some account of the historical significance of the Catholic church. New ed. '08(S12) O. pap., 20 c. Longmans.

Development and electrical distribution of water power. Lyndon, L. **$3 net. Wiley.

Development of Christianity. Pfleiderer, O. $1.50 net. B: W. Huebsch.

Development of Germany as a world power. American Academy of Political and Social Science. 50 c. Am. Acad. Pol. Sci.

Development of modern Europe. *See* Robinson, Ja. Harvey.

Development of nestling feathers. Jones, L. 50 c. L. Jones.

Development of religion. King, I. **$1.75 net. Macmillan.

Development of school support in Colonial Massachusetts. Jackson, G: L. $1; 75 c. Teachers' Coll.

Development of the brain of the American alligator. Reese, A. M. Smith. Inst.

Development of the chick. Lillie, F. R. **$4 net. Holt.

Development of the District of Columbia. Davis, H: E. (Add. Superintendent for price.) U. S., Supt. of Docs.

Development of the English law of conspiracy. Bryan, J. W. 75 c. Johns Hopkins.

Development of the state. Dealey, J. Q. $1.50. Silver.

Development of theology in Germany since Kant. Pfleiderer, O. *$2.75 net. Macmillan.

Devens, R: Miller, ["Frazar Kirkland,"] and Chase, C: W.
Glory of our youth. '10(Ja29) c. pors. 8°, $3.75. C. A. Nichols.

Devereaux, Anna W.
Outline of a year's work in the kindergarten. 4th ed. '08(D) c. 14+161 p. il. 12°, 70 c. M. Bradley.

Devereaux, G. R. M.
Etiquette for men.—Etiquette for women '10(O) 12°, ea., 50 c. Fenno.

Devereux, Mary.
From kingdom to colony. '08(My.) c. 12°, (Popular ed. of recent fiction.) †75 c. Little, B. & Co.
Up and down the sands of gold. '08(My.) c. 12°, (Popular ed. of recent fiction.) †75 c. Little, B. & Co.

Devereux, W:
Henry of Navarre; romantic play in four acts. '09(Mr13) c. 12°, pap., 50 c. Knickerbocker Press.

—, and Lovell, Stephen.
Raleigh; romance of Elizabeth's court; founded on the successful drama "Sir Walter Raleigh" as played by Lewis Waller. '10(Ap16) c. D. $1. Lippincott.

Devil (The). *See* Molnar, Ference;—Westrum, Adriaan Schade van.

Devil in London. Sims, G: R. $1. Dodge.

Devil in search of a wife, by a Boston lady; [verses.] '08(N) c. no paging. il. S. pap., gratis. J: R. Anderson.

Devil in the church: [anti-Catholic.] '08(N) 500 p. il. $1. L. J. King.

Devil worshiper. Ray, F: A. $1.50. C. M. Clark.

Devil's bride. Stine, M. H: $1. Minter.

Devil's motor. *See* Corelli, Marie.

Devil's note book. Bainbridge, O. $1. Cochrane.

Devil's pulpit. Watson, H: B. M. †$1.50. Dodd.

Devil's rebellion. May, C: F. $1.25. M., L. & I.

Devine, E: T:
Misery and its causes. '09(My15) D. (American social progress ser.) **$1.25 net. Macmillan.
Report on the desirability of establishing an employment bureau in the City of New York. '09(Mr13) c. il. tabs., 8°, (Russell Sage foundation pubs.) (Priv. pr.) Charities Pub.
Social forces; from the editor's page of *The Survey.* '09(D25) c. D. $1.25. Charities Pub.

Devine, H: C.
People's co-operative banks: for workers in towns, and small holders, allotment cultivators. '08(D5) *35 c. net. Cassell.

De Vinne, Thdr. Low.
Notable printers of Italy during the fifteenth century; il. with facsimiles from early editions and with remarks on early and recent printing. '10(Jl2) c. pors. f°, $15. Grolier Club.

Devious ways. Cannan, G. $1.50. Duffield.

Devlin, Rob. T:
Treaty power under the Constitution of the United States: commentaries on the treaty clauses of the Constitution; construction of treaties; extent of treaty making power, [etc.;] with appendices cont. regulation of Dept. of State relative to extradition of fugitives from justice, [etc.] '08(Jl) c. 70+864 p. Q. shp., $6. Bancroft-W.

Devney, Raymond Smith.
Brand new doctor. '08, [1909.] (Mr) c. 9-176 p. il. por. 12°, $1.25. R. S. Devney.

De Voe, Wa.
Doors of life; or, studies in self-healing. '09(N6) c. D. $1. Funk.

Devon pillow lace. Moody, A. P. *$1.50 net. Cassell.

DEVONIAN AGE.
See **Paleontology.**

Devonic fishes of the New York formations. Eastman, C: R. $1.25. N. Y. State Educ.

DEVONSHIRE, England.
Harper, C: G. North Devon coast. *$6 net. Scribner.
Knight, F. A., *and* Dutton, L. M. Devonshire. 45 c. net. Putnam.
Stabb, J: Some old Devon churches. *$3 net. Scribner.

Devotional commentaries; ed. by A: Rob. Buckland. 12°, *$1 net. Am. S. S.
—Buckland. First Epistle to the Thessalonians.—St. Paul's second Epistle to the Thessalonians.

Devotional commentary on the Gospel of St. Matthew. Horton, R. F. *$1 net. Revell.

DEVOTIONAL EXERCISES AND MEDITATIONS.
Angelus and Regina Cæli. 25 c. Longmans.
Beissel, S. Lord's prayer and the Hail Mary: points for meditation. *90 c. net. Herder.
Book of the divine consolation of Saint Angela Da Foligno. *$2.50 net. Duffield.
Bronchain, C: L: L. Meditations for every day in the year according to the doctrine and spirit of St. Alphonsus Mary de Liguori. 2 v. $5 net. Herder.
Eaton, R. Auxilium infirmorum: manual for the sick. *45 c. net. Herder.
For love of our Lord: series of devotional papers. *40 c. net. Young Churchman.
Geirmann, P: Private retreat for religious. *$1.50 net. Benziger.
Gottheil, G. Sun and shield: devout thoughts for every day use. *$1 net. Bloch.
Lasance, F. X. My prayer-book. $1.25. Benziger.
M., G. With the beloved: book of private devotion in verse. *60 c. net. Young Churchman.
More, G. Holy practices of a divine lover. *75 c. net. Herder.
Mortimer, A. G. Shadows of the valley; [to be used in the visitation of the sick.] $1.50 net. Jacobs.
Newman, J: H: Meditations and devotions. In 3 pts. ea., *40 c. net. Longmans.
Pepper, G: W. The way: devotional book for boys. *40 c. net; $1.05. Longmans.
Prayer-meeting talks. $1.25. Pub. Ho. of Evangelical Assoc.
Smith, C: E., *comp.* Altar devotions. **25 c. net. Longmans.
Thomas *à Kempis.* Imitation of Christ. *45 c. net. Putnam.
Well spent quarters: fifteen-minute meditations. 85 c. Chr. Press.
Wilson, J. R. Chapel in every home. (Priv. pr.) J. R. Wilson.
Young, J. B., *comp.* Helps for the quiet hour. $1. Eaton & M.
See also Bibles; — Calendars and year-books; — Christian life; — Consolation; — Cross; — Good Friday; — Hymns; — Jesus Christ; — Lent; — Lord's prayer; — Lord's supper; — Prayer; — Prayer-meetings; — Prayers; — Sermon on the Mount; — Worship.

Devotional hours with the Bible. Miller, J. R. In 8 v. v. 4. ea., $1.25 net. Doran.

Devotional hours with the Sunday-school lesson. *See* Miller, Ja. Russell.

Devotional ser. 50 v. 1909. S. 16°, ea.. vellum, 50 c. Altemus.

Devotional ser. 16°. Un. B. Pub.
—Bowman. Bible doctrine of devotion. *20 c. net.

Devourers (The). Chartres, A. V. $1.25 Putnam.

De Vries, D.
Calculation of clange-wheels for screw-cutting on lathes. '09(Ap3) il. 8°, $1.25. Spon.

De Vries, Hugo.
Intracellular pangenesis, incl. paper on fertilization and hybridization; tr. from the German by C. Stuart Gager. '10(Jl2) c. 8°, $3. Open Court.
Mutation theory. In 2 v. v. 1. '09(O23) il. in col.; v. 2. '10(D31) ea., $4 net. Open Court.

De Vries, W: Levering.
Foundation stone book, Washington Cathedral, A.D. 1907. '08(Je.) 157 p. pors. plans, 8°, $1.50. Cathedral.

De Walsh, Faust C:
Grillparzer as a poet of nature. '10(N19) 8°, (Columbia Univ. pubs.) pap., $1 net. Lemcke.

Dewar, Douglas.
Birds of the plains: [India.] '08(O24) il. O. *$4 net. Lane.
Indian birds; being a key to the common birds of the plains of India. '10(Ap30) D. $2 net. Lane.

—, and Finn, Fk.
Making of species. '09(Ag28) il. O. *$2.50 net. Lane.

Dewar, G: Albemarle Bertie.
The airy way. '10(O22) 12°, $1.75 net. Macmillan.
Book of the dry fly. New ed., with contribs. by the Duke of Rutland and J. E. Booth. '10(O8) col. il. 12°, $2.50 net. Macmillan.
Life and sport in Hampshire. '08(N21) il. O. *$3 net. Longmans.

De Waters, Mrs. Lillian Stephenson.
Glad tidings. [1910] (F) c. '09. 307 p. 12°, $1.25. L. S. De Waters.
Thinking heavenward. '08(D) c. 42 p. 12°, 50 c. L. S. De Waters.

Dewdrop on ocean wave. Browne, H. A. $1. J. M. Williams.

Dewe, Rev. Juhl Adalbert.
History of economics. '08(My9) c. O. $1.50. Benziger.
Psychology of politics and history. '10 (Ap2) D. $1.75 net. Longmans.

De Weese, Truman A.
Principles of practical publicity. 2d ed. '08 (N14) c. il. D. **$2 net. Jacobs.

Dewey, Mrs. Byrd Spilman.
Bruno. New ed. '08(F22) c. il. 12°, †50 c. Little, B. & Co.

Dewey, Daisy.
Problems of your generation. '10(Je11) c. D. $1. Arden.

Dewey, Davis Rich.
Financial history of the United States. 3d ed. '08(Ap25) charts, 12°, (American citizen ser.) **$2 net. Longmans.
See also Holdsworth, J: Than.

—, and Chaddock, Rob. Emmet.
State banking before the Civil War, by Davis R. Dewey, and The safety fund banking system in New York, 1829-1866, by Rob. E. Chaddock. '10(N) 388 p. fold. map, fold. diagr., 8°. Gov. Pr. Off.
Bibliographic footnotes.

Dewey, J:
Ethics: a lecture. '08(D12) c. 8°, 25 c. Columbia Univ.
How we think. '10(Je4) c. 12°, $1. Heath.
Influence of Darwin on philosophy, and other essays in contemporaneous thought. '10(My7) c. D. $1.40 net. Holt.
Moral principles in education. '09(Ag14) c. 12°, (Riverside educational monographs.) **35 c. net. Houghton M.

—, and Small, Albion Woodbury.
My pedagogic creed by Prof. J: Dewey, and The demands of sociology upon pedagogy, by Prof. Albion W. Small. '10 (Jl30) S. (Teachers' manuals.) pap., 15 c. Flanagan.

—, and Tufts, Ja. Hayden.
Ethics. '08(O17) c. O. (American science ser.) $2. Holt.

—, Woodbridge, F: Ja. Eug., Adler, Felix, and others.
Essays philosophical and psychological in honor of William James, professor in Harvard University; by his colleagues at Columbia University. '08(My16) c. por. tabs., O. **$3 net. Longmans.

Dewey, Katharine Fay.
Star people. '10(O22) c. il. O. $1.50. Houghton M.

Dewey, L: Marinus.
James Rising of Suffield, Conn., and some of his descendants. '09, [1910.] (Ap) 11 p. 8°, 50 c. N. E. Hist.

Dewey, T: Emmet.
Poetry in song, and some other studies in literature. '07, [1908.] (Ag) 11-192 p. por. 4°, $1.50. C: M. Harger.

Dewey, Willis Alonzo.
Essentials of homœopathic materia medica and homœopathic pharmacy; being a quiz compend upon the principles of homœopathy, homœopathic pharmacy, and homœopathic materia medica; arranged and compiled especially for the use of students of medicine. 4th rev. ed. '08, [1909.] (Mr) c. 9+13-372 p. 12°, *$1.75 net; flex. mor., *$2 net. Boericke & T.

Dewhirst, J: Mark.
Elements of bookkeeping; designed for class instruction. '10(N19) c. 4°, $1. Wagoner.

Dewhurst, E: Bury.
Science of lawn tennis. '10(N12) c. il. 8°, $2.50. Innes.

De Windt, Harry.
Finland as it is. New and rev. ed. '10 (O8) il. 12°, $1.50 net. Dutton.
Through savage Europe; being the narrative of a journey, undertaken as special correspondent of the *Westminster Gazette,* throughout the Balkan states and European Russia. New popular ed. '10 (D3) il. 8°, $1.50 net. Lippincott.

Dewing, Arth. Stone.
Life as reality; philosophical essay. '10 (Je11) c. D. $1.25 net. Longmans.

Dewing, Eliz. Bartol.
Other people's houses. '09(N6) c. D. †$1.50. Macmillan.

De Witt, C: Howard.
Laboratory guide and outlines in histology. Rev. ed. '08(D) c. 174 p. il. 8°. (Add. author for price.) C: H. De Witt.

Dewitt, D: Miller.
Assassination of Abraham Lincoln and its expiation. '09(F6) c. O. $2.25. Macmillan.

De Witt, Norman Wentworth.
Dido episode in the Æneid of Virgil. '08 (Mr21) 8°, pap., $1. W: Briggs.

De Witt, Wa.
Family genealogical record book. '08(F) c. 12°, **$1.25 net. Grafton Press.

De Wulf, Maurice.
Hist. of medieval philosophy. 3d ed.; tr. by P. Coffey. '09(D25) O. *$3 net. Longmans.

Dey, Frederic van Rensselaer.
Gentleman of quality. '09(Ap3) c. il. D. $1.50. L. C. Page.

De Zulueta, Fs. M.
Early steps in the fold; instructions for converts, and enquirers. '10(D3) c. O. $1. Kenedy.

Dhalla, Manckji Nuisservanji.
Nyaishes or Zoroastrian litanies: Avestan text with the Pahlavi, Sanskrit, Persian and Gujarati versions; ed. together and tr., with notes; Khordah Avesta, pt. 1. '09(F27) 8°, (Columbia Univ. Indo-Iranian ser.) **$2 net. Lemcke.

DIABETES.
See Bright's disease.

DIAGNOSIS.
Abrams, A. Diagnostic therapeutics. $5. Rebman.
Atkinson, T: G. Functional diagnosis. $1.50. Chic. Med. Bk.
Butler, G. R. Diagnostics of internal medicine. $6. Appleton.
Cabot, R: C. Physical diagnosis. *$3 net. Wood.
Children's dialogues and entertainments. 40 c.; 25 c. Penn Pub. Co.
Da Costa, J: C. Principles and practice of physical diagnosis. *$3.50 net Saunders.
Dennis, J: K., *and others.* Comic dialogues. 50 c.; 30 c. Penn Pub. Co.
Emerson, C: P. Clinical diagnosis. $5. Lippincott.
Faught, F. A. Essentials of lab'y diagnosis design for students and practitioners. $2. Davis.
Fyfe, J: W: Specific diagnosis and specific medication. $5; $6. Scudder.
Greene, C: L. Medical diagnosis. *$3.50 net. Blakiston.
Hawes, A. T. Observation of symptoms. *$1 net. Whitcomb.
Knox, E. B. Aids to microscopic diagnosis. $1 net. Wood.

DIAGNOSIS.—*Continued.*
Leftwick, R. W. Index of symptoms. $2.25 net. Wood.
Savill, T: D. System of clinical medicine dealing with the diagnosis, prognosis, and treatment of diseases. *$7 net. Longmans.
Schmidt, R. Pain: its causation and diagnostic significance in internal diseases. **$3 net. Lippincott.
Slade, C: B. Physical examination and diagnostic anatomy. $1.25. Saunders.
Todd, J. C. Manual of clinical diagnosis. *$2 net. Saunders.
Webster, R. W. Diagnostic methods. chemical, bacteriological and microscopical. *$6 net; *$7.50 net. Blakiston.
Wilson, J. C. Hdbk. of medical diagnosis. $6. Lippincott.
Wood, F. C. Chemical and microscopical diagnosis. $5. Appleton.
See also Blood;—Breathing;—Children;—Gynecology;—Nervous system;—Smallpox;—Surgery;—Tuberculosis;—Urine and urinary organs;—Venereal diseases;—Veterinary medicine and surgery;—*also* names of diseases.

Diagrams for designing reinforced concrete structures. Dodge, G. F. $4 net. M. C. Clark.
Dialectic of Plotinus. Overstreet, H. A. 25 c. Univ. of Cal.

DIALOGUES.
Denton, C. J., *comp.* Program book; collection of new recitations, dialogues, drills and choruses for boys and girls. 40 c. J. Fisher.
See also Entertainments;—Readers;—Recitations.

Dialogus, Agricola, and Germania. *See* Tacitus, Caius Cornelius.

Diamant, Sidney.
Curves for calculating beams, channels and reactions; manual for engineers, architects, designers, draughtsmen, builders and contractors. '08, [1909.] (F) c. 3+13 p. il. *$2 net. McGraw.

Diamond master. Futrelle, J. †$1. Bobbs-M.
Diamond spider. Butler, E. B. $1.25 net. A. Harriman

DIAMONDS.
Arkansas. *Bureau of Mines, Manufactures and Agriculture.* Descriptive catalogue of the diamond bearing rock to accompany exhibit of peridotite rock. gratis. G. B. Tucker.
Arkansas Diamond Co. Brief account of the discovery and investigation and the official repts. of geologist and mining engineer on the occurrence of diamonds in Pike Co., Ark. (Not for sale.) S: W. Reyburn.
Chester, C. B. Science of diamonds. 50 c. Chester & B.
Crookes, *Sir* W: Diamonds. *75 c. net. Harper.
Holt, S. T., *ed.* The diamond. gratis. F. Holt.
Schneider, P. F. Preliminary rept. on the Arkansas diamond field. (Add. pubs. for price.) Cen. Pr.

Diamonds cut paste. Castle, *Mrs.* A. S. †$1.50. Dodd.
Diana dethroned. Letts, W. M. $1.50. Lane.
Diana of Dobson's. Hamilton, C. M. †$1.50. Century Co.
Diana of the Crossways. *See* Meredith, G:
Diana's diary. Schafer, F. W. 50 c.; 25 c. Laird.

DIARIES.
See Almanacs and annuals.

DIARRHOEA.
Illoway, H. Summer diarrhea of infants. *$1 net. W: R. Jenkins.

Diary kept at the siege of Louisberg. Stearns, B: 25 c. S: A. Green.
Diary of a bachelor. Shea, C. A. $1. Bachelor Pub.
Diary of a birthday doll. Dow, E. C. $1.25. Stern.
Diary of a Daly débutante; being passages from the journal of a member of Augustin Daly's famous company of players. '10 (Ap2) c. il. pors. facsim. D. $1.25 net. Duffield.
Diary of a district messenger. Metcalfe, J. S. 25 c. Life Pub. Co.
Diary of a lady-in-waiting. Bury, *Lady* C: S. M. C. 2 v. *$7.50 net. Lane.
Diary of a looker-on. Hind, C: L. $2. Lane.
Diary of a lost one. Böhme, M., *ed.* $1.50. Hudson Press.
Diary of a mining investor. Vigouroux, G: E. $1. Quick News.
Diary of a Modernist. Palmer, W: S. $1.40 net. Longmans.
Diary of a refugee. Fearn, *Mrs.* F. H., *ed.* $1.25 net. Moffat.
Diary of a shirtwaist striker. Malkiel, T. S. 50 c. Co-operative Press.
Diary of a show-girl. Irwin, G. L. $1. Moffat.
Diary of a visit to the United States. Russell, C: R., *Baron.* $3. Benziger.
Diary of a young officer. Favill, J. M. **$1.50 net. Donnelley.
Diary of an enlisted man. Bush, H. M. 50 c.; 25 c. E: T. Miller.
Diary of an enlisted man. Van Alstyne, L. $2. Tuttle, M. & T.
Diary (The) of an exiled nun; with preface by François Coppée; auth. tr. '10(Jl2) c. 12°, $1. Herder.
Diary of my honymoon; anonymous. '10 (N19) c. front. 12°, $1.20. Macaulay.
Diary of the home. Griffith, J. E. $4; $6. Griffith-S.
Diary of verse and philosophy. Lehmann, J: A. 50 c. J: A. Lehmann.

DIATHEKE.
See Bible. N. T.

DIATHESIS.
Ramsay, A. M. Diathesis and ocular diseases. $2 net. Wood.

Diaz, Mrs. Abby Morton.
Flatiron and the red cloak. '08(S19) c. front. D. (Bimbi ser.) bds., **40 c. net. Crowell.

DIAZ, Porfirio, *President of Mexico.*
Fornaro, C. de. Diaz, czar of Mexico. $1.50. C. de Fornaro.
Godoy, J. F. Porfirio Diaz, president of Mexico. **$2 net. Putnam.
Zayas Enriquez, R. de. Porfirio Diaz, [president of Mexico.] **$1.50 net. Appleton.

DIAZO-COMPOUNDS.
See Chemistry.

Dibble, Sheldon.
Hist. of the Sandwich Islands. '09(O23) fold. map, D. *$1.75 net. Burrows.

D'IBERVILLE, P. L., *Sieur.*
See Iberville, P. L., *Sieur* d'.

Di Bruno, Jos. Faà, D.D.
Catholic belief; or, short simple exposition of Catholic doctrine. Author's American ed.; ed. by Rev. J: A. Lambert. '10(Ja1) c. T. (Lib. of popular instruction.) pap., 10 c.; 10 copies, $1; 50 copies, $5; 100 copies, $10. Benziger.

Dicey, Albert Venn.
Introd. to the study of the law of the constitution. 7th ed. '08(O24) 8°, *$3.50 net. Macmillan.

Dick, Harris B., ed.
Games of patience; or, solitaire with cards. 2d ser. '08(Ag29) c. 12°, $1; bds., 75 c. Dick.

Dick, Rev. S: Medary.
Psychotherapy; or, the ministry of the church to the body: five sermons del. in Wesley Methodist Episcopal Church, Minneapolis, Minn. '09(Je12) c. por. O. pap., 25 c. S: M. Dick.

Dick, Stewart.
Cottage homes of England. '09(N13) col. il. O. *$7 net, boxed. Longmans.

Dick, W: Brisbane, ["Trumps."]
American Hoyle: hdbk. of games; to which is appended an elaborate treatise on the doctrine of chances. 19th ed. '09(Jl3) c. 16°, $1.50; bds., 75 c.; pap., 50 c. Dick.

Dick among the Lumberjacks. Dimock, A. W. $1.50. Stokes.

Dick and Dolly. Wells, C. †$1.50. Dodd.

Dick and Dolly's adventures. Wells, C. $1.25. Dodd.

Dick & Fitzgerald plays. v. 1-16. '09(S4); v. 17-28. '10(O15) D. ea., pap., 25 c. Dick.

Dick Haley. Whitaker, O. B. 80 c. Chr. Pub. Assoc.

Dick Hamilton ser. *See* Garis, Howard Roger.

Dick in the Everglades. Dimock, A. W. †$1.50. Stokes.

Dick Randall. Clark, E. H. $1.50. Bobbs-M.

Dickens, C:
Library Dickens; complete works. 30 v. '10(D31) 12°, ea., $1 net; per set, $30 net; ¾ mor., $90 net. Little, B. & Co.

Works. De luxe ed. 15 v. '10(N) il. levant, $45. Crowell.

Works. 15 v. New imperial lib. ed. '10 (D) il. 8°, ea., $1.25; hf. cf., $2.25; New il. sterling ed., ea., $1. (Sets only.) Estes.

Works. In 15 v. Piccadilly ed. '09(Ap17) il. hf. leath., $52. Funk.

Works. De luxe ed. 17 v. '10(D) 16°, ea., mor., $1.50 net. (Sets only.) Nelson.

[Works.] In 20 v. '08(N14) pors. 12°, (Oxford Dickens,) ea., 80 c.; limp leath., $1.25; lambskin, $1.50; per set, $16; limp leath., $25; lambskin, $30; India paper ed., in 17 v., lambskin, ea., $1.75; per set, lambskin, $35; red rutland, $40, (sold only in sets;) red Russia, $70, (sold only in sets;) sealskin, $75, (sold only in sets.) Oxford Univ.

Works. Centenary ed. in 36 v. v. 1-2, Sketches by Boz; v. 3, American notes for general circulation and pictures from Italy; v. 4, The adventures of Oliver Twist; v. 5, 6, The posthumous papers of the Pickwick Club; v. 7, Child's history of England; v. 8, 9, The old curiosity shop; v. 10, Christmas books. '10(D24) il. 8°, ea., $1. Scribner.

Works. Gadshill ed.; ed. by And. Lang. In 38 v. '08(D12) 8°, ea., $1.50; per set, $57; hf. cf., $110 net; hf. mor., $150 net. Scribner.

Works; with the life of Dickens by Fk. T. Marzials, J: Forster, Mamie Dickens, and Adolphus W. Ward; introds. by And. Lang, Hamilton W. Mabie, C: Dickens, the younger, and E: Everett Hale; essays, critical comments, arguments, and notes by Frederic G. Kitton and others; J: H. Clifford, managing editor. [Booklovers ed.] '09(Ap3) c. 30 v., il. pors. 12°, per set, $27.50; hf. leath., $37.50; limp leath., $47.50. Univ. Soc.

American notes; introd. by G. K. Chesterton. '08(F22) 16°, (Everyman's lib.) *35 c. net; leath., *70 c. net. Dutton.

Boys and girls from Dickens; twenty of the most famous children from the works of C: Dickens; ed. by Boughton Scott. '10(N12) c. il. O. $2. Macaulay.

Children's Dickens; stories sel. from the various tales. '10(D) col. il. 4°, bds., 75 c. Doran.

Child's history of England; introd. by G. K. Chesterton. '08(F22) 16°, (Everyman's lib.) *35 c. net; leath., *70 c. net. Dutton.

Chimes (The). '08(N21) c. il. O. †$2. Baker & T.

Chimes. '10(D31) front. 32°, (Ariel booklets.) leath., 75 c., boxed. Putnam.

Christmas books. In 5 v. '08(Ja18) 12°, per set, $5. Dutton.

Christmas carol. New ed. '08(D19) il. 75 c.; holiday ed., $1.25. Caldwell.

Christmas carol; with a biographical sketch, list of references, and notes. '08(S5) c. 12°, (Crane classics.) 25 c.; pap., 15 c. Crane.

Christmas carol in prose; being a ghost story of Christmas. '09(N6) c. 12°, (Rubric ser.) **60 c. net. Duffield.

Christmas carol; introd. and notes by E. Gordon Browne. '08(Ap18) D. (Classbooks of English literature.) *36 c. net. Longmans.

Christmas carol. '10(D17) por. Ff. (Oxford moment ser.) silk or limp leath., 40 c. net. Oxford Univ.

Christmas carol; in the amanuensis style of phonography by Benn Pitman and Jerome B. Howard. '10(Je) 85 p. S. pap., 35 c. Phonograph.

Christmas stories. '09(N) 14+708 p. 12°, (Everyman's lib.) *35 c. net; leath., *70 c. net. Dutton.

Dickens, C:—*Continued.*

David Copperfield. '08(O10) 12°, ("Best books" ser.) leath., *$1 net. Dutton.

David Copperfield; ed. by E: Chauncey Baldwin. '10(Je11) c. S. (Lake English classics.) 50 c. Scott, F. & Co.

Dickens dictionary: characters and scenes of the novels and miscellaneous works alphabetically arranged by Alex. J. Philip. '09(Mr27) 8°, $3. Dutton.

Dickens-Kolle letters; ed. by Harry B. Smith; supp. to letters from C: Dickens to Maria Beadnell. '10(Jl16) facsims., pors. 8°. (Pr. for members only. 483 copies.) Bibliophile.

Dickens' stories about children every child can read; ed. by Rev. Jesse Lyman Hurlbut, D.D. '10(Ja1) c. por. il. D. (Winston's every child's lib.) 75 c. Winston.

Edwin Drood [and] Master Humphrey's clock. '09(N) 10+354 p. 12°, (Everyman's lib.) *35 c. net; leath., *70 c. net. Dutton.

Hard times; introd. by G. K. Chesterton. '08(F22) 16°, (Everyman's lib.) *35 c. net; leath., *70 c. net. Dutton.

Harry Furniss Dickens. In 14 v. '10(Je4) c. il. 12°, $30. J. T. Gleason.

Holly Tree Inn, and A Christmas tree. '08(Ja18) il. O. $2. Baker & T.

Little Dorrit; introd. by G. K. Chesterton. '08(F22) 16°, (Everyman's lib.) *35 c. net; leath., *70 c. net. Dutton.

Mr. Pickwick and his friends. '10(D10) col. il. 4°, $5 net; ed. de luxe, $20 net. Doran.

Mugby Junction and other stories; printed in the corresponding style of Pitman's shorthand. 20th century ed. '09(N6) S. pap., 50 c. Pitman.

Our mutual friend; introd. by G. K. Chesterton. '08(F22) 16°, (Everyman's lib.) *35 c. net; leath., *70 c. net. Dutton.

Our mutual friend. '09(Mr27) il. 12°, (Illustrated pocket classics.) $1; leath., $1.50. Macmillan.

Parisian scenes from A tale of two cities; ed., with notes, by J. H. Lobban. '10 (Je4) 12°, 30 c. net. Putnam.

Posthumous papers of the Pickwick Club. '10(Ap9) 16°, (Everyman's lib.) 35 c. net; leath., 70 c. net. Dutton.

Posthumous papers of the Pickwick Club; with 43 original il. and 223 additional pictures of originals of characters and places, scenes and incidents, curious topical allusions, references and analogies and facsimiles; collected and annotated by C. Van Noorden. [Topical ed.] In 2 v. '10(Ap9) O. $7 net. Scribner.

Reprinted pieces. '09(N) 12+302 p. 12°, (Everyman's lib.) *35 c. net; leath., *70 c. net. Dutton.

Scenes and characters from the works of C: Dickens; being 866 pictures printed from the original wood blocks engraved for the Household ed. by Fred Barnard, "Phiz," J. Mahony, C: Green, A. B. Frost, Gordon Thompson, Sir Luke Fildes. '08 (D19) 8°, *$3 net. Scribner.

Speech del. at Gore House, Kensington, May 10, 1851; printed from the original autograph manuscript. '09(D) c. 17 p. 8°. (Not for sale.) Bibliophile.

Tale of two cities; ed., with an introd. and notes, by Julian W. Abernethy. '08(Ap4) c. por. 16°, (Merrill's English texts.) 50 c. C: E. Merrill.

Tale of two cities; ed., with notes and introd., by F: W: Roe. '10(Jl2) c. D. (Longmans' English classics.) 25 c. net. Longmans.

Uncommercial traveller. '09(N) 22+370 p. 12°, (Everyman's lib.) *35 c. net; leath., *70 c. net. Dutton.

Wisdom of Dickens; collected and arr. from his writings and letters by Temple Scott. '08(O17) c. il. 24°, *$1 net. M. Kennerley.

—, and Winter, Mrs. Maria Beadnell.

Charles Dickens and Maria Beadnell ["Dora"]; private correspondence; ed. by G: Pierce Baker. '08(D) c. 9-30+152 p. il. pors. facsims. (Priv. pr.) Bibliophile.

DICKENS, Charles.

Browne, H. B., *comp.* Short plays from Dickens. *$1 net. Scribner.

Furniss, H. Book of Dickens illustrations. $1. J. T. Gleason..

Jackson, A. F., *ed.* David Copperfield; retold.—Little Nell; retold. ea., 75 c. net. Jacobs.

Kitton, F. G: Charles Dickens. *$3.50 special net. Appleton.

Leffmann, H: About Dickens. *50 c. net. H: Leffmann.

Miner, W. H. Dickens' ball. $2. W. H. Miner.

Shore, W: T. Charles Dickens and his friends. *$1.75 net. Cassell.

Smith, M. S. C., *ed.* Studies in Dickens. $1.25. Chautauqua Pr.

Dickerman, C:, and Boyer, Fs. Howard.

Refrigeration. '09(F20) c. il. 8°, (American School of Correspondence pubs.) $1. Am. Sch. Corr.

Dickert, Rev. T: Wilson.

Hist. of St. Stephen's Reformed Church, Reading, Pa., 1884-1909. '09, [1910.] (F) c. 12+17-392 p. il. pors. 12°, $1.25. T: W. Dickert.

Dickey, Helene Louise.

See Leland, Claude G.

Dickey, Luther S:

Hist. of the 103d Regiment, Pennsylvania Veteran Volunteer Infantry, 1861-1865. '10(Jl) 14+400 p. il. pors. maps (1 fold) plans, 4°, $5. L. S: Dickey.

Dickie, Ja. F., D.D.

In the Kaiser's capital. '10(O15) c. il. O. $2 net. Dodd.

Dickins, Mrs. Edith Pratt.

Port o' dreams. '09(Mr27) c. S. **$1 net. Putnam.

Dickins, Lilian, and Stanton, Mary, eds.
Eighteenth-century correspondence; being the letters of Deane Swift, Pitt, the Lyttletons and the Grenvilles, Lord Dacre, Robert Nugent, Charles Jenkinson, the Earls of Guilford, Coventry and Hardwicke, Sir Edward Turner, Mr. Talbot of Lacock, and others to Sanderson Miller, Esq., of Radway. '10(Ag20) il. pors. O. $3.50 net. Duffield.

Dickinson, Arth. Lowes.
Accounting practice and procedure; instruction paper. '09(D4) c. 8°, (American School of Correspondence pubs.) 50 c. Am. Sch. Corr.
See also Lybrand, W: M.

Dickinson, E:
New musical education; popular course on Chopin, for use in schools and homes: Lesson 1-v, complete course. '10(Ap23) c. 12°, $1. Aeolian Co.
Study of the history of music; with an annotated guide to music literature. Rev. and enl. ed. '09(My22) c. 8°, **$2.50 net. Scribner.

Dickinson, Fs. Arth.
Lake Victoria to Khartoum, with rifle and camera; with introd. by the Rt. Hon. Winston Churchill. '10(Ja15) O. *$4 net. Lane.

Dickinson, G: A., M.D.
Your boy, his nature and nurture. '09 (N13) il. D. *$1 net. Doran.

Dickinson, Goldsworthy Lowes.
Is immortality desirable?; Ingersoll lecture, 1908. '09(My22) c. D. **75 c. net. Houghton M.
Justice and liberty: political dialogue. '08 (D5) c. D. **$1.20 net. McClure.

Dickinson, H. N.
Sir Guy and Lady Rannard. '09(S11) 12°, $1.50. Duffield.

Dickinson, Mrs. Herbert.
See Ward, *Mrs.* Eliz. Stuart Phelps.

Dickinson, Jacob McGavock.
Address to the graduating class of the United States Military Academy, West Point, N. Y., June 11, 1909. '09, [1910.] (F) c. 8 p. 8°. West Point.

Dickinson, Martha Gilbert.
See Bianchi, *Mrs.* M. G. D.

Dickinson, T. Herb., comp.
See Pyre, Ja. Fs. Augustine, *comp.*

—, and Roe, F: W., eds.
Nineteenth century English prose; ed., with introds. and notes. '09(Ja23) c. D. $1. Am. Bk.

Dick's sweetheart. Hungerford, *Mrs.* M. H. 50 c. Hurst.

Dicksee, Lawrence Rob.
A B C of bookkeeping. '09(Mr20) tabs., D. 80 c. Longmans.
Auditing; ed. by Rob. H. Montgomery. Authorized American ed., rev. and enl. '10(Ja8) 8°, $5. Ronald Press.
Business organization. '10(O1) D. (Longmans' commercial ser.) $1.50. Longmans.

Dickson, D:, and Smith, Ja. M.
David Dickson's and James M. Smith's farming. '10(Ag) c. 255 p. il. 12°, 50 c. Cultivator Pub.

Dickson, J. G.
See Vincent, *Sir* Edg.

Dickson, Sallie O'Hear.
Ralph Fabian's mistakes. '08(Ap11) c. D. $1. B'way Pub.

Dickson, W: Elliot Carnegie, M.D.
Bone-marrow: a cytological study; forming an introduction to the normal and pathological histology of the tissue, more especially with regard to blood formation, blood destruction, etc. '08(O3) il. F. *$12 net. Longmans.
See also Beattie, J. M.

Dicky bird book; il. in col. by W. Foster. '09 (D) $1. Doran.

Dicky Delightful in Rainbow Land. Naylor, J. B. $1. Saalfield.

DICOTYLEDONS.
See Botany.

DICTATION.
See Spellers;—Spelling.

Dictation day by day. *See* Van Wagenen, Kate.

Dictation to reporting shorthand. Chartier, E: M. $1.50. E: M. Chartier.

DICTIONARIES.
See Encyclopædias;—Vest pocket reference book ser.;—Webster, Noah;—*also* names of languages and subjects.

Dictionary of chemical and metallurgical machinery, appliances and material manufactured or sold by advertisers in *Electrochemical and Metallurgical Industry.* '09 (O16) c. 12°, 50 c. Electrochemical Pub.

Dictionary of metallurgical and chemical machinery, appliances and material, manufactured or sold by advertisers in *Metallurgical and Chemical Engineering.* 2d ed. [1910.] c. 4+219 p. 12°, 50 c. Metallurgical.

Dictionary of terms used in architecture and building. '09(S18) il. 12°, 50 c. Indust. Bk.

Did your child say this? Preble, G: H., *comp.* 50 c. J. W. Luce.

Diderot, Denis.
Selections from Diderot; ed., with an introd. and notes, by W. F. Giese. '08 (Je6) c. S. (Modern lang. ser.) 50 c. Heath.

Didier, Eugene Lemoine.
Poe cult, and other papers. '08(D19) c. pors. 12°, $1.50. Am. Press.
Poe cult and other Poe papers; with a new memoir. '09(Ag) 301 p. il. 12°, $1.50. B'way Pub.
Way to keep him. '08(N) D. (Everybody's booklets.) pap., 10 c. Am. Press.
Way to win her: a booklet for every woman. '08(Jl) c. (Everybody's booklets.) pap., 10 c. Am. Press.
Way to win him. '08(N) D. (Everybody's booklets.) pap., 10 c. Am. Press.

Dido episode in the Æneid. De Witt, N. W. $1. W: Briggs.

Didwin, I:, pseud.
See Sturdy, W: A.

Diederichs, Herman.
See Carpenter, Rolla Clinton.

Diefendorf, Allen Ross, M.D.
See Clark, L. Pierce.

Diefendorf, Mary Riggs.
Historic Mohawk. '10(D31) c. il. 8°, $2 net. Putnam.

Dieffenbach, W: Hermann.
Hydrotherapy: brief summary of the practical value of water in disease for students and practicians of medicine. '09 (Je) 16+267 p. il. 8°, $3. Rebman.

DIEGNENO INDIANS.
See Indians.

Diehl, Alice M.
Life of Beethoven. '08(D) 8°, $3. Clode.
Life of Beethoven. '09(D) por. 8°, *$3 net. Doran.

Diemer, Hugo.
Automobiles. '09(My8) c. il. diagrs., 8°, (American School of Correspondence pubs.) $1.50. Am. Sch. Corr.
Factory organization and administration. '10(O1) c. il. (forms) 8°, $3. McGraw-H.

Dienst, G: Elias.
What to do for the stomach. '08(Ja18) 16°, $1. Boericke & T.

DIES.
See Printers and printing;—Seals.

Dies und das. Fick, H. H. 25 c. Am. Bk.
Dies und das aus dem leben eines ostindischen missionars. Zorn, C. M. $1.25. Concordia Pub.

Dieserud, Juul.
Scope and content of the science of anthropology: hist. review, library classification and select, annot. bibliography. '08(Je13) c. D. *$2 net. Open Court.

DIET.
See Cookery;—Food.

Dietrich, Gideon.
Biology of the sex problem according to the latest facts disclosed by biology and evolution. '09(D25) c. D. 50 c. Educ. Press.

Dietrich, W:
Swine; breeding, feeding and manageagement. '10(Ap) c. 312 p. por. il. 8°, $1.50. Saunders Pub.

Dieudonné, A.
Bacterial food poisoning: concise exposition of the etiology, bacteriology, pathology, symptomatology, prophylaxis, and treatment of so-called ptomaine poisoning; tr. and ed., with additions, by C: F: Bolduan; author. translation. '09(Mr) 9-128 p. 8°, *$1 net. Treat.

Diffenderffer, Fk. Ried.
Hist. of the Farmers' Bank of Lancaster, the Farmers' National Bank, and the Farmers' Trust Company of Lancaster, 1810-1910. '10(Ap) c. 228 p. il. pors., facsims. 4°, gratis. Farmers' Trust Co.

Different types of modern engines. Myers, M. C. $1. M. C. Myers.

DIFFERENTIAL CALCULUS.
See Calculus.

DIFFERENTIAL EQUATIONS.
See Equations.

Difficult labor. Herman, G: E. $2.50 net. Wood.

Digby, Sir Kenelm.
See Browne, *Sir* T:

Digest of literature. Davenport, B: R., *ed.* 3 v. (Add. pubs. for price.) Hist. Pub. Co., (Pa.)

DIGESTION.
Adams, E. O. Diseases of the digestive system. $2. Cleveland Homeopath.

DIGESTION.—*Continued.*
Billings, F., *ed.* Diseases of the digestive system. $6. Appleton.
Blackwood, A. L. Food tract, its ailments and disease of the peritoneum. $1.50. Boericke & T.
Colinheim, P. Diseases of the digestive canal: esophagus, stomach, intestine. *$4 net. Lippincott.
Moynihan, B. G: A. Pathology of the living and other essays. $2 net. Saunders.
Robertson, T. B. On the synthesis of paranuclein through the agency of pepsin and the chemical mechanics of the hydrolysis and synthesis of proteins through the agency of enzymes. (Add. Univ. for price.) Univ. of Cal.
See also Food;—Intestines;—Stomach.

Diggle, Bp. J: W:
Home life. '08(My23) D. (Christian life ser.) *60 c. net. Cassell.

Diggs, Mrs. Annie Le Porte.
Story of Jerry Simpson. '08(Je27) c. pors. 12°, $1.10. J. Simpson.

Digressions of V. Vedder, E. $6 net. Houghton M.

Dike, Fs. Harold, comp.
Scientific French reader; comp., with notes and vocab. Rev. and enl. ed. '09(Ja23) c. il. 12°, (Ser. of modern lang. textbks.) $1. Silver.

Dilemma (A). Andreyev, L. $1. Brown Bros.
Dilemma (The). Chesney, *Sir* G. $1.50. Abbatt.

Dilg, Howard Wills, comp.
Liability investigator's handbook. '08(S12) c. 16°, $1.50. Spectator.

Dill, Jacob Smiser.
Isaac Taylor Tichenor, the home mission statesman. '08(Jl18) c. il. pors. 12°, 50 c.; pap., 25 c. S. S. Bd. So. Bapt.

Dill, Ja. B.
See New Jersey. **Statute and case law of the state.**

Dill, W: F.
See Pa. **Constables' guide.**

Diller, Jos. Silas.
Geology of the Taylorsville region, California. '09(Mr6) il. maps, 8°, (U. S. Geol. Survey, bull.) (Add. Superintendent for price.) U. S., Supt. of Docs.

Dilley, Arth. Urbane.
Oriental rugs. '09(Ag) c. 80 p. il. map, 8°, 50 c. Dilley.

Dillingham's magic picture books for children: [Mother Goose rhymes.] '08(D) 4°, 6 titles, ea., 25 c.; in 1 v., $1. G: W. Dillingham.

DILLMAN FAMILY.
See Genealogies: Houser, W: W.

Dillon, E:
Arts of Japan. 2d ed. '09(O9) il. S. (Little books on art.) *$1 net. McClurg.
Porcelain and how to collect it. '10(D10) 12°, $2 net. Dutton.

Dillon, J: M.
Motor days in England. '08(Je20) c. il. O. **$3 net. Putnam.

Dillon, Mrs. Mary C. Johnson.
Patience of John Morland. '09(Jl17) c. il. in col. D. †$1.50. Doubleday, P.

Dillon, Patricia.
Earl or chieftain?; romance of Hugh O'Neill. '10(Jl) 4+139 p. front. 35 c. net. Herder.

Dilworth, Hiram Powers.
Ode to prophesy. [1910.] (D) c. 13 p. 12°, 25 c. H. P. Dilworth.

Diman, Louise.
Stories from Greek history for children. [1910.] c. '09. 235 p. il. 12°, (Graded supplementary reading ser.) 40 c. C: E. Merrill.

Dimensional idea as an aid to religion. Tyler, W. F. 50 c.. Fenno.

Diminished dollar and railway rates. Newcomb, H. T. 35 c. North American.

Dimock, Anthony Weston.
Dick among the Lumberjacks. '10(S10) c. il. (Boy explorers ser.) $1.50. Stokes.
Dick in the Everglades. '09(O16) c. il. D. (Boy explorer ser.) †$1.50. Stokes.

— and Julian Anthony.
Florida enchantments. '08(N7) c. il. O. *$3 net. Outing.

Dimock, Julian Anthony.
See Dimock, Anthony Weston.

Dimock, Rev. Nathaniel.
Christian doctrine of sacerdotium as contained in the Scriptures and taught in our formularies. Memorial ed.; with introd. note by the Rt. Rev. H. C. G. Moule. '10 (Ag6) D. 75 c. net. Longmans.
Christian unity; some considerations on the subject. Memorial ed.; with introd. note by the Rt. Rev. H. C. G. Moule. '10(Je11) D. 50 c. net. Longmans.
Doctrine of the Lord's supper: two lectures; with appendix on the augmentation theory. Memorial ed.; with introd. note by the Rt. Rev. H. C. G. Moule. '10(Je11) D. 50 c. net. Longmans.
Doctrine of the sacraments in relation to the doctrines of grace as contained in the scriptures, taught in our formulas, and upheld by our reformers. New ed. '08(D12) D. 60 c. Longmans.
Hist. of the Book of Common Prayer in its bearing on present eucharistic controversies. Memorial ed.; with introd. note by the Rt. Rev. H. C. G. Moule. '10(Ag6) D. 75 c. net. Longmans.
Our one Priest on high; or, the present sacerdotal function of Christ in Heaven. Memorial ed.; with introd. note by Rt. Rev. H. C. G. Moule. '10(Je18) D. 50 c. net. Longmans.
Ritual; its use and misuse. Memorial ed.; with introd. note by the Rt. Rev. H. C. G. Moule. '10(O15) D. 75 c. net. Longmans.
Sacerdotium of Christ. Memorial ed.; with an introd. note by the Rt. Rev. H. C. G. Moule. '10(O22) D. 75 c. net. Longmans.

Dinah. *See* Whiffen, Edn. T: Jeptha sacrificing.

Dinanderie. Perry, J: T-. $5.50 net. Macmillan.

D'Indy, Paul Marie Théodore Vincent.
César Franck; tr. from the French, with introd. by Rosa Newmarch. '09(D25) pors. pls. O. *$2.50 net. Lane.

Dinger, Lieut. H: C.
Hdbk. for the care and operation of naval machinery. '08(D5) il. 16°, *$2 net. Van Nostrand.

Dingwell, Ja. Davidson.
Christus centuriarum. '09(N6) c. D. $1. Badger.

DINING.
Wilson, E: S. Poetry of eating. 50 c. E: S. Wilson.
See also Cookery;—Food;—Toasts.

Dinkelspiel, pseud.
See Hobart, G: Vere.

Dinkins, Ja.
Genealogical: the Dinkins and Springs families. '08(Jl) 24 p. pors. O. pap., gratis. J. Dinkins.

DINKINS FAMILY.
See Genealogies.

Dino, Duchesse de.
See Talleyrand-Perigord, Dorothée von B., *Duchesse* de.

Dinsmore, J: Wirt.
Teaching a district school: a book for young teachers. '08(Ag8) c. D. $1. Am. Bk.

Dinsmore, Julia Stockton, (F. V.)
Verses and sonnets. '10(Ap23) c. O. $1.25 net, boxed. Doubleday, P.

Dionne, Narcisse Eutrope, M.D., ed.
Le parler populaire des Canadiens français, ou, lexique des canadianismes, acadianismes, anglicismes, americanismes, mots anglais les plus en usage au sein des familles canadiennes et acadiennes françaises; avec preface par Raoul de la Grasserie. '09(Je12) O. *$3.50 net. Stechert.

Dionysius of Halicarnassus.
Dionysius of Halicarnassus on literary criticism; being the Greek text of the De compositione verborum; ed., with introd., tr., notes, glossary and appendices, by W. Rhys Roberts. '10(Ap9) 8°, $3 net. Macmillan.

DIPHTHERIA.
Geddings, H: D. Precis on the management of outbreaks of smallpox, diphtheria and scarlet fever. (Add. Superintendent for price.) U. S., Supt. of Docs.
Goodman, H. M. Duration and disappearance of passive diphtheric immunity.—Experimental studies on diphtheric immunity. ea., 25 c. H. M. Gorman.
Nuttall, G: H:, *and* Graham-Smith, G:, *eds.* Bacteriology of diphtheria. *$7 net. Putnam.

DIPLOMACY.
American foreign policy; by a diplomatist. **$1.25 net. Houghton M.
Barclay, *Sir* T: Problems of international practice and diplomacy. $6.50. Boston Bk.
Escott, T: H. S. Story of British diplomacy. *$4 net. Jacobs.
Hart, A. B. Manual of American history, diplomacy, and government. $2. Harvard Univ.
Van Dyne, F: Our foreign service: the "A B C" of American diplomacy. $2.50. Lawyers' Co-op.
See also Ambassadors;—Arbitration;—Consuls;—International law;—Peace; — Spanish-American war.

Diplomatic memoirs. Foster, J: W. 2 v. **$6 net. Houghton M.

Diplomatist's wife in many lands. Fraser, M. C. 2 v. $6 net. Dodd.

DIPTERA.
See Flies.

Direct- and alternating-current machine design. Crocker, F. B. *$5 net. McGraw.

Direct and alternating currents. Bedell, F. *$2 net. Van Nostrand.

Direct legislation. White, J: Z. 5 c.; per doz., 40 c.; per 100, $2. Timby.

Direction of a line. Davis, J. B. 75 c. Wahr.

Direction of desire. Bligh, S. M. 70 c. net; $1. Oxford Univ.

DIRECTOIRE.
See France.

DIRECTORIES.
See names of places and subjects;—*also* Newport social index.

DIRECTORS.
See Business.

Directory of booksellers, newsdealers and stationers in the United States and Canada. 5th ed. '09(Mr6) Q. $5. H. W. Wilson.

Directory of directors in the city of New York. [1909, 10th ed.] '09(Ag21) c. O. $5. Audit Co.

Directory of libraries in the United States and Canada. 6th ed. '08(D5); 7th ed. '10 (O15) f°, bds., ea., *$5 net. H. W. Wilson.

Directory of manufacturers of and dealers in engineers' and contractors' machinery and supplies. 1908 ed. '08(O) 162 p. 16°, pap., gratis. McGraw.

Directory of publishers, 1907. '08(Jl18) O. leatherette, $1. Pub. Weekly.

Dirks, R.
Komical Katzenjammers. '08(Ag8) c. il. obl. Q. (Stokes' comic juveniles.) bds., 60 c. Stokes.

Disappearance of the small landowner. Johnson, A. H. $1.75. Oxford Univ.

Disappearing eye. Hume, F. W. †$1.25. G: W. Dillingham.

Disbrow, C: W.
Analysis of the banking and currency system of the United States indicating the cause of periodic panics and suggesting a remedy. '10(Ap16) c. 8°, pap., gratis. U. S. Fidelity.

Disciple of chance. Dean, S. $1.50. Stokes.

DISCIPLES OF CHRIST.
Garrison, J. H. Story of a century; brief hist. sketch and exposition of the religious movement inaugurated by Thomas and Alexander Campbell, 1809-1909. $1. Chr. Pub. Co.

Hayden, W. L. Centennial addresses delivered in 1909; [centenary of the founding of the Disciples of Christ.] 50 c. W. L. Hayden.

Hill, J: L. As others see us, and as we are: plea of the Disciples of Christ. 75c. Standard Pub.

Moore, W: T: Comprehensive history of the Disciples of Christ. *$3.50 net; *$4.50 net; *$6 net. Revell.

DISCIPLES OF CHRIST.—*Continued.*
Warren, W. R. Program of the international centennial celebration and conventions of the Disciples of Christ. $1. Am. Ch. Miss.
See also Campbell, Alexander.

DISCIPLINE.
See Teachers and teaching.

Discontented stuffed cat. Thurston, C. B. $1.25. Saalfield.

DISCOUNT.
See Banks and banking.

Discourses and sermons. Gibbon, J. $1. Murphy.

Discourses of Jimmy. Newhall, R. De S. 50 c. Circular Adv.

DISCOVERIES AND DISCOVERERS.
See Explorers;—Voyages and travels.

Discoveries which make mental therapeutics and the transmission of mental communications an exact science. Starrett, D. W: $1.75. D. W: Starrett.

Discovery of discoveries. Mason, E. L. $1.25. E. L. Mason.

Discovery of North Pole. Mowbray, J. H: $1.50. G: W. Bertron.

Discovery of self. Ludlow, J. M. 35 c. net. Revell.

Discovery of the soul. Wilson, F. B. $1. Fenno.

Discussion of methods for determining the availability of phosphoric acid. Leavens, G: D. (Add. pubs. for price.) Coe-M.

Discussion of the eclipses of Jupiter's satellites. Sampson, R. A. $1. Harvard Univ.

DISEASES.
See Children; — Dairy;—Diathesis;—Diet;—Fasting;—Homeopathy; — Infectious diseases;—Insects; — Milk; — Mosquitoes;—Nervous system; —Pathology;—Veterinary medicine and surgery; —*also* names of diseases.

Diseases of a gasolene automobile. Dyke, A. L. $1. A. L. Dyke.

Diseases of children; ed. by Dr. M. Pfaundler and Dr. A. Schlossmann; Eng. tr. by H: L. K. Shaw and Linnæus La Fetra; with an introd. by L. Emmett Holt. '08(Je20) c. 4 v., il. tabs., 8°, $20. Lippincott.

Diseases of cultivated plants and trees. Massee, G: $2.25 net. Macmillan.

Diseases of economic plants. Stevens, F. L. $2 net. Macmillan.

Diseases of occupation. Oliver, T: *$2.50 net. Dutton.

Diserens, Paul.
See Breckenridge, Lester Paige.

Disinfection of sewage. Phelps, E. B. (Add. Superintendent for price.) U. S., Supt. of Docs.

Disinherited (The). Wallace, G: $1. J. S. Ogilvie.

DISLOCATION.
See Fracture.

DISPENSATORIES.
See Pharmacy.

Disposal of West Side railroad tracks: report to the Merchants' Association of New York by its committee on disposal of West Side railroad tracks, Nov. 25, 1908. '09 (Ap3) map, O. pap., gratis. Merchants' Assoc.

Disposition of decedent's real property. Noble, W: N. $3.50. Banks & Co.

Disputed handwriting. Lavay, J. B. $3. Harvard Bk.

Disraeli, B:, [Earl of Beaconsfield.]
Novels; each with introd. by the Earl of Iddesleigh. Uniform ed. In 9 v. '08 (Je27) 24°, *$4.50 net; flex. leath., *$6.50 net. Lane.

DISRAELI, Benjamin, [*Earl* of Beaconsfield.]
Monypenny, W: F. Life of Benjamin Disraeli, Earl of Beaconsfield. In 4 v. v. 1. $3 net. Macmillan.

Dissatisfied soul. Slosson, *Mrs.* A. T. *75 c. net. Bonnell.

DISSECTION.
See Anatomy.

Dissemination of disease by dairy products, and methods for prevention. '10(Jl) 57 p. il. 8°, (U. S., Dept. of Agriculture, Bu. of Animal Industry, cir.)

DISSERTATIONS.
Carnegie Institution of Washington. *Dept. of Historical Research.* List of doctoral dissertations in progress, Dec., 1909. Carnegie.

Dissociation of a personality. Prince, M. **$2.80 net. Longmans.

Dissolving circle. Lillibridge, W: O. †$1.50. Dodd.

DISTILLATION.
Normandy, F. Sea water distillation. *$2 net. Lippincott.

Distinctive functions of university, college and normal school in the preparation of teachers. Brown, E. E. (Add. author for price.) E. E. Brown.

Distinctive homes of moderate cost. Saylor, H: H., *ed.* $2 net. McBride, W.

Distribution and functions of mental imagery. Betts, G: H. $1; 75 c. Teachers' Coll.

Distribution and movements of desert plants. Spalding, V. M. $2. Carnegie.

Distribution of gas. Hole, W. *$6 net. Spon.

Distribution of ownership. Underwood, J. H. *$2 net; *$1.50 net. Macmillan.

Distributors (The). Partridge, A. †$1.50. McClure.

District convention. *See* Dumont, Fk. Caught with the goods.

District of Columbia: concise biographies of its prominent and representative contemporary citizens. '08(My23) c. 8°, (American biographical directories.) $6; hf. mor., $7.50. Potomac Press.

District of Columbia. Corporation law, annot., with index; by F: S. Tyler. '10(Mr) c. 86 p. O. pap., 75 c. Byrne.

District of Columbia. *Ct. of appeals.* Repts.; (C: Cowles Tucker.) v. 30. '08(Ag); v. 31 (O); v. 32. '09(Je); v. 33. '10(F); v. 34 (S) c. O. shp., ea., *$5 net. Lawyers' Co-op.

District of Columbia. Extracts from the code of the District of Columbia and the Constitution of the U. S. '09, [1910.] (Je) 118 p. T. pap., 25 c. Collins, H. & Co.

District of Columbia. Index digest of cases; being a complete digest of cases decided by the court of appeals, D. C., from 1893 to Mar. 1, 1908, and reported in vs. 1 to 29 of the appeal cases D. C.; and also of reported decisions of the Sup. Ct., D. C., rendered during that period and reported in the Washington law reports; and of cases decided by the Sup. Ct. of the U. S. on appeals from the ct. of appeals; by W: S. Torbert. '08(N) c. O. shp. (Add. pubs. for price.) Byrne.

DISTRICT OF COLUMBIA.
Davis, H: E. Development of the District of Columbia. (Add. Superintendent for price.) U. S., Supt. of Docs.
Dodd, W. F. Government of the District of Columbia. $1.50. Byrne.
Montgomery, W. S. Historical sketch of education for the colored race in the District of Columbia, 1807-1905. 25 c. Smith Bros.
Morrison, A. J. District of Columbia in the xviiith century. 50 c. Lowdermilk.
Ridgely, H. W., *ed.* Historic graves of Maryland and the District of Columbia. **$2 net. Grafton Press.
Shoemaker, L: P. Shall the government of the District of Columbia be American in form or un-American? (Add. pubs. for price.) Judd & D.
Tindall, W: Origin and government of the District of Columbia. (Add. Superintendent for price.) U. S., Supt. of Docs.
See also Evangelical Lutheran Church, Georgetown;—Washington.

Ditchfield, Rev. P: Hampson.
Charm of the English village. '08(D5) il. 4°, *$3 net. Scribner.
Manor houses of England. '10(Je4) 8°, $3 net. Scribner.
Old-time parson. '09(My22) 8°, *$2.50 net. Dutton.

Ditman, Norman E:
Education and its economic value in the field of preventive medicine; the need for a school of sanitary science and public health. '08(N21) il. 8°, (Columbia Univ. Quarterly, Supplement.) (Add. pubs. for price.) Columbia Univ.

Ditmars, Raymond Lee.
Reptiles of the world, tortoise and turtles, crocodilians, lizards and snakes of the eastern and western hemispheres. '10 (Jl30) c. col. front. il. O. $5 net. Sturgis & W.

Ditmas, C: Andrew.
Historic homesteads of Kings County. '09 (D11) il. in col. f°, vellum, $5. C: A. Ditmas.

Ditson's dollar books of piano music. Q. $1. Ditson.
—Gottschalk. Piano composition.

Div-a-let. Vail, W: H: 25 c. W. H. Vail.

Diva's ruby. Crawford, F. M. †$1.50. Macmillan.

Diven, T: J.
Aztecs and Mayas. In 2 v. v. 1. '09(Je5) c. D. $1. Antiquarian.

Diver, Maud.
Candles in the wind. '09(N20) D. $1.50. Lane.
Captain Desmond, V. C. '08(Mr21) D. †$1.50. Lane.
Great amulet. '08(Je6) D. †$1.50. Lane.

Divers, W. H.
Spring flowers at Belvoir Castle; with directions for cultivation and notes on the gardens by W. H. Divers, head gardener to his grace the Duke of Rutland. '09 (N20) il. O. *$1.80 net. Longmans.

Diversions in Sicily. Jones, H: F. *$1.25 net. Scribner.

Diverting adventures of Maurin. Aicard, J. $1.50. Lane.

DIVIDENDS.
See Interest (*on money*).

Divine and moral songs for children. Watts, I: $1. L. C. Page.

Divine challenge. Dawson, W: J. 50 c. Doran.

Divine comedy *See* Dante Alighieri.

Divine Craftsman. Selby, T: G. *$1.25 net. Eaton & M.

Divine credentials of the Bible. Lewis, T: H. $1.25. Meth. Protestant.

Divine friendship. Brett, J. *$1 net. Longmans.

DIVINE HEALING.
Dresser, H. W. Physician to the soul. **$1 net. Putnam.
Harbin, R. M. Health and happiness. **90 c. net. Am. Bapt.
Lowrie, A. W: Vision of Father, Son and three judges at the throne of the heavenly globe. $1.50. A. W: Lowrie.
Prather, C: E. Spiritual healing. $1.25. Power Pub.
See also Christian science;—Faith cure.

Divine immanence. McConnell, F. J. 75 c. Eaton & M.

Divine in man. Hubbard, E. 10 c. Roycrofters.

Divine in man. Schofield, A. T. *75 c. net. Armstrong.

Divine lover. Hollings, G: S. 40 c. Longmans.

Divine minstrels. Bailly, A. *$1.25 net. Scribner.

Divine praises. Graham, W: *75 c. net. Wagner.

Divine right of individuality in religion. Jones, A. T. 25 c. A. T. Jones.

Divine right of mission. Mabie, H: C. **50 c. net. Am. Bapt.

Divine seal. Orcutt, E. L. $1.50. C. M. Clark.

Divine story. Holland, C. J. $1; 50 c. J. M. Talley.

Divine time table. Hicks, J: S. S. 50 c.; 30 c. J: S. S. Hicks.

Divine weeks of Josuah Sylvester. Du Bartas, G. de S., *Seigneur.* $2. H. M. Youmans.

Divine worker in creation and Providence. Dykes, J. O. $2.25. Scribner.

Divinity of our Lord and Saviour Jesus Christ. Liddon, H: P. $1.25. Longmans.

Division and reunion, 1829-1909. Wilson, W. $1.25. Longmans.

DIVORCE.
Biddle, C. S. Principles, pleading and practice obtaining in the court of chancery of New Jersey in divorce and other causes matrimonial. $3. Soney.

DIVORCE.—*Continued.*
Donovan, J. M. Law of marriage, annulment, domicile, divorce. $1. J. M. Donovan; Med. Pr
Lichtenberger, J. P. Divorce. **$1.50 net. Longmans.
Martin, F. J. G. Divorce. 25 c. Jackson Print.
Phillips, J: B. Increase of divorce. 25 c. Univ. of Col.
United States. *Bureau of the Census.* Marriage and divorce, 1867-1906. 2 v.
Wilkins, H. J. Hist. of divorce and remarriage for English churchmen. $1.25 net. Longmans.
See also **Marriage.**

Divorcons. Sardou, V. $1.25. Dramatic.

Diwan of Abu'l-ala: tr. by H: Baerlein. '08 (S19) 16°, (Wisdom of the East.) *40 c. net. Dutton.

Dix, Beulah Marie.
Allison's lad, and other martial interludes; being six one-act dramas. '10(F19) D. **$1.35 net. Holt.
Rose o' Plymouth-town; romantic comedy in four acts. '08, [1909.] (F) c. 9-161 p. 8°, $1.25. Dramatic.

Dix, Irving Sidney.
The comet, and other verses. '10(Jl16) c. S. pap., 15 c. I. S. Dix.

Dixie Hart. Harben, W: N. $1.50. Harper.

Dixie Kitten. Tappan, E. M. $1. Houghton M.

Dixie rose. Kortrecht, A. $1.50. Lippincott.

Dixon, Mrs. Clarissa Belknap.
Janet and her dear Phebe. '09(F13) c. D. $1. Stokes.

Dixon, Jos.
New harvest mouse from Petaluma, California. '09(S18) Q. (Univ. of Cal. pubs.; Zoology.) pap., 5 c. Univ. of Cal.

Dixon, Roland Burrage.
Chimariko Indians and language. '10(O1) Q. (Univ. of Cal. pubs.; Am. archæology and ethnology.) pap., $1. Univ. of Cal.
See also Saper, E:

Dixon, T:, jr.
Comrades: story. '09(Ja23) c. il. D. †$1.50. Doubleday, P.

Dixon, W: Macneile, and Grierson, Herbert J: Clifford, comps.
English Parnassus; anthology of longer poems; with introd. and notes. '10(Ja1) D. $1.50. Oxford Univ.

Dixson, Claiborne.
Abbeys of Great Britain. '09(F13) il. D. *$1.50 net. Scribner.

Do it to a finish. Marden, O. S. *30 c. net. Crowell.

Do not spit. New York [City.] *Dept. of Health.* gratis. N. Y. Dept. Health.

Do the dead depart? Bates, E. K. $1.50. Dodge.

Do we need Christ for communion with God? Lemme, L. *40 c. net. Eaton & M.

Do we want an asset currency? Marburg, T. 10 c. Dulany.

Do you remember? Harrison, J. 60 c. **Cochrane.**

Doak, Alson M.
How to be rich; short studies in the things that are worth while. '10(D17) c. 12°, $1. Jennings.

Doan, Fk.
See Mexico. Richardson's manual.

Doan, Fk. Carleton.
Religion and the modern mind, and other essays in modernism. '09(N20) c. D. *$1.10 net. Sherman, F.

Doane, Rennie Wilbur.
Insects and disease; popular acct. of the way in which insects may spread or cause some of our common diseases. '10 (N5) c. il. D. (American nature ser.: Group IV., Working with nature.) $1.50 net. Holt.

Dobson, G.
St. Petersburg. '10(Ag13) il. map, 8°, (Color books ser. of travel and description.) $2.50 net. Macmillan.

Dobson, H: Austin.
De libris: prose and verse. '08(O31) c. il. O. $1.50. Macmillan.
Old Kensington Palace, and other papers. '10(D17) il. por. facsim., D. $1.50 net. Stokes.
Proverbs in porcelain and other poems. '09 (D) 4°, (Lyric garland.) 50 c.; Japan vellum, *$1 net. T: B. Mosher.

Dobson, W: Hervie.
Modern medicine in China. '08(Je6) 8°, (George Washington Univ. pubs., Medical science ser.) pap. (Not for sale.) George Washington Univ.

DOBYNS FAMILY.
See **Genealogies.**

Doc, pseud.
The Christ way. '10(Mr26) c. S. bds., 75 c. Good Thoughts.

Dock, Christopher.
Life and works; with a translation of his works into the English language by Martin G. Brumbaugh, and an introd. by S: W. Pennypacker. '08(Ap25) il. O. **$5 net. Lippincott.

Dock, G:, M.D., and Bass, C: Cassedy.
Hookworm disease; etiology, pathology, diagnosis, prognosis, prophylaxis, and treatment. '10(S) c. 250 p. il. 8°, $2.50. Mosby.
—, **ed.** Diseases of the heart, by L. von Schrotter, Th. von Jürgensen, L. Krehl, H. Vierordt; ed., with additions, by G: Dock. '08(Ja4) il. 8°, (American ed. of Nothnagel's practice.) *$5 net; hf. mor., *$6 net. Saunders.

Dock, Lavinia L.
Hygiene and morality; manual for nurses and others; giving an outline of the medical, social, and legal aspects of the venereal diseases. '10(Je18) c. D. $1.25. Putnam.

Dockery, A. V.
Black bass and other fishing in North Carolina. '09(Jl) c. 3-176 p. il. 12°, 75 c. Commercial Pr. Co.

DOCKS.
Sikes, G: C. Rept. on the Chicago dock problem. (Add. pubs. for price.) Chic. Harbor Com.

Dr. Ellen. Tompkins, J. W. †$1.50. Baker & T.

Dr. Faustus. *See* Marlowe, Christopher.

Dr. Johnson and Mrs. Thrale. Broadley, A. M. *$5 net. Lane.

Dr. Morgan. Renard, P. $1.50. C. M. Clark.

Dr. Paul McKim. Spivey, T: S. $1.50. Neale.

Doctor Rast. Oppenheim, J. $1.50. Sturgis & W.

Doctor says: book of advice for the household, with practical hints for the preservation of health and the prevention of disease. '09(Ap10) c. O. **$1 net. Jacobs.

Dr. Thorne. *See* Trollope, Anthony.

Dr. Thorne's idea. Mitchell, J: A. $1 net. Doran.

Doctor's Christmas Eve. Allen, J. L. $1.50. Macmillan.

Doctor's daughter. Walter, W: W. $1.25. W: W. Walter.

Doctor's lass. Booth, E: C. $1.30 net. Century Co.

DOCTORS.
See **Physicians.**

Doctors (The). Hubbard, E. $2. Roycrofters.

Doctrine and doctrinal disruption. Mallock, W: H. *$1.50 net. Macmillan.

Doctrine of the Church of England on the holy communion. Meyrick, F: $1. Longmans.

Doctrine of the Lord's supper. Dimock, N. 50 c. net. Longmans.

DOCTRINES.
See **Theology.**

Doctrines and discipline of the Methodist-Episcopal church. Goodsell, D. A. 30 c. Jennings.

Doctrines of grace. Bishop, G: S. $1.50. Gospel Pub.

Documentary history of American Industrial Society. Commons, J. R., *and others, eds.* In 10 v. *$50 net. A. H. Clarke.

Documentary history of Chelsea. Chamberlain, M. 2 v. $5. Mass. Hist. Soc.

Documentary source book of American history. MacDonald, W:, *ed.* *$1.75 net. Macmillan.

Dodd, Mrs. Anna Bowman Blake.
Falaise, the town of the Conqueror. [New ed.] '10(S10) c. il. D. $1.50 net, boxed. Little, B. & Co.
In and out of a French country-house. '10 (O22) c. il. O. $2.25 net. Dodd.
In and out of three Normandy inns. Rev. and corrected ed. '10(O1) c. il. D. $2.50 net, boxed. Little, B. & Co.
On the knees of the gods. '08(F8) c. D. †$1.50. Dodd.

Dodd, Ira Seymour.
Brother and the brotherhood. '08(O10) c. D. **$1.50 net. Dodd

Dodd, Loring Holmes.
Glossary of Wulfstan's homilies. '08(D12) 8°, (Yale studies in English.) **$1 net. Holt

Dodd, Marg. Eliot.
Chemistry of the household. '10(Je18) c. il. 12°, $1.25. Am. Sch. Home Economics.

Dodd, Wa. Fairleigh.
Government of the District of Columbia; a study in federal and municipal administration. '09(O) c. 298 p. 8°, $1.50. Byrne.
Bibliographical note (7 p.).
Revision and amendment of state constitutions. '10(N) c. 17+350 p. O. $2. Johns Hopkins.
—, **comp.** Modern constitutions: fundamental laws of twenty-two of the most important countries of the world, with historical and biographical notes. '09(Ja23) c. O. *$5 net, boxed. Univ. of Chic.

Dodd, W: E:
Jefferson Davis. '08(Ja11) por. D. (American crisis biographies.) **$1.25 net. Jacobs

Dodge, A. Johnson.
Practical embalmer. Rev. ed., with an appendix of 400 questions and answers on anatomy, embalming and sanitary science. '08, [1909.] (S) c. '07. 23+257 p. il. por. 8°, $3. A. J. Dodge.

DODGE, Augustus Cæsar.
Pelzer, L: Augustus Cæsar Dodge. $2. State Hist., Ia.

Dodge, D: L.
War inconsistent with the religion of Jesus Christ. [1910.] (My) 12°, (International lib.) 50 c. net. Ginn.

Dodge, G: M.
Telegraph instructor. Rev. ed. '08(My9) c. il. 12°, $1. G: M. Dodge.

Dodge, Gordon Floyd.
Diagrams for designing reinforced concrete structures, incl. diagrams for reactions and strengths of steel beams. '10(Ap9) c. il. obl. f°, $4 net. M. C. Clark.

Dodge, Grenville Mellen.
How we built the Union Pacific Railway, and other railway papers and addresses. '10(Jl) 136 p. il. pors. 8°. Gov. Pr. Off.

Dodge, J:
Narrative of Mr. John Dodge during his captivity at Detroit; reproduced in facsimile from the 2d ed. of 1780; with introd. note by Clarence Monroe Burton. '09(D4) por. Q. $5, boxed. Torch Press.

Dodge, Lawrence G.
Farm management in northern potato-growing sections. '09(D) 31 p. il. 8°, (U. S., Dept. of Agriculture, farmers' bull.) pap. (Add. Superintendent for price.) U. S., Supt. of Docs.

Dodge, Mrs. Mary Mapes.
Hans Brinker; or, the silver skates. '09 (N13) col. il. O. 50 c. McLoughlin.

Dodge, Ozias.
Experiments in producing printing surfaces. '08(D) 29 p. 12°. (Add. pubs. for price.) De Vinne.

Dodge lib.; new ser. of classics, with pors. from drawings by Lionel Heath. 7 v. '10 (N) 12°, $1.25; ooze, $2. Dodge.
Contents: Emerson's essays, 1st ser., 2d ser.; Poetry of earth; Milton, Paradise lost; Lamb, Essays of Elia; Thoughts of Marcus Aurelius; Sunlit road.

Dodge's geographical ser. il. maps, 8°. Rand, McN. & Co.
—Widtsoe *and* Peterson. Dodge's geography of Utah. *35 c. net.

Dodgson, C: Lutwidge, ["Lewis Carroll."]
Alice in Wonderland; il. by C: Robinson. [New and cheaper ed.] '10(D) il. (partly col.) $1. Cassell.
Alice in Wonderland. '08(O17) il. 12°, $1.25. Duffield.
Alice in Wonderland. '10(N5) col. il. O. bds., $2; $2.50. Tuck.
Alice's adventures in Wonderland. Popular ed. '08(D5) il. $1.50. Cassell.
Alice's adventures in Wonderland. '08 (Je6) 16°, *50 c. net. Macmillan.
Alice's adventures in Wonderland. '09, [1910.] (F) il. 4°, $3. Nelson.
Hunting of the Snark. '09(O) c. 10+15-119 p. il. 8°, 50 c. Altemus.
Hunting of the Snark; an agony in eight fits. '10(D17) il. 16°, 50 c. net. Macmillan.
Through the looking-glass. '09(Ag) c. 8+185 p. il. (partly col.) 8°, $1.50. Dodge.
Through the looking glass. '08(O24) il. 16°, *50 c. net. Macmillan.

DODGSON, Charles Lutwidge.
Maybank, T: Alice's adventures in Wonderland [in words of one syllable]. 50 c. Dutton.
Moses, B. Lewis Carroll in Wonderland and at home. $1.25 net. Appleton.

Dodgson, J: Wallis.
See Hanson, E: Kenneth.

Dods, Rev. Marcus.
Footsteps in the path of life. [1910.] (My) 215 p. 12°, $1.25 net. Doran.
Christ and man. [1910.] (My) 275 p. 12°, $1.50 net. Doran.

Dodsley, Rob.
Economy of human life, from an English copy of 1765; rev. by Clifford Anderson Owens. '10(Je25) c. 8°, $1.50. C. A. Owens.

DODSLEY, Robert.
Straus, R. Robert Dodsley, poet, publisher and playwright. $6.50 net. Lane.

Doerflinger, C: H.
Prospectus of the People's New Education Advanced Common School, embracing kindergarten, primary, elementary and advanced education; based on the pedagogical thought and practice of progressive modern education, (1869 to 1907.) '09(My8) pors. O. pap., 25 c. C: H. Doerflinger.

Does Christ say go to church? O'Neill, D. D. 5 c. D. D. O'Neill.

DOFOBS.
See Society of Dofobs.

DOG.
Archer, F. M. Dog in health and disease. 50 c. Fenno.
Axtell, E: Boston terrier and all about it. $1.50. Dogdom Pub.
Barton, F. T. Dog in health, accident and disease. $1. Altemus.
Barton, F. T. Non-sporting dogs. $1.75.—Sporting dogs. $2.50.—Toy dogs. $1. W: R. Jenkins.

DOG.—*Continued.*
Barton, F. T. Terriers, their points and management. *$1.60 net. M. Kennerley.
Brown, J: Our dogs. 50 c. Altemus.
Bryce, C. A. Gentleman's dog; his rearing, training and treatment. $1. So. Clinic Pr.
Caldwell, F. W. Wolf, the storm leader. $1.60 net. Dodd.
English foxhound kennel stud book of America. v. 1. (Priv. pr.) F. L. Wiles.
Gask, L. True stories about dogs. $1.50. Crowell.
Gersbach, R., *and* Jager, T. F. Police dog in word and picture. $1.50. T. F. Jager.
H., H. Scientific education of dogs. $1.75. W: R. Jenkins.
Harshbarger, J. A. Gentleman Don; story of a dog. $1. Crane.
Hartley, O. Hunting dogs. 60 c. A. R. Harding.
Holiday, E. How to train horses and dogs. $1. Dodge City.
Hutchinson, W. N. Dog breaking. *$1 net. Scribner.
Leighton, R. Dogs and all about them. $1.50 net. Cassell.
Lyman, M. B. Only a dog. 25 c. Am. Humane.
Merwin, H: C. Dogs and men. 60 c. net. Houghton M.
Mills, W. How to keep a dog in the city. 25 c. W: R. Jenkins.
Mooney, H: J: How to train your own dogs. 50 c. Saalfield.
Müller, G., *and* Glass, A. Diseases of the dog and their treatment. *$5 net. Franklin Press, (Pa.)
Police and work dogs in Europe by H: W. Diederich and H: Albert Johnson. '09 (Je) 16 p. il. 8°, pap., 5 c. U. S., Supt. of Docs.
Senour, C. Master St. Elmo: autobiography of a celebrated dog. *$1 net. Juvenile Bk.
Smith, A. C. Everyman's book of the dog. $1.50 net. Doran.
Smith, A. N. Bobtail Dixie: autobiography of a dog. 60 c. Educ. Pub.
Watson, J. Dog book. 2 v. in 1. $5 net. Doubleday, P.
Whitcomb, C. G. N. Autobiograph of Jeremy L., the actor dog. 50 c. net. Bassette.
Whitford, C. B. Training the bird dog. *$1.25 net. Outing.
Williams, *Mrs.* L. Manual of toy dogs. 60 c. net. Longmans.
See also Rabies.

Dog Crusoe and his master. Ballantyne, R. M. $1. Bowman.
Dog day. Emanuel, W., *pseud.* 50 c. Dutton.
Dog of Flanders. La Ramée, L. de. **40 c. net. Crowell.
Dog pit: how to breed, train and handle pit bulls. '08(Je6) c. il. por. (Fox's athletic lib.) pap., 25 c. R: K. Fox.
Dog World and Anti-Cat Review. Emanuel, W., *pseud.* **25 c. net. Stokes.

Dogaressas of Venice. Staley, E. $3.50 net. Scribner.

DOGMA.
See Theology.

Dogmatic theology. *See* Hall, Fs. Jos.

DOGMATICS.
See Theology.

Dogmatism and evolution. Laguna, T. de S. $1.75 net. Macmillan.

Doherty, Ja. Jos.
Household baker. '07, [1908.] (Ap.) c. 190 p. por. 16°, $1.50. J. J. Doherty.

Doing over. Huschart, F. M. $1.50. Clarke.
Doktor Kritikus. Nida, A. $1. A. Nida.

Dolan, Rev. T: Stanislaus.
Papacy and the first councils of the church. '10(Ja22) 8°, *75 c. net. Herder.
See of Peter and the voice of antiquity; critical notes on Bishop Coxe's "Ante-Nicene fathers"; with a preface by His Eminence, Ja., Cardinal Gibbons. '08 (N) c. 11+106 p. 12°, *60 c. net. Herder.

Dolbeer, Rev. W: H.
The benediction; introd. by Prof. D. H. Bauslin. '08(Ja11) 12°, 75 c. Lutheran Pub.

DOLCI, Carlo.
Hay, G: Carlo Dolci. *65 c. net. Stokes.

Dole, C: Fletcher, D.D.
The coming people. New ed. '10(D) 75 c. Crowell.
Coming religion. '10(Jl9) c. D. $1 net. Small.
Ethics of progress; or, the theory and practice by which civilization proceeds. '09 (S4) c. O. $1.50. Crowell.
Hope of immortality: our reasons for it. '08(O10) c. D. (What is worth while ser.) bds., **30 c. net. Crowell.
Noble womanhood. '09(O9) c. D. bds., $1, boxed. Caldwell.
What we know about Jesus. '08(Ag1) bds., *75 c. net. Open Court.

Dole, Nathan Haskell.
The Pilgrims, and other poems. '08(Ja18) O. bds. (Priv. pr.) N. H. Dole.
Teacher of Dante, and other studies in Italian literature. '08(Ap11) c. D. **$1.75 net. Moffat.
See also Browne, G: Waldo.

Dole, R: Bryant.
Quality of surface waters in the United States. pt. 1, Analyses of waters east of the one hundredth meridian. '10(Mr12) 8°, (U. S., Dept. of the Interior, Water-supply paper.)

Dolin, Stanislow.
Evolution of the spiritual world; new discovery which reveals mysteries of the Bible. '09(D) 15 p. O. pap., 15 c. C. D. Raymer.

Doll, W: F:
Money and democracy. '10(Ap) c. 7-40 p. 4°, 25 c. W: F: Doll.

Dollar hen. Hastings, M. M. $1. Arcadia Press.
Doll's house. *See* Ibsen, Henrik.
Doll's house that glue built. Williams, C. A. $1. Stokes.

DOLLS.
Bowers, M. B. Dorothy and her ward-robe. 35 c. Davis Press.
Gates, *Mrs.* J. S. April fool doll. †$1.25. Bobbs-M.
Starr, L. B. Doll book. *$2 net. Stokes.
Young, S. Letty Lane paper family. $1. Jacobs.

Dolls and toy balloons. Jenkins, F. $1. B'way Pub.

Dolls' story-book. Lovejoy, M. I., *ed.* 50 c. Wilde.

Dolly Drake. Weiderseim, G. G. 50 c. Stokes.

Dolly reforming herself. Jones, H: A. S: French.

Dolly's college experiences. Jones, M. C. $1.50. C. M. Clark.

Dolmage, Cecil G.
Astronomy of to-day. '08(N7) il. D. (Popular scientific ser.) *$1.50 net. Lippincott.

DOLOMITE MOUNTAINS, Italy..
Hamer, S. H. The Dolomites. $3 net. Lane.

Domain of belief. Coke, G. H: J: $2.50 net. Macmillan.

Domer, Harry Tennyson.
Citizens of no mean city; address del. at joint Thanksgiving-Day service of Third Lutheran church and Church of the Reformation, Baltimore, Md., Nov. 28, 1907. '07, [1908.] (Mr.) c. 30 p. 16°. (Add. pubs. for price.) Lutheran Pub.

DOMESTIC ANIMALS.
Armsby, H: P. Principles of animal nutrition; with special reference to the nutrition of farm animals. $4. Wiley.
Burkett, C: W: Farm stock: treatise on horses, cattle, sheep and swine. *$1.50 net. Judd.
Burkett, C: W., *ed.* Domestic animals. *$3.50 net. Ginn.
Davenport, E. Domesticated animals and plants. $1.25.—Principles of breeding. $2.50. Ginn.
Jordan, W. H. Feeding of animals. **$1.50 net. Macmillan.
McConnell, P. Live stock. *60 c. net. Cassell.
Moncrieff, A. R. H. Beasts of business. $1.50. Macmillan.
North-West Mills Company. Saccharine feeds and feeding. gratis. North-West Mills.
United States. *Superintendent of Documents. Animal Industry Bureau.* Repts., bulletins and circulars rel. to animal industry. gratis. U. S., Supt. of Docs.
Wilcox, E. V., *and* Smith, C. B. Farmer's cyclopedia of live stock. $4.50; $5.50. Judd.
See also Animals;—Cattle; — Ensilage; — Feeding and feeding stuffs;—Meat;—Parasites;—Poultry;—Veterinary medicine and surgery;—*also* names of domestic animals.

Domestic architecture of England. *See* Garner, T:

DOMESTIC ECONOMY.
Benton, C. F., *pseud.* Living on a little. $1.25. Estes.
Coldwater, C: H: Helping hand for every day's want. $1.50. C: H: Coldwater.

DOMESTIC ECONOMY.—*Continued.*
Dodd, M. E. Chemistry of the household. $1.25. Am. Sch. Home Economics.
Gist, E. Gist of domestic science. 75 c. E. Gist.
Goessling, A. O., *comp.* Housekeeper's reference book and domestic counselor. 50 c. Phelps.
Good Housekeeping manual of home handicraft. (Add. pubs. for price.) Phelps.
Hamilton, J: Farmers' institute for women. (Add. Superintendent for price.) U. S., Supt. of Docs.
Hays, W. M. Agriculture, industries and home education in our public schools. gratis. Nat. Educ. Assoc.
Hewitt, *Mrs.* E. C. How to live on a small income. 50 c. Jacobs.
Household economist. Popular ed., 35 c.; Standard ed., $1.25; $1.50. Davis-G.
Hunt, C. L. Home problems from a new standpoint. *$1 net. Whitcomb.
James, A. L. Housekeeping for two. **$1.25 net. Putnam.
Johnson, A. A., *ed.* Household companion. $1.50. Uplift.
Johnson, C. When mother lets us help. **75 c. net. Moffat.
Kinne, H. Equipment for teaching of domestic science. 30 c. Columbia Univ.
Krout, M. H. Platters and pipkins. 75 c. net. McClurg
Langworthy, C: F. U. S. government publications as sources of information for students of home economics. (Add. Assoc. for price.) Am. Home Economics Assoc.
Little helps for home-makers. $2. Chapple Pub.
Morse, S. L. Household discoveries: recipes and processes. (Add. pubs. for price.) Success.
Tatum, J., *comp.* Information of great value to newly married people. gratis. H. K. Palmer.
Terhune, *Mrs.* M. V. H. Houskeeper's week. **$1.50 net. Bobbs-M.
Van de Water, *Mrs.* V. T. From kitchen to garret. 75 c. net. Sturgis & W.
Vulté, H. T., *and* Goodell, G: A. Lab'y notes in household chemistry. $1.25. Chemical.
Wilkinson, J: W. Institute hdbk. on agriculture and domestic science; for teachers. 30 c. Oklahoma Bk.
See also Bacteria;—Cleaning;—Cookery;—Dairy;—Dressmaking;—Family;—Food; — Furniture;—Gardens and gardening;—Girls;—House decoration;—Hygiene;—Insects; — Laundry work;—Needlework;—Repairing;—Wall decoration.

Domestic employment: handbook. '09(Je5) S. pap., per 100, $4; per 300, $10; per 500, $16. Legal Aid.

Domestic Engineering directory of jobbers and manufacturers of plumbing, heating, lighting, engine, mining and mill supplies. 15th ed. In 2 pts. '08(Mr) c. 1274 p. 16°, leath., $5. Domestic Engineering.

Domestic jobbing. Hasluck, P. N., *ed.* 50 c. McKay.

DOMESTIC RELATIONS.
Tiffany, W. C. Hdbk. on the law of persons and domestic relations. $3.75. West Pub.
See also Divorce;—Family;—Marriage;—Woman.

Domestic sanitary **engineering and plumbing.** Raynes, F. W. ***$3 net. Longmans.**

DOMESTIC SCIENCE.
***See* Domestic economy.**

DOMICILE.
***See* Marriage.**

Dominant dollar. Lillibridge, W: O. $1.50. McClurg.

DOMINICAN REPUBLIC, West Indies.
International Bureau of American Republics. Dominican Republic; general descriptive data. (Add. pubs. for price.) Int. Bu. Am. Republics.

Dominican tertiaries' guide. McKenna, C: H., *comp.* 75 c.; $1.25. Rosary.

Dominion and power. Patterson, C: B. $1.20 net. Funk.

DOMINION OF CANADA.
***See* Canada.**

Dominion of dreams. *See* Macleod, Fiona, *pseud.*

Dominion of New Zealand. Douglas, *Sir* A. P. *$3 net. Little, B. & Co.

Dommasch, Otto.
Neuer englischer lehr gang; mit aussprachebezeichnung zum schul-, privat- und selbstunterricht. '09(Ja9) c. D. 50 c. Stechert.

Domville-Fife, C: W.
Great states of South America. '10(D31) il. maps, 8°, $4.50 net. Macmillan.

Don. Besier, R. $1 net. Duffield.

Don Basilio. Schilling, J. *$1 net. Holt.

Don-Carlos, Mrs. Louisa Cooke.
See Carlos, *Mrs.* Louisa Cooke Don-.

Don Coronado through Kansas. Stowell, J: $1.50. Don Coronado.

Don MacGrath. Parrish, R. $1.50. McClurg.

DON PEDRO, *of Castile.*
Storer, E: Peter the Cruel; life of the notorious Don Pedro of Castile. $4 net. Lane.

Don Quixote. *See* Cervantes Saavedra, Miguel de.

Don vascaeno: the fruit. Cole, S. $1.50. Connoisseurs' Press.

Donahey, Mrs. Mary Dickerson.
Castle of Grumpy Grouch: fairy story. '08 (O24) c. il. Q. $1.25. Stern.
Down Spider Web lane; a fairy tale. '09 (N6) c. il. Q. $1.25, boxed. Stern.
Through the little green door. '10(N12) c. il. D. $1. Stern.

Donahoe, Dan. Jos., ed.
Early Christian hymns; translations of the verses of the most notable Latin writers of the early and middle ages. '08(D) c. 12+271 p. 12°, *$2 net. Grafton Press.

Donahoe, Marg. Frances.
Manual of nursing. '10(D) c. 10+489 p. il. 12°, $2. Appleton.
Text-book of nursing. '09, [1910] (My) 400 p. il. $1.75 net. Appleton.

Donakin circus. Cort, H. R. $1. Stokes.

Donaldson, Fs.
Pract. shaft sinking. '10(N19) c. il. 8°, $2. McGraw-H.

Donaldson, O. F.
Workingman's view of the Bible. '09 (D11) c. D. *$1.20 net. Sherman, F.

Donaldson, Orren Madison.
Common honesty; study of fundamental principles and their relation to the labor problem. '10(Mr5) c. 12°, 50 c. Van-American.

Donaldson, Stuart Alex., D.D.
Church life and thought in North Africa, A.D. 200. '10(Ja22) 200 p. 12°, *$1.25 net. Putnam.

DONATUS, Ælius.
Basore, J: W: Scholia on hypokrisis in the Commentary of Donatus. gratis. Johns Hopkins.

Dondlinger, P: Tracey.
Book of wheat: economic history and practical manual of the wheat industry. '08 (D) 11+369 p. front. 12°, *$2 net. Judd.

Donegal memories. *See* Johnston, J. N.

Donellan lectures. *See* Astley, Hugh J: Dukinfield.

Donkey John of the toy valley. **Morley, M. W.** $1.25. **McClurg.**

Donnelly, C: Fs.
Roma, and other poems. '09, [1910.] (Ap) 16+63 p. por. 8°. (Priv. pr.) J. T. White & Co.

DONNELLY, Charles Francis.
Conway, K. E., *and* Cameron, M. W. Charles Francis Donnelly. (Priv. pr.) J. T. White & Co.

Donovan, J: P., ["Westerner."]
Handling the hog from start to finish. [1910.] (S) c. 150 p. 12°, $3. Butchers Advocate.

Donovan, Jos. Mitchell.
Law of marriage, annulment, domicile, divorce. 8th ed., 1908. '08(Je); 9th ed. '09(N) c. S. pap., ea., $1. J. M. Donovan; Med. Pr.

Donovan, Jos. Wesley.
Modern jury trials and advocates. 4th rev. ed., enl. '08(Je) c. 21+720 p. O. $4.50. Banks.

Donovan, Mary.
Very first book. '10(D31) 8°, 20 c.; pap., 10 c. Hinds.

Donovan, Mike, [Michael Jos. O'Donovan.]
Roosevelt that I know; ten years of boxing with the President—and other memories of famous fighting men; ed. by F. H. N. '09(Mr6) c. il. D. *$1 net. B. W. Dodge.

Don't fret ser. T. 50 c. Dodge.
—Pennington. All is well.—Be strong.

Don't kill the laying hen. Potter, T. F. $1. T. F. Potter.

Don'ts for bachelors and old maids. Antrim, *Mrs.* M. T. $1; 50 c. Altemus.

Don'ts in bridge Emery, *Mrs.* B. B. 50 c. net. W: R. Jenkins.

Donworth, Grace.
Down home with Jennie Allen. '10(S17) c. il. D. $1.50. Small.
Letters of Jennie Allen to her friend Miss Musgrove. '08(N14) c. il. D. †$1.50. Small.

D'Ooge, Martin Luther.
Acropolis of Athens. '09(Ja23) il. figs. plans, O. *$4 net, boxed. Macmillan.

"Dooley, Mr.," pseud.
See Dunne, Finley P:

Dooley, W: H:
Textiles for commercial, industrial evening and domestic arts schools. '10(D24) c. il. 8°, $1. Heath.

Dooling, J: C.
Equitable remedies of creditors in Michigan. '08(Je) c. 11+347 p. O. $4. Drake Law Bk.

Doolittle, B:, and Jones, C: Colcock, jr.
Short narrative of mischief done by the French and Indian enemy, on the western frontiers of the province of the Massachusetts-Bay; from the beginning of the French war; drawn up by the Rev. Mr. Doolittle; biographical sketch of the Honorable Major John Habersham of Georgia, by C: C. Jones, jr.; [*Magazine of History* with *Notes and Queries;* extra no.] '10(My21) 4°, to subscribers, $1.75. Abbatt.

Doolittle, Eric.
Catalogue and remeasurement of the 648 double stars discovered by Professor G. W. Hough. '08(My9) F. (Univ. of Penn. pub., Astronomical ser.) pap. (Add. pubs. for price.) Univ. of Penn.; [Appleton.]

Doolittle, G. M.
Year's work in an out-apiary; or, an average of 114½ pounds of honey per colony, in a poor season. '09(Ja2) O. pap., 50 c. A. I. Root.

DOOLITTLE, James Rood.
Mowry, D. Appreciation of James Rood Doolittle. 15 c. State Hist., Wis.

Doomed city. Carling, J: R. $1.50. Clode.

Door of darkness. Annesley, *Mrs.* M. †$1.50. Lane.

Door where the wrong lay. Greene, *Mrs.* M. E. B. $1.50. C. M. Clark.

Doors of life. De Voe, W. $1. Funk.

Doran, Beverley.
Breath of the mountains: [poems.] '08 (F1) c. 12°, $1. Badger.

Dore, S. Ernest.
See Morris, Malcolm.

Doré lectures. Troward, T. 50 c. Roger Bros.

Dorée, Nadage.
Is your soul progressing? '08(Je6) c. por. 12°, $1. Am. News.

Doremus, Philip.
Reminiscences of Montclair, [N. J.,] with some account of Montclair's part in the Civil War. '08, [1909.] (Mr) 111 p. il. pors. 8°, $1. P. Doremus.

"Doria, Clara," pseud.
See Rogers, *Mrs.* Clara Kathleen Barnett.

Dorian days. Stafford, W. P. **$1.25 net. Macmillan.

Dorland, W: Alex. Newman, M.D.
Age of mental virility: inquiry into the records of achievement of the world's chief workers and thinkers. '08(O3) c. D. **$1 net. Century Co.

American il. medical dictionary; a new and complete dictionary of the terms used in medicine, surgery, dentistry, pharmacy, chemistry, nursing, and kindred branches, with the pronunciation, derivation and definition, incl. much collateral information of an encyclopedic character. 5th ed., rev. and enl. '09(Ag) c. 876 p. il. (partly col.) 8°, *$4.50 net; with thumb index, *$5 net. Saunders.

—, **ed.** Am. pocket medical dictionary; cont. the pronunciation and definition of all the principal terms used in medicine and the kindred sciences. 6th ed., rev. and enl. '09 (Je) c. 5-598 p. 16°, *$1 net; with thumb index, *$1.25 net. Saunders.

Dorner, Herman Bernard.
Window gardening. '08(My9) c. il. D. **$1 net. Bobbs-M.

Dornröschen. Fisher, E. *25 c. net. Crowell.

Dornville-Fife, C: W.
See Fife, C: W. Dornville-.

Dorothy and her ward-robe. Bowers, M. B. 35 c. Davis Press.

Dorothy and the wizard in Oz. Baum, L. F. $1.25. Reilly & B.

Dorothy at Oak Knowe. Raymond, *Mrs.* E. H. 60 c. Chatterton.

Dorothy Brooke's school days. Sparhawk, F. C. $1.50. Crowell.

Dorothy Brooke's vacation. Sparhawk, F. C. $1.50. Crowell.

Dorothy Brown. Rhodes, N. †$1.50. Lothrop, L. & S.

Dorothy Dainty in the country. Brooks, A. †$1. Lothrop, L. & S.

Dorothy Dainty's gay times. Brooks, A. †$1. Lothrop, L. & S.

Dorothy Dainty's winter. Brooks, A. $1. Lothrop, L. & S.

Dorothy Dale, a girl of to-day. Penrose, M. 60 c. Cupples & L.

Dorothy Dale and her chums. Penrose, M. 60 c. Cupples & L.

Dorothy Dale at Glenwood school. Penrose, M. 60 c. Cupples & L.

Dorothy Dale's great secret. Penrose, M. 60 c. Cupples & L.

Dorothy Dale's queer holidays. Penrose, M. 60 c. Cupples & L.

Dorothy in California. Raymond, *Mrs.* E. H. 60 c. Chatterton-P.

Dorothy of Anglewood. Nicolovius, L. 75 c. B'way Pub.

Dorothy on a house boat. Raymond, *Mrs.* E. H. 60 c. Chatterton-P.

Dorothy on a ranch. Raymond, *Mrs.* E. H. 60 c. Chatterton-P.

Dorothy's schooling. Raymond, *Mrs.* E. H. 60 c. Chatterton-P.

Dorothy's travels. Raymond, *Mrs.* E. H. 60 c. Chatterton-P.

Dorr, Mrs. Julia Caroline Ripley.
Beyond the sunset; latest poems. '09, [1910.] (F) 9+94 p. 12°, *$1.25 net. Scribner.
See also Nadaud, Gustave.

Dorr, Mrs. Rita Childe.
What eight million women want. '10(D10) c. il. pors. O. $2 net. Small.

Dorrance, Mrs. Ethel Arnold Smith.
Maid and a man. '09(S25) c. il. in col. O. **$1.50 net. Moffat.

Dorrington, Alb., and Stephens, A. G.
Our Lady of Darkness. '10(My14) il. 12°, $1.50. Macaulay.

Dorris, C: Elias Webb, ed.
Interesting correspondence; discussion between C. E. W. Dorris and Miss Nora Yount (Christians) and A. E. Clement, W. H. Lovell, Chas. W. Galloway, and Geo. W. Nackles (Methodists); appendix by editor. '10(Je) c. 2-289 p. 12°, $1. C: E. W. Dorris.

Dorris, G. Preston.
See Dyke, And. Lee.

D'ORSAY, *Comte* A. G.
See Orsay, *Comte* A. G. d'.

Dorset, G.
A successful wife; a story. '10(S3) c. il. D. $1.50. Harper.

Dorset, Marion.
Hog cholera. '09, [1910.] (F) 23 p. il. 8°, (U. S., Dept. of Agriculture, farmers' bull.) pap.

DORSET, England.
Heath, S. South Devon and Dorset coast. $2.25 net. Stokes.
Salmon, A. L. Dorset. 45 c. net. Putnam.

Dose book of specific medicines: their history, characteristics, [etc.;] and a glossary of indicated remedies and disease names and definitions, by V. L. Bell, M.D. '08(Ja11) S. pap. (Add. pubs. for price.) Lloyd Bros.

Dosia. Durand, *Mme.* A. M. C. F. 45 c. Heath.

DOSIOLOGY.
See Medicine.

Dot. Zimmerman, L. M. $1. L. M. Zimmerman.

Dotty Seaweed. Cornell, H. $2. Philosopher Press.

Douanier (Le) de mer. Berthet, É. 60 c. Oxford Univ.

Double cross. Willets, G. $1.50. G: W: Dillingham.

Double fortune. Hoskins, B. L. $1.25. Neale.

Double life. Leroux, G. $1.50. Kearney

Double play. Barbour, R. H: †$1.50. Appleton.

Doubleday, Mrs. Nellie Blanchan De Graff, [Mrs. Fk. Nelson Doubleday.]
See Blanchan Neltje, *pseud.*

Doubleday, Roman.
Hemlock Avenue mystery. '08(F29) c. il. D. †$1.50. Little, B. & Co.
Red House on Rowan Street. '10(Mr26) c. il. D. †$1.50. Little, B. & Co.

DOUBT.
See Agnosticism;—Faith;—Skepticism.

Doudney, Sarah.
Shadow and shine. '08(D26) D. $1.50. Jennings.

Dougall, Lily:
Paths of the righteous. '08(O24) 12°, $1.50. Macmillan.

Dougherty, Michael.
Prison diary of Michael Dougherty, late Co. B, 13th Pa. Cavalry, while confined in Pemberton, Barrett's, Libby, Andersonville, and other southern prisons; sole survivor of 127 of his regiment captured the same time, 122 dying in Andersonville. '08, [1909.] (Mr) c. 75 p. por. 12°. (Not for sale.) C: A. Dougherty.

Doughty, C: Montagu.
Wanderings in Arabia; arr. with introd. by E: Garnett. '08(My16) 2 v., il. 8°, $4.50. Scribner.

Doughty, H: Montagu.
Chronicles of Theberton, a Suffolk village; with introd. and notes by the Rev. W. W. Skeat. '10(D24) il. 8°, $2.50 net. Macmillan.

Douglas, A. H.
Elements of commercial law. '09(Ag7) D. (Pitman's practical primers of business.) 50 c. Pitman.

Douglas, Amanda Minnie.
Helen Grant, graduate. '08(N14) c. il. D. (Helen Grant books.) †$1.25. Lothrop, L. & S.
Helen Grant, teacher. '09(S11) c. il. D. (Helen Grant ser.) $1.25. Lothrop, L. & S.
Helen Grant's decision. '10(Ag20) c. il. D. (Helen Grant books.) $1.25. Lothrop, L. & S.
Little girl in old Pittsburg. '09(O9) c. D. (Little girl ser.) †$1.50. Dodd.
Little girl in old Salem. '08(O10) c. D. ("Little girl" ser.) †$1.50. Dodd.

Douglas, And. Halliday.
Philosophy and psychology of Pietro Pomponazzi; ed. by C: Douglas and R. P. Hardie. '10(O29) O. $2.50 net. Putnam.

Douglas, Sir Arth. Percy.
Dominion of New Zealand. '10(F19) il. fold. map, O. *$3 net. Little, B. & Co.

Douglas, Eliz.
Cake and biscuit book. '08(O31) S. (New cookery books.) 50 c. McKay.
Pudding and pastry book. '08(O31) S. (New cookery book.) 50 c. McKay.
Soup and sauce book. '08(O31) S. (New cookery books.) 50 c. McKay.

Douglas, Gavin.
How to make money. '10(O8) 12°, 50 c. net. Dutton.

Douglas, Hudson, pseud.
See Aitken, Rob.

Douglas, Hugh A.
Venice and her treasures; with notes on the pictures by Maud Cruttwell. '10 (Mr26) il. S. *$1.50 net. Scribner.

Douglas, Ja.
Adventures in London. '09(O23) c. por. O. **$1.75 net. Cassell.
Untechnical addresses on technical subjects. 2d ed., with additional addresses. '08 (O3) c. 12°, $1. Wiley.

Douglas, J: C.
See Harrison, C:

Douglas, Loudon M.
Refrigeration in the dairy. '08(N21) royal 8°, $1. Nickerson & C.

Douglas, Marian.
In the poverty year: story of life in New Hampshire in 1816. '08(S19) c. front. D. (Bimbi ser.) bds., **40 c. net. Crowell.

Douglas, R:
Surgical diseases of the abdomen, with special reference to diagnosis. 2d ed., rev. and enl. by R: A. Barr. '09(Mr) 900 p. il. 8°, *$6 net. Blakiston.

Douglas, R: Leroy, comp.
Manufactures; hist. of manufactures in the Kansas district. [1910.] (D) 135 p. il. pors. 8°, gratis State Hist., Kan.

DOUGLAS, Stephen Arnold.
Carr, C. E. Stephen A. Douglas. *$2 net. McClurg.
Fish, D. Legal phases of the Lincoln and Douglas debates. (Priv. pr.) D. Fish.
Johnson, A. Stephen A. Douglas. **$2.50 net. Macmillan.
Sparks, E. E., *and others, eds.* Semi-centennial of the Lincoln-Douglas debates in Illinois, 1858-1908: suggestions for school entertainments. 35 c. Phillips Bros.

Douglas, Wa. Jules.
Practical hints for concrete constructors. '08(Ja11) il. 12°, (Engineering News reprints.) pap., 25 c. Engineering News.

Douglas-Lithgow, Rob. Alex., M.D.
Dict. of American-Indian place and proper names in New England. '09(Ag7) c. por. O. $7. Salem Press.

DOUGLASS, Ephraim.
Burton, C. M. Ephraim Douglass and his times. $1.85 Abbatt.

Douglass, Harlan Paul.
Christian reconstruction in the South. '09 (N6) c. il. O. *$1.50 net. Pilgrim Press.

Douglass, J: Jordan.
Girdle of the great: story of the new South. '08(Ap11) c. il. D. $1.50. B'way Pub.

DOUGLASS FAMILY.
See Genealogies: Cisco, J. G.

Doumic, René.
George Sand; some aspects of her life and work; tr. by Alys Hallard. '10(Je4) c. pors. fac. 8°, $3.50. Putnam.

Dounce, Harry Esty.
Cliartho Philanders: very ancient idyll newly refurbished for another spring. '10(F19) c. 8°, pap., 25 c. G: W: Browning.

Douris and the painters of Greek vases. Pottier, E. $2.50. Dutton.

Douthat, Rob. W:
Latin synonyms defined from two standpoints. '08(Ja18) D. $1. R. W: Douthat.

Douthit, Jasper Lewis.
Jasper Douthit's story. '09(Ap10) D. *$1.25 net. Am. Unitarian.

Dove, Patrick E:
Theory of human progression; abr. by Julia A. Kellogg. '10(Jl16) c. D. pap., 25 c. Blanchard.

Dove in the eagle's nest. *See* Yonge, Charlotte Mary.

DOVER, Mass.
Smith, F. Biographical sketch of the residents of that part of Dedham which is now Dover, who took part in King Philip's war. (Priv. pr.) F. Smith.
Smith, F. Founders of the First parish, Dover, Mass. $1. J: H. Faulk.
Vital records of Dover, Mass., to 1850 $1.50. N. E. Hist.

Dow, Albert Gallatin.
Dow, C. M., *comp.* Albert Gallatin Dow. gratis. Journal Pr.

Dow, Arth. Wesley.
Composition; standard treatise for art teachers and students. New ed., rev. and enl. '10(O) 160 p. il. 4°, $2.50 net. Baker & T.
Theory and practice of teaching art. '08 (O3) c. figs. 8°, $1. Teachers' Coll.

Dow, Carl Stephen.
See Newell, W: S.

Dow, C: M., comp.
Albert Gallatin Dow, 1808-1908. '08(N) 7-78 p. 4°, gratis. Journal Pr.

Dow, Ethel Constance.
Diary of a birthday doll. '08(O24) c. il. O. $1.25, boxed. Stern.
Mother's hero. '10(N12) c. col. il. O. $1.25. Stern.
Proud Roxana. '09(N6) c. il. O. $1.25, boxed. Stern.

Dow, G: Fs.
Old wood engravings, views and buildings in the county of Essex, [Mass.] '08, [1909.] (Jl) 14 p. il. 4°. (Priv. pr.) G: F. Dow.

Dowd, Willis Bruce.
James Grant, a model American. '10(Mr5) c. il. pors. 8°, 75 c. Riverdale Press.

Dowden, E:
Essays, modern and Elizabethan. '10(Jl30) 8°, $2 net. Dutton.
—, **ed.** *See* Shakespeare, W:

Dowding, H: Wallace.
Man from Mars; or, service for service's sake. '10(D3) $1.50. Cochrane.

Dowler, J. S., & Co.
Coffee calculator; (intended for wholesale coffee trade and bankers dealing in the article.) '07, [1908.] (Mr) c. 31 p. tabs., 16°. (Add. pub. for price.) J. S. Dowler & Co.

Dowling, Marg. Caroline.
Easy Spanish for beginners: series of progressive reading lessons arr. to supply material for systematic lessons in speaking and writing. '10(Ap9) 8°, 40 c. G: Dowling.

Dowman, Fs.
Great English painters. '09, [1910.] il. 12°, **$1.50 net. boxed. Jacobs

Down, P. D., comp.
"Electrician" handy copper wire tables and formulae. '08(Je20) c. 16°, *$1 net. Van Nostrand.

Down at Cross Timbers. McGeeney, P. S. $1. Angel Press.
Down at Stein's Pass. McGeeney, P. S. $1. Angel Press.
Down home with Jennie Allen. Donworth, G. $1.50. Small.
Down in Porto Rico. Fowles, G: M. 75 c. Eaton & M.
Down on the old plantation. Scogin, *Mrs.* S. M. C. 25 c. J: D. Howe.
Down Spider Web lane. Donahey, *Mrs.* M. D. $1.25. Stern.
Down the road with a tramp writer. Wright, J: L. $1. Black Lion.
Down to the sea. Grenfell, *Sir* W. T. $1 net. Revell.
Down Wild Goose Canyon. Upton, C: E. 75 c. C: E. Upton.

Downer, Arth. Cleveland, D.D.
Mission and ministration of the Holy Spirit. '10(Je4) 8°, $3 net. Scribner.

Downer, B: Ja., comp.
See United States. Compilation of laws rel. to trust companies.

Downes, Constance, comp.
Sunshine and roses; book of happiness and good cheer. '10(O8) c. O. pap., 75 c., boxed; ooze, $1.50, boxed. Platt & P.

Downes, Louise.
New democracy. '10(D10) c. 8°, $2. Sherman, F.

Downey, E. H.
Hist. of labor legislation in Iowa. '10 (Jl30) O. (Iowa economic hist. ser.) $2. State Hist. Ia.

Downey, June Etta.
Control processes in modified handwriting. '08, [1909.] (O) 7+148 p. facsims. 4°, (Studies from the Psychological Laboratory of the University of Chicago.) $1.50. Psychological Review.

Downey, Sheridan, comp. and ed.
See Wyoming. *Sup. ct.* Complete digest.

Downey, W:
Thoughts on themes from Patmos. v. 1. '10(Je11) c. D. $1.25. Downey.

Downie, Ja. Walker.
Clinical manual for the study of diseases of the throat. 2d ed., rev. and in a large measure rewritten. '09(N) 18+432 p. il. O. *$3.25 net. Macmillan.

Downs, Mrs. Sarah Eliz. Forbush.
See Sheldon, *Mrs.* Georgie.

Downs, T: Nelson.
Art of magic; ed. by J: Northern Hilliard. '09(Ap3) c. il. pors. 8°, $5. W. S. Edwards.

Doyle, Sir Arth. Conan.
Crime of the Congo. '09(D11) c. O. 50 c.; pap., 25 c. Doubleday, P.
Round the fire stories. '08(N7) c. D. †$1.50. McClure.
Through the magic door: [essays on books.] '08(My9) c. D. **$1.25 net. McClure.

Doyle, E:
The comet: a play of our times. '08(N21) c. D. bds., $1.25. Badger.

Doyle, Gregory, M.D.
Incidents of European travel. Souvenir ed. '10(Ag6) c. il. pors. O. $1.50. G. Doyle.

Doyle, J:
World's great character builder and practical thoughts for every day living. '08, [1909.] (Mr) c. 19+21-270 p. 12°, 50 c. J: Doyle.

Doyle, Mrs. Martha Claire MacGowan, ["Martha James."]
Hero of Pigeon Camp. '08(S5) il. D. (Pigeon Camp ser.) †$1.25. Lothrop, L. & S.
Mint Julip. '09(D4) c. col. il. front. O. $2.50. W. D. Lane.

Doyle, Mary E.
Standard Catholic readers: First reader. '09(Ag21); second reader. '09(S4); third reader; fourth reader, for fourth and fifth grades; fifth reader, for sixth, seventh and eighth grades. '09(S11) c. il. D. 1st reader, 20 c.; 2d reader, 30 c.; 3d reader, 40 c.; 4th reader, 50 c.; 5th reader, 60 c. Am. Bk.

Doyle, W: S.
New instruction book on ocean bathing, swimming and boating. '10(Ag13) c. 24°, 25 c. W. S. Doyle.

Drafting-room practice. '08(My23) c. il. 8°, (Machinery's reference ser.) pap., 25 c. Indust. Press.

Drage, Geoffrey.
Austria-Hungary. '09(Ag21) il. 8°, maps, $6. Dutton.

Dragendorff, Johann Georg Noël.
Plant analysis, qualitative and quantitative; tr. from the German by H: G. Greenish. '10(F19) tabs., O. (Anastatic reprint.) *$3.50 net. Stechert.

Dragnet (The). Barnett, E. S. $1.50. B: W. Huebsch.

Drag-net (The). Bohan, E. B. $1.50. C. M. Clark.

Dragon Portland cement. [1910. ed.] '10 (N) 194 p. il. 8°. Lawrence Cement.

Dragon's blood. Rideout, H: M. **$1.20 net. Houghton M.

Dragon's silk. Herring, P. $1.50. Cassell.

DRAGS.
See Hydrography.

DRAINAGE.
Brown, C: F. Drainage of irrigated lands. U. S., Supt of Docs.
Fortier, S:, *and* Cone, V. M. Drainage of irrigated lands on the San Joaquin Valley, Cal. (Add. Superintendent for price.) U. S., Supt. of Docs.
Ontario, Canada. Drainage acts. $5. A. Pool.
See also Farms and farming;—Hydraulic engineering; — Irrigation; — Plumbing; — Sewage and sewerage;—Water supply;—*also* names of states.

Drake, Allison Emery, Ph. D.
Discoveries in Hebrew, Gaelic, Gothic, Anglo-Saxon, Latin, Basque, and other Caucasic languages; showing fundamental kinship of the Aryan tongues and of Basque with the Semitic tongues. '08 (Ja18) facsims., O. ¾ mor., *$6 net. Herrick.
Supplementary discoveries showing Aryo-Semitic cognation. '10(N) c. no paging, O. (With Discoveries in Hebrew, Gaelic, Gothic, Anglo-Saxon, Latin, Basque, and other Caucasic languages.) pap., $6 net. Herrick.

Drake, B. F.
Progressive drawing. 7 bks. '09(Ja16) il. obl. S. pap., bks. 1, 2, 3, ea., 20 c.; bks. 4, 5, 6, 7, ea., 25 c. Union Pub., (Nashville.)

Drake, Dan.
Notices concerning Cincinnati. 2 v. in 1. '09(Mr) 8°, (Historical and Philosophical Society of Ohio pubs.) (Not for sale.) Hist. and Phil. Soc., O.

DRAKE, Daniel.
Juettner, O. Daniel Drake and his followers. $5. Harvey Pub.

Drake, Mrs. Emma Frances Angell, M.D.
What a woman of forty-five should know. '10(Je4) 16°, (Self and sex ser.) $1. Vir Pub.
What a young wife ought to know. New rev. ed. '08(O17) c. por. 16°, (Self and sex ser.) *$1 net. Vir Pub.

Drake, F. W.
Way of fellowship. '10(O22) D. $1 net. Longmans.

DRAKE, *Sir* Francis.
Bacon, E. M. Boys' Drake. $1.50 net. Scribner.
Brereton, R. M. Question: did Sir Francis Drake land on any part of the Oregon coast? *25 c. net. Gill.
Hague, J. D. Drake medal. gratis. W. D. Pagan.

Drake, Mrs. J. B., comp.
See Bourhill, *Mrs.* E. J.

Drake, J: N., comp.
See New York [State.] Tax law.

Drake, S: Adams.
Book of New England legends and folk lore in prose and poetry. New and rev. ed. '10(S10) c. il. O. $1.50 net, boxed. Little, B. & Co.
Old Boston taverns and tavern clubs. '10 (My14) 4°, pap., 50 c. W. A. Butterfield.

Drake: an English epic. Noyes, A. **$1.50 net. Stokes.

DRAMA AND DRAMATISTS.
Bruner, J. D. Compression in the French classical drama. 10 c. J. D. Bruner.
Caffin, C: H: Appreciation of the drama. **$1.50 net. Baker & T.
Crowley, T. J. Character-treatment in the mediæval drama. $1; 75 c. Univ. Press, (Notre Dame.)
Eaton, W. P. American stage. **$1.50 net. Small.
Evanston, Ill., Public Library. The drama; catalogue of books on dramatic literature. Evanston Pub. Lib.
Faxon, F: W., *ed.* Dramatic index for 1909; 1910. ea., $3.50 net. Boston Bk.
Garnett, P. Bohemian jinks. *$1.50 net. Garnett.
Gildersleeve, V. C. Government regulation of the Elizabethan drama. *$1.25 net. Lemcke.
Grau, R. Forty years' observation of music and the drama. $5. B'way Pub.
Hill, H. W. Sidney's Arcadia and the Elizabethan drama. (Add. Univ. for price.) Univ. of Nev.
Jebb, *Sir* R: C. Samson Agonistes and the Hellenic drama. 35 c. Oxford Univ.
Klein, D: Literary criticism from the Elizabethan dramatists. $1.50 net. Sturgis & W.
Kueffner, L. M. Development of the historic drama. 50 c. net. Univ. of Chic.
Lanier, S. Shakespeare and his forerunners.. $1.60. Doubleday, P.
Mantzius, K. History of the theatrical art. In 5 v. v. 4, 5. ea., *$3.50 net. Lippincott.
Marks, J. A: English pastoral dramas (1660-1798). *$1.50 net. Stechert.

DRAMA AND DRAMATISTS.—*Continued.*
Matthews, J. B. Study of the drama. **$1.50 net. Houghton M.
Mulliken, C. A. Reading list on modern dramatists: D'Annunzio, Hauptmann, Ibsen, Maeterlinck, Phillips, Rostand, Shaw and Suderman. 20 c. Boston Bk.
Murray, J: T. English dramatic companies, 1558-1642. 2 v. $7.50 net. Houghton M.
Price, W: T. Analysis of play construction. $5. W: T. Price.
Rees, K. Rule of three actors in the classical Greek drama. *75 c. net. Univ. of Chic.
Ristine, F. H. English tragicomedy; its origin and hist. $1.50. Lemcke.
Schelling, F. E. Elizabethan drama, 1558-1642. 2 v. **$7.50 net. Houghton M.
Swinburn, A. C: Age of Shakespeare. **$2 net. Harper.
Symons, A. Plays, acting and music. **$2 net. Dutton.
Thorndike, A. H. Tragedy, [English.] **$1.50 net. Houghton M.
Thorndike, A. H., *comp.* Minor Elizabethan drama. 2 v. ea., 35 c. net; 70 c. net. Dutton.
Vaughan, C: E. Types of tragic drama. *$1.60 net. Macmillan.
Walkley, A. B. Drama and life. *$1.75 net. Brentano's.
Watt, L. M. Attic and Elizabethan tragedy. *$2 net. Dutton.
Witkowski, G. German drama of the nineteenth century. $1. Holt.
Wright, H: B. Recovery of a lost Roman tragedy. $1.50. Yale Univ.
See also Actors and actresses;—Costume;—Operas;—Pantomime;—Plays;—Theatre;—*also* names of dramatists;—Temple dramatists.

Drama and life. Walkley, A. B. *$1.75 net. Brentano's.
Drama in sunshine. Vachell, H. A. *$1 net. Fenno.
Drama of Saint Helena. Frémeaux, P. $3 net. Appleton.
Dramatic art of magic. Haley, L: C. $1.15. L: C. Haley.
Dramatic French reader. Ashleman, L. A. 75 c. Flanagan.
Dramatic reader for grammar grades. Knight, M. 50 c. Am. Bk.
Dramatis personæ. *See* Browning, Rob.
Dramatization in the Grammar grades. Woodbury, S. E. 30 c. S. E. Woodbury.

Drane, Augusta Theodosia.
Christian schools and scholars; or, sketches of education from the Christian era to the Council of Trent. '10(Jl30) O. (Anastatic reprint of the 2d ed. pub. in London, 1881.) $6 net. Stechert.

Drannan, W: F.
Capt. W. F. Drannan, chief of scouts, as pilot to emigrant and government trains, across the plains of the wild West of fifty years ago. '10(N12) c. il. pors. 8°, $1. Rhodes & M.

"Dranoel," pseud.
See Leonard, Josiah Sloan.

Draper, Andrew Sloan.
Adaptation of the schools to industry and efficiency; address before the National Education Association, June, 1908. '09 (Ja23) O. pap., gratis. A. S. Draper.
Addresses and papers, 1908-1909. '09(My8) O. pap. (Add. pubs. for price.) N. Y. State Educ.
Agriculture and its educational needs. '10 (Ap30) S. 50 c. Bardeen.
American education; with introd. by N: Murray Butler. '09(D18) c. O. **$2 net. Houghton M.
Industrial and trades schools; addresses by the Commissioner of Education. '08, [1909.] (S) 5-67 p. 8°. (Add. Dept. for price.) N. Y. State Educ.
Our children, our schools, and our industries. '08(Ap25) D. 50 c. Bardeen.
Rescue of Cuba: marking an epoch in the growth of free government. '10(My21) c. il. D. $1. Silver.

Draper, G: Otis.
More: a study of financial conditions now prevalent. '08(F29) c. D. **$1 net. Little, B. & Co.

Draper, W: Franklin.
Recollections of a varied career. '08(O3) c. il. O. **$3 net. Little, B. & Co.

Draper ser. il. D. State Hist., Wis.
—Thwaites *and* Kellogg, *eds.* Revolution on the upper Ohio. $1.50.

DRAPERIES.
See House decoration;—Upholsterery.

Drapery and drapers' accounts. Beynon, R: $1. Pitman.

DRAUGHTING.
See Architectural drawing;—Mechanical drawing.

DRAUGHTS.
See Checkers.

Drawbridge, Rev. C. L.
Is religion undermined? 2d ed. '08(O31) D. pap., 50 c. Longmans.
Old beliefs and new knowledge. New and cheaper ed. '08(O31) D. pap., 25 c. Longmans.
Religious education. [Cheaper ed.] '08 (F29) O. price reduced from *$1.25 net to *90 c. net; pap., 50 c. Longmans.

DRAWING.
Bailey, H: T., *ed.* Nature drawing from various points of view. $1.50. Davis Press.
Colby, L. E. Talks on drawing, painting, making, decorating, for primary teachers. $1.50. Scott, F. & Co.
Daniels, F: H. School drawing. $1.20. M. Bradley.
Dow, A. W. Theory and practice of teaching art. $1. Teachers' Coll.
Everett, H. E;, *and* Lawrence, W: H: Freehand and perspective drawing. $1. Am. Sch. Corr.
Haney, J. P., *ed.* Art education in the public schools of the United States. $3.50. Am. Art.
Hartmann, S. Landscape and figure composition. $3 net. Baker & T.
Neus, E. General instructions in drawing. 50 c. Sch. Liberal Arts.
Norton, D. M. Freehand perspective and sketching. $3. D. M. Norton.

DRAWING.—*Continued.*
Rankine, W. F. Nature study and brush work. *$1.25 net. Cassell.
Rawson, W. W. Manual of drawing. pt. 1. 90 c. net. Longmans.
Ruskin, J: Elements of drawing. *$1 net. Dutton.
Solomon, S. J. Practice of oil painting and of drawing as associated with it. $1.75 net. Lippincott.
Trimble, E. D. Teachers' art manual. $1.25. Carnahan.
See also Anatomy for artists;—Architectural drawing;—Book illustration; — Caricature;—Decoration and ornament;—Engineering;—Fine arts;—Mechanical drawing;—Perspective;—Topographical drawing.

DRAWING BOOKS.
Drake, B. F. Progressive drawing. 7 bks. bks. 1, 2, 3, ea., 20 c.; bks. 4, 5, 6, 7, ea., 25 c. Union Pub. Co., (Nashville.)
Seegmiller, W., *ed.* Applied arts drawing book. 6 v. v. 1-2, ea., 10 c.; v. 3-6, ea., 15 c. Atkinson, M. & G.

Drawing standards and conventions: University of Michigan, Department of Engineering, Mechanical Department. '08 (Ap11) c. il. Q. pap., 25 c. Wahr.

DRAWINGS.
Bachelor belles; with il. by H. Fisher. **$3 net. Dodd.
Book of sweethearts. $2.50. Bobbs-M.
Christy, H. C. Book of drawings. **$3 net. Moffat.
Fisher, H. American beauties. $3. Bobbs-M.
Fisher, H., *il.* American girl.—Pictures in color. ea., $3.50 net. Scribner.
Fisher, H., *il.* Garden of girls. $3.50. Dodd.
Flagg, J. M. City people. **$3.50 net. Scribner.
Hutt, H: Henry Hutt picture book. **$3 net. Century Co.
Hutt, H:, *il.* Girls. $3 net. Scribner.
Judge. Yours truly, and 100 other orig. drawings by American artists. $1.25. Judge.
Spare, A. O. Book of satyrs. *$6 net. Lane.
Underwood, C. F. Girls of to-day. **$3 net. Stokes.
See also Architecture;—Caricature;—Cartoons.

Drawings by the great masters ser. il. Q. *$2.50 net. Scribner.
—Bell. Drawings of Rembrandt.
—Hind. Drawings of Leonardo da Vinci.
—Stannus. Drawings of Alfred Stevens.
—Uzanne. Watteau.

Drawings made for commercial use. Westermann, L. A., Company. gratis. Westermann.

DRAWNWORK.
See Needlework.

DRAWYERS PRESBYTERIAN CHURCH, Odessa, Del.
Higgins, A. Historical address delivered before the "Friends of Old Drawyers" Presbyterian Church, near Odessa, Delaware. 40 c. Delaware Hist. Soc.

Dream adventures of Little Bill. Goldsborough, E. K., *jr.* $1.25. B'way Pub.

Dream and story. Carrington, H: B. *75 c. net. Pilgrim Press.
Dream blocks. Higgins. A. C. $2. Duffield.
Dream child. Huntley, *Mrs.* F. C. $1. Indo-Am. Bk.
Dream of a throne. Embree, C: F. †75 c. Little, B. & Co.
Dream of Gerontius. *See* Newman, *Cardinal* J: H:
Dream of love. Abbey, H: 75 c. Riverside Press.
Dream-road. Goold, W: D. $1 net. Sherman, F.
Dreamer (The). Stanard, *Mrs.* M. M. P. N. *$1.50 net. Bell Bk.
Dreaming back. Crawford, F. N. $1. B'way Pub.
Dreaming river. Moses, W: J: B. $1. Stokes.

DREAMS.
Xanto, *Mme.* Dream books. 50 c. Penn Pub. Co.
See also Fortune tellers.

Dreams. Ranum, *Mrs.* L. C. $1. Badger.
Dreams and realities. Corpies, L. B. (Priv. pr.) Pub. Ho. of M. E. Ch., So.
Dreams of Tommy Dimplecheek. Evans, I. C. I. $1. Neale.
Dreams of yesterdays. Matthews, *Mrs.* F. E. M. $1. Cochrane.
Dreamthorp. Smith, A. 50 c.; 75 c. Dutton.

DRED SCOTT CASE.
Ewing, E. W: R. Legal and historical status of the Dred Scott decision. $3. Cobden.
Gresham, O. Dred Scott case. (Add. author for price.) O. Gresham.

Dredging. United States. Engineer Dept. Gov. Pr. Off.

Dreier, T:
Heroes of insurgency. '10(D31) c. D. 50 c. Human Life.

Drescher, Martin.
Gedichte. '09(N) c. 219 p. por. 8°, $2. Columbia Pr.

DRESS.
See Costume;—Dressmaking;—Hygiene.

Dresser, Horatio Willis.
Greatest truth and other discourses and interpretations. '07, [1908.] (D) 10+234 p. 16°. 90 c. Progressive Lit.
Message to the well, and other essays and letters on the art of health. '10(F26) c. D. (Inner life ser.) **$1.25 net. Putnam.
Philosophy of the spirit. '08(Je6) c. O. **$2.50 net. Putnam.
Physician to the soul. '08(O17) c. D. **$1 net. Putnam.

Dressing of minerals. Louis, H: *$8.50 net. Longmans.

DRESSMAKING.
Berge, *Mme.* Every woman her own dressmaker. *$1.25 net. Doran.
Merwin, P. American system of dressmaking. $20. Am. Coll. Dressmaking.
Williams, W. R. Science of skirt drafting. $10. Gazette Co.

DREW, Daniel.
White, B., *ed.* Book of Daniel Drew. $1.50 net. Doubleday, P.

Drew sermons, 1909. Tipple, E. S., *ed.* *$1.25 net; for 1910. *$1 net. Eaton & M.

Drewry, W: Fs.
Correlation of the physician and the layman: address of the president; [del. before the Medical Society of Virginia. '09 (Ap10) 12°. (Priv. pr.) Williams Pr.

Drexel, Arnold.
Progressive barber; a book for the apprentice and for the barber. '09(S) c. 72 p. 16°, $1. Wis. State Barbers' Bd.

Driesch, Hans.
Science and philosophy of the organism: Gifford lectures, 1907. In 2 v. v. 1. '08 (Je13); v. 2. '09(Ja16) il. 8°, ea., *$3 net. Macmillan.

Drifted in. Carleton, W. $1.50. Moffat.
Drifting thistledown. Barnett, *Mrs.* P. A., *and another.* 90 c. net. Longmans.
Driftwood. De Cerkez, F. E. $1.50. Badger.
Drill jigs. '08(My23) c. il. 8°, (Machinery's reference ser.) pap., 25 c. Indust. Press.
Drill regulations. Sletzer, W: H:, *comp.* *$1 net. Lilley.

DRILLS (*fancy*).
Kellogg, A. M., *ed.* Fancy drills and marches. 50 c.; 30 c. Penn Pub. Co.
Newhall, W: B. English ball drill. 10 c. Bassette.
Reilly, F: J. "Right-dress"; simple drill regulations. 50 c. Educ. Pub.
See also Entertainments;—Freemasonry;—Songs.

DRILLS (*machinery*).
See Machinery.

Drinker, Cecil K.
See Sutton, Howard A.

Drinker, H: Sturgis, jr.
Treatise on the interstate commerce act and digest of decisions construing the same. 2 v. '09(Mr) c. 22+563; 565-1140 p. O. $10.—Supp. v. 3. '10(D) c. O. $5. Bisel.

DRINKS.
See Beverages;—Liquors.

Driver, S: Rolles, D.D.
Introd. to the literature of the Old Testament. New [10th] ed., rev. [1910.] '10 (Mr26) O. (International theological lib.) *$2.50 net. Scribner.
Modern research as illustrating the Bible; Schweich lectures, 1908. '09(N13) O. $1.20. Oxford Univ.
See also International critical commentary.

—, and Sanday, W:, D.D.
Christianity and other religions. '08(D19) 8°, 50 c. Longmans.

Dromina. Ayscough, J:, *pseud.* †$1.50. Putnam.
Drop forging. Woodworth, J. V. $2.50. Henley.
Drop forging. '09(Ag14) c. il. 8°, (Machinery's reference ser.) 25 c. Indust. Press.
Dropped from the clouds. *See* Verne, Jules.

Droste-Hülshoff, Annette Elizabeth, Freiin von.
Die Judenbuche; with introd., notes and vocab. by Dr. Ernst O. Eckelmann. '10 (Jl30) c. il. por. D. (Oxford German ser.) 60 c. Oxford Univ.

DROWNING.
United States. *Treasury Dept. Life-saving Service.* Directions for restoring the apparently drowned. (Add. Superintendent for price.) U. S., Supt. of Docs.

Druce, G: Claridge, comp.
List of British plants containing the *Spermophytes, Pteridophytes* and *Charads* found either as natives or growing in a wild state in Britain, Ireland, and the Channel Isles. '08(My23) D. pap., 85 c. Oxford Univ.

Drugging a nation Merwin, S: *$1 net. Revell.

DRUGGISTS.
Mason, H. B., *ed.* Window displays for druggists. $1. E. G. Swift.

Druggists' and dispensers' practical show-card instructor. Thompson, W: A. $1. W: A. Thompson.

DRUGS.
See Materia medica; — Medicine; — Pharmacy; — Poisons;—Stimulants and narcotics.

Drummer boy. Cuming, M. A. $1. M. A. Cuming.

Drummer boy of Shiloh. Reinhardt, V. 25 c. V. Reinhardt.

Drummers' yarns. Schofield, R. J. 25 c. Excelsior.

Drummond, And. Lewis.
True detective stories. '09(Jl31) c. por. D. $1.50. G: W. Dillingham.

Drummond, H:
Greatest thing in the world. '08(O3) D. (What is worth while ser.) leatherette, **30 c. net. Crowell.

Drummond, I. M.
See Kirkaldy, J. W.

Drummond, Josiah Hayden.
Maine masonic text book, for the use of lodges; rev. by Herbert Harris. 6th ed. '10(Je) c. 5-389 p. 16°, $1.50. Berry.

Drummond, Rob. J., D.D.
Faith's certainties. '09(D) 16+403 p. D. *$1.50 net. Doran.

Drummond, Mrs. Sara King Wiley.
Dante and Beatrice. '09(D18) c. S. **$1.25 net. Macmillan.

Drummond, W: H:, M.D.
Great fight: poems and sketches; ed., with a biographical sketch, by May Harvey Drummond. '08(O10) c. il. D. **$1.25 net. Putnam.

Drum's story. Miller, D. S. $1. Hungerford-H.

Drums of war. Stackpoole, H: D. V. $1.20 net. Duffield.

DRUNKENNESS.
See Temperance.

Drury, Bp. T: Wortley.
See Moule, Handley Carr Glyn.

DRY FARMING.
See Agriculture;—Farms and farming.

Dry farming in Wyoming. Cooke, V. T. gratis. V. T. Cooke.

DRY-GOODS.
See Bookkeeping;—Business.

Dryden, Ja.
Syllabus of illustrated lecture on the production and marketing of eggs and fowls. '09(My) 20 p. 8°, (U. S., Dept. of Agriculture, Office of Experiment Stations, Farmers' Institute lecture.) pap., 5 c.

Dryden, J:
Poetical works. Cambridge ed. '09(Ap3) c. por. O. $3. Houghton M.

Dryden, J:, and Villiers, G:, Duke of Buckingham.
Sel. dramas of John Dryden, with the rehearsal by G: Villiers, Duke of Buckingham; ed., with introd. and notes, by G: R. Noyes. '10(D3) c. O. $2. Scott, F. & Co.

DRYDEN, John.
Virgil Maro, P. Dryden's Æneid of Virgil. 75 c.; $1.25. Cassell.

Dryden, J: Fairfield.
Addresses and papers on life insurance and other subjects. '10(Ag6) por. O. (Priv. pr.) Prudential Insurance.

Drysdale, A. H., D.D.
Christ invisible our gain. '09(O30) D. *$1.25 net. Armstrong.

Drysdale, C. V.
Foundations of alternate current theory. '10(Je11) il. figs. O. $2.50 net. Longmans.

Drysdale, W:
Beach patrol; a story of the Life-Saving Service. '09(O9) c. il. D. (Brain and brawn ser.) †$1.50. Wilde.
Fast mail; the story of a train boy. '09 (O9) c. il. D. (Brain and brawn ser.) †$1.50. Wilde.
Young reporter; a story of Printing House Square. '09(O) c. il. D. (Brain and brawn ser.) †$1.50. Wilde.
Young supercargo; a story of the Merchant Marine. '09(O9) c. il. D. (Brain and brawn ser.) †$1.50. Wilde.
See also Adventures in field and forest.

Dual mind. Page, H. L. $1. Green Leaf.

Dualism of fact and idea. Talbert, E. L. 50 c. net. Univ. of Chic.

Duane, Alex.
New classification of the motor anomalies of the eye. [1910.] (Mr) *$1.25 net. W: R. Jenkins.
Formerly published by E. R. Pelton.

DU BARRY, Jeanne Bécu, *Comtesse.*
Hayes, H. K., *ed.* Du Barry, enchantress. 75 c. Estes.
Williams, H. N. Madame du Barry. *$3.50 net. Scribner.

Du Bartas, Guillaume de Salluste, Seigneur.
Divine weeks of Josuah Sylvester; mainly tr. from the French of William de Saluste, lord of the Bartas; ed., with introd., notes, emendations and excisions, by Theron Wilber Haight; collated with the quarto editions of 1608, 1611 and 1613, and the folios of 1621, 1633 and 1641. '08(D12) c. il. por. O. $2. H. M. Youmans.

DUBLIN.
See Trinity College.

Dublin book of Irish verse. Cooke, J:, *ed.* $1.75; $2.50; $3.50. Oxford Univ.

Dublin University Press ser. O. Longmans.
—Whittaker. Hist. of the theories of æther and electricity. $4.50 net.

Dubois, —, and De Geer, —.
Lectures et conversations. '09(Ja16) c. D. 75 c. W: R. Jenkins.

Du Bois, Constance Goddard.
Religion of the Luiseño Indians of southern California. '08(Ag1) il. Q. (Univ. of Cal. pubs., Am. archæology and ethnology.) pap., $1.25. Univ. of Cal.

Du Bois, Hamilton Graham.
Soul of the singer: [poems.] '08(Jl) c. 7-44 p. D. $1. Badger.

Du Bois, Ja. T.
Fun and pathos of one life. '08(D) $1. Neale.

Dubois, Louis François Alphonse Paul.
See Paul-Dubois, Louis François Alphonse.

Du Bois, Mary Constance.
Lass of the silver sword. '09(O2) c. il. D. †$1.50. Century Co.
League of the Signet Ring. '10(O1) c. il. D. $1.50. Century Co.

Du Bois, Mary R. J., comp.
Pleasant thought year book. '08(O17) c. S. **$1 net. Holt.
Poems for travelers. '08(Ag1) S. *$1.50 net. Holt.

Du Bois, Patterson.
Fire builders; true tales of child character building. '10(Jl2) c. D. bds., 35 c. net. F. M. Barton.
Point of contact in teaching. 4th ed., rev. and enl. '08(N21) 12°, 75 c. Dodd.

Dubois, Paul, M.D.
Nervous states, their nature and causes; author. tr. by E: G. Richards. '10(Ap16) D. 75 c. net. Funk.
Psychic treatment of nervous disorders; tr. and ed. by Smith Ely Jelliffe, M.D., and W: A. White, M.D. 6th ed., rev. '09(Jl17) c. O. **$3 net. Funk.
Self-control and how to secure it, (L'Education de soi-même;) author. tr. by Harry Hutcheson Boyd. '09(Ap10) c. D. **$1.50 net. Funk.

DUBOIS, Toussaint.
See Dubois Co., Ind.

Du Bois, W: E: Burghardt.
John Brown. '09(O2) c. por. maps, D. (American crisis biographies.) **$1.25 net. Jacobs.
—, ed. Economic co-operation among negro Americans; rept. of a social study made by Atlanta Univ., under the patronage of the Carnegie Institution of Washington, D. C.; together with the proceedings of the 12th conference for the study of the negro problems, held at Atlanta University. '08(Ag1) tabs., O. (Atlanta Univ. pubs.) pap., $1. Atlanta Univ.
Efforts for social betterment among negro Americans; rept. of special study made at Atlanta Univ. under the patronage of the trustees of the John F. Slater Fund; together with proceedings of the 14th Annual Conference for the Study of Negro Problems, held at Atlanta Univ., Tuesday, May 24th, 1909. '10(Jl2) O. (Atlanta Univ. pubs.) pap., 75 c. Atlanta Univ.

DUBOIS COUNTY, Ind.
Wilson, G: R. Hist. of Dubois County from its primitive days to 1910; incl. biographies of Capt. Toussaint Dubois and the Very Rev. Joseph Kundeck. $4. G: R. Wilson.

Du Bose, Horace Mellard.
Francis Asbury; biographical study. '09 (N20) c. por. D. (Methodist founders' ser.) $1. Pub. Ho. of M. E. Ch., So.
Life at its best: series of studies in the vital doctrines of consciousness; ideal and effort. '08(N) c. 152 p. 12°, 50 c. net. Pub. Ho. of M. E. Ch., So.
Men of Sapio Ranch. '09(Jl3) c. il. D. $1. Pub. Ho. of M. E. Ch., So.

Du Bose, Joel Campbell.
Alabama history. '08(D) c. 432 p. il. 12°, 75 c. B. F. Johnson.

Du Bose, W: Porcher.
High priesthood and sacrifice: exposition of the Epistle to the Hebrews. '08(Je13) c. D. (Bishop Paddock lectures, 1907-1908.) **$1.50 net. Longmans.

Du Cane, Florence.
Flowers and gardens of Japan. '08(O24) il. 8°, (Color books.) *$6 net. Macmillan.
Flowers and gardens of Madeira. '09(D25) col. il. sq. 8°, (Color books ser.) *$2 net. Macmillan.

Du Cerceau, Jacques Androuet.
French chateaux and gardens in the XVIth century; sel. and described with an account of the artist and his works by W. H. Ward. '09(Je26) il. plans, F. bds., *$10 net. Scribner.

Duchesne, Abbé Louis Marie Oliver.
Churches separated from Rome; author. tr. from the French by Arnold Harris Mathew. '08(F15) O. (International Catholic lib.) *$2 net. Benziger.
Early history of the Christian church, from its foundation to the end of the third century: rendered into English from the 4th ed. '09(Je5) O. *$2.50 net. Longmans.
Roman church before Constantine. '09 (Je19) pap., 10 c Cathedral Lib.

Duchess (The), pseud.
See Hungerford, *Mrs.* Marg. Hamilton.

Duchess of dreams. Macvane, E. †$1.50. Lippincott.

Duchess of Malfi. *See* Webster, J:

Ducklings go a-swimming. Jewett, J: H. 75 c. Small.

DUCKS.
Bradford, C: Wild-fowlers; or, duck shooting in the great lagoon. *$1 net. Nassau Press.
Ducks and geese. 3d ed.; hist. of the water fowl industry of America; articles by foremost breeders, the ablest poultry writers and the best poultry artists; complete instructions regarding the breeding, rearing, feeding, housing, marketing and exhibiting of these profitable fowls. Rev. 1910-1915 Standard ed. '10(Ap) c. 104 p. il. 4°, 75 c. Reliable Poultry Journ.
Nourse, H. A. Turkeys, ducks and geese. 50 c. Webb.

Duckworth, Fs. Robinson Gladstone.
The Cotswolds. '08(Je13) il. map, 12°, (Color books.) *$2.50 net. Macmillan.

Duclaux, Mme. Agnes Mary Frances Robison Darmesteter.
See Darmesteter, *Mme.* Agnes Mary Frances Robison.

Dudden, F: Homes, D.D.
In Christ's name: four addresses del. to candidates for ordination in the chapel of Fulham Palace, Advent, 1907; with preface by the Lord Bishop of London. '08(Ap11) O. *60 c. net. Longmans.

Dudeney, H: Ernest.
Canterbury puzzles and other curious problems. '08(Mr21) il. 12°, *$1.25 net. Dutton.

Dudeney, Mrs. H: Ernest.
Rachel Lorian. '09(Mr20) c. D. †$1.50. Duffield.
Shoulder knot. '09, [1910.] (Ja) front. 12°, $1.50. Cassell
Trespass. '09(S18) D. $1.25, fixed. Small, M.

Dudevant, Mme. Armandine Lucile Aurore Dupin.
See Sand, George, *pseud.*

Dudley, Albertus True.
At the home plate. '10(Ag20) c. il. D. (Stories of the Triangular League.) $1.25. Lothrop, L. & S.
A full-back afloat. '08(N14) c. il. D. (Phillips Exeter ser.) †$1.25 Lothrop, L. & S.
School four. '09(S11) c. il. D. (Stories of the Triangular League.) $1.25. Lothrop, L. & S.
Yale cup. '08(Ap4) c. D. (Phillips Exeter ser.) †$1.25. Lothrop, L. & S.

Dudley, Carl Hermon.
And this is war. '10(My21) 12°, $1. Cochrane.

Dudley, Edg. S.
Military law, and the procedure of courts-martial. 2d ed., rev. and enl. '09(Ja30); 3d ed., rev. '10(Ap) 12°, ea., $2.50 net. Wiley.

Dudley, E: Lawrence.
Isle of Whispers: tale of the New England seas. '10(Mr5) c. D. †$1.50. Holt.

Dudley, Emilius Clark, M.D.
Principles and practice of gynecology. 5th ed., rev. '08(Ag29) c. il. 8°, *$5 net; leath., *$6 net; hf. mor., *$6.50 net. Lea.

—, and Bachellé, Cecil von, eds.
Gynecology. '08(O17) c. il. 12°, (Practical medicine ser.) $1.25. Year Bk.

Dudley, Georgiana Eliz. Moncrieffe, Countess of, comp.
Dudley book of cookery and household recipes. '09(My8) O. *$2 net. Longmans.

Dudley, Gertrude, and Kellor, Frances Alice.
Athletic games in the education of women. '09(F27) c. D. **$1.25 net. Holt.

DUDLEY, *Lady* Jane.
See Gray, *Lady* Jane.

DUDLEY, Robert, *Earl of Leicester.*
Richardson, *Mrs.* A. Lover of Queen Elizabeth. *$3.50 special net. Appleton.

DUDLEY, Mass.
Vital records of Dudley, Mass., to the end of the year 1849. (Add. pub. for price.) F. P. Rice.

Due process of law. Schroeder, T. (Add. pubs. for price.) Free Speech.

Dueckelmann, Anna Fischer-.
See Fischer-Dueckelmann, Anna.

Duff, Alex. Wilmer, and Ewell, Arth. Woolsey.
Physical measurements. 2d ed., rev. and enl. '10(O8) c. il. O. (Blakiston science ser.) $1.50 net. Blakiston.

—, and Guthe, Karl Eugen.
Mechanics and the properties of matter, by A. Wilmer Duff, and Heat, by K. E. Guthe; from the 2d ed. of "A text-book of physics"; ed. by A. Wilmer Duff. '10 (O15) c. il. 8°, (Blakiston's science ser.) $1.60. Blakiston.

—, Guthe, Karl Eugen, Hallock, W:, [and others.]
Text-book of physics; ed. by Alex. Wilmer Duff. '08(S19) c. il. O. (Science ser.) *$2.75 net. Blakiston.

—, ed. Text-book of physics. 2d ed., rev. '09(S4) c. il. O. (Blakiston's science ser.) *$2.75 net. Blakiston.

Duff, Archibald, D.D.
Hints on Old Testament theology. '08 (Je13) 12°. *$1 net. Macmillan.
Hist. of Old Testament criticism. '10(O22) c. il. pors. S. (Hist. of the sciences.) 75 c. net. Putnam.

Duff, J: Wight.
Literary history of Rome; from the origin to the close of the Golden Age. '09 (Jl31) $4. Scribner.

Duff, Nora.
Matilda of Tuscany, la gran donna d' Italia. '09(D18) il. 8°, *$3.50 net. Dutton.

Duff, Orva S., comp.
See Lewis, H: Harrison.

Duff lectures. *See* Speer, Rob. Elliott.

Dufferin, F: Temple Blackwood, Lord.
Letters from high latitudes; with introd. by Jon Stefansson. '10(D10) il. 16°, (Everyman's lib.) 35 c. net; leath., 70 c. net. Dutton.

Duffey, Arth. F., ed.
How to sprint. '09(Jl3) front. il. 16°, (Spalding's athletic lib.) pap., 10 c. Am. Sports.

Duffy, R:
Adventure in exile. '08(D12) c. D. $1.50. B. W. Dodge.

Dufour, Fk. O.
Bridge engineering; roof trusses. '08(N21) c. il. 8°, (American School of Correspondence pubs.) $3. Am. Sch. Corr.

Dugan, W: Ja.
Manual of electro-therapeutics. '10(Jl) c. 10+242 p. il. 8°, $2. Davis.

Duggan, F. J., M.D.
Infinity, or nature's God: [verse.] '09 (Jl17) c. obl. T. leath., $1.50. F. J. Duggan.

Duggar, B: Minge.
Fungous diseases of plants; with chapters on physiology, culture methods and technique. '10(Ap9) c. il. 8°, (Country life education ser.) $2. Ginn.

Duggar, J: F:
Agriculture for southern schools. '08 (Je13) c. il. 12°, *75 c. net.—Virginia supp. '08(Ag22) c. 12°, pap., *12 c. net. Macmillan.

Dugmore, Arth. Radclyffe.
Camera adventures in the African wilds; being an acct. of a four months' expedition in British East Africa, for the purpose of securing photographs of the game from life; with 140 photographs from life by the author. '10(Mr12) c. Q. **$6 net. Doubleday, P.

Duke, Fk. Williamson.
See Colaw, J: Marvin.

Duke, T: S:
Celebrated criminal cases of America. '10 (D10) c. pors. O. $3 net. Barry.

DUKE FAMILY.
See **Genealogies: Smyth, S: G.**

Duke of Gandia. Swinburne, A. C: **$1.25 net. Harper.

Duke's motto. McCarthy, J. H. †$1.50. Harper.

Duke's price. Brown, D. V. **$1.20 net. Houghton M.

Dukesmith, Fk. Hutchinson.
Modern air-brake practice. 5th ed. '08(D) c. 419+35 p. il. 8°, $1.50. Drake.

Dulac, Edm.
Lyrics, pathetic and humorous, from A to Z. '09(O2) c. il. in col. Q. **$2 net, boxed. Warne.

Dulci fistula. Branham, G. B., *ed.* 75 c. R. F. Mason.

Dulles, Allen Macy.
True church. '08(Ja18) 12°, *$1.25 net. Revell

Dulles, C: Winslow, M.D.
Accidents and emergencies. 7th ed., thoroughly rev. and enl. '09(Ap17) c. il. figs. D. *$1 net. Blakiston.

Dulon, Julie T.
See Baker, Franklin T:

DUMA.
See **Russia.**

Dumas, Alexandre.
Works. 10 v. '10(D) $30. Crowell.
Works. 15 v. New imperial lib. ed. '10 (D) il. 8°, ea., $1.25; hf. cf., $2.25. New il. sterling ed., ea., $1. (Sets only.) Estes
Works. In 15 v. v. 1, Three musketeers; with introd. by And. Lang. '10(D10) front. 16°, (New century lib.) limp leath., $1.25. Nelson.
Ascanio. Illustrated Cabinet ed. '08(N14) 2 v. c. il. 12°, $3. Estes.
Celebrated crimes. In 4 v. v. 3, The crimes of the Marquis de Brinvilliers and others; with an introd. by R. S. Garnett. '08 (F15); v. 4, The crimes of Ali Pacha and others; with an introd. by R. S. Garnett. '08(Mr7) il. 12°, ea., $1.75. Macmillan.
Chicot the jester. '10(Ap2) 16°, (Everyman's lib.) 35 c. net; leath., 70 c. net. Dutton.
Count of Monte Cristo. 2 v. '10(D) il $2.50, boxed. Crowell.
Count of Monte Cristo. 2 v. '09(O30) 12°, (Everyman's lib.) ea., *35 c. net; leath., *70 c. net. Dutton.
Episodes from Les trois mousquetaires; ed., with introd., notes and vocab., by I. H. B. Spier. '10(D) 5+188 p. por. maps, 16°, (Heath's modern language ser.) 45 c. net. Heath.

Dumas, Alexandre.—*Continued.*
The forty-five. '10(Ap2) 16°, (Everyman's lib.) 35 c. net; leath., 70 c. net. Dutton.
Le Comte de Monte-Cristo; l'emprisonment; l'évasion; la découverte du trésor; ed., with notes, exercises and vocab., by C. Fontaine. '09(Ag7) c. map, 40 c. Am. Bk.
L'evasion, épisode tiré de Vingt ans après; abrgd. and ed. by R. T. Currall. '09(O16) S. (Crowell's shorter French texts.) *25 c. net. Crowell.
Man in the iron mask. '08(Jl11) 12°, (Magnolia lib.) 50 c. Hurst.
Marguerite de Valois. '08(S19) 16°, (Everyman's lib.) *35 c. net; leath., *70 c. net. Dutton.
My memoirs; tr. by E. M. Waller; with an introd. by And. Lang. In 6 v. v. 3. '08(Mr7); v. 4 (Je27); v. 5 (O24); v. 6. '09(Je19) front. 12°, ea., *$1.75 net. (Sold in sets only.) Macmillan.
My pets; newly tr. by Alfred Allinson. '09(O30) il. D. *$1.75 net. Macmillan.
Olympe de Cleves. Illustrated cabinet ed. 2 v. '08(D19) c. il. 12°, $3. Estes.
Pages choisies par B. L. Templeton. '10 (D24) D. (Cours de français et d'allemand.) 50 c. Oxford Univ.
Récits tirés des Impressions de voyage (Le midi de la France); ed. by J. E. Mansion. '09(O16) S. (Crowell's shorter French texts.) *25 c. net. Crowell.
Tales; Le voyage des Mousquetaires, Le dîner de Porthos, Le bastion de Saint-Gervais; with notes and vocab. '10(D24) c. il. 16°, 25 c. net. Macmillan.
Three musketeers. '08(O10) 12°, ("Best books" ser.) leath., *$1 net. Dutton.
Three musketeers. '10(O) il. 8°, $1.50. Fenno.
Twenty years after. '08(O10) 12°. ("Best books" ser.) leath., *$1 net. Dutton.
Twenty years after. '10(O) il. 8°, $1.50. Fenno.

Du Maurier, Guy L: Busson.
Englishman's home: a play. '09(Ap24) c. O. $1.25. Harper.

DUMB.
See **Deaf and dumb.**

DUMB BELLS.
Bojus, G. H. Dumb bell exercises. 10 c. Am. Sports.

Dumesnil, Amant H: Ohmann, M.D.
Diseases of the skin. 3d ed. '08, [1910.] (O) 593 p. il. 8°, $4. Mosby.

Dummelow, Rev. J: Roberts, ed.
Commentary on the Holy Bible, by various writers; with general articles and maps. Complete in 1 v. '09(Mr6) c. O. **$2.50 net. Macmillan.

Dummkopf (Der). Fulda, L. 35 c. Holt.

Dumont, Fk.
Caught with the goods: a sketch in one act; The district convention: a burlesque; The half-breed: a western drama. '08 (N7) D. pap., ea., 15 c. Penn Pub. Co.
Girl from "L Triangle" Ranch: a drama; The night riders: a melodrama; The old New Hampshire home: a melodrama. '08 (N7) c. D. pap., ea., 25 c. Penn Pub. Co.

Dumont, H:
A golden fancy, and other poems. '10(S) c. 114 p. por. 8°, $1.25. Chapple Pub.

DUMOURIEZ, Charles Francois.
Rose, J. H. Dumouriez and the defense of England against Napoleon. *$5 net. Lane.

Dumpy books for children. il. T. †50 c. Stokes.
—Bannerman. Story of little black Quasha.
—Layard. Harriet Hare.

Dunbar, Booth C:
See Verrill, Harry Mighels.

Dunbar, J: Brown.
"White man's foot in Kansas": address at the Pawnee Village, Republic County, Kansas, Sept. 27, 1906, celebrating the 100th anniversary of the flag in Kansas. '09(Ag7) il. fold. maps, O. pap., gratis. State Hist., Kan.

Dunbar, Paul Laurence.
Lyrics of lowly life; with an introd. by W: Dean Howells. '08(N14) c. il. O. **$1.60 net. Dodd.

Dunbar, W. H.
See Alleman, Herbert Christian.

Dunbar, W: Philipps.
Principles of sewage treatment; tr., with the author's sanction, by H. T. Calvert. '08(D19) il. 8°, *$4.50 net. Lippincott.

Duncan, Carson S.
See Denney, Jos. Villiers.

Duncan, D:
Life and letters of Herbert Spencer. '08 (Je6) c. 2 v., pors. O. **$5 net. Appleton.

Duncan, F. Martin.
Denizens of the deep. '07, [1909.] (Jl) 8+151 p. il. $1.75. Cassell.

Duncan, Frances.
When mother lets us garden. '09(Ap24) c. il. O. **75 c. net. Moffat.

Duncan, Isadora.
The dance. Authorized ed. '09(D4) c. pors. Q. pap., 50 c.; bds., $1. Forest Press.

Duncan, J: Garrow.
Exploration of Egypt and the Old Testament. '09(Mr6) 12°, *$1.50 net. Revell.

Duncan, Canon Jos.
Popular hymns. '10(D24) 12°, $2 net. Whittaker.

Duncan, Norman.
Billy Topsail and Company. '10(Jl16) c. 12°, $1.50. Revell.
Christmas eve at Topmast Tickle. '10 (S17) c. 12°, (Idyll envelope ser.) pap., 25 c., in envelope. Revell.
Every man for himself. '08(S26) c. il. D. †$1.50. Harper.
Going down from Jerusalem; the narrative of a sentimental traveller. '09(O23) c. il. O. **$1.50 net. Harper.
Higgins: a man's Christian. '09(N20) c. por. S. 50 c. Harper.
Suitable child. '09(O23) c. il. D. bds., *60 c. net; decorated bds., *$1 net. Revell.

Duncan, R. Howard.
Pract. curve tracing, with chapters on differentiation and integration. '10(My21) il. O. $1.60 net. Longmans.

DUNCAN, William.
Arctander, K. J. L. W. A. Apostle of Alaska: story of William Duncan of Metlakhtla. *$1.50 net. Revell.

Duncon, J:
Lady Lettice, Viscountess Falkland; ed., with introd., by M. F. Howard. '08 (My9) il. pors. 12°, *$2 net. Dutton.

Dungan, D: Roberts.
Outline studies in the life of Christ. '09, [1910.] (Mr) c. 94 p. 12°, 25 c. D: R. Dungan.

Dunglison, R: Ja.
New school physiology and hygiene. '08 (D5) c. il. 12°, (Werner educational ser.) *$1 net. Am. Bk.

Dunham, Mrs. Anna Cross, [Tabitha Ann Cross.]
Corduroy road; tale of pioneer life in the middle west in the early 40's. '10(Ja22) c. 234 p. il. O. $1.25. Werner Co.

Dunham, Curtis.
Gambolling with Galatea. '09(Je5) c. il. D. **$1.15 net. Houghton M.

Dunham, W: Russell, M.D.
Science of human life; the world's postponed problem the operative plan of vital force. '10(D3) c. D. $1. Badger.

Dunkerley, S.
Hydraulics. In 2 v. v. 2, The resistance and propulsion of ships. '08(Ag1) O. $3. Longmans.

Dunlap, Boutwell.
See Cowan, Rob. Ernest.

Dunlap, C: Eug.
Non-sectarian peacemaker and the churches at Frictionville. '10(Ap) 200 p. 16°, 50 c. C: E. Dunlap.

Dunlap, Lina.
Candlelight tea; book of recipes. '10(D17) c. 8°, $1. Transylvania.
Contents: Beverages; Salads; Sandwiches.
Heart of the wheat; book of recipes. '10 (D17) c. 8°, $1. Transylvania.
Contents: Breads; Cakes; Pies.
Out of the blue grass; book of recipes. '10 (D17) c. 8°, $1. Transylvania.
Contents: Soups; Meats; Vegetables.

Dunlop, W:, M.D.
Recollections of the war of 1812; with a biographical sketch of the author by A. H. U. Colquhoun. 2d ed. '08(D5) D. por. (U. E. ser.) $1. Hist. Pub.

Dunmore, Wa. T.
Federal regulation of railway rates. '08 (D5) **$1 net. Houghton M.

DUNMORE'S EXPEDITION.
See Point Pleasant (Battle of).

Dunn, Arth. W:
Civics, the community and the citizen; rev. by the State Text-book Committee and approved by the State Board of Education. '10(N12) il. 12°, (California state ser.) 50 c. Cal. Dept. Pub. Instruction.

Dunn, Byron Archibald.
With Lyon in Missouri. '10(O22) c. D. (Young Missourian ser.) $1.25. McClurg.

Dunn, Eliza.
Rugs in their native land. '10(D10) c. il. (partly in col.) O. $2.50 net. Dodd.

Dunn, Jacob Piatt.
Greater Indianapolis; hist., the industries, the institutions, and the people of a city of homes. 2 v. '10(N12) c. il. pors. 4°, $20. Lewis Pub. Co.
True Indian stories; with glossary of Indiana Indian names. '08(N7) c. il. por. maps, 12°, $1. Sentinel.

—, and Wrigley, Mrs. Sarah A. Finley.
Word Hoosier, by Jacob Piatt Dunn and John Finley, by Mrs. Sarah A. Wrigley, (his daughter.) '07, [1909.] (Mr) 37 p. 8°, (Indiana Historical Society pubs.) *50 c. net. Bobbs-M.

DUNN, John Ainsworth.
Cary, S. C., *comp.* John Ainsworth Dunn. Gardner, Mass. (Not for sale.) S. C. Cary.

Dunn, L: Vincent.
Catholic church in Clinton County, Iowa; facts learned from pioneer records. '08 (Ag1) il. pors. 8°, $2. Torch Press.

Dunn, Rob. Lee.
William Howard Taft, American. '08 (Ag8) $1. Chapple Pub.

Dunn, W:
See Marsh, C: Fleming.

Dunn-Pattison, Reginald Philipson.
Black Prince. '10(Jl30) il. maps, plans, 4°, $2.50 net. Dutton.
Napoleon's marshals. '09(O2) il. O. *$3 net. Little, B. & Co.

Dunne, Finley P:, ["Mr. Dooley."]
Mr. Dooley says. '10(S17) c. D. $1 net. Scribner.

Dunnell, Mark Boothby.
See Minnesota digest.

Dunning, Ja. Edm.
Master builders. '09(Je19) c. front. D. †$1.50. Appleton.

Dunning, Ralph Cheever.
Hyllus; a drama. '10(Jl30) D. $1.25 net. Lane.

Dunraven, Earl of, [T: Wyndham-Quin Windham.]
Self-instruction in the practice and theory of navigation. Rev. and enl. ed. In 3 v. '08(F29) il. 8°, per set, *$8 net. Macmillan.

Duns, Mary Amelia.
Pract. care and feeding of children. 2d ed., rev. and enl. '09, [1910.] c. 150 p. por. 12°, $1.50. Chic. Med. Bk.

Dunseath, Ja. R.
See Arizona Territory. *Sup. ct.* Repts.

Dunton, Edith Kellogg.
See Warde, Marg., *pseud.*

Dunton, Lucy, pseud.
See Cable, Lucy Leffingwell.

Dunwoodie books of games. D. Brentano's.
—Ayres. Bridge. *$1 net.

DUODENUM.
See Intestines.

Dupe (The). Biss, G. †$1.50. Brentano's.

Du Plantz, Marguerite.
See Owen, Marg. Cuncliffe.

Duplicate death. Fox-Davies, A. C: $1.50. Macaulay.

Du Pont de Nemours, E. I., Powder Co.
Useful information for practical men. '08 (Ap18) il. tabs., S. leath., $1. Du Pont de Nemours.

Du Pont de Nemours, Philip Fs.
Currente calamo: [poems.] '08(Ja18) por. 8°, $1.50. Patterson & W.

Du Puis, Brother Fs.
Life and legend of the lady Saint Clare; tr. from the French version (1563) by Charlotte Balfour; with introd. by Father Cuthbert. '10(D3) il. D. $1.25 net. Longmans.

Dupuy, Rev. B: Hunter.
Huguenot Bartholomew Dupuy and his descendants. '08(My16) c. 8°, $6.50. B: H. Dupuy.

DuPuy, C: Meredith.
Genealogical hist. of the Dupuy family, by C: Meredith DuPuy; with additions by his son Herbert DuPuy. '10(Jl) 9+165 p. col. front. (coat of arms) il. pors. map, facsims., fold. tabs., 4°. (Priv. pr.) H. DuPuy.
Contains genealogical notes of the Haskins, Richards, Evans, Richardson, Loockermans, Hostetter and Rickey families.

DUPUY FAMILY.
See Genealogies.

Durable satisfactions of life. Eliot, C: W. $1. Crowell.

Durand, A.
Childhood of Jesus Christ according to the canonical Gospels; with historical essay on the brethren of the Lord; author. tr. from the French; ed. by Rev. Jos. Bruneau. '10(Je4) c. 12°, $1.50 net. McVey.

Durand, Mme. Alice Marie Céleste Fleury, ["Henry Gréville."]
Dosia; ouvrage couronné par L'Académie Française; with introd., notes and vocabulary by Thdr. E. Hamilton. '10(F12) c. S. (Heath's modern lang. ser.) 45 c. Heath.

Durand, Sir H: Mortimer.
Nadir Shah. '09(Je5) il. 8°, *$3 net. Dutton.

Durand, Ja. Benedict.
Songs in the night, and other poems; also a memoir of the author by Silas H. Durand. '09(Jl) 66 p. por. 12°, 50 c. S. H. Durand.

Durand, Ralph.
Oxford, its buildings and gardens. '10 (D24) col. il. Q. $5 net. Duffield.

Durand, W: F:
Researches on the performance of the screw propeller. '08(J4) il. Q. (Carnegie Institution of Washington pub.) pap., 75 c. Carnegie.
Resistance and propulsion of ships. 2d ed., rev. '09(F20) c. 8°, $5. Wiley.

Duras, Victor Hugo.
Universal peace. '08(Je20) c. por. O $2. B'way Pub.

Duration and disappearance of passive diphtheric immunity. Goodman, H. M. 25 c. H. M. Goodman.

Durell, Clement V.
Course of plane geometry for advanced students. pt. 1. '09(Ap3) diagrs., 8°, *$1.50 net; pt. 2. '10(Jl16) il. 8°, $2.40 net. Macmillan.

Durell, Fletcher.
Logarithmic and trigonometric tables. '10 (My14) 8°, 75 c. C: E. Merrill.
Plane trigonometry. '10(My14) c. il. 8°, $1; bound with Logarithmic and trigonometric tables, $1.25. C: E. Merrill.
Durell, J. C.
Self-revelation of our Lord. '10(Ag27) 8°, $2 net. Scribner.
Dürer, Albrecht.
Masterpieces. '09(D25) il. T. (Painters' ser.) leath., *75 c. net; pap., *25 c. net. Stokes.
DÜRER, Albrecht.
Furst, H. E. A. Dürer. $1.50 net. Stokes.
Duret, Theodore.
Manet and the French impressionists; tr. by J. E. Crawford Flitch. '10(F19) 4°, *$3.75 net. Lippincott.
Durgin, G: Fs.
Letters from Labrador. '08(My9) c. il. por. 12°, gratis. Rumford Pr.
Durham, Mary Edith.
High Albania. '09(D4) il. O. *$4 net. Longmans.
Durham, Rob. Lee.
Call of the South. '08(Ap4) c. D. $1.50. L. C. Page.
"Durham, Victor G.," pseud.
Submarine boys and the middies; or, the prize detail at Annapolis. '10(D) il. 12°, (Submarine boys ser.) $1. Altemus.
Submarine boys and the spies; or, dodging the sharks of the deep. '10(D) il. 12°, (Submarine boys ser.) $1. Altemus.
Submarine boys for the flag; or, deeding their lives to Uncle Sam. '10(D) il. 12°, (Submarine boys ser.) $1. Altemus.
Submarine boys' lightning cruise; or, the young kings of the deep. '10(D) il. 12°, (Submarine boys ser.) $1. Altemus.
Submarine boys on duty; or, life on a diving torpedo boat. '09(D18) c. il. 12°, $1. Altemus.
Submarine boys' trial trip; or, "making good" as young experts. '10(D) il. 12°, (Submarine boys ser.) $1. Altemus.
Durham, Willard Higley.
See MacCracken, H: Noble.
Düring, Mrs. Stella M.
End of the rainbow. '10(O8) c. front. D. $1.50. Lippincott.
Love's privilege. '09(My22) c. il. D. †$1.50. Lippincott.
During the Reign of Terror. Elliott, G. D. $1.50 net. Sturgis & W.
Durkee, Fk. W:
Experiments in general inorganic chemistry. 2d ed., rev. '10(F12) 50 c. Tufts Coll.
Durkee, Rev. Jacob Hilton, ed. and comp.
Hist. of the World's Temperance Centennial Congress; and memorial of Dr. Billy J. Clark, held at Saratoga Springs, N. Y., June 14-23, 1908. '08(N) c. 199 p. il. pl. 8°, $1. J. H Durkee.
DURKEE, Ruel.
Browne, G: W. Ruel Durkee [fiction]. $1.50. Badger.
Durley, Ella Hamilton.
My soldier lady. '08(D12) il. 12°, $1.50. C. M. Clark.

Durning-Lawrence, Sir Edn.
Bacon is Shakespeare; together with a reprint of Bacon's Promus of the formularies, and elegancies, collated, with the orig. ms. by the late E. B. Bickley and rev. by F. A. Herbert. '10(O8) c. il. pors. facsims., O. $1 net. J: McBride.
Durrant, W: Scott.
Cross and dagger; Crusade of the children. '10(O8) il. D. $1.50. Lane.
Durrett, Reuben T:
Traditions of the earliest visits of foreigners to North America, the first formed and first inhabited of the continents. '08 (Ap18) c. por. il. 4°, (Filson Club pubs.) pap., $4. Morton.
Duruy, Jean Victor.
Hist. of France. 2 v. '10(D) il. $2.50, boxed. Crowell.
Dushaw, Amos I.
Proselytes of the Ghetto. '09(O) c. 128 p. 8°, 75 c. J. Heidingsfeld.
DUST.
See Hygiene;—Roads.
Dustless roads. Smith, J. W. *$3.50 net. Lippincott.
Dustman, Urias M.
Book of plans and building construction for general contractors and home builders. 2d ed. '10(D3) c. obl. O. $2. C: C. Thompson.
DUTCH ART.
See Painters and painting.
Dutch bulbs and gardens. Silberrad, U. L. *$2 net. Macmillan.
Dutch ditties for children. Terhune, A. $1.25. Schirmer.
DUTCH IN THE UNITED STATES.
Huizinga, G: F. What the Dutch have done in the west of the United States. (Priv. pr.) E: Bok.
Netherland Chamber of Commerce in America, New York City, 1609-1909; the Dutch in New Netherland and the United States. 75 c. Netherland Chamber of Com.
Dutch nation. Motley, J: L. $1.75. Harper.
Dutch New York. Singleton, E. *$3.50 net. Dodd.
Dutch painters ser. T. leath., *75 c. net; pap., *25 c. net. Stokes.
—Israels. Masterpieces.
—Jordaens. Masterpieces.
—Maris. Masterpieces.
—Mauve. Masterpieces.
—Metsu. Masterpieces.
—Ostade. Masterpieces.
—Steen. Masterpieces.
—Van der Weyden. Masterpieces.
—Vermeer. Masterpieces.
DUTCH REFORMED CHURCH.
See Reformed church.
DUTCH REFORMED CHURCH, Port Richmond, S. I.
See New York City.
Dutch standard in the U. S. tariff law. (Add. Superintendent for price.) U. S., Supt. of Docs.
DUTCHESS COUNTY, N. Y.
Book of the supervisors of Dutchess County, N. Y., 1718-1722. (Add. pubs. for price.) Vassar Bros.

DUTCHESS COUNTY, N. Y.—*Continued.*
Hasbrouck, F., *ed.* Hist. of Dutchess County, New York. $15. S. A. Matthieu.
Old miscellaneous records of Dutchess County: the second book of the supervisors and assessors. '09, [1910.] (Ap) 80+91-195 p. il. Q. pap. (Priv. pr.) Vassar Bros.

Dutchie doings. Parkinson, E. $1. Dodge.

Duthie, Arth. L:
Decorative glass processes. '09(Mr13) il. 8°, (Westminster ser.) **$2 net. Van Nostrand.
Ornamental window glass work. '08(D5) il. 8°, (Westminster ser.) *$2 net. Van Nostrand.
Practical church decoration: guide to the design and execution of decoration of churches, chapels and other ecclesiasical structures. '08(Mr21) il. 12°, (Decorator ser. of practical books.) $1.25. Painters' Mag.

Duthie, Rev. D. Wallace, ed.
Bishop in the rough '09(Je12) il. 8°, *$2 net. Dutton.

DUTIES.
See Tariff.

Duties and beauties of life. Rowe, F: L: $2.50; $3.50. F: L: Rowe.

Duties and liabilities of bank directors. Alcorn, E. G. $1.50. Financial Pub.

Duties of the heart. Bachye, *Rabbi.* *40 c. net. Dutton.

Du Toit, A. L.
See Rogers, Arth. W.

Dutt, W: Alfr.
Norfolk. '09, [1910.] (F) 8+156 p. 8°, (Cambridge county geographies.) *45 c. net. Putnam.
Norfolk and Suffolk coast. '10(D17) O. (County coast ser.) $2.25 net. Stokes.
Suffolk. '09, [1910.] (F) 8°, (Cambridge county geographies.) *45 c. net. Putnam.

Dutton, A. I., ed.
How to sell an Overland; collection of strong and effective selling points for the benefit of dealers selling Overland automobiles, used successfully by some of the best motor-car salesmen in America; ed. by A. I. Dutton. [1910.] (Jl) c. 144 p. il. 8°, $2. Willys-Overland.

Dutton, L. M.
See Knight, Fs. A.

Dutton, Maude Barrows, comp.
Tortoise and the geese, and other fables of Bidpai. '08(O17) c. il. D. $1. Houghton M.

Dutton, S: Train, and Snedden, D: S:
Administration of public education in the United States; with an introd. by N: Murray Butler. '08(O17) 12°, *$1.75 net. Macmillan.

Dutton's ancient cities; ed. by B. C. A. Windle. il. 12°, *$1.75 net. Dutton.
—Holmes. Wells and Glastonbury.

Dutton's best books ser. 16°, *$1 net. Dutton.
—Addison. *The Spectator.* 4 v.
—Antoninus. Meditations.
—Augustine, *St.* Confessions.

Dutton's best books ser.—Continued.
—Austen. Emma.—Mansfield Park.—Northanger Abbey, and Persuasion.—Pride and prejudice.—Sense and sensibility.
—Bacon. Essays.
—Bible. Old Testament. 4 v.—New Testament.
—Blackmore. Lorna Doone.
—Boswell. Life of Johnson. 2 v.
—Browning. Poems and plays, 1833-1844.—1844-1864.
—Bulwer-Lytton. Last days of Pompeii.
—Burns. Poems and songs.
—Carlyle. Hist. of the French Revolution.—Sartor resartus.—Heroes and hero worship.
—Chaucer. Canterbury tales.
—Craik. John Halifax.
—Dante. Divine comedy.
—Dickens. David Copperfield.
—Dumas. Three musketeers.—Twenty years after.
—Eliot. Adam Bede.—Romola.—Silas Marner.
—Emerson. Essays: 1st and 2d ser.
—Evelyn. Diary. 2 v.
—Gaskell. Cranford.
—Goldsmith. Vicar of Wakefield.
—Holmes. Autocrat of the breakfast table.—Professor of the breakfast table.
—Irving. Sketch book.
—Keats. Poetical works.
—Kingsley. Westward ho!
—Lamb. Essays of Elia.—Tales from Shakespeare.
—Macaulay. Essays.—Hist. of England. 3 v.
—Malory. Le morte d' Arthur. 2 v.
—Manning. Household of Sir Thomas More.
—Motley. Rise of the Dutch Republic. 3 v.
—Palgrave. Golden treasury.
—Pepys. Diary. 2 v.
—Plato. The republic.
—Prescott. Conquest of Peru.
—Reade. Cloister and the hearth.
—Robertson. Sermons on Bible subjects.—Sermons on Christian doctrine.—Sermons on religion and life.
—Ruskin. Elements of drawing.—Ethics of the dust.—Modern painters. 5 v.—Pre-Raphaelitism.—Sesame and lilies.—Seven lamps of architecture.—Stones of Venice. 3 v.—Unto this last.
—Scott. Ivanhoe.
—Shakespeare. Comedies.—Histories and poems.—Tragedies.
—Shelley. Poetical works.
—Sheridan. Plays.
—Sismondi. History of the Italian republics.
—Stanley. Memorials of Canterbury.
—Tennyson. Poems, 1830-1863.
—Thackeray. History of Henry Esmond.
—Thoreau. Walden.
—Trollope. Barchester Towers.—Framley Parsonage.—The warden.
—Wordsworth. Longer poems.—Shorter poems.

Dutton's children's heroes ser.; ed. by J: Lang. il. 16°, 50 c. Dutton.
—Marshall. Story of Cromwell.—Story of Napoleon.

Dutton's English lib. 16°, *75 c. net. Dutton.
—Harris, *comp.* First printed translations into English of the great foreign classics.
—Zielinski. Our debt to antiquity.

Dutton's English masterpieces ser. 16°, 50 c.; pap., 25 c. Dutton.
—Browning. Sonnets from the Portuguese.
Dutton's every child's lib. il. 16°, 50 c. Dutton.
—Addison. Sir Roger de Coverley.
—Cartwright. Brave Beowulf.—One for Wod and one for Lok.
—Old, old myths of Greece and Rome.
—Reynard the fox.
—Seven champions of Christendom.
—Sigurd the dragon slayer.
—Sterne. My Uncle Toby.
Dutton's everyman's lib. See Everyman's.
Dutton's holiday annual; ed. by Alfr. C. Playne: with stories by W. H. D. Rouse, E. Nesbit, G. A. Henty, [and others.] '08 (N7); '10(D) il. Q. ea., $2; bds., $1.25. Dutton.
Dutton's miniature reference lib. 32°, padded leath., 50 c. Dutton.
—Baylee. Gazetteer of the world.
—Bower. Dictionary of economic terms.
—Brown *and* Martin. French and English dictionary.
—Butler. Dictionary of philosophical terms.
—Dawson. Book of the saints.—Nicknames and pseudonyms.
—Feller. New pocket dictionary of German-English and English-German.
—Hensman *and* Webb. When and where of famous men and women.
—Hyamson. Dictionary of artists and art terms.—Newspaper reader's campanion.
—Schwann. German-French and French-German pocket dictionary.
—Sonnenschein. Five thousand words frequently misspelt.
—Tucker. Book of anniversaries.
—Villiers. Dict. of foreign and American literature.
—Vivian. Dictionary of literary terms.
—Wesseley *and* Gray. English-Italian dictionary.
—Woodhouse. Dictionary of classical mythology.
Dutton's new lib. of medicine. 8°, *$2.50 net. Dutton.
—Oliver. Diseases of occupation.
—Schofield. Functional nerve diseases.
Dutton's new universal lib. 12° and 16°, *50 c. net; leath., *75 c. net. Dutton.
—Addison *and* Steele. The spectator. v. 1-6.
—Ainsworth. Crichton.—Flitch of bacon.—Guy Fawkes.—Miser's daughter.—The spendthrift.
—Aristophanes. Plays.
—Bulwer-Lytton. Rienzi.
—Caine. Cobwebs of criticism.
—Coleridge. Complete poetical works.—Lectures and notes on Shakespeare.
—Comte. General view of positivism.
—Galt. Annals of the parish.
—Guérin. Journal.
—Hazlitt. Lectures on the English poets.
—Irving. Sketch book.
—Knight. Shadows of the old booksellers.
—Lyall. Poems.
—Mill. Auguste Comte.—Utilitarianism.
—Muller. Comparative mythology.
—Patterson. Essays.
—Ruskin. Crown of wild olive.—Ethics of the dust.
Dutton's new universal lib.—Continued.
—Sainte-Beuve. Causeries du lundi. v. 2-7.
—Seeley. Ecce homo.
—Smith. Dreamthorp.
—Sophocles. Tragedies.
—White. Poems, letters and prose fragments.
Dutton's oval ser. 12°, 50 c. Dutton.
—Hearne. Motoring.
—Holland. How to use a camera.
Dutton's popular lib. of art. il. 16°, *75 c. net; leath., *$1 net. Dutton.
—Chesson. Cruikshank.
—Sickert. Whistler.
Dutton's stories from history ser.; ed. by J: Lang. il. T. 50 c. Dutton.
—Dalkeith. Stories from Roman history.
—Kelman, Stories from the Crusades.
—Macgregor. Stories of the Vikings.
—Skae. Stories from English history.
Dutton's told to the children ser.; ed. by Louey Chisholm. il. 16°, 50 c. Dutton.
—Æsop. Fables.
—Andersen. Fairy tales.
—Bunyan. Pilgrim's progress.
—Cameron. Stories of the ballads.
—Chisholm. Simple Susan.—Stories from Shakespeare. 2d ser.
—Dalkeith. Little plays.
—Dante. Stories from Dante.
—Defoe. Robinson Crusoe.
—Chisholm, *ed.* Nursery rhymes.
—Grimm. Stories from Grimm.
—Hawthorne. Tanglewood tales.
—Kingsley. The heroes.
—Lang. Stories from Shakespeare. 1st ser.
—MacGregor. Stories from Dante.—Stories from the ballads.—Stories of Siegfried.—Stories of three saints.—Undine.
—Marshall. Stories of Beowulf.—Stories of Guy of Warwick.—Stories of Roland.
—Smith. Stories from Wagner.
—Steedman. Nursery tales.
—Stowe. Uncle Tom's cabin.
—Thackeray. Rose and the ring.
DUTY.
See **Conduct of life;—Ethics.**
Duty of altruism. McConnell, R. M. $1.50 net. Macmillan.
Duty of being beautiful. Hubbard, *Mrs.* S. A. 50 c. McClurg.
Duty of happiness. Lubbock, *Sir* J: 40 c.; 75 c. Caldwell.
DUXBURY, Mass.
Bradford, L. Historic Duxbury in Plymouth County, Mass. $1. G. Bradford.
Duyckinck, Whitehead Cornell, and Cornell, Rev. J:
Duyckinck and allied families. '08, [1909.] (F) $5. T. A. Wright.
DUYCKINCK FAMILY.
See **Genealogies.**
Dweller on the borderland. Lanza, C. H., *Marquise.* $1.50. McVey.
Dwellers ser. 6 v. '10(Mr26) il. 8°, ea., *50 c. net. Jacobs.
DWELLINGS.
See Architecture.
Dwigg ser. See Dwiggins, Clare Victor.

Dwiggins, Clare Victor.
Wants. '09, [1910.] (S) il. 16°, (Dwigg ser.) $1; ooze cf., $1.50. Winston.
—, comp. and il. Toasts. '08(S19) shaped, 35 c., boxed. Winston.

Dwight, E: L.
See United States statute citer-digest.

Dyar, Muriel Campbell.
Davie and Elisabeth. '08(O17) c. front. D. †$1. Harper.

Dyar, Ralph E.
Hicks at college: comedy in three acts. '09(N) 16°, pap., 25 c. Dramatic.

Dye, J: T.
Ideals of democracy. '09(Ap24) c. D. **90 c. net. Bobbs-M.

DYEING.
Baird, H: C. Pract. dry cleaner, scourer and garment dyer. *$2.50 net. Baird.
Farrell, F. Dyeing and cleaning. (Add. pubs. for price.) Lippincott.
Knecht, E., *and others.* Manual of dyeing. 2 v. *$12 net. Lippincott.
Mathews, J. M. Laboratory manual of dyeing and textile chemistry. $3.50. Wiley.
Mulliken, S: P. Method for the identification of pure organic compounds. v. 3, Identification of the commercial dyestuffs. $5. Wiley.
Olney, L: A. Textile chemistry and dyeing $3. Am. Sch Corr.
Owen, F. A., *and* Standage, H. C. Dyeing and cleaning of textile fabrics. $2. Wiley.
Pawlie, E: Pract. hdbk. of garment dyeing and cleaning. $3.75. M. M. Frank.
Prag, E: Course in dyeing for garment dyers. $5. Modern Dyer.
See also Spectra.

Dyer, Fk. Lewis, and Martin, T: Commerford.
Edison, his life and inventions. In 2 v. '10(N19) c. il. pors. O. $4. Harper.

Dyer, F: H., comp.
Compendium of the war of the rebellion; comp and arranged from official records of the Federal and Confederate armies. '08(Ag1) 8°, hf. mor., *$10 net. Torch Press.

Dyer, I: W., comp.
See Maine corporation law.

Dyer, Wa. Alden.
Lure of the antique; being a book of ready reference for collectors of old furniture, china, mirrors, candlesticks, silverware, pewter, glassware, copper utensils, clocks, and other household furnishings of our American forefathers. '10(O15) c. il. O. $2.40 net. Century Co.

Dygert, H. Arth.
Crops that pay: pecans, mangoes, avocados, pineapples: what they are; where and how they grow; what profit they give. '08(Jl4) c. 12°, pap., 10 c. Am. Nut & Fruit Co.

Dyke, And. Lee.
Anatomy of the automobile. '08(Ap11) c. il. 12°, $2. A. L. Dyke.
Course of automobile engineering in 24 lessons. '09(My8) c. il. $10. A. L. Dyke.
Troubles, remedies and repairs of the automobile and gasoline engine. '09(Ap10) c. il. D. $2. A. L. Dyke.

Dyke, And. Lee, and Dorris, G. Preston.
Diseases of a gasolene automobile and how to cure them. [Rev. ed.] '08(Ap11) c. il. D. $1. A. L. Dyke.

Dyke, Oliver Opp-.
See Opp-Dyke, Oliver.

Dyke's automobile and gasoline engine encyclop. '10(D17) il. 4°, $3. A. L. Dyke.

Dyke's Corners. Oakley, E. C. $1.50. Badger.

Dykes, Ja. Oswald.
Divine worker in creation and Providence. '10(Ja22) $2.25. Scribner.

Dyllington, J: W. Anthony.
Green domino: a comedy. '08(O24) 12°, $1.50. Lane.
Unseen thing; novel. '10(Jl30) D. $1.20 net. J: W. Luce.

Dymond, C: W.
Key to the theory and methods of linear perspective. '10(D17) 12°, 75 c. Spon.

Dynamic meteorology. Bjerknes, V. F. K. Carnegie.

Dynamic school of to-morrow. Hildebrand, F. A. $2. Aberdeen.

Dynamic theory of life and mind. Alexander, J. B. $2.75. J. B. Alexander.

Dynamical theory of sound. Lamb, H. *$3.50 net. Longmans.

DYNAMICS.
Ferry, E. S. Brief course in elementary dynamics for students of engineering. *$1.25 net. Macmillan.
Lunn, A. C. Differential equations of dynamics. (Add. author for price.) A. C. Lunn.
Reeve, S. A. Energy, work, heat and transformations. *$2 net. McGraw-H.
See also Electricity;—Heat;—Mechanics;—Physics;—Sound;—Statics.

Dynamics of organism. Terry, S. B. (Add. pubs. for price.) Terry.

Dynamiter. Stevenson, R. L. 50 c. Hurst.

Dynamo, motor, and switchboard circuits. Bowker, W: R. *$2.50 net. Van Nostrand.

DYNAMOS AND MOTORS.
Ashford, C. E., *and* Kempson, E. W. E. Elem. theory of direct current dynamo electric machinery. *$1 net. Putnam.
Care and repair of dynamos and motors. 25 c. Indust. Press.
Crocker, F. B. Dynamo-electric machinery. $1.50. Am. Sch. Corr.
Crocker, F. B., *and* Arendt, M. Electric motors. $2.50 net. Van Nostrand.
Franklin, W: S., *and* Esty, W: Dynamo laboratory manual. **$1.75 net.—Dynamos and motors. *$4 net. Macmillan.
Hawkins, C: C., *and* Wallis, F. The Dynamo. *$5.50 net. Macmillan.
Hird, W. B. Elementary dynamo design. *$2.50 net. Cassell.
Hobart, H: M. Electric motors. $5.50 net. Macmillan.
Hobart, J: M., *and* Ellis, A. G. High-speed dynamo electric machinery. **$6 net. Wiley.
Kahl, J: C., *and* Cole, L. A. Electrical connections, [for dynamos and motors.] 25 c. W. R. C. Smith.
Lummis-Paterson, G. W. Management of dynamos. $1.50. Henley.

DYNAMOS AND MOTORS.—*Continued.*
Meade, N. G. Electric motors. *$1 net. McGraw.
Powell, F. E. Small dynamos and motors. 25 c. Spon.
Raymond, E: B. Tracing of direct-current and alternating-current motor troubles. $1.50. Hill Pub.
Weed, A. J. Dynamo building for amateurs. $1; 50 c. Henley.
See also Alternating currents;—Automobiles;—Boats;—Electrical engineering;—Engines;—Hydraulic engineering; — Machinery; — Steam engine.

Dynasts (The). Hardy, T: pt. 3. *$1.50 net. Macmillan.

Dyson, C. C.
Life of Marie Amelie, last queen of the French, 1782-1866. '10(O8) il. por. O. $3.50 special net. Appleton.
Madame de Maintenon, her life and times, 1635-1710. '09(N6) il. por. O. *$4 net. Lane.

Dyson, Fk. Watson.
Astronomy. '10(S) il. 16°, (Appleton's scientific primers.) 50 c. net. Appleton.

DYSPEPSIA.
Fenwick, W: S. Dyspepsia. $3. Saunders.

E., C. E.
House of Hell: a ballad of Blackfoot. '09 (Je5) c. S. pap. (Add. author for price.) C. E. E.

E., J. and S., H., comps.
Golden threads of life. '10(O29) S. (Quiet hour ser.) 50 c. Stokes.
Life's common way. '08(Ag8) T. 50 c.; leath., $1. Stokes.

E., O. N., pseud.
Vocabulary for young fathers, by O. N. E. '08(Je20) c. D. bds., 75 c. Dodge.

Each for all and all for each. Parsons, J: *$1.50 net. Sturgis & W.

Each in his own tongue. Carruth, W: H. **$1 net. Putnam.

Eades, Jacob Allen.
Sword of the spirit. '08, [909.] (S) 133 p. por. 16°, $1.50. Skelton.

Eadie, Andrew.
See Eadie, Rob.

Eadie, Rob. and Andrew.
Physiology and hygiene for young people. '09, [1910.] (F) c. 6+353 p. il. 12°, 65 c. Scribner.

Eagan, Alice Livingstone.
Released: poem. '08(Ja25) 12°, 75 c. B'way Pub.

Eagar, J. H. L.
Courtship under contract. '10(Ag) $1.20 net. Health-Culture.

Eagle, Wa. Ja., ed.
See American negligence digest.

Eagle badge. Day, H. F: †$1.25. Harper.

Eagle lib. O. Brooklyn Eagle.
—Brooklyn Daily Eagle almanac, 1910. 50 c.
—Government cook book. 10 c.

Eagle's feather. Post, *Mrs.* E. P. $1.50. Dodd.

Eagle's nest. McAulay, A. $1.50. Lane.

Eakle, Arth. Starr.
Notes on some California minerals. '08 (D26) figs. Q. (Univ. of Cal. pubs., Geology.) pap., 15 c. Univ. of Cal.

"Ealer, Rev.," pseud.
Education unmasked. pt. 1, Common sense; pt. 2, Public schools of New York City. '10(D) 32 p. pap., 25 c. Critic & G.

Eales, Irving Ja., M.D.
Healthology (health study). '08(Ja18) pors. D. $1.50. I. J. Eales.

Eames, Edn. Hubert.
See Graves, C: Burr.

Eames, H: Edg.
Military maps explained. '08(O) 143 p. maps, 16°, $1. Hudson.
Rifle in war. '08(D) c. 104 p. tabs., 8°. (Add. pubs. for price.) Staff Coll.
Rifle in war. 2d ed. '09(N) c. 9+331 p. il. 8°, $2. U. S. Cavalry.

EAR.
American Medical Assoc. Papers presented before section on laryngology and otology. 1908. $1.50; 1909. (Add. pubs. for price.) Am. Medical.
Bacon, G. Manual of otology. *$2.25 net. Lea.
Ballinger, W: L. Treatise on medical and surgical diseases of the nose, throat and ear. *$5.50 net. Lea.
Bárány, R. Physiology and pathology of the semicircular canals. $1 net. Hoeber.
Barr, T: *and* J. S. Manual of diseases of the ear; incl. those of the nose and throat in relation to the ear. *$4.50 net. Macmillan.
Barrett, J. A. A B C of good hearing. 25 c. J. A. Barrett.
Bezold, F., *and* Siebenmann, F. Text-book of otology. *$3.50 net. Colegrove.
Bishop, S. C. Diseases of the nose, throat and ear. $4.50; $6. Davis.
Dench, E. B. Diseases of the ear. $5. Appleton.
Gleason, E: B. Manual of diseases of the nose, throat and ear. $2.50. Saunders.
Gray, A. A. Ear and its diseases. $4.25 net. Wood.
Heine, B. Operations on the ear. *$3 net. Wood.
Jones, J. A. Short practice of aural surgery. *$1.75 net. Lane.
Knight, C: H., *and* Bryant, W. S. Diseases of the nose, throat and ear. *$4.50 net; *$6 net. Blakiston.
Kopetzky, S: J. Surgery of the ear. $4. Rebman.
Lake, R: Hdbk. of diseases of the ear for students and practitioners. **$2.75 net. Wood.
Lamb, W: Pract. guide to the diseases of the nose, throat and ear. *$3 net. Wood.
Maxwell, S: S. Experiments on the functions of the internal ear. Univ. of Cal.
Meyer, M. F. Introduction to the mechanics of the inner ear. *$1 net. Univ. of Mo.
Murray, A. N: Minor ophthalmic and aural technique. $3. Cleveland Press.
Packard, F. R. Text-book of diseases of the nose, throat and ear. subs., **$3.50 net; **$4 net. Lippincott.
Politzer, A. Text-book of the diseases of the ear. *$8 net. Lea.

EAR.—*Continued.*
West, C: E., *and* Scott, S. R. Operations of aural surgery, together with those for the relief of the intracranial complications of suppurative otitis media. *$2 net. Blakiston.
Witkowski's atlas of the mechanism of hearing. *$2 net. W: R. Jenkins.
Wood, C. A., *and others, eds.* Eye, ear, nose and throat. $1.50. Year Bk.
See also Deaf and dumb;—Lip-reading;—Nervous system;—Nurses and nursing.

Eardley-Wilmot, Sainthill.
Forest life and sport in India. '10(O22) il. O. $3.50 net. Longmans.

Earhart, Lida Belle.
Systematic study in the elementary schools. '08(S5) c. tabs., 8°, (Columbia Univ., Teachers' Coll., contribs. to education.) pap., $1. Teachers' Coll.
Teaching children to study. '09(O23) c. O. (Riverside educational monographs.) 60 c. Houghton M.

Earhart, Will.
Art songs for high schools. '10(Ag27) Q. 80 c. Am. Bk.

Earl, I. P.
Childhood, and other verse. '08(O24) 12°, pap., 50 c. Cochrane.

Earl, J: Prescott.
Captain of the school team. '10(D3) c. il. D. $1.25. Penn Pub. Co.
On the school team. '08(Ag8) c. il. 12°, †$1.25. Penn Pub. Co.
School team in camp. '09(N13) c. il. D. †$1.25. Penn Pub. Co.

Earl or chieftain? Dillon, P. 35 c. net. Herder.

Earland, Ada.
Ruskin and his circle. '10(My14) il. O. $1.75 net. Putnam.

Earle, Mrs. Alice Morse.
Two centuries of costume in America, 1620-1820. New ed. 2 v. in 1. '10(O8) il. 8°, $2.50 net. Macmillan.

Earle, Franklin Sumner.
Southern agriculture. '08(My2) c. il. D. **$1.25 net. Macmillan.

Earle, Mrs. Teda Morgan.
See Morgan, Earlaine, *pseud.*

Earley, Carrie L.
Poems. '09(My) c. 7-81 p. por. 12°, 50 c. G: G Earley.

Earlham College bull. 8°. Earlham Coll.
—Kelly. Influence of Friends on American education. 25 c.

Earliest cosmologies. Warren, W: F. *$1 50 net. Eaton & M.
Earliest sources for the life of Jesus. Burkitt, F. C. **50 c. net. Houghton M.
Earliest version of Babylonian deluge story. Hilprecht, H. V. 75 c. net. Holman.
Earliest years at Vassar. Wood, F. A. 50 c. F. A. Wood.

Earls, Michael.
Chorister's Christmas eve; little play for the Christmas days, with a modern legend and the old Christmas carols. '10 (F) 62 p. 8°, pap., 25 c. Herder.
Melchior of Boston. '10(D3) c. D. $1. Benziger.

Early age of Greece. Ridgeway, W: v. 1. *$5 net. Putnam.
Early American novel. Loshe, L. D. *$1 net. Lemcke.
Early bird. Chester, G: R. $1.50. Bobbs-M.
Early Christian hymns. Donahoe, D. J., *ed.* *$2 net. Grafton Press.
Early Christianity. Slack, S. B. *40 c. net. Open Court.
Early church history. Gwatkin, H: M. *$5.25 net. Macmillan.
Early day railroading from Chicago. Prescott, D. W. C. $1.50. D: B. Clarkson.
Early days of monasticism on Mount Athos. Lake, K. $2.90. Oxford Univ.
Early days of Santa Barbara. Hawley, W. A: $1. W. A: Hawley.
Early days on Boston common. Ayer, M. F. $4 net. C: E. Goodspeed.
Early Devonic history of New York and eastern North America. pt. 1. Clarke, J: M. $2.50. N. Y. State Educ.
Early education of children. Plaisted, L. L. $1.50. Oxford Univ.
Early English colonies in America. Ingram, A. F. W. *$2 net. Young Churchman.
Early English lyrics; sel. and arr. with introd. and annotations by A. T. Quiller-Couch. '08(D19) (Early English classics.) 10 c. Oxford Univ.
Early English proverbs. Skeat, W. W:, *comp.* $1.15. Oxford Univ.
Early English romances in verse; done into modern English by Edith Rickert. [v. 1,] Romances of friendship; [v. 2,] Romances of love. '09(F20) 16°, (New medieval lib.) pigskin, ea., *$2 net. Duffield.
Early Greek philosophy. Benn, A. W. *50 c. net. Dodge.
Early Greek philosophy. Burnet, J. *$3 net. Macmillan.
Early history of the Christian church. Duchesne, L. M. O. *$2.50 net. Longmans.
Early London. Besant, *Sir* W. *$7.50 net. Macmillan.
Early mile-stones leading from Boston. Green, S: A. 25 c. S: A. Green.
Early morning scenes in the Bible. Nash, L. L. $1 net. Revell.
Early New England towns. MacLear, A. B. *$1.50 net. Longmans.
Early New York. MacCoun, T. $5. T. MacCoun.
Early physicians of Germantown. Willits, I. Pearson. (Not for sale.) Site and Relic.
Early religion of Israel. Paton, L. B. 50 c. net. Houghton M.
Early Rhode Island. Weeden, W: B. $2.50. Grafton Press.
Early South American newspapers. Winship, G: P. $1. Am. Antiquarian.
Early Spanish cartography. Stevenson, E: L. 50 c. Davis Press.
Early steps in the fold. De Zulueta, F. M. $1. Kenedy.
Early traditions of Genesis. Gordon, A. R. *$2.25 net. Scribner.
Earning power of railroads, 1908. Mundy, F. W., *comp. and ed.* $2 Metropolitan Adv.

Earning power of railroads. Mundy, F. W., *comp. and ed.* 1909, $1; 1910, $2.50. J. H. Oliphant.

Earp, Edn. L.
Social aspects of religious institutions. '08 (F1) c. D. *75 c. net. Eaton & M.

EARTH (The).
Becker, G: F. Age of the earth. 5 c. Smith. Inst.
Hemiup, *Mrs.* M. R. Our world, the earth a revolving engine with a central propelling power. $2. Hemiup.
Rogers, J. E. Earth and sky every child should know. $1.20 net. Doubleday, P.
Suess, E. Face of the earth. v. 3, $5.75; v. 4, $7.75. Oxford Univ.
Taber, C: A. M. Our periodic earth. 75 c.; 50 c. G. H. Ellis.
See also Creation; — Geodesy; — Meteorology; — Physical geography;—Universe.

Earth (The). Fagan, J. B. $1 net. Duffield.

Earth cry. Garrison, *Mrs.* T. P. $1 net. M. Kennerley.

Earth movements in the California earthquake of 1906. Hayford, J: F. pap., 15 c. U. S., Supt. of Docs.

Earth poem. Dalliba, G. **$2 net. Putnam.

Earth songs. Smith, *Mrs.* M. C. $1.25. Badger.

EARTHENWARE.
See Ceramics.

Earthly footprints of Jesus. Sweetapple, H. D. S. *$2 net. Whittaker.

EARTHQUAKES.
Brooklyn Public Library. Earthquakes and volcanoes: list of books with reference to periodicals in the Library. gratis. Brooklyn Lib.
Caine, W: R. H. Cruise of the "Port Kingston": [earthquake at Kingston, Jamaica.] (Add. author for price.) W: R. H. Caine.
California earthquake of April 18, 1906. 2 v. and atlas. v. 1, pts. 1, 2, with atlas. $17; v. 2, $2. Carnegie.
Derleth, C: Destructive extent of the California earthquake. *$1.25 net. A. M. Robertson.
Elliott, J. Earthquakes: their causes. 25 c. J. Elliott.
Hayford, J: F., *and* Baldwin, A. Le S. Earth movements in the California earthquake of 1906. 15 c. U. S., Supt. of Docs.
Jones, C. M. Earthquakes. (privately pr.) C. M. Jones.
Jordan, D: S., *ed.* California earthquake of 1906. *$3.50 net. A. M. Robertson.
Knott, C. G. Physics of earthquake phenomena. $4.75. Oxford Univ.
Miller, J. M. World's greatest disaster: the complete story of the Italian earthquake horror. $1.50. Monarch.
Wilson, J. F. Earthquakes and volcanoes —hot springs. $1.25. J. F. Wilson.
See also Volcanoes;—*also* Kingston;—Messina disaster.

Earth's bounty. Saint Maur, *Mrs.* K. V. **$1.75 net. Macmillan.

EARTHWORK.
Crockett, C: W. Methods of earthwork computations. *$1.50 net. Wiley.
Grace's earthwork tables for calculating the cubical contents of cuttings. $5. Spon.
Henderson, R. S. Earthwork tables. $1. Engineering News.
McGee, G. C. McGee's tables; hdbk. of excavation and embankment tables. $2.50. G. C. McGee.
Prelini, C: Graphical determination of earth slopes, retaining walls and dams. **$2 net. Van Nostrand.
See also Retaining walls.

Easby-Smith, Ja. Stanislaus.
See Smith, Ja. Stanislaus Easby-.

Easdale, W. C.
Sewage disposal works; their design and construction. '10(N12) 8°, $4. Spon.

EAST (The).
See Orient.

EAST AFRICA.
See Africa;—Mammalia.

EAST AFRICAN PROTECTORATE.
See Nandi.

East end of Europe. Upward, A. *$4 net. Dutton.

East Granby, Conn. Congregational Church. Records of the Congregational church in Turkey Hills, now the town of East Granby, Conn., 1776-1858. '07, [1908.] (Je.) 158 p. 8°, (Turkey Hill ser.) $3.50. A. C. Bates.

EAST INDIA COMPANY.
Saintsbury, E. B., *comp.* Calendar of the court minutes, etc., of the East India Company, 1640-1643. $4.15. Oxford Univ.

East London visions. Lawler, O: W. $1.75 net. Longmans.

EAST PLYMOUTH, Ct.
Pond, E. L. Tories of Chippeny Hill, Conn. **$1 net. Grafton Press.

Easter, Arth. Miller.
Songs of sentiment and faith. '10(D31) c. por. D. $1.50 net. Eichelberger.

EASTER.
Angelus and Regina Cæli. 25 c. Longmans.
Archibald, A. W. Easter hope. $1. S. D. Towne.
Book of Easter. **$1.50 net, boxed. Macmillan.
Kent, A. Origin of the Easter festival. 25 c. C. E. Kent.
Moody, P. D. First Easter sermon. 30 c. Northfield Press.
Schmid, J. Die Osterfestberechnung in der abendländischen kirche vom I. allgemeinen konzil zu Nicäa bis zum ende des VIII. jahrhunderts. *80 c. net. Herder.
Spencer, C. B. Easter reflections. $1. Jennings.
See also Holy Week;—Jesus Christ.

Easter eggs. Schmid, C. v. $1.25. Macmillan.

EASTER LILY.
Oliver, G: W. Production of Easter lily bulbs in the United States. 15 c. U. S., Supt. of Docs.

Easter tidings. Bugbee, W. N. 25 c. Dick.

Easterday, Levi Fast M.
History of the Easterday family. pt. 1. '08(Mr) c. 32 p. O. pap., $2. L. F. M. Easterday.

EASTERDAY FAMILY.
See Genealogies.

EASTERN CHURCH.
See Church history.

Eastern Ill. State Normal School bull. 8°. Eastern Ill. State Normal Sch.
—Bagley. Education and utility. gratis.

Eastern Kentucky papers. Connelley, W: E. $2. W: E.. Connelley.

Eastern lion in the West. Nicolovius, L. 75 c. B'way Pub.

EASTERN QUESTION.
See Balkans;—Turkey.

EASTERN STAR, ORDER OF THE.
See Freemasonry.

Eastland, Florence Martin.
His tribute. '09(N6) c. front. D. *60 c. net. Jennings.
Matt of the water-front. '09(My15) c D. *60 c. net. Jennings.

Eastman, C: Alex., M.D., ["Ohiyesa,"] and Mrs. Elaine Goodale.
Smoky Day's wigwam evenings; Indian stories retold. '10(D17) c. il. D. 60 c. Little, B. & Co.
Wigwam evenings; Sioux folk tales retold. '09(O9) c. il. D. †$1.50. **Little, B. & Co.**
School edition of "Wigwam evenings." Supplementary reading (1 p.).

Eastman, C: Rochester.
Devonic fishes of the New York formations. '07, [1908.] (D) 2+235 p. 8°, (New York State Museum memoir.) $1.25. N. Y. State Museum.
Bibliographical footnotes.

Eastman, Crystal.
Work-accidents and the law. '10(Je18) c. il. diagrs., O. (Russell Sage foundation pubs.; Pittsburgh Survey; findings.) $1.50. Charities Pub.

Eastman, Mrs. Elaine Goodale.
Little Brother o' Dreams. '10(Mr5) c. D. **$1 net. Houghton M.

Eastman, Fk. Marshall.
Supp. to 2d ed. of Eastman on private corporations, [in Pennsylvania.] '09(D) c. O. $1.50 Bisel.
Treatise on the law rel. to private corporations [in Pennsylvania.] 2d ed., rev. and enl. '08(My.) c. 2 v., 33+830; 32+331 p. O. (Add. pubs. for price.) Bisel.

Eastman, Harold B:
Experiments with railway cross-ties. '08 (Ag1) il. tabs., 8°, (U. S., Dept. of Agriculture, Forest Service, circular.) pap., 15 c. U. S., Supt. of Docs.

Eastman, J: Robie.
Hist. of the town of Andover, New Hampshire, 1751-1906. '10(D17) il. pors. fold maps, 8°, $3; hf. leath., $3.75. Andover (N. H.) Com. Hist.

Eastside boys. Kagay, D. M. $1. Roxburgh.

Eastwood, Carlin.
Master road. '10(O22) c. D. $1.35 net. A. Harriman.

Easy arrangement of the Spanish verb. Seide, J. N. $2. J. N. Seide.

Easy catechetics for the first school year. Urban, A. 60 c. Wagner.

Easy French cookery. Mario, A. **60 c. net. Cassell.

Easy French prose composition. Guerber, H. A. pt. 1. 25 c. Am. Bk.

Easy French selections for sight translation. Mansion, J. E., *comp.* 15 c. Heath.

Easy German stories. Levi, H. *40 c. net. Crowell

Easy German stories. Ries, C. E. 35 c. Am. Bk.

Easy method for Croatians to learn the English language. Lochmer, A. *$1.50 net. Caspar.

Easy money. Atkey, B. †$1.50. Estes.

Easy Spanish. Dowling, M. C. 40 c. G: Dowling.

EATING.
See Cookery;—Food.

Eaton, Amasa Mason, and Craig, Clara E.
Roger Williams; with suggestions for study in schools. '09(Ap3) O. (R. I. educational circulars; historical ser.) pap., gratis. R. I. Dept. Educ.

Eaton, Rev. Arth. Wentworth Hamilton.
Hist. of Kings County, Nova Scotia, heart of the Acadian land; with many genealogies. '10(O1) c. 8°, $7. Salem Press.

Eaton, Dan. Cady.
Handbook of modern French painting. '09 (My15) c. il. D. **$2 net. Dodd.

Eaton, Elon Howard.
Birds of New York. In 2 v. v. 1. '10 (Jl16) il. map, 4°, (N. Y. State Museum, memoir.) $3. N. Y. State Educ.

Eaton, Ethel Mason.
Kindergartens in the public schools. '09 (O16) S. pap., 5 c. Pub. Ed. Assoc.

Eaton, F. M.
See Van Winkle, Walton.

Eaton, Isabel Graham.
By the shores of Arcady. '09(F6) c. D. $1.25. Outing.

Eaton, Ja. Shirley.
Education for efficiency in railroad service. '10(Mr26) 8°, (United States, Bu. of Education, bull.)

Eaton, Paul Webster.
The treasure. '09(N13) c. il D. $1.50. Fenno.

Eaton, Rob.
Auxilium infirmorum: manual for the sick. '09(Jl) 12°, 8+202 p. *45 c. net. Herder.
Night thoughts for the sick and desolate. '09(O) 18+237 p. 16°, *45 c. net. Herder.

Eaton, Seymour, ["Paul Piper."]
Prince Domino and "Muffles." '10(N12) c. il. O. $1.25. Stern.
Teddy B. and Teddy G., Roosevelt bears abroad. '08(O24) c. il. Q. (Roosevelt bears ser.) hf. cf., $1.50. Stern.
Teddy-B and Teddy-G, the bear detectives. '09(N6) Q. $1.50, boxed. Stern.

Eaton, Wa. Prichard.
American stage of to-day. '08(D19) c. O. **$1.50 net. Small.
At the New Theatre and others; the American stage; its problems and performances, 1908-1910. '10(N5) c. D. $1.50 Small.

—, and Underhill, Elsie Morris.
Runaway place. '09(My22) c. D. †$1.25. Holt.

Eaton juvenile classics. il. 12°. Eaton & Co.
—Hood. Story of Puck. 35 c.; 50 c.

Eaves, A. Osborne.
Mastery of death. '09(S) 96 p. 12°, (Psychic lib.) bds., *$1 net. Badger.

Eaves, Lucile.
Hist. of California labor legislation, with introd. sketch of the San Francisco Labor Movement. '10(O1) c. O. (Univ. of Cal. pubs.; Economics.) pap., $4. Univ. of Cal.

Eayrs, G:, ed.
See Townsend, W. J., *D.D.*

Ebb and Flo. Hillier, *Mrs.* A. W. $1. J. M. Williams.

Ebbinghaus, Hermann.
Psychology: elem. text-book; tr. and ed. by Max Meyer. '08, [1909.] (Ja) c. 8+215 p. il. 12°, $1.20. Heath.

Ebbutt, M. I.
Hero-myths and legends of the British race. '10(O1) il. O. $2 net. Crowell.

Eberhardt, C: C.
Indians of Peru. '10(Ja1) por. 8°. (Add. Inst. for price.) Smith. Inst.

Eberhart, Noble Murray.
Brief guide to vibratory technique. 2d ed., rev. and enl. '10(My14) c. D. $1. New Med.
Practical X-ray therapy. 2d ed., rev. and enl. '09(D) c. 256 p. il. 12°, $1.50. New Med.

Ebers, Georg Moritz.
The emperor. '08(Je27) 12°, (Magnolia lib.) 50 c. Hurst.

Ebner von Eschenbach, Marie.
Lotti, die uhrmacherin; ed., with introd. and notes, by G: H: Needler. '08(N21) c. S. 35 c. Holt.

Ebright, W. H., comp.
Bethlehem's star: a service for Christmas. '08(N7) c. O. pap., *$2 net per 100. Eaton & M.

Eby, Anson Doner.
Showers of blessing. '08, [1909.] (Mr) c. 268 p. 12°, 15 c. A. D. Eby.

Eby, Elias Grant.
Handy tables by which over 500,000 problems of the busy man are already solved. [3d ed.] '09(Ag7) c. nar. Q. leath., $2.50. J. F. Smith.

Eby, H: Harrison.
Observations of an Illinois boy in battle, camp and prisons—1861 to 1865. '10 (My) c. 284 p. il. por. map, 12°, $1. H: H. Eby.

Ecce homo. *See* Muller, G. A.—Nietzsche, Friedrich Wilhelm.—Seeley, *Sir* J: R.

Eccles, Fs. Yvon.
Century of French poets; being a selection illustrating the hist. of French poetry during the last hundred years; with introd., biographical and critical notices of the writers represented; summary of the rules of French versification and a commentary. '10(Je18) 8°, $3 net. Dutton.

Eccles, Lewis Franklin.
Plain analysis of socialism. '08(My16) c. 12°, 25 c. L. F. Eccles.
Trumpet voice from the throne "it is done"; The secret of the ages; The box of oil. '08(My16) c. 12°, 25 c. L. F. Eccles.

Eccles, W: McAdam.
Elem. anatomy and surgery for nurses. '10(D) 15+158 p. 12°, $1. W: R. Jenkins.
Hernia: its etiology, symptoms and treatment. 3d ed. '08(F15) il. 8°, *$2.50 net. Wood.

Ecclesia discens. Peile, J. H. F. *$1.60 net. Longmans.

ECCLESIASTICAL ARCHITECTURE.
See **Church architecture.**

ECCLESIASTICAL BIOGRAPHY.
See **Christian biography.**

ECCLESIASTICAL HISTORY.
See **Church history.**

ECCLESIASTICAL NEEDLEWORK.
See **Needlework.**

ECCLESIASTICAL POLITY.
See **Church polity.**

ECCLESIOLOGY.
See **Church history.**

ECHINODERMS.
Clark, A. H. On a collection of feather stars, or comatulids, from Japan. 15 c. U. S., Supt. of Docs.
McClendon, J. F. *Ophiurans* of the San Diego region. 30 c. Univ. of Cal.
Mortensen, T. On some West Indian echinoids. Gov. Pr. Off.
Pack, R. W. Notes on the *echinoids* from the tertiary of California. 10 c. Univ. of Cal.
Slocom, A. W. New crinoids from the Chicago area.—New echinoids from the Ripley group of Mississippi. ea., 50 c. Field Museum.
Weaver, C: E. New *echinoids* from the Tertiary of California. 5 c. Univ. of Cal.
See also **Crustaceans.**

Echoes. Strong, F. 50 c. Werner Co.

Echoes and prophecies. Hyde-Vogl, V. D. $1. Ariel.

Echoes from Bharatkhand. Ward, E. F. 75 c. Free Meth.

Echoes from Edinburgh. Gairdner, W. H. T. $1 net. Revell.

Echoes from M. A. C. Hall, M. K. 50 c. Rep.-Courier.

Echoes from Oak Street. Benjamin, R. 50 c. Donahue.

Echoes from the beat. Hair, Dell. 3 v. (Add. pubs. for price.) N. B. Newton.

Echoes from the frontier. Powell. A. M. **$1 net. Wessels.

Echoes from the *Oxford Magazine;* being reprints of seven years. '09(Je19) 16°, (Oxford lib. of prose and poetry.) 90 c. Oxford Univ.

Echoes from the prairie and the hills. Knapp, H. L. (Add. pubs. for price.) Wichita.

Echoes of long ago. Gunnett, A. H. 50 c. Mayhew.

Echoes of myself. Narodny, I. $2. Liberty Pub.

Echoes of Naples. Favilli, M. $1.25. Ditson.

Echoes of Pawnee Rock. Perkins, M., *comp.* 50 c. Goldsmith-W.

Echoes of the Emancipation Proclamation. Reed. W: B. 15 c. W: B. Reed.

Eckard, Jean, and Naundorff, Karl Wilhelm.
King who never reigned; being memoirs upon Louis XVII.; with a preface by Jules Lemaitre, together with introd. and notes by Maurice Vitrac and Arnould Galopin, to which is added Joseph Turquan's New light upon the fate of Louis XVII. '09 (Je5) il. pors. O. *$3.50 net. J: McBride.

Eckel, Rev. E: H:
Chronicles of Christ Church parish, Williamsport, Pa., 1840-1896; pub. by direction of the vestry of Christ Church and brought down to April, 1910, the 70th anniversary of the first Episcopal Church service held in Williamsport. '10(D) c. 7+155 p. pls., pors. 8°, $2. Christ Ch.

Eckel, Edn. Clarence.
Portland cement industry from a financial standpoint. '09(Ap24) c. il. map, 8°, $2. Moody's Mag.

Eckles, C. H.
See Shaw, Roscoe Hart.

Eckloff, Christian F:
Memoirs of a Senate page, (1855-1859;) ed. by Percival G. Melbourne. '09(My8) c. D. $1. B'way Pub.

Eckman, G: Peck, D.D.
Passion week sermons. [1910.] (F) c. 262 p. 12°, (Christian festivals ser.) $1. Jennings.
Studies in the gospel of John. 2d ser., chapters XIII-XXI. '08(N14) c. O. *$1 net. Jennings.

Eckstein, Ernst, and Wildenbruch, Ernst v.
Der besuch im karzer: von Ernst Eckstein; Das edele blut, von Ernest von Wildenbruch; with notes, vocab., and exercises by Herbert C: Sanborn. '08(S19) c. il. S. (Internat. modern lang. ser.) 50 c. Ginn.

Eclectic Eng. classics. 12°. Am. Bk.
—Bible. O. T. Old Testament narratives. 20 c.
—College entrance requirements in English, 1909-1915. 90 c.
—Thackeray. Henry Esmond. 60 c.

Eclectic practice in diseases of children. Mundy, W: N. $3. Scudder.

Eclectic readings. il. D. Am. Bk.
—Baldwin. Another fairy reader. 35 c.—Stories of Don Quixote. 50 c.—Stories of the king. 50 c.
—Davis *and* Chow-Leung. Chinese fables and folk stories. 40 c.
—Farmer. Nature myths of many lands. 45 c.
—Foote *and* Skinner. Makers and defenders of America. 60 c.
—Guerber. Story of old France. 65 c.
—Haight, *comp.* Adventures of Pathfiender.—Last of the Mohicans. ea., 35 c.
—Lucia. Stories of American discoverers for little Americans. 40 c.
—Swift. Gulliver's travels. 35 c.

Eclogues (The). *See* Virgil, Maro, Publius.

ECOLOGY.
See Botany;—Zoology.

Economic annals of the nineteenth century. Smart, W: $6.50 net. Macmillan.

Economic aspects of lengthening human life. Fisher, I. (Add. pubs. for price.) Com. of One Hundred.

Economic causes of great fortunes. Youngman, A. $1.50 Bankers' Pub.

Economic conditions of Bolivia. Calderon, I. (Priv. pr.) W. F. Roberts.

Economic co-operation among negro Americans. Du Bois, W: E. B., *ed.* $1. Atlanta Univ.

Economic functions of vice. McElroy, J: 50 c. Nat. Tribune.

ECONOMIC GEOLOGY.
See Geology.

Economic heresies. Nathan, *Sir* N. *$3 net. Houghton M.

Economic history of anthracite tide water canals. Jones, C. L. $1.50. Univ. of Penn.; [Appleton.]

Economic influences upon educational progress in the United States. Carlton, F. T. 50 c. Wisconsin Hist.

Economic interpretation of history. Rogers, J. E. T. *$1.50 net. Putnam.

Economical interpreter, for Italians to learn English. Bolognese, S. 50 c. Caspar.

ECONOMICS.
See Political economy.

Economics of manual training. Rouillion, L. $2. Van Nostrand.

Economics of railway operation. Byers, M. L. *$5 net. Engineering News.

Economics of railway transport. Williams, S. C: *$1.25 net. Macmillan.

Economy and training of memory. Watt, H: J. 50 c. Longmans.

Economy cook book. '10(Ap9) 12°, 50 c. Inter Aid.

Economy factor in steam power plants. Hawkins, G: W. $3. Hill Pub.

Economy of education. Sturdy, W: A. $1. J. D. Bonnell.

Economy of human life. Dodsley, R. $1.50. C. A. Owens.

ECUADOR, South America.
International Bureau of American Republics. Ecuador; general descriptive data. Int. Bu. Am. Republics.
See also Manabi.

Eddy, Arth. Jerome.
Ganton & Co. '08(S26) c. il. O. $1.50. McClurg.

Eddy, C:
Hole in the coat: [novel.] '08(F29) il. 12°, $1.50. Cassell.
Mrs. Bailey's debts. '08(D12) front. D. $1.50. Cassell.

Eddy, Clarence.
Twenty-five organ recital programmes. '09 (N) c. 32 p. D. pap., gratis. Schuberth.

Eddy, Mrs. Mary Morse Baker Glover.
Christian science vs. pantheism and other messages to the Mother Church. '09, [1908.] (D) 94 p. 8°, 26 c. A. V. Stewart.
Manual of the mother church, First church of Christ, scientist in Boston, Mass. 73d ed. '08(Ag) 137 p. 12°, $1. A. V. Stewart.
No and yes. 72d ed. '08(D12) c. 12°. (Add. pubs. for price.) A. V. Stewart.

Eddy, Mrs. Mary Morse Baker Glover.—*Cont.*
Personal contagion; also, What our leader says. '10(Ja15) c. 16°, pap., 10 c. Chr. Sci.
Poems. '10(D31) c. 16°, $1.50. A. V. Stewart.
Rudimental divine science. '08(D12) c. 8°. (Add. pubs. for price.) A. V. Stewart.
Unity of good. 91st ed. '08(D12) c. 8°. (Add. pubs. for price.) A. V. Stewart.

EDDY, *Mrs.* Mary Morse Baker Glover.
Brisbane, A. Mary Baker G. Eddy. *$1 net. Ball Pub.
Milmine, G. Life of Mary Baker G. Eddy. **$2 net. Doubleday, P.
Norton, C. Woman's cause: [essay on Mrs. Eddy's influence in uplifting women.] **75 c. net. Estes.
O'Brien, *Mrs.* S. W. Life of Mary Baker Eddy. $3. Concord Pub.
Wilbur, S. Life of Mary Baker Eddy. $3. Concord Pub.
See also Christian Science.

Eddy, Wa. Hollis.
Text-book in general physiology and anatomy. '08(Ja11) il. D. $1.20. Am. Bk.

Eddy (The). Cullen, C. L. $1.50. G: W. Dillingham.

Eddyite (The). Loutitt, G: W: $1. Colonial Press, (Ind.)

Ede, Dean W: Moore, D.D.
Clergy and social service. '10(Mr26) D. 90 c. Longmans.

Edele (Das) blut. Wildenbruch, E. v. *See* Eckstein, Ernst. Der besuch im karzer.

Edelmann, R:
Text-book of meat hygiene, with special consideration of ante-mortem and post-mortem inspection of food-producing animals; author. tr., with additions, by J: Robbins Mohler and Adolph Eichhorn. '08(N21) c. il. 8°, $4.50. G: E. Howard.

EDEMA.
Fischer, M. H: Œdema. $2. Wiley.

Eden, F. S.
School history of the County Palatine of Durham. '09(Je19) il. D. 50 c. Oxford Univ.

Eden, T: Watts, M.D.
Manual of midwifery. '08(O31) il. *$3.50 net. Chic. Med. Bk.

Edes, Marcia Josephine and S: Harcourt, comps.
Book of old Newport; old drawings and photographs of Newport, New Hampshire; embellished by Martin W. Nourse. '09, [1910.] (F) c. 53 p. il. f°, $1. M. J. Edes.

Edes, Rob. Thaxter, M.D.
Parson Gay's three sermons; or, Saint Sacrement. '08(My23) c. D. $1.50. Cochrane.

Edes, S: Harcourt, comp.
See Edes, Marcia Josephine, *comp.*

Edgar, Albert E.
How to advertise a retail store. '08(My2) c. il. por. 8°, $3.50. Outing Press.

Edgar, J: A:
Heroes of England. '10(N12) 16°, (Everyman's lib.) 35 c. net; leath., 70 c. net. Dutton.

Edgar, J: G:
Runnymede, and Lincoln Fair. '08(S19) 16°, (Everyman's lib.) *35 c. net; leath., *70 c. net. Dutton.

Edgar, Madalen G., comp.
Treasury of verse for little children. '08 (O31) il. O. $2.50. Crowell.

Edgar. Hammerstein-Gesmold, L. K. W. v. *$1.25 net. Herder.

Edgcumbe, Kenelm.
Industrial electrical measuring instruments. '09(My) 219 p. il. 8°, *$2 net. Van Nostrand.

Edgcumbe, R:
Byron: the last phase. '09(D11) O. *$3 net. Scribner.

EDGECOMBE Co., N. C.
Lichtenstein, G. Visit to Young's Pier at Atlantic City, N. J.; also, When Edgecombe was a-borning, The word sheriff, and Products of colonial North Carolina. (Add. author for price.) G. Lichtenstein.

Edgerly, Asa Sanborn.
He did it; or, the life of a New England boy, written in his adopted state, California. '09, [1910.] (Ja) 139 p. il. pors. 12°, $1. A. S. Edgerly.

Edgerly, Webster, ["Edm. Shaftsbury."]
Book of glame; complete course in life electricity, the source of vitality. '08, [1909.] (Mr) c. 319 p. por. 8°, $4. Ralston Univ.
Book of the Psychic Society: study of the fourteen unseen powers that control human life. '09(Ja16) c. 8°, $2. Ralston Univ.
Operations of the other mind; incl. the science of all phenomena and the practice of all forms of human control over others; in twenty-five cycles of knowledge. '09(Mr) $25. Ralston Univ.
Private lessons in the cultivation of sex magnetism, teaching the development and wonderful enlargement of those powers and influences that nature has implanted in every human life. '10(Ap) c. 500 p. 8°, $25. Ralston Univ.

Edgett, Grace Lawrence.
Exercises in geometry. '09(D4) c. 12°, 40 c. Heath.

Edgeworth, Maria.
Castle Rackrent, and The absentee. '10 (Ap) 16°, (Everyman's lib.) 35 c. net; leath., 70 c. net. Dutton.
Tales; with introd. by Austin Dobson. '08 (D19) il. O. †$1.50. Stokes.
Tales that never die; ed. by C: Welsh, with introd. by C: Eliot Norton. '08(N7) c. il. por. D. $1.25. Caldwell.

EDGEWORTH, Maria.
Hill, C. Maria Edgeworth and her circle in the days of Buonaparte and Bourbon. *$6 net. Lane.

Edghill, Ernest Arth.
Faith and fact; study of Ritschlianism; essay for the Norrison prize, 1908; with preface by the Bishop of Southwark. '10(Ap9) 12°, $1.60 net. Macmillan.
Spirit of power as seen in the Christian church of the second century. '10(D24) D. $1.40 net. Longmans.

Edicts of Asoka. *See* Asoka, or Pinyadasi, *Emperor of India.*

Edina bibelots. 6 v. '10(D) 24°, limp ooze, ea., $1, boxed. Caldwell.

EDINBURGH, Scotland.
Masson, R. Edinburgh. 75 c. net. Macmillan.
Stevenson, R. L: Edinburgh; picturesque notes. *$1.75 net. Scribner.
Watkeys, F: W: Old Edinburg. 2 v. $3. L. C. Page.
See also International World Missionary Conference.

EDINBURGH AND LEITH CORPORATIONS.
See Granton.

Edinburgh lecture ser. D. Roger Bros.
—Troward. Doré lectures. 50 c.

Edinburgh lectures on mental science. Troward, T: 75 c. Roger Bros.

EDISON, Thomas Alva.
Dyer, F. L., *and* Martin, T: C. Edison, his life and inventions. 2 v. $4. Harper.
Jones, F. A. Thomas Alva Edison. **$2 net. Crowell.

Editha series. v. 1-36. '09(O2); v. 37-46. '10 (N) il. 12°, ea., 50 c. Caldwell.

Edkins, J. S.
See Beddard, A. P.

Edler, A. B., rep.
See Utah. *Sup. ct.* Repts.

Edminster, Clothier Franklin.
Structural drawing. '08(Ja4) il. obl. 12°, $2.50. D: Williams.

Edmison, J: P.
Stories from the Noresland. '09(N13) c. il. D. (Classic stories for boys and girls.) †$1.25. Penn Pub. Co.

Edmonds, Franklin Spencer, and Perrine, W:
Thomas Balch and the Geneva tribunal; speech by Franklin Spencer Edmonds and article by William Perrine. '09(N) 11 p. 4°. (Add. author for price.) F. S. Edmonds.

Edmonds, J. W.
Spiritualism. 9th ed. 2 v. '09(D) 741 p. $3.50. Austin.

Edmondson, C: Howard.
Lab'y guide in invertebrate zoology. [1910.] c. '09. 64 p. 8°, 25 c. C. H. Edmondson.

Edmunds, Albert Jos.
Buddhist and Christian gospels now first compared from the originals: being "Gospel parallels from Pali texts;" reprinted with additions. 4th ed.; being the Tokyo ed. rev. and enl.; ed., with English notes on Chinese versions dating from the early Christian centuries by Masaharu Anesaki. In 2 v. v. 1. '08(S19); v. 2. '09(My8) c. O. pap., ea., *$2 net. A. J. Edmunds.
Quaker literature in the libraries of Philadelphia. '08(N21) (Add. author for price.) A. J. Edmunds.

Edmunds, G: Franklin.
Income tax; a former Vermont senator describes the power of taxation and defines difference between property taxes, duties and imposts. '10(Ap) 4 p. 8°, pap. U. S., Supt. of Docs.

Edser, Edn.
Heat for advanced students. '08(D12) il tabs., 12°, *$1 net. Macmillan.

Edson, And. Wheatley.
Bibliography of a course on school administration, summer session, Teachers' College, 1910. '10(Jl16) c. 8°, (Columbia Univ., Teachers' College, syllabi.) 10 c. Teachers' Coll.

EDUCATION.
Alston, L. Education and citizenship in India. $1.25 net. Longmans.
Anderson, L. F. History of common school education. $1.25. Holt.
Andrews, B: R: Museums of education. 30 c. Teachers' Coll.
Armstrong, H. E. Teaching of scientific method. $1.75 net. Macmillan.
Armstrong, J. E. Advantages of limited sex segregation in the high school. pap., 15 c. J. E. Armstrong.
Armstrong, S: C. Ideas on education. (Add. pubs. for price.) Hampton Inst.
Bagley, W: C. Education and utility. gratis. Eastern Ill. State Normal Sch.
Baker, J. H. Educational aims and civic needs. (Add. pubs. for price.) Univ. of Col.
Benson, A. C. The schoolmaster: commentary upon the aims and methods of an assistant-master in a public school. *$1.25 net. Putnam.
Blandin, *Mrs.* I. M. E. History of the higher education of women in the South prior to 1860. *$3 net. Neale.
Bolton, F. E. Principles of education. $3. Scribner.
Brooks, E. C. Comparison of school systems. Trinity Coll.
Brown, E. E. Government by influence and other addresses. $1.25. Longmans.
Brown, G: P. Physiology and psychology of education. pt. 1, Elem. education. 25 c. Public Sch. Pub.
Brownlee, J. Moral training in the public schools. 10 c. Holden Pat. Bk.
Brumbaugh, M. G. Philanthropy and public education. gratis. Phil. Trades School.
Buffalo Public Library. Means of education and self-culture offered day-workers by the city of Buffalo. gratis. Buffalo Pub. Lib.
Burke, C. E. Child study and education. 75 c. Benziger.
Burnham, W: H:, *and* Suzzallo, H: History of education as a professional subject. 50 c. Teachers' Coll.
Burstall, S. A. Impressions of American education in 1908. *$1.25 net. Longmans.
Butler, N: M., *ed.* Education in the United States. $2.50. Am. Bk.
Carlton, F. T. Economic influence upon educational progress in the United States, 1820-1850. 50 c. Wisconsin Hist.
Carlton, F. T. Education and industrial evolution. *$1.25 net. Macmillan.
Carnegie Foundation for the Advancement of Teaching. Standard forms for financial reports of colleges, universities and technical schools. gratis. Carnegie.
Classical Conference, Ann Arbor, Mich. Value of humanistic, particularly classical, studies as a preparation for the study of theology. Univ. of Mich.

EDUCATION.—*Continued.*

Cole, P. R:, *comp.* Later Roman education in Ausonius, Capella and the Theodosian code. 25 c. Columbia Univ.

Conference for the Study of the Problems of Rural Life. 2d, Charlottesville, Va., 1909. Addresses del. at the Univ. of Va. summer school. B. R. Payne.

Conover, J. P. Personality in education. **$1.25 net. Moffat.

Cooke, M. L. Academic and industrial efficiency. Carnegie.

Coursault, J. H. Learning process. *$1 net. Teachers' Coll.

Crane, R: T. Utility of all kinds of higher schooling. $1.—Crane's reply to criticisms on his book. gratis. R: T. Crane.

Cubberley, E. P. Changing conceptions of education. **35 c. net. Houghton M.

Davenport, E. Education for efficiency. $1. Heath.

De Garmo, C: Principles of secondary education. v. 2, 3. ea., *$1 net. Macmillan.

Dewey, J:, *and* Small, A. W. My pedagogic creed. 15 c. Flanagan.

Draper, A. S. Addresses and papers [on education.] (Add. pubs. for price.) N. Y. State Educ.

Draper, A. S. American education. **$2 net. Houghton M.

Dutton, S: T., *and* Snedden, D: S: Adminstration of public education in the United States. *$1.75 net. Macmillan.

Ealer, *Rev., pseud.* Education unmasked. 25 c. Critic & G.

Edson, A. W. Bibliography of a course on school administration, summer session. 10 c. Teachers' Coll.

Educational Settlement Committee, England. Towards educational peace. 36 c. net. Longmans.

Eliot, C: W: Education for efficiency and the new definition of the cultivated man. 35 c. Houghton M.

Ellis, C: C. Lancasterian schools in Philadelphia. (Not for sale.) Univ. of Penn.

Emerson, R. W. Education: an essay. **35 c. net. Houghton M.

Fleshman, A. C. Educational process. $1.25. Lippincott.

Flury, E. Pract. hints on education to parents and teachers. 75 c. net. Benziger.

Folwell, W: W. University addresses. *$1 net. H. W. Wilson.

Gallinger, J. H. General education board; memorandum. U. S., Supt. of Docs.

Gayley, C: M. Idols of education. **50 c. net. Doubleday, P.

Goodspeed, F. L. True aims of education. 15 c. F. L. Goodspeed.

Graves, F. P. History of education before the Middle Ages.—Hist. of education during the Middle Ages and the transition to modern times. ea., **$1.10 net. Macmillan.

Graves, F. P. Introduction to history of education. pt. 1. Univ. of Mo.

Grice, *Mrs.* M. V. M. Home and school united in widening circles of inspiration and service. 60 c. Sower.

EDUCATION.—*Continued.*

Haney, J: D. Registration of city school children. $1.50. Teachers' Coll.

Harris, C: A: Rapid survey of the Massachusetts educational system. 40 c. C: A: Harris.

Heck, W. H. Mental discipline and educational values. **$1 net. Lane.

Henderson, E. N. Textbk. of the principles of education. $1.75 net. Macmillan.

Hobhouse, W. Theory and practice of ancient education. *$1 net. Stechert.

Hodgson, G. Studies in French education. $1.10. Putnam.

Holst, B. P., *and others, eds.* Pract. home and school methods of study and instruction in the fundamental elements of education. $3.25. Holst.

Hoyt, C: O. Studies in the history of modern education. $1.50. Silver.

Jones, A. J. Syllabus for the study of the hist. of education. 25 c. R. I. Normal.

Jordan, D: S. Care and culture of men. $1.25. Whitaker & R.

Kansas. *Committee on Course of Study.* Course of study for the common schools of Kansas. 10 c. Crane.

Kant, I. Educational theory. $1.25. Lippincott.

Kentucky. *Dept. of Education.* Elem. course of study. gratis. Kentucky Dept. Educ.

Kerr, J: Scottish education. $2 net. Putnam.

Key, E. K. S. Education of the child. **75 c. net. Putnam.

King, H: C., *and others.* Education and national character. *$1.50 net. Rel. Educ.

Knowlson. T: S. Century student's manual. **$1 net. Warne.

Laurie, S. S. Institutes of education. *$1.90 net. Macmillan.

MacCracken, H: M. Tercentenary announcements, 1609-1909; "Three epochs in education in New York City." gratis. N. Y. Univ.

McIlwaine, R: Addresses and papers bearing chiefly on education. $1. R: McIlwaine.

Maennel, B. Auxiliary education, the training of backward children. $1.50. Doubleday, P.

Magnus, *Sir* P. Educational aims and efforts, 1880-1910. $2.25 net. Longmans.

Marrs, S. M. N. Educational miscellany. 15 c. S. M. N. Marrs.

Milton, G: F. Compulsory education in the South. gratis. Nat. Child Labor.

Milton, J: Treatise on education. 5 c. Old South Work.

Monroe, P. Syllabus of a course of study on the history and principles of education. 20 c. Teachers' Coll.

Mott, J: R. Chinese student migration to Tokyo. 5 c. Y. M. C. A.

Munroe, J. P. Educational ideal. $1. Heath.

Munroe, J. P. Specialist blight on American education. (Add. author for price.) J. P. Munroe.

EDUCATION.—*Continued.*

Murphy, T: E: Popular errors about classical studies. St. Mary's Coll.

National Society for the Scientific Study of Education. Eighth year book. In 2 pts. ea., *75 c. net.—Ninth year book. pt. 1. 75 c. net. Univ. of Chic.

New York State. *Education Dept.* Course of study and syllabus for elem. schools. N. Y. State Educ.

New York [State.] Education law. (Add. pubs. for price.) N. Y. State Educ.

Northrop, C. Addresses, educational and patriotic. $1.80 net. Univ. of Minn.

Norton, A. O. Readings in the history of education. 85 c. Harvard Univ.

O'Shea, M. V. Social development and education. $2. Houghton M.

Oxford and working-class education: being rept. of a joint committee of university and working-class representatives on the relation of the university to the higher education of work people. 35 c. Oxford Univ.

Patterson, C: B. New way to educate children. 25 c. New Way.

Paulsen, F. German education past and present. *$1.25 net. Scribner.

Plaisted, L. L. Early education of children. $1.50. Oxford Univ.

Publishers' Weekly. American educational list. 1908; 1909; 1910. ea., 50 c. Pub. Weekly.

Randolph, C. F. Rept. of a visit to European schools, incl. England, Wales, Scotland, Holland and Germany, 1909. 75 c. C. F. Randolph.

Raub, A. D. World an educational unit with centralized education as the controlling force. 25 c. A. D. Raub.

Raymond, G: L. Fundamentals in education, art, and criticism. $1.40 net. Funk.

Rietz, H. L., *and* Shade, I. Correlation of efficiency in mathematics and efficiency in other subjects. 35 c. Univ. of Ill.

Ruediger, W: C. Principles of education. **$1.25 net. Houghton M.

Sachs, J., *ed.* Studies in secondary education. 30 c. Teachers' Coll.

Sandys, J: E. Hist. of classical scholarship. In 3 v. v. 2, 3. ea., *$2.75 net. Putnam.

Scott, C. A. Social education. $1.25. Ginn.

Stevenson, A. E. Education and business leadership. (Add. pubs. for price.) Univ. Extension.

Strong, J: Hist. of secondary education in Scotland. $2.50. Oxford Univ.

Sturdy, W: A. Economy of education. $1. J. D. Bonnell.

Swift, E. J. Mind in the making. **$1.50 net. Scribner.

Talbot, M. Education of women. $1.25 net. Univ. of Chic.

Taylor, W: J. Syllabus of the history of education. $1. Heath.

Tear, D. A. Logical basis of educational theory from the standpoint of "instrumental" logic. 50 c. Univ. of Chic.

EDUCATION.—*Continued.*

Thum, W: Forward step for the democracy of to-morrow. $1.50. Twentieth Century Club.

Thwing, C: F. Education in the Far East. **$1.50 net.—Hist. of education in the United States since the Civil War. $1.25 net. Houghton M.

United States. *Bureau of Education.* Bibliography of education for 1908-9.—List of publications, 1867-1910.

United States. *Bureau of Education.* Teacher's professional library: classified list of one hundred titles. (Add. Superintendent for price.)

United States. *Dept. of the Interior. Bu. of Education.* Index to the Reports of the Commissioner of Education, 1867-1907. (Add. Superintendent for price.)

United States. *Superintendent of Documents.* Education; list of government publications. gratis.

Walsh, J. J. Education, how old the new. $2. Fordham Univ.

Washington. *Dept. of Education.* Hist. of education in Washington; preliminary ed. issued for distribution at the A.-Y.-P. exposition. (Add. Superintendent for price.) Wash. Supt. Sch.

Watts, T: T. Thoughts on education: a protest against our present system.]Priv. pr.] T: T. Watts.

Webster, W: F., *and* Heeter, S. L. Our present needs; the lagging half [backward children]. (Priv. pr.) W: F. Webster.

Wendell, B. Mystery of education and other performances. **$1.25 net. Scribner.

Wisconsin Free Public Library. Study outlines for the use of clubs and reading associations. gratis. Wisconsin Free Lib.

Wyer, J. I., *and* Phelps, M. L., *comps.* Bibliography of education for 1907. (Add. Superintendent for price.) U. S., Supt. of Docs.

Yetter, J: M. Educational system of Pennsylvania. $1. Cochrane.

Young Men's Christian Associations. *Educational Dept.* Outlines of courses of study. 50 c.; 35 c. Y. M. C. A.

See also Agriculture;—Alaska-Yukon-Pacific Exposition;—Boys;—Children;—Classical literature; — Colleges and universities; — Country life; — Culture;—Ethics;—Examinations;—Fine arts;—Friends (*Society of*);— Games;—Girls;—Gymnastics and physical culture;—Home study;—Idealism; — Imagination; — Indians;—Jews; — Kindergarten;—Language;—Librarians and libraries; — Manual training; — Mathematics; — Medicine; — Memory; — Nature; — Negroes;—Psychology;—Railroads; — Religious education; — Schools; — Songs; — Statistics; — Sunday-school; — Superstitions; — Teachers and teaching; — Technical education; — Vocational education;—*also* Hegel, G. W. F.;—Montaigne, M. E. de; — Pestalozzi, J. H.; — *also* names of states.

Education and its economic value in the field of preventive medicine. Ditman, N. E. (Add. pubs. for price.) Columbia Univ.

Education and problems of the Protestant ministry. Hill, D: S. $1. Stechert.

Education and railroad men; [list of books applying to railroad work.] '09(Mr13) pap., 25 c. Y. M. C. A.
Education (L') de soi-même. *See* Du Bois, Paul.
Education law, 1909. '09(Jl10) O. (N. Y. State Educ. Dept. bull.) pap. (Add. pubs. for price.) N. Y. State Educ.
Education of Jacqueline. De Pratz, C. $1.50. Duffield.
Education of nurses; the function of the hospital. '10(Jl) 57 p. 8°, (Teachers' College record.) 30 c. Teachers' Coll.
Education of the will. Knowlson, T: S. *$1.50 net. Lippincott.
Education of the will. Payot, J. **$1.50 net. Funk.
Education of Uncle Paul. Blackwood, A. $1.50. Holt.
Education of workers in the shoe industry. Dean, A. D. 10 c. Nat. Soc. Promotion Indust. Educ.
Education through music. Farnsworth, C: H. $1. Am. Bk.
Educational advantages for American students in France. Geddes, J., *jr.* 25 c. J. Geddes.
Educational ideal in the ministry. Faunce, W: H. P. **$1.25 net. Macmillan.
Educational issues in the kindergarten. Blow, S. E. **$1.50 net. Appleton.
Educational meaning of manual arts and industries. Row, R. K. $1.25. Row, P. & Co.
Educational organizations promoting international friendship. Mead, *Mrs.* L. T. A. per 100, $3. Int. Sch. of Peace.
Educational process. Fleshman, A. C. $1.25. Lippincott.

EDUCATIONAL PSYCHOLOGY.
See Psychology.

Educational Settlement Committee, England. Towards educational peace; plan of re-settlement in English elementary education. '10(Jl2) Q. pap., 36 c. net. Longmans.
Educational standards with other papers on nursing. Robb, I. A. H. $1.25. Koeckert.
Educational statesmanship in the South. Smith, C: A. gratis. C: A. Smith.
Educational theory. *See* Kant, Immanuel.
Educational woodworking for home and school. Park, J. C. *$1 net. Macmillan.
Educative value of Bible study. Conley, J: W. 5 c.; per 100, $2.50. Am. Bapt.
Educator ser. 8°. Educator.
—Robinson. History of South Dakota. 75 c.

EDUCATORS.
See Teachers and teaching.

EDWARD, *Prince of Wales (called* Black Prince).
Dunn-Pattison, R. P. Black Prince. $2.50 net. Dutton.

EDWARD VI., *King of England.*
Froude, J. A. Edward VI. *35 c. net; *70 c. net. Dutton.
Markham, *Sir* C. R. King Edward VI. *$3 net. Dutton.

EDWARD VII., *King of England.*
Boyle, J. King Edward VII. as a man and a monarch. 60 c.; 25 c. A. H. Smythe.
Escott, T: H. S. King Edward and his court. *$4 net. Jacobs.

EDWARD VII., *King of England.—Continued.*
Holt-White, W: E: B: People's king; short life of Edward VII. $1.25 net. Lane.
Where's master? 50 c. net. Doran.

Edward and I and Mrs. Honeybun. Horn, K. $1.50. Brentano's.
Edward Garrett. Porter, H. $1.25. Lincoln Pub. Co.

Edwardes, Tickner.
Lift-luck on southern roads. '10(Je11) il. D. $1.50 net. Macmillan.
Lore of the honey-bee. '09(Jl) 23+281 p. il. 12°, *$2.40 net. Scribner.

Edwardian inventories for Buckinghamshire; ed. by F. C. Eeles, from transcripts by Rev. J. E. Brown. '08(D5) Q. (Alcuin Club collections.) *$6 net. Longmans.
Edward's dream. Busch, W. *$1 net. Open Court.

Edwards, Arth. Robin, M.D.
Treatise on the principles and practice of medicine. 2d ed., rev. '09(S) 1246 p. il. 8°, *$5.50 net. Lea.

Edwards, Clarence, pseud.
See Hearn, E: C.

Edwards, D: W:
Up the grade. '10(F19) c. il. 12°, $1.50. C. M. Clark.

Edwards, Deltus Malin.
Toll of the Arctic seas. '10(D3) c. il. O. fold. map, $2.50 net. Holt.

Edwards, Ernest.
Personal information for boys. '09(O23) c. D. (Personal purity pubs.) 50 c. Fenno.
Personal information for young women. '09(D18) c. 12°, (Personal purity pubs.) 50 c. Fenno.

Edwards, G: Wharton.
Brittany and the Bretons. '10(O22) il. (partly in col.) O. $6 net. Moffat.
Holland of to-day. '09(O23) c. il. Q. **$6 net, boxed. Moffat.

Edwards, J: Harrington, D.D.
God and music. New ed. '08(Ag8) c. D. **$1.25 net. Baker & T.
Primer of homiletics. '08(D26) D. *75 c. net. Jennings.

Edwards, Matilda Barbara Betham-.
See Betham-Edwards, Matilda Barbara.

Edwards, Owen Morgan.
Short history of Wales. '08(Ap4) geneal. tab., maps, 12°, *75 c. net. Univ. of Chic.

Edwards, R: H:, ed.
Business morals. '10(O1) c. D. (Studies in American social conditions.) pap., 10 c. R: H: Edwards.
Concentrated wealth. '10(F19) c. D. (Studies in American social conditions.) pap., 10 c. R: H: Edwards.
Immigration. '09(Mr13) c. D. (Studies in American social conditions.) pap., 10 c. R: H: Edwards.
Labor problem. '09(Je12) c. D. (Studies in American social conditions.) pap., 10 c. R: H: Edwards.
Liquor problem. '09(Ja2) c. D. (Studies in American social conditions.) pap., 10 c. R: H: Edwards.
Negro problem. '09(Ja23) c. D. (Studies in American social conditions.) pap., 10 c. R: H: Edwards.

Edwards, R: H:—*Continued.*
Poverty. '09(Ag28) D. (Studies in American social conditions.) pap., 10 c. R: H: Edwards.
Edwards, R: Kemble.
Mystery of the miniature. '09(Ap3) c. il. D. $1.50. C. M. Clark.
Edwards, Rob. T:
Short Methodist stories. '09(Je26) c. D. *$1 net. Cochrane.
Edwards, Ward Hampton.
Parts of speech; suggested definitions for a logical grammar of the English language. '09, [1910.] (F) 24 p. 8°, 25 c. W. H. Edwards.
Bibliography (2 p.).
Edwards, W: Seymour, D.D.
Christian view of childhood. '08(Ap18) c. S. bds., *25 c. net. Jennings.
In to the Yukon. 3d ed. [1910.] (D) various paging, il. maps, 12°. Jennings.
On the Mexican highlands. 2d ed. '10 (F) $1.50. Jennings.
Edwin Drood. *See* Dickens, C:
Eeden, Frederik Willem van.
Practical communism, work and bread: address del. before the Civic Forum; with biographical note. '08(D5) por. 12°, (Civic Forum addresses.) pap., 10 c. Civic Forum.
Ysbrand; a tragicomedy; auth. tr. from the orig. Dutch; with photographs of the author and the original American cast. '10(Mr) c. 82 p. pors. 8°, 25 c. Lawrence Journ.
Eeles, Fs. Carolus.
Traditional ceremonial and customs connected with the Scottish liturgy. '10 (D17) O. (Alcuin Club collections.) bds., $6 net. Longmans.
—, ed. *See* Edwardian inventories.
Eells, E:
Mission to hell. '09(N6) c. D. *80 c. net. Sherman, F.
Eells, Myron, D.D.
Marcus Whitman: pathfinder and patriot. '09(S11) c. il. pors. map, O. *$2.50 net. A. Harriman.
Effect of a constant stimulus upon touch localization. Lurie, L: A. (Add. University for price.) Univ. of Cin.
Effective industrial reform. Reid, D: C. $1.35. D: C. Reid.
Effective magazine advertising. Bellamy, F., *ed.* *$5 net. M. Kennerley.
Effective speaking. Phillips, A. E: *$1.50 net. Newton Co.
Effects of the rays of radium on plants. Gager, C. S. $2. N. Y. Botanical.
Effects of war on property. Latifi, A. *$1.50 net. Macmillan.
Efficiency as a basis for operation and wages. Emerson, H. $2. Engineering Mag.
Efficient citizen ser. il. D. Ginn.
—Allen. Civics and health. $1.25.
Effinger, J: R.
See Thieme, Hugo P.
Efforts for social betterment among negro Americans. Du Bois, W: E: B. 75 c. Atlanta Univ.
Efird, C. M., rep.
See South Carolina. *Sup. ct.* Repts.

Egan, Ja. W:
Five practical chapters on retail advertising. '08, [1909.] (F) c. 48 p. 16°. (Add. pubs. for price.) J. W: Egan.
Egan, Maurice Fs.
Wiles of Sexton Maginnis. '09(Ap3) c. il. D. †$1.50. Century Co.
Egbert, Ja.
Alexander Campbell and Christian liberty; centennial volume on his controlling ideas—enforced by his own words. Centennial ed., 1809-1909. '09(D4) c. por. 12°, $1.50. Chr. Pub. Co.
Egbert, Seneca, M.D.
Manual of hygiene and sanitation. 5th ed. '10(O) 508 p. il. 12°, $2.25 net. Lea.
Egerton, Hakluyt.
Liberal theology and the ground of faith. '08(S19) 8°, *$1.25 net. Dutton.
Eggeling, Otto, and Ehrenberg, F:
Freshwater aquarium and its inhabitants. '08(D26) c. il. O. (American nature ser.; group IV, Working with nature.) **$2 net. Holt.
Egger, Jos. S. J.
Are our prayers heard? '10(Ag) 64 p. 8°, pap., 15 c. Herder.
Eggerth, Werner.
My own philosophy, and other poems and dramas. '09(Jl17) c. O. $1.50. W. Eggerth.
Eggleston, E:, and Seelye, Mrs. Lillie Eggleston, [Mrs. E. Seelye.]
Montezuma and the conquest of Mexico. '08(N21) c. front. 12°, (Famous American Indians.) †$1.25. Dodd.
Eggleston, G: Cary.
Hist. of the Confederate War; its causes and its conduct. In 2 v. '10(Ap30) c. O. $4 net, boxed. Sturgis & W.
Irene of the Mountains: a romance of old Virginia. '09(S11) c. il. D. †$1.50. Lothrop, L. & S.
Recollections of a varied life. '10(Ap30) por. O. $2.75 net. Holt.
Two gentlemen of Virginia: a novel. '08 (S5) c. il. D. †$1.50. Lothrop, L. & S.
Warrens of Virginia: a novel founded on the play of W: C. de Mille. '08(Ag29) c. il. D. †$1.50. G: W. Dillingham.
Westover of Wanalah; story of love and life in old Virginia. '10(Ag20) il. D. $1.50. Lothrop, L. & S.
EGGS.
Kelley, F: Treatise on food and egg production. $1. F: Kelley.
Pearl, R., *and* Surface, F. M. Biometrical study of egg production in the domestic fowl. 15 c. U. S., Supt. of Docs.
Wiley, H. W., *and others.* Preliminary study of the effects of cold storage on eggs, quail, and chickens. (Add. Superintendent for price.) U. S., Supt. of Docs.
See also Poultry.
Eginton, Libbie J.
First practice reader. '08(Ap11) c. il. D. 30 c. Silver.
Egleston-Hinman, Mrs. Eliz. Trowbridge.
Naya; story of the Bighorn country. '10 (D3) c. il. D. $1.50. Rand, McN. & Co.
Egoists. Huneker, J. G. **$1.50 net. Scribner.

Egy, Willard Leo.
See Clement, J. K.

EGYPT.
Al-Kindi, A. U. M. History of the governors of Egypt. pt. 1. **$1 net. Lemcke.
Al-Kindi, A. U. M., *comp.* History of the Egyptian cadis. *$3.50 net. Stechert.
Baedeker, K. Egypt and the Sudan. *$4.50. net. Scribner.
Baikie, J. Story of the Pharaohs. $2 net. Macmillan.
Breasted, J. H: Hist. of Egypt from the earliest times to the Persian conquest. **$5 net.—History of the ancient Egyptians. **$1.25 net. Scribner.
Buttles, J. R. Queens of Egypt. *$3 net. Appleton.
Capart, J. Une rue de tombeaux à Saggarah. In 2 v. $15. Stechert.
Carson, B. M. From Cairo to the Cataract. $2.50. L. C. Page.
Churchward, A. Signs and symbols of primordial man: being an explanation of the evolution of religious doctrines from the eschatology of the ancient Egyptians. $8 net. Dutton.
Clymer, R. S. Mystery of Osiris: Egyptian mythology. $5. Philosophical.
Cromer, *Earl* of. Modern Egypt. In 2 v. **$6 net. Macmillan.
Davis, T. M. Excavations: Biban el Moluk; the funeral papyrus of Iouiya. *$12.50 net. Dutton.
Davis, T. M., *and others.* Tomb of Iouiya and Touiyou. *$12.50 net. Dutton.
Duncan, J: G. Exploration of Egypt and the Old Testament. *$1.50 net. Revell.
Farman, E. E. Egypt and its betrayal. **$2.50 net. Grafton Press.
Finney, F: N. Letters from across the sea. (Priv. pr.) F: N. Finney.
Hichens, R. S. Egypt and its monuments. **$6 net. Century Co.
Kelly, R. T. Egypt. *75 c. net. Macmillan.
Lane, E: W: Account of the manners and customs of the modern Egyptians. *35 c. net; *70 c. net. Dutton.
Linforth, I. M. Epaphos and the Egyptian apis. 10 c. Univ. of Cal.
Lorimer, N. By the waters of Egypt. *$4 net. Pott.
McManus, B. Our little Egyptian cousin. 60 c. L. C. Page.
Maspero, G. C. C. New light on ancient Egypt. *$4 net. Appleton.
Müller, W. M. Egyptological researches. v. 2. $9. Carnegie.
Muschler, R. Manual flora of Egypt. $6. Lemcke.
Neville, E. Old Egyptian faith. $1.50 net. Putnam.
People of Egypt. $1.75 net. Macmillan.
Petrie, W: M. F. Arts and crafts of ancient Egypt. $1.75 net. McClurg.
Petrie, W: M. F. Personal religion in Egypt before Christianity. **75 c. net. Harper.
Pier, G. C. Inscriptions of the Nile monuments. **$5 net. Putnam.
Sladen, D. B. W. Queer things about Egypt. $5 net. Lippincott.

EGYPT.—*Continued.*
Thackeray, L. Light side of Egypt. *$2.50 net. Macmillan.
Viaud, L. M. J. Egypt. **$2.50 net. Duffield.
Watson, C: R. In the valley of the Nile. *$1 net. Revell.
Weigall, A. E: P. Guide to the antiquities of Upper Egypt, from Abydos to the Sudan frontier. $2.50 net. Macmillan.
Withers, P. Egypt of yesterday and to-day. $1.75 net. Stokes.
Wymper, C: Egyptian birds. *$6 net. Macmillan.
Yusuf Ibn Taghri Birdi. Annals, entitled An-nujûm Az-zâhira fî mulûk misr val-kâhira. 2 v. ea., $1.50. Univ. of Cal.
See also Kharga;—Manuscripts; — Mythology; — Nile river;—Pyramids;—Soudan.

Egypt and how to see it. '08(Mr14) c. il. S. bds., **$1.40 net. Doubleday, P.
Egypt and Israel. Brewer, W. $2 net. Torch Press.

EGYPT CHURCH, Egypt, Pa.
Roberts, C: R., *and* Schindel, J. D. Hist. of Egypt Church, [Egypt, Pa.] 27 c. Lehigh Co. Hist. Soc.

Egypt Exploration Fund, Græco-Roman Branch. Fragment of an uncanonical gospel from Oxyrhynchus; ed., with translation and commentary, by Bernard Pyne Grenfell and Arthur Surridge Hunt. '08(Ja18) il. O. pap., 40 c. Oxford Univ.
Egypt in Asia. Cormack, G: *$3 net. Macmillan.
Egyptian literature: comprising Egyptian tales, hymns, litanies, invocations, Book of the dead, and Cuneiform writings; with introd. by Epiphanius Wilson. '08(Je27) c. il. 8°, $1.75; hf. mor., $3.50. Lamb Pub.
Egyptian oasis. Beadnell, H. J. L. $3.50. Dutton.

EGYPTIAN PHILOSOPHY.
See Philosophy.

Ehrenberg, F:
See Eggeling, Otto.

Ehrenfeld, C: Lewis.
Brief story of the founding of the Southwestern State Normal School at California, Pa., incl. the hist. of the change of financial policy of the state toward all her normal schools, consequent upon the action of the Legislature of 1872, with an appendix by C. L. Ehrenfeld, ex-principal. '10(Ag) 8+105 p. il. pors. 12°, 75 c. New Era Print.

Ehrlich, Paul, M.D.
Experimental researches on specific therapeutics: three lectures del. before the Royal Institute of Public Health, London. '09(Mr) 100 p. por. *$1 net. Hoeber.
Studies in immunity; collected and tr. by Dr. C: F. Bolduan. '10(Je18) c. 8°, $6. Wiley.

Ehrmann, Mary B.
Child's song garden. '08, [1910.] (Mr) 85 p. il. 4°, $1. W: H. Willis.
Child's song treasury. '10(Mr5) il. 4°, $2. W: H. Willis.

Ehrmann, Max.
Complete poems. '10(D17) 12°, $1.50 net. Dodge.

Eichhorn, Adolph.
See Mohler, J: Robbins.

Eickemeyer, Carl.
Cinderella. '09(Mr) 25 c. C. Eickemeyer.
Giant killer. '09(Ap24) c. por. S. pap., 25 c. C. Eickemeyer.

Eickmann, Wa.
See Luther, Martin.

Eiesland, J: Arndt.
Advanced algebra for technical schools and colleges. '10(F26) c. il. 8°, $2. J: A. Eiesland.

Eifel, Aloysius J., tr.
See Jüngest, Antonie.

Eigenmann, Carl H.
Cave vertebrates of America: study in degenerate evolution. '09(Jl17) il. Q. (Carnegie Inst. of Wash. pubs.) pap., $5. Carnegie.

Eigensinn. Benedix, R. J. 15 c. Oxford Univ.

Eight hour primer. McNeill, G: E. (Add. author for price.) G: E. McNeill.

813. Leblanc, M. $1.20. Doubleday, P.

1872: letters written by a gentleman in Boston. Murdock, H., *ed.* *$5 net. Houghton M.

1869-1909; forty years of advertising. Ayer, N. W., & Son. (Add. pubs. for price.) Ayer.

Eighteen sermons on great themes. Wright, L. $1. Chr. Un.

Eighteen years in Uganda and East Africa. Tucker, A. R. *$8.50 net. Longmans.

Eighteenth century correspondence. Dickins, L., *ed.* $3.50 net. Duffield.

Eighteenth century literature; Oxford miscellany. '10(Ja1) 8°, $1.35. Oxford Univ.

Ein nordischer held. Roth, R. 35 c. Am. Bk.

Eiselen, F: Carl.
Prophecy and the prophets in their historical relations. '09(O23) c. *$1.50 net. Eaton & M.

—, and Barclay, W. C.
Worker and his Bible. '09(N) c. 236 p. maps, 12°, (Worker and his work ser.) 55 c. Bd. S. S. M. E. Ch.

Eisenhart, Luther Pfahler.
Treatise on the differential geometry of curves and surfaces. '09(O23) c. il. O. $4.50. Ginn.

Eisner, Alf. Wolf-.
See Wolf-Eisner, Alfr.

Eke, Alfr. J.
Elements of insurance; a guide to the principles and practice of accident, fire, marine and life insurance. '09(O2) D. (Pitman's practical business primers.) 50 c. Pitman.

Ekern, G: L., comp.
See Wisconsin. Insurance laws.

Ekin, T. C.
Water pipe and sewer discharge diagrams. '09(My1) tabs., 4°, *$3 net. Van Nostrand.

ELAGABALUS.
See Heliogabalus.

ELASTICITY.
See Physics.

Elba and elsewhere. Seitz, D. C. $1.25 net. Harper.

"Elbertus, Fra," pseud.
See Hubbard, Elbert.

ELBOW.
See Arm.

Elder, Benedict, comp.
See Oklahoma. General statutes.

Elder, Cyrus.
Poems. '10(Ja1) c. 12°, **$1.25 net. Lippincott.

Elder, D: Paul, comp.
Friendship. '10(Ap16) c. front. 8°, 50 c. P. Elder.

Elder, T: L.
See Gilbert, E: Holmes.

Elder Boise. Tomlinson, E. T. **50 c. net. Am. Bapt.

Elderton, Ethel M.
See Elderton, W. Palin.

Elderton, W. Palin and Ethel M.
Primer of statistics. '10(F19) il. 12°, *60 c. net. Macmillan.

EL DORADO COUNTY, California.
California. *State Mining Bureau.* Map of El Dorado County, Cal., showing boundaries of the national forests; comp. from data furnished by the U. S. Forest Service. '09(O) map, f°, pap., 20 c. Cal. State Mining.

El dorado "29." Maule, F. I. $1 net. Winston.

Eldred, Warren L.
Boys of Brookfield Academy. '10(Ap30) c. il. D. $1.50. Lothrop, L. & S.
Crimson ramblers. '10(Ag20) c. il. O. (St. Dunstan ser.) $1.50. Lothrop, L. & S.
Lookout Island campers. '09(S11) c. il. O. †$1.50. Lothrop, L. & S.

Eldredge, Zoeth Skinner, and Molera, Eusabius J.
March of Portola and the discovery of the Bay of San Francisco by Z. S. Eldredge; and, The log of the "San Carlos," by E. J. Molera. '09(N) 71 p. il. 8°, 50 c. Cal. Promotion.

Eldridge, E: H.
Shorthand dictation exercises. Graham ed.; Gregg ed.; Isaac Pitman ed.; Benn Pitman ed.; Edition without shorthand outlines; designed for use by students of any system of shorthand. '10(Ja8); ed. (Ja22) c. Q. pap., ea., 65 c. Am. Bk.

Eldridge, G: Dyre.
In the potter's house. '08(Mr28) c. O. †$1.50. Doubleday, P.
See also Landis, Abb.

Eldridge, W: Tillinghast.
American princess. '09(O9) c. front. D. $1.50. Sturgis & W.
Meryl. '08(My2) c. front. D. †$1.50. Dodd.

ELECTIONS.
Glasson, W: H: Australian voting system. 20 c. W: H: Glasson.
Griffin, A. P. C., *comp.* Library of Congress select list of references on corrupt practices in elections. (Add. Supt. for price.) U. S., Supt. of Docs.
Ingram, T: D. Plan for a direct election law. 15 c. T: D. Ingram.
Jewett, F. G. Manual for election officers and voters in the state of N. Y. $3; $2.50; $2. M. Bender.
Kansas. General election laws. 50 c. Crane.

ELECTIONS.—*Continued.*
King, J: Electoral reform. *85 c. net. Wessels.
Massachusetts. Laws of the commonwealth rel. to qualifications and registration of voters. 1908; 1910. ea., 35 c. R: L. Gay.
Mohr, E. J: Advisability of electing United States senators by popular ballot. (Priv. pr.) Georgetown Univ.
Rhode Island manual for voters. (Add. pubs. for price.) Green, H. & A.
Schaffner, M. A. The recall. 5 c. Wisconsin Free Lib.
See also Citizenship;—Primaries;—Referendum;—Suffrage;—United States;—*also* names of states.

Electoral reform. King, J. *85 c. net. Wessels.

ELECTRA.
See Elektra.

Electra. Hoffmannstal, H. H. v. **$1.25 net. Brentano's.

Electra. *See* Sophocles.

ELECTRIC ANESTHESIA.
See Death.

ELECTRIC BATTERIES.
Bubier, E: T. How to make electric batteries. 50 c.; 25 c. Bubier.
Watson, A. E. Storage batteries. $1.50. Bubier.

Electric blasting apparatus and explosives. Maurice, W: $3.50. Van Nostrand.

ELECTRIC CABLES.
See also Electrical engineering;—Electric wires.

ELECTRIC CAR.
See Electric railroads.

ELECTRIC CURRENTS.
See Alternating currents;—Electricity.

ELECTRIC DYNAMOS.
See Dynamos and motors.

ELECTRIC FURNACES.
See Furnaces.

ELECTRIC HEATING.
See Heating.

Electric ions and their use in medicine. Leduc, S. *$1 net. Hoeber.

ELECTRIC LAMPS.
See Electric light.

ELECTRIC LIGHT.
Amrine T: H. Comparative tests of carbon, metallized carbon and tantalum filament lamps. (Add. Univ. for price.) Univ. of Ill.
Amrine, T: H., *and* Guell, A. Tests of tungsten lamps. gratis. Univ. of Ill.
Barrows, W: E: Electrical illuminating engineering. *$2 net. McGraw.
Floy, H: Compilation of records of the Colorado Springs lighting controversy. $4. Illuminating Engineering.
Huels, F: W: Comparison of the effects of frequency on the light of incandescent and Nernst lamps. 25 c. Univ. of Wis.
Ives, H. E. Volt scale for a watts-per-candle meter. Gov. Pr. Off.
Knox, C: E., *and* Shaad, G: C. Electric wiring and lighting. $1. Am. Sch. Corr.
Lighting country homes by private electric plants. gratis. Univ. of Ill.
Maycock, W: P. Electric lighting and power distribution. In 2 v. v. 1. *$1.90 net. Macmillan.
Solomon, M. Electric lamps. *$2 net. Van Nostrand.

ELECTRIC LIGHT.—*Continued.*
Taylor, F. H. How to use electric light. 25 c.—Private house electric lighting. 50 c. Spon.
Walker, S. F. Pocket book of electric lighting and heating. $3. Henley.
Ziedler, J., *and* Lustgarten, J. Electric arc lamps: their principles, construction and working. *$2 net. Van Nostrand.
See also Electric wires.

ELECTRIC MACHINERY.
See Machinery.

ELECTRIC METERS.
Hutchinson, C. T. Rept. upon types of electric meters in use in N. Y. City. gratis. N. Y. Pub. Service Com.
Shepard, W: M., *and* Jones, A. G. Watt hour meter. $2. Technical Pub. Co.

ELECTRIC MOTORS.
See Automobiles;—Boats;—Dynamos and motors.

Electric power plant engineering. Weingreen, J. $5. McGraw-H.

Electric power plants. Murray, T: E: (Priv. pr.) T: E: Murray.

ELECTRIC RAILROADS.
Conway, T:, *jr.* Traffic problems of interurban electric railroads. gratis. Univ. of Penn.
Davies, F. H. Electric power and traction. *$2 net. Van Nostrand.
Dawson, P. Electric traction on railways. $9 net. Van Nostrand.
Gutmann, L. Motorman and his duties. *$1 net. McGraw.
Kirkman, M. M. Electricity applied to railways. $5. C. Phillips.
Livermore, V. B:, *and* Williams, J. R. How to become a competent motorman. **$1 net. Van Nostrand.
Lowe, P. M. Electric railway troubles and how to find them. $1.50. Drake.
Modern electric railway practice. 4 v. $22.50. W. V. Wheat.
Parham, E. C., *and* Shedd, J: C. Miscellaneous tests of electric car equipment.—Shop tests on electric car equipment for inspectors and foremen. ea., $1. McGraw-H.
Pease, C: S. Freight transportation on trolley lines. $1. McGraw-H.
Small, S. A. Electrical railroading. $3.50.—How to become a successful motorman. $1.50. Drake.
Swingle, C. F. Electric railway power stations. $2. Drake.
See also Bookkeeping;—Street railroads;—Transportation.

ELECTRIC RAILWAYS.
See Street railroads.

ELECTRIC SWITCHBOARDS.
Baxter, W:, *jr.* Switchboards for power, light and railway service. $1.50. Henley.
Connan, J: C. Switchboard measuring instruments. $2. Spon.

ELECTRIC TOYS.
See Toys.

ELECTRIC TRACTION.
See Electric railroads.

ELECTRIC TRANSFORMERS.
Grondahl, L. O. Synchronous commutation as a method for alternating-current—direct-current transformation. 20 c. Johns Hopkins.

ELECTRIC WAVE TELEGRAPHY.
See Wireless telegraphy.

ELECTRIC WIRES.
Auerbacher, L: J: Electrical contracting. $2. McGraw-H.
Branch, J. G. Electric wiring. $2. Branch.
Coyle, D., *and* Howe, F. J. O. Electric cables, their construction and cost. *$5 net. Spon.
Cushing, H. C. Standard wiring for electric light and power as adopted by the fire underwriters of the United States. $1. H. C. Cushing, Jr.
Down, P. D., *comp.* "Electrician" handy copper wire tables. *$1 net. Van Nostrand.
Harrison, N. Electric wiring diagrams and switchboards. $1.50. Henley.
Ibbetson, W. S. Theory and practice of electric wiring. $2. Spon.
Knox, G: E., *and* Shaad, G: C. Electric wiring and lighting. $1. Am. Sch. Corr.
Pratt, H. Wiring a house. 25 c. Henley.
Rosenthal, L. W. Practical calculator of transmission lines, for distribution of direct and alternating currents by means of overhead, underground, and interior wires. $2. McGraw.
Russell, A. Theory of electric cables and networks. *$3 net. Van Nostrand.
See also Electric light;—Electricity;—Telegraphy;—Telephones.

Electrical activities of the human body. Goodson, G: A. 75 c. G: A. Goodson.
Electrical connections. Kahl, J: C. 25 c. W. R. C. Smith.

ELECTRICAL ENGINEERING.
American Institute of Electrical Engineers, Library. Catalogue of the Wheeler gift of books, pamphlets and periodicals. $8. Am. Inst. Elec. Eng.
Auerbacher, L: J: Electrical contracting. $2. McGraw-H.
Barr, J A. Principles of direct current electrical engineering. *$3.25 net. Macmillan.
Berg, E. J. Electrical energy, its generation, transmission, and utilization. *$2.50 net. McGraw.
Bottone, S. R. Electrical engineering for students. 2 v. ea., 75 c. McKay.
Bowker, W: R. Dynamo, motor and switchboard circuits. *$2.50 net. Van Nostrand.
Clayton, W: B., *and* Craig, J. W. Questions and answers about electrical apparatus. 50 c.; 35 c. Clayton & C.; T: P. Nichols.
Del Mar, W: A. Electric power conductors. *$2 net. Van Nostrand.
Electrical solicitor's handbook. [2d ed.;] editorial committee: Arth. Williams, chairman; Otis Allen Kenyon, Norman G. Meade, Adolph Hertz. '09. [1910.] (F) c. 3-282 p. il. 16°, $2. Nat. Elec.
Floy, H: High-tension underground electric cables. $2. Elec. Pub.
Foster, H. A. Electrical engineers' pocket book. $5 net. Van Nostrand.
Freedman, W: H. Types of dynamo-electric machinery; direct current instruction paper. Am. Sch. Corr.

ELECTRICAL ENGINEERING.—*Continued.*
General Electric Company. Instructions for testing electrical apparatus. '09, [1910.] (Ap) 5-424 p. il. 12°. (Add. pubs. for price.) General Electric.
Hall, H. Young electrician. $1.50 net. Macmillan.
Handbook ser. In 4 v. ea., 10 c. Sampson.
Hartpence, A. Introd. course of continuous current engineering. *$2.50 net. Van Nostrand.
Haslam, A. P. Electricity in factories and workshop. $2.50. Henley.
Hay, A. Electrical distributing networks and transmission lines. $3.50 net. Cassell.
Henderson, J: Electrotechnics. $1.20. Longmans.
Horstmann, H: C. Modern electrical construction. $1.50. Drake.
Ibbettson, W. S. Pract. electrical engineering for elem. student in trade and technical schools. $1.50. Spon.
Karapetoff, V. Experimental electrical engineering. **$6 net; In 2 v. v. 1, $3.50. Wiley.
Kempe, H. R. Hdbk. of electrical testing. $6. Spon.
Koester, F. Steam-electric power plants. **$5 net. Van Nostrand.
Lyndon, Lamar. Development and electrical distribution of water power. *$3 net. Wiley.
Lyon, W. V. Problems in electrical engineering. *$1.50 net. McGraw.
Montgomery, J. H. Specifications for electrical construction. $1. Wahr.
Murray, T: E: Electric power plants. (Priv. pr.) T: E: Murray.
National Electric Light Association. Electrical solicitors' hdbk. (Not for sale.) Nat. Electric.
Norris, H: H. Introd. to the study of electrical engineering. **$2.50 net. Wiley.
Onken, W: J., *jr., and* Baker, J: B. Harper's how to understand electrical work. $1.75. Harper.
Oulton, L., *and* Wilson, N. J. Pract. testing of electrical machines. *$1.40 net. Macmillan.
Rosenthal, L. W. Pract. calculation of transmission lines for distribution of direct and alternating currents. *$2 net. McGraw.
Rowland, A. J., *and* Creagmile, W: B. Experiments in applied electricity. $1.25. McGraw-H.
St. John, T: M. Electrical handicraft. $1. T: M. St. John.
Simmons, H. H. Outlines of electrical engineering. *$6 net. Cassell.
Sloane, T. O. Electricians' handy book. $3.50. Henley.
Sloane, T: O. Elementary electrical calculations. $2. Van Nostrand.
Specification for electrical construction. $1. Wahr.
Standard hdbk. for electrical engineers. $4 net. McGraw-H.
Steinmetz, C: P. General lectures on electrical engineering. $2 net. Robson.

ELECTRICAL ENGINEERING.—*Continued.*
Steinmetz, C: P. Theoretical elements of electrical engineering. *$4 net. McGraw-H.
Stone & Webster. Current literature references, [electrical engineering,] 1907. (Add. pubs. for price.) Stone & W.
Swingle, C. F. Twentieth century hdbk. for steam engineers and electricians. $3. Drake.
Thomälen, A. Text-book of electrical engineering. *$4.20 net. Longmans.
United States. *Dept. of Commerce and Labor. Bu. of Census.* Electrical industries of Porto Rico. (Add. Superintendent for price.)
Weingreen, J. Electric power plant engineering. $5. McGraw-H.
Whittaker's arithmetic of electrical engineering. 50 c. Macmillan.
See also Chemistry;—Dynamos and motors;—Electric light;—Electric switchboards;—Electricity;—Elevators; — Engineering; — Hydraulic engineering;—Telegraphy.

Electrical installations of the United States navy. Walling, B. T. $6; $6.85. U. S. Naval Inst.

ELECTRICAL MEASUREMENTS.
Anthony, W: A. Lecture notes on the theory of electrical measurements. $1. Wiley.
Edgcumbe, K. Industrial electrical measuring instruments. *$2 net. Van Nostrand.
Richardson, S. S. Magnetism and electricity and the principles of electrical measurement. *$2 net. Van Nostrand.
See also Physics.

ELECTRICAL TRACTION.
See Electric railroads.

Electrical treatment. Harris, W. $2 net. Funk.
"Electrician" handy copper wire tables. Down, P. D., *comp.* *$1 net. Van Nostrand.
Electrician ser. il. 8°, $3.50. Van Nostrand.
—Maurice. Electric blasting apparatus and explosives.

ELECTRICITY.
Agnew, P. G. Approximate experimental method for the analysis of E. M. F. waves. (Add. Superintendent for price.) U. S., Supt. of Docs.
Albe, E. E. F. d'. Electron theory. $1.25 net. Longmans.
American School of Correspeondence. Cyclopedia of applied electricity. 6 v. $36. Am. Sch. Corr.
Ashcroft, E. A. Study of electrothermal and electrolytic industries. In 3 pts. pt. 1. *$2 net. McGraw.
Ashe, S. W. Electricity experimentally and practically applied. $2 net. Van Nostrand.
Ayrton, W: E: Pract. electricity. $2.50 net. Cassell.
Barus, C. Condensation of vapor as induced by nuclei and ions. 75 c. Carnegie.
Bates, P. A. Equipment of country houses with electricity. 25 c. Franklin Inst.
Bottone, S. R. Amateur electrician's workshop. 75 c. McKay.

ELECTRICITY.—*Continued.*
Branch, J. G. Conversations on electricity. $2. Rand, McN. & Co.
Broadbent, F. Chats on electricity. $1.25 net. Lippincott.
Bull, P. G: Simple experiments in static electricity. 25 c. Spon.
Bullard, W: H. G. Naval electricians' textbook. $6.50. U. S. Naval Inst.
Burlington, Ia. Public Library. Pract. books in the library on electricity, engineering, railroading and other subjects. Burlington Pub. Lib.
Campbell, N. R. Modern electrical theory. *$2.25 net. Putnam.
Coblentz, W: W. Note on the thermoelectric properties of tantalum and tungsten. Gov. Pr. Off.
Cohen, L: Coefficient of reflection of electrical waves at a transition point. [1910.] (Jl) 549-554 p. 8°. Gov. Pr. Off.
Corbin, T: W. "How does it work" of electricity. 75 c. Fenno.
Crocker, F. B., *and others.* Pract. lessons in electricity. $1.50. Am. Sch. Corr.
Cummings, G: W. Electricity and magnetism in telephone maintenance. $1.50. McGraw.
Decker, W. Complete condensed electricity. In 3 pts. ea., $4; per set, $12. Barnes Mfg. Co.
Foster, G: C., *and* Porter, A. W. Elem. treatise on electricity and magnetism. $3.50. Longmans.
Franklin, W: S., *and* MacNutt, B. Elements of electricity and magnetism. *$1.60 net. Macmillan.
Gibson, C: R. Autobiography of an electron. $1.50 net. Lippincott.
Hall, H. Young electrician. $1.50 net. Macmillan.
Hawkins, N. Electrical dict. $3.50.—New catechism of electricity. $2. Audel.
Hibbert, W. Popular electricity. *$1.25 net. Cassell.
Hobart, H: M. Electricity. $2 net. Van Nostrand.
Iles, G: Electricity uncovers a law of evolution. gratis. G: Iles.
Jeans, J. H. Mathematical theory of electricity and magnetism. *$4.50 net. Putnam.
Karapetoff, V. Electric circuit. $1.50. Andrus.
Kerr, E. W. Power and power transmission. $2. Wiley.
Kobbé, B. Introd. to electricity. *$3 net. Lippincott.
Lodge, *Sir* O. J. Modern views of electricity. *$1.25 net. Macmillan.
Lorentz, H. A. Theory of electrons. *$2.50 net. Stechert.
Lowe, P. E. Vest-pocket compendium of applied electricity. 25 c.; 50 c. McKay.
McClung, R. K. Conduction of electricity through gases and radio-activity. *$1.50 net. Blakiston.
Marshall, P. Workshop wrinkles and recipes. 50 c. Spon.
Millikan, R. A., *and* Mills, J: Short university course in electricity, sound and light. $2. Ginn.

ELECTRICITY.—*Continued.*
Munro, J: Story of electricity. 92 c. S. S. McClure.
O'Reilly, M. F., *and* Welsh, J. J. Makers of electricity. *$2 net. Fordham Univ.
Schneider, N. H. Electric circuits and diagrams. In 2 pts. ea., 25 c. Spon.
Shepardson, G: D.. Electrical catechism. *$2 net. McGraw.
Sloane, T: O. Arithmetic of electricity. $1.
—Standard electrical dict. $3. Henley.
Small, C: S. A-. Elem. electricity up-to-date. $1. Drake.
Steel, R. E. Pract. electricity. 50 c. net. Macmillan.
Steinmetz, C: P. Theory and calculations of transient electric phenomena and oscillations. $5. McGraw.
Swoope, C. W. Lessons in pract. electricity. $2 net. Van Nostrand.
Taylor, F. H. Guide to the electrical examinations. 75 c. Spon.
Timbie, W: H: Elements of electricity. $2 net. Wiley.
Tompkins, J. C. S. Electricity explained in simple language. $1. Cochrane.
Tunzelman, G. W. de. Treatise on electrical theory and the problem of the universe. $4.50 net. Lippincott.
Tyndall, C: H. Electricity and its similitudes. *$1 net. Revell.
Underhill, C: R. Solenoids, electromagnets and electromagnetic windings. $2 net. Van Nostrand.
Verschoyle, W. D. Electricity: what is it? *$1 net. Macmillan.
Walker, S. F. Electricity in mining. $3.50. Van Nostrand.
Whittaker, E. T. Hist. of the theories of æther and electricity. $4.50 net. Longmans.
See also Agricultural chemistry;—Alternating currents;—Armatures;—Dynamos and motors;—Electric batteries;—Electric light;—Electric engineering;—Galvanometer; — Induction coils;—Lightning;—Machinery;—Magnetism; —Medical electricity;—Physics;—Radio-activity;—Radium; —Roentgen rays;—Telegraphy; — Telephone;—Toys;—Wireless telegraphy;—*also* entries beginning with Electric, Electro.

Electrification of railway terminals. Chicago. *City Council. Committee on Local Transportation.* (Add. pubs. for price.) Donnelley.

ELECTRO-CHEMISTRY.
Jacobson, C. A. Conductivity and ionization of electrolytes in aqueous solutions as conditioned by temperature, dilution and hydrolysis. 60 c. Johns Hopkins.
Monell, S: H. Rudiments of modern electrical chemistry. *$1 net. W: R. Jenkins.
Richards, T. W:, *and others.* Electrochemical investigation of liquid amalgams of thalium, indium, tin, zinc, cadmium, lead, copper and lithium. 50 c. Carnegie.
See also Spectrum.

Electro-magnetic ore separation. Gunther, C: G. *$2 net. Hill Pub.

ELECTRO-METALLURGY.
Kershaw, J. B. C. Electro metallurgy. *$2 net. Van Nostrand.
Macmillan, W. Electro-metallurgy. $4 net. Lippincott.

ELECTRO-MOTIVE FORCE.
See Electricity.

ELECTRO-PHYSIOLOGY.
See Medical electricity;—Physiology.

ELECTRO-PLATING.
Bedell, W: L. D: Practical electro-plating. $2. Hansom & V.
Gentry, G: Pract. electro-plating. 50 c. Spon.

ELECTRO-TECHNICS.
See Electrical engineering.

ELECTRO-THERAPEUTICS.
See Medical electricity.

ELECTRO-TYPING.
Partridge, C: S. Electrotyping. $2. Inland Pr.

ELECTRO-VITAL FORCE.
See Universe.

ELECTROLYTIC INDUSTRIES.
See Electricity.

ELECTRONS.
See Electricity.

ELECTROTHERMAL INDUSTRIES.
See Electricity.

Elegy on the much-to-be-deplored death of that never-to-be-forgotten person, the Reverend Nathaniel Collins. Mather, C. $3. Baumgardt.

Elegy written in a country churchyard. *See* Gray, T:

ELEKTRA (*opera*).
Hutcheson, E. Elektra; guide to the opera. *75 c. net. Schirmer.

Elementary commercial class-books. D. Macmillan.
—Gow. Marine insurance. $1.10 net.

Elements (The). Tilden, *Sir* W: A: 75 c. net. Harper.

ELEVATORS.
Baxter, W:, *jr.* Hydraulic elevators. $2.50 net. McGraw-H.
Bolton, R. P. Elevator service. *$5 net. R. P. Bolton.
Swingle, C. F. Elevators, hydraulic and electric. $1. Drake.

Eleventh hour. Potter, D: †$1.50 Dodd.

Elfer, W: André.
Breeding minks in Louisiana for their fur; profitable industry. '09(N) c. 64 p. il. 12°. 75 c. Gessner.

Elford, Percy, and Heaton, S:
Pract. school gardening. '09(D18) il. 12°, *70 c. net. Oxford Univ.
—, comps. School garden note book. '09 (Ap3) D. 25 c. Oxford Univ.

ELGIN BOTANIC GARDEN, New York City.
Brown, A. Elgin Botanic Garden, its history and relation to Columbia College. $1. A. Brown.

Elimination of pupils from school. Falkner, R. P. 10 c. R. P. Falkner.

Elimination of the tramp. Kelly, E. **$1 net. Putnam.

Eliot, Sir C: Norton Edgecumbe, ["Odysseus."]
Turkey in Europe. '08(Ap25) maps, O. $2.50. Longmans.

Eliot, C: W:
College taxation: remarks before the Joint Committee on Taxation, Massachusetts legislature, March 13, 1907. '07. [1908.] (F) O. pap., gratis. Harvard Univ.

Eliot, C: W:—*Continued.*
Conflict bet. individualism and collectivism in a democracy; three lectures (University of Virginia, Barbour-Page Foundation). '10(D10) c. D. 90 c. net. Scribner.
Durable satisfactions of life. '10(Ag13) c. D. $1. Crowell.
Education for efficiency and the new definition of the cultivated man. '09(Jl3) c. D. (Riverside educational monographs.) 35 c. Houghton M.
Fruits of medical research with the aid of anæsthesia and ascepticism. '09, [1910.] (Mr) 19 p. 8°. (Not for sale.) Mass. Gen. Hospital.
Future of trades-unionism and capitalism in a democracy; being the Larwill Lectures for 1909. '10(Jl2) c. D. $1 net. Putnam.
Lawlessness: address. '09(My15) c. por. D. (Civic Forum addresses.) pap., 10 c. Civic Forum.
Religion of the future. '09(D25) D. *50 c. net. Ball Pub.
Religion of the future. '09(N6) por. D. 75 c. J: W. Luce.
Religion of the future; lecture del. at close of 11th session of the Harvard Summer School of Theology, July 12, 1909. '10 (Ja8) D. bds., **50 c. net. Stokes.
University administration. [Norman Wait Harris lectures.] '08(N21) c. O. **$1.50 net. Houghton M.
—, **ed.** *See* Harvard classics.

ELIOT, Charles William.
Kuehnemann, E. Charles W. Eliot, president of Harvard University. **$1 net. Houghton M.

Eliot, George, [pseud. for Mrs. J: W. Cross.]
Works. 10 v. '10(D) $30. Crowell.
Works. [Crowell's thin-paper sets.] 8 v. '09(O9) 16°, flex. leath., $10. Crowell.
Works. Personal ed. 12 v. '10(D17) il. 12°, ea., $1.50; per set, $18; hf. leath., $24. Doubleday, P.
Works. 8 v. New imperial lib. ed. '10 (D) il. 8°, ea., $1.25; hf. cf., $2.25; New il. sterling ed., ea., $1. (Sets only.) Estes.
Works. Uniform ed. 4 v. now ready. '08(Je27) 24°, *$2 net; flex. leath., *$3 net. Lane.
Works. De luxe ed. 12 v. '10(D) 16°, ea., mor., $1.50 net. (Sets only.) Nelson.
Writings. [Large pap. ed.] '08(N21) c. 25 v., il. pors. 8°, per set, $125 to $600. (750 copies.) Houghton M.
Adam Bede. '08(O10) 12°, (Best books ser.) leath., *$1 net. Dutton.
Felix Holt. '09(Mr27) 16°, (Everyman's lib.) *35 c. net; leath., *70 c. net. Dutton.
Mill on the Floss. Luxembourg ed. '08 (S5) il. O. $1.50, boxed. Crowell.
Mill on the Floss. '08(S19) 16°, (Everyman's lib.) *35 c. net; leath., *70 c. net. Dutton.
Romola. '08(O10) 12°, (Best books ser.) leath., *$1 net. Dutton.
Romola. In 2 v. '09(Ag28) il. S. (Ideal classics.) flex. leath., ea., $1.25. Winston.

Eliot, George.—*Continued.*
Scenes of clerical life; with introd. by Grace Rhys. '10(D10) c. 16°, (Everyman's lib.) 35 c. net; leath., 70 c. net. Dutton.
Scenes of clerical life; with introd. by Annie Matheson. '09(My15) 16°, (World's classics.) 40 c.; leath., 75 c. Oxford Univ.
Silas Marner. '08(O10) 12°, (Best books ser.) leath., *$1 net. Dutton.
Silas Marner. '10(O8) il. 12°, (Queen's treasure ser.) $1. Macmillan.
Silas Marner, the weaver of Ravelo; ed., with an introd. and notes, by Cornelia Beare. '08(O10) c. por. 12°, (Merrill's English texts.) **40 c. net. C: E. Merrill.
Silas Marner; ed. by F. T. Baker. '10 (D3) 16°, (Scribner's English classics.) 25 c. net. Scribner.
Two lovers. '09(N6) c. col. il O. **$1 net. Moffat.

ELIOT, George.
Davidson, *Mrs.* H. A. N. Study of Romola. 50 c. H. A. Davidson.
Olcott, C: S. George Eliot. $2 net. Crowell.

Eliot, S: Atkins.
Heralds of a liberal faith. In 3 v. v. 1, The prophets; v. 2, The pioneers; v. 3, The preachers. '09(N20) ea., *$1 net; per set, *$3 net. Am. Unitarian.

ELIZABETH, *Empress of Austria.*
Küchler, C. Elizabeth, Empress of Austria. *60 c. net. McClurg.

ELIZABETH, Philippine Marie Helene, *Madame.*
Scott, *Mrs.* M. M. M-. Madame Elizabeth de France. *$3.50 net. Longmans.

ELIZABETH, *Princess Palatine.*
Godfrey, E., *pseud.* Sister of Prince Rupert: Elizabeth Princess Palatine. *$4 net. Lane.

ELIZABETH, *Queen of England.*
Hume, M. A. S. Two English queens and Philip. *$4.50 net. Putnam.
Laneham, R. Letter: describing a part of the entertainment unto Queen Elizabeth at the castle of Kenilworth. *$1.75 net. Duffield
Mumby, F. A., *comp.* Girlhood of Queen Elizabeth. **$3 net. Houghton M.

Elizabeth Crane. Curtis, H: E. B'way Pub.
Elizabeth Davenay. De Pratz, C. $1.50. M. Kennerley.

ELIZABETH (PA.) METHODIST EPISCOPAL CHURCH.
Wiley, R: T. Elizabeth Methodist Episcopal Church. 50 c. R: T. Wiley.

Elizabeth of Boonesborough. Witherspoon, *Mrs.* P. F. $1.50. Badger.

ELIZABETH STUART, *Queen of Bohemia.*
Green, M. A. E. Elizabeth, Queen of Bohemia and Electress Palatine. *$3.50 net. Dutton.
Hay, M. Winter queen; being the unhappy hist. of Elizabeth Stuart, Electress Palatine, Queen of Bohemia. $4 net. Houghton M.

Elizabeth visits America. Glyn, *Mrs.* E. S. †$1.50. Duffield.

ELIZABETHAN DRAMA.
See Drama and dramatists.

Elizabethan parish. Ware, S. L. 50 c. Johns Hopkins.

Elizabethan people. Stephenson, H: T. **$2 net. Holt.

Elizabeth's story. Pierce, G. H. 50 c. G. H. Pierce.

ELIZABETHTOWN QUADRANGLE.
See New York State.

Elkington, Ernest Way.
Canada: land of hope. '10(D31) il. maps, 8°, $1.75 net. Macmillan.

ELKS, BENEVOLENT AND PROTECTIVE ORDER OF.
See Freemasonry.

Elkus, Abram I., and Glenn, Garrard.
Treatise on secret liens and reputed ownership, 1910. '10(Jl) c. O. $3.50. Baker, V. & Co.

Elkus, Savilla Alice.
Concept of control. '08(My9) 8°, (Archives of philosophy.) 40 c. Science Pr., (N. Y.)

Ellen. *See* Battell, Jos.

Ellett, A. H.
Federal Union and Mississippi; civil government for use in grammar grades of the public schools. '10(Ag6) c. 12°, 75 c. B. F. Johnson.

Ellett, Fk. Gates.
Making the up grade. '09(D11) c. il. por. D. $1. F. G. Ellett.

ELLICOTT, Andrew.
Mathews, C. Van C. Andrew Ellicott: his life and letters. **$2.50 net. Grafton Press.

Ellicott, Bp. C: J:
Bible commentary for English readers. In 12 v. Pocket ed. '10(My21) ea., 75 c. net; leath., $1.25 net. Cassell.

Ellington, Rev. W. S.
See Boyd, R. H.

Elliot, G: Fs. Scott.
Botany of to-day; popular account of recent notable discoveries. '09(D4) il. D. *$1.50 net. Lippincott.
Wonders of the plant world. '10(Ja1) il. 12°, 75 c. Lippincott.

Elliott, Berton E., and Ward, P. R.
Motor craft encyclopedia. '10(D31) c. il. fold. chart, 12°, $1. Motor Craft.

Elliott, Byron K. and W: F.
Law of railroads, together with their duties, rights, liabilities, etc. 2d ed. 5 v. v. 1, The corporation; v. 2, Governmental control, location, construction; v. 3, Operation; v. 4, The carrier; v. 5, Table of cases. Index. '07, [1908.] (Mr.) c. 8°, $27. Bobbs-M.

Elliott, C: Burke.
Principles of the law of public corporations; rev., [etc.,] by J: E. Macy. '10 (Mr) c. O. $4. Callaghan.

Elliott, C: Gleason.
Practical farm drainage. 2d ed., rewritten. '08(N7) figs. 12°, $1.50. Wiley.

Elliott, E: Graham.
Biographical story of the constitution; study of the growth of the American union. '10(F12) c. O. **$2 net. Putnam.

"Elliott, Emilia," pseud.
See Jacobs, Caroline Emilia.

Elliott, Frances B.
Old court life in France. [New and cheaper ed.] 2 v. in 1. '10(D10) il. sq. 16°, $1.50 net. Brentano's.
Old court life in Spain. [New and cheaper ed.] 2 v. in 1. '10(D10) sq. 16°, $1.50 net. Brentano's.

Elliott, Mrs. Grace Dalrymple.
During the Reign of Terror; journal of my life during the French Revolution; with introd. and notes; tr. from the French by E. Jules Meras. '10(Ap16) c. il. pors. D. (Court ser. of French memoirs.) $1.50 net. Sturgis & W.
In the shadow of the guillotine; ed. by Helen Kendrick Hayes. '09(Ap10) por. D. 75 c. Estes.

Elliott, Ja.
Earthquakes: their causes. '08(D5) map, O. pap., 25 c. J. Elliott.
Nebular hypothesis untenable. '08(Mr28) O. 25 c. J. Elliott.
Solar heat, non-solar. '09(Jl3) O. pap., 25 c. J Elliott.
Sun spots, their cause and the cause of their periodicity. '08(Mr28) O. 25 c. J. Elliott.

Elliott, J:
Resurgam: [poem.] '08(Mr28) c. front. 12°, **$1 net. Lane.

Elliott, J:, 1865-, ed.
See Connecticut. Sales act.—New Jersey. Sales act.

Elliott, Mrs. J:
See Howe, Maud.

Elliott, J: H:, D.D.
Brook in the pasture. '10(My14) c. S. (Inner circle ser.) bds., 25 c. Un. Soc. C. E.

Elliott, Marietta M. S.
As they came to me: [poems.] '08(S12) c. il. por. D. $1. M. M. S. Elliot.

Elliott, Sophronia Maria.
Household bacteriology. [Text-book ed.] '10(Ag27) c. il. por. 12°, $1.50. Am. Sch. Home Economics.
Household hygiene. [Text book ed.] '10 (D3) il. 12°, $1.25. Am. Sch. Home Economics.

Elliott, W. H.
A B C of railroad signaling; lecture del. before the Harvard School of Business Administration. '10(Jl9) c. il. 12°, $1. Mackenzie-K.

Elliott, W: F.
See Elliott, Byron K.

Ellis, Mrs.
See Hubbard, Mina Benson.

Ellis, A. G.
See Hobart, H: Metcalf.

Ellis, Carlos Bent.
Practical bookkeeping. '08(F29) c. O. $1.35. Allyn & B.
Reference book for use with Ellis's Practical bookkeeping. '08(My2) c. 12°, 75 c. Allyn & B.

Ellis, C: Calvert.
Lancasterian school in Philadelphia. '09 (Ap) 88 p. 8°. (Not for sale.) Univ. of Penn.
Bibliography (6 p.).

Ellis, C: E:
Authentic hist. of the Benevolent and Protective Order of Elks. '10(N) c. 473 p. il. pors. maps, 4°, $5; hf. mor., $7.50; mor., $10. C: E: Ellis.
Bound with this: "The official history of Chicago Lodge no. 4, B. P. O. E., C: E: Ellis. Chicago, Ill.

Ellis, D:
Outlines of bacteriology; (technical and agricultural.) '09(N13) il. O. *$2.50 net. Longmans.

Ellis, E. E.
See Gregory, Herbert Ernest.

Ellis, Edith M. O. Lees, [Mrs. Havelock Ellis.]
Steve's woman. '09(N) c. 259 p. col. il. 12°, $1.50. J: McBride.
Three modern seers—James Hinton, Nietzsche, Edward Carpenter. '10(D17) 12°, $1.25 net. M. Kennerley.

Ellis, E: Sylvester.
Alden among the Indians; or, the search for the missing pony express rider. '10 (Ja1) c. il. 12°, (Overland ser.) $1; per set, $2, boxed. Winston.
Alden, the pony express rider; or, racing for life. '10(Ja1) c. il. 12°, (Overland ser.) $1; per set, $2, boxed. Winston.
Captain of the camp; or, Ben, the young boss. '10(Ag6) c. il. D. (Catamount Camp ser.) $1. Winston.
Catamount Camp. '10(Ag6) c. il. D. (Catamount Camp ser.) $1; with the above, $2, boxed. Winston.
Fire, snow and water; or, life in the lone land. '08(O3) c. il. D. †75 c. Winston.
Guida per gl' immigranti Italiani negli Stati Uniti d'America; [tr. into Italian by Constantino M. Panunzio.] '09(Mr13) nar. T. pap., gratis. C. M. Panunzio.
Library of American hist. from the discovery of America to the present time. [Ed. de luxe.] In 9 v. '10(N12) c. il. 4°, $56. Jones Bros.
Low twelve: incidents illustrative of the fidelity of Free Masons to one another. '08(Ap18) c. 8°, $1.50. Niglutsch.
Off the reservation. '08(O3) c. il. D. (Arizona ser.) †$1. Winston.
P. Q. & G.; or, "as the twig is bent the tree's inclined." '08(O17) c. il. D. $1.25. Estes.
Phantom auto. '08(O3) c. il. D. †75 c. Winston.
The round-up. '08(O3) c. il. O. (Arizona ser.) †$1. Winston.
Story of Red Feather; tale of the American frontier. '08, [1909.] (Ap) c. 3-132 p. il. 8°, 50 c. McLoughlin.
Trailing Geronimo. '08(O3) c. il. D. (Arizona ser.) †$1. Winston.
Unlucky Tib. '09(O2) c. il. D. †$1.25. Estes.
Upside down; automobile story for boys. '10(Ja1) c. il. D. 75 c. Winston.
Work and win; story of a country boy's success. '10(S17) c. il. 12°, $1. Burt.
Young pioneers; or, better to be born plucky than rich. '09(My) c. '08. 280 p. il. 12°, †$1. Burt.
—, ed. Hist. of our country from the discovery of America to the present time. 8 v. '10(D17) c. il. pors. maps, 4°, $48. Jones Bros.

Ellis, E: Sylvester, and Snyder, H:
Brief hist. of New Jersey. '10(Je25) c. il. pors. D. 60 c. Am. Bk.

Ellis, Eliz.
Fair moon of Bath. '08(Ap11) c. front. D. †$1.50. Dodd.
Girl who won. '10(Jl2) c. il. D. $1.50. Dodd.

Ellis, G:
Modern practical joinery. '08(Je20) il. Q. *$6 net. Scribner.

Ellis, H: Havelock.
The criminal. 3d ed., rev. and enl. '10 (D24) il. 12°, (Contemporary science ser.) $1.50. Scribner.
Evolution of modesty; the phenomena of sexual periodicity, auto-erotism. 3d ed., rev. and enl. '10(Ag) 15+352 p. diagrs., 8°, (Studies in the psychology of sex.) $2. Davis.
Soul of Spain. '08(My2) front. O. *$2 net. Houghton M.
Studies in the psychology of sex. v. 6, Sex in relation to society. '10(Ap) 16+656 p. 8°, $3. Davis.

Ellis, Mrs. H: Havelock.
See Ellis, Edith M. O. Lees.

Ellis, J: Breckenridge.
Arkinsaw cousins. '08(F29) c. D. †$1.50. Holt.
Fated to win (The soul of a serf). '10 (D31) c. D. $1. Laird.
Soul of a serf; romance of love and valor among the Angles and Saxons. '10(Jl2) c. il. D. Library ed., extra cl., $1.50. Laird.
Twin Starrs: a novel. '08(Ap18) c. D. $1. Mayhew.

Ellis, Katharine Ruth Ellis.
Wide Awake girls. '08(O3) c. il. D. (Wide Awake girls ser.) †$1.50. Little, B. & Co.
Wide Awake girls at college. '10(O1) c. il. D. (Wide Awake girls ser.) $1.50. Little, B. & Co.
Wide Awake girls in Winsted. '09(S25) c. D. (Wide Awake girls ser.) †$1.50. Little, B. & Co.

Ellis, Lynn Webster.
Minor articles of farm equipment. '10 (Mr) 15 p. 8°, (U. S., Dept. of Agriculture, Bu. of Plant Industry, circular.) pap.

Ellis, Mrs. Olyette.
Autumn leaves: [poems.] '08, [1909.] (Ja) c. 256 p. il. 8°, $1 hand col. il., $1.25. Times Pub. Co., (Wis.)

Ellis, Robinson.
Lecture on Professor Birt's ed. of the Vergilian catalepton. '10(D3) 8°, pap., 40 c. net. Oxford Univ.

Ellis, S. M.
William Harrison Ainsworth and his friends. '10(D10) il. O. $10 net. Lane.

Ellis, Wade Hampton, ed.
See Ohio. Municipal code.

Ellis, W: T:
Men and missions; with a foreword by J: B. Sleman, jr., and with a statistical and historical appendix comp. by Abigail J. Davies. '10(Je18) c. D. 60 c. net. S. S. Times.

ELLIS LANDING, Cal.
Nelson, N. C. Ellis Landing shellmounds. 75 c. Univ. of Cal.

Ellis Publishing Co. Student's guide to accompany the Ellis cabinet system of teaching bookkeeping and business practice. Rev. ed. '10(F19) c. forms, 4°, (Learning by doing ser.) $1.50. Ellis Pub.

Ellis Publishing Co. Student's guide to accompany the Ellis tablet method of teaching bookkeeping and business practice; complete course. '10(S) c. 149 p. forms, 4°, $1. Ellis Pub.

Ellison, Dan. Ja., D.D.
Italy through the stereoscope. '08(Je6) c. maps, 12°, $1.90. Underwood.

Ellison, Mrs. Edith Nicholl.
Blossoming of the waste. '08(My23) c. front. O. $1.50. Calkins & Co.
Burnt offering. '09(Ja2) 12°, $1.25. B'way Pub.

Ellison, F. O'B.
See Alcock, N. H.

Ellwanger, W: De Lancy.
Snuff box full of trees and some apocryphal essays. '09(D25) c. 8°, **$2 net. Dodd.

Ellwood, C: Abram.
Sociology and modern social problems. '10 (D10) c. D. $1. Am. Bk.

Elm-tree fairy book. Johnson, C., *ed.* †$1.50. Little, B. & Co.

Elmore, Ja. Buchanan.
Love among the mistletoe and poems. '08, [1909.] (Ap) c. 7+ 223 p. por. il. 12°, $1. J. B. Elmore.

Elmore, Jefferson.
Book of Latin prose composition for the use of colleges and advanced classes in schools. '09(N20) 12°, (Students' ser. of Latin classics.) $1. B: H. Sanborn.

Elo the eagle. Bralliar, F. $1. Pacific Press.

ELOCUTION.
Fulton, R. I., *and* Trueblood, T: C. Essentials of public speaking for secondary schools. 90 c. Ginn.
Kleiser, G. How to develop power and personality in speaking. **$1.25 net.—Teachers' key to How to speak in public. 50 c. Funk.
Morgan, A. Art of speech and deportment. *$1.50 net. McClurg.
Phillips, A. E: Natural drills in expression, with selections. $1.25.—Tone system in public speaking and reading. $1. Newton Co.
Powers, L. T. *and Mrs.* C. H. Talks on some fundamentals of expression. $1.25. L. Powers Sch.
Shoemaker, J. W. Practical elocution. $1.25. Penn Pub. Co.
Webber, J. P. Elements of elocution. (Priv. pr.) J. P. Webber.
See also Debating;—Lecturing;—Orators and oratory; — Preaching;—Pronunciation;—Readers;—Reading;—Recitations;—Rhetoric;—Voice.

ELOQUENCE.
See Orators and oratory;—Preaching.

Eloquent sons of the South. Graves, J: T., *and others, eds.* $2. Chapple Pub.

Elsden, Ja. Vincent.
Principles of chemical geology. '10(Ag13) 8°, $1.60 net. Macmillan.

Elsee, Rev. C:
Neoplatonism in relation to Christianity. '08(D19) 8°, *75 c. net. Putnam.

Elsewhere land. Mallette, G. E. 50 c. Univ. Bk. Store.

Elshemus, L: Michael.
Companionship: [poems.] '10(F) 15 p. 8°, *$1.25 net. Dreamers Press.
Thoughts at night-time. [1910.] (Je) 16 p. O. pap., $1.25. Dreamers Press.

Elsie and the Arkansaw bear. Paine, A. B. $1. Altemus.

Elson, Arth.
Music club programs from all nations. '08 (Ja18) pors. 8°, (Music students' lib.) $1.25. Ditson.

Elson, H: W:
Child's guide to American history. '09 (Ag21) c. il. O. **$1.25 net. Baker & T.
Comets, their origin, nature, and history. '10(Ap9) c. il. S. 50 c. net. Sturgis & W.
Hist. of the United States of America. Reissue in 5 v. '08(O10) il. maps, 8°, *$7.50 net. Macmillan.
Star-gazer's hand-book; a brief guide for amateur students of astronomy. '09(O2) c. D. *50 c. net. Sturgis & W.

Elson, L: C:
Curiosities of music: facts regarding the music of ancient and savage nations. '08 (S12) c. 12°, $1. Ditson.
Mistakes and disputed points in music and music teaching. '10(D31) c. 8°, $1.25. T. Presser.
Pocket music dict. '10(Mr19) c. nar. S. 35 c. Ditson.

Elson, Rob.
The magnate. '09(Ap10) D. †$1.50. Brentano's.

Elson, W: H.
See Short, Rob. L:

—, and Keck, Christine.
Grammar school reader. Bk. 2. '10(N12) c. D. 50 c.; Bk. 3 (Ap30); Bk. 4 (My21) ea., 60 c. Scott, F. & Co.

Elston, T: Sidney.
See Hall, Elmer Edg.

Eltinge, Le Roy.
See Munson, E: Lyman.

Eltringham, H.
African mimetic butterflies. '10(O8) il. F. $15. Oxford Univ.

Eltzbacher, Paul.
Anarchism; tr. by Steven T. Byington. '08 (Ap11) c. 16°, $1.50. B: R. Tucker.

Eltzholtz, Carl Frederik.
John Wesley's Conversion and sanctification. '08(Ap18) c. S. *25 c. net. Jennings.

Elusive Isabel. Futrelle, J. †$1.50. Bobbs-M.

Elusive pimpernel. Orczy, E. M. R. M. J. B., *Baroness.* †$1.50. Dodd.

Elwang, W: Wilson.
Social function of religious belief. '08 (My23) c. Q. (Univ. of Mo. studies, Social science ser.) pap., $1. Univ. of Mo.

Elwell, Jos. Bowne.
Practical bridge. '08(Mr28) c. il. S. **$1.50 net. Scribner.
Principles, rules and laws of auction bridge. '10(O8) c. S. $1.25 net. Scribner.

Ely, R: Thdr.
Outlines of economics; rev. and enl. by the author and T: S. Adams, Max O. Lorenz, Allyn A. Young. '08(S26) tabs., *$2 net. Macmillan.

Ely, Simpson.
Sermons, essays and outlines, by Simpson Ely; comp. by his son Marcellus R. Ely. '10(O8) c. por. 12°, $1. Standard Pub.

Ely, Wilmer Mateo.
Young pearl hunters. '09(My) 304 p. il. 12°, †$1. Burt.
Young plume hunters. '10(S17) c. il. 12°, (Boy chum ser.) $1. Burt.

ELY, Eng.
Conybeare, J: W: E: Highways and byways in Cambridge and Ely. $2 net. Macmillan.

Elzas, Barnett Abraham.
Leaves from my historical scrap book. 2d ser. '08(Ag) 44 p. 8°, $1. B. A. Elzas.

Elzevir library. [1910.] (My) 16°, hf. vel., 60 c.; mor., $1. Reilly & B.
Contents: Fancy and humor of C: Lamb; Wit and imagination of B: Disraeli; Vignettes from Oliver Goldsmith; Wit and sagacity of Dr. S: Johnson; Insight and imagination of J: Ruskin; Vignettes of London life from C: Dickens; Vignettes of country life from C: Dickens; Eighteenth century vignettes from W: M. Thackeray; Wisdom and humor of T: Carlyle.

EMANCIPATION.
See Slavery.

Emancipation. Savay, N. L-. (Priv. pr.) Kinckerbocker Press.

EMANUEL, David.
Hühner, L. First Jew to hold the office of governor of one of the United States. 25 c. Bloch.

Emanuel, Wa., pseud.
Dog World and Anti-Cat Review; written and illustrated by dogs for dogs. '09 (D25) c. 8°, pap., **25 c. net. Stokes.

—, and Aldin, Cecil C: Windsor.
Conceited puppy. '09(O2) il. 24°, bds., 50 c. Dutton.
Dog day; or, an angel in the house. '08 (D19) il. sq. 16°, 50 c. Dutton.

Emanuel movement, with sermons from promiment ministers and opinions of laymen. '08(Ag8) c. pap., 10 c. Brooklyn Eagle.

EMBALMING.
Dodge, A. J. Practical embalmer. $3. A. J. Dodge.
Myers, E. Champion text-book on embalming. $5; $5.50; $6. Champion Chemical.

EMBOSSING.
See Printers and printing.

Embree, C: Fleming.
Dream of a throne. '08(My.) c. 12°, (Popular ed. of recent fiction.) †75 c. Little, B. & Co.

EMBRIOGENY.
See Embryology.

EMBROIDERY.
Brown, N. C., *and* Locke, E. I., *eds.* Priscilla Hardanger book; designs in embroidery. 25 c. Priscilla.
Cartier-Bresson, *Mme.* How to work embroidery stitches. 25 c. Mills & G.
Hall, M. R. English church needlework. *$3 net. Gorham.
Heminway, M., & Sons Silk Co. Treatise on embroidery. 15 c. Heminway.
Huish, M. B. Samplers and tapestry embroideries. $17. Longmans.
Lay, L. F., *and* Buckle, M. Art in needlework: embroidery. *$2 net. Scribner.
National Society of Fine Arts. Tapestries, textiles, and embroideries. (Add. pub. for price.) Nat. Soc. of Fine Arts.
Priscilla Pub. Co. Wallachian embroidery. 15 c. Priscilla.
Townsend, W. G. P., *and* Pesel, L. F. Embroidery, or the craft of the needle. *$1.50 net. Stokes.
See also Needlework.

EMBRYOLOGY.
Bailey, F: R., *and* Miller, A. M. Text-book of embryology. *$4.50 net; *$5.50 net. Wood.
Bryce, T: H., *and others.* Contributions to the study of the early development and imbedding of the human ovum. *$4 net. Macmillan.
Budgett, J: S: Work of John Samuel Budgett: collection of his zoological papers. *$7 net. Putnam.
Jenkinson, J. W. Experimental embryology. *$4.15 net. Oxford Univ.
Keibel, F., *and* Mall, F. P. Manual of human embryology. v. 1. $7.50 net. Lippincott.
Keith, A. Human embryology and morphology. $3.50 net. Longmans.
Lillie, F. R. Development of the chick; an introd. to embryology. **$4 net. Holt.
Marshall, F. H. A. Physiology of reproduction. $6 net. Longmans.
Minot, C: S. Laboratory text book of embryology. $3.50. Blakiston.
Przibram, H. Embryogeny: laws governing the development of the animal egg. *$2.50 net. Putnam.
Reese, A. M. Introd. to vertebrate embryology; based on study of frog, chick and mammal. $1.50 net. Putnam.
Ritter, W: E., *and* Bailey, S: E. On the weight of developing eggs. 10 c. Univ. of Cal.
See also Biology;—Cells.

Embury, Aymar, 2d.
One hundred country houses; modern American examples. '09(O2) c. il. Q. **$3 net, boxed. Century Co.

Emerald city of Oz. Baum, L. F. $1.25. Reilly & B.

EMERGENCIES.
See Accidents.

Emergency surgery. Sluss, J: W: *$3.50 net. Blakiston.

Emeritus ser. 40 v. '10(N) il. ea., $1.50 boxed. Caldwell.

Emerson, Arth. I., and Weed, Clarence Moores.
Our trees: how to know them: photographs from nature, by Arth. I. Emerson; with a guide to their recognition at any season of the year and notes on their characteristics, distribution, and culture by Clarence M. Weed. '08(Mr7) c. il. O. $3. Lippincott.

Emerson, C: Phillips, M.D.
Clinical diagnosis. 2d ed. '08(N) c. 25+17-686 p. il. pls. 8°, $5. Lippincott.
Essentials of medicine. '08(D19) c. il. figs. O. **$2 net. Lippincott.

Emerson, C: Wesley.
Six lectures. '09(Ag7) c. por. D. leath., $2; bds., $1.15, boxed. C: W. Emerson.

Emerson, E: Randolph.
Beverages, past and present: historical sketch of their production, with a study of the customs connected with their use. '09(Ja30) c. 2 v., O. **$5 net, boxed. Putnam.

Emerson, Edn., jr.
Comet lore: Halley's comet in hist. and astronomy. '10(Ap23) c. il. pls. por. 8°, 25 c. E. Emerson.

Emerson, F: Valentine.
Manual of physical geography. '10(Ja1) c. O. **$1.40 net. Macmillan.

Emerson, G: Douglas.
Niagara campaign of 1759. 2d ed. '09 (S) c. 81 p. por. plan, 8°, $1.50. G: D. Emerson.

Emerson, Gilbert D.
Bookbinding for libraries. '09, [1910.] (Ap) 22 p. 16°, gratis. G. D. Emerson (Phil.)

Emerson, Harrington.
Efficiency as a basis for operation and wages. '09(N6) c. il. 12°, (Works management lib.) $2. Engineering Mag.

Emerson, H: Pendexter, and Bender, Ida C.
English spoken and written. Bk. 1, Lessons in language for primary grades. '09 (O16) il. 12°, *$1.50 net; Bk. 2, Lessons in language, literature, and composition; Bk. 3, Pract. lessons in English grammar and composition. '10(Je18) c. il. 12°, bk. 2, 50 c. net; bk. 3, 60 c. net. Macmillan.
Bk. 2, formerly published under series title "Words spoken and written."
Modern English. Bk. 1, Elementary lessons in English. '08(Ag8) *35 c. net; Southern ed., N. Y. ed., ea., *40 c. net; Bk. 2, Pract. English grammar with exercises in composition. (Ag22) il. 12°, *60 c. net; N. Y. State ed., 60 c. net. Macmillan.

Emerson, Nathaniel Bright.
Unwritten literature of Hawaii; the sacred songs of the hula collected and tr., with notes and an account of the hula. '09 (D18) il. 8°, (Smithsonian Institution, Bu. of Am. Ethnology, bull.) pap. (Add. Superintendent for price.) U. S., Supt. of Docs.

Emerson, Philip.
See Weed, Clarence Moores.

Emerson, Ralph Waldo.
Earlier poems; ed., with introd. and notes, by Oscar C: Gallagher. '08(Ag8) c. por. 24°, (Pocket Amer. and Eng. classics.) *25 c. net. Macmillan.
Education: an essay, and other selections. '09(Ap17) c. D. (Riverside educational monographs.) **35 c. net. Houghton M.
Emerson day by day; ed. by H. Smith. '10 (D) 12°, (Day by day ser.) 60 c.; ooze, $1. Crowell.
Essay on self-reliance. '08, [1909.] (Mr) 59 p. por. 8°, $2. Roycrofters.
Essays. 1st and 2d ser. '08(O10) 12°, (Best books ser.) leath., *$1 net. Dutton.
Essays, (selected;) ed., with an introd. and notes, by Edna H. L. Turpin. '08(Ja4) por. 16°, (Eng. texts.) 30 c. C: E. Merrill.
Essays: (Experience, Manners, Prudence, Self-reliance.) '10(O31) front. 32°, (Ariel booklets.) leath., 75 c., boxed. Putnam.
Journals of Ralph Waldo Emerson, with annotations; ed. by E: Waldo Emerson and Waldo Emerson Forbes. [v. 1,] 1820-1824; [v. 2,] 1824-1832. '09(D4); [v. 3,] 1833-1835; [v. 4,] 1836-1838. '10 (D3) c. il. pors. O. ea., $1.75 net. Houghton M.
Nature. '09(N6) c. 12°, (Rubric ser.) **60 c. net. Duffield.
Nature, and The conduct of life. '08(S19) 16°, (Everyman's lib.) *35 c. net; leath., *70 c. net. Dutton.
Pocket Emerson; ed. by W. T. S. Sonnenschein. New ed. '09, [1910.] (F) 16°, (Wayfaring books.) leath., *$1.25 net. Dutton.
Poems. '10(D) 12°, (Autograph poets.) $1; hf. leath., $1.50. Houghton M.
Power; Success; and Greatness; with an introd. by R: Watson Gilder. '08(O10) por. T. (Thumb-nail ser.) leath., $1. Century Co.
Representative men; introd. by Ernest Rhys. '08(F22) 16°, (Everyman's lib.) *35 c. net; leath., *70 c. net. Dutton.
Wisdom of Emerson. '09, [1910.] (F) sq. 16°, (Wisdom ser.) *$1 net. Brentano's.
Worldly wisdom from Emerson; ed. and arranged by F. S. Bigelow. '08, [1909.] (Mr) c. 95 p. 24°, (World's wisdom ser.) $1, boxed. Altemus.
See also Cicero, Marcus Tullius.

—, and Furness, W: H:
Records of a lifelong friendship; [correspondence bet. Emerson and Furness;] ed. by Horace H. Furness. Riverside Press ed. '10(D10) il. pors. facsims., sq. 8°, $5 net. (750 copies.) Houghton M.

EMERSON, Ralph Waldo.
Chapman, J: J. Emerson, and other essays. **$1.25 net. Moffat.
Cooke, G: W., *comp.* Bibliography of Ralph Waldo Emerson. **$5 net. Houghton M.
Harrison, J: S. Teachers of Emerson. $1.50 net. Sturgis & W.
Thoreau, H: D. Emerson's obituary. 10 c. E. B. Hill.

Emerson, Rob. Leonard.
Legal medicine and toxicology. '09(Jl) 13+593 p. il. 8°, $5. Appleton.

Emerson, Willis G:
The smoky god; or, a voyage to the inner world; with il. by J: A. Williams. '08 (Ag22) c. D. $1. Forbes.

Emery, Mrs. Bell Bowman.
Don'ts in bridge; latest rules and penalties simplified and condensed. Rev. ed. '10 (Jl16) c. col. il. T. 50 c. net. W: R. Jenkins.

Emery, Cyrene.
The way that He willeth for me. '09(D18) c. 24°, 25 c. Reid Pub.

Emery, Frederic B.
Elementary chemistry. '09(O) 14+666 p. il. tabs., 12°, $1.50. Chemical.

Emery, Grenville E.
See Bradbury, W: Frothingham.

Emery, W: D'Este, M.D.
Immunity and specific therapy. '09(Ag) 14+436 p. il. *$3.50 net. Hoeber.

Emigrant (The). Jager, A. (Add. pubs. for price.) Southern California Pr.

Emigrant trail. Bonner, G. $1.50. Duffield.

EMIGRATION.
See Immigration.

Émigré (L') *See* Bourget, Paul Charles Joseph.

EMILIA, Italy.
See Italy.

Emily Bellefontaine. Yerf, C. $1.25. Conkey.

Emily Fox-Seton. Burnett, *Mrs.* F. H. †$1.50. Stokes.

EMINENT DOMAIN.
See Real property.

Eminent Household of Columbian Woodmen.
Authentic ritual; opening of the feast; closing of the feast; reception to the household; installation of officers; establishing household; order of business. '10(Je) c. 35 p. il. 8°. (Not for sale.) J. B. Frost.

Emma. *See* Austen, Jane.

EMMANUEL CHURCH, Boston.
Baker, R. S. New ideals in healing. **85 c. net. Stokes.
Boyd, T: P. How and why of the Emmanuel movement. *$1 net. Whitaker & R.
Laurence, H. Letter of hope. **50 c. net. Moffat.
McComb, S: Healing ministry of the church. 25 c. S: McComb.
Macomber, W: History of the Emmanuel movement. **25 c. net. Moffat.
MacDonald, R. Mind, religion and health; with an appreciation of the Emmanuel movement. **$1.30 net. Funk.
Powell, L. P. Emmanuel Church Movement in a New England town [Northampton, Mass.] **$1.25 net. Putnam.
Witmer, L. Mental healing and the Emmanuel Movement. 25 c. Psychological Clinic.
Worcester, E., *and* McComb, S: Christian religion as a healing power. **$1 net. Moffat.
Worcester, E., *and others.* Religion and medicine. **$1.50 net. Moffat.
See also Psychotherapy.

Emmet, Alida Chandler.
Psyche sleeps and other poems. '10(Ag13) c. 12°, bds., $1. Moffat.

EMMET, Robert.
Blum, E. C. Robert Emmet's wooing. $1. Cochrane.
Gwynn, S. L. Robert Emmet. *$1.50 net. Macmillan.

Emmet, T: Addis, M.D.
Ireland under English rule. 2d ed., rev. and in large part rewritten. 2 v. '08 (D12) c. 8°, **$5 net. Putnam.

Emmons, G: Thornton.
Chilkat blanket; with notes on the blanket designs by Franz Boas. '08(O10) il. f°, (Memoirs of the Am. Museum of Natural History.) $2. Am. Museum.

Emmons, W: Harvey.
Reconnaissance of some mining camps in Elko, Lander, and Eureka counties, Nevada. '10(My) 130 p. maps, il. 8°, (U. S Geolog. Survey, bull.)
Bibliography (2 p.).
Some ore deposits in Maine and the Milan mine, New Hampshire. '10(N) 62 p. il. map, diagrs., 8°, (U. S., Dept. of the U. S. Interior, Geolog. survey; bull.)
Bibliography (3 p.).

Emotionalist (The). Olmsted, S. †$1.50. Appleton.

Empedocles.
The fragments; tr. into English verse by W: Ellery Leonard. '09(Ja30) c. il. 8°, $1. Open Court.

EMPEDOCLES.
Millerd, C. E. On the interpretation of Empedocles. 75 c. Univ. of Chic.

Emperor (The). *See* Ebers, Georg Moritz.

Emperor's candlesticks. Orczy, E. M. R. M. J. B., *Baroness.* 50 c. Doscher.

Empire of the East. Montgomery, H. B. *$2.50 net. McClurg.

Empire story. Marshall, H. E. *$2.50 net. Stokes.

EMPLOYERS' LIABILITY.
See Insurance;—Negligence.

EMPLOYMENT.
See Labor and laboring classes.

EMPLOYMENT AGENCIES.
Devine, E: T: Report on the desirability of establishing an employment bureau in the city of New York. (Priv. pr.) Charities Pub.

Empty house. Phelps, *Mrs.* E. S. $1.20 net. Houghton M.

ENAMEL.
Dawson, *Mrs.* N. Enamels. *$1 net. McClurg.
Day, L. F. Enamelling. *$3 net. Scribner.
Grampp, O. Pract. enameler. $10. D: Williams.
Grünwald, J. Enameling on iron and steel. *$2 net. Lippincott.
Jewellery enamelling. 25 c. Spon.

Enault, Louis.
Le chien du capitaine; ed. by Marg. de G. Verrall. '10(Ap30) S. bds., 45 c. net. Putnam.

Enchanted castle. Bland, *Mrs.* E. N. †$1.25. Harper.

Enchanted forest. Andrews, *Mrs.* M. R. S. $1.50. Dutton.

Enchanted ground. Smith, J. H. $1.50. Houghton M.
Enchanted hat. Macgrath, H. †$1.50. Bobbs-M.
Enchanted island. Noyes, A. $1.25 net. Stokes.
Enchanted ship. Andom, R. $1.25. Cassell.
Enchanted wood. Hamer, S. H. 75 c. Estes.
Enchanters of men. Mayne, E. C. *$3.50 net. Jacobs.
Encyclopedia and dictionary of medicine, surgery and the specialties; ed. by J. W. Ballantyne, M.D. In 10 v. v. 6, 7. '08(My16) c. il. 8°, ea., *$5 net. Chic. Med. Bk.
Encyclopedia of railroading. 6 v. '10(D17) c. 8°, leath., $36.50. Nat. Text Bk.

ENCYCLOPAEDIAS.
Aiton's encyclopedia. 5 v. $20. Welles.
Americana: universal reference library; arts and sciences, literature, history, [etc.] 16 v. (Add. pubs. for price.) Scientific American.
Appleton's new pract. cyclopedia. 6 v. $18; $24. Appleton.
Beach, C. B., *and* McMurry, F. M., *eds.* New students' reference work for teachers, students and families. $16.50. Compton.
Champlin, J: D. Young folks' cyclopædia of persons and places. **$3 net. Holt.
Chandler, W: H:, *ed.* New complete condensed encyclopedia. $3.75; $5. Collier.
Cornyn, J. H. Mexican topics prep. for The new student's reference work [by Chandler B. Beach and others.] With New student's reference work. $25. Compton.
Current cyclopedia of reference. 8 v. $25; $36. Syndicate Pub.
Everybody's encyclopedia. $5. De Bower-C.
Holst, B. P., *and* Roark, R. N., *eds.* New Teachers' and pupils' cyclop. 5 v. $18.75. Holst.
Houghtaling, C: E., *comp.* Revised hdbk. of useful information. 50 c. C: E. Houghtaling.
La Salle extension university encyclop. $5. De Bower-C.
Minter, L. Compendium of every day wants. $1.90; $2.75. Minter.
Morris, C:, *ed.* Cyclopedia, dictionary and atlas of the world. $3.50; $4.50; $5.50. Hampden Pub.
Morris, C:, *and others, eds.* Imperial reference library; comprising a general encyclopædia of literature, hist., art, science, invention and discovery. 6 v. $55. Syndicate Pub.
Neil, H: Columbia encyclopedia of useful knowledge. $2.50. Columbia Pub.
Practical home encyclopedia; dict. of universal knowledge; editor-in-chief, G: J. Hagar. 8 v. '09, [1910.] (N) il. maps, 8°. Hamilton Bk.
Published also under title: "The new standard encyclopedia."
Ruoff, H: W., *ed.* Standard dictionary of facts. $4.90; $5.50; $6.25; $6.75. Frontier Press.
Twentieth century household library. $3.50. Holman.

ENCYCLOPAEDIAS.—*Continued.*
United editors encyclopedia and dictionary. 40 v. $90. Un. Editors.
Villiers, A., *ed.* Routledge's everyman's cyclop. $1.50 net. Dutton.
Werner encyclopædia. 25 v. $65; $85. Werner Co.
Winston's encyclopedia. 8 v. $6. Winston.
World-wide encyclopedia and gazetteer. 12 v. $13.50. Chr. Herald.
Wright, C. D., *ed.* New century book of facts. $7.50. King-R.
See also under special subjects.

End of dreams. Wilson, W. L. $1.50. M. Kennerley.
End of the game. Mayer, O. S. $1. Moods.
End of the rainbow. Düring, *Mrs.* S. M. $1.50. Lippincott.
End of the road. Hyatt, S. P. †$1.50. Appleton.
End of the world. Howard, H. F. $1.50. Meader's.

Endell, Ja.
Love story of Empress Josephine '09 (O23) il. 8°, *$2.50 net; ¾ levant, *$5 net. Pott.

Enelow, H. G.
What do Jews believe? '08, [1909.] (My) 11 p. 8°, (Jewish tracts, issued by the Central Conference of American Rabbis.) pap., gratis. J. Morgenstern.

Enemies and evidences of Christianity. Quackenbos, J: D. $1.50. Eaton & M.
Energies of men. James, W: **25 c. net. Moffat.
Energy, work, heat and transformation. Reeve, S. A. $2. McGraw-H.
Enforcement of the statutes of labourers during the first decade after the Black Death. Putnam, B. H. pap., $4. Longmans.

ENGADINE.
See Switzerland.

Engaged girl sketches. Blake, E. C. $1. Forbes.
Engaged girl's record book. *See* Swan, Mabel M., *comp.*
Engaging Janet. Bates, E. W. 15 c. Penn Pub. Co.

Engel, Carl.
Music of the most ancient nations; particularly of the Assyrians, Egyptians, and Hebrews; with special reference to the recent discoveries in western Asia and Egypt. '10(Je4) il. 8°, $3.50 net. Scribner.
Musical instruments. New and rev. ed. '10(D24) il. 12°, $1.25 net. Scribner.

Engelhardt, Zephyrin.
Holy man of Santa Clara; or, life, virtues and miracles of Fr. Magin Catala, O. F. M. '09(N) 197 p. il. 12°, 75 c. Barry.
Missions and missionaries of California. v. 1, Lower California. '08(O24) c. O. *$2.50 net. G. Engelhardt.

Engeln, Oscar Diedrich von.
At Cornell. '09(Ag14) c. il. pors. O. $1.50. Artil Co.
See also Tarr, Ralph Stockman.

Engels, F:
See Marx, Karl.

Engineer School, U. S. Army, occasional papers. 8°. (Not for sale.) Engineer Sch.
—Meyer. Library of Congress. Select list of references on inland waterways of Europe.
—United States. *Engineer School.* Corps of military engineers and pioneers in German.
—Winslow. Lectures on seacoast defense.
—Wooten. Provisional battalion of engineers in the Philippines. (Priv. pr.)
—Youngberg. Hist. of engineer troops.

ENGINEER TROOPS.
See United States Army.

ENGINEERING.
American School of Correspondence. Cyclopedia of civil engineering. 8 v. $18.60. Am. Sch. Corr.
American School of Correspondence. Cyclopedia of mechanical engineering. 7 v. $18.60. Am. Sch. Corr.
Ball, W. V. Law affecting engineers. *$2 net. Van Nostrand.
Brightmore, A. W. Structural engineering. *$3.75 net. Cassell.
Burlington (Ia.) Public Library. Pract. book in the library on electricity, engineering, railroading and other subjects. Burlington Pub. Lib.
Church, I. P. Mechanics of engineering. $6. Wiley.
Colvin, F. H., *and* Cheney, —. Engineer's arithmetic. 50 c. Henley.
Corbin, T: W. Engineering of to-day. $1.50 net. Lippincott.
Crane, W. R: Index of mining engineering literature. **$4 net; **$5 net. Wiley.
Crane, W: E: American stationary eugineering. $2. Henley.
Cunningham, B. Treatise on the principles and practice of harbour engineering. *$5 net. Lippincott.
Cyclcp. of engineering. 7 v. $2.60. Am. Sch. Corr.
Derr, L:, *ed.* Cyclopedia of engineering. 6 v. (Add. pubs. for price.) Am. Sch. Corr.
Dict. of metallurgical and chemical machinery. 50 c. Metallurgical.
Encyclopedia of pract. engineering and allied trades. In 5 v. v. 5. per set, $25. Henley.
Farnum, J: S. Pract. points, questions and answers; hdbk. for stationary, locomotive and marine engineers, firemen, electricians, motormen and machinists. $1.50. Laird.
Fowler, C: E. Law and business of engineering and contracting. *$2.50 net. McGraw.
Gebhardt, G: F: Steam power plant engineering. $6 net. Wiley.
Gillette, H. P., *and* Dana, R: T. Cost keeping and management engineering. $3.50. M. C. Clark.
Golding, H: A. Engineers' and machinists' hdbk. $1.50 net. Fenno.
Gunsaulus, F. W., *ed.* Modern engineering practice. 12 v. $29.80. Am. Sch. Corr.
Gurley's manual of the principal instruments used in American engineering and surveying. 50 c. W. & L. E. Gurley.

ENGINEERING.—*Continued.*
Hall, C. "How does it work" of model making. 75 c. Fenno.
Harcourt, L. F. V. Civil engineering as applied in construction. $5 net. Longmans.
Harrington, J: L. Necessity for individual engineering libraries and for continuing study after graduation. 10 c. J: L. Harrington.
Holmes, U. T. Notes on experimental engineering. $1.50. U. S. Naval Inst.
Hopkinson, B. Vibrations of systems having one degree of freedom. 75 c. net. Putnam.
Horner, J. G., *and others, eds.* Henley encyclop. of pract. engineering and allied trades. In 5 v. ea., $6; per set, $25. Henley.
Jenkins, C: F. Engineering science. 35 c. Oxford Univ.
Larard, C. E., *and* Golding, H. A. Practical calculations for engineers. *$2 net. Lippincott.
Lewis, M. H: Water-proofing; engineering problem. 50 c. Engineering News.
Looff, M. Engineers' pocket dictionary of technical terms: French-English. 60 c. Spon.
McCullough, E. Engineering contractors' pocket book. (Add. pubs. for price.)—Engineering work in towns and cities. *$3 net. M. C. Clark.
McLaren, R. S. Mechanical engineering for beginners. *$1.75 net. Lippincott.
Molesworth, *Sir* G. L. Pocket-book of useful formulæ and memoranda for civil, mechanical and electrical engineers. $2. Spon
Moore, S. H. Mechanical engineering and machine shop practice. *$4 net. Hill Pub.
National Association of Stationary Engineers of America. Five years questions and answers. $2. Nat. Assoc. Stationary Engineers.
Ostrup, J: C. Standard specifications for structural steel—timber—concrete and reinforced concrete. $1. McGraw-H.
Peddle, J: B. Construction of graphical charts. $1.50. McGraw-H.
Polk's architects', engineers', builders' and contractors' directory. 2 v. $5. Polk.
Porter, C: T. Engineering reminiscences. *$3 net. Wiley.
Reed's hdbk. to the Board of Trade examinations. $5. Spon.
Reynolds Library, Rochester, N. Y. Catalogue of works on engineering and allied subjects in Library. Reynolds Lib.
Sames, C: M. Pocket-book of mechanical engineering. $2. C: M. Sames.
Shelford, F. Pioneering for engineers. $1.25. Spon.
Smith, E. B. Mechanical engineering laboratory manual. $2. E. B. Smith.
Spangler, H. W., *and others.* Elements of steam engineering. $3. Wiley.
Swingle, C. F. Catechism of steam, gas, and electric engineering. $1.50. Drake.
Trautwine, J: C. Civil engineer's pocket-book. *$5 net. Wiley.
Tucker, J. I. Contracts in engineering. $3. McGraw-H.

ENGINEERING.—*Continued.*
United States. *Superintendent of Documents.* Engineering; mechanics; government documents. gratis.
Waddell, J: A. L., *and* Wait, J: C. Specifications and contracts. *$1 net. Spon.
Wakeman, W: H: Manual of steam engineering. gratis. N. Y. Belting and Packing.
Warren, W: H: Engineering construction in steel and timber. $5 net. Longmans.
Waterbury, L. A. Vest-pocket hdbk. of mathematics for engineers. **$1.50 net. Wiley.
Watts, W. B. Engineers' quiz books. $1. Democracy and Civil Service.
West, A. C. Pract. stationary engineering in form of questions and answers. $5. A. C. West.
Williams, A. How it is done, or, victories of the engineer. $1.25. Nelson.
Woods, R. J. Theory of structures. *$3 net. Longmans.
See also **Aerial navigation;—Air brake;—Alternating currents;—American Society of Mechanical Engineers; — Arches; — Architecture; — Bridges; — Building; — Building materials; —Chemistry; — Concrete;—Curves;—Dams; — Dynamics;—Earthwork;—Electrical engineering; —Elevators;—Engines; — Furnaces;—Gages;— Gas and gasfitting; — Geodesy; — Geometry; — Hydraulic engineering; — Irrigation;—Locomotives; — Machinery; — Marine engineering; — Mathematics;—Mechanical drawing;—Mechanical engineering;—Mechanics;—Mines and mining;—Pumps; — Railroads; — Refrigeration; — Reservoirs; — Roads;—Sanitary engineering; — Ships and shipbuilding;—Singer Building;—Statistics;—Steam engine;—Steel; — Strength of materials;—Surveying;—Tunnels and tunneling; —Turbines;—Water supply.**
Engineering descriptive geometry. Bartlett, F. W. $1.50 net. Wiley.
Engineering index annual for 1908. '09(My); for 1909. '10(Je4) c. 8°, ea., $2. Engineering Mag.
Engineering News reprints. il. 12°. *Engineering News.*
—Douglas. Practical hints for concrete constructors. 25 c.
Engineering thermodynamics. Hirschfeld, C. F. 50 c. Van Nostrand.
ENGINEERS.
Kelly's directory of the engineers and iron and metal trades and colliery proprietors. *$10 net. Kelly.
See also **Astronomy.**
Engineers' pocketbook of reinforced concrete. Heidenreich, E. L. $3. M. C. Clark.
Engineers' pocket dictionary of technical terms: French-English. Looff, M. 60 c. Spon.
Engineers' quiz book. Watts, W. B. $1. Democracy and Civil Service.
ENGINES.
Allen, J: R., *and* Bursley, J: A. Heat engines. $3. McGraw-H.
Audel's gas engine manual: treatise rel. to the theory and management of gas, gasoline and oil engines. $2. Audel.
Brown, C. W. Petrol engine. 50 c. Spon.
Butler, E. Carburettors, vaporizers, and distributing valves, used in internal combustion engines. *$2 net. Lippincott.
Carpenter, R. C., *and* Diedrichs, H. Internal combustion engine. $5 net. Van Nostrand.

ENGINES.—*Continued.*
Clerk, D. Gas, petrol and oil engine. v. 1. *$4 net. Wiley.
Corbin, T: W. "How does it work" of modern engines. 75 c. Fenno.
Dyke, A. L. Automobile and gasoline engine encyclopedia. $3.—Troubles, remedies and repairs of the automobile and gasoline engine. $2. A. L. Dyke.
Ewing, J. A. Steam-engine and other heat engines. $3.75 net. Putnam.
Faurote, F. L. Boy's text book on gas engines. (Add. author for price.) F. L. Faurote.
Goldingham, A. H. Design and construction of oil engines. $2.50.—Gas engine in principle and practice. *$1.50 net. Spon.
Grover, F: Modern gas and oil engines. $2. Spon.
Guldner, H. Design and construction of internal combustion engines. $10 net. Van Nostrand.
Hiscox, G. D. Gas, gasoline, and oil engines, incl. gas producer plants. *$2.50 net. Henley.
Hogle, W: M. Internal combustion engine. *$3 net. McGraw.
Jones, F. R. Gas engine. $4. Wiley.
Junge, F. E. Gas power. $5. Hill Pub.
Levin, A. M. Modern gas engine and the producer gas. $4. Wiley.
Lieckfeld, G. Oil motors. *$4.50 net. Lippincott.
Longanecker, E. W. Pract. gas engineer. *$1 net. Longanecker.
Mehrtens, A. C. Gas engine theory and design. $2.50. Wiley.
Model book of engines. 50 c. Dutton.
Myers, M. C. Different types of modern engines and their valve setting. $1. M. C. Myers.
Peabody, C. H. Thermo-dynamics of the steam-engine and other heat-engines. $5. Wiley.
Poole, C. P. Gas engine. *$1 net. Hill Pub.
Ripper, W: Heat engines. 90 c. net. Longmans.
Spooner, H: J: Notes on the drawings of a four-cylinder petrol engine. 75 c. Longmans.
Stephenson, J. H., *and others.* Farm engines and how to run them. $1. Drake.
Strength of cylinders. 25 c. Indust. Pub.
Von Culin, C. How to run and install gasoline engines. 25 c. Van Nostrand.
Walker, S. F. Steam boilers, engines and turbines. *$3.50 net. Van Nostrand.
Willard, W. C. Why the gas engine goes. 75 c. Penton.
Wimperis, H. E. Internal combustion engine. *$3 net. Van Nostrand.
See also **Boilers;—Locomotives;—Marine engineering;—Shaft governors;—Steam engine;—Turning;—Valves.**

England, Bp. J:
Works; ed., with introd., notes, and index under the direction of the Most Reverend Sebastian G. Messmer. '08(O10) c. 7 v., pors. 8°, per set, *$30 net. H. Clark.

ENGLAND.

Abram, A. Social England in the xvth century. *$1 net. Dutton.

Adams, *Mrs.* H., *and* Browne, E. A., *eds.* Social calendar, 1910. $1.25. Macmillan.

Adams, W. I. L. Photographing in old England. $2.50 net. Baker & T.

Allen, J. W. Wheel magic; or, revolutions of an impressionist: [cycling in England.] *$1.25 net. Lane.

Andrews, C: M., *and* Davenport, F. G. Guide to the manuscript materials for the hist. of the U. S. to 1783, in the British Museum, in minor London archives, and in the libraries of Oxford and Cambridge. $2. Carnegie.

Andrews, W: Old English towns. *$2 net. Pott.

Anglo-Saxon chronicle. *$2 net. Macmillan.

Anson, *Sir* W: R. Law and custom of the constitution. In 3 v. v. 2, pt. 1. $3.40. v. 2. pt. 2. $2.90. Oxford Univ.

Arnold-Forster, H. O. Hist. of England. 2 v. per set, $2 net. Cassell.

Ashley, W: J., *ed.* British industries. *$1.50 net. Longmans.

Atlay, J. B. Victorian chancellors. In 2 v. v. 2. *$4 net. Little, B. & Co.

Auvergne, E. B. d'. Castles of England. *$2 net; *$4 net. Pott.

Babson, R. W. Printed bankers' directory for England. $7.50. R. W. Babson.

Barfield, T. C. Longmans' historical illustrations. In 6 portfolios. ea., 90 c. net. Longmans.

Bevan, T: Stories from British hist. 50 c. net. Little, B. & Co.

Bradley, A. G. English lakes. $1.25, boxed. Estes.

Bradley, A. G. Rivers and streams of England. *$6 net. Macmillan.

British historical portraits. v 1. $2.90. Oxford Univ.

Callender, G. A. R. Sea kings of Britain. 75 c. Longmans.

Cannon, H: L. Reading references for English history. $2.50. Ginn.

Carse, R. Monarchs of merry England: humorous rhymes. $1.50. Stokes.

Cathedrals of England and Wales. 2 v. ea., *25 c. net. Stokes.

Chambers, A. M. Constitutional history of England. *$1.40 net. Macmillan.

Chapman, A. B. W. *and* M. W. Status of women under the English law. *75 c. net. Dutton.

Cheney, C: E: Second Norman conquest of England. (Not for sale.) Chic. Lit. Club.

Cheyney, E: P. Readings in English history. $1.80. Ginn.

Clarke, H. A. Browning's England. **$2 net. Baker & T.

Collier, P. England and the English from an American point of view. **$1.50 net. Scribner.

Cook, T: T. Gardens of England. *$2.50 net. Macmillan.

Cunningham, W. English industry and commerce in modern times. In 2 pts. *$5.25 net. Putnam.

ENGLAND.—*Continued.*

Dale, L. Landmarks of British hist. 90 c. net. Longmans.

Dick, S. Cottage homes of England. *$7 net. Longmans.

Dickens, C: Child's history of England. *35 c. net; *70 c. net. Dutton.

Dillon, J: M. Motor days in England. **$3 net. Putnam.

Ditchfield, P: H. Charm of the English village.—Manor houses of England. ea., $3 net. Scribner.

Eden, F. S. School history of the County Palatine of Durham. 50 c. Oxford Univ.

Edgar, J: A: Heroes of England. 35 c. net; 70 c. net. Dutton.

Edwardes, T. Lift-luck on southern roads. $1.50 net. Macmillan.

Erasmus, D. Selections; principally from his Epistles; [Latin.] 90 c. Oxford Univ.

Finnemore, J: England. *75 c. net. Macmillan.

Firth, C: H. Last years of the Protectorate. In 2 v. *$7 net. Longmans.

Fletcher, C: R. L. Introductory history of England. In 4 v. v. 3, 4. ea., *$1.50 net. Dutton.

Fortescue, J: W: County lieutenancies and the army, 1803-1814. *$3 net.—Hist. of the British Army. In 6 v. v. 5, 1803-1807; v. 6, 1807-1809. ea., $6 net. Macmillan.

Fox, F. Ramparts of empire: view of the navy from an imperial standpoint. $2.25 net. Macmillan.

Fraser, E: "Londons" of the British fleet. **$1.50 net. Lane.

Froissart, J. Chronicles of England, France and Spain. $2.50. Dutton.

Gairdner, J. Lollardy and the Reformation in England. 2 v. *$6.50 net. Macmillan.

Galloway, W: J. Musical England. $1.50 net. Lane.

Garner, T:, *and* Stratton, A. Domestic architecture of England during the Tudor period. In 3 pts. pts. 1, 2. subs., ea., *$16 net; per set, *$48 net. Scribner.

Gasquet, F. A. Black death of 1348 and 1349. *$2 net. Macmillan.

Gasquet, F. A. Greater abbeys of England. **$3.50 net. Dodd.

Gilliat, E. Heroes of Elizabethan England. $1.50 net. Lippincott.

Gratacap, L: P. Evacuation of England: the twist in the Gulf Stream: [fiction.] †$1.25. Brentano's.

Green, J: R: Short hist. of the English people. 3 v. $5.25; $10.50. Lamb Pub.

Greenwood, A. D. Lives of the Hanoverian queens of England. v. 1. *$3.50 net. Macmillan.

Grierson, E. Children's tales of English minsters. *$2 net. Macmillan.

Gwyther, G. M. English history in the class-room. 80 c. Longmans.

Hackwood, F: W: Inns, ales and drinking customs of old England. *$2.50 net. Sturgis & W.

Hall, H. Studies in English official historical documents. $3.75. Putnam.

ENGLAND.—*Continued.*

Hall, H., *ed.* Formula book of English official historical documents. pt. 1, $2; pt. 2, $2.50. Putnam.

Harding, S: B. *and* W: F. Story of England. 60 c. Scott, F. & Co.

Hime, H: W. L. History of the Royal Regiment of Artillery. *$2 net. Longmans.

Hissey, J. J: Charm of the road.—English holiday with car and camera. ea., $3 net. Macmillan.

History of England in words of one syllable. 50 c. Dutton.

Holdsworth, W. S. History of English law. v. 1. *$4 net. Little, B. & Co.

Holland, C. From the Foreland to Penzance. *$3.50 net. Duffield.

Holme, C: Art in England during Elizabethan and Stuart periods. *$3 net. Lane.

Holme, C:, *ed.* Gardens of England in the midland and eastern counties. *$3 net. Lane.

Holmes, T: R. E: Ancient Britain and the invasions of Julius Cæsar. $6.75. Oxford Univ.

Home, G. C. Motor routes of England. $1.50; $2.25.—What to see in England. *$1 net. Macmillan.

Howells, W: D: Seven English cities. *$2 net. Harper.

Huish, M. B. American pilgrim's way in England. $6; $15. W. E. Jones, Baltimore.

Huish, M. B. Happy England. *$6 net. Macmillan.

Hunt, W:, *and* Poole, R. L., *eds.* Political hist. of England. In 12 v. v. 6-9. ea., $2.60 net. Longmans.

Hurlbert, E: B. English Reformation and Puritanism. *$2.50 net. Univ. of Chic.

Jerrold, W. C. Shakespeare-land. $1.25. Estes.

Jusserand, J. A. A. J. Little hist. of the English people. In 3 v. v. 3, pt. 2. *$3.50 net. Putnam.

Lang, E. M. Some old English abbeys. 60 c.; $1. Stokes.

Laprade, W: T: England and the French Revolution, 1789-1797. 75 c. Johns Hopkins.

Leo, S. L. French Renaissance in England. $2.50 net. Scribner.

Lippincott, *Mrs.* S. J. C. Merrie England: travels, descriptions, tales, [etc.] 40 c. Ginn.

Lloyd-George,, D: Better times: speeches. $1 net. Doran.

Low, S. J. M., *and* Pulling, F: S., *eds.* Dict. of English hist. $3.50 net. Cassell.

Lowell, A. L. Government of England. 2 v. **$4 net. Macmillan.

Macartney, M. E. English houses and gardens in the seventeenth century. *$6 net. Scribner.

Macartney, M. E., *ed.* Recent English domestic architecture. *$3.50 net. Scribner.

Macaulay, T: B., *Lord.* Hist. of England. 3 v. ea., 35 c. net; 70 c. net; $1 net. Dutton.

Macaulay, T: B., *Lord.* Hist. of England, chap. III. 50 c. Oxford Univ.

ENGLAND.—*Continued.*

McKilliam, A. E. Hist. of England for elem. and secondary schools. 60 c. net. Macmillan.

Macphail, A. Essays in politics: [England.] *$1.80 net. Longmans.

Magnus, *Sir* P. Educational aims and efforts, 1880-1910. $2.25 net. Longmans.

Maitland, F: W: Constitutional hist. of England. **$3.50 net. Putnam.

Marriott, J: A. R. English political institutions. $1.10. Oxford Univ.

Marshall, H. E. An island story; hist. of England. $2.75 net. Stokes.

Maxwell, *Sir* H. E. Century of empire, 1801-1900. In 3 v. v. 1, 2. ea., $4 net. Longmans.

Meredith, H. O. Outlines of the economic history of England. $2. Pitman.

Middlemore, J: T. The navy in the House of Commons. 50 c.; 30 c. Longmans.

Mitford, M. R. Sketches of English life and character. $1.75 net. McClurg.

Moran, T: F. Theory and practice of the English government. **$1.20 net. Longmans.

Mortimer, J. H. Sprig of Plantagenet; or, the national debt of England. $1.50. Independent Pub.

Murphy, T: D. In unfamiliar England. $3; $7. L. C. Page.

Neville, *Lady* D. F. W. Under five reigns. $5 net. Lane.

Oman, C: W: C., *ed.* Hist. of England. In 7 v. v. 1. $3 net. Putnam.

Paget, H: L. Home life in England. 75 c. net. Longmans.

Pierce, W: Historical introduction to the Marprelate tracts. *$3 net. Dutton.

Powell, E. T: Essentials of self-government, (England and Wales.) *$1.50 net. Longmans.

Previté-Orton, C. W. Political satire in English poetry. $1.50 net. Putnam.

Ramsay, *Sir* J. H: Dawn of the constitution; or, the reigns of Henry III. and Edward I. *$2.75 net. Macmillan.

Rawnsley, H. D. Round the Lake Country. *$1.50 net. Macmillan.

Reynolds, K. B. Outline lessons in English hist. 75 c. Putnam.

Rise and progress of the British explosives industry. *$5.25 net. Macmillan.

Robinson, H. P. Twentieth century American: comparative study of the peoples of the two great Anglo-Saxon nations. **$1.75 net. Putnam.

Rose, J. H. Dumouriez and the defense of England against Napoleon I. *$5 net. Lane.

Shadwell, A. Industrial efficiency; comparative study of England, Germany and America. *$2 net. Longmans.

Shelley, H: C: Untrodden English ways. $1.50 net; **$3 net. Little, B. & Co.

Sherrill, C: H. Stained glass tours in England. *$2.50 net. Lane.

Skae, H. T: Stories from English history. 50 c. Dutton.

South, R: Moths of the British Isles. 2d ser. *$3 net. Warne.

ENGLAND.—*Continued.*

Sparrow, W. S. English house. *$2 net. Lane.

Sparrow, W. S. Old England. *$6 net; *$10 net. Pott.

Stawell, *Mrs.* R. Motor tours in the west country. $1.75 net. Doran.

Steele, R., *comp.* Tudor and Stuart proclamations, 1485-1714. In 2 v. $34. Oxford Univ.

Stephens, K., *ed.* Stories from old chronicles. $1.50. Sturgis & W.

Stephenson, H: T. Elizabethan people. **$2 net. Holt.

Story, A. T: American shrines in England. *$2 net. Macmillan.

Stowe, M. A. English grammar schools in the reign of Queen Elizabeth. *$1.50 net. Teachers' Coll.

Stowell, E. C. Consular cases and opinions from the decisions of the Eng. and Am. courts. $5. Byrne.

Supervision of street railways in England and Prussia. (Add. pubs. for price.) Lyon

Swinburne, H. L. Royal navy. *$6 net. Macmillan.

Synge, M. B. Great Victorian age. *$1 net. Doran.

Tearle, C. Rambles with an American. $2.50 net. Duffield.

Toynbee, A. Lectures on the industrial revolution of the eighteenth century in England. $1. Longmans.

Traill, H: D., *and* Mann, J. S., *eds.* Social England. 12 v. ea., $3 net; per set, $35 net. Putnam.

Trenholme, N. M. Outline of English hist. for use in high schools and colleges. 50 c. Ginn.

Trevelyan, G: M. England in the age of Wycliffe. **$2 net. Longmans.

Turpin, E. H. L. English history stories. *50 c. net. C: E. Merrill.

Victoria history of the counties of England. In 174 v. (Add. pubs. for price.) Dutton.

Vinogradoff, P. G. English society in the eleventh century. $5.25. Oxford Univ.

Visit to the homeland of Washington's ancestors. gratis. P: Henderson.

Wallis-Chapman, A. B. *and* M. Status of woman under English law. *75 c. net. Dutton.

Walpole, *Sir* S. Hist. of twenty-five years, 1856-1880. In 4 v. v. 3-4. $8. Longmans.

Ward, B. Dawn of the Catholic revival in England, 1781-1803. 2 v. *$7 net. Longmans.

Warner, A. Seeing England with Uncle John: [fiction.] †$1.50. Century Co.

Watson, F. English grammar schools to 1660. *$2 net. Putnam.

Webb, S. *and Mrs.* B. P. English local government. [v. 3, 4.] The manor and the borough. 2 v. *$7 net.—English poor law policies. *$2.50 net. Longmans.

Welsford, J. W: W. Strength of England. *$1.75 net. Longmans.

Wharton, *Mrs.* A. H. English honeymoon. **$1.50 net. Lippincott.

White, A. B. Making of the English constitution, 449-1485. **$2 net. Putnam.

ENGLAND.—*Continued.*

Williams, E. B. England's story for children. $1.50. Stokes.

Williamson, C: N., *and Mrs.* A. M. L. Set in silver: [motor trip through England; fiction.] †$1.50. Doubleday, P.

Wilson, W: R. A. Journeys of the Kit-Kat Club; England. **$2 net. Appleton.

Winstanley, D. A. Personal and party government; chapter in the political hist. of the reign of George III., 1760-1766. $1.50 net. Putnam.

See also Abingdon; — Agriculture; — Architecture; — Avon River; — Banks and banking; — Berkshire; — British empire; — Buckingham; — Buckinghamshire; — Cambridge; — Cambridge University; — Canterbury; — Cathedrals;—Chancery; — Church architecture; — Church of England; — Civil law; — Colonial government; — Cornwall; — Costume; — Cotswold (The); — Coventry; — Devonshire; — Dorset;—Drama and dramatists;—Education;— Ely; — Essex; — Eton College; — Furniture;— Gardens and gardening;—Glastonbury;—Great Britain;—Hampshire;—Herfordshire;—House of Commons;—Isle of Man;—Isle of Wight;— Jews;—Journalism; — Kent;—Law;—Leeds; — London; — Malta; — Marprelate controversy; — Middlesex;—Names (*geographical*);—Norfolk;— Northumberland; — Nunburnholme; — Order of the Garter;—Oxford;—Oxford Museum;—Oxford University;—Palaces;—Parliament;— Peninsular War;—Political economy;—Railroads; —Reformation;—Socialism; —Somerset;—South Devonshire; — Southampton; — Stratford-on-Avon;—Street railroads;—Suffolk;—Surrey; — Sussex;—Thames River;—Trafalgar campaign; —Wells;—Westmoreland; — Wiltshire; — Winchester; — Windsor;—Windsor Castle;—Worcester;—Worcestershire;—Wye river;—Yorkshire; *also* Anne, *Queen;*—Catherine *of Braganza;*— Charles II.;—Dumouriez, Charles Francois;— Edward VI., VII.;—George I.-IV.;—Henry VIII.; —Lecky, William Edward Hartpole;—Napoleon I.;—Shakespeare, William;—Stuart, Henry;— Victoria, *Queen;*—William *the Conqueror.*

English, Douglas.

"Wee tim-rous beasties": studies of animal life and character. 3d ed. '08(My16) O. $1.50. Cassell.

English and Scottish popular ballads. Witham, R. A., *comp.* 40 c. Houghton M.

English-Arabic conversation dictionary; with a grammar, a collection of phrases and an Arabic-English vocabulary. '09(Ap3) Tt. (Nutt's conversation dictionaries.) $1.50. Lemcke.

ENGLISH ARTISTS.
See Artists.

English as we speak it in Ireland. Joyce, P. W. $1 net. Longmans.

English ball drill. Newhall, W: B. 10 c. Bassette.

English catalogue of books, for 1907: giving in one alphabet, under author and title, the size, price, month of publication, and publisher of books issued in the United Kingdom. '08(Mr7); for 1908. '09(Mr13); for 1909. '10(Ap9) Q. ea., *$1.50 net. Pub. Weekly.

English children in the olden time. Godfrey, E., *pseud.* *$3 net. Dutton.

ENGLISH CHURCH.
See **Church of England.**

English Church manuals; ed. by Rev. J. C. Wright, Rev. Dawson Walker, Rev. J. E. Watts-Ditchfield and Rev. F. S. Guy Warman. v. 1-14. '08(D26); v. 15. '09 (Mr); v. 16-18 (N20); v. 19. '10(S); v. 20-23 (O8) S. pap., ea., 4 c. net; assorted, per doz., 36 c. net; assorted, per 100, $3 net. Longmans.

English church needlework. Hall, M. R. *$3 net. Gorham.

English churchman's library. '09(Ap10) ea., *40 c. net. Young Churchman.
Contents: Whitham, A. R., Christian use of the Psalter; Staley, Rev. Vernon, Practical religion; Lacey, Rev. T. A., Mysteries of grace; Bickersteth, Rev. Cyril, Letters to a godson, first ser. (Old Testament subjects); Bickersteth, Rev. Cyril, Letters to a godson, second ser. (Christian doctrine.)

English classics. *See* Heath's.—Scribner's.

ENGLISH COMPOSITION.
See English language;—Rhetoric.

English costume. Clinch, G: $2.50 net. McClurg.

English Episcopal palaces. Rait, R. S., *ed.* $2.50 net. Pott.

English factories in India. *See* Foster, W:

English figure skating. Benson, E: F. *$2.50 net. Macmillan.

English foxhound kennel stud book of America. v. 1; comp. and ed. for the Masters of Foxhounds Association of America by Alex. H: Higginson. '09(Ap) 12°. (Priv. pr.) F. L. Wiles.

English gold lustres. Clarke, J: M. (Add. author for price.) J: M. Clarke.

ENGLISH GRAMMAR.
See English language.

English grammar schools in the reign of Queen Elizabeth. Stowe, M. A. *$1.50 net. Teachers' Coll.

ENGLISH HISTORY.
See England.

English holiday with car and camera. Hissey, J. J: $3. Macmillan.

English home. Fletcher, B. F. $4 net. Scribner.

English honeymoon. Wharton, *Mrs.* A. H. **$1.50 net. Lippincott.

English house. Sparrow, W. S. *$2.50 net. Lane.

English houses and gardens. Macartney, M. E. *$6 net. Scribner.

English humorists. Thackeray, W: M. **25 c. net. Macmillan.

English idylls ser. il. 12°, $2. Dutton.
—Austen. Mansfield Park.—Sense and sensibility.

English industry and commerce. Cunningham, W. In 2 pts. *$5.25 net. Putnam.

English lakes. Bradley, A. G. $1.25, boxed. Estes.

ENGLISH LANGUAGE.
Arnold, S. L., *and* Kittredge, G: L. Mother tongue. 2 bks. bk. 1, 45 c.; bk. 2, 60 c.; with composition, 70 c. Ginn.
Barré, F. T. English accentuation. 60 c. Kenedy.
Bell, R. H. Changing values of English speech. $1.25. Hinds.
Bierce, A. Write it right. *50 c. net. Neale.
Blakely, G. S. Teachers' outlines for studies in English. 50 c. Am. Bk.
Bowen, E. W. Questions at issue in our English speech. $1. B'way Pub.
Brown, G. Institutes of English grammar. 80 c. Wood.
Brubaker, A. R., *and* Snyder, D. High school English. $1.10. C: E. Merrill.
Buck, G. "Make believe grammar." (Priv. pr.) Univ. of Chic.

ENGLISH LANGUAGE.—*Continued.*
Burk, F., *and* McFadden, E. B. Course of study in grammar. 30 c. San F. St. Normal.
Callaway, M., *jr.* Incidental teaching of English. 15 c. Univ. of Tex.
Choate, A., *and* Hartman, G. Exercises for parsing and analysis. $1. A. Choate.
Clarkson's standard Am. dict. of the Eng. language. $7.75. D: B. Clarkson.
Cody, S. Art of writing and speaking the English language. 50 c. Old Greek Pr.
Comprehensive standard dict. of the English language. $1.50. Funk.
Concise Standard Dictionary of the English language. 60 c. Funk.
Coone, H: H. Draughon's pract. speller and dict. for use in commercial colleges and high schools. 60 c. Draughon's.
Crandall, H. E. First year English book. $1. Atkinson, M. & G.
Dommasch, O. Neuer, englischer lehrgang; [in German.] 50 c. Stechert.
Edwards, W. H. Parts of speech; suggested definitions for a logical grammar of the English language. 25 c. W. H. Edwards.
Emerson, H: P., *and* Bender, I. C. English spoken and written. Bks. 1-3. bk. 1, $1.50; bk. 2, 50 c. net; bk. 3, 60 c. net. Macmillan.
Emerson, H: P., *and* Bender, I. C. Modern English. Bk. 1. *35 c. net; Southern ed., *40 c. net; New York ed., *40 c. net; Bk. 2, 60 c. net; N. Y. State ed., 60 c. net. Macmillan.
Evans, L. B. Elements of English grammar. 40 c.—Introductory language lessons. 30 c. Am. Bk.
Fernald, J. C. Working grammar of the English language. **$1.50 net. Funk.
Fowler, H: W. *and* F. G: King's English. 40 c. Oxford Univ.
Frank, M. M. Constructive exercises in English. 50 c. Longmans.
Gjerset, K. English grammar. 60 c. Lutheran Pub.
Gowdy, C. English grammar. 80 c. Allyn & B.
Guthrie, J. D. Byrne duplex English, punctuation and correspondence. $1. Byrne Pub.
Hagar, H. A. Applied business English. $1.25. Gregg Pub.
Hanson, C: L. English composition. 80 c. Ginn.
Harris, J. H. Course of study and teachers' manual in elem. English. In 2 pts. pt. 1, 25 c.; pt. 2, 35 c. Northwestern Sch.
Harris, T: G. Spiral course in English. 2 bks. bk. 1, 35 c.; 30 c.; bk. 2, 60 c.; 50 c. Heath.
Hartog, P. J., *and* Langdon, *Mrs.* A. H. Writing of English. 60 c. Oxford Univ.
Heath, F. R. A manual of language lessons. $1. Phonograph.
Henderson, G. W. English grammar by parallelism and comparison. 75 c. H. H. Henderson.

English language.—*Continued.*

Hitchcock, A. M. Words and sentences, including a review of grammar. 35 c. Holt.

Howland, G: C. Advanced lessons in English. 60 c.—Elem. lessons in English. 40 c. McClurg.

Huelin y Arssu, C. Technological dict. $4. Spon.

Hughs, G: S. Grammar of English. $1. G: S. Hughs.

Hülshof, J: L. Reading made easy for foreigners. 1st reader, 30 c.; 2d reader, 40 c.; 3d reader, 50 c. Hinds.

Jesperson, O. Modern English grammar on historical principles. pt. 1. *$3 net. Stechert.

Jonson, B. English grammar. *75 c. net. Sturgis & W.

Krapp, G: P. Elements of English grammar. **80 c. net.—Modern English. **$1.25 net. Scribner.

Lee, A. S. Ten weeks in English grammar. 65 c. A. S. Lee.

Leonard, M. H. Grammar and its reasons. *$1.50 net. Barnes.

Lochmer, A. Easy methods for Croatians to learn the English language without a teacher. *$1.50 net. Caspar.

Lounsbury, T: R. Standard of usage in English. **$1.50 net. Harper.

McFadden, E. B. Course of study in language for grammar grades.—Course of study in primary language. ea., 30 c.—Course of study in language for elem. schools and hdbk. to accompany the California States series text. 55 c.; 30 c. San F. St. Normal.

McNichols, J: P. Fundamental English. 80 c.—Teachers' handbook to accompany Fundamental English. $1.50. Schwartz, K. & F.

Maestro, S. New grammar for Italians to speedily learn the English language. *$1 net. Caspar.

March, F. A. Thesaurus dict. of the Eng. language. (Add. pubs. for price.) Stanley & W.

Marsh, H. A. Grammar in a nutshell. 35 c. Hammond Pub.

Maxwell, W: H: J., *and others.* Speaking and writing. Bk. 1. 20 c.; Bk. 2. 23 c. Am. Bk.

Metcalf, R. C., *and* Rafter, A. L. A language series; bk. 1. 40 c.; bk. 2, 60 c. Am. Bk.

Miller, J. W: English composition and essay writing. 60 c. Longmans.

Modern dict. of the English language. 60 c. net. Macmillan.

Murray, J. A: H:, [*and others,*] *eds.* New English dict.; reissue in quarterly parts. Apr. pt. of v. 6. $1.25.—Ja. pt. of v. 7. $1.90.—July pt. of v. 8. $1.25.—Oct. pt. of v. 6. 60 c.—Jan., Oct. pts. of v. 7. ea., $1.43.—Apr., July pts. of v. 8. ea., 94 c.—Jan. pt. of v. 8; April pt. of v. 8. ea., 60 c.—July pt. of v. 8. $1.25.—Oct. pt. of v. 8. 94 c. Oxford Univ.

English language.—*Continued.*

O'Brien, S. R. English for foreigners. 50 c. Houghton M.

Palmer, G: H. Self cultivation in English. **10 c. net. Crowell.

Palmer, G: H. Self-cultivation in English. **35 c. net. Houghton M.

Payne, W: M. Quarter-century English literature. (Priv. pr.) Chic. Lit. Club.

Peterson, H. C. First steps in English composition. 40 c. Flanagan.

Pierce, R. M., *ed.* Dict. of hard words. $1.20 net. Dodd.

Pitman's commercial dictionary of the English language. 25 c. Pitman.

Prince, J: T. Pract. English grammar for upper grades. 60 c. Ginn.

Reed, A. Word lessons for intermediate and grammar grades. 25 c. C: E. Merrill.

Rine, G: W. Essentials of English. 75 c. Pacific Press.

Roberts, P: English for coming Americans. Teachers' manual. 50 c.; 35 c. Students' lesson leaves. [4 ser.] per ser., 5 c. Y. M. C. A.

Roget, P: M. Thesaurus of English words and phrases. *$1.60 net. Longmans.

Rossman, M. B., *and* Mills, M. W. Graded sentences for analysis. 30 c. M W. Mills.

Russell, T: H. Faulty diction. 25 c.; 50 c. McKay.

Sawin, R. L., *and* Palmer, F. H., *eds.* Right-at-hand stories for dictation in the school-room. 80 c. Palmer Co.

Schleif, O. Technique of English. 75 c. O. Schleif.

Scott, A. C. Practical English. 80 c. Row, P. & Co.

Scott, F. N., *and* Denney, J. V. Elem. English composition. 80 c. Allyn & B.

Shackford, M. H., *and* Judson, M. Composition, rhetoric, literature. $1.12. B: H. Sanborn.

Sharp, A. E. Forms for analysis and parsing. 75 c. W: R. Jenkins.

Simmons, R. J. H. Practical English grammar for common schools. 50 c. R. J. H. Simmons.

Sisk, B: F. Elements of English grammar. —Grammar as a science. (Add. pubs. for price.) So. Sch. Bk.

Sisk, B: F., *and* MacDonald, M. E. First steps in English grammar. (Add. pubs. for price.) So. Sch. Bk.

Skeat, W. W: Etymological dict. of the English language. $11.75. Oxford Univ.

Smith, C. J. Popular dict. for common use. 50 c. Powers.

Smith, O. C. Vox musarum: rules and suggestions for developing the power, beauty and sublimity of the English language by the proper application of the various sounds, signs, [etc.] $1. O. C. Smith.

Snell, F. M. Essentials of English syntax. 50 c. Longmans.

Standard dictionary of the English language. 2 v. $12. Funk.

ENGLISH LANGUAGE.—*Continued.*

Stebbins, C: M. Progressive course in English. 60 c.—Progressive course in English; third book. *85 c. net.—Sentence improvement: practice book in applied grammar. 75 c. Sibley.

Stevens, C: M., *ed.* Standard home and school dictionary. $3. Judge.

Students' ed. of a Standard dict. of the English language. $2.50; $5, boxed. Funk.

Sypherd, W. O., *and* Messersmith, G: S. High school course in English. gratis. Del. College.

Thorley, W. C. Primer of English for foreign students. 60 c. net. Macmillan.

Universal self-pronouncing dictionary of the English language. $1.75. Winston.

Upham, A. H. French influence in English literature. *$2 net. Lemcke.

Van Wagenen, K. Dictation day by day. 2d-5th yrs. 2d, 3d yr., ea., *18 c. net; 4th, 5th yr., ea., *20 c. net. Macmillan.

Wallach, *Mrs.* I. R. Second book in English for foreigners. 50 c. Silver.

Ware, J. R. Passing English of the Victorian era. *$3 net. Dutton.

Webster, N. Collegiate dictionary. $5.—New international dictionary of the English language. $12; $14; $14.50; $17.50; $18; $20; in 2 v., $12; $14.—Pract. dictionary. 80 c. G. & C. Merriam.

Webster, N. Imperial dictionary. $6; $9; $12. G: W. Ogilvie; Saalfield.

Webster, N. Intercollegiate dict. of the English language. $2.45 with *Success Magazine* for 1 yr. E. M. Dunbar.

Webster, N. Intercollegiate dict: of the English language. $1.75; $2.50.—Universal dictionary. $10; $15. Saalfield.

Webster, N. Laird & Lee's new standard dictionary. 75 c.—Laird & Lee's Webster's new standard dictionary. $1.50. Laird.

Webster, N. School and office dict. 50 c.—Universal self-pronouncing dictionary. (Add. pubs. for price.) Winston.

Webster, N. Unabridged dict. $2.50. Reilly & B.

Webster, W: F., *and* Cooley, *Mrs.* A. W. Essentials of grammar and composition. **55 c. net. Houghton M.

White, R: G. Every day English. $2. Houghton M.

White, T. W. Grammar for thinkers. 20 c. Tuft's Coll.

Williams, M. A. Report on the teaching of English in the United States. $1. Bardeen.

Willoughby, J. E. Written exercises on direct and indirect quotations. 35 c. Am. Sch. Deaf.

Wood, T: Pract. grammar and composition. 70 c. Appleton.

Worcester, J. E. Academic dictionary. $1.50.—Lippincott's business and office dict. $1.50.—Lippincott's correspondence dict. $1.—Lippincott's handy dict. 75 c. Lippincott.

Wyld, H: C. K. Elem. lessons in English grammar. 50 c. Oxford Univ.

ENGLISH LANGUAGE.—*Continued.*

Zeitlen, J. Accusative with infinitive and some kindred constructions in English. **$1 net. Macmillan.

See also Abbreviations; — Americanisms;—Anglo-Saxon;—Ireland;—Letter writing; — Phonetics; —Pronunciation; — Punctuation; — Rhetoric; — Slang; — Spellers; — Spelling (Simplified); — Words;—*also* Pocket reference lib.

English lead work. Weaver, L. $10 net. Scribner.

English library ser. *See* Dutton's.

ENGLISH LITERATURE.

Baines, C. E. Short hist. of English literature. *$1 net. Longmans.

Calish, E: N. Jew in English literature. *$2 net. Bell Bk.

Chapman, E: M. English literature in account with religion, 1800-1900. **$2 net. Houghton M.

Cole, G: W., *comp.* Catalogue of books consisting of English literature and miscellanea. 2 v. $75. Dodd.

Coleridge, C. R. Story of English literature. $1.25 net. Cassell.

Conant, M. P. Oriental tale in England in the eighteenth century. **$2 net. Lemcke.

Cook, A. S., *and* Tinker, C. B., *eds.* Select translations from Old English prose. $1.25. Ginn.

Cousin, J: W. Short biographical dict. of English literature. 35 c. net; 70 c. net. Dutton.

Craik, G: L. Manual of English literature. *35 c. net; *70 c. net. Dutton.

Cunliffe, J: W: Century readings for a course in English literature. $2.50. Century Co.

Eighteenth century literature. $1.35. Oxford Univ.

Garnett, R:, *and* Gosse, E. W: English literature. In 4 v. $12; $20. Grosset.

Gowans A. L., *comp.* Characteristic passages from the hundred best English prose writers. 35 c. Crowell.

Hadow, G. E. *and* W: H: Oxford treasury of English literature. v. 3, Jacobean to Elizabethan. 90 c. Oxford Univ.

Heydrick, B: A. One year course in English and American literature. $1. Hinds.

Hooker, E. R. Study book in English literature from Chaucer to the close of the romantic period. $1. Heath.

Long, W: J. English literature. $1.35. Ginn.

Macpherson, W: Principles and method in the study of English literature. 60 c. Putnam.

Magnus, L. English literature in the nineteenth century. *$2 net. Putnam.

Manly, J: M., *comp. and ed.* English prose, (1137-1890.) $1.50. Ginn.

Marshall, H. E. Child's English literature. *$2.50 net. Stokes.

Moody, W: V., *and others.* First view of English and American literature. $1.25 net. Scribner.

Morley, H: First sketch of English literature. $2.50 net.—Library of English literature. 5 v. ea., $2.50 net. Cassell.

Newcomer, A. G., *and* Andrews, A. E. Twelve centuries of English poetry and prose. $1.75. Scott, F. & Co.

ENGLISH LITERATURE.—*Continued.*

Pancoast, H: S. Study lists, chronological tables and maps to accompany An introduction to English literature. 50 c. Holt.

Pancoast, H: S., *and* Shelly, P. V. First book in English literature. $1.25. Holt.

Pearson, P: H: Questions for interpretive and literary study. 16 v. ea., 7 c. P: H: Pearson.

Pyre, J. F. A., *and others, comps.* Century outlines for a course in English literature. 75 c. net. Century Co.

Raub, A. N. Studies in Eng. and Am. literature from Chaucer to present time. $1.50. Stradling.

Schelling, F. E. English literature during the lifetime of Shakespeare. $2.50. Holt.

Studies in English and comparative literature by former and present students at Radcliffe College, 1894-1909. $1.50. Ginn.

Taine, H. A. Hist. of English literature. 3 v. $5.25; $10.50. Lamb Pub.

Taine, H. A. History of English literature. 4 v. $6; $12. Altemus.

Thomas, C: S. How to teach English classics. 15 c. Houghton M.

Toynbee, P. J. Dante in English literature. 2 v. *$5 net. Macmillan.

Walker, H. Literature of the Victorian era. $3.50 net. Putnam.

Ward, A. W:, *and* Waller, A. R., *eds.* Cambridge hist. of English literature. In 14 v. v. 1-6. ea., **$2.50 net; subs., per set, **$31.50 net. Putnam.

Ware, A. Plan of literature study of grammar grades. 30 c. San F. State Normal.

Warren, K. M., *comp. and ed.* Treasury of English literature; from the beginning to the 18th century. $2. Dodge.

Wiebalk, A. Course of study in composition. 30 c. San F. State Normal.

See also American literature;—Authors;—Ballads; — Bibliographies; — Criticisms; — Fiction; — Poetry; — Poets; — Proverbs; — Quotations; — Translations;—Wit and humor;—*also* Arthur, *King.*

English literature for schools. *See* Putnam's.

English local government. *See* Webb, Sidney.

English men of letters ser.; ed. by J: Morley. D. **75 c. net. Macmillan.

—Carpenter. Walt Whitman.

—Macaulay. James Thomson.

—Noyes. William Morris.

English men of science ser.; ed. by Dr. J. Reynolds Green. 12°, *$1 net. Dutton.

—Gray. Lord Kelvin.

English narrative poems. Fuess. C. M., *ed.* *25 c. net. Macmillan.

English nativity plays. Heminway, S: B., *ed.* *$2.50; $2. Holt.

English Parnassus. Dixon, W: M. $1.25. Oxford Univ.

English pastoral drama. Marks, J. A: *$1.50 net. Stechert.

English philosophy. Forsyth, T: M. $1.75 net. Macmillan.

English poems. *See* Baldwin, E: C.—Bronson, Wa. Cochrane, *ed.*

ENGLISH POETRY.
See Poetry.

English prices with German equivalents. St. Koczorowski, —. 50 c. Spon.

English prices with Russian equivalents. Adriassewich, A. 50 c. Spon.

English prose fiction: selected list of about 800 titles cataloged by author and title, with annotations. '09(My8) 16°, pap., 15 c. H. W. Wilson.

English readings. *See* Holt's.

English settlement in the Illinois. Sparks, E. E., *ed.* $2.50. Torch Press.

English shop-fronts old and new. Dan, H. $6. Helburn.

English socialism of to-day. Arnold-Forster, H. O. *$1.25 net. Dutton.

English society in the eleventh century. Vinogradoff, P. G. $5.25. Oxford Univ.

ENGLISH SPARROW.
See Sparrow.

English spelling and spelling reform. Lounsbury, T: R. **$1.25 net. Harper.

English student's wander-year in America. Bowden-Smith, A. G. $1.50 net. Longmans.

English tragicomedy. Ristine, F. H. $1.50. Lemcke.

English vegetable garden; written by experts. '09(Ag7) il. 8°, ("Country Life" lib.) *$3 net. Scribner.

English voyages of adventure. Bacon, E. M. $1.50. Scribner.

English voyages of the sixteenth century. Raleigh, W. A. $3.50 net. Putnam.

Englishman in Ireland. Scott-James, R. $2 net. Dutton.

Englishman in Italy. Wollaston, G: H., *comp.* *$1.75 net. Oxford Univ.

Englishman's castle. Loane, M. $2. Longmans.

Englishman's home. Du Maurier, G. L: B. $1.25. Harper.

ENGRAVERS AND ENGRAVINGS.

Anderson, W: Japanese wood engravings. *$1 net. Dutton.

Austin, S. E. History of engraving. *$1.50 net. Scribner.

Baker, W: H. Dictionary of engraving. bds., 75 c. W: H: Baker.

Banner, G. A. Practical engineering on metal. $1.25. Van Nostrand.

Burch, R. M. Color printing and color printers. $3 net. Baker & T.

Fischel, O., *and* Von Boehm, M. Modes and manners of the XIXth century as represented in the pictures and engravings of the time. *$7 net. Dutton.

Grolier Club, New York. Catalogue of an exhibition of early American engraving upon copper. (Add. Club for price.) Grolier Club.

Hind, A. M. Short history of engraving and etching. *$5 net. Houghton M.

Holme, C:, *ed.* Old English colour-prints. *$3 net. Lane.

Kampmann, C. Die graphischen künste, mit gahrbreichen abbildungen und beilagen dritte. 20 c. Stechert.

ENGRAVERS AND ENGRAVINGS.—*Continued.*
Keppel, F: Golden age of engraving. $3.50 net; $7 net. Baker & T.
Lawrence, R: H., *comp.* Catalogue of the engravings issued by the Society of Iconophiles of the City of New York. (Priv. pr.) R: H. Lawrence.
Layard, G: S. Suppressed plates: wood engravings, etc. *$4 net. Macmillan.
Meadon, J., *ed.* Graphic arts and crafts year book, [1909.] $5. Oswald.
Nevill, R. French prints of the eighteenth century. $5. Macmillan.
Rembrandt van Rhyn, P. Etchings. *$2.50 net. Scribner.
Seidlitz, W. von. Hist. of Japanese color prints. $6.50 net. Lippincott.
Thomas, T. H. French portrait engraving of the XVIIth and XVIIIth centuries. $5.50 net. Macmillan.
Vallance, A., *and* Salaman, M. C: Art in England during Elizabethan and Stuart periods, with note on The first century of English engraving. *$2.50 net; *$3 net. Lane.
Weitenkampf, F. How to appreciate prints. **$1.50 net. Moffat.
See also Photo-engraving;—*also* Foster, John;—Isabey, J. B.;—*also* names of engravers.

ENGRAVINGS.
See Engravers and engravings.

Engstrom, Dag Agnar.
Bevel gear tables; tables and necessary explanation to enable anyone to figure bevel gears without the use of trigonometry. 2d ed. '09(Ap17) c. il. O. $1. Henley.

Enid. *See* Tennyson, Alfr., *Lord.*
Enlarged practice-book in English composition. Hitchcock, A. M. $1. Holt.
Enlarged small talks on bridge. Meyer. V. M. K. 50 c. Ruledge.
Enlarged small talks on skat. Meyer, V. M. K. 75 c. Ruledge.
Enlisted specialists examiner. Cloke, H. E:, *comp.* *$2 net. Wiley.

Ennis Graham, pseud.
See Molesworth, *Mrs.* Mary Louise Stewart.

Ennis, W: Duane.
Applied thermodynamics for engineers. '10 (N12) c. il. 8°, $4.50. Van Nostrand.
Linseed oil and other seed oils; industrial manual. '10(Ap23) c. il. plans, (partly fold.,) 8°, $4. Van Nostrand.

ENNIUS QUINTUS.
Woodruff, L. B. Reminiscences of Ennius in Silius Italicus. 40 c. net. Macmillan.

Eno, Joel Nelson.
Thomas Lillibridge of Newport, R. I., and his descendants. '09, [1910.] (Ap) 11 p. 8°, (Register reprints, ser.) 50 c. N. E. Hist.

Eno, W: Phelps.
Street traffic regulation. '10(Ja15) il. plans, facsim., Q. $2. Rider & D.

Enoch Arden. *See* Tennyson, Alfr., *Lord.*

Enock, C. Reginald.
Andes and the Amazon; life and travel in Peru. New ed. '10(N12) c. il. 8°, $1.50 net. Scribner.
Farthest West; life and travel in the United States. '10(D17) il. map, O, $4 special net. Appleton.

Enock, C. Reginald.—*Continued.*
Great Pacific coast; being an acct. of life and travel in the western states of North and South America, from California, British Columbia and Alaska to Mexico, Panama, Peru and Chili; and a study of their physical and political conditions. '10(Je4) il. map, 8°, $4 net. Scribner.
Mexico; its ancient and modern civilization, history and political conditions, topography and natural resources, industries and general development; with an introd. by Martin Hume. '09(Ag7) il. map, 8°, (South American ser.) $3. Scribner.
Peru; its former and present civilization, history and existing conditions; with an introd. by Martin Hume. '08(D5) il. 8°, *$3 net. Scribner.

Enological studies. Alwood, W: B. U. S., Supt. of Docs.

Enright, Maurice, M.D.
Ridgefield tavern: romance of Sarah Bishop, hermitess. '08(Je27) il. 12°, $1.25; pap., 75 c. Brooklyn Eagle.

Enright, T:
King of Nobody's Island. '09(Jl17) c. D. $1. Gibson Pub.

ENSILAGE.
Modern silage methods. 10 c. Silver Manufacturing.

ENTELODONTIDAE.
See Monkeys.

Entering the kingdom. Allen J. 15 c. Fenno.

ENTERTAINMENTS.
Bartholemew, E. House book to the hostess [record of fêtes, festivals, etc.]. $1.50 net; $2.50 net. Dodge.
Bugbee, W. N. Easter tidings: entertainment for girls. 25 c. Dick.
Chase, F. E. Club and lodge-room entertainments. 25 c. W. H. Baker.
Jackson, M. M. Artistic entertainments. 25 c. Flanagan.
Kellogg, A. M., *comp.* Special day exercises: for school celebrations.—Spring and summer school celebrations. ea., 50 c.; 30 c. Penn Pub. Co.
Leverton, W. Little entertainments and how to manage them. 50 c. Fenno.
Revell, E. I., *comp.* Arbor day exercises for the school-room. 25 c. Educ. Pub.
Riley, A. C. D., *and* Gaynor, J. L. Welcome spring!: spring or Easter program for Sunday or day schools. 25 c. C. F. Summy Co.
Stern, R. B. Neighborhood entertainments. 75 c. net. Sturgis & W.
Yale, *Mrs.* E. D. When mother lets us give a party. **75 c. net. Moffat.
Yendes, L. A., *and* Brown, W. F. A., *eds.* Entertainments for every occasion. $1.25. Hinds.
See also Amusements;—Charades;—Christmas;—Dancing;—Dialogues; — Drills;—Games;—Memorial day;—Pantomime;—Plays;—Recitations;—Riddles;—Washington's birthday;—*also* Lincoln, Abraham.

ENTOMOLOGY.
See Insects.

Entre bastidores o' hasta hallarla. Walton, *Mrs.* O. F. 50 c. Am. Tr.

ENTRÉES.
See Cookery.

Envelope books. v. 1-3. '08(D19) nar. 16°, leath., ea., *$1.25 net; pap., *25 c. net; v. 4-10. [1910.] (D) col. il. ea., $1 net; pap., 25 c. net. Jacobs.

Envelope edition of booklets. '08(O17); '09 (O); '10(D) D. pap., ea., *35 c. net, in envelope. Pilgrim Press.
Contents: The blue cure, Porter; The child Jesus took, Smyth; The face angelic, Haydn; The gospel of good health, Brown; The keen joy of living, Park; The land of delight, Gordon; The love watch, Knight; The practice of immortality, Gladden; The signs in the Christmas fire, Knight; The song of our Syrian guest, Knight; The valley of troubling, Goodwin; Whence cometh help, Buckram; The shepherd of Jebel-Nur, Knight; The spirit of truth, Gordon; The mystery of peace, Smart; The golden bond, Smart, *ed.*; The Sermon on the Mount, Park; A man's faith, Grenfell; The deacon's week, Cook; Quest for health and happiness, Hawkins.

Envelope ser. *See* Revell's.

ENZYMES.
See Fermentation.

Eothen. *See* Kinglake, Alex. W:

Epaphos and the Egyptian apis. Linforth, I. M. 10 c. Univ. of Cal.

Eparde, Tirza.
Two ends of a house-boat. '09(D) il. $1.25. B'way Pub.

Ephemer aeternitatis. Kelman, J: $1.25 net. Doran.

Epic and romance. Ker, W: P. $1.50. Macmillan.

Epic of heaven. Creamer, E: S. $1. B'way Pub.

EPIC POETRY.
See Poetry.

Epictetus.
Moral discourses; ed. by Eliz. Carter and W. H. D. Rouse. '10(Ap16) 16°, (Everyman's lib.) 35 c. net; leath., 70 c. net. Dutton.
Noble thoughts of Epictetus; selected and ed. by Dana Estes; with essay on The discourses by Canon F. W: Farrar. '09 (Jl) c. 15+89 p. front. 16°, (Noble thoughts of the world's greatest minds; ed. by D. Estes.) hf. parchment, $1.50; parchment, $5, boxed. Estes.

EPICUREANISM.
See Philosophy.

EPIGRAMS.
Haultain, T: A. Hints for lovers. **$1 net. Houghton M.
Inglehart, M., *comp.* Catchwords of worldly wisdom. *75 c. net; *$1.25 net; *$1 net. McClurg.
Jameson, *Mrs.* H. T. Pippins and peaches: [epigrams.] $1. Reilly & B.
Joyce, J: A. Truth. $1. J: A. Joyce.
Mackail, J: W:, *ed.* Select epigrams from Greek anthology. *75 c. net; *$1 net. Longmans.
Pulitzer, W. Cupid's pack of cards. $1. J: W. Luce.
"Theocratus," *pseud.* Legacy of a man who wanted to do his duty. 50 c. Corona Pub.
See also Aphorisms;—Maxims;—Mottoes;—Quotations;—Toasts.

EPIPHYSES.
See Fractures.

EPISCOPAL CHURCH.
See Catholic church; — Church of England; — Methodist Episcopal church;—Protestant Episcopal church.

Episodes from an unwritten history. Bragdon, C. 15 c. Manas Press.

Episodes in the doings of the dualized. Mason, E. L. 50 c. E. L. Mason.

EPISTLES.
See Bible.

EPITAPHS.
Andrews, F. D., *comp.* Inscriptions on the grave stones in the old "New England Town" burying ground, Fairton, N. J. 25 c. F. D. Andrews.
Pleasants, H: Hist. of the Old Eagle School, Tredyffrin, in Chester County, Pennsylvania, with alphabetical lists of interments in the graveyard. $2. Winston.
Rice, F. P., *comp.* Marlborough, Mass., burial ground inscriptions. $3. F. P. Rice.
Ridgely, H. W., *ed.* Hist. graves of Maryland and the District of Columbia, with inscriptions appearing on the tombstones. **$2 net. Grafton Press.

Epitome of gynecology. Child, C: G., *jr.* *$1 net. Lea.

Epitome of the *Aeronautical Annual;* ed. by Ja. Means. '10(Jl30) c. il. pors. 8°, $1. W: B. Clarke.

Epler, Percy Harold.
Master minds at the commonwealth's heart. '10(Ja29) c. il. pors. 8°, $2. F. S. Blanchard.

Epoch in the spiritual life. Curtis, C: N. *$1.25 net. Eaton & M.

Epoch-making contributions to medicine, surgery and the allied sciences. Camac, C: N. B., *comp.* *$4 net. Saunders.

Epoch maps illustrating American history. Hart, A. B. 60 c. Longmans.

Epochs and phases of Christian experience. Whitney, W: $1. Observer.

Epochs in Baptist history. Griffiths, E. C. (Add. pubs. for price.) Advance.

Epochs in the life of Paul. Robertson, A. T: **$1.25 net. Scribner.

Epochs of American history; ed. by Albert Bushnell Hart. il. S. Longmans.
—Hart. Formation of the Union, 1750-1829. $1.25.
—Thwaites. The colonies, 1492-1750. $1.25.
—Wilson. Division and reunion. $1.25.

Epochs of philosophy; ed. by J: Grier Hibben. Scribner.
—Hibben. Philosophy of the enlightenment. **$1.50 net.
—Hicks. Stoic and Epicurean. **$1.50 net.

Eppendorff, Lina.
Handwork construction. '09(Ap3) c. figs. O. $1.58. L. Eppendorff.

Epsom mystery. Grainger, F. E. *$1 net. Fenno.

EPWORTH LEAGUE.
Brummitt, D: B. Notes on the Epworth League devotional meeting topics. 2d ser., 1908; 1st ser., 2d ser., 1909; 1st ser., 2d ser., 1910. ea., *15 c. net; per doz., *$1.20 net. Eaton & M.

Equal pay for equal work. Strachan, G. C. B: F. Buck.

Equal suffrage. Summer, H. L. **$2 net. Harper.
Equality of rights for all citizens black and white alike. Grimke, F. J. 5 c. F. J. Grimke.
Equality of the states and the Hague conferences. Hicks, F: C: (Add. author for price.) F: C: Hicks.
EQUATIONS.
Birkhoff. G: D: Asymptotic properties of the solutions of ordinary linear differential equations. (Add. author for price.) G: D: Birkhoff.
Bôcher, M. Introd. to the study of integral equations. *75 c. net. Putnam.
Lunn, A. C. Differential equations of dynamics. (Add. author for price.) A. C. Lunn.
See also Algebra.
EQUESTRIAN POLO.
See Polo.
Equipment for teaching of domestic science. Kinne, H. 30 c. Columbia Univ.
Equipment of country houses with electricity. Bates, P. A. 25 c. Franklin Inst.
EQUITABLE LIFE ASSURANCE SOCIETY.
Day, W: A. Address at 50th anniversary of the founding of the society. Equitable Life.
Equitable Life Assurance Society of the United States. First fifty years of the Equitable Life Assurance Society of the United States, 1859-1909. '09(Jl) 127 p. il. pors. 8°. (Add. pubs. for price.) W. F. Powers.
Equitable remedies of creditors in Michigan. Dooling, J: C. $4. Drake Law Bk.
Equitable Union. Badgley, N. E. $1.50. N. E. Badgley.
EQUITY.
Abbott, N. T. Cases on the law of equity jurisprudence and trusts. $6. Flood.
Bispham, G: T. Principles of equity; treatise on the system of justice administered in courts of chancery. $6. Banks.
Illustrative cases in equity. $2. West Pub.
Langdell, C. C. Brief survey of equity jurisdiction. (Add. pub. for price.) Harvard Law.
Lewis, W: D. Equity jurisdiction torts. (Add. pubs. for price.) Int. Pr.
Maitland, J. W. Equity. *$4 net. Putnam.
Rush, G: F: Manual of equity pleading, state and federal. (Add. pubs. for price.) Chic. Legal News.
See also Actions at law;—Chancery.
Equity jurisdiction, trespass to real property. Lewis, W: D. $1. W: D. Lewis.
Er soll dein herr sein. Heyse, P. J. L. 30 c. Am. Bk.
Era of conscience. Folk, J. W. 10 c. Civic Forum.
Era of progress and promise. Hartshorn, W. N. $5.75. Priscilla.
Erasmian pronunciation of Greek. Bywater, I: 35 c. Oxford Univ.
Erasmus, Desiderius.
Altera colloquia Latina adapted from Erasmus; with notes and vocabulary by G. M. Edwards. '08(Je6) por. S. (Pitt Press ser.) *40 c. net. Putnam.

Erasmus, Desiderius.—*Continued.*
Ciceronianus; or, a dialogue on the best style of speaking; tr. by Izora Scott; with an introd. by Paul Monroe. '08 (S5) c. 8°, (Columbia Univ., Teachers' Coll., contribs. to education; historical ser.) pap., $1. Teachers' Coll.
Opvs epistolarvm; denvo recognitvm et avctvm per P. S. Allen. v. 2, 1514-1517. '10(My14) O. $5.75. Oxford Univ.
Treatise on war. '07, [1908.] (D) (Humanist's lib.) bds., *$6 net. Merrymount.
Selections; principally from his Epistles, by P. S. Allen. '08(O24) por. S. 90 c. Oxford Univ.
ERASMUS, Desiderius.
Faulkner, J: A. Erasmus: the scholar. *$1 net. Jennings.
Ercilla y Zúñiga, Alonso de.
Historia de la virgen madre de dios Maria; desde su purissima Concepcion sin pecado original, hasta su gloriosa assumpcion; poema heroyco [facsim.] 2 v. '03 [1909.] (N) 104; 105-248 p. 8°, ea., $6. Hispanic Soc.
La aravca [facsim.] '02 [1909.] 7+17+392 p. 8°, $12.50 (200 copies). Hispanic Soc.
Segvnda parte de la Aravcana de Don Alonso de Erzilla y Çuñiga, que trata la porfiada guerra entre los Españoles, y Araucanos, co algunas cosas notables que en aquel tiempo sucedieron. '03, [1909.] 335 p. 8°, $12.50. (200 copies.) Hispanic Soc.
Erckmann, Emile, and Chatrian, Alexandre.
The Conscript, and Waterloo. '09(Mr27) 16°, (Everyman's lib.) *35 c. net; leath., *70 c. net. Dutton.
Hist. of a conscript of 1813. '10(D10) D. $1.50 net. Macmillan.
Le trésor du vieux seigneur; ed., with introd., notes, exercises and vocabulary, by W. M. Daniels. '09(O23) S. (Shorter French texts.) *25 c. net. Crowell.
Madame Thérèse; ed., with introd., notes and vocabulary, by E: Manley. '10 (Mr19) c. S. (Heath's modern language ser.) 40 c. Heath.
See also Wilson-Green, A.
Erdman, W: Jacob.
Holy Spirit and Christian experience. [3d ed., rev.] '09(Ag) c. 51 p. 12°, pap., 25 c. Gospel Pub.
Erecting work. Collins, H. E. $1. Hill Pub.
Erewhon. Butler, S: $1.25 net. Dutton.
Erewhon revisited. Butler, S: $1.25 net. Scribner.
Eric. Waggaman, *Mrs.* M. T. 75 c. Kilner.
Eric. *See* Farrar, F: W:
Erichsen, Nelly.
See Ross, *Mrs.* Janet Ann Duff-Gordon.
Erickson, Matilda.
Temperance torchlights. '10(Ap30) il. D. 50 c. Review and Herald Pub.

ERIE CANAL.
Hepburn, A. B. Artificial water-ways and commercial development, with a history of the Erie Canal. **$1 net. Macmillan.

ERIE COUNTY, Pa.
Miller, J: Twentieth century hist. of Erie Co. 2 v. $18. Lewis Pub.

ERIE RAILROAD.
Hubbard, E. Romance of the railroad; being a story of the Bergen Cut on the Erie. 10 c. Roycrofters.

Erixon, Alexandre.
Vale of shadows. '08(D12) c. front. D. $1.50. B'way Pub.

Ernest, Otto, pseud.
See Schmidt, Otto Ernest.

Erni, H:
Chemical determinative mineralogy and physical determinative mineralogy; being pts. 1 and 2 of Erni's "Mineralogy simplified." 4th ed., rev., rearranged, and with the add. of entirely new matter by Amos Peaslee Brown. '08(D) c. 209-392 p. il. 16°. (Add. pubs. for price.) Baird.
Mineralogy simplified: easy methods of identifying minerals, including ores, by means of the blow-pipe, by flame reactions, by humid chemical analysis and by physical tests. 4th ed., rev., rearranged, and with the addition of entirely new matter, by Amos Peaslee Brown. '08 (N21) c. il. 12°, leath., *$2.50 net. Baird.

ERNODEA.
See Botany.

Ernst, Alfr.
The new flora of the volcanic island of Krakatau; tr. by A. C. Seward. '08, [1910.] (F) 74 p. il. map, 4°. (Add. pubs. for price.) Putnam.
Bibliography (2 p.).

Ernstes und heiteres. Schrakamp, J., *ed.* 35 c. Am. Bk.

Errett, I:
Querists' drawer; discussion of difficult subjects and passages of the Scriptures; arranged and ed. by Z. T. Sweeny. '10 (Jl30) c. 8°, $1.50. Standard Pub.

Errors in magnetic testing with ring specimens. Lloyd, M. G. (Add. Superintendent for price.) U. S., Supt. of Docs.

Errors of mind healing compared with the miracles of Christ. Willman, R. $1. Advocate Pub.

Errors of Romanism. Cox, W: J. E: $1. Dearing.

Erskine, Beatrice, [Mrs. Steuart Erskine.]
Royal cavalier; the romance of Rupert, Prince Palatine. '10(O15) il. pors. O. $3.75 special net. Appleton.

Erskine, Helen.
See Erskine, J:

Erskine, J:
Leading American novelists. '10(My14) c. pors. O. (Biographies of leading Americans.) $1.75 net. Holt.

—, and Helen.
Written English; guide to the rules of composition. '10(N5) c. T. 40 c. net. Century Co.

Erskine, Payne.
When the gates lift up their heads: story of the South in the seventies. '08(My.) c. 12°, (Popular ed. of recent fiction.) †75 c. Little, B. & Co.

Erskine, Mrs. Steuart.
See Erskine, Beatrice.

Erskine-Murray, Ja. D.
Wireless telephones and how they work. '10(My21) il. $1. Henley.

Erstes lesebuch. Werner-Spanhoofd, A. 75 c. Heath.

Eruption of Pelée. Heilprin, A. $4. Geographical Soc.

Erwin, Fk. Alex.
Cases on sales of personal property. 2d ed. '09(Mr) c. 15+701 p. O. $3.50. Banks.

Erwood, W: Jos.
Essentials of psychic development; being number two of Lessons of progress. '10(My21) c. 8°, 50 c. W: J. Erwood.
Living thought: book of essays. '09(Jl10) c. por. D. $1. W: J. Erwood.
Mediumship: its use and abuse; being number three of Lessons of progress. '10(My21) c. 8°, 50 c. W: J. Erwood.
The rational life; being a book of essays on vital themes. '10(Je18) c. por. 12°, $1. W: J. Erwood.

ERYSIPHE CICHORACEARUM.
See Fungi.

Erzälende dichtungen, gedichte und aphorismen. Schlapp, G: *$1.50 net. Caspar.

Esarey, Sol H., rep.
See Indiana. *Appellate ct.* Repts.—*Sup. ct.* Repts.

Escapades of an American youngster. Berwick, M. H. $1. Brentano's.

Escapades of Condy Corrigan. Healy, C. 50 c. Soc. Divine Word.

Escape from East Tennessee to the federal lines. Ragan, R. A. $1. Dony.

Escher, Franklin.
Elements of foreign exchange; foreign exchange primer. '10(Jl2) c. 8°, $1. Bankers Pub.

Escott, T: Hay Sweet.
Edward Bulwer, first Baron Lytton of Knebworth. '10(Ap23) 4°, $2.50 net. Dutton.
King Edward and his court. '08(Ag15) 8°, *$4 net. Jacobs.
Story of British diplomacy. '08(Ag15) 8°, *$4 net. Jacobs.

Escott-Inman, Rev. Herbert.
See Inman, Herbert Escott-.

Esenwein, Jos. Berg.
Writing the short-story: hdbk. on the rise, structure, writing and sale of the modern short-story. '09(My15) c. D. $1.25. Hinds.

Eshelman, H: Fk.
Lancaster County Indians; annals of the Susquehannocks and other Indian tribes of the Susquehanna territory from about the year 1500 to 1763, the date of their extinction. '10(F26) c. 8°, $2. H: F. Eshelman.

Esmond, Darwin W:, comp.
Poetry of childhood; Paul's lilies, some written, some loved, by the boy. '08, [1909.] (My) c. 108 p. il. pors. 12°, $1.50. B'way Pub.

ESOPHAGUS.
See Digestion;—Throat.

ESOTERISM.
Marsland, A. E. What esoterism is. 35 c. Oriental Esoteric.
See also Theosophy.

España and Émaux et camées. *See* Gautier, Théophile.

ESPERANTO.
Baker, A. Introd. to Esperanto. 10 c. Am. Esperantist.
Defoe, D. Robinsono Kruso; [in Esperanto.] 50 c. Altemus.
Franks, A. Esperanto for the English. 50 c. McKay.
Kellerman, I. Complete grammar of Esperanto. $1.25. Heath.
Lawrence, E. A., *comp.* First reader; Esperanto. *25 c. net. Revell.
Marx, K., *and* Engels, F: Manifests of the communist party: [text in Eng. and Esperanto.] 50 c. Kerr.
Privat, E. Esperanto at a glance. *15 c. net.—Esperanto in fifty lessons. *50 c. net. Revell.
Rhodes, J. English-Esperanto dictionary. *$2 net. Revell.
Underhill, J. Esperanto and its availability for scientific writings. 50 c. Colo. Sci. Soc.

Esque, Jean L: de.
Betelguese. '08(Ag8) 12°, $1.25. Connoisseurs' Press.
Flight of a soul: poetical tragedy in four parts. '08(Ag8) c. 12°, $1.50. Connoisseurs' Press.
Seasons and other poems. '08(Ag8) c. 12°, $1. Connoisseurs' Press.

Esquemeling, J.
Buccaneers of America: true acct. of the remarkable assaults committed of late years upon the coasts of the West Indies by the buccaneers of Jamaica and Tortuga, (both English and French.) '10 (Ap2) il. 4°, $4 net. Dutton.

Essay on distribution of livelihood. Stanton, R. *$1.50 net. Farwell.
Essay on self-reliance. *See* Emerson, Ralph Waldo.
Essay on the governing causes of the natural rate of interest. *See* Massie, Jos.
Essay on the human understanding. *See* Locke, J:
Essay on the life of our patriotic admiral, Christopher Columbus. Kitchen, M. L. K. 50 c. R. Kitchen.
Essay on ways and means for raising money for the support of the present war. *See* Farquier, Fs.

ESSAYISTS.
See Authors.

ESSAYS.
Acton, J: E. E: D.-A., *Lord.* History of freedom and other essays. *$3 net. Macmillan.
Alden, H: M. Magazine writing and the new literature. **$2 net. Harper.
Bacon, A. S. Woolly horse: [papers on timely topics.] $1. A. S. Bacon.
Bacon, F., *Lord.* Essays. *$1 net. Dutton.
Bacon, F., *Lord.* Essays; or, counsels civil and moral. *35 c. net. Heath.

ESSAYS.—*Continued.*
Bacon, F., *Lord.* Essays. *40 c. net; *30 c. net. Houghton M.
Bacon, F., *Lord.* Essays. **$1.25 net. Scribner.
Bacon, F., *Lord.* Essays and Wisdom of the ancients. *40 c. net. Little, B. & Co.
Bagby, G: W. Old Virginia gentleman. $1.50 net. Scribner.
Beerbohm, M. Yet again. *$1.50 net. Lane.
Belloc, J. H. P. On anything.—On everything.—On nothing and kindred subjects. ea., $1.25 net. Dutton.
Bennett, E. A. How to live on 24 hours a day. 50 c. net.—Human machine: ser. of studies. 75 c. net.—Reasonable life. 50 c. net. Doran.
Benson, A. C. At large.—Silent isle. ea., $1.50 net. Putnam.
Benson, A. C. Until the evening. **30 c. net. Crowell.
Benson, E: F. A reaping. $1.25, fixed. Doubleday, P.
Bierce, A. Shadow on the dial, and other essays. *$2 net. A. M. Robertson.
Bisland, E. At the Sign of the Hobby Horse. $1.25 net. Houghton M.
Bland, H. N. Happy moralist. *$1.25 net. M. Kennerley.
Boyden, E. Odd moments. 75 c.; 50 c. Cochrane.
Bradley, A. C., *comp.* Essays and studies by members of the English Association. $1.75. Oxford Univ.
Carson, J. D. In nature's temple. $1.25. Oldach.
Chapman, J: J. Emerson, and other essays. **$1.25 net. Moffat.
Chesterton, G. K. All things considered. *$1.50 net. Lane.
Chesterton, G. K. Tremendous trifles. *$1.20 net.—What's wrong with the world. $1.50. Dodd.
Clark, G: L. Notions of a Yankee parson. $1 net. Sherman, F.
Colby, F. M. Constrained attitudes. $1.20 net. Dodd.
Cole, M. E. G. Essays. $1. B'way Pub.
Coles, R: T: Events and reflections. 50 c. Mayhew.
Conner, C: C. From nature to man. 75 c. Hampden Pub.
Crothers, S: M. Among friends.—By the Christmas fire. ea., **$1.25 net. Houghton M.
Davidson, J: The man forbid. $1.25 net. Ball Pub.
Dawson, W: J. Quest of the simple life. $1.50. Dutton.
Dawson, W: J. *and* Coningsby W: Great English essayists. *$1 net. Harper.
Didier, E. L. Poe cult and other papers. $1.50. Am. Press.
Dobson, H: A. Old Kensington Palace and others papers. $1.50 net. Stokes.
Dowden, E: Essays, modern and Elizabethan. $2 net. Dutton.
Ellwanger, W: D. Snuff box full of trees and some apocryphal essays. **$2 net. Dodd.

ESSAYS.—*Continued.*

Ely, S. Sermons, essays and outlines. $1. Standard Pub.

Emerson, R. W. Essays: 1st and 2d ser. *$1 net. Dutton.

Emerson, R. W. Essays, (selected.) 30 c. C: E. Merrill.

Emerson, R. W. Essays. 75 c. Putnam.

Emerson, R. W. Power, success and greatness. *$1 net. Century Co.

Erwood, W: J. Living thought. $1. W: J. Erwood.

Fadner, G: M. Pound of brains; thirty years' observation, or horse sense. $1. G: M. Fadner.

Fairbank, J. A. In town and other conversations. $1.25 net. McClurg.

Fellers, J: E. Crossing familiar paths. 80 c. Booklovers' Assoc.

Frank, E. Essays. $1. B'way Pub.

Franklin, F. People and problems: addresses and editorials. **$1.50 net. Holt.

Froude, J. A. Short studies on great subjects. 5 v. ea., *60 c. net. Scribner.

Gasquet, F. A. Old English Bible, and other essays. *$2.25 net. Macmillan.

Gibson, R. A. College days essays. $1. Nixon-J.

Goldsmith, O. Selected essays. 40 c. net. Putnam.

Gould, G: M. Infinite Presence. $1.50 net. Moffat.

Graham, H: G. Literary and historical essays. *$2 net. Macmillan.

Graham, J: E. Mere hints, moral and social. $1. Mercy.

Guthrie, W: N. Vital study of literature and other essays. Sergel.

Hall, B. Life, love, and peace. $1. Arcadia.

Harrison, F: Realities and ideals. **$1.75 net. Macmillan.

Harvey, G: B. M. Women, etc.: essays. **$1 net. Harper.

Hawthorne, H. Women and other women. $1.20. Duffield.

Hazlitt, W: Table talk. *35 c. net; *70 c. net. Dutton.

Herridge, W: T: Coign of vantage. *$1 net. Revell.

Hewlett, M. H: Letters to Sanchia. 90 c. net. Scribner.

Hind, C: L. Diary of a looker-on. $2. Lane.

Horton, R. F. Great issues. **$1.50 net. Macmillan.

Howard, J: R., *comp.* Best American essays. 35 c. Crowell.

Howells, W: D. Imaginary interviews. $2 net. Harper.

Huxley, T: H: Selected essays and addresses. 25 c. net. Macmillan.

James, H: Views and reviews. *$1.50 net; *$2.50 net. Ball Pub. Co.

Joline, A. H. At the library table. $1.50. Badger.

Kane, R. Sermon of the sea and other studies. *$1.50 net. Longmans.

Kieffer, J. S. Head and heart. *$1.50 net. Ref. Ch. Pub.

ESSAYS.—*Continued.*

King, W: Sure possession and other thoughts of a layman. $1.50. A. B. Caldwell.

Kreymborg, A. Love and life and other studies. **$1 net. Grafton Press.

Lamb, C: Essays of Elia.—Last essays of Elia. ea., *40 c. net. Little, B. & Co.

Lamb, C: Essays of Elia. 50 c. C: E. Merrill.

Lamb, C: Select essays of Elia. 40 c. Am. Bk.

Leacock, S. B. Literary lapses. $1.25 net. Lane.

Lee, V., *pseud.* Laurus nobilis. *$1.50 net. Lane.

Le Gallienne, R: Attitudes and avowals. $1.50 net. Lane.

Le Gallienne, R: October vagabonds. $1.50 net. M. Kennerley.

Lloyd, H: D. Mazzini, and other essays. $1.50 net. Putnam.

Lubbock, Sir J: Peace and happiness. **$1.50 net. Macmillan.

Lucas, E. V. One day and another. *$1.25 net. Macmillan.

Mabie, H. W., *ed.* Essays that every child should know. **90 c. net; **$1.50 net. Doubleday, P.

Macaulay, T: B., *Lord.* Essays. 2 v. ea., *$1 net. Dutton.

Macaulay, T: B., *Lord.* Essay on Lord Clive.—Essay on Warren Hastings. ea., 25 c. net. Longmans.

Macaulay, T: B., *Lord.* Miscellaneous essays. 35 c. net; 70 c. net. Dutton.

Macphail, A. Essays in fallacy. $1.50 net. Longmans.

Manning, F. Scenes and portraits. *$1.75 net. Putnam.

Mansfield College essays; testimonial volume presented to Principal Fairbairn upon his 70th birthday. *$3 net. Doran.

Martin, E. M. Wayside wisdom. *$1.50 net. Longmans.

Martin, E: S. In a new century. **$1.50 net. Scribner.

Matthews, J. B. American of the future, and other essays. **$1.25 net. Scribner.

Meynell, A. C. T. Ceres' runaway, and other essays. *$1.25 net. Lane.

Monahan, M. Palms of papyrus. $2.50 net. M. Kennerley.

Montaigne, M. E. de. Essays. 35 c. net; 70 c. net. Dutton.

More, P. E. Shelburne essays. $1.25 net. Putnam.

Morgan, M. H. Addresses and essays. $1.50. Am. Bk.

Morley, C: London at prayer. *$2.50 net. Dutton.

Morley, J: Critical miscellanies. v. 4. **$1.50 net. Macmillan.

Müller, J. Hindrances of life. *$1.50 net. M. Kennerley.

Munger, T. T. On the threshold. $1. Houghton M.

Nicoll, *Sir* W: R. Round the clock. $1.25 net. Doran.

Paine, H. E. Old people. $1.25 net. Houghton M.

ESSAYS.—*Continued.*

Patterson, C: E. Mysteries of life revealed; truth in verse as came through spiritual consciousness. $1. C: E. Patterson.

Pattison, M. Essays. 50 c.; 75 c. Dutton.

Peacock, W., *comp.* Selected English essays. *40 c. net; *75 c. net. Oxford Univ.

Pearson, C: W: Literary and biographical essays. *$1.25 net. Sherman, F.

Raymond, C: F. Happy life. 75 c.; $1.25. Dodge.

Read, H. E. Beggar or a king. 30 c. Business Pub.

Repplier, A. Happy half-century. **$1.10 net. Houghton M.

Rhodes, J. F. Historical essays. **$2.25 net. Macmillan.

Ritchie, A. I. T., *Lady.* Blackstick papers. **$1.75 net. Putnam.

Sedgwick, H: D. New American type, and other essays. **$1.50 net. Houghton M.

Seneca, L. A. Selected essays. *60 c. net. Macmillan.

Sheehan, P. A. Parerga: [essays.] **$1.60 net. Longmans.

Showerman, G. With the professor. **$1.50 net. Holt.

Smith, E. B. Essays and addresses. *$2.50 net. McClurg.

Snow, *Mrs.* J. F. Afternoons. $1.20; $1.25. Ulbrich.

Spender, J: A. Comments of Bagshot. **$1.25 net. Holt.

Spingarn, J. E., *ed.* Critical essays of the seventeenth century. In 3 v. v. 3. $1.75. Oxford Univ.

Stebbing, W. Three essays. 20 c. Oxford Univ.

Stewart, C: D: Essays on the spot. $1.25 net. Houghton M.

Strauss, J. V. Ideas of a plain country woman. **$1 net. Doubleday, P.

Street, G: S. People and questions. $1.50 net. M. Kennerley.

Taylor, W: H: De quibus: discourses and essays. $1.50. Bell Bk.

Temple, *Sir* W: Essays on ancient and modern learning and on poetry. 85 c. Oxford Univ.

Thomas, E: Rest and unrest. $1 net. Dutton.

Thomas, J. M. Idylls of the beautiful. $1. J. M. Thomas.

Thompson, E. Book of hours. $1.50. Forest Press.

Thompson, F. Renegade poet. $1.25 net. Ball Pub.

Trent, W: P. Longfellow, and other essays. $1.50. Crowell.

Van Dyke, H: J. Counsels by the way. **$1 net. Crowell.

Vaughan, J: S. Dangers of the day. $1. Ave Maria.

Walpole, *Sir* S. Essays: political and biographical. *$3 net. Dutton.

Wedgwood, J. Nineteenth century teachers and other essays. *$3 net. Doran.

Wells, H. G: First and last things. **$1.50 net. Putnam.

ESSAYS.—*Continued.*

Whiteing, R: Little people. *$1.50 net. Cassell.

Wilkinson, W: C. Good of life and other little essays. $1.25 net. Funk.

Willcox, *Mrs.* L. C. Human way. **$1.25 net. Harper.

Wilson, J. New views on old subjects. $1.50. Lemcke.

Yoxall, J. H: Wander years. *$2 net. Dutton.

See also Authors;—Criticism;—History;—Ireland;—Plato;—Poetry;—Political science;—Renaissance;—*also* under special subjects.

Essays, biographical and chemical. Ramsay, *Sir* W: *$2.50 net. Dutton.

Essays in municipal administration. Fairlie, J: A. **$2.50 net. Macmillan.

Essays in politics. Macphail, A. *$1.80 net. Longmans.

Essays of American essayists: incl. biographical and critical sketches [of B: Franklin, Channing, Irving, Prescott, Hawthorne, Motley, Walt Whitman and others;] with introd. by Chauncey C. Starkweather. '08 (Je27) c. il. 8°, $1.75; hf. mor., $3.50. Lamb Pub.

Essays of British essayists: incl. biographical and critical sketches [of Bacon, Rob. Burton, J: Locke, Addison, Hume, Goldsmith and others.] '08(Je27) c. 2 v., il. 8°, $3.50; hf. mor., $7. Lamb Pub.

Essays of Elia. *See* Lamb, C:

Essays of French, German and Italian essayists: incl. biographical and critical sketches [of Montaigne, Voltaire, Lessing, Wieland, Lavater, Goethe, Schiller, Leopardi and others.] '08(Je27) c. il. 8°, $1.75; hf. mor., $3.50. Lamb Pub.

Essays on evolution. Poulton, E: B. *$4 net. Oxford Univ.

Essays on literature. Caird, E: $1.75. Macmillan.

Essays philosophical and psychological. Dewey, J: **$3 net. Longmans.

Essence of religion. Bowne, B. P. $1.50 net. Houghton M.

Essential Calvinism. Strong, J. S. *75 c. net. Pilgrim Press.

Essential life. Stanton, S. B. **$1 net. Scribner.

Essential nature of law. Pattee, W: I. $2.50. Callaghan.

Essential needs of the soul. Reed, J. 75 c. Badger.

Essentials. Jefferson, C: E: 35 c. Y. M. C. A.

Essentials in mediæval history. Harding, S: B. $1. Am. Bk.

Essentials of character. Sisson, E: O. $1 net. Macmillan.

Essentials of descriptive geometry. Phillips, J. D: $1. Tracey, G. & Co.

Essentials of lettering. French, T: E. $1. Varsity Supply.

Essentials of milk hygiene. Jensen, C. O. **$2 net. Lippincott.

Essentials of pianoforte playing. Johns, C. $1.50. Ditson.

Essentials of self government. Powell, E. T: *$1.50 net. Longmans.

Essentials of the Five Scapulars. Lynch, J. S. M. 25 c. Cathedral Lib.

ESSEX, England.

Bosworth, G: F. Essex. 45 c. Putnam.

Moncrieff, A. R. H. Essex. *$6 net. Macmillan.

Weston, W. H. School hist. of Essex. 50 c. Oxford Univ.

ESSEX, Mass.

Vital records of Essex, Mass., to the end of the year 1849. (Add. pubs. for price.) Essex Inst.

ESSEX COUNTY, Mass.

Dow, G: F. Old wood engraving, views and buildings in the county of Essex. (Priv. pr.) G: F. Dow.

ESSEX COUNTY, N. J.

See Sewage and sewerage.

Essig, C: Ja., M.D., and Koenig, A:, M.D.

Dental metallurgy. 6th ed., thoroughly rev. '09(Jl) 355 p. il. 12°, *$2 net. Lea.

Essig, Montgomery F., comp.

See Bible. [Selections.]

Establishing boundary line between Colorado and New Mexico and Oklahoma. United States. *Congress. House. Committee on the Judiciary.* 5 c. U. S., Supt. of Docs.

Estabrook, Alma Martin.

Rule of three. '09(My1) c. il. D. †$1.25. Small.

Estabrook, J: Davis.

Three generations of Northboro Davises, 1781-1894. '09(Ag7) il. pors. facsim., O. pap., $3. J: D. Estabrook.

Estabrooke, W: Ludlow.

See Baskerville, C:

Estate fences. Vernon, A. $3.50. Spon.

ESTATES.

See Executors and administrators;—Land;—Property; — Real property; — Wills;—*also* names of states.

Estêbanez, Don Joaquin, pseud.

See Tamayo y Baus, *Don* Manuel.

Estes, Gustavus Kendall.

See O'Neil, Rob. Kingsley.

ESTHETICS.

See Æsthetics.

Estimates and agents' companion. Brown, J. N. $1; $1.50. Rough Notes.

Estimating. Nichols, E: $1. Am. Sch. Corr.

Estimating frame and brick houses. Hodgson, F: T. $1. D: Williams.

Estimating tactical situations. Fitch, R. S. (Priv. pr.) Staff Coll.

Estimating the cost of buildings. Joslin, A. W. $1. D: Williams.

Estimator's price book. Hicks, I: P. $1. D: Williams.

Estournelles de Constant, Paul Henri Benjamin, Baron d'.

See Hill, D: Jayne.

Estranjero (El). Waters, R. J. $1.50 net. Rand, McN. & Co

Esty, W:

Alternating-current machinery. '09(My8) c. il. por. 8°, (American School of Correspondence pubs.) $3. Am. Sch. Corr.

See also Franklin, W: Suddards.

ETCHING.

See also Engravers and engraving;—*also* Whistler, James A. M.

Etchings of the East. Moore, J: M. *$1 net. Pub. Ho. of M. E. Ch., So.

Etchings of the Master. McFarland, J: T. *$1.25 net. Eaton & M.

Eternal boy. *See* Johnson, Owen M.

Eternal epistle. Long, S. P: $2.50. S. P: Long.

Eternal fires. Cory, V. $1.50. M. Kennerley.

Eternal fires. Schoonmaker, N. M. $1.50. B'way Pub.

Eternal hills. Keller, C: E. 25 c. C: E. Keller.

Eternal rose. Chater, M. $1 net. Revell.

Eternal values. Münsterberg, H. **$2.50 net. Houghton M.

Eternity of matter. Farrar, L. B. $2. N. E. Stevens.

Ethel Vale. Phelps, G. F. $1. Chr. Witness.

Ethel Wright. Corwin, M. L. $1. Cochrane.

ETHER.

Lodge, *Sir* O. J. Ether of space. **75 c. net. Harper.

May, C. E. Oxygen ethers of the type—N: C. (O R), derived from certain nitrogen heterocycles. (Add. author for price.) C. E. May.

Whittaker, E. T. Hist. of the theories of æther and electricity. $4.50 net. Longmans.

Ethic of Jesus. Stalker, J. *$1.75 net. Armstrong.

Ethical and religious significance of the state. Dealey, J. Q. **10 c. net. Am. Bapt.

Ethical aspects of evolution. Benett, W. $2. Oxford Univ.

Ethical end of Plato's theory of ideas. Cavenagh, F. A. 50 c. Oxford Univ.

Ethical obligations of the lawyer. Archer, G. L. $3 net. Little, B. & Co.

ETHICS.

Aristotle. Nicomachean ethics. bk. 6. *$1.75 net. Putnam.

Buckham, M. H: Moral conditions in intellectual attainment. gratis. M. H: Buckham.

Cabot, *Mrs.* E. L. Ethics for children. $1.25. Houghton M.

Clark, H: W. Christian method of ethics. *$1.25 net. Revell.

Clark, J: K. Systematic moral education. $1 net. Barnes.

Cronin, M. Science of ethics. *$4.50 net. Benziger.

Davies, A. E. Moral life; study in genetic ethics. *$2 net. Psychological Review.

Dewey, J: Ethics. 25 c. Columbia Univ.

Dewey, J: Moral principles of education. **35 c. net. Houghton M.

Dewey, J:, *and* Tufts, J. H. Ethics. $2. Holt.

Dole, C: F. Ethics of progress. $1.50. Crowell.

Eliot, C: W: Lawlessness: address. 10 c. Civic Forum.

Every-day ethics. $1.25 net. Yale Univ.

Fitch, M. H. Physical basis of mind and morals. $1. Kerr.

Flack, A. G. Moral education. 50 c. Cochrane.

ETHICS.—*Continued.*

Hart, J. K. Critical study of current theories of moral education. 50 c. net. Univ. of Chic.

Hastings, J., *ed.* Encyclopedia of religion and ethics. In 10 or 12 v. v. 1, 2. ea., $7; $9. (Sold in sets only.) Scribner.

Hatch, D: P. Straight goods in philosophy. $1. Rogers Bros.

Hayden, E. A. Social will. $1. Psychological Review.

Jordan, D. S. Strength of being morally clean. $1, boxed. Caldwell.

King, H: C. Ethics of Jesus. **$1.50 net. Macmillan.

Krause, F. H. Manual of moral and humane education. $1.25. Donnelley.

Lloyd, J: W: Life's beautiful battle. $1.25. J: W: Lloyd.

McConnell, R. M. Duty of altruism. $1.50 net. Macmillan.

Meakin, F: Function, feeling, and conduct. **$1.50 net. Putnam.

Moore, J: H. New ethics. *$1 net. Bloch.

Mortensen, A. C. Law of transformation in nature of natural bodies: [science applied to man's moral development.] 50 c. A. C. Mortensen.

Murray, J: C. Hand-book of Christian ethics. *$2.25 net. Scribner.

Nicholson, A. M. Concept standard; historical survey of what men have conceived as constituting or determining life values. $1.50. Teachers' Coll.

Palmer, G. H. Ethical and moral instruction in schools. **35 c. net. Houghton M.

Perry, R. B. Moral economy. **$1.25 net. Scribner.

Rand, B:, *comp.* Classical moralists. **$3 net. Houghton M.

Read, C. Natural and social morals. *$2.75 net. Macmillan.

Royce, J. Philosophy of loyalty. **$1.50 net. Macmillan.

Sadler, M. E., *ed.* Moral instruction and training in schools. 2 v. ea., **$1.50 net. Longmans.

Sera, L. G. On the tracks of life; immorality of morality. *$2.50 net. Lane.

Sharp, F. C. Study of the influence of custom on the moral judgment. 30 c. Univ. of Wis.

Slater, T: Manual of moral theology for English speaking countries. *$2.75 net. Benziger.

Spiller, G. Faith in man: [faith in moral endeavor.] *75 c. net. Macmillan.

Spinoza, B. Ethics, and De intellectus emendatione. 35 c. net; 70 c. net. Dutton.

Taylor, C: K. Basic cause; discussion of modern morals. 25 c. net. Staton Bros.

Westermarck, E: Origin and development of the moral ideas. In 2 v. v. 2. *$3.50 net. Macmillan.

See also Amusements;—Business;—Character;—Charities; — Cheerfulness; — Christian life; — Christianity; — Children; — Conduct of life; — Conscience;—Courage;—Crime and criminals;—Culture; — Divorce;—Education;—Etiquette;—Family;—Friendship;—Happiness;—Heredity;—Liberty;—Manners and customs;—Marriage;—Optimism;—Patriotism;—Painters and painting;—Peace; — Philosophy; — Politics;—Poor;—Religion; — Religious education; — Sex; — Sin;—Social science;—Success;—Temperance;—Temptation; — War; — Will;—Young men;—Young people;—*also* Plato.

Ethics of Christian life. Haering, T. v. *$3 net. Putnam.

Ethics of conservation. Fletcher, H: F. 10 c. H: F. Fletcher.

Ethics of force. Warner, H. E. 50 c. net. Ginn.

Ethics of St. Paul. Alexander, A. B. D. $2 net. Macmillan.

Ethics of the dust. *See* Ruskin, J:

Ethics of the practice of law. Hughes, T: (Add. pubs. for price.) Daily Record.

Ethno-geography of the Pomo and neighboring Indians. Barrett, S: A. $3.25. Univ. of Cal.

ETHNOGRAPHY.
See Ethnology.

Ethnologic dict. of the Navaho language. '10 (Je25) c. il. 8°, $5 (200 copies.) Franciscan Fathers (Ariz.)

ETHNOLOGY.

Boas, F. Anthropology: [lectures.] 25 c. Macmillan.

Bruner, F. G. Hearing of primitive peoples: experimental study of the auditory acuity and the upper limit of hearing of Whites, Indians, Filipinos, Ainu and African Pigmies. $1. Science Pr., (N. Y.)

Dieserud, J. Scope and content of the science of anthropology. *$2 net. Open Court.

Fisher, H. N. Ethnography and commercial importance of Latin America and the West Indies in 1906. (Add. Superintendent for price.) U. S., Supt. of Docs.

Fraser, J: F. Quaint subjects of the king. *$1.25 net. Cassell.

Frobenius, L. Childhood of man. *$3 net. Lippincott.

Gehring, A. Racial contrasts: distinguishing traits of the Græco-Latins and Teutons. **$1.50 net. Putnam.

Haddon, A. C. Races of man and their distribution. *50 c. net. Stokes.

Hrdlicka, A. Skeletal remains suggesting or attributed to early man in North America. 25 c. U. S., Supt. of Docs.

Johnston, *Sir* H. H., *and others.* Living races of mankind. In 2 v. *$10 net. Bowman.

Joyce, T. A., *and* Thomas, N. W., *eds.* Women of all nations. In 24 pts. pt. 1, 25 c. Cassell.

Kroeber, A. L: Ethnography of Cahuilla Indians. 75 c. Univ. of Cal.

Keane, A: H: World's peoples. *$2 net. Putnam.

McCabe, J. Prehistoric man. 50 c. net. Stokes.

Marett, R. R., *ed.* Anthropology and the classics: six lectures. $2. Oxford Univ.

Nelson, N. C. Ellis Landing shellmounds. 75 c.—Shellmounds of the San Francisco Bay region. 50 c. Univ. of Cal.

Parmelee, M. Principles of anthropology and sociology in their relation to criminal procedure. *$1.25 net. Macmillan.

ETHNOLOGY.—*Continued.*
Putnam anniversary volume; anthropological essays. $8 net. Stechert.
Sinclair, W: J. Recent investigations bearing on the question of the occurrence of neocene man in the auriferous gravels of the Sierra Nevada. 35 c. Univ. of Cal.
Standard library of natural history, embracing living animals of the world and living races of mankind. 5 v. $16.50; $19.50. Univ. Soc.
Thomas, W: I: Source book for social origins. *$4.50 net. Univ. of Chic.
United States. *Superintendent of Documents.* Ethnology; titles and prices of those published documents of the United States Bureau of American Ethnology which are now available for distribution. [2d ed.] '09(Je) 14 p. 8°, pap., gratis.
Weale, B. L. P., *pseud.* Conflict of colour. $2 net. Macmillan.
See also Archæology;—Aryan language;—Aryans;—Cliff dwellers;—Eugenics;—Evolution;—Folk lore;—Indians;—Kafirs; — Language;—Man;—Mexican languages;—Mythology; — Negroes;—Philippine Islands;—Totemism; — Voyages and travels.

Etiology of cholera infantum, typhoid fever and appendicitis. Tilden, J: H: $5. Merchants' Pub.

ETIQUETTE.
Antrim, *Mrs.* M. T. Don'ts for bachelors and old maids. $1; 50 c. Altemus.
Clark, J. W. Desk book on the etiquette of social stationery. $1. Eaton, C. & P.
Collier, W: Book of etiquette entitled "Don't do that." v. 1. 50 c. Bennett.
Correct social usage. 2 v. ea., $1.95; per set, $2.95; $3.95. H. A. Lewis.
Devereaux, G. R. M. Etiquette for men.—Etiquette for women. ea., 50 c. Fenno.
Glover, E. H. "Dame Curtsey's" book of etiquette. *50 c. net. McClurg.
Hall, *Mrs.* F. M. H. Hdbk. of hospitality for town and country. $1.50. Estes.
Hardy, E. J. How to be happy though civil. *$1 net. Scribner.
Palmer, A. S. Ideal of a gentleman. *$1.50 net. Dutton.
Ravenbyrne, E. M. Good health and good manners. 25 c. Ainsworth.
Sangster, *Mrs.* M. E. M. Good manners for all occasions. $1.25. Cupples & L.
Sheldon, R. L. Social silhouettes. 50 c. S. W. Anderson.

Etiquette for Americans by a woman of fashion. New and rev. ed. '09(S11) 16°, *$1.50 net. Duffield.
Eton algebra. Scoones, P. pt. 1. *50 c. net. Macmillan.

ETON COLLEGE, Eton, Eng.
Greg, W. W., *comp.* Descriptive catalogue of the early editions of the works of Shakespeare in the library of Eton College. $1.10. Oxford Univ.
Greg, W. W., *comp.* Descriptive catalogue of the early eds. of the works of Shakespeare preserved in the library of Eton College. $1.20. Oxford Univ.
Stone, C. Eton. *$2 net. Macmillan.

ETRURIA.
See Tuscany.

Ettinger, W: L.
See Burchill, Georgine.

Etudes of life. Winn, E. L. $1.50. Fischer.
Etymological dict. of the English language. Skeat, W. W: $11.75. Oxford Univ.

ETYMOLOGY.
See Words.

Etzenhouser, Rudolph.
Engravings of prehistoric specimens from Michigan, U. S. A. '10(N) c. 39 p. il. por. 4°. R. Etzenhouser.

EUCALYPTUS.
Graves, W: E., *comp. and ed.* Studies in eucalyptus. $1. W: E. Graves.

EUCHARIST (The).
See Lord's supper.

EUCHRE.
Van Rensselaer, *Mrs.* J: K. Nonsuch euchre and kindred games. $2. Bond.

Eucken, Rudolf Christof.
Christianity and the new idealism; study in the religious philosophy of to-day; tr. [from the 3d German ed.] by Lucy Judge Gibson and W. R. Boyce Gibson. '10 (Ja29) 12°, (Harper's lib. of living thought.) *75 c. net. Harper.
Life of the spirit; introd. to philosophy; tr. by F. L. Pogson. '09(Ja30) D. (Crown theological lib.) *$1.50 net. Putnam.
Meaning and value of life. '09(D25) 12°, *$1.40 net. Macmillan.
Problem of human life as viewed by the great thinkers from Plato to the present time; tr. from the German by Williston S. Hough and W. R. Boyce Gibson. '09 (S11) c. O. **$3 net. Scribner.

Euclid.
Elements; 13 books; tr. by T: L. Heath. 3 v. '09(Ap24) *$13.50 net. Putnam.

Euclid shorthand manual. Curry, J. S: $1.50. Burrows.

EUGENE, Prince.
See François. Eugène de Savoie-Carignan.

EUGENE ONEGIN (*opera*).
Tschaikowsky, P. I. Eugene Onégin. $3.50; $2.50. Schirmer.

EUGENICS.
American Academy of Political and Social Science. Race improvement in the United States. $1. Am. Acad. Pol. Sci.
Bell, A. G. Few thoughts concerning eugenics. 25 c. Nat. Geog.
Davenport, C: B. Eugenics. 50 c. net. Holt.
Hatch, W. M. Ideal family: manual on the science of procreation. $1. W. M. Hatch.
Muncie, *Mrs.* E. H. Four epochs of life. $1.50 net. Greaves.
Saleeby, C. W. Parenthood and race culture: an outline of eugenics. **$2.50 net. Moffat.
Schultz, A. P. Race or mongrel. $2.50. L. C. Page.
Whetham, W: C. D. *and* Catherine D. Family and the nation. *$2.50 net. Longmans.
See also Woman.

EUGENIE, Marie de Montijo, *Empress of the French.*
Holm, E. Eugénie: Empress of the French. 50 c. net. McClurg.
Legge, E: Empress Eugénie, 1870-1910. $2 net. Scribner.
Loliée, F. A. Life of an empress: Eugénie de Montijo. *$4 net. Dodd.
Eugenie Grandet. *See* Balzac, Honoré de.
Eugenius, the star child. Nicolovius, L. 75 c. B'way Pub.
Eumenides. *See* Æschylus.
Eunice Loyd. Moody, R. N. $1.50. F: L: Rowe.
"Eureka." Washburn, E. J. $1. Sun.
Eureka rate tables. Patchel, G: $50. G: Patchel.
Euripides.
The Bacchae; tr. into Eng. rhyming verse, with explanatory notes, by Gilbert Murray. 2d ed. '08(My2) D. 50 c. Longmans.
Euripides: tr. into English rhyming verse by G: Gilbert Aimé Murray. 4th ed. '08 (O31) il. D. $2. Longmans.
Evripidis fabvlae; recognovit brevique adnotatione critica instrvxit Gilbertvs Murray. Tomvs 3; insvnt, Helena, Phoenissae, Orestes, Bacchae, Iphigenia Avlidensis, Rhesus. '10(Mr26) D. $1.10. Oxford Univ.
Hippolytus; tr. into Eng. rhyming verse, with explanatory notes, by Gilbert Murray. 5th ed. '08(My2) D. 50 c. Longmans.
Iphigenia in Tauris; tr. into English rhyming verse, with explanatory notes, by Gilbert Murray. '10(My21) c. D. 75 c. net. Oxford Univ.
Phœnissæ; ed. by A. C. Pearson. '09, [1910.] (F) 246 p. 8°, (Pitt Press ser.) *$1.25 net. Putnam.
Plays; tr. by Shelley, Dean Milman, Potter and Woodhull. v. 2. '08(F22) 16°, (Everyman's lib.) *35 c. net; leath., *70 c. net. Dutton.
The revellers; the choruses of the Bacchai of Euripides, and the third book of Lucretius; tr. into English verse by Rev. R. E. McBridge. '09(Ag7) c. 12°, $1. B'way Pub.
EURIPIDES.
Harry, J. E: Question of divination, (Medea 240, [by Euripides.])—Studies in Euripides; Hippolytus. (Add. Univ. for price.) Univ. of Cin.
EUROPE.
Abraham, G: D. Complete mountaineer. *$4.80 net. Doubleday, P.
Bailey, J. W. First impressions of Europe. **$1.25 net. Grafton Press.
Blanchard, A. E. Journey of joy: [fiction.] †$1.50. Estes.
Burt, W: Europe and Methodism. 35 c. Jennings.
Crocker, H: G. Situation in southeastern Europe (Add. pub. for price.) B. S. Adams.
Cust, N. Gentlemen errant: journeys and adventures of four noblemen in Europe during the XV. and XVI. centuries. *$4 net. Dutton.
EUROPE.—*Continued.*
Dale, *Mrs.* L. Stories from European hist. 50 c. net. Longmans.
De Windt, H. Through savage Europe. $1.50 net. Lippincott.
Doyle, G. Incidents of European travel. $1.50. G. Doyle.
Du Bois, M. R. J., *comp.* Poems for travelers. *$1.50 net. Holt.
Finney, F: N. Letters from across the sea. (Priv. pr.) F. N. Finney.
Foster, A. G. By the way; travel letters. $1.50. P. Elder.
Foster, H. D., *and* Fay, S. B. Syllabus of European hist. 50 c. E. P. Storrs.
Frazar, *Mrs.* M. D. Practical European guide. $1.50. Small.
Froissart, J. Chronicles of England, France, Spain and adjoining countries. 2 v. $3.50; $7. Lamb Pub.
Frye, W: E: After Waterloo; reminiscences of European travel. (Add. pubs. for price.) P. R. Reynolds.
Gallichan, W. M. Old continental towns. $2 net. Pott.
Gompers, S: Labor in Europe and America. $2 net. Harper.
Good, J. I. Famous places of the reformed churches. $1.50. Heidelberg.
Guthridge, A. S. From capitol to Kremlin. $1.25 net. Neale.
Hallam, H: Hist. of Europe during the Middle Ages. 3 v. $5.25; $10.50. Lamb Pub.
Hassall, A. European hist. chronologically arr. $1.50 net. Macmillan.
Hazen, C: D. Europe since 1815. $3. Holt.
Hood, C: N. Europe, the second trail. 50 c. Rolling Stone.
Humphrey, L. H., *comp.* Poetic old-world. **$1.50 net. Holt.
Jane, L. C. From Metternich to Bismarck; text-book of European hist. $1.10. Oxford Univ.
Johnson, A. J., *ed.* Six ages of European hist. 6 v. ea., *90 c. net. Macmillan.
Lodge, R. B. Bird-hunting through wild Europe. $2.50 special net. Appleton.
McPherson, L. G. Transportation in Europe. $1.50 net. Holt.
Mayer, L. W. Mining methods in Europe. $2.50. Hill Pub.
Mayne, J: Journal during a tour on the continent upon its reopening after the fall of Napoleon, 1814. *$4 net. Lane.
Moryson, F. Itinerary of Fynes Moryson. In 4 v. v. 3 and 4. ea., *$3.25 net. Macmillan.
Munroe, W: B. Government of European cities. **$2.50 net. Macmillan.
Newnham-Davis, N. Gourmet's guide to Europe. *$1.50 net. Brentano's.
Nichol, J: Tables of European history, literature, science and art; and of American history, literature and art. *$2.25 net. Macmillan.
Osborne, T: M. Adventures of a green dragon. [European travel.] (Priv. pr.) Auburn Pub.

EUROPE.—*Continued.*
Poe, C. H. Southerner in Europe. 75 c. Mutual Pub. Co.
Presbrey, F. Motoring abroad. *$2 net. Outing.
Rees, T: Sixty days in Europe and what we saw there. $1.25. State Register.
Reich, E. Foundations of modern Europe. **$1.50 net. Macmillan.
Robinson, J. H., *and* Beard, C: A. Development of modern Europe. 2 v. v. 1, $1.50; v. 2, $1.60.—Readings in modern European history. v. 1, $1.40; v. 2, $1.50; 2 v. in 1, abrg. ed., $1.50. Ginn.
Royland, H: C. Across Europe in a motor boat. **$2 net. Appleton.
Satchel guide for the vacation tourist in Europe, 1909, 1910. ea., **$1.50 net. Houghton M.
Seitz, D. C. Elba and elsewhere. $1.25 net. Harper.
Snider, D. J. European history. $1.50. Sigma.
Snowden, J. H: Summer across the sea. *$1 net. Revell.
Stedman, E. C. *and* T: L., *eds.* Complete pocket guide to Europe. $1.25 net. W: R. Jenkins.
Stratton, C. R. Picturesque Europe. $1. Nat. Pub. Co.
Thompson, R. L. Glimpses of medical Europe. **$2 net. Lippincott.
Trenholme, N. M. Syllabus for the history of western Europe. In 2 pts. ea., 40 c. Ginn.
Vinogradoff, P. G. Roman law in mediæval Europe. *75 c. net. Harper.
Wood, A. T. *and* B. R. Ribbon roads. $2.50 net. Putnam.
Woods, H. C. Washed by four seas; travels in the Near East. *$2.50 net. Wessels.
See also Balkans;—Cities;—Inland navigation;—Mediterranean Sea;—Middle Ages;—Mines and mining;—Napoleonic wars;—Painters and painting; — Renaissance; — *also* names of separate countries.

European hero stories. Tappan, E. M. **65 c. net. Houghton M.

European larch (*larix europaea*). '09(N) 3 p. 8°, (U. S., Dept. of Agriculture, forest service, forest planting leaflet.) pap. (Add. Superintendent for price.)

Euster, W: Tell.
Philosophy of church building: how to build a beautiful modern church or parsonage at half price. '08(Je13) c. il. por. 8°, full leath., $3.50. Pendleton.

Euthenics. Richards, *Mrs.* E. H. S. $1 net. Whitcomb & B.

Euthyphro (The). *See* Plato.

Euwer, J: Hays.
Silver cross. '07, [1908.] (Mr.) c. 15 p. il. 12°. (Add. author for price.) J: H. Euwer.

Eva Garvey publishing fund. 12°. S. S. Bd. So. Bapt.
—Frost. Our church life. 90 c.

Eva Mary, Sister.
Little pilgrimage to holy places. '09, [1910.] (Jl) c. 80 p. 12°. Order Transfiguration.

Evacuation of England: the twist in the Gulf Stream. Gratacap, L: P. †$1.25. Brentano's.

Evalena. Dawson, *Mrs.* B. P. C. 60 c. Cochrane.

Evan Grayle's daughters. Robson, I. S. 75 c. McKay.

Evangel. Hamilton, W: W. *20 c. net; *15 c. net. Am. Bapt.

Evangel (The) first standard teacher training course; approved by the Committee on Education of the International Sunday School Association; general introd. by Franklin McElfresh, D.D. '10(O1) c. S. pap., 35 c. F. M. Barton.

Evangelical invasion of Brazil. Gammon, S: R. 75 c. Presb. Pub.

EVANGELICAL LUTHERAN CHURCH, Georgetown, D. C.
Waring, L. H. Hist. of the Evangelical Lutheran Church of Georgetown, D. C. 35 c. L. H. Waring.

Evangelical Lutheran Church in North America. An explanation of the Common service; with appendices on Christian hymnody and liturgical colors, and a glossary of liturgical terms. 2d rev. and enl. ed. '08(Ap18) c. sq. D. 75 c. Gen. Council.

Evangeline. *See* Longfellow, H: Wadsworth.

EVANGELISM.
See Conversion;—Missions and missionaries;—Revivals.

Evangelistic sermons, together with practical suggestions for the conduct of the after-meeting; comp. by the Evangelistic Committee of the Presbyterian Church in the U. S. A. '09(Je) c. 5-293 p. 12°, 75 c.; pap., 35 c. P. E. Zartmann.

EVANGELIZATION.
See Conversion.

Evans, Alex. W:, and Nichols, G: Elwood.
Bryophytes of Connecticut: [mosses.] '08 [1909.] (Mr) 5-203 p. 8°, (Conn. state geol. and natural hist. survey bull.) 30 c. Conn. Lib.

Evans, Alvin E.
Roman law studies in Livy. '10(Ag13) 8°, (Univ. of Mich. studies; Humanistic ser.) pap., 46 c. net. Macmillan.

Evans, Arth. J:
Scripta Minoa; written documents of Minoan Crete with special reference to the archives of Knossos. v. 1. '10 (Mr26) F. $12.75. Oxford Univ.

Evans, Augusta Jane.
See Wilson, *Mrs.* A. J.

Evans, C. E.
School buildings. '10(D) 61 p. il. plans, 8°, (Conference for education in Texas bull.) gratis. C. E. Evans.

Evans, C:
American bibliography: chronolog. dict. of books, pamphlets and periodical pubs pr. in U. S. fr. 1639 to 1820; with bibliog. notes. In 6 v. v. 5, 1774-1778. '09(Je12); v. 6, 1779-1785. '10(Ag27) Q. per v., $15. (Priv. pr.) C: Evans; [Blakely Press.]

—, and Bunn, Clinton Orrin.
Study of civil government, incl. "Constitution and enabling act of the state of Oklahoma." '08(Jl) c. 8+12 p. 8°, pap., 55 c. Bunn.

Evans, C: T.
Essays: practical hints for retail jewelers by one of them; articles reprinted from *The Manufacturing Jeweler.* '08(Ap18) c. por. 12°. (Add. pubs. for price.) W. B. Frost.

Evans, D: J., M.D.
Obstetrics; a manual for students and practitioners. 2d ed., rev. and enl. '09(O) c. 9+17-440 p. il. 8°, $2.25. Lea.

Evans, Edn.
How to compose within the lyric form. '09 (Je5) D. *$1 net. Scribner.

Evans, F. Cridland.
Rose of Eden: a drama in four acts. '08 (N7) c. D. pap., 25 c. Penn Pub. Co.

Evans, Mrs. Florence.
Purity, birth and sexual problems for mothers. '08(Ap18) c. il. D. (Add. pubs. for price.) Purity Pub.

Evans, G: Fullerton.
College freshman's don't book. '10(Ag13) c. il. front. nar. 12°, 75 c. P. Elder.

Evans, H: Ridgely.
House of the sphinx. '08(Ja4) D. $1.50. Neale.
Old and the new magic. New and enl. ed. '09(O23) il. $2. Open Court.

Evans, Holden A.
Trade follows the flag. '08(Je6) 8°, pap., 15 c. U. S., Supt. of Docs.

Evans, Howard.
Sir Randal Cremer, his life and work; published for the International School of Peace. '10(My21) c. por. map, D. $1.40 net. Ginn.

Evans, I. C. I.
Dreams of Tommy Dimplecheek. '08(N7) c. front. D. $1. Neale.

Evans, J. H.
Ornamental turning; work of pract. instruction in the above art. In 3 v. '10(Jl30) D. ea., $1. McKay.

Evans, J: H:
Birth of Mormonism in picture: scenes and incidents in early church hist. from photographs. '10(Ap16) c. il. obl. D. pap., 75 c. Deseret S. S. Un.
One hundred years of Mormonism; hist. of the Church of Jesus Christ of Latter-day Saints from 1805 to 1905. 3d ed. '10(Mr26) c. D. $1.25. Deseret News.

Evans, Lawton Bryan.
Elements of English grammar. '08(F1) c. D. 40 c. Am. Bk.
Essential facts of American hist. '10(F5) c. il. pors. 12°, $1. B: H. Sanborn.
First lessons in American history. '10 (Ag6) c. il. pors. maps, 12°, 70 c. B: H. Sanborn.
History of Georgia for use in schools. '09 (My22) c. il. double map, 12°, (State history ser.) *$1 net. Am. Bk.
Introductory language lessons. '08(F1) c. il. D. 30 c. Am. Bk.

Evans, M. A. B.
Monthly sonata, and other verses. '10 (D31) 8°, $1.25. Putnam.

Evans, Marshall Blakemore.
High school course in German. Rev. ed. '09(S4) 12°, (Univ. of Wis. bull.; High school ser.) pap. (Add. Univ. for price.) Univ. of Wis.

—, and Prokosch, Eduard.
German exercises book. '08(D19) c. O. bds., 30 c. Ginn.

Evans, May Garrettson, comp.
Questions and answers on the elements of music. '08(Mr.) c. 82 p. 12°, 80 c. M. G. Evans.

Evans, Nellie Seelye, [Mrs. Dudley Evans.]
September roses: [poems.] '08(F) 12°, $1. D. Evans.

Evans, Powell.
Address on fire prevention del. before the National Association of Manufacturers, May 20, 1908, New York. '08(Jl18) c. 8°. (Add. author for price.) P. Evans.

Evans, Robley Dunglison.
An admiral's log; being continued recollections of naval life. '10(Mr12) c. il. por. O. **$2 net. Appleton.

Evans, Sebastian, tr.
See High history of the Holy Graal.

Evans, W:
How to memorize. '09(My) c. 95 p. 12°, *50 c. net. Bible Inst.
Personal soul-winning. [1910.] (D) c. 192 p. 8°, $1. Bible Inst.

Evanston, Ill. Public Library. The drama; catalogue of books on dramatic literature contained in the Evanston Public Library; Gertrude L. Brown, comp. '09, [1910.] (D) 32 p. 8°. Evanston Pub. Lib.

EVAPORIMETER.
See Refrigeration.

Evarts, J: Wesley.
Light of life; mystery unveiled by a personal visit of Christ; science brings revolution of religion and law. '10(Mr26) c. pors. D. $2. L. Evarts.

Eva's choice. Browne, L. G. 60 c. Cochrane.

Evasion (L') épisode tiré de Vingt ans aprés. Dumas, A. *25 c. net. Crowell.

Eve, G: W.
Decorative heraldry: hdbk. of its artistic treatment. '08(Mr21) il. 12°, *$2 net. Macmillan.
Heraldry as art: its development and practice, chiefly in England. '08(Mr14) il. 8°, *$5 net. Scribner.

Eve. Sherlock, S. M. 90 c. net. Longmans.

Eve and the evangelist. Rice, H. E. $1.25. Roxburgh.

Evelina. *See* Arblay, *Mme.* Frances B. d'.

Evelyn, J:
Diary. 2 v. '08(O17) 16°, (Best books ser.) leath., ea., *$1 net. Dutton.
Diary of John Evelyn; with introd. and notes by Austin Dobson. Globe ed. '08 (My9) 12°, $1.50. Macmillan.

Evening (The) Capital, Annapolis, Md. Hist. and industrial ed., portraying the glories past and future possibilities of Annapolis, Md.; ed. and comp. by Albert E. Walker. '08(Je) c. f°, pap., 20 c. Evening Capital.

Evening Post. Real estate values: compendium of real estate considerations in Manhattan from January, 1904, to April, 1908. '08(Je27) c. 16°, pap., 25 c. N. Y. Eve. Post.

Evening Post book of bank reports; **cont.** complete repts. at the close of business, February 14, 1908, of all the National Banks of New York, Boston, Philadelphia, Chicago and Pittsburgh, and of the leading banks of the principal banking centres of U. S. [*Also*] Repts. of Canadian banks. '08(Ap4) c. pap., 15 c. N. Y. Eve. Post.

EVENING SCHOOLS.
See Technical education.

Evening telegram cook book. Telford, E. P. 75 c.; 35 c. Cupples & L.

Evening thoughts. Miller, J. R. **65 c. net; **85 c. net. Crowell.

Events and reflections. Coles, R: T: 50 c. Mayhew.

Everett, Bert Noland.
Accomplished through sacrifice. '10(Jl) c. 120 p. por. 12°, 50 c. Review Press, (Ill.)

Everett, C: Carroll, D.D.
Theism and the Christian faith. '09(O9) 8°, *$3.50 net. Macmillan.

Everett, Herbert E:, and Lawrence, W: H:
Freehand and perspective drawing; pt. 1, Freehand drawing; pt. 2, Perspective drawing. '09(F20) il. 8°, (American School of Correspondence pubs.) $1. Am. Sch. Corr.

Everett, Leolyn Louise.
Closed book and other poems. '10(Ag27) c. D. $1.25 net. Wessels & B.

Everett, Marshall, pseud.
See Neil, H:

Everett, Mrs. Ruth.
That man from Wall Street. '08(Je20) c. front. D. $1.50. G: T. Long.

Everett-Green, Evelyn.
See Green, Evelyn Everett-.

EVERGLADES.
See **Florida.**

EVERGREENS.
Dallimore, W. Holly, yew and box. $2.50. Lane.
Weed, C. M. Study of the evergreens in the public schools. gratis. F. W. Rane.

Everhart, Elfrida.
Hdbk. of United States public documents. '10(Je4) c. 8°, $2.50 net. H. W. Wilson.

Everly, Lu Lester, Blount, Ralph Earle, and Walton, Calvin Levi.
Laboratory lessons in physical geography. '08(F22) c. il. maps, O. pap., 56 c. Am. Bk.

Evermann, Barton Warren.
Fishes of Alaska. '07, [1908.] (F) 140 p. il. 4°, pap., $1. U. S., Supt. of Docs.

Evers, J: J., and Fullerton, Hugh S.
Touching second; the science of baseball. '10(Je4) il. por. D. c. $1.25. Reilly & B.

Eversley ser. 12°, $1.50 Macmillan.
—Ker. Epic and romance.
—Morley. Life of Richard Cobden. 2 v.

Everts, Katherine Jewell.
Speaking voice: principles of training simplified. '08(N14) c. D. **$1 net. Harper.

Every boy's and girl's ser. il. 12°, **75 c. net. Macmillan.
—Craik. Little lame prince.
—Fortescue. Story of a red deer.

Every boy's lib.; companion ser. to *Editha ser.* 35 v. '10(N) il. 12°, ea., 50 c. Caldwell.

Every child should know ser. il. D. Doubleday, P.
—Bacon. Pictures that every child should know. **$1.20 net.
—Burt, *ed.* Prose that every child should know. **90 c. net; **$1.50 net.
—Kipling. Stories and poems every child should know. $1.20.
—Lorenzini. Adventures every child should know; Pinocchio. **90 c. net.
—Mabie, *ed.* Essays that every child should know. **90 c. net; **$1.50 net.—Folk tales every child should know. 90 c.
—Mabie *and* Stephens, *eds.* Heroines that every child should know. **90 c. net; **$1.50 net.
—Rogers. Earth and sky every child should know.—Trees that every child should know. ea., **$1.20 net.
—Stack. Wild flowers every child should know. $1.20.

Every child's library. *See* Dutton's.—Winston's.

Every-day business for women. Wilbur, M. A. $1.25 net. Houghton M.

Every-day diseases of children. Candler, G: H: $1. Clinic.

Every-day English. White, R: G. $2. Houghton M.

Every-day ethics; addresses del. in the Page lecture series, 1909, before the senior class of the Sheffield Scientific School, Yale University. '10(Ap16) c. O. $1.25 net. Yale Univ.

Every-day evangelism. Leete, F: D. *$1 net. Jennings.

Every day girls. Lippmann, J. M. †75 c. McKay.

Every-day Japan. Lloyd, A. *$4 net. Cassell.

Every day ser. 2 v. '10(D) col. il. ea., bds., 40 c. Cassell.

Every girl's library. Fitzhugh, P. K., *ed.* 10 v. $4. Pearson Pub. Co.

Every man for himself. Duncan, N. †$1.50. Harper.

Every man his chance. Stone, M. W. $1.50. Badger.

Every man's lawyer. Bolles, A. S. 3 v. $3. Doubleday, P.

Every woman her own dressmaker. Berge, *Mme.* *$1.25 net. Doran.

Everybody's booklets. D. pap., 10 c. Am. Press.
—Didier. Way to win her.
—Jones. Strange adventures of an author in search of a publisher.

Everybody's cat book. Champion, D. B. $2. D. B. Champion.

Everybody's encyclopedia; editorial staff, C: Higgins, assisted by a large corps of specialists and experts. '09(D25) c. col. il. maps, 4°, $5. De Bower-C.

Everybody's lonesome. Laughlin, C. E. 75 c. net. Revell.

Everybody's secret. Calthrop, D. M. †$1.50. G: W. Dillingham.

Everyday poems. Wells, A. R. $1.25 net. Revell.

Everyman: a morality play; ed. with introd., notes and bibliography by Montrose J. Moses. '08(Jl18) c. il. 12°, cl., *$1 net. M. Kennerley.

Everyman: a morality play; with an introd. by A. T. Quiller-Couch. '08(D19) S. (Select English classics.) 10 c. Oxford Univ.

Everyman, and other mystery plays. '09 (Mr27) 16°, (Everyman's lib.) *35 c. net; leath., *70 c. net. Dutton.

Everyman's book of the dog. Smith, A. C. $1.50 net. Doran.

Everyman's encyclopædia. *See* Villiers, A.

Everyman's history of the English church. Dearmer, P. *75 c. net; *$1 net; *50 c. net. Warne.

Everyman's lib.; ed. by Ernest Rhys. 16°, *35 c. net; leath., *70 c. net. Dutton.
—Abbott. Rollo at work, and Rollo at play.
—Aimard. Indian scout.
—Ainsworth. Tower of London.
—Annals of Fairyland; reign of King Cole. —Reign of King Oberon.
—Arblay. Evelina.
—Aristophanes. The Acharnians.
—Arnold. On the study of Celtic literature. —Poems, 1840-1866.
—Atlas of literary and historical geography.
—Aucassin and Nicolette.
—Ballantyne. Ungava.
—Balzac. Cat and Racket.—Catherine de Medici.—The Chouans.—Christ in Flanders.—Cousin Pons.—Quest of the absolute.
—Bates. Naturalist on the Amazon.
—Bede, *the Venerable.* Ecclesiastical hist. of the English nation.
—Berkeley. New theory of vision.
—Blackmore. Lorna Doone.—Springhaven.
—Boswell. Tour in the Hebrides with Dr. Johnson.
—Brontë. Jane Eyre.—Shirley.—The professor.—Villette.
—Brooke. Theology in the English poets.
—Bulfinch. Age of fable.
—Bulwer-Lytton. Pilgrims of the Rhine.
—Burke. Reflections on the French Revolution.—Speeches and letters on American affairs.
—Burton. First footsteps in East Africa.
—Byron, *Lord.* Complete poetical and dramatic works. 3 v.
—Carlyle. Letters and speeches of Cromwell. 3 v.—Sartor resartus.
—Cervantes. Don Quixote. 2 v.
—Chaucer. Canterbury tales.
—Cicero. Select letters and orations.
—Collins. Woman in white.
—Converse. Long Will.
—Cousin. Short biographical dict. of English literature.
—Craik. Manual of English literature.
—Creasy. Fifteen decisive battles of the world.
—Curtis. Prue and I, and Lotos eating.
—Dante. Divine comedy.
—Daudet. Tartarin of Tarascon [and] Tartarin on the Alps.
—Defoe. Journal of the plague year.—Memoirs of a cavalier.

Everyman's lib.—Continued.
—Dickens. American notes.—Child's history of England.—Christmas stories.—Edwin Drood [and] Master Humphrey's clock.—Hard times.—Little Dorrit.—Our mutual friend—Pickwick papers.—Reprinted pieces. —Uncommercial traveller.
—Dufferin. Letters from high latitudes.
—Dumas. Chicot the jester.—Count of Monte Cristo. 2 v.—Forty-five.—Marguerite de Valois.
—Edgar. Heroes of England.—Runnymede, and Lincoln Fair.
—Edgeworth. Castle Rackrent, and The absentee.
—Eliot, *pseud.* Felix Holt.—Mill on the Floss.—Scenes of clerical life.
—Emerson. Nature, and The conduct of life. —Representative men.
—Epictetus. Moral discourses.
—Erckmann *and* Chatrain. Conscript, and Waterloo.
—Euripides. Plays.
—Everyman and other mystery plays.
—Fielding. Hist. of the adventures of Joseph Andrews.—Tom Jones. 2 v.
—First and second prayer books of King Edward VI.
—Francis of Assisi, *St., and* Bonaventura. Little flowers, and Mirror of perfection; also Life of St. Francis.
—Franklin. Memoirs.—Narrative of a journey to the shores of the Polar seas, 1819-22.
—Froude. Edward VI.—Henry VIII. 3 v.—Mary Tudor.
—Galt. Annals of a parish.
—Gaskell. Life of Charlotte Brontë.
—Gibbon. Decline and fall of the Roman Empire. 6 v.
—Gilfillan. Literary portraits.
—Giraldus Cambrensis. Itinerary and description of Wales.
—Gleig. Life of Wellington.
—Goethe. Faust. pts. 1-2.
—Goldsmith. Poems and plays.—Vicar of Wakefield.
—Hakluyt. Voyages. 8 v.
—Harvey. Anatomical disquisition on the motion of the heart and blood in animals.
—Hawthorne. Marble faun.
—Hazlitt. Comic writers of Great Britain.—Lectures on English poets, and the spirit of the age.—Table talk.
—Helps. Life of Columbus.
—Herbert. The temple.
—Herodotus. Rawlinson's Herodotus. In 2 v.
—Herrick. Hesperides, and Noble numbers.
—High hist. of the Holy Graal.
—Homer. Iliad.—Odyssey.
—Hugo. Les miserables. 2 v.—Notre Dame de Paris.
—Hutchinson. Memoirs of Col. Hutchinson.
—Huxley. Lectures and lay sermons.
—Ibsen. Doll's house, Wild duck, Lady from the sea.
—Irving. Conquest of Granada.
—James. Richelieu.
—Jonson. Complete plays.
—Kinglake. Eothen.

Everyman's lib.—Continued.
—Kingsley. Alton Locke.—Geoffrey Hamlyn.—Hereward the Wake.—Water babies; and Glaucus.
—Koran.
—Lamb. Letters. v. 2.—Tales from Shakespeare.
—Lane. Account of the manners and customs of the modern Egyptians.
—Le Sage. Adventures of Gil Blas de Santillane. 2 v.
—Lewes. Life of Goethe.
—Longfellow. Poems.
—Lützkow. Bohemia.
—Macaulay. Hist. of England. 3 v.—Miscellaneous essays.—Speeches on politics.
—Machiavelli. History of Florence.—The prince.
—Manning. Mary Powell, and Deborah's diary.
—Marlowe. Plays and poems.
—Marryat. Perceval Keene.—Settlers in Canada.
—Martineau. Feats of Fjord.
—Masefield, *comp.* Chronicles of the Pilgrim fathers.
—Melville. Omoo.
—Merivale. History of Rome.
—Mill. Utilitarianism, liberty, representative government.
—Milman. History of the Jews. 2 v.
—Milton. Poems.
—Montaigne. Essays.
—More. Utopia and the dialogue of comfort against tribulations.
—Nibelungenlied (The). Fall of the Nibelungs.
—Parkman. Conspiracy of Pontiac.
—Peacock. Headlong Hall and Nightmare Abbey.
—Plato *and* Xenophon. Socratic discourses.
—Plutarch. Lives. 3 v.
—Poe. Tales of mystery and imagination.
—Polo. Travels.
—Prescott. Conquest of Mexico. 2 v.—Conquest of Peru.
—Prothero. Psalms in human life.
—Ramayana (The), and The Mahabharata.
—Reade. Peg Woffington; and Christie Johnson.
—Ruskin. Crown of wild olive.—Ethics of the dust.—Time and tide.
—Scott. Lives of the novelists.—Woodstock.
—Seeley. Ecce homo.
—Smith. Life of William Carey.—Smaller classical dictionary.—Wealth of nations. 2 v.
—Spenser. Faerie Queene. 2 v.
—Spinoza. Ethics.
—Spyri. Heidi.
—Stevenson. Kidnapped.—Treasure Island.
—Stowe. Uncle Tom's cabin.
—Swedenborg. Heaven and hell.
—Swift. Tale of a tub.
—Tacitus. [Selected works.] 2 v.
—Thackeray. Christmas books.—Newcomes. 2 v.—Pendennis. 2 v.—Vanity fair.
—Thomas à Kempis. Imitation of Christ.
—Thoreau. Walden.
—Thorndike. Minor Elizabethan drama, 2 v.
—Thucydides. Hist. of Peloponnesian war.

Everyman's lib.—Continued.
—Tolstoi. Master and man.
—Trollope. Dr. Thorne.—Last chronicle of Barset. 2 v.—Small house at Arlington.
—Trotter. Bayard of India.—Hodson of Hodson's Horse.—Life of Warren Hastings.
—Verne. Abandoned.—Dropped from the clouds.—Secret of the island.—Twenty thousand leagues under the sea.
—Villehardouin *and* Joinville. Chronicles of the crusades.
—Voltaire. History of Charles XII.
—Woolman. Journals and other papers.
—Wordsworth. Longer poems.
—Wyss *and* Montolieu. Swiss family Robinson.
—Yonge. Book of golden deeds.—Dove in the eagle's nest.—Heir of Redclyffe.—Little duke.

Everything behind the engine. McArdle, F. $2. F. McArdle.

EVESTHES JORDANI.
See Paleontology.

EVIDENCE.
Best, W: M. Principles of the law of evidence. $3.50. Boston Bk.
Camp, E. W., *and* Crowe, J: F., *eds.* Encyclopædia of evidence. v. 12-14. ea., $6. L. D. Powell.
Camp, E. W., *and others, eds.* 1st biennial supplement to the encyclopedia of evidence. $6. L. D. Powell.
Hammon, L: L. On evidence covering burden of proof, presumptions, judicial notice, judicial admissions, and estoppel. $6. Keefe-D.
Jones, B. W. Law of evidence in civil cases. (Add. pub. for price.) Bancroft-W.
Moore, C: C. Treatise on facts, or the weight and value of evidence. v. 1, 2. $12. E: Thompson.
Ohio. Outline of the law of evidence. $1. R. Metzler.
Osborn, A. S. Typewriting as evidence. (Add. pubs. for price.) Genesee.
Wigmore, J: H: Pocket code of the rules of evidence in trials at law. **$4 net. Little, B. & Co.
See also Logic;—Trials.

Evidences of Christianity. Hopkins, M. $1.25. T. R. Marvin.

EVIL.
Burton, M. L. Problem of evil. $1.25. Open Court.
See also Sin.

Evinson, Elmer.
Amateur performance. '09(Jl31) 12°, $1. B'way Pub.

EVOLUTION.
Benett, W. Ethical aspects of evolution. $2. Oxford Univ.
Bourne, G. C: Herbert Spencer and animal evolution. 50 c. Oxford Univ.
Burns, J. D. What is man?; or, creationism vs. evolutionism. $2. Cochrane.
Darwin, C: R. Foundations of the origin of species; two essays. *$2.50 net. Putnam.
Depéret, C: Transformation of the animal world. *$1.75 net. Appleton.

EVOLUTION.—*Continued.*
Dewar, D., *and* Finn, F. Making of species. *$2.50 net. Lane.
Fifty years of Darwinism. **$2 net. Holt.
Gerard, J: Old riddle and the newest answer. 20 c. Longmans.
Haeckel, E. H. Evolution of man. 2 v. $5 net. Putnam.
Hall, F. J. Evolution and the fall. **$1.50 net. Longmans.
Iles, G: Electricity uncovers a law of evolution. gratis. G: Iles.
Laguna, T. d'L. *and* G. A. de. Dogmatism and evolution. $1.75 net. Macmillan.
Lewis, A. M. Evolution: social and organic. 50 c. Kerr.
Lock, R. H. Recent progress in the study of variation, heredity and evolution. $2 net. Dutton.
McCabe, J. Evolution. *50 c. net. Stokes.
Macnamara, N. C. Evolution and function of living purposive matter. $1.75 net. Appleton.
Moore, J: H. Universal kinship. $1. Kerr.
Poulton, E: B. Essays on evolution. *$4 net. Oxford Univ.
Rogers, L. W. Hidden side of evolution. 10 c. Theosophical Bk.
Smith, L. Evolution: fantasy [poems]. $1.25. Lane.
Sorley, W: R. Interpretation of evolution. v. 4. 60 c. Oxford Univ.
Thompson, H: C. New reading of evolution. *$1.60 net. New Reading.
Thomson, J: A. Darwinism and human life. $1.50 net. Holt.
Tyler, J: M. Man in the light of evolution. **$1.25 net. Appleton.
Wasmann, E. Berlin discussion of the problem of evolution. *$1.60 net. Herder.
See also Biology;—Botany;—Children;—Embryology;—Ethnology;—Eugenics; — Heredity;—Lady-beetle;—Man;—Religion and science;—Universe;—Vertebrates;—Woman.

Evolution (L') de l'arbitrage international. Balch, T: W. $2. Allen, L. & S.
Evolution of a "damn." Frederick, H. 10 c.; 25 c. H. M. Bones.
Evolution of forces. Le Bon, G. *$1.75 net. Appleton.
Evolution of Italian art. Allen, G. *$3.50 net. Wessels.
Evolution of Italian sculpture. Balcarres, *Lord.* *$6 net. Dutton.
Evolution of law. Scott, H: W. $3; $4. Wilson Pub. Co.
Evolution of mammalian molar teeth. Osborn, H: F. *$2 net. Macmillan.
Evolution of mind. McCabe, J. $2 net. Macmillan.
Evolution of modern Germany. Dawson, H. *$4 net. Scribner.
Evolution of modern orchestration. Coerne, L: A. *$3 net. Macmillan.
Evolution of modesty. Ellis, H: H. $2. Davis.
Evolution of money. Kinnaird, P. $1; 50 c. P. Kinnaird.
Evolution of printing. Pfizenmayer, P. gratis. P. Pfizenmayer.
Evolution of property Lafargue, P. 50 c. Kerr.
Evolution of religion. Hinckle, W: A. 80 c. net. Sherman, F.
Evolution of Rose. Snow, E. 50 c. Badger.
Evolution of Seward's Mexican policy. Callahan, J. M. 75 c. Univ. of W. Va.
Evolution of the American flag. Canby, G: $1. Ferris.
Evolution of the anti-tuberculosis crusade. Hutt, W: H. gratis. W: H. Hutt.
Evolution of the atmosphere. Phinn, J: *$1.25 net. Indust.
Evolution of the constitution of West Virginia. Callahan, M. F. 50 c. Univ. of W. Va.
Evolution of the Messianic idea. Oesterley, W: O. E. *$1.25 net. Dutton.
Evolution of the sciences. Houllevigue, L. $2 net. Van Nostrand.
Evolution of the spiritual world. Dolin, S. 15 c. C. D. Raymer.
Evolution of worlds. Lowell, P. **$2.50 net. Macmillan.
Evolutionary socialism. Bernstein, E: *$1 net. B: W. Huebsch.

Ewald, Carl.
Old room; tr. from the Danish by Alexander Teixeira de Mattos. '08(Mr28) c. D. †$1.25. Scribner.
Queen bee, and other nature stories; tr. from the Danish by G. C. Moore-Smith. '08(Mr21) il. O. $1.25. Nelson.

Ewart, J: Spencer.
Kingdom of Canada: imperial federation, the colonial conferences, the Alaska boundary and other essays. '08(Ag22) il. maps, O. $2.50. Morang.

Ewart, Jos. Archibald, Filed, Wilbur Stanwood, and Morrison, Adelbert Harland.
Civil service manual. In 3 v. '08(D5) c. D. $2.50. Home Corr. Sch.

Ewart, Nellie Eliz.
Daily living: manual designed to simplify the work of the housekeeper; being a pract. cook book adapted to families of moderate and small means, introducing food principles, marketing, cooking and serving; furnishing menus and recipes for 365 consecutive days. '09(Mr) c. '08. 14+579 p. il. 12°, *$1.84 net.. H. P. Hood.

Ewell, Arth. Woolsey.
Text-book of physical chemistry; theory and practice. '09(O30) c. il. tabs., O. *$2.25 net. Blakiston.
See also Buff, Alex. Wilmer.

Ewell, Marshall Davis.
Manual of medical jurisprudence for the use of students at law and of medicine. 2d ed. '09(D) c. 10+407 p. 12°, (Students' ser.) $2.50. Little, B. & Co.

Ewing, Elbert W: Robinson.
Hist. and law of the Hayes-Tilden contest before the electoral commission, the Florida case, 1876-77. '10(F12) c. S. $1.50. Cobden.
Legal and historical status of the Dred Scott decision; history of the case and an examination of the opinion delivered by the Supreme Ct. of the U. S., Mar. 6, 1857. '09(Je) c. 228 p. por. O. $3. Cobden.

Ewing, H: Ellsworth.
Oribatoidea of Illinois. '09, [1910.] (Je) 52 p. il. 4°, (Ill. State Lab'y Natural Hist. bull.) pap., 50 c. Ill. Lab'y Nat. Hist.
Systematic and biological study of the *acarina* of Illinois. [1910.] (My) 120 p. il. O. (University of Illinois bulletin; University studies.) pap., $1. Univ. of Ill.

Ewing, Ja. Alfr.
Mechanical production of cold. '08(N21) 8°, *$3.25 net. Putnam.
Steam-engine and other heat engines. 3d ed., rev. and enl. '10(O22) c. figs. fold. diagrs., O. $3.75 net. Putnam.

Ewing, Jos. Grant.
Poems. '09, [1910.] (Ap) c. 8+32 p. 12°. (Not for sale.) J. G. Ewing.

Ewing, Mrs. Juliana Horatia Gatty.
Works. New library ed; a life of the author by her sister, Marg. E. Gatty. In 11 v. '08(S19) c. per v., $1. Little, B. & Co.
The brownies and other tales. '10(Je18) il. 12°, (Macmillan's queen's treasure ser.) $1. Macmillan.
Flat iron for a farthing. '09(Ja16) il. 12°, (Queen's treasures ser.) $1. Macmillan.
Jan of the windmill. '09(Ap3) il. 12°, (Queen's treasures ser.) $1. Macmillan.
Lob Lie-by-the-Fire; or, the luck of Lingborough, and other tales. '09(D25) il. 12°, (Queen's treasure ser.) *$1 net. Macmillan.
Mrs. Overtheway's remembrances. '09 (Jl3) il. 12°, (Queen's treasures ser.) $1. Macmillan.
Six to sixteen. '08(D5) 12°, (Queen's treasures ser.) $1. Macmillan.
We and the world '10(O8) il. 12°, (Queen's treasure ser.) $1. Macmillan.

Ewing, Rev. W., and Thompson, J. E. H., D.D.
Temple dict. of the Bible. '10(Ap2) il. maps, 8°, $4 net. Dutton.

Ewyn, Janan.
Memories of Cuba, and other poems. '08 (O24) c. D. $1. Badger.

Examination and repair of simple highway bridges. Sherrill, C. O. 25 c. Staff Coll.

Examination of water. Leffmann, H: $1.25. Blakiston.

EXAMINATIONS.
Cloke, H. E:, *comp.* Enlisted specialists' examiner. *$2 net. Wiley.
College Entrance Examination Board. Questions set at the examinations held June 15-20, 1908. 60 c. Ginn.
Goepp, R. M. State Board questions and answers: [examinations in medicine.] (Add. pubs. for price.) Saunders.
Lusby, J. W: County examiner. $1. Teacher's Supply.
New York State Education Department. Professional examination papers, 1908-9. N. Y. State Educ.
Pollock, H. M., *and* Rowell, G: C. American examination and review book. $1.50. N. Y. Educ. Co.
State Board examination questions and answers. $3 net. Wood.
See also Civil service;—Engineering;—Medicine;—Physical geography.

Examples of calculating designs. '08(D5) c. diagrs., 8°, (Machinery's reference ser.) pap., 25 c. Indust. Press.

Excalibur. Cram, R. A. $2; $10. Badger.

EXCAVATIONS.
See Archæology;—Earthwork.

Excavations: Biban el Moluk. Davis, T. M. *$12.50 net. Dutton.

Excavations in an Erie Indian village. Parker, A. C. 30 c. U. S. State Educ.

Excavations of the Island of Pseira. Seager, R: B. $5. Univ. of Penn.

Excelsior art series. 18 v. '09(D18) 16°, leath., ea., $1, boxed; pap., ea., 50 c., boxed. Cupples & L.

Excerpta Cypria. Cobham, C. D., *ed.* *$6.30 net. Putnam.

EXCHANGE.
Escher, F. Elements of foreign exchange. $1. Bankers' Pub.
Fortune, W: H. Costs in currency of British, German, French and Austrian cotton goods; tariff, August 5, 1909. $4. W: H: Fortune.
See also Money;—Stocks.

EXCHANGES.
See Stocks.

Excursions of a booklover. Marvin, F. R. $1.50 net. Sherman, F.

Executioner's knife. *See* Sue, M. J. E.

EXECUTORS AND ADMINISTRATORS.
Baugh, F: H:, *and* Schmeisser, W: C. Theory and practice of estate accounting for accountants, lawyers, [etc.] $4. Curlander.
Hartich, F: F. Hints; simple treatise on the duties and obligations of executors and administrators. $2. F. C. Hill.
Indiana. Statutes rel. to the settlement of estates, descent of property, wills, [etc.] $2. Independent.
Long, J. R. Notes of lectures on the law of wills and administration. $1. Michie.
Rockel, W: M. Guide for administrators and executors in the settlement of estates of deceased persons in Ohio. $1.50. W. H. Anderson.
Ruston, J: E: Decedents estates. $2. E. W. Whitfield.
Stockbridge, H: Law of executors and administrators. $1.25. C. A. Haskel.
United States. *Treasury Dept.* Estates of American citizens dying abroad.
See also Bookkeeping;—Wills.

Exegetical commentary on the Gospel according to St. Matthew. Plummer, A. *$3 net. Scribner.

Exell, Rev. Jos. S.
Biblical illustrator; Isaiah, v. 2. '09(Mr6) 8°, *$2 net. Revell.

Exercise in education and medicine. McKenzie, R. T. *$3.50 net; *$5 net. Saunders.

Exercises in French composition. Koren, W: 75 c. Holt.

Exile of St. Helena. Gonnard, P. *$3.50 net. Lippincott.

Ex-meridian attitude. Rust, A. $5. Wiley.

EXODUS.
See Bible. O. T.

EXOGAMY.
***See* Totemism**

EXOPHTHALMUS.
See Eye.

Expansion of Christendom. Carus-Wilson, M. L. G. P. $1.50 net. Doran.

Expansion of New England. Mathews, L. K. **$2.50 net. Houghton M.

Expansion of races. Woodruff, C: E: $4. Rebman.

Expensive Miss du Cane. Macnaughtan, S. $1.50. Dutton.

Experience of grace. Frost, J. M., *ed.* 40 c.; 25 c. S. S. Bd. So. Bapt.

Experiences of a boy. Hartshorn, E. F. $2. Baker Pr.

Experiential psychology of music. Feininger, K. $2. A. Gemünder.

Experiment in colonization of the house martin. Miller, C: W. gratis. Worthington Soc.

Experimental applied mechanics. Maxim, J. L. 60 c. Longmans.

Experimental embryology. Jenkinson, J. W. *$4.15 net. Oxford Univ.

Experimental object lessons. Gray, C. E. 75 c. net. Revell.

Experimental pharmacology. Greene, C: W. *$1 net. Blakiston.

Experimental researches on specific therapeutics. Ehrlich, P. *$1 net. Hoeber.

Experimental study of dementia præcox. Gatewood, L. C. 75 c. Psychological Review.

Experimental study of fatigue. Yoakum, C. S. $1.35. Psychological Review.

Experimental study of sleep. Sidis, B. *$1 net. Badger.

Experiments on the generation of insects. Redi, F. $2. Open Court.

Experiments on the sub-human. Greene, J. M. (Add. pubs. for price.) N. Y. Anti-Vivisection.

Exploits of a physician detective. Butler, G: F. $1. Clinic.

Exploration of the air. Clayton, H: H. $1. Harvard Univ.

EXPLORATIONS.
See Voyages and travels;—*also* names of countries.

Explorer (The). Maugham, W: S. †$1.50. Baker & T.

Explorer's adventures in Tibet. Landor, A. H: S. $1.50. Harper.

EXPLORERS.
Coe, E. D. Reminiscences of a pioneer in the Rock River country. 35 c. State Hist., Wis.
Crowell, K. R. Call of the waters: study of the frontier. *50 c. net; *30 c. net. Revell.
Crowell, K. R. Fair America. $2 net. Doran.
Crowell, K. R. Pioneers. 40 c.; 25 c. Willett Press.
Durrett, R. T: Traditions of the earliest visits of foreigners to North America. $4. Morton.
Hutchinson, F: W. Men who found America. $1.50. Stern.

EXPLORERS.—*Continued.*
Kelsey, D. M. Exploration, discovery and conquest of the New World. $1. Nat. Pub. Co.
Lucia, R. Stories of American discoverers for little Americans. 40 c. Am. Bk.
Moncrieff, A. R. H. Adventurers in America. $1.75. Macmillan.
Mulhall, *Mrs.* M. M. Explorers in the New World before and after Columbus. *$2.25 net. Longmans.
Shaw, L. True hist. of some of the pioneers of Colorado. $1. L. Shaw.
Wood, E. Famous voyages of the great discoverers. $1.50. Crowell.
See also Voyages and travels;—*also* names of explorers.

EXPLOSIONS.
See Mines and mining.

EXPLOSIVES.
Guttmann, O. Manufacture of explosives. *$1.10 net. Macmillan.
Munroe, C: E:, *and* Hall, C. Primer on explosives for coal miners. Gov. Pr. Off.
Rise and progress of the British explosives industry. *$5.25 net. Macmillan.
United States. *Interstate Commerce Commission.* Regulations for the transportation of explosives, as rev. and amended April 13, 1909. '09(Je) 32 p. 8°, pap.
United States. *Interstate Commerce Commission.* Regulations for the transportation of explosives, Jan. 15, 1910. Gov. Pr. Off.
Weaver, E. M. Notes on military explosives. $3 net. Wiley.
Wisser, J: P. Explosive materials. 50 c. Van Nostrand.
See also Artillery;—Blasting;—Firearms;—Guncotton;—Gunpowder;—Mines and mining.

Export commission houses, New York City. Directory comp. by the editorial staff of the *American Exporter;* complete list of the export commission merchants of N. Y. City, together with data as to their foreign branches, foreign agents, [etc.] '08(My9) c. 8°, $2. Am. Exporter.

Export tariffs of foreign countries. Stone, N. I: (Add. Superintendent for price.) U. S., Supt. of Docs.

Exporters' encyclopedia. Pigott, C., *comp.* $5. Exporters' Enc.

EXPORTING.
See Commerce.

EXPORTS.
See Commerce.

EXPOSITION.
See Rhetoric.

Exposition and illustration in teaching. Adams, J: **$1.25 net. Macmillan.

Expositions of Holy Scriptures. *See* Maclaren, Alex.

Expositor's Greek Testament. *See* Nicoll, *Sir* W: Robertson, *ed.*

Expository essays in Christian philosophy. 8°, $1. Herder.
—Windle. What is life?

EXPRESS.
Colorado Manufacturers' Association, *comp.* Pocket ed. of 25,000 freight and express rates, covering Colo., Idaho, Kan., Mont., Neb., N. M., Utah, Wyoming. $3. Colo. Manuf.

EXPRESS.—*Continued.*
United States. *Interstate Commerce Commission.* Regulations governing the construction and filing of tariff and classifications of express companies; administrative rulings and opinions. (Add. Superintendent for price.)
Visscher, W: L. Thrilling and truthful history of the pony express. 75 c. Rand, Mc.N. & Co.
"Express." Briggs, J. S. $2. Express.
Expressive voice culture. Southwick, *Mrs.* J. E. 60 c. J. E. Southwick.
Exquisite ser. 4 v. '10(N) fronts. 12°, ea., $1 net. Dodge.
Contents: Friendship outstays the hurrying flight of time; Thoughts for you; Kind thoughts; Remembrance.
Extempore speaking. Shurter, E. Du B. $1. Ginn.
Exterior painting. Maire, F: 60 c. Drake.
Extermination of mosquitoes. Levey, E. C. gratis. Richmond Dept. of Health.
Exton Manor. Marshall, A. †$1.50. Dodd.
Extract from Captain Stormfield's visit to Heaven. *See* Clemens, S: Langhorne.
EXTRADITION.
See Crime and criminals.
Extraordinary adventures of Arsène Lupin. *See* Leblanc, Maurice.
Exuviation, autotomy and regeneration in ceratium. Kofoid, C: A. 50 c. Univ. of Cal.
EYE.
Albrecht, J. F. E. Primer of eye diseases. (Add. pubs. for price.) Ware.
Alger, E. M. Refraction and motility of the eye. $1.50. Davis.
American Medical Assoc. Papers before section on ophthalmology, June 2-5, 1908. $1.50.—1909. (Add. pubs. for price.) Am. Medical.
Axenfeld, J. Bacteriology of the eye. *$6 net. Wood.
Bacon, V. V., *and* Booth, F: Refraction: essentials of systematized, condensed and elucidated. 75 c. Chic. Med. Bk.
Ball, J. M. Modern ophthalmology. *$7 net; *$8.50 net. Davis.
Beard, C: H. Ophthalmic surgery. $5. Blakiston.
Claiborne, J. H. Cataract extraction. *$2 net. Wood.
Duane, A. New classification of the motor anomalies of the eye. *$1.25 net. W: R. Jenkins.
Fernald, G. M. Effect of achromatic conditions on the color phenomena of peripheral vision. $1. Psychological Review.
Fox, L. W. Pract. treatise on ophthalmology. $6. Appleton.
Fuchs, E. Text book of ophthalmology. *$6 net. Lippincott.
Gould, G: M. Biographic clinics: essays concerning the influence of visual function, pathologic and physiologic, upon the health of patients. v. 6. *$1 net. Blakiston.
Gould, G: M. Righthandedness and lefthandedness. **$1.25 net. Lippincott.
Greeff, R: Atlas of external disease of the eye. $10. Rebman.

EYE.—*Continued.*
Haab, O. Atlas and epitome of ophthalmoscopy and ophthalmoscopic diagnosis. —Atlas of the external diseases of the eye. ea., $3. Saunders.
Harman, N. B. Aids to ophthalmology. *$1 net. Wood.
Henderson, F. L. Lessons on the eye for undergraduate students. $1.50. Blakiston.
Henderson, T. Glaucoma. $3 net. Longmans.
Herbert, H. Cataract extraction. *$3.75 net. Wood.
Howe, L. Muscles of the eye. In 2 v. v. 2. *$4.25 net. Putnam.
Hubbell, A. A. Development of ophthalmology in America, 1800 to 1870. *$1.75 net. Chic. Med. Bk.
Leatham, J: G. Elem. theory of the symmetrical optical instrument. *75 c. net. Putnam.
Lewis, J. J: Pocket optical dictionary. $1.25 J. J: Lewis.
Making of a mechanical optician; pract, treatise on the mechanical work of optometrists and opticians. [1910.] (Ap) c. '09. 111 p. il. 8°, $1. Keystone Pub.
May, C: H: Manual of the diseases of the eye. *$2 net. Wood.
Meller, J. Ophthalmic surgery. *$3 net. Blakiston.
Murray, A. N: Minor ophthalmic and aural technique. $3. Cleveland Press.
Onodi, A. Optic nerve and the accessory senses of the nose. $3.50 net. Wood.
Parker, H. C. Hdbk. of diseases of the eye. $2. Davis.
Percival, A. S. Prescribing of spectacles. $2 net. Wood.
Ramsay, A. M. Diathesis and ocular diseases. $2 net. Wood.
Schuster, A. Introd. to the theory of optics. $4. Longmans.
Schweinitz, G: E. de. Diseases of the eye. $6.50 net.—Pulsating exophthalmus. *$2 net. Saunders.
Shoemaker, W: T., *and* Swan, J: M. Retinitis pigmentosa: [disease of the retina.] *$2 net. Lippincott.
Shute, D. K. Reflex neuroses with particular reference to eyestrain. (Not for sale.) George Washington Univ.
Souter, W: N. Refractive and motor mechanism of the eye. $2. Keystone Pub.
Southall, J. P. C. Principles and methods of geometrical optics. $5.50 net. Macmillan.
Talbot, C. W. Diseases of the eye and how recognized. $1. Boger.
Thorington, J. Refraction and how to refract. *$1.50 net. Blakiston.
Weeks, J. E. Treatise on diseases of the eye. $6 net. Lea.
Witkowski's atlas of the mechanism of vision. *$2 net. W: R. Jenkins.
Wood, C. A. System of ophthalmic therapeutics. subs., $7. Cleveland Press.
Wood, C. A., *and* Woodruff, T: A. Commoner diseases of the eye. *$2.50 net. Chic. Med. Bk.

EYE.—*Continued.*
Wood, C. A., *and others, eds.* Eye, ear, nose and throat. $1.50. Year Bk.
Wright, J: W. Text book of ophthalmology. *$3 net. Blakiston.
See also Blind;—Lenses;—Light;—Nervous system;—Nurses and nursing;—Spectacles;—Tuberculosis.

Eyes of a child. Fôster, A. G. 60 c. Book & Art; Seymour.

Eyre, Archibald.
Girl in waiting. New ed. '10(D) 75 c. Grosset.

Ezekiel. Pratt, L †$1. Doubleday, P.

EZRA (Book of).
See Bible. O. T.

F., C. R. L.
See Fletcher, C: Rob. Leslie.

F., M. J.
Making of Jim O'Neill; story of seminary life. '10(D) 4+140 p. front. 12°, 35 c. net. Herder.

Fabian essays in socialism. Shaw, G: B., *ed.* *50 c. net. Ball Pub. Co.

Fabian socialist ser. por. D. Lane.
—Shaw. Socialism and superior brains. 75 c. net.

FABLES.
Æsop. Fables. $20 net. Doran.
Æsop. Fables. 50 c. Dutton.
Æsop. Fables from Æsop. 50 c.; †$1.50. Stokes.
Alcott, L. M. Flower fables. $1. McLoughlin.
Andersen, H. C. Fairy tales. $3. Dutton.
Bulfinch, T: Age of fable. 35 c. net; 70 c. net. Dutton.
Davis, M. H., *and* Chow-Leung. Chinese fables and folk stories. 40 c. Am. Bk.
Dutton, M. B., *comp.* Tortoise and the geese, and other fables of Bidpai. $1. Houghton M.
Favorite fairy tales. $1.50. Harper.
Gardner, M. Work that is play: dramatic reader based on Æsop's fables. 35 c. Flanagan.
Ingelow, J. Mopsa, the fairy. $1.50. Lippincott.
La Fontaine, J. de. Fables. $2. Putnam.
La Fontaine, J. de. Fables told in easy French. 50 c. net. Jacobs.
Montenegro, C. Two travelers: book oı fables. $1.25. Badger.
Phillpotts, E. Flint heart. $1.50. Dutton.
Richards, *Mrs.* L. E. H. Pig brother, and other fables. **40 c. net. Little, B. & Co.
Wollaston, *Sir* A. N., *comp.* Tales within tales; adapt. from Fables of Pilpai. *$1 net. Dutton.
See also Fairy tales;—Folklore;—Manuscripts;—Mythology.

FACE.
Marshall, J: S. Manual of the injuries and surgical diseases of the face, mouth and jaws. $6.50. White Dental.
Rawley, J. P. Character reading dict. gleaned from the books of all ages. $1. J. P. Rawley.

Face of China. Kemp, E. G. *$6 net. Duffield.

Face of Christ in art. Larson, J. H: $1. J. H: Larson.

Face of the earth. *See* Suess, E.

Faces and phases of German life. Liefeld, E. T. $1.50 net. Fowler & W.

Facheux (Les). Fontaine, M. L. P. 25 c. W: R. Jenkins.

Facsimile of the first issue of the *Gazeta de Lima.* Brown University. $2. Brown Univ.

Facsimile reproduction in ten sheets of the map of 1502 of Nicolo de Caneirio. Stevenson, E: L. $20. Hispanic Soc.

Fact of conversion. Jackson, G: *$1.25 net. Revell.

Fact of sin. Stroup, N. W. *$1 net. Jennings.

Factor tables for the first ten millions. Lehmer, D. N. $20. Carnegie.

FACTORIES.
American School of Correspondence. Factory accounts. $1.50. Am. Sch. Corr.
Carpenter, C: U. Profit making in shop and factory management. $2. Engineering Mag.
Church, A. H. Production factors in cost accounting and works management. $2.
—Proper distribution of expense burden: [factory management.] $1. Engineering Mag.
Diemer, H. Factory organization and administration. $3. McGraw-H.
Foster, W: English factories in India, 1622-1623.—1624-1629.—1630-1633. ea., $4.15. Oxford Univ.
George, W. L. Labor and capital at Port Sunlight: [account of an experiment in the conduct of a manufacturing enterprise.] *$1.40 net. Scribner.
Gesundheit, M. Cost reduction: [factory management.] (Not for sale.) M. Gesundheit.
Haslam, A. P. Electricity in factories and workshop. $2.50. Henley.
Matheson, E. Depreciation of factories, mines and industrial undertakings and their valuation. $4. Spon.
Nicholson, J. L. On factory organization and costs. $12.50. Kohl Technical.
Smith, T: A. Power and its transmission; pract. hdbk. for the factory works manager. $1. Spon.
Stabler, H., *and* Pratt, G. H. Purification of some textile and other factory wastes. U. S., Supt. of Docs.
Whitin, E. S. Factory legislation in Maine. $1. Longmans.
Wilson, G: B. Air-conditioning: treatise on the humidification, ventilation, cooling, and the hygiene of textile factories. $1.50. Wiley.
See also Business;—Flour-mills;—Shoes;—Tuberculosis;—*also* names of states.

Facts, figures and formulas for irrigation engineers. Buckley, R. B. $4.25. Spon.

Facts of faith. Smith, C: E: *80 c. net. Sherman, F.

Fadner, G: M.
Pound of brains: thirty years' observation; or, horse sense. '08(O) 415 p. por. 8°, $1. G: M. Fadner.

Fads or facts? Rayon, M. 75 c. M. S. Pub.

Faelten, Reinhold, comp.
Catechism of the Faelten system: [pianoforte.] '08(Ap.) c. 24 p. 12°, 50 c. A. P: Schmidt.

Faerber, Rev. Friedrich Wilhelm.
Catechism for the Catholic parochial schools of the United States. '10(Je4) c. 12°, 40 c. Svovoda.

Faerie Queene. *See* Spenser, Edm.

Faery Queen and her knights. Church, A. J: $1.50. Macmillan.

Fagan, Ja. Bernard.
The earth: modern play in four acts. '10 (Ag20) por. D. (Plays for to-day and to-morrow.) $1 net. Duffield.

Fagan, Ja. Octavius.
Confessions of a railroad signalman. '08 (O10) c. il. D. $1. Houghton M.
Labor and the railroads. '09(N13) c. D. *$1 net. Houghton M.

Fagots of cedar. Swift, I. $1.25. Willows Shop.

Fair, Agnes Thecla.
Sour dough's Bible. '10(Jl) 57 p. 12°, 50 c. Trustee.

Fair, Albert, pseud.
See Peker, C: Godfrey.

Fair, J:, ed.
The new life. In 4 v. '08(D5) D. v. 1, 2, 3, ea., $2; mor., $5; v. 4, 25 c.; per set, $6.25; mor., $15.25. Fair Pub.

Fair, W: Cooper.
People's home stock book. '10(N) 5+315 p. il. (partly col.) por. 4°, (People's home lib.) $3. R. C. Barnum.

Fair America. Crowell, K. R. $2 net. Doran

Fair Mississippian. Murfree, M. N. †$1.50. Houghton M.

Fair moon of Bath. Ellis, E. †$1.50. Dodd.

Fair women at Fontainbleau. Hamel, F. *$3.50 net. Brentano's.

Fairall, C: H.
See California. Code of civil procedure.

Fairbairn, Andrew Martin, D.D.
Studies in religion and theology; the church; in idea and in history. '10(F12) O. *$3.50 net. Macmillan.

FAIRBAIRN, Andrew Martin, *D.D.*
Mansfield College essays; testimonial volume presented to Principal Fairbairn upon his 70th birthday. *$3 net. Doran.

Fairbank, Janet Ayer.
In town and other conversations. '10 (D17) c. il. D. bds., $1.25 net. McClurg.

Fairbanks, Rev. Alonzo Deming.
Christ's second coming. '10(Je11) c. por. D. $1. Roxburgh.

Fairbanks, Arth.
Athenian lekythoi, with outline drawing in glaze varnish on a white ground: [vases for wine or oil.] '08(Ap4) c. il. 4°, (Univ. of Mich. studies, Humanistic ser.) $4. Macmillan.

Fairbanks, Mrs. Charles Mason, comp.
See Thackeray, W: Makepeace.

Fairbanks, Harold Wellman.
Stories of our mother earth. Rev. ed. '09 (S) c. '08. 197 p. il. 12°, *25 c. net. Educ. Pub.

Fairchild, Herman Le Roy.
Glacial waters in central New York. '09 (Ag) 66 p. il. maps, 8°, (N. Y. State Museum bull.) pap., 40 c. N. Y. State Educ.
See also Clarke, J: Mason.

Fairfield, H. P.
Examples of machine shop practice. '08 (Je13) c. il. 8°, (Machinery's reference ser.) pap., 25 c. Indust. Press.

Fairfield, Oliver Jay.
Stories from the New Testament. '09(N) c. 6+70+15 p. 8°, (Beacon ser.) 35 c.; pap., 25 c.; Teachers' ed., 65 c. Unitarian S. S.

FAIRFIELD, Ct.
Child, F. S: Fairfield, ancient and modern. 50 c.—Old New England church, established religion in Connecticut. $1. Fairfield Hist.

Fairies-of-sorts. Molesworth, *Mrs.* M. L. S. $1.50. Macmillan.

Fairlie, J: Archibald.
Essays in municipal administration. '08 (F1) c. O. **$2.50 net. Macmillan.
Some suggested changes in the constitution of Michigan. '07, [1908.] (O) 11 p. 4°, 25 c. J: A. Fairlie.

Fairman, Lucy.
Blue calf, and other tales of Peter. '08 (D) c. 143 p. il. 12°, 75 c. Griffith-S.

Fairmount girls ser. *See* Baker, *Mrs.* Etta Anthony.

FAIRMOUNT PARK, Philadelphia.
Schirmer, R: C. Philadelphia Fairmount park. 50 c. R: C. Schirmer.

FAIRTON, N. J.
Andrews, F. D., *comp.* Inscriptions on the grave stones in the old "New England Town" burying ground, Fairton. 25 c. F. D. Andrews

Fairweather, Rev. W:
Background of the Gospels; or, Judaism in the period between the Old and New Testaments; twentieth ser. of the Cunningham lectures. '09(My15) O. *$3 net. Scribner.

Fairy book ser. *See* Lang, And., *ed.*

Fairy changeling. Spofford, *Mrs.* H. E. P. $1 net. Badger.

Fairy flights ser. *See* Campbell, A. M. Stokes.

Fairy-land of living things. Kearton, R: *$1.25 net. Cassell.

Fairy latch-key. Horsfall, M. $1.25. Fenno.

Fairy ring. Wiggin, K. D. S. $1.25 net. Doubleday, P.

Fairy surprises. Cape, E. P. *75 c. net. E. P. Cape.

Fairy tale plays. Bell, *Lady* F. E. O. $1.50. Longmans.

FAIRY TALES.
Andersen, H. C. Fairy tales. $1. Bowman.
Andersen, H. C. Fairy tales. *$1.50 net. Dodge.
Andersen, H. C. Fairy tales. 50 c.; $1.25. Dutton.
Andersen, H. C. Fairy tales; told in easy French. *50 c. net. Jacobs.

FAIRY TALES.—*Continued.*

Andersen, H. C. Fairy tales. $1.50. Lippincott.

Andersen, H. C. Ugly duckling and other stories: [phonography.] 25 c. Phonograph.

Andrews, *Mrs.* M. R. S. Enchanted forest. †$1.50. Dutton.

Annals of Fairyland; reign of King Cole. —Reign of King Oberon. ea., *35 c. net; *70 c. net. Dutton.

"Aunt Naomi," *pseud.* Jewish fairy tales and fables. *$1 net. Bloch.

Baldwin, J. Another fairy reader. 35 c. Am. Bk.

Bates, L. Fairy tale of a dog and an old dame by the sea. 15 c. Longmans.

Baum, L. F. American fairy tales. †$1.25. Bobbs-M.

Benson, I. E. Yellow princess. 25 c. McLoughlin.

Bigham, M. A. Overheard in Fairyland. †$1.50. Little, B. & Co.

Bland, *Mrs.* E. N. Enchanted castle. †$1.25. Harper.

Boston. Public Library. Finding lists of fairy tales and folk stories in books at the branches of the Public Library of the city of Boston. 5 c. Boston Pub. Lib.

Bourhill, *Mrs.* E. J., *and* Drake, *Mrs.* J. B., *comps.* Fairy tales from South Africa. $1.50. Macmillan.

Burnett, *Mrs.* F. H. Spring cleaning. †60 c. Century Co.

Burnham, *Mrs.* C. L. R. Flutterfly. †75 c. net. Houghton M.

Butler, E. B. Diamond spider and other stories. $1.25 net. A. Harriman.

Cape, E. P. Fairy surprises for little folks. *75 c. net. E. P. Cape.

Dasent, *Sir* G: W., *ed.* Norse fairy tales. $1.75. Lippincott.

Donahey, *Mrs.* M. D. Castle of Grumpy Grouch.—Down Spider Web lane. ea., $1.25. Stern.

Dow, E. C. Proud Roxana. $1.25. Stern.

Fairyland stories. $1.50. Tuck.

Father Tuck's Picture land. $1. Tuck.

Graves, A. P. Irish fairy book. $1.50. Stokes.

Grierson, E. W. Scottish fairy book. $1.50 net. Stokes.

Griffis, W: E. Fire-fly's lovers. †$1. Crowell.

Grimm, J. L. K. *and* W. K. Fairy tales. $1. Bowman.

Grimm, J. L. K. *and* W. K. Fairy tales. *$1.50 net. Dodge.

Grimm, J. L. K. *and* W. K. Fairy tales. *$6 net; *$20 net. Doubleday, P.

Grimm, J. L. K. *and* W. K. Fairy tales. $1.25. Dutton.

Grimm, J. L. K. *and* W. K. Fairy tales; told in easy French. *50 c. net. Jacobs.

Grimm, J. L. K. *and* W. K. Fairy tales from Grimm $1.50. Stern.

Grimm, J. L. K. *and* W. K. Fairy tales. $2 net. Stokes.

Grimm, J. L. K. *and* W. K. House in the wood and other fairy tales. $1.35 net. Warne.

FAIRY TALES.—*Continued.*

Grimm, J. L. K. *and* W. K. Household stories. $1.25. Cassell.

Grimm, J. L. K. *and* W. K. Stories from Grimm. 50 c. Dutton.

Harper, *Mrs.* B. W. Flora's fairies. 50 c. Cochrane.

Hauf, W. Fairy tales. $2.50. Dutton.

James, G., *comp.* Green Willow and other Japanese fairy tales. $5.50 net. Macmillan.

Johnson, C., *ed.* Elm-tree fairy book. †$1.50. Little, B. & Co.

Ker, A. Papuan fairy tales. $1.50 net. Macmillan.

Kern, J. R. *and* M. M., *eds.* German stories retold: (Grimm's märchen.) 30 c. Am. Bk.

Kingsley, C: Water babies; and Glaucus. *35 c. net; *70 c. net. Dutton.

Kolle, F: S. Fifty and one tales of modern Fairyland. $1.25. Fenno.

Laboulaye, E. R. L. Fairy tales. $2.50. Dutton.

Lang, A., *ed.* Beauty and the beast; Forty thieves. ea., *75 c. net.—Invisible prince; Three dwarfs; Twelve huntsmen. ea., **60 c. net.—Lilac fairy book. $1.60 net. Longmans.

Lansing, M. F., *comp. and ed.* Fairy tales. 2 v. ea., 35 c. Ginn.

Lapen, F. Brownyboo. $1.25. Saalfield.

Lazare, J., *ed.* Les plus jolis contes de fées. 35 c. Ginn.

Lee, H. Legends from Fairyland. $1.50. Lippincott.

Lewis, C. Almost fairy children. $1.25. Bobbs-M.

MacDonald, G: Light princess. **40 c. net. Crowell.

Molesworth, *Mrs.* M. L. S. Fairies-of-sorts. $1.50. Macmillan.

Naylor, J. B. Dicky Delightful in Rainbow Land. $1. Saalfield.

Nixon-Roulet, M. F. Japanese folk stories and fairy tales. 40 c. Am. Bk.

Paquin, S: S. Garden fairies. **$1 net. Moffat.

Perrault, C. Fairy tales, told in easy French. 50 c. net. Jacobs.

Pitman, N. H. Chinese fairy stories. $1. Crowell.

Reader, E. Story of the little mer-man. *$1.25 net. Macmillan.

Singleton, E. Wild flower fairy book. $1.25. Dodd.

Spielmann, *Mrs.* M. H. Rainbow book. **$1.50 net. Warne.

Sowerby, M. *and* G. Bumbletoes: fairy tale in verse. †75 c. Duffield.

Steedman, A. Nursery tales. 50 c. Dutton.

Sutton, A. L. Mushroom fairies. $1.25. Saalfield.

Thackeray, W: M. Rose and the ring. 50 c. Dutton.

Thackeray, W: M. Rose and the ring. *50 c. net. Macmillan.

Thackeray, W: M. Rose and the ring. $1.25. Stokes.

Thomas, W. J. Welsh fairy-book. $1.50. Stokes.

FAIRY TALES.—*Continued.*
Upton, F. K. Adventures of Borbee and the Wisp. *$1.50 net. Longmans.
Volkmann-Leander, R. v. Traumereien an französischen kaminen. 40 c. Ginn.
Washburne, *Mrs.* M. F. Old fashioned fairy tales. †$1.25. Rand, McN. & Co.
Webb, E. C. *and* D. The littlest fairy. $1.50. Dodge.
Weeden, L. L. Fairy tales in wonderland. $1.50. Dutton.
Welsh, C:, *comp. and ed.* Fairy tales children love. $1.25. Dodge.
Wiggin, K. D. S., *and* Smith, N. A., *eds.* Fairy ring. $1.25 net.—Tales of wonder. †$1.50. Doubleday, P.
Wiggin, K. D. S., *and* Smith, N. A., *eds.* Tales of laughter. †$1.50. McClure.
Williams, H. Fairy tales from folk lore. **$1 net. Moffat.
See also Fables;—Folk-lore;—Heroes;—Mythology;—Story-telling;—*also* Arabian night's entertainment.

Fairy tales of all nations; famous stories from the English, German, French, Italian, Arabic, Russian, Swedish, Danish, Norwegian, Bohemian, Japanese and other sources; tr. and ed. by Logan Marshall. '10(D10) c. col. il. O. $2. Winston.

Fairyland stories. '09(N13) col. il. F. bds., $1.50. Tuck.

FAITH.
Benson, M. Venture of rational faith. *$2 net. Macmillan.
Coke, H: J: Domain of belief. $2.50 net. Macmillan.
Costin, W: W. Introduction to the genetic treatment of the faith-consciousness in the individual. *65 c. net. Williams & W.
Gibson, W. R. B. God with us. *$1.40 net. Macmillan.
Grenfell, W. T. Man's faith. *50 c. net. Pilgrim Press.
Inge, W. R. Faith and its psychology. *75 c. net. Scribner.
Moule, H. C. G. Faith; its nature and works. *$1.25 net. Cassell.
Reed, M. Sea of faith. *80 c. net. Am. Unitarian.
Rickett, J. C. Origins and faith. *$1.50 net. Revell.
Rowland, E. H. Right to believe. **$1.25 net. Houghton M.
Smith, C: E: Facts of faith. *80 c. net. Sherman, F.
Stettheimer, E. Will to believe as a basis for the defense of religious faith. $1. Science Pr., (N. Y.)
Tomkins, F. W. Faith and life of a Christian. *75 c. net. Am. S. S.
See also Agnosticism;—Creeds;—Religion;—Skepticism;—Theology;—Truth.

Faith and fact. Edghill, E. A. $1.60 net. Macmillan.

Faith and life of a Christian. Tomkins, F. W. *75 c. net. Am. S. S.

Faith and works of Christian Science. Paget, S. *$1.25 net. Macmillan.

FAITH CURE.
Dearmer, P. Body and soul: effect of religion on health. *$1.50 net. Dutton.

FAITH CURE.—*Continued.*
Fitzgerald, D: B: Law of Christian healing. *75 c. net. Revell.
Towne, W: E. Way to perfect healing. 50 c. W: E. Towne.
See also Christian science; — Divine healing; — Mind and body.

Faith-healer. *See* Moody, W: V.

Faith-Hope. Cole, *Mrs.* D. R. B. $1. G. O. Tubby.

Faith, hope, love. Strand, G. B., *comp.* 50 c. net. McClurg.

Faith in man. Spiller, G. *75 c. net. Macmillan.

Faith of a layman. Osborne, W: F: $1.25. Cassell.

Faith of a modern Christian. Orr, J. $1.50 net. Doran.

Faith of a modern Protestant. Bousset, W. **75 c. net. Scribner.

Faith of Catholics. Berington, J., *comp.* $6 net. Pustet.

Faith of his fathers. Jacomb, A. E. †$1.50. Dodd.

Faithfull, Rev. R. C.
My place in the world and other sermons. '10(D24) 12°, $1.40 net. Whittaker.

Faith's certainties. Drummond, R. J. *$1.50 net. Doran.

FALAISE, France.
Dodd, *Mrs.* A. B. B. Falaise, the town of the conqueror. $1.50 net. Little, B. & Co.

Falconer, Rev. J. W.
Three crosses. '08(D20) front. O. *75 c. net. Jennings.

Falconnet, H.
See Seeligmann, Thdr.

Falk, Myron S:
See Burr, W: Hubert.

Falkiner, Caesar Litton.
Essays rel. to Ireland; biographical, historical, and topographical; with a memoir of the author by E. Dowden. '09(D11) O. $3.50. Longmans.

FALKLAND, Lettice, *Viscountess.*
Duncon, J: Lady Lettice, Viscountess Falkland. *$2 net. Dutton.

Falkner, Roland Post.
Elimination of pupils from school; review of recent investigations. '09(N) 255-275 p. 8°, 10 c. R. P. Falkner.
Retardation: its significance and its measurement; [repr. from the *Educational Review,* New York, Sept., 1909.] '09, [1910.] (Mr) 122-131 p. 8°. (Add. pubs. for price.) Educ. Review.
Some uses of statistics in the supervision of schools. '09(N) 8 p. 8°. (Add. author for price.) R. P. Falkner.
What can and do school reports show?; [the *Psychological Clinic* reprint from v. 4.]. '10(Jl16) 8°, 20 c. R. P. Falkner.

FALL (The).
See Sin.

Fall of Babylon. Fitzpatrick, F. W. gratis. Shaw Bros.

Fall of David's tabernacle, rebuilt by Christ. Benjamin, C: T: 75 c. Reliance.

Fall of the Nibelungs. Nibelungenlied (The). *35 c. net; *70 c. net. Dutton.

Fall of the old order. Plunket, I. L. $1.10. Oxford Univ.

Fall River, Mass.
Lincoln, J. T. City of the Dinner-pail. **$1.25 net. Houghton M.
Fallacies of Christian Science. Wood, J. G. $1. J. G. Wood.
Fallacies of protection. Bastiat, F. *$1 net. Putnam.
Fallina. Mumma, R. M. $1. Roxburgh.
Fallow, Lance.
An ampler sky. '09(D25) 12°, *$1 net. Macmillan.
Fallows, Alice Katharine.
Mental hygiene in everyday living. '09 (My8) c. S. (Making the best of things ser.) bds., *35 c. net. McClurg.
Point of view. '09(My8) c. S. (Making the best of things ser.) bds., *35 c. net. McClurg.
Talk on relaxation. '09(My8) c. S. (Making the best of things ser.) bds., *35 c. net. McClurg.
Fallows, Bp. S:, D.D.
Health and happiness; or, religious therapeutics and right living. '08(N14) c. D. *$1.50 net. McClurg.
Falls, De Witt Clinton.
The journey book. '10(O1) c. il. O. bds., $1. Century Co.
False position. Reynolds, *Mrs.* L. B. $1.50. Brentano's.
False science in the schools; how physiology is mistaught by the makers of text-books. '08, [1909.] (My) 7 p. 16°, pap., gratis. U. S. Brewers' Assoc.
Fame's pathway. Taylor, H. C. C-. †$1.50. Duffield.
Familiar friends ser. front. D. $1. Sturgis & W.
—Kingsley. The heroes.
—Ward. Gypsy Breynton.
Familiar nursery jingles. '08(O17) c. il. Q. $1.25. Stokes.
Familiar Swiss flowers. Hulme, F: E: *$3 net. Cassell.
Families.
See Genealogies.
Family.
Abbott, E. H. On training of parents. **$1 net. Houghton M.
Griffith, J. E. Diary of the home: [family record book.] $4; $6. Griffith-S.
Jackson, C: H., *comp.* Cases on the law of domestic relations. Thompson & Co.
Kane, R. Plain gold ring. 90 c. net. Longmans.
Klykken, O. Our homes and our children. 75 c. Lutheran Pub.
Maryland. Law of domestic relations. $3. Balto. Pr.
Mordecai, S: F. Domestic relations. (Add. author for price.) S: F. Mordecai.
New York. Law of domestic relations in the state. $5. M. Bender.
Rabbino, B. **Domestic Relations Court; plea for the preservation of the home. 25 c. Hebrew Standard.**
Savage, C: A. Athenian family: sociological and legal study. *$1.50 net; *$1.25 net. Lord Balto. Pr.
Snyder, E. W: Questions and answers on domestic relations. 50 c. Sprague.

Family.—*Continued.*
Stocking, J. T. Dearest spot on earth: [essays on the home.] $1. Caldwell.
See also **Children;—Divorce;—Domestic economy;** —Ethics;—Eugenics; — Genealogies;—Genealogy; — Home; — Marriage; — Mother;—Names (*personal*); — Race suicide; — Socialism; — Woman.
Family and the nation. Whetham, W: C. D. *$2.50 net. Longmans.
Family at Misrule. Turner, E. †$1.50. McKay.
Family books. D. **$1 net. Penn Pub. Co.
—Chance. Care of the child.
—Priestman. Home decoration.
—Solis-Cohen. Family health.
Family chronicle. Lyster, G., *ed.* *$5 net. Dutton.
Family doctor. Barrett, E. $1.25 net. Dutton.
Family health. Solis-Cohen, M. **$1 net. Penn Pub. Co.
Family names and their story. Baring-Gould, S. *$3 net. Lippincott.
Family record. Mason, T. W. (Priv. pr.) Grafton Press.
Famine and the bread. Johnston, H. A. (Add. pubs. for price.) Y. M. C. A.
Famous American Indians. 12°. †$1.25. Dodd.
—Eggleston *and* Seelye. Montezuma.
Famous blue-stockings. Wheeler, E. R. $4 net. Lane.
Famous books. 8°, $1. Grosset.
—Habberton. Helen's babies.
Famous books for girls. New ed. 32 v. '10 (N) il. 12°, ea., 75 c. Caldwell.
Famous cathedrals. Singleton, E., *comp. and ed.* **$1.60 net. Dodd.
Famous cavalry leaders. Johnston, C: H. L. $1.50. L. C. Page.
Famous fanatics. Hayler, G. 60 c. Funk.
Famous French salons. Hamel, F. *$3.50 net. Brentano's.
Famous fugitive poems. Johnson, E. R., *comp.* $1.25 net. Holt.
Famous hymns of the world. Sutherland, A. 6 v. ea., 50 c.; 75 c. Stokes.
Famous impostors. Stokes, B. $2 net. Sturgis & W.
Famous Indian chiefs. Johnston, C: H. L. $1.50. L. C. Page.
Famous Indian chiefs I have known. Howard, O. O. *$1.50 net. Century Co.
Famous leaders ser. il. pors. O. L. C. Page.
—Johnston. Famous scouts. $1.50.
Famous men of modern times. Haaren, J: H: 50 c. Am. Bk.
Famous modern orations. West, E. E., *comp.* 35 c. Werner.
Famous old receipts. Smith, *Mrs.* J. H., *comp.* **$2 net. Winston.
Famous places of the reformed churches. Good, J. I. $1.50. Heidelberg.
Famous poems explained. Barbe, W. $1. Hinds.
Famous scouts. Johnston, C: H. L. $1.50. L. C. Page.
Famous sculpture. Singleton, E., *comp. and ed.* $1.60 net. Dodd.
Famous stories. Jones, S: P. *$1 net. Revell.

Famous voyages of the great discoverers. Wood, E. $1.50. Crowell.

Famous women of Florence. Staley, E. $3.50. Scribner.

FAMULUS.
See Terence Afer, Publius.

FANATICS.
See Biography.

Fancy cheese in America. Publow, C: A. 75 c. Am. Sheep.

Fanning, Clara Eliz., comp.
Selected articles on capital punishment. '10 (F26) 12°, (Debaters' hdbk. ser.) $1. H. W. Wilson.
Selected articles on the election of United States senators. '10(Je4) 12°, (Debaters' hdbk. ser.) $1. H. W. Wilson.
Selected articles on the enlargement of the United States Navy. 3d and enl. ed. '10 (D10) 12°, (Debaters' hdbk. ser.) $1. H. W. Wilson.

Fanning, F. W. Burton-.
See Burton-Fanning, F. W.

Fanning, W: H. W.
Historical sketch of the St. Louis University. '09(Jl) 64 p. il. por. 8°, (St. Louis Univ. bull.) pap., gratis. St. L. Univ.

Fanny Lambert. Stacpoole, H: De V. $1.50. Fenno.

FANS.
Hubbard, C: L. Fans, ventilation and heating. 25 c. Indust. Press.
Rhead, G: W. Hist. of the fan. *$25 net. Lippincott.

Fantasy of Mediterranean travel. Bayne, S: G. **$1.25 net. Harper.

FAR EAST.
Angier, A. G. Far East revisited. *$4.20 net. Scribner.
Binyon, L. Painting in the Far East. *$6 net. Longmans.
Browne, G: W., *and* Dole, N. H. New America and the Far East. $36.25; $49.75. M. Jones.
Grew, J. C. Sport and travel in the Far East. $3 net. Houghton M.
Millard, T. F. F. America and the Far Eastern question. **$4 net. Moffat.
Moore, J: M. Etchings of the East. *$1 net. Pub. Ho. of M. E. Ch., So.
Peck, E. M. H. Travels in the Far East. $3. J. S. Peck.
Ronaldshay, L. J: L. D., *Earl of*. Wandering student in the Far East. *$8.40 net. Scribner.
Smith, F. D. Blue waters and green and the Far East to-day. $1.50. Crane.
Thwing, C: F. Education in the Far East. **$1.50 net. Houghton M.
Weale, B. L. P., *pseud.* Coming struggle in eastern Asia. *$3.50 net. Macmillan.
Zwemer, S: M., *and* Brown, A. J. Nearer and farther East. **50 c. net. Macmillan.
See also Burma;—China;—Corea;—India;—Japan;—Legends;—Persia;—Philippine Islands;—Russia;—Russo-Japanese War;—Siam;—Siberia.

Far from the madding crowd. *See* Hardy, T:

Far north in India. Anderson, W: B. 50 c. Bd. For. Miss.

Farabee, W: Curtis.
Some customs of the Macheyengas; [repr. from the Proceedings of the Amer. Antiquarian Society for Oct., 1909.] '10 (Jl16) 4°, 50 c. Davis Press.

Farce (La) de Paquin fils. *See* **Lailavoix, L.**

FARCES.
See Plays.

Farewell address. *See* Washington, G:

Faris, J: Thomson.
Sunday school in the country. '08(D) c. 47 p. S. pap. (Add. pubs. for price.) Westminster.
Winning their way: boys who learned self-help. '09(S11) c. il. D. $1.50. Stokes.

Faris, Lillie.
Study of the Quaker poet [Whittier]; arr. for primary grades. '08(O17) c. il. por. 8°, 25 c. Athens Pr.

Faris, Rev. W: Wallace.
How to talk with God. '09(Ja25) c. S. *50 c. net. S. S. Times.

Farley, Archbp. J: Murphy.
History of St. Patrick's Cathedral, [New York City.] '08(My2) 12°. (Add. Society for price.) Soc. for Propagation of Faith.

Farley, Jos. Pearson.
Three rivers, the James, the Potomac, the Hudson; retrospect of peace and war. '10(F5) c. il. in col. O. *$2 net. Neale.

Farlow, Alfr.
Relation of government to the practice of Christian science. '10(F5) c. 8°, ea., 3 c.; per 100, $3. A. Farlow.

FARM ANIMALS.
See Domestic animals.

Farm babies. Aldin, C. $1.25. Doran.

Farm bacteriology. Palmer, W: C. 15 c. W: C. Palmer.

Farm book. Smith, E. B. $1.50 net. Houghton M.

Farm book-keeping. Lamb, H: G. $1. H: G. Lamb.

Farm, cottage, camp and canoe in maritime Canada. Silver, A. P. *$2 net. Dutton.

Farm dairy. Gurler, H: B: $1. Breeders' Gazette.

FARM ENGINES.
See Agricultural machinery;—Engines.

Farm festivals. Carleton, W. $1.25. Harper.

FARM IMPLEMENTS.
See Farms and farming.

Farm poultry. Watson, G: C. **$1.25 net. Macmillan.

Farm that glue made. Williams, C. A. $1. Stokes.

Farman, Elbert Eli.
Egypt and its betrayal: account of the country during the periods of Ismail and Tewfik, Pashas, and of how England acquired a new empire. '08(Ap18) 12°, **$2.50 net. Grafton Press.

FARMAR FAMILY.
See Genealogies: Billopp, C: F., *comp.*

Farmer, Florence Virginia.
Nature myths of many lands. '10(Ap30) c. il. D. (Eclectic readings.) 45 c. Am. Bk.

Farmer, Ja. Albin.
Trial manual of personal injury laws; Illinois. '10(Mr) O. limp leath., $4. Fiske & Co.

Farmer, M. M.
See Farmer, R. C.

Farmer, R. C. and M. M.
Four-figure logarithms on a new graphic system, dispensing with interpolations, for the use of teachers, students, engineers, chemists, etc. '10(N12) D. 20 c. net. Longmans.

Farmer and his relation to the country. Flowers, W: T: 50 c. W: T: Flowers.

Farmer George. Melville, L. 2 v. *$7.50 net. Brentano's.

Farmer's cyclopedia of domestic animals. Wilcox, E. V. $4.50; $5.50. Judd.

Farmer's year. Haggard, H: R. $1.50. Longmans.

FARMERS' EDUCATIONAL AND CO-OPERATIVE UNION OF AMERICA.
See Farms and farming.

Farmers' Republic, Somerville, N. J. Book of the Farmers' Republic. '09(O2) D. 50 c. Farmers' Repub.

Farmers' shipping associations; plans of organization of shipping associations for fruit and vegetable growers; rules and regulations of some of the best shipping associations in the United States; arranged by the *Fruit-Grower.* '09(Ja) c. 38 p. T. ("Brother Jonathan" ser.) pap., gratis. Fruit-Grower.

FARMERS' TRUST COMPANY OF LANCASTER, Lancaster, Pa.
Diffenderffer, F. R. Hist. of the Farmers' Bank of Lancaster; the Farmers' Bank and the Farmers' Trust Co. gratis. Farmers' Trust Co.

Farmers' veterinarian. Burkett, C: W: *$1.50 net. Judd.

Farming it. Shute, H: A: *$1.20 net. Houghton M.

FARMINGDALE, Me.
Vital records of Farmingdale, Me., to the year 1892. $1. H. S. Webster.

FARMS AND FARMING.
About the farm; illustrated description of the New Boston diary and other industries at Valley View, Muzzey, and Hutchinson farms. gratis. J. R. Whipple.
Ashe, W: W. Terracing of farm lands. 6 c. Uzzell.
Atwater, J. American farmer's figurer enl. 50 c.; 75 c.; $1. Atwater.
Bailey, L. H. State, and the farmer. **$1.25 net. Macmillan.
Bailey, L. H. Training of farmers. **$1 net. Century Co.
Barrett, C: S. Mission, hist. and times of the Farmers' Union. (Add. author for price.) C: S. Barrett.
Bexell, J: A. Business side of farming. 50 c. J: A. Bexell.
Bolton, E. S. Farm life a century ago. (Priv. pr.) C: K. Bolton.

FARMS AND FARMING.—*Continued.*
Bonner, J. C. Plans and methods used under Bonner farm cost system. (Add. pubs. for price.) Bonner
Briggs, L. J., *and* Belz, J. O. Dry farming in relation to rainfall and evaporation. Gov. Pr. Off.
Buffum, B. C. Arid agriculture. $1.50. B. C. Buffum.
Butterfield, K. L. Chapters in rural progress. *$1.25 net. Univ. of Chic.
Carpenter, D. Facts for farmers. 10 c. D. Carpenter.
Cobleigh, R. Handy farm devices and how to make them. *$1.50 net. Judd.
Cooke, V. T. Dry farming in Wyoming. gratis. V. T. Cooke; Wyo. State Dry Farming.
Cotton, J: S. Improvement of pastures in eastern New York and the New England states. U. S., Supt. of Docs.
Dickson, D: David Dickson's and James M. Smith's farming. 50 c. Cultivator Pub.
Elliott, C: G. Practical farm drainage. $1.50. Wiley.
Ellis, L. W. Minor articles of farm equipment. Gov. Pr. Off.
Green, F. E. Small holding. *$1 net. Lane.
Haggard, H: R. Farmer's year: being his commonplace book for 1898. $1.50. Longmans.
Hall, B. Garden yard: hdbk. of extensive farming. $1. McKay.
Hall, B. Little land and a living. $1. Arcadia.
Hamilton, J:, *and* Stedman, J: M. Farmers' institutes for young people. Gov. Pr. Off.
Hays, W. M. Farm development. $1.50. Judd.
Jardine, J. T. Coyote-proof pasture experiment. (Add. Superintendent for price.) U. S., Supt. of Docs.
McConnell, P. Complete farmer. $1.50 net. —Farm equipment. 60 c. net. Cassell.
Macdonald, W. Dry-farming. **$1.20 net. Century Co.
McLennan, J: Manual of pract. farming. $1.50 net. Macmillan.
Miller, C. H., *comp.* Garden and farm almanac. 25 c. Doubleday, P.
Modern silage methods. 10 c. Silver Manufacturing.
New York [State.] *Dept. of Agriculture.* Agricultural advantages of New York State. gratis.—List of farms occupied and unoccupied for sale or rent. (Add. pubs. for price.) N. Y. Dept. Agri.
Ohio farm laws. 25 c. Rural Pub.
Parkinson, E: K. Guide to the country home. *$1 net. Outing.
Saint Maur, *Mrs.* K. V. Earth's bounty. **$1.75 net. Macmillan.
Sanders Publishing Co., Chicago. Farm buildings. $2. Sanders Pub
Scofield, C. S., *and* Rogers, S. J. Truckee-Carson experiment farm. (Add. Superintendent for price.) U. S., Supt. of Docs.

FARMS AND FARMING.—*Continued.*
Sheldon, J. P. Farm and the dairy. *$1 net. Macmillan.
Shute, H: A: Farming it. [fiction.] **$1.20 net. Houghton M.
Smith, C. B., *and* Froley, J: W: Replanning a farm for profit. (Add. Superintendent for price.) U. S., Supt. of Docs.
Smurr, T. W. Treatise on the law of farm drainage founded on the laws and judicial decisions of the state of Illinois. (Add. pubs. for price.) Bobbs-M.
Steiner, H. L. How to keep farm accounts. $1. Steiner & Co.
Thomas, T. G: First aid to shipping fruits, vegetables, butter, eggs and game for profit, to market. $1. T. G: Thomas.
Waldin, W. Truck farming in the Everglades. $1. W. Waldin.
Warren, G: F., *and* Livermore, K. C. Lab'y exercises in farm management. 80 c. net. Macmillan.
Williams, W: K. Indiana farm laws with business forms and model business letters. $1.50. Rural Pub.
Woll, F. W., *and others.* Hdbk. for farmers and dairymen. $1.50. Wiley.
See also Agricultural machinery;—Agriculture;—Alfalfa;—Birds;—Cattle;—Clover;—Commerce;—Concrete;—Corn;—Cotton;—Dairy;—Domestic animals;—Domestic economy;—Ensilage;—Fertilizers;—Insects;—Irrigation;—Plowing;—Potato;—Poultry;—Prices;—Soils;—Veterinary medicine and surgery;—*also* Wyoming.

Farnell, Lewis R:
Cults of the Greek states. In 5 v. v. 5. '10(Ja1) il. O. $6. Oxford Univ.

Farnham, H: P., ed.
See Lawyers' repts. annot.

Farnsworth, C: Hubert.
Education through music. '09(N20) c. D. $1. Am. Bk.

Farnsworth, E: Clarence.
Mementos and sea pictures. '09(Jl) c. 91 p. por. 8°, $1.50. Smith & S.
Saint Helena, and other poems. '10(S) c. 6+71 p. por. 8°, $1. Smith & S.
Sophistries of Christian science. '09(D25) c. 8°, $1.25. Smith & S.

Farnum, J: S.
Practical points, questions and answers; hand book for stationary, locomotive and marine engineers, firemen, electricians, motormen and machinists; rev. by D. Holland. '10(D31) c. il. por. 16°, $1.50. Laird.

Farquhar, Arth. B.
Tariff revision from the manufacturers' standpoint; address made before the American Association for the Advancement of Science, Johns Hopkins University. '09(F6) O. pap. (Add. author for price.) A. B. Farquhar.

Farrar, F. A.
Old Greek nature stories. '10(S10) il. O. $1.50 net. Crowell.

Farrar, Dean F: W:
Bells and pomegranates; ed. by Eric Farrar. '10(D24) 12°, $1.50 net. Whitaker.
Eric; or, little by little. '09(S18) il. 12°, 75 c. Macmillan.
Julian Home: a tale of college life. '09(S18) il. 12°, 75 c. Macmillan.

Farrar, Dean F: W:—*Continued.*
Life of Christ. 2 v. '10(D) il. $2.50, boxed. Crowell.
Life of lives: further studies in the life of Christ. Popular ed. '08(My23) O. *$1.25 net. Cassell.
St. Winifred's; or, the world of school. '09(S18) il. 12°, 75 c. Macmillan.

Farrar, Ja. McNall, D.D.
Junior congregation, 1884-1908: [addresses.] '08(O10) D. **$1.20 net. Funk.
Little talks to little people. 10(O1) c. D. $1.20 net. Funk.

Farrar, Lockhart Brooks.
Eternity of matter; series of discussions affirming the eternity of matter as a primal postulate. '10(Jl16) c. por. 8°, $2. N. E. Stevens.

Farrell, Arth.
How to play ice hockey. '10(Mr26) c. il. por. 16°, (Spalding's athletic lib.) pap., 10 c. Am. Sports.

Farrell, E: D.
See Niver, Harmon.

Farrell, Fs. D:
Dry-land grains in the Great Basin. '10(S) 39 p. il. tabs., 8°, (U. S., Dept. of Agriculture, Bu. of Plant Industry circular.)

Farrell, Fk. J.
Dyeing and cleaning. '08(N7) il. D. (Griffin's technological handbooks.) (Add. pubs. for price.) Lippincott.

Farrer, Reginald J.
Alpines and bog plants. '08(N14) il. O. $2.50. Longmans.
In a Yorkshire garden. '09(N20) O. il. $3.50. Longmans.
In old Ceylon. '08(N14) il. O. $4. Longmans.
Ways of rebellion. '08(Ap18) D. †$1.50. Longmans.

Farrington, Arth. M.
Need of state and municipal meat inspection to supplement federal inspection. [1910.] (Je) 14 p. il. 8°, (U. S., Dept. of Agriculture, Bu. of Animal Industry circular.)

Farrington, E. A., comp.
See Bancroft, Marg.

Farrington, E. C.
See Maine. Railroad laws.

Farrington, E: Holyoke, and Woll, Fritz, Wilhelm.
Testing milk and its products. 18th rev. and enl. ed. '08(Ap4) c. il. por. tabs., D. $1. Mendota.

Farrington, Ernest Albert, M.D.
Clinical materia medica: course of lectures del. at the Hahnemann Medical College, Phil.; with memorial sketch of the author, by Aug. Korndœrfer, M.D. 4th ed., rev. and enl. '08(Ag15) c. 8°, $6; hf. mor., $7. Boericke & T.

Farrington, Fk.
Back in the harness: sequel to "Talks by the old storekeeper." '08(D19) c. front. D. 50 c. Merchants' Help.
Retail advertising—complete. '10(Je11) c. D. $1. Byxbee Pub.

Farrington, Frederic Ernest.
French secondary schools; acct. of the origin, development, and present organization of secondary education in France. '10(My21) O. $2.50. Longmans.

Farrington, Herbert M.
Gates that shall not prevail. '08(Ap25) D. †$1.50. Lane.

Farrington, Marg. Vere.
Fra Lippo Lippi: a romance. 4th ed. '08 (My2) c. il. O. **$1.75 net. Putnam.

Farrington, Oliver Cummings.
Meteorite studies, II. '09(D) 19 p. il. (Field Museum of Natural History pubs.; Geological ser.) 50 c. Field Museum.

—, and Tillotson, Edn. Ward.
Notes on various minerals in the museum collection. '08, [1910.] (Ap) 131-163 p. il. 8°, (Field Columbian Museum pubs.; Geological ser.) Field Museum.

Farrow, G: E:
Adventures of a dodo. '08(Jl11) il. 12°, $1.25. Wessels.
Zoo babies; with short interviews. '08 (S5) il. Q. bds., $1.25. Stokes.

Farthest west. Enock, C. R. $4 special net. Appleton.

Fascinating Duc de Richelieu. Williams, H. N. $4 net. Scribner.

Fascinating Mrs. Halton. Benson, E: F. 1.20, fixed. Doubleday, P.

Fascination of London ser. il. 16°, *90 c. net. Macmillan.
—Besant, *and others.* Storeditch and the East End.
—Mitton. Hackney and Stoke Newington.

Fashionable adventures of Joshua Craig. Phillips, D: G. †$1.50. Appleton.

Fassig, Oliver Lanard.
Climate and weather of Baltimore. '08 (Ag8) il. charts, 4°, (Maryland Weather Service, Special pub.) pap., *$2.50 net. Maryland Geol.

Fassler, Adolphe.
See Persona, *pseud.*

Fast game. Parson, K. $1.25. Roxburgh.

Fast mail. Drysdale, W: †$1.50. Wilde.

FASTING.
Carrington, H. Vitality, fasting and nutrition. $5. Rebman.
Eales, I. J. Healthology (health study). $1.50. I. J. Eales.
Hazzard, L. B. Fasting for the cure of disease. $1.50. L. B. Hazzard.

FASTS AND FEASTS.
Bell, C. C. Children's round of fast and festival. *40 c. net. Young Churchman.
Kellner, K. A. H. Heortology; hist. of the Christian festivals. *$3 net. Herder.
See also Christmas;—Easter;—Good Friday;—Holy Week;—Lent.

Fäststämning, en samlung originella dialoger. Liljengren, A. 50 c. A. Liljengren.

Fatal barter. Watkinson, W: L. *$1 net. Revell.

Fatal ruby. Garvice, C: $1.50. Doran.

Fate and the butterfly. Halsey, F. $1.50. B. W. Dodge.

Fate of Iciodorum. Jordan, D: S. **90 c. net. Holt.

Fated five. Biss, G. $1.50. Brentano's.

Fated to win (The soul of a serf). Ellis, J: B. $1. Laird.

Fate's a fiddler. Pinkham, E. G: †$1.50. Small.

Father (The). Strindberg, J. A. *$1 net. J: W. Luce.

Father Abraham. Tarbell, I. M. **50 c. net. Moffat.

Father and child. *See* Bible. Selections.

Father Brighthopes. Trowbridge, J: T. 50 c. Hurst.

Father Crow and his crew. Olmsted, F. H: †$1. B. W. Dodge.

Father Jim. R., J. G. 10 c. Ave Maria.

Father Kelly of the Rosary. Rose, E: E. 50 c. Rosary.

Father to his son. Swain, J: D. *50 c. net. Yale Pub.

Father Tuck's annual; stories and poems by Rosa Nouchette Carey, E. Nesbit, Norman Gale, the editor, etc.; ed. by Edric Vredenburg. '09(N13) O. $2.50; bds., $1.75. Tuck.

Father Tuck's Picture Land. '09(N13) col. il. Q. $1. Tuck.

FATHERS OF THE CHURCH.
Bardenhewer, O. Patrology: lives and works of the fathers of the church. *$3.75 net. Herder.
Budge, E. A. W., *ed.* Paradise or garden of the holy fathers. *$4 net. Duffield.
Robinson, E. A. Short studies of the heroes of the early church. *50 c. net. Jennings.
See also Francis, *St.*;—Saints;—*also* names of fathers and saints;—*also* Texts and studies, ed. by J. A. Robinson.

FATIGUE.
Yoakum, C. S. Experimental study of fatigue. $1.35. Psychological Review.

FATS.
See Oils and fats.

Faught, Fs. Ashley.
Essentials of laboratory diagnosis, designed for students and practitioners. '09(Ap) *$1.50 net; 2d rev. ed. '10(Jl) c. il. pls. 8°, $2. Davis.

Faulding, G. M.
Old man's beard, and other tales. '10(Ja22) col. il. 12°, $2. Dutton.

Faulkner, Herbert W.
Homes of the men of 1830; [paintings] by Alexis Jean Fournier. '10(Je) c. 3-75 p. il. 8°. (Priv. pr.) W: Schaus.

Faulkner, J: Alfr., D.D.
Erasmus: the scholar. '08(Mr7) c. D. (Men of the kingdom.) *$1 net. Jennings.

Faults and follies. Hughes, G: W. 75 c. G: W. Hughes.

Faulty diction. Russell, T: H. 25 c.; 50 c. McKay.

Faunce, Dan. Worcester, D.D.
Mature man's difficulties with his Bible. '08(Mr28) c. D. **75 c. net. Am. Bapt.

Faunce, W: Herbert Perry.
Educational ideal in the ministry: the Lyman Beecher lectures at Yale University in the year 1908. '08(N21) c. D. **$1.25 net. Macmillan.

Fauquier, Fs.
Essay on ways and means for raising money for the support of the present war without increasing the public debts; London, 1756. '08(F22) 8°, (Reprints of economic tracts.) subs., per set of 4 tracts, pap., *$2 net. Johns Hopkins.

Faurote, Fay Leone.
Boy's text book on gas engines. '08(Ap18) c. il. S. (Add. author for price.) F. L. Faurote.

Faust, Albert Bernhardt.
German element in the United States; with special reference to its political, moral, social, and educational influence. In 2 v. '09(D18) c. il. pors. facsims., maps, O. **$7.50 net, boxed. Houghton M.

FAUST (*by Goethe*).
Hauhart, W: F. Reception of Goethe's Faust in England in the first half of the nineteenth century. *$1 net. Lemcke.
Hitch, M. Goethe's Faust: a fragment of socialist criticism. 50 c. Kerr.
See also Goethe, J. W. v.;—Marlowe, Christopher. Dr. Faustus.—Phillips, Stephen;—Taylor, Bayard.

Faustine, Madeline, and Wagner, Mary E.
New reader for evening schools; adptd. for foreigners; with introd. by H. C. Missimer. '10(Ja8) c. il. 12°, 50 c. Hinds.

Fauth, Philip.
Moon in modern astronomy; tr. by Jos. McCabe; with an introd. by J. Ellard Gore. '09(Jl17) il. 8°, *$2 net. Van Nostrand.

Favard, Berthe des Combes.
See Knowles, Mary H.

Faversham, Mrs. Julie Opp.
Squaw man; a novel adapted from the play by Edn. Milton Royle. '10(D) il. 75 c. Grosset.

Favill, H: Baird, ed.
See Butler, G: Fk., *ed.*

Favill, Josiah Marshall.
Diary of a young officer serving with the armies of the United States during the war of the rebellion. '09(N) 298 p. il. pors. 8°, *$1.50 net. Donnelley.

Favilli, Mario.
Echoes of Naples; (thirty Neapolitan songs.) '10(Mr12) c. F. pap., $1.25. Ditson.

Favorite and favors of the sacred Heart of Jesus. Berry, L. C. *75 c. net. Chr. Press.

Favorite fairy tales; childhood choice of representative men and women. New ed. '10 (N5) c. il. O. $1.50. Harper.

Favorite fish and fishing. Henshall, J. A. *$1.25 net. Outing.

Favorite of Napoleon. George, *Mlle.* *$2.50 net. J: McBride.

Favorite operas from Mozart to Mascagni. Hadden, J. C. $2.25. Stokes.

Favorite poems of famous people. Varney, G: L., *ed.* $1.50. Vaughan Pub.

Favorite song pantomimes. Irish, M. 30 c. Flanagan.

Favorites of Henry of Navarre. "Petit Homme Rouge," *pseud.* $3 net. Badger.

Favorites of the French court ser. 8°. Badger.
—"Petit Homme Rouge," *pseud.* Favorites of Henry of Navarre. $3 net.

Favre de Coulevain, Mlle, ["Pierre de Coulevain."]
On the branch; [tr.] from the French by Alys Hallard. '10(Ja) c. 406 p. 12°, $1.25. Dutton.

Favreau, J. Arth.
La grande semaine; fêtes du troisième centenaire de la découverte du lac Champlain. '09(D4) c. il. maps, O. $1.25. Belisle Pr.

Fawcett, E: Douglas.
The individual and reality. '09(D4) O. *$4.25 net. Longmans.

Fawcett, H:
Manual of political economy. 8th ed. '08 (D12) 12°, *$2.60 net. Macmillan.

Faxon, F: Winthrop, comp.
Check-list of American and English periodicals. '08(Mr28) c. 8°, pap. (Priv. pr.) Boston Bk.
—, ed. Dramatic index for 1909; covering articles and illustrations concerning the stage and its players in the periodicals of America and England; with record of books on the drama and of texts of plays published during 1909; comp. with the cooperation of 24 librarians. '10(Ap9) O. $3.50 net.—Bound with Annual magazine subject index. $5.50 net. Boston Bk.

Faxon, Grace B.
Popular recitations and how to recite them; collection of the best selections for recitation, incl. several pantomimes, with complete directions for their delivery. 4 v. '09(D) c. 12°, $1. F. A. Owen.

Fay, C: Ryle.
Co-operation at home and abroad. '08 (O24) 8°, *$3 net. Macmillan.

Fay, Sidney Bradshaw.
See Foster, Herbert Darling.

Fayant, Fk.
Some thoughts on speculation. '09(Jl31) O. pap. (Priv. pr.) Baruch.

Fayrer, C:, ed.
Venomous snakes; poison of venomous snakes and the methods of preventing death from their bite; reprinted papers by the late Sir Jos. Fayrer, Sir Lauder Brunton and Major Leonard Rogers. '09 (Mr27) 8°, *75 c. net. Macmillan.

Fearn, Mrs. Frances Hewitt, ed.
Diary of a refugee. '10(O22) c. il. D. $1.25 net. Moffat.

FEASTS.
See Fasts and feasts.

FEATHER STARS.
See Echinoderms.

FEATHERS.
See Birds.

Feats on the Fjord. *See* Martineau, Harriet.

February boys. Molesworth, *Mrs.* M. L. S. $1.50. Dutton.

Federal and state aid to education in Iowa. Buffum, H. S. $1. Univ. of Ia.

Federal civil service as a career. Foltz, E. B. K. **$1.50 net. Putnam.

FEDERAL CODE.
See United States.

Federal control of trusts. French, H: F. (Add. pubs. for price.) Kohn & P.

FEDERAL COURTS.
See Courts.

FEDERAL EQUITY.
See United States.

FEDERAL GOVERNMENT.
See United States.

FEDERAL LAW.
See United States.

Federal regulation of industry. American Academy of Political and Social Science. $1. Am. Acad. Pol. Sci.

Federal reporter. *See* United States. *Courts.*

Federal spice standards. Brooks, R. O. 50 c. Spice Mill.

Federal Union and Mississippi. Ellett, A. H. 75 c. B. F. Johnson.

Federal usurpation. Fierce, F. **$1.50 net. Appleton.

Federalist (The); by Alex. Hamilton, J: Hay and Ja. Madison; interpreting the Constitution as agreed upon by the Federal Convention, September 17, 1787; with introd. by Goldwin Smith. '08(Je27) c. 8°, $1.75; hf. mor., $3.50. Lamb Pub.

Federalists party in Massachusetts to the year 1800. Morse, A. E. *$2 net. Princeton Univ.

Fee, Mary H.
Woman's impressions of the Philippines. '10(Ap9) c. il. D. $1.50 net. McClurg.

FEEBLE-MINDED.
See Idiocy

FEED-WATER.
See Water.

FEEDING AND FEEDING STUFFS.
Armsby, H. P. Feeding for meat production. 10 c. U. S., Supt. of Docs.
Brode, J. L. Oil-seed products and feed stuffs. Gov. Pr. Off.
Haywood, J: K., *and* Warner, H. J. Commercial feeding stuffs of the U. S. 25 c. U. S., Supt. of Docs.
Henry, W: A. Feeds and feeding. $2.25. W: A. Henry.
Jordan, W. H. Feeding of animals **$1.50 net. Macmillan.

Feet of the years. Hyde, J: D. $1.25 net. Metropolitan Press, (N. Y.)

Feierliche (Das) gelübde als ehehindernis in seiner geschichtlichen entwicklung dargestellt. Scharnagl, A. *$1.50 net. Herder.

Feine, Karl Eduard Paul.
St. Paul as a theologian. In 2 pts. '08 (Mr14) c. S. (Foreign religious ser.) ea., *40 c. net. Eaton & M.

Feininger, Karl.
An experiential psychology of music. '09 (O30) c. por. figs. facsim., D. $2. A. Gemünder.
First series of four essays on the experimental psychology of reproductive music. no. 1, Mechanism and expression; no. 2, Teacher as a moral factor; no. 3, Music as a luxury; no. 4, Music as a necessity. '08(D) c. 106 p. il. 8°. (Add. pubs. for price. 25 City Hall Place, N. Y.) Business Press.

Felice. Long, J: L. †$1. Moffat.

Felicia. Gould, E. L. $1. Penn Pub. Co.

Felicia visits. Gould, E. L. $1 net. Penn Pub. Co.

Felicia's friends. Gould, E. L. †$1. Penn Pub. Co.

Felicita. Hare, C. †$1.25. Stokes.

Félise. *See* Swinburne, Algernon C:

Felix, Mildred.
Our children: [play.] '10(Je) c. 82 p. D. pap., 50 c. Phœnix.

Felix Holt. *See* Eliot, G:

Felkin, Mrs. Alfr. Laurence.
See Fowler, Ellen Thorneycroft.

Feller, F. E.
New pocket dict. of German-English and English-German; rev. by M. A. Curle. '08(Jl18) 32°, (Miniature reference lib.) 50 c. Dutton.

Fellers, J: Elmer.
Crossing familiar paths: a collection of notes, comments, and suggestions concerning persons, places, things and miscellaneous. 3d ed. '08(Ag15) c. por. 12°, 80 c. Booklovers' Assoc.

Fellows, C:
Selection of dishes and the Chef's reminder; high class culinary text book. 9th ed., rev. '09, [1910.] (Ja) c. 220 p. por. obl. 16°, $1. Hotel Monthly.

Fellows Gear Shaper Co. Stub-tooth gear. '09(F20) c. il. O. pap., gratis. Fellows Gear.

Fellowship in the life eternal. Findlay, G: G. *$2.50 net. Doran.

Fellowship songs. Albertson, R., *comp.* 25 c. Public Pub.

Felt, Ephraim Porter.
Control of flies and other household insects. '10(Mr12) il. O. (New York State Educ. Dept. bull.) pap. 15 c. N. Y. State Educ.
Control of household insects. '09(My22) O. (N. Y. State Museum bull.) (Add. pubs. for price.) N. Y. State Educ.

Felt. Timmerman, J: F., *comp.* 50 c. Am. Sch. Corr.

Felter, Lottie Schoolcraft.
Landscapes and waterscapes. '08, [1909.] (F) 7-120 p. 12°, *$1 net. Cannon City Record.

Felton, R. Forester.
British floral decoration. '10(Je18) il. (partly col.) 8°, (Color books, miscellaneous.) $2.50 net. Macmillan.

FENCE-POSTS.
See Concrete.

Fenceless France. Coyle, R. M. (Priv. pr.) Buchanan.

FENCES.
Vernon, A. Estate fences. $3.50. Spon.

Fénelon, François de Salignac de La Mothe-Fénelon.
Spiritual counsels from the letters of Fénelon; first and second series in 1 v.; sel. by Lady Amabel Kerr. '10(O) 6+102+4+104 p. 16°, 45 c. net. Herder.

Fenn, Courtenay H.
Over against the treasury; or, companions of the present Christ; a vision. '10(Je4) c. 12°, 50 c. Westminster.

Fennel and rue. Howells, W: D. †$1.50. Harper.

Fenneman, Nevin Melancthon.
Physiography of the St. Louis area. '09, [1910.] (N) 10+83 p. il. maps, 8°, (Ill. State Geolog. Survey bull.) Univ. of Ill.

Fenollosa, Mrs. Mary McNeil, [Mrs. Ernest F. Fenollosa.]
See McCall, Sidney, *pseud.*

Fenton, H: J: Horstman.
Outlines of chemistry; with practical work. pt. 1. '09(O9) 8°, *$3 net. Putnam.

FENTON FAMILY.
See Genealogies.

Fenwick, Frances de Wolfe.
Arch-satirist. '10(Ap30) c. il. D. $1.50. Lothrop, L. & S.

Fenwick, W: Soltau.
Dyspepsia, its varieties and treatment. '10 (Ag) 485 p. il. 8°, $3. Saunders.
"Literature" (8 p.).

Ferguson, Alex. McGowen, and Lewis, Lowery Laymon.
Elem. principles of agriculture: a text book for the common schools. '08(Ag8) c. il. D. $1. Ferguson Pub. Co.

Ferguson, Emily.
Janey Canuck in the West. '10(D3) il. $1.20 net. Cassell.

Ferguson, Esther Baldwin.
Lump of gold. [1910.] (N) c. 5+229 p. 12°, $1.50. Gilmartin.

Ferguson, J: W.
Way to win. '10(F5) c. D. $1.50. Neale.

Ferguson, Stirling Price.
See Clayton, H: Helm.

Ferguson, W: Blair Morton.
Zollenstein. '08(My16) c. front. D. †$1.50. Appleton.

Fergusson, E. Morris.
For home department workers. '09(F6) c. S. pap., 10 c. Westminster.

Ferina, C:, D.D., comp.
Saint Rita's prayer book, together with a short life of the saint. '08(O) c. 387 p. front. (Add. pub. for price.) C: Ferina.

FERMENTATION.
Alwood, W: B. Fermenting power of pure yeasts and some associated fungi. 15 c. U. S., Supt. of Docs.
Bayliss, W: M. Nature of enzyme action. *$1 net. Longmans.
Cook, F. C. Comparison of beef and yeast extracts of known origin. Gov. Pr. Off.
See also Bacteria;—Digestion.

Fernald, C: A:, M.D.
Universal international genealogy and of the ancient Fernald families, with chronology from creation found in the discovered lost rolls, primitive Bible, squares. '10(Ap) c. 432 p. il. pors. facsims., 4°, $5; $15. C: A: Fernald.

Fernald, C: H:
Genera of the *tortricidæ* and their types. '08, [1909.] (Jl) 67 p. 8°, pap., 75 c. C: H: Fernald.

Fernald, F: Atherton.
Index guide to Buffalo and Niagara Falls; arranged alfabetically. '10(Je) 224 p. il. D. pap., 25 c. Fernald.

Fernald, Grace Maxwell.
Effect of achromatic conditions on the color phenomena of peripheral vision. '09, [1910.] (Mr) 4+91 p. il. tabs., 4°, (Psychological monographs; studies from the Psychological Laboratory of the University of Chicago.) $1. Psychological Review.
Bibliography (7 p.).

Fernald, Ja. Champlin.
Working grammar of the Eng. language. '08(D26) c. D. **$1.50 net. Funk.

Fernald, Rob. Heywood.
Recent development of the producer-gas power plant in the U. S. '10(Mr12) il. fold. maps (in pocket,) 8°, (U. S., Geolog. Survey, bull.) Gov. Pr. Off.

—, Smith, C. D., and others.
Incidental problems in gas-producer tests. '09(D) 29 p. il. 8°, (U. S., Dept. of the Interior, Geological Survey, bull.) (Add. Superintendent for price.)

FERNALD FAMILY.
See Genealogies.

Fernández Juncos, Manuel, comp.
Lecturas escogidas, collección de obras de autores eminentes. '10(N19) c. pors. 12°, 90 c. Silver.

Fernley lectures. D. Eaton & M.
—Telford. Man's partnership with divine providence. *$1.25 net.

Fernow, Bernard Eduard.
Brief hist. of forestry in Europe, the United States and other countries. '10(Mr5) c. D. $2.50. Forestry Quarterly.
Care of trees in lawn, street and park; with list of trees and shrubs for decorative use. '10(My7) c. il. D. (American nature ser., group IV., Working with nature.) $2 net. Holt.

FERNS.
Beecroft, W. I., *comp.* Who's who among the ferns. *$1 net. Moffat.
Conard, H: S. Structure and life-history of the hay-scented fern. 50 c. Carnegie.
Graves, C: B., *and others.* Catalogue of the flowering plants and ferns of Connecticut. 75 c. Conn. Lib.
Hemsley, A. Book of fern culture. *$1 net. Lane.
Marshall, R. Ferns of the Dells of the Wisconsin River. 25 c. R. Marshall.
Step, E. Wayside and woodland ferns. *$2.25 net. Warne.
Willis, J: C. Manual and dict. of the flowering plants and ferns. *$2.75 net. Putnam.

Ferree, Ja. Barr.
Sentiment as a national asset: an oration del. at the Fourth of July celebration in Tenafly, N. J., 1908. '08(Ag22) 8°, pap., gratis. J. B. Ferree.

FERRER, Francisco.
Haeckel, E. H., *and others.* Francisco Ferrer. 25 c. Francisco Ferrer Assoc.

Ferreres, Juan B.
Decree on daily communion: historical sketch and commentary; tr. by H. Jimenez. '09(My) 168 p. 8°, *75 c. net. Herder.

Ferreri, Giulio.
Am. institutions for the education of the deaf. '08(D) 159 p. por. 8°. (Add. Inst. for price.) Penn. Inst.

Ferrero, Felice.
Valley of Aosta; descriptive and historical sketch of an Alpine valley noteworthy in story and in monument. '10(Jl2) c. il. maps, O. $2 net. Putnam.

Ferrero, Guglielmo.
Characters and events of Roman history from Cæsar to Nero; Lowell lectures of 1908; tr. by Frances Lance Ferrero. '09(Je5) c. O. **$2.50 net. Putnam.
Greatness and decline of Rome. v. 3; tr. by Rev. H. J. Chaytor. '08(N7); v. 4 (D5); v. 5. '09(Mr27) O. ea., *$2.50 net. Putnam.

Ferri, Enrico.
Socialism and modern science, (Darwin, Spencer, Marx;) tr. by Rob. Rives La Monte. 3d ed. '09(Ap3) c. D. $1. Kerr.

Ferris, Carrie Sivyer.
Sunday kindergarten, game, gift and story; a manual for use in the Sunday schools and in the home. '09(S4) c. il. O. (Constructive Bible studies; Elementary ser.) *$1.25 net. Univ. of Chic.

Ferris, R:
How it flies; or, the conquest of the air. '10(D24) c. il. D. $1.20 net. Nelson.

Ferro Machine and Foundry Co., Cleveland, O. Marine gasoline engines and equipment; treatise on correct design, construction, installation and operation of power boats. '09(Je19) c. il. f°, 25 c. Ferro.

Ferry, Ervin Sidney.
Brief course in elementary dynamics for students of engineering. '08(Ag29) il. 8°, *$1.25 net. Macmillan.
—, and Jones, Arth. Taber.
Manual of practical physics. v. 1, Fundamental measurements and properties of matter; heat. '08(F8) c. il. tabs., O. $1.75. Longmans.

Ferry, J: Farwell.
Catalogue of a collection of birds from Costa Rica. '10(D10) 8°, (Field Museum of Natural Hist. pubs.; Ornithological ser.) pap., 50 c. Field Museum.

Ferryman, A: Ferryman Mockler-.
See Mockler-Ferryman, A: Ferryman.

Fertility of soils. Gardner, F. D. 15 c. U. S., Supt. of Docs.

FERTILIZATION (plants).
See Botany.

FERTILIZERS.
American fertilizer handbook, 1908; 1909; 1910. ea., $3. Ware.
Battle, H. B., *and* Gascoyne, W: J: Chemical conversion tables for use in the analysis of commercial fertilizers. $2.50. Williams & W.
Beavers, J. C. Farm practice in the use of commercial fertilizers in the south Atlantic states. Gov. Pr. Off.
Bowker, W: H. Plant food; its sources, conservation, preparation and application. 25 c.; pap., gratis. W: H. Bowker.
Gardner, F. D. Fertility of soils as affected by manures. 15 c. U. S., Supt. of Docs.

FERTILIZERS.—*Continued.*
Hall, A. D. Fertilizers and manures. **$1.50 net. Dutton.
Leavens, G: D. Discussion of methods for determining the availability of phosphoric acid.—Remarkable fertilizer: Thomas phosphate powder. (Add. pubs. for price.) Coe-M.
MacKnight, F: E. Fertilizer and acid plants. 50 c. Insurance Press.
Minns, E: R. Barnyard manure, its value and uses. gratis. Sears Roebuck.
Murray, J. A. Soils and manures. $2 net. Van Nostrand.
Schreiner, O., *and* Skinner, J. J: Some effects of a harmful organic soil constituent. Gov. Pr. Off.
Seeds, R. S. Lecture, "How God made the soil fertile." (Add. author for price.) R. S. Seeds.
Snyder, H. Soils and fertilizers. *$1.25 net. Macmillan.
Ville, G. Artificial manures. *$3 net. Longmans.
Vivian, A. First principles of soil fertility. *$1 net. Judd.
Voorhees, E: B. Fertilizers: source, character and composition of natural home-made and manufactured fertilizers. **$1.25 net. Macmillan.
Wendel, J: A. Mineral-fertilizer. 25 c. J: A. Wendel.
Whitney, M. Composition of commercial fertilizers. Gov. Pr. Off.
Whitney, M. Fertilizers for cotton soils. U. S.. Supt. of Docs.
See also Agricultural chemistry;—Alfalfa;—Biology;—Soils;—Wheat.

Fess, Simeon Davidson.
History of political theory and party organization in the United States. '10 (Ag20) c. il. pors. D. $1.50. Ginn.
History of political theory and party organization in the United States. '08(F1) c. 12°, $1.50. World's Events.

Fetch over the canoe. Visscher, W: L. (Not for sale.) W: L. Visscher.

Fetherolf, Ja. Milton.
Forest planting on the northern prairies. '08(Ag1) diagrs., 8°, (U. S., Dept. of Agriculture, Forest Service, circular.) pap., 15 c. U. S., Supt. of Docs.

Fetherston, Rev. Sir G: Ralph.
Secret signatures of my friends. '10 (S10) S. (Thumb-o-graph ser.) 50 c. net. Stokes.

Feuchtersleben, Ernst Baron von, M.D.
Health and suggestion; the dietetics of the mind; tr. and ed. by Ludwig Lewisohn. '10(My7) c. D. $1 net. B: W. Huebsch.
See also Pollak, Gustav.

Feuilerat, Albert.
John Lyly; contribution à l'histoire de la Renaissance en Angleterre. '10(My7) c. 12°, $4 net. Putnam.

FEVER.
Wilcox, R. W. Manual of fever nursing. $1. Blakiston.
Wilson, J. C. Fever-nursing. $1 net. Lippincott.
See also Hay fever;—Malaria;—Scarlet fever;—Skin;—Typhoid fever;—Yellow fever.

Few scraps, oily and otherwise. Smiley, A. W. $1. A. W. Smiley.

Fewkes, Jesse Wa.

Antiquities of the Mesa Verde National Park; Spruce-tree House. '09(O2) il. plan, O. (Smithsonian Institution, Bu. of Am. Ethnology bull.) (Add. Superintendent for price.) U. S., Supt. of Docs.

—, ed. Journal of American ethnology and archæology. v. 5, Hopi songs, by B: Ives Gilman. '08(D26) O. (Hemenway southwestern expedition.) bds., **$2 net. Houghton M.

Feyerabend, Karl, comp.

Complete Hebrew-English pocket-dictionary of the Old Testament. '08(D12) S. (Toussaint-Langenscheidt methods.) 75 c. Lemcke.

Fez, Morocco.

See Hafid, Mulai.

Ffoulke, C: Mathew.

Monograph on the Judith and Holofernes series, consisting of 8 Flemish tapestries with original borders. '07, [1908.] (Mr.) 2+28 p. pls. 8°. (Add. author for price.) C: M. Ffoulke.

ffoulkes, C:

Armour and weapons; with a preface by Viscount Dillon. '09(D4) il. O. bds., $2.15. Oxford Univ.

Ffoulkes, Constance Jocelyn, and Maiocchi, Rodolfo, D.D.

Vincenzo Foppa of Brescia, founder of the Lombard School: his life and his work. '09(Ja16) il. 4°, *$25 net. Lane.

Fiancés (Les) du Spitzberg. Marmier, X. 75 c. Oxford Univ.

Fichte, Johann Gottlieb.

Vocation of man. '10(Je) 12°. (Religion of science lib.) pap., 30 c. Open Court.

Fick, H. H.

Dies und das: ein buch für die kleinen; '08(O10) c. il. D. 25 c. Am. Bk.

Ficke, Arth. Davison.

Breaking of bonds; drama. '10(O22) c. D. bds., $1 net. Sherman, F.

Ficklen, J: Rose.

History of Reconstruction in Louisiana (through 1868). '10(Ag6) c. O. (Johns Hop[illegible] Univ. studies in historical and political science.) $1.50; pap., $1. Johns Hopkins.

Fiction.

Allison, Y. E. Delicious vice: [novel reading;] (first and second ser.) ea., **55 c. net. Burrows Bros.

Best stories by foremost Catholic authors. Given with one $2 sub. to *Benziger's Magazine* and $1 extra, or free with 2 subs. Benziger.

Burton, R: Masters of the English novel. $1.25. Holt.

Canby, H: S. Short story in English. $1.60. Holt.

Chester, G: R. Art of short story writing. $3.50. Pub. Syndicate.

Dawson, W: J. *and* Coningsby W:, *comps.* Great English short-story writers. In 2 v. ea., **$1 net. Harper.

English prose fiction: selected list. 15 c. H. W. Wilson.

Fiction.—*Continued.*

Gerwig, G: W: Art of the short story. *75 c. net. Percy Pub.

Hamilton, C. M. Materials and methods of fiction. **$1.50 net. Baker & T.

Hawthorne, J., *ed.* Library of the world's best mystery and detective stories. 6 v. $6.50. Review of Reviews.

Horne, C: F. Technique of the novel. **$1.50 net. Harper.

Jeffers, L. R. List of editions selected for economy in book buying. 25 c. A. L. A.

Jeffers, L. R., *comp.* Reference list of titles suggested for a special library binding. N. Y. Pub. Lib.

Johnson, J. G. Southern fiction prior to 1860. $2. Michie.

Loshe, L. D. Early American novel. *$1 net. Lemcke.

Matthews, J. B., *ed.* The short-story: specimens illustrating its development. $1. Am. Bk.

Nead, B: M. Some hidden sources of fiction. (Priv. pr.) Jacobs.

Patten, W:, *ed.* International short stories. $2.10. Collier.

Ransome, A. Hist. of story-telling. $3 net. Stokes.

Utica, N. Y. Public Library. Sel. list of historical fiction. gratis. Utica Lib.

Whitmore, C. H. Woman's work in English fiction, from the Restoration to the mid-Victorian period. $1.25 net. Putnam.

Wigmore, J: H: List of legal novels. 40 c. Ill. Law Review.

Young, D. F. Fiction writer's workshop. 50 c. Editor Co.

See also Authors;—Authorship;—Criticism;—Fables;—Fairy tales;—Folk lore;—German literature;—Legends;—Story telling.

Fiction catalog: a selected list catalogued by author and title with annotations. '08(D) 147 p. 12°, pap., 25 c. H. W. Wilson.

Fiction catalog; selected list of 2000 titles cataloged by author and titles, with annotations. '09, [1910.] (Ap) 171 p. 16°, pap., 25 c. H. W. Wilson.

Published also in abr. ed.; 1200 titles, 20 c.; 800 titles. 15 c.; 350 titles, 5c.

Fiddle sticks. Hall, F. C. 50 c. W. F. Roberts.

Fiddles.

See Violins.

Fido. Wiederseim, *Mrs.* G. G. 50 c. Stokes.

Fieberger, Gustave Jos.

Text-book on field fortification. 2d ed. '08 (O3) c. maps, 8°, *$2 net. Wiley.

Field, Claud.

Tales of the caliphs. '09(Ap17) 8°. (Romance of the East ser.) *$1 net. Dutton.

Field, Cyril.

Story of the submarine. '10(Ja1) 8°, *$2 net. Lippincott.

Field, E: Salisbury, ["Childe Harold."]

Cupid's understudy. '09(D4) c. il. D. $1.25, boxed. W. J. Watt.

In pursuit of Priscilla. '08(F15) c. il. D. 50 c.; ooze cf., $1. Altemus.

Sapphire bracelet. '10(O22) c. il. O. $1.25, boxed. W. J. Watt.

Field, Eug.
Cradle lullabies; with an introd. by Edn. Osgood Grover. '09(Je12) c. por. O. bds., 50 c. Canterbury Co.
Poems. Complete ed. '10(D10) c. por. O. $2 net. Scribner.
Sister's cake, and other stories. '08(Ag1) c. 16°, (Ansonia classics.) 50 c. Hurst.
—, and Senour, Caro S.
Musical poems for school, kindergarten and home: poems by Eugene Field; music by Caro S. Senour. '08(Je20) c. pors. F. bds., $1. Scribner.
Field, Louise Maunsell.
Katherine Trevelyan. '08(Ap4) c. D. †$1.50. McClure.
Field, Michael, pseud.
See Bradley, Catherine, *and* Cooper, Edith.
Field, Wa. Taylor.
What is success? '10(N5) c. D. pap., 25 c. net, in envelope. Pilgrim Press.
Field and forest ser. il. 12°. Educ. Pub.
—Chase. Plant babies and their cradles. 40 c.
Field and woodland plants. Furneaux, W: S. *$1.50 net. Longmans.
Field book for railroad surveying. Crandall, C: L. $2. Wiley.
Field day and play picnic for country children. Scudder, M. T. 10 c. Charities Pub.
Field Museum of Natural History pubs. il. 8°, pap. Field Museum.
—Cory. Birds of Illinois and Wisconsin. (Zoölogical ser.) $4.—Birds of Leeward Islands, Caribbean Sea. (Ornithological ser.) 50 c.
—Dall, Description of two new pulmonate mollusks. (Zoölogical ser.) 50 c.
—Dearborn. Catalogue of a collection of birds from British East Africa.—Catalogue of a collection of birds from Guatemala. (Ornithological ser.) ea., 50 c.
—Farrington. Meteorite studies, II. (Geological ser.) 50 c.—Notes on various minerals in the museum collection. (Geological ser.)
—Ferry. Catalogue of a collection of birds from Costa Rica. (Ornithological ser.) 50 c.
—Greenman. New or noteworthy spermatophytes from Mexico. (Botanical ser.) 50 c.
—Meek. Batrachians and reptiles from British East Africa.—Notes on batrachians and reptiles from the islands north of Venezuela.—Notes on fresh-water fishes from Mexico and Central America.—New species of fishes from tropical America.—Zoology of lakes Amatitlan and Atitlan. (Zoölogical ser.) ea., 50 c.
—Meek *and* Hildebrand. Synoptic list of the fishes known to occur within fifty miles of Chicago. (Zoological ser.) $1.
—Millspaugh. Prænunciæ Bahamenses. (Botanical ser.) 50 c.
—Osgood. Diagnosis of new East African mammals.—Further new mammals of Brit. East Africa.—Mammals from the coast and islands of northern South America.—Peculiar bear from Alaska. (Zoological ser.) ea., 50 c.

Field Museum of Natural History pubs.—Continued.
—Slocum. New crinoids from the Chicago area.—New echinoids from the Ripley group of Mississippi. (Geology ser.) ea., 50 c.
—Wolcott. Notes on some cleridæ of Middle and North America. (Zoological ser.)
Field practice of railway location. Beahan, W. $3. Engineering News.
Field trips in the Boston Basin. Getchell, E. L. 60 c. net. Little, B. & Co.
Fielding, H:
Works. 7 v. New imperial lib. ed. '10 (D) il. 8°, ea., $1.25; hf. cf., $2.25; New il. sterling ed., ea., $1. (Sets only.) Estes.
Fielding: [selections;] ed. by G: Saintsbury. '09(N6) por. 12°, (Masters of literature.) *$1.10 net. Macmillan.
Hist. of the adventures of Joseph Andrews and his friend Mr. Abraham Adams; with introd. by G: Saintsbury. '10(D10) c. 16°, (Everyman's lib.) 35 c. net; 70 c. net. Dutton.
History of Tom Jones, a foundling. '08 (F22) 2 v., 16°, (York lib.) $1.60; leath., $2.50. Macmillan.
Tom Jones; introd. by G: Saintsbury. 2 v. '09(Mr27) 16°, (Everyman's lib.) ea., *35 c. net; leath., *70 c. net. Dutton.
Wise sayings and favorite passages from the works, including his Essay on conversation. Pocket ed. '09(Ap3) c. 16°, 50 c. Torch Press.
FIELDING, Henry.
Godden, G. M. Henry Fielding; memoir, incl. newly discovered letters and records. $5. Barse & H.
Fiero, Ja. Newton, comp.
See New York [State.] Practice in special actions.
—, rep. *See* New York [State.] *Ct. of appeals.* Repts.
Fife, C: W., Domville-.
See Domville-Fife, C: W.
Fifteen decisive battles of the world. *See* Creasy, *Sir* E: Shepherd.
Fifteen lessons on the stall bars. Nissen, H. 30 c. Bassette.
Fifteen reasons why no-license is better than license. Alden, G: W. 10 c. G: W. Alden.
Fifteen years among the top-knots. Underwood, *Mrs.* L. H. $1.50. Am. Tr.
FIFTH AVENUE PRESBYTERIAN CHURCH, New York City.
Jessup, H: W. History of the Fifth Avenue Presbyterian Church, New York City. $1. Barnes.
Fifty and one tales of modern Fairyland. Kolle, F: S. $1.25. Fenno.
Fifty common birds around the capital. Heywood, E. E. 25 c. Crane.
Fifty fables for teachers. Bardeen, C: W., *comp.* $1. Bardeen.
54-40 or fight. Hough, E. †$1.50. Bobbs-M.
Fifty house plans designed for home builders in the Southwest. '10(Mr5) c. il. plans, 8°, 50 c. Assoc. Architects.
Fifty lessons in training for service. Moninger, H. H. *40 c. net; *25 c. net. Standard Pub.

Fifty pictures of Gothic altars. Dearmer, P. $6 net. Longmans.
Fifty songs. Grieg, E. H. $2.50; $1.50. Ditson.
Fifty-three years in Syria. Jessup, H: H. In 2 v. **$5 net. Revell.
Fifty-two nature rambles. Westell, W. P. $1.50. Dodge.
Fifty years in camp and field. Hitchcock, E. A. **$4 net. Putnam.
Fifty years in Constantinople. Washburn, G: **$3 net. Houghton M.
Fifty years in Wall Street. Clews, H: *$3 net. H: Clews.
Fifty years of Darwinism: modern aspects of evolution; centennial addresses in honor of Charles Darwin, before the American Association for the Advancement of Science, Baltimore, Friday, Jan. 1, 1909. '09 (My8) c. O. **$2 net. Holt.
Fifty years of modern painting. Phythian, J: E. *$3.50 net. Dutton.
Fifty years of new Japan. Okuma, *Count* S. 2 v. *$7.50 net. Dutton.
Figgis, Darrell.
Vision of lime: poems; with an introd. by Gilbert K. Chesterton. '09 (Ag21) D. *$1.25 net. Lane.
Figgis, J: Neville.
Gospel and human needs. '09 (Ap24) D. (Hulsean lectures.) *$1.25 net. Longmans.
Fight for conservation. Pinchot, G. 60 c. net. Doubleday, P.
Fight for your life. Hanford, B: 25 c. Wiltshire Bk.
Fighter (The). Terhune, A. P. $1.50. Lovell.
FIGHTING.
See Battles;—Military art and science;—Naval art and science.
Fighting Joe. Adams, W: T. 50 c. Hurst.
Fighting saint. Stifler, J. M. *75 c. net. Revell.
Fighting the Mill Creeks. Anderson, R. A. 50 c. Chico Record.
Fighting the slave-hunters. Swann, A. J. *$3.50 net. Lippincott.
Fighting the traffic in young girls. *See* Bell, Ernest Albert.
Fighting the Turk in the Balkans. Smith, A. D. H. **$1.75 net. Putnam.
Fighting with Fremont. McNeil, E. $1.50. Dutton.
FIGS.
Van Velzer, A. C. Fig culture. $1.50. Dealy.
Figueroa, Francisco de.
Obras de Francisco de Figveroa. laureado pindara Español. [facsim.] '03, [1909.] (N) 64 p. 8°, $3.50. (200 copies.) Hispanic Soc.
FIGURES.
See Numerals.
Figyelmessy, Mrs. Elisa Haldeman.
Two boys in the tropics. '10 (O8) c. il. D. $1.35 net. Macmillan.
File no. 113. *See* Gaboriau, E.
Filed, Wilbur Stanwood.
See Ewart, Jos. Archibald.
Files and filing. '09 (O16) c il. 8°, (Machinery's reference ser.) pap., 25 c. Indust. Press.

Filippi, Filippi de.
Ruwenzori: [account of the expedition of the Duke of the Abruzzi to the snow range of central Africa.] '08 (D19) il. 4°, *$8 net. Dutton.
Fille (La) de Roland. Bournier, *Vicomte* H. de. 30 c. Heath.
Fillebrown, C: Bowdoin.
A B C of taxation; with Boston object lessons, private property in land, and other essays and addresses. '09 (Mr13) c. D. $1.20. Doubleday, P.
Genealogy of the Fillebrown family, with biographical sketches. '10 (My) c. 13+178+15 p. il. facsims., 8°, $5. C: B. Fillebrown.
A 1909 single tax catechism, together with notices of the A B C of taxation. 4th ed. '09, [1910.] (Mr) c. 20 p. 16°, pap., 5 c. C: B. Fillebrown.
Fillebrown, Mrs. Rebekah Huddell Miller.
Rhymes of happy childhood. '09 (My1) c. il. O. **$2 net. Winston.
FILLEBROWN FAMILY.
See Genealogies.
Fillmore, Millard.
Addresses, private correspondence and miscellaneous writings; ed. by Frank H. Severance. '08 (F1) 2 v., il. 8°, (Buffalo Historical Society pubs.) *$7 net. Buffalo Hist. Soc.
Fillmore, Parker Hoysted.
The hickory limb. '10 (S3) c. il. D. 50 c. net. Lane.
Filson, J:
See Phillips, P. L.
Filson Club publications. f°. Morton.
—Durrett. Traditions of the earliest visits of foreigners to North America. $4.
—Townsend. Life of James Francis Leonard. $4.
—Young. Prehistoric men of Kentucky. $4.50.
Final faith. Mackenzie, W: D. $1.75 net. Macmillan.
Finality of the Christian religion. Foster, G: B. pt. 1. *$2.50 net. Univ. of Chic.
Davies, A. E. Money and the stock market. 50 c. Pitman.
Finality of the higher criticism. Riley, W: B. $1. W: B. Riley.
FINANCE.
American Academy of Political and Social Science. Lessons of the financial crisis. $1. Am. Acad. Pol. Sci.
Andrew, A. P., *comp.* Financial diagrams. Gov. Pr. Off.
Bagehot, W. Lombard Street; description of the money market. $1.25 net. Dutton.
Cleveland, F: A. Bank and the treasury. **$2 net. Longmans.
Columbia University. Currency problem and the present financial situation. *$1.25 net. Lemcke.
Dewey, D. R. Financial history of the United States. **$2 net. Longmans.
Financial diary, 1908. $3.50. Financial Calendar.
Ford, H: J. Cost of our national government. $1.50 net. Columbia Univ.
Hanna, H. S. Financial history of Maryland, (1789-1848.) 75 c. Johns Hopkins.

FINANCE.—*Continued.*
Jevons, W: S. Investigations in currency and finance. *$3 net. Macmillan.
King, C. F. Light of four candles: [concerning a legal fight with T. W. Lawson.] $1.50. C. F. King.
New York [City.] *Bu. of Municipal Research.* How should public budgets be made? 10 c. Bu. Municipal.
New York [City.] *Dept. of Finance.* Manual of accounting and business procedure of the city of New York. (Priv. pr.) M. B. Brown.
Noyes, A. D. Forty years of American finance. *$1.50 net. Putnam.
Plehn, C. C. Introduction to public finance. **$1.75 net. Macmillan.
Shea, C. A. Financial diary, 1908. $3.50. Financial Calendar.
United States. *National Monetary Commission.* Rept. to the National Monetary Commission on the fiscal systems of the United States, England, France, and Germany. '10(Jl) 86 p. 8°.
United States. *Superintendent of Documents.* Finance; public documents now available. gratis.
United States. *Treasury Department.* Report of Hon. Robert J. Walker, Secretary of the Treasury, on the state of the finances, dated Dec. 3, 1845. (Add. Superintendent for price.) U. S., Supt. of Docs.
See also Advertising; — Banks and banking; — Bonds;—Business;—Commerce; —Corporations; —Credit;—Exchange;—Interest; —Investments; — Money; — Negotiable instruments; — New York City;—Panics;—Prices;—Stocks; —Tariff; —Taxation;—Wealth.

Finances of Sir John Kynnersley. Fox-Davies, A. C: †$1.50. Lane.
Financial advertising. Borosdi, W:, *ed.* $2. Adv. Cyclo.
Financial advertising. Lewis, E. S. $5. Levey.
Financial and administrative hist. of Milwaukee. Larson, L. M. 50 c. Univ. of Wis.
Financial and trade situation, past, present and future. Clews, H: (Add. pubs. for price.) H: Clews.
Financial diary, 1908: diary of past financial events from the beginning of financial hist. in U. S. to the present time; diary of future financial events for the year 1908. '08(F8) c. tabs., D. leath., $3.50; 1909. '09(Ap3) $4. Financial Calendar.
Financial gatling gun. Vallette, J. C. 50 c. J. C. Vallette.
Financial history of the United States. Dewey, D. R. **$2 net. Longmans.
Financial legislation in principle and history. Taylor, W: G: L. $1. Univ. of Neb.
Financing an enterprise. Cooper, F. $4. Ronald Press.

Finberg, Alex. J.
Ingres. '10(D17) col. il. O. (Masterpieces in color.) bds., 65 c. net. Stokes.
Turner's sketches and drawings. '10(Je4) 8°, (Scribner's classics in art ser.) $4 net. Scribner.

Finch, Edn. Ward, M.D.
Frontier, army and professional life of Edwin Ward Finch, M.D., with suggestive thoughts from his own personal experiences in the treatment of pneumonia, etc. '09(Jl) c. 8+119 p. por. 12°, $1. Simmons, M. & D.

Finch, Fs. Miles.
Blue and the gray, and other verse; with preliminary word by And. D. White. '09 (F27) c. por. D. **$1.30 net. Holt.

Finch, W: Coles-.
See Coles-Finch, W:

Finck, H: Theophilus.
Grieg and his music. '09(Je5) c il. pors. O. **$2.50 net. Lane.
Massenet and his operas. '10(D10) c. pors. D. $1.50 net. Lane.
Success in music and how it is won; with a chapter on tempo rubato by Ignace Jan Paderewski. '09(N20) c. O. **$2 net. Scribner.

Finding Christ in ourselves. Cady, E. H. 15 c. Roger Bros.

Findlay, G: G., D.D.
Fellowship in the life eternal; exposition of the Epistles of St. John. '09(D) 15+422 p. O. *$2.50 net. Doran.

Findley, Palmer, M.D.
Gonorrhea in women. '08, [1910.] 118 p. 8°, $2. Mosby.

Fine, H: Burchard, and Thompson, H: Dallas.
Co-ordinate geometry. '09(S18) il. D. *$1.60 net; Answers. '10(My14) pap., 20 c. Macmillan.

Fine art juveniles. il. 8°. Stokes.
—Darton. Wonder book of birds and beasts. $1.50.

FINE ARTS.
Addison, *Mrs.* J. De We. G. Arts and crafts in the Middle Ages. $3. L. C. Page.
Allen, J. R. Celtic art in Pagan and Christian times. *$3 net. Jacobs.
Babbitt, I. New Laokoon; essay on the confusion of the arts. $1.25 net. Houghton M.
Balch, E. S. Art in America before the Revolution. (Add. author for price.) E. S. Balch.
Barnes, E. Child study in relation to elementary art education. (Add. pubs. for price.) Am. Art.
Brinton, S. Renaissance in Italian art. 9 pts. $9 net. Scribner.
Buckley, E., *and others, eds.* The fine arts. (Add. pub. for price.) Nat. Art. Soc.
Carotti, G. History of art. v. 1, 2. ea., *$1.50 net. Dutton.
Carter, C: M. Art; outline study, elem. schools. gratis. Colo. Supt. Sch.
Collmann, S. M. Art talks with young folks. $1.50. Young Israels.
Columbia University lectures on science, philosophy and art, 1907-1908. *$5 net. Lemcke.
Conway, A. E., *and* Martin, *Sir* W: Children's book of art. *$2 net. Macmillan.
Cosgrove, *Mrs.* H. C. J. Amateur art. $1. Donnelley.

FINE ARTS.—*Continued.*

Cram, R. A., *ed.* Christian art. 3 v. *$15 net. Badger.

Crouch, J. Puritanism and art. $3.75 net. Cassell.

De Garmo, C: Laboratory exercises in art appreciation. 40 c. Bardeen.

Froehlich, H. B., *and* Snow, B. E. Progressive lessons in art education. In 8 v. ea., 15 c. Prang.

G., A. E. Modern art at Venice. $2 net. Bowles.

Gareschè, M. R. Art of the ages. $1.25. Prang.

General Federation of Women's Clubs. Hdbk. of art in our own country. 25 c. E. W. Pattison.

Goodyear, W: H: Renaissance and modern art. *$1 net. Macmillan.

Griggs, E: H. Art and the human spirit. *50 c. net; *25 c. net. Huebsch.

Holme, C: Art in England during the Elizabethan and Stuart periods. *$3 net. Lane.

Holme, C:, *ed.* Peasant art in Sweden, Lapland and Iceland. $3 net. Lane.

Howard, W: G. Ut pictura poesis. $1. Grandgent.

Jameson, F: Art's enigma. $2 net. Lane.

Jerningham, C: E. W. Art and curio collector's guide to London. 35 c. net. Cassell.

Johnson, W: M. The W. Martin Johnson School of Art. Elementary instruction in color, perspective, pen drawings, [etc.] $1.50. W: M. Johnson.

Levy, F. N. American art annual. v. 7. $5. Am. Art.

New York City Art Commission. Catalogue of the works of art belonging to the City of New York. gratis. Art Com. of N. Y.

Okakura, K. Ideals of the East; with ref. to the art of Japan. *$1.50 net. Dutton.

Powers, H. H., *and others.* Outlines for the study of art [Italian]. 2 v. ea., $1.50. Bu. Univ. Travel.

Ricci, C. Art of northern Italy. $1.50 net. Scribner.

Sarotti, G. History of art. v. 1, Ancient art. *$1.50 net. Dutton.

Shaw, G: B. Sanity of art. 75 c. B: R. Tucker.

Sturgis, R. Artists' way of working in the various handicrafts and arts of design. $5 net. Dodd.

United States. *Dept. of Commerce and Labor. Bu. of Manufactures.* Municipal art commissions and street lighting in European cities. '10(Jl) 30 p. 8°.

Vallance, A., *and* Salaman, M. C: Art in England during the Elizabethan and Stuart periods. *$2.50 net; *$3 net. Lane.

Weiss, A. Introd. to the philosophy of art. 50 c. Univ. of Cal.

Whistler, J. A. M. "Ten o'clock": [Art lectures.] *$1 net. E. D. North.

Williams, L. Arts and crafts of ancient Spain. 3 v. *$4.50 net. McClurg.

FINE ARTS.—*Continued.*

Yerkes, C: T. Catalogue de luxe of ancient rugs, sculptures, tapestries, costly furniture and other objects belonging to estate of late Charles T. Yerkes. $20. Am. Art Assoc.

See also Archæology;—Æsthetics;—Anatomy for artists;—Architecture;—Artists;—Book-plates;—Bronzes;—Caricature;—Cartoons;—Ceramics; —China painting; — Classification; — Color; —Criticism;—Decoration and ornament;—Drawing; — Egypt; — Embroidery; — Enamel;—Engravers and engravings;—Fans;—Furniture;—Heraldry;—House decoration;—Jewelry;—Lace; — Landscape painting; — Lead; — Lettering; — Librarians and libraries;—Manuscripts;—Metal work;—Miniatures; — Modelling; — Munich;—Music;—Needlework;—Painters and painting;—Perspective;—Photography; — Plastering; —Portraits;—Sculpture;—Silver;—Singing; —Stained glass;—Symbols;—Tapestry;—Wall decoration; —Water-color painting;—*also* Boston Museum of Fine Arts;—British Institution;—Metropolitan Museum, N. Y.;—National Gallery;—*also* Mary, *Virgin.*

Finegan, T: E:

Textbook on New York school law. 5th ed., rev. to Jan. 1, 1908. '08(F) c. D. canvas, $1. M. Bender.

See also New York. Text-bk. of school law.

Finella in Fairyland. Brown, D. V. 50 c. net. Houghton M.

Finer grain. *See* James, H:

Finerty, J: F:

Ireland: people's hist. of Ireland. In 2 v. New ed. '09(D) il. 8°, *$2.50 net, boxed. Dodd.

Finger play reader. Davis, J: W. pts. 1 and 2. ea., 35 c.; teachers' ed., ea., 50 c. Heath.

FINGER PRINTS.

Brayley, F. A: Arrangement of finger prints identification and their uses. $2. Worcester Press.

Hall, J: D. Suggestions on taking finger prints; prep. under direction of the Bureau of Navigation. Gov. Pr. Off.

Fink, Bruce.

Lichens of Minnesota. '10(Ag) 8+269 p. il. pls. 8°, (Smithsonian Institution; United States National Museum bull.) Gov. Pr. Off.

Bibliographies (2 p.) (18 p.).

Fink, Karl.

Brief history of mathematics: author. tr. of "Geschichte der elementar-mathematik." 2d rev. ed. '09(Mr) 12+343 p. *$1.50 net. Open Court.

Finkel, B: Franklin.

Mathematical solution book; cont. systematic solutions of many of the most difficult problems, taken from the leading authors on arithmetic, and algebra, [etc.] 4th ed., rev. and enl. '09(Je) c. 16+549 p. il. pors. 8°, $2. Kibber.

Finklea, Mrs. A. B.

Col. Wilton's daughter. '09(D) $1.25. B'way Pub.

FINLAND.

De Windt, H. Finland as it is. $1.50 net. Dutton.

Scott, A. M. Through Finland. *$1.25 net. Dutton.

Thomson, M. P. Finland. *75 c. net. Macmillan.

Waineman, P. Summer tour in Finland. *$2.50 net; *$5 net. Pott.

Finlay, Ja. Ralph.
Cost of mining; exhibit of the results of important mines throughout the world. '09(D4) c. il. maps, O. *$5 net. McGraw-H.

Finlayson, T. Campbell, D.D.
Ship's engines: a parable. '08(Ag22) T. pap., **15 c. net. Eaton & M.

FINLEY, John.
Dunn, J. P., *and* Wrigley, *Mrs.* S. A. F. Word Hoosier, and John Finley. *50 c. net. Bobbs-M.

Finley, J: Huston, and Sanderson, J: Franklin.
American Executive and executive methods. '08(D12) c. D. (American state ser.) **$1.25 net. Century Co.

Finn, Fk.
Wild beasts of the world. In 2 v. '10 (My14) il. in col. 4°, $8 net. Dodge.
See also Dewar, Douglas.

Finn the wolfhound. Dawson, A. J. $1.50. Lippincott.

Finnemore, J:
England. '08(O24) il. map, 12°, (Peeps at many lands ser.) *75 c. net. Macmillan.
His first term. '10(Ja1) il. 12°, $1.50. Lippincott.
Holy Land. '08(S19) il. map, 12°. (Peeps at many lands ser.) *75 c. net. Macmillan.
Lone patrol. '10(D31) il. 12°, $1.50. Lippincott.
Morocco. '08(Ag22) il. 12°, (Peeps at many lands ser.) *75 c. net. Macmillan.
Story of a scout. '08(N7) il. 12°, $1.50. Macmillan.
Story of Robinhood and his merry men. '09(D25) col. il. 12°, (Color books for boys and girls.) *$1.50 net. Macmillan.
Switzerland. '08(S19) il. map, 12°, (Peeps at many lands ser.) *75 c. net. Macmillan.
Teddy Lester's chums. '10(D31) il. 12°, $1.50. Lippincott.
Two boys in war-time. '08(N7) il. 12°, $1.50. Macmillan.
Wolf patrol: tale of Baden-Powell's boy scouts. '08(N7) il. 12°, $1.50. Macmillan.

FINNEY, Charles Grandison.
Cochran, W: C. Charles Grandison Finney; memorial address del. at the dedication of the Finney Memorial Chapel. (Priv. pr.) Lippincott.

Finney, F: Norton.
Letters from across the sea, 1907-1908. '09, [1910.] (Je) 13+244 p. il. pors. 8°. (Priv. pr.) F: N. Finney.

Finot, Jean.
Philosophy of long life; tr. from the French by Harry Roberts. '09(My15) O. *$2.50 net. Lane.

Finsbury technical manuals. il. 8° Spon.
—Darling. Heat for engineers. $5.

FIORILLO, Federigo.
Winn, E. L. How to study Fiorillo. 75 c. Fischer.

Fippin, E. O.
See Lyon, T: L.

Fir and the palm. Briggs, O. M. †$1.50. Scribner.

FIRDUSI (Abul Kasin Mansur.)
Renninger, E. D. Story of Rustem and other Persian hero tales from Firdusi. **$1.50 net. Scribner.

FIRE.
Crosby, E. U., *and* Fiske, H: A. Crosby-Fiske hdbk. of fire protection. $4. Insurance Field.
Evans, P. Address on fire prevention del. before Nat. Ass'n of Manufactures, May 20, 1908. (Add. author for price.) P. Evans.
Jenness, H. T. Bucket brigade to flying squadron. $1.50. H. T. Jenness.
Maris, C. Dangers and chemistry of fire. Ohio State Fire Marshal.
National Board of Fire Underwriters. Fire engine tests and fire stream tables. gratis. Nat. Bd. Fire.
New York State. *Public Service Commission, 2d District.* In the matter of fire prevention along lines of railroads in the Adirondacks forest preserves. (Add. pubs. for price.) N. Y. Pub. Service Com.
Rane, F. W: We must stop forest fires in Massachusetts. (Add. author for price.) F. W: Rane.
See also Building materials;—Forests and forestry;—Heat.

Fire builders. Du Bois, P. 35 c. net. F. M. Barton.

FIRE DEPARTMENT, New York City.
Merchants' Association of New York. Investigation of the Fire Department of New York. gratis. Merchants' Assoc.

FIRE-ENGINES.
See Fire.

Fire-fly's lovers. Griffis, W: E. †$1. Crowell.

FIRE INSURANCE.
See Insurance.

Fire insurance in New England for ten years, Dec. 31, 1899-Dec. 31, 1908, inclusive; comp. from the statements filed with the various New England insurance departments. [10th ed.] '09(Jl) c. 202 p. 12°, $3.50. Standard Pub. Co.

FIRE PREVENTION.
See Fire.

Fire-resistive properties of various building materials. Humphrey, R: L. (Add. Superintendent for price.) U. S., Supt. of Docs.

Fire, snow and water. Ellis, E: S. †75 c. Winston.

Fire tax and waste of structural materials. Wilson, H. M. Gov. Pr. Off.

FIREARMS.
Browne, B. H. Guns and gunning. 30 c.; 20 c. J. Stevens.
Sawyer, C: W. Firearms in American hist. C: W. Sawyer.
See also Artillery;—Rifle;—Shooting.

FIREFLY.
Ives, Herb. Eug., *and* Coblentz, W: Weber. Luminous efficiency of the firefly. 10 (Jl) 321-336 p. il. 8°. Gov. Pr. Off.

FIRELESS COOKERY.
See Cookery.

Fireman's preparatory instruction. Baker, G: H: 3 v. $20. Railway Educ.

FIREMEN.
O'Reilly, J. J: E: How to become a fireman. 75 c. Chief.
Fireproof construction, for houses and other buildings of moderate cost. 2d ed. '09, [1910.] (My) 93 p. il. O. pap., gratis. Nat. Fire Proofing.
Fireside encyclopedia of poetry. Coates, H: T., *comp.* $2-$7.50. Winston.
Fireside travels. *See* Lowell, Ja. Russell.
FIREWOOD.
See Wood.
Firing line. Chambers, R. W. †$1.50. Appleton.
FIRST AID (*to the injured*).
See Accidents;—Red Cross Society.
First aid in nursery ailments. Coolidge, E. L. $1. E. L. Coolidge.
First aid to shipping fruits, vegetables, [etc.] Thomas, T. G: $1. T. G: Thomas.
First aid to the child. Young, D. H. $1.25. Dutton.
First aid to the sick. Young, D. H. $1.25 net. Dutton.
First aid to the sick by the use of domestic remedies. Vorbeck, J. C. $1. J. C. Vorbeck.
First and last things. Wells, H. G: **$1.50 net. Putnam.
First and second prayer book of King Edward VI. '10(Ap23) 16°, (Everyman's lib.) 35 c. net; leath., 70 c. net. Dutton
First at the North Pole. Stratemeyer, E: $1.25. Lothrop, L. & S.
First at the Pole. Shaw, F. H. $1.50. Cassell.
FIRST BAPTIST CHURCH, Providence, R. I.
King, H: M., *comp. and ed.* Historical catalogue of members of the First Baptist Church in Providence, Rhode Island. $2. F. H. Townsend.
First book of stories for the story-teller. Coe, F. E. 80 c. Houghton M.
First century of Lake Champlain. Royce, *Mrs.* C. H. B. 25 c. C. H. B. Royce.
FIRST CHURCH, Pembroke, Mass.
Litchfield, H: W. First church in Pembroke, 1708-1908. 25 c. G: E: Lewis.
First Church of Christ, Hartford, Ct. Commemorative exercises of the First Church of Christ in Hartford, on the 100th anniversary of the dedication of the meeting-house and the 275th anniversary of the founding of the church, Dec. 1-3, 1907. '08, [1909.] (Je) 81 p. 8°. (Add. pubs. for price.) First Church of Christ.
First Easter sermon. Moody, P. D. 30 c. Northfield Press.
FIRST ENGLISH EVANGELICAL CHURCH, Pittsburgh, Pa.
Gongaware, G: J., *ed.* History of the First English Evangelical Lutheran Church in Pittsburgh. $1. First Eng. Evan. Luth. Ch.
First fifty years of the Equitable Life Assurance Society. Equitable Life Assurance Society. (Add. pubs. for price.) W. F. Powers.
First governess of the Netherlands. Tremayne, *Mrs.* E. E. *$3 net. Putnam.
First great Canadian. Reed, C: B. $2 net. McClurg.
First impressions of Europe. Bailey, J. W. **$1.25 net. Grafton Press.
First love. Van Vorst, M. $1.50. Bobbs-M.
First map of Kentucky. Phillips, P. L. *$2.50 net. Torch Press.
First negro priest on southern soil. Bragg, G: F. 75 c. Church Advocate.
First page of the Bible. Bettex, F. 25 c. Germ. Lit. Bd.
First Plymouth marriage. Shaw, R. H. 35 c. R. H. Shaw.
FIRST PRESBYTERIAN CHURCH, Albany, N. Y.
Paltsits, V. H. First Presbyterian Church founded in 1763, Albany, New York. gratis. Albany First Presb. Ch.
First principles of Christian citizenship. Swift *Rev.* A. *75 c. net. Revell.
First printed translations into English of the great foreign classics. Harris, W: J., *comp.* *75 c. net. Dutton.
First records of Marlborough, Mass. '09, [1910.] (F) 47 p. 8°, (Systematic history fund pubs.) pap., $1. F. P. Rice.
First revolutionary step [in France.] Christophelsmeier, C. H. $1. Univ. of Neb.
First round. Lucas, St. J. W. $1.25 net. Dutton.
First siege of Louisburg. Baker, H: M. (Priv. pr.) H: M. Baker.
First sketch of English literature. Morley, H: $2.50 net. Cassell.
First steps in organizing playgrounds. Hanmer, L. F. 10 c. Charities Pub.
First two years of Kansas. Martin, G: W. gratis. G: W. Martin.
First written grammar of the Bontoc Igorot language. Seidenadel, C. W. $5. Open Court.
Firth, C: Harding.
House of Lords during the Civil War. '10 (D3) O. $2.60 net. Longmans.
Last years of the Protectorate, 1656-1658. In 2 v. v. 1, 1656-1657; v. 2, 1657-1658. '09(D11) O. *$7 net. Longmans.
Milton as a historian; from the proceedings of the British Academy. v. 3. '09(Ja23) O. pap., 40 c. Oxford Univ.
Firth, Franklin Jones.
Christian unity in effort; something about the religious faiths, creeds, and deeds of people of the United States and elsewhere in their relation to Christian unity in effort. '10(Mr26) c. D. **$1.50 net. Lippincott.
Fischel, Oscar, and Von Boehm, Max.
Modes and manners of the XIXth century as represented in the pictures and engravings of the time; tr. by M. Edwards; introd. by Grace Rhys. 3 v. '09(D18) 8°, silk, **$7 net. Dutton.
Fischelis, Philipp.
See Broomell, I: Norman.
Fischer, Emil.
Introd. to the preparation of organic compounds; tr. with author's sanction from the new (8th) German ed. by R. V. Stanford. '10(Ag13) il. 12°, $1.25 net. Van Nostrand.
Fischer, Heinrich.
Landeskunde der Vereinigten Staaten von Nordamerika. 2 v. '08(O24) il. tabs., map, S. 40 c. Stechert.

Fischer, H: W., ed.
Memoirs of Prince John de Guelph; with introd. '10(D) 8°, $2. B. W. Dodge.

Fischer, H: W: Hubert.
Private lives of Kaiser William II. and his consort; secret hist. of the court of Berlin, from the papers and diaries of Ursula, Countess von Eppinghoven, dame du palais to Her Majesty, the empress, queen. 3 v. [Connoisseur ed.] [1910.] (Ja) c. '09. il. pors. facsims., 8°, $12. (500 copies.) W. C. Adams.

Fischer, L:, M.D.
Diseases of infancy and childhood. 2d ed. '08(Ag29); 3d ed. '10(Je) c. il. 8°, sub., ea., *$6.50 net; hf. mor., *$8 net. Davis.

Fischer, Martin H:
Œdema; study of the physiology and the pathology of water absorption by the living organism; the 1909 Nathan Lewis Hatfield prize essay of the College of Physicians of Philadelphia. '10(Ag) 209 p. il. diagrs. 8°, $2. Wiley.

Fischer-Dueckelmann, Anna, M.D.
Wife as the family physician: practical work of ref. for the family in health and sickness, with special attention to diseases of women and children, married life, sexual hygiene, child-birth, care of children, family hygiene, etc. '08(Ap4) c. por. Q. $5. Int. Medical.

Fish, Carl Russell.
Some phases of the economic history of Wisconsin, 1860-70. '08(Ap18) 12°, pap., 35 c. State Hist., Wis.

Fish, Dan.
Legal phases of the Lincoln and Douglas debates; annual address before the State Bar Association of Minnesota at Minneapolis, July 14, 1909. '09, [1910.] (Ap) 15 p. 16°. (Priv. pr.) D. Fish.

Fish, Stuyvesant.
Address before the Economic Club of Boston, March 24, 1908. Under what conditions will the railroads of the United States best serve the public? '09(F6) 8°, pap., gratis. S. Fish.

Fish, Theophilus.
Tonalt Camembile of the exchange; up-to-date newspaper story; ed. by E. Clement D'Art. '10(Ap) c. 70 p. D. pap., 25 c. House of Fun.

Fish, Williston.
Last will. '08(D) c. 17 p. 16°, 40 c. A. Bartlett.
Legacy to mankind. '08(Mr14) 8°, pap. (Priv. pr.) Univ. Press., (Camb.)

Fish and fishing.
Balch, T: W. La question des pêcheries de l'Atlantique. $1.25. Allen, L. & S.
Barnes, O. P. Fly fishing in wonderland; [Yellowstone National Park.] $1. O. P. Barnes.
Borchardt, E. M., *comp.* North Atlantic coast fisheries arbitration. Gov. Pr. Off.
Bradford, C: B. Angler's guide: hdbk. of the haunts and habits of the popular game fish, inland and marine. $1; 50 c. —Angler's secret. *$1 net.—Determined angler. 60 c. Nassau Press.
Briggs, E. E: Angling and art in Scotland. *$4 net. Longmans.

Fish and fishing.—*Continued.*
Camp, S: G. Fishing kits and equipment. $1 net. Outing.
Dennis, O. M. Some reasons for failure of fish protective legislation. Gov. Pr. Off.
Dewar, G: A. B. Book of the dry fly. $2.50 net. Macmillan.
Dockery, A. V. Black bass and other fishing in North Carolina. 75 c. Commercial Pr. Co.
Evermann, B. W. Fishes of Alaska. $1. U. S., Supt. of Docs.
Forbes, S. A. On the general interior distribution of Illinois fishes. $1. Ill. Lab'y Nat. Hist.
Forbes, S. A., *and* Richardson, R. E. Fishes of Illinois. Exchange or gratis. Ill. Lab'y Nat. Hist.
Frazer, P. D. Rodmaking for beginners. $1. Forest.
Fryer, C: E: International regulations of the fisheries on the high seas. Gov. Pr. Off.
Gill, T. N: Contributions to the life history of fishes. (Add. pubs. for price.) Smith. Inst.
Held, R. J., *and* Rice, E: B., *eds.* Angler's guide. 50 c. Field and Stream.
Henshall, J. A. Favorite fish and fishing. *$1.25 net. Outing.
Hodgson, W: E. Angler's season. *$1.50 net. Macmillan.
Holder, C: F: Big game at sea. *$2 net. Outing.
Holder, C: F: Method of studying the life hist. of fishes.—Plan for an educational exhibit of fishes. Gov. Pr. Off.
Holder, C: F: Recreations of a sportsman on the Pacific Coast. $2 net. Putnam.
Holder, C: F:, *and* Jordan, D: S. Fish stories, alleged and experienced. **$1.75 net. Holt.
Hoover, M. H. Wild ginger, wood sorrel and sweet cicely; [sportsmen's stories.] $1.50. B'way Pub.
International Fisheries Commission (U. S. and Gt. Brit.). Protection and preservation of food fishes in international boundary waters of the U. S. and Canada; message from the President of the United States, transmitting a rept. by the Secretary of State submitting a system of uniform and common international regulations for the protection and preservation of the food fishes which have been prepared by the International Fisheries Commission. '10(Ap) 19 p. 8°, pap. Gov. Pr. Off.
Jordan, D: S. Fishes. **$6 net. Holt.
Jordan, D: S. Work of the International Fisheries Commission of Great Britain and the United States. Gov. Pr. Off.
Meek, S. E. New species of fishes from tropical America.—Notes on fresh-water fishes from Mexico and Central America. —Zoölogy of lakes Amatitlan and Atitlan, Guatemala, with special reference to ichthyology. ea., 50 c. Field Museum.
Meek, S. E., *and* Hildebrand, S. F. Synoptic list of the fishes known to occur within fifty miles of Chicago. $1. Field Museum.

FISH AND FISHING.—*Continued.*

Muller, J. W., *and* Knowlson, A. Fishing around New York. 50 c.; 25 c. Knowlson & M.

New York [State.] Forest, fish and game laws, 1908. 50 c. M. Bender.

Newberry, A. S. Caught on the fly: fugitive notes of sport. (Priv. pr.) A. S. Newberry.

Olsen, O. T. International regulations of the fisheries on the high seas. Gov. Pr. Off.

Randall, W., *ed.* Angler's guide. 60 c.; 50 c. Field and Stream.

Rhead, L: J: Book of fish and fishing. **$1.50 net. Scribner.

Sharp, G. E. Fly-leaves from a fisherman's diary. $1.40 net. Longmans.

Sölling, A. Improved and pract. method of packing fish for transportation. Gov. Pr. Off.

Stevenson, C: H. International regulations of the fisheries on the high seas. Gov. Pr. Off.

United States. *Dept. of Commerce and Labor. Bureau of the Census.* Instructions to special agents; Census of the fishing industry (Add. Superintendent for price.) U. S., Supt. of Docs.

United States. *Dept. of Commerce and Labor. Bureau of Fisheries.* List of publications of the Bu. of Fisheries available for distribution. gratis.—National aspects of angling and the protection of game fishes.

United States. **Fishes; in the United States public documents great attention is given to fishes and fisheries; documents cont. information on these subjects are sold at cost of paper, printing, and binding, and delivered free, by the Superintendent of** Documents. '09(O) 61 p. 8°, gratis.

Walton, I., *and* Cotton, C. Complete angler. *$1.50 net. Lane.

See also Aquarium; — Bass; — Cookery;—Crustaceans; — Echinoderms; — Fisheries; — Game laws;—Gold fish;—Jellyfish;—Marine zoology; — Mollusks; — Mosquitoes; — Paleontology; — Salmon;—Sculpin;—Trout;—Whales and whaling.

Fishe, Marian H.

My Father's business; or, the life and work of Miss Agnes Gibson. '09(Mr) 60 c. China Inland.

"Fisher, Bud," pseud.

See Fisher, H. C.

Fisher, Cassius Asa.

Geology of the Great Falls coal field, Montana. '09(My) 85 p. il. 8°, (Dept. of Interior, U. S. Geol. Survey bull.) pap., 20 c.

See also Ashley, G: Hall.

Fisher, C: A.

Minstrel with the self-same song, and other poems. 2d ed. '08(S5) c. D. $1. F. Fisher.

Fisher, Dan. Webster, D.D.

A human life: autobiography, with excursuses. '09(D) c. 325 p. 12°, *$1.50 net. Revell.

Fisher, Emma.

Dornröschen: ein märchenspiel. '09(Ag28) S. (Modern language ser.) *25 c. net. Crowell.

La belle au bois dormant; féerie en quatre tableaux; ed. by F. G. Harriman. '10 (Ja29) S. (Crowell's shorter French texts.) *25 c. net. Crowell.

Fisher, H. C., ["Bud Fisher."]

Mutt and Jeff cartoons. '10(O15) c. obl. T. bds., 50 c. net. Ball Pub.

Fisher, Harrison, il.

American beauties. '09(O30) c. col. il. Q. $3, boxed. Bobbs-M.

American girl; [colored drawings of twelve types of American women;] with a foreword by James B. Carrington. '09(N6) c. por. f°, bds., *$3.50 net. Scribner.

Garden of girls. '10(O15) c. il. in col. por. F. bds., $3.50. Dodd.

Pictures in color. '10(O8) c. F. $3.50 net, boxed. Scribner.

Fisher, Herbert Albert Laurens.

Bonapartism: six lectures del. in the University of London. '08(Ap11) 8°, *$1.15 net. Oxford Univ.

Frederick William Maitland, Downing professor in the laws of England; biographical sketch. '10(O1) O. $1.65 net. Putnam.

Fisher, Herbert Wescott.

Making life worth while; book on health —and more. '08(O8) c. D. $1.20 net. Doubleday, P.

Fisher, Horace Newton.

Ethnography and commercial importance of Latin America and the West Indies in 1906. '09(My) 4 p. chart. 8°, pap. U. S., Supt. of Docs.

Fisher, Irving.

Bulletin of the Committee of One Hundred on National Health; being a rept. on national vitality, its wastes and conservation; prep. for the National Conservation Commission. '09(N) 9+138 p. 8°. (Add. Superintendent for price.) U. S., Supt. of Docs.

Economic aspect of lengthening human life: address del. before the Association of Life Insurance Presidents, New York, Feb. 5, 1909. '09(Jl10) O. pap. (Add. pubs. for price.) Com. of One Hundred.

National vitality, its wastes and conservation. '10(Je) 619-751 p. diagr., 8°. Gov. Pr. Off.

Fisher, J. W., comp.

See Texas. Laws.

Fisher, Jerome B., rep.

See New York [State.] *Sup. ct.* Repts.

Fisher, J: I.

Added interest tables. 1909 ed. '09(Je) 152 p. 8°, $5 J: I. Fisher.

Bank instalment system: tables for instalment loans at bank discount. '09(Je) 62 p. il. 4°, $25. J: I. Fisher.

20th century tables: all-purpose interest book. New and enl. ed. $2.50. J: I. Fisher.

Fisher, Martin L., and Cotton, Fassett Allen.

Agriculture for common schools. '09(O30) c. il. 12°, $1. Scribner.

Fisher, Mary.
Journal of a recluse; tr. from the orig. French. '09(O9) c. 11+334 p. front. D. $1.25. Crowell.

Fisher, Mary A.
Ghost in the garret and other stories. '10 (Ag27) D. $1. Aberdeen.
Young Doctor Hamilton. '08(D12) il. 12°, 75 c. Cochrane.

Fisher, Sydney G:
Struggle for American independence. '08 (My16) c. 2 v., il. pors. facsim., maps, O. **$4 net. Lippincott.

Fisher, Willard Ja.
See Blaker, Ernest.

Fisher, W: Darius.
From dawn to dusk. '09(Ag) c. 38 p. il. por. 8°, 50 c. McDonald & Co.

FISHERIES.
Special agreement bet. the United States and Great Britain. '09(My) 11 p. 8°, pap. (Add. Superintendent for price.) U. S., Supt. of Docs.

FISHERMEN.
See Fish and fishing.

FISHING.
See Fish and fishing.

Fishleigh, Wa. Turner.
Problems in descriptive geometry for class and drawing room. '10(O8) c. il. 4°, $1. W. T. Fishleigh.

Fiske, G: Wa.
Boy life and self-government. '10(S3) c. 12°, $1. Y. M. C. A.

Fiske, H: A.
See Crosby, Everett U.

Fiske, J. Parker B.
See Bragdon, Claude.

Fiske, J:
Meaning of infancy. '09(My22) c. 12°, (Riverside educational monographs.) **35 c. net. Houghton M.
Unpublished orations: "The discovery of the Columbia River, and the Whitman controversy"; "The Crispus Attucks memorial," and "Columbus memorial." '10 (Mr12) c. por. 12°. (Priv. pr.) 489 copies.) Bibliophile.

Fiske fund prize dissertation. 8°. Snow & F.
—Palmer. Has surgical treatment lessened the mortality from appendicitis? 50 c.

FISKE ICELANDIC COLLECTION, Cornell University, Ithaca, N. Y.
Cornell University. Islandica: annual rel. to Iceland and the Fiske Icelandic collection. v. 1-3. ea., $1 net. Cornell Univ.

Fit for work. Schofield, A. T. *$1.25 net. Armstrong.

Fitch, Anthony.
Ballads of the western mines and others. '10(Je) 69 p. il. 12°, 75 c. Cochrane.

Fitch, Asahel Norton.
New commercial law. 3d ed., rev. '10 (F) c. 262 p. O. (Williams & Rogers ser.) $1.05. Am. Bk.

Fitch, G:
The automobile. '10(Mr12) c. il. 12°, 35c. Collier.
Big strike at Siwash. '09(N6) c. il. S. (Little comic masterpieces.) †50 c. Doubleday, P.

Fitch, G:—*Continued.*
Bridge whist. '10(Mr12) c. il. 16°, 35 c. Collier.
Golf for the beginner. '10(Mr12) c. il. 16°, 35 c. Collier.

Fitch, Michael Hendrick.
Physical basis of mind and morals. 2d ed., with numerous additions and emendations. '09(Ap17) c. D. (International lib. of social science.) $1. Kerr.

Fitch, Roger Stanley.
Estimating tactical situations and composing field orders. '09, [1910.] (Ap) 30 p. O. pap. (Priv. pr.) Staff Coll.

Fitch, W: Clyde.
Beau Brummel: a play: written for Richard Mansfield. '08(O10) c. il. por. O. **$1.50 net. Lane.
Wave of life. '09(D25) c. 8°, $1.50. M. Kennerley.

FITCH, William Clyde.
Bell, A. Clyde Fitch I knew. $1. B'way Pub.

Fitchett, Rev. W: H:, ["Vedette."]
Beliefs of unbelief. '08(F29) c. D. *$1.25 net. Eaton & M.
Pawn in the game: [a novel.] '08(Ag29) c. $1.25. Eaton & M.

Fite, Mrs. Eliz. Mitchell Stephenson, ed.
Lovers' year-book. '10(O8) c. front. D. (Day by day ser.) 60 c., boxed; leath., $1, boxed. Crowell.

Fite, Emerson D:
Social and industrial conditions in the North during the Civil War. '10(Mr26) c. O. **$2 net. Macmillan.

Fitt, Arth. Percy.
All about Northfield; brief hist. and guide. [1910.] (Jl) c. 166 p. il. maps, facsims., 12°, $1. Northfield Press.

Fitz, G: Wells, M.D.
Principles of physiology and hygiene. '08 (O10) c. il. figs. D. $1.12. Holt.

Fitz, Leslie Arth.
Handling wheat from field to mill. '10(D) 12 p. 8°, (U. S., Dept. of Agriculture, Bu. of Plant Industry circular.)

Fitzgerald, D: Bruce.
Law of Christian healing. '08(O3) c. 12°, *75 c. net. Revell.

FitzGerald, J: Driscoll, 2d.
Rambles in Spain. '10(O15) c. map, O. $3 net, boxed. Crowell.

Fitzgerald, Rob.
Statesmen snowbound. '09(Ag7) c. il. D. *$1.25 net. Neale.

Fitzgerald, T: W. H., comp. and ed.
Ireland and her people; biography, together with a popular history; to which is added an appendix of copious notes and useful tables; supplemented with a dictionary of proper names in Irish mythology, geography, genealogy, etc. In 10 or 12 v. v. 1. '09(Je5); v. 2. '10 (Ap16) c. pors. 8°, ea., $3; ¾ mor., $5; full mor., $9. Fitzgerald Bk.

FITZHERBERT, *Mrs.* Maria Anne Smythe.
Wilkins, W: H: Mrs. Fitzherbert and George IV. $5. Longmans.

Fitzhugh, Percy Keese.
Galleon treasure. '08(O3) c. D. (Crowell's young people ser.) †75 c. Crowell.
King Time; or, the mystical Land of the Hours. '08(O31) c. il. O. $1.25. Caldwell.
—, **ed.** Every girl's library; collection of appropriate and instructive reading for girls of all ages from best authors of all times with general introd. by the editor and critical and interpretive essays by Ella Wheeler Wilcox, Margaret E. Sangster, Stella George Stern Perry. 10 v. '10 (Ap16) c. pors. 16°, per set, $4. Pearson Pub.

Fitzhugh, T:
Prolegomena to the history of Italico-Romanic rhythm. '08(Ag8) c. O. pap., 25 c. Anderson.
Sacred tripudium, the accentual and rhythmic norm of Italico-Romanic speech and verse. [2d ed.] '09, [1910.] c. 59 p. 8°, (Univ. of Va., bull. of the School of Latin.) 75 c. Anderson.

Fitzmaurice-Kelly, Ja.
Chapters on Spanish literature. '09(N20) 8°, $1.75. Hispanic Soc.

Fitzpatrick, Ernest Hugh.
Coming conflict of nations; or, the Japanese-American war; narrative. Library ed. '10(Ja15) c. 12°, $2. H. W. Rokker.
Magdalene of France: an historical drama. '08(Mr.) 62 p. il. 8°. (Add. pubs. for price.) Sentinel Pub.

Fitzpatrick, F. W.
Fall of Babylon; scenario of a spectacular drama. '10(D) c. 18 p. il. O. pap., gratis. Shaw Bros.

FitzPatrick, Hugh Louis.
Equestrian polo. '10(O) c. 62 p. por. il. 16°, (Spalding's athletic lib.) pap., 10 c. Am. Sports.

Fitzpatrick, Sir Ja. Percy.
Jock of the Bushveld. Abridged ed. '09 (Ap3) il. D. *50 c. net; prize ed., *90 c. net. Longmans.

Fitz-Patrick lectures. *See* Moore, Norman.

Fitz Simon, Vincent Alphonso.
Christ of promise in Homer, Hesiod, Vergil, Ovid, Horace, etc. '09(Je12) c. 8°, $3. G: W. Dillingham.

Five chums ser. D. Lothrop, L. & S.
—Brainerd, *pseud.* Winning the Eagle prize. $1.25.

Five cousins in California. Reinertsen, E. M. A. $1.50. C. M. Clark.

Five essays on the art of Ignacio Zuloaga. Utrillo, *Don* M. 50 c. Hispanic Soc.

Five foot shelf. ***See* Harvard classics.**

Five hundred (*card game*).
See Cards.

Five journeys around the world. Peebles, J. M. $1.75. Peebles.

Five knots. White, F. M. †$1.50. Little, B. & Co.

Five months in the Himalayas. Mumm, A. L: *$6 net. Longmans.

Five months on a derelict. Houston, E. J. †$1.25. Am. Bapt.

Five nations. *See* Kipling, Rudyard.

Five new rodents. Heller, E. Smith Inst.

Five nights. Cory, V. $1.50. M. Kennerley.

Five-place logarithmic and trigonometric tables. Conant, L. L., *ed.* 50 c. Am. Bk.

Five practical chapters on retail advertising. Egan, J. W: (Add. pubs. for price.) J. W: Egan.

Five Stuart princesses. Rait, R. S., *ed.* *$3.50 net. Dutton.

5000 facts about Canada. Yeigh, F., *comp.* 25 c. Canadian Facts.

Five thousand miles underground. Rockwood, R., *pseud.* 60 c. Cupples & L.

Five thousand words frequently misspelt. Sonnenschein, W. S. 50 c. Dutton.

Five to twelve series. 6 v. '09(O2) il. D. ea., 75 c. Caldwell.

Five years of railroad regulation by the states. Huebner, G. G. 25 c. Am. Acad. Pol. Sci.

Flack, Anna Graham.
Democracy. '10(O15) c. 12°, 50 c. Cochrane.
Moral education. '10(S3) c. 12°, 50 c. Cochrane.

Flack, Horace Edg.
Adoption of the fourteenth amendment. '08 (D19) c. O. $2. Johns Hopkins.

Flagellates.
See Botany.

Flagg, Ja. Montgomery.
All in the same boat: [humorous verses.] '08(N14) c. il. D. bds., 75 c. Life Pub. Co.
City people; [cartoons of life in the city and suburbs;] sketches and caricatures of types of dwellers in cities. '09(N6) c. obl. 4°, bds., **$3.50 net. Scribner.

Flagg, J: H:
Lyrics of New England, and other poems. '09(D) c. 7-142 p. 8°, $1. W: J. Taylor.

Flags.
Bowron, E M. B. Our flag: its history. 50 c. H: S. Bowron.
Canby, G: Evolution of the American flag. $1. Ferris.
Champion, S. E. B. Our flag. $1. Tuttle, M. & T.
Fow, J: H: True story of the American flag. *50 c. net. W: J. Campbell.
Horner, H. H., *ed.* American flag. gratis. N. Y. State Educ.
Parry, O. R. Betsy Ross and the United States flag. 20 c.; 10 c. T. W. Worrall.
United States. *Congress Senate. Committee on Military Affairs.* American flag; hearing on bills to prevent desecration. '08, [1909.] (O) 15 p. 8°. (Add. Superintendent for price.) U. S., Supt. of Docs.
Waters' pocket flag manual, containing flags of American and Canadian yacht clubs. (Add. pubs. for price.) J. K. Waters Co.

Flame dancer. Mathews, F. A. †$1.50. G: W. Dillingham.

Flaming sword. Harrison, *Mrs.* E. O. *$1.25 net. McClurg.

Flamini, Francesco.
Introd. to the study of the Divine comedy; tr. by Freeman M. Josselyn; tr. rev. and augm. by the author. '10(D3) c. il. D. $1.25. **Ginn.**

Flamma, Ario.
Dramas. '10(Ja1) c. por. O. pap., $2. Flamma.

Flamsted Quarries. Waller, M. E. $1.50. Little, B. & Co.

Flanagan's library of travel. il. D. Flanagan.
—Koch. Little journey to northern wilds. 50 c.
—White *and* Smith. Little journey to South Africa. 50 c.

Flanders, Erwin Bixby.
Which? beer privilege anarchy or liberty with justice and prohibition? '08(Jl4) c. O. pap., 10 c. Flanders.

Flanders, Ralph E:
Bevel gearing. '09(Ag14) c. il. 8°, (Machinery's reference ser.) 25 c. Indust. Press.
Gear-cutting machinery; complete review of contemporary American and European practice. '09(Jl31) c. figs. 12°, $3. Wiley.

Flandrau, C: Macomb.
Viva Mexico!: [description of Mexico and Mexicans.] '08(O10) c. D. **$1.25 net. Appleton.

Flanigan, D: Willis, and Parker, C. I., comps.
Vaughan's practical review for law students; questions and answers. '09(My) c. 66 p. 12°, $5. D: W. Flanigan.

Flashlights from real life. Dale, J: T. $1. Fairfax Pub.

Flashlights of truth. Folk, D: H: $1. D: H: Folk.

Flashlights on evangelical history. Stapleton, *Rev.* A. $1. A. Stapleton.

FLATBUSH, N. Y.
See New York City.

FLATHEAD Co., Montana.
Views of the Mission Mountains, Flathead Lake and Valley, Montana; with pictures from the Flathead Indian reservation. $1. M. J. Elrod.

Flathead Indian reservation; acts relating to the reservation providing for the opening of the same to settlement. the construction of irrigating systems, and the disposal of the timber lands. '09(Ag21) 8°, pap. (Add. Superintendent for price.) U. S., Supt. of Docs.

Flather, J: Jos.
Transmission of power by leather belting, fibrous ropes and toothed gearing. '08 (Mr.14) c. il. 8°, *$1.35 net. H. W. Wilson.

Flatiron and the red cloak. Diaz, *Mrs.* A. M. **40 c. net. Crowell.

Flatiron for a farthing. *See* Ewing, *Mrs.* Juliana Horatia Gatty.

FLATS.
See Apartments;—Architecture.

Flaubert, Gustave.
Salammbô; ed. by E. Lauvrière. '09(Mr6) por. S. (Oxford higher French ser.) $1.15. Oxford Univ.
Stories by Flaubert; ed. by Arth. Ransome. '10(O8) 12°, (World's story teller ser.) 40 c. net. Dutton.
Temptation of St. Anthony; tr. by Lafcadio Hearn. '10(D17) c. D. $1.25. A. Harriman.

Flaw in the sapphire. Snyder, C: M. $1. Metropolitan Press, (N. Y.)

Flaws in classical research. Postgate, J: P. *$1.40 net. Oxford Univ.

FLAX.
Carter, H. R. Modern flax, hemp, and jute spinning and twisting. *$3 net. Van Nostrand.

FLEAS.
McCoy, G: W. Experimental investigation of biting of man by fleas, from rats and squirrels. (Add. Superintendent for price.) U. S., Supt. of Docs.

Fleay, F: Gard.
Chronicle hist. of the London stage, 1559-1642. Anastatic reprint of the London ed., 1890. '09(N20) tabs., O. *$6 net. Stechert.

Fleckenstein, Ninon Traver.
Widow's wisdom. '09(S18) c. il. S. 75 c. Caldwell.

Fleet street. Davidson, J: *$1 net. M. Kennerley.

Fleetwood, H:
Secret of life, death and immortality. '10 (Ja15) c. front. 12°, $1. H: Fleetwood.

Fleischmann, Maximilian C:
After big game in Arctic and tropic; sportsman's note-book of the chase off Greenland and Alaska; in Africa, Norway, Spitzbergen, and the Cassair. '09, [1910.] (Je) c. 247 p. il. 4°. (Priv. pr.) M. C: Fleishmann.

Fleisher's knitting and crocheting manual; complete illustrated hdbk. of the art, cont. clear instructions for every step—from the simplest stitches to elaborate garments; authoritative fashion book of articles made of yarns. 8th ed. '10(N) 189 p. il. 8°, 25 c. Fleisher.

Flem, pseud.
See Fleming, G: T.

Fleming, D: Hay.
The Reformation in Scotland; causes, characteristics and consequences; Stone lectures for 1907-1908. '10(D) 8°, $3 net. Doran.

Fleming, G:, pseud.
See Fletcher, Julia Constance.

Fleming, G: Elliott.
A beggar in evening dress. '08(S) c. 93 p. 8°. (Add. author for price.) G: E. Fleming.

Fleming, G: T., ["Flem."]
Flem's views of old Pittsburgh, precious with memories. '08, [1909.] (F) 80 p. 4°, 25 c. Flem Pub.

Fleming, H: Stuart.
Report on the present and future of the bituminous coal trade. '08(Ap.) c. 87 p. tabs., diagrs., 4°, bds., $5. H: S. Fleming.

Fleming, J: Ambrose.
Elem. manual of radiotelegraphy and radiotelephony. '08(N7) il. figs. O. *$2 net. Longmans.

FLEMING, Marjorie.
Wiley, K. Pet Marjorie and Sir Walter Scott. *$1 net; *75 c. net. Cochrane.

Fleming, Wa. Lynwood.
Ex-slave pension frauds; repr. from the *South Atlantic Quarterly.* '10(O) 15 p. 8°, (Louisiana State Univ. bull.) La. State Univ.
Jefferson Davis at West Point; repr. from publications of the Mississippi Historical Society. 10(Jl2) O. (Louisiana State Univ. bull.) pap. La. State Univ.
Jefferson Davis, the negroes and the negro problem. '08(D5) 8°, (La. State Univ. bull.) gratis. Wa. L. Fleming.
Religious and hospitable rite of feet washing; repr. from the *Sewanee Review* for January, 1908. '08(Ap11) 8°, gratis. W. L. Fleming.
Religious life of Jefferson Davis; repr. from the *Methodist Review.* '10(Jl2) O. (Louisiana State Univ. bull.) pap. La. State Univ.

Fleming, W: F., comp. and ed.
Physical culture classics. 4 v. '09(D25) c. il. 8°, per set, $15. E. R. Dumont.

Fleming, W: H:
Tariff, civil service, income tax, imperialism, the race problem, and other speeches. '09(Ap3) c. 4°, *$2.50 net. A. B. Caldwell.

FLEMISH ARTISTS.
See Artists;—Painters and painting.

Flemming, L: Andrew.
Pract. tanning. 2d ed., in great part rewritten, thoroughly rev. and much enl. '10(Ap9) c. il. 8°, $6 net. Baird.
Receipts and remedies; useful hints for everyone on health, beauty, clothing, food. '08(O3) c. S. (Popular handbooks.) 50 c. Penn Pub. Co.

Flesh and matter. Murray, S. V. 50 c. S. V. Murray.

Fleshless diet. Buttner, J. L. $1.35 net. Stokes.

Fleshman, Arth. Cary.
Educational process. '08(Jl18) c. D. (Lippincott's education ser.) $1.25. Lippincott.

Fletcher, Bannister F. and Herbert Phillips.
The English home; with introd. by the Duke of Argyll. '10(D3) il. 8°, $4 net. Scribner.

Fletcher, Beaumont.
Richard Wilson, R.A. '08(Je20) il. por. D. (Makers of British art.) *$1.25 net. Scribner.

Fletcher, C: Rob. Leslie, ["C. R. L. F.," pseud.]
Introductory history of England. In 4 v. [v. 3,] From the Restoration to the beginning of the great war; [v. 4,] The great European war. '09(Jl10) fold. maps, plans, O. ea., *$1.50 net. Dutton.
Mr. Gladstone at Oxford, 1890. '08(S19) 16°, *$1 net. Dutton.

Fletcher, Ella Adelia.
Law of the rhythmic breath; teaching the generation, conservation, and control of vital force. '08(N7) c. D. *$1 net. Fenno.

Fletcher, Giles and Phineas.
Poetical works; ed. by F: S: Boas. In 2 v. v. 1. '08(D12); v. 2. '09(My) facsims., 12°, (Cambridge English classics.) ea., *$1.50 net. Putnam.

Fletcher, H: F.
Ethics of conservation. '10(D24) c. D. pap., 10 c. H: F. Fletcher.

Fletcher, Herb. Phillips.
See Fletcher, Bannister, F.

Fletcher, Horace.
Optimism, a real remedy; with a foreword by W: Dana Orcutt. '08(F1) c. por. nar. D. 75 c. McClurg.

Fletcher, J. W.
Poems of the nineteenth century. '10(F19) c. por. D. 50 c. J. W. Fletcher.

Fletcher, J:
See Beaumont, Fs.

Fletcher, Jos. Smith.
Book about Yorkshire. '08(D19) il. O. (English countryside ser.) *$2 net. Doubleday, P.
Harvest moon. '08(N21) 12°, $1.50. J: McBride.
Mothers in Israel. '08(Mr14) c. D. †$1.50. Moffat.

Fletcher, Julia Constance, ["George Fleming."]
Kismet. '08(My.) c. 12°, (Popular ed. of recent fiction.) †75 c. Little, B. & Co.

Fletcher, Phineas.
See Fletcher, Giles.

Fletcher, R. A.
Steamships: the story of their development to the present day. '10(D3) il. 8°, $3.75 net. Lippincott.

Fletcher, W: And.
Rebel private, front and rear: experiences from the early fifties and through the Civil War. '08(S) c. 193 p. por. 8°, $1. Greer Pr.

Fletcher, W: I:, ed.
Annual library index, 1907. '08(Je6) c. O. **$3.50 net; 1908. '09(Ap10) $5 net; 1909. '10(Ap23) $5 net. Pub. Weekly.

—, and Poole, Mary, comps.
Poole's index to periodical literature; fifth supplement from January 1, 1902, to January 1, 1907. '08(Je20) c. 4°, $10; shp., $12; hf. mor., $14. Houghton M.

Fletcher, W: Meade.
See Illinois. Treatise on the incorporation and management of corporations.

Flexner, Abraham.
American college: a criticism. '08(N7) c. D. **$1 net. Century Co.
Medical education in the United States and Canada; rept. to the Carnegie Foundation; with introd. by H: S. Pritchett. '10(Jl2) c. Q. pap. Carnegie Found.

Flick, Alex. Clarence.
Rise of the mediæval church and its influence on the civilization of western Europe, from the first to the thirteenth century. '09(D11) c. O. **$3.50 net. Putnam.

Flick, Lawrence F., M.D.
Tuberculosis, a curable and preventable disease. '10(D) pap., 10 c. Winston.

FLIES.
Felt, E: P. Control of flies and other household insects. 15 c. N. Y. State Educ.
Hine, J. S. Robberflies of the genus *Asilus*. 50 c. J. S. Hine.
Merchants' Association of New York. House fly at the bar. gratis. Merchants' Assoc.
Miller, C: W. Occurrence of the larvæ of a parasitic fly, *Protocalliphora chryorrhoea* Meigen, in bird nests in the vicinity of Shawnee, Pa. gratis. Worthington Soc.
Townsend, C: H: T. Taxonomy of the *Muscoidean* flies. 60 c. Smith. Inst.
Williston, S: W. Manual of North American *Diptera*. $4. J. N. Hathaway.

FLIGHT.
See Aerial navigation;—Flying.

Flight of a soul. Esque, J. L: de. $1.50. Connoisseurs' Press.
Flights and fancies. Wickliffe, E. L. $2. E. L. Wickliffe.
Flights o' fancy. Simmons, L. $1; $1.75. Atlantis Press.
Flighty Arethusa. Foster, D: S. $1.50. Lippincott.

Fling, Fred Morrow.
Mirabeau and the French revolution. In 3 v. v. 1, The youth of Mirabeau. '08 (S12) c. il. pors. O. **$3.50 net. Putnam.
—, ed. Source studies on the French Revolution; tr. by Helen Dresser Fling. 2d ed. '07, [1908.] (Mr) c. 8°, 50 c. F. M. Fling.

Flint, G: Elliott.
Short cut. '09(My) c. 292 p. D. $1.50. Romance.

Flint, Lillian Cecilia.
Small gardens for small gardeners; or, what little hands can do with plants. '10 (My21) c. il. S. 50 c. Flanagan.

Flint heart. Phillpotts, E. $1.50. Dutton.
Flitch of bacon. Ainsworth, W: H. 50 c.; 75 c. Dutton.

Flom, G: Tobias.
History of Scandinavian studies in American universities; with a bibliography. '08(Ag8) 8°, (Iowa studies in language and lit.) pap., 50 c. Univ. of Ia.
Norwegian immigration to the United States. '09(N) (Priv. pr.) G: T. Flom.
—, ed. *See* Tegnér, Esaias.

Flood, L. L.
See Loughlin, Burren.

FLOODS.
Carnegie Library, Pittsburgh. Floods and flood protection. 15 c. Carnegie Lib.
Gibson, H: H. Oak flooring. 50 c. Hardwood Record.
Hall, W: L., *and* Maxwell, H. Surface conditions and stream flow. Gov. Pr. Off.
See also Meteorology.

FLOORS.
See Concrete.

FLORA.
See Botany.

Flora's fairies. Harper, *Mrs.* B. W. 50 c. Cochrane.

FLORE, *Madame*.
Jackson, F. Life of Madame Flore. *$1 net. Herder.

FLORENCE, Italy.
Biagi, G. Men and manners of old Florence. *$3.50 net; *$6.50 net. McClurg.
Cruttwell, M. Guide to the paintings in the churches and minor museums of Florence. *$1.25 net. Dutton.
Del Lungo, I. Women of Florence. *$2.25 net. Doubleday, P.
Hare, A: J: C. Florence; [also] Venice. $2. Macmillan.
Hutton, E: Country Walks about Florence. $1.50. Scribner.
Kellogg, V. L. In and out of Florence. $2.50 net. Holt.
Machiavelli, N. History of Florence. *35 c. net; *70 c. net. Dutton.
Machiavelli, N. Hist. of Florence. $1.75; $3.50. Lamb Pub.
Singleton, E., *comp. and ed.* Florence as described by great writers. $1.60 net. Dodd.
Staley, E. Famous women of Florence. $3.50. Scribner.
See also Medici, Lorenzo de.

Florence Gardiner sings. Milbank, J. H. $1.50. Goerck.
Florentine frame. Robins, E. †$1.50. Moffat.
Florentine painters. Berenson, B. **$1.50 net. Putnam.
Florentine sculptors of the Renaissance. Bode, W. *$4 net. Scribner.
Florentine tragedy. Wilde, O. *$1.25 net. J: W. Luce.

FLORICULTURE.
See Gardens and gardening.

Florida. *Supreme ct.* Digest of the decisions. vs. 40 to 57; by G: A. Choate. '10(D) c. O. shp., $12. F. H. Thomas.

FLORIDA.
Dimock, A. W. *and* Julian A. Florida enchantments. *$3 net. Outing.
Packard, W. Florida trails as seen from Jacksonville to Key West and from November to April, inclusive. $3 net. Small.
Short, P. Brief acct. of journeys in the western country, 1809-1812. Hist. and Phil. Soc. O.
Smith, S: R. Reclamation of the Florida everglades. gratis. Miami Pr.
Standard guide, Florida. '10(Ap) c. 100 p. il. fold. map, 8°, 25 c. Foster & R.
Willson, *Mrs.* M. M-. Seminoles of Florida. **$1.25 net. Moffat.
See also St. Augustine.

Florida. *See* Apuleuis, Lucius. Apologia.
Floridian sonnets. Venable, W: H: $1. Badger.
Florist's scrap book. '09(Ap10) c. S. pap., $1. J: C. Moninger.

Flory, Jacob Stoner.
Love's sweet dream fully realized through holy matrimony and a sanctified home. '08, [1909.] (My) c. 5-174 p. 12°, 50 c. Higher Life.

Flory, J: S:
Literary activity of the German Baptist Brethren in the eighteenth century. '08 (Ag1) c. 8°, $1.25. Brethren Pub. Ho.

Flosser, Fk.
Brief hist. of the U. S. Soldiers' Home, Washington, D. C. '09, [1910.] (F) 11+5 p. 12°, pap., 25 c. H. B. Darling.

FLOUR.
Bates, J. H: Miller's guide book. $1. Dixie Miller.
United States. *Dept. of Commerce and Labor.* Flour and wheat trade in European countries and the Levant. (Add. Superintendent for price.)
See also Commerce.

FLOUR-MILLS.
Lawson, P. V. Invention of the roller flour mill. 25 c. State Hist., Wis.

Flow of water. Schmeer, L: **$3 net. Van Nostrand.

Flower, B: Orange.
Christian science as a religious belief and a therapeutic agent. '10(Ja29) c. 12°, $1. Twentieth Century.

Flower, Jessie Graham.
Grace Harlowe's plebe year at high school; or, the merry doings of the Oakdale freshman girls. '10(D24) il. 12°, (High school girls ser.) $1. Altemus.

Flower and thorn. Mifflin, L. $1. Oxford Univ.
Flower fables. Alcott, L. M. $1. McLoughlin.
Flower family. Middleton, C. S. 60 c. Aberdeen.
Flower o' the grass. Murray, A. F. $1.25 net. Harper.
Flower o' the Orange. Castle, *Mrs.* A. S. †$1.50. Macmillan.
Flower of destiny. Mordecai, M. $1.50 net. Putnam
Flower of the dusk. *See* Reed, Myrtle.
Flower of the mind. Meynell, *Mrs.* A. C. T. $1.50 net. Lane.
Flower Queen. Barri, O. 20 c. Am. Bk.

Flowerdew, Herb.
Second elopement. '10(N5) D. $1.50. Brentano's.

Flowers, W: T:
Farmer, and his relation to the country, the manufacturing, the speculative and political world. '08, [1909.] (F) c. 111 p. 8°, pap., 50 c. W: T: Flowers.

FLOWERS.
Armfield, C. Flower book. $2. Warne.
Baily, W: L. Trees, plants and flowers. 60 c. Lippincott.
Beecroft, W. I., *comp.* Who's who among the wild flowers. **$1.20 net. Moffat.
Curtis, C: H. Book of the flower show. $1 net. Lane.
Felton, R. F. British floral decoration. $2.50 net. Macmillan.
Florist's scrap book. $1. J: C. Moninger.
Hastings, S. Summer flowers on the high Alps. $2.50 net. Dutton.
Hulme, F: E: Familiar Swiss flowers. *$3 net. Cassell.
Keeler, H. L. Our garden flowers. $2 net. Scribner.
Longyear, B. O. Rocky Mountain wild flower studies. $1. Merchants' Pub.
Ramaley, F. Wild flowers and trees of Colorado. $1.25; $1. A. A. Greenman.

FLOWERS.—*Continued.*
Reed, C. A. Flower guide: wild flowers east of the Rockies. $1 net.—Wild flowers. $2.50 net. Doubleday, P.
Stack, F. W: Wild flowers every child should know. $1.20. Doubleday, P.
Wright, H. J. *and* W. P. Beautiful flowers and how to grow them. $8 net. Dodge.
Wright, W. P. Popular garden flowers. $2 net. Clode.
See also Alphabets;—Bindweed;—Botany;—Clover;—Daffodils;—Easter lily;—Gardens and gardening;—Orchids; — Pansies;—Peonies;—Roses;—Sweet peas;—Violets;—*also* California.

Flowers (The). Gerry, M. S. 50 c. net. Harper.
Flowers and gardens of Madeira. Du Cane, F. *$2 net. Macmillan.
Flowers of Parnassus. il. 6°. Lane.
—Phillips. Marpessa. 50 c. net; 75 c. net.

Floy, H:
Compilation of the records of the Colorado Springs lighting controversy. '08(F) c. 327 p. il. diagrs., 8°, $4. Illuminating Engineering.
High-tension underground electric cables. '09(My22) c. il. tabs., 12°, $2. Elec. Pub.

Floyd, F: Clark.
History of the Fortieth (Mozart) regiment, New York Volunteers, which was composed of four companies from New York, four companies from Massachusetts and two companies from Pennsylvania. '09 (Ap3) c. il. facsims., pors. O. $3. F: C. Floyd.

Floyd, G. C.
See Gale, Norman Bingham Clifton.

Fluch (Der) der schönheit. Riehl, W. H. v. 40 c. Ginn.

Fluegel, Maurice.
Exodus, Moses and the Decalogue legislation; central doctrine and regulative organum of Mosaism. '10(Mr5) c. 8°, $2. M. Fluegel.
Humanity, benevolence and charity legislation of the Pentateuch and the Talmud; in parallel with the laws of Hammurabi, the doctrine of Egypt, the Roman XII tables and modern codes. '08(Ag29) c. 8°, *$2 net. M. Fluegel.

FLUORSPAR.
Fohs, F. J. Fluorspar deposits in Kentucky; with notes on the production, mining and technology of the mineral in the U. S. 80 c. Kentucky State Lib.

Flurscheim, A.
Working hints for suction gas producers. '09(Mr13) il. 12°, bds., *50 c. net. Spon.

Flürscheim, Michael.
Economic and social problem. '09(D) 277 p. por. 8°, 25 c. Jefferson.

Flury, Elise.
Pract. hints on education to parents and teachers; tr. from her orig. German work. '10(Jl30) 12°, 75 c. net. Benziger.

FLUTE.
Boehm, T. Flute and flute playing. $1.50. D. C. Miller.

Flute of the gods. Ryan, *Mrs.* M. E. M. **$1.50 net. Stokes.

Flutterfly. Burnham, *Mrs.* C. L. R. †75 c. Houghton M.

Flux, Alfr. W:
Swedish banking system. '10(Ag) 248 p. diagr. 8°. Gov. Pr. Off.

Fly-aways and other seed travelers. Fultz, F. M. 60 c. Pub. Sch. Pub.

Fly fishing in wonderland. Barnes, O. P. $1. O. P. Barnes.

Fly-leaves from a fisherman's diary. Sharp, G. E. $1.40 net. Longmans.

Fly on the wheel. Thurston, *Mrs.* K. C. †$1.50. Dodd.

Fly wheels. '09(Jl31) c. diagrs., 8°, (Machinery's reference ser.) pap., 25 c. Indust. Press.

FLYING.
Dewar, G: A. B. Airy way. $1.75 net. Macmillan.
See also Aerial navigation.

Flying death. Adams, S: H. †$1.50. McClure.

Flying Dutchman. Hadden, J. C., *comp.* 50 c.; $1. Stokes.

FLYING MACHINES.
See Aerial navigation.

Flying Mercury. Ingram, E. M. $1.50. Bobbs-M.

Flying Plover. Roberts, G: E: T. $1. L. C. Page.

Flynn, Paul Vincent.
History of St. John's church, Newark; a memorial of the golden jubilee of its consecration; with a retrospect of the progress of Catholicity. '09(Ap10) c. il. pors. 8°, $3. P. V. Flynn.

Flynt, Josiah, [pseud. for Josiah Flynt Willard.]
My life; with an introd. by Arth. Symons. '08(O24) c. pors. O. *$2 net. Outing.

FODDER.
See Clover; — Ensilage; — Farms and farming; — Feeding and feeding stuffs.

Fogarty, Ja. H:
Priest and parson. '08(Je13) c. 12°, *$1.25 net. Chr. Press.

Fogazzaro, Antonio.
Pereat Rochus, and Un' idea di Ermes Torranza; ed., with introd., notes and vocabulary. '09(My15) c. S. (Modern lang. ser.) 40 c. Heath.
The politician; tr. by G. Mantellini. '08 (F8) c. D. $1.50. J: W. Luce.

Fogg, Mrs. Adna James, ed.
Fogg family in America. '07, [1908.] (Ag) front. 8°, hf. mor., $1.58. J. L. M. Willis.

Fogg, Mary Lape, comp.
See Bible. N. T. Life of Christ.

FOGG FAMILY
See Genealogies.

Foght, Harold Waldstein.
American rural school; its characteristics, its future and its problems. '10(My14) c. D. $1.25 net. Macmillan.

Fogle, Humphrey Marshall.
Palace of death; or, the Ohio Penitentiary Annex; human-interest story of the incarceration and execution of Ohio's murderers, with a detailed review of the incidents connected with each case. '08, [1909.] (My) c. 278 p. il. pors. 8°, $1. Fogle.

Fohlin, Ernest V.
Salt Lake City, past and present. '09(S11) c. il. pors. 8°, $1.25; pap., 75 c. E. V. Fohlin.

Fohs, F. Julius.
Fluorspar deposits of Kentucky; with notes on the production, mining, and technology of the mineral in the United States, also some data concerning barite deposits. '07, [1909.] (S) 3-4+296 p. maps, 4°, (Kentucky geological survey.) 80 c. Kentucky State Lib.

Folcarinia. Warner, A. D. (Add. pubs. for price.) Smith-B

Folded meanings. Hosmer, S. H. C. $1. Badger.

Foley, G: Cadwalader.
Anselm's theory of the atonement; the Bohlen lectures, 1908. '09(F6) c. D. **$1.50 net. Longmans.

Foley, Ja. W:
Verses; songs with silver linings. [1910.] (Je) c. 100 p. 4°, $2 net. Hoskins.
Verses; Sunshine and song. '09, [1910.] (F) c. 87 p. 4°. o. p. J. W: Foley.

Foley, J: Thaddeus, ["Consistency."]
With King James' Bible as exclusive authority can the Protestant Christian question the eucharist? '09(Ag21) c. D. $1.50. Pilot Co.

Foli, P. R. S.
Fortune telling by cards. '10(O) 12°, 50 c. Fenno.

Foligus, Caesare.
Padua. '10(Ap23) il. 12°, (Mediæval towns ser.) $1.75 net; leath., $2.25 net. Dutton.

Folk, D: H:
Flash lights of truth. [1910.] (D) 155 p. O. pap., $1. D: H: Folk.

Folk, Edg. Estes.
Baptist principles; letters to my son. '09 (D) c. 308 p. por. 12°, $1. S. S. B., So. Bapt.

Folk, Mrs. H: B.
See Folk, Martha F.

Folk, Jos. Wingate.
Era of conscience: address del. before the Civic Forum. '08(D5) por. 12°, (Civic Forum addresses.) pap., 10 c. Civic Forum.

Folk, Martha F., [Mrs. H: B. Folk.]
Heart thoughts: papers and addresses. '09 (Ja16) c. por. D. **75 c. net. Am. Bapt.

FOLK DANCING.
See Dancing.

FOLK LORE.
Boston Public Library. Finding lists of fairy tales and folk stories in books at the branches of the Public Library of the City of Boston. 5 c. Boston Pub. Lib.
Dayrell, E. Folk stories from Southern Nigeria. $1.50. Longmans.
Gask, L. Folk tales from many lands. $1.50 net. Crowell.
Grierson, *Mrs.* E. W. Children's book of Celtic stories. *$2 net. Macmillan.
Honey, J. A. South African folk-tales. $1 net. Baker & T.
Judson, K. B., *comp.* Myths and legends of the Pacific northwest. $1.50 net. McClurg.

FOLK LORE.—*Continued.*
Kidd, D. Bull of the Kraal and the heavenly maidens. *$2 net. Macmillan.
Kurtz, B: P. Studies in the marvellous. $2. Univ. of Cal.
Lawson, J. C. Modern Greek folklore and ancient Greek religion. $4 net. Putnam.
Mabie, H. W., *ed.* Folk tales every child should know. 90 c. net. Doubleday, P.
Marshall, F. Cat school: folk lore story. —Nixie well; the goat and the troll. ea., *30 c. net. Educ. Pub.
O'Sheridan, M. G Gaelic folk tales. 60 c. M. G. O'Sheridan.
Ruskin, J: Dame Wiggins and her seven wonderful cats. *30 c. net. Educ. Pub.
Williams, H. Fairy tales from folk-lore. **$1 net. Moffat.
See also Archæology; — Fables; — Fairy tales; — Games;—Japan;—Legends;—Manners and customs;—Mythology;—New England.

Folk-lore ser. il. 12°, *30 c. net. Educ. Pub.
—Marshall. Cat school.—Nixie well.
—Ruskin. Dame Wiggins and her seven wonderful cats.

Folk-memory. Johnson, W. $4.15. Oxford Univ.

FOLK MUSIC.
See Music.

FOLK-SONGS.
See Songs.

Folks back home. Wood, E. †$1.50. McClure.

Follett, Mary Parker.
Speaker of the House of Representatives; with introd. by Alb. Bushnell Hart. '09, [1910.] (Jl) 26+378 p. 12°, $1.75 net. Longmans.

Follett, Mrs. Susan Jennette.
The two Marys: a retrospect; a tribute. '09(S) c. 46 p. 16°, 75 c. Arts and Crafts.

Following the color line. Baker, R. S. **$2 net. Doubleday, P.

Following the Conquistadores. *See* Mozans, H. J., *pseud.*

Following the flag. Coffin, C: C. 50 c. Hurst.

Follows, G: Herbert.
Essentials of descriptive geometry. '08 (O10) il. 8°, *$2 net. Hill Pub.

Folly of building temples of peace with untempered mortar. Bigelow, J: $1 net. B: W. Huebsch.

Folsom, C: Follen.
Studies of criminal responsibility and limited responsibility. '09(Ag7) pors. 8°. (Priv. pr.) C: F. Folsom.

Foltz, El Bie Kean.
Federal civil service as a career. '09 (Mr20) c. D. **$1.50 net. Putnam.

Folwell, Amory Prescott.
Sewerage: designing, construction and maintenance of sewerage systems. 6th ed., rev. and enl. 10(Jl30) c. il. 8°, $3. Wiley.

Folwell, W: Watts.
Minnesota, the North Star state. '08(O24) c. map, D. (American commonwealths.) **$1.25 net. Houghton M.
University addresses. '10(Mr12) c. 12°, *$1 net H. W. Wilson.

Fontaine, Lamar.
My life and my lectures. '08(Je6) c. por. O. $3. Neale.

Fontaine, Marie Louise P.
Les facheux: comédie en un acte. '08(F29) c. 12°, pap., 25 c. W: R. Jenkins.

FONTAINEBLEAU, France.
See France.

Fontes prosae nvmerosae. Clark, A. C., *comp.* $1.50. Oxford Univ.

FONTS
See Church decoration and ornament.

FOOD.
Abel, *Mrs.* M. W. H. Care of food in the home. Gov. Pr. Off.
American School of Home Economics. Food values; pract. methods in diet calculations. 10 c. Am. Sch. Home Economics.
Benedict, A. L. Golden rules of dietetics. $3. Mosby.
Bevier, I., *and* Usher, S. Food and nutrition. *$1 net. Whitcomb.
Bigelow, W. D. Food legislation during the year ended June 30, 1907. (Add. Superintendent for price.) U. S., Supt. of Docs.
Brown, G. Scientific nutrition simplified. *75 c. net. Stokes.
Brown, *Mrs.* L. N. Scientific living for prolonging the term of human life. $1. Health-Culture.
Browne, *Sir* J. C.- Parcimony in nutrition. **75 c. net. Funk.
Carrington, H. Vitality, fasting and nutrition. $5. Rebman.
Clayton, E. G., *comp.* Compendium on food microscopy. *$4 net. Wood.
Eales, I. J. Healthology (health study). $1.50. I. J. Eales.
Fletcher, H. Optimism, a real remedy. 75 c. McClurg.
Food and diet: priced list of public documents rel. to food and diet issued by scientific bureaus of the United States Government. 2d ed. '08, [1909.] (My) 27 p. 8°, pap., gratis. U. S., Supt. of Docs.
Frear, W:, *and others.* Breakfast foods: investigation of breakfast foods, [etc.] Harrisburg Pub.
Friedenwald, J., *and* Ruhräh, J. Diet in health and disease. $4.—Dietetics for nurses *$1.50 net. Saunders.
Gibbs, W. S. Lessons in proper feeding of the family. 25 c. Assoc. Imp. Con. Poor.
Greenish, H: G: Microscopical examination of food and drugs. $3. Blakiston.
Hall, W. S. Nutrition and dietetics. **$2 net. R. Appleton.
Hills, J. L., *and others.* Dietary studies in rural regions in Vermont, Tennessee and Georgia. Gov. Pr. Off.
Hogan, L. E. S. Children's diet in home and school. 75 c. net. Doubleday, P.
Hunt, C. L. Daily meals of children. (Add. Superintendent for price.) U. S., Supt. of Docs.
James, A. Catering for two. $2; $5. Putnam.

FOOD.—*Continued.*

Jamestown Exposition. Eleventh annual conference of the Association of State and National Food and Dairy Departments, held at Jamestown Tercentennial Exposition. $3. Wiley.

Kelley, F: Treatise on food and egg production. $1. F: Kelley.

Kellogg, J: H. Battle Creek Sanitarium diet list. 25 c. Modern Medicine.

Leach, A. E. Food inspection and analysis. $7.50. Wiley.

Lusk, G. Elements of the science of nutrition. *$3 net. Saunders.

Macewen, H. A. Food inspection. $2.50 net. Van Nostrand.

Moss, J. A. Story of a troop mess. 75 c. U. S. Infantry.

Norton, *Mrs.* A. P. Food and dietetics. $1.25. Am. Sch. Home Economics.

Organization work, and publications of food and nutrition investigations. gratis. U. S., Supt. of Docs.

Pattee, A. F. Pract. dietetics with ref. to diet in disease. $1.50 net. A. F. Pattee.

Pope, A. E., *and* Carpenter, M. L. Essentials of dietetics in health and disease. *$1 net. Putnam.

Read, C. S. On fads and feeding. *$1 net. Dutton.

Rhode Island pure food and drug act. (Add. pubs for price.) E. L. Freeman.

Richards, *Mrs.* E. H. S. Cost of food. $1. Wiley.

Richards, *Mrs.* E. H. S., *and* Woodman, A. G. Air, water, and food from a sanitary standpoint. $2. Wiley.

Sherman, H: C., *and others.* Calcium, magnesium, and phosphorus in food and nutrition. Gov. Pr. Off.

Snyder, H. Human foods and their nutritive value. *$1.25 net. Macmillan.

Snyder, S. P., *comp.* Treatise on foods and their effects upon health and the physical and moral life. $1. Health.

Strohecker, C. Royal road to health. $1. C. Strohecker.

Sutherland, G. A., *ed.* System of diet and dietetics. *$9.25 net. Oxford Univ.

Thompson, W. G. Practical dietetics, with reference to diet in diseases. $5. Appleton.

United States. *Dept. of Agriculture. Bu. of Chemistry.* Bulletins, circulars and food inspection decisions of the Chemistry Bureau. gratis.

United States. *Dept. of Agriculture.* Influence of sodium benzoate on the nutrition and health of man. (Add. Superintendent for price.)

United States. *Dept. of Agriculture. Office of Experiment Stations.* Dietary studies in public institutions in Philadelphia, Pa.

United States. *Dept. of Commerce and Labor. Bu. of Labor.* Increase in cost of food and other products.

United States. *Superintendent of Documents.* Food and diet; price list. gratis.

FOOD.—*Continued.*

Yeo, I. B. Food in health and disease. $2.50 net. Funk.

See also Bacteria;—Beans;—Beef trust;—Beverages;—Bread;—Butter;—Cereals;—Children;—Cookery;—Digestion;—Domestic animals;—Fasting;—Fruit;—Hygiene;—Meat;—Metabolism;—Milk;—Nuts;—Oysters;—Preserving;—Prices;—Proteids;—Spices;—Temperance;—Vegetarianism.

FOOD ADULTERATION.

United States. *Dept. of Agriculture. Board of Food and Drug Inspection.* Regulations and decisions concerning guaranties and serial numbers, and their use. [1910.] (Je) 13 p. 8°.

Wells, E. M. Guide to legal labels in compliance with the Food and Drug Act. $3. E. M. Wells.

See also Maple syrup.

Food and nutrition investigations of the Office of Experiment Stations—organization and publication. '10(D) 22 p. 8°, (U. S., Dept. of Agriculture; Office of Experiment Stations; circular.)

Food as a medicine in the cure of disease. '09(Ap17) S. pap., 25 c.; 12 nos., $2. H. A. Yergin.

Food preservation: statement of facts in the case, together with references to the authorities. '10(Jl16) 12°, 50 c. Pub. Health.

Food tract, its ailments and disease. Blackwood, A. L. $1.50. Boericke & T.

Fool of quality. Brooke, H: 2 v. *$1 net. Lane.

Fool (A) there was. Browne, P. E. $1.50. H. K. Fly.

Foolish questions. Goldberg, R. L. **50 c. net. Small.

Foord, Alfr. Stanley.

Springs, streams and spas of London-history and associations. '10(N19) il. O. $3.50 net. Stokes.

Foot, Constance M.

Insect wonderland. '10(My14) il. D. $1.25 net. Lane.

Foot, F: Norman.

Baking powder and other leavening agents. [1910.] (Ja) c. '09. 7-86 p. il. 12°, $1.50. Spice Mill.

FOOT.

Witkowski's atlas of bones of foot. *$3 net. W: R. Jenkins.

FOOT-AND-MOUTH DISEASE.

See Veterinary medicine and surgery.

FOOT-BALL.

Camp, W. C. Book of foot-ball. $2 net. Century Co.

Camp, W. C., *ed.* How to play foot ball. —Official foot ball guide, 1908, 1909. ea., 10 c. Am. Sports.

Graham, T: W. Universal foot ball and hand ball. 20 c. T: W. Graham.

"Old International," *pseud.* How to play Rugby. 10 c. Am. Sports.

Short, C: W., *jr.* Digest of the foot ball rules for 1910. 10 c. Am. Sports.

Spalding's official Rugby foot ball guide. '10(N) front., il. pors. 16°, (Spalding's athletic lib.) 10 c. Am. Sports.

Foot prints on the sands of time. Alexander, J. B. 50 c. J. B. Alexander.

Football boys of Lakeport. Stratemeyer, E: †$1.25. Lothrop, L. & S.

Foote, Allen Ripley.
Speech del. before Wisconsin legislature, June 5, 1907: [public utilities bills of Wisconsin and New York.] '07, [1908.] (Mr.) 21 p. 8°. (Add. author for price.) A. R. Foote.
Foote, Anna Eliz., and Skinner, Avery Warner.
Makers and defenders of America. '10 (D17) c. D. (Eclectic readings.) 60 c. Am. Bk.
Foote, E: Milton.
Text-book of minor surgery. 2d ed.; il. by 407 engravings from original drawings and photographs. '09(D) 7+27-752 p. il. 8°, *$5 net. Appleton.
Foote, J: Alexander.
Essentials of materia medica and therapeutics for nurses. '10(O) c. 5-7+9-194 p. 12°, $1.25. Lippincott.
Foote, Mrs. Mary Hallock.
Royal Americans. '10(Ap16) c. D. $1.25 net. Houghton M.
Footlight rhymes. Hines, *Mrs.* E. R. $1. B'way Pub.
Footprint (The). Morris, G: †$1.50. Scribner.
Footprints in the snow. Tatham, H. F. W. $1.50 net. Macmillan.
Footprints of Abraham Lincoln. Hobson, J. T. 50 c. Un. B. Pub.
Footprints of the centuries. Gearhart, G: A. $1. L. L. Gearhart.
Footsteps in a parish. Stone, J: T. **75 c. net. Scribner.
Footsteps in the path of life. Dods, M. $1.25 net. Doran.
Footsteps in the ward. Capes, H. M. 50 c. net. Herder.
Footsteps of Scott. Crockett, S: R. *$1.25 net. Jacobs.
FOPPA, Vincenzo.
Ffoulkes, C. J., *and* Maiocchi, R. Vincento Foppa of Brescia, founder of the Lombard School. *$25 net. Lane.
For Charles the Rover. Wynne, M. $1.50. Fenno.
For Christmas day. Bushnell, C. C. 50 c.; 40 c. C. C. Bushnell.
For God and the people. Rauschenbusch, W. $1 net. Pilgrim Press.
For high schools; part songs. Aiken, W. H., *comp. and ed.* 65 c. Am. Bk.
For home department workers. Fergusson, E. M. 10 c. Westminster.
For Jacinta. Bindloss, H. †$1.50. Stokes.
For joy's sake. Seekings, H. S. *50 c. net. Jennings.
For Lilias. Carey, R. N. 50 c. Hurst.
For love of our Lord: series of devotional papers. '09(Ap10) *40 c. net. Young Churchman.
For love of you. Tuck, C. E. 75 c. B. F. Bowen.
For my name's sake. Campol, F. $1.10. Herder.
For the gaiety of nations. Rice, W. de G. C., *comp.* *50 c. net. Dodge.
For the interest of the traveller ser. See James, Juliet Lumbard.
For the King's sake. Blanchard, F. Q. 35 c. F. Q. Blanchard.
For the liberty of Texas. Stratemeyer, E: †$1.25. Lothrop, L. & S.
For the life that now is. Lyon, M. H. 75 c. Revell.
For the love of Lady Margaret. Wilson, W: T. $1.50. Stone & B.
For the Norton name. Godfrey, H. †$1.25. Little, B. & Co.
For the stars and stripes. Tomlinson, E. T. †$1.50. Lothrop, L. & S.
For you and for me. Hale, A., *pseud.* *$1.25 net. Campion.
Forbes, Mrs. A. S. C.
See Forbes, Harrie Rebecca Piper Smith.
Forbes, Edg. Allen.
Land of the white helmet; lights and shadows across Africa. '10(D10) c. 8°, $1.50 net. Revell.
Forbes, G:
Hist. of astronomy. '09(D11) c. pors. S. (Hist. of the sciences.) **75 c. net. Putnam.
Forbes, Harrie Rebecca Piper Smith, ["Mrs. A. S. C. Forbes."]
Mission tales in the days of the dons. '09 (Ap17) c. il. O. $1.50. McClurg.
Forbes, Ja.
See Harding, J: W:
Forbes, Stephen Alfr.
On the general and interior distribution of Illinois fishes. '09, [1910.] (Je) 56 p. 4°, (Ill. State Lab'y of Natural Hist. bull.) pap., $1. Ill. Lab'y Nat. Hist.
—, and Richardson, Rob. Earl.
The fishes of Illinois. '09(O) 131+357 p. il. f°, (Natural History Survey of Illinois; State Laboratory of Natural History.) With atlas. Exchange or gratis. Ill. Lab'y Nat Hist.
Forbes, W. B., ["Maintop."]
Hounds, gentlemen, please. '10(D) il. 8°, $3.75 net. Doran.
Forbes-Leith, W:
See Leith, W: Forbes-.
Forbidden ground. Watson, G. $1.35. Lane.
Forbidden guests. *See* Corbin, J: Husband.
Forbidden road. Anbanesi, E. A. M. 75 c. Cupples & L.
Forbush, W: Byron.
Broadening path: treasure book for boys and girls, together with Firelight and children's faces: book of help for fathers and mothers; with editorial assistance by G. L. Howe. In 2 v. '08(Ap4) c. il. pors. O. $5; hf. leath., $8. B. F. Bowen.
Church work with boys. '10(N5) c. D. bds., 50 c. net. Pilgrim Press.
—, and Masseck, Fk. Lincoln.
Boys' round table; manual of the international Order of the Knights of King Arthur. 8th ed., rewritten. '10(Je) c. 202 p. il. plan, 8°, 90 c. Knights King Arthur.
Boys' round table; a manual of the international order of the Knights of King Arthur. 6th ed. '08(D) c. 188 p. il. 12°, $1. F. L. Masseck.
Force of the wind. Chatley, H. *$1.25 net. Lippincott.

Forchheimer, F:, M.D.
Prophylaxis and treatment of internal diseases. '08(F1); 2d ed. '10(O) c. tabs., 8°, subs., ea., $5. Appleton.

Forcing book. Bailey, L. H. **$1.25 net. Macmillan.

Ford, Abbie A.
John Pierpont; biographical sketch. '09 (N) 25 p. pl. pors. 4°. (Priv. pr.) J. A. Crosby.

Ford, E. A.
Blessed Joan of Arc; complete story of her wonderful life, her tragic death, her rehabilitation, her beatification. '10 (Ap) il. 12°, $1 net. Chr. Press.

Ford, Fs. Chipman.
Hdbk. of regional anatomy. '10(O) 193 p. 12°, $1.50. F. C. Ford.

Ford, G: B.
See Marsh, B: Clarke.

Ford, H:
600 business law points for the business man, banker, lawyer, professional man, and farmer. '10(Jl16) c. 8°, $3.50. H: Ford.

Ford, H: Jones.
Cost of our national government. '10 (D31) 12°, (Columbia Univ. lectures, George Blumenthal foundation.) $1.60 net. Lemcke.

Ford, Julia Ellsworth.
King Solomon and the fair Shulamite: a poetic idyl arranged in sequence. '08 (My16) c. il. *$1.50 net. F. F. Sherman.
Simeon Solomon: an appreciation. '09(Ag) 77 p. il. 4°, *$3.50 net. F. F. Sherman.

Ford, Sewell.
Cherub Devine. '10(D) il. 75 c. Grosset.
Cherub Devine. '09(My8) c. D. $1.50. M. Kennerley.
Honk, honk!!, Shorty McCabe at the wheel. '09(D4) c. front. il. S. 50 c. M. Kennerley.
Just horses. '10(My21) c. D. $1 net. M. Kennerley.
Side-stepping with Shorty. '08(My9) c. 12°, $1.50. M. Kennerley.

Ford, Stephen V. R., ed.
See Methodist year book.

Ford, Webster.
Songs and sonnets. '10(O15) c. D. bds., $1. Rooks Press.

Ford, W: Ebenezer.
See Dana, E: Salisbury.

Ford, Worthington Chauncey.
Campaign of 1844; [repr. from the Proceedings of the Amer. Antiquarian Society, Oct., 1909.] '10(Jl16) 8°, 50 c. Davis Press.
George Washington. '10(D17) c. T. (Beacon biographies.) 50 c. net. Small.

—, and Matthews, Albert.
Bibliography of the laws of the Massachusetts Bay, 1641-1776. '07, [1909.] (Mr) 5+186 p. 8°. (Priv. pr.) Univ. Press, (Camb.)

—, ed. *See* United States. Continental Congress. Journals.

Forder, Archibald.
Adventures among the Arabs in desert, tent, and town. '09(Jl) 12°, $1. Gospel Pub.

Fordham University Press ser. O. Fordham Univ.
—O'Reilly *and* Walsh. Makers of electricity. *$2 net.

Ford's travelers' and shippers' guide book "A" of New York State. '10(Je) c. 124 p. 16°, $1.50. H. M. Ford.

Fordyce, Dingwall.
Hygiene of infancy and childhood and the underlying factors of disease. '10(N) 300 p. 8°, $2.50 net. Wood.

Fore! the call of the links. Webling, W. H. 75 c. Caldwell.

FOREIGN EXCHANGE.
See Exchange.

Foreign mission study courses. il. 12°. Young People's Miss.
—Neely. South America. 50 c.; 35 c.

FOREIGN MISSIONS.
See Missions and missionaries.

Foreign religious ser.; ed. by R. J. Cooke. S. *40 c. net. Eaton & M.
—Bachmann. New message of Jesus.
—Barth. Gospel of St. John.
—Beth. Miracles of Jesus.
—Feine. St. Paul as a theologian.
—Grützmacher. Virgin birth.
—Lemme. Do we need Christ in communion with God?
—Meyer. Sinlessness of Jesus.
—Müller. Our Lord: belief in the deity of Christ.
—Orelli. Peculiarity of the religion of the Bible.
—Riggenbach. Resurrection of Jesus.
—Von Hase. New Testament parallels in Buddhistic literature.

Foreign trade and yacht club directory. National Association of Engine and Boat Manufacturers. (Not for sale.) Nat. Assoc. Engine and Boat Manufact.

Foreigner (The). Gordon, C: W: $1.50. Doran.

Forel, Auguste Henri, M.D.
Hypnotism; or, suggestion and psychotherapy; tr. from the 5th German ed., by H. W. Armit. Am. ed., rev. and cor. '08 (Ja4) 8°, $2.50. Rebman.
Sexual question; Eng. adaptation by C. F. Marshall. '08(Je6) c. il. O. *$5 net. Rebman.

FORENSIC PRACTICE.
See Law.

Forerunners of Dante. Butler, A. J:, *ed.* $2. Oxford Univ.

"Forest, Gale," pseud.
See Reinertsen, Emma May Alexander.

Forest and town. De Merril, A. N. $1.25 net. Torch Press.

Forest foundling. Hamer, S. H. $1. Estes

FOREST INSECTS.
See Insects.

Forest land of Penn. Spangenberg, *Mrs.* F. I. $1.50. Badger.

Forest life and sport in India. Eardley-Wilmot, S. $3.50 net. Longmans.

Forest runners. Altsheler, J. A. †$1.50. **Appleton.**

FORESTS AND FORESTRY.
Ammons, E. M. Forest reservations. Gov. Pr. Off.
Carter, E: E. Methods of increasing forest productivity. Gov. Pr. Off.
Cary, A. Manual for northern woodsmen. *$2 net. Harvard Univ.
Chittenden, H. M. Forests and reservoirs in their relation to stream flow. $1.50. Am. Soc. Civil Engineers.
Cleveland, T., *jr.* Status of forestry in the United States. (Add. Superintendent for price.) U. S., Supt. of Docs.
Cook, H. O. How to make improvement thinnings in Mass. woodlands. F. W. Rane.
Fernow, B. E. Brief hist. of forestry in Europe, the United States and other countries. $2.50. Forest Quarterly.
Fetherolf, J. M. Forest planting on the northern prairies. 15 c. U. S., Supt. of Docs.
Foreign trade of the United States in forest products, 1851-1908. '09, [1910.] (Mr) 32 p. tabs., 8°, (U. S., Dept. of Agriculture, Bu. of Statistics, bull.) pap.
Graves, H: S. Protection of forests from fire. Gov. Pr. Off.
Hawes, A. F. Forest fires in Vermont. gratis. A. F. Hawes.
Holmes, J: S., *and* Foster, J. H. Study of forest conditions of southwestern Miss., Jan., 1908. 25 c. Brandon Pr.
Kellogg, R. S. Forests of Alaska.—Forest planting in Illinois. Gov. Pr. Off.
Langdell, R. S. Forest nursery and reforestation work in Massachusetts. F. W. Rane.
Massachusetts. Forest laws. (F. W. Rane.) (Add. pub. for price.) F. W: Rane.
Maw, P. T. Practice of forestry. $7. Scribner.
Minnesota. *Forestry Commissioner.* Plan of reforestration. (Add. Commission for price.) Minn. Forestry Com.
Minnesota State Board of Immigration. Minnesota's timber lands. (Add. pubs. for price.) Minn. State Bd. Immigration.
New York [State.] Forest, fish and game laws, 1908. 50 c. M. Bender.
Pinchot, G. Conservation of natural resources: [forestry.] 10 c. U. S., Supt. of Docs.
Practical assistance to owners of forest land and to tree planters. (Add. Superintendent for price.) U. S., Supt. of Docs.
Price, O. W., *and others.* Forests of the U. S.: their use. Gov. Pr. Off.
Rane, F. W: Forestry from a commercial standpoint.—We must stop forest fires in Massachusetts (Add. author for price.) F. W: Rane.
Schenck, C. A. Forest finance. $1. C. A. Schenck.
Schenck, C. A Forest protection. $1.50. Inland Press.
Trentham, P. Practice of forestry. $7 net. Scribner.

FORESTS AND FORESTRY.—*Continued.*
United States. *Congress. House. Committee on the Judiciary.* Power of federal government to acquire lands for national forest purposes. (Add. Superintendent for price.)
United States. *Dept. of Agriculture.* Education of forest students; letter from the Secretary of Agriculture, with statement of the amount of money expended under the direction of the forester in the education of students. '10(Jl) 3 p. 8°.
United States. *Dept. of Agriculture.* Forestry in nature study.
United States. Forest service. '10(Ag) 27 p. 8°. Gov. Pr. Off.
United States. Forest Service: bulletins, circulars, maps, and silvical leaflets rel. to forests; Agriculture Department, U. S. A.; for sale by the Superintendent of Documents. '09(O) 18 p. 8°, gratis.
United States. *Superintendent of Documents.* Forest Service; bulletins, circulars, etc.
Wadsworth, J. W., *jr.* Forest preservation and conservation of water supply. gratis. J. W. Wadsworth.
See also Climate;—Commerce;—Fire;—Floods;—Meteorology;—Natural resources;—Nature;—Pine trees;—Trees;—Wood;—*also* Arkansas;—El Dorado Co., Cal.;—Placer Co., Cal.;—White Mts., N. H.

Forewarners (The). Cena, G. $1.50. Doubleday, P.

Forgan, Ja. Berwick.
Should national bank deposits be guaranteed by the government or by a deposit with the government—in either case the necessary fund to be raised by taxing all the banks on their deposits?: address del. before the annual meeting of group 2 of the Bankers' Association of the State of Ill. held at Peoria June 11, 1908. '09(Je) 28 p. pap. (Add. author for price.) J. B. Forgan.

FORGE (The).
Bacon, J: L. Elem. forge practice. $1.50. Wiley.
Bacon, J: L. Forging. $1. Am. Sch. Corr.
Drop forging. 25 c. Indust. Press.
Littlefield, J. D. Notes for forge shop practice. 80 c. Taylor-H.

FORGERIES.
Hingston, W: E: Forgeries and false entries. $1. Roxburgh.
Osborn, A. S. Questioned documents. $5.25. Lawyers' Co-op.

Forget it not; book consisting of the initiatory and the three subordinate lodge degrees, the ceremony of admission by card, the form of installation for subordinate lodge officers and the charges for instituting subordinate lodges, unwritten work added. '09(D) c. 111 p. 16°, $1.50. Bullis & H.
Forget-me-nots. McFalls, *Mrs.* C. A. P. $1.50. Badger.
Forget-me-nots of the Civil War. Battle, L. E. L. $1.50. J. M. Battle.

Forgive and forget. Lingen, E. $1.50. Benziger.

Forgiveness of sins. Hall, A. C. A. **$1 net. Longmans.

Forgotten prime meridian. Ware, H. E. (Priv. pr.) H. E. Ware.

Foringer, W. S.
How to breathe and how to be well. '10 (D31) S. leath., $1. B'way Pub.

Form in music. Macpherson, C: C. $2.25. Schirmer.

Form of baptism in sculpture and art. Christian, J: T. $1. J: T. Christian.

Formal discipline. Bennett, C: J. C. 50 c. Teachers' Coll.

Forman, Emily Shaw.
Guess work: 101 charades. '08(Ag) c. 62 p. D. bds., $1. Badger.

Forman, H: Ja.
In the footprints of Heine. '10(N5) c. il. O. $2 net. Houghton M.

Forman, Justus Miles.
Bianca's daughter. '10(Ap9) c. front. D. $1.50. Harper.
Jason: a romance. '09(Jl31) c. D. †$1.50. Harper.

Forman, Maurice Buxton, comp.
George Meredith; some early appreciations. '10(Ja22) 12°, $1.50. Scribner.

Forman, S: Eagle.
Essentials in civil government. '09(Ja23); New Jersey ed. (O23) c. il. D. ea., 60 c. Am. Bk.
Hist. of the United States for schools. '10(D24) c. il. por. maps, O. $1 net. Century Co.

Formation of the union.. Hart, A. B. $1.25. Longmans.

Formby, J:
American Civil War; concise hist. of its causes, progress and results. '10(Je25) O. with book of maps, $4.50 net. Scribner.

Formont, Maxime.
Child of chance. '08(Je13) D. †$1.50. Lane.

FORMS.
See Business.

FORMS (*in law*).
Bates, C. Pleading, practice, parties and forms under the code. 3 v. $18. W. H. Anderson.
Cann, G: T. Requests to charge in civil and criminal cases; with citations of authorities and forms for instructions to petit juries, [etc.] $6.25. Harrison Co.
Jones, L. A. Legal forms; incl. forms in conveyancing, together with general legal and business forms. $6. Bobbs-M.
Pitman, B., *and* Howard, J. B. Legal forms in amanuensis style of phonography. (Add. pubs. for price.) Phonograph.
See also Commercial law;—*also* names of states.

Forms of discourse. Cairns, W: B. $1.15. Ginn.

Formula book of English official historical documents. Hall, H., *ed.* pt. 1, $2; pt. 2, $2.50. Putnam.

Fornaro, Carlo de.
Diaz, czar of Mexico: an arraignment, with an open letter to Theodore Roosevelt. '09(Jl17) c. por. 8°, $1.50. C. de Fornaro.
Mexico tal cual es; comentarios. '09(Jl17) c. por. 8°, $2.50; pap., $1. C. de Fornaro.

Forrest, Joshua Rhodes.
Student cavaliers. '08(S5) c. il. D. *$1 net. Fenno.

FORREST, Nathan Bedford.
Morton, J: W. Artillery of Nathan Bedford Forrest's cavalry. $2.50. Pub. Ho. of M. E. Ch., So.

Forrest, W: Mentzel.
India's hurt, and other addresses. [1910] (Ap) c. '09. 9-171 p. 12°, 50 c. Chr. Pub. Co.

Forrester, Izola L.
Polly Page Yacht Club. '10(D17) il. D. $1.25. Jacobs.
Those Preston twins. '10(N5) c. il. D. $1.25. Wilde.

Forsaken (The). Trepoff, I., *pseud.* $1. Cochrane.

Forse, W: Harry, jr.
Electric railway auditing and accounting. '08(N21) c. il. O. *$2 net. McGraw.

Forsslund, Louise, pseud.
See Waddell, *Mrs.* C: Carey.

Forster, Hugh Oakeley Arnold-.
See Arnold-Forster, Hugh Oakeley.

Forsyth, D:, M.D.
Children in health and disease. '09(N) c. 19+362 p. 8°, *$3 net. Blakiston.

Forsyth, T: M.
English philosophy; study. '10(D24) 8°, $1.75 net. Macmillan.

Forsythe, Mary Isabella.
Beginnings of New York: old Kingston, the first state capital. '09(N6) c. D. pap., 25 c. Badger.

Forsythe, P: Taylor, D.D.
Cruciality of the cross. '09(N13) O. *$1.50 net. Doran.
Missions in state and church: sermons and addresses. '08(D5) O. *$1.75 net. Armstrong.
Person and place of Jesus Christ; Congregational Union lecture for 1909. '10 (Mr5) O. *$1.50 net. Pilgrim Press.
Work of Christ. '10(D) 12°, $1.50 net. Doran.

Forsythe, Rob.
Blast furnace and the manufacture of pig iron. '08(Mr21) il. 8°, $3. D: Williams.

Fort, C:
Outcast manufacturers. '09(Ap10) c. D. $1.50. B. W. Dodge.

FORT ANCIENT, Ohio.
Peabody, C:, *and* Moorehead, W. K. Exploration of Bushey cavern, pt. 1; Fort Ancient, the great prehistoric earthwork of Warren Co., O., pt. 2. 75 c. Andover.
Randall, E. O. Masterpieces of the Ohio mound builders; the hill-top fortifications, incl. Fort Ancient. $1. Ohio Archæolog.

Fort Dearborn year book. Hardy, L. A. 50 c. net. McClurg.

FORT SANDOSKI, Ohio.
See Ohio.

Fortescue, J: W:
County lieutenancies and the army, 1803-1814. '09(Mr6) O. *$3 net. Macmillan.
Hist. of the British Army in 6 v. v. 5, 1803-1807; second part continued; from the renewal of the war to the evacuation of Rio de la Plata. v. 6, 1807-1809; from the Expedition to Egypt, 1807, to the Battle of Coruna, January, 1809. '10 (N19) maps, 8°, ea., $6 net. Macmillan.
Story of a red deer. '08(Mr21) front. 12°, (Every boy's and every girl's ser.) *75 c. net. Macmillan.

Fortescue-Brickdale, J. M., M.D.
Pract. guide to the newer remedies. '10 (N) 281 p. 12°, $2 net. Wood.
See also Francis, Fs.

Fortier, Alcée, ed.
Louisiana; comprising sketches of countries, towns, events, institutions, persons; arranged in cyclop. form. In 2 v., with a supplementary volume of contemporary biography. '10(F12) c. por. 4°, $48. S. A. Brant.

Fortier, S:
Irrigation of alfalfa. '09, [1910.] (F) 48 p. il. tab., 8°, (U. S., Dept. of Agriculture; farmers' bull.) pap.
Irrigation of orchards. '10(Ag) 36 p. il. 8°, (U. S., Dept. of Agriculture; Farmers' bull.) Gov. Pr. Off.

—, and Cone, Victor M.
Drainage of irrigated lands in the San Joaquin Valley, Cal. '09(D) 58 p. il. fold. maps, 8°, (U. S., Dept. of Agriculture, Office of Experiment Stations, bull.) pap. (Add. Superintendent for price.)

—, and others.
Irrigation in the Sacramento Valley, Cal. '09(My) 99 p. il. map, 8°, (U. S., Dept. of Agriculture, Experiment Stations bull.) pap. (Add. Superintendent for price.) U. S., Supt. of Docs.

FORTIFICATION.
Hobson, R. P. Fortifications bill: speech. U. S., Supt. of Docs.
Woodruff, J. A. Applied principles of field fortification. $1. Staff Coll.

Fortune, W: H:
Costs in currency of British, German French and Austrian cotton goods; tariff, August 5, 1909; made up with duties and a given rate of expenses, showing the costs, "regular" by the yard, also, the dividing lines bet. each rate of duty and the dividing lines showing where the specific rate advances into the ad valorem rate. '10(D17) c. tabs., 8°, $4. W: H: Fortune.

Fortune. Snaith, J: C. $1.50. Moffat.

Fortune and men's eyes. Peabody, J. P. $1.25. Houghton M.

Fortune hunter. Vance, L. J. †$1.50. Dodd.

FORTUNE TELLERS.
Foli, P. R. S. Fortune telling by cards. 50 c. Fenno.
Xanto, *Mme.* Fortune telling. 50 c. Penn Pub. Co.
See also Astrology;—Dreams;—Phrenology.

Fortune telling birthday book. Ghesiri, *Mme.* $1; $2. Platt & P.

FORTUNES.
See Wealth.

Fortunes of Betty. Spooner, C. 50 c. J. S. Ogilvie.

Fortunes of eight. Robson, I. S. 75 c. McKay.

Fortunes of life. Nonnen, E. 50 c. Engberg-H.

Fortunes of the Farrells. Vaizey, J. B. †$1.50. Jacobs.

Forty-five. *See* Dumas, Alexandre.

Forty-four French folk-songs. Tiersot, J., *comp.* $2; $1. Schirmer.

Forty-mile quadrangle, Yukon-Tanana region. Prindle, L. M. (Add. Superintendent for price.) U. S., Supt. of Docs.

Forty minutes late. Smith, F. H. †$1.50. Scribner.

Forty-one years in India. Roberts, F: S., *Earl.* $2. Longmans.

Forty thieves. *See* Lang, Andrew, *ed.*

Forty years' observation of music and the drama. Grau, R. $5. B'way Pub.

Forty years of American finance. Noyes, A. D. *$1.50 net. Putnam.

FORUM, Rome.
Huelsen, C. Roman Forum: its history and its monuments. *$1.75 net. Stechert.
Lanciani, R. Roman forum. $1.50 net. Stechert.

FORUM JUDICUM.
See Visigothic code.

Forward mission study courses. il. 12°, 50 c.; pap., 35 c. Young People's Miss.
—Brown. Why and how of foreign missions.
—Gale. Korea in transition.
—Helm. Upward path.
—Hubbard. Under marching orders.
—Platt. The frontier.
—Strong. Challenge of the city.

Forward movement hymnal; missionary and devotional hymns, for use in missionary meetings, Sunday-school, mission concerts, mision circles, and young people's societies. '08(D) 72 p. 8°, pap., **15 c. net. Am. Bapt.

Forward Movement Mission studies, (graded series.) Bk. 1, (primary grades,) The children of mission lands; by W. C: Griggs, M.D. '09(Jl3); Bk. 2 (primary grades), Mission children, their teachers and friends, by W: C. Griggs, M.D. (N20); Bk. 4. Heroes of modern missions, by C. P. Chipman; Bk. 5 (for intermediate dept.), Men of mark in modern missions, by Howard B. Grose. '10(Ag27); Bk. 6 (for intermediate dept.), The story of our Baptist missionary work, by Lorilla E. Bushnell. '09(O30) c. il. D. pap., ea., **15 c. net. Am. Bapt.

Forward pass. Barbour, R. H: †$1.50. Appleton.

Forward step for the democracy of to-morrow. Thum, W: $1.50. Twentieth Century Club.

Fosdick, C: Austin.
See Castlemon, Harry, *pseud.*

Fosdick, Harry Emerson.
Second mile: [reflections upon the conduct of life.] '08(D) c. 51 p. 12°, *40 c. net. Y. M. C. A.

Fosdick, Morris Archibald.
Pertinent, penetrating pen points and peculiar parodies by a perhaps im-pertinent polytechnic professor; or, Dear Richard's almanac; v. 1; being a collection of droll sayings, wise saws, pointed stories and sermonettes, or simple principles of the philosophy of Morris Brewster, by his friend "Morris Junior," author of The career of Morris Brewster (now being written.) '08, ['909.] (Mr) 111 p. il. 12°, $1. Neuner.

Foss, C. W., comp.
Lord will provide: stories for children. '08 (D12) il. O. 35 c. Augustana.
—, **ed.** Masterpieces from Swedish literature in English form. 2 v. '09(Jl) c. '06. pors. 12°, 75 c. Augustana.

Fossard, Adelaide Rawnsley, comp.
See Thackeray, W: Makepeace.

FOSSILS.
See Cat;—Paleontology;—Peacock.

Foster, Agness Greene.
By the way; travel letters. [Rev. and enl. ed.] '10(S17) c. il. D. $1.50 net. P. Elder.
Eyes of a child. [1910.] (Ap) 60 c. Book & Art.
Eyes of a child. '09(D) il. 60 c. Seymour.
To friendship. '10(Ap23) c. front. 8°, 35 c. P. Elder.
You and some others; poems. '09(D18) c. front. 16°, Rosemary ed., flex. fabriano, *75 c. net; Friendship ed., fabriano bds., *$1.25 net. P. Elder.

Foster, Birket.
Birket Foster. '10(N19) col. il. 8°, (Great painters ser.) $1 net. Macmillan.

Foster, Burnside, M.D.
Suggestion concerning the increased longevity of life insurance policy-holders; address delivered before the Association of Life Insurance Presidents, New York, April 2, 1909. '09(O2) O. pap., gratis. Assoc. Life.

Foster, C:
Story of the Bible from Genesis to Revelation, told in simple language. '08(N) c. 704 p. il. 8°, $1.50. C: Foster.
Story of the Gospel; or, our Saviour's life on earth, told in words easy to read and understand. '09(Ag) c. 366 p. il. 12°, 75 c. C: Foster.

Foster, D: Skaats.
Flighty Arethusa. '10(O29) c. il. D. $1.50. Lippincott.

Foster, Edith Fs.
Marigold's winter. '08(O17) c. il. D. †$1.25. Estes.

Foster, E: Powell.
Ro: international language based on classification of ideas with stem-words on the "a priori" or philosophic plan using letters as figures are used in the science of mathematics. [2d ed.] '10(D3) c. 16°, $1. Ro Co.

Foster, Ellsworth.
Cyclopedia of civil government. '08(D3) c. il. 8°, $2.50. College Pub.

Foster, Eug. Clifford.
Boy and the church. '09(Ag7) c. S. *75 c. net. S. S. Times.
Conventions and how to care for them. '08(Jl18) c. 16°, pap., *25 c. net. S. S. Times.
Starting to teach; for the leaders of boys' Bible classes. '10(Jl30) c. 12°, 40 c. Y. M. C. A.

Foster, Frances G. Knowles-.
See Knowles-Foster, Frances G.

Foster, G: Burman.
Finality of the Christian religion. pt. 1. New ed. '09(N20) 8°, *$2.50 net. Univ. of Chic.
Function of religion in man's struggle for existence. '09(My8) S. *$1 net. Univ. of Chic.

Foster, G: Carey, and Porter, Alfr. W.
Elem. treatise on electricity and magnetism; founded on Joubert's "Traité elementaire d'électricité." 3d ed. '10(Mr5) O. $3.50. Longmans.

Foster, Herbert Darling, and Fay, Sidney Bradshaw.
Syllabus of European history, 375-1870. 3d ed. pt. 1, 375-1500; pt. 2, 1500-1870. '10 (Mr26) c. D. bds., 50 c. E. P. Storrs.

Foster, Horatio A.
Electrical engineers' pract. book. 6th ed. '10(N) 1636 p. il. 8°, leath., $5 net. Van Nostrand.

Foster, J. H.
See Holmes, J: Simcox.

Foster, J:
Shakespeare word-book: glossary of archaic forms and varied usages of words employed by Shakespeare. '08(N21) 8°, hf. mor., *$3 net. Dutton.

FOSTER, John.
Green, S: A. John Foster, the earliest American engraver. $2. Mass. Hist. Soc.

Foster, J: Buckingham, ed.
Spalding's official base ball record, 1909. '09 (Ja16); 1910. '10(Mr26) c. il. pors. S. (Spalding's athletic lib.) pap., ea., 10 c. Am. Sports.

Foster, J: McGaw.
To know and believe: studies in the Apostles' Creed. '08(N21) c. D. **90 c. net. Longmans.

Foster, J: Watson.
Diplomatic memoirs. In 2 v. '09(D4) c. il. pors. facsims., O. **$6 net, boxed. Houghton M.
War not inevitable. '10(D) 15 p. O. (International School of Peace pamphlets.) pap., per 100, $3. Int. Sch. of Peace.

Foster, Joshua Hill.
The judgment day; story of the seven years of great tribulation. '10(Jl c. 139 p. front. 12°, 75 c. Bapt. World.

Foster, Joshua Ja.
Chats on old miniatures. '08(O17) il. O. ("Chats" ser.) $2. Stokes.

Foster, Leonard Gurley.
Blossoms of nature: [poems.] '08(Ag22) c. il. por. D. $1. L. G. Foster.

Foster, Louise Nellis.
Songs of the Alps. '08, [1909.] (F) c. 51 p. il. por. 8°, $1.25. W. Y. Foote.

Foster, Mrs. Mary Jane Chisholm.
Mother the child's first Bible teacher. '08 (Ap18) c. S. bds., *25 c. net. Jennings.

Foster, Mary Story-Maskelyne Arnold-.
See Arnold-Foster, Mary Story-Maskelyne.

Foster, Maximilian.
Corrie who? '08(N14) c. il. D. †$1.50. Small.

Foster, Nancy Kier.
Not of her race. '10(D31) c. D. $1.50. Badger.

Foster, Olive Hyde.
Cookery for little girls. '10(D10) c. il. D. 75 c. net. Duffield.

Foster, Rob. F:
Auction bridge. '09(F6) c. il. 12°, **$1 net. Stokes.
Auction bridge up to date; cont. official laws of auction bridge as adopted 1910 by the Whist Club of New York. [Rev. ed.] '10(O29) c. il. D. $1 net. Stokes.
Bridge manual: complete system of instruction in the game, to which is added dummy bridge and duplicate bridge, with the complete text of the American laws of bridge, repr. by permission of the Whist Club of N. Y. New ed., rev. and enl. '08(Ap11) c. il. 16°, $1.25. Brentano's.
Cab no. 44. '10(F5) c. D. †$1.25. Stokes.
Complete Hoyle: encyclopedia of games. New rev. and enl. ed. '09(Ja23) c. il. O. **$2.50 net. Stokes.
Encyclopedia of games; including all the indoor games played at the present day. 8th ed. '09(Mr13) c. il. D. $1.25; 75 c.; pap., 50 c. Stokes.
Skat up to date. '09(Mr13) c. D. pap., 25 c. Dick.

Foster, Rob. O.
Social game. '10(Jl) c. 16 p. O. pap., 10 c. R. O. Foster.

References (¼ p.).

Foster, Roger.
Treatise on federal practice, civil and criminal, including practice in bankruptcy, admiralty, patent cases, foreclosure of railway mortgages, suits upon claims against the U. S. equity pleading and practice, receivers and injunctions in the state courts. 4th ed., rev. and enl. In 3 v. v. 1. '09(Ap); v. 2 (Jl); v. 3 (O) c. 17+952 p. O. ea., $6.50; per set, $19.50. Callaghan.

Foster, Stephen A., ed.
See Chicago. Municipal court.

Foster, W:
English factories in India, 1622-1623. '08 (O24); 1624-1629. '09(Je26); 1630-1633. '10(Jl30) map, O. ea., $4.15. Oxford Univ.

Foster, W: Trufant.
Argumentation and debating. '08(Jl11) c. D. **$1.25 net. Houghton M.

Fothergill, W. E., M.D.
Manual of diseases of women. '10(D) 452 p. il. 8°, $3 net. Wood.

Fouard, Abbé Constant Henri.
Christ, the son of God; trans. from the 5th ed., with the author's sanction, by G: F. X. Griffith; with an introd. by His Eminence Cardinal Manning. New and cheaper ed., omitting the notes and appendices. '08(D26) c. O. pap., 25 c. Longmans.

Foulché-Delbosc, Raymond.
Bibliographie hispanique, 1905, 1906. '09 (N20) 12°, ea., $1.25. Hispanic Soc.

Foulk, C: W:
Introductory notes on quantitative chemical analysis. 2d ed., rev. and enl. '10 (D17) c. il. 8°, $2.50. Heer.

Foulke, Roland R.
See Pennsylvania. Treatise on the rules against perpetuities.

Foulke, W. Dudley.
Quaker boy; tale of the outgoing generation as it appears chronicled in the autobiography of Robert Barclay Dillingham, [*pseud.*] '10(O15) c. map, 12°, $1.50. Cochrane.

Found by the circus. Kaler, J. O. $1. Crowell.
Found in friendship's fields. Parsons, L. B., *comp.* $1.25. L. B. Parsons.
Foundation and the superstruction. De Mill, R: M. **$3 net. Putnam.
Foundation stone book, Washington Cathedral. De Vries, W: L. $1.50. Cathedral.
Foundation stones of success. Sharpe, E. A. 3 v. $8; $12. Howard S.

FOUNDATIONS.
See Earthwork;—Masonry.

Foundations of alternating current theory. Drysdale, C. V. $2.50 net. Longmans.
Foundations of American grape culture. Munson, T. V. $3. Judd.
Foundations of German. Kayser, C. F. 80 c. Am. Bk.
Foundations of mathematics. Carus, P. *75 c. net. Open Court.
Foundations of modern Europe. Reich, E. **$1.50 net. Macmillan.
Foundations of the nineteenth century. 2 v. Chamberlain, H. S. $10 net. Lane.
Foundations of the origin of species. Darwin, C: R. *$2.50 net. Putnam.
Founders and rulers of united Israel from the death of Moses to the division of the Hebrew kingdom. Kent, C: F. **$1 net. Scribner.
Founders of the first parish, Dover, Mass. Smith, F. $1. J: H. Faulk.
Founding of the church. Bacon, B: W. 50 c. Houghton M.
Founding the South Side Library. Nuesse, G: C. 50 c. Enterprise Pr.

FOUNDRIES.
Penton's foundry list, 1908. $10. Penton.
Richards, W: A. Text-book of elem. foundry practice for the use of students in college and secondary schools. $1.25 net. Macmillan.
Sharp, J: Modern foundry practice. $8. Spon.
Stimpson, W: C. Foundry work. $1. Am. Sch. Corr.
Tate, J. M., *and* Stone, M. O. Foundry practice. $2. Wiley.
See also Furnaces;—Iron;—Machinery.

Fountain (The) of life, to Catholic teachers, by one. '09(D25) S. pap., *35 c. net. Longmans.

FOUNTAINS ABBEY, Ripon, Eng.
Oxford, A. W. Ruins of Fountains Abbey. $1.40 net. Oxford Univ.

Four and the fire. Day, T: F. $1. Rudder.

Four boys and a fortune. Tomlinson, E. T. $1.50. **Lothrop, L. & S.**

Four boys on the Mississippi. Tomlinson, E. T. †$1.50. Lothrop, L. & S.

Four champions of Great Britain and Ireland. Mord, W. $1.50. Stokes.

Four Christmases. Ayres, M. M. 50 c. M. M. Ayres.

Four Corners abroad. Blanchard, A. E. †$1.50. Jacobs.

Four Corners at school. Blanchard, A. E. †$1.50. Jacobs.

Four Corners in camp. Blanchard, A. E. $1.50. Jacobs.

Four daughters of God. Traver, H. $1. Winston.

Four epochs of life. Muncie, *Mrs.* E. H. $1.50 net. Greaves.

Four fascinating French women.. Bearne, *Mrs.* C. M. C. $3.50 net. Brentano's.

Four-flusher. Hazzard, J: E: †$1. G: W. Dillingham.

Four Georges. *See* Thackeray, W: Makepeace.

Four hundred good stories. Whiting, R. R., *comp.* $1. Baker & T.

Four little Fosters. Verhoeff, C. $1.15. A. H. Crist.

Four million. Henry, O., *pseud.* 75 c. Burt.

Four philanthropists. Jepson, E. 75 c. Cupples & L.

Four plays for children. Chapman, J: J. **$1 net. Moffat.

Four-Pools mystery. Webster, J. †$1.50. Century Co.

Four score and more. Russell, G: B. $1.25. Ref. Ch. S. S. Bd.

Four-square. Rickaby, J. *60 c. net. Wagner.

Four Victorian poets. Brooke, S. A: **$1.75 net. Putnam.

Four years in Europe with Buffalo Bill. Griffin, C: E. $1. C: E. Griffin.

Four years with five armies. Gause, I: *$2 net. Neale.

FOURTH DIMENSION.
See Mathematics.

FOURTH OF JULY.
Coolidge, A. C. Christmas vs. Fourth of July. 25 c. A. C. Coolidge.
Moore, J. H. Our national beginnings. J. H. Moore.

Fourtner, S:
Cause of our financial panics and how they may be averted. '08(D12) c. por. T. pap., 50 c. S: Fourtner.

Fouse, Levi Garner.
Recent developments in the life insurance business. '09, [1910.] 578-583 p. 8°, (American Academy of Political and Social Science pubs.) pap., 15 c. Am. Acad. Pol. Sci.

Fout, H. H.
See Weekley, *Bp.* W: Marion.

Fow, J: H:
True story of the American flag. '08(O17) il. pap., *50 c. net. W: J. Campbell.

Fowke, Gerard.
Antiquities of central and south-eastern Missouri; (rept. on explorations made in 1906-'07 under the auspices of the Archæological Institute of America.) '10(D17) il. fold. map, O. (Smithsonian Institution, Bu. of Am. Ethnology, bull.) 40 c. Smith. Inst.

Fowle, F. E., jr.
See Abbot, C: Greeley.

Fowle, Fk. F.
Protection of railroads from overhead transmission line crossing. '09(S11) il. 12°, *$1.50 net. Van Nostrand.

Fowler, C: Evan.
Law and business of engineering and contracting. '09(Mr13) c. O. *$2.50 net. McGraw.

Fowler, Bp. C: H:
Addresses on notable occasions; with an introd. by R. J. Cooke, D.D. '08(O3) c. por. D. bds., *$1.50 net. Jennings.
Patriotic orations; prep. for publication by his son, Carl Hitchcock Fowler; with introd. by J: Wesley Hill. '10(Mr12) c. pors. O. *$1.50 net. Eaton & M.

Fowler, Ellen Thorneycroft, [Mrs. Alfr. Laurence Felkin.]
Miss Fallowfield's fortune. '08(N14) c. front. D. †$1.50. Dodd.

Fowler, Fs. G:
See Fowler, H: Watson.

Fowler, G: Little.
Locomotive breakdowns, emergencies and their remedies; rev. and enlarged by W: W. Wood. 5th ed., rev. and enl. '08 (Ap4) c. il. 16°, $1. Henley.

—, and Mellin, Carl J.
Locomotive design. '09(F13) c. diagrs., 8°, (Machinery's reference ser.) pap., 25 c. Indust. Pres.

—, and Wood, W: Wallace.
Locomotive breakdowns, emergencies and their remedies. 6th rev. ed. '10(Ja15) c. il. $1. Henley.

Fowler, Harold North, Wheeler, Ja. Rignall, and Stevens, Gorham Phillips.
Hdbk. of Greek archæology. '09(O2) c. il. D. (Greek ser. for colleges and schools.) $2. Am. Bk.

Fowler, H: Watson and Fs. G:
King's English; abr. for school use. '08 (D19) D. 40 c. Oxford Univ.

Fowler, Jessie Allen.
Brain roofs and porticos: psychological study of mind and character. '08(Jl11) c. 8°, *$1 net. Fowler & W.

Fowler, Rev. Montague.
Morality of social pleasures. '10(D3) D. $1.25 net. Longmans.

Fowler, Nathaniel Clark, jr.
Starting in life; what each calling offers ambitious boys and young men. [New ed.] '10(O17) c. il. pors. O. $2. Little, B. & Co.

Fowler, Orson Squire and Lorenzo Niles.
Hereditary descent, its laws and facts applied to human improvement. '08(D12) c. 12°. (Add. pubs. for price.) Fowler & W.

Fowler, Rob. Ludlow.
See New York [State.] Real property law.
—, ed. *See* New York [State.] Digested treatise and compendium of law.—Personal property law.

Fowler, W: K., ed.
Suggestive exercises for special day programs for the use of the public schools. '09(D) c. 164 p. il. pors. 8°, 25 c. Univ. Pub.

Fowler, W: Warde.
Social life at Rome in the age of Cicero. '09(Mr6) c. fold. map, O. **$2.25 net. Macmillan.

Fowler-Chumos, Mrs. O. S.
Something for you to look into: [tobacco question.]. [1910.] (S) 65 p. D. pap., 25 c. Fowler-Chumos.

Fowles, Ernest.
Key to the questions and exercises in "Studies in musical graces." '08(S19) c. O. 75 c. Boston Music.

Fowles, G: Milton.
Down in Porto Rico. Rev. ed. '10(My7) c. il. fold. map, 12°, 75 c. Eaton & M.

Fowlkes, B: Plumer.
Co-operation the solution of the so-called negro problem. '08(D) c. 8+9-181 p. il. por. 8°. (Add. pubs. for price.) Novelty.

FOWLS.
See Poultry.

Fowre hymnes. Spenser, E. *50 c. net. Putnam.

Fox, Alice Wilson.
Hearts and coronets; story for young people. '10(O1) c. D. $1.50. Macmillan.

Fox, Frances Marg.
Carlota: story of the San Gabriel Mission. '08(O3) c. il. D. (Roses of St. Elizabeth ser.) $1. L. C. Page.
Seven Christmas candles. '09(N20) c. il. D. (Roses of St. Elizabeth ser.) $1. L. C. Page.
Seven little wise men. '10(D3) c. col. il. D. (Roses ser.) $1. L. C. Page.

Fox, Fk.
Australia. '10(D24) col. il. maps, 8°, (Color books of travel and description.) $6 net. Macmillan.
Ramparts of empire; view of the navy from an imperial standpoint. '10(O15) il. 12°, (Color book ser.; misc.) $2.25 net. Macmillan.

Fox, J:, D.D.
Round the world for the American Bible Society: twelve letters descriptive of a visit to the Society's agencies in the Far East. '08(Ap11) c. il. 8°, gratis. Am. Bible.

Fox, J:, jr.
Trail of the lonesome pine. '08(O17) c. il. D. †$1.50. Scribner.

Fox, L. Webster.
Pract. treatise on ophthalmology. '10, [1909.] (D) 25+807 p. il. 8°, $6. Appleton.

Fox, Marion.
Hand of the north. '10(N19) D. $1.50. Lane.

Fox, Page.
One thousand ways to make money; old and new opportunities for fortune; a storehouse of facts in all kinds of business, and hundreds of trade secrets. 3d ed. '08(Ag8) c. D. 50 c. B'way Pub.

Fox, Philip.
See Hale, G: Ellery.

Fox, R: Kyle.
Life and battles of Jack Johnson, champion pugilist of the world; together with the complete records of John L. Sullivan, James J. Corbett, Robert Fitzsimmons, James J. Jeffries, Tommy Burns and Peter Jackson. '09(Jl) c. 15-71 p. por. 16°, (Fox's athletic lib.) 25 c.; pap., 10 c. R: K. Fox.

Fox, Simeon M.
Early hist. of the Seventh Kansas cavalry. [1910.] (D) 16 p. 8°. State Hist. Kan.

Fox, William Johnson.
Garnett, R: Life of W. J. Fox. *$5 net. Lane.

Fox-Davies, Arth. C:
Complete guide to heraldry. '09(Ag28) il. 8°. *$4 net. Dodge.
Duplicate death. '10(My14) c. il. 12°, $1.50. Macaulay.
Finances of Sir John Kynnersley. '08 (Ap18) c. D. †$1.50. Lane.

Fox.
Carlisle, R. H: Fox hunting past and present. *$1.50 net. Lane.
Higginson, A. H:, *and* Chamberlain, J. I. Hunts of the United States and Canada; their masters, hounds and histories. *$10 net; *$30 net. F. L. Wiles.
Seton, E. T. Biography of a silver-fox: [fiction.] $1.50. Century Co.
Taylor, W. P., *and* Dixon, J. Two new rodents; northern coast form of the California gray fox. 20 c. Univ. of Cal.
Vyner, R. Notitia venatica; treatise on fox hunting. 2 v. $10 net. Dutton.
See also Hunting.

FOX INDIANS.
See Indians.

FOX RIVER VALLEY, Wisconsin.
Hobbs, W: H., *and* Leith, C: K. Pre-Cambrian volcanic and intrusive rocks of the Fox river valley. 25 c. Univ. of Wis.

Foxcroft, H. C.
See Clarke, T. E. S.

Foxe, J:
Christian martyrs of the world. Newly rev. and il. '07, [1908.] (Ap.) c. 590 p. 8°, $1.50. C: Foster.

FOXHOUND.
See Dog.

Fox's athletic lib. il. S. pap. R: K. Fox.
—Dog pit. 25 c.
—Fox. Life and battles of Jack Johnson. 25 c.; 10 c.
—Gotch. Wrestling and how to train. 10 c.
—McFadden. Blocking and hitting. 10 c.
—McGraw. Scientific baseball. 25 c.; 10 c.
—Smith. Official basket ball guide. 10 c.

Foxy Grandpa and his boys. Schultze, C. E. 60 c. Stokes.

"Fra Elbertus," pseud.
See Hubbard, Elbert.

Fra Lippo Lippi. Farrington, M. V. **$1.75 net. Putnam.

Fractionation of crude petroleum. Cram, M. P. 50 c. Johns Hopkins.

Fractionation of crude petroleum by capillary diffusion. Gilpin, J. E. 10 c. U. S., Supt. of Docs.

FRACTURE.
Cotton, F. J. Dislocations and joint fractures. $6. Saunders.
Stimson, L. A. Pract. treatise on fractures and dislocations. $5 net. Lea.
Walton, A. J. Fractures and separated epiphyses. $3 net. Longmans.
See also Arm.

Fradryssa, G. V.
Roman Catholicism capitulating before Protestantism: [a vindication of Christ by a Catholic priest;] tr. from the Spanish. '09(Ja23) c. D. $1.50. Southern Pub. (Ala.)

Fragments from Græco-Jewish writers. Stearns, W. N., *ed.* *75 c. net. Univ. of Chic.

FRAGONARD, Jean Honoré.
Macfall, H. Fragonard. *65 c. net; *$1.50 net. Stokes.

Frame, And. Jay.
Insuring bank deposits is purely theoretical, impractical, revolutionary and fatal to conservatism; history condemns it; as presented at the annual banquet of the Cincinnati Bankers' Club, Feb. 8, 1908. '09(My) 15 p. 8°, pap., 15 c. A. J. Frame.

Frame, Virginia Woodson, comp.
Girls' college record to serve as a treasury for pleasant memories of student days. '08(D12) linen, *$1.50 net, boxed; leath., *$6 net, boxed. P. Elder.

Framing. Radford, W: A. $1. Radford Architectural.

Framley parsonage. *See* Trollope, Anthony.

France, Alice.
Sung in the shadow: poems. '08(S) c. 94 p. por. 8°, $1. Sketch Bk.

France, Anatole, [pseud. for Jacques Anatole Thibault.]
Works. Complete limited edition in 15 v. [v. 1,] Mother of pearl; [v. 2,] The garden of Epicurus; [v. 3,] The red lily. '08(Ag29); [v. 4,] The crime of Sylvestre Bonnard; tr. by Lafcadio Hearn; [v. 5,] Well of Saint Clare; tr. by Alfr. Allinson; [v. 6,] Balthasar; tr. by Mrs. J: Lane. '09(Ja23); [v. 7,] Thaïs; tr. by Rob. B. Douglas. '09(Ap10); [v. 8,] The white stone; tr. by C: E. Roche. (O16); [v. 9,] Penguin Island; tr. by A. W. Evans; [v. 10-11,] The Life of Joan of Arc; tr. by Winifred Stephens; [v. 12,] The merrie tales of Jacques Tournebroche, and Child life in town and country; tr. by Alfr. Allinson. '09(N6); [v. 13,] The elm tree on the mall; chronicle of our own times; tr. by M. P. Willcocks; [v. 14,] The wicker-work woman; chronicle of our own times; tr. by M. P. Willcocks; '10(Jl9) [v. 15,] On life and letters; first series, tr. by A. W. Evans. '10(N19) O. ea., $2; except v. 10-11, $8. Lane.

FRANCE, Anatole.
Brandes, G: Anatole France. *75 c. net. McClure.

FRANCE.
Allinson, A. Days of the Directoire. *$5 net. Lane.
Anderson, F. M., *comp.* Constitutions and other select documents illustrative of the history of France, 1789-1907. *$2.50 net. H. W. Wilson.
Baedeker, K. Northern France. *$2.25 net. Scribner.
Barker, E: H. France of the French. *$1.50 net. Scribner.
Behm, B. Hist. of some French kings. $2 net. Macmillan.
Berry, W. G. France since Waterloo. *$1.50 net. Scribner.
Betham-Edwards, M. B. French vignettes. **$3 net. Brentano's.
Betham-Edwards, M. B. Unfrequented France. $3 net. Stokes.
Bracq, J. C. France under the Republic. $1.50 net. Scribner.
Bumpus, T: F. Cathedrals of northern France. $2. Pott.
Carson, *Mrs.* N. B. From Irish castles to French chateaux. $1.50 net. Small.
Commercial convention bet. France and Canada; collated by N. I: Stone; with rept. by Fk. H. Mason. '09(Je) 35 p. 8°, pap. (Add. Superintendent for price.) U. S., Supt. of Docs.
Coyle, R. M. Fenceless France: the story of an automobile ride. (Priv. pr.) Buchanan.
Dalkeith, L. Stories from French hist. *50 c. net. Dutton.
Dodd, *Mrs.* A. B. B. In and out of a French country-house. $2.25 net. Dodd.
Du Cereau, J. A. French chateaux and gardens in the XVII. century. *$10 net. Scribner.
During, J. V. Hist. of France. 2 v. $2.50 boxed. Crowell.
Elliott, F. B. Old court life in France. 2 v. in 1. $1.50 net. Brentano's.
Farrington, F. E. French secondary schools. $2.50. Longmans.
Fisher, H. A. L. Bonapartism. *$1.15 net. Oxford Univ.
Fricero, K. Our visit to France. $1. Dodge.
Froissart, J: Chronicles of England, France and Spain. $2.50. Dutton.
Geddes, J., *jr.* Educational advantages for American students in France. 25 c. J. Geddes.
George, W. L. France in the twentieth century. *$1.75 net. Lane.
Graham, J., *and* Oliver, G: A. S. French commercial practice connected with the export and import trade to and from France, and the French colonies. pt. 2. *$1 net. Macmillan.
Guerber, H. A. Story of old France. 65 c. Am. Bk.

FRANCE.—*Continued.*
Guizot, F. P. Hist. of France. 8 v. $24. Crowell.
Guthrie, A. Letters from France and Italy. *$1.25 net. McClurg.
Hall, J: R. Bourbon restoration. *$4 net. Houghton M.
Hamel, F. Dauphines of France. $4 net. Pott.
Hamel, F. Fair women at Fontainebleau. —Famous French salons. ea., *$3.50 net. Brentano's.
Hammerton, J. A. In the track of R. L. Stevenson and elsewhere in old France. *$1.50 net. Dutton.
Hanotaux, G. Contemporary France. In 4 v. v. 4, (1877-1882.) *$3.75 net. Putnam.
Hodgson, G. Studies in French education. $1.10. Putnam.
Home, G. C. Motor routes of France. $2 net; $2.25 net. Macmillan.
Jerrold, L. Real France. $1.50 net. Lane.
Klein, F. American student in France. *$2.50 net. McClurg.
Lawton, F: Third French Republic. *$3.50 net. Lippincott.
Michelet, J. Histoire de France; selections. $1. Holt.
Patet, F. J. Précis d'histoire de France. $1.50. F. J. Patet.
Pears, C: From the Thames to the Seine. $4 net. Jacobs.
Peixotto, E. C. Through the French provinces. **$2.50 net. Scribner.
Pennell, *Mrs.* E. R. French cathedrals, monasteries and abbeys, and sacred sites of France. **$5 net. Century Co.
Perkins, C. C. French cathedrals and chateaux. 2 v. *$5 net. Holt.
Prothero, R. E. Pleasant land of France. *$2 net; *$3.50 net. Dutton.
Qui etes-vous? [Who are you?] Annuaire des contemporains, 1908. *$2 net. Lemcke.
Qui etes-vous? [Who are you?] Annuaire des contemporains, 1909. $2. Stechert.
Quinnet, E. France et Allmagne. $1.15. Oxford Univ.
Sabatier, P. Open letter to His Eminence, Cardinal Gibbons, apropos of his interview on the separation of church and state in France. *60 c. net. Sherman, F.
Sherrill, C: H. Stained glass tours in France. **$1.50 net. Lane.
Sterne, L. Sentimental journey through France and Italy. $1.25 net. Brentano's.
Sterne, L. Sentimental journey through France and Italy. $1.50. Lippincott.
Sterne, L. Sentimental journey through France and Italy. $3. Putnam.
Sumichrast, F: C. J: M. S: R. de. Church and state in France. 25 c. E. H. Robson.
Talleyrand-Périgord, D. v. B., *Duchesse* de. Memoirs of the Duchesse de Dino. $2.50 net. Scribner.
Tardieu, A. P. G. A. France and the alliances. **$1.50 net. Macmillan.
Thompson, J. W. Wars of religion in France, 1559-1576. *$4.50 net. Univ. of Chic.

FRANCE.—*Continued.*
Waddington, *Mrs.* M. A. K. Chateau and country life in France. **$2.50 net. Scribner.
Wharton, *Mrs.* E. N. J. Motor flight through France. **$2 net. Scribner.
See also Alsace; — Banks and banking; — Brittany; — Burgundy; — Cathedrals; — Falaise;— French Academy;—French and Indian war;— French Revolution; — Huguenots; — Malta; — Mentone; — Modernism; — Morocco; — Napoleonic wars;—Normandy;—Painters and painting; — Palaces; — Paris; —Parks;—Peninsular war; — Port Royalists; — Provence; — Renaissance;—Riviera;—Rouen;—Songs;—Theatre; — Touraine;—Versailles; — Waterloo (Battle of); —Waterloo;—*also* Angouleme, *Duchess of;*— Bonaparte family;—Bourbon, Charles Duc de; —Catherine de Medici;—Danton, G. J.;—Du Barry, J. B., *Comtesse;*—Elizabeth Charlotte, *Duchess of Orleans;*—Elizabeth, Philippine Marie Helen, *Madame;*—Joan *of Arc;*—Josephine, *Empress;*—Louis XII., XIV., XVII.;—Louis Philippe; — Maintenon, Francoise; —Marie Antoinette; — Marie de Medici; — Marie Louise, *Empress of France;*—Mirabeau, H. G. R., *Comte* de;—Napoleon I., III.;—Robespierre, M. M. I.

FRANCHISE.
See Public utilities;—Suffrage.

Franchise facts. **Peters, J. W. S. $1. J. W. S. Peters.**

FRANCIA, Francesco Raibolini.
Carmichael, M. Francia's masterpiece. *$2 net. Dutton.

FRANCIS JOSEPH I., *of Austria.*
Rumbold, *Sir* H. Francis Joseph and his times. **$4 net. Appleton.
Weindel, H. de. Real Francis Joseph. *$4 special net. Appleton.

Francis of Assisi, St.
Little flowers of St. Francis of Assisi; newly revised and augmented version of the tr. by T. W. Arnold; with introd. by Dr. Guido Biagi. '08(O17) il. cr. 8°, (Art and letters lib.) *$3 net. Duffield.

—, and Bonaventura, St., [Bp. of Albany.]
The little flowers, also The Mirror of perfection, by St. Francis of Assisi; tr. by Rob. Steele; and Bonaventura's Life of St. Francis; tr. by E. Gurney Salter. '10(D10) 16°, (Everyman's lib.) 35 c. net; leath., 70 c. net. Dutton.

Francis, Mrs.
Matthew Strong. '08(N7) il. O. $2. Lippincott

Francis, Alex.
Americans: an impression. '09(S4) O. *$1.50 net. Appleton.

Francis, C: Kenworthy.
See Parr, S: Wilson.

Francis, Fs., and Fortescue-Brickdale, J. M.
Chemical basis of pharmacology. '08 (Ap25) O. *$4 net. Longmans.

Francis, J: Reynolds.
Home Circle Fraternity; evolution of a new religion. '10(D3) c. D. $1. Progressive Thinker.

Francis, M. E., pseud.
See Blundell, Mary E. Sweetman.

Francis, Rev. Paul Ja., and Jones, Rev. Spencer.
Prince of the apostles; [argument favoring the union of the Catholic and Anglican churches.] '08(Mr14) D. **75 c. net. Lamp Pub.

Francis, T. E., rep.
See Missouri, *St. Louis,* Kansas City, etc. Courts.

FRANCIS OF ASSISI, *St.*
Bailly, A. Divine minstrels; narrative of the life of St. Francis of Assisi with his companions: [fiction.] *$1.25 net. Scribner.
Goff, *Mrs.* R. Assisi of St. Francis; together with The influence of the Franciscan legend on Italian art. *$6 net. Dodd.
Heins, M. A. Story of St. Francis of Assisi. *75 c. net. Benziger.
Jewett, S. God's troubadour: [child's life of St. Francis.] $1.25 net. Crowell.
Thomas *of Celano, Brother.* The lives of S. Francis of Assisi. *$2 net. Dutton.
See also **Sassetta. Stefano.**

Francis Kane's fortune. Smith, *Mrs.* E. T. 50 c. Hurst.

Francisca reina. Truesdell, A. W. (Priv. pr.) Badger.

Franciscan days of vigil. De Bary, R: $1.50 net. Longmans.

Franciscan Sisters of Perpetual Adoration, La Crosse, Wis. Geography briefly told. '09(N) c. various paging, il. 8°, 80 c. Franciscan Sisters.

FRANCISCANS.
Muzzey, D: S. Spiritual Franciscans. gratis. D: S. Muzzey.

Francisco, our little Argentine cousin. Brooks, E. C. 60 c. L. C. Page.

FRANCK, César.
D'Indy, V. César Franck. *$2.50 net. Lane.

Franck, Harry Alverson.
Vagabond journey around the world; narrative of personal experience. '10(Mr26) c. il. O. **$3.50 net. Century Co.

FRANCO-AUSTRIAN CAMPAIGN.
Petre, F. L. Napoleon and the Archduke Charles: hist. of the Franco-Austrian campaign. *$4 net. Lane.

FRANCO-PRUSSIAN WAR.
See **Paris.**

François, Victor Emmanuel.
Key to François' French prose composition, introductory and advanced. '09(S11) c. D. 80 c. Am. Bk.
—, **ed.** Easy standard French; ed., with English exercises, notes and vocab. '10(O1) c. S. 40 c. Am. Bk.

FRANÇOIS EUGÈNE DE SAVOIE-CARIGNAN, *Prince.*
Würdig, L. Prince Eugène. 50 c. net. McClurg.

FRANÇOIS I. *of France.*
Haggard, A. C: P. Two great rivals (François I. and Charles V.) and the women who influenced them. $4 special net. Appleton.

François le champi. *See* Sand, G., *pseud.*

Frank, Edith.
Essays. [1910.] (My) c. 70 p. 12°, $1. B'way Pub.

Frank, H:
Mastery of mind in the making of a man. '08(O3) c. por. D. $1. Fenno.
Modern light on immortality. '09(Ag14) c. O. *$1.85 net. Sherman, F.
Tragedy of Hamlet: psychological study. '10(O1) c. pors. O. $1.50 net. Sherman, F.

Frank, Maude M.
Constructive exercises in English. '09 (Ap10) c. D. 50 c. Longmans.

Frank, Rob. J:
Commentary on the science of organization and business development. Rev. ed. '09 (Jl17) c. 8°, mor., $2.75; shp., $3. Chic. Commercial; S: A. Bloch.

Frank in the woods. Castlemon, H., *pseud.* 50 c. Hurst.

Frank Merriwell stories. *See* Standish, B. L.

Frank Merriwell's champions. Standish, B. L. †75 c. McKay.

Frank Merriwell's courage. Standish, B. L. †75 c. McKay.

Frank Merriwell's daring. Standish, B. L. †75 c. McKay.

Frank Merriwell's loyalty. Standish, B. L. †75 c. McKay.

Frank Merriwell's return to Yale. Standish, B. L. †75 c McKay.

Frank Merriwell's secret. Standish, B. L. †75 c. McKay.

Frank Merriwell's skill. Standish, B. L. †75 c. McKay.

Frank on the prairie. Castlemon, H., *pseud.* 50 c. Hurst.

Frankau, Mrs. Julia.
See Danby, Fk., *pseud.*

Frankel, Lee Kaufer, and Dawson, Miles Menander.
Workingmen's insurance in Europe. '10 (O15) c. 8°, (Russell Sage Foundation pubs.) $2.50. Charities Pub.

Frankish, C: Goodwin.
Beautiful San Antonio canyon; choice collection of superb half-tones from recent photographs. '09(S) c. 65 p. il. 4°, 50 c. C: G. Frankish.

Frankland, Fs. W: Barrett.
Theories of parallelism; historical critique. '10(My7) c. 16°, 90 c. net. Putnam.

Franklin, B:
Autobiography; with selections from his other writings; ed., with comments, notes, bibliography, and topics for study, by H. A. Davidson. '08(N21) c. pors. map, 16°, 50 c. Heath.
Autobiography; the unmutilated and correct version; comp. and ed., with notes, by J: Bigelow. '10(Mr26) por. O. $1.50. Putnam.
Autobiography; ed. by Nathaniel E. Griffin. '08(F1) c. 16°, (Lake Eng. classics.) 30 c. Scott, F. & Co.
Memoirs of the life and writings; ed. by W. A. MacDonald. '08(S19) 16°, (Everyman's lib.) *35 c. net; leath., *70 c. net. Dutton.
Poor Richard's almanac. '08(O17) c. nar. 12°, (Rubric ser.) bds., **60 c. net. Duffield.
Wisdom of Franklin. '09(Je) c. 32°, leath., **$1 net. Brentano's.
Worldly wisdom from Benjamin Franklin; sel. and arr. by F. S. Bigelow. '08(N21) c. 24°, cf., $1, boxed. Altemus.
See also Stories of humor.

FRANKLIN, Benjamin.
Alford, F., *comp.* Wit of Lincoln, the wisdom of Franklin. 25 c. Scott-M.
American Philosophical Society. Calendar of the papers of Benjamin Franklin in the library of the American Philosophical Society. (Not for sale.) Am. Philosophical Soc.
Hart, C: H: Original portrait of Doctor Franklin painted by Joseph Wright, 1782. *$2.50 net. C: H: Hart.
Mangasarian, M. M. Religion of Washington, Jefferson and Franklin. 10 c. Independent Religious.
Pennsylvania University Library. Calendar of the papers of Benjamin Franklin in the library of the University of Penn. $1.50. Univ. of Penn.; [Appleton.]
Rotch, A. L. Benjamin Franklin and the first balloons. (Not for sale.) A. L. Rotch.
Swift, L. Benjamin Franklin. 50 c. net. Small.

Franklin, Fabian.
Life of Daniel Coit Gilman. '10(My21) c. pors. O. $3.50 net. Dodd.
People and problems: addresses and editorials. '09(Ja16) c. D. **$1.50 net. Holt.

Franklin, Sir J:
Narrative of a journey to the shores of the Polar Sea in the years 1819, '20, '21, '22. '10(Ap23) 16°, (Everyman's lib.) 35 c. net; leath., 70 c. net. Dutton.

Franklin, J: Henderson.
Rebuilding of King Solomon's temple. '10 (O29) c. il. map, D. $1.50. J: H. Franklin.

Franklin, Moses.
Reward of capital. '08(D) 25 c. M. Franklin.

Franklin, Seneca Ely.
Address on freemasonry del. at Sunbright, Tenn., December 27, 1891. '07, [1908.] (Je.) c. 42 p. 8°, 75 c. Ebbert & R.

Franklin, W: Suddards.
Electric waves; advanced treatise on alternating-current theory. '09(D18) c. il. 8°, **$3 net. Macmillan.

—, Crawford, C. M., and Macnutt, Barry.
Practical physics. In 3 v. v. 1, Precise measurements; v. 2, Elem. and advanced measurements in electricity and magnetism. '08(F1); v. 3, Photometry. (F29) c. il. 8°, v. 1, 2, ea., *$1.25 net; v. 3, *90 c. net. Macmillan.

—, and Esty, W:
Dynamo laboratory manual for colleges and technical schools. [Rev. ed.] v. 1, Direct-current studies and tests. '09(O2) c. il. O. **$1.75 net. Macmillan.
Dynamos and motors. '09(S4) il. 8°, *$4 net. Macmillan.

—, and MacNutt, Barry.
Elements of electricity and magnetism: text-book for colleges and technical schools. '08(Ag22) c. por. il. *$1.60 net. Macmillan.
Light and sound. '09(Jl31) c. il. O. **$1.60 net. Macmillan.
Mechanics and heat. '10(Ag13) il. 8°, $1.75 net. Macmillan.

FRANKLIN (Battle of).
Banks, R. W. Battle of Franklin, Nov. 30, 1854, [Civil War.] $1.25. Neale.
See also Civil War.

Franklin Winslow Kane. **Sedgwick, A. D.** $1.50. **Century Co.**

FRANKPLEDGE SYSTEM.
Morris, W: A. Frankpledge system. $1.75. **Longmans.**

Franks, A.
Esperanto for the English. '09(My8) 12°, 50 c. McKay.

Franz, Shepherd Ivory.
Psychology and the medical school. '08 (Je6) 8°, (George Washington Univ. pubs., Medical science ser.) pap. (Not for sale.) George Washington Univ.

Franz von Sickingen. Lasalle, F. J. G. $1. N. Y. Labor News.

Fraprie, Fk. Roy.
See Ansell, Florence Jean.

Frary, Marie Harriette, and Stebbins, C: M.
The crystal palace, and other legends: retold. '10(Mr12) c. il. D. 60 c. Stebbins.

Fraser, Alex. Campbell.
Berkeley. '09(Jl31) 12°, (Philosophies ancient and modern from Pythagoras to Spencer.) *50 c. net. Dodge.

Fraser, D:
Short cut to India: record of a journey along the route of the Baghdad railway. '09(Je26) il. fold. map, O. *$5 net. Scribner.

Fraser, E:
"Bellerophon," "the bravest of the brave." '10(S10) il. O. $2. Stokes.
"Londons" of the British fleet. '08 (Ag22) il. (partly col.) D. **$1.50 net. Lane.

Fraser, Georgia.
Crow-Step. '10(D3) c. D. $1.50. Witter & K.
Stone house at Gowanus; scene of the Battle of Long Island; Stirling's headquarters; Cornwallis's redoubt; occupied by Washington; colonial residence of Dutch architecture built by Nicholas Vechte, 1609. '09(D25) il. pors. O. $2.50. Witter & K.

Fraser, Mrs. Hugh.
See Fraser, *Mrs.* Mary Crawford.

Fraser, J: Foster.
Australia: making of a nation. '10(O1) 8°, $1.75. Cassell.
Life's contrasts. '08(D5) front. *$1.75 net. Cassell.
Quaint subjects of the king; [account of strange tribes in the British Empire.] '09(Ap24) il. D. *$1.25 net. Cassell.

Fraser, Mrs. Mary Crawford, ["Mrs. Hugh Fraser."]
Diplomatist's wife in many lands. 2 v. '10(D10) c. por. O. $6 net, boxed. Dodd.
Giannella. '09(O) 4+355 p. 8°, $1.50. Herder.
Heart of a Geisha. '08(N14) c. il. D. †$2. boxed. Putnam.

Fraser, W: H:, and Van der Smissen, W: H:
German grammar, for schools and colleges. '09(N20) c. map, 12°, (Modern language ser.) $1.10. Heath.

Fraternal society law. *See* Hardy, Carlos S.

Fraternalism and the church; by a devotee to both. '10(Mr5) c. D. $1. Chamberlin.

FRATERNITIES.
See Secret societies.

Fraternity. Galsworthy, J: **$1.35 net. Putnam.

Fraternity: a romance. [New ed.] '10(O15) D. $1 net. Harper.

Frau von Colson's Christmas eve. Musson, *Mrs.* L. W. 75 c. Rust-Craft.

Frayser, Nannie Lee.
Little prodigals. '10(Jl2) c. D. bds., 35 c. net. F. M. Barton.

Frazar, Mrs. Mae D.
Practical European guide. 3d ed. '08 (Ap11) c. S. $1.50. Small.
Pract. guide to Great Britain and Ireland; preparation, cost, routes, sightseeing. 2 v. '09(D18) c. S. (Pract. guide ser.) ea., **$1 net. Small.

Frazer, Ja. G:
Adonis, Attis, Osiris: studies in the history of Oriental religion. 2d ed., rev. and enl. '08(Ja11) 8°, *$3.25 net. Macmillan.
Psyche's task: [influence of superstition on the growth of institutions.] '09(Ap24) 8°, *80 c. net. Macmillan.
Totemism and exogamy; treatise on certain early forms of superstition and society. In 4 v. '10(Je18) 8°, $16 net. Macmillan.

Frazer, Perry D.
Rodmaking for beginners. '08(Je6) c. il. S. (Angler's workshop.) $1. Forest.

Frazer, Persifor, and Brown, Amos Peaslee.
Tables for the determination of minerals by physical properties ascertainable with the aid of a few field instruments based on the system of the late Professor Doctor Albin Weisbach. 6th ed., rev. to date. '10(Jl16) c. 8°, $2.50. Lippincott.

Frear, W:, M.D., Given, G. C., M.D., and Broomell, A. W., M.D.
Breakfast foods: cont. the results of an investigation of breakfast foods and pancake flours on sale in the markets of Pennsylvania. '08(My16) 8°, pap. (Add. pubs. for price.) Harrisburg Pub.

Freda. Hinkson, *Mrs.* K. T. $1.20 net. Cassell.

Freddie and Santa Claus in circus land. Aye, O. 30 c. Laird.

Freddy Carr. Garrold, R. P. 85 c. Benziger.

FREDERICK *the Great.*
Carlyle, T: Life of Frederick the Great. *$1.50 net. McClurg.
Carpenter, *Mrs.* K. E. R. Story of Frederick the Great for boys and girls. $1. Lothrop, L. & S.

FREDERICK WILLIAM, *Elector of Brandenburg.*
Schmidt, F. Youth of the great Elector, [Frederick William, of Brandenburg.] *60 c. net. McClurg.

Frederick, Fk. Forrest.
Simplified mechanical perspective; for the use of high schools, technical and manual training high schools, evening industrial schools and art schools. '09(D18) c. figs. Q. 75 c. Manual Arts.
Wash method of handling water colour. '09(Ja23) c. il. 8°, 50 c. Manual Arts.

Frederick, H.
Evolution of a "damn." '08(S) c. 15 p. S. pap., 10 c.; Holiday ed., 25 c. H. M. Bones.

Frederick, Oliver D.
See Whigham, Wallace Hugh.

FREDERICKSBURG, Va.
Quin, S. J. History of the city of Fredericksburg, Virginia. $1.50. R. L Knox.
Walker, A. E., *comp. and ed.* The *Free Lance-Star* historical and industrial number, portraying the glorious past and future possibilities of Fredericksburg. 20 c. Free Lance-Star.

FREDERICKSBURGH, [Patterson,] N. Y.
Patrick, L. S. Washington's headquarters and the Revolutionary army at Fredericksburgh. 10 c. Quaker Hill.

Fredet, Rev. P:
Modern history; rev. and enl. by C: H. McCarthy. '10(S17) c. il. pors. maps, 12°, $1.50. Murphy.

Free coinage and a self-adjusting ratio. Balch, T: W. (Not for sale.) T: W. Balch.

Free hide text book. National Association of Tanners. (Add. pubs. for price.) Nat. Assoc. Tanners.

Free Lance-Star historical and industrial number. Walker, A. E., *comp. and ed.* 20 c. Free Lance-Star.

Free life. Wilson, W. **75 c. net. Crowell.

Free Methodist Church. Doctrines and discipline of the Free Methodist Church. '07, [1908.] (Mr.) c. 278 p. 24°, pap., 40 c. Free Meth.

FREE METHODIST CHURCH.
See Methodist Episcopal church.

Free press anthology. *See* Schroeder, T. *comp.*

Free rangers. Altsheler, J. A. †$1.50. Appleton.

Free Sewing Machine Co. Free family sewing machine. '08(Ag) c., 168 p. il. 12°, $1.50. Free Sewing.

FREE TRADE.
See Reciprocity;—Tariff.

Freear, Rob. L:
Nancy Hart. '08(N14) c. il. D. $1.50. C. M. Clark.

Freebooters of the wilderness. Laut, A. C. $1.35 net. Moffat.

Freece, Hans P.
Letters of an apostate Mormon to his son. '09(Jl) c. '08. 73 p. il. por. 8°, 50 c. H. P. Freece.

Freedman, W: Horatio.
Types of dynamo-electric machinery, direct-current; instruction paper. '10 (Ja15) c. il. 8°, pap., 50 c. Am. Sch. Corr.

FREEDOM OF THE PRESS.
See Liberty of the press.

Freehand and perspective drawing. Everett, H. E: $1. Am. Sch. Corr.

Freehand perspective and sketching. Norton, D. M. $3. D. M. Norton.

Freeman, A. C., ed. and rep.
See American state repts.

Freeman, Douglas Southall.
Calendar of Confederate papers, with a bibliography of some Confederate publications; prepared under the direction of the Confederate Memorial Literary Society. '08(D20) c. O. $2.50. Confederate Museum.

Freeman, J: Dolliver.
Concerning the Christ. '08(D5) D. *$1 net. Armstrong.

Freeman, Rev. J: Haskell.
Oriental land of the free; or, life and mission work among the Laos of Siam, Burma, China and Indo-China. '10 (Je25) c. il. map, D. 50 c. Westminster.

Freeman, J: Ripley.
Lock canal at Panama. '09(Je) 12 p. 8°, pap. (Add. Superintendent for price.) U. S., Supt. of Docs.
See also Arnold, Bion Jos.

Freeman, Mrs. Mary Eleanor Wilkins.
Green door. '10(D3) col. il. O. 75 c. net. Moffat.
Shoulders of Atlas. '08(Je20) c. front. D. †$1.50. Harper.
Winning lady. '09(N13) c. il. D. †$1.25. Harper.

Freeman, Sarah Jane.
Syllabus of a course on elem. bookmaking and bookbinding. '10(Ap16) il. 8°, (Columbia Univ., Teachers' College, syllabi) 30 c. Teachers' Coll.

Freeman, W: Neely.
Saint Mammon: a novel. '08(D12) c. il. D. $1.50. B'way Pub.

Freemantle, Eliz.
The One and I. '08(Ag29) c. il. D. †$1.50. Jacobs.

Freemasonry.
Anthony, A. L. Hist. of Calvary Commandery for fifty years. $5. A. L. Anthony.
Barratt, N. S., *and* Sachse, J. F. Freemasonry in Pennsylvania. *$5 net.. J. F. Sachse.
Brockaway, C: A. Ancient accepted Scottish rite; one hundred years of Aurora grata. $1. Aurora Grata.
Buck, J. D. Lost word found in the great work: [freemasonry.] 50 c. Indo-Am. Bk.
Burton, A. J. Eastern Star; a collection of historic papers, reminiscences, poems, essays, etc., etc., rel. to the Eastern Star. 75 c. A. J. Burton.
Callahan, C: H. Memorial to Washington the Mason, to be erected at Alexandria, Virginia. $1. Alexandria-Washington.
Carpenter, H. M. Bom-tu floor work. $1. H. M. Carpenter.
Chilcott, L. S. Templar tactics and manual. $1.50. L. S. Chilcott.
Davis, G. H. One hundred years of masonry in the Oranges, 1809-1909. $2. Chronicle Pub.
Drummond, J. H. Maine Masonic text book. $1.50. Berry.
Ellis, C: E: Authentic hist. of the Benevolent and Protective Order of Elks. $5; $7.50; $10. C: E: Ellis.

Freemasonry.—*Continued.*
Ellis, E: S. Low twelve: incidents illustrative of the fidelity of Free Masons to one another. $1.50. Niglutsch.
Forget it not. $1.50. Bullis & H.
Franklin, S. E. Address on freemasonry. 75 c. Ebbert & R.
Hempstead, F. Poems by [the] poet laureate of freemasonry. $3; $5. F. Hempstead.
Howard, P. Odd fellowship up to date. $1; 50 c. Dick.
Huie, W: G. Bible application of Freemasonry. $1.50. W: G. Huie.
Ketler, W: H. Why he is an elk. 5 c. H. B. Ketler.
Kruse, C: H: Transition of masonry. $1. C: H: Kruse.
Lowe, F. Odd Fellows' vest pocket guide. 50 c. F. Lowe.
Mackey, A. G. Lexicon and hist. of freemasonry. $6. T. A. McClure.
Masonic chronicles catechism rel. to masonic law and usage. 75 c.; 50 c. Masonic Chronicler.
Masonic code of Minnesota; cont. constitution, general regulations and resolutions, with annot. decisions of the Grand Lodge of A. F. & A. M. of Minnesota; rev. ed., comp. and rearranged with copious general index by W: P. Roberts, H: R. Wells and W: P. McGonagle. '10(Jl) c. 381 p. 12°. Grand Lodge.
Monitor of the work, lectures and ceremonies of ancient craft masonry in the jurisdiction of the Grand Lodge of the State of New York. [1910.] (Je) c. 143 p. 16°, $1. E: M. L. Ehlers.
Official Pythian lodge directory. $2. H. H. Richardson.
Oppenheim, S: Jews and masonry in the United States before 1810. 50 c. S: Oppenheim.
Order of the Eastern Star. O. E. S.; standard ritual containing the degree of the Eastern star, the Queen of the South, the Amaranth, the Matron's administrative, and all forms and ceremonies of the order, by S. G. Watkins. '09, [1910.] (Ap) c. 155 p. il. 16°, 75 c. S. G. Watkins.
Pierce, J: A. Why the secrets of Freemasonry are withheld from members. 10 c. J: A. Pierce.
Pimbley, A. F. Baltimore Conference of Grand Masters, together with acct. of dedication week. $2.50. A. F. Pimbley.
Preuss, A., *ed.* Study in American freemasonry. *$1.50 net.. Herder.
Rowell, B: W., *and* Richardson, A. L., *comps.* Massachusetts consistory of sublime princes of the royal secret thirty-second degree of the Ancient and Accepted Scottish Rite for the northern jurisdiction of the United States. (Priv. pr.) B: W. Rowell.
Ronayne, E. Master's carpet; or, Masonry and Baal worship identical. 75 c. T. B. Arnold.
Sletzer, W: H:, *comp.* Drill regulations, uniform rank, Knights of the Maccabees of the world. *$1 net. Lilley.

FREEMASONRY.—*Continued.*
Taylor, W: M. Taylor-Hamilton monitor of symbolic masonry. $1. Coyle.
Vail, C: H. Ancient mysteries and modern masonry. $1. Macoy Pub.
Wright, R. C. Indian masonry. $1.50. Tyler Pub.
See also Pike, Albert
Freer-Logion, Das. Gregory, C. R. 65 c. Lemcke.
Freese, Nettie Isabel.
Without credentials. '08, [1909.] (F) c. 22 p. D. pap., 35 c. N. I. Freese.
Freeston, C: L.
High roads of the Alps; motoring guide to 100 mountain passes. '10(D3) il. maps, $3. Scribner.
FREEVILLE, N. Y.
See George Junior Republic.
FREIGHT.
Am. Assoc. of Local Freight Agts.' Assocs. Compilation of convention topics. $1.50. Am. Assoc. Freight.
Colorado Manufacturers' Assoc., *comp.* Pocket ed. of 25,000 frieght and express rates. $3. Colo. Manuf.
Kenly, A. C. Why freight is lost or damaged. 10 c. Baughman Sta. Co.
Ketchum, E. S. Freight economics; how traffic experts save freight money. $1. Shipper's Freight.
Pease, C: S. Freight transportation on trolley lines. $1. McGraw-H.
Weld, L: D. H. Private freight cars and American railways. *$1.50 net. Longmans.
See also Bills of lading;—Carriers;—*also* New York City.
FREIGHT RATES.
See Carriers;—Railroads.
Frémeaux, Paul.
Drama of Saint Helena; tr. from the French by Alf. Rieu and the author. '10(Ap2) O. $3 net. Appleton.
French, Alice.
See Thanet, Octave, *pseud.*
French, Allen.
See Story of Grettir the Strong.
French, C. H., and Osborn, G.
Elementary algebra. '08(D5) 8°, *$1.50 net. Putnam.
French, Mrs. C: Ellis.
See Warner, Anne.
French, C: Sheldon.
Worship of the golden calf: a story of wage-slavery in Massachusetts. '08(O) c. 189 p. 8°, $1. C: S. French.
French, Donald Graham.
Points about poetry. '10(Je25) c. 12°, 60 c. Editor Co.
FRENCH, Edwin Davis.
Brainerd, I. H., *ed.* Edwin Davis French: [American designer of bookplates.] (Priv. pr.) De Vinne.
French, G:
Art and science of advertising. '09(Mr20) c. il. O. **$2 net. Sherman, F.
French, H: Findlay.
Federal control of trusts and combinations in restraint of trade under the commerce clause of the Constitution. '09(My) c. 28 p. O. pap. (Add. pubs. for price.) Kohn & P.
French, Herbert, M.D.
Medical laboratory methods and tests. 2d ed. '08(Mr28) il. 16°, limp leath., *$1.75 net. Chic. Med. Bk.
French, Howard Barclay, comp.
Genealogy of the descendants of Thomas French who came to America from Nether Heyford, Northamphire, England, and settled in Berlinton (Burlington) in the province and country of west New Jersey. 2 v. '09(Je12) il pors. facsims., 4°, ea., $8. H. B. French.
French, Ja. Magoffin, M.D.
Text-book of the practice of medicine for students and practitioners. 4th rev. ed.; rev. by C: Spencer Williamson. '10 (S) 1323 p. il. 8°, $5.50 net; leath., $6.50 net. Wood.
French, Lester Gray.
First principles of theoretical mechanics. '08(Mr14) c. il. 8°, (Machinery's reference ser.) pap., 25 c. Indust. Press.
French, Lillie Hamilton.
House dignified; its design and its decoration. '08(O10) c. il. Q. **$5 net, boxed. Putnam.
French, Nora May.
Poems. '10(Je) c. 91 p. por. 16°. $1.25. Strange.
French, T: Ewing, and Meiklejohn, Rob.
Essentials of lettering; manual for students and designers. 2d ed. '10(Ap16) c. il. 16°, $1. Varsity Supply.
FRENCH ACADEMY, Paris.
Robertson, D. M. Hist. of the French Academy, 1635(4)-1910, with outline sketch of the Institute of France. $3 net. G: W. Dillingham.
FRENCH AND INDIAN WAR.
American Antiquarian Society. Manuscript records of the French and Indian war in the library of the society. $2.50. Am. Antiquarian.
Emerson, G: D. Niagara campaign of 1759. $1.50. G: D. Emerson.
Hadden, J. Washington's expedition (1753-1754) and Braddock's expedition (1775). $1. J. Hadden.
Sylvester, H. M. Indian wars of New England. 3 v. $15 net; $50; $1000. W. B. Clarke.
FRENCH ARTISTS.
See Painters and painting.
FRENCH AUTHORS.
See Authors.
French-Canadian in prose and verse. Amsbary, W. B. 25 c. La Salle Extension.
French cathedrals and chateaux. Perkins, C. C. 2 v. *$5 net. Holt.
French cathedrals, monasteries and abbeys. Pennell, *Mrs.* E. R. **$5 net. Century Co.
French chateaux and gardens. Du Cerceau, J. A. *$10 net. Scribner.
French classics for English readers. See Putnam's.
French dishes for English tables. Pratz, C. de. $1. McKay.
FRENCH FAMILY.
See Genealogies.
FRENCH HISTORY.
See France.
French household cooking. Keyzer, *Mrs.* F. *60 c. net. Scribner.

FRENCH IN THE UNITED STATES.
Belote, T. F: Scioto speculation and the French settlement at Gallipolis. 75 c. Univ. of Cin.
French influence in English literature. Upham, A. H. *$2 net. Lemcke.
FRENCH LANGUAGE.
About, E. F. V. La mère de la marquise. 25 c. W: R. Jenkins.
About, E. F. V. Les jumeaux de l'Hotel Corneille. *25 c. net. Crowell.
Andersen, H. C. Fairy tales; told in easy French. *50 c. net. Jacobs.
Angellier, A. Page choisies. $1.15. Oxford Univ.
Arabian nights' entertainments; told in easy French. *50 c. net. Jacobs.
Armstrong, E: C. Syntax of the French verb. 90 c. Holt.
Ashleman, L. A. Dramatic French reader. 75 c. Flanagan.
Auzas, A., *ed.* Poemes Napolēoniens. *25 c. net. Crowell.
Balzac, H. de. César Birotteau. 60 c.—Eugénie Grandet. 85 c.—Une ténébreuse affaire. 60 c. Oxford Univ.
Balzac, H. de. Le médecin de campagne. *90 c. net. Putnam.
Banderet, P., *and* Reinhard, P. First lessons in French. *50 c. net. Crowell.
Bawr, S. de C., *Baroness* de. Michel Perrin. *25 c. net. Crowell.
Bazin, R. Contes choisis. 35 c. Heath.
Bellot, J. R. Journal d'un voyage aux mers polaires. 60 c. Oxford Univ.
Bernard, C. de. L'anneau d'argent. 35 c. net. Macmillan.
Berthet, É. Le douanier de mer. 60 c. Oxford Univ.
Berthon, H. E., *and* Starkey, V. G. Tables synoptiques de phonologie de l'ancien français. 85 c. Oxford Univ.
Biart, L. Monsieur Pinson. 35 c. net. Macmillan.
Bigot, M. H. La petite princesse. 35 c. Am. Bk.
Blanchaud, R. de, *comp. and ed.* One thousand common French words. *25 c. net. Crowell.
Blanchaud, R. de, *comp.* Progressive French idioms. 60 c. Heath.
Blanchaud, R. de, *ed.* Quatre contes des Mille et une nuits. *25 c. net. Crowell.
Boileau-Desperéaux, N. Satires epitres et l'art poëtique. *$1 net. Putnam.
Boileau-Despréaux, N. Selections. 50 c. Heath.
Boname, L. C. Study and practice of French in school for beginners. pt. 1. 60 c.; pt. 2, 90 c. L. C. Boname.
Bouët-Willaumez, *Comte* L. E. Batailles de terre et de mer. 60 c. Oxford Univ.
Bourget, P. C. J. Un saint. 35 c. net. Macmillan.
Bournier, *Vicomte* H. de. La fille de Roland. 30 c. Heath.
Brown *and* Martin. French and English dictionary. 50 c. Dutton.
Bruce, M. S. Lectures faciles. 60 c. Heath.
Brueys, D. A. de., *and* Palaprat, J. L'avocat Patelin. *25 c. net. Crowell.

FRENCH LANGUAGE.—*Continued.*
Campan, *Mme.* J. L. H. G. Mémoires. 85 c. Oxford Univ.
Carter, B: F. French word-lists. 25 c. Holt.
Chardenal, C. A. Complete French course. $1. Allyn & B.
Chouville, L. Histoires courtes et longues pour lecture expliquée et reproduction. 60 c. Oxford Univ.
Claretie, A. A. Pierrille. 40 c. Holt.
Clarke, C: C. Common difficulties in reading French. $1. W: R. Jenkins.
Colin, H. L. T., *and* Sérafon, A. Pract. lessons in French grammar. $1.12. B: H. Sanborn.
Collot, A. S. French-English and English-French dict. $2.75 net. W: R. Jenkins.
Comfort, W: W. Exercises in French prose composition. 25 c.—Les maîtres de la critique littéraire au XIXme siècle 50 c. Heath.
Compayré, J. G. Yvan Gall, le pupille de la marine. 35 c. Holt.
Coppée, F. Contes choisis.—Pour la couronne. ea., 35 c. net. Holt.
Corneille, P. Le Cid. 45 c. Am. Bk.
Corneille, P. Nicomiède. 35 c. net. Macmillan.
Cousin, V. La société française en XVIIe siècle. $1.15. Oxford Univ.
Daniels, W. M., *comp. and ed.* Choix de poésies faciles. *25 c. net. Crowell.
Daudet, A. Choix de contes. 30 c. Heath.
Daudet, A. Jack. pt. 1.—Lettres de mon moulin.—La Tour des Maures. ea., 35 c. Macmillan.
David, J. Le serment. 40 c. Oxford Univ.
Defoe, D. Robinson Crusoe; told in easy French. *50 c. net. Jacobs.
De La Rochelle, P. Guide to French pronunciation. *50 c. net.—New study of French verbs. *$1.50 net. Stechert.
De La Rochelle, P. New and progressive study of French verbs, with idiomatic expressions in French and English. $1.50. F. K. Kane.
Delpit, L. L'age d'or de la litterature française. 90 c. Heath.
Desnoyers, L. C. J. F. Les mésaventures de Jean-Paul Choppart. 40 c. Heath.
Diderot, D. Selections from Diderot. 50 c. Heath.
Dike, F. H., *comp.* Scientific French reader. $1. Silver.
Dionne, N. E., *ed.* Le parler populaire des Canadiens français. *$3 net. Stechert.
Dubois *and* De Geer. Lectures et conversations. 75 c. W: R. Jenkins.
Dumas, A. Episodes from Les trois mousquetaires. 45 c. net. Heath.
Dumas, A. Le Comte de Monte Cristo. 40 c. Am. Bk.
Dumas, A. L'evasion épisode tiré de Vingt ans aprés.—Récits tirés des Impressions de voyage. ea., *25 c. net. Crowell.
Dumas, A. Tales; Le voyage des Mousquetaires, Le dîner de Porthos, Le bastion de Saint-Gervais. 25 c. net. Macmillan.

FRENCH LANGUAGE.—*Continued.*

Durand, Mme. A. M. C. F. Dosia. 45 c. Heath.

Enault, L. Le chien du capitaine. 45 c. net. Putnam.

Erckmann, E., *and* Chatrian, A. Le trésor du vieux seigneur. *25 c. net. Crowell.

Erckmann, E., *and* Chatrain, A. Madame Thérèse. 40 c. Heath.

Fisher, E. La belle au bois dormant. *25 c. net. Crowell.

Flaubert, G. Salambô. $1.15. Oxford Univ.

Fontaine, M. L. P. Les facheux: comedie. 25 c. W: R. Jenkins.

François, V. E. Key to French prose composition. 80 c. Am. Bk.

François, V. E., *ed.* Easy standard French. 40 c. Am. Bk.

Gautier, T. España and Emaux et camées. 70 c.—Voyage en Espagne. 60 c. Oxford Univ.

Gay, A. G. Mon livre de petites histoires. $1. W: R. Jenkins.

Giese, W: F., *and* Cool, C: D., *comps.* French anecdotes arranged for translation. 40 c. Heath.

Globe English-French pocket dict. 75 c. net. Lippincott.

Grimm, J. L. K. *and* W. K. Fairy tales. *50 c. net. Jacobs.

Guerber, H. A. Easy French prose composition 1re part. 25 c.—Joan of Arc. 30 c. Am. Bk.

Halévy, L. Un mariage d'amour. 25 c. Heath.

Harmanson, S. T. M., *comp.* French verb form. 35 c. Ginn.

Healy, E., *comp.* La comédie classique en France. 50 c. Am. Bk.

Hein, G. Exercises in French conversation. *40 c. net. Crowell.

Hélein, J. H. J. Pract. French conversation in thirty easy progressive lessons. 85 c. W: R. Jenkins.

Hénin, B: L. A. French verb drill. 35 c. W: R. Jenkins.

Huelin y Arssu, C. Technological dict. $4. Spon.

Hugo, V. La bataille de Waterloo. *25 c. net. Crowell.

Hugo, V. Les misérables. $1.25.—Ruy Blas. 65 c. Holt.

Hugo, V. Notre-dame de Paris. $1.15.—Préface du Cromwell. 85 c. Oxford Univ

Hugo, V. Selected poems. 80 c. Heath.

James, W., *and* Molé, A. Dictionary of the French and English languages. *$1.50 net. Macmillan.

Johnson, A. S. Six short French plays; for the use of preparatory schools. 50 c. Longmans.

Josselyn, F. M., *and* Talbot, L. R., *eds.* Elem. reader of French history. 30 c. Ginn.

King, L. Le petit bon-homme Pierre. 50 c. Longmans.

Knowles, M. H., *and* Favard, B. C. Perfect French possible. 35 c. Heath.

FRENCH LANGUAGE.—*Continued.*

Koren, W: Exercises in French composition for schools and colleges. 75 c. Holt.

La Bédollière, E. G. de. Histoire de la Mère Michel et de son chat. *35 c. net. Macmillan.

Laboulaye, E. R. L. Le chateau de la vie. *25 c. net. Crowell.

La Fontaine, J. de. Fables, told in easy French. 50 c. net. Jacobs.

Lailavoix, L. La farce de Paquin fils. *25 c. net. Crowell.

Lamartine, A. M. L. Jocelyn. $1.—Tailleur de pierres de Saint-Point. 60 c. Oxford Univ.

Lamy, G. Voyage du novice Jean-Paul a travers la France d'Amerique. 35 c. net. Macmillan.

Landell, G. J. G. de la. Une haine a bord. 75 c. Oxford Univ.

Latham, E: French-English and English-French dictionary. 50 c. Dutton.

Laurie, A., *pseud.* Une année de collège à Paris. 35 c. net. Macmillan.

Lazare, J., *ed.* Les plus jolis contes de fées. 35 c. Ginn.

Lemaître, J. Contes extrait de Myrrha. 30 c. Heath.

Lewis, L. R. Vocab. of French words and idioms. 35 c. Tufts Coll.

Looff, M. Engineers' pocket dictionary of technical terms: French-English. 60 c. Spon.

Luquiens, F: B. Introduction to old French phonology and morphology. *$1.50 net. Yale Univ.

Macé, J. Contes du petit château. *25 c. net. Crowell.

Maistre, X. de. Les prisonniers du Caucase. 30 c. Ginn.

Mansion, J. E., *comp.* Easy French selections for sight translation. 15 c. Heath.

Marchand, C: M. Elem. course in practical French for beginners. **60 c. net. Brentano's.

Marique, P. J., *and* Gilson, H: B. Exercises in French composition. 40 c. Ginn.

Marivaux, P. C. de C. de. Le jeu de l'amour et du hasard. 35 c. net. Macmillan.

Marmier, X. Les fiancés du Spitzberg. 75 c. Oxford Univ.

Martin, C. F. French verb, its conjugation and idiomatic use. $1.25. Am. Bk.

Méras, B. *and* E. J. French verbs and verbal idioms in speech. *60 c. net. Sturgis & W.

Mérimée, P. Contes et nouvelles. 70 c.—La chronique du règne de Charles IX. $1. Oxford Univ.

Michelet, J. Histoire de France. $1. Holt.

Michelet, J. L'oiseau. 70 c. Oxford Univ.

Moffitt, B. L. Drill in French pronunciation. *15 c. net.—French pronoun drill. *25 c. net. W: R. Jenkins.

Molière, J. B. P. de. L'Avare: comédie. *50 c. net. Macmillan.

Molière, J. B. P. de. L'avare.—Le bourgeois gentilhomme.—Le médecin malgré lui. ea., *25 c. net. Crowell.

FRENCH LANGUAGE.—*Continued.*

Molière, J. B. P. de. Le bourgeois gentilhomme. 35 c. Holt.

Moreau, H. Contes à ma sœur. *25 c. net. Crowell.

Musset, L. C. A. de. Croisilles. *25 c. net. Crowell.

Pascal, B., *and others.* Pensées, maximes et réflexions. *40 c. net. Macmillan.

Passy, J., *and* Rambeau, A. Chrestomathie française. *$1.25 net. Stechert.

Peloubet, S. S. Students' law dict. of words and phrases in law Latin, law French and Anglo-Saxon. $1.50; $2. Peloubet.

Perrault, C. Fairy tales, told in easy French. 50 c. net. Jacobs.

Pitman, *Sir* I: International mercantile letters: English-French. 85 c. Pitman.

Post, M. A. My little French book. 50 c. Dutton.

Prentys, E. P. French for daily use. 50 c.; 75 c. W: R. Jenkins.

Racine, J. B. Andromaque.—Britannicus. ea., 35 c. Holt.

Reichenbach, M. Deux comédies enfantines, (Le petit chaperon rouge; Jean et Marguerite.) *25 c. net. Crowell.

Rostand, E. La Princesse Lointaine. 40 c. Heath.

Roth, E: Conversationaliste français. $1. E: Roth.

Roux, L: A. Lessons in [French] grammar and composition. 18 c. Heath.

Rozan, C. Les petites ignorances de la conversation. *25 c. net. Crowell.

Sainte-Beuve, C. A. Causeries du lundi. v. 5. 50 c.; 75 c. Dutton.

Sainte-Beuve, C. A. Trois portraits litteraires. 85 c. Oxford Univ.

Sainte-Hilaire, M. de. Anecdotes sur Napoléon. *25 c. net. Crowell.

Sand, G., *pseud.* François le champi. 85 c. —La petite Fadette. 60 c.—Les maîtres sonneurs. $1.15. Oxford Univ.

Sandeau, L. S. J. Sacs et Parchensins. 35 c. net. Macmillan.

Sandeau, L. S. J. Un heritage. 60 c. Oxford Univ.

Schwann, H. German-French and French-German pocket dictionary. 50 c. Dutton.

Scribe, A. E. Mon étoile. *25 c. net. Crowell.

Scribe, A. E., *and* Legouvé, G. J. B. E. W. Bataille de dames. 30 c. Am. Bk.

Sébillot, P. Choix de contes populaires de la Haute-Bretagne.—Contes des marins de la Haute-Bretagne. ea., *25 c. net. Crowell.

Siepmann, O. Short French grammar. *60 c. net. Macmillan.

Sismondi, J. C. L. de. Marignan: conquêt et perte du Milanais.—Pavie et le sac de Rome. ea., 50 c. Oxford Univ.

Spiers, I. H: B. Manual of elem. French. 50 c.—Exercises on Manual. 50 c. Ginn.

Staël-Holstein, A. L. G. N., *Baronne* de. De l'Allemagne. 85 c. Oxford Univ.

Taine, H. A. Voyage aux Pyrénées. 60 c. Oxford Univ.

Talbot-Tournier, E. La méthode Tournier. $1.25. Belisle Pr.

FRENCH LANGUAGE.—*Continued.*

Thieme, H. P., *and* Effinger, J: R. French grammar. *$1.25 net. Macmillan.

Thierry, J. N. A. Les Normands en Angleterre et en France. 60 c. Oxford Univ.

Tocqueville, A. C. H. C. de. Voyage en Amérique. 40 c. Heath.

Tolhausen, A., *ed.* Technological dictionary in French, English and German. In 3 v. ea., *$2.75 net. Macmillan.

Töpfer, R. Le lac de Gers. *40 c. net. Macmillan.

Tricoche, G: N. Some stumbling blocks of the French language. 75 c.—Vade mecum du professeur de français. $1.50. G: N. Tricoche.

Tuckerman, J. Simplicité: reader of French pronunciation. 50 c. Am. Bk.

Vigny, A. V., *Comte* de. Chatterton. $1. —Servitude et grandeur militaires. 60 c. Oxford Univ.

Voltaire, F. M. A. de. Zaïre; tragedy in verse. 30 c. Heath.

Weill, F., *ed.* Historical French reader. 40 c. Am. Bk.

Willcox, C. De W. French-English military technical dict. Gov. Pr. Off.

Williams-White, H., *and* Robichez, E. French vocabularies. 50 c. Longmans.

Wilson-Green, A. Exercises on Erckmann-Chatrian's Waterloo. *30 c. net. Putnam.

See also Handy pronouncing dictionary;—Tauchnitz manuals of conversation;—Tauchnitz pocket dictionaries.

FRENCH LITERATURE.

Gribble, F. H: Passions of the French Romantics. $3.75 net. Scribner.

Konta, *Mrs.* A. L. Hist. of French literature. **$2.50 net. Appleton.

Pellissier, G. J. M., *comp.* Anthologie des prosateurs français contemporains. v. 1. $1.20 net. Lemcke.

Stephens, W. French novelists of to-day. $1.50. Lane.

Tales from the old French. $1.25 net. Houghton M.

Vreeland, W. U., *and* Michaud, R., *comps.* Anthology of French prose and poetry. $1.40. Ginn.

Wells, B: W. Modern French literature. **$1 net. Little, B. & Co.

Wilmot-Buxton, E. M. Stories from old French romance. 75 c. net. Stokes.

See also Authors;—Manuscripts.

French men of letters; ed. by Alex. Jessup. por. D. **$1.50 net. Lippincott. —Harper. Sainte-Beuve.

French method of intensive cultivation and asparagus forcing. Herrmann, H. $1. H: L. Freking.

French novelists, Stephens, W. $1.50. Lane.

FRENCH PAINTING.

See Painters and paintings.

French pastellists of the eighteenth century. Macfall, H. *$10.50 net. Macmillan.

FRENCH POETRY.

Bailey, J: C. Claims of French poetry. $2.50. M. Kennerley.

Bonnier, C., *comp.* La ligneé des poètes au XIXe siècle. $1. Oxford Univ.

FRENCH POETRY.—*Continued.*

Eccles, F. Y. Century of French poets. $3 net. Dutton.

Lucas, S. W. L., *comp.* Oxford book of French verse; XIII. to XIX. century. *$1.75 net; *$2.40 net; *$3 net. Oxford Univ.

French portrait engraving. Thomas, T. H. $5.50 net. Macmillan.

French prints of the eighteenth century. Nevill, R. $5. Macmillan.

French procession. Darmesteter, *Mme.* A. M. F. R. D. **$3.50 net. Duffield.

FRENCH REVOLUTION.

Acton, J: E. E: D.-A. Lectures on the French Revolution. $3.25 net. Macmillan.

Aulard, F. V. A. French Revolution; political history, 1789-1804. 4 v. per set, $8 net. Scribner.

Burke, E. Reflections on the French Revolution. 35 c. net; 70 c. net. Dutton.

Carlyle, T: French Revolution. 2 v. $2.50; $3. Crowell.

Carlyle, T: French Revolution. 2 v. $3.50; $7.50. Lamb Pub.

Carlyle, T: French Revolution. 3 v. ea., $1.25. Winston.

Carlyle, T: History of the French Revolution. 2 v. ea., *$1 net. Dutton.

Christophelsmeier, C. H. First revolutionary step [in France,] (June 17, 1789.) $1. Univ. of Neb.

Elliott, *Mrs.* G. D. During the Reign of Terror. $1.50. Sturgis & W.

Elliott, *Mrs.* G. D. In the shadow of the guillotine. 75 c. Estes.

Fling, F. M., *ed.* Source studies on the French Revolution. 50 c. F. M. Fling.

Gosselin, L. L. T. Romances of the French Revolution. 2 v. *$6 net. Brentano's.

Gosselin, L. L. T. Tribunal of the terror. *$3.50 net. Lippincott.

Johnston, R. M. The French Revolution. **$1.25 net. Holt.

Kropotkin, *Prince* P. A. Great French Revolution. *$2.25 net. Putnam.

Laprade, W: T: England and the French Revolution. 75 c. Johns Hopkins.

Terry, H., *ed.* French song and verse for children. 50 c. Longmans.

Warwick, C: F. Napoleon and the end of the French Revolution. $2.50 net. Jacobs.

See also France;—*also* Batz, *Baron* de;—Danton, Georges Jacques;—Mirabeau, Honore G. R., *Comte* de.;—Napoleon I.

French secondary schools. Farrington, F. E. $2.50. Longmans.

French vignettes. Betham-Edwards, M. B. **$3 net. Brentano's.

Frênilly, Auguste François Faveau, Marquis de.

Recollections of Baron de Frênilly peer of France, (1768-1828:) ed., with an introd. and notes by Arthur Chuquet; tr. from the French by Frederic Lees. '09(F27) por. O. *$3 net. Putnam.

Frenssen, Gustav.

Peter Moor's journey to southwest Africa: narrative of the German campaign; tr. from the orig. with the consent of the author by Marg. May Ward. '08(S26) c. D. †$1.25. Houghton M.

Frere, F. H.

Permanent way diagrams, giving the spread of crossings for turnouts of any radius: [chart.] '09(Je19) in case, $1.25. Spon.

Frere, Rev. Wa. Howard, and Illingworth, A. L., eds.

Sursum corda: handbook of intercession and thanksgiving; with preface by the Bishop of Southwick. '09(Ap10) *55 c. net *75 c. net. Young Churchman.

Frescati. Daingerfield, *Mrs.* N. G. *$1 net. Neale.

FRESCO PAINTING.

See Wall decoration.

Fresenborg, —.

Thirty years in hell: [account of the author's thirty years as a priest; anti-Catholic.] '08(N) 400 p. $1. L. J. King.

Fresh-air book. Müller, J. P. *85 c. net. Stokes.

Fresh fields and legends old and new. Day, S. J. **$1.25 net Putnam.

Fresh leaves and green pastures. Panton, *Mrs.* J. E. F. *$3.50 net. Brentano's.

Fresh posies. Brown, A. F. $1.50. Houghton M.

Fresh water aquarium and its inhabitants. Eggeling, O. **$2 net. Holt.

Fresh water *Cyclops* of Long Island. Byrnes, E. F. 80 c. Brooklyn Inst.

Fresh water from old wells. Seymour, R. G. **80 c. net. Am. Bapt.

Freshman co-ed. Lee, A. L. $1.25. Penn Pub. Co

FRESNO COUNTY, Cal.

See California.

Freston, Eliz. Helene.

Poems. '08(D) c. 3+143 p. 12°, $1. B'way Pub.

FRET SAW.

See Woodwork.

Fretz, Rev. Abraham Ja.

Genealogical record of the descendants of Andrew Newbaker of Hardwick township, Warren Co., N. Y. '08(D) 4+5-40 p. il. pors. 8°, $1.50; pap., 65 c. Union Times.

Genealogical record of the descendants of Benjamin Chamberlain of Sussex Co., N. J.; with an introd. by Raymond Chamberlain. '07, [1908.] (D) 14+104 p. il. pors. 8°, $1.25; pap., 75 c. A. J. Fretz.

Genealogy of the Moyer family. '09, [1910.] (Je) 144 p. il. pors. 8°, $2.25. A. J. Fretz.

Freud, Sigmund.

Selected papers on hysteria and other psychoneuroses: auth. tr. by A. A. Brill. '09, [1910.] (F) $2. Jour. Nervous Disease

Freyer, P. Johnston, M.D.

Clinical lectures on the surgical diseases of the urinary organs. '08(My16) il. 8°, *$4 net. Wood.

Freytag, Gustav.

Debit and credit; tr. by L. C. Cummings; with a preface by Chevalier Christian C. J. Bunsen. '09(Ag28) D. *$1.50 net. Abbatt.

Die journalisten; lustspiel in vier akten; ed., with introd., notes and vocabulary, by Calvin Thomas. 2d ed., rev. '09(D) c. 10+224 p. 16°, 35 c. Holt.

Friar observant. Brookfield, F. M. $1.50. Herder.

Fricero, Kate I.
Little French people. '10(D) 4°, $1.25. Dodge.
Our visit to France. '09(Ag28) il. f°, $1. Dodge.

Frick, C.
Cursus philosophicus; in usum scholarum. 4th ed. v. 1, Logica. '08, [1909.] (Mr) 12+326 p. 8°, hf. mor., *$1.10 net. Herder.

Friday and Saturday. Byron, M. 50 c. Stokes.

Friedberger, Franz, and Fröhner, Eugen.
Veterinary pathology, (author. tr.;) tr. by Matthew Horace Hayes; with notes on bacteriology by R: Tanner Hewlett. 6th ed., (rev. and enl.) '09(Ja16) 2 v., 8°, *$8 net. Chic. Med. Bk.

Friedenwald, Julius, and Ruhräh, J:
Diet in health and disease. 3d ed., thoroughly rev. and enl. '09(Je) c. 765 p. il. tabs., 8°, $4. Saunders.
Dietetics for nurses. 2d ed., rev. and enl. '09(Je) c. 3-395 p. il. tabs., 8°, *$1.50 net. Saunders.

Friedlander, Ludwig.
Roman life and manners under the Early Empire, v. 1; authorized tr. of the 7th enl. and rev. ed. "Sittengeschichte Roms"; tr. by J. H. Freese and L. A. Magnus. '08(N21); v. 2. '09(Jl17); v. 3 (D) 12°, ea., *$1.50 net. Dutton.

Friedmann, M.
See Gierlich, **Nickolaus.**

Friedrich der Grosse, und Der Siebenjährige Krieg. Schrader, F. 35 c. net. Macmillan.

Friend, J. Albert Newton.
Introd. to the chemistry of paints. '10 (O1) il. D. $1.20 net. Longmans.
Theory of valency: [chemical combination.] '09(F20) figs. D. (Text-books of physical chemistry.) $1.60. Longmans.

Friend, J: Wesley.
Legal aphorisms. '08(D) c. 255 p. 8°, $5. Whittet.

Friend in the kitchen. Colcord, *Mrs.* A. L. 50 c.; 25 c. Review and Herald.

Friendly craft. Hanscom, E. D., *ed.* **$1.25 net. Macmillan.

Friendly library. In 8 v. '09(D25) 16°, ea., *$1.25 net; leath., ea., *$1.75 net. Macmillan.
Contents: The book of Christmas; The book of friendship; Hansome, Elizabeth D., The friendly craft; Lucas, E. V., *ed.,* The gentlest art; The ladies' pageant; Second post; Some friends of mine; Martin, E. S., The wayfarer in New York.

Friendly life. Cope, H: F. *35 c. net. Revell.

Friendly little house. Taggart, M. A. $1.25. Benziger.

FRIENDLY SOCIETIES.
See **Benefit societies.**

Friends, Society of. The Friends' hymnal. Rev. ed. '08(My2) c. O. (Add. pubs. for price.) Funk.

FRIENDS (*Society of*).
Braithwaite, J. B. A "Friend" of the nineteenth century. $2.50 net. Doran.
Edmunds, A. J. Quaker literature in the libraries of Philadelphia. (Add. author for price.) A. J. Edmunds.
Grubb, E: Authority and the light within. *80 c. net. Winston.
Gummere, *Mrs.* A. M. Quaker in the forum. **$1.50 net. Winston.
Gummere, *Mrs.* A. M. Witchcraft and Quakerism. $1. Biddle Press.
Kelly, R. L. Influence of Friends on American education. 25 c. Earlham Coll.
Lampson, *Mrs.* G. L., ***comp.* and *ed.*** Quaker post-bag; letters to Sir John Rodes of Barlbrough Hall, in the county of Derby, Baronet, and to John Gratton, of Monyash, 1693-1742. $2.50 net. **Longmans.**
Moon, J. H. Why Friends (Quakers) do not baptize with water. 25 c. J. H. Moon.
Stephen, C. E. Light arising: [papers from Quaker periodicals.] **90 c. net. Winston.
***See also* Jay, Allen.**

Friends and friendships. Hearn, E: C. 25 c. E: C. Hearn.

Friends from the Book of books. Mord, W. $1.50. Stokes.

Friends of the hunted. Jewett, J: H. $1. Dodge.

FRIENDSHIP.
Addingley, A., *comp.* In friendship's meditation. 75 c.; $1.50. Platt & P.
Black, H. Friendship booklets. 6 v. ea., 35 c. net. Revell.
Book of friendship. $1.25 net; $1.75 net. Macmillan.
Brooks, R:, *comp.* Old friends are best. $1.25; $2. Dodge.
Catchwords of friendship. *50 c. net. McClurg.
Cicero, M. T. Essay on friendship. 50 c. Newton & C.
Cicero, M. T., *and* Emerson, R. W. On friendship, by Cicero; Friendship, by Emerson. **$2.50 net. Putnam.
Connolly, M., *ed.* Friendship year book. 60 c.; $1. Crowell.
Cope, H: F: Friendly life. *35 c. net. Revell.
Elder, D: P., *comp.* Friendship. 50 c. P. Elder.
Foster, A. G. To friendship. 35 c. P. Elder.
Glasspool, R:, *comp.* To have a friend, be one. $1; $2. Platt & P.
Grayson, D:, *pseud.* Adventures in friendship. $1.20, fixed. Doubleday, P.
Hearn, E: C. Friends and friendships. 25 c. E: C. Hearn.
Kauffman, R. W., *comp.* Book of friendship. 75 c. Altemus.
King, H: C. Laws of friendship—human and divine. *$1.25 net. Macmillan.
M., A. D., *comp.* Friendship tried is ever true. 30 c. Stokes.
Ransome, A., *comp.* Book of friendship. $2.50 net. Stokes.

FRIENDSHIP.—*Continued.*
Rice, W. de G. C. *and* F. Wealth of friendship. $1.25; $2; $2.50. Barse & H.
Rice, W. G. *and* F., *comps.* Little book of friendship. 35 c.; $1. Reilly & B.
Shaffner, L. Love and friendship. 25 c. P. Elder.
Shayler, J. In friendship's garden. $1.25; $2. Stokes.
Stevenson, R. L: Meaning of friendship. 50 c. Canterbury Co.
Thoreau, H: D. Friendship. 75 c. Putnam.
Warren, I. R., *comp.* Book of friendship. $1.50 net. Jacobs.
Woolard, S: F., *ed.* Beauties of friendship. *50 c. net; *$1.25 net. Goldsmith-W.
Friendship outstays the hurrying flight of time. '09(Ag) 41 p. front. in col., 12°, *50 c. net. Dodge.
Friendship ser. 10 v. '10(N) ea., 25 c.; ooze, 75 c., boxed. Crowell.
Friendship through the year. Lander, M. J., *comp.* $1; $1.50. Dodge.
Friendship village. Gale, Z. †$1.50. Macmillan.
Friendship village love stories. Gale, Z: †$1.50. Macmillan.
Fries, Jan August.
Methods and standards in bomb calorimetry: investigations in co-operation with the Institute of Animal Nutrition of the Pennsylvania State College. '10(O) 32 p. tabs., 8°, (U. S., Dept. of Agriculture, Bu. of Animal Industry, bull.)
See also Armsby, H: Prentiss.
FRIESIAN CATTLE.
See Cattle.
Frink, Fred Goodrich.
See Hall, Arth. Graham.
Frink, Mrs. Maria, ["Grace Gold,"] comp.
How to be happy; gems of thought from the world's greatest writers. '08(Mr7) c. il. por. D. $1; pap., 25 c. Laird.
Fripp, Sir Alfr. Downing.
Human anatomy for the art student. '10 (D10) il. 8°, (New art lib.) $1.75 net. Lippincott.
Fritch, G. M., ed.
Baby's history; record of the first eventful year in the life of our dear child. '10 (Ap9) c. il. 4°, 60 c. G. M. Fritch.
Frithiof's saga. *See* Tegnér, Esaias.
Fritsch, W. A.
Aus Amerika: alte und neue heimath. '08 (Ap11) S. pap., 40 c. Lemcke.
Fritts, J: P.
Port Jervis [N. Y.]; ed. by W. H. Nearpass and Ja. Bennett. '08(O) c. 47 p. 4°, 25 c. E. L. Parks.
Fritz auf ferien. Arnold, H. 25 c. Am. Bk.
Fritz in Germany. McDonald, *Mrs.* E. A. B. 60 c. Little, B. & Co.
Fritzi. Daulton, *Mrs.* A. M. †$1.50. Century Co.
Frobenius, Leo.
Childhood of man: account of the lives, customs and thoughts of the primitive races tr. by A. H. Keane. '08(O10) il. O. *$3 net. Lippincott.

FROEBEL, Friedrich Wilhelm August.
Wiebé, E: Golden jubilee edition of The paradise of childhood; incl. a life of Froebel, by H: W. Blake. $2. M. Bradley
Froeberg, Sven.
Relation between the magnitude of stimulus and the time of reaction. '08(Ap11) il. tabs., O. (Archives of psychology.) pap., 35 c. Science Press, (N. Y.)
Froehlich, Hugo B., and Snow, Bonnie E.
Progressive lessons in art education. In 8 v. '10(Jl 2) c. il., partly col., ea., 15 c. Prang.
FROG.
Meek, S. E. Batrachians and reptiles from British East Africa.—Notes on batrachians and reptiles from the islands north of Venezuela. ea., 50 c. Field Museum.
University of Michigan. Laboratory directions for general biology; the frog. 25 c. Wahr.
See also Embryology.
Frogs o' Poolo. Crowell, J. F. $1.50. Dutton.
Frogville wheelman. Beadle, M. L. S. $1. M. L. S. Beadle.
Frohne, H. W.
See Desmond, H: W.
Fröhner, Eugen.
See Friedberger, Franz.
Froissart, Jean.
Chronicles of England, France and Spain. '08(O24) il. 12°, $2.50. Dutton.
Chronicles of England, France, Spain and the adjoining countries; tr. from the French by T: Johnes. [Also] Voltaire's Charles XII.; tr. by Tobias Smollett, with special introd. by Justin McCarthy. '08 (Je27) c. 2 v., il. 8°, $3.50; hf. mor., $7. Lamb Pub.
Frolics at Fairmount. Baker, *Mrs.* E. A. $1.50. Little, B. & Co.
From a book lover's notes. Simpson, K. D., *comp.* 60 c. Cloister.
From Bull Run to Appomattox. Hopkins, L. W. $1. L. W. Hopkins.
From Cairo to the Cataract. Carson, B. M. $2.50. L. C. Page.
From canoe to tunnel. Jersey City, N. J., Free Public Library. gratis. Jersey City Lib.
From Capitol to Kremlin. Guthridge, A. S. J. $1.25 net. Neale.
From Damascus to Palmyra. Kehnan, J: *$6 net. Macmillan.
From darkness to light. Helm, M. *50 c. net; *30 c. net. Revell.
From dawn to dusk. Fisher, W: D. 50 c. McDonald & Co.
From day to day with Longfellow. Longfellow, H: W. 75 c. Barse & H.
From day to day with Stevenson. Stevenson, R. L: 75 c. Barse & H.
From day to day with Tennyson. Tennyson, A., *Lord.* 75 c. Barse & H.
From day to day with Whittier. Whittier, J: G. 75 c. Barse & H.
From Eden to the Jordan. Medbury, C: S. 50 c.; 30 c. Standard Pub.

From Edinburgh to India and Burmah. Burn-Murdoch, W. G. *$3.50 net. Dutton.
"—— from cellar to garret": textbook on household science. '09(My8) c. obl. Ff. pap., 10 c. Carbona.
From here and there. Giddings, J. W. 75 c. Cochrane.
From incarnation to reincarnation. Ingalese, R: $2. Occult.
From Irish castles to French chateaux. Carson, *Mrs.* N. B. $1.50 net. Small.
From keel to kite. Hornibrook, I. †$1.50. Lothrop, L. & S.
From kingdom to colony. Devereux, M. †75 c. Little, B. & Co.
From kitchen to garret. Van de Water, *Mrs.* V. T. 75 c. net. Sturgis & W.
From Lincoln to Taft. Smith, C: E., *comp.* (Add. pubs. for price.) Hammerling.
From log cabin to the White House. Thayer, W: M. 50 c. Hurst.
From lotos to cherry blossom. Morrison, S. G. $1.50. Cochrane.
From Metternich to Bismarck. Jane, L. C. $1.10. Oxford Univ.
From my youth up. Sangster, *Mrs.* M. E. M. *$1.50 net. Revell.
From nature to man. Conner, C: C. 75 c. Hampden Pub.
From passion to peace. Allen, J. 50 c. net. Crowell.
From Peking to Mandalay. Johnston, R. F. *$5 net. Dutton.
From Pekin to Sikkim. Lesdain, *Count* de. *$4 net. Dutton.
From pillow to throne. Jacobs, C: W. 50 c. M. A. Johnson.
From poet to premier. Slicer, T: R. *$3 net. Grolier Club.
From prospect to mine. Ritter, E. A. $2. Mining Science.
From quiet valleys. Jones, T: S., *jr.* $1.25. G: W: Browning.
From Ruwenzori to the Congo. Wollaston, A. F. R. *$5 net. Dutton.
From sea to sea. *See* Kipling, Rudyard.
From Sioux to Susan. Daulton, *Mrs.* A. M. †$1.50. Century Co.
From sketch-book and diary. Butler, *Lady* E. *$2.50 net. Macmillan.
From slavery to freedom. Macy, S. B. $1.25 net. Longmans.
From smithy to senate. Hodgson, G: B. *$1.75 net. Cassell.
From text to talk. Ballard, A. $1.20 net. Sherman, F.
From the book of life. Burton, R: **$1.25 net. Little, B. & Co.
From the bottom up. Irvine, A. F. **$1.50 net. Doubleday, P.
From the cup of silence. Huntington, H. M. G. $1. Putnam.
From the earth to the moon. Verne, J. 50 c. Hurst.
From the Eastern Sea. Noguchi, Y. $1 net. M. Kennerley.
From the evidence presented. Stone, D. C. 25 c. Saginaw.
From the foothills of song. Packard, C. M. $1. Badger.
From the Foreland to Penzance. Holland, C. *$3.50 net. Duffield.
From the heart of the hills. Scollard, C. $1. G: W. Browning.
From the Jordan to the throne of Saul. Medbury, C: S. 25 c. Standard Pub.
From the jungle through Europe with Roosevelt. O'Laughlin, J: C. 25 c. Chapple Pub.
From the plains to the pulpit. Anderson, J: W. $1. J: W. Anderson.
From the Thames to the Seine. Pears, C: $4 net. Jacobs.
From their point of view. Loane, M. $2. Longmans.
From Virginia to Texas. Gray, W: F. (Not for sale.) A. C. Gray.
From youth into manhood. Hall, W. S. 50 c. Y. M. C. A.

Frommel, Emil.
Mit ränzel und wanderstab: eine schülerwanderung durch den nördlichen Schwarzwald; ed., with exercises, notes and vocab., by Dr. Wilhelm Bernhardt. '09(Mr13) c. il. por. S. (Modern lang. ser.) 35 c. Heath.

Frontenoy, Mme. la Marquise de.
See Owen, Marg. Cunliffe.

Frontier (The). Platt, W. 50 c.; 35 c. Young People's Miss.
Frontier army and professional life. Finch, E. W. $1. Simmons, M. & D.
Frontier ballads. Hanson, J. M. $1.50. McClurg.
Frontier boys. Roosevelt, W. 60 c. Chatterton-P.
Frontier boys in Colorado. Roosevelt, W. 60 c. Chatterton-P.
Frontier boys in Hawaii. Roosevelt, W. 60 c. Chatterton-P.
Frontier boys in the Rockies. Roosevelt, *Captain* W. 60 c. Chatterton-P.
Frontier boys in the saddle. Roosevelt, W. 60 c. Chatterton.
Frontier boys in the Sierras. Roosevelt, W. 60 c. Chatterton-P.
Frontier boys on the coast. Roosevelt, *Captain* W. 60 c. Chatterton-P.
Frontiers. Curzon, G: N., *Baron.* 50 c. Oxford Univ.
Frontiers of Baluchistan. Tate, G. P. *$5 net. Scribner.
Frontiersman (The). Cody, H. A. $1.20 net. Doran.

Frost, E. L.
See Frost, T: G.

Frost, F: J. Tabor.
See Arnold, Channing.

Frost, Harwood.
Art of roadmaking. '10(N12) il. por. 8°, $3. H. Frost.

Frost, Ja. Marion.
The memorial supper of our Lord: a plea for organic church life. '08(Mr) c. 282 p. il. 12°, 90 c. S. S. Bd. So. Bapt.
Our church life; serving God on God's plan. '09(N) c. 269 p. front. 12°, (Eva Garvey Publishing Fund.) 90 c. S. S. Bd. So. Bapt.
—, ed. Experience of grace, three notable instances: Saul of Tarsus, John Jasper, Edward Everett Hale, jr. '08(Jl4) c. 16°, 40 c.; pap., 25 c. S. S. Bd. So. Bapt.

Frost, T: Gold.
Man of destiny. '09(Ag7) c. il. D. $1.50. Gramercy.
Treatise on guaranty insurance and compensated suretyship; including therein as subsidiary branches the law of fidelity, commercial and judicial insurance, [etc.] 2d ed., rev. and enl. '09(Mr) c. 54+802 p. O. $6. Little, B. & Co.
Treatise on the business corporation law of the state of New York. '09(Ag) c. 20+1097 p. O. $6. M. Bender.
Treatise on the incorporation and organization of corporations, created under the "business corporation acts" of all the states and territories of the U. S. 3d ed., enl. and rev. to Jan. 1, 1908. '08(Ap) c. O. **$5 net. Little, B. & Co.
— and E. L.
Frost family in England and America. '09 (N) 195 p. $3. Russell Pr.
Frost, W: Dodge, and McCampbell, Eug. Franklin.
Text-book of general bacteriology. '10(D) c. 17+340 p. il. D. $1.60 net. Macmillan.
FROST.
See Meteorology.
FROST FAMILY.
See Genealogies.
Frothingham, Arth. Lincoln.
Monuments of Christian Rome, from Constantine to the Renaissance. '08(D12) c. il. O. (Handbooks of archæology and antiquities.) **$2.25 net. Macmillan.
Roman cities in Italy and Dalmatia. '10 (Je) c. il. O. $1.75 net. Sturgis & W.
Frothingham, R:
Rise of the republic of the United States. 10th ed. '10(S10) c. O. $2. Little, B. & Co.
Froude, Ja. Anthony.
Edward VI.; introd. by Llewellyn Williams. '09(Mr27) 16°, (Everyman's lib.) *35 c. net; leath., *70 c. net. Dutton.
Henry VIII.; introd. by Llewellyn Williams. 3 v. '09(Mr27) 16°, (Everyman's lib.) ea., *35 c. net; leath., *70 c. net. Dutton.
Mary Tudor; introd. by Llewellyn Williams. '10(N12) 16°, (Everyman's lib.) 35 c. net; leath., 70 c. net. Dutton.
Short studies on great subjects. In 5 v. '08(D5) 16°, ea., *60 c. net. Scribner.
Frozen fortune. Pollock, F. L. $1.20 net. Macaulay.
Frozen grail. Barker, E. $1.25 net. Duffield.
Frozen Northland. Mason, W. S. $1. Jennings.
Frugality in the spiritual life. Watkinson, W: L. *$1 net. Revell.
FRUIT.
American Pomological Society. Fruits recommended by the American Pomological Society for cultivation in the various sections of U. S. and Canada. (Add. Superintendent for price.) U. S., Supt. of Docs.
Bailey, L. H. Principles of fruit-growing. **$1.50 net. Macmillan.
Bealby, J: T. Fruit ranching in British Columbia. *$1.50 net. Macmillan.

FRUIT.—*Continued.*
Dygert, H. A. Crops that pay: pecans, mangoes, avocados, pineapples. 10 c. Am. Fruit & Nut Co.
Farmer's shipping associations; plans of organization of shipping associations for fruit and vegetable growers. gratis. Fruit-Grower.
Fortier, S: Irrigation of orchards. Gov. Pr. Off.
Gould, H. P. Fruit growing for home use in the central and southern Great Plains. U. S., Supt. of Docs.
Green, S: B. Popular fruit growing. $1. Webb.
Hume, H. H. Citrus fruits and their culture. $2.50 net. Judd.
Kains, M. G., *comp.* Making horticulture pay; experiences in gardening and fruit growing. $1.50. Judd.
Los Angeles. Public Library. California, United States and experiment station documents of interest to California horticulturists. (Add. Library for price.) Los Angeles Lib.
Paddock, W., *and* Whipple, O. B. Fruit-growing in arid regions. $1.50 net. Macmillan.
Thornton, A: W. Suburbanite's hdbk. of dwarf fruit tree culture. 50 c. A: W. Thornton.
Wickson, E: J. California fruits and how to grow them. $3. Pacific Rural.
See also Agriculture;—Apples;—Berries;—Cookery;—Fertilizers;—Fig;—Gardens and gardening;—Grafting; — Grapes;—Lemon;—Mangoes;—Moth;—Oranges;—Preserving;—Trees.
Fruit of desire. Demarest, V., *pseud.* $1.20 net. Harper.
Fruits of the devotion to the Sacret Heart. Graham, W: S. 75 c. Wagner.
Fruits of the tree. Bryan, W: J. 35 c. net. Revell.
Fry, Mrs. Anna M. Gayle.
Memories of old Cahaba, [Ala.] '08, [1909.] (S) c. '05. 128 p. il. 12°, $1. Pub. Ho. of M. E. Ch., So.
Fry, R:
Scheme for a paper currency; together with two petitions written in Boston Gaol in 1739-1740; with an introd. by And. McFarland Davis. '08(N7) $3.75. Club for Colonial Reprints.
Fry, W: H:
New Hampshire as a Royal Province. '09 (F27) c. O. (Columbia Univ. studies in hist., economics and public law.) pap., $3. Longmans.
Frye, Alexis Everett.
First book in geography. '10(Ag27) il. maps, O. 50 c. Ginn.
Grammar school geography. pt. 1. '10 (Je4) c. il. maps, 8°, 80 c. Ginn.
Frye, Prosser Hall.
Literary reviews and criticisms. '08(O3) c. D. **$1.25 net. Putnam.
Frye, W: E:
After Waterloo; reminiscences of European travel, 1815-1819; ed., with a preface and notes, by Salomon Reinach. '09(Jl31) 8°. (Add. pubs. for price.) P. R. Reynolds.

Fryer, C: E:
International regulations of the fisheries on the high seas; from bulletin of the Bureau of Fisheries, volume XXVIII, 1908. '10(Mr26) 4°, (U. S., Bu. of Fisheries, bull.)

Fryer, J:
Admission of Chinese students to American colleges. '09(Jl3) 8°, (U. S., Bureau of Education, bull.) pap. (Add. Superintendent for price.)

FUCACEAE.
See **Seaweeds.**

Fuchs, Ernest, M.D.
Text book of ophthalmology; authorized tr. from the 11th German ed. by Alex. Duane. 3d Eng. ed. '08(Mr7) c. 8°, *$6 net. Lippincott.

Fucus histriomastix. *See* Ward, Rob.

FUEL.
Baker, G: H. Locomotive fuel economy. $1. R'way Educ.
Booth, W: H., *and* Kershaw, J. B. C. Smoke prevention and fuel economy. $2.50. Henley.
Fernald, R. H., *and others.* Incidental problems in gas-producer tests. (Add. Superintendent for price.) U. S., Supt. of Docs.
Goss, W: F. M. Utilization of fuel in locomotive practice. (Add Superintendent for price.) U. S., Supt. of Docs.
Jüptner von Jonstorff, H. Heat energy and fuels. *$3 net. McGraw.
Lewes, V. B. Liquid and gaseous fuels. *$2 net. Van Nostrand.
Sexton, A. H. Fuel and refractory materials. $2.50 net. Van Nostrand.
Snodgrass, J: M. Fuel tests with house-heating boilers. gratis. Univ. of Ill.
Strong, R. M. Commercial deductions from comparisons of gasoline and alcohol tests on internal-combustion engines. U. S., Supt. of Docs.
White, M. Fuels of the household. *75 c. net. Whitcomb.
See also Coal;—Gases;—Locomotives;—Petroleum.

Fuertes, Ja. Hillhouse.
See Soper, G: Alb.

Fuess, Claude Moore, and Sanborn, H: N., eds.
English narrative poems. '09(O9) 24°, (Pocket Am. and Eng. classics.) *25 c. net. Macmillan.

Fugitive freshman. Paine, R. D. $1.50. Scribner.

Fugitives (The). Nonnen, E. 50 c. Engberg-H.

FUGUE.
See **Music.**

Fuhrmann Henshel. Hauptman, G. $1.25. Dramatic.

Fujiwara, Sadaiye, comp.
Hundred verses from old Japan; being a tr. of the Hyakunin-isshiu by W: N. Porter. '10(F19) il. S. (Oxford lib. of prose and poetry.) 90 c. Oxford Univ.

Fuld, Leonhard Felix.
Police administration; critical study of police organizations in the United States and abroad. '10(F5) c. il. tabs., pors. O. **$3 net. Putnam.

Fulda, Ludwig.
Der dummkopf, lustspiel in fünf augzügen; ed., with introd. and notes, by W: Kilborne Stewart. '10(D3) c. S. 35 c. Holt.

Fulfillment (The). Raphael, F. P. $1.50. Sturgis & W.

Full allegiance. Knight, G. H. *$1 net. Armstrong.

Full-back afloat. Dudley, A. T. †$1.25. Lothrop, L. & S.

Full blessing of Pentecost. Murray, A. *75 c. net. Revell.

Full fathom five. Melville, H. $1.50 net. Macmillan.

Full glory of Diantha. Mighels, E. S. $1.50. Forbes.

Fuller, Arth. Franklin.
Poems. [1910] (Ap) c. '09, 69 p. 16°, 35 c. Solar Lit.
A man and his neighbors. [1910.] (F) c. '09. il. pors. 8°, 35 c. Solar Lit.
Odd soldiery. [1910.] (Je) c. 116 p. il. pors. O. pap., 25 c. Solar Lit.

Fuller, Arth. W:
Complete manual for 1908 of questions and answers for examination on the standard code of railroad rules and train rights. '08(Ag22) c. S. $1. A. W. Fuller.

Fuller, Eva Greene, comp.
Up-to-date sandwich book. '09(N13) c. D. bds., *$1 net. McClurg.

Fuller, F: D.
Analysis of Paris green, 1908. '09, [1910.] (Mr) 32 p. 8°, (Commonwealth of Pennsylvania, Dept. of Agriculture, bull.) pap. Penn. Dept. of Agriculture.
Preliminary report on results of analysis of Paris green. '08(O10) 8°, (Penn., Dept. of Agriculture, bull.) (Add. pubs. for price.) Penn. Dept. of Agriculture.

Fuller, Harvey Austin.
Beauties of the gloaming. '08(D) c. 5-66 p. il. 8°, $1; pap., 30 c. H. A. Fuller.

Fuller, H: Blake.
Waldo Trench, and others: stories of Americans in Italy. '08(S5) c. D. †$1.50. Scribner.

Fuller, Hubert Bruce.
Speakers of the House. '09(S25) c. por. O. **$2 net. Little, B. & Co.

Fuller, Paul Edn.
Use of windmills in irrigation in the semi-arid west. '10(Jl) 44 p. il. 8°, (U. S. Dept. of Agriculture; farmers' bull.)

Fuller, Rob. Higginson.
Government by the people: laws and customs regulating the election system and the formation and control of political parties in the United States. '08(My2) c. D. **$1 net. Macmillan.
South Africa at home. '08(D5) il. 12°, *$1.75 net. Scribner.

Fuller, Rufus.
Circle and square; ancient problem arranged in four parts. '08, [1909.] (Jl) c. '07. 46 p. il. 8°, $1. R. Fuller.

Fuller, S: R:
See Brainerd, Norman, *pseud.*

Fuller, Sir T: Ekins.
Right Honourable Cecil John Rhodes; monograph and reminiscence. '10(Je4) il. O. $1.60 net. Longmans.

Fuller, T: O.
Twenty years in public life, 1890-1910, North Carolina-Tennessee. '10(O) c. 279 p. il. pors. 12°, $1.25. Nat. Bapt. Pub.

Fuller, W: Hyslop, comp.
Genealogy of some descendants of Edward Fuller of the "Mayflower." '08(N) 306 p. il. pors. 8°, $4. W: H. Fuller.
Genealogy of some descendants of Dr. Samuel Fuller of the Mayflower; to which is added a Supp. to the Genealogy of some descendants of Edward Fuller of the Mayflower pub. in 1908. '10(D) 263 p. il. pors. 8°, $5. W: H. Fuller.

Fuller, W: Oliver.
"An old town by the sea." 2d ed. '09, [1910.] (Ag) 16 p. il. 16°, 5 c. W: O. Fuller.

FULLER FAMILY.
See Genealogies.

FULLER'S OHIO BRIGADE.
See Ohio.

Fullerton, A. R., comp.
Life insurance law chart, 1908-1909; summary of state [New York] laws applicable to life ins. companies of other states. '08(O) c. (Add. pub. for price.) Spectator.

Fullerton, Edith Loring.
Lure of the land; history of a market-garden and dairy plot developed within eight months upon Long Island's idle territory, long designated as "scrub oak waste," and "pine barrens," being a true story of the work carried on by the Long Island Railroad Co. at Experimental Stations Numbers One and Two, to which in this the second edition has been added the aftermath, bringing the story from September, '05, to September, '09. '09, [1910.] (Ap) c. 9+142 p. 8°. Long Island R. R.

Fullerton, Lady Georgiana Levenson Gower.
Constance Sherwood: an autobiography of the sixteenth century. '08(Ag8) 8°, 40 c. Connoisseurs' Press.

Fullerton, Hugh S.
See Evers, J: J.

Fulmer, Clark Adelbert.
State and local government of Nebraska. [1910.] (My) c. '09. 112 p. 12°, 50 c. Ginn.

Fulness of Christ, Talbot, E. S. *50 c. net. Macmillan.

Fulness of the gospel. Moody, D. L. *50 c. net. Revell.

Fulton, C: Herman.
Principles of metallurgy; introd. to the metallurgy of the metals. '10(O8) c. il. tabs., diagrs., 8°, $5. McGraw-H.

Fulton, Edn. Giles.
Vegetarian cook-book; substitutes for flesh foods. '10(Jl16) c. il. tabs., por. 12°, $1. Pacific Press.

Fulton, Ja. A.
Other side of the money question. '08 (Ap18) c. D. pap., 25 c. Hutchinson & B.

Fulton, Rob.
Life of Robert Fulton, and information regarding the business transactions by the Fulton Trust Co. of New York [2d ed.] '08, [1909.] (F.) c. '06, 23 p. il. pors., O. pap., gratis. Fulton Trust Co.

FULTON, Robert.
Brooklyn Public Library. List of books and magazine articles on Henry Hudson and the Hudson River, Robert Fulton and early steam navigation. gratis. Brooklyn Lib.
Hall, E. H. Hudson and Fulton. (Add. pubs. for price.) Hudson-Fulton.
Horner, H. H., *comp. and ed.* Hudson-Fulton celebration, Sept. 25 to Oct. 9, 1909. (Add. pubs. for price.) N. Y. State Educ.
Hudson-Fulton Celebration Commission, New York. Hudson and Fulton. (Not for sale.) Hudson-Fulton.
Miller, P. F. Story of Robert Fulton. $1. P. F. Miller.
Sutcliffe, *Mrs.* A. C. Robert Fulton and the "Clermont." **$1.20 net. Century Co.
See also Hudson-Fulton celebration.

Fulton, Rob. Irving, and Trueblood, T: Clarkson.
Essentials of public speaking for secondary schools. '09(Je26) c. il. D. 90 c.; 2d ed. '10(N12) c. il. D. $1. Ginn.

Fultz, Fs. Marion.
Fly-aways and other seed travelers. '09 (Ag7) il. 16°, 60 c. Pub. Sch. Pub.
Out of door studies in geography. In 2 pts. pt. 1, The making of the surface and soils of the upper Mississippi region; pt. 2, The formation of mountain ranges. '09(Ag7) il. 12°, ea., 60 c. Pub. Sch. Pub.

FUMIGATION.
Woglum, R. S. Fumigation investigations in California. 15 c. U. S., Supt. of Docs.

Fun and pathos of one life. Du Bois, J. T. $1. Neale.
Fun in a doctor's life. Clevenger, S. V. $1. Evolution Pub.
Fun in the school-room. Shelland, H: E. 15 c. Dick.
Fun on the farm. Craveison, O. $1.25. Kuyahora Press.
Function, feeling, and conduct. Meakin, F: **$1.50 net. Putnam.
Function of a school of pedagogy. Horne, H. H. gratis. Sch. Pedagogy.
Function of criticism. Smith, D: N. 35 c. Oxford Univ.
Function of religion in man's struggle for existence. Foster, G: B. *$1 net. Univ. of Chic.
Function of state historian of New York. Paltsits, V. H. gratis. N. Y. State Hist.
Functional diagnosis. Atkinson, T: G. $1.50. Chic. Med. Bk.
Functional nerve diseases. Schofield, A. T. *$2.50 net. Dutton.
Fundamental English. McNichols, J: P. 80 c. Schwartz, K. & F.
Fundamental facts of elementary physics. Bardeen, C: W:, *ed.* $1. Bardeen.
Fundamental fallacies of socialism. Preuss, A. *$1 net. Herder.

Fundamental theorems of the differential calculus. Young, W: H: 75 c. net. Putnam.
Fundamental truths of the Christian religion. Seeberg, R. *$1.50 net. Putnam.
Fundamentals and requirements of health and disease. Powell, T: $5. Powell Pub.
Fundamentals in education, art and criticism. Raymond, G: L. $1.40 net. Funk.
Fundamentals of child study. Kirkpatrick, E. A. *$1.25 net. Macmillan.

FUNERALS.
De Long, A. H. Pastor's ideal funeral book. $1. Jennings.
See also Burial;—Cremation.

FUNGI.
Buller, A. H. R. Researches on fungi. *$4 net. Longmans.
Clements, F. E: Genera of fungi. $2. H. W. Wilson.
Duggar, B: M. Fungous diseases of plants. $2. Ginn.
Lloyd, C. G. Synopsis of the known phalloids. (Not for sale. Apply to author for terms.) Lloyd Lib.
Patterson, *Mrs.* F. W., *and others.* Some fungous diseases of economic importance. Gov. Pr. Off.
Reed, G: M. Infection experiments with *erysiphe cichoracearum:* [mildews.] 35 c. Univ. of Wis.
Setchell, W: A. Genus Sphaerosoma. 15 c. Univ. of Cal.
White, E: A. Second rept. on the hymeniales of Conn. 35 c. Conn. Lib.
See also Bacteria;—Fermentation.

Funk, Franz Xavier.
Manual of church hist.; auth. tr. from the 5th German ed. by Luigi Cappadelta. v. 1. '10(Jl) 16+396 p. 8°, $2.75 net. Herder.

Funk, I: Kaufman, D.D.
Next step in evolution: the present step. 4th ed. '08(Ap25) c. front. S. **50 c. net. Funk.
—, ed. *See* Standard dictionary.

Funk, W. R.
See Mills, Job Smith.

Funny bone. Kieffer, H: M. 75 c.; $1. Dodge.

FUR.
Harding, A. R. Fur farming. 60 c. A. R. Harding.
See also Minks.

Furetière, Antoine.
Poésies diverses; tr. by Isabella Bronk. '08(Ag) c. 162 p. por. 8°, pap., $1.50. Furst.
Poésies diverses; partial reprint from the edition of 1664; ed., with introd., notes and glossary, by Isabelle Bronk. '08 (D19) por. Q. *$1.75 net. Stechert.

Furlong, C: Wellington.
Gateway to the Sahara; observations and experiences in Tripoli. '09(O9) c. il. (partly col.) O. **$2.50 net. Scribner.

Furlong, J: Ryan.
Is Ingersoll in hell? 2d ed., enl. '10(Ag) 183 p. por. 12°, $1. Boulder Pub.

Furman, Howard Van F.
Manual of pract. assaying; rev. by W: D. Pardoe. 6th ed. '08(N7); 7th ed., rev. and enl. '10(N5) c. il. tabs., 8°, ea., $3. Wiley.

Furnace of gold. Mighels, P. V. $1.20. FitzGerald.

FURNACES.
Borchers, J. A. W. Electric furnaces. *$2.50 net. Longmans.
Forsythe, R. Blast furnace and the manufacture of pig iron $3. D: Williams.
Harbison-Walker Refractories Co., Pittsburg. Study of the open hearth. $1. R. S. Davis.
Kershaw, J: B. C. Electric furnace in iron and steel production. **$2.50 net. Van Nostrand.
King, A. S. Electric furnace for spectroscopic investigations. (Add. Institution for price.) Carnegie.
Kirk, E: Cupola furnace. $3.50. Baird.
Morgan, J. J. Blast furnace practice. *75 c. net. Lippincott.
Nagel, O. Producer gas fired furnaces. *$2 net. O. Nagel.
Smith, M. H. Furnaceman's hdbk. 50 c. Master Sheet Metal.
Stansfield, A. Electric furnace: its evolution and practice. $2. Hill Pub.
See also Boilers.

Furneaux, W: S.
Field and woodland plants. '09(D4) col. il. D. (Outdoor world ser.) *$1.50 net. Longmans.

Furness, Horace Howard, ed.
See Shakespeare, W:

Furness, W: H:
See Emerson, Ralph Waldo.

Furness, W: H:, 3d.
Island of stone money; Uap of the Carolines. '10(O15) c. il. map, O. $3.50 net. Lippincott.

Furnishing of a modest home. Daniels, F. H. $1. Davis Press.

Furniss, Harry.
Book of Dickens illustrations; now published complete in one volume; first printed in fourteen volumes of Dickens' works by the same publisher. '10(Jl2) c. 12°, $1. J. T. Gleason.

FURNITURE.
Baroggio, A. Two hundred seating furniture in historical styles. $12. A. Gerbel.
Bell, J. M., *comp.* Furniture designs of Thomas Chippendale.—Furniture designs of George Hepplewhite. ea., $6 net. Scribner.
Benn, H. P., *and* Bolwock, W. C. Characteristics of old furniture styles in England. *$1 net. Scribner.
Binstead, H. E. Furniture styles; with a chapter on modern mission and craftsman furniture. $2. Trade Periodical.
Brigham, L. Box furniture. **$1.60 net. Century Co.
Dyer, W. A. Lure of the antique; being a book of ready reference for collectors of old furniture, china, mirrors, etc., and other household furnishings of our American forefathers. $2.40 net. Century Co.
Glidden, A. G. Hand made furniture and how to make it. $1. Hand Made Furniture.

FURNITURE.—*Continued.*
Hessling, E., *ed.* Louis XV. furniture in the Louvre. $10.—Louis XV. furniture in the Museum of Decorative Art at Paris. $12.—Renaissance furniture. $21. Hessling.
Hessling, E. *and* W. Louis XIV. furniture in the Louvre and the Museum of Decorative Arts, (Paris.) $13.40. Hessling.
Hodgson, F: T: Pract. cabinet maker and furniture designer's assistant. $2. Drake.
Jacquemart, A. History of furniture. *$7.50 net. Scribner.
Lenygon, F. Decoration and furniture of English mansions during the seventeenth and eighteenth centuries. *$1 net. Scribner.
Lockwood, L. V. Collection of English furniture of the XVII. and XVIII. centuries. (Not for sale.) Tiffany Studios.
Macquoid, P. History of English furniture. In 4 v. v. 4 $15. Putnam.
Polley, G: H:, *comp.* Gothic architecture, furniture and ornament of England from the 11th to the 16th century. $40. Polley.
Salvatore, S. Italian architecture: interiors and furniture during 14th, 15th, 16th and 17th centuries. $25. Polley.
Sheraton, T: Furniture designs of Thomas Sheraton. $6 net. Scribner.
Singleton, E. Furniture of our forefathers. **$5 net. Doubleday, P.
Spanish colonial architecture: interiors and furniture during the 17th, 18th and 19th centuries. $30. Polley.
Wheeler, G. O. Old English furniture of the 17th and 18th centuries. $3. Scribner.
Windsor, H. H., *ed.* Mission furniture. pts. 1, 2. ea., 25 c. Popular Mechanics.
See also Cabinet work;—Church furniture;—Concrete;—House decoration; — Mantels; — Upholstery;—Woodcarving.

Furnivall, F: J., and Munro, J:
Shakespeare, life and work. '09(Je19) il. por. map, facsim., 16°, (Century Shakespeare.) *35 c. net; leath., *65 c. net. Cassell.
—, ed. *See* Laneham, Rob.—Rogues and vagabonds.—Shakespeare, W:

Furry, W: Davis.
Æsthetic experience: its nature and function. '08(My16) c. 8°, (Johns Hopkins Univ. studies in philosophy and psychology.) $1.60. Johns Hopkins.

FURS.
Wallace, A. F. Sorting, grading and curing furs. $1. A. F. Wallace.

Fursac, Joseph Rogues de, M.D.
See Rogues de Fursac, Joseph.

Furst, Herbert E. A.
Dürer. '10(Jl30) il. D. (Masterpieces in color.) bds., 65 c. net; leath., $1.50 net. Stokes.

Furst, S: Willis.
Mensuration, with special application of the prismoidal formula; designed for supplementary work in normal schools, high schools, academies, and advanced classes in grammar and common schools. '09(D) c. 10+72 p. il. 12°, 50 c. Sower.

Further advances in physiology. Hill, L., *ed.* *$4.20 net. Longmans.
Further adventures of Quincy Adams Sawyer. Pidgin, C: F. $1.50. L. C. Page.
Further experiences of an Irish R. M. Somerville, E. A. O. $1 net. Longmans.
Further studies of solution tension and toxicity in lipolysis. Pond, R. H. 25 c. N. Y. Botanical.
Furze the cruel. Trevena, J: †$1.50. Moffat.

Futrelle, Jacques.
Diamond master. '09(O23) c. il. D. †$1. Bobbs-M.
Elusive Isabel. '09(My8) c. il. D. †$1.50. Bobbs-M.
Simple case of Susan. '08(My2) c. front. D. †$1.25. Appleton.
Thinking machine on the case. '08(Mr21) c. front. D. †$1.50. Appleton.

Future leadership of the church. Mott, J: R. $1. Y. M. C. A.

FUTURE LIFE.
Anstadt, P: Recognition of our friends in heaven. $1; $1.50. Anstadt.
Björklund, J. G. Death and resurrection from the point of view of the cell-theory. $1 net. Open Court.
Gardner, F: Future life. 25 c. F: Gardner.
Gatty, *Mrs.* M. S. Life beyond. 25 c. net. Revell.
Gordon, G: A. Crossing the bar: a lyric of life everlasting. *50 c. net. Pilgrim Press.
Gottschall, A. H. Visions of heaven and hell. 75 c. A. H. Gottschall.
Gray, J. Progress in the life to come. 25 c. net. Revell.
Gwynne, W. Some purposes of paradise: on the life of the soul between death and resurrection. *75 c. net. Gorham.
Hawthorne, J. Lovers in heaven. 25 c. New Church.
Howard, H. F. End of the world and the opening of the book of life. v. 1. $1.50. Meader's.
Howatt, J. R. Next life; light on the worlds beyond. *$1 net. Revell.
Howells, W: D., *and others.* In after days. **$1.25 net. Harper.
Hyslop, J. H. Psychical research and the resurrection. **$1.50 net. Small.
Jensen, J. C. Square look into eternity. 25 c.; $1. J. C. Jensen.
Kelman, J: Ephemeraeternitatis; short studies in life here and hereafter. $1.25 net. Doran.
Kempson, F. C. Future life and modern difficulties. *$1.25 net. Dutton.
Keppel, D: That ye may know; the question, how may I know that I have eternal life? *35 c. net. Eaton & M.
Lees, R. J. Through the mists. $1.50. Badger.
Lombroso, C. After death—what? **$2.50 net. Small.
McDonald, D. W: What we are and what we will be. $1.50. D. W: McDonald.
Mercer, J: E: Science of life and the larger hope. $1.20 net. Longmans.
Mills, L. H. Avesta eschatology compared with the books of Daniel and Revelations. 50 c.; 75 c. Open Court.

FUTURE LIFE.—*Continued.*
Paterson-Smyth, J: Gospel of the hereafter. $1 net. Revell.
Paul, J: H. The hereafter. 50 c. Pentecostal.
Peebles, J. M. Immortality and our employment hereafter. $1.25; 75 c. Austin.
Randall, E: C. Future of man, metapsychic. *$1.50 net. Ulbrich.
Rogers, L. W. Scientific evidence of future life. 10 c. Theosophical Bk.
Spalding, J. H. Spiritual world; as described in the writings of Emanuel Swedenborg. *40 c. net; *60 c. net. Warne.
Stanton, H. C. Starry universe, the Christian's future empire. *$1.50 net. Revell.
Staudt, C. K. Idea of the resurrection in the ante-Nicene period. *50 c. net. Univ. of Chic.
Stephens, C: A. Natural salvation: immortal life on earth. $1.75. Laboratory Co.
Swedenborg, E. Heaven and hell. *35 c. net; *70 c. net. Dutton.
Whiting, L. Life transfigured. $1.25 net. Little, B. & Co.
Whiting, L. Lilies of eternal peace: [Easter booklet.] **75 c. net; **$1.50 net. Crowell.
See also Death;—Heaven;—Immortality;—Psychical research; — Reincarnation; — Salvation; — Soul;—Spiritualism;—Theosophy; — *also* Swedenborg, E.

Future of astronomy. Pickering, E: C: E: C: Pickering.
Future of man. Randall, E: C. *$1.50 net. Ulbrich.
Future of rail and water transportation. Hill, J. J. (Add. author for price.) J. J. Hill.
Future of war. Bloch, J. de. 50 c. net. Ginn.

Fyfe, C: A.
Steamship coefficients, speeds and powers. '08(F8) c. il. 8°, leath., $4. Spon.

Fyfe, J: W:, M.D.
Specific diagnosis and specific medication; together with abstracts from the writings of J: M. Scudder, M.D., and other leading authors. '10(Ja15) c. O. $5; shp., $6. Scudder.

Fyvie, J:
Tragedy of the Georgian era. '09(My8) il. 8°, *$4 net. Dutton.
Wits, beaux and beauties of the Georgian era. '09(S4) il. pors. O. *$4 net. Lane.

G., A. E.
Modern art at Venice and other notes. '10(Ap23) il. $2 net. (175 copies.) Bowles.

Gaboriau, Emile.
File no. 113. '08(Je27) 12°, (Magnolia lib.) 50 c. Hurst.

Gabriel, C: H., ed.
The victory: collection of popular Sunday school songs. '08(Je6) c. O. 20 c. Jennings.

Gadow, Hans Frederich.
Through southern Mexico: travels of a naturalist. '08(D19) il. maps, 8°, *$6 net. Scribner.

Gaebelein, Rev. Arno Clemens.
Prophet Joel; exposition, with a foreword by C. I. Scofield. '10(Je4) 12°, 75 c. Our Hope Office.

Gaelic folk tales. O'Sheridan, M. G. 60 c. M. G. O'Sheridan.

GAELIC LANGUAGE.
See Language.

Gaffney, T: Clery, comp. and ed.
Bible symbols designed and arranged to familiarize the child with the great events of Bible history. '10(Ag6) c. il. 8°, $2. J: A. Hertel.

Gage, Fred. W:
Modern presswork. '09(Je) c. 138 p. 12°, $2. Inland Pr.

Gage, R. B.
See Kümmel, H: Barnard.

Gage, Simon H:
The microscope: an introd. to microscopic methods and to histology. 10th ed., rev. '08(N21) c. il. 8°, $1.50. Comstock Pub.

Gage, Stephen De Meritte.
See Clark, Harry Willard.

Gager, C: Stuart.
Effects of the rays of radium on plants. '08, [1909.] (O) 8+278 p. il. tabs., diagrs. Q. (N. Y. Botanical Garden memoirs.) pap., $2. N. Y. Botanical.

GAGES.
Woodworth, J. V. Gages and gaging systems. $2. Hill Pub.

Gaige, Roscoe Crosby, and Harcourt, Alfr., comps.
Books and reading. '08(O24) c. D. (Humanity essays.) **$1.50 net. Baker & T.

Gailor, T: Fk., D.D.
Christian church and education; Bedell Lectures, 1909. '10(Jl2) c. D. $1 net. Whittaker.

Gaines, Clement Carrington, ed.
Simplified phonetic shorthand. Rev. of 1908. '10(My14) c. 8°, $2. C. C. Gaines.

Gaines, Franklin Wilks.
Oregon and her politicians vs. honest politics. '08(Je) c. 103 p. 8°, pap., 25 c. F. W. Gaines.

Gaines, Mrs. Nettie Viola Stewart, comp.
Pathway to western literature. '10(O8) c. 12°, 75 c. N. S. Gaines.

Gainsborough, Sir T:
Masterpieces. '09(D25) il. 24°, (Painters' ser.) leath., *75 c. net; pap., *25 c. net. Stokes.

GAINSBOROUGH, *Sir* Thomas.
Grieg, J. Gainsborough. *$15 net. Macmillan.
Rothschild, M. Gainsborough. *65 c. net. Stokes.

Gairdner, Ja.
Lollardy and the Reformation in England. '08(O24) 2 v., 8°, *$6.50 net. Macmillan.

Gairdner, W. H. T.
D. M. Thornton: study in missionary ideals and methods. '09(Je19) c. 12°, *$1.25 net. Revell.
Echoes from Edinburgh: acct. of the International World Missionary Conference. '10(D10) 12°, $1 net. Revell.

Gairy, Richardson A.
Poets' vision and the noblest struggle. '09 (Jl) pap., 25 c. N. Y. Age.

Gait of American trotter and pacer. Jordan, R., *jr.* $3.50. W: R. Jenkins.

Gaius, [or Caius.]
Institutes (extracts); The digest, title 45; 1, De verborum obligationibus; tr. by J. Graham Trapnell. '09(Ja16) 12°, (New classical lib.) leatherette, *$1 net. Macmillan.

Galabin, Alfr. Lewis, M.D., and Blacker, G:, M.D.
Practice of midwifery; being the 7th ed. of Dr. Galabin's Manual of midwifery, greatly enl. and extended. '10(Jl) 31+1123 p. il. O. $6 net. Macmillan.

Galahad Jones. Adams, A. H. $1.50. Lane.

GALATEA COLLECTION.
See **Boston Public Library.**

GALATIANS (Epistle to the).
See **Bible. N. T.**

Galbreath, C: Burleigh, comp.
Ohio emblems and monuments. '08(Je6) il. 8°, pap., gratis. C: B. Galbreath.

Gale, Albert Liscomb, and Kline, G: Washington.
Bryan the man, the great commoner at close range: [an appreciation from a Republican viewpoint.] '08(S12) c. il. pors. 12°, $1. Thompson Pub.

Gale, Edwards J.
Pewter and the amateur collector. '09 (D4) c. il. O. **$2.50 net. Scribner.

Gale, Ja. Scarth.
Korea in transition. '09(Ag) 11+270 p. il. map, 12°, (Forward mission study courses.) 50 c.; pap., 35 c. Young People's Miss.

Gale, Marie Josephine.
Alice Brenton. '09(Je12) c. il. 12°, $1.50. C. M. Clark.

Gale, Norman Bingham Clifton, and Floyd, G. C.
My playtime book. '09(N13) il. Q. bds., 50 c. Tuck.

Gale, Oliver Marble, and Wheeler, Harriet Martha.
Knight of the wilderness. '09(N6) c. il. D. $1.50. Reilly & B.

Gale, Zona.
[Works.] In 3 v. v. 1, Friendship Village; v. 2, Friendship Village love stories; v. 3, The loves of Pelleas and Etarre. '10(O22) 12°, ea., $1.50. Macmillan.
Friendship village. '08(N14) c. O. †$1.50. Macmillan.
Friendship village love stories. '09(D4) c. D. †$1.50. Macmillan.

GALICIA, Spain.
Wood, W. Corner in Spain. $2 net. Pott.

GALILEE.
See **Palestine.**

Gallagher, Antonia Mercedes ["Rev. R: W. Alexander."]
Missionary's notebook. '08(Je6) c. D. $1. Cath. Standard and Times.

Gallagher, Fs. E.
See Cameron, Fk. Kenneth.

GALLAGHER, Joseph Astley.
Conway, K. E., *comp.* Story of a beautiful childhood. $1. C. M. Clark.

Gallatin, Fs. Dawson.
Unfinished divorce. '09(Ap24) c. D. $1.50. Cochrane.

Galleon treasure. Fitzhugh, P. K. †75 c. Crowell.

Gallerani, Rev. Alex.
Jesus all good; tr. and ed. by F. Loughnan. '09(Mr) 254 p. 16°, 50 c.; $1. Kenedy.

Galley, Henrietta, and Arnold, Jesse Oglevee.
Hist. of the Galley family with local and old-time sketches in the Yough region. '08(D) c. 13-271 p. il. pors. 8°. (Add. pubs. for price.) Phila. Pr.

GALLEY FAMILY.
See **Genealogies.**

Gallic war. *See* Cæsar, Caius Julius.

Gallichan, Wa. M.
Modern woman and how to manage her. '10(Je11) 12°, $1.50 net. Lane.
Old continental towns. '10(N19) il. 8°, $2 net. Pott.

Gallichan, Mrs. Wa. M.
See Hartley, Catherine Gasquoine.

Gallico, Paolo, comp. and ed.
Most popular piano instructor. '09(D4) c. Q. pap., 75 c. Hinds.

Gallinger, Jacob Harold.
General education board: memorandum along the lines of the promotion of pract. farming in the southern states; the development of a system of public high schools in the southern states; and the promotion of higher education throughout the U. S. '10(Je) 15 p. charts, 8°. Gov. Pr. Off.

Gallizier, Nathan.
Court of Lucifer; tale of the Renaissance. '10(N5) c. il. O. $1.50. L. C. Page.

Gallon, Tom.
Dead man's love. '10(My21) D. $1.50. Brentano's.

Galloway, G:
Principles of religious development. '09 (D25) 8°, *$3 net. Macmillan.

Galloway, G: Washington.
The Arkansas sharpshooter. '10(S) c. 105 p. por., 12°, 50 c. Smith.

Galloway, T: Walton.
First course in zoology. 2d ed. '09(My) c. 12+481 p. 8°, *$2 net. Blakiston.
Text-book of elem. zoology, for secondary educational institutions. '10(Je) 20+418 p. il. 12°, $1.25 net. Blakiston.

Galloway, W: Johnson.
Musical England. '10(Jl9) O. $1.50 net. Lane.

GALLOWAY.
See **Scotland.**

GALLS.
See **Insects.**

Gallup, Mrs. Eliz. Wells.
Bi-literal cypher of Sir Francis Bacon. pt. 3, Deciphered secret story, 1622 to 1671; The lost manuscripts, where they were hidden. '10(D24) c. il. pors. O. pap., $2. Howard.
Concerning the bi-literal cypher of Francis Bacon; pros and cons of the controversy; explanations, reviews, criticisms and replies. '10(D24) por. facsims., O. pap., 75 c. Howard.

Gallwey, Sir Ralph W: Payne-.
See Payne-Gallwey, *Sir* Ralph W:

Galsworthy, J:
A commentary; [indictment of modern social conditions.] '08(S5) D. $1.50. Putnam.
A motley. '10(Je25) c. D. $1.20 net. Scribner.
Fraternity. '09(Mr20) c. D. **$1.35 net. Putnam.
Island pharisees. '08(Je13) c. D. *$1.50 net. Putnam.
Justice; tragedy in 4 acts. '10(O15) c. D. 60 c. net. Scribner.
Plays: The silver box; Joy; Strife. '09 (Je19) c. D. *$1.35 net, fixed. Putnam.
Villa Rubein: [a novel.] '08(Jl11) c. D. †$1.50. Putnam.

Galt, J:
Annals of the parish. '10(Ap2) 16°, (Everyman's lib.) 35 c. net; leath., 70 c. net. Dutton.
Annals of the parish; with an introd. and glossary by J: McInnes. '08(N21) 16°, (New universal lib.) 50 c.; leath., 75 c. Dutton.
Annals of the parish; ed., with introd. and glossary, by G. S. Gordon. '09(Je19) 16°, (Oxford lib. of prose and poetry.) 90 c. Oxford Univ.

Galton, Fs.
Memories of my life. '09(Ap17) il. 8°, *$3.50 net. Dutton.

GALVANOMETER.
Wenner, F. Theoretical and experimental study of the vibration galvanometer. U. S., Supt. of Docs.

GAMBETTA, Leon.
Gheusi, P. B. Gambetta. $3.50 special net. Appleton.

Gamble, Eleanor Acheson McCulloch.
Study in memorising various materials by the reconstruction method. '09, [1910.] (Mr) 12+210 p. tabs., 4°, (Psychological monographs; Wellesley College studies in psychology.) $2.25. Psychological Review.

Gamble, F: W:
Animal life. '08(O10) 12°, *$2 net. Dutton.

GAMBLING.
Hubbard, E. Pasteboard proclivities. 10 c. Roycrofters.
Nevill, R. Light come, light go. *$4.50 net. Macmillan.
See also Lotteries.

Gambolling with Galatea. Dunham, C. **$1.15 net. Houghton M.

Gambrill, J: Montgomery.
See Andrews, C: McLean.

Game and the candle. Ingram, E. M. †$1.50. Bobbs-M.

GAME FOWL.
See Birds.

GAME LAWS.
New York [State.] Forest, fish and game laws, 1908. 50 c. M. Bender.

Game of draughts. Richmond, J. L. 50 c. Warne.

Game of life. Hall. B. 20 c. Breslow.

Game of the golden ball. Johnson, E. $1.50. Macaulay.

GAME-PRESERVING.
Jones, O. Ten years of game-keeping. *$3 net. Longmans.
Jones, O., *and* Woodward, M. Gamekeeper's note-book. $2.10 net. Longmans.
National bird and mammal reservations in Alaska in charge of the U. S. Department of Agriculture. U. S., Supt. of Docs.
Palmer, T. S. Private game preserves and their future in the United States. Gov. Pr. Off.

Gamertsfelder, S. J.
Bible study on prayer. '08(My16) c. S. (Albright ser.) 40 c. Evangelical Assoc.

GAMES.
Angell, E. D. Play; comprising games for the kindergarten, playground, schoolroom and college. $1.50 net. Little, B. & Co.
Bancroft, J. H. Games for the playground. **$1.50 net. Macmillan.
Barker, J. S. Games for the playground. 60 c. net. Longmans.
Barse, *Mrs.* M. E. S. Games for all occasions. 60 c. Barse & H.
Beard, L. *and* A. B. Little folks' handy book. 75 c. Scribner.
Burchenal, E., *ed.* Folk-dances and singing games. $2.50; $1.50. Schirmer.
Crawford, C. Folk dances and games. $1.50. Barnes.
Dick, W: B. American Hoyle. $1.50; 75 c.; 50 c. Dick.
Foster, R. F: Complete Hoyle: encyclopedia of games. **$2.50 net.—Encyclopedia of games. $1.25; 75 c.; 50 c. Stokes.
Hoyle, E. Standard games and bridge whist, [etc.;] also billiards, pool, [etc.] 75 c.; 25 c. Laird.
Johnson, G: E. What to do at recess. 25 c. Ginn.
Lucas, E: V. *and* E. Three hundred games and pastimes [for children]. $2 net. Macmillan.
Model book of games. 50 c. Dutton.
Newton, M. B. Graded games and rhythmic exercises. **$1.25 net. Barnes.
Parsons, B. R. Plays and games for indoors and out. $1.50. Barnes.
Phillips, B., *comp.* Standard Hoyle. $1; 75 c.; 50 c. Excelsior.
Scudder, M. T. Field day and play picnic for country children. 10 c. Charities Pub.
Vail, W: H: Div-a-let; division by letters. 25 c. W. H. Vail.
Yendes, L. A., *and* Broun, W. F. A., *eds.* Entertainments for every occasion. $1.25. Hinds.
See also Amusements; — Athletics; — Baseball; — Billiards; — Bowling; — Cards; — Checkers; — Chess; — Croquet; — Euchre; — Football; — Golf; — Gymnastics and physical culture; — Hockey; — Kindergarten; — Lacrosse; — Lawn tennis; — Pool; — Puzzles; — Skat; — Tennis; — Water polo.

Games of drawing room hockey, laws of Badminton, garden hockey, golf croquet, lawn hockey, wicket polo, tether ball, hand tennis, volley ball, basket goal, hand polo. '10(Jl2) c. il. 12°, (Spalding's athletic lib.) pap., 10 c. Am. Sports.

Games that glue played. Williams, C. A. $1. Stokes.

GAMEWELL, Mary Porter.
Hubbard, E. D. Under marching orders; story of Mary Porter Gamewell. *50 c. net. Young Peoples' Miss.

Gammans, Harold Winsor.
Broken statue de Fontange; dramatic day. '10(F5) c. 16°, leath., 60 c.; pap., 40 c. Ruebush-E.

GAMMELL FAMILY.
See Genealogies: Whittier, C: C.

Gammon, S: R., D.D.
Evangelical invasion of Brazil; or, a half century of Evangelical missions in the Land of the Southern Cross. '10(Mr26) c. il. pors. map, O. 75 c. Presb. Pub.

Gancel, Jos.
Ready reference of menu terms; glossary of over 5000 names. '10(Ap16) c. 16°, $1. J. Gancel.

Gandy, J. P.
Elements of banking. '09(S25) D. (Practical primers of business.) 50 c. Pitman.

Gang (The). Brasted, F. $1.25. Griffith.

Ganong, W: Fs.
Laboratory course in plant physiology. 2d ed., extended to form a hdbk. of experimentation for educational use. '09(Ja23) c. O. $1.75. Holt.

Teaching botanist: manual of information upon botanical instruction; incl. outlines and directions for a synthetic general course. 2d ed. '10(Je18) c. D. $1.25 net. Macmillan.

Gansey, R. Johnston.
See Ainsworth, J: H.

Gant, S: Goodwin.
Constipation and intestinal obstruction (obstipation). '09(Mr) c. 11-559 p. il. 8°, *$6 net. Saunders.

Ganton & Co. Eddy, A. J. $1.50. McClurg.

Gantt, H: Laurence.
Work, wages, and profits; their influence on the cost of living. '10(Ag13) c. fold. charts, 12°, (Works management lib.) $2. Engineering Mag.

Ganz, H: F. W.
Practical hints on modelling, design and mural decoration; with foreword by Alf. Gilbert. '08(Jl18) il. O. *$1 net. Lippincott.

Gapen, J. K., comp.
Poems and plays of William Shakespeare arranged in the order of their first appearance. '08, [1909.] (Mr) c. 5+9-56 p. 8°. (Add. author for price.) J. K. Gapen.

GARAGE.
Radford, W: A., *comp.* Garages and how to build them. $1. Radford Architectural.

GARBAGE.
See Refuse and refuse disposal.

Garbe, Richard v.
Akbar, Emperor of India. '09(O23) il. *50 c net. Open Court.

Garbe, Rob.
Application of highly superheated steam to locomotives; ed. by Leslie S. Robertson. '09(D) c. 70 p. 8°, *$2.50 net. Henley.

Garber, Aaron Leedy.
Bibleopathy: a system of diet, healing and living based on the Bible and nature, and a guide to the modest life. '08(O) c. 208 p. 12°, $1. Restitution.

Garber, J: Palmer.
Settlements on the Delaware prior to the coming of William Penn: written for the City History Soc. of Phil. and read at the meeting of Nov. 13, 1907. '09, [1910.] (Je) 129-161 p. fold. map, Q. (City History Soc. of Phil. pubs.) (Sold to members only.) City Hist. Phil.

Garbett, Arth. Selwyn, comp.
Gallery of musical celebrites; collection of 70 portrait-biographies of the world's foremost composers, singers, pianists, violinists, organists and teachers who have lived during the last 200 years. '09, [1910.] (F) c. 143 p. pors. 8°, 75 c. T. Presser.

Garbett, Canon, and Martin, Rev. S., eds.
Family prayer-book, morning and evening prayers for every day. '08(D5) il. 4°, *$1.50 net. Cassell.

Garceau, Edg.
Renal, ureteral, perirenal and adrenal tumors, and actinomycosis and echinococcus of the kidney. '09(N) c. 13+421 p. il. 8°, $5. Appleton.

GARCIA, Manuel.
MacKinlay, M. S. Manuel Garcia. *$4 net. Appleton.

Garden, Rob. I.
History of Scott Township, Mahaska Co., Iowa. [Also] War reminiscences, [1861-1865.] [Also] Did the buffalo ever inhabit Iowa? '08(Ap18) il. por. 12°, $1.25. Shockley Bros.

Garden at 19. Jepson, E. $1.20 net. Wessels & B.

Garden-craft ser. See Macmillan's.

Garden fairies. Paquin, S: S. **$1 net. Moffat.

Garden flowers in color; ed. by R. Hooper Pearson. il. O. bds., 65 c. net. Stokes.
—Cuthbertson. Pansies, violas and violets.
—Jacob. Daffodils.
—Wright. Sweet peas.

GARDEN FURNITURE.
See Concrete.

Garden game. Hidden, J. A. 75 c. M. Bradley.

Garden in the wilderness. Ver Beck, H. R. **$1.50 net. Baker & T.

Garden lib. il. D. Doubleday, P.
—Barnes. House plants and how to grow them. $1.10.

Garden muse. Bradley, W: A., *comp. and ed.* $1.25 net. Sturgis & W.

Garden of Eden. Hodges, G: $1.50. Houghton M.

GARDEN OF EPICURUS.
See France, Anatole.

Garden of fate. Norton, R. $1.50. W. J. Watt.

Garden of girls. Fisher, H., *il.* $3.50. Dodd.

Garden of girls. Hilton, M. A. $1.50. Tandy-T.

Garden of God. Brett, J. *$1.20 net. Longmans.

Garden of Grey Ledge. Hazelwood, C. W. $1.25 net. Sherman, F.

Garden ser. for children. il. 12°, 75 c. C. M. Clark.

—Warren. Little Danny Dandelion.—Little Goldie Goldenrod.—Little Polly Primrose and her friends.

Garden yard. Hall, B. $1. McKay.

Gardenhire, S: Major.

Purple and homespun: a novel. '08(Ap25) c. D. †$1.50. Harper.

GARDENING.

See Gardens and gardening.

GARDENS AND GARDENING.

Albee, *Mrs.* H. R. Hardy plants for cottage gardens. $1.60 net. Holt.

American Fork & Hoe Company, Cleveland, O. Gardening for health and recreation. Am. Fork.

Arnott, S. Gardening in the north. *$1 net. Cassell.

Babcock, E. B. Suggestions for garden work in California schools. Univ. of Cal.

Bailey, L. H. Forcing book: cultivation of vegetables. **$1.25 net.—Garden making. **$1.50 net.—Horticulturists' rule-book. 75 c.—Manual of gardening. **$2 net.—Principles of vegetable gardening. **$1.50 net. Macmillan.

Baker, T. Yard and garden: information for the amateur gardener. **$2 net. Bobbs-M.

Batson, *Mrs.* H. M. Summer garden of pleasure. $3.50. McClurg.

Bennett, I. D. Vegetable garden. **$1.50 net. McClure.

Biggle, J. Garden book. 50 c. W. Atkinson.

Blanchan, N., *pseud.* American flower garden. $5; $10. Doubleday, P.

Bray, *Mrs.* M. M. My grandmother's garden. $1. Badger.

Brooks, S. W. Garden with a house attached. $1.50 net. Badger.

Calthrop, D. C. Charm of gardens. $2.50 net. Macmillan.

Cecil, A. M. T. A. Hist. of gardening in England. $3.50 net. Dutton.

Cook, E: T. Gardens of England. *$2.50 net. Macmillan.

Davidson, *Mrs.* K. L. Gardens past and present. *$1.50 net. Scribner.

Divers, W. H. Spring flowers at Belvoir Castle. *$1.80 net. Longmans.

Dorner, H. B. Window gardening. **$1 net. Bobbs-M.

Du Cane, F. Flowers and gardens of Japan. *$6 net. Macmillan.

Duncan, F. When mother lets us garden. **75 c. net. Moffat.

Elford, P., *and* Heaton, S: Pract. school gardening. *70 c. net. Oxford Univ.

Elford, P., *and* Heaton, S:, *comps.* School garden note book. 25 c. Oxford Univ.

English vegetable garden. *$3 net. Scribner.

Farrer, R. J. In a Yorkshire garden. $3.50. Longmans.

GARDENS AND GARDENING.—*Continued.*

Flint, L. C. Small gardens for small gardeners. 50 c. Flanagan.

Greene, M. L. Among school gardens. $1.25. Charities Pub.

Hays, H. A. Little Maryland garden. **$1.75 net. Putnam.

Higgins, M. M. Little gardens for boys and girls. **$1.10 net. Houghton M.

Holme, C:, *ed.* Gardens of England in the midland and eastern counties. *$3 net. Lane.

Hulme, F: E: That rock garden of ours. **$3 net. Jacobs.

Jeffery, J. A. Elem. laboratory study in crops. gratis. Mich. Supt. Pub. Instruction.

Jekyll, G. Children and gardens. *$2 net. —Color in the flower garden. *$3.75 net. Scribner.

Jekyll, G. Home and garden.—Wood and garden. ea., $2 net. Longmans.

Kains, M. G., *comp.* Making horticulture pay; experiences in gardening and fruit growing. $1.50. Judd.

Lodeman, E. G. Spraying of plants; for the purpose of destroying insects and fungi. **$1.25 net. Macmillan.

Lounsberry, A. Garden book for young people. **$1.50 net.—Gardens near the sea. $4.20 net. Stokes.

Lowell, Mass. City Library. Gardens and gardening: list of books in Lowell City Library. gratis. Lowell Lib.

Macartney, M. E. English houses and gardens in the 17th and 18th centuries. *$6 net. Scribner.

McLaren, J: Gardening in California, landscape and flower. *$3.75 net. A. M. Robertson.

Maynard, S: T. Small country place. **$1.50 net. Lippincott.

Maxwell, *Sir* H. E. Scottish gardens. *$6 net. Longmans.

Meyer, F. W. Rock and water gardens. $2. Scribner.

Miller, C. H., *comp.* Garden and farm almanack. 25 c. Doubleday, P.

Oklahoma. *Dept. of Education.* Some suggestions in school gardening. gratis. Oklahoma Dept. Educ.

Oliver, G: W. Plant culture. $1.50. De La Mare.

Osborne, C: F., *ed.* Historic houses and their gardens. $6. Winston.

Palmer, C. F. Elem. horticulture for California schools. 50 c. C. F. Palmer.

Parsons, H: G. Children's gardens for pleasure, health and education. $1 net. Sturgis.

Pearson, R. H. Book of garden pests. *$1 net. Lane.

Rawson, W. W. Success in market gardening. $1.10 net. Doubleday, P.

Rexford, E. E. Home garden: vegetable and small-fruit growing. **$1.25 net. Lippincott.

Richmond, *Mrs.* In my lady's garden. **$3.50 net. Jacobs.

Scott, T., *comp.* In praise of gardens. $1.25. Baker & T.

GARDENS AND GARDENING.—*Continued.*
Shafer, *Mrs.* S. A. White-paper garden. $2.50 net. McClurg.
Sidgwick, *Mrs.* C. U., *and* Paynter, *Mrs.* Children's book of gardening. *$2 net. Macmillan.
Silberrad, U. L., *and* Lyall, S. Dutch bulbs and gardens. *$2 net. Macmillan.
South Carolina. Trucking industry in South Carolina. gratis. State Co.
Tabor, G., *and* Teall, G. Garden primer. $1. McBride, W.
Thomas, H. H. Gardening difficulties solved. 60 c. net.—Ideal garden. $2 net. —Little gardens: how to make the most of them. *40 c. net. Cassell.
Thomas, H. H. Gardening in town and suburb. $1. Longmans.
Thonger, C: Book of the cottage garden. *$1 net. Lane.
Underwood, L. Garden and its accessories. $1 net. Little, B. & Co.
Underwood, L. Garden diary and country home guide. **$3.25 net. Stokes.
Verplanck, *Mrs.* V. E. E. Year in my garden. $1. W: E. Verplanck.
Weathers, J: Practical guide to school, cottage, and allotment gardening. $1. Longmans.
Weed, C. M., *and* Emerson, P. School garden book. $1.25. Scribner.
Wolseley, *Hon.* F. G. Gardening for women. *$1.75 net. Cassell.
Wright, W. P. Cassell's A B C of gardening. *$1.25 net. Cassell.
Wright, W. P. Garden week by week throughout the year. *$2 net. Doubleday, P.
Wright, W. P. Perfect garden. *$2 net. Lippincott.
Wright, W. P. Popular garden flowers. $2 net. Clode.
Wright, W. P., *ed.* Cassell's dict. of gardening. In 2 v. $10 net. Cassell.
See also Agriculture;—Beans;— Birds;—Botany; —California;—Farms and farming;—Fertilizers; —Flowers; — Forests and forestry; — Fruit;— Grafting;—Greenhouses;—Indoor gardening;— Landscape gardening; — Lawns; — Madeira; — Parks;—Potatoes;—Roses;—Spraying; — Trees; —Vegetables.

Gardens old and new: the country house and its garden environment; ed. by H. Avray Tipping. '08(D5) 3 v., il. f°, ea., *$12 net. Scribner.

Gardiner, E: Norman.
Greek athletic sports and festivals. '10 (S24) il. D. (Hdbks. of archæology and antiquities.) $2.50 net. Macmillan.

Gardiner, Marg. Doane.
Universal neurasthenia. '09(My22) c. il. O. bds., *$1 net. F. F. Sherman.

Gardner, Abbie Peckham.
Mews and musings. '10(O8) c. il. 12°, 75 c. Cochrane.
See also Sharp, *Mrs.* Abigail Gardner.

Gardner, C: Morris.
See Gardner, *Mrs.* Lillian May Stickney.

Gardner, Edm. Garratt.
St. Catherine of Siena. '08(Ja18) il. sq. demy 8°, *$4 net. Dutton.
See also Cell of self-knowledge.

Gardner, Elmer Elsworth.
American Pitmanic shorthand. '08(O17) c. 12°. $1.25. Am. Pitmanic.

Gardner, Ernest Arth.
Religion and art in ancient Greece. '10 (Ag13) 16°, (Harper's lib. of living thought.) 75 c. net. Harper.
Six Greek sculptors. '10(Je4) il. 12°, $2 net. Scribner.

Gardner, Fk. Augustine, M.D.
Glover's Marblehead regiment in the War of the Revolution. '09 (O) 25 p. Q. 50 c. Salem Press.
—, comp. and ed. Thomas Gardner, planter (Cape Ann, 1623-1626; Salem, 1626-1674), and some of his descendants, giving Essex County, Mass., and northern New England lines to the eighth generation and Nantucket lines through the fourth generation. '07, [1909.] (Mr) 4+343 p. por. 8°, $3.50. Essex Inst.

Gardner, Fk. Duane.
Fertility of soils as affected by manures. '08(Je6) il. tabs., 8°, (U. S. Dept. of Agriculture, Bureau of Soils, bull.) pap., 15 c. U. S., Supt. of Docs.

Gardner, F:
Future life; extract from thought transmission and consciousness. '10(Ap) 24 p. nar. D. pap., 25 c. F: Gardner.

Gardner, H. Bellamy.
Surgical anæsthesia. '09(N) 250 p. il. 12°, *$2.25 net. Wood.

Gardner, H: Alfr.
See Cushman, Allerton Seward.

Gardner, Ja. Browne.
Massachusetts memorial to her soldiers and sailors who died in the Department of No. Carolina, 1861-1865, dedicated at New Bern, No. Carolina, Nov. 11, 1908. '09, [1910.] (Ja) c. 7-102 p. il. pors. 8°, $3.25. Gardner & T.

Gardner, Ja. P:
Moneys of the world. '09(My22) c. 24°, (Bankers handy ser.) 50 c. Bankers Pub.

Gardner, Mrs. Lillian May Stickney and C: Morris.
Gardner history and genealogy. '07, [1908.] (Mr.) c. 450 p. 8°. (Add. pubs. for price.) Erie Pr.

Gardner, Marg. A.
Scale and chord helps. '09(O) 12 p. 12°, 20 c. M. A. Gardner.

Gardner, Marg. Doan.
House of rest: [play.] '09(D) c. '08. 29 p. il. 12°, *$1 net. F. F. Sherman.

Gardner, Mary.
Work that is play: dramatic reader based on Æsop's fables. '08(N7) il. D. 35 c. Flanagan.

Gardner, Mary Tracy and W: E:
Winners of the world. '09(S) c. 16+238 p. 24°, pap., 35 c. Old Corner.
Winners of the world during twenty centuries. '10(Ap9) c. 16°, 60 c. net; pap., 30 c. net. Revell.

Gardner, Nathaniel Lyon.
Leuvenia; new genus of flagellates. '10 (Je) 97-106 p. Q. (Univ. of Cal. pubs.; Botany.) pap., 10 c. Univ. of Cal.
Bibliography (2 p.).
New *chlorophyceae* from California. '09 (My15) il. Q. (Univ. of Cal. pubs.; Botany.) pap., 10 c. Univ. of Cal.

Gardner, Nathaniel Lyon.—*Continued.*
Variations in nuclear extrusion among the Fucaceae. '10(S) 121-136 p. il. Q. (Univ. of Cal. pubs.; Botany.) pap., 15 c. Univ. of Cal.

Gardner, Percy.
Modernity and the churches. '10(Je4) 12°, (Crown theological lib.) $1.50 net. Putnam.

Gardner, Sarah M. H.
Quaker idyls. Enl. ed. '10(Mr26) c. front. S. **$1 net. Holt.

Gardner, W: Amory.
In Greece with the classics. '08(My9) c. front. D. **$1.50 net. Little, B. & Co.

Gardner, W: E:
See Gardner, Mary Tracy.

Gardner, W: Ja.
Hist. of Jamaica from its discovery by Christopher Columbus to the year 1872, incl. account of its trade and agriculture; sketches of the manners, habits and customs of all classes of its inhabitants, and narrative of the progress of religion and education on the island. New ed. '09 (D11) fold. map, 8°, *$2.50 special net. Appleton.

GARDNER FAMILY.
See Genealogies.

Garesché, Marie R.
Art of the ages; compendium of the hist. and development of art in western civilization from the earliest times down to the present; pt. 1. '10(Jl16) c. il. maps, 8°, $1.25. Prang.

GARFIELD, Harry Augustus.
Williams College, Williamstown, Mass. Williams College; induction of Harry Augustus Garfield, LL.D., into the office of president, Oct. 7, 1908. $1. L. W. Spring.

GARFIELD, James Abram.
Thayer, W: M. From log cabin to the White House: life of James A. Garfield. 50 c. Hurst.
Vincent, E. La V. Story of Garfield. 15 c. L. H. Nelson.

Garforth, W: E:
Suggested rules for recovering coal mines after explosions and fires. '09, [1910.] (F) 71 p. il. 12°, *$1.50 net. Van Nostrand.

GARIBALDI, Guiseppe.
Trevelyan, G: M. Garibaldi and the thousand. *$2.25 net. Longmans.

Garis, Howard Roger.
Dick Hamilton's cadet days. '10(D31) c. il. 12°, (Dick Hamilton's ser.) 60 c. Grosset.
Dick Hamilton's fortune; or, the stirring doings of a millionaire's son. '09(S) c. 6+275 p. il. 12°, 60 c. Grosset.
Johnnie and Billy Bushytail. '10(O) il. 8°, (Bed-time stories.) 60 c. Fenno.
Larry Dexter's great search; or, the hunt for the missing millionaire. '09(S) 6+247 p. il. 12°, (Great newspaper ser.) 60 c. Grosset.

Garis, Howard Roger.—*Continued.*
Sammie and Susie Littletail. '10(O29) c. col. il. D. (Bed-time stories.) 60 c. Fenno.
Those Smith boys; or, the mystery of the thumbless man. '10(O29) c. il. O. $1.25. Fenno.

Garity, Mary E., ["Betty."]
Real letters to a real girl. '09(Je26) 12°, $1.25. C. M. Clark.

Garland, Claude Mallory.
See Clement, J. K.—Hudson, C. S.

Garland, D: S., ed.
See American and English annot. cases;—Am. and Eng. encyclop. of law.—Digest. —*also* McKinney, W: M., *ed.*

Garland, Hamlin.
[Works.] '09(Jl3) Harper.
Contents. Boy life on the prairie, $1.50; The eagle's heart, $1.50; Jason Edwards, $1.25; A little Norsk, 50 c.; Main-travelled roads, $1.50; Prairie folks, $1.50; Rose of Dutcher's Coolly, $1.50; A spoil of office, $1.25; The trail of the gold-seekers, $1.50; A wayside courtship, $1.25.
Cavanagh, forest ranger. '10(Ap2) c. D. $1.50. Harper.
Moccasin Ranch; a story of Dakota. '09 (S18) c. front. D. †$1. Harper.
Other main-travelled roads. '10(O1) c. D. $1.50. Harper.
Shadow world. '08(O17) c. D. $1.35. Harper.

Garland, H: L.
See Louisiana. Code of practice.

Garland, Ja. S., ed.
See Massachusetts town law.

Garland for girls. Alcott, L. M. †$1.50. Little, B. & Co.

Garland to Sylvia. MacKaye, P. W. $1.25 net. Macmillan.

Garman, C: E:
Letters, lectures and addresses: a memorial volume; prepared with the co-operation of the class of 1884, Amherst College, by Eliza Miner Garman. '09(Jl3) c. pors. O. **$3 net. Houghton M.

GARMENT CUTTING.
Ardleigh, H. American garment cutter. $15. Am. Fashion.
Gordon, S. S. Gordon's work on cutting men's garments. $10. S. S. Gordon.
Rude, C: B. A. D. Rude "great modern system" for designing and cutting men's garments. $12.50. A. D. Rude.
Townend, *Mrs.* F. B. Plain needlework and cutting out. 75 c. net. Cassell.
See also Dressmaking;—Tailoring.

Garner, Ja. Wilford.
Introd. to political science: treatise on the origin, nature, functions, and organization of the state. '10(Je25) c. O. $2.50. Am. Bk.

Garner, T:, and Stratton, Arth.
Domestic architecture of England during the Tudor period. In 3 pts. pt. 1. '08 (Je20); pt. 2. '09(Mr20); pt. 3. '10 (Je4) f°, portfolio, subs., ea., *$16 net; per set, *$48 net. Scribner.

Garnett, Christopher B., comp.
See Virginia. Business man's code.

Garnett, Ja. Mercer.
Genealogy of the Mercer-Garnett family of Essex County, Virginia; supposed to be descended from the Garnetts of Lancashire, Eng.; comp. from original records, and from oral and written statements of members of the family. '10(N) c. 62 p. il. pors. 8°, $1. J. M. Garnett.

Garnett, Mrs. Louise Ayres.
Muffin shop: [story in rhyme.] '08(D) il. 4°, $1.50. Rand, McN. & Co.
Rhyming ring. '10(N12) c. col. il. Q. $1.25. Rand, McN. & Co.

Garnett, Lucy Mary Jane.
Home life in Turkey. '09(S18) il. pors. D. *$1.75 net. Macmillan.

Garnett, Martha Roscoe, [Mrs. R. S. Garnett.]
Infamous John Friend. '09(Jl31) c. D. †$1.50. Holt.

Garnett, Porter.
Bohemian jinks. '08(Ag8) c. il. diagrs., D. bds., *$1.50 net. P. Garnett.
—, ed. *See* San Francisco Committee of Vigilance.

Garnett, Mrs. R. S.
See Garnett, Martha Roscoe.

Garnett, R:
Life of W. J. Fox, public teacher and social reformer, 1786-1864; by the late R: Garnett; concluded by E: Garnett. '09(D11) il. pors. O. *$5 net. Lane.
—, and Gosse, Edm. W:
English literature; illustrated record. In 4 v. '10(Je4) il. 8°, per set, $12; hf. mor., $20. Grosset.

Garnett, Thdr. Stanford.
J. E. B. Stuart, (Major-General,) commander of the Cavalry Corps, Army of Northern Virginia, C. S. A. '08(Ja4) por. D. $1. Neale.

Garnett, W: Hubert Stuart.
Turbines. [1910.] (D) il. 8°, $1.60 net; (formerly $2.75 net.) Macmillan.

GARNETT FAMILY.
See Genealogies.

Garno, B:
Modern billiards; complete text-book of the game, containing plain and practical instruction how to play and acquire skill at this scientific amusement. New ed. '09(O) c. 382 p. il. 12°, $1. Brunswick-B.

Garretson, Beulah C.
Breen villagers. '10(O1) c. D. $1. B'way Pub.

Garrett, A. E.
Periodic law. '09(O23) fold. tabs., D. (Internat. scientific ser.) *$1.75 net. Appleton.

Garrett, A. H.
Hydraulic tables and diagrams for pract. engineers. '09(Jl3) obl. O. $5. Longmans.

GARRETT, Edmund.
Cook, E: T. Edmund Garrett. *$3 net. Longmans.

Garrett, S: Bond.
Hist. of Welcome Garrett and his descendants, from his birth in 1758 down to a recent date. '09, [1910.] (Ja) c. 141 p. por. diagr. 8°, $5. S: B. Garrett.

GARRETT FAMILY.
See Genealogies.

GARRETTSON, Freeborn.
Tipple, E. S. Freeborn Garrettson. *25 c. net. Eaton & M.

Garrison, C: Lloyd.
How to conduct a successful shoe store. '08(Jl) c. 7-70 p. 8°, $1. Boot & Shoe.

Garrison, Elisha Ely.
Accounting every business man should know. '09(N20) c. D. **$1.20 net. Doubleday, P.

Garrison, Ja. Harney.
Story of a century; brief hist. sketch and exposition of the religious movement inaugurated by Thomas and Alexander Campbell, 1809-1909. '09(D18) c. front. pors. 12°, $1. Chr. Pub.

Garrison, Rev. S. Olin.
Probationer's hdbk.; religious, historical, doctrinal, disciplinary, and practical; with an introd. by Rev. J. O. Peck. Rev. ed. '09(Je) c. 80 p. 16°, per doz., pap., 75 c.; cl., $1.25. Jennings.

Garrison, Mrs. Theodosia Pickering.
Earth cry and other poems. '10(D17) 16°, $1 net. M. Kennerley.
Joy o' life. '09(My15) c. S. *$1 net. M. Kennerley.

Garrison, Wendell Phillips.
Letters and memorials. '08(D12) por. 8°, *$1.50 net. Nation.

Garrod-Thomas, R. N.
See Richards, Thdr. W:

Garrold, Rev. R. P.
Freddy Carr and his friends; day school story. '10(N19) c. front. D. 85 c. Benziger.

Garryowen. Stacpoole, H: De V. $1.50. Duffield.

Garstang, J:
Land of the Hittites; acct. of the recent explorations and discoveries in Asia Minor; with introd. by A. H. Sayce. '10 (Jl30) il. maps, plans, 4°, $4 net. Dutton

Garvey, Ina.
Comedy of Mammon. '08(My16) c. O. †$1.50. Estes.

Garvice, C:
Ashes of love. '10(Ap9) 12°, pap., 25 c. J. S. Ogilvie.
Fatal ruby. '10(Ap23) c. D. $1.50. Doran.

Garvie, Alfr. Ernest, D.D.
The Christian certainty and modern perplexity. '10(D) 8°, $2 net. Doran.
Gospel for to-day. '10(D) 12°, $1.50 net. Doran.

Gary, Anstiss Curtiss.
The unforgotten: [poems.] '09(Je) c. 93 p. 12°, $1. De Laurence, S.

GARY, Ind.
Moore, W. H. "If I had known" about Gary in 1909. $1. P. E. Moore.

GAS AND GAS-FITTING.
Allen, H. Modern power gas producer. *$2.50 net. Van Nostrand.
American School of Correspondence. Gas producers. $1. Am. Sch. Corr.
Clement, J. K. On the rate of formation of carbon monoxide in gas producers. Univ. of Ill.

GAS AND GAS-FITTING.—*Continued.*

Fernald, R. H. Recent developments of the producer-gas power plant in the United States. Gov. Pr. Off.

Flurscheim, A. Working hints for suction gas producers. *50 c. net. Spon.

Gas Educational Fund, New York. Catechism of central station gas engineering in the United States. $5. Gas Educ. Fund.

Gerhard, W: P. American practice of gas piping and gas lighting in buildings. *$3 net. McGraw.

Herring, W. R. Granton gas works of Edinburgh and Leith Corporations. **$6.50 net. Spon.

Hole, W. Distribution of gas. *$6 net. Spon.

Junge, F. E. Gas power. $5. Hill Pub.

Latta, M. N-. American producer gas practice and industrial gas engineering. *$6 net. Van Nostrand.

Miller, J: C. Power gas and gas producer. $1. Popular Mechanics.

Robson, P. W. Power gas producers. *$3 net. Longmans.

Royle, H. M. Chemistry of gas manufacture. $4.50. Henley.

Ruggles, F. A. Massachusetts gas companies. (Priv. pr.) F. A. Ruggles.

Smith, C. A. Suction gas plants. *$1.75 net. Lippincott.

Stone, C: H: H. Practical testing of gas meters $3.50. Wiley.

Webber, W: H. Y. Town gas and its uses. *$2 net. Van Nostrand.

See also Engines.

Gas Educational Fund, New York. Catechism of central station gas engineering in the United States; comp. from the questions and answers sent out to the practical class, Trustees Gas Educational Fund. '10(F5) c. il. 8°, $5. Gas Educ. Fund.

GAS ENGINE.
See Engines.

Gas Traction Co., Minneapolis. Modern farming; the passing of the horse. '09(N) 9-54 p. il. pls. 8°, gratis. Gas Traction.

GAS TURBINES.
See Turbines.

Gascon royalist in revolutionary Paris. Gosselin, L. L. T. $3.50 net. Dodd.

Gascoyne, W: J:
See Battle, Herbert B.

Gascoyne-Cecil, Rev. Lord R. W. E.
See Cecil, *Rev. Lord* R. W. E. Gascoyne-.

GASES.

Buckingham, E. On the definition of the ideal gas. Gov. Pr. Off.

Chamberlin, R. T: Gases in rocks. 50 c. Carnegie.

Gill, A: H. Gas and fuel analysis. $1.25. Wiley.

Haber, F. Thermodynamics of technical gas-reactions. *$3 net. Longmans.

Harris, G. D. Oil and gas in Louisiana. Gov. Pr. Off.

Harris, G. D., *and others.* Oil and gas in northwestern Louisiana. La. Geol. Survey.

GASES.—*Continued.*

Schmidt, C. L. A. Table of H+O H—concentrations corresponding to electromotive forces determined in gas chain measurements. 10 c. Univ. of Cal.

United States. *Dept. of the Interior. U. S. Geological Survey.* Known productive oil and gas fields of the United States in 1908.

See also Acetylene;—Coal;—Electricity;—Fuel;—Furnaces;—Light;—Mines and mining.

Gasiorowski, Waclaw.

Tragic Russia; tr. by the Viscount de Busancy. '08(D12) il. pors. O. *$2.50 net. Cassell.

Gask, G: E.
See Spencer, Wa. G.

Gask, Lilian.

Folk tales from many lands; retold. '10 (S3) il. O. $1.50 net. Crowell.

In nature's school. '09(Ag7) il. D. $1.50. Crowell.

Quest of the white merle. '10(Ag6) il. D. $1.50. Crowell.

True stories about dogs. '10(S10) il. O. $1.50. Crowell.

Wonders of the zoo. '09(Ag28) il. 12°, $1.25. Dodge.

Gask, Stuart.
See Hardy, E. S.

Gaskell, Mrs. Eliz. Cleghorn Stevenson.

Cousin Phillis; with a preface by T: Seccombe. '08(O31) 12°, (Queen's treasures ser.) $1. Macmillan.

Cranford. '08(O17) 16°, (Best books ser.) leath., *$1 net. Dutton.

Cranford. Holiday ed. '10(S10) por. D. hf. leath., $1.10 net. Houghton M.

Cranford. '09(D25) col. il. 12°, (Queen's treasures ser.) $1. Macmillan.

Cranford; with introd. and notes by Marg. A. Eaton. '09(S) c. 248 p. *40 c. net. Educ. Pub.

Cranford; ed., with introd., notes and suggestive questions, by H. E. Coblentz. '10(Ap16) c. il. por. D. (Riverside literature ser.) 40 c. Houghton M.

Cranford; ed., with introd. and notes, by Katherine E. Forster. '10(Ag13) c. pors. 16°, (Scribner English classics.) 25 c. Scribner.

Cranford; ed. for school use by Alb. Elmer Hancock. '10(N5) c. S. (Lake English classics.) 35 c. Scott, F. & Co.

Life of Charlotte Brontë. '08(S19) 16°, (Everyman's lib.) *35 c. net; leath., *70 c. net. Dutton.

North and south; with introd. by Clement Shorter. '09(My15) 16°, (World's classics.) *40 c. net; leath., *75 c. net. Oxford Univ.

Sylvia's lovers; with preface by T: Seccombe. '10(D10) col. il. D. $1.50 net. Macmillan.

Sylvia's lovers. '10(Je4) 16°, (World's classics.) 35 c. net; mor., 65 c. net. Oxford Univ.

Gaskell, Wa. Holbrook.

Origin of vertebrates. '08(N7) figs. O. *$6 net. Longmans.

Gaskin, Mrs. Arth.
Tale of six little travellers. '07. [1909.] (Jl) il. in col. 12°, bds., 50 c. Jacobs.

GASOLINE ENGINES.
See Engines.

"GASPEE (The)."
Knox, H. B. Destruction of the "Gaspee": [British schooner destroyed by people of Rhode Island, 1772.] gratis. R. I. Dept. Educ.

Gasquet, Abbot Fs. Aidan, D.D.
Black death of 1348 and 1349. 2d ed. '08 (Mr14) 12°, *$2 net. Macmillan.
Greater abbeys of England. '08(O24) c. il. O. **$3.50 net. Dodd.
Last abbot of Glastonbury, and other essays. '08(Ap4) il. 12°, *$2 net. Macmillan.
Old English Bible, and other essays. New ed. '08(Ag1) 12°, *$2.25 net. Macmillan.

—, and Bishop, Edm.
Bosworth psalter. '09(My1) 4°, *$4.50 net. Macmillan.

Gass, Sherlock Bronson.
English composition. '10(O15) c. 12°, $1. Scott, F. & Co.

GASSENDI, Pierre.
Brett, G. S. Philosophy of Gassendi. *$3 net. Macmillan.

Gaston de Latour. *See* Pater, Wa.

GASTRIC DISEASES.
See Stomach.

GASTRONOMY.
See Dining.

Gate beautiful. Miller, J. R. **85 c. net. Crowell.

Gate of peace. Carman, B. subs., *$5 net. Village Press.

Gatehouse, Fk. B.
Handbook for cement workers. '08(D5) il. 8°. *$1.75 net. Lippincott.

Gates, Burton Noble.
Miscellaneous papers on apiculture; bee keeping in Massachusetts. '09(Ag) 81-109 p. map, il. 8°, (U. S., Dept. of Agriculture; Bu. of Entomology.) pap., 5 c.

Gates, Eleanor, [Mrs. R: Walton Tully.]
The justice of Gideon. '10(N12) c. il. D. $1.20 net. Macaulay.

Gates, Mrs. Ellen Maria Huntington.
To the unborn peoples, and other poems. '10(Ag13) c. O. $1. Baker & T.

Gates, Herb. Wright.
Heroes of the faith. [1910.] (D) c. 3+235 p. il. 12°, (Bible study union (Blakeslee) graded lessons.) 50 c. Bible Study.

Gates, Mrs. Josephine Scribner.
April fool doll. '09(N13) c. il. O. †$1.25. Bobbs-M.
Little Girl Blue lives in the woods till she learns to say please. '10(O15) c. col. il. S. bds., 50 c. net. Houghton M.
Live dolls' party days. '10(D31) c. il. O. $1.25. Bobbs-M.
Live dolls' play days. '08(O24) c. il. O. †$1.25. Bobbs-M.
Sunshine Annie. '10(D31) c. O. $1.25. Bobbs-M.

Gates, Mary C. Bishop, [Mrs. Merrill E. Gates.]
Hymns of nature and songs of the spirit: poems. '08(O24) c. 12°, *$1.25 net. Revell.

Gates, Mrs. Susa Young.
John Stevens' courtship; story of the Echo Canyon war. '09(N) c. 8+377 p. front. 12°, $1. Deseret News.

Gates and keys to Matthew. Robinson, L. 50 c. Pentecostal.

Gates of India. Holdich, *Sir* T: H. $3.25 net. Macmillan.

Gates of life. Stoker, B. 75 c. Cupples & L.

Gates of twilight. Harman, H: E. Stone & B.

Gates that shall not prevail. Farrington, H. M. †$1.50. Lane.

Gateway ser. of English texts; ed. by Henry Van Dyke. S. Am. Bk.
—Copeland *and* Rideout, *eds.* Selections from Byron, Wordsworth, Shelley, Keats and Browning. 40 c.
—Lamb. Select essays of Elia. 40 c.

Gateway to Shakespeare. '09, [1910.] (F) il. 4°, $2. Nelson.

Gateway to the Sahara. Furlong, C: W. **$2.50 net. Scribner.

Gatewood, Ja. Duncan.
Naval hygiene; prep. by direction of the Bureau of Medicine and Surgery and pub. by permission of the Navy Department. '09(O16) c. il. 8°, $6. Blakiston.

Gatewood, Lee C.
Experimental study of dementia præcox; [repr. from the *Psychological Review.*] '10(My14) tabs., 4°, (Ohio State Univ., Psychological studies.) 75 c. Psychological Review.

Gathered fragments. Lewis, J: H:, *comp.* 50 c. Lewis & W.

Gathered leaves. *See* Coleridge, Mary Eliz.

Gathman, H.
American soaps: treatise on the manufacture of soap. 2d ed. '08(My16) c. il. 8°, $15. H. Gathman.

Gattiker, Emma, comp.
Sel. list of German books recommended for a small public library; adopt. for use by the League of Library Commissions. '08 (F1) D. (A. L. A. Publishing Board foreign book list.) pap., 50 c. A. L. A.

Gatty, Mrs. Alfr.
See Gatty, *Mrs.* Marg. Scott.

Gatty, Mrs Marg. Scott, [Mrs. Alfr. Gatty.]
Life beyond. '10(D31) 16°, (Revell's idyll envelope ser.) 25 c. net. Revell.
Parables from nature. New ed. '10(N19) col. il. 8°, $2 net. Macmillan.

GATUN DAM.
See Dams.

Gaunt, Mary.
The uncounted cost. '10(Ag20) D. $1.20 net. Clode.

Gause, I:
Four years with five armies: army of the frontier, army of the Potomac, army of the Missouri, army of the Ohio, army of the Shenandoah. '08(F15) c. pors. O. *$2 net. Neale.

Gauss, H: Colford.
American government: organization and officials; with the duties and powers of federal office holders. '08(F22) c. O. hf. leath., $5. Hamersly.

Gaut, Helen Lukens.
Trails to peace. '10(Ap2) c. il. nar. O. pap., 50 c. H. L. Stanton.

Gautier, Théophile.
España and Émaux et camées; ed. by C. Edm. Delbos. '09(Mr6) por. S. (Oxford higher French ser.) 70 c. Oxford Univ.
Stories by Gautier; tr. by Lafcadio Hearn. '08(Ag15) 16°, (World's story-tellers' ser.; ed. by A. Ransome.) *40 c. net. Dutton.
Tales; tr. by Lafcadio Hearn and Myndart Verelst. '09(D4) c. S. (Wayside lib.) leath., $1. Brentano's.
Trois grotesques; ed. by H. J. Chaytor. '09(Mr6) por. S. (Oxford higher French ser.) 70 c. Oxford Univ.
Voyage en Espagne; ed. by Gerald Goodridge. '09(Mr6) map, D. (Oxford modern French ser.) 60 c. Oxford Univ.
See also Good stories.

Gay, Agnes Godfrey.
Mon livre de petites histoires. '10(F19) c. il. O. bds., $1. W: R. Jenkins.

Gay, Carl W.
Timely hints to horse breeders. '09, [1910.] (Mr) 24 p. 8°, (Commonwealth of Pennsylvania, Dept. of Agriculture, bull.) pap. Penn. Dept. of Agriculture.

Gay, Mrs. Maude Clarke.
Paths crossing: a romance of the plains. '08(Ag15) c. il. D. $1.50. C. M. Clark.

Gay, R: Lewis, comp.
See Massachusetts. Laws of the commonwealth.—Laws of Mass.

Gay Gnani of Gingalee. Huntley, *Mrs.* F. C: $1. Indo-Am. Bk.

Gay gods and merry mortals. Shores, R. J. B'way Pub.

GAY LECTURES.
See Whitley, W. T.

Gay Lord Waring. Townley, H. $1.50. W. J. Watt.

Gayley, C: Mills.
Idols of education. '10(Mr5) c. D. **50 c. net. Doubleday, P.

Gaynor, Jessie L.
Elements of musical expression. '08(O) 116 p. $1.25. C. F. Summy Co.
See also Riley, Alice C. D.

Gayworthys. Whitney, *Mrs.* A. D. T. 50 c. Hurst.

GAZETA DE LIMA (*periodical*).
Brown University. Facsimile of the first issue of the *Gazeta de Lima.* $2. Brown Univ.

GAZETTEERS.
Baylee, J: T. Gazetteer of the world. 50 c. Dutton.
See also Atlases;—Geography.

Gear, H. L., rep.
See California. *District cts.* Repts.—*District cts of appeal.* Repts.

Gearhart, Anna Frances.
Story of Moses adapt. for primary grades. '08(D5) front. D. pap., 10 c. Flanagan.

Gearhart, G: Adelbert.
Footprints of the centuries. '09, [1910.] (F) 64 p. por. 12°, $1. L. L. Gearhart.

GEARS AND GEARING.
Engstrom, D. A. Bevel gear tables. $1. Henley.
Fellows Gear Shaper Co. Stub-tooth gear. gratis. Fellows Gear.
Flanders, R. E: Bevel gearing. 25 c. Indust. Press.
Flanders, R. E: Gear-cutting machinery. $3. Wiley.
Logue, C: H. American machinist gear book. $2.50 net. McGraw-H.
Spiral gearing.—Spur gearing. ea., 25 c. Indust. Press.
See also Valves.

Gebhard, Eliz. Louisa.
Parsonage between two manors; annals of Clover-Reach. '09, [1910.] (Ja) 23+15 p. il. pors. 12°, $1.50. E. L. Gebhard.

Gebhardt, G: F:
Steam power plant engineering. '08(O3); 2d ed. '09(O30); 3d ed. '10(O22) c. il. figs. 8°, ea., *$6 net. Wiley.

Geddes, Ja., jr.
Educational advantages for American students in France. '09(Ap3) O. pap., 25 c. J. Geddes.

Geddes Burns. *See* Burns, Rob.

Geddings, H: D.
Precis on the management of outbreaks of smallpox, diphtheria and scarlet fever. '09(My15) 8°. (Add. Superintendent for price.) U. S., Supt. of Docs.

Geden, Alfr. S., D.D.
Outlines of introduction to the Hebrew Bible. '09(My15) facsims.. O. *$3.50 net. Scribner.

Gedichte. Drescher, M. $2. Columbia Pr.

GEESE.
Ducks and geese. 75 c. Reliable Poultry Journ.
Nourse, H. A. Turkeys, ducks and geese. 50 c. Webb.

Geeting, J: F. and H. C., reps.
See American criminal repts.

Geheimnis (Das) der gestalt. Hauptmann, C. F. M. (Add. pubs. for price.) R. Tombo.

Gehring, Albert.
Basis of musical pleasure, together with a consideration of the opera problem and the expression of emotions in music. '10 (D3) c. 8°, $1.50. Putnam.
Racial contrasts; distinguishing traits of the Græco-Latins and Teutons. '08(S19) c. O. **$1.50 net. Putnam.

Geiermann, Rev. P:
Margaret's influence; secret of the confessional. '10(Je4) c. 8°, $1. Herder.
Mission remembrance of the Redemptorist fathers. '08(Mr28) c. front. Tt. leath., 50 c. Benziger.
Private retreat for religious; enriched with reflections and select readings taken from the spiritual writings of St. Alphonsus. '09(Jl3) c. D. *$1.50 net. Benziger.

Geikie, Sir Archibald.
Charles Darwin as geologist; Rede lecture given at the Darwin Centennial Commemoration on June 24, 1909. '09, [1910.] (F) 91 p. 16°, 75 c. Putnam.

Geil, W: Edg.
Great wall of China. '10(Ja1) c. il. maps, 8°, $5. Sturgis & W.

Gellibrand, Emma.
J. Cole. '08(Ag1) 16°, (Ansonia classics.) 50 c. Hurst.

Gelston, Willis Lord.
Organization for boys. '10(Ja29) c. S. pap., 10 c. Presb. Bd.

GEMS.
See Precious stones.

Gems of German songs. Rev. ed. '09(D4) c. 4°, pap., $1. Ditson.

Gems of immortality. Allen, E. A. $2.25; $2.75; $3.75. Central Pub.

Gems of life. White, *Mrs.* A. 60 c. Pillar of Fire.

Gems of thought. Damon, H: B., *comp.* (Priv. pr.) H: B. Damon.

Gems of thought. Thompson, A. $1.50. A. Thompson.

Genealogical and family history of the state of Maine. Little, G: T:, *ed.* 4 v. $25. Lewis Pub.

Genealogical miniatures; ed. by M. T. R. Washburn. 8°. Allaben.
—Washburn. Ancestry of William Howard Taft. $1.

GENEALOGIES.
Abbe, C., *and* Nichols, *Mrs.* Townsend genealogy. $2. Allaben.
Alden, F. W., *comp.* John Alden of Ashfield, Mass., and Chautauqua County, New York. $1.50. F. W. Alden.
Allaben, F. Ancestry of Leander Howard Crall; monographs on the Crall, Haff, Beatty, [etc.,] families. **$50 net. Grafton Press.
Allen, J: K. George Morton of Plymouth Colony and some of his descendants. (Priv. pr.) J: K. Allen.
Allen, O. P. Allen memorial. 2d ser., 1640-1907. $3.75.—Descendants of Nicholas Cady of Watertown, Mass. $5. O. P. Allen.
Allyn, A. B., *comp.* Black Hall traditions and reminiscences, [Griswold family.] $1. A. B. Allyn.
Alvord, S: M., *comp.* Genealogy of the descendants of Alexander Alvord, early settler of Windsor, Conn., and Northampton, Mass. *$5 net. S: M. Alvord.
Babcock, W: E., *comp.* Hess-Higbee genealogy. $2. W: E. Babcock.
Badger, J: C. Giles Badger and his descendants. $1. J: C. Badger.
Baker, E. T:, *comp.* Geneal. of Eber and Lydia Smith Baker of Marion, Ohio, and their descendants. 50 c. L. A. Copeland.
Baldwin, T: W. Patten geneal.; William Patten of Cambridge, 1635, and his descendants. $5. T: W. Baldwin.
Ballou, *Mrs.* A. A. P., *and* Cooper, W: F. Dobyns-Cooper and allied families of Ballou, Bramble, Coulter, Credit, Duval, Henry, Kemp, Larew, Lyon, Norwood, Perry, Pierce and Taylor. 50 c. W: F. Cooper.
Barbour, *Mrs.* F. C. W. Spelman geneal. $5. Allaben.

GENEALOGIES.—*Continued.*
Barbour, S. Reminiscences, by Sylvester Barbour, a native of Canton, Conn. $1. S. Barbour.
Barclay, C. B. Our American Barclays. (Priv. pr.) Grafton Press.
Bare, D. M. *and* R. B., *comps.* Geneal. of Johannes Baer, 1749-1910. $2 net. Cen. Pr. & Pub.
Barnard, E. K. Early Maltby; with some Rhoades hist. and that of the Maulsby family in America. $6.25. S: N. Rhoades.
Beam, E. Family history, [Hyder family.] 50 c. Carroll Record Co.
Bellet, L. P. du. Some prominent Virginia families: [Edward Jaquelin-Martha Carey; their descendants.] 4 v. $10. J. P. Bell.
Boggs, M. A., *ed.* Alexander letters. (Priv. pr.) G: J. Baldwin.
Booth, C: E. One branch of the Booth family. $5. C: E. Booth.
Boyd, L., *comp.* The Irvines and their kin; also short sketches of their kindred: Carlisles, McDowells, Johnstons, Maxwells, McElroys. $5; $10; $25. Donnelley.
Brainard, L. A. Genealogy of the Brainerd-Brainard family in America, 1647-1908. 3 v. $15. L. A. Brainard.
Brenan, G., *and* Staham, E. P. House of Howard. 2 v. *$6 special net. Appleton.
Brown, W: B. Family hist. of Jeremiah Fenton and his descendants. $3.50. W: B. Brown.
Browning, E: F. Genealogy of the Brownings in America. $7.50. E: F. Browning.
Buck, A. H: Bucks of Wethersfield, Connecticut. (Priv. pr.) A. H: Buck.
Butler, W: D., *and others.* Butler family in America. $2.50; $5. Shallcross.
Cain, W. S. Autobiography of Captain W. S. Cain; biographical sketches of relatives. (Priv. pr.) W: S. Cain.
Caldwell, C: T. William Coaldwell, Caldwell or Coldwell of England, Massachusetts, Connecticut and Nova Scotia. Judd & D.
Campbell, F. Robert Campbell genealogy. $3.25. F. Campbell.
Carpenter, S. D. Genealogical notes of the Carpenter family. $5. G: N. Kreider.
Carter, *Mrs.* C. M. R. John Reddington of Topsfield, Mass., and some of his descendants; with notes on the Wales family. (Add. pubs. for price.) J. G. Leach.
Carter, W: G. H. Giles Carter of Virginia. *$2.50 net. Lord Balto. Pr.
Chaffee, W: H: Chaffee genealogy. *$15 net. Grafton Press.
Chaffin, W: L. Biographical hist. of Robert Randall and his descendants. *$5 net. Grafton Press.
Christie, *Mrs.* S. C. Cantrill-Cantrell genealogy. **$5 net. Grafton Press.
Cisco, J. G. Historic Sumner Co., Tenn., with genealogies of the Bledsoe, Cage and Douglas families, and genealogical notes of other Sumner Co. families. $2. J. G. Cisco.

GENEALOGIES.—*Continued.*

Clark, H: S., *comp. and ed.* Record of the lands and past descendants of Henry and Anne Clark. 50 c. H: S. Clark.

Colcock, C: J. Hist. of the progenitors and some South Carolina descendants of Col. Ann Hawkes Hay. (Priv. pr.) C: J. Colcock.

Cole, A. S., *comp.* Scott family of Shrewsbury, N. J. $2. A. S. Cole.

Cole, E. B. Descendants of James Cole of Plymouth, 1633. *$7 net. Grafton Press.

Colver, F. L. Colver-Culver geneal. $5. Allaben.

Cope, G., *comp. and ed.* Genealogy of the Darlington family. *$4 net. C. D. Heydecker.

Crandall, *Mrs.* R. R. N. Neil family, Sweden-America, 1718-1908. (Add. pubs. for price.) R. R. N. Crandall.

Deas, A. S. Recollections of the Ball family of South Carolina and the Comingtee plantation. $5. A. Ball.

Dewey, L: M. James Rising of Suffield, Conn., and some of his descendants. 50 c. N. E. Hist.

Dinkins, J. Genealogical: the Dinkins and Springs families. gratis. J. Dinkins.

Dupuy, B: H. Huguenot Bartholomew Dupuy and his descendants. $6.50. B: H. Dupuy.

Du Puy, C: M. Genealog. hist. of the Dupuy family. (Priv. pr.) H. Du Puy.

Duyckinck, W. C., *and* Cornell, J: Duyckinck and allied families. $5. T. A. Wright.

Eno, J. N. Thomas Lillibridge of Newport, R. I., and his descendants. 50 c. N. E. Hist.

Easterday, L. F. M. Hist. of the Easterday family. pt. 1. $2. L. F. M. Easterday.

Estabrook, J: D. Three generations of Northboro Davises, 1781-1894. $3. J: D. Estabrook.

Fernald, C: A: Universal international genealogy and of the ancient Fernald families, with chronology. $5; $15. C: A: Fernald.

Fillebrown, C: B. Geneal. of Fillebrown family. $5. C: B. Fillebrown.

Fogg, *Mrs.* A. J. Fogg family in America. $1.58. J. L. M.

French, H. B., *comp.* Genealogy of the descendants of Thomas French. 2 v. ea., $8. H. B. French.

Fretz, A. J. Genealogical record of the descendants of Benjamin Chamberlain of Sussex Co., N. J. $1.25; pap., 75 c.—Genealogy of the Moyer family. $2.25. A. J. Fretz.

Frost, T: G. *and* E. L. Frost family in England and America. $3. Russell Pr.

Fuller, W: H., *comp.* Geneal. of some descendants of Dr. Samuel Fuller of the "Mayflower." $5.—Geneal. of some descendants of Edward Fuller of the "Mayflower." $4. W: H. Fuller.

Galley, H., *and* Oglevee, A. J. Hist. of the Galley family. Phila. Pr.

Gardner F. A. Thomas Gardner, planter, and some of his descendants. $3.50. Essex Inst.

Gardner, *Mrs.* L. M. S. *and* C: Morris. Gardner hist. and geneal. Erie Pr.

GENEALOGIES.—*Continued.*

Garnett, J. M. Genealogy of the Mercer-Garnett family of Essex County, Virginia. $1. J. M. Garnett.

Garrett, S: B. Hist. of Welcome Garrett and his descendants. $5. S: B. Garrett.

Genealogical record of the descendants of Andrew Newbaker of Hardwick township, Warren Co., N. J. $1.50; 65 c. Union Times.

Gentry, R: Gentry family in America. *$5 net. Grafton Press.

Gibbon, F. P. Lawrences of the Punjaub. *$1.50 net. Dutton.

Gift, A. K., *comp.* Hist. of the Gift, Kern and Royer families. $1.50. Herald Pr.

Goodspeed, W. A. Hist. of the Goodspeed family. $10; $15. W. A. Goodspeed.

Gray, G: A., *comp.* Holmes geneal. *$5 net. G: A. Gray.

Hale, O. F., *comp.* Ancestry and descendants of Josiah Hale, fifth in descent from Samuel Hale of Hartford, Conn., 1637. $2. O. F. Hale.

Hamlin, *Mrs.* M. L. S. Eleazer Hamlin and his descendants. $1. C: S. Hamlin.

Harding, W: J. Ancestry in the line of her fathers of Adelia Chamberlain Harding, daughter of Rev. Hiram Chamberlain, and Anna Aaelia Griswold. $1. E. Putnam.

Harris, J. S. Collateral ancestry of Stephen Harris. *$3 net. W: J. Campbell.

Herr, T. W. Geneal. record of Rev. Hans Herr. $10; lineal descent, $5. T. W. Herr.

Hess, T: Jonathan and Hannah Steelman; family tree. $3.50. T: Hess.

Heydecker, C. T. Geneal. of Samuel Gourley and his descendants. 75 c. C. T. Heydecker.

Holman, D. E. Holmans in America. v. 1. *$7 net. Grafton Press.

Honeyman, A. V. D. Honeyman family. $6.—Van Doorn family. $10. Honeyman.

Hooker, E: Descendants of Rev. Thomas Hooker, Hartford, Connecticut. $10. M. H. Hooker.

Houser, W: W., *comp.* Geneal. of the Houser, Rhorer, Dillman, Hoover families. $2. W: W. Houser.

Huntting, T. D., *comp.* Descendants of Abraham Huntting. (Priv. pr.) T. D. Huntting.

Hurd, *Mrs.* D. D. S. Hist and geneal. of the family of Hurd in the U. S. $10; $15. D. D. S. Hurd.

Jewett, F. C. Hist. and genealogy of the Jewetts of America. **$20 net. Grafton Press.

Johnson, A. V. V. Gimm family. Gillespie & L.

Jones, E. C. B. Brewster genealogy. 2 v. *$15 net. Grafton Press.

Kennan, T: L. Geneal. of the Kennan family. $2.50. T: L. Kennan.

Lea, J. H., *and* Hutchinson, J. R. Ancestry of Abraham Lincoln. $10, boxed. Houghton M.

Leach, J. G., *ed.* Some acct. of the Tree family and its connections in England and America. (Priv. pr.) Lippincott.

GENEALOGIES.—*Continued.*

Learned, M. D. Abraham Lincoln, American migration. *$3 net. W: J. Campbell.

Lewis, G: A. Edmund Lewis of Lynn, Massachusetts, and some of his descendants. $3. Essex Inst.

Livingston, E. B. Livingstons of Livingston manor. $10. J: H: Livingston.

McAleer, G:, *comp.* Study in the origin and signification of the surname McAleer. $3.50. G: McAleer.

McPike, E. F. Extracts from British archives on the families of Halley, Hawley, Parry, Pyke, etc. (Priv. pr.) E. F. McPike.

Martin, R: A. Castor family, Holmesburg branch. $2 net. Martin & A.

Mason, F. C. Hist. of the Barton and Mason families in Europe and America. $3.25. Rep. Pr. Co.

Mason, T. W. Family record of our line of descent from Major John Mason of Norwich, Ct. (Priv. pr.) Grafton Press.

Mendoza, D. H. de. Life of Lazarillo de Tormes; with notice of the Mendoza family. *$1.25 net. Macmillan.

Merrill, S: P. My loves and my lovers, [incl. Merrill and Wilcox genealogies.] $1. Marion Press.

Middlebrook, L: F. Register of the Middlebrook family. $6. L: F. Middlebrook.

Miller, W: H. Hist. and geneal. of the families of Miller, Woods, Harris, Wallace, Moupin, Oldham, Kavanaugh and Brown. $5. W: H. Miller.

Moffat, R. B. Moffat genealogies. (Priv. pr.) R. B. Moffat.

Moon, R. C. Morris family of Philadelphia. 3 v. $20. R. C. Moon.

Morris, S. Hale family in Connecticut. (Priv. pr.) Clapp.

Mowry, W: A: Descendants of John Mowry of Rhode Island. $3. Preston.

Murdock, W: G. Brady family reunion. $1.25. W: G. Murdock.

Nicholls, W. Sergeant Francis Nicholls of Stratford, Ct., 1639, and the descendants of his son, Caleb Nicholls. $5. Grafton Press.

Northrup, A. J. Northrup-Northrop geneal. **$10 net. Grafton Press.

Norton, W. W. Some descendants of John Norton of Branford, 1622-1709. (Add. pubs. for price.) Journal Press, (Ct.)

Nutting, J. K. Nutting genealogy. $5. Bardeen.

Nye, G: H., *and* Best, F. E., *comps.* Genealogy of Nye family. (Add. pubs. for price.) Nye.

Onderdonk, E. Geneal. of the Onderdonk family in America. $6. A. J. Onderdonk.

Parks, F. S., *comp.* Genealogy of the Parke families of Massachusetts. $5.25. F. S. Parks.

Peabody, R. E. Derbys of Salem, Mass. (Priv. pr.) Essex Inst.

Peck, T: B. William Slade of Windsor, Conn., and his descendants. $3.50. Sentinel (N. H.)

GENEALOGIES.—*Continued.*

Perrine, H. D., *comp.* Daniel Perrin, "The Huguenot," and his descendants in America, of the surnames Perrine, Perine and Prine. $10 net. H. D. Perrine.

Poole, M. E. Hist. of Jan Van Cleef of New Utrecht, L. I., and some of his descendants. (Add. pubs. for price.) Ithaca Journ.

Pope, C: H:, *and* Hooper, T:, *comps.* Hooper geneal. *$7 net. C: H. Pope.

Prosch, T: W. Conklin-Prosch family, with some reference to the Dotter, Roe, Reynolds, Brooks, Mapes, Elder, McCarver and other connections. (Priv. pr.) T: W. Prosch.

Putnam, E. Putnam lineage. $15. Salem Press.

Read, H. P. Rossiana: papers and documents rel. to the hist. and genealogy of the ancient and noble house of Ross, of Ross-shire, Scotland, $10. H. P. Read.

Reade, P. H., *comp.* First generation of the name of Hildreth in Middlesex Co., in Mass. $1.25. P. Reade.

Risley, E. H. Risley family hist. $5. Grafton Press.

Rix, G. S. Hist. and geneal. of the Ricks family in America. $5. J. Ricks.

Russell, G. W. Acct. of some of the descendants of John Russell, the emigrant from Ipswich, England. $4. Conn. Hist.

Schaeffer, C. Memoirs and reminisc.; with notes and genealog. record of the Schaeffer family. (Priv. pr.) W: M. Johnson.

Seilhamer, G: O. Bard family. $10. Kittochtinny.

Sellers, E. J. Genealogy of the De Carpentier family of Holland. $3.—Genealogy of the Jaquett family. $5. E. J. Sellers.

Sharpe, E: S. Descendants of the pioneers, [Salem Co., N. J.] 10 c. Salem Co. Hist. Soc.

Sinnett, C: N. Richard Pinkham of old Dover, N. H., and his descendants East and West. $5.—Sinnett genealogy: Michael Sinnett of Harpswell, Maine. $4. C: N. Sinnett.

Slocum, C: E. Hist. of Francis Slocum, the captive; [with genealogy of her descendants.] $2.50. Slocum Pub.

Slocum, C: E. Hist. of the Slocums, Slocumbs and Slocombs of America, genealogical and biographical, from 1637 to 1908. 2 v. (Add. pubs. for price.) Tuttle Co.

Smith, L. B. Jesse Smith, his ancestors and descendants. $4; $6. Allaben.

Smyth, S: G., *comp. and ed.* Genealogy of the Duke-Shepherd-Van Metre family. $3. S: G. Smyth.

Stackpole, E. S. Macomber genealogy. $5. E. S. Stackpole.

Sterling, A. M. Sterling geneal. *$50 net; *$25 net. Grafton Press.

Stevens, P. Stephens-Stevens genealogy. $5. Allaben.

GENEALOGIES.—*Continued.*

Stratton, H. R., *comp.* Book of Strattons: collection of records from England and Scotland. v. 1. **$8 net. Grafton Press.

Sutliff, S: M. Hist. of the American and puritanical family of Sutliff or Sutliffe. $2. S: M. Sutliff.

Tagliapietra, M. T., *comp.* Townsend-Townshend, 1066-1909: the hist., genealogies and alliances of the English and American house of Townsend. $10. M. T. Tagliapietra.

Talmadge, A. W. Talmadge, Tallmadge, and Talmade geneal. *$10 net. Grafton Press.

Terrell, E. H. Further genealog. notes on the Tyrrell-Terrell family of Va. (Priv. pr.) E. H. Terrell.

Tillinghast, J. A. *and* F: W. Little journeys to the home of Elder Pardon Tillinghast. (Not for sale.) J: A. Tillinghast.

Trowbridge, F. B. Trowbridge genealogy. $15; $17.50. F. B. Trowbridge.

Turk, W. A. C. Beatty-Asfordby.; ancestry of John Beatty and Susanna Asfordby. $4. Allaben.

Ulrich, B. A., *comp.* Von Reisenkampff-Ulrich family hist. 10 c. Co-operative Pr. Co.

Van Benschoten, W: H: Concerning the Van Bunschoten or Van Benschoten family in America. $4. Haight.

Vreeland, N. G., *ed.* Hist. and geneal. of the Vreeland family. $5. Hist. Pub. Co., (N. J.)

Walker, G. K. Memoirs of the Graham family. $2. T. A. Wright.

Ward, G: K., *comp.* Andrew Warde and his descendants, 1597-1910. $10. De La Mare.

Washburn, L. A. Richard Webber family; genealogy from the first settlement in America. (Priv. pr.) A. I. Root.

Washburn, M. T. R. Ancestry of William Howard Taft. $1. Allaben.

Waters, T: F. Candlewood; [with genealogies of John Brown, William Fellows, Robert Kinsman.] $1.50. Salem Press.

Waters, T: F. Old Bayroad from Saltonstall's Brook and Samuel Appleton's farm; [also] A genealogy of the Ipswich descendants of Samuel Appleton. 25 c. Ipswich Hist.

Watson, *Mrs.* A. W. R. "Of sceptred race" [families of royal descent; Watson family.] $10. Early.

Wells, F: H., *comp.* William Wells and his descendants. $3.25. F: H. Wells.

Wheeler, G., *comp.* Geneal. of a branch of the Wheelers. $1. G. Wheeler.

Wheeler, W: O., *comp.* Ogden family in America. (Priv. pr.) Lippincott.

Whitcher, W: F: Descendants of Chase Whitcher of Warren, N. H. *$3.50 net. W: F: Whitcher.

White, A. L. Genealogy of the ancestors and descendants of John White of Wenham and Lancaster, Mass., 1574-1909. In 4 v. ea., $5; per set, $28. A. L. White.

GENEALOGIES.—*Continued.*

White, J: B. Geneal. of the descendants of Thomas Gleason of Watertown, Mass. $7.50. Nichols Print.

Whittier, C: C. Urann family of New England, including the descendants of Margaret (Urann) Gammell. 75 c. C: C. Whittier.

Wickwire, A. M. Genealogy of the Wickware family. $6. A. M. Wickwire.

Williams, C. S. Descendants of Thomas White of Weymouth, Mass. C. S. Williams

Wilson, L. M., *ed.* Barber geneal. Section 1, Descendants of Thomas Barber of Windsor, Conn.; section 2, Descendants of John Barber of Worcester, Mass. $10. J: B. White.

Wise, J. C., *comp.* Digested index and genealogical guide to Bishop Meade's "Old churches, ministers and families of Virginia"; embracing 6,900 proper names. Bell Bk.

Witwer, G:, *and* A. C., *comps.* Witwer geneal. $2.25. L. P. Hardy.

Wood, A. A. Luther Sisson of Easton, Mass., his ancestry and descendants. 50 c. A. A. Wood.

Woodruff, F. E. Woodruffs of New Jersey. **$5 net. E. Woods.

Woods, H: E. Woods family of Groton, Mass. (Priv. pr.) H: E. Woods.

Wright, C: W. Wright ancestry of Caroline, Dorchester, Somerset and Wicomico counties. *$2.25 net. C: W. Wright.

Wright, *Mrs.* E. F. R. Reed-Read lineage; Captain John Reed of Providence, R. I., and Norwalk, Ct., and his descendants through his sons, John and Thomas. $10. Mattatuck Press.

Wyand, E. C. Brief hist. of the Andrew Putman (Buttman, Putnam), Christian Wyandt (Weyandt, Weygandt, Voint, Wyand), and Adam Snyder families (Schneider) of Washington County, Maryland. $1. E. C. Wyand.

Wyman, *Mrs.* M. E. T. Genealogy of the descendants of Lawrence and Mary Antisell of Norwich and Willington, Conn.; incl. some records of Christopher Antisell of Sraduff, Birr, (Kings Co.,) Ireland. $5. L. Wyman.

Yale, R. H. Yale geneal. and hist. of Wales. $5. R. H. Yale.

Zartman, R. C. Zartman family. $1.50. Lyon & A.

See also Chapin Family Association pubs; — Cohasset, Mass.;—Genealogy;—Maine;—Massachusetts;—Medford, Mass.;—Middlesex Co., Mass.;—Names (*personal*);—New Hampshire;—New York State;—Pendleton Co., W. Va.;—Salem Co., N. J.;—Shenandoah Valley.

GENEALOGY.

Burk, *Sir* J: B. *and* A. P: Genealogical and heraldic hist. of the peerage and baronetage. *$12 net. Putnam.

Crozier, W: A., *ed.* Virginia heraldica: registry of Virginia gentry entitled to coat armor. $3. Genealog. Assoc.

Cutter, W: R:, *ed.* Genealogical and family hist. of northern New York. $25. Lewis Pub.

De Witt, W. Family genealogical record book. **$1.25 net. Grafton Press.

GENEALOGY.—*Continued.*
Hanson, J. C. M., *comp.* American and English genealogies in the Library of Congress. $1.05. Gov. Pr. Off.
Smith, F. M. Colonial families of America. $2. Allaben.
Waters, H: F.-G. Genealogical gleanings in England. 2 v. $10. N. E. Hist.
See also Biography;—Epitaphs;— Genealogies;—*also* names of families, persons and towns.

Genealogy of morals. *See* Nietzsche, Friedrich.

Genée, Franz Friedrich Richard.
See Zell, F.

Genera of fungi. Clements, F. E: $2. H. W. Wilson.

Genera of the *tortricidæ* and their types. Fernald, C: H: 75 c. C: H: Fernald.

General character of the proteins. Schryver, S: B. *80 c. net. Longmans.

General Church of the New Jerusalem. Liturgy. '08(Ag) c. 5+814 p. 8°, $2; mor., $3.50. Acad. Bk. Room.

General Federation of Women's Clubs. Hdbk. of art in our own country; comp. by G. F. W. C. art committee, 1906-1908; ed. by Mrs. Everett W. Pattison. '08(Je) c. 54 p. 8°, 25 c. E. W. Pattison.

General history of Macon County, Missouri. '10(Ag20) c. il. pors. f°, $15. H. Taylor & Co.

General history of western nations. *See* Reich, Emil.

General lectures on electrical engineering. Steinmetz, C: P. *$2 net. Robson.

General lumber tariff. Walker, J: R., *comp.* $5. Lumbermen's Pub.

General surgical technique. Gray, H. M. W. *See* Colum, Rowland W. Practice of anæsthetics.

General theory of law. Korkunov, N. M. $3.50. Boston Law.

GENERATIVE ORGANS.
Ballenger, E. G. Genito-urinary diseases and syphilis. *$3 net. E. W. Allen.
Caspar, L. Text-book of genito-urinary diseases. *$5 net. Blakiston.
Gilchrist, T: C. Outline of skin diseases. 75 c. Students' Bk.
Greene, R. H., *and* Brooks, H. Diseases of the genito-urinary organs and the kidney. *$5 net. Saunders.
Keyes, E. L., *jr.* Disease of the genito-urinary organs. $6 net; $7 net. Appleton.
Kreissl, F. Urogenital therapeutics. $5. Cleveland Press.
Watson, F. S., *and* Cunningham, J: H., *jr.* Diseases and surgery of the genito-urinary system. 2 v. *$12 net; *$17 net. Lea.
White, J. W:, *and* Martin, E: Genito-urinary surgery and venereal diseases. $6. Lippincott.
Witkowski's Atlas of female reproductive organs.—Atlas of male reproductive organs. ea., *$3 net. W: R. Jenkins.
See also **Gynecology;—Midwifery;—Sex;—Urine and urinary organs;—Venereal diseases.**

GENESEE VALLEY.
See **New York State.**

GENESIS (Book of).
See **Bible. O. T.**

Genesis; manual for instruction of children. Talmey, B. S. $1.50. Practitioner's Pub.

Genesis of speech. Scott, F. N. (Add. pubs. for price.) Modern Lang. Assoc.

GENETIC ETHICS.
See **Ethics.**

Genetic psychology. Kirkpatrick, E. A. **$1.25 net. Macmillan.

GENETICS.
See **Heredity.**

GENEVA, Switzerland.
Gribble, F. Geneva. *$2 net. Macmillan.

GENEVA-OVID QUADRANGLES.
See **New York State.**

Genial idiot. Bangs, J: K. †$1.25. Harper.

GENITO-URINARY DISEASES.
See **Generative organs.**

GENOA, Italy
Carden, R. W. City of Genoa. *$2.50 net; *$5 net. Pott.

Genthe, Martha Krug.
Valley towns of Connecticut. '07, [1908.] (N) c. 32 p. il. maps, 8°, 50 c. Am. Geog. Soc.

Gentistoria, the new system (an encyclopedia): orig. and practical method of self-instruction. '08(Ag15) c. 3 v., il. charts, 4°. (Add. pub. for price.) Home Educ.

Gentle grafter. Henry, O., *pseud.* †$1. McClure.

Gentle knight of Old Brandenburg. Major, C: $1.50. Macmillan.

Gentleman (The). Ollivant, A. **$1.50 net. Macmillan.

Gentleman Don. Harshbarger, J. A. $1. Crane.

Gentleman from East Blueberry. Marshall, B. 50 c. Capital City Press.

Gentleman from Mississippi. Wise, T: A. *50 c. net. J. S. Ogilvie.

Gentleman of quality. Dey, F: V. $1.50. L. C. Page.

Gentleman of Virginia. Brebner, P. J: $1.50. Macmillan.

Gentleman's dog. Bryce, C. A. $1. So. Clinic Pr.

Gentlemen errant. Cust, *Mrs.* N. *$4 net. Dutton.

Gentry, G:
Pract. electro-plating; pract. hdbk. on the apparatus and processes employed in the electro-deposition of metals. '10(D17) 12°, bds., 50 c. Spon.

Gentry, R:
Gentry family in America, 1676 to 1909, inclusive. '10(Ja8) il. 8°, *$5 net. Grafton Press.

GENTRY FAMILY.
See **Genealogies.**

GEODESY.
Molitor, D: A. Geodetic surveying for the use of students in the College of Civil Engineering, Cornell University. 30 c. D: A. Molitor.
United States. *Dept. of Commerce and Labor. Coast and Geodetic Survey.* Geodesy; supp. investigation in 1909 of the figure of the earth and isostasy. '10 (Jl) 80 p. charts, 4°.
See also **Astronomy;—Surveying.**

Geoffrey Hamlyn. *See* Kingsley, H:

Geographical distribution of the investments of life insurance companies. Cox, R. L. gratis. Assoc. Life.

Geographical essays. Davis, W: M. $2.75. Ginn.

Geographical library. il. O. Doubleday, P.
—Abraham. Complete mountaineer. *$4.80 net.
—Cook. To the top of the continent. **$2.50 net.

GEOGRAPHY.

Archer, R: L., *and others.* Teaching of geography in elem. schools. $1.10 net. Macmillan.

Atlas of literary and historical geography. 35 c. net; 70 c. net. Dutton.

Benziger's elem. geography for Catholic schools. 54 c. Benziger.

Calmerton, G. Geography—history. (Not for sale.) Fort Wayne Sch. Bd.

Chamberlain, J. F. How we travel. *40 c. net. Macmillan.

Davis. W: M. Geographical essays. $2.75. Ginn.

Dunton, L. School-children the world over. $1.50. Stokes.

Franciscan Sisters of Perpetual Adoration. Geography briefly told. 80 c. Franciscan Sisters.

Frye. A. E. First book in geography. 50 c. —Grammar school geography. pt. 1. 80 c. Ginn.

Fultz, F. M. Out of door studies in geography. In 2 pts. ea., 60 c. Pub. Sch. Pub.

Herbertson, A. J. Physiographical introd. to geography. 40 c. Oxford Univ.

Herbertson, A. J. *and* F. L. D. R. Senior geography. 75 c. Oxford Univ.

Herbertson, F. L. D. R. Elementary geography. v. 1, 2, 3. ea., 30 c.; v. 4, 40 c.; v. 7, 60 c. Oxford Univ.

Kirk, F. M. Senior geography questions. 25 c. Oxford Univ.

Lyde, L. W. Man in many lands. 65 c. net.—School text-book of geography. *$1 net. Macmillan.

McMurry, C: A. Central topics in geography. In 2 v. ea., 10 c. Flanagan.

Mill, H. H., *ed.* International geography. **90 c. net. Appleton.

Morris, C: Industrial and commercial geography, for use in schools. $1.10 net. Lippincott.

Murphy, D. C. Recreations in history and geography. *30 c. net. Educ. Pub.

Niver, H. B., *and* Farrell, E: D. Geographies; 6A and 6B grades, 80 c.; 6A, 55 c.; 6B, 55 c. Noble.

Pattillo, H: Geographical catechism. 75 c. Univ. of N. C.

Scantlebury. E. E. Homes of the world's babies. 50 c. Flanagan.

Schmucker, S: C. Columbia elem. geography. 60 c. Hinds.

Sutherland, W: J. Teaching of geography. $1.25. Scott, F. & Co.

Tarr, R. S., *and* McMurry, F. M. Advanced geography. $1. Cal. Supt. Pub. Instruction.

GEOGRAPHY.—*Continued.*

Tarr, R. S., *and* McMurry, F. M. Geographies. 5 bk. ser. pt. 2, Earth as a whole. **55 c. net.—New geographies. In 2 bks. bk. 1, complete, 65 c. net; bk. 2, complete, $1.10 net. Macmillan.

Unstead, J. F. Practical geography. pts. 1, 2, ea., 40 c.; pts. 1-2, bound together, 60 c. Oxford Univ.

Ware, A. Course of study and teacher's manual in map geography. 30 c. San F. St. Normal.

Winslow, I: O. Geography readers. 5 v. ea., 50 c. net. Heath.

Wyss, C. v. Child's world in pictures. 75 c. net. Macmillan.

See also Altitudes;—Antarctic regions;—Arctic regions;—Atlases;—Commerce; — Ethnology; — Evolution;—Explorers; — Gazetteers;—Maps; — —Physical geography; — Surveying; — Voyages and travels;—*also* names of places and countries.

Geography and dialects of the Miwok Indians. Barrett, S: A. 50 c. Univ. of Cal.

Geological and Natural History Survey of Minnesota report, botanical ser. il. 8°. F: E. Clements.
—Tilden. Minnesota algae. $1.

GEOLOGICAL SOCIETY, London, Eng.

Centenary of the Geological Society of London. *75 c. net. Longmans.

Woodward, H. B. History of the Geological Society of London. *$2.60 net. Longmans.

GEOLOGY.

Babbitt, J. B. Physical history of the earth in outline. $1.50. E. E. Sherman.

Chamberlin, R. T. Gases in rocks. 50 c. Carnegie.

Chamberlin, T: C., *and* Salisbury, R. D. College text-book of geology. **$3.50 net. Van Nostrand.

Corder, G: A. Miner's geology and prospector's guide. $2. Spon.

Elsden, J. V. Principles of chemical geology. $1.60 net. Macmillan.

Gregory, H. E., *and* Robinson, H: H. Preliminary geological map of Connecticut. (Add. pubs. for price.) Conn. Lib.

Gregory, J: W. Geology. 50 c. net. Appleton.

Grew, E. S. Romance of modern geology. *$1.50 net. Lippincott.

Hayes, C: W. Hdbk. for field geologists. **$1.50 net. Wiley.

Hayes, C: W., *and* Lindgren, W. Contributions to economic geology. 1907. pt. 1. —1908. pt. 1. U. S., Supt. of Docs.

Hickling, G: Geology. 50 c. net. Stokes.

Hillebrand, W: F., *and* Schaller, W. T. Mercury minerals from Terlingua. Gov. Pr. Off.

Houston, E. J. Boy geologist at school and in camp: [fiction.] †$1. Altemus.

Joly, J: Radioactivity and geology. *$3 net. Van Nostrand.

Kemp, J. F. Geology: [lecture.] 25 c. Macmillan.

Kemp, J. F. Hdbk. of rocks, for use without the microscope. **$1.50 net. Van Nostrand.

Knopf, A. Probable tertiary land connection bet. Asia and North America. 10 c. Univ. of Cal.

GEOLOGY.—*Continued.*

Lake, P., *and* Rastall, R. H. Text-book of geology. $4.50 net. Longmans.

Merriam, J: C. Skull and dentition of a primitive ichthyosaurian from the middle Triassic. 10 c. Univ. of Cal.

Nickles, J: M. Bibliography of North American geology for 1908. Gov. Pr. Off.

Phalen, W: C. Economic geology of the Kenova quadrangle; Kentucky, Ohio and West Virginia. (Add. Superintendent for price.) U. S., Supt. of Docs.

Ries, H. Economic geology, with special reference to the United States. $3.50 net. Macmillan.

Salisbury, R. D., *ed.* Outlines of geologic hist. $1.50 net. Univ. of Chic.

Schwarz, E. H. L. Causal geology. $2.50. Van Nostrand.

Studies from the geological department, [University of Illinois.] 75 c. Univ. of Ill.

Taber, C: A. M. Cause of geologic periods. 75 c. Ellis.

United States *Dept. of the Interior. U. S. Geological Survey.* Publications; (not incl. topographical maps.) gratis.

United States. *Dept. of the Interior, U. S. Geological Survey.* Publications of the United States Geological Survey.

United States. *Dept. of the Interior, U. S. Geological Survey.* Technologic publications of the United States Geological Survey. gratis.

Walcott, C: D. Cambrian geology and paleontology. Nos. 1, 2, 3, 4, 5, 6, 7. no. 1, 5 c.; no. 2, 25 c.; nos. 3, 4, 5 (Add. pubs. for price); no. 6, 70 c.; no. 7, 10 c. Smith. Inst.

Wheeler, J. T. Zonal-belt hypothesis: new explanation of the cause of the ice age. **$2.50 net. Lippincott.

Woodward, H. B. Geology of water-supply. $2.50. Longmans.

See also Alaska;—Cape Colony;—Africa;—Clay;—Coal; — Copper;—Crystallography; — Earth; — Earthquakes; — Ethnology; — Evolution;—Glaciers;—Granite;—Magnesite;—Mineralogy;—Paleontology;—Petroleum;—Physical geography;—Rocks;—Salts;—Soils;—Stone;—*also* California;—Chihuahua; — Fox river valley; — Georgia;—Goldfield, Nev.;—Leadville; — Louisiana;—Mississippi valley;—Missouri;—Montana;—Morgan Co., Mo.;—New England;—New York City;—New York State; — North America; — North Carolina;—Orangia;—Oregon;—Pike Co., Mo.;—San Pablo, Cal.; — Texas; — Vermont;—*also* Geological Society, London.

GEOMETRICAL DRAWING.

Auerbach, M. Elem. course in graphic mathematics. 35 c. Allyn & B.

GEOMETRY.

Achimedes. Geometrical solution derived from mechanics. 50 c. Open Court.

Anthony, G. C., *and* Ashley, G: F: Descriptive geometry. $2. Heath.

Askwith, E: H. Analytical geometry of the conic sections. *$2.60 net. Macmillan.

Bartlett, F. W., *and* Johnson, T. W. Engineering descriptive geometry. $1.50 net. Wiley.

Bruce, W: H., *and* Cody, C. C. Elem. of plane geometry. 75 c. Southern Pub. (Tex.)

GEOMETRY.—*Continued.*

Bush, W. N., *and* Clarke, J: B. Elements of geometry. $1.25. Silver.

Candy, A. L. Elements of plane and solid analytic geometry. *$2 net. Heath.

Carus, P. Foundations of mathematics: philosophy of geometry. *75 c. net. Open Court.

Coolidge, J. L. Elements of non-Euclidean geometry. *$5 net. Oxford Univ.

Davison, C:, *and* Richards, C. H. Plane geometry. *$1 net. Putnam.

Durell, C. V. Course of plane geometry for advanced students. pt. 1. *$1.50 net; pt. 2. $2.40 net. Macmillan.

Edgett, G. L. Exercises in geometry. 40 c. Heath.

Eisenhart, L. P. Treatise on the differential geometry of curves and surfaces. $4.50. Ginn.

Euclid. Elements: 13 books. *$13.50 net. Putnam.

Fine, H: B., *and* Thompson, H: D. Coordinate geometry. *$1.60 net.—Answers. 20 c. Macmillan.

Fishleigh, W. T. Problem in descriptive geometry for class and drawing room. $1. W. T. Fishleigh.

Follows, G: H. Essentials of descriptive geometry. *$2 net. Hill Pub.

Godfrey, C:, *and* Siddons, G. W. Modern geometry. *50 c. net. Putnam.

Hime, H: W. L. Anharmonic co-ordinate. $3 net. Longmans.

Hood, G: J. Descriptive geometry problems. 85 c. G: J. Hood.

Keller, S: S. Mathematics for engineering students: plane and solid geometry. *$1.25 net. Van Nostrand.

Keller, S: S., *and* Knox, W. F. Mathematics for engineering students: analytical geometry and calcuius. $2. Van Nostrand.

Lyman, E. A. Plane and solid geometry. $1.25.—Plane geometry.—Solid geometry. ea., 75 c. Am. Bk.

McLeod, C. H. Elem. descriptive geometry. $1.50. Wiley.

Newton, F. E., *and* Lynde, L. E: Syllabus of plane geometry. $1. Andover.

Nichols, E: W. Analytic geometry. $1.25. Heath.

Phillips, J. D:, *and* Millar, A. V. Essentials of descriptive geometry. $1. Tracy, G. & Co.

Phillips, J. D:, *and* Millar, A. V. Notes on descriptive geometry. $1. A. V. Millar.

Picksford, A. G. Elem. projective geometry. $1.25 net. Putnam.

Raymond, W: G. Railroad field geometry. $2. Wiley.

Riggs, N. C. Analytic geometry. $1.60 net. Macmillan.

Robbins, E: R. Key to Plane and solid geometry. $1. Am. Bk.

Scott, C. A. Introductory acct. of certain modern ideas and methods in plain analytical geometry. *$2.50 net; *$3 net. Macmillan.

Slaught, H. E., *and* Lennes, N. J. Plane geometry. $1. Allyn & B.

GEOMETRY.—*Continued.*
Smith, E. R. Plane geometry. 75 c. Am. Bk.
Smith, P. F., *and* Granville, W: A. Elem. analysis. $1.50. Ginn.
Stamper, A. W. Hist. of the teaching of elem. geometry. $1.50; $1.15. Teachers' Coll.
Stone, J: C., *and* Millis, J. F. Elem. geometry, plane. 80 c. B: H. Sanborn.
Strout, C: H: Plane geometry. $1. C: H: Strout.
Wells, W. New plane and solid geometry. $1.25. Heath.
Wentworth, G: A. Plane geometry. 80 c. Ginn.
Wilson, V. T. Descriptive geometry. **$1.50 net. Wiley.
See also Curves;—Mechanical drawing;—Mensuration;—Perspective; — Projection; — Surveying; Trigonometry.

Geonica. Ginzberg, L: 2 v. (Add. pubs. for price.) Jewish Theological.

GEORGE I. *of England.*
Melville, L. First George in Hanover and England. 2 v. *$6 net. Scribner.

GEORGE III., *of England.*
Melville, L. Farmer George: life and character of George III. 2 v. *$7.50 net. Brentano's.
Willson, H: B. George III., as man, monarch and statesman. *$3 net. Jacobs.

GEORGE IV., *of England.*
Bury, *Lady* C. S. M. C. Diary of a lady-in-waiting. 2 v. *$7.50 net. Lane.
Wilkins, W: H: Mrs. Fitzherbert and George IV. $5. Longmans.

GEORGE I., II., III., IV., *of England.*
Boulton, W: B. In the days of the Georges. $4. Pott.
Thackeray, W: M. Four Georges. $2 net. Macmillan.

George, Mlle., [Marguerite-Josephine Weymer, called "Mlle. George."]
Favorite of Napoleon: memoirs; ed. from the original manuscript by Paul Cheramy. '09(Je5) por. O. *$2.50 net. J: McBride.

George, D: Lloyd.
See Lloyd-George, D:

George, Earl B.
See Dickinson, Hobert C:

George, Rev. E: A:
Seventeenth century men of latitude: forerunners of the new theology. '08(My9) c. pors. D. **$1.25 net. Scribner.

George, Florence A.
Vegetarian cookery. '08(D5) D. $1.25. Longmans.

George, Rev. Hereford Brooke.
Historical evidence. '09(N13) D. 75 c. Oxford Univ.

George, Llewellyn.
A to Z horoscope delineator; pract. information, lessons, and interpretations rel. to the science of astrology. '10 (Jl16) c. il. 16°, $2. Portland (Ore.) Sch. Astrology.

George, Marian M.
Character building. [In 2 v.] v. 1, Ethical lessons in kindness, industry, obedience, thankfulness and humane education; v. 2, Ethical lessons in charity, self-control, honesty, cheerfulness, truthfulness, courtesy, cleanliness and humane education. '09(Ag14) c. il. pors. O. ea., $1.25. Flanagan.

George, W. L.
France in the twentieth century. '08(D12) D. *$1.75 net. Lane.
Labor and housing at Port Sunlight. '09 (Jl) 6+218 p. 12°, *$1.40 net. Scribner.

George, W:
Law of apartments, flats and tenements. '08(Jl) c. 489 p. O. $4. Fallon.

George, W: Reuben.
Junior Republic, its hist. and ideals; with introd. by T: M. Osborne. '10(F10) c. il. por. facsims., D. **$1.50 net. Appleton.

George Blumenthal lectures. *See* Blumenthal, (George.)

George Junior Republic, Freeville, N. Y. Nothing without labor. 7th ed. '09(D) 12 p. il. por. 12°, gratis. George Jr. Repub.

GEORGE JUNIOR REPUBLIC, Freeville, N. Y.
George, W: R. Junior Republic. **$1.50 net. Appleton.

GEORGE, LAKE.
See Lake George.

George Washington Univ. pubs., Medical science ser. 8°. (Not for sale.) George Washington Univ.
—Dobson. Modern medicine in China.
—Franz. Psychology and the medical school.
—Shute. Philosophical foundations of charlatanry.—Reflex neuroses.
—White. Hospitals and asylums of Europe.

George Watson, the trials of a stammerer. Bryant, F. A: 10 c. F. A: Bryant.

GEORGETOWN, D. C.
See Evangelical Lutheran Church;—Mozes, Zebina; —Washington, D. C.

GEORGETOWN UNIVERSITY, District of Columbia.
Smith, J. S. E-. Georgetown University in the District of Columbia, 1789-1907. 2 v. $30. Lewis Pub.

Georgia (Colony.) Commons House of Assembly, Journal, January 7, 1755, to . . .; comp and pub. under authority of the legislature by Allen D. Candler. '08(Ag15) 8°, per v., $3. Franklin-T.

Georgia. *Ct. of appeals.* Repts. v. 2; (Stevens and Graham.) '08(Mr); v. 3 (Jl); v. 4. '08, [1909.] (Ja); v. 5 (Ag); v. 6. '10 (Mr); v. 7 (O) c. O. shp., ea., $1.75. Georgia Lib.

Georgia. Encyclopedic digest of repts.; (T: Johnson Michie.) v. 15, 16. '10(Jl) c. O. shp., ea., $7.50. Michie.

Georgia. Executive Council, 1777-1789. Minutes of the Executive Council, from Jan. 14, 1778, to Jan. 6, 1785, and Journal of the Land Court from Apr. 6 to May 26, 1784. '08(N) 883 p. 4°, (Revolutionary records of the state of Georgia.) $3. Franklin-T.

Georgia. Journal of the House of Assembly, from August 17, 1781, to February 26, 1784. '08(O10) 4°, (Revolutionary records of the state of Georgia.) $3. Franklin-T.

Georgia. *Supreme ct.* Repts.; (Stevens and Graham.) v. 129. '08(Ap); v. 130 (O); v. 131. '09(My) ea., $5; v. 132, 133. '10 (Je); v. 134 (D) c. O. shp., ea., $1.75. Georgia Lib.

Georgia. *Supreme ct.* Repts. v. 64, 65, annot.; (Jackson and Lumpkin.) '07, [1908.] c. (My.) O. shp., ea., $3. Michie.

GEORGIA.
Candler, A. D., *comp.* Revolutionary records of the state of Georgia. $1.50. Franklin-T.
Crane, E. A., *and* Soderholtz, E. E. Examples of colonial architecture in South Carolina and Georgia. $16. Hessling.
Evans, L. B. History of Georgia for use in schools. *$1 net. Am. Bk.
Goetchius, H: R. Litigation in Georgia during the reconstruction period. 25 c. H: R. Goetchius.
Hühner, L. **Jews of Georgia from the outbreak of the American Revolution to the** close of the 18th century. 25 c. Bloch.
Jones, C: E. Georgia in the war, 1861-65. $1. C: E. Jones.
M'Call, H. Hist. of Georgia. $5. A. B. Caldwell.
McCallie, S: W. Preliminary rept. on the marbles of Georgia. 13 c. S: W. McCallie.
MacIntyre, W: I. Legislative reminiscences. 25 c. W: I. MacIntyre.
Manley, W. D., *comp. and ed.* Georgia country banker. $1.25. Mutual Pub. Co.
Northen, W: J., *ed.* Men of mark in Georgia. In 6 v. v. 2. per set, $50; $100. A. B. Caldwell.
Ryman, D. E. Compilation of words and phrases judicially defined by the Sup. Ct. of Georgia and the Ct. of Appeals. $6. Harrison Co.
Van Epps, H. Georgia form book. $6. Harrison Co.
Veatch, O. Second rept. on the clay deposits of Georgia. gratis. S: W. McCallie.
Watson, T: L. Preliminary rept. on manganese deposits of Georgia. 12 c. S: W. McCallie.
Wylly, C: S. Seed that was sown in the colony of Georgia. $1.25 net. Neale.
See also Indians;—Schools;—*also* Emanuel, David;—Habersham, John.

Georgia Geological Survey bulletin. 4°, pap. S: W. McCallie.
—McCallie. Preliminary rept. on the marbles of Georgia.
—Veatch. Second rept. on the clay deposits of Georgia. gratis.
—Watson. Preliminary rept. on manganese deposits of **Georgia**. 12 c.

Georgia laws made plain; compiled by R. O. Jones, approved by H. A. Hall, Att'y Gen. for Ga. [1910.] (D) c. 100 p. D. pap., gratis. Bankers' Law Pub.

Georgian pageant. Moore, F. F. $3.50. Dutton.

Gephart, W: Franklin.
Transportation and industrial development in the Middle West. '09(Jl3) c. il. maps, O. (Columbia Univ. studies in history, economics and public liw.) pap., $2. Longmans.

Gepp, C: Granville, and Haigh, A. E.
Latin English dictionary. '09(S11) S. $1.10. Longmans.

Gerald de Barry.
See Giraldus Cambrensis.

Gerard, Dorothea, [Mme. Longard de Longgarde.]
Pomp and circumstance. '08(N14) c. il. D. $1.50. B. W. Dodge.

Gerard, Baron François Pascal.
Masterpieces. '10(D17) il. 24°, (Painters' ser.) leath., 75 c. net; pap., 25 c. net. Stokes.

Gerard, Ja. Watson, comp.
See New York [State.] Digested treatise and compendium of law.

Gerard, J:
Old riddle and the newest answer. 5th and cheaper ed. '08(Mr14) O. pap., 20 c. Longmans.

Gerard, Louise.
Golden centipede. '10(Ag6) D. $1.25 net. Dutton.

Gerberding, G: H:, D.D.
Lutheran catechist; companion book to "The Lutheran pastor." '10(Ap23) c. 8°, $1.50. Lutheran Pub.
Vägen till frälsning enligt den Lutherska **kyrkans uppfattning af Guds ords lära.** '08, [1909.] (S) c. 240 p. 12°, $1. Augustana.

Gerda in Sweden. McDonald, *Mrs.* E. A. B. 60 c. Little, B. & Co.

Gerhard, W: Paul.
American practice of gas piping and gas lighting in buildings. '08(Je13) c. tabs., O. *$3 net. McGraw.
Guide to sanitary inspections. 4th ed., entirely rev. and enl. '09(Ja30) 12°, $1.50. Wiley.
Modern baths and bath houses. '08(F8) figs. 8°, *$3 net. Wiley.
Sanitation and sanitary engineering. 2d rev. and enl. ed. '09(My8) D. $1.50. W: P. Gerhard.
Sanitation, water supply and sewage disposal of country houses. '09(Je5) c. il. fold. map, 12°, $2. Van Nostrand.
Water supply, sewerage, and plumbing of modern city buildings. '09(D) 32+491 p. il. figs. 8°, *$4 net. Wiley.

Germaine. Rowland, H: C. $1.50. Lane.

GERMAN-AMERICANS.
Bosse, G. V. Deutsche (Das) element in den Vereinigen Staaten. $3. Lemcke.
Helbig, R: E. German-American researches: growth of collection in N. Y. Public Library, 1906-07. gratis. N. Y. Pub. Lib.
Rosengarten, J. G: German archives as sources of German-American history. (Not for sale.) J. G: Rosengarten.
Skal, G. von. Hist. of German immigration to the United States. $10; $15. G. von Skal.
See also Germans in the U. S.

GERMAN ART.
See Painters and paintings.
German bracelet. Graydon, J. F. $1.50. Neale.
German Christmas Eve. Seidel, H. 50 c.; 25 c. Abbey Co.
German drama of the nineteenth century. Witkowski, G. $1. Holt.
German Emperor and the German government. Burgess, J: W: (Add. pubs. for price.) Columbia Univ.
German Evangelical Synod of North America. Gesangbuch der evangelischen kirche. '08(Je13) c. 24°, leath., 50 c.; $1; flex. mor., $1.50; $2; Small ed., with notes, 90 c.-$3.50; Large ed., with notes, $1.25-$2.50. Eden Pub.
GERMAN HISTORY.
See Germany.
German Hospital, New York City. Festschrift zur vierzigjährigen stiftung des Deutschen hospitals; herausgegeben von dem Medical Board im auftrage der aerzte des Deutschen hospitals und dispensary in der Stadt New York. '09(N20) il. fold. tabs., Q. pap., $2.80. Lemcke.
German Kali Works. Tobacco culture. '08 (Ag) 98 p. il. 8°, pap., gratis. Germ. Kali.
GERMAN LANGUAGE.
Allen, P. S., *ed.* Herein! first German readings. 70 c. Holt.
Arndt, E. M. Deutsche patrioten in Ruszland zur zeit Napoleons. 30 c. Heath.
Arnold, H. Fritz auf ferien. 25 c. Am. Bk.
Arnold, M. Hdbk. of German construction and complete verb scheme 60 c. Flanagan.
Auerbach, B. Brigitta. 40 c. Ginn.
Bacon, P. V. Im vaterland. $1.25. Allyn & B.
Baker, G: M., *comp. and ed.* German stories. 40 c. Holt.
Bartram, J. W. Longmans' illustrated first conversational German reader. 80 c. Longmans.
Baumbach, R. Augewählte märchen und gedichte. 45 c.—Das Habictsfräulein. 40 c.—Der schwiegersohn. 40 c. Ginn.
Baumbach, R. Der schwiegersohn; eine schneidergeschichte. 40 c. Holt.
Becker, H. K., *and* Rhoades, L. A. Elements of German. $1. Scott, F. & Co.
Betz, F:, *ed.* Die Schildbürger ihre wisheit und grosze torheit. 35 c. Heath.
Bierwirth, H. C. Beginning German. 90 c. —German inflections. 40 c. Holt.
Buchheim, E. S. Der ungebetene gast. 15 c. Oxford Univ.
California Assoc. of Teachers of German. Four years' course in German for secondary schools. 25 c. H. K. Schilling.
Chalmers, W. P., *comp. and ed.* Deutsche gedichte zum auswendiglernen. *40 c. net. Crowell.
Deutsch, S. Medical German. *$2 net. W: R. Jenkins.
Deutsch-englische lesebücher für katholische schulen. In 3 v. v. 1, 13½c.; v. 2, 16⅔c.: v. 3, 25 c. Benziger.
Droste-Hülshoff, A. E., *Frelin* v. Die Judenbuche. 60 c. Oxford Univ.

GERMAN LANGUAGE.—*Continued.*
Eckstein, E., *and* Wildenbruch, E. v. Der besuch im karzer, and Das edle blut. 50 c. Ginn.
Evans, M. B. High school course in German. (Add. University for price.) Univ. of Wis.
Evans, M. B., *and* Prokosch, E. German exercise book. 30 c. Ginn.
Feller, F. E. New pocket dictionary of German-English and English-German. 50 c. Dutton.
Fick, H. H. Dies und das. 25 c. Am. Bk.
Fisher, E. Dornrösen: ein märchen-spiel. *25 c. net. Crowell.
Fraser, W: H:, *and* Van der Smisson, W: H: German grammar. $1.10. Heath.
Frommel, E. Mit ränzel und wanderstab. 35 c. Heath.
Fulda, L. Der dummkopf, lustspiel in fünf aufzügen. 35 c. Holt.
Gerstäcker, F. W. C. Germelshausen. 30 c. Am. Bk.
Goebel, F. Rübezahl. 35 c. net. Macmillan.
Goethe, J. W. v. Goethe in Italy.—Vicar of Sesenheim. ea., 35 c. Holt.
Goethe, J. W. v. Götz von Berlichingen mit der eisernen hand.—Torquato Tasso. ea., 80 c. Ginn.
Grillprazer, F. König Ottokars glück und ende. 60 c. Holt.
Gutzkow, K. F. Uriel Acosta. 35 c. Holt.
Ham, R. J., *and* Leonard, A. N. Brief German grammar. $1. Ginn.
Hauff, W. Lichtenstein. 80 c. Holt.
Hein, G. Aus wahl deutscher prosa der gegenwart. 70 c. Oxford Univ.
Heine, H. Die Harzreise. 50 c. Am. Bk.
Heine, H. Die Harzreise. 45 c. Heath.
Herders konversations-lexicon. 8 v. *$28 net. Herder.
Heyse, P. J. L. Anfang und ende. 35 c. Ginn.
Heyse, P. J. L. Anfang und ende. 40 c. Holt.
Heyse, P. J. L. Er soll dein herr sein. 30 c. Am. Bk.
Hillern, *Frau* W. B. v. Höher als die kirche. 50 c. C: E. Merrill.
Holzwarth, F. J. German students' manual. $1.35. H. Rees.
Howe, G: M. First German book. 90 c. Holt.
Huelin y Arssu, C. Technological dict. $4. Spon.
James, W: Dict. of the English and German languages. *$1.50 net. Macmillan.
Jensen, W. Die braune Erica: novelle. 35 c. Heath.
Kayser, C. F., *and* Monteser, F. Foundations of German. 80 c. Am. Bk.
Kellogg, R. J. German verb blank. 35 c. Ginn.
Kern, J. R. *and* M. M., *eds.* German stories retold: (Grimm's Märchen.) 30 c. Am. Bk.
Kettner, L. My little German travelling companion. 25 c. net. Cassell.
Lambert, M. B. Alltägliches: ein konversations- und lesebuch. 75 c. Heath.

GERMAN LANGUAGE.—*Continued.*

Lambert, M. B. Hdbk. of German idioms. 40 c. Holt.

Lessing, G. E. Minna von Barnhelm. 60 c. Oxford Univ.

Levi, H. Easy German stories. *40 c. net. Crowell.

Ludwig, O. Der orbförster. 35 c. net. Holt.

Lutz, F: Elem. German reader. $1. Silver.

McCollom, M. L., *comp.* German verb form: [blank-book.] 30 c. Am. Bk.

Moltke, *Count* H. K. B. v. Die beiden freunde. *35 c. net. Holt.

Moser, B. von. Der bibliothekar. Schwank in vier akten. 40 c. Holt.

Moser, G. v. Ultimo, lustspiel in fünf akten. 35 c. Holt.

Nichols, A. B., *comp.* Easy German reader. 40 c.—Modern German prose: reader for advanced classes. $1. Holt.

Osthaus, C. W. F., *and* Biermann, E. H. Key to German prose composition. 65 c. Am. Bk.

Osthaus, C. W. F., *and* Biermann, E. H., *eds.* German prose composition. 65 c. Am. Bk.

Picard, L. B. Der neffe als onkel. **35 c. net. Holt.

Pitman, *Sir* I: International mercantile letters: [English-German.] 85 c. Pitman.

Pope, P. R. German composition. 90 c. Holt.

Rauser, F. C. "Siegfried Bergmann": dramatisches volksstück. 25 c. Schaefer & K.

Reichenbach, M. Das Rothkäppchen: spiel. *25 c. net. Crowell.

Riehl, W. H. v. Der fluch der schönheit. 40 c. Ginn.

Ries, C. E. Easy German stories. 35 c. Am. Bk.

Roth, R. Ein nordischer held. 35 c. Am. Bk.

Schiller, J. C. F. v. Jungfrau von Orleans. 70 c.—Selections from ballads and lyrics. 60 c. Am. Bk.

Schiller, J. C. F. v. Jungfrau von Orleans. 70 c.—Maria Stuart. 75 c. Ginn.

Schmidt, O. E. Überwunden. 30 c. Holt.

Schrader, F. Friedrich der Grosse und Der Siebenjährige Krieg. 35 c. net. Macmillan.

Schrakamp, J., *ed.* Ernstes und heiteres; tales by modern German writers. 35 c. Am. Bk.

Schwann, H. German-French and French-German pocket dictionary. 50 c. Dutton.

Spyri, *Mrs.* J. H. Was der grosmutter lehre bewirkt. 25 c. net. Heath.

Stökl, *Mrs.* H. B. Alle fünf! 30 c. Heath.

Storm, T. Auf der universität. 35 c. Holt.

Storm, T. Der schimmelreiter. 70 c. Ginn.

Storm, T., *and others.* Immensee, by Storm; Germelshausen, by Gerstäcker; Der lindenbaum, by Seidel. 40 c. Scott, F. & Co.

Sudermann, H. Heimat. 35 c. Heath.

Till Eulenspiegels. 30 c. Heath.

GERMAN LANGUAGE.—*Continued.*

Tolhausen, A., *ed.* Technological dictionary in French, English and German. In 3 v. ea., *$2.75 net. Macmillan.

Tuckerman, J. Am aufang. 50 c. Holt.

Volkmann-Leander, R. v. Traumereien an französischen kaminen. 40 c. Ginn.

Wachenhusen, H. Vom ersten bis zum letzten schuss; Kriegserinnerungen. 35 c. net. Macmillan.

Wallentin, I. G. Introd. to scientific German. $1. Times Pub. Co., (Pa.)

Werner-Spanhoofd, A. Erstes lesebuch. 75 c. Heath.

Whitney, M. P., *and* Stroebe, L. L. Exercises in German syntax and composition for advanced students. 90 c. Holt.

Wildenbruch, E. von. Neid. 35 c. Heath.

Wright, J. Hist. German grammar. $2.40. Oxford Univ.

Zastro, K. Wilhelm der Siegreiche. 35 c. net. Macmillan.

Zschokke, J. H. D. Der zerbrochene krug; Das wirtshaus zu Cransac. *50 c. net. Allyn & B.

See also Gothic language;—Handy pronouncing dictionaries;—Tauchnitz manuals of conversation;—Tauchnitz pocket dictionaries.

GERMAN LITERATURE.

Arnold, R. S. Allgemeine bücherkunde zur neueren deutschen literaturgeschichte. $2.25. Stechert.

Brooklyn Public Library. German books in the Brooklyn Public Library. 5 c. Brooklyn Lib.

Buffalo Public Library. Books in German, printed by the German Young Men's Association. gratis. Buffalo Pub. Lib.

Collitz, K. H., *comp.* Selections from early German literature. $1. Am. Bk.

Ebner von Eschenbach, M. Lotti, die uhrmacherin. 35 c. Holt.

Flory, J: S: Literary activity of the German Baptist Brethren in the eighteenth century. $1.25. Brethren Pub. Ho.

Gattiker, E., *comp.* Sel. list of German books recommended for a small public library. 50 c. A. L. A.

Goodnight, S. H. German literature in American magazines prior to 1846. 50 c. Univ. of Wis.

Haertel, M. H: German literature in American magazines, 1846 to 1880. 50 c. Univ. of Wis.

Könnecke, G. Deutcher Literaturatlas. *$1.50 net. Stechert.

Phillips, M. E. Hdbk. of German literature. *$1 net. Macmillan.

Priest, G: M. Brief hist. of German literature. **$1.50 net. Scribner.

Shottenfels, G. R. Parzival, and other stories from the German. 50 c. Educ. Pub.

Thomas, C. Anthology of German literature. $2.25. Heath.

Thomas, C. History of German literature. **$1.50 net. Appleton.

Wernaer, R. M. Romanticism and the romantic school in Germany. *$2 net. Appleton.

Witkowski, G. German drama and dramatists of the nineteenth century. $1. Holt.

GERMAN POETRY.
Bithell, J. The Minnesingers. v. 1. $2. Longmans.
German (A) Pompadour. Hay, M. $1.50. Scribner.
German schlagball. Pertuch, A. R. 15 c. McVey.
GERMAN THEOLOGIANS.
See Theology.
Germania. *See* Tacitus, Caius Cornelius. Agricola.
Germanische bibliotek. D. Stechert.
—Jesperson. Modern English grammar. pt. 1. *$3 net.
Germanistic Society of America pubs. O. pap. R. Tombo.
—Hauptmann. Das geheimnis der gestalt.
Germanistische Gesellschaft. *See* University of Wisconsin.
Germann, G: B.
See Bailey, Middlesex A.
GERMANS IN THE UNITED STATES.
Faust, A. B. German element in the United States. 2 v. **$7.50 net. Houghton M.
Heinrici, M., *ed.* Das buch der Deutschen in Amerika. $5. M. Heinrici.
Skal, G. v. Hist. of German immigration in the United States and successful German-Americans and their descendants. $10. F. T. Smiley.
GERMANTOWN, Pa.
Learned, M. D. Life of Francis Daniel Pastorius, founder of Germantown. *$5 net. W: J. Campbell.
Willits, I. P. Early physicians of Germantown. (Not for sale.) Site and Relic.
See also Philadelphia.
GERMANY.
American Academy of Political and Social Science. Development of Germany as a world power. 50 c. Am. Acad. Pol. Sci.
Atkinson, C. T: Hist. of Germany, 1715-1815. *$4 net. Jacobs.
Babson, R. W. Printed bankers' directory for Germany. $5. R. W. Babson.
Baedeker, K. Northern Germany as far as the Bavarian and Austrian frontiers. *$2.40 net.—Southern Germany. $1.80 net. Scribner.
Barker, J. E. Modern Germany. *$3 net. Dutton.
Berry, R. Germany of the Germans. $1.50 net. Scribner.
Carnegie Foundation for Advancement of Teaching. Financial status of the professor in America and in Germany. gratis. Carnegie Found.
Chamberlain, A. H. Conditions and tendencies of technical education in Germany. 50 c. Bardeen.
Civil code of the German empire, as enacted on Aug. 18, 1896 (in effect June 1, 1900); tr. by Wa. Loewy. '10(Ap) 71+689 p. $5. Boston Bk.
Dawson, H. Evolution of modern Germany. *$4 net. Scribner.
Hislam, P. A. Admiralty of the Atlantic: enquiry into the development of German sea power. *$2 net. Longmans.
Holzwarth, F. J. German students' manual of the literature, land and people of Germany. $1. Am. Bk.

GERMANY.—*Continued.*
Janssen, J. Hist. of the German people at the close of the Middle Ages. v. 9-14. *$18.75 net. Herder.
Kampffmeyer, P. Changes in the theory and tactics of the (German) social democracy. 50 c. Kerr.
Liefeld, E. T. Faces and phases of German life. $1.50 net. Fowler & W.
Paulsen, F. German education past and present. *$1.25 net. Scribner.
Quinnet, E. France et Allemagne. $1.15. Oxford Univ.
Savory, D. L., *comp.* Deutsches reformlesebuch. 60 c. Oxford Univ.
Schauffler, R. H. Romantic Germany. **$3.50 net. Century Co.
Shadwell, A. Industrial efficiency: comparative study of England, Germany and America. *$2 net. Longmans.
Sidgwick, *Mrs.* C. U. Germany. *75 c. net.—Home life in Germany. *$1.75 net. Macmillan.
Small, A. W. The Cameralists; pioneers of German social polity. *$3 net. Univ. of Chic.
Stubbs, W: Germany in the Middle Ages, 476-1250. *$2 net.—Germany in the later Middle Ages, 1200-1500. *$2.25 net. Longmans.
Thompson, R. J:, *comp.* Suggestions for the development of American export trade to Germany. gratis. Nat. Business.
United States. *Dept. of State.* German manufactures; message from the President of the U. S. transmitting, in response to Senate resolution no. 55 of June 4, 1909, all correspondence which passed bet. the Dept. of State and the German government having relation to German manufactures furnished by the German government to the U. S. '09(Ag) 20 p. 8°, pap. (Add. Superintendent for price.)
United States. *Dept. of State.* Wages in Germany; message from the President of the U. S., transmitting a letter from the acting secretary of state with accompanying papers furnished by the German government on the subject of wages paid to German workmen. '09(S) 134 p. 8°. (Add. Superintendent for price.)
United States. *Engineer School.* Corps of military engineers and pioneers in Germany, from "Revue du génie militaire," vol. XXXIV, no. 2, 1907; practice maneuvers of engineers in Germany, from "Revue militaire des armees etrangeres," June, 1907; tr. by H: E. Haferkorn. '09, [1910.] (Mr) 31 p. fold. map, 8°, (Occasional papers, Engineer school U. S. Army.) Engineer Sch.
Viereck, G: S. Confessions of a barbarian. $1.25 net. Moffat.
See also Alsace; — Banks and banking; — Berlin;—Black Forest;—Blind (The);—Castle of Brucksales;—Commerce;—Germans in the U. S.;—Leipzig campaign;—Munich;—Oberammergau;—Prussia;—Reformation; — Rhine river;—Rothenburg;—Songs; — Theology;—Weimar;—*also* Frederick *the Great;*—Frederick William, *Elector of Brandenburg;* — William I.; — William II.

Germelshausen. *See* Gerstäcker, F. W. C.—Storm, Theodor.

Gernsback, Hugo.
Wireless telephone. '10(Je4) c. il. 12°, 25 c. Modern Electrics.

Gerrard, Rev. T: J.
Cords of Adam: [devotional essay.] '08 (Je13) D. *$1.50 net. Longmans.

Gerrish, F: H., M.D.
See Prince, Morton, *M.D.*

Gerry, Margarita Spalding.
The flowers. '10(Ap9) c. il. O. 50 c. net. Harper.
Toy shop: romantic story of Lincoln the man. '08(S19) c. front. S. **50 c. net. Harper.

Gersbach, Rob., and Jager, Thdr. F.
Police dog in word and picture; the trainer's hdbk., the breeder's guide. '10(Ap) c. 7+172 p. il. 12°, $1.50. T. F. Jager.

Gerson, Oscar.
Our colonial history, from the discovery to the Revolution. '08(O17) c. il. maps, 12°, 50 c. Hinds.

Gerstäcker, Friedrich Wilhelm Christian.
Germelshausen; ed., with notes, exercises, and vocab., by A. Busse. '10(Mr26) c. S. 30 c. Am. Bk.
See also Storm, Theodor.

Gerstenberg, Alice.
Little world: [plays for girls.] '08(D) $1.25. Dramatic.

Gertrude Elliot's crucible. Sheldon, *Mrs.* G. †$1.50. G: W. Dillingham.

Gerwig, G: W:
Art of the short story. '10(F12) S. *75 c. net. Percy Pub.

Gesangbuch. *See* German Evangelical Synod of North America.

Geschæftliche (Die) seite der religion. Roche, J. T: *10 c. net; per 100, $6.50. Wiltzius.

Gesenius, Friedrich Heinrich Wilhelm.
Hebrew grammar, as ed. and enl. by the late E. Kautzsch. 2d English ed., rev. in accordance with the 28th German ed. (1909), by A. E. Conley; with facsimile of the Siloam inscription by J. Euting and a table of alphabets by M. Lidzbarski. '10(D17) O. $5.25 net. Oxford Univ.

Gesmold, Ludwig K. W. Hammerstein-, von.
See Hammerstein-Gesmold, Ludwig K. W. von.

Gest, J: Marshall.
Influence of Biblical texts upon English law; address before the Phi Beta Kappa and Sigma Xi societies, June 14th, 1910. '10(Ag) c. 32 p. 8°. (Priv. pr.) Buchanan.
Practical suggestions for drawing wills and the settlement of estates in Pennsylvania. '09(N) 20+152 p. 8°, *$2 net. T. & J. W. Johnson.

Gest of Robin Hood. Clawson, W: H. $1. Univ. of Toronto.

GESTATION.
See Pregnancy.

Gestefeld, Ursula Newell.
Joyous birth. '10(D17) c. 12°, $1. Exodus.

Gesundheit, Maurice.
Cost reduction: [factory management;] paper read before the Metal Manufacturers' Association of Philadelphia. '08(My.) c. 12 p. 8°. (Not for sale.) M. Gesundheit.

Get-rich-quick Wallingford. Chester, G: R. †$1.50. Altemus.

"Get the hook." Miner, H. C. gratis. H: C. Miner.

Getchell, Everett Lamont.
Field trips in the Boston Basin. '10(D17) 12°, 60 c. net. Little, B. & Co.

Getman, F: Hutton.
Introd. to physical science. '09(Ag21) c. figs. 12°, **$1.50 net. Wiley.
Laboratory exercises in physical chemistry. 2d ed., rev. '08(Mr28) c. figs. tabs., 12°, **$2 net. Wiley.

Gettell, Raymond Garfield.
Introd. to political science. '10(D3) c. O. $2. Ginn.

Getting and holding. Hamby, W: H. 50 c. net. S. S. Times.

Getting of wisdom. Richardson, H. H., *pseud.* $1.50. Duffield.

Getting on. Marden, O. S. $1 net. Crowell.

Gettner, Florence I.
Joan of Arc; monologue. '10(Je4) c. il. 16°, 40 c. F. I. Gettner.

GETTYSBURG, Pa.
Miller, R. C. Historic views of Gettysburg. 50 c. J. I. Mumper.

GETTYSBURG (Battle of).
Cowell, A. T. Tactics at Gettysburg as described by participants. 25 c. A. T. Cowell.
Haskell, F. A. Battle of Gettysburg. $1. Wis. Hist.
Knox, P. C. Memorial address on the battlefield of Gettysburg, May 30, 1908. (Add. author for price.) P. C. Knox.
Mosby, J: S. Stuart's cavalry in the Gettysburg campaign. **$2 net. Moffat.
Norton, O. W. Strong Vincent and his brigade at Gettysburg, July 2, 1863. (Not for sale.) O. W. Norton.
Spear, W: E. North and the South at Antietam and Gettysburg. $1. W: E. Spear.

Gettysburg address. *See* Lincoln, Abraham.

Getz, J:
Catalogue of the Macomber collection of Chinese pottery. '09(Jl31) il. O. bds., $1.25. Boston Museum.

Geyserland. Hatfield, R:, *ed.* $3. R: Hatfield.

Ghent, W: Ja.
Socialism and success; some uninvited messages. '10(O29) c. D. $1 net. Lane.

Gher, Alphonso Moser.
Missing empire; tale of the "Kittatinnies." 2d ed. '09(D18) c. T. pap., 35 c. A. M. Gher.
Old trail and the new; tales of the Kittatinnies. '09(D4) il. por. S. 75 c.; pap., 50 c. A. M. Gher.
Ghesiri, Mme.
Fortune telling birthday book. '10(O8) c. O. $1, boxed; leath., $2, boxed. Platt & P.
Gheusi, P. B.
Gambetta: life and letters; auth. tr. by Violette M. Montagu. '10(O15) pors. O. $3.50 special net. Appleton.
GHIRLANDAJO, Il, *originally* Domenico Bigordi, *or* Corradi.
Davies, G. S. Ghirlandaio. *$4 net. Scribner.
GHIZEH, Egypt.
See Pyramids.
Ghost in the garret. Fisher, M. A. $1. Aberdeen.
GHOSTS.
Bruce, H: A. B. Historic ghosts and ghost hunters. **$1.25 net. Moffat.
Hawkins, J., *comp.* Ghost stories and tales of the supernatural: [bibliography.] Boston Bk.
Podmore, F. Telepathic hallucinations: the new view of ghosts. *50 c. net. Stokes.
Ghosts (The). *See* Ingersoll, Rob. Green.
"Ghosts or devils." Moore, F. M. $1. F. M. Moore.
Giannella. Fraser, M. C. $1.50. Herder.
Giant (The). Smith, A. W: 75 c. Andrus.
Giant American causeway. Case, G: A. 15 c. G: A. Case.
Giant and the star. Cawein, M. J. **$1 net. Small.
Giant days. Shipp, J. E. D. $3. Americus.
Giant killer. Eickemeyer, C. 25 c. C. Eickemeyer.
Giant-land. Quiz, R. *$2 net. Putnam.
Giant of the treasure caves. Mulliken, *Mrs.* G. E. $1.50. Estes.
Gibbon, E:
Autobiography of Edward Gibbon, as originally edited by Lord Sheffield; with an introd. by J. B. Bury. '08(Ap4) 16°, (World's classics.) 50 c.; leath., 75 c. Oxford Univ.
Decline and fall of the Roman Empire; ed. by O. Smeaton. In 6 v. vs. 1-3. '10 (Ap2): v. 4-6 (D10) 16°, (Everyman's lib.) ea., 35 c.; leath., 70 c. net. Dutton.
Gibbon, F: P.
Lawrences of the Punjaub. '08(D12) 12°, (Temple biographies.) *$1.50 net. Dutton.
Gibbon, J. M., ed.
See Annals of fairyland.
Gibbon, Perceval.
Salvator. '09(Ap17) c. D. †$1.50. Doubleday, P.
Gibbons, Cardinal Ja.
Discourses and sermons for every Sunday and the principal festivals of the year. '09(Ja16) c. D. $1. Murphy.
True manhood. '09(Ap3) c. D. bds., 50 c. McClurg.
Formerly published by Doxey Book Shop Co.
GIBBONS, *Cardinal* James.
Sabatier, P. Open letter to His Eminence, Cardinal Gibbons, apropos of his interview on the separation of church and state in France. *60 c. net. Sherman, F.
Gibbons, Willard S., ed.
See New York [State.] *Surrogate's cts.* Repts.
Gibbs, G: Fort.
Tony's wife. '10(Ap9) c. il D. $1.50. Appleton.
Gibbs, Josiah Fs.
Lights and shadows of Mormonism. [1910.] (F) c. '09. 53 p. il. pors. 8°, $1.25. Salt Lake Trib.
Gibbs, Philip H.
King's favorite; the love story of Robert Carr and Lady Essex. '09, [1910.] (F) 446 p. il. 8°, *$4 net. Jacobs.
Romance of George Villiers, first Duke of Buckingham. '08(F29) pors. O. *$3.50 net. Putnam.
Street of adventure. '10(Je4) 8°, $1.25 net. Dutton.
Gibbs, Wa. M.
Spices and how to know them. '10(Ja15) c. il. maps, O. $3.50. W. M. Gibbs.
Gibbs, W: E.
Textbook of physics. Pt. 1. '10(My7) c. il. 12°, (Carnegie Technical Schools textbooks.) $1.50. Van Nostrand.
Gibbs, Winifred S.
Lessons in the proper feeding of the family. '09(Je19) O. pap., 25 c. Assoc. Imp. Con. Poor.
Gibbs' travellers' route and reference book of the United States and Canada. (Map ed.,) for the use of commercial travellers, merchants, and others. '09(Mr) c. 127 p. maps, 8°, $3. Gibbs Bros. & M.
GIBRALTAR.
Lang, J. Gibraltar and the West Indies. *$2 net. Stokes.
GIBSON, Agnes.
Fishe, M. H. My Father's business; or, the life and work of Miss Agnes Gibson. 60 c. China Inland.
Gibson, Alfr.
London and the girl. '10(S) il. 8°, $1.50. Cassell.
Gibson, Arnold Hartley.
Hydraulics, and its application. '09(Ja16) 8°, *$5 net. Van Nostrand.
Water hammer in hydraulic pipe lines; with a chapter on the speed regulation of hydraulic turbines. '09(Jl17) il. 12°, *$2 net. Van Nostrand.
Gibson, Arth. H.
Human economics. '09(Je19) O. *$3.50 net. Longmans.
Gibson, C:
Wounded Eros; sonnets; with an introd. by W: Stanley Braithwaite. '08(N) c. 33+129 p. front. 8°, *$2.50 net. C: Gibson.
Gibson, C: R.
Autobiography of an electron. '10(D31) il. 8°, $1.50 net. Lippincott.
How telegraphs and telephones work. '09 (Je5) il. O. *75 c. net. Lippincott.

Gibson, C: R.—*Continued.*
Romance of modern manufacture. '09(O2) il. O. (Romance ser.) *$1.50 net. Lippincott.
Scientific ideas of to-day. '08(N7) il. D. (Popular scientific ser.) *$1.50 net. Lippincott.

Gibson, Charlotte Chaffee.
In the golden East: geog. reader. '08 (F22) c. 12°, *60 c. net. Little, B. & Co.

Gibson, Clarence B.
Reflections of nature with affection taught; book including fiction, story telling, and science. '10(O15) c. il. 12°, 60 c. C. B. Gibson.

Gibson, Bp. Edg. C: Sumner, D.D.
The three creeds. '08(My2) D. (Oxford lib. of pract. theology.) *$1.40 net. Longmans.

Gibson, G: Howard.
People's hour and other themes. '09(N6) c. D. $1. Englewood Pub.

Gibson, Harvey.
Biology. '10(S) il. 16°, (Appleton's scientific primers.) 50 c. net. Appleton.

Gibson, H: H.
Oak flooring; being an outline of correct methods of manufacture, handling, laying and finishing; with an analysis of widths, thickness and grades. '09(N) 38 p. 8°, 50 c. Hardwood Record.

Gibson, J: W:
Junior history of the United States. '08 (Ja4) il. maps, D. 60 c. Flanagan.

Gibson, P:, ["Mario Malanotte."]
The Medici viola: a legend. '09(O9) c. front. D. $1. P: Gibson.

Gibson, Reuben Alonzo.
College days essays. '10(N19) c. 12°, $1. Nixon-J.

Gibson, Rob. E: Lee.
Miracle of St. Cuthbert and sonnets. '09 (Je19) c. O. bds., $1. Morton.

Gibson, T:
Cycles of speculation. 2d ed. '09(Jl31) il. 12°, $1.50. Moody's Mag.
Increasing gold supply and its effect on security values; with an appendix. '09 (My8) c. tabs., 12°, $1. Gibson Pub.
Market letters for 1907. '08(My23) c. il. tabs., D. $1. T: Gibson.
Special market letters, 1908. '09(My8) c. 12°, $1. Gibson Pub.
Thomas Gibson's weekly market letters, 1908. 2 v. '09(N) charts, 12°, ea., $1. Gibson Pub.

Gibson, W. Herbert.
See Webb, Wa. Loring.

Gibson, Walcot.
Geology of coal and coal-mining. '08(Jl18) il. tabs., maps, D. (Arnold's geological ser.) $2.50. Longmans.

Gibson, Rev. Wa. Ernest.
Marital messenger. '10(D3) c. D. $1.50. Neale.

Gibson, W: Ralph Boyce.
God with us: study in religious idealism. '09(Jl17) 12°, *$1.40 net. Macmillan.
—, **and Klein, Augusta.**
Problem of logic. '08(Ag22) diagrs., 8°, *$4.50 net. Macmillan.

Giddings, Franklin H:
Sociology: [a lecture.] '08(N21) c. 8°, pap. (Add. pubs. for price.) Columbia Univ.

Giddings, J. Wight.
From here and there. '10(O1) c. 12°, 75 c. Cochrane.

Giddings, Thaddeus Philander.
School music teaching; for superintendents, music supervisors, and grade teachers. '10(Je4) c. 8°, $1. C. H. Congdon.

Gidley, Ja. Williams.
Notes on a collection of fossil mammals from Virgin Valley, Nevada. '08(D20) figs. Q. (Univ. of Cal. pubs., Geology.) pap., 10 c. Univ. of Cal.

Gielow, Mrs. H: J.
See Gielow, Martha S.

Gielow, Martha S., ["Mrs. H: J. Gielow."]
Old Andy, the moonshiner. '10(Mr12) c. il. 16°, 50 c. W. F. Roberts.

Gierlich, Nikolaus, and Friedmann, M.
Studies in paranoia; periodic paranoia and the origin of paranoid delusions by Nikolaus Gierlich; Contributions to the study of paranoia by M. Friedmann; ed. by Smith Ely Jelliffe, M.D. '08, [1909.] (Ag) c. 4+78 p. 8°, (Nervous and mental disease monograph ser.) $1. Journal Nervous Disease.

Giese, W: Frederic, and Cool, C: Dean, comps.
French anecdotes arranged for translation, conversation and composition. '10(Je18) c. S. (Heath's modern language ser.) 40 c. Heath.
Spanish anecdotes; arranged for translation and conversation. '09(Mr27) c. S. (Modern lang. ser.) 60 c. Heath.

Giesecke, Alb. Anthony.
American commercial legislation before 1789. '10(D17) c. 12°, (Publications of the Univ. of Penn.; series in political economy and public law.) $1.50. Appleton.

Giesecke, F: Ernest.
Mechanical drawing. pts. 1 and 2. 3d ed. '08(N) c. il. 8°, ea., $1. E. Dietzgen.

Giffin, W: Milford.
Todd and his friends; being the biography of a family pet bull dog. '09(Ap3) c. il. D. 25 c. Flanagan.

Gifford, Mrs. Augusta Hale.
New Italy; her people and their story. '09 (My15) c. il. pors. O. **$1.20 net. Lothrop, L. & S.

Gifford lectures. *See* Adam, Ja.;—Driesch, Hans.

Gift, Aaron Kern, comp.
History of the Gift, Kern and Royer families. '09(My22) c. il. pors. 8°, $1.50. Herald Pr.

GIFT FAMILY.
See **Genealogies.**

Gift of friendship. Grover, E. O. 50 c. Canterbury.

Gift of influence. Black, H. *$1.25 net. Revell.

Gift-wife. Hughes, R. $1.35. Moffat.

Gigliucci, Clara Anastasia Novello, Countess.
See Novello, Clara Anastasia.

Gihr, Rev. N:
Holy sacrifice of the mass; tr. from the 6th German ed. 3d ed. '08(D5) 12°, hf. mor., *$1 net. Herder.
Gil Blas. *See* Le Sage, Alain René.
Gilbert, Mrs. Ann Taylor.
See Taylor, Jane.
Gilbert, Barry.
See **Mechem, Floyd Russell.**
Gilbert, C: Benajah.
See Gleason, C: H.—Hallock, Ella B.
Gilbert, Edg.
History of Salem, N. H. '08(Ja18) il. pors. maps, charts, 8°, $3; hf. cf., $4. Rumford Pr.
Gilbert E: Holmes, and Elder, T: L.
The varieties of the United States cents of 1796. '09(D) c. il. f°, $1. T: L. Elder.
Gilbert, Fk. Bixby.
See New York [State.] Annot. code.—Annot. consolidated laws.—Bender's supervisors' [etc.] manual.—Court rules.
—, **comp.** Manual for supervisors, county and town officers with decisions, annots., [etc.] 4th ed. '08(O) c. 7+1139 p. O. $6.30. M. Bender.
See also New York [State.] Highway code.
—, **ed.** *See* Collier, W: Miller.—New York [State.] Consolidated laws.
Gilbert, G: Holley, D.D.
Interpretation of the Bible. '08(Mr7) c. 12°, **$1.25 net. Macmillan.
—, **ed.** *See* Bible.
Gilbert, Grove Karl, and Brigham, Albert Perry.
Introd. to physical geography. '08(Jl11) il. maps, D. (Twentieth century textbooks.) **$1.25 net. Appleton.
Gilbert, Ja. Zacchaeus.
Evesthes Jordani; primitive flounder from the Miocene of California. '10(Je) 405-411 p. il. Q. (Univ. of Cal. pubs., Geology.) pap., 15 c. Univ. of Cal.
Gilbert, Marie Dolores Eliza Rosanna, *known as* "Lola Montez."
Auvergne, E. B. d'. Lola Montez. *$4 net. Lane.
Gilbert, Paul Ja.
King's greatest business. '09(S11) c. 12°, *75 c. net. Revell.
Gilbert, Rob. Warren.
Golden rod and lilies. '08(Jl) c. 188 p. D. $1.50. Badger.
Gilbert, Sir W: Schwenk.
Pinafore picture book. '08(O3) il. O. *$2 net. Macmillan.
Savoy operas. [First series.] Pirates of Penzance; Patience; Princess Ida; The yeomen of the guard. '09(O9); Second series: Iolanthe; The Mikado; The Gondoliers; Ruddigore. '10(N19) col. il. 4°, ea., $5 net, boxed. Macmillan.
Gilbert, W: Williams.
The root-rot of tobacco caused by *Thielavia basicola.* '09(D) 55 p. il. 8°, (U. S., Dept. of Agriculture, Bureau of Plant Industry, bull.) pap. (Add. Superintendent for price.)
Gilbert Islands.
Bingham, H. Gilbertese-English dictionary. $1.50. Am. Bd. For. Miss.
Gilbert Neal. Harben, W: N. †$1.50. Harper.
Gilbertese-English dictionary. Bingham, H. $1.50. Am. Bd. For. Miss.
Gilbey, Sir Wa., and Cuming, E: W: Dirom.
George Morland: his life and works. '08 (Ja25) il. 8°, *$6 net. Macmillan.
Gilbreth, Fk. Bunker.
Bricklaying system. '09(N6) il. charts, 8°, *$3 net. M. C. Clark.
Concrete system. '08(Je13) c. il. tab., 8°, *$5 net. Engineering News.
Field system. '08(Ag1) c. il. tabs., 16°, flex. leath., *$3 net. M. C. Clark.
—, **Worden, C. A., and others.**
Pract. talks on contracting; being reprints from the *Contractor* of valuable papers. '10(Ap16) c. il. 8°, $1.50. Contractor Pub.
Gilchrist, Beth Bradford.
Life of Mary Lyon. '10(Ap30) c. il. por. O. $1.50 net. Houghton M.
Gilchrist, T: Caspar.
Outline of skin diseases, prepared for the use of students at the Johns Hopkins Medical School, Baltimore. '10(D) c. 4-20+16 p. il. 12°, 75 c. Students' Bk.
Gilchrist, W: Wallace.
See McLaughlin, Ja. M.
Gilded beauties of the Second Empire. Loliée, F. $4 net. Brentano's.
Gilded chair. Post, M. D. $1.50. Appleton.
Gilded way. Mapes, V. $1.50. Neale.
Gilder, Jeannette Leonard, ed.
Masterpieces of the world's best literature. 8 v. '10(Ap9) c. 16°, $3. O. T. Harris.
Gilder, R: Watson.
Grover Cleveland. '10(O29) c. O. $1.80 net. Century Co.
Lincoln the leader, and Lincoln's genius for expression. '09(O16) c. D. $1. Houghton M.
Poems. [Household ed.] '08(N14) c. por. O. $1.50. Houghton M.
Gildersleeve, Basil Lanneau.
Hellas and Hesperia; or, the vitality of Greek studies in America; three lectures. '09(S11) c. por. D. (Univ. of Virginia, Barbour-Page foundation.) *$1 net. Holt.
Gildersleeve, Virginia Crocheron.
Government regulation of the Elizabethan drama. '08(Ag22) il. maps, 8°, (Columbia Univ. Studies in English.) *$1.25 net. Lemcke.
Gildersleeve-Lodge Latin ser. 12°. Heath.
—Barse. Writing Latin. bk. 1. 50 c. net.
—Cecero. Cato Maior de senectvte.—Laelivs de amicitia. ea., 75 c. net.
—Sallustius Crispus. Bellum Catilinae. $1.
Gilds.
See **Guilds.**
Giles, Rev. Chauncey.
Chauncey Giles year book. '10(Ag6) c. 12°, $1.25. Lippincott.
Giles, Herbert Allen.
Ancient China. '07, [1909.] (Ap) 8°, (Religions ancient and modern.) *40 c. net. Open Court.

Giles, J. E:, and others.
Nursing in diseases of the eye, ear, nose, and throat, by the committee on nurses of the Manhattan Eye, Ear, and Throat Hospital: J. Edward Giles, Arth. B. Duel, Harmon Smith; assisted by J: R. Shannon, J: R. Page; with chapters by Herbert B. Wilcox, Eugenia D. Ayers. '10(Jl) c. 5-281 p. il. 8°, $1.50. Saunders.

Gilfillan, G:
Literary portraits; introd. by Robertson Nicoll. '09(Mr27) 16°, (Everyman's lib.) *35 c. net; leath., *70 c. net. Dutton.

Gill, A: Herman.
Gas and fuel analysis for engineers. 5th ed., rev. '08(O3) c. 12°, $1.25. Wiley.
Short hand-book of oil analysis. 5th ed., rev. and enl. '09(F20) c. figs. tabs., O. **$2 net. Lippincott.

Gill, C: G., rep.
See Louisiana. *Sup. ct.* Repts.

Gill, G: Creswell.
Beyond the blue-grass: a Kentucky novel. '08(Ag1) c. D. $1.50. Neale.

Gill, J: Kaye, comp.
Dictionary of the Chinook jargon; with examples of use in conversation and notes upon tribes and tongues. 15th ed. '09 (Ap10) c. T. pap., 50 c. Gill.

Gill, Thdr. N:
Contributions to the life histories of fishes. '09(Jl) il. 8°. (Add. pubs. for price.) Smith. Inst.

Gillette, Frederika B., comp.
Title index to the works of Honoré de Balzac. '09(My8) O. pap., 25 c. Boston Bk.

Gillette, Halbert Powers.
Hdbk. of cost data for contractors and engineers: reference book giving methods of construction and actual cost of materials and labor on numerous engineering works. 2d ed. '10(Jl16) c. il. D. leath., $5 net. M. C. Clark.

—, and Dana, R: T.
Cost keeping and management engineering; treatise for engineers, contractors and superintendents engaged in the management of engineering construction. '10 (F19) c. il. forms, 8°, $3.50. M. C. Clark.

—, and Hill, C: S.
Concrete construction. '08(Je13) c. il. 8°, *$5 net. M. C. Clark.

Gillette, J: Morris.
Vocational education. '10(Ap30) c. D. $1. Am. Bk.

Gillette, King Camp.
World corporation. '10(O8) c. por. O. $1. World Corporation.

Gillette's industrial solution. Severy, M. L. *$1.50 net. Ball Pub.

Gilliam, D: Tod.
Text book of practical gynecology for practitioners and students. 3d rev. ed. '08, [1909.] (Mr) c. 16+642 p. il. 8°, subs., *$4.50 net; hf. mor., *$6 net. Davis.

Gilliam, E: Winslow, M.D.
Ravenswood. '08(Je27) c. D. $1.25. Neale.

Gilliat, Rev. E:
Heroes of Elizabethan England. '10(D31) il. 8°. (Hero ser.) $1.50 net. Lippincott.
Heroes of modern crusades: true stories of the undaunted chivalry of champions of the downtrodden in many lands. '08 (N7) il. D. (Hero ser.) *$1.50 net. Lippincott.
Heroes of modern India. '10(Ja1) 8°, $1.50. Lippincott.

Gillie, R. C., D.D.
Kinsfolk and friends of Jesus. New ed. '08(O3) il. 12°, *$1.50 net. Macmillan.

Gillilan, Strickland W.
Including Finnigin. '10(F12) c. D. $1. Forbes.
Formerly published by Pearson Bros.

Gillis, Ja. L.
See California. State Library, Sacramento.

Gillman, H:
Hassan, a fellah: a romance of Palestine. '08(My.) c. 12°, (Popular ed. of recent fiction.) †75 c. Little, B. & Co.

Gillmore, Mrs. Inez Haynes.
June jeopardy. '08(Je6) c. D. $1.50. B: W. Huebsch.
Maida's little shop. '10(Ja29) c. front. D. $1.25. B: W. Huebsch.
Phœbe and Ernest. '10(N5) c. il. D. $1.50. Holt.

Gilman, Albert F.
Laboratory outline for determinations in quantitative chemical analysis. '08(My16) c. forms, 16°, *90 c. net. Chemical.

Gilman, Arth.
My Cranford: a phase of the quiet life. '09(Mr20) c. D. **$1.25 net. Houghton M.

Gilman, B: Ives.
See Fewkes, Jesse Wa.

Gilman, Bradley, D.D.
Son of the desert. '09(O2) c. il. D. †$1.50. Century Co.

Gilman, Dan. Coit.
Daniel Coit Gilman, first president of the Johns Hopkins University, 1876-1901. '09 (Mr27) por. 8°, (Johns Hopkins Univ. circular, new ser.) pap., gratis. Johns Hopkins.
Fasciculi of the Memorial Symposium of the class of Yale, 1852, academic, held on their classmate Daniel Coit Gilman, who died October 13, 1908. '10(Jl9) O. E. Cutter.

GILMAN, Daniel Coit.
Franklin, F. Life of Daniel Coit Gilman. $3.50 net. Dodd.

Gilman, Lawrence.
Aspects of modern opera. '08(D12) c. D. **$1.25 net. Lane.
Edward MacDowell: a study. '09(Ja2) c. pors. D. **$1.50 net. Lane.

Gilman, W: C.
Memoir of Daniel Wadsworth Coit of Norwich, Connecticut, 1787-1876. '09(S18) por. D. $1.25. W: C. Gilman.

Gilmore, Albert Field.
Birds through the year. '10(My21) c. il. D. 50 c. Am. Bk.

Gilmore, C: Whitney.
Smithsonian exploration in Alaska in 1907 in search of *Pleistocene* fossil vertebrates. '08(Je13) map, O. (Smithsonian miscellaneous collections.) pap. (Add. Institution for price.) Smith. Inst.

Gilmore, Eug. Allen.
Cases on the law of partnership; sel. from decisions of Eng. and Am. cts.; J: Brown Scott, ed. '08(D) c. 16+638 p. O. (Am. casebook ser.) $3.75. West Pub.

—, rep. *See* Wisconsin. *Sup. ct.* Repts.

Gilmore, Marion Forster.
Virginia; a tragedy, and other poems. '10(Jl9) c. 8°, $1. Morton.

Gilpin, E. N.
Last campaign: cavalryman's journal, [account of Gen. James H. Wilson's Cavalry campaign in Alabama and Georgia.] '09(Ap) 617-675 p. il. por. 8°, 50 c. U. S. Cavalry.

Gilpin, Jos. Elliott, and Cram, Marshall P.
Fractionation of crude petroleum by capillary diffusion; under the supervision of D: T. Day. '09(Mr6) il. 8°, (U. S. Dept. of the Interior, Geol. Survey, bull.)

Gilson, C: Ja. L:
The refugee; strange story of Nether Hall. '10(S17) c. il. D. $1.25 net. Century Co.

Gilson, H: Brockway.
See Marique, Pierre Joseph.

Gilson, Marjary L.
See Dana, J: Cotton.

Gilson, Roy Rolfe.
Wistful years. '09(N13) il. D. †$1.50. Baker & T.

GIMM FAMILY.
See **Genealogies: Johnson, A. V. V.**

"Ginger," pseud.
See Irwin, Wallace Admah.

Ginger and Pickles. Potter, B. 50 c. Warne.

Gingerich, Solomon Fs.
Wordsworth: a study in memory and mysticism. '08(Mr.) 205 p. 12°, $1.20. Mennonite.

GINKO TREE.
Maury, S. W. Ginko tree. 25 c. net. Lane.

Ginn's international modern language ser. D. and S. Ginn.
—Auerbach. Brigitta. 40 c.
—Baumbach. Der schweigersohn. 40 c.
—Becquer. Legends, tales and poems. $1.
—Eckstein *and* Wildenbruch. Der besuch im karzer, and Das edle blut. 50 c.
—Goethe. Götz von Berlichingen.—Torquato Tasso. ea., 80 c.
—Heyse. Anfang und ende. 35 c.
—Josselyn *and* Talbot. Elementary reader of French history. 30 c.
—Lazare. Les plus jolis contes de fées. 35 c.
—Maistre. Les prisonniers du Caucase. 30 c.
—Marique. Exercises in French composition. 40 c.
—Pereda. Pedro Sánchez. $1.
—Riehl. Der fluch der schönheit. 40 c.
—Schiller. Jungfrau von Orleans. 70 c.—Maria Stuart. 75 c.
—Storm. Der schimmelreiter. 70 c.
—Volkmann-Leander. Träumereinen an französischen Kaminen. 40 c.

Ginn's language readers. il. D. Ginn.
—Wade *and* Sylvester. Fifth reader. 65 c.

Ginn's mathematical texts; ed. by Percy F. Smith. il. O. Ginn.
—Granville. Plane and spherical trigonometry. $1.25.

Ginn's standard English classics. D. Ginn.
—Bunyan. Grace abounding. 35 c.
—Goldsmith *and* Gray. Deserted village, and Elegy in a country churchyard. 25 c.
—Lodge. Rosalynde. 35 c.
—Macaulay. Essays on Clive and Hastings. 35 c.
—Shakespeare. Midsummer night's dream. 35 c.

GINSENG.
See Botany.

Ginzberg, Louis.
Geonica. 2 v. '10(Ap23) 8°, (Texts and studies of the Jewish Theological Seminary of America.) (Add. pubs. for price.) Jewish Theological.
Contents: **I, The Geonim and their Halakic writings; II, Genizah studies.**

Legends of the Jews; tr. from the German manuscript by Henrietta Szold. In 4 v. v. 1. '09(Je5); v. 2. '10(Je18) c. O. ea., $2. Jewish Pub.

Giorgione (Giorgio Barbarelli).
See Carpaccio, Vittore.

Giotti, Angiolotto di Bondone.
Masterpieces of Giotto (1276-1336). '10 (S10) il. T. (Painters' ser.) leath., 75 c. net; pap., 25 c. net. Stokes.

Gipsy count. Wynne, M. $1.50. J: McBride.

Giraldus Cambrensis, [or Gerald de Barry.]
Itinerary and description of Wales; introd. by W. Llewellyn Williams. '08(Mr7) (Everyman's lib.) *35 c. net; leath., *75 c. net. Dutton.

Girard, Mrs. Mary Augusta Gage Brown.
Vocal art. '10(Ja29) c. 12°, $1. Cuneo.

Girders for electric overhead cranes. Branston, J: W: 25 c. Indust. Press.

Girdle of the great. Douglass, J: J. $1.50. B'way Pub.

Girdlestone, Rev. Rob. Baker.
Old Testament theology and modern ideas. '09(Ap10) D. (Anglican Church handbooks.) *40 c. net. Longmans.
See also Moule, Handley Carr Glyn.

Girl and the bill. Merwin, H: B. †$1.50. Dodd.

Girl and the detective. Blaney, C: E: 25 c. J. S. Ogilvie.

Girl and the game. Williams, J. L. †$1.50. Scribner.

Girl and the man. Yorke, C., *pseud.* $1.50. Estes.

Girl and the motor. Ward, H. $1. Gas Engine.

Girl from Dixie. Rodney, M. $1. Cochrane.

Girl from his town. Van Vorst, M. †$1.50. Bobbs-M.

Girl from "L Triangle" Ranch. Dumont, F. 25 c. Penn Pub. Co.

Girl from Montana. Lutz, *Mrs.* G. L. H. $1. Golden Rule.

Girl from Texas. Blaney, C: E: 25 c. J. S. Ogilvie.

Girl from the Marsh Croft. Lagerlöf, S. O. L. $1.50. Little, B. & Co.
Girl from Vermont. Saunders, M. *$1.25 net. Griffith.
Girl graduate: her own book; designed and il. by Louise Perrett and Sarah K. Smith. '09(Ap24) O. $1.50, boxed; flex. mor., $3, boxed.—Commencement ed. [1910.] (My) $6. Reilly & B.
Girl I left behind me. Mills, W. J. $2 net. Dodd.
Girl I loved. Riley, J. W. $2; $3. Bobbs-M.
Girl in question. Honk, L. C. V. †$1.50. Lane.
Girl in waiting. Eyre, A. 75 c. Grosset.
Girl of the fourth. Irvine, A. M. 75 c. McKay.
Girl of the Limberlost. Porter, G. S.- †$1.50. Doubleday, P.
Girl of Virginia. Thruston, L. M. †75 c. Little, B. & Co.
Girl question. Harding, J: W: †$1. G: W. Dillingham.
Girl wanted. Waterman, N. $1.25. Forbes.
Girl who earns her own living. Richardson, A. S. *$1 net. B. W. Dodge.
Girl who lived in the woods. Cooke, M. B. $1.50. McClurg.
Girl who won. Ellis, E. $1.50. Dodd.
Girlhood of Queen Elizabeth. Mumby, F. A., *comp.* **$3 net. Houghton M.
Girl's annual, 1910. '10(D) $1.50. Cassell.
GIRLS.
Boston Public Library. Brief list of books for home reading for boys and girls in the Library. gratis. Boston Pub. Lib.
Chance, M. S. B. Mother and daughter. $1 net. Century Co.
Creighton, *Mrs.* L. Art of living, and other addresses to girls. *50 c. net. Longmans.
Edwards, E. Personal information for young women. 50 c. Fenno.
Latimer, C. W. Girl and woman. **$2 net. Appleton.
McKeever, W: A. Better crop of boys and girls.—Training the girl to keep at home. ea., gratis. W: McKeever.
Paret, A. P., *ed.* Harper's handy book for girls. $1.75. Harper.
Sangster, *Mrs.* M. E. M. Happy school days: [advice to schoolgirls.] $1.25. Forbes.
Saunders, F. W. Letters to a business girl. $1.25. Laird.
Slattery, M. Girl in her teens. 50 c. net. S. S. Times.
Sweet, F. H. Illustrious girls of many lands. 50 c. McLoughlin.
Trades for London girls. *25 c. net. Longmans.
Walker, E. E. Pretty girl papers. $1.25 net. Little, B. & Co.
Wetzel, F. X. Guide for girls in the journey of life. 40 c. Herder.
Wood-Allen, *Mrs.* M. What a young girl ought to know. $1. Vir.
See also Agriculture;—Children;—Education;—Etiquette;—Hygiene;—Woman;—Young people.
Girls. Hutt, H:, *il.* $3 net. Scribner.
Girls of Fairmount. Baker, E. A. †$1.50. Little, B. & Co.
Girls of the forest. Smith, *Mrs.* E. T. †$1. Burt.
Girls of to-day. Underwood, C. F. **$3 net. Stokes.
Girls' college record. Frame, V. W., *comp.* *$1.50 net; *$6 net. P. Elder.
Girls' own authors series. '08(D19) il. 12°, ea., †$1. Estes.
Contents: The girl rough riders, Prentiss Ingraham; The story-book house, Honor Walsh; Maid Sally, Harriet A. Cheever; Lou, Harriet A. Cheever; The brass bound box, Evelyn Raymond; The doings of Nancy, Evelyn Raymond; Two girls abroad, Nellie M. Carter; Two Altheas, Edith Horsman; Marigold's winter, Foster; Flossie's play days, Hall; Chums, Pool.
Girls' own lib. il. D. 75 c. McKay.
—Green. Carol Carew.
—Hutchinson. Ways of a girl.
—Irvine. Girl of the fourth.
—Lippmann. Every day girls.
—Moore. Sydney Lisle.
—Robson. Evan Grayle's daughters.—Fortunes of eight.
—Smith. Betty Vivian.—School favorite.
—Turner. Family at misrule.—Little mother Meg.—Miss Bobbie.—Seven little Australians.—That girl.—Three little maids.
Girty, G: Herbert.
Fauna of the Caney shale of Oklahoma. '09, [1910.] (Ja.) 106 p. il. 8°, (U. S., Dept. of the Interior; U. S. Geological Survey, bull.) pap., 25 c.
Guadalupian fauna. '09(Ap3) il. map, Q. (U. S. Dept. of the Interior, Geol. Survey, professional papers.) pap., $1.50.
Gissing, F: T.
Commercial peat, its uses and its possibilities. '10(F19) 8°, *$2 net. Lippincott.
Gist, Eliz.
Gist of domestic science. Rev. ed. '09 (Je) 168 p. 8°, 75 c. E. Gist.
Gist of domestic science. Gist, E. 75 c. E. Gist.
Gist of Nietzsche. Nietzsche, F. W. 60 c. net. J: W. Luce.
Gist of the lesson. *See* Torrey, R. A.
Giuseppina. Marvel, T: L. 25 c. Dramatic.
Give up your gods. Rees, A. D. **$1 net. Lippincott.
Giveen, Clement Martin, ed.
Chronology of municipal history and election statistics, Waterville, Maine, 1771-1908, designed for a book of reference. '08, [1909.] (Ap) c. 278 p. il. pors., 8°, $1.50. Maine Farmer.
Given, G. C., M.D.
See Frear, W:
Givens, Rob. T., ed.
Has it ever occurred to you? '09(Jl) 8°, 55 c. R. T. Givens.
Giving a man another chance. Smith, W. M. *$1 net. Revell.
GIZEH, Egypt.
See Ghizeh.
Gjerset, Knut.
English grammar. '08(N7) c. D. 60 c. Lutheran Pub.
Glacial epoch and the Noachian deluge. Magoun, H. W. 25 c. H. W. Magoun.

GLACIERS.
Fairchild, H. L. Glacial waters in central New York. 40 c. N. Y., State Educ.
Sherzer, W: H. Glaciers of the Canadian Rockies and Selkirks. Smith. Inst.

Glad lady. Blanchard, A. E. $1.50 Estes.

Glad tidings. De Waters, *Mrs.* L. S. $1.25. L. S. De Waters.

Glad tidings. Thomas, R. $1.25. Pilgrim Press.

Gladden, Washington, D.D.
Church and modern life. '08(Mr28) c. D. **$1.25 net. Houghton M.
Lord's prayer; seven homilies. '08(D) 192 p. 12°, $1. Houghton M.
Nation and the kingdom; annual sermon before the American Board of Commissioners for Foreign Missions; del. at Plymouth Church, Minneapolis, Minn., Oct. 13, 1909. '09, [1910.] (Je) 24 p. 8°, gratis. Am. Bd. For. Miss.
Recollections. '09(O30) c. por. O. **$2 net. Houghton M.

Gladney, Fk. Young.
Restraints of trade in patented articles. '10 (N) 7+405 p. 8°, $3.50. Mazda.

Gladstone, W: Ewart.
Correspondence on church and religion; sel. and arr. by D. C. Lathbury. '10 (O1) c. il. O. $5, boxed. Macmillan.

GLADSTONE, William Ewart.
Brooklyn. Public Library. William Ewart Gladstone; list of books and of references to periodicals. gratis. Brooklyn Lib.
Fletcher, C: R. L. Mr. Gladstone at Oxford in 1890. *$1 net. Dutton.

Gladwin, W: Zachary.
See Zollinger, Gulielma, *pseud.*

Gladys, the angel of the good. Smith, J: R. $1. Jewel Pub.

GLANDS.
Sajous, C: E. de M. Internal secretions and the principles of medicines. 2 v. $12. Davis.
See also Parathyroid gland;—Thyroid gland.

Glasenapp, Maximilian.
Plaster, overburnt gypsum and hydraulic gypsum; tr. by Dr. W. Michaelis, jr. '10(Jl9) c. il. 8°, 50 c. Cement & Engineering.

Glasgow, Ellen Anderson Gholson.
Ancient law. '08(F1) c. O. †$1.50. Doubleday, P.
Romance of a plain man. '09(My22) c. D. †$1.50. Macmillan.

Glasgow gallery. '08(N7) il. T. (Great art galleries.) bds., 35 c.; limp calfskin, $1. Caldwell.

Glaspell, Susan.
Glory of the conquered. '09(Mr13) c. D. †$1.50. Stokes.

Glass, Alex.
See Müller, Georg.

Glass, Arth. Wellington.
Justifiable falsehood: story of love and mystery. '09(My) c. '08. 192 p. 12°, $1. A. W. Glass.

Glass, D: Rose.
Lightning legible shorthand. for use in all fields of labor where the highest degree of speed and legibility is demanded. 2d ed. '09(N) c. 9-86 p. il. 12°. (Add. author for price.) D: R. Glass.

Glass, Montague.
Potash & Perlmutter; their business ventures and adventures. '10(Ag13) c. il. 12°, $1.50. Doubleday, P.

GLASS.
Duthie, A. L: Decorative glass processes. *$2 net. Van Nostrand.
Kümmel, H: B., *and* Gage, R. B. Glass-sand industry of New Jersey. (Add. author for price.) H: B. Kümmel.
Lovejoy, O. R. Children in the glass industry in Pennsylvania. (Add. pubs. for price.) Nat. Child Labor.
Rosenhain, W. Glass manufacture. *$2 net. Van Nostrand.
See also Stained glass.

Glass house. Kingsley, *Mrs.* F. M. †$1.50. Dodd.

Glasson, W: H:
Australian voting system; sketch of its history and principles—why N. Carolina and S. Carolina and Georgia should adopt it. '09(O) 13 p. 8°, pap., 20 c. W: H: Glasson.

Glasspool, R:, comp.
To have a friend, be one. '10(O1) c. O. $1, boxed; leath., $2, boxed. Platt & P.

GLASTONBURY, England.
Holmes, T: S. Wells and Glastonbury. *$1.75 net. Dutton.

Glaucoma. Henderson, T. $3 net. Longmans.

Glaucus. *See* Kingsley, C: Water babies.

Glazebrook, Michael G:, D.D.
Studies in the Book of Isaiah. '10(D3) fold. map, D. $1.90. Oxford Univ.

GLAZES.
See Ceramics.

Gleam o' dawn. Goodrich, A. F: †$1.50. Appleton.

Gleams of sunshine for hearts in shadow. '09 (D4) c. 12°, 35 c. Good Tidings.

Gleanings. Hendrix, L. E. G. 75 c.; 30 c. L. E. G. Hendrix.

Gleanings. Sherman, *Mrs.* M. J. M. 65 c. M. J. M. Sherman.

Gleanings gathered from many sources. Morgan, K. K. 80 c. Book & Art.

Gleanings of quiet hours. Thompson, P. J., (Add. author for price.) P. J. Thompson.

Gleason, C: H., and Gilbert, C: Benajah.
Gilbert arithmetics. 3 v. '10(D24) c. il. 12°, bk. 1, 36 c. net; bk.. 2, 40 c. net; bk. 3, 45 c. net. Macmillan.

Gleason, E: Baldwin.
Manual of diseases of the nose, throat, and ear. 2d ed., thoroughly rev. '10(O) 11-563 p. il. 12°, $2.50. Saunders.

GLEASON FAMILY.
See Genealogies: White, J: B.

Gleig, C:
Middy of the "Blunderbore." '10(D31) il. 12°, $1.50. Lippincott.

Gleig, Rev. G: Rob.
Life of Wellington. '09(Mr27) 16°, (Everyman's lib.) *35 c. net; leath., *70 c. net. Dutton.

Glen Ellyn. Montagu, G. $1.50. G. Montagu.

GLEN RIDGE, N. J.
Nolen, J: Plan for the Borough of Glen Ridge. $1 net. J: Nolen.

GLENESK, Algernon Borthwick, *Lord.*
Lucas, R. J. Lord Glenesk and the "*Morning Post.*" $6 net. Lane.

Glenloch girls. Remick, G. M. †$1.25. Penn Pub. Co.

Glenloch girls abroad. Remick, G. M. $1.25. Penn Pub. Co.

Glenn, Fk. A., and Byrne, H: E:
Speller and dictionary. 3d ed. '08(Je) c. 81 p. 24°, 25 c. Byrne Pub.

Glenn, Garrard.
See Elkins, Abram I.

Glenn, Laurence Mell.
Harking back. '08, [1909.] (My) c. 80 p. por. 24°. (Priv. pr.) Furman Univ.

Glenn, Pressley Adams.
See Hunter, S: J:

GLENS FALLS, N. Y.
Holden, J. A. Glens Falls, N. Y. 60 c. Glens Falls Pub.

Gli Americani nella vita moderna. Pecorini, A. $1.25. F. Tocci.

Glidden, Alb. G.
Hand made furniture and how to make it. '10(Jl9) c. il. 8°, $1. Hand Made Furniture.

GLIDERS.
See **Aërial navigation.**

GLIDING MACHINE.
See **Aerial navigation.**

Glimpse (The). Bennett, E. A. †$1.50. Appleton.

Glimpse of love. Lindsay, F. A. 60 c. Lindsay.

Glimpse of the isles of the Pacific. Wheeler, W: W. (Not for sale.) Hardman.

Glimpse of Utah. Colborn, E: F. gratis. Denver & Rio Grande.

Glimpses around the world. Stein, G. M. $2 net. Winston.

Glimpses into the life of the Indian schools. Hare, W: H. (Add. author for price.) W: H. Hare.

Glimpses of a strange world. Stollnitz, H: S. $1.50. H: S. Stollnitz.

Glimpses of India. Swain, C. A. $1.25. Woman's For. Miss.

Glimpses of medical Europe. Thompson, R. L. **$2 net. Lippincott.

Glimpses of the Alaska-Yukon-Pacific Exposition, Seattle, Wash., and the great Northwest. '09(My8) obl. T. 75 c., boxed; pap., 25 c. Laird.

Glimpses of the heavenly life. Miller, J. R. **50 c. net. Crowell.

Glimpses of the life of Samuel Morris. Morris, H. P. 75 c. S: N. Rhoads.

Glints of wisdom. Colville, W: W. J. 40 c. Macoy Pub.

Globe English-French pocket dict. '10(O8) 32°, 75 c. net. Lippincott.

Globe ser. *See* Chancellor, W: Estabrook.

Gloria. Turner, G. F. $1.50. Dodd.

Gloria crucis. Beibitz, J. H. $1. Longmans.

Glorious company of the apostles. Jones, J: D. *75 c. net. Doran.

Glorious mother. Woolard, S: F., *comp.* *50 c. net; *$1.25 net. Goldsmith-W.

Glory and the abyss. Brown, V. $1.25 net. Dutton.

Glory of his country. Landis, F: †$1. Scribner.

Glory of our youth. Devens, R: M. $3.75. C. A. Nichols.

Glory of the conquered. Glaspell, S. †$1.50. Stokes.

Glory of the Shia world. Sykes, P. M., *tr. and ed.* $3.50 net. Macmillan.

Gloryville or Hellburg, which? Davey, J: 20 c. J: Davey.

Glossemata. *See* Prudentius, Aurelius Clemens.

GLOUCESTERSHIRE, Eng.
See **Cotswold (The).**

Glover, Ellye Howell, ["Dame Curtsey."]
"Dame Curtsey's" book of etiquette. '09 (N20) c. front. S. bds., *50 c. net. McClurg.
"Dame Curtsey's" book of guessing contests. '08(Ag29) c. S. bds., *50 c. net. McClurg.
"Dame Curtsey's" book of recipes. '09 (N20) c. il. S. *$1 net. McClurg.

Glover, Terrot Reaveley.
Conflict of religions in the early Roman Empire. 3d ed. '09(D11) O. *$2.50 net. Scribner.

Glover's Marblehead regiment in the war of the Revolution. Gardner, F. A. 50 c. Salem Press.

GLUCOSIDES.
See **Chemistry.**

Glue ser. *See* Williams, Clara Andrews.

Glyn, Mrs. Elinor Sutherland.
Beyond the rocks. '08(My9) c. D. †$1.50. Duffield.
Damsel and the sage. '08(My9) c. O. bds., †$1.25. Duffield.
Elizabeth visits America. '09(My22) 12°, †$1.50. Duffield.
His hour. '10(O) c. 304 p. front. D. $1.50. Appleton.
Reflections of Ambrosine. '08(My9) c. D. †$1.50. Duffield.
Sayings of grandmamma. '08(My9) c. T. $1.25. Duffield.
Vicissitudes of Evangeline. '08(My9) c. D. †$1.50. Duffield.
See also Metcalfe, Ja. Stetson.

Glyn, Marg. H.
Analysis of the evolution of musical form. '09(F27) O. *$3.50 net. Longmans.

Go (*game*).
Smith, A. Game of Go, the national game of Japan. **$2.50 net. Moffat.

Go forth and find. Pittman, *Mrs.* H. D. $1.50. Badger.

Go forward. Miller, J. R. **50 c. net. Crowell.

Go-to-bed stories. Bell, L. $1. Gospel Pub.

Go to it. Hobart, G: V. †75 c. G: W. Dillingham.

Goal of life. Butler, H. E. $2. Esoteric.

GOATS.

Case for the goat, by "Home Counties." $1.25. Dutton.

Immel, A. A. Scientific sheep and goat breeding [astrology]. $1. E. E. Hahn.

Thompson, G: F. Angora goat. 5 c. U. S., Supt. of Docs.

GOD.

Abbott, L. Seeking after God. $1. Crowell.

Ainslie, P: God and me: relationship of the believer with God. 45 c. Temple Seminary.

Barwell, J. W. Science, the mind, revelation, the heart of God. 25 c. Jacobs & H.

Bavinck, H. **Philosophy of revelation.** **$2 net. **Longmans.**

Brett, J. Divine friendship: [papers on God's love.] *$1 net. Longman's.

Cady, H. E. God a present help. 60 c. Roger Bros.

Carus, P. God: inquiry into the nature of man's highest ideal. *$1 net. Open Court.

Clarke, W: N. Christian doctrine of God. **$2.50 net. Scribner.

De Laurence, L. W: God, the Bible, truth and Christian theology. $3.50.—Immanence of God. $3.25. De Laurence, S.

Dykes, J. O. Divine worker in creation and Providence. $2.25. Scribner.

Edwards, J: H. God and music. **$1.25 net. Baker & T.

Everett, C: C. Theism and the Christian faith. *$3.50 net. Macmillan.

Hall, J: A. Nature of God. $1.25. Lutheran Pub.

Hammond, E., *comp.* Splendor of God: extracts from sacred writings of the Bahais. *60 c. net. Dutton.

Heisley, C: W. Providence and calamity. *$1.10 net. Sherman, F.

Hill, L. Two great questions; the existence of God and the immortality of the soul. $2. L. Hill.

Hood, J: Beauty of God as revealed in His works. *$1.25 net. Lanahan.

Huizinga, F. v. C. P. Belief in a personal God. *50 c. net. Sherman, F.

Ingram, A. F. W. Joy in God. *60 c. net. Whittaker.

"Justus," *pseud.* Prolegomena to theism. $2. A. H. Kellogg.

Lyman, A. J. Underneath are the Everlasting Arms. 50 c. net. Pilgrim Press.

McConnell, F. J. Diviner immanence. 75 c. Eaton & M.

Meagher, J. L. Wonders of the universe; what science says of God. $1. Chr. Press.

Nichols, G. P. Preciousness of God's thoughts. *$1.25 net. Revell.

Pigou, A. C. Problems of theism, and other essays. *$1 net. Macmillan.

Randall, J: H. The real God. $1.25. Caldwell.

Rhodes, L. R. Circumstantial evidence: using the revealed truths of the infinite as a basis from which to demonstrate a God of design. 75 c. L. R. Rhodes.

GOD.—*Continued.*

Russell, M. At home with God. $1.25 net. Longmans.

Scull, D: Union with God in thought and faith. **$1 net. Winston.

Shumaker, E. E. God and man. **$2 net. Putnam.

Smith, D: Man's need of God. $1.50 net. Doran.

Van Ness, T: Search for God traced in Hebrew and Christian sources. 30 c. Unitarian S. S.

Veach, R. W. King and His kingdom. *60 c. net; *35 c. net. Revell.

Wilt, D. W. Man's influence with God. 75 c. D. W. Wilt.

Worcester, E. Living word. **$1.50 net. Moffat.

See also Bible; — Holy Spirit; —Incarnation;—Jesus Christ; — Monotheism; — Philosophy; —Religion;—Theology;—Trinity.

God a present Help. Cady, H. E. $1. Rogers Bros.

God bless you. Tilly, F: E., *ed.* 25 c. E. Kaufmann.

God enthused man. Harrington, C: H: 75 c. J: A. Davis.

God-man; or, the life and works of Jesus. Losch, H: $1.50. Badger.

God of clay. Bailey, H: C. †$1.50. Brentano's.

God of love. McCarthy, J. H. †$1.50. Harper.

God of our fathers. Belasco, G: S. *$1.20 net. Bloch.

God-parents. Mason, *Mrs.* G. S. **$1.10 net. Houghton M.

God with us. Gibson, W. R. B. *$1.40 net. Macmillan.

Godbey, S: Macginis.

Bible and problem of poverty. '08(O24) 12°, *$1 net. Revell.

Goddard, Harold Clarke.

Chaucer's Legend of good women; repr. from the *Journal of English and German Philology.* '09(Je19) pap. (Add. author for price.) H. C. Goddard.

Studies in New England transcendentalism. '08(Ap18) 8°, (Columbia Univ. studies in English.) *$1 net. Lemcke.

Goddard, Jos.

Rise of music: being a careful enquiry into the development of the art from its primitive puttings forth in Egypt and Assyria to its triumphant consummation in modern effect. '08(D12) figs. D. *$2.50 net. Scribner.

Goddard, Oscar Elmo.

Manual of missions for laymen. '08(Mr.) c. '07. 124 p. 12°. (Add. author for price.) O. E. Goddard.

Goddard, Pliny Earle.

Kato texts. '09(D25) por. Q. (Univ. of Cal. pubs.; American archæology and ethnology.) pap., $2.50. Univ. of Cal.

Godden, G. M.

Henry Fielding; memoir, incl. newly discovered letters and records. '10(D) 13+325 p. il. facsims. $5. Barse & H.

Godée-Molsbergen, E. C., comp.
Hist. of South Africa; for use in schools; comp. at the request of the Zuid-Afrikaanse Taalbond, the Zuid-Afrikaanse Onderwijers Unie, and the Afrikaanse Christelike Vrouwen Vereniging. '10 (Ap30) maps, D. 90 c. net. Longmans.

GODETIA.
See Botany.

Godfrey, C:, and Siddons, A. W.
Modern geometry. '08(N7) 8°, *50 c. net. Putnam.

Godfrey, Eliz., [pseud. for Jessie Bedford.]
Cradle of a poet. '10(Ag27) D. $1.50. Lane.
English children in the olden time. '08(F8) il. 8°, *$3 net. Dutton.
Sister of Prince Rupert: Elizabeth, Princess Palatine and Abbess of Hertford. '09(Ap24) por. il. O. *$4 net. Lane.

Godfrey, Hollis.
Elem. chemistry. '09(Jl17) c. il. D. $1.10. Longmans.
For the Norton name. '09(O2) c. il. D. (Young captains of industry.) †$1.25. Little, B. & Co.
Health of the city. '10(Je4) c. D. $1.25 net. Houghton M.
Jack Collerton's engine. '10(O1) c. D. (Young captains of industry.) $1.25. Little, B. & Co.
Lab'y manual to accompany Godfrey's "Elem. chemistry." '10(Ap23) c. D. bds., 36 c. Longmans.
Man who ended war. '08(O17) c. il. D. †$1.50. Little, B. & Co.

Godley, Alfr. Denis.
Oxford in the eighteenth century. '08(N14) il. O. *$2.25 net. Putnam.

Godlover, Hugh Bliss.
Science of minds fundamentally treated. '08 (Ap.) c. 48+3 p. 12°, $1. H. B. Godlover.

Godly self-control. Pierson, A. T. *50 c. net. Armstrong.

Godoy, José Francisco.
Porfirio Diaz, president of Mexico; master builder of a great commonwealth. '10 (Mr5) c. il. maps, O. **$2 net. Putnam.

Godrycz, J: A., D.D.
Doctrine of modernism and its refutation. '08(Je6) *75 c. net. McVey.

God's country. Mitchell, D. H. $6. Ebbert & R.
God's garden. Brown, C: *$1 net. Eaton & M.
God's hand. Cady, H. E. 10 c. Roger Bros.
God's heroes. Barney, L. C. $3 net. Lippincott.
God's troubadour. Jewett, S. $1.25 net. Crowell.
Gods (The). *See* Ingersoll, Rob. Green.
Gods and heroes of the north. *See* Zimmern, Alice.

Godwin, Mrs. Mary Wollstonecraft.
Love letters of Mary Wollstonecraft to Gilbert Imlay; with a prefatory memoir by Roger Ingpen. '08(O3) pors. S. *$1 net. Lippincott.

Goebel, Ferdinand.
Rübezahl: ed. by D. B. Hurley. '10(D24) 16°, (Macmillan's new ser.) of German texts.) 35 c. net. Macmillan.

Goepp, Rudolph Max, M.D.
State board questions and answers. [examinations in medicine.] '07, [1908.] (Mr.) 800 p. 8°. (Add. pubs. for price.) Saunders.

Goerens, Paul.
Introd. to metallography; tr. by Fred Ibbotson. '08(Ap25) il. O. *$2.50 net. Longmans.

Goessling, Adeline O., comp.
Housekeeper's reference book and domestic counselor. '10(Mr12) c. il. 12°, 50 c. Phelps.

Goetchius, H: R.
Litigation in Georgia during the reconstruction period; the president's annual address before the fourteenth annual session of the Georgia Bar Association. '10 (Ap) 42 p. 8°, pap., 25 c. H: R. Goetchius.

Goetchius, Mrs. Marie Louise.
Anne of Tréboul. '10(My21) c. D. $1 net. Century Co.

Goethals, G: Washington.
Isthmian canal. '09(My) 23 p. 8°, pap. U. S., Supt. of Docs.

Goethe, Johann Wolfgang v.
Works. 7 v. New imperial lib. ed. '10 (D) il. 8°, ea., $1.25; hf. cf., $2.25. New il. sterling ed., ea., $1. (Sets only.) Estes.
Faust. pts. 1 and 2; tr. by A. G. Latham. '08(S19) 16°, (Everyman's lib.) *35 c. net; leath., *70 c. net. Dutton.
Goethe in Italy; extracts from Goethe's Italienische reise for classroom use; ed., with notes and introd., by A. B. Nichols. '09(Ap17) c. front. S. 35 c. Holt.
Götz von Berlichingen mit der eisernen hand; ein schauspiel; together with Zu Shakespeares namenstag; with introd., notes and appendix by J. A. C. Hildner. '10(N5) c. il. por. S. (International modern language ser.) 80 c. net. Ginn.
Hermann und Dorothea; ed. for the use of students, with notes and vocab. by Waterman T: Hewett. '08(Ag22) c. il. S. 60 c. Am. Bk.
Hermann und Dorothea; ed., with introd., notes and vocab., by R: A. von Minckwitz. '08(Ag8) c. il. por. 12°, (Merrill's German texts.) 60 c. C: E. Merrill.
Hermann and Dorothea. '10(D) front. 32°, (Ariel booklets.) leath., 75 c., boxed. Putnam.
Poems and prose. '08(O3) il. Q. bds., *$2.50 net, boxed. Stokes.
Poetry and truth of my own life; rev. tr. by Minna Steele Smith; with introd. and bibliography by Karl Breul. '08(Je6) 2 v., 16°, ea., 80 c.; leath., $1.25. Macmillan.
Torquato Tasso; ein schauspiel; ed., with introd., notes, repetitional exercises, and vocab., by J: Firman Coar. '08(My9) c. S. (Internat. modern lang. ser.) 80 c. Ginn.
Vicar of Sesenheim; extracts from books IX-XII. of Goethe's "Dichtung und wahrheit"; with an introd., appendix, notes and vocab. by A. B. Nichols. '08(Mr7) c. front. S. 35 c. Holt.

GOETHE, Johann Wolfgang v.
Bielschowsky, A. Life of Goethe. In 3 v. v. 3. **$3.50 net. Putnam.
Lewes, G: H: Life of Goethe. *35 c. net; *75 c. net. Dutton.
Pinger, W. R. R. Der junge Goethe und das publikum. 50 c. Univ. of Cal.
Santayana, G: Three philosophical poets: Lucretius, Dante, and Goethe. $2.25. Harvard Univ
See also Faust;—Weimar.

Goetia; or, the lesser key of Solomon the King. '10(D) $1. Occult Pub. Co.

Goetschius, Percy.
Exercises in elem. counterpoint. '10(My21) c. O. $1.50 net. Schirmer.

Goff, Clarissa, [Mrs. Rob. C: Goff.]
Assisi of St. Francis; together with The influence of the Franciscan legend on Italian art, by J. Kerr Lawson. '09(D25) col. il. 8°, *$6 net, boxed. Dodd.

Goff, Mrs. Rob. C:
See Goff, Clarissa.

Goff, Rob. Remington.
Preparation for United States civil service examinations. '10(Ap16) c. 8°, $3. Clerk Agency.

Goggin, Rev. T. E.
Man's great charter: exposition of the first chapter of Genesis. New ed. '09(Mr27) 12°, *$1.75 net. Gorham.

Gogol, Nikolai Vasilevich.
Revizór, a comedy; tr. for the Yale University Dramatic Association by Max S. Mandell; with introd. by W: Lyon Phelps. '08(My.) c. 12+10+72 p. por. 8°, $1; pap., 50 c. C. P. Franchot.

Going, C: Buxton.
Methods of the Santa Fe; economy in the manufacture of transportation. '09(S4) c. il. 8°, $1. Engineering Mag.
Star-glow and song. '09(Ap17) c. D. *$1.20 net. Harper.

Going down from Jerusalem. Duncan, N. **$1.50 net. Harper.
Going some. Beach, R. E. $1.25. Harper.
Going some. "Windy Bill," *pseud.* 10 c. J. S. Ogilvie.

Goins, J: B.
American waiter. 2d ed., rev. and enl. '08 (Ag) c. 152+4 p. il. nar. 16°, $1. Hotel Monthly.

Gold, Grace, pseud.
See Frink, *Mrs.* Maria.

GOLD.
Adams, W: J. Hints on amalgamation and the general care of gold mills. $2. Mining and Scientific.
Crane, W. R: Gold and silver: economic history of mining. **$5 net. Wiley.
Laney, F. B. Gold Hill mining district of North Carolina. N. C. Geolog. Survey.
Launay, L. de. World's gold: its geology. extraction and political economy. **$1.75 net. Putnam.
Meade, E: S. Story of gold. **75 c. net. Appleton.
Rose, T: K. Precious metals: gold, silver and platinum. **$2 net. Van Nostrand.
See also Cyanide process;—*also* Alaska;—Idaho;—Klondike.

GOLD (*as money*).
Brace, H. H. Gold production and future prices. $1.50. Bankers' Pub.
Gibson, T: Increasing gold supply and its effect on security values. $1. Gibson Pub.
Morgan, A. T. Passing of gold; or, what is lawful money. $1. J: A. Anderson.
See also Coins and medals;—Money.

Gold brick. Whitlock, B. $1.50. Bobbs-M.
Gold dust. New ed. '10(D) 50 c., boxed; limp leath., $1. Barse & H.
Gold-gated West. Simpson, S: L. $2. Lippincott.
Gold hunters. Curwood, J. O. †$1.50. Bobbs-M.

GOLD MILLS.
See Gold.

Gold, prices, and wages under the greenback standard. Mitchell, W. C. $5. Univ. of Cal.
Gold trail. Bindloss, H. $1.30 net. Stokes.

Goldberg, Reuben Lucius.
Foolish questions. '09(Je26) c. il. 16°, **50 c. net. Small.

Goldberger, Jos.
Straw itch (Dermatitis Schambergi); a disease new to American physicians. '10 (Ag) 8 p. il. 8°. Gov. Pr. Off.

Golden, D: W:
Steam engine science. '08, [1909.] (F) c. '06. 26 p. il. 8°, $1. Sutton.

Golden, G: Fuller.
My Lady Vaudeville and her White Rats: [history of the organization known as the White Rats.] '09(My8) c. il. pors. O. $1. White Rats.

Golden, Rev. Meletios, ed.
Conversion of a high priest into a Christian worker. '09, [1910.] (F) c. 15+17-144 p. il. pors. 8°, $1. M. Golden.

Golden age of engraving. Keppel, F: $3.50 net; $7 net. Baker & T.
Golden anthologies. 16°, 50 c.; leath., 75 c. Dutton.
—Cullen. Hundred best hymns in the English language.
Golden bond. Smart, G: T:, *ed.* *35 c. net. Pilgrim Press.
Golden books. 30 v. '10(N) 16°, ea., 50 c., boxed. Barse & H.
Golden books for children; ed. by Clifton Johnson. il. D. Baker & T.
—Arabian nights. $1 net.
—Robin Hood. $1 net.
Golden candlestick. Nichols, J: H. 10 c.; per doz., $1. Smith & L.
Golden centipede. Gerard L. $1.25 net. Dutton.
Golden classics. il. 12°. Rand, McN. & Co.
—Brown. Rab and his friends. 50 c.
—Hathaway. Little Corsican, Napoleon Bonaparte. $1.
—Ruskin. King of the Golden River.—Mystery of life. ea., 50 c.
Golden council series. New ed., 1909. 27 v. '09(O2) il. S. ea., 75 c., boxed. Caldwell.
Golden curves. Wright, F. J. 25 c. net. Hills & H.
Golden fancy. Dumont, H: $1.25. Chapple Pub.
Golden galleon. Harrison, *Mrs.* M. S. L. K. $1.20. Doran.

Golden girdle. Mockler-Ferryman, A: F. $1.50. Macmillan.
Golden gleanings. Sloane, J. R., *comp.* $1. J. R. Sloane.
Golden heart. Barbour, R. H: $2. Lippincott.
Golden hour. Lewis, P., *comp.* $1. Bobbs-M.
Golden hour ser. 12°, 40 c. Educ. Pub.
—Hix, *comp.* Book of lullabies.
—Stevenson. Child's garden of verses.
Golden hours with the saints. 2 v. '10(D) front. ea., 50 c. net. Doran.
"Golden Hynde." Noyes, A. **$1.25 net. Macmillan.
Golden ladder. Potter, M. H. †$1.50. Harper.
Golden legend. *See* Longfellow, H: Wadsworth.
Golden month ser. 4 v. '10(D) col. fronts. ea., 50 c. Doran.
Golden opportunity. Lunt, E. M. (Priv. pr.) Towle Mfg.
Golden road. Allen, F. W. $1.50 net. Wessels & B.
Golden rod and lilies. Gilbert, R. W. $1.50. Badger.
Golden rose. Rives, A. †$1.25. Harper.
Golden rule cock book. *See* Sharpe, *Mrs.* M. R. L., *comp.*
Golden rule republic no Utopia. Randall, W: H: 25 c. Co-operative Pr. Co.
Golden rules of dietetics. Benedict, A. L. $3. Mosby.
Golden season. Kelly, M. $1.20. Doubleday, P.
Golden ser. of il. juvenile books. il. 12°, $1.50. Macmillan.
—Bourhill *and* Drake. Fairy tales from South Africa.
—Molesworth. Fairies-of-sorts.
Golden Square High School. Baldwin, M. $1.25. Lippincott.
Golden staircase. Chisholm, L., *comp.* *$1.50 net; *$1 net. Putnam.
Golden text book, 1909; 1910. *See* McFarland, J: T.
Golden text ser. 16°. T: B. Mosher.
—Arnold. Thyrsis and the Scholar gipsy. 40 c.; 60 c.; $1.
Golden thoughts from the Hebrew prophets. Bible. O. T. *50 c. net; *75 c. net. Lane.
Golden thoughts lib. 16°, *50 c. net; *75 c. net. Lane.
—Bible. O. T. Golden thoughts from the Hebrew prophets.
Golden threads. E., J., *comp.* 50 c. Stokes.
Golden town. Barnett, L. D., *comp.* *$1 net. Dutton.
Golden treasury. *See* Palgrave, Fs. Turner, *comp.*
Golden treasury. Hickman, S. H., *comp.* $1. B'way Pub.
Golden treasury of music. F. Schirmer.
—Brahms. [Songs:] collection of fifty songs. $2 net.
Golden treasury ser.; ed. by Fs. Turner Palgrave. 16°, $1. Macmillan.
—Æschylus. Suppliant maidens.
—Brown. Poems.
—Huxley. Aphorisms and reflections.

Golden treasury ser.—Continued.
—Masson. La lyre française.
—Page, *ed.* Golden treasury of American songs and lyrics.
—Palgrave, *comp.* Golden treasury. $1.50.
—Palgrave, *ed.* Latin anthology.
Golden week ser. '10(D) ea., 25 c. Doran.
Golden words fitly spoken. Wood, H. W., *comp.* $1.50 net. Lippincott.
Goldenrod. Carr, S. $1. S. Carr.

GOLDFIELD, Nev.
Ransome, F: L. Geology and ore deposits of Goldfield, Nev. (Add. Superintendent for price.) U. S., Supt. of Docs.

GOLDFISH.
Mulertt, H. Goldfish and its systematic culture. $2. H. Mulertt.
Smith, H. M. Japanese gold fish. $2. W. F. Roberts.
Wolf, H. T. Gold fish breeds and other aquarian fishes. $3. Innes.

Goldin, Hyman Elias.
First year in Hebrew, with exercises and vocab. '10(Ag27) O. 40 c. Druckerman.
—, and Silk, B.
Second year in Hebrew. '10(Ag27) O. 60 c. Druckerman.

Golding, Harry, ed.
Book of animals for boys and girls. '08 (Ag8) il. Q. bds., $1.50. Stokes.
See also Saalfield's annual.—Stokes' wonder book.

Golding, H: A.
Engineers' and machinists' hdbk..; complete guide for turners, fitters, screw-cutters and all machinists. '10(Je18) il. 16°, leath., $1.50 net. Fenno.
See also Larnard, C: E.

Goldingham, Arth. Hugh.
Design and construction of oil engines; with full directions for erecting, testing, installing, [etc.] 3d ed., rev. and enl. '10(Ap16) c. il. tabs., 12°, $2.50. Spon.
Gas engine in principle and practice. '08 (F8) c. il. 8°, *$1.50 net. Spon.

Goldman, Emma.
Anarchism and other essays; with a biographical sketch by Hippolyte Havel. '10(D31) D. $1 net. Mother Earth.

Goldmark, Josephine.
See Brandeis, L: D.

Goldsborough, Edm. Kennedy, jr.
Dream adventures of Little Bill. '10(Jl2) il. $1.25. B'way Pub.

Goldschmidt, Rudolf.
Alternating current commutator motor and The leakage of induction motors. In 1 v. '09. [1910.] (F) 220 p. il. 8°, *$3 net. Van Nostrand.

Goldsmith, Oliver.
Works; ed. by P: Cunningham; with a biograph. and critical introd. by Horatio Sheafe Krans. In 10 v. [The Turks' Head ed.] '08(Ag22) c. 10 v., il. por. 8°, **$50 net. Putnam.
Deserted village. '10(O15) col. il. Q. bds., $4.50 net, boxed. Dodd.
Good-natured man; a comedy. '10(N19) col. il. O. $2.50 net, boxed. Putnam.

Goldsmith, Oliver.—*Continued.*
Good-natured man; She stoops to conquer; ed., with introd. and notes, by T: H. Dickinson. '09(Ap10) c. por. D. (Riverside literature ser.) 40 c.; bound separately, ea., pap., 15 c. Houghton M.
Poems; with biographical and critical introd. by Horatio Sheafe Krans. '10(N12) c. il. O. $1.50 net. Putnam.
Poems and plays; ed. by Austin Dobson. '10(Ap2) 16°, (Everyman's lib.) 35 c. net; leath., 70 c. net. Dutton.
Selected essays; ed., with introd. and notes, by J. H. Lobban. '10(Ap2) S. (English literature for schools.) 40 c. net. Putnam.
She stoops to conquer; a comedy. '10 (N19) col. il. O. $2.50 net, boxed. Putnam.
Traveller and The deserted village; ed., with introd. and notes, by Horatio Nelson Drury. '09(Je19) c. por. 12°, (Twentieth century textbooks.) **30 c. net. Appleton.
Vicar of Wakefield; introd. by J. M. D. '08(Mr7) 16°, (Everyman's lib.) *35 c. net; leath., *70 c. net. Dutton.
Vicar of Wakefield. '08(O10) 12°, (Best books ser.) leath., *$1 net. Dutton.
Vicar of Wakefield. '10(D31) il. 8°, $1.50; leath., $2.50 net. Putnam.
See also Gray, T:

—, and Gray, T:
Goldsmith's The deserted village; Gray's Elegy in a country churchyard; ed., with introd. and notes, by Louise Pound. '10 (Ap9) c. S. (Standard English classics.) 25 c. Ginn.
Traveller, and The deserted village, and Gray's Elegy in a country churchyard; ed. by Rose M. Barton. '09(D18) pors. 12°, (English classics.) 25 c. Heath.
Traveller and Deserted village, also T: Gray's Elegy in a country churchyard; ed. by Warren Fenno Gregory. '09(N) c. 5+94 p. por. 16°, (Students' ser. of English classics.) 25 c. Sibley.

GOLDSMITH, Oliver.
Buckland, E. S. L. Oliver Goldsmith. *50 c. net. Macmillan.
Merington, M. Vicar of Wakefield; play founded on Oliver Goldsmith's novel. $1.25. Duffield.

Goldston, Will.
More tricks and illusions without mechanical apparatus. '10(D10) il. 12°, 50 c. Dutton.
Tricks and illusions for amateur and professional conjurors. '08(N21) il. 8°, *$1.25 net. Dutton.

Goldsmith, W: M.
Stones in a life. '08(Ag22) c. por. 12°, 65 c. W: M. Goldsmith.

Goldthwait, Ja. Wa.
Physical features of the Des Plaines Valley. '09, [1910.] (F) 10+103 p. il. maps, 8°, (Illinois, State Geological Survey bull.) pap. Univ. of Ill.

Goldthwait, Joel Ernest, M.D., Painter, C: Fairbank, M.D., and Osgood, Rob. Bayley, M.D.
Diseases of the bones and joints; clinical studies. '09(Ag) 7+13+685 p. il. 8°, $6. Heath.

GOLF.
Allerton, M., *and* Browning, R. Golf made easy. 35 c. net. Cassell.
Braid, J. Advanced golf. *$3 net. Jacobs.
Braid, J. Ladies' field golf book. *40 c. net. Scribner.
Fitch, G: Golf for the beginner. 35 c. Collier.
Haultain, T. A. Mystery of golf. $5. Houghton M.
Haultain, T. A. Mystery of golf. $1.75 net. Macmillan.
Kennedy, D. E. Golf in Sapphira's days. 60 c. Queen's Shop.
Official year book and directory of golf and automobiling, 1909. $5. Stettiner.
Simpson, H. Seven stages of golf: [pictures and verse.] *75 c. net. Lippincott.
Stoddard, W. L., *comp.* New golfer's almanac. **90 c. net. Houghton M.
Travis, W. Practical golf. *$2 net. Harper.
Vaile, P. A. Modern golf. *$2.25 net. Macmillan.
Whitlatch, M. Golf. $2 net. Outing.

GOLF LINKS.
See Lawns.

Golf rules as amended by N. Y. G. A., Feb. 17, 1909. [Pocket ed.] '09(Ap17) pap., 5 c. Lent & G.

Gollancz, Rev. Hermann.
Sermons and addresses; setting forth the teachings and spirit of Judaism. '09 (Ap10) royal 8°, *$3.60 net. Bloch.
—, tr. Translations from Hebrew and Aramaic; being The Targum to the Song of songs; The book of the apple; The ten Jewish martyrs; A dialogue on games of chance. '09(Ja23) 12°, *$2 net. Bloch.

Gollancz, Israel.
Pocket lexicon concordance to the Temple Shakespeare. '10(Je4) 16°, 60 c. net; leath., 75 c. Dutton.

Golliwogg books. 12 v. Upton, B. ea., $1 net. Longmans.

Golliwogg in the African jungle. Upton, B. $1.50. Longmans.

Gomez de Avellaneda y Arteaga, Gertrudis.
Baltasar: biblical drama in verse; ed., with introd., notes and vocab., by Carlos Bransby. '08(Ag22) c. S. 65 c. Am. Bk.

Gompers, S:
Injunction data filed by S: Gompers. '08 (Ag8) 8°, pap., 25 c. U. S., Supt. of Docs.
Labor in Europe and America; personal observations from an American viewpoint of life and conditions of working men in Great Britain, France, Holland, Germany, Italy, etc. '10(My14) c. por. O. $2 net. Harper.

Gompers, S:, and Gutstadt, Herman.
Meat, vs. rice: American manhood against Asiatic Coolieism; which shall survive?; published by American Federation of Labor; reprinted with introd. and appendices. '08(O10) O. pap. (Add. pubs. for price.) Asiatic Exclusion.

Goncourt, Edmond Louis Antonie Huot de.
Confidantes of a king; the mistresses of Louis xv.; tr. from the French by Ernest Dowson. In 2 v. '09(D11) il. 8°, *$4 special net. Appleton.

Gongaware, G: J., ed.
History of the First English Evangelical Lutheran church in Pittsburgh, 1837-1909. '09, [1910.] (F) c. 13+230 p. il. pors. plan, 8°, $1.
First Eng. Evan. Luth. Ch.

Gonnard, Philippe.
Exile of St. Helena, the last phase in fact and fiction; from the French of Philippe Gonnard. '09(N20) il. pors. O. *$3.50 net. Lippincott.

GONORRHEA.
See Syphilis;—Venereal diseases.

GONVILLE AND CAIUS COLLEGE, Cambridge University, Eng.
James, M. R. Descriptive catalogue of the manuscripts in the library of Gonville and Caius College. In 2 v. *$3.50 net. Putnam.

Gooch, Fk. Austin, and Browning, Philip Embury.
Outlines of qualitative chemical analysis. 2d ed., rev. '09(O30) 8°, **$1.25 net. Wiley.

Good, D. Clare.
See Pennsylvania. Index to cases.
—, ed. *See* Constables' guide.

Good, Ja. I:, D.D.
Famous places of the reformed churches; religious guidebook to Europe; together with a chapter by Rev. Marcus A. Brownson, *D.D.* '10(Jl30) il. pors. 12°, $1.50. Heidelberg.
See also Richards, G: W.

Good citizenship. Cleveland, S. G. 50 c. Altemus.

Good citizenship. Richman, J. 45 c. Am. Bk.

Good fellowship. Woolard, S: F., *comp.* *$1 net. Goldsmith-W.

GOOD FRIDAY.
Clow, W. M. Day of the cross. *$1.50 net. Doran.
Larrabee, E: A. Calls of the conqueror: Good Friday addresses. *60 c. net. Young Churchman.
Richardson, G. L. Travail of His soul: three hours' devotion for Good Friday. *60 c. net. Young Churchman.

Good health. Ravenbyrne, E. M. 30 c. Ainsworth.

Good health and good manners. Ravenbyrne, E. M. 25 c. Ainsworth.

Good health and how we won it. Sinclair, U. B., *jr.* **$1.20 net. Stokes.

Good Housekeeping lib. il. 8°. Phelps.
—Maddocks, M., *ed.* Good Housekeeping family cook book. 50 c.

Good Housekeeping manual of home handicraft. '08(Mr.) c. 144 p. il. 8°. (Add. pubs. for price.) Phelps.

Good housekeeping woman's home cook book. Curtis, *Mrs.* I. G., *comp.* 60 c. Reilly & B.

Good-living, a practical cookery-book. Van Buren, S. $2.50. Putnam.

Good-luck book. Bang, O., *ed.* $1. Brandu's.

Good manners for all occasions. Sangster, *Mrs.* M. E. M. $1.25. Cupples & L.

Good men and true. Rhodes, E. M. $1 net. Holt.

Good-natured man. *See* Goldsmith, Oliver.

Good-night stories. Parkhurst, L. F. 50 c. Eaton & M.

Good night stories. Sittig, *Mrs.* F. $1.50. Crombie & Co.

Good of life. Wilkinson, W: C. $1.25 net. Funk.

Good Roads Party from states of Arkansas, Oklahoma, Louisiana, Texas, on tour of inspection through eastern states. '10 (Je18) il. pors. D.
St. Louis and San Francisco R.R.

Good Shepherd. Body, G: *80 c. net. Whittaker.

Good Shepherd. Shaw, C. $1.50. Fenno.

Good Shepherd; narratives and poems for young people; collected and tr. by O. V. H. '09(N20) il. D. bds., 25 c. E. Kaufmann.

Good sport with famous packs. Bradley, C. $5 net. Dutton.

Good stories by Rudyard Kipling, Edg. Allan Poe, Washington Irving, Théophile Gautier, Rob. L: Stevenson, and others. '08(D12) c. 2 pt. in 1 v. por. D. †75 c. Doubleday, P.

Good sword Belgarde. Curtis, A. C: †$1.50. Dodd.

Good (The), the beautiful, the true. Brown, C: G. $1. C: G. Brown.

Good things to eat. Wilson, E. L. $3. Pub. Ho. of M. E. Ch., So.

Good things to eat and how to prepare them; more than two hundred and fifty choice recipes comp. especially for customers and friends of the Larkin Co. by the Larkin kitchen laboratory department. 9th ed., rev. '10(O) 78 p. il. 12°, pap., 15 c. Larkin.

Good value books. 8°, 50 c. Grosset.
—Habberton. Helen's babies.

Good wolf. Burnett, *Mrs.* F. H. **$1 net. Moffat.

Goodchild, Wilbert.
Precious stones; with a chapter on artificial stones by Rob. Dykes. '08(D5) il. 8°, (Westminster ser.) *$2 net. Van Nostrand.

Goodall, Agnes M.
Portugal. '09(D25) col. il. map, 12°, (Peeps at many lands.) *75 c. net. Macmillan.

Goodall, Edn., M.D.
See Savage, G. H:, *M.D.*

Goodell, G: Arth.
See Vulté, Hermann Thdr.

Goodenough, G: Alfr.
See Townsend, Edg. Jerome.

—, and Moore, Lewis Eug.
Strength of chain links. '07, [1909.] (Ap) 73 p. il. 8°, (Univ. of Ill. bull.; Engineering experiment station.) pap. (Add. University for price.) Univ. of Ill.

Goodhart, Ja. Frederic, M.D., and Still, G: Frederic, M.D.
Diseases of children. 9th ed. '10(Jl) 16+931 p. il. 8°, $5. Blakiston.

Goodloe, Abbe Carter.
The star-gazers. '10(O1) c. front. D. $1 net. Scribner.

Goodman, Frederic Simeon.
Evangelism through Bible study: plea for a winning method of enlisting men for Christian life. '09(O2) c. D. pap., *25 c. net. S. S. Times.

Goodman, Herbert Marcus.
Duration and disappearance of passive diphtheric immunity. '08, [1909.] (Je) 184-202 p. il. tabs., 8°, pap., 25 c. H. M. Goodman.
Experimental studies on diphtheric immunity. '08, [1909.] (Je) 509-540 p. tabs., 8°, pap., 25 c. H. M. Goodman.

Goodman, Paul.
Synagogue and the church: contribution to the apologetics of Judaism. '08(N21) 12°, *$1.50 net. Dutton.

Goodmann, Gustav.
Probate proceedings and administration of estates. '09(S11) c. S. bds., 25 c. G. Goodmann.

Goodnight, Scott Holland.
German literature in American magazines prior to 1846. '08(Je6) O. (Univ. of Wis. bull., Philology and literature ser.) pap., 50 c. Univ. of Wis.

Goodnow, Eliz.
The market for souls. '10(F) c. 155 p. D. *$1.25 net. M. Kennerley.

Goodnow, Fk. Johnson.
Municipal government. '09(S4) c. O. **$3 net. Century Co.

Goodrich, Alfr. J:
Music as a language; meaning of musical sounds; illustrated with characteristic examples from the works of Bach, Haendel, Gluck, Haydn, Mozart, Cherubini, Beethoven. [2d and rev. ed.] '09(Mr27) c. 8°, $1. Schirmer.

Goodrich, Arth. F:
Gleam o' dawn. '08(Je6) c. il. D. †$1.50. Appleton.
Lady without jewels. '09(Je12) c. D. †$1.50. Appleton.
The yardstick man. '10(O1) c. front. D. $1.50. Appleton.

Goodrich, Asa Stanley.
Normal class manual of Old Testament history. '08(Je27) c. 12°, *50 c. net. Revell.

Goodrich, C: Landon.
Profitable cotton farm. '09(O) 23 p. il. 8°, (U. S., Dept. of Agriculture: Farmer's bull.) pap. (Add. Superintendent for price.) U. S., Supt. of Docs.

Goodrich, Clarence Leon, and Stanley, Fk. Arth.
Accurate tool work. '09(Ja16) il. *$2 net. Hill Pub.
Automatic screw machines and their tools. '09(My1) il. 12°, *$2 net. Hill Pub.

Goodsell, Alfr. Taylor.
Vocalists' and pianists' companion: text book devoted to musical information. New rev. ed. '09(Ap10) c. Tt. leath., 50 c. A. T. Goodsell.

Goodsell, Bp. Dan. Ayres, Hingeley, Jos. B., and Buckley, Ja. Monroe, eds.
Doctrines and discipline of the Methodist Episcopal church, 1908. '08(O17) c. S. 30 c. Jennings.

Goodsell, Willystine.
Conflict of naturalism and humanism. '10 (N) 7+183 p. 8°, (Columbia Univ. contributions to education; Teachers' College ser.) $1.50. Teachers' Coll.

Goodson, G: Arth.
Electrical activities in the human body. '09 (Je12) c. il. D. 75 c. G: A. Goodson.

Goodspeed, Edg. Johnson.
Chicago literary papyri. '08(Ag29) c. 8°, pap., *50 c. net. Univ. of Chic.

Goodspeed, Fk. Lincoln.
"True aims of education"; Mills College founders' day, May 4, 1910. [1910.] (Ag) 16 p. 12°, pap., 15 c. F. L. Goodspeed.

Goodspeed, Weston Arth.
History of the Goodspeed family. '08(Ja18) il. tabs., 4°, hf. mor., $10; mor., $15. W. A. Goodspeed.

GOODSPEED FAMILY.
See Genealogies.

Goodwin, Elliot Hersey.
Merit system: letter in defense of the Civic League's detailed provision for a new city charter. '10(My7) 8°, 25 c. Civic League.

Goodwin, Emma E.
Course in sewing; pract. instruction in needlework for use in schools and at home. 3 v. '10(D10) c. il. 8°, $1.50. Beattys.

Goodwin, Fk. Elbert.
Cost accounting pathfinder. '10(My7) c. por. 12°, 50 c. Midland Pub. Co.

Goodwin, Harry Manly.
Elements of the precision of measurements and graphical methods. 2d ed. '08(Mr.) c. 79 p. diagrs., 8°, 85 c. Maclachlan.

Goodwin, Jos. H:
Improved book-keeping and business manual. 27th ed. 1909-1910. '09(Jl) c. 3-301 p. por. 4°, $3. J. H: Goodwin.

Goodwin, Mrs. Maud Wilder.
Veronica Playfair. '09(S25) c. il. D. $1.50. Little, B. & Co.
White aprons. '08(My.) c. 12°, (Popular ed. of recent fiction.) †75 c. Little, B. & Co.

Goodwin, Wilder.
The up grade. '10(Ja8) c. D. †$1.50. Little, B. & Co.

Goodwin, Rev. W: Archer Rutherford.
Bruton Parish Church restored, and its historic environment. 1907 memorial ed. '08(Ja11) il. plans, O. $2.61. W: A. R. Goodwin.

Goodyear, Lloyd E.
Progressive business accounting; elem. course in bookkeeping practice, forms and usages for commercial schools and individual reference. '10(F26) c. forms, 4°, $2. Waterloo.
See also Goodyear, S: H.

Goodyear, S: Horatio.
Goodyear's advanced accounting, with business practice by office and tablet methods. '10(Ja29) c. 24°, $1. Goodyear-M.

— and Lloyd E.
Higher accounting. '08(My16) c. forms, 8°, 90 c. Goodyear-M.
Modern inductive bookkeeping with business practice by office and tablet methods. Regular ed.—Theory introduction. '08 (My16) c. 90 c. Goodyear-M.
Railway accounting, with routine for office training. '08(My16) c. forms, 8°, 30 c. Goodyear-M.
Wholesale accounting. '08(My16) c. forms, 8°, 30 c. Goodyear-M.

Goodyear, W: H:
Desirable projection of art museums as suggested by the desirable classification of art libraries. '09, [1910.] (Ag) 93-115 p. 8°. (Priv. pr.) W: H: Goodyear.
Renaissance and modern art. '08(D12) c. il. 12°. *$1 net. Macmillan.

Gookin, F: W:
Our defective American banking system. '09(My1) 12°, (Club papers.) (Priv. pr.) Chic. Lit. Club.

Goold, Mary.
New England cook book. '09, [1910.] (Ja) c. 12°, 75 c. M. G. Buckley.

Goold, W: Dwight.
The dream-road, and other verses. '10 (O22) c. D. bds., $1 net. Sherman, F.

GOOSE.
See **Geese.**

Goose girl. MacGrath, H. †$1.50. Bobbs-M.

Goosie-gander rhymes. **Lowenheim, G. $1. Saalfield.**

Gorbach, August Bernhard.
Unter der mitternachtssonne; abenteuer aus dem leben der Klondyke-gold gräber. '08(O) c. 194 p. il. por. 12°. (Add. author for price.) A. B. Gorbach.

Gordon, Alex. Reid.
Early traditions of Genesis. '08(Mr14) O. $2.25. Scribner.

Gordon, Alfr.
Diseases of the nervous system. '08(N) c. 12+487 p. il. 8°, $2.50. Blakiston.

Gordon, Armistead Churchill.
Robin Aroon. '08(O17) c. D. *$1.25 net. Neale.
William Fitzhugh Gordon: his life, times and contemporaries, (1787-1858.) '10 (Ja15) c. por. O. *$3 net. Neale.

Gordon, Bertha F.
Overtones; little book of verses. '09, [1910.] (My) no paging, S. pap., 25 c. McClurg.

Gordon, C: H:
See Lindgren, Waldemar.

Gordon, C: W:, ["Ralph Connor."]
[Works.] Author's de luxe ed. in 6 v. [v. 1,] Black Rock; [v. 2,] The sky pilot. '08(N14) c. il. O. ea., $2. Revell.
Angel and the star. '08(N7) c. il. D. *50 c. net; pap., *25 c. net, in envelope. Revell.
Beyond the marshes. '09(D11) c. front. D. pap., *25 c. net, in envelope. Revell.
Dawn by Galilee; story of the Christ. '10 (F12) c. col. il. 12°, 35 c. Doran.
The foreigner; tale of Saskatchewan. '09 (N20) c. D. $1.50. Doran.
Life of James Robertson, missionary superintendent in the northwest territories. '08 (D26) c. il. O. *$1.50 net. Revell.
Recall of love; message of hope. '10(D10) il. in col. D. pap.., 35 c. net; bds., 50 c. net. Doran.

Gordon, Eliz. M.
Mighty hunter in Toyland. '08(O3) c. il. obl. O. bds., $1. Dodd

Gordon, G: Angier, D.D.
Beatrice, the insight of love. '10(D31) c. D. bds., 50 c.. Pilgrim Press.
Claims of the ministry on strong men. '09 (Mr) 19 p. 12°, (Claims and opportunities of the Christian ministry.) 10 c. Y. M. C. A.
Crossing the bar: lyric of life everlasting. '09(N13) D. bds., *50 c. net. Pilgrim Press.
The great assurance. '10(Mr12) c. D. bds., *50 c. net. Pilgrim Press.
Land of pure delight. '08, [1909.] (Mr) c. 24 p. 12°, *35 c. net. Pilgrim Press.
Religion and miracle. New and enl. ed. '10(N5) c. D. $1.30 net. Houghton M.
Sure and living faith. '08(O10) c. D. (What is worth while ser.) bds., **30 c. net. Crowell.

GORDON, George Angier, D.D.
Record and celebration by the Old South Church and society of the 25th anniversary of the installation of Rev. George A. Gordon, D.D., April, 1909. '09(O) 144 p. 8°, 50 c. Univ. Press, (Camb.)

Gordon, H. Laing, M.D.
Modern mother; guide to girlhood, motherhood and infancy. '09(O23) il. O. $2. Fenno.

Gordon, Hanford Lennox.
Indian legends, and other poems. '10 (Jl16) c. pors. 8°, $1.50. Salem Press.
Laconics. '10(S) c. 209 p. por. 8°, $1.50. Salem Press.

Gordon, H: Evarts, ed.
See Trueblood, T: Clarkson, *ed.*

Gordon, Ja.
Old plantation, and other poems. '09(Ag) 166 p. por. 12°, $1.25. J. Gordon.

Gordon, J: Houston.
Experiments in supplemental irrigation with small water supplies in Cheyenne, Wyo., in 1909. '10(Je) 11 p. il. 8°, (U. S., Dept. of Agriculture; Office of Experiment Stations, circular.)

Gordon, Kate.
Esthetics. '09(O30) c. D. $1.50. **Holt.**

GORDON, Leon.
Rhine, A. B. Leon Gordon; an appreciation. 75 c. Jewish Pub.

Gordon, Lina Duff, [Mrs. Aubrey Waterfield.]
Home life in Italy; letters from the Apennines. '08(O24) il. 12°, *$1.75 net. Macmillan.

Gordon, Mrs. Mary Kilgore.
See Gordon, *Rev.* S. Dickey.

Gordon, Mary Lindsay.
Cinderella owl book. '07, [1909.] (Jl) il. in col. 16°, bds., 50 c. Jacobs.

Gordon, Rev. S: Dickey.
Crowding out the Christ-child; quiet talk. '10(D10) c. D. (Idyll envelope ser.) pap., 25 c. net, in envelope. Revell.
Quiet talks about the tempter. '10(S17) c. 16°, 75 c. net. Revell.
Quiet talks with world winners. '08(D5) c. D. **75 c. net. Armstrong.

— and Mrs. Mary Kilgore.
Quiet talks on home ideals. '09(D11) c. D. *75 c. net. Revell.
The quietest talk; footnote to Quiet talks on home ideals. '10(Ap9) c. 16°, pap., 10 c. net. Revell.

Gordon, Selden Smith.
Gordon's work on cutting men's garments, complete treatise on the art and science of delineating all garments for men, especially prepared for self-instruction. '10 (My) c. 176 p. il. 8°, $10. S. S. Gordon.
"Standard" work on cutting ladies' tailor-made garments. Rev. ed. '08(Ap.) c. 224 p. il. f°, $10. J: J. Mitchell.

Gordon, W. J.
Our home railways [English]; how they began and how they are worked. '10 (D10) il. (partly col.) 8°, 2 v., $4.50 net; hf. mor., $7.50 net. Warne.

Gordon, W: Andrew.
Gordon's Texas corporation manual. [1910.] (O) c. 92 p. O. W: A. Gordon.

GORDON, William Fitzhugh.
Gordon, A. C. William Fitzhugh Gordon, a Virginian of the old school. *$3 net. Neale.

Gordon, Winifred.
Book of days. '09(O2) 24°, *60 c. net. Dutton.

Gordy, Wilbur Fisk.
American leaders and heroes; preliminary text-book in United States history. Indiana ed. '09(O23) c. il. maps, 12°, 60 c. Scribner.
Colonial days: hist. reader. '08(D5) c. il. maps, 12°, *50 c. net. Scribner.
Elem. hist. of the United States. '09, [1910.] (My) c. 17+315 p. il. pors. maps, 12°, 65 c. net. Scribner.

Gore, Bp. C:
New Theology and the old religion. '08 (F8) 12°, *$2 net. Dutton.
Orders and unity. '10(F19) 12°, *$1.35 net. Dutton.

Gore, Herbert C:
Apparatus for use in the determination of volatile acids in wines and vinegars. '09 (O) 2 p. il. 8°, (U. S., Dept. of Agriculture, Bu. of Chemistry; circular.) pap.

Gore, Ja. Howard, comp.
American members of foreign orders. '10 (D17) c. O. $2. W. F. Roberts.

Gore-Booth, Eva.
See Booth, Eva Gore-.

Gorgas, Ferdinand Ja. S:
Dental medicine; manual of dental materia medica and therapeutics. 8th ed., rev. and enl. '09(Je) 10+627 p. il. 8°, $4. Blakiston.

Gorgas, W: Crawford, M.D.
Annual rept. of the Department of Sanitation of the Isthmian Canal Commission for the year 1907. '08(Je.) 78 p. D. pap., 15 c. U. S., Supt. of Docs.

Gorgeous Borgia. McCarthy, J. H. †$1.50. Harper.

Gorgeous isle. Atherton, *Mrs.* G. F. H. **90 c. special net. Doubleday, P.

Gorham, Fs.
Lone trail at thirty: [poems.] '09(Ap24) nar. O. $1. Black Lion.

Goring-Thomas, A. R.
Mrs. Gramercy-Park. '09(Je26) D. $1.50. Lane.

Górky, Maxim, [pseud. for Alexéi Maximovitch Pyeschkôff.]
The spy; author. tr. by T: Seltzer. '08 (D5) c. D. $1.50. B: W. Huebsch.
Tales from Gorky. '10(D) 12°, (Wayside lib.) limp. leath., $1. Brentano's.

Gorse, F.
School algebra course. In 3 pts. pt. 1, To simple simultaneous equations, with appendix; pt. 2, Factors to quadratic equations, with appendix; pt. 3, Surds to the binominal theorem, with appendix. '08 (F1) 8°, bds., ea., *25 c. net. Putnam.

Gorsline, Ernest Elisha.
Study of the Claisen condensation. '08, [1910.] (Ap) 54 p. 8°, pap., 55 c. Johns Hopkins.

Gorst, Sir J: Eldon.
New Zealand revisited: recollections of the days of my youth. '08(Ag29) il. 12°, *$4 net. Pitman.

Gorton, F: Russell.
High school course in physics. '10(O8) il. pors. 12°, (Twentieth century text-books.) $1.25. Appleton.

Gortzis, Nicholas.
See Vlasto, Solon J.

Gosling's picnic. Jewett, J: H. 75 c. Small.

Gospel and human needs. Figgis, J: N. *$1.25 net. Longmans.

Gospel and the church. Loisy, A. *$1 net. Scribner.

Gospel and the modern man. Mathews, S. $1.50 net. Macmillan.

Gospel at work in modern life. Whitaker, R. 50 c. net. Griffith.

Gospel cheer messages. Swift, P. H. *$1.25 net. Jennings.

Gospel for to-day. Garvie, A. E. $1.50 net. Doran.

Gospel in athletic phrases. Waite, R: A., *jr.* 25 c. Y. M. C. A.

Gospel in Latin lands. Clark, F. E: **50 c. net. Macmillan.

Gospel in literature. Greene, J. N. 75 c. Jennings.

Gospel in the church. Gwynne, W. 40 c. Gorham.

Gospel lessons and life history. Sewell, E. G. *$1.15 net. McQuiddy.

Gospel of freedom. Herrick, R. $1.50. Macmillan.

Gospel of good health. Brown, C: R. *75 c. net; *35 c. net. Pilgrim Press.

Gospel of grace. Jones, J: D. *$1.25 net. Doran.

Gospel of greed. McDermott, C: H. $1. Chapple Pub.

Gospel of Jesus the Son of God. Knox, G: W: 50 c. Houghton M.

Gospel of optimism. Lacey, T: J. $1. Red Diamond.

Gospel of pain. Hardy, T: J: *$1.25 net. Macmillan.

Gospel of reconciliation. Walker, W: L. *$2 net. Scribner.

Gospel of the hereafter. Paterson-Smyth, J: $1 net. Revell.

Gospel of the kingdom. Savage, H: E: $3.50. Longmans.

Gospel of the left hand. Young, D. T. *$1.25 net. Doran.

Gospel songs. Alexander, C: M., *comp.* *15 c. net; *30 c. net. Revell.

GOSPELS.
See Bible.

Goss, C: Frederic, D.D.
That other hand upon the helm. '10(D17) c. 12°, 75 c. Jennings.

Goss, W: Freeman Myrick.
Comparative tests of run-of-mine and briquetted coal on locomotives, incl. torpedo-boat tests and some foreign specifications for briquetted fuel. '09(Mr6) il. 8°, (U. S. Dept. of the Interior, Geol. Survey, bull.) 15 c.

High steam-pressures in locomotive service. '08(F29) il. tabs., O. (Carnegie Institution of Washington pubs.) pap., $1.25. Carnegie.

Superheated steam in locomotive service. '10(D31) tabs., diagrs., fold. diagrs., Q. pap., $1.25. Carnegie.

Utilization of fuel in locomotive practice. '09(D) 28 p. il. 8°, (U. S., Dept. of the Interior, Geological Survey, bull.) (Add. Superintendent for price.)

Gossamer thread. Seibert, V. $1 net. Small.

Gosse, Edm. W.
Henrik Ibsen. '08(F1) c. D. (Literary lives.) **$1 net. Scribner.
See also Garnett, R:

Gosselin, Louis Léon Théodore, ["G. Lenôtre."]
Daughter of Louis XVI., Marie Thérèse-Charlotte de France, Duchess d'Angoulême; tr. by J. Lewis May. '08(Ag1) por. O. *$4 net. Lane.

Gascon royalist in revolutionary Paris; [tr.] from the French by Mrs. Rodolph Stowell. '10(D10) il. 8°, $3.50 net. Dodd.

Romances of the French Revolution. 2 v. il. 8°, *$6 net. Brentano's.

Tribunal of the terror; study of Paris in 1793-1795; from the French by F: Lees. '10(F19) il. facsim., pors. 8°, *$3.50 net. Lippincott.

Gossip, G: Hatfield Dingley.
See Trepoff, Ivan, *pseud.*

Gostling, Mrs. Frances M. Parkinson.
Bretons at home; with an introd. [in French] by Anatole Le Braz. '09(S25) il. O. *$2.50 net. McClurg.

Gotch, Fs.
Two Oxford physiologists: Richard Lower, 1631 to 1691; John Mayow, 1643 to 1679. '08(Ag15) pors. 8°, (Oxford Univ. Extension Summer Meeting, 1907.) pap., 35 c. Oxford Univ.

Gotch, Fk.
Wrestling and how to train. '08(Jl) c. 163 p. pors. 16°, (Fox's athletic lib.) pap., 10 c. R: K. Fox.

Gotch, J: Alfr.
Growth of the English house; short hist. of its architectural development from 1100 to 1800. '10(Mr26) il. O. *$3 net. Scribner.

Gotham and other stories. Stone, E. D. *40 c. net. Macmillan.

GOTHIC ARCHITECTURE.
See Architecture.

GOTHIC LANGUAGE.
Wright, J. Grammar of the Gothic language, and the Gospel of St. Mark; selections from the Second Epistle to Timothy. $1.75. Oxford Univ.
See also Language.

GOTHS.
Jordanes. Origin and deeds of the Goths. 50 c. C: C. Mierow.

Gott und sein volk. Anschütz, E: $1.50. Germ. Bapt.

Gottes botschaft an die menscheit; die Bibel in predigten dargelegt. por. 8°. Germ. Bapt.

—Anschütz. Gott und sein volk. $1.50.

Gottheil, Rev. Gustav.
Sun and shield: book of devout thoughts for every day use. '09(Ja9) 16°, *$1 net. Bloch.

Gottschalk, Louis Moreau.
Piano compositions. In 2 v. v. 1; with biog. introd. by W: Arms Fisher. '08 (D5) c. Q. (Ditson's dollar books of piano music.) pap., $1. Ditson.

Gottschall, Amos H.
Abolished rites; or, spiritual, not ceremonial worship. 8th ed. '10(F26) c. 16°, 75 c. A. H. Gottschall.

—, **comp.** Visions of heaven and hell; what men and women claim to have seen in the world beyond; gleaned from various works. '10(F26) c. 16°, 75 c. A. H. Gottschall.

Gotty and the gov'ner. Copping, A. E. $1.50. M. Kennerley.

Gotty in furrin parts. Copping, A. E. $1.50. M. Kennerley.

Goucher, J: Franklin, D.D.
Christianity and the United States. '08 (Jl4) c. por. D. *50 c. net. Eaton & M.

Goudy, H:
Trichotomy in Roman law. '10(D3) O. $1.35. Oxford Univ.

Gould, Alfr. Pearce.
Elements of surgical diagnosis. Enl. ed. [1910.] (My) 600 p. 8°, $2 net. Funk.

Gould, C: Newton.
Geography of Oklahoma. '09(O) c. 13+178 p. il. fold. map, 12°, 75 c. Bunn.

Gould, Eliz. Lincoln.
Admiral's little housekeeper. '10(D3) c. il. D. $1. Penn Pub. Co.
Barbara and the five little Purrs. '08(O31) il. D. 75 c. Caldwell.
Felicia. '08(O3) c. il. D. $1. Penn Pub. Co.
Felicia visits. '10(D3) c. D. $1 net. Penn Pub. Co.
Felicia's friends. '09(N13) c. D. †$1. Penn Pub. Co.

Gould, Ezra Palmer.
Biblical theology of the New Testament. '09(Ap3) 12°, (New Testament handbooks.) Price raised from *75 c. net. to *$1 net. Macmillan.

Gould, F. J.
Conduct stories: volume of stories for the moral instruction of children; issued by the Normal Education League of London. '10(Ap9) 12°, $1. Macmillan.

Gould, G: Milbry, M.D.
Biographic clinics: essays concerning the influence of visual function, pathologic and physiologic, upon the health of patients. v. 6. '09(N) 8+492 p. 12°, *$1 net. Blakiston.
Bibliography of the contributions of G: M. Gould, M.D., to ophthalmology, general medicine, literature, etc. '09(N) 62 p. O. pap., gratis. Andrus.
Borderland studies. v. 2, Miscellaneous addresses and essays pertaining to medicine and the medical profession. '08(S5) c. D. $2. Blakiston.
Concerning Lafcadio Hearn; with a bibliography by Laura Stedman. '08(My9) c. por. D. **$1.50 net. Jacobs.
Illustrated dict. of medicine, biology and allied sciences. 6th ed., with additions and corrections and a supp. incl. upwards of 38,000 additional words based upon recent scientific literature. '10(S) 16+17-1633+571 p. il. 4°, mor., $14. Blakiston.
The Infinite Presence. '10(O1) c. D. $1.50 net. Moffat.
Pocket medical dict.; giving the pronunciation and definition of the principal words used in medicine and the collateral sciences. 5th ed. '09, [1910.] (F) 7+9-863 p. 16°, leath., *$1 net; thumb index, *$1.25 net. Blakiston.
Practitioner's medical dict. 2d ed., rev. '10 (N) 16+1043 p. il. 8°, flex. leath., $4; with thumb index, $4.50. Blakiston.
Righthandedness and lefthandedness. '08 (Je6) c. il. D. **$1.25 net. Lippincott.
See also Stedman, Laura.

Gould, Harris Perley.
Fruit growing for home use in the central and southern Great Plains. '10(My) 23 p. il. 8°, (U. S., Dept. of Agriculture, Bu. of Plant Industry, circular.)

Gould, Ja.
Treatise on the principles of pleading; comprising rules of practice and a description of forms of action and adapted to the modern codes of procedure. 6th ed., by Arth. P. Will. '09(Mr) c. 66+634 p. O. $6.50. Banks & Co.

Gould, Jos.
Story of the 48th: record of campaigns of the 48th regiment Pa. Veteran Volunteer Infantry during the four eventful years of its service in the war for the preservation of the Union. '08(N) c. 471 p. il. pors. 8°, $4. J. Gould.

Gould, Sabine Baring-.
See Baring-Gould, Sabine.

Gould, W. Reid.
Greater New York and state lawyers' diary for 1908. '08(F); 1909. '09(Ja); 1910. '10(F) c. S. ea., $1. W. R. Gould.

Goulder, W: Armistead.
Reminiscences; incidents in the life of a pioneer in Oregon and Idaho. '09(My) c. 376 p. por. 12°, $3. T. Regan.

Gouraud, Aimée Crocker, [Mrs. Jackson Gouraud.]
Moon madness and other fantasies. '10 (D31) c. por. D. $1. B'way Pub.

Gouraud, Mrs. Jackson.
See Gouraud, Aimée Crocker.

Gourlay, C:
Construction of a house; presented by means of a set of 40 plates containing plans and detail drawings, with letterpress, of a design for a country house, incl. motor house and chauffeur's lodge. '10(N19) F. $2.75 net. Lane.

Gourley, Reginald.
See Adventures of pirates.

Gourley, S: Birch.
Colloquy, and other poems. Souvenir ed. '09(Ap10) c. por. O. pap., boxed. (Add. author for price.) S: B. Gourley.

GOURLEY FAMILY.
See Genealogies: Heydecker, C. T.

Gourmet's guide to Europe. Newnham-Davis, N. *$1.50 net. Brentano's.

Gourmet's guide to London. Newnham-Davis, N. *$1.50 net. Brentano's.

GOURNIA, Crete.
See Crete (*Island of*).

GOUT.
Strauss, H. Gout. $1. Treat.
See also Arthritis;—Metabolism.

Governance of empire. Silburn, P. A. B. $3 net. Longmans.

GOVERNMENT.
See Colonial government;— Municipal government; —Political science;—*also* names of countries, states and places.

Government by influence. Brown, E. E. $1.25 net. Longmans.

Government cook book; economical use of meat in the home, by C. F. Langworthy and Caroline L. Hunt, and Preparation of vegetables for the table, by Maria Parloa. '10(O22) 4°, (Eagle lib.) pap., 10 c. Brooklyn Eagle.

Government employ. Chase, F. N. 15 c. F. N. Chase.

GOVERNMENT LAND.
See Land.

Government of the District of Columbia. Dodd, W. F. $1.50. Byrne.

Government of the people of the state of Michigan. King, J. A. 50 c. Hinds.

GOVERNMENT OWNERSHIP.
Bigelow, J: Substitute for the tariff upon imports and a provision for an equitable distribution of the wealth of nations. (Priv. pr.) J: Bigelow.
Sells, E. W. Corporate management compared with government control. gratis. Haskins & S.
Van Wagener, A. Government ownership of railways. $1.25. Putnam.
See also Carriers;—Railroads.

Government positions. Hopkins, E. P. 25 c. Wash. Civil Service.

Government reclamation work in foreign countries. Gray, E: D. M. (Add. Superintendent for price.) U. S., Supt. of Docs.

Government regulation of the Elizabethan drama. Gildersleeve, V. C. *$1.25 net. Lemcke.

Governmental action for social welfare. Jenks, J. W. $1 net. Macmillan.

Governor and the boss. Bragdon, G. F. 25 c. J. S. Ogilvie.

Governor's special message transmitting the rept. of the Commission on Occupational Diseases to the Forty-Sixth General Assembly, April, 1900. '10(Ap2) O. pap., gratis. Ill. State Journ.

Governors (The). Oppenheim, E: P. †$1.50. Little, B. & Co.

Governors of Maryland. Buchholz, H. E. $2.50. Williams & W.

Gow, W:
Marine insurance; hdbk. [4th ed., rev. and enl.] '10(Ap9) D. (Elem. commercial class-books.) $1.10 net. Macmillan.

Gowans, Adam L., comp.
Characteristic passages from the hundred best English prose writers. '10(Ag6) c. por. S. (Handy volume classics, pocket ed.) 35 c. Crowell.

Gowdy, Chestine.
English grammar. '09(Jl) 8+293 p. 12°, 80 c. Allyn & B.

Gowen, Rev. Herbert H:
Hawaiian idylls of love and death. '08 (Ag29) c. front. O. $1. Cochrane.
Revelation of "the things that are": an exposition of Revelation IV. and V. '08 (N7) c. D. *50 c. net. Whittaker.

Gower, Rowland, Lord Sutherland-.
See Sutherland-Gower, Rowland, *Lord.*

Gowing, Clara.
Alcotts as I knew them. '10(Ja1) c. il. por. 12°, $1.25. C. M. Clark.

GOWRIE CONSPIRACY.
Skotlands rimur: Icelandic ballads on the Gowrie conspiracy. $1.15. Oxford Univ.

Goya y Lucientes, Francisco.
Masterpieces. '09(D25) il. 24°, (Painters' ser.) leath., *75 c. net; pap., *25 c. net. Stokes.

GOYA Y LUCIENTES, Francisco.
Calvert, A. F: Goya. *$1.25 net. Lane.

Grabau, Amadeus W:, and Shimer, Hervey Woodburn.
North American index fossils, invertebrates. In 2 v. v. 1.. '09(D); v. 2. '10 (O15) c. il. 8°, ea., $6 net. Seiler.

Grabill, Ethelbert Warren.
Mechanics of piano technic. '09(Je12) c. il. D. $1.25. A. W. Hunt.

GRACE.
See Salvation.

Grace abounding. *See* Bunyan, J:

Grace Harlowe's plebe year at high school. Flower, J. G. $1. Altemus.

Grace's earthwork tables for calculating the cubical contents of cuttings. '08(Jl4) 4°, $5. Spon.

Gracie and her pets. Hunter, M. L. 75 c. Cochrane.

GRACILARIOPHILA.
See Parasites.

Graded art readers. il. D. Ginn.
—Cyr. Story of three great artists. 50 c.

Graded dictation. Rasmussen, W. $1. Gregg Pub.

Graded games. Newton, M. B. **$1.25 net. Barnes.

Graded Sunday-school in principle and practice. Meyer, H: H. 75 c. net. Eaton & M.

Graded supplementary reading ser. *See* Merrill's.

"Grades of steel." Parrock, H. P. $1. H. P. Parrock.

Grading simplified: teacher's aid. Webb, L. T. 75 c. Hackney.

Grady, B: Franklin.
Sectionalism and some of its fruits. '09 (N) 40 p. 8°, 25 c. B: F. Grady.

Grady, H: Woodfin.
Complete orations and speeches. '10(Ap16) $1.50. South-West Pub.

Graefe, Julius A. Meyer-.
See Meier-Graefe, Julius A.

Graetz, Heinrich.
Hist. of the Jews. De luxe ed. 6 v. [1910.] (My) 8°, per set, $18. Jewish Pub.

Grafoni. Hitlofi, I. 50 c. I. Hitlofi.

GRAFTING.
Couts, C: O. Cleft grafting. 50 c. C: O. Couts.

Grafton, Bp. C: Chapman.
Catholic atlas; digest of Catholic theology. '08(F8) c. Q. **$2.50 net. Longmans.
Christian and Catholic. [3d ed.] '10 (F19) c. D. **$1.50 net. Longmans.
Journey Godward of Doulos Iesou Christou, (a servant of Jesus Christ.) '10 (F19) il. pors. O. $2.50. Young Churchman.

Grafton historical ser.; ed. by F. H. Hitchcock and H: R: Stiles. il. 12°. Grafton Press.
—Carpenter. Roger Williams. **$2 net.
—Ridgely. Historic graves of Maryland and the District of Columbia. **$2 net.
—Taylor. Witchcraft delusion in colonial Connecticut. **$1.50 net.
—Weeden. Early Rhode Island. $2.50.

Grafton medical books. il. 8°. Grafton Press.
—Kolle. Subcutaneous hydrocarbon protheses. **$2.50 net.

Graham, —, rep.
See Georgia. *Ct. of appeals.* Repts.—*Sup. ct.* Repts.

Graham, Alb. B.
Centralized schools in Ohio. '09, [1910.] (Je) 24 p. il. maps, 8°, (Ohio State Univ., Agricultural College extension bull.) pap., gratis. A. B. Graham.
Country schools of Ohio. '10(N) 40 p. il. maps, 8°, (Ohio State Univ., Agricultural College Extension bull.) Ohio State Univ.

Graham, D: Wilkie.
Way to win, and other poems. '09(Ja) 126 p. 12°, $1.10. B'way Pub.

Graham, E: Arth. Pancras.
Mystery of Naples. '09(O) 9+349 p. il. 8°, $1.50. Herder.

"Graham, Ennis," pseud.
See Molesworth, *Mrs.* Mary Louise Stewart.

Graham, Harry J. C., ["Col. D. Streamer."]
Bolster book: book for the bedside; (compiled from the occasional writings of Reginald Drake Biffin.) '10(S3) D. $1.50 net. Duffield.
Deportmental ditties. '09(D4) c. il. D. bds., $1. Duffield.
Group of Scottish women. '08(O17) il. 8°, *$3.50 net. Duffield.

Graham, Harry Jefferson.
Civil service self-instructor. '08(Ja18) il. tabs., 8°, $2.50. H. J. Graham.

Graham, H: Grey.
Literary and historical essays. '08(My2) por. 8°, *$2 net. Macmillan.
Scottish men of letters of the eighteenth century. '08(N21) pors. 8°, *$2 net. Macmillan.

Graham, Ja.
See Hooper, F:

—, and Oliver, G: A. S.
French commercial practice connected with the export and import trade to and from France, the French colonies, and the countries where French is the recognized language of commerce. pt. 2. '08(O24) 12°, *$1 net. Macmillan.

Graham, J:, and Clark, Ellery Harding.
Pract. track and field athletics. '10(My21) c. il. pors. 8°, $1. Duffield.

Graham, Rev. J: E.
Mere hints, moral and social. '10(O22) c. O. $1. Mercy.

Graham, Llewellyn J., rep.
See Kansas. *Sup. ct.* Repts.

Graham, Stephen.
Vagabond in the Caucasus, with some notes of his experiences among the Russians. '10(N5) il. maps, O. $4 net. Lane.

Graham, T: W.
Universal foot ball and hand ball: rules of the game revised. 2d ed.; with an appendix containing rules, diagram and other descriptional matter rel. to foot base ball, by the same author. '08(My9) c. il. O. pap., 20 c. T: W. Graham.

Graham, W: Jos.
Romance of life insurance; its past, present and future, with particular reference to the epochal investigation era of 1905-1908. '09, [1910.] (Ja) c. 271 p. il. por. 12°, $1.50. World To-day.

Graham, Rev. W: S.
Divine praises; addresses to Holy Name societies. '09(Mr) c. '08. 113 p. 8°, *75 c. net. Wagner.
Duty; twelve conferences to young men. '10(D3) c. 8°, 75 c. Wagner.
Fruits of the devotion to the Sacred Heart; course of sermons for the first Fridays. '10(Mr12) c. 12°, 75 c. Wagner.
Phases of the sacred passion: Lenten course. '09(My) c. 58 p. 8°, pap., *40 c. net. Wagner.

Graham-Smith, G: Stuart, ed.
See Nuttall, G: H:

GRAHAM FAMILY.
See Genealogies, Walker, A. K.

Grahame, Kenneth.
Wind in the willows. '08(O17) c. front. D. †$1.50. Scribner.

GRAIN.
Atwater, J. American grain computator. $3.50. Atwater.
See also Cereals;—Corn;—Milo.

GRAIN ITCH.
See Straw itch.

Grainger, Fs. E:, ["Headon Hill."]
The avengers. '08(Ap11) c. 12°, (Popular priced copyrights.) 50 c. B. W. Dodge.
Epsom mystery. '08(Mr7) front. D. *$1 net. Fenno.
Hate of man. '08(D12) front. 12°, $1.50. Cassell.
Monksglade mystery. '10(Je18) il. D. $1.50. Fenno.
One who saw. '08(Ap11) il. 12°, (Popular priced copyrights.) 50 c. B. W. Dodge.
Traitor's wooing. '09(S4) front. D. $1.50. Kearney.
Unmasked at last. '09(F13) front. D. *$1 net. Fenno.

Grainger, M. Allerdale.
Woodsmen of the West. '08(N14) il. O. $2.50. Longmans.

GRAMMAR.
See names of languages.

Grammar of lettering. Lyons, A. W. *$2.50 net. Lippincott.
Grammar school geography. Frye, A. E. pt. 1, 80 c. Ginn.

Grampp, Otto.
Practical enameler; manual for self-instruction for those engaged or interested in the trade, giving the latest and most approved methods of enameling sheet-steel and cast iron ware. '10(Je18) $10. D: Williams.

GRANADA, Spain.
Calvert, A. F: Granada: present and bygone. *$2.50 net. Dutton.
Irving, W. Chronicle of the conquest of Granada. 35 c. Oxford Univ.

Granbery, J: Cowper.
Outline of New Testament Christology; study of genetic relationships within the Christology of the New Testament period. '10(My7) 8°, (Univ. of Chic. historical and linguistic studies in literature rel. to the New Testament, 2d ser.) 50 c. Univ. of Chic.

Grand Army flag day, Rhode Island, February twelfth, 1909. '09(Ap) 51 p. por. 8°. (Add. pub. for price.) R. I. Dept. Educ.

Grand Army man. O'Higgins, H. J. †$1.50. Century Co.

Grand Army of the Republic. *Dept. of Georgia.* Services in commemoration of the 100th anniversary of the birth of Abraham Lincoln, arranged by Union and Confederate veterans under the auspices of O. M. Mitchel Post no. 1, Trinity Methodist Episcopal Church South, Atlanta, Ga., Feb. 14, 1909. '09(Ag) 48 p. por. 8°. (Add. pubs. for price.) D. I. Carson.

Grand Army of the Republic. *Dept. of Massachusetts. John A. Rawlins Post, no.* 43. Story of the John Brown bell. [1910.] (S) 19 p. il. pors. 8°, 25 c. J: A. Rawlins Post.

GRAND CANYON, Arizona.
James, G: W. Grand Canyon of Arizona. $1.50 net. Little, B. & Co.
See also Colorado river.

Grande (La) semaine. Favreau, J. A. $1.25. Belisle Pr.

Grandin, Egbert H:, Jarman, G: Wallace, M.D., and Marx, Simon.
Text-book on practical obstetrics by Egbert H: Grandin, with the collaboration of G: W. Jarman and Simon Marx. 4th ed., rev. and enl. '09(Je) c. 16+538 p. il. 8°, $4. Davis.

Grandma's cook book. Lloyd, *Mrs.* E. B. $1.25. Jennings.

Grandmother Goose stories. *See* Jewett, J: Howard.

Grandmother's favorite ser. 6 v. [1910.] (F) il. 12°, ea., 75 c. Dutton.
Contents: Birthday present, retold by Olive Allen; Fairchild family, retold by Jeanie Lang; Margot and the goldfish, retold by Amy Steedman; Holiday House, retold by Olive Allen; Apple pie, retold by Amy Steedman.

Grandpa's little girls and their friends. Curtis, A. T. †$1. Penn Pub. Co.

Grandpa's little girls at school. Curtis, A. T. †$1. Penn Pub. Co.

Grandpa's little girls' house-boat party. Curtis, A. T. $1. Penn Pub. Co.

Granger, Anna D.
Skat and how to play it. '08(D12) 12°, $1. Brentano's.

Granger, I. P.
Law of liberty. '10(Je11) c. D. pap., 20 c. I. P. Granger.

GRANITE.
Dale, T: N. Chief commercial granites of Massachusetts, New Hampshire and Rhode Island. (Add. Superintendent for price.) U. S., Supt. of Docs.
Dale, T: N. Granites of Vermont. Gov. Pr. Off.

Grant, Mrs. Anne Macvicar.
Memoirs of an American lady. New and cheaper ed. '09(D) 8°, *$2.50 net. Dodd.

Grant, Arth. Hastings, comp.
List of defunct municipal lighting plants. 3d ed., rev. and enl. '08(Ap) c. 31 p. 8°, pap., 40 c. Municipal Ownership.

Grant, C. M., D.D.
Between the Testaments. '09(O2) 12°, *75 c. net. Revell.

Grant, Mrs. Colquhoun.
Louise Renée de Kérouaile, Duchess of Portsmouth. '09(D11) il. pors. 8°, *$4 special net. Appleton.
Quaker and courtier: life and work of William Penn. '08(F22) il. 8°, *$3.50 net. Dutton.

Grant, Mrs. Ethel.
See Mumford, Ethel Watts-.

GRANT, James.
Dowd, W. B. James Grant, a model American. 75 c. Riverdale Press.

Grant, J: Wesley.
Out of the darkness: [story of negro life.] '09(Je5) c. O. $1.10. Nat. Bapt. Pub.

Grant, J: W: Davis.
How to market ability: a pract. treatise on employment, telling how advertising methods may be applied to the securing of positions. '08(O10) c. D. pap., 50 c. Advancement Co.

Grant, Mary Leonard.
See Buchanan, Frances Grant.

Grant, Percy Stickney, D.D.
Observations in Asia. '09(Ap24) c. D. bds., **$1.25 net. Brentano's.
Search of Belisarius. '08(F8) c. D. bds., **$1.50 net. Brentano's.

Grant, Rob.
The Chippendales. '09(Ap10) c. D. $1.50. Scribner.

GRANT, *General* Ulysses Simpson.
Cannon, J. G. Speech of Hon. Joseph G. Cannon before the Middlesex Club, Boston, Mass. Gov. Pr. Off.
Knox, T: W. Boy's life of General Grant. $1.25. Saalfield.
Nicolay, H. Boy's life of Ulysses S. Grant. $1.50. Century Co.
Sawyer, G: H: V. Grant's campaign in Virginia. *$1.60 net. Macmillan.
Shrady, G: F: General Grant's last days. (Priv. pr.) De Vinne.
Smith, N: G. Grant, the man of mystery. *$1.50 net. Young Churchman.

Grant Vernon. Stanton, E. B. $1. Roxburgh.

GRANTON, Scotland.
Herring, W. R. Granton gas works of Edinburgh and Leith Corporations. *$6.50 net. Spon.

GRANVILLE, *Sir* Richard.
Granville, R., *comp.* King's general in the west: life of Sir Richard Granville. *$4 net. Lane.

Granville, Rev. Roger, comp.
King's general in the west: life of Sir Richard Granville, Bart., 1600-1659. '08 (Ap25) il. pors. maps, O. *$4 net. Lane.

Granville, W: Anthony.
Plane and spherical trigonometry; and four-place tables of logarithms. '09 (Jl17) il. O. (Mathematical texts.) $1.25. Ginn.
Plane trigonometry and Four-place tables of logarithms, bound separately, *$1 net; Four-place tables of logarithms, bound separately, *50 c. net.
See also Smith, Percey Franklyn.

GRAPES.
Hedrick, U. P., *and others.* Grapes of New York. (Not for sale.) Lyon.
Munson, T. V. Foundations of American grape culture. $3. Judd.

Grapes and thorns. Tincker, M. A. $1. Chr. Press.

Graphic arts and crafts year book. Meadon, J., *ed.* $5. Oswald.

Graphic history. Roch, A. L. $3. Dixon.

GRAPHIC STATICS.
See Statics.

Graphical determination of earth slopes. Prelini, C: **$2 net. Van Nostrand.

GRAPHICS.
Spangler, H: W. Graphics. $1.50. McVey.
Turner, G. C. Graphics: applied to arithmetic, mensuration and statics. *$1.25 net. Macmillan.
See also Geometrical drawing;—Machinery;—Mechanical drawing.

Graphischen (Die) künste. Kampmann, C. 20 c. Stechert.

GRAPHOLOGY.
See Handwriting.

GRASS.
See Alfalfa;—Canada bluegrass;—Lawns;—Milo;—Quitch-grass.

Grasset, Jos., M.D.
Marvels beyond science (L' occultisme hier et aujourd'hui; le merveilleux prescientifique); record of the progress made in the reduction of the occult phenomena to a scientific basis; with preface by Emile Faguet; auth. tr. of the 2d rev. and enl. French ed. by René Jacques Tubeuf. '10(O15) c. O. $1.75 net. Funk.

Grassi, Gius.
See James, W:

Gratacap, L: Pope.
Evacuation of England: the twist in the Gulf Stream. '08(Ag15) c. D. †$1.25. Brentano's.
Geology of the city of New York. 3d ed., enl. '09(Jl17) c. il. fold. maps, O. $2.50. Holt.
Mayor of New York; romance of days to come. '10(N19) c. D. $1.50. G: W: Dillingham.
Protection: a reasonable doctrine. '09 (Ag7) 16°, pap., 20 c. Twentieth Century Pub.

Graton, L: Caryl.
See Lindgren, Waldemar.

Grattan, Fs. W:
With those that were; stories of two wars. '09(My8) c. il. D. $1.50. B'way Pub.

Grattan, Rob.
Glossary of technical words, phrases, maxims and abbreviations found in the text of the popular or students' ed. of the Cyclopedia of law and procedure. '09 (Ag) 230 p. 16°, $1.50. Am. Law Bk.
See also New York. Bender's village laws.

Gratz, Herman.
Making of ice cream, ices, frozen fruits, [etc.;] every detail belonging to the ice cream business plainly and conscientiously described. '09(Jl) c. 3-85 p. 12°, $5. H. Gratz.

Gratz, T: D.
Palmistry made easy. '09(Je26) c. figs. D. **25 c. net. Winston.

Grau, Rob.
Business man in the amusement world; volume of progress in the field of the theatre. '10(D3) c. il. pors. O. $5, boxed. B'way Pub.
Forty years' observation of music and the drama. '09(N20) c. pors. 8°, $5. B'way Pub.

Grautoff, Ferdinand Heinrich, ["Parabellum."]
Banzai! '09(Ja2) c. il. map, D. †$1.50. Baker & T.

GRAVENITZ, Wilhelmine von.
See Von Gravenitz, Wilhelmine.

Graves, Alfr. Perceval.
Irish fairy book. '09(D25) il. 8°, $1.50. Stokes.
Irish poems; with a foreword by Douglas Hyde. In 2 v. '08(O24) 16°, *$1.50 net; leath., *$2.25 net. (Sold in sets only.) Macmillan.

Graves, Algernon.
British Institution, 1806-1867: complete dictionary of contributors and their work. '08(Je27) 4°, *$18 net. Macmillan.

Graves, C: Burr, M.D., Eames, Edn. Hubert, M.D., Bissell, C: Humphrey, and others.
Catalogue of the flowering plants and ferns of Connecticut, growing without cultivation. '10(My21) O. (Connecticut State Geological and Natural History Survey bull.) pap., 75 c. Conn. Lib.

Graves, C: Larcom.
Life and letters of Alex. Macmillan. '10 (D10) pors. O. $3.50 net. Macmillan.

Graves, Etta Merrick.
Year of primary occupation work. '10 (D17) c. il. 8°, 50 c. Educ. Pub.

—, and Watkins, Amelia Warfield.
Year book for primary grades, based on Froebel's mother plays; [with] music by Rupert W. Graves. '08(Je27) c. 8°, $1.25. M. Bradley.

Graves, Fk. Pierrepont.
History of education before the Middle Ages. '09(F20) c. D. **$1.10 net. Macmillan.
Hist. of education during the Middle Ages and the transition to modern times. '10 (O8) c. D. $1.10 net. Macmillan.
Introd. to the history of education. pt. 1. '08(Je6) c. 8°, pap., 60 c. Univ. of Mo.

Graves, H: Solon.
Protection of forests from fire. '10(S) 48 p. il. 8°, (U. S., Dept. of Agriculture, Forest Service, bull.)

Graves, J: Temple, Howell, Clark, and Williams, Wa., eds.
Eloquent sons of the South: hdbk. of Southern oratory. 2 v. '09(N) c. pors. 16°, $2. Chapple Pub.

Graves, W: Elliott, comp. and ed.
Studies in eucalyptus. '10(Ap9) c. il. 8°, $1. W: E. Graves.

GRAVES' DISEASE.
See Thyroid gland.

GRAVESTONES.
See Epitaphs.

Gray, Alb. A., M.D.
Ear and its diseases. '10(Ag) 402 p. il. 8°, with stereoscope in pocket, $4.25 net. Wood.

Gray, Alex.
See Davidson, J:

Gray, Alonzo.
Cavalry tactics as illustrated by the war of the rebellion, together with many interesting facts important for cavalry to know. pt. 1. '10(D17) c. 8°, $1.50. U. S. Cavalry.

Gray, And.
Lord Kelvin: an account of his scientific life and work. '08(Jl18) 12°, (English men of science ser.) *$1 net. Dutton.

Gray, Asa.
New manual of botany; rearranged and extensively rev. by B: Lincoln Robinson and Merrill Lydon Fernald. 7th ed. '08 (O3) c. il. O. $2.50.—'08(D26) c. D. leath., $3. Am. Bk.

Gray, C. Earl.
See Rogers, Lore Alford.

Gray, Charlotte Elvira.
Experimental object lessons; Bible truths simply taught. '10(My7) c. 12°, 75 c. net. Revell.

Gray, D:
Mr. Carteret and others. '10(Mr26) c. il. D. **$1 net. Century Co.

Gray, E: D. McQueen.
Government reclamation work in foreign countries; comp. from consular repts. and official documents. '09(Ag) 4+115 p. 8°, pap. (Add. Superintendent for price.) U. S., Supt. of Docs.

Gray, Eliz. H.
Old ninety-nine's cave. '09(Je12) c. il. 12°, $1.50. C. M. Clark.

Gray, Eunice T.
Winning of Fuji: Japanese play in one act. '09(N) 16°, pap., 25 c. Dramatic.

Gray, F. H. T.
See Wesseley, J. E.

Gray, G: Arth., comp.
Holmes genealogy: a genealogical record to 1908 of the descendants of George Holmes of Roxbury, Mass., baptized in 1594 in the Old Nazing Church, Eng., and who emigrated to America in 1637; to which is appended the descendants of John Holmes of Woodstock, Conn., by the late E. Holmes Bugbee of Killingly, Conn. Limited ed. '08(D) 10+432 p. front. 8°, *$5 net. G: A. Gray.

Gray, H. M. W.
General surgical technique; ed. by Ja. Cantlie. '09(D) 392 p. il. 12°, *$3 net. Wood.

See also Collum, Rowland, W.

Gray, H:
Anatomy, descriptive and surgical. New American ed. (17th), enl. and rev. '08 (Ag29); 18th ed. '10(S) c. il. imp. 8°, ea., *$6 net; leath., *$7 net. Lea.

Gray, J. J.
Reclaimed; or, the mountain castle mystery. '08(F29) c. D. $1.50. B'way Pub.

Gray, Ja. M., M.D.
Great epochs of sacred history and the shadows they cast; popular Bible studies on the first twelve chapters of Genesis, showing the bearing of primeval history on present and coming events. '10(Je4) c. 12°, 50 c. Revell.

Gray, Ja. M., M.D.—*Continued.*
Progress in the life to come. '10(Ag20) c. 16°, bds., 25 c. net. Revell.
Satan and the saint; or, the present darkness and the coming light; popular Bible studies on the personality of Satan, the evil of Christian Science, the power behind the medium, the heresies of the "millennial dawn," the characteristics of the age end, and the second coming of Christ. '09(My) c. 9-124 p. 12°, 25 c. Bible Inst.

Gray, J: Cameron.
Number by development; method of number instruction; primary. '10(Mr5) c. il. D. **$1 net. Lippincott.

Gray, J: Chipman.
Nature and sources of the law. '09(N) c. 12+232 p. O. (Columbia University lectures.) *$1.50 net. Lemcke.

—, **comp.** Select cases and other authorities on the law of property. 2d ed. v. 5. '08 (Ap); v. 6 (Ag) c. O. ea., $3.50. G: H. Kent.

Gray, L: H.
Indo-Iranian phonology. '09(F6) 8°, (Columbia Univ. Indo-Iranian ser.) price reduced from $3 to $2. Lemcke.

Gray, Mary Agatha.
Turn of the tide; story of humble life by the sea. '10(O29) c. D. $1.25. Benziger.

Gray, T:
Poetical works. Cabinet ed. '08(D19) 12°, (British poets ser.) $1.50. Estes.
Buried city of Kenfig. '09, [1910.] (My) 348 p. il. fold. maps, facsims., 8°, $3.50 net. Appleton.
Elegy in a country churchyard, and other poems; ed., with an introd. and notes, by Cornelia Beare. '09(D) c. 55 p. por. 16°, (Merrill's English texts.) 30 c. C. E. Merrill.
Elegy written in a country churchyard. '10(O) 22 p. front. 12°, $2. (200 copies.) F. J. Trezise.
Poems published in 1768. '10(F19) S. (Oxford lib. of prose and poetry.) 90 c. Oxford Univ.
See also Goldsmith, Oliver. Traveller and Deserted village.

—, **and Cowper, W:**
Elegy written in a country church-yard, and other poems by T: Gray; together with The diverting history of John Gilpin and other poems by W: Cowper; ed. by J. H. Castleman. '09(S18) 24°, (Pocket Am. and Eng. classics.) *25 c. net. Macmillan.

—, **and Goldsmith, Oliver.**
T: Gray's elegy written in a country churchyard and other poems; Oliver Goldsmith's The deserted village, The traveller, and other poems ed., with notes and an introd., by Ja. F. Hosic. '10(D10) c. D. (Longmans' English classics.) 25 c. Longmans.

GRAY, Thomas.
Cook, A. S., *ed.* Concordance to the English poems of Thomas Gray. **$2.50 net. Houghton M.

Gray, W: Beall, and Ball, C: Backus.
Plumbing. '09(F20) c. il. 8°, (American School of Correspondence pubs.) $1.50. Am. Sch. Corr.

Gray, W: F.
From Virginia to Texas, 1835; diary of Col. Wm. F. Gray giving details of his journey to Texas and return in 1835-1836 and second journey to Texas in 1837; with preface by A. C. Gray; printed for the information of his descendants. '09(D) c. 8+230 p. 8°. (Not for sale.) A. C. Gray.

Graydon, Judith Farrer.
German bracelet. '09(Ja23) c. D. $1.50. Neale.

Graydon, S:
Some notes on catalog making. '09(Jl3) front. O. bds., $1 Trow Press.

Grayson, D:, pseud.
Adventures in friendship. '10(N19) c. il. O. $1.20, fixed. Doubleday, P.

Grayson, Justine.
Tenderfoot abroad. '08(F1) c. O. $1. W. A. Butterfield.

Great adventurer. Sampter, J. E. 75 c. R. Kerr.

Great (The) aeroplane. Brereton, F: S. $1.25. Caldwell.

Great American industries. Rocheleau, W: F. Bk. 4. 60 c. Flanagan.

Great American lawyers. *See* Lewis, W: Draper, *ed.*

Great American universities. Slosson, E. E. $2.50 net. Macmillan.

Great amulet. Diver, M. †$1.50. Lane.

Great and greater Britain. Barker, J. E. *$3 net. Dutton.

Great apostasy. Talmage, J. E: 60 c. Deseret News.

Great archbishop of Dublin. King, W: *$1.60 net. Longmans.

Great art galleries ser. il. T. bds., 35 c.; limp calfskin, $1. Caldwell.
—Glasgow gallery.
—Wallace collection.

Great artist ser. il. Q. *$2 net. Doran.
—Baldry. Sir Joshua Reynolds.
—Bell. Sir Edward Burne-Jones.
—Davey. Botticelli.
—Radford. Dante Gabriel Rosetti.
—Staley. Raphael.

Great assurance. Gordon, G: A. *50 c. net. Pilgrim Press.

Great autobiographies. Griggs, E: H. *50 c. net; *25 c. net. B: W. Huebsch.

GREAT BRITAIN.
Abraham, G: D. Complete mountaineer. *$4.80 net. Doubleday, P.
Alton, H. King's customs: account of maritime revenue and contraband traffic in England, Scotland and Ireland from earliest times to year 1800. *$3.50 net. Dutton.
Baedeker, K. Hdbk. of Great Britain. $3 net. Scribner.
Barker, J. E. Great and greater Britain. *$3 net. Dutton.
Barnard, C. H. British Isles in pictures. 75 c. net. Macmillan.

GREAT BRITAIN.—*Continued.*
Berkeley, G: George Berkeley on several queries proposed to the public, 1735-37. $1. Lord Balto. Pr.
Bonhote, J. L. Birds of Britain. *$6 net. Macmillan.
Burke, *Sir* J. B. *and* A. P: Genealogical and heraldic hist. of the peerage and baronetage. *$12 net. Putnam.
Carter, C. E: Great Britain and the Illinois country. $1.50. Am. Hist.
Cooper, C. S., *and* Westell, W. P. Trees and shrubs of the British Isles. 2 v. *$7 net. Dutton.
Dixon, C. Abbeys of Great Britain. *$1.50 net. Scribner.
Druce, G: C., *comp.* List of British plants containing the *Spermophytes, Pteridophytes* and *Charads.* 85 c. Oxford Univ.
Escott, T: H. S. Story of British diplomacy. *$4 net. Jacobs.
Frazar, *Mrs.* M. D. Pract. guide to Great Britain and Ireland. 2 v. **$1 net. Small.
Herbertson, A. J., *and* Jowett, L., *eds.* British Isles; descriptive geography. *75 c. net. Macmillan.
Johnson, W. Folk-memory; or, the continuity of British archæology. $4.15. Oxford Univ.
Kelly's directory of the engineers and iron and metal trades and colliery proprietors, [Great Britain.] *$10 net. Kelly.
Leland, J: Itinerary, 1535-1543. pts. 4, 5. *$4 net. Macmillan.
Millais, J: G. Natural hist. of British game birds. *$60 net. Longmans.
Moore, N. History of the study of medicine in the British Isles. $3.40. Oxford Univ.
Murphy, T: D. British highways and byways from a motor car. $3; $7. L. C. Page.
South, R: Moths of the British Isles, first series. *$3 net. Warne.
Step, E: Wayside and woodland trees: guide to British sylva. *$1.75 net. Warne.
Taylor, C: M. British Isles through an opera glass. *$1.25 net. Jacobs.
Tomlinson, E. T. British Isles. **60 c. net.—Young Americans in the British Isles. $1.50. Houghton M.
United States. *Dept. of Commerce and Labor. Bureau of Labor.* Woman and child wage earners in Great Britain.
United States. *Dept. of Commerce and Labor. Bureau of Manufactures.* British iron and steel industry. (Add. Superintendent for price.)
Wilkinson, H: S. Britain at bay. *$1.50 net. Putnam.
See also Birds;—British Empire;—Civil Service;—Country life;—England;—Fisheries;—House of Commons;—House of Lords;—Hunting;—Ireland;—Mythology;—Parliament;—Scotland;—Sports;—Tariff;—Wales;—*also* names of colonies.

Great buildings and how to enjoy them. *See* Browne, Edith A.

Great cities in America. Wilcox, D. F. $1.25 net. Macmillan.

Great cities of the world. New uniform ed. '10(D) col. il. 8°. Estes.
Contents: Reynolds-Ball, Paris, 2 v., $3; Holiday ed., $5; hf. lev., $10; Clement, Rome, 2 v., $3; Holiday ed., $6; Johnson, Florence, $1.50; Holiday ed., $3; Clement, Constantinople, $1.50; Holiday ed., $3; Reynolds-Ball, Cairo, $1.50; Holiday ed., $3; Cairo of yesterday and to-day, Tourists' ed., 75 c. net; Johnson, Genoa, $1.50; Holiday ed., $3; Clement, Venice, $1.50; Holiday ed., $3; Clement, Naples, $1.50; Holiday ed., $3.

Great crisis in the life of Christ. Scott, L. W. $1. F: L: Rowe.
Great design of Henry IV. Sully, *Duc* de. **50 c. net. Ginn.
Great discovery of four worlds and their inhabitants. Holley, *Rev.* C: D. 75 c. C: D. Holley.
Great divide. Moody, W: V. **$1.25 net. Macmillan.
Great English letter-writers. *See* Dawson, W: J.
Great English novelists. Dawson, W: J. $1 net. Harper.
Great English novelists. Jackson, H. **$1.50 net. Jacobs.
Great English painters. Dowman, F. **$1.50 net. Jacobs.
Great English poets. Hill, J. $1.50. Jacobs.
Great English portrait painters of the 18th century: Reynolds, Gainsborough, and Romney; ed. by T. Leman Hare. '09(O) 239 p. col. il. O. *$2 net. Stokes.
Great English short-story writers. Dawson, W: J., *comp.* 2 v. ea., **$1 net. Harper.
Great epochs of sacred history. Gray, J. M. 50 c. Revell.
Great etchers ser. See Scribner's.
Great events in the life of Christ. McConaughy, J. 75 c.; 50 c. Y. M. C. A.
Great experiment. Morgan, A. 50 c. Seymour.
Great fight. Drummond, W: H: **$1.25 net. Putnam.
Great five. Crook, I: *25 c. net. Jennings.
Great French Revolution. Kropotkin, *Prince* P. A. *$2.25 net. Putnam.
Great galleries of Europe ser. v. 5-7. '10(D) il. 24°, ea., bds., 35 c.; limp leath., 75 c. Caldwell.
Contents: Glasgow Gallery; Wallace Gallery of London; Kensington Gallery of London.

Great god gold. Le Queux, W: $1.50. Badger.
Great hymns of the middle ages. Brainerd, E. W., *comp.* $1. Century Co.
Great infidels. *See* Ingersoll, Rob. Green.
Great issue. Walter, E. $1.50. Doscher.
Great issues. Horton, R. F. **$1.50 net. Macmillan.

GREAT LAKES.
Channing, E:, *and* Lansing, M. F. Story of the Great Lakes. **$1.50 net. Macmillan.
Curwood, J. O. Great Lakes. **$3.50 net. Putnam.
Green, F. W., *comp.* Mitchell & Co.'s hdbk. of the Great Lakes. $1.50. Mitchell & Co.
Law, W: H. Among the lighthouses of the Great Lakes. 10 c. W. H. Law.
Mills, J. C. Our inland seas. $1.75 net. McClurg.

GREAT LAKES.—*Continued.*
United States. *Navy Dept.* Status of naval vessels on the Great Lakes.
United States. *Steamboat Inspection Service.* Pilot rules for the Great Lakes and their connecting and tributary waters.
See also Inland navigation.

Great marvel ser. See Rockwood, Roy, *pseud.*
Great masters of Dutch and Flemish painting. Bode, W. *$2 net. Scribner.
Great masters of landscape painting. Michel, F. E. $7.50 net. Lippincott.
Great ministry. Horr, G: E. *$1 net; Sunday-school ed., *75 c. net. Bible Study.
Great Miss Driver. Hawkins, A. H. †$1.50. McClure.
Great moments in a woman's life. Blake, E. C. 75 c. Forbes.
Great musicians. Oldmeadow, E. $1.50. Jacobs.
Great musicians' art and glory. Crawford, R. $2.50. D. W. Newton.
Great natural healer. Clark, C: H. 50 c. Jacobs.
Great newspaper ser. See Garis, Howard Roger.
Great operas ser. See Hadden, J. Cuthbert.
Great operas told for children. Prendergast, J: $1.50. Stokes.
Great Pacific coast. Enock, C. R. $4 net. Scribner.
Great painters ser. 8°. Macmillan.
—Foster. Birket Foster. $1 net.
Great pictures as moral teachers. Jackson, H: E. $1.50. Winston.
Great portraits. *See* Hale, Philip L.
Great possessions. Ward, *Mrs.* J. M. H.-S. **$1.35 net. Putnam.
Great problem. Burke, J: J. *$1 net. Herder.
Great pyramid of Jeezeh. McCarty, L: P. $5; $6. McCarty.
Great Ralegh [*sic.*] Sélincourt, H. de. *$3.50 net. Putnam.
Great red dragon. Chester, *Lord, pseud.* 75c.; 35 c. Guiding Star.
Great rivers of the world. Singleton, E., *comp.* **$1.60 net. Dodd.

GREAT SALT LAKE, Utah.
Lambourne, A. Our inland sea. $2.50. A. Lambourne.

Great salvation. Bowman, T: 50 c. Pub. Ho. of Evangelical Assoc.
Great salvation. Wilson, P. *$1.25 net. Jennings.
Great sea horse. Anderson, I. *$2 net; **$15 net. Little, B. & Co.
Great secret. Oppenheim, E: P. †$1.50. Little, B. & Co.
Great short stories. Patten, W: $2.25. Collier.
Great states of South America. Domville-Fife, C: W. $4.50 net. Macmillan.
Great texts of the New Testament. Greenhough, J. G. *$1 net. Eaton & M.
Great (A) thinker. Haseltine, M. W. 3 c. Mass. New-Ch. Un.
Great treason. Hoppus, M. A. M. $1.50. **Macmillan.**

Great triumvirate: Jefferson, Hamilton, Aaron Burr. See Pidgin, C: Felton.
Great Victorian age. Synge, M. B. $1. Doran.
Great wall of China. Geil, W: E. $5. Sturgis & W.
Great wet way. Dale, A., *pseud.* **$1.50 net. Dodd.
Great White North. Wright, *Mrs.* H. S. S. $2.50 net. Macmillan.
Great white plague. Otis, E: O. **$1 net. Crowell.
Great (The) within. Larson, C. D. 50 c. Eternal Progress.
Great world mystery: [poem.] Nicholovius, L. $1. B'way Pub.
Great writers ser. 42 v. [1910.] (Jl) ea., 40 c. Simmons.
Great writers ser. 8°. Scribner.
—Wyngate. Life of John Ruskin. $1.
Greater abbeys of England. Gasquet, F. A. **$3.50 net. Dodd.
Greater America. Paine, R. D. *$1.50 net. McClurg.
Greater love. Sholl, A. McC. $1.50. Outing.
Greater mischief. Westrup, M. †$1.50. Harper.

GREATER NEW YORK.
See New York City.

Greater power. Bindloss, H. **$1.30 net. Stokes.

GREATER SEATTLE.
See Seattle.

Greatest good of mankind. Wenzlick, W: 75 c. W: Wenzlick.
Greatest men of the Christian church. Walker, W. $1.50. Univ. of Chic.
Greatest thing in the world. *See* Drummond, H:
Greatest things in religion. Antrim, E. M. 75 c. Jennings.
Greatest trust in the world. Russell, C: E: 50 c. B. W. Dodge.
Greatest truth. Dresser, H. W. 90 c. Progressive Lit.
Greatest wish in the world. Thurston, E. T. $1.50. M. Kennerley.

Greathouse, C: Howard, comp.
Historical sketch of the U. S. Department of Agriculture. '08(My16) il. pors. 8°, pap., 25 c. U. S., Supt. of Docs.

Greatness and decline of Rome. *See* Ferrero, Guglielmo.

GRECO, El, Domenico Theotocopuli, *called.*
Calvert, A. F:, *and* Hartley, C. G. El Greco: account of his life and works. *$1.50 net. Lane.

Gredt, Jos.
Elementa philosophiæ Aristotelico-Thomisticæ. v. 1, Logica; philosophia moralis. '09(N) 25+496 p. 8°, *$2.45 net. Herder.

GREECE.
Abbott, G: F:, *ed.* Greece in evolution. $1.50 net. Wessels & B.
Adam, J. Religious teachers of Greece. *$4 net. Scribner.
Allinson, F. G. *and* A. C. E. Greek land and letters. **$2.50 net. Houghton M.
Anderson, W: J., *and* Spiers, R. P. Architecture of Greece and Rome. *$7.50 net. Scribner.
Baedeker, K. Greece. *$2.40 net. Scribner.

GREECE.—*Continued.*
Blümner, H. Home life of the ancient Greeks. $2 net. Cassell.
Browne, E. A. Greece. *75 c. net. Macmillan.
Bureau of University Travel, Boston. Cruises of the Athena in Greece and the eastern Mediterranean, 1910. gratis. Bu. Univ. Travel.
Bury, J: B. Ancient Greek historians. $2.25. Macmillan.
Diman, L. Stories from Greek history for children. 40 c. C: E. Merrill.
Farnell, L. R: Cults of the Greek states. In 5 v. v. 5. $6. Oxford Univ.
Farrar, F. A. Old Greek nature stories. $1.50 net. Crowell.
Fowler, H. N., *and others.* Handbook of Greek archæology.. $2. Am. Bk.
Gardiner, E: N. Greek athletic sports and festivals. $2.50 net. Macmillan.
Gardner, E. A. Religion and art in ancient Greece. 75 c. net. Harper.
Gardner, W: A. In Greece with the classics. **$1.50 net. Little, B. & Co.
Guide to Greece, the Archipelago, Constantinople, coasts of Asia Minor, Crete, and Cyprus. *$2.75 net. Macmillan.
Jones, W: H: S: Malaria: a neglected factor in the history of Greece and Rome. *80 c. net. Macmillan.
Lawson, J: C. Modern Greek folklore and ancient Greek religion. $4 net. Putnam.
Lewis, L. B. Pupils' notebook and study outline in Oriental and Greek history. 25 c. Am. Bk.
Mahaffy, J: P. What have the Greeks done for modern civilization? **$2.50 net. Putnam.
Marquand, A. Greek architecture. **$2.25 net. Macmillan.
Miller, W: Latins in the Levant; a history of Frankish Greece. *$5 net. Dutton.
Moore, M. Days in Hellas. **$2 net. Jacobs.
Nixon-Roulet, M. F. Our little Grecian Cousin. 60 c. L. C. Page.
O'Connor, J: B. Chapters in the history of actors and acting in ancient Greece. $1. Univ. of Chic.
Quinn, D. Helladian vistas: [essays on Greece.] $1.50. D. Quinn.
Ridgeway, W: Early age of Greece. v. 1. *$5 net. Putnam.
Rose, A. Christian Greece and living Greek. $1. Stechert.
Seyffert, O. Dictionary of classical antiquities; abr. *$1 net. Macmillan.
Stories of Greece and Rome. **65 c. net. Century Co.
Sullivan, T: R. Lands of summer: Italy, Sicily and Greece. **$1.50 net. Houghton M.
Tappan, E. M. Story of the Greek people. $1.50; **65 c. net. Houghton M.
Thucydides. History. 3 v. $10.50. Tandy-T.
Walden, J: W: H: Universities of ancient Greece. **$1.50 net. Scribner.
See also Apostles;—Archæology;—Athens;—Crete;—Heroes;—Mythology;—Painters and painting;—Peloponnesian war.

Greeff, Richard.
Atlas of external diseases of the eye for physicians and students; only authorized English tr., by P. W. Shedd. '09(N) c. 8+140 p. col. pl. 4°, $10. Rebman.

Greek and Roman methods of painting. Laurie, A. P. 75 c. net. Putnam.

GREEK ARCHITECTURE.
See Architecture.

GREEK ART.
See Ceramics.

Greek buildings represented by fragments in the British Museum. Lethaby, W: R: *$4.20 net. Scribner.

GREEK CHURCH.
Adeney, W. F: Greek and Eastern churches. *$2.50 net. Scribner.
See also Armenian church.

GREEK DRAMA.
See Drama and dramatists.

Greek gospel. Usher, E: P. $1. E: P. Usher.

Greek heroes. Niebuhr, B. G. 50 c. Cassell.

GREEK HISTORY.
See Greece.

GREEK LANGUAGE.
Buck, C. D. Introd. to the study of Greek dialects. $2.75. Ginn.
Bywater, I. Erasmian pronunciation of Greek and its precursers. 35 c. Oxford Univ.
Euripides. Fabvlae. 90 c. Oxford Univ.
Herodotus. Bks. 7, 8. $1.75; Text ed., 40 c. Am. Bk.
Herodotus. Herodoti historiæ. v. 1, 2. ea., $1.10. Oxford Univ.
Homer. Iliad: first three books. 40 c. Am. Bk.
Jackson, J. Iambica; English-Greek and Greek-English vocab. for writers of Iambic verse. *$1.50 net. Macmillan.
Kaegi, A. Advanced lessons in Greek. *70 c. net.—First lessons in Greek. *80 c. net. Herder.
Menardos, S. Value of Byzantine and modern Greek in Hellenic studies. 35 c. Oxford Univ.
Norton, F: O. Lexicographical and historical study of Diathekes. *75 c. net. Univ. of Chic.
Pausanias. The Attica. $1.65. Ginn.
Plato. Apology of Socrates. *50 c. net. Macmillan.
Plato. Apology of Socrates and Crito; with extracts from the Phaedo and Symposium and from Xenophon's Memorabilia. $1.40. Ginn.
Plato. The Euthyphro. 60 c. Oxford Univ.
Robertson, A. T: Short grammar of the Greek New Testament. $1.50. Armstrong.
Rose, A. Medical Greek: collection of papers on medical onomatology and a grammatical guide to learn modern Greek. $1. Stechert.
Sturtevant, E. H. Studies in Greek noun-formations. 25 c. net. Univ. of Chic.
Thackeray, H: S. Grammar of the Old Testament in Greek. v. 1. *$2.75 net. Putnam.

GREEK LANGUAGE.—*Continued.*
Theophrastus. Characteres. 90 c.; 75 c. Oxford Univ.
Thompson, E. F. *Metanoeo* and *metamelei* in Greek literature until 100 A.D., including discussion of their cognates and of their Hebrew equivalents. *25 c. net. Univ. of Chic.
Thucydides. Histories. bk. IV. 90 c.; Notes only, 60 c. Oxford Univ.
Vincent, *Sir* E., *and* Dickson, J. G. Hdbk. of modern Greek. *$1.90 net. Macmillan.
Williams, C: B. Participle in the book of Acts. *50 c. net. Univ. of Chic.
See also Bible;—*also* names of Greek authors.

GREEK LETTER SOCIETIES.
See Secret societies.

GREEK LITERATURE.
Allinson, F. G. *and* A. C. E. Greek lands and letters. **$2.50 net. Houghton M.
Gildersleeve, B. L. Hellas and Hesperia: the vitality of Greek studies in America. *$1 net. Holt.
Havell, H. L., *comp.* Stories from the Greek tragedy; retold. $1.50. Dodge.
Mackail, J: W:, *ed.* Select epigrams from Greek anthology. *75 c. net; *$1 net. Longmans.
Murray, G: G. A. Interpretation of ancient Greek literature. 35 c. Oxford Univ.
Stearns, W. N., *ed.* Fragments from Græco-Jewish writers. *75 c. net. Univ. of Chic.
Tyrrell, R. Y. Essays on Greek literature. *$1.25 net. Macmillan.
Wilamowitz-Moellendorff, E. F. W: U. v. Greek historical writings and Apollo. 70 c. Oxford Univ.
See also Drama and dramatists;—Greek poetry;—Orators and oratory;—Papyri;—*also* names of authors.

GREEK PHILOSOPHY.
See Philosophy.

Greek Pilgrim's progress. Cebes. $1. Monsalvat.

GREEK POETRY.
Headlam, W. G: Book of Greek verse: [translations.] *$1.75 net. Putnam.
Lane, M. C. Index to the fragments of the Greek Elegiac and Iambic poets as contained in the Hiller-Crusius ed. of Bergk's Anthologia lyrica. 80 c. Longmans.
Mackail, J: W: Lectures on Greek poetry. $3 net. Longmans.
Ogden, C: J. De infinitivi finalis vel consecutivi constructione apud priscos poetas Græcos. **$1.25 net. Lemcke.

Greek ser. for colleges and schools; ed. by Herbert Weir Smith. il. D. Am. Bk.
—Fowler, *and others.* Handbook of Greek archæology. $2.
—Herodotus. [Histories:] bks. 7, 8. $1.75; Text ed., 40 c.
—Homer. Iliad. 40 c.
—Xenophon. Hellenica. $1.65; Text ed., 40 c.

Greek studies. *See* Pater, Wa.

Greely, Major-General Adolphus Washington.
Hdbk. of Alaska. '09(Je5) c. il. maps, O. **$2 net. Scribner.
Hdbk. of polar discoveries. 4th ed., rev. and enl. '09(D11); 5th ed. '10(My) c. maps, por. O. ea., **$1.50 net. Little, B. & Co.
Polar bibliography (7 p.).

Green, Alice Sophia Amelia Stopford, [Mrs. J: R: Green.]
Making of Ireland and its undoing, 1200-1600. '08(Ag1) map, 8°, *$2.50 net. Macmillan.

Green, Allen Ayrault.
Land of Lost. '08(D5) c. il. Q. †$1.25. Small.

Green, Rev. And.
Bells of Atchison, and other poems. '08 (S) c. 8+126 p. 8°, 75 c. A. Green.

Green, Anna Katharine.
See Rohlfs, *Mrs.* Anna Katharine Green.

Green, Arth. Octavius, comp.
Modern Arabic stories, ballads, proverbs and idioms; collected, transliterated and translated. In 2 pts. '09(N13) D. pt. 1, $1.75; pt. 2, $1.50. Oxford Univ.
Pract. Arabic grammar. 4th ed., enl. and rev. 2 v. '09(D) il. 12°, v. 1, $2.15; v. 2, $3. Oxford Univ.

Green, Arth. Wilson-.
See Wilson-Green, Arth.

Green, Bennett Wood.
How Newport's News got its name. '08 (Ap11) 8°, gratis. W: E. Jones.

Green, Bernard R.
Book stack and shelving for libraries. '08 (O) c. 160 p. il. plans. gratis. Snead & Co.

Green, Edm. Fk.
Verses. [1910.] (My) c. 15-211 p. 12°, $1 net. A. M. Robertson.

Green, Edm. Samson, comp.
Complete index to California codes and laws now in force. '10(Ag) c. O. shp., $6.40. Bancroft-W.
—, ed. *See* American state repts.

Green, Evelyn Everett-.
Carol Carew; or, was it imprudent? '10 (Je4) il. D. (Girls' own lib.) 75 c. McKay.
City of the Golden Gate. '09(Ag28) il. 12°, $1.25. Dodge.

Green, F. E.
Small holding. '08(S19) il. plans, S. (Country handbooks.) *$1 net. Lane.

Green, F:
Cases of the law of carriers; sel. from decis. of Eng. and Amer. courts. '10(S) c. 614 p. Q. (Amer. casebook ser.) $4. West Pub.

Green, F: W:, comp.
"Mitchell & Co.'s hdbk. of the Great Lakes," containing complete information regarding the construction of American and Canadian vessels. names and addresses of their owners, lists of steamships corporations, also information concerning docks and harbors of the Great Lakes, etc. '09(N) c. 8°, $1.50. Mitchell & Co.

Green, Hans L.
Waste merchants standard code; combines quantity, material and price in one word; alphabetically arranged in English-French-German. '10(Mr) c. 190 p. 8°, $5. H. L. Green.

Green, Helen.
Maison de Shine: more stories of the actors' boarding house. '08(N14) c. D. $1. B. W. Dodge.
Mr. Jackson. '09(D25) c. front. 12°, $1.25. B. W. Dodge.

Green, Ja.
Personal recollections of Daniel Henry Chamberlain, once governor of South Carolina. '08(D) c. 15 p. pors. pap., 25 c. Davis & B.

GREEN, James, *D.D.*
Wirgman, A. T. Life of James Green. *$6 net. Longmans.

Green, J: Alb.
Tone and technique of the violin. '07, [1908.] (Ap.) c. 24 p. 8°, $1. J: A. Green.

Green, J: R:
Short history of the English people; with introd. by Albert C. Cook. In 3 v. v. 3 contains Guizot's History of civilization in Europe; tr. by W: Hazlitt; with introd. by Paul van Dyke. '07(Je27) c. 3 v., il. 8°, $5.25; hf. mor., $10.50. Lamb Pub.

Green, Mrs. J: R:
See Green, Alice Stopford.

Green, Jos. Reynolds.
Botany. '10(S) il. 16°, (Appleton's scientific primers.) 50 c. net. Appleton.
Hist. of botany, 1860-1900; being a continuation of Sachs' Hist. of botany, 1530-1860. '10(Ja1) D. $3.15. Oxford Univ.

Green, Mrs. Mary Anne Everett Wood.
Elizabeth Queen of Bohemia and Electress Palatine. '09(D18) 8°, *$3.50 net. Dutton.

Green, Max, M.D.
Jewish question and the key to its solution. '08(O3) c. **75 c. net; pap., **40 c. net. —Yiddish ed. '09(S) c. 25 c. Jacobs.

Green, Olive, pseud.
See Reed, Myrtle [*now Mrs.* Myrtle Reed McCullough.]

Green, Oscar Olin.
Normal evangelism; introd. by Prof. Byron H. De Ment. '10(Jl9) c. 12°, $1 net. Revell.

Green, Rev. P:
How to deal with lads; hdbk. of church work; with introd. by the Rt. Rev. Bishop of Gloucester. '10(O22) D. 80 c. net. Longmans.

Green, S: Abbott.
Colonel William Prescott and Groton soldiers in the battle of Bunker Hill. '09, [1910.] (Ap) 10 p. 8°, 35 c. S: A. Green.
Early mile-stones leading from Boston; and mile-stones at Groton. '09(Jl) 27 p. il. 8°, 25 c. S: A. Green.
John Foster, the earliest American engraver. '09. 5+149 p. il. pors. 8°, silk, $2. Mass. Hist. Soc.
Memoir of Abbott Lawrence. '08, [1909.] (Ap) 9 p. por. 8°, 35 c. S: A. Green.

Green, S: Abbott.—*Continued.*
Slavery at Groton, Massachusetts, in provincial times. '09(Je19) 8°, pap., 25 c. S: A. Green.
Three historical addresses at Groton, Mass. '08(O17) 8°, $2.50. Littlefield.

Green, S: Bowdlear.
Popular fruit growing. '09(Jl) 298 p. il. 12°, $1. Webb.

Green, S: Gosnell, D.D.
Gospel of St. Mark: [commentary.] '09 (F13) c. 16°, (Westminster New Testament.) *75 c. net. Revell.

Green, S: Swett.
Worcester, England, and Worcester, Massachusetts. '09(F6) il. pors. Q. pap., gratis. S: S. Green.

GREEN, Samuel Swett.
Coombs, Z. W. Samuel Swett Green, Worcester Lib., 1871-1909. (Add. Lib. for price.) Worcester Pub. Lib.

Green, T: E:, D.D.
In praise of valor: address made at Denver at the close of the Spanish-American war under auspices of the Col. Soc. of Sons of the Revolution. '08(Ja18) bds., $3; with hand-illumined initial, $5. Torch Press.

Green, W. Curtis.
Old cottages and farmhouses in Surrey. '08(Ag1) $8.40. Helburn.

GREEN BAY, Wis.
See Kellogg Public Library.

GREEN BUG.
See Parasites.

Green carnation. Hichens, R. S. $1. M. Kennerley.
Green cloak. Davis, Y., *pseud.* $1.50. Sturgis & W.
Green domino. Dyllington, A. $1.50. Lane.
Green door. Freeman, *Mrs.* M. E. W. 75 c. net. Moffat.
"Green Finch" cruise. Kempson, F. C. $1.75. Longmans.
Green Fund book ser. D. Am. S. S.
—Huntington. Charms of the old Book. *90 c. net.
—MacPhail. Magnetism of the Bible. *75 c. net.
—Rice. Commentary on the gospel according to Matthew. $1.25.
—Roads. Rural christendom. *90 c. net.
—Tomkins. Faith and life of a Christian. *75 c. net.
Green ginger. Morison, A. †$1.50. Stokes.
Green leaves from life's garden. Hinman, *Mrs.* L. $1. Badger.
Green mouse. Chambers, R. W: $1.50. Appleton.
Green mummy. Hume, F. W. †$1.25. G: W. Dillingham.
Green patch. Hutten, *Baroness* B. v. $1.50. Stokes.
Green Willow. James, G., *comp.* $5.50 net. Macmillan.

Greenaway, Kate.
Marigold garden; pictures [in color] and rhymes by Kate Greenaway. '10(N12) O. bds., $1.50 net. Warne.
Under the window; pictures and rhymes for children. '10(Ag20) il. in col. O. $1.50. Warne.
See also Brown, Rob. Pied piper.

Greenbarry, Harry.
The sermon. '10(Mr26) c. T. bds., 50 c. Good Thoughts.

Greendlinger, Leo.
Accountancy problems, with solutions; with introd. by J: R. Loomis. '09(My) 8°, *$5 net. Accountancy.
Accountancy problems with solutions. 2d ed., rev. and enl., with an introd. by J: R. Loomis. '10(Ap) 410 p. 8°, $5. Business Bk.

Greene, Arth. Maurice, jr.
See Spangler, H. Wilson.

Greene, C: Lyman.
Medical diagnosis; manual for students and practitioners. 3d ed., rev. '10(F) c. 19+725 p. il. diagrs., 12°, (Leather bound ser. of medical manuals.) leath., *$3.50 net. Blakiston.

Greene, C: Wilson.
Experimental pharmacology; laboratory guide for the study of the physiological action of drugs. 3d ed., rev. '09(Je) c. 10+76 p. il. 8°, *$1 net. Blakiston.

Greene, E: Lee.
Landmarks of botanical hist.; study of certain epochs in the development of the science of botany. pt. 1, prior to 1562 A.D. '09, [1910.] (Ap) 329 p. O. (Smithsonian miscellaneous collections.) pap., 65 c. Smith. Inst.

Greene, Evarts Boutell, ed.
See Illinois State Historical Library.

Greene, Frances Nimmo.
Into the night: story of New Orleans. '09 (O2) c. il. D. **$1.20 net. Crowell.

Greene, Fs. Vinton.
Lincoln as commander-in-chief. [1910.] (Je) 12 p. 8°, 50 c. F. V. Greene.
Niagara Falls in 1907: paper read before the American Civic Association at the annual convention, Providence, R. I., Nov. 19, 1907. '08(F) c. 8°. (Add. pubs. for price.) Ontario Power.

Greene, Fk. L., comp.
Vermont, the Green Mountain state: past, present, prospective; pub. by the Vermont Commission to the Jamestown Tercentennial Exposition. '07, '08(Je) 80 p. il. 8°, gratis. C: S. Forbes.

GREENE, George Sears.
In memoriam; George Sears Greene, Brevet Major General, U. S. Volunteers, 1861-1899. [1910.] (Ap) D. E. Sickles.

Greene, Harry Irving.
Yozondè of the wilderness. '10(O8) c. front. D. $1 net. FitzGerald.

Greene, Harry Noyes, ed.
See Am. and Eng. annot cases.—Digest.

Greene, Homer.
Lincoln conscript. '09(Ap24) c. il. D. †$1.50. Houghton M.

Greene, Jos. Morse.
Experiments on the sub-human: are they justifiable? 2d ed. '08, [1909.] (Jl) 3-28 p. 8°, pap. (Add. pubs. for price.) N. Y. Anti-Vivisection.

Greene, Jos. Nelson.
Gospel in literature. '10(D17) c. 12°, 75 c. Jennings.

Greene, Maria Louise.
Among school gardens. '10(My14) c. il. D. (Russell Sage Foundation pubs.) $1.25. Charities Pub.

Greene, Mrs. Mary Ellen Brown.
Door where the wrong lay. '09(Je26) c. front. D. $1.50. C. M. Clark.

Greene, R: Arnold.
Saint Peter. '09(My22) c. D. *75 c. net. Sherman, F.

Greene, Rob.
Pandosto; or, Dorastus and Fawnia: being the original of Shakespeare's "Winter's tale"; ed. by P. G. Thomas. '08(O31) facsim. 16°, (Shakespeare lib.: Shakespeare classics.) bds., *$1 net; Persian, *$1.60 net; lib. ed., hf. parchment, 12°, *$1.70 net. Duffield.
Robert Greene: [plays;] ed., with introd. and notes, by T: H. Dickinson. '09(D11) front. D. (Mermaid ser.) *$1 net. Scribner.

Greene, Rob. Holmes, and Brooks, Harlow.
Diseases of the genito-urinary organs and the kidney. '08(N) c. 9-605 p. il. chart, 8°, *$5 net. Saunders.

Greene, W: Houston.
Lessons in chemistry. 4th ed., thoroughly rev., by Harry F. Keller. '08(D19) c. il. 12°, $1. Lippincott.

Greene County [Ohio] Home Coming Association. Greene County, 1803-1908. '08(O) c. 10+226 p. il. 8°, $1.20. Greene Co. Home.

Greener, W: Wellington.
Gun and its development. New and rev. ed. (9th), rewritten. '10(D3) il. 8°, $4 net. Scribner.

Greenhough, Rev. J. G.
Mind of Christ in St. Paul. '09(D) 16+310 p. O. *$1.50 net. Doran.
See also Brown, C:

—, Brown, C:, Walker, W. L., and others.
Great texts of the New Testament. '09 (N20) D. *$1 net. Eaton & M.

GREENHOUSES.
Dean, M. System of greenhouse heating for steam or hot water. $2. Domestic Engineering.
Hasluck, P. N., *ed.* Greenhouse and conservatory construction and heating. *$1 net. Cassell.

Greenish, H: G:
Microscopical examination of foods and drugs; designed for the use of analysts, pharmacists, and students. 2d ed., rev. '10(N) 17+386 p. il. 8°, $3. Blakiston.

GREENLAND.
See Arctic regions.

Greenman, Jesse More.
New or noteworthy spermatophytes from Mexico, Central America and the West Indies. '07, [1908.] (My.) 247-287 p. 8°, (Field Columbian Museum pub., Botanical ser.) pap., 50 c. Field Museum.

Greenough, Mrs. Jeanie Ashley Bates, comp.
Year of beautiful thoughts. '10(Ag13) c. D. $1. Crowell.

Greenslet, Ferris.
Life of Thomas Bailey Aldrich. '08(O10) c. il. pors. O. **$3 net; large pap. ed., **$5 net. Houghton M.

GREENVILLE (Treaty of).
Wilson, F. E. Peace of Mad Anthony; acct. of the subjugation of the northwestern Indian tribes and the treaty of Greenville, Ohio. $1.25. F. E. Wilson.

GREENWICH, N. J.
Andrews, *Mrs.* B. A. Colonial and old houses of Greenwich, N. J. $1; 50 c. B. A. Andrews.
Andrews, F. D. Tea-burners of Cumberland County, [N. J.,] who showed their resistance to British tyranny. 30 c. F. D. Andrews.

Greenwood, Alice Drayton.
Lives of the Hanoverian queens of England. '09(Ag14) v. 1, 8°, *$3.50 net. Macmillan.

Greenwood, Grace, pseud.
See Lippincott, *Mrs.* Sarah Jane Clarke.

Greenwood, Granville G:
In re Shakespeare; Beeching v. Greenwood; rejoinder on behalf of the defendant. '09(My8) D. *$1 net. Lane.
Shakespeare problem restated. '08(Ag1) front. O. *$5 net. Lane.

Greenwood, I: J:
The circus; its origin and growth prior to 1835, with a sketch of negro minstrelsy. [2d ed.] '09(S4) c. il. pors. O. *$5 net. Abbatt.

Greenwood, Major, jr.
Physiology of the special senses. '10(Ap2) il. O. $2.40 net. Longmans.

Greenwood, W:
Auxilium: summary of Latin essentials. '07, [1908.] (Mr) c. 32 p. por. 8°, *40 c. net; polychrome ed., *30 c. net. W: Greenwood.

Greenwood, W: H:
Iron; its sources, properties and manufacture; rev. and partly rewritten by A. Humgoldt Sexton. '08(Ag8) c. il. 12°, (Technical instruction manuals.) $1. McKay.

Greer, Jos. H.
Social evil; its cause, effect and cure. '10 (F19) c. 12°, 50 c. J. H. Greer.

Greg, Wa. Wilson, comp.
Descriptive catalogue of the early editions of the works of Shakespeare preserved in the library of Eton College. '10(D24) O. $1.20. Oxford Univ.

Gregg, Rev. Arth. Eug.
Quest of the Holy Grail. '09(Jl31) c. il. O. pap., 25 c. F. L. Masseck.

Gregg, Fred Marion.
Hdbk. of parliamentary law. '10(My7) c. S. 50 c. Ginn.

Gregg, J: Robert.
The Gregg reporter. '09(N) c. 7+111 p. 12°, $1.50. Gregg Pub.

GREGORIAN CHANTS.
See Church music.

GREGORY VII., *Pope.*
Smith, E. A. Hildebrand: the builder. *$1 net. Jennings.

Gregory, Sister, comp.
Queen of flowers, and her maids of honor. '08(D) c. 50 p. il. 12°, 50 c. Sisters of St. Joseph.

Gregory, Alva Adam.
Spinal adjustment; auxiliary method of treatment designed for the use of those who believe in and appreciate the true principle of progress in the healing art. '10(My) c. 487 p. il. 8°, $5. A. A. Gregory.

Gregory, Lady Augusta.
See Yeats, W: Butler.

Gregory, Caspar René, D.D.
Das Freer logion. '08(Je27) il. facsims., O. pap., 65 c. Lemcke.
Die griechischen handschriften des Neuen Testaments. '08(D5) O. (Versuche u. Entwürfe.) pap., $3.30. Lemcke.

Gregory, C: Lawson.
Alcoholism and insanity; with introd. by J. B. Gambrell. '10(N19) c. por. 12°, $1.50. Von Boeckmann-J.

Gregory, C: Noble.
Samuel Freeman Miller. '08(Ja18) il. pors. 8°, (Iowa biographical ser.) $2. State Hist. Ia.
Samuel Freeman Miller, associate justice of the Supreme Court of the United States, 1862-1890. '08(N21) 8°, *$2 net. Torch Press.

Gregory, Herbert Ernest, and Ellis, E. E.
Underground water resources of Connecticut; by Herbert E. Gregory; with a study of the occurrence of water in crystalline rock by E. E. Ellis. '09(N) 200 p. il. maps, tabs., O. (U. S., Dept. of the Interior, Geolog. Survey; Water supply papers.) pap. (Add. Superintendent for price.) U. S., Supt. of Docs.

—, Keller, Albert Golloway, and Bishop, Avard Longley.
Physical and commercial geography; study of certain controlling conditions of commerce. '10(Ap30) c. maps, O. $3. Ginn.

—, and Robinson, H: Hollister.
Preliminary geological map of Connecticut. '08(Ja4) il. map, O. (Connecticut state geolog. and natural hist. survey bull.) pap. (Add. pubs. for price.) Conn. Lib.

Gregory, Ja. J. H.
Cabbages and cauliflowers: how to grow them; pract. treatise, giving full details, incl. keeping and marketing the crop. Rev. ed. '08, [1909.] (F) c. 93 p. il. 12°, 30 c. J. J. H. Gregory.

Gregory, J: Wa.
Geology. '10(S) il. 16°, (Appleton's scientific primers.) 50 c. net. Appleton.

Gregory, Louise Fanshawe.
Mamma Nelly and I: story of a thinking doll. '08(O24) c. il. Q. $1.25. Stern.

Gregory, R: Arman, and Hadley, H: E.
Class book of physics. '10(F19) il. 12°, *$1 net. Macmillan.

Gregory, W: B:
Selection and installation of machinery for small pumping plants. '10(D) 40 p. il. 8°, (U. S., Dept. of Agriculture, Office of Experiment Stations, circular.)

Gregory, W: King.
Orders of mammals. '10(Je4) il. 8°, (American Museum of Natural Hist.) $5. Am. Museum.

Greig, Ja. Weir.
Game of bowling on the green or lawn bowls. '10(Jl2) c. il. pors. plan, 12°, (Spalding's athletic lib.) pap., 10 c. Am. Sports.

Grenell, Zelotes.
Church clerk; hdbk. for clerks of Baptist churches. '09(Je) c. 46 p. 12°, pap., 25 c. Am. Bapt.

Grenfell, Bernard Pyne, ed.
See Egypt Exploration Fund, Græco-Roman Branch.—Hellenica Oxyrhynchia.

GRENFELL, *Rev.* George.
Hawker, G: Life of George Grenfell. *$2 net. Revell.
Johnston, *Sir* H. H. George Grenfell and the Congo. 2 v. $7.50 special net. Appleton.

Grenfell, Wilfred Thomason, M.D.
Adrift on an ice-pan. '09(Je26) c. il. por. D. **75 c. Houghton M.
Down to the sea. '10(S17) c. D. $1 net. Revell.
Man's faith. '09(Ja9) c. D. bds., *50 c. net. Pilgrim Press.
A man's helpers. '10(O1) c. D. bds., 50 c. net. Pilgrim Press.
What life means to me. '10(Mr19) c. D. bds., *35 c. net. Pilgrim Press.

—, and others.
Labrador; the country and the people. '09 (N20) c. il. map, D. **$2.25 net. Macmillan.

Gresham, Otto.
Dred Scott case. '08(Jl) 45 p. O. pap. (Add. author for price.) O. Gresham.

Gresham, Rob. Jesse.
Sentiment and story. '08(F15) c. D. $1.50. Neale.

GRESHAM, *Sir* Thomas.
See Money.

Gress, Edm. Geiger.
Art and practice of typography; manual of American printing, incl. brief hist. up to the 20th century, with reproductions of the work of early masters of the craft and an extensive review and elaborate showing of modern commercial typographic specimens. '10(Ap9) c. il. (partly col.) facsims., (partly col.,) S. $5. Oswald.

"Gretchen," pseud.
See Wright, Fannie J.
—, comp. At the feet of Jesus: short prayers and texts for Lent, Holy Week, and Eastertide. '08(Mr7) S. pap., *25 c. net. Hills & H.

Greth, J: C: W:
Water purification facts for steam users. '10(My) c. 15 p. 8°, gratis. Scaife.

Greuze, Jean Baptiste.
Masterpieces of Greuze (1725-1895). '10 (S10) il. T. (Painters' ser.) leath., 75 c. net; pap., 25 c. net. Stokes.

GREUZE, Jean Baptiste.
Macklin, A. E. Greuze. *65 c. net. Stokes.

"Gréville, Henry," pseud.
See Durand, *Mme.* Alice Marie Céleste Fleury.

Grew, Edn. Sharpe.
Romance of modern geology. '08(N7) il. D. (Romance ser.) *$1.50 net. Lippincott.

Grew, Jos. Clark.
Sport and travel in the Far East. '10 (My21) c. il. O. $3 net. Houghton M.

GREY, Barbarina, *Lady.*
Lyster, G. Family chronicle. *$5 net. Dutton.

Grey, H:
Key to the Waverley novels in chronological sequence; with index of the principal characters. '10(Mr12) D. $1. Bowman.

GREY, *Lady* Jane.
Davey, R: Nine days' queen. *$3.50 net. Putnam.
Taylor, I. A. Lady Jane Grey and her times. *$4 special net. Appleton.

Grey, Maxwell, pseud.
See Tuttiett, Mary Gleed.

Grey, Zane.
Heritage of the desert: a novel. '10(S17) c. front. D. $1.50. Harper.
Last of the plainsmen: [trip across the Arizona Desert with "Buffalo Jones."] '08(S5) c. O. *$1.50 net. Outing.
Last trail. '09(Ap10) c. il. 12°, †$1. Burt.
Short-stop. '09(Jl10) c. il. D. $1.25. McClurg.
Young forester. '10(O15) c. front. D. $1.25. Harper.

Grey knight. De la Pasture, *Mrs.* E. B. †$1.50. Dutton.

Greylock, Godfrey, pseud.
See Smith, J. E. A.

GREYLOCK MOUNTAIN.
See **Berkshire Hills, Mass.**

Gribben, D: Sharpe.
Mathematics made easy. v. 1. '07, [1908.] (Mr.) c. 126 p. D. $1. D: S. Gribben.

Gribble, Fs. H:
Chateaubriand and his court of women. '09 (D11) pors. O. *$3.75 net. Scribner.
Geneva. '08(O24) il. 8°, (Color books.) *$2 net. Macmillan.
Lake of Geneva. '09(O2) il. map. 12°. (Color book ser.) *$6 net. Macmillan.
Lausanne. '09(My15) 8°, (Color books.) *$3 net. Macmillan.
Love affairs of Lord Byron. '10(D3) il. pors. 8°, $3.75 net. Scribner.
Montreux. '08(Je6) il. (Color books.) *$2.50 net. Macmillan.
Passions of the French romantics. '10 (Jl2) 4°, $3.75 net. Scribner.
Rousseau and the women he loved. '08 (D5) 8°, *$3.75 net. Scribner.

Grice, Mrs. Mary Van Meter.
Home and school united in widening circles of inspiration and service—home—school—community—nation; with pref. notes by Elmer Ellsworth Brown and Martin Grove Brumbaugh. '10(Ja15) c. il. 24°, 60 c. Sower.

Griechische handschriften des Neuen Testaments. Gregory, C. R. $3.30. Lemcke.

Grieg, Edvard Hagerup.
Fifty songs; ed by H: T. Finck for high voice. '09(F20) c. por. Q. (Musicians' lib.) $2.50; pap., $1.50. Ditson.
Larger piano compositions; ed. by Bertha Feiring Tapper. '09(F20) c. por. Q. (Musicians' lib.) $2.50; pap., $1.50. Ditson.
Piano lyrics and shorter compositions; ed. by Bertha Feiring Tapper; with a preface by S: Swift. '10(O22) c. F. (Musicians' lib.) $2.50; pap., $1.50. Ditson.

GRIEG, Edvard Hagerup.
Finck, H: T. Grieg and his music. **$2.50 net. Lane.
Lee, E. M. Grieg. 50 c.; $1. Macmillan.

Grieg, Ja.
Gainsborough. '10(F19) col. il. 8°, *$15 net. Macmillan.

Grier, Ja. Alex.
Pastoral homilies delivered as commencement addresses to the graduating classes of the Allegheny Theological Seminary; introd. by J: McNaugher. '10(F19) c. por. 12°, $1. Un. Presb. Bd.

Grier, T: Graham.
On the canal zone, Panama. '08(Ag22) c. il. por. fold. map, 8°, $1. Wagner & H.

Grierson, Mrs. Eliz. W.
Children's book of Celtic stories. '08(D12) il. 8°, (Color books for boys and girls.) *$2 net. Macmillan.
Children's tales of English minsters. '09 (D25) il. 12°, (Color books for boys and girls.) *$2 net. Macmillan.
Scottish fairy book. '10(D17) il. O. $1.50 net. Stokes.
Tales of English minsters. In 7 v. '10 (D10) il. (partly col.) D. bds., ea., 50 c. net. Macmillan.

Grierson, Fs.
Valley of shadows: recollections of the Lincoln country, 1858-1863. '09(Ap24) c. O. **$2 net. Houghton M.

Grierson, Herbert J: Clifford, comp.
See Dixon, W: Macneile, *comp.*

Griffin, Appleton Prentiss Clark, comp.
Bibliography of American historical societies (the United States and the Dominion of Canada). 2d ed., rev. and enl. '08 (Ap18) 8°, (American Historical Association, Annual report.) $1. U. S., Supt. of Docs.
Library of Congress list of books, (with reference to periodicals,) rel. to the eight-hour working day and to limitation of working hours in general. '08(Mr7) Q. pap., 15 c. U. S., Supt. of Docs.
Library of Congress list of books, (with references to periodicals,) rel. to postal savings banks. '08(Mr7) O. pap., 15 c. U. S., Supt. of Docs.
Library of Congress list of references on international arbitration. '09(Ja23) c. Q. pap., 20 c. U. S., Supt. of Docs.
Library of Congress list of works rel. to deep waterways from the Great Lakes to the Atlantic Ocean. '08(Je6) Q. pap., 25 c. U. S., Supt. of Docs.
Library of Congress list of works rel. to the first and second banks of the United States. '08(Je6) Q. pap., 25 c. U. S., Supt. of Docs.

Griffin, Appleton Prentiss Clark.—*Continued.*
Library of Congress list of works rel. to government regulation of insurance, U. S. and foreign countries. 2d ed. '08 (O10) O. pap. (Add. Supt. for price.) U. S., Supt. of Docs.
Library of Congress list of works rel. to political parties in the U. S. '07. [1908.] (F) Q. pap., 10 c. U. S., Supt. of Docs.
Library of Congress select list of books, (with references to periodicals,) rel. to currency and banking, with special regard to recent conditions. '08(Ap18) 8°, pap., 25 c. U. S., Supt. of Docs.
Library of Congress select list of references on corrupt practices in elections. '08 (O10) O. pap. (Add. Supt. for price.) U. S., Supt. of Docs.
Library of Congress select list of references on workingmen's insurance; general, United States, Great Britain, Germany, France, Belgium. '08(O10) O. pap. U. S., Supt. of Docs.

Griffin, Austin B., ed.
See New York [State.] Annot. code.

Griffin, C: Eldridge.
Four years in Europe with Buffalo Bill: a descriptive narrative of the big American show's successful tour in foreign lands. '08, [1909.] (Mr) c. 94 p. il. pors. 8°, $1. C: E. Griffin.

Griffin, C: Lewis.
Machine design. '08(Je13) il. (American School of Correspondence pubs.) $1.50. Am. Sch. Corr.

Griffin, Grace Gardner, comp.
Writings on American history, 1906: a bibliography of books and articles on United States and Canadian history published during the year 1906. '08(O3); 1907. '09 (Je19); 1908. '10(Je11) O. ea., **$2.50 net. Macmillan.

Griffin, Martin Ignatius Jos.
Catholics and the American Revolution. In 2 v. v. 2. '09(Ja9) il. 8°, $3. M. I. J. Griffin.
General Stephen Moylan, muster-master general, secretary and aide-de-camp to General Washington, quartermaster-general, colonel of Fourth Pennsylvania Light Dragoons, the first and last president of the Friendly Sons of St. Patrick; also contains The Moylans in the Revolution, John, James and Jasper. '09 (Ap3) il. 8°, $1.50. M. I. J. Griffin.
Story of Commodore John Barry, "the father of the American navy," [1745-1803.] '08(Ap4) c. il. 8°, $1; pap., 50 c. M. I. J. Griffin.

Griffin, Russell B.
Pianoforte telegraphy, (Morse telegraph code.) '08(Ja4) f°, $1. Morse Art.

Griffin, W. Hall.
Life of Robert Browning; with notices of his writings, his family, and his friends; completed and ed. by Harry Christopher Minchin. '09(D10) il. pors. O. $3.50 net. Macmillan.

Griffin's scientific text-books. il. D. Lippincott.
—Chatley. Force of the wind. *$1.25 net.
—Smith. Suction gas plants. *$1.75 net.
—Stewart. Elementary text-book of physics. pt. 2, 3. ea., *$1.50 net.

Griffin's technological handbooks. il. D. Lippincott.
—Farrell. Dyeing and cleaning. (Add. pubs. for price.)
—Ingle. Elementary agricultural chemistry. *$1.50 net.

Griffis, W: Elliott.
Fire-fly's lovers, and other fairy tales of old Japan. '08(O10) c. il. D. †$1. Crowell.
Story of New Netherland; the Dutch in America. '09(Ap24) c. il. D. **$1.25 net. Houghton M.

Griffith, A. Hume-.
See Hume-Griffith, A.

Griffith, Elmer Cummings.
Epochs in Baptist history. '09(My8) D. pap. (Add. pubs. for price.) Advance.

Griffith, Helen Sherman.
Help wanted: a comedy. '08(N7) c. D. pap., 15 c. Penn Pub. Co.
Letty and the twins. '10(Jl2) c. il. front. 12°, 60 c. Penn Pub. Co.
Patty of the circus. '09(N13) c. il. D. 60 c. Penn Pub. Co.

Griffith, Ira S:
Essentials of woodworking. '08(N21) c. il. D. $1.25; Rev. ed. '09(D) il. 12°, $1. Manual Arts.

Griffith, Ja. Bray.
Administrative and industrial organization; instruction paper. '09(D4) c. il. charts, 4°, (American School of Correspondence pubs.) pap., 50 c. Am. Sch. Corr.
Advertising and sales organization; instruction paper. [1910.] (Ap) c. 64 p. il. map, forms, 8°, (American School of Correspondence pubs.) 50 c. Am. Sch. Corr.
Corporation accounts; instruction paper. '09(D4) c. forms, 8°, (American School of Correspondence pubs.) 50 c. Am. Sch. Corr.
Credit organization; instruction paper. [1910.] (Ap) c. 54 p. forms, 8°, (American School of Correspondence pubs.) 50 c. Am. Sch. Corr.
Purchasing and stores department; instruction paper. '09(D4) c. il. forms, 8°, (American School of Correspondence pubs.) 50 c. Am. Sch. Corr.
Records of labor and manufacturing orders; instruction paper. '09(D4) c. il. forms, 8°, (American School of Correspondence pubs.) 50 c. Am. Sch. Corr.
Shipping department; instruction paper. '10 (O1) c. forms, 8°, (Am. School of Correspondence pubs.) (Priv. pr.) Am. Sch. Corr.
Single entry bookkeeping—comparative statements; instruction paper. '09(D4) c. forms, 8°, (American School of Correspondence pubs.) 50 c. Am. Sch. Corr.

Griffith, Ja. Bray.—*Continued.*
Single proprietors' and partners' accounts; instruction paper. '09(N20) c. forms, 8°, (American School of Correspondence pubs.) 50 c. Am. Sch. Corr.
Voucher system accounting charts; instruction paper. '09(D4) c. il. forms, 8°, (American School of Correspondence pubs.) 50 c. Am. Sch. Corr.
Wholesale, commission, and storage accounts. '09(D25) c. forms, 8°, (American School of Correspondence pubs.) 50 c. Am. Sch. Corr.
See also Am. Sch. of Correspondence.

—, and Sweetland, C: A:
Trustees', executors', and stock brokers' accounts. '09(D25) c. forms, 8°, (American School of Correspondence pubs.) 50 c. Am. Sch. Corr.

Griffith, Ja. Eveleth.
Diary of the home: journal of the everyday doings of the family. '08(Je20) c. Q. $4; full lev., $6. Griffith-S.

Griffith, Mrs. M. E. Hume-.
See Hume-Griffith, *Mrs.* M. E.

Griffith, Michael Jos., D.D.
Meaning of the mass: adapted to the doctrinal, moral and historical explanations of the holy mass. '09(Mr) c. 248 p. 12°, *$1 net. Kenedy.

Griffiths, D:
Protected stock range in Arizona. '10 (Je) 28 p. il. map, 8°, (U. S., Dept. of Agriculture; Bureau of Plant Industry bull.)

Griffiths, T: Michael.
Non-secret formulas. 2d ed. [1910.] (N) 514 p. 8°, $5. Interstate Pr.

Griggs, E: Howard.
Art and the human spirit. '08(D5) c. O. *50 c. net; pap., *25 c. net. B: W. Huebsch.
Great autobiographies: types and problems of manhood and womanhood. '08(F1) c. D. *50 c. net; pap., *25 c. net. B: W. Huebsch.
Human equipment, its use and abuse. '09 (O30) c. S. (Art of life ser.) *50 c. net. B: W. Huebsch.

Griggs, Sutton Elbert.
Needs of the South. '09(Ap17) c. D. pap., 10 c. Orion Pub.
Pointing the way. '08(S19) c. D. $1. Orion Pub.
Race question in a new light. '09(Ap17) c. D. pap., 15 c. Orion Pub.

Griggs, W: C:, M.D.
See Forward Movement Mission studies.

Grillparzer, Franz.
König Ottokars glück und ende; trauerspiel in fünf aufzügen; ed., with introd. and notes, by Carl Edg. Eggert. '10 (Jl2) c. il. pors. map, D. 60 c. Holt.

GRILLPARZER, Franz.
De Walsh, F. C: Grillparzer as a poet of nature. $1 net. Lemcke.
Williamson, E: J: Grillparzer's attitude toward Romanticism. 50 c. net. Univ. of Chic.

Grills, Merton W.
Alpha; a few poems collected to commemorate the first home-coming of Richsquare, Aug. 22, 1908. '08(D) 38 p. il. 12°, pap., 25 c. M. W. Grills.

Grime, J. H.
Hist. of alien immersion and valid baptism, involving researches from different viewpoints, by various writers. '09(S18) D. pap., *15 c. net. Bapt. Bk.

Grimes, Rev. Wa. B.
Water wagon, and other poems; with ten new temperance rally songs. '09(Ag21) c. O. pap., 15 c. W. B. Grimes.

Grimké, Archibald H:
Modern industrialism and the negroes of the United States. '09(Mr6) 8°, (Occasional papers.) pap., 15 c. Am. Negro Acad.

Grimke, Rev. Fs. Ja.
Christianity and race prejudice; two discourses delivered in the Fifteenth Street Presbyterian Church, Washington, D. C., May 29th and June 5th, 1910. [1910.] (S) 29 p. 8°, 15 c. F. J. Grimke.
Equality of rights for all citizens, black and white alike: discourse del. in the 50th St. Presbyterian Church, Washingtón, D. C., Sunday, March 7th, 1909. '09 (Jl) 19 p. 8°, pap., 5 c. F. J. Grimke.
Progress and development of the colored people of our nation; address del. before the American Missionary Association, October 21, 1908, at Galesburg, Ill. '09 (Jl3) 8°, pap., 10 c. F. J. Grimke.

Grimm, Albert Friedrich Wilhelm, ["Alfr. Ira."]
Im zuckerbusch; eine erzählung aus Wisconsins vergangenheit. 2 v. '09(D) c. il. 12°, $1.75. Antigo.

Grimm, Carl Rob.
Secondary stresses in bridge trusses. '08 (Je20) c. tabs., 8°, $2.50. Wiley.

Grimm, Jakob Ludwig Karl and Wilhelm Karl.
Animal stories. '09(N6) il. 4°, $1.50. Duffield.
Fairy tales. '09(Ag) 336 p. il. 8°, *$1.50 net. Dodge.
Fairy tales; ed. by Wa. Jerrold. '10(D) 12°, (Children's classics.) $1.25. Dutton.
Fairy tales; sel. and retold by Githa Sowerby. '10(S10) col. il. O. $2 net. Stokes.
Fairy tales for children and the household; a new tr. by N. J. Davidson. '08(O10) il. D. (Bowman's illustrated lib. of world-favorite books.) $1. Bowman.
Fairy tales from Grimm; ed., with an introd., by Hamilton W. Mabie. '09(N6) c. il. Q. $1.50, boxed. Stern.
Fairy tales of the brothers Grimm; il. by Arthur Rackham; tr. by Mrs. Edgar Lucas. '10(Ja22) O. hf. cl., *$6 net, boxed; ed. de luxe, *$20 net, boxed. Doubleday, P.
Fairy tales told in easy French by Kathleen Fitzgerald. '09, [1910.] (Ja) col. il. sq. 16°, (Children's favorites.) *50 c. net. Jacobs.
House in the wood, and other fairy stories. '10(D31) col. il. 8°, bds., $1.35 net. Warne.

Grimm, Jakob Ludwig Karl and Wilhelm Karl.—*Continued.*
Household stories; ed. by J. R. Monsell. '08(D5) $1.25. Cassell.
Stories from Grimm, told to the children, by Amy Steedman. '08(Je6) il. 16°, (Told to the children ser.) 50 c. Dutton.
See also Kern, Ja. R.
Grimm, Wilhelm Karl.
See Grimm, Jakob Ludwig Karl.
Grimm lib. 12°. Scribner.
—Boswell. Irish precursor of Dante. *$3.50 net.
Grimsdale, G. E.
See Corbion, W: Amelius.
Grimshaw, Beatrice Ethel.
In the strange south seas. '08(N7) il. O. *$3.50 net. Lippincott.
New New Guinea. '10(D10) il. 8°, $3.50 net. Lippincott.
Vaiti of the Islands. '08(N14) c. il. D. †$1.50. Wessels.
Grimshaw, Rob.
Engine runner's catechism; work cont. answers to direct questions on how to erect, adjust, and run the principal steam engines used in the United States; being a sequel to the author's "Steam engine catechism." 7th ed. '10(D17) c. il. 16°, $2. Henley.
Modern workshop hints. '10(Jl30) D. $2. McKay.
Locomotive catechism. 27th ed., entirely rev., enl. and reset. '08(Mr14) c. il. 12°, $2.50. Henley.
GRINDING.
Commercial grinding. 25 c. Brown & S.
Grinding and lapping. '09(Je5) c. il. 8°, (Machinery's reference ser.) pap., 25 c. Indust. Press.
Grinnell, Fordyce, jr.
Quarternary myriopods and insects of California. '08. 207-215 p. il. Q. (Univ. of Cal. pubs., Geology.) pap., 10 c. Univ. of Cal.
Grinnell, G: Bird.
Jack the young explorer. '08(S5) c. D. †$1.25. Stokes.
Grinnell, Hilda Wood.
See Grinnell, Jos.
Grinnell, Jos.
Bibliog. of California ornithology. '09(S) 166 p. 4°, (Cooper Ornithological Club of California; Pacific coast avifauna.) $1.50. W. L. Chambers.
Biota of the San Bernardino Mountains. '09(Ja16) il. map, Q. (Univ. of Cal. pubs.; Zoology.) pap., $2. Univ. of Cal.
New cowbird of the genus *molothrus;* with note on the probable genetic relationships of the North American forms. '09. [1910.] (F) 275-281 p. Q. (Univ. of Cal. pubs.; Zoology.) pap., 5 c. Univ. of Cal.
Three new song sparrows from California. '09(My15) Q. (Univ. of Cal. pubs.; Zoology.) pap., 5 c. Univ. of Cal.
Two heretofore unnamed wrens of the genus *Thryomanes;* Savannah sparrow of the Great Basin; second record of the spotted bat (*Euderma maculatum*) for

Grinnell, Jos.—*Continued.*
California. '10(Ap) 307-320 p. Q. (University of California pubs.; Zoology.) pap., 15 c. Univ. of Cal.
See also Heller, Edm.
— and Hilda Wood.
Reptiles of Los Angeles County, Cal. '08 (O) 64 p. il. 8°, (Throop Institute bull., Science ser.) pap., gratis. Throop Poly. Inst.
Grisewood, Rob. Norman.
Zarlah the Martian. '09(Ag7) c. front. D. $1. Fenno.
Grismer, Jos. Rhode.
'Way down east. '09(Ap) 190 p. il. 12°. 75 c. J. S. Ogilvie.
Grissom, Irene Welch.
The superintendent. '10(D17) c. D. $1.35 net. A. Harriman.
Griswold, Grace.
Love and the year and other poems. '10 (D17) c. D. bds., 60 c. net. Duffield.
GRISWOLD FAMILY.
See Genealogies, Allyn, A. B.
Gritman, C:
See Chicago law directory.
Grizzly bear. Wright, W. H. **$1.50 net. Scribner.
Groat, B: Feland.
New methods in backwater computations; with additions. '09(S) c. 15 p. 4°, 25 c. (o. p.) Univ. of Minn.
GROCERS.
Tupman, W. F. Grocery. $1. Pitman.
Groenings, Ja.
History of the passion of our Lord Jesus Christ. 2d rev. ed. '08(D5) 8°, *$1.25 net. Herder.
Groff, J: Eldred.
Materia medica for nurses; and questions for self-examination. 4th rev. ed., rearranged by Lucy C. Ayers; sections on therapeutics rewritten by Herman C. Pitts. '08(Je); 5th ed. '09(N) c. 12°, ea., *$1.25 net. Blakiston.
Grohman, W: Adolph Baillie.
See Baillie-Grohman, W: Adolph.
Grohusko, Jacob Abraham.
Jack's manual: treatise on the care and handling of wines and liquors: recipes for fancy mixed drinks, and when and how to serve. '08(O) c. 58 p. 12°, $1. J. A. Grohusko.
Jack's manual on the vintage and production, care and handling of wines, liquors, etc.; hdbk. of information for home, club, or hotel; recipes for fancy mixed drinks and when and how to serve. '10(Ap) c. 5-87 p. il. por. 12°, $1. J. A. Grohusko.
GROLIER, Jean, *Vicomte* d' Aguisy.
Le Roux de Lincy, A. J. V. Researches concerning Jean Grolier, his life and his library. (Add. Club for price.) Grolier Club.
Grolier Club, New York.
Catalogue of an exhibition of early American engraving upon copper, 1727-1850, at the Grolier Club, January 24 to February 15, 1908. '08(Mr) c. 100 p. por. 12°. (Add. Club for price.) **Grolier Club.**

GROLIER CLUB, New York.
See **Printers and printing.**

Gronau, Georg, comp.
Masterpieces of sculpture; 120 examples. In 2 v. v. 1, From the earliest times to Michelangelo; v. 2, From Michelangelo to the present day. '10(D17) T. pap., ea., 25 c. net. Stokes.

Grondahl, Lars Olai.
Synchronous commutation as a method for alternating-current—direct-current transformation. '09(N) 19 p. il. 8°, pap., 20 c. Johns Hopkins.

Groner, Augusta.
Joe Muller, detective; being the acct. of some adventures in the professional experience of a member of the Imperial Austrian Police; [tr. by] Grace Isabel Colbron. '10(My21) c. D. $1.50. Duffield.

Groom, Percy.
Trees and their life histories. '08(D12) il. 4°, *$10 net. Cassell.

Groot, Jan Jakob Maria de.
See De Groot, J. J. M.

Gros, Raymond, ed.
T. R. in cartoon. '10(Ag6) c. il. 8°, $1. Saalfield.

Grose, E: Fabrique.
Centennial history of the village of Ballston Spa, incl. the towns of Ballston and Milton; incl. an unpublished history of the late J: C. Booth: souvenir of the centennial celebration held June 22-25, 1907. '08(Jl4) c. il. pors. 4°, $2. E: F. Grose.

GROSS, *Rev.* Carl.
Gross, C., *jr. and* E: M. Auxiliarium: predigtentwürfe aus der fünfzigjährigen amtszeit dès seligen pastor C. Gross, sen. 45 c. C. Gross.

Gross, Carl, jr., and E: M., eds.
Auxiliarium; predigtentwürfe aus den fünfzigjährigen amtszeit dès seligen pastor C. Gross, sen. '08, [1909.] (Mr) c. 40 p. por. 8°, 45 c. C. Gross.

Gross, F: L:
Law of real estate brokers; with forms: manual for the use of lawyers and real estate operators. '10(D) 473 p. 8°, $4. Ronald Press.

GROSS, Samuel Eberly.
Plagiarism of The merchant prince of Cornville, by Cyrano de Bergerac. (Not for sale.) Rand, McN. & Co.

Grosscup, P: Stenger.
Celebration of Abraham Lincoln's birthday and second anniversary of institution of General James Shields Council no. 967, Knights of Columbus, February 12, 1907: address. '08(Je6) 8°. (Add. author for price.) P: S. Grosscup.

Grossman, Rabbi Rudolph, D.D.
Brief manual regarding Jewish faith and life. '09(My) c. 24 p. 12°, pap., 12 c. Bloch.

Children's services; arranged for each week of the month, holidays and for patriotic occasions. '09(Ap17) c. 12°, pap., 10 c. Bloch.

Grossvaters jugenderinnerungen. Zorn, C. M. 2 v. $2. Northwestern Pub.

Grosvenor, Gilbert Hovey, ed.
Scenes from every land: illustrations from the *National Geographic Magazine;* with short bibliography of gazetteers, atlases, and books descriptive of foreign countries and natural history. '08(Mr7) c. 8°, $1; leath., $2.50; Second ser. '10(Ja8) c. 8°, $2. Nat. Geographic Soc.

Grosvenor, Sarah E.
See Whitcomb, Ida Prentice.

Grosvenor Library, Buffalo, N. Y. Catalogue of the books rel. to music in the Grosvenor Library. '10(Ja15) 8°, gratis. Grosvenor Lib.

Grosvenor Library, Buffalo, N. Y. Index-catalogue of books in the department of local history and genealogy. Ed. of 1908. '08(Je) 65 p. 8°, pap., 25 c. Grosvenor Lib.

Grosvenor Library, Buffalo, N. Y. Reading list on birds and bird study. '09(O) 14 p. 8°, pap., gratis. Grosvenor Lib.

Groszmann, Maximilian Paul Eugen.
Classification of exceptional children as a guide in determining segregation. [1910.] (N) 12 p. 8°. Groszmann.

Groszmann School for Nervous and Atypical Children, founded April 1, 1900, maintained by the National Association for the Study and Education of Exceptional Children, Maximilian P. E. Groszmann, Ph.D., director. '09, [1910.] 24 p. por. 8°. Groszmann.

Grotenfelt, Gösta.
Principles of modern dairy practice from a bacteriological point of view; authorized American ed. by F. W. Woll. 3d ed., rev. '08(D) 6+286 p. il. 12°, $2. Wiley.

Groth, Lorentz Alb.
Welding and cutting of metals by aid of gases or electricity. '09(Ag14) il. 8°, **$3 net. Van Nostrand.

Groton, Rev. W: Mansfield, and others, eds.
Sunday-school teacher's manual. '09(Ja30) c. O. **$1 net. Jacobs.

GROTON, Ct.
Burgess, C: F., *ed.* Historic Groton. $2. C: F. Burgess.

GROTON, Mass.
Green, S: A. Slavery at Groton, Mass., in provincial times. 25 c. S: A. Green.
Green, S: A. Three historical addresses at Groton, Mass. $2.50. Littlefield.
See also Prescott, William.

GROUND-SQUIRRELS.
See Squirrels.

Ground tumbling. Worth, H: W. 10 c. Am. Sports.

Grounds and rudiments of law. *See* Hughes, W: Taylor.

Group of English essayists of the early nineteenth century. Winchester, C. T: **$1.50 net. Macmillan.

GROUSE.
Malcolm, G:, *and* Maxwell, A. Grouse and grouse moors. $2.75 net. Macmillan.
See also Birds.

Grousset, Paschal.
See Laurie, André, *pseud.*

Grove, Sir G:, ed.
Dictionary of music and musicians; ed. by J. A. Fuller Maitland. In 5 v. v. 4. '08 (Je13); v. 5. '10(Ag6) c. il. pors. O. ea., **$5 net. (Subs. only.) Macmillan.

Grover, Edn. Osgood.
Gift of friendship and other verses. '10 (O) c. 30 p. 12°, 50 c. Canterbury.
—, and Wellman, Harry Richmond, comps.
Songs of Dartmouth College. '10(Ja22) c. '98, '09. Q. (Songs of Dartmouth College ser.) *$1.20 net. Grover & W.
—, ed. Book of good cheer: [quotations.] '09(My) 16°.—Book of good fellowship; "a plate of toasts." '09(Mr) c. 63 p. ea., $1. Volland.
Grover, F:
Modern gas and oil engines. 5th ed., rev. and enl. '10(Je4) c. il. 12°, $2. Spon.
Grover, Nahum Wesley.
Catechetical Bible lessons. '10(Jl2) c. T. pap., 10 c. Winona.
Groves, Ernest W. Hey.
Synopsis of surgery. '08(D19) 12°, *$2.50 net; 2d ed., rev. '10(Ap) il. 12°, $3.25 net. Wood.
Groves, J. W.
See Belden, A. W.
Groves-Showell, P.
Definitions in navigation and nautical astronomy: together with descriptions of the various instruments used for the purpose of navigation; also tables of weights and measures and complete list of formulæ for determining areas and volumes. '08(Jl18) maps, D. *$1.25 net. Lippincott.
Growing church. McAfee, C. B. *50 c. net. Northfield Press.
Growing South. Alderman, E. A. 10 c. Civic Forum.
Growth in silence. Cocroft, S. 60 c. Physical Culture Ex.
Growth of corporate wealth. Hanks, C: S. 50 c. Authors' Pub.
Growth of large fortunes. Watkins, G: P. $1. Macmillan.
Growth of Philippine children. Bobbitt, J: F. (Add. author for price.) J. F. Bobbitt
Growth of the English house. Gotch, J: A. *$3 net. Scribner.
Growth of the Gospels. Petrie, W: M. F. 90 c. net. Baker & T.
Grubb, E:
Authority and the light within: [talks on Quaker doctrine.] '08(S26) D. *80 c. net. Winston.
Gruber, Calvin Luther.
Government of the state of Pennsylvania, incl. local government. '09(Jl) c. 9-173 p. il. 8°, $1.50. C. L. Gruber.
Government of the United States. '09 (My) c. 6+7-446 p. il. map, 8°, $1.50. C. L. Gruber.
Grumbine, Harvey Carson.
Love, faith and endeavor: [poems.] '09 (O) 3-76 p. 12°, *$1 net. Sherman, F.
Grumbine, Jesse C: Fremont.
Telepathy; or, the science of thought transference. '10(Je25) c. 12°, 50 c. Order of White Rose (Mass.)
Grundy, Mrs. Mabel Sarah Barnes-.
See Barnes-Grundy, *Mrs.* Mabel Sarah.
Grüne sklaven. Schrader, G: H. F. *$1 net. Stechert.
Gruner, O. C., M.D.
Studies in puncture fluids. '09(Mr) c. 18+287 p. 8°, *$3 net. Blakiston.
Grünwald, Julius.
Enamelling on iron and steel. '10(F19) 8°, *$2 net. Lippincott.
Gruse, E:
Poems. '09(Jl31) c. 12°, $1. B'way Pub.
Spirit of the woods: comedy. '09(Jl31) c. 12°, $1 B'way Pub.
Grützmacher, R: Heinrich.
Virgin birth. '08(Ja4) S. (Foreign religious ser.) *40 c. net. Eaton & M.
GRYLLUS.
See Crickets.
GUADALOUPE MOUNTAINS, New Mexico.
Girty, G: H. Guadaloupian fauna. $1.50. U. S., Supt. of Docs.
GUAM, Ladrone Islands.
Bible. N. T. Four Gospels and the Acts of the apostles of the New Testament of our Lord and Savior Jesus Christ and the Psalms; [tr. into Chamorro.] pap., 30 c. Am. Bible.
Safford, W. E. Chamorro language of Guam, grammar of the idiom spoken by the inhabitants of the Marianne, or Ladrone Islands. *$1 net. Lowdermilk.
GUANAJUATO, Mexico.
Myers, C. B. G. City of dreams, (Guanajuato,) [Mexico.] 50 c. P. M. Myers.
Guarantee of bank deposits. Herrick, M. T. gratis. M. T. Herrick.
GUARANTIES AND SURETIES.
Bunker, R. E., *ed.* Cases on suretyship. $3.50. Wahr.
Guaranty of bank deposits. Laughlin, J. L. (Add. pubs. for price.) Johnson, K. & Q.
Guaranty of bank deposits. Revell, A. H. (Add. author for price.) A. H. Revell.
GUATEMALA, Central America.
Dearborn, N. Catalogue of a collection of birds from Guatemala. 50 c. Field Museum.
Defense of the government of Guatemala before the Central American Court of Justice at Cartago, in the case of Honduras. (Add. pubs. for price.) Int. Bu. Am. Republics.
International Bureau of American Republics. Guatemala; general descriptive data. (Add. pubs. for price.) Int. Bu. Am. Republics.
Meek, S. E. Zoölogy of lakes Amatitlan and Atitlan, Guatemala, with special reference to ichthyology. 50 c. Field Museum.
Winter, N. O. Guatemala and her people of to-day. $3. L. C. Page.
See also Mosses;—Peten.
Guay, Marcellin.
See Colin, *Father.*
GUELL, Antonio.
See Amrine, T: Hamer.
Guéranger, Prosper L: Paschal.
Religious and monastic life explained; authorized version from the French; [tr.] by Rev. Jerome Veth. '08, [1909.] (Mr) c. 113 p. 16°, *50 c. net. Herder.

Guerber, Hélène Adeline.
Easy French prose composition; based on Contes et legendes, 1re partie. '09(Je26) c. D. 25 c. Am. Bk.
Joan of Arc; French composition; with notes and vocabulary. '10(S17) c. D. 30 c. Am. Bk.
Stories of Shakespeare's comedies. '10 (O22) c. il. D. $1.25 net. Dodd.
Story of old France. '10(S17) c. il. D. (Eclectic readings.) 65 c. Am. Bk.
Guerilla chief and other tales. Reid, M. $1. Dutton.
Guérin, Eugénie de.
Journal. '08(O17) 24°, (New universal lib.) 50 c.; leath., 75 c. Dutton.
Guerini, Vincenzo.
Hist. of dentistry from the most ancient times until the end of the 18th century. '09(S) 375 p. il. 8°, *$6 net. Lea.
Guess work. Forman, E. S. $1. Badger.
GUESSING CONTESTS.
See Amusements.
Guest, Edgar Albert.
Home rhymes, from "Breakfast table chat." '09(D11) c. 12°, $1. H. R. Guest.
Guest at the gate. Thomas, E. M. $1.50. Badger.
GUEST BOOKS.
Book of hospitalities and a record of guests; with a foreword on old house mottoes. $1.50 net. P. Elder.
Guiterman, A. Guest book. *$7.50 net; *$15 net. P. Elder.
Guest of Quesnay. Tarkington, N. B. †$1.50. McClure.
Gueth, Oswald.
Refrigerating engineer's pocket manual. '08 (O12) c. il. por. 12°, $1.50. O. Gueth.
Guggisberg, F: Gordon.
See Guggisberg, *Mrs.* Lilian Decima Moore.
Guggisberg, Mrs. Lilian Decima Moore and F: Gordon.
We two in West Africa. '09(My22) il. maps, 8°, *$3.50 net. Scribner.
Guida per gl' immigranti Italiani. Ellis, E: S. gratis. C. M. Panunzio.
GUIDE BOOKS.
See Automobiles;—Railroads;—Voyages and travels;—*also* names of countries and places.
Guide for girls in the journey of life. Wetzel, F. X. 40 c. Herder.
Guide ser., (formerly Child's guide ser.) il. D. $1.25 net. Baker & T.
—Caffin. Guide to pictures.
—Clarke. Guide to mythology.
—Elson. Guide to American history.
—Macy. Guide to reading.
—Mason. Guide to music.
—Singleton. Guide to great cities; Northwestern Europe.
—Stevenson. Guide to biography for young readers.
Guide to Belgium, incl. the Ardennes and Luxemburg. 5th ed., rev. and enl. '10 (Ag27) il. map, S. (Slip-in-the-pocket guide books.) $1 net. Platt & P.
Guide to French pronunciation. De La Rochelle, P. *50 c. net. Stechert.
Guide to Greece, the Archipelago, Constantinople, the coasts of Asia Minor, Crete, and Cyprus. '08(Je6) maps, plans, 16°, (Macmillan's guides.) *$2.75 net. Macmillan
Guide to high school observation. Whipple, G. M. 40 c. Bardeen.
Guide to Holland. '10(Ag27) il. map, plans, S. (Slip-in-the-pocket guide books.) $1 net. Platt & P.
Guide to modern opera. Singleton, E. **$1.50 net. Dodd.
Guide to Paris and its environs. 8th ed., rev. '10(Ag27) map, plan, S. (Slip-in-the-pocket guide books.) $1 net Platt & P.
Guide to sanitary inspections. Gerhard, W: P. $1.50. Wiley.
Guide to successful squab raising. Jones, M. O. 50 c. M. O. Jones.
Guide to Switzerland. 6th ed., rewritten and reillustrated. '10(Ag27) il. map, S. (Slip-in-the-pocket guide book.) $1 net. Platt & P.
Guide to technical writing. Rickard, T: A. $1. Mining and Scientific.
Guide to the country home. Parkinson, E: K. *$1 net. Outing.
Guide to the materials for the history of the United States in Spanish archives. Shepherd, W: R. 50 c. Carnegie.
Guide to the mushrooms. Cole, E. T. $1.50 net. Doubleday, P.
Guide to the study and use of reference books. Kroeger, A. B. *$1.25 net. A. L. A.
Guide to the teachers' mastery of texts. Buck, E. C. 85 c. E. C. Buck.
Guide to the twelve tissue remedies of biochemistry. Anshutz, E: P. 75 c. Boericke & T.
GUIDES (*English regiment*).
Younghusband, G: J: Story of the Guides. *$2.25 net. Macmillan.
Guiding hand. Kidd, J. N: $1.50. J. N: Kidd.
Guiding voices. Jenison, S. A. 35 c. S. A. Jenison.
Guigou, Paul.
Animal trainer. '10(N5) col. il. obl. D. $1.25. Duffield.
Animals in the Ark; tr. from the French by Edgar Mills. '09(N6) col. il. $1.25. Duffield.
Guilday, P: K.
See Barton, G:
GUILDS.
Morse, H. B. Gilds of China. *$1.20 net. Longmans.
Unwin, G: Gilds and companies of London. *$2 net. Scribner.
See also Trade-unions.
GUILFORD COURT HOUSE (Battle of).
Morehead, J. M. Battle of Guilford Court House, North Carolina. gratis. J. M. Morehead.
Smith, C: A. Significance of hist. in a democracy. Guilford Battle.
Guillotine Club. Mitchell, S. W. $1.50. Century Co.
Guilty? Arctander, K. J. L. W. A. $1.25. Cochrane.
Guiness, H: Grattan, D.D.
"On the rock"; the certainties of religion contrasted with the speculations of philosophy. '09(O23) 12°, *$1 net. Revell.

Guiney, Louise Imogen.
Happy ending. '09(D25) c. front. O. **$3 net, boxed. (500 copies.) Houghton M.

Guinness, Geraldine.
Peru: its story, people and religion. '09 (Mr6) 8°, *$2.50 net. Revell.

Guiterman, Arth.
Guest book; pages for the bright chronicles of hospitality. '08(D12) Golden fabric ed., *$7.50 net, boxed; pigskin, *$15 net. P. Elder.
See also Leconte de Lisle, Charles Marie René.

Guizot, François Pierre Guillaume.
History of civilization in Europe. *See* Green, J: R: Short hist. of the English people. v. 3.
Hist. of England. 4 v. New imperial lib. ed. '10(D) il. 8°, ea., $1.25; hf. cf., $2.25; New il. sterling ed., ea., $1. (Sets only.) Estes.
Hist. of France. 8 v. '10(D) $24. Crowell.
Hist. of France. 8 v. New imperial ed. '10 (D) il. 8°, ea., $1.25; hf. cf., $2.25; New il. sterling ed., ea., $1. (Sets only.) Estes.

Guldner, Hugo.
Design and construction of internal combustion engines; tr. and rev. by H. Diederich. '10(Ag6) il. 4°, $10 net. Van Nostrand.

GULF OF MEXICO.
United States. *Hydrographic Offices.* Navigation of the Gulf of Mexico and Caribbean Sea. v. 1. 6th ed.; the West India Islands; incl. the Bermuda Islands and the Bahama Banks, [and Supplement.] 2 v. '09(Je) 8°, (U. S. Hydrographic Office pubs.) pap. (Add. Superintendent for price.) U. S., Supt. of Docs

Gulf songs. Robertson, S: L. (Add. author for price.) S: L. Robertson.

Gulick, Mrs. Charlotte Emily Vetter.
Emergencies. '09(Jl3) c. il. D. (Gulick hygiene ser.) 40 c. Ginn.

Gulick, E: L.
See Gulick, Sidney Lewis.

Gulick, Luther Halsey, M.D.
Healthful art of dancing. '10(O8) c. il. D. $1.40 net Doubleday, P.
Mind and work. '08(N14) c. D. **$1.20 net. Doubleday, P.

—, and Ayres, Leonard P.
Medical inspection of schools. '08(N14) c. O. (Russell Sage foundation.) $1. Charities Pub.

Gulick, Sidney Lewis, D.D., and E: L.
Outline studies of the growth of the kingdom of God. '10(Jl2) c. D. 50 c. net. Pilgrim Press.

Gulick hygiene ser.; ed. by Luther Halsey Gulick, M. D. il. D. Ginn.
—Gulick. Emergencies. 40 c.
—Jewett. Body and its defenses. 65 c.—Body at work. 50 c.—Control of body and mind. 50 c.

Gull, Cyril Arth. E: Ranger.
See Thorne, Guy, *pseud.*

Gulliver, Gilbert H:
Metallic alloys: their structure and constitution. '08(D19) il. 12°, *$2 net. Lippincott.

Gulliver, Lucile.
Over the Nonsense Road. '10(N12) c. col. il. O. $1.50 net. Appleton.

Gulliver's travels. *See* Swift, Jonathan.

Gummere, Mrs. Amelia Mott.
City of Penn; being a brief account of the history of Philadelphia from 1683 to 1908. '08(N) c. 29 p. il. 12°, 20 c. Biddle Press.
Quaker in the forum. '10(F26) c. il. O. **$1.50 net. Winston.
Witchcraft and Quakerism: study in social history. '09(My22) $1. Biddle Press.

Gummere, Fs. Barton.
See Hinchman, Wa. S.

Gummey, H: Riley, jr., D.D.
Consecration of the eucharist. '08(Mr) c. 34+459 p. 8°, *$2 net. Anners.

Gun Club boys of Lakeport. Stratemeyer, E: †$1.25. Lothrop, L. & S.

GUN COTTON.
Munroe, C: E: Detonation of gun cotton. (Priv. pr.) Am. Philosophical.

Gun-runner (The). Stringer, A. J: A. $1.50. B. W. Dodge.

Gunn, Ja.
Pract. design of motor cars. '10(O1) il. Q. $3 net. Longmans.

Gunn, Rob. Alex.
Bruce Douglas, a man of the people. '10 (Mr5) 12°, $1.50. Mayhew.

Gunners' examiner. Cloke, H. E: $1.50. Wiley.

Gunnett, A. H.
Echoes of long ago. '08, [1909.] (Mr) c. 5+54 p. il. 12°, bds., 50 c. Mayhew.

Gunnison, Royal Arch.
Condition of natives of Alaska: paper presented by Mr. Teller, containing the charge of Judge Royal A. Gunnison, before the grand jury, in the district court, at Juneau, Alaska. '08(Ap18) 8°, pap., 10 c. U. S., Supt. of Docs.

GUNPOWDER.
Du Pont de Nemours, E. I., Powder Co. Useful information for practical men: [manufacture and uses of gunpowder.] $1. Du Pont de Nemours.

GUNS.
Askins, C: American shotgun. $2 net. Outing.
Greener, W: W. Gun and its development. $4 net. Macmillan.
Rausenberger, F. Theory of the recoil of guns with recoil cylinders. *$4.50 net. Van Nostrand.
See also **Artillery;—Rifle;—Shooting.**

Guns and gunning. Browne, B. H. 30 c.; 20 c. J. Stevens.

Gunsaulus, Fk. Wakeley, ed.
Modern engineering practice. 12 v. '09 (Je5) c. pors. tabs., 8°, (American School of Correspondence pubs.) $29.80. Am. Sch. Corr.

Gunther, C: Godfrey.
Electro-magnetic ore separation. '09(My8) il. *$3 net. Hill Pub.

Gurler, H: B:
Farm dairy. '09(F6) c. il. por. 12°, $1. Breeders' Gazette.

Gurley's handbook for the use of sealers of weights and measures. 2d ed. '09(Jl17) c. il. tabs., S. 50 c. W. & L. E. Gurley.

Gurley's manual of the principal instruments used in American engineering and surveying, manufactured by W. & L. E. Gurley. 43d ed. '09(Jl10) c. il. pors. S. 50 c. W. & L. E. Gurley.

Gurney, Rev. T: A.
Nunc dimittis: the song of the watcher for the Lord's Christ. '08(Ja25) D. price changed from *$1 net to *60 c. net. Longmans.

GUSTAVUS II., Adolphus, *King of Sweden.*
Monroe, *Mrs.* H. E. Hist. of the life of Gustavus Adolphus II., the hero-general of the Reformation. 40 c. Lutheran Pub.

Guthe, Karl Eugen.
See Duff, Alex. Wilmer.

Guthridge, Anna Sterling, [Mrs. Jules Guthridge.]
From Capitol to Kremlin. '10(Ap2) c. por. D. $1.25 net. Neale.

Guthrie, Arth., ["Anthony Rowley."]
Letters from France and Italy. '09(O2) il. D. *$1.25 net. McClurg.

Guthrie, Ben Eli, rep.
See Missouri. *St. Louis and Kansas City Cts. of appeals.* Repts.—Cases.

Guthrie, J. Denton.
Byrne duplex English punctuation and correspondence. '08(Je) c. 5-109 p. 8°, $1. Byrne Pub.
Sidelights on Byrne simplified shorthand. '08(O) c. 100 p. 12°, 75 c. Byrne Pub.

Guthrie, Rev. Kenneth Sylvan.
Message of Philo Judæus of Alexandria. '09(S18) c. D. $1. Open Court.
Philosophy of Plotinos; his life, times, and philosophy; [bound with this: Selections from Plotino's Enneads.] '10(Jl16) c. 8°, $1. Prophet Pub.
Plotinus, his life, times and philosophy. '09(O23) 50 c. Open Court.
Spiritual message of literature; or, prophetic art. '09(O23) $1. Open Court.

Guthrie, T: Anstey, ["F. Anstey."]
Travelling companions. '09(O30) 16°, *$1 net. Dutton.

Guthrie, W: Anderson.
McDuffie's discovery of the natural causes for the variations of the magnetic needle of the compass. '10(Mr12) c. por. 12°, 50 c. W: A. Guthrie.

Guthrie, W: Norman.
Vital study of literature and other essays. '09(S18) 12°, $1.50. Sergel.

Gutiérrez, Antonio Garciá.
El trovador; ed., with notes and vocab., by H. H. Vaughan. '08(Ap18) c. S. (Modern lang. ser.) 40 c. Heath.

Gutmann, Ludwig.
Motorman and his duties. 6th ed., rev. and enl. by Lawrence E. Gould. '08(S5) c. il. figs. D. *$1 net. McGraw.

Gutstadt, Herman.
See Gompers, S:

GUTTA PERCHA.
See India rubber.

Guttmann, Oscar.
Manufacture of explosives; four Cantor lectures del. at the Royal Society of Arts in Nov. and Dec., 1908. '09(Ap3) il. O. *$1.10 net. Macmillan.

Gutzkow, Karl Ferdinand.
Uriel Acosta; trauerspiel in fünf aufzügen; ed., with introd. and notes, by S. W. Cutting and A. C. von Noé. '10(D3) c. S. 35 c. Holt.

Guy Fawkes. *See* Ainsworth, W: H.

Guy Hunter. Stark, W: W. $1.50. Cochrane.

Guy Mannering. *See* Scott, *Sir* Wa.

GUY *of Warwick.*
Marshall, H. E. Stories of Guy of Warwick. 50 c. Dutton.

Guyer, Michael Frederic.
Deficiencies of the Chromosome theory of heredity. '09, [1910.] (Je) 19 p. O. (Univ. of Cin. studies.) Univ. of Cin.
Bibliography (2 p.).

Guyot, Yves.
Socialistic fallacies. '10(Ag13) 12°, $1.50 net. Macmillan.

Gwathmey, Ja. T.
Tumbling for amateurs. '10(O) c. 61 p. por. il. 16°, (Spalding athletic lib.) pap., 10 c. Am. Sports.

Gwatkin, H: Melville.
Early church history to A.D. 313. In 2 v. fold. map, O. *$5.25 net. Macmillan.

Gwen Wynn. Reid, M. †$1. Dutton.

Gwenda. Barnes-Grundy, *Mrs.* M. S. $1.50. Baker & T.

Gwyer, Maurice Linford.
See King, Jos.

Gwynn, Stephen Lucius.
Holiday in Connemara. '09(Jl3) il. 12°, *$2 net Macmillan.
Robert Emmet; historical romance. '10 (F19) 12°, *$1.50 net. Macmillan.

Gwynne, Paul.
Nightshade. '10(D3) D. $1.35 net. Brentano's.

Gwynne, Rev. Walker.
Gospel in the church: a manual of instruction. '09(F20) il. 16°, (Ser. of instruction books for schools and families.) 40 c. Gorham.
Some purposes of paradise: life of the soul between death and resurrection. 2d ed., rev. '08(Ag29) c. 12°, *75 c. net. Gorham.

Gwyther, G. M.
English hist. in the classroom. '09(O30) fold. map, fold. chart, D. 80 c. Longmans.

Gymnasium handbook. '09(Ap17) S. pap. (Add. pubs. for price.) Bassette.

GYMNASTICS AND PHYSICAL CULTURE.
Anderson, H: S., *and* Schell, S. Artistic work and gymnastic games. 75 c. Werner.
Borden, G: R. Physical training for the school and class room. 10 c. Am. Sports.
Bowen, W. P. Teaching of elem. school gymnastics. $1. Bassette.

GYMNASTICS AND PHYSICAL CULTURE.—*Cont.*
Brooklyn. Public Library. Personal hygiene and physical development. gratis. Brooklyn Lib.
Buffington, F. C. Physical training for Filipinos. $1. Heath.
Checkley, E. Natural method of physical training. **$1.25 net. Baker & T.
Cromie, W: J. Parallel bar exercises.—Pyramid building. ea., 10 c. Spalding.
Fleming, W: F., *comp. and ed.* Physical culture classics. 4 v. per set, $15. E. R. Dumont.
Gymnasium hand book. (Add. pubs. for price.) Bassette.
Gymnastic nomenclature of the Young Men's Christian Associations of North America. 5th ed.; rev. and ed. by the Nomenclature Committee of the Physical Directors Society of the Young Men's Christian Associations. '10(D) 9+157 p. il. 12°, $1. Y. M. C. A.
Harris, W: T. Physical training in and out of school. 30 c. Bardeen.
Inter-Collegiate Association of Amateur Gymnasts of America. Constitution, by-laws, and records, 1899-1909. 10 c. Am. Sports.
James, A. R. Ball games and breathing exercises. 40 c. Longmans.
McKenzie, R. T. Exercise in education and medicine. *$3.50 net; *$5 net. Saunders.
Nissen, H. Fifteen lessons on the stall bars.—Twenty gymnastic lessons on the boom. ea., 30 c. Bassette.
Nolan, G. V., *comp.* My lady's toilet; complete up-to-date treatise on the toilet; also a systematic course of physical culture instruction. $1. People's News.
Schatz, W: J. Club swinging for physical exercise and recreation. $1. Am. Gymnasia.
Seymour, H. R. Physical training. *$1 net. W: R. Jenkins.
Skarstrom, W: Gymnastic kinesiology. *$1.25 net. Bassette.
Stecher, W: A. Hdbk. of graded lessons in physical training and games. *35 c. net. McVey.
Storey, T: A. Department of physical instruction, [College of the City of New York.] 50 c. T: A. Storey.
Taylor, C: K. Physical training for boys, and a word or two for their parents. $1. Staton Bros.
Warman, E: B Twenty minute exercises. 10 c. Am. Sports.
Wide, A. Home gymnastics according to the Ling system. *50 c. net. Funk.
Winjum, A. R. T. Manual of physical exercises. $1.75. Modern Medicine.
Young Men's Christian Association. Gymnastic nomenclature of the Y. M. C. A.'s of North America. $1. Y. M. C. A.
See also Anthropometry;—Athletics;—Boxing;—Dancing; — Drills (*fancy*); — Dumbbells; — Games;—Hygiene;—Indian clubs;—Jiu-jitsu;—Running;—Sports and sportsmen;—Swimming;—Wrestling.

GYMNOSPERMS.
See Botany.

Gynecological diagnosis. Burrage, W. L. $6. Appleton.

GYNECOLOGY.
Aarons, S. J. Gynæcological therapeutics. $2 net. Wood.
Allbutt, T: C. System of medicine and gynæcology. In 12 v. v. 7, 8. ea., $6; $7; $8. (Subs. only.) Macmillan.
Ashton, W: E. Text-book on the practice of gynecology. $6.50. Saunders.
Bandler, S: W. Medical gynecology. *$5 net; *$6.50 net. Saunders.
Bell, W. B. Principles of gynæcology. $6 net. Longmans.
Child, C: G., *jr.* Epitome of gynecology. *$1 net. Lea.
Cragin, E. B. Essentials of gynecology. $1. Saunders.
Cullen, T: S. Adenomyoma of the uterus. *$6.50 net. Saunders.
Davis, E: P. Obstetric and gynecologic nursing. *$1.75 net. Saunders.
Dudley, E. C. Principles and practice of gynecology, for students and practitioners. *$5 net; *$6 net; *$6.50 net. Lea.
Dudley, E. C., *and* Bachellé, C. von, *eds.* Gynecology. $1.25. Year Bk.
Fothergill, W. E. Manual of diseases of women. $3 net. Wood.
Gilliam, D: T. Text book of practical gynecology for practitioners and students. *$4.50 net; *$6 net. Davis.
Herman, G. E. Student's hdbk. of gynecology. *$2.50 net. Wood.
Jewett, C: Syllabus of gynecology. $1.25. C: Jewett.
Kelly, H. A. Medical gynecology. $6; $7. —Operative gynecology. 2 v. $15. Appleton.
Kelly, H. A., *and* Cullen, T. S. Myomata of the uterus. *$7.50 net; *$9 net. Saunders.
Kelly, H. A., *and* Noble, C: P., *eds.* Gynecology and abdominal surgery. v. 2. *$8 net; *$9.50 net. Saunders.
Kisch, E. H. Sexual life of woman in its physiological, pathological and hygienic aspects. $5. Rebman.
Macfarlane, C. Reference hdbk. of gynecology for nurses. *$1.25 net. Saunders.
McKay, W. J. S. Operations upon the uterus, perineum and round ligaments. *$6 net. Wood.
Massey, G: B. Conservative gynecology and electrotherapeutics. *$4 net. Davis.
Rice, M. C. Electricity in gynecology. $1. Laing.
Stewart, N., *and* Young, J. Pract. gynecology. *$2 net. Wood.
Winter, G., *and* Ruge, C. Text-book of gynecological diagnosis. $6. Lippincott.
See also Embryology;—Midwifery;—Pregnancy.

GYPSUM.
See Cement.

Gypsy Breynton. *See* Ward, *Mrs.* Eliz. Stuart Phelps.

Gypsy moth. Martin, J: F. B'way Pub.

"H & S." lib. [Standard books by prominent authors upon subjects of importance to ministers, teachers and laymen.] 30 v. '10 (D) 12°, ea., 50 c. net. Doran.

H., H.
Scientific education of dogs. '10(D31) 12°, $1.75. W: R. Jenkins.

Haab, Otto.
Atlas and epitome of ophthalmoscopy and ophthalmoscopic diagnosis. 2d American ed. from the 5th rev. and enl. German ed.; ed. by G: Edm. Schweinitz. '09 (Je) c. 94 p. il. diagrs., 12°, (Saunders' medical hand atlases.) $3. Saunders.
Atlas of the external diseases of the eye, incl. brief treatise on the pathology and treatment; author. tr. from the German 3d ed., rev.; ed. by G: Edm. Schweinitz. '09(Je) c. 244 p. il. 12°, (Saunders' medical hand-atlases.) $3. Saunders.

HAAR, Chateau of, Netherlands.
Cuypers, B. J. H. Chateau of Haar. $40. Hessling.

Haaren, J: H:, and Poland, Addison B.
Famous men of modern times. '09(Ap24) c. D. 50 c. Am. Bk.

Habakkuk. *See* **Bible.**

Habberton, J:
Budge and Toddie. '09(Ja23) c. il. D. $1. Grosset.
Helen's babies. '08(D) c. 187 p. il. 16°. (Add. pubs. for price.) Altemus.
Helen's babies. '08(Ag1) c. 8°, (Famous books.) $1; (Good value books.) 50 c. Grosset.
Who was Paul Grayson?. '09(My22) c. il. 16°, (Harper's young people ser.) 60 c. Harper.
Worst boy in town. '08(D12) c. il. 12°, $1. Jacobs.

HABEAS CORPUS.
Sellery, G: C. Lincoln's suspension of habeas corpus as viewed by Congress. 35 c. Univ. of Wis.

Haber, Fritz.
Thermodynamics of technical gas-reactions; tr. by Arth. B. Lamb. '08(Mr7) il. O. *$3 net. Longmans.

HABERSHAM, John.
Doolittle, B:, *and* Jones, C: C., *jr.* Short narrative of mischief done by French and Indian enemy [and] Biograph. sketch of Hon. Major John Habersham of Georgia. To subscribers. $1.75. Abbatt.

Habershon, S: Herb.
Diseases of the stomach. '09(D) 565 p. il. (partly col.) 12°, $2.50. Chic. Med. Bk.

Habichtsfräulein (Das). Baumbach, R. 40 c. Holt.

Habit formation and the science of teaching. Rowe, S. H: **$1.50 net. Longmans.

Hackes, Sidney, comp.
Fairchild's rapid letterer and show-card maker. '10(D17) c. f°, $2. Fairchild Co.

Hackett, Fk. Warren.
Deck and field: addresses before the United States Naval War College and on commemorative occasions. '09(Je) c. 11+222 p. 12°, *$1.25 net. Lowdermilk.

Hackley, Sarah Bell.
Tobacco tiller: tale of the Kentucky tobacco fields. '09(N6) c. il. 12°, $1.50. C. M. Clark.

Hackney, Mrs. Alice Jane Herdman, comp.
Cullings of forty years, from musical lanes and hedges. '10(Ap23) c. 12°, $1. Bapt. Bk.

HACKNEY, Eng.
See London.

Hackwood, F: W:
Inns, ales, and drinking customs of old England. '09(D18) il. O. *$2.50 net. Sturgis & W.

Hadden, Ja.
Washington's expeditions (1753-1754) and Braddock's expedition (1775); with hist. of Tom Fausett, the slayer of General Edward Braddock. '10(Ag13) c. il. pors. D. $1. J. Hadden.

Hadden, Ja. Cuthbert.
Favorite operas from Mozart to Mascagni. '10(D17) col. il. O. $2.25. Stokes.
Master musicians. '10(D) il. pors. 8°, $1.75. Barse & H.
Operas of Wagner; their plots, music and history. '08(O3) il. O. $2.25. Stokes.
—, **comp.** Flying Dutchman; [from Wagner's opera.] col. il. T. (Great operas ser.) 50 c.; leath., $1. Stokes.
Meistersingers; [from Wagner's opera.] '08(D19) il. T. (Great operas ser.) 50 c.; leath., $1. Stokes.
Ring of the Nibelung; [from Wagner's opera.] '08(D19) il. T. (Great operas ser.) 50 c.; leath., $1. Stokes.
Tristan and Isolde; [from Wagner's opera.] '08(D19) il. T. (Great operas ser.) 50 c. Stokes.

Haddock, Fk. Channing.
Business power; pract. manual in financial ability. In 4 pts: The personal factors, Economic laws and business maxims, Psychology in business, Business in fact. '10(S) c. 19+556 p. 8°, $3. Power-Bk.
Culture of courage; pract. companion-book for unfoldment of fearless personality through the white life of reason and harmony. '10(N19) c. 8°, $3. Power-Bk.
The personal atmosphere: studies in poise and power. '08(Mr.) c. 86 p. 12°, $1. Power-Bk.
Power for success through culture of vibrant magnetism; specialized gymnasium in magnetic personality embracing four divisions: psychic magnetism—physical rationale—prevention of waste—the body magnetic and twenty-eight practical new-thought lessons in success magnetism. 2d ed., rev., with alterations and new matter. '10(Jl) c. 450 p. 8°, $10. Power-Bk.
Power of will: companion-book for unfoldment of selfhood through direct personal culture. 3d ed., rev., with alterations and new matter. '09(Mr6) c. 8°, $3. Power-Bk.

Haddon, Alfr. Cort.
Magic and fetishism. '07, [1909.] (Ap) 8°, (Religions ancient and modern.) *40 c. net. Open Court.
Races of man and their distribution. '10 (Mr26) il. D. (Twentieth century science ser.) *50 c. net. Stokes.

Hadley, Chalmers R.
Why do we need a public library?; material for a library campaign; adopted for state use by the League of Library Commissions. '10(My14) 12°, (A. L. A. Pub. Board, Library tract no. 10.) 5 c. A. L. A.

Hadley, E: S.
Railway working and appliances; to which are added a chapter and diagram on railway sketching. '09(Ap10) figs. D. *50 c. net. Longmans.

Hadley, H: E.
See Gregory, R: A.

Hadley, L: D.
How to get eggs from your own hens during the winter months. '10(Ag20) c. il. 8°, $1. L: D. Hadley.

Hadley, Wa. B:
Selections of harmony for the cheerful or sad: [poems.] '09(Jl3) S. 75 c.; in 2 pts., ea., pap., 25 c. R: Bylsma.

Hadlock, Edn. Harvey.
Press correspondence and journalism; complete system and course of instruction for students. '10(Ap23) c. por. 8°, $3. Un. Press.
Profitable authorship; how to write and where to sell short stories and other manuscripts. '10(Ap23) c. por. 8°, $3. Un. Press.

Hadow, Gerald Elliott and W: H:
Oxford treasury of English literature. v. 3. Jacobean to Victorian. '08(N14) cr. 8°, 90 c. Oxford Univ.

Hadow, W: H:
See Hadow, Gerald Elliott.

Haebler, O.
Stil-lehre; study of style for colored surface decoration, incl. textiles, wall paper, etc. '10(Ap16) il. 4°, $8. Hessling.

Haeckel, Ernst Heinrich.
Evolution of man; popular scientific study; tr. from the fifth (enl.) ed. by Jos. McCabe. v. 1, Embryology or ontogeny; v. 2, The evolution of the species or phylogeny. '10(Je11) il. figs. O. $5 net. Putnam.

—, and others.
Francisco Ferrer; his life work and martyrdom. '10(D) 12°, pap., 25 c. Francisco Ferrer Assoc.

HAEMATOLOGY.
See Blood.

Haering, Theodor v.
Ethics of Christian life; tr. from the 2d German ed. by Ja. S. Hill; with introd. by Rev. W. D. Morrison. '09(F27) 8°, (Theological translation lib.) *$3 net. Putnam.

Haertel, Martin H:
German literature in American magazines, 1846 to 1880. '09(F6) O. (Univ. of Wis. bull.; Philology and literature ser.) pap., 50 c. Univ. of Wis.

Haffey, Mrs. Marg. Higgins.
See Higgins, G: H:

HAFID, Mulai.
Harris, L. With Mulai Hafid at Fez. $3 net. Badger.

Hafiz, Shams ed-din Muhammad.
Rubaiyat of Hafiz; tr., with introd., by Syed Abdul Majid; rendered into English verse by L. Cranmer Byng. '10 (D10) 16°, (Wisdom of the East ser.) 60 c. net. Dutton.

Hagar, Alex. T:
See Hagar, Marshall S.

Hagar, Hubert Adonley.
Applied business English. '09(N) c. 6+278 p. 4°, $1.25. Gregg Pub.
Applied business punctuation and business forms. '10(Ja29) c. 4°, 40 c. Gregg Pub.

Hagar, Marshall Spring and Alex. T:
Forms, rules and general orders in bankruptcy. '10(O) c. O. $6.50. M. Bender.

Hage, Rev. Hyacinth.
Life of Blessed Gabriel of Our Lady of Sorrows, Gabriel Possenti, of the Congregation of the Passion; rewritten and enl. by Rev. N: Ward; with an introd. by Cardinal Gibbons. '10(My) c. 3-295 p. por. pl. 12°, 50 c.; pap., 25 c. Kilner.

Hagedoorn, Arend L.
Inheritance of yellow color in rodents. '09 (My15) Q. (Univ. of pubs.; Physiology.) pap., 5 c. U. S., Supt. of Docs.
Origin of two new retrogressive varieties by one mutation in mice. '08, [1909.] (F.) Q. (Univ. of Cal. pubs., Physiology.) pap. (Add. University for price.) Univ. of Cal.

Hagedorn, Hermann, jr.
Horse thieves; comedy in one act. '10 (Je4) il. 8°, 60 c. net. Harvard Co-op.
Silver blade: a drama. '08(Mr14) O. bds., *$1.10 net. Harvard Co-op.
Troop of the guard, and other poems. '09(N6) c. D. **$1.10 net. Houghton M.
Woman of Corinth: tale in verse. '08(D19) c. D. **$1 net. Houghton M.

Hagenbeck, Carl.
Beasts and men; being Carl Hagenbeck's experiences for half a century among wild animals; an abridged tr. by Hugh S. R. Elliot and A. G. Thacker; with introd. by P. Chalmers Mitchell. '09 (D25) il. por. O. *$3.50 net. Longmans.

Hager, Rev. Levi Lewis.
Sixty years with the muse: poems. '09 (Mr) c. '08. il. 12°, 60 c. Un. B. Pub.

Hagerling, F: Ja.
Training and treatment of the horse. '10 (Ag20) c. il. 12°, 50 c. Hagerling.

Haggard, Andrew C: Parker.
Amours of Henri de Navarre and of Marguerite de Valois. '10(D10) il. 8°, $4.50 net. Brentano's.
Louis XVI. and Marie Antoinette. 2 v. '09 (D11) il. 8°, *$6 special net. Appleton.
Two great rivals (Francois I. and Charles V.) and the women who influenced them. '10(O22) il. O. $4 special net. Appleton.

Haggard, D. A., ed.
See Nebraska synoptical digest.

Haggard, H: Rider.
Farmer's year: being his commonplace book for 1898. '08(Jl18) il. maps, D. (Silver lib.) $1.50. Longmans.
Lady of the heavens. '09(My15) c. D. $1.50. Lovell.
Morning Star. '10(Je4) c. il. D. $1.50. Longmans.
Queen Sheba's ring. '10(S10) c. il. col. front. D. $1.50. Doubleday, P.

Haggard, H: Rider.—*Continued.*
Winter pilgrimage: being an account of travels through Palestine, Italy, and the island of Cyprus. [Cheaper re-issue.] '08 (Ap18) il. D. (Silver lib.) $1.50. Longmans.
Yellow god. '08(D5) c. D. 75 c. Cupples & L.

HAGIOLOGY.
See **Catholic church.**

Hagood, Johnson.
Memoirs of the war of secession; from the orig. manuscripts of Johnson Hagood, brigadier-general, C. S. A. I. Hagood's 1st 12 months S. C. V.; II. Hagood's brigade; [ed. by U. R. Brooks.] '10(D10) c. il. por. maps, 8°, $3. State Co.

Hague, G:
Banking and commerce; pract. treatise for bankers and men of business, together with the author's experiences of banking life in England and Canada during fifty years. '08, [1909.] (Mr) c. 11+386 p. por. 8°, $3. Bankers Pub.
Pract. treatise on banking and commerce. '09(Mr27) c. por. 8°, $3. Bankers Pub.

Hague, Ja. Duncan.
Drake medal. '09(Ap) 21 p. il. maps, 8°, pap., gratis. W. D. Pagan.

Hague, Wa.
Death ends all; or, the nature of death logically, naturally and experimentally revealed. 2d rev. ed. '10(Mr5) D. 75 c.; pap., 40 c. Timby.

HAGUE PEACE CONFERENCES.
Choate, J. H., *and others.* American addresses at the Second Hague Peace Conference. $1.50. Ginn.
Davis, G: B. Elements of international law; incl. results of second Peace Conference at The Hague. $3. Harper.
Hicks, F: C: Equality of the states and the Hague conferences. (Add. author for price.) F: C: Hicks.
Higgins, A. P. Hague Peace Conferences. $5 net. Putnam.
Hill, D: J., *and others.* Second Hague peace conference. 15 c. U. S., Supt. of Docs.
Hull, W: I. Two Hague conferences and their contributions to international law. $1.65. Ginn.
Mead, E. D. Results of the two Hague conferences and the demands upon the third conference. per 100, $3. Int. Sch. of Peace.
Scott, J. B. Hague Peace Conference of 1899 and 1907. In 2 v. $5. Johns Hopkins.
Scott, J. B. Work of the second Hague conference. gratis. Assoc. Inst. Conciliation.
Scott, J. B., *ed.* Texts of the Peace conference. $2. Ginn.
United States. *Naval War College,* Newport, R. I. International law situations with solutions and notes. (Add. Superintendent for price.) U. S., Supt. of Docs
See also **Diplomacy.**

Hahn, Rev. B. Florian.
Collection of easy hymns, Salvete Christi vulnera. '09(Jl) 18 p. 8°, pap., 35 c. St. Boniface's.

Haig, Alex.
Uric acid in the causation of disease. 7th ed. '08, [1909.] (Mr) 12+940 p. il. 8°, *$4 net. Blakiston.

Haig, Harold Axel.
The plant cell; its modifications and vital processes; manual for students. '10(Ap9) il. 12°, $2 net. Lippincott.

Haigh, A. E.
See Gepp, C: Granville.

Haight, C: Sherwin, and Marsh, Arth. Merwin.
Questions and answers for bar-examination review. 2d ed. '09(Ap) c. 52+585 p. O. $4. Baker, V. & Co.

Haight, Marg. N., comp.
Adventures of Pathfinder; adapt. from J Fenimore Cooper's Pathfinder. '09(Je19) c. il. D. (Eclectic readings.) 35 c. Am. Bk.
Last of the Mohicans; adapt. from J. Fenimore Cooper's "The last of the Mohicans." '09(Jl3) c. il. D. (Eclectic readings.) 35 c. Am. Bk.

Haight, Theron Wilber.
Three Wisconsin Cushings; sketch of the lives of Howard B., Alonzo H. and William B. Cushing, children of a pioneer family of Waukesha County. '10(Je) c. 14+109 p. pors. facsims., 8°, (Wisconsin History Commission: original papers.) $1. Wisconsin Hist.

Haile, Martin.
Life of Reginald Pole. '10(Je18) pors. O. $5.25 net. Longmans.

Hailes, C: J.
See New York [State.] Banking law.—*Ct. of appeals.* Rules.—Penal law.—Public service commissions law.
—, **comp.** *See* New York [State.] Banking law.—Code of civil procedure.—Penal code.
—, **ed.** *See* New York [State.] Statutory rev. of laws.—Tax law.

Hailey, J:
Hist. of Idaho. '10(Mr5) c. por. 8°, $3. Syms-York.

Hainbach, Rudolf.
Pottery decorating; tr. from the German by C: Salter. '09(Ap24) il. 12°, *$3 net. Van Nostrand.

Haine (Une) a bord. *See* Landelle, Guillaume Joseph Gabriel de la.

Haines, Alice Calhoun.
Cock-a-doodle Hill; being further chronicles of the Dudley Grahams. '09(N20) c. il. D. †$1.50. Holt.

Haines, C: Grove.
Conflict over judicial powers in the United States to 1870. '09(Jl17) c. O. (Columbia Univ. studies in history, economics and public law.) pap., $1.50. Longmans.

Haines, Elijah Middlebrook.
See Illinois. Compilation of the laws.

Hains, Thornton Jenkins.
Bahama Bill, mate of the wrecking sloop "Sea-horse." '08(Ap4) il. D. $1.50. L. C. Page.

Hainsselin, M. T.
Isle of Maids. '08(Ap25) †$1.50. Lane.

Hair, Dell.
Echoes from the beat: [poems.] 3 v. '08 (N) c. 17-156 p. por. il. 8°, (Add. pubs. for price.) N. B. Newton.

HAIR.
Robinson, T. Baldness and grayness. *$1 net. W: R. Jenkins.
Walsh, D: Hair and its diseases. *$1 net. Chic. Med. Bk.

HAITI, West Indies.
International Bureau of American Republics. Haiti; general descriptive data. Int. Bu. Am. Republics.

Hakluyt, R:
Voyages. In 8 v. vs. 3, 4. '08(Mr7); v. 5, 6. '08(S19); v. 7, 8. '09(My27) 16°, (Everyman's lib.) ea., *35 c. net; leath., *70 c. net. Dutton.
Voyages of Drake and Gilbert; select narratives from the Principal navigations; ed. by E: J: Payne; with additional notes, maps, etc., by C. R. Beazley. '09 (Ag14) 8°, 60 c. Oxford Univ.

HAKLUYT, Richard.
Bacon, E. M. Boy's Hakluyt. $1.50. Scribner.

Halberstadt, Baird.
General map of the bituminous coal fields of Pennsylvania, 1907; [also] List of mines, operators and purchasing agents. '07, [1908.] (Ag) 24+12 p. 8°, $6. B. Halberstadt.

Halcyon song-book. Marshall, L. B., *comp.* 75 c. Silver.

Haldeman, I: Massey.
Christian Science in the light of Holy Scripture. '09(Mr27) c. O. *$1.50 net. Revell.
Mental assassination; or, Christian Science a physical, intellectual, moral and spiritual peril. [1910.] (Ap) 10 c. C: C. Cook.
New religion; or, Athenian culture and Christianity. [1910.] (Ap) 30 p. 16°, pap., 10 c. C: C. Cook.
Thinking above what is written; or, the exaltation of human wisdom above the word of God. [1910.] (Ap) 30 p. 16°, pap., 10 c. C: C. Cook.

Halden, G: Mason.
Setting out of tube railways. '08(F8) c. il. 4°, *$4 net. Spon.

Hale, A. Creighton.
Art of massage. '10(D) 18+144 p. 8°, $2. W: R. Jenkins.

Hale, Albert.
Savings bank investments. 4th ed. '08 (Ap4) c. Tt. leath., $1.50. A. Hale.

Hale, Albert Barlow, M.D.
Pract. guide to Latin America; incl. Mexico, Central America, the West Indies and South America; preparation, cost, routes, sightseeing. '09(D18) c. S. (Pract. guide ser.) **$1 net. Small.

Hale, And., [pseud. for Catharine Hall Wetherill.]
For you and for me: book of verse. '09 (Jl17) c. D. *$1.25 net. Campion.

Hale, Mrs. Annie Riley.
Rooseveltian fact and fable. '10(O8) c. il. por. D. $1. A. R. Hale.

Hale, E: Everett, D.D.
Man without a country; with notes and introd. by Norris H. Laughton. '08, [1909.] (Mr) c. 96 p. 24°, (Altemus' classics ser.) $1, boxed. C. M. Clark.
Man without a country; with introd. and notes by E. Isabel Revell. '10(Je4) c. 12°, 25 c. Educ. Pub.
Man without a country; tr. into Greek by N. A. Fletorides. '08(Ap.) c. 113 p. 12°, 75 c. N. A. Fletorides.
Man without a country; ed., with introd. and notes, by S: Marion Tucker. '10 (N19) il. 24°, (Pocket Am. and Eng. classics.) 25 c. net. Macmillan.
Man without a country. '10(O1) col. il. D. 75 c., boxed; leath., $2, boxed. Platt & P.

—, and Brewer, D: Josiah.
Mohonk·addresses; with introd. by Edn. D. Mead. '10(N19) c. il. pors. 12°, $1. Int. Sch. of Peace.

—, ed. Lights of two centuries: artists, sculptors, prose writers, composers, poets and inventors. '08(F22) c. pors. 12°, $1.50. Little, B. & Co.
Modern achievement; or, making of the modern world. '10(My14) 8°, $9. Westminster (Chic.)

Hale, E: Everett, jr.
William H. Seward. '10(O15) c. por. D. (American crisis biographies.) $1.25 net. Jacobs.

HALE, Edward Everett, *jr.*
Frost, J. M., *ed.* Experience of grace, three notable instances: Saul of Tarsus. John Jasper. Edward Everett Hale, jr. 40 c. S. S. Bd. of Bapt.

Hale, G: Ellery.
Preliminary note on the rotation of the sun as determined from the motions of the hydrogen *flocculi.* '08(Jl4) il. 4°, (Contributions from the Mount Wilson solar observatory.) pap. (Not for sale.) Carnegie.
Study of stellar evolution. '08(Je6) c. il. Q. (Univ. of Chic. decennial pubs.) *$4 net. Univ. of Chic.
Tower telescope of the Mount Wilson solar observatory. '08(Jl18) il. 4°, (Contributions from the Mount Wilson solar observatory.) pap. (Not for sale.) Carnegie.

—, and Adams, Wa. Sydney.
Photography of the "flash" spectrum without an eclipse. [1910.] (F) il. 4°, (Contributions from the Mount Wilson Solar Observatory.) Carnegie.

—, and Fox, Philip.
Rotation period of the sun, as determined from the motions of the *calcium flocculi.* '08(D5) il. tabs., Q. pap., 40 c. Carnegie.

Hale, Rev. Harris Grafton, and Hall, Newton Marshall, D.D., comps.
Biblical dramas, for use especially in young people's meetings and the evening services of the church. 12 v. '10(D) pap., ea., 15 c. Pilgrim Press.
Contents: v. 1, The story of Joseph and his brethren; v. 2, The story of Jacob; v. 3, Moses the Liberator; v. 4, Samuel and Saul; v. 5, David the King; v. 6, The story of David and Jonathan; v. 7, The story of Solomon; v. 8, The story of Job; v. 9, The story of Elijah; v. 10, The messages of the prophets; v. 11, Nehemiah the builder; v. 12, Paul, the prisoner of the Lord.

Hale, Mrs. Louise Closser.
The actress. '09(Mr6) c. il. D. †$1.50. Harper.

Hale, Oscar Fitzalan, comp.
Ancestry and descendants of Josiah Hale, fifth in descent from Samuel Hale of Hartford, Conn., 1637; to which is added an epistolary appendix showing other lines of descent. '10(S17) facsims., O. $2. O. F. Hale.

Hale, Philip Leslie.
Great portraits: children. '10(Ja29) c. il. Q. $1.50, boxed. Bates & G.
Great portraits: women. '10(Ja29) c. il. Q $1.50, boxed. Bates & G.
The Madonna [in art.] '09(Ap3) c. il. 4°, $1. Bates & G.

Hale, W: Bayard.
Week in the White House with Theodore Roosevelt. '08(Je6) c. pors. il. D. bds., *$1.25 net Putnam.

Hale, W: Gardner, Beeson, C: H:, and Carr, Wilbert Lester.
Latin composition. 4th ed. '10(Ap23) c. 12°, 60 c. Atkinson, M. & G.

Hale, W: Jay.
Calculations of general chemistry; with definitions, explanations, and problems. '09(N20); 2d ed., rev. '10(Jl30) c. 12°, ea., $1. Van Nostrand.

HALE FAMILY.
See Genealogies, Morris, S.

Halévy, Ludovic.
Un mariage d' amour; ed., with notes and vocab., by Richmond Laurin Hawkins. '08(Ap18) c. S. (Modern lang. ser.) 25 c. Heath.

Haley, L: Coleman.
Dramatic art of magic; series of artistic conjuring experiments fully explained in detail. '10(S17) c. por. 8°, $1.15. L: C. Haley.

Haley, M. J.
See Page, Ja. Madison.

Half a chance. Isham, F. S. †$1.50. Bobbs-M.
Half Breed. *See* Dumont, Fk. Caught with the goods.
Half-breed dance. Kemp, R. H. 25 c. Kemp & H.
Half century of Minneapolis. Hudson, H. B. $15. Hudson Pub.
Half-hour talks on character building. Kirtley, J. S. $2. Hamming.
Half hours with highwaymen. Harper, C: G: 2 v. *$16.80 net. Scribner.
Half in earnest. Hine, M. $1.50. Lane.
"Half moon" (The). Hueffer, F. M. †$1.50. Doubleday, P.
Half-smart (The) set: a novel. '08(My23) c. il. D. †$1.50. Stokes.
Half the battle in Burmese. Brown, R: G. $2. Oxford Univ.
Halfway House. Hewlett, M. H: †$1.50. Scribner.

Halfyard, S: Follet.
Spiritual basis of man and nature. [1910.] (F) c. 252 p. 12°, $1. Jennings.

Haliburton, Marg. Winifred.
Drill book. '09(Mr) 64 p. 12°, 18 c. B. F. Johnson.
Phonics in reading: manual. '09(Mr) 64 p. 12°, 40 c. B. F. Johnson.

HALIMEDA.
See Seaweeds.

Hall, A. G., and Frink, F. G.
Hall and Frink's trigonometry. New ed., incl. spherical trigonometry. '10(D31) 8°, (Mathematical ser.) $1.25. Holt.

Hall, Alfr. Bates, and Chester, Clarence L.
Panama and the canal. '10(Mr5) c. il. D. 60 c. Newson.

Hall, Alfr. Daniel.
Fertilizers and manures. '10(Ja22) 8°, **$1.50 net. Dutton.
Soil (The): an introd. to the scientific study of the growth of crops. '08(D) il. 12°, *$1.50 net. Dutton.

HALL, Angeline Stickney.
Hall, A. Astronomer's wife; biography of Angeline Hall. $1. Nunn.

Hall, Angelo.
Astronomer's wife: biography of Angeline Hall. '09(Ja23) c. il. pors. O. $1. Nunn.

Hall, Anna Maria Fielding, [Mrs. S: Carter Hall.]
Tales of Irish life and character. '10(O1) il. D. $1.75 net. McClurg.

Hall, Arnold, and Heywood, Fk.
Shipping: a guide to the routine in connection with the shipment of goods and the clearance of vessels inwards and outwards, with numerous reproductions of actual shipping forms. '09(S4) D. (Practical primers of business.) 50 c. Pitman.

Hall, Bp. Arth. Crawshay Alliston.
Apostolic ministry; charge; del. at the annual convention of the diocese, 1910; with notes and appendices. '10(Jl2) O. pap., 25 c. Longmans.
Forgiveness of sins. '08(F29) c. D. **$1 net. Longmans.

Hall, Arth. Graham, and Frink, Fred Goodrich.
Trigonometry. '09(Jl3) c. il. O. (Mathematical ser. of college text-books.) $1.40. Holt.

Hall, Bolton.
Game of life; with an introd. written for this ed. by ex-Governor Lucius F. C. Garvin. '09(My) c. 9-230 p. 16°, 20 c. Breslow.
Garden yard: hdbk. of intensive farming; with an introd by N. O. Nelson; rev. by Herbert W. Collingwood and S: Fraser. '09(Je5) c. D. $1. McKay.
Life, and love and peace; with introd. by the late Bishop Huntington. '09(Je26) c. D. $1. Arcadia.
Little land and a living; with a letter as an introd. by W: Borsodi. '08(Je6) front. D. $1. Arcadia.

Hall, C: Cuthbert, D.D.
Christ and the eastern soul; Barrows lectures, 1906-1907. '09(My1) c. O. **$1.25 net. Univ. of Chic.
Silver cup: simple messages to children. '09(Ap3) c. D. **$1.25 net. Houghton M.

Hall, Clarence.
See Munroe, C: E:

—, and Snelling, Wa. O.
Coal-mine accidents: their causes and prevention; with introd. by Jos. Austin Holmes. '07, [1908.] (Jl.) 21 p. 8°, (U. S. Geological survey bull.) pap., 5 c. U. S., Supt. of Docs.

Hall, Clayton Colman, ed.
Narratives of early Maryland, 1633-1684. '10(O22) c. il. maps, O. (Orig. narratives of early American hist.) $3 net. Scribner.

Hall, Cyril.
"How does it work" of model making. '10 (Ag13) il. D. (How does it work ser.) 75 c. Fenno.

Hall, Mrs. D: Prescott.
See Hall, *Mrs.* Florence Marion Howe.

Hall, Miss E. V.
See Tallentyre, S. G., *pseud.*

Hall, Edith H.
Decorative art at Crete in the bronze age: a dissertation. '07, [1909.] (Mr) 47 p. il. fold. tab., 4°. (Add. pubs. for price.) Winston.

Hall, E: Hagaman.
Brief hist. of the City Hall Park of New York City; with an appeal for its preservation. '10(Je4) 4°, pap., gratis. (2000 copies.) Am. Scenic.
Hudson and Fulton; with suggestions designed to aid the holding of general commemorative exercises and children's festivals during the Hudson-Fulton celebration in 1909. 3d ed. '09(Ag28) c. il. O. pap. (Add. pubs. for price.) Hudson-Fulton.

Hall, Eliza Calvert, [pseud. for Mrs. Eliza Caroline Calvert Obenchain.]
Land of long ago. '09(S18) c. il. D. †$1.50. Little, B. & Co.
Sally Ann's experience. '10(S10) c. front. D. 50 c. net. Little, B. & Co.

Hall, Elmer Edg., and Elston, T: Sidney.
Physical measurements in properties of matter and heat. '08(N) c. 94 p. 8°, $1. E. E. Hall.

Hall, Mrs. Florence Marion Howe, [Mrs. D: Prescott Hall.]
Hdbk. of hospitality for town and country. '09(N20) c. D. $1.50. Estes.

Hall, Fs. Cadwalader.
Fiddle sticks; verse. '09(Mr) c. 110 p. 16°, 50 c. W. F. Roberts.

Hall, Fs. Jos., D.D.
Dogmatic theology. In 10 v. v. 2, Authority, ecclesiastical and biblical. '08(Ap4); v. 3, The being and attributes of God. '09(Ap3); v. 4, The Trinity. '10(D17) c. D. ea., $1.50 net. Longmans.
Evolution and the fall; [Bishop Paddock lectures, 1909-10.] '10(Ja29) c. D. **$1.50 net. Longmans.

Hall, Fk. Oliver, D.D.
Soul and body; book of sermons. '09 (D25) c. S. *$1 net. Universalist.

Hall, F: Smith.
Scholarships for working children. '08, [1909.] (S) 4 p. 8°, (National Child Labor Committee pubs.) (Add. pubs. for price.) Nat. Child Labor.

Hall, Gertrude.
Legend of Sainte Cariberte des Oies done into verse. '09(Je5) c. il. 4°, $3. Badger.
Unknown quantity. '10(Mr5) c. D. †$1.50. Holt.

Hall, Grace.
Letters from G. G. '09(N13) c. S. $1.25. Holt.

Hall, H. A.
See Georgia laws.

Hall, H. R.
Days before history. [New ed.] '10(Ag6) il. O. $1.50. Crowell.

Hall, Hammond
Young electrician. '10(D3) il. D. $1.50 net. Macmillan.

Hall, Harvey Monroe.
Compositae of southern California. '08 (Ja11) il. map, Q. (Univ. of Cal. pubs., Botany.) pap., $3. Univ. of Cal.
Studies in ornamental trees and shrubs. '10(Ap9) Q. (Univ. of Cal. pubs.; Botany.) pap., 75 c. Univ. of Cal.

Hall, H:
How money is made in security investments. 3d ed. '08(N21); 4th ed. '09 (Jl31) c. il. tabs., 8°, ea., $1.50. H: Hall.

Hall, H: Fielding.
Inward light: [exposition of Buddhism.] '08(F1) c. O. **$1.75 net. Macmillan.
One immortality. '09(Ja30) c. D. †$15.0. Macmillan.

Hall, Hillman Allyn.
Hist. of the Sixth New York Cavalry, (Second Ina Harris Guard;) Second Brigade, First Division, Cavalry Corps, Army of the Potomac, 1861-1865; comp. from letters, diaries, recollections and official records. '08, [1909.] (Mr) c. 575 p. il. pors. maps, 8°, $5. F. A. Easton.

Hall, Hubert, ed.
Formula book of English official historical documents. pt. 1, Diplomatic documents. '10(My) 8°, $2; pt. 2, Ministerial and judicial records selected and transcribed by a seminar of the London School of Economics. '10(Mr26) O. $2.50. Putnam.
Studies in English official historical documents. '08(D5) royal 8°, $3.75. Putnam.

Hall, J. G.
See Stevens, Fk. Lincoln.

HALL, James.
James, D. L. Judge James Hall; literary pioneer of the Middle West. Heer.

Hall, Ja. A:
Starving on a bed of gold; or, the world's longest fast. '09(Ag) 149 p. il. pors. 8°, $1. J. A: Hall.

Hall, J: And., D.D.
Nature of God; series of lectures. '10 (Jl16) c. 12°, $1.25. Lutheran Pub.

Hall, J: D.
Suggestions on taking finger prints, prepared under direction of the Bureau of Navigation; [repr. from *United States Naval Medical Bulletin,* v. 4, no. 1.] '10(Mr) 6 p. 2 il. 8°. (Add. Superintendent for price.) U. S., Supt. of Docs.

Hall, J: Manley, ed.
United States: account of past and contemporary conditions and progress. '08 (My9) c. 12°, $1.50. J: M. Hall.

HALL, J: Newton.
Barker, W. M., *and* Hall, L. J. S. Memoirs of Eld. J. N. Hall, the peerless defender of the Baptist faith. $1.50. J. N. Hall.

Hall, J: R.
Bourbon restoration. '09(D4) pors. O. *$4 net. Houghton M.

Hall, J: W.
See Harboard, F. W.

Hall, Lillian J. Smith.
See Barker, W. M.

Hall, Mabel Kinney.
Echoes from M. A. C. '09(Je) c. 7-31 p. 8° 50 c. Rep.-Courier.

Hall, Maud R.
English Church needlework. '09(Mr27) il. 4°, *$3 net. Gorham.

Hall, Newton Marshall, comp.
See Hale, Harris Grafton, *comp.*

Hall, Prescott Farnsworth, ed.
See Massachusetts. Law of landlord and tenant.—Massachusetts business corporations law.

Hall, R: Nicklin.
Prehistoric Rhodesia; examination of the historical, ethnological, and archæological evidences as to the origin and age of the rock mines and stone buildings. '10(Je4) 8°, $3.50 net. Jacobs.

Hall, Mrs. S: Carter.
See Hall, Anna Maria Fielding.

Hall, S: Roland.
How to get a position and how to keep it. '08(Ag8) c. S. **50 c. net. Funk.

Hall, Sharlot Mabridth.
Cactus and pine; songs of the Southwest. '10(D17) c. D. $1.50 net. Sherman, F.

Hall, T: Cuming, D.D.
Hist. of ethics within organized Christianity. '10(S24) c. O. $3 net. Scribner.
Social solutions in the light of Christian ethics. '10(F19) c. D. *$1.50 net. Eaton & M.

Hall, Thornton.
Love intrigues of royal courts. '10(D10) il. 8°, $3.50 net. Dodd.

Hall, Wilbur J.
See Home, Edg. F.

Hall, W: E:
Treatise on international law. 6th ed.; ed. by J. B. Atlay. '10(Mr26) O. $6. Oxford Univ.

Hall, W: Logan, and Maxwell, Hu.
Surface conditions and stream flow. '10 (Mr15) 8°, (U. S., Dept. of Agriculture, Forest Service, circular.)

Hall, Winfield Scott, M.D.
From youth into manhood. '09(S18) 16°. pap., 50 c. Y. M. C. A.
Nutrition and dietetics; manual for students of medicine, for trained nurses, and for dietetians in hospitals and other institutions. '10(F5) c. il. O. **$2 net. Appleton.

HALL-MARKS.
See Silver.

Hallam, H:
Hist. of Europe during the Middle Ages; with introd. by Arth. Richmond Marsh. In 3 v. v. 3 contains Jules Michelet's "Modern history," with introd. by W: MacDonald. '08(Je27) c. il. 8°, $5.25; hf. mor., $10.50. Lamb Pub.

Hallberg, Carl Svantē Nicanor, M.D., and Salisbury, Jerome H:, M.D., comps.
Physicians' manual of the Pharmacopeia and the national formulary. 2d ed., rev. '08(My); 3d ed., rev. '09(My) c. 16°, ea., 40 c. Am. Medical.

Hallenbeck, Edn. F., D.D.
Passion for men; plea for endeavor in soul winning. '10(Ap9) c. 16°, 40 c. net. Revell.

Haller, G: Fs., and Cunningham, Elmer Tiling.
Tesla high frequency coil, its construction and uses. '10(N12) c. il. 12°, $1.25. Van Nostrand.

HALLEY FAMILY.
See Genealogies: McPike, E. F.

HALLEY'S COMET.
See Astronomy

Halliburton, W: Dobinson.
Essentials of chemical physiology, for the use of students. '09, [1910.] (F) 11+280 p. figs. O. $1.50. Longmans.

Hallock, C:
Peerless Alaska. '08(D19) c. il. D. $1.25. B'way Pub.

Hallock, Ella B., and Gilbert, C: B.
Some living things: primary lessons in physiology. '08(N7) c. il. D. 36 c. Barnes.

Hallock, W:
See Duff, Alex. Wilmer.

Halloway, W: Whiteman, D.D.
Resolutions in honor of William Whiteman Halloway, D.D., for thirty-three years pastor of the Memorial Presbyterian Church of Dover, New Jersey, with extracts from four of his sermons; to which are added six of his poems. '10 (Je) c. 39 p. por. 8°. (Priv. pr.) De Vinne.

Hallowell, Ja. Mott.
Taxation of domestic manufacturing corporations in Massachusetts; rept. to the Mass. Manufacturers' Association to investigate the subject of the taxation of domestic manufacturing industries in Massachusetts. [1910.] (F) 61 p. 8°, gratis. J. M. Hallowell.
See also Harvey, G:

Hallowell, Me.
Nason, *Mrs.* E. H. Old Hallowell on the Kennebec. $3.50. E. H. Nason.
Halocynthia Johnsoni. Ritter, W: E. 50 c. Univ. of Cal.
Halpin, Rev. Patrick Albert.
Christian pedagogy; or, the instruction and moral training of youth. '09(D) c. 15+229 p. 8°, $1.50. Wagner.
Hals, Franz.
Staley, E. Franz Hals. *65 c. net. Stokes.
Halse, E:
Dict. of Spanish and Spanish-American mining, metallurgical and allied terms; to which some Portuguese and Portuguese-American (Brazilian) terms are added. '08(Je6) il. D. *$3.50 net. Lippincott.
Halsey, Forrest.
Fate and the butterfly. '09(My) c. D. $1.50. B. W. Dodge.
Halsey, Fs. Whiting.
See Lodge, H: Cabot.
Halsey, Henrietta A.
See Halsey, Rena I.
Halsey, Mina Deane.
Tenderfoot in California. '08(D) c. 13-149 p. il. 12°, $1. M. D. Halsey.
Halsey, Rena I. and Henrietta A.
One hundred new songs for primary schools. '10(D31) 8°, $1. Hinds.
Halsham, J:
Idlehurst: a journal kept in the country. 2d ed. '08(Mr21) 12°, *$1.50 net. Dutton.
Halsted, Leonora B.
Victorious life. '10(Je11) c. col. front. D. $1.50. Metropolitan Press, (N. Y.)
Haltigan, Ja.
Irish in the American Revolution, and their early influence in the colonies. '08(My9) c. il. pors. 8°, $2. Haltigan.
Ham, Roscoe Ja., and Leonard, Arth. Newton.
Brief German grammar. '09(Mr6) c. S. $1. Ginn.
Ham and his immediate descendants. Hayne, J. E. (Add. pubs. for price.) Weltz Press.
Hambledon men. Lucas, E: V., *ed.* 90 c. Oxford Univ.
Hambleton, Ja. C.
Genus *corizus;* with a review of the north and middle American species. '09(Ag) 133-147 p. il. 4°, (Univ. of Ohio contributions from the Dept. of Zoology and Entomology.) pap., 25 c. Univ. of O.
Hamburg-American Line. Unveiling of a Lincoln memorial tablet on board the S. S. "President Lincoln" of the Hamburg-American line, at the piers, Hoboken, N. J.; under the auspices of the Grand Army of the Republic. '08(D12) il. por. 4°, pap. Hamburg-American Line.
Hamby, W: H.
Getting and holding; how to get, teach and entertain a Sunday-school class; for Sunday-school teachers and those who ought to be. '10(O1) c. D. ("Times" hdbks. for Sunday-school workers.) 50 c. net. S. S. Times.
Hamel, Fk.
Dauphines of France. '10(N19) il. pors. 8°, $4 net. Pott.
Fair women at Fontainbleau. '09(Jl3) 8°, *$3.50 net. Brentano's.
Famous French salons. '08(Ag15) pors. O. *$3.50 net. Brentano's.
Hamer, Sam Hield.
The Dolomites. '10(N12) col. il. O. $3 net. Lane.
Enchanted wood. '10(S17) il. D. 75 c. Estes.
Forest foundling. '10(S17) il. O. $1. Estes.
Magic wand. '09, [1910.] (F) col. il. 4°, $1. Estes.
Peter Pink-eye. '09, [1910.] (F) col. il. 12°, 75 c. Estes.
Princess and the dragon. '09, [1910.] (F) col. il. 4°, $1. Estes.
Transformations of the Truefitts. '08(D5) il. 75 c.; bds., 60 c. Cassell.
Wonderful isles. '09, [1910.] (F) col. il. 4°, $1.25. Estes.
Hamilton, Alex.
See Federalist (The).
Hamilton, Alexander.
Hamilton, A. M. Intimate life of Alexander Hamilton. $3.50 net. Scribner.
Oliver, F: S. Alexander Hamilton. *75 c. net; *$1.25 net; *$2.50 net. Putnam.
Hamilton, Allan McLane, M.D.
Intimate life of Alexander Hamilton, based upon orig. family letters and other documents, many of which have never before been published. '10(O15) c. il. facsims., O. $3.50 net. Scribner.
Hamilton, And., comp.
See New York [State] insurance laws.—Statutory rev. of laws.
Hamilton, Burritt.
See Michigan. Modern law of general business corporations.
Hamilton, Cecily Mary.
Diana of Dobson's. '08(Je20) c. front. D. †$1.50. Century Co.
Hamilton, C: Hadley.
Chart of the law of automobiles. '10(F26) c. fold. chart, 16°, $1. C: H. Hamilton.
—, ed. *See* Wisconsin. *Sup. ct.* Supplement.
Hamilton, Cicely Mary.
Marriage as a trade. '09(Ag28) c. D. **$1.25 net. Moffat.
Hamilton, Clarence Grant.
Outlines of music history. '08(Mr14) c. O. (Music students lib.) $1.50. Ditson.
Piano teaching; its principles and problems. '10(D31) c. il. O. $1.25. Ditson.
Hamilton, Clayton Meeker.
Materials and methods of fiction; with an introd. by Brander Matthews. '08(Je6) c. D. **$1.50 net. Baker & T.
Theory of the theatre and other principles of dramatic criticism. '10(Ap30) c. D. $1.50 net. Holt.
Hamilton, Cosmo.
Blindness of virtue. '09(Jl3) 12°, $1.50. Brentano's.
Sense of humor: a novel. '09(Jl31) $1.50. Brentano's.

HAMILTON, Elizabeth Gunning, *Duchess of.*
Bleackley, H. W: Story of a beautiful duchess. *$5 net. Dutton.

HAMILTON, Emma Lyon, *Lady.*
Moorhouse, E. H. Nelson's Lady Hamilton. *$3 net. Brentano's.

Hamilton, Eug. Lee-.
See Lee-Hamilton, Eug.

Hamilton, Fs. Marion.
Perceptual factors in reading: quantitative study of the psychological processes involved in word perception. '08(Ap11) tabs., O. (Archives of psychology.) pap., 50 c. Science Pr., (N. Y.)

Hamilton, Green Polonius.
Bright side of Memphis: compendium of information concerning the colored people of Memphis, Tenn. '09(F20) c. il. pors. 8°, $2.50. G. P. Hamilton.

Hamilton, H: E:
Biographical sketch of Gurdon Saltonstall Hubbard, read before the Chicago Historical Society, Tuesday evening, Apr. 16, 1907, on the occasion of the unveiling of a bronze tablet in [his] memory. '08, [1909.] (Ap) 28 p. por. 8°, 50 c. Chic. Hist.

Hamilton, Isabel.
Palatial homes in the city of New York and the dwellers therein; arranged for the convenience of the passerby. '10 (Ap30) il. D. pap., 15 c.; bds., 25 c. I. Hamilton.

Hamilton, Ja. Shelley.
Butt Chanler, freshman. '08(O10) c. il. D. †$1.50. Appleton.
New sophomore. '09(O16) c. il. D. †$1.50. Appleton.

Hamilton, J:
Address on a better agriculture and how to get it; del. before the meeting of the Pa. State Board of Agriculture, held at Harrisburg, Pa., Jan. 22 and 23, 1908. '08, [1909.] (My) 18 p. 8°. (Add. pubs. for price.) N. B. Critchfield.
Farmers' institutes for women. '09(D) 16 p. 8°, (U. S., Dept. of Agriculture, Office of Experiment Stations, circular.) pap. U. S., Supt. of Docs.
Progress in agricultural education extension. '10(Ag) 12 p. 8°, (U. S., Dept. of Agriculture, Office of Experiment Stations, circular.) Gov. Pr. Off.

—, and Stedman, J: Moore.
Farmers' institutes for young people. '10 (D) 40 p. 8°, (U. S., Dept. of Agriculture, Office of Experiment Stations, circular.)

Hamilton, J: Judson.
Dethronement of the city boss; being a study of the commission plan as begun in Galveston; developed and extended in Des Moines, and already taken up by many other cities, East and West. '10 (Je4) c. D. $1.20 net. Funk.

Hamilton, Jos.
Transfigured. '10(O15) c. front. 8°, $1. Am. Tr.

Hamilton, Joseph Grégoire de Roulhac.
Presentation of portrait of Governor Abner Nash to the state of North Carolina in the hall of the House of Representatives, at Raleigh, Nov. 15, 1909, by the North Carolina Society of the Sons of the Revolution; address by J. G. de Roulhac Hamilton. [1910.] (Ap) 15 p. 8°. (Not for sale.) J. G. R. Hamilton.
See also Riley, Franklin Lafayette.

Hamilton, M. A.
Junior history of Rome. '10(Ag20) c. 8°, $1.10. Oxford Univ.

Hamilton, Nain Delf.
See Parr, S: W:, *jr.*

Hamilton, P: Jos.
Colonial Mobile; historical study, largely from original sources, of the Alabama-Tombigbee Basin and the old South West from the discovery of the Spiritu Santo in 1519 until the demolition of Fort Charlotte in 1821. Rev. and enl. ed. '10(Ap30) c. il. pors. maps, facsims., O. $3.50 net. Houghton M.

Hamilton, S:
Complete arithmetic. '08(Je6) c. D. 60 c. Am. Bk.
Elem. arithmetic. '08(Je6) c. il. D. 35 c. Am. Bk.
Key to Hamilton's arithmetics; intermediate, school, elementary, and complete. '08(O3) c. tabs., D. 80 c. Am. Bk.

Hamilton, W: Wistar, D.D.
Evangel: [song book.] '09(Mr) 224 p. bds., *20 c. net; pap., *15 c. net. Am. Bapt.
How to grow in the Christian life. Vest pocket ed. '08(D19) leath., *25 c. net; pap., *10 c. net. Am. Bapt.
Sane evangelism. '09(Ja16) c. O. **75 c. net. Am. Bapt.
Worldly amusements. '09(Jl3) c. nar. T. leath., **10 c. net. Am. Bapt.

HAMILTON, Mass.
Vital records of Hamilton, Mass., to the end of the year 1849. (Add. pubs. for price.) Essex Inst.

Hamilton's second marriage. *See* Clifford, *Mrs.* W. K. Three plays.

HAMLET.
See Shakespeare, William.

Hamlin, Alfr. Dwight Foster.
Text-book of the hist. of architecture. 8th ed. '09(O30) il. figs. D. (College histories of art.) $2. Longmans.

Hamlin, F: W:
Manual of practical obstetrics. '08(Je) c. 480 p. 12°, $2.50. Boericke & R.

HAMLIN, Hannibal.
Connor, S. Address to commemorate the 100th anniversary of the birth of Hannibal Hamlin. (Not for sale.) C: Hamlin.

Hamlin, L. Belle, ed.
Selections from the Follett papers, 1.; arr. and ed. by L. Belle Hamlin. [1910.] (D) 4°, (Historical and Philosophical Society of Ohio pubs.) Hist. and Phil. Soc., O.

Hamlin, Mrs. Myra Louise Sawyer.
Eleazer Hamlin and his descendants; their homes. '09(Mr) c. 7-46 p. il. 8°, $1. C: S. Hamlin.
Persis Putnam's treasure. '08(N7) c. D. il. †$1.25. Little, B. & Co.

HAMLIN FAMILY.
See Genealogies.

Hammarsten, Olof.
Text-book of physiological chemistry; author. tr. from the author's enl. and rev. 6th German ed. by J: A. Mandel. '08 (Ja25) 8°, $4. Wiley.

Hammarström, Nanny.
Adventures of two ants; tr. from the Swedish by A. E. B. Fries. '10(S10) c. il. O. $1. Stokes.

"Hammed." Le Fevre, F. S. $1.50. Belgravia.

Hammell, G: M., D.D., ed.
Passing of the saloon; authentic and official presentation of the anti-liquor crusade in America. '08, [1909.] (F) c. 3-12+436 p. pors. 4°, $2; hf. mor., $2.75; mor., $3.50. Tower Press.

Hammer, Bonaventura, comp.
Mary, help of Christians, and the fourteen saints invoked as holy helpers; instructions, legends, novenas, and prayers, with thoughts of the saints for every day in the year; to which is added an appendix on the reasonableness of Catholic ceremonies and practices. 09(S) 497 p. il. 8°, *$2 net. Benziger.

Hammers, Eliz., ed.
Toyland; toyland, joyland, little-girl-and-boy-land. '07, [1908.] (Jl.) 16-288 p. il. 8°, (Juvenile tales.) (Add. pub. for price.) E. B. Holmes.

Hammerstein-Gesmold, Ludwig K. W. von.
Edgar; or, from atheism to the full truth; tr. from the German at the Georgetown Visitation Convent; pref. by Rev. J: A. Conway. 2d ed. '08(F22) 8°, *$1.25 net. Herder.

Hammerton, J: Alex.
George Meredith in anecdote and criticism. '09(Ag14) c. il. 8°, *$4 net. M. Kennerley.
In the track of R. L. Stevenson and elsewhere in old France. '08(Je20) il. 8°, *$1.50 net. Dutton.

Hammock, A. G.
See Hammock, Claude S.

Hammock, Claude S. and A. G.
Manual arts for elementary schools; drawing, design, construction. Shop work. '10(D31) c. il. diagrs., 4°, per doz., $3. Heath.
Manual arts for elem. schools; drawing, design, construction. 8 v. '10(D31) c. il. diagrs., D. and O. vs. 1-3, ea., pap., per doz., $1.50; vs. 4-8, ea., pap., per doz., $2.25. Heath.
Teachers' manual, to accompany The manual arts for elem. schools. '10(D31) c. forms, T. pap., gratis. Heath.

Hammon, L: Lougee.
On evidence covering burden of proof, presumptions, judicial notice, judicial admissions, and estoppel. '08(Ja4) O. shp., $6. Keefe-D.

Hammond, Eleanor Prescott.
Chaucer: a bibliographical manual. '08 (O17) 8°, *$3 net. Macmillan.

Hammond, Mrs. Emily Vanderbilt Sloane, comp.
Looking upward day by day. '10(Ja8) 16°, *$1 net. Dutton.

Hammond, Eric, comp.
Splendor of God; extracts from the sacred writings of the Bahaïs; with an introd. by Eric Hammond. '09(Jl17) 16°, (Wisdom of the East ser.) *60 c. net. Dutton.

Hammond, H. W.
Style-book of business English; designed for use in business colleges, high schools, and for self-instruction. '08(Mr28) O. 60 c.; 3d rev. ed. '09(D11) il. O. 85 c. Pitman.

—, Beygrau, F. R., and Mason, W. L.
Pitman's progressive dictator; selections of original letters relating to twenty-seven different lines of business, arranged with vocabularies and engraved shorthand outlines and phrases. '09(O16) D. 85 c. Pitman.

Hammond, Harold.
West Point; its glamour and its grind. '10 (Ap16) c. il. D. $1.25. Cupples & L.

Hammond, Ja. T., comp.
See Utah. Compiled laws.

Hammond, Rev. Jos.
Magister moritur; our Lord's last hours. '10(Mr5) 12°, *$2 net. Whittaker.

Hammond, Stephen Tillinghast, ["Shadow."]
My friend the partridge. '08(Je6) c. por. S. $1. Forest.

Hammond's atlas of New York City and the metropolitan district; containing new maps of each borough on large scale. '08(Ag29) Q. pap., 25 c. C. S. Hammond.

Hammond's guide map of Brooklyn Borough, N. Y.; showing all streets, subways, tunnels, ferries, elevated and surface railroads, parks, parkways, etc. '08(Ag22) c. pap., 15 c. C. S. Hammond.

Hammond's handy atlas of the world. '08 (N21) c. il. 8°, $1; leath., $1.50; pap., 50 c. C. S. Hammond.

Hammond's pictorial atlas of the world; new series of over one hundred maps; accompanied by an index-gazetteer of cities and towns, and a descriptive gazetteer of the states, countries and physical features of the globe. '08(N21) c. il. f°, $5. C. S. Hammond.

Hammond's road map of the country around New York. '08(Ag22) c. pap., 25 c. C. S. Hammond.

Hamp, Sidford F:
Coco Bolo, king of the Floating Islands. '10(O29) c. il. D. $1. Badger.
Trail of the badger: story of the Colorado border thirty years ago. '08(O17) c. il. D. †$1.50. Wilde.

HAMPSHIRE, Eng.
Clarke, F. School hist. of Hampshire. 50 c. **Oxford Univ.**
Dewar, G: A. B. Life and sport in Hampshire. *$3 net. Longmans.
Read, D. H. M. Highways and byways in Hampshire. $2. Macmillan.
Varley, T. Hampshire *$6 net. Macmillan.

Hampton, Celwyn Emerson.
Twenty-first's trophy of Niagara. '09(S) c. 19 p. il. 4°, $1. C. E. Hampton.

HAMPTON, Va.
Church, J. W. The crucible, a Southerner's impression of Hampton. gratis. Hampton Inst.

Hampton arithmetic. Low, F. F. $1. Hampton Inst.

Hancock, Albert Elmer.
Bronson of the rabble. '09(O23) c. front D. †$1.50. Lippincott.
John Keats. '08(O17) c. il. O. **$2 net. Houghton M.

Hancock, E: Lee.
Applied mechanics for engineers. '09 (Ja23) c. figs. D. **$2 net. Macmillan.

Hancock, Eliz. Hazelwood.
See Neale, Wa.

Hancock, Eug. T:
Notes accompanying the lectures on geology applied to mining; course given at Michigan College of Mines. '10(Ap9) c. il. tabs., 8°, $1. New Era Pr.

Hancock, Harrie Irving.
High school captain of the team; or, Dick & Co. leading the athletic vanguard. '10 (D) il. 12°, (High school boys ser.) $1. Altemus.
High school freshmen; or, Dick & Co.'s first year pranks and sports. '10(D) il. 12°, (High school boys ser.) $1. Altemus.
High school left end; or, Dick & Co. grilling on the football gridiron. '10(D) il. 12°, (High school boys ser.) $1. Altemus.
High school pitcher; or, Dick & Co. on the Gridley diamond. '10(D) il. 12°, (High school boys ser.) $1. Altemus.
Motor Boat Club and the wireless; or, the dot, dash and dare cruise. '09(D18) c. il. 12°, $1. Altemus.
Motor Boat Club at Nantucket; or, the mystery of the Dunstan heir. [1910.] (D) il. 12°, $1. Altemus.
Motor Boat Club at the Golden Gate; or, a thrilling capture in the great fog. '10 (F19) c. il. 12°, †$1. Altemus.
Motor Boat Club in Florida; or, laying the ghost of Alligator Swamp. '10(F19) c. il. 12°, †$1. Altemus.
Motor Boat Club of the Kennebec; or, the secret of Smugglers' Island. '09(D18) c. il. 12°, $1. Altemus.
Motor Boat Club off Long Island; or, a daring marine game at racing speed. '09 (D18) c. il. 12°, $1. Altemus.
Uncle Sam's boys in the ranks; or, two recruits in the United States Army. '10 (D31) c. pls. 12°, (Boys of the army ser.) $1. Altemus.

Hancock, Harris.
Lectures on the theory of elliptic functions. v. 1, Analysis. '10(Je4) figs. $5. Wiley.

Hancock, Jos. L.
Nature sketches in temperate America. '10 (D17) il. (12 in col.) 8°, $2.75 net. McClurg.

Hancock, Mary S.
Children of history. In 2 v. '09(D25) il. 12°, ea., **50 c. net. Little, B. & Co.

HAND.
Gould, G: M. Righthandedness and lefthandedness. **$1.25 net. Lippincott.
Kroeger, E. R. Hand expansions and contractions. $1.25. Ditson.
Witkowski's atlas of the bones of the hand. *$2 net. W: R. Jenkins.
See also Finger prints.

Hand loom linen weavers of Ireland. White, J. (Add. pubs. for price.) Irish Hand-Woven.

Hand-loom weaving. Hooper, L. $2.25 net. Macmillan.

Hand made furniture. Glidden, A. G. $1. Hand Made Furniture.

Hand-made gentleman. Bacheller, I. A. †$1.50. Harper.

Hand of Ethelberta. *See* Hardy, T:

Hand of God. Stephenson, C. B. $1.50. Ball Pub. Co.

Hand of the north. Fox, M. $1.50. Lane.

Hand on the latch. Cholmondeley, M. †$1.25. Dodd.

HAND WORK.
See Manual training.

Handbook of learned societies and institutions: America. '08(Jl18) O. (Carnegie Institution of Washington pub.) pap., $4. Carnegie.

Handbook of penmanship; manual for teachers and students of free-arm movement writing; complete development of rapid writing for all grades; arranged in 3 pts. '10(D10) c. il. obl. D. pap., 25 c. net. Macmillan.

Handbook ser. In 5 v. '08. c. T. pap., ea., 10 c. Sampson.
Contents: 1, Houghton, W: C., Small electric motor to be built without castings; 2, O'Donnell, T. E., How to make an annunciator; 3, Cole, M., How to grind and set edge tools; 4, Cole, M., Making and fixing electric bells and batteries. 5, Cole, M., Tempering steel, annealing and case hardening iron.

Handbooks for animal owners. See Altemus.

Handbooks for the clergy; ed. by Arth. W. Robinson, *D.D.* D. *90 c. net. Longmans.
—Carter. Preaching.
—Clayton. Church defense.

Handbooks of American government. See Macmillan's.

Handbooks of archaeology and antiquities. See Macmillan's.

Handbooks of art history of all countries and all ages; ed. by *Sir* E: J: Poynter and T. Roger Smith. 12°, $1.25. Gorham.
—Buxton. Painting: English and American. —Painting: German, Flemish and Dutch.
—Poynter. Painting: Classic and Italian.
—Redford. Sculpture: Egyptian, Assyrian, Greek and Roman.
—Redgrave. Water-color painting in England.
—Scott. Sculpture: Gothic, Renaissance and modern.
—Smith. Painting: Spanish and French.
—Smith *and* Slater. Architecture: classic and early Christian.—Architecture: Gothic and Renaissance.

Handbooks of English Church expansion; ed. by Rev. Canon Dodson and Rev. G. R. Bullock-Webster; with a general preface by the Bishop of St. Albans. 6 v. '09(Ap10) ea., 80 c. Young Churchman.
Contents: 1, Bickersteth, Mrs., Japan; 2, Tucker, Rev. Canon Norman, Western Canada; 3, Norris, Rev. F. L., China; 4, David, Rev. A. E., Australia; 5, Baynes, Bp. Hamilton, South Africa; 6, Andrews, Rev. C. F., North India.

Handbooks of practical gardening. See Lane's.

HANDEL, Georg Frederich.
Streatfield, R: A. Handel. **$2.50 net. Lane.

Handicap (The). Knowles, R. E. $1.20 net. Revell.

Handicapped. Pottle, E. B. †$1.50. Lane.

HANDICRAFTS.
See Decoration and ornament;—Leather;—Manual training;—Mechanics.

Handler, Blanche.
Sea-scamps: [verses for children.] '08 (Ag8) il. obl. S. (Ainslie booklets.) bds., 50 c. Stokes.

Handley, L. de B.
How to play water polo. '10(S3) c. il. 12°, (Spalding's athletic lib.) 10 c. Am. Sports.

Handlin, W: Wallace.
Speling book, gramar and reder ov the American language. '09, [1910.] (Jl) 155 p. il. pors. 16°, $1. H: J. Brauer.

Hands and how to read them. René, E. 50 c. Fenno.

Hands of compulsion. Barr, *Mrs.* A. E. H. †$1.50. Dodd.

Handwork construction. Eppendorff, L. $1.58. L. Eppendorff.

Handwork in wood. Noyes, W: $2. Manual Arts.

HANDWRITING.
Booth, M. H. How to read character in handwriting. 50 c. Winston.
Thorndike, E: L. Handwriting. 30 c. Columbia Univ.
See also Abbreviations;—Autographs;—Forgeries;—Penmanship.

Handy Bible encyclopedia. Hurlbut, J. L., *ed.* $3. Winston.

Handy book of American government. Bartlett, W: H. 50 c. Crowell.

Handy book for brewers. Wright, H. E. *$5 net. Van Nostrand.

Handy book of proverbs. Walker, J., *comp.* 50 c. Crowell.

Handy farm devices. Cobleigh, R. *$1.50 net. Judd.

Handy hand-books. 15 v. '10(D) nar. 12°, ea., 50 c. Platt & P.
Contents: Graham, Athletics of to-day; Humphrey, A word to women, How to be pretty, Manners for girls, Beauty adorned, Manners for men, Manners for women; Hardy, Concerning marriage; Nissen, Health, exercise and home gymnastics; Wood, Recitations, comic and otherwise; Applause reciter; Masters, Book of stitches; Coo-ee reciter; Knollys, Gentle art of good talking; What shall I say? (letter writer for ladies).

Handy Happy Hooligan. Opper, F: B. 60 c. Stokes.

Handy information ser. See Crowell's.

Handy Jack book of navigation. Rudder (The). $1. Rudder.

Handy man's enquire within. Hasluck, P. N., *ed.* *$2.50 *net.* Cassell.

Handy man's workshop and laboratory. Bond, A. R., *comp. and ed.* $2. Munn.

Handy manual of social reform. '08(D) 25 c. Funk.

Handy pronouncing **dictionaries.** 3 v. '09 (O9) 16°, ea., *$1.25 **net.** Little, B. & Co.

Handy tables. Eby, E. G. $2.50. J. F. Smith.

Handy volume classics. See Crowell's.

Haney, Ja. Parton.
Vocational training and trade teaching in the public schools. '09(Je19) 8°, (Am. Acad. of Pol. and Soc. Science pubs.) pap., 15 c. Am. Acad. Pol. Sci.
—, ed. Art education in the public schools of the United States: symposium prepared under the auspices of the American committee of the third International Congress for the Development of Drawing and Art Teaching. '08(D5) c. il. 8°, $3.50. Am. Art.

Haney, J: Dearling.
Registration of city school children; consideration of the subject of the city school census. '10(N19) c. il. forms, 8°, (Columbia Univ., Teachers' College; contribs. to education.) $1.50. Teachers' Coll.

Haney, J: L:
Monsieur D'Or; dramatic fantasy. '10 (D24) c. D. $1.20 net. Egerton Press.

Haney, Lewis H:
Congressional history of railways in the United States to 1850. '08(D) 273 p. maps, 8°, (Univ. of Wisconsin bull. economics and political science ser.) 50 c. Univ. of Wis.
Congressional history of railways in the United States, 1850-1887. '10(O) 6+7-335 p. maps, tabs., fold tab., 8°, (Univ. of Wis. bull.; Economic and political science ser.) 50 c. Univ. of Wis.

Hanford, B:
Fight for your life!; recording some activities of a labor agitator. '09(My) c. 127 p. 12°, pap., 25 c. Wiltshire Bk.

Hanish, Otoman Zar-Adusht-.
Mazdaznan encyclop. of dietetics and home cook book; cooked and uncooked foods, what to eat and how to eat it. 5th ed. '09(D) c. 230 p. 12°, $1.25. Mazdaznan.

Hankins, Fk. Hamilton.
Adolphe Quetelet as statistician. '08(D12) 8°, (Studies in history, economics and public law.) pap., *$1.25 net. Longmans.

Hanks, Austin Kimball.
Pract. suggestions regarding the selection and use of a photographic equipment; written from actual experience; il. by author. '10(Ap9) c. 8°, $1. A. K. Hanks.

Hanks, C: Stedman, ["Niblick."]
Benefit of the Hepburn law to the banker, broker, shipper and the public: address del. before the Fitchburg Board of Trade, April 3. '07. [1908.] (F) 38 p. 16°, pap., 50 c. Authors' Pub.
Growth of corporate wealth and its effect upon us as individuals. '07, [1908.] (Mr.) 40 p. 16°, 50 c. Authors' Pub.
Our Plymouth forefathers. '09(My1) c. il. pors. maps, O. $1.50. Estes.

Hanly, J. Fk.
My Lord and Savior Jesus Christ; address del. before the 51st Ohio State Sunday School Convention held in Cleveland, O., June 15, 1910. '10(D31) c. 12°, 85 c. Hollenbeck Press.

Hanmer, Lee F.
First steps in organizing playgrounds. '08 (Jl18) il. D. (Russell Sage foundation pub.) pap., 10 c. Charities Pub.

Hanna, Hugh Sisson.
Financial history of Maryland, (1789-1848.) '08(F8) O. (Johns Hopkins Univ. studies in historical and pol. science.) pap., 75 c. Johns Hopkins.

Hanna, Marcus Alonzo, Monument Association. Dedication of the monument erected to the memory of Marcus A. Hanna, University Circle, Cleveland, May 23, 1908. '08(N) 56 p. 8°. (Priv. pr.) Burrows.

Hanna, Matthew Elting.
Tactical principles and problems. [1910.] (Je) c. 8+459 p. il. fold. maps, 8°, $2.50. M. E. Hanna.

Hanna, Septimus J.
Christian science: the religion of the Bible: a lecture. '09(Mr27) c. 16°, pap., 6 c. Chr. Sci.

Hannahs, Eliz. Helen.
Lessons in psychology. '08(Je6) c. 12°, $1. E. H. Hannahs.

Hannele. Hauptmann, G. **$1 net. Doubleday, P.

HANNINGTON, *Bp.* James.
Berry, W. B. Bishop Hannington and the story of the Uganda mission. *$1 net. Revell.

Hanotaux, Gabriel.
Contemporary France; tr. from the French by E. Sparvel-Bayly. In 4 v. v. 4, (1877-1882.) '09(Jl3) pors. O. *$3.75 net. Putnam.

HANOVER, N. H.
See **Rochester reprints.**

HANOVERIAN QUEENS.
See **England.**

Hans and sister Hilda. Jewett, J: H. 50 c. Dutton.

Hans Brinker. Dodge, *Mrs.* M. M. 50 c. McLoughlin.

Hansbrough, Mrs. Lucinda Victoria Blair.
Life of Rev. R. Downey Blair, with sketches of his pastorates and tributes by friends who knew and loved him for his noble Christian character and his sturdy type of moral manhood. '08, [1909.] (Mr) c. 248 p. il. pors. 12°, $1.50. L. V. B. Hansbrough.

Hanscom, Eliz. Deering, ed.
Friendly craft: a collection of American letters. '08(D12) c. S. **$1.25 net. Macmillan.

Hansen, H. C., Type Foundry.
Book of types, borders, ornaments, brass rule, printing materials and the like for printerdom, 1909. '08, [1909.] (Mr) c. 384 p. il. f°. (Not for sale.) H. C. Hansen.

Hansen, Niels Ebbesen.
Wild alfalfas and clovers of Siberia; with a perspective view of the alfalfas of the world. '09(Ag) 31 p. fold map, 8°, (U. S., Dept. of Agriculture; Bu. of Plant Industry bull.) (Add. Superintendent for price.) U. S., Supt. of Docs.

Hansey, Jennie A., comp.
See Lee, W: H:

Hanson, C: Lane.
English composition. '08(My9) c. D. 80 c. Ginn.

Hanson, E: Kenneth, and Dodgson, J: Wallis.
Intermediate course of laboratory work in chemistry. '09(F20) figs. O. *$1.20 net. Longmans.

Hanson, E: Smith.
Cement pipe and tile. '09(Ap10) c. il. 12°, $1. Cement Era.

Hanson, Haldor Johan, comp.
English-Norwegian-Danish dict.; comp. for "Skandinaven." '09(N) c. 334 p. 16°, 50 c. J: Anderson.

Hanson, Ja. Christian Meinich.
Subject catalogs of the Library of Congress; [from the Proceedings of the American Library Association annual meeting, 1909.] '10(O1) 8°. H. W. Wilson.
—, **comp.** American and English genealogies in the Library of Congress; preliminary catalogue. '10(D) 805 p. Q. $1.05. Gov. Pr. Off.

Hanson, Jos. Mills.
Conquest of the Missouri; being the story of the life and exploits of Captain Grant Marsh. '09(N6) c. O. il. map, O. *$2 net. McClurg.
Frontier ballads. '10(D3) c. col. il. O. $1. McClurg.
With Sully into the Sioux land. '10(D3) c. il. O. (Among the Sioux ser.) $1.50. McClurg.

Hanstein, Herman.
Constructive drawing. 3d ed. '08(O) c. 73 p. diagrs., 8°, $1. Keuffel.

Hanus, Paul H:
Beginnings in industrial education, and other educational discussions. '08(S26) c. D. **$1 net. Houghton M.

Hapgood, G:
Solitaire and patience: fifty games. '08 (S5) c. il. S. (Popular handbooks.) 50 c. Penn Pub. Co.

Hapgood, Hutchins.
Anarchist woman. '09(My22) 12°, *$1.25 net. Duffield.
Spirit of the Ghetto. Rev. ed. '09(D) il. 12°, *$1.25 net. Funk.
Types from city streets. '10(Je4) c. il. D. $1.50 net. Funk.

Hapgood, Mrs. Hutchins.
See Boyce, Neith, *pseud.*

Hapgood, Thdr. Brown.
Bookplates. '08(Ja18) il. por. 8°, (Monographs on American book-plate designers.) set of 12 brochures, per set, $18; Japan pap., $30. Goodspeed.

Happenings of future years foretold in the Welsh almanacs; with introd. by H: Blackwell. '10(Mr19) pap., 25 c. H: Blackwell.

HAPPINESS.
Ainsworth, P. C. Heart of happiness. $1 net. Revell.
Al Ghazzali, A. H. M. Alchemy of happiness. 60 c. net. Dutton.
Barrows, M. M., *ed.* Value of happiness. $1.50; $2; $2.50; $4; $5. Caldwell.
Chapple, J. M. Happy habit. $1.50. Chapple Pub.
Eliot, C: W: Durable satisfactions of life. $1. Crowell.
Frink, *Mrs.* M. How to be happy: [selections.] $1; 25 c. Laird.
Hilty, C. Happiness: essays on the meaning of life. 75 c. Grosset.
Jennings, N. I., *comp.* Latch-string to happiness. 50 c. Lone Star.
Joslyn, R. W. Philosophy of happiness. $1. Normalist.
Hutton, W. S. Pathway to happiness. 50 c. net. Dutton.
Lubbock, *Sir* J: Duty of happiness. 40 c.; 75 c. Caldwell.
Patterson, C: B. New way to happiness. *25 c. net. Rogers Bros.
Slicer, T: R. Way to happiness. *$1 net. Sturgis & W.
Smith, *Mrs.* H. W. Christian secret of a happy life. *$1 net. Revell.
Sunderland, J. T: Oh, to be rich and young. $1. Am. Unitarian.
Wayt, H. True source of a happy life. 50 c. Chr. Pub. Co.
Williams, H: S. Science of happiness. $2 net. Harper.
See also **Cheerfulness.**

Happy book. Sowerby, G. 40 c. net. Doran.
Happy chaps. Wells, C. $1.50. Century Co.
Happy Child-Town. Middleton, C. S. 60 c. Aberdeen.
Happy ending. Guiney, L. I. **$3 net. Houghton M.
Happy England. Huish, M. B. *$6 net. Macmillan.
Happy family. Bower, B. M. $1.25. G: W. Dillingham.
Happy habit. Chapple, J. M. $1.50. Chapple Pub.
Happy half-century. Repplier, A. **$1.10 net. Houghton M.
Happy Hawkins. Wason, R. A. †$1.50. Small.
Happy hour paint book. Schaeffer, A. J. 50 c. Saalfield.
Happy hour ser. il. D. bds., 50 c. Wilde.
—Hoyt. Little chum club.
—Hoyt, *ed.* Little folks in the country.—Play days.
—Lovejoy, *ed.* Dolls' story-book.
Happy hours for the boys and girls. Lewis, D. E. 50 c. S. S. Times.
Happy hunting grounds. Hightower, J. $1.25. J. Hightower.
Happy Island. Lee, J. $1. Century Co.
Happy life. Raymond, C: F. 75 c.; $1.25. Dodge.
Happy little time. Richards, *Mrs.* L. E. H. $1.25. Estes.
Happy moralist. Bland, H. N. *$1.25 net. M. Kennerley.
Happy night. Clarke, W. J. P. $1.50. Cochrane.
Happy prince. *See* Wilde, Oscar.
Happy school days. Sangster, *Mrs.* M. E. M. $1.25. Forbes.
Happy Sunday hours. *See* Bible.
Happy teacher. Anderson, M. B. 60 c. net. B: W. Huebsch.

Harbaugh, C: Hamilton.
Causes of disability as applied under accident and health insurance policies. '09 (Ap17) c. il. 8°, $6. Spectator.

Harbaugh, T: Chalmers, ed. and comp.
Centennial history; Troy, Piqua and Miami County, Ohio, and representative citizens. '09, [1910.] (Mr.) 11-857 p. il. pors., 4°, mor., $16. Richmond-A.

Harben, W: Nathaniel, ["Will N."]
Dixie Hart. '10(O15) c. front. D. $1.50. Harper.
Gilbert Neal: a novel. '08(O10) c. front. D. †$1.50. Harper.
Pole Baker. '10(D) 75 c. Burt.
Redemption of Kenneth Galt. '09(O9) c. front. D. †1.50. Harper.

Harbin, Rob. Maxwell, M.D.
Health and happiness; or, an analogical study of disease and sin. '08(Je6) c. D. **90 c. net. Am. Bapt.

Harbison-Walker Refractories Co., Pittsburg.
Catalogue; cont. useful information in connection with the use of silica, magnesia, chrome and fire clay brick and various refractories, as furnished by the Harbison-Walker Refractories Co. [1910.] (Ap) il. 16°. (Add. pubs. for price.) Harbison-W.

Harbison-Walker Refractories Co., Pittsburg. Study of the open hearth; treatise on the open hearth furnace and the manufacture of open hearth steel. '09, [1910.] (Mr) c. 9-91 p. il. 16°, $1. R. S. Davis.

Harbord, F. W., and Hall, J. W.
Steel: its metallurgy and mechanical treatment. 3d ed., rev. '08(Ag29) il. 8°, *$9 net. Lippincott.

HARBORS.
Cunningham, B. Treatise on the principles and practice of harbour engineering. *$5 net. Lippincott.
United States. *Office of Naval Intelligence.* Coaling, docking and repairing facilities of the ports of the world. 5th ed. '09 (O) 239 p. 8°. (Add. Superintendent for price.) U. S., Supt. of Docs.
United States. *Treasury Dept.* Balances of appropriations for river and harbor improvements. (Add. Superintendent for price.) U. S., Supt. of Docs.
See also Inland navigation;—*also* Chicago.

Harbottle, T: Benfield.
Dict. of Latin quotations. '10(F19) 12°, *$1 net. Macmillan.

—, and Dalbiac, Philip Hugh.
Dictionary of quotations, (Italian.) [New ed.] '09(Jl3) 12°, *$1.25 net. Macmillan.

Harbour, Jefferson Lee.
Marcia and the major. '08(S19) c. front. D. (Bimbi ser.) bds., **40 c. net. Crowell.

Harcourt, Alfr., comp.
See Gaige, Roscoe Crosby.

"Harcourt, C:," pseud.
See Lindsay, C: Harcourt Ainslie Forbes-.

Harcourt, Leveson Fs. Vernon-.
Civil engineering as applied in construction. 2d ed., rev. by H: Fidler. '10(Ap9) il. O. (Civil engineering ser.) $5 net. Longmans.

Hard, Miron Elisha.
Mushroom, edible and otherwise, its habitat and its time of growth. '08(D19) c. il. por. 4°, $4.75: ¾ lev., $6; mor., $7.50. Mushroom Pub.

Hard, W:, and others.
Injured in the course of duty; repr. with some additions, from *Everybody's Magazine;* being an exposition and some conclusions on the subject of industrial accidents. '10(Jl30) S. pap., gratis. Ridgway.

Hard pressed. White, F. M. $1.50. Fenno.

Hard rock man. Bechdolt, F: R. $1 net. Moffat.

Hard times. Dickens, C: *35 c. net; *70 c. net. Dutton.

Hard times edition. Walton, M. A. 25 c. S. Walton.

HARDANGER NEEDLEWORK.
See Needlework.

Hardcastle, Ella.
See Knight, C: R.

Hardcastle, Mrs. Minnie A.
Word signs made easy, Graham phonography. '08(Jl) c. 88 p. 12°, $1. Word Sign.

Harden, E: Walker.
Cost of living to railways; from the *Outlook,* Apr. 9, 1910. '10(Je11) O. pap. E: W. Harden.

Hardenberg, Friedrich Leopold, Freiherr von, ["Novalis."]
Devotional songs of Novalis: German and English, collected and ed. by Bernhard Pick. '10(Je4) c. por. 12°, $1. Open Court.

Hardening and tempering. '09(Ag28) c. il. diagrs., 8°, (Machinery's reference ser.) pap., 25 c. Indust. Press.

Harder, Edm. Cecil.
Manganese deposits of the United States with sections on foreign deposits, chemistry, and uses. '10(N) 298 p. il. maps, diagrs., 8°, (U. S., Dept. of the Interior, U. S. Geolog. survey; bull.)
Bibliography (5 p.).

Hardesty, Irving.
Laboratory guide for histology; laboratory outlines for the study of histology and microscopic anatomy; with a chapter on laboratory drawing by Adelbert Watts Lee. '08(D) c. 7+193 p. il. 8°, *$1.50 net. Blakiston.

Hardey, Mother Mary Aloysia.
Mary Aloysia Hardey, religious of the Sacred Heart, 1809-1886; with introd. by the Rev. T: J. Campbell. '10(D24) c. il. pors. O. $2. Am. Press.

Hardie, C: Martin.
John Pettie. '08(D12) il. 8°, (Color books.) *$6 net. Macmillan.

Hardie, G: Rob.
Where to go in the Adirondacks. '09(My) il. pap., 25 c. G: R. Hardie.

Hardie, Ja. Keir.
India; impressions and suggestions. '09 (S11) D. bds., *$1 net. B: W. Huebsch.

Harding, Arth. Rob.
Fur farming: information about fur bearing animals, enclosures, habits, care, etc. '09(My22) c. il. S. 60 c. A. R. Harding.
Ginseng and other medicinal plants. '08 (S12) c. il. por. S. $1. A. R. Harding.
Wolf and coyote trapping. '09(O23) c. il. D. 60 c. A. R. Harding.

Harding, J: W:
Chorus lady; novelized from the play by Ja. Forbes. '08(Mr28) c. il. D. †$1.50. G: W. Dillingham.
City of splendid night. '09(Mr13) c. il. D. †$1.50. G: W. Dillingham.
Girl question, founded on the play of Will M. Hough and Fk. R. Adams. '08(N14) c. il. D. †$1. G: W. Dillingham.
Paid in full; novelized from the play by Eug. Walter. '08(Je6) c. il. D. †$1.50. G: W. Dillingham.
The time, the place and the girl; fr. the play of Will M. Hough and Fk. R. Adams; il. by Gordon Grant. '08(Ag29) c. D. †$1. G: W. Dillingham.

Harding, S: Bannister.
Essentials in mediæval history (from Charlemagne to the close of the fifteenth century); in consultation with Albert Bushnell Hart. '09(Ap3) c. il. maps, O. hf. leath., $1. Am. Bk.

—, **comp. and ed.** Select orations illustrating American political hist. with an introd. on oratorical style and structure, and notes by J: Mantel Clapp. '09(O9) c. D. **$1.25 net. Macmillan.

— **and W: Fletcher.**
Story of England; elem. hist. for sixth and seventh grades. '09(D4) c. il. S. (Lake history stories.) 60 c. Scott, F. & Co.

Harding, W:
Mental nursing. '10(D) 8+91 p. 16°, 50 c. W: R. Jenkins.

Harding, W: Fletcher.
See Harding, S: Bannister.

Harding, W: Ja.
Ancestry in the line of her father of Adelia Chamberlain Harding, daughter of Rev. Hiram Chamberlain and Anna Adelia Griswold; also the ancestry of Capt. Hiram S. Chamberlain in the line of Leander, son of Peleg Chamberlain. '08 (Ap18) por. 8°, $1. (Priv. pr.) E. Putnam.

Harding's luck. Bland, *Mrs.* E. N. $1.50. Stokes.

Hardman, W:
Hist. of Malta during the period of the French and British occupations, 1798-1815; ed., with an introd. and notes, by J. Holland Rose. '09(N13) front. O. *$6.50 net. Longmans.

HARDWARE.
Rating register hardware merchants United States and Canada; comp. by the *Hardware Dealers' Magazine.* '10(N) c. 8°, $5. Mallett.
Who makes what; book of reference for buyers; directory of manufacturers, products, foreign and wholesale hardware merchants, [etc.] $1. Mallett.

HARDWARE STORE.
See Business.

Hardware window dressing. Bird, T: A., *comp. and ed.* $2.50. Merchants' Record.

Hardy, Arth. Lemuel.
Clutch of circumstance. '09(D4) c. por. 12°, $1. Mayhew.

Hardy, Blanche Christabel.
Princesse de Lamballe. '09(My22) il. 8°, *$3.50 net. Appleton.

Hardy, Carlos S.
Fraternal Society law, embracing the statute law and a digest of the decisions of the courts of last resort, [etc.,] concerning fraternal beneficiary societies. Rev. ed. '10(O) c. 680 p. O. $10. R. Smith.
—, **comp.** Fraternal society law, embracing the statute law and a digest of the decisions of the court of last resort of the several states concerning fraternal beneficiary societies. Ed. for 1907. '08(My) c. 1159 p. O. *$10 net. C. S. Hardy.

HARDY, Dudley.
Johnson, A. E. Dudley Hardy, R.I., R.M.S. *$1.75 net. Macmillan.

Hardy, E. S., and Gask, Stuart.
Three bold pirates. '10(Ap23) il. 16°, (Little mother ser.) bds., 50 c. Dutton.

Hardy, Rev. E: J:
How to be happy though civil: book on manners. '09(O16) D. *$1 net. Scribner
John Chinaman at home. New and pop. [2d] ed. '08(Mr14) il. 12°, *$1.50 net. Scribner.

Hardy, Godfrey Harold.
Course of pure mathematics. '08(N7) 8°, *$4 net. Putnam.

Hardy, Lawrence Abbott.
Fort Dearborn year book. '10(D17) il. 50 c. net. McClurg.

Hardy, T:
Desperate remedies; novel. [Thin paper ed.] '10(O15) front. 12°, $1.25; leath., $1.25 net. Harper.
The dynasts: drama of the Napoleonic wars; in 19 acts and 30 scenes. In 3 pts. pt. 3. '08(Je27) 12°, *$1.50 net. Macmillan.
Far from the madding crowd. [Thin paper ed.] '10(My14) 16°, $1.25; leath., $1.25 net. Harper.
Hand of Ethelberta; comedy in chapters. [Thin paper ed.] '10(S17) front. 12°, $1.25; leath., $1.25 net. Harper.
Jude the obscure. [Thin paper ed.] '10 (My14) front. 16°, $1.25; leath., $1.25 net. Harper.
A Laodicean; story of to-day. [Thin paper ed.] '10(Ag13) 16°, $1.25; leath., $1.25 net. Harper.
Mayor of Casterbridge. Thin paper ed. '10(D10) 12°, $1.25; leath., $1.25 net. Harper.
Pair of blue eyes. Thin paper ed. '10 (D10) front. maps, 12°, $1.25; leath., $1.25 net. Harper.
Return of the native. [Thin paper ed.] '10(Mr12) front. 16°, leath., $1.25. Harper.
Tess of the D'Urbervilles. [Thin paper ed.] '09(My22) 16°, $1.25; leath., *$1.25 net Harper.

Hardy, T:—*Continued.*
Time's laughingstocks, and other verses. '10(Ja15) 12°, *$1.50 net. Macmillan.
Under the greenwood tree. [Thin paper ed.] '10(My14) 16°, $1.25; leath., $1.25 net. Harper.

Hardy, T: J:
Gospel of pain. '08(Je6) 12°, *$1.25 net. Macmillan.

Hardy plants for cottage gardens. Albee, *Mrs.* H. R. $1.60 net. Holt.

Hare, Anne.
The Wollopors. '10(N12) il. S. bds., 50 c. Saalfield.

Hare, A: J: Cuthbert.
Florence; [also] Venice; rev. by St. Clair Baddeley. 7th ed. '08(F22) il. maps, plan, 16°, $2. Macmillan.

"Hare, Christopher," pseud.
Charles de Bourbon, High Constable of France, "The Great Condottiere." '10 (O8) il. front., O. $4 net. Lane.
Courts and camps of the Italian renaissance; being a mirror of the life and times of the ideal gentleman, Count Baldassare Castiglione; derived largely from his own letters and other contemporary sources, to which is added an epitome of his famous work, "The book of the courtier"; with appreciations and annotations. '08(D5) il. 8°, *$2.50 net. Scribner.
Felicita; romance of old Siena. '09(O30) D. (Little novels of famous cities.) †$1.25, boxed. Stokes.
Romance of a Medici warrior; study in heredity; being the true story of Giovanni Delle Bande Nere, to which is added the life of his son, Cosimo I., Duke of Tuscany. '10(D3) il. 8°, $2.50 net. Scribner.

Hare, Hobart Amory, M.D.
Text-book of practical therapeutics. 13th ed., thoroughly rev. '09(O) 951 p. il. 8°, *$4 net; leath., *$5 net; hf. mor., *$5.50 net. Lea.
—, **and Beardsley, E: J: Gillespie.**
Medical complications, accidents and sequels of typoid fever and other exanthemata. 2d ed., rev. and enl. '09(N) 398 p. il. 8°, *$3.25 net. Lea.
—, **and others.**
National standard dispensatory. 2d ed., thoroughly rev. and much enl. '09 (Ja16) c. il. 4°, $8. Lea.

Hare, T: Truxtun.
Junior in the line. '09(N13) c. il. D. †$1.25. Penn Pub. Co.
Senior quarter-back. '10(D3) c. il. D. $1.25. Penn Pub. Co.
Sophomore half-back. '08(O3) c. il. D. (College athletic ser.) †$1.25. Penn Pub. Co.

Hare, W. Loftus.
Watts. '10(D17) col. il. O. (Masterpieces in colour.) bds., 65 c. net. Stokes.

Hare, Bp. W: Hobart.
Glimpses into the life of the Indian schools in South Dakota. '08, [1909.] (F) 15 p. il. 16°. (Add. author for price.) W: H. Hare.

Haremlik. Brown, D. V. **$1.25 net. Houghton M.

Hargrave, Basil.
Origins and meanings of popular phrases and names. '10(D10) 12°, $1.50 net. Lippincott.

Haring, Clarence H:
Buccaneers in the West Indies in the xviiith century. '10(D10) il. maps, 8°, $3.50 net. Dutton.

Haring, Fred Benson.
Manual of procedure; law of conditional sales, cont. the essential features of the laws concerning conditional sales in every state and territory of the United States, also approved forms for conditional contracts of sale, acknowledgements, etc. Interleaved ed. of 1909. '09 (My) c. 370 p. O. $5. Ronald Press.

Harker, Alfr.
Natural history of igneous rocks. '09 (Je19) il. O. *$3 net. Macmillan.
Petrology for students: an introd. to the study of rocks under the microscope. 4th ed. '08, [1909.] (My) 336 p. il. 12°, (Cambridge geological ser.) *$2 net. Putnam.

Harker, Mrs. Lizzie Allen.
His first leave. '08(Mr28) D. †$1.50. Scribner.
Miss Esperance and Mr. Wycherly. '08 (S19) c. D. †$1.50. Scribner.
Romance of the nursery. Rev. and enl. ed. '09, [1910.] c. 410 p. front. 12°, $1.25. Scribner.

Harker, Ray Clarkson.
Christian Science. '08(O3) c. D. *50 c. net. Jennings.

Harking back. Glenn, L. M. (Priv. pr.) Furman Univ.

Harlan, H: D:
See Maryland. Law of domestic relations.

Harlan, Mrs. M. R., ["Marie Cottrell."]
In the land of extremes. '09(Jl3) c. D. *$1.50 net. Cochrane.

Harlan, R: Davenport.
Two pre-requisites for the permanent improvement of the American consular service; new law and a special training school; an address. '08(O) 16 p. 8° (Add. pub. for price.) Nat. Business.

Harland, H:
Royal end: a romance. '09(Ap10) c. 12°, †$1.50. Dodd.

Harland, Marion, pseud.
See Terhune, *Mrs.* Mary Virginia Hawes.

Harlow, W. E.
Mental and moral therapeutics. '10(F19) c. por. 8°, $1.50. W. E. Harlow.

Harman, G. W.
Twenty lessons in free-arm movement writing: supplement to accompany Smith's "Practice books." '09(My1) il. obl. 12°, pap., 25 c. Macmillan.

Harman, H: E.
Gates of twilight; [poems.] '10(D31) c. il. O. Stone & B.

Harman, Nathaniel Bishop.
Aids to ophthalmology. 4th ed. '08(Ag22) c. il. 16°, *$1 net. Wood.

Harmanson, S. T. M., comp.
French verb form. '09(N20) c. obl. O. pap., 35 c. Ginn.

Harmen Pols. Schwartz, J. M. W. V. der P. $1.35 net. Lane.

Harmer, Sidney F:, and Shipley, Arth. Everett, eds.
Cambridge natural history. In 10 v. v. 3, Molluscs, by H. A. Cooke; Recent brachiopods, by A. E. Shipley; Fossil brachiopods, by F. R. C. Reed; v. 4, Spiders, mites, scorpions, etc., by C. Warburton; Trilobites, etc., by M. Laurie; Pycnogonds, by D'Arcy W. Thompson; Lingulatulidæ and tardigrada, by A. E. Shipley; Crustacea, by Geoffrey Smith; v. 6, Insects, pt. 2, by D. Sharp; v. 10, Mammalia, by F. E. Reddard. '09(Ag14) il. 8°, v. 3, *$3.25 net; v. 4, *$4.25 net; v. 6, $3.50 net; v. 10, *$4 net. Macmillan.

Harmonial philosophy. Davis, A. J. 27 v. $30. Austin.

Harmonic analysis.
See Mathematics.

Harmonic booklet ser. D. 50 c. Indo-Am. Bk.
—Buck. Lost word found in the great work.
—Huntley. Who answers prayer.

Harmonic fiction ser. D. $1. Indo-Am. Bk.
—Huntley. Dream child.—Gay Gnani of Gingalee.

Harmonies. Howe, M. A. D. **$1.10 net. Houghton M.

Harmony.
Bradley, K. McP. Harmony and analysis. $1.50. C. F. Summy Co.
Clarke, H. A. Harmony on the inductive method. $1. Ditson.
Landon, C: W. First steps in harmony. 50 c. Church.
Leighton, G: A. Harmony. $1.25. Willis Music.
Loewengard, M. J. Harmony modernized. $1.25 net. Schirmer.
Oslin, S. J. Eureka harmony method. 60 c. Eureka.
Parkhurst, H. E. Complete system of harmony. $2. Fischer.
Schaaf, E: A 20th century harmony textbook compend system. $1. Schirmer.
Schwartz, G: F. Catechism of harmony. 50 c. White-S.
Shepherd, F. H. Key to "Harmony simplified." $1.25. Schirmer.
Van Der Velpen, J. B. H. Harmony and thorough bass. In 2 v. v. 1. C. F. Summy Co.
White, W: A. Harmony and ear-training. $1.50. Silver.
See also Counterpoint;—Music.

Harmsworth, Cecil Bisshopp.
Pleasure and problem in South Africa. '08 (S12) il. D. *$1.50 net. Lane.

Harn, G: U.
John Sherman. '08, [1909.] (Ja) (Add. pubs. for price.) P. J. Herr.

Harn, O. C.
How to protect structural metal; pract. hdbk. upon the mixing and application of paint to iron or steel, tin, and galvanized iron, together with a brief explanatory discussion of the causes of corrosion and remedies for it. '09(N) c. 5-37+4 p. 8°, pap., gratis. Nat. Lead.

Harnack, Carl Gustav Adolf, D.D.
Constitution and law of the church in the first two centuries. '10(D31) (Crown theological lib.) $1.75 net. Putnam.
Mission and expansion of Christianity in the first three centuries tr. and ed. by Ja. Moffatt. 2d enl. and rev. ed. '09(Ja30) 2 v., fold. maps, (Theological translation lib.) *$7 net. Putnam.
Monasticism: its ideals and history and the Confessions of St. Augustine; tr. by E. E. Hellet and F. H.. Marseille. '10 (O8) 8°, (Crown theological lib.) $1.50 net. Putnam.
New Testament studies: II., the sayings of Jesus, the second source of St. Matthew and St. Luke; tr. by the Rev. J: R: Wilkinson. '08(D12); III., The Acts of the Apostles; tr. by Rev. J. R. Wilkinson. '09(Ja30) 12°, (Crown theological lib.) ea., *$1.75 net. Putnam.

HARNETT, Cornelius.
Connor, R. D. W. Cornelius Harnett; essay in North Carolina hist. $1.50. R. D. W. Connor.

Harney, W: Wallace.
Spirit of the South. '09(Je19) c. D. $1.50. **Badger.**

HARNEY BASIN REGION.
See Oregon.

Harnwell, Mrs. Anna Jane Wilcox.
Locks to pick; key at rear; book of charades. '09(D4) c. D. bds., $1. Badger.

Harper, And. M., comp.
See Canada. Digest.

Harper, Mrs. B. W.
Flora's fairies. '08(N21) il. 12°, pap., 50 c. Cochrane.

Harper, C: G:
Half hours with the highwaymen: picturesque biographies and traditions of the "Knights of the road." '09(Ap3) 2 v., O. *$16.80 net. Scribner.
North Devon coast. '08(D5) il. 8°, *$6 net. Scribner.
Somerset coast. '09(Je26) il. map. O. *$6. net. **Scribner.**
Tower of London; fortress, palace and prison. '09, [1910.] (D) il. 12°, *$2.50 net. Jacobs.

Harper, G: McLean.
Charles-Augustin Sainte-Beuve. '09(Ap24) c. por. (French men of letters.) **$1.50 net. Lippincott.

Harper, H: Howard.
Journey in southeastern Mexico; narrative of experiences, and observations on agricultural and industrial conditions. '10 (Ap) 13+100 p. front. 8°. (Priv. pr.) H: H. Harper.

Harper, Mrs. Ida A. Husted.
Life and work of Susan B. Anthony. In 3 v. v. 3. '08(Je27) c. O. $2.50; per set, $7.50. Nat. Am. Woman Suffrage.
Woman suffrage throughout the world. '07, [1908.] (Jl) 16 p. 8°, pap. (Add. author for price.) I. A. H. Harper.

Harper, J: Murdock.
Champlain: a drama; with an introd. entitled Twenty years and after. Anglo-American ed. '09(Ja23) c. D. *$1.75 net. Lane.

Harper, Olive.
Chinatown trunk mystery. '09(D) 120 p. il. 12°, pap., 25 c. J. S. Ogilvie.
Convict's sweetheart. '09(S4) il. 12°, pap., 25 c. J. S. Ogilvie.
Creole slave's revenge. '08(Ag8) il. 12°, pap., 25 c. J. S. Ogilvie.
It's never too late to mend. '08(Mr) il. 12°, pap., 25 c. J. S. Ogilvie.
Jack Sheppard, the bandit king. '08(S5) il. 12°, pap., 25 c. J. S. Ogilvie.
King of bigamists. '09(S4) il. 12°, pap., 25 c. J. S. Ogilvie.
Millionaire and the policeman's wife. '08, [1909.] (Mr) 128 p. il. 12°, pap., 25 c. J. S. Ogilvie.
On trial for his life. '08(Ag15) il. 12°, pap., 25 c. J. S. Ogilvie.
Opium smugglers of 'Frisco. '08(O3) il. 12°, pap., 25 c. J. S. Ogilvie.
Queen of the outlaw's camp. '09(D) 120 p. il. 12°, pap., 25 c. J. S. Ogilvie.
Queen of the secret seven. '09(S4) il. 12°, pap., 25 c. J. S. Ogilvie.
River pirates. '09(S4) il. 12°, pap., 25 c. J. S. Ogilvie.
Sal, the circus gal. '09(S4) il. 12°, pap., 25 c. J. S. Ogilvie.
Shadow behind the throne. '08(Mr) il. 12°, pap., 25 c. J. S. Ogilvie.
Through Death Valley. '08(Mr) il. 12°, pap., 25 c. J. S. Ogilvie.
Tony the bootblack. '08(Mr) il. 12°, pap., 25 c. J. S. Ogilvie.
Wanted by the police. '09(O30) il. 12°, pap., 25 c. J. S. Ogilvie.
Workingman's wife. '09(S4) il. 12°, pap., 25 c. J. S. Ogilvie.

Harper, Rob. Almer.
Organization of certain *coenobic* plants. '09(F6) il. tabs., O. (Univ. of Wis. bull.; Science ser.) pap., 40 c. Univ. of Wis.

Harper, Rob. Fs.
Assyrian and Babylonian letters belonging to the Kouyunjik collections of the British Museum. v. 9. '10(D31) 8°, $6 net. Univ. of Chic.
—, **Brown, Fs., D.D., and Moore, G: Foot, D.D., eds.**
Old Testament and Semitic studies in memory of William Rainey Harper. '08 (F1) c. 2 v., 8°, subs., *$10 net. Univ. of Chic.

Harper, S: Northrup.
New electoral law for the Russian Duma. '08(F8) c. D. (Univ. of Chic. studies in political science.) pap., *25 c. net. Univ. of Chic.

Harper, Wa. B:
Utilization of wood waste by distillation. '08(F8) c. 4°, $3. St. L. Lumberman.

HARPER, William Rainey.
Harper, R. F., *and others, eds.* Old Testament and Semitic studies in memory of William Rainey Harper. 2 v. *$10 net. Univ. of Chic.

Harper's athletic ser. il. D. 60 c. Harper.
—Boys on the railroad.
—Making good. 60 c.
—On track and diamond.
—On the gridiron.
—Runaway flying-machine.

Harper's book of little plays. Briscoe, M. S. $1. Harper.

HARPER'S FERRY, W. Va.
See **Brown, John.**

Harper's handy book for girls. Paret, A. P., *ed.* $1.75. Harper.

Harper's how to understand electrical work. Onken, W: H:, *jr.* $1.75. Harper.

Harper's indoor book for boys. Adams, J. H: $1.75. Harper.

Harper's library of living thought. 16°, *75 c. net. Harper.
—Arrhenius. Life of the universe. 2 v.
—Becker. Christianity and Islam.
—Bertholet. Transmigration of souls.
—Crookes. Diamonds.
—Eucken. Christianity and the new idealism.
—Gardner. Religion and art in ancient Greece.
—Hawes. Crete.
—Lodge. Ether of space.
—Meyer. Jesus or Paul.
—Mott. Brain and voice in speech and song.
—Petrie. Personal religion in Egypt before Christianity.
—Seeberg. Revelation and inspiration.
—Swinburne. Three plays of Shakespeare.
—Tilden. The elements.
—Vinogradoff. Roman law in mediæval Europe.
—Weiss. Paul and Jesus.
—Wrede. Origin of the New Testament.

Harper's machinery book for boys. Adams, J. H: $1.75. Harper.

Harper's modern ser. of supplementary readers for the elementary schools; ed. by Percival Chubb. il. D. 50 c. Harper.
—Clemens. Travels at home.—Travels in history.
—Howells. Boy life.

Harper's novelettes; ed. by W: Dean Howells *and* H: M. Alden. 12°, †$1. Harper.
—Howells *and* Alden, *eds.* Life at high tide.

Harper's practical books for boys. D. il. $1.75. Harper.
—Adams. Harper's indoor book for boys.—Harper's machinery book for boys.
—Onken *and* Baker. Harper's how to understand electrical work.

Harper's young people's ser. il. D. 60 c. Harper.
—Adventures at sea.
—Adventures in field and forest.
—Adventures with Indians.
—Adventures with pirates.
—Habberton. Who was Paul Grayson?
—Kaler. Toby Tyler.
—King of the plains; stories of ranch, Indian and mine.
—Musset. Mr. Wind and Madam Rain.
—Young detectives.

Harraden, Beatrice.
Interplay. '08(D19) c. D. †$1.50. Stokes.

Harriet Hare. Layard, A. 50 c. Stokes.

Harriman, Mrs. Alice.
Man of two countries. '10(D31) c. D. $1.50. A. Harriman.
Songs o' the Olympics. '09(S4) c. il. O. bds., $1; leath., $2; limp leath., $2.50. A. Harriman.

Harriman, J: Emery, jr., ["John Arrima."]
Mystic ride of the somnial bride: [a poem.] '09(Je12) c. D. pap., $1. Cycle Press.

Harrington, Rev. C: H:
God enthused man: life story of Evangelist Rev. John A. Davis. '08(Jl18) c. il. pors. facsims., 8°, 75 c. J: A. Davis.

Harrington, J: Lyle.
Necessity for individual engineering libraries and for continuing study after graduation. '09(Ap) 24 p. 8°, pap., 10 c. J: L. Harrington.

Harrington, W., and O'Rourke, Stephen G.
Latin bones; easier method in Latin. [1910.] (D) 7-88 p. 12°. Cen. Pr.

Harriott, Mrs.
See Morris, Clara.

Harris, C: A:
Rapid survey of the Massachusetts educational system. [1910.] (N) c. 100 p. 12°, 40 c. C: A: Harris.

Harris, Corra May White, [Mrs. L. H. Harris.]
Circuit rider's wife. '10(Ag13) il. $1.50. Altemus.

Harris, Elmo Golightly.
Compressed air; theory and computations. '10(O8) c. il. 8°, $1.50 net. McGraw-H.

Harris, Frances Helen.
Plays for young people. '10(D) $1. Cassell.

Harris, Fk.
The bomb. '09(F20) c. D. $1.50. M. Kennerley.
Man Shakespeare and his tragic life story. '09(N13) c. O. *$2.50 net. M. Kennerley.
Montes the matador, and other stories. '10 (Je4) c. 12°, $1 net. M. Kennerley.

Harris, Gilbert Dennison.
Cartography of southwestern Louisiana; with special reference to the Jennings sheet. '07, [1908.] (Ap.) 24 p. maps. O. (Louisiana Geological survey bull.) pap. (Add. author for price.) G. D. Harris.
Notes on the geology of the Winnifield sheet. '07, [1908.] (Ap.) 36 p. il. maps, O., (Louisiana Geological survey bull.) pap. (Add. author for price.) G. D. Harris.
Oil and gas in Louisiana; with a brief summary of their occurrence in adjacent states. '10(D) 5-192 p. il. maps, diagrs., 8°, (U. S., Dept. of the Interior, U. S. Geolog. Survey, bull.)

—, Maury, J. C., and Reinecke, L.
Rock salt, its origin, geological occurrences and economic importance in the state of Louisiana, together with brief notes and references to all known salt deposits and industries of the world. '09(Jl31) il. maps, 8°, (Louisiana; Geol. Survey, bull.) pap. (Add. pubs. for price.) La. Geol. Survey.

—, Perrine, I., and Hopper, W. E.
Oil and gas in northwestern Louisiana, with special reference to the Caddo Field. '09, [1910.] (Jl) 52 p. O. (La. Geol. Survey, bull.) La. Geol. Survey.

Harris, Ja. H.
Course of study and teachers' manual in elem. English. 2 pts. '09(N) c. 12°, pt. 1, 25 c.: pt. 2, 35 c. Northwestern Sch.

Harris, Mrs. Jane Yancey.
Thoroughly tested: a drama in six acts. '07, [1908.] (O.) c. 56 p. 8°, 25 c. J. Y. Harris.

Harris, Joel Chandler, ["Uncle Remus."]
Bishop and the boogerman; being the story of a little truly-girl, who grew up. '09 (F6) c. il. D. **$1 net. Doubleday, P.
Little Mr. Thimblefinger stories. '10(O1) c. il. D. (Riverside literature ser.) 40 c. Houghton M.
Shadow between his shoulder-blades. '09 (S25) c. il. D. **50 c. net. Small.
Uncle Remus and the Little Boy. '10(S17) c. il. O. $1.25. Small.
Uncle Remus, his songs and his sayings. New and rev. ed. '08(D5) c. il. 12°, $2. Appleton.
—, ed. *See* Alderman, Edn. Anderson.

HARRIS, Joel Chandler.
Lee, I. L., *comp.* "Uncle Remus" Joel Chandler Harris as seen and remembered by a few of his friends. (Priv. pr.) I. L. Lee.

Harris, Jos. Smith.
Collateral ancestry of Stephen Harris, born September 4, 1798, and of Marianne Smith, born April 2, 1805. '09(F20) tabs., 4°, *$3 net. W: J. Campbell.

Harris, Lawrence.
With Mulai Hafid at Fez; behind the scenes in Morocco. '10(Je4) il. O. $3 net, boxed. Badger.

Harris, Rabbi Maurice H:
Modern Jewish hist. from the Renaissance to the Russian exodus. '10(Je18) c. il. 8°, bds., 30 c. net. Bloch.
Thousand years of Jewish hist.; from the days of Alexander the Great to the Moslem conquest of Spain. New ed., rev. and enl. '10(D17) c. O. $1. Bloch.

Harris, Bp. Merriman Colbert.
Christianity in Japan. '08(Mr7) c. S. (Little books on missions.) *35 c. net. Jennings.

Harris (Norman Wait) lecture. *See* Bowne, Borden Parker.—Eliot, C: W:

Harris, Rollin Arth.
Manual of tides, 1894-1908. 5 v. in 6. '08 (Jl.) il. tabs., charts, 4°. (Add. Superintendent for price.) U. S., Supt. of Docs.

Harris, Thdr.
Banker's views on religious and other important subjects. '08(Je) c. 24+329 p. por. 8°. (Add. pub. for price.) W. P. Harvey.

Harris, T: Green.
Spiral course in English. '08(F15) c. 2 bks., il. 12°, bk. 1, 35 c.; bds., 30 c.; bk. 2, 60 c.; bds., 50 c. Heath.

Harris, Wilfred, M.D.
Electrical treatment. '10(My) 384 p. il. 8°, (Modern methods of treatment.) $2 net. Funk.

Harris, W: C:, and Bean, Tarleton Hoffman.
The basses, fresh-water and marine; ed. and il. by L: Rhead. [New ed.] '10 (Jl16) c. O. $3 net. Stokes.

Harris, W: Ja., comp.
First printed translations into English of the great foreign classics. '09(Jl17) 16°, (English library ser.) *75 c. net. Dutton.

Harris, Rev. W: Shuler.
Hell before death. '08(S5) c. il. 12°, $1. Minter.
Sermons by the devil. '08(F) c. '07. 207 p. il. 12°, $1; lib. ed., $1.50; full mor., $2. Minter.
Sparks of truth; or, living truth in full flames. '10(F) c. '09. 304 p. il. 8°, $1. Minter.

Harris, W: Torrey.
Physical training in and out of school. '10 (D17) D. bds., 30 c. Bardeen.
Question of recess. '10(D17) D. bds., 30 c. Bardeen.

HARRIS FAMILY.
See Genealogies.

Harris-Burland, J: Burland.
See Burland, J: Burland Harris-.

Harrison, Alfr. H.
In search of a polar continent, 1905-1907. '08(N14) il. map, O. *$3.50 net. Longmans.

Harrison, Birge.
Landscape painting. '09(N6) c. il D. **$1.50 net. Scribner.

Harrison, Mrs. Burton.
See Harrison, *Mrs.* Constance Cary.

Harrison, Mrs. Carter H:
See Harrison, Edith Ogden.

Harrison, C:, and Douglas, J: C.
Photographer's handbk. '08(Ag22) S. (Country handbooks.) **$1 net. Lane.

Harrison, Mrs. Constance Cary, [Mrs. Burton Harrison.]
Count and the congressman; il. by Alex. O. Levy. '08(Ag8) c. D. 75 c. Cupples & L.
See also My favorite novelist.

Harrison, Edith Ogden, [Mrs. Carter H: Harrison.]
Flaming sword, and other legends of the earth and sky. '08(O10) c. il. O. *$1.25 net. McClurg.
Ladder of moonlight; Cotton myth. '09 (O9) c. col. il. D. (Biblical stories retold for children.) bds., *50 c. net. McClurg.
Mocking-bird; Sunrise and sunset. '09(O9) c. col. il. D. (Biblical stories retold for children.) bds., *50 c. net. McClurg.
Polar star; Aurora borealis. '09(O9) c. col. il. D. (Biblical stories retold for children.) bds., *50 c. net. McClurg.
Princess Sayrane; romance of the days of Prester John. '10(N5) c. col. il. O. $1.35 net. McClurg.

Harrison, E: Philip.
Course of pract. physics. '10(D31) diagrs., D. $1.50 net. Longmans.

Harrison, Mrs. Eliz.
Misunderstood children; sketches taken from life. '10(F19) D. $1.25. Central Pub.

Harrison, Eveleen.
Jeweled crown. '10(Je4) c. il. 8°, $1. Gospel Pub.

Harrison, Florence.
In the fairy ring. '09(O2) Q. $2. Caldwell.
Rhyme of a run, and other verse. '08(D19) il. obl. 8°, $2. Caldwell.

Harrison, Frederic.
My Alpine jubilee: articles [on mountaineering.['08(My9) 8°, *$1.25 net. Dutton.
National and social problems. '08(My9) O. **$1.75 net. Macmillan.
Realities and ideals. '08(O17) c. O. **$1.75 net. Macmillan.
—, **ed.** New calendar of great men: biographies of the 558 worthies of all ages and nations in the positivist calendar of Auguste Comte. '08(Ag15) 8°, *$2.50 net. Macmillan.

Harrison, H. H.
Model steam turbines; how to design and build them. '09(D18) 12°, pap., 25 c. Spon.

Harrison, Jane Ellen.
Ancient Greece. '07, [1909.] (Ap) 8°, (Religions ancient and modern.) *40 c. net. Open Court.
Prolegomena to the study of Greek religion. 2d ed. '08(Mr28) 8°, *$6 net. Putnam.

Harrison, Jennie.
Do you remember? '09(D) c. 61 p. 12°, 60 c. Cochrane.

Harrison, J: Ellis.
Parliamentary usage of the general conference, M. E. Church, South. '08(O); 2d rev. ed. '09(O23) c. 16°, ea., 25 c. Pub. Ho. of M. E. Ch., So.

Harrison, J: Smith.
Teachers of Emerson. '10(Je4) c. D. $1.50 net. Sturgis & W.

Harrison, Mrs. Mary St. Leger Kingsley, ["Lucas Malet."]
Golden galleon. '10(D3) c. D. $1.20. Doran.
Little Peter: Christmas morality for children of any age. New ed. '09(D) col. il. *$1.50 net. Doran.
The score; [Out in the open.—Miserere nobis.] '09(Ag21) c. D. †$1.50. Dutton.

Harrison, Newton.
Electric wiring diagrams and switchboards. '09(D) c. 272 p. il. 12°, $1.50. Henley.
Making wireless outfits. '09(Ap3) c. il. 12°, (Model lib.) 50 c.; pap., 25 c. Spon.
Wireless telephone construction for receiving and sending. '09(Je19) c. il. 12°, (Model lib.) pap., 25 c. Spon.

Harrison, R: Compton.
Manual of New York corporation law; cont. the important statutes regulating business incorporations, digest of these statutes and the principal forms used by corporations operating in the State of New York. 2d ed., rev. and enl. '09 (Je) 511 p. 8°, $4.25. Ronald Press.

Harrison, Virginia Bioren.
Whisper of destiny, and other poems. '09 (N) 12+144 p. 16°, *$1.25 net. Dutton.

HARRISON COUNTY, W. Va.
Haymond, H: Hist. of Harrison County, West Virginia. $3.50. Acme.

Harrison Safety Boiler Works, Philadelphia.
Purification of water for boiler feeding; comp. by the Harrison Safety Boiler Works for the confidential information of its agents and employees. '09, [1910.] (Ap) c. 105 p. il. tabs., 8°. (Priv. pr.) Harrison.
Bibliography (1 p.).

Harrod, S: Glenn.
Latin terms of endearment and of family relationship; lexicographical study based on v. VI of the Corpus inscriptorum Latinarum. '10(F19) O. pap., 75 c. Princeton Univ.

Harry, Jos. E:
Problems in the Prometheus. '07. [1908.] (F) 6-48 p., 8°, (University studies.) 50 c. Univ. of Cin.
Question of divination, (Medea 240, [by Euripides.]) '09(F6) O. (University studies.) pap. (Add. University for price.) Univ. of Cin.
Studies in Euripides: Hippolytus. '09 (Ag28) O. (Univ. of Cin. studies.) pap. (Add. Univ. for price.) Univ. of Cin.

"HARRY KNOWLTON" (The).
See "Larchmont" (The).

Harry Richmond. *See* Meredith, G:

Harry's island. Barbour, R. H: †$1.50. Century Co.

Harshbarger, Jessie A.
Gentleman Don; the life story of a good dog. '10(N19) c. il. 8°, $1. Crane.

Hart, Albert Bushnell.
Actual government as applied under American conditions. 3d ed., rev. '08(S12) c. il maps, facsims., O. $2.25 Longmans.
Epoch maps illustrating American hist. 4th rev. ed. '10(O22) c. maps, obl. D. 60 c. Longmans.
Formation of the union, 1750-1829. Rev. ed. '10(D10) c. maps, S. (Epochs of American hist.) $1.25. Longmans.
Manual of American history, diplomacy, and government, for class use. '08(Je6) c. 8°, $2. Harvard Univ.
Southern South. '10(My21) c. tabs., D. $1.50 net. Appleton.
—, **Higginson, T: Wentworth, Van Tyne, Claude Halstead, and others.**
Decisive battles of America; ed. by Ripley Hitchcock. '09(N6) c. il. maps, D. $1.50. Harper.
—, **ed.** American nation: hist. from original sources. In 27 v. v. 27, Analytic index covering every important event, noted person and historical fact mentioned in the preceding 26 vols.; comp. by D: Maydole Matteson. '08(F8) c. 8°, **$2 net. Harper.
Extracts from official papers rel. to the Isthmian canal, 1515-1909. '10(Jl16) 12°, (Am. hist. leaflets.) 10 c. Simmons.

Hart, C: H:
Benjamin West's family; with unpublished letters of West. '08(N21) por. 4°. (Add. author for price.) H: C. Hart.
Original portrait of Doctor Franklin painted by Joseph Wright, 1782, belonging to the Royal Society, London; portraits of Franklin attributed to Duplessis, in the Corcoran gallery of art, Washinton, D. C., and to Greuze in the Public Library, Boston, Mass., shown to be by Joseph Wright. '09(Ap3) por. 8°, *$2.50 net. C: H: Hart.
—, **ed.** Register of portraits painted by Thomas Sully, 1801-1871; with an introd. and notes. '09(S) c. 198 p. pors. 8°. (Priv. pr.) C: H: Hart.

Hart, C: Hopwood, D.D.
Joan, the Maid of France. '10(Jl30) il. 8°, $1.25. Dutton.

Hart, Fs. Russell.
Attack upon Cartagena by the French in 1697. '08(N) 6 p. map, 4°, 50 c. Assoc. Pub.
Attacks upon the Spanish Main by Admiral Vernon: [siege of Cartagena, Colombia.] '08(N) 24 p. il. maps, 4°, 50 c. Assoc. Pub.

Hart, G: H.
Rabies and its increasing prevalence. '08 (Ag1) 8°, (U. S., Dept. of Agriculture, Bureau of Animal Industry, circular.) pap., 15 c. U. S., Supt. of Docs.

Hart, Gordon.
Woman and the race. '08, [1909.] (Ag) 280 p. il. 16°, $1. Ariel.

Hart, Hastings Hornell.
Cottage and congregate institutions for children. '10(D17) c. il. plans, tabs., 8°, (Russell Sage Foundation pubs.) $1; pap., 50 c. Charities Pub.
—, **ed.** Juvenile court laws in the United States; summary by states, by T: J. Homer; topical abstract, by Grace Abbott; and the new juvenile court law of Monroe County, N. Y. '10(D17) c. 8°, (Russell Sage Foundation pubs.) $1.50. Charities Pub.

Hart, H: Martyn, D.D.
Tragedy of Hosea and other sermons. '09 (D) (Add. pubs. for price.) Whittaker.

Hart, I. W., rep.
See Idaho. *Sup. ct.* Repts.

Hart, J. Wesley.
In the iron time. '08(D26) D. $1.50. Jennings.

Hart, Jerome Alfr.
Vigilante girl. '10(Ap16) c. il. O. $1.50. McClurg.

Hart, Jos. Kinmont.
Critical study of current theories of moral education. '10(My21) c. O. pap., 50 c. net. Univ. of Chic.

HART, *Sir* Robert.
Bredon, J. Sir Robert Hart. ***$1.75 net. Dutton.**

Hart, S:
Book of common prayer. '10(Jl2) c. 12°, (Sewanee theological lib.) $1.50. Univ. Press, (Sewanee.)

Hart, Wa. Morris.
Ballad and epic: study in the development of the narrative art. '09(Ja23) 8°. (Harvard studies and notes in philology and literature.) $2.50. Ginn.

Harte, Fs. Bret.
Poems. '10(D) 12°, (Autograph poets.) $1; hf. leath., $1.50. Houghton M.
Salomy Jane. '10(O15) c. col. il. O. $1 net. Houghton M.
See also Stories of humor.
—, and Kozlay, C: Meeker.
Lectures of Bret Harte; comp. from various sources; to which is added The piracy of Bret Harte's fables, by C: Meeker Kozlay. '09(O23) c. il. por. **facsim. D. *$1.50 net. C: M. Kozlay.**

Harte, May Jerome.
Light of His countenance; tale of Rome in the second century after Christ. '10 (Ap30) c. front. D. $1.25. Benziger.

Hartel, August, comp. and ed.
Altars and pulpits. 3d ed. '10(Ag6) il. f°, (in portfolio,) $10.70. Hessling.

Hartford, I: Ja.
Original treatise on electro-vital force; giving the source of vital force and its action upon both the animal and vegetable kingdoms. '08(O10) c. il. por. O. $2. I: J. Hartford.

HARTFORD, Ct.
Andrews, F. D., *ed.* Business men of the city of Hartford (Ct.) in the year 1799. 35 c. F. D. Andrews.
Wright, G: E: Crossing the Connecticut: [at Hartford.] $5. Smith-Linsley.

HARTFORD THEOLOGICAL SEMINARY, Hartford, Ct.
Paton, L. B., *ed.* **Recent Christian progress; studies in Christian thought and work during the last seventy-five years; by professors and alumni of Hartford Theological Seminary, in celebration of its seventy-fifth anniversary. **$3 net. Macmillan.**

Hartich, F: F.
Hints; simple treatise on the duties and obligations of executors and administrators. '09(D) c. 39 p. T. pap., $2. F. C. Hill.

Hartley, Catherine Gasquoine, [Mrs. Wallis M. Gallichan.]
Stories from the Greek legends. '10(Ja1) 12°, *$1.25 net. Lippincott.
Things seen in Spain. '10(D10) 16°, 75 c. Dutton.
See also Calvert, Albert F:

Hartley, Oliver.
Hunting dogs. '09(S) 253 p. 12°, 60 c. A. R. Harding.

Hartley, Percy J.
My lady of Cleeve. '08(F8) c. il. D. †$1.50. Dodd.

Hartley House cook book. Pierce, E. A. 60 c. net. Wessels & B.

Hartman, E: Randolph.
Socialism versus Christianity. '09(Je5) c. D. $1.50. Cochrane.

Hartman, Gertrude.
See Choate, Augusta.

Hartman, J. F., comp.
Monologues and parodies; unique collection of monologues, epigrams, epitaphs and parodies. '10(D10) c. il. 12°, 75 c. T: J. Carey.

Hartmann, Fs. M.
Elem. mechanics for engineering students. '10(S) c. 11+171 p. figs. $1.25 net. Wiley.

Hartmann, Franz.
Life and doctrines of Philippus Theophrastus Bombast of Hohenheim, known by the name of Paracelsus. New ed. '10 (D17) 8°, $2.50. Theo. Pub. Co.

Hartmann, H: August G:
Tales of Aztlan; the romance of a hero of our late Spanish-American war: [memorial to Captain William Owen O'Neill, U. S. V.] [Rev. ed.] '09(Jl31) c. por. 12°, $1. **B'way Pub.**

Hartmann, Sadakichi, ["Sidney Allan."]
Composition in portraiture. '09(F6) c. il. O. $3. E: L. Wilson.
Landscape and figure composition. '10 (S24) c. il. Q. $3 net, boxed. Baker & T.
Schopenhauer in the air: twelve stories. '08 (O17) 50 c. S. Hartmann.
Whistler book; monograph of the life and position in art of James McNeill Whistler, together with careful study of his more important works. '10(N5) c. il. O. $2.50, boxed. L. C. Page.

Hartnagel, C. A.
See Newland, D: Hale.

Hartness, Ja.
Hartness flat turret lathe manual; hdbk. for operators. '10(Je) c. 5+219 p. il. diagrs., 8°, gratis. Jones & Lamson.
Machine building for profit, and the Hartness flat turret lathe. '09(O) 5-253 p. il. 8°, gratis. Jones & Lamson.

Hartog, Phillippe Jos., and Langdon, Mrs. Amy H.
Writing of English. 2d ed. '08(Ja18) D. 60 c. Oxford Univ.

Hartpence, Alanson.
Poisoned lake, and other poems.. '08 (Ap25) c. 12°, $1. B'way Pub.

Hartpence, J: A., comp.
See New Jersey lawyers' diary.

Hartshorn, Edm. F.
Experiences of a boy, by his father's son. '10(D10) c. 12°, $2. Baker Pr.

Hartshorn, W: Newton, and Penniman, G: W., eds.
Era of progress and promise, 1863-1910; the religious, moral, and educational development of the American negro since his emancipation. '10(Je4) c. il. pors. 4°, $5.75. Priscilla.

Hartt, Rollin Lynde.
People at play; excursions in the humor and philosophy of popular amusements. '09(Je5) c. il. D. **$1.50 net. Houghton M.

Hartung, Harry Hall, M.D.
First aid to the injured. Pocket ed. '09 (Mr27) c. il. S. pap., 50 c. H. H. Hartung.

HARTZ MOUNTAINS.
See Heine, Heinrich.

HARVARD, John.
Davis, A. McF. John Harvard's life in America. (Not for sale.) A. McF. Davis.

Harvard, Valery, M.D.
Manual of military hygiene for the military service of the United States. '09(My) 498 p. il. 8°, *$4 net. Wood.

Harvard classics: ed. by C: W: Eliot. In 50 v. v. 1-23. '10(F); v. 24-32 (Je18); v. 33-43 (D17) c. il. pors. facsims., 8°, subs., $100; ¾ mor., $195; mor., $345. Collier.
Contents: [v. 1,] Æschylus, Sophocles, Euripides and Aristophanes; nine Greek dramas; by E. D. A. Morshead, E. M. Plumptre, Gilbert Murray and B. B. Rogers. [v. 2,] Arabian nights; stories from the Thousand and one nights; tr. by E. W. Lane. [v. 3,] St. Augustine and Thomas à Kempis; Confessions of St. Augustine and The imitation of Christ, by Thomas à Kempis. [v. 4,] Bacon, Francis, *Lord*, Milton, J., and Browne, *Sir* T:; Essays civil and moral and The new Atlantis by Bacon; Areopagitica and Tractate on education, by John Milton; Religio medici, by Sir Thomas Browne. [v. 5,] Burke, Edmund, On taste; On the sublime and beautiful; Reflections on the French Revolution; Letter to a noble lord. [v. 6,] Burns, Rob. Poems and songs. [v. 7,] Cicero, Marcus Tullius *and* Plinius Caecilius Secundus, Gaius. Letters of Cicero; with his treatises on friendship and old age, and letters of Gaius Plinius Caecilius Secundis. [v. 8,] Dana, R: H: Two years before the mast and Twenty years after. [v. 9,] Dante Alighieri. Divine comedy. [v. 10,] Darwin, C: Rob. Origin of species. [v. 11,] Darwin, C: Rob. Voyage of the Beagle. [v. 12,] Emerson, Ralph Waldo. Essays and English traits. [v. 13,] English essays from Sir Philip Sidney to Macaulay. [v. 14,] Folk-lore and fable: Æsop, Grimm, Andersen. [v. 15,] Franklin, B:, Woolman, J:, *and* Penn, W: Autobiography of Franklin; Journal of John Woolman; Fruits of solitude, by Penn. [v. 16,] Goethe, Johann W. von, *and* Marlowe, Christopher. Faust, pt. 1, Egmont, Hermann and Dorothea, by Goethe; Doctor Faustus, by Marlowe. [v. 17,] Homer. Odyssey; tr. by S. H. Butcher and A. Lang. [v. 18,] Manzoni, Alessandro. I promessi sposi (The betrothed). [v. 19,] Mill, J: Stuart, *and* Carlyle, T: Autobiography; Essay on liberty, by Mill; Characteristics, Inaugural address, Essay on Scott, by Carlyle. [v. 20,] Milton, J: Complete poems. [v. 21,] Modern English drama: Dryden, Sheridan, Goldsmith, Shelley, Browning, Byron. [v. 22,] Plato, Epictetus, *and* Antoninus, Marcus Aurelius. Apology, Phædo, and Crito of Plato; Golden sayings of Epictetus; Meditations of Marcus Aurelius. [v. 23,] Smith, Adam. Inquiry into the nature and causes of the wealth of nations; [v. 24,] Chronicle and romance Froissart, Malory, Holinshed; [v. 25,] French and English philosophers: Descartes, Rousseau, Voltaire, Hobbes; [v. 26,] Scientific papers: physics, chemistry, astronomy, geology; [v. 27,] Cervantes Saavedra, Miguel de. The first part of the most delightful history of the most ingenious knight Don Quixote of the Mancha; tr. by T: Shelton; [v. 28,] Literary and philosophical essays: French, German and Italian; [v. 29,] Essays, English and American; [v. 30,] Continental drama: Calderon, Corneille, Racine, Molière, Lessing, Schiller; [v. 31,] Cellini, Benvenuto, Autobiography; tr. by J. Addington Symonds; [v. 32,] Voyages and travels, ancient and modern; [v. 33] Preface and prologues to famous books; [v. 34-36,] English poetry, 3 v.; [v. 37,] American historical documents, 1900-1904; [v. 38,] English philosophers of the seventeenth and eighteenth centuries: Locke, Berkeley, Hume; [v. 39,] Scientific papers: physiology, medicine, surgery, geology; [v. 40,] Pascal, Blaise, Thoughts, tr. by W. F. Trotter; Letters, tr. by M. L. Booth; Minor works, tr. by O. W. Wright; [v. 41,] Epic and saga: Beowulf; The song of Roland; The destruction of Dá Derga's hostel; The story of the Volsungs and Niblungs; [v. 42, 43,] Sacred writings. In 2 v. v. 1, Confucians, Hebrews, Christian. pt. 1, v. 2, Christian; pt. 2, Buddhist, Hindu, Mohammedan.

Harvard economic studies. O. Houghton M.
—Daggett. Railroad reorganization. **$2 net.
—Wright. Wool-growing and the tariff. $2 net.

Harvard historical studies. O. Longmans.
—Morris. Frank pledge system. $1.75.

HARVARD LAMPOON.
Wheelwright, E. M. Lampy's early days, by an old Lampooner. $5. Harvard Lampoon.

Harvard lectures. *See* Bury, J: B.

Harvard Monthly. *See* Selected poems.

Harvard Oriental ser. ed. by C: Rockwell Lanman. 4°. Ginn.
—Pañchatantra. $1.50.

Harvard studies and notes in philology and literature. 8°. Ginn.
—Hart Ballad and epic. $2.50.

Harvard studies in comparative literature; ed. by W: H: Schofield. 8°. Harvard Univ.
—Santayana. Three philosophical poets. $2.25.

Harvard University. Associated Harvard Clubs. *Committee on Public School Administration.* Reform in city school administration; rept. of the Committee on public school administration, prepared for consideration and discussion at the annual meeting of the Associated Harvard Clubs, Cincinnati, May 28th and 29th. '09, [1910.] (Mr) 33 p. 8°. Assoc. Harvard Clubs.

Harvard University. Class of 1868. Harvard College, class of 1868: 40th anniversary, secretary's rept. no. 8, 1868-1908. '09(S) 6+261 p. il. pors. 8°. (Not for sale.) E. O. Cockayne.

HARVARD UNIVERSITY, Cambridge, Mass.
Kent, G: H: Ware collection of Blaschka glass flower models: [in the Agassiz Museum.]. 35 c. G: H. Kent.
Peabody, F. G. Social museum as an instrument of university teaching; a classified list of the collections in the Social Museum of Harvard University to Jan., 1908. gratis. F. G. Peabody.

Harvard University Astronomical Observatory. Catalogue of 36,682 stars fainter than the magnitude 6.50 observed with the 4-inch meridian phonometer forming a supplement to the Revised Harvard photometry. '08, [1909.] (My) 280 p. 4°, (Harvard Univ. Astronomical Observatory annals.) pap., $2. Harvard Univ.

Harvard University Astronomical Observatory. Revised Harvard photometry: catalogue of the positions, photometric magnitudes and spectra of 9110 stars, mainly of the magnitude 6.50, and brighter; observed with 2 and 4 inch meridian photometers. '08(O) 4+252 p. tabs., 8°, (Annals of Astronomical Observatory of Harvard Univ.) $2. Harvard Univ.

Harvard University Astronomical Observatory annals. 4°, pap. Harvard Univ.
—Bailey. Peruvian meteorology. $1.50.
—Campbell. Comparison stars for 252 variables of long period. (Add. pubs. for price.)
—Cannon. Maxima and minima of variable stars of long period. $1.
—Clayton *and* Ferguson Exploration of the air with balon-sondes. $1.
—Pickering. Durckmusterung zones.—Researches of the Boyden department.—Search for a planet beyond Neptune. ea., $1.
—Wendell. Photometric observations made with the fifteen inch east equatorial during the years 1892 to 1902. $1.

Harvard University Department of Social Ethics, pubs. 8°. Harvard Univ.; F. G. Peabody.
—Cole. Motives and results of the social settlement movement. (Add. pubs. for price.)
—Peabody. Social museum as an instrument of university teaching. gratis.

HARVARD UNIVERSITY LAW SCHOOL, Cambridge, Mass.
Warren, C. Hist. of the Harvard Law School and of early legal conditions in America 3 v, $25. Lewis Pub.

Harvard University lectures on protection to home industry. Thompson, R. E. $1. Am. Protective.

Harvard University Peabody Museum of American Archaeology and Ethnology memoirs. il. 4°, pap. Peabody Museum.
—Maler. Explorations in the Department of Peten Guatemala. $4.

HARVEIAN ORATION.
See Savage, G: H:

Harvest moon. Fletcher, J. S. $1.50. J: McBride.

HARVEST MOUSE.
See Mice.

Harvest within. Mahan, A. T. **$1.50 net. Little, B. & Co.

Harvey, Edn. Lawrence.
Sermons on Bible characters. '10(Ja29) c. por. 12°, 50 c. Metropolitan Ch. Assoc.

Harvey, Mrs. Emma May Bates.
My wonder book; pages from the life of Lewis Benton Bates. '09, [1910.] (Mr) c. 9+206 p. il. pors., facsim. 12°, $1. Chapple Pub.

Harvey, Eustace J.
Land law and registration of title; comparison of the old and new methods. '10(N) 10+278 p. $2.60 net. Longmans.

Harvey, G: Brinton McClellan.
Women, etc.; some leaves from an editor's diary. '08(O24) c. D. **$1 net. Harper.

Harvey, Lorenzo Dow.
Practical arithmetic. In 2 books. Bk. 1. '08(D5) c. tabs., D. 35 c.; Bk. 2. '09 (Mr27) c. D. 50 c. Am. Bk.

Harvey, Lula Martha.
Priscilla Irish crochetbook; collection of new and original designs with stitches and lessons for working. '10(F26) c. il. 4°, 25 c. Priscilla.

Harvey, May Louise.
American normal readers. Bk. 3. '08, [1909.] (Mr) 224 p. il. 50 c. Silver.

Harvey, Nathan Alb.
Mental ontogeny; the psychology of infancy, childhood and adolescence. '10 (Je11) c. pap., 50 c. N. A. Harvey.
Principles of teaching. '10(My14) c. il. 12°, $1.25. Row, P. & Co.
Thinking process. '10(My21) O. pap., 40 c. N. A. Harvey.

Harvey, Oscar Jewell.
Hist. of Wilkes-Barré, Luzerne Co., Pa. from its first beginnings to the present time; incl. chapters of newly discovered early Wyoming Valley history, together with many biographical sketches and much genealogical material. '09(Ag) 3 v. il. pors. maps, facsims., 4°, ea., $5. O. J. Harvey.

Harvey, R: Selden.
Rights of the minority stockholder. '09 (Jl) c. 164 p. O. $2. Baker, V. & Co.

Harvey, Thdr. Lee.
In antescript, two presidential nominees; one Unitarian—W. H. Taft; the other Trinitarian—W. J. Bryan. The great tribulation that is surely coming; in postscript, political parties, the Lord's government by injunction. '09(Ap17) c. O. pap., 25 c. T. L. Harvey.

Harvey, W:, 1578-1657.
Anatomical disquisition on the motion of the heart and blood in animals; tr. from the Latin by Rob. Willis, [with introd. by E. A. Parkyn.] [1910.] (F) 30+239 p. 16°, (Everyman's lib.) *35 c. net; leath., *70 c. net. Dutton.

Harvey, W:, comp.
Irish life and humor in anecdote and story. '09(N20) col. il. D. *$1.50 net. Lippincott.

Harvey, W: L., comp.
See Kansas. General elections laws.

Harvey-Jellie, Mrs.
Into the sunshine. '09, [1910.] (F) 200 p. 12°, $1. Northfield Press.

Harvey Society, New York. Harvey lectures. '08(Je6); '09(O9) c. il. O. ea., **$2 net. Lippincott.

Harwood, H: Hamilton.
Prohibition victorious: then—what? '10 (Jl30) S. $1.50. H: H. Harwood.
Two of the most remarkable and interesting of the sonnets of Francis Bacon, the true Shakespeare; a compilation, arrangement, and composition. '09(F6) c. por. 8°, $1. H: H. Harwood.

Harwood, W: Sumner.
Life and letters of Austin Craig; introd. and reminiscences of Antioch College by E: Everett Hale. '09(Ja30) c. il. pors. facsims., O. *$1.50 net. Revell.

Harza, Leroy Fs.
Investigation of the hydraulic ram. '09 (F13) il. tabs., O. (Univ. of Wis. bull., Engineering ser.; Researches in hydraulics.) pap., 25 c. Univ. of Wis.

Harzreise (Die). *See* Heine, Heinrich.

Has a negro the right to vote? Adriaans, J: H: (Add. author for price.) J: H: Adriaans.

Has it ever occurred to you? Givens, R. T., *ed.* 55 c. R. T. Givens.

Has surgical treatment lessened the mortality from appendicitis? Vale, F. P. 50c. Snow & F.

Hasbrouck, Fk., ed.
Hist. of Dutchess County, N. Y. '10(Je4) il. pors. maps, (partly fold.,) 8°, $15. S. A. Matthieu.

Haselden, Florence Taylor.
Marion: [a story.] '09(Ja23) c. 12°, $1. B'way Pub.

Haseltine, Mayo Williamson.
Great thinker; repr. of articles pub. in the New York *Sun*, Sept. 6 and 13, 1908, on Emanuel Swedenborg. '10(Mr5) 40 p S. pap., 3 c. Mass. New-Ch. Un.

Haselwood, J: Adam.
See Hatch, Kirk Lester.

Hash. Wheeler, M. P. 75 c.; 50 c. M. P. Wheeler.

Hasheesh eater. Ludlow, F. 50 c. B. W. Dodge.

Haskell, Franklin Aretas.
Battle of Gettysburg. '09(Ap3) por. O. (Wisconsin History Commission reprints.) $1. Wis. Hist.

Haskell, Helen Eggleston.
O-Heart-San: the story of a Japanese girl. '08(N14) c. il. D. (Roses of St. Elizabeth ser.) †$1. L. C. Page.

Haskell, Mrs. Juliana.
Bayard Taylor's translation of Goethe's "Faust." '08(O10) c. 8°, pap., *$1 net. Lemcke.

Haskell, Stephen Nelson.
Story of Daniel the prophet. '08(Mr) c. 359 p. il. 8°, $1; $1.25; $1.50; $1.75. Bible Training.

Haskell lectures. *See* Macdonald, Duncan Black.

HASKINS & SELLS ATHLETIC ASSOCIATION.
See Athletics.

Haslam, Arth. Pirrie.
Electricity in factories and workshops; its cost and convenience. '09(D) c. 312 p. il. 8°, $2.50. Henley.

Hasluck, Paul Nooncree, ed.
Cabinetwork and joinery. '08(My23) il. O. $3. McKay.
Cassell's cyclopedia of mechanics. 5 v. '09 (My22) il. 8°, ea., *$2.50 net. Cassell.
Cassell's house decoration. '09(Jl3) il. O. *$3 net. Cassell.
Domestic jobbing: repair of household articles. '08(Je6) il. 12°, ("Work" handbooks.) 50 c. McKay.
Greenhouse and conservatory construction and heating. '09(Je19) il. 12°, *$1 net. Cassell.
Handyman's enquire within, making, mending, renovating. '09(My15) il. 8°, *$2.50 net. Cassell.
Tinplate work. '08(Mr7) il. S. ("Work" handbooks.) 50 c. McKay.
Wood carving. '08(My23) il. O. $3. McKay.

Hassall, Arth.
European history, chronologically arr., 476-1910. New ed. '10(D24) c. 12°, $1.60 net. Macmillan.

Hassan. Gillman, H: †75 c. Little, B. & Co.

Hasse, Adelaide Rosalia.
Index of economic material in documents of the states of the U. S.: Massachusetts, 1789-1904. '08(O10) Q. pap., $2.25; New York, 1789-1904. '08(Mr21) pap., $3.75; Rhode Island, 1789-1904. '08(My9) pap., 75 c.; California, 1849-1904. '09(Ja2) pap., $2.25; Illinois, 1809-1904. '09(S11) pap., $5; Delaware, 1789-1904. '10(Je18) pap., $1.50; Kentucky, 1792-1904. '10(Mr26) Q. pap., $5. Carnegie.
Materials for a bibliography of the public archives of the thirteen original states: covering the colonial period and the state period to 1789. '08(D26) O. (Add. Superintendent for price.) U. S., Supt. of Docs.

Hassler, Harriot E., comp.
Graded list of stories for reading aloud. '08(D) 34 p. 12°, pap., gratis. Indiana Lib.

Hastain, E., comp.
Index to Choctaw-Chickasaw [Indians] deeds and allotments. '09(Ja30) c. 8°, $100. E. Hastain.

Hastings, Edn. G:
See Russell, Harry Luman.

Hastings, G. W.
Vindication of Warren Hastings. '09 (My15) il. pors. O. $2. Oxford Univ.

Hastings, Ja., D.D., ed.
Dictionary of the Bible. [Complete in 1 v.] '09(F6) c. double map, Q. **$5 net. Scribner.
Dictionary of Christ and the gospels; ed. by Ja. Hastings, with the assistance of J: A. Selbie, D.D., and J: C. Lambert, D.D. In 2 v. v. 2. '08(My16) c. map, plan, 4°, $6; hf. mor., $8. Scribner.
Encyclopedia of religion and ethics. In 10 or 12 v. v. 1. '08(D12); v. 2. '10(F12) 8°, subs., per v., $7; hf. mor., $9. (Sold in sets only.) Scribner.

Hastings, Milo Milton.
Cold-storage evaporimeter. '09(D) 8 p. il. 8°, (U. S., Dept. of Agriculture, Bu. of Animal Industry, circular.) pap. (Add. Superintendent for price.)
Dollar hen. '09(Ag28) il. 12°, $1. Arcadia.

Hastings, Mrs. Rosetta Butler.
Coffin nails; the story of Jane McGregor. '08(N) c. 264 p. 12°, 50 c. Dispatch Pub.

Hastings, Somerville.
Summer flowers on the high Alps. '10 (Jl30) 4°, $2.50 net. Dutton.

HASTINGS, Warren.
Hastings, G. W. Vindication of Warren Hastings. $2. Oxford Univ.
Macaulay, T: B., *Lord.* Essays on Clive and Hastings. 35 c. Ginn.
Macaulay, T: B., *Lord.* Essays on Lord Clive and Warren Hastings. 40 c. Houghton M.
Macaulay, T: B., *Lord.* Essay on Warren Hastings. 40 c. Allyn & B.
Macaulay, T: B., *Lord.* Essay on Warren Hastings. 15 c. Houghton M.
Macaulay. T: B., *Lord.* Essay on Warren Hastings. 25 c. Longmans.
Trotter, L. J. Life of Warren Hastings. 35 c. net; 75 c. net. Dutton.

Hastings, W: Wa.
Physical director as a hygienist. '09(Ap17) O. (Hygiene and physical education ser.) pap., 10 c. Bassette.

Hatch, D: Patterson, ["Paul Karishka."]
Straight goods in philosophy. '10(Je4) c. 12°, $1. Roger Bros.
Twentieth century Christ. '10(N) 12°, $1 net. Fenno.
The under world and its women. '10 (My7) c. 12°, 15 c. Roger Bros.

Hatch, D. S.
Aërial navigation. '10(D10) c. il. 8°, $1. Am. Sch. Corr.

Hatch, Dorus Reuben.
Civil government of Colorado. 14th ed. '10(S) 68 p. 12°, 60 c. Herrick.

Hatch, F: H:
Text book of petrology. 5th ed. '09 (Mr27) il. 12°, *$1.90 net. Macmillan.

—, and Vallentine, E. J.
Mining tables: comparison of the units of weight, measure, currency, mining area, etc., of different countries; with tables, constants and other data. '08(Ja25) 8°, *$1.90 net. Macmillan.
Weights and measures of international commerce: tables and equivalents. '08(Ja11) 8°, *80 c. net. Macmillan.

Hatch, Kirk Lester.
Simple exercises illustrating some applications of chemistry to agriculture. '08 (Ag) 22 p. il. 8°, (U. S. Dept. of Agriculture, Office of Experiment Stations, bull.) pap., 15 c. U. S., Supt. of Docs.
See also Benkendorf, Gustavus H: W:

—, Haselwood, J: Adam, and Keffer, C: Albert.
Elementary agriculture of Tennessee, with practical arithmetic. '09(N) c. 185 p. il. fold. map, 12°, 40 c. Row, P. & Co.

Hatch, Willis Marion.
Ideal family: a private manual on the science of procreation. '08(Mr.) c. 136 p. 16°, $1. W. M. Hatch.

Hatcher, Rob. Anthony, and Wilbert, Martin I.
Pharmacopeia and the physician. 2d rev. ed. '08(My.) c. 485 p. 12°, $1. Am. Medical.

Hatcher, W: Eldridge.
Along the trail of the friendly years. '10 (Jl16) c. 8°, $1.50 net. Revell.
John Jasper: the unmatched negro philosopher and preacher. '08(S12) c. 12°, *$1 net. Revell.

Hate of man. Grainger, F. E: $1.50. Cassell.

Hatfield, Fk., pseud.
Realm of light: a novel. '08(Ag22) c. D. $1.50. Reid Pub.

Hatfield, H: Rand.
Modern accounting. '09(Ap3) c. D. **$1.75 net. Appleton.

Hatfield, Montraville Lawson.
How to stop stammering. '10(My14) c. por. 12°, $1.50. M. L. Hatfield.

Hatfield, R:, ed.
Geyserland: empiricisms in social reform. Tentative ed. '08(Je27) c. front. O. $3. R: Hatfield.

HATFIELD, Mass.
Wells, D. W. *and* R. F. Hist. of Hatfield, Mass., 1660-1910. F. C. H. Gibbons.
Wight, C. A. Hatfield book. $1.35. C. A. Wight.

Hathaway, C: E., and Griffith, Ja. Bray.
General expense and cost summaries; instruction paper. '09(D4) c. forms, 8°, (American School of Correspondence pubs.) 50 c. Am. Sch. Corr.

Hathaway, Esse Virginia.
Little Corsican, Napoleon Bonaparte; with introd. and notes. '09(N20) c. il. por. 12°, (Golden classics.) $1. Rand, McN. & Co.

Hathaway, S., comp.
Appeal to common sense and words that tell; guide to temperance on safe and sane lines; prohibition fallacies exposed. '10(S17) c. 12°, 50 c. Common Sense Pub.

HATS.
See Millinery.

Hatt, Jos. Arth. H:
The colorist; designed to correct the commonly held theory that red, yellow, and blue are the *primary* colors. '09(My1) c. il sq. O. $1.50. Van Nostrand.

Hatton, H:, and Plate, Adrian.
Magicians' tricks: how they are done; with contributions by Felicien Trewey, Karl Germain, Will Goldston, and others. '10 (O29) c. il. D. $1.60 net. Century Co.

Hatton, R: G.
Craftsman's plant-book: figures of plants selected from the XVI century herbals. '10(Ap23) f°, $7.50 net. Dutton.

Hauck, Albert, ed.
See New Schaff-Herzog encyclopedia.

Hauenstein, Minnie Ferris.
Songs from the silence. '09, [1910.] (F) c. 11-111 p. 8°, $1.25. M. F. Hauenstein.

Hauff, Wilhelm.
Fairy tales. '10(D) 344 p. il. in col. 12°, $2.50. Dutton.
Lichtenstein; romantische sage aus der württembergischen geschichte; abr. and ed., with introd. and notes, by Ja. Percival King. '10(Ap2) c. por. map, S. 80 c. Holt.

Hauhart, W: Frederic.
Reception of Goethe's Faust in England in the first half of the nineteenth century. '09(Jl17) 8°, (Columbia Univ. Germanic studies.) pap., $1 net. Lemcke.

Haultain, Thdr. Arnold.
Hints for lovers. '09(N6) c. D. **$1 net. Houghton M.
Mystery of golf: briefe account of games in generall, their origine, antiquitie, and rampancie, and of the game ycleped golfe in particular. '08(N21) $5. Houghton M.
Mystery of golf. 2d ed., rev. and enl. '10 (D17) c. O. $1.75 net. Macmillan.

Haunted house. Spencer, H: P. $1. Badger.

Haunted king. Moore, T: E. $1.50. C. M. Clark.

Haunts of ancient peace. Austin, A. *$2 net. Macmillan.

Haupt, W: G:
Art of business college soliciting. '10(Je) c. 89 p. por. 16°, $2. W: G: Haupt.

Hauptmann, Carl Ferdinand Maximilian.
Das geheimnis der gestalt, (The secret form;) vortag gehalten vor der Germanistischen gesellschaft von Amerika, 2. Dezember, 1908. '09(Jl17) O. (Publications of the Germanistic Society of America.) pap. (Add. pubs. for price.) R. Tombo.

Hauptmann, Gerhart.
Fuhrmann Henshel: play in five acts. '09 (N) 12°, $1.25. Dramatic.
Hannele: a dream poem; rendered into Eng. verse and prose by C: H. Meltzer. '08(Ap4) c. D. **$1 net. Doubleday, P.

Hauser, I. L.
Caste; a novel. '08(D) c. 199 p. 8°. (Add. author for price.) I. L. Hauser.

Hauskins, J. E.
A new world: theological treatise. '08(O) c. D. pap. (Add. author for price.) J. E. Hauskins.

Hausmann, E.
See Sheldon, S:

Have Congregationalists abandoned the Bible? Peace, D. $1; pap., 50 c. S. D. Towne.

Havell, Ernest Binfield.
Benares, the sacred city. '08(D19) il. 8°, $3. Caldwell.
Indian sculpture and painting; with an explanation of their motives and ideals. '09 (Mr20) il. Q. *$25 net. Scribner.

Havell, H. L., comp.
Stories from Don Quixote. '09(Ag21) 16°, (Told through the ages ser.) $1.50. Dodge.
Stories from the Æneid. '09(Ag21) 16°, (Told through the ages ser.) $1.50. Dodge.
Stories from the Greek tragedy. '09(Ag21) 16°, (Told through the ages ser.) $1.50. Dodge.
Stories from the Iliad. '09(Ag21) 16°, (Told through the ages ser.) $1.50. Dodge.
Stories from the Odyssey. '09(Ag21) 16°, (Told through the ages ser.) $1.50. Dodge.

Haven, Curtis.
Complete manual of practical phonography. New ed. '09(Mr27) il. 8°, $2. C. Haven.

Haven (The). Phillpotts, E. †$1.50. Lane.

HAVERFORD COLLEGE, Haverford, Pa.
Barton, G: A., *ed.* Haverford [College] Library collection of cuneiform tablets or documents from the Temple Archives of Telloh. In 2 pts. pt. 2. $5 net. Winston.

Haverford essays: studies in modern literature, prep. by some former pupils of Prof. Fs. B. Gummere. '09(Jl) $1.25. Haverford Coll.

Haverford verse, by Haverfordians past and present, commemorating the 75th anniversary of the founding of the [Haverford] college. '08(N) c. 5-94 p. 8°, **$1.25 net. Winston.

Havergal, Fs. Ridley.
Bells across the snow. '09(D25) il. F. pap., 25 c. Stokes.

HAVERHILL, Mass.
Vital records of Haverhill, Mass. Topsfield Hist. Soc.

Haverson, Ja. Percival.
Sour sonnets of a sorehead and other songs of the street. '08(Jl18) c. S. 50 c. Caldwell.

Haverstick, Alex. C.
Churchman's ready reference; with introd. by Rev. Leighton Coleman. '09 (Je) $1. Young Churchman.

Haviland, M. D.
Lives of the fur folk. '10(O15) il. D. $1.35 net. Longmans.

Havton timorvmenos. *See* Terentius Afer, Publius.

Haw, G:
Lad of London. '10(S) il. 8°, $1.25. Cassell.

Hawaiian annual for 1909. 35th issue. '09 (F6) 8°, pap., 85 c. Thrum.

HAWAIIAN ISLANDS.
Baldwin, C: W. Geography of the Hawaiian Islands. 60 c. Am. Bk.
Brigham, W: T. Ancient Hawaiian house. $3. Bishop Museum.
Dibble, S. History of the Sandwich Islands. *$1.75 net. Burrows.

HAWAIIAN ISLANDS.—*Continued.*
Gowen, H. H: Hawaiian idylls of love and death. $1. Cochrane.
Hitchcock, C: H: Hawaii and its volcanoes. $2. Hawaiian Gazette.
Newell, F: H. Hawaii, its natural resources. 10 c. U. S., Supt. of Docs.
Taylor, C: M. Vacation days in Hawaii and Japan. *$1.25 net. Jacobs.
Territory of Hawaii; statements before the Committee on Pacific Islands and Porto Rico, United States Senate, on certain bills pending before the committee rel. to the territory of Hawaii. '08, [1909.] (S) 38 p. 8°. (Add. Superintendent for price.) U. S., Supt. of Docs.
Thrum, T: G., *comp.* Hawaii; almanac and annual for 1910. 75 c. Thrum.
Thrum, T. G., *comp. and tr.* Stories of the Menehunes; Hawaiian traditions. 50 c. net. McClurg.
Walker, F. D. Log of the Kaalokai; being a description of the small islands, shoals and reefs lying w. n. w. of the Hawaiian group proper. $1. Hawaiian Gazette.
See also Kilauea;—Mauna Loa.

HAWAIIAN LITERATURE.
Emerson, N. B. Unwritten literature of Hawaii. (Add. Superintendent for price.) U. S., Supt. of Docs.
Hawaiian memories: [poems.] Wenner, B. H. 50 c. Cochrane.

Haweis, Hugh Reginald.
Memories of a musical life. '09(Jl) c. 185 p. 12°. (Add. pubs. for price.) Fischer.

Hawes, Alfr. Taylor, M.D.
Care of the patient. '10(D) 7+173 p. il. 12°, $1 net. Blakiston.
Observation of symptoms; arranged for the use of nurses. '08(N7) c. O. *$1 net. Whitcomb.

Hawes, Austin F.
Forest fires in Vermont. [1910.] (Jl) 48 p. il. maps, 8°, (Vt. Forest Service pub.) pap., gratis A. F. Hawes.

Hawes, C: H: and Mrs. Harriet A. Boyd.
Crete, the forerunner of Greece; with preface by Arth. J. Evans. '10(F19) il. map, plans, 16°, (Harper's lib. of living thought.) *75 c. net. Harper.

Hawes, Mrs. Harriet A. Boyd, Williams, B. E., Seager, R. B., and others.
Gournia, Vasiliki and other prehistoric sites on the Isthmus of Hieraptera, Crete: excavations of the Wells-Houston-Cramp expeditions in 1901, 1903, 1904. '08(D12) il. f°, $26; in portfolio, $25. C. H. Hawes.
See also Hawes, C: H:

Hawk, Philip Bovier.
Practical physiological chemistry; book designed for use in courses in practical physiological chemistry in schools of medicine and of science. 2d ed., rev. and enl. '09(Mr); 3d ed., rev. and enl. '10 (N) il. (partly col.) 8°, ea., $2.50. Blakiston.
Bibliographical footnotes.

Hawk (The). Legge, R. $1.50. J: McBride.
Hawk Eye. Smith, L. R. 30 c. Flanagan.

Hawker, G:
Life of George Grenfell. '09(Ag7) 8°, *$2 net. Revell.

Hawkes, Clarence.
Black bruin: biography of a bear. '08 (S19) c. D. †$1.50. Jacobs.
Shovelhorns; the biography of a moose. '09(O9) c. il. D. $1.50. Jacobs.
Wilderness dog; biography of a gray wolf. '10(S17) c. il. D. $1.50. Jacobs.

Hawkes, Herbert Edn., Luby, W: Arth., and Touton, Fk. C:
First course in algebra. '10(Ap30) c. D. $1. Ginn.

Hawkins, Anthony Hope, ["Anthony Hope."]
Adventure of Lady Ursula; comedy in four acts. '10(Jl) c. 7-137 p. 12°, 50 c. S: French.
Great Miss Driver. '08(O3) c. il. D. †$1.50. McClure.
Love's logic, and other stories. '08(Ap4) c. D. †$1.50. McClure.
Pilkerton's peerage: comedy in four acts. '08, [1909.] (Mr) 112 p. 12°, 50 c. S: French.
Second string. '10(N5) c. D. $1.50. Doubleday, P.

Hawkins, C: Augustine.
Legal counselor and form book: hdbk. of business law and legal forms, [etc.] Rev. ed. '10(Ap) c. O. shp., $3.75. Ziegler.

Hawkins, C: Caesar, and Wallis, F.
The dynamo: its theory, design and manufacture. 4th ed. '08(Ag15) 8°, *$3.25 net; 5th ed., rewritten, rev. and enl. In 2 v. '09(N20) il. O. *$5.50 net. Macmillan.

Hawkins, Chauncey J.
Quest for health and happiness. '09(Ja9) c. D. bds., *50 c. net. Pilgrim Press.

Hawkins, Flora Legler-.
Unfinished melody. '09(Mr) c. '08. 9-36 p. 12°, 50 c. Denrich.

Hawkins, G: H: E:
Poster advertising. '10(D31) col. il. por. 4°, $3. G: H: E: Hawkins.

Hawkins, G: Wa.
Economy factor in steam power plants. '09 (Ja23) diagrs., 8°, $3. Hill Pub.

Hawkins, Jean, comp.
Ghost stories and tales of the supernatural: [bibliography.] '09(My22) O. (Bulletin of bibliography pamphlets.) pap., 20 c. Boston Bk.

Hawkins, Rev. Sir J: C.
Horae synopticae; contribs. to study of the synoptic problems. 2d ed., rev. and supplement. '10(Ja1) O. $3.40. Oxford Univ.

Hawkins, Nehemiah, ["William Rogers."]
Electrical dict.; cyclop. of words, terms, phrases and data used in the electric arts, trades and sciences; incl. standardization rules of the American Institute of Electrical Engineers. '10(My14) c. 8°, $3.50. Audel.
Mechanical dictionary. '09(Je19) c. 8°, $3.50. T. Audel.
New catechism of electricity. '08(Ag8) c. il. 16°, leath., $2. Audel.
Practical treatise on the steam engine indicator. '08(Ag8) c. 8°, $1. Audel.

Hawkins, Wa. Everett.
Chords and discords. '09(N) c. 81 p. por. 12°, $1.25. Murray Bros. Press.

Hawks, Earl Bedford.
Incubation and brooding; thorough and practical text. '09(N) c. 52 p. il. 12°, 50 c. E. B. Hawks.
Science and art of poultry culture. '09 (Mr27) c. il. 12°, $2.75. E. B. Hawks.

Hawley, Wa. A:
Early days of Santa Barbara, California, from the first discoveries by Europeans to December, 1846. '10(My) c. 105 p. il. 8°, $1. W. A: Hawley.

HAWLEY FAMILY.
See Genealogies: McPike, E. F.

Hawn, W:
All around the civil war; or, before and after. '08(Ag1) c. O. 75 c. W: Hawn.

Haworth, Ira.
Reminiscences about Abraham Lincoln; also an address delivered before the Washingtonian Temperance Society, at the Second Presbyterian Church, Springfield, Illinois, February 22, 1842, by Abraham Lincoln. [Souvenir ed.] '10 (N) 31 p. il. 8°, 25 c. E. F. Heisler.

Hawthorne, Hildegarde.
Women and other women: essays in wisdom '08(F15) c. S. $1.20. Duffield.

Hawthorne, Julian.
Lovers in heaven. '10(Ja15) c. il. O. bds., 25 c. New Church.
Secret of Solomon. '09, [1910.] (Ap) c. 22 p. 16°, pap. J. Hawthorne.
—, **ed.** Library of the world's best mystery and detective stories. '08(S19) c. 6 v., fronts. 12°, $6.50. Review of Reviews.
Lock and key library; classic mystery and detective stories; ed. by Julian Hawthorne. 10 v. '09, [1910.] (Je) fronts. 12°, with sub. to *Review of Reviews.* $10.50. Review of Reviews.
Contents: North Europe; Mediterranean; German: Classic French: Modern French; French novels; Old time English; Modern English; American Real life.

Hawthorne, Nathaniel.
Works. De luxe ed. 8 v. '10(N) il. levant, $24. Crowell.
House of the seven gables; ed., with an introd. and notes, by J. H. Castleman. '08 (Ja4) por. 16°, (Eng. texts.) 40 c. C: E. Merrill.
Letters of Hawthorne to William D. Ticknor, 1851-1864. 2 v. '10(S) c. facsims., 12°. (Not for sale.) Carteret.
Marble faun; with introd. by Leslie Stephen. '10(Ap2) 16°, (Everyman's lib.) 35 c. net; leath., 70 c. net. Dutton.
Mosses from an old manse; sel. and ed., with introd. and notes, by C: Elroy Burbank. '08(S19) 24°, (Pocket Am. and Eng. classics.) *25 c. net. Macmillan.
Stories by Hawthorne. '09(F13) 16°, (World's story tellers ser.) *40 c. net. Dutton.
Stories of classical fables: a wonder book for boys and girls. '08(Ag1) c. il. 8°, 35 c. McLoughlin.
Tanglewood tales, told to the children, by C. E. Smith. '08(Je6) il. 16°, (Told to the children ser.) 50 c. Dutton.

Hawthorne, Nathaniel.—*Continued.*
Wonder book. '08(O3) c. il. Q. (Dandelion classics for children.) †$1.50. Stokes.
Wonder book, and Tanglewood tales '10 (Mr26) il. in col. 8°, $2. Jacobs.
Wonder book and Tanglewood tales for girls and boys; with pictures by Maxfield Parrish. '10(N5) c. O. $2.50. Duffield.
Wonder book for boys and girls, and Tanglewood tales. '10(N5) c. col. il. 12°, $2.50. Dutton.

HAWTHORNE, Nathaniel.
Clarke, H. A. Hawthorne's country. $2.50 net. Baker & T.
Sanborn, F. B: Hawthorne and his friends. $3. Torch Press.

Hawtrey, C:
Private secretary: farcical comedy in three acts. '07, [1909.] (Mr) 90 p. 12°, 25 c. S: French.

Hay, Alfr.
Electrical distributing networks and transmission lines. '10(S) il. 8°, $3.50 net. Cassell.
Introd. course of continuous current engineering. '08(Ap25) il. 8°, *$2.50 net. Van Nostrand.

Hay, G:
Bellini. '08(F22) il. O. (Masterpieces in colour.) bds., *65 c. net. Stokes.
Carlo Dolci. '08(D19) il. O.(Masterpieces in colour.) il. bds., *65 c. net. Stokes.

Hay, Rev. H: Clinton.
See Reed, Ja.

Hay, H: Johnson.
Colorado poems. '08(Ag) c. 32 p. il. obl. S. pap., 75 c. H: J. Hay.

Hay, Ian, [pseud. for Ian Hay Beith.]
A man's man. '10(O8) front. D. $1.20 net. Houghton M.
Right stuff. '10(Ap30) c. front. D. $1.20 net. Houghton M.

Hay, J:
Poet in exile; early letters of J: Hay; ed. by Caroline Ticknor. '10(Je18) c. por. facsim., 8°, $5. (440 copies.) Houghton M.
See also Federalist (The).

Hay, Marie, [now Baroness Hindenburg.]
German Pompadour; being the true hist. of Wilhelmine von Gravenitz, Landhofmeisterin of Würtemberg; romance of the XVIIIth century. '10(Jl2) il 8°, $1.50. Scribner.
Winter queen; being the unhappy history of Elizabeth Stuart, Electress Palatine, Queen of Bohemia; romance. '10(D3) pors. O. $4 net. Houghton M.

Hay, Oliver Perry.
Fossil turtles of North America. '08(S19) il. tabs., O. (Carnegie Institution of Washington pub.) pap., $9. Carnegie.

HAY.
Clark, C: C., *comp.* Hay crops of the United States, 1866-1906. 15 c. U. S., Supt. of Docs.
McClure, H. B. Conditions affecting the value of market hay. (Add. Superintendent for price.) U. S., Supt. of Docs.
See also Clover.

HAY FAMILY.
See Genealogies: Colcock, C: J.

HAY FEVER.
Yonge, E. I. Hay fever and paroxysmal sneezing. $2 net. Wood.

HAY-SCENTED FERN.
See Ferns.

Hayden, Arth.
Chats on old earthenware. '09(O9) il., col. front. O. $2; ¾ levant, $5. Stokes.

Hayden, Edn. And.
Social will. '09(Jl) 4+93 p. 4°, (Psychological monographs.) $1. Psychological Review.

Hayden, Warren Luce.
Centennial addresses delivered in 1909; [centenary of the founding of the Disciples of Christ.] '09(D4) c. il. pors. O. 50 c. W. L. Hayden.

HAYDN, Franz Joseph.
Runciman, J: F. Haydn. *50 c. net; *$1 net. Macmillan.

Haydon, Arth. Lincoln.
Riders of the plains; adventures and romance with the North-West Mounted Police, 1873-1910. '10(S17) il. O. $2.75 net. McClurg.

Stories of King Arthur; with four col. pls. and other il. by Arth. Rackham. '10(D) 94 p. 12°, 50 c. Cassell.

Hayen, Eberhard.
Negro question: an essay. '08(D5) c. Q. pap., 25 c. E. Hayen.

Hayens, Herbert.
Red Caps of Lyons; story of the French Revolution. '09(O9) il. D. †$1.50. Appleton.

Hayes, Alice M.
Horsewoman; pract. guide to side-saddle riding and hunting. 3d ed., rev. and enl. '10(D24) il. 8°, $5 net. Scribner.

Hayes, Carlton Huntley.
Introd. to the sources relating to the Germanic invasions. '09(Jl3) D. (Studies in history, economics and public law.) pap., $1.50. Longmans.

Hayes, C: Willard.
Hdbk. for field geologists. 2d ed., thoroughly rev. '09(Jl3) c. figs. 16°, mor., **$1.50 net. Wiley.

—, and Lindgren, Waldemar.
Contributions to economic geology, 1907. pt. 1. '08(O10); 1908. pt. 1. '09(N) il. maps, O. (Dept. of the Interior, U. S. Geolog. Survey bull.) pap. (Add. Supt. for price.)

Hayes, Ellen.
Letters to a college girl. '09(Ag) 68 p. 12°. 60 c. E. Hayes.

Hayes, Helen Kendrick, ed.
Du Barry, enchantress. '09(Ap10) pors. D. 75 c. Estes.

Hayes, Hiram Wallace.
Paul Anthony, Christian. '08(Ag29) c. D. $1.50. Reid Pub.

The peacemakers. '09(N13) c. front. D. $1.50. Reid Pub.

Royal good fellow. '10(N19) c. il. D. 75 c. net. Howerton.

Hayes, J: Russell.
In memory of Whittier: [poems.] '10 (Jl2) il. 12°, 50 c. Biddle Press.

Old meeting houses. '09(Je12) c. il. 12°, $1. Biddle Press.

Hayes, S:
Justice practice of Iowa, civil and criminal; with examples of original papers and docket entries in civil actions. '09(Mr) c. 18+340 p. O. $4.25. Flood.

HAYES-TILDEN CONTEST.
Ewing, E. W: R. Hist. and law of the Hayes-Tilden contest. $3. Cobden.

Hayford, J: Fillmore, and Baldwin, Albert Le Seur.
Earth movements in the California earthquake of 1906. Appendix no. 3; rept. for 1907. '08(Jl18) maps, wide 4°, pap., 15 c. U. S. Supt. of Docs.

—, and Pike, Lilian.
Hypsometry: precise leveling in the United States, 1903-1907, with a readjustment of the level net and resulting elevations. '09 (Jl) 280 p. tabs., fold. chart, 4°, pap., 45 c. U. S., Supt. of Docs.

Hayler, Guy.
Famous fanatics, historical and religious. '10(Jl30) D. 60 c. Funk.

Haymes, Rob., and Rose, Dorothy.
Little Miss Quixote. '08(O3) il. D. $1.50. Longmans.

Haymond, H:
Hist. of Harrison County, West Virginia; from the early days of northwestern Virginia to the present. '10(Mr12) c. il. 12°, $3.50. Acme.

Hayne, Jos. Elias, M.D., D.D.
Ham and his immediate descendants, and their wonderful achievements. '09(O) c. 4+44 p. por. 8°. (Add. pubs. for price.) Weltz Press.

President Taft measured by his most remarkable speech on the Hamitic race question, and the duty of the American people to this race. '10(D17) il. pors. 8°, 35 c. J. E. Hayne.

Hayne, Rob. Young.
Speech on Foot's resolution, in the U. S. Senate, Jan. 21-25, 1830; in the reporting style of phonography, by Benn Pitman and Jerome B. Howard. '08(My.) 53+8 p. S. pap. (Add. pubs. for price.) Phonograph.

HAYNE, Robert Young.
Jervey, T: D. Robert Y. Hayne. **$3 net. Macmillan.

Haynes, G: H:
Charles Sumner. '09(D18) c. 12°, (American crises biographies.) **$1.25 net. Jacobs.

Haynes, Jack E.
Official guide, Yellowstone National Park; descriptive, geological, historical. 25th ed., rev. annually. '10(Je) c. 141 p. il. fold. map, 16°, 25 c. J. E. Haynes.
Bibliography (1 p.).

Haynes, Ja. B.
Economic aspects of prohibition; analysis of industrial and material conditions in Kansas and other states, proving the

policy of prohibition to be highly detrimental. '09, [1910.] (N) 24 p. 8°, 15 c. J. B. Haynes.

Hays, Gilbert Adams, comp.

Under the red patch: story of the 63d Regiment, Pennsylvania Volunteers, 1861-1864; with personal narrative by W: H. Morrow, Company A. '08(N) c. 476 p. il. pors. 8°, $2. G. A. Hays.

Hays, Helen Ashe.

Antietam and its bridges; annals of an historic stream. '10(Je18) c. il. Q. $3.50. Putnam.

Little Maryland garden. '09(My1) c. il. D. **$1.75 net, boxed. Putnam.

Hays, Mrs. Marg. Parker Gebbie.

Kiddie Land. '10(S3) c. il. Q. bds., $1.25. Jacobs.

Turr'ble tales of Kaptin Kiddo. '10(N12) c. il. obl. Q. pap., 35 c. net. Stern.

Hays, Milton D.

My grandfather's best brand; and A parent's mistake. 320 p. il. 16°, $1. M. D. Hays.

Hays, Willet Martin.

Agriculture, industries, and home economics in our public schools: an address. '08 (N) 37 p. il. 8°, gratis. Nat. Educ. Assoc.

Cooperation in agriculture; rev. form of paper read before the Southern States Association of Agriculture and other agricultural workers, October, 1907, at Columbia, S. C. '10(Ap) 10 p. 8°, pap. Gov. Pr. Off.

Education for country life. '09(O) 40 p. il. 8°, (U. S., Dept. of Agriculture; Office of Experiment Stations; circular.) pap.

Farm development; introd. book on agriculture. '10(D31) c. il. 12°, $1.50. Judd.

Haytol ser. of text books for industrial education; ed. by F. E. Mathewson. il. 12°. Taylor-H.

—Holton. Shop mathematics. $1.25.

—Littlefield. Notes for forge shop practice. 80 c.

Hayward, Fs. Sidney.

Helen Ayr. '08(N21) il. 12°, $1.50. Cochrane.

Hayward, J. W.

Essentials of a convenient, comfortable and healthy house. '10(Je4) 8°, $4. Spon.

Hayward, Roland.

Classification of the families of the *Coleoptera* of America, north of Mexico. '09, [1910.] (F) 37 p. 8°, 50 c. Am. Entomol.

Hayward, Mrs. Sidney Willard.

See Herford, Beatrice Brooke.

Hayward, Wa. Brownell.

Bermuda, past and present; descriptive and historical acct. of the Somers Islands. '10(S24) c. il. D. $1.25 net. Dodd.

Haywood, J: Campbell.

Silver cleek. '08(D5) il. $1. M. Kennerley.

Haywood, J: Kerfoot, and Warner, H. J.

Commercial feeding stuffs of the United States: their chemical and microscopical examination; with the collaboration of B. J. Howard. '08(Je6) tabs., il. 8°, (U. S. Dept. of Agriculture, Bureau of Chemistry, bull.) pap., 25 c.

Injury to vegetation and animal life by smelter wastes. '10(Ag) 63 p. il. 8°, (U. S., Dept. of Agriculture, Bu. of Chemistry, bull.) Gov. Pr. Off.

Haywood, Kate Harper.

Torchbearers on the King's highway; with prefatory note by Rev. Everett P. Smith. '09(Ap10) c. D. pap., 20 c. Young Churchman.

Haywood, Marshall De Lancey.

Lives of the bishops of North Carolina from the establishment of the episcopate in that state down to the division of the diocese. '10(My7) c. pors. 8°, $1.50. A. Williams.

HAYWOOD CASE.

See **Moyer and Haywood case.**

Hazard, Caroline.

Brief pilgrimage in the Holy Land; recounted in a series of addresses del. in Wellesley College chapel. '09(N13) c. il. D. **$1.25 net. Houghton M.

College year; vesper addresses in Wellesley College Chapel by the president, Caroline Hazard. '10(My21) C. D. $1.25 net. Houghton M.

Scallop shell of quiet: [poems.] '08(Mr7) c. front. D. **$1 net. Houghton M.

Hazard, R. H.

House on stilts; a novel. '10(Ag20) c. il. D. $1.50. G: W. Dillingham.

Hazeldine, Norton F. W.

Sufism of the Rubáiyát; or, the secret of the great paradox. 2d ed. '08(O) c. 56 p. por. 16°, $1. N. F. W. Hazeldine.

Therapeutics dietetics; or, the science of health foods and their medicinal values. 2d ed. '08(N) c. 68 p. por. 12°, $1. N. F. W. Hazeldine.

Hazell's annual for 1910; cyclopædic record of men and affairs for use in 1910; rev. to November 30th, 1909; ed. by Hammond Hall. 25th year of issue. '10(Mr26) D. *$1.50 net. Scribner.

Hazeltine, Horace.

City of encounters. '08(D5) c. il. 12°, $1.50. M. Kennerley.

Hazeltine, Mary Emogene, ed.

Anniversaries and holidays; references and suggestions for picture bulletins. '09 (D4) D. pap., 25 c. Wisconsin Free Lib.

Hazelton, G: Cochrane, jr.

The raven: the love story of Edgar Allan Poe, ('twixt fact tnd fancy.) '09(F27) c. D. †$1.50. Appleton.

Hazelwood, Charlotte Williams.

Garden of Grey Ledge and other poems. '10(D17) c. D. $1.25 net. Sherman, F.

Hazen, Allen.

See Williams, Gardner Stewart.

Hazen, C: Downer.

Europe since 1815. '10(Jl2) c. maps, O. (American historical ser.) $3. Holt.

Hazlehurst, Ja. Nisbet.
Towers and tanks for water-works. 3d ed., rev. and enl. '08(Ag1) c. il. 8°, $2.50. Wiley.

Hazlitt, W:, (1778-1830.)
Characters of Shakspere's plays; ed., with introd. and notes, by J. H. Lobban. '09 (My) 23+280 p. 16°, (Cambridge English literature for schools.) *40 c. net. Putnam.
Comic writers of Great Britain; ed. by W. E. Henley. '10(Ap16) 16°, (Everyman's lib.) 35 c. net; leath., 75 c. net. Dutton.
Lectures on English poets, and the spirit of the age; with introd. by A. R. Waller. '10(D10) 16°, (Everyman's lib.) 35 c. net; leath., 70 c. net. Dutton.
Lectures on the English poets. '08(Mr7) 12°, (New universal lib.) 50 c.; leath., 75 c. Dutton.
Table talk. '08(S19) 16°, (Everyman's lib.) *35 c. net; leath., *70 c. net. Dutton.

Hazlitt, W:
See New York [State.] Code of civil procedure.

Hazzard, J: E:
The four-flusher. '08(N14) c. D. †$1. G: W. Dillingham

Hazzard, Linda Burfield.
Fasting for the cure of disease. [2d ed.] '10(N.) 161 p. 16°, $1.50. L. B. Hazzard.

He can who thinks he can. Marden, O. S. **$1 net. Crowell.

He did it. Edgerly, A. S. $1. A. S. Edgerly.

He goeth before you. Conwell, R. H. 50 c. F. M. Barton.

He is a Jew. Ketler, W: H. 10 c. H. B. Ketler.

He restoreth my soul. W., A. H. (Canada.) $1.50 net. Putnam.

Heacock, W: A.
Best way to start a mail order business: a complete system and set of lessons for beginners. '08. c. 64 p. il. 4°, $3. W: A. Heacock.

Head, Gustavus P., ed.
See Wood, Casey Alb., *ed.*

Head, Idress.
Historical and interesting places of Saint Louis. '09, [1910.] c. 136 p. il. 12°, pap., 25 c. Missouri Hist.

Head, Ja. W:
Hist. and comprehensive description of Loudoun County, Va. [1910.] (Ja) 186 p. por. 8°, $1. J. W. Head.

HEAD.
Cunningham, D. J:, *and others.* Imperial stereoscopic anatomy of the head and neck. $10. Imperial Pub.
Kebler, L. F., *and others.* Harmfulness of headache mixtures. pap., 10 c. U. S., Supt. of Docs.
See also Brain;—Ear;—Eye; — Face; — Hair; — Mouth;—Nose.

Head and heart. Kieffer, J. S. *$1.50 net. Ref. Ch. Pub.

Head coach. Paine, R. D. $1.50. Scribner.

Head of Iron. Patterson, B. S. *$1.20 net. T. M. Walker.

HEADACHE.
See Head.

Headden, W: Parker.
Occurrence of arsenic in soils, plants, fruits and animals. 345-360 p. 8°, 50 c. Colo. Sci. Soc.

Headlam, Rev. Arth. Cayley, D.D.
History, authority, and theology. '10 (Ap30) D. $2 net. Young Churchman.

Headlam, Cecil.
Inns of Court. '09(Jl3) il. map, 8°, (Color books.) *$2 net. Macmillan.
Venetia and northern Italy. '08(O24) il. map, 8°, (Old world travel ser.) *$2.50 net. Macmillan.

Headlam, Wa. G:
Book of Greek verse. '08(F1) 8°, *$1.75 net. Putnam.

Headland, I: Taylor.
Court life in China; capital, its officials and people. '09(O23) c. il. O. *$1.50 net. Revell.

Headley, Russel, ed.
Hist. of Orange Co., N. Y. '08, [1909.] (My) 10+17-997 p. il. pors. 8°, $15. Van Deusen & E.

Headlong Hall. Peacock, T: L. *35 c. net; *70 c. net. Dutton.

Heads of families at the first census, 1790. United States. *Dept. of Commerce and Labor. Bureau of Census.* $1. U. S., Supt. of Docs.

Heald's Pitman-Graham shorthand. Barnes, L. E. $1.25. E: P. Heald.

Healey, Horace G.
Healey system of free arm movement writing. In 10 nos. '10(Je18) c. obl. D. pap., ea., 10 c. Am. Bk.

Healing ministry of the church. McComb, S: **25 c. net. Moffat.

HEALTH.
See Hygiene

Health and beauty hints. Mixter, M. $1. Cupples & L.

Health and happiness. Fallows, S: *$1.50 net. McClurg.

Health and happiness. Harbin, R. M. **90 c. net. Am. Bapt.

Health and longevity. Richardson, J. G. $12. Stanley Inst.

Health and suggestion. Feuchtersleben, E. v. $1 net. B: W. Huebsch.

Health and wealth. Hubbard, E. $2. Roycrofters.

Health and wealth from within. Towne, W: E. $1. E. J. Towne.

Health culture; how to live, what to eat, to wear, to do, in health, in sickness, in youth, in middle life, in old age, to achieve perfect bodily and mental vigor, abounding health and longevity. '09(N20) c. il. 12°, $1. Polk.

Health from knowledge. Colville, W: W. J. 50 c. Macoy.

Health of the city. Godfrey, H. $1.25 net. Houghton M.

Health, progress and administration in the West Indies. Boyce, *Sir* R. W. $3.50 net. Dutton.

Healthful art of dancing. Gulick, L. H. $1.40 net. Doubleday, P.

Healthful spirit. Bate, H. N. *90 c. net. Longmans.

Healthology. Eales, I. J. $1.50. I. J. Eales.

Healy, Cahir.
Escapades of Condy Corrigan; amusing series of Irish fireside stories. '10(F) c. 9-172 p. il. 12°, 50 c. Soc. Divine Word.

Healy, Edith, comp.
La comédie classique en France; arr. as a reader, with vocab. '08(Mr7) c. S. 50 c. Am. Bk.

Healy, Archbishop J:
Papers and addresses: theological, philosophical, biographical, archæological. '10 (Ja22) por. facsim., *$2.25 net. Herder.

HEARING.
Bruner, F. G. Hearing of primitive peoples. $1. Science Pr., (N. Y.)
Peterson, J. Combination tones and other related auditory phenomena. $1.50. Psychological Review.
See also Ear.

Hearn, Rev. E: C., ["Clarence Edwards."]
Friends and friendships: a New Year sermonette. '08(Mr) c. D. (Holly ser. of booklets.) pap., 25 c. E: C. Hearn.

Hearn, Lafcadio.
Japanese letters of Lafcadio Hearn; ed., with introd., by Eliz. Bisland. '10(D17) c. il. pors. O. $3 net. Houghton M.
—, tr. *See* France, Anatole;—Gautier, Théophile.

HEARN, Lafcadio.
Gould, G: M. Concerning Lafcadio Hearn. **$1.50 net. Jacobs.

Hearne, Herbert Clement.
Tables of stresses in roof trusses, including tables of compression and tension members, and extracts from the building laws of various cities. '09(Jl17) c. 4°, *$4 net. Hill Pub.

Hearne, R. P.
Aerial warfare; with an introd. by Sir Hiram Maxim. '09(Ja30) il. maps, figs. O. *$2.50 net. Lane.
Airships in peace and war; being the 2d ed. of "Aerial warfare"; with 7 new chapters; with introd. by Sir Hiram Maxim. '10(F12) O. *$3.50 net. Lane.
Motoring. '08(O17) 12°, (Oval ser.) 50 c. Dutton.

HEART.
Bishop, L: F. Heart diseases, blood pressure. $3. Treat.
Dock, G:, *ed.* Diseases of the heart. *$5 net; *$6 net. Saunders.
Harvey, W: Anatomical disquisition on the motion of the heart and blood in animals. *35 c. net; *70 c. net. Dutton.
Hirschfelder, A. D. Diseases of the heart and aorta. $6 net. Lippincott.
Neusser, E. v. Clinical treatises on the symptomology and diagnosis of disorders of respiration and circulation. pt. 3, Angina pectoris. $1. Treat.
Satterthwaite, T: E: Diseases of the heart and aorta. *$3 net. W: R. Jenkins.
See also Arteries;—Blood.

Heart of a child. Danby, F., *pseud.* †$1.50. Macmillan.

Heart of a Geisha. Fraser, *Mrs.* M. C. †$2. Putnam.

Heart of Abraham Lincoln. Whipple, W. 50 c. Biddle Press.

Heart of Central Africa. Springer, J: M. *$1 net. Jennings.

Heart of desire. Dejeans, E. $1.50. Lippincott.

Heart of gold. Smith, *Mrs.* E. T. 50 c. Hurst.

Heart of happiness. Ainsworth, P. C. $1 net. Revell.

Heart of hope. Darling, J. T. (Not for sale.) J. T. Darling.

Heart of India. Barnett, L. D. *60 c. net. Dutton.

Heart of Kentucky. Pittman, *Mrs.* H. D. $1.50. Neale.

Heart of our country. Murray-Aaron, E. $11; $12.50; $15. G: F. Cram.

Heart of Scotland. Moncrieff, A. R. H. *$3 net. Macmillan.

Heart of silence. Cramp, W. S: $1.50. C. M. Clark.

Heart of the Antarctic. Shackleton, *Sir* E. H. **$10 net. Lippincott.

Heart of the Old Testament. Sampey, J: R: 50 c. S. S. Bd. So. Bapt.

Heart of the people. Abarbanell, J. R. $1.50. C. M. Clark.

Heart of the red firs. Anderson, *Mrs.* A. W. †$1.50. Little, B. & Co.

Heart of the singer. Whitney, F: $1.25. F. Whitney.

Heart of the South. Hoffer, C. M. 50 c. C. M. Hoffer.

Heart of the stranger. McLeod, C. $1.25. Revell.

Heart of the wheat. Dunlap, L. $1. Transylvania.

Heart of Washington. Knox, D. H. $1.50. Neale.

Heart poems. Sigbee, A. E. 75 c. B'way Pub.

Heart songs; [collection of favorite songs voted on by 20,000 persons.] '09(N) $2.50. Chapple Pub.

Heart thoughts. Folk, M. F. **75 c. net. Am. Bapt.

Heart throbs. Stuart, I. B., *jr.* 75 c. Charter Oak.

Heart to heart letters. Bottome, *Mrs.* M. $1. Doran.

Heartbreak Hill. Vielé, H. K. †$1.50. Duffield.

Hearts and coronets. Fox, A. W. $1.50. Macmillan.

Hearts are trumps. Otis, A. $1.50. J: McBride.

Hearts atour. Chetwood, E. $1.50. Evening Post.

Hearts contending. Loose, K. R. $1.50. Harper.

HEAT.
Berry, C: W: Temperature-entrophy diagram. $2. Wiley.
Clement, J. K., *and* Egy, W. L. Thermal conductivity of fire-clay at high temperatures. gratis. Univ. of Ill.

HEAT.—*Continued.*

Clement, J. K., *and* Garland, C. M. Study in heat transmission. Univ. of Ill.

Darling, C: R. Heat for engineers. $5. Spon.

Dickinson, Hobert C., Mueller, Eug. F., *and* George, Earl B. Specific heat of some calcium chloride solutions between —35° C and +20° C. '10(Jl) 379-408 p. il. 4°. Gov. Pr. Off.

Easer, E. Heat for advanced students. *$1 net. Macmillan.

Elliott, J. Solar heat, non-solar. 25 c. J. Elliott.

Ennis, W: D. Applied thermodynamics for engineers. $4.50. Van Nostrand.

Franklin, W: S., *and* Macnutt, B. Mechanics and heat. $1.75 net. Macmillan.

Haber, F. Thermodynamics of technical gas-reactions. *$3 net. Longmans.

Hirschfeld, C. F. Engineering thermodynamics. 50 c. Van Nostrand.

Jüptner von Jonstorff, H. Heat energy and fuels. *$3 net. McGraw.

Marks, L. S., *and* Davis, H. N. Diagrams; reproduced from tables and diagrams of the thermal and properties of saturated and superheated steam. **40 c. net. Longmans.

Mills, J: Introd. to thermodynamics. $2. Ginn.

Reeve, S. A. Energy, work, heat and transformations. $2. McGraw-H.

Spangler, H: W. Applied thermodynamics. $2.50. McVey.

Spangler, H: W. Notes on thermodynamics. $1. Wiley.

Sheehy, J. Heat and cold. $1.75. J. Sheehy.

Stewart, R. W. Elem. text-book of physics. pt. 4, Heat. *$1.50 net. Lippincott.

Tillman, S: E. Elem. lessons in heat. **$1.50 net. Wiley.

Trevor, J. E. Lectures on thermodynamics. $1. J. E. Trevor.

Young, G. A. Elem. notes on thermodynamics. $1. G. A. Young.

See also Calorimeter; — Chemistry; — Dynamics; — Heating; — Physics; — Radio-activity; — Steam; — Sun.

HEAT ENGINES.
See Engines.

Heath, Dudley.
Miniatures. '08(D19) il. Q. (Connoisseurs' lib.) *$7.50 net, boxed. Putnam.

Heath, Franklin Reinhardt.
Manual of language lessons. '08(Je13) c. D. $1. Phonograph.

Heath, Sidney H.
South Devon and Dorset coast. '10(D17) il. O. (County coast ser.) $2.25 net. Stokes.

Heather. Trevena, J: †$1.50. Moffat.

Heath's English classics. 16°. Heath.
—Bacon. Essays. *35 c. net.
—Goldsmith *and* Gray. Goldsmith's The traveller and The deserted village, and Gray's Elegy in a country churchyard. 25 c.
—Lamb. Essays of Elia. *40 c. net.

Heath's modern language ser. D. and S. Heath.
—Arndt. Deutsche patrioten in Ruszland zur zeit Napoleons. 30 c.
—Arrom de Ayala. Un serviton y un liberalito ō tres almas de dios. 50 c.
—Bazin. Contes choisis. 35 c.
—Bernhardt, *ed.* Der weg zum glück. 40 c.
—Betz, *ed.* Die Schildbürger ihre wisheit und ungrosze torheit. 35 c.
—Blanchard, *comp.* Progressive French idioms. 60 c.
—Böhlen. Ratsmädelschichten. 40 c.
—Boileau-Despréaux. Selections. 50 c.
—Bruce. Lectures faciles. 60 c.
—Cervantes. Selections from Don Quixote. 80 c.
—Comfort. Exercises in French prose composition. 25 c.—Les maitres de la critique littéraire au XIXme siècle. 50 c.
—Dante. La divina commedia. v. 1. $1.25.
—Daudet. Choix de contes. 30 c.
—Delpit. Age d'or de la litterature française. 90 c.
—Desnoyes. Les Mésaventures de Jean-Paul Choppart. 40 c.
—Diderot. Selections. 50 c.
—Dumas. Episodes from Les trois mousquetaires. 45 c. net.
—Durand. Dosia. 45 c.
—Erckmann *and* Chatrian. Madame Thérèse. 40 c.
—Fogazzaro. Pereat Rochus and Un' idea di Ermes Torranza. 40 c.
—Fraser *and* Van der Smissen. German grammar. $1.10.
—Frommel. Mit ränzel und wanderstab. 35 c.
—Giese *and* Cool. French anecdotes. 40 c.—Spanish anecdotes. 60 c.
—Gutiérrez. El trovador. 40 c.
—Halévy. Un mariage d' amour. 25 c.
—Heine. Die Harzreise. 45 c.
—Hugo. Selected poems. 80 c.
—Jensen. Die braune Erica. 35 c.
—Lambert. Alltägliches. 75 c.
—Lemaire. Contes extraits de Myrrha. 30c.
—Mansion. Easy French selections for sight translations. 15 c.
—Palacio Valdés. José. 90 c.
—Racine. Phèdre. 30 c.
—Remy, *comp. and ed.* Spanish composition. 60 c.
—Rostand. Princesse Lointaine. 40 c.
—Roux. Lessons in [French] grammar. 18c.
—Spyri. Was der grosmutter lehre bewirkt. 25 c.
—Stökl. Alle fünf! 30 c.
—Sudermann. Heimat. 35 c.
—Thomas. Anthology of German literature. $2.25.
—Tamayo y Baus. Lo positivo. 45 c.
—Till Eulenspiegls. 30 c.
—Tocqueville. Voyage en Amérique. 40 c.
—Valera. Pepita Jiménez. 90 c.
—Voltaire. Zäire; tragedy in verse. 30 c.
—Werner-Spanhoofd. Erstes lesebuch. 75c.
—Windenbruch. Neid. 35 c.

Heath's pedagogical lib. 12°. Heath.
—Laing. Reading. $1.
—Munroe. Educational ideal. $1.
—Tracy *and* Stimpfl. Psychology of childhood. $1.20.
Heath's science text-books. il. 12°. Heath.
—Newell. Descriptive chemistry. $1.20.
Heath's technical drawing ser. 12°. Heath.
—Anthony. Machine drawing. $1.50.
—Anthony *and* Ashley. Descriptive geometry. $2.

HEATING.
American School of Correspondence. Cyclopedia of heating, plumbing and sanitation. $12.—Heating and ventilation. pt. 1. $1.50. Am. Sch. Cor.
Baldwin, W: J. St. J. Hot water heating and fitting. *$4 net. McGraw.
Baldwin, W: J. St. J. On heating. $2.50. Wiley.
Carpenter, R. C. Heating and ventilating buildings. $4. Wiley.
Chaimovitch, I: Tables for calculating sizes of steam pipes for low pressure heating. $2. Domestic Engineering.
Dean, M. Steam fitters' computation and price book. $3.—System of green house heating for steam or hot water. $2. Domestic Engineering.
Hoffman, J. D:, *and* Raber, B: F: Hdbk. for heating and ventilating engineers. $3.50. J. D: Hoffman.
Hubbard, C: L. Fans, ventilation and heating. 25 c. Indust. Press.
Hubbard, C: L. Heating and ventilation. $1.50. Am. Sch. Corr.
Hubbard, C: L. Power, heating and ventilation. 3 v. $5 net. Technical Press.
King, A. G. Practical steam and hot water heating and ventilation. $3. Henley.
Lincoln, H. C. Pract. steam and hot-water fitting. $1. D: Williams.
Richey, N. G. Building mechanics' ready reference. Plumbers', steam-fitters' and tinners' ed. **$1.50 net. Wiley.
Snow, W: G. Pract. and comprehensive treatise on warming buildings with hot air. $1.75. D: Williams.
Walker, S. F. Pocket book of electric lighting and heating. $3. Henley.
White, W. L. *and* G. M. Heating engineers quantities. $4.25. Spon.
See also Coal;—Furnaces;—Greenhouses;—Heat;—Steam pipes;—Valves;—Ventilation.

Heaton, S:
See Elford, Percy.

Heaton, Willis E.
See New York [State.] Surrogates' cts.

HEAVEN.
Robinson, A. M. Heaven: what and where? 50 c.; 25 c. Pub. Ho. of M. E. Ch., So.
Walpole, G: H: S. Kingdom of heaven; what it is and how we enter it. *$1 net. Dutton.

Heaven and hell. *See* Swedenborg, Emanuel.
Heavenly heretics. Powell, L. P. **$1.25 net. Putnam.
Heavenly Jervsalem: a mediæval song of the joys of the chvrch trivmphant; with annot. by W: Loring Andrews. '08(D5) c. il. 8°, **$14 net. Scribner.
Heavenly life. Allen, J. 50 c.; 15 c. Fenno.
Heavenly pilgrim. Pierce, D: R. $1. D: R. Pierce.
Heaven's recent wonders. Boissarie, P. G. $1.50. Pustet.
Heavenward. Remensnyder, J. B: 50 c. Lutheran Pub.
Heavenwards. Loyola, *Mother* M. $1.25 net. Kenedy.

Heazlitt, Clarence Watt.
When skies are gray with a rift or two: verses. '09(Ap24) D. $1. Neale.

Hebberd, Stephen Southric.
Impending anarchy. '08(D) c. 93 p. 12°. (Add. pubs. for price.) Maspeth.

Hebrew beginnings. *See* Stebbins, *Mrs.* E. W. H., *and* Saunderson, H: H.

HEBREW BOOKS.
See **Printers and printing.**

Hebrew history. *See* Stebbins, *Mrs.* E. W. H., *and* Saunderson, H: H.

HEBREW LANGUAGE.
Adams, J: Sermons in syntax: studies in the Hebrew text. *$1.50 net. Scribner.
Feyerabend, K., *comp.* Complete Hebrew-English pocket-dictionary of the Old Testament. 75 c. Lemcke.
Gesenius, F. H. W. Hebrew grammar. $5.25 net. Oxford Univ.
Goldin, H. E. First year in Hebrew. 40 c. Druckerman.
Goldin, H. E., *and* Silk, B. Second year in Hebrew. 60 c. Druckerman.
Neuhausen, S. A. Tables of declension and conjugation. 15 c. Druckerman.
See also Semitic language.

Hebrew literature: comprising Talmudic treatises, Hebrew melodies, and the Kabbalah unveiled; with introd. by Epiphanius Wilson. '08(Je27) c. il. 8°, $1.75; hf. mor., $3.50. Lamb Pub.

HEBREW LITERATURE.
Cantrell, E: A. Bible and modern literature; comparing the literature of to-day with the ancient Jewish scriptures. 50 c. Los Angeles Liberal.
Ginzberg, L: Geonica. 2 v. Jewish Theological.
Gollancz, H., *tr.* Translations from Hebrew and Aramaic; Targum to the Song of songs; Book of the apple; Ten Jewish martyrs; Dialogue on games of chance. *$2 net. Bloch.
Newcomb, G: T: Simple method of translating Hebrew. (Not for sale.) G: T: Newcomb.
Simon, L., *ed* Aspects of the Hebrew genius; essays on Hebrew literature and thought. $1. Bloch.
Slouschz, N. Renaissance of Hebrew literature. $1.25. Jewish Pub.
Yerushalmi fragments from the Genizah. v. 1. Jewish Theological.
See also Semitic literature.

Hebrew prophecy. Zollars, E. V. $1. Standard Pub.

HEBREW RELIGION.
See **Jews.**

HEBREWS.
See **Jews.**

HEBRON LUTHERAN CHURCH, Madison Co., Va.
Huddle, W: P: Hist. of the Hebron Lutheran Church, Madison Co., Va. $2. W: P: Huddle.

HECH-HECKY VALLEY, Cal.
See Yosemite Valley.

Hecht, Solomon.
How to become a letter carrier or postal clerk. '10(O) c. 80 p. 12°, 50 c. Police Chronicle.

Heck, Fk.
Secrets of expert exhibitors and easy lessons in judging; exposition of the methods employed by breeders of standard bred fowls in preparing their birds for poultry shows, incl. many dishonest schemes which are occasionally practiced. '09(D18) c. il. 12°, $2. F. Heck.

Heck, Rob. Culbertson Hays.
Notes on elem. kinematics. '10(My7) c. il. 8°, $1. Van Nostrand.
Notes on the graphics of machine forces. '10(S17) c. il. 8°, $1. Van Nostrand.

Heck, W. H.
Mental discipline and educational values. '09(N13) c. D. **$1 net. Lane.

Hecker, Eug. Arth.
Short hist. of the progress of woman's rights from the days of Augustus to the present time; with special reference to the record in England and the United States. '10(D31) 8°, $1.50 net. Putnam.
Teaching of Latin in secondary schools. '10(F19) c. D. 80 c. Schoenhof.

Heckewelder, J: Gottlieb Ernestus.
Narrative of the mission of the United Brethren among the Delaware and Mohegan Indians from its commencement in the year 1740 to the close of the year 1808; ed. by W: Elsey Connelley. '08 (O10) pors. facsims., maps, 4°, *$30 net. Burrows.

Hecox, Clarence W.
Students' manual for machine shop practice. '10(N19) c. il. tabs., 8°, $2. C. W. Hecox.

Hedges, Florence Edythe Blake-.
I am; novel of psychotherapy. '10(D3) c. col. il. D. $1.50. Roxburgh.
See also Blake-Hedges, Florence Edythe.

Hedges, Job. Elmer.
Common sense in politics. '10(D10) c. D. $1.25. Moffat.

Hedin, Sven Anders.
Overland to India. 2 v. '10(D31) col. il. 8°, $7.50 net. Macmillan.
Trans-Himalaya; discoveries and adventures in Tibet. In 2 v. '09(D18) c. il. O. **$7.50 net, boxed. Macmillan.

Hedley, J:
Tramps in dark Mongolia. '10(N12) il. 8°, $3.50 net. Scribner.

Hedrick, C: C.
Cotton spinning. '09(My8) c. il. 8°, (American School of Correspondence pubs.) $3. Am. Sch. Corr.

Hedrick, Earle Raymond.
Algebra for secondary schools. '08(S12) c. diagrs., D. hf. leath., $1. Am. Bk.

—, and Kellogg, Oliver Dimon.
Applications of the calculus to mechanics. '10(My21) c. O. $1.25. Ginn.

Hedrick, Ulysses P., and others.
Grapes of New York; [rept. of the New York Agricultural Experiment Station for the year 1907.] '08, [1909.] (My) 15+564 p. il. f°. (Not for sale.) Lyon.

Heess, J: Karl.
Practical methods for the iron and steel works chemist. '08(Ap.) c. 60 p. 8°, $1. Chemical.

Heeter, Silvanus Laurabee.
See Webster, W: Franklin.

Hegan, Alice Caldwell.
See Rice, *Mrs.* Alice Caldwell Hegan.

Hegel, Georg Wilhelm Friedrich.
Phenomenology of mind; tr., with introd. and notes, by J. B. Baillie. 2 v. '10(D10) O. (Lib. of philosophy.) $5.50 net. Macmillan.
Philosophy of history; with prefaces by C: Hegel and the translator, J. Sibree. '08 (Je27) c. il. 8°, $1.75; hf. mor., $3.50. Lamb Pub.

HEGEL, Georg Wilhelm Friedrich.
Adams, G: P. Mystical element in Hegel's early theological writings. 35 c. Univ. of Cal.
Cunningham, G. W. Thought and reality in Hegel's system. $1.25. Longmans.
Mackenzie, M. Hegel's educational theory and practice. $1. Bardeen.

HEGLER, Edward C.
In memory of Edward C. Hegler. '10(Jl) no paging, O. por. pap., gratis. Open Court.

Hegner, Rob. Wilhelm.
Introd. to zoology. '10(D10) c. il. pors. D. $1.90 net. Macmillan.

Hegyessy, Ja.
Must women suffer everlastingly? [1910.] (S) c. 246 p. por. 8°, $2.50. J. Hegyessy.

Heidenrich, Eyvind Lee.
Engineers' pocket book of reinforced concrete. '08(D26); il. tabs., 12°, *$3 net. M. C. Clark.

Heidi. *See* Spyri, Johanna.

Heil, Adolf, and Esch, W.
Manufacture of rubber goods. '09(Je19) il. O. *$3.50 net. Lippincott.

Heil, Esch W.
See Heil, Adolf.

Heilbron, W: Caspar.
Convict life at the Minnesota State Prison, Stillwater, Minnesota. '09(S18) c. il. por. D. pap., 25 c. W: C. Heilbron.
Convict life at the Minnesota State Prison, Stillwater, Minnesota. 2d ed. '10(Jl30) c. il. pors. 12°, pap., 25 c. H. L. Taylor.

Heilbroner, L:, comp.
Baseball blue book; reliable directory of all leagues and clubs and official playing schedules of leagues working under the national agreement, 1910. '10(Je18) c. O. pap., $1. L: Heilbroner.

Heilprin, Angelo.
Eruption of Pelée: summary and discussion of the phenomena and their sequels. '08(Ag1) c. il. por. f°, $4. Geographical Soc.

Heimat. *See* Sudermann, Hermann.

Hein, Gustav.
Auswahl deutscher prosa der gegenwart, mit lebensbeschreibungen der verfasser und ammerkungen; verlagerechtlicheausgabe. '10(Mr26) D. 70 c. Oxford Univ.

Exercises in French conversation and composition; with notes and vocab. '09 (Ag28) D. (Modern language ser.) *40 c. net. Crowell.

Heindel, Rev. J: Elmer.
Short history of the English Evangelical Lutheran church of the Redeemer. '08 (My.) c. 31 p. il. obl. 12°, pap., 50 c. J: E. Heindel.

Heindel, Max.
Rosicrucian cosmo-conception; or, Christian occult science; elem. treatise upon man's past evolution, present constitution and future development. 2d ed., rev. and enl. [1910.] (D) c. 542 p. il. 12°, $1. Donohue.

Rosicrucian cosmo-conception; or, Christian occult science; elem. treatise upon man's past evolution, present constitution and future development. [1910.] (Ja) c. '09. 536 p. il. 12°, $1. M. Heindel.

Rosicrucian philosophy in questions and answers. '10(D3) c. il. 12°, $1. Rosicrucian.

Heine, Bernhard.
Operations on the ear; operation for suppurative otitis media and its intracranial complications; tr. and ed. from the 2d German ed. by W. Lombard Murphy. '08 (D26) il. 8°, *$3 net. Wood.

Heine, Heinrich.
Die Harzreise; ed., with notes and vocab. by Parke R. Kolbe. '08(D5) c. il. map, S. 50 c. Am. Bk.

Die Harzreise; ed., with introd., notes and vocab., by J: Vos. '08(F15) c. il. 16°, (Modern lang. ser.) 45 c. Heath.

Heinrich Heine's memoirs; from his works, letters and conversations; ed. by Gustav Karpeles; English tr. by Gilbert Cannan. 2 v. '10(D3) pors. O. $5 net. Lane.

Several poems; tr. by F. K. Ball. '09, [1910.] (F) c. 32 p. 16°, pap., *25 c. net. W: B. Clarke.

Songs and lyrics of Heine; tr. by C: G. Leland. '10(D31) front. 32°, (Ariel booklets.) leath., 75 c., boxed. Putnam.

HEINE, Heinrich.
Forman, H: J. In the footprints of Heine. $2 net.. Houghton M.
Scott, H: B. The Lorelei and other poems with prose settings. $1. Werner Co.

Heineman, Thdr. W:
Physical basis of civilization. '08(My2) c. D. $1.25. Forbes.

Heinemann, H. E. O.
Rule of "not too much"; being a collection of articles written during the past few years in discussing the principle of temperance, with special reference to the use of fermented beverages. Enlarged ed. '09(D4) c. D. pap., 25 c. H. E. O. Heinemann.

Heinrich, Max.
Correct principles of classical singing; cont. essays on choosing a teacher, the art of singing, etc.; together with an interpretative key to Handel's "Messiah" and Schubert's "Die schöne müllerin." '10(N19) c. O. $1.50 net. Lothrop, L. & S.

Heinrici, Max, ed.
Das buch der Deutschen in Amerika; hrsg. unter den auspicien des Deutsch-Amerikanischen National-Bundes. '10(Ag20) c. il. 4°, $5. M. Heinrici.

Heins, M. Alice.
Story of St. Francis of Assisi; with a preface by Father Cuthbert. '08, [1909.] (Mr) 80 p. il. *75 c. net. Benziger.

Heir of Redclyffe. *See* Yonge, Charlotte Mary.

Heir of the ages. Moore, A. 75 c. Doran.

Heiress of Cranham Hall. Junior, M. $1.25. B'way Pub.

Heisley, C: Wesley.
Providence and calamity. '09(Je12) c. D. *$1.10 net. Sherman, F.

Heistand, H: Olcot Sheldon.
Abraham Lincoln; being an address del. before the Men's League of the Broadway Tabernacle, Feb. 13, 1908. '09(N) 40 p. por. 16°. (Priv. pr.) H: O. S. Heistand.

Heitland, W: Emerton.
Roman republic. 3 v. '10(Ja22) 8°, per set, *$10 net. Putnam.

Heitmann, H:
Course in the theory and practice of higher accounting prepared for students of Eastman College. '10(S3) c. 8°, $2. Eastman Coll.

Helbig, R: Ernest.
German American researches: growth of the German American collection of the New York Public Library during 1906-1907. '09(Ja16) Q. gratis. N. Y. Pub. Lib.

Held, R. Johnson, M.D., and Rice, E: Baldwin, eds.
Angler's guide. 6th annual ed., 1910. '10(Mr26) c. il. D. pap., 50 c. Field and Stream.

Helderberg harmonies. Merritt, *Mrs.* M. I. L. $1.25. M. I. L. Merritt.

Hélein, Jacques Henri Jules.
Pract. French conversation in thirty easy progressive lessons. First book. '10 (D31) c. 12°, 85 c. W: R. Jenkins.

Helen. Wheat, *Mrs.* L. †$1.50. Grafton Press.

Helen Ayr. Hayward, F. S. $1.50. Cochrane.

Helen Grant books. *See* Douglas, Amanda Minnie.

Helen with the high hand. Bennett, A. $1.20 net. Doran.

Helen's babies. *See* Habberton, J:

Helianthus. La Ramée, L. de. †$1.50. Macmillan.

Heliocentric astrology. Merton, H. W. $1.50. McKay.

HELIOGABALUS.
Butler, O. F. Studies in the life of Heliogabalus. $1.25. Macmillan.

Heliographic positions of sun-spots. Peters, C. H. F. $2.50. Carnegie.

Hell before death. Harris, W: S. $1. Minter.

Hell-fire Harrison. Wattles, W. D. $1. L. C. Page.

Helladian vistas. Quinn, D. $1.50. D. Quinn.

Hellas and Hesperia. Gildersleeve, B. L. *$1 net. Holt.

Hellencia Oxyrhyncia cum Theopompi et Cratippi fragmentis; recognoverunt brevique adnotatione critica instruxerunt, Bernardus P. Grenfell et Arthurus S. Hunt. '09(S11) D. $1.10. Oxford Univ.

Hellenica: selections. Xenophon. $1.65; Text ed., 40 c. Am. Bk.

Heller, Albert H:
Stresses in structures and the accompanying deformations. 2d ed. '08(Ag1) c. il. 8°, $3. Wiley.

Heller, Edm.
Five new rodents from British East Africa. '10(Mr19) il. O (Smithsonian misc. collections.) pap. (Add. Inst. for price.) Smith. Inst.

—, and Grinnell, Jos.
Mammals of the 1908 Alexander Alaska expedition; with descriptions of the localities visited and notes on the flora of the Prince William Sound region. '10 (Ap16) Q. (Univ. of Cal. pubs.; Zoology.) pap., $1. Univ. of Cal.

"Hellespont," pseud.
Complete auction bridge. '10(D31) 12°, $1.25 net. Lippincott.

Hellman, G: Sidney.
The Hudson and other poems. '09, [1910.] (F) c. 9+144 p. 12°, $1.50. Putnam.

Helm, Mary.
From darkness to light: story of negro progress. '09(Je19) c. 16°, *50 c. net; pap., *30 c. net. Revell.
Longtail monkey and other stories. '10 (D17) c. D. 75 c. Pub. Ho. M. E. Ch., So.
Upward path: the evolution of a race. '09 (Ag) 333 p. il. pors. maps, 12°, (Forward mission study courses.) 50 c.; pap., 35 c. Young People's Miss.

Helm, W: H:
Jane Austen and her country-house comedy. '10(F19) por. facsim., O. *$3.50 net. Lane.

Helmholtz, Anna Augusta.
Indebtedness of Samuel Taylor Coleridge to August Wilhelm von Schlegel. '08 (F1) O. (Univ. of Wis. bull., Philology and literature ser.) pap., 40 c. Univ. of Wis.

Helmholtz, H:
See McArdle, Fred.

Help to self-help, 1908. '09(F) 167 p. fold map, S. pap., gratis. People's Univ.

Help wanted. Griffith, H. S. 15 c. Penn Pub. Co.

Helpful hints as business helpers. Hubbard, E. 10 c. Roycrofters.

Helping hand. Bible. **25 c. net; **15 c. net. Am. Bapt.

Helping hand for every day's wants. Coldwater, C: H: $1.50. C: H: Coldwater.

Helping up the man who is down. Kolb, C: B. 25 c. C: B. Kolb.

Helps, Sir Arth.
Life of Columbus. '10(D17) 16°, (Everyman's lib.) 35 c. net; leath., 70 c. net. Dutton.

Helps for skat players. McColl, F. S. 35 c. W: R. Jenkins.

Helps for the quiet hour. Young, J. B., *comp.* $1. Eaton & M.

Helps for worship; for use in the Sunday school, the prayer meeting and the home. '08(D) c. various paging, D. pap. (Add. pubs. for price.) Presb. Bd.

Helps for young mothers. Miller, M. W. 50 c. Jacobs.

Helps toward nobler living. Tomkins, F. W. **50 c. net; **75 c. net. Jacobs.

Helter Skelters. Daulton, G: †$1.25. Stokes.

HELYAS.
See Legends.

Heman, P.
See Smith, Lyman D.

Hematological atlas. Schleip, K. F. W. $10. Rebman.

HEMATOLOGY.
See Blood.

Hemenway southwestern expedition. O. Houghton M.
—Fewkes, *ed.* Journal of American ethnology and archæology. v. 5, Hopi songs. **$2 net.

Hemingway, S: Burdett, ed.
English nativity plays; ed., with introd., notes and glossary. '09(Je12) O. (Yale studies in English.) $2.50; pap., $2. Holt.

Heminway, M., & Sons Silk Co.
Treatise on embroidery. Ed. de luxe. '08 (Ja4) il. O. (Art needlework ser.) pap., 15 c. Heminway.

Hemiup, Mrs. Maria Remington.
Our world, the earth a revolving engine with a central propelling power. '08 (Ja18) il. por. O. $2. Hemiup.

Hemlock Avenue mystery. Doubleday, R. †$1.50. Little, B. & Co.

HEMOGLOBINS.
See Blood.

HEMORRHAGE.
See Blood.

HEMP.
Carter, H. R. Modern flax, hemp, and jute spinning and twisting. *$3 net. Van Nostrand.

Hemphill, Ja. Calvin, ed.
Men of mark in South Carolina. v. 1. '07, [1908.] (Mr.) c. pors. 8°, $10. Men of Mark.

Hempstead, Fay.
Poems by Fay Hempstead, poet laureate of freemasonry. '08, [1909.] (Mr) c. 18 p. il. por. 8°, $3; mor., $5. F. Hempstead.

Hemsley, Alfr.
Book of fern culture. '08(N7) il. D. (Handbooks of practical gardening.) *$1 net. Lane.

Hemstreet, C: and Marie.
Nooks and corners of old London. '10 (O15) c. il. 16°, $1. Pott.

Hemstreet, Marie.
See Hemstreet, C:

Henderschott, F. C.
See Nelson, *Mrs.* Dora.

Henderson, Anna Wilson, ["Mrs. A. H. Macpherson,"] and Palen, Hasbrouck Osterhoudt.
What and how: systematized course of hand work, for primary grades. '09(F13) c. il. 8°, $2. M. Bradley.

Henderson, Bernard W:
Civil war and rebellion in the Roman empire, A.D. 69-70. '08(Je13) S°, *$2.60 net. Macmillan.

Henderson, C: Hanford.
Lighted lamp: a novel. '08(O10) c. D. †$1.50. Houghton M.

Henderson, C: Richmond, D.D.
Industrial insurance in the United States. '09(F13) c. O. *$2 net. Univ. of Chic.
Reasonable social policy for Christian people; pub. for the Social Service Committee of the Northern Baptist Convention. '09(Jl17) c. 12°, (Social service ser.) pap., 10 c. Am. Bapt.
Social duties from the Christian point of view. '09(Mr27) c. D. (Constructive Bible studies: Advanced and supplementary ser.) $1.25. Univ. of Chic.
—, ed. Correction and prevention. In 4 v. v. 1, Prison reform, ed. by C: Richmond Henderson, and Criminal law in the United States, by Eug. Smith; v. 2, Penal and reformatory institutions, by 16 leading authorities; v. 3, Preventive agencies and methods, by C: Richmond Henderson; v. 4, Preventive treatment of neglected children, by Hastings H. Hart; with special papers by leading authorities. '10(D24) c. il. pors. diagrs., O. (Russell Sage Foundation pubs.) ea., $2.50; per set, $10. Charities Pub.

Henderson, Ernest Flagg.
Lady of the old régime. '09(O23) c. il. pors. O. **$2.50 net. Macmillan.

Henderson, Ernest Norton.
Text-book on the principles of education. '10(D10) c. O. $1.75 net. Macmillan.

Henderson, Fk. L., M.D.
Lessons on the eye for undergraduate students. 4th ed., rev. '10(D) 13+238 p. il. 12°, $1.50. Blakiston.

Henderson, G. W., M.D.
English grammar by parallelism and comparison. '10(S17) c. D. 75 c. H. H. Henderson.

Henderson, Rev. H: F.
With Dante on the mountain; guide through the circles of the Purgatorio. '10 (D17) c. 12°, 75 c. Jennings.

Henderson, Ja. Darlington MacNary.
Oak amongst the pines and other poems. '10(F19) c. D. $1.50. Badger.

Henderson, J:
Electrotechnics. '10(F5) D. (Physical and electrical engineering lab'y manuals.) $1.20. Longmans.

Henderson, J:
Jamaica. '09(D25) il. map, (Peeps at many lands ser.) *75 c. net. Macmillan.

Henderson, Jos. Melville.
Onomatopoeia: [poems;] il. by Tom Brown. [1910.] (Je) c. 76 p. il. 16°, 50 c. Enterprise Pub.

Henderson, Percy E., ["Selim."]
British officer in the Balkans. '09(Mr13) il. map, O. *$3.50 net. Lippincott.

Henderson, Reuben Stewart.
Earthwork tables. '08(D26) f°, pap., $1. Engineering News.

Henderson, Thomson, M.D.
Glaucoma; inquiry into the physiology and pathology of intra-ocular pressure. '10 (O) 15+222 p. figs. O. $3 net. Longmans.

Henderson, Wa. G:
Norah Conough. '09(Ap17) c. D. $1.50. Outing.

Henderson, W: Ja.
See On the gridiron;—*also* Stevens, Rowan.

Hendrick, W. A.
Joysome hist. of education. '09(D) 35 c. Point of View.

Hendricks, Eldo Lewis.
History and civil government of Indiana. '08(Ag22) c. il. 12°, *40 c. net. Macmillan.
See also Ashley, Roscoe Lewis.

Hendrix, Bp. Eug. Russell.
Christ's table talk: study in the method of our Lord. '08(Jl4) 12°, *$1 net. Pub. Ho. of M. E. Ch., So.

Hendrix, Lily Eliz. Graves.
Gleanings; a book of poems. '08(O) c. 163 p. il. por. 12°, 75 c.; pap., 30 c. L. E. G. Hendrix.

HENEY, Francis Joseph.
Calhoun, P. Some facts regarding Francis J. Heney, Esq. gratis. United R. R. of S. F.

Hénin, Benjamin Louis Antoine.
French verb drill. '09(Ap3) bds., 35 c. W: R. Jenkins.

Henius, Jos.
Maisies' music. '10(D24) c. F. $1.25 net. Schirmer.

Henius, Max.
See Wahl, Rob.

Henke, F: Goodrich.
Study of the psychology of ritualism; dissertation submitted to the faculty of the Graduate School of Arts and Literature in candidacy for the degree of Doctor of Philosophy. '10(N19) c. 8°, pap., $1 net. Univ. of Chic.

Henkel, Alice.
American medicinal barks. '09(Ag) 59 p. il. 8°, (U. S., Dept. of Agriculture; Bu. of Plant Industry bull.) pap., 15 c.

Henland, Cecil.
Christmas book. '08(Ag15) 16°, *50 c. net. Jacobs.

Henley, W: Ernest.
London voluntaries and other poems. '10 (Jl16) 12°, (Lyric garland ser.) bds., 50 c.; Japan vellum, $1. T: B. Mosher.
Rhymes and rhythms and Arabian nights' entertainment. '09(D) 4°, (Lyric garland.) *50 c. net; Japan vellum, *$1 net. T: B. Mosher.

Henley school-boy ser. *See* Channon, Fk. E.

Henley's encyclopedia of practical engineering. Horner, J. G., *and others.* 5 v. ea., $6; per set, $25. Henley.

Henley's twentieth century book of receipts, formulas and processes. Hiscox, G. D., *ed.* $3; $4. Henley.

Henney, W: F.
Songs of the times. '10(Je18) c. 12°, $1. Cochrane.

Hennibique Construction Co. Hennibique armored concrete system, patented Oct. 4, 1898. '08(Ap) c. 95 p. il. 4°, pap., 50 c. Hennibique.

Henrich, Harrison Crockett.
Types of California beauties; photographic reproductions of sepia drawings. '10 (F26) c. il. 4°, $50. H. Heywood.

Henriques, H. S. Q.
Jews and the English law. '08(D5) 8°, *$3.50 net. Bloch.

HENRY IV., *King of France.*
Haggard, A. C: P. Amours of Henri de Navarre and of Marguerite de Valois. $4.50 net. Brentano's.
"Petit Homme Rouge," *pseud.* Favorites of Henry of Navarre. $3 net. Badger.
Sully, *Duc* de. Great design of Henry IV. **50 c. net. Ginn.

Henry VIII., King of England.
Assertio septem sacramentorum; or, defence of the seven sacraments; re-ed., with an introd., by Rev. L: O'Donovan; preface by His Eminence Ja. Cardinal Gibbons. '08(F29) c. O. *$2 net. Benziger.

HENRY VIII., *King of England.*
Froude, J. A. Henry VIII. 3 v. ea., *35 c. net; *70 c. net. Dutton.
Tree, *Sir* H. B. Henry VIII. and his court. 50 c. net. Cassell.

Henry, Agnes, [Mrs. C: Philip Henry.]
Skat made easy. '09(Ap3) c. S. **50 c. net. Jacobs.

Henry, Alfr. Judson.
Lightning and lightning conductors. '09 (O) 20 p. il. 8°, (U. S., Dept. of Agriculture; Farmers' bull.) (Add. Superintendent for price.) U. S., Supt. of Docs.

Henry, Mrs. C: Philip.
See Henry, Agnes.

Henry, G: Garr.
How to invest money. '08(My9) c. D. **75 c. net. Funk.

Henry, G: M., ed.
See Pennsylvania. Monaghan's cumulative annual digest.

Henry, G: W.
Hist. of the Jumpers; or, shouting, genuine and spurious; a hist. of the outward demonstrations of the spirit. '09(My) c. 379 p. il. pors. 12°, $1. Metropolitan Ch. Assoc.

Henry, J: Norman, M.D.
Nurse's handbook of medicine. 2d ed. '09 (Ap24) c. il. chart, D. **$1.50 net. Lippincott.

Henry, O., [pseud. for W: Sydney Porter.]
Four million. '10(D) 75 c. Burt.
Gentle grafter. '08(N14) c. il. D. †$1. McClure.
Let me feel your pulse; adventures in neurasthenia. '10(N5) c. S. (Little comic masterpieces.) 50 c. Doubleday, P.
Options. '09(N6) c. il. D. †$1.50. Harper.
Roads of destiny. '09(My15) c. D. †$1.50. Doubleday, P.
Strictly business; more stories of the four million. '10(Mr5) c. D. $1.20, fixed. Doubleday, P.
Voice of the city. '08(Je13) c. D. †$1. McClure.
Whirligigs. '10(O8) c. D. $1.20, fixed. Doubleday, P.

HENRY, William.
Jordan, F., *jr.* Life of William Henry of Lancaster, Pennsylvania, patriot, military officer, inventor of the steamboat. $1.25 net. Boulton Pub.

Henry, W: Arnon.
Feeds and feeding; hdbk. for the student and stockman. 10th ed., rev. and entirely rewritten. '10(D17) c. 8°, $2.25. W: A. Henry.

Henry Esmond. *See* Thackeray, W: Makepeace.

Henry in search of a wife. Courlander, A. $1.50. Brentano's.

Henry of Navarre. Devereux, W: 50 c. Knickerbocker Press.

Henry of Navarre. Wynne, M. †$1.50. Putnam.

Henry Phipps Institute. Fourth annual rept., for the study, treatment, and prevention of tuberculosis, 1906-1907; ed. by Jos. Walsh. '08(D) 430 p. (Add. pubs. for price.) Henry Phipps Inst.

HENS.
See Poultry.

Hensel, Harry C.
Knight of the twentieth century. '09(Jl10) c. O. bds., $1. H. C. Hensel.

Henshall, Ja. Alex., M.D.
Favorite fish and fishing. '08(My2) c. il. D. *$1.25 net. Outing.

Henshaw, Fred F.
See Stevens, J: Cyprian.

Henshaw, Helen Hinman.
Passing of the word. '10(Ap9) c. 12°, $1.50. Torch Press.

Henshaw, Nevil Gratiot.
Aline of the Grand Woods: story of Louisiana. '09(F20) c. O. $1.50. Outing.

Henslowe, E Colin.
See Behnke, Kate Emil.

Hensman, Howard, and Webb, Clarence.
When and where of famous men and women. '08(O10) Tt. (Miniature reference lib.) leath., 50 c. Dutton.

Henson, Canon Herbert Hensley.
Liberty of prophesying; Lyman Beecher lectures delivered 1909, and three sermons. '09(D18) c. D. *$1.50 net. Yale Univ.
National church: essays on its history and constitution: [Church of England]; with an introd. by the Rev. J. Llewelyn Davies. '08(F29) 8°, *$1.50 net. Macmillan.
Westminster sermons. '10(D) $1.25 net. Doran.

Henton, Ja.
Mystery of pain: book for the sorrowful. '10(D) front. 32°, (Ariel booklets.) leath., 75 c., boxed. Putnam.

Henty, G: Alfr.
Curse of Carnes' Hold. '08(Jl4) 12°, (Henty ser.) 50 c. Hurst.
Hidden foe. '08(Ag1) 12°, (Henty ser.) 50 c. Hurst.

Henty ser. *See* Henty, G: Alfr.

Hentz, J: P., D.D.
Hist. of the Lutheran version of the Bible. '10(O22) por. D. $1.25. J: P. Hentz.

Heortology. Kellner, K. A. H: *$3 net. Herder.

Hepburn, Alonzo Barton.
Artificial water-ways and commercial development, (with a history of the Erie Canal.) '09(Ja30) c. D. **$1 net. Macmillan.

Hepburn, W. Bruce.
Notes on dental metallurgy; for the use of dental students and practitioners. '10(D) 221 p. 12°, $2 net. Wood.

HEPBURN RATE LAW.
See Railroads.

HEPPLEWHITE FURNITURE.
See Furniture.

Hepworth, G: Hughes.
Hiram Golf's religion; or, the "shoemaker by the grace of God." '10(N5) c. il. 12°, $1.25. Dutton.

Hepworth, Melville Willis Campbell.
Notes on maritime meteorology. '08(Ag1) 12°, *$1.25 net. Van Nostrand.

Her book. Swan, M. M., *comp.* $2 net. Houghton M.

Her cave-man's letters. Swift, L. $1.25. Gillam's.

Her faithful knight. Cooke, W. B. $1.50. Cassell.

Her Highness; an Adirondack romance. '10 (O15) c. front. 12°, $1.50. Badger.

Her ladyship. Hinkson, *Mrs.* K. T. †$1.25. McClurg.

Her sacrifice. Mitchell, E. 50 c. Grafton Pub.

Her scarlet slippers. Thompson, A. C. 15 c. Penn Pub. Co.

Her strange marriage. Nelson, *Mrs.* D. 25 c. J. S. Ogilvie.

Her wedding night. Whiteside, G. K. 50 c. G. K. Whiteside.

Herakles. Lodge, G: C. **$1.25 net. Houghton M.

HERALDRY.
Eve, G: W. Decorative heraldry. *$2 net. Macmillan.

HERALDRY.—*Continued.*
Eve, G: W. Heraldry as art. *$5 net. Scribner.
Fox-Davies. A. C: Complete guide to heraldry. *$4 net. Dodge.
Milbourne, J. S. Heraldry for amateurs. $1.40. Scribner.
Pimbley, A. F. Dictionary of heraldry. A. F. Pimbley.
Zieber, E. Heraldry in America. $5. Bailey, B. & B.
See also Genealogy.

Heralds of a liberal faith. Eliot, S: A. 3 v. ea., *$1 net; per set, *$2.50 net. Am. Unitarian.

Heralds of the morning. Tait, A. O. $2; $3.50. Pacific Press.

Herb, Ferdinand, M.D.
Gonorrhea and sexual debility in men. '08 (Je6) c. il. 8°, $2.50. R & S Pub.

HERBALS.
See Decoration and ornament.

Herbermann, C: G., ed.
See Catholic encyclopedia.

Herbert, Agnes.
Isle of Man; with a foreword by A. W. Moore. '09(S11) il. O. *$3.50 net. Lane.

—, and "A Shikári," pseud.
Two Dianas in Alaska. '08(O24) il. O. *$4 net. Lane.

Herbert, Alice.
Measure of our youth. '09(Ap10) D. $1.50. Lane.

Herbert, Auberon.
Voluntaryist creed; being the Herbert Spencer lecture del. at Oxford, June 7, 1906, and A plea for voluntaryism. '08(N21) O. 80 c. Oxford Univ.

Herbert, Frances.
Visit of Humpty. '10(D) col. il. sq. 16°, 30 c. Jacobs.

Herbert, G:
Priest of the temple; or, the country parson; introd. and notes by the Rt. Rev. J. B. Cheshire. '08(O10) c. D. *75 c. net. Whittaker.
The temple: sacred poems; introd. by E: Thomas. '08(Mr7) 16°, (Everyman's lib.) *35 c. net; leath., *70 c. net. Dutton.

Herbert, H.
Cataract extraction. '08(D5) il. 8°, *$3.75 net. Wood.

Herbert, Lucas.
We preach Christ crucified: considerations and meditations for boys. '08(N21) 8°, *$1 net. Herder.

Herbert, Mrs. Nellie Candee Tucker.
Lyrics and idyls. '08(F1) c. D. $1.25. Badger.

Herbert, S.
First principles of heredity. '10(N19) il. 8°, $1.75 net. Macmillan.

Herbert Spencer lecture. *See* Spencer (Herbert) lecture.

Herbertson, Agnes Grozier.
Heroic legends: stories of St. George and the dragon, Robin Hood, Richard and Blondel, and other legends. '08(D12) il. 8°, $2. Caldwell.

Herbertson, And. J.
Physiographical introd. to geography. '10 (Ag27) il. maps, D. (Oxford geographies.) 40 c. Oxford Univ.

—, and Fanny Louisa Dorothea Richardson.
Senior geography. 3d ed. '10(My21) maps, D. (Oxford geographies.) 75 c. Oxford Univ.

—, and Jowett, Lettice, eds.
British Isles; descriptive geography from orig. sources. '10(F19) il. 12°, *75 c. net. Macmillan.

Herbertson, Fanny Louisa Dorothea Richardson.
Elementary geography. v. 1, A first physiography; v. 2, In and about our islands. '09(D4); v. 3, Europe, excluding the British Isles. '09(S11) ea., 30 c.; v. 4, Asia. '10(Ja1); v. 7, The British Isles. (Ja22) il. maps, D. (Oxford geographies; ed. by A. J. Herbertson.) v. 4, 40 c.; v. 7, 60 c. Oxford Univ.
See also Herbertson, And. J.

Herbs and apples. Whitney, *Mrs.* H. H. $1.25 net. Lane.

HERCULANEUM, Italy.
Barker, E. R. Buried Herculaneum. *$3 net. Macmillan.
Waldstein, C:, *and* Shoobridge, L. Herculaneum: past, present and future. *$5 net. Macmillan.

HERCULES (*god*).
Winter, J: G. Myth of Hercules at Rome. 50 c. net. Macmillan.

Herd (The). Ward, J. O. P. $1.50. Cochrane.

HERDER, Johann Gottfried von.
See Weimar.

Herders konversations-lexikon. 3 aufl., reich illustriert durch textabbildungen, tafeln und karten. '08(Ap11) 8 v., il. por. maps, plans, facsim., tabs., 4°, *$28 net. Herder.

Here then is a preachment. Hubbard, E. 10 c. Roycrofters.

Hereafter (The). Paul, J: H. 50 c. Pentecostal.

Heredia, José-Maria de.
Les trophées (the sonnets); tr. by H: Johnson. '10(D31) c. 12°, $1.75. F. W. Chandler.

HEREDITY.
Bateson, W: Mendel's principles of heredity. *$3.50 net.—Methods and scope of genetics. 50 c. Putnam.
Cannon, W: A. Studies in heredity. (Add. Institution for price.) Carnegie.
Castle, W: E., *and others.* Studies of inheritance in rabbits. 75 c. Carnegie.
Darbishire, A. D. Breeding and the Mendelian discovery. $1.75 net. Cassell.
De Vries, H. Intracellular pangenesis, incl. a paper on fertilization and hybridization. $3. Open Court.
Fowler, O. S., *and* Niles, L. Hereditary descent, its laws and facts applied to human improvements. (Add. pubs. for price.) Fowler & W.
Guyer, M. F. Deficiencies of the chromosome theory of heredity. Univ. of Cin.
Herbert, S. First principles of heredity. $1.75 net. Macmillan.

HEREDITY.—*Continued.*
Influence of heredity on disease. *$1.50 net. Longmans.
Lock, R. H. Recent progress in the study of variation, heredity and evolution. $2 net. Dutton.
Moore, A. R. Biochemical conception of dominance. pap. Univ. of Cal.
Ott, E: A. "Sour grapes"; or, heredity and marriage. $1. Lyceumite.
Punnett, R. C. Mendelism. 50 c. Wilshire Bk.
Reid, G: A. O. Laws of heredity. $5.50 net. Macmillan.
Spillman, W: J. Application of some principles of heredity to plant breeding. Gov. Pr. Off.
Thompson, J: A. Heredity. *$3.50 net. Putnam.
Walker, C: E. Hereditary characters and their modes of transmission. $2.40 net. Longmans.
See also Biology;—Eugenics;—Evolution;—Poultry;—Rodents;—Silk-worms.

Hereford, W: R:
The demagog. '09(N20) c. D. †$1.50. Holt.

Hereford. Sparrow, *Mrs.* M. D. $1. Badger.

Herein! Allen, P. S., *ed.* 70 c. Holt.

Here's to you. Alderson, W: A., *comp.* $1.25; $2. Dodge.

Heretics and heresies. *See* Ingersoll, Rob. Green. Humboldt.

Hereward, the Wake. *See* Kingsley, C:

Herford, Beatrice Brooke, [Mrs. Sidney Willard Hayward.]
Monologues. '08(My16) c. D. $1.25. Scribner.

Herford, Oliver.
Simple jography; or, how to know the earth and why it spins, by Peter Simple, F. T. G., (Fellow of the Terrestrial Globe.) '08(N14) c. D. $1. J: W. Luce.
See also Molnar, Ferenc;—Mumford, Ethel Watts-.

—, and Clay, J: Cecil, comps.
Cupid's almanac and guide to hearticulture, for this year and next. '08(O3) c. il. nar. O. bds., **90 c. net. Houghton M.
Cupid's cyclopedia; comp. for Daniel Cupid. '10(O1) c. il. in col. S. bds., $1 net. Scribner.

—, and Collins, Sewell.
Smoker's year book. '08(D19) c. il. 8°, **$1 net. Moffat.

—, Mumford, Ethel Watts-, [now Mrs. Grant,] and Mizner, Addison.
Complete cynic; being bunches of wisdom culled from the calendars of Oliver Herford, Ethel Watts Mumford, Addison Mizner '10(Jl30) c. col. il. 12°, 75 c. P. Elder.

Heritage, Lizzie.
Cassell's household cookery; with an introd. by J. L. W. Thudichum. '09(Ag) il., $1.50. Cassell.

Heritage (Un). Sandeau, J. 60 c. Oxford Univ.

Heritage of the desert. Grey, Z. $1.50. Harper.

Herkomer, Sir Hubert von.
The Herkomers. '10(N19) il. 8°, $2.50 net. Macmillan.
My school and my gospel. '08(Ag22) il. Q. *$7.50 net. Doubleday, P.

Herman, G: Ernest.
Difficult labor; guide to its management, for students and practitioners. 5th rev. ed. '10(Jl) 569 p. il. 12°, $2.50 net. Wood.
Student's hdbk. of gynecology. '08(Je6) il. 12°, *$2.50 net. Wood.

Hermann, H: Bernard Meyer, comp.
Library of Congress list of works rel. to the Supreme Court of the United States. '09(Jl17) Q. pap., 20 c. U. S., Supt. of Docs.

Hermann und Dorothea. *See* Goethe, Johann Wolfgang v.

Hermannsson, Halldór.
See Islandica.

Hermit and the wild woman. Wharton, *Mrs.* E. N. J. †$1.50. Scribner.

Hermit of Capri. Tarkington, J: S. $1.25. Harper.

HERNDON, William Henry.
Newton, J. F. Lincoln and Herndon. $3. Torch Press.

HERNIA.
Eccles, W: M. Hernia: its etiology, symptoms and treatment. *$2.50 net. Wood.
Miller, C: C. Cure of rupture by paraffin injections. C: C. Miller.
Murray, R. W. Hernia; its cause and treatment. $1.75. Blakiston.

Hero and Leander. *See* Marlowe, Christopher.—Schütze, M.

Hero-myths and legends of the British race. Ebbutt, M. I. $2 net. Crowell.

Hero of Pigeon Camp. Doyle, *Mrs.* M. C. M. †$1.25. Lothrop, L. & S.

Hero of Sedan. Brereton, F: S. $1.25. Caldwell.

Hero of Trent. Isaac, E. M. 75 c. Chr. Witness.

Hero ser.. il. 8°, $1.50 net. Lippincott.
—Dawson. Heroines of missionary adventure.
—Gilliatt. Heroes of Elizabethan England.
—Heroes of modern crusades.
—Wright. Adventures among the red Indians.

Hero tales from American life. Miller, F. T. $1. Chr. Herald.

Hero tales of the far North. Riis, J. A. $1.35 net. Macmillan.

Herodotus.
Herodoti historiae; recognovit brevique adnotatione critica instruxit. v. 1. '08 (O24); v. 2. '09(My15) D. (Scriptorum classicorum bibliotheca Oxoniensis.) ea., $1.10. Oxford Univ.
[Histories:] books VII. and VIII.; ed., with introd. and notes, by C: Forster Smith and Arth. Gordon Laird. '08(O24) c. front. D. (Greek ser. for colleges and schools.) $1.75.—*Same.* Text ed. pap., 40 c. Am. Bk.
[Histories:] seventh, eighth and ninth books: tr., with introd., text, apparatus, commentary, appendices, maps by Reginald W. Mecan. In 2 v. v. 1 in 2 pts. '08(Je6) 8°, *$9 net. Macmillan.
History; tr. from the ancient Greek by G: Rawlinson. [Olympic ed.] '09(D18) c. il. 8°, (Historians of Greece.) $14. Tandy-T.
Rawlinson's Herodotus; ed. by E. H. Blakeney. In 2 v. '10(Ap23) 16°, (Everyman's lib.) ea., 35 c. net; leath., 70 c. net. Dutton.

HEROES.
Carlyle, T: Lectures on heroes, hero-worship, and the heroic in history. 50 c. Oxford Univ.
Carlyle, T: Sartor resartus, and Heroes and hero worship. *35 c. net; *70 c. net. Dutton.
Davis, *Mrs.* O. S. Hero tales. $1.25 net. Pilgrim Press.
Gates, H. W. Heroes of the faith. 50 c. Bible Study.
Gilliat, E: Heroes of Elizabethan England. $1.50 net. Lippincott.
Kingsley, C: The heroes. 50 c.; $2.50. Dutton.
Kingsley, C: The heroes. 50 c. Stokes.
Kingsley, C: The heroes; Greek fairy tales for my children. $1. Sturgis & W.
Lang, L. B. Red book of heroes. *$1.60 net. Longmans.
Miller. F. T. Hero tales from American life. $1. Chr. Herald.
Renninger, E. D. Story of Rustem and other Persian hero tales from Firdusi. **$1.50 net. Scribner.
Tappan, E. M. European hero stories. **65 c. net. Houghton M.
See also Explorers;—India;—Missions and missionaries;—Mythology;—Saints;—*also* Wagner, Wilhelm Richard.

Heroes and crises of early Hebrew history from the creation to the death of Moses. Kent, C: F. **$1 net. Scribner.

Heroes and greathearts. Dale, J: T., *comp.* $1. Fairfax.

Heroes and happenings of Egypt, Assyria, Greece. Myers, S. E. 80 c. S. E. Myers.

Heroes and martyrs of faith. Peake, A. S: $1.50 net. Doran.

Heroes in gray. Sherrill, S: W. 30 c. C. J. Bell.

Heroes of American history. *See* Ober, F: Albion.

Heroes of California. James, G: W. $2 net. Little, B. & Co.

Heroes of England. Edgar, J: A: 35 c. net; 70 c. net. Dutton.

Heroes of insurgency. Dreier, T: 50 c. Human Life.

Heroes of Israel. *See* Bible. O. T.

Heroes of modern crusades. Gilliat, E: *$1.50 net. Lippincott.

Heroes of modern India. Gilliat, E: $1.50. Lippincott.

Heroes of the nations ser.; ed. by E. A. Abbott. il. D. **$1.35 net; hf. leath., **$1.60 net. Putnam.
—MacNutt. Fernando Cortes.
—Putnam. Charles the Bold.
—Stenton. William the Conqueror.

Heroes of the polar seas. Maclean, J. K. $1.50. Lippincott.
Heroic legends. Herbertson, A. G. $2. Caldwell.
Heroic life and exploits of Siegfried. Madeley, D. F. $1.50. Crowell.
Heroic (A) priest. Boyton, *Mrs.* P., *comp.* $1. G: C. Tilyou.
Heroic Spain. O'Reilly, E. B. $2.50 net. Duffield.
Heroine (The). Barrett, E. S. 90 c. Oxford Univ.
Heroine of the strait. Crowley, M. C. †75 c. Little, B. & Co.
Heroines of a school room. Tannenforst, W. †$1.25. Winston.
Heroines of missionary adventure. Dawson, *Rev.* E. C. *$1.50 net. Lippincott.
Heroines that every child should know. Mabie, H. W., *ed.* **90 c. net; **$1.50 net. Doubleday, P.

Heron, Ja., D.D.
Short history of Puritanism. '08(D19) 16°, *50 c. net. Scribner.

Heron-Allen, E:
Manual of cheirosophy; by means whereof the past, the present, and the future may be read in the formations of the hands, preceded by an introd. argument upon the science of cheirosophy and its claims to rank as a physical science. '08(D19) il. D. $1.75. Putnam.

Herr, Horace Dumont.
The tenters; mountain-side stories told in verse. '09(F13) c. il. S. wood veneer, *50 c. net. A. M. Adams.

Herr, Thdr. Witmer, comp.
Genealogical record of Rev. Hans Herr and his direct lineal descendants from his birth, A.D. 1639, to the present time; containing the names, etc., of 13,223 persons. '08(N) 12+785 p. il. pors. 8°, $10; lineal descent, $5. T. W. Herr.

HERR FAMILY.
See Genealogies.

Herrick, Clay.
How to increase the business of a trust company. '08(Ja18) sq. 24°, (Bankers handy ser.) bd's., 50 c. Bankers Pub.
Trust companies, their organization, growth and management. '09(S11) c. 8°, hf. leath., *$4 net. Bankers Pub.

Herrick, Myron T.
Guarantee of bank deposits: address before Nebraska Bankers' Association at Lincoln, Neb., Sept. 25, 1908. '09(Je) 19 p. 8°, gratis. M. T. Herrick.

Herrick, Rob., 1591-1674.
Hesperides, and Noble numbers; introd. by Ernest Rhys. '08(Mr7) 16°, (Everyman's lib.) *35 c. net; leath., *70 c. net. Dutton.

HERRICK, Robert, 1591-1674.
Moorman, F. W: Robert Herrick. $5 net. Lane.

Herrick, Rob., 1868-.
The common lot. '08(N7) 12°, $1.50. Macmillan.
Gospel of freedom. '08(N7) 12°, $1.50. Macmillan.
Jock O' Dreams. '08(N7) 12°, $1.50. Macmillan.

Herrick, Rob., 1868.—*Continued.*
Life for a life. '10(Je11) c. D. $1.50. Macmillan.
Master of the inn. '08(My2) c. D. bds., **50 c. net. Scribner.
Memoirs of an American citizen. '08(N7) il. 12°, $1.50. Macmillan.
Together. '08(Jl18) D. †$1.50. Macmillan.
Web of life. '08(N7) 12°, $1.50. Macmillan.

Herrick, S:
Manual of the U. S. homestead and other public land laws. '09, [1910.] (F) 227 p. D. pap., 50 c. A. Harriman.
Formerly published by the Ivy Press.

Herrick, Mrs. Sophia McIlvaine Bledsoe.
Public school physiology; perversion of truth and science in the name of temperance. '08, [1909.] (My) 8 p. 16°, pap., gratis. U. S. Brewers' Assoc.

Herridge, W: T:, D.D.
Coign of vantage: [essays.] '08(O10) c. 16°, *$1 net. Revell.

Herring, Paul.
Dragon's silk. '08(My16) front. D. $1.50. Cassell.

Herring, W. R.
Granton gas works of the Edinburgh and Leith Corporations. '08(Jl4) il. f°, *$6.50 net. Spon.

Herringshaw, T: W:, and others.
National lib. of American biography; contains 35,000 biographies of the acknowledged leaders of life and thought of the United States. 5 v. [1910.] (Ap) c. il. pors. 8°, ea., $10. Am. Pub. Assoc.

Herriott, Hallie Irene.
Jungle jingle book. [1910.] (D) c. 50 p. il. 16°, 25 c. Carnahan.

Herrman, H.
French method of intensive cultivation and asparagus forcing; treatise on the French method of gardening. '10(Je) c. 9-50 p. il. 8°, $1. H: L. Freking.

Herrmann, Gustav.
See Weisbach, Julius.

Herron, W. W.
See Texas.—Supp. to Sayles' annot. civil statutes.—Supp. to Willson's annot.

Herschel, Bouton Lazell, rep.
See Michigan. *Sup. ct.* Repts.

Herschell, G: Arieh.
Soured milk and pure cultures of lactic acid bacilli in the treatment of disease. '09(N) 4+36 p. front. 8°, *50 c. net. Chic. Med. Bk.

Hersey, Fk. Wilson Cheney, comp. and ed.
See **Copeland, C: Townsend.**

Herter, Christian Archibald, M.D.
Imagination and idealism in the medical sciences. '10(Mr) (Not for sale.) Am. Medical.
On infantilism from chronic intestinal infection, characterized by the overgrowth and persistence of flora of the nursling period: study of the clinical course, bacteriology, chemistry and therapeutics of arrested development in infancy. '08 (D5) 12°, *90 c. net. Macmillan.

HERTFORDSHIRE, Eng.
Lydekker, R: **Hertfordshire.** 45 c. Putnam.

Hertiginnan of Finland. Topelius, Z. $1; 75 c. Engberg-H.

Hertwig, Oscar, and Campbell, H: Johnstone.
The cell: outlines of general anatomy and physiology. '09(Ap3) il. 8°, *$2.25 net. Macmillan.

Herty, C: Holmes.
Per cent. tables for oil in cottonseed products, with method of analysis. '08(O) 50 p. 8°, $2. C: H. Herty.

Hervey, Wa. Lowrie.
Picture work. '08(F15) c. 16°, pap., *30 c. net. Revell.

—, and Hix, Melvin.
First reader. '09(Ap10) c. il. D. (Horace Mann readers.) 30 c. Longmans.
Primer. '08(F15) il. D. (Horace Mann readers.) 30 c. Longmans.
Second reader. '09(S11) c. il. D. (Horace Mann readers.) 40 c. Longmans.
Third reader. '10(N19) c. il. (partly in color.) D. (Horace Mann readers.) 48 c. Longmans.

HERZEGOVINA.
Holbach, *Mrs.* M. M. Bosnia and Herzegovina. *$1.50 net. Lane.

Herzog, Johann Jakob.
See New Schaff-Herzog encyclopedia.

Herzog, Maximilian Jos., M.D.
Text-book on disease-producing microörganisms, especially intended for the use of veterinary students and practitioners. '10(D) c. 11+644 p. il. 8°, $4.75 net. Lea.
See also Robertson, W:

Herzogenberg, Elisabet v. and Heinrich v.
See Brahms, Johannes.

Hesiod.
Poems and fragments; done into English prose, with introd. and appendices, by A. W. Mair. '08(D19) D. $1. Oxford Univ.

Hesketh-Prichard, Hesketh Vernon.
See Prichard, Hesketh Vernon Hesketh-.

Hesper-phosphor. Scholl, J: W. 75 c. Wahr.

Hesperides. Herrick, R. *35 c. net; *70 c. net. Dutton.

Hesperides. Pomroy, G: 80 c. G: Pomroy.

Hess, Fk. Lee.
Magnesite deposits of California. '09(Mr6) il. map, 8°, (U. S. Dept. of the Interior, Geol. Survey, bull.) (Add. Superintendent for price.) U. S., Supt. of Docs.

Hess, Mrs. Gertrude Fox, comp.
List of books for teachers in the Seattle Public Library. '10(S) 22 p. 12°, (Seattle Public Lib.: reference list.) pap., gratis. Seattle Pub. Lib.

Hess, Harold Miner.
Philosophy and methods of operation of the analytic system for the measurement of relative fire hazard (mercantile classes) papers read before the Fire Insurance Club of Chicago, 1908-09. '09(O9) c. il. tabs., 12°, pap., gratis. H. M. Hess.

Hess, T:
Jonathan and Hannah Steelman; family tree or record of the descendants of their four children. '10(My) c. 176 p. il. pors. 8°, $3.50. T: Hess.

HESS FAMILY.
See Genealogies: Babcock, W: E.

Hessian (The). Marble, T: L. 15 c. Penn Pub. Co.

Hessling, Bruno.
See Behrens, C.

Hessling, Egon and Waldemar.
Louis XIV. furniture in the Louvre and the Museum of Decorative Arts (Paris). '09(Je19) il. f°, $13.40. Hessling.

—, ed. Louis XV. furniture in the Museum of Decorative Art at Paris. '10(Ag6) il. f°, (in portfolio,) $12. Hessling.
Renaissance furniture; masterpieces of old French furniture, art, carpentry, and decorative wood work from the collection of the Musee de Cluny. '10(Ag6) il. f°, (in portfolio,) $21. Hessling.

—, and Waldemar, eds.
Applied bronze work in the style Louis XVI; collection of documents and photographs after the orig. pieces in the Musée des Arts Decoratifs of Paris. '10(Ap16) il. 4°, $8. Hessling.

Hessling, Waldemar.
See Hessling, Egon.

Hester ser. *See* Baird, Jean Katherine.

Hester's counterpart. Baird, J. K. $1.20. Lothrop, L. & S.

Heston, Winifred, M.D.
A bluestocking in India; her medical wards and messages. '10(Jl16) c. $1 net. Revell.

HETEROPTERA.
See Insects.

Hettich, Lola Burks, ed.
Priscilla crochet book. '08(Mr.) c. 48 p. il. 8°, pap., 25 c. Priscilla.

Hevor, the Gaul. Timayenis, T. T: 50 c. T. T: Timayenis.

Heward, E: Vincent.
St. Nicotine. '09(My22) 12°, *$1.50 net. Dutton.

Hewett, Edg. Lee.
Ancient ruins of the Southwest. '09, [1910.] (Ap) c. 24 p. il. maps, 8°. Denver & Rio Grande.

Hewitt, C: E:
The spirit of Penn. '09(Jl3) front. 12°, $1. J. S. Ogilvie.

Hewitt, Mrs. Emma Churchman.
How to live on a small income. '09(Jl10) c. S. 50 c. Jacobs.
How to train children. '08(Jl18) c. S. 50 c. Jacobs.

Hewitt, W:
Bleichert system of aerial tramways; reversible aerial tramways; aerial tramways of special design. '09(D18) c. il. 8°, gratis. Trenton Iron Co.

Hewitt, W: P. H., ed.
Hist. of the diocese of Syracuse, established 1886; with an introd. by the Rt. Rev. Mgr. J. S. M. Lynch; Story of the parishes, 1615-1909, ed. by W: P. H. Hewitt. '09, [1910.] (Mr) c. 5-67 p. 8°, $2. W. P. H. Hewitt.

Hewlett, Graham.
Sea terms and phrases, English-Spanish: Spanish-English; términos marítimos, inglés-español: español-inglés. '08, [1909.] (O) 368 p. fold tab., 32°, *$1.25 net. Lippincott.

Hewlett, Maurice H:
Artemision: idylls and songs. '09(Ap24) S. *$1 net. Scribner.
Halfway House. '08(Je27) c. D. †$1.50. Scribner.
Letters to Sanchia upon things as they are; extracted from the correspondence of Mr. John Maxwell Senhouse. '10 (My14) c. D. 90 c. net. Scribner.
Open country: a comedy with a sting. '09 (S11) c. D. †$1.50. Scribner.
Rest harrow; comedy of resolution. '10 (S3) c. il. D. $1.50. Scribner.
Ruinous face. '09(O23) c. il O. †$1. Harper.
Sacrifice at Prato; an old-fashioned narrative. '08(N) c. 22 p. il. 16°, $2.50. Hillside.
Spanish jade. '08(My16) c. il. D. **90 c. net. Doubleday, P.

HEWLETT, Maurice Henry.
Bronner, M. Maurice Hewlett; being a critical review of his prose and poetry. $1.25 net. J: W. Luce.

Heydecker, Christian T.
Genealogy of Samuel Gourley and his descendants, 1784-1909; and acct. of Gourley re-union, 1908. '10(Ja8) c. il. por. 8°, 75 c. C. T. Heydecker.

Heydrick, B: Alex.
One year course in English and American literature; with reading lists and references for further study. '09(Mr27) c. il. pors. 12°, $1. Hinds.

Heyl, Rev. Fs.
Battle of Germantown. '09(D) 41-64 p. il. (City Hist. Society of Philadelphia pub.) 25 c. (Sold to members only.) City Hist., Phil.

Heylin, H: Brougham.
Cotton weaver's handbook. '08(Jl18) il. D. *$2.50 net. Lippincott.

Heyny, W:
Modern lettering, artistic and practical. '10 (Ja8) c. obl. D. $2. W: T. Comstock.

Heyse, Paul Johann Ludwig.
Anfang und ende; ed., with introd., notes, exercises, and vocab., by A. Busse. '10 (F5) c. por. S. (International modern language ser.) 35 c. Ginn.
Anfang und ende; novelle; ed., with exercises, notes, and vocab., by Lawrence A. McLouth. '10(D17) c. 16°, 40 c. Holt.
Er soll dein herr sein; ed., with introd., notes, exercises and vocab., by Martin H. Haertel. '08(Ag22) c. S. 30 c. Am. Bk.

Heyser, O. E.
Mermaid of the magic city. '08(D12) 12°, 75 c. Cochrane.

Heysinger, I: Winter, M.D.
Spirit and matter before the bar of modern science. '10(Je4) O. $3.75 net. Lippincott.

Heywood, Edna Eliz.
Fifty common birds around the capital, [Topeka, Kan.] '09(Jl) c. 64 p. 12°, 25 c. Crane.

Heywood, Fk.
See Hall, Arnold.

Heywood, J: W.
Hints on exporting; suggestions for the guidance of millers and others who wish to embark in the export trade. 8th ed. '10(Ap) c. 75 p. il. tabs., 8°. (Not for sale.) Northwestern Miller.

Heywood, W:
History of Perugia; ed. by R. Langton Douglas. '10(My) il. map, (fold.,) O. (Historic states of Italy.) $3.50 net. Putnam.

Hiawatha. *See* **Longfellow, H: Wadsworth.**

Hiawatha alphabet. Holbrook, F. 75 c. Rand, McN. & Co.

Hiawatha entertainments. Schell, S., *ed.* 35 c. Werner.

Hiawatha's black-robe. Leahy, E. 35 c. net. Herder.

Hibben, J: Grier.
Philosophy of the enlightenment. '10 (Mr26) c. O. (Epochs of philosophy.) **$1.50 net. Scribner.

Hibbert, E.
See Knecht, Edm.

Hibbert, Wa.
Popular electricity. '09(Je12) il. *$1.25 net. Cassell.

Hibbert lectures. *See* James, W:

Hichborn, Franklin.
Story of the session of the California legislature of 1909. '09(O2) tabs., $1.25. Barry.

Hichens, Rob. Smythe.
Bella Donna. '09(O23) c. D. †$1.50. Lippincott.
Egypt and its monuments. '08(N7) c. il. Q. **$6 net, boxed. Century Co.
Green carnation. '08(Mr28) c. 8°, $1. M. Kennerley.
The Holy Land. '10(O29) c. il. Q. $6 net. Century Co.
Spirit in prison. '08(S19) c. il. D. †$1.75. Harper.

Hickey, Fk. S., comp.
See Coyle, H:

Hickey, Ja. H., ed.
See New York [State.] **Digested treatise** and compendium of law.

Hickling, G:
Geology. '10(S) il. diagrs., 16°, (Twentieth century science ser.) 50 c. net. Stokes.

Hickman, Albert.
Unofficial love story. '09(N6) c. il. D. †$1. Century Co.

Hickman, Stella Hadley, comp.
Golden treasury from gifted minds, selected and arranged by Stella Hadley Hickman. [1910.] (My) c. '09. 111 p. por. 12°, $1. B'way Pub.

Hickory limb. Fillmore, P. H. 50 c. net. Lane.

Hickox, W: Eug.
Correspondent's manual for stenographers, typewriter operators, and clerks. Rev. and enl. ed. '09(Mr13) c. S. 50 c. Lothrop, L. & S.

Hicks, F: C:
Equality of the states and the Hague conferences. '08(D5) Q. pap. (Add. author for price.) **F: C: Hicks.**

Hicks, I: Perry.
Builders' guide; comprising an easy, pract. system of estimating material and labor for carpenters, contractors and builders. Rev. and enl. '10(Je18) il. $1. D: Williams.
Building plans and how to draw them; pract. lessons on architectural drawing. 3d ed. '09(Jl31) c. il. sq. 8°, 50 c. Indust.
Estimator's price book and pocket companion. Rev. and enl. ed. '10(D17) tabs., 16°, $1. D: Williams.
Simple treatise on architectural perspective for beginners. '09(Jl31) c. il. sq. 8°, 50c. Indust.

Hicks, J:
Something about Singlefoot; chapters in the life of an Oshkosh man. '10,(My14) c. 12°, $1.50. Cochrane.

Hicks, J: Solomon Soules.
Divine time table. '10(Mr5) c. S. 50 c. pap., 30 c. J: S. S. Hicks.

Hicks, Reese Victor, comp. and ed.
Tricks of the poultry trade. Rev. ed. '10(S) 61 p. il. 8°, 50 c. Poultry Culture.

Hicks, Rob. Drew.
Stoic and Epicurean. '10(Mr26) c. O. (Epochs of philosophy.) **$1.50 net. Scribner.

Hicks, Warren E.
Champion spelling book for public and private schools. '09(My22). In 2 pts. (Jl31) c. D. ea., 18 c. Am. Bk.

Hicks, Rev. W:
Bible thoughts; with questions and answers. 2d ed. '08(O) 87 p. S. pap., 25 c. Nat. Bapt. Pub.

Hicks at college. Dyar, R. E. 25 c. Dramatic.

HIDALGO Y COSTILLO, **Miguel.**
Noll, A. H., *and* McMahon, A. P. Life and times of Miguel Hidalgo y Costilla. $1 net. McClurg.

HIDATSA INDIANS.
See Indians.

Hidden, Julia A.
Garden game, and other songs. '09(Jl31) bds., 75 c. M. Bradley.

Hidden chains; [tr.] from the German by C. Thdr. Benze. '10(Jl30) c. D. $1.50. Erie Pr.

Hidden foe. Henty, G: A. 50 c. Hurst.

Hidden life. Orr, C: E. 60 c. Gospel Trumpet Co.

Hidden princess. Jackson, F. $1.50. Jacobs.

Hidden signatures of Francesco Colonna and Francis Bacon. Booth, W: S. $1.50 net. W. A. Butterfield.

Hidden water. Coolidge, D. $1.35 net. McClurg.

Hide and seek in Forestland. Chambers, R. W. **40 c. net. Appleton.

HIDES.
See Leather.

HIERAPETRA (*Isthmus of*).
See Crete (*Island of*).

Hiero-Salem. Mason, *Mrs.* E. L. $2. E. L. Mason.

Hierro, Baltasar del.
Libro y primera parte, delos victoriosos hechos del muy valeroso cavallero dom Alvaro del Baça; señor delas villas d'l Uifo, y fãcta Cruz. [facsim.] '03, [1909.] (N) no paging, 8°, $7. (200 copies.) Hispanic Soc.

Higby, Clinton D.
Government of Pennsylvania and the nation. '08, [1909.] (Ja) c. 4+241 p. il. 12°, 70 c. Heath.

Higgins, Aileen Cleveland.
Dream blocks. '08(O17) c. il. 4°, $2. Duffield.
Little princess of the pines. '10(D3) c. il. D. $1.25. Penn Pub. Co.
Little princess of Tonopah. '09(N13) il. D. †$1.25. Penn Pub. Co.
Thekla: a drama. '08(Mr14) c. 12°, $1. Badger.

Higgins, Alex. Pearce.
Hague Peace Conferences and other international conferences concerning the laws and usages of war; texts of conventions with commentaries. '10(D) 14+632 p. 8°, $5 net. Putnam.

Higgins, Anthony.
Historical address delivered before the "Friends of Old Drawyers" Presbyterian Church, near Odessa, Del., on Sunday, June 7, A.D. 1908, at the two hundredth anniversary of the establishment of the congregation. '09(Ap17) por. O. (Papers of the Historical Society of Delaware.) pap., 40 c. Delaware Hist. Soc.

Higgins, C:, ed.
See La Salle Extension Univ. encyclop.

Higgins, C: M.
Brooklyn's neglected battle ground. '10 (Ag6) c. il. O. pap., 35 c. Witter & K.

Higgins, D: Williams.
Mystic spring, and other tales of western life. New and rev. ed. '09(Ja2) il. 12°, $1.50. B'way Pub.

HIGGINS, *Rev.* Francis Edmund.
Duncan, N. Higgins; a man's Christian. 50 c. Harper.

Higgins, G: H:, and Haffey, Mrs. Marg. Higgins.
Tract number 3377; romance of the oil region. '09(D) c. 382 p. il. 12°, $1.50. C. M. Clark.

Higgins, Lothrop Davis.
Simple experiments in physics. [1910.] (My) c '09. 6+114 p. il. 12°, 35 c. Ginn.

Higgins, Myrta Marg.
Little gardens for boys and girls. '10 (Mr19) il. D. **$1.10 net. Houghton M.

Higginson, Alex. H:, and Chamberlain, Julian Ingersoll.
Hunts of the United States and Canada; their masters, hounds and histories. '08 (D19) c. il. pors. 8°, subs., *$10 net; limited ed., ¾ mor., $30. F. L. Wiles.

Higginson, Mrs. Ella Rhoades.
Alaska, the great country. '08(D5) c. il. map, D. $2.50. Macmillan.

Higginson, Fs.
New England's plantation, with the Sea Journal and other writings. '09(Mr) 133 p. 8°, bds. (Not for sale.) Essex Bk.

Higginson, T: Wentworth.
Carlyle's laugh and other surprises. '09 (N13) c. D. **$2 net. Houghton M.
Things worth while. '08(My9) c. D. (Art of life ser.) *50 c. net. B: W. Huebsch.
See also Hart, Albert Bushnell.

High, Ja. L.
Treatise on the law of receivers. 4th ed., by Shirley T. High. '10(Ap) c. O. $7.50. Callaghan.

High adventure. De Sélincourt, H. †$1.50. Lane.
High Albania. Durham, M. E. *$4 net. Longmans.
High calling. Jowett, J. H. *$1.25 net. Revell.
High chair. Cooke, E. V. $1. Dodge.
High Court of Parliament. McIlwain, C: H. $2.50 net. Yale Univ.
High frequency currents. Crook, H. E. *$2 net. Wood.
High-frequency currents. Strong, F: F. *$3 net. Rebman.
High frequency electric currents. Monell, S: H. *$4 net. W: R. Jenkins.
High history of the Holy Graal; [by Perceval le Gallois;] tr. by Dr. Sebastian Evans. '10(Ap23) 16°, (Everyman's lib.) 35 c. net; leath., 70 c. net. Dutton.
High masonry dam design. Morrison, C: E: $1.50. Wiley.
High priest and sacrifice. Du Bose, W: P. **$1.50 net. Longmans.
High school boys ser. *See* Hancock, Harrie Irving.
High school course in Latin composition. Baker, C: M. $1. Macmillan.
High school girl ser. il. 12°. Altemus.
—Flower. Grace Harlow's plebe year at high school. $1.
High school song book. Zeiner, E. J. A., *comp.* *85 c. net. Macmillan.
High school word book. Sandwick, R: L. 40 c. Heath.

HIGH SCHOOLS.
See Schools.

High-speed dynamo electric machinery. Hobart, H: M. **$6 net. Wiley.
High-speed steel. Becker, O. M. $4. McGraw-H.
High steam pressures in locomotive service. Goss, W: F. M. $1.25. Carnegie.
High-tension underground electric cables. Floy, H: $2. Elec. Pub.

HIGHER CRITICISM (*of the Bible*).
Day, T: F. New Bible-country. 30 c. Crowell.
Duff, A. Hist. of Old Testament criticism. 75 c. net. Putnam.
McGarvey, J: W: Short essays in Biblical criticism. $1.50. Standard Pub.
Nash, H: S. History of the higher criticism of the New Testament. *$1 net. Macmillan.
Riley, W: B. Finality of the higher criticism. $1. W: B. Riley.

HIGHER CRITICISM.—*Continued.*
Wishard, S: E. Testimony of the Bible concerning the assumption of destructive criticism. 60 c. S. E. Wishard.

Higher life in art. La Farge, J: **$2.50 net. Doubleday, P.
Higher sacrifice. Jordan, D: S. *80 c. net. Am. Unitarian.
Highlanders of the South. Thompson, S: H. 50 c. net. Eaton & M.

Highley, Mont Frederic, comp.
See Oklahoma. Form book.

Hightower, Ja.
Happy hunting grounds. '10(Ag6) c. il. por. 16°, $1.25. Hightower.

Highway construction. Byrne, A. T. $1. Am. Sch. Corr.
Highway engineering. Morrison, C: E: $2.50. Wiley.
Highway of mission thought. Ray, T. B., *ed.* 75 c. S. S. Bd. So. Bapt.

HIGHWAYMEN.
Harper, C: G: Half hours with highwaymen. 2 v. *$16.80 net. Scribner.

HIGHWAYS.
See Roads.

Highways and byways ser. il. 12°, 8°, *$2 net. Macmillan.
—Jerrold. Highways and byways of Kent.—Highways and byways of Middlesex.
—Johnson. Highways and byways of the Pacific coast.—Highways and byways of the Rocky Mountains.
—Parker. Highways and byways in Surrey.
—Read. Highways and byways in Hampshire.
—Shorter. Highways and byways in Buckinghamshire.
Highways of Japan. Lawson, *Lady.* $3.75 net. Stokes.
Highways of progress. Hill, J. J. $1.50 net. Doubleday, P.
Highways of success. Macmurray, T: J. $1. Progress Co.

Higinbotham, J: U.
Three weeks in Holland and Belgium. '08 (My16) c. il. D. $1.50. Reilly & B.

Higley, Elmer Ellsworth, D.D.
Homespun religion. '09(S18) c. D. (What is worth while ser.) leatherette, **30 c. net. Crowell.

HIGSBEE FAMILY.
See Genealogies: Babcock, W: E.

Hilary on her own. Barnes-Grundy, *Mrs.* M. S. †$1.50. Baker & T.
Hilary Thornton. Wales, H., *pseud.* †$1.50. Estes.
Hilda of the hippodrome. Paine, D. C. $1 net. Reilly & B.
Hilda's mascot. Neland, *Mrs.* M. E. H. $1. Saalfield.
Hilda's wish. Hoxie, B. D. †50 c. Estes.

Hildebrand, Fk. Alonzo.
Dynamic school of tomorrow; rationalism in teaching the aesthetic element in education. '10(N5) c. il. 8°, $2. Aberdeen.

Hildebrand, Ira P.
See Warren, E: H.

Hildebrand, S. F.
See Meek, Seth Eug.

HILDEBRAND, *St.*
See Gregory VII.

Hildebrandt, Alfr.
Airships past and present; tr. by W. H. Story. '08(F8) il. 8°, *$3 net. Van Nostrand.

Hildreth, E:
Edward Hildreth: in memoriam, 1833-1907. '08(S) c. 56 p. il. por. 12°. (Not for sale.) Donnelley.

HILDRETH FAMILY.
See Genealogies: **Reade, P. H.,** ***comp.***

Hilgard, Eug. Woldemar, and Osterhout, W. J. V.
Agriculture for schools of the Pacific Slope. '10(Mr26) c. il. D. **$1 net. Macmillan.

Hilgers, Jos.
Roman index and its latest historian: critical review of "The censorship of the church of Rome," by G: Haven Putnam; with introd. note by Arth. Preuss. '08 (D5) 8°, pap., *10 c. net. Herder.

Hilkey, C: Jos.
Legal development in colonial Massachusetts, 1630-1686. '10(S10) c. O. (Studies in history, economics and public law.) pap., $1.25. Longmans.

Hill, Alex.
Body at work: treatise on the principles of physiology. '09(F20) il. figs. O. *$4.50 net. Longmans.

Hill, Arth. F.
See Hill, W. H:

Hill, Arth. G:
Architectural history of the Christian church. '09(Ap10) il. 12°, *60 c. net. Young Churchman.

Hill, C:
Manual of normal histology and organography. 2d ed., thoroughly rev. '09, [1910.[(Ja) 9-468 p. il. 12°, $2. Saunders.

Hill, C: Shattuck.
Concrete inspection; manual of information for inspectors of concrete work; with standard and typical specifications. '09 (O23) il. 16°, *$1 net. M. C. Clark.
See also Gillette, Halbert Powers.

Hill, Constance.
Maria Edgeworth and her circle in the days of Buonaparte and Bourbon. '09 (N6) il. pors. O. *$6 net. Lane.

Hill, D: Jayne, Estournelles de Constant, Paul Henri Benjamin, Baron d', and Scott, Ja. Brown.
Second Hague peace conference. '08(Je6) 8°, (U. S. Senate document.) pap., 15 c. U. S., Supt. of Docs.

Hill, D: R.
Philosophy of Christianity and the philosophy of government, together with a criticism of God's word, history and reason applied to false teachers; embellished with songs and poetry. '08, [1909.] (Mr) c. 301 p. 12°, $1.50. Tribune Co.

Hill, D: Spence.
Education and problems of the Protestant ministry. '08(Je20) c. pap., $1. Stechert.

Hill, Edn. B.
Henry Thoreau's mother. '08(D26) 24°, (Collectanea.) pap., 10 c. E. B. Hill.

Hill, Everett Merrill.
Story the crocus told. '10(Mr5) c. por. D. *$1 net. Uplook Pub.

Hill, Frederic Stanhope.
Romance of the American Navy as embodied in the stories of certain of our public and private armed ships from 1775 to 1909. '10(Mr26) c. il. pors. O. **$2.50 net. Putnam.

Hill, F: Trevor.
Lincoln's legacy of inspiration. '09(N20) c. front. 12°, 50 c. Stokes.
On the trail of Washington: narrative hist. of Washington's boyhood and manhood, based on his own writings, authentic documents and other authoritative information. '10(F12) c. il. O. (National holiday ser.) **$1.50 net. Appleton.
Story of a street: narrative history of Wall Street from 1644 to 1908. '08(N14) c. il. O. **$1.60 net. Harper.

Hill, G. F.
One hundred masterpieces of sculpture; from the sixth century, B.C., to the time of Michelangelo; with introd. by G. F. Hill. '10(O8) il. O. $4 net. Lane.

Hill, H. W.
See Winslow, Kenelm.

Hill, Headon, pseud.
See Grainger, Fs. E:

Hill, H: Wayland.
Historical review of waterways and canal construction in New York State. '09 (Je5) c. 8°, (Buffalo Historical Society pubs.) $5; pap., $4. Buffalo Hist. Soc.

Hill, Herbert Wynford.
Sidney's Arcadia and the Elizabethan drama. '09(Mr13) 8°, (Univ. of Nev. studies.) (Add. University for price.) Univ. of Nev.

Hill, I: W:
See McBain, Howard Lee.

Hill, J. Stacy.
Ways of an aristocrat. '08(Mr) c. 93 p. 12°. (Add. author for price.) J. S. Hill.

Hill, J. Woodroffe.
Diseases of the cat. '10(D) 123 p. il. 8°, $1.25. W: R. Jenkins.

Hill, Ja.
Synopsis of draughts openings: [checkers.] 5th ed. '09(Ap24) D. 50 c. Warne.

Hill, Ja. Jerome.
Address del. before the Farmers' National Congress, Madison, Wis., Sept. 24, 1908. '10(F) 22 p. 8°, gratis. Farmers' Nat.
Future of rail and water transportation: letter read at The-Lakes-to-the-Gulf Deep Waterway Association convention, Chicago, Ill., Oct. 7th-9th, 1908. '09 (Je12) O. pap. (Add. author for price.) J. J. Hill.
Highways of progress. '10(Je25) c. O. $1.50 net. Doubleday, P.

Hill, Mrs. Janet McKenzie.
Cooking and serving en casserole and things we relish. '10(O) c. 48 p. il. 16°, 10 c. Int. Silver.
Cooking for two. '09(Je5) c. il. O. **$1.50 net. Little, B. & Co.
See also Parloa, Maria.

Hill, J: L.
As others see us, and as we are: the plea and position of the Disciples of Christ. '08(O17) c. 12°, 75 c. Standard Pub.
The transition. '09(Jl31) 12°, $1.50. B'way Pub.

Hill, Julian.
Great English poets. '08(Ag15) 12°, $1.50. Jacobs.

Hill, Leonard.
See Beddard, A. P.
—, ed. Further advances in physiology. '09 (Je5) il. O. *$4.20 net. Longmans.
Recent advances in physiology and bio-chemistry. '08(Ap25) il. O. *$5 net. Longmans.

Hill, Luther B.
History of the state of Oklahoma. 2 v. '09 (Ap17) c. pors. map, 4°, $20. Lewis Pub.

Hill, Lysander.
The two great questions; the existence of God and the immortality of the soul. '09 (D18) c. il. D. $2. L. Hill.

Hill, R.
See Vest pocket reference book ser.

Hill, Rob. Tudor.
Public domain and democracy; study of social, economic and political problems in the United States in relation to western development. '10(S10) c. O. (Columbia Univ. studies in history, economics and public law.) pap., $2. Longmans.

Hill, Rowland Gardner.
English-Spanish manual, by Major C. G. Morton. 4th ed., rev. and enl. '09(Jl31) 16°, $1. Hudson.

Hill, Vernon.
Arcadian calendar; 12 designs descriptive of the months. '10(F19) f°, *$1.50 net. Lane.

Hill, W. H:, Arth. F. and Alfr. E.
Antonio Stradivari; his life and work, (1644-1737;) with an introd. by Lady Huggins. 2d ed. '09(D11) il. O. *$2.50 net. Macmillan.

Hill-Lutz, Mrs. Grace Livingston.
See Lutz, *Mrs.* Grace Livingston Hill-.

HILL COUNTY, Texas.
See Baptist church.

Hill kink books. Colvin, F. H., *comp.* 10 v. ea., 50 c. Hill Pub.

Hill o' dreams. Lanyon, H. $1 net. Lane.

Hill Rise. Maxwell, W: B. 75 c. Cupples & L.

Hillebrand, W: Fs.
Analysis of silicate and carbonate rocks; revision of Bulletin 305. '10(Jl) 239 p. il. 8°, (U. S., Dept. of the Interior, U. S. Geological Survey, bull.)
—, **and Schaller, Waldemar Thdr.**
Mercury minerals from Terlingua, Texas. '09, [1910.] (Mr) 174 p. il. 8°, (U. S., Dept. of the Interior, U. S. Geological Survey, bull.) pap.

Hiller, Mrs. Eliz. O., comp.
Pract. cook book. '10(O15) c. por. 12°, $1. Doherty Op.

Hillern, Frau Wilhelmine Birch von.
Höher als die kirche; eine erzählung aus alter zeit; ed., with introd., notes, exercises in syntax and vocab., by F: W. J. Heuser. '10(Mr) c. 184 p. map, il. por. 12°, (Merrill's German texts.) 90 c. C: E. Merrill.
"Collateral reading" (1 p.).

Hillier, Alfr. P:, M.D.
The commonweal; study of the federal system of political economy. '09(N20) D. *$1.50 net. Longmans.

Hillier, Mrs. Amelia Willard.
Ebb and Flo, and other short stories. '08 (N21) c. D. $1. J. M. Williams.

Hilliers, Ashton.
As it happened. '09(S18) D. *$1.35 net. Putnam.
The master-girl; romance. '10(Ap30) c. D. $1.25 net. Putnam.

Hillquit, Morris.
Hist. of socialism in the United States. Rev. ed. '09(D); 5th rev. and enl. ed. '10(Je4) 8°, ea., *$1.50 net. Funk.
Recent progress of the socialist and labor movements in the United States. '08 (O10) 12°, pap., 10 c. Kerr.
Socialism in theory and practice. '09 (Mr6) c. D. *$1.50 net. Macmillan.

Hills, A. T.
Commercial law. '08(Ag) c. 308 p. O. Practical Text-Book Co.

Hills, Elijah Clarence, and Reinhardt, Louise, eds.
Spanish short stories; ed., with introd., notes and vocab. '10(O22) c. D. $1. Heath.
—, ed. Spanish tales for beginners; ed., with notes and vocabulary. '09(Je19) c. S. $1.10. Holt.

Hills, Jos. Lawrence, Wait, C: Edm., and White, H: Clay.
Dietary studies in rural regions in Vermont, Tennessee, and Georgia. '09, [1910.] Mr) 142 p. tabs., il. 8°, (U. S., Dept. of Agriculture, Office of Experimental Stations, bull.) pap.

Hilprecht, Rev. Herman Volrath.
Earliest version of the Babylonian deluge story, and The Temple Library of Nippur. '10(My14) il. (Univ. of Penn., Babylonian expedition, ser. D., Cuneiform texts.) 75 c. net. Holman.
Hilprecht anniversary volume; studies in assyriology and archæology; dedicated to H. V. Hilprecht by his colleagues, friends and admirers; ed. by Carl Wilhelm Seidenedel. 457 p. il. 4°, $5. Open Court.
So-called Peters-Hilprecht controversy; cont. record of the proceedings and rept. of the committee appointed by the Univ. of Penn., to investigate the charges against Prof. Hilprecht and his reply to his critics. '08(My16) c. O. *75 c. net. Holman

HILPRECHT, *Rev.* Herman Volrath.
Peters, J: P. Hilprecht's answer: [analysis of "so-called Peters-Hilprecht controversy."] (Priv. pr.) J: P. Peters.

Hilton, Harold.
Introd. to the theory of groups of finite order. '08(D19) 8°, *$4.75 net. Oxford Univ.

Hilton, Marian A.
Garden of girls. '09(Ap17) c. il. D. $1.50. Tandy-T.

Hilty, Carl.
Happiness: essays on the meaning of life; tr. by Fs. Greenwood Peabody. '09 (Mr6) c. D. 75 c. Grosset.

HIMALAYA MOUNTAINS, Asia.
Bruce, C: G. Twenty years in the Himalaya. $4.20 net. Longmans.
Mumm, A. L: Five months in the Himalaya. *$6 net. Longmans.
Workman, *Mrs.* F. B. *and* W: H. Peaks and glaciers of Nun Kun. *$4.50 net. Scribner.
See also Tibet.

Hime, H: W: Lovett.
Anharmonic co-ordinates. '10(Ag6) O. $3 net. Longmans.
History of the Royal Regiment of Artillery, 1815-1853. '08(N21) O. *$2 net. Longmans.

Himmels-harfe. Sprunger, J: A., *comp.* 35 c. Light and Hope.

Himmelwright, Abraham Lincoln Artman.
Pistol and revolver. '08(Ap11) c. il. S. $1; full mor., $1.50; pap., 60 c. U. S. Revolver.

Hinchman, Anne.
Poems. '10(Jl) 51 p. 12°. (Priv. pr.) Riverside Press.

Hinchman, Wa. Swain.
Tintagel, and other verses. '10(D) 101 p. 16°, $1. Groton Sch.

—, and Gummere, Fs. Barton.
Lives of great English writers, from Chaucer to Browning. '08(Ap11) c. pors. map, D. **$1.50 net. Houghton M.

Hinckle, W: Alb., M.D.
Evolution of religion. [2d ed.] '10(D24) c. D. 80 c. net. Sherman, F.

Hinckley, G: Wa.
Some Good Will boys. '10(Jl2) c. front. por. 12°, 75 c. Good Will.

Hinckley, H: Barrett.
Poems. '09(N) 39 p. 4°, pap., 50 c. Nonotuck.
Notes on Chaucer: commentary on the Prolog and six Canterbury tales. '07, [1908.] (Mr.) c. 11+324 p. 8°, $3. Nonotuck.

Hind, A. M.
Short history of engraving and etching; with full bibliography, classified list and index of engravers. '08(O24) il. O. *$5 net. Houghton M.

Hind, C: Lewis.
Augustus Saint-Gaudens; special extra number of *The International Studio,* 1908. '08(O10) c. il. Q. **$5 net; pap., **$2.50 net. Lane.
Constable. '09(O30) il. D. (Masterpieces in colour.) bds., *65 c. net; leath., *$1 50 net. Stokes.
Diary of a looker-on. '08(My16) D. $2. Lane.

Hind, C: Lewis.—*Continued.*
Drawings of Leonardo da Vinci. '08(D5) il. f°, (Drawings of the great masters.) *$2.50 net. Scribner.
Hogarth. '10(D17) col. il. O. (Masterpieces in color.) bds., 65 c. net. Stokes.
Watteau. '10(S10) col. il. O. (Masterpieces in colour.) bds., 65 c. net; leath., $1.50 net. Stokes.

Hindenburg, Baroness.
See Hay, Marie.

HINDI COTTON.
See Cotton.

Hindle, E:
Life hist. of *trypanosoma dimorphon,* Dutton & Todd. '10(F) 127-144 p. pls. figs. Q. (University of California pubs., Zoology.) pap., 50 c. Univ. of Cal.

Hindrances of life. Müller, J. *$1.50 net. M. Kennerley.

Hindrances to good citizenship. Bryce, J. *$1.15 net. Yale Univ.

Hinds, J: Iredelle Dillard.
Qualitative chemical analysis from the standpoint of solubilities, ionization and mass action. '10(N5) c. 8°, $2. Chemical.

Hinds, W: Alfr.
American communities and co-operative colonies. 2d rev. '08(F15) c. il. pors. D. $1.50. Kerr.

Hindu classics: literature of India; with critical and biographical sketches by Epiphanius Wilson. '08(Je27) c. il. 8°, $1.75; hf. mor., $3.50. Lamb Pub.

HINDU LITERATURE.
See Sanskrit literature.

Hindu-Yogi science of breath. Atkinson, W: W. 75 c.; 50 c. Yogi Pub.

HINDUISM.
Barnett, L. N. Heart of India: sketches in hist. of Hindu religion. *60 c. net. Dutton.
Bloomfield, M. Religion of the Veda. **$1.50 net. Putnam.
De Laurence, L. W: Mystic test book of "The Hindu occult chambers;" The magic and occultism of India; Hindu and Egyptian crystal gazing; The Hindu magic mirror. $2. De Laurence, S.
Fletcher, A. E. Law of the rhythmic breath, [as taught in ancient Hindu philosophy.] *$1 net. Fenno.
Mylne, L: G: Missions to Hindus. *$1.20 net. Longmans.
Noble, M. E. Indian study of love and death. 75 c. Longmans.
Paramananda, *Swami.* Principles and purposes of Vedanta. 25 c. Paramananda.
Paramânanda, *Swâmi.* Vedanta in practice. **$1 net. Baker & T.
Rajan Iyengar, T. C. Hindu-Aryan theory on evolution and involution; or, the science of raja-yoga. **$1.50 net. Funk.
See also Krishna (*God*);—Reincarnation;—Theosophy;—Upanishads;—*also* Benares.

Hine, C: Cole.
Book of forms (fire insurance) for the use of agents and others. 4th ed.; rev. and enl. by S: R. Weed. '09(Jl31) c. O. $2. C: C. Hine.

Hine, C: Gilbert.
Hist. and legend; fact. fancy and romance of the Old Mine Road, Kingston, N. Y., to the mine holes of Pahaquarry. '08, [1909.] (N) various paging, 8°, (Hine's annual, 1908.) $1.25. Hine Bros.
Story of Martha's Vineyard. '08(Je27) c. il. map, sq. D. $1.50. Hine Bros.

Hine, Ja. Stewart.
Robberflies of the genus *Asilus.* '10(F) 136-170 p. il. 4°, (Ohio State University; contributions from the Department of Zoology and Entomology.) pap., 50 c. J. S. Hine.

Hine, Muriel.
Half in earnest. '10(My21) D. $1.50. Lane.

Hinemon, J: H.
Geography of Arkansas. '08(Ap18) c. il. maps, sq. O. 50 c. Rand, McN. & Co.

Hines, Mrs. Earle Remington.
Footlight rhymes. '10(Je11) c. il. pors. D. $1. B'way Pub.

Hines, E: Warren.
Abstracts of cases decided by the federal cts. rel. to the 14th amendment upon the power of states to regulate rates of railroads and other public utilities, as reported in v. 1-155 of the federal reporter, and in v. 1-206 of the U. S. Sup. Ct. reports. '08(Mr) c. 11+248 p. O. *$5. Morton.

Hines, Fk. T:, and Ward, Franklin Wilmer.
Service of coast artillery; publication auth. by the War Department. '10(Je11) c. il. 8°, $3.50 net. Goodenough & W.

Hingham, Mass. First Parish. Two hundred and twenty-fifth anniversary of the opening of the old meeting house in Hingham, Mass., for public worship, January 20, 1907: 1682-1907. '07, [1908.] (Mr.) 44 p. front. 12°, pap., 50 c. L. C. Cornish.

Hingley, S. H.
Hints on advanced bridge. '10(Ap9) S. leath., 75 c. net. Macmillan.

Hingston, W: E:
Forgeries and false entries. '09(Jl31) 12°, $1. Roxburgh.

Hinke, W: J:
New boundary stone of Nebuchadrezzar I. from Nippur, with a concordance of proper names and a glossary of the Kudurru inscriptions thus far published. '09 (Ap3) il. 4°, (Babylonian expedition of the Univ. of Penn.; ser. D: Researches and treatises.) $3.50. Univ. of Penn.

Hinkeley, Jos. B.
See Goodsell, Dan. Ayres.

Hinkende bote am Mississippi: volks-kalender, 1909: 54 jahrgang. '08(D5) il. 4°, pap., 5 c.; per doz., 30 c.; per gross, $3. Herder.

Hinkle, F: Wallis.
Army rifles: paper read before the Ohio Commandery of the Loyal Legion, Feb. 5, 1908. '08(Je6) 8°, pap. (Not for sale.) F: W: Hinkle.

Hinkson, Mrs. Katharine Tynan, [formerly Katharine Tynan.]
Freda. '10(D10) col. front. 12°, $1.20 net. Cassell.
Her ladyship. '08, [1909.] (Je) 6+305 p. 12°, $1.25. McClurg.
Ireland. '09(D25) il. map, 12°, (Peeps at many lands ser.) *75 c. net. Macmillan.
Little book for John O'Mahony's friends. '09(D) 32°, (Ideal ser. of little masterpieces.) *50 c. net; *$1 net. T: B. Mosher.
Lost angel. '08(S26) D. †$1.50. Lippincott.
Mary Gray. '09(Jl3) c. il. D. $1.50. Cassell.
Peggy, the daughter. '09(N13) front. D. $1.50. Cassell.

Hinman, Mrs. Eliz. Trowbridge Egleston-.
See Egleston-Hinman, Eliz.

Hinman, Harold J.
See American bankruptcy repts. Digest.
—, ed. *See* Street railway repts.

Hinman, Mrs. Lilian.
Green leaves from life's garden: [poems.] '10(Mr26) c. D. $1. Badger.

Hinsdale, Guy.
Hydrotherapy; work on hydrotherapy in general, its application to special affections, the technic or processes employed, and the use of waters internally. '10(S) c. 7-466 p. il. 8°, $3.50. Saunders.

Hinton, Howard, ["Ralph Morley."]
My comrades; or, School-days at Mt. Pleasant; story of the Hudson, incl. traditions and legends of the hill-country bordering the east bank of that historic river; reissued as appropriate tribute on the part of the Mount Pleasant Academy to the Hudson-Fulton celebration. '09, [1910] (Ja) c. 329 p. il. 12°, $1.25. C. F. Brusie.

HINTON, James.
Ellis, E. M. O. L. Three modern seers: James Hinton, Nietzsche, Edward Carpenter. $1.25 net. M. Kennerley.

Hints. Hartich, F: F. $2. F. C. Hill.

Hints for carpenters. Peker, C: G. 50 c. Indust. Bk.

Hints for crystal drawing. Reeks, M. *$1.10 net. Longmans.

Hints for hunters and trappers, cont. game laws, trapping secrets, camping hints, cooking recipes, etc. '09(Ag) 64 p. S. pap. (Add. pubs. for price.) A. R. Harding.

Hints for lovers. Haultain, T. A. **$1 net. Houghton M.

Hints of contemporary life in the writings of Thomas Shepard. (Priv. pr.) A. McF. Davis.

Hints on advanced bridge. Hingley, S. H. 75 c. net. Macmillan.

Hints on amalgamation and the general care of gold mills. Adams, W: J. $2. Mining and Scientific.

Hints on exporting. Heywood, J: W. (Not for sale.) Northwestern Miller.

Hints on forwarding, finishing and ruling. Linton, C. B. $2. Burt Pub.

Hints on house furnishing. Sparrow, W. S. *$2.50 net. Lane.

Hints on Old Testament theology. Duff, A. *$1 net. Macmillan.

Hints on revolver shooting. Winans, W. **50 c. net. Putnam.
Hints to young students of occultism. Rogers, L. W. 25 c. Theosophical Bk.
Hintze, L:
Atlas of Norman Co., Minn. '07, [1909.] (Mr.) c. 28 maps, f°, cl., $10. L: Hintze.
Hippodrome (The). '10(D) col. il. 75 c. Saalfield.
HIPPOLOGY.
See Horse.
Hippolytus. *See* Euripides.
HIPPOPOTAMUS.
Miller, G. S. Description of a new species of hippopotamus. 10 c. Smith. Inst.
Hiram Golf's religion. Hepworth, G: H. $1.25. Dutton.
Hird, Fk.
Deeper stain. '09(O9) c. D. †$1.50. Appleton.
Victoria, the woman. '08(Ap11) c. il. pors. facsim., O. **$2.50 net. Appleton.
Hird, W. Benison.
Elem. dynamo design. '09(Jl3) O. *$2.50 net. Cassell.
Hirsch, Adolph.
Science of commercial bookkeeping. '10 (Ap9) 12°, $2. J. S. Ogilvie.
Hirsch, C. E.
Art and craft of the author. '08(F) c. '07. 12°, **$1.50 net. Grafton Press.
Hirsch, Fritz.
Castle of Brucksales; das Brucksaler schloss-aus anlass der renovation, (1900-1909;) published under the patronage of the Ministry of Finance of the Grand Duchy of Baden. '10(Ap16) il. f°, $25. Hessling.
Hirschfeld, Albert Martin.
Standard hdbk. on wines and liquors. '08 (Ja18) 8°, $1.50. Popper.
Hirschfeld, C. F.
Engineering thermodynamics. 2d ed. '10 (Ag6) 16°, (Van Nostrand science ser.) bds., 50 c. Van Nostrand.
Hirschfelder, Arth. Douglass.
Diseases of the heart and aorta; with introd. note by Lewellys F. Barker. [1910.] (S) c. 23+632 p. il. col. front. 8°, $6 net. Lippincott.
Bibliographies at end of chapters.
Hirschler, Diana.
Art of retail selling; textbk. for salespeople. '10(O) 165 p. il. 12°, $1. N. Y. Inst. Mercantile.
Formerly $2.
Hirschman, L: J.
Hdbk. of diseases of the rectum. '09(O) c. 5+374 p. il. (partly col.) 8°, $4. Mosby.
Hirschy, Noah Calvin.
Artaxerxes III Ochus and his reign, with special consideration of the Old Testament sources bearing upon the period. '09(Je19) c. 8°, pap., *75 c. net. Univ. of Chic.
Hirshberg, Leonard Keene, ed.
What you ought to know about your baby; text book for mothers on the care and feeding of babies, with questions and answers especially prep. by the ed. '10 (Je) c. 97 p. 8°, 25 c. Butterick.
Hirst, Barton Cooke.
Text-book of obstetrics. 6th ed., rev. and enl. '09(O) c. 9-992 p. il. 8°, $5. Saunders.
Hirst, Marg. E.
Life of Friedrich Liszt and selections from his writings; with an introd. by F. W. Hirst. '09(Jl31) 12°, *$2 net. Scribner.
Hirst, W: Alfr.
Argentina; with introd. by Martin Hume. '10(N12) il map, 8°, (South American ser.) $3 net. Scribner.
Hirth, Friedrich.
Ancient history of China to the end of the Chóu dynasty. '08(Mr7) c. map, tabs., 8°, **$2.50 net. Lemcke.
His better self. Jayhews, T: $1.50. Saalfield.
"His birthday." Le Feuvre, A. *35 c. net. Armstrong.
His first leave. Harker, *Mrs.* L. A. †$1.50. Scribner.
His first term. Finnemore, J: $1.50. Lippincott.
His hour. Glyn, *Mrs.* E. S. $1.50. Appleton.
His model wife. Bagg, H. F. 15 c. Penn Pub. Co.
His struggle magnificent. Bond, W: S. $1.50. Cochrane.
His tribute. Eastland, F. M. *60 c. net. Jennings.
Hiscox, Gardner Dexter.
Compressed air, its production, uses, and applications. 5th ed., rev. and enl.. '09 (F20) c. il. tabs., 8°, $5. Henley.
Gas, gasoline and oil engines, incl. gas-producer plants. 18th ed., rev. '09(D) c. 484 p. il. 8°, *$2.50 net. Henley.
Hydraulic engineering. '08(My2) il. tabs., 8°, $4. Henley.
Mechanical appliances, mechanical movements and novelties of construction. 2d ed. In 2 v. v. 2. '09(D) c. 400 p. 8°, $2.50. Henley.
Mechanical movements, powers and devices. 11th ed. '10(My21) 8°, $2.50. Henley.
—, ed. Henley's twentieth century book of receipts, formulas and processes. '09(D) c. il. 8°, $3; hf. mor., $4. Henley.
Hisgen, T: L.
Biographical sketch of Thomas L. Hisgen; fr. the Boston *Transcript.* '08(Ag22) 16°, pap., gratis. T: L. Hisgen.
Hislam, Percival A.
Admiralty of the Atlantic: inquiry into the development of German sea power, past, present and prospective. '08(Ap25) il. map, O. *$2 net. Longmans.
Hispanic Society of America. Catalogue of paintings by Ignacio Zuloaga exhibited by the Hispanic Society of America, March 21 to April 11, 1909; with introd. by Christian Brinton. '09(N20) il. 12°, 50 c. Hispanic Soc.
Hispanic Society of America. Catalogue of paintings by Joaquin Sorolla y Bastida exhibited by the Hispanic Society of America, Feb. 8 to Mar. 8, 1909; with introd. by Leonard Williams. '09(Ap) c. 154 p. il. por. 12°, pap., 25 c. Hispanic Soc.

Hispanic Society of America. Eight essays on Joaquín Sorella y Bastida; printed on the occasion of the exhibition of paintings by Señor Sorolla at the invitation of the Hispanic Society of America, New York City, Feb. 4 to Mar. 9, 1909. '09(O2) c. 2 v., il. pors. O. *$7.50 net. Hispanic Soc.

Hisperica famina; ed. with a short introd. and index verborum by Fs. J: H: Jenkinson. '09(Mr) 40+95 p. facsims., O. cl., *$1.75 net. Putnam.

Hiss, Philip Hanson, jr., and Zinsser, Hans.
Text-book of bacteriology; pract. treatise for students and practitioners of medicine. '10(O) c. 14+745 p. il. 8°, $3.75. Appleton.
Bibliographical foot-notes.

Hissey, Ja. J:
Charm of the road; England and Wales. '10(N19) il. 8°, $3 net. Macmillan.
English holiday with car and camera. '08 (N7) il. map, 8°, $3. Macmillan.

Histoire de la Mère Michel. La Bédollière, E. G. de. *35 c. net. Macmillan.

Histoires courtes et longues pour lecture expliquée et reproduction. Chouville, L. 60 c. Oxford Univ.

HISTOLOGY.
Bailey, F: R. Text-book of histology. $3.50 net. Wood.
Dahlgren, U. Text-book of principles of animal histology. *$3.75 net. Macmillan.
De Witt, C: H. Laboratory guide and outlines in histology. (Add. author for price.) C: H. De Witt.
Gage, S. H: The microscope; introd. to microscopic methods and to histology. $1.50. Comstock Pub.
Hardesty, I. Laboratory guide for histology. *$1.50 net. Blakiston.
Hill, C: Manual of normal histology and organography. $2. Saunders.
Leroy, L: Essentials of histology. *$1 net. Saunders.
Piersol, G: A. Normal histology, with special reference to the structure of the human body. $3.50. Lippincott.
Radasch, H: E. Compend of histology. *$1 net; *$1.25 net. Blakiston.
Schäfer, E: A. Essentials of histology. $3.50 net. Lea.
See also Anatomy;—Bones;—Cells.

HISTORIANS.
Littell, J: S. Historians and the English Reformation. $2.50 net. Young Churchman.

Historians of Greece. il. 8°. Tandy-T.
—Herodotus. History. 4 v. $14.
—Thucydides. History. 3 v. $10.50.
—Xenophon. History. 5 v. $15.

Historians' home study ser. 8°. Dixon.
—Rocheleau. Pract. hist. of the world. 8 v. $26.75.

Historic boyhoods. Holland, R. S. *$1.50 net. Jacobs.

Historic dress in America, 1800-1870. McClellan, E. $6 net. Jacobs.

Historic episcopate. Thompson, R. E. $1.50. Westminster.

Historic ghosts. Bruce, H: A. B. **$1.25 net. Moffat.

Historic girlhoods. Holland, R. S. $1.50 net. Jacobs.

Historic graves of Maryland and the District of Columbia. Ridgely, H. W., *ed.* **$2 net. Grafton Press.

Historic homes and places. 4 v. Cutter, W: R:. *ed.* (Add. pubs. for price.) Lewis Pub.

Historic homesteads. Ditmas, C: A. $5. C: A. Ditmas.

Historic houses and their gardens. Osborne, C: F., *ed.* $6. Winston.

Historic Indiana. Levering, J. H. **$2.50 net. Putnam.

Historic ministry and the present Christ. Slattery, C: L. **50 c. net. Longmans.

Historic Mohawk. Diefendorf, M. R. $2 net. Putnam.

Historic old Rhinebeck. Morse, H. H. *$3 net. H. H. Morse.

Historic rivers ser. *Now* American waterways.

Historic states of Italy; ed. by E: Armstrong and R. Langston Douglas. il. O. Putnam.
—Allen. Hist. of Verona. $3.50.
—Heywood. Hist. of Perugia. $3.50 net.

Historic Sullivan. Taylor, O. $2.50. King Pr.

Historic views of Gettysburg. Miller, R. C. 50 c. J. I. Mumper.

Historical and linguistic studies in literature related to the New Testament; issued under the direction of the Department of Biblical and Patristic Greek: second series. v. 1. '09(Jl31) c. 8°, *$3 net; v. 2, pt. 1 (D25) pap., *50 c. net. Univ. of Chic.

Historical and Philosophical Society of Ohio pubs. 4°. Hist. and Phil. Soc., O.
—Bradford, *ed.* James McBride manuscripts.
—Drake. Notices concerning Cincinnati.
—Hamlin, *ed.* Selections from the Follett papers.
—Short. Brief accts. of journeys in the western country.

Historical and religious value of the fourth Gospel. Scott, E. F. 50 c. Houghton M.

Historical Bible. *See* Kent, C: Foster.

Historical character of St. John's gospel. Robinson, J. A. 25 c. Longmans.

Historical collections of the Essex Institute. pap. (Priv. pr.) Essex Inst.
—Peabody. Derbys of Salem.

Historical digest of the provincial press. Weeks, L. H., *comp. and ed.* subs., per v., $7.50; per set, $150. Soc. Americana.

Historical, dramatic and romantic ballads. Lothrop, G: E. (Add. author for price.) G: E. Lothrop.

Historical evidence. George, H. B. 75 c. Oxford Univ.

Historical French reader. Weill, F., *ed.* 40 c. Am. Bk.

Historical geography of the British colonies. Lucas, C: P. Oxford Univ.

Historical German grammar. Wright, J. $2.40. Oxford Univ.

Historical guide to the city of New York. Kelley, F. B., *comp.* **$1.50 net Stokes.

Historical Man of Nazareth. Bryant, W. F. 75 c. W. F. Bryant.

Historical, Natural History and Library Society of South Natick. Historical collections of the Historical, Natural History and Library Society. v. 1. '09, [1910.] (Ap) il. 8°, 50 c.
Hist. Soc., (So. Natick.)

Historical review of waterways and canal construction in New York State. Hill, H: W. $5; $4. Buffalo Hist. Soc.

Historical ser. for Bible students; ed. by C: F. Kent and Fk. K. Sanders. D. **$1.25 net. Scribner.
—Breasted. History of the ancient Egyptians.

Historical stories of the ancient world and the Middle Ages, retold from *St. Nicholas Magazine.* il. D. **65 c. net. Century Co.
—Stories of chivalry.
—Stories of classic myths.
—Stories of Greece and Rome.
—Stories of royal children.
—Stories of the ancient world.
—Stories of the Middle Ages.

Historical tales. Morris, C: 15 v. (Sold by subs. only.) Angelus Univ.

History.

Acton, J: E. E: D.-A., *Lord.* Cambridge modern history. In 12 v. v. 5, Age of Louis XIV. *$4 net; v. 6, The eighteenth century; v. 11, Growth of nationalities. ea., **$4 net; v. 12. $4 net.—Historical essays and studies. *$3 net. Macmillan.

American Historical Association. Study of hist. in the elementary schools. 50 c. Scribner.

Anderson, A. Course of study in history. 30 c. San F. St. Normal.

Andrews, C: M., *and others.* Bibliography of history for schools and libraries. 60 c. net. Longmans.

Burdick, J. E., *ed.* General index [to The history of nations.] $2.75; $3.75; $5. J: D. Morris.

Chamberlain, H. S. Foundations of the nineteenth century. In 2 v. $10 net. Lane.

Chamberlin, J. E. Ifs in history. $1. Altemus.

Clare, I. S. Illustrated history of all nations. 15 v. (Add. pubs. for price.) Chr. Herald.

Dewe, J. A. Psychology of politics and history. $1.75 net. Longmans.

Frankland, W: B. Theories of parallelism; an historical critique. 90 c. net. Putnam.

Fredet, P: Modern history. $1.50. Murphy.

Gasquet, F. A. Last abbot of Gladstonbury, and other essays. *$2 net. Macmillan.

George, H. B. Historical evidence. 75 c. Oxford Univ.

Harding, S: B. Essentials of mediæval history. $1. Am. Bk.

Hegel, G. W. F. Philosophy of history. $1.75; $3.50. Lamb Pub.

Herodotus. [Histories:] seventh, eighth and ninth books. In 2 v. v. 1 in 2 pts. *$9 net. Macmillan.

Herodotus. History. 4 v. $14. Tandy-T.

History.—*Continued.*

Historical, Natural History and Library Society of South Natick. Historical collections of the Historical, Natural History and Library Society. 50 c. Hist. Soc., (So. Natick.)

Hocking, W: E. On the law of history. 20 c. Univ. of Cal.

Johnson, H: Problem of adapting history to children in the elementary school. 30 c. Teachers' Coll.

Keatinge, M. W. Studies in the teaching of history. $1.60 net. Macmillan.

Kemp, E. W. Outline history for the grades. $1.25. Ginn.

Kerney, M. J. Compendium of history, ancient and modern. *$1.25 net. Murphy.

Lamborn, E. A. G. Perspective history chart. $2.90. Oxford Univ.

Leadbetter, F. E. Outlines and studies to accompany Meyers' General hist. 35 c. Ginn.

Lecky, W: E: H. Historical and political essays. $1.60 net; *$3.50 net. Longmans.

McCarthy, J. Short history of our own times. $1.50. Harper.

Morris, C: Historical tales. 15 v. (Sold by subs. only.) Angelus Univ.

Murphy, D. C. Recreations in history and geography. *30 c. net. Educ. Pub.

Myers, S. E. Heroes and happenings of Egypt, Assyria, Greece. 80 c. S. E. Myers.

Plunket, I. L. Fall of the old order: textbook of European history, 1763-1815. $1.10. Oxford Univ.

Rawlinson, G: Ancient hist. fr. the earliest times to the fall of the Western Empire. $1.75; $3.50. Lamb Pub.

Reade, W: W. Martyrdom of man. $1.50 net. Lane.

Reich, E. General history of western nations from 5000 B.C. to 1900 A.D. pt. 1, Antiquity. 2 v. *$4 net. Macmillan.

Reimensnyder, J: M. Ancient history and the Bible. 35 c.; 20 c. Lutheran Pub.

Renouf, V. A. Outlines of general history. *$1.30 net. Macmillan.

Rhodes, J. F. Historical essays. **$2.25 net. Macmillan.

Ridpath, J: C. Hist. of the world. 9 v. $65. Jones Bros.

Robarts, E. True stories from hist. 60 c. Dodge.

Robinson, J. H. History: [a lecture.] (Add. pubs. for price.) Columbia Univ.

Rocheleau, W: F., *ed.* Pract. hist. of the world. 8 v. $26.75. Dixon.

Rogers, J. E. T. Economic interpretation of history. *$1.50 net. Putnam.

Roosevelt, T. Biological analogies in hist. 60 c.; 35 c. Oxford Univ.

Smith, C: A. Significance of hist. in a democracy. Guilford Battle.

Stories of the ancient world. **65 c. net. Century Co.

Terhune, A. P. World's great events. **$1.20 net. Dodd.

Terhune, *Mrs.* M. V. H. Where ghosts walk. $2.50 net. Putnam.

HISTORY.—*Continued.*
Upward, A. Secrets of the past; [historical narratives.] $1.50. Brentano's.
Vinogradoff, P., *ed.* Oxford studies in social and legal hist. v. 1. $4.15. Oxford Univ.
See also Archæology;—Architecture;—Battles;—Bible; — Biography; — Church history;—Civilization;—Costumes; — Crusades; — Education;—Ethnology;—Finance;—Geography;—Historians;—Inquisition; — Inscriptions;—Jews;—Liberty;—Middle Ages;—Military art and science;—Naval art and science;—Political science;—Reformation;—Renaissance;—Sailors;—Slavery; —Social science; —Statistics;—Wealth;—Woman;—Words;—*also* names of persons, countries and places.

History, authority and theology. Headlam, A. C. $2 net. Young Churchman.
History making; story of a great nation, the national departments and their duties. '10 (N19) c. 8°, $2. Chapple.
History of a conscript of 1813. Erckmann, E. $1.50 net. Macmillan.
History of a strange case. Abbott, D: P. (Add. pubs. for price.) Open Court.
History of Aythan Waring. Jacob, V. **$1.25 net. Dutton.
History of Christianity in Japan. Cary, O. In 2 v. ea., *$2.50 net. Revell.
History of civilization. Allen, E. A. 8 v. $21. Ferguson-A.
History of cumulative voting and minority representation in Illinois. Moore, B. F. 50 c. Univ. of Ill.
History of England in words of one syllable; il. after famous paintings by Holbein, Cope and others. '09(N) 11+94 p. 8°, 50 c. Dutton.
History of English poetry. Courthope, W: J: In 6 v. v. 5, 6. ea., $3.25 net. Macmillan.
History of freedom. Acton, J: E. E: D.-A., *Lord.* *$3 net. Macmillan.
History of medieval philosophy. De Wolf, M. C. J. *$3 net. Longmans.
History of Mr. Polly. Wells, H. G: $1.50. Duffield.
History of story-telling. Ransome, A. $3 net. Stokes.
History of the adventures of Joseph Andrews and his friend Mr. Abraham Adams. *See* Fielding, H:
History of the Cavendish Laboratory, 1871-1910. '10(D24) il. pors. O. $2.60 net. Longmans.
History of the Red River Valley, past and present; incl. acct. of the counties, cities, towns and villages of the valley from the times of their first sttlement and formation, by various writers. In 2 v. '10(My7) il. pors. 4°, $15. Herald Pr., (N. Dak.)
History of the sciences. S. **75 c. net. Putnam.
—Duff. Hist. of Old Testament criticism.
—Forbes. Hist. of astronomy.
—Thorpe. Hist. of chemistry. 2 v.
History of Tom Jones. Fielding, H: 2 v. $1.60; $2.50. Macmillan.
History of twenty-five years. Walpole, *Sir* S. In 4 v. v. 3-4. $8. Longmans.

Hitch, Marcus.
Goethe's Faust: a fragment of socialist criticism. '08(My16) c. S. (Standard socialist ser.) 50 c. Kerr.

Hitchcock, Albert Wellman.
Psychology of Jesus: study of the development of His self-consciousness. '08 (My23) c. 12°, *$1.25 net. Pilgrim Press.

Hitchcock, Alfr. Marshall.
Enlarged practice-book in English composition. '09(Mr6) c. il. D. $1. Holt.
Theme-book in English composition. '10 (Ap2) c. D. 50 c. Holt.
Words and sentences, including a review of grammar. '08(Mr7) c. D. 35 c. Holt.

Hitchcock, C: H:
Hawaii and its volcanoes. '09(N20) c. il. O. $2. Hawaiian Gazette.

Hitchcock, E:, and Nelligan, R: Fs.
Wrestling, 'catch-as-catch-can' style. '10 (S) c. 43 p. por. il. 16°, (Spalding's athletic lib.) pap., 10 c. Am. Sports.

Hitchcock, Ethan Allen.
Fifty years in camp and field; diary; ed. by W. A. Croffut. '10(F5) c. por. O. **$4 net. **Putnam.**

Hitchcock, Rev. F. R. Montgomery.
Christ and his critics. '10(D10) 12°, $1 net. Revell.

Hitchcock, Ja. Ripley Wellman, ed.
See Hart, Albert Bushnell.

Hitchcock, Mary E., [Mrs. Roswell D. Hitchcock.]
Tales out of school about naval officers (and others) by a woman who has lived on a man-of-war. '08(Je13) c. il. D. $1. Gotham Press.

Hitchcock, Romyn.
Automatic telegraphy; "study of the commercial aspects of machine telegraphy." '10(Ap23) il. 8°. Gov. Pr. Off.

Hitchcock, Mrs. Roswell D.
See Hitchcock, Mary E.

Hitchener, Eliz.
See Shelley, Percy Bysshe.

Hitchens, Edn. Lockhart.
Bible and labor: an economic interpretation of the Scriptures. '08(N) c. 80 p. por. D. pap., 25 c. Baker & B.

Hite, Maxwell H.
Lessons in how to become a successful moving picture machine operator. '10 (My21) c. figs. O. pap., $1. M. H. Hite.

Hitherto untold. Anderson, G. $1. Cochrane.

Hitlofi, Iven.
Grafoni; new phonography, a world-shorthand for universal adoption; complete instructor. [3d ed.] '10(Ap) c. 17+20-48 p. 16°, 50 c. I. Hitlofi.

Hitt, Rodney, comp.
See Adams, Braman B.

Hix, Melvin.
First year in United States history. Bks. 1 and 2. '08(D5) c. il. 12°, ea., 40 c. Hinds.
See also Hervey, Wa. Lowrie.
—, **comp.** Book of lullabies. '09(Ag21) c. 12°, (Golden hour ser.) 40 c. Educ. Pub.
Brief outline of the books I have read. [New ed.] '09(Ag7) c. O. pap., 25 c. **Hinds.**

Hixon, Hiram W.
Notes on lead and copper smelting and copper converting; rev. with accounts of twelve years' experiment and development. 4th ed. '09(My22) c. il. 8°, $3. Hill Pub.

Ho! to the land of sunshine. New Mexico Territory. *Bu. of Immigration.* (Not for sale.) N. M. Bu. of Immigration.

Hoadley, G: Arth.
Elements of physics. '08(S12) c. il. tabs., D. $1.20. Am. Bk.
Physical laboratory handbook. '09(Ap3) c. figs. D. 50 c. Am. Bk.
Teachers' manual to accompany Elements of physics. '05(D5) c. il. D. pap., 25 c. Am. Bk.

Hoag, Ernest Bryant.
Health studies; applied physiology and hygiene; with prefatory note by D: Starr Jordan. '09(D18) c. il. 12°, 75 c. Heath.

HOAGLAND MEMORIAL PRESBYTERIAN CHURCH, Dover, N. J.
See Halloway, W: Whiteman.

Hoare, Rev. E.
Communion and communicant. '08(My16) Fe. *20 c. net. Am. S. S.
Shall I go to confession? '08(My16) Fe. *20 c. net. Am. S. S.

Hoare, Lady Katharine L.
Art of tatting; with introd. by the Queen of Roumania. '10(D10) il. Q. $7 net. Longmans.

Hobart, Alvah Sabin, D.D.
Our silent partner. '08(Mr21) c. 12°, *75 c. net. Revell.
Tillage of the heart; or, the cultivation of goodness. '10(Ja15) c. por. 16°, 50 c. Am. Bapt.

Hobart, Edn. L.
Semi-hist. of a boy-veteran of the 28th Regiment Illinois Infantry Volunteers; [with The truth about Shiloh.] '10 (Ap23) il. front. pors. 8°, $1.25. E. L. Hobart.
Story of Vicksburg and Jackson; "Lest we forget"; dispatches of Charles A. Dana; General John A. McClernand, General Jacob G. Lauman; rept. of Colonel I: Pugh; rept. of Colonel G: E. Bryant; rept. of Captain F: E. Prime; "All about Jackson," by S: M. Howard; comp. from the official records of the Union and Confederate armies; [appended: "Shiloh"; and History of the 13th Illinois.] [1910.] (Ap23) 28 p. il. 8°, pap., 25 c. E. L. Hobart.

HOBART, Garret Augustus.
Magie, D: Life of Garret Augustus Hobart, twenty-fourth Vice-President of the United States. **$2.50 net. Putnam.

Hobart, G: Vere, ["Dinkelspiel;" "Noah Lott;" "Hugh McHugh."]
Dinkelspiel's letters to Looey. '08(My2) c. il. nar. D. 75 c. G: W. Dillingham.
Go to it. '08(Mr28) c. il. D. †75 c. G: W. Dillingham.

Hobart, H: Metcalf.
Electric motors; continuous, polyphase, and single-phase motors. 2d ed., entirely rewritten, rev. and enl. '10(O8) il. 8°, $5.50 net. Macmillan.
Electricity. '10(Ag6) 8°, $2 net. Van Nostrand.

—, and Ellis, A. G.
High-speed dynamo electric machinery. '08 (Ag1) c. diagrs., 8°, **$6 net. Wiley.

Hobart, Ja. Fs.
Millwrighting. '09(Mr27) il. *$3 net. Hill Pub.

Hobbes, T:
Leviathan; repr. from the ed. of 1651, with an essay by the late W. G. Pogson Smith. '09(N13) D. 85 c. Oxford Univ.

HOBBES, Thomas.
Taylor, A. E: Hobbes. *50 c. net. Dodge.

Hobbs, W: Herbert, and Leith, C: Kenneth.
Characteristics of the inland-ice of the Arctic regions. '10(N19) c. il. maps, 8°, $2. Am. Philosophical.
Pre-Cambrian volcanic and intrusive rocks of the Fox River valley, Wisconsin. '08(F1) il. maps, O. (Univ. of Wis. bull., Science ser.) pap., 25 c. Univ. of Wis.

Hobhouse, Rev. Wa.
The church and the world in idea and in history; eight lectures preached before the University of Oxford in the year 1909 on the foundation of the late Rev. John Bampton, Canon of Salisbury. '10 (Jl16) 8°, $3.25 net. Macmillan.
Theory and practice of ancient education. '09(D25) O. bds., *$1 net. Stechert.

Hoblyn, R: D.
Dict. of terms used in medicine and the collateral sciences. 14th ed., rev. throughout, with numerous additions by J: A. P. Price. '09, [1910.] (F) 12+868 p. 12°, *$3 net. Macmillan.

Hobson, J: Atkinson.
Industrial system; inquiry into earned and unearned income. '10(Ap2) O. $2.50 net. Longmans.

Hobson, Jonathan Todd.
Footprints of Abraham Lincoln; presenting many interesting facts, reminiscences and illustrations never before published. '09(Je) c. 114 p. il. pors. 12°, 50 c. Un. B. Pub.

Hobson, R. L.
Porcelain: oriental, continental and British; book for handy reference for collectors. '10(S10) il. front. in col. O. $2.15 net. Stokes.

Hobson, Richmond Pearson.
Fortifications bill; speech in the House of Representatives, Thursday, Feb. 18, 1909. '09(My) 23 p. 8°., pap. (Add. Superintendent for price.) U. S., Supt of Docs.
In line of duty. '10(O8) c. il. D. $1.50. Appleton.

Hockenberry, J: Coulter.
Rural school in the United States. '08 (S19) c. 4°, 75 c. J: C. Hockenberry.

Höcker, Gustav.
Arnold of Winkelried; tr. from the German by G: P. Upton. '08(O10) c. il. S. (Life stories for young people.) *60 c. net. McClurg.

HOCKEY.
Farrell, A. How to play ice hockey. 10 c. Am. Sports.
White, E. E. Complete hockey player. **$2 net. Jacobs.
See also Games.

Hocking, Jos.
Chariots of the Lord. '09(Je19) il. D. $1.50. Eaton & M.
Sword of the Lord: romance of the time of Martin Luther. '09(My15) c. 12°, $1.25. Dutton.

Hocking, Rev. Silas Kitto.
Who shall judge? '10(S) il. 8°, $1.50. Cassell.

Hocking, W: Ernest.
On the law of history. '09(O16) Q. (Univ. of Cal. pubs.; Philosophy.) pap., 20 c. Univ. of Cal.
Two extensions of the use of graphs in elementary logic. '09(Je12) figs. Q. (Univ. of Cal. pubs.; Philosophy.) pap., 15 c. Univ. of Cal.

Hodell, C: Wesley.
Old yellow book: source of Browning's "The ring and the book," in complete photo-reproduction; with translation, essay, and notes. '08(S19) il. por. Q. (Carnegie Institution of Washington pub.) pap., $7. Carnegie.

Hodgdon, Jeanette Rector.
First course in American history. In 2 bks. '08(D5) c. il. 12°, ea., 65 c. net. Heath.

Hodge, R: Morse.
New Testament authors and their works. '09(S) c. 63 p. 8°, pap., *30 c. net. Seiler.

Hodge, W: H:
Intuitive perception; presented by a new philosophy of natural realism: in accord with universally accepted truths. '10 (My14) 8°, $1.50. Wickersham.

Hodges, Almon Danforth.
Almon Danforth Hodges and his neighbors; autobiographical sketch of a typical old New Englander; ed. by Almon D. Hodges, jr.; presented by Amory G. Hodges and Almon D. Hodges, jr. '09, [1910.] (Mr) 7-353 p. il. pors., facsim. 8°, o. p. A. D. Hodges.

Hodges, Dean G:
Apprenticeship of Washington, and other sketches of significant colonial personages. '09(F20) c. D. **$1.25 net. Moffat.
Baccalaureate sermon preached before the candidates for degrees in Columbia University, June 9, 1907. '07, [1908.] (Mr.) 12 p. 8°, pap., gratis. G: Hodges.
Garden of Eden; stories from the first nine books of the Old Testament. '09(O2) c. il. O. $1.50. Houghton M.
Independence of the ministry. '10(Je) c. 18 p. 12°, (Claims and opportunities of the Christian ministry.) 10 c. Y M. C. A.
Year of grace, Trinity to Advent. '10 (Je4) c. D. $1.25 net. Whittaker.

Hodges, Dean G:, comp.
When the King came: stories from the four Gospels. '08(S26) c. il. D. **$1.25 net. Houghton M.

Hodges, H: Clay, ["Alvidas."]
Science and key of life; planetary influences in 6 v. v. 4-6. '10(Ap9) il. por. O. ea., $2. Astro Pub.

Hodges, Leigh Mitchell, comp.
Poems we love. '08(N14) c. 8°, $1.50. Dodge.

Hodges, W: Romaine.
Carl Wimar: biography. '08(D) c. 37 p. il. 8°, $1.25; $1.50. C. Reymershoffer.

Hodgetts, E: Arth. Brayley.
Court of Russia in the nineteenth century. '08(Je20) 2 v., pors. tabs., O. *$6 net. Scribner.

Hodgman, Fs.
Surveyor's tables. '07, [1908.] c. 6+124 p. 16°, Star ed., $1.50; Regular ed., $1. Hodgman.

Hodgson, Ernest Franklin.
Wigwam portable houses. '08(O) c. 42 p. il. 4°. (Add. author for price.) E. F. Hodgson.

Hodgson, F: T:
A B C of the steel suare and its uses. '08 (N) c. 136 p. il. 12°, 50 c. Drake.
Carpenters and joiners pocket companion; handy reference book; to which is prefixed thorough treatise on "Carpenters' geometry." '10(Je25) c. il. tabs., 12°, 50 c. Indust. Bk.
Estimating frame and brick houses, barns, stables, factories, and outbuildings. 8th ed., enl., amended and modernized. '10 (Je18) il. $1. D: Williams.
Light and heavy timber framing made easy; balloon framing, mixed framing, heavy timber framing, houses, factories, bridges, barns, rinks, timber-roofs, and all other kinds of timber buildings. '09(N20) c. il. 8°. $2. Drake.
Practical bricklaying self-taught. '08(F1) il. plans, 12°, $1. Drake.
Pract. cabinet maker and furniture designer's assistant; with essays on hist. of furniture, taste in design, color and materials; with full explan. of the canons of good taste in furniture. '10(F26) c. il. 12°, $2. Drake.
Pract. steel construction; dealing with all phases in the construction of our modern steel buildings. '10(D17) c. il. 12°, $1. Drake.
Practical stonemasonry self-taught. '08 (Ja11) il. plans, tables, 12°, $1. Drake.
—, ed. Treatise on the five orders of architecture; comp. from the works of Sir W: Chambers, Palladio, Vignola, Gwilt and others; comp., rev. and ed. by F: T. Hodgson. '10(S17) c. il. 12°, $2. Drake.

Hodgson, G: B.
From smithy to senate: life story of James Annand, journalist and politician: with introd. by the Earl of Aberdeen; a chapter of reminiscences by Aaron Watson. '08(D5) il. pors. 8°, *$1.75 net. Cassell.

Hodgson, Geraldine.
Studies in French education from Rabelais to Rousseau. '08(O17) D. $1.10. Putnam.

Hodgson, W: Earl.
Angler's season. '09(Jl17) il. 12°, *$1.50 net. Macmillan.

Hodgson, W: Hope.
Carnacki, the ghost finder, and a poem. '10(F26) c. 8°, 25 c. P. R. Reynolds.

Hodson, A. L.
Letters from a settlement. '09(Ap24) il. D. $1.50. Longmans.

Hodson, Fred, ed.
Broad lines in science teaching; with introd. by M. E. Sadler. '10(F19) O. *$1.25 net. Macmillan.

Hodson of Hodson's Horse. *See* Trotter, Lionel H.

Hoe, Rob.
Catalogue of books of emblems. '09(Mr) (Priv. pr.) R. Hoe.

Hoenshel, Elmer Ulysses.
My three days in Gilead. '09(Jl17) por. S. 50 c.; pap., 30 c. E. U. Hoenshel.

Hofer, Mari Ruef.
Music for the child world. 2 v. v. 1, Characteristic scenes and sketches; v. 2, Rhythms, marches and games. '08(O) c. v. 1, $1.25; v. 2, $1.50. C. F. Summy Co.

Hoff, Arth. Bainbridge.
Battle ship's order book. '08(Ap.) c. 96 p. 12°, $1. U. S. Naval Inst.

Hoffer, Cora Mickle.
Heart of the South. '10(Ap23) c. por. 8°, 50 c. C. M. Hoffer.

Hoffert, Franklin Pierce, comp.
Hufford family hist., 1729-1909. '09(O23) c. il. pors. f°, $3. F. P. Hoffert.

Höffding, Harold.
History of modern philosophy. '08(Je6) 2 v., price increased from $7.50 to *$9 net. Macmillan.

Hoffman, C: Fenno.
Stories. '08(Ag15) 16°, (World's story-teller's ser.; ed. by A. Ransome.) *40 c. net. Dutton.

Hoffman, E: Fenno.
Proceedings to obtain inspection of books and papers in aid of suits at law or in equity. '08(Ap.) c. 21 p. O. pap., 25 c. E: F. Hoffman.

Hoffman, Fk. Sargent.
Sphere of religion: consideration of its nature and of its influence upon the progress of civilization. '08(F15) c. D. **$1.75 net. Putnam.

Hoffman, Ja. D:
Course of instruction in elementary machine design. '09(My1) c. il. 8°, *$2.50 net. J. D: Hoffman.

—, and Raber, B: F:
Hdbk. for heating and ventilating engineers. '10(N5) c. il. plans, 12°, $3.50. J. D: Hoffman.

Hoffman, Otto Sichel, ed.
Optimistic voices; introd. by Horace Fletcher. New ed., rev. and enl. '09 (Ag28) c. D. pap., *35 c. net. O. S. Hoffman.

Hoffman, R:
Some musical recollections of fifty years; with biograph. sketch by his wife. '10 (Ap16) c. pors. O. $1.50 net. Scribner.

Hoffman, Rob. Fulkerson.
Mark Enderby, engineer. '10(N12) c. il. O. $1.50. McClurg.

Hoffmann, Mrs. Aline Lydia Rossier, [Mrs. Adolphe Hoffmann.]
Before marriage: mother's parting counsel to her son on the eve of his marriage. '08(Ap11) c. por. S. **35 c. net. Vir Pub.
Social duty of our daughters: a mother's talk with mothers and their grown daughters. '08(Ap11) c. por. S. **35 c. net. Vir Pub.

Hoffmann, F: L., rep.
See Ohio. *Sup. ct.* Repts.

Hofmann, Josef.
Piano playing: book of simple suggestions. '08(N7) c. il. D. **75 c. net. McClure.
Piano questions answered; little book of direct answers to 250 questions asked by piano students. '09(O30) c. D. **75 c. net. Doubleday, P.

Hoffmannstal, Hugo Hofmann von.
Electra; tr. by Arth. Symons. '08(Ap11) c. 12°, **$1.25 net. Brentano's.

Hofmeister, Christopher W., and Spencer, P. J.
Acturi: a synopsis of human progress; or, the theocracy of the Almighty evolved in the democracy of humanity; historic, prophetic and scientific. '08(S) c. 137 p. D. pap., 25 c. C. W. Hofmeister.

Hog.
Coburn, F. D. Swine in America. *$2.50 net. Judd.
Dietrich, W: Swine. $1.50. Saunders Pub.
Donovan, J: P. Handling the hog from start to finish. $3. Butchers' Advocate.
Dorset, M. Hog cholera. Gov. Pr. Off.
Knapp, S. A. Hog raising in the south. U. S., Supt. of Docs.

Hogan, Albert Edmond.
Pacific blockade. '08(N21) O. $2. Oxford Univ.

Hogan, Mrs. J. L.
See Hogan, Louise E. Shimer.

Hogan, Louise E. Shimer, [Mrs. J. L. Hogan.]
Children's diet in home and school; with classified recipes and menus. New ed. '10(D3) 12°, 75 c. net. Doubleday, P.
How to feed children. 9th ed., newly rev. '09(Jl17) c. il. D. **$1 net. Lippincott.

Hogan, Wilber Fisk, ["Ino."]
The story of sixty years. '08(Ag) c. 112 p. 8°, 50 c. W. F. Hogan.

Hogarth, D: G:
Accidents of an antiquary's life. '10(My7) il. 8°, $2.50 net. Macmillan.
Ionia and the East: six lectures del. before the University of London. '09(My15) map, O bds., $1.15. Oxford Univ.

Hogarth, W:
Analysis of beauty. '09(My8) c. il. D. *$1.50 net. Silver Lotus.
Marriage à la mode; (7 plates and letter-press.) '10(F19) il. f°. Dutton.
Masterpieces of Hogarth (1697-1764). '10 (S10) il. T. (Painters ser.) leath., 75 c.; pap., 25 c. net. Stokes.

HOGARTH, William.
Hind, C: L. Hogarth. 65 c. net. Stokes.
Hogarth's London. Wheatley, H: B: *$4.80 net. Dutton.
Hogg, C: Edg.
Pleading and forms; pract. treatise on the system of common law pleading, supplemented with numerous precedents of declarations, pleas, replications, and court orders, now in use in the state of West Virginia. 3d ed. '08, [1909.] (Ja) c. 56+719 p. O. shp., $6. Clarke.
Treatise and forms for use in justices' courts and upon appeals therefrom to the circuit ct.; also in proceedings of lunacy and bastardy, and before coroners, etc., adapted to the state of West Virginia. '09(Ap) c. 48+879 p. O. $7.50. W. H. Anderson.
Hogle, W: M.
Internal combustion engines. '09(Ap17) c. figs. O. *$3 net. McGraw.
Höher als die kirche. Hillern, *Frau* W. B. v. 50 c. C: E. Merrill.
Hoile, Ja. T., and Brown, W: C.
Correspondence between James T. Hoile, secretary Manufacturers' Association of N. Y., and William C. Brown, senior vice-president N. Y. Central lines, on railway freight rates. '08(S) 28 p. D. pap. (Add. pubs. for price.) Manufacturers' Assoc.
HOISTING MACHINERY.
Böttcher, A. Cranes. *$10 net. Van Nostrand.
Branston, J: W: Girders for electric overhead cranes. 25 c. Indust. Press.
Design of electric overhead cranes. 25 c. Indust. Press.
Theory of crane design. 25 c. Indust. Press.
See also Machinery.
Holbach, Mrs. Maude M.
Bosnia and Herzegovina; some wayside wanderings. '09(N20) il. map, D. *$1.50 net. Lane.
Holbein, Hans.
Masterpieces of Holbein the younger; reproductions of photographs. '08(F22) il. T. (Painters' ser.) pap., *25 c. net; leath., *75 c. net. Stokes.
HOLBEIN, Hans.
Bensusan, S: L. Holbein. *65 c. net. Stokes.
Holborn Hill. Tearle, C. $1.20. Clode.
Holbrook, D: Leverett.
Panorama of creation, as presented in Genesis. '09(Ja23) c. il. D. *50 c. net. S. S. Times.
Holbrook, Evans.
Cases on judicial opinions and precedents. '10(Ap) c. O. pap., 75 c. West Pub.
Holbrook, Florence.
Hiawatha alphabet. '10(N12) c. col. il. Q. 75 c. Rand, McN. & Co.
Holbrooke, G: Otis.
Aryan word-building. '10(D10) c. 8°, $2. Knickerbocker Press.
Holcomb, I: Mason.
See Thoburn, Jos. Bradfield.
Holcombe, Arnold.
Odd man. '09(N20) D. $1.50. Lane.
Holcombe, Chester.
Real Chinaman. New ed. '09(D) il. 8°, *$2 net. Dodd.
Holden, Rev. G. F.
Holy Ghost, the comforter; with an introd. by the Bishop of London. '08(F15) D. *90 c. net. Longmans.
Holden, Ja. Austin.
Glens Falls, New York, "the Empire City"; our part and place in history: descriptive and illustrative ed. introducing to the readers the Empire city of the state and her citizens, past and present. '08, [1909.] (Je) 16+32 p. il. pors. f°, 60 c. Glens Falls Pub.
Holden, Rev. J: Stuart.
Pre-eminent Lord and other sermons. '09 (N13) O. *$1.25 net. Doran.
Price of power. '08(F15) c. 16°, *50 c. net. Revell.
Redeeming vision. '09(Mr6) 12°, *$1.25 net. Revell.
Supposition and certainty. '08(Ag15) 12°, *75 c. net. Revell.
Holder, C: F:
Big game at sea. '08(Mr28) c. il. O. *$2 net. Outing.
Channel Islands of California; book for the angler, sportsman and tourist. '10 (Je11) c. il. maps, . $2 net. McClurg.
The marooner. '08(D12) c. D. $1.50. B. W. Dodge.
Method of studying the life history of fishes; paper presented before the Fourth International Fishery Congress, Washington, Sept. 22 to 26, 1908. '10(Jl) 1137-1141 p. 4°. Gov. Pr. Off.
Plan for an educational exhibit of fishes; paper presented before the Fourth International Fishery Congress, held at Washington, Sept. 22 to 26, 1908. '10 (Jl) 1309-1314 p. 8°. Gov. Pr. Off.
Recreations of a sportsman on the Pacific Coast. '10(My7) c. il. O. $2 net. Putnam.
—, and Jordan, D: Starr.
Fish stories, alleged and experienced; with a little history natural and unnatural. '09(Mr13) c. il. Q. (American nature ser.; group 5, diversions from nature.) **$1.75 net. Holt.
Holdich, Sir T: Hungerford.
Gates of India; historical narrative. '10 (Ap16) maps, O. $3.25 net. Macmillan.
Holdsworth, J: Thom, and Dewey, Davis Rich.
First and second banks of the United States. '10(O) 311 p. fold. tabs., 8°. Gov. Pr. Off.
Holdsworth, W. S.
History of English law. In 3 v. v. 1. '08 (Je27); v. 2, 3. '09(O) 8°, ea., $4 net. Little, B. & Co.
Hole, Rev. C:
Manual of English church hist.; with preface by the Very Rev. H: Wace. '10(N5) D. $1.25 net. Longmans.
Hole, Wa.
Distribution of gas. '08(Jl4) il. 8°, *$5 net; New ed. '10(Je4) c. $6. Spon.
Hole book. Newell, P: $1.25. Harper.
Hole in the coat. Eddy, C: $1.50. Cassell.

Holiday, E.
How to train horses and dogs. '10(O1) il. O. pap., $1. Dodge City.
Holiday and social happenings. Salisbury, M. E., *comp.* $1.50; $2.50. Barse & H.
Holiday booklets ser. 3 v. '10(D) 16°, ea., 25 c. net. Dodd.
Holiday plays. Merington, M. $1.25. Duffield.
Holiday study of cities and ports. Peabody, R. S. $1. Boston Soc. Architects.
Holiday tales. Oliver, E. A. 75 c. Yonkers Pub.
Holiday touch. Loomis, C: B. **$1.25 net. Holt.
Holiday with the birds. Marks, J. A. 75 c. Harper.
HOLIDAYS.
Blair, M., *comp.* Our holidays: recitations and exercises. 50 c. McLoughlin.
Hazeltine. M. E., *ed.* Anniversaries and holidays. 25 c. Wisconsin Free Lib.
Tittle, W., *comp.* Colonial holidays. $2.50 net. Doubleday, P.
See also Arbor day;—Christmas;—Easter;—Fourth of July;—Memorial day;—Thanksgiving day;—Washington's birthday;—*also* Lincoln, Abraham.
Holidays in Connemara. Gwynn, S. L. *$2 net. Macmillan.
HOLINESS.
See Christian life;—Salvation.
Holinshed, Raphael.
Shakespeare's Holinshed: the Chronicle and the historical plays compared by W. G. Boswell-Stone. '08(Ja18) O. (Shakespeare lib.: Shakespeare's England.) *$3.50 net. Duffield.
Holland, Clive.
From the Foreland to Penzance: ports and harbors of the south coast [England]. '08(O17) il. 8°, *$3.50 net. Duffield.
How to use a camera. '08(O17) 12°, (Oval ser.) 50 c. Dutton.
Things seen in Japan. '08(O17) 24°, ("Things seen" ser.) *75 c. net; leath., *$1 net. Dutton.
Tyrol and its people. '09(D4) il. map, 12°, *$2.50 net, boxed. Pott.
Holland, Rev. Cornelius Jos.
Divine story; short life of our blessed Lord, written especially for young people. 4th ed. '10(Je11) c. il. 8°, lib. ed., $1; popular ed., 50 c. J. M. Tally.
Holland, Eliz. Vassall, Lady.
Journal of Elizabeth, Lady Holland, 1791-1811: ed. by the Earl of Ilchester. In 2 v. '08(N14) pors. O. *$6 net. Longmans.
Spanish journal of Elizabeth Lady Holland; ed. by the Earl of Ilchester. '10 (D17) map, por. O. $4.20 net. Longmans.
Holland, H: Hurst.
See Atton, H:
Holland, H: Scott.
Optimism of Butler's "Analogy." '08(O24) O. (Romanes lecture.) pap., 70 c. Oxford Univ.
Holland, Ja. W:, M.D.
Textbook of medical chemistry and toxicology. 2d ed., rev. and enl. '08(D) c. 9-655 p. il. 8°, *$3 net. Saunders.
Urine and clinical chemistry of the gastric contents, the common poisons and milk. '09(Ja23) c. 12°, *$1 net. Blakiston.
Holland, Josephine Park.
Calhoun Strout: psychic. '09(Je) 9-70 p. 12°, 50 c. J. P. Holland.
Holland, Rob. Afton, D.D.
Commonwealth of man: Slocum lectures, 1894. New ed. '08(Je13) c. 12°, *$1 net. Young Churchman.
Holland, Rob. W., and Nixon, Alfr.
Banking law. '08(D19) D. (Longmans' commercial ser.) $1.75. Longmans.
Holland, Rupert Sargent.
Builders of united Italy. '08(S12) c. D. **$2 net. Holt.
Historic boyhoods. '09(N20) c. 12°, *$1.50 net. Jacobs.
Historic girlhoods. '10(D17) c. O. $1.50 net. Jacobs.
Man in the tower. '09(O9) c. il. D. †$1.50. Lippincott.
Holland, T: Erskine.
Elements of jurisprudence. 11th ed. '10 (S) c. 451 p. O. $2.50. Oxford Univ.
Laws of war on land, (written and unwritten.) '08(O24) O. $1.50. Oxford Univ.
Letters to *The Times* upon war and neutrality, (1881-1900;) with some commentary. '09(N13) O. *$1.75 net. Longmans.
Valedictory retrospect (1874-1910); being lecture del. at All Souls' College, June 17, 1910. '10(Ag27) O. pap., 35 c. Oxford Univ.
HOLLAND.
See Netherlands.
HOLLAND, Mich.
Huizinga, G: F. What the Dutch have done in the west of the United States. (Priv. pr.) E: Bok.
HOLLAND HOUSE, London.
Sanders, L. Holland House circle. *$3.50 net. Putnam.
HOLLAND SOCIETY, N. Y.
Bogert, H: L. Year book of the Holland Society of New York. $5. Knickerbocker Press.
Hollander, Bernard, M.D.
Hypnotism and suggestion in daily life, education and medical practice. '10(O1) D. $1.75. Putnam.
Holleman, Arnold Frederik.
Text-book of inorganic chemistry; issued in Eng. in co-operation with Hermon C: Cooper. 3d Eng. ed., partly rewritten. '08(S12) il. 8°, $2.50. Wiley.
Text-book of organic chemistry; ed. by A. Jamieson Walter, assisted by Owen E. Mott, with the co-operation of the author. 3d English ed., partly rewritten. '10(S17) il. 8°, $2.50. Wiley.
Holley, Rev. C: Dan.
Great discovery of four worlds and their inhabitants: the external world, the world of mind within us, the world of eternity, and world of everlasting punishment. '08(Ag15) c. 12°, 75 c. C: D. Holley
Holley, Clifford Dyer.
Lead and zinc pigments. '09(Ag14) c. figs. 8°, **$3 net. Wiley.
—, and Ladd, Edn. Fremont.
Analysis of mixed paints, color pigments, and varnishes. '08(F8) c. il. 12°. $2.50. Wiley.

Holley, Marietta, ["Josiah Allen's wife."]
Samantha on children's rights. '09(O23) c. il. O. †$1.50. G: W. Dillingham.

Hollick, C: Arth., and Jeffrey, E: C.
Studies of Cretaceous coniferous remains from Kreischerville, N. Y. '09(S) 8+138 p. il. 4°. (N. Y. Botanical Garden memoirs.) $2. N. Y. Botanical.

Holliday, Carl.
Once upon a time. '09(N20) c. 12°, 75 c. B'way Pub.
—, **comp.** Three centuries of southern poetry, (1607-1907.) '08(N) c. 267 p. 12°, *$1 net. Pub. Ho. of M. E. Ch., So.

Hollinger, Mrs. J. A.
See Hollinger, L. Israel.

Hollinger, L. Israel, [Mrs. J. A. Hollinger.]
Threads from three lives. '09(Mr) 6-338 p. 12°, $1. L. I. Hollinger.

Hollings, G: Seymour.
Divine lover, and other poems. '08(D5) S. 40 c. Longmans.

Hollingworth, Harry Levi.
Inaccuracy of movement; with special reference to constant errors. '09(Ag7) il. tabs., O. (Archives of psychology.) pap., 80 c. Science Pr., (N. Y.)

Hollis, Alfr. Claud.
The Nandi, [East African tribe]: their language and folk-lore; with introd. by Sir C: Eliot. '09(Ap3) il. fold. map, O. $5.25. Oxford Univ.

Hollis, H. P.
Chats about astronomy. '10(F19) 12°, *$1.25 net. Lippincott.

Hollister, Horace Adelbert.
High school administration. '09(S) c. 11+379 p. 12°, $1.50. Heath.
Public school buildings and their equipment: with special reference to high schools. '10(My21) il. plans, O. (Univ. of Ill., School of Education, bull.) pap., gratis. Univ. of Ill.

Hollister, Ned.
Mammals collected by John Jay White in British East Africa. '10(Ap) 12 p. il. O. (Smithsonian miscellaneous collections.) pap. Smith. Inst.

Holliston, Mass. Vital records of Holliston, Mass., to the year 1850. '08(Ag) 358 p. 8°, $4.50. N. E. Hist.

Hollmann, G.
Jewish religion in the time of Jesus. '09 (N20) *$1 net. Am. Unitarian.

Hollow needle. Leblanc, M. $1.20, fixed. Doubleday, P.

Hollow tree snowed-in book. Paine, A. B. $1.50. Harper.

Holloway, Jane.
At Flower Farm. '09(N20) il. bds., $1. Stern.

Holloway, T: Beaver.
See Schweinitz, G: Edm. de.

HOLLY.
See Evergreens.

Holly (The). Maury, S. W. 25 c. Lane.

Holly House and Ridges Row. Baldwin, M. $1.50. Lippincott.

Holly ser. of booklets. See Hearn, E: C.

Holly Tree Inn. *See* Dickens, C:

Holm, Eric, [pseud. for Clara Tschudi.]
Eugénie: Empress of the French; tr. from the German by G: P. Upton. '10(O22) c. il. S. (Life stories for young people.) 50 c. net. McClurg.

Holman, D: Emory, M.D.
Holmans in America. v. 1, The descendants of Soloman Holman. '09(My22) il. 8°, *$7 net. Grafton Press.

Holman, Emily Eliz.
Picturesque camps, cabins and shacks. '08 (Mr.) c. 32 p. il. plans, obl. 4°, $2. E. E. Holman.
Picturesque suburban houses; thirty designs from $3000 to $10,000; designed by E. E. Holman. '07, [1909.] (F) c. 32 p. il. plans, f°, $2. E. E. Holman.

Holman, H:
Pestalozzi: account of his life and works. '08(O3) il. D. *$1.10 net. Longmans.

Holman, M. L.
Conservation idea as applied to the American Society of Mechanical Engineers; presidential address. '09(My) 41 p. 8°, pap., 30 c. Am. Soc. Mech. Engineers.

Holman, Worthington C.
Talking points and selling arguments. '08 (Jl) c. 2 v., 11+259; 261-514 p. 8°, $5. Salesmanship.

HOLMAN FAMILY.
See Genealogies.

Holme, C:
Art in England during the Elizabethan and Stuart periods: special extra number of the *International Studio.* '08(Je27) f°, *$3 net. Lane.
—, **ed.** Colour photography, and other recent developments of the art of the camera; special summer number of *The Studio.* '08 (S5) il. Q. pap., *$3 net. Lane.
Gardens of England in the midland and eastern counties; special winter number of *The Studio.* '09(F6) il. 4°, *$3 net. Lane.
Old English colour-prints; text by Malcolm C: Salaman; [special winter number of the *International Studio.*] '10 (F12) col. il. Q. pap., *$3 net. Lane.
Peasant art in Sweden, Lapland and Iceland; autumn number of the *International Studio.* '10(D10) col. il. O. pap., $3 net. Lane.
Portrait miniatures; text by G: C. Williamson; [special spring number of the *International Studio.*] '10(Je11) il. (mostly in col.) Q. $3 net; pap., $2.50 net. Lane.
Sketching grounds; [special extra number of the *International Studio.*] '09(S18) il. Q. *$3 net. Lane.
Water colors of J. M. W. Turner; text by W. G. Rawlinson and A. J. Finberg; foreword by Sir C: Holroyd; [special spring number of the *International Studio,* 1909.] '09(Jl3) il. Q. pap., *$3 net. Lane.

Holmes, Mrs. Bettie Fleischmann.
The log of the "Laura" in polar seas. '07, [1908.] (Mr.) c. 137 p. il. map, 4°. Univ. Press, (Camb.)

Holmes, C: J:
Notes on the science of picture-making. '10(My14) 8°, $3 net. Appleton.

Holmes, Christian R.
Modern hospitals, with special reference to our new municipal hospital and its relation to medical education in Cincinnati. '08, [1909.] (Je) 22 p. il. maps, 8°, pap., gratis. Univ. of Cin.

Holmes, Dan. H:
Under a fool's cap; songs. '10(N19) c. 12°, $1. T: B. Mosher.

Holmes, Canon Ernest E:
The church; her books and her sacraments; course of instructions given at All Saints, Margaret Street, in Lent, 1910. '10(N12) D. $1 net. Longmans.
Immortality. '09(Mr13) D. (Oxford lib. of practical theology.) *$1.40 net. Longmans.

Holmes, Gordon.
By force of circumstances. '09(F20) c. D. $1.50. Clode.
The de Bercy affair. '10(N12) c. il. D. $1.50. Clode.

Holmes, J: Simcox, and Foster, J. H.
Study of forest conditions of southwestern Mississippi, Jan., 1908. '10(Jl16) fold. map, 8°, (Miss. State Geol. Survey, bull.) 25 c. Brandon Pr.

Holmes, Mrs. Mary Jane Hawes.
Chateau d'Or; Norah and Kitty Craig, as published in the *New York Weekly,* vol. 31, no. 19. '08(N21) c. front. 12°, †$1. G: W. Dillingham.
Tempest and sunshine. '09(Je19) c. 12°, $1. Rand, McN. & Co.

Holmes, Oliver Wendell.
Complete poetical works. Cabinet ed. '08 (D) c. 12+453 p. por. 12°, $1; hf. cf., $2.25; hf. mor., $3; flex. levant, $3.50. Houghton M.
Poems. '10(D) 12°, (Autograph poets.) $1; hf. leath., $1.50. Houghton M.
Autocrat of the breakfast table. '08(O10) 12°, (Best books ser.) leath., *$1 net. Dutton.
Professor at the breakfast table. '08(O10) 12°, (Best books ser.) leath., *$1 net. Dutton.
See also Stories of humor.

HOLMES, **Oliver Wendell.**
Brooklyn Public Library. **Oliver Wendell** Holmes, 1809-1894; list of books with references to periodicals in the Library. gratis. Brooklyn Lib.
Crothers, S. M. Oliver Wendell Holmes, the autocrat, and his fellow boarders. **75 c. net. Houghton M.

Holmes, Sir R: Rivington.
Windsor. '08(My2) il. 8°, (Color books.) price reduced from *$3 net to *$2.50 net. Macmillan.

Holmes, R: Sill.
The victor. '08(N14) c. O. $1.50. Revell.

Holmes, Stanley Harry.
See Walton, G: A:

Holmes, T:
Known to the police. '08(D5) O. *$3 net. Longmans.

Holmes, T: Rice E:
Ancient Britain and the invasions of Julius Cæsar. '08(Ja18) il. maps, O. $6.75. Oxford Univ.

Holmes, T: Scott.
Wells and Glastonbury. '09(My22) 12°, (Ancient cities ser.) *$1.75 net. Dutton.

Holmes, Urban Tigner.
Notes on experimental engineering, for the instruction of midshipmen at the U. S. Naval Academy. '08(Ja18) il. 8°, $1.50. U. S. Naval Inst.

HOLMES FAMILY.
See Genealogies: Gray, G: A.

Holmgren, C: J: A:
Story of twentieth century Christianity: the road to Jericho. '09(Je12) c. por. O. pap. (Add. pubs. for price.) Forum of Conscience.

Holms, A. Campbell.
Practical shipbuilding: treatise on the structural design and building of modern steel vessels. 2d [and cheaper] ed. In 2 v. v. 1, Text; v. 2, Diagrams and illustrations. '08(My16) O. and F°, *$10 net. Longmans.

Holst, Bernhart Paul, and Roark, Ruric Nevel, eds.
New Teachers' and pupils' cyclop.; reference lib. of hist., geography, biography, literature, economics, civics, arts, sciences, discoveries and inventions. 5 v. '10(F26) c. il. pors. maps, 4°, $18.75. Holst.

—, and others, eds.
Pract. home and school methods of study and instruction in the fundamental elements of education. '10(O15) c. il. 4°, $3.25. Holst.

Holstein-Friesian Association of America. Outlines of the advanced registry system of the Holstein-Friesian Association of America and rules for officially authenticated butter fat tests; with introd. article on Holstein-Friesian cattle and tables showing highest records to date. 4th ed., prep. for students of agricultural schools and others interested. '09(D) 44 p. il. por. 8°. (Add. pubs. for price.) Transcript.

Holt, Hamilton.
Commercialism and journalism. '09(D25) c. D. **$1 net. Houghton M.

Holt, Harrison Jewell.
Calendared isles: romance of Casco Bay. '10(Je18) c. D. $1.50. Badger.

Holt, Luther Emmett, M.D.
Care and feeding of children; catechism for the use of mothers and children's nurses. 5th ed., rev. and enl. '09(O) 195 p. il. 16°, 75 c. Appleton.
Diseases of infancy and childhood, for the use of students and practitioners of medicine. 5th ed., rev. and enl. '09(Jl) 17+1171 p. il. 8°, $6. Appleton.

Holt, Rosa Belle.
Rugs, oriental and occidental, antique and modern. New and enl. ed., entirely reset. '08(O31) c. il. map, Q. *$5 net, boxed. McClurg.

Holt, Sidney T., ed.
The diamond; short and snappy account of its occurrence, characters and applications in jewelry. '09(D) c. 35 p. 12°, gratis. F. Holt.

Holt, W: Leland, and Robinson, W: Josephus, M.D.
Venereal peril; popular treatise on venereal diseases: their nature, course, symptoms and prevention. '09(Mr) c. 58 p. 12°, 50 c.; pap., 25 c. Altrurians.

Holt-White, W: E: Bradden.
Crime club. '10(Ap23) c. 12°, $1.50. Macaulay.
People's king; short life of Edward VII. '10(O8) pors. D. $1.25 net. Lane.

Holton, E: Ellsworth.
Shop mathematics. '10(N19) c. il. 12°, (Haytol ser. of text books for indust-education.) $1.25. Taylor-H.

Holton, Susan.
Little stories about little animals for little children. '09(Jl17) c. il. T. bds., 60 c. Children's Pub.

Holt's English readings. S. Holt.
—Bible. O. T. Old Testament narratives. 60 c.
—Johnson. Selections. 40 c.
—Poe. Selections from critical writings. **75 c. net.

Holtz, F: Leopold.
Nature-study. '08(Je20) c. il. D. **$1.50 net. Scribner.

Holtzclaw, W: Jeziah.
Women of to-day; introd. by J. A. Leavitt, D.D. '09(Jl3) c. por. D. *75 c. net. Bapt. Bk.

Holvik, Johan Andreas.
Beginner's book in Norse. '10(D) c. 284 p. 8°, $1.25. Augsburg.

HOLY COMMUNION.
See Lord's supper.

HOLY EUCHARIST.
See Lord's supper.

HOLY GHOST.
See Holy Spirit.

HOLY GRAIL.
High hist. of the Holy Graal. 35 c. net; 70 c. net. Dutton.

HOLY LAND.
See Palestine.

HOLY LEAGUE.
See **Provence.**

Holy man of Santa Clara. Engelhardt, Z. 75 c. Barry.
Holy mount. Brett, J. *60 c. net. Young Churchman.
Holy Mountain. Reynolds, S. $1.50. Lane.
Holy orders. Corelli, M. †$1.50. Stokes.
Holy practices of a divine lover. More, G. *75 c. net. Herder.
Holy sacrifice of the mass. Gihr, N: *$1 net. Herder.

HOLY SCRIPTURES.
See Bible.

Holy Scriptures, with commentary. D. Jewish Pub.
—Bible. O. T. Micah. 75 c.

HOLY SPIRIT.
Barry, J. G. H. Meditations on the office and work of the Holy Spirit. *$1.50 net. Young Churchman.
Davison, W: T. Life spiritual. $1.50 net. Doran.
Downer, A. C. Mission and ministration of the Holy Spirit. $3 net. Scribner.
Erdman, W: J. Holy Spirit and Christian experience. 25 c. Gospel Pub.

HOLY SPIRIT.—*Continued.*
Holden, G. F. Holy Ghost, the comforter. *90 c. net. Longmans.
McKaig, R. N. Life and times of the Holy Spirit. v. 1. 50 c. Chr. Witness.
Myers, C. Real Holy Spirit. *50 c. net. Revell.
Swete, H: B. Holy Spirit in the New Testament. *$2.60 net. Macmillan.
Torrey, R. A. Person and work of the Holy Spirit as revealed in the Scriptures and in personal experience. $1 net. Revell.
Winstanley, E: W: Spirit in the New Testament, and a survey of the evidence concerning the Holy Spirit. *$1.10 net. Putnam.
See also Trinity.

Holy water and its significance for Catholics. Theiler, H: 50 c. Pustet.

HOLY WEEK.
Beibitz, J. H. Gloria crucis: addresses del. in Lichfield Cathedral Holy Week and Good Friday. $1. Longmans.
Eckman, G: P. Passion week sermons. $1. Jennings.
Ochsenford, S. E. Passion story as recorded by the four evangelists; together with psalms and prayers suitable for the services of Holy Week. 75 c. Gen. Council.
See also Lent.

Holyday prayers; new ritual for New Year and Day of Atonement. 2 v. '09(N) c. 8°, $2. Bloch.

Holzwarth, Franklin Ja.
German students' manual. '08(N) c. 256 p. il. fold. map, 12°, $1.35. H. Rees.
German students' manual of the literature, land and people of Germany. '10(Ap9) c. map, D. $1. Am. Bk.

Homan, Rev. J. A.
Prohibition, the enemy of temperance. '10 (Jl30) O. $1; pap., 50 c. Christian Liberty.

Homans, J. E., ed.
See Patten, W:, *ed.*

Homans, Ja. E:
Self-propelled vehicles; pract. treatise on the theory, construction, operation, care and management of all forms of automobiles. [7th ed., rev.] '09(D25) c. il. 8°, $2. Audel.

Home, Andrew.
Bravo, Bob!; school story. '10(Ja1) il. 12°, $1.50. Lippincott.

Home, C. M.
Under the ban; tale of the interdict. '10 (Ag) 191 p. 8°, pap., 60 c. Herder.

Home, Gordon Cochrane.
Along the rivieras of France and Italy. '08(O10) il. O. (Old world travel.) *$3 net. Macmillan.
Motor routes of England; southern section. '09(O30) il. maps, O. $1.50; leath., $2.25. Macmillan.
Motor routes of France. '10(Je18) il. 8°, (Color books, miscellaneous.) $2 net; leath., $2.25 net. Macmillan.
Romance of London. '10(Ag13) il. map, 8°, (Color books ser. of travel and description.) $1 net. Macmillan.

Home, Gordon Cochrane.—*Continued.*
What to see in England. New ed. '08 (Je6) il. maps, 12°, *$1 net. Macmillan.
Yorkshire vales and wolds. '08(Jl11) il. map, 8°, (Color books.) *$3 net. Macmillan.

HOME.
Cope, H: F: Home as the school for social living. 15 c. Am. Bapt.
Jekyll, G. Home and garden. $2 net. Longmans.
Stocking, J. T. Dearest spot on earth. $1. Caldwell.
See also Domestic economy;—Family;—House decoration.

Home afloat. Townsend, T. $1. Athenia Pub.
Home again with me. Riley, J. W. $2; $3. Bobbs-M.
Home and school ser. for young folks. il. D. Flanagan.
—Rocheleau. Great American industries. Bk. 4. 60 c.
Home and school united in widening circles. Grice, *Mrs.* M. V. M. 60 c. Sower.
Home builder. Abbott, L. **75 c. net. Houghton M.
Home Candy Makers, Canton, O. Art of home candy making. 2d ed. [1910.] (Ja) c. '09. 5-107 p. il. 8°, $2. Home Candy.
Home-comers. Kirkland, W. $1.20 net. Houghton M.
"Home Counties," pseud.
See Robertson-Scott, J. W.

HOME DECORATION.
See House decoration.

Home from sea. Wasson, G: S. †$1.50. Houghton M.
Home garden. Rexford, E. E. **$1.25 net. Lippincott.
Home gymnastics. Wide, A. *50 c. net. Funk.
Home, health and success. Nelson, T. $1. Gospel Trumpet Co.
Home letters. Sherman, W: T. **$2 net. Scribner.
Home library of law: *See* Bolles, Albert S. Every man's lawyer.
Home life. Diggle, J: W: *60 c. net. Cassell.
Home life in all lands. Bk. 2. Morris, C: **$1 net. Lippincott.
Home life in America. Busbey, K. G. $2 net. Macmillan.
Home life in England. Paget, H: L. 75 c. net. Longmans.
Home life in Germany. Sidgwick, *Mrs.* C. *$1.75 net. Macmillan.
Home life in Ireland. Lynde, R. $2.50 net. McClurg.
Home life in Italy. Gordon, L. D. *$1.75 net. Macmillan.
Home life in Spain. Bensusan, S: L. $1.75 net. Macmillan.
Home life in Turkey. Garnett, L. M. J. *$1.75 net. Macmillan.
Home life of the ancient Greeks. Blümner, H. $2 net. Cassell.
Home made hash. Lloyd, J. A. $1.25. J. A. Lloyd.
Home-made ice-cream. Metzgar, C: M. $1; 50 c. Metzgar.
Home made jingles. Sorenson, G. $1. Douglas Pr.
Home memories. Barber, E. $1.50. Badger.
Home mission ser. 12°, *50 c. net; pap., *30 c. net. Revell.
—Crowell. Call of the waters.
Home mission stories. il. D. †$1.25. Am. Bapt.
—Tomlinson. Sifting of Philip.

HOME MISSIONS.
See Missions and missionaries.

Home nursing. Hufton-Windust, F. *50 c. Macmillan.
Home occupations for boys. Johnston, B. 50 c. Jacobs.
Home of the Soul. Wagner, C: **$1.20 net. Funk.
Home problems from a new standpoint. Hunt, C. L. *$1 net. Whitcomb.
Home rhymes. Guest, E. A. $1. E. A. Guest.

HOME RULE.
See Ireland.

Home school ser. il. 8°. College Assoc. Pub.
—Nave. Theology for young people. $1.25.
Home ser. 12°, 50 c. Hurst.
—Alcott. Modern Cinderella.
—Alger. Bertha's Christmas vision.
—Carey. For Lilias.—Nellie's memories.—Search for Basil Lyndhurst.
—Clarke. Little Prudy's Dotty Dimple.—Little Prudy's story book.
—John. Baliff's maid.—In the Schillingscourt. —Lady with the rubies.
—Molesworth. Marrying and giving in marriage.—Us.
—Smith. Francis Kane's fortune.—How it all came about.—Heart of gold.
—Walford. Baby's grandmother.
—Whitney. Gayworthys.
—Yonge. Dove in the eagle's nest.

HOME-STUDY.
Gentistoria, the new system (an encyclopedia); original and practical method of self-instruction. 3 v. (Add. pub. for price.) Home Educ.
Skinner, H. M., *ed.* Collegiate course for home study. 12 v. $29.95; $39.95; $57. Cree.

Home-study in vital science. 12 v. '08(D) ea., $1; per set, $10. Psychic World.
Home training bull. *See* McKeever, W: Archibald.
Homemaker ser. *See* Putnam's.

HOMEOPATHY.
Allen, H: C. Materia medica of the nosodes with provings of the X-rays. $4. Boericke & T.
Blackwood, A. L. Contagious, constitutional and blood diseases. $1.75. Boericke & T.
Boenninghausen, C. M. F. v., *M.D.* Lesser writings; comp. by T: Lindsay Bradford, M.D. $1.50. Boericke & T.
Dewey, W. A. Essentials of homœopathic materia medica and homœopathic pharmacy. *$2 net. Boericke & T.
Nash, E. B. Regional leaders. $1.50. Boericke & T.
Rademacher, J. G. W. Universal and organ remedies. $1. Boericke & T.

HOMEOPATHY.—*Continued.*
Shedd, P. W: Clinic repertory; including a repertory of time modalities. $1.50. Boericke & T.
Ward, J. W: Agnostic in medicine. (Priv. pr.) Murdock Press.
See also Materia medica;—Medicine;—Surgery.

Homer, [Gk. Homeros.]
Iliad: first three books and selections; ed. for the use of schools by J. R. Sitlington Sterrett. Text ed. '08(Je6) c. il. D. (Greek ser. for colleges and schools.) pap., 40 c. Am. Bk.
Iliad; tr. by the Earl of Derby; introd. by F. M. Stawell. '10(N5) 16°, (Everyman's lib.) 35 c. net; leath., 70 c. net. Dutton.
The Iliad; tr. into English hexameter verse by Prentiss Cummings; abridgment which includes all the main story and the most celebrated passages. In 2 v. '10(S10) c. D. $3 net. Little, B. & Co.
Iliad; tr. into English prose by F. H. Blakeney. v. 1, bks. I-XII. '10(Ja8) 12°, (Bohn's lib.) *$1 net. Macmillan.
Odysseia. '09(N13) no paging, Q. bds., $33.60, boxed. Oxford Univ.
Odyssey; W: Cowper's tr.; with notes by F. M. Stawell. '10(D10) 16°, (Everyman's lib.) 35 c. net; leath., 75 c. net. Dutton.
Odyssey; tr. by G. Herbert Palmer. Abridged school ed. '09(Ap10) fold. map, 12°, (Riverside literature ser.) *75 c. net. Houghton M.
See also Perry, W. C.

HOMER, [*Gk.* Homeros.]
Agar, T: L.- Homerica; emendatione and elucidatione of the Odyssey. $4.75. Oxford Univ.
Havell, H. L., *comp.* Stories from the Iliad; retold.—Stories from the Odyssey; retold. ea., $1.50. Dodge.
Lang, A. World of Homer. $2.25 net. Longmans.
Stawell, F. M. Homer and the Iliad. *$3 net. Dutton.

Homer, N. Y., pseud.
See Stienback, Leroy Lindley.

Homerica. Agar, T: L-. $4.75. Oxford Univ.

HOMES.
See Architecture;—Domestic economy;—Family;—Home;—House decoration;—Wall decoration.

Homes of character. Newson, J: H: $1. J: H: Newson.

Homes of the world's babies. Scantlebury, E. E. 50 c. Flanagan.

Homespun. Parker, L. B. †$1.50. Holt.

Homespun religion. Higley, E. E. **30 c. net. Crowell.

HOMESTEAD LAW.
See Land.

Homestead of a colonial dame. Sutcliffe, *Mrs.* A. C. 50 c. A. C. Sutcliffe.

Homesteaders (The). Boyles, K. $1.50. **McClurg.**

HOMILETICS.
See Preaching;—Sermons.

HOMONYMS.
See Words.

HONDURAS, Central America.
Defense of the government of Guatemala before the Central American Court of Justice at Cartago, in the case of Honduras. (Add. pubs. for price.) Int. Bu. Am. Republics.
International Bureau of American Republics. Honduras; general descriptive data. Int. Bu. Am. Republics.

Hone, Percy F.
Southern Rhodesia. '09(D4) il. maps, 8°, *$3.50 net. Macmillan.

Hone, Philip.
Diary of Philip Hone, 1828-1851; ed., with an introd., by Bayard Tuckerman. [New ed.] '10(S24) c. O. $3.50 net. Dodd.

Honesty's garden. Creswick, P. $1.25. Putnam.

Honey, Ja. Alb., M.D.
South-African folk-tales. '10(D17) c. S. $1 net. Baker & T.

Honeyman, Abraham Van Doren.
Honeyman family (Honeyman, Honyman, Hunneman, etc.) in Scotland and America, 1548-1908. '09(Ap17) c. pors. il. 4°, $6. Honeyman.
Justice of the peace: practice and forms in New Jersey. '08(S) 8°, $6. Honeyman.
Van Doorn family; (including Van Dorn, Van Doren, etc., A.D. 1088-1908,) in Holland and America. '09(Ap17) il. 4°, $10. Honeyman.
See also New Jersey. Index-analysis.

HONEYMAN FAMILY.
See Genealogies.

Honeymoon confidences, by the bride herself. '09(N) c. 206 p. front. 12°, $1.25. Hudson Press.

Honk, honk!!. Ford, S. 50 c. M. Kennerley.

Honnold, Arth. B.
Powers and duties of justices of the peace in civil, criminal and special cases in the state of Oklahoma, with forms and proceedings complete; also the law on general subjects. '09(Ja) c. 9+727 p. O. (Add. pubs. for price.) Flood.

HONOLULU, H. I.
See Pacific Scientific Institution.

Honor of a Lee. Travers, *Mrs.* L. M. $1.50. Cochrane.

Honoring God with our substance. Moore, T: V. *5 c. net. Presb. Bd.

Hood, C: Newton, ["A Rollingstone."]
Europe, the second trail; being an acct. of a second experimental trip to Europe, of 80 days' duration, for the purpose of outlining the best second trip to Europe, to cost not over $325, or $4 per day. '10(My21) c. il. D. pap., 50 c. Rolling Stone.

Hood, G: Jüssen.
Descriptive geometry problems. '09(Ap) c. 69 p. diagrs., 16°, 85 c. G: J. Hood.

Hood, J:
Beauty of God as revealed in His works, His written word, and the living word through the ministry of life and light and love. '08, [1909.] (F) c. 372 p. 12°, *$1.25 net. Lanahan.

Hood, Jos. Godfrey.
Trick and fancy pool shots exposed. '08, [1909.] (Mr) c. 96 p. il. 12°, pap., 50 c. Exposé.

Hood, Mary L.
Story of Puck. '07, [1908.] (N) c. 57 p. il. 12°, (Eaton juvenile classics.) 35 c.; Trade ed., 50 c. Eaton & Co.

Hood, T:
Poetical works; with memoir by R: Monkton Milnes. Illustrated Cabinet ed. 3 v. '08(N14) il. 12°, $4.50. Estes.

HOOD, Thomas.
Jerrold, W. C. Thomas Hood: his life and times. *$5 net. Lane.

Hoodman Grey, Christian. Raeburn, D: $1.50. Cassell.

HOOD'S TEXAS BRIGADE.
See **Civil War (United States).**

Hooker, Brian.
Right man. '08(O17) c. il. O. †$1.50. Bobbs-M.

Hooker, E:
Descendants of Rev. Thomas Hooker, Hartford, Ct., 1586-1908; ed. by Marg. Huntington Hooker. '09(D18) c. por. 8°, $10. M. H. Hooker.

Hooker, Eliz. Robbins.
Study book in English literature from Chaucer to the close of the romantic period. '10(Mr12) c. map, 12°, $1. Heath.

HOOKER, Richard.
Paget, F. Introd. to the fifth book of Hooker's treatise of the laws of ecclesiastical polity. $1.75. Oxford Univ.

Hooker, W: Brian.
Two burglars: farce. '08(S19) c. 12°, pap., 25 c. Dick.

HOOKER FAMILY.
See **Genealogies.**

HOOKWORM DISEASE.
Dock, G:, *and* Bass, C: C. Hookworm disease. $2.50. Mosby.
Stiles, C: W. Hookworm disease in its relation to the negro.—Soil pollution and its relation to hookworm disease and typhoid fever.—Treatment of hookworm disease.
See also **Medicine.**

Hooper, F:, and Graham, Ja.
Import and export trade; (formerly known as "Modern business methods";) being a guide to the operations incidental to the trade of the United Kingdom. '08 (D12) tabs., 8°, (Modern manuals of commerce.) *$1 net. Macmillan.

Hooper, J:
See Wells, Percy A.

Hooper, Louisa M.
Selected list of music and books about music for public libraries. '10(Ja15) 8°, 25 c. A. L. A.

Hooper, Luther.
Hand-loom weaving; plain and ornamental; with line drawings by the author and Noel Rooke. '10(D10) il. D. (Artistic crafts ser. of technical hdbks.) bds., $2.25 net. Macmillan.

Hooper, T:, comp.
See Pope, C: H:

HOOPER FAMILY.
See Genealogies: Pope, C: H:

Hoople, Mrs. Carrie Munson.
Along the way, with pen and pencil: [poems.] '10(Ja8) il. 12°, *$1.50 net. Grafton Press.

Hoosier romance. *See* **Riley, Ja. Whitcomb.**

Hoosier widow. Spivey, T: S. $1.50. Neale.

Hoover, Bessie Ray.
Opal. '10(N5) c. il. D. $1.20 net. Harper.
Pa Flickinger's folks. '09(Ag28) c. il. D. †$1. Harper.

Hoover, Herb. Clark.
Principles of mining. '09(My1) il. O. $2.50. Hill Pub.

Hoover, Matthew, H:
Wild ginger, wood sorrel and sweet cicely; [sportsmen's stories.] '10(Ja15) c. il. 12°, $1.50. B'way Pub.

HOOVER FAMILY.
See Genealogies: Houser, W: W.

Hopalong Cassidy. Mulford, C. E: $1.50. McClurg.

Hope, A. P.
Poems. '10(Ja15) c. por. D. $1.25. Neale.

"Hope, Anthony," pseud.
See Hawkins, Anthony Hope.

Hope, Ascott Rob., pseud.
See Moncrieff, Ascott Rob. Hope.

Hope, Isabel.
Treasure and the field. '08(D) 8+189 p. 12°, *$1 net. Herder.

Hope, Laurence, [pseud. for Mrs. Malcolm Nicolson.]
Complete works. Uniform ed. In 3 v. '08 (Je27) 12°, *$4.50 net; hf. mor., *$12 net. Lane.
Songs from the garden of Kama. '09 (Mr27) il. 4°, *$3 net. Lane.

Hope of immortality. Dole, C: F. **30 c. net. Crowell.

Hope Ranch. Steel, J. K. $1.25. Pacific Improvement.

Hopf, Ludwig.
Human species; considered from the standpoints of comparative anatomy, physiology, pathology and bacteriology. Authorized English ed. '09(Ap3) il. O. *$3 net. Longmans.

Hopi. Jewett, M. 30 c. Educ. Pub.

HOPI INDIANS.
See Indians.

Hopkins, Mrs. A. J.
See **Briscoe, Marg. Sutton.**

Hopkins, Albert Allis, comp. and ed.
Scientific American hdbk. of travel; with hints for the ocean voyage, for European tours, and a pract. guide to London and Paris. '10(Ap30) c. il. maps, D. $2 net; leath., $2.50 net. Munn.

Hopkins, Alphonso Alva.
Profit and loss in man: [plea for prohibition.] '09(Ja16) c. D. **$1.20 net. Funk.

Hopkins, And. Delmar.
Insect injuries to the wood of living trees. '10(D) 4 p. 8°, (U. S., Dept. of Agriculture, Bu. of Entomology circular.)

Hopkins, Cyril G:
Soil fertility and permanent agriculture. '10(Ap16) c. il. pors. tabs., maps, O. (Country life education ser.) $2.75. Ginn.
Story of the soil, from the basis of absolute science to real life. '10(D31) D. $1.50. Badger.

Hopkins, Earl Palmer.
Government positions and how to secure them. 7th ed. '09, [1910.] (Mr) 63 p. il. 8°, pap., 25 c. Wash. Civil Service.

Hopkins, Rev. Herbert Müller.
Poems. '10(D31) por. 12°, bds., $1 net. Badger.
Priest and pagan. '08(Mr28) c. front. D. †$1.50. Houghton M.

Hopkins, Ja. F:, comp. and ed.
Decorating fabrics by stenciling. '08(Jl18) c. il. O. (Art-crafts booklets.) pap., 25 c. Hirshberg.

Hopkins, J: W:, and Underwood, Patrick Healey.
New arithmetics: advanced book. [New rev. ed.] '08(Ja25) il. 12°, *50 c. net. Macmillan.

Hopkins, Luther W.
From Bull Run to Appomattox: a boy's view. '08(D5) c. pors. maps, D. $1. L. W. Hopkins.

Hopkins, Mark.
Evidences of Christianity; lectures before the Lowell Institute, rev. as a text-book, with a supplementary chapter considering some attacks on the critical school, the corroborative evidence of recently discovered manuscripts, etc., and the testimony of Jesus on his trial. Presentation ed., on the Bross foundation, Lake Forest College. '09(N) 3-371 p. 8°, (Bross lib.) $1.25. T. R. Marvin.

Hopkins, T: Cramer.
Elements of physical geography. '08(Je20) c. il. maps, D. $1.35. B: H. Sanborn.
—, and Clark, B. W.
Laboratory manual in physical geography. '09(Ap24) c. D. 50 c. B: H. Sanborn.

Hopkins, Tighe.
Women Napoleon loved. '10(Ag20) 8°, $4.50 net. Little, B. & Co.

Hopkins, W: J:
Meddlings of Eve. '10(Ag20) c. D. $1 net. Houghton M.
Old Harbor. '09(N20) c. O. **$1.35 net. Houghton M.
The sandman: his sea stories. '08(N7) c. il. D. (Sandman stories.) $1.50. L. C. Page.

Hopkinson, Bertram.
Vibrations of systems having one degree of freedom. '10(Ag6) c. 8°, (Cambridge engineering tracts.) pap., 75 c. net. Putnam.

Hopper, Ja. Marie.
Trimming of Goosie. '09(S25) c. D. **$1.10 net. Moffat.
—, and Bechdolt, F: R.
"9009." '08(O10) c. D. †$1.25. McClure.

Hopper, W. E.
See Harris, Gilbert Dennison.

Hoppin, Ja. Mason, ed.
See Buckley, Edm.

Hoppus, Mary A. M., [now Mrs. Marks.]
A great treason; story of the War of Independence. [New ed.] '10(O1) D. $1.50. Macmillan.

HOPS.
Horst, E. C. Duty on hops. gratis. Horst.
Stockberger, W. W. Necessity for new standards of hop valuation. (Add. Superintendent for price.) U. S., Supt. of Docs.

Horace, [Quintus Horatius Flaccus.]
Horace, the greatest of lyric poets: account of his life, a translation in prose or verse of the best of all his writings. '08(F8) c. por. 8°, $1. W: Greenwood.
Roman poet presented to modern readers; ed. by Dr. C: Loomis Dana and J: Cotton Dana. '08(My16) c. il. pors. O. $3. Elm Tree Press.
The satires; with an introd. and notes by E: P. Morris. '09(Ag7) c. D. (Morris and Morgan's Latin ser.) $1.—Text ed. pap., 30 c. Am. Bk.
Saturarum, liber II.; ed. by Ja. Gow. '09, [1910.] (F) 12°, 50 c. Putnam.

HORACE, [Quintus Horatius Flaccus.]
Medley, W. Interpretations of Horace. $3. Oxford Univ.

Horace Mann readers. See Hervey, Wa. Lowrie, *and* Hix, Melvin.

Horae subsecivae. *See* Brown, J:

Horae synopticae. *See* Hawkins, *Sir* J: C.

Hord, H: F., rep.
See Porto Rico. *United States district ct.* Repts.

Horder, W. Garrett, ed.
Sunlit road. '10(D) $1.25. Dodge.

Horine, J: Winebrenner.
Catechist's hdbk.; being also an exposition of Luther Small's catechism for laymen, based on the Katechismus of Dr. Theodor Kaftan. '10(Je4) c. 12°, 90 c. Gen. Council.

Horn, Mrs. Delia H.
Timely aid: [analysis of Christian Science and Spiritualism in form of fiction.] '09 (S11) il. pors. 12°, $1.25. Austin.

Horn, E: Traill.
Summer sermons. '08(Je27) c. 12°, *$1 net. Pilger.

Horn, Kate.
Edward and I and Mrs. Honeybun. '10 (N12) D. $1.50. Brentano's.
Ships of desire. '09(Ap24) il. D. $1.50. Cassell.

Horn, Paul Whitfield.
The life of our schools; address del. to the City Teachers' Institute of Houston, Texas, Sept. 19, 1908, just before the opening of the schools for the year 1908-09. '09(N) 32 p. 16°, pap., 15 c. Cargill.
See also McCallum, Arth. Newell.

Hornaday, W: Temple.
Camp-fires on desert and lava. '08(D19) c. il. O. **$3 net. Scribner.
See also New York Zoological Park.

Hornbeck, Stanley Kuhl.
Juvenile courts. '09(Mr6) D. (Comparative legislation bull.) pap., 25 c. Wisconsin Free Lib.

Hornblow, Arth.
By right of conquest. '09(My22) c. il. D. †$1.50. G: W. Dillingham.
The profligate: a novel. '08(Je13) c. D. †$1.50. G: W. Dillingham.
See also Klein, C:

Hornbook ser. O. West Pub.
—Black. Hdbk. of American constitutional law. $3.75.
—Tiffany. Hdbk. on the law of persons.—Hdbk. of the law of sales. ea., *$3.75 net.

Hornbrooke, Fs. Bickford, D. D.
Ring and the book, by Robert Browning; an interpretation. '09(N20) c. D. **$1.50 net. Little, B. & Co.

Horne, C: F.
Technique of the novel. '08(My16) c. D **$1.50 net. Harper.
—, ed. *See* Bible.

Horne, Herman Harrell.
Function of a school of pedagogy. '10(Ap) 6 p. 8°, pap., gratis. Sch. Pedagogy.
Idealism in education; or, first principles in the making of men and women. '10 (D10) c. D. $1.25 net. Macmillan.

Horner, Harlan Hoyt, comp. and ed.
Hudson-Fulton celebration, Sept. 25 to Oct. 9, 1909: brochure for the use of the schools. '09(Jl10) il. pors. facsims., fold. map, Q. pap. (Add. pubs. for price.) N. Y. State Educ.
—, ed. American flag; New York State Education Dept., 6th annual rept.; supp. volume. '10(O1) il. Q. gratis. N. Y. State Educ.

Horner, H: R., rep.
See South Dakota. *Sup. ct.* Repts.

Horner, Jos., D.D.
Gospels of Matthew and Luke: vindication of their agreement and accuracy as to certain dates and order of events; also a tentative theory of the baptism for the dead. '08(Ja11) por. D. *60 c. net; pap., *40 c. net. J. Horner.
Supp. to his book "The Gospels of Matthew and Luke," in further vindication of their historical agreement from the vision of Zacharias to the beginning of the ministry of John and Jesus. '10(Je11) c. S. pap., 10 c. J. Horner.

Horner, Jos. Gregory.
Principles of fitting. [4th ed., rev. and enl.] '09(S18) il. 12°, *$1.75 net. Macmillan.
Principles of pattern making. 4th ed. '09 (Je5) il. 16°, *90 c. net. Macmillan.
—, [and others,] eds.
Henley's encyclop. of pract. engineering and allied trades. In 5 v. '10(My21) il. 4°, ea., $6; per set, $25. Henley.

Hornibrook, Isabel.
From keel to kite. '08(N14) c. il. D. †$1.50. Lothrop, L. & S.

Hornung, Ernest W:
Mr. Justice Raffles. '09(O2) c. D †$1.50. Scribner.

Hornyold, Bp. J: Jos.
Commandments and sacraments explained in 52 discourses. '10(Je18) 12°, 75 c. Chr. Press.

Horr, G: Edn., D.D.
Great ministry. '09(Ap) c. 6+209 p. il. 12°, *$1 net; Sunday-school ed., *75 c. net. Bible Study.
Training of the chosen people. '08(O10) il. D. 75 c.; $1. Bible Study.

Horsburgh, E. L. S.
Lorenzo the Magnificent, and Florence in her Golden Age. '08(N14) il. maps, O. *$4.50 net. Putnam.

HORSE.
Alexander, A. S. Horse secrets. 25 c. W. Atkinson.
Apperley, C: J. Condition of hunters: [horses.] *$4 net. Putnam.
Barton, F. T. The horse: ailments and accidents. $1. Altemus.
Barton, F. T. The horse: its selection and purchase. *$2.50 net. Chic. Med. Bk.
Battell, J. American stallion register. $5. Am. Pub. Co., (Vt.)
Biggle, J. Biggle horse book. 50 c. W. Atchinson.
Bosvile, G. Horses, horsemen and stable management. *$2 net. Dutton.
Carlson, G: L. Studies in horse breeding. $2. G: L. Carlson.
Davenport, H. C. My quest of the Arab horse. **$2 net. B. W. Dodge.
Gay, C. W. Timely hints to horse breeders. Penn. Dept. of Agriculture.
Hagerling, F: J. Training and treatment of the horse. 50 c. F: J. Hagerling.
Holiday, E. How to train horses and dogs. $1. Dodge City.
Jenkins' brief description of the horse; its external and internal organization. 50 c. W: R. Jenkins.
Johnstone, J. H. S. The horse: practical treatise on the American horse breeding industry. $2. Sanders Pub.
Jordan, R., *jr.* Gait of American trotter and pacer. $3.50. W: R. Jenkins.
Marshall, F. C. Elements of hippology. $1.25. Hudson.
Mohler, J: R. Infectious anemia, or swamp fever of horses. 5 c. U. S., Supt. of Docs.
Official horse show blue book. $5; $6.50. J. W. Waring.
Richardson, C: New book of the horse. 2 v. (Subs. only.) Cassell.
Rommel, G: M. Regeneration of the Morgan horse. Gov. Pr. Off.
United States. Mounted Service School, Fort Riley, Kan. Army horse in accident and disease, 1909 ed.; manual prep. for the use of students of the Training School for Farriers and Horseshoers, by the training school instructors. '09, [1910.] (F) 3-112 p. il. 8°, pap. Gov. Pr. Off.
Von Oettingen, B. Horse breeding in theory and practice. $15 net. Little, B. & Co.
Wolcott, E. F., *comp.* Army horses: remount systems abroad, improvements suggested at home. $1. U. S., Supt. of Docs.
See also Domestic animals; — Horsemanship; — Horseshoeing; —Loco plant; — Stables;—Statistics;—Veterinary medicine and surgery.

Horse and hound. Williams, R. D. $2.50 net. Outing.
Horse marines. *See* Kipling, Rudyard.
HORSE POWER.
See Mechanics.
HORSE-SHOWS.
See Horse.
Horse thieves. Hagedorn, H. 60 c. net. Harvard Co-operative.
HORSEMANSHIP.
Anderson, E: L. Horses and riding. $1. U. S. Cavalry.
Hayes, A. M. The horsewoman. $5 net. Scribner.
Horsemen of the plains. Altsheler, J. A. $1.50. Macmillan.
HORSESHOEING.
Magner, D. A B C guide to sensible horse shoeing. $1. Saalfield.
Russell, W: On scientific horseshoeing. $4. Krehbiel.
Horsewoman (The). Hayes, A. M. $5 net. Scribner.
Horsfall, M.
Fairy latchkey. '10(O) il. col. front. 12°, $1.25. Fenno.
Horsley, Albert E.
See Orchard, Harry, *alias*.
Horsley, Reginald.
New Zealand. '09(O9) il. in col. map, O. (Romance of history ser.) *$2 net. Stokes.
Horsley, Sir Victor Alex. Haden, and Sturge, Mary D., M.D.
Alcohol and the human body; with a chapter by Arth. Newsholme. 2d ed. '09 (Ja9) il. 8°, *$1.50 net. Macmillan.
Horst, E. Clemens.
Duty on hops: revised report of hearing given before the Committee on Ways and means on Thursday, November 19th, 1908, to E C. Horst, hop grower, of San Francisco, on application of the California Tariff Revision Committee for increased duty on hops. '09(Ap3) 8°, pap., gratis. E. C. Horst.
Horstmann, H: C:, and Tousley, Victor Hugo.
Modern electrical construction; showing the latest approved methods of installing work of all kinds according to the safety rules of the National Board of Fire Underwriters. 2d ed., rev. and enl. '08 (N21) c. il. 12°, leath., $1.50. Drake.
Practical armature and magnet winding: a comprehensive treatise for the workers; fully illustrating the theoretical principles and shop practice of armature and magnet work. '09(S) c. 5+231 p. il. 16°, $1.50. Drake.
Hort, E. C.
Rational immunization in the treatment of pulmonary tuberculosis and other diseases. '09(Je) il. 4°, *$1.50 net. Wood.
Hort, Fenton J: Antony, D.D.
Epistle of St. James; Greek text, with introd.; commentary as far as chap. 4, verse 7, and addtional notes. '10(Ja15) 8°, *$1.10 net. Macmillan.
HORTICULTURE.
See Flowers;—Fruit;—Gardens and gardening.
Horton, C. B., ed.
Reaching the boys of an entire community. '09(Jl3) c. 12°, $1. Y. M. C. A.
Horton, Rob. Forman, D.D.
Devotional commentary on the Gospel of St. Matthew. '09(My1) 12°, *$1 net. Revell.
Great issues. '09(D18) c. D. **$1.50 net. Macmillan.
Making the best of both worlds. '10(D31) 25 c. net, in envelope. Union Press.
My belief: answers to certain religious difficulties. '08(Ag15) 12°, *$1.25 net. Revell.
Triumphant life. '09(Ag21) 12°, 50 c. Revell.
HOSIERY.
See Advertising.
Hoskins, Bertha Ladd.
Double fortune. '09(My8) D. $1.25. Neale.
Hoskins, Leander Miller.
Theoretical mechanics. 3d ed. '08(F8) c. figs. O. $3. Stanford Univ. Bkstore.
Hosmer, G: Leonard.
Azimuth. '09(My8) c. figs. 16°, mor., $1. Wiley.
Text-book on pract. astronomy. '10(D3) c. figs. 8°, $2 net. Wiley.
See also Breed, C: Blaney.
Hosmer, Susan Harris Coleman.
Folded meanings: a book of charades. '09 (S) $1. Badger.
Hospitality; mine host. McGovern, J: $1. Hotel Monthly.
HOSPITALS.
Aikens, C. A. Hospital housekeeping. $1.25. Nat. Hospital.
Holmes, C. R. Modern hospitals. gratis. Univ. of Cin.
White, W: A. Hospitals and asylums of Europe. (Not for sale.) George Washington Univ.
Woodbridge, S: H. Air and the hospital. 20 c. Maclachan.
See also German Hospital, N. Y.
Hot air, vibration and, high frequency currents. Monell, S: H. *$15 net. W: R. Jenkins
Hot coals. Vincent, E. L. V. $1.50. C. M. Clark.
"Hot stuph." Laws, R. D. $1.50. Yellow Jacket.
Hot water for domestic use. Allen, J: K., *ed.* 50 c. Domestic Engineering.
Hot water heating and fitting. Baldwin, W: J. S. *$4 net. McGraw.
Hotchkiss, Chauncey Crafts.
Prisoner of the sea. '08(O31) c. D. $1.50. J: McBride.
Hotchkiss, S:
Progressive age of reason. '10(O15) c. 12°, $1.75. S: Hotchkiss.
Hotchkiss, W: H., ed.
See Collier, W: Miller.
HOTELS.
Goins, J: B. American waiter. $1. Hotel Monthly.
Hotel Red Book. 1909 ed. '09(Ag); 1910 ed. '10(S) ea., $3. Hotel Red Book.
Leahy's hotel guide of America. $1. Am. Hotel.

HOTELS.—*Continued.*
Palmer, M. E. B. Guide to hotel housekeeping. $1. M. E. B. Palmer.
Vehling, P. Die moral des hotels. $1. Didion.

See also Inns.

Houck, L:
History of Missouri. [In 3 v.] '08(D26) c. O. $18, boxed. Donnelley.
—, **ed.** Spanish régime in Missouri; collection of papers and documents rel. to upper Louisiana, principally within the present limits of Missouri, during the dominion of Spain, from the archives of the Indies at Seville, etc.; tr. from the orig. Spanish into English; and incl. also some papers concerning the supposed grant to Col. G: Morgan at the mouth of the Ohio, found in the Congressional Library; ed., with an introd. and notes, biograph. and explanatory. In 2 v. '10(Mr12) c. pors. O. $12, boxed; in 3 v., $18, boxed. Donnelley.

HOUDIN, Jean Eugéne Robert.
Houdini, H. Unmasking of Robert Houdin. $2. Conjurers Mag.
Houdini, H. Unmasking of Robert Houdin. 2 v. in 1. $1.50 net. Dutton.

Houdini, Harry.
Unmasking of Robert Houdin. '08(Ap18) c. D. $2. Conjurers Mag.
Unmasking of Robert Houdin, and Handcuff secrets. 2 v. in 1. '10(Ap23) 8°, $1.50 net. Dutton.

Houdlette, Edith Laura.
Charles Estienne Houdelette (Charles Estienne) Huguenot; the Houdlette family, 1707-1909. '09(Jl) c. 14 p. 8°. (Not for sale.) E. L. Houdlette.

HOUDLETTE FAMILY.
See Genealogies.

Hough, B: Olney.
Elem. lessons in exporting; to which is added an exporter's gazetteer of the world. '09(My22) c. facsims., O. $3. Johnston Export.

Hough, Emerson.
54-40 or fight. '09(Ja16) c. D. †$1.50. Bobbs-M.
Purchase price. '10(N19) c. il. D. $1.50. Bobbs-M.
Singing mouse stories. '10(D17) c. S. $1. Bobbs-M.
The sowing; "Yankee's" view of England's duty to herself and to Canada. '10(O1) il. pors. 12°, $1.25. Vanderhoof-G.
Story of the outlaw. '10(D) 75 c. Burt.
Young Alaskans. '08(N7) c. il. D. †$1.25. Harper.

Hough, S: Strickler, ed.
Church in earnest: call for the training necessary for world achievements; a word of preparation by Bp. G. M. Mathews. '08(D26) c. D. 25 c. For. Miss. Soc. of Un. B.
See also Mills, Job Smith.

Hough, Will M:
See Harding, J: W:

Houghtaling, C: E., comp.
Revised hand book of useful information. '10(D17) c. il. 24°, 50 c. C: E. Houghtaling.

Houghton, Alb. Allison.
Concrete floors and side-walks. '10(D17) c. il. 12°, (Concrete worker's reference books.) 50 c. Henley.
Concrete from sand molds. '10(My21) il. $2. Henley.
Concrete wall forms. '10(D17) c. il. 12°, (Concrete worker's reference books.) 50 c. Henley.
Ornamental concrete without molds. '10 (Je25) c. il. 12°, $2. Henley.

Houghton, C: Edn.
Elements of mechanics of materials: a text for students in engineering courses. '09 (Ag28) c. il. 8°, **$2 net. Van Nostrand.

Houghton, Mrs. Louise Seymour.
Telling Bible stories; with introd. by Rev. T. T. Munger. 2d ed.; with an appendix. '08(D5) c. 12°, **$1.25 net. Scribner.

Houk, L. C. Violett.
Girl in question. '08(My23) c. D. †$1.50. Lane.

Houk, Russell Whitelaw, comp.
Authentication, acknowledgment and proof of written instruments under the various laws which have been in force in Texas from her earliest hist. to the present time. 2d ed. '08(Mr.) c. 631 p. 8°, $5.50. Bancroft-W.

Houllevigue, Aimé Louis Charles.
Evolution of the sciences. '10(My14) 8°, $2 net. Van Nostrand.

Houmas, Mount.
Strange record: [a novel.] '08(Je27) c. D. $1.50. Neale.

Hound of heaven. *See* Thompson, Fs.

Hounds, gentlemen, please. Forbes, W. B. $3.75 net. Doran.

House, E: J:
Hunter's camp-fires. '09(N13) c. il. O. **$5 net. Harper.

House, Homer Doliver.
North American species of the genus *Ipomoea*. '08, [1909.] (Ap) 81-263 p. 8°, (Columbia Univ. contributions from the Dept. of Botany.) pap., 35 c. Columbia Univ.
Studies in the North American *convolvulaceae*. IV., The genus *Exogonium*. '08, [1909.] (Mr) 97-107 p. il. 8°, (Contributions from the New York botanical garden.) 25 c. N. Y. Botanical.

House between the trees. Lane, J: R. †$1.50. C. M. Clark.

House-boating on a colonial waterway. Hutchins, F. $2.50. L. C. Page.

House book to the hostess. Bartholomew, E. $1.50 net; $2.50 net. Dodge.

House by the lock. Williamson, *Mrs.* A. M. L. 50 c. B. W Dodge.

House chimneys; ser. of articles and letters on chimney troubles and their remedies. 3d ed., rev. and enl. '10(D17) il. pap., 25 c. D: Williams.

HOUSE DECORATION.
Daniels, F. H. Furnishing of a modest home. $1. Davis Press.
Fletcher, B. F. *and* H. P. English home. $4 net. Scribner.
French, L. H. House dignified. **$5 net. Putnam.

HOUSE DECORATION.—*Continued.*
Hasluck, P. N., *ed.* Cassell's house decoration. *$3 net. Cassell.
Keith, H. P., *and* Cummings, E. A. Pract. studies in interior decoration and furnishing. $1. M. L. Keith.
Keith, M. L., *comp.* Interior beautiful. $1. M. L. Keith.
Latham, C: In English homes. v. 3. $15 net. Scribner.
Lenygon, F. Decoration and furniture of English mansions during the seventeenth and eighteenth centuries. *$1 net. Scribner.
Priestman, D. T. Home decoration. **$1 net. Penn Pub. Co.
Priestman, M. T. Art and economy in home decoration. **$1.50 net. Lane.
Priestman, M. T. Artistic homes. $2 net. McClurg.
Sabin, A. H. House painting, glazing, paper hanging and white-washing. $1. Wiley.
Shackleton, R. *and* E. Adventures in home making. $1.75. Lane.
Sparrow, W. S. Hints on house furnishing. *$2.50 net. Lane.
Sparrow, W. S., *ed.* Our homes and how to make the best of them. $3.50 net. Doran.
Studio year book of decorative art, 1908. *$5 net; 1909. **$2.50 net; 1910. $3 net. Lane.
Your house and its decoration. $2. Sherwin-W.
See also Carpets;—Decoration and ornament;—Floors;—Furniture; — Mantels;—Paintings; — Plastering; — Rugs; — Upholstery; — Wall decoration.

House dignified. French, L. H. **$5 net. Putnam.

HOUSE FLY.
See Flies.

House in the water. Roberts, C: G: D. $1.50. L. C. Page.
House in the wood. Grimm, J. L. K. *and* W. K. $1.35 net. Warne.

HOUSE MARTIN.
Miller, C: W. Experiment in colonization of the house martin. gratis. Worthington Soc.

House of Arden. Bland, E. N. $1.50. Dutton.
House of bondage. Kauffmann, R. W. $1.25 net. Moffat.
House of brick. Clay Products Association of America. 50 c. Rogers & M.
House of brick for ten thousand dollars. Rogers, A. D. 25 c. Rogers & M.
House of brick of moderate cost: the practicability and stability of the brick house—its value as an investment—as a thing of beauty which will be a joy forever; thoughts concerning these matters are here submitted for consideration. [1910.] (N) c. 95 p. il. plans, 4°, 50 c. Rogers & M.
House of Chimham. Work, E. W. 75 c. Am. Tr.

HOUSE OF COMMONS (*English*).
Middlemore, T: D. The navy in the House of Commons. 50 c.; 30 c. Longmans.
Redlich, J. Procedure of the House of Commons. $10 net. Dutton.

House of falling leaves. Braithwaite, W: S. *$1 net. J: W. Luce.
House of Hell. E., C. E. (Add. author for price.) C. E. E.
House of Howard. Brenan, G. 2 v. *$6 special net. Appleton.
House of lies. Warwick, S. $1.50. Cassell.

HOUSE OF LORDS (*English*).
Firth, C: H. House of Lords during the Civil War. $2.60 net. Longmans.

House of mystery. Irwin, W: H: **$1.15 net. Century Co.
House of prayer. Converse, F. *$1.50 net. Dutton.

HOUSE OF REPRESENTATIVES.
See **United States.**

House of rest. Gardner, M. D. *$1 net. F. F. Sherman.
House of Rimmon. Van Dyke, H: J. *$1 net. Scribner.
House of the heart. Mackay, C. D. **$1.10 net. Holt.
House of the lost court. Savallo, T. de. †$1.50. McClure.
House of the seven gables. *See* Hawthorne, Nathaniel.
House of the sphinx. Evans, H: R. $1.50. Neale.
House of the Whispering Pines. Rohlfs, *Mrs.* A. K. G. $1.50. Putnam.
House of whispers. Le Queux, W: $1.50. Brentano's.
House on Cherry Street. Barr, *Mrs.* A. E. H. †$1.50. Dodd.
House on stilts. Hazard, R. H. $1.50. G: W. Dillingham.
House on the marsh. James, *Mrs.* F. A. P. 50 c. Hurst.
House on the north shore. Washburne, *Mrs.* M. F. $1.25. McClurg.
House painting, glazing, paper hanging, and white-washing. Sabin, A. H. $1. Wiley.

HOUSE PLANTS.
See **Indoor gardening.**

House that a Jap built. Weaver, G. C. 75 c. Reilly & B.
House that Jack built. '09(Ag7) il. shaped book, mounted on bds., 25 c. Curtis Adv.
House with no address. Bland, *Mrs.* E. N. †$1.50. Doubleday, P.
Houseboat days in China. Bland, J. O. P. $5. Longmans.
Household bacteriology. Elliott, S. M. $1.50. Am. Sch. Home Economics.
Household baker. Doherty, J. J. $1.50. J. J. Doherty.
Household catechism on the Decalogue. Walker, S. G. 25 c.; 40 c. S. G. Walker.
Household companion. Johnson, A. A., *ed.* $1.50. Uplift.
Household discoveries. *See* Morse, S. L.
Household economist, the system that leads to plenty; the most simple home account book '09(Ag14) 4°, pap., 35 c.; Standard ed., f°, $1.25; hf. leath., $1.50. Davis-G.

HOUSEHOLD ECONOMY.
See Domestic economy.

Household hygiene. Elliott, S. M. $1.25. Am. Sch. Home Economics.

HOUSEHOLD INSECTS.
See **Insects.**

Household of Sir T: More. Manning, A. *$1 net. Dutton.

Household physician, twentieth century medica; pract. description in plain language of all the diseases of men, women and children; by a corps of eminent specialists, practising physicians and surgeons: Herbert E. Buffum, A. T. Lovering, Ira Warren, A. E. Small, W: Thorndike, J. Heber Smith, C: P. Lyman. New ed. '09(D) c. 1464 p. il. 4°, $8. Woodruff Pub.

HOUSEHOLD SCIENCE.
See Domestic economy.

Household stories. Grimm, J. L. K. $1.25. Cassell.

Housekeeper pudding book. Bacheller, D., *comp.* 50 c. Housekeeper Corp.

Housekeeper's reference book and domestic counselor. Goessling, A. O., *comp.* Phelps.

Housekeeper's week. Terhune, *Mrs.* M. V. H. **$1.50 net. Bobbs-M.

HOUSEKEEPING.
See Domestic economy.

Houser, W: Wesley, M.D., comp.
Genealogy of the Houser, Rhorer, Dillman, Hoover families. '10(D) 239 p. il. pors. O. $2. W: W. Houser.

HOUSER FAMILY.
See Genealogies.

HOUSES.
See Architecture;—Concrete;—Domestic economy; —House decoration;—Wall decoration.

Houses of glass. Mackay, *Mrs.* H. G. E. **$1 net. Duffield.

Housing conditions in St. Louis. Civic League of St. Louis. *Housing Committee.* (Add. pubs. for price.) Civic League.

Housing reform. Veiller, L. $1.25. Charities Pub.

Housley, W. H.
All kinds of gems of prose and verse. '10 (D31) c. D. B'way Pub.

Housman, Laurence.
Chinese lantern: a play. '08(D5) c. 12°. (Priv. pr.) Brentano's.

Houston, Edn. Ja.
At school in the Cannibal Islands. '09 (S25) c. D. (Pacific ser.) †$1.25. Griffith.
Boy geologist at school and in camp. '08 (F8) c. il. D. †$1. Altemus.
Chip of the old block; or, at the bottom of the ladder. '10(O8) c. il. D. (Young mineralogist ser.) $1.25. Griffith.
Five months on a derelict. '08(Ag1) c. il. maps, O. (Pacific ser.) †$1.25. Am. Bapt.
In captivity in the Pacific. '09(F13) c. il. O. (Pacific ser.) †$1.25. Am. Bapt.
Land of drought; or, across the Great American Desert. '10(O15) c. front. map, O. (Young mineralogist ser.) $1.25. Griffith.
Wonder book of light. '08(D5) c. il. D. (Wonder books of science.) **$1.50 net. Stokes.
Wonder book of magnetism. '08(N7) c. il. D. (Wonder books of science.) **$1.50 net. Stokes.

Houston, Edn. Ja.—*Continued.*
Wonder book of the atmosphere. '08(Ap4) c. D. (Wonder books of science.) $1.50. Stokes.
Wrecked on a coral island. '08(D5) c. il. O. (Pacific ser.) †$1.25. Am. Bapt.

HOUSTON, Texas.
See Shearn Church, Houston.

Houtin, Albert.
A married priest; tr. from the French by J: R: Slattery. '10(Mr12) c. D. *70 c. net. Sherman, F.

Houtz, Rev. Alfr.
Master's call to service. '10(Je18) c. 12°, 60 c. Ref. Ch. Pub.
Ties that bind. pt. 1, Ties that bind on earth; pt. 2, Ties that bind in heaven. '08(N) c. 117 p. 12°, 50 c. I. M. Beaver.

Hovey, Edm. Otis.
Geological reconnaissance in the western Sierra Madre of the state of Chihuahua, Mexico. '07, [1908.] (My.) c. 401-442 p. il. maps, 8°, pap., 45 c. E. O. Hovey.

Hovey, Horace Carter, D.D.
Hdbk. of the Mammoth Cave of Kentucky; pract. guide to the regulation routes. '09, [1910.] (F) c. 63 p. il. maps, D. pap., 25 c. Morton.

Hovey, R:
To the end of the trail: [poems;] ed., with notes, by Mrs. R: Hovey. '08(My9) c. por. S. **$1.25 net. Duffield.

Hovis, W: Forney.
Quality folks; practical meditations. '09 (Ap3) c. 12°, *$1 net. Jennings.

How, F: Douglas.
Clerical humour of olden times; sketches of some clerical humorists between 12th and 18th centuries. '08(Ag) 263 p. front. por. 12°, $2. Pitman.
Oxford. '10(Jl30) col. il. O. (Beautiful England ser.) bds., $1.25, boxed. Estes.

How Abraham Lincoln became president. Davis, J: M. *75 c. net. J: M. Davis.

How Americans are governed. Marriott, C. $1.75. Harper.

How and what to dance. Lamb, W: 50 c. Fenno.

How and where to sell mss. Cochrane, C: H. 50 c. Cochrane.

How and why of the Emmanuel movement. Boyd, T: P. $1. Whitaker & R.

How Bee Martin became king of the birds, and Kingbird's coronation. Lang, O. 10 c. Flanagan.

"How books." See System "how books."

How can God answer prayer? Biederwolf, W: E: *75 c. net. Revell.

How Canada was won. Brereton, F: S. $1.25. Caldwell.

How Dexter paid his way. Clark, K. U. **40 c. net. Crowell.

How does it feel to be old? Marsdon, E: $1. Scribner.

How does it work ser. il. 12°, 75 c. Fenno.
—Corbin. "How does it work" of electricity.
—"How does it work" of modern engines.
—Hall. "How does it work" of model making.

How does the death of Christ save us? Mabie, H: C. **50 c. Am. Bapt.

How fortunes are made in advertising. Lewis, H: H. $1. Publicity.
How God made the soil fertile. Seeds, R. S. (Add. author for price.) R. S. Seeds.
How great men succeed. Larson, C. D. 50 c. Progress Co.
How I know that the dead return. Stead, W: T: *75 c. net. Ball Pub. Co.
How it all came about. Smith, *Mrs.* E. T. 50 c. Hurst.
How it flies. Ferris, R: $1.20 net. Nelson.
How it is done. Williams, A. $1.25. Nelson.
How it is made. Williams, A. $1.25. Nelson.
How may I know the voice of God in my soul? Bates, *Mrs.* V. B. 35 c. Presb. Bd.
How money is made in security investments. Hall, H: $1.50. H: Hall.
How Newport's News got its name. Green, B. W. gratis. W. E. Jones.
How protection grows. Perris, G: H. 10 c. Cassell.
How Richard won out. Potter, M. K. †75 c. Wilde.
How shall the little ones sew? Johnson, F. K. 10 c. People's Univ.
How telegraphs and telephones work. Gibson, C: R. *75 c. net. Lippincott.
How the Indian suit ran away. *See* Bird, Mary Herrick.
How the public can own and control new railroads. Jaros, S: (Add. pubs. for price). Jaros Co.
How the public will solve our problems of science teaching. Woodhull, J. F: gratis. C: P. Cary.
How the world is clothed. Carpenter, F. G: 60 c. Am. Bk.
How they went to the seaside. Prager, S. R. $1. Stokes.
How to advertise a retail store. Edgar, A. E. $3.50. Outing Press.
How to appreciate prints. Weitenkampf, F. **$1.50 net. Moffat.
How to argue and win. Kleiser, G. $1.25 net. Funk.
How to be a good salesman. Quinn, F. O. 50 c. Harper-Adams.
How to be happy. Frink, *Mrs.* M. $1; 25 c. Laird.
How to be happy though civil. Hardy, E. J. *$1 net. Scribner.
How to be rich. Doak, A. M. $1. Jennings.
How to become a citizen of the United States. '10(My) 10 p. pors. S. pap., gratis. Y. M. C. A.
How to become a competent motorman. Livermore, V. B: **$1 net. Van Nostrand.
How to become a detective. Bradford, M. C. $2. Globe Pr., (Wash., D. C.)
How to become a fireman. O'Reilly, J. J: E: 75 c. Chief.
How to become a law stenographer. Mason, W. L., *comp.* $1; 75 c. Pitman.
How to become a letter carrier. Lachaussee, C: A. 25 c. Chief.
How to become a letter carrier or postal clerk. Hecht, S. 50 c Police Chronicle.
How to become a patrolman. O'Reilly, J. J: E: 50 c. Chief.
How to become a successful motorman. Small, S. A-. $1.50. Drake.
How to become an inspector on public works. Seely, W. (Add. pubs. for price.) C. M. Clark.
How to breathe and how to be well. Foringer, W. S. $1. B'way Pub.
How to build a 20 ft. bi-plane glider. Morgan, A. P. 50 c. Spon.
How to build an aeroplane. Petit, R. $1.50 net. Van Nostrand.
How to build up a heavy laying strain. Van Arsdale, L. F: 50 c. Poultry Monthly.
How to catch. Sullivan, J. E: 10 c. Am. Sports.
How to collect continental china. Wylde, C. H. $2. Macmillan.
How to compose within the lyric form. Evans, E. *$1 net. Scribner.
How to conduct a successful shoe store. Garrison, C: L. $1. Boot & Shoe.
How to cook fish. Reed, M. **90 c. net. Putnam.
How to cook for the sick and convalescent. Sachse, H. V. $1.25. Lippincott.
How to cook meat and poultry. Reed, M. **$1 net. Putnam.
How to cook vegetables. Reed, M. **$1 net. Putnam.
How to deal with lads. Green, P: 80 c. net. Longmans.
How to design an aeroplane. Chatley, H. 50 c. Van Nostrand.
How to design and construct a power boat; repr. from the *Rudder*. '10(F26) c. il. f°, $1. Rudder.
How to develop power and personality in speaking. Kleiser, G. **$1.25 net. Funk.
How to develop self-confidence in speech and manner. Kleiser, G. $1.25 net. Funk.
How to do business by letter. Cody, S. $1. Sch. of Eng.
How to double the day's work. Lennen, F W. $2. System.
How to dress a doll. Morgan, *Mrs.* M. E. H. 50 c. Altemus.
How to enter the postal service. Lachaussee, C: A. 50 c. Chief.
How to feed children. Hogan, L. E. S. **$1 net. Lippincott.
How to get a better situation. Walker, H: C. $2. Opportunity.
How to get a position and how to keep it. Hall, S: R. **50 c. net. Funk.
How to get eggs from your own hens during the winter. Hadley, L. D. $1. L. D. Hadley.
How to get on the police force [in New York City; ed. by D: L. Kaufmann.] '08(D) c. 4+152 p. S. pap., 50 c. Police Chronicle.
How to get registered. Mason, H. B. pap., 50 c. C: L. Mason.
How to grow in the Christian life. Hamilton, W: W. *25 c. net; *10 c. net. Am. Bapt.
How to grow mushrooms for market. '09 (My8) c. il. O. pap., 50 c. U. S. Mushroom.
How to grow one hundred bushles of corn. Smith, W: C. $1. W: C. Smith.

How to help. Conyngton, M. *$1.50 net. Macmillan.
How to hold an audience. *See* Kleiser, Grenville. Humorous hits.
How to identify the stars. Milham, W. I. **75 c. net. Macmillan.
How to increase the business of a trust company. Herrick, C. 50 c. Bankers Pub.
How to increase your sales: plans that have won new buyers; how to develop trade and keep it; 125 selling plans used and proved by 54 salesman and salesmanagers. 3d rev. ed. '09(O) 128 p. il. 12°, $2. System.
How to invest money. Henry, G: G. **75 c. net. Funk.
How to judge a book. Shuman, E. L. $1.25 net. Houghton M.
How to keep a dog in the city. Mills, W. 25 c. W: R. Jenkins.
How to keep bees for profit. Lyon, D. E. $1 net. Macmillan.
How to keep farm accounts. Steiner, H. L. $1. Steiner & Co.
How to keep fit. Schofield, A. T. 75 c. Moffat.
How to keep hens for profit. Valentine, C. S. $1.50 net. Macmillan.
How to keep well. Blaisdell, A. F. 45 c. Ginn.
How to keep well and live long. Matthews, S. C. $1. S. C. Matthews.
How to keep well and live long. Terry, T. B. $1. Farmer Co.
How to know architecture. Wallis, F. E. $2 net. Harper.
How to know the holy Bible. Limerick, D. T., *ed.* 20 c. Praise Pub.
How to know the trees. Irving, H: $1.25 net. Cassell.
How to live longer. Kealing, H. T. 35 c.; 45 c. H. T. Kealing.
How to live on a small income. Hewitt, *Mrs.* E. C. 50 c. Jacobs.
How to live on 24 hours a day. Bennett, E. A. 50 c. net. Doran.
How to make a living. Packard, *Mrs.* L. H. 75 c. S. S. Packard.
How to make baby Irish crochet. Cartier-Bresson, *Mme.* 25 c. Mills & G.
How to make electric batteries. Bubier, E: T. 50 c.; 25 c. Bubier.
How to make Irish crochet lace. Cartier-Bresson, *Mme.* 25 c. Mills & G.
How to make money. Douglas, G. 50 c. net. Dutton.
How to make things go. Peters, M. C. 25 c. Laird.
How to make wireless instruments; treatise for the experimenter and amateur on the construction of wireless instruments and apparatuses, by twenty wireless experts; 25 different instruments, 75 illustrations. '10 (Ap) c. 94 p. 12°, 25 c. H. Gernsback.
How to market ability. Grant, J: W: D. 50 c. Advancement.
How to memorize. Evans, W: *50 c. net. Bible Inst.
How to nurse sick children. West, C: *40 c. net. Longmans.
How to obtain our own. True, H. B., *ed.* $1. Roger Bros.
How to plant and cultivate an orange orchard. Canada, J: W: 50 c. J: W: Canada.
How to play base ball. Murnane, T. H. 10 c. Am. Sports.
How to play bridge. Tinkham, E. A. $1. E. A. Tinkham.
How to play first base. Wray, J. E:, *ed.* 10 c. Am. Sports.
How to play ice hockey. Farrell, A. 10 c. Am. Sports.
How to play lawn tennis. Paret, J. P. 10 c. Am. Sports.
How to play shortstop. Wray, J. E:, *ed.* 10 c. Am. Sports.
How to play third base. Wray, J: E., *ed.* 10 c. Am. Sports.
How to play water polo. Handley, L. d'B. 10 c. Am. Sports.
How to preach with power. Young, W: H: $1. How Pub.
How to prepare for Kreutzer. Winn, E. L. $1. Fischer.
How to reach men. Hudson, M. A. *50 c. net. S. S. Times.
How to read character in handwriting. Booth, M. H. 50 c. Winston.
How to read plans. Peker, C: G. 50 c. Indust.
How to relieve the depression. Johannsen, N: A. L. J. (Add. author for price.) N: Johannsen.
How to run and install gasoline engines. Von Culin, C. 25 c. Van Nostrand.
How to run 100 yards. Morton, J. W. 10 c. Am. Sports.
How to sell real estate. Melberg, P: L. $2.50. P: L. Melberg.
How to series. See Macmillan's.
How to speak effectively without notes. Speer, R. E. 10 c. Nat. Bible.
How to sprint. Duffey, A. F., *ed.* 10 c. Am. Sports.
How to stay young. Larson, C. D. $1. Eternal Progress.
How to stop stammering. Hatfield, M. L. $1.50. M. L. Hatfield.
How to study. McMurry, F. M. **$1.25 net. Houghton M.
How to study birds. Job, H. K. $1.50 net. Outing.
How to study Fiorillo. Winn, E. L. 75 c. Fischer.
How to study Kreutzer. Winn, E. L. 75 c. Fischer.
How to study the stars. Rudaux, L. *$2 net. Stokes.
How to succeed as an inventor. Smith, G. B. 10 c. Inventors.
How to successfully keep railroad accounts. Shorter, R. G. $2.50. R. K. Shorter.
How to take care of a wife. Keith, M. C. 50 c. Keith & G.
How to take part in the services of the Episcopal church. Johnson, G: B. per 100, $3. Young Churchman.
How to talk with God. Faris, W: W. 50 c. S. S. Times.
How to teach English classics. Thomas, C: S. 15 c. Houghton M.
How to teach reading. Clark, S. H: $1. Scott, F. & Co.

How to teach reading. Coon, C: L. gratis. N. C. Dept. Pub. Instruct.

How to think music. Seymour, H. A. $1. H. W. Gray.

How to train children. Hewitt, *Mrs.* E. C. 50 c. Jacobs.

How to train horses and dogs. Holiday, E. $1. Dodge City.

How to train your own dogs. Mooney, H. J. 50 c. Saalfield.

How to understand the words of Christ. Butler, A. A: *90 c. net. Whittaker.

How to use a camera. Holland, C. 50 c. Dutton.

How to use concrete. Boynton, W. C. $1. Concrete Pub.

How to use electric light. Taylor, F. H. 25 c. Spon.

How to use slide rules. Petri-Palmedo, D. 50 c. Kolesch.

How to use water power. Chatley, H. *$1 net. Van Nostrand.

How to walk before God. Vaubert, T. F. 40 c. Herder.

How to wrestle. Toombs, F: R., *ed.* 10 c. Am. Sports.

How to write a business letter. Wiers, C: R. $1. C: R. Wiers.

How to write letters that win; 247 vital pointers gathered from a study of 1200 actual letters. '09(D) c. 128 p. il. 12°, with sub. to *System*, $2. System.

How two hundred children live and learn. Reeder, R. R. $1.25. Charities Pub.

How we are governed in Alabama. McBain, H. L. 65 c. Bell Bk.

How we are governed in Tennessee and the nation. McBain, H. L. 55 c. Southern Sch. Supply.

How we are governed in Virginia. McBain, H. L. 55 c. H. L. McBain.

How we are governed in Virginia and the nation. McBain, H. L. 65 c. Bell Bk.

How we think. Dewey, J: $1. Heath.

How we travel. Chamberlain, J. F. *40 c. net. Macmillan.

How West Virginia was made. Lewis, V. A., *ed.* (Priv. pr.) News-Mail Co.

How words grow. Mead, W: L. 50 c. Crowell.

HOWARD, Bronson.
In memoriam. Bronson Howard, 1842-1908; founder and president of the American Dramatists Club; addresses del. at the memorial meeting, Sunday, Oct. 18, 1908, at the Lyceum Theatre, New York, with a brief biography and other appreciations and records of his dramatic works, incl. a list of his plays with the original casts. '10(Ag) 130 p. pors. 8°. (Not for sale.) Marion Press.

Howard, Clifford.
The Passover: an interpretation. '10(Ag13) 16°, $1 net. Fenno.

Howard, Dan.
American history, government and institutions. '09(Ap3) c. il. maps, D. 65 c. D. Howard.

Howard, Fk. Ward, comp.
Merrill's story books: Banbury Cross stories. '09(My) c. 123 p. il. 12°, 25 c. C: E. Merrill.
Merrill's story books: Dick Whittington and other stories. '09(My) c. 167 p. il. 12°, 30 c. C: E. Merrill.

Howard, G: Elliott.
Biography of American statesmanship; analyt. reference syllabus. '09, [1910.] (Mr) 75 p. 8°, pap., 50 c. Univ. of Neb.

Howard, G: Ellsworth.
See McGrew, T: Fletcher.

Howard, Harry F.
End of the world and the opening of the book of life. v. 1. '08(Jl) c. 400 p. por. 8°, $1.50. Meader's.
Last testament. v. 1. '10(Je) c. il. 12°, $1. Howard Pub. Co., (N. H.)

Howard, Rev. H:
Raiment of the soul, and other studies. '08 (N14) por. D. *$1.25 net. Eaton & M.
Summits of the soul. '10(Ag27) c. D. $1.25 net. Eaton & M.

Howard, H: L., pseud.
See Wells, C: Jeremiah.

Howard, Jerome Bird.
Progressive dictation exercises; designed to accompany The phonographic amanuensis. '08, [1909.] (S) 56 p. 12°, pap., 25 c. Phonograph.
See also Pitman, Benn.

Howard, J: Raymond, comp.
Best American essays. '10(Ag6) c. por. S. (Handy volume classics, pocket ed.) 35 c. Crowell.
Best American orations. '10(Ag6) c. por. S. (Handy volume classics, pocket ed.) 35 c. Crowell.

Howard, Leland Ossian.
Economic loss to the people of the United States through insects that carry disease. '09(My) 40 p. 8°, (U. S., Dept. of Agriculture, Bu. of Chemistry bull.) pap. 10 c. U. S., Supt. of Docs.

Howard, Major General Oliver Otis.
Famous Indian chiefs I have known. '08 (S19) c. il. D. *$1.50 net. Century Co.

Howard, Percy.
Odd fellowship up to date. '09(N13) c. S. $1; pap., 50 c. Dick.

Howard, Philip Eug.
What a superintendent can do. '08(D) c. 46 p. S. pap. (Add. pubs. for price.) Westminster.

Howard, Timothy E:
Hist. of St. Joseph County, Indiana. 2 v. '07, [1908.] (O.) il. pors. map, 4°, $18. Lewis Pub.

Howard, W: Guild.
Ut pictura poesis; repr. from the Publications of the Modern Language Association. '09(Ap) $1. Grandgent.
—, **ed.** Laokoon: Lessing, Herder, Goethe; selections ed. with an introd. and a commentary. '10(D3) c. front. D. $1.50. Holt.

Howard, W: Lee, M.D.
Lila Sari. '08(D5) c. D. $1.50. Badger.
Plain facts on sex hygiene. '10(O1) c. D. $1 net. Clode.
Start your child right; confidential advice to parents and teachers. '10(S17) c. 12°, 75 c. net. Revell.

HOWARD Co., Ind.
Morrow, J. Hist. of Howard Co., Ind. 2 v. $18. B. F. Bowen.

HOWARD FAMILY.
Brenan, G., *and* Statham, E. P. House of Howard. 2 v. *$6 special net. Appleton.

Howatt, Rev. J. Reid.
Next life: light on the worlds beyond. '10(F12) c. 12°, *$1 net. Revell.

Howden, Jos. Russell.
Boys' book of locomotives. [3d ed.] '09 (Jl3) c. il. tabs., O. $2. Stokes.
Boys' book of railways. '10(Jl30) c. il. O. $2. Stokes.
Boys' book of steamships. '08(O10) il. O. $2. McClure.
Boys' book of warships. '10(D3) il. 8°, $2. Stokes.

Howe, Edg. F., and Hall, Wilbur Jay.
Story of the first decade in Imperial Valley, Cal. '10(N5) c. il. 8°, $3. E. F. Howe.

Howe, Edn. D., ed.
See New York [State.] Village laws.

Howe, Ernest.
Landslides in the San Juan Mountains, Colo., incl. consideration of their causes and their classification. '09(D) 58 p. il. 4°, (U. S., Dept. of the Interior, Geological Survey; Professional paper.) pap.

Howe, F. J. O.
See Coyle, D.

Howe, Frederic Clemson.
Privilege and democracy in America. '10 (Mr19) c. O. **$1.50 net. Scribner.

Howe, G: Maxwell.
First German book. '08(O10) c. D. 90 c. Holt.

Howe, Herbert Alonzo.
Elements of descriptive astronomy. Rev. ed. '09(N6) c. il. maps, O. $1.25. Silver.

Howe, J: Dicks.
See Scogin, *Mrs.* Samuel Martha Caldwell.

Howe, Mrs. J: Elliott.
See Howe, Maud.

Howe, Mrs. Julia Ward.
At sunset. '10(D24) c. por. D. $1.25 net. Houghton M.
—, comp. Original poems and other verse set to music as songs. '08(S19) por. Q. pap., $1.50; Ed. de luxe, $5. Boston Music.

Howe, Lucien, M.D.
Muscles of the eye. In 2 v. v. 2. '08(D12) il. 8°, *$4.25 net. Putnam.

Howe, Mark Antony De Wolfe.
Boston common: scenes from four centuries. Special limited ed. '10(D10) il. 4°, $6 net. (500 copies.) Houghton M.
Harmonies; book of verse. '09(N13) c. O. **$1.10 net. Houghton M.
Life and letters of George Bancroft. In 2 v. '08(Ap25) c. pors. O. per set, **$4 net, boxed. Scribner.

Howe, Marshall Avery.
Phycological studies. III., Further notes on *halimeda* and *avrainvillea.* '08, [1909.] (Mr) 491-516 p. il. 8°, 25 c. N. Y. Botanical.

Howe, Maud, [Mrs. J: Elliott.]
Roma beata: letters from the Eternal City. [Popular ed.] '09(S18) il. O. **$1.50 net, boxed. Little, B. & Co.
Sicily in shadow and in sun; the earthquake and the American relief work. '10 (D3) c. il. fold. map, O. $3 net, boxed; leath., $5.50 net, boxed. Little, B. & Co.
Sun and shadow in Spain. '08(N14) c. il. O. **$3 net. Little, B. & Co.
Two in Italy. [New popular ed.] '09(S18) c. O. **$1.50 net, boxed. Little, B. & Co.

Howe, P. P.
Repertory theatre. '10(D17) 12°, $1 net. M. Kennerley.

Howe, S: Gridley.
Letters and journals; ed. by his daughter, Laura E. Richards; with notes by F. B. Sanborn. [v. 2, The servant of humanity.] '09(Je19) c. por. O. **$3 net. Estes.

Howe, Will D:
See Thomas, C: Swain.

Howe baseball scoring record, schedule and rule book, containing blanks to carry complete scoring and playing record of major league team for the entire season of 1910. '10(My) c. 96 p. il. 16°, 10 c. Howe & B.

Howel Dda, the Good.
Welsh medieval law; being a text of the laws of Howel the Good, namely the British Museum Harleian ms. 4353 of the 13th century, with translation, introd., apdendix, glossary and a map, by A. W. Wade-Evans. '09(Ap3) D. $2.90. Oxford Univ.

Howell, C. M. Hinds.
See Wilson, Harold W.

Howell, E: Beach.
Lode and placer claims: a manual of mining law in the states and territories of the U. S.; with forms. '08(Je) c. 202+7 p. D. $1. Keefe.

Howell, Logan Douglass.
Howell primer. '10(My7) c. D. 25 c. Hinds.

Howell, Mary Hubbard.
Through the winter; written for Am. Sunday-School Union. '09(Je) c. 399 p. il. 12°, 80 c. Am. S. S.

Howell, W: H:
Text-book of physiology for medical students and physicians. 3d ed., thoroughly rev. '09(N) c. 998 p. il. (partly col.) 8°, $4. Saunders.

Howells, W: Dean.
Boy life: stories and readings selected from the works of William Dean Howells; arranged for supplementary reading in elementary schools by Percival Chubb. '09 (S18) c. il. D. (Harper's modern ser. of supplementary readers for the elementary schools.) 50 c. Harper.
Children of the summer. '09(N) il. 8°, *$1.35 net. Harper.
Christmas every day. '08(O24) c. Q. †$1.75. Harper.

Howells, W: Dean.—*Continued.*
Fennel and rue: a novel; '08(Mr21) c. O. †$1.50. Harper.
Imaginary interviews. '10(O22) c. il. O. $2 net. Harper.
Mother and the father: dramatic passages. '09(Je12) c. il. O. **$1.20 net. Harper.
My Mark Twain: reminiscences and criticisms. '10(S17) c. il. pors. O. $1.40 net. Harper.
Rise of Silas Lapham; with an introd. '10(O22) c. '84. D. (Riverside literature ser.) 40 c. Houghton M.
Roman holidays, and others. '08(D12) c. il. O. **$3 net. Harper.
Seven English cities. '09(N6) il. O. *$2 net. Harper.

—, and Alden, H: Mills, eds.
Life at high tide. '09(My) c. '07. 268 p. 12°, (Harper's novelettes.) †$1. Harper.

—, James, H:, Bigelow, J:, and others.
In after days; thoughts on the future life. '10(F19) c. pors. D. **$1.25 net. Harper.

Howes, Abby Willis.
Primer of American literature. '09(Jl31) c. pors. 16°, **50 c. net. Heath.

Howes, Edith.
Sun's babies; [nature study.] '10(D) $1.25 net. Cassell.

Howie, H. M.
Bobo's adventures. '09(S) 16 p. il. in col. Q. (Baby ser.) bds., 35 c. Stokes.

Howland, Franklyn.
Centennial history of the first Methodist Episcopal Church of New Bedford, Fairhaven and Acushnet, Mass. '07. [1908.] (My) c. 67 p. il. pors. $2. E. H. Howland.
History of the town of Acushnet, Bristol County, state of Massachusetts. '07 [1908.] (My.) c. 398 p. il. pors. 4°, $5. E. H. Howland.

Howland, G: C.
Advanced lessons in English. '10(D10) c. il. 60 c. McClurg.
Elem. lessons in English. '10(D10) c. il. 40 c. McClurg.

Howland, Marion R.
Woman's world cook book; cont. hundreds of invaluable recipes. '10(F5) c. il. 12°, 10 c. Currier.

How's your health? McIntyre, *Mrs.* L. L. $1.25. L. L. McIntyre.

Hoxie, Bertha Davidson.
Hilda's wish, Christmas in Denmark. '08 (D19) c. il. 12°. (Christmas in many lands ser.) †50 c. Estes.

Hoxie, G: Howard, M.D.
Practice of medicine for nurses; with chap. on the technic of nursing by Pearl L. Laptad. '08(Ap4) c. il. 8°, *$1.50 net. Saunders.
Symptomatic and regional therapeutics. '10(S) c. 8+499 p. il. 8°, $4. Appleton.

Hoyle, Edmond.
Games modernized; [by] Prof. Hoffman. New ed., rev. to 1909 by Ernest Bergholt. '09(D) 16+476 p. 16°, *75 c. net. Dutton.
Standard games and bridge whist, 500, fan tan, solo hearts and card tricks, [etc.;] also billiards, pool, American ten pins and bowling, [etc.] '08(Mr7) c. il. D. bds., 75 c.; pap., 25 c. Laird.

HOYLE, Edmond.
Foster, R. F: Complete Hoyle: encyclopedia of games. **$2.50 net. Stokes.
Lowe, P. E., *comp.* Hoyle's card games. 15 c. Ottenheimer.
Phillips, B., *comp.* Standard Hoyle. $1; 75 c.; 50 c. Excelsior.

Hoyle's games of cards; the latest ed; the most popular games of cards played in the English-speaking world, with rules and directions for the most successful methods of play. '09, [1910.] (Ja) c. 208 p. il. 12°, 25 c. Ottenheimer.

Hoyt, Anne.
See Bisland, Eliz.

Hoyt, Arth. Stephen, D.D.
Call of the country church. '09(Mr) c. 11 p. 12°. (Claims and opportunities of the Christian ministry.) 5 c.; per 100, $4. Y. M. C. A.
The preacher: his person, message, and method. '09(F20) c. D. **$1.50 net. Macmillan.

Hoyt, C: Oliver.
Studies in the history of modern education. '08(D26) c. il. pors. map, O. $1.50. Silver.

Hoyt, Dan. Mansfield.
Practical therapeutics and prescription writing. '09(N) c. 20+291 p. il. 8°, $3.50. Dolbey.

Hoyt, Elisabeth, ed.
Little Chum Club. '10(N5) c. il. D. (Happy hour ser.) bds., 50 c. Wilde.
Little folks in the country. '09(O9) c. il D. (Happy hour ser.) †50 c. Wilde.
Play days. '09(O9) c. il. D. (Happy hour ser) †50 c. Wilde.

Hoyt, Rev. Wayland.
Some of the reasons why I cannot accept the results of the destructive criticism of the Old Testament. '08, [1909.] (Mr) c. 32 p. 12°, pap., 10 c. Am. Bapt.

Hrbek, Jeffrey Dolezal.
Linden blossoms. '08, [1909.] c. 126 p. por. 8°, $1.50. Torch Press.

Hrdlicka, Ales, [i.e., **Alois Ferdinand.**]
New examples of American Indian skulls with low forehead. '08, [1909.] (F) 171-175 p. il. O. pap. (Add. Superintendent for price.) U. S., Supt. of Docs.
On the stature of the Indians of the Southwest and of northern Mexico. '10 (Ap16) 4°, 50 c. Torch Press.
Physiological and medical observation among the Indians of southwestern United States and northern Mexico. '09 (F6) il. chart, tabs., O. (Smithsonian Institution, Bu. of American Ethnology bull.) (Add. Superintendent for price.) U. S., Supt. of Docs.
Skeletal remains suggesting or attributed to early man in North America. '08(F1) il. O. (Smithsonian Inst., Bu. of Am. Ethnology bull.) 25 c. U. S., Supt. of Docs.
Tuberculosis among certain Indian tribes of the United States. '09(Ag7) il. O. (Smithsonian Institution, Bu. of American Ethnology bull.) (Add. Superintendent for price.) U. S., Supt. of Docs.

Hrebelianovich, Prince Lazarovich-.
See Lazarovich-Hrbelianovitch, *Prince.*

Hsaio Ching.
Book of filial duty; tr. by Ivan Chên. '09 (F13) 16°, (Wisdom of the East ser.) *40 c. net. Dutton.

Hsiang Yuan-P'ien.
Chinese porcelain; sixteenth-century colored il. with Chinese MS. text; tr. and annot. by Stephen Wootton Bushell. '08 (N14) il. F. limp silk, $34, boxed. Oxford Univ.

Hubbard, Mrs. Alice Moore.
Life lessons. '10(F12) c. pors. 8°, hf. ooze, $3. Roycrofters.
Woman's work. '08(My2) c. por. 8°, $5; $7.50; $10; $25. Roycrofters.

Hubbard, C: Lincoln.
Fans, ventilation and heating. '09(Je5) c. il. 8°, (Machinery's reference ser.) pap., 25 c. Indust. Press.
Heating and ventilation. '08(N21) c. il. 8°, (American School of Correspondence pubs.) $1.50. Am. Sch. Corr.
Power, heating and ventilation; treatise for designing and constructing engineers, architects and students. In 3 v. v. 1, Boiler room equipment; v. 2, Power and lighting; v. 3, Heating and ventilation. '10(My14) il. 8°, $5 net. Technical Press.

Hubbard, Elbert, ["Fra Elbertus."]
Cigarettist; being a preachment. [1910.] (Ap) 14 p. 8°, pap., 10 c. Roycrofters.
Closed or open shop? '10(My) c. 3-37 p. 8°, 10 c. Roycrofters.
Divine in man. '09(Ag) c. 6 p. 12°, 10 c. Roycrofters.
The doctors; satire in four seizures. '10 (F12) c. il. 8°, limp leath., $2. Roycrofters.
Health and wealth. '08(N) c. 9-162 p. por. 12°, bds., $2. Roycrofters.
Helpful hints for business helpers; written in a sincere and kindly desire to help the young who do not know, and the older ones who sometimes forget. [1910.] c. '09. 18 p. 8°, 10 c. Roycrofters.
Here then is a preachment entitled, a business necessity, the same having been written with one hand. '10(Ap) c. 5-16 p. 8°, 10 c. Roycrofters.
Little journey to a great dentist. '09(D) c. 43 p. 8°, 25 c. Roycrofters.
Little journeys to the homes of famous women. '08(D) c. 9-313 p. pors. 4°. (Add. pubs. for price.) Roycrofters.
Little journeys to the homes of good men and great. '08(D) c. 9-348 p. pors. 8°. (Add. pubs. for price.) Roycrofters.
Little journeys to the homes of great business men. '09(My) c. '08. 12°, bds., $2; limp leath., $3; ¾ ooze, $5; ¾ levant, $10. Roycrofters.
Man of Sorrows: being a little journey to the home of Jesus of Nazareth. '09 (Mr27) c. front. 12°, $2. Roycrofters.
The mintage; being ten stories and one more. '10(D3) c. por. 12°, $2. Roycrofters.
Motto book; being a catalogue of epigrams, by Fra Elbertus, [*pseud.,*] assisted at times by Solomon, Ruskin, Shakespeare, Joaquin Miller, Benjamin Franklin, Walt Whitman, Ali Baba, and Felix Cyrenius. [1910.] (Ja) c. '09. 50 p. il. 8°, 10 c. Roycrofters.
Pasteboard proclivities. [1910.] (Mr) c. '09. 13 p. 12°, 10 c. Roycrofters.
Romance of the railroad; being a story of the Bergen Cut on the Erie. '10(Ag) 31 p. pl. 8°, 10 c. Roycrofters.
So here cometh White hyacinths: a book of the heart; an attempt to body forth ideas and ideals for the betterment of men, eke women. '08(Mr14) c. pors. 12°, limp leath., $2. Roycrofters.
Standard Oil Company; being a repr. from *The Fra Magazine.* '10(Ap9) c. O. pap., 10 c. Roycrofters.
Tale of two tailors, which the same has the unique quality of being true. '09(Ap) c. 29 p. por. 12. (Add. pubs. for price.) Stein, B.
This then is a William Morris book. '08 (Ap25) c. pors. facsim., 8°, $2. Roycrofters.
See also Clarke, Jos. Ignatius Constantine.

—, and Albertson, Rev. C: Carroll.
Joint debate Hubbard-Albertson; question: resolved "That Christianity is declining"; the debaters, Elbert Hubbard, foreman of the Roycroft Shop, East Aurora, N. Y.—yes; Rev. Dr. C. C. Albertson, pastor of the Central Presbyterian Church, Rochester, N. Y.—no. '09(Ag) 32 p. 12°, 25 c. Roycrofters.

Hubbard, Ethel Daniels.
Under marching orders; story of Mary Porter Gamewell. '09(O) 12+222 p. il. pors., map, facsim. 12°, (Forward mission study courses.) *50 c. net. Young People's Miss.

Hubbard, F. C.
Through library windows. '10(F) $1.25. B'way Pub.

HUBBARD, Gurdon Saltonstall.
Hamilton, H: E: Biographical sketch of Gurdon Saltonstall Hubbard. 50 c. Chic. Hist.

Hubbard, H: Lewis.
Summing it up; treatise on economical, moral and religious conditions of the present time, showing how they have been evolved through the centuries, with suggestions as to how the mistakes can be rectified, and universal happiness and equality assured. '09(O2) c. D. 50 c. J. S. Ogilvie.

Hubbard, J: Milton.
Notes of a private. '09(Ag) 189 p. il. por. 12°, $1. E. H. Clarke.

Hubbard, Mrs. Leonidas, jr.
See Hubbard, Mina Benson.

Hubbard, Mina Benson, [formerly Mrs. Leonidas Hubbard, jr., now Mrs. Ellis.]
Woman's way through Labrador: account of the exploration of the Nascaupee and George rivers. '08(O10) c. il. pors. map, O. **$1.50 net. McClure.

Hubbard, Prévost.
Dust preventives and road binders. '10 (My14) figs. 8°, $3 net. Wiley.

Hubbard, Mrs. Sara Anderson.
Duty of being beautiful. '08(My23) c. nar. D. bds., 50 c. McClurg.

Hubbard, W: Lines, ed.
American history and encyclopedia of music. In 10 v. '08(O3) ea., $3.50; $4.50; $6. Squire-C.

Hubbell, Alvin Allace.
Development of ophthalmology in America, 1800 to 1870: address del. in abstract before the section of ophthalmology of the American Medical Association, June 4, 1907; rev. and enl. '08(Ap4) c. il. pors. 12°, *$1.75 net. Chic. Med. Bk.

Hubbell, G: Allen.
Horace Mann, educator, patriot and reformer; study in leadership. '10(Mr12) c. por. D. $1.50. Fell.

Hubbell, J: H:, ed. and comp.
Legal directory for lawyers and business men, cont. the names of one or more of the leading and most reliable attorneys in over 4000 cities and towns in the U. S. and Canada. [etc.,] 1909. '08(D) c. 1428+400 p. O. $5. Hubbell.

Hubel, Henni.
Blätter und blüten; gedichte und sprüche. '10(F5) c. 16°, $1. Brentano's.

Hubley, Adam.
Adm. Hubley, jr., Lt. Col. Comdt. 11th Penna. Regt., his journal, commencing at Wyoming, July 30th, 1779; by J: W. Jordan; (repr. from the *Pennsylvania Magazine of History and Biography* for April, July and Oct., 1909.) '09, [1910.] (My) 57 p. facsims., 8°, $1. Hist. Soc. Penn.

HUBNER, Baron Joseph Alexander von.
Sartow, *Sir* E. M. Austrian diplomat in the fifties: [Baron Joseph von Hübner.] 50 c. Putnam.

Huck, Olive.
Otis Hamilton's quest. '10(N5) c. D. $1 net. Am. S. S.

Huckel, Rev. Oliver.
Mental medicine; five conferences with students at the Johns Hopkins Medical School; with an introd. by Lewellys F. Barker, M.D. '09(Jl10) c. D. **$1 net. Crowell.
See also Wagner, Wilhelm Richard.

Huddle, Rev. W: P:
Hist. of the Hebron Lutheran church, Madison Co., Va., 1717 to 1907. '08(Je) c. 11+116 p. il. pors. 8°, $2. W: P: Huddle.

Huddy, Xenophon Pearce.
Law of automobiles. 2d ed. '09(My) c. 26+364 p. O. $3.50. M. Bender.

Hudgins, Rev. C: Buckner.
The convert. '08(F15) c. D. $1.50. Neale.

Hudgins, C: D.
Transferred identity; or, the unsolvable mystery in the life of John McFarland. '09(Ag7) c. D. pap., 25 c. J. S. Ogilvie.

Hudson, Bernard.
Aids to medicine. '09, [1910.] (F) 260 p. 16°, (Students' aid ser.) *$1.25 net. Wood.

Hudson, C. S., and Garland, C. M.
Tests of a liquid air plant. '08(Je) 20 p. il. 8°, (Univ. of Ill. bull.) pap., gratis. Univ. of Ill.

HUDSON, Henry.
Brooklyn Public Library. List of books and magazine articles on Henry Hudson and the Hudson River, Robert Fulton and early steam navigation. gratis. Brooklyn Lib.
Chamberlain, F. Hudson tercentenary; an historical retrospect regarding the object and quest of an all-water route from Europe to India. (Add. pubs. for price.) Lyon.
Clarke, J. I. C., *and* Hubbard, E. Manhattan, an ode; Henry Hudson, an essay. $2. Roycrofters.
Hall, E: H. Hudson and Fulton. (Add. pubs. for price.) Hudson-Fulton.
Horner, H. H., *comp. and ed.* Hudson-Fulton celebration, Sept. 25 to Oct. 9, 1909. (Add. pubs. for price.) N. Y. State Educ.
Hudson-Fulton Celebration Commission, New York. Hudson and Fulton. (Not for sale.) Hudson-Fulton.
Janvier, T: A. Henry Hudson. **75 c. net. Harper.
Murphy, H: C. Henry Hudson in Holland. *$2.50 net. Tice & L.

Hudson, Horace Bushnell.
Half century of Minneapolis. '09(My15) c. il. pors. Q. hf. mor., $15. Hudson Pub.

Hudson, Marshall Alonze.
How to reach men; to hold men; to teach men; to win men; how it has been done. '08(N14) c. D. *50 c. net. S. S. Times.

Hudson, Mrs. Susan E. Johnson.
Washington's home, (by permission of the *Colonial Magazine;*) hist. of the "Mount Vernon Association." '08, [1909.] (Jl) 12 p. il. 16°. (Add. pubs. for price.) Hanzsche.

Hudson, W: Cadwalader.
J. P. Dunbar: a story of Wall Street. '08(Ap11) c. 12°, (Popular priced copyrights.) 50 c. B. W. Dodge.

Hudson, W: H:
Herbert Spencer. '09(Jl31) 12°. (Philosophies ancient and modern from Pythagoras to Spencer.) *50 c. net. Dodge.
Introd. to the study of literature. '10(D24) 12°, $1.25 net. Heath.
Land's End: a naturalist's impression in West Cornwall. '08(O10) il. O. *$3 special net. Appleton.
Shepherd's life impressions of the South Wiltshire Downs. '10(D10) il. 8°, $2.50 net. Dutton.

HUDSON, N. Y.
Bradbury, *Mrs.* A. R. Hist. of the city of Hudson, N. Y. $1.50. A. R. Bradbury.

Hudson and other poems. Hellman, G: S. $1.50. Putnam.

HUDSON-FULTON CELEBRATION.
Adams, E: D. Hudson-Fulton medal. E: D. Adams.
Burdick, E. E., *comp.* Hudson-Fulton celebration; catalogue of historical exhibition held by Free Public Library of Jersey City, Sept.-Dec., 1909. Jersey City Pub. Lib.

Hudson-Fulton Celebration. Catalogue of an exhibition held in the Metropolitan Museum of Art, [New York City,] commemorative of the tercentenary of the discovery of the Hudson river by Henry Hudson, 1609, and the centenary of the use of steam in the navigation of said river by Robert Fulton, 1807. In 2 v. '09(D4) c. il. 4°, bds., $5. Metropolitan Museum.

Hudson-Fulton Celebration Commission, New York. Historical pageant; Hudson-Fulton celebration, Sept. 25 to Oct. 9, 1909. [1910.] c. '09. 64 p. il. 4°, 50 c. Redfield.

Hudson-Fulton Celebration Commission, New York. Hudson and Fulton. '09(Ag14) 8°. (Not for sale.) Hudson-Fulton.

Hudson-Fulton Celebration Commission. Official programme Hudson-Fulton celebration, Sept. 25 to Oct. 9, 1909. '09(S25) c. il. F. pap., 25 c. Hudson-Fulton.

HUDSON RIVER, N. Y.
Farley, J. P. Three rivers, the James, the Potomac, the Hudson; a retrospect of peace and war. *$2 net. Neale.
Jersey City Free Public Library. From canoe to tunnel. gratis. Jersey City Lib.
Johnson, C. Picturesque Hudson. **$1.25 net. Macmillan.
Jones, W: B. Hudson river outlet from the Erie canal to the sea. (Not for sale.) W: B. Jones.
Mack, A. C. Palisades of the Hudson. *75 c. net. Palisades Press.
Miller, E. W., *comp.* Sail and steam: historical sketch showing New Jersey's connection with Hudson-Fulton celebration. gratis. Jersey City Lib.
Verplanck, W: E:, *and* Collyer, M. W. Sloops of the Hudson. **$1.50 net. Putnam.
See also Mount Pleasant Academy, N. Y.

HUDSON TUNNELS.
See Hudson River.

HUDSON'S BAY COMPANY.
Reed, C: B. Masters of the wilderness; study of the Hudson's Bay Company. 50 c. Chic. Hist.
See also Canada.

Huebinger, Melchoir.
Map and guide for river to river road; three hundred and eighty miles dragged highway across Iowa from Council Bluffs to Davenport, originated and carried to completion by the Des Moines Daily Capital. [1910.] (O) c. 140 p. il. maps, 12°, 50 c. Iowa Pub.

Huebner, Grover Gerhard.
Five years of railroad regulation by the states. '08(O) 138-156 p. tabs., 8°, (Am. Acad. of Pol. and Sciences pubs.) 25 c. Am. Acad. Pol. Sci.

Huebschmann, J: Simon.
Boys, youths, men. '09(D) c. 7+80 p. 12°, 50 c. Central.

Hueffer, Ford Madox.
The "Half Moon": a romance. '09(Jl3) c. D. †$1.50. Doubleday, P.
See also Hutchings, W. W.

Hueffer, Oliver Madox.
Book of witches. '09(Je5) front. O. *$2.50 net. J: McBride.

Huelin y Arssu, Carlos.
Technological dict. in Spanish-French-English-German. '10(N5) 12°, $4. Spon.

Huels, F: W:
Comparison of the effects of frequency on the light of incandescent and Nernst lamps. '08(F1) figs. tabs., O. (Univ. of Wis. bull., Engineering ser.) pap., 25 c. Univ. of Wis.

Huelsen, Christian.
Roman Forum: its history and its monuments; tr. by Jesse Benedict Carter. 2d ed., rev. and enl. '09(Mr6) il. S. *$1.75 net. Stechert.

Huey, Edm. Burke.
Psychology and pedagogy of reading; with review of the hist. of reading and writing, and of methods, texts, and hygiene in reading. '08(F8) c. il. 12°, *$1.40 net. Macmillan.

Huey, Maud Morrison.
Marjorie Moxie: her experiences. '10 (N12) c. il. D. $1.25. Rand, McN. & Co.

Huffcut, Ernest Wilson, ed.
Law of negotiable instruments; statutes, cases and authorities. 2d ed., rev. and enl., by F: D. Colson. '10(O) c. O. $4.50. Baker, V. & Co.

Huffman, Jasper Abraham.
Old Testament messages of the Christ. '09 (N) c. 181 p. por. 8°, 75 c. Bethel Pub.

HUFFORD FAMILY.
See Genealogies: Hoffert, F. P., *comp.*

Hufton-Windust, Florance.
Home nursing and hygiene. '08(Je6) 12°, *50 c. net. Macmillan.

Hügel, Baron Friedrich v.
Mystical element in religion, as studied in St. Catherine of Genoa and her friends. '08(D) 2 v., 18+466; 6+422 p. 8°, *$6 net. Dutton.

Hugh, D: Douglas.
Bulletin concerning rural schools and their consolidation. '09, [1910.] (Je) 38 p. il. pors., plans, D. (State Normal School bull.) pap. Colo State Normal.
Bibliography (6 p.).

Hughes, A. A.
Pract. dictation; junior course arranged to accompany Pract. spelling by the same author. '10(My21) S. 20 c. Longmans.
Pract. spelling; junior course arr. to accompany Pract. dictation, by the same author. '10(My21) D. 15 c. Longmans.

Hughes, C. H.
Terra cotta hollow tiles for walls of houses. [1910.] (My) 12 p. il. O. pap., gratis. Nat. Fire Proofing.

Hughes, C: E.
Book of the Black Forest. '10(Jl16) il. maps, 8°, $3 net. Dutton.

Hughes, C: Evans.
Addresses and papers, 1906-1908; with an introd. by Jacob Gould Schurman. '08 (My2) c. por. D. $1.50. Putnam.
Conditions of progress in democratic government. '10(Je11) c. D. (Yale lectures on the responsibilities of citizenship.) $1.15 net. Yale Univ.
Speech of Hon. C: E. Hughes at the Lincoln dinner of the Republican Club at the Waldorf-Astoria, N. Y., Feb. 12, 1908. '08(O) 10 p. 4°, 25 c. Law Reporting.

—, and Brewer, D: Josiah.
Idea of Public Office: address by C: E. Hughes [and] Public office in relation to public opinion; address, by D: J. Brewer; del. before the Civic Forum. '08(D5) pors. 12°, (Civic Forum addresses.) pap., 10 c. Civic Forum.

Hughes, Dickie.
Pudgy. '10(Ap23) il. 16°, (Little mother ser.) bds., 50 c. Dutton.

Hughes, Bp. Edn. Holt.
Teaching of citizenship. '09(O9) c. D. $1.25. Wilde.
Thanksgiving sermons. '09, [1910.] (F) 246 p. 12°, (Christian festivals ser.) *$1 net. Eaton & M.; Jennings.

Hughes, G: Washington.
Faults and follies as mirrored in a series of lectures. '08(N) c. 5-303 p. 12°, 75 c. G: W. Hughes.

Hughes, Rev. H. G.
Jesus Christ and human life; course of Lenten sermons. [1910.] (Ap) c. 46 p. 8°, 40 c. net. Wagner.

Hughes, H: Clay.
Philosophy of the federal constitution. '08 (S19) c. D. *$1.50 net. Neale.

Hughes, Ja. Laughlin.
Teaching to read. '09(Je26) c. S. 50 c. Barnes.

Hughes, M. L.
Manual of chiropody. [1910.] (Mr) *25 c. net. W: R. Jenkins.
Formerly published by E. R. Pelton.

Hughes, Mrs. Mary E.
Answer to "Three years in Arkansas." '08 (Ja4) por. 12°, pap., 25 c. Wiley & W.

Hughes, Rupert.
Gift-wife. '10(O22) c. il. D. $1.35. Moffat.
The Lakerim cruise. '10(O1) c. il. D. $1.50. Century Co.

Hughes, T:
Ethics of the practice of law. '09(Ja) c. 92 p. O. cl. (Add. pubs. for price.) Daily Record.
Tom Brown's school days. '08(O10) il. D. (Bowman's illustrated lib. of the world-favorite books.) $1. Bowman.
Tom Brown's school days; ed., with introd. and notes, by C: Swain Thomas. '08 (O24) front. 24°, (Pocket Am. and Eng. classics.) *25 c. net. Macmillan.

Hughes, T: Aloysius.
History of the Society of Jesus in North America, colonial and federal. In 6 v.: 3 of text and 3 in 2 of the accompanying documents. v. 1, pt. 1, nos. 1-140, 1605-1838. '08(O10); v. 1, pt. 2, nos. 141-224, 1605-1838. '10(Ap23) maps, facsims., Q. ea., *$4.50 net. Burrows.

Hughes, W: Taylor.
Grounds and rudiments of law. v. 1. '08 (F); v. 2 (Ag); v. 3, 4. '08, [1909.] (Ja) c. O. ea., $4. Usona.

Hughs, G: Shelley.
Grammar of English; on the theory that this is the first; complete for schools, colleges and universities, for private study, for reference, and for teaching by correspondence. '10(N19) c. 8°, $1. G: S. Hughs.

Hughson, Rev. Shirley Carter.
Warfare of the soul; pract. studies in the life of temptation; with preface by the Rev. Alfr. G. Mortimer. '10(F19) c. D. **$1.20 net. Longmans.

Hughson, Wa., comp.
Church's mission to the mountaineers of the south, by Archdeacon Neve of Va., Archdeacon Spurr, of W. Va., [etc.] '08 (N) c. 10+131 p. il. pors. 12°, (Soldier and servant ser.) 75 c.; pap., 50 c. Church Missions.

Hugo, G: B., and Carey, Ja. F.
Socialism, "the creed of despair"; joint debate in Faneuil Hall, March 22, 1909, G: B. Hugo, affirmative, and Ja. F. Carey, negative. '09(Ag7) c. O. 75 c. G: B. Hugo.

Hugo, T. W.
Digest-index of "Morals and dogma," of Albert Pike 33°. [1910.] (Ja) c. '09. 200 p. por. 8°, $1. T. W. Hugo.

Hugo, Victor.
Complete works. In 20 v. '08(Je27) $25; hf. mor., $40. Lamb Pub.
Works. De luxe ed. 8 v. '10(N) il. levant, $24. Crowell.
Works. 10 v. New imperial lib. ed. '10 (D) il. 8°, ea., $1.25; hf. cf., $2.25; New il. sterling ed., ea., $1. (Sets only.) Estes.
[Works.] In 8 v. v. 1, 2, The history of a crime; v. 3, Napoleon the Little; v. 4, 5, Poems; v. 6, 7, 8, Dramatic works. Handy library ed. '09(Ap3) fronts. 12°, ea., **$1 net; per set, **$8 net; hf. mor., **$20 net; Library ed., *$8 net; **$10 net; hf. mor., **$20 net. Little, B. & Co.
Works. De luxe ed. 8 v. '10(D) 16°, ea., mor., $1.50 net. (Sets only.) Nelson.
Novels. In 8 v. '09(Je19) fronts. 16°, (New century lib.) limp leath., ea., $1.25. Nelson.
La Bataille de Waterloo; (extrait des Misérables;) ed. by R. P. Jago. '10 (Ja29) map, S. (Crowell's shorter French texts; ed. by J. E. Mansion.) *25 c. net. Crowell.
Les misérables. 2 v. '10(D) il. $2.50, boxed. Crowell.
Les misèrables. 2 v. '09(Mr27) 16°, (Everyman's lib.) *35 c. net; leath., *70 c. net. Dutton.
Les miserables; ed., with introd., notes and vocab., by Douglas Labaree Buffum. '08 (N21) c. S. $1.25. Holt.
Les miserables. New library ed. In 5 v. '08(O24) il. 12°, *$5 net. McKay.
Les misérables. '10(O1) D. 50 c. net; leath., $1 net, boxed. Platt & P.

Hugo, Victor.—*Continued.*
Les misérables. In 3 v. '09(My1) S. (Ideal classics.) leath., $3.75, boxed. Winston.
Notre Dame de Paris. '10(Ap2) 16°, (Everyman's lib.) 35 c. net; leath., 70 c. net. Dutton.
Notre-Dame de Paris; ed. by Leon Delbos. '09(Mr6) por. S. (Oxford higher French ser.) $1.15. Oxford Univ.
Poèmes choisis, 1822-1865; préface de L. Aguettant. '09(Mr6) por. S. (Les classiques français.) leath., *$1 net. Putnam.
Préface du Cromwell; ed. by Edmond Wahl. '09(My15) por. S. (Oxford higher French ser.) 85 c. Oxford Univ.
Ruy Blas; with an introd. and notes by Kenneth McKenzie. '09(Jl10) c. por. S. 65 c. Holt.
Selected poems; ed., with introds. and notes, by Albert Schinz. '08(My23) c. por. S. (Modern lang. ser.) 80 c. Heath.
Selected poems; ed., with introd. and notes, by H. W. Eve. '08(F1) 8°, (Pitt Press ser.) *50 c. net. Putnam.

HUGO, Victor.
Bruner, J. D. Studies in Victor Hugo's dramatic characters. $1. Ginn.

Huguenot Bartholomew Dupuy. Dupuy, B: H. $6.50. B: H. Dupuy.

HUGUENOTS.
Thompson, J. W. Wars of religion in France, 1559-1576. *$4.50 net. Univ. of Chic.

Hühner, Leon.
First Jew to hold the office of governor of one of the United States. '09(O) 187-195 p. 8°, 25 c. Bloch.
Jews of Georgia from the outbreak of the American Revolution to the close of the 18th century. '09(O) 89-108 p. 8°, 25 c. Bloch.
Jews of Newport; address del. on the occasion of unveiling the memorial tablet in the old Jewish synagogue at Newport, R. I., Sept. 7, 1908. '09(N) 11 p. 24°, pap. (Add. author for price.) L. Hühner.
Some Jewish associates of John Brown; [reprinted from the *Magazine of History* with notes and queries, September, 1908.] '09(Ap3) 8°, pap., o. p. L. Hühner.

Huie, W: Green.
Bible application of Freemasonry. '08 (My23) c. por. D. $1.50. W: G. Huie.

Huish, Marcus Bourne.
American pilgrim's way in England, to homes and memorials of the founders of Virginia, the New England States and Pennsylvania, the Universities of Harvard and Yale, the first president of the United States, and other illustrious Americans. '09(F) 376 p. il. 4°, $6; ltd. ed., 312 p. f°, hf. cf., $15. [London, Fine Arts Society.] W. E. Jones, Baltimore.
Happy England. '10(F19) col. il. sq. 8°, (Color book ser.) *$6 net. Macmillan.
Samplers and tapestry embroideries; also the stitchery of the same, by Mrs. Head. '09(Ag7) il. Q. price increased from $14 to $17. Longmans.

Huizinga, A. v. C. P.
Belief in a personal God. '10(Mr12) c. D. *50 c. net. Sherman, F.

Huizinga, G: Ford.
What the Dutch have done in the west of the United States. '09, [1910.] (Mr) 13-52 p. 8°. (Priv. pr.) E: Bok.

Hulbert, Archer Butler.
Niagara River. '08(O17) c. il. maps, O. **$3.50 net, boxed. Putnam.
—, **comp. and ed.** Crown collection of photographs of American maps, [in the British Museum, London.] In 5 v. v. 4, 5. '09 (D25) f°, ea., $100. A. H. Clark.

Hulbert, Eri Baker, D.D.
English Reformation and Puritanism, with other lectures and addresses: memorial; ed. by A. R. E. Wyant. '08(F1) c. por. O. *$2.50 net. Univ. of Chic.

Hulburd, Ebenezer Wallace, comp.
Life of little Justin Hulburd, medium, actor, and poet. '09(Jl17) c. 3 v., pors. O. ea., $1.75; per set, $5. E. W. Hulburd.

Hulfish, D: Sherrill.
Motion picture, its making and its theater. '09(D25) c. il. 12°, 50 c. Elec. Mag.

Hull, Eleanor.
Boys' Cuchulain; heroic legends of Ireland. '10(Ag6) col. il. O. $1.50 net. Crowell.

Hull, Ernest R.
Formation of character; with preface by the Bp. of Salford. '10(Jl) 4+123 p. 12°, pap., 15 c. net. Herder.

Hull, J: Wellington.
Alpha and omega. [1910.] (Ap) c. '09. 123 p. il. por. 16°, 50 c. J: W. Hull.

Hull, Paul.
See Adventures of pirates.—On the gridiron.

Hull, W: I:
Two Hague conferences, and their contributions to international law; published for the International School of Peace. '08 (N14) c. D. $1.65. Ginn.

HULL HOUSE, Chicago.
Addams, J. Twenty years in Hull House. $2.50 net. Macmillan.

Hulme, F: E:
Familiar Swiss flowers. '08(My16) D. *$3 net. Cassell.
That rock garden of ours. '09, [1910.] (D) c. il. 12°, **$3 net. Jacobs.

Hulse, Mrs. Olive M.
Two hundred recipes for making salads, with thirty recipes for dressings and sauces. '10(D31) c. 8°, $1. Hopewell Press.

Hulsean lectures. *See* Figgis, J: Neville.—Masterman, *Rev.* J: H. B.

Hülshof, J: Ludwig.
Reading made easy for foreigners; First reader; Second reader; Third reader. '09(Je5) c. D. 1st reader, 30 c.; 2d reader, 40 c.; 3d reader, 50 c. Hinds.

Hülshoff, Annette Elizabeth, Frelin von Dröste-.
See Droste-Hülshoff, A. E., *Frelin* von.

Hult, Gottfried Emanuel.
Reveries and other poems. '10(F19) c. 12°, **$1.25 net. Putnam.

Human, all too human. Nietzsche, F. W. 50 c. Kerr.

HUMAN ANATOMY.
See Anatomy.

Human anatomy for art students. Fripp, *Sir* A. D. $1.75 net. Lippincott.

Human beings vs. things. Coolidge, A. C. $1. Hungerford-H.

Human body. Martin, H: N. **$2.50 net. Holt.

Human body a volume of divine revelations. Tanner, H: S: 35 c. H: S: Tanner.

Human body and health. Davison, A. 40 c.; 50 c. Am. Bk.

Human cobweb. Weale, B. L. P., *pseud.* †$1.50. Dodd.

Human economics. Gibson, A. H. *$3.50 net. Longmans.

Human equipment. Griggs, E: H. *50 c. net. B: W. Huebsch.

Human foods and their nutritive value. Snyder, H. *$1.25 net. Macmillan.

Human (A) life. Fisher, D. W. *$1.50 net. Revell.

Human life. Knight, S. S. $1. Fenno.

Human machine. Bennett, E. A. 75 c. net. Doran.

Human nature a revelation of the divine. Robinson, C: H: 25 c.; 40 c. net. Longmans.

Human nature in politics. Wallas, G. *$1.50 net. Houghton M.

Human nature in selling goods. Collins, J. H. 50 c. Altemus.

Human physiology. Ritchie, J: W. 80 c. World Bk.

Human pilgrimage. Spyker, J: A., *comp.* 75 c. Hammond Pr. Co.

Human species. Hopf, L. *$3 net. Longmans.

Human speech. Macnamara, N. C. *$1.75 net. Appleton.

Human way. Willcox, *Mrs.* L. C. **$1.25 net. Harper.

Humane movement. McCrea, R. C. $2 net. Lemcke.

HUMANISM.
See Philosophy.

Humanists' lib.; ed. by Lewis Einstein. 8°, *$6 net. Merrymount.
—Erasmus. Treatise on war.
—Nolhac. Petrarch and the ancient world. $6.
—Sidney. Defence of poesie.

Humanity. Denifle, H: *$1.25 net. Pustet.

Humanity, benevolence and charity legislation of the Pentateuch and the Talmud. Fluegel, M. *$2 net. Fluegel.

Humanity essays. D. Baker & T.
—Gaige *and* Harcourt. Books and reading. **$1.50 net.

Humbler poets. Rice, W. *and* G. C. $1.50. net. McClurg.

Humboldt, Archibald, pseud.
See March, G: Otis, *comp.*

HUMBOLDT, Friedrich Heinrich Alexander von.
Ingersoll, R. G. Humboldt and Heretics and heresies. 25 c. Farrell.

HUMBOLDT Co., Nev.
Ransome, F: L. Notes on some mining districts in Humboldt County, Nevada. U. S., Supt. of Docs.

Hume, Fergus W.
Amethyst cross. '09(Ap24) front. D. $1.50. Cassell.
Disappearing eye. '09(Ag28) c. D. †$1.25. G: W. Dillingham.
Green mummy. '08(Ag29) c. D. †$1.25. G: W. Dillingham.
Peacock of jewels. '10(Ag20) c. front. D. $1.25. G: W. Dillingham.
Red scull. '08(D) c. 319 p. il. 12°, $1.50. Dodge.
Sacred herb. '08(Mr7) c. front. D. †$1.25. G: W. Dillingham.
Sealed message. '08(Mr14) c. front. D. †$1.25. G: W. Dillingham.
Solitary farm. '09(My22) c. front. 12°, †$1.25. G: W. Dillingham.

Hume, Harold Hardrada.
Citrus fruits and their culture. [3d ed.] '10(Ag20) il. 12°, $2.50 net. Judd.
Pecan and its culture. 2d ed. '10(D3) il. 12°, $1.50. H. H. Hume.

Hume, Martin And. Sharp.
Two English queens [Mary and Elizabeth] and Philip. '08(D5) 8°, *$4.50 net. Putnam.

Hume-Griffith, A.
See Hume-Griffith, *Mrs.* M. E.

Hume-Griffith, Mrs. M. E. and A.
Behind the veil in Persia and Turkish Arabia: account of an Englishwoman's eight years' residence amongst the women of the East. '09(Mr13) il. map, O. *$3.50 net. Lippincott.

HUMERUS.
See Arm.

HUMILIATI.
See Church history.

HUMILITY.
Marett, R. R. Birth of humility. 35 c. Oxford Univ.

Humming bird. Johnson, O. M. 50 c. Baker & T.

HUMOR.
See Wit and humor.

Humor of the heart for faith. Pierce, C: C. *$1 net. Young Churchman.

HUMORISTS.
See Biography.

Humorous hits. Kleiser, G. **$1 net. Funk.

Humorous masterpieces; pictures by Phil May. '08(O24) T. pap., *25 c. net. Stokes

Hump Tree stories. Jones, M. J. $1. P. Elder.

Humphrey, Harriette Zephine.
Over against Green Peak. '08(Ap18) c. D. †$1.25. Holt.

Humphrey, Lucy Henderson, comp.
Poetic new-world. '10(Jl30) c. S. $1.50 net; leath., $2.50 net. Holt.
Poetic old-world: book for tourists: [poems.] '08(Ag1) c. S. **$1.50 net. Holt.

Humphrey, R: Lewis.
Fire-resistive properties of various building materials. '09(Jl31) il. O. (U. S., Dept. of the Interior, Geol. Survey bull.) pap. 30 c. U. S., Supt. of Docs.
Strength of concrete beams; results of tests of 108 beams (first series) made at the structural-materials testing laboratories. '08(O10) tabs., O. (Dept. of the Interior, U. S. Geolog. Survey bull.) pap. (Add. Supt. for price.) U. S., Supt. of Docs.

Humphrey Bold. Strang, H. †$1.50. Bobbs-M.

Humphreys, Arth. L.
Salt and sincerity. '09(Ag28) 12°, $1. Dodge.

Humphries, Sydney.
Oriental carpets, runners and rugs, and some Jacquard reproductions. '10(Ap9) il. pors. O. $10.50 net. Macmillan.

Humpty Dumpty ser. 4 v. '10(D) col. il. ea., 15 c. Saalfield.

Hun, Marcus T.
See New York [State.] *Cts. of record.* General rules.

Hundred best hymns. Cullen, J:, *comp.* 75 c. Dutton.

"**Hundred** best" ser.; [treasury of poetry in various tongues.] 6 v. [1910.] (D) ea., 50 c. net; leath., 75 c. net. Jacobs.

Hundred verses from old Japan. Fujiwara, S., *comp.* 90 c. **Oxford Univ.**

Huneker, Ja. Gibbons.
Egoist: book of supermen: Stendhal, Baudelaire, Flaubert, Anatole France, Huysmans, Barrès, Nietzsche, Blake, Ibsen, Stirner and Ernest Hello. '09(Ap3) c. por. facsim., D. **$1.50 net. Scribner.
Promenades of an impressionist. '10(Ap2) c. D. $1.50 net. Scribner.

HUNGARIAN LANGUAGE.
Yolland, A. H. Dictionary of the Hungarian and English language. pt. 1, Eng. Hungarian. *$4.50 net. Caspar.
Zeisler, A. Hungarian-English self pronouncing pocket interpreter. (Add. pub. for price.) Nyitray.

HUNGARIAN LITERATURE.
Campbell, J. M., *comp.* Sel. list of Hungarian books. 15 c. A. L. A.

HUNGARIANS IN THE UNITED STATES.
Az Amerikai magyar népszava jubileumi diszalbuma. $5. G. D. Berko.

HUNGARY.
Alden, P., *ed.* Hungary of to-day. *$3 net. Brentano's.
Bovill, W. B. F. Hungary and the Hungarians. *$2 net. McClure.
Nixon-Roulet, M. F. Our little Hungarian cousin. 60 c. L. C. Page.
Stokes, A. Hungary. *$6 net. Stokes.
Temperley, H. W: V., *and* Marczali, H. Hungary in the 18th century. $2.50 net. Putnam.
United States. *Dept. of State.* Affairs of Hungary, 1849-1850; message from the President of the United States, transmitting correspondence with A. Dudley Mann, (1849-1850,) in response to Senate resolution no. 85, of Dec. 7, 1909, rel. to affairs of Hungary. '10(Mr) 29 p. 8°, pap.
See also Austria-Hungary.

Hungerford, Mrs. Marg. Hamilton, ["The Duchess," formerly Mrs. Argles.]
Airy fairy Lilian. '08(Ag1) 12°, (Magnolia lib.) 50 c. Hurst.
Dick's sweetheart. '08(Ag8) 12°, (Magnolia lib.) 50 c. Hurst.

Hungry heart. Phillips, D: G. †$1.50. **Appleton.**

Hunnewell, Ja. Frothingham.
Collectors: address read to the Club of Odd Volumes at its annual meeting, Boston, Dec. 18, 1907. '08(Jl4) c. 12°. (Priv. pr.] Club Odd Vol.

Hunt, Arth. Surridge, ed.
See Egypt Exploration Fund, Græco-Roman Branch.—Hellenica Oxyrhynchia.

Hunt, Caroline Louisa.
Daily meals of children. '09(Jl17) 62 p. il. 8°, (U. S., Bu. of Education, bull.) pap. U. S., Supt. of Docs.
Home problems from a new standpoint. '08(S5) c. D. *$1 net. Whitcomb.
See also Langworthy, C: Ford.—Whitaker, G: Mason.

Hunt, Cecil.
See Davies, Randall.

Hunt, E. W.
Conserving and increasing the fertility of the soil. '09(S) 11 p. 8°, pap., gratis. C. Hildredth.

Hunt, Enid Leigh, [Mrs. Derek E: Thornton.]
Advent of Arthur. '08(N7) il. O. $2. Lippincott.

Hunt, Gaillard.
John C. Calhoun. '08(Ag29) c. por. D. (Am. crisis biographies.) $1.25. Jacobs.

Hunt, Ja. H: Leigh.
See Browning, Rob.

HUNT, James Henry Leigh.
Miller, B. Leigh Hunt's relations with Byron, Shelley and Keats. $1.25 net. Lemcke.

Hunt, Mary Amelia.
Universal bible, his-tory and her-story; human nature. [1910] (F) c. '09. 205 p. 8°, $1.50. M. A. Hunt.

Hunt, S: Furman.
Orations and historical addresses; ed. by the members of his family; biog. essay by Calvin Dill Wilson. '08(Ag8) c. por. O. **$2.50 net. Clarke.

Hunt, Violet B.
White rose of weary leaf. '08(Ag15) c. D. †$1.50. Brentano's.
Wife of Altamont. '10(Je4) D. $1.50. Brentano's.

Hunt, Rev. W:, ed.
See Stephens, W: R: W., *ed.*

—, and Poole, Reginald Lane, eds.
Political hist. of England. In 12 v. v. 6, Hist. of England from the accession of Edward VI. to the death of Elizabeth (1547-1603); by G. F. Pollard. '10(O15); v. 7, From the accession of James I. to the Restoration (1603-1660,) by F. C. Montague; v. 8, The history of England from the Restoration to the death of William III., (1660-1702,) by R: Lodge. '10(Ap2); v. 9, History of England from the accession of Anne to the death of George II., (1702-1760,) by I: Saunders Leadam. '09(Je5) fold. maps, O. ea., $2.60 net. Longmans.

Hunt, Rev. W: H:, ed.
See Mission preaching for a year.

HUNT, William Holman.
Coleridge, M. E. Holman Hunt. *65 c. net. **Stokes.**

"Hunt" coal and ore handling machinery, designed and manufactured by the C. W. Hunt Co. [Engineer's ed.] '09(Je) c. 88 p. il. 8°, gratis. C. W. Hunt.

Hunter, Alex.
Huntsman in the South. v. 1, Virginia and North Carolina. '08(F15) c. il. por. D. *$1.50 net. Neale.

Hunter, Byron.
Clover seed production in the Willamette Valley, Oregon. '09(Jl) 15 p. 8°, (U. S., Dept. of Agriculture; Bu. of Plant Industry circular.) pap. (Add. Superintendent for price.) U. S., Supt. of Docs.

—, and Jayne, Stephen Oscar.
Suggestions to settlers on the sandy soils of the Columbia River Valley. '10(Ag) 23 p. il. 8°, (U. S., Dept. of Agriculture, Bu. of Plant Industry, circular.)
"Bulletins of value to farmers in the Columbia River Valley" (2 p.).

Hunter, J:, D.D.
De profundis clamavi, and other sermons. '08(Ag29) 12°, *$1.50 net. Macmillan.

Hunter, Marg. L.
Gracie and her pets. '09(Je26) D. 75 c. Cochrane.

Hunter, S: J:, and Glenn, Pressley Adams.
Green bug and its enemies; study in insect parasitism, by S. J. Hunter; Influence of climate on the green bug and its parasite, by P. A. Glenn. '09, [1910.] (Mr) 9+221 p. il. maps, tabs., 8°, (Univ. of Kansas, Dept. of Entomology; contributions.) pap., gratis. S: J: Hunter.

Hunter, Wa. D:, and Mitchell, Jos. D.
Practical demonstration of a method for controlling the cattle tick. '09(Je) 4 p. 8°, (U. S., Dept. of Agriculture, Bu. of Animal Industry circular.) pap. (Add. Superintendent for price.)

Hunter, Wiles Rob.
The crisis: the unions and the courts, the tyranny of injunctions, the power of unity. '09(Ap3) sq. S. pap., 10 c. S: A. Bloch.
Socialists at work. '08(Ap18) c. D. **$1.50 net. Macmillan.

Hunter, W:, M.D.
Severest anæmias: their infective nature, diagnosis and treatment. v. 1, with historical schemes, charts and plates. '09 (Je) 15+226 p. il. Q. *$3.25 net. Macmillan.
Bibliography (21 p.).

Hunter, W: C.
Brass tacks; "capsule optimism." '10 (S17) c. por. S. 50 c. net. Reilly & B.

Hunter's camp-fires. House, E: J: **$5 net. Harper.

HUNTERS.
See Horse.

Hunting, H: Gardner.
Cave of the Bottomless Pool. '09(O30) c. il. D. †$1.50. Holt.
Silver canoe: the story of the secret that had to be kept. '09(S4) c. il. D. $1.25. McClurg.
Witter Whitehead's own story about a lucky splash of whitewash; some stolen silver, and a house that wasn't vacant. '09(Mr27) c. il. D. †$1.25. Holt.

HUNTING.
Bradley, C. Good sport with famous packs. $5 net. Dutton.
Browne, B. H. Guns and gunning. 30 c.; 20 c. J. Stevens.
Brunner, J. Tracks and tracking. *$1.25 net. Outing.
Chapman, A. On safari: big game hunting in British East Africa. *$4.50 net. Longmans.
Coaten, A. W., *ed.* British hunting. $65 net. Little, B. & Co.
Fleishmann, M. C: After big game in Arctic and tropic. (Priv. pr.) M. C: Fleischmann.
Herbert, A., *and* A. Shirkâri, *pseud.* Two Dianas in Alaska. *$4 net. Lane.
Hints for hunters and trappers. (Add. pubs. for price.) A. R. Harding.
Hoover, M. H: Wild ginger, wood sorrel and sweet cicely; [sportsmen's stories.] $1.50. B'way Pub.
Hornaday, W: T. Campfires on desert and lava. **$3 net. Scribner.
House, E: J: Hunter's camp-fires. **$5 net. Harper.
Martindale, T: With gun and guide. $2 net. Jacobs.
Miller, J. M. Hunting big game in the wilds of Africa. $1.50. Nat. Pub. Co.
Newberry, A. S. Caught on the fly: fugitive notes of sport. (Priv. pr.) A. S. Newberry.
Niedieck, P. With rifle in five continents: [travelling and hunting experiences.] *$5 net. Scribner.
Peer, F. S. Hunting field with horse and hound in America, the British Isles and France. $5. M. Kennerley.
Prichard, H. V. H. Hunting camps in wood and wilderness. $4 net. Sturgis & W.
Randolph, E. F. Inter-ocean hunting tales. $1. Forest.
Roosevelt, T. African game trails. $4 net. Scribner.
Russan, A. Mighty hunters. [fiction.] **$1.35 net. Longmans.
Surtees, R. S. Hunts with Jorrocks. *$5 net. Doubleday, P.
Surtees, R. S. Jorrocks on 'unting. 50 c. Dutton.
Tjäder, R: Big game of Africa. $3 net. Appleton.
Turberville, G: Booke of hunting, 1576. $2.50. Oxford Univ.
Wallace, A. F. Land cruising and prospecting: book of valuable information for hunters, trappers, [etc.] 60 c. A. R. Harding.
Wallace, H. F. Stalks abroad: being some account of the sport obtained during a two years' tour of the world. *$3.50 net. Longmans.
Whitney, H. Hunting with the Eskimos. $3.50 net. Century Co.
Williams, R. D. Horse and hound. $2.50 net. Outing.
Wright, S. H. Adventures among wild beasts. *$1.50 net. Lippincott.

HUNTING.—*Continued.*
York, E: P., *Duke* of. Master of game. *$4 net. Duffield.
See also Africa;—Dog;—Fish and fishing;—Fox; — Game laws; — Game preserving; — India; — Mink;—Rifle; — Sea-otter;—Shooting;—Sports and sportsmen; — Trapping; — *also* Roosevelt, Theodore.

Hunting of the snark. *See* **Dodgson, C: Lutwidge.**

Huntington, Annie Oakes.
Poison ivy and swamp sumach. '08(Ap18) c. il. O. bds., 75 c. O. Huntington.
Studies of trees in winter; deciduous trees of northeastern America; introd. by C: S. Sargent. '10(Ja1) il. 8°, *$2.25 net. J: R. Anderson.
Studies of trees in winter. New, rev. and enl. ed. '10(D3) col. il. 8°, $2.50. Estes.

Huntington, Archer Milton.
Sonnets. '08(Jl) c. 21 p. 16°. (Not for sale.) De Vinne.
See also Poem of the Cid.

Huntington, Mrs. Archer Milton.
See Huntington, Helen Manchester Gates.

Huntington, E. V., comp.
Four place table of logarithms and trigonometric functions. Unabridged ed. '08 (O3) 8°, 60 c. Harvard Co-op.

Huntington, Ellen Alden.
Fireless cooker. '09(Je5) il. fold. tab., O. (Univ. of Wis. bull.; University extension ser.) pap., 25 c. Univ. of Wis.

Huntington, Rev. G:
Charms of the old Book; or, a study of the attractions of the Bible; a prize book. '09(D11) c. D. (Green Fund book ser.) *90 c. net. Am. S. S.

Huntington, Helen Manchester Gates, [Mrs. Archer Milton Huntington.]
Apprentice to truth. '10(F26) c. D. $1.50. Putnam.
From the cup of silence, and other poems. '10(F19) 12°, $1. Putnam.
Sovereign good. '08(S26) c. D. †$1.50. Putnam.

Huntington, Ida M.
Peter Pumpkin in Wonderland. '08(D12) c. O. $1.25. Rand, McN. & Co.

Huntley, Mrs. Florence Chance.
Dream child. '09(Ja2) c. 12°, (Harmonic fiction ser.) $1. Indo-Am. Bk.
Gay Gnani of Gingalee; or, discords of devolution; a tragical entanglement of modern mysticism and modern science. '09(Ja2) c. D. (Harmonic fiction ser.) $1. Indo-Am. Bk.
—, ed. Who answers prayer? '08(D26) c. S. (Harmonic booklet ser.) 50 c. Indo-Am. Bk.

Hunts of the United States and Canada. Higginson, A. H. *$10 net; *$30 net. F. L. Wiles.

Hunts with Jorrocks. *See* Surtees, R. S.

Huntsman in the South. Hunter, A. v. 1. *$1.50 net. Neale.

Huntting, Teunis Dimon, comp.
Descendants of Abraham Huntting, the sixth in line from John Huntting, the first of the name in America. '10(S) 11 p. coat of arms, 8°, pap. (Priv. pr.) T. D. Huntting.

HUNTTING FAMILY.
See **Genealogies.**

Hurd, Mrs. Dena D. Soekland.
History and genealogy of the family of Hurd in the United States, and a partial history of the New England families of Heard and Hord, including a treatise on nomenclature, heraldry and coat armour, and ancestry. '10(My) c. 6+339 p. il. pors. 4°, $10; $15. D. D. S. Hurd.

Hurd, H. F., rep.
Porto Rico. *United States District ct.* Repts.

Hurd, Harvey B., comp. and ed.
See Illinois. Revised statutes.

Hurd, Marian Kent, and Wilson, Jean Bingham.
When she came home from college. '09 (N13) c. il. D. **$1.35 net. Houghton M.

HURD FAMILY.
See **Genealogies.**

Hurlburt, Rufus Prentiss.
At Cloudy Pass. '08(D12) il. 12°, $1.50. C. M. Clark.

Hurlbut, Edm.
What was nominated on the bond?; the gold standard in the crucible of facts; thou shalt not bear false witness; some oratorical gems of the 45th Congress, secured from library vaults, to inform and inspire the youth of America. '08(D) c. 129 p. tabs., 8°. (Add. pubs. for price.) Baur.

Hurlbut, Jesse Lyman, D.D.
Bible atlas; manual of Biblical geography and history; especially prepared for the use of teachers and students of the Bible, and for Sunday school instruction. '10 (Je4) c. il maps, plans, fold. map, 4°, $2.75. Rand, McN. & Co.
Organizing and building-up the Sunday school. '10(Jl30) c. D. (Modern Sunday school manuals.) 65 c. net. Eaton & M.
Story of our country every child can read. '10(Ag6) c. il. D. (Every child's lib.) 75 c. Winston.
—, ed. Handy Bible encyclopedia; prepared in simple language. '08, [1909.] (Mr) 6+390 p. il. maps, 8°, $1.50; hf. mor., $2; thin pap. ed. de luxe, $3. Winston.
Lives of our presidents. '08(O3) c. pors. D. (Every child's lib.) 75 c. Winston.
Stories about children of all nations. '08 (N14) c. il. D. (Every child's lib.) 75 c. Winston.
Stories of great Americans. '08(O3) c. front. D. (Every child's lib.) 75 c. Winston.
Stories of our naval heroes. '08(N14) c. il. D. (Every child's lib.) 75 c. Winston.
Story of Jesus and the early church. '08 (O3) c. il. D. (Every child's lib.) 75 c. Winston.
Sunday half hours with great preachers: a sermon for every Sunday in the year. '08 (Ja11) pors. 8°, $1.50. Winston.
Superintendent's helper for 1909. '08(N7); for 1910. '09(N13); for 1911. '10(D3) c. nar. T. leath., ea., *25 c. net. Eaton & M.
Teacher-training lessons for the Sunday-school. '08(Ag15) c. il. maps, D. pap., *30 c. net; *50 c. net. Eaton & M.

Hurlbut, W: J.
See Marshall, E:

Hurst, Harold Edn., and Lattey, Rob. Tabor.
Text-bk. of physics. '10(D) 8°, $3. Van Nostrand.

Hurst, J. W.
Life story of a fowl. '08(O24) il. 8°, (Animal autobiographies.) *$2 net. Macmillan.

Hurst, W: Hudson.
Silagrafy; new system of short-hand, invented by William Hudson Hurst; arr. for self-instruction and colleges. '10 (O8) c. 8°, $1.50. Hurst.

Hurt, Wa.
The scarlet shadow. '08(Ja11) D. $1.50. Appeal.

Hurtt, J: Milton.
Addenda to dividend law. '10(N) c. 23 p. O. pap., 50 c. J: H. Lee.
Dividend law and some of its applications: the John Milton Hurtt system. '09(S4) O. $2.50. J: M. Hurtt.

Hurwitz, G:
New teacher of ladies' home tailoring. '10 (Ag20) c. por. fold. chart, f°, $10. G: Hurwitz.

HUS, John.
Lützow, F. H. H. V., *Graf v.* Life and times of Master John Hus. *$4 net. Dutton.

Husband, A. P.
Roosevelt bears visit Llanerch: account of their possible experiences on such a trip. '08, [1909.] (F) c. 11-39 p. pors. 12°. (Add. author for price.) A. P. Husband.

Husband, Marg. Fair Anderson.
Dict. of the characters in the Waverley novels of Sir Wa. Scott. '10(D10) 8°, $3 net. Dutton.

Husband and The forbidden guests. Corbin, J: $1.25 net. Houghton M.

Husband by proxy. Steele, J. $1.50. FitzGerald.

Husband's story. Phillips, D: G. $1.50. Appleton.

HUSBANDS AND WIVES.
See Domestic relations;—Marriage.

Husbands of Edith. McCutcheon, G: B. †$1.25. Dodd.

Huschart, Fk. Michael.
Doing over: tour eastward around the world. '08(Ja11) il. 12°, $1.50. Clarke.

Husselman, Cal.
Southern poultry guide. '09(Mr27) c. il. por. 12°, $1. Southern Planter.

Hussey, Eyre.
Polly Winford. '09(Mr20) D. $1.50. Longmans.

Hutcheson, Ernest.
Elektra; guide to the opera; with musical examples from the score. '10(F12) c. D. *75 c. net. Schirmer.

Hutchings, W. W., and Hueffer, Ford Madox.
London Town past and present; with a chapter on the future of London by Ford Madox Hueffer. '09(O23) 2 v., il. Q. ea., *$3 net. Cassell.

Hutchins, Fk. and Mrs. Cortelle.
Houseboating on a colonial waterway. '10 (Jl9) c. il. D. $2.50, boxed. L. C. Page.

Hutchinson, Alfr. L.
Storm bound. ser. of character sketches and scenes from life. '09(D) c. 3-115 p. front. 12°, $1. Cochrane.

Hutchinson, Arth. Stuart Menteth.
Once aboard the lugger—; the history of George and his Mary. '09(S) c. '08. 327 p. 12°, $1.50. M. Kennerley.

Hutchinson, Cary Talcott.
Rept. upon types of electric meters in use in New York City; submitted Feb. 19, 1909; Public Service Commission for the first district, New York. '09(N) 34 p. 8°, pap., gratis. N. Y. Pub. Service Com.

Hutchinson, Mrs. C: L.
See Hutchinson, Frances Kingsley.

Hutchinson, Frances Kingsley, [Mrs. C: L. Hutchinson.]
Motoring in the Balkans; along the highways of Dalmatia, Montenegro, the Herzegovina and Bosnia. '09(O9) c. il. map, O. *$2.75 net. McClurg.

Hutchinson, F: Winthrop.
Men who found America. '09(N6) c. col. il. Q. $1.50, boxed. Stern.

Hutchinson, J. R.
See Lee, Ja. H:

HUTCHINSON, John.
Hutchinson, *Mrs.* L. Colonel Hutchinson, Roundhead. 75 c. Estes.
Hutchinson, *Mrs.* L. Memoirs of Col. Hutchinson. *35 c. net; *70 c. net. Dutton.

Hutchinson, Sir Jonathan.
Syphilis. New and enl. ed. '10(My) 600 p. il. 8°, $3 net. Funk.

Hutchinson, Mrs. Lucy.
Colonel Hutchinson, Roundhead; ed. by Helen Kendrick Hayes. '09(Ap10) pors. D. 75 c. Estes.
Memoirs of Col. Hutchinson with an introd. by F. P. G. Guizot. '08(S19) 16°, (Everyman's lib.) *35 c. net; leath., *70 c. net. Dutton.

Hutchinson, M. F.
Captain Ferrercourt's widow. '10(O15) D. $1.50. Longmans.
Ways of a girl; or, the story of one year. '10(Je4) D. (Girls' own lib.) 75 c. net. McKay.

Hutchinson, Reno.
See Bosworth, E: Increase.

Hutchinson, Rob., M.D.
Applied physiology. '08(O3) D. *$2 net. Longmans.
Lectures on diseases of children. 2d ed., rev. and enl. '09, [1910.] (F) 12+426 p. il. D. *$2.40 net. Longmans

—, and Collier, Horace Stansfield, eds.
Index of treatment; rev. and ed. to conform with American practice by Warren Coleman, M.D. '08 (Mr14) il. 8°, *$6 net; hf. mor., *$7.50 net. Wood.

—, and Rainy, Harry, M.D.
Clinical methods: guide to the pract. study of medicine. New and rev. ed. '10 (My) 632 p. il. 8°, $2.50 net. Funk.

Hutchinson, W. M. L.
Orpheus with his lute; stories of the world's springtime. '09(N20) il. D. *$1.40 net. Longmans.

Hutchinson, W. N.
Dog breaking; the most expeditious, certain, and easy method, whether great excellence or only mediocrity be required, with odds and ends for those who love the dog and gun. Popular ed. '09(S4) il. O. *$1 net. Scribner.

Hutchinson, Woods, M.D.
Conquest of consumption. '10(Mr19) c. il. D. **$1 net. Houghton M.
Instinct and health. '08(N7) c. D. **$1.20 net. Dodd.
Preventable diseases. '09(D4) c. D. **$1.50 net. Houghton M.

Hutt, H:, il.
Girls; [il. in color] by H: Hutt. '10(O8) c. Q. $3 net, boxed. Scribner.
Henry Hutt picture book: [82 full-page plates of the follies and foibles of American girls.] '08(O17) c. Q. **$3 net, boxed. Century Co.

Hutt, W: H., M.D.
Evolution of the anti-tuberculosis crusade. '08(Ag8) 8°, pap., gratis. W: H. Hutt.

Hutten, Baroness Bettina von.
Araby. '08(Ap11) c. il. 12°, (Popular priced copyrights.) 50 c. B. W. Dodge.
Beechy; or, the lordship of love. '09(O16) c. front. D. †$1.50. Stokes.
Green patch. '10(O22) c. D. $1.50. Stokes.
Kingsmead: a novel. '09(Ap3) c. front. D. †$1.50. Dodd.

HUTTEN, Ulrich von.
Jordan, D: S. Ulrich von Hutten. 60 c. Am. Unitarian.

Huttern, Johann.
Rationelle hydromechanik. [1910.] (N) c. 41 p. il. 4°. Little & I.

Hutton, E:
Country walks about Florence. '08(D12) il. S. $1.50. Scribner.
Giovanni Boccaccio: biographical study. '09(N20) il. O. *$5 net. Lane.
In unknown Tuscany; with notes by W: Heywood. '09(Ag21) il. 8°, *$2.50 net. Dutton.
Rome. '09(N6) col. il. D. *$2 net. Macmillan.
Siena and southern Tuscany. '10(N19) col. il. 12°, $2 net. Macmillan.

Hutton, Frederic Remsen.
Mechanical engineering of steam power plants. 3d ed., rewritten. '08(O3) c. 8°, $5. Wiley.

Hutton, J: Alex.
Authority and person of our Lord. '10 (Ag20) c. 16°, 50 c. net. Revell.

Hutton, W. S.
Pathway to happiness; comprising the philosophy of the sunny side of life. '10 (D10) 12°, 50 c. net. Dutton.

Hutton, W: Holden, D. D.
Age of revolution: being an outline of the church from 1648-1815. '08(Je6) 8°, (Church universal ser.) *$1.50 net. Macmillan.

Huxley, T: H:
Aphorisms and reflections; selected by Henrietta A. Huxley. '08(Ja25) por. 16°, (Golden treasury ser.) $1. Macmillan.

Huxley, T: H:—*Continued.*
Autobiography and selected essays; ed., with introd. and notes, by Ada L. F. Snell. '09(O23) c. D. (Riverside literature ser.) 40 c. Houghton M.
Lectures and lay sermons; (contains in full Huxley's 8 remarkable illustrated lectures on the Vertebrate skull;) with introd. by Sir Oliver Lodge. '10(D10) c. 16°, (Everyman's lib.) 35 c. net; leath., 70 c. net. Dutton.
Selected essays and addresses; ed., with notes and introd., by Philo Melvyn Buck, jr. '10(Je4) T. (Macmillan's Am. and Eng. pocket classics.) 25 c. net. Macmillan.

Hverdagsfolk. Ager, W. T. 25 c. Fremad.

Hyaku-nin-isshiu. *See* Fujiwara, Sadaiye, *comp.*

Hyamson, Albert M.
Dictionary of artists and art terms. '08 (D19) 32°, (Miniature reference lib.) 50 c. Dutton.
Newspaper reader's companion. '08(D19) 32°, (Miniature reference lib.) leath., 50 c. Dutton.

Hyans, E: M.
Theory of accounts for accountant students. '09, [1910.] (Ja) c. 11-208 p. forms, tab., 8°, $5. Universal Business.

Hyatt, A. H., ed.
Winds of heaven: an anthology. '08(N21) 16°, (Wayfaring books.) *$1 net. Dutton.

Hyatt, E:
School architecture and school improvement, from the 23d biennial rept.; prep. at the request of the Tahoe convention of superintendents. '09, [1910.] (F) 151 p. il. O. pap. Cal. Dept. of Pub. Inst.
—, comp. Conservation of natural resources; from the 23d biennial rept. of the Superintendent of Public Instruction. '10(F19) il. O. pap. Cal. Dept. of Pub. Inst.

Hyatt, Nathaniel Irving.
Twenty Father Goose melodies. Ditson ed. '10(N) 13 p. 4°, pap., 75 c. Ditson.

Hyatt, Stanley Portal.
Biffel: a trek ox. '10(D24) il. 12°, $1.50 net. Dodge.
End of the road. '09(Ag21) c. D. †$1.50. Appleton.
Little brown brother. '08(S12) c. D. †$1.50. Holt.
People of position. '10(O1) c. front. D. $1.20 net. Wessels & B.

Hyde, Aurelia.
A primer. '08(S19) c. il. D. 25 c. Am. Bk.

Hyde, E: Selden.
Progress from experience. '10(Je4) c. 12°, $1.25. Cochrane.

Hyde, Rev. Ja.
Bibliography of the works of Emanuel Swedenborg, original and translated. '09 (Ag7) 8°, $10. New Church.

Hyde, Ja. Nevins, M.D.
Practical treatise on diseases of the skin. for the use of students and practitioners. 8th and rev. ed. '09(N) c. 27+17-1126 p. il. 8°, *$5 net; leath., *$6 net. Lea.

Hyde, J: Dalison.
Feet of the years. '10(D) 298 p. D. $1.25 net. Metropolitan Press, (N. Y.)

Hyde, W: De Witt, D.D.
Abba Father; or, the religion of everyday life: [prayers for every day.] '08(O24) c. 12°, bds., *50 c. net. Revell.
Self-measurement: scale of human values with directions for personal application. '08(D26) c. D. (Art of life ser.) *50 c. net. B: W. Huebsch.
Sin and its forgiveness. '09(N13) c. S. (Modern religious problems.) 50 c. Houghton M.
The teacher's philosophy in and out of school. '10(Ag20) c. D. (Riverside educational monographs.) 35 c. Houghton M.

Hyde, W: H:
Telephone troubles and how to find them on both the magneto and central energy (common battery) system and manual of construction, cost units for estimate work. 14th ed. '10(Jl) c. 56 p. il. tabs., 16°, 25 c. W: H: Hyde.

Hyde-Vogl, Mrs. Virginie Douglass.
Echoes and prophecies. '09(N) 12°, $1. Ariel.

HYDE PARK, London.
Tweedie, *Mrs.* E. B. H. Hyde Park. *$7.50 net. Pott.

HYDER FAMILY.
See Genealogies: Beam, E.

Hydraulic elevators. Baxter, W:, *jr.* $2.50 net. McGraw-H.

HYDRAULIC ENGINEERING.
Ball, R. S. Natural sources of power. *$2 net. Van Nostrand.
Barr, W: M. Pumping machinery. $5. Lippincott.
Bligh, W: G: Pract. design of irrigation. *$6 net. Van Nostrand.
Chatley, H. How to use water power. *$1 net. Van Nostrand.
Dunkerley, S. Hydraulics. In 2 v. v. 2. $3. Longmans.
Garrett, A. H. Hydraulic tables and diagrams for practical engineers. $5. Longmans.
Gibson, A. H. Hydraulics and its application. *$5 net.—Water hammer in hydraulic pipe lines. *$2 net. Van Nostrand.
Greene, F. V. Niagara Falls in 1907. (Add. pubs. for price.) Ontario Press.
Groat, B: F. New methods in backwater computations. 25 c. (o. p.) Univ. of Minn.
Harza, L. F. Investigation of the hydraulic ram. 25 c. Univ. of Wis.
Hiscox, G. D. Hydraulic engineering. $4. Henley.
Jerrett, H. D. Hydraulic tables and memoranda. $1.50. Hicks-J.
Koester, F. Hydroelectric developments and engineering. *$5 net. Van Nostrand.
Lea, F: C: Hydraulics for engineers and engineering students. *$4.25 net. Longmans.
Lyndon, L. Development and electrical distribution of water power. **$3 net. Wiley.

HYDRAULIC ENGINEERING.—*Continued.*
Mead, D. W. Relations of experimental results to the theory of the tangential water wheel. 40 c. Univ. of Wis.
Mead, D. W. Water power engineering. *$6 net. McGraw.
Molitor, D: A. Hydraulics of rivers, weirs and sluices. **$2 net. Wiley.
Player, P. Notes on hydro-electric developments. *$1 net. McGraw.
Porter, D. Notes on hydraulic measurements, for use of students in Mass. Inst. of Technology. $1.50. D. Porter.
Russell, G: E. Text-book on hydraulics. $2.50. Holt.
Schmeer, L: Flow of water. **$3 net. Van Nostrand.
Schon, H. A. E. C. v. Hydro-electric practice. **$6 net. Lippincott.
Stewart, C. B. Investigation of flow through large submerged orifices and tubes. pt. 1. 25 c. Univ. of Wis.
Turneaure, F: E., *and* Black, A. Hydraulic engineering. $1. Am. Sch. Corr.
United States. *Dept. of the Interior. Geological Survey.* Public utility of water powers and their governmental regulation.
Williams, G. S., *and* Hazen, A. Hydraulic tables. $1.50. Wiley.
See also Dams;—Drainage; — Engineering; — Hydromechanics;—Irrigation;—Mines and mining; — Pumps; — Reservoirs; — Turbines;—Water-supply.

HYDRO-ELECTRIC ENGINEERING.
See Hydraulic engineering.

Hydro-electric practice. Schon, H. A. E. C. v. **$6 net. Lippincott.

HYDROGEN.
Kemble, W: F., *and* Underhill, C: R. Periodic law and the hydrogen spectrum. 50 c. Van Nostrand.

HYDROGRAPHIC SURVEYING.
See Nautical surveying.

HYDROGRAPHY.
Bjerknes, V. F. K., *and others.* Dynamic meteorology and hydrography. Carnegie.
Heck, N. H. Description of long wire drag. '10(Jl) 21 p. il. f°. Gov. Pr. Off.
McEwen, G: F. Preliminary rept. on the hydrographic work carried on by the Marine Biological Station of San Diego. 15 c. Univ. of Cal.

HYDROMECHANICS.
Huttern, J. Rationelle hydromechanik. Little & I.

HYDROPATHY.
See Water cure.

HYDROPHOBIA.
See Rabies.

HYDROSTATICS.
Jessop, C: M., *and* Caunt, G: W: Elements of hydrostatics. 60 c. net. Macmillan.

HYDROTHERAPY.
See Water cure.

HYGIENE.
Achorn, J: W. Nature's help to happiness. **50 c. net. Moffat.
Allen, W: H. Broader motive for school hygiene. (Priv. pr.) W: H. Allen.
Allen, W: H. Civics and health. $1.25. Ginn.

HYGIENE.—*Continued.*

Balch, L. Manual for boards of health and health officers; also the public health law. *$1.50 net. Banks & Co.

Ballou, G: D. Seven essentials to life and health. $1.50 net. G: D. Ballou.

Barry, W. F. Hygiene of the schoolroom. $1.50. Silver.

Barwick, A. J. Manual of physiology and hygiene in primary grades. gratis. N. C. Dept. Pub. Instruct.

Bergey, D: H. Principles of hygiene. $3. Saunders.

Bishop, *Mrs.* E. M. Daily ways to health. $1.50 net. B: W. Huebsch.

Blaisdell, A. F. How to keep well; text-book of physiology and hygiene. 45 c. Ginn.

Boeckmann, P. v. Physique; treatise on deep breathing, [etc.] $1. P. v. Boeckmann.

Brewer, I: W. Personal hygiene in tropical and semi-tropical countries. *$1 net. Davis.

Brewer, I: W. Rural hygiene. **$1.25 net. Lippincott..

Brooklyn. Public Library. Personal hygiene and physical development. gratis. Brooklyn Lib.

Bryce, A. Laws of health. $2 net. Lippincott.

Clarke, J: H. Vital economy. 50 c.; 30 c. Wessels.

Conn, H. W: Elementary physiology and hygiene. *60 c. net. Silver.

Conn, H. W:, *and* Budington, R. A. Advanced physiology and hygiene. $1.10. Silver.

Currier, C: G. Outlines of pract. hygiene. $2 net. Treat.

Davison, A. Dust as a carrier of disease in the schoolroom. 10 c. A. Davison.

Davison, A. Health lessons. 2 bks. bk. 1, 35 c.; bk. 2, 60 c.—Human body and health. 40 c.; 50 c. Am. Bk.

Dock, L. L. Hygiene and morality. $1.25. Putnam.

Dunglison, R: J. New school physiology and hygiene. *$1 net. Am. Bk.

Eadie, R. *and* A. Physiology and hygiene for young people. 65 c. Scribner.

Edgerly, W. Book of glame: complete course in life electricity; the source of vitality. $4. Ralston Univ.

Egbert, S. Manual of hygiene and sanitation. $2.25 net. Lea.

Elliott, S. M. Household hygiene. $1.25. Am. Sch. Home Economics

Fallows. A. K. Talk on relaxation. *35 c. net. McClurg.

Fisher, H. W. Making life worth while. $1.20 net. Doubleday, P.

Fisher, I. Bulletin of the Committee of One Hundred on national health.—National vitality, its wastes and conservation. U. S., Supt. of Docs.

Fitz, G: W. Principles of physiology and hygiene. $1.12. Holt.

Flemming, L: A. Receipts and remedies. 50 c. Penn Pub. Co.

HYGIENE.—*Continued.*

Foringer, W. S. How to breathe and how to be well. $1. B'way Pub.

Garber, A. L. Bibleopathy, a system of diet, healing and living based on the Bible and nature. $1. Restitution.

Gatewood, J. D. Naval hygiene. $6. Blakiston.

Godfrey, H. Health of the city. $1.25 net. Houghton M.

Hastings, W: W. Physical director as a hygienist. 10 c. Bassette.

Health culture; how to live, what to eat, to wear, to do, in health, in sickness. $1. Polk.

Hoag, E. B. Health studies. 75 c. Heath.

Home-study in vital science. 12 v. ea., $1; per set, $10. Psychic World.

Hutchinson, W. Instinct and health. **$1.20 net. Dodd.

Jewett, *Mrs.* F. G. Body and its defenses. 65 c. Ginn.

Kealing, H. T. How to live longer. 35 c.; 45 c. H. T. Kealing.

Kirkham, S. D. Philosophy of self-help. **$1.25 net. Putnam.

Knight, A. P. Hygiene for young people. 60 c. C: E. Merrill.

Kober, G: M. Industrial and personal hygiene. 50 c. President's Home Com.

Krohn, W: O. Graded lessons in hygiene. *60 c. net. Appleton.

Larson, C. D. How to stay young. $1. Eternal Progress.

Latson, W. R. C. Attainment of efficiency. $1. Health-Culture.

Law, H. Viavi hygiene. $1. Viavi.

Lindley, E. M. Health in the home. $1. Health-Culture.

Long, J: I. T. Lines from a doctor to his son. $1. J: I. T. Long.

Lorand, A. Old age deferred. $2.50. Davis.

MacCarthy, F. H. Hygiene for mother and child. $1.25 net. Harper.

MacFie, R. Air and health. *$2.50 net. Dutton.

McIntyre, *Mrs.* L. L. How's your health? $1.25. L. L. McIntyre.

McIsaac, I. Hygiene for nurses. *$1.25 net. Macmillan.

McIsaac, I., *comp.* Elements of hygeine for schools. **60 c. net. Macmillan.

Martin, G: H. School hygiene in Massachusetts. gratis. G: H: Martin.

Mayberry, J. W. Physiology and hygiene. 60 c. Southern Pub. (Tex.)

Metchnikoff, E. Prolongation of life. *$2.50 net. Putnam.

Millard, C. N. Building and care of the body. 40 c. net. Macmillan.

Mills, J. P. Health. $2. Brentano's.

Mixter, M. Health and beauty hints. $1. Cupples & L.

Moras, E. R. Autology (study thyself) and autopathy (cure thyself). $12. E. R. Moras.

Müller, J. P. Fresh-air book. *85 c. net. Stokes.

HYGIENE.—*Continued.*

National public health; papers, opinions, letters, etc., relative to the national public health, in the consideration of Senate bill (S. 6049) "A bill establishing a Department of Public Health, and for other purposes." '10(O) 240 p. diagrs. 8°. Gov. Pr. Off.

New York State. Bender's health officer's manual and public health law. $2. M. Bender.

New York State. Public health law. $2.50. Banks & Co.

Notter, J. L. Theory and practice of hygiene. *$7 net. Blakiston.

Parkes, L: C., *and* Kenwood, H: R: Hygiene and the public health. *$3 net. Blakiston.

Patch, F. W. Individual responsibility. **50 c. net. Moffat.

Patterson, C: B. New way to health. 25 c. Roger Bros.

Patterson, J: A. The breaking dawn; or, how long we live in the body. $1. Chronicle Pub.

Peabody, S. W. Historical study of legislation regarding public health in the states of New York and Massachusetts. $1. Journal of Infectious Diseases.

Pennsylvania. Rules and regulations of the Department of Health. (Add. pubs. for price.) Penn. Dept. of Health.

Porter, C: Sanitary law, in question and answer, for the use of students of public health. 90 c. net. Longmans.

Powell, T: Fundamentals and requirements of health and disease. $5. Powell Pub.

Price, G: M. Epitome of hygiene and public health. $1 net. Lea.

Prudden, T. M. Dust and its dangers. 75 c. Putnam.

Pyle, W. L., *and others.* Manual of personal hygiene. $1.50 net. Saunders.

Ralston Health Club. Personal book of the Ralston Health Club. $1.25. Ralston Univ.

Ralston Health Club. Universal system of the Ralston Health Club. $2.50. Ralston Health.

Ravenbyrne, E. M. Good health. 30 c.—Good health and good manners. 25 c. Ainsworth.

Richards, *Mrs.* E. H. C. Cost of cleanness. $1. Wiley.

Ritchie, J: W. Primer of sanitation. 60 c.—Sanitation and physiology. $1.20. World Bk.

Ritchie, J: W., *and* Caldwell, J. S. Primer of hygiene. 40 c. World Bk.

Ritchie, J: W., *and* Purcell, M. A. Primer of sanitation for the tropics. 60 c. World Bk.

Robertson, G. Money value of good health. 10 c. G. Robertson.

Rogers, J. F. Life and health. $1 net. Lippincott.

Rohe, G: H:, *and* Robin, A. Text-book of hygiene. *$3.50 net. Davis.

Rossiter, F: M. Pract. guide to health. $3; $5. Review and Herald Pub.

HYGIENE.—*Continued.*

Sadler, W: S: Science of living. $1.50 net. McClurg.

Saleeby, C. W. Health, strength and happiness. *$1.50 net. Kennerly.

Salud y hogar. $3. Pacific Press.

Schofield, A. T. Fit for work; or, health in Christian service. *$1.25 net. Armstrong.

Schofield, A. T. How to keep fit. 75 c. Moffat.

Shoemaker, J: V. Health and beauty. *$3 net. Davis.

Simon, S. J. Physical perfection. $3; $5. MacGerald.

Simpson, W: J: R. Principles of hygiene as applied to tropical and sub-tropical climates. *$5 net. Wood.

Sinclair, U. B., *jr., and* Williams, M. Good health and how we won it. **$1.20 net. Stokes.

Smith, A. W., *comp.* Selected bibliography of sanitary science. *50 c. net. Stechert.

Smith, F: W. Essentials of practical hygiene. $2. G: K. Smith.

Solis-Cohen, M. Family health. **$1 net. Penn Pub. Co.

Terry, T. B. How to keep well and live long. $1. Farmer Co.

Tuttle, T: D. Principles of public health. 50 c. World Bk.

Tyrell, C: A. Royal road to health. (Not for sale.) Tyrell's Hygienic Inst.

United States Public Health and Marine Hospital Service. Publications. Gov. Pr. Off.

Warman, E: B. Health influenced by Underwear. 10 c. Am. Sports.

Watkins, L. B. Natural life in the human world. 10 c. L. B. Watkins.

Whipple, G. M. Questions in school hygiene. 60 c. Bardeen.

Whitelegge, B: A., *and* Newman, G: Hygiene and public health. $1.75 net. Funk.

Wyman, W. Present organization and work for the protection of health in the United States. Gov. Pr. Off.

See also Anatomy; — Bacteria; — Beauty; — Boys;—Children; — Contagion; — Education: —Fasting; — Food; — Girls; — Gymnastics and physical culture; — Hair; — Hypnotism; —Jiu-jitsu;—Labor and laboring classes;—Longevity; —Meat;—Medicine;—Mental science;—Military hygiene; — Milk; — Mind and body; — New thought;—Nurses and nursing;—Outdoor life; —Pathology;—Physiology;—Plumbing; — Quarantine;—Rat;—Sanitary engineering;—Schools; —Sex;—Temperance;—Tropical diseases;—Veterinary medicine and surgery; — Water; — Woman;—Worry.

Hygiene and physical education ser. O. and S. pap. Bassette.

—Burnham. One session a day or two in the public schools? 10 c.

—Hastings. Physical director as a hygienist. 10 c.

—Newhall. English ball drill. 10 c.

—Nissen. Fifteen lessons on the stall bars. —Twenty gymnastic lessons on the boom. ea., 30 c.

Hygiene lib. 8°, *$2.50 net. Dutton.

—MacFie. Air and health.

Hygiene of the nose. Burnham, W: H: W: H: Burnham.

Hygiene of the soul. Pollak, G. $1.20 net. Dodd.

Hylacomylus.
See Waldseemüller, Martin.

Hylas. Dargan, E. P. **Badger.**

Hyllus. Dunning, R. C. $1.25 net. Lane.

Hymenaeus. Moore Smith, G: C. *$1.10 net. Putnam.

HYMNS AND HYMN WRITERS.
Alexander, C: M., *comp.* Gospel songs. *15 c. net; *30 c. net. Revell.
Bernard *of Cluny.* Source of "Jerusalem the golden"; together with other pieces. $1.25 net. Univ. of Chic.
Bible readings and hymns for school use. 50 c. Wahr.
Bilhorn, P: P., *and others, eds.* Hymns of His grace. 30 c.; per 100, $25. Bilhorn.
Brainerd, E. W., *comp.* Great hymns of the Middle Ages. $1. Century Co.
Campbell, E. F. R. The hymn "Jesus of Nazareth passeth by," its history, and other verses. $1.25. M. E. Munson.
Christ in song. $1. Review and Herald Pub.
Christian science hymnal. $1.15; $3.50. Chr. Sci. Pub.
Coffin, H: S., *and* Vernon, A. W., *eds.* Hymns of the kingdom of God. $1.50 net. Barnes.
Cullen, J:, *comp.* Hundred best hymns in the English language. 50 c.; 75 c. Dutton.
Dann, H. School hymnal. 50 c. Am. Bk.
Dann, H., *comp. and ed.* Christmas carols and hymns for school and choir. 45 c. Am. Bk.
Donahue, D. J., *ed.* Early Christian hymns. *$2 net. Grafton Press.
Duncan, J. Popular hymns. $2 net. Whittaker.
Forward movement hymnal. **15 c. net. Am. Bapt.
Friends, Society of. Friends' hymnal. (Add. pubs. for price.) Funk.
Gabriel, C: H., *ed.* The victory: Sunday school songs. 20 c. Jennings.
German Evangelical Synod of North America. Gesangbuch. 50 c.-$2; 90 c.-$3.50; $1.25-$2.50. Eden Pub.
Hahn, B. F. Collection of easy hymns. 35 c. St. Boniface's.
Ives, C: T., *and* Woodman, R. H., *eds.* Hymns of the living church. $1.50. Century Co.
Julian, J:, *ed.* Dictionary of hymnology. *$7 net. Scribner.
Lowry, S. C. Hymns and spiritual songs. $1 net. Longmans.
Noble, G. C., *ed.* Most popular hymns. 50 c. Hinds.
Oxford hymn book. 30 c.; 50 c.; with music, $1.15. Oxford Univ.
Patton, J:, *and* Rosecrans, J. H. Gospel hymns. 35 c.; per doz., $4; per 25, $8. Showalter-P.
Pick, B., *comp.* Hymns and poetry of the Eastern church. *$1 net. Eaton & M.
Reformed Episcopal Church. Book of common praise. 90 c. Armstrong-K.

HYMNS AND HYMN WRITERS.
Sacred songs. $1. Ditson.
Seipt, A. A. Schwenkfelder hymnology. $2. Americana Germanica.
Smith, S: F. My country; illustrated and illuminated version. *$3 net. Tandy-T.
Sprunger, J: A., *and* Dyck, H. J. Himmels-harfe für sonntag-schulen. 35 c. Light and Hope.
Sutherland, A. Famous hymns of the world, [their origin and romance.] 6 v. ea., 50 c.; 75 c. Stokes.
Tileston, *Mrs.* M. W. F., *comp.* Stronghold of hope; hymns of comfort. $1 net. Little, B. & Co.
Towner, D. B., *ed.* Ideal song and hymn book. 35 c. net; 30 c. net; 15 c. net. Revell.
Warren, H: W., *comp.* Fifty-two memory hymns. *50 c. net. Jennings.
Watts, I: Divine and moral songs for children. $1. L. C. Page.
Zelie, J: S. "Lead kindly light." 75 c. Dodd.
See also Church music;—Sunday-school.

Hymns of nature. Gates, M. C. B. *$1.25 net. Revell.

Hymns of worship and service. 20th ed.; [with this is bound Selections from the Scriptures; ed. by C. C. Albertson.] '09 (D11) c. 8°, $1.50. Century Co.

Hyne, C: J: Cutcliffe Wright.
Sandy Carmichael. '08(N7) il. O. †$2. Lippincott.

Hyperbolic functions. *See* Trigonometry.

HYPEREMIA.
See Blood.

HYPNOTISM.
Bramwell, J: M. Hypnotism and treatment by suggestion. $1.75 net. Funk.
Forel, A. H. Hypnotism; or, suggestion and psychotherapy. $2.50. Rebman.
Hollander, B. Hypnotism and suggestion in daily life, education and medical practice. $1.75. Putnam.
Lathrop, L. C. Use and abuse of hypnotism. 50 c. L. C. Lathrop.
Moll, A. Hypnotism. $1.50. Scribner.
Page, H. L. Dual mind. $1. Green Leaf.
Podmore, F. Mesmerism and Christian Science. *$1.50 net. Jacobs.
Quackenbos, J: D. Hypnotic therapeutics in theory and practice. **$2 net. Harper.
Savage, G: H: Harveian oration on experimental psychology and hypnotism. 40 c. Oxford Univ.
Wingfield, H. E. Introd. to the study of hypnotism; experimental and therapeutic. $2 net. Wood.
See also Ghosts;—Mind and body;—Personality;—Psychical research;—Suggestion (*Mental*).

Hypocrites (The). Jones, H: A. 75 c.; 50 c. S: French.

Hypsometry: precise leveling in the United States. Hayford, J: F. 45 c. U. S., Supt. of Docs.

Hyrst, H. W. G., pseud.
See Wright, Sidney Harry.

Hyslop, Ja. Hervey.
Psychical research and the resurrection. '08 (Je20) c. D. **$1.50 net. Small.

HYSTERIA.
Freud, S. Selected papers on hysteria; and other psychoneuroses. $2. Journal Nervous Diseases.
Saville, T: D. Lectures on hysteria and allied vaso-motor conditions. *$2.50 net. Wood.
I am. Hedges, F. E. B. $1.50. Roxburgh.
"I am reminded." Allen, G: H. 5 c. G: H. Allen.
I and my true love. Keays, *Mrs.* H. A. M. C. †$1.50. Small.
I choose. Whitney, *Mrs.* G. C. $1 net. Sherman, F.
I have a little money. Davis, W: E., *jr.* $1. W: E. Davis.
I married a soldier. Lane, *Mrs.* L. S. $1 net. Lippincott.
"I rule the house." Cooke, E. V. $1 net. Dodge.
Iambica. Jackson, J. *$1.50 net. Macmillan.
Ibañez, Vincent Blasco.
See Blasco Ibáñez, Vincente.
Ibbetson, A.
Tea from grower to consumer. '10(Mr26) il. maps, D. (Pitman's common commodities of commerce.) 75 c. Pitman.
Ibbettson, W. S.
Pract. electrical engineering for elem. students in trade and technical schools. '10 (D31) 12°, $1.50. Spon.
Theory and practice of electric wiring. '09 (Je19) il. 12°, $2. Spon.
Ibershoff, Adolph.
See Bárány, Robert.
IBERVILLE, Pierre Le Moyne, *Sieur* d'.
Reed, C: B. The first great Canadian. $2 net. McClurg.
Iblis in Paradise. Roe, G: $1.25. Altemus.
Ibsen, Henrik.
Collected works; [rev. and ed., with introds., by W: Archer.] Copyright ed. In 11 v. v. 1, Lady Inger of Östråt; The feast at Solhoug; Love's comedy. '08 (F1) c. D. $1. Scribner.
Brand, et dramatisk digt.; ed., with introd. and notes, by Julius Emil Olson. '08 (Ag22) c. pors. 12°, $1.50. J: Anderson.
Doll's house, The wild duck, and The lady from the sea; with introd. by R. Farquharson Sharp. '10(D10) 16°, (Everyman's lib.) 35 c. net; leath., 70 c. net. Dutton.
Doll's house; with notes and introd. by M: L. Mencken. '08(D5) 16°, (Player's Ibsen.) *75 c. net. J: W. Luce.
John Gabriel Borkman: play; tr. by W: Archer. '09(D) 16°, $1. Duffield.
Letters; tr. by J: Nilsen Laurvik and Mary Morison. '09(D) por. 8°, *$2.50 net. Duffield.
Little Eyolf: play; tr. by W: Archer. '09 (D) 16°, $1. Duffield.
Little Eyolf; with notes and introd. by H: L. Mencken. '08(D5) 16°, (Players' Ibsen.) *75 c. net. J: W. Luce.
On the heights (Paa vidderne): tragedy in lyrical ballads; English version in the form of the original by W: Norman Guthrie. '10(F19) c. 12°, 25 c. (250 copies.) Univ. Extension Dept.
Speeches and new letters; tr. by Arne Kildal; with introd. by Dr. Lee M. Hollander, and bibliographical appendix. '10 (Ja15) c. por. O. *$3 net. (500 copies.) Badger.
When we dead awaken: play; tr. by W: Archer. '09(D) 16°, $1. Duffield.
IBSEN, Henrik.
Gosse, E. W: Henrik Ibsen. **$1 net. Scribner.
Moses, M. J. Henrik Ibsen: the man and his plays. *$1.50 net. M. Kennerley.
Shaw, G: B. Quintessence of Ibsenism. $1. Brentano's.
ICE.
See Antarctic regions;—Arctic regions;—Glaciers;—Refrigeration;—Water.
Ice-bound heights of the Mustagh. Workman, F. B. *$5 net. Scribner.
ICE CREAM.
Gratz, H. Making of ice cream. $5. H. Gratz.
Metzgar, C: M: Home-made ice cream and candy. $1; 50 c. Metzgar.
Miller, V. Standard recipes for ice cream makers. $1; $1.50. Laird.
See also Cookery.
ICE HOCKEY.
See Hockey.
ICE SKATING.
See Skating.
ICELAND.
Islandica: annual relating to Iceland and Fiske Icelandic collection in Cornell University library. v. 1-3. ea., $1 net. Cornell Univ.
Leith, *Mrs.* D. Iceland. *75 c. net. Macmillan.
Zoëga, G. T. Concise dict. of old Icelandic. $3.40. Oxford Univ.
See also Fine arts.
ICHTHYOLOGY.
See Fish and fishing.
ICHTHYOSAURIA.
Merriam, J: C. Triassic *ichthyosauria:* [extinct reptiles.] $3. Univ. of Cal.
See also Geology.
Iconographia parasitorum hominis. Ward, H: B. 50 c. Univ. of Neb.
Idaho. Revised codes. v. 1, Political and civil; prepared by J: F. MacLane. '08 (Ag) c. O. pap. (Add. pub. for price.) Syms-York.
Idaho. *Supreme ct.* Digest of decisions, v. 1-13; (Ja. F. Ailshie and Edn. Snow.) '08(O) c. O. shp., $8. Bancroft-W.
Idaho. *Supreme ct.* Repts.; (I. W. Hart.) v. 13. '08(My); v. 14 (N); v. 15. '09 (Jl); v. 16. '10(Ap) c. 8°, shp., ea., $4.25. Bancroft-W.
IDAHO.
Goulder, W: A. Reminiscences; incidents in the life of a pioneer in Oregon and Idaho. $3. T. Regan.
Hailey, J: Hist. of Idaho. $3. Syms-York.
Jellum, S. P. Some central Idaho gold districts. 50 c. Northwest Mining.
Stephenson, J., *jr.* Irrigation in Idaho. U. S., Supt. of Docs.
See also Indians;—Irrigation;—West.

Iddings, Jos. Paxson.
Igneous rocks. v. 1, Their chemical and mineral composition. '09(Je26) c. il. figs. 8°, $5. Wiley.

Idea of creation: its origin and value. Caldwell, W: 50 c. W: Caldwell.

Idea of public office. Hughes, C: E. 10 c. Civic Forum.

Idea of resurrection in the ante-Nicene period. Staudt, C. K. *50 c. net. Univ. of Chic.

Idea of the soul. Crawley, A. E. *$2.25 net. Macmillan.

Ideal Christian life. Norton, W: H. $1. W: H. Norton.

Ideal (The) collection of the world's great art; board of eds.: J: La Farge, W: Rankin, Sir Martin Conway; advisory council: Lorado Taft, Halsey C. Ives, W: M. Chase; member from England: Frank Brangwyn. [In 12 parts lettered A-L, in portfolio.] [1910.] c. 63 l. 60 pl. 8°, subs. (Add. pubs. for price.) Doubleday, P.

Ideal commonwealths: comprising More's Utopia; Bacon's New Atlantis; Campanella's City of the sun; and Harrington's Oceana; with introds. by H: Morley. '08 (Je27) c. 8°, $1.75; hf. mor., $3.50. Lamb Pub.

Ideal family. Hatch, W. M. $1. W. M. Hatch.

Ideal garden. Thomas, H. H. $2 net. Cassell.

Ideal metrology. Wood, H. G. $1.50. H. G. Wood.

Ideal ministry. Johnson, H. *$1.75 net. Revell.

Ideal of a gentleman. Palmer, A. S. *$1.50 net. Dutton.

Ideal of Christian worship. Delany, S. P. *50 c. net. Young Churchman.

Ideal ser. of classics. See Winston's ideal classics.

Ideal song and hymn book. Towner, D. B., *ed.* 35 c. net; 30 c. net; 15 c. net. Revell.

Ideal teacher. Palmer, G: H. 35 c. Houghton M.

Ideal tour. '10(Ag) c. 92 p. il. 8°, gratis. Pierce.

IDEALISM.

Ball, J. W. Absolute idealism and immortality. (Add. pubs. for price.) Woodruff-C.

Barrett, H. D. Pantheistic idealism. $1. H. D. Barrett.

Brierley, J. Life and the ideal. $1.25 net. Houghton M.

Buchanan, U. Ideals and conduct. $1. Cochrane.

Eucken, R. C. Christianity and the new idealism. *75 c. net. Harper.

Horne, H. H. Idealism in education. $1.25 net. Macmillan.

Jones, H: Idealism as a practical creed. *$2 net. Macmillan.

Upward, A. New word; an open letter on the meaning of the word idealist. $1.50. M. Kennerley.

See also Medicine.

Ideals and principles of church reforms. Barry, J. C. $1.25 net. Scribner.

Ideals for every day living. Porter, D. L. 75 c. net. Pilgrim Press.

Ideals of charity. Crawford, V. M. *75 c. net. Herder.

Ideals of democracy. Dye, J: T. **90c. net. Bobbs-M.

Ideals of the East. Okakura, K. *$1.50 net. Dutton.

Ideals of the republic. Schouler, J. **$1.50 net. Little, B. & Co.

IDEAS.

See Psychology.

Ideas of a plain country woman. Strauss, J. U. **$1 net. Doubleday, P.

Ideas on education. Armstrong, S: C. (Add. pubs. for price.) Hampton Inst.

Identification of the manuscripts of Catullus. Ullman, B. L: 75 c. B. L: Ullman.

IDIOCY.

Seguin, E: Idiocy; and its treatment by the physiological method. $2. Teachers' Coll.

Idiomatic ear training. Jewett, A. D. $1. A. D. Jewett.

Idle hours of a busy lawyer. Peadro, R. M. $1. Shelley Co. Leader.

Idle moments. Templeton, F. 35 c. F. Templeton.

Idle songs of an idle soldier. Moreland, G: M. 50 c. G: M. Moreland.

Idlehurst. Halsham, J: *$1.50 net. Dutton.

Idolatry. Perrin, A. R. †$1.50. Duffield.

Idols. Locke, W: J: 75 c. Burt.

Idols of education. Gayley, C: M. **50 c. net. Doubleday, P.

Idyll envelope ser. See Revell's.

Idyll of All fool's day. Bacon, *Mrs.* J. D. D. †$1.25. Dodd.

Idylls of Greece. *See* Sutherland, H. V.

Idylls of the beautiful. Thomas, J. M. $1. J. M. Thomas.

Idylls of the king. *See* Tennyson, Alf., *Lord.* —*also* Spence, W.

Idyls of Lakeside, by the O'Byrnes, [children of Christopher O'Byrne of Friendsville;] with preface by Rev. P: C. Winters. [1910.] (F) c. '09. 17+167 p. il. 8°, $1. Servants Immaculate Heart.

If David knew. Mathews, F. A. $1.50. G: W: Dillingham.

"If I had known" about Gary in 1909. Moore, W. H. $1. P. E. Moore.

If I should meet the Master. Smart, G: T: 50 c. net. Pilgrim Press.

If I were a boy. Keeler, L. E. *$1 net. Revell.

Ifs of history. Chamberlin, J. E. $1. Altemus.

Igneous rocks. v. 1. Iddings, J. P. $5. Wiley.

Ignition, timing and valve setting. Russell, T: H. $1; $1.50. C: C. Thompson.

IGOROT LANGUAGE.

See Philippine Islands.

Il trionfo. Bracco, R. (Add. pub. for price.) V. Ciocia.

Ilbert, Sir Courtenay Peregrine.
Government of India; being a digest of the statute law rel. thereto; with historical introd. and explanatory matter; with a supp. chapter on the Indian Councils Act of 1900. 2d ed. '10(D17) 8°, $3.75 net; supp. chapter separately, pap., 35 c. net. Oxford Univ.

Iles, Mrs. Frances Rawlins.
Poems. '08(D19) c. D. $1.25 Badger.

Iles, G:
Electricity uncovers a law of evolution. '09 (Jl31) O. pap., gratis. G: Iles.

—, **ed.** Little masterpieces of autobiography. In 6 v. v. 1, Greatest Americans; v. 2, Soldiers and explorers; v. 3, Men of science; v. 4, Writers; v. 5, Artists and composers; v. 6, Actors. '08(N14) pors. S. ea., **75 c. net; per set, **$4.50 net. Doubleday, P.

Iliad (The). *See* Homer.

Iliad of the East. Macdonald, *Mrs.* F: R., *comp.* *$1.50 net. Lane.

Iliowizi, H:
Revelation: worlds mystic and realistic. '10 (D10) 12°, $2 net. Dutton.

Illegal trial of Christ. *See* Bacon, A. S:

Illingworth, A. L., ed.
See Frere, Wa. Howard.

Illinois. *Appellate cts.* Repts. v. 129; (W. Clyde Jones and Keene H. Addington.) '08(Ja25); v. 130; with a directory of the judiciary. '08(F); v. 131. '08(Mr); v. 132. '08(My) c. O. shp., ea., $3.75; v. 133, 134 (Jl); v. 135 (Ag); v. 136, 137 (S); v. 138 (O); v. 139, 140 (N); v. 141. '09 (Mr); v. 142 (Je); v. 143 (S); v. 144 (O); v. 145 (D); v. 146. '10(Ja); v. 147 (My); v. 148 (Jl); v. 149 (S) ea., $3.50. Callaghan.

Illinois. Compilation of the laws rel. to township organization and management of county affairs, [etc.;] by Elijah Middlebrook Haines. 26th ed., rev. '10(Ap) c. O. shp., $4. Legal Adv.

Illinois. *Courts.* Repts. of cases decided in the circuit, superior, criminal, probate, county and municipal cts., and incl. the unrep. decisions of the sup. ct., and the federal courts of Ill.; ed. and annot. by Fs. E. Matthews, Hal Crumpton Bangs, and D: F. Rosenthal. v. 2. '08(Ag) c. O. shp. Flood.

Illinois. Cyclopedic digest. v. 10, (Supplement.) '08(D); v. 11. '09(Ap) c. O. shp. (Add. pubs. for price.) Keeefe-D.

Illinois. Cyclopedic digest finding list. '09 (Ag) c. O. pap. (Add. pubs. for price.) Keefe-D.

Illinois. Cyclopedic digest, selected subject. v. 1-3; being an abridgment from the Ill. Cyc. Digest, vs. 1-9. '09(N) c. ea., $2. Keefe-D.

Illinois. Educational Commission. Bulletins, nos. 1-8. '09(Je) 8°, pap. (Add. pubs. for price.) Ill. Educ. Com.
Contents: no. 1, Tentative plan for a state board of education, 38 p.; no. 2, Tentative plan for a county board of education, with some suggestions in regard to the county superintendency, 53 p.; no. 3, Tentative plan for the certification of teachers, 32 p.; no. 4, Tentative plan for making the township the unit of school organization, 47 p.; no. 5, Tentative recommendations concerning county teachers' institutes, 7-57 p.; no. 6, General school law of Illinois as revised, simplified and condensed and codified by the Illinois Educational Commission, 87 p.; no. 7, Tentative recommendations in regard to minimum salaries for teachers, 7-37 p.; no. 8, Bills providing for a state board of education, the certification of teachers, and township organization of rural schools, 8 p.

Illinois. Illinois at Vicksburg; pub. under authority of an act of the Forty-fifth General Assembly by the Illinois-Vicksburg Military Park Commission. '07, [1908.] (My.) 709 p. il. pors., maps, 4°, $4; leath., $5. Blakely.

Illinois. Law of corporations, [etc.;] by R. Waite Joslyn. [1910.] (N) c. O. $5. Flood.

Illinois. Legal rights of married women. '08, [1909.] (Ja) c. 45 p. pap. (Add. pub. for price.) F: R. Young.

Illinois. Notes on the repts.; cyclop. of Illinois law comprising a digest of the supreme and appellate court decisions, [etc.;] by W. Clyde Jones and Keene H. Addington, and Donald J. Kiser. v. 1. '10(Ap); v. 2 (Je); v. 3 (S) c. O. ea., $7.50. Callaghan.

Illinois. Personal injury cases, Illinois; incl. cases under dram-shop act and assault and battery; law and the facts alphabetically arr. by Joslyn R. Waite. '08(Ap.) c 70+688 p. O. *$6 net. Flood.

Illinois. Revised statutes of the state, 1908, cont. all the general statutes of the state in force Jan. 1, 1909, [etc.]; comp. and ed. by Harvey B. Hurd, [etc.] '08(N) c. por. O. shp., $5; 1909. '10(My) $6. Chic. Legal News.

Illinois. *Supreme ct.* Repts. v. 229; (I: Newton Phillips.) '08(Mr); v. 230 (Ap); v. 231 (My); v. 232 (Je); v. 233 (Jl); v. 234 (S); v. 235. '09(F); v. 236 (Mr); v. 237 (Ap); v. 238 (Je); v. 239 (Ag); v. 240 (O); v. 241. '10(F); v. 242 (My); v. 243 (Je); v. 244 (Jl); v. 245 (D) c. O. shp., ea., $2.25. Phillips.

Illinois. Treatise on the incorporation and management of corporations; by W: Meade Fletcher. '10(N) c. O. $7.50. Callaghan.

ILLINOIS.
Barrows, H. H. Geography of the middle Illinois Valley. 10 c. Univ. of Ill.
Bartow, E: Chemical and biological survey of the waters of Illinois. gratis.—Municipal water supplies of Illinois. Univ. of Ill.
Bartow, E:, *and others.* Mineral content of Illinois water. gratis. Univ. of Ill.
Biographical and reminiscent history of Richland, Clay and Marion Counties, Ill. '09, [1910.] (N) 17-608 p. il. pors. 4°. B. F. Bowen.
Boggess, A. C. Settlement of Illinois, 1778-1830. $3 Chic. Hist.
Bowman, I., *and* Reeds, C. A. Water resources of East St. Louis district, [Illinois.] (Add. pub. for price.) Univ. of Ill.
Campbell, W: H. Illinois hist. stories. 55 c. Appleton.
Carter, C. E: Great Britain and the Illinois country. $1.50. Am. Hist.

ILLINOIS.—*Continued.*

Chemical and biological survey of Illinois. Rept. from Sept. 1, 1906, to Dec. 31, 1907, E: Bartow. '08, [1909.] (Je) 88 p. il. 8°, (Univ. of Ill. bull.; Water Survey ser.) pap., gratis. Univ. of Ill.

Chipman, G: E., *ed.* Illinois cases, common law pleading. $2. Callaghan.

Cory, C. B. Birds of Illinois and Wisconsin. $4. Field Museum.

Farmer, J. A. Trial manual of personal injury laws; Illinois. $4. Fiske & Co.

Fenneman, N. M. Physiography of the St. Louis area. Univ. of Ill.

Forbes, S. A., *and* Richardson, R. E. Fishes of Illinois. Exchange or gratis. Ill. Lab'y Nat. Hist.

Hasse, A. R. Index of economic material in documents of the states of the U. S.; Illinois, 1809-1904. $5. Carnegie.

Hobart, E. L. Semi-hist. of a boy-veteran of the 28th Regiment Illinois Infantry Volunteers. $1.25. E. L. Hobart.

Invitation serieuse aux habitants des Illinois, by Un Habitant des Kaskaskias. $2.50. Club for Colonial Reprs.

Jones, L. E. Decisive dates in Illinois hist. $2. Ill. Pr.

Jones, T: Complete hist. of 46th regiment, Ill. Volunteer Infantry. $2.25. W. H. Wagner.

Kellogg, R. S. Forest planting in Ill. Gov. Pr. Off.

Kuehl, G: W. Automobile guide book of Ill. $2 net. Caspar.

Marsh, C: W. Recollections, 1837-1910. $1.50. Farm Impl. News.

Moore, B. F. History of cumulative voting and minority representation in Illinois, 1870-1908. 50 c. Univ. of Ill.

Nida, W: L. Story of Illinois and its people. 80 c. E. P. Barnes.

Olson, E. W., *ed.* History of the Swedes of Illinois. In 2 v. *$20 net; *$25 net. Engberg-H.

Parr, S: W., *and* Francis, C: K. Modification of Illinois coal by low temperature distillation. gratis. Univ. of Ill.

Pooley, W: V. Settlement of Illinois from 1830 to 1850. 75 c. Univ. of Wis.

Robinson, L. E., *and* Moore, I. History of Illinois. 60 c. Am. Bk.

Rolfe, C: W., *and others.* Paving brick and paving brick clays of Illinois. (Add. pubs. for price.) Univ. of Ill.

Schuyler, R. L. Transition in Illinois from British to American government. *$1.25 net. Lemcke.

Sharp, K. L. Illinois libraries. p. 3, College, institutional and special libraries, (excepting Chicago,) public school libraries; pt. 4, Chicago libraries; pt. 5, Buildings. ea., $1. Univ. of Ill.

Slocom, A. W. New crinoids from the Chicago area. 50 c. Field Museum.

Sparks, E. E., *ed.* English settlement in the Illinois. $2.50. Torch Press.

Waller, E. Brief hist. of Illinois. 40 c. Wagoner.

ILLINOIS.—*Continued.*

Winchell, S: R., *comp. and ed.* Civic manual for Chicago, Cook County and Illinois. 50 c. Flanagan.

See also **Altitudes;—Chicago;—Des Plaines Valley;—Insects;—Marion Co.;—Mississippi Valley;—Woodford Co.**

Illinois cases common law pleading; ed. by G: E. Chapman. 2d ed. '09(Je) c. 241 p. O. (Add. pubs. for price.) Callaghan.

Illinois. Dept. of Public Instruction circular. 8°, pap., 35 c. Phillips Bros.

—Sparks, E. E., *ed.* Semi-centennial of the Lincoln-Douglas debates in Illinois.

Illinois State Geological Survey bull. il. 8°. Univ. of Ill.

—Barrows. Geography of the middle Illinois Valley. 10 c.

—Bartow, *and others.* Mineral content of Illinois waters. gratis.

—Bowman. Water resources of the East St. Louis district.

—Carman. Mississippi Valley between Savanna and Davenport.

—Fenneman. Physiography of the St. Louis area.

—Goldthwait. Physical features of the Des Plaines Valley.

—Rolfe, *and others.* Paving brick and paving brick clays of Illinois.

Illinois State Historical Library. Collections of the Illinois State Historical Library. v. 1; ed. by H. W. Beckwith. '08, [1909.] (Ag) o. p.; v. 4, Executive ser. v. 1, The governors' letter-books, 1818-1834; ed. with introd. and notes by Evarts Boutell Greene and Clarence Walworth Alvord. '09 (Ag14) pors. O. (Add. pubs. for price.) Ill. State Hist. Lib.

Illinois State Historical Library. Collections of the Illinois State Historical Library. v. 2: Virginia ser., v. 1, Cahokia records, 1778-1790; ed., with introd. and notes, by Clarence Walworth Alvord. '08(Mr28); v. 3; Lincoln ser., v. 1, The Lincoln-Douglas debates of 1858; ed., with introd. and notes, by Edw. Erle Sparks. '08(O3) c. il. pors. facsim., map, O. (Not for sale.) Ill. State Hist. Lib.

Illinois State Laboratory of Natural History bull. 4°. Ill. Lab'y Nat. Hist.

—Baker. Ecology of the Skokie Marsh area. 60 c.

—Ewing. Oribatoidea of Illinois. 50 c.

—Forbes. On the general and interior distribution of Illinois fishes. $1.

Illinois State Normal School, Charleston. List of books in the schoolroom libraries of the first six grades in the Eastern Illinois State Normal School. '09, [1910.] (Je) 35 p. 12°. Ill. State Normal.

Illinois supplement to Brickwood's Sackett on instructions to juries, [etc.;] by Albert W. Brickwood. '10(Mr) c. O. $2.50. Callaghan.

Illinois Water Survey ser. 8°. Univ. of Ill.

—Bartow, *and others.* Mineral content of Illinois waters. gratis.

Illoway, H., M.D.

Summer diarrhea of infants. [1910.] (Mr) *$1 net. W: R. Jenkins.

Formerly published by E. R. Pelton.

Illuminated manuscripts. Bradley, J: W. *$1 net. McClurg.

ILLUMINATING.
See Electric light;—Light;—Lighting.

Illustrated Bible dictionary. Piercy, W: C., *ed.* *$5 net. Dutton.

Illustrated guide to flowering plants. Stevens, G: T: $2.50 net. Dodd.

Illustrated history of all nations. Clare, I. S. (Add. pubs. for price.) Chr. Herald.

Illustrated history of the Yellowstone Valley, embracing the counties of Park, Sweet Grass, Carbon, Yellowstone, Rosebud, Custer and Dawson, State of Montana. '07, [1908.] (O.) 21+669 p. il. pors. 4°, mor., $4.50. Western Hist.

Illustrated phonics. Ives, M. I. 40 c. Longmans.

Illustrated photogravure books. See Winston's.

ILLUSTRATIONS.
See Drawings.

ILLUSTRATIONS (*religious*).

Bomberger, J: H., *comp.* Three thousand practical illustrations in religion and morals, for preachers, platform speakers, Sunday school superintendents and teachers. $2. Central.

Carradine, B. Living illustrations. $1. Chr. Witness.

Jeffs, A. Art of sermon illustration. *$1 net. Revell.

Marshall, L. Rivets for truth. 60 c. Chr. Pub. Co.

Prather, C: H: Hdbk. of classics. $1. Pub. Ho. M. E. Ch., So.

Illustrative cases in equity; sel. by W: Sullivan Pattee. 4th ed. '08, [1909.] (Ja) c. 9+230 p. O. $2. West Pub.

Illustrious boys of many lands. Sweet, F. H. 50 c. McLoughlin.

Illustrious girls of many lands. Sweet, F. H. 50 c. McLoughlin.

Illustrious prince. Oppenheim, E: P. $1.50. Little, B. & Co.

Im vaterland. Bacon, P. V. $1.25. Allyn & B.

Image of Eve. Briscoe, M. S. †$1.25. Harper.

IMAGERY.
See Psychology.

Imaginary conversations. Landor, W. S. 75 c. Putnam.

Imaginary interviews. *See* Howells, W: Dean.

Imaginary portraits. *See* Pater, Wa.

IMAGINATION.

Buckham, M. H: Culture of the imagination. (Add. author for price.) M. H: Buckham.

Rhoades, J. Training of the imagination. *75 c. net. Lane.

See also Medicine.

Imagination in business. Deland, L. F. **50 c. net. Harper.

Imber, Naphtali Herz.

Treasures of two worlds; unpublished legends and traditions of the Jewish nation. '10(Ag13) c. 12°, 50 c. Citizens Pr.

Imhaus, N: E:

Hand book on some minerals and rocks. '08(Je6) c. 8°, 50 c. Ryder Bros.

Imitation of Christ. *See* Thomas *à Kempis.*

IMLAY, Gilbert.
See Godwin, *Mrs.* Mary Wollstonecraft.

Immanence of God. De Laurence, L. W: $3.25. De Laurence, S.

Immel, A. A., M.D.

Scientific sheep and goat breeding; in accordance with the natural laws of reproduction. '10(S) c. 31 p. nar. S. pap., $1. E. E. Hahn.

Immensée. *See* Storm, Theodor.

IMMERSION.
See Baptism.

Immigrant and the community; addresses, papers and resolutions of the fourth annual conference of the Society for the Promotion of Social Service in the Young Men's Christian Association, Montclair, March 31, April 1 and 2, 1910, with a bibliography on immigration. '10(N5) c. il. front. map, 8°, 75 c. Y. M. C. A.

Immigration. '09(My22) D. (Univ. of Wis. bull.) pap., gratis. Univ. of Wis.

IMMIGRATION.

Edwards, R: H:, *ed.* Immigration. 10 c. R: H: Edwards.

Immigrant and the community. 75 c. Y. M. C. A.

Lodge, H: C. Speech on immigration. U. S., Supt. of Docs.

Ray, M. K. Immigration problem: bibliography. 25 c. Wis. Free Lib.

Restriction of immigration. Univ. of Wis.

Roberts, P: Immigrant races in North America. 50 c. Y. M. C. A.

Steiner, E: A. Immigrant tide. *$1.50 net. Revell.

United States. *Dept. of Commerce and Labor. Bu. of Immigration and Naturalization.* Catalogue of books and blanks used by the Immigration Service, July, 1909. '09(D) 14 p. 8°. (Add. Superintendent for price.)

United States. *Dept. of Commerce and Labor. Bu. of Immigration and Naturalization; Division of Information.* Information for immigrants. '09(S) 26 p. 24°, pap. (Add. Superintendent for price.) U. S., Supt. of Docs.

United States. *Dept. of Commerce and Labor. Bureau of Immigration and Naturalization.* Immigration laws and regulations, July, 1907. 15 c.

United States. *Immigration Commission.* Statement relative to the work and expenditures of the Immigrant Commission created under section 39 of the immigration act of Feb. 20, 1907. '09(My) 44 p. 8°, pap. (Add. Superintendent for price.)

United States. Immigration laws and regulations of July 1, 1907. 6th ed., approved June 7, 1909. '09(Ag) 86 p. 8°, pap.

Watson, E. J. Addresses on immigration. gratis. State Co.

See also Anthropometry;—Naturalization;—Ships and shipbuilding;—Yellow peril;—*also* names of different nationalities in the U. S.

Immorality and foolishness of prohibition. Paul, H. A. C. 20 c. H. A. C. Paul.

Immortal memories. Shorter, C. K. $1.50. Harper.
Immortal moment. Sinclair, M. †$1.50. Doubleday, P.
Immortal soul. Mallock, W: H. †$1.50. Harper.
IMMORTALITY.
Albe, E. E: F. d'. New light on immortality. *$1.75 net. Longmans.
Ball, J. W. Absolute idealism and immortality. (Add. pubs. for price.) Woodruff-C.
Berry, J: B. Some assurances of immortality. $1. Fenno.
Bigelow, W: S. Buddhism and immortality. **75 c. net. Houghton M.
Burney, C: F. Israel's hope of immortality. $1. Oxford Univ.
Dickinson, G. L. Is immortality desirable? **75 c. net. Houghton M.
Dole, C: F. Hope of immortality. **30 c. net. Crowell.
Frank, H: Modern light on immortality. *$1.85 net. Sherman, F.
Hill, L. Two great questions; the existence of God and the immortality of the soul. $2. L. Hill.
Holmes, E. E: Immortality. *$1.40 net. Longmans.
Koplowitz, I. Al-moveth; or, immortality of the soul. 75 c. Bloch.
Lodge, *Sir* O. J. Immortality of the soul. *$1 net. Ball Pub. Co.
Lodge, *Sir* O. J. Science and immortality. *$2 net. Moffat.
McKennan, F. B. Man's incarnation: key to life eternal. $1. McKennan.
Palmer, F. Winning of immortality. $1 net. Crowell.
Smyth, N. Modern belief in immortality. **75 c. net. Scribner.
See also Death;—Future life;—Heaven;—Philosophy;—Psychical research;—Soul.
Immortality. *See* Comstock, Warren E. Days of long ago.
Immortality and our employment hereafter. Peebles, J. M. $1.25; 75 c. Austin.
Immune sera. Bolduan, C: F: $1.50. Wiley.
IMMUNITY.
See Infectious diseases;—Serum.
Immunity of the Japanese chestnut to bark disease. Metcalf, H. 5 c. U. S., Supt. of Docs.
Imola, Benvenuto da.
See Vernon, W: Warren.
Impending anarchy. Hebberd, S. S. (Add. pubs. for price.) Maspeth.
Imperator ad se ipsum. *See* Antoninus, Marcus Aurelius.
Imperial gazetteer of India. New ed., published under the authority of His Majesty's Secretary of State for India in Council. In 26 v. v. 5-14. '08(N14); v. 15-25; v. 26, atlas. '09(My15) maps, 8°, v. 5-25, ea., $2; hf. mor., $2.50; v. 26, $5; hf. mor., $5.75; subs., per set., $30; hf. mor., $37. Oxford Univ.
Imperial marriage. Marchmont, A. W. $1.20 net. Dodge.
Imperial reference library. Morris, C:, *ed.* 6 v. $55. Syndicate Pub.
Imperial ritual of magic. Clymer, R. S. $1. Philosophical.
Imperial stereoscopic anatomy of the head and neck. Cunningham, D. J: $10. Imperial Pub.
IMPERIAL VALLEY, Cal.
Howe, E. F., *and* Hay, W. J. Story of the first decade in Imperial Valley, Cal. $3. E. F. Howe.
IMPERIALISM.
Cromer, *Earl* of. Ancient and modern imperialism. 90 c. net. Longmans.
Nicholson, J. S. Project of empire; critical study of economics of imperialism. *$2.25 net. Macmillan.
Impersonator (The). Taylor, M. I. 75 c. Little, B. & Co.
Import and outlook of socialism. Mann, N. M. $1.50 net. J. H. West.
IMPORT DUTIES.
See Tariff.
Importance of the mining industry. Cantwell, H. J. gratis. H. J. Cantwell.
Important events in musical history. Bloomfield, D. 25 c. Presser.
Importers ready reference tables. Motley, J. $1.25. Motley Press.
IMPORTS.
See Commerce.
Impostor (The). Scott, J: R: $1.50. Lippincott.
IMPOSTORS.
See Biography.
IMPRESSIONISM.
See Painters and painting.
Impressions of a layman. Markoe, R. J. $1.50. Willwerscheid.
Impressions of American education in 1908. Burstall, S. A. *$1.25 net. Longmans.
Impressions of Henry Irving. Pollock, W. H. **$1 net. Longmans.
Impressions of India. Craik, *Sir* H. *90 c. net. Macmillan.
Imprisoned midshipmen. Seawell, M. E. †$1.25. Appleton.
Improper Prue. Manning, G. $1.50. B. W. Dodge.
Impropriety of taxing returns to life insurance policy-holders. Cox, R. L. gratis. R. L. Cox.
Improved book-keeping. Goodwin, J. H: $3. J. H: Goodwin.
IMPROVED ORDER OF RED MEN.
Robinson, C: A. This book contains one hundred reasons why I am a Red Man and some nuggets of gold. 50 c. C: A. Robinson.
In a monk's cassock. Moran, P. V. A. $1. Conkey.
In a mysterious way. Warner, A. †$1.50. Little, B. & Co.
In a new century. Martin, E: S. **$1.50 net. Scribner.
In a roundabout way. Mulholland, C. *75 c. net. Benziger.
In a Yorkshire garden. Farrer, R. J. $3.50. Longmans.
In Africa. McCutcheon, J: T. $3. Bobbs-M.
In after days. Howells, W: D. **$1.25 net. Harper.
In amber lands. McInnes, T. $1. B'way Pub.

In ambush. Van Vorst, M. †$1.50. Lippincott.
In American fields and forests; H: D: Thoreau, J: Burroughs, J: Muir, Bradford Torrey, Dallas Lore Sharp, Olive Thorne Miller. '09(Mr20) c. il. D. **$1.50 net. Houghton M.
In and around the old St. Louis Cathedral of New Orleans. Chambon, C. M. 50 c. C. M. Chambon.
In and out of a French country-house. Dodd, *Mrs.* A. B. B. $2.25 net. Dodd.
In and out of Florence. Kellogg, V. L. $2.50 net. Holt.
In and out of three Normandy inns. Dodd, *Mrs.* A. B. B. $2.50 net. Little, B. & Co.
In antescript, two presidential nominees. Harvey, L. 25 c. T. L. Harvey.
In Calvert's Valley. Montague, M. P. †$1.50. Baker & T.
In captivity in the Pacific. Houston, E. J. †$1.25. Am. Bapt.
In Christ's name. Dudden, F: H. *60 c. net. Longmans.
In closed territory. Bronson, E. B. *$1.75 net. McClurg.
In crystal hills. Allen, F: J. 50 c. F: J. Allen.
In Cupid's realm. Buchanan, F. G. $1.15. F. G. Buchanan.
In David's town. Burrell, D: J. 50 c. Am. Tr.
In defense of liberty. Chipman, W: P. †$1. Burt.
In English homes. Latham, C: v. 3. $15 net. Scribner.
In forbidden seas. Snow, H. J. $3.50 net. Longmans.
In four continents. Williams, H: F. 50 c. Presb. Pub.
In friendship's garden. Shaylor, J. $1.25; $2. Stokes.
In friendship's meditation. Addingley, A., *comp.* 75 c.; $1.50. Platt & P.
In God's orchard. Learmont, J. *$1 net. Eaton & M.
In Greece with the classics. Gardner, W: A. **$1.50 net. Little, B. & Co.
In Indian Mexico. Starr, F: *$5 net. Forbes.
In Korea with Marquis Ito. Ladd, G: T. **$2.50 net. Scribner.
In life's sweet afternoon. Lindsay, C. A. (Priv. pr.) Jacobs.
In line of duty. Hobson, R. P. $1.50. Appleton.
In Lockerbie Street. Daggett, M. P. 50 c. B. W. Dodge.
In Lotus land. Ponting, H. G. $6 net. Macmillan.
In love's garden. Anderson, I. F. $1. Arroyo Guild.
In Mary's reign. Orczy, E. M. R. M. J. B., *Baroness.* 75 c. Cupples & L.
In memoriam. *See* Tennyson, Alfr., *Lord.*
In Morocco with General D'Amade. Rankin, J. R. L. *$2.50 net. Longmans.
In my lady's garden. Richmond, *Mrs.* **$3.50 net. Jacobs.
In nature's garden. Shaylor, J., *comp.* $1.25; $2. Stokes.
In nature's school. Gask, L. $1.50. Crowell.
In nature's temple. Carson, J. D. $1.25. Oldach.
In old Ceylon. Farrar, R. J. $4. Longmans.
In old Kentucky. Marshall, D. E: $1.50. G: W. Dillingham.
In old Quivira. McCarter, M. H. 50 c. Crane.
In our country's service. Phillips, M. J. $1. E: T. Miller.
In our town. White, W: A. $1.50. Macmillan.
In peanut land. Dean, E. $1.75; $1.25. Fenno.
In praise of books. Swan, H. 50 c. Dutton.
In praise of gardens. Scott, T., *comp.* $1.25. Baker & T.
In praise of valor. Green, T: E: $3; $5. Torch Press.
In pursuit of Priscilla. Field, E: S. 50 c.; $1. Altemus.
In quest of prosperity. Rawie, H: 25 c. H: Rawie.
In re Shakespeare. Greenwood, G. G: *$1 net. Lane.
In search of a polar continent. Harrison, A. H. *$3.50 net. Longmans.
In ship and prison. Chipman, W: P. $1.50. Saalfield.
In Spain. Lomas, J: *$2 net. Macmillan.
In Starland with a three-inch telescope. Olcott, W. T. **$1 net. Putnam.
In Texas with Davy Crockett. McNeil, E. $1.50. Dutton.
In the Abruzzi. Macdonell, A. *$2 net. Stokes.
In the beginning. *See* Macy, S. B.
In the bend of the Estataue. Sparks, S: J. 75 c. B'way Pub.
In the border country. Bacon, *Mrs.* J. D. D. **$1, fixed. Doubleday, P.
In the Catskills. Burroughs, J: $1.50 net. Houghton M.
In the clouds for Uncle Sam. Lamar, A. 60 c. Reilly & B.
In the country God forgot. Charles, F. †75 c. Little, B. & Co.
In the crucible. Williams, I. C. 85 c. Kenedy.
In the dark and cloudy day. Knight, G. H. $1.25 net. Doran.
In the days of the Georges. Boulton, W: B. $4. Pott.
In the dead of night. McIntyre, J: T: †$1.50. Lippincott.
In the desert. Phillips, L. M. $2. Longmans.
In the Fairy Ring. Harrison, F. $2. Caldwell.
In the footprints of Heine. Forman, H: J. $2 net. Houghton M.
In the forbidden land. Landor, A. H: S. $3. Harper.
In the front office; plans and suggestions for writing more fire insurance, effective means for advertising the fire insurance business, schemes for making the office more productive at less cost. '10(Jl16) c. il. fold. tab., (in pocket,) 8°, $2. RoughNotes.
In the golden East. Gibson, C. C. *60 c. net. Little, B. & Co.

In the grip of the nyika. Patterson, J: H: **$2 net. Macmillan.
In the heart of Africa. Mecklenburg-Strelitz, A. F., *Duke* of. $5 net. Cassell.
In the iron time. Hart, J. W. $1.50. Jennings.
In the Kaiser's capital. Dickie, J. F. $2 net. Dodd.
In the land of extremes. Harlan, *Mrs.* M. R. *$1.50 net. Cochrane.
In the land of the blue gown. Little, A. B. $2.50 net. Appleton.
In the land of the mosques and minarets. Miltoun, F., *pseud.* $3; $7. L. C. Page.
In the land of to-morrow. Cranke, J. P. $1.50. B'way Pub.
In the light of the cross. Mortimer, A. G. **80 c. net. Whittaker.
In the Master's country. Tarbell, M. 50 c. net. Doran.
In the mountain's shadow. Rodney, M. $1.50. C. M. Clark.
In the open. Kirkham, S. D. **$1.75 net. P. Elder.
In the open. Stoddard, W: O. †60 c. Harper.
In the potter's house. Eldridge, G: D. †$1.50. Doubleday, P.
In the poverty year. Douglas, M. **40 c. net. Crowell.
In the Schillingscourt. John, E. 50 c. Hurst.
In the school of Christ. McDowell, W: F. $1.25 net. Revell.
In the service of the princess. Rowland, H: C. $1.50. Dodd.
In the shadow of God. Jamieson, G. A. **$1 net. Fenno.
In the shadow of San Juan. Armstrong, M. M. $1. Pueblo Pub.
In the shadow of the guillotine. Elliott, Mrs. G. D. 75 c. Estes.
In the shadow of the peaks. Couch, S. B. $1.50. Cochrane.
In the shadow of the pines. Damon, F. A. $1. F. A. Damon
In the South Seas. Stevenson, R. L: *$1 net; *$1.25 net. Scribner.
In the strange south seas. Grimshaw, B. E. *$3.50 net. Lippincott.
In the torrid Sudan. Tangye, H. L. $3 net. Badger.
In the track of R. L. Stevenson. Hammerton, J: A. *$1.50 net. Dutton.
In the twilight zone. Craven, R. C. $1.50. C. M. Clark.
In the valley of the Nile. Watson, C: R. *$1 net. Revell.
In the valley of the shadows. Woolwine, T: L. †$1. Doubleday, P.
In the wake of the green banner. Metour, E. P. †$1.50. Scribner.
In the woods and on the shore. Ware, R: D. $2. L. C. Page.
In three legations. Bunsen, *Mme.* C. de. $3.50. Scribner.
In Togo's country. Schwartz, H: B. *$1.50 net. Jennings.
In town. Fairbank, J. A. $1.25 net. McClurg.
In treaty with honor. Crowley, M. C. 75 c. Little, B. & Co.
In unfamiliar England. Murphy, T: D. $3; $7. L. C. Page.
In unknown Tuscany. Hutton, E: *$2.50 net. Dutton.
In various moods. Bacheller, I. A. $1 net. Harper.
In West Point gray. Russel, *Mrs.* F. K. $1.50. L. C. Page.
In whaling days. Tripp, H. †$1.50. Little, B. & Co.
In wild Africa. Knox, T: W. †$1.50. Wilde.
In wildest Africa. MacQueen, P: $3. L. C. Page.
Inaccuracy of movement. Hollingworth, H. L. 80 c. Science Pr., (N. Y.)

INCANDESCENT LAMP.
See Electric light.

Incarnate love. Brett, J. 75 c. Longmans.

INCARNATION.
Angelus and the Regina Cæli. 25 c. Longmans.
Case, C. D. Incarnation and modern thought. *50 c. net. Univ. of Chic.
Grützmacher, R: H. Virgin birth. *40 c. net. Eaton & M.
Streatfeild, G: S. The incarnation. *40 c. net. Longmans.
See also Jesus Christ.

Incarnation of the snow. Bain, F. W: †$1.25. Putnam.

INCAS.
Markham, *Sir* C. R. Incas of Peru. $3 net Dutton.

INCENSE.
See Worship.

Inchbald, Mrs. Eliz. Simpson.
Simple story; with an introd. by G. L. Strachey. '09(My15) S. (Oxford lib. of prose and poetry.) 90 c. Oxford Univ.

Inchbold, Mrs. A. Cunnick, [Mrs. Stanley Inchbold.]
Lisbon and Cintra. '08(O17) il. 8°, *$3.50 net. Duffield.

Incidental teaching of English. Callaway, M., *jr.* 15 c. Univ. of Tex.
Incidents of European travel. Doyle, G. $1.50. G. Doyle.
Including Finnigin. *See* Gillilan, S. W.
Incognito. Berlage, H. J. (Add. author for price.) H. J. Berlage.

INCOME TAX.
See Taxation.

Incomparable Siddons. Parsons, *Mrs.* C. *$3.50 net. Putnam.
Incompatibilities in prescriptions. Ruddiman, E. A. $2. Wiley.

INCORPORATION.
See Corporations.

Increase in cost of food. United States. *Dept. of Commerce and Labor. Bu. of Labor.*
Increase of divorce. Phillips, J: B. 25 c. Univ. of Col.
Increasing gold supply. Gibson, T: $1. Gibson Pub.
Incrusting *chilostomatous bryozoa* of west coast of North America. Robertson, A. $1. Univ. of Cal.
Incubation and brooding. Hawks, E. B. 50 c. E. B. Hawks.

INCUNABULA.
De Vinne, T. L. Notable printers of Italy during the 15th century. $15. Grolier Club.
Josephson, A. G. S. Incunabula in the Senn collection at the John Crerar Library. (Priv. pr.) Am. Medical.
Independence of the ministry. Hodges, D. 10 c. Y. M. C. A.
INDEX EXPURGATORIUS.
Betten, F. S. Roman index of forbidden books. *35 c. net. Herder.
Index of symptoms. Leftwich, R. W. $2.25 net. Wood.
Index of treatment. Hutchison, R., *ed.* *$6 net; *$7.50 net. Wood.
INDEXES.
American Institute of Mining Engineers. General alphabetical and analytical index: Transactions. v. 1-35. $5; $6. Am. Inst. Mining Eng.
Annual magazine subject index. v. 1, Magazine subject index to Dec. 31, 1907. *$3 net; *$4 net; v. 2, 1908, $3; v. 3, 1909, $5.50 net. Boston Bk.
Ballard, E. E. Complete index to Ballard's Law of real property. v. 1-12. $6.50. Flood.
Burdick, J. E., *ed.* General index [to The history of nations.] $2.75; $3.75; $5. J: D. Morris.
Crane, W. R: Index of mining engineering literature. **$4 net; **$5 net. Wiley.
Cumulative index for current law. v. 1-9. (Add. pubs. for price.) Keefe-D.
Engineering index annual, 1909. $2. Engineering Mag.
Fletcher, W: I:, *ed.* Annual library index, 1907. **$3.50 net; 1908.—1909. ea., *$5 net. Pub. Weekly.
Fletcher, W: I:, *and* Poole, M., *eds.* Poole's index to periodical literature. $10; $12; $14. Houghton M.
General index of the statutes contained in Burns' annot. Indiana statutes of 1908. 18; $20. Bobbs-M.
Gillette, F. B., *comp.* Title index to the works of Honoré de Balzac. 25 c. Boston Bk.
Hasse, A. R. Index of economic material in documents of states of the U. S.: California. $2.25.—Delaware. $1.50.—Illinois. $5.—Kentucky. $5.—Massachusetts. $2.25.—New York. $3.75.—Rhode Island. 75 c. Carnegie.
Hastain, E., *comp.* Index to Choctaw-Chickasaw [Indians] deeds and allotments. $100. E. Hastain.
Jacobs, H:. *comp.* "Where to find it"; index to sources of information. 50 c. H: Jacobs.
Lane, M. C. Index to the fragments of the Greek Elegiac and Iambic poets as contained in the Hiller-Crusius ed. of Bergk's Anthologia lyrica. 80 c. Longmans.
Missouri. Index to the revised statutes for 1899 and the session acts of 1901-1907. $1.25. Vernon Law Bk.

INDEXES.—*Continued.*
Payne, W: W., *comp.* General index to *Sidereal Messenger,* v. 1-10; *Astronomy and Astro-Physics,* v. 1-3; *Popular Astronomy,* v. 1-16. $1.50. Popular Astronomy.
Richardson, E. C., *comp. and ed.* Alphabetical subject index and index encyclopædia to periodical articles on religion, 1890-1899. $10. Hartford Sem., [Scribner.]
Technical press index. *$3 net. Engineering News.
Wayland, J: W. Complete index to "The German element in the Shenandoah Valley of Virginia." 30 c. J: W. Wayland.
Winternitz, M. Index to the names and subject matter of the sacred books of the East. $5.75. Oxford Univ.
Wise, J. C., *comp.* Digested index and genealogical guide to Bishop Meade's "Old chuches, ministers and families of Virginia"; embracing 6,900 proper names. $2 net. Bell Bk.
See also Classification;—Railroads;—Readers.
INDEXING.
Beak, G. B. Indexing and précis writing. *50 c. net. Macmillan.
INDIA.
Allen, J. C. Heroes of Indian hist. 50 c.—Narrative of Indian history. 90 c. Longmans.
Alston, L. Education and citizenship in India. $1.25 net. Longmans.
Anderson, W: B., *and* Watson, C: R. Far north in India. 50 c. Bd. For. Miss.
Andrews, C. F. Christ in India. $1.50 net. Doran.
Asoka. Edicts of Asoka. $6.75. Oxford Univ.
Atkinson, W: W. Inner teachings of the philosophies and religions of India. *$1 net. Yogi Pub.
Bloomfield, M. Religion of the Veda. **$1.50 net. Putnam.
Bruce, H: Letters from Malabar, and on the way. *$2 net. Dutton.
Burn-Murdoch, W. G. From Edinburgh to India and Burmah. *$3.50 net. Dutton.
Chailley-Bert, J. Administrative problems of British India. $3.25 net. Macmillan.
Chamberlain, J. Kingdom in India. *$1.50 net. Revell.
Craik, *Sir* H: Impressions of India. *90 c. net. Macmillan.
Crawford, W: H:, *ed.* Thoburn and India. *$1 net. Eaton & M.
Dewar, D. Birds of the plains: [India.] *$4 net.—Indian birds. $2 net. Lane.
Eardley-Wilmot, S. Forest life and sport in India. $3.50 net. Longmans.
Foster, W: English factories in India, 1622-1623. — 1624-1629. — 1630-1633. ea., $4.15. Oxford Univ.
Gilliat, E: Heroes of modern India. $1.50. Lippincott.
Hardie, J. K. India; impressions and suggestions. *$1 net. B: W. Huebsch.
Havell, E. B. Indian sculpture and painting. *$25 net. Scribner.

INDIA.—*Continued.*
Heston, M. Bluestocking in India: [fiction.] $1 net. Revell.
Holdich, *Sir* T: H. Gates of India. $3.25 net. Macmillan.
Ilbert, *Sir* C. P. Government of India. $3.75 net; supp. chapter separately, 35 c. net. Oxford Univ.
Imperial gazetteer of India. In 26 v., v. 5-25; v. 26, atlas. v. 5-25, ea., $2; $2.50; v. 26, $5; $5.75; subs., per set, $30; $37. Oxford Univ.
Jones, J: P: India: its life and thought. **$2.50 net. Macmillan.
Kelman, J. H. Children of India. 60 c. net. Revell.
Ketkar, S. V. Hist. of caste in India. v. 1. Taylor & C.
Manucci, N. Storia do Mogor; or, Mogul India, 1653-1708. v. 3, 4. ea., *$3.50 net. Dutton.
Morley, J: Indian speeches, (1907-1909.) *$1 net. Macmillan.
Noble, M. E. Web of Indian life. *$1.75 net. Holt.
O'Donnell, C: J. Causes of present discontent in India. **85 c. net. Wessels.
Oman, J: C. Cults, customs and superstitions of India. **$3.50 net. Jacobs.
Oswell, G. D. Sketches of rulers of India. v. 1-4. ea., 70 c. Oxford Univ.
People of India. $1.75 net. Macmillan.
Reynolds-Ball, E. A. Tourist's India. *$2 net. Brentano's.
Richter, J. History of missions in India. *$2.50 net. Revell.
Roberts, F: S., *Earl.* Forty-one years in India. 2 v. in 1. $2. Longmans.
Smith, V. A. Early history of India. $4.75.
—Oxford students' history of India. 60 c. Oxford Univ.
Stebbing, E: P. Jungle by-ways in India. $4 net. Lane.
Steel, *Mrs.* F. A. W. India through the ages. *$1.25 net. Dutton.
Stratton, W: A. Letters from India. *$3.50 net. Dutton.
Surridge, V. India. *$2 net. Stokes.
Swain, C. A. Glimpses of India. $1.25. Woman's For. Miss.
Watt, *Sir* G: Commercial products of India. *$5 net. Dutton.
Webb, M. de P. India and the empire: consideration of the tariff problem. *$1.20 net. Longmans.
Wilson-Carmichael, A. Lotus buds; [children of India.] *$5 net. Armstrong.
Younghusband, G: J: Story of the Guides: [English regiment.] *$2.25 net. Macmillan.

See also Akbar; — Asoka; — Benares;—Bengal;—Bhutan; — Buddha and Buddhism; — Burma;—Burmese language; — East India Company; —Hinduism; — Mahabharata; — Painters and painting; — Sanskrit literature; — Sculpture;—Sikh religion;—Sikhim;—Tibet;—Yellow peril; — Yunnan, China; — *also* Outram, *Gen. Sir* James.

INDIA RUBBER.
Heil, A., *and* Esch, W. Manufacture of rubber goods. *$3.50 net. Lippincott.
International Bu. of Am. Republics. Rubber and its relatives. (Add. Superintendent for price.) U. S., Supt. of Docs.

INDIA RUBBER.—*Continued.*
Pearson, H: C. Crude rubber and compounding ingredients. $10. India Rubber.
Pearson, H: C., *comp.* Rubber trade directory. $3. India Rubber.
Seeligmann, T., *and others.* India rubber and gutta percha. $5 net. Van Nostrand.
Terry, H. L. India-rubber and its manufacture. *$2 net. Van Nostrand.
Indian and scout. Brereton, F: S. $1.25. Caldwell.
Indian captivities ser. S. Huntting.
—Captivity of Mrs. Johnson. $3; $5.
—Steele. Indian captive. $2.50; $5.
—Williams. Redeemed captive. $2.50; $5.
INDIAN CHARITY SCHOOL, Hanover, N. H., and Lebanon, Ct.
See **Rochester reprints.**
INDIAN CLUBS.
Camann, H: B. Indian clubs exercises and exhibition drills. 75 c. H: B. Camann.
Warman, E: B. Indian club exercises. 10 c. Am. Sports.
Indian dust. Rothfeld, O. *$1.50 net. Lane.
Indian legends and other poems. Gordon, H. L. $1.50. Salem Press.
Indian Rights Association. Addresses del. at the 27th annual meeting of the Association, Dec. 17, 1909. '10(My7) 8°, (Indian Rights Assoc. pubs., 2d ser.) gratis. Indian Rights Assoc.
Indian scout. *See* Aimard, G.
Indian speeches. Morley, J: *$1 net. Macmillan.
Indian study of love and death. Noble, M. E. 75 c. Longmans.
Indian texts ser. 8°, *$3.50 net. Dutton.
—Manucci. Storia do mogor. v. 3, 4.
Indiana. *Appellate ct.* Repts.; (G: W. Self and Sol. H. Esarey.) v. 40. '08(Jl); v. 41. '08, [1909.] (F); v. 42 (O) ea., $4; v. 43-44. '10(D) c. O. ea., shp., $1.50. Burford.
Indiana. Burns' annot. statutes, showing the general statutes in force, Jan. 1, 1908; embracing the revision of 1881 as amended, and all permanent, general and public acts of the general assembly passed since the adoption of that revision; cont. also the U. S. and Ind. constitutions; annot. by Harrison Burns. In 3 v. v. 1. '08(Mr); v. 2, 3 (Je) c. O. per set, $18. Bobbs-M.
Indiana. Complete guide for township officers. 4th ed., by W. W. Thornton. '09 (Jl) c. 37+625 p. O. $4. W. H. Anderson.
Indiana. Complete index to notes to statutes; covering the years 1903 to 1908, inclusive, v. 1-6. '08, [1909.] (Ja) c. 110+8 p. O. $2. Nat. Annot.
Indiana. General index of the statutes cont. in Burns' annot. Ind. statutes, 1908; (Harrison Burns.) '08(Jl) c. 378 p. O. $18; shp., $20. Bobbs-M.
Indiana. Laws concerning taxation. 25 c. W: H. Sheiman.
Indiana. Laws of negligence; (G: Shirts.) '08(O) c. 56+1250 p. O. (Add. pubs. for price.) Callaghan.)
Indiana. Statutes of state rel. to the settlement of estates, descent of property, wills, [etc.;] by R. C. Brown. '10(Ag) c. O. $2. Independent.

Indiana. *Supreme and Appellate cts.* Second supp. to new citations; (J: Wesley Thompson.) '08(Ja11) O. **$7.50 net. Bobbs-M.

Indiana. *Supreme ct.* Repts.; (G: W. Self and Sol. H. Esarey.) v. 167. '08(Ja4); v. 168. '08(Mr); v. 169 (N); v. 170. '08, [1909]; v. 171. '09, [1910.] (F); v. 172 (S) c. O. shp., ea., $3.50. Aetna Pr.; Burford.

INDIANA.
Clopper, E: N: Child labor in Indiana. gratis. Nat. Child Labor.
Election law of Indiana (in force Sept. 1, 1908), with instructions to voters and election officers. '09(Jl) 247 p. 8°, pap., 25 c. Burford.
Hendricks, E. L. Hist. and civil government of Indiana. *40 c. net. Macmillan.
Levering, J. H. Historic Indiana. **$2.50 net. Putnam.
Lindley, H. Government of Ind. 50 c. Ginn.
McDonald, D: Treatise on the laws of Indiana pertaining to the powers and duties, [etc.,] of justices of the peace, [etc.] $7.50. W. H. Anderson.
Perry, O., *comp.* Indiana in the Mexican war. (Add. author for price.) O. Perry.
Rand, McNally & Co.'s new ideal state and county survey and atlas; cont. a large county and railway map of Indiana. (Subs. only.) Rand, McN. & Co.
Sanders, D: W. Manual of civil government of Ind. 50 c. Manual Pub. Co.
Stott, W: T. Indiana Baptist history. $2. W: T. Stott.
Thornton, W: W. Indiana negligence. 2 v. $12.—Law governing cities and towns in Indiana. $7.50. W. H. Anderson.
White, E: M. Indiana laws made plain. $1. Bankers' Law Pub.
Williams, W: K. Indiana farm laws, with business forms and model business letters. $1.50. Rural Pub.
See also Clark Co.;—Dubois Co.;—Gary;—Howard Co.; — Indianapolis; — Marshall Co.; — St. Joseph's Co.;—Sullivan Co.;—Tippecanoe Co.

Indiana. McKnight, L. A. 50 c. L. A. McKnight.

Indiana corporation law, [etc.;] with complete forms; by Harrison Burns. '10(N) c. O. $7.50. Bobbs-M.

Indiana Historical Society pubs. 8°. Bobbs-M.
—Browning. Lockerbie's assessment list of Indianapolis. 25 c.
—Dunn *and* Wrigley. Word Hoosier; and John Finley. *50 c. net.

Indiana law stamps from the earliest issue of the Ind. reports to the year 1910; comp. by W. G. Pilkinton. '10(My) c. S. pap., $5. Law Stamp.

INDIANAPOLIS, Ind.
Browning, E. G. Lockerbie's assessment list of Indianapolis. 25 c. Bobbs-M.
Dunn, J. P. Greater Indianapolis. 2 v. $20. Lewis Pub.

Indianapolis blue book of selected names of Indianapolis and suburban towns, 1910. '09 (N) c. 8°, $5. Dau.

INDIANS.
Abel, A. H. Indians in the Civil War. (Not for sale.) Am. Hist. Review.
Abel, A. H. Proposals for an Indian state, 1778-1878. Gov. Pr. Off.
Adventures with Indians. 60 c. Harper.
Affairs of the five civilized tribes in Oklahoma; statement of Commissioner J. G: Wright. '09(My) 44 p. 8°. (Add. Superintendent for price.) U. S., Supt. of Docs.
Alexander, H. B. Religious spirits of the American Indian as shown in the development of his religious rites and customs. 30 c. Open Court.
Anderson, R. A. Fighting the Mill Creeks; campaigns against Indians. 50 c. Chico Record.
Angel, M. La piedra pintada; painted rock of California. $1.25. Grafton Pub.
Balance due loyal Creek Indians; rept. '09 (My) 5 p. 8°, pap. (Add. Superintendent for price.) U. S., Supt. of Docs.
Barrett, S: A. Ethno-geography of the Pomo and neighboring Indians. $3.25.—Material culture of the Klamath Lake and Modoc Indians of northwestern Cal. and southern Ore. 75 c.—Pomo Indian basketry. $1.75. Univ. of Cal.
Barrett, S: A., *and* Kroeber, A. L: Geography and dialect; [also] On the evidence of the occupation of certain regions by the Miwok Indians. 50 c. Univ. of Cal.
Bledsoe, S. T. Indian land laws. $6. Pipes-R.
Bloomfield, J. K. The Oneidas. *$2.25 net. Alden Bros.
Brooks, D. Stories of the red children. 40 c.; 30 c. Educ. Pub.
Burton, C. M. Ephraim Douglass and his times. $1.85. Abbatt.
Bushnell, D: I., *jr.* The Choctaw of Bayou Lacomb, St. Tammany Parish, Louisiana. U. S., Supt. of Docs.
Brown, A. F., *and* Bell, J. M. Tales of the Red Children. †$1. Appleton.
Carrington, *Mrs.* F. C. My army life and the Fort Phil. Kearney massacre. $2 net. Lippincott.
Carrington, H. B. Indian question. *60 c. net; *30 c. net. DeWolfe.
Catlin, G: Boy's Catlin; my life among the Indians. **$1.50 net. Scribner.
Converse, *Mrs.* H. M. C. Myths and legends of the New York State Iroquois. 75 c.; 50 c. N. Y. State Educ.
Coon, F. L. Coeur d'Alene Indian Reservation, Kootenai Co., Idaho. 25 c. Inland Pr. Co.
Curtis, E: S. North American Indian. (Add. author for price, per v. or set.) E: S. Curtis.
Delaware Indians; Mr. Clark of Wyoming presented the following memorial and accompanying papers, praying that such legislation be enacted as will provide for the issuing to the Delaware Indians and their descendants land warrants as bounties, etc. '09(S) 25 p. 8°. (Add. Superintendent for price.) U. S., Supt. of Docs.

INDIANS.—*Continued.*

Densmore, F. Chippewa music. 45 c. Smith. Inst.

Dixon, R. B. Chimariko Indians and language. $1. Univ. of Cal.

Douglas-Lithgow, R. A. Dict. of American-Indian place and proper names in New England. $7. Salem Press.

Du Bois, C. G. Religion of the Luiseño Indians. $1.25. Univ. of Cal.

Dunn, J. P. True Indian stories. $1. Sentinel Pub. Co.

Eastman, C: A. *and Mrs.* E. G. Smoky Day's wigwam evenings. 60 c.—Wigwam evenings; Sioux folk tales retold. †$1.25. Little, B. & Co.

Eberhardt, C: C. Indians of Peru. Smith. Inst.

Emmons, G: T. Chilkat blanket. $2. Am. Museum.

Equalization of Creek allotments; hearing before the Committee on Indian Affairs, House of Representatives, Mar. 19, 1908. '08, [1909.] (Je) 52 p. 8°, pap. (Add. Superintendent for price.) U. S., Supt. of Docs.

Eshleman, H: F. Lancaster County Indians. $2. H: F. Eshleman.

Ethnological dict. of the Navaho language. $5. Franciscan Fathers (Ariz.)

Etzenhouser, R. Engravings of prehistoric specimens from Michigan. R. Etzenhouser.

Farabee, W: C. Some customs of the Macheyengas. 50 c. Davis Press.

Fewkes, J. W., *ed.* Journal of American ethnology and archæology. v. 5, Hopi songs, by B: Ives Gilman. **$2 net. Houghton M.

Flathead Indian reservation; acts rel. to reservation providing for opening to settlement, [etc.] (Add. Superintendent for price.) U. S., Supt. of Docs.

Gill, J: K., *comp.* Dictionary of the Chinook jargon. 50 c. Gill.

Goddard, P. E. Kato texts. 50 c. Univ. of Cal.

Gunnison, R. A. Condition of natives of Alaska. 10 c. U. S., Supt. of Docs.

Hare, W: H. Glimpses in the life of the Indian schools in South Dakota. (Add. author for price.) W: H. Hare.

Hastain, E., *comp.* Index to Choctaw-Chickasaw [Indians] deeds and allotments. $100. E. Hastain.

Hearings before the Senate Committee on Indian affairs on matters rel. to the Osage tribe of Indians, [Ap. 29, 1908-Jan. 26, 1909.] '09(My) 281 p. tabs., 8°, pap. (Add. Superintendent for price.) U. S., Supt. of Docs.

Heckewelder, J: G. E. Narrative of the mission of the United Brethren among the Delaware and Mohegan Indians. *$30 net. Burrows.

Hightower, J. Happy hunting grounds. $1.25. J. Hightower.

Howard, O. O. Famous Indian chiefs I have known. *$1.50 net. Century Co.

INDIANS.—*Continued.*

Hrdlicka, A. New examples of American Indian skulls with low forehead.—Physiological and medical observation among the Indians of southwestern United States and northern Mexico.—Tuberculosis among certain Indian tribes of the United States. (Add. Superintendent for price.) U. S., Supt. of Docs.

Hrdlicka, A. On the stature of the Indians of the Southwest and of northern Mexico. 50 c. Torch Press.

Indian depredations; hearings before the Committee on Indian Affairs, House of Representatives, Feb. 27-Mar. 4, 1908. '08, [1909.] (Je) 56 p. 8°, pap. (Add. Superintendent for price.) U. S., Supt. of Docs.

Indian Rights Association. Addresses del. at the 27th annual meeting, 1909. gratis. Indian Rights Assoc.

James, G: W. What the white race may learn from the Indian. *$1.50 net. Forbes.

James, J. A. Indian diplomacy and the opening of the Revolution in the West. 25 c. State Hist. Wis.

Johnston, C: H. L. Famous Indian chiefs. $1.50. L. C. Page.

Kellogg, L. P. Fox Indians during the French régime. 35 c. State Hist., Wis.

Kinnicutt, L. N. Indian names of places in Plymouth County, Massachusetts. $2. N: J. Bartlett.

Kroeber, A. L: Chumash and Costanoan languages. 35 c.—Ethnography of Cahuilla Indians. 75 c.—Mission record of the California Indians. 25 c.—Notes on Shoshonean dialects of southern California. 35 c. Univ. of Cal.

Leupp, F. E. Indian and his problem. $2 net. Scribner.

Libby, O. G. Typical villages of the Mandans, Arikara, and Hidatsa in the Missouri Valley, North Dakota. (Add. pubs. for price.) State Hist., N. D.

Lipps, O. H. The Navajos. *$1 net. Torch Press.

Littleheart, O. Lure of the Indian country. $1; 25 c. A. Abbott.

Long, F: J., *comp.* Dictionary of the Chinook jargon. 25 c. Lowman.

Lummis, C: F. Pueblo Indian folk-stories. $1.50. Century Co.

Lumpkin, W. Removal of the Cherokee Indians from Georgia. 2 v. Dodd.

McBeth, K. C. Nez Percés Indians since Lewis and Clark. *$1.50 net. Revell.

McClintock, W. Old North Trail; or, life, legends and religion of the Blackfeet Indians. $4 net. Macmillan.

McKenzie, F. A. Indian in relation to the white population of the United States. $1; 50 c. A. McKenzie.

McLaughlin, J. My friend the Indian. $2.50 net. Houghton M.

Meany, E. S., *comp.* Indian geographical names of Washington. 25 c. Hyatt-F.

Memorial of Choctaw Indians; against reopening the Choctaw and Chickasee rolls. U. S., Supt. of Docs.

INDIANS.—*Continued.*

Merriam, C. H., *ed.* Dawn of the world; myths and tales of Mewan Indians, California. $3.50. A. H. Clark.

Mission record of the California Indians. Univ. of Cal.

Mitchell, D. H. God's country. $6. Ebbert & R.

Morehouse, G: P. Kansa, or Kaw Indians, and their history. (Add. pubs. for price.) G: Martin.

Morton, J. S. White Cow and other tales; being some anecdotes about Indian orators of the territorial period of Nebraska. (Priv. pr.) P. Morton.

Navaho-English catechism of Christian doctrine for the use of Navaho children. $1. Franciscan Fathers.

Osage civilization fund; hearing on joint resolution no. 67. '09(My) 59 p. 8°, pap. (Not for sale.) U. S., Supt. of Docs.

Parkman, F. Conspiracy of Pontiac. 2 v. ea., *35 c. net; *70 c. net. Dutton.

Pepper, G: H., *and* Wilson, G. L. Hidatsa shrine and beliefs respecting it. 50 c. Am. Anthropological.

Revenues, etc., of the Choctaw, Chickasaw, Cherokee, Creek and Seminole tribes; letter from the Sec'y of the Interior transmitting, in response to Senate resolution and by direction of the President, a detailed statement. '09(My) 42 p. 8°, pap. (Add. Superintendent for price.) U. S., Supt. of Docs.

Roberts, G: E: T. Flying Plover: stories. $1. L. C. Page.

Robinson, D. Sioux Indians: hist. of Dakota or Sioux Indians. $2. Torch Press.

Ruyl, B. B. Little Indian maidens at work and play. †$1. Dutton.

Ryan, *Mrs.* M. E. M. Flute of the gods: [fiction.] **$1.50 net. Stokes.

St. Mary's Industrial School. Noble lives of a noble race. $2. St. Mary's Indust.

Sanders, H. F. Trails through western woods. $2 net. A. Harriman.

Sapir, E: Takelma texts. $2.50. Univ. of Penn.

Sapir, E:, *and* Dixon, R. B. Yana texts; together with Yana myths. $2.50. Univ. of Cal.

Scott, H. L. Testimony regarding trouble on the Navajo reservation. (Add. Superintendent for price.) U. S., Supt. of Docs.

Sharp, *Mrs.* A. G. Hist. of the Spirit Lake massacre and captivity of Miss Abbie Gardner. $1.25. A. G. Sharp.

Shaw, G: C. Chinook jargon and how to use it. (Add. pubs. for price.) Rainier Pr.

Short, P. Brief accts. of journeys in the western country, 1809-1812. Hist. and Phil. Soc., O.

Sparkman, P. S. Culture of the Luiseño Indians. 50 c. Univ. of Cal.

Speck, F. G. Creek Indians of Taskigi Town, Oklahoma. 55 c. Am. Anthropological.

INDIANS.—*Continued.*

Speck, F. G. Ethnology of the Yuchi Indians. $2.50. Univ. of Penn.

Spinden, H. J. Nez Percé Indians. 95 c. Am. Anthropological.

Starr, F: In Indian Mexico. *$5 net. Forbes.

Steele, Z. Indian captive: captivity and sufferings of Zadoc Steele. $2.50; $5. Huntting.

Sylvester, H. M. Indian wars of New England. In 3 v. $50; $15 net; $1000. W. B. Clarke.

Tanner, H: S: Pre-historic man: the first settlers on the western continent Oriental free masons. 25 c. H: S: Tanner.

Thomas, J. D., *comp. and ed.* The Osages; their names, allotment, numbers, ages and sex. 50 c. J. D. Thomas.

United States. *Dept. of the Interior. General Land Office.* Opening of Indian reservations. (Add. Superintendent for price.) U. S., Supt. of Docs.

United States. *Dept. of the Interior.* Lands of the Choctaw and Chickasaw Indians; letter from the Secretary of the Interior transmitting, by direction of the President and pursuant to Senate resolution no. 171, answers to certain questions therein. '09(My) 6 p. 8°, pap. (Add. Superintendent for price.)

United States. Investigation of Indian contracts. '10(Ag) 34 p. 8°. Gov. Pr. Off.

United States. *Office of Indian Affairs.* Indian treaties; message from the President of the United States, transmitting agreements concluded with certain Indian tribes for the commutation of their perpetual annuities under treaty stipulations, together with draft of a bill providing for the ratification of said agreements, etc. '10(Ap) 43 p. 8°, pap.

United States. *Office of Indian Affairs.* Instructions and regulations governing inspecting and investigating officials of the Office of Indian affairs, June 19, 1909. '09(S) 10 p. 8°. (Add. Superintendent for price.) U. S., Supt. of Docs.

United States. *Office of Indian Affairs.* Manual for Indian schools; brief discussion of principles and methods of education with reference to a few changes found desirable in the present system of Indian education. '10(S) 15 p. 8°. Gov. Pr. Off.

United States. Regulations governing the execution of leases of Indian allotments on the Umatilla Reservation in Oregon; approved by the Secretary of the Interior, Sept. 15, 1909. '09(D) 7 p. 8°. (Add. Superintendent for price.) U. S., Supt. of Docs.

United States. *Superintendent of Documents.* Indians; price list of public documents. gratis.

United States. *Treasury Dept.* Eastern Cherokees against the United States.

Waddell, W: The red-man; or, the destruction of a race. 85 c. W: Waddell.

INDIANS.—*Continued.*
Walker, T: B. Descriptive catalogue with reproductions of life-size bust portraits of famous Indian chiefs, great medicine men, [etc.;] with biograph. sketch of each and brief hist. of tribes they represent. (Not for sale.) Hahn.
Wall, O. G. Recollections of the Sioux massacre. $1.50. M. C. Russell.
Warman, C. Weiga of Temagami: [Indian tales.] $1.50; $2.50. Caldwell.
Waterman, T. T. Religious practices of the Diegneño Indians. 80 c. Univ. of Cal.
Wheeler, C. F. *and* J. R. Life of Scout Two Braids, (Thomas Stringer.) 25 c. Wood-B.
Williams, J: Redeemed captive: [account of the author's Indian captivity.] $2.50; $5. Huntting.
Williams, J: L. Our brother in red: synopsis of the Indian life. 25 c. Pub. Ho. of M. E. Ch., So.
Willson, *Mrs.* M. M. Seminoles of Florida. **$1.25 net. Moffat.
Wilson, E. N: Among the Shoshones. $1.25. Skelton.
Wright, R. C. Indian masonry. $1.50. Tyler Pub.
Wright, S. H. Adventures among the red Indians. $1.50 net. Lippincott.
Zeisberger, D: Hist. of northern American Indians. $2. Ohio Archæolog.
See also Aztecs;—Black Hawk war;—Flathead Co., Montana;—French and Indian war;—Grenville (Treaty of); — Incas; — Lincoln Co., Kan.; — Mayas;—Ouachita Valley;—Ripley;—Songs;—Sullivan's Indian campaign;—Tippecanoe (Battle of);—Yosemite Valley;—Yukon;—*also* Samoset, *Indian chief;* — Slocum, Francis; — *also* Narratives of captivities series;—Rochester reprints.
India's hurt. Forrest, W: M. 50 c. Chr. Pub. Co.
INDICATORS.
See Marine engineering;—Steam engine.
Indices to Diatessarica. Abbott, E. A. *$1.25 net. Macmillan.
INDICTMENTS.
Joyce, H. C. Treatise on the law governing indictments. $7.50. M. Bender.
INDIGESTION.
See Digestion.
Indispensable book. Moore, W. W: 75 c. net. Revell.
Individual and reality. Fawcett, E: D. *$4.25 net. Longmans.
Individual development of man. Beary, H. R. $1. Hartman Pub.
Individual evangelism. Beach, C: F. *$1 net. Allen, L. & S.
Individual recipes in use at Drexel Institute. Spring, H. M. 50 c. Winston.
Individual responsibility. Patch, F. W. **50 c. net. Moffat.
Individual singing exercises. *See* Abbott, Arth. J.
Individual sovereignty. Lorentz, A. M. $1. Mayhew.
INDIVIDUALISM.
Clews, H: Individualism versus socialism. (Add. author for price.) H: Clews.
Jordan, W: G: Crown of individuality. *$1 net. Revell.

INDIVIDUALISM.—*Continued.*
Kidd, B: Individualism and after: lecture. 35 c. Oxford Univ.
La Monte, R. R., *and* Mencken, H: L: Men *versus* the man. **$1.35 net. Holt.
Parsons, J: Each and all; study of the mutual influence of the individual and society. *$1.75 net. Sturgis & W.
See also Children;—Communism;—Social science;—Socialism;—Voluntaryism.
INDO-IRANIAN LANGUAGE.
Gray, L: H. Indo-Iranian phonology. $2. Macmillan.
INDO-IRANIANS.
See Aryans.
INDOOR GARDENING.
Barnes, P. T. House plants and how to grow them. $1.10. Doubleday, P.
Rexford, E. E. Indoor gardening. **$1.50 net. Lippincott.
Indoor target practice. Parker, J: H: $1. Arms and the Man.
INDUCTION COILS.
Armagat, H. Theory, design and construction of induction coils. *$2 net. McGraw.
Collins, A. F: Design and construction of induction coils. *$3 net. Munn.
Haller, G: F., *and* Cunningham, E. T. Tesla high frequency coil. $1.25. Van Nostrand.
Pike, J: Practical induction coil construction. 50 c. Spon.
Induction, development and heritability of fascinations. Knox, A. A. *See* Cannon, W. A. Topography of the *chlorophyll* apparatus.
Inductive method of learning stonework. Barr, J: W: $3.50. J: W: Barr.
Industrial and commercial geography. Morris, C: $1.10 net. Lippincott.
Industrial and personal hygiene. Kober, G: M. 50 c. President's Home Com.
INDUSTRIAL ARTS.
See Useful arts.
INDUSTRIAL CHEMISTRY.
See Chemistry.
INDUSTRIAL EDUCATION.
See Technical education.
Industrial efficiency. Shadwell, A. *$2 net. Longmans.
Industrial electrical measuring instruments. Edgcumbe, K. *$2 net. Van Nostrand.
INDUSTRIAL GEOGRAPHY.
See Geography.
Industrial handbooks. pap. Popular Mechanics.
—Windsor, *ed.* Mission furniture. pts. 1, 2. ea., 25 c.
INDUSTRIAL INSURANCE.
See Insurance.
INDUSTRIAL INSURANCE COMMISSION.
See Insurance.
Industrial organization. Woods, C. E. 3 v. $24. Woods.
Industrial problems. Richardson, N. A. $1. Kerr.
Industrial studies. Allen, N. B. 65 c. Ginn.
Industrial system. Hobson, J: A. *$2.50 net. Longmans.
INDUSTRIAL TRAINING.
See Technical education.

INDUSTRIES.
See Transportation;—Useful arts.

Indy, Vincent d'.
See D'Indy, Vincent.

INEBRIATES.
See Stimulants and narcotics;—Temperance.

Inequalities in the motion of the moon. Brown, E. W: *$2 net. Putnam.

INFALLIBILITY.
Simpson, W: J: S. Roman Catholic opposition to papal infallibility. $2 net. Young Churchman.

Infamous John Friend. Garnett, M. R. S. †$1.50. Holt.

Infant fairy-readers. See Longmans'.

Infant feeding by artificial means. Sadler, S. H. *$1.25 net. Dutton.

INFANT MORTALITY.
See Children.

INFANTILISM.
See Children.

INFANTRY.
Lloyd, E. M. Review of the history of infantry. *$2 net. Longmans.
Moss, J. A. Non-commissioned officers' manual. $1.50.—Privates' manual. 50 c. U. S. Infantry.
Norwood, J: W. Instructions for the infantry private of the National Guard. 25 c. Arms and the Man.
Norwood, J: W. Instructions for the non-commissioned officer. (Add. pubs. for price.) E: T. Miller.
Stewart, M. B. Hdbk. for non-commissioned officers of infantry. 50 c. Hudson.
See also Food.

INFANTS.
See Children.

Infatuation. Osbourne, L. †$1.50. Bobbs-M.

Infection experiments with *erysiphe cichoracearum*. Reed, G: A. 35 c. Univ. of Wis.

INFECTIOUS DISEASES.
Bordet, J. Studies in immunity. $6. **Wiley.**
Chapin, C: V. Sources and modes of infection. $3 net. Wiley.
Death in the kiss: treatise on infection. 25 c. B'way Pub.
Ehrlich, P. Experimental researches on specific therapeutics. *$1 net. Hoeber.
Ehrlich, P. Studies in immunity. $6. Wiley.
Emery, W. D'E. Immunity and specific therapy. *$3.50 net. Hoeber.
Hort, E. C. Rational immunization in the treatment of pulmonary tuberculosis and other diseases. *$1.50 net. Wood.
McCampbell, E. F. Lab'y methods for the experimental study of immunity. $1.25. Heer.
Muir, R. B., *and others*. Studies in immunity. *$3 net. Oxford Univ.
Wilson, J. C., *ed.* Infectious diseases. $6. Appleton.
Wright, *Sir* A. E: Studies on immunization and their application to the diagnosis and treatment of bacterial infections. **$5 net. Wood.
See also Contagion;—Fever;—Serum;—*also* names of diseases.

Inferences at bridge. Dalton, W: *40 c. net. Lippincott.

Infinite Presence. Gould, G: M. $1.50 net. Moffat.

INFINITESIMAL CALCULUS.
See Calculus.

Infinity, or nature's God. Duggan, F. J. $1.50. F. J. Duggan.

INFLAMMATION.
Adami, J: G: Inflammation; introd. to the study of pathology. *$1.50 net. Macmillan.

Influence of acidity of cream on the flavor of butter. Rogers, L. A. (Add. Superintendent for price.) U. S., Supt. of Docs.

Influence of alcohol and other drugs on fatigue. Rivers, W. H. R. *$1.70 net. Longmans.

Influence of Biblical texts on English law. Gest, J: M. (Priv. pr.) Buchanan.

Influence of bodily posture on mental activities. Jones, E. E. 50 c. Science Pr., (N. Y.)

Influence of Darwin on philosophy. Dewey, J: $1.40 net. Holt.

Influence of Friends on American education. Kelly, R. L. 25 c. Earlham Coll.

Influence of heredity on disease, with special reference to tuberculosis, cancer and diseases of the nervous system: discussion; introductory address, Sir W: S. Church; diseases of the nervous system, Sir W: R. Gowers; tuberculosis, Arth. Latham; cancer, E. F. Bashford; from the proceedings of the Royal Society of Medicine, 1909. '09(My22) il. Q. *$1.50 net. Longmans.

Influence of muscular and mental work on metabolism. Benedict, F. G. 15 c. U. S., Supt. of Docs.

Influence of sodium benzoate on the nutrition and health of man. United States. *Dept. of Agriculture*. $1. U. S., Supt. of Docs.

Influence of the Franciscan legend on Italian art. *See* Goff, *Mrs.* Rob. Assisi of St. Francis.

Influence of wealth in imperial Rome. Davis, W: S. $2 net. Macmillan.

Information of great value to newly married people. Tatum, J., *comp.* gratis. H. K. Palmer.

Ingalese, Isabella.
See Ingalese, R:

Ingalese, R:
Art of self-control; chapter from "The history and power of mind." '09(Ja23) c. 12°, $1. Occult.
— **and Isabella.**
From incarnation to re-incarnation. Rev. ed. '08(Je27) c. 8°, $2. Occult.

Ingalls, Helen Anabel.
Revel of the toys. '10(N12) c. O. $1.25. Ball Pub. Co.

Ingalls, Ja. Shelden.
Slaves to the trust. '08(D26) c. 16°, pap., 10 c. Social Justice.

INGALLS, John James.
Connelley, W: E. Ingalls of Kansas. $2. W: E. Connelley.

Ingalls, Wa. Renton.
Lead and zinc in the U. S. '08(Je13) c. il. 8°, *$4 net. Hill Pub.

Inge, W: Ralph, D.D.
Faith and its psychology. '10(F5) D. (Studies in theology.) *75 c. net. Scribner.

Ingelow, Jean.
Mopsa, the fairy. '10(N12) c. col. il. O. $1.50. Lippincott.

Poems; sel. and arr. by And. Lang. Pocket ed. '08(Je20) S. (Longmans' pocket lib.) *75 c. net. Longmans.

Inger, Archie J.
Revealed translation of John's Revelation. '09(Ag) 266 p. 12°, 50 c. A. J. Inger.

Ingersoll, Ernest.
Conquest of the North; authentic account of the finding of the North Pole, by Dr. Frederick A. Cook, Com. R. E. Peary, U. S. N., together with biographies of the explorers and a brief hist. of Arctic discovery. '09(N) c. 40 p. il. maps, 8°, pap., 10 c. C. S. Hammond.

Ingersoll, Rob. Green.
The ghosts. '10(Jl)) pap., 25 c. Farrell.
The gods. '10(Jl) pap., 25 c. Farrell.
The great infidels. '10(Jl) pap., 25 c. Farrell.

Humboldt and Heretics and heresies. '10 (Jl) pap., 25 c. Farrell.
Toward humanity; arr. by Anne Montgomerie Traubel. '08(N21) c. 24°, (Vest pocket ser.) 40 c.; flexible leath., 75 c.; pap., 25 c. T: B. Mosher.

INGERSOLL, Robert Green.
Furlong, J: R. Is Ingersoll in hell? $1. Boulder Pub.

Ingersoll lectures. *See* Bigelow, W: S.

INGHAM, Samuel Delucenna.
Ingham, W: A. Samuel Delucenna Ingham. (Priv. pr.) W: A. Ingham.

Ingham, W: Armstrong.
Samuel Delucenna Ingham. '10(F) 15 p. por. 8°. (Priv. pr.) W: A. Ingham.

Ingle, Herbert.
Elem. agricultural chemistry. '09(F20) D. (Griffin's technological handbooks.) *$1.50 net. Lippincott.

Ingleby, Clement Mansfield, comp.
See Munro, J. J., *ed.*

Ingleby, Leonard Cresswell.
Oscar Wilde. '08(O10) por. O. *$3.50 special net. Appleton.

Inglehart, Mary, comp.
Catchwords of worldly wisdom; little book of epigrams. '09(O16) c. S. (Upward and onward ser.) bds., *75 c. net; ooze cf., *$1.25 net, boxed; limp cf., *$1 net. McClurg.

Inglis, Alex. Ja.
See Baker, C: McCoy.

Inglis, Ja. S.
Illustrated catalogue of oil and water color paintings by Dutch, French, English, American and Italian artists belonging to the estate of the late James S. Inglis, to be sold at unrestricted public sale on [March 9th and 10th, 1910]; sale will be conducted by Mr. Thomas E. Kirby, of the American Art Association, managers. '10(My) 175 p. il. 8°, $1; $5. Am. Art. Assoc.

Ingpen, Mrs. Ada de la Mare, comp. and ed.
Women as letter-writers: collection of letters. '10(Ap2) pors. S. $1.25 net. Baker & T.

Ingram, Bp. Arth. Foley Winnington.
Early English colonies in America; with a preface by the Bishop of London. '08 (Je13) *$2 net. Young Churchman.

Into the fighting line; sermons. '10(D31) 12°, $1.50 net. Whittaker.

Joy in God. '10(Ja8) *60 c. net. Whittaker.

Love of the Trinity. '08(S12) 12°, *60 c. net. Whittaker.

Mysteries of God. '10(N12) D. $1. Young Churchman.

Ingram, Eleanor Marie.
Flying Mercury. '10(N12) col. il. O. $1.50. Bobbs-M.

Game and the candle. '09(O16) c. il. D. †$1.50. Bobbs-M.

Ingram, Harry M., ed.
See New York [State.] Penal law.

Ingram, J: H.
True Chatterton. '10(D24) il. por. 8°, $3 net. Scribner.

Ingram, T: Darlington, M.D.
Plan of a direct election law for determining true primary and final elections by the will of a concurring majority of all the voters concerned and at one direct voting. '09(My22) c. 8°, pap., 15 c. T: D. Ingram.

INGRES, Jean Auguste Dominique.
Finberg, A. J. Ingres. 65 c. net. Stokes.

Inherent law of life. Kleinschrod, F. $1.25 net. Macmillan.

INHERITANCE.
See Chancery;—Heredity.

Inheritance in canaries. Davenport, C: B. 80 c. Carnegie.

Inheritance in silkworms. Kellogg, V. L. $1. Stanford Univ.

Inheritance of characteristics in domestic fowl. Davenport, C: B. $4.50. Carnegie.

INHERITANCE TAX.
See Taxation.

Initiation and its results. Steiner, R. $1.25. Macoy.

INITIATIVE.
See Referendum.

INJECTORS.
Kneass, S. L. Practice and theory of the injector. $1.50. Wiley.

INJUNCTIONS.
American Federation of Labor, Wash., D. C. Buck's Stove and Range Co. injunction suit and contempt proceedings. 25c. Trades Unionists.
Charnock, S. Injunctions in labor disputes and the remedy. 10 c. S. Charnock.
Gompers, S: Injunction data filed by S: Gompers. 25 c. U. S., Supt. of Docs.
Joyce, H. C. Treatise on the law relating to injunctions. In 3 v. $19. M. Bender.

INJUNCTIONS.—*Continued.*
Knaus, H: Judicial usurpation: open letter to Congress showing this in the injunctions in labor disputes. (Add. author for price.) H: Knaus.
Lewson, J: Monopoly and trade restraint cases, incl. conspiracy, injunction, [etc.] 2 v. (Add. pubs. for price.) Flood.
Schaffner, M. A. Effect of the recent boycott decisions. 25 c. Am. Acad. Pol. Sci.
See also Trade-unions.

Injured in the course of duty. Hard, W: gratis. Ridgway.

INJURIES.
See Accidents;—Damages;—Mines and mining;—Negligence;—Railroads.

Injuries and diseases of the knee-joint. Bennett, *Sir* W: H: *$2 net. Wood.

Injuries of nerves. Sherren, J. *$2 net. Wood.

INK.
Ruxton, P., Inc. Printing inks. $2. Ruxton.

INLAND NAVIGATION.
American Academy of Political and Social Science. American waterways. $1. Am. Acad. Pol. Sci.
Atlantic Deeper Waterways Association. 1st annual convention, Baltimore, 1908. gratis. Atlantic Deeper Waterways.
Atlantic Deeper Waterways conference held at Philadelphia, Nov. 18-20, 1907; rept. of the proceedings. gratis. Book Pr.
Burk, A. B., *and* Schaff, W. H., *comps.* Project of the Atlantic Deeper Waterways Association. gratis. A. B. Burk.
Griffin, A. P. C., *comp.* Library of Congress list of works rel. to deep waterways from the Great Lakes to the Atlantic. 25 c. U. S., Supt. of Docs.
Hepburn, A. B. Artificial waterways and commercial development; (with a history of the Erie Canal.) **$1 net. Macmillan.
Hill, H: W. Hist. review of waterways and canal construction in New York state. $5; $4. Buffalo Hist. Soc.
List of works rel. to deep waterways from the Great Lakes to the Atlantic Ocean, with some other related works, books, articles in periodicals, U. S. documents; comp. under the direction of Appleton Prentiss Clark Griffin. '08, [1909.] (My) 59 p. 4°, pap. (Add. Superintendent for price.) U. S., Supt. of Docs.
Long, C. E. Lake steam-manship and guide to the marine board examinations. *$2 net. C. E. Long.
Meese, W: A: Abraham Lincoln: incidents in his life relating to waterways. 40 c. W: A: Meese.
Meyer, H. H: B., *comp.* Select list of references on inland waterways of Europe. Engineer Sch.
National Rivers and Harbors Congress. Proceedings of the 3d annual convention. gratis. Ebbert & R.
New York, Brockton and Boston canal; its importance to Mass. industries. (Add. pub. for price.) E. B. Mellen.
Peabody, R. S. Holiday study of cities and ports. $1. Boston Soc. Architects.

INLAND NAVIGATION.—*Continued.*
Quick, J: H. American inland waterways. **$3.50 net. Putnam.
Rochester, N. Y. Chamber of Commerce. Waterways development. gratis. Wegman.
United States. *Steamboat Inspection Service.* Pilot rules for the Great Lakes and their connecting and tributary waters. '09(Ag) 19 p. il. 8°. (Add. Superintendent for price. U. S., Supt. of Docs.
United States. *Steamboat Inspection Service.* Pilot rules for the inland water of the Atlantic and Pacific coasts. (Add. Superintendent for price.)
United States. *Steamboat-Inspection Service.* Pilot rules for the rivers whose waters flow into the Gulf of Mexico and their tributaries and the Red River of the North; ed. March 20, 1909. '09(N) 20 p. il. 8°. (Add. Superintendent for price.) U. S., Supt. of Docs.
White, J. Josiah White's history; [canal navigation and use of anthracite coal in Penn.] (Add. pubs. for price.) Lehigh Coal.
See also Canals;—Hudson river;—Rivers.

Inland voyage. *See* Stevenson, Rob. L: Travels with a donkey.

INLAND WATERWAYS.
See Inland navigation.

Inman, Rev. Herbert Escott-.
Quest of Douglas Holms. '09(Ja30) il. D. $1.50. Warne.
Wulnoth the wanderer: a story of King Alfred of England. '08(O10) c. il. O. $1.50. McClurg.

Inn of the Silver Moon. Viele, H. K. $1.25. Duffield.

Inner circle ser. S. Un. Soc. C. E.
—Elliott. Brook in the pasture. 25 c.

Inner consciousness. Atkinson, W: W. 50 c. Advanced Thought.

Inner life. Bjerregaard, C. H. A. $2. Theo. Pub. Co.

Inner life of the United States. Vay de Vaya and Luskod, *Count.* *$4 net. Dutton.

Inner life ser. D. Putnam.
—Dresser. Message to the well. **$1.25 net.

Inner shrine. King, B. †$1.50. Harper.

Inner teachings of the philosophies and religions of India. Atkinson, W: W. *$1 net. Yogi Pub.

Innes, Norman.
Lonely guard. '09(O2) front. D. *$1.25 net. Jacobs.
My lady's kiss. '08(N21) c. il. $1.50. Rand, McN. & Co.

INNOCENT III., *Pope,* (Giovanni Lothario Conti.)
See Catholic church.

Innocent murderers. Johnston, A. W: $1.50. Duffield.

INNS.
Dodd, *Mrs.* A. B. B. In and out of three Normandy inns. *$2.50 net. Little, B. & Co.
Drake, S: A. Old Boston taverns and tavern clubs. 50 c. W. A. Butterfield.

INNS.—*Continued.*
Hackwood, F: W: Inns, ales, and drinking customs of old England. *$2.50 net. Sturgis & W.
Shelley, H: C: Inns and taverns of old London. $3. L. C. Page.
Wood, S. G. Taverns and turnpikes of Blandford, 1733-1833. *$2 net. S. G. Wood.
See also Hotels.
INNS OF COURT, London, Eng.
Headlam, C. Inns of Court, [London.] *$2 net. Macmillan.
Ringrose, H. Inns of Court. *$2 net. Lawyers' Co-op.
Innumerable company. Jordan, D: S. *50 c. net. Am. Unitarian.
Ino, pseud.
See Hogan, Wilber Fisk.
INORGANIC CHEMISTRY.
See Chemistry.
Inquirer's guide. Canevin, J. F. R. 10 c.; per 100, $5. Cath. Church Extension.
INQUISITION.
Adler, E. N. Auto de fé and Jew: [sketches of the effects of the Inquisition in Spain and Portugal.] $1.75. Oxford Univ.
Lea, H: C: Inquisition in the Spanish dependencies. **$2.50 net. Macmillan.
Vacandard, E. The Inquisition. *$1.50 net. Longmans.
INSANITY.
Barrus, C. Nursing the insane. **$2 net. Macmillan.
Beers, C. W. The after care of the insane. gratis. C. W. Beers.
Beers, C. W. Mind that found itself. $1.50 net. Longmans.
Church, A., *and* Peterson, F: Nervous and mental diseases. *$6.50 net. Saunders.
Dana, C: L. Text-book of nervous diseases and psychiatry. *$5 net; *$6 net. Wood.
Gatewood, L. C. An experimental study of dementia præcox. 75 c. Psychological Review.
Gierlich, N., *and* Friedmann, M. Studies in paranoia. $1. Journal Nervous Disease.
Gregory, C: L. Alcoholism and insanity. $1.50. Von Boeckmann-J.
Jung, C. Psychology of dementia præcox. $2. Journal Nervous Disease.
Patrick, H. T., *and* Mix, C: L:, *eds.* Nervous and mental diseases. $1.25. Year Bk.
Potts, C: S. Nervous and mental diseases. *$2.50 net. Lea.
Prince, M., *ed.* My life as a disassociated personality. 50 c. Badger.
Rogues de Fursac, M. H. J. P. Manual of psychiatry. $2.50. Wiley.
Savage, G: H:, *and* Goodall, E. Insanity and allied neuroses. $2.75 net. Funk.
Schofield, A. T. Christian sanity: [religious mania.] *$1 net. Armstrong.
Sidis, B. Psychopathological researches. *$3 net. Badger.
Sommer, H. J. Index of 1180 post-mortems of the insane; State Hospital for the Insane, Norristown, Pa. (Add. pubs. for price.) State Hospital Insane.

INSANITY.—*Continued.*
Stoddart, W. H. B. Mind and its disorders. *$4 net. Blakiston.
Storring, G. Mental pathology in its relation to normal psychology. *$2.75 net. Macmillan.
Talmey, M. Psyche; concise and easily comprehensible treatise on the elements of psychiatry and psychology for students of medicine and law. $2.50. Medico-Legal.
Tredgold, A. F. Mental deficiency. *$4 net. Wood.
White, W: A. Outlines of psychiatry. $2. Journal Nervous Disease.
Younger, E. G. Insanity in every-day practice. $1.25 net. Chic. Med. Bk.
See also Brain;—Hospitals;—Hysteria;—Idiocy;—Medical jurisprudence;—Mind and body;—Nervous system.
INSCRIPTIONS.
Armstrong, H: H. Autobiographic elements in Latin inscription. 40 c. Macmillan.
Pier, G. C. Inscriptions of the Nile monuments. **$5 net. Putnam.
Prentice, W: K. Greek and Latin inscriptions. **$10 net. Century Co.
Tolman, J. A., *jr.* Study of the sepulchral inscriptions in Buecheler's "Carmina Epigraphic Latina." 75 c. net. Univ. of Chic.
See also Epitaphs;—Letters.
Inscrutable woman. Baron, E: D: $1.50. B'way Pub.
INSECTS.
Banks, N. Catalogue of the nearctic *Hemiptera-Heteroptera.* $1. Am. Entomol.
Banks, N. Directions for collecting and preserving insects. (Add. Superintendent for price.)—List of works on North American entomology. Gov. Pr. Off.
Bertelli, L. Prince and his ants. $1.35 net. Holt.
Bremner, O. E. Destructive insects and their control. gratis. State Horticultural.
Doane, R. W. Insects and disease. $1.50 net. Holt.
Felt, E. P. Control of flies and other household insects. 15 c. N. Y. State Educ.
Foot, C. M. Insect wonderland. $1.25 net. Lane.
Grinnell, F., *jr.* Quaternary myriopods and insects of California. 10 c. Univ. of Cal.
Hambleton, J. C. Genus corizus. 25 c. Univ. of O.
Hayward, R. Classification of the families of the *Coleoptera* of America, north of Mexico. 50 c. Am. Entomol.
Hopkins, A. D. Insect injuries to the wood of living trees. Gov. Pr. Off.
Howard, L. O. Economic loss to the people of the U. S. through insects that carry disease. 10 c. U. S., Supt. of Docs.
Kellogg, V. L. American insects. **$5 net.—Insect stories. **$1.50 net. Holt.
Marks, J. A., *and* Moody, J. Little busybodies: life of crickets, ants, bees, beetles and other busy bodies. 75 c. Harper.

INSECTS.—*Continued.*

New York State. *Education Dept.* Twenty-fifth rept. of the state entomologist on injurious and other insects of the state of N. Y. 35 c. N. Y. State Educ.

Pearson, R. H. Book of garden pests. *$1 net. Lane.

Pierce, W: D. Monographic revision of the twisted winged insects comprising the order *Strepsiptera* Kirby. Gov. Pr. Off.

Redi, F. Experiments on the generation of insects. $2. Open Court.

Selous, E. Wonders of the insect world. 75 c. Lippincott.

Smith, J: B. Our insect friends and enemies. **$1.50 net. Lippincott.

Some insects injurious to truck crops. Gov. Pr. Off.

Stebbins, F. A. Insect galls of Springfield, Massachusetts, and vicinity. $1.50. Springfield Mu. of Nat. Hist.

Thomas, E: Some British butterflies and insects. *$2 net. Doran.

United States. Entomology Bureau; bulletins, circulars and technical series relating to insects; Agriculture Dept., U. S. A.; for sale by the Superintendent of Documents. '09(N) 24 p. 8°, pap., gratis.

United States. *Superintendent of Documents.* Entomology Bureau; bulls., circulars, [etc.]

Weed, C. M. Farm friends and farm foes. 90 c. Heath.

Westell, W. P. Insect book. *$1 net. Lane.

See also Ants;—Bees;—Beetles;—Birds;—Butterflies;—Cattle tick;—Crickets;—Firefly;—Fleas;—Flies;—Lady beetles;—Mites;—Mosquitoes;—Moths;—Parasites;—San José scale;—Weevil;—Zoology.

Inside history of the White House. Willets, G. $1. Chr. Herald.

Inskip, G: D.

New manual of squares and logarithms from 0' to 100' advancing by 32ds of inches; logarithms of natural numbers from 0 to 10,000; logarithmic trigonometrical functions for every minute of the quadrant and the auxiliary trigonometrical functions S and T for the calculation of the logarithms of sines, tangents and co-tangents of the angles from 0 to 3600 seconds, [etc.;] natural sines and co-sines. '09(D11) c. 12°, $3. M. C. Clark.

INSOMNIA.
See Sleep.

Inspectors' handbook of reinforced concrete. Ballinger, W. F. $1. Engineering News.

INSPIRATION (*of the Bible*).
See Bible;—Higher criticism.

Inspiration of poetry. Woodberry, G: E: *$1.25 net. Macmillan.

Inspiration of prophecy. Joyce, G. C. $1.40. Oxford Univ.

Inspired millionaires. Lee, G. S. $1.25. Mt. Tom Press.

Instinct and health. Hutchinson, W. **$1.20 net. Dodd.

Institute for Colored Youth, Cheyney, Pa. Applied domestic science: daily menus for the school year and dietary study for October; three well balanced and wholesome meals daily at 21 cents per day. '09(Jl) c. 48 p. 8°, 50 c. Inst. Colored Youth.

INSTITUTE OF FRANCE.
See French Academy.

Institute song book. Bryant, L. 30 c. Barnes.

Institute songs. McCollins, J. E. 15 c. Am. Bk.

Institutes of education. Laurie, S. S. *$1.90 net. Macmillan.

Institutes of English grammar. Brown, G. 80 c. Wood.

Institutes of Gaius. *See* Gaius.

Institutional church and the public library. Keogh, A. (Add. author for price.) A. Keogh.

Institutional history of Virginia in the seventeenth century. Bruce, P. A. $6 net. Putnam.

Instruction of Ptah Hotep; and the Instruction of Ke Gemni, the oldest books in the world; tr. by Battiscombe G. Gunn. '08 (Je6) 16°, (Wisdom of the East.) *40 c. net. Dutton.

Instructions for the non-commissioned officer. Norwood, J: W. (Add. pubs. for price.) E: T. Miller.

Instructor entertainment ser. 12°. F. A. Owen.

—Little plays and exercises. 35 c.

INSTRUMENTAL MUSIC.
See Church music;—Flute;—Music;—Orchestral music;—Organ and organists;—Pianoforte;—Violin;—Violoncello.

Instrumentation. Prout, E. 75 c. Ditson.

Instruments of the modern orchestra. Schlesinger, K. 2 v. $6 net. Scribner.

INSULATION.
See Refrigeration.

INSURANCE.

Allen, F. W. T. Insurance enactments. $10. Law Reporting.

American School of Correspondence. Insurance and real estate methods. $1.50. Am. Sch. Corr.

Bonham, A. N. Misconceptions of life insurance policy holders. $3. A. N. Bonham.

Brown, J. N. Estimates and agents' companion. $1: $1.50. Rough Notes.

Cox, R. L. Geographical distribution of the investments of life insurance companies.—Life insurance and legislation in 1909.—Taxation of life insurance in the U. S. ea., gratis. Assoc. Life.

Cox, R. L. Impropriety of taxing returns to life insurance policy-holders. gratis. R. L. Cox.

Critchell, R. S. Recollections of a fire insurance man; incl. experiences in U. S. Navy during the Civil War. $1.25. R. S. Critchell.

Dawson, M. M. Comparative reserve tables.—Survivorship annuity tables. ea., $25. Chronicle Co.

Deitch, G. A. Digest of insurance cases. v. 1-20; with general index. 6 v. $36.—Digest of insurance cases. v. 20-22. ea., $3. Rough Notes.

INSURANCE.—*Continued.*

De Leon, E. W., *comp.* Manual of liability insurance. $2. Spectator.

Dilg, H. W., *comp.* Liability investigator's hdbk. $1.50. Spectator.

Dryden, J: F. Addresses and papers on life insurance. (Priv. pr.) Prudential.

Eke, A. J. Elements of insurance; guide to the principles of fire, accident, marine and life insurance. 50 c. Pitman.

Fire insurance in New England for ten years, 1899-1908. $3.50. Standard Pub. Co.

Fire insurance laws, taxes and fees; cont. a digest of the statutory requirements in the U. S. and Canada, [etc.;] also a compilation of county and municipal taxes and fees; rev. to Aug. 1, 1909. '09(O); rev. to Aug. 15, 1910. '10(O) c. O. shp., ea., $5. Spectator.

Fouse, L. G. Recent developments in the life insurance business. 15 c. Am. Acad. Pol. Sci.

Frankel, L. K., *and* Dawson, M. M. Workingmen's insurance in Europe. $2.50. Charities Pub.

Frost, T: G. Treatise on guaranty insurance and compensated suretyship. $6. Little, B. & Co.

Gow, W: Marine insurance. $1.10 net. Macmillan.

Graham, W: J. Romance of life insurance. $1.50. World To-day.

Griffin, A. P. C., *comp.* Library of Congress list of works rel. to government regulations of insurance, U. S. and foreign countries.—Library of Congress select list of references on workingmen's insurance. (Add. Supt. for price.) U. S., Supt. of Docs.

Handy chart of casualty, surety and other miscellaneous insurance companies in America; showing their financial standing and business for the ten years ending Dec. 31, 1907. '08, [1909.] (My) c. 36 p. 8°, 25 c. Spectator.

Harbaugh, C: H. Causes of disability as applied under accident and health insurance policies. $6. Spectator.

Hard, W:, *and others.* Injured in the course of duty. gratis. Ridgway.

Henderson, C: R. Industrial insurance in the United States. *$2 net. Univ. of Chic.

Hess, H. M. Philosophy and methods of operation of the analytic system for the measurements of relative fire hazard. gratis. H. M. Hess.

Hine, C: C. Book of forms (fire insurance). $2. C: C. Hine.

How to sell more fire insurance; 67 business getting plans used and improved by 38 agents. '09, [1910.] (Mr) 128 il. 12°, gratis, with subscription to *System.* System.

Hubbard, E. Here then is a preachment entitled, a business necessity. 10 c. Roycrofters.

In the front office; plans and suggestions for writing more fire insurance. $2. Rough Notes.

INSURANCE.—*Continued.*

Johnson, E. C. Our best mutual friend; life insurance explained and its principles simplified. 75 c. E. C. Johnson.

Landis, A., *and* Eldridge, G. D. Tables based upon the National Fraternal Congress table of mortality and various rates of interest. $25. C. C. Hine.

Law, F. E. Method of deducting liability rates. $1. Spectator.

Law Reporting Company. Insurance enactments of 1907. $10. Law Reporting.

Lewis, F. W. State insurance. *$1.25 net. Houghton M.

Lure of inadequate rates. 10 c. Fraternal Monitor.

McCune, W: G: Fire insurance agency for profit. $1. Northern Pub.

McKitrick, R. Accident insurance for workingmen. 25 c. Wisconsin Free Lib.

Matthews, W: D. Manual of inspections; ref. book for use of fire underwriters. $3. Insurance Field.

New York [State.] Insurance law; by Amasa J. Parker, jr. $3. Banks.

New York [State.] New York insurance law. $2.50. Banks & Co.

Niblack, W: C. Abstracters and title insurance, 1908. *$2 net. Callaghan.

Price, W: H. Life insurance reform in New York. 75 c. Am. Economic Assoc.

Ramsey, M. E. Practical life insurance examinations. **$1.25 net. Lippincott.

Reform in life insurance taxation. gratis. Assoc. Life.

Rept. of the Industrial Insurance Commission to the Governor of Illinois. gratis. J. A. Rose.

Richards, G: Selection of cases on the law of insurance. $3.50.—Treatise on the law of insurance in all its branches. $6.75. Banks.

Singer, I., *ed.* International insurance encyclop. In 4 v. v. 1, $6; $8; $10; v. 2, 3, 4, ea., $12; $15; $18; per set, in advance, $35; $45; $55. Am. Encyclopedic.

Spectator Co. Annual and deferred dividends. $1.50. Spectator.

Steeb, G: V. Special agents' and adjusters' handbooks. $1.50. Spectator.

United States. *Dept. of the Interior. U. S. Geolog. Survey.* Fire tax and waste of structural materials in the United States.

United States. Fire insurance laws, taxes and fees. (Add. pubs. for price.) Spectator.

Webb, E. G: Comparisons simplified; or, how to select the "best" life insurance company. $2.—Comparisons simplified; unique and comprehensive insurance statistics. $3. E. G: Webb.

Webb, E. G:, *comp.* Comparisons simplified: dealing with life insurance companies. $3. Bassette.

Wessels, E. J. Struggle everlasting. *$3 net. E. J. Wessels.

Who is who in insurance? $5; $7. Singer.

Wolfe, S. H. Examination of insurance companies. $3. Insurance Press.

INSURANCE.—*Continued.*
Young, M. Science and art of writing life insurance. $2. N. Y. Insurance.
Zartman, L. W:, *ed.* Yale readings in insurance. In 2 v. ea., *$2.25 net. Yale Univ.
See also Benefit societies;—Equitable Life Assurance Soc.;—Fertilizers;—Fire; — Longevity; — Sulphuric acid;—*also* names of states.

Insurance engineering ser. il. 8°. Insurance Press.
—MacKnight. Fertilizer and acid plants. 50 c.

INSURGENCY.
See Biography.

Insuring bank deposits. Frame, A. J. 15 c. A. J. Frame.

Insurrections. Stephens, J. *40 c. net. Macmillan.

INTEGRAL CALCULUS.
See Calculus.

INTEGRAL EQUATIONS.
See Equations.

Integrals of mechanics. Lester, O. C. 80 c. Ginn.

INTELLECT.
See Brain;—Insanity;—Mind;—Psychology.

Intellectual pup. Wood, H. E. 50 c. H. Wood.

"Intelligent labor." Woods, C. A. (Add. pubs. for price.) State Co.

INTEMPERANCE.
See Temperance.

Inter-Collegiate Association of Amateur Athletes of America. Constitution, by-laws and laws of athletics adopted by the convention held at New York Feb. 28, 1891, as amended in convention Feb. 27, 1892-Feb. 26, 1910. '10(Je11) S. (Spalding's athletic lib.) pap., 10 c. Spalding.

Inter-Collegiate Association of Amateur Gymnasts of America. Constitution, by-laws and records of the Association, 1899-1909; ed. by P. R. Carpenter; rev. according to a vote of the Association. '09(D18); 1899-1910. [1910.] (D) c. il. pors. 16°, (Spalding's athletic lib.) pap., ea., 10 c. Am. Sports.

Intercollegiate debates. Pearson, P. M., *ed.* $1.50. Hinds.

INTEREST (*on money*).
Bankers and merchants perpetual maturity guide, for the purpose of quickly determining the accurate number of days between any two given dates—both inclusive. $5. Bankers Pub. Co.
Fisher, J: I. Added interest tables, 1909. $5—Fisher bank instalment system: tables for instalment loans at bank discount. $25—20th century tables. $2.50. J: I. Fisher.
Hurtt, J: M. Addenda to dividend law. 50 c. J: H. Lee.
Hurtt, J: M. Dividend law and some of its applications. $2.50. J: M. Hurtt.
Massie, J. Essay on the governing causes of the natural rate of interest. (Reprint of economic tracts.) subs., per set of 4 tracts, *$2 net. Johns Hopkins.
Potter, W. W. Law of interest in Michigan. $2.50. Drake Law Bk.
Robinson, J. W. Robinsonian building-loan interest tables. $5. J. W. Robinson.
See also Investments;—Loans;—Usury.

Interest of America in international conditions. Mahan, *Captain* A. T. $1.50 net. Little, B. & Co.

INTERIOR DECORATION.
See Furniture;—House decoration;—Rugs;—Wall decoration.

Interior painting. Maire, F: 60 c. Drake.

Interiors beautiful. Keith, M. L., *comp.* $1. M. L. Keith.

Interloctury motions in the United States Patent Office. Stoddard, E. J. $1. E. J. Stoddard.

Interlude (An). Barton, C. J. $1.50. C. J. Barton.

Interludes. Jones, T. S. *50 c. net. G: W: Browning.

Interludes and poems. Abercrombie, L. *$1.25 net. Lane.

Interludes, ethical, social and theological. Whiton, J. M. *$1.40 net. Whittaker.

Intermedial spelling blank. Smith, L. D. *60 c. net. Macmillan.

Intermediate and grammar methods. Rocheleau, W: F. 2 v. $6.50 Interstate Sch. Corr.

Intermediate course in Isaac Pitman phonography. 75 c. Blythebourne Pub.

Intermediate course of laboratory work. Hanson, E: K. *$1.20 net. Longmans.

INTERNAL COMBUSTION ENGINES.
See Engines.

INTERNAL REVENUE.
See Taxation.

Internal secretion and the principles of medicine. Sajous, C: E. de M. *$6 net. Davis.

International (The) accountants' manual; or, twentieth century bookkeeping and business practice. '10(Jl2) c. il. 4°, $3. Business Man's Pub.

International art ser. *See* Brentano's.

International Bureau of American Republics, Washington, D. C. Argentine Republic. '09(Ag); Bolivia. '09(Ag); Brazil. '09 (S); Colombia. '09(S); Costa Rica. '09 (S); Cuba. '09(Ag28); Dominican Republic. '09(S); Ecuador. '09(S); Guatemala. '09(S); Haiti. '09(S); Honduras. '09(S); Mexico. '09(S); Nicaragua. '09 (S); Panama. '09(Ag28); Paraguay. '09 (S); Salvador. '09(S); Uruguay. '09 (S); Venezuela. '09(S); il. 8°, ea., pap. (Add. pubs. for price.) Int. Bu. Am. Republics.

International Bureau of American Republics, Washington, D. C. Cotton, the most widely used staple in the world; (repr. of an article from the Monthly Bulletin of the International Bureau of American Republics, April, 1909.) '09, [1910.] (Mr) 599-613 p. il. 8°. Gov. Pr. Off.

International Bureau of American Republics. Washington, D. C. List of Latin American history and description in the Columbus Memorial Library, [Washington, D. C.] '08 (F22) 8°, pap., gratis. Int. Bu. Am. Republics.

International Bureau of the American Republics, Washington, D. C. List of publications published or distributed by the International Bureau of American Republics. '09(N20) 8°, gratis. Int. Bu. Am. Republics.

International Bureau of the American Republics, Washington, D. C. Municipal organizations in Latin America; [articles repr. from the *Monthly Bulletin* of the International Bureau of American Republics.] no. 1, Buenos Aires, Argentine Republic; no. 2, Lima, Peru; no. 3, Rio de Janeiro, Brazil; no. 4, Santiago de Chile. '09(N) il. 8°. (Add. pubs. for price.) Int. Bu. Am. Republics.

International Bureau of American Republics, Washington, D. C. Rubber and its relatives; (repr. of an article from the Monthly Bulletin of the International Bureau of American Republics, December, 1908.) '09, [1910.] 990-1010 p. il. 8°, pap. Gov. Pr. Off.

International Bureau of American Republics, Washington, D. C. Tentative programme for the fourth Pan-American conference to be held at Buenos Aires, Argentina, May, 1910. '09(S18) O. pap., gratis. (Also in Spanish.) Int. Bu. Am. Republics.

International Bureau of American Republics, Washington, D. C., *comp.* Chile: a hdbk. '09(Ag7) il. fold. map, O. $1. Int. Bu. Am. Republics.

International cable directory of the world, 1908. 10th annual ed. '08(D19) $15. Int. Cable.

International Catholic lib.; ed. by J. Wilhelm, D.D. In 11 v. v. 9. '08(F15); v. 2, 4, 8, 10, 11. '08, [1910.] (Je) 12°, ea., $2 net. Benziger.

V. 2, Hist. of the books of the New Testament, by L'Abbé Jacquier, in 2 v., v. 2, The synoptic Gospels; v. 4, Catholic church, the Renaissance, Protestantism, by Alfred Banderillart; v. 8, Great schism of the West, by L. Salembier; v. 9, Churches separated from Rome; v. 10, Finding of the cross, by Louis de Combes; v. 11, Temporal sovereignty of the Popes, by L. Duchesne.

International Claim Agency, Pittsburgh, Pa. Next of kin, heirs at law, legatees, etc.; list of families who have been advertised for to claim money and property in Great Britain and all parts of the world. [2d ed.] '09(Jl) c. 249 p. 8°, $1. Int. Claim.

International Commission on Zoological Nomenclature. Opinions rendered by the International Commission on Zoological Nomenclature. In 2 v. v. 1, Opinions 1-25. '10(S) 61 p. O. pap. Smith. Inst.

International Conference on State and Local Taxation. State and local taxation; third international conference, Louisville, Ky., Sept. 21-24, 1909; addresses and proceedings. '10(Je) 387 p. 8°, $2. Int. Tax.

International Congress for the History of Religions. Transactions of the third International Congress. '09(Ja23) 2 v., il. figs. Q. $6.75. Oxford Univ.

International Congress of Arts and Science. International university lectures. Cambridge ed. In 12 v. '10(Ja22) c. il. pors. 8°, per set, $49.50. Univ. Alliance.

International Congress on Tuberculosis. Transactions of the sixth International Congress on Tuberculosis, Washington, Sept. 28 to Oct. 5, 1908, with an account and catalogue of the tuberculosis exhibition, Washington, Sept. 21 to Oct. 12, 1908. 8 v. '08, [1909.] (N) il. tabs., (partly fold.,) 4°, pap., per set, $10. Nat. Assoc. Tuberculosis.

INTERNATIONAL CO-OPERATION.
See **Political science.**

International Correspondence Schools, Scranton, Pa. Tratado de aritmética mercantil, arreglado especialmente para los estudiantes de las Escuelas internacionales por correspondencia. [1910.] (N) c. 321 p. 8°. Int. Textbk.

International Correspondence Schools, Scranton, Pa. Tratado elemental de matemáticas y mecánica, arreglado especialmente para los estudiantes de las Escuelas internacionales por correspondencia. [1910.] (Jl) c. 287 p. il. 8°. (Priv. pr.) Int. Correspondence.

INTERNATIONAL COUNCIL OF WOMEN.
Aberdeen, I. M., *Countess of.* Our lady of the sunshine and her international visitors; [acct. of visit of International Council of Women to Canada.] 50 c. net. Dutton.

International critical commentary on the Holy Scriptures of the Old and New Testament; ed. by C: A. Briggs, D.D., S. Rolles Driver, D.D., and Alfred Plummer, D.D. [v. 15,] Ecclesiastes, by G: Aaron Barton; [v. 16,] Esther, by Lewis Bayles Paton, '08(D5); [v. 17,] Amos and Hosea, by W. R. Harper; [v. 18,] Psalms. 2 v. [1910.] (Je); [v. 19,] Critical and exegetical commentary on Genesis, by J: Skinner; [v. 20,] Critical and exegetical commentary on the Book of Chronicles, by E: Lewis Curtis, D.D., and Albert Alonzo Madsen. '10(Je25) c. O. v. 15-16, ea., **$2.25 net; v. 17-20, ea., $3 net. Scribner.

International dictionary. *See* Webster, Noah.

International directory of booksellers [1909] and bibliophile's manual; incl. lists of the public libraries of the world, publishers, book collectors, learned societies and institutions, universities and colleges; also bibliographies of book and library catalogues, concordance, bookplates, etc.; ed. by Ja. Clegg. [8th ed.] '10(Ja1) D. $2. Dodd.

International documents; collection of international conventions and declarations of a law-making kind; ed., with introd. and notes, by E. A. Whittuck. '08(Jl11); Reissue, with additions. '09(O16) O. ea., *$3.50 net. Longmans.

International education ser.; ed. by W. T. Harris. 12°, **$1.50 net. Appleton.
—Blow. Educational issues in the kindergarten.

International exchange. Margraff, A. W: $5. Int. Exchange.

INTERNATIONAL FISHERIES COMMISSION.
See **Fish and fishing.**

International geography. Mill, H. R., *ed.* **90 c. net. Appleton.

International incidents for discussion in conversation classes. Oppenheim, L. *$1 net. **Putnam.**

International Institute of Agriculture. International crop-reporting service; rept. presented by Dr. Traugott Müller, delegate of the German empire, adopted by the General Assembly Dec., 1909, concerning the establishment of an international crop-reporting service for the staples of agriculture for 1910-1911, etc. '10(Ap) 28 p. 8°. Gov. Pr. Off.

INTERNATIONAL INSTITUTE OF AGRICULTURE, Rome, Italy.
Lubin, D: International Institute of Agriculture at Rome; letter. (Add. Superintendent for price.) U. S., Supt. of Docs.

INTERNATIONAL LANGUAGES.
See Esperanto;—Ro.

INTERNATIONAL LAW.
Barclay, *Sir* T: Problems of international practice and diplomacy, with special reference to the Hague conferences. $6.50. Boston Bk.
Baty, T: International law. *$2.75 net. **Longmans.**
Davis, G: B. **Elements of international** law. $3. **Harper.**
Hall, W: E: Treatise on international law. $6. Oxford Univ.
Hogan. A. E. Pacific blocade. $2. Oxford Univ.
Holland, T: Erskine. Valedictory retrospect, (1874-1910.) 35 c. Oxford Univ.
International documents: collection of international conventions and declarations. *$3.50 net. Longmans
Internoscia, J. New code of international law. $12. Int. Code.
Lawrence, T: J. Principles of international law. $3 net. Heath.
Oppenheim, L. International incidents for discussion in conversation classes. $1 net. Putnam.
Takahashi, S. International law applied to the Russo-Japanese war. *$8 net. Bank.
Walker, T: A. Manual of public international law. *$2.50 net. Macmillan.
Westlake, J: International law. pt. 2. *$3 net. Putnam.
Wilson, G. G. Hdbk. of international law. $3.75. West Pub.
Wilson, G: G., *and* Tucker, G: F. International law. $2.50. Silver.
See also Ambassadors;—Arbitration (international); — Citizenship; — Consuls;—Diplomacy;— Hague Peace Conference;—Monroe doctrine;— Naturalization; — Peace; — Spanish-American war;—Wars.

International library. vs. 7-13. '08(O24) T. leath., *75 c. net; pap., *25 c. net. Stokes.
Contents: 7, Goblin market and other poems, Rosetti; 8, Les chefs-d'œuvre lyriques de Pierre de Ronsard et son école; 9, Les chef-d'œuvre lyriques de Alfred de Musset; 10, Alladine and Palomides, Maeterlinck: 11 Les chef d'œuvre lyriques de André Chénier; 12, Le cid, Corneille; 13, Intérior, Maeterlinck.

International lib.; ed. by Edn. D. Mead. 12°. Ginn.
—Bloch. Future of war. 50 c. net.
—Bridgman. World organization. 50 c. net.
—Dodge. War inconsistent with the religion of Jesus Christ. 50 c. net.
—Sumner. Addresses on war. 50 c. net.
—Walsh. Moral damage of war. 90 c. net.
—Warner. Ethics of force. 50 c. net.

International lib. of social science. 12°, $1. Kerr.
—Fitch. Physical basis of mind and morals.

International (The) library of technology. [Architectural lib. 10 v.] Textbks. for engineering professors and trades; or, for those who desire information concerning them. '10(O22) c. '09. il. plans, O. ea., ¾ mor., $5. Int. Textbk.

International (The) library of technology. [Chemistry lib. 11 v.] Series of textbks. for persons engaged in the engineering professions and trades; or, for those who desire information concerning them. '10(D3) c. il. plans, O. ea., ¾ mor., $5, boxed. Int. Textbk.

International (The) library of technology. [Navigation lib. 8 v.] Series of textbks. for persons engaged in the engineering professions and trades; or, for those who desire information concerning them; cont. numerous practical examples and their solutions. '10(N19) c. il. plans, O. ea., ¾ mor., $5, boxed. Int. Textbk.

International manuscripts; [facsimiles of royal historical and diplomatic documents from the originals in the British Museum; with descriptions and translations by G: F. Warner.] 3 pts. '10(D) per set, $1.50 net. Brentano's.

International medical annual, 1909. 27th year. '09(O) il. 8°, *$3.50 net. **Treat.**

International mercantile letters. Pitman, *Sir* I: 85 c. Pitman.

International modern language ser. See Ginn's.

International motor cyclopædia; year book. '08(My16) c. il. 8°, $10. Int. Motor.

INTERNATIONAL PEACE.
See Peace.

International peace lib. D. Ginn.
—Sully. Great design of Henry IV. **50 c. net.

International Reform Bureau. Patriotic studies for men's leagues, young people's societies and civic clubs; incl. extracts from bills, acts and documents of U. S. Congress rel. to moral and social reforms, 1888-1908. 20th anniversary ed. '08(S) 294 p. il. 4°, 75 c.; pap., 35 c. Int. Ref. Bu.

International regulations of the fisheries on the high seas. *See* Fryer, C: E.; Olsen, O. T.; Stevenson, C: H.

International relations of the Chinese Empire. Morse, H. B. $6 net. Longmans.

International School of Peace pamphlet ser. pap., per 100, $3. Int. Sch. Peace.
—Brewer. Mission of the U. S. in the cause of peace.
—Foster. War not inevitable.
—Mead, E. D. Literature of the peace movement.—Results of the two Hague conferences.
—Mead, L. T. A. Educational organizations promoting international friendship.
—Ralston. Some supposed just causes of war.
—Waste of militarism.

International scientific ser. See Appleton's.

International short stories. Patten, W:, *ed.* 3 v. $2.10. **Collier.**

International Studio. *See* Hind, C: Lewis.—Holme, C:—Studio year book.

International Sunday-school lessons. Lesson handbook, 1909: a concise commentary on the International Sunday-school lessons. '08(N7) c. maps, nar. T. (Berean ser.) *20 c. net; leath., *25 c. net. Eaton & M.

International system of magnetic (alchemic) therapeutics. Clymer, R. S. gratis. R. C. Clymer.

International system of ophthalmic practice; ed. by W. L. Pyle. 8°. Blakiston.

—Darier. Therapeutics. $4.

International theological lib.; ed. by C: A. Briggs and Stewart D. F. Salmond. O. Scribner.

—Adeney. Greek and Eastern Churches. *$2.50 net.

—Clarke. Christian doctrine of God. *$2.50 net.

—Cunningham. Christianity and social questions 75 c. net.

—Driver. Introd. to the literature of the Old Testament. *$2.50 net.

International World Missionary Conference.

Gairdner, W. H. T. Echoes from Edinburgh. $1 net. Revell.

Internationalism. Crafts, W. F. 40 c.; 25 c. Int. Ref. Bu.

Internoscia, Jerome.

New code of international law. '10(D) c. $12. Int. Code.

In 3 columns English, French and Italian.

Inter-ocean hunting tales. Randolph, E. F. $1. Forest.

Interplay. Harraden, B. †$1.50. Stokes.

Interpretation of ancient Greek literature. Murray, G. G: A. 35 c. Oxford Univ.

Interpretation of evolution. Sorley, W: R. v. 4. 60 c. Oxford Univ.

Interpretation of life. Mars, G. C. **$3 net. Appleton.

Interpretation of radium. Soddy, F: * $1.75 net. Putnam.

Interpretation of the Bible. Gilbert, G: H. **$1.25 net. Macmillan.

Interpretation of the character of Christ to non-Christian races. Robinson, C: H: *$1.20 net. Longmans.

Interpretation of topographic maps. Salisbury, R. D. (Add. Superintendent for price.) U. S., Supt. of Docs.

"Interpretations" of the bishops and their influence on Elizabethan episcopal policy. Kennedy, W. M. 50 c. Longmans.

Interpreter's commentary on the New Testament. *See* Abbott, Lyman.

Interrupted friendship. Voynich, *Mrs.* E. L. B. $1.50. Macmillan.

Interrupted kiss. Marsh, R: $1.50. Cassell.

Inter-Scholastic Athletic Association of the Middle Atlantic States. Official hdbk. [1910;] ed. by W: A. Joiner and Edn. B. Henderson. '10(Je11) S. (Spalding's athletic lib.) pap., gratis. Am. Sports.

Interstate commerce.

See Commerce; — Commercial law; — Express; — Railroads.

Interstate transportation.

See Transportation.

Interview (An). Church, D. W. $1. B. Carey.

Intestinal autointoxication. Combe, A. *$4 net. Rebman.

Intestines.

Bosanquet, W. C., *and* Clogg, H. S. Stomach, intestines and pancreas. *$4 net. Wood.

Deaver, J: B., *and* Ashhurst, A. P. C. Surgery of the upper abdomen: stomach and duodenum. v. 1. *$5 net. Blakiston.

Kemp, R. C. Diseases of the stomach and intestines. *$6 net. Saunders.

Schmidt, A. Examination of the function of the intestines by means of the test diet. *$1.50 net. Davis.

See also Autointoxication;—Constipation;—Digestion.

Intimate life of Alexander Hamilton. Hamilton, A. M. $3.50 net. Scribner.

Intimate recollections of Joseph Jefferson. Jefferson, *Mrs.* E. P. **$3.50 net. Dodd.

Intimations of immortality. *See* Wordsworth, W:

Into the fighting line. Ingram, A. F. W. $1.50 net. Whittaker.

Into the night. Greene, F. N. **$1.20 net. Crowell.

Into the primitive. Bennet, R. A. $1.50. McClurg.

Into the Yukon. Edwards, W: S. Jennings.

Intoxicated ghost. Bates, A. †$1.50. Houghton M.

Intoxicating drinks and drugs in all lands and times. Crafts, W. F. 75 c. Int. Ref. Bu.

Intoxicating liquors.

See Liquors.

Intracellular pangenesis. De Vries, H. $3. Open Court.

Introducing Corinna. Kirkland, W. *$1 net. Revell.

Introduction to Christian missions. Johnson, T: C. 75 c. Presb. Pub.

Introduction to Shakespeare. MacCracken, H: N. 90 c. net. Macmillan.

Introduction to the rarer elements. Browning, P. E. *$1.50 net. Wiley.

Introduction to the sources relating to the Germanic invasions. Hayes, C. H. $1.50. Longmans.

Introduction to the study of biology. Kirkaldy, J. W. $1.60. Oxford Univ.

Introductions to notable poems. Mabie, H. W. $2. Dodd.

Intruding angel. Marriott, C: $1.50. Lane.

Intrusion of Jimmy. Wodehouse, P. G. $1.50. W. J. Watt.

Intuitive perception. Hodge, W: H: $1.50. Wickersham.

Invaders. Morgan, J. L. $1.50. Fenno.

Invariants of quadratic differential forms. Wright, E. J. *75 c. net. Putnam.

Inventa Italorum. Clark, A. C. $3. Oxford Univ.

Invention of the roller flour mill. Lawson, P. V. 25 c. State Hist., Wis.

Inventions.

Burns, E. E. Story of great inventions. $1.25. Harper.

Marks, G: C. Inventions, patents and designs. *$1 net. Van Nostrand.

INVENTIONS.—*Continued*
Smith, G. B. How to succeed as an inventor. 10 c. Inventors.
Wright, F. B. Inventions, how to protect, sell and buy them. 25 c. Spon.
See also Patents;—Trade-marks.

Inventory of the contents of Mount Vernon, 1810; with pref. note by Worthington Chauncey Ford. '10(F5) facsims., 8°. (Priv. pr.) Univ. Press.

INVERTEBRATES.
See Crustaceans; — Insects; — Jellyfish;—Marine zoology;—Mollusks;—Paleontology; —Reptiles; —Zoology.

Investigation of flow through large submerged orifices and tubes. Stewart, C. B. pt. 1. 25 c. Univ. of Wis.
Investigation of the hydraulic ram. Harza, L. F. 25 c. Univ. of Wis.
Investigations in currency and finance. Jevons, W: S. *$3 net. Macmillan.

INVESTMENTS.
Babson, R. W. Business barometers: textbook on fundamental statistics for investors. $2; $3.—Investments: what and when to buy. $2. R. W. Babson.
Commercial and Financial Chronicle. Hdbk. of securities; Jan., 1910; description; income; prices; dividends; comp. by the *Commercial and Financial Chronicle.* '10 (Mr) c. 192 p. obl. 16°, $1. Dana.
Hall, H: How money is made in security investments. $1.50. H: Hall.
Henry, G: G. How to invest money. **75 c. net. Funk.
Moody, J: Investor's primer. *$1.50 net. Moody Corporation.
Mortimer, F. C. Investment of trust funds. 75 c.; $2. R. C. Ayres.
Nicholas, F. C. Mining investments and how to judge them. *$1.50 net. Moody Corporation.
Poor's handbook of investors' holdings. $15. Poor's.
Reynolds, M. M. Investor's catechism. $1. Moody's Mag.
Robinson, J. W. Robinsonian bond and investment tables. $5. J. W. Robinson.
Rollins, M. Money and investments. $2 net. Estes.
Ruhl, O. Rationale of investment in zinc mining. 25 c. Mining News.
Sprague, C: E. Amortization: guide to the ready computation of the investment value of bonds. 50 c.—Text-book of the accountancy of investment. $4. C: E. Sprague.
See also Bonds;—California;—Corporations;—Insurance; — Interest; —Loans;—Mines and mining; — Mortgages; — Railroads; — Stocks; — Wall Street.

Investor's catechism. Reynolds, M. M. $1. Moody's Mag.
Investors' library. See Moody's.
Invisible glory. Wilkinson, G: H. *$2 net. Young Churchman.
Invisible island. Macdonald, A. $1.25. Caldwell.
Invisible links. Lagerlöf, S. O. L. †$1.50. Little, B. & Co.
Invisible prince. *See* Lang, Andrew, *ed.*
Invisible world about us. Rogers, L. W. 10 c. Theosophical Bk.

Invitation serieuse aux habitants des Illinois, by Un Habitant des Kaskaskias; repr. in facsimile from the original ed. published at Philadelphia in 1772; with introd. and bibliographical notes by Clarence W. Alvord and Clarence E. Carter. '08(Ap18) 8°, pap., $2.50. Club for Colonial Reprs.
Invocation of saints. Stone, D. *40 c. net. Longmans.
Involuntary chaperon. Cameron, M. †$1.50. **Harper.**
Inward light. Hall, H. F. **$1.75 net. Macmillan.

Ioannis Saresberiensis. *See* John *of Salisbury.*

IONIA.
See Orient (The).

Ionic surgery in the treatment of cancer. Massey, G: B. $3. Chatterton.
Ionization in closed vessels. Strong, W: W. 25 c. Johns Hopkins.
Iorio, Adrian J., comp.
My school life; [school or college memory book.] '10(D) 8°, $1; mor., $2.50. Caldwell.

Iowa. Reference work on justice practice, by Leonard B. Robinson. '08(Je) c. 55+609 p. 8°, *$6.50 net. Callaghan.
Iowa. State Historical Society. Proceedings of the fiftieth anniversary of the constitution of Iowa, held under the auspices of the State Historical Society of Iowa; ed. by B: F. Shambaugh. '08(Je13) il. pors. 8°, $3. State Hist., Ia.
Iowa. Statistical abstract of Iowa railroads: (supp. to railroad assessment rept.;) comp. by Arth. H. Davison and Almer U. Swan. '07, [1908.] (Jl) 63 p. 8°, pap., gratis. A. H. Davison.
Iowa. Supplement to the code of Iowa; ed. by C. N. Jepson. '07, [1908.] (My.) c. 226+1552 p. 4°, $3. W. C. Hayward.
Iowa. *Supreme ct.* Digest of decisions from the organization of the territory, [etc.;] (Emlin McClain.) v. 1, 2. '08, [1909.] (Ja); v. 3 (Mr); v. 4 (Ap) c. O. (McClain's new Iowa digest.) (Add. pubs. for price.) Callaghan.
Iowa. *Supreme ct.* Repts.; (W. W. Cornwall.) v. 134. '07, [1908.] (Mr); v. 135 (Ag); v. 136 (D); v. 137. '08, [1909.] (Mr); v. 138 (Je); v. 139 (O); v. 140. '09, [1910.] (F); v. 141, 142 (Je); v. 143 (N) c. O. shp., ea., $3. Flood.

IOWA.
Bender, W. H. Iowa. *20 c. net. Macmillan.
Buffum, H. S. Federal and state aid to education in Iowa. $1. Univ. of Ia.
Downey, E. H. Hist. of labor legislation in Iowa. $2. State Hist., Ia.
Garden, R. I. History of Scott Township, Mahaska Co., Iowa. [Also] War reminiscences. [Also] Did the buffalo ever inhabit Iowa? $1.25. Shockley Bros.
Hayes, S: Justice practice of Iowa. $4.25. Flood.
Huebinger, M. Map and guide for river to river road. 50 c. Iowa Pub.
Kearny, S. W. The 1820 journal of Stephen Watts Kearny. *$1 net. Missouri Hist.

IOWA.—*Continued.*

Lazell, F: J: Some summer days in Iowa. $1.50. Torch Press.

Riggs, J: F. Next step in school legislation; annual address del. before the Iowa State Teachers' Assoc., Dec. 3, 1908. (Add. author for price.) J: F. Riggs.

Shambaugh, B: F. Second report on the public archives, [Iowa.] (For private distribution.) Hist. Dept. of Ia.

Spooner, J: C. Beeman versus Jackman: [suit in equity brought under the provisions of the prohibitory law of Iowa.] (Add. author for price.) J: C. Spooner.

Stanton, G. S. "When the wildwood was in flower": [ranch life in Iowa.] *$1 net. J. S. Ogilvie.

Toof, M. D. Assessor's manual for Iowa. 25 c. M. D. Toof.

Ware, E. F. Lyon campaign in Missouri: hist. of the First Iowa Infantry [in the Civil War.] $1. Crane.

Weaver, S. M. Iowa, its constitution and laws. *40 c. net. C: E. Merrill.

Wood, J. Iowa justice's form book and constable's guide. $1.50. Fidlar & C.

See also Amana Community;—Clinton Co.;—Mississippi Valley;—Pella;—Sioux County;—Spirit Lake.

Iowa biographical ser.; ed. by B: F. Shambaugh. pors. 8°, $2. State Hist., Ia.
—Gregory. Samuel Freeman Miller.
—Parish. John Chambers.
—Pelzer. Augustus Cæsar Dodge.
—Reid. Thomas Cox.

Iowa economic history ser. O. **State Hist., Ia.**
—Downey. Hist. of labor **legislation** in Iowa. $2.

Iowa State University. Constructive and rebuttal speeches of the representatives of the State University of Iowa in the intercollegiate debates. 2 v. '10(My14) pors. O. pap., ea., $1. Forensic.

Iowa studies in language and literature. **8°,** pap., 50 c. **Univ. of Ia.**
—Flom. Hist. of **Scandinavian studies** in Am. universities.

Iowa University. College of Medicine. Contributions from the Dept. of Pathology and Bacteriology, (incl. the Bacteriological Laboratory of the State Board of Health.) v. 1. '08, [1909.] (Mr) il. tabs., 8°, (Univ. of Ia., bull.; new ser.) pap., 25 c. Univ. of Ia.

Iphigenia in Tauris. *See* Euripides.

IPOMOEA.
See Botany.

IPSWICH, Mass.

Waters, T: F. Candlewood; an ancient neighborhood in Ipswich. $1.50. Salem Press.

Waters, T: F. Old Bay road from Saltonstall's Brook and Samuel Appleton's farm. 25 c. Ipswich Hist.

Ipswich Historical Society pubs. 8°. Ipswich Hist.
—Waters. Old Bay road. 25 c.

"Ira, Alfr.," pseud.
See Grimm, Albert Friedrich Wilhelm.

Ireland, Archbp. J:
Church and modern society: lectures and addresses. 2 v. '08(Ag8) 8°, *$3 net. Herder.

Ireland, Mrs. Mary Eliza Haines.
Hilda's mascot; tale of "Maryland, my Maryland." '10(D3) c. il. D. $1. Saalfield.
Otterbrook people. '08(Mr14) c. S. 35 c. Un. B. Pub.

IRELAND.

Bagwell, R: Ireland under the Stuarts and during the interregnum. In 2 v. $10.50. Longmans.

Barlow, J. Irish idylls. $2 net. Dodd.

Black's [A. & C.] guide to Ireland. $1.75. Macmillan.

Brown, S. J. Reader's guide to Irish fiction. $1.25 net. Longmans.

Carson, *Mrs.* N. B. **From Irish castles to** French châteaux. **$1.50 net.** **Small.**

Corkey, A. Truth about Ireland. 75 c. Schockley Bros.

Curtis, W: E. One Irish summer. **$3.50 net. Duffield.

Dease, A. Beckoning of the wand: sketches of a lesser-known Ireland. $1. Herder.

Emmet, T: A. Ireland under English rule. 2 v. **$5 net. Putnam.

Falkiner, C. L. Essays rel. to Ireland. $3.50. Longmans.

Finerty, J: F. Ireland. 2 v. *$2.50 net. Dodd.

Fitzgerald, T. W. H., *comp. and ed.* Ireland and her people. In 10 or 12 v. v. 1, 2. ea., $3; $5; $9. Fitzgerald Bk.

Frazar, *Mrs.* M. D. Pract. guide to Great Britain and Ireland. In 2 v. **$1 net. Small.

Graves, A. P. Irish fairy book. $1.50. Stokes.

Green, A. S. A. S. Making of Ireland and its undoing, 1200-1600. *$2.50 net. Macmillan.

Hall, A. M. F. Tales of Irish life and character. $1.75 net. McClurg.

Harvey, W:, *comp.* Irish life and humor in anecdote and story. *$1.50 net. Lippincott.

Hinkson, *Mrs.* K. T. Ireland. *75 c. net. Macmillan.

Hull, E. Boys' Cuchulain; heroic legends of Ireland. $1.50 net. Crowell.

Jones, P. F. Shamrock land. **$2 net. Moffat.

Joyce, P. W. Concise history of Ireland. $1.25.—English as we speak it in Ireland. $1 net. Longmans.

Joyce, P. W., *ed.* Old Irish folk music and songs. *$3.50 net. Longmans.

Lennox, P. J. Early printing in Ireland. (Add. pubs. for price.) Cath. Univ.

Loomis, C: B. Just Irish: [humorous account of travels in Ireland.] $1; $1.50 net. Badger.

Lynd, R. Home life in Ireland. $2.50 net. McClurg.

Macdonough, M. Irish life and character. *$1.50 net. Whittaker.

Madden, D. H. Some passages in the early history of classical learning in Ireland. $1. Longmans.

IRELAND.—*Continued.*
Mason, R. Song lore of Ireland. $2 net. Wessels & B.
O'Brien, W: Olive branch in Ireland. $3.25 net. Macmillan.
O'Donnell, F. H. M. Hist. of the Irish parliamentary party. 2 v. $5 net. Longmans.
O'Donnell, W: C:, *jr.* Around the Emerald Isle. $1. Roxburgh.
O'Neill. Irish folk music. $2. Regan.
O'Sheridan, M. G. Gaelic folk tales. 60 c. M. G. O'Sheridan.
Paul-Dubois, L. F. A. Contemporary Ireland. *$2 net. Baker & T.
Plummer, C: Vitae sanctorum Hiberniae. In 2 v. $9.75. Oxford Univ.
Plunkett, *Sir* H. Ireland in the new century. *40 c. net. Dutton.
Redmond, J: E: Home rule speeches of John Redmond, M.P. $2.50 net. Stokes.
Reynolds, J. B. Ireland; elem. rational geography. 50 c. net. Macmillan.
Rhys, *Sir* J: Notes on the Coligny calendar. $4.20. Oxford Univ.
Scott-James, R. An Englishman in Ireland. $2 net. Dutton.
Shoemaker, M. M. Wanderings in Ireland. **$2.50 net. Putnam.
Somerville, E. A. O., *and* Ross, M., *pseud.* All on the Irish shore.—Further experiences of an Irish R. M.—Some experiences of an Irish R. M.—Some Irish yesterdays. ea., $1 net. Longmans.
Sutherland, H. Ireland yesterday and today. $1. North American, (Phil.)
White, J. Hand loom linen weavers of Ireland. (Add. pubs. for price.) Irish Hand-Woven.
See also Church architecture;—Connemara;—Irish poetry;—Music;—Scotch-Irish in the U. S.;—Wexford.

Irenaeus testimony to the fourth Gospel. Lewis, F. G. *50 c. net. Univ. of Chic.
Irene Liscomb. Lamb, *Mrs.* M. E. J. $1.50. B'way Pub.
Irene of the Mountains. Eggleston, G: C. †$1.50. Lothrop, L. & S.

Ireton, Rob. Emmett.
Central bank; [concise statement of facts in relation to our present currency system.] '10(F26) c. 12°, $1.60. A. Stumpf.

Irish, Marie.
Favorite song pantomimes; 26 of our old and favorite songs pantomimed and arranged to be produced by one or more persons. '09(N6) c. D. pap., 30 c. Flanagan.
Patriotic celebrations: monologues, recitations, motion songs, song pantomimes, exercises, drills and dialogues for all patriotic occasions, suitable for all ages. [1910.] c. 120 p. il. 12°, 25 c. T. S. Denison.

—, Denton, Clara J., Smith, Laura R., and others.
Thirty new Christmas dialogues and plays. '09(N20) c. D. pap., 30 c. Flanagan.

IRISH CROCHET LACE.
See Lace.

Irish ecclesiastical architecture. Champneys, A. C. $7.50 net. Macmillan.
Irish fairy book. Graves, A. P. $1.50. Stokes.
Irish folk music. O'Neill, F. $2. Lyon & H.; McClurg.
Irish idylls. Barlow, J. $2 net. Dodd.
Irish in the American Revolution. Haltigan, J. $2. Haltigan.
Irish life and character. Macdonough, M. *$1.50 net. Whittaker.
Irish life and humor in anecdote and story. Harvey, W:, *comp.* *$1.50 net. Lippincott.
Irish melodies. Moore, T: 50 c.; 75 c. Dutton.
Irish poems. Graves, A. P. 2 v. *$1.50 net; *$2.25 net. Macmillan.

IRISH POETRY.
Cooke, J:, *ed.* Dublin book of Irish verse. $1.75; $2.50; $3.50. Oxford Univ.

Irish precursor of Dante. Boswell, C. S. *$3.50 net. Scribner.
Irish R. M. ser. See Somerville, E. A. O., *and* Ross, M.
Irish toasts. Na Gael, S., *pseud.* 50 c. Caldwell.
Irish wit and humor: anecdote biography of Swift, Curran, O'Leary and O'Connell. '08 (D5) c. S. 50 c. Pustet.
Irma in Italy. Reed, H. L. †$1.25. Little, B. & Co.

"Iron, Ralph," pseud.
See Schreiner, *Mrs.* Olive.

IRON.
American Iron & Steel Association. Directory to the iron and steel works of the U. S. $12.—Canadian supp. (Add. pubs. for price.) Am. Iron and Steel.
Armes, E. Story of coal and iron in Alabama. $5. Ala. Chamber of Com.
Blair, A. A. Chemical analysis of iron. **$4 net. Lippincott.
Cole, M. Tempering steel; annealing and case hardening iron. 10 c. Sampson.
Cushman, A. S. Preservation of iron and steel. 10 c. U. S., Supt. of Docs.
Cushman, A. S., *and* Gardner, H: A. Corrosion and preservation of iron and steel. $4 net. McGraw-H.
Forsythe, R. Blast furnace and the manufacture of pig iron. $3. D: Williams.
Greenwood, W: H: Iron: its sources, properties and manufacture. $1. McKay.
Heess, J: K. Practical methods for the iron and steel works chemist. $1. Chemical.
Kelly's directory of the engineers and iron and metal trades and colliery proprietors, [Great Britain.] *$10 net. Kelly.
Macfarlane, W. Laboratory notes on iron and steel analyses. *$2.50 net. Longmans.
Newland, D: H., *and* Hartnagel, C. A. Iron ores of the Clinton formation in New York state. 35 c. N. Y. State Educ.
Sang, A. Corrosion of iron and steel. $1. McGraw-H.
Smith, J. R. Story of iron and steel. **75 c. net. Appleton.
Spencer, A. C. Magnetite deposits of the Cornwall type in Pennsylvania. (Add. Superintendent for price.) U. S., Supt. of Docs.

IRON.—*Continued.*
Stansbie, J. H. Iron and steel. *$2 net. Van Nostrand.
Talbot, A. N. Tests of cast-iron and reinforced concrete culvert pipe. pap., gratis. Univ. of Ill.
Turner, T: Metallurgy of iron. *$1.25 net. Lippincott.
United States. *Dept. of Commerce and Labor. Bureau of Manufactures.* British iron and steel industry and Luxemburg iron and steel wages by C: M. Pepper; with suppl. article on English chain manufacture by Alb. Halstead. '09 (Je) 37 p. 8°, pap. (Add. Superintendent for price.) U. S., Supt. of Docs.
United States. *Dept. of the Interior. Geological Survey.* Iron ore produced and manufactured in United States, 1908; letter from the Secretary of the Interior, inclosing reply from the Director of the Geological Survey; with information requested by Senate resolution no. 289, 60th Congress, 2d session, relative to iron ore. '09(Je) 9 p. tabs., 8°, pap. (Add. Superintendent for price.)
United States. Iron and steel products; estimates of increases and reductions in duties of H. R. 1438. (Add. Superintendent for price.) U. S., Supt. of Docs.
West, T: D. Metallurgy of cast iron. $3. Gardner Pr.
See also Blacksmithing;—Foundries;—Furnaces;—Magnetism; — Painting (*Mechanical*); — *also* Pennsylvania.

Iron arrow head. *See* Sue, Marie Joseph Eugène.
Iron cardinal. McCabe, J. *$3.50 net. J: McBride.
Iron collar. *See* Sue, Marie Joseph Eugène.
Iron Heel. London, J. †$1.50. Macmillan.
Iron (The) lord. Crockett, S: R. 75 c. Cupples & L.
Iron muse. Underwood. J: C. $1.25 net. Putnam.
Iron ore resources of the world; summary comp. upon the initiative of the Executive Committee of the XI. International Geological Congress, Stockholm, 1910, with the assistance of geological surveys and mining geologists of different countries; ed. by the general secretary of the congress; accompanied by an atlas of 42 maps. '10(Jl9) il. 8°, $20. Lemcke.
Iron pincers. *See* Sue, Marie Joseph Eugène.
Ironmaster (The). Ohnet, G. 50 c. Warne.

"Ironquill," pseud.
See Ware, Eug. Fitch.

Irons, Geneviève.
Maiden up to date: a novel. '08(N21) 8°, *$1.60 net. Herder.
Torn scrap book: talks and tales illustrative of the "Our Father"; with preface by Rev. Rob. Hugh Benson. '08(Ap25) D. $1. Longmans.

Ironside, J:
Red symbol. '10(Ap23) c. il. D. $1.50. Little, B. & Co.

IROQUOIS INDIANS.
See Indians.

Irresistible current. Lowenberg, *Mrs.* I. $1.25. B'way Pub.
Irresolute Catherine. Jacob, V. †$1. Doubleday, P.

IRRIGATION.
Audenried, W: G., *jr.* Irrigation. (Add. pub. for price.) Rep. Bank Note.
Bligh, W: G: Practical design of irrigation. *$6 net. Van Nostrand.
Bowie, A: J., *jr.* Practical irrigation: its value and cost. *$3 net. McGraw.
Buckley, R. B. Facts, figures and formulas for irrigation engineers. $4.25. Spon.
Buffum, B. C. Arid agriculture. $1.50. B. C. Buffum.
Elliott, E. C. G: Pract. farm drainage. $1.50. Wiley.
Fortier, S:, *and others.* Irrigation in the Sacramento Valley, Cal. 15 c. U. S., Supt. of Docs.
Gordon, J: H. Experiments in supplemental irrigation with small water supplies at Cheyenne, Wyo. Gov. Pr. Off.
King, F. H. Irrigation and drainage. **$1.50 net. Macmillan.
Price, C: R. Irrigated lands of U. S., Canada and Mexico. 30 c. Scenic America.
Price, C: R., *and* Power, J. C. Irrigated lands of United States, Canada and Mexico. 50 c. Pan-Pacific.
Putney, A. H., *and others.* Manufactures, mining; irrigation; real estate. $4. Cree.
United States. *Dept. of Agriculture. Office of Experiment Stations.* Organization, work and publications of irrigation investigations. '09(S) 12 p. 8°, gratis.
United States. Irrigation projects of the U. S. Reclamation Service; national reclamation of arid lands. '09(D) 16 p. il. 8°. (Add. Superintendent for price.)
Wyoming. Irrigation laws. (Add. pub. for price.) C. T. Johnston.
See also Alfalfa;—Cereals;—Drainage;—Land;—Orchards;—Reservoirs;—Water-supply; —Windmills;—*also* names of states.

Irvine, A. M.
Girl of the fourth; story of an unpopular school girl. '10(Je4) front. D. (Girls' own lib.) 75 c. McKay.

Irvine, Alex. Fitzgerald.
From the bottom up; life story of Alexander Irvine. '10(Mr12) c. il. D. **$1.50 net. Doubleday, P.

Irvine, Alonzo Blair.
See Utah. *Sup. ct.* Repts.

IRVINE FAMILY.
See Genealogies: Boyd, L., *comp.*

Irving, H:
How to know the trees. '10(Jl9) il. 8°, $1.25 net. Cassell.

Irving, Sir H: Brodrib.
Theatre in its relation to the state. '08 (Ja11) por. D. 50 c. E. H. Bacon.

IRVING, *Sir* Henry Brodrib.
Brereton, A. Life of Henry Irving. 2 v. *$6.50 net. Longmans.
Pollock, W. H. Impressions of Henry Irving. **$1 net. Longmans.

Irving, Mrs. Margaret.
Nature's truths told to a little maid. '10 (O) 48 p. 12°, 75 c. Aberdeen Pub. Co.

Irving, Washington.
Works. De luxe ed. 10 v. '10(N) il. levant. $30. Crowell.
Works. 12 v. Handy volume ed. [on Bible paper.] '10(D) ea., $1.50 net; per set, $18 net. Macmillan.
Works. Handy vol. ed. in 12 v. '10(D17) limp leath., ea., $1.50 net; per set, $18 net. Putnam.
The Alhambra; with an introd. by Eliz. Robins Pennell. '08(O31) il. 16°, (Pocket classics.) 80 c.; leath., $1.25. Macmillan.
Bachelors. '09(N) 32 p. il. 16°, 50 c. Dutton.
Child's Rip Van Winkle. '08(D19) c. il. O. $1.50. Stokes.
Christmas, Christmas eve, Christmas day. '10(F5) 16°, leath., *35c. net. Macmillan.
Chronicle of the conquest of Granada from the manuscript of Fray Antonio Agapida. '10(D17) 12°, (World's classics.) 35 c. Oxford Univ.
Conquest of Granada; with introd. by Ernest Rhys. '10(D10) 16°, (Everyman's lib.) 35 c. net; leath., 70 c. net. Dutton.
Knickerbocker's history of New York. [Bks. 3-7;] ed., with notes and an introd., by Edn. A. Greenlaw. '09(My1) 24°, (Pocket Am. and Eng. classics.) *25 c. net. Macmillan.
Legend of Sleepy Hollow, and other essays. '08(S5) c. 12°, (Crane classics.) 25 c.; pap., 15 c. Crane.
Legends of the Alhambra; with an introd. by Hamilton Wright Mabie. '09(N20) c. col. pls. O. **$2.50 net, boxed. Lippincott.
Life of Washington. 2 v. '10(D) il. $2.50, boxed. Crowell.
Old Christmas. '10(Ja1) il. 8°, *$2 net. Dodd.
Old English Christmas. '10(D10) col. il. nar. 12°, $1.25 net. Jacobs.
Old fashioned Christmas day; il. (in col.) by Cecil Aldin. '10(D) 50 c. net. Doran.
Old fashioned Christmas eve; il. [in col.] by Cecil Aldin. '10(D) 50 c. net. Doran.
Rip Van Winkle. '09(My1) c. il. 16°, 40 c. Altemus.
Rip Van Winkle. '09(N13) c. col. pls. nar. O. bds., 75 c., boxed. J: W. Luce.
Rip Van Winkle, and The legend of Sleepy Hollow. '08(O31) il. 16°, (Pocket classics.) 80 c.; leath., $1.25. Macmillan.
Selected tales from Tales of a traveller; ed. by Jennie F. Chase. '09(Je12) c. T. (Pocket Am. and Eng. classics.) **25 c. net. Macmillan.
Selections from Bracebridge Hall; ed., with notes and introd., by S: Thurber, jr. '10 (Ap16) c. por. D. (Riverside literature ser.) 25 c. Houghton M.
Selections from the Sketch book; ed. with teaching material by Lewis Worthington Smith. '10(Ja1) c. il. 16°, 25 c. Flanagan.
Sketch book, and Bracebridge Hall. '08 (Mr21) front. S. (New century lib.) $1; limp leath., $1.25. Nelson.

Irving, Washington.—*Continued.*
Sketch book of Geoffrey Crayon. '08(O17) 16°, (Best books ser.) leath., *$1 net. Dutton.
Sketch book of Geoffrey Crayon. '08(O24) 24°, (New universal lib.) 50 c.; leath., 75 c. Dutton.
Sketch book of Geoffrey Crayon, gent. 2 v. in 1. '08(D5) c. il. por. D. (Thin paper ser. of popular classics.) limp leath., $1.25. Lippincott.
Tales from the Alhambra; adpt. by Josephine Brower. '10(N19) c. col. il. D. $1.25 net. Houghton M.

—, and Steele, Sir R:
Widows. '09(N) 32 p. il. 16°, 50 c. Dutton.
Wives. '09(N) 32 p. il. 16°, 50 c. Dutton.

Irwin, Grace Luce, [Mrs. Wallace Irwin.]
Diary of a show-girl. '09(Ap10) c. il. D. $1. Moffat.

Irwin, Louise Godfrey.
Secret of old Thunderhead. '09(O30) c. il. D. †$1.50. Holt.

Irwin, S: Pashley.
Auto roads from Chicago to points in central Ill. and St. Louis; return routes described. '10(Ag) c. 137 p. fold. front. maps, 8°, $1.50. Pantagraph.

Irwin, Mrs. Wallace.
See Irwin, Grace Luce.

Irwin, Wallace Admah, ["Ginger."]
A bird cage: [alphabet book of verse.] '08(N7) c. il. Q. $1.50. B. W. Dodge.
Letters of a Japanese schoolboy, ("Hashimura Togo.") '09(Mr20) c. il. D. †$1.50. Doubleday, P.
Love sonnets of a car conductor; with a harmless and instructive introd. by Wolfgang Copernicus Addleburger. '08(Ap18) c. front. sq. D. bds., **50 c. net. P. Elder.
The Teddysee. '10(D17) c. il. O. bds., 75 c. net. B: W. Huebsch.

Irwin, W: H:
Confessions of a con man. '09(Ag14) c. il. D. *$1 net. B: W. Huebsch.
House of mystery; episode in the career of Rosalie Le Grange, clairvoyant. '10 (Mr26) c. il. D. **$1.15 net. Century Co.
Pictures of Old Chinatown. '08(D12) c. O. **$1 net. Moffat.
The readjustment. '10(D10) c. D. $1.20 net. B: W. Huebsch.
Warrior the untamed: the story of an imaginative press agent. '09(S11) c. il. D. †50 c. Doubleday, P.

Is immortality desirable? Dickinson, G. L. **75 c. net. Houghton M.
Is Ingersoll in hell? Furlong, J: R. $1. Boulder Pub.
Is mankind advancing? Martin, *Mrs.* J: $2 net. Baker & T.
Is Mars habitable? Wallace, A. R. *60 c. net. Macmillan.
Is religion undermined? Drawbridge, C. L. 50 c. Longmans.
Is Shakespeare dead? Clemens, S: L. **$1.25 net. Harper.
Is your soul progressing? Dorée, N. $1. Am. News.

Isaac, Rev. E. M.
Hero of Trent; or, saved from the jaws of hell. '10(O8) c. 12°, 75 c. Chr. Witness.

Isaacs, Abram S:
Step by step; story of the early days of Moses Mendelssohn. '10(D17) D. 75 c. Jewish Pub.

Isabel, the pearl of Cuba. Townsend, C: 25 c. Dick.

ISABEY, Jean Baptiste.
Basily-Callimaki, *Mme.* de. J.-B. Isabey, sa vie, son temps, 1767-1855. *$80 net. Lemcke.

ISAIAH.
See Bible. O. T.

Isaman, Mrs. Sara White.
Tourist tales of California. '09, [1910.] (F) il. *$1 net. Reilly & B.

Isham, Frederic Stewart.
Half a chance. '09(S25) c. D. †$1.50. Bobbs-M.
Lady of the Mount. '08(F29) c. il. D. †$1.50. Bobbs-M.
Social bucaneer. '10(O22) c. D. $1.50. Bobbs-M.

ISLAM.
See Mohammed and Mohammedanism.

Islam lands. Shoemaker, M. M. $2.50 net. Putnam.

Island of Regeneration. Brady, C. T. †$1.50. Dodd.

Island of stone money. Furness, W: H., 3*d*. $3.50 net. Lippincott.

Island pharisees. Galsworthy, J: *$1.50 net. Putnam.

Island providence. Niven, F: $1.50 net. Lane.

Island secret. McAllister, E. C. †$1.50. Estes.

Island story. Marshall, H. E. $2.75 net. Stokes.

Island traders. MacDonald, A. $1.25. Caldwell.

Islandica: an annual relating to Iceland and the Fiske Icelandic collection in Cornell University library; ed. by G: W: Harris. v. 1, Bibliography of the Icelandic sagas and minor tales, by Halldor Hermannsson. '08(Jl4); v. 2, The Northmen in America, by Halldór Hermannsson. '09(Jl17); v. 3, Bibliography of the sagas of the kings of Norway and related sagas and tales, by Halldór Hermannsson. '10(Je11) c. 8°, pap., ea., $1 net. Cornell Univ.

Islands of the Pacific. Alexander, J. M. $1.50. Am. Tr.

Isle of dead ships. Marriott, C. **$1 net. Lippincott.

Isle of Maids. Hainsselin, M. T. †$1.50. Lane.

ISLE OF MAN, England.
Cane, W. R. H. Isle of Man. *$2 net. Macmillan.
Herbert, A. Isle of Man. *$3.50 net. Lane.

Isle of temptation. Colleton, A. S. $1.50. Stuyvesant Press.

Isle of Whispers. Dudley, E: L. †$1.50. Holt.

ISLE OF WIGHT, England.
Moncrieff, A. R. H. Isle of Wight. *$2.50 net. Macmillan.

ISLE ROYAL, Lake Superior, Mich.
Adams, C: C. Ecological survey of Isle Royal. 85 c. Mich. Geol.

Isolation of harmful organic substances from soils. Schreiner, O. (Add. Superintendent for price.) U. S., Supt. of Docs.

Isolée (L'). *See* Bazin, René.

ISOMETRY.
See Poetry.

ISRAEL.
See Jews.

Israel Bruna. Deutsch, G. $1.25. Badger.

ISRAELITES.
See Jews.

Israels, Josef.
Masterpieces of Israels; reproductions from his most renowned pictures. '08(O24) T. (Dutch painters.) leath., *75 c. net; pap., *25 c. net. Stokes.
Rembrandt. '08(F22) il. O. (Masterpieces in colour.) bds., *65 c. net. Stokes.

Israel's ideal. Adams, J: $1.50 net. Scribner.

Isthmian Canal: message from the President transmitting report of the Board of Engineers appointed to accompany ex-Secretary of War William H. Taft to the Isthmian Canal to look into the condition of canal work and report upon the feasibility and safety of the Gatun Dam, etc. '09(Je19) 8°, pap. (Add. Superintendent for price.) U. S., Supt. of Docs.

Istoria ton enomenon politeion tes Amerikes. Vlasto, S. J. $2. Atlantis Pub.

ISTRIA.
See Austria-Hungary.

It never can happen again. De Morgan, W: F. †$1.75. Holt.

ITALIAN ARCHITECTURE.
See Architecture.

ITALIAN ART.
See Fine arts;—Painters and painting.

Italian highways and byways. Miltoun, F., *pseud.* $3. L. C. Page.

Italian hours. James, H: **$7.50 net. Houghton M.

ITALIAN LANGUAGE.
Arbib-Costa, A. Italian lessons. $1 Tocci.
Bolognese, S. Economical interpreter for Italians to learn English. 50 c. Caspar.
Bracco, R. Il trionfo. (Add. pub. for price.) C. Ciocia.
Dante Alighieri. La divina commedia. v. 1, Inferno. $1.25. Heath.
Fogazzaro, A. Pereat Rochus and Un' idea di Ermes Torranza. 40 c. Heath.
James, W:, *and* Grassi, G. Dict. of English and Italian languages. *$1.50 net. Macmillan.
Maestro, S. New grammar for Italians to speedily learn the English language. *$1 net. Caspar.
Marinoni, A., *comp. and ed.* Italian reader. 90 c.; 75 c. W: R. Jenkins.
Moore, S. W. Libro illustrato di lingua inglese: illustrated English-Italian language book and reader. 35 c. Heath.
Padovina, P. Laird & Lee's standard vest pocket English-Italian, Italian-English dict. 50 c.; 75 c. Laird.

ITALIAN LANGUAGE.—*Continued.*
Pitman, *Sir* I: International mercantile letters: English-Italian. $1. Pitman.
Sergio, A. Logical method to learn the Italian language. $1. Italian Sch.
Valgimigli, A. Tourists' vade mecum of Italian colloquial conversation. 40 c. Pitman.
Wesseley, J. E., *and* Gray, F. H. T. English-Italian and Italian-English dictionary. 50 c. Dutton.
See also **Tauchnitz pocket dictionaries.**

ITALIAN LITERATURE.
Dole, N. H. Teacher of Dante, and other studies in Italian literature. **$1.75 net. Moffat.

ITALIAN PAINTING.
See Painters and painting.

ITALIAN POETRY.
Butler, A. J:, *ed.* Forerunners of Dante. $2. Oxford Univ.
Lucas, St. J. W. L., *comp.* Oxford book of Italian verse, XIII century-XIX century. $2 net; $2.50 net. Oxford Univ.

ITALIAN SCULPTURE.
See **Sculpture.**

Italian vignettes. Arms, M. W. *$1.25 net. M. Kennerley.

ITALIANS IN THE UNITED STATES.
See **Naturalization.**

Italians of to-day. Bazin, R. **$1.25 net. Holt.
Italica. Thayer, W: R. **$1.50 net. Houghton M.

ITALY.
Arms, M. W. Italian vignettes. *$1.25 net. M. Kennerley.
Baedeker, K. Central Italy and Rome. $2.25.—Italy from the Alps to Naples. $2.40 net.—Southern Italy and Sicily. *$1.80 net. Scribner.
Bazin, R. Italians of to-day. **$1.25 net. Holt.
Boulting, T: Woman in Italy. $4 net. Brentano's.
Bumpus, T: F. Cathedrals and churches of northern Italy. $2.50. L. C. Page.
Carr, *Mrs.* C. North Italian folk. 50 c. net. Macmillan.
Chi è; annuario biografico italiano. $1. Stechert.
Ellison, D. J. Italy through the stereoscope. $1.90. Underwood.
Frothingham, A. L. Roman cities in Italy and Dalmatia. $1.75 net. Sturgis & W.
Gordon, L. D. Home life in Italy: letters from the Apennines. *$1.75 net. Macmillan.
Gifford, *Mrs.* A. H. New Italy. **$1.20 net. Lothrop, L. & S.
Guthrie, A. Letters from France and Italy. *$1.25 net. McClurg.
Haggard, H. R. Winter pilgrimage: travels through Palestine, Italy, and the island of Cyprus. $1.50. Longmans.
Hare, C. Courts and camps of the Italian renaissance. *$2.50 net. Scribner.
Headlam, C. Venetia and northern Italy, being the story of Venice, Lombardy and Emilia. *$2.50 net. Macmillan.
Holland, R. S. Builders of united Italy. **$2 net. Holt.

ITALY.—*Continued.*
Howe, M. Two in Italy. **$1.50 net. Little, B. & Co.
James, H: Italian hours. **$7.50 net. Houghton M.
Jordan, L: H:, *and* Labanca, B. Study of religion in Italian universities. $2.40. Oxford Univ.
Jörgensen, J. Pilgrim walks in Franciscan Italy. *75 c. net. Herder.
Lanciani, R. A. Wanderings in the Roman Campagna. *$5 net. Houghton M.
Lee, V., *pseud.* Studies of the eighteenth century in Italy. *$6 net. McClurg.
Macdonell, A. In the Abruzzi. *$2 net. Stokes.
Mario, *Mme.* J. W. Birth of modern Italy. *$3.50 net. Scribner.
Mason, *Mrs.* C. A. Spell of Italy. $2.50. L. C. Page.
Miltoun, F., *pseud.* Italian highways and byways from a motor car. $3. L. C. Page.
Pais, E. Ancient Italy: hist. and geograph. investigations. *$5 net. Univ. of Chic.
Peet, T. E. Stone and bronze ages in Italy and Sicily. $5.25. Oxford Univ.
Ricci, C. Art of northern Italy. $1.50 net. Scribner.
Salvatore, S. Italian architecture. $25. Polley.
Schauffler, R. H., *comp.* Through Italy with the poets. **$2 net. Moffat.
Seeley, E. L., *comp.* Artists of the Italian Renaissance.—Stories of the Italian artists from Vasari. ea., *$3 net. Duffield.
Sismondi, J. C. L. de. History of the Italian republics. *$1 net. Dutton.
Steedman, A. Legends and stories of Italy for children. $2.50 net. Putnam.
Sterne, L. Sentimental journey through France and Italy. $1.25 net. Brentano's.
Sterne, L. Sentimental journey through France and Italy. $1.50. Lippincott.
Sterne, L. Sentimental journey through France and Italy. $3. Putnam.
Stevens, T: W. Book of words: pageant of the Italian renaissance. 50 c. Antiquarian Soc.
Sullivan, T: R. Lands of summer: Italy, Sicily and Greece. **$1.50 net. Houghton M.
Supplementary commercial agreement bet. the U. S. and Italy. (Add. Superintendent for price.) U. S., Supt. of Docs.
Symonds, M. Days spent on a Doge's farm. *$2.50 net. Century Co.
Symons, A. Cities of Italy. $2. Dutton.
Thayer, W: R. Italica: studies in Italian life and letters. **$1.50 net. Houghton M.
Vernon, *Mrs.* K. D. E. Italy from 1494 to 1790. *$1.75 net. Putnam.
Villari, P. Mediæval Italy. $3.75. Scribner.
Whiting, Lilian. Italy, the magic land. $1.50 net. Little, B. & Co.
Wollaston, G: H., *comp.* Englishman in Italy: collection of verses written by some of those who have loved Italy. *$1.75 net. Oxford Univ.

ITALY.—*Continued.*
Zangwill, I. Italian fantasies. $2 net. Macmillan.
See also Aosta Valley;—Apostles;—Assisi;—Bologna; — Corsica;—Dolomite Mountains;—Florence;—Genoa;—Herculaneum; — Messina disaster;—Milan;—Modernism;—Naples;—Napoleonic wars;—Padua; —Palestina;—Perugia;—Pisa; — Pompeii; — Printers and printing; — Renaissance; — Riviera; —Rome;—Sardinia;—Sculpture; — Sicily;—Siena;—Tuscany;—Urbino;—Venice;—Verona; —Vincenzo;—*also* Garibaldi, Guiseppe;—Joanna I.;—Medici (The).

Italy, my Italy. Browning, R. 50 c. net; $1 net. T: B. Mosher.

Italy's great horror of earthquake and tidal wave. Mowbray, J. H:, *comp.* $1. Nat. Pub. Co.

ITHACA, N. Y.
See Cornell University.

Ithomites, Apostle.
New Greece, pedagogic and instructive psychology. '10(N19) c. il. 16°, 75 c. A. Ithomites.

Itinerary (The). *See* Leland, J:

Itinerary and description of Wales. Giraldus Cambrensis. *35 c. net; *70 c. net. Dutton.

Itinerary of Azariah Frejolity. Augustine, W: A. (Add. author for price.) W: A. Augustine.

Itinerary of Fynes Moryson. *See* Moryson, Fynes.

It's great to be crazy. Stein, J. J. 15 c. Penn Pub. Co.

It's never too late to mend. Harper, O. 25 c. J. S. Ogilvie.

ITO, Hirombumi, *Prince.*
Ladd, G: T. In Korea with Marquis Ito. **$2.50 net. Scribner.
Nakamura, K. Prince Ito. $1. Anraku.

Itoma. Alexander, T. $1. Kuyhora Press.

Ivanhoe. *See* Scott, *Sir* Wa.

Ivatts, E. B.
Railway management at stations. '10(D) 8°, $2.50. Van Nostrand.

Ives, C: Taylor, and Woodman, Raymond Huntington, eds.
Hymns of the living church. '10(D31) 8°, hf. mor., $1.50. Century Co.

Ives, Ella Gilbert.
Out door music; songs of birds, trees, flowers, the road, love, religion. '08 (O) c. 144 p. 16°, $1. Arakelyan.

Ives, Herb. Eug.
Volt scale for a watts-per-candle meter. [1910.] (Jl) 543-547 p. 8°. Gov. Pr. Off.

Ives, Mary Isaphene.
Illustrated phonics: a text-book for schools. '09(O2) c. il. D. 40 c. Longmans.

Ivey, T: Neal.
Bildad Akers: his book; the notions and experiences of a quaint rural philosopher who thinks for himself; ed. by T: N. Ivey. [1910] (F) c. '09. 10+205 p. 12°, $1. Mutual Pub.

Ivimey, J: W:
Complete version of ye three blind mice. '09(Ap3) c. il. obl. D. bds., *50 c. net. Warne.

Ivimy, A. M.
Woman's guide to Paris. '10(Jl30) 16°, $1.25 net. Brentano's.

Ivins, Lester S.
Agriculture in the public schools. '10 (Ja22) c. il. S. pap., 35 c. March.

Ivins, W: Mills, and Mason, Herbert Delavan.
Control of public utilities in the form of an annotation of the public service commissions law of the state of New York and covering all important Am. cases, together with the text of the federal interstate commerce act, and the rapid transit act of New York, [etc.] '08(N) c. 79+1149 p. O. *$7 net. Baker, V. & Co.

Ivory booklets. 6 v. [1910.] (D) ea., 25 c. Jacobs.

"J. B.," pseud.
See Bierley, J.

J. Cole. Gellibrand, E. 50 c. Hurst.

J. P. Dunbar. Hudson, W: C. 50 c. B. W. Dodge.

"J. S. of Dale," pseud.
See Stimson, Frederic Jesup.

Jacberns, Raymond.
Attic boarders. '10(Ja1) 12°, $1.50. Lippincott.
Becky Compton, ex-dux. '10(Ja1) 12°, $1.50. Lippincott.
Boy and a secret. '08(D26) il. D. $1.25. Lippincott.
Poor Uncle Harry. '10(D3) col. il. 12°, $1.50. Lippincott.
Schoolgirl's battlefield. '10(D10) col. il. 12°, $1.50. Dutton.
Three amateur scouts. '10(D3) col. il. 12°, $1.50. Lippincott.

Jack, W: R., M.D.
See Wheeler, Alex.

Jack. *See* Daudet, Alphonse.

Jack Collerton's engine. Godfrey, H. $1.25. Little, B. & Co.

Jack Frost jingles. Earle, T. M. 75 c. C. M. Clark.

Jack Hall at Yale. Camp, W. C. †$1.50. **Appleton.**

Jack Harvey's adventures. Smith, R. P. $1.50. L. C. Page.

Jack Lorimer's holidays. Standish, W., *pseud.* L. C. Page.

Jack Lorimer's substitute. Standish, W. $1.50. L. C. Page.

Jack Morning's treasure. Millard, B. *$1 net. Clode.

Jack Ranger ser. *See* Young, Clarence.

Jack Roostand. Zagel, H. H. $1. Lange.

Jack Sheppard, the bandit king. Harper, O. 25 c. J. S. Ogilvie.

Jack South and some other Jacks. Bearne, D: $1. Herder.

Jack Spurlock, prodigal. Lorimer, G: H. †$1.50. Doubleday, P.

Jack the Giant Killer: operetta. Clark, F. A. 40 c. Ditson.

Jack the runaway. Webster, F. V. 35 c. Cupples & L.

Jack the young explorer. Grinnell, G: B. †$1.25. Stokes.

Jackman, Abi S.
Prince of spendthrifts. '08(S19) il. 12°, pap., 25 c. J. S. Ogilvie.

Jackman, W. J.
A B C of the motor cycle. '10(My21) c. il. D. (Thompson ser. of home study books.) $1; flex. leath., $1.50. C: C. Thompson.

—, and Russell, T: Herbert.
Flying machines, construction and operation; with introd. chapter by Octave Chanute. '10(Je25) c. D. (Thompson ser. of home study books.) $1; flex. leath., $1.50. C: C. Thompson.

Jack's manual. Grohusko, J: A. $1. J: A. Grohusko.

Jacks, Lawrence Pearsall.
Mad shepherds and other human studies. '10(S10) front. D. $1.20 net. Holt.

Jackson, Abraham Valentine Williams.
Philology: a lecture. '08(O3) O. 25 c. Columbia Univ.

JACKSON, Alice.
Speer, R. E. Memorial of Alice Jackson. 75 c. Revell.

Jackson, Alice F., ed.
David Copperfield: retold. '10(D10) col. il. 12°, (Children's Dickens.) bds., 75 c. net. Jacobs.
Ivanhoe; retold. '10(D10) col. il. 12°, (Children's Scott.) bds., 75 c. net. Jacobs.
Little Nell; retold. '10(D10) col. il. 12°, (Children's Dickens.) bds., 75 c. net. Jacobs.
The talisman; retold. '10(D10) col. il. 12°, (Children's Scott.) bds., 75 c. net. Jacobs.

Jackson, Alma Drayer.
Study of Ohio forms of the genus *Lepidocyrtus.* [1910.] (Ap) 525-538 p. il. 8°, (Ohio State Univ.; contribs. from the Dept. of Zoology and Entomology.) gratis. Ohio State Univ.

Jackson, And.
Statesmanship of Andrew Jackson as told in his writings and speeches; ed. by Fs. Newton Thorpe. '09(My22) c. O. (Principles of American statesmanship.) $2.50. Tandy-T.

Jackson, Caroline Ruth, and Daugherty, Amelia Crum, [Mrs. L. S. Daugherty.]
Agriculture through the laboratory and school garden. '08(O17) c. il. 12°, *$1.50 net. Judd.

Jackson, C: E.
Bird lyrics and other poems. '10, [1910.] (M.) c. 104 p. 12°, $1. Smith & S.

Jackson, C: H., comp.
Cases on the law of domestic relations. '10 (Je) O. Thompson & Co.

Jackson, C: Tenney.
Day of souls. '10(Mr12) c. il. D. †$1.50. Bobbs-M.
My brother's keeper. '10(O22) c. il. D. $1.50. Bobbs-M.

Jackson, Cyril.
Unemployment and trade unions; with preface by Rt. Hon. Viscount Milner. '10(O1) D. 50 c. net. Longmans.

Jackson, E. Hilton.
Law Latin; a treatise in Latin with legal maxims and phrases, as a basis of instruction. 3d ed. '10(N) c. D. $1.50. Byrne.

Jackson, Emily, [Mrs. F. Nevill Jackson.]
Toys of other days. '09(Mr13) il. Q. ("Country Life" lib.) *$7.50 net. Scribner.

Jackson, Mrs. F. Nevill.
See Jackson, Emily.

Jackson, Frances.
Life of Madame Flore, second superior-general of the Ladies of Mary. '08(Ag8) il. 8°, *$1 net. Herder.

Jackson, Fk. H.
Monograph of the Boston Opera House, 1909. '10(Ja1) c. il. pors. Q. bds. (Add. pub. for price.) W. A. Butterfield.

Jackson, Fred.
Hidden princess: modern romance. '10 (S10) c. col. front. D. $1.50, boxed. Jacobs.

Jackson, F: Hamilton.
Shores of Adriatic: the Austrian side, the Küstenlande, Istria and Dalmatia. '08(D) 16+420 p. 8°, *$6 net. Dutton.

Jackson, Mrs. Gabrielle Emilie Snow.
Adventures of Tommy Postoffice; true story of a cat. '10(N5) c. il. 12°, $1.25. Dutton.
Captain Polly of Annapolis. '10(N5) il. 8°, $1.50. Dutton.
Dawn of womanhood. '08(S12) c. 12°, *$1.25 net. Revell.
Little Miss Crickett at school. '08(O24) c. il. D. †$1.25. Appleton.
Three little women. '08(D12) c. il. 12°, †$1. Winston.
Three little women at work; story for girls. '10(Ja1) c. il. D. $1. Winston.
Three little women's success; story for girls. '10(D10) c. il. 12°, $1. Winston.
Wee Winkles at the mountains. '08(O3) c. il. O. †$1.25. Harper.

Jackson, Rev. G:
Fact of conversion: Cole lectures. '08 (S12) c. 12°, *$1.25 net. Revell.

Jackson, G:
Sixty years in Texas. 2d ed. '09(Ja23) il. pors. O. $1.50. G: Jackson.

Jackson, G: Leroy.
Development of school support in colonial Massachusetts. '10(Ja22) c. 8°, (Teachers' College; Contributions to education.) $1; pap., 75 c. Teachers' Coll.

Jackson, G: T:, M.D.
Diseases of the skin: ready-reference handbook. 6th ed. '08(Ag29) il. 8°, *$3 net. Lea.

Jackson, Mrs. Helen Maria Fiske Hunt.
Nelly's silver mine; story of Colorado life. '10(N5) c. col. il. D. $2. Little, B. & Co.

Jackson, H:, rep.
See Georgia. *Sup. ct.* Repts.

Jackson, H: Ezekiel.
Great pictures as moral teachers. '10 (My21) c. il. 8°, $1.50. Winston.
Message of the modern minister; introd. by Amory H. Bradford. '08(O24) c. 12°, *50 c. net. Revell.

Jackson, Holbrook.
Great English novelists. '09, [1910.] (Ja) c. 312 p. il. 12°, **$1.50 net, boxed. Jacobs.

Jackson, J.
Iambica; English-Greek and Greek-English vocab. for writers of Iambic verse. '10 (Ja15) 12°, *$1.50 net. Macmillan.

Jackson, Ja. W:
Lost letter; or, the triumph of patience; story for boys. '09(Jl) c. 181 p. 12°, 75 c. Standard Pub.

Jackson, Jos.
Catalogue of the flowering plants and ferns of Worcester Country, Mass. 3d ed. rev. and enl. '09, [1910.] (S) 5+102 p. il. 8°, $1. Western Nat. Hist.

Jackson, Lambert Lincoln.
See Young, Jacob W: Albert.

Jackson, Loulia.
Nameless woman; story of my life. '10 (Je) c. 675 p. 8°, $2.50. L. Jackson.

Jackson, M. Katherine
Outlines of the literary history of colonial Pennsylvania. '08(F1) 8°, (Columbia Univ. studies in English.) *$1.25 net. Lemcke.

Jackson, Maude M.
Artistic entertainments: six new drills and entertainments. '08(My16) c. D. pap., 25 c. Flanagan.

Jackson, S: Alex.
Among the maples. '08(O) c. 4+204 p. 12°, *90 c. net. Un. Presb. Bd.

Jackson, S: Trevena.
Lincoln's use of the Bible. '09(Ja23) c. por. S. limp bds., *25 c. net. Eaton & M.

JACKSON, Sheldon.
Stewart, R. L. Sheldon Jackson, pathfinder and prospector of the missionary vanguard in the Rocky Mountains and Alaska. *$2 net. Revell.

JACKSON, *General* Thomas Jonathan, [*known as* "Stonewall Jackson."]
White, H: A. Stonewall Jackson. *$1.25 net. Jacobs.

Jackson, Vincent, ed.
English melodies from the XIII to XVIII centuries; 100 songs, with music; ed., with introd. and historical notes. '10 (D10) 8°, $3 net. Dutton.

Jackson, Wilfrid Scarborough.
Trial by marriage. '09(O30) D. $1.50. Lane.

JACKSON, Mississippi.
Hobart, E. L. Story of Vicksburg and Jackson. 25 c. E. L. Hobart.

Jacob, Mrs. Arth.
See Jacob, Violet.

Jacob, Rev. Jos.
Daffodils; preface by Rev. W. Wilks. '10 (D31) col. il. O. (Garden flowers in colors.) bds., 65 c. net. Stokes.

Jacob, son of Aaron, High priest of the Samaritans.
Messianic hope of the Samaritans; tr. from the Arabic by Abdullah Ben Kori; ed., with an introd. by W: Eleazar Barton. '08(Mr7) il. por. O. pap., 25 c. Open Court.

Jacob, Violet, [Mrs. Arthur Jacob.]
History of Aythan Waring. '08(F8) c. D. **$1.25 net. Dutton.
Irresolute Catherine. '09(Mr27) D. †$1. Doubleday, P.

Jacob Faithful. Marryat, F: 50 c. Hurst.

Jacob the heel-grasper. Williams, L. M. $1. L. M. Williams.

Jacobi, Abraham.
Dr. Jacobi's works; collected essays, addresses, scientific papers and misc. writings; ed. by W: J. Robinson, M.D. 8 v. '09, [1910.] (Ja) c. fronts. il. pors. 8°, $15. Critic & G.

—, ed. Diseases of children; authorized tr. from "Die deutsche klinik" under the general editorial supervision of Julius L. Salinger, M.D. '10, [1909.] (D) c. 17+828 p. il. 8°, (Modern clinical medicine.) $6. Appleton.

Jacobi, Eduard.
Portfolio of dermochromes; English adaptation of text of the 1st and 2d eds. by J. J. Pringle. 3d rev. and enl. ed. '09 (S); 4th ed., rev. and enl. [1910.] (Jl) c. il. (partly col.) 4°, ea., $24. Rebman.

Jacob's sons. Petrie, G: L. $1.25. Neale.

Jacobs, Caroline Emilia, ["Emilia Elliott."]
Joan's jolly vacation. '09(N20) 12°, †$1.50. Jacobs.
Patricia. '10(S17) c. col. front. D. $1. Jacobs.
Texas Blue Bonnet. '10(D3) c. il. D. $1.50. L. C. Page.

Jacobs, C: W.
From pillow to throne; Miss Lizzie L. Johnson, invalid missionary worker. [1910.] (Ag) c. 110 p. il. pors. 12°, 50 c. M. A. Johnson.

Jacobs, H:, comp.
"Where to find it"; index to sources of information on all subjects of general interest. '09(O16) c. D. pap., 50 c. H: Jacobs.

Jacobs, H: W:
Betterment briefs; collection of published papers on organized industrial efficiency: [railroads.] '08(S) 240 p. il. tabs., 8°, $3.50. Crane.
Betterment briefs: collection of published papers on organized industrial efficiency: [railroads.] [2d ed.] '09(Ap17) c. il. tabs., 8°, $3.50. Wiley.

Jacobs, Jos., and Appleborne, L:
New York bar examination, questions and answers. 2d ed. '10(Ja) c. O. $4. Banks.

Jacobs, Lawrence Merton.
Bank acceptances. '10(O) 20 p. 8°. Gov. Pr. Off.

Jacobs, Michael.
Notes on the Rebel invasion of Maryland and Pennsylvania, and the battle of Gettysburg. [7th ed., rev. and enl.] '09 (Jl3) fold. map, O. $1; pap., 25 c. G. E. Jacobs.

Jacobs, Philip P., comp.
Campaign against tuberculosis in the United States; incl. a directory of institutions dealing with tuberculosis in the United States and Canada; comp. under the direction of the National Association for the Study and Prevention of Tuberculosis. '08(O10) c. chart, O. (Russell Sage foundation pub.) $1. Charities Pub.

Jacobs, Thornwell.
Law of the white circle. '08(D) c. 253 p. il. 12°, $1.25. Taylor-T.

Jacobs, W: Wymark.
Sailors' knots. '09(N20) c. il. D. †$1.50. Scribner.
Salthaven. '08(O24) c. il. D. †$1.50. Scribner.

—, and Parker, L: Napoleon.
Beauty and the barge; farce in three acts. '10(D) c. 148 p. plans, 12°, 50 c. S: French.

Jacobson, Carl Alfr.
Conductivity and ionization of electrolytes in aqueous solutions as conditioned by temperature, dilution and hydrolysis. '08, [1909.] (S) 60 p. 8°, pap., 60 c. Johns Hopkins.

Jacobus, C:, ed.
Croquet and its rules, thoroughly revised. '08(Ag1); '10(S3) c. il. por. 16°, (Spalding's athletic lib.) pap., ea., 10 c. Am. Sports.

Jacobus, Melancthon Williams, D.D., ed.
Roman Catholic and Protestant Bibles compared: Gould prize essays. 2d ed., rev. and supplemented with appendices originally accompanying the essays and a composite bibliography covering the general literature of the subject. '08(F15) c. D. **$1.25 net. Scribner.

—, Nourse, E: Everett, D.D., Zenos, Andrew Constantinedes, D.D., and others, eds.
Standard Bible dictionary designed as a comprehensive guide to the Scriptures. '09(F13) c. il. maps, Q. $6; hf. mor., $10; full mor., $12; indexed, 50 c. extra. Funk.

Jacoby, Harold.
Astronomy. '08(F29) c. 8°, pap., 25 c. Macmillan.

Jacoby, H: Sylvester.
Structural details; or, elements of design in heavy framing. '09(O9) c. 8°, **$2.25 net. Wiley.

Jacomb, A. E.
Faith of his fathers; a story of some idealists. '09(S18) c. D. †$1.50. Dodd.

JACQUARD WEAVING.
See Weaving.

Jacqueline of the carrier-pigeons. Seaman, A. H. *$1.25 net. Sturgis & W.

Jacquemart, Albert.
History of furniture; ed. by Mrs. Bury Palliser. 2d ed. '08(Je20) Q. *$7.50 net. Scribner.

JAQUETT FAMILY.
See Genealogies: Sellers, E. J.

Jacquette. Cody, G. E. †$1.25. Duffield.

Jaekel, Frederic Blair.
The lands of the tamed Turk; or, the Balkan states of to-day. '10(O15) c. fold. map, D. $2.50, boxed. L. C. Page.

Jaffa, Myer E:
Nuts and their uses as food. '08, [1909.] (My) 28 p. 8°, (U. S., Dept. of Agriculture; farmers' bull.) pap. (Add. Superintendent for price.)
See also Ward, Archibald Robinson.

Jaffray, Rob.
Two knights of the swan; Lohengrin and Helyas; study of the legend of the Swan-Knight, with special reference to its two most important developments. '10(Ap30) c. il. O. $1.25 net. Putnam.

Jager, A.
Emigrant; the life, experience and humorous adventures of A. Jager, emigrant to South America in 1882, to Australia in 1885, and to California in 1908. '08, [1909.] (Ja) c. 14+15-408 p. il. por. tabs., 12°. (Add. pubs. for price.) Southern California Pr.

Jager, Thdr. F.
See Gersbach, Rob.

Jagger, J: Ernest.
Elem. text-book on mechanical drawing. '10(O8) il. 4°, $3.50 net. Lippincott.

Jake—or Sam. Block, R. E. 50 c. FitzGerald.

Jallade, Etienne Jean.
A vol d'oiseau; poésies diverses. '09(D) c. 204 p. 8°, $1. W: R. Jenkins.

JAMAICA (Island of).
Gardner, W: J. Hist. of Jamica. *$2.50 special net. Appleton.
Henderson, J: Jamaica. *75 c. net. Macmillan.
See also Kingston.

James I., King of Scotland.
King's quair and The quare of jelusy; ed., with introd., notes, appendix and glossary by Alex. Lawson. '10(D24) il. 8°, $2 net. Macmillan.

James, Alice L.
Catering for two. '08(Ag22) c. Everyday ed., 16°, $2; Bridal ed., 4°, silk, $5. Putnam.
Housekeeping for two. '09(D4) c. S. **$1.25 net. Putnam.

James, Alice R.
Ball games and breathing exercises; with preface by Harry Campbell. '08(S12) il. D. 40 c. Longmans.

James, C: F.
Struggle for religious liberty in Virginia. '08(N) 272 p. $1.25. Review and Herald Pub.

James, Davis L.
Judge James Hall; literary pioneer of the Middle West; repr. from Ohio Archæological and Historical Publications. '09, [1910.] (F) 468-483 p. O. pap. Heer.

James, Edith E. Coulson.
Bologna, its history, antiquities and art. '10(M26) il. fold. map, O. $4.80. Oxford Univ.

James, Mrs. Florence Alice Price, ["Florence Warden."]
Dazzling Miss Davison. '10(D17) 12°, $1.50. H. K. Fly.
House on the marsh. '08(Ag1) 12°, (Magnolia lib.) 50 c. Hurst.
Life's arrears. '09(Jl3) il. D. $1.50. Cassell.

James, G: Payne Rainsford.
Richelieu. '09(Ap3) 16°, (Everyman's lib.) *35 c. net; leath., *70 c. net. Dutton.

James, G: Watson, jr.
Bride of the violin and other poems. '10 (F) c. 19 p. nar. O. pap., 50 c. G: W. James, Jr.

James, G: Wharton.
Grand Canyon of Arizona; how to see it. '10(S10) c. il. D. $1.50 net. Little, B. & Co.
Heroes of California; story of the founders of the Golden State as narrated by themselves or gleaned from other sources. '10(D3) c. il. O. $2 net. Little, B. & Co.
Through Ramona's country. '08(D12) c. O. **$2 net. Little, B. & Co.
What the white race may learn from the Indian. '08(Je6) c. il. O. *$1.50 net. Forbes.
See also Stoddard, C: Warren.

James, Gertie de S. Wentworth-.
See Wentworth-James, Gertie de S.

James, Grace.
Joan of Arc. '10(N5) il. 8°, $3.50 net. Dutton.
—, comp. Green Willow and other Japanese fairy tales. '10(D10) col. il. $5.50 net. Macmillan.

James, H:
The finer grain. '10(O15) c. D. $1.25 net. Scribner.
Italian hours; with il. in col. by Jos. Pennell. '09(D4) c. Q. **$7.50 net, boxed. Houghton M.
Julia Bride. '09(O9) c. il. O. †$1.25. Harper.
Novels and tales; [with special prefaces by the author.] New York ed. In 24 v. v 2, The American. '08(F1); vs. 3 and 4, The portrait of a lady; vs. 5 and 6, The Princess Casamassima. '08(Mr7); vs. 7 and 8, The tragic muse. '08(Ap18); v. 9, The awkward age; v. 10, Spoils of Poynton; v. 11, What Maisie knew; v. 12, The aspern papers. '08(D5); v. 13, Lady Barbarina, The siege of London, etc.; v. 14, The reverberator, Madame de Mauves, etc. '09(F6); v. 15, The lesson of the master, The death of the lion, The next time, The figure in the carpet, The Coxon fund; v. 16, The author of Beltraffio, The middle ages, Greville Fane, Broken Wings, The tree of knowledge, The abasement of the Northmores, The great good place, Four meetings, Paste, Europe, Miss Gunton of Poughkeepsie. '09(Ap3); v. 17, The altar of the dead; The beast in the jungle; The birthplace; The private life; Owen Wingrave; The friends of the friends; Sir Edmund Orme; The real right thing; The jolly corner; Julia Bride; v. 18, Daisy Miller; Pandora; The Patagonia; The marriage; The real thing; Brooksmith; The Beldonald Holbein; The story in it; Flicker bridge; Mrs. Merwin. '09(My1); v. 19 and 20, The wings of a dove; v. 21 and 22, The ambassadors. '09(Je19); v. 23, 24, The golden bowl. (Ag21) c. fronts. 12°, subs., ea., $2; hf. levant, $4. Scribner.
Views and reviews; introd. by Le Roy Phillips. '08(Je6) c. D. *$1.50 net; parchment, *$2.50 net. Ball Pub.
See also Howells, W: Dean.

James, Howard.
Wraith of Knopf. '08(D) c. 2+117 p. 12°, $1. B'way Pub.

James, Ja. Alton.
Indian diplomacy and the opening of the Revolution in the West; [from the Proceedings of the State Historical Society of Wisconsin for 1909.] '10(Ap9) O. pap., 25 c. State Hist., Wis.
—, **and Sanford, Albert Hart.**
American history. '09, [1910.] (F) c. 17+565 p. il. maps, double map, 12°, **$1.40 net. Scribner.
References at end of chapters.
—, ed. *See* Sparks, Edn. Erle.

JAMES, Joshua.
Kimball, S. I. Joshua James, life-saver. *60 c. net. Am. Unitarian.

James, Juliet Lumbard, [Mrs. M. C. James, comp.]
Twenty English cathedrals. '08(Je13) c. T. (For the interest of the traveller.) hf. cl., $1. M. C. James.

James, Lewis.
Twelve steps to success. '08(D12) c. D. bds., $1. A. Harriman.

James, Mrs. M. C.
See James, Juliet Lumbard.

James, Martha, pseud.
See Doyle, *Mrs.* Martha Claire MacGowan.

James, Mrs. Mary Ingles.
Scientific tone production. '08(Mr.) c. 96 p. por. pls. D. *$1.25 net. C: W. Thompson.

James, Montague Rhodes.
Descriptive catalogue of the manuscripts in the library of Gonville and Caius College. In 2 v. '08(Je6) Q. ea., *$3.50 net. Putnam.

James, R. A. Scott-.
See Scott-James, R. A.

James, Rita Bell.
See Bell, Lucia Chase.

James, T. Campbell.
See Sudborough, J: Jos.

James, W:
Dict. of the English and German languages. 4th ed., entirely rewritten and greatly enl. '08(Je13) 12°, *$1.50 net. Macmillan.
—, **and Grassi, Gius.**
Dict. of the English and Italian languages; with the Italian pronunciation and the accentuation of every word in both languages. 13th ed. '08(Jl11) 12°, *$1.50 net. Macmillan.
—, **and Molé, A.**
Dictionary of the French and English languages. New ed., completely rewritten and greatly enl. by L: Tolhausen and G: Payn, assisted by E. Heymann. '08(Mr7) 12°, *$1.50 net. Macmillan.

James, W:, 1842-1910.
Energies of men. '08(D12) c. D. (Religion and medicine publications.) pap., **25 c. net. Moffat.
Meaning of truth; sequel to "Pragmatism." '09(O30) c. O. *$1.25 net. Longmans.
Pluralistic universe; Hibbert lectures at Manchester College on the present situation in philosophy. '09(Ap24) c. O. **$1.50 net. Longmans.
See also Begbie, Harold.

JAMES, William.
Dewey, J:, *and others*. Essays philosophical and psychological in honor of William James. **$3 net. Longmans.
JAMES, Epistle of St.
See Bible. N. T.
JAMES RIVER, Va.
Farley, J. P. Three rivers, the James, the Potomac, the Hudson; retrospect of peace and war. *$2 net. Neale.
Hutchins, F. *and Mrs.* C. Houseboating on a colonial waterway. $2.50. L. C. Page.
Jameson, Mrs. Anna Brownell Murphy.
Legends of the Madonna, as represented in the fine arts. '10(Mr12) il. S. $1.25. Bowman.
Shakespeare's heroines. '09(Ap17) 16°, (York lib.) *80 c. net; leath., *$1.25 net. Macmillan.
Jameson, E. M.
Pendleton twins. '08(F29) il. D. $1.25. Jennings.
Jameson, F:
Art's enigma. '10(N12) il. O. $2 net. Lane.
Jameson, Mrs. Helen Follett, ["Madame Qui Vive."]
Pippins and peaches. '09(Ap10) c. il. D. bds., $1. Reilly & B.
Jameson, J: Franklin, ed.
Narratives of New Netherland, 1609-1664. '09(S25) c. maps, facsims., O. (Original narratives of early American history.) **$3 net. Scribner.
Jameson, Jos. Moore.
Elem. pract. mechanics. '09, [1910.] c. 12+321 p. il. 12°, $1.60. Longmans.
Jamestown Exposition. Eleventh annual convention of the Association of State and National Food and Dairy Departments, held at Jamestown Tercentennial Exposition, July 16-19, 1907. '08(Ap25) c. 8°, $3. Wiley.
JAMESTOWN EXPOSITION.
New Jersey. Official souvenir, the New Jersey Commission to the Jamestown tercentennial exposition. gratis. E. M. Jackson.
Jamieson, Guy Arth.
In the shadow of God. '10(Mr26) c. D. **$1 net. Fenno.
Jamieson, M. M., jr.
Jolly tars. '10(D) 28 p. il. (partly col.) 24°, (Little mother ser.) bds., 50 c. Dutton.
Warriors brave: story of the little lead soldiers. '08(N7) il. Tt. (Little mother ser.) bds., 50 c. Dutton.
Jamison, Ja. Carson.
With Walker in Nicaragua; or, reminiscences of an officer of the American phalanx. '10(F5) pors. D. $1.50. J. C. Jamison.
Jan of the windmill. *See* Ewing, *Mrs.* Juliana Horatia Gatty.
Jane, Lionel Cecil.
From Metternich to Bismarck; textbook of European hist., 1815-1878. '10(D10) maps, plans, 8°, $1.10. Oxford Univ.
Jane Eyre. *See* Brontë, C.
Jane Hamilton's recipes. **Poindexter, *Mrs.* C. M.**, *comp.* $1. **McClurg.**
Jane Jones and some others. King, B: F. $2. Forbes.
Janet and her dear Phebe. Dixon, *Mrs.* C. B. $1. Stokes.
Janet at odds. Ray. A. C. †$1.50. Little, B. & Co.
Janet of the dunes. Comstock, *Mrs.* H. T. †$1.50. Little, B. & Co.
Janet Vardoff. Clark, *Mrs.* S. R. G. $1.50. Griffith.
Janey Canuck in the West. Ferguson, E. $1.20 net. Cassell.
Janssen, Johannes.
Hist. of the German people at the close of the Middle Ages; tr. from the German by A. M. Christie. v. 9-14. '09(O) 8°, *$18.75 net. Herder.
Janvier, T: Allibone.
Henry Hudson: brief statement of his aim and his achievements, to which is added a newly-discovered partial record now first published of the trial of the mutineers by whom he and others were abandoned to their death. '09(Ag28) c. il. D. **75 c. net. Harper.
—, comp. Legends of the City of Mexico. '10(Ja22) c. il. O. **$1.30 net. Harper.
JAPAN.
American Academy of Political and Social Science. Commercial relations bet. the U. S. and Japan. Am. Acad. Pol. Sci.
Anderson, W: Japanese wood engravings. *75 c. net; *$1 net. Dutton.
Andrews, R. W. Japan mission of the American church. $1; 50 c. Church Missions.
Angus, D. C. Japan. $1 net. Cassell.
Cary, O. History of Christianity in Japan. In 2 v. ea., *$2.50 net. Revell.
Clark, A. H. On a collection of feather stars, or *comatulids* from Japan. 15 c. U. S., Supt. of Docs.
D'Autremer, J. Japanese empire and its economic condition. $3 net. Scribner.
Davidson, A. M. C. Present-day Japan. *$1.50 net. Scribner.
De Becker, J. E. Nightless city; or, the hist. of the Yoshiwara Yukwaku. *$10 net. Wessels.
Dillon, E. Arts of Japan. *$1 net. McClurg.
Du Cane, F. Flowers and gardens of Japan. *$6 net. Macmillan.
Harris, M. C. Christianity in Japan. *35 c. net. Jennings.
Holland, C. Things seen in Japan. *75 c. net; *$1 net. Dutton.
Ladd, G: T. Rare days in Japan. $2.25 net. Dodd.
Lampe, W. E. Japanese Social organization. 75 c.; 50 c. Princeton Univ. Press.
Lawson, *Lady.* Highways of Japan. $3.75 net. Stokes.
Lloyd, A. Every-day Japan. *$4 net. Cassell.
Lloyd, A. Wheat among the tares: studies of Buddhism in Japan. *$1.10 net. Macmillan.
Longford, J. H. Story of old Japan. $1.75 net. Longmans.
Master singers of Japan. 60 c. net. Dutton.

JAPAN.—*Continued.*
Miglon, G. In Japan. *$1.50 net. Lippincott.
Miyakawa, M. Life of Japan. $1.50 net. Neale.
Montgomery, H. B. Empire of the East. *$2.50 net. McClurg.
Norman, *Sir* H: Real Japan. *$1.50 net. Scribner.
Okakura, K. Ideals of the East; with ref. to the art of Japan. *$1.50 net. Dutton.
Okuma, *Count* S., *comp.* Fifty years of new Japan. 2 v. $7.50 net. Dutton.
Ozaki, Y. T. Warriors of old Japan. **$1.25 net. Houghton M.
Ponting, H. G. In Lotus-land: Japan. $6 net. Macmillan.
Pontius, A. W., *comp.* Protection extended to patents, designs, trade-marks and copyrights in China, Japan and Korea. (Add. Superintendent for price.) U. S., Supt. of Docs.
Redesdale, A. B. F.-M., *Lord.* Tales of old Japan. 50 c. net. Macmillan.
Schwartz, H: B. In Togo's country. *$1.50 net. Jennings.
Smelser, F. L. *and* M. E. L. Miracles of grace in Japan. (Add. pubs. for price.) Hudson.
Smith, A. Game of go, the national game of Japan. **$2.50 net. Moffat.
Smith, R: G. Ancient tales and folk lore of Japan. *$6 net. Macmillan.
Stratton, C. R. Picturesque Japan. $1. Nat. Pub. Co.
Taylor, C: M. Vacation days in Hawaii and Japan. *$1.25 net. Jacobs.
Thompson, A. M. Japan for a week. $1.50 net. Lane.
Tyndale, W. Japan and the Japanese. $5 net. Macmillan.
Uyehara, G. E. Political development of Japan, 1867-1909. $3 net. Dutton.
Women and wisdom of Japan. *40 c. net. Dutton.
See also Bass;—China;—Corea;—Fairy tales;—Far East;—Mineral waters;—Painters and painting;—Port Arthur;—Russo-Japanese war;—Shintoism;—Yellow peril.

Japan in New York. '08(Mr14) c. il. pors. O. Pap., 50 c. Anraku.
Japanese artist in London. Markino, Y. $2 net. Jacobs.
Japanese folk stories. Nixon-Roulet, M. F. 40 c. Am. Bk.
Japanese gold fish. Smith, H. M. $2. W. F. Roberts.

JAPANESE IN THE UNITED STATES.
American Academy of Political and Social Science. Chinese and Japanese in America. $1. Am. Acad. Pol. Sci.

JAPANESE LITERATURE.
Fujiwara, S., *comp.* Hundred verses from old Japan. 90 c. Oxford Univ.
Persian literature; including Japanese literature. 2 v. $3.50; $7. Lamb Pub.

JAPANESE PRINTS.
See Engravers and engravings.

JAPANESE-RUSSIAN WAR.
See Russo-Japanese war.

Japanese sword guards. Okabe-Kakuya. $1.25. Boston Museum.
Japanese wood engravings. Anderson, W: *75 c. net; *$1 net. Dutton.

Japhet in search of a father. Marryat, F. 50 c. Hurst.

JAQUELIN FAMILY.
See Genealogies: Bellet, L. P. du.

Jardine, Ja. T.
Coyote-proof pasture experiment, 1908. '09 (D) 40 p. il. tabs., 8°, (U. S., Dept. of Agriculture, forest service; circular.) pap. (Add. Superintendent for price.)

Jardine, Rob., M.D.
Clinical obstetrics. 3d ed. '10(F) 745 p. il. 8°, *$6.50 net; hf. mor., *$7.50 net. Wood.

Jarman, G: Wallace, M.D.
See Grandin, Egbert H:

Jaros, S:
How the public can own and control new railroads: by public ownership and government supervision. '08(O) c. 27 p. 8°. (Add. pubs. for price.) Jaros Co.

Jason. Forman, J. M. †$1.50. Harper.

JASPER, John.
Frost, J. M., *ed.* Experience of grace, three notable instances: Saul of Tarsus, John Jasper, Edward Everett Hale, jr. 40 c. S. S. Bd. So. Bapt.
Hatcher, W: E. John Jasper: the unmatched negro philosopher and preacher. *$1 net. Revell.

Jasper, Wa.
Susanna: drama. '08(My9) c. D. bds. (Priv. pr.) Mayhew.

Jasper Hunnicutt of Jimpsonhurst. Votaw, C. E. $1.50. Union Bk.

Jastro, Jos.
Qualities of men; essay in appreciation. '10(O15) c. D. $1 net. Houghton M.

Jataka (The). Buddhaghosha. v. 6. *$4 net. Putnam.

JAWS.
See Mouth.

Jay, Allen.
Autobiography of Allen Jay; born 1831, died 1910. '10(Jl2) c. il. pors. O. $1.50 net. Winston.

Jayhawker (The). Martin, J: A. $1.50. C. M. Clark.

Jayhews, T:
His better self; novel. '10(D10) c. 12°, $1.50. Saalfield.

Jayne, Stephen Oscar.
See Hunter, Byron.

Jayne, W:
Abraham Lincoln, personal reminiscences of the martyred president: address del. to the Grand Army Hall and Memorial Association February 12, 1900. '08(Ag1) c. pors. 12°, pap., 25 c. Grand Army.

Jean Armour Burns Club, Washington, D. C.
Speeches and essays, by Prof. John Wilson, Rev. Dr. Wallace, Gen. Ja. A. Garfield, [and others;] with poems on Burns, by Montgomery, Halleck, Campbell, Mrs. W: R. Smith, and others, and eighty appreciations of Robert Burns. 4th ed., enl. '10 (F5) pors. 12°, gratis. Gibson Bros.

Jean-Christophe. *See* Rolland, Romain.

Jean et Marguerite. *See* Reichenbach, M. Deux comédies enfantines.

JEANNE D'ARC.
See Joan *of Arc.*

Jeanne of the marshes. Oppenheim, E: P. †$1.50. Little, B. & Co.

Jeannie's journal. Randolph, A. $1. Bonnell.

Jeanrenaud, Henriette.
Duke of Brittany; tr. from the German by G: P. Upton. '08(S19) c. il. S. (Life stories for young people.) *60 c. net. McClurg.

Jeans, Ja. Hopwood.
Mathematical theory of electricity and magnetism. '08(Mr28) 8°, *$4.50 net. Putnam.

Jebb, Camilla.
Star of the salons: Julie de Lespinasse. '08 (Ap4) O. *$3.50 net. Putnam.

Jebb, Sir R: Claverhouse.
Attic orators from Antiphon to Isaeus. 2 v. 1876, '08(Ag15) 8°, *$5.50 net. Macmillan.
Samson Agonistes and the Hellenic drama. '10(F19) O. pap., 35 c. Oxford Univ.
See also Theophrastus. Characters.
—, tr. *See* Aristotle.

Jedge Waxem's pocket-book of politics. Lampton, W: J. 50 c. G: W. Dillingham.

JEEZEH, Egypt.
See **Ghizeh.**

JEFFERIES, **John Richard.**
Thomas, E: Richard **Jefferies; his life** and work. *$3 net. Little, B. & Co.

Jefferies, R:
Life of the fields. '08(N7) il. D. *$1.50 net. Lippincott.
Nature near London. '08(D5) il. 12°, *$1.50 net. Lippincott.
Open air. '08(N7) il. D. *$1.50 net. Lippincott.

Jeffers, Mrs. Helen Eliz. Van Sickle, ["Elizabeth von Zicklen."]
Little Prince Charming. '09(Je) c. 258 p. il. 12°, $1.35. Reid Pub.

Jeffers, Le Roy.
List of editions sel. for economy in book buying. '10(N19) c. 8°, 25 c. A. L. A.
—, comp. Reference list of titles suggested for a special library binding. '10(Mr5) 8°. N. Y. Pub. Lib.

Jefferson, C: E:, D.D.
Building of the church. '10(O1) c. D. $1.25 net. Macmillan.
Character of Jesus. '08(O10) c. O. **$1.50 net. Crowell.
Christmas builders. '09(S11) c. front. D. bds., **50 c. net. Crowell.
Congregationalism. '10(N5) c. D. bds., 25 c. net. Pilgrim Press.
Essentials: address on the fundamentals of Christian faith and service. '08(Je6) c. D. bds., 35 c. Y. M. C. A.
Minister as preacher. '09(Mr) c. 12 p. 12°, (Claims and opportunities of the Christian ministry.) 5 c.; per 100, $4. Y. M. C. A.
My Father's business: series of sermons to children. '09(O9) c. il. O. **$1.25 net. Crowell.
Next step: [to be used in following up the results of evangelistic campaigns.] '09 (Mr13) 35 c.; condensed, 5 c. Y. M. C. A.

Jefferson, C: E:—*Continued.*
Original year. '10(N5) c. D. bds., 50 c. net. Pilgrim Press.
Talks on high themes for young Christians. '09(N13) c. D. bds., *75 c. net. Pilgrim Press.

Jefferson, Mrs. Eugénie Paul.
Intimate recollections of Joseph Jefferson. '09(D4) c. il. pors. O. **$3.50 net. Dodd.
Right-Motive Club. '08(O3) c. 12°, *$1 net; with hand-illuminated initials, *$2 net. Washington Bk.

JEFFERSON, Joseph.
Jefferson, *Mrs.* E. P. Intimate recollections of Joseph Jefferson. **$3.50 net. Dodd.

Jefferson, T:
Jefferson Bible. '08(D) c. '04. 23+161 p. 25 c.; 50 c. McKay.

JEFFERSON, Thomas.
Mangasarian, M. M. Religion of Washington, Jefferson and Franklin. 10 c. Independent Religious.

Jefferson, Wilson Ja.
Verses. '09(D4) c. D. bds., $1. Badger.

Jefferson, Me. Centennial celebration of the town of Jefferson, Lincoln Co., Me., Ag. 21, 1907; comp. by Alberto A. Bennett. '08 (N) 61 p. il. por. 8°. (Add. pub. for price.) F. E. Jackson.

Jeffery, Jos. Alex.
Elem. laboratory study in crops for the schools of Michigan. '07, [1908.] (Je.) c. 28 p. il. 8°, pap., gratis. Mich. Supt. Pub. Instruction.
Elem. laboratory study in soils, for the schools of Michigan. '08(Je) c. '07. 36 p. il. 8°, pap., gratis. Mich. Supt. Pub. Instruction.

Jefferys, W: Hamilton, M.D., and Maxwell, Ja. L., M.D.
Diseases of China, incl. Formosa and Korea. '10(D) 16+716 p. il. maps, 8°, $6. Blakiston.

Jeffords, Sydney G., ed.
Series of notable debates by men of the hour; dry—wet. '09, [1910.] (Ja) c. 128 p. il. pors. 8°, 50 c. S. G. Jeffords.

Jeffs, A.
Art of sermon illustration. '09(S11) 12°, *$1 net. Revell.

Jehanne of the golden lips. Knowles-Foster, F. G. $1.50. Lane.

Jekyll, Gertrude.
Children and gardens. '08(D19) il. 8°, ("Country Life" lib.) *$2 net. Scribner.
Colour in the flower garden. '08(D5) il. 8°, *$3.75 net. Scribner.
Home and garden; notes and thoughts, pract. and critical, of a worker in both. New ed. '01, [1910.] (S) 14+301 p. O. price reduced from $3.50 to $2 net. Longmans.
Wood and garden; notes and thoughts, pract. and critical, of a working amateur. '10(S10) il. O. $2 net. Longmans.

Jelfs, G: F:
Commentaries on sin. '10(S17) c. D. $1 net. Sherman, F.

Jellett, H:, M.D.
Manual of midwifery for students and practitioners. 2d ed. [1910.] (Je) 1220 p. il. 8°, $6 net: leath., $7 net. Wood.

Jellett, H:, 1821-1901.
Sermons on special and festival occasions; with introd. by J. H. Bernard. '08(Ja25) por. D. *$1.20 net. Longmans.

Jellie, Mrs. Harvey-.
See Harvey-Jellie, *Mrs.*

Jelliffe, R. A., comp.
See Percival, Milton.

Jelliffe, Smith Ely, M.D., comp.
See Reissig, Carl.

Jellum, S. P.
Some central Idaho gold districts. '09, [1910.] 84 p. il. maps, 8°, 50 c. Northwest Mining.

JELLYFISH.
Mayer, A. G. Medusæ of the world. 3 v. ea., $6; per set, $18. Carnegie.
Torrey, H. B. *Leptomedusae* [jellyfish] of the San Diego region. 20 c. Univ. of Cal.

JENA CAMPAIGN.
Maude, F. N. Jena campaign. *$1.60 net. Macmillan.

Jenckes, Adaline Louise.
Origin, the organization and the location of the staple of England. '08(D) 83 p. maps, 8°, pap. (Add. pubs. for price.) Univ of Penn.

Jenison, Sarah A.
Guiding voices; decorated by Emma M. Moseley. [1910.] c. '09 (Ja) 29 p. il. 16°, 35 c. S. A. Jenison.

Jenkin, C: Frewen.
Engineering science: lecture. '08(D12) O. pap., 35 c. Oxford Univ.

Jenkins, C: Fs., and Depue, Oscar B.
Hdbk. for motion picture and stereopticon operators. '08(My9) c. il. 16°, $2.50. Knega.

Jenkins, F. J: H:, ed.
See Hisperica famina.

Jenkins, Floyd, McGraw, Donald, and Darrow, R: Putnam, comps.
Dolls and toy balloons; musical comedy up to date. '10(Je11) c. D. $1. B'way Pub.

Jenkins, Fk. E., D.D.
See Baker, Smith.

—, Atkinson, H: A., Baker, Smith, and others.
Anglo-Saxon Congregationalism in the South. '08, [1909.] (Ja) 300 p. il. pors. 12°. (Add. pubs. for price.) Franklin-T.

Jenkins, Stephen.
Princess and another. '08(My9) c. front. D. price changed to $1.50. B: W. Huebsch.

Jenkins' brief description of the horse; its external and internal organization. '08 (Ag22) c. il. 12°, 50 c. W: R. Jenkins.

Jenkins' manual of photoengraving. *See* Amstutz, N. S.

Jenkinson, Eleanor L.
Ocklye cookery book. '10(S) 8°, 60 c. net. Cassell.

Jenkinson, Emily.
Silverwool. '10(D31) D. $1.50. Baker & T.

Jenkinson, J. W.
Experimental embryology. '09(O) 341 p. figs. 8°, *$4.15 net. Oxford Univ.

Jenks, E:, ed.
Digest of English civil law. Bk. 2. pts. 1, 2, 3. '10(S) c. O. ea., pap., $1.25. Boston Bk.

Jenks, G: C.
The climax; from the celebrated play of the same name, by E: Locke. '10(Ja15) c. il. D. $1.50. H. K. Fly.
The climax. '10(D) il. 75 c. Grosset.

Jenks, Jeremiah Whipple.
Governmental action for social welfare. '10 (Je18) c. D. (American social progress ser.) $1 net. Macmillan.
Life questions of high school boys. '10 (My14) c. 12°, 40 c. Y. M. C. A.
Principles of politics from the viewpoint of the American citizen. '09(My22) 12°, (Columbia Univ. lectures, George Blumenthal foundation.) *$1.50 net. Lemcke.

Jenks, Orrin Roe.
Last prophets of Israel. '09(O) c. 81 p. il. 8°, 35 c. Our Hope.

Jenks, Tudor.
Chemistry for young people. '10(Ja1) c. il. D. **$1.50 net. Stokes.
Photography for young people. '08(S5) c. D. **$1.50 net. Stokes.
When America became a nation. '10(S3) c. il. pors. map, D. $1.25. Crowell.
When America won liberty; patriots and loyalists. '09(S18) c. il. D. $1.25. Crowell.

Jenne, Eldred Llewellyn.
Papers on deciduous fruit insects and insecticides; the codling moth in the Ozarks. '09(Ag) 32 p. il. tabs., 8°, (U. S., Dept. of Agriculture, Bu. of Entomology bull.) pap. (Add. Superintendent for price.) U. S., Supt. of Docs.

Jenner, Mrs. Katharine Lee Rawlings, [Mrs. H: Jenner.]
Christian symbolism. '10(O8) c. il. S. (Little books on art.) $1 net. McClurg.
Our Lady in art. '10(D3) il. T. (Little books on art.) $1 net. McClurg.

Jenner, W: A.
The octopus: reaching for books; considerations upon the pending copyright bills. '09(Ja16) O. pap., gratis. W: A. Jenner.
Publisher against the people; plea for the defense: examination of the proposed new copyright law. '09(Ja16) 8°, gratis. W: A. Jenner.

—, and Wilson, H: E.
Cæsar's first campaign; beginner's Latin book. '10(D10) c. il. 12°, $1 net. Appleton.

Jenness, Herbert Thdr.
Bucket brigade to flying squadron; fire fighting past and present. '10(Ag13) c. il. pors. facsims., 8°, $1.50. H. T. Jenness.

Jenness, Ja. Freeman.
Our rich inheritance. '08(Ap18) c. D. (What is worth while ser.) **30 c. net. Crowell.

Jennett, Norman E.
Monkey shines of Marseleen. '09(D18) il. 4°, bds., 60 c. Cupples & L.

Jennings. Edn. B.
People and their property; [also] The people and the trusts. '08(Ag8) c. D. $1. B'way Pub.

Jennings, Janet.
Abraham Lincoln, the greatest American. '09(Ag28) c. il. 16°, 50 c. Jennings.

Jennings, Nina Isabel, comp.
The latch-string to happiness; little book for your heart when it's heavy. '09(D) c. 61 p. 8°, 50 c. Lone Star.
Man and his mate: [love songs and letters.] '08(S5) c. facsim., O. pap., 50 c.; limp leath., $1.50. Lone Star.
When we're in love; little book for your heart when it's full. '10(Ag20) c. 8°, 50 c. Lone Star.

Jennings, Oscar, M.D., ed.
Morphia habit and its voluntary renunciation; (personal relation of a suppression after twenty-five years' addiction;) with notes and additional cases by Oscar Jennings. '09(N) 502 p. 12°, *$2 net. Wood.

Jenny's bird house. Merriam, L. F. $1. C. M. Clark.

Jensen, Carl Arth.
See New York. Treatise on the mechanics lien law.

Jensen, Carl Oluf.
Essentials of milk hygiene. 2d ed., rev. '09(F20) c. il. figs. O. **$2 net. Lippincott.

Jensen, C: A.
Seasonal nitrification as influenced by crops and tillage. '10(Jl) 31 p. il. 8°, (U. S. Dept. of Agriculture; Bu. of Plant Industry; bull.)

Jensen, G: H.
Elem. industrial work. '10(Jl30) c. il. $1. G: H. Jensen.

Jensen, J. C.
Square look into eternity. '09(N) c. 54 p. 12°, 25 c.; 2d rev. ed. '10(Ap30) c. S. $1. J. C. Jensen.

Jensen, Wilhelm.
Die braune Erica; novelle; ed., with introd. and notes, by E: S. Joynes. '09(F6) c. 16°, (Modern lang. ser.) 35 c. Heath.

Jephtha sacrificing. Whiffen, E. T: **$1 net. Grafton Press.

Jepson, C. N., ed.
See Iowa. Supplement.

Jepson, Edg.
Four philanthropists. '08(Je20) c. il. D. 75 c. Cupples & L.
Garden at 19. '10(Je11) c. il. D. $1.20 net. Wessels & B.
Tangled wedlock. '08(Mr14) D. †$1.50. McClure.

—, and Leblanc, Maurice.
Arsène Lupin; from the play. '09(N13) c. il. D. †$1.50. Doubleday, P.

Jepson, G:
Elem. principles of industrial drawing. [1910.] c. '09 (Ja) 28 p. obl. 16°, 50 c. G: Jepson.

Jepson, Willis Linn.
Flora of California; to be completed in about 15 pts. pts. 1, 2. '09(D25) 12°, pap., pt. 1, 90 c.; pt. 2, 80 c. Cunningham, C. & W.

Jepson, Willis Linn.—*Continued.*
Synopsis of the North American godetias. '08(Ja11) il. Q. (Univ. of Cal. pubs., Botany.) pap., 40 c. Univ. of Cal.
Trees of California. '10(Ja22) il. 16°, *$2.50 net. Cunningham, C. & W.

Jerd Cless. Daley, M. $1.50. Cochrane.

JEREMIAH.
See Bible.

Jernegan, Prescott Ford.
"1001" questions and answers on Philippine history and civil government. '08(F1) c. S. (Philippine question books.) pap. Philippine Educ.

Jerningham, C: E: Wynne, ["Marmaduke."]
Art and curio collector's guide to London. '10(O1) 12°, 35 c. net. Cassell.
Bargain book. '10(D31) front. 8°, $3.50 net. Warne.
Marmaduke maxims. '10(F19) *$1.25 net. Brentano's.
See also Nevill, Ralph.

Jerome, Jerome Klapka.
Passing of the third floor back. '08(N14) c. S. †$1. Dodd.
They and I. '09(O23) c. D. †$1.50. Dodd.

Jerrett, Herman Dan.
Hydraulic tables and memoranda. '08 (O10) c. il. 16°, $1.50. Hicks-J.

Jerrold, Clare.
Beaux and the dandies: Nash, Brummell, and D'Orsay, with their courts. '10(D10) il. O. $5 net. Lane.

JERROLD, Douglas William.
Jerrold, W. C. Douglas Jerrold and *Punch*. $4 net. Macmillan.

Jerrold, Laurence.
Real France. '10(D17) D. $1.50 net. Lane.

Jerrold, Mrs. Maud F.
Francesco Petrarca: poet and humanist. '09(O30) 8°, *$4 net. Dutton.

Jerrold, Walter Copeland, ["Walter Copeland."]
Babes and blossoms. '09(O2) il. D. (Riddle and puzzle bks.) bds., 75 c. Caldwell.
Cake shop: verses. '08(D12) il. 48°, bds., 25 c. Dutton.
Douglas Jerrold and *Punch*. '10(D31) il. 8°, $4 net. Macmillan.
Highways and byways in Kent. '08(Ja11) il. map, 12°, (Highways and byways ser.) $2. Macmillan.
Highways and byways of Middlesex. '10 (Ja1) il. map, 12°, (Highways and byways ser.) *$2 net. Macmillan.
Shakespeare-land. '10(Jl30) col. il. O. (Beautiful England ser.) bds., $1.25, boxed. Estes.
Thomas Hood: his life and times. '09 (My1) il. pors. facsim., O. *$5 net. Lane.

—, ed. Book of living poets. '09(Ap17) c. D. *$2.50 net. Lane.
See also Annals of fairyland.

—, and Robinson, C:
Little book of other people. '09(Jl17) il. in col. 48°, bds., 25 c. Dutton.
Little book of sailors. '09(Jl17) il. in col. 48°, bds., 25 c. Dutton.
Little book of soldiers. '09(Jl17) il. in col. 48°, bds., 25 c. Dutton.
Mother Goose's nursery rhymes. '09 (Ag28) il. in col. 8°, *$1.50 net. Dodge.

Jersey, Marg. Eliz. Leigh Villiers, Countess of.
Augustus; or, the adventures of a little boy in search of his own way. '10(S10) il. S. 50 c. Stokes.

JERSEY CATTLE.
See Cattle.

Jersey City, N. J., Free Public Library. From canoe to tunnel: a sketch of the history of transportation between Jersey City and New York, 1661-1909; a souvenir of Tunnel Day, July 10, 1909. '09(Ag28) O. pap., gratis. Jersey City Lib.

JERSEY CITY, N. J.
Muirheid, W. G., *ed.* Jersey City of today. $10. F. Stevens.
See also Church of the Redeemer.

Jersey jingles. Robbins, L. H. $1. Vance.

JERUSALEM.
Conder, C. R. City of Jerusalem. *$4 net. Dutton.
Duncan, N. Going down from Jerusalem. **$1.50 net. Harper.
Merrill, S. Ancient Jerusalem. *$6 net. Revell.
Paton, L. B. Jerusalem in Bible times. $1. Univ. of Chic.
Smith, G: A. Jerusalem from earliest times to A.D. 70. 2 v. *$7.50 net. Armstrong.
See also Palestine.

Jerusalem delivered. Tasso, T. $1.75; $3.50. Lamb Pub.

Jerusalem the golden. *See* Bernard *of Cluny.*

Jervey, Thdr. Dehon.
Robert Y. Hayne. '09(My15) c. pors. O. **$3 net. Macmillan.

Jesperson, Otto.
Modern English grammar on historical principles. pt. 1, Sounds and spellings. '09(Ag14) D. (Germanische bibliotek.) *$3 net. Stechert.

Jessica Trent's inheritance. Raymond, *Mrs.* E. H. 75 c. McKay

Jessop, C: Minshall, and Caunt, G: W:
Elements of hydrostatics. '10(D24) c. il. 12°, 60 c. net. Macmillan.

Jessup, H: Harris, D.D.
Fifty-three years in Syria; introd. by Ja. S. Dennis, *D.D.* In 2 v. '10(Mr19) c. il. pors. O. **$5 net, boxed. Revell.

Jessup, H: Wynans.
History of the Fifth Avenue Presbyterian Church of New York City, New York, from 1808 to 1908, together with an account of its centennial anniversary celebration, December 18-23, 1908. '09 (My15) c. il. pors. fold. tab., 8°, $1. Barnes.
Law and practice in the surrogates' courts in the state of New York. 3d ed. '09 (N) c. O. $10. Banks.

Jester Life and his marionettes. Antrim, *Mrs.* M. T. $1. Altemus.

Jester men. Mann, C. $1.50. Weed-Parsons.

Jester's sword. Johnston, *Mrs.* A. F. 50 c.; 35 c. L. C. Page.

Jesters (The). Zamacoïs, M. **$1 net. Brentano's.

JESTS.
See Wit and humor.

Jesuit (The). Clark, F. B. $1.25. Eaton & M.

JESUITS.
See Jesus (*Society of*).

Jesup, Morris Ketchum.
Resolutions in appreciation of Morris K. Jesup by the trustees of the Am. Museum of Natural History, the Scientific Staff of the Am. Museum of Natural History, the N. Y. Acad. of Sciences, [etc.] '08 (N) por. 4°. (Not for sale.) Am. Museum.

JESUP, Morris Ketchum.
Brown, W: A. Morris Ketchum Jesup. $2.50 net. Scribner.

Jesup lectures. *See* Columbia Univ. lectures.

JESUS (*Society of*).
Hughes, T: A. History of the Society of Jesus in North America. In 6 v. v. 1; pts. 1, 2. ea., *$4.50 net. Burrows.

JESUS CHRIST.
Abbott, E. Message of the Son of Man. *$1.75 net. Macmillan.
Andrews, C. F. Christ in India. $1.50 net. Doran.
Bachman, P. New message in the teaching of Jesus. *40 c. net. Eaton & M.
Bacon, A. S: Illegal trial of Christ. 25 c. A. S: Bacon.
Benjamin, C: T: Fall of David's tabernacle, rebuilt by Christ. 75 c. Reliance.
Berry, L. C. Favorite and favors of the Sacred Heart of Jesus. *75 c. net. Chr. Press.
Beth, K. Miracles of Jesus. *40 c. net. Eaton & M.
Bible. N. T. Life of our Lord; chronologically arranged. *30 c. net; *60 c. net. Dutton.
Bishop, C: M. Jesus the worker. $1.25 net. Revell.
Blackstone, W: E. Jesus is coming. *50 c. net; *25 c. net. Revell.
Body, G: The Good Shepherd. *80 c. net. Whittaker.
Bond, A. R. Master preacher. $1 net. Am. Tr.
Boone, I. Conquering Christ. 50 c. Bible Study.
Borneman, F. W. B., *and others.* Jesus as a problem, teacher, personality and force. $1 net. Funk.
Bradley, S: C. Jesus of Nazareth: a life *$2 net. Sherman, F.
Brett, J. Holy mount: meditations on the transfiguration of our Lord as revealing the life of prayer. *60 c. net. Young Churchman.
Brett, J. Incarnate love: meditations on the love of Jesus. 75 c. Longmans.
Briggs, C: A: Virgin birth of our Lord. *25 c. net. Whittaker.
Broadus, E. H. Book of the Christ child. $1.75. Appleton.
Broderick, M. Trial and crucifixion of Jesus Christ of Nazareth. *$1.25 net. Longmans.
Bryan, W: J. Prince of peace. 35 c. Reilly & B.
Bryant, W. F. The historical Man of Nazareth. 75 c. W. F. Bryant.

JESUS CHRIST.—*Continued.*

Burgess, I: B., *ed.* Life of Christ. $1. Univ. of Chic.

Burkitt, F. C. Earliest sources for the life of Jesus. **50 c. net. Houghton M.

Burton, E. D., *and* Mathews, S. Life of Christ, for the use of classes in secondary schools. $1. Univ. of Chic.

Butler, A. A: How to understand the words of Christ. *90 c. net. Whittaker.

Cady, H. E. God a present help: [interprets the teachings of Jesus.] $1. Roger Bros.

Capecelatro, A. Christ, the church and man. *55 c. net. Herder.

Chandler, W. M. Trial of Jesus from a lawyer's standpoint. 2 v. *$5 net. Empire Pub.

Clark, H: W: Christ from without and within. *$1.25 net. Revell.

Clow, W. M. Secret of the Lord. $1.50 net. Doran.

Creel, G: Quatrains of Christ. **75 c. net. P. Elder.

Crooker, J. H: Jesus brought back. *75 c. net. Sherman, F.

Crucifixion, by an eye-witness: letter written seven years after the crucifixion. $1. Indo-Am. Bk.

Delitzsch, F. Whose son is Christ? *80 c. net. Am. Unitarian.

Denney, J. Jesus and the Gospel. **$2 net. Armstrong.

Dimock, N. Our one Priest on high. 50 c. net.—Sacerdotium of Christ as taught in Holy Scriptures. 75 c. net. Longmans.

Dods, M. Christ and man. $1.50 net. Doran.

Dole, C: F. What we know about Jesus. *75 c. net. Open Court.

Drysdale, A. H. Christ invisible our gain. *$1.25 net. Armstrong.

Dudden, F: H. In Christ's name. *60 c. net. Longmans.

Dungan, D: R. Outline studies in the life of Christ. 25 c. D: R. Dungan.

Durand, A. Childhood of Jesus Christ according to the canonical Gospels. $1.50 net. McVey.

Durell, J. C. Self-revelation of our Lord. $2 net. Scribner.

Farrar, F: W: Life of Christ. $2.50. Crowell.

Farrar, F: W: Life of lives: studies in the life of Christ. *$1.25 net. Cassell.

Fitz Simon, V. A. The Christ of promise in Homer, Hesiod, Vergil, Ovid, Horace, etc. $3 G: W. Dillingham.

Forsyth, P: T. Person and place of Jesus Christ. *$1.50 net. Pilgrim Press.

Forsythe, P: T. Work of Christ. $1.50 net. Doran.

Fouard, C. Christ, the son of God. 25 c. Longmans.

Freeman, J: D. Concerning the Christ. *$1 net. Armstrong.

Gallerani, A. Jesus all good. 50 c.; $1. Kenedy.

Gillie, R. C. Kinsfolk and friends of Jesus. *$1 net. Macmillan.

Gordon, C: W: Angel and the star: [story of Christ's birth.] *50 c. net. Revell.

Gordon, G: A. Great assurance. *50 c. net. Pilgrim Press.

Graham, W: Phases of the sacred passion. *40 c. net. Wagner.

Granbery, J: C. Outline of New Testament Christology. 50 c. Univ. of Chic.

Groenings, J. History of the passion of our Lord Jesus Christ. *$1.25 net. Herder.

Hall, C: C. Christ and the eastern soul. **$1.25 net. Univ. of Chic.

Hammond, J. Magister moritur; our Lord's last hours. *$2 net. Whittaker.

Hanly, J. F. My Lord and Savior Jesus Christ. 85 c. Hollenbeck Press.

Hastings, J., *ed.* Dict. of Christ and the Gospels. In 2 v. v. 2. $8. Scribner.

Hendrix, E. R. Christ's table talk. *$1 net. Pub. Ho. of M. E. Ch., So.

Herbert, L. We preach Christ crucified. *$1 net. Herder.

Hitchcock, A. W. Psychology of Jesus. *$1.25 net. Pilgrim Press.

Hitchcock, F. R. M. Christ and His critics. $1 net. Revell.

Holland, C. J. Divine story; short life of our blessed Lord. *$1 net; 50 c. J. M. Tally.

Horr, G: E. Great ministry. *$1 net; Sunday-school ed., *75 c. net. Bible Study.

Hubbard, E. Man of Sorrows; being a little journey to the home of Jesus of Nazareth. $2. Roycrofters.

Huffman, J. A. Old Testament messages of the Christ. 75 c. Bethel Pub.

Hughes, H. G. Jesus Christ and human life. 40 c. net. Wagner.

Hurlbut, J. L., *ed.* Story of Jesus and the early church. 75 c. Winston.

Hutton, J: A. Authority and person of our Lord. 50 c. net. Revell.

Jefferson, C: E: Character of Jesus. **$1.50 net. Crowell.

Jones, E. F. Story of Jesus told for children. $1. Crowell.

Kaye, J: B. Trial of Christ. [Blank verse.] *$1 net. Sherman, F.

King, H: C. Ethics of Jesus. **$1.50 net. Macmillan.

Kingsford, A. B., *and* Maitland, E. Perfect way; or, the finding of Christ. $2.50. Theo. Pub. Co.

Knox, G: W: Gospel of Jesus the Son of God. 50 c. Houghton M.

Lagerlöf, S. O. L., *comp.* Christ legends. **$1.25 net. Holt.

Larson, J. H: Face of Christ in art. $1. J. H: Larson.

Lawis, J: F. Life of our Lord. 60 c. Dutton.

Lēmann, —. Jesus before the Sanhedrim. 50 c. J. Magath.

Lemme, L. Do we need Christ for communion with God? *40 c. net. Eaton & M.

Leonard, W: E. Poet of Galilee. *$1 net. B: W. Huebsch.

Lepin, M. Christ and the Gospel. $2. McVey.

"Levi," *pseud., comp.* Aquarian gospel of Jesus the Christ. $2. E. S. Dowling.

JESUS CHRIST.—*Continued.*
Liddon, H: P. Divinity of our Lord and Saviour Jesus Christ. $1.25. Longmans.
Life of Christ for children. **$1 net. Longmans.
Life of Jesus of Nazareth. $4. Nelson.
Little, E. S. Works of Jesus. $1.25; 75 c. P. Elder.
Lodge, *Sir* O. J., *and others.* Jesus or Christ. *$1.50 net. Sherman, F.
Losch, H: God-man; or, the life and works of Jesus. $1.50. Badger.
McClelland, T. C. Mind of Christ. **$1.25 net. Crowell.
McConaughy, J. Great events in the life of Christ. 75 c.; 50 c. Y. M. C. A.
McDowell, W: F. In the school of Christ. $1.25 net. Revell.
McFarland, J: T. Etchings of the Master. *$1.25 net. Eaton & M.
Mangasarian, M. M. Truth about Jesus; is he a myth? $1; 50 c. Independent Religious.
Mangasarian, M. M., *and* Crapsey, A. S. Debate: Resolved that the Jesus of the New Testament is an historical personage. (Add. pub. for price.) T. Brentano.
Marvin, F: R. Christ among the cattle: a sermon. 50 c. Pafraets.
Mary Josephine, *Sister.* Story of our Lord's life told for children by a Carmelite nun. $1. Cathedral Lib.
Meissner, *Mme.* de. Words of our Lord and Savior Jesus Christ, spoken from the cross. 25 c. Woodward & L.
Merrell, E: H. Person of Christ. 90 c. net. Bibliotheca Sacra.
Merrick, M. V. Life of Christ. *50 c. net. Herder.
Meschler, M. Life of our Lord Jesus Christ. 2 v. *$4.75 net. Herder.
Meyer, A. Jesus or Paul? *75 c. net. Harper.
Meyer, L. R., *comp.* Jesus; selections. *10 c. net. Jennings.
Meyer, M. Sinlessness of Jesus. *40 c. net. Eaton & M.
Miller, J. R. Bethlehem to Olivet: life of Jesus Christ. **$1.50 net.—The Master's friendships. 50 c. net; **30 c. net. Crowell.
Milton, W: H. Cure of souls: Christ's treatment of the individual. *$1 net. Whittaker.
Montefiore, C. G. Some elements of the religious teaching of Jesus. 75 c. net. Macmillan.
Morgan, G: C. Mountains and valleys in the ministry of Jesus. *25 c. net. Revell.
Muller, E. F. K. Our Lord: belief in the deity of Christ. *40 c. net. Eaton & M.
Myers, C. The boy Jesus. **60 c. net. Am. Bapt.
Nolloth, C: F: Person of our Lord and recent thought. *$1.25 net. Macmillan.
Oesterley, W: O. E. Evolution of the Messianic idea. *$1.25 net. Dutton.
Orr, J. Resurrection of Jesus. *$1.50 net. Jennings.

JESUS CHRIST.—*Continued.*
Otten, B. J. What think you of Christ? 25 c. Herder.
Otto, R. Life and ministry of Jesus. 50 c. Open Court.
Park, C: E. Jesus of Nazareth. 40 c.; 30 c.; 65 c. Unitarian S. S.
Philip, *Brother.* Meditations on the passion of Our Lord Jesus Christ. $1. La Salle Bureau.
Pick, B. Paralipomena: remains of gospels and sayings of Christ. *75 c. net. Open Court.
Pratt, S: W. Deity of Jesus Christ according to the Gospel of John. 50 c. S. S. Times.
Remy, J. S. Story of Jesus told for little children in words of one syllable. 50 c. Altemus.
Riggenbach, E. Resurrection of Jesus. *40 c. net. Eaton & M.
Robinson, C: H: Interpretation of the character of Christ to non-Christian races. *$1.20 net.—Studies in the resurrection of Christ. *$1.25 net. Longmans.
Robinson, E. A. Short studies of Christ. 50 c. Eaton & M.
Rominger, C. A. Coming kingdom. $1. C. A. Rominger.
Rumball, E. A. Jesus and modern religion. *75 c. net. Open Court.
Russell, E. Jesus of Nazareth in the light of to-day. **60 c. net. Winston.
Sanday, W: Christologies ancient and modern. $1.75. Oxford Univ.
Sanday, W: Outlines of the life of Christ. **$1.25 net. Scribner.
Schechter, S. Studies in Judaism. 2d ser. $2. Jewish Pub.
Schuré, E. Jesus the last great initiate. *$1.25 net. Badger.
Schuyler, H: C. Charity of Christ.—Courage of Christ. ea., *50 c. net. P: Reilly.
Schweitzer, A. Quest of the historical Jesus. $3.50 net. Macmillan.
Scott, L. W. Great crisis in the life of Christ. $1. F: L: Rowe.
Seeley, *Sir* J: R. Ecce homo. *35 c. net; *70 c. net. Dutton.
Segal, J. Wanderings of Jesus: [in verse.] $2.50. J. Segal.
Ségur, S. R., *Comtesse* de. Life of Christ for children. $1. Herder.
Selbie, W. B. Aspects of Christ. $1.50 net. Doran.
Seymour, R. F. Christ in Flanders. $1.25; $5. Seymour.
Sharman, H: B. Teaching of Jesus about the future. *$3 net. Univ. of Chic.
Shaw, C. Good Shepherd. $1.50.—Suffer little children; child's life of Christ. $2.50. Fenno.
Simpson, J. G. Christus crucifixus. $1.50 net. Doran.
Smart, G: T: If I should meet the Master! 50 c. net. Pilgrim Press.
Smith, D. Days of His flesh. $2 net. Doran.
Smith, H. L. Christian race: [course of lessons on the life of Christ.] 75 c. Y. M. C. A.

JESUS CHRIST.—*Continued.*
Smith, J. T. S. The perfect Man. *10 c. net. Revell.
Speer, R. E. Deity of Christ. *25 c. net. Revell.
Stalker, J. Ethic of Jesus according to the synoptic Gospels. *$1.75 net. Armstrong.
Stalker, J. Life of Jesus Christ. *60 c. net. Revell.
Stafford, E: R. Shop talks; ser. of addresses on Jesus Christ and His disciples. 75 c. Jennings.
Steedman, A. Little child's life of Jesus. $1. Stokes.
Stevens, G: B. Teaching of Jesus. *$1 net. Macmillan.
Strong, J., *ed.* Studies in the Gospel of the Kingdom; series no. 1. 75 c. Am. Inst. Social Service.
Sweetapple, H. D. S. Earthly footprints of Jesus. *$2 net. Whittaker.
Swete, H: B. Appearances of our Lord after the Passion. *80 c. net. Macmillan.
Tait, A. J. Christ and the nations. $1.50 net. Doran.
Talbot, E. S. Fulness of Christ. *50 c. net. Macmillan.
Taylor, M. Life of Christ. $1.25. Acme.
Thompson, J. M. Jesus according to Saint Mark. $1.50 net. Dutton.
Torrey, R. A. Studies in the life and teachings of our Lord. $1.50. Bible Inst.
Twining, A. G. Childhood of our blessed Lord Jesus Christ. *60 c. net. Young Churchman.
Walker, W: L. Teaching of Christ in its present appeal. *$1 net. Scribner.
Wallace, L. Boyhood of Christ. $1.50. Harper.
Walser, G: H. Life and teachings of Jesus. *$1.35 net. Sherman, F.
Warneck, J. L. Living Christ and dying heathenism. *$1.75 net. Revell.
Weiss, J. Paul and Jesus. *75 c. net. Harper.
Wendling, G: R. Man of Galilee. *$3 net; *$1 net. Olcott.
Whitcomb, I. P., *and* Grosvenor, S. E. Christ-child in legend and art. $1 net. Dodd.
Whitcomb, I. P., *and* Grosvenor, S. E. Christ-child in story, legend, art and song. 75 c. B'way Pub.
Whitteker, J: E. Separated life: Biblical defense of the divinity of Christ. $1. Gen. Council.
Wright, E. D. Psychology of Christ. *$1 net. Cochrane.
Yoder, J: O. Journeys of Jesus, with charts and harmony. 90 c. Lutheran Pub.

See also Apostles;—Atonement;—Beatitudes;—Bible;—Christian life;—Christianity;—Christmas;—Cross;—Easter;—God;—Good Friday;—Holy Spirit; — Holy week; — Incarnation; — Lent;—Lord's prayer;—Lord's supper;—Mary, *Virgin;*—Messiah;—Miracles; —Palestine; — Parables;— Prayers;—Salvation;—Second Advent;—Sermon on the Mount;—Trinity;—War.

Jesus, Hernando de.
Exposicion de los siete psalmos penitenciales del Real Profeta David: covn acto de contricion, y conuersion, y lagrymas del pecador [facsim.] '03 [1909.] (N) no paging, 4°, $3 (200 copies). Hispanic Soc.

Jett, Ann Searcy, ["Ann Se Arcy."]
A Kentucky girl; or, a question unanswered. '09, [1910.] (D) c. 111 p. il. por. 12°, $1. Berea.

Jeu (Le) de l'amour et du hasard. Marivaux, P. C. d. C. d. 35 c. net. Macmillan.

Jevons, Fk. Byron.
Introd. to the study of comparative religion. '08(N7) c. D. (Hartford-Lamson lectures on the religions of the world.) **$1.50 net. Macmillan.

Jevons, W: Stanley.
Investigations in currency and finance; ed., with an introd., by H. S. Foxwell. New ed., abridged, with a preface by H. Stanley Jevons. '09(My15) il. 8°, *$3 net. Macmillan.
Studies in deductive logic. '08(Ap4) diagrs., 12°, *$1.60 net. Macmillan.

Jeweled crown. Harrison, E. Gospel Pub.

Jewell, Ja. Ralph.
Agricultural education, incl. nature study and school gardens. 2d ed., rev. '08. [1909.] (My) 148 p. 8°, (U. S. Bureau of Educ. bull.) pap. (Add. Superintendent for price.) U. S., Supt. of Docs.

Jewellery enamelling; dealing with various processes in vogue for the embellishment of metals by means of vitreous enamels. '10(Je4) il. 12°, (Art craftsman ser.) pap., 25 c. Spon.

JEWELRY.
Davenport, C. Jewellery. *$1 net. McClurg.
Evans, C: T. Essays: practical hints for retail jewelers. (Add. pubs. for price.) W. B. Frost.
Lunt, E. M. Golden opportunity. (Priv. pr.) Towle Mfg.
Rathbone, R. L. B. Simple jewelry. $2 net. Van Nostrand.
Smith, H. C. Jewellery. *$7.50 net. Putnam.

Jewels from my casket. Winslow, *Mrs.* A. J. F. $1.25. A. J. Winslow.

Jewett, Albert Dewey.
Idiomatic ear training: text book for use in class, to awaken pupils to the use of the listening ability, one of the most important fundamental steps in the study of music. '09(My1) c. il. O. $1. A. D. Jewett.

Jewett, C:, M.D.
Syllabus of gynecology. '09(N) c. 3+5-191 p. 12°, $1.25. C: Jewett.

Jewett, Mrs. Frances Gulick.
Body and its defenses. '10(Ap30) c. il. D. (Gulick hygiene ser.) 65 c. Ginn.
Body at work. '09(My8) c. il. D. (Gulick hygiene ser.) 50 c. Ginn.
Control of body and mind. '09(Ja30) c. il. figs. D. (Gulick hygiene ser.) 50 c. Ginn.

Jewett, Frederic Clarke.
History and genealogy of the Jewetts of America. 2 v. '09(My22) il. pors. 4°, **$20 net. Grafton Press.

Jewett, Freeborn G.
Election manual for election officers and voters in the state of N. Y. 18th ed., rev. and enl. by Melvin Bender and H. J. Hinman. '10(S) c. $2.50; pap., $2. M. Bender.
Manual for election officers and voters in the state of New York. 16th ed. '08 (Ag) c. 10+504 p. 8°, $2.50; $3; pap., $2. M. Bender.

Jewett, J: Howard, ["Hannah Warner."]
Ducklings go a-swimming. '08(D5) c. il. sq. S. (Grandmother Goose stories.) 75 c. Small.
Friends of the hunted. '09(Je26) c. il. D. $1. Dodge.
Gosling's picnic. '08(D5) c. il. sq. S. (Grandmother Goose stories.) 75 c. Small.
Hans and sister Hilda. '10(D) 12 p. 8°, bds., 50 c. Dutton.
Kittens and the bear. '08(D5) c. il. sq. S. (Grandmother Goose stories.) 75 c. Small.
Tame bunnies and wild, Bunn, Rabb and Pudgy. '08(N7) il. T. (Little mother ser.) bds., 50 c. Dutton.
What happened to the little chicks. '08 (D5) c. il. sq. S. (Grandmother Goose stories.) 75 c. Small.

Jewett, Mrs. Louise Rogers.
History of Italian painting. '09(Ja23) c. O. pap., 60 c. Mt. Holyoke Coll.

Jewett, Martha.
Hopi, the cliff-dweller. '10(Ap16) c. il. 12°, 30 c. Educ. Pub.

Jewett, Mary.
Reminiscences of my life in Persia. '09 (D18) il. por. $1. Torch Press.

Jewett, Sarah Orne.
Stories and tales. In 7 v. v. 1, Deephaven; v. 2, Tales of New England; v. 3, A country doctor; v. 4, The queen's twin and other stories; v. 5, The life of Nancy; v. 6, A native of Winby; v. 7, The country of the pointed firs. '10(D3) 16°, $7 net. (Sold in sets only.) Houghton M.

Jewett, Sophie, ["Ellen Burroughs."]
God's troubadour; story of St. Francis of Assisi. '10(Ag6) c. il. O. $1.25 net. Crowell.
Poems. Memorial ed. '10(D24) c. por. D. $1.25 net. Crowell.
See also Pearl (The).

JEWETT FAMILY.
See Genealogies.

Jewish fairy tales and fables. "Aunt Naomi." *pseud.* *$1 net. Bloch.

JEWISH HISTORY.
See Jews.

JEWISH LITERATURE.
See Hebrew literature.

Jewish question and key to its solution. Green, M. **75 c. net; **40 c. net. Jacobs.

Jewish religion in the time of Jesus. Hollmann, G. *$1 net. Am. Unitarian.

Jewish story book. Myers, J. M. 30 c. Bloch.

Jewish tracts, issued by the Central Conference of American Rabbis. 8°, pap. J. Morgenstern.
—Enelow. What do the Jews believe? gratis.
—Philipson. Jew in America. gratis.

Jews. Newly improved prayer book entitled Yoreh-Malkosh U'Marveh; improved guide for the teaching to young and old the art of properly reading the Hebrew language, by Rabbi Sabbath Check. '08, [1909.] c. v. 1, 8°, $1. S. Check.

JEWS.
Abernethy, A. T. The Jew a negro. 50 c. Dixie.
Adler, C., *and* Casanowicz, I. M. Collection of Jewish ceremonial objects in the U. S. National Museum. (Add. Supt. for price.) U. S., Supt. of Docs.
Adler, E. N. Auto de fé and Jew: [sketches of the effect of the Inquisition in Spain and Portugal.] $1.75. Oxford Univ.
Adler, H. M., *and* Davis, A., *eds.* Service of the synagogues. 6 v. (Add. author for price.) H. D. Buegeleisen.
American Jewish year book, 1908, 1909, 1910. ea., 75 c. Jewish Pub.
Blum, I. Jews of Baltimore. $3. Hist. Review.
Brewer, W. Egypt and Israel. $2 net. Torch Press.
Burney, C: F. Israel's hope of immortality. $1. Oxford Univ.
Calisch, E: N. Jew in English literature. *$2 net. Bell Bk.
Chicago Hebrew Institute. Program of celebrations during Lincoln week; [Abraham Lincoln and the Jewish spirit: address.] 5 c. Chic. Hebrew Inst.
Clay, A. T. Amurru, the home of the northern Semites. $1.25. S. S. Times.
Collmann, S. M. Jews in art. $1.50. Bacharach.
Cook, S. A. Religion of ancient Palestine. *40 c. net. Open Court.
Cooke, P. Our misunderstanding concerning the Jews. (Add. author for price.) P. Cooke.
Davis, N. D. Notes on the hist. of the Jews in Barbados. $1. Bloch.
Deutsch, G. Hist. of the Jews. 60 c. Bloch.
Dushaw, A. I. Proselytes of the Ghetto. 75 c. J. Heidingsfeld.
Elzas, B. A. Leaves from my historical scrap book: [hist. of S. C. with especial ref. to Jewish affairs.] $1. B. A. Elzas.
Enelow, H. G. What do the Jews believe? gratis. J. Morgenstern.
Fairweather, W: Background of the Gospels; or, Judaism in the period between the Old and New Testaments. *$3 net. Scribner.
Fleugel, M. Humanity, benevolence and charity legislation of the Pentateuch and the Talmud; in parallel with the laws of Hammurabi, the doctrines of Egypt, the Roman XII tables and modern codes. *$2 net. H. Fleugel.
Ginzberg, L: Legends of the Jews. In 4 v. v. 1, 2. ea., $2. Jewish Pub.

JEWS.—*Continued.*

Goodman, P. Synagogue and the church. $1.50. Dutton.

Graetz, H. Hist. of the Jews. 6 v. $18. Jewish Pub.

Grant, C. M. Between the Testaments. *75 c. net. Revell.

Green, M. Jewish question and key to its solution. **75 c. net; **40 c. net; 25 c. Jacobs.

Grossman, R. Brief manual regarding Jewish faith and life. 12 c.—Children's services. 10 c. Bloch.

Hapgood, H. Spirit of the Ghetto. *$1.25 net. Funk.

Harris, M. H: Modern Jewish hist. from the Renaissance to the Russian exodus. 30 c. net.—Thousand years of Jewish hist. $1. Bloch.

Henriques, H. S. Q. Jews and the English law. *$3.50 net. Bloch.

Hollmann, G. Jewish religion in the time of Jesus. *$1 net. Am. Unitarian.

Holy day prayers. $2. Bloch.

Horr, G: E. Training of the chosen people. 75 c. Bible Study.

Hühner, L. Jews of Georgia from the outbreak of the American Revolution to the close of the 18th century. 25 c. Bloch.

Hühner, L. Jews of Newport. (Add. author for price.)—Some Jewish associates of John Brown. o. p. L. Hühner.

Imber, N. H. Treasures of two worlds; legends and traditions of Jewish nation. 50 c. Citizens Pr.

Jenks, O. R. Last prophets of Israel. 35 c. Our Hope.

Joseph, M. Judaism as creed and life. *$1.25 net. Macmillan.

Kabbala denudata. Kabbalah unveiled. $3.50. Theo. Pub. Co.

Ketler, W: H. He is a Jew. 10 c. H. B. Ketler.

Kisch, H. J. Religion of the civilized world and Judaism. 40 c. Bloch.

Krauskopf, J. Prejudice [against the Jews]; its genesis and exodus. 75 c.; 35 c. Bloch.

Loisy, A. Religion of Israel. $1.50. Putnam.

Macaulay, T: B., *Lord.* Essay and speech on Jewish disabilities. $1 net. Bloch.

Milman, H: H. History of the Jews. $1.50. Bloch.

Milman, H: H. Hist. of the Jews. 2 v. ea., *35 c. net; *70 c. net. Dutton.

Myers, J. M. Story of the Jewish people. In 2 v. v. 1. *60 c. net. Bloch.

Nathaniel ibn al-Fayyumi. Bustan al-ukul: [account of the Jews of southern Arabia in the Middle Ages.] *$2.50 net. Lemcke.

Oesterley, W: O. E., *and* Box, G: H. Religion and worship of the Synagogue. *$3 net. Scribner.

Oppenheim, S: Early hist. of the Jews in New York, 1654-1664. $1.—Jews and masonry in the United States before 1810. 50 c. S: Oppenheim.

Paton, L. B. Early religion of Israel. 50 c. net. Houghton M.

Peters, M. C. Justice to the Jew. $1. Trow Press.

Peters, M. C. Justice to the Jew: what he has done for the world. **75 c. net. McClure.

Philipson, D. Jew in America. gratis. J. Morgenstern.

Rogers, R. W: Religion of Babylonia and Assyria, especially in its relation to Israel. *$2 net. Eaton & M.

Schechter, S. Some aspects of Rabbinic theology. **$2.25 net. Macmillan.

Schomer, A. S. Primary cause of antisemetism. $1. A. S. Schomer.

Shatzke, J. S. Unseen dangers behind humanity; or, the real causes why the Jew is hated. $2.50. New Humanity.

Shearer, J: B. Hebrew institutions, social and civil. 60 c. net. Presb. Pub.

Silber, M. Jewish achievement. $1. Modern View.

Simon, A. Principle of Jewish education in the past. 25 c. A. Simon.

Stearns, W. N. Primer of Hebrew history. *40 c. net. Eaton & M.

Strack, H. L. Jew and human sacrifice. *$3 net. Bloch.

Sulzberger, M. Am Ha-Aretz; ancient Jewish parliament. 75 c. net. J. H: Greenstone.

Wagner, W. R. Judaism in music. $1.25 net. Scribner.

See also Bible;—Hebrew language;—Hebrew literature; —Inquisition;—Monotheism;—Prayers; — Prophets (Hebrew); — Samaritans;—Semitic languages;—Semitic religions;—Talmud;—Temple; — *also* Congregation Mikve Israel; — *also* Emanuel, David.

JIGS.

See Machinery.

Jim Hands. Child, R: W. $1.50. Macmillan.

Jim Hardy. Showalter, L. P. (Add. author for price.) L. P. Showalter.

Jim Mortimer. Bell, W. $1.50. Macmillan.

Jimbo. Blackwood, A. †$1.25. Macmillan.

Jimmie Moore of Bucktown. Trotter, M. E. *75 c. net. Revell.

Jimmy. Adams, J. J. 75 c. J. J. Adams.

Jimpy stories. Parsons, H. G. †$1.25. Dutton.

Jiu jitsu, the effective Japanese mode of self-defense; il. by snapshots of K. Koyama and A. Minami, well known native experts. '10(S3) c. 12°, (Spalding's athletic lib.) 10 c. Am. Sports.

Joab, Albert E.

Robert Burns, peasant, poet, patriot; oration, del. before the Caledonian and St. Andrew's societies of Tacoma, Washington, on the 138th anniversary of the poet's nativity. '10(Ap9) pors. O. pap., 50 c. A. E. Joab.

JOAN *of Arc.*

Bangs, M. R. Jeanne D'Arc: the Maid of France. $1.25 net. Houghton M.

Ford, E. A. Blessed Joan of Arc. $1 net. Chr. Press.

Guerber, H. A. Joan of Arc. 30 c. Am. Bk.

Hart, C: H. Joan, the Maid of France. $1.25. Dutton.

James, G. Joan of Arc. $3.50 net. Dutton.

JOAN *of Arc.—Continued.*
Lang, A. Maid of France: life and death of Jeanne d' Arc. *$3.50 net. Longmans.
Michelet, J. Jeanne D'Arc. 50 c. Oxford Univ.
Murray, T. D., *ed.* Jeanne D'Arc, maid of Orleans. *$3.50 net. McClure.
See also France, Anatole, *pseud.* Works. v. 10-11.
Joan of Arc; monologue. Gettner, F. I. 40 c. F. I. Gettner.
Joan of Garioch. Kinross, A. †$1.50. Macmillan.
Joan of the hills. Clegg, T: B. $1.50. Lane.
JOANNA I., *Queen of Naples.*
Steele, F. M. F. Beautiful queen, Joanna I. of Naples. $3.50 net. Dodd.
Joan's jolly vacation. Jacobs, C. E. †$1.50. Jacobs.
Job, Herbert Keightley.
How to study birds; pract. guide for amateur bird-lovers and camera-hunters. '10 (My14) c. il. O. $1.50 net. Outing.
Sport of bird-study. '08(Je6) c. O. *$2 net. Outing.
JOB (Book of).
See Bible.
Jocelyn. *See* Lamartine, Alphonse Marie Louis.
Jock O' Dreams. Herrick, R. $1.50. Macmillan.
Jock of the Bushveld. Fitzpatrick, *Sir* J. P. *50 c. net; *90 c. net. Longmans.
Joe Muller. Groner, A. $1.50. Duffield.
Joe Sap's tales. Sappington, J. $1. Embree Pr.
JOEL.
See Bible. O. T.
Johannine writings. Sehmiedel, P. W. *$1.50 net. Macmillan.
Johannsen, Albert.
Determination of rock-forming minerals. '08(Mr14) il. figs. 8°, $4. Wiley.
Johannsen, N: A. L. J.
How to relieve the depression: suggestion for railroad men and bankers. '08(S19) 8°, pap. (Add. author for price.) N: Johannsen.
Neglected point in connection with crises. '08(O17) c. chart, 8°, $1.50. Bankers Pub.
JOHN, *St., Gospel of.*
See Bible.
John, Eugenia, ["E. Marlitt."]
Baliff's maid. '08(Je13) 12°, (Home ser.) 50 c. Hurst.
In the Schillingscourt. '08(Je13) 12°, (Home ser.) 50 c. Hurst.
Lady with the rubies. '08(Jl18) 12°, (Home ser.) 50 c. Hurst.
John, Lewis Franklin, D.D.
Life of Ezekiel Boring Kephart, statesman, educator, preacher, bishop of the church of the United Brethren in Christ; with an introd. by Bishop N. Castle, D.D. '08 (Mr14) c. il. pors. facsim., D. $1.25. Un. B. Pub.
John, of Worcester.
Chronicle of John of Worcester, 1118-1140; being the continuation of the "Chronicon ex chronicis" of Florence of Worcester; ed. from a manuscript in the Library of Corpus Christi College, Oxford, by J. R. H. Weaver. '08, [1909.] (O) 72 p. facsims., 8°, (Anecdota oxoniensia; mediæval and modern ser.) *$1.90 net. Oxford Univ.
John and Betty's history visit. Williamson, M. $1.25. Lothrop, L. & S.
John Arrowsmith. Bushnell, *Mrs.* B. J. $1.50. Torch Press.
John Bargreave's gold. Brereton, F: S. $1.25. Caldwell.
John Brody's astral body. Bardeen, C: W: $1. Bardeen.
John Chinaman and a few others. Parker, E: H. *$1.25 net. Dutton.
John Chinaman at home. Hardy, E. J. *$1.50 net. Scribner.
John Crerar Library, Chicago, Ill. Catalogue rules; supplementary to "Catalog rules, author and title entries compiled by committees of the American Library Association and the (British) Library Association." American ed. '10(Ja22) 8°. (Not for sale.) John Crerar Lib.
John Crerar Library, Chicago, Ill. List of current medical periodicals and allied serials, December, 1909. '10(My) 25 p. 4°, 10 c. John Crerar Lib.
JOHN CRERAR LIBRARY, SENN COLLECTION.
Josephson, A. G. S. Incunabula in the Senn collection at the John Crerar Library. (Priv. pr.) Am. Medical.
John de Guelph. *See* Fisher, H: W., *ed.*
John Gabriel Borkman. *See* Ibsen, Henrik.
John Gilpin. Cowper, W: *See* Gray, T:
John Glayde's honor. Sutro, A. 50 c. S: French.
John H. Converse lectures. *See* Converse, (John H.,) lectures.
John Halifax, gentleman. *See* Craik; *Mrs.* Dinah Maria Mulock.
John Holden. De Leon, T: C. $1.50. G: W. Dillingham.
John Marsh's millions. Klein, C: $1.50. G: W. Dillingham.
John Marvel, assistant. Page, T: N. †$1.50. Scribner.
John Montcalm, heretic. Rupp, F: A: $1. I. M. Beaver.
John of Salisbury, Bp. of Chatres.
Joannis Saresberiensis, Episcopi Carnotensis Policratici sive de nvgis cvrialivm et vestigiis philosophorvm, libri VIII; recognovit et prolegomenis, apparatvcritico, commentario, indicibvs instrvxit, Clemens C. I. Webb. In 2 v. '09(N13) O. $11. Oxford Univ.
John of the woods. Brown, A. F. †$1. Houghton M.
John Silence, physician extraordinary. Blackwood, A. $1.50. J: W. Luce.
John Stevens' courtship. Gates, *Mrs.* S. Y. $1. Deseret News.
John the Baptist. Sudermann, H. *$1.50 net. Lane.
John the unafraid. '10(Mr19) c. S. bds., $1, boxed. McClurg.
John Winterbourne's family. Brown, A. $1.35 net. Houghton M.
Johnnie and Billy Bushytail. Garis, H. R. 60 c. Fenno.
Johnny Crow's party. Brooke, L. L. $1 net. Warne.

Johnny Hep. Sayler, H. L. 35 c.. Reilly & B.

Johns, Rev. C: Alex.
Birds in their haunts; with a glossary of common and provincial names and technical terms; ed., rev. and annot. by Jean A. Owen. '09(Ap17) il. 8°, *$3 net. Dutton.

Johns, Claude Hermann Wa.
Ur-Engur, a bronze of the fourth millennium, in the library of J. Pierpont Morgan. 38 p. il. 16°, hf. vellum. (Priv. pr.) F. F. Sherman.

Johns, Clayton.
Essentials of pianoforte playing; pract. system of mind and finger training. '09 (D4) c. il. O. $1.50. Ditson.

Johns Hopkins University. *Psychological Laboratory.* Studies; communicated by Professor G: Malcolm Stratton. '09(Je19) il. 4°, (Psychological Review monograph supplements.) $1. Psychological Review.

Johns Hopkins University circular, new ser. pap. Johns Hopkins.
—Gilman. Daniel Coit Gilman. gratis.

Johns Hopkins Univ. studies in hist. and polit. science. O. pap. Johns Hopkins.
—Andrews. British committees, commission, and councils of trade and plantations. 75 c.
—Bryan. Development of the English law of conspiracy. 75 c.
—Campbell. Neutral rights and obligations in the Anglo-Boer war. 75 c.
—Ficklen. Hist. of Reconstruction in Louisiana. $1.50; $1.
—Hanna. Financial history of Maryland, (1789-1848.) 75 c.
—Laprade. England and the French Revolution. 75c.
—Matthews. Legislative and judicial history of the Fifteenth Amendment. (Add. pubs. for price.)
—Motley. Apprenticeship in American trade unions. 50 c.
—Myers. Self-reconstruction of Maryland. 50 c.
—Spedden. Trade union label. 50 c.
—Ware. Elizabethan parish. 50 c.

Johns Hopkins Univ. studies in philosophy and psychology. il. 4°. Johns Hopkins.
—Burrow. Determination of the position of a momentary impression. 65 c.
—Furry. Æsthetic experience. $1.60.

JOHNSON, *Mrs.*
Captivity of Mrs. Johnson. $3; $5. Huntting.

Johnson, A. E.
Dudley Hardy, R.I., R.M.S.; containing 56 examples of the artist's work in brush, pen and pencil. '10(F19) col. il. 12°, *$1.75 net. Macmillan.
Lawson Wood. '10(D17) col. il. 8°, (Brush, pen and pencil ser.) $1.75 net. Macmillan.
Tom Browne, R. I. '09(My8) il. O. (Brush, pen and pencil ser.) *$1.50 net. Macmillan.

Johnson, A. J., ed.
Six ages of European history. In 6 v. v. 1, Dawn of mediæval Europe, 476-918, by the Rev. J. H. B. Masterman; v. 2, Central period of the Middle Age, 918-1273, by Beatrice A. Lees; v. 3, End of the Middle Age, 1273-1453, by Eleanor C. Lodge; v. 4, Europe in Renaissance and Reformation, 1453-1650, by Mary A. Hollings; v. 5, Age of the enlightened despots, 1660-1789, by A. H. Johnson; v. 6, Remaking of modern Europe, 1789-1878, by J: Arth. Ransome Marriott. '10(Ja15) maps, 12°, ea., *90 c. net. Macmillan.

Johnson, A. S.
Six short French plays; for the use of preparatory schools. '10(N12) il. S. 50 c. Longmans.

Johnson, A. T.
Chickens and how to raise them. '09(N13) c. il. S. (Red letter ser.) pap., 25 c. Penn Pub. Co.
Chickens and how to raise them; all about chickens, how to hatch, house, feed and fatten them, and cure their diseases. '10 (D3) c. il. T. 50 c. Penn Pub. Co.

Johnson, Adrian.
See Johnson, Eliz.

Johnson, Alex. Bryan.
Surgical diagnosis. '09(Ag) 3 v., il. 8°, per set, $18. Appleton.

Johnson, Alice A., ed.
Household companion; comprising a complete cook book—pract. household recipes, aids and hints for household decorations; care of domestic plants and animals and a treatise on domestic medicine, incl. a chapter on tuberculosis by Dr. Lawrence F. Flick. [1910.] (Je) c. '09. il. 8°, $1.50. Uplift.

Johnson, Allen.
Stephen A. Douglas. '08(Ap18) c. O. **$2.50 net. Macmillan.

Johnson, Mrs. Alta Leonard.
Only a boy: [in memory of Wilbur Warren Johnson.] '08(Ja4) por. 8°, pap. (Not for sale.) A. L. Johnson.

Johnson, Alvin Saunders.
Introd. to economics. '09(S18) c. 12°, $1.50. Heath.
Introductory economics. '08(Ap18) c. D. $1.50. Sch. of Liberal Arts.

Johnson, Anna, ["Hope Daring."]
Education by doing: occupations and busy work for primary classes. '09, [1910.] (O) 109 p. 16°, 50 c. net. Barnes.
Virginian holiday. '10(Ja1) c. il. D. $1. Am. Tr.

Johnson, Arth. H:
Disappearance of the small landowner; Ford lectures, 1908. '09(N13) fold. maps, O. $1.75. Oxford Univ.

Johnson, Augusta Virginia Voigt, [Mrs. R. E. Johnson.]
Gimm family, hist. and genealogy. '10(F) c. '09. 8+15-45 p. front. por. fold. tab., 8°. Gillespie & P.

Johnson, Ben W.
Coping saw work. '09(O2) c. il. O. (Manual training reprints.) pap., 20 c. Manual Arts.

Johnson, Burges.
Rhymes of home: 1, Mating; 2, Building; 3, Year in and year out; 4, Little folk. '10(S3) c. D. $1 net. Crowell.
—, **ed.** *See* Johnson, Constance, *ed.*

Johnson, C: F:
Shakespeare and his critics. '09(Mr20) c. O. **$1.50 net. Houghton M.

Johnson, C: L.
Saw directory; the builder's guide; how to buy good saws and saw-fitting tools; how to take out bends, kinks and bumps; the care, selection and proper fitting of hand saws. 2d ed., rev. '09(N13) il. O. pap., $1. C: L. Johnson.

Johnson, C: Morris.
Rapid methods for the chemical analysis of special steels, steel-making alloys, and graphite. '09(Ja30) 8°, $3. Wiley.

Johnson, C: Nelson, ed.
Text book of operative dentistry, by various authors. '08(D); 2d ed., rev. and enl. '10(S) c. il. 8°, ea., *$6 net; shp., *$7 net. Blakiston.

Johnson, Clifton.
Highways and byways of the Pacific coast. '08(N7) c. il. O. (American highways and byways ser.) **$2 net. Macmillan.
Highways and byways of the Rocky Mountains. '10(N12) c. il. O. (Am. highways and byways ser.) $2 net. Macmillan.
Picturesque Hudson. '09(S25) c. S. (Picturesque river ser.) **$1.25 net. Macmillan.
Picturesque St. Lawrence. '10(My14) c. il. S. (Picturesque river ser.) $1.25 net. Macmillan.
Tale of a black cat. '09(Ag) 84 p. il. 32°, 60 c. Dodge.
—, ed. Elm-tree fairy book. '08(N14) c. il. O. †$1.50. Little, B. & Co.
Songs every one should know. '08(D12) c. O. 50 c. Am. Bk.

Johnson, Constance.
When mother lets us cook: book of simple receipts for little folk with important cooking rules in rhyme. '08(N7) c. il. O. **75 c. net. Moffat.
When mother lets us help; many practical suggestions to little folk who want to be useful about the house; with several important rules in rhyme. '09(D18) c. il. D. **75 c. net. Moffat.
— and Burges, eds.
Year book of humor; collection of jovial quotations from many English and American writers of the past and present. '10 (O1) c. por. D. (Day by day ser.) 60 c., boxed; leath., $1, boxed. Crowell.

Johnson, E. Bird.
Dict. of the University of Minnesota. '08 (Ag15) c. il. pors. 8°, 75 c.; pap., 50 c. E. B. Johnson.

Johnson, E:
Wonder-working providence, 1628-1651; ed. by J. Franklin Johnson. '10(Ap16) c. map, facsims., O. (Original narratives of early American hist.) $3 net. Scribner.

Johnson, Edn. Rossiter.
Hist. of the War of the Secession, 1861-1865. 5th ed., rev. and enl. '10(N12) c. maps, O. $2 net. Wessels & B.

Johnson, Edn. Rossiter.—*Continued.*
Story of the Constitution of the United States. '10(Je11) c. D. $1 net. Wessels & B.
—, comp. Famous fugitive poems. '09, [1910.] (My) 364 p. 12°, $1.25 net. Holt.
Originally pub. as Famous single and fugitive poems.
—, ed. Authors digest; the world's great stories in brief, prepared by a staff of literary experts, with the assistance of many living novelists; Rossiter Johnson, ed.-in-chief. [Authors' Club ed.] 20 v. '09(N) c. il. pors. 8°. (Add. author for price.) E. R. Johnson.

Johnson, Mrs. Edn. Rossiter.
See Johnson, Helen Kendrick.

Johnson, Eliz. and Adrian.
Game of the golden ball. '10(My7) c. il. 12°, $1.50. Macaulay.

Johnson, Emory R:
American railway transportation. 2d rev. ed. '08(D5) c. il. maps, chart, 12°, (Appleton's business ser.) **$1.50 net. Appleton.
Elements of transportation. '09(O16) c. il. D. **$1.50 net. Appleton.
Trend of governmental regulation of railroads: an address. '08(N) 5 p. 8°, (Am. Acad. of Pol. and Social Science pubs.) pap., 15 c. Am. Acad. Pol. Sci.

Johnson, Enoch.
Captain of industry. '08(O10) c. il. D. $1.50. C. M. Clark.

Johnson, Ernest Clifton.
Our best mutual friend; life insurance explained and its principles simplified, together with much other information bearing upon the subject. '09(S) c. 96 p. 12°, 75 c. E. C. Johnson.

Johnson, Florence Kendrick.
How shall the little ones sew? '10(Ap2) c. T. pap., 10 c. People's Univ.
Large meals for little money. '09(Mr6) c. T. pap., 10 c. People's Univ.

Johnson, F: W:
Prevention of accidents. 3d ed., entirely rewritten. '10(Ap16) c. il. 12°, 25 c. McGraw-H.

Johnson, G. L.
Photographic optics and color photography; incl. the camera, kinematograph, optical lantern, and the theory and practice of image formation. '09, [1910.] (F) 314 p. il. 8°, *$3 net. Van Nostrand.

Johnson, Rev. G: B.
How to take part in the services of the [Protestant] Episcopal church. '08 (Ap11) 24°, pap., per 100, $3. Young Churchman.

Johnson, G: Ellsworth.
What to do at recess. '10(Je25) c. il. D. 25 c. Ginn.

Johnson, G: Sands.
Ballads of the season. '10(Jl2) $1.50. Aberdeen.

Johnson, Mrs. Grace Pettis.
Historical sketch. Museum of Natural History, 1859-1909. '10(O) 58 p. front. il. pors. 8°, 50 c.; pap., 25 c. Springfield Lib. Assoc.

Johnson, Helen Kendrick, [Mrs. Edn. Rossiter Johnson.]
Woman and the Republic: survey of the woman-suffrage movement in the United States. New and enl. ed., with an index. '09(Ap10) c. D. pap., 35 c. Nat. League.

Johnson, H:
Life and voyages of Joseph Wiggins, F.R.G.S., modern discoverer of the Kara Sea route to Siberia. '08(F8) il. 8°, *$5 net. Dutton.

Johnson, H:, 1867-.
Problem of adapting history to children in the elementary school. '09(Ap24) 8°, (Teachers College record.) pap., 30 c. Teachers' Coll.

Johnson, H:, 1855-.
Seer, and other poems. '10(D31) c. 12°, $1.50. F. W. Chandler.

Johnson, H: Herbert.
Teeth: their growth and preservation. '09, [1910.] (F) c. 81 p. il. 16°, 75 c. H: H. Johnson.

Johnson, Herrick, D.D.
Ideal ministry. '08(My23) c. 12°, *$1.75 net. Revell.

Johnson, Hugh S:
Williams of West Point. '08(S26) c. il. D. †$1.50. Appleton.
Williams on service. '10(O29) c. il. D. $1.50. Appleton.

Johnson, Rev. J. B.
Spiritual verses as aids to mental prayer. '08(My2) D. 75 c. Longmans.

Johnson, J. P.
Geological and archæological notes on Orangia. '10(Ap16) il. O. $3 net. Longmans.
Ore deposits of South Africa; with a chapter on hints to prospectors. '10(My21) il. 8°, $2. Henley.
Stone implements of South Africa. 2d ed., rev. and enl. '08(O10) il. O. $3.25. Longmans.

JOHNSON, Jack.
Fox, R: K. Life and battles of Jack Johnson, champion pugilist of the world. 25 c.; 10 c. R: K. Fox.

Johnson, Ja. Gibson.
Southern fiction prior to 1860: an attempt at a first-hand bibliography. '09(O) c. 7+126 p. 8°, $2. Michie.

Johnson, Jeremiah Monroe.
Hand book on infant baptism. '08(Ag22) c. 12°, 25 c. J. M. Johnson.

JOHNSON, John Albert.
Day, F. A., *and* Knappen, T. M. Life of John Albert Johnson, three times governor of Minnesota. $3.50; $5. Forbes.

Johnson, J: Butler.
Theory and practice of surveying; designed for the use of surveyors and engineers generally, but especially for the use of students in engineering. 17th ed., rewritten by Leonard S. Smith. '10(D3) il. maps, tabs., 8°, $3.50 net. Wiley.

—, Bryan, C: Wa., and Turneaure, F: Eug.
Theory and practice of modern framed structures. In 3 pts. pt. 1, Stresses in simple structure. 9th ed., rewritten. '10 (My7) c. il. 8°, $3 net. Wiley.

Johnson, Jos. French.
Canadian banking system. '10(N) 191 p. fold. tabs., fold. forms, fold. diagrs., 8°. Gov. Pr. Off.
Bibliography (1 p.).

Johnson, Lewis Jerome.
Reinforced concrete. '10(Jl30) il. $1 net. Moffat.
Statics by algebraic and graphic methods. 2d ed., rev. and enl. '08(N7) il. figs. 8°, $2. Wiley.

JOHNSON, Lizzie L.
Jacobs, C: W. From pillow to throne. 50 c. M. A. Johnson.

Johnson, L: Diffendorf.
Billy Wise, with illustrations; or, observations of daily life. '08(N) 335 p. il. D. $1.50. L: D. Johnson.

Johnson, Mrs. Mary Kellogg.
Moloch: [argument against vivisection.] '08(S12) c. 16°, *50 c. net. W. B. Clarke.

Johnson, Maurice.
Songs of a cripple. '09(My) c. 11+103 p. il. obl. 32°, **$1 net. Grafton Press.

Johnson, Merle, comp.
Bibliography of the work of Mark Twain. '10(D31) c. 8°, $5. (500 copies.) Harper.

Johnson, Myrtle Eliz.
Quantitative study of the development of the salpa chain in *salpa fusiformis-runcinata.* '10(My) 145-176 p. il. fold. tab., Q. (Univ. of Cal. pubs.; Zoology.) pap., 35 c. Univ. of Cal.
"Literature" (1 p.).

Johnson, Owen McMahon.
The humming bird. '10(Je4) c. il. D. 50 c. Baker & T.
Prodigious Hickey; a Lawrenceville story. '10(Ag13) c. il. D. $1.50. Baker & T.
Published in 1909 as "The eternal boy."
The varmint. '10(Jl30) c. il. D. $1.50. Baker & T.

Johnson, Reginald Brimley.
Cambridge colleges. '09, [1910.] (Ja) c. il. 32°, leath., **90 c. net. Jacobs.

Johnson, Rob. Underwood.
Poems. 2d ed. '08(My16) c. D. **$1.20 net. Century Co.
Saint-Gaudens; ode and other verse; being the 3d ed. of his Poems. '10(Mr5) c. D. **$1.20 net. Century Co.

Johnson, Rossiter.
See Johnson, Edn. Rossiter.

Johnson, Mrs. Rossiter.
See Johnson, Helen Kendrick.

Johnson, Roswell H.
Determinate evolution in the color-pattern of the lady-beetles. '10(Jl9) O. pap., $1. Carnegie.

Johnson, S:
Johnson on Shakespeare: essays and notes sel. and set forth with an introd. by Walter Raleigh. '08(S26) 8°, 85 c. Oxford Univ.
Selections from works; ed., with introd. and notes, by C: Grosvenor Osgood. '09 (D18) c. por. S. (English readings.) 90 c. Holt.

JOHNSON, Samuel.
Boswell, J. Life of Johnson. 2 v. $2.50; $3. Crowell.

JOHNSON, Samuel.——*Continued.*
Boswell, J Life of Johnson. In 6 v. $5. Dodge.
Boswell, J. Life of Johnson. 2 v. ea., *$1 net. Dutton.
Boswell, J. **Life of Samuel Johnson. In 2 v. *$6 net. Sturgis & W.**
Broadley, A. M. Doctor Johnson and Mrs. Thrale. *$5 net. Lane.
Brooklyn Public Library. Samuel Johnson, 1709-1784; a list of books with references to periodicals in the library. gratis. Brooklyn Lib.
Carlyle, T:, *and* Macaulay, T: B., *Lord.* Robert Burns, by T: Carlyle; Samuel Johnson, by Lord Macaulay. 30 c.; 20 c. Newson.
Macaulay, T: B., *Lord.* Life and writings of Addison; Samuel Johnson. **25 c. net. Scribner.
Raleigh, W. A. Samuel Johnson. *35 c. net.—Six essays on Johnson. $1.75. Oxford Univ.
Yale University Library. Catalogue of an exhibition of mss., first editions, early engravings and various literature rel. to Samuel Johnson, 1709-1784.—List of books and articles rel. to Samuel Johnson. ea., 25 c. Yale Univ. Lib.

Johnson, S: L., D.D.
Absolute necessity of baptism. '10(F12) 16°, pap., *10 c. net. Revell.
Revival sermons; ed. by M. W. Gilbert. '09(D) c. 192 p. 12°, *$1 net. Revell.

Johnson, Thdr. Woolsey.
See Bartlett, Fk. W.

Johnson, T: Cary.
Introd. to Christian missions. '09(F6) c. O. 75 c. Presb. Pub.

Johnson, V. E.
Theory and practice of model aeroplanning. '10(D31) il. 12°, $1.50. Spon.

Johnson, Wa.
Folk-memory; or, the continuity of British archæology. '08(D12) il. O. $4.15. Oxford Univ.

JOHNSON, Wilbur Warren.
Johnson, *Mrs.* A. L. Only a boy: [in memory of Wilbur Warren Johnson.] (Not for sale.) A. L. Johnson.

JOHNSON, *Sir* William.
New York State Library. Calendar of the Sir William Johnson manuscripts in the New York State Library. $1. N. Y. State Educ.

Johnson, W: Fs.
See Pa. Practice; sections at law.

Johnson, W: H:
King's henchman: a chronicle of the sixteenth century. '08(My.) c. 12°, (Popular ed. of recent fiction.) †75 c. Little, B. & Co.

Johnson, W: Martin.
The W. Martin Johnson School of Art; elementary instruction in color, perspective, lights and shadows, pen drawing and composition. [1910.] (Ap) c. '09. 112 p. por. il. 8°, $1.50. W: M. Johnson.

Johnson, W: Trimble, jr.
See Ayers, S: H:

Johnson, W: Woolsey.
Differential and integral calculus. Differential abridged ed. 2 v. in 1. '08(N14) c. 8°, $2.50. Wiley.
Elem. treatise on the differential calculus. '08(O3) c. figs. $1.50. Wiley.

Johnson ser. il. D. B. F. Johnson.
—Colaw, *and others.* School arithmetic. 35 c.

Johnson ser. of English classics. 16°. B. F. Johnson.
—Addison. Sir Roger de Coverley papers. 25 c.

Johnston, Alex.
Hist. of American politics; **rev. and enl.** by W: M. Sloane, continued by Winthrop More Daniels. '10(Jl2) c. **90 c. Holt.**

Johnston, Mrs. Annie Fellows.
Jester's sword. '09(Jl17) c. S. 50 c.; bds., 35 c. L. C. Page.
Little Colonel's good times book. '10(Ja1) c. por. 12°, (Little Colonel ser.) $1.50; mor., $3. L. C. Page.
Mary Ware in Texas. '10(D3) c. il. D. (Little Colonel ser.) $1.50. L. C. Page.
Mary Ware, the Little Colonel's chum. '08 (N7) c. il. D. (Little Colonel ser.) $1.50. L. C. Page.
Rescue of the Princess Winsome: a fairy play. '08(O3) c. S. front. (Johnson jewel ser.) 50 c.; bds., 35 c. L. C. Page.
See also Johnston, Mary Gardner.

Johnston, Arth.
Myths and facts of the American Revolution; commentary on United States hist. as it is written. '10(Ap16) 8°, $1.50 net. W: B. Clarke.

Johnston, Bertha, and Chapin, Fanny.
Home occupations for boys and girls. '08 (N7) c. S. 50 c. Jacobs.

Johnston, C:
See Mahabharata.

Johnston, C: Haven Ladd.
Famous cavalry leaders. '08(O3) c. il. pors. O. $1.50. L. C. Page.
Famous Indian chiefs; their battles, treatises, sieges, and struggles with the whites for the possession of America. '09(D4) c. pors. O. $1.50. L. C. Page.
Famous scouts, incl. trappers, pioneers, and soldiers of the frontier; their hazardous and exciting adventures in the mighty drama of the white conquest of the North American continent. '10(D3) c. il. pors. O. (Famous leaders ser.) $1.50. L. C. Page.

Johnston, Christopher N.
St. Paul and his mission to the Roman Empire. '09(O2) 12°, *75 c. net. Revell.

Johnston, E:
Manuscript and inscription letters; [16 charts] for schools and classes and for the use of craftsmen. '10(F19) il. 4°, *$1.25 net. Macmillan.

Johnston, Emma L.
See Maxwell, W: H:

Johnston, Gansey R.
Some comments on the 1907 annual rept. of Am. Telephone and Telegraph Co. '08 (N) c. 24 p. 8°, 10 c. Int. Independent.

Johnston, Geneva R.
See Bentley, Alys E

Johnston, Sir Harry Hamilton.
George Grenfell and the Congo; hist. and description of the Congo Independent State and adjoining districts of Congoland; together with some acct. of the native peoples and their languages, the fauna and flora; and similar notes on the Cameroons and the Island of Fernando Pô; founded on the diaries and researches of the late Rev. G: Grenfell. In 2 v. '10(Ap2) il. maps, O. $7.50 special net. Appleton.
Negro in the New World. '10(O8) il. maps, 4°, $6 net. Macmillan.

—, Lydekker, R:, Keane, A: H:, and others.
Living races of mankind. New ed. In 2 v. '10(Mr26) il. 4°, hf. mor., *$10 net. Bowman.

Johnston, Howard Agnew.
Famine and the bread. '08(D) c. 11-146 p. il. 12°. (Add. pubs. for price.) Y. M. C. A.
Victorious manhood; introd. by Ira Landrith. '09(Jl31) c. 12°, *75 c. net. Revell.

Johnston, Ja. Nicoll.
Donegal memories. '08(Je) c. 6-29 p. il. por. 8°. (Priv. pr.) Matthew-N.
Donegal memories and other poems. [New and enl. ed.] '10(F19) c. por. O. $2; mor., $5. J. N. Johnston.

Johnston, Ja. Perry.
Told in the smoker; these stories are based on actual happenings, and give the author's personal experience during 35 years of hustling. '08(D) c. 338 p. il. 8°. (Add. pubs. for price.) Thompson & T.

Johnston, Lena E.
China. '10(Ja1) col. il. map, 12°, (Peeps at many lands ser.) *75 c. net. Macmillan.

Johnston, Mary.
Lewis Rand. '08(O3) c. il. O. †$1.50. Houghton M.

Johnston, Mary Gardner.
Little Colonel doll book; representing characters and costumes from the books of the *Little Colonel series,* by Annie Fellows Johnston. '10(D17) c. il. 4°, bds., $1.50. L. C. Page.

Johnston, Mercer Green.
Plain American talk in the Philippines. '07, [1908.] (Ag.) 198 p. 12°, $1.25. J: R. Edgar.

Johnston, Rev. R. E.
Mission of woman: sermon preached before His Majesty the King on Lady Day, 1906. '09(Ja9) T. 40 c. Longmans.

Johnston, R. F.
From Peking to Mandalay. '08(S19) il. 4°, *$5 net. Dutton.
Lion and dragon in northern China. '10 (D10) il. map, 8°, $5. Dutton.

Johnston, Ralph W.
To-day's pictorial story of Alexander Campbell and the Christian churches. '10 (Ja8) c. il. pors. 4°, 75 c. R. W. Johnston.

Johnston, Rob. Matteson.
French Revolution. '09(Jl17) c. front. D. **$1.25 net. Holt.
Napoleon. [New ed.] '09(Jl17) c. front. maps, D. **$1.25 net. Holt.

Johnston, W: And., and West, Paul.
Innocent murderers. '10(My7) c. front. D. $1.50. Duffield.

JOHNSTON FAMILY.
See Genealogies: Boyd, L., *comp.*

Johnston jewel ser. See Johnston, *Mrs.* Annie Fellows.

Johnstone, J. Alfr.
Touch, phrasing and interpretation. '08 (D19) 12°, *$1.40 net. Scribner.

Johnstone, Ja.
Conditions of life in the sea: account of quantitative marine biological research. '08(O17) il. maps, O. (Cambridge biological ser.) $3. Putnam.

Johnstone, Ja. Hope Stewart.
Horse book: practical treatise on the American horse breeding industry as allied to the farm. '08(Ja11) il. 12°, $2. Sanders Pub.

JOINERY.
See Cabinetwork;—Carpentry.

JOINTS.
See Bones.

Joinville, Jean de.
See Villehardouin, Geoffroi de.

JOKES.
See Wit and humor.

Jokes that we meet; humorous illustrations for the writer, talker, and public speaker. '10(Ap16) 65 c. South-West.

Joline, Adrian Hoffman.
At the library table. '10(F12) c. O. $1.50. Badger.
Method and conduct of the reorganization of corporations; two lectures del. before the School of Business Administration of Harvard Univ., April 4 and 6, 1910. '10 (Ag) 103 p. 8°. (Priv. pr.) A. H. Joline.

Jolly, Austin H., D.D.
Ruling elders' hdbk.; specially prepared for the ruling elders of the Presbyterian church in the U. S. Rev. ed. '08(My23) c. S. 50 c. Presb. Bd.

Jolly bachelors. Bugbee, W. N. 25 c. Dick.

Jolly face ser. 4 v. '10(D) ea., 25 c. Saalfield.

Jolly ghost. Lent, E. M. *$1 net. Werner.

Jolly half dozen. Culter, *Mrs.* M. M. $1 net. Jennings.

Jolly in Germany. Copping, A. E. $1.25 net. Doran.

Jolly tars. Jamieson, M. M., *jr.* 50 c. Dutton.

Joly, J:
Radioactivity and geology; account of the influence of radioactive energy on terrestrial history. '09(O16) il. 12°, *$3 net. Van Nostrand.

JONATHAN.
Spaulding, A. W. Man of valor: story life of Jonathan, son of Saul. 75 c. Review and Herald Pub.

Jonathan and David. Ward, *Mrs.* E. S. P. **50 c. net. Harper.

Jonathan Twigg. Davis, L. E. $1. O. P. Davis.

Jones, A. Clement, and Blomfield, C. H.
Elem. mechanics of solids and fluids. '10 (O1) D. $1.30. Longmans.

Jones, A. Hamilton.
Strange adventures of an author in search of a publisher. '09(F) 4 p. D. (Everybody's booklets.) pap., 10 c. Am. Press.

Jones, A. R.
See Buffington, Bertha Elinor.

Jones, Adam Leroy.
Logic, inductive and deductive; an introdtion to scientific method. '09(O30) c. il. D. **$1 net. Holt.

Jones, Alice Johnson.
Some minor chords. '10(My14) c. 12°, $1. Eaton & M.

Jones, Alice M.
Paul Merritt; tale for school boys. '09 (Jl) c. 197 p. 12°, $1. Washington Bk.

Jones, Allen Green.
See Shepard, W: Martin.

Jones, Alonzo Trévier.
Church federation and the kingdom of God. '10(Ap30) c. S. pap., 25 c. A. T. Jones.
Divine right of individuality in religion; or, religious liberty complete. '08(Ag15) c. 16°, 25 c. A. T. Jones.

Jones, Amanda Theodosia.
Psychic autobiography. '10(S) c. il. por. $2. Alden Bros.

Jones, Arth. Gordon.
Amazing adventures of an inventor. '08 (O3) c. D. †$1.50. Winston.

Jones, Arth. Julius.
Syllabus for the study of the history of education; treatment of present educational needs, problems, and tendencies, as explained and clarified by the educational practice of the past. '10(Jl) 30 p. 8°, (Rhode Island Normal School bull.) 25 c. R. I. Normal.
Bibliography (2 p.).

Jones, Arth. Taber.
See Ferry, Ervin Sidney.

Jones, B: Washington.
Under the stars and bars; a hist. of the Surry Light Artillery; recollections of a private soldier in the war between the states. '09(Ag) 13+297 p. 12°, $1. B: W. Jones.

Jones, Burr W.
Law of evidence in civil cases. 2d ed. '08(O) c. 29+1368 p. O. (Add. pub. for price.) Bancroft-W.

JONES, C. Rodman.
Jones, C: H: In memoriam: C. Rodman Jones. (Priv. pr.) C: H: Jones.

Jones, Caleb and Julia Anna.
Opisthorphorus; or, the man who walked backward. '09(Je19) c. il. pors. D. $1.25. Conkey.

Jones, C: Colcock, jr.
See Doolittle, B.

Jones, C: Edgeworth.
Georgia in the war, 1861-65. '09(D4) c. S. pap., $1. C: E. Jones.

Jones, C: H:
In memoriam: C. Rodman Jones, born Aug. 14, 1875, died Je. 25, 1909. '09, [1910.] (My) 60 p. pors. 8° (Priv. pr.) C: H: Jones.
Life and public services of J. Glancy Jones. 2 v. '10(Jl2) por. 8°, $7.50 net. Lippincott.

Jones, C: H:—*Continued.*
Whitemarsh; address del. before the Pennsylvania Society of Sons of the Revolution at Whitemarsh, Montgomery Co., Pa., June 19, 1909. '09(Ag) 20 p. il. 8°. (Add. author for price.) C: H: Jones.

Jones, Chester Lloyd.
Economic hist. of the anthracite tidewater canals. '09(D) $1.50. Univ. of Penn.; [Appleton.]

Jones, Mrs. Christine Elisabeth Hesson.
Story of the wonderland under the stainless flag; or, a woman's reverie. '09 (Ag) 46 p. 8°, 25 c. Kansas Prohibitionist.

Jones, Clarence Miller.
Earthquakes; supplementary to "From rime to reason." '08(Ja11) O. pap. (Priv. pr.) C. M. Jones.
Science and art. '08(Ja11) O. pap. (Add. author for price.) C. M. Jones.

Jones, Claud P.
Countersign; story of Tibet. '09(N20) c. front. D. $1.50. Badger.

Jones, Dan.
Chart of English speech sounds; with key-words and notes. '08(O24) D. pap., 15 c. Oxford Univ.
Pronunciation of English; phonetics and phonetic transcriptions. '09, [1910.] (F) 12°, 90 c. Putnam.

Jones, D: Rhys.
Course of study in primary arithmetic and hdbk. to the state ser. text. '09(Mr) 4°, (San Francisco State Normal School bulls.; new ser.) pap., 30 c. San F. St. Normal.
See also McClymonds, J: W:

Jones, Dora Duty.
Technique of speech; a guide to the study of diction according to the principles of resonance. '09(O23) c. col. il. fold. D. **$1.25 net. Harper.

Jones, E. F.
Story of Jesus told for children. '10(Ag13) c. il. D. $1. Crowell.

Jones, Edm. A.
Needed school legislation: address read before the School Improvement Federation, Dec. 28, 1908. '09(Ag) 11 p. 8°. (Add. author for price.) E. A. Jones.

Jones, E: Groves, and Stephens, Rob. Grier.
Outlines of physiology. 2d ed., rev. '08 (F15) c. il. 12°, *$1.50 net. Blakiston.

Jones, E: R:
Notes on drainage. '08(Ap4) c. il. 12°, $1.25. E: R: Jones.

Jones, Elmer Ellsworth.
Influence of bodily posture on mental activities. '08(Ja18) tabs., 8°, (Archives of psychology.) pap., 50 c. Science Pr., (N. Y.)

Jones, Emma C. Brewster.
Brewster genealogy. 2 v. '09(My22) il. 8°, *$15 net. Grafton Press.

Jones, F. L., and Talty, J: A.
Questions, answers and whys on the locomotive. '08(Je6) c. 16°, (Add. pub. for price.) F. L. Jones.

Jones, F. T.
See Crew, H:

Jones, Florence Nightingale.
Boccaccio and his imitators in German, English, French, Spanish, and Italian literature: "The Decameron." '10(Ja29) c. O. pap., *50 c. net. Univ. of Chic.

Jones, Forrest Rob.
Gas engine. '09(F13) c. figs. 8°, $4. Wiley.
Machine design. pt. 1, Kinematics of machinery. 4th ed., rev. '08(N7) figs. 8°, $1.50. Wiley.

Jones, Fs. Arth.
Thomas Alva Edison: sixty years of an inventor's life. '08(F15) c. il. O. **$2 net. Crowell.

Jones, G: W.
Braille or New York point?; discussion of the two systems of tactile print at a public hearing conducted by a committee of the Board of Education of New York City, March 24, 1909. '09(D18) 8°, gratis. G: W. Jones.

Jones, Harry.
Prince Boohoo and little Smuts. '09(O9) il. O. $1.50. Stokes.

Jones, Harry Clary.
Introd. to physical chemistry. '10(Ap9) il. 12°, $1.60 net. Macmillan.

—, and Anderson, J: A.
Absorption spectra of solutions of certain salts of cobalt, nickel, copper, iron, chromium, neodymium, praseodymium, and erbium in water, methyl alcohol, ethyl alcohol and acetone, and in mixtures of water with the other solvents. '09(Ap17) il. Q. $3.50. Carnegie.

—, and Strong, W: Walker.
Study of absorption spectra of solutions of certain salts of potassium, cobalt, nickel, copper, chromium, erbium, praseodymium. '10(D31) il. tabs., Q. $5. Carnegie.

Jones, H:
Idealism as a practical creed; lectures on philosophy and modern life del. before the University of Sydney. '09(Jl17) D. *$2 net. Macmillan.
Tennyson; from the Proceedings of the British Academy. v. 4. '10(Mr26) O. pap., 40 c. Oxford Univ.
Working faith of the social reformer, and other essays. '10(Ap9) 8°, $2.40 net. Macmilan.

Jones, H:, M.D.
Radical cure for the swarming habit of bees. '09(D) c. 21 p. 16°, 25 c. H: Jones.

Jones, H: Arth.
Case of rebellious Susan; comedy in three acts. '10(Ja15) c. 8°, 75 c.; pap., 50 c. S: French.
Dolly reforming herself; comedy in four acts. '10(N) c. 95 p. 8°. S: French.
The hypocrites: a play. '08(Je27) c. plans, 8°, 75 c.; pap., 50 c. S: French.
The masqueraders: play. '09(N20) c. 8°, 50 c. S: French.

Jones, H: Festing.
Diversions in Sicily. '09(D11) D. *$1.25 net. Scribner.

Jones, H: Stuart.
Roman empire, B.C. 29-A.D. 476. '08(Jl18) il. maps, D. (Story of the nations.) **$1.35 net; hf. leath., **$1.60 net. Putnam.

Jones, Horace Leonard.
Poetic plural of Greek tragedy in the light of Homeric usage. '10(O1) O. (Cornell Univ. studies in classic philology.) bds., 80 c. Longmans.

Jones, J. Arnold, M.D.
Short practice of surgery '08(Ap4) il. D. (Practitioner's handbooks.) *$1.75 net. Lane.

JONES J. Glancy.
Jones, C: H: Life and public services of J. Glancy Jones. 2 v. $7.50 net. Lippincott.

Jones, Ja., and Hodgson, S. M.
Tramp machinist, by two tramps. '07, [1908.] (Mr.) c. 7+109 p. il. 12°. (Add. author for price.) Ja. Jones.

JONES, Jason.
Martin, J. Jason Jones: life story of an American politician. $2. Chronicle Pub.

Jones, Jenkin Lloyd.
See McCutcheon, J: T.

Jones, Rev. J: Cooper.
Words of consolation and encouragement for the sorrowing. '08(Je) c. 320 p. por. 8°, $2.75. J: C. Jones.

Jones, Rev. J: Dan.
Birthday of hope. '09(D11) c. front. D. pap., *25 c. net, in envelope. Revell.
Glorious company of the apostles. '09 (N13) D. *75 c. net. Doran.
Gospel of grace. '09(N13) D. *$1.25 net. Doran.
Model prayer; series of expositions on the Lord's prayer. 3d ed. '09(N20) D. *75 c. net. Doran.

Jones, J: Logan.
Sunshine and shadow; some promiscuous writings. '10(F19) 8°, $1.50. Hudson.

Jones, J: P:, D.D.
India: its life and thought. '08(N7) c. il. O. **$2.50 net. Macmillan.
Modern missionary challenge; study of the present day world missionary enterprise; its problems and results. '10(D10) 8°, $1.50 net. Revell.

Jones, Johnny, pseud.
Book of nature; by Johnny Jones; spelling by his mother. '09(D18) flex., *25 c. net; School ed., carmbric, *50 c. net. P. Elder.

Jones, Julia Anna.
See Jones, Caleb.

Jones, Leonard A:
Legal forms; incl. forms in conveyancing, together with general legal and business forms, and precedents for ordinary use and for unusual cases. 6th ed., rev., extended and greatly enl. '09(N) c. 59+1131 p. 8°, $6. Bobbs-M.
Treatise on the law of mortgages on personal property. 5th ed., rev. and enl. '08(O) c. 95+1088 p. O. (Add. pubs. for price.) Bobbs-M.

Jones, Lester Bartlett, ed.
See Shepardson, Fs. Wayland.

Jones, Lionel M.
Practical physics. '09(Mr13) figs. D. $1. Longmans.

Jones, Lottie E.
Decisive dates in Illinois hist.; story of the state, told in a record of events which have determined the history of Illinois and of the nation. '09, [1910.] (Ap) 276 p. il. pors. map, 8°, $2. Ill. Pr.
Bibliography (7 p.).

Jones, Lynds.
Development of nestling feathers. '07, [1908.] (Ag.) il. 8°, 50 c. L. Jones.

Jones, Mabel Cronise.
Dolly's college experiences. '09(D) c. 276 p. il. 12°, $1.50. C. M. Clark.

Jones, Mary Best.
Songs of seasons. '09(Ap10) c. O. 25 c. Am. Bk.

Jones, Mary Joss.
Hump Tree stories; High-hopper Grasshopper, Big Bill Brown Bird, Bumble Buster, Dickey Swift, Black Brother, Winkey Pink, and other folks of the Hump Tree colony. '10(O29) c. il. O. bds., $1. P. Elder.

Jones, Matt Bushnell.
History of the town of Waitsfield, Vt., 1782-1908; with family genealogies. '09 (Je12) il. maps, plans, 8°, $5. Littlefield.

Jones, Rev. Maurice.
St. Paul the orator: critical historical and explanatory commentary on the speeches of St. Paul. '10(D) 12°, $1.50 net. Doran.

Jones, Mettie M. Ware, [Mrs. W. F. Jones,] ed.
San Rafael cook book, 1906. '07, [1908.] (Mr.) c. 222 p. 8°, $1. W. F. Jones.

Jones, Milton Osman.
Guide to successful squab raising. '09 (Je12) c. il. D. pap., 50 c. M. O. Jones.

Jones, Morgan D.
Nest of vipers. '10(D31) c. por. D. B'way Pub.

Jones, Olivia Mary, Leary, Eleanor Gertrude, and Quish, Agnes E.
Teaching children to study; the group system applied. '09(Je19) c. il. D. **80 c. net. Macmillan.

Jones, Owen.
Ten years of game-keeping. '09(N13) il. O. *$3 net. Longmans.

—, and Woodward, Marcus.
Gamekeeper's note-book. '10(N12) il. O. $2.10 net. Longmans.

Jones, Paul.
Lady of the lotus. '07, [1908.] (Mr.) c. 30 p. 12°. (Add. pubs. for price.) Runyan & H.
See also Page, W: Herbert.

Jones, Philip Lovering.
Restatement of Baptist principles. '09 (Ap17) c. D. **50 c. net. Am. Bapt.

Jones, Plummer Flippen.
Shamrock land: ramble through Ireland. '08(O31) c. il. O. **$2 net. Moffat.

Jones, R. G.
See Buffington, Bertha Elinor.

Jones, R. Llewellyn.
Arthritis deformans; comprising rheumatoid arthritis, osteo-arthritis, and spondylitis deformans. '09(S) c. il. 8°, *$4 net. Wood.

Jones, R. O.
See Georgia laws.

Jones, Rob. Dorsey, comp. and ed.
With the American fleet from the Atlantic to the Pacific. '08(S5) c. Q. $3; hf. mor., $4; mor., $5. Harrison Pub.

Jones, Rufus Matthew.
Studies in mystical religion. '09(Je12) 8°, *$3.50 net. Macmillan.

Jones, S. Carleton.
Out of Drowning Valley. '10(N5) c. D. $1.50. Holt.

Jones, S: Porter.
Famous stories; reproduced in the language in which Sam Jones uttered them, by G: Rutledge Stuart. '08(D5) c. 12°, *$1 net. Revell.
Popular lectures; ed. by Walt Holcomb. '09(Je12) c. por. 12°, *75 c. net. Revell.

Jones, Sidney Wa.
Treatise on the law of insolvent and failing corporations. '08(D) c. 25+1011 p. 8°, $6.50. Vernon Law Bk.

Jones, Rev. Spencer.
See Francis, Paul Ja.

Jones, T: B.
Complete hist. of 46th Regiment, Ill. Volunteer Infantry. '07, [1908.] (N) 379 p. pors. fold. map, 8°, $2.25. W. H. Wagner.

Jones, T: S:, jr.
Ave atque vale. '09(Ag28) T. pap., 25 c. G: W: Browning.
From quiet valleys: [poems.] '08(My16) c. D. bds., $1.25. G: W: Browning.
Interludes: [poems.] '08(N) c. 23 p. D. pap., *50 c. net. G: W: Browning.
Rose-jar. [2d ed., enl.] '10(Ja15) c. D. bds., *$1 net; autographed and numbered, $3.50. G: W: Browning.
Sonnets. '09(Ag28) T. pap., 25 c. G: W: Browning.
See also Scollard, Clinton.

Jones, T: Wallace, comp.
Scenic treasures of California, incl. Grand Canyon of Arizona; comp., engraved, printed by Tom Jones; made expressly and exclusively for Fred Harvey, Kansas City, Mo. '08, [1909.] (F) c. 40 p. il. f°, 50 c. F. Harvey.

Jones, Mrs. W. F., ed.
See Jones, Mettie M. Ware.

Jones, Wa. Clyde, ed.
See Illinois. *Appellate cts.* Repts.—Notes on the repts.

Jones, Wharton Stewart.
Pract. arithmetic. [1910.] (D) c. '09. 308 p. il. 12°, 50 c. Am. Bk.

Jones, W: Boucher.
Hudson river outlet from the Erie canal to the sea; address del. at the Atlantic Deeper Waterways Conference, Philadelphia, Nov. 18, 1907. '07, [1908.] (Mr.) 18 p. 8°. (Not for sale.) W: B. Jones.

Jones, W: C.
Birch-rod days, and other poems. '10 (Mr12) c. il. por. 8°, $1. Cuneo.

Jones, W: H: S:
Malaria: a neglected factor in the history of Greece and Rome; with introd. by Major R. Ross and concluding chapter by G. G. Ellett. '08(Ja25) 12°, *80 c. net. Macmillan.

Jones, Willis H.
Telegraphy for beginners, the standard method; authoritative book of instruction in the methods and forms most approved, with lessons; incl. the Morse and continental codes. '10(S17) c. il. 12°, 50 c.; pap., 25 c. Spon.

Jones-Bacon, Mrs. Eugenie.
See Bacon, *Mrs.* Eugenie Jones-.

Jones & Laughlin's Standard steel construction: manual for architects, engineers and contractors; containing useful tables, formulas, and other information rel. to the use of beams, channels, and structural shapes; rev. by F. L. Garlinghouse. 6th ed. '08(D) c. 305 p. il. tabs., 16°. (Add. pubs. for price.) Jones & Laughlin.

Jones' Index to legal periodicals. 2 v. '09 (N) hf. mor., $20. Boston Bk.

Jonson, Ben.
Complete plays; introd. by Felix E. Schelling. In 2 v. '10(D10) 16°, (Everyman's lib.) ea., 35 c. net; leath., 70 c. net. Dutton.
English grammar; ed., with introd. and notes, by Alice Vinton Waite. '09(O2) D. *75 c. net. Sturgis & W.
The New Inn; or the light heart; ed., with introd., notes, and glossary, by G: Bremner Tennant. '08(Mr14) O. (Yale studies in English.) $2.50; pap., $2. Holt.

Jonson, G. C. Ashton.
Hdbk. to Chopin's works. New and rev. ed. '08(D19) 12°, **$1.50 net; New and rev. ed. '10(D24) 12°, $2 net. Scribner.
Formerly published by Doubleday, Page & Co.

Jordaens, Jacob.
Masterpieces. '08(D12) T. (Dutch painters.) leath., *75 c. net; pap., *25 c. net. Stokes.

JORDAENS, Jacob.
Rooses, M. Jacob Jordaëns, his life and work. *$12.50 net. Dutton.

Jordan, D: Starr.
Call of the nation; plea for taking politics out of politics. '10(D3) c. D. bds., $1. Am. Unitarian.
Care and culture of men. '10(Jl30) c. front. por. 8°, $1.25. Whitaker & R.
Fate of Iciodorum; being the story of a city made rich by taxation. '09(Ap17) c. S. **90 c. net. Holt.
Fishes. '08(Ja25) il. Q. (American nature ser.; group 1, Classification of nature.) **$6 net. Holt.
Higher sacrifice. '08(O10) c. D. bds., *80 c. net. Am. Unitarian.
Innumerable company. New ed. '08 [1908,] (Je) 40 p. 12°, *50 c. net. Am. Unitarian.
Philosophy of hope. '08, [1909.] (Je) 45 p 12°, *75 c. net. Am. Unitarian.
Religion of a sensible American. '09(O2) c. D. bds., *80 c. net. Am. Unitarian.

Jordan, D: Starr.—*Continued.*
Story of Matka; tale of the Mist-Islands. '10(F5) il. map, 12°, $1. Whitaker & R.
Strength of being morally clean. New ed. 08, [1909.] (Je) 45 p. *50 c. net. Am. Unitarian.
Strength of being morally clean; study of the quest for unearned happiness; a white cross address. '09(O9) c. D. bds., $1, boxed. Caldwell.
Ulrich von Hutten; "Knights of the Order of Poets." '10(D3) c. D. bds., 60 c. Am. Unitarian.
Work of the International Fisheries Commission of Great Britain and the United States; paper presented before the Fourth International Fishery Congress, Washington, Sept. 22-26, 1908. '10 (Mr26) 8°, (United States, Bu. of Fisheries, bull.)

—, **ed.** California earthquake of 1906; articles by D: Starr Jordan, J: Casper Branner, [etc.] '08(Ja4) il. O. *$3.50 net. A. M. Robertson.
Leading American men of science. '10 (N10) c. pors. O. (Biographies of leading Americans.) $1.75 net. Holt.

—, **and Kellogg, Vernon Lyman.**
Scientific aspects of Luther Burbank's work. '09(Mr6) c. il. por. O. *$1.75 net. A. M. Robertson.

—, **and Richardson, Rob. Earl.**
Review of the serranidæ or sea bass of Japan. '10(F) 421-473 p. O. pap. Gov. Pr. Off.

—, **and Thompson, W: Fs.**
Description of a new species of deep-water sculpin (*triglopsis Ontariensis*); from Lake Ontario; with notes on related species. '10(My) 75-78 p. O. pap. Gov. Pr. Off.

Jordan, Edn. Oakes.
Text-book of general bacteriology. '08(D); 2d ed., thoroughly rev. '10(O) c. il. fold. charts, 8°, ea., *$3 net. Saunders.

Jordan, Fs., jr.
Life of William Henry, of Lancaster, Pa., 1729-1786, patriot, military officer, inventor of the steamboat; contribution to Revolutionary history. '10(S) 7+185 p. il. pors. 12°, $1.25. Boulton.

Jordan, Rev. L: H:
Modernism in Italy: its origin, its incentive, its leaders and its aims. '09(N13) Q. pap., 50 c. Oxford Univ.

—, **and Labanca, Baldassare.**
Study of religion in the Italian universities. '09(N13) D. $2.40. Oxford Univ.

Jordan, Rudolf, jr.
Gait of the American trotter and pacer. '10(Jl9) c. il. 8°, $3.50. W: R. Jenkins.

Jordan, W. G., D.D.
Biblical criticism and modern thought. '09 (My22) 12°, *$3 net. Scribner.

Jordan, Whitman Howard.
Feeding of animals. 5th ed. '08(Ap11) c. il. 12°. (Rural science ser.) **$1.50 net. Macmillan.

Jordan, W: G:
Crown of individuality. '09(O23) c. D. *$1 net. Revell.
Little problems of married life; the Baedeker to matrimony. '10(Ag27) c. D. $1 net. Revell.
Power of purpose. '10(S17) c. 16°, (Right living ser.) bds., 35 c. net. Revell.

Jordanes.
Origin and deeds of the Goths, in English version; by C: Christopher Mierow, jr. '08, [1909.] (Mr) 100 p. 8°, 50 c. C: C. Mierow.

Jordon, Eliz. Grover.
Many kingdoms. '08(N7) front. D. †$1.50. Harper.

Jörgensen, Johannes.
Pilgrim walks in Franciscan Italy. '09 (Ja16) *75 c. net. Herder.

Jorrocks on 'unting. *See* Surtees, Rob. S.

Josaphare, Lionel.
Sovereign in the street, and other poems. '07, [1908.] (S) c. 7-31 p. 16°, *50 c. net. A. M. Robertson.
World of suckers. '09(N) c. 6+109 p. D. bds., $1. Danner.

José. Palacio Valdés, A. 90 c. Heath.

"Joseffy."
See Magic and magicians.

Joseph, Rev. Morris.
Judaism as creed and life. 2d and rev. ed. '10(F19) D. *$1.25 net. Macmillan.

Joseph and his brethren. Wells, C: J. 35 c. Oxford Univ.

Josephine, *Empress of the French.*
Endell, J. Love story of Empress Josephine. *$2.50 net; *$5 net. Pott.
Roberts, W. J. Love story of Empress Josephine. *$3.50 net; *$7 net. Pott.
Sergeant, P. W. Empress Josephine. In 2 v. *$6.50 net. Dodd.

Josephson, Aksel Gustav Salomon.
Incunabula in the Senn collection at the John Crerar Library. '09, [1910.] (Ag) 6 p. 8°. (Priv. pr.) Am. Medical.

Joshua to Ruth. Mayer, E. 30 c. E. Mayer.

"Josiah Allen's wife," pseud.
See Holley, Marietta.

Joslin, Arth. W.
Estimating the cost of buildings. '10(Ag13) c. il. 12°, $1. D: Williams.

Joslin, Elliott Proctor.
See Benedict, Fs. Gano.

Joslyn, Rodolphus Waite.
Philosophy of happiness; consideration of normalism. '10(Mr12) D. $1. Normalist.
See also Illinois. Law of corporations.

Josselyn, Alice Amanda.
Thoughts of a thinker; or, science and health under the limelight. '08(O3) c. 12°, *75 c. net. Fowler & W.

Josselyn, Freeman Marshall, and Talbot, Lester Raymond, eds.
Elem. reader of French history. '09(My8) c. maps, S. (Internat. modern lang. ser.) 30 c. Ginn.
—, tr. *See* Flamini, Francesco.

Jourdain, M.
Old lace: hdbk. for collectors. '09(My15) il. O. $4.50. Scribner.

Journal d'un voyage aux mers polaires. Bellot, J. R. 60 c. Oxford Univ.

Journal of a missionary tour. Cram, J. $1.50. G: P. Humphrey.

Journal of a neglected wife. Urner, M. H. *$1.10 net. B. W. Dodge.

Journal of a recluse. Fisher, M. $1.25 Crowell.

Journal of an expedition across Venezuela and Columbia, 1906-1907. Bingham, H. *$2.25 net. Yale Pub.

Journal of the debates in the convention which framed the Constitution. Madison, J., *comp.* 2 v. *$4.50 net. Putnam.

Journal of the plague year. *See* Defoe, Dan.

Journalism.
Hadlock, E. H. Press correspondence and journalism. $3. Un. Press.
Holt, H. Commercialism and journalism. **$1 net. Houghton M.
Prize articles on promoting and conducting the affairs of college and high school annuals. $1. Stafford Engraving.
Salisbury, W: Career of a journalist: [fiction.] *$1.50 net. B. W. Dodge.
Williams, J. B. History of English journalism to the foundation of the *Gazette.* *$3 net. Longmans.
See also Liberty of the press;—Newspapers.

Journalisten (Die). Freytag, G. 35 c. Holt.

Journey book. Falls, DeW. C. $1. Century Co.

Journey God-ward. Grafton, C: C. $2.50. Young Churchman.

Journey in southeastern Mexico. Harper, H: H. (Priv. pr.) H: H. Harper.

Journey in Southern Siberia. Curtin, J. **$3 net. Little, B. & Co.

Journey of joy. Blanchard, A. E. †$1.50. Estes.

Journey through Bookland. Sylvester, C: H. 10 v. $22.50; $29.50. Thompson Pub. Co. (Chic.)

Journeys of Jesus. Yoder, J: O. 90 c. Lutheran Pub.

Journeys of observation. Rickard, T: A. $3.50. Dewey Pub.

Journeys of the Kit-Kat Club; England. Wilson, W: R. A. **$2 net. Appleton.

Jowett, G: T:, D.D.
Apocalypse of St. John; brief contribution to the controversy as to the date and authorship thereof, with a short history of its interpretation. '10(D24) S. 40 c. Oxford Univ.

Jowett, J. H:, D.D.
The high calling: meditations on St. Paul's letter to the Philippians. '09(S11) c. 12°, *$1.25 net. Revell.
Our blessed dead. '10(My7) 16°, bds., 25 c. net. Revell.
School of Calvary. '10(D31) S. 50 c. net. Pilgrim Press.
The transfigured church. '10(S17) 12°, $1.25 net. Revell.

Jowett, Lettice, ed.
See Herbertson, Andrew J.

Joy. *See* Galsworthy, J: Plays.

Joy-bells. Snead, G. T. *$1 net. Gorham.

Joy in God. Ingram, A. F. W. *60 c. net. Whitaker.

Joy o' life. Garrison, *Mrs.* T. P. *$1 net. M. Kennerley.
Joy of Bible study. Lees, H. C. *40 c. net. Longmans.
Joy of work. Babcock, M. D. 35 c. net. Revell.
Joyce, G. C.
Inspiration of prophecy. '10(Ag20) c. 8°, $1.40. Oxford Univ.
Joyce, G: Hayward.
Principles of logic. '08(D12) O. $2.50. Longmans.
Joyce, Howard C.
Law of intoxicating liquors, [etc.] '10(Jl) c. O. $7.50. M. Bender.
Treatise on the law governing indictments with forms. '08(Je) c. 92+916 p. O. $7.50. M. Bender.
Treatise on the law relating to injunctions. In 3 v. '09(My) c. 26+1004; 27-47; 1905-2075; 2077-2484 p. O. $16.50; after July 1, $19. M. Bender.
Joyce, J: Alex.
Robert Burns. '10(Ja15) c. pors. D. $1. J: A. Joyce.
Truth. '08(Je6); 2d ed. '09(Ap10) c. por. D. ea., $1. J: A. Joyce.
Joyce, Jos. Asbury.
Treatise on franchises, especially those of public service corporations; cont. also in an appendix the public service commissions law of New York, and the public utility law of Wisconsin. '09(Ap) c. 126+1130 p. O. $6.50. Banks.
Joyce, Patrick Weston.
Concise history of Ireland. [New ed.] '08 (Ja25) il. map, facsim., D. $1.25. Longmans.
English as we speak it in Ireland. '10 (Ap30) D. $1 net. Longmans.
—, ed. Old Irish folk music and songs; ed., with annotations, for the Royal Society of Antiquaries of Ireland. '09(Ap3) O. *$3.50 net. Longmans.
Joyce, Rob. Dwyer.
Ballads of Irish chivalry; ed., with annotations, by his brother, P. W. Joyce. '08 (N14) S. 90 c. Longmans.
Joyce, T. Athol, and Thomas, N. W., eds.
Women of all nations. In 24 pts. '08(My2) il. Q. pap., ea., 25 c. Cassell.
For original entry giving details of scope of work *see* "Weekly Record," May 2, [1491.]
Joynt, Rev. R. C.
Pastoral work. '09(Mr6) D. (Anglican Church handbooks.) *40 c. net. Longmans.
Joyous birth. Gestefeld, U. N. $1. Exodus.
Joyous days. Marriner, H: L. 50 c. Western Press.
Joys of earth. Wilcox, H: S. $1. Wilcox Bks.
Joys of life. Shaylor, S. J., *comp.* $2. Barse & H.
Joys that live. De Long, J: E. 75 c. J: E. De Long.
Joysome history of education. Hendrick, W. A. 35 c. Point of View.
JUDAISM.
See Jews.
Judaism in music. Wagner, W. R. $1.25 net. Scribner.
Judd, Aspinwall.
Practical points in the use of X-ray and high-frequency currents. '09(N) c. 13+189 p. il. 8°, $1.50. Rebman.
Judd, C: Hubbard.
Psychology. In 3 v. v. 2, 3. '08(D5) c. 12°, v. 2, *75 c. special net; v. 3, *$1.50 special net. Scribner.
Judd, Wilbur Webster.
Birds of Albany County, [N. Y.] '08(F22) il. 8°, $2.50. A. M. Allen.
Jude, Alex.
Steam turbine. 2d ed., rev. throughout and rewritten. '10(D17) il. 8°, $6 net. Lippincott.
Jude the obscure. *See* Hardy, T:
Judenbuche (Die). **Droste-Hulshoff, A. E.,** *Frelin* v. 60 c. **Oxford Univ.**
Judge.
Yours truly, and one hundred other original drawings, by celebrated American artists. 2d ed. '07, [1908.] (My.) c. 93 p. f°, $1.25. Judge.
Judge Fritznoodle. Strouse, M. W. $1.25. Roxburgh.
Judge West's opinion. Ludlow, J. M. *$1 net. Revell.
JUDGES.
Brooks, U. R. South Carolina bench and bar. v. 1. *$1.50 net. State Co.
Holbrook, E. Cases on judicial opinions and precedents. 75 c. West Pub.
Illinois. *Appellate cts.* Repts.; with a directory of the judiciary. v. 130, 131. ea., $3.75. Callaghan.
JUDGMENT (Day of).
See Future life.
Judgment day. Foster, J. H. 75 c. Bapt. World.
Judgment of Eve. Sinclair, M. †$1.25. Harper.
Judicial usurpation. Knaus, H: (Add. author for price.) H: Knaus.
Judith. Schütze, M. $1.25 net. Holt.
Judith of the Cumberlands. MacGowan, A. †$1.50. Putnam.
Judson, F: Newton.
Labor decisions of Judge Taft. '07, [1908.] (Mr.) 16 p. 8°. (Add. author for price.) F: N. Judson.
Judson, Harry Pratt.
Young American; civic reader. Rev. ed. '08, [1909] (Mr) c. 259 p. il. 12°, (Graded supplementary reading ser.) *60 c. net. C: E. Merrill.
Judson, Katharine Berry.
Montana, "the land of shining mountains." '09(My15) c. D. *75 c. net. McClurg.
—, comp. Myths and legends of the Pacific northwest, especially of Washington and Oregon. '10(N5) c. il. pors. O. $1.50 net. McClurg.
Judson, Marg.
See Shackford, Martha Hale.
Judson, W: Pierson.
City roads and pavements suited to cities of moderate size. 4th ed. '09(Mr) c. 197 p. il. 8°, *$2 net. Engineering News.
Road preservation and dust prevention. '08 (Ag29) c. il. 12°, *$1.50 net. Engineering News.

Judy pioneer girl. Patterson, E. 50 c. McLoughlin.

Juengst, Antonie.
Brother's sacrifice; adpt. by Aloysius J. Eifel. '10(Mr26) c. D. 50 c. Soc. Divine World.

Juettner, Otto, M.D.
Daniel Drake and his followers. '09(Je12) c. pors. O. $5. Harvey Pub.

Julia Bride. James, H: $1.25. Harper.

Julian, A.
See Dimock, A. W.

Julian, J:, D.D., ed.
Dictionary of hymnology. Rev. ed.; with new supplement. '08(D5) 8°, *$7 net. Scribner.

Julian Home. *See* Farrar, F: W:

Julie. *See* Rousseau, Jean-Jacques.

Julien, Fanny.
See Davis, J: Wa.

Julien, Joseph François B. D.
Julienno Provencalo. '10(Jl16) (Not for sale.) M. C. Julien.

Julie's diary: a personal record. '08(Jl4) D. $1.50. J: W. Luce.

Julius, Willem Henri.
Anomalous refraction phenomena investigated with the spectroheliograph. '09 (My) 11 p. il. 4°, (Contributions from the Mount Wilson solar observatory.) pap. (Not for sale.) Carnegie.

Jumbo and his family. Mayer, H. 50 c. Dutton.

Jumeaux (Les) de l'Hotel Corneille. About, E. F. V. *25 c. net. Crowell.

JUMPERS (*religious sect*).
Henry, G: W. Hist. of the Jumpers. $1. Metropolitan Ch. Assoc.

June jeopardy. Gillmore, *Mrs.* I. $1.50., B: W. Huebsch.

Jung, C.
Psychology of dementia præcox. '09, [1910.] (F) $2. Journal Nervous Disease.

Jungborn dietary. Just, A. 75 c. net. Dutton.

Junge, Franz Erich.
Gas power: study of the evolution of gas power. '08(Ag1) c. diagrs., 8°, $5. Hill Pub.

Junge (Der) Goethe und das publikum. Pinger, W. R. R. 50 c. Univ. of Cal.

Jungfrau von Orleans. *See* Schiller, Johann Cristoph Friedrich v.

Jungle by-ways in India. Stebbing, E: P. $4 net. Lane.

Jungle folk of Africa. Milligan, R. H. *$1.50 net. Revell.

Jungle-jangle. Newell, P: 15 c. Harper.

Junior history of Methodism. Koons, G: W: 25 c. Eaton & M.

Jungle jingle book. Herriott, H. I. 25 c. Carnahan.

Jüngst, Antonie.
See Juengst, Antonie.

Junior, Meredith.
Heiress of Cranham Hall. '10(D31) c. D. $1.25. B'way Pub.

Junior congregation. Farrar, J. M. **$1.20 net. Funk.

Junior in the line. Hare, T: T. †$1.25. Penn Pub. Co.

Junior officer of the watch. Zogbaum, R. F. †$1.50. Appleton.

Junior Republic. George, W: R. **$1.50 net. Appleton.

JUPITER (*planet*).
Sampson, R. A. Discussion of the eclipses of Jupiter's satellites, 1878-1903. Harvard Univ.

Jüptner von Jonstoff, Hanns.
Heat energy and fuels: pyrometry, combustion, analysis of fuels and manufacture of charcoal, coke and fuel gases; tr. by Oskar Nagel. '09(F6) c. figs. O. *$3 net. McGraw.

Jurgenson, Gerhard Martin.
Social mirror: [on suffragettes.] '09(Je26) c. il. por. D. $1.50. O. L. Panzer.

Jurisdiction of the court of claims of the state of New York. Cardozo, B: N. $3. Banks & Co.

JURISPRUDENCE.
See Law.

JURY.
Bierly, W. R. Juries and jury trials, state and federal. (Add. pubs. for price.) Welsh.
Brickwood, A. W. Sackett on instructions to juries. 3 v. $19.50. Callaghan.
Cann, G: T. Requests to charge in civil and criminal cases; with citation of authorities and forms for instructions to petit juries, [etc.] $6.25. Harrison Co.
Cranston, L. A. Instruction to juries. In 3 v. $22.50. Flood.
Donovan, J. W. Modern jury trials and advocates. $4.50. Banks.
Illinois supplement to Brickwood's Sackett on instructions to juries. $2.50. Callaghan.
See also Trials;—*also* names of states.

Jusserand, Jean Adrien Antoine Jules.
Literary hist. of the English people. In 3 v. v. 3, pt. 2. '09(D4) front. O. *$3.50 net. Putnam.

Just, Adolf.
Jungborn dietary; vegetarian cookery book. '10(O8) il. 12°, 75 c. net. Dutton.

Just between ourselves. Warner, A. $1.50. Little, B. & Co.

Just boys. Wood, M. B. **75 c. net. Revell.

"Just folks." Laughlin, C. E. $1.50. Macmillan.

Just for a change. Byron, M. 25 c. Stokes.

Just for two. Cutting, *Mrs.* M. S. D. **$1 fixed. Doubleday, P.

Just friends. Todd, M. I. $1. M. I. Todd.

Just horses. Ford, S. $1 net. M. Kennerley.

Just Irish. Loomis, C: B. $1; $1.50 net. Badger.

Just kids. Lewis, E. C., *comp.* 50 c. Caldwell.

Just one blue bonnet. Randleson, *Mrs.* S. A. $1. A. N. Ingersoll.

Just so stories. *See* Kipling, Rudyard.

Justice, Thdr.
Tariff: wool and wool goods; statement of Tariff Committee, National Assoc. of Wool Manufacturers; statement of Erben-Harding Co., of Phila., and J: G. Wright; item from the Boston News Bureau of Nov. 20, 1909; address of W: Whitman. '10(Je) 29 p. 8°. Gov. Pr. Off.

JUSTICE.
See Equity.

Justice. Galsworthy, J: 60 c. net. Scribner.

Justice and liberty. Dickinson, G. L. **$1.20 net. McClure.

Justice of Gideon. Gates, E. $1.20 net. Macaulay.

Justice of the Mexican war. Owen, C: H: **$1.25 net. Putnam.

Justice practice of Iowa. Hayes, S: $4.25. Flood.

Justice to the Jew. *See* Peters, Madison Clinton.

JUSTICES OF THE PEACE.
Bryant, E. E. Treatise on the civil and criminal jurisdiction of justices of the peace ,and the powers and duties of constables in executing process in the state of Wis. *$6.50 net. Callaghan.
Colorado justice manual. $4. Courtright.
Honeyman, A. Van D. Justices of the peace: practice and forms in New Jersey. $6. Honeyman.
Ohio. Treatise on laws pertaining to the powers and duties of and practice, [etc.,] before justices of the peace. $6.50. W. H. Anderson.
See also Magistrates;—*also* names of states.

Justifiable falsehood. Glass, A. W. $1. A. W. Glass.

Justin, Jennie, comp.
Little content: [poems.] '09(N6) D. pap., 20 c. Edwards Bk.

Justinian I., [Flavius Anicius Justinianus.]
Digest of Justinian; tr. by C: H: Monro. v. 2. '09(Je12) 8°, *$4 net. Putnam.

"Justus," pseud.
Prolegomena to theism. '10(D17) c. 8°, $2 A. H. Kellogg.

JUTE.
Carter, H. R. Modern flax, hemp and jute spinning and twisting. *$3 net. Van Nostrand.

JUVENILE COURTS.
Hart, H. H., *ed.* Juvenile court laws in the United States. $1.50. Charities Pub.
Hornbeck, S. K. Juvenile courts. 25 c. Wisconsin Free Lib.
Lindsey, B: B., *and* O'Higgins, H. J. The beast. $1.50 net. Doubleday, P.
Travis, T: Young malefactor: study in juvenile delinquency. **$1.50 net. Crowell.
See also Probation system.

Juvenile crime and reformation. MacDonald, A. 50 c. U. S., Supt. of Docs.

JUVENILE DELINQUENTS.
See Children;—Crime and criminals.

Juvenile speaker. Baum, L. F., *comp.* $1.25. Reilly & B.

Juvenile tales. il. 8°. E. B. Holmes.
—Hammers. Toyland. (Add. pub. for price.)

KAALOKAI (schooner).
See Hawaiian Islands.

Kabbala denudata. Kabbalah unveiled; cont. the following books of the Zohar: 1, The book of concealed mystery; 2, The greater holy assembly; 3, The lesser holy assembly; tr. into English from the Latin version of Knorr von Rosenroth, and collated with the original Chaldee and Hebrew text by S: L. MacGregor Mathers. 3d impression. '08(Ap11) O. $3.50. Theo. Pub. Co.

Kaegi, Adolf.
Advanced lessons in Greek; comp. the verbs in mi, the irregular verbs, and the chief rules of syntax; author. Eng. ed. by Ja. A. Kleist. 3d ed. '08(D5); 4th ed. '10(Ag) 8°, ea., *70 c. net. Herder.
First lessons in Greek; comp. the noun and the regular verb in ō; author. Eng. ed. by Ja. A. Kleist. 3d ed. '08(D5) 8°, *80 c. net. Herder.

Kaenders, Rev. P.
Lucius Flavus: a drama; adapt. from Father Spillmann's story. '08(D5) 8°, pap., *25 c. net. Herder.

Kaeppelin, Charles Eugène Rodolphe.
Alsace throughout the ages; done into English by Mary Louise Hendee. '09 (My1) c. D. ¾ mor., $1.50. C: Miller.

Kaessman, Fred G.
Cure of consumption, coughs and colds. '08 (D5) c. nar. S. pap., 10 c. Health-Wealth.

KAFIRS.
Kidd, D. Kafir socialism and the dawn of individualism. *$2.75 net. Macmillan.

Kagay, Daniel Martin.
Eastside boys. '10(Ja15) c. 12°, $1. Roxburgh.

Kagey, C: Claudius.
Land survey and land titles; text book for schools and students in the laws of real property. '10(O) 155 p. maps, 8°, $1.12. C: C. Kagey.

Kahl, J: Corliss, and Cole, Lindon Albertia.
Electrical connections; pract. instructions on the connection, operation and management of direct current dynamos and motors. '09(Jl3) c. diagrs., S. pap., 25 c. W. R. C. Smith.

Kahlenberg, L:
Lab'y exercises in general chemistry. 2d ed., rev. '09(D4) c. D. 90 c. L: Kahlenberg.
Outlines of chemistry. '09(O30) c. figs. O. **$2.60 net. Macmillan.

Kahn, Alex. N:
Printers' vade mecum: indispensable desk book for printers, stationers, paper dealers and all large users of printing or buyers of printing materials. '08. c. 45 p. il. charts, forms, f°, $5. A. N: Kahn.

Kahn, Amy.
Barnes' first year book; silhouette reader. '10(Ap9) c. il. D. 30 c. net. A. S. Barnes.

Kahn system standards: a hdbk. of pract. calculation and application of reinforced concrete; comp. by the Engineering Dept., Trussed Concrete Steel Co. 2d ed., rev. and enl. '08(Je6); 3d ed., rev. and enl. '09(N6) c. il. D. pap., ea., $1.50; 4th ed., rev. and enl. '10(D17) 50 c. Trussed Concrete.

Kaib, Rev. Dan. Jos.
Bookkeeping for parish priests; treatise on accounting, business forms and business laws; designed for the use of the Catholic clergy and as a text-book in seminaries. '10(S17) c. il. forms, 8°, $1.25. Wiltzius.

Kaibara, Ekken.
Women and wisdom of Japan; with an introd. by Shingoro Takaishi. '08(Je26) 64 p. 16°, (Wisdom of the East ser.) *40 c. net. Dutton.

Kains, Maurice Grenville.
Profitable poultry production. '10(D3) c. il. 12°, $1.50. Judd.
—, comp. Making horticulture pay. '10(Ja1) c. il. 12°, $1.50. Judd.

KAIROUAN, Tunis.
See Tunis.

Kaiser, Paul.
The law in the light of the gospel: a series of sermons on the precepts of Christ concerning the law in the Sermon on the Mount; tr. from the German. '09(Ag) 146 p. 12°, 85 c. Germ. Lit. Bd.

Kaler, Ja. Otis, ["James Otis."]
Afloat in freedom's cause: story of two boys in the war of 1812. '08(Ap4) c. il. 12°, †$1. Burt.
Calvert of Maryland; story of Lord Baltimore's colony. '10(Je25) c. il. D. 35 c. Am. Bk.
Cruise of the "Phœbe." '08(O24) c. il. O. (Business venture ser.) †$1.50. Estes.
Cruise of the "Pickering." '09(Ap10) c. 12°, †$1. Burt
Cruise of the "Sally D." '10(D3) c. il. D. 60 c. Penn Pub. Co.
Found by the circus. '09(Ag14) c. il. D. $1. Crowell.
Geography of Maine. '10(D) c. 23 p. D. pap. (Priv. pr.) J. O. Kaler.
Mary of Plymouth; story of the Pilgrim settlement. '10(Mr26) c. il. D. 35 c. Am. Bk.
Minute boys of Boston. '10(Jl16) c. il. 12°, $1.25. Estes.
Minute boys of Long Island. '08(O17) c. il. D. †$1.25. Estes.
Minute boys of New York City; written by Adam Skidmore. '09(O2) c. il. D. †$1.25. Estes.
Peter of New Amsterdam; story of old New York. '10(Ap30) c. il. D. 35 c. Am. Bk.
Richard of Jamestown; story of the Virginia Colony. '10(Mr26) c. il. D. 35 c. Am. Bk.
Ruth of Boston; story of the Massachusetts Bay colony. '10(Mr26) c. il. D. 35 c. Am. Bk.
The "Sarah Jane," Dicky Dalton, captain; story of tugboating in Portland Harbor. '09(O2) c. il. O. (Business venture ser.) †$1.50. Estes.
Stephen of Philadelphia; story of Penn's colony. '10(Ap30) c. il. D. 35 c. Am. Bk.
Struggle for freedom; the story of young Amos Dunkel, oarsman in the whale boat navy, in 1776. '09(Ag14) c. il. 12°, $1. Burt.

Kaler, Ja. Otis.—*Continued.*
Toby Tyler. '09(My22) c. 12°, (Harper's young people ser.) 60 c. Harper.
Two stowaways aboard the "Ellen Maria." '08(O3) c. il. D. (Crowell's young people ser.) †75 c. Crowell.
Wireless station at Silver Fox Farm. '10 (S3) c. il. O. $1.50. Crowell.
With Grant at Vicksburg; boy's story of the siege of Vicksburg. '10(S17) c. il. $1. Burt.

Kallmeyer, C:
Pract. legal and business manual; in English and German. 2d ed., rev. and enl. '09(N) c. 79+47 p. S. 75 c. C: Kallmeyer.

KALSOMINING.
See Calcimining.

Kaminer, Siegfried, ed.
See Senator, Hermann.

Kampen mod taering. Knopp, S. A. 25 c. Amerika Pub.

Kampffmeyer, Paul.
Changes in the theory and tactics of the (German) social-democracy; tr. by Winfield R. Gaylord. '08(Jl11) c. S. 50 c. Kerr.

Kampmann, C.
Die graphischen Künste, mit gahrlreichen abbildungen und beilagen dritte, vermehrte und verbesserte aufslage. '10 (S10) (Sammlung goschen.) 20 c. Stechert.

Kandel, I: Leon.
Training of elem. school teachers in Germany. '10(N19) c. 8°, (Columbia Univ., Teachers' Coll.; contribs. to education.) $1.50. Teachers' Coll.

Kander, Mrs. Simon.
"Settlement" (Jewish) cook book. 3d ed. '08(Je) c. 12°, *$1 net. Caspar.

Kane, Matthew J., rep.
See Oklahoma. *Sup. ct.* Repts.

Kane, Rev. Rob.
Plain gold ring; lectures on home. '10 (D17) D. 90 c. net. Longmans.
Sermon of the sea, and other studies. '10 (F5) D. *$1.50 net. Longmans.

Kaneko, Josephine Conger.
Little sister of the poor. '10(Jl16) 25 c. Progressive Woman.

Kanen, C: F.
See New Mexico. Kanen's corporation laws.

KANSA INDIANS.
See Indians.

Kansas. *Committee on Course of Study.*
Course of study for the common schools of Kansas. '09, [1910.] (F) c. 113 p. 12°, pap., 18 c. Crane.
Bibliography (2 p.).

Kansas. Digest, annot. In 5 v. v. 1. '09 (N); v. 2-4. '10(F); v. 5 (Mr) c. O. (Am. digest system, state ser.) ea., $6. West Pub.

Kansas. General election laws, including the primary election law of 1908; (G. C. Clemens; rev. by W: L. Harvey.) '08 (Jl) c. 97 p. O. pap., 50 c. Crane.

Kansas. General statutes, 1909; by C. F. W. Dassler. '10(Ap) c. O. shp., $6.50. Crane.

Kansas. Manual of the law of roads and highways in the state, with forms and record entries. 11th ed., by G. C. Clemens; rev. by W: L. Harvey. '09(Ag) c. 113 p. O. pap., 50 c. Crane.

Kansas. *Supreme ct.* Repts.; (Llewellyn J. Graham.) v. 74. '08(Ja4); v. 75. '08 (Ap); v. 76. '08(Ag) c. O. ea., $3.50. State Pr., (Kan.)

KANSAS.
Bark, D. H. Irrigation in Kansas. 10 c. U. S., Supt. of Docs.
Benton, H. O., *and* B. J:, *comps and eds.* Aid to Kansas history to be used in connection with Noble L. Prentis' "History of Kansas." 25 c. H. O. Benton.
Bergin, A. Swedish settlements in central Kansas. gratis. Kansas State Hist.
Boyle, J. E. Financial history of Kansas. 50 c. Univ. of Wis.
Clemens, G. C. Township officers' guide; manual of the laws concerning townships and township officers in Kansas. 50 c. Crane.
Connelley, W: E. Ingalls of Kansas. $2. W: E. Connelley.
Douglas, R: L. Manufactures. gratis. State Hist., Kan.
Dunbar, J: B. White man's foot in Kansas. gratis. State Hist., Kan.
Fox, S. M. Early hist. of the Seventh Kansas cavalry. State Hist., Kan.
Heywood, E. E. Fifty common birds around the capital, [Topeka, Kan.] 25 c. Crane.
Marshall, J: Kansas druggists' intoxicating liquor law. $1.25; 50 c. State Temperance.
Martin, G: W. Boundary lines of Kansas. gratis. State Hist., Kan.
Martin, G: W. First two years of Kansas. gratis. G: W. Martin.
Prentis, N. L. Hist. of Kansas. 60 c. C. Prentis.
Stowell, J. Don Coronado through Kansas. $1.50. Don Coronado.
Warren, J. A. Notes on the number and distribution of native legumes in Nebraska and Kansas. (Add. Superintendent for price.) U. S., Supt. of Docs.
See also Lincoln Co.

KANSAS CITY, Mo.
Palmer, C. S. Index to Kansas City charter, 1908. (Add. pub. for price.) Pipes-R.
Peters, J. W. S. Franchise facts. $1. J. W. S. Peters.
Tuttle, F. W. Tuttle and Pike's atlas of Kansas city and vicinity. $60. Tuttle & P.

Kansas rhymes. Atwood, F: J. $1. Crane.

Kant, Immanuel.
Critique of practical reason, and other works on the theory of ethics; tr. by T: Kingsmill Abbott. 6th ed.; with memoir and portrait. '09(Ap3) O. $4.50. Longmans.
Critique of pure reason; with introd. by the translator, J. M. D. Meiklejohn, and special introd. by Brandt V. B. Dixon. '08 (Je27) c. il. 8°, $1.75; hf. mor., $3.50. Lamb Pub.

Kant, Immanuel.—*Continued.*
Educational theory; tr. and ed. with an introd. by E: Franklin Buchner. '08 (D19) c. 12°, (Lippincott educational ser.) $1.25. Lippincott.
Philosophy of Kant, as contained in extracts from his own writings; sel. and tr. by J: Watson. New ed. '08(Ap18) 12°, *$1.75 net. Macmillan.

KANT, Immanuel.
Caird, E: Critical philosophy of Immanuel Kant. *$6.25 net. Macmillan.
Prichard, H. A. Kant's theory of knowledge. $2.15. Oxford Univ.
Watson, J: Philosophy of Kant explained. *$3.75 net. Macmillan.

Kaplan, A. O.
New baby's biography. '08(D19) c. il. Q. $2.50, boxed. Brentano's.

Kaplan, Jacob Hyman.
Psychology of prophecy: study of the prophetic mind as manifested by the ancient Hebrew prophets. '08(D) c. 12+148 p. 8°, *$1.50 net. J. H. Greenstone.

Kapp, Gisbert.
Transformers for single and multiphase currents. 2d rev. and enl. ed. '08(D12) diagrs., 8°, *$3 net. Macmillan.

Kapteyn, Jacobus Cornelius.
On certain statistical data which may be valuable in the classification of the stars in the order of their evolution. [1910.] 12 p. 8°, (Contribs. from the Mt. Wilson Solar Observatory.) pap., gratis. Carnegie.
On the absorption of light in space. '09 (My) 9 p. 4°, (Contributions from Mount Wilson Solar Observatory.) pap. (Not for sale.) Carnegie.

Karadja, Princess Mary.
Towards the light: mystic poem. '09(Ap3) c. nar. D. **50 c. net. Dodd.

Karapetoff, Vladimir.
The electric circuit. '10(S17) c. il. 8°, $1.50. Andrus.
Experimental electrical engineering and manual for electrical testing. '08(Ja18) figs. 8°, *$6 net; 2d ed., corr. In 2 v. v. 1. '10(O22) il. 8°, $3.50 net. Wiley.

KAREN HILLS.
See Burma.

Karishka, Paul, pseud.
See Hatch, D: Patterson.

Karma. *See* Besant, *Mrs.* Annie Wood.

KASHMIR.
Pirie, P. Kashmir, the land of streams and solitudes. *$5 net. Lane.
Younghusband, *Sir* F. E: Kashmir. *$6 net. Macmillan.
See also Mustagh Range.

Kasmar, M. K.
First lessons in aeronautics. '09(D4) c. il. D. hf. leath., $2. Am. Aero. Soc.

Kassabian, Mihran Krikor.
Röntgen rays and electro-therapeutics, with chapters on radium and phototherapy. 2d ed. [1910.] (Jl) c. 40+5-540 p. il. charts, tabs., 8°, (Lippincott's new medical ser.) $3.50. Lippincott.

Katahdin and Chesuncook. *See* Thoreau, H: D:

Katherine Trevelyan. Field, L. M. †$1.50. McClure.
Kathleen in Ireland. McDonald, *Mrs.* E. A. B. 60 c. Little, B. & Co.
Kato texts. Goddard, P. E. 50 c. Univ. of Cal.
Katrine. Lane, *Mrs.* E. M. †$1.50. Harper.
Katz, Eliz.
Poems. '09(Ap10) c. D. $1. E. Katz.
Kauffman, Reginald Wright.
House of bondage. '10(S3) c. D. $1.25 net. Moffat.
My heart and Stephanie. '10(Mr26) c. il. D. $1.50. L. C. Page.
What is socialism? '10(F19) c. D. **$1.25 net. Moffat.
See also Viereck, G: Sylvester.
—, **comp.** Book of friendship. '09(O16) c. 24°, 75 c. Altemus.
Book of gratitude. '09(O16) c. 24°, 75 c. Altemus.
Book of love; little manual of affection. '09(D18) c. 24°, 75 c. Altemus.
Kaufman, Herbert.
The winning fight. '10(O1) c. 8°, $1.50. H. Kaufman.
Kaufman, Nettie M., comp.
Our sisters' recipes, comp. in Pittsburgh, Penna. '09(My) c. 224 p. il. 8°, $1. J. A. Perley.
Kaun, Hugo, comp.
Das deutsche lied; 55 ausgewählte männerchore. '07, [1909.] (Ja.) 139 p. 12°, $1. Rohlfing.
Kaupp, B: Franklyn.
Animal parasites and parasitic diseases. '08(N7): 2d ed., rev. '10(Mr) c. il. 12°, ea., $2.25. A. Eger.
Kautsky, Karl.
The class struggle (Erfurt program); tr. by W: E. Bohn. '10(My21) c. S. (Standard socialist ser.) 50 c.; pap., 25 c. Kerr.
Road to power; authorized tr. by A. M. Simons. 09(O23) c. D. 50 c.; pap., 25 c. S: A. Bloch.
Kavanagh, Marcus A.
Proof of design in creation; tested by the established rules of evidence. '10(My21) D. pap., 10 c. Flanagan.
KAVANAUGH FAMILY.
See Genealogies: Miller, W. H.
KAW INDIANS.
See Indians.
Kawai, Unkichi.
Crown-imperial. 2 v. '10(Jl) 16°. McClurg.
KAY COUNTY, Okla.
Standard atlas of Kay County, Oklahoma, including a plat book of the villages, cities and townships of the county; map of the state, United States and world; patrons directory, reference business directory and departments devoted to general information; analysis of the system of U. S. land surveys, digest of the system of civil government, etc., etc.; comp. and published by G: A. Ogle & Co. '10(Mr) 31 p. col. maps, il. f°, $15. Ogle.
Kaye, J: Brayshaw.
Trial of Christ in seven stages. '09(N20) c. D. *$1 net. Sherman, F.
Kaye, Percy Lewis.
Readings in civil government. '10(N5) c. D. $1.20 net. Century Co.
Kaye-Smith, Sheila.
Spell Land; story of a Sussex farm. '10 (D10) D. $1.75 net. Macmillan.
Starbrace. '09(Jl3) 12°, *$1.50 net. Macmillan.
Tramping Methodist. '08(N7) 12°, $1.50. Macmillan.
Kayser, Carl Friedrich, and Monteser, Frederick.
Foundations of German. '09(S5) c. D. 80 c. Am. Bk.
Keable, B. B.
Coffee, from grower to consumer. '10 (Mr26) il. map, D. (Pitman's common commodities of commerce.) 75 c. Pitman.
Kealing, Hightower T.
How to live longer: the gospel of good health, for the school, the home and the general reader. '08, [1909.] (F) c. 63 p. 16°, 35 c.; 45 c. H. T. Kealing.
Keane, A: H:
World's peoples: their bodily and mental characters, beliefs, traditions, political and social institutions. '08(F8) il. O. *$2 net. Putnam.
See also Johnston, *Sir* Harry Hamilton.
Keane, C: Alex.
Modern organic chemistry. '09(Je26) il. D. (Contemporary science ser.) *$1.50 net. Scribner.
Keane, J: Augustin.
Brambles and twigs of song. '10(Ag6) c. 12°, $1. B'way Pub.
Kearny, Stephen Watts.
1820 journal of Stephen Watts Kearny; comprising a narrative account of the Council Bluff-St. Peter's military exploration and a voyage down the Mississippi river to St. Louis; ed. by Valentine Mott Porter. '08(D) 54 p. il. por. map, 8°, pap., *$1 net. Missouri Hist.
Kearton, R:
Fairy-land of living things. '08(My16) il. D. *$1.25 net. Cassell.
Keatinge, Maurice Wa.
Studies in the teaching of hist. '10(Je4) 12°, $1.60 net. Macmillan.
Keats, J:
Complete poetical works. '08(D19) 12°, (Crowell's thin paper poets.) ooze leath., $1.75, boxed. Crowell.
Poetical works. '08(O10) 12°, ("Best books" ser.) leath., *$1 net. Dutton.
Poetical works. Cabinet ed. In 2 v. '08 (D19) 12°, (British poets ser.) ea., $1.50. Estes.
Poems published in 1820; ed., with introd. and notes, by M. Robertson. '10(Ja22) D. (Oxford lib. of prose and poetry.) 90 c. Oxford Univ.
John Keats; unpublished poem to his sister Fanny, April, 1818. '10(Mr12) facsim. 8°, $10.25. (Priv. pr.) (489 copies.) Bibliophile.
Keats day by day; ed. by Constance M. Spender. '10(O8) c. por. D. (Day by day ser.) 60 c., boxed; leath., $1, boxed. Crowell.

Keats, J:—*Continued.*
Lyrics. '09(Ap1c) front. 32°, (Ariel booklets.) leath., 75 c., boxed. Putnam.
Odes, sonnets, and lyrics; with a preface by Edm. Clarence Stedman, and a note by R: Watson Gilder. '08(O10) c. T. (Thumb-nail ser.) leath., $1, boxed. Century Co.

KEATS, John.
Hancock, A. E. John Keats. **$2 net. Houghton M.
See also Hunt, James Henry Leigh.

Keays, Mrs. Hersilia A. Mitchell Copp, [Mrs. C: H: Keays.]
I and my true love. '08(O17) c. D. †$1.50. Small.

Kebler, Lyman Frederic.
Drug legislation in the United States, rev. to July 15, 1908. '09(Je) 8°, (U. S., Dept. of Agriculture, Bu. of Chemistry bull.) pap., 35 c. U. S., Supt. of Docs.
Habit-forming agents: their indiscriminate sale and use a menace to the public welfare. '10(Jl) 19 p. il. 8°, (U. S., Dept. of Agriculture; farmers' bull.)

—, Morgan, F. P., and Rupp, Philip.
Harmfulness of headache mixtures. '09 (D) 16°, 8°, (U. S., Dept. of Agriculture; farmers' bull.) pap., 10 c.

Kecht, Bp. F. J.
Child's Bible history adpt. from the works of J. Schuster and G. Mey; tr. from the German. 16th and 17th eds. '10(Ag) 104 p. il. 12°, 25 c. Herder.
Pract. commentary on Holy Scripture, for the use of those who teach Bible hist.; tr. and adapted from the 16th German ed.; preface by the Very Reverend M. F. Glancy. 3d rev. ed. '10(O) 32+840 p. il. maps, 8°, $4.20 net. Herder.

Keck, Christine.
See Elson, W: H:

Kedar Kross. Shurts, J. V. $1.50. Badger.

Keeble, S: E., ed.
Social teaching of the Bible; ed. for the Wesleyan Methodist Union for Social Service. '09(N20) D. *$1 net. Eaton & M.

Keeler, Bronson C.
Short history of the Bible. [New ed.] '09 (Je5) c. D. 75 c.; pap., 50 c. Farrell.

Keeler, Mrs. Clarissa Olds.
American bastiles; with introd. by E: E. Richardson. '10(D) 61 p. il. O. pap., 25 c. C. O. Keeler.

Keeler, Harriet Louise.
Our garden flowers; popular study of their native lands, their life histories, and their structural affiliations. '10(Je4) c. il. D. $2 net. Scribner.

Keeler, Lucy Elliot.
If I were a boy. '08(N7) c. D. *$1 net. Revell.
Old Fort Sandoski of 1745 and the Sandusky country. '09(Ja16) maps, pors. 25 c. L. E. Keeler.

Keen, Adelaide, comp.
With a saucepan over the sea: quaint and delicious recipes from the kitchens of foreign countries. [New ed.] '10(O1) c. il. D. $1.50 net. Little, B. & Co.

Keen, Ja. T., ed.
See Campbell, Rob.

Keen, W: Williams, M.D., ed.
Surgery: its principles and practice. In 5 v. v. 3, 4. '08(Ja4); v. 5. '09, [1910.] (F) il. 8°, ea., *$7 net; hf. mor., *$8 net. Saunders.

Keep, Austin Baxter.
History of New York Society Library; with an introd. chapter on libraries in colonial New York, 1698-1776. '09(Ja9) c. 8°, $7.50. Scribner.

Keep-sake books. 5 v. '10(D) ea., 50 c. Platt & P.

Keep up your courage. Ayer, M. A., *ed.* **$1 net; **$2 net. Lothrop, L. & S.

Keesey, Rev. Wilbur Ruth.
Six modern devils. '09(O2) c. S. bds., *35 c. net. Jennings.

Keffer, C: Albert.
See Hatch, Kirk Lester.

Kehoe, W: Jos.
Manual of the Kehoe stenographic writer; thorough exposition of the method of writing the English language in syllables by means of dots and dashes; also an appendix showing the limits of pen stenography. '10(S) c. 111 p. il. 12°, $1. W. F. Roberts.

Keibel, Franz, and Mall, Franklin Paine.
Manual of human embryology. In 2 v. v. 1. '10(S) c. 566 p. il. 8°, $7.50 net. Lippincott.

Keidanz, H., comp. and ed.
Rice gambit; supplement to 4th ed. '09 (Jl31) il. 8°, pap., 17 c. Am. Chess.

Keidel, G: C:
Hist. of French fable manuscripts. '09 (N) 207-219 p. 8°, $1. Modern Lang. Assoc.

Keigwin, C: Alb.
Precedents of pleading at common law; with annots. '10(F) c. O. $5. Byrne.

Keirle, Nathaniel Garland.
Studies in rabies; collected writings of Nathaniel Garland Keirle; with an introd. by W: H. Welch and a biographical sketch by Harry Friedenwald. Testimonial ed. '09(D) 386 p. por. 8°. (Not for sale.) H. Friendenwald.

Keith, Arth.
Human embryology and morphology. 2d ed., rev. and enl. '10(N) 11+402 p. il. O. $3.50 net. Longmans.

Keith, Arth. Berriedale, ed.
The Aitareya Aranyaka; ed. from the ms. in the Indian Office and the library of the Royal Asiatic Society; with introd., tr., notes, indexes, and an appendix cont. the portion hitherto unpublished of the Sankhayana Aranyaka. '09(D4) facsim., O. (Anecdota Oxoniensis Aryan ser.) pap., $7.75. Oxford Univ.

Keith, C: Kenneth.
See Van Hise C: R:

Keith, G: E., M.D.
See Keith, Skene.

Keith, Henrietta P., and Cummins, Eleanor A.
Pract. studies in interior decoration and furnishing. 2d ed. '10(F5) il. 8°, $1. M. L. Keith.

Keith, J: Rob.
See Brand, Alex. Thdr.

Keith, Marian.
Treasure valley. '09(N13) c. D. $1.50. Doran.

Keith, Max L., comp.
Interiors beautiful. 2d ed. '10(F5) il. 4°, $1. M. L. Keith.

Keith, Melville Cox.
How to take care of a wife. 2d ed., rev., enl. '08(S12) c. il. por. D. pap., 50 c. Keith & G.
Marriage bed; medical and philosophical treatise on the marital habits of the human race and the rights of sexual compact between the sexes; the law and testimony. 3d ed. rev and enl. '10 (Ja) c. 5-14-419 p. por. il. 8°, $3.50. Keith & G.

Keith, Skene, M.D., and G: E., M.D.
Cancer: relief of pain and possible cure. '08(Ap18) c. 12°, **$1.25 net. Macmillan.

Keith of the border. Parrish, R. $1.35 net. McClurg.

Keller, Albert Galloway.
Colonization: study of the founding of new societies. '08(S19) c. maps, O. $3. Ginn.
See also Gregory, Herbert Ernest.

Keller, C: Eli.
Eternal hills: a bit of idealism. '09(Je19) c. por. O. pap., 25 c. C: E. Keller.

Keller, Helen Adams.
Song of a stone wall. '10(O29) c. pors. O. bds., $1.20 net. Century Co.
World I live in. '08(D5) c. por. D. $1.20. Century Co.

Keller, H: G.
See Kellogg, Eliz.

Keller, S: Smith.
Mathematics for engineering students: algebra and trigonometry. 2d ed., rev. '08 (D12) c. diagrs., 8°, (Carnegie Technical School's text books.) **$1.75 net. Van Nostrand.
Mathematics for engineering students: plane and solid geometry. 2d ed., rev. '08(D12) c. diagrs., 8°, (Carnegie Technical School's text books.) leath., **$1.25 net. Van Nostrand.

—, and Knox, W. F.
Mathematics for engineering students: analytical geometry and calculus. 2d ed., rev. '08(D12) c. diagrs., 8°, (Carnegie Technical School's text books.) $2. Van Nostrand.

Kellerman, Ivy.
Complete grammar of Esperanto, the international language; with graded exercises for reading and translation, together with full vocabularies. '10(S17) c. D. $1.25. Heath.

Kellerman, Karl Frederic, and Whittaker, H. A.
Farm water supplies of Minnesota; by Karl F. Kellerman and H. A. Whittaker, in co-operation with the Minnesota State Board of Health. '09, [1910.] 87 p. il. 8°, (U. S., Dept. of Agriculture, Bureau of Plant Industry, bull.) pap.

Kellerstrass, Ernest.
Kellerstrass way of raising poultry. '10 (F) c. 93 p. il. 4°, $1. E. Kellerstrass.

Kelley, A: Hill, and Morse, Herbert W.
Natural speller. '09(Ap17) c. front. 12°, **25 c. net. Scribner.

Kelley, Fk. Bergen, comp.
Historical guide to the city of New York; comp. from original observations and contributions made by members and friends of the City History Club of New York. 09(O16) c. il. maps, S. **$1.50 net. Stokes.

Kelley, F:
Treatise on food and egg production. '09 (My1) c. 12°, $1. F: Kelley.

Kelley, H: Harrison.
Pract. directions for marking and adjusting the Corliss valve gear with one and two eccentrics. '08, [1909.] (Je) 31 p. diagrs., 8°. Included with subs to *Southern Engineer* at $1. Southern Engineer.

Kelley, S: Wa., M.D.
Surgical diseases of children; modern treatise on pediatric surgery. '09(My) c. 11+15-765 p. il. 8°, *$5 net. Treat.

Kellner, K. A. H.
Heortology: history of the Christian festivals from their origin to the present day; tr. with the author's permission from the 2d German ed. by a priest of the diocese of Westminster. '09(Mr27) 8°, *$3 net. Herder.

Kellner, Oskar.
Scientific feeding of animals; tr. by W: Goodwin. '10(O8) 12°, $1.90 net. Macmillan.

Kellogg, Alice Maude, ed.
Fancy drills and marches. '08(O3) c. il. D. 50 c.; pap., 30 c. Penn Pub. Co.
Spring and summer school celebrations: exercises, recitations, pantomimes, tableaux, [etc.] '08(O3) c. D. 50 c.; pap., 30 c. Penn Pub. Co.

Kellogg, Amos Markham, comp.
Special day exercises: programs for school celebrations. '08(O3) c. il. D. 50 c.; pap., 30 c. Penn Pub. Co.

Kellogg, Brainerd, ed.
See Reed, Alonzo,

Kellogg, Eliz.
Merry Xmas!: farce comedy in two scenes. '10(O15) D. pap., 50 c., in envelope. U. P. James.

—, and Keller, H: G.
Thirteen good animals: [pictures for coloring, and rhymes.] '08, [1909.] (F) 4°, 75 c. Davis Press.

Kellogg, Mrs. Ella Eaton.
Studies in character building: book for parents. '09(Mr6) c. il. D. $1. Modern Medicine.

Kellogg, Fk. Eug.
Young duck-shooters in camp. '10(S10) c. il. D. $1.25. Stokes.

Kellogg, Ja. Lawrence.
Shell-fish industries. '10(F19) c. il. D. (American nature ser.; group IV.) **$1.75 net. Holt.

Kellogg, J: Azor.
Capture and escape: narrative of army and prison life. '09(F6) por. O. (Wisconsin History Commission, original papers.) bds., $1. Wisconsin Hist.

Kellogg, J: Harvey, M.D.
Battle Creek Sanitarium diet list. '09(Jl3) c. S. pap., 25 c. Modern Medicine.

Light therapeutics; pract. manual of phototherapy for the students and the practitioner, with special reference to the incandescent electric-light bath. '10(Je) c. 217 p. il. 8°, $2.50. Good Health.

Miracle of life. '09(Mr6) il. O. $1.50. Modern Medicine.

Rational hydrotherapy; manual of the physiological and therapeutic effects of hydriatic procedures, and the technique of their application in the treatment of disease. 4th rev. ed. '10(S) c. 31+21-1247 p. il. 8°, subs., $6 net; hf. rus., $7.50 net. Davis.
Bibliography (11 p.).

The stomach: its disorders, and how to cure them. '09(Mr6) c. il. D. $1.50; ¾ leath., $2. Modern Medicine.

Kellogg, Louise.
Rodent fauna of the late tertiary beds at Virgin Valley and Thousand Creek, Nevada. '10(Jl) 421-437 p. pls. O. (Univ. of Cal. pubs.; Geology.) 15 c. Univ. of Cal.

Kellogg, Louise Phelps.
Fox Indians during the French régime. '08 (Je6) 8°, pap., 35 c. State Hist., Wis.

Organization, boundaries, and names of Wisconsin counties; from the Proceedings of the State Historical Society of Wisconsin for 1909. '10(Ap) 184-231 p. O. pap., 35 c. State Hist., Wis.

—, ed. *See* Thwaites, Reuben Gold.

Kellogg, Mrs. Lucy Jane Cutler.
Memoirs of Rev. Timothy Foster Rogers; prep. for the 100th anniversary of the ordination, Sept. 19, 1909. [1910.] (N) 14 p. plan, 8°. (Priv. pr.) W. H. Pierce.

Kellogg, Oliver Dimon.
See Hedrick, Earle Raymond.

Kellogg, Rob. J.
German verb blank. '10(F19) c. Q. pap., 35 c. Ginn.

Kellogg, Royal Shaw.
Forest planting in Illinois. '10(Mr) 32 p. il. tabs., 8°, (U. S., Dept. of Agriculture, Forest Service, circular.) pap.

Forests of Alaska. '10(Ag) 24 p. il. map, (fold. map) 8°, (U. S., Dept. of Agriculture; Forest Service; bull.)

Timber supply of the U. S. '09(S) 24 p. map, tabs., 8°, (U. S., Dept. of Agriculture, Forest Service circular.) pap. (Add. Superintendent for price.)

See also Price, Overton Westfeldt.

Kellogg, Vernon Lyman, ["Max Vernon."]
American insects. 2d ed., rev. '08(Jl4) c. Q. (American nature ser., group 2, Classification of nature.) **$5 net. Holt.

In and out of Florence; new introd. to a well-known city. '10(Je18) c. il. O. $2.50 net, boxed. Holt.

Insect stories. '08(Ag15) c. O. (Amer. nature ser.; group 5, Diversions from nature.) **$1.50 net. Holt.

See also Jordan, D: Starr.

—, and Smith, Mrs. Ruby Green.
Inheritance in silkworms, by Vernon L. Kellogg; with the partial collaboration of Ruby Green Smith. '09(F20) il. 4°, (Leland Stanford Junior Univ. pubs., University ser.) pap., $1. Stanford Univ.

KELLOGG PUBLIC LIBRARY, Green Bay, Wis.
Martin, D. B. Local history story hour; rept. of an experiment in the Kellogg Public Library at Green Bay. 10 c. State Hist. Wis.

Kells, Rob. A.
Stereopticon lecture on shorthand. '10 (N5) il. D. pap., 25 c. Pitman.

Kelly, Aloysius Oliver Jos., M.D.
Practice of medicine; guide to the nature, discrimination and management of disease. '10(O) c. 19+945 p. il. diagrs., 8°, $4.75 net. Lea.

Kelly, Edmond.
Elimination of the tramp; by the introduction into America of the labor colony system. '08(F15) c. D. (Questions of the Day.) **$1 net. Putnam.

Twentieth century Socialism; what it is not; what it is; how it may come. '10 (Je11) c. D. $1.75 net. Longmans.

Kelly, Mrs. Florence Finch, [Mrs. Allan Kelly.]
Delafield affair. '09(Mr13) c. il. $1.50. McClurg.

Rhoda of the Underground. '09(D4) c. il. D. $1.50. Sturgis & W.

Kelly, Howard Atwood, M.D.
Appendicitis and other diseases of the vermiform appendix. [New ed.] '09(Mr) 28+502 p. il. 4°, $6. Lippincott.

Medical gynecology. '08(Je13) c. 8°, $6; hf. mor., $7. Appleton.

Operative gynecology. 2 v. 2d ed., rev. and enl. '08, [1909.] (F) c. il. 4°, $15. Appleton.

—, and Cullen, T: Stephen, M.D.
Myomata of the uterus. '09(O) c. 19+723 p. col. il. 8°, *$7.50 net; hf. mor., *$9 net. Saunders.

—, and Noble, C: Percy, M.D., eds.
Gynecology and abdominal surgery. v. 2. '08(Ja4) il. 8°, *$8 net; hf. mor., *$9.50 net. Saunders.

Kelly, Howard Clinton.
See Russell, Waterman S. C.

Kelly, J. Fitzmaurice-.
See Fitzmaurice-Kelly, J.

Kelly, Ja. Paul.
Prince Izon; romance of the Grand Canyon. '10(Ap9) c. col. il. O. $1.50. McClurg.

Kelly, Myra, [Mrs. Allan McNaughton.]
American public school as a factor in international conciliation. '10(Jl2) 12°, (Amer. Assoc. International Conciliation pubs.) gratis. Am. Assoc. Int. Conciliation.
Golden season. '10(Ja22) c. il. D. $1.20. Doubleday, P.
Little aliens. '10(Ap16) c. il. D. $1.50. Scribner.
New faces. '10(Ag20) c. il. D. $1.50. G: W. Dillingham.
Rosnah. '08(N21) c. il. O. †$1.50. Appleton.

Kelly, R. Talbot.
Burma. '08(Ag22) il. map, 12° (Peeps at many lands ser.) *75 c. net. Macmillan.
Egypt. '08(O24) il. map, 12°, (Peeps at many lands ser.) *75 c. net. Macmillan.

Kelly, Rob. Lincoln.
Influence of Friends on American education. '09, [1910.] (Ag) 16 p. 8°, (Earlham College bull.) 25 c. Earlham Coll.

Kelly's directory of the engineers and iron and metal trades and colliery proprietors; comprising every trade and profession in any way connected with the above trades throughout England, Scotland and Wales, and the principal towns in Ireland, the Channel Islands, and Isle of Man. [11th ed.] '09(Jl31) 4°, *$10 net. Kelly.

Kelman, Janet Harvey.
Children of India. '10(N5) 12°, 60 c. net. Revell.
Stories from the Crusades. '08(Mr28) il. 24°, (Stories from history ser.) 50 c. Dutton.

Kelman, J:, D.D.
Courts of the temple. '10(S17) 16°, bds., 35 c. net. Revell.
Ephemera eternitatis; short studies in life here and hereafter. '10(D) 12°, $1.25 net. Doran.
From Damascus to Palmyra. '08(D12) il. map, 8°, (Color books.) *$6 net. Macmillan.
The Holy Land. '09(S18) 8°, *$1.75 net. Macmillan.

Kelsey, D. M.
Exploration, discovery and conquest of the New World; cont. the thrilling adventures of Christopher Columbus, Americus Vespucius, John and Sebastian Cabot, etc.; with introd. by Murat Halstead. '10(Jl9) c. il. 8°, $1. Nat. Pub. Co.

Kelsey, Fs. Willey.
Problem of religious instruction in the state universities. '09(Ap17) O. pap. (Add. author for price.) F. W. Kelsey.

Kelsey, Harlan Page.
See Olmsted, F: Law.

Kelsey, Rayner Wickersham.
United States consulate in California. '10 (Jl16) c. O. (Academy of Pacific coast history pubs.) pap. (Free to Fellows of the Academy.) Univ. of Cal.

Keltie, J. Scott, ed.
See Statesman's year-book.

Kelty, R: Albert.
Quaker Jim. '09(N20) c. 12°, $1.50. B'way Pub.

Kelvin, W: Thomson, Lord.
Mathematical and physical papers. v. 4, Hydrodynamics and general dynamics. '10(Je4) 4°, $6.40 net. Putnam.

Kelvin, William Thomson, *Lord.*
Gray, A. Lord Kelvin: an account of his scientific life and works. *$4 net. Dutton.
King, *Mrs.* E. T. Lord Kelvin's early home. *$2.60 net. Macmillan.
Thompson, S. P. Life of William Thomson. $7.50 net. Macmillan.

Kelynack, Thdr. N., M.D., ed.
Tuberculosis in infancy and childhood: its pathology, prevention and treatment; by various writers. '08(N21) il. 8°, *$4 net. Wood.

Kemble, Dunston.
Teaching of the holy Scriptures. '08(O3) c. S. *40 c. net. Am. S. S.

Kemble, W: Fretz, and Underhill, C: Reginald.
Periodic law and hydrogen spectrum. '09 (Jl31) c. il. 8°, 50 c. Van Nostrand.

Kemp, E. G.
Face of China; travels in east, north, central and western China; with some account of the new schools, universities, missions and the old religious sacred places of Confucianism, Buddhism and Taoism. '09(N6) col. il. 4°, *$6 net. Duffield.

Kemp, Ellwood Wadsworth.
Outline of history for the grades. '09(Jl17) c. D. $1.25. Ginn.

Kemp, Ja. Furman.
Geology. '08(F29) c. 8°, pap., 25 c. Macmillan.
Hdbk. of rocks, for use without the microscope; with a glossary of the names of rocks and of other lithological terms. 4th ed., rev. '08(Ag1) c. il. 8°, **$1.50 net. Van Nostrand.

—, and Ruedemann, Rudolf.
Geology of the Elizabethtown and Port Henry quadrangles. '10(Jl) 5-173 p. il. fold. maps, fold. plan, 8°, (New York State Educ. Dept., bull.) 40 c. N. Y. State Educ.
Bibliography (4 p.).

Kemp, Oliver.
Wilderness homes: book of the log cabin. '09(Ja30) c. il. O. wood veneer, *$1.25 net. Outing.

Kemp, Randall Harold.
Half-breed dance, and other far western stories; based on the experiences of the author. '09(Jl17) c. il. 12°, 35 c. Kemp & H.

Kemp, Rob. Coleman, M.D.
Diseases of the stomach and intestines. '10(Mr) 750 p. il. 8°, *$6 net. Saunders.

Kempe, H. R.
Hdbk. of electrical testing. 7th ed., rev. and enl. '09(Mr13) il. 8°, $6. Spon.

Kempson, E. W. E.
See Ashford, C. E.

Kempson, F: Claude.
Church in modern England: study of the place in Christendom and the distinctive mission to the world of the Anglican communion. '08(S19) 8°, *$1.25 net. Dutton.
Future life and modern difficulties. '08 (Ag15) 12°, *$1.25 net. Dutton.
"Green Finch" cruise. '09(Ap24) il. O. $1.75. Longmans.
Misadventures of a hack cruiser. '10(O29) il. O. $1.75 net. Longmans.

Kempthorne, W. Oke.
Principles of railway stores management. '08(F8) c. 8°, *$4 net. Spon.
Railway stores' price-book; being a hdbk. of prices of stores and materials for railways. '10(Je4) 8°, $4. Spon.

KEN, *Bp.* Thomas.
Marston, E: Thomas Ken and Izaak Walton. *$2 net. Longmans.

Kendall, Ezra Fremont.
Top soil, rich in wit and humor, relating the happenings to one "Sandy Loam," a Simon pure Hoosier character. '09(Jl) 192 p. il. 12°, 50 c. Cleveland News.
Vinegar buyer; sharp sayings of sharp people, by Ezra Kendall; founded on James Whitcomb Riley's poem "Jap Miller." '09(D) c. 188 p. il. 12°, 50 c. Cleveland News.

Kenealy, Arabella.
Whips of time. '09(Ap3) c. il. D. †$1.50. Little, B. & Co.

KENFIG, Wales.
Gray, T: Buried city of Kenfig. $3.50 net. Appleton.

Kenilworth, Wa. Winston.
Psychic control through self-knowledge. '10(Mr26) c. O. $2. Fenno.

Kenilworth. *See* Scott, *Sir* Wa.

Kenison, Ervin.
Mechanical drawing: instruction paper. '10 (Ja8) c. il. 8°, (Am. School of Correspondence pubs.) 50 c. Am. Sch. Corr.

Kenly, Albert Clark.
Why freight is lost or damaged. '09(Ja9) c. 8°, pap., 10 c. Baughman Sta. Co.

Kennan, G:
Tent life in Siberia. [Rev. and enl. ed.] '10(Ap30) c. il. O. $2.50 net. Putnam.

Kennan, Kossuth Kent.
Income taxation. '10(D31) c. tabs., 8°, $3.50. Burdick.

Kennan, T: Lathrop.
Genealogy of the Kennan family. '08(O10) c. il. pors. 8°, $2.50. T: L. Kennan.

KENNAN FAMILY.
See Genealogies.

Kennard, Howard Percy, M.D.
Russian peasant. 08(Mr7) il. pors. D. *$1.50 net. Lippincott.

Kennedy, A. M.
Essentials of phonography; to accompany Course in Isaac Pitman shorthand. '08 (N) 20 p. O. pap., 20 c. Pitman.

Kennedy, C: Rann.
Servant in the house. '08(Ap25) c. il. D. †$1.25. Harper.
The winterfeast: [a play.] '08(D26) c. il. O. $1.25. Harper.

Kennedy, D. Ross.
Aeroplane portfolio; consisting of nine large sheets of scaled drawings of biplane and mono-plane machines, with descriptive book in envelope. '10(Je4) 50 c. net. Spon.

Kennedy, Dan. Edwards.
Golf in Sapphira's days. '10(S3) c. D. pap., 60 c. Queen's Shop.
Philip the forester. '09(Je19) c. 8°, $4.50. Queen's Shop.

Kennedy, E: G., comp.
Etched work of Whistler; with introd. by Royal Cortissoz. '10(Mr26) c. il. 3 portfolios of pls., f°, $100. (404 copies.) Grolier Club.

Kennedy, H: Clinton.
Damphool in the Kentucky legislature. '09 (Jl) c. 5-190 p. il. 12°, $1. Conkey.

Kennedy, J. M.
Quintessence of Nietzsche. '10(Ag20) por. D. $1.50 net. Duffield.

Kennedy, Ja. Boyd.
Beneficiary features of American trade unions. '09(F6) c. O. (Johns Hopkins Univ. studies in hist. and pol. science.) pap., 50 c. Johns Hopkins.

Kennedy, Ja. Mackintosh.
Valve-setter's guide; treatise on the construction and adjustment of the principal valve gearings used on American locomotives. '10(Mr5) c. il. 12°, 50 c. A. Sinclair.

Kennedy, Mrs. M. G.
Our boys and girls; how to interest and instruct them in Bible study. '09, [1910.] (F) 7-122 p. 12°, 75 c. Wilde.

Kennedy, Mrs. Sara Beaumont Cannon.
Told in a little boy's pocket. '08(O3) c. il. D. †75 c. Moffat.

Kennedy, W. M.
"Interpretations" of the bishops and their influence on Elizabethan episcopal policy, (with an appendix of the original documents.) '08(D19) Q. (Alcuin Club tracts.) 50 c. Longmans.

Kennelly, Arth. Edn.
Wireless telegraphy and wireless telephony. 2d ed. '09(Ap24) c. figs. D. (Present day primers.) **$1 net. Moffat.

Kennett, Canon Rob. Hatch.
Church's gain from modern thought as shown in Old Testament study. '10(Je4) D. pap., 20 c. net. Longmans.

KENOVA QUADRANGLE.
See Geology.

Kent, Rev. Alex.
Origin of the Easter festival.. '09(O9) por. Q. pap., 25 c. C. E. Kent.

Kent, C: Foster.
Founders and rulers of united Israel fr. the death of Moses to the division of the Hebrew kingdom. '08(Ag8) c. D. (Hist. Bible.) **$1 net. Scribner.
Heroes and crises of early Hebrew history fr. the creation to the death of Moses. '08(Ag8) c. maps, D. (Hist. Bible.) **$1 net. Scribner.
Kings and prophets of Israel and Judah. '09(My22) c. 12°, (Historical Bible.) **$1 net. Scribner.

Kent, C: Foster.—*Continued.*
Sermons, epistles and apocalypses of Israel's prophets, from the beginning of the Assyrian period to the end of the Maccabean struggle. '10(Ap2) c. maps, charts, O. (Students' Old Testament.) $2.75 net. Scribner.

Kent, C: W:, ed.
See Alderman, Edn. Anderson.

—, and Patton, J: Shelton, eds.
Book of the Poe centenary; record of the exercises at the Univ. of Va., January 16-19, 1909, in commemoration of the 100th birthday of Edgar Allan Poe. '09 (Je19) c. 12°, $1. J: S. Patton.

Kent, Eliza.
Manual of arithmetic: outline of work in number for use in school for the deaf. '08(Jl18) c. il. 12°, 65 c. Atkinson, M. & G.

Kent, Ernest Beckwith.
Constructive interests of children: [manual training.] '08(F8) O. pap., 50 c. Teachers' Coll.

Kent, G: H:
Ware collection of Blaschka glass flower models, [at Harvard Univ.] '08(Je20) c. il. S. pap., 35 c. G: H. Kent.

KENT, James.
Coxe, M. Chancellor Kent at Yale, 1777-1781. (Priv. pr.) M. Coxe.

Kent, Otis Beall.
Advisability of repealing the Fifteenth Amendment of the Constitution of the United States. '08, [1909.] (My) 17 p. 8°, pap., gratis. Georgetown Univ.

Kent, W:
Mechanical engineeer's pocket-book. 8th ed., rewritten and enl. '10(S) 40+1461 p. 16°, mor., $5 net. Wiley.

KENT, England.
Bosworth, G: F. Kent. 45 c. Putnam.
Jerrold, W. C. Highways and byways of Kent. $2. Macmillan.

Kentucky. *Dept. of Education.* Elementary course of study. '09(N)3-31 p. 8°, (Bulletin of Kentucky Dept. of Education; new ser.) pap., gratis. Kentucky Dept. Educ.

KENTUCKY.
Connelley, W: E. Eastern Kentucky papers. $2. W: E. Connelley.
Cook, J. F. Old Kentucky. *$3 net. Neale.
Fohs, F. J. Fluorspar deposits of Kentucky. 80 c. Kentucky State Lib.
Hasse, A. R. Index of economic material in the documents of the United States; Kentucky. $5. Carnegie.
McDonald, C: M. Kentucky forms; cont. all legal forms under the Ky. code of practice. $4.50. J. E: Hughes.
McElroy, R. M. Kentucky in the nation's history. **$5 net. Moffat.
Matson, G: C. Water resources of the Blue Grass region, Kentucky. (Add. Superintendent for price.) U. S., Supt. of Docs.
Phillips, P. L. First map of Kentucky, by J: Filson: a bibliographical account. *$2.50 net. Torch Press.

KENTUCKY.—*Continued.*
Young, B. H. Prehistoric men of Kentucky. $4.50. Morton.
See also Mammoth Cave.

KENTUCKY BLUEGRASS.
See Seed.

KENTUCKY CAMPAIGN.
See Civil War.

Kentucky eloquence. Young, B. H., *ed.* $5. B: La Bree.

Kentucky Geological Survey bull. 4°. Kentucky State Lib.
—Fohs. Fluorspar deposits of Kentucky.

Kentucky girl. Jett, A. S. $1. Berea.

Kentucky of Kentucky. Kniffin, T: H. $1.25. Cochrane.

Kentucky statutes. 4th ed.; (J: D. Carroll.) '09(Mr) c. 2100 p. O. shp., $10. Courier-Journ.

Kentucky statutes; systematized and annotated; cont. all general laws not incl. in the codes of practice, and incl. the acts of the general assembly, session of 1908; codified, simplified, fully annot., [etc.;] comp. by Lev Russell. '09(Mr) c. 79+1661 p. O. shp., $10. J. E. Hughes.

Kenwood, H: R:
See Parkes, L: Coltman.

Kenyon-Warner, Mrs. Ellen E.
Character building readers. 8 v. First reader, pt. 1, Parental love, pt. 2, Industry; Second reader, pt. 1, Co-operation and helpfulness, pt. 2, Courage; Third year, Personal responsibility; Fourth year, Thoughtfulness and devotion; Fifth year, Adaptability; Sixth year, Fidelity and justice; Seventh year, Aspiration and self-reliance; Eighth year, Self and duty. '10(D31) 16°, 1st reader, pt. 1 and 2, ea., 25 c.; Teachers' ed., 35 c.; 2d reader, pt. 1, 30 c.; pt. 2, 35 c.; 3d and 4th years, ea., 45 c.; 5th-8th years, ea., 50 c. Hinds.

Keogh, And.
Institutional church and the public library. '07, [1908.] (Mr.) 259-263 p. 8°, pap. (Add. author for price.) A. Keogh.

KEPHART, *Bp.* Ezekiel Boring.
John, L. F. Life of Ezekiel Boring Kephart. $1.25. Un. B. Pub.

Kephart, Horace.
Camp cookery. '10(Je4) c. il. D. $1 net. Outing.

Kepner, W: A.
See Dahlgren, Ulric.

Keppel, D:
That ye may know; question, how may I know that I have eternal life? answered from the First Epistle of St. John. '09 (O16) c. S. *35 c. net. Eaton & M.

Keppel, F:
Christmas in art; the Nativity as depicted by artists of the 15th and 16th centuries. '09(N6) il. 8°, *$2.50 net. Duffield.
Golden age of engraving; specialist's story about fine prints. '10(N19) c. il. O. $3.50 net; de luxe ed., bds., $7 net. Baker & T.

Keppel, W: H.
999 points in law, court decisions, and business guide. '08(My.) c. 64 p. T. pap., 25 c. Keppel Pub.

Ker, Annie.
Papuan fairy tales. '10(Ap9) il. O. $1.50 net. Macmillan.

Ker, D:
Lost among white Africans; boy's adventures on the Upper Congo. [New ed.] '09(O23) col. il. D. $1.25. Cassell.

Ker, W: Paton.
Epic and romance: essays on medieval literature. '08(Ap18) 12°, (Eversley ser.) $1.50. Macmillan.
On the hist. of the ballads 1100-1500; from the Proceedings of the British Academy. v. 4. '10(My21) O. pap., 60 c. Oxford Univ.
Tennyson; the Leslie Stephen lecture, del. in the Senate House, Cambridge, on 11 Nov., 1909. '10(Mr26) D. 30 c. Putnam.

KERAMICS.
See Ceramics.

Kerley, C: Gilmore, M.D.
Short talks with young mothers on the management of infants and young children. 2d ed., rev. and enl. '09(Ag7) c. il. 12°, *$1 net. Putnam.
Treatment of the diseases of children. 2d ed., rev. '09(Je) c. 9-629 p. il 8°, $5. Saunders.

Kerlin, Rob. T:
Theocritus in English literature. '10(N12) 8°, pap., $1.50. J. P. Bell.

Kern, Ja. R. and Minna M., eds.
German stories retold: (Grimm's Märchen;) ed. for school use. '08(F22) c. S. 30 c. Am. Bk.

Kern, J: Adam.
Study of Christianity as organized, its ideas and forms. '10(Jl2) c. 8°, $2.50. Pub. Ho. of M. E. Ch., So.

Kern, Mary Root.
See Chamberlin, Georgia Louise.

Kern, Minna M., ed.
See Kern, Ja. R.

KERN FAMILY.
See Genealogies: Gift, A. K., *comp.*

Kerney, Martin Jos.
Compendium of history, ancient and modern, for schools and colleges. [New ed.;] rev. and enl. by C: H. McCarthy. '09(Ag21) il. maps, O. *$1.25 net. Murphy.

Kernodle, P: Jefferson.
Lives of Christian ministers; over two hundred memoirs. '09(N) c. 11+408 p. pors. 8°. (Add. author for price.) P: J. Kernodle.

Kerr, Lady Annabel Cowper.
Short life of Christopher Columbus. '08 (D) 198 p. il. 12°, *$1 net. Herder.

Kerr, Estelle M.
Little Sam in Volendam: rhymes. '08(O31) c. Q. **$1.25 net. Moffat.

Kerr, Eug. Wycliff.
Power and power transmission. 2d ed., rev. '08(Ja25) figs. 8°, $2. Wiley.

Kerr, G: W., comp.
Sweet peas up-to-date, with complete description of all known varieties, incl. novelties for 1910. '10(Jl) c. 80 p. il. por. 12°, 10 c. Burpee.

Kerr, Ja. M.
Treatise on the law of mechanics' liens; with annot. forms, rev., corrected, brought down to date and completed. '08 (D) c. 96+1048 p. O. (Add. pubs. for price.) Bender-M.
—, ed. *See* California. Codes.

Kerr, J:
Scottish education; school and university. '10(My7) c. 8°, $2 net. Putnam.

Kerr, J: Graham, ed.
See Budgett, J: S:

Kerr, J: M. Munro.
Operative midwifery. '08(O10) il. 8°, *$6 net. Wood.
See also Bryce, T: H.

Kerr, J: W.
Hist., development, and statistics of milk charities in the United States. '10(D) 22 p. 8°. Gov. Pr. Off.

Kerr, Le Grand, M.D.
Baby, its care and development; for the use of mothers. '08(Ag15) c. il. 12°, *$1 net. A. T. Huntington.
Care and training of children. '10(O1) D. 75 c. net. Funk.

Kerr, Rob. Jos.
Hdbk. of Mexican law; being an abridgment of the principal Mexican codes. '09 (Ag) c. 260 p. O. $3.50. Pan-Am. Law.
Translation of the mining law of Mexico. '10(F) c. O. $1.50. Pan-Am. Law.

Kerr, S. Parnell.
George Selwyn and the wits. '09(Jl31) il. 8°, *$3.50 net. Brentano's.

Kerr, Winfield Scott.
John Sherman: his life and public services. '08(Ap11) c. 2 v., pors. O. *$4 net. Sherman, F.

Kerr lectures. *See* Law, Rob.

Kershaw, J: Baker Cannington.
Electric furnace in iron and steel production. '08(Ag1) il. 12°, *$2.50 net. Van Nostrand.
Electro metallurgy. '08(D5) il. 8°, (Westminster ser.) *$2 net. Van Nostrand.
See also Booth, W: H.

Ketcham, Rev. Kneeland Platt.
Organized Christianity. '08. 12°, 75 c. K. P. Ketcham.

KETCHIKAN, Alaska.
See Alaska.

Ketchum, Elvin Sydney.
Beginning and development of American railroads. '10(O15) c. 8°, 25 c. La Salle Extension.
Construction of classifications and tariffs. '10(My21) c. 8°, 25 c. La Salle Extension.
Freight economics; how traffic experts save freight money. '09(F6) c. 8°, $1 Shippers Freight.
Interstate commerce law. '10(Mr) c. O. pap., 25 c. La Salle Extension.

Ketchum, Irma A.
Our story reader. '08(D5) c. 12°, *35 c. special net. Scribner.

Ketchum, Milo Smith.
Design of highway bridges and the calculation of stresses in bridge trusses. '08 (D12) c. il. tabs., 8°, *$4 net. Engineering News.
Design of steel mill buildings and the calculation of stresses in framed structures. 1st ed. '08(Ag22) c. $3. Engineering News.

Ketkar, Shridhar Venkatesh.
History of caste in India; evidence of the Laws of Manu on the social conditions in India during the third century A.D. v. 1. '09(D4) c. D. *$1.50 net. Taylor & C.

Ketler, I: Conrad.
The pilgrims; epical interpretation. '10 (S17) c. 12°, $1.50 net. Revell.

Ketler, W: H.
He is a Jew; with introd. by Rabbi H: Berkowitz. '08(Jl) c. 6+12 p. S. pap., 10 c. H. B. Ketler.
Why he is an Elk; written by him the day after the parade. '09(F) c. '08. 6 p. T. pap., 5 c. H. B. Ketler.

Kettle, Rosa Mackenzie.
Mistress of Langdale Hall; a romance of West Riding. '09(S25) front. D. †$1.25. Estes.
Under the grand old hills; romance. '09 (O9) front. D. †$1.25. Estes.

Kettner, Ludwig.
My little German travelling companion. New ed. '10(S) 25 c. net. Cassell.

KEW GARDENS, London.
Bean, W: J. Royal Botanic Gardens, Kew. *$7.50 net. Cassell.
Moncrieff, A. R. H. Kew Gardens. *$2.50 net. Macmillan.

Key, Ellen Karolina Sofia.
Century of the child. '09(Mr6) c. por. D. **$1.50 net. Putnam.
Education of the child; repr. from author. Am. ed. of "The century of the child"; with introd. note by E: Bok. '10(Mr5) c. D. **75 c. net. Putnam.

Key, Fs. Scott, 3rd.
Our flag. '09(O9) il. in col. O. pap., 25 c. H. C. Brown.

Key of the unknown. Carey, R. N. †$1.50. Lippincott.

Key to animals on which wolf and coyote bounties are often paid Bailey, V. (Add. Superintendent for price.) U. S., Supt. of Docs.

Key to German prose composition. Osthaus, C. W. F. 65 c. Am. Bk.

Key to health, wealth and love. Sears, J. S. 25 c. Sears Invest.

Key to indexing and précis writing. Beak, G. B. *50 c. net. Macmillan.

Key to New England trees. Collins, J. F. 40 c. Preston.

[Key] to noted names in history, science, mythology, literature, art and fiction, with their description and pronunciation. '10 (Ap23) c. nar. S. bds., 25 c. Funk.

Key to succession in the presidency of the church. Sanders, P: J. $1.50. P: J. Sanders.

Key to the Bible and our looking-glass. Lastinger, C. $1.50. Tribune Pr. Co., (Fla.)

Key to the theory and methods of linear perspective. Dymond, C: W. 75 c. Spon.

Key to the world's progress. Devas, C: S. 20 c. Longmans.

Key to yesterday. Buck, C: N. $1.50. W. J. Watt.

Keyes, E: Loughborough, jr., M.D.
Diseases of the genito-urinary organs considered from a medical and surgical standpoint, including a description of gonorrhea in the female and conditions peculiar to the female urinary organs. '10(My) c. 17+975 p. il. 8°, $6 net; hf. leath., $7 net. Appleton.
Syphilis. '08(Ap25) c. il. 8°. (Add. pubs. for price.) Appleton.

Keyes, T: Bassett, M.D.
Renewal of life; arguments for subcutaneous injections of oil in the cure and prevention of senility and disease; for the making of the acme of abundant health, stamina, vigor, vitality and constitution; for the cure of consumption and other diseases, particularly those of a chronic nature. '09(S18) c. pors. O. $2. Tubercle Press.

Keys, Gwen, ed.
Priscilla knitting book. '08. c. 48 p. il. 8°, 25 c. Priscilla.

Keyser, Cassius Jackson.
Mathematics. '08(F29) c. 8°, pap., 25 c. Macmillan.

Keyser, Harriette A.
Bishop Potter, the people's friend. '10 (Ap9) c. por. D. $1 net. Whittaker.

Keyser, Leander Sylvester.
Our bird comrades. '08(Ja18) il. 8°, $1.25; vellum, $1.75. Rand, McN. & Co.
Rational test; Bible doctrine in the light of reason. '08, [1909.] (Mr) 9-189 p. 12°, 75 c.; pap., 60 c. Lutheran Pub.

Keyzer, Mrs. Frances.
French household cooking, with a number of recipes from the best Paris chefs, simple and inexpensive. '09(F13) O. (Country life lib.) *60 c. net. Scribner.

Keziah Coffin. Lincoln, J. C. †$1.50. Appleton.

KHARGA, Egypt.
Beadnell, H. J. L. An Egyptian oasis: an account of the oasis of Kharga. $3.50. Dutton.

KHARTOUM, Africa.
See **Africa.**

Kidbook series. '09(Ag7) il. oblong. bds., ea., 75 c. Curtis Adv.
Contents: no. 1, Danny Dime's bank book; no. 2, Timothy Trim's clock book.

Kidd, B:
Individualism and after; Herbert Spencer lecture. '08(O24) O. pap., 35 c. Oxford Univ.

Kidd, Dudley.
Bull of the Kraal and the heavenly maidens: tale of black children. '08(D12) 8°, (Color books for boys and girls.) *$2 net. Macmillan.
Kafir socialism and the dawn of individualism: introduction to the study of the native problem. '08(My2) 8°, *$2.75 net. Macmillan.
South Africa. '08(O10) il. map, 12°, (Peeps at many lands ser.) *75 c. net. Macmillan.

Kidd, Fk.
Urinary surgery; review. '10(N) 16+429 p. il. O. $2.60 net. Longmans.

Kidd, Ja. Harvey.
Personal recollections of a cavalryman with Custer's Michigan cavalry brigade in the Civil War. '09(Mr6) c. pors. maps, O. $2. J. H. Kidd.

Kidd, Josiah N:
Guiding hand; rev. ed. of the author's former work, entitled Sylvanus and Ruth; or, the operations of Providence with respect to matrimony. '08, [1909.] (Ag) 252 p. por. 12°, $1.50. J. N. Kidd.

Kidder, Fk. Eug.
Architect's and builder's pocket-book. 15th ed., rev. '08(Ap25) c. figs. 16°, mor., $5. Wiley.
Building construction and superintendence; rev. and enl. by T: Nolan: pt. 1, Masons' work; 9th ed., rev. '09(My8) c. figs. tabs., O. $6. W: T. Comstock.
Churches and chapels; their arrangements, construction and equipment. 4th ed. '10 (Ag13) c. 179 p. il. plans, obl. 12°, $3. W. T. Comstock.

Kiddie Land. Hays, M. P. G. $1.25. Jacobs.

Kiddie of the camp. Leighton, R. $1. Lippincott.

Kidnapped. *See* Stevenson, Rob. L:

Kidnapped campers. Canfield, *Mrs.* F. A. C. †$1.25. Harper.

KIDNEYS.
Garceau, E. Renal, ureteral, perirenal and adrenal tumors. $5. Appleton.
Greene, R. H., *and* Brooks, H. Diseases of the genito-urinary organs and the kidney. *$5 net. Saunders.
Longyear, H. W. Nephrocoloptosis; description of the nephrocolic ligament and its action in the causation of nephroptosis. $3. Mosby.
Wilson, H. W. Movable kidney. *$1.25 net. Longmans.
See also Bright's disease;—Urine and urinary organs.

Kids of many colors. Boylan, *Mrs.* G. D. $1. Hurst.

Kiefer, Rev. W: R., and Mack, Newton H,
Hist. of the 153d Regiment Pennsylvania Volunteers Infantry, which was recruited in Northampton Co., Pa., 1862-1863. '09, [1910.] (F) 352 p. il. pors. map, 8°, $2. Chemical.

Kieffer, Rev. H: Martyn, comp.
Funny bone. '10(My14) 24°, bds., 75 c.; ooze leath., $1. Dodge.

Kieffer, Jos. Spangler.
Head and heart. '10(Ja22) c. por. O. *$1.50 net. Ref. Ch. Pub.

KILAUEA, Hawaii.
Brigham, W: T. Volcanoes of Kilauea and Mauna Loa. $3.50: $4.50. Bishop Museum.

Kilbourn, Dwight C.
Bench and bar of Litchfield County, Conn. (1709-1909). '09(N) 540 p. il. pors. 8°, $5. Kilbourn.

Kilburn, Harriet Mason, comp. and ed.
Calendar of the fellowship, 1910. '09(N6) O. bds., *75 c. net. Little, B. & Co.

Kilby, Quincy, comp.
See Tompkins, Eug.

Kildal, Arne, comp.
Selected list of Norwegian and Danish books recommended for a small public library; adopted for use by the League of Library Commissions '09(Mr27) 12°, (A. L. A. Publishing Board, foreign book list.) pap., 25 c. A. L. A.

Kilgore, Rev. Elias Gaston.
Trials and triumphs of a young preacher; with additional notes; autobiography. '08, [1909.] (Ap) c. 421 p. por. 12°, *$1 net. Pub. Ho. of M. E. Ch., So.

Killebrew, Jos. P.
Tobacco districts and types. '09, [1910.] (F) 16 p. 8°, (U. S., Dept. of Agriculture, Bureau of Statistics, circular.) pap.

Kilmeny of the orchard. Montgomery, L. M. $1.25. L. C. Page.

Kilpatrick, Van Evrie.
Departmental teaching in elementary schools. '08(Ap18) c. il. 16°, *60 c. net. Macmillan.

Kilroy, Marg.
Little torment. '10(D31) il. 12°, $1. Lippincott.

Kilvert, B: Sayre Cory.
Kite book. '09(O23) c. il. in col. Q. **$1.25 net. Dodd.

Kim. Kipling, R. **$1.50 net. Doubleday, P.

Kim Su Bang. Wagner, E. C. 50 c. Pub. Ho. M. E. Ch., So.

Kimball, Dexter Simpson, and Barr, J: H:
Elements of machine design. '09(O30) il. 8°, $3. Wiley.

Kimball, E: Ancel.
Christian Science; a lecture del. in Queen's Hall, London, England, May 22, 1908. '08 (N21) c. 16°, pap., 6 c.; per dozen, 60 c.; per 25, $1.15; per 50, $2.25. Chr. Sci.
Christian Science, (La science chrétienne;) le pouvoir de l'homme sur le mal. '09 (S) c. 28 p. 16°, pap., 6 c. Chr. Sci.
Christian Science, (La science chrétienne;) ses bienfaits pour l'humanité. '09(S) c. 50 p. 16°, pap., 6 c. Chr. Sci.

Kimball, Sumner Increase.
Joshua James: life-saver. '09(O2) c. D. (True American types ser.) *60 c. net. Am. Unitarian.

Kimber, Diana Clifford.
Text book of anatomy and physiology for nurses. 3d ed.; rev. by Caroline E. Gray. '09(O9) il. 8°, *$2.50 net. Macmillan.

Kimberley, C: Hubbell.
See Stanislaus, Ignatius Valerius Stanley.

Kimm, Silas Conrad, ed.
Questions in physical geography given at examinations held by the Regents of New York. '08, [1909.] (Mr) c. 9-138 p. il. maps, 12°, with key, $1 Bardeen.

Kimmell, Mary Forward.
Tantalus. '10(F19) c. 12°, $1.50. C. M. Clark.

Kimono ballads. Stoddard, C: C. *50 c. net. Calkins & Co.

KINAESTHETIC SENSATION.
See Psychology.

Kincaid's battery. Cable, G: W. †$1.50. Scribner.

Kind, J: L:
Edward Young in Germany: historical surveys; influence upon German literature. '08(My16) 8°, (Columbia Univ. Germanic studies.) *$1.25 net. Lemcke.

Kinder, T: S:
Rube's twenty years' adventures. '09(Ap3) c. D. 50 c.; pap., 25 c. Laird.

KINDERGARTEN.
Abt, I: A. Inquiry into the status of the kindergarten. 50 c. I: A. Abt.
Ayres, M. M. Playing house in kindergarten. 50 c. M. M. Ayres.
Blow, S. E. Educational issues in the kindergarten. **$1.50 net. Appleton.
Devereaux, A. W. Outline of a year's work in the kindergarten. 70 c. M. Bradley.
Eaton, E. M. Kindergartens in the public schools. 5 c. Pub. Ed. Assoc.
Graves, E. M., ***and*** **Watkins, A. W.** Year book for primary grades based on Froebel's mother plays. $1.25. M. Bradley.
Hidden, J. A. Garden game and other songs [for kindergarten.] 75 c. M. Bradley.
Newman, C. S. Kindergarten in the home. $1.50. L. C. Page
Vanderwalker, N. C. Kindergarten in American education. **$1.25 net. Macmillan.
Wiebé, E: Golden jubilee ed. of The paradise of childhood. $2. M. Bradley.
Woodford, A. L. Practical system in folding, cutting, modeling, etc. 75 c. B'way Pub.
See also Drills;—Games;—Manual training;—Music;—Story-telling;—Sunday-school.

Kindergarten stories for the Sunday school and home. Cragin, L. E. $1.25 net. Doran.

KINDERHOOK, N. Y.
Village beautiful, Kinderhook, N. Y. $3. Fellowcraft Shop.

Kinderlehre. Luther, M. 50 c. W. Eickmann.

Kindle, E: Martin.
Devonian fauna of the Ouray limestone. '09, [1910.] (Mr) 60 p. il. 8°, (U. S., Dept. of the Interior, U. S. Geological Survey, bull.) pap.

KINEMATICS.
See Mechanics.

KINESIOLOGY.
See Gymnastics and physical culture.

KINETICS.
See Mechanics.

King, Alb. Freeman Africanus, M.D.
Manual of obstetrics. 11th ed. '10(S) 713 p. il. (some in col.) 12°, $2.75 net. Lea.

King, Alfr. Grant.
Practical steam and hot water heating and ventilation. '08(My2) c. diagrs., 8°, $3. Henley.

King, Alix.
Romance of a monk. '10(D17) c. D. $1.20 net. Metropolitan Press, (N. Y.)
Romance of a nun. [1910.] (Ap) 330 p. D. $1.50. Kearney.

King, Anna E.
See Lane, *Mrs.* J:

King, Arth. Scott.
Correspondence between Zeeman effect and pressure displacement for the spectra of iron, chromium, and titanium. [1910.] (D) 26 p. tabs., 4°, (Contribs. from the Mount Wilson Solar Observatory.) Carnegie.
Electric furnace for spectroscopic investigations, with results for the spectra of titanium and vanadium. '09(Mr13) il. 4°, (Contributions from the Mt. Wilson Solar Observatory.) pap. (Add. Institution for price.) Carnegie.
Further study of the H and K lines of calcium. '09(O) 9 p. il. 4°, (Contributions from the Mt. Wilson Solar Observatory.) pap. (Add. Institution for price.) Carnegie.
On the separation in the magnetic field of some lines occurring as doublets and triplets in sun-spot spectra. '09(My) 8 p. il. 4°, (Contributions from Mount Wilson Solar Observatory.) pap. (Not for sale.) Carnegie.
Relative intensities of the yellow, orange and red lines of calcium in electric furnace spectra. '09(My) 8 p. il. 8°, (Contributions from Mount Wilson Solar Observatory.) pap. (Not for sale.) Carnegie.
Zeeman effect for titanium. '09(N) 13 p. il. 4°, (Contributions from the Mt. Wilson Solar Observatory.) pap. (Add. Institution for price.) Carnegie.

King, Basil.
Inner shrine. '09(My15) c. '08. il. D. †$1.50. Harper.
Wild olive; novel. '10(Je4) c. il. D. $1.50. Harper.

King, B: Franklin.
Jane Jones and some others. '09(N6) c. col. il. O. $2, boxed. Forbes.

King, Cardenio Flournoy.
Light of four candles. '08(D19) c. por. D. $1.50. C. F. King.

King, General C:
Lanier of the cavalry. '09(Ap24) c. il. 12°, †$1.25. Lippincott.
To the front: sequel to "Cadet days." '08 (F22) c. il. D. †$1.25. Harper.

King, Sir C: Simeon, ed.
See King, W:

King, Bp. E:
Love and wisdom of God; sermons; ed. by B. W. Randolph. '10(D31) O. $1.75 net. Longmans.
Requirements for the ministry; an address. '10(D24) O. pap., 15 c. Oxford Univ.

King, Rev. Elisha Alonzo, and Meyer, Rev. F: Brotherton.
Clean and strong; book for young men. '10(F5) c. D. $1. Un. Soc. C. E.

King, Mrs. Eliz. Thomson.
Lord Kelvin's early home; recollections of sister; together with some family letters and suppl. chapter by the ed., Eliz. Thomson King. '10(Ja1) il. O. *$2.60 net. Macmillan.

King, Mrs. Florence Palmer.
See Palmer, Florence Ursula.

King, Franklin Hiram.
Irrigation and drainage principles and practice of their cultural phases. 5th ed. '08 (Mr7) c. il. 12°, (Rural science ser.) **$1.50 net. Macmillan.
Ventilation for dwellings, rural schools and stables. '09(Ja23) c. front. figs. D. 75 c. F. H. King.

King, F: Alwin.
Suggestion note-book; prep. especially for teachers visiting foreign schools. '09 (N) c. 29+250 p. 16°, $1. F. A. King.

King, Georgiana Goddard.
Bryn Mawr spelling book. '10(F5) c. 12°, 25 c. G. G. King.
Way of perfect love: [allegorical poem.] '08(O10) 12°, bds., $1.25. Macmillan.

King, Gertrude.
The landlubbers. '09(Ap10) c. il. D. †$1.50. Doubleday, P.

King, H: Churchill, D.D.
Ethics of Jesus; [William Belden Noble lectures, 1909.] '10(F19) c. D. (New Testament handbooks.) **$1.50 net. Macmillan.
Laws of friendship—human and divine. '09 (Ap3) D. *$1.25 net. Macmillan.
Letters on the greatness and simplicity of the Christian faith; rev. ed. of "Letters to Sunday-school teachers." '09(N13) c. D. bds., *75 c. net. Pilgrim Press.
Seeming unreality of the spiritual life: Nathaniel William Taylor lectures for 1907. '08(O3) c. D. **$1.50 net. Macmillan.

—, Peabody, Fs. Greenwood, Abbott, Rev. Lyman, and others.
Education and national character; [papers read at the fifth general convention of the Religious Education Association, held at Washington, D. C., Feb. 11-13, 1908.] '08, [1909.] (Je) 319 p. 8°, *$1.50 net. Rel. Educ.

King, Rev. H: Melville.
Sir Henry Vane, Jr.; Governor of Massachusetts and friend of Roger Williams and Rhode Island. '09(O16) c. D. $1.25. Preston.
—, comp. and ed. Historical catalogue of the members of the First Baptist Church in Providence, Rhode Island. '09(Ap10) il. pors. Q. buckram, $2. F. H. Townsend.

King, Irving.
Development of religion; study in anthropology and social psychology. '10(Mr5) c. O. **$1.75 net. Macmillan.

King, Jos.
Electoral reform: inquiry into our system of parliamentary representation; with a preface by L. Harcourt. '08(Jl11) 16°. *85 c. net. Wessels.

—, Bigham, F. T. R., Gwyer, Maurice Linford, and others.
Management of private affairs. '08(N21) D. 85 c. Oxford Univ.

King, Jos. L.
Hist. of the San Francisco Stock and Exchange Board, by the chairman. '10 (Jl16) c. il. pors. facsims., O. $2. J. L. King.

King, Julia Anne.
Government of the people of the state of Michigan. Rev. ed. '09(D18) c. il. 12°, 50 c. Hinds.

King, Leonard W:
Hist. of Babylonia and Assyria. In 3 v. v. 1, History of Sumer and Akkad. '10 (Jl9) il. 8°, $4.80 net. Stokes.

King, Lottie.
Le petit bon-homme, Pierre; sa cousine, Marie et leurs amis. '10(O1) il. D. 50 c. Longmans.

KING, Richard.
Bates, R. O. Billy and Dick from Andersonville prison to the White House. 50 c. Sentinel Pub., (Cal.)

King, Sidney J., comp.
Official route guide; touring guide to the best and most reliable routes in the Central West. '10(Jl16) c. il. maps, 8°, $2. S. J. King.

King, Archbishop W:
Great archbishop of Dublin, William King, D.D., 1650-1729: his autobiography, family, and a selection from his correspondence; ed. by Sir C: Simeon King. '08 (D19) il. O. *$1.60 net. Longmans.

King, W:, M.D.
Sure possession and some thoughts of a layman. '09, [1910.] (Ap) c. 238 p. por. 8°, $1.50. A. B. Caldwell.

King Alfred's jewel. Trask, K. N. *$1.25 net. Lane.
King and His kingdom. Veach, R. W. *60 c. net; *35 c. net. Revell.
King and no king. *See* Beaumont, Fs. Knight of the burning pestle.
KING AND QUEEN COUNTY, Va.
Bagby, A. King and Queen county, Virginia. *$3.50 net. Neale.
King Blackjack and his sword. Stainer, C. L. *$2.40 net. Oxford Univ.
King Cotton. Watkins, J. L. $1.50. J. L. Watkins.
KING GEORGE'S WAR.
Doolittle, B:, *and* Jones, C: C., *jr.* Short narrative of mischief done by the French and Indian enemy, on the western frontiers of the province of the Massachusetts-Bay [and] biograph. sketch of Major John Habersham. to subscribers, $1.75. Abbatt.
See also Louisburg Siege.
King in khaki. Webster, H: K. †$1.50. Appleton.
King of Arcadia. Lynde, F. †$1.50. Scribner.
King of bigamists. Harper, O. 25 c. J. S. Ogilvie.
King of Nobody's Island. Enright, T: $1. Gibson Pub.
King of Rome. Kubinyi, V. v. (For private circulation.) Knickerbocker Press.
King of the air. Strang, H. †$1.50. Bobbs-M.
King of the Golden River. *See* Ruskin, J:
King of the plains; stories of ranch, Indian and mine by Til Tilford and others. '10 (O29) c. il. D. (Harper's young people's ser.) 60 c. Harper.

King of U-Kan. Reynolds, R. G: $1.50. R. G: Reynolds.

KING PHILIP'S WAR.
Bicknell, T: W., *ed.* Addresses and poem in commemoration of the Captain Michael Pierce fight, Mar. 26, 1676, [at Central Falls, R. I.] (Add. pub. for price.) T: W. Bicknell.

King Solomon and the fair Shulamite. Ford, J. E. *$1.50 net. F. F. Sherman.

King Spruce. Day, H. F. †$1.50. Harper.

King Time. Fitzhugh, P. K. $1.25. Caldwell.

King who never died. Senior, D. $1.50. Macmillan.

King who never reigned. Eckard, J. *$3.50 net. J: McBride.

Kingdom in India. Chamberlain, J. *$1.50 net. Revell.

Kingdom of Canada. Ewart, J: S. $2.50. Morang.

Kingdom of earth. Partridge, A. †$1.50. Little, B. & Co.

Kingdom of heaven. Walpole, G: H: S. *$1 net. Dutton.

Kingdom of slender swords. Rives, H. E. †$1.50. Bobbs-M.

Kingdom parables and their teaching. Broughton, L. G. 75 c. net. Revell.

Kinglake, Alex. W:
Eothen; with an introd. by Harold Spender. '08(S19) 16°, (Everyman's lib.) *35 c. net; *70 c. net. Dutton.

King's choice. Levi, R. 15 c. Bloch.

King's conquest. Luce, F. W. $1. Jennings.

King's customs. Atton, H: *$3.50 net. Dutton.

King's English. Fowler, H: W. 40 c. Oxford Univ.

King's favorite. Gibbs, P. H. *$4 net. Jacobs.

King's general in the west. Granville, R., *comp.* *$4 net. Lane.

King's (The) greatest business. Gilbert, P. J. *75 c. net. Revell.

King's henchman. Johnson, W: H: †75 c. Little, B. & Co.

King's mark. Bangs, E. M. $1.50. C. M. Clark.

King's palace. Strong, A. L. 50 c. Oak Leaves.

King's quair. *See* James I., *King of Scotland.*

KINGS.
See names of kings.

KINGS (Book of).
See Bible. O. T.

Kings and prophets of Israel. Kent, C: F. **$1 net. Scribner.

KINGS COUNTY, Cal.
See California.

KINGS COUNTY, N. Y.
Ditmas, C: A. Historic homesteads of Kings County. $5. C: A. Ditmas.

KINGS COUNTY, Nova Scotia.
Eaton, A. W. H. Hist. of Kings County, Nova Scotia, heart of the Acadian land. $7. Salem Press.

Kings in exile. Roberts, C: G: D. †$1.50. Macmillan.

Kings of Israel. Mord, W. 35 c. Stokes.

Kings' favorites. Bickley, F. $3.50. Lane.

Kingsford, Anna Bonus, M.D., and Maitland, E:
Perfect way; or, the finding of Christ. 6th ed. '08(Ap11) c. D. $2.50. Theo. Pub. Co.

Kingsford, quarter. Barbour, R. H: $1.50. Century Co.

Kinglake, Alex. W:
Eothen; with introd. by D. G. Hogarth and notes by V. H. Collins. '10(D10) front. map, 8°, 60 c. Oxford Univ.

Kingsley, Rev. C:
Works. De luxe ed. 5 v. '10(D) 16°, ea., mor., $1.50 net. (Sets only.) Nelson.
Alton Locke. '08(N14) front. S. (New century lib.) padded leath., $1.25. Nelson.
Alton Locke, tailor and poet; with introd. by Ernest Rhys. '10(D10) c. 16°, (Everyman's lib.) 35 c. net; leath., 70 c. net. Dutton.
At last; Christmas in the West Indies. '10 (D24) c. il. 16°, 50 c. net. Macmillan.
Hereward, the Wake. '10(Ag6) il. pors. O. (Luxembourg illustrated lib.) $1.50, boxed. Crowell.
Hereward the Wake; introd. by Ernest Rhys. '08(Mr7) 16°, (Everyman's lib.) *35 c. net; leath., *70 c. net. Dutton.
Hereward the Wake. '08(N14) front. S. (New century lib.) padded leath., $1.25. Nelson.
The heroes. '10(D) 296 p. il. $2.50. Dutton.
Heroes, told to the children by Mary Macgregor. '08(Je6) il. 16°, (Told to the children ser.) 50 c. Dutton.
The heroes. '08(O3) il. T. (Books for the young.) 50 c. Stokes.
The heroes; Greek fairy tales for my children. '10(Ja1) il. 12°, (Familiar friends ser.) $1. Sturgis & W.
Two years ago. '08(N14) front. S. (New century lib.) padded leath., $1.25, boxed. Nelson.
Water-babies; pictured by G: Soper. '10 (Je11) O. $1.50. Baker & T.
Water babies; and Glaucus; introd. by Rose Kingsley. '08(F22) 16°, (Everyman's lib.) *35 c. net; leath., *70 c. net. Dutton.
Water babies. '08(O24) il. 8°, $2.50. Dutton.
Water babies; fairy tale for a land-baby. New ed. '10(N19) col. il. 8°, $2 net. Macmillan.
Water-babies; fairy tale for a land-baby. '09(D11) col. il. Q. *$5 net, boxed. Macmillan.
Westward ho! '08(O17) 16°, (Best books ser.) leath., *$1 net. Dutton.

Kingsley, Mrs. Florence Morse.
And so they were married. '08(O3) c. il. front. S. †$1. Dodd.
Glass house. '09(Ap17) c. il. D. †$1.50. Dodd.
Star of love. '09(O16) c. il. O. $2. Appleton.
Those Brewster children. '10(Mr26) c. il. D. $1. Dodd.

Kingsley, H:
Geoffrey Hamlyn. '10(Ap2) 16°, (Everyman's lib.) 35 c. net; leath., 70 c. net. Dutton.

Kingsley, H: Ross, comp.
Patriotic and American songs. 2d ed. '09, [1910.] (O) c. '09. 24 p. S. pap., 10 c. H: R. Kingsley.

Kingsley, Rose Georgina.
Roses and rose growing; with a chapter on "How to grow roses for exhibition," by Rev. F. Page-Roberts. '09(Ja9) il. 8°, *$2 net. Macmillan.

Kingsley English texts. 16°, pap. Palmer Co.
—Addison, *and others.* Sir Roger de Coverley papers. 40 c.
—Bible. O. T. Narrative episodes from the Old Testament. 25 c.
—Coleridge. Rime of the ancient mariner. 25 c.
—Longfellow. Evangeline. 40 c.
—Lowell. Vision of Sir Launfal. 25 c.
—Shakespeare. Julius Cæsar.—Macbeth. ea., 25 c.

Kingsmead. Hutten, *Baroness* B. v. †$1.50. Dodd.

KINGSTON, Jamaica.
Caine, W: R. H. Cruise of the "Port Kingston": [earthquake at Kingston.] W: R. H. Caine.

Kinkade, F:
My lady's fortune hunt. '08(Mr) c. 378 p. il. 12°, $1.50. C. M. Clark.

Kinkaid, Mrs. Mary Holland McNeish.
Man of yesterday. '08(Mr28) c. il. D. †$1.50. Stokes.

Kinkead, Edg. Benton, Black, S: L., and Williams, Loyd T., comps.
Complete law quizzer; self-preparation for final examination, [etc.] 4th ed., rev. '09, [1910.] (Mr.) c. 16+1055 p. O. buckram, $4.50. W. H. Anderson.

KINKS.
See Machinery.

Kinks for boss weavers. Textile World Record. 75 c. Lord & N.

Kinks for cotton superintendents. Textile World Record. (Sold to subscribers of Textile World Record only.) Lord & N.

Kinks for wool and worsted finishers. Textile World Record. 75 c. Lord & N.

Kinnaird, Percy.
Evolution of money. '09(S18) c. D. $1; pap., 50 c. P. Kinnaird.

Kinne, Helen.
Equipment for teaching of domestic science; with chapter on the School of Household Arts, Teachers' College, Columbia University, by B: R. Andrews. '10(N5) il. plans, 8°, (Columbia Univ., Teachers' College record.) pap., 30 c. Columbia Univ.

Kinnear, P:
Wrecking the nation: the crime of 1907-8. '08(Mr) c. 44 p. 12°, pap. (Add. pubs. for price.) Co-operative Pub. Co.

Kinney, Asa Stephen.
Views of Mount Holyoke College, South Hadley, Mass. '09, [1910.] (Ap) 4 p. por. 8°, 50 c. A. S. Kinney.

Kinnicutt, Leonard Parker, Winslow, Charles-Edward Amory, and Pratt, Rob. Winthrop.
Sewage disposal. '10(O22) c. figs. 8°, $3 net. Wiley.

Kinnicutt, Lincoln Newton.
Indian names of places in Plymouth, Middleborough, Lakeville and Carver, Plymouth County, Mass.; with interpretations of some of them. '09(D18) 8°, $2. N. J. Bartlett.

Kinross, Albert.
Joan of Garioch. '08(N14) c. il. D. †$1.50. Macmillan.

Kinsey, Rob. Baldwin.
Serious question, what is true repentance? '09(N) c. 215 p. por. 12°, $1. R. B. Kinsey.

Kinsfolk and friends of Jesus. Gillie, R. C. *$1 net. Macmillan.

Kinship of God and man. Lanier, J: J. 3 v. ea., $1.50; per set, $3.50. J: J. Lanier.

Kinsley, A. T.
Text book of veterinary pathology, for students and practitioners. '10(D) 8+19-400 p. il. tabs., 4°, $4; hf. leath., $4.50. A. Eger.

Kinsman, Bp. F: Jos.
Principles of Anglicanism. '10(D31) c. D. $1 net. Longmans.

KINTON, Ada Florence.
Randleson, *Mrs.* S. A. Just one blue bonnet: life story of Ada Florence Kinton [of the Salvation Army.] $1. A. N. Ingersoll.

Kintzing, Pearce, M.D.
Long life and how to attain it. '08(Je20) c. D. **$1 net. Funk.

Kipling, Rudyard.
Works. Library ed. 10 v. '09(Ap) 8°, per set, $7.50; ¾ mor., $12.50. Fenno.
Abaft the funnel. '09(O16) c. D. †$1.50. B. W. Dodge.
Actions and reactions. [Outward bound ed.] 09(O16) c. il. O. †$1.50. Doubleday, P.
Actions and reactions. '09(D4) c. D. (Pocket Kipling.) limp leath., **$1.50 net. Doubleday, P.
Birthday book; comp. by Jos. Finn, (authorized by Rudyard Kipling.) '09 (Mr13) il. D. (Pocket Kipling.) limp leath., **$1.50 net. Doubleday, P.
Collected verse. '10(N5) c. col. il. Q. $3.50 net, boxed; leath., $10 net, boxed; limited ed. of 125 autographed and numbered copies on large paper, $20 net, boxed. Doubleday, P.
Day's work. '08(My2) c. 12°, (Pocket Kipling.) leath., **$1.50 net. Doubleday, P.
Departmental ditties, *and* Ballads and barrack room ballads. '08(Ag22) c. (Pocket Kipling.) leath., **$1.50 net. Doubleday, P.
Five nations. '09(Mr27) c. D. (Pocket Kipling.) leath., **$1.50 net. Doubleday, P.
From sea to sea. '09(Jl17) c. D. (Pocket Kipling.) limp leath., **$1.50 net. Doubleday, P.

Kipling, Rudyard.—*Continued.*
Horse marines. '10(D17) c. 8°, 50 c. Doubleday, P.
Just so stories. '09(Je5) c. il. D. (Pocket Kipling.) leath., **$1.50 net. Doubleday, P.
Kim. '08(My2) D. (Pocket Kipling.) leath., **$1.50 net. Doubleday, P.
Life's handicap. '08(D26) c. D. (Pocket Kipling.) leath., **$1.50 net. Doubleday, P.
Light that failed. Rev. ed. '08(S12) c. D. (Pocket Kipling.) leath., **$1.50 net. Doubleday, P.
Many inventions. '08(D26) c. D. (Pocket Kipling.) leath., **$1.50 net. Doubleday, P.
Plain tales from the hills; with a biographical sketch by C: Eliot Norton. Rev. ed. '08(S5) c. D. (Pocket Kipling.) leath., **$1.50 net. Doubleday, P.
Puck of Pook's Hill. '09(Mr13) c. D. (Pocket Kipling.) limp leath., **$1.50 net. Doubleday, P.
Rewards and fairies. '10(O15) c. il. O. $1.50. Doubleday, P.
Seven seas. '08(D26) c. D. (Pocket Kipling.) leath., **$1.50 net. Doubleday, P.
Soldier tales. '09(Je) 12°, (Wayside lib.) limp leath., $1. Brentano's.
Song of the English. '10(Ja22) c. il., **$7.50 net, boxed. Doubleday, P.
Stalky & Co. '09(Ap17) c. D. (Pocket Kipling.) leath., **$1.50 net. Doubleday, P.
Stories and poems every child show know; ed. by Mary E. Burt and W. T. Chapin. '09(My15) c. D. (Every child should know ser.) $1.20. Doubleday, P.
Under the deodars; The phantom 'rickshaw; Wee Willie Winkie. '09(Mr27) c. D. (Pocket Kipling.) leath., **$1.50 net. Doubleday, P.
With the night mail. '09(Ap10) c. il. D. †$1. Doubleday, P.
See also Good stories.

—, and Balestier, C: Wolcott.
The Naulahka. '09(Je12) c. D. (Pocket Kipling.) limp leath., **$1.50 net. Doubleday, P.

Kipper, Herman Brunswick.
Life; inorganic, organic, immortal. '08 (D) c. 10+49 p. 12°. (Add. pubs. for price.) Univ. Press, (Camb.)

Kirbye, J. E:
Puritanism in the South. '09(Ap10) c. 12°, bds., 75 c. Pilgrim Press.

Kirk, Mrs. Alice Gitchell.
People's home recipe book. '10(D3) c. il. por. 4°, (People home lib.) $3. R. C. Barnum.

Kirk, E:
Cupola furnace; pract. treatise on the construction and management of foundry cupolas. 3d ed., thoroughly rev. and partly rewritten. '10(Ag27) il. 8°, $3.50. Baird.

"Kirk, Eleanor," pseud.
See Ames, *Mrs.* Eleanor Maria Easterbrook.

Kirk, F. M.
Senior geography questions. '10(D17) c. 8°, (Oxford geographies.) pap., 25 c. Oxford Univ.

Kirk, Rev. J:
Biographies of English Catholics in the 18th century; being part of his projected continuation of Dodd's Church history; ed. by J: Hungerford Pollen and Edn. Burton. '09(Jl) 16+293 p. pors. 8°, *$2.75 net. Benziger.
—, comp. *See* Berington, Jos., *comp.*

Kirk, W:, ed.
Modern city: Providence, Rhode Island, and its activities. '09(O16) c. il. tabs.. O. *$2.50 net. Univ. of Chic.

Kirkaldy, J. W., and Drummond, I. M.
Introd. to the study of biology. '09(N13) il. D. $1.60. Oxford Univ.

Kirkes, W: Senhouse, M.D.
Hdbk. of physiology. 21st ed., rev. and enl. by W. D. Halliburton. '08, [1909.] (Mr) 19+916 p. il. 12°, $3; leath., *$3.75 net. Blakiston.
Hdbk. of physiology; rev. and rewritten by C: Wilson Greene. 7th American revision. '10(O) 9+761 p. il. (partly col.) diagrs., 8°, $3. Wood.

Kirkham, Stanton Davis.
In the open: studies and appreciations of nature. '08(O17) c. il. O. **$1.75 net. P. Elder.
Mexican trails: record of travel in Mexico. '09(Mr27) c. il. O. **$1.75 net. Putnam.
Philosophy of self-help: application of practical psychology to daily life. '09(Ja30) c. D. **$1.25 net. Putnam.
Resources; interpretation of the well-rounded life. '10(F19) c. D. **$1.25 net. Putnam.

Kirkland, Caroline.
Some African highways: a journey of two American women to Uganda and the Transvaal. '08(Ag8) c. il. map, O. $1.50. Estes.

"Kirkland, Frazar," pseud.
See Devens, R: Miller.

Kirkland, Winifred.
The home-comers. '10(O1) c. il. D. $1.20 net. Houghton M.
Introducing Corinna. '09(O9) c. il. D. *$1 net. Revell.

Kirkman, G: Wycherly.
See Putney, Albert Hutchinson.

Kirkman, Marshall Monroe.
Romance of Alexander the king. '09(N6) c. il. map, D. (Alexandrian romances.) $1.50. C. Phillips.
Romance of Alexander the prince. '09 (N6) c. il. map, D. (Alexandrian romances.) $1.50. C. Phillips.
Romance of Alexander and Roxana. '09 (N6) c. il. D. (Alexandrian romances.) $1.50. C. Phillips.
Science of railways; rev. and enl. ed., 1908. [v. 1,] Air brake: its construction and working; [v. 2,] Supplement to the volume Air brake; [v. 3,] Operating trains; [v. 4,] Cars, their construction, handling and supervision, in 2 books; [v. 5,] Electricity applied to railways; [v. 6,] Loco-

motive appliances. '08(D19); [v. 7.] In 2 bks. Bk. 1, Locomotive, engine failures; Bk. 2, Motive power department. '08, [1909.] (Ja); [v. 8,] Engineers' book. '09(Ag28) il. tabs., 12°, $36. (Sold in sets only.) C. Phillips.

Science of railways. Rev. and enl. ed., 1910. [v. 1,] Air brake. '10(Mr26); [v. 3,] Operating trains (Jl16); [v. 5,] Electricity applied to railways. Ed. 1910. [v. 6,] Locomotive appliances (S); [v. 7,] The locomotive. In 2 bks. Bk. 1, Engine failures; Bk. 2, Motive power department. '10(Mr26); [v. 9,] Air brake portfolio (Ap9); [v. 10,] Shops and shop practice. 2 v. '10(Ja1) il. tabs., 12°, per set, $36. (Sold in sets only.) C. Phillips.

"Science of railways" portfolio. '10(Jl16) c. f°, $5. C. Phillips.

Kirkpatrick, Edn. Asbury.
Fundamentals of child study. New ed., rev. '08(D12) 12°, *$1.25 net. Macmillan.
Genetic psychology. '09(Je5) c. D. **$1.25 net. Macmillan.
—, ed. Studies in development and learning; contributions from the department of psychology and child study in the Fitchburg Normal School. '09(Ap17) figs. O. (Archives of psychology.) pap., $1. Science Pr., (N. Y.)

Kirkpatrick, G: Ross.
War—what for? '10(S3) c. il. 8°, $1.20. G: R. Kirkpatrick.

Kirkpatrick, Howard.
Applied vocalization. '09(Mr13) c. S. 50 c. H. Kirkpatrick.

Kirkup, T:
History of Socialism. 4th ed. '09(Je19) 12°, *$2.25 net. Macmillan.
Primer of Socialism. '08(D19) D. *40 c. net. Macmillan.

Kirlin, Jos. L. J.
Catholicity in Philadelphia from the earliest missionaries down to the present time. '09(O16) c. pors. 8°, $3.50. McVey.

Kirsch, W:
Scientific magical experiments. '09(N20) c. il. O. pap., 50 c. W: Kirsch.

Kirtley, Ja. S:, D.D., ed.
Half-hour talks on character building by self-made men and women; with special introd. by H: Hopkins; also special autograph articles on true success and character building by ex-President Roosevelt, Senator Albert J. Beveridge and many other noted men and women. '10(D3) c. il. pors. $2. Hamming.

Kirwan, T:, ["William Wonder."]
Reciprocity (social and economic) in the thirtieth century, the coming co-operative age; forecast of the world's future. '10 (F19) c. D. *$1 net. Cochrane.

Kisch, Enoch Heinrich.
Sexual life of woman in its physiological, pathological and hygienic aspects; only auth. tr. into the English language from the German by M. Eden Paul, M.D. '10 (Ap) c. 11+686 p. il. 4°, $5 Rebman.

Kisch, H. J.
Religion of the civilized world and Judaism. '10(Je4) 8°, 40 c. Bloch.

Kiser, Donald J.
See Illinois. Notes on the repts.

Kiser, S: Ellsworth.
Sonnets of a chorus girl. '09(My1) c. il. S. bds., 50 c. Dodge.

Kismet. Fletcher, J. C. †75 c. Little, B. & Co.

Kiss of Helen. Marriott, C: $1.50. Lane.

KISSING.
See Infectious diseases.

Kitchen, Maria Louisa Kindt, [Mrs. R. Kitchen.]
Essay on the life of our patriotic admiral, Christopher Columbus. '09(Ap) c. '08. 22 p. il. 8°, 50 c. R. Kitchen.

KITCHEN.
See Cookery;—Domestic economy.

Kite book. Kilvert, B: S. C. **$1.25 net. Dodd.

KITES.
Miller, C: M. Construction and flying of kites. 20 c. Manual Arts.
Miller, C: M. Kite craft. (Not for sale.) Davis Press.

Kitson, C: Herbert.
Studies in fugue. '10(Ja1) 8°, $1.50. Oxford Univ.

Kittens and the bear. Jewett, J: H. 75 c. Small.

Kitton, Frederic G:
Charles Dickens. '08(O10) il. O. *$3.50 special net. Appleton.

Kittredge, Dan. Wright.
Memoirs of a failure. '08(D19) c. D. *$1.25 net. U. P. James.

Kittredge, G: Lyman.
See Arnold, Sarah Louise.

Kittredge, J: Herbert.
Method of impressions and bites: [for false teeth.] '07, [1908.] (My.) c. 123 p. il. 8°, $3.50. J: H. Kittredge.

Kittrell, Norman Goree.
Primer of the government of Texas, for use as a text book in schools. '09, [1910.] (F) c. 216 p. front. 12°, 40 c. Southern Pub., (Tex.)

Kitty kat Kimmie. Patteson, *Mrs.* S. L. $1.25. Jacobs.

Kitty-puss. Wiederseim, *Mrs.* G. G. 50 c. Stokes.

Klaber, W:
On certain 7-nitro-4-quinazolones. '07, [1908.] (My.) 8°. (Add. author for price.) W: Klaber.

"Klahowga," pseud.
See Barnes, Orange Perry.

KLAMATH LAKE INDIANS.
See Indians.

Klarmann, Rev. And. F.
Life in the shadow of death; art and purpose of living. '10(O22) c. D. $1 net. Pustet.
Nizra, the flower of the Parsa, the visit of the Wisemen. '08(N21) 12°, *$1 net. Herder.

Klauser, Julius.
Nature of music; orig. harmony in one voice. '10(Ap9) c. por. O. $2.50. Houghton M.

Kleber, J: C.
Master spirit. '10(My14) c. 12°, $1.50. Cochrane.

Kleberg, Rudolph, rep.
See Texas. *Ct. of criminal appeals.* Repts.

Klebs, Arnold Carl, ed.
Tuberculosis; treatise by American authors on its etiology, pathology, frequency, semeiology, diagnosis, prognosis, prevention, and treatment. '09(N) 29+939 p. il. 8°, $6. Appleton.

Kleeberger, F. L,
See Torrey, H. B.

Klein, Augusta.
See Gibson, W. R. Boyce.

Klein, C:
Music master; novelized from the play as produced by D: Belasco. '09(Mr27) c. il. D. †$1.50. Dodd.

—, and Hornblow, Arth.
John Marsh's millions; novel. '10(Ag20) c. il. O. $1.50. G: W. Dillingham.
Third degree: narrative of metropolitan life. '09(N20) c. il. D. †$1.50. G: W. Dillingham.

Klein, D:
Literary criticism from the Elizabethan dramatists, repertory and synthesis; with introd. note, by J. E. Spingarn. '10(Jl30) c. D. $1.50 net. Sturgis & W.

Klein, Felix, Abbé.
American student in France. '08(Ap25) c. il. O. *$2.50 net. McClurg.

Klein, H. J.
Star atlas; maps of all stars from 1 to 6.5 magnitude between North Pole and south declination; tr. and brought up to date by Edm. McClure. New ed. '10(D) 81 p. charts, 4°, $3.50 net. Gorham.

Klein, Hermann.
Unmusical New York; brief criticism of triumphs, failures and abuses. '10(Ap2) por. D. $1.50 net. Lane.

Klein, Jacob.
Situation at present: a plain explanation of Socialism. '08(Ag22) 16°, pap., 10 c. J. Klein.

Kleinschmidt, R. A., comp.
See Oklahoma. Form book.

Kleinschrod, Franz.
Inherent law of life: new theory of life and disease; tr. from the German and ed. by Louise C. Appel. '10(D17) 12°, $1.25 net. Macmillan.

Kleiser, Grenville.
How to argue and win. '10(N5) c. D. $1.25 net. Funk.
How to develop power and personality in speaking; with an introd. by Lewis O. Brastow. '09(Ja9) c. D. **$1.25 net. Funk.
How to develop self-confidence in speech and manner. '10(N5) c. D. $1.25 net. Funk.
Humorous hits, and How to hold an audience. '08(Mr28) c. D. **$1 net. Funk.
Teacher's key to How to speak in public. '09(My15) c. 12°, 50 c. Funk.
—, comp. World's greatest sermons; introd. by Lewis O. Brastow, D.D. In 10 v. '08 (D19) c. S. subs., $7.50; hf. mor., $10, boxed. Funk.
World's great sermons; introd. by Lewis O. Brastow. In 10 v. '10(My14) per set, $2.75. Westminster, (Chic.)

Klette, C: Herman Bruno.
Lost mine of the Mono. '09(D) $1.50. Cochrane.

Kline, G: Washington.
See Gale, Albert Liscomb.

Kline, R. E. Pattison.
Argumentation and debate. '10(Mr) c. 23 p. O. pap., 25 c. La Salle Extension.

Klingman, G: Adam.
Church hist. for busy people. '09(D18) c. 12°, $1. F: L: Rowe.

KLONDIKE, Alaska.
Gorbach, A. B. Unter der mitternachtssonne; abenteuer aus dem leben der Klondyke-goldgräber. (Add. author for price.) A. B. Gorbach.
MacDonald, A. The White trail: early days in the Klondike: [fiction.] $1.25. Caldwell.

Klugh, Maria Catherine.
Tales from the Far North. '09(Ag28) il. D. 6c c. Flanagan.

Klykken, O.
Our homes and our children; lectures; tr. from the Norwegian by Peer Stromme. '09(D18) c. 12°, 75 c. Lutheran Pub.

Knack of it. Loomis, C: B. *75 c. net. Revell.

Knapp, Adeline.
Well in the desert. '08(S5) c. D. †$1.50. Century Co.

Knapp, G: Leonard.
Scales of justice. '10(O1) c. col. il. D. $1.50. Lippincott.

Knapp, Harriet Loretta.
Echoes from the prairie and the hills: [poems.] '08(D) c. 75 p. pors. D. (Add. pubs. for price.) Wichita.
Miriam's tower. [2d ed.] '10(F26) c. pors. 12°, $1.25. Wichita.

Knapp, Marg. Lizzie.
But still a man. '09(F13) c. D. †$1.50. Little, B. & Co.

Knapp, Seaman Asahel.
Cotton, the greatest of cash crops. '10 (My) 10 p. 8°. (U. S., Dept. of Agriculture, circular.)
Demonstration work on southern farms. '10(D) 19 p. il. 8°. (U. S., Dept. of Agriculture, farmers' bull.)
Hog raising in the south. '09(D) 8 p. 8°, (U. S., Dept. of Agriculture, Office of the Secretary, circular.) (Add. Superintendent for price.)

Knapp, Shepherd.
History of the Brick Presbyterian Church in the city of New York. '09(Mr13) il. pors. maps, 8°, $5. Scribner.

Knappen, Thdr. M.
See Day, Fk. A.

Knappenberger, Ja. Buchanan.
Exposition of the book of Revelation. '08 (Je27) c. por. O. $1. J. B. Knappenberger.

Knaus, H:
Judicial usurpation: an open letter to Congress showing this in the injunctions in labor disputes. '08(My16) c. 8°, pap. (Add. author for price.) H: Knaus.

Kneass, Strickland Landis.
Practice and theory of the injector. 3d ed., rev. and enl. '10(Ap9) c. il. tabs., 8°, $1.50. Wiley.

Knecht, Edm., Rawson, Christopher, and Lowenthal, R:
Manual of dyeing. 2d ed. In 2 v. '10 (F19) 8°. *$12 net. Lippincott.

KNEE.
Bennet, *Sir* W: H: Injuries and diseases of the knee-joint. *$2 net. Wood.

Knickerbocker ser. il. 12°. Putnam.
—Munroe. Cab and caboose. $1.25.

Knickerbocker's history of New York. *See* Irving, Washington.

Kniffin, T: Henderson.
Kentucky of Kentucky; romance of the blue grass region. '09(D) 5-163 p. il. 12°, $1.25. Cochrane.

Kniffin, W: H:, jr., comp.
New York Savings Bank cases. [Loose leaf ed.; limited to 200 copies.] '10 (Mr) c. Q. $5. Haedrich.

Knight, Adele Ferguson.
Mademoiselle Celeste; romance of the French Revolution. '10(My14) c. front. D. $1.50. Jacobs.

Knight, Archibald Patterson.
Hygiene for young people. '09(N20) c. il. 12°, 60 c. C: E. Merrill.

Knight, Austin Melvin.
Modern seamanship. 5th ed., rewritten and enl. '10(D) 13+540 p. il. 8°, $7.50. Van Nostrand.

Knight, C:
Shadows of the old booksellers. '08(Jl18) 16°, (New universal lib.) 50 c.; leath., 75 c. Dutton.

Knight, C: Huntoon, and Bryant, W: Sohier.
Diseases of the nose, throat and ear. 2d ed., rev. '09(N) c. 19+631 p. il. 8°, *$4.50 net; hf. mor., *$6 net. Blakiston.

Knight, C: Rob.
Animals of the world, for young people; with an introd. by Tudor Jenks. '08(N7) il. O. **$2 net. Stokes.

—, and Hardcastle, Ella.
Birds of the Bible for young people. '10 (F5) 8°, $2. Stokes.
Birds of the world for young people. '10 (Ja1) c. il. (partly col.) O. **$2 net. Stokes.

Knight, E: F:
Awakening of Turkey: history of the Turkish revolution. '09(Je19) pors. O. *$3 net. Lippincott.

Knight, Fs. A.
Somerset. [1910.] (My) 12+192 p. 8°, (Cambridge county geographies.) 45 c. Putnam.

—, and Dutton, L. M.
Devonshire. '10(Jl9) c. 8°, (Cambridge county geographies.) 45 c. net. Putnam.

Knight, Rev. G. H.
Full allegiance. '09(N20) D. *$1 net. Armstrong.
In the dark and cloudy day. '10(D) 12°, $1.25 net. Doran.

Knight, J. H.
Motor repairing for amateurs. '08(Jl4) il. 12°, *$1 net. Spon.

Knight, Jos., comp.
Smoker's reveries; companion book to pipe and pouch. '09(O9) c. S. $1; leath., $1.75, boxed. Caldwell.

Knight, Marietta.
Dramatic reader for grammar grades. '10 (Ap30) c. il. D. 50 c. Am. Bk.

Knight, Ora Willis.
Birds of Maine. Subscription ed. '08(N) c. 17+19-693 p. il. map, 8°, $3.50. Glass.

Knight, Sherwood Sweet.
Human life. '10(O15) 12°, $1. Fenno.

Knight, Rev. W: Allen.
No room in the inn. '10(O15) c. il. D. bds., 50 c. Pilgrim Press.
Shepherd of Jebel Nur. '09(N13) c. front. D. bds., *50 c. net. Pilgrim Press.
Signs in the Christmas fire. '08(O10) front. vellum, *50 c. net; envelope ed., *35 c. net; bds., *35 c. net. Pilgrim Press.

Knight, W: Angus.
Six lectures on some nineteenth century artists, English and French, del. at the Art Inst. of Chicago; being the Scammon lectures for the year 1907. '10 (Mr5) c. il. por. 8°, $2. Art. Inst. of Chic.
—, **ed.** Poets on Christmas. '08(Je27) 12°, *$1 net. Gorham.

Knight errant and his doughty deeds. Davidson, N. J., *ed.* $1.50. Lippincott.

Knight in homespun. Spoth, J: C: $1.50. C. M. Clark.

Knight of the burning pestle. *See* Beaumont, Fs.

Knight of the highway. Scollard, C. $1. G: W: Browning.

Knight of the twentieth century. Hensel, H. C. $1. H. C. Hensel.

Knight of the West Side. Sheppard, W: H: P. †60 c. Penn Pub. Co.

Knight of the wilderness. Gale, O. M. $1.50. Reilly & B.

Knight Templar's pilgrimage to the Holy Land. Wilson, T: W. $1.50; $2. T: W. Wilson.

Knighthood in germ and flower. Cox, J: H. $1.25. Little, B. & Co.

Knight's tale. *See* Chaucer, Geoffrey. The prologue.

Knights (The). *See* Aristophanes.

KNIGHTS HOSPITALLERS.
See Knights of St. John of Jerusalem.

KNIGHTS OF COLUMBUS.
Mugan, E. L. Side lights K. of C. as reviewed from without. Donohue.

KNIGHTS OF KING ARTHUR.
Dennen, E. J. Knights of King Arthur. 25 c. E. J. Dennen.
Forbush, W: B., *and* Masseck, F. L. Boys' round table. 90 c. Knights King Arthur.

KNIGHTS OF PYTHIAS.
See Freemasonry.

KNIGHTS OF ST. JOHN OF JERUSALEM.
Belabre, *Baron* de. Rhodes of the knights: [describes monuments of the Knights of St. John still standing in Rhodes.] $9.75. Oxford Univ.

Knights of the golden horseshoe, and other lays. Stewart, R. A. 50 c. R. A. Stewart.

Knights of the horseshoe. Caruthers, W: A. $1. Burt.

Knights of the Silver Shield. *See* Alden, Raymond MacDonald. Why the chimes rang.

KNIGHTS TEMPLAR.
See Freemasonry.

Knipe, Alden Arth.
Captain of the eleven. '10(O1) c. il. D. $1.25. Harper.
Red magic book. '10(O8) c. il. O. $1.25 net. Doubleday, P.
See also Knipe, *Mrs.* Emilie Benson.

Knipe, Mrs. Emilie Benson and Alden Arth.
Little Miss Fales. '10(Ap16) c. front. D. $1.25. Harper.

Knit goods finishing. Metcalf, M. A., *comp.* 50 c. Am. Sch. Corr.

KNITTING.
Fleisher's knitting and crocheting manual. 25 c. Fleisher.
Keys, Gwen, *ed.* Priscilla knitting book. 25 c. Priscilla.
McCormack, M. A. Spool knitting. *$1 net. Barnes.
Metcalf, M. A. Knitting: [machinery.] $3. Am. Sch. Corr.
Metcalf, M. A., *comp.* Knit goods finishing. 50 c. Am. Sch. Corr.
Textile World Record. Kinks on cost finding in knitting mills. 75 c. net. Lord & N.

KNIVES.
Treatise on the care of saws and knives. $2 net. Baldwin.

Knobel, E:
Wild animals of North America. '09(N) il. obl. 4°, $2.50. Lovell.

Knocks and kinks. Collins, H. E. $1. Hill Pub.

Knopf, Adolph.
Geology of the Seward Peninsula tin deposits, Alaska. '09(Mr6) il. map, 8°, (U. S. Geol. Survey, bull.) pap., 15 c.
Probable tertiary land connection bet. Asia and North America. '10(Je) 413-420 p. Q. (Univ. of Cal. pubs.; Geology.) pap., 10 c. Univ. of Cal.
See also Moffit, Fred Howard.

Knopf, Siegmund Adolph, M.D.
Kampen mod tæring, med tillæg omhanlende sundhedsregler for hjemmet og skolen, tilstelning af sanatorium-behandling i hjemmet samt en historisk oversigt over kampen mod tæring i de Forenede Stater; oversat fram engelsk af A. C. Amundson. '08(D5) il. 8°, 25 c. Amerika Pub.
Tuberculosis a preventable and curable disease. '09(Jl17) c. il. por. D. **$2 net. Moffat.

Knorr, G: Washington.
Consolidated rural schools and organization of a county system. '10(N) 99 p. il. tabs., diagrs., 8°, (U. S., Dept. of Agriculture, Office of Experiment Stations bull.)

Knott, Cargill Gilston.
Physics of earthquake phenomena. '08 (D5) il. figs. O. $4.75. Oxford Univ.

Knott, H:
Destroyer; man to demon; the devastation of a life by strong drink. '08(D) c. 222 p. il. 8°, 75 c. Vansant.

Know thy neighbor. Wiggins, *Mrs.* L. K. $1.25. J. L. Nichols.

Know thyself. Burch, *Mrs.* A. E. S. $1. A. E. S. Burch.

Know thyself ser. *See* Cocroft, Susanna.

Knowing and teaching the scholar. Schauffler, A. F: 50 c. S. S. Times.

KNOWLEDGE.
Coursault, J. H. Learning process. *$1 net. Teachers' Coll.
Stoner, J: R. Logic and imagination in perception of truth. $1.50. Cochrane.
Wodehouse, H. Presentation of reality. $1 net. Putnam.
See also Culture;—Education;—Philosophy;—Psychology;—Science.

Knowledge, life and reality. Ladd, G: T. $3.50. Dodd.

Knowles, Dan. Clark, D. D.
Chapel talks. '10(F19) c. por. D. *$1 net. Eaton & M.

Knowles, Frederic Lawrence, comp.
Year book of famous lyrics; selections from the British and American poets arranged for daily reading or memorizing. '10(Ag20) c. il. pors. D. $1.50, boxed; anniversary ed., $3, boxed; limp leath., $3. Caldwell.

Knowles, Mrs. Mary Henrietta, and Favard, Berthe des Combes.
Perfect French possible; some essential and adequate helps to French pronunciation and rhythm. '10(O1) c. D. 35 c. Heath.

Knowles, Rob. E:
Attic guest. '09(O23) c. D. *$1.20 net. Revell.
The handicap; novel of pioneer days. '10 (O29) c. D. $1.20 net. Revell.
Web of time. '08(N14) c. D. $1.50. Revell.

Knowles-Foster, Frances G.
Jehanne of the golden lips. '10(O22) D. $1.50. Lane.

Knowlson, Arth.
See Muller, Julius Washington.

Knowlson, T: Sharper.
Art of sympathy. '10(S10) D. $1. Warne.
Business!; pract. hints for master and man. '10(Ja22) D. pap., *40 c. net. Warne.
Century student's manual. '10(Ja29) c. D. **$1 net. Warne.
Education of the will. '09(Jl31) D. *$1.50 net. Lippincott.
Origins of popular superstitions and customs. '10(D31) 8°, $1.75 net. Pott.

Knowlton, Fk. Hall.
Birds of the world; with a chapter on the anatomy of birds by Frederic A. Lucas; the whole ed. by Rob. Ridgway. '09 (Ap3) c. il. Q. (American nature ser.; group 1, Natural history.) **$7 net, boxed. Holt.

Known to the police. Holmes, T: *$3 net. Longmans.

Knox, Alice Adelaide.
See Cannon, W. A.

Knox, C: Edn., and Shaad, G: C.
Electric wiring and lighting; pt. 1, Electric wiring, by C: E. Knox; pt. 2, Electric lighting, by G: C. Shaad. '09(F20) c. il. 8°, (American School of Correspondence pubs.) $1. Am. Sch. Corr.

Knox, Dorothea Heness.
Heart of Washington. '09(Ag7) c. D. $1.50. Neale.

Knox, E. M.
Bible lessons for schools: Exodus. '08 (Ja11) il. map, 16°, *40 c. net. Macmillan.

Knox, Ernest Blake, M.D.
Aids to microscopic diagnosis. '10(Jl) 16°, $1 net. Wood.

Knox, G: H.
Leadership: [business success.] '09(Jl) c. 13-311 p. por. 12°, (Personal help lib.) $1.40; leath., $2.80. Personal Help.

Knox, G: W:
Gospel of Jesus the Son of God: interpretation for the modern man. '09(N13) c. S. (Modern religious problems.) 50 c. Houghton M.

Knox, Horatio B.
Destruction of the "Gaspee": [British schooner destroyed by citizens of Rhode Island, 1772.] '09(Ap3) O. (R. I. educational circulars; historical ser.) pap., gratis. R. I. Dept. Educ.

Knox, Philander Chase.
Future of commerce: address before the Chamber of Commerce of Pittsburgh, Feb. 12, 1908. '08(F) O. pap. (Add. author for price.) P. C. Knox.
Memorial address on the battlefield of Gettysburg, May 30, 1908. '09(Ag21) 8°, pap. (Add. author for price.) P. C. Knox.
People, the railroads and the national authority; address del. before the Civic Forum. '08(D5) por. 12°, (Civic Forum addresses.) pap., 10 c. Civic Forum.
Remarks at a dinner given to the Pennsylvania delegation in Congress by Hon. Jos. C. Sibley, Dec. 4, 1907. '08(F) O. pap. (Add. author for price.) P. C. Knox.

KNOX, Philander Chase.
Burke, J. F. Some of the public services of Philander Chase Knox. (Add. author for price.) J. F. Burke.

Knox, T: Wallace.
Boy's life of General Grant. '09(Ap3) il. por. 12°, $1.25. Saalfield.
In wild Africa; adventures of two youths in a journey through the Sahara desert. [New ed.] '09(O9) c. il. D. (Travel-Adventure ser.) †$1.50. Wilde.

Knox, W. F.
See Keller, S: Smith.

KNOX COLLEGE, Galesburg, Ill.
Mather, R. Commemoration address of the 17th anniversary of [its] founding. (Priv. pr.) R. G. Cooke.

Knudson, Albert Cornelius, D.D.
Old Testament problem. '08(Ap25) c. S. *35 c. net. Jennings.

Knuth, Paul.
Hdbk. of flower pollination: based upon Hermann Müller's work, The fertilization of flowers by insects; tr. by J. R. Ainsworth Davis. v. 1, Introduction and literature; v. 2, Observations on flower pollination made in Europe and the Arctic regions on species belonging to the natural orders: Ranunculaceæ to Stylidicæ. '08(My23) il. por. O. v. 1, $6.75; v. 2, $10.75; v. 3. '09(D4) pors. O. $9.75. Oxford Univ.

KOATI ISLAND.
Bandelier, A. F. A. Islands of Titicaca and Koati. $5. Hispanic Soc.

Kober, G: Martin.
Industrial and personal hygiene. '08, [1909.] (Mr) 8-175 p. 8°, 50 c. President's Home Com.

Koch, Felix J:
Little journey to northern wilds. '09(Ja9) c. il. D. (Library of travel.) 50 c. Flanagan.

Koch, Richard.
German imperial banking laws; together with the German stock exchange regulations. '10(S) 5+330 p. fold. forms, 8°. Gov. Pr. Off.

Koch, Thdr. Wesley.
Hdbk. of the libraries of the University of Michigan. '10(Mr12) S. pap., 10 c. Wahr.

Koebel, W. H.
Portugal, its land and people. '10(F19) col. il. 8°, *$4 net. Dodd.

Koehler, S. R.
See Buxton, *Rev.* Harry J: Wilmot.

Koenig, A:, M.D.
See Essig, C: J.

Koerner, Gustave Philipp.
Memoirs of Gustave Koerner, (1809-1896); ed. by T: J. McCormack. 2 v. '09(D18) 8°, $10 net. Torch Press.

Koester, Fk.
Hydroelectric developments and engineering. '09(Jl17) il. tabs., 4°, *$5 net. Van Nostrand.
Steam-electric power plants. '08(My16) c. il. 8°, **$5 net. Van Nostrand.

Kofoid, C: Atwood.
Exuviation, autotomy and regeneration in *Ceratium;* [also,] Notes on some obscure species of *Ceratium* [Fish.] '08(Je6) il. Q. (Univ. of Cal. pubs., Zoology.) pap., 50 c. Univ. of Cal.
Revision of the genus *ceratocorys,* based on skeletal morphology. '10(Je) 177-187 p. Q. (Univ. of Cal. pubs.; Zoology.) pap., 10 c. Univ. of Cal.

Köhler, Christian Louis Heinrich.
Little school of velocity without octaves. Op. 242 (Farrar). Ditson ed. '10(D) 28 p. F. pap., 50 c. Ditson.

Kohler, Ja. Pollock.
About panics, hardtimes, the cause and the cure. 2d ed., cor. and enl. '08, [1910.] (Mr) 6+86 p. il. por. 12°, 15 c. Outing.

Kohler, Max Ja.
Un-American character of race legislation. '09(D18) (Publications of the American Academy of Political and Social Science.) pap., 25 c. Am. Acad. Pol. Sci.

Kolb, C: B.
Helping up the man who is down; or, seven years in the slums. 2d ed. '10(N) 37 p. il. por. 8°, 25 c. C: B. Kolb.

Kolbe, Bruno.
Introd. to electricity: being a translation of the 2d ed. of Einführung in die Elektrizitatslehre; with corrections and additions by the author; tr. by Jos. Skellon. '08(Je13) il. figs. O. *$3 net. Lippincott.

Kolle, F: Strange.
Fifty and one tales of modern Fairyland. New ed. '10(Ag13) il. 12°, $1.25. Fenno.
Subcutaneous hydrocarbon protheses. '08, [1909.] (Ag) c. 153 p. il. 8°, (Grafton medical books.) **$2.50 net. Grafton Press.

Kolle, Mrs. Loretto Ellen Duffy.
The blue lawn. '10(Ag13) il. 12°, $1 net. Fenno.

Komical Katzenjammers. Dirks, R. 60 c. Stokes.

KONGO FREE STATE.
See Congo Free State.

König Ottokars glück und ende. Grillparzer, F. 60 c. Holt.

Konkle, Burton Alva.
James Wilson and the Constitution: opening address in the official series of events known as the James Wilson memorial; del. before the Law Academy of Philadelphia. '07, [1908.] (My.) 40 p. il. por. facsim., 8°, gratis. Law Acad.

Könnecke, Gustav.
Deutscher literaturatlas; mit einer Einführung von Christian Muff. '08(D19) il. f°, *$1.50 net. Stechert.

Konody, Paul G.
Brothers Van Eyck. '08(Ja25) il. 16°, (Bell's miniature ser. of great painters.) 50 c.; leath., $1. Macmillan.
Chardin. '09(O9) il. in col. O. (Masterpieces in colour ser.) bds., *65 c. net; limp leath., *$1.50 net. Stokes.
Raphael. '08(D19) O. (Masterpieces in colour.) il. bds., *65 c. net. Stokes.
—, ed. *See* National Gallery.

Konta, Mrs. Annie Lemp.
Hist. of French literature, from the oath of Strasburg to Chanticler. '09(D18) c. O. **$2.50 net. Appleton.

Koogle, Effie Louise, comp.
The Christmas collation: up-to-date collection of the choicest original and selected recitations, songs, dialogs, and other exercises, furnishing full and ample provision for the Christmas program; for all ages. '09(N) c. 12°, pap., 25 c. March.

Koons, Rev. W: G:
Junior history of Methodism; with an introd. by Rob. R. Doherty. '09(My22) c. il. 12°, 25 c. Eaton & M.

Koopman, Harry Lyman.
Librarian of the desert: poem. '08(Jl) c. 12+73 p. 12°, $1. Everett.
—, ed. *See* Brown, Rob. Perkins.

KOOTENAI COUNTY, Idaho.
See Indians.

Kopetzky, S: Jos.
Surgery of the ear. '08(D) c. 17+368 p. il. charts, 8°, $4. Rebman.

Koplik, H:
On diseases of children; text-book for use of students and practitioners. 3d ed., enl. and thoroughly rev. [1910.] (Ap) 944 p. il. $5 net. Lea.

Koplowitz, Isidore.
Al-moveth; or, immortality of the soul. '09(N) c. 79 p. por. 12°, 75 c. Bloch.

Koran; Rodwell's translation; introd. by Rev. G: Margoliouth. '09(Ap3) 16°, (Everyman's lib.) *35 c. net; leath., *70 c. net. Dutton.

KORAN.
Wollaston, *Sir* A. N. Religion of the Koran. *40 c. net. Dutton.

KOREA.
See Corea.

Koren, W:
Exercises in French composition for schools and colleges. '09(O30) c. D. 75 c. Holt.

Korkunov, N. M.
General theory of law; tr. by W. G. Hastings. '09(D18) 8°, $3.50. Bost. Law.

Kornicker, J. S., comp.
See Century Code Co.

Kortrecht, Augusta.
Dixie rose. '10(O8) c. col. front. D. $1.50. Lippincott.

Kosmos: poem. *See* Morris, J. C.

KOTSINA-CHITINA REGION.
See Alaska.

Kozlay, C: Meeker.
See Harte, Fs. **Bret.**

Kraemer, H:
Text-book of botany and pharmacognosy. 3d ed., rev. and enl. '08(N); 4th rev. and enl. ed. '10(D3) c. il. figs. 8°, ea., **$5 net. Lippincott.

Kraft, Fk.
Sex of offspring; a modern discovery of a primeval law. '08(Ag) c. 112 p. 12°, $2. Barsuette.

Kraft, Mary Jane, M.D.
Suggestions to the expectant mother. '07, [1908.] (Mr.) c. 94 p. D. $2. M. J. Kraft.

KRAKATOA.
Ernst, A. New flora of the volcanic island of Krakatau. Putnam.

Kramer, Harold Morton.
Castle of Dawn. '08(Ap4) c. il. D. †$1.50. Lothrop, L. & S.
The chrysalis. '09(Ap10) c. il. D. †$1.50. Lothrop, L. & S.

Krankenseelsorge (Die). Untraut, H. J. 60 c. Wiltzius.

Krans, Horatio Sheafe, ed.
English love poems, old and new. '09(D4) c. S. **$1.25 net, boxed. Putnam.
Lincoln tribute book: appreciations by statesmen, men of letters, and poets at home and abroad; together with a Lincoln centenary medal from the second design made for the occasion by Roiné. '09(F27) c. il. S. **$1.75 net. Putnam.
Lost art of conversation; selected essays; ed., with an introd. and notes. '10(My14) c. D. $1.50 net. Sturgis & W.

Krapp, G: Philip.
Authority of law in language. '09(My15) O. (Univ. of Cin. studies.) pap., 50 c. Univ. of Cin.
Elements of English grammar. ''08(Je20) c. D. *80 c. net. Scribner.
Modern English: its growth and present use. '09(S4) c. D. **$1.25 net. Scribner.

Krause, Fedor.
Surgery of the brain and spinal cord, based on personal experiences; tr. by Herman A. Haubold. '09(D) c. il. 4°, $6. Rebman.

Krause, Flora Helm.
Manual of moral and humane education. '10(N19) c. il. 8°, $1.25. Donnelley.

Krauskopf, Jos., D.D.
Prejudice: its genesis and exodus; [treats of prejudice against Jews.] '09(Ja9) c. 12°, 75 c.; pap., 35 c. Bloch.

Krecht, Edm., and Hibbert, Eva.
New reduction methods in volumetric analysis. '10(D31) D. $1 net. Longmans.

Krehbiel, E: B:
The interdict, its hist. and its operation, especial attention to the time of Pope Innocent III, 1198-1216. '09(N) c. 8+184 p. 12°, (Prize essays of the American Historical Association.) $1.50. Am. Hist.

Krehbiel, H: E:
Book of operas; their histories, their plots and their music. '09(D18) c. il. pors. D. **$1.75 net. Macmillan.
Chapters of opera: records concerning the lyric drama in New York from its earliest days down to the present time. '08 (D26) c. il. pors. O. **$3.50 net. Holt.
—, ed. Songs from the operas for alto. '10 (Ja29) c. F. (Musicians' lib.) $2.50; pap., $1.50. Ditson.
Songs from the operas for mezzo soprano. '08(O17) c. il. 4°, (Musicians' lib.) $2.50; pap., $1.50. Ditson.
Songs from the operas for soprano. '08 (F22) c. pors. Q. (Musicians' lib.) $2.50; pap., $1.50. Ditson.
Songs from the operas for tenor. '10(N19) F. (Musicians' lib.) $2.50; pap., $1.50. Ditson.

Kreider, Eug. G.
See Washington. Index to Remington & Ballinger's codes.

Kreidler, C: R., ed.
See New York. Kreidler's analyzed citations.

KREISCHERVILLE, N. Y.
Hollick, C: A. Studies of Cretaceous coniferous remains from Kreischerville, N. Y. $2. N. Y. Botanical.

Kreisinger, H:
See Ray, Wa. T.

Kreissl, Filipp.
Urogenital therapeutics, medical and surgical. '08(My.) c. 461 p. il. 8°, $5. Cleveland Press.

Kremer, Mrs. Ida.
Struggle for a royal child, Anna Monica Pia, Duchess of Saxony: my experiences as governess in the house of the Countess Montignoso during 1906. '08(Ja18) por. 8°. $1.50. M. Kennerley

Kreps, Elmer Harry.
Camp and trail methods; interesting information for all lovers of nature: what to take and what to do. '10(S3) c. il. S. 60 c. A. R. Harding.
Science of trapping; describes the fur bearing animals, their nature, habits and distribution, with practical methods for their capture. '09(Ag) c. 245 p. il. por. 16°, 60 c. A. R. Harding.

KREUTZER, Rodolphe.
Winn, E. L. How to prepare for Kreutzer. $1.—How to study Kreutzer. 75 c. Fischer.

Kreutzer sonata. *See* Tolstoi, *Count* Lyoff Nikolaievich.

Kreymborg, Alfr.
Apostrophes; book of tributes to masters of music. '10(O8) c. D. bds., 50 c. Grafton Press.
Love and life, and other studies. '08(Ap4) c. D. bds., **$1 net. Grafton Press.

KRISHNA (*god*).
Schuré, E. Orpheus and Krishna. *$1.25 net. Badger.

Kroeber, Alfr. L:
Chumash and Costanoan languages. '10 (D10) O. (Univ. of Cal. pubs.; American archæology and ethnology.) pap., 35 c. Univ. of Cal.
Ethnography of the Cahuilla Indians. '08 (Jl4) il. Q. (Univ. of Cal. pubs., American archæology and ethnology.) pap., 75 c. Univ. of Cal.
Mission record of the California Indians, from a manuscript in the Bancroft library. '08(Je6) Q. (Univ. of Cal. pubs., Am. archæology and ethnology.) pap., 25 c. Univ. of Cal.
Notes on Shoshonean [Indian] dialects of southern California. '09(O16) Q. (Univ. of Cal, pubs. in American archæology and ethnology.) pap., 35 c. Univ. of Cal.
See also Barrett, S: Alfr.

Kroeger, Alice Bertha.
Guide to the study and use of reference books. 2d ed., rev. and enl. '09(Ja30) c. O. *$1.25 net. A. L. A.
—, and Cattell, Sarah Ware.
Aids in book selection. '09(Ap3) 12°, (A. L. A. Publishing Board; library handbooks.) pap., 15 c. A. L. A.

Kroeger, E. R.
Hand expansions and contractions. (1910.] (F) $1.25. Ditson.

Krohn, J: Alb.
The walk of colonial Jack; story of a long-distance walker. '10(S) c. 127 p. por. il. 8°. 25 c. J: A. Krohn.

Krohn, W: Otterbein, M.D.
Graded lessons in hygiene. '08(Jl11) c. il. D. *60 c. net. Appleton.
Graded lessons in physiology and hygiene. '08(Jl11) c. il. D. *60 c. net. Appleton.

Kropotkin, Prince Piotrievitch Alexeievitch.
Great French revolution, 1789-1793; tr. from the French by N. F. Dryhurst. '09 (D11) O. *$2.25 net. Putnam.

KROPOTKIN, *Prince* Piotrievitch Alexeievitch.
Robinson, V. Comrad Kropotkin. $1. Altrurians.

Krout, Mary Hannah.
Memoirs of Hon. Bernice Pauahi Bishop '09(Mr13) c. il. pors. 8°. (Not for sale.) Putnam.
Platters and pipkins. '10(N5) c. S. bds., 75 c. net, boxed. McClurg.

"Kru-Cha," pseud.
See Kruse, C: H:

Kruger, Gustav.
The Papacy; the idea and its exponents. '09(Jl3) 12°, (Crown theological lib.) $1.50. Putnam.

Krull, Rev. Virgilius Herman.
Alphabetical oddities; [warnings against abuses of Catholic practices; arranged alphabetically.] '09, [1910.] (My) 31 p. D. V. H. Krull.
Common-sense view of Christian science. '08(S5) c. D. parchment, 15 c.; 2d ed. '08, [1910.] (My) T. pap., 25 c. V. H. Krull.

Krumreig, E: Ludwig, D.D.
Shadowing wing. '10(F5) c. por. D. $1.50. E: L. Krumreig.

Kruse, C: H:, ["Kru-Cha."]
Transition of masonry. '09, [1910.] (Ap) c. 76 p. il. por. 12°, $1. C: H: Kruse.

Kubinyi, Victor von.
King of Rome. '08(F8) il. pors. 8°. (For private circulation.) Knickerbocker Press.

Küchler, Carl Gottlieb Friedrich.
Elizabeth, Empress of Austria and Queen of Hungary; tr. from the German by G: P. Upton. '09(S11) c. pors. S. (Life stories for young people.) *60 c. net. McClurg.
Queen Maria Sophia of Naples; a forgotten heroine; tr. from the German by G: P. Upton. '10(O22) c. il. S. (Life stories for young people.) 50 c. net. McClurg.

Kueffner, Louise Mallinckrodt.
Development of the historic drama; its theory and practice; study based chiefly on the dramas of Elizabethan England and of Germany; a dissertation. '10 (O) 95 p. O. pap., 50 c. net. Univ. of Chic.

Kuehl, G: W.
Automobile guide book of Illinois; descriptions of the best automobile touring routes; routes extending into Iowa, Mo., Minn., Wis., Ind., Mich., O., N. Y., Penn. and Canada. '10(Je) c. 226 p. 12°, $2 net. Caspar.
Automobile blue book of Wisconsin. '09 (F6) 12°, *$2 net. G: W. Kuehl.

Kuehnemann, Eugen.
Charles W. Eliot, president of Harvard University, (May 19, 1869-May 19, 1909.) '09(Je12) c. O. **$1 net. Houghton M.

Kuhn, H. A.
Substantial prosperity; illustrated by diagrams showing panics, periods of depression and logical forecast of the future, coal production and exhaustion of coal, with special reference to Pittsburgh coal district. '07(My23) c. obl. Q. pap., $2. Pittsburgh-W.

Kuhn, Walt.
Little bird told me! '09(Je12) il. D. bds., 75 c Life Pub. Co.

Kuhns, Levi Oscar.
Love of books and reading. '10(S24) c. D. $1. net. Holt.
Sense of the infinite: study of the transcendental element in literature, life and religion. '08(S12) c. D. **$1.50 net. Holt.
Switzerland: its scenery, history, and literary associations. '10(O1) il. c. map, O. $2 net. Crowell.

Kullmer, C. J.
Star maps and star facts. 2d enl. ed. '10 (N12) c. 8°, pap., 15 c. net. C. J. Kullmer.

Kümmel, H: Barnard, and Gage, R. B.
Glass-sand industry of New Jersey. '08 (Je13) il. O. (New Jersey, Geological survey.) pap. (Add. author for price.) H. B. Kümmel.

Kummer, Clare Beecher-.
Bible rhymes for the not too young. '10 (My14) col. il. 4°, 75 c. net. B. W. Dodge.

KUNDECK, Joseph.
See **Dubois Co., Ind.**

Kunou, C: A.
Manual of cardboard construction for third, fourth and fifth grades. 3d rev. ed. '07, [1908.] (S) 84 p. il. tab., 8°, 35 c. Jones' Bk. Store.

Kunst, Earle.
Mystery of Evangeline Fairfax. '10(Ap23) c. il. 12°, $1. Metropolitan Press, (N. Y.)

Kunz, G: F:
History of the gems found in North Carolina. '08(My16) 8°, (N. C. Geological and economic survey.) (Add. pubs. for price.) Uzzell.

—, and Stevenson, C: Hugh.
Book of the pearl: the history, art, science and industry of the queen of gems. '08 (O17) c. il. Q. **$12.50 net, boxed. Century Co.

Kunz, Martin.
Physiology of the blind (the vicariate of the senses). '08, [1910.] (F) 31 p. 8°, (Volta Bureau; reprints of useful knowledge.) 50 c. Volta.

Kurnel, The, pseud.
See Cole, Rob. Jermain.

Kuropatkin, General Alexei Nicolaevitch.
Russian army and the Japanese war; tr. by Capt. A. B. Lindsay; ed. by Major E. D. Swinton. '09(My15) 2 v., il. maps, pors. O. *$7.50 net. boxed. Dutton.

Kurtz, B: Putnam.
Studies in the marvellous. '10(Ap9) Q. (Univ. of Cal. pubs.; Modern philology.) pap., $2. Univ. of Cal.

Kurzgefasste vergleichende grammatik der semitischen sprachen. Brockelmann, C. $3. Lemcke.

KÜSTENLANDE.
See Austria-Hungary.

Kutter, Hermann.
They must; or, God and the social democracy: a frank word to Christian men and women. '09(Ag21) c. D. $1. Co-operative Pr. Co.

Kybalion (The): a study of the hermetic philosophy of ancient Egypt and Greece, by three initiates. '08(Ag8) c. 12°, $1.08. Yogi Pub.

Kyle, D: Braden, M.D.
Diseases of the nose and throat. 4th ed., rev. '08(Ja4) il. 8°, *$4 net; hf. mor., *$5.50 net. Saunders.

Kynnersley, E. M. Sneyd-.
See Sneyd-Kynnersley, E. M.

La vida es sveño. **Calderon de la Barca, P.** Univ. of Toronto.

Labanca, Baldassare.
See Jordan, L: H:

La Bédollière, Emile Gigault de.
Histoire de la Mère Michel et de son chat; adapt. and ed. by Eugène Pellissier. '08 (Ap18) 16°, (Siepmann's primary French ser.) *35 c. net. Macmillan.

LABELS.
See Food adulteration.

Labor and housing at Port Sunlight. George, W. L. *$1.40 net Scribner.

LABOR AND LABORING CLASSES.
American Academy of Political and Social Science. Labor and wages.—Settlement of labor disputes. ea., $1. Am. Acad. Pol. Sci.
American Association for Labor Legislation. Review of labor legislation of 1909. gratis. Parsons Pr.
Beveridge, W: H: Unemployment. *$2.40 net. Longmans.
Chapin, R. C. Standard of living among workingmen's families in New York City. $2. Charities Pub.
Chapman, S. J: Work and wages. pt. 2. $4. Longmans.
Collins, J. H. Art of handling men. 50 c. Altemus.
Commons, J. R., *and others, eds.* Documentary hist. of American industrial society. In 10 v. *$50 net. A. H. Clarke.
Crosby, E. H. Labor and neighbor: appeal to first principles. 25 c. L: F. Post.
Debs, E. V. Debs: his life, writings and speeches. $2. Appeal.
Donaldson, O. M. Common honesty; study of fundamental principles and their relation to the labor problem. 50 c. Van-American.
Edwards, R: H:, *ed.* Labor problem. 10 c. R: H: Edwards.
French, C: S. Worship of the golden calf: a story of wage-slavery in Mass. $1. C: S. French.

LABOR AND LABORING CLASSES.—*Continued.*
Gantt, H: L. Work, wages and profits. $2. Engineering Mag.
Gompers, S: Labor in Europe and America. $2 net. Harper.
Griffin, A. P. C., *comp.* Library of Congress list of books rel. to the eight-hour working day. 15 c. U. S., Supt. of Docs.
Harris, W. S. Hell before death. $1. Minter.
Hitchens, E. L. Bible and labor. 25 c. Baker & B.
Jones, J., *and* Hodgson, S. M. Tramp machinist. (Add. author for price.) Ja. Jones.
Judson, F: N. Labor decisions of Judge Taft. (Add. author for price.) F: N. Judson.
Knaus, H: Judicial usurpation: open letter to Congress showing this in the injunctions in labor disputes. (Add. author for price.) H: Knaus.
Labor question; U. S. public documents rel. directly or indirectly to the wage-workers and their welfare. '09(My) 31 p. 8°, pap., gratis. U. S., Supt. of Docs.
Langdon, *Mrs.* E. F. Labor's greatest conflicts. [Moyer, Haywood and Pettibone case.] 50 c. E. F. Langdon.
Lloyd, H: D. Men, the workers. **$1.50 net. Doubleday, P.
McCallen, R. S. Master and slave. $1.50. Nat. Bk.
McNeill, G: E. Eight hour primer. (Add. author for price.) G: E. McNeill.
Overlock, M. G: Working people; their health and how to protect it. $2. M. G: Overlock.
Oxford and working-class education: being the rept. of a joint committee of university and working-class representatives on the relation of the university to the higher education of work people. 35 c. Oxford Univ.
Putnam, B. H. Enforcement of the statutes of labourers during the first decade after the Black Death, 1347-1359. $4. Longmans.
Rea, R. Imports and employment. 10 c. Cassell.
Schaffner, M. A. Labor contract from individual to collective bargaining. 50 c. Univ. of Wis.
Schlesinger, A. Labor amendment our next great job. $1.50. N. Y. Medical.
Stelzle, C: Church and labor. **50 c. net. Houghton M.
Stelzle, C: Letters from a workingman. *$1 net. Revell.
Thompson, C. B. Churches and the wage earners. **$1 net. Scribner.
True, E. I. Labor problem; bibliography. 25 c. Wis. Free Lib.
United States. *Dept. of Commerce and Labor. Bureau of Labor.* Labor laws of the United States. (Add. Superintendent for price.) U. S., Supt. of Docs.

LABOR AND LABORING CLASSES.—*Continued.*
United States. *Dept. of Commerce and Labor. Bu. of Manufactures.* Industrial conditions in Europe; by H: Studniczka, special agent. '10(Ag) 8°.
See also Accidents;—Capital and labor;—Children;—Church;—Communism; — Co-operation;—Employment agencies; — Factories; — Girls; — Guilds; — Immigration; —Injunctions;—Insurance;—Labor colonies;—Negligence;—Negroes; — Pathology; — Political economy; — Poor; — Railroads;—Servants; — Slavery; — Social science;—Socialism; — Strikes;—Trade unions;—Wages; — Woman; — Yellow peril;—*also* New York City;—*also* names of states.

Labor and neighbor. Crosby, E. H. 25 c. L: F. Post.

Labor and the railroads. Fagan, J. O. *$1 net. Houghton M.

LABOR COLONIES.
Kelly, E. Elimination of the tramp: by the introd. into America of the labor colony system. **$1 net. Putnam.

Labor history of the Cripple Creek district. Rastall, B. M. 50 c. Univ. of Wis.

Labor or the money god! which? Pidgin, C: F. $1.50. Mayhew.

LABOR UNIONS.
See Trade-unions.

Laboratory arts. Woollatt, G: H: *$1 net. Longmans.

Laboratory botany. Clute, W. N. 75 c. Ginn.

Laboratory directions in general biology: (zoological half,) first semester. '08(Je13) c. il. O. pap., 50 c. Wahr.

Laboratory directions in general zoology. Sigerfoos, C: P: 65 c. H. W. Wilson Co.

Laboratory exercises in art appreciation. De Garmo, C: 40 c. Bardeen.

Laboulaye, Edouard René Lefebvré de.
Fairy tales. 09(O2) il. 8°, $2.50. Dutton.
Le château de la vie; ed. by R. T. Currall. '10(Ja29) S. (Crowell's shorter French texts.) *25 c. net. Crowell.

LABRADOR.
Browne, P. W: Where the fishers go: the story of Labrador. $1.75. Cochrane.
Durgin, G: F. Letters from Labrador. gratis. Rumford Pr.
Grenfell, W. T. Adrift on an ice-pan. **75 c. net. Hougton M.
Grenfell, W. T. Down to the sea. $1 net. Revell.
Grenfell, W. T., *and others.* Labrador. **$2.25 net. Macmillan.
Hubbard, L. B. Woman's way through Labrador. **$1.50 net. McClure.
Townsend, C: W. Labrador spring. $1.50. Estes.
See also Navigation.

Lac (Le) de Gers. Töpffer, R. *40 c. net. Macmillan.

LACE.
Carità. Lacis; instructions in filet brodé or darning on net. *$3.50 net. Lippincott. Lippincott.
Cartier-Bresson, *Mme.* How to make baby Irish crochet.—How to make Irish crochet lace. ea., 25 c. Mills & G.
Designs and instructions for Irish crochet lace. '10(F) c. 32 p. il. 4°, 25 c.. Buettner.

LACE.—*Continued.*
Harvey, L. M. Priscilla Irish crochetbook. 25 c. Priscilla.
Jourdain, M. Old lace. $4.50. Scribner.
Lowes, *Mrs.* E. L. Chats on old lace and needlework. $2. Stokes.
Moody, A. P., *and* Tompkins, A. E. Devon pillow lace. *$1.50 net. Cassell.
Old lace manual. $1. A. M. Kohlsaat.
Pollen, M. M. Seven centuries of lace. *$9 net. Macmillan.
United States. *Dept. of Commerce and Labor.* Lace industry in England and France; by W. A. Graham Clark. '09 (My) 59 p. il. 8°, pap. (Add. Superintendent for price.) U. S., Supt. of Docs.
See also Needlework.

Lacey, Rev. T. A.
Roman diary and other documents rel. to the papal inquiry into English ordinations, 1896. '10(D17) O. $3.50 net. Longmans.
—, ed. Bishop's letters. '09(Ap10) 8°, pap., *50 c. net. Young Churchman.

Lacey, Rev. T: Ja.
Beginning at Jerusalem; studies in historic communions of Christendom. '10(Ja1) c. S. 60 c. Gorham.
Gospel of optimism, and other sermons. '08 (D) c. 88 p. 12°, $1. Red Diamond.

Lachaussee, C: Alfr.
Custom house and internal revenue services; how to enter them. '08(O) c. 57 p. 16°, 25 c. Chief.
How to become a letter carrier or post office clerk; explanation of civil service requirements, rules for the 13 U. S. civil service districts, postal regulations governing the service, etc.; written for the *Chief*, journal of the civil service. '08 (Mr7) c. 16°, pap., 25 c. Chief.
How to enter the postal service. 4th ed. '09(O2) c. S. 50 c. Chief.

Lacis. Carità. **$3.50 net. Lippincott.

Laconics. Gordon, H. L. $1.50. Salem Press.

La Croix, Arda.
Lucky Jim: story of love and adventure founded upon Jos. Santley's new play by W: G. Beckwith and Jos. Santley; novelized by Arda La Croix. '08, [1909.] (Mr) 128 p. il. 12°, (Play book ser.) pap., 25 c. J. S. Ogilvie.
Yankee Doodle detective. '09(S4) il. 12°, pap., 25 c. J. S. Ogilvie.

Lacroix, J. V.
See Campbell, Delwin Morton.

LACROSSE.
United States Inter-Collegiate Lacrosse League. Constitution, by-laws and playing rules, 1908-1910. ea., 10 c. Am. Sports.

LACTARIA.
See Mushrooms.

LACTIC ACID.
See Milk.

Lacy, Ernest.
Bard of Mary Redcliffe. Il. autograph ed. '10(Je) 21+205 p. il. 12°, $5. Sherman.

Lad of London. Haw, G: $1.25. Cassell.

Ladd, Edn. Fremont.
See Holley, Clifford Dyer.

Ladd, Frederic Pierpont.
Lady of Shenipsit; novel of New England. '10(S10) c. il. D. $1.25 net. Sturgis & W.
One fair daughter. '09(Mr13) c. il. 8°, $1.50. M. Kennerley.
Woman pays; il. by Gordon Grant. '08 (Je) c. 278 p. 8°, cl., $1.50. M. Kennerley.

Ladd, G: Trumbull.
In Korea with Marquis Ito. pt. 1, A narrative of personal experiences; pt. 2, A critical and historical inquiry. '08(Mr7) c. il. por. O. **$2.50 net. Scribner.
Knowledge, life and reality; essay in systematic philosophy. '10(Ja1) c. 8°; $3.50. Dodd.
Rare days in Japan. '10(O15) c. il. O. $2.25 net. Dodd.

Ladd, Horatio Oliver.
Trend of scientific thought away from religious beliefs. '09(D4) c. D. bds., 75 c. Badger.

Ladder of moonlight. Harrison, E. O. *50 c. net. McClurg.
Ladies fair and frail. Bleackley, H. W: *$5 net. Lane.
Ladies' field golf book. Braid, J. *40 c. net. Scribner.
Ladies' pageant. Lucas, E: V., *ed.* **$1.25 net. Macmillan.

LADRONE ISLANDS.
See Guam.

Lady, The. Putnam, *Mrs.* E. J. S. $2.50 net. Sturgis & W.
Lady Athlyne. Stoker, B. $1.50. Lovell.

LADY-BEETLES.
Johnson, R. H. Determinate evolution in the color-pattern of the lady-beetles. $1. Carnegie.

Lady Dean's daughter. Noot, J. $1.50. Cochrane.
Lady from the sea. *See* Ibsen, Henrik. Doll's house.
Lady Geraldine's courtship. *See* Browning, *Mrs.* Eliz. Barrett.
Lady Good-for-Nothing. Couch, *Sir* A. T: Q. $1.20 net. Scribner.
Lady in gray. Laughlin, C. E. *50 c. net. Revell.
Lady in the car. Le Queux, W: †$1.50. Lippincott.
Lady in the white veil. O'Neill, R. C. †$1.50. Harper.
Lady Julia's emerald. Colville, H. H. †$1.50. Lane.
Lady Méchante. Burgess, F. G. **$1.50 net. Stokes.
Lady Merton, colonist. Ward, *Mrs.* M. A. A. $1.50. Doubleday, P.
Lady nurse of Ward E. Stearns, A. A. **$1.20 net. Baker & T.
Lady of Big Shanty. Smith, F. B. †$1.20. Doubleday, P.
Lady of France. Conly, *Mrs.* E. H. S. $1.50. Homewood.
Lady of Shenipsit. Ladd, F. P. $1.25 net. Sturgis & W.
Lady of the Blackfriars. Ross, C. $2 net; $5. C. Ross.
Lady of the Dynamos. Shaw, A. M. †$1.50. Holt.
Lady of the green scarf. Sharpe-Patterson, *Mrs.* V. 35 c. Flanagan.
Lady of the heavens. Haggard, H: R. $1.50. Lovell.
Lady of the Lake. *See* Scott, *Sir* Wa.
Lady of the lotus. Jones, P. (Add. pubs. for price.) Runyon & H.
Lady of the Mount. Isham, F. S. †$1.50. Bobbs-M.
Lady of the old régime. Henderson, E. F. **$2.50 net. Macmillan.
Lady of the spur. Potter, D: $1.50. Lippincott.
Lady of the tower. Barton, G: $1.25. Benziger.
Lady with the rubies. John, E. 50 c. Hurst.
Lady without jewels. Goodrich, A. F: †$1.50. Appleton.
Laelia. Smith, G. C. M., *ed.* $1.10 net. Putnam.
Laelivs de amicitia. *See* Cicero, M. T.

Lafar, Francz.
Technical mycology. v. 2, Eumycetic fermentation. pt. 2. '10(D) 748 p. 8°, $4 net. Lippincott.

La Farge, J:
Higher life in art: lectures on the Barbizon School of France, inaugurating the Scammon course at the Art Institute of Chicago. '08(D26) c. il. O. **$2.50 net. Doubleday, P.

Lafargue, Paul.
Evolution of property from savagery to civilization. '10(My21) S. (Standard socialist ser.) 50 c. Kerr.

LA FAYETTE MARIE MADELEINE PIOCHE DE LA VERGNE, COMTESSE DE.
Rea, L. Life and times of Marie Madeleine, Countess of La Fayette. '09(Je) il. 8°, *$3.50 net. Brentano's.

Lafayette-Savay, Norbert.
See Savay, Norbert Lafayette-.

Laflin, Ellen P.
Poems. '09(Ap) c. 33 p. il. 8°. (Not for sale.) Grafton Press.

La Fontaine, Jean de.
Fables; told in easy French by Kathleen Fitzgerald. '10(D) il. sq. 16°, (Children's favorites.) 50 c. net. Jacobs.
Fables; with a preface by Jules Claretie. In 2 v. '10(Je4) por. 16°, $2. Putnam.

Laforet, N: Jos.
Causes and cure of unbelief; ed. by Cardinal Gibbons, with chapter by the Rev. Dr. P. J. Ryan. '10(Ap16) c. 16°, 60 c.; pap., 30 c. Kilner.

Lagden, Sir Godfrey Yeatman.
The Basutos: mountaineers and their country; narrative of events rel. to the tribe from its formation early in the nineteenth century to the present day. In 2 v. '10(O29) il. maps, O. $6 special net. Appleton.

Lagerlöf, Selma Ottiliana Lovisa.
Girl from the Marsh Croft; tr. from the Swedish by Velma Swanston Howard. '10(My14) c. D. $1.50. Little, B. & Co.
Invisible links; tr. from the Swedish by Pauline Bancroft Flach. New ed. '09 (Je19) 12°, †$1.50. Little, B. & Co.
Miracles of anti-Christ; tr. from the Swedish by Pauline Bancroft Flach. New ed. '09(Je19) 12°, †$1.50. Little, B. & Co.
Story of Gósta Berling. New il. ed. '10 (D10) 8°, $2 net. Little, B. & Co.
—, **comp.** Christ legends; tr. from the Swedish by Velma Swanston Howard. '08(N21) c. il. D. **$1.25 net, boxed. Holt.

Laggards in our schools. Ayres, L. P. $1.50. Charities Pub.

Lagrange, Jos. Louis.
Lectures on elementary mathematics; tr. from the French by T: J. McCormack. 2d ed. '09(Mr) 172 p. *$1 net. Open Court.

LA GRANGE MILITARY ACADEMY, La Grange, Ala.
Wyeth, J: A. Hist. of La Grange Military Academy and cadet corps. $2. M. S. Wyeth.

Laguna, Grace Andrus de.
See Laguna, Thdr. de Leo.

Laguna, Thdr. de Leo and Grace Andrus de.
Dogmatism and evolution; studies in modern philosophy. '10(N12) O. $1.75 net. Macmillan.

Lailavoix, L.
La farce de Paquin fils. '10(Ja29) S. (Crowell's shorter French texts.) *25 c. net. Crowell.

Laing, Gordon Jennings.
See Smith, Minnie Louise.

Laing, Mary E.
Reading: manual for teachers; rev. and enl. '08, [1909.] (Ja) 8+216 p. 12°, (Heath's pedagogical lib.) $1. Heath.

Lair, Jules.
Louise de La Vallière and the early life of Louis XIV. from unpublished documents; tr. from the 4th French ed. by Ethel Coburn Mayne. '08(S5) il. pors. O. (Memoir ser.) *$3.50 net. Putnam.

Laird, Jos. Packard.
Story of the violets and the rose, and other poems. '09, [1910.] (N) c. 4+49 p. 24°. Knickerbocker Press.

Laird & Lee's diary and time-saver; incl. territorial acquisitions and the Panama Canal. 10th annual ed., 1909. '08(S5); 11th annual ed., 1910. '09(O9); 12th annual ed., 1911. '10(D10) c. maps, nar. T. leath., ea., 25 c. Laird.

Laird & Lee's standard vest pocket English-Italian, Italian-English dictionary. Padovani, P. 50 c.; 75 c. Laird.

Laird & Lee's Webster's dict. *See* Webster, Noah.

Lake, C: S.
Locomotives of 1907: supp. to his large work of "World's locomotives." '08(Jl4) il. obl. 8°, bds., 50 c. Spon.

Lake, Edm. Fs.
Composition and heat treatment of steel. '10(N12) c. il. 8°, $2.50. McGraw-H.

Lake, Fred Perrine.
Uncle Sim. '09(D) c. 457 p. il. 12°, $1.50. C. M. Clark.

Lake, Rev. Kirsopp.
Early days of monasticism on Mount Athos. '10(Ja22) maps, O. $2.90. Oxford Univ.

Lake, Philip, and Rastall, R. H.
Text-book of geology. '10(D3) O. (Arnold's geological ser.) $4.50 net. Longmans.

Lake, R:
Hdbk. of diseases of the ear for students and practitioners. 3d ed. '10(Mr) il. col. pls. 8°, *$2.75 net. Wood.

LAKE AMATITLAN.
See Guatemala.

Lake and rail transportation. Barry, C: E. 25 c. La Salle Extension.

LAKE ATITLAN.
See Guatemala.

LAKE CHAMPLAIN, N. Y.
Crockett, W. H. History of Lake Champlain. 75 c. Shanley.
Favreau, J. A. La grande semaine; [tercentenary celebration.] $1.25. Belisle Pr.
New York State. *Education Dept.* Lake Champlain tercentenary; dates and places of formal exercises, [July 4-10, 1909.] '09 (S) 32 p. il. map, 4°. (Add. pubs for price.) N. Y. State Educ.
Reid, W: M. Lake George and Lake Champlain. $3.50 net. Putnam.
Royce, *Mrs.* C. H. B. First century of Lake Champlain. 25 c. C. H. B. Royce.
Scollard, C. Song for the tercentenary of Lake Champlain. 50 c. G: W: Browning.

Lake Champlain tercentenary, [July 4-10, 1909.] '09(Jl17) il. map, Q. pap. (Add. pubs. for price.) N. Y. State Educ.

Lake classical ser. D. Scott, F. & Co.
—Cicero *and* Sallustus. Selected orations and The Catiline. $1.
—Livy. Selections from the first decade. 60 c.

Lake English classics; ed. by Lindsay Todd Damon. 16°. Scott, F. & Co.
—Browning. Selections. 40 c.
—Chaucer. Selections. 40 c.
—De Quincy. Selections. 25 c.
—Dickens. David Copperfield. 50 c.
—Franklin. Autobiography. 30 c.
—Gaskell. Cranford. 35 c.
—Longfellow. Narrative poems. 40 c.
—Macaulay. Essays on Clive and Hastings. 35 c.
—Poe, Longfellow *and* Whittier. Three American poems: The raven; Courtship of Miles Standish; Snowbound. 25 c.
—Scott. Quentin Durward. 45 c.
—Shakespeare. Henry the Fifth.—Midsummer night's dream. ea., 25 c.
—Stevenson. Inland voyage and travels with a donkey. 35 c.
—Washington, Webster *and* Lincoln. Washington, Webster and Lincoln: selections for the college entrance English requirements. 25 c.

LAKE GENEVA, Switzerland.
Gribble, F. H: Lake of Geneva. *$6 net. Macmillan.

LAKE GEORGE, N. Y.
Reid, W: M. Lake George and Lake Champlain. $3.50 net. Putnam.

Lake German classics. 12°. Scott, F. & Co.
—Becker *and* Rhoades. Elements of German. $1.
—Lessing. Minna von Barnhelm. 50 c.
—Storm. Gerstacker. Seidel, Immensee. Germelshausen, Der lindenbaum. 40 c.

Lake history stories. il. 4°. Scott, F. & Co.
—Harding. Story of England. 60 c.

LAKE LOUISE, Canada.
See Rocky mountains.

LAKE ONTARIO.
See Sculpin.

Lake ship yard methods of steel ship construction. Curr, R. $2. Penton.

Lake steam-manship and guide to the marine board examinations. Long, C. E. $2. C. E. Long.

LAKE VICTORIA.
See Africa.

Lakeport ser. *See* Stratemeyer, E:

Lakerim cruise. Hughes, R. $1.50. Century Co.

LAKES.
See Inland navigation.

Lakeside classics. il. 12°, *50 c. net. Ainsworth.
—Dante. Divine comedy.

Lakeside ser. of English readings. 12°, pap. Ainsworth.
—Scott. Lady of the lake. 20 c.

LAKEVILLE, Mass.
See Plymouth County, Mass.

LALA-LAMBA LANGUAGE.
See Rhodesia, South Africa.

Lamar, Ashton.
Aeroplane express; or, the boy aeronaut's grit. '10(D10) c. il. D. (Aeroplane boys ser.) 60 c. Reilly & B.
Boy aeronaut's club; or, flying for fun. '10 (D17) c. il. D. (Aeroplane boys ser.) 60 c. Reilly & B.
In the clouds for Uncle Sam; or, Morey Marshall of the signal corps. '10(Ap9) c. il. 12°, (Aeroplane boys ser.) 60 c. Reilly & B.
Stolen aeroplane; or, how Bud Wilson made good. '10(Ap9) il. 12°, (Aeroplane boys ser.) 60 c. Reilly & B.

Lamartine, Alphonse Marie Louis.
Jocelyn: ed. by Émile Legouis. '09(Mr6) por. S. (Oxford higher French ser.) $1. Oxford Univ.
Le tailleur de pierres de Saint-Point; ed. by W. Robertson. '10(Ag20) c. (Oxford modern French ser.; ed. by Leon Delbos.) 60 c. Oxford Univ.

Lamb, C:
Works. 5 v. New imperial lib. ed. '10 (D) il. 8°, ea., $1.25; hf. cf., $2.25; New il. sterling ed., ea., $1. (Sets only.) Estes.
Works. Elia ed.; with memoir by Alfr. Ainger. In 12 v. '08(Je27) c. il. bds., $30; hf. mor. or cf., $60. Lamb Pub.
Essays of Elia. '08(N21) 16°, (Best books ser.) leath., *$1 net. Dutton.

Lamb, C:—*Continued.*
Essays of Elia selected and ed. by Harry Evan Coblentz. '09(Ap3) c. il. por. 16°, (English classics.) *40 c. net. Heath.
Essays of Elia; Last essays of Elia. '08 (Je27) c. 2 v., 8°, $4. Lamb Pub.
Essay of Elia.—Last essays of Elia. '09, [1910.] (F) 12°, ea., *40 c. net. Little, B. & Co.
Essays of Elia; ed., with introd. and notes, by J. H. Castleman. '08(Ap4) c. por. 16°, (Merrill's English texts.) 50 c. C: E. Merrill.
Letters. 2 v. '09(Ap3) 16°, (Everyman's lib.) ea., *35 c. net; leath., *70 c. net. Dutton.
Select essays of Elia; ed. by J: F. Genung. '10(Ja1) c. por. S. (Gateway ser.) 40 c. Am. Bk.
Wisdom of Charles Lamb; selected with an introd. by Temple Scott. '09(Jl31) c. 16°, (Wisdom ser.) limp leath., **$1 net. Brentano's.

— and Mary.
Works in prose and verse. Oxford ed. In 2 v. '09(Ag14) pors. D. ea., 75 c. Oxford Univ.
Tales from Shakespeare; il. by G: Soper. '10(Je11) O. $1.50. Baker & T.
Tales from Shakespeare. '08(O10) il. D. (Bowman's illustrated lib. of world-favorite books.) $1. Bowman.
Tales from Shakespeare. '08(O10) 12°, (Best books ser.) leath., *$1 net. Dutton.
Tales from Shakespeare. '10(Ap2) il. 16°, (Everyman's lib.) 35 c. net; leath., 70 c. net. Dutton.
Tales from Shakespeare; il. by Arth. Rackham. '09(D18) il. 8°, *$2.50 net; Limited large paper ed., *$7.50 net. Dutton.
Tales from Shakespeare. '08(Je27) c. 2 v., il. 8°, $4. Lamb Pub.
Tales from Shakespeare. 2 v. in 1. '08 (D5) il. por. D. (Thin paper ser. of popular classics.) limp leath., $1.25, boxed. Lippincott.
Tales from Shakespeare; introd. preface by And. Lang. '08(N7) il. D. $1.50. Lippincott.

Lamb, C: F., rep.
See Wisconsin. *Sup. ct.* Repts.

Lamb, Edn. Gifford.
Social work of the Salvation Army. '09, [1910.] (Ap) c. 143 p. 8°, $1. E. G. Lamb.
Bibliography (4 p.).

Lamb, Fs. Jones.
Miracle and science: Bible miracles examined by the methods, rules and tests of the science of jurisprudence. '09(Jl17) c. D. *$1.50 net. Bibliotheca Sacra.

Lamb, H: Grant.
Farm book-keeping. '08(N) 8+69 p. 12°, $1. H: G. Lamb.

Lamb, Horace.
Dynamical theory of sound. '10(Mr12) figs. O. *$3.50 net. Longmans.

Lamb, Mary.
See Lamb. C:

Lamb, Mrs. Mary Eliz. Jordan.
Irene Liscomb. '09(Ja2) 12°, $1.50. B'way Pub.

Lamb, W:
How and what to dance. '10(O) 12°, 50 c. Fenno.

Lamb, W:, M.D.
Practical guide to the diseases of the nose, throat and ear. 2d rev. and enl. ed. '09 (F6) il. 12°, *$3 net. Wood.

LAMBALLE, Marie Thérèse Louise de Savoie-Carignan, *Princesse* de.
Hardy, B. C. Princesse de Lamballe. *$3.50 net. Appleton.

Lambert, J: C., D.D.
Missionary heroes in Africa. '10(Ja1) 8°, *75 c. net. Lippincott.
Missionary heroes in Asia. '08(N7) il. D. *75 c. net. Lippincott.
Missionary heroes in Oceanica. '10(D31) il. 8°, 75 c. Lippincott.

—, Greenough, J. G., Selby, T: G., and others.
Great texts of the Old Testament. '09 (N20) D. *$1 net. Eaton & M.

Lambert, Rev. L: Aloisius.
Christian science before the bar of reason; ed. by Rev. Aloysius Stanislaus Quinlan. '08(Je6) c. 12°, *$1 net. Chr. Press.

Lambert, Marcus Bachman.
Alltägliches: ein konversations-und lesebuch. '08(Ap11) c. D. (Modern lang. ser.) 75 c. Heath.
Hdbk. of German idioms. '10(D3) c. D. 40 c. Holt.

Lambert, W: Harrison.
Abraham Lincoln, 1809-1909; Lincoln literature; address before the Commandery of the state of Pa., Military Order of the Loyal Legion memorial meeting, Feb. 3, 1909. '09(Je) 16 p. 12°. (Not for sale.) W: H. Lambert.
1809-1909. Abraham Lincoln; address del. before the Union League of Philadelphia, Feb. 12, 1909. [1910.] (F) 24 p. por. 8°. (Not for sale.) W: H. Lambert.
Gettysbury address; when written, how received, its true form. '09, [1910.] (F) 27 p. facsims., 8°. (Priv. pr.) W: H. Lambert.

"Lambkin-Sphinx," pseud.
See Crittenton, Celia Louise.

Lamborn, E. A. Greening.
Perspective history chart. '09(N20) $2.90. Oxford Univ.
School history of Berkshire; with an introd. by C. R. L. Fletcher. '08(O24) il. D. 50 c. Oxford Univ.
Stories from the history of Berkshire. '08 (N21) il. D. bds., 25 c. Oxford Univ.

Lambourne, Alfr.
Our inland sea; the story of a homestead: [Great Salt Lake.] '09(My) c. 256 p. il. 8°, $2.50. A. Lambourne.

Lambuth, Wa. Russell.
Side lights on the Orient. '09(Mr6) c. il. D. *75 c. net. Pub. Ho. of M. E. Ch., So.

La Monte, Rob. Rives, and Mencken, H: L:
Men *versus* the man; correspondence between Robert Rives La Monte, socialist, and H. L. Mencken, individualist. '10 (Mr26) c. D. **$1.35 net. Holt.

Lamoreaux, Mrs. Antoinette Abernethy.
Unfolding life: study of development with reference to religious training; with introd. by Marion Lawrance. '08(Ap18) c. D. 75 c. Rel. Pub.
See also Schauffler, Adolphus F:

La Motte Fouqué, Friedrich Heinrich Karl, Freiherr de.
Sintram and his companions; tr. by A. C. Farquharson. '10(Ja1) 8°, *$2.50 net. Lippincott.
Sintram and his companions and Undine; with an introd. by Charlotte M. Yonge. '09(O2) il. O. $1.50. Stokes.
Undine; adapted from the German by W. L. Courtney and il. [in color] by Arthur Rackham. '09(D4) O. **$2 net. Doubleday, P.
Undine; tr. from the German by G: P. Upton. '08(O3) c. il. S. (Life stories for young people.) *60 c. net. McClurg.

Lampe, W. E.
Japanese social organization. '10(Jl16) c. 12°, 75 c.; pap., 50 c. Princeton Univ.

Lampson, Sophy Felicité De Rodes Locker-, [Mrs. Godfrey L. T. Locker-Lampson.]
Quaker post-bag; letters to Sir John Rodes of Barlbrough Hall, in the county of Derby, Baronet, and to John Gratton of Monyash, 1693-1742; with preface by Augustine Birrell. '10(O15) pors. facsims., O. $2.50 net. Longmans.

Lampton, W: Ja.
Jedge Waxem's pocket-book of politics; owned by Jedge Wabash Q. Waxem, member of Congress from Wayback. '08 (Ap11) c. nar. S. pocket-book style, leath., 50 c. G: W. Dillingham.
Trolley car and the lady: trolley trip from Manhattan to Maine. '08(Ag22) c. il. 16°, pap., 25 c. Badger.

Lampy's early days. Wheelwright, E. M. $5. Harvard Lampoon.

Lamson, Zachary Gage.
Autobiography; with introd. and historical notes by O. T. Howe. '09(Ja9) c. front. facsim., 8°, *$1.25 net. W: B. Clarke.

Lamy, George.
Voyage du novice Jean-Paul a travers la France d'Amerique; ed. by D. Devaux. '10(D24) c. 16°, (Macmillan's new ser. of French texts.) 35 c. net. Macmillan.

Lancaster, F. Hewes.
Marie of Arcady. '09(S25) c. front. D. †$1.25. Small.

Lancaster, G. B.
Altar stairs. '08(O17) D. †$1.50. Doubleday, P.

Lancaster, W: Jos. Cosens, ["Harry Collingwood."]
Blue and gray. '08(D5) il. $1.25. Cassell.

LANCASTER, Pa.
See **Farmers' Trust Company.**

LANCASTER COUNTY, Pa.
See **Indians.**

Lancasterian schools in Philadelphia. Ellis, C: C. (Not for sale.) Univ. of Penn.

Lanchester, F. W.
Aerial flight. v. 1, Aerodynamics; v. 2, Aerodonetics. '09, (My) 2 v., 442; 448 p. il. 8°, *$6 net. Van Nostrand.

Lanciani, Rodolfo Amedo.
Roman forum; photographic description of its monuments. '10(My14) Q. $1.50 net. Stechert.
Wanderings in the Roman Campagna. '09 (D4) c. il. maps, O. *$5 net, boxed. Houghton M.

LAND.
Acts of Congress rel. to the public lands passed by the 60th Congress, 2d session; with notes, indexing, etc.; comp. by S: Herrick. '09(Jl) c. 22 p. 8°, pap. (Add. Superintendent for price.) U. S., Supt. of Docs.
Bledsoe, S. T. Indian land laws. $6. Pipes-R.
Collings, J. Land reform, occupying, ownership, peasant proprietary, and rural education. $1. Longmans.
Donaldson, O. M. Common honesty; study of fundamental principles and their relation to the labor problem. 50 c. Van-American.
Dove, P. E: Theory of human progression. 25 c. Blanchard.
Gray, E: D. M. Government reclamation work in foreign countries. (Add. Superintendent for price.) U. S., Supt. of Docs.
Harvey, E. J. Land law and registration of title. $2.60 net. Longmans.
Herrick, S: Manual of the United States Homestead and other public land laws. 50 c. A. Harriman.
Johnson, A. H. Disappearance of the small landowner. $1.75. Oxford Univ.
Kagey, C: C. Land survey and land titles. $1.12. C: C. Kagey.
Martin, T. Mining law and land office procedure. (Add. pubs. for price.) Bender-M.
Mieir, W: O. Possible method of reclamation for the arid West. 25 c. W: O. Mieir.
Pegram, H: Land title registration. (Not for sale.) H: Pegram.
Puter, S. A. D., *and* Stevens, H. Looters of the public domain. $3. Portland.
Rawie, H: Wages and the price of land. 25 c. H: Rawie.
Reclamation of alluvial lands in southern Louisiana. gratis. La. Meadow.
Reform of the land laws; conservation of national resources; extracts from recommendations of the President, the Secretary of the Interior, and the Commissioner of the General Land Office, etc. '10(Mr) 80 p. 8°, pap.
Rood, J: R., *comp.* Decisions, statutes, etc., concerning the law of estates in land. $4. Callaghan.
Rountree, B. S. Land and labor; lessons from Belgium. $3.50 net. Macmillan.
Sampson, F. W: Natural revegetation of depleted mountain grazing lands. (Add. Superintendent for price.) U. S., Supt. of Docs.
Soul of the world: [fiction; advocating balanced land tenure.] $1. Equitist.

LAND.—*Continued.*
Thompson, H. Cost of clearing logged-off land for farming in the Pacific northwest. U. S., Supt. of Docs.
Treat, P. J. National land system. $2 net. Treat.
United States. *Dept. of the Interior. General Land Office.* Regulations concerning the selection of desert lands by certain states and territories under the act of Congress approved Aug. 18, 1894. with amendments, and the making of final proof for desert lands segregated thereunder. '09(Je) 15 p. 8°, pap. (Add. Superintendent for price.)
United States. *Dept. of the Interior. General Land Office.* Suggestions to homesteaders and persons desiring to make homestead entries; approved Apr. 10, 1909. '09(Je) 40 p. 8°, pap. (Add. Superintendent for price.)
United States. *Dept. of the Interior.* Reclamation projects.
United States. *Dept. of the Interior.* Unappropriated public lands of the United States. (Add. Superintendent for price.)
United States. *General Land Office.* Suggestions to homesteaders and persons desiring to make homestead entries. 10 c.
United States. Instructions relative to publication of final-proof notices and concerning the discretionary authority of registers in the selection of newspapers for that purpose. '09(D) 12 p. 8°. (Add. Superintendent for price.)
United States. Statutes and regulations governing entries and proof under the desert land laws, together with suggestions to persons desiring to make entries under said laws; approved Nov. 30, 1908, (with amendment of August 21, 1909.) '09(D) 18 p. 8°. (Add. Superintendent for price.) U. S., Supt. of Docs.
United States. *Superintendent of Documents.* Lands; United States public documents rel. to lands, and more especially to the public lands of the national domain. [3d ed.] '10(Ag) 39 p. 8°, gratis.
United States vacant lands, located by states, territories, districts and countries. 25 c. Webb.
See also Agriculture;—Democracy;—Landlord and tenant;—Property;—Real property;—Surveying;—Taxation;—Titles (law);—*also* names of states.

Land and the Book. Thomson, W: M. $7.50; $12. Harper.
Land babies and sea babies at play. Shore, E. $1. Stokes.
Land cruising and prospecting. Wallace, A. F. 60 c. A. R. Harding.
Land (The); its Lord and sacred lore. Loomis, B. J. 75 c. Stoneman.
Land lover and his land. Williams, M. M. (Priv. pr.) E. W. Sells.

LAND NATIONALIZATION.
See Political economy.

Land of drought. Houston, E. J. $1.25. Griffith.

Land of enchantment. Whiting, L. **$1.50 net. Little, B. & Co.
Land of fortune. Steel, E. T: 75 c. E. T: Steel.
Land of frozen suns. Sinclair, B. W: $1.50. G: W. Dillingham.
Land of heart's desire. Yeats, W: B. *$1.50 net. T: B. Mosher.
Land of living men. Trine, R. W. $1.25. Crowell.
Land of long ago. Hall, E. C., *pseud.* †$1.50. Little, B. & Co.
Land of Lost. Green, A. A. †$1.25. Small.
Land of Never Was. Olmstead, M. $1. Jacobs.
Land of Nod and what Tinkie and Tess found there. McSpadden, J. W. †$1.50 Crowell.
Land of promise. De Bary, R: *$1.50 net. Longmans.
Land of pure delight. Gordon, G: A. *35 c. net. Pilgrim Press.
Land of purple shadows: Strobridge, I. M. $1.75; $6.75; $10. Artemesian.
Land of really true. Olmsted, M. $1. Jacobs.
Land of romance. Lang, J. $2.50 net. Dodge.
Land of the Blue Flower. Burnett, *Mrs.* F. H. **75 c. net. Moffat.
Land of the golden trade. Lang, J: $2 net. Stokes.
Land of the Hittites. Garstang, J: $4 net. Dutton.
Land of the lion. Rainsford, W: S. **$3.80 net. Doubleday, P.
Land of the living. Warren, M. R. †$1.50. Harper.
Land of the white helmet. Forbes, E. A. $1.50 net. Revell.
Land teaching. Stockbridge, H. E: $1. Southern Ruralist.

Landacre, Fs. Leroy.
Protozoa of Sandusky Bay and vicinity. '08 (Je.) 423-472 p. 8°, pap., 35 c. Ohio Acad. of Sci.

Bibliography.

Landau, Leo A.
Big cinch; society and financial novel. '10(Mr) c. 305 p. il. D. $1.50. Franklin.

Landelle, Guillaume Jos. Gabriel de la.
Une haine a bord; ed. by R. E. A. Chessex. '09(Mr6) S. (Oxford modern French ser.) 75 c. Oxford Univ.

Landels, T: Durley.
Visions: [poems.] '10(Ag6) c. D. $1 net. Sherman, F.

Lander, Mamie Jones, comp.
Friendship through the year: [selections for each day.] '09(Je26) c. D. $1; leath., $1.50. Dodge.

Landes, Sarah Windle.
Elem. domestic science; text-book for schools. pt. 1, Food and cookery. '10 (Mr12) c. O. pap., 54 c. S. W. Landes.

Landeskunde der Vereinigten Staaten. Fischer, H. 2 v. 40 c. Stechert.

Landis, Abb, and Eldridge, G: Dyre.
Tables based upon the National Fraternal Congress table of mortality and various rates of interest, also combined disability and mortality tables based on the American experience and National Fraternal Congress tables of mortality. '09(O) 40+222 p. 4°, $25. C. C. Hine.

Landis, D: Rogers.
Pastorate of Martin Wentz. '08(O24) c. D. *$1 net. Elmcroft.

Landis, F:
Angel of Lonesome Hill; story of a president. '10(My7) c. front. D. bds., 50 c. net. Scribner.
Glory of his country. '10(Mr12) c. D. †$1. Scribner.

LANDLORD AND TENANT.
McAdam, D: Rights, duties, remedies and incidents belonging and growing out of the relation of landlord and tenant. 3 v. $19.50. Baker, V. & Co.
Tiffany, H. T. Law of landlord and tenant. 2 v. $6.50. Keefe-D.
Underhill, H. C. Treatise on the law of landlord and tenant. 2 v. $12. Flood.
See also names of states.

Landlubbers. King, G. †$1.50. Doubleday, P.

Landmann, Julius.
Swiss banking law; study and criticism of the Swiss legislation respecting banks of issue. '10(My) 269 p. fold. tabs., 8°. Gov. Pr. Off.

Landmanns (Des) geflügel-buch. Sevenich, J. M. 40 c. Excelsior Pub.
Landmarks in Russian literature. Baring, M. $1.75 net. Macmillan.
Landmarks of botanical history. Greene, E: L. 65 c. Smith. Inst.
Landmarks of British history. Dale, L. 90 c. Longmans.

Landon, C: Woodworth.
First steps in harmony. '08(Mr) c. 93 p. 12°, 50 c. Church.

Landor, Arnold H: Savage.
Explorer's adventures in Tibet. '10(Ap30) c. il. O. $1.50. Harper.
In the forbidden land; account of a journey into Tibet. [Popular ed.] '09(N20) c. fold. map, O. $3. Harper.

Landor, Wa. Savage.
Imaginary conversations (selected). '10 (D) front. 32°, (Ariel booklets.) leath., 75 c. Putnam.

LAND'S END, Eng.
See Cornwall.

Lands of sacred story. Nichols, J. T: $1.25. Chr. Un.
Lands of summer. Sullivan, T: R. **$1.50 net. Houghton M.
Lands of the tamed Turk. Jaekel, F. B. $2.50. L. C. Page.

Landsberg, Grace F.
A B C of philosophy. '09(Jl3) c. D. 75 c. Fenno

LANDSCAPE ARCHITECTURE.
See Towns.

LANDSCAPE GARDENING.
Nolen, J: Repton's art of landscape gardening. $3 net. J: Nolen.
Parsons, S: Landscape gardening. $2 net. Lane.
Waugh, F. A. Landscape beautiful; study of the utility of the natural landscape. $2. Judd.

LANDSCAPE PAINTING.
Felter, L. S. Landscapes and waterscapes. *$1 net. Cannon City Record.
Harrison, B. Landscape painting. **$1.50 net. Scribner.
Hartmann, S. Landscape and figure composition. $3 net. Baker & T.

LANDSLIDES.
See San Juan Mts.

Landsman. Raff, L. E. 50 c. Rudder.

Lane, Alfr. Church.
Mine waters; (with chemical assistance especially of Dr. G. Fernekes.) '08, [1909.] (My) 90 p. il. 8°. (Not for sale.) A. J. Yungbluth.

Lane, Mrs. C. A.
See Lane, Martha Allen Luther.

Lane, Clarence Bronson.
Business of dairying: how to conduct dairy farming for the largest profit. '09(Mr27) c. il. tabs., 12°, *$1.25 net. Judd.
Medical milk commissions and the production of certified milk in the United States. '08(Ag1) il. 8°, (U. S. Dept. of Agriculture, Bureau of Animal Industry, bull.) pap., 15 c.

—, and Parks, Karl E.
Improved methods for the production of market milk by ordinary dairies. [1910.] (Je) 12 p. il. 8°, (U. S., Dept. of Agriculture, Bu. of Animal Industry.)

—, and Weld, Ivan C.
Competitive exhibitions of milk and cream; with rept. of exhibition held at Pittsburg, Pa., in co-operation with the Pittsburg Chamber of Commerce. '09(D) 36 p. tabs., 8°, (U. S., Dept. of Agriculture, Bu. of Animal Industry, circular.) pap. (Add. Superintendent for price.)

Lane, E: W:
Account of the manners and customs of the modern Egyptians; introd. by Ernest Rhys. '08(Mr7) il. 16°, (Everyman's lib.) *35 c.; leath., *70 c. net. Dutton.

Lane, Mrs. Elinor Macartney.
Apple-tree Cottage. '10(Ap16) c. il. D. 50 c. net. Harper.
Katrine. '09(Mr27) c. D. †$1.50. Harper.

Lane, Mrs. J:, [formerly Anna Fichberg King.]
According to Maria. '10(Ap2) c. il. D. $1.50. Lane.

Lane, J: Haden.
Birth of liberty: story of Bacon's Rebellion. '09(Ag7) c. 12°, *$1 net. Bell Bk.

Lane. J: Russell.
House between the trees. '09(Ap3) c. il. D. $1 50. C. M. Clark.

Lane, J: Veasey.
Marching with Morgan. '09(Je19) c. il. O. $1.50. L. C. Page.

Lane, Leasure Porter.
Tone, silence and time: comprehensive and logical treatment of the true meaning of characters that represent music. '08(Ja11) por. O. $1.75. L. P. Lane.

Lane, Mrs. Lydia Spencer.
I married a soldier; or, old days in the old army New ed. '10(D) 12°, $1 net. Lippincott.

Lane, Martha Allen Luther, ["Mrs. C. A. Lane."]
First book of religion. '09(N) c. 71+25 p. pls. 8°, (Beacon ser.) 35 c.; pap., 25 c.; Teachers' ed., 65 c. Unitarian S. S.

Lane, Mary Corwin.
Index to the fragments of the Greek Elegiac and Iambic poets as contained in the Hiller-Crusius edition of Bergk's Anthologia lyrica. '08(Jl18) O. (Cornell studies in classical philology.) bds., 80 c. Longmans.

Lane that had no turning. Parker, *Sir* G. $1.50. Harper.
Lane to Sleepy Town. Wilkinson, E. H. $1.25. E. H. Wilkinson.

Laneham, Rob.
Letter; describing a part of the entertainment unto Queen Elizabeth at the castle of Kenilworth in 1575; ed., with introd., by F. J. Furnivall. '08(Ja18) il. O. (Shakespeare lib.: Shakespeare's England.) *$1.75 net. Duffield.

Lane's handbooks of practical gardening ser.; ed. by Harry Roberts. il. D. *$1 net. Lane.
—Crane. Book of the pansy.—Book of the sweet pea.
—Curtis. Book of the flower show.
—Hemsley. Book of fern culture.
—Pearson. Book of garden pests.
—Thonger. Book of the cottage garden.

Lane's new pocket lib. 34 v. '10(D24) 32°, ea., 50 c. net; leath., 75 c. net. Lane.
Contents: Borrow, G:, Works, 5 v.; Disraeli, B:, Works, 9 v.; Eliot, George, Works, 4 v.; Trollope, Anthony, Works, 16 v.

Laney, Fs. Baker.
Gold Hill mining district of North Carolina. '10(N) 137 p. il. maps, 4°, (North Carolina, Geological and Economic Survey bull.) pap., 15 c. N. C. Geolog. Survey.
Bibliography (19 p.).

—, and Wood, Katharine Hill.
Bibliography of North Carolina geology, mineralogy and geography, with a list of maps. '09, [1910.] (O) 428 p. 4°, (North Carolina Geological and Economic Survey, bull.) 25 c. N. C. Geolog. Survey.

Lang, And.
Maid of France: story of the life and death of Jeanne d'Arc. '08(D12) pors. map, O. *$3.50 net. Longmans.
Making of religion. 3d ed. '10(Ap2) D. $2. Longmans.
Origin of terms in human relationship; from the Proceedings of the British Academy. v. 3. '09(Je12) O. pap., 40 c. Oxford Univ.
Sir George Mackenzie, king's advocate, of Rosehaugh: his life and times, 1636 (?)-1691. '09(F27) il. por. O. *$4.20 net. Longmans.
Sir Walter Scott and the border minstrelsy. '10(O15) O. $1.60 net. Longmans.
World of Homer. '10(D3) il. O. $2.25 net. Longmans.

—, comp. Tales of King Arthur and the round table; with introd., notes, etc., by J. C. Allen. '10(F5) il. D. (Longmans' class-books of English literature.) 30 c. Longmans.

Lang, And., ed.
Beauty and the Beast, and other stories from the "fairy books"; ed. by Andrew Lang. '09(D11) c. il. D. **75 c. net. Longmans.
Forty thieves, and other stories from the "Fairy books." '09(D11) c. il. D. **75 c. net. Longmans.
Invisible prince, and other stories from the "Fairy books"; ed. by Andrew Lang. '09 (D11) c. il. D. **60 c. net. Longmans.
Lilac fairy book. '10(O22) c. col. il. D. (Fairy book ser.) $1.60 net. Longmans.
Three dwarfs, and other stories from the "Fairy books"; ed. by Andrew Lang. '09 (D11) c. front. D. **60 c. net. Longmans.
Twelve huntsmen, and other stories from the "Fairy books"; ed. by Andrew Lang. '09(D11) c. il. D. **60 c. net. Longmans.

Lang, Mrs. And.
See Lang, Leonora Blanche.

Lang, Elsie M.
Oxford colleges. '10(D10) il. 32°, leath., 90 c. net. Jacobs.
Some old English abbeys. '08(O17) Tt. (Old England ser.) 60 c.; leath., $1. Stokes.

Lang, George.
Pixy's holiday journey; tr. from the German by Mary E. Ireland. '08(Ag1) c. il. D. $1. Saalfield.

Lang, Jean.
Land of romance: the Border; its history and legend. '10(O22) il. O. $2.50 net. Dodge.

Lang, Jeanie.
More stories from Shakespeare. '10(D10) col. il. 24°, 50 c. net. Dutton.
Stories from Shakespeare. [1910.] (F) col. il. 12°, (Told to the children ser.) *50 c. net. Dutton.

Lang, J:
Gibraltar and the West Indies; or, outposts of empire. '09(O9) il. in col. O. (Romance of history ser.) *$2 net. Stokes.
Land of the golden trade (West Africa). '10(S10) col. il. maps, O. (Romance of history ser.) $2 net. Stokes.

Lang, Leonora Blanche, [Mrs. And. Lang.]
Book of princes and princesses; ed. by And. Lang. '08(O10) c. il. D. **$1.60 net. Longmans.
Red book of heroes; ed. by And. Lang. '09(O16) il. D. *$1.60 net. Longmans.

Lang, Ossian.
Bee Martin, king of the birds, and other tales. '08(N7) c. il. D. 30 c. Flanagan.
How Bee Martin became king of the birds, and Kingbird's coronation; il. by Marg. Ely Webb. '08(Ag8) c. D. pap., 10 c. Flanagan.

Lang, W. H.
Australia. '09(O9) il. in col. maps, O. (Romance of history ser.) *$2 net. Stokes.

Langbein, Georg.
Complete treatise on the electro-deposition of metals: comprising electro-plating and galvanoplastic operations, [etc.;] tr. from the 6th German ed., with additions by W: T. Brannt. '09(My8) c. il. 8°, *$4 net. Baird.

Langbein, G: F. and J. C. Julius, comps.
See New York [City.] *Municipal ct.* Law and practice.

Langdell, Christopher Columbus.
Brief survey of equity jurisdiction; being a series of articles reprinted from the *Harvard Law Review.* 2d ed., enl. '08(O) shp. (Add. pub. for price.) Harvard Law.

Langdell, R. S.
Forest nursery and reforestation work in Massachusetts, by R. S. Langdell, under the direction of F. W. Rane. '10(Jl) 6 p. pls. O. pap. F. W. Rane.

Langdon, Mrs. Amy H.
See Hartog, Phillippe Jos.

Langdon, Mrs. Emma Florence.
Labor's greatest conflicts. [Moyer, Haywood and Pettibone case, etc.] '08, [1909.] (F) $1; pap., 50 c. E. F. Langdon.

Langdon, Rev. Stephen Herbert, comp.
Sumerian and Babylonian psalms. '09 (Ap3) O. hf. leath., $6. Stechert.

Langdon, W: H:, and Markham, Edwin.
Struggle between graft and democracy, [in San Francisco;] address by W: H. Langdon, [and] The vermin in the dark, a poem by Edn. Markham; del. before the Civic Forum. '08(D5) pors. 12°, (Civic Forum addresses.) pap., 10 c. Civic Forum.

Langford, Augustine.
Voyage of the Wenonah. '09(My22) c. il. double map. 12°, $1.50. C. M. Clark.

Langland, Ja., ed.
Chicago Daily News almanac and yearbook, 1909. 25th year. '09(Ja23) c. il. pors. maps, 40 c. Chic. Daily News.

Langley, S: Pierpont.
Researches and experiments in aerial navigation. '08(Ag15) O. (Smithsonian Inst. bulletins.) pap. (Add. pubs. for price.) U. S., Supt. of Docs.

Langstroth, Lorenzo Lorraine.
On the hive and honey bee; rev. by Dadant. Twentieth century ed. '09(Ap3) c. il. pors. 12°, $1.20. Dadant.

Langton, H. H., ed.
See Wrong, G: McKinnon, *ed.*

LANGUAGE.
Connecticut Acad. of Arts and Sciences. Transactions. v. 15, July, 1909, To the Univ. of Leipzig on the occasion of the 500th anniversary of its foundation; [twelve monographs on linguistic subjects.] $3.50. Yale Univ.
Drake, A. E. Discoveries in Hebrew, Gaelic, Gothic, Anglo-Saxon, Latin, Basque, and other Caucasic languages. —Supplementary discoveries showing Aryo-Semitic cognation. ea., $6 net. Herrick.
Jackson, A. V. W. Philology: a lecture. 25 c. Columbia Univ.
Krapp, G: P. Authority of law in language. 50 c. Univ. of Cin.
Scott, F. N. Genesis of speech. (Add. pubs. for price.) Modern Lang. Assoc.

LANGUAGE.—*Continued.*
Studies in philology. v. 2-5. ea., 50 c. Univ. of N. C.
Worthington, L. N: Polyglot phrases. *$1.10 net. Macmillan.
See also Abbreviations; — Classical philology; — Criticism; —Elocution; — Esperanto;—Phonetics;—Pronunciation;—Prosody: — Punctuation; —Rhetoric;—Ro;— Slang;—Speech;—Spellers; —Words;—*also* names of languages.

Language of Richard Wagner's Ring des Nibelungen. Schuler, J: (Priv. pr.) Steinman & F.

Language reader ser. *See* Macmillan's.

Language readers. *See* Ginn's.

Language ser. *See* Metcalf, Rob. C.

Langworthy, C: Ford.
U. S. government publications as sources of information for students of home economics. '09(D) 227-252 p. O. pap. (Add. Assoc. for price.) Am. Home Economics Assoc.

—, and Hunt, Caroline Louisa.
Economical use of meat in the home. '10 (My) 543 p. 8°, (U. S., Dept. of Agriculture; Farmers' bull.)

Lanier, J: Jabez.
Kinship of God and man; the new and old theology: attempt to formulate a thorough-going trinitarian theology; with an introd. by the Rt. Rev. C. K. Nelson. 2d ed., rev. and enl. In 3 v. v. 1, Harmony; v. 2, Good and evil; v. 3, Salvation of man. '10(Ag) 12°, ea., $1.50; per set, $3.50. J: J. Lanier.

Lanier, Sidney.
Poem outlines. '08(O3) c. D. **$1 net. Scribner.
Shakspere and his forerunners: studies in Elizabethan poetry and its development from early English. '08(D19) c. 2 pt. in 1 v., por. O. $1.60. Doubleday, P.

LANIER, Sidney.
Carroll, C: C. Synthesis and analysis of the poetry of Sidney Lanier. 25 c. C: C. Carroll.

Lanier of the cavalry. King, C: †$1.25. Lippincott.

Lankester, Sir Edn. Ray, ed.
Treatise on zoology. In 10 pts. pt. 1, Introduction and protozoa; 1st fascicle, by S. J. Hickson, J. J. Lister, F. W. Gamble, A. Willey, H. M. Woodcock, W. F. R. Weldon and E. Ray Lankester. '09 (Mr6); pt. 2, Porifera and coelentera, by E. A. Minchin, G. H. Fowler and G. C. Bourne; pt. 3, Echinoderma, by F. A. Bather, J. W. Gregory and E. S. Goodrich; pt. 4, Platyhelmia, mesozoa and nemertini, by Prof. Benham. '10(D); pt. 5, Mollusca, by P. Pilseneer. '09(D); pt. 7, Appendiculata, third fascicle crustacea. '10(D); pt. 9, Vertebrata craniata (first fascicle: cyclostomes and fishes). '10(Ja8) il. 8°, pts. 1, 3, 4, 5, 7, ea., $5.25 net; pt. 2, $5.50 net; pt. 9, $6.50 net. Macmillan.

Lanphear, Emory.
Surgical therapeutics. '08(N) c. 396 p. 12°, $1. Clinic.

Lansdell, H:
Sacred tenth; or, studies in tithe-giving, ancient and modern; cont. a bibliography on tithe-giving, lists of crown grantees, and modern lay owners of English alienated tithes, etc. 2 v. '08(N) 8°, *$6 net. Gorham.

Lansdowne, Jane.
Shadow of Eversleigh. '08(N14) c. D. $1.25. Benziger.

Lansing, Marion Florence.
Life in the greenwood. '09(O23) c. il. S. (Open road lib. of juvenile literature.) 35 c. Ginn.
—, comp. Page, esquire knight; book of chivalry. '10(Je18) c. il. S. (Open road lib. of juvenile literature.) 35 c. Ginn.
—, comp. and ed. Fairy tales. v. 1. '08(F1); v. 2 (S19) c. S. (Open road lib. of juvenile literature.) ea., 35 c. Ginn.
Tales of old England in prose and verse. '09(Ja23) c. il. S. (Open road lib. of juvenile literature.) 35 c. Ginn.
See also Channing, E:

Lanslots, D. I.
Hdbk. of canon law for congregations of women under simple vows. '09(My) D. *$1.25 net. Pustet.

Lantern of luck. Aitken, R. $1.50. W. J. Watt.

Lantz, D: Ernest.
Brown rat in the U. S. '09(Ag) 54 p. il 8°, (U. S., Dept. of Agriculture, Biological Survey bull.) pap. (Add. Superintendent for price.)
How to destroy rats. '09(D) 20 p. il. 8°, (U. S., Dept. of Agriculture, farmers' bull.) pap. (Add. Superintendent for price.) U. S., Supt. of Docs.

Lanyon, Helen.
Hill o' dreams: [Irish verses.] '10(O1) D. bds., $1 net. Lane.

Lanza, Clara Hammond, Marquise.
Dweller on the borderland. '10(F12) c. D. $1.50. McVey.

Lâo-Tsze.
Book of the simple way; with introd. and commentary by Wa. Gorn Old. '09(S) 186 p. 12°, (Psychic lib.) *$1.25 net. Badger.
Sayings of Lao-Tzu; tr. by Lionel Giles. '08(Je6) 16°, (Wisdom of the East.) *40 c. net. Dutton.

Laodicean. *See* Hardy, T:

Laokoon. Howard, G., *ed.* $1.50. Holt.

Lapen, Florence.
Brownyboo: [fairy story.] '08(O24) c. Q. bds., $1.25. Scribner.

LAPLAND.
Le Blond, *Mrs.* A. Mountaineering in the land of the midnight sun. *$3.50 net. Lippincott.
See also Fine arts.

Laprade, W: T:
England and the French Revolution, 1789-1797. '10(Mr5) c. O. (Johns Hopkins Univ. studies in historical and political science.) pap., 75 c. Johns Hopkins.

La Ramée, Louise de, ["Ouida."]
Dog of Flanders. '08(S19) c. front. D. (Bimbi ser.) bds., **40 c. net. Crowell.

La Ramée, Louise de.—*Continued.*
Dog of Flanders, The Nüremberg stove, and other stories. '09(N20) c. col. il. O. †$1.50. Lippincott.
Helianthus. '08(O17) c. D. †$1.50. Macmillan.
Little earl. '08(S19) c. front. D. (Bimbi ser.) bds., **40 c. net. Crowell.
Moths. '08(Jl11) 12°, (Magnolia lib.) 50 c. Hurst.
Nürnberg stove. '08(S19) c. front. D. (Bimbi ser.) bds., **40 c. net. Crowell.

Larard, C. E., and Golding, H. A.
Practical calculations for engineers. '08 (Mr7) il. tabs., D. *$2 net. Lippincott.

LARCH.
See Trees.

"LARCHMONT" DISASTER (The).
United States. *Steamboat Inspection Service.* Findings in investigation of collision between steamer "Larchmont" and schooner "Harry Knowlton." 25 c. U. S., Supt. of Docs.

Larden, Wa.
Recollections of an old mountaineer. '10 (D3) il. O. $4 net. Longmans.

Large, Mary Harriott.
Twelfth juror. '08(N14) c. front. D. $1.50. C. M. Clark.

Large meals for little money. Johnson, F. K. 10 c. People's Univ.

Large print lib. O. Doubleday, P.
—Reade. Love me little, love me long. †$1.50.

Larger piano compositions. Grieg, E. H. $2.50; $1.50. Ditson.

Larimer, Ja. McCormick.
Bucyrus, the railroad wrecker. '09(D) c. 96 p. 16°, 25 c. Muskogee.

Larison, Cornelius Wilson, M.D.
The sol: hwens?—hwither? '08(Je27) c. O. $1.50. Fonic.

LARKIN, Thomas Oliver.
Kelsey, R. W. The United States consulate in California. Univ. of Cal.

Larned, C: W:
Athletics from a historical and educational standpoint. '09(N) 9 p. 8°. (Add. pubs. for price.) Am. Phys. Educ.

La Rochefoucauld, 6th Duc de, Prince de Marsillac.
See Pascal, Blaise.

Larrabee, Rev. E: Allan.
Calls of the Conqueror: being Good Friday addresses on the seven words from the cross. '08(Ap11) c. S. *60 c. net. Young Churchman.

Larry Burke, freshman. Odell, F. I. $1.25. Lothrop, L. & S.

Larry Dexter's great search. Garis, H. R. 60 c. Grosset.

Larson, Christian Daa.
The great within. '07, [1908.] (Mr.) c. 99 p. 16°, 50 c. Eternal Progress.
How great men succeed. '10(Je4) c. 16°, (Progress ser.) 50 c. Progress Co.
How to stay young. '08. c. 211 p. 12°, $1. Eternal Progress.
Ideal made real; or, applied metaphysics for beginners. '09(My) 264 p. 8°. (Not for sale.) Progress Co.

Larson, Christian Daa.—*Continued.*
Mastery of self. '07, [1908.] (Mr.) c. 97 p. 16°, 50 c. Eternal Progress.
On the heights. '08, [1909.] (F) c. 9-74 p. 16°, 50 c. Progress Co.
See also McKay, G: Lewis.

Larson, Ja. H:
Face of Christ in art. '09(N) c. 5-44 p. 12°, $1. H: J. Larson.

Larson, Laurence Marcellus.
Financial and administrative hist. of Milwaukee. '08(D) 8°, (Univ. of Wisconsin bull.) pap., 50 c. Univ. of Wis.

Larsson, Gustaf.
Sloyd for the three upper grammar grades. Teachers' ed. '08(Jl18) c. il. obl. S. $1.25. Ellis.

Larwill lectures. *See* Eliot, C: W:

LARYNGOLOGY.
See Throat.

Lasalle, Ferdinand Johann Gottlieb.
Franz von Sickingen; tragedy in five acts; from the German. '10(My7) c. 12°, $1. N. Y. Labor News.

La Salle Extension University encyclop.; editorial staff, C: Higgins, assisted by a large corps of specialists and experts. '09, [1910.] (Ja) c. 1367 p. il. maps, 4°, $5. De Bower-C.

Lasance, Rev. Fs. Xavier.
My prayer-book: prayers and devotions. '08(D5) c. T. leath., $1.25. Benziger.
Young man's guide; counsels, reflections, and prayers for Catholic young men. '10 (Ap9) c. front. nar. T. 75 c.; levantum, $1; American seal, $1.25. Benziger.

Lasar, C: A.
Pract. hints for art students. '10(F19) c. il. S. **$1 net. Duffield.

Lash (The). Lyman, O. L. $1.50. Badger.

Laskowski, P: E.
Art of baking. '10(Ap) c. 233 p. por. 16°, $1. P: E. Laskowski.

Lass of the silver sword. Du Bois, M. C †$1.50. Century Co.

Lassar-Cohn, Dr.
Chemistry in daily life; tr. by M. M. Pattison Muir. 4th ed., rev. and augmented. '09(Ja30) 12°, *$1.75 net. Lippincott.

Last American frontier. Paxon, F. L. **$1.50 net. Macmillan.

Last abbot of Glastonbury. Gasquet, F. A. *$2 net. Macmillan.

Last campaign. Gilpin, E. N. 50 c. U. S. Cavalry.

Last chronicle of Barset. *See* Trollope, Anthony.

Last days of Charles II. Crawfurd, R. $1.75. Oxford Univ.

Last days of Papal Rome. De Cesare, R. *$3.50 net. Houghton M.

Last days of Pompeii. *See* Bulwer-Lytton, *Sir* E: G:, Earle Lytton.

Last days of St. Pierre. Smirnow, L: $1.50. C. M. Clark.

Last duchess of Belgrade. Seawell, M. E. †$1.25. Appleton.

Last Egyptian: a romance of the Nile. '08 (Ap18) c. D. $1.50. Stern.

Last hurdle. Bacon, E: (Not for sale.) D. G. Bacon.

Last journals. Walpole, H. *$7.50 net. Lane.
Last king of Poland. Bain, R. N. *$3 net. Putnam.
Last of the chiefs. Altsheler, J. A. $1.50. Appleton.
Last of the Houghtons. Buckley, R: W. $1.50. Neale.
Last of the Mohicans. *See* Cooper, Ja. Fenimore.—Haight, M. M., *comp.*
Last of the plainsmen. Grey, Z. *$1.50 net. Outing.
Last phase of the league in Provence. Wilkinson, M. *$1.50 net. Longmans.
Last prophets of Israel. Jenks, O. R. 35 c. Our Hope.
Last salute. Roberts, C. M. $1.50; $1. C. M. Roberts.
Last testament. Howard, H. F. v. 1. $1. Howard Pub. Co., (N. H.)
Last trail. Grey, Z. †$1. Burt.
Last voyage of the "Donna Isabel." Parrish, R. $1.50. McClurg.
Last will. Fish, W. 40 c. A. Bartlett.
Last woman. Beeckman, R. $1.50. W. J. Watt.
Last years of the Protectorate. Firth, C: H. 2 v. *$7 net. Longmans.

Lastinger, Clayton.
Key to the Bible and our looking-glass. '08 (N) c. 381 p. 8°, $1.50. Tribune Pr. Co., (Fla.)

Latch-string to happiness. Jennings, N. I., *comp.* 50 c. Lone Star.
Later Roman education. Cole, P. R:, *comp.* 25 c. Teachers' Coll.
Later years of Catherine de Medici. Sichel, E. *$3 net. Dutton.

Latham, Arth., M.D.
Dict. of treatment. '09(Mr) 6+325 p. 12°, *$2 net. Blakiston.

Latham, C:
In English homes; internal character, furniture and adornments of some of the most notable houses of England accurately depicted from photographs specially taken. v. 3; the letterpress edited and an introd. written by H. Avray Tipping. '10(Ap2) F. $15 net. Scribner.

Latham, E:
French-English and English-French dict. '10(O8) 48°, cl. or im. mor., 50 c. Dutton.

Latham, Mrs. Ettie J.
Hist. of the town of Pownal, [Me.,] written for its centennial, Sept. 2, 1908. '09(F) 40 p. 12°, 30 c. Lewiston Journ.

Lathbury, Albert A:
Life in two worlds. 2d ed. '08, [1909.] (F) c. '02. 7+327 p. il. por. 12°. (Add. author for price.) A. A: Lathbury.

Lathbury, Eva.
Long gallery. '09(Je12) c. D. †$1.50. Holt.
Sinking ship. '09(D4) c. D. †$1.50. Holt.

Lathe and planer tools. '08(Je20) c. il. 8°, (Machinery's reference ser.) pap., 25 c. Indust. Press.

LATHES.
See Turning.

Lathrop, Lester Cassius.
Use and abuse of hypnotism. '09(Ap24) c. S. pap., 50 c. L. C. Lathrop.

Latifi, Almá.
Effects of war on property; studies in international law and policy; with a note on belligerent rights at sea by J: Westlake. '09(F13) O. *$1.50 net. Macmillan.

Latimer, Caroline Wormeley, M.D.
Girl and woman; book for mothers and daughters; with an introd. by Howard A. Kelly. '10(F19) c. O. **$2 net. Appleton.

Latimer, H: Randolph.
Virginia Dare, and other poems. '08(Ap18) c. O. pap. (Add. pubs. for price.) Lord Balt. Pr.

Latimer, Ja. Brandt.
Railway signaling in theory and practice. '09(N20) il. por. 8°, $2.50. Mackenzie-K.

Latimer, Rob. Sloan.
Liberty of conscience **under three Tsars.** '09(O2) 12°, *$1.50 net. **Revell.**

LATIN AMERICA.
See Spanish-America.

Latin classics. See Macmillan's.

LATIN LANGUAGE.
Allen, B. M., *and* Phillips, J: L. Latin composition. $1. Allyn & B.
Antoninus, M. A. Imperator ad se ipsum. 75 c. Oxford Univ.
Arnold, E: V. Corthurnulus: three short Latin historical plays. *35 c. net. Macmillan.
Avellanus, A. Palaestra: primer of Tusculan system of learning to speak Latin. In 3 pts. pt. 1, no. 1. .25 c. A. Avellanus.
Baker, C: M., *and* **Inglis, A. J. High** school course in Latin composition. $1. In 2 v. and 3 pts. v. 1, pts. 1, 2, *60 c. net; v. 2, pt. 3, *55 c. net. **Macmillan.**
Barss, J: E. Writing Latin. bk. 1. 50 c. net. Heath.
Bennett, C: E. First year Latin. $1.—Latin grammar. 80 c. Allyn & B.
Browne, G: H: Vest-pocket memory-test Latin word-list. 75 c.; also, A memory-test note-book. 15 c. Ginn.
Bunse, F: J. Latin grammar. (Not for sale.) F: J. Bunse.
Bushnell, C. C. Readings from Latin verse. 75 c. Allyn & B.
Byrne, L. Syntax of high school Latin. *75 c. net. Univ. of Chic.
Cæsar, C. J. Cæsar in Britain. 25 c. Oxford Univ.
Cæsar, C. J. Expeditions to Britain. De bello Gallico IV. 20-36; v. 1-23. 50 c.—[Gallic war.] Preparatory Cæsar; De bello Gallico, book II., *40 c. net; books 2 and 3, 50 c. Longmans.
Cæsar, C. J. Four books of Cæsar's Gallic war. $1. Am. Bk.
Cæsar, C. J. Gallic War; bks. I-VII. **$1.25 net. Macmillan.
Caldecott, W. Exercises on Edward's The story of the kings of Rome. 15 c. net. Putnam.
Carter, H. P. First exercises in Latin. 60 c. B. S. Adams.
Cicero, M. T. De finibus bonorum et malorum. *$2.40 net. Longmans.
Cicero, M. T. Laelivs de amicitia.—M. Tvlli Ciceronio Cato Maior de senectvte. ea., 75 c. net. Heath.

LATIN LANGUAGE.—*Continued.*

Cicero, M. T. Phillipic orations, I, 2, 3, 5, 7. 90 c. Oxford Univ.

Cicero, M. T. Six orations. $1. Ginn.

Cicero, M. T. Tusculan disputations, I, II, V. $1.50. Allyn & B.

Douthat, R. W: Latin synonyms defined from two standpoints. $1. R. W: Douthat.

Elmore, J. Book of Latin prose composition. $1. B: H. Sanborn.

Erasmus, D. Altera colloquia Latina. *40 c. net. Putnam.

Fitzhugh, T: Prolegomena to the history of Italico-Romanic rhythm. 25 c.—Sacred tripudium; accentual and rhythmic norm of Italico-Romanic speech and verse. 75 c. Anderson.

Gepp, C: G., *and* Haigh, A. E. Latin-English dictionary. $1.10. Longmans.

Greenwood, W: Auxilium: summary of Latin essentials. *40 c. net; *30 c. net. W: Greenwood.

Hale, W: G., *and others.* Latin composition. 60 c. Atkinson, M. & G.

Harrington, W., *and* O'Rourke, S. G. Latin bones; easier method in Latin. Cen. Pr.

Harrod, S: G. Latin terms of endearment and of family relationship. 75 c. Princeton Univ.

Hecker, E. A. Teaching of Latin in secondary schools. 80 c. Schoenhof.

Horace, Q. H. F. Satires. $1; Text ed., 30 c. Am. Bk.

Jackson, E. H. Law Latin. $1.50. Byrne.

Jenner, W: A., *and* Wilson, H: E. Cæsar's first campaign. $1 net. Appleton.

Livy; bk. IX. *75 c. net. Putnam.

Livy. Selections from the first decade. 60 c. Scott, F. & Co.

Livy. [Works:] book I and selections from books 2-10. *60 c. net. Macmillan.

Locke, R. H: Latin forms and syntax. *$1 net. McVey.

Lodge, G. Vocab. of high school Latin. *$1.50 net. Teachers' Coll.

Lothman, D. W: Latin lessons for beginners. $1. Ginn.

Martial. Selected epigrams. $1.50. Ginn.

Martin, H: Notes on the syntax of the Latin inscriptions found in Spain. $1. Furst.

Meader, C. L. Usage of idem, ipse and words of related meanings. 50 c. net. Macmillan.

Merrill, W: A: On the contracted genetive in I in Latin. 25 c. Univ. of Cal.

Mitchell, G: W. Latin composition, based on Cæsar. *60 c. net. Macmillan

Mood, J. R. Some figurative usages of *venire* and *ire.* gratis. Johns Hopkins.

Murphy, E: J. Latin pronounced for altar boys. *50 c. net.—Latin pronounced for church services. *75 c. net. Chr. Press.

Ogden, C: J. De infinitivi finalis. $1 net. Lemcke.

Paetow, L: J. Arts course at medieval universities. $1. Univ. of Ill.

Pearson, H: C. Key to essentials of Latin for beginners. 25 c.—Latin prose composition. 50 c. Am. Bk.

LATIN LANGUAGE.—*Continued.*

Peloubet, S. S. Students' law dict. of words and phrases in law Latin, law French and Anglo-Saxon. $1.50; $2. Peloubet.

Plautus, T. M. The Trinummus. *60 c. net. Macmillan.

Potter, F. H. Elem. Latin course. [Also] A new method for Cæsar. $1.12. B: H. Sanborn.

Reiley, K. C. Studies in the philosophical terminology of Lucretius and Cicero. *$1.25 net. Lemcke.

Ritchie, F. First steps in Latin. 60 c.—Second steps in Latin. 75 c. Longmans.

Sallustius Crispus, C. Bellum Catalinae. $1. Heath.

Scott, H: F., *and* Van Tuyl, C: H. Cæsar composition book. 40 c. Scott, F. & Co.

Seneca, L. A. Three tragedies. *60 c. net. Macmillan.

Sidey, F: K. Participle in Plautus, Petronius, and Apuleius. *50 c. net. Univ. of Chic.

Smith, M. L., *and* Laing, G. J. First Latin lessons. $1. Allyn & B.

Smith, M. L. S. Supplementary exercises on "Ora maritina," by E. A. Sonnenschein. 35 c. net. Macmillan.

Smith, W. W. Course in first year Latin. $1. W: R. Jenkins.

Stewart, M. A. Latin abstract substantives. 40 c. Macmillan.

Stone, E. D. Gotham, and other stories: Latin reading book. *40 c. net. Macmillan.

Sturmer, J. W: Rudiments of Latin, with special reference to the nomenclature of the U. S. pharmacopœia. $1. J. W: Sturmer

Swan, F: T. Use of the adjective as a substantive in the De rerum natura of Lucretius. Macmillan.

Tacitus, C. C. The Agricola. **40 c. net. —Tacitus' histories. bks. I and 2. 60 c. net. Macmillan.

Taylor, H. D. Latin and English idiom. *60 c. net. Putnam.

Terence Afer, P. Comedies. **$1.50 net. Oxford Univ.

Terence Afer, P. Phormio. 60 c. Scott, F. & Co.

Terence Afer, P. Phormio, simplified for the use of schools. 50 c.—Terenti Afri Havton temorvmenos. $1. B: H. Sanborn.

Tyng, E. M. Latin prose exercises. 60 c. Longmans.

Virgil, P. M. Æneid; bks. I-VI. $1.40. B: H. Sanborn.

Whittemore, L. D. Latin reading book. 75 c. O. P. Barnes.

See also Cursus;—*also* names of Latin authors.

LATIN LITERATURE.

Brown, A. C. B., *ed.* Selections from the Latin literature of the Early Empire. $1.10. Oxford Univ.

Clark, A. C., *comp.* Fontes prosae nvmerosae. $1.50. Oxford Univ.

Cowles, W: L., *ed.* Selections from Ennius, Calullus, Tibullus and Propertius. 60 c. W: L. Cowles.

LATIN LITERATURE.—*Continued.*
Duff, J: W. Literary history of Rome. $4. Scribner.
Harbottle, T: B. Dict. of Latin quotations. *$1 net. Macmillan.
Lipscomb, H. C. Aspects of the speech in the later Roman epic. $1. Furst.
See also names of Latin authors.

LATIN POETRY.
Butler, H. E. Post-Augustan poetry from Seneca to Juvenal. $2.90. Oxford Univ.
Palgrave, F. T., *ed.* Latin anthology. *$1 net. Macmillan.

Latin ser. See Macmillan's.

LATINI, Brunetto.
Dole, N. H. Teacher of Dante. **$1.75 net. Moffat.

Latins in the Levant. Miller, W: *$5 net. Dutton.

LATITUDE.
Porter, J. G. Variations of latitude, 1899 to 1906. $1. Univ. of Cin.

Latitude and departure calculations of land made easy and self proving. Randabaugh, I. F. $1.25; $1.50; $2. I. F. Randabaugh.

La Tourette, Clara, and McDaniel, C: Foster.
Commercial art typewriting; touch method producing typewriting artists. '10(O) c. 48 p. 8°, 65 c. C: F. McDaniel.

Latson, W. R. C.
Attainment of efficiency. '10(Ag) $1. Health-Culture.

Latta, Ja. W:
Was secession taught at West Point?; read at the meeting [of the Military Order of the Loyal Legion of the United States, Pennsylvania Commandery,] May 5, 1909. '09(S18) O. pap., $1. M. O. L. L., (Pa.)

Latta, M. Nisbet-.
American producer gas practice and industrial gas engineering. '10(F19) il. 8°, *$6 net. Van Nostrand.

Latter-day problems. Laughlin, J. L. **$1.50 net. Scribner.

LATTER-DAY SAINTS.
See Mormonism.

Latter day sinners and saints. Ross, E: A. 50 c. net. B: W. Huebsch.

Latter rain covenant. Myland, D: W. 50 c. Evangel.

Lattey, Rob. Tabor.
See Hurst, Harold Edn.

Lauck, Blanche Morris.
The picnic, and other verses. '09(D) c. 40 p. 16°, 50 c. Cochrane.

Laughlin, Annie, ed.
The reappear: a book of choice recipes. '08(O17) c. 12°, 60 c. A. Laughlin.

Laughlin, Clara Eliz.
Death of Lincoln: story of Booth's plot, his deed and the penalty. '09(F6) c. il. map, D. **$1.50 net. Doubleday, P.
Everybody's lonesome. '10(Jl16) c. 12°, bds., 75 c. net. Revell.
"Just folks." '10(O29) c. D. $1.50. **Macmillan.**
Lady in gray. '08(O10) c. 12°, bds., *50 c. net. Revell.

Laughlin, Ja. Laurence.
Guaranty of bank deposits; address before the State Bankers' Assoc. of Nebraska, at Lincoln, Neb., Sept. 25, 1908. '08, [1909.] (Mr) 16 p. 8°. (Add. pubs. for price.) Johnson, K. & Q.
Latter-day problems. '09(N6) c. D. **$1.50 net. Scribner.

Laughter, Victor Hugo.
Operator's wireless telegraph and telephone hand-book. '09(Je19) c. il. 12°, $1. Drake.

—, and Morgan, Alfr. P.
Wireless telegraphy made simple; embodying in addition helpful information on wireless telephone receivers, and construction of a wireless transformer, by Alfr. P. Morgan. '09(D) c. 31 p. il. 8°, 25 c. Popular Electricity.

Laughter of life. Albanesi, *Mrs.* E. A. M. 75 c. Cupples & L.

Launay, L. de.
World's gold: its geology, extraction, and political economy; tr. by Orlando Cyprian Williams; with an introd. by C: A. Conant. '08(N21) c. O. (Science ser.) **$1.75 net. Putnam.

LAUNDRY WORK.
Townsend, C: F. Chemistry for launderers. $1. Nat. Laundry.

Launspach, C: W. L.
State and family in early Rome. '08(Ag15) 8°, *$2.50 net. Macmillan.

"LAURA," The.
See Arctic regions.

Laureate series of the poets. 34 v. '09(O9) il. S. ea., $1, boxed. Caldwell.

LAUREL BRIGADE.
See Ashby cavalry.

Laureled leaders. Phillips, M. E. $2. Lothrop, L. & S.

Laurie, André, [pseud. for Paschal Grousset.]
Une année de collège à Paris; ed. by Fabian Ware. '10(D24) 16°, (Macmillan's new ser. of French texts.) 35 c. net. Macmillan.

Laurie, Arth. Pillans.
Greek and Roman methods of painting; some comments on the statements made by Pliny and Vitruvius about wall and panel painting. '10(O29) D. 75 c. net. Putnam.

Laurie, Simon Somerville.
Institutes of education; introd. to rational psychology. 3d ed. '09(Je19) 8°, *$1.90 net. Macmillan.

Laurus nobilis. **Lee, V., *pseud.* *$1.50 net. Lane.**

LAUSANNE, Switzerland.
Gribble, F. H: Lausanne. *$3 net. Macmillan.

Laut, Agnes Christina.
Canada, the empire of the north. '09(D4) c. il. pors. map, O. **$1.75 net. Ginn.
Conquest of the great Northwest: being the story of the adventurers of England known as Hudson's Bay Co. '09(O) c. il. pors. maps, facsims. 8°, $5. Moffat.
Formerly published by Outing Pub. Co.
Freebooters of the wilderness. '10(D3) c. D. $1.35 net. Moffat.

LAUZUN, *Duke of.*
Sanders, M. F. Duke of Lauzun: courtier and adventurer. 2 v. *$6 net. Brentano's.

LA VALLIÈRE, Françoise Louise de La Baume Le Blanc, *Duchesse* de.
Lair, J. Louise de La Vallière and the early life of Louis XIV. *$3.50 net. Putnam.

Lavarack, F: C:
Locking: elem. treatise on the mechanisms in interlocking lever machines by which the movements of the levers are restricted to certain predetermined ways, rendering it impossible to operate conflicting switches and signals on railways. '08 (Ja11) il. 8°, $2. F: C: Lavarack.

Lavay, Jerome Buell.
Disputed handwriting. '09(Ap24) c. il. 8°, $3. Harvard Bk.

Lavender. Taylor, E: R. $2. P. Elder.

Lavender and rosemary. Stevens, E., *comp.* 75 c.; $1.50. Platt & P.

Lavinder, Claude H.
Prophylaxis of pellagra. '09, [1910.] (Ap) 13 p. 8°. (Add. Superintendent for price.) U. S., Supt. of Docs.

—, Williams, C. F., and Babcock, Ja. Woods.
Prevalence of pellagra in the U. S.: a statistical and geographical note with bibliog. '09(S) 6 p. 8°. (Add. Superintendent for price. U. S., Supt. of Docs.

Law, E: F.
Alloys and their industrial applications. '09 O. *$4 net. Lippincott.

Law, Emma Norine.
Shame of a great nation; story of the "white slave trade." '10(Ap9) c. por. 8°, $1. E. N. Law.

Law, Fk. E.
Method of deducting liability rates. '08(D) 24 p. fold. tab., 12°, $1. Spectator.

Law, Frederic Stanley.
Operatic tales. '08(Ja11) 12°, $1.50. Hatch.

Law, F: Houk.
Ad Miriam: [poems.] '09(Jl3) c. D. **$1 net. Putnam.
Sister Clementia. '10(O15) 12°, $1.50. Fenno.

Law, Hartland.
Viavi hygiene.. [Rev. ed.] '08(D) c. 11-416 p. 12°, $1. Viavi.

Law, Rev. Rob.
Test of life: study of the first Epistle of St.John; being the Kerr lectures for 1909. '09(Ap3) O. *$3 net. Scribner.

Law, W:
Liberal and mystical writings of William Law: with an introd. by W: Scott Palmer and a preface by W. P. DuBose. '08 (My2) O. *$1 net. Longmans.

Law, W: Hainstock.
Among the lighthouses of the Great Lakes. '08(Ap11) c. il. O. pap., 10 c. W: H. Law.

LAW.
Abbott, N. T. Cases on the law of equity, jurisprudence and trusts. (Add. pubs. for price.) Flood.
American Academy of Political and Social Science. Administration of justice in the United States. $1. Am. Acad. Pol. Sci.
American decisions. v. 5, 6, 7. ea., $6.50.—Extra annot. vs. 21-40. ea., $2.75; per set, $55. Bancroft-W.; Lawyers' Co-op.
American law and procedure. In 14 v. La Salle Extension.

LAW.—*Continued.*
American law digest and legal directory, 1908-09. (Add. pubs. for price.) Bankers' Pub. Co.
Archer, G. L. Law office and court procedure. *$3 net. Little, B. & Co.
Baylies, E. Test questions for law students on law, equity, practice, pleadings and evidence, with answers. (Add. pubs. for price.) M. Bender.
Becker, F. S. Bender's code citations analyzed, 1907. $1. M. Bender..
Bender's practice time-table, consisting of the times required for each step in the practice of law in the state of N. Y. $2. M. Bender.
Berlinicke, H. R. Legal information. 25 c. Berlinicke & A.
Bolles, A. S. Every man's lawyer. 3 v. $3. Doubleday, P.
Campbell, R., *ed.* Ruling cases. v. 27. $5.50. Boston Bk.
Chadman, C: E. Concise legal directory. $6. Am. Corr. Sch. Law.
Chadman, C: E., *ed.* Cyclopedia of law. 12 v. $60. Am. Corr. Sch. Law.
Clark, W: L., *comp.* Elementary law. $5. —Quiz book. (Add. pubs. for price.) Am. Law Bk.
Constantineau, A. Treatise on De Facto Doctrine in its relation to public officers, [etc.] $6. Lawyers' Co-op.
Cooley, R. W., *ed.* Brief making and the use of law books. $2. West Pub.
Credit corporation of America. Law and bank list. $2. Credit Corporation.
Cumulative index for current law. v. 1-9. (Add. pubs. for price.) Keefe-D.
Danaher, F. M. Bar examinations, (N. Y.) $4. Lyon.
Flanigan, D: W., *and* Parker, C. I., *comps.* Vaughn's practical review for law students. $5. D: W. Flanigan.
Foster, R. Treatise on federal practice, civil and criminal, incl. practice in bankruptcy. In 3 v. v. 3. $6.50. Callaghan.
Friend, J: W. Legal aphorisms. $5. Whittet.
Gest, J: M. Influence of Biblical texts on English law. (Priv. pr.) Buchanan.
Grattan, R. Glossary of technical words, phrases, etc., found in the Cyclopedia of law and procedure. $1.50. Am. Law Bk.
Gray, J: C. Nature and sources of the law. *$1.50 net. Macmillan.
Hawkins, C: A. Legal counselor and form book. $3.75. Ziegler.
Hoffman, E: F. Proceedings to obtain inspection of books and papers in aid of suits at law or in equity. 25 c. E: F. Hoffman.
Holdsworth, W. S. History of English law. In 3 v. ea., $4 net. Little, B. & Co.
Holland, T: E. Elements of jurisprudence. $2.50. Oxford Univ.
Howel Dda, *the Good.* Welsh medieval law. $2.90. Oxford Univ.
Hughes, T: Ethics of the practice of law. (Add. pubs. for price.) Daily Record.
Hughes, W: T. Grounds and rudiments of law. v. 1-4. ea., $4. Usona.

LAW.—*Continued.*

Kallmeyer, C: Pract. legal and business manual. 75 c. C: Kallmeyer.

Keppel, W: H. 999 points in law, court decisions, and business guide. 25 c. Keppel Pub.

King, J. B., *and others.* Management of private affairs. 85 c. Oxford Univ.

Kinkead, E. B., *and others, comps.* Complete law quizzer; self preparation for final examination. $4.50. W. H. Anderson.

Kohler, M. J. Un-American character of race legislation. 25 c. Am. Acad. Pol. Sci.

Korkunov, N. M. General theory of law. $3.50. Bost. Law.

Lawyers' repts., annot. Index; new ser. vs. 19-23. Lawyers' Co-op.

Lobingier, C: S. People's law. **$4 net. Macmillan.

Lorenzen, E. G. Cases on the conflict of laws sel. from decisions of Eng. and Am. courts. $4.50. West Pub.

MacDonald, G: A. Light side of the law. $1.75 net. Cassell.

Mack, W:, *ed.* Cyclopedia of law and procedure. Popular ed. Bks. 1-9. ea., $7.50. (Sold only in sets of 12 v.) Am. Law Bk.

Mack, W:, *and* Blashfield, D. C., *eds.* Cyclop. of law and procedure; cyc. annots., 1-34 cyc. Canadian cases. $6.60. Am. Law Bk.

Mack, W:, *and* Blashfield, D. C., *eds.* Cyc. annots. to Cyclopedia of law and procedure, 1-27. subs., $4.60. Am. Law Bk.

Mack, W:, [*and others,*] *eds.* Cyclopedia of law and procedure. In 40 v. v. 28-36. subs., per v., $7.50. Am. Law Bk.

McKinney, W: M., *and* Garland, D: S., *eds.* American and English encyclopædia of law and practice. v. 1-5. ea., $7.50. E: Thompson.

Maitland, J. W. Equity: also, The forms of action at common law; two courses of lectures. *$4 net. Putnam.

Martindale's American law directory (annual), 1908. $15; 1910. $15.50. Martindale.

Mayes, E: Ribs of the law. (Add. pubs. for price.) Lex.

Monaghan, J. P. Complete legal advertising form book. (Add. pubs. for price.) Legal.

Mordecai, S: F. Law lectures: treatise from a North Carolina standpoint on those portions of the 1st and 2d books of the commentaries of Sir W: Blackstone which have not become obsolete. $10. Edwards.

Mordecai, S: F., *and* McIntosh, A. C. Remedies by selected cases. $6. State Journ. Co.

Morris, M. F. Introd. to the history of the development of law. $2. Byrne.

Nichols, J. L., *and* Goodrich, H. H. Robinson's business points: a compendium of legal and business forms. $1. J. L. Nichols.

Pattee, W: I. Essential nature of law. $2.50. Callaghan.

LAW.—*Continued.*

Peloubet, S. S. Students' law dict. of words and phrases in law Latin, law French and Anglo-Saxon. $1.50; $2.—Peloubet's legal maxims. $1.50; $2. Peloubet.

Putney, A. H. Foreign laws. $5.—Law library. 12 v. subs., $57. Cree.

Putney, A. H., *ed.* Popular law lib. 12 v. ea., $5. Cree.

Robinson, W: C. Elem. law. *$3.50 net. Little, B. & Co.

Rood, J: R. Leading and illustrative cases; with notes on the law of judgments, attachments, garnishments and executions. $3. Wahr.

Russell, L. Statute law and how to find it. (Add. pub. for price.) J. E. Hughes.

Ryman, D. E. Compilation of words and phrases judicially defined by the Sup. ct. of Georgia. $6. Harrison Co.

Schroeder, T. Due process of law. (Add. pubs. for price.) Free Speech.

Scott, H: W. Evolution of law. $3; $4. Wilson Pub. Co.

Select essays in Anglo-American legal history, by various authors; comp. and ed. by a committee of the Association of American Law Schools. 3 v. per set, **$12 net. Little, B. & Co.

Shive, R. J. Handy digest (civil); key to the books that contain the law. $4.75. State Cap.

Smith, E. M. Jurisprudence. 25 c. Columbia Univ.

Stimson, F. J. Popular law-making. $2.50 net. Scribner.

Taylor, H. Science of jurisprudence. $3.50. Macmillan.

Thayer, J. B. Legal essays. *$3.50 net. Boston Bk.

Townes, J: C: Law books and how to use them. $2.50. Austin Pr.

Wilgus, H. L. Legal education in the United States. (Not for sale.) Mich. Law. Rev.

Woodbine, G: E. Four thirteenth century law tracts. $1.20 net. Yale Univ.

See also Accidents;—Actions at law;—Admiralty;—Advertising;—Apartments;—Arbitration (International);—Attorneys;—Automobiles;—Banks and banking;—Bankruptcy;—Benefit societies;—Bonds;—Boycotting;—Building laws;—Business;—Capital punishment;—Carriers;—Chancery;—Children;—Church of England;—Civil law;—Coal;—Commerce;—Commercial law;—Conspiracy;—Constitutional law;—Constitutions;—Consuls;—Contracts;—Conveyancing;—Copyright;—Corporations;—Courts;—Courts martial;—Criminal law;—Damages;—Debts;—Detectives;—Divorce;—Domestic relations;—Drainage;—Elections;—Engineering;—Equity;—Evidence;—Executors and administrators;—Factories;—Family;—Farms and farming;—Fish and fishing;—Food;—Food adulteration;—Forests and forestry;—Forgery;—Forms (*in law*);—Game laws;—Guarantees and sureties;—Habeas corpus;—Harvard University Law School;—History;—Hygiene;—Immigration;—Injunctions;—Insurance;—Interest;—International law;—Inventions;—Irrigation;—Jews;—Judges;—Jury;—Justices of the peace;—Juvenile courts;—Labor and laboring classes;—Land;—Landlord and tenant;—Lawyers;—Liquors;—Magistrates;—Marriage;—Mechanics' liens;—Medical jurisprudenc;—Mercantile law;—Mines and mining;—Money;—Mortgages;—Naturalization;—Negligence;—Negotiable instruments;—Negroes;—Notaries;—Nuisance;—Parliamentary law;—Partnership;—Patents;—Periodicals;—Personal property;—Pharmacy;

— Pleading and practice; — Police; — Poor; — Principal and agent; — Prison; — Property;—Public utilities;—Railroads;—Real property;—Receivers; — Roads; — Sales;—Schools;—Servants; — Speculation; — Slavery;—Stenography;—Stocks;—Supervisors; —Taxation;—Telephone;—Temperance;—Titles; — Torts;—Town officers; — Trade-marks;—Trade-unions;—Trespass;—Trials;—Trusts;—Trusts and trustees;—Villages; — Visigothic code; — Water-rights;—Wills;—Woman;—*also* Douglas, Stephen Arnold; — Hayes-Tilden contest; — Lincoln, Abraham; — Maitland, Frederick William; — *also* Litchfield Co., Ct.;—Massachusetts Bay;—*also* National reporter ser.;—*also* names of states.

Law and custom of the constitution. Anson, *Sir* W: R. In 3 v. v. 1, *$3.40 net; v. 2, pt. 1, $3.40; pt. 2, $2.90. Oxford Univ.

Law and love. Boyd, F. L. *90 c. net. Longmans.

Law and the prophets. Westphal, A. $2.75 net. Macmillan.

Law in the light of the gospel. Kaiser, P. 85 c. Germ. Lit. Bd.

Law Latin. Jackson, E. H. $1.50. Byrne.

Law of Christian healing. Fitzgerald, D: B. *75 c. net. Revell

Law of Christian marriage. Stone, D. 10 c. Longmans.

Law of church and grave. Scanlan, C: M. $1.35. Benziger.

Law of liberty. Granger, I. P. 20 c. I. P. Granger.

Law of love. St. Morris, C: $1.50. C. M. Clark.

LAW OF NATIONS.
See **International law.**

LAW OF PERSONS.
See Domestic relations.

Law of prayer. Ostrom, H: 50 c. Praise Pub.

Law of success. Cushing, J: J. $1. Jenckes.

Law of the range. Barrows, W. G. $1.50. C. M. Clark.

Law of the rhythmic breath. Fletcher, A. E. *$1 net. Fenno.

Law of the white circle. Jacobs, T. $1.25. Taylor-T.

Law of transformation in nature of natural bodies. Mortensen, A. C. 50 c. A. C. Mortensen.

Law Reporting Company. Insurance enactments of 1907. 3d ed. '08(Je6) Q. $10. Law Reporting.

LAW STAMPS.
See **Indiana;—Ohio;—Pennsylvania.**

Lawis, Rev. J: F.
Life of our Lord; chronologically arr. '09, [1910.] (F) 16°, 30 c.; leath., 60 c. Dutton.

Lawler, O'Dermid W.
East London visions. '10(Ap2) D. $1.75 net. Longmans.

Lawless wealth. Russell, C: E: $1.50. B. W. Dodge.

Lawlessness. Eliot, C: W: 10 c. Civic Forum.

LAWN TENNIS.
See Tennis.

LAWNS.
Thornburn, J. M., & Co. Seeding and preservation of golf links. (Add. pubs. for price.) J. M. Thorburn.

Lawrance, Marion.
Working manual of a successful Sunday school. '08(Je27) c. 12°, pap., *25 c. net. Revell.

See also Schauffler, Adolphus F:

Lawrence, Albert Lathrop.
Travels of Phœbe Ann. '09(Ap3) il. 12°, $1.50. C. M. Clark.

The Wolverine. '08(My.) c. 12°. (Popular ed. of recent fiction.) †75 c. Little, B. & Co.

Lawrence, C. E.
Much ado about something. '09(D11) D. *$2.40 net. Scribner.

Lawrence, E. A., comp.
First reader intended for those who are beginning the study of Esperanto. '09 (Ap24) c. 16°, *25 c. net. Revell.

Lawrence, Sir Edn. Durning-.
See Durning-Lawrence, *Sir* Edn.

Lawrence, Edn. Gordon.
Power of speech and how to acquire it. '09 (D11) c. D. $1.25. Hinds.

Lawrence, H: Carter.
Making him buy: the selling end of it. '10(S3) c. 12°, $2. Consol. Pub.

Making him pay; exemplifying the evolution of conciliation; [debt collecting.] '08 (D) c. 19-271 p. 12°, $2. Consol. Pub.

"Lawrence, Hope," [pseud. for Amelia Grant Schwarz.]
Letter of hope; with a preface by Rev. Elwood Worcester. '08(N7) c. front. D. **50 c. net. Moffat.

Light beyond the shadows; with a foreword by A. C. Hall, D.D. '09(S4) c. bds., *50 c. net. Moffat.

Lawrence, J:
Hist. of the Grand Army of the Republic and New Brunswick's representation in the civil war. '09(D) 8 p. il. 8°. (Not for sale.) Times Pub. Co.

Lawrence, Rev. J: B:
Power for service; introd. by Rev. B. H. Carroll. '09(Jl) c. 14+261 p. 12°, $1.15. C: O. Chalmers.

Lawrence, Jos. B.
Accidents and emergencies. [1910.] (Mr) *75 c. net. W: R. Jenkins.
Formerly published by E. R. Pelton.

Lawrence, R: Hoe, comp.
Catalogue of the engravings issued by the Society of Iconophiles of the City of New York, MDCCCXCIV-MCMVIII; with an introd. by W: Loring Andrews. '09(Jl10) il. 4°. (Priv. pr.) R: H. Lawrence.

Lawrence, Rob. Means, M.D.
Primitive psychotherapy and quackery. '10 (D17) c. O. $2 net. Houghton M.

Lawrence, Sir T:
Sir Thomas Lawrence, the English portrait painter; with an introd. by R. S. Clouston. '08(Ja18) il. 8°, (Newnes' art lib.) bds., *$1.25 net. Warne.

LAWRENCE, *Sir* Thomas.
Bensusan, S: L. Lawrence. $1.50 net. Stokes.

Clouston, R. S. Sir Thomas Lawrence. *$1.25 net. Warne.

Lawrence, T: Jos.
Principles of international law. 4th ed., rev. and rewritten. '10(D17) c. 8°, $3 net. Heath.

Lawrence, W: H:
Principles of architectural perspective. 3d ed., rev. '08(D12) diagrs., 8°. (Add. pubs. for price.) W: B. Clarke.
See also Everett, Herbert E:

LAWRENCE EXPERIMENT STATION.
See Sewage and sewerage.

LAWRENCE FAMILY.
Gibbon, F. P. Lawrences of the Punjaub. *$1.50 net. Dutton.

Laws, Clarence R.
Manual for the collection of commercial paper. '08(S19) c. O. pap., 50 c. C. R. Laws.

Laws, Romulus Don.
"Hot stuph; or, *The Yellow Jacket* boiled down." '09(Je5) c. il. por. O. $1.50. Yellow Jacket.

Laws, Wallace.
Life of a tramp; not a work of fiction, but true incidents. '10(Mr5) c. il. por. 12°, 25 c. Donohue.

Laws of auction bridge; as adopted by the Whist Club; also the etiquette of the game. '10(Jl30) 24°, 50 c. Whist Club.

Laws of friendship. King, H: C. *$1.25 net. Macmillan.

Laws of health. Bryce, A. $2 net. Lippincott.

Laws of heredity. Reid, G: A. O. $5.50 net. Macmillan.

Laws of the inner kingdom. Clark, H: W. *$1.25 net. Revell.

Laws of the King; or, talks on the Commandments, by a religious of the Society of the Holy Child Jesus. '10(Je18) c. il. S. 60 c. Benziger.

Lawson, J. Kerr.
See Goff, *Mrs.* Rob.

Lawson, J: C.
Modern Greek folklore and ancient Greek religion; study in survivals. '10(Ap23) 12°, $4 net. Putnam.

Lawson, Lady Kate.
Highways of Japan. '10(D24) 8°, $3.75 net. Stokes.

Lawson, Publius Virgilius.
Invention of the roller flour mill. '08(Je20) por. 8°, pap., 25 c. State Hist., Wis.
Paper-making in Wisconsin; [from the proceedings of the State Historical Society of Wisconsin for 1909.] '10(Ap2) il. O. pap. State Hist., Wis.

LAWSON, Thomas William.
King, C. F. Light of four candles; [concerning a legal fight with T. W. Lawson.] $1.50. C. F. King.

Lawson, X.
Sydney Carrington's contumacy. '08(Ag1) c. 12°, $1.25. Pustet.

Lawton, F:
Balzac. '10(D17) il. pors. O. $4 net. Wessels & B.
François-Auguste Rodin. '08(D12) il. pors. 16°, *$1 net. M. Kennerley.
Third French Republic. '09(Ap17) il. O. *$3.50 net. Lippincott.

Lawton, Wilbur.
Boy aviators in Africa; or, an aerial ivory trail. '10(O8) c. front. D. (Boy aviators ser.) 50 c. Hurst.
Boy aviators in Nicaragua; or, in league with the insurgents. '10(Ap9) c. 12°, (Boy aviators ser.) 35 c. Hurst.
Boy aviators in record flight; or, the rival aeroplane. '10(O8) c. front. D. (Boy aviators ser.) 50 c. Hurst.
Boy aviators on secret service. '10(Ag20) c. il. 12°, (Boy aviators ser.) 50 c. Hurst.
Boy aviators' polar dash; or, facing death in the Antarctic. '10(D) c. il. 12°, (Boy aviators ser.) 35 c. Hurst.
Boy aviators' treasure quest; or, the golden galleon. '10(O8) c. front. D. (Boy aviators ser.) 50 c. Hurst.

Lawyer's brief on the atonement. Morgan, C: C. 75 c. C: C. Morgan.

Lawyer's guide. Crane, H. S., *comp.* $1. F. T. Riley.

LAWYERS.
American Adjusters Co. Directory of reliable lawyers and banks in the U. S. and Canada. 1908; 1910. ea., $5.50. **Am. Adjusters.**
Archer, G. L. Ethical obligations of the lawyer. $3 net. Little, B. & Co.
Bailey, H. R. Attorneys and their admission to the bar of Mass. $2.50. W: J. Nagel.
Banks' New York state lawyers' diary for 1908; 1909; 1910. ea., $2. Banks & Co.
Bender's national lawyers' diary and directory for the state of New York, 1908; 1909; 1910. ea., $2. M. Bender.
Benton, J. H: Lawyers' official oath and office. $1.50. Boston Bk.
Brooks, U. R. South Carolina bench and bar. v. 1. *$1.50 net. State Co.
California and Nevada. Attorneys' and bankers' directory, 1908-09. $2. C. A. Murdock.
Chicago law directory, 1910. $1. Gritman.
Cope, E: A., *and* Robins, H. W. H. Solicitor's office organization, management and accounts. $2. Pitman.
Coxe, R. D. Legal Philadelphia. $2. W. J. Campbell.
Gould, W: R. Greater New York and state lawyers' diary for 1908; 1909; 1910. ea., $1. W: R. Gould.
Haight, C: S., *and* Marsh, A. M. Questions and answers for bar-examination review. $4. Baker, V. & Co.
Hubbell, J: H:, *ed.* Legal directory. 1909, 1910. ea., $5. Hubbell.
Jacobs, J., *and* Appleborne, L: New York bar examination, questions and answers. $4. Banks.
Lewis, W: D., *ed.* Great American lawyers. In 8 v. (Add. pubs. for price.) Winston.
Martindale, J. B. Am. law directory, (annual,) 1908, 1909. subs., ea., $15.50. Martindale.
Massachusetts lawyers' diary for 1910. $1.50; $2.50; $2. Standard Diary.
New Jersey lawyers' diary and bar directory, 1908; 1909; 1910. ea., $1.50. Soney.

LAWYERS.—*Continued.*
Putney, A. H. Bar examination review. $4. Ill. Bk.
Sharp & Alleman Co.'s lawyers' and bankers' directory for 1908. Jan. ed.—July ed.; for 1909. Jan. ed.—July ed.; for 1910. Jan. ed.—July ed.; for 1911, Jan ed. ea., $5. Sharp & A.
Smyth, P. G., *comp.* Told out of court. $1. P. G. Smyth.
Torrey, G: A. Lawyer's recollections in and out of court. $1.50 net. Little, B. & Co.
Zimmerling, C: B., *comp.* Directory of members of Philadelphia bar. gratis. Guarantee.
See also names of places and states.

Lawyers' list; selected list of general practitioners, corporation and trial lawyers of the United States of America, [etc.] '08 (Ag15); '09(Je); '10(Je) c. D. ea., $3.25; $5.25; $10.25. H. R. Brown.

Lawyers' reports annot. New ser., book 11; Burdett A. Rich, H: P. Farnham, eds., 1908. '08(F); bk. 12 (Ap); bk. 13 (Je); bk. 14 (Ag); bk. 15 (N); bk. 16. '08, [1909.] (Ja); bk. 17 (Mr); bk. 18 (Je); bk. 19 (Ag); bk. 20 (O); bk. 21 (N); bk. 22. '10(F); bk. 23 (Mr); bk. 24 (Je); bk. 25 (Ag); bk. 26 (O); bk. 27, 28 (D) c. O. shp., ea., $4. (Sold only in sets.)—Digest; new ser., bk. 12. '08(Je); bks. 13-18; with full index to annots. '09(Jl) c. Q. ea., $2.—Digest; new ser. vs. 1-24, with full index. (Jl), $4.—Index; new ser. vs. 19-23 (Mr) c. O. pap. Lawyers' Co-op.

Lay, W: August.
Age to come; brief review of "The age that was," "The age that is," and "The age to come"; together with comprehensive and elaborate chart embracing the periods from "Paradise lost to Paradise restored." '09, [1910.] (F) 52 p. chart, 8°, 25 c. W: A. Lay.

Lay of the land. Sharp, D. L. **$1.25 net. Houghton M.

Layard, Arth.
Harriet Hare. '08(Ag8) il. T. (Dumpy books for children.) bds., 50 c. Stokes.

Layard, G: Somes.
Suppressed plates: wood engravings, etc. '08(Ja25) il. 8°, *$4 net. Macmillan.

Lays of a lazy dog. Stevens, D. K. 50 c. J: W. Luce.

Lays of ancient Rome. *See* Macaulay, T: B., *Lord.*

Lays of the Grays. Parker, B. $1.50. **Stokes.**

Layton, Katherine Alberta W.
Nibelungen of Wagner. '10(Mr5) c. O. (Univ. of Ill. bull., University studies.) pap., 75 c. Univ. of Ill.

Lazare, Jules, ed.
Les plus jolis contes de fées; ed., with vocab. '08(F1) S. (Internat. modern lang. ser.) 35 c. Ginn.

Lazarillo de Tormes. *See* Mendoza, Diego Hurtado de.

Lazarovich-Hrebelianovich, Prince and Princess Eleanor Hulda Calhoun.
Servian people; their past glory and their destiny. 2 v. '10(N5) c. il. map, O. $5 net, boxed. Scribner.

Lazell, F: J:
Isaiah as a nature-lover. '10(D10) c. front. 16°, (Torch ser.) 60 c. Torch Press.
Some spring days in Iowa. '08, [1909.] c. 69 p. 8°, $1.50. Torch Press.
Some summer days in Iowa. '10(Ja8) c. il. 8°, $1.50. Torch Press.

Lazell, Herschel Bouton, rep.
See Michigan. *Supreme ct.* Repts.

Lazy John. Steedman, C: $1.50. Jacobs.

Lea, F: C:
Hydraulics. '08(Mr14) il. O. *$4.25 net. Longmans.

Lea, H: C:
Inquisition in the Spanish dependencies: Sicily, Naples, Sardinia, Milan, the Canaries, Mexico, Peru, New Granada. '08 (F8) c. O. **$2.50 net. Macmillan.

LEA, Henry Charles.
Baumgarten, P. M. Henry Charles Lea's historical writings. *90 c. net. Wagner.

Lea, General Homer.
Valor of ignorance; with specially prepared maps. '09(N6) c. por. O. **$1.80 net. Harper.
Vermillion pencil: a romance of China. '08 (Mr21) c. front. D. †$1.50. McClure.

Lea, Ja. H:, and Hutchinson, J. R.
Ancestry of Abraham Lincoln. '09(Mr6) c. il. pors. facsims., tabs., map, Q. hf. leath., $10, boxed. Houghton, M.

Lea, J:
Mr. Whistler and the Wimples. '09(S) col. il. Q. (Wimple ser.) bds., 35 c. Stokes.
Romance of bird life. '08(N7) il. D. (Romance ser.) *$1.50 net. Lippincott.
Uncle Wisdom's parlor tour. '10(D) col. il. 4°, bds., $1. Stokes.
Wimple children. '09(S) col. il. Q. (Wimple ser.) bds., $1. Stokes.
Winnie Wimple and ragged robin. '09(S) col. il. Q. (Wimple ser.) bds., 35 c. Stokes.
See also Coupin, Henri Eugène Victor.

Lea, S: Hill.
Irrigation in South Dakota. '09(Je) 60 p. map, 8°, (U. S., Dept. of Agriculture; Office of Experiment Stations bull.) pap.

Leach, Albert Ernest.
Food inspection and analysis; for the use of public analysts, health officers, sanitary chemists, and food economists. 2d ed., rev. and enl. '09(D11) c. tabs., 8°, $7.50. Wiley.

Leach, Arth. Fs.
Milton as a schoolboy and schoolmaster; from the Proceedings of the British Academy. v. 3. '09(Ap3) O. pap., 40 c. Oxford Univ.

Leach, Josiah Granville, ed.
Some account of the Tree family and its connections in England and America. '08 (My9) c. il. pors. 8°. [priv. pr.] Lippincott.

Leacock, Stephen Butler.
Literary lapses. '10(D10) D. $1.25 net. Lane.

LEAD.
Betts, A. G. Lead refining by electrolysis. $4 Wiley.
Buckley, E. R. Geology of the disseminated lead deposits of St. Francois and Washington counties, [Mo.] (Add. pubs. for price.) H. Stephens.
Hixon, H. W. Notes on lead and copper smelting. $3. Hill Pub.
Ingalls, W. R. Lead and zinc in the United States. *$4 net. Hill Pub.
Weaver, L. English lead work. $10 net. Scribner.
See also Paints;—Solder.

Lead glazed pottery. Barber, E. A. pt. 1. **90 c. net. Doubleday, P.

Lead of honour. Richardson, N. $1.50. L. C. Page.

Leadbetter, Florence Eugénie.
Outlines and studies to accompany Meyers' General history; students' notebook. [1910.] c. '08. 6+66 p. 8°, 35 c. Ginn.

Leaders in respiratory organs. Nash, E. B. $1.50. Boericke & T.

Leaders of socialism. Taylor, G. R. S. $1 net. Duffield.

Leaders of the English Pre-Raphaelites: Holman Hunt, Rossetti and Millais; ed. by T. Leman Hare. '09(O) 235 p. col. il. O. *$2 net. **Stokes.**

LEADERSHIP.
Brent, C: H: Leadership. **$1.25 net. Longmans.
Knox, G: H. Leadership. $1.40; $2.80. Personal Help.
Mumford, E. Origins of leadership. *50 c. net. Univ. of Chic.

Leadership of Shakespeare. Davenport, A. 10 c. A. Davenport.

Leading American essayists. Payne, W: M. $1.75 net. Holt.

Leading American men of science. Jordan, D: S. $1.75 net. Holt.

Leading American novelists. Erskine, J: $1.75 net. Holt.

Leading facts of history ser. il. D. Ginn.
—Montgomery. Leading facts of American hist. $1.

LEADVILLE, Colo.
United States. *Dept. of the Interior. U. S. Geolcg. Survey.* Pleistocene geology of the Leadville quadrangle. 30 c.

LEADWORK.
See Lead.

Leaf and tendril. Burroughs, J: **$1.10 net. Houghton M.

Leaflets. Snow, L. $1.25. B'way Pub.

League of American Municipalities. Book of American municipalities. '08(N) $2; '09 (D18) $3.50; '10(Ap16) pors. 4°, pap., $3.50. League Am. Municipalities.

League of Library Commissions. Small library buildings: a collection of plans; introd and notes by Cornelia Marvin. '08 (N21) il. plans, 8°, $1.25. A. L. A.

League of the Signet Ring. Du Bois, M. C. $[illegible]0. Century Co.

Leahy, E.
Hiawatha's black-robe. '10(Jl) 4+135 p. front. 12°, 35 c. net. Herder.

Leahy, G: Vincent, ["Catholicus."]
Astronomical essays. '10(Je) 9+274 p. 12°, $1. G: V. Leahy.

Leahy's hotel guide of America; cont. a complete list of hotels in all the principal cities of the United States and Canada. Rev. ed., no. 13. '09(O) c. 43 p. f°, $1. Am. Hotel.

Leale, C: A:
Lincoln's last hours; [address del. before the commandery of the state of New York, Military Order of the Loyal Legion of the United States, at the regular meeting, Feb., 1909, city of New York, in observance of the 100th anniversary of the birth of President Abraham Lincoln.] '09(N) c. 16 p. 8°. (Add. author for price.) C: A: Leale.

Lear, E:
Book of limericks. New ed. '08(S19) c. 12°, $1.50. Little, B. & Co.
Letters to Chichester Fortesque, Lord Carlingford and Frances, Countess Waldegrave; ed. by Lady Strachey. '08(O17) il. por. 12°, *$3.50 net. Duffield.

Learmount, Rev. Ja.
In God's orchard; being courses of talks to the young folk. '09(D4) D. *$1 net. Eaton & M.

Learned, Marion Dexter.
Abraham Lincoln; American migration; family English not German. '09(D18) c. il. por. facsim., map, O. *$3 net. W: J. Campbell.
Life of Francis Daniel Pastorius, the founder of Germantown, [Pa.;] with an appreciation of Pastorius by S: Whitaker Pennypacker. '08(N7) il. 8°, *$5 net. W: J. Campbell.

LEARNED SOCIETIES.
Handbook of learned societies and institutions: America. $4. Carnegie.

Learning by doing ser. 4°. Ellis Pub.
—Ellis Publishing Co. Students' guide to accompany the Ellis cabinet system of teaching bookkeeping and business practice. $1.50.

Learning process. Coursault, J. H. ***$1 net. Teachers' Coll.**

Leary, Eleanor Gertrude.
See Jones. Olive M.

Lea's ser. of medical epitomes. 12°. Lea.
—Child. Epitome of gynecology. *$1 net.

Leathem, J: Gaston.
Elem. theory of the symmetrical optical instrument. '08(N7) 8°, (Cambridge tracts in mathematics and mathematical physics.) pap., *75 c. net. Putnam.

LEATHER.
Bennett, H. G. Manufacture of leather. $4.50 net. Van Nostrand.
Flemming, L: A. Pract. tanning. $6 net. Baird.
Leland, C. G. Leather work. *$1.50 net. Macmillan.
National Association of Tanners. Free hide text book. (Add. pubs. for price.) Nat. Assoc. Tanners.

LEATHER.—*Continued.*
Procter, H: R. Leather industries laboratory book of analytical and experimental methods. $7.50. Spon.
Roycroft leather-book. 10 c. Roycrofters.
Trotman, S. R. Leather trades chemistry. *$4.50 net. Lippincott.
Wilson, W. H. Leather work. $1. M. B. Willcox.

Leather bound ser. of medical manuals. il. 12°, leath. Blakiston.
—Greene. Medical diagnosis. $3.50.

Leathersmith lib.; favorite authors bound in hand-tooled leath; embossed title medallions. 16 v. '10(N) 16°, ea., $1.50 net. Dodge.
Titles: Barrack-room ballads; Borrowings; Courtship of Miles Standish; Evangeline; Favorite poems; For friendship's sake; Emerson's Friendship; Love; Self-reliance; Compensation; More borrowings; Irving's Old Christmas; Pippa passes; Rubaiyat; Shakespeare's Sonnets; Sesame and lilies.

Leatherstocking tales. *See* Cooper, Ja. Fenimore.

Leathes, J: Beresford.
The fats. '10(O1) O. (Monographs on biochemistry.) bds., $1.25 net. Longmans.

Leathes, Stanley Mordaunt, ed.
See Acton, J: E. E: D.-A., *Lord.*

Leaven of love. Burnham, *Mrs.* C. L. R. †$1.50. Houghton M.

Leavens, G: D.
Discussion of methods for determining the availability of phosphoric acid in Thomas phosphate powder (basic slag phosphate). '09(N20) c. il. tabs., O. pap. (Add. pubs. for price.) Coe-M.
Remarkable fertilizer: Thomas phosphate powder (basic slag phosphate) and its uses. '09(O9) c. D. pap. (Add. pubs. for price.) Coe-M.

Leaves from a life. Panton, *Mrs.* J. E. *$3.50 net. Brentano's.

Leaves from a Madeira garden. Thomas-Stanford, C: $1.50. Lane.

Leaves from my historical scrapbook. Elzas, B. A. $1. B. A. Elzas.

Leaves from the note book. Nevill, *Lady.* D. F. W. *$3.75 net. Macmillan.

Leaves of grass. *See* Whitman, Walt.

Leaves of gold. *See* Bruce, Wallace.

Leaves of life. Lyle, S: H., *jr.* $1.25. McGregor Co.

Leaves of truth. Meakin, J: P. $1.50. J: P. Meakin.

Leavitt, Ezekiel.
Songs of grief and gladness and "Deborah"; with appreciation of Leavitt by Gotthard Deutsch and foreword; tr. by Alice Stone Blackwell. '07, [1908.] (Mr.) c. 2+76 p. por. 12°. (Add. pubs. for price.) Modern View.

Leavitt, J: McDowell, D.D.
Bible League essays in Bible defence and exposition. '09(Ja23) c. D. $1. Bible League.
Our flag, our rose and our country; with other poems. '09(Ja23) c. D. $1.50. Bible League.

Leavitt, Sheldon.
"As ye will": [mental healing.] '08(Mr.) c. 235 p. il. por. 8°, 1.50. Magnum Bonum.
Better part, in metre. '10(F19) c. il. 8°, $2.50. Magnum Bonum.
Paths to the heights. '08(Ap25) c. D. **$1 net. Crowell.
Psychic solution of the problem of cure. '08(O10) c. il. 12°, $3. Magnum Bonum.

LEBANON, Ct.
See Indian Charity School.

LEBANON COUNTY, Pa.
Croll, P. C. Lebanon County imprints and bibliography. 25 c. P. C. Croll.

Lebanon County Historical Society papers. 8°. C. P. Croll.
—Croll. Lebanon County imprints. 25 c.

Leblanc, Maurice.
Arsene Lupin, gentleman burglar. '10 (Je18) 12°, 75 c.; pap., 25 c. J. S. Ogilvie.
Arsène Lupin versus Herlock Sholmes; tr. from the French by G: Morehead. '10 (F26) c. 12°, (Extraordinary adventures of Arsène Lupin.) 25 c. Donohue.
Arsene Lupin versus Sherlock Holmes. '10 (Je18) 12°, 75 c.; pap., 25 c. J. S. Ogilvie.
813; tr. by Alex. Teixeira de Mattos. '10 (D17) c. 12°, $1.20. Doubleday, P.
Extraordinary adventures of Arsène Lupin, gentleman-burglar; tr. from the French by G: Morehead. '10(F26) c. 12°, 25 c. Donohue.
Extraordinary adventures of Arsene Lupin, gentleman burglar; preface by Jules Claretie; tr. by Olive Harper. '10(Jl2) c. 12°, 75 c. J. S. Ogilvie.
Hollow needle; further adventures of Arsène Lupin; tr. by Alexander Teixeira de Mattos. '10(O8) c. il. D. $1.20, fixed. Doubleday, P.
See also Jepson, Edg.

Le Blond, Eliz. Alice Frances Hawkins-Whitshed, [Mrs. Aubrey Le Blond.]
Mountaineering in the land of the midnight sun. '08(O3) il. map, O. *$3.50 net. Lippincott.

Le Bon, Gustave, M.D.
Blonde lady; being a record of the duel of wits between Arsène Lupin and the English detective; tr. by Alex. Teixeira de Mattos. '10(My14) c. il. front. 12°, 50 c. Doubleday, P.
The crowd; study of the popular mind. '10 (Je4) 12°, $1.50 net. Macmillan.
Evolution of forces. '08(D5) il. 12°, (International scientific ser.) *$1.75 net. Appleton.

LE BRUN, Marie Anne Elizabeth Vigée.
Macfall, H. Vigée Le Brun. *65 c. net. Stokes.

Le Burke, Montmorency Hill.
The she-devil; romance of the Spanish-American war. '10(N) 7-357 p. 12°, $1.50. C. E. Apgar.

Leckey, Phoebe Fabian.
Beckoning heights. '08(Ap18) c. il. D. $1.50. Neale.

Leckie, Rev. J. H.
Authority in religion. '10(Mr26) O. *$2 net. Scribner.

Lecky, Elisabeth van Dedem, [Mrs. W: E: Hartpole Lecky.]
Memoir of the Right Hon. William Edward Hartpole Lecky, M.P., O.M., LL.D., D.C.L., Litt.D. '09(N13) c. pors. D. **$2.50 net. Longmans.

Lecky, Squire Thornton Stratford.
Wrinkles in practical navigation. 15th ed., rev. and enl. by W: Allington. '08(Ag1) 8°, *$8 net. Van Nostrand.

Lecky, W: E: Hartpole.
Historical and political essays. '08(O31) O. *$3.50 net; New ed. '10(N12) D. $1.60 net. Longmans.
Old-age pensions; reprinted from *The Forum.* '08(Ag22) 8°, pap., 25 c. Longmans.

LECKY, William Edward Hartpole.
Lecky, E. Van D. Memoir of the Right Hon. William Edward Hartpole Lecky. *$2.50 net. Longmans.

Lecky, Mrs. W: E: Hartpole.
See Lecky, Elisabeth van Dedem.

Le Clerc, J. Arth., and Wahl, Rob.
Chemical studies of American barleys and malts. '09(Je) 75 p. front. 8°, (U. S., Dept. of Agriculture; Bu. of Chemistry bull.) pap., 20 c. U. S., Supt. of Docs.

Leconte de Lisle, Charles Marie René.
Orestes: drama in 2 pts; adapted by Andre Tridon and A. Guiterman. '09(N) 35 p. pap., 50 c. A. Tridon.

Lectionary. Baudot, J. $1 net. Herder.
Lecturas escogidas, colleción de obras de autores eminentes. Fernãndez, J. M., *comp.* 90 c. Silver.
Lecture on diseases of children. Hutchinson, R. *$2.40 net. Longmans.
Lectures et conversations. Dubois. 75 c. W: R. Jenkins.
Lectures faciles. Bruce, M: S. 60 c. Heath.
Lectures on hysteria. Saville, T: D. *$2.50 net. Wood.
Lectures on the English poets. Hazlitt, W: 50 c.; 75 c. Dutton.

LECTURING.
Lewis, A. M. Art of lecturing. 25 c. Kerr.

Ledford, Preston Lafayette.
Reminiscences of the civil war, 1861-1865. '09(N) c. 104 p. 32°, 25 c. News Pr. Ho.

Ledos de Beaufort, Raphaël.
Franz Liszt, the story of his life; to which are added Franz Liszt in Rome, by Nadine Helbig, list of the composer's chief works, summary of his compositions, and a list of his noted pupils. '10(N19) c. pors. D. $1.25. Ditson.

Ledoux, L: Vernon.
Yzdra; a tragedy. '09(O16) c. D. **$1.25 net. Putnam.

Leduc, Stephen.
Electric ions and their use in medicine; tr. by R. W. Mackenna; with an appendix by the translator. '09(Mr) 80 p. *$1 net. Hoeber.

"Lee," pseud.
Clare Loraine; or, little leaves from a little life. '10(My7) c. D. 85 c. Benziger.

Lee, Mrs. Agnes.
Border of the lake; [poems.] '10(S10) c. D. $1 net. Sherman, F.

Lee, Albert.
Pie and the pirate. '10(Mr12) c. il. 16°, 50 c. Collier.

Lee, Albert Sherman.
Hist. of West Virginia; the facts condensed. '10(Ap) 31 p. 8°, 20 c. A. S. Lee.
Ten weeks in arithmetic. '09, [1910.] (F) c. 3-255 p. il. 12°, (Condensed ser.) $1. A. S. Lee.
Ten weeks in English grammar. '08(Mr) c. 137 p. por. 12°, 65 c. A. S. Lee.

Lee, Alice Louise.
Freshman co-ed. '10(D3) c. il. D. $1.25. Penn Pub. Co.

Lee, Edn.
Text-book of experimental chemistry. '08 c. il. tabs., O. *$1.50 net. Blakiston.

Lee, Eliz. Batts.
Talks on successful gowning. '10(Ap) c. 205 p. por. 12°, $1.50. E. B. Lee.

Lee, Ernest Markham.
Grieg. '08(M21) il. por. 16°, (Bell's miniature ser. of musicians.) 50 c.; leath., $1. Macmillan.
Story of opera. '10(Je4) il. pors. 12°, (Music story ser.) $1.25 net. Scribner.

Lee, Fs. Bazley, ed.
Genealogical and memorial hist. of the state of New Jersey. 4 v. '10(N19) c. il. pors. 4°, $25. Lewis Pub.
Genealogical and personal memorial of Mercer County, New Jersey. '07, [1908.] (My.) c. 2 v. 432; 433-916 p. il. pors. 8°, $18. Lewis Pub.

Lee, Rev. Fk. T.
Sidelights on the Bible. '08(O3) c. il. O. **$1 net. Winston.

Lee, Frederic Schiller.
Physiology. '08(F29) c. 8°, pap., 25 c. Macmillan.

Lee, G: Taylor.
Virginia feud: story of a mountain lassie. '08(F15) c. D. $1.50. Neale.

Lee, Gerald Stanley.
Inspired millionaires. '08(Je27) c. D. $1.25. Mt. Tom Press.

Lee, Mrs. Gerald Stanley.
See Lee, Jennette.

Lee, Guy Carleton, and others, eds.
World's orations. In 10 v. '08(F29) price reduced from $3.50 to $1.50. Putnam.

Lee, Holme.
Legends from Fairy Land; narrating the history of Prince Glee and Princess Trill, the cruel persecutions and condign punishment of Aunt Spite; introd. by Effie H. Freemantle. '08(N7) il. D. $1.50. Lippincott.

Lee, Ivy Ledbetter.
Railroad valuation. '07, [1908.] (Jl.) 8°, pap. (Not for sale.) Bankers Pub.
—, comp. "Uncle Remus"; Joel Chandler Harris as seen and remembered by a few of his friends; incl. a memorial sermon by the Rev. Ja. W. Lee, and a poem by Fk. L. Stanton. '09(F13) c. il. pors. facsims., 4°. (Priv. pr.) I. L. Lee.

Lee, Jennette, [Mrs. Gerald Stanley Lee, formerly Jennette Barbour Perry.]
Happy Island; new "Uncle William" story. '10(Je4) c. col. front. D. $1. Century Co.
Simeon Tetlow's shadow. '09(Mr6) c. D. †$1.50. Century Co.

LEE, Jesse.
Meredith, W: H: Jesse Lee, a Methodist apostle. *25 c. net. Eaton & M.

Lee, J: T:
Bibliography of Carver's travels; [from the proceedings of the State Historical Society of Wisconsin for 1909.] '10(Ap9) il. O. pap., 35 c. State Hist., Wis.

Lee, Lawrence H., rep.
See Alabama. *Sup. ct.* Repts.

Lee, Marion Beveridge.
Barselma's kiss. '08(D) 332 p. il. 12°, $1.50. C. M. Clark.

LEE, *General* Robert Edward.
Arkansas. *Dept. Pub. Instruction.* Suggestive program for the schools of Arkansas for use in celebration of Robert E. Lee day, Jan. 9th. gratis. Arkansas Dept. Pub. Instruct.
Darling, J. T. Cold facts; the pen of Col. Lee writes the indictment against the sword of General Lee. $1.50 per 100 copies. J. T. Darling.
Page, T: N. Robert E. Lee. *$1.25 net. Scribner.

Lee, Sidney Lazarus.
French Renaissance in England: acct. of the literary relations of England and France in the sixteenth century. '10 (N12) O. $2.50 net. Scribner.
Life of William Shakespeare. New and rev. ed., with a new preface. '09(My1) c. il. facsims., D. **$2.25 net. Macmillan.
—, **ed.** Play of King Leir and his three daughters. '09(S11) front. 16°, (Shakespeare lib.: Shakespeare classics.) bds., *$1 net; Persian, **$1.60 net; Lib. ed., *$1.70 net. Duffield.
See also Stephen, *Sir* Leslie, *ed.*

Lee, Mrs. Susan Richmond.
See Yorke, Curtis, *pseud.*

Lee, Vernon, [pseud. for Violet Paget.]
Works. Uniform set. In 8 v. '08(Je27) 12°, *$12 net. Lane.
Althea; dialogues on aspirations and duties. New ed. '10(Ap30) D. $1.50 net. Lane.
Countess of Albany. [2d ed.] '09(O30) pors. D. *$1.50 net. Lane.
Laurus nobilis; chapters on art and life. '09(O30) 12°, *$1.50 net. Lane.
Renaissance fancies and studies. [2d ed.] '09(O23) D. *$1.50 net. Lane.
Studies of the eighteenth century in Italy. 2d ed., with a new preface. '08(O17) il. O. *$6 net. McClurg.
Vanitas; polite stories, incl. hitherto unpublished story entitled A frivolous conversion. '10(O22) D. $1.50 net. Lane.

Lee, W: H:, and Hansey, Jennie A., comps.
Standard domestic science cook book. '08 (S26) c. O. washable keratol ed., $1.75; in tray, $1.90; leath., $2.50, boxed. Laird.

Lee-Hamilton, Eugene.
Mimma Bella; sonnet sequence written on the death of a little child. '09(O16) $1.25. Duffield.
Mimma Bella; in memory of a little life. '09(D) sq. 16°, pap., *75 c. net; Japan vellum, *$1.50 net. T: B. Mosher.

Leech, S:
Thirty years from home; or, a voice from the main deck; being the experience of Samuel Leech, who was for six years in the British and American navies. '10 (Je11) front. 8°, $3.25. Abbatt.

LEECH, Samuel.
Maclay, E. S. Youthful man-o'-warsman; from the diary of an English lad who served in the British frigate "Macedonian." $1.50. Navy Blue.

Leech, Rev. S: Vanderlip.
Raid of John Brown at Harper's Ferry as I saw it. '09, [1910.] (F) 24 p. por. 8°, 40 c. S: V. Leech.

Leechman, D.
Making of a motor car. '08(Ag1) il. 12°, 50 c. Spon.

Leeder, S. H.
Desert gateway: Biskra and thereabouts. '10(D31) 8°, $1.75 net. Cassell.

Leedham-Green, C:, M.D.
Treatment of gonorrhœa in the male. 2d ed. '08(Je27) il 8°, *$2 net. Wood.

Leeds, C: Carley.
Mechanical drawing for trade schools. High-school ed. '08(Ag1) c. diagrs., obl. 4°, (Carnegie Technical Schools text books.) **$1.25 net. Van Nostrand.
Mechanical drawing for trade schools. Machinery trades ed. '09(My15) c. diagrs., 4°, (Carnegie Technical Schools text books.) *$2 net. Van Nostrand.

Leeds, Fk. H:, and Butterfield, W. J. Atkinson.
Acetylene: principles of its generation and use; pract. hdbk. on the production, purification, and subsequent treatment of acetylene for the development of light, heat and power. 2d ed. '10(Ap9) 12°, $2.75 net. Lippincott.

LEEDS, England.
Price, A. C. Leeds and its neighborhood. 90 c. Oxford Univ.

Lees, Dorothy Neville.
Tuscan feasts and Tuscan friends. '08 (Ap11) il. 8°, *$1.75 net. Dodd.

Lees, Frederic.
Summer in Touraine. '09(My15) il. map, O. *$2.75 net. McClurg.

Lees, Rev. G: Robinson.
Life and adventure beyond Jordan. '09 (D11) c. il. 12°, **$1.75 net. Appleton.
Witness of the wilderness, the Bedawin of the desert: their origin, history, home life, strife, religion, and superstitions in their relation to the Bible. '09(F27) il. D. $1.25. Longmans.

Lees, Rev. Harrington C.
Joy of Bible study. '09(Mr6) D. (Anglican Church handbooks.) *40 c. net. Longmans.

Lees, Ja.
Complete guide to the game of draughts. 9th ed.; with improvements of play by J. Richards. '09(Je19) il. S. 50 c. Warne.

Lees, Rob. Ja.
Through the mists. '09(S) 385 p. 12°, (Psychic lib.) bds., $1.50. Badger.

Leete, F: De Land, D.D.
Every-day evangelism; personal, trained, co-operative. '09(Ap3) c. D. *$1 net. Jennings.

LEEWARD ISLANDS, Caribbean Sea.
Cory, C: B. Birds of the Leeward Islands. 50 c. Field Museum.

Le Feuvre, Amy.
"His birthday"; Christmas sketch. '09 (D11) D. bds., *35 c. net. Armstrong.

Le Fevre, Fk. Stiles.
"Hammed," a tale of the crusades; arr. from the memoirs of a warrior-monk. '08(O) c. 314 p. 8°, $1.50. Belgravia.

Lefferts, Marshall Clifford.
Alexander Pope; notes toward a bibliography of early editions of his writings; catalogue of Marshall C. Lefferts's great collection of first and later editions of the works of Alexander Pope, with the autograph manuscript of "An essay on man." '10(My21) facsims., O. bds., $2.50; pap., without facsims., gratis. Dodd.

Lefferts, Sara Tawney.
Christmas letter. '08(O3) il. 4°, (One family ser.) pap., 60 c. Cupples & L.
Pansy wedding. '09(S) 85 p. il. 16°, 60 c. Cupples & L.
Patriotic jubilee. '10(D) il. 4°, (One family ser.) pap., 60 c. Cupples & L.

Leffingwell, Albert, M.D.
American meat; its methods of production and influence on public health. '10 (My14) 12°, $1.25 net. T. E. Schulte.
Vivisection question. 2d ed. '09(F20) 8°, o. p. S. R. Taber.

Leffmann, H:, M.D.
About Dickens: essays on a few themes suggested by the novels. '08(D5) 16°, *50 c. net. H: Leffmann.
Consolidation of Philadelphia; written for the City History Society of Philadelphia and presented at the meeting of Jan. 9, 1907. '08. [1909.] (N) 25-40 p. il. map, 4°, (Publications of the City History Society of Philadelphia.) pap., 25 c. (Sold to members only.) City Hist. Phil.
Examination of water for sanitary and technic purposes, by chemical and bacteriological methods. 6th ed., rev. and enl. '09(F20) c. il. 12°, $1.25. Blakiston.
Notes on the secret service of the revolutionary army operating around Philadelphia; written for the City History of Phil. and read at the meeting of Jan. 12, 1910. '10(Je) 165-173 p. facsim. Q. (City History Soc. of Phil. pubs.) pap., 25 c. (to members only). City Hist. Phil.
Philadelphia celebrations. '09(D) 65-82 p. (City Hist. Society of Philadelphia pub.) 25 c. (Sold to members only.) City Hist., Phil.

Left hand autograph book. Moulder, M., *comp.* *50 c. net. Stokes.

LEFTHANDEDNESS.
See Hand.

Leftwick, Ralph Winnington, M.D.
Index of symptoms; with diagnostic methods. 4th ed. [1910.] (Je) 12°, $2.25 net. Wood.

Legacy of a man who wanted to do his duty. "Theocratus," *pseud.* pt. 1. 50 c. Corona Pub.

Legacy to mankind. Fish, U. [priv. pr.] Univ. Press, (Camb.)

LEGAL ADVERTISING.
See Law.

Legal and commercial transactions dated in the Assyrian, Neo-Babylonian and Persian periods. Clay, A. T. $6. Univ. of Penn.

Legal and historical status of the Dred Scott decision. Ewing, E. W: R. $3. Cobden.

Legal aphorisms. Friend, J: W. $5. Whittet.

Legal development in colonial Massachusetts. Hilkey, C: J. $1.25. Longmans.

LEGAL DIRECTORIES.
See Lawyers.

Legal education in the United States. Wilgus, H. L. (Not for sale.) Mich. Law Rev.

LEGAL FORMS.
See Forms (*in law*).

Legal medicine. Emerson, R. L. $5. Appleton.

Legal medicine. Stewart, G. H. $5. Bobbs-M.

Legal phases of the Lincoln and Douglas debates. Fish, D. (Priv. pr.) D. Fish.

Legal secretary. Moore, W: V. $3. Boger.

Legal status of rural high schools in the United States. Snyder, E. R. $1.50. Teachers' Coll.

Legalized outlaw. Artman, S: R. $1. Business Men's.

Le Gallienne, R:
Attitudes and avowals. '10(O29) c. D. $1.50 net. Lane.
Love-letters of the king; or, the life romantic. '08(My.) c. 12°, (Popular ed. of recent fiction.) †75 c. Little, B. & Co.
October vagabonds. '10(D17) c. il. 12°, bds., $1.50 net. M. Kennerley.
Omar repentant: [poem.] '08(Jl18) c. hf. cl., *75 c. net. M. Kennerley.
New poems. '09(O16) D. *$1.50 net. Lane.
Orestes; a tragedy. '10(My7) 12°, $1 net. M. Kennerley.
Painted shadows. '08(My.) c. 12°, (Popular ed. of recent fiction.) †75 c. Little, B. & Co.
Retrospective reviews; literary log. 2 v. '10(D17) 12°, $3.50 net. Lane.

Legend of Bethlehem. Smith, D: 50 c. Doran.

Legend of Jerusalem. Smith, D: 50 c. net. Doran.

Legend of Montrose. *See* Scott, *Sir* Wa.

Legend of Sainte Cariberte des Oies. Hall, G. $3. Badger.

Legend of Sleepy Hollow. *See* Irving, Washington.

Legend of the Holy Fina, Virgin of Santo Gimignano; now first tr. from the trecento Italian of Fra Giovanni di Coppo; with introd. and notes by M. Mansfield. '08 (O24) 12°, (New mediæval lib.) pigskin, *$2.50 net. Duffield.

Legendary ballads. Sidgwick, F., *ed.* *$2 net. Stokes.

LEGENDS.

Aucassin and Nicolette, and 15 other mediæval romances and legends. 35 c. net; 70 c. net. Dutton.

Becquer, G. A. D. Romantic legends of Spain. **$1.50 net. Crowell.

Brailsford, E: J. Spiritual sense in sacred legends. $1.25 net. Eaton & M.

Brooks, E: Wonder stories from the Mabinogions. †$1.25. Penn Pub. Co.

Campbell, L. E. Age of gold; being a collection of northland tales, song, sketch and narrative. *$1.25 net. Whitaker & R.

Carus, P. Bride of Christ: a study in Christian legend lore. *75 c. net. Open Court.

Converse, *Mrs.* H. M. C. Myths and legends of the New York State Iroquois. 75 c.; 50 c. N. Y. State Educ.

Conwell, R. H. He goeth before you. 50 c. F. M. Barton.

Frary, M. H., *and* Stebbins, C: M. Crystal palace, and other legends. 60 c. Stebbins.

Ginzberg, L. Legends of the Jews. In 4 v. v. 1, 2. ea., $2. Jewish Pub.

Herbertson, A. G. Heroic legends: [St. George and the dragon, Robin Hood, etc.] $2. Caldwell.

Islandica. v. 3, Bibliog. of the sagas of the kings of Norway and related sagas and tales. $1 net. Cornell Univ.

Jaffray, R. Two knights of the swan. $1.25 net. Putnam.

Janvier, T: A., *comp.* Legends of the City of Mexico. **$1.30 net. Harper.

Klugh, M. C. Tales from the Far North [Scandinavian countries]. 60 c. Flanagan.

Legend of the Holy Fina, Virgin of Santo Gimignano. *$2.50 net. Duffield.

Morris, W: Story of Sigurd the Volsung. 50 c. Longmans.

Rich, O. V. Prophecy of Yah-Ma-Sun; [Indian legend.] 50 c. A. Harriman.

Sheldock, M. L. Collection of Eastern stories and legends. 50 c. net. Dutton.

Stoddard, F. J. As old as the moon: Cuban legends. **$1 net. Doubleday, P.

Tegnér, E. Frithiof's saga. *$2 net. Engberg-H.; E. B. Shaw.

See also Ballads; — Fables; — Fairy tales;—Folklore;—Italy; — Mary, *Virgin;* — Mythology; — New England;—Nibelungenlied.

Legends from Fairy Land. Lee, H. $1.50. Lippincott.

Legends of the Alhambra. *See* Irving, Washington.

Legends, tales and poems. Becquer, G. A. D. $1. Ginn.

Leger, Raymond Alfr.
See McDonald, Raymond, *pseud.*

Legg, J. Wickham.
Popular use of the Athanasian creed. '10 (F5) D. *60 c. net; pap., *40 c. net. Longmans.

Legge, E:
Empress Eugenie, 1870-1910; Her Majesty's life since "The Terrible Year," together with the statement of her case; the Emperor's own story of Sedan; account of his exile and last days, and reminiscences of the Prince Imperial from authentic sources. '10(Jl2) il. facsim., 8°, $2 net. Scribner.

Legge, Ronald.
The "Hawk": story of aerial war. '09 (My15) c. D. $1.50. J: McBride.

LEGISLATION.
See Law;—Political science;—*also* names of places, states and countries;—*also* for legislation on special subject, *see* name of subject.

Legislative reference bull. 8°. **R. I. State Lib.**

—Sherwood. Summary of the general banking laws of the commercial states. gratis.

Legislative reminiscences. MacIntyre, W: I. 25 c. W: I. MacIntyre.

Legislature of the province of Virginia. Miller, E. I. *$2 net; *$1.50 net. Lemcke.

Legler, E: Eduard.
Books for the people. '08(My9) 16°, pap., gratis. H: E. Legler.

Legler-Hawkins, Flora.
See Hawkins, Flora Legler-.

Legouvé, Gabriel Jean Baptiste Ernest Wilfred.
See Scribe, Augustin Eugène.

LEGUMES.
Warren, J. A. Notes on the number and distribution of native legumes in Nebraska and Kansas. (Add. Superintendent for price.) U. S., Supt. of Docs.
See also Beans.

Lehman, F: Martin.
The white slave hell, or, with Christ at midnight in slums of Chicago; slum data furnished by Rev. N. K. Clarkson. '10 (S) c. 7+9-418 p. il. pors. 12°, $1.50. Chr. Witness.

Lehman, H: Harvey.
Poultry doctor: treatise on poultry diseases; written in plain language for the farmer and poultry raiser. '09(D) c. 96 p. il. por. 12°, 75 c. H: H. Lehman.

Lehmann, F: W:
Abraham Lincoln: addresses at Memorial Hall, Chicago, Feb. 12, 1908. '09(Ap10) 16°, pap., 25 c. Umbdenstock-F-P.

Lehmann, J: Alb.
Diary of verse and philosophy. [1910.] (Je) c. 24 p. 8°, 50 c. J: A. Lehmann.

Lehmann, Rudolph Chambers.
Complete oarsman. '08(D19) il. 8°, *$3 net. Jacobs.

Memories of half a century. '09(My) (Add. pubs. for price.) Scribner.

Lehmer, Derrick Norman.
Factor tables for the first ten millions; cont. the smallest factor of every number not divisible by 2, 3, 5 or 7 between the limits of 0 and 10017000. '10(Ap2) obl. F. hf. leath., $20. Carnegie.

Leibnitz, Gottfried Wilhelm von.
Philosophical works; tr. from the orig. Latin and French, with notes by G: Martin Duncan. 2d ed. '08(Ap4) 8°, $2.50. Tuttle, M. & T.

LEICESTER, Mass.
See Second Congregational Church.

Leidel, E: F.
See Poetsch, C: J.

Leidigh, Arth. H.
See Ball, Carleton Roy.

Leiding, Harriette Kershaw.
"Street cries of an old southern city"; with music and illustrations. '10(Ap) c. 12 p. 8°, 25 c. H. K. Leiding.

Leigh, Florence.
Mac; his book: story of a Scotch terrier. '08(O3) il. Q. $1.50. Stokes.

Leighter, H. Clough-.
See Clough-Leighter, H.

LEIGHTON, Frederic, *Lord*, of Stretton.
Baldry, A. L. Leighton. *65 c. net. Stokes.

Leighton, G: Arth.
Harmony; text book. '10(D17) c. fold. chart, 8°, $1.25. Willis Music.

Leighton, Gerald, M.D.
Scientific Christianity; study of the biology of character. '10(O1) D. $1.25 net. Moffat.

Leighton, Marshall Ora, ed.
Surface water supply of the United States, 1907-8. pt. 1, North Atlantic coast, by H. K. Barrows and R. H. Bolster; pt. 2, South Atlantic coast and eastern Gulf of Mexico; pt. 3, Ohio River basin, by A. H. Horton, M. R. Hall and R. H. Bolster; pt. 4, St. Lawrence River basin, by H. K. Barrows, A. H. Horton and R. H. Bolster; pt. 5, Upper Mississippi River and Hudson Bay basins, by A. H. Horton, E. F. Chandler and R. H. Bolster; pt. 6, Missouri River basin, by Rob. Follansbee and J. E. Stewart. '10(S); pt. 7, Lower Mississippi basin, by W: B. Freeman and others. (D); pt. 8, Western Gulf of Mexico, by W. B. Freeman, W. A. Lamb and R. H. Bolster; pt. 9, Colorado River basin, by W. B. Freeman and R. H. Bolster; pt. 10, The Great Basin, by E. C. La Rue, and others. (D); pt. 11, California, by W. B. Clapp and W. F. Martin (N); pt. 12, North Pacific Coast, by J. C. Stevens and F. F. Henshaw. '10 (Jl) O. (U. S., Dept. of the Interior, U. S. Geolog. Survey; water-supply paper.) pap., pt. 1, 5 c.; pt. 3, 20 c.; pt. 4, 20 c.; pt. 5, 15 c.; pt. 6, 30 c.; pt. 7, 15 c.; pt. 8, 20 c.; pt. 9, 25 c.; pt. 10, 15 c.; pt. 11, 30 c.; pt. 12, 35 c. Gov. Pr. Off.

Leighton, Rob.
"Coo-ee." '10(D31) il. 12°, $1. Lippincott.
Dogs and all about them. '10(Je4) il. D. $1.50 net. Cassell.
Kiddie of the camp. '10(D31) il. 12°, $1. Lippincott.

Leighton, Archbp. Rob.
Rules and instructions for a holy life and prayers and meditations; selected and ed., with an introd., by the Rev. Ja. Dinwoodie and a pref. note by the Rt. Rev. H. C. G. Moule, D.D. '10(F5) S. *60 c. net. Longmans.

LEIPZIG, Germany.
See University of Leipzig.

LEIPZIG CAMPAIGN.
Maude, *Col.* F. N. Leipzig campaign. *$1.60 net. Macmillan.

Leiser, Jos.
Canaway and the Lustigs. '09(S11) c. il. D. $1. Young Israels.

Leisure moments. Maclean, S. $1. B'way Pub.

Leitch, B. M.
Mariposa grove of big trees, California. '10 (My) c. 32 p. il. 4°, 50 c. B. M. Leitch.

Leith, C: Kenneth.
See Hobbs, W: Herbert.—Van Hise, G: R:

Leith, Mrs. Disney.
Iceland. '08(O10) il. map, 12°, (Peeps at many lands ser.) *75 c. net. Macmillan.

Leith, W. Compton.
Apologia diffidentis. '08(M7) 8°, *$2.50 net. Lane.

Leith, W: Forbes.
Memoirs of Scottish Catholics during the XVIIth and XVIIIth centuries; selected from hitherto inedited mss. In 2 v. v. 1, The reign of King Charles I., 1627-1649; v. 2, From the Commonwealth to emancipation, 1674-1793. '09(O2) il. O. *$7 net. Longmans.

Lejars, Félix.
Urgent surgery; tr. from the 6th French ed. by W: S. Dickie. In 2 v. v. 1. '09 (D); v. 2. '10(S) il. 8°, per set, $14 net; hf. mor., $16 net. Wood.

Leland, Arth. and Lorna Higbee.
Plans and specifications for playground construction and playground apparatus. '10(F5) c. il. 8°, 25 c. Bassette.
—, eds. Playground technique and playcraft. v. 1. '10(Mr19) c. il. plans, O. $2.50. Bassette.

Leland, C: Godfrey.
Leather work. 3d ed. '08(O24) il. *$1.50 net. Macmillan.
Mystic will. '08(D) 119 p. 50 c. Progress Co.

Leland, Claude G., Dickey, Helene Louise McRae, Anna Mont, and others.
Library and the school. '10(Ja29) front. D. 50 c. Harper.

Leland, J:
Itinerary, 1535-1543; with an appendix of extracts from Leland's Collectanea; ed. by Lucy Toulmin Smith. v. 2, cont. pts. 4 and 5. '08(Mr7); v. 4; cont. pts. 7 and 8. '09(Ap3) map, 8°, ea., *$4 net. Macmillan.
For v. 3, Itinerary in Wales, see Am. Catalog, 1905-07.

Leland, Lorna Higbee.
See Leland, Arth.

Leland, S: Phelps.
World making: scientific explanation of the birth, growth and death of worlds. 17th ed., enl. and rev. '06, [1910.] c. '98, 166 p. il. D. 75 c. S: P. Leland.

Leland. Waldo Gifford.
See Van Tyne, Claude Halstead.

Leland, Wa. S.
Boiler accessories. '08(N21) c. il. 8°, (American School of Correspondence pubs.) $1. Am. Sch. Corr.
Steam turbines. '10(Jl30) c. il. 8°, (Amer. School of Correspondence pubs.) $1.50. Am. Sch. Corr.

Leland Stanford Junior University pubs. See Stanford (Leland) Junior University pubs.

Lelen, Rev. Jos. Mary.
Towards the altar; papers on vocations to the priesthood. '10(Jl) c. 125 p. 16°, 15 c. Herder.
Towards the eternal priesthood; treatise on the divine call, comp. from approved sources. '10(Jl) c. 115 p. 16°, 15 c. Herder.
"List of books for seminarians' spiritual reading" (1 p.).

Lely, J. M., ed.
See Best, W. M.

Lemaître, Jules.
Contes extraits de Myrrha; ed., with notes and vocab., by E. Riville-Rensch. '08 (O3) (Modern lang. ser.) 30 c. Heath.

Lémann, —.
Jesus before the Sanhedrim; tr. from the French by Julius Magath. 7th ed. '10 (Mr26) S. 50 c. J. Magath.

Lemme, Ludwig.
Do we need Christ for communion with God? '08(Mr14) c. S. (Foreign religious ser.) *40 c. net. Eaton & M.

LEMON.
Powell, G: H., *and* Chace, E: M. Italian lemons. (Add. Superintendent for price.) U. S., Supt. of Docs.
True, R. H., *and* Severs, A. F. Some factors affecting the keeping qualities of American lemons. (Add. Superintendent for price.) U. S., Supt. of Docs.

Le Moyne, L: Valcoulon.
Country residences in Europe and America. c. il. F. $7.50. Doubleday, P.

Lena, Pedro Rodríguez de.
Libro del passo honroso defendido por el Excelente Cauallero Suero de Quiñones. [facsim.] '02, [1909.] (N) 139 p. 8°, $6.50. (200 copies.) Hispanic Soc.

LENCLOS, Anne (called Ninon de).
Rowsell, M. C. Ninon de l'Enclos and her century. $3.75 net. Brentano's.

Lenington, Norman Gallileo.
Seven principles of successful salesmanship. '08(S19) c. S. (Commercial science ser.) $1. Commercial Sci.

LENJE LANGUAGE.
See Rhodesia, So. Africa.

Lenk, Heinrich von.
Marie Antoinette's youth; tr. from the German by G: P. Upton. '08(S19) c. il. S. (Life stories for young people.) *60 c. net. McClurg.

Lennard, Vivian R.
Passiontide and Easter: (sermons.) '09 (F20) 12°, 80 c. Whittaker.

Lennawood's monologues. Wood, L. $1. Holliswood.

Lennen, Philip W.
How to double the day's work; how to systematize yourself and your desk: managing your work to-day—planning your work of to-morrow—handling your routine and correspondence—saving time and multiplying results. 5th rev. ed. '09 (D) c. 128 p. il. 12°, with sub. to *System*, $2. System.

Lennes, Nels Johann.
See Slaught, Herbert Ellsworth.

Lennox, Patrick Jos.
Early printing in Ireland; [repr. from the *Catholic University Bulletin*.] '09(Ag) 233-248+380-399 p. 8°. (Add. pubs. for price.) Cath. Univ.

Lenora. Martin, W. D. 75 c. Pub. Ho. of M. E. Ch., So.

Lenotre, G., pseud.
See Gosselin, Louis Léon Théodore.

LENOX, William.
See American Revolution.

LENSES.
Nutting, P. G. Resolving power of objectives. Gov. Pr. Off.

Lent, Evangeline M.
Jolly ghost: pantomimed song; words and pantomime by Evangeline M. Lent; music by Frances M. Slater. '09(Ag7) c. il. F. pap., *$1 net. Werner.

LENT.
Abbott, E. H. What they did with themselves: [lenten readings.] **30 c. net. Crowell.
Behold the Lamb of God: Lententide sermons. 85 c. Germ. Lit. Bd.
Gretchen, *pseud.*, *comp.* At the feet of Jesus: [prayers and texts for Lent.] *25 c. net. Hills & H.
Hughes, H. G. Jesus Christ and human life; course of Lenten sermons. 40 c. net. Wagner.
McGowan, F. X. Two series of lenten sermons. 75 c. Pustet.
Snyder, A. W. Through the forty days. *$1 net. Whittaker.
Williams, J. H. Village sermons for Lent. *80 c. net. Whittaker.
See also Easter;—Good Friday;—Holy week.

Lentala of the south seas. Morrow, W: C. †$1.50. Stokes.

Lenygon, Francis.
Decoration and furniture of English mansions during the seventeenth and eighteenth centuries. '09(D11) il. F. *$1 net. Scribner.

Leon, Luis de.
Exposicion del Miserere. [facsim.] '03, [1909.] (N) no paging, 4°, $3. (200 copies.) Hispanic Soc.

LEON, Spain.
Calvert, A. F: Leon, Burgos and Salamanca. *$1.25 net. Lane.

LEONARD, *St.*
Da Masserano, G. M. Life of St. Leonard of Port Maurice. $1.50. Kilner.

Léonard, [Léonard Autié.]
Recollections of Léonard, hairdresser to Queen Marie-Antoinette; tr. by E. Jules Méras. '10(Ja1) c. pors. D. (Court ser. of French memoirs.) *$1.50 net. Sturgis & W.

Leonard, Adna Wright.
Roman Catholic Church at the fountain head, in the light of the Fairbanks-Roosevelt-Vatican incidents. '10(D17) c. 12°, 15 c. Jennings.

Leonard, Arth. Newton.
See Ham, Roscoe Ja.

Leonard, Fk. H.
Christian Science: demonstrable religion; a lecture. '09(Ja16) c. 16°, pap., 6 c. Chr. Sci.

LEONARD, James Francis.
Townsend, J: W. Life of James Francis Leonard, the first practical sound-reader of the Morse alphabet. $4. Morton.

Leonard, J: W.
Hist. of the city of New York, 1609-1909. '10(D31) c. il. pors. Q. $15. Journal of Commerce.
Who's who in Pennsylvania. '09(Jl) 596 p. 8°, $5. Hamersly.

Leonard, Josiah Sloan, ["Dranoel."]
Some experiences and meditations of a jack-ass. '09(Je) c. 46 p. 8°, $1.25. Metropolitan Press, (Ore.)

Leonard, Mary Hall.
Grammar and its reasons. '08(Ap25) c. D. *$1.50 net. Barnes.
Moral training in public schools. '08 (Ag15) c. 12°, (Monographs on education.) pap., 25 c. Palmer.

Leonard, R. M., comp.
See Pageant of English poetry.

Leonard, Rob. Josselyn.
Manual of cardboard construction. '08 (Mr) c. 32 p. il. 8°. (Add. pubs. for price.) Bd. of Educ., Berkeley, (Cal.)

Leonard, W: Ellery Channing.
Byron and Byronism in America. '08(F1) 8°, (Columbia Univ. studies in English.) pap., *$1 net. Lemcke.
Poet of Galilee. '10(Ja8) c. D. bds., *$1 net. B: W. Huebsch.

Leonard, W: S:
Machine shop tools and methods. 5th ed., rev. and enl. '08(Ap25) c. figs., 8°, $4. Wiley.

Leonora. Rumsey, F. $1.50. Appleton.

Leonore Stubbs. Walford, *Mrs.* L. B. C. $1.50. Longmans.

Leopard and the lily. Bowen, M., *pseud.* $1.25, fixed. Doubleday, P.

LEOPOLD, *King of the Belgians.*
Rappoport, A. S. Leopold the Second, King of the Belgians. $3 net. Sturgis & W.

Lepelletier, Edmond Adolphe de Bouhelier.
Life of Paul Verlaine. '09(O16) il. 8°, **$3.50 net. Duffield.

Lepers of Molokai. Stoddard, C: W. 75 c. Ave Maria.

LEPIDOCYRTUS.
See **Moths.**

Lepin, Rev. Marius.
Christ and the Gospel; or, Jesus the Messiah and Son of God. '10(D17) c. 8°, $2. McVey.

LEPROSY.
Currie, D. H. Second International Conference on Leprosy. (Add. Superintendent for price.) U. S., Supt. of Docs.

LEPROSY.—*Continued.*
United States. Studies upon leprosy. 6 nos. '08, [1909.] (D) il. 8°. (Add. Superintendent for price.) U. S., Supt. of Docs.

LEPTOMEDUSAE.
See Jellyfish.

Le Queux, W:
The closed book. '08(Ap11) c. 12°, (Popular priced copyrights.) 50 c. B. W. Dodge.
Great god gold. '10(O15) c. D. $1.50. Badger.
House of whispers. '10(S10) D. $1.50. Brentano's
Lady in the car. '08(Je27) D. †$1.50. Lippincott.
Pauper of Park Lane. '08(Je20) c. D. 75 c. Cupples & L.

Le Rossignol, Ja. E:
Little stories of Quebec. '08(D26) c. D. *$1.25 net. Jennings.

—, and Stewart, W: Downie.
State Socialism in New Zealand. '10(D3) c. map, D. $1.50 net. Crowell.
Taxation in New Zealand. '10(Jl30) 8°, (Univ. of Neb. studies.) 75 c. Univ. of Neb.

Leroux, Gaston.
Double life. '10(Ja1) c. D. $1.50. Kearney.
Mystery of the yellow room. '08(Jl4) c. front. D. †$1.50. Brentano's.
Perfume of the lady in black. '09(Mr27) c. D. †$1.50. Brentano's.

Le Roux de Lincy, Adrien Jean Victor.
Researches concerning Jean Grolier, his life and his library, with a partial catalogue of his books; ed. by Baron Roger Portalis; tr. and rev. by Carolyn Shipman. '08(F1) c. pls. 4°, pap. (Add. Club for price.) Grolier Club.

Leroy, L:
Essentials of histology; arr. with questions following each chapter. 4th ed., rev. and enl. '09(O) 11-284 p. il. 12°, (Saunders' question-compends.) *$1 net. Saunders.

Le Sage, Alain René.
Adventures of Gil Blas de Santillane. In 2 v. '10(Ap23) 16°, (Everyman's lib.) ea., 35 c. net; leath., 70 c. net. Dutton.
Adventures of Gil Blas de Santillana; tr. by Tobias Smollett; with an introd. and notes by Ja. Fitzmaurice Kelly. Pocket ed. '08(My16) 2 v., por. S. (World's classics.) ea., 40 c. Oxford Univ.

Lesdain, Count de.
From Pekin to Sikkim through the Ordos, the Gobi desert, and Tibet. '08(Ag15) il. maps, 8°, $4. Dutton.

LESLEY, J. Peter.
Ames, *Mrs.* M. L., *ed.* Life and letters of Peter and Susan Lesley. 2 v. Putnam.

LESLEY, Susan.
See **Lesley, J. Peter.**

Leslie Stephen lecture. *See* Stephen (Leslie) lecture.

LESPINASSE, Julie Jeanne Eléonore de.
Jebb, C. Star of the salons: Julie de Lespinasse. *$3.50 net. Putnam.

Less than kin. Miller, *Mrs.* A. D. †$1.25. Holt.

"Lessing, Bruno," pseud.
See Block, Rudolph Edgar.

Lessing, Gotthold Ephraim.
Minna von Barnhelm; oder, das soldatenglück; ein lustspiel in fünf aufzügen; ed., with introd. notes and vocab., by Josef Wiehr. '10(Jl30) c. (Oxford German ser.) 60 c. Oxford Univ.
Minna von Barnhelm; odor, soldatengluck; ed., with introd. and notes, by Otto Heller; vocab. and exercises by Ernest L. Wolf. '09(N) 293 p. D. (Lake German classics.) 50 c. Scott, F. & Co.

Lesson in marriage. Björnson, B. 50 c. net. Brandu's.
Lessons for Methodists. Vaughan, D: D. $1. Jennings.
Lessons in living. Towne, *Mrs.* E. J. $1. E. J. Towne.
Lessons in truth. Cady, H. E. $1; 50 c. Unity Tr.
Lessons of the financial crisis. American Academy of Political and Social Science. $1. Am. Acad. Pol. Sci.

Lester, C: C., rep.
See New York [State.] *Cts. of record.* Misc. repts.

Lester, Katherine Morris.
Clay work. '09(F6) c. il. D. $1.25. Manual Arts.

Lester, Oliver Clarence.
Integrals of mechanics. '09(Je26) c. figs. O. 80 c Ginn.

Let me feel your pulse. Henry, O., *pseud.* 50 c. Doubleday, P.
Let the nation arise. Theodul, C. $1. Balance.
Let the roof fall in. Danby, F., *pseud.* $1.50. Appleton.

LETCHWORTH PARK.
See **New York State.**

Lethaby, W: R:
Greek buildings represented by fragments in the British Museum. '09(Ap3) figs. O. *$4.20 net. Scribner.

Letitia. Macfarlane, C: A. $1.50. C. M. Clark.

LE TOURNEUR, Pierre.
Cushing, M. G. Pierre Le Tourneur. **$1.50 net. Lemcke.

Letson, S: Brisbin.
Christian Science as it is; an analysis. '10(O) c. no paging, O. pap., 25 c.; leath., 50 c. S: B. Letson.

Letter of hope. Laurence, H. **50 c. net. Moffat.

LETTER-WRITING.
Atkins, G: S. Business getters. 75 c. Cochrane.
Bannon, A. Letter writing and model letters. 50 c. Bardeen.
Marohnic, J. English-Croatian letter-writer. $1. J. Marohnic.
Villiers, A. Complete letter-writer for ladies and gentlemen. 50 c. net. Dutton.
See also **Commercial correspondence; — Letters (Correspondence); —Penmanship;—Rhetoric;— Stenography.**

LETTERING.
American School of Correspondence. Architectural drawing and lettering. $1. Am. Sch. Corr.

LETTERING.—*Continued.*
Bergling, J: M. Art monograms and lettering. In 3 v. ea., $1.50; v. 1 and 2, $3; 3 vs. in same cover, $4.25. J: M. Bergling.
French, T: E., *and* Meiklejohn, R. Essentials of lettering. $1. Varsity Supply.
Hackes, S., *comp.* Fairchild's rapid letterer and show-card maker. $2. Fairchild Co.
Heyny, W: Modern lettering, artistic and pract. $2. W: T. Comstock.
Johnston, E: Manuscript and inscription letters. *$1.25 net. Macmillan.
Lyons, A. W. Grammar of lettering. *$2.50 net. Lippincott.
Meinhardt, T: F. Practical lettering for beginners, draughtsmen, architects, [etc.] 60 c. Stechert.
Smith, P. J. Lettering and writing. $1.50. Scribner.
Thompson, W: A. Druggist and dispensers practical show card instructor. $1. W: A. Thompson.
See also **Alphabets.**

LETTERS (Correspondence).
Campbell, J: D. S., *Duke* of Argyll, *ed.* Intimate society letters of the eighteenth century. $10. Lane.
Dawson, W: J. *and* Coningsby W: Great English letter writers. In 14 v. v. 1, 2. ea., *$1 net. Revell.
Dickins, L., *and* Stanton, M., *eds.* An eighteenth-century correspondence; letters of Dean Swift, Pitt, etc. $3.50 net. Duffield.
Ingpen, A. M., *comp. and ed.* Women as letter-writers. $1.25 net. Baker & T.
Lampson, *Mrs.* G. L., *comp. and ed.* Quaker post-bag; letters to Sir John Rodes of Barlbrough Hall in the county of Derby, Baronet. $2.50 net. Longmans.
Lucas, E: V. Second post. $1.25; $1.75 net. Macmillan.
Record of letters. 75 c. Reilly & B.
Strachey, L., *ed.* Love letters of famous royalties and commanders. *$2.50 net. J: McBride.

Letters from a settlement. Hodson, A. L. $1.50. Longmans.
Letters from a workingman. Stelzle, C: *$1 net. Revell.
Letters from across the sea. Finney, F: M. (Priv. pr.) F: N. Finney.
Letters from an ocean tramp. McFee, W: *$1.50 net. Cassell.
Letters from China. Conger, S. P. *$2.75 net. McClurg.
Letters from Colonial children. Tappan, E. M. $1.50. Houghton M.
Letters from France and Italy. Guthrie, A. *$1.25 net. McClurg.
Letters from G. G. Hall, G. $1.25. Holt.
Letters from high latitudes. Dufferin, F: T. B., *Lord.* 35 c. net; 70 c. net. Dutton.
Letters from India. Stratton, W: A. *$3.50 net. Dutton.
Letters from Labrador. Durgin, G: F. gratis. Rumford Pr.
Letters from Malabar. Bruce, H: *$2 net. Dutton.
Letters from Queer Street. Abbott, J. H. M. *$1.75 net. Macmillan.

Letters from the teacher (of the Order of the 15). Curtiss, F. H., *ed.* $1.10. Curtiss.
Letters of a Dakota divorcee. Burr, J. $1. Roxburgh.
Letters of a Japanese schoolboy. Irwin, W. A. †$1.50. Doubleday, P.
Letters of Alcuin. Page, R. B. $1; 50 c. Forest Press.
Letters of an apostate Mormon to his son. Freece, H. P. 50 c. H. P. Freece.
Letters of Jennie Allen to her friend Miss Musgrove. Donworth, G. †$1.50. Small.
Letters of Junius. *See* **Pownall, Thomas.**
Letters of Mildred's mother to Mildred. Price, E. D. 25 c. J. S. Ogilvie.
Letters on the greatness and simplicity of the Christian faith. King, H: C. *75 c. net. Pilgrim Press.
Letters patent of Elizabeth and James the First, addressed to the university. Clark, J: W., *ed.* 75 c. Putnam.
Letters that collect; or, how to get money by mail; ser. of collection letters used in actual business practice. '10(N19) c. 8°, $1. Modern Mercantile.
Letters to a business girl. Saunders, F. W. 25 c.; $1.25. Laird.
Letters to a college girl. Hayes, E. 60 c. E. Hayes.
Letters to a neurologist. Collins, J. *$1 net. Wood.
Letters to a salmon fisher's sons. Chaytor, A. H: $3 net. Houghton M.
Letters to Cassite kings. Radau, H., *ed. and tr.* $6. Univ. of Penn.
Letters to His Holiness Pope Pius x, by a Modernist. '10(My14) c. por. D. $1.25. Open Court.
Letters to my son. '10(Je4) c. D. $1 net. Houghton M.
Letters to salesmen. '10(F26) c. 12°, $1. Col. Tool Steel.
Letters to Sanchia. Hewlett, M. H: 90 c. net. Scribner.
Letters to *The Times* upon war and neutrality. Holland, T: E. *$1.75 net. Longmans.
Lettres de mon moulin. *See* Daudet, Alphonse.
Letts, Mrs. Albina Marilla Brockway.
By grandsire's well, and other poems. '09 (S) c. 5-123 p. por. 12°, $1. Kellogg-B.
Letts, W. M.
Diana dethroned. '09(Je26) D. $1.50. Lane.
Letty and the twins. Griffith, H. S. 60 c. Penn Pub. Co.
Letty Lane paper family. Young, S. $1. Jacobs.
Leuba, Ja. H.
Psychological origin and nature of religion. '09(O23) 8°. (Religious ancient and modern.) *40 c. net. Open Court.
Leupp, Fs. Ellington.
The Indian and his problem. '10(Ap2) c. O. $2 net. Scribner.
Leutner, Winifred G:
Article in Theocritus. '08(S5) 8°, pap., gratis. Johns Hopkins.
LEUVENIA.
***See* Botany.**

LEVANT (*The*).
***See* Orient.**
Level plan for church union. Brown, W: M. $1.50 net. Whittaker.
Leveller (The). McArthur, A. $1.50. Doscher.
Levels of living. Cope, H: F: *$1 net. Revell.
Lever, C: Ja.
Works. De luxe ed. 4 v. '10(D) 16°, ea., mor., $1.50 net. (Sets only.) Nelson.
Levering, Julia Henderson.
Historic Indiana. '09(Mr6) c. il. pors. map, O. **$2.50 net. Putnam.
Leverton, Waldemar.
Little entertainments and how to manage them. '10(O) 12°, 50 c. Fenno.
Levey, J:
Refrigeration memoranda; collection of useful information relating to ice making and refrigerating. '08(N21) flexible leath., 75 c. Nickerson & C.
"Levi," pseud.
Aquarian philosophy: the twenty-two truisms of the great masters, with notes and comments. '09(O23) Q. pap., $1. (Printed as manuscript.) E. S. Dowling.
—, comp. Aquarian gospel of Jesus the Christ: the philosophic and practical basis of the religion of the Aquarian age of the world and of the church universal. '09 (S18) c. O. $2. E. S. Dowling.
"Levi, Eliphas," pseud.
See Constant, Alphonse L:
Levi, Hedwig.
Easy German stories; ed., with notes and vocab., by Mrs. Luise Delp. '09(Je19) D. (Modern lang. ser.) *40 c. net. Crowell.
Levi, L: Emanuel, and Manuel, Earle Vincent.
Tanners' and chemists' hdbk. '09(D) c. 363 p. tabs., 12°, $5. L: E. Levi.
Levi, Ruth.
King's choice; Purim sketch. '10(Mr26) c. D. pap., 15 c. Bloch.
Leviathan. *See* Hobbes, T:
Levin, A. M.
Modern gas engine and the gas producer; with formulas, tables and examples from a designer's computation record-book. '09 (D) 18+485 p. 8°, $4. Wiley.
LEVINGTON, William.
Bragg, G: F. First negro priest on southern soil. 75 c. Church Advocate.
Levitt, Dorothy.
Woman and the car: hdbk. for all women who motor or who want to motor; ed., with introd. articles, by C. Byng-Hall. '09(Ap24) il. D. *$1 net. Lane.
Levy, Ernest Coleman.
Exterminator of mosquitoes. '08(O) 14 p. il. 8°, gratis. Richmond Dept. of Health.
Levy, Florence N.
American art annual, 1909-10. Limited ed. v. 7. '10(Ap16) c. il. por. 12°, $5. Am. Art.
Levy, Reeva Huson, comp.
See Phillips, *Mrs.* Fannie Frank.
Lew Ott. Totten, *Mrs.* M. B. $1. M. B. Totten.

Lewes, G: H:
Life of Goethe; introd. by Havelock Ellis. '08(F22) 16°, (Everyman's lib.) *35 c. net; leath., *70 c. net. Dutton.

Lewes, Vivian Byam.
Liquid and gaseous fuels. '08(Mr7) il. tabs., O. (Westminster ser.) *$2 net. Van Nostrand.

Lewin, F. G.
A B C book for good boys and girls. '10 (O29) Q. bds., $1.50. Stokes.
Rhymes of ye olde sign boards. '10 (O29) nar. F. bds., $1.50. Stokes.

Lewis, Abram Herbert.
Spiritual Sabbathism. '10(Jl2) c. por. 8°, $1.50. Am. Sabbath Tr. Soc.

Lewis, Alfr. H:
An American patrician: Aaron Burr. '08 (Mr7) c. il. D. **$2 net. Appleton.
Wolfville folks. '08(My16) c. front. D. †$1.50. Appleton.

Lewis, Arth. G.
Stub ends of thought and verse. '09, [1910.] (Ja) c. 107 p. por. 16°, $1. Bohemian Soc.

Lewis, Arth. Morrow.
Art of lecturing. '08(F1) D. pap., 25 c. Kerr.
Evolution: social and organic. '08(Ap4) S. (Standard socialist ser.) 50 c. Kerr.
Ten blind leaders of the blind. '09(F6) c. 16°, 50 c. Kerr.
Contents: Benjamin Kidd; Henry George; Immanuel Kant; Prof. Richard T. Ely; Cesare Lombroso; Max Stirner; Thomas Carlyle; Albert Schäffle; August Comte; Bishop Spalding.
Vital problems in social evolution. '09 (Ap3) S. 50 c. Kerr.

Lewis, B.
Medical vademecum in German and English; with preface by A. Politzer. '10 (Ap) 15+559 p. 8°, $5 net. Blakiston.

Lewis, Caleb, pseud.
Almost fairy children; or, the cozy evenings of brother and sister. '09(D11) c. il. D. $1.25. Bobbs-M.

Lewis, Dan. Elwood.
Happy hours for the boys and girls. '10 (Ja29) D. *50 c. net. S. S. Times.

Lewis, E. C., comp.
Ain't it awful. '10(D) 16°, 50 c. Caldwell.
Just kids. '10(D) 16°, 50 c. Caldwell.
Smile, don't worry: compilation of humorous matter that will cheer. '09(Ap3) c. sq. T. 50 c. Mutual Bk.

Lewis, E. I.
Inorganic chemistry. '08(F1) 8°, *$1.25 net. Putnam.

Lewis, E. W., rep.
See Arizona Territory. *Sup. ct.* Repts

LEWIS, Edward Gardner.
Madden, E. C: U. S. government's shame: the great Lewis case. 50 c. Nat. Bk. Co.

Lewis, Elias St. Elmo.
Financial advertising, for commercial and savings banks, trust, title insurance, and safe deposit companies, investment houses. '09(Mr27) c. il. 4°, $5. Levey.

Lewis, Emily Sargent.
Little singer, and other verses. '10(N19) c. D. $1 net. Lippincott.

Lewis, Florence Jane.
Climbing up to nature: [a novel.] '08 (My16) c. il. D. $1.50. C. M. Clark.

Lewis, Fk. Grant.
Irenaeus testimony to the fourth Gospel. '08(Ag29) c. 8°, pap., *50 c. net. Univ. of Chic.

Lewis, Fk. W.
State insurance: social and industrial need. '09(Mr20) c. fold. tabs., O. **$1.25 net. Houghton M.

Lewis, G: Harlan.
Edmund Lewis of Lynn, Massachusetts, and some of his descendants. '08, [1909.] (N) 151 p. 8°, $3. Essex Inst.

Lewis, Mrs. Harrison C.
See Cameron, Marg.

Lewis, Harry Reynolds.
Poultry lab'y guide; manual for the study of pract. poultry keeping. '10(D24) il. 12°, 65 c. net. Macmillan.

Lewis, H: Harrison, and Duff, Orva S., comp.
How fortunes are made in advertising; [also] Great successes. Twentieth century ed. '09(Mr27) c. il. pors. 24°, $1. Publicity.

Lewis, Ja. J:
Pocket optical dictionary. 3d ed., rev. and enl. '08(Ap18) c. il. nar. S. leath., $1.25. J. J: Lewis.

Lewis, J:
Eminent domain. 3d ed. 2 v. '09(O) *$13 net. Callaghan.

Lewis, J: H., and Cupper, Percy A.
Irrigation in Oregon. '09(Je) 67 p. diagrs., map, 8°, (U. S., Dept. of Agriculture; Office of Experiment Stations bull.) pap. 15 c. U. S., Supt. of Docs.

Lewis, J: H:, comp.
Gathered fragments. '09(Ap10) c. S. 50 c. Lewis & W.

Lewis, Jos. Vance.
Out of the ditch; true story of an ex-slave. '10(N) 154 p. il. pors. 8°, $1.50. Jos. Vance Lewis.

Lewis, Jos. Volney.
Origin and relations of the Newark rocks; The Newark (Triassic) copper ores of New Jersey; Properties of trap rocks for road construction. '08(Je13) il. maps, O. (New Jersey, Geological survey.) pap. (Add. author for price.) J. V. Lewis.

Lewis, L. B.
Pupil's notebook and study outline in Oriental and Greek history. '09(O16) c. O. pap., 25 c. Am. Bk.

Lewis, Lawrence.
Advertisements of *The Spectator;* being a study of the literature, history and manners of Queen Anne's England as they are reflected therein, as well as an illustration of the origins of the art of advertising; with appendix of representative advertisements now for the first time reprinted, and an introd. note by G: Lyman Kittredge. '09(Je26) c. fold. facsim., O. $2. Houghton M.

Lewis, Leo Rich.
Vocab. of French words and idioms; with verb-list and grammar-syllabus, for use in high school and college. 3d ed. '10 (F12) 35 c. Tufts Coll.
See also Cole, S: Winkley.

Lewis, LeRoy, M.D.
Anatomy and physiology for nurses. 2d ed. '10(F) 342 p. *$1.75 net. Saunders.

Lewis, Lowery Laymon.
See Ferguson, Alex. McGowen.

Lewis, Montgomery Hill.
Utility speller for elementary and advanced grades. pts. 1, 2. '09(Je) c. 90 p. 12°, 30 c. Educ. Pub.

Lewis, Myron H:
Popular hdbk. for cement and concrete users. '10(My21) il. 12°, $2.50. Henley.
Waterproofing: an engineering problem; paper read before the Municipal Engineers of the City of New York, Nov. 25, 1908. '09(Jl17) il. 8°, 50 c. Engineering News.

Lewis, Prudence, comp.
Golden hour; stories and poems. '10(D31) c. D. $1. Bobbs-M.

Lewis, Rev. T: Hamilton.
Divine credentials of the Bible. '08, [1909.] (Mr) 6+3-295 p. 8°, $1.25. Meth. Protestant.
Fraternal address to the General Conference of the M. E. Church, South; del. at Asheville, N. C., 1910. '10(Ag27) D. pap. Pub. Ho. M. E. Ch., So.

Lewis, Virgil Anson.
Hist. of the battle of Point Pleasant, fought between white men and Indians at the mouth of the Great Kanawha River (now Point Pleasant, West Virginia), Monday, Oct. 10th, 1774; the chief event of Lord Dunmore's war; (abridged from the author's manuscript "History of Lord Dunmore's war".) '09(N) c. 4+131 p. pors. 8°, $1.50. Tribune Pr. Co., (W. Va.)
—, **ed.** How West Virginia was made; proceedings of the first convention of the people of northwestern Virginia at Wheeling, May 13, 14 and 15, 1861, and the journal of the second convention of the people of northwestern Virginia at Wheeling, which assembled June 11th, 1861; with appendixes and an introd., annotations and addenda. '10(Ag20) front. 8°. (Priv. pr.) News-Mail Co.

Lewis, W: Draper, ed.
Great American lawyers: history of the legal profession in America. In 8 v. v. 1. '08(O3); v. 2, 3, 4. '09(F20) University ed. c. pors. O. (Add. pubs. for price.) Winston.
See also Pepper, G: Wharton.
—, comp. *See* Pennsylvania legislation on associations.
—, and McConnell, Miriam.
Equity jurisdiction torts; a coll. of cases with notes. '08(O) c. (Add. pub. for price.) Int. Pr.
Equity jurisdiction, trespass to real property. '08(Je) c. 207-306 p. 8°, $1. W: D. Lewis.

Lewis, W. J.
See Archer, R: Lawrence.

Lewis, W: Walford.
Typewriting. '10(N5) c. il. forms, 12°, $1. D. L. Musselman.

LEWIS FAMILY.
See Genealogies.

Lewis Rand. Johnson, M. †$1.50. Houghton M.

Lewisohn, Ludwig.
Broken snare. '08(O10) c. D. $1.50. B. W. Dodge.
A night in Alexandria: dramatic poem. '10 (Ap) c. '09. 16 p. 8°, pap., 50 c. Moods.

LEWISTOWN COAL FIELD.
See Montana.

Lewkowitsch, Julius Isidor.
Chemical technology and analysis of oils, fats and waxes. 4th ed. '09(Je12) 3 v., il. 8°, *$15 net. Macmillan.

Lewson, J:
Monopoly and trade restraint cases, incl. conspiracy, injunction, quo warranto, pleading and practice and evidence. '08 (Ag) c. 2 v., 66+396; 397-835 p. O. buck., $10. Flood.

Lex in corde. Barnes, W. E. $1.50 net. Longmans.

Lexer, Erich.
General surgery; presentation of the scientific principles upon which the practice of modern surgery is based. American ed.; ed. by Arth. Dean Bevan; auth. tr. of the 2d German ed. by Dean Lewis. '10(My) c. 29+1041 p. il. 4°, $6 net; hf. leath., $7 net. Appleton.
Bibliographical notes interspersed.

Lexicographical and historical study of Diatheke. Norton, F: O. *75 c. net. Univ. of Chic.

LEXICONS.
See names of languages and subjects.

LEXINGTON, Mass.
Piper, F. S. Lexington; birthplace of American liberty. 25 c. Lexington Hist. Soc.

Leyden-Agar, T:
See Agar, T: Leyden-.

LIABILITY.
See Insurance;—Negligence.

Lias, J. J.
Nicene creed; manual for the use of candidates for holy orders. '10(Jl16) 12°, $1.75 net. Macmillan.

Liautard, A., M.D.
Animal castration. 10th ed., rev. and enl. (D) 165 p. il. por. 8°, $2. W: R. Jenkins.

Libbey, Laura Jean.
Works. '10(O) 12°, ea., 50 c. J. S. Ogilvie.
Contents: The alphabet of love; A beautiful coquette; The crime of Hallowe'en; Daisy Brooks; Daisy Gordon's folly; Dora Miller; Flirtations of a beauty; A forbidden marriage; Gilberta, the beauty; He loved but was lured away; Junie's love test; Little Leafy; Little Rosebud's lovers; Little romp Edda; Lyndall's temptations; Madolin Rivers; A master workman's oath; Miss Middleton's lover; Pretty Freda's lovers; Wilful Gaynell.
Novels. '08(Mr) 12°, pap., ea., 25 c. J. S. Ogilvie.
Titles: All for love of a fair face; Beautiful Ione's lover; Beautiful Victorine's folly; Daisy Brooks; Gilberta the beauty; Happy-Go-Lucky Lotty; Heiress of Cameron Hall; Junie's love test; Leonie Locke; Little romp Edda; Little Rosebud's lovers; Madolin Rivers; Struggle for a heart. Formerly published by George Munro Sons.

Libby, C: Thornton.
Cash, panics and industrial depressions. '08 (My9) 8°, gratis. C: T. Libby.

Libby, Orin Grant.
Typical villages of the Mandans, Arikara and Hidatsa in the Missouri Valley, North Dakota. '09(D) 21 p. il. map, 8°. State Hist., N. D.

Liberal and mystical writings. Law, W: *$1 net. Longmans.

Liberal theology. Egerton, H. *$1.25 net. Dutton.

Liberalism and the social problems. Churchill, W. L. S. *$1.50 net. Doran.

Liberators (The). Stevens, I: N. $1.50. B. W. Dodge.

LIBERIA.
United States. *Commission to Liberia.* Affairs in Liberia; message from the President of the United States. [1910.] (Jl) 37 p. 8°. Gov. Pr. Off.

Liberma, Marco Fs.
Story of Chantecler; critical analysis of Rostand's play. '10(S3) il. D. 75 c. net. Moffat.

LIBERTY.
Cecil, *Lord* H. R: H. Liberty and authority. $1. Longmans.
Dawbarn, C. Y. C. Liberty and progress. *$3 net. Longmans.
Mackinnon, J. History of modern liberty. In 8 v. v. 3. *$5 net. Longmans.
See also Declaration of Independence;—Democracy;—Slavery.

Liberty of conscience under three Tsars. Latimer, R. S. *$1.50 net. Revell.

Liberty of prophesying. Henson, H. H. *$1.50 net. Yale Univ.

LIBERTY OF THE PRESS.
Reedy, W: M. Myth of a free press. W: M. Reedy.
Schroeder, T., *comp.* Free press anthology. $2. Free Speech; Truth Seeker.
See also Journalism;—Newspapers.

Liberty or death. Pollard, E. F. †$1.50. Dodd.

Librarian of the desert. Koopman, H. L. $1. Everett.

LIBRARIANS AND LIBRARIES.
Alabama. *Dept. of Education.* Alabama library day. (Not for sale.) Ala. Supt. Educ.
Baker, F. T:, *and* Abbot, A. Bibliog. of children's reading; [also] The use of the school library. 60 c. Teachers' Coll.
Bostwick, A. E. American public library. $1.50 net. Appleton.
Brown, Z. M., *comp.* Buying list of books for small libraries. gratis. N. Y. State Educ.
Buffalo Public Library. Class-room libraries for public schools. 25 c. Buffalo Pub. Lib.
Clark, J: W. Care of books. *$2.50 net. Putnam.
Connecticut. Public Library. Helps in library work with children. gratis. Conn. Pub. Lib.
Dana, J: C. Library primer. $1. Lib. Bu.

LIBRARIANS AND LIBRARIES.—*Continued.*
Dana, J: C. Modern American library economy, as illustrated by the Newark, N. J., Free Public Library. pt. 1, Lending department; section 1, Work of the registration desk. 25 c.—pt. 5, School department; section 2, Course of study for normal school pupils on the use of a library, by M. L. Gilson. 75 c. Elm Tree Press.
Directory of libraries in the United States and Canada. $5 net. H. W. Wilson.
Fletcher, W: I:, *ed.* Annual library index, 1907, *$3.50 net; 1908, 1909, ea., $5 net. Pub. Weekly.
Green, B. R. Book stack and shelving for libraries. gratis. Snead & Co.
Hadley, C. R. Why do we need a public library? 5 c. A. L. A.
Keogh, A. Institutional church and the public library. (Add. author for price.) A. Keogh.
League of Library Commissions. Small library buildings. $1.25. A. L. A.
Legler, E: E. Books for the people. gratis H: E. Legler.
Leland, C. G., *and others.* Library and the school. 50 c. Harper.
Pearson, E. L. Library and the librarian. $1.50.—Old librarian's almanack. per set of 6 v. $5. Elm Tree Press.
Savage, E. A. Story of libraries and book-collecting. *75 c. net. Dutton.
Sharp, K. L. Illinois libraries. pts. 3, 4, 5. ea., $1. Univ. of Ill.
United States. *Bureau of Education.* Statistics of public, society, and school libraries having 5000 volumes and over in 1908. (Add. Superintendent for price.) U. S., Supt. of Docs.
Washington, D. C. Public Library. Work of the public library with the children of Washington. gratis. Washington Pub. Lib.
World's best books; suggestions for the selection of a home library. 50 c. Globe-W.
See also Bibliographies;—Book-prices;—Bookbinders and bookbinding;—Books and reading;—Cataloguing;—Children;—Classification;—*also* Boston Public Library;—Carnegie Library;—Library of Congress;—New York Public Library;—New York Society Library;—Newark, N. J., Free Public Library;—University of Michigan.

Librarians ser.; ed. by J. Cotton Dana *and* H: W. Kent O. Elm Tree Press.
—Pearson. Library and the librarian. $1.50. —Old librarian's almanack. per set of 6 v., $5.

LIBRARIES.
See Librarians and libraries.

Library Association of California. *Committee on Pictures for Libraries.* Picture list; [annotated list of 500 well-known pictures.] '09(Ap17) 8°, (Publications of the California Lib. Assoc.) pap., 25 c. Cal. L. A.

LIBRARY ECONOMY.
See Librarians and libraries.

LIBRARY FURNISHINGS.
See Librarians and libraries.

Library of art. *See* Scribner's.

LIBRARY OF CONGRESS, Washington, D. C.
Hanson, J. C. M. Subject catalogs of the Library of Congress. H. W. Wilson.
Small, H., *comp.* Hdbk. of the Library of Congress. 30 c. Curtis & C.
Sonneck, O. G: T. Music division of the Library of Congress. (Add. author for price.) O. G: T. Sonneck.

Library of Congress list of references on reciprocity; comp. under the direction of the chief bibliographer. 1st ed., Appleton Prentiss Clark Griffin. 2d ed., with additions, H. H. B. Meyer. '10(D3) O. pap., 15 c. Gov. Pr. Off.

Library of early novelists; Picaresque section. 12°, $2. Dutton.
—Rojas. Celestina.

Library of economics and politics. See Crowell's.

Library of English literature. 5 v. Morley, H: ea., $2.50 net. Cassell.

Library of genetic science and philosophy. 12°. Psychological Review.
—Baldwin. Darwin and the humanities. $1.50.

Library of golden thoughts. por. T. Lane.
—Pauline. Golden thoughts of Carmen Sylva, Queen of Roumania. 50 c. net.

Library of literary criticism. *See* Moulton, C: W., *ed.*

Library of literary history. See Scribner's.

Library of living thought. See Harper's.

Library of philosophy. See Macmillan's.

Library of science for the workers. S. 50 c. Kerr.
—Nietzsche. Human, all too human.

Library of southern literature. Alderman, E. A., *and others, eds.* In 15 v. vs. 1-7. per set, $80-$200. Martin & H.

Library of the world's best mystery and detective tales. Hawthorne, J., *ed.* 6 v. $6.50. Review of Reviews.

Library of travel. See Flanagan's.

Library of Tribune extras. O. pap., 25 c. Tribune Assoc.
—Tribune almanac and political register, 1908; 1909; 1910.

Library of useful stories. See Appleton's.

Library of valuable knowledge. 12°. S. S. McClure.
—Munro. Story of electricity. 92 c.
—Willson. Story of rapid transit. 92 c.

Libro de los Engaños y los asayamientos de las mugeres publícalo Adolfo Bonilla y San Martín. '04, [1909.] (N) 19-72 p. (Bibliotheca hispanica.) $1. Hispanic Soc.

Libro de los Tres Reyes de Oriente; published in facsimile from the ms. in the Library of the Escorial by Archer M. Huntington. '04, [1909.] (N) no paging, $6. (100 copies.) Hispanic Soc.

Libro illustrato di lingua inglese. Moore, S. W. 35 c. Heath.

LICHENS.
Fink, B. Lichens of Minnesota. Gov. Pr. Off.

Lichtenberg, Georg Christoph.
Reflections; sel. and tr. by Norman Alliston. '08(D19) 12°, $1. Scribner.

Lichtenberger, Ja. P.
Divorce; study in social causation. '09 (N20) c. O. (Columbia University, studies in history, economics and public law.) pap., **$1.50 net. Longmans.

Lichtenstein, Gaston.
Visit to Young's Pier at Atlantic City, N. J.; also. When Edgecombe was a-borning, The word sheriff, and Products of colonial North Carolina. '08, [1909.] (Ag) 15 p. 8°. (Add. author for price.) G. Lichtenstein.

Lichtenstein. Hauff, W. 80 c. Holt.

Liddell, T. Hodgson.
China, its marvel and mystery. '10(Ap30) il. Q. $6.50 net. Lane.

Liddon, H:. Parry, D.D.
Divinity of our Lord and Saviour Jesus Christ: 8 lectures preached before the University of Oxford in the year 1866. Cheaper reissue. '08(Ap11) D. (Bampton lectures for 1866.) $1.25. Longmans.

Lieber, Fs.
Manual of political ethics. New ed.; ed. by T. D. Woolsey. 2 v. '10(D17) 8°, $5.50 net. Lippincott.

Liebich, Louise, [Mrs. Franz Liebich.]
Claude-Achille Debussy. '08(Mr7) il. por. D. (Living masters of music.) *$1 net Lane.

Liebknecht, Wilhelm.
Karl Marx biographical memoirs; tr. by Ernest Untermann. '08(My16) c. S. (Standard socialist ser.) 50 c. Kerr.

Lieckfeld, G.
Oil motors: their development, construction and management. '08(D19) 8°, *$4.50 net. Lippincott.

Liedtke, Friedrich Wilhelm.
A B C des Skat in Deutsch und Englisch. '09(Mr6) c. T. 50 c. Schaefer & K.

Liefeld, E. Theophilus.
Faces and phases of German life. '10(Je18) $1.50 net. Fowler & W.

LIÈGE, Belgium.
Omond, G: W: T. Liège and the Ardennes. *$3 net. Macmillan.

LIENS.
Elkins, A. I., *and* Glenn, G. Treatise on secret liens and reputed ownership, 1910. $3.50. Baker, V. & Co.

LIFE.
See Biology:—Christian life;—Conduct of life;—Death;—Ethics;—Future life:—Hygiene;—Longevity;—Man;—Philosophy;—Vital force.

Life and adventure beyond Jordan. Lees, G: R. **$1.75 net. Appleton.

Life and adventures of A-no. 1. Livingston, L. R. 25 c. Self Mastery.

Life and adventures of Robinson Crusoe. *See* Defoe, Dan.

Life and health. Rogers, J. F: $1 net. Lippincott.

Life and power from within. Colville, W. J. $1 net. Fenno.

Life and song. Childe, N. S. 50 c. H. Childe.

Life and sport in Hampshire. Dewar, G: A. B. *$3 net. Longmans.

Life and the great forever. Chesney, E., *comp.* *$1.50 net. Lane.

Life and the ideal. Brierley, J. $1.25 net. Houghton M.

Life as reality. Dewing, A. S. $1.25 net. Longmans.
Life at high tide. Howells, W: D., *ed.* †$1. Harper.
Life at its best. Du Bose, H. M. *50 c. net. Pub. Ho. of M. E. Ch., So.
Life beyond. Gatty, *Mrs.* M. S. 25 c. net. Revell.
Life for a life. Herrick, R. $1.50. Macmillan.
Life histories of familiar plants. Ward, J: J. *$1.75 net. Cassell.
Life-histories of northern animals. Seton, E. T. In 2 v. *$18 net. Scribner.
Life history of the salmon. Malloch, P. D. $3.50 net. Macmillan.
Life in His name. McIntyre, D: M. $1.25. Armstrong.
Life in old Virginia. McDonald, J. J. $1.50. Old Virginia.
Life in the greenwood. Lansing, M. F. 35 c. Ginn.
Life in the navy. Beyer, T: 25 c. Laird.
Life in the Orient. Basmajian, K. H. $1 net. Am. Tr.
Life in the Roman world of Nero and St. Paul. Tucker, T: G: $2.50 net. Macmillan.
Life in the shadow of death. Klarmann, A. F. $1 net. Pustet.
Life in the Word. Mauro, P. *50 c. net. Revell.
Life in two worlds. Lathbury, A. A: (Add. author for price.) A. A: Lathbury.
Life, inorganic, organic, immortal. Kipper, H. B. (Add. pubs. for price.) Univ. Press, (Camb.)

LIFE INSURANCE.
See Insurance.

Life lessons. Hubbard, *Mrs.* A. M. $3. Roycrofters.
Life, love and peace. Hall, B. $1. Arcadia.
Life melodious. Baldwin, F: C. $1.25. F: C. Baldwin.
Life of a fossil hunter. Sternberg, C: H. **$1.60 net. Holt.
Life of a tramp. Laws, W. 25 c. Donohue.
Life of an enclosed nun; by a Mother Superior. '10(O22) por. S. $1 net. Lane.
Life of Christ for children. '10(F5) c. il. O. **$1 net. Longmans.
Life of Japan. Miyakawa, M. $1.50 net. Neale.
Life of Jesus of Nazareth [80 facsimiles in color of water color drawings by W: Hole: with Bible narrative]. '09, [1910.] (F) $4. Nelson.
Life of lives. Farrar, F: W: *$1.25 net. Cassell.
Life of me. Shakelford, E. $1.50. Dodge.
Life of Saint Clare ascribed to Fr. Thomas of Celano of the Order of Friars Minor, A.D. 1255-1261; tr. and ed. from the earliest mss. by Fr. Paschal Robinson, of the same Order; with appendix cont. the rule of Saint Clare. '10(Ap2) c. il. D. $1. Dolphin Press.
Life of the fields. Jefferies, R: *$1.50 net. Lippincott.
Life on the ocean. Little, G: $2. Lippincott.
Life of the spirit. Eucken, R. C. *$1.50 net. Putnam.
Life of the universe. Arrhenius, S. A. 2 v. *75 c. net. Harper.
Life on God's plan. Mackintosh, H. R. $1.50 net. Doran.
Life pictures of Calvin. Richards, G: W. 25 c. Heidelberg.
Life preservers on motor vessels. '09(Je) 4 p. 8°, pap. (Add. Superintendent for price.) U. S., Supt. of Docs.
Life questions of high school boys. Jenks, J: W. 40 c. Y. M. C. A.
Life spiritual. Davison, W: T. $1.50 net. Doran.
Life stories for young people; tr. by G: Putnam Upton. il. S. *60 c. net. McClurg.
--Höcker. Arnold of Winkelried.
—Holm. Eugénie, Empress of the French.
—Jeanrenaud. Duke of Brittany.
—Küchler. Elizabeth, Empress of Austria.—Queen Maria Sophia of Naples.
--La Motte Foqué. Undine.
—Lenk. Marie Antoinette's youth.
—Merz. Louise, Queen of Prussia.
—Schmidt. Charlemagne.—Youth of the great Elector.
—Walter. Emperor William First.
—Würdig. Prince Eugene.
Life story of a college boy. Taylor, *Mrs.* L. E. $1. Chr. Witness.
Life story of a fowl. Hurst. J. W. *$2 net. Macmillan.
Life sublime. Rogers, L. W. 10 c. Theosophical Bk.
Life thoughts in rhyme. Treadwell, A: $1.50. A: Treadwell.
Life transfigured. Whiting, L. $1.25 net. Little, B. & Co.
Life with a purpose. Wright, H: B. $1.50. Revell.
Life's arrears. James, *Mrs.* F. A. P. $1.50. Cassell.
Life's beautiful battle. Lloyd, J: W: $1.25. J: W: Lloyd.
Life's chequer-board. Wallace, H. $1.50. Cassell.
Life's common way. E., J., *and* S., H., *comps.* 50 c.; $1. Stokes.
Life's contrasts. Fraser, J: F. *$1.75 net. Cassell.
Life's day. Bainbridge, W: S. **$1.35 net. Stokes.
Life's handicap. *See* Kipling, Rudyard.
Life's little day. O'Neill, D. J. S., *comp.* 25 c. Soc. Divine Word.
Life's new psalms. Warnack, H: C. $1; 30 c. Roger Bros.
Life's to-morrow. Millard, J. W: **75 c. net. Am. Bapt.
Life's understudies. Rozant, I. $1.50. M. Kennerley.
Lift-luck on Southern roads. Edwardes, T. $1.50 net. Macmillan.
Lifted bandage. Andrews, *Mrs.* M. R. S. **50 c. net. Scribner.

LIGAMENTS.
See Bones.

LIGHT.
Franklin, W. S., *and* McNutt, B. Light and sound. **$1.60 net. Macmillan.
Houston, E. J. Wonder book of light. **$1.50 net. Stokes.
Kapteyn, J. C. On the absorption of light in space. (Not for sale.) Carnegie.
MacLaurin, R: C. Light. **$1.50 net. Lemcke.
MacLaurin, R: C. Theory of light. *$2.75 net. Putnam.
Millikan, R. A., *and* Mills, J: Short university course in electricity, sound and light. $2. Ginn.
Morris, M. Light and X-ray treatment of skin diseases. *$1.50 net. Funk.
Poynting, J: H: Pressure of light. 75 c. net. Gorham.
Rentschler, H. C. **New method for measuring the index of refraction of a gas for different light-waves and the results obtained for several gases.** 20 c. Johns Hopkins.
Thompson, S. P. Light, visible and invisible. $2 net. Macmillan.
Wickenden, W: E. Illumination and photometry. *$2 net. McGraw-H.
Woodruff, W: L. Therapeutics of light vibration. *$1.50 net. J. F. Elwell.
See also Color;—Electric light;—Eye;—Gas;—Lenses; —Perspective; — Photography;—Radioactivity;—Radium;—Roentgen rays;—Spectrum.

Light and heavy timber framing made easy. Hodgson, F: T: $2. Drake.
Light and truth ser. Am. Bapt.
—Cooke. Johann Gerhard Oncken. **50 c. net. Am. Bapt.
Light arising. Stephen, C. E. **90 c. net. Winston.
Light beyond the shadows. Lawrence, H. **50 c. net. Moffat.
Light come, light go. Nevill, R. *$4.50 net. Macmillan.
Light fingered gentry. Phillips, D: G. 75 c. Grosset.
Light from the ancient East. Deissmann, G. A. $4 net. Doran.
Light Horse Harry's legion. Tomlinson, E. T. $1.50. Houghton M.
Light in dark places. Bachman, N. 60 c. net. Presb. Pub.
Light of Asia. *See* Arnold, *Sir* Edn.
Light of four candles. King, C. F. $1.50. C. F. King.
Light of His countenance. Hart, M. J. $1.25. Benziger.
Light of life. Evarts, J: W. $2. L. Evarts.
Light of stars. Bohannon, H. D. *$1 net. Fenno.
Light of the world. *See* Arnold, *Sir* Edn.
Light on dark places at Panama. Chatfield, M. A. $1.50. B'way Pub.
Light on the path. M. C., *pseud.* 75 c. Theo. Pub. Co.
Light princess. MacDonald, G: **40 c. net. Crowell.
Light side of Egypt. Thackeray, L. *$2.50 net. Macmillan.
Light side of the law. MacDonald, G: A. $1.75 net. Cassell.
Light that failed. *See* Kipling, Rudyard.
Light that never fails. Bateman, M. E. S. 60 c. Cochrane.
Light through the valley. MacLafferty, J. H: 50 c. net. P. Elder.
Lighted lamp. Henderson, C: H. †$1.50. Houghton M.

Lighthall, W: Douw.
Master of life: romance of the Five Nations. '09(Ag21) il. O. $1.50. McClurg.

LIGHTING.
Bowles, J. D. Acetylene for lighting country houses. Univ. of Mo.
Pond, G: G. Calcium carbide and acetylene. gratis. Penn. State Coll.
Steinmetz, C: P. Radiation, light and illumination. *$3 net. McGraw-H.
See also Electric light;—Electrical engineering;—Railroads.

LIGHTNING.
Henry, A. J. **Lightning and lightning conductors. (Add. Superintendent for price.) U. S., Supt. of Docs.**

LIGHTNING CONDUCTORS.
See Lightning.

Lightning estimator. Bradt, H. J. $1. Bradt.
Lightning legible shorthand. Glass, D: R. (Add. author for price.) D: R. Glass.
Lights and shadows. Sands, H. $1.25. Cochrane.
Lights and shadows of life on the Pacific coast. Woods, S. D. $1.20 net. Funk.
Lights and shadows of Mormonism. Gibbs, J. F. $1.25. Salt Lake Trib.
Lights of two centuries. Hale, E: E., *ed.* $1.50. Little, B. & Co.
Lignée (La) des poètes au XIXe siècle. Bonnier, C., *comp.* $1. Oxford Univ.

Liguori, St. Alphonsus.
On retreats; tr. by Rev. E. H. Buckland. '09(O) 8°, 23 p. pap., 6 c. net. Herder.

Lila Sari. Howard, W: L. $1.50. Badger.
Lilac fairy book. Lang, A., *ed.* $1.60 net. Longmans.
Lilac girl. Barbour, R. H: $2. Lippincott.
Lilies (The). Spencer, H: P. $1. Badger.
Lilies of eternal peace. Whitney, L. **75 c. net; **$1.50 net. Crowell.

Liljengren, Adolph.
Fästämning, en samling originella dialoger, passande alt uppläsas vid ungdomsfäster och särskilda högtider; med bidrag af Leonard Stromberg. '09(Ap) 89 p. il. por. 12°, 50 c. A. Liljengren.

Lilley, A. E. V., and Midgley, W.
Book of studies in plant form; with some suggestions for their application to design. Enl. ed. '08(D5) il. 8°, *$2 net. Scribner.

Lilley, Alfr. Leslie.
Modernism. '08(D5) 8°, *$1.75 net. Scribner.

Lilley, Henrietta M.
Second school year; course of study with detailed selection of lesson material arranged by months and correlated. [New ed.] '09(O23) c. il. D. (School year books.) 60 c. Flanagan.

Lillibridge, W: Otis.
Dissolving circle. '08(Ap11) c. front. D. †$1.50. Dodd.
Dominant dollar. '09(S25) c. il. O. $1.50. McClurg.
Quercus Alba, the veteran of the Ozarks. '10(O1) c. front. D. bds., 50 c., boxed. McClurg.
Quest eternal. '08(O10) c. front. D. †$1.50. Dodd.

LILLIBRIDGE FAMILY.
See Genealogies: Eno, J. N.

Lillie, Fk. Rattray.
Development of the chick; introd. to embryology. '09(Ja16) c. il. fold. tab., 8°, **$4 net. Holt.

Lilts and lyrics for the school room. Riley, A. C. D. $1. C. F. Summy Co.

LIMA, Peru.
See International Bureau of American Republics, Washington, D. C. Municipal organizations.

Limerick, Dudley T., ed.
How to know the holy Bible. '08(O17) il. S. bds., 20 c. Praise Pub.

LIMERICKS.
See Parody;—Poetry.

LIMES.
See Cement.

LINACRE, Thomas.
Osler, W: Thomas Linacre. *75 c. net. Putnam.

Linacre lecture. *See* Osler, W:

Linch, C: Sutteiley.
Marine engine indicating; complete treatise on the indicator and indicator diagrams as applied to marine engines. '10 (Je4) c. il. 8°, $2. Am. Steam Gauge.

Lincoln, Abraham.
Life and works. Centenary ed.; ed. by Marion Mills Miller. '08(Ja11) 9 v., pors. 12°, $14. Current Lit.
Works; introds. and special articles by Thdr. Roosevelt, W: H. Taft and others; managing eds.: J: H. Clifford, Marion W. Miller. 8 v. '09(Ap3) c. il. pors 16°, $6; hf. leath., $8. University Soc.
Abraham Lincoln: tributes from his associates: reminiscences of soldiers, statesmen and citizens: with introd. by W: Hayes Ward. [New ed.] '09(Ja30) c. por. D. (Astor prose ser.) 60 c. Crowell.
Anthology of the epigrams and sayings of Abraham Lincoln, collected from his writings and speeches; ed. by Fs. D. Tandy. '08(N21) c. O. 75 c. F. D. Tandy.
Emancipation proclamation. Special ed. '09(Mr13) **$4 net. Houghton M.
First and second inaugural addresses; message, July 5, 1861; proclamation, Jan. 1, 1863; Gettysburg address, Nov. 19, 1863. '09, [1910.] (Jl) 40 p. 8°. Gov. Pr. Off.
Inaugurals, addresses, and letters (selections); ed., with introd. memoir and notes. '10(N5) c. D. (Longmans' English classics.) 25 c. Longmans.
Selections from Lincoln's speeches and letters. arr. for learners of Munson phonography by Bertha Crocker. '10(Ag) c. 128 p. 12°, 75 c. S. S. Packard.

Lincoln, Abraham.—*Continued.*
Selections from the addresses, inaugurals, and letters of Abraham Lincoln; ed., with an introd. and notes, by Percival Chubb. '09(D11) c. por. S. (Macmillan's pocket Am. and Eng. classics.) 25 c. Macmillan.
Selections from the writings and addresses of Abraham Lincoln; ed., with introd. and notes, by Cornelia Beare. '10(My7) c. por. 12°, (Merrill's English texts.) 25 c. C: E. Merrill.
Table talk of Abraham Lincoln; ed. by W: Osborn Stoddard. (Centenary ed.) '09 (F6) c. front. S. 50 c. Stokes.
Versions of the Gettysburg address cited by Major William H. Lambert in his paper entitled "The Gettysburg address—when written, how received, its true form." '10(Je4) 16°, pap. (Priv. pr.) W: H. Lambert.
Wisdom of Abraham Lincoln; sel. and ed., with introd., by Temple Scott. '08(D5) c. Tt. (Wisdom ser.) leath., **$1 net. Brentano's.
Wisdom of Abraham Lincoln: being extracts from the speeches, state papers, and letters. '08(N7) c. T. **50 c. net; limp leath., **75 c. net. Wessels.
Worldly wisdom from Abraham Lincoln; ed. and arr. by F. S. Bigelow. '08(D12) c. T. leath., $1, boxed. Altemus.
See also Washington, G:

LINCOLN, Abraham.
Alford, F., *comp.* Wit of Lincoln, the wisdom of Franklin. 25 c. Scott-M.
Allen, L. W. Abraham Lincoln: a poem. **$1.25 net. Putnam.
Andrews, *Mrs.* M. K. S. Perfect tribute: [story dealing with Lincoln's Gettysburg speech.] †$1. Scribner.
Atkins, S. D. Abraham Lincoln. gratis. Journal Pr., (Ill.)
Atkinson, E. Boyhood of Lincoln.—Lincoln's love story. ea., **50 c. net. Doubleday, P.
Baker, D: C: Lincoln vs. liquor. (Add. pubs. for price.) Baker Pub.
Bancroft, G: Abraham Lincoln. **60 c. net. Wessels.
Barrett, F. W. Z. Mourning for Lincoln. **$1 net. Winston.
Beale, J. F. Abraham Lincoln; a brief biography. $1. Strawbridge & C.
Bergold, L. C. Abraham Lincoln centennial. 40 c. Educ. Pub.
Binns, H. B. Life of Abraham Lincoln. *$1.50 net. Dutton.
Boston Public Library. Abraham Lincoln, Feb. 12, 1809-Apr. 15, 1865: short list of books for school use cont. in the Library. gratis. Boston Pub. Lib.
Branigan, W: H: Abraham Lincoln. (Add. pubs. for price.) M. L. Morrison.
Brooklyn Public Library. Abraham Lincoln: list of Lincoln's writings and works rel. to Lincoln in the Library. gratis. Brooklyn Lib.
Browne, R. H: Abraham Lincoln and the men of his time. 2 v. $3. Blakely-O.

LINCOLN, Abraham.—*Continued.*

Campbell, H. Life of Abraham Lincoln. *25 c. net. Educ. Pub.

Carr, M. B. Abraham Lincoln. 25 c. Williams Pr., (N. Y.)

Chafin, E. W. Lincoln, the man of sorrows. 50 c. Lincoln Temperance.

Chicago Hebrew Institute. Program of celebrations during Lincoln week. 5 c. Chic. Hebrew Inst.

Chicago. Public Library. List of books and magazine articles on Abraham Lincoln. gratis. Chic. Pub. Lib.

Chittenden, L. E. Lincoln and the sleeping sentinel. **50 c. net. Harper.

Choate, J. H. Abraham Lincoln and other address in England. $2 net. Century Co.

Church, D. W. An interview. $1. B. Carey.

Cowen, B: R. Abraham Lincoln. *$1 net. Clarke.

Creelman, J. Why we love Lincoln. *$1.25 net. Outing.

Darling, J. T. Heart of hope: [lecture on Lincoln.] (Not for sale.) J. T. Dearborn.

Davis, J: M. How Abraham Lincoln became president. *75 c. net. J: M. Davis.

Dewitt, D: M. Assassination of Abraham Lincoln and its expiation. $2.25. Macmillan.

Fish, D. Legal phases of the Lincoln and Douglas debates. (Priv. pr.) D. Fish.

Flag day, one hundredth anniversary of the birth of Abraham Lincoln, 1809-1909; program of exercises, New Mexico, Feb. 12, 1909. '09(My) 39 p. 8°, pap., gratis. J. E. Clark.

Gerry, M. S. Toy shop: story of Lincoln: [fiction.] **50 c. net. Harper.

Gilder, R: W. Lincoln, the leader and Lincoln's genius for expression. $1. Houghton M.

Grand Army flag day, Rhode Island, February twelfth, 1909. (Add. pub. for price.) R. I. Dept. Educ.

Grand Army of the Republic. *Dept. of Georgia.* Services in commemoration of the 100th anniversary of the birth of Abraham Lincoln. (Add. pubs. for price.) D. I. Carson.

Greene, F. V. Lincoln as commander-in-chief. 50 c. F. V. Greene.

Grosscup, P: S. Celebration of Abraham Lincoln's birthday. (Add. author for price.) P: S. Grosscup.

Hamburg-American Line. Unveiling of a Lincoln memorial tablet on board the S. S. "President Lincoln." (Add. pubs. for price.) Hamburg-American Line.

Haworth, I. Reminiscences about Abraham Lincoln. 25 c. E. F. Heisler.

Heistand, H: O. S. Abraham Lincoln. (Priv. pr.) H: O. S. Heistand.

Hill, F: T. Lincoln's legacy of inspiration. 50 c. Stokes.

Hobson, J. T. Footprints of Abraham Lincoln. 50 c. Un. B. Pub.

Jackson, S. T. Lincoln's use of the Bible. *25 c. net. Eaton & M.

Jayne, W: Abraham Lincoln. 25 c. Grand Army.

Jennings, J. Abraham Lincoln. 50c. Jennings

LINCOLN, Abraham.—*Continued.*

Krans, H. S., *ed.* Lincoln tribute book. **$1.75 net. Putnam.

Lambert, W: H. Abraham Lincoln, 1809-1909; Lincoln literature: address. (Not for sale.)—1809-1909; Abraham Lincoln. (Not for sale.)—Gettysburg address. (Priv. pr.) W: H. Lambert.

Laughlin, C. E. Death of Lincoln. **$1.50 net. Doubleday, P.

Leale, C: A: Lincoln's last hours. (Add. author for price.) C: A: Leale.

Learned, M. D. Abraham Lincoln, American migration. *$3 net. W: J. Campbell.

Lehmann, F: W: Abraham Lincoln; address at Memorial Hall, Chicago. 25 c. Umbdenstock-F.-P.

Lincoln story-calendar, 1911. $1.25. Dutton.

Long, J: D. Abraham Lincoln. 25 c. net. W: B. Clarke.

Love, J: L. Lincoln the emancipator. 15 c. J: L. Love.

Lowell (Mass.) City Library. List of Lincoln's writings and works rel. to Lincoln in the Library. gratis. Lowell Lib.

MacChesney, N. W:, *ed.* Abraham Lincoln; the tribute of a century, 1809-1909. $2.75 net. McClurg.

McElroy, J: Soul growth of Abraham Lincoln. 10 c. J: McElroy.

Mackaye, P. W. Ode on the centenary of Abraham Lincoln. *75 c. net. Macmillan.

Markens, I: Abraham Lincoln and the Jews. $1. I: Markens.

Meese, W: A: Abraham Lincoln: incidents in his life relating to waterways. 40 c. W: A: Meese.

Middling, T. Lincoln in the Black Hawk war. $1.25. Sigma.

Military Order of the Loyal Legion of the United States. *New York Commandery.* Addresses del. at the regular meeting held Feb. 3, 1909, at Delmonico's, in observance of the 100th anniversary of the birth of Abraham Lincoln. (Add. pubs. for price.) M. O. L. L., (N. Y.)

Military Order of the Loyal Legion of the United States. *Pennsylvania Commandery.* Abraham Lincoln memorial meeting. (Add. pubs. for price.)—Abraham Lincoln. 15 c.—Celebration of the 100th anniversary of the birth of Abraham Lincoln, American Academy of Music, Feb. 12, 1909; programme. '09(S) c. 3 p. 8°, $1.50. M. O. L. L., (Pa.)

Miller, F. T. Portrait life of Lincoln. $2. Patriot.

Mitchell, W. B. Abraham Lincoln. 50 c. Smith & S.

Moores, C: W. Life of Abraham Lincoln. **60 c. net; *Same* (in Riverside literature ser.) **25 c. net; **15 c. net. Houghton M.

Morgan, J. Abraham Lincoln, the boy and the man. **$1.50 net. Macmillan.

Mott, E: H. Lincoln: brief biographical sketch. (Not for sale.) M. B. Brown.

New York Institution for the Instruction of the Deaf and Dumb. 100th anniversary of the birth of Abraham Lincoln. N. Y. Inst. Deaf and Dumb.

LINCOLN, Abraham.—*Continued.*
Newton, J. F. Lincoln and Herndon.—Abraham Lincoln; essay. ea., $3. Torch Press.
Noyes, I: P. Ode on Lincoln. 10 c. I: P. Noyes.
Oakleaf, J. B., *comp.* Analysis of the Gettysburg address [of Lincoln.] gratis. J. B. Oakleaf.
Oldroyd, O. H., *comp.* Centenary of the birth of Abraham Lincoln. (Add. author for price.) O. H. Oldroyd.
One hundredth anniversary of the birth of Abraham Lincoln; issued by Fs. G. Blair for the schools of Illinois. '08, [1909.] (My) 45 p. il. por. 8°, pap., gratis. F. G. Blair.
Pennell, O. H:, *comp.* Religious views of Abraham Lincoln. 75 c.; 25 c. Timby.
Peters, M. C. Abraham Lincoln's religion. 75 c. Badger.
Phillips, I: N. Lincoln. $1. McClurg.
Pickens, W: Abraham Lincoln. 15 c. W: Pickens.
Pickett, W: P. Negro problem: Abraham Lincoln's solution. **$2.50 net. Putnam.
Public exercises by the citizens of Worcester, Massachusetts, in commemoration of the one-hundredth anniversary of the birth of Abraham Lincoln, held in Mechanics' Hall, Friday evening, February 12th, 1909. '09, [1910.] (F) 37 p. por. O. pap. Worcester.
Putnam, G: H. Abraham Lincoln. **$1.25 net. Putnam.
Rantoul, R. S: Abraham Lincoln: an address. 50 c. Essex Inst.
Reiter, H. G. Story of Lincoln. 5 c. Paine.
Revell, E. I. Lincoln's birthday; exercises for the schoolroom. 25 c. Educ. Pub.
Rice, A. T., *comp. and ed.* Reminiscences of Abraham Lincoln. **$2 net. Harper.
Ross, R. R. Abraham Lincoln. 50 c. R. R. Ross.
Rothschild, A. Lincoln, master of men. **$1.50 net. Houghton M.
Russell, L. E. Abraham Lincoln: [bibliography.] 50 c. Torch Press.
Schauffler, R. H., *ed.* Lincoln's birthday. **$1 net. Moffat.
Schechter, S. Abraham Lincoln: memorial address. (Add. author for price.) S. Schechter.
Selby, P. Abraham Lincoln. 50 c. Chic. Hist.
Sellery, G: C. Lincoln's suspension of habeas corpus as viewed by Congress. 35 c. Univ. of Wis.
Sheppard, M. Abraham Lincoln. (Add. author for price.) M. Sheppard.
Sindelar, J. C:, *ed.* Lincoln Day entertainments. 25 c. Flanagan.
Snider, D. J. Abraham Lincoln: interpretation in biography. $1.50. Sigma.
Some Lincoln correspondence with southern leaders before the outbreak of the Civil War from the collection of Judd Stewart. '10(Mr19) c. 8°, pap. (Priv. pr.) J. Stewart.

LINCOLN, Abraham.—*Continued.*
Sparks, E. E., *and others, eds.* Semi-centennial of Lincoln-Douglas debates in Illinois, 1858-1908; circular of suggestions for school celebrations. 35 c. Phillips Bros.
Staples, E. L. Man of destiny; being the story of Abraham Lincoln: epic poem. $1; $2; 75 c. Lincoln.
Storey, M. Abraham Lincoln. (Priv. pr.) M. Storey.
Sumner, E: A. Abraham Lincoln. 50 c.; 25 c. Tandy-T.
Tarbell, I. M. Father Abraham. **50 c. net. Moffat.
Walsh, W: S. Abraham Lincoln and the London *Punch:* cartoons. **$1 net. Moffat.
Wanamaker primer on Abraham Lincoln. gratis. Wanamaker.
Warfield, E. D. Abraham Lincoln: a memorial address. 25 c. E. D. Warfield.
West Virginia. *Dept. of Free Schools.* Program for Lincoln day and suggestions for the observance of the birthdays of other eminent men; prep. by T: C. Miller. '09(My) 48 p. il. pors. 8°. (Add. pubs. for price.) Tribune Pr. Co., (W. Va.)
Wettstein, C. T., *comp. and ed.* Was Abraham Lincoln an infidel? $1.25. C. M. Clark.
Whipple, W. Heart of Lincoln. 50 c. Biddle Press.
Whipple, W. Story life of Lincoln. **$1.75 net. Winston.
White, H. Abraham Lincoln in 1854. gratis. State Hist., Ill.
Whitlock, B. Abraham Lincoln. **50 c. net. Small.
Whitney, H: C. Life of Lincoln. 2 v. **$2.50 net. Baker & T.
Williams, F. H. Burden bearer: an epic of Lincoln. **$2.50 net. Jacobs.

Lincoln, Azariah T:, and Walton, Ja. Henri, jr.
Exercises in elem. quantitative chemical analysis for students of agriculture. '08 (Ja11) il. tabs., 8°, *$1.50 net. Macmillan.

Lincoln, C: Z., ed.
See New York State. State of N. Y. messages from the governors.

Lincoln, Eldridge B.
Art of securing better teaching positions; hdbk. for teachers. '10(Ag20) c. D. pap., 60 c. Progress Club.

Lincoln, H. C.
Pract. steam and hot-water fitting; text book for the student and mechanic. '10(D17) 8°, $1. D: Williams.

Lincoln, Jonathan Thayer.
City of the Dinner-pail. '09(O2) c. D. **$1.25 net. Houghton M.

Lincoln, Jos. Crosby.
Cy Whittaker's place. '08(O10) c. il. D. †$1.50. Appleton.
Depot master. '10(My21) c. il. D. $1.50. Appleton.
Keziah Coffin. '09(O2) c. il. D. †$1.50. Appleton.
Our village. '09(Ap24) c. il. D. **$1.50 net. Appleton.

Lincoln, Varnum.
The deserted farm house, and other poems. 2d ed. '09(D) c. 123 p. il. por. 8°, $1. Gilson.

LINCOLN, Mass.
Vital records of Lincoln, Mass., to 1850. $2.25. N. E. Hist.

Lincoln centenary, Feb. 12, 1909: a prospectus for the schools of the state; comp. by Harlan Hoyt Horner. '09(Mr) 31 p. O. pap., gratis. N. Y. State Educ.

Lincoln centennial medal; presenting the medal of Abraham Lincoln by Jules Edouard Roiné, together with papers on the medal; its origin and symbolism by G: N. Olcott, and the Lincoln Centennial commemoration by R: Lloyd Jones, and certain characteristic utterances of Abraham Lincoln. '08(D5) c. D. medal in bronze, **$5 net, boxed; leath., medal in silver, **$12 net, boxed. Putnam.

Lincoln conscript. Greene, H. $1.50. Houghton M.

LINCOLN COUNTY, Kansas.
Bernhardt, C. Indian raids in Lincoln County, Kansas, 1864 and 1869. 50 c. Lincoln Sentinel.

LINCOLN FAMILY.
See Genealogies, Lea, J. H:; Learned, M. D.

Lincoln Fair. *See* Edgar, J: G: Runnymede.

Lincoln Fellowship. Proceedings at the first annual meeting and dinner of the Lincoln Fellowship, held at Delmonico's, New York City, Wednesday, February 12th, 1908. '08 (D5) c. por. 8°. (Not for sale.) Lincoln Fellowship.

Lincoln, Lee, Grant and other biographical addresses. *$2 net. Neale.

LINCOLN PARK, Portland, Me.
Dedication of Lincoln Park; being the public exercises held in the Payson Memorial Church and at Lincoln Park, Feb. 12, 1909, in observance of the 100th anniversary of the birth of Abraham Lincoln. '09, [1910.] (Je) 35 p. il. pors. plan, 8°, $1.25. Smith & S.

Lincoln story-calendar, 1911; [comp. by Wayne Whipple.] '10(D17) c. il. 4°, $1.25. Dutton.

Linden, Leon Mathias.
Concord of sweet notes. '08(Mr) c. 159 p. por. 12°, $1. Hyland.

Linden blossoms. Hrbek, J. D. $1.50. Torch Press.

Lindenbaum (Der). Seidel, H. *See* Storm, Theodor.

Lindgreen, Waldemar.
See Hayes, C: Willard.

Lindgren, C:
New salesmanship and how to do business by mail. '10(Ja22) c. il. D. $1.50; hf. leath., $2. Laird.

Lindgren, Waldemar.
See Hayes, C: Willard.

—, Graton, L: Caryl, and Gordon, C: H:
Ore deposits of New Mexico. '10(N) 361 p. il. maps, 4°, (U. S., Geological Survey, Professional paper.)

LINDISFARNE GOSPELS.
See Anglo-Saxon language.

Lindley, E. Marguerite.
Health in the home; pract. work on the promotion and preservation of health; with il. descriptions of Swedish gymnastic exercise for home and club practice. New and rev. ed. '09(Je) c. 14+414 p. il. 12°, $1. Health-Culture.

Lindley, Harlow.
Government of Indiana. [1910.] (My) c. '09. 110 p. 12°, 50 c. Ginn.
Bibliography (1 p.).

Lindsay. Arth. Adolphus.
Mind the builder: "The new psychology" continued. '09(Mr13) c. por. S. leath., $1. Lindsay Pub. Co.
New psychology. '08(Je27) c. por. 8°, $1.50; pap., $1. Lindsay Pub. Co.

Lindsay, Clara A.
In life's sweet afternoon; rhymes of the quiet hour. '09, [1910.] (Ja) c. 203 p. 12°. (Priv. pr.) Jacobs.

Lindsay, Flora Alice.
Glimpse of love; or, the doctor's wooing. '10(Jl2) c. por. 16°, 60 c. Lindsay.

Lindsay, Forbes, ["Boston," "Charles Harcourt."]
Bridge, and how to play it. '08(S5) c. il. S. (Popular handbooks.) 50 c. Penn Pub.
Daniel Boone, backwoodsman. '08(S26) c. il. D. $1.50. Lippincott.
Panama and the canal to-day; historical acct. of the canal project from the earliest times, with special references to the enterprises of the French company and the United States. '10(N5) c. il. maps, O. $3, boxed. L. C. Page.
Washington: the city and the seat of government. '08(N7) c. il. O. (Illustrated photogravure books.) $3, boxed; mor., $7. Winston.

Lindsay, Harry C., rep.
See Nebraska. *Sup. ct.* Repts.

Lindsay, N: Vachel.
Tramp's excuse and other poems. '09(O9) O. pap., gratis. N: V. Lindsay.

Lindsey, B: Barr, and O'Higgins, Harvey Jerrold.
The beast. '10(My7) c. por. D. $1.50 net. Doubleday, P.

Lindsey, W:
Severed mantle. '09(O23) c. col. il. O. **$1.35 net. Houghton M.

Lindsley, Philip.
Hist. of greater Dallas and vicinity. '09 (D) il. pors. 4°, $20. Lewis Pub.

LINEAR PERSPECTIVE.
See Perspective.

Linebarger, C: Estes.
Text-bk. of physics. '10(D24) c. il. 12°, $1.25. Heath.

LINEN.
See Weaving.

Lines from a doctor to his son. Long, J: I. T. $1. J: I. T. Long.

Linforth, Ivan Mortimer.
Epaphos and the Egyptian apis. '10(S) 81-92 p. Q. (Univ. of Cal. pubs.; Classical philology.) pap., 10 c. Univ. of Cal.

Lingen, Ernest.
Forgive and forget. '09(Mr6) c. D. $1.50. Benziger.

Lingley, C: Ramsdell.
Transition in Virginia from colony to commonwealth. '10(Jl9) c. (Columbia Univ. studies in hist., economics and public law.) pap., $1.50 net. Longmans.

LING'S SYSTEM.
See Gymnastics and physical culture.

LINGUISTICS.
See Language.

LINK MOTION.
See Valves.

Linn, Allen Dawson.
Instructions in vapor process drying. '10 (Ag) c. 71 p. il. fold. plans, 8°. A. D. Linn.

Linn, Rev. S:
Seven parables of the kingdom. '08(Jl18) c. 24°, 40 c. S: Linn.

LINOTYPE MACHINE.
Thompson, J: S. Mechanism of the linotype. $2. Inland Pr.

LINSEED OIL.
See Oils and fats.

Linton, Chester Burton.
Hints on forwarding, finishing and ruling. '10(D31) c. il. 16°, $2. Burt Pub.

Lion and dragon in northern China. Johnston, R. F. $5. Dutton.

Lionberger, I: H.
See Missouri. Laws governing manufacturing.

LIONS.
See Africa.

LIP-READING.
Nitchie, E: B. Lessons in lip-reading. *$1.25 net. Surdus.

Lipman, Jacob Goodale.
Bacteria and country life. '08(O10) il. 12°, (Rural science ser.) *$1.50 net. Macmillan.

LIPPI, *Fra* Filippo.
Anderson, A. J. Romance of a friar and a nun. *$2.50 net. Dodd.

Lippincott, Mrs. Sara Jane Clarke, ["Grace Greenwood."]
Merrie England; travels, descriptions, tales and historical sketches. '09(Ja23) c. il. 16°, 40 c. Ginn.

Lippincott's educational ser.; ed. by M. G. Brumbaugh. D. $1.25. Lippincott.
—Fleshman. Educational process.
—Kant. Educational theory.
—Schmucker. Study of nature.

Lippincott's new art lib.; ed. by H. H. Spielmann and P. G. Konody. il. 8°, $1.75 net. Lippincott.
—Fripp. Human anatomy for the art student.
—Solomon. Practice of oil painting.
—Toft. Modelling and sculpture.

Lippincott's new medical dict. Thomas, Q. $5 net. Lippincott.

Lippincott's new medical ser.; ed. by Fs. Randolph Packard. il. 8°. Lippincott.
—Kassabian. Röntgen rays and electro-therapeutics. $3.50.
—Packard. Text-book of diseases of the nose, throat and ear. subs., **$3.50 net; **$4 net.

Lippincott's thin paper ser. of popular classics. D. $1.25, boxed. Lippincott.
—Defoe. Life and adventures of Robinson Crusoe.
—Irving. Sketch book.
—Lamb. Tales from Shakespeare.
—Morris. King Arthur and the knights of the round table.—Tales from Shakespeare.

Lippincott's wonder lib. il. 8°. Lippincott.
—Selous. Wonders of the insect world. 75 c.

Lippman, F. W., ed.
See National Gallery.

Lippmann, Julie Mathilde.
Every day girls. '09(Je5) c. front. D. (Girls' own lib.) †75 c. McKay.

Lipps, Oscar Hiram.
The Navajos. '09(My) c. 136 p. il. map, 8°, (Little histories of North American Indians.) *$1 net. Torch Press.

LIPS.
See Mouth.

Lips of music. Porter, C. $1.25. Crowell.

Lipscomb, D:
Queries and answers; ed. by J. W. Shepherd. '10(Je) c. 458 p. por. 8°, $1.50. J. W. Shepherd.

Lipscomb, Herbert Cannon.
Aspects of the speech in the later Roman epic. '09(Ag) 48 p. 8°, $1. Furst.

Lipscomb, T. H.
Conscience and its culture; or, through conscience to Christ. '10(N5) c. D. $1. Pub. Ho. of M. E. Ch., So.

LIQUEURS.
See Liquors.

LIQUID AIR.
Hudson, C. S., *and* Garland, C. M. Tests of a liquid air plant. gratis. Univ. of Ill.

Liquid and gaseous fuels. Lewes, V. B. *$2 net. Van Nostrand.

LIQUORS.
American Academy of Political Science. Regulation of the liquor traffic. $1. Am. Acad. Pol. Sci.
Artman, S: R. Legalized outlaw: [liquor traffic.] $1. Business Men's.
Baker, D: C: Lincoln vs. liquor. (Add. pubs. for price.) Baker Pub.
Blow, B. E. Revenue law and the retail liquor dealer. $1. R. M. Wood.
Bonfort's wine and spirit trade directory. $3. Leoser Bros.
Crafts, W. F., *and others.* Intoxicating drinks and drugs in all lands and times. 75 c. Int. Ref. Bu.
Edwards, R: H:, *ed.* Liquor problem. 10 c. R: H: Edwards.
Flanders, E. B. Which? beer privilege anarchy or liberty with justice and prohibition? 10 c. E. B. Flanders.
Grohusko, J. A. Jack's manual on the vintage and production, care and handling of wines, liquors, etc. $1. J. A. Grohusko.
Hirschfeld, A. M. Standard handbook on wines and liquors. $1.50. Popper.
Joyce, H. C. Law of intoxicating liquors. $7.50. M. Bender.
Marshall, J: Kansas druggists' intoxicating liquor law. $1.25; 50 c. State Temperance.

LIQUORS.—*Continued.*
Matthews, A. Retail liquor dealers' manual of United States internal revenue laws. 75 c. J. M. Wolfe.
New Jersey. Laws rel. to the regulation and traffic in intoxicating liquors. $2. Soney.
United States. To regulate interstate commerce in intoxicating liquors, etc.; report from the Committee on the Judiciary, with hearings held by a subcommittee of said Committee, on bills to limit the effect of the regulations of commerce between the several states in certain cases. '09(O) 48+277 p. 8°. (Add. Superintendent for price.) U. S., Supt. of Docs.
Warner, H. S. Social welfare and the liquor problem. $1. Intercoll. Prohibition.
Woollen, W. W., *and* Thornton, W. W. Intoxicating liquors. $13.50. W. H. Anderson.
Wright, H. S., *comp.* Old time recipes for home made wines, cordials, and liqueurs. $1.50. Estes.
See also Beer;—Beverages;—Brewing;—Cider;—Taxation;—Temperance; — Temptation;—Whiskey;—Wine;—*also* names of states.

LISBON, Portugal.
See Portugal.

Lischer, Benno E:
Elements of orthodontia; lab'y note book for students and beginners, comprising a series of exercises in orthodontia technology. '09, [1910.] (Ja) c. 96 p. il. obl. 16°, $1. Mosby.

Lisk, Jos. P.
A B C of the steam engine; with description of the automatic governor. 2d ed. '10(Je4) il. 12°, 50 c. Spon.

LIST, Friedrich.
Hirst, M. E. Life of Friedrich List. *$2 net. Scribner.

List of books for college and high school libraries. '09(Jl) 63 p. 8°, pap. (Add. pubs. for price.) Eau Claire Bk.

Listen to me stories. Aspinwall, *Mrs.* A. $1.50. Dutton.

Lister, A. Lindsay, ["Badsworth."]
Principles of auction bridge; with the latest developments and the laws of the game; with cases and decisions by the committee of the Portland Club. '10 (O8) il. 16°, $1.25 net. Putnam.

Lister, Jos. Lister, Baron.
Collected papers of Joseph Baron Lister. 2 v. '10(Ag20) il. pors. Q. $10. Oxford Univ.

LISZT, Franz.
Ledos de Beaufort, R. Franz Liszt. $1.25. Ditson.

Litchfield, Grace Denio.
Baldur, the beautiful; [poem.] '10(D31) 8°, $1 net. Putnam.
Narcissus, and other poems. '08(Ap18) c. S. **$1 net. Putnam.
Supreme gift. '08(Mr28) c. front. D. †$1.50. Little, B. & Co.

Litchfield, H: Wheatland.
First church in Pembroke, [Mass.,] 1708-1908. '08, [1909.] (Ag) 21 p. front. 12°, 25 c. G: E: Lewis.

LITCHFIELD COUNTY, Ct.
Kilbourn, D. C. Bench and bar of Litchfield County, Conn. $5. Kilbourn.

Literary activity of the German Baptist Brethren in the eighteenth century. Flory, J: S $1.25. Brethren Pub. Ho.

Literary and biographical essays. Pearson, C: W: *$1.25 net. Sherman, F.

Literary and historical essays. Graham, H: G. *$2 net. Macmillan.

Literary appreciations. Smiley, A. J. 60 c. A. J. Smiley.

Literary by-paths in old England. Shelley, H: C: **$1.50 net. Little, B. & Co.

LITERARY CRITICISM.
See Criticism.

Literary history of Rome. Duff, J: W. $4. Scribner.

Literary history of the Adelphi and its neighborhood. Brereton, A. $3.50. Duffield.

Literary lapses. Leacock, S. B. $1.25 net. Lane.

Literary lives; ed. by W. Robertson Nicoll. D. **$1 net. Scribner.
—Gosse. Henrik Ibsen.
—Lubbock. Samuel Pepys.

Literary man's Bible. *See* Bible. O. T.

Literary portraits. *See* Gilfillan, G:

Literary reviews and criticism. Frye, P. H. **$1.25 net. Putnam.

Literary taste. Bennett, E. A. 75 c. net. Doran.

LITERATURE.
Babbitt, I. Literature and the American college. **$1.25 net. Houghton M.
Caird, E: Essays on literature. $1.75. Macmillan.
Chautauqua Literary and Scientific Circle. Studies in European literature. $1.50. Chautauqua Pr.
Cox, J: H. Literature in the common schools. **90 c. net. Little, B. & Co.
Davenport, B: R., *ed.* Digest of literature. 3 v. (Add. pubs. for price.) Hist. Pub. Co., (Pa.)
Gilder, J. L., *ed.* Masterpieces of the world's best literature. 8 v. $3. O. T. Harris.
Haverford essays: studies in modern literature. $1.25. Haverford Coll.
Hudson, W: H: Introd. to the study of literature. . $1.25 net. Heath.
Jackson, M. K. Outlines of the literary history of colonial Pennsylvania. *$1.25 net. Macmillan.
Ker, W: P. Epic and romance: essays on medieval literature. $1.50. Macmillan.
Lodge, H: C., *and* Halsey, F. W., *eds.* Best of the world's classics. $7.50; $20. Funk.
Lucas, E: V., *ed.* Some friends of mine [descriptions of characters from various authors.] **$1.25 net. Macmillan.
More, P. E. Shelburne essays. 5th ser. —6th ser. ea., **$1.25 net. Putnam.
Peck, H. T. Literature: [a lecture.] (Add. pubs. for price.) Columbia Univ.
Peck, H. T. Studies in several literatures. **$1.20 net. Dodd.

Little helps for home-makers; wealth of personal pract. knowledge in home-making, chosen from contributions made by ten thousand women of America to the *National Magazine.* '10(F19) c. 8°, $2. Chapple Pub.
Little heroine at school. Curtis, A. T. $1.25. Lothrop, L. & S.
Little heroine of Illinois. Curtis, A. T. †$1.25. Lothrop, L. & S.
Little heroine ser. il. D. †$1.25. Lothrop, L. & S.
—Curtis. Little heroine of Illinois.
Little histories of North American Indians. il. 8°, *$1 net. Torch Press.
—Lipps. The Navajos.
Little history of the English people. Jusserand, J. A. A. J. In 3 v. v. 3, pt. 2. *$3.50 net. Putnam.
Little Indian maidens at work and play. Ruyl, B. B. †$1. Dutton.
Little Indian tales. Roy, L. E. $1. E: S. Whaples.
Little journey to a great dentist. Hubbard, E. 25 c. Roycrofters.
Little journey to northern wilds. Koch, F. J: 50 c. Flanagan.
Little journey to South Africa. White, R. J. 50 c. Flanagan.
Little journey to Switzerland. '10(D) il. 50 c. net. Cassell.
Little journeys to ancient sanctuaries. Magill, H. B. *$1 net. Little Journeys.
Little journeys to the homes of famous women. Hubbard, E. (Add. pubs. for price.) Roycrofters.
Little journeys to the homes of good men and great. Hubbard, E. (Add. pubs. for price.) Roycrofters.
Little journeys to the homes of great business men. Hubbard, E. $2; $3; $5; $10. Roycrofters.
Little king. Major, C: $1.50. Macmillan.
Little Knight of the X Bar B. Maule, *Mrs.* M. K. $1.50. Lothrop, L. & S.
Little lady at the fall of Quebec. Barnes, A. M. †$1.25. Penn Pub. Co.
Little lame prince. *See* Craik, *Mrs.* D. M. M.
Little land and a living. Hall, B. $1. Arcadia.
Little letters to boys grown tall. "Uncle Ned," *pseud.* 80 c.; 50 c. Abbey.
Little lower than the angels. Parkhurst, C: H: *$1.25 net. Revell.
Little maid in Toyland. Sutton, A. L. $1. Saalfield.
Little maid Marian. Blanchard, A. E. †$1. Jacobs.
Little maid of Boston town. Lothrop, *Mrs.* H. M. S. $1.50. Lothrop, L. & S.
Little maid who danced to every mood. Nyblom, H. †75 c. Estes.
"Little man from Chicago." Meminger, *Mrs.* L. S. $1. Alliance Press.
Little Maryland garden. Hays, H. A. **$1.75 net. Putnam.
Little masqueraders. '08(D5) 12°, pap., 20 c. Laird.
Little masterpieces of autobiography. Iles, G:, *ed.* 6 v. **75 c. net; per set, **$4.50 net. Doubleday, P.
Little Maude and her mamma. Loomis, C: B. †50 c. Doubleday, P.
Little Miss Cricket at school. Jackson, *Mrs.* G. E. S. †$1.25. Appleton.
Little Miss Evangeline. Raymond, *Mrs.* E. H. †$1.25. Penn Pub. Co.
Little Miss Fales. Knipe, *Mrs.* E. B. $1.25. Harper.
Little Miss Quixote. Haymes, R. $1.50. Longmans.
Little Mr. Thimblefinger stories. Harris, J. C. 40 c. Houghton M.
Little Mother Meg. Turner, E. †75 c. McKay.
Little mother ser. il. 24°, bds., 50 c. Dutton.
—Hardy *and* Gask. Three bold pirates.
—Hughes. Pudgy.
—Jamieson. Jolly tars.—Warriors brave.
—Jewett. Tame bunnies and wild.
—Mayer. Jumbo and his family.
Little Ned Happy and Flora. Smith, G. **$1.30 net. Harper.
Little Nell. *See* Dickens, C:
Little Nemo in Slumberland. McKay, W. 60 c. Cupples & L.
Little novels of famous cities. il. D. Stokes.
—Hare. Felicita; romance of old Siena. †$1.25.
Little old New York. '10(N) 32 p. il. fold. plan, 16°, 10 c. Oxford Pub.
Little old outlaws. Miller, *Mrs.* A. A. 75 c. net. McClurg.
Little old-time Sunday. Allen, C. S. 75 c. C. S. Allen.
Little patch o' blue. Sharp, G. S. $1. Badger.
Little people. Whiteing, R: *$1.50 net. Cassell.
Little people everywhere. See McDonald, *Mrs.* Etta Blaisdell.
Little people's recitation series. 4 v. '09(O2) c. D. ea., 75 c. Caldwell.
"Little perfect hour." McLaughlin, W., *comp.* 75 c. W. McLaughlin.
Little Perkie. May, S. 30 c. Jacobs.
Little Peter. Harrison, *Mrs.* M. S. K. *$1.50 net. Doran.
Little pilgrimage ser. il. D. L. C. Page.
—Crawford. St. Botolph's Town. $2.50; $6.
—Tozier. Susan in Sicily. $2.
Little plays. Dalkeith, L. 50 c. Dutton.
Little plays and exercises; incl. drills and music for younger children; by various authors. '10(Ja8) c. 12°, (Instructor entertainment ser.) 35 c. F. A. Owen.
Little plays for little people. Noyes, *Mrs.* M. I. O. 35 c. Ginn.
Little Polly Primrose and her friends. Warren, C. F. 75 c. C. M. Clark.
Little Prince Charming. Jeffers, *Mrs.* H. E. V. $1.35. Reid Pub.
Little princess of the pines. Higgins, A. C. $1.25. Penn Pub. Co.
Little princess of Tonopah. Higgins, A. C. †$1.25. Penn Pub. Co.
Little problems of married life. Jordan, W: G: $1 net. Revell.
Little prodigals. Frayser, N. L. 35 c. net. F. M. Barton.
Little Prudy books. See Clarke, Rebecca Sophia.

Little red fox. Ames, *Mrs.* E. †60 c. Estes.

Little red hen ser. 5 v. '09(D) col. il. ea., bds., 50 c. Doran.
Contents: **Little small red hen; Princess in the ragged gown; Story of Roger; Little green door; Mother Goose nursery rhymes.**

Little red mare. Young, O. E. 15 c. Dick.

Little Red Riding Hood, and The three little bears; pictured [in color] by J: R. Neill. '10(D17) c. D. (Turnover books.) 60 c. Reilly & B.

Little revolution: a politico-social romance; by the author of "None so pretty," "A discrepant world," etc. 2d impression. '08 (Mr14) D. †$1.75. Longmans.

LITTLE ROCK, Ark.
Ohlander, M., *comp.* Little Rock and Pulaski County, Arkansas, illustrated. 50 c. M. Ohlander.

Little Sam in Volendam. Kerr, E. M. **$1.25 net. Moffat.

Little sermons on the Sunday Gospels. Wakeford, J: $1.50 net. Longmans.

Little shepherd of Provence. Stein, E. $1. L. C. Page.

Little singer. Lewis, E. S. $1 net. Lippincott.

Little sister of the poor. Kaneko, J. C. 25 c. Progressive Woman.

Little sister Prue. Brooks, A. †$1. Lothrop, L. & S.

Little sister Snow. Little, F., *pseud.* **$1 net. Century Co.

Little sky high. Butterworth, H. **40 c. net. Crowell.

Little songs for two. Cooke, E. V. *$1 net; *$1.50 net. Dodge.

Little stings. Crosland, T: W: H. *75 c. net. J: W. Luce.

Little stories about little animals. Holton, S. 60 c. Children's Pub.

Little stories for boys and girls: [Greek heroes and heroines.] '09(Ag) il. $1.50. (600 copies.) Seymour.

Little stories of Quebec. Le Rossignol, J. E: *$1.25 net. Jennings.

Little talks to little people. Farrar, J. M. $1.20 net. Funk.

"Little ten minutes." Bayley, F. *$1 net. Revell.

Little terror. Blaney, C: E: 25 c. J. S. Ogilvie.

Little tin soldier. Mar, G. $1. Lippincott.

Little torment. Kilroy, M. $1. Lippincott.

Little tot lib.; il. by Fk. Adams. 2 v. '10 (N) 8°, ea., 75 c. Dodge.

Little tots' lib. 6 v. '09, [1910.] (F) 18°. (Add. pubs. for price.) Dutton.

Little treasury ser. of devotional books. 9 v. '10(D) col. il. ea., 25 c. Doran.

Little violinist. Aldrich, T: B. 25 c. Phonograph.

Little wee bear and Golden Hair. Byron, M. 25 c. Stokes.

Little wizard of White Cloud Hill. Crichton, F. E. $1.25. Longmans.

Little women. Alcott, L. M. **63 c. net. Little, B. & Co.

Little workers. Lowe, C. M. $1. Dutton.

Little world. Gerstenberg, A. $1.25. Dramatic.

Littlefield, C: Wentworth.
Twelve vitalized tissue remedies for private and domestic use; constituting a new science in the work of health and healing. '10(O1) c. 8°, (Companion life ser.) $2.50. C: W. Littlefield.

Littlefield, Ja. Drake.
Notes for forge shop practice; course for high schools. '10(D3) c. il. 8°, (Haytol ser. of textbooks for industrial education.) 80 c. Taylor-H.

Littlefield, Milton Smith.
Hand-work in the Sunday-school; with an introd. by Patterson Du Bois. '08(Ag8) c. il. maps, D. *$1 net. S. S. Times.

Littleheart, Oleta.
Lure of the Indian country, and a romance of its great resort. '09(Je26) c. il. S. moccasin skin, $1; pap., 25 c. A. Abbott.

Littlest fairy. Webb, E. C. $1.50. Dodge.

LITURGIES.
See Worship;—*also* names of churches.

Live dolls' party days. Gates, *Mrs.* J. S. $1.25. Bobbs-M.

Live dolls' play days. Gates, *Mrs.* J. S. †$1.25. Bobbs-M.

LIVE STOCK.
See Cattle;—Domestic animals.

LIVELIHOOD.
See Political economy.

Lively, Rev. W: Irven.
Cloud rifts: poems. '08(Ag22) c. por. 12°, $1. Lively.

LIVER.
White, W: H. Common affection of the liver. *$2 net. Wood.

Livermore, Kenneth Carter.
See Warren, G: F.

Livermore, Virgil B:, and Williams, Ja. R.
How to become a competent motorman. '08(Ag1) c. il. 12°, **$1 net. Van Nostrand

Livery of heaven. Sawyer, R. H. $1.50. C. M. Clark.

Lives of Christian ministers. Kernodle, P: J. (Add. author for price.) P: J. Kernodle.

Lives of great Altrurians. 16°. Altrurians.
—Robinson. Comrad Kropotkin. $1.

Lives of great English writers. Hinchman, W. S. **$1.50 net. Houghton M.

Lives of illustrious men. *See* Plutarch.

Lives of the bishops of North Carolina. Haywood, M. D. $1.50. A. Williams.

Lives of the British architects. Chancellor, E. B. $2 net. Scribner.

Lives of the fur folk. Haviland, M. D. $1.35 net. Longmans.

Lives of the novelists. Scott, *Sir* W. 35 c. net; 70 c. net. Dutton.

Living anatomy and pathology. Rotch, T: M. $6 net. Lippincott.

Living atonement. Champion, J: B: $1.25. Griffith.

Living Bible. Wells, A. R. 75 c. Un. Soc. C. E.

Living Christ and dying heathenism. Warneck, J. L. *$1.75 net. Revell.

Living Church annual, and Whittaker's churchman's annual; a church cyclopedia and almanac, 1909; 56th year of Whittaker's almanac, 28th year of Living Church annual, first year of consolidation. '08(D26); 1910. '10(Ja1); 1911. '10(D31) pors. D. ea., 75 c.; pap., 50 c. Young Churchman.
Living fire. Rogers, J. $1.50. Occult Pub. Co.
Living ideals. Del Mar, E. $1. Progressive Lit.
Living illustrations. Carradine, B. *$1. Chr. Witness.
Living masters of music ser.; ed. by Rosa Newmarch. il. D. *$1 net. Lane.
—Liebich. Claude-Achille Debussy.
—Newmann. Richard Strauss.
Living mummy. Pratt, A. †$1.50. Stokes.
Living on a little. Benton, C. F., *pseud.* $1.25. Estes.
Living races of mankind. Johnston, *Sir* H. H. 2 v. *$10 net. Bowman.
Living teachers. Slattery, M. *35 c. net. F. M. Barton.
Living thought. Erwood, W: J. $1. W: J. Erwood.
Living universe. Bray, H: T. $3.50. Truro.
Living word. Worcester, E. **$1.50 net. Moffat.

Livingston, Alice Muriel.
See Williamson, C: Norris.

Livingston, Edn. Brockholst.
Livingstons of Livingston Manor; being the hist. of that branch of the Scottish house of Callendar which settled in the English province of New York during the reign of Charles the Second; and also incl. an acct. of Robert Livingston of Albany, "The nephew," a settler in the same province, and his principal descendants. '10(Ap) 33+590 p. il. pors. map, facsim. fold. geneal. tab., 8°, $10. J: H: Livingston.

Livingston, Leon Ray.
Life and adventures of A-no. 1, America's most celebrated tramp; written by himself. '08(My16) il. por. 8°, 25 c. Self Mastery.

Livingston, Luther S., comp.
American book prices current, Sept. 1, 1907, to Sept. 1, 1908. v. 14. '08(O10); Sept. 1, 1908, to Sept. 1, 1909. v. 15. '10(F5) O. ea., **$6 net; Large pap., ed., **$15 net. Dodd.
Bibliography of the first editions in book form of the writings of Henry Wadsworth Longfellow; comp. largely from the collection formed by the late Jacob Chester Chamberlain, with assistance from his notes and memoranda. '08(D5) c. O. (Chamberlain bibliographies.) *$3 net; on Van Gelder pap., *$10 net (Priv. pr.) Dodd.

LIVINGSTON FAMILY.
See Genealogies.

Livy [Livius Patavinus, Titus].
[Works:] book 1 and selections from books 2-10; ed. by Wa. Dennison. '08(F8) map, 16°, (Macmillan's Latin classics.) *60 c. net. Macmillan.
Ab vrbe condita; liber IX.; ed., with introd. and notes, by T. Nicklin. '10(My14) D. 75 c. Oxford Univ.

Livy [Livius Patavinus, Titus].—*Continued.*
Book IX; ed., with introd., notes, etc., by W. B. Anderson. '09(O9) 8°, (Pitt Press ser.) *75 c. net. Putnam.
Evans, A. E. Roman law studies in Livy. 40 c. net. Macmillan.
Selections from the first decade; ed. by Omera Floyd Long. '09(Ja23) c. map, D. (Lake classicsal ser.) 60 c. Scott, F. & Co.

Lloyd, Alfr. H:
Will to doubt: essay in philosophy for the general thinker. '08(F8) c. 12°, *$1.25 net. Macmillan.

Lloyd, Rev. Arth., 1852-.
Every-day Japan: introd. by Count Havashi. '09(Ap24) il. O. *$4 net. Cassell.
Wheat among the tares: studies of Buddhism in Japan. '08(Ag1) 12°, *$1.10 net. Macmillan.

Lloyd, Rev. Arth. Selden, 1857-.
Christianity and the religions; three lectures del. at the summer school of Harvard University, 1908. '09(My8) 12°, **75 c. net. Dutton.

Lloyd, Curtis Gates.
Synopsis of the known phalloids; with an illustration of each species. '09, [1910.] (Mr) 96 p. il. por. 8°. (Not for sale. Apply to author for terms.) Lloyd Lib.

Lloyd, Mrs. Ella Bentley.
Grandma's cook book; collection of tried recipes. '10(My14) c. 12°, $1.25. Jennings.

Lloyd, Emily, pseud.
See Maurer, *Mrs.* Ruth D. Johnson.

Lloyd, Ernest Marsh.
Review of the history of infantry. '08 (Je13) O. *$2 net. Longmans.

Lloyd, Fs. Ernest.
Physiology of stomata. '08(Mr28) il. tabs., Q. (Carnegie Institution of Washington pub.) pap., $1.50. Carnegie.
—, and Bigelow, Maurice Alpheus.
Teaching of biology in the secondary school. '08(D12) 8°, (American teachers' ser.) $1.50. Longmans.

Lloyd, Frederic E. J., D.D., comp.
Church musician's directory, 1910; blue book of the church musicians of America. '10(D3) c. O. $3.50. Ritzmann, B. & Co.

Lloyd, H: Demarest.
Lords of industry. '10(D3) c. D. $1.50 net. Putnam.
Mazzini, and other essays. '10(D31) c. 8°, $1.50 net. Putnam.
Men, the workers. '09(S11) c. por. O. **$1.50 net. Doubleday, P.

Lloyd, J:, pseud.
See Morgan, Jacque Lloyd.

Lloyd, J: Uri.
Eclectic alkaloids, resins, resinoids, oleoresins and concentrated principles; incl. portraits and biographies of John King, William Stanley Merrell, Alexander Wilder, William Tully, Grover Coe, Robert Stafford Newton, Edward S. Wayne, Calvin Newton and John Coakley Lettsom. [1910.] (Jl) c. 7+54 p. pors. 4°, (Lloyd Library of Botany, Pharmacy and Materia Medica, bull.) $1. Lloyd Lib.

Lloyd, J: W:
Life's beautiful battle; or, the human soul before pain; study in the reconciliation. '10(Jl16) c. 12°, $1.25. J: W: Lloyd.

Lloyd, Julius A.
Home made hash; or, scraps from old feasts; menagerie of ideas, original, rare and exotic. 2d ed., rev. and enl. '09 (My) c. 320 p. il. por. 12°, $1.25. J. A. Lloyd.

Lloyd, Morton Githens.
Errors in magnetic testing with ring specimens. '09(Je) 435-452 p. diagrs. 4°, pap. U. S., Supt. of Docs.

Lloyd-George, D:
Better times; speeches. '10(D10) D. $1 net. Doran.

Lloyd Library of Botany, Pharmacy, and Materia Medica bull. 4°, $1. Lloyd Pub.
—Life and medical discoveries of Samuel Thomson. (Reproduction ser.)
—Lloyd. Eclectic alkaloids, resins, resinoids, oleo-resins and concentrated principles.

Lo Ammi, Israel.
Nungasser, I. M. Israel Lo Ammi. 75 c. B'way Pub.

Loaded dice. Clark, E. H. †$1.50. Bobbs-M.

Loane, M.
Englishman's castle: [articles on the British poor.] '09(Ap10) D. $2. Longmans.
From their point of view: [studies among the poor in England.] '08(Je13) D. $2. Longmans.
Neighbours and friends. '10(Ap2) D. $2. Longmans.
Next street but one: [studies of the Eng. poor.] New and cheaper ed. '08(My2) D. $1.25. Longmans.
Queen's poor: life as they find it in town and country. [New and cheaper ed.] '08(My2) D. $1.25. Longmans.

Loans.
Bureau of Social Research, New York. Chattle loan business. 25 c. Charities Pub.
Wassam, C. W. Salary loan business in New York City. 75 c. Charities Pub.
See also Finance;—Investments.

Lob Lie-by-the-Fire. *See* Ewing, *Mrs.* J. H. G.

Lobben, Peder.
Machinists' and draftsmen's hdbk. 2d and enl. ed. '10(O1) c. il. tabs., 8°. $2.50. Van Nostrand.

Lobingier, C: Sumner.
The people's law; or, popular participation in law-making, from ancient folk-moot to modern referendum; with an introd. by G: Elliott Howard. '09(D18) c. O. **$4 net. Macmillan.

Lobstein, P.
Introd. to Protestant dogmatics; auth. tr. from the orig. French ed. by Arth. Maxon Smith. [2d ed.] '10(D3) c. D. $1.50 net. Univ. of Chic.

Local and state government in Nebraska. Wilson, E. P. 20 c. Univ. Pub.

Local government.
Chandler, A. D. Local self-government. (Priv. pr.) A. D. Chandler.

Local government.—*Continued.*
Powell, E. T: Essentials of self-government, (England and Wales.) *$1.50 net. Longmans.
See Cities; — Municipal government;—Towns;—Villages.

Local history story hour. Martin, D. B. 10 c. State Hist. Wis.

Loch, C: Stewart.
Charity and social life; short study of religious and social thought in relation to charitable methods and institutions. '10 (Jl30) D. $2 net. Macmillan.

Lochmer, A.
Easy method for Croatians to learn the English language without a teacher; with pronunciation of the English in Croatian phonetic equivalents. '09(D18) 12°, bds., *$1.50 net. Caspar.

Lock, C: G. Warnford.
Miners' pocket-book. 5th ed., entirely rewritten. '09(Mr13) il. 12°, limp leath., *$4 net. Spon.

Lock, Rob. Heath.
Recent progress in the study of variation, heredity and evolution. New and enl. ed. '10(Ap23) il. 8°, $2 net. Dutton.

Lock and key library. *See* Hawthorne, Julian, *ed.*

Lockard, J: Ready.
Bee hunting. '08(N7) c. 16°, pap., 25 c. A. R. Harding.

Lockard, Lorenzo B.
Tuberculosis of the nose and throat. '08 (D) 400 p. il. *$5 net. Mosby.

Locke, Elma Iona, ed.
See Brown, Nellie Clarke, *ed.*

Locke, Ja.
Plotting of Frances Ware. '09(My15) c. D. †$1.50. Moffat.
Stem of the crimson dahlia. '08(F15) il. D. †$1.50. Moffat.

Locke, J:
Essay on the human understanding; with the notes and illustrations of the author and an analysis of his doctrine of ideas. New and rev. ed. '09(Ap17) 8°, *$1.50 net. Dutton.

Locke, John.
Alexander, S: Locke. *50 c. net. Dodge.

Locke, Rob. H:
Latin forms and syntax. '08(D) c. 206 p. 8°, *$1 net. McVey.

Locke, W: J:
Works. Uniform ed. In 10 v. '08(Je27) 12°, $15. Lane.
Christmas mystery; the story of three wise men. '10(O22) c. il. O. 75 c. net. Lane.
Idols. '10(D) 75 c. Burt.
Septimus. '09(Ja2) c. il. D. †$1.50. Lane.
Simon the jester. '10(Je11) c. il. D. $1.50. Lane.

Locker-Lampson, S. F. D.
See Lampson, S. F. D. Locker-.

Lockerbie, George Murray.
Browning, E. G. Lockerbie's assessment list of Indianapolis. 25 c. W. K. Stewart.

Lockhart, Arth. J:
Birds of the cross, and other poems. '09, [1910.] (F) c. 9-239 p. 16°, $1. C. R. Lougee.

Lockhart, J: Gibson.
Selections from Lockhart's life of Sir Walter Scott; ed. by A. Barter, with notes. '10(D24) 12°, 30 c. net. Macmillan.

Locking. Lavarack, F: C. $2. F: C. Lavarack.

LOCKJAW.
See Tetanus.

Locks to pick. Harnwell, A. J. W. $1. Badger.

Lockwood, Luke Vincent.
Collection of English furniture of the XVII. and XVIII. centuries. '09(Ja30) c. il. 4°. (Not for sale.) Tiffany Studios.

Lockyer, Sir Jos. Norman and Winifred L., comps.
Tennyson as a student and poet of nature; with introd. and notes. '10(D10) D. $1.50 net. Macmillan.

Lockyer, Winifred L.
See Lockyer, *Sir* Jos. Norman.

LOCO PLANT.
Marsh, C: D. Loco-weed disease of the plains. 25 c. U. S., Supt. of Docs.
United States. *Dept. of Agriculture.* Loco-weed disease.

LOCOMOTIVES.
American Railway Master Mechanics' Association. Locomotive dict. $16. Railroad Age.
Fowler, G: L. Locomotive breakdowns. $1. Henley.
Fowler, G: L., *and* Mellin, C. J. Locomotive design. 25 c. Indust. Press.
Fowler, G: L., *and* Wood, W: W. Locomotive breakdowns, emergencies and their remedies. $1. Henley.
Garbe, R: Application of highly superheated steam to locomotives. *$2.50 net. Henley.
Goss, W: F. M. High steam pressures in locomotive service.—Superheated steam in locomotive service. ea., $1.25. Carnegie.
Grimshaw, R. Locomotive catechism. $2.50. Henley.
Howden, J. R. Boys' book of locomotives. $2. Stokes.
Jeffrey, H. S. Boilers of locomotives of interstate commerce; statement from Mr. H. S. Jeffrey in support of the bill to promote the safety of employees and travelers upon railroads by compelling common carriers engaged in interstate commerce to equip their locomotives with safe and suitable boilers and appurtenances thereto. [1910.] (Jl) 14 p. 8°. Gov. Pr. Off.
Jones, F. L. Questions, answers and whys on the locomotive. (Add. pub. for price.) F. L. Jones.
Kirkman, M. M. Science of railways. [v. 6,] Locomotive appliances. per set, $36. (Sold in sets only.) [v. 7,] The locomotive. In 2 bks. $3.50.—[v. 8,] Engineers' and firemen's hdbk.—"Science of railways" portfolio. $5. C. Phillips.
Lake, C: S. Locomotives of 1907. 50 c. Spon.

LOCOMOTIVES.—*Continued.*
McArdle, F., *and* Helmholtz, H:, *eds.* Locomotive text for engineers and firemen. $2.50. McArdle & H.
National Correspondence School of Railroading. Locomotive text for engineers. Nat. Corr. Sch. R. R.
Pendred, V. Railway locomotive. *$2 net. Van Nostrand.
Perrigo, C: O. E. Change gear devices. $1. Henley.
Reilly, T. S. Locomotive firing. 50 c. Crandall Pub.
Rhodes, J: C., *comp.* Questions and answers in the use of coal and oil fuels and locomotive operation. $2. J: C. Rhodes.
Schmidt, O. C., *ed.* Pract. railroading. 6 v. $20. Stanley Inst.
Sinclair, A. Locomotive engine running and management. $2. Wiley.
Swingle, C. F. Locomotive fireman's boiler instructor. $1.50. Drake.
Taylor, A. T. Modern British locomotives. *$2 net. Spon.
Turner, E:, *pseud.* Standard guide for locomotive engineers and firemen. 75 c. Laird.
Wood, W: W. Walschaert locomotive valve gear. $1.50. Henley.
See also Air-brake;—Coal;—Fuel;—Railroads;—Steam engine.

Locy, W: Albert.
Biology and its makers. '08(Ag15) c. il. O. **$2.75 net. Holt.

Lode and placer claims. Howell, E: B. $1. Keefe.

Lodeman, E. G.
Spraying of plants: hist., principles and practice of the application of liquids and powders to plants for the purpose of destroying insects and fungi; with a preface by B. T. Galloway. '08(Mr21) c. il. 12, (Rural science ser.) **$1.25 net. Macmillan.

Lodge, G: Cabot.
Herakles: [a play.] '08(D12) c. D. **$1.25 net. Houghton M.
Soul's inheritance, and other poems. '09 (D18) c. D. **$1 net. Houghton M.

Lodge, Gonzalez.
Vocab. of high school Latin: vocab. of Cæsar's Gallic wars, books 1-5; Cicero against Catiline, on Pompey's command, for the poet Archais; Vergil's Æneid, books 1-6; arr. alphabetically and in the order of occurrence. '08(F8) c. O. (Columbia Univ., Teachers' Coll., contrib. to education.) *$1.50 net.—Rev. ed. '09 (D18) $1.50. Teachers' Coll.

Lodge, H: Cabot.
Short history of the English colonies in America. Rev. ed. '09(My22) c. map, 8°, $3. Harper.
Speech on immigration before the Boston City Club, Boston, Mass., on Mar. 20, 1908. '08(D) 9 p. 8°. (Add. Superintendent for price.) U. S., Supt. of Docs.

Lodge, H: Cabot.—*Continued.*
Speeches and addresses, 1884-1909. [2d ed.] '09, [1910.] (F) c. 10+462 p. 8°, $2.50. Houghton M.
See also United States. Investigation relative to wages.

—, and Halsey, Fs. Whiting, eds.
The best of the world's classics; restricted to prose; with an introd., biographical and explanatory notes, etc. In 10 v. '09 (D4) c. S. per set, $7.50; full levant, $20, boxed. Funk.

Lodge, Sir Oliver Jos.
Ether of space. '09(Je5) c. front. figs. S. (Harper's lib. of living thoughts.) **75 c. net. Harper.
Immortality of the soul. '08(Je6) c. D. *$1 net. Ball Pub.
Modern views of electricity. 3d ed. '08 (Ja11) il. 12°, *$1.25 net. Macmillan.
Parent and child; treatise on the moral and religious education of children. '10(S17) c. D. 50 c. net. Funk.
Reason and belief. '10(D17) c. D. $1.25 net. Moffat.
Science and mortality. '08(O31) c. O. **$2 net. Moffat.
Survival of man; study in unrecognized human faculty. '09(D18) c. O. **$2 net. Moffat.

—, Campbell, Rev. Reginald J:, Tyrrell, Rev. G:, and others.
Jesus or Christ? [by Father Tyrrell, Father Jos. Rickaby, Principal Garvie, Prof. Percy Gardner, etc.] '09, [1910.] (F) 8°, *$1.50 net. Sherman, F.

Lodge, R. B.
Bird-hunting through wild Europe. '10 (My14) c. il. $2.50 special net. Appleton.

Lodge, R:
See Hunt, *Rev.* W: Polit. hist. of Eng. v. 8.

Lodge, T:
Rosalynde: being the original of Shakespeare's "As you like it"; ed. by W. W. Greg. '08(O17) 16°, (Shakespeare lib.: Shakespeare classics.) bds., *$1 net; Persian, *$1.60 net; Lib. ed., hf. parchment, 12°, *$1.70 net. Duffield.
Rosalynde or, Euphues' golden legacy; ed., with introd. and notes, by E: Chauncey Baldwin. '10(D31) c. S. (Standard English classics.) 35 c. Ginn.

Lodger overhead. Davis, C: B. †$1.50. Scribner.

Loeb, Ja.
Loeb collection of Arretine pottery, catalogued; with introd. and descriptive notes by G: H. Chase. '08(N) 8+167 p. il. 4°, $10. Harvard Co-op.
Collection is in the Fogg Museum of Art, Harvard University.

Loehe, Wilhelm.
Three books concerning the church, offered to friends of the Lutheran Church for consideration and discussion; tr. from the German by E: T. Horn. '08, [1909.] (F) c. 13+202 p. 12°, $1. Pilger.

Loewengard, Max Julius.
Harmony modernized; tr. from the 6th augmented and thoroughly rev. German ed. by Dr. Th. Baker. '10(O8) c. O. $1.25 net. Schirmer.

Loewy, Wa., tr.
See Germany. Civil code.

Lofthouse, W. F.
Bible, its origin and authority. '10(F19) S. *50 c. net. Eaton & M.

Log cabin to White House ser. 12°. Hurst.
—Thayer. From log cabin to White House. 50 c.

Log cabins.
See Architecture.

Log of the Kaalokai. Walker, F. D. $1. Hawaiian Gazette.

Log of the "Laura." Holmes, *Mrs.* B. F. Univ. Press, (Camb.)

Log of the voyage of the Atlantic fleet, Dec. 16, 1907-Feb. 22, 1909. '09(N) c. 47 p. 12°, 25 c. Navy Pub.

Log of three across the sea. Smeeth, H. M. $1. Henneberry.

Logan, G: Wood.
Elements of hydrographic surveying. '08 (F) c. '07. 176 p. il. 12°. (Add. pubs. for price.) U. S. Naval Inst.

Logan, Mrs. Indiana Washington Peddicord.
Kelion Franklin Peddicord of Quirk's Scouts, Morgan's Kentucky Cavalry, C. S. A.: biographical and autobiographical; together with a general biographical outline of the Peddicord family. '08(Jl4) c. pors. O. *$2 net. Neale.

Logan, Mrs. J: A., ed.
See Logan, Mary Simmerson Cunningham.

Logan, Mary Simmerson Cunningham, [Mrs. J: A. Logan,] ed.
Our national government; life and scenes in our national capital. '09(My8) c. il. pors. facsims., 8°, $3.25; hf. mor., $3.75; full mor., $4.25. Baldwin.

Logan, Maurice S.
Musicology. '09(D11) c. figs. O. $1.25. Hinds.

Logan, W: Newton.
Clays of Mississippi. pt. 1, Brick clays and clay industry of northern Mississippi. '08 (O3) il. map, O. (Mississippi State Geol. Survey bull.) pap. (Add. pub. for price.) Brandon Pr.
Pottery clays of Mississippi. [1910.] (Jl) 228 p. il. 8°, (Miss. State Geolog. Survey, bull.) pap., 50 c. Miss. Geol. Survey.

Logarithms.
Castle, Fk. Logarithmic and other tables. *20 c. net. Macmillan.
Conant, L. L., *ed.* Five-place logarithmic and trigonometric tables. 50 c. Am. Bk.
Durell, F. Logarithmic and trigonometric tables. 75 c. C: E. Merrill.
Farmer, R. C. *and* M. M. Four-figure logarithms on a new graphic system. 20 c. net. Longmans.
Huntington, E. V., *comp.* Four place table of logarithms and trigonometric functions. 60 c. Harvard Co-op.
Inskip, G: D. New manual of squares and logarithms. $3. M. C. Clark.
Saxton, E. Logs for four-place work. $3. E. Saxton.

LOGARITHMS.—*Continued.*
Smoley, C. Tables containing parallel tables of logarithms and squares of feet, inches and fractions of interest. $2.50. Engineering News.
Sprague, C: E. Logarithms to 12 places. $3. C: E. Sprague.
Use of logarithms and logarithmic tables. 25 c. Indust. Press.
Wallace, J. Logarithmic land measurement. $2. Spon.
Woodward, C. J. A B C of five-figure logarithms for general use. $1.25. Spon.

LOGIC.
Atkinson, W: W. Art of logical thinking; or, the laws of reasoning. $1. Progress Co.
Baldwin, J. M. Thoughts and things: study of genetic logic. v. 2. *$2.75 net. Macmillan.
Bode, B. H: Outline of logic. $1. Holt.
Creighton, J. E. Introductory logic. *$1.40 net. Macmillan.
Gibson, W. R. B., *and* Klein, A. Problem of logic. *$4.50 net. Macmillan.
Hocking, W: E. Two extensions of the use of graphs in elementary logic. 15 c. Univ. of Cal.
Jevons, W: S. Studies in deductive logic. *$1.60 net. Macmillan.
Jones, A. L. Logic, inductive and deductive. **$1 net. Holt.
Joyce, G: H. Principles of logic. $2.50. Longmans.
Pillsbury, W. B. Psychology of reasoning. $1.50 net. Appleton.
Taylor, W: J. Elem. logic. $1.25. Scribner.
See also Evidence;—*also* Mill, John Stuart.

Logic and imagination in perception of truth. Stoner, J. R. $1.50. Cochrane.

Logic of will. Wodehouse, H. *$1.10 net. Macmillan.

Logical basis of educational theory from the standpoint of the "instrumental" logic. Tear, D. A. 50 c. Univ. of Chic.

Logue, C: H.
American machinist gear book; simplified tables and formulas for designing, and pract. points in cutting all commercial types of gears. '10(Ag20) il. 8°, $2.50 net. McGraw-H.

LOHENGRIN.
See Legends.

Loisy, Abbé Alfr.
Gospel and the Church; tr. by Christopher Home. New ed., with an introd. by Newman Smyth. '09(Mr6) D. *$1 net. Scribner.
Religion of Israel; tr. by Arth. Galton. '10 (D17) 12°, (Crown theological lib.) $1.50. Putnam.

Loliée, Frédéric Auguste.
Gilded beauties of the Second Empire. '10 (S) il. 8°, $4 net. Brentano's.
Life of an empress; Eugénie de Montijo. '10(Ja1) il. 8°, *$4 net. Dodd.

LOLLARDS.
See Reformation.

Lomas, J:
In Spain. '08(Je6) il. map, 8°, *$2 net. Macmillan.

Lomax, J: Avery, comp.
Cowboy songs; introd. by Barrett Wendell. '10(D3) 12°, $1.50 net. Sturgis & W.

Lombard, L:
Observations of a bachelor. '10(Ag6) c. il. por. D. $1. Estes.
Vicious virtuoso. '10(Ag6) c. D. 75 c. Estes.

Lombard Street; description of the money market. Bagehot, W. $1.25 net. Dutton.

Lombardic architecture. Rivoira, G. T. $20. Helburn.

LOMBARDY.
See Italy.

Lombroso, Cesare.
After death—what?: spiritistic phenomena and their interpretation rendered into English by W: Sloane Kennedy. '09(O9) c. il. O. **$2.50 net. Small.

Lomer, Gerhard R:
Concept of method. '10(Ag6) c. 8°, (Teachers' College, Columbia Univ., contribs. to education.) $1. Teachers' Coll.

London, Jack.
Burning Daylight. '10(O15) c. il. D. $1.50. Macmillan.
Iron heel. '08(F29) c. D. †$1.50. Macmillan.
Lost Face. '10(Mr12) c. il. D. $1.50. Macmillan.
Martin Eden. '09(O9) c. front. D. †$1.50. Macmillan.
Revolution. '09(N6) T. pap., 5 c.; 60 copies, $1; 100, $1.50; 1,000, $10. Kerr.
Revolution and other essays. '10(Ap30) c. D. $1.50 net. Macmillan.
Theft; play in four acts. '10(D3) c. S. $1.25 net. Macmillan.

LONDON, Eng.
Babson, R. W. Stock brokers and bond dealers of London. $5. R. W. Babson.
Baedeker, K. London and its environs. *$1.80 net. Scribner.
Besant, *Sir* W: Early London.—London city—London in the nineteenth century. ea., *$7.50 net. Macmillan.
Besant, *Sir* W., *and others.* Shoreditch and the East End. *90 c. net. Macmillan.
Brereton, A. Literary hist. of the Adelphi and its neighborhood. $3.50. Duffield.
Bumpus, T. F: London churches. 2 v. *$4 net; *$8 net. Pott.
Campbell, W. S. "Passerby" in London. *$1.75 net. Scribner.
Cassell's guide to London. 25 c. Cassell
Chancellor, E. B. Private palaces of London—past and present. *$5 net. Lippincott.
Chancellor, E. B. Wanderings in London. *75 c. net. Pott.
Coburn, A. L. London. $6. Brentano's.
De Milt, A. R. Ways and days out of London. $2.50 net. Baker & T.
Douglas, J. Adventures in London. **$1.75 net. Cassell.
Foord, A. S. Springs, streams and spas of London-hist. and associations. $3.50 net. Stokes.
Hemstreet, C: *and* M. Nooks and corners of old London. $1. Post.

LONDON, Eng.—*Continued.*
Home, G. C. Romance of London. $1 net. Macmillan.
Hutchings, W. W., *and* Hueffer, F. M. London Town past and present. *$3 net. Cassell.
Jerningham, C: E. W. Art and curio collector's guide to London. 35 c. net. Cassell.
Lawler, O. W. East London visions. $1.75 net. Longmans.
Lucas, E: V. Wanderer in London. $2.50 net. Macmillan.
Lucy, *Sir* H: W. Sixty years in the wilderness: [reminiscences of life in London.] *$3 net. Dutton.
Lyons, A. N. Sixpenny pieces: [a doctor's experiences in London's slums.] $1.50. Lane.
Maps of old London. *$1.75 net. Macmillan.
Markino, Y. Japanese artist in London. $2 net. Jacobs.
Melville, H. *and* L. London's lure. *$1.25 net. Macmillan.
Milne, J. My summer in London. $1.50 net. Dutton.
Mitton, G. E. Hackney and Stoke Newington. *90 c. net. Macmillan.
Moncrieff, A. R. H. London. $2.50 net. Macmillan.
Morley, C: London at prayer. *$2.50 net. Dutton.
Nevill, R., *and* Jerningham, C: E: W. Piccadilly to Pall Mall: morals, manners and men. *$3.50 net. Dutton.
Newnham-Davis, N. Gourmet's guide to London. *$1.50 net Brentano's.
Ogilvy, J. S. Relics and memorials of London city. $5 net. Dutton.
Pennell, *Mrs.* E. R. Our house and the people in it. $1.25 net. Houghton M.
Pictorial and descriptive guide to London. $1 net. Platt & P.
Rickett, A. C. London life of yesterday. *$2.50 net. Dutton.
Rook, C. London sidelights. *$1.70 net. Longmans.
Stow, J: Survey of London. *75 c. net. Dutton.
Stow, J: Survey of London. 2 v. $9.25. Oxford Univ.
Symons, A. London; book of aspects. (Not for sale.) E. D. Brooks.
Wheatley, H: B: Hogarth's London. *$4.80 net. Dutton.
See also Blackfriars theatre;—British Institution;—British Museum;—Geological Society;—Guilds;—Holland House;—Hyde Park;—Inns of Court;—Kew Gardens;—London Hospital;—National Gallery;—Royal Academy;—St. Bartholomew-the-Great;—St. Paul's Cathedral;—Theatre;—Tower of London;—Wallace collections;—Westminster Abbey.

London and the girl. Gibson, A. $1.50. Cassell.

LONDON HOSPITAL, London.
Morris, E. W. Hist. of the London hospital. $1.75 net. Longmans.

London lib. 8°, *$1 net. Dutton.
—Burton. Bookhunter.
—Trench. Notes on the miracles of our Lord.

London Municipal Society. Case against socialism; with prefatory letter by A. J. Balfour. '08(Je13) 12°, *$1.50 net Macmillan.

London voluntaries. Henley, W: E. 50 c.; $1. T: B. Mosher.

"Londons" of the British fleet. Fraser, E: **$1.50 net. Lane.

Lone patrol. Finnemore, J: $1.50. Lippincott.

Lone ranch. *See* Reid, Mayne.

Lone Star defenders. Barron, S: B. *$2 net. Neale.

Lone trail at thirty. Gorham, F. $1. Black Lion.

Lonely God. Stephens, J. $1.50 net. Macmillan.

Lonely guard. Innes, N. *$1.25 net. Jacobs.

Lonely lovers. Newte, H. W. G. $1.50. M. Kennerley.

Lonesome trail. Bower, B. M., *pseud.* †$1.25. G: W. Dillingham.

Long, C: Albert.
Solution of interests dependent upon money, subsidiary money, currency, emergency currency, and banking for every nation. '10(Ap30) c. por. D. O. $1. Aberdeen.

Long, C: Massie.
Virginia county names. '09(Ja23) c. map, O. *$1.50 net. Neale.

Long, Clarence E.
Lake steam-manship and guide to the marine board examinations; for pilots' and masters' licenses. v. 1. '08, [1909.] (Mr) c. il. 8°, $2. C. E. Long.

Long, Eli H., M.D.
Text-book of dental materia medica, therapeutics and prescription writing. 3d ed., rev. '09(S) 311 p. il. 8°, *$2.75 net. Lea.

Long, F: J., comp.
Dict. of the Chinook jargon, English-Chinook. '09(Ag14) c. S. pap., 25 c. Lowman.

Long, Harold C., and Percival, J:
Common weeds of the farm and garden. '10(Jl30) il. O. $2 net. Stokes.

Long, J: Davis.
Abraham Lincoln; address at the centennial in Symphony Hall, Boston, February 12, 1909. '09, [1910.] (O) 35 p. 8°, 25 c. net. W: B. Clarke.

Long, J: Harper.
Text-book of physiological chemistry for students of medicine. 2d ed., rev. '09 (O) c. 8+396 p. il. 8°, $2.50. Blakiston.

Long, J: Ignatius Thdr.
Lines from a doctor to his son; or, knowledge vs. ignorance. '10(Mr) 216 p. por. 12°, $1. J: I. T. Long.

Long, J: Luther.
Felice. '08(N7) c. front. D. †$1. Moffat.

Long, Jos. Ragland.
Notes of lectures on the law of wills and administration. '10(Je) c. O. pap., $1. Michie.
Outline of the jurisdiction and procedure of the federal courts. '10(Mr) O. shp., $1.50. Michie.

Long, Jos. Schuyler.
Out of the silence; book of verse. '09 (Mr) c. 11-137 p. 12°, $1.25. J. S. Long.
Sign language; descriptive vocab. of signs used by the deaf in the United States and Canada. '10(Je11) c. il. 8°, $2. J. S. Long.

Long, Maxwell Budd.
New commandment: a comedy. '08(My23) c. D. pap., 75 c. M. B. Long.

Long, Rev. Simon P:
Eternal epistle; sermons on the epistles for the church year; Miss Florence May Welty, rep. '08, [1909.] (Mr) c. 893 p. por. 8°, $2.50. S. P: Long.
Prepare to meet thy God. 4th ed. '08, [1909.] (Mr) c. 87 p. por. 12°, 35 c. S. P: Long.
Way made plain; few plain sermons to busy adults who think they have not the time to take a thorough course of catechetical instruction. '08, [1909.] (Mr) c. 194 p. por. 12°, $1. S. P: Long.
Wounded word. '08, [1909.] (Mr) c. 35 c. S. P: Long.

Long, Solomon Levy.
Child slaves and other poems. '09(D4) por. 12°, $1.25. Courier Press.

Long, W: Jos., D.D., ["Peter Rabbit."]
English literature; its history and its significance for the life of the English-speaking world: text-book for schools. '09(O9) c. il. facsims., pors. map, D. $1.35. Ginn.
Northern trails. Bks. 1 and 2. '08(S19) c. il. D. (Woodfolk ser., bks. 6-7.) ea., 45 c. Ginn.

Long arm of Mannister. Oppenheim, E: P. †$1.50. Little, B. & Co.

Long gallery. Lathbury, E. †$1.50. Holt.

Long Island (Battle of).
Fraser, G. Stone house at Gowanus; scene of the battle of Long Island. $2.50. Witter & K.
Higgins, C: M. Brooklyn's neglected battle ground. 35 c. Witter & K.

Long Island, N. Y.
Braislin, W: C. List of the birds of Long Island. 75 c. Linnaean.
Byrnes, E. T. Fresh water *Cyclops* of Long Island. 80 c. Brooklyn Inst.
Fullerton, E. L. Lure of the land. Long Island R. R.
Ruther, F: Long Island to-day. $2. F: Ruther.

Long life and how to attain it. Kintzing, P. **$1 net. Funk.

Long, long story ser. 6 v. '10(D) col. il. ea., bds., 25 c. Cassell.

Long odds. Bindloss, H. †$1.50. Small.

Long shadow. Bower, B. M., *pseud.* †$1.25. G: W. Dillingham.

Long Will. Converse, F. *35 c. net; *70 c. net; $1.50 net. Dutton.

Longan, Mrs. Emma Lard.
Parliamentary rules made easy. 4th ed. '10(N) c. 127 p. 16°. Hudson.

Longanecker, E. W., M.D.
Practical gas engineer. 6th ed. '08(Ag22) c. *$1 net. Longanecker.

Longarde, Mme. Longard de.
See Gerard, Dorothea.

Longest, W: Butler.
Whys and wherefores of the modern motor car. '09(Ap24) c. il. 12°, 50 c. W: B. Longest.

Longevity.
Bersford, T: Theories and facts for students of longevity and health. $1. T: Bersford.
Eaves, A. O. Mastery of death. *$1 net. Badger.
Finot, J. Philosophy of long life. *$2.50 net. Lane.
Fisher, I. Economic aspects of lengthening human life. (Add. pubs. for price.) Com. of One Hundred.
Foster, B. Suggestion concerning the increased longevity of life insurance policy holders. gratis. Assoc. Life.
Kintzing, P. Long life and how to attain it. **$1 net. Funk.
Lorand, A. Old age deferred. $2.50 net. Davis.
Marden, O. S. Why grow old? **30 c. net. Crowell.
Marston, E: How does it feel to be old? $1. Scribner.
Matthews, S. C. How to keep well and live long. $1. S. C. Matthews.
Metchnikoff, E. Prolongation of life. **$1.75 net; *$2.50 net. Putnam.
Minot, C: S. Problem of age, growth and death. **$2.50 net. Putnam.
Patterson, J: A. The breaking dawn; or, how long may we live in the body. $1. Chronicle Pub.
Ostrom, H: Rich in yesterdays; message to the aged. 75 c. Praise Pub.
See also Food;—Hygiene.

Longfellow, H: Wadsworth.
Complete poetical works. '08(D19) 12°, (Crowell's thin paper poets.) ooze leath., $1.75, boxed. Crowell.
Poetical works; with explanatory notes. '08(Mr21) por. S. (New century lib.) $1; limp leath., $1.25. Nelson.
Works. 10 v.; [ed. by C: Welsh. Ed. de luxe.] '09(N) c. il. 8°. (Add. pubs. for price.) W. D. Lane.
Addresses and poem read at Bowdoin College, June 26, 1907, in commemoration of the centenary of the birth of Henry Wadsworth Longfellow of the class of 1825. '07, [1908.] (Mr.) 35 p. 8°, pap., 25 c. Bowdoin College.
Building of the ship. '10(D) 16°, (Abbey classics.) pap., 25 c., boxed; bds., 50 c. boxed; limp leath.. $1, boxed. Abbey Co.
Formerly published by Paul Elder.
Children's Longfellow. '08(O3) c. il. O. $3, boxed. Houghton M.
Courtship of Miles Standish; with notes by M. A. Eaton. '08(F22) il. por. S. 25 c. Educ. Pub.
Courtship of Miles Standish and other poems; with introd. by Austen T. Kempton. '10(N5) c. il. 8°, $1. Grosset.
Courtship of Miles Standish. '09(Ap10) front. 32°, (Ariel booklets.) leath., 75 c., boxed. Putnam.

Longfellow, H: Wadsworth.—*Continued.*
Evangeline. '08(N14) c. nar. O. bds., 75 c., boxed. J: W. Luce.
Evangeline. '09(O30) c. il. 12°, (Neill gift book ser.) $1.25, boxed. Reilly & B.
Evangeline; ed., with notes, outline study and examination questions by Maud Elma Kingsley and Frank Herbert Palmer. '09(O) c. 11+116+27 p. 16°, (Kingsley English texts.) 40 c. Palmer Co.
From day to day with Longfellow; comp. by Olive Van Buren. '10(Ag20) c. front. 12°, 75 c. Barse & H.
Golden legend. '10(D3) col. il. Q. $2.50 net, boxed. Doran.
Hiawatha. '09(O30) c. il. D. (Neill gift book ser.) $1.25, boxed. Reilly & B.
Longfellow. '10(D17) por. Ff. (Oxford moment ser.) silk or limp leath., 40 c. net. Oxford Univ.
Longfellow day by day; ed. by Anna H. Smith. '10(O8) c. por. D. (Day by day ser.) 60 c., boxed; leath., $1, boxed. Crowell.
Narrative poems; ed. for school use by J: Rush Powell. '09(F6) c. 16°, (Lake English classics.) 40 c. Scott, F. & Co.
Poems; introd. by Katherine Tynan. '09 (Ap3) 16°, (Everyman's lib.) *35 c. net; leath., *70 c. net. Dutton.
Poems. '10(D) 12°, (Autograph poets.) $1; hf. leath., $1.50. Houghton M.
Song of Hiawatha. '08(D19) il. 12°, $1, boxed; presentation ed., $1.25, boxed; ed. de luxe, flexible ooze leath., $1.75, boxed. Rand, McN. & Co.
Story of Hiawatha adptd. from Longfellow, by Winston Stokes, with the original poem. '10(O29) c. col. il. O. $2 net. Stokes.
Tales from Longfellow, by Gertrude Ruth Schottenfels. '10(Ja15) c. il. por. 12°, 50 c. Educ. Pub.
Tales of a wayside inn; with notes. '08 (My16) c. 3 v., 12°, (Crane classics.) ea., 25 c.; pap., 15 c. Crane.
Tales of a wayside inn; with introd. and notes by M. A. Eaton. '08(Ap4) c. 16°, (Classic lib.) 25 c.; pap., 15 c. Educ. Pub.
Wind mill. '09(Ag7) booklet mounted on shaped bds., 25 c. Curtis Adv.
See also Poe, Edg. Allan.
—, **ed.** Poems of New England. '08(O10) c. S. limp leath., $1.25. Houghton M.

LONGFELLOW, Henry Wadsworth.
Clarke, H. A. Longfellow's country. **$2 net. Baker & T.
Livingston, L. S., *comp.* Bibliography of the first editions in book form of the writings of Henry Wadsworth Longfellow. *$3 net; *$10 net. Dodd.
Schell, S., *ed.* Hiawatha entertainments. 35 c. Werner.
Trent, W: P. Longfellow and other essays. $1.50. Crowell.

Longford, Jos. H.
Story of old Japan. '10(N19) fold. map, O. $1.75 net. Longmans.

LONGITUDE.
Ware, H. E. Forgotten prime meridian. (Priv. pr.) H. E. Ware.

Longley, W: Raymond.
See Smith, Percy Franklin.

Longmans' civil engineering ser. O. Longmans.
—Harcourt. Civil engineering as applied in construction. $5 net.
—Warren. Engineering construction in steel and timber. $5 net.

Longmans' class-books of English literature. D. Longmans.
—Defoe. Adventures of Robinson Crusoe. *50 c. net.
—Dickens. Christmas carol. *36 c. net.
—Lang, *comp.* Tales of King Arthur and the round table. 30 c.
—Morris. Story of Sigurd the Volsung. 50 c.
—Zimmern. Gods and heroes of the North. *36 c. net.

Longmans' commercial ser.; ed. by Alfr. Nixon. D. Longmans.
—Bithell. Handbook of German commercial correspondence. $1.25.
—Dicksee. Business organization. $1.50.
—Holland *and* Nixon. Banking law. $1.75.
—Warren. Spanish grammar. $1.

Longmans' English classics; ed. by G: Rice Carpenter. 31 v. '09(Mr13) D. price reduced from *40 c. net to 25 c. Longmans.

Longmans' English classics; ed. by G: Rice Carpenter. D. 25 c. Longmans.
—Arnold. Sohrab and Rustum.
—Dickens. Tale of two cities.
—Gray *and* Goldsmith. Elegy written in a country churchyard, and Deserted village.
—Lincoln. Inaugural addresses and letters.
—Macaulay. Essay on Lord Clive.—Essay on Warren Hastings.
—Parkman. Oregon trail.
—Scott. Quentin Durward.
—Stevenson. Treasure Island.
—Thoreau. Walden.

Longmans' historical illustrations. Barfield, T. C. In 4 portfolios. ea., 90 c. net. Longmans.

Longmans' illustrated first conversational German reader. Bartram, J. W. 80 c. Longmans.

Longmans' infant fairy-readers. S. limp cl., 15 c. Longmans.
—Bates. Fairy tale of a dog and an old dame by the sea.

Longmans' physical and electrical engineering laboratory manuals. D. Longmans.
—Henderson. Electrotechnics. $1.20.

Longmans' pocket lib. S. Longmans.
—Arnold. Light of the world. *75 c. net.
—Ingelow. Poems. *75 c. net.
—Morris. Poems by the way. 75 c. net; $1 net.
—Newman. Church of the fathers.—University teaching.

Longmans' text-books of physical chemistry; ed. by Sir W: Ramsay. il. D. Longmans.
—Desch. Metallography. $3 net.
—Friend. Theory of valency. $1.60.
—Smiles. Relations between chemical constitution and some physical properties. $4 net.
—Thomsen. Thermochemistry. $2.50.
—Young. Stoichiometry. $2.
Longshore boys. Stoddard, W: O. †$1.50. Lippincott.
Longtail monkey. Helm, M. 75 c. Pub. Ho. M. E. Ch., So.
LONGUEVILLE, Anne Geneviève de Bourbon-Condé, *Duchesse* de.
Williams, H. N. Princess of intrigue, Anne Geneviève de Bourbon. 2 v. *$6.50 net. Putnam.
Longueville, T:
Curious case of Lady Purbeck; by the author of The life of Sir Kenelm Digby. '09(Ap10) O. $2. Longmans.
First Duke and Duchess of Newcastle-upon-Tyne. '10(O22) il. pors. O. $3.50 net. Longmans.
Longyear, Burton O.
Rocky Mountain wild flower studies; an account of the ways of some plants that live in the Rocky Mountain region. Author's ed. '09(S18) c. il. 12°, $1. Merchants Pub.
Longyear, Howard Williams, M.D.
Nephrocoloptosis; description of the nephrocolic ligament and its action in the causation of nephroptosis, with the technic of the operation of nephrocolopexy, in which the nephrocolic ligament is utilized to immobilize both kidney and bowel. '10(O) 5-251 p. il. 8°, $3. Mosby.
Looff, M.
Engineers' pocket dictionary of technical terms: French-English. '08(Jl18) 16°, 60 c. Spon.
Look on the brighter side. Rutherford, W. R. 75 c.; $1.25. Dodge.
Looking forward. Todd, J. 50 c. Highlands.
Looking upward day by day. Hammond, E. V., *comp.* *$1 net. Dutton.
Lookout Island campers. Eldred, W. L. †$1.50. Lothrop, L. & S.
Loom of the desert. Strobridge, I. M. $1.75. Artemisia.
Loomis, Bennett Jonathan.
The land; its Lord and sacred lore; story told in verse of the life of the Lord Jesus. '10(D17) c. il. 12°, 75 c. Stoneman.
Loomis, C: Battell.
Holiday touch, and other tales of undaunted Americans. '08(O17) c. il. D. **$1.25 net. Holt.
Just Irish. '09(Ap17) $1; [New ed.] '10 (D31) c. il. D. $1.50 net. Badger.
Knack of it: some essays in optimism. '08 (S12) c. 16°, *75 c. net. Revell.
Little Maude and her mamma. '09(O23) c. il. S. (Little comic masterpieces.) †50 c. Doubleday, P.
Looms of life. Scheffauer, H. C: $1.25. Neale.
Loose, Katherine Riegel, ["Georg Schock."]
Hearts contending. '10(Ap23) c. D. $1.50. Harper.
Loose leaf system of laboratory notes. Schaffer, T. H. *75 c. net. Blakiston.
Looters of the public domain. Puter, S. A. D. $3. Portland.
Lorand, Arnold, M.D.
Old age deferred. '10(D24) c. O. $2.50 net. Davis.
Lord, Eleanor Louisa, comp.
See Abel, Annie Heloise.
Lord, Everett W:
Child labor and the public schools. '09 (Je) 12 p. 8°, (National Child Labor Committee pubs.) pap. (Add. pubs. for price.) Nat. Child Labor.
Topics and suggestions for debates on child labor. '09(Mr27) O. pap., gratis. Nat. Child Labor.
Lord, G: W.
Boiler troubles and their treatment. Rev. ed. [1910.](Je) c. 80 p. 12°, gratis. G: W. Lord.
Lord Alistair's rebellion. Upward, A. $1.50. M. Kennerley.
Lord and Thomas' pocket dict. of the American press for 1910; complete list of newspapers, magazines and periodicals published in the United States, Canada, Porto Rico, Hawaiian and Philippine Islands. '10 (Je11) c. nar. S. leath., $2. Lord.
Lord Loveland discovers America. Williamson, C: N. $1.20, fixed. Doubleday, P.
Lord of lands. Benson, P. R. †$1.50. Holt.
Lord of the sea. Strang, H. $1 net. Doran.
Lord of the world. Benson, R. H. †$1.50. Dodd.
Lord Ormont and his Aminta. *See* Meredith, G:
Lord will provide. Foss, C. W., *comp.* 35 c. Augustana.
LORD'S PRAYER.
Aked, C: F. Lord's prayer. $1. Revell.
Gladden, W. Lord's prayer; seven homilies. $1. Houghton M.
Irons, G. Torn scrap book: talks and tales illustrative of the "Our Father." $1. Longmans.
Jones, J: D. Model prayer. *75 c. net. Doran.
Richards, W: R. Study of the Lord's prayer. 75 c. Presb. Bd.
See also Devotional exercises and meditations.
LORD'S SUPPER.
Alston, E. A., *and* Turton, Z. H. Origines eucharisticae. *35 c. net. Whittaker.
Dimock, N. Doctrine of the Lord's supper. 50 c. net. Longmans.
Ferreres, J. B. Decree on daily communion. *75 c. net. Herder.
Foley, J: T. With King James' Bible as exclusive authority can the Protestant Christian question the eucharist? $1.50. Pilot Co.
Frost, J. M. Memorial supper of our Lord. 90 c. S. S. Bd. So. Bapt.
Gihr, N: Holy sacrifice of the mass. *$1 net. Herder.
Griffith, M. J. Meaning of the mass. *$1 net. Kenedy.
Gummey, H: R., *jr.* Consecration of the eucharist. *$2 net. Anners.
Hoare, E. Communion and communicant. *20 c. net. Am. S. S.

LORD'S SUPPER.—*Continued.*
Lowrie, W. A. Abba, Father: comment on the Lord's prayer. *$1 net. Longmans.
Meschler, M. Sublimity of the holy eucharist. 75 c. net. Herder.
Meyrick, F: Doctrine of the Church of England on the holy communion. $1. Longmans.
Neumann, A. J. R., *comp.* Sacrament of the altar. 30 c. Germ. Lit. Bd.
Newbolt, W: C: E. Sacrament of the altar. *$1.40 net. Oxford Univ.
O'Connell, C. J. Holy Eucharist and frequent daily communion. *60 c. net. Benziger.
Pourrat, P. Teaching of the fathers on the real presence of Christ in the holy eucharist. 15 c. Cathedral Lib.
Smith, C: E., *comp.* Altar devotions. **50 c. net. Longmans.
Stone, D. History of the doctrine of the holy eucharist. 2 v. *$8.50 net. Longmans.
Waggett, P. N. Holy eucharist. *$1.25 net. Young Churchman.
Zulueta, F. M. de. Ministry of daily communion. 60 c.—Spouse of Christ and daily communion. 30 c. Herder.
See also Book of common prayer.

Lords and lovers. **Dargan, O. T.** ****$1.50 net.** **Scribner.**
Lords of high decision. Nicholson, M. †$1.50. Doubleday, P.
Lords of industry. Lloyd, H: D. $1.50 net. Putnam.
Lore of the honey-bee. Edwards, T. *$2.40 net. Scribner.
Lorelei. Scott, H: B. $1. Werner Co.

Lorentz, Hendrik Antoon.
Theory of electrons and its applications to the phenomena of light and radiant heat: lectures del. in Columbia University. '09 (Je19) O. (B. G. Teubner's mathematische wissenschaften.) *$2.50 net. Stechert.

Lorenz, Albert Michael.
Individual sovereignty; being a revised edition of "Pleasure and progress." '10 (Ja22) c. 12°, $1. Mayhew.

Lorenz, Edm. Simon.
Practical church music. '09(My1) c. 12°, *$1.50 net. Revell.

Lorenzen, Ernest Gustav.
Cases on the conflict of laws, sel. from decisions of English and American courts. '09(Mr) c. 21+784 p. O. (Am. case book ser.) $4.50. West Pub.

Lorenzini, Carlo, ["C. Collodi."]
Adventures every child should know; Marvellous adventures of Pinocchio; ed. by Mary E. Burt; from an orig. tr. by A: G. Caprani. '09(F20) c. D. (Every child should know ser.) **90 c. net. Doubleday, P.
Pinocchio: the adventures of a little wooden boy; tr. by Jos. Walker. '09(S11) c. il. D. $1. Crowell.
Pinocchio; the aventures of a marionette; tr. from the Italian by Wa. S. Cramp, with ed. revision by Sarah E. H. Lockwood. [New holiday ed.] '09(D4) c. il. O. ****$1 net.** Ginn.

Lorimer, G: Horace.
Jack Spurlock, prodigal. '08(Je6) c. D. †$1.50. Doubleday, P.

Lorimer, Norma.
By the waters of Egypt. '09(N6) il. 8°, ***$4 net.** Pott.

Lorimer of the northwest. Bindloss, H. †$1.50. Stokes.
Lorna Doone. *See* Blackmore, Rob. Doddridge.

Lorraine, Rupert.
Woman and the sword. '09(Jl3) D. 75 c. **McClurg.**

Los Angeles, [Cal.] Penal ordinances of the city; comp. by Emmet H. Wilson; indexed by M. L. Germain. [1910.] (Jl) c. 418 p. O. pap., $2. Los Angeles Pub.

Los Angeles, Cal., Public Library. California, United States and experiment station documents of interest to California horticulturists; comp. for the San Jose meeting of the California Library Association. '08(N) [1909.] 16 p. 8°. (Add. Library for price.) Los Angeles Lib.

LOS ANGELES, Cal.
Robinson, C: M. City beautiful. $1. Municipal Art Com.
See also Temple Baptist Church.

LOS ANGELES Co., California.
Grinnell, J. *and* H. W. Reptiles of Los Angeles Co. gratis. Throop Poly. Inst.

Los Angeles Normal School bull. il. 8°. C. F. Palmer.
—Palmer. Elem. horticulture for California schools. 50 c.

Losch, Rev. H:
God-man; or, the life and works of Jesus the Christ and son of God; a poem in fifteen parts. 2d rev. and enl. ed. '09 (S) c. 6-182 p. il. por. 12°, $1.50. Badger.

Loshe, Lillie Deming.
Early American novel. '08(F1) 8°, (Columbia Univ. studies in English.) pap., ***$1 net.** Lemcke.

Losing game. Payne, W. †$1.50. **G: W. Dillingham.**
Lost ambassador. Oppenheim, E. P. $1.50. Little, B. & Co.
Lost among white Africans. Ker, D: $1.25. Cassell.
Lost angel. Hinkson, *Mrs.* K. T. †$1.50. Lippincott.
Lost art of conversation. Krans, H. S., *ed.* $1.50. Sturgis & W.
Lost borders. Austin, *Mrs.* M. H. †$1.25. Harper.
Lost cabin mine. Niven, F: †$1.50. Lane.
Lost Christ. Smith, R. *25 c. net. Doran.
Lost clue. Walton, *Mrs.* O. F. $1.25. Am. S. S.
Lost Face. London, J. †$1.50. Macmillan.
Lost garden. Bell, L. $1.25 net. Doran.
Lost goddess. Barron, E: †$1.50. Holt.
Lost guide. Norvell, J. E. $1. Chr. Witness.
Lost joy and other dreams. *See* Schreiner, *Mrs.* O.
Lost legion. Mathews, R. V. **$1. E. C. Hill.**
Lost Lenore. Reid, M. †$1. Dutton.
Lost letters. Jackson, J. W: 75 c. Standard Pub.
Lost millionaire. Davidson, L. C. $1.50. Cassell.

Lost mine of the Mono. Klette, C. H. B. $1.50. Cochrane.
Lost tales of Miletus. *See* Bulwer-Lytton, *Sir* E: G: **Earle Lytton.**
"Lost;" trap-shooter's guide. Shaw, C: E:, *jr.* 75 c. C: E: Shaw.
Lost word found in the great work. Buck, J. D. 50 c. Indo-Am. Bk.
Lothar, Rudolph.
Tiefland (The lowland): music drama in a prelude and two acts; text after Angel Guimerá by Rudolph Lothar; English version by Rosie Helen Elkin; music by Eugene d'Albert. '08(N) c. 74 p. 8°, vocal score, Eng. and German, $5; piano score, $4; libretto, Eng. and German, 35 c. Boosey.
Lothman, Dan. W:
Latin lessons for beginners. '08(O31) c. il. O. $1. Ginn.
Lothrop, Almira Strong, [Mrs. G: Van Ness Lothrop.]
Court of Alexander III.; letters of Mrs. Lothrop, wife of the late Honorable George Van Ness Lothrop, former minister plenipotentiary and envoy extraordinary of the United States to Russia; ed. by W: Prall. '10(Jl9) c. il. pors. O. $1.50 net. Winston.
See also Lothrop, Almira Strong.
Lothrop, G: Edn., jr.
Historical, dramatic and romantic ballads. 2 v. '08(D) c. 12°. (Add. author for price.) G: E. Lothrop.
Lothrop, Mrs. G: Van Ness.
See Lothrop, Almira Strong.
Lothrop, Mrs. Harriet Mulford Stone, ["Marg. Sidney."]
Little maid of Boston Town. '10(D17) c. il. 12°, $1.50. Lothrop, L. & S.
"Loti, Pierre," pseud.
See Viaud, Louis Marie Julien.
Lotos eating. *See* **Curtis, G: W. Prue and I.**
Lott, Noah, pseud.
See Hobart, G: Vere.
LOTTERIES.
Brown University. Three proclamations concerning the lottery for Virginia, 1613-1621. (Add. pubs. for price.) Brown Univ.
Lotti die uhrmacherin. Ebner von Eschenbach, M. 35 c. Holt.
Lotus buds. Wilson-Carmichael, A. *$5 net. Armstrong.
Lotus lib. 7 v. '10(D) limp leath., $1 net. Brentano's.
Contents: Daudet, Sappho; Gaboriau, The black-mailers; Daudet, The nabob; Beckford, Vathek; Lemaitre, Their majesties: the kings; Ohnet, Deep abyss; Bourget, Our lady of lies.
LOUDOUN Co., Va.
Head, J. W. **Hist. and comprehensive description of Loudoun County, Va. $1.** J. W. Head.
Lougheed, Victor.
Vehicles of the air; popular exposition of modern aeronautics with working drawings. '09(D11) c. il. O. *$2.50 net. Reilly & B.
Loughlin, Burren, and Flood, L. L.
Brightwits, Prince of Mogadore. '09(O9) c. il. O. 75 c. Caldwell.
Loughnan, R. A.
New Zealand at home. '08(D5) il. 12°, *$1.75 net. Scribner.
LOUIS XIII., *King of France.*
Patmore, K. A. Court of Louis XIII. *$3.50 net. Brentano's.
Taylor, I. A. Making of a king. $3.50 net. Dodd.
LOUIS XIV., *King of France.*
Lair, J. Louise de La Vallière and the early life of Louis XIV. *$3.50 net. Putnam.
Major, C: The little king; story of the childhood of Louis XIV. $1.50. Macmillan.
Williams, H. N. Madame de Montespan and Louis XIV. $2. Scribner.
LOUIS XV., *King of France.*
Goncourt, E. L. A. H. de. Confidantes of a king. In 2 v. *$4 special net. Appleton.
Louis XV. furniture in the Louvre. '10(Ag6) il. f°, (in portfolio,) $10. Hessling.
Louis XV. furniture in the Museum of Decorative Art. Hessling, E., *ed.* $12. Hessling.
LOUIS XVI., *King of France.*
Cléry, J. B. C.-H. Royal family in the Temple Prison. $1.50. Sturgis & W.
Haggar, A. C: P. Louis XVI. and Marie Antoinette. 2 v. *$6 special net. Appleton.
Louis XVI. painting. Behrens, C. $8 Hessling.
LOUIS XVII., *King of France.*
Eckard, J., *and* Naundorff, K. W. King who never reigned, (Louis XVII.) *$3.50 net. J: McBride.
Welch, C. Little dauphin: [the son of Louis XVI. *and* Marie Antoinette.] *$1.50 net. Scribner.
LOUIS XVIII., *King of France.*
Sandars, M. F. Louis XVIII. $4 net; $7 net. Pott.
Stenger, G. Return of Louis XVIII. *$3 net. Scribner.
LOUIS PHILIPPE, *King of France.*
Arnaud, R. Louis Philippe and his sister. *$4.20 net. Scribner.
Louis, H:
Dressing of minerals. '09(My22) il. fold. plans, Q. *$8.50 net. Longmans.
Louis Chiswick's mission. Adams, W: T. $1. Lothrop, L. & S.
Louis' every woman's cook book. Muckenstrum, L: J. $1.50. Caldwell.
LOUISBURG (Siege of).
Baker, H: M. First siege of Louisburg. (Priv. pr.) H: M. Baker.
Peppernell, *Sir* W: Journal of Sir William Peppernell kept during the expedition against Louisbourg, Mar. 24-Aug. 22, 1745. $1. Am. Antiquarian.
Stearns, B: Diary kept at the siege of Louisburg. 25 c. S: A. Green.
LOUISE, *Queen of Prussia.*
Merz, H. Louise, Queen of Prussia. *60 c. net. McClurg.
Louisiana. Annots. to the acts of the general assembly of the state; comp. by Thdr. Cotonio. '09(N) c. O. $15. La. Pub. Co.

Louisiana. Annotations to the constitution of the state; comp. under direction of Thdr. Cotonio. '10(Ap) c. O. $5. La. Pub. Co.

Louisiana. Annotations to the revised statutes of the state; comp. under direction of Thdr. Cotonio. '10(Ap) c. O. $5. La. Pub. Co.

Louisiana. Code of practice, with annots. of H: L. Garland, jr., [etc.;] comp. and ed. by Solomon Wolf. [3d ed.] '10(D) c. O. shp., $15. Hansell.

Louisiana. Constitution and rev. laws, [etc.;] supp. to ed. in 2 v. [v. 3;] comp. and annot. by Solomon Wolff. '10(Ap) c. O. shp., $12. Hansell.
For ed. in 2 v. *see* American Catalog, 1900-1905.

Louisiana. [*Courts.*] Repts. Annot. ed. Bk. 23. '10(N) c. O. $7.50. (Sold only in sets. Repr. backwards.) West Pub.

Louisiana. Rev. civil code, with amendments, [etc.,] to 1908; ed. by E. D. Saunders. '09 (D) c. D. $6; shp., $6; im. mor., $7; mor., $10. Hansell.

Louisiana. *Supreme ct.* Repts. Annot. ed., unabr. Bk. 43, cont. a verbatim repr. of v. 36 of the La. repts. '07, [1908.] (F); Bk. 42, repr. of v. 35. (Mr); Bks. 41-40, repr. of v. 34-33. (Ap); Bk. 39, repr. of v. 32. (Jl); Bks. 38-37, repr. of v. 31-30. (N); Bk. 36, repr. of v. 29. (D); Bk. 35, repr. of v. 28. '09(My); Bk. 34, repr. of v. 26, 27; Bk. 33, repr. of v. 25. (N) c. O. shp., ea., $7.50. (Sold only in complete sets. Repr. backwards.) West Pub.

Louisiana. *Supreme ct.* Repts.; (C: G. Gill.) v. 119. '08(Ap); v. 120 (O); v. 121 (D); v. 122. '09(S) c. Q. shp., ea., $8; v. 123. '09, [1910.] (F); v. 124 (Je); v. 125 (S) c. O. buckram, ea., $4.50. West Pub.

Louisiana. *Supreme ct. and superior ct. of the territory of La.* Repts. Annot ed. Bk. 32. '09, [1910.] (Ja); Bks. 31-28 (Ap); Bks. 26, 27 (Je); Bk. 25 (Jl); Bk. 24 (Ag); Bks. 23-21 (D) c. O. ea., $7.50. (Sold only in sets. Repr. backwards.) West Pub.

LOUISIANA.
Ficklen, J: R. Hist. of Reconstruction in Louisiana. $1.50; $1. Johns Hopkins.
Fortier, A., *ed.* Louisiana. In 2 v. $48. S. A. Brant.
Harris, G. D. Cartography of southwestern Louisiana.—Notes on the geology of the Winnfield sheet: [Louisiana.] (Add. author for price.) G. D. Harris.
Harris, G. D., *and others.* Rock salt, its origin, geological occurrences and economic importance in Louisiana. (Add. pubs. for price.) La. Geol. Survey.
Illinois Central Railroad Co. Louisiana reclaimed lands make fertile farms; pamphlet full of information concerning the prairie marshes and cypress swamp lands of Louisiana and how they are being reclaimed; comp. by J. F. Merry. '09, [1910.] (Mr) 28 p. il. 8°. (Add. pubs. for price.) Ill. Central R. R.
Magruder, H. Hist. of Louisiana. 65 c. Heath.

LOUISIANA.—*Continued.*
Morris, A. Studies in the civil government of the state of Louisiana and the Constitution of the United States. 50 c. Natchitoches Times.
Reclamation of alluvial lands in southern Louisiana. gratis. La. Meadow.
See also Gases;—Missouri;—New Orleans;—Oils and fats;—Ouachita Valley.

Louisiana Geological Survey bull. O. La. Geol. Survey.
—Harris. Cartography of southwestern Louisiana.—Notes on the geology of the Winnfield sheet. (Add. author for price.)
—Harris, *and others.* Oil and gas in northwestern Louisiana.—Rock salt. (Add. pubs. for price.)

Louisiana State Univ. bull. 8° La. State Univ.
—Boyd. General W. T. Sherman as a college president. gratis.
—Fleming. Ex-slave pension frauds.—Jefferson Davis at West Point.—Jefferson Davis, the negroes and the negro problem. gratis.—Religious life of Jefferson Davis.
—Read. Southern R.

Louisville, Ky. Free Public Library. List of practical books in the library on electricity, machine shop practice, foundry practice, plumbing and woodworking; comp. for the Southern Electrical and Industrial Exposition, Louisville, April, 1909. '09(Ag7) S. pap. (Add. pubs. for price.) Louisville Pub. Lib.

Lounsberry, Alice.
Garden book for young people. '08(Ap18) c. il. O. **$1.50 net. Stokes.
Gardens near the sea. '10(N19) c. il. (8 in col.) O. $4.20 net. Stokes.

Lounsbury, T: Raynesford.
English spelling and spelling reform. '09 (O16) c. D. **$1.25 net. Harper.
Shakespeare as a dramatic artist. '08(Je20) c. O. (Shakespearean wars.) **$2 net. Scribner.
Standard of usage in English. '08(Ap25) c. D. **$1.50 net. Harper.

LOURDES, France.
See Miracles.

Louttit, G: W:
Eddyite (The): a Christian Science tale. '08(N) c. 223 p. 12°, $1. Colonial Press, (Ind.)

Louvre (The) [Paris]; ed. by T. Leman Hare; text by Paul G. Konody and Maurice W. Brockwell; [reproductions in color of 54 selected masterpieces.] '10(D17) 4°, $5 net. Dodge.

LOUVRE (The), Paris.
Hessling, E. *and* W. Louis XIV. furniture in the Louvre. $13.40.—Louis XV. furniture in the Louvre. $12. Hessling.

Lovable degenerate. Stoddard, W: B. $1. Cochrane.

Love, E. L.
Trip to the unknown, and other poems. '10(Jl2) c. 12°, 75 c. Cochrane.

Love, Ja. Franklin, D.D.
Unique message and the universal mission of Christianity. '10(D10) 12°, $1.25 net. Revell.

Love, J: L.
Lincoln the emancipator; address del. before the Excelsior Club, Guthrie, Okla., Feb. 12, 1909. '09(Je) 21 p. 8°, pap., 15 c. J: L. Love.

LOVE.
Anderson, L. H. Mystery of love scientifically and philosophically considered. $2. L. H. Anderson.
Drummond, H: Greatest thing is the world. *30 c. net. Crowell.
Gordon, G: A. Beatrice, the insight of love. 50 c. Pilgrim Press.
Jennings, N. I., *comp.* Man and his mate: [love songs and love letters.] 50 c.; $1.50.—When we're in love. 50 c. Lone Star.
Kauffman, R. W., *comp.* Book of love. 75 c. Altemus.
Krans, H. S., *ed.* English love poems. **$1.25 net. Putnam.
Moore, W: T: Supremacy of the heart life. *$1.25 net. Revell.
Pogue, J: F. Philosophy of living, which is loving. $1. Krehbiel.
Richardson, F. Love; and all about it: [satirical essays.] *75 c. net. M. Kennerley.
Schaffner, L. Love and friendship. 35 c. net. P. Elder.
Talmey, B. S. Woman: treatise on normal and pathological emotions of feminine love. $3. Practitioners' Pub.
Willoughby, L., *ed.* Love in all ages. 50 c. Volland.
See also Friendship;—Marriage;—Woman.

Love affairs of Lord Byron. Gribble, F. H. $3.75 net. Scribner.
Love affairs of Napoleon. Turquan, J. *$5 net. Lane.
Love among the chickens. Wodehouse, P. G. $1.50. Circle Pub.
Love among the mistletoe. Elmore, J. B. $1. J. B. Elmore.
Love and honor. D'Avenant, *Sir* W: *60 c. net. Heath.
Love and life. Kreymborg, A. **$1 net. Grafton Press.
Love and the ironmonger. Randall, F. J. †$1.50. Lane.
Love and the year. Griswold, G. 60 c. net. Duffield.
Love and wisdom of God. King, E: $1.75 net. Longmans.
Love enthroned. Steele, D. $1.20. Eaton & M.
Love, faith and endeavor. Grumbine, H. C. *$1 net. Sherman, F.
Love, friendship and good cheer. Strand, G. B., *comp.* 50 c. net. McClurg.
Love in the valley. *See* Meredith, G:
Love in the weaving. Orthwein, E. H. $1.50. B'way Pub.
Love intrigues of royal courts. Hall, T. $3.50 net. Dodd.
Love is all Booth, E. 30 c. Reliance.
Love letters. Godwin, *Mrs.* M. W. *$1 net. Lippincott.
Love letters from the Nile. Randolph, M. $1.50. Knickerbocker Press.
Love letters of famous poets and novelists. Strachey, L., *ed.* *$2 net. J: McBride.
Love letters of famous royalties and commanders. Strachey, L., *ed.* *$2.50 net. J: McBride.
Love-letters of the king. Le Gallienne, R: †75 c. Little, B. & Co.
Love me little, love me long. Reade, C: †$1.50. Doubleday, P.
Love never faileth. Powers, J. D. O. 50 c. A. Harriman.
Love of books and reading. Kuhns, L. O. $1 net. Holt.
Love of the Trinity. Ingram, A. F. W. *60 c. net. Whittaker.
Love of the wild. McKishnie, A. P. $1.20. FitzGerald.
Love poems. Robbins, R. C. R. C. Robbins.
Love poems XVIII century. '09(O2) il. Q. bds., *$2.50 net, boxed. Stokes.
Love songs and lyrics. Middleton, J. A. *75 c. net. J: W. Luce.
Love sonnets of a car conductor. Irwin, W. A. **50 c. net. P. Elder.
Love story of Empress Josephine. Endell, J. *$2.50 net; *$5 net. Pott.
Love story of Empress Josephine. Roberts, W. J. *$3.50 net; *$7 net. Pott.
Love tales of the nations. New ed. In 5 v. '08(D19) 16°, ea., *50 c. net. Jacobs.
Contents: American love tales; German love tales; Irish love tales: Scotch love tales; English love tales.
Love test. Brady, C. T. *$1.25 net. Young Churchman.
Love the criminal. Burland, J: B. H-. 75 c. Cupples & L.
Love, the judge. Carey, W. †$1.50. Dodd.
Love thrives in war. Crowley, M. C. †75 c. Little, B. & Co.

Lovejoy, Mary Isabella, ed.
Doll's story-book. '08(N14) c. il. D. (Happy hour ser.) bds., 50 c. Wilde.

Lovejoy, Owen R.
Children in the glass industry in Pennsylvania. 3d ed., rev. '09(Jl) 15 p. il. 16°, (National Child Labor Committee pubs., smaller ser.) pap. (Add. pubs. for price.) Nat. Child Labor.

Loveland stories in verse. MacKay, E. M. $1.25. L. Washington.

"Lovell, Ingraham," pseud.
See Bacon, *Mrs.* Josephine Dodge Daskam.

Lovell, Stephen.
See Devereux, W:

Lovell, W: H.
Plane table and its use in surveying. '08 (Ag8) c. il. D. *$1 net. McGraw.

Lovely Mrs. Blake. Marsh, R: $1.20 net. Cassell.
Lovely woman; pictured by famous American artists. '10(D31) c. O. $2.50, boxed. Bobbs-M.

Loveman, Rob.
Blushful South and Hippocrene; being songs by Robert Loveman. '09(D11) c. 12°, **$1 net. Lippincott.

Lover of Queen Elizabeth. Richardson, *Mrs.* A. *$3.50 special net. Appleton.

Loveridge, Rose Taylor.
Twins in twain. '09(N) c. 180 p. 8°, $1.50. R. T. Loveridge.

Lover's complaint. *See* Shakespeare, W: Sonnets.

Lover's diary. Parker, *Sir* G. $1.25. Harper.

Lover's tragedy. *See* Auringer, Obadiah Cyrus. Twin poems of the Revolution.

Lovers in heaven. Hawthorne, J. 25 c. New Church.

Lovers year-book. Fite, *Mrs.* E. M. S., *ed.* 60 c.; $1. Crowell.

Love's logic. Hawkins, A. H. †$1.50. McClure.

Love's privilege. Düring, *Mrs.* S. M. †$1.50. Lippincott.

Love's rainbow dream. Popham, W: L. 50 c. W: L. Popham.

Love's sweet dream fully realized. Flory, J. S. 50 c. Higher Life.

Love's young dream. Crockett, S: R. $1.50. Macmillan.

Lovett, Ja. De Wolf.
Old Boston boys and the games they played. New ed. '08(S19) c. il. 12°, *$1.50 net. Little, B. & Co.

Lovett, Rob. Morss.
See Moody, W: Vaughan.

Lovewell, Mrs. Caroline Forbes Barnes, Whittemore, Mrs. Frances Dean Davis, and Lyon, Mrs. Hannah Wright.
Fireless cooker: how to make it, how to use it, what to cook. '08(S12) c. il. D. $1. Home Pub. Co. (Kan.)

Loving cup. Nesbit, W. D., *ed.* 50 c. Volland.

Low, Albert Howard.
Technical methods of ore analysis. 3d ed., rev. and enl. '08(Ja18); 4th ed. '09 (N6) 8°, ea., $3. Wiley.

Low, Alfr. Maurice.
America at home. '08(D5) il. 12°, *$1.75 net. Scribner.
The American people: study in national psychology. '09(O30) c. O. **$2.25 net. Houghton M.

Low, D: Allan.
Applied mechanics; embracing strength and elasticity of materials, theory and design of structures, theory of machines and hydraulics. '09(N20) il. O. $2.75. Longmans.

Low, Flora Frances.
Hampton arithmetic. '09(N) c. 302 p. il. 12°, $1. Hampton Inst.

Low, F: Rollins.
Steam engine indicator. 3d ed., rev. and enl. '10(O1) c. il. tabs., 8°, $1.50. McGraw-H.

Low, May Austin.
Confession, and other verses. '09(O) 11-47 p. 12°, *80 c. net. Sherman, F.

Low, Sidney, Ja. Mark, and Pulling, S: Sanders, eds.
Dict. of English hist. New and rev. ed. '10(D3) pors. 8°, $3.50 net. Cassell.

Low, Will Hicok.
Chronicle of friendships, 1873-1900. '08 (D19) c. il. pors. facsims., O. **$3 net. Scribner.
Painter's progress; being partial survey along the pathway of art in America and Europe, with sundry examples and precepts culled from personal encounter with existing conditions and reference to the careers of many artists, both ancient and modern; six discourses forming the fifth annual series of the Scammon lectures, del. before the Art Institute of Chicago, April, 1910. '10(N5) c. il. D. $1.50 net Scribner.

Low-cost suburban homes: designs and pictures of suburban houses that have been built at costs ranging from $1,000 to $10,000; by representative architects. '08(N) 62 p. il. plans, O. (House and garden illustrated books.) pap., 25 c. Winston.

Low to high gear ser.; by E: Sylvester Ellis. 8 v. '10(D) il. 12°, ea., 75 c. Estes.
Contents: From high to low gear; Lost dragon; P. Q. & G.; Plucky Jo; Patriot and Tory; True blue; Lucky Ned; Unlucky Tib.

Low twelve. Ellis, E: S. $1.50. Niglutsch.

Lowater, Mrs. Ninette Maine.
Songs from the wayside: book of verse. '09(Mr) c. '02. 121 p. il. por. 12°, $1. Sun Press.

Lowber, Ja. W:
Struggles and triumphs of the truth. 3d ed. '10(Jl) c. 15+533 p. pors. 8°, $2. Standard Pub.

Lowe, C. M.
Little workers: [book of rhymes and illustrations about various trades and industries.] '10(Ap23) il. 4°, bds., $1. Dutton.

Lowe, C:
Prince's pranks. '09(Jl10) D. $1.50. Lane.

Lowe, Fs. J.
Around Africa and across the Andes. '10 (Jl9) c. il. O. pap., 50 c. International Press.

Lowe, Fk.
Odd Fellows vest pocket guide. '09(Jl3) c. Tt. 50 c. F. Lowe.

Lowe, Houston.
Paints for steel structures. 5th ed. '09 (D) 115 p. 12°, $1. Wiley.

Lowe, Paul E., comp.
Hoyle's card games; the most popular games of cards played in the English-speaking world, with rules and directions for the most successful methods of play. '09(D) c. 127 p. 12°, 15 c. Ottenheimer.

Lowe, Paul Emilius.
Electric railway troubles and how to find them; comprehensive treatise on motors, motor operation, motor repairs, car break-downs, control systems, repairing of control, air brakes, air brake troubles, and electric railway operation generally. '09(O9) c. il. 12°, $1.50. Drake.
Vest-pocket compendium of applied electricity. '10(O15) c. il. nar. T. 25 c.; leath., 50 c. McKay.
—, **ed.** Twentieth century book of toasts; gems of thought from master minds. '10 (Je4) c. D. 50 c. McKay.

Lowe, Rev. W: H:
Systemization of the Russian verb. '09, [1910.] (F) 8°, *$1.50 net. Putnam.

Lowell, Abbott Lawrence.
Government of England. '08(Je6) c. 2 v., tabs., O. per set, **$4 net. Macmillan.

Lowell, Mrs. Carrie Thompson, comp.
Impressions in and about Portland, Maine. '10(S) c. 46 p. il. 16°, 50 c. A. W. Lowell.

Lowell, Ja. Russell.
Poems; with a biographical sketch by Nathan Haskell Dole. '09(O2) c. D. (Crowell's thin paper poets.) limp leath., $1.25, boxed; ooze, $1.75, boxed. Crowell.
Poems. '10(D) 12°, (Autograph poets.) $1; hf. leath., $1.50. Houghton M.
The courtin'; set to pictures. '09(O9) c. il. facsim., O. bds., *$1.50 net. Houghton M.
Fireside travels; with an introd. by E. V. Lucas. '10(Ja22) S. (Oxford lib. of prose and poetry.) 90 c. Oxford Univ.
Lowell day by day; ed. by Lucy L. Cable. '10(D) 12°, (Day by day ser.) 60 c.; ooze, $1. Crowell.
Vision of Sir Launfal. '10(D) 16°, (Abbey classics.) pap., 25 c., boxed; bds., 50 c., boxed; limp leath., $1, boxed. Abbey Co.
Formerly published by Paul Elder.
Vision of Sir Launfal; ed., with introd., notes, outline study and examination questions, by Maud Elma Kingsley and Fk. Herbert Palmer. '10(Ap9) c. 16°, (Kingsley English texts.) 25 c. Palmer Co.
Vision of Sir Launfal. '10(D) front. 32°, (Ariel booklets.) leath., 75 c., boxed. Putnam.
Vision of Sir Launfal, and other poems; ed., with an introd. and notes, by Julian W. Abernethy. '09(Ja30) c. por. 16°, (Merrill's English texts.) 25 c. C: E. Merrill.

Lowell, Percival.
Evolution of worlds. '09(D11) c. il. O. **$2.50 net, boxed. Macmillan.
Mars, as the abode of life. '08(D19) c. il. O. **$2.50 net, boxed. Macmillan.
See also Wallace, Alfr. Russel.

Lowell, Mass. City Library. Gardens and gardening: list of books rel. to gardens and gardening in the Lowell City Library. '10(Je4) 12°, gratis. Lowell Lib.

Lowell, Mass. City Library. List of Lincoln's writings and works rel. to Lincoln in the Lowell City Library. '09(Mr) 18 p. pap., gratis. Lowell Lib.

Lowell, Mass. City Library. Textiles: list of books rel. to textiles in the Library. '10(Ja8) 12°, pap., gratis. Lowell Lib.

Lowell lectures. *See* Ferrero, Guglielmo.—Mahaffy, J: Pentland.

Lowenberg, Mrs. I.
Irresistible current. '08(Ag8) c. il. D. $1.25. B'way Pub.
A nation's crime; novel. '10(D3) c. D. $1.50. Neale.

Lowenheim, Gertrude.
Goosie-gander rhymes. '09(O30) c. col. il. obl. D. bds., $1. Saalfield.

Lowenthal, R:
See Knecht, Edm.

Lower, Richard.
Gotch, F. Two Oxford physiologists: Richard Lower, 1631 to 1691; John Mayow, 1641 to 1679. 35 c. Oxford Univ.

Lower California.
North, A. W. Mother of California: hist. sketch of the little known land of Baja California. **$2 net. P. Elder.

Lowes, Mrs. Emily Leigh.
Chats on old lace and needlework. '08 (O17) il. O. ("Chats" ser.) $2. Stokes.
Chats on old silver. '09(O30) O. ("Chats" ser.) **$2 net; ¾ levant, *$5 net. Stokes.

Lowndes, Arth., D.D.
Century of achievement: hist. of the New York Bible and Common Prayer Book Society for one hundred years. 2 v. '10 (Jl30) 8°, $5. Gorham.
Vindication of Anglican orders. 3d ed., rev. and enl. '09(Mr27) 2 v., 8°, *$3.50 net. Gorham.

Lowndes, Mrs. Marie Adelaide Belloc-.
See Belloc-Lowndes, *Mrs.* Marie Adelaide.

Lowndes, Mary E.
Nuns of Port Royal as seen in their own narratives. '10(Ja1) il. 8°, $4.15. Oxford Univ.

Lownhaupt, F:
Investment bonds, their issue and their place in finance. '08(D5) c. O. **$1.75 net. Putnam.
Series on bonds; facts regarding their issue and their security. 6 v. v. 1, Railroad bonds; v. 2, Public utility bonds; v. 3, Industrial bonds; v. 4, Municipal bonds; v. 5, Irrigation bonds; v. 6, Timber bonds. '10(D17) ea. 24°, pap., 10 c. Moody's Mag.

Lowrie, Alfr. W:
Vision of Father, Son and three judges at the throne of the heavenly globe. '10 (Je11) il. por. O. $1.50. A. W: Lowrie.

Lowrie, Wa.
Abba, Father: a comment on the Lord's prayer. '08(N21) D. *$1 net. Longmans.

Lowry, Edith Belle, M.D.
Confidences: talks with a young girl concerning herself. '10(N5) c. S. 50 c. net. Forbes.

Lowry, S. C.
Hymns and spiritual songs. '10(D17) D. $1 net. Longmans.

Loyal little subject. Pomeroy, S. G. 50 c. Estes.

Loyalists of Massachusetts. Stark, J. H: $5. W: B. Clarke.

Loyalty.
See Ethics.

Loyd, W: H.
Early courts of Pennsylvania. '10(D) c. 9+287 p. D. $3.50. Boston Bk.

Loyola, Ignatius de (Inigo Lopez de Recalde).
Thompson, F. Saint Ignatius Loyola. *$3.25 net. Benziger.

Loyola, Mother Mary.
Heavenwards; ed. by Father Thurston. '10(Jl2) il. 12°, $1.25 net. Kenedy.

Lubarsky, L: H:, ed.
Elementary algebra: manual of examinations in mathematics; regents' questions and answers. '09(F6) c. 8°, $1.50. Engineering News.

Lubbock, Alfr. Basil.
Deep sea warriors. '10(F5) c. D. †$1.50. Dodd.

Lubbock, Sir J:, [Lord Avebury.]
Duty of happiness. '10(Ag20) por. T. (Remarque ser. of literary masterpieces.) 40 c., boxed; limp leath., 75 c., boxed. Caldwell.
Peace and happiness: [essays.] '09(F13) c. D. **$1.50 net. Macmillan.
Value of time. '10(Ag20) por. T. (Remarque ser. of literature masterpieces.) 40 c., boxed; limp leath., 75 c., boxed. Caldwell.

Lubbock, Percy.
Samuel Pepys. '10(Mr26) il. pors. D. (Literary lives.) *$1 net. Scribner.

Lubin, D:
International Institute of Agriculture at Rome; letter written to Hon. G: C. Perkins and Hon. Fk. P. Flint. '09(S) 6 p. 8°. (Add. Superintendent for price.) U. S., Supt. of Docs.

Luby, Ja. Patrick Kenyon.
Black cross clove. '10(D10) c. D. $1.20 net. B: W. Huebsch.

Luby, W: Arth.
See Hawkes, Herbert Edn.

Luby, W: Jeremiah.
The vandal; or, half a Christian; novel on Irish-American life. '09(N) c. 344 p. 12°, $1.25. Hyland.

Lucas, Sir C: Prestwood.
Historical geography of the British colonies. v. 1, The Mediterranean and eastern colonies. 2d ed., rev. and brought up to date by R. E. Stubbs. v. 2, The West Indies. 2d ed., rev. and brought up to date by C. Atchley. v. 3, West Africa. 2d ed., rev. to the end of 1899. v. 4, South and East Africa, pt. 1, Historical. v. 5, Canada, pt. 1, New France; pt. 2, Historical, by Hugh E. Egerton; v. 6, Australasia, by J. D. Rogers; pt. 1, Historical. '08(N21) maps, D. v. 1, $1.25; v. 2, $1.90; v. 3, $2; v. 4, pt. 1, $2.40; v. 5, pt. 1, $1.50; v. 6, $1.90. Oxford Univ.
History of Canada, 1763-1812. '09(Ap17) fold. maps, O. $4.15. Oxford Univ.

Lucas, Clarence.
Story of musical form. '08(D12) por. D. (Music story ser.) *$1.25 net. Scribner.

Lucas, E: Verrall.
Anne's terrible good nature, and other stories for children. '08(N21) il. 12°, $1.75. Macmillan.
Mr. Ingleside. '10(O15) c. D. $1.35 net. Macmillan.
One day and another. '09(O2) S. *$1.25 net. Macmillan.
Over Bemerton's: an easy-going chronicle. '08(O17) c. D. †$1.50. Macmillan.
Second post; companion to "The gentlest art." '10(N5) c. S. (Friendly lib.) $1.25, boxed; leath., $1.75 net, boxed. Macmillan.

Lucas, E: Verrall.—*Continued.*
The slowcoach. '10(D3) c. D. $1.50 net. Macmillan.
Wanderer in Holland. New ed. '10(O22) col. il. map, 12°, limp leath., $2.50 net. Macmillan.
Wanderer in London. New ed. '10(O22) col. il. 12°, limp leath., $2.50 net. Macmillan.
Wanderer in Paris. '09(O2) c. map, D. **$1.75 net; New ed. '10(O22) col. il. 12°, limp leath., $2.50 net. Macmillan.

— and Eliz.
Three hundred games and pastimes; or, what shall we do now?; suggestions for children's games and employments. '10 (My10) il. 8°, $2 net. Macmillan.

—, ed. Hambledon men: being a new ed. of John Nyren's young cricketer's tutor, together with a collection of other matter drawn from various sources, all bearing upon the great batsmen and bowlers before round-arm came in. '09(My15) il. S. (Oxford lib. of prose and poetry.) 90 c. Oxford Univ.
Ladies' pageant: [selections in verse and prose in praise of women.] '08(O24) c. S. **$1.25 net. Macmillan.
Some friends of mine; rally of men. '09 (O30) c. S. **$1.25 net. Macmillan.

Lucas, Eliz.
See Lucas, E: Verrall.

Lucas, St. John Welles Lucas.
First round. '10(Ap23) 8°, $1.25 net. Dutton.

—, comp. Oxford book of French verse; XIII to XIX century. '08(D19) cr. 8°, *$1.75 net; India paper ed., *$2.40 net; mor., *$3 net. Oxford Univ.
Oxford book of Italian verse, XIII century-XIX century. '10(D17) 8°, $2 net; Oxford India pap., $2.50 net. Oxford Univ.
Rose-winged hours: English love lyrics. '08(N21) front. S. *$1.40 net. Longmans.

Lucas, Mrs. Lewis Clarke.
See Lucas, Paula Easby-Smith.

Lucas, Paula Easby-Smith (Mrs. Lewis Clarke Lucas,) ["Lady Polly."]
All about salads. '08(My9) 75 c. Cathedral Lib.

Lucas, Reginald Jaffray.
Colonel Saunderson, M.P.: a memoir. '08 (Jl11) 8°, *$4 net. Dutton.
Lord Glenesk and the *"Morning Post."* '10(Jl30) front. por. O. $6 net. Lane.

Luce, Rev. Fk. Wellington.
King's conquest; addresses and sermons. '10 (D17) c. por. 8°, $1. Jennings.

Lucia, Rose.
Stories of American discoverers for little Americans. '10(F26) c. D. (Eclectic readings.) 40 c. Am. Bk.

Lucian, [Latin Lucianus Samosatensis.]
Dialogues; prep. for schools with short notes in Greek by W. H. D. Rouse. '09 (D4) D. 50 c.; notes to accompany above, 87 p. D. bds., 50 c. Oxford Univ.
See also Codex Taurinensis (Y).

Lucier, Alvin Jos.
The machine: political satire. '08(O17) c. il. 12°, $1. Mayhew.

Lucius Flavus. Kaenders, P. *25 c. net. Herder.

Lucky Jim. La Croix, A. 25 c. J. S. Ogilvie.

Lucretius Carus, Titus.
De rerum natura; selection from the fifth book (1-782); ed., with introd., analysis and notes, by W. D. Lowe. '10(My14) D. 90 c. Oxford Univ.
Lucretius on the nature of things; tr. by by Cyril Bailey. '10(Mr26) D. $1. Oxford Univ.
On the nature of things; tr. by H. A. J. Munro; with an introd. by J. D. Duff. '08(Mr14) 12°, (Bohn's classical lib.) *$1.50 net. Macmillan.

LUCRETIUS CARUS, Titus.
Masson, J: Lucretius: epicurean and poet. [v. 2, supplementary.] **$2 net. Dutton.
Merrill, W: A. Cicero's knowledge of Lucretius's poem. 10 c. Univ. of Cal.
Santayana, G: Three philosophical poets; Lucretius, Dante, and Goethe. $2.25. Harvard Univ.
Swan, F: T. Use of the adjective as a substantive in the De rerum natura of Lucretius. 40 c. Macmillan.

Lucy, Sir H: W., ["Toby, M. P."]
Memories of eight parliaments. pt. 1, Men; pt. 2, Manners. '08(My9) O. *$2.50 net. Putnam.
Sixty years in the wilderness: [reminiscences of London.] '09(Jl17) 8°, *$3 net. Dutton.

Lucy Arlyn. Trowbridge, J: T. 50 c. Hurst.

Ludlow, Fitzhugh.
Hasheesh eater. '08(Ap11) c. 12°, (Popular priced copyrights.) 50 c. B. W. Dodge.

Ludlow, Ja. Meeker, D.D.
Discovery of self. '10(D10) c. 12°, (Right living ser.) bds., 35 c. net. Revell.
Judge West's opinion, reported by a neighbor. '08(O31) c. D. *$1 net. Revell.

Ludovici, Anthony M.
Nietzsche, his life and works; with preface by Dr. Oscar Levy. '10(D24) 12°, (Philosophies ancient and modern from Pythagoras to Spencer.) 50 c. net. Dodge.

LUDWIG II., *King of Bavaria.*
Tschudi, C. Ludwig, the second king of Bavaria. *$2.50 net. Dutton.

Ludwig, Otto.
Der erbförster; ein trauerspiel in fünfe aufzügen; ed., with introd. and notes, by Norton C. Stewart. '10(O1) c. S. 35 c. net. Holt.

Ludy, Rob. B., ed.
Answers to questions prescribed by medical state boards. 4th ed., rewritten and enl. '10(O) 7+768 p. 8°, $1.50. McVey.

Luffmann, Carl Bogue.
Quiet days in Spain. '10(Ag20) O. $2 net. Dutton.

Lühe, M.
See Braun, Maximilien Gustav.

Luini, Bernardino.
Masterpieces. '10(Ja) 24°, (Painters' ser.) leath., *75 c. net; pap., *25 c. net. Stokes.

LUINI, Bernardino.
Mason, J. Bernardino Luini. *65 c. net. Stokes.

Luise. Rudolph, J. F. S. 30 c. J. F. S. Rudolph.

LUISEÑO INDIANS.
See Indians.

Luke, T: D., M.D.
Manual of natural therapy. '08(D) 317 p. il. *$2.50 net. Wood.

LUKE (*Gospel of*).
See Bible. N. T.

Luke the physician. Ramsay, *Sir* W: M. *$3 net. Armstrong.

Lukens, Victor Herbert, and Russell, Ja. Elmer.
Presbyterian church membership. '08(D) 16 p. S. pap. (Add. pubs. for price.) Westminster.

LULLABIES.
See Songs.

Lullabies of many lands. Withington, E., *comp.* 50 c. Caldwell.

Luman, J: A., ed.
Comprehensive arithmetic for grammar, high and commercial schools. 4th ed., rev. '08(O) c. 367 p. il. 4°, (Peirce ser.) $1.50. Peirce Sch

LUMBER.
Daniel, J: W. Lumber schedule; paper entitled Data on the lumber schedule; also a sworn statement of the difference in the wage scale of U. S. and Canada. U. S., Supt. of Docs.
Linn, A. D. Instructions in vapor process drying. A. D. Linn.
Lumber saved by using odd lengths. '10 (S) 5 p. tabs., 8°, (U. S., Dept. of Agriculture, Forest Service, circular.)
National Lumber Exporters' Association. Car service storage, switching, and other terminal rules. (Priv. pr.) Nat. Lumber.
Prescott, D. C. Evolution of modern band saw mills for sawing logs. gratis. Prescott.
Register of sawmill and planing mill auxiliary equipment for 1910. 3d ed. '10 (Jl) c. 593 p. 16°. (Not for sale.) Am. Lumberman.
Saley, M. L. Book of lumber shed construction for retail lumber yards. $1.50. Am. Lumberman.
United States. *Interstate Commerce Commission.* Memorandum on lumber reparation cases. (Add. Superintendent for price.) U. S., Supt. of Docs.
Walker, J: R., *comp.* General lumber tariff. $5. Lumbermen's Pub.
See also Forests and forestry;—Wood.

Lumberjack, A., pseud.
See Phillips, T: Whitefield.

Lummis, C: Fletcher.
Pueblo Indian folk-stories. '10(D17) c. il. 12°, $1.50. Century Co.

Lummis-Paterson, G. W.
Management of dynamos; hdbk. of theory and practice. 4th ed. '09(D) c. 292 p. il. 12°, $1.50. Henley.

Lump of gold. Ferguson, E. B. $1.50. Gilmartin.

Lumpkin, Wilson.
Removal of the Cherokee Indians from Georgia; ed. by Wymberley Jones De Renne from manuscripts in his possession. '08(My16) c. 2 v., pors. 8°. (Add pubs. for price.) Dodd.

Lumsden, Carlos B.
Dawn of modern England: being a hist. of the Reformation in England, 1509-1525. '10(D3) O. $3 net. Longmans.

Lumsden, Leslie L.
What the local health officer can do in the prevention of typhoid fever. '10(Ap) 14 p. 8°, pap. Gov. Pr. Off.

LUNACY.
See Insanity.

Lunarian professor. Alexander, J. B. $1. J. B Alexander.

LUNCHEON.
365 luncheon dishes. **50 c. net; **40 c. net. Jacobs.

Lundeberg, Axel, and Seymour, F:
Great Roosevelt African hunt and the wild animals of Africa. '10(Je25) c. il. 8°, $1.75. D. B. McCurdy.

LUNDY'S LANE, BATTLE OF.
See War of 1812.

Lunge, G:
Coal, tar and ammonia. 2 v. 4th ed. '09, [1910.] (F) 1210 p. il. 8°, *$15 net. Van Nostrand.
General methods used in technical analysis; English tr. rev. by C: A. Keane. In 3 v. v. 1, in 2 pts. '09(My1) il. 8°, *$15 net. Van Nostrand.
Manufacture of sulphuric acid and alkali: theoretical and pract. treatise. 3d ed. much enl. In 3 v. v. 2, Sulphate of soda, hydrochloric acid, leblanc soda. '09 [1910.] (F); v. 3, Ammonia soda (Ag) 840 p. il. $15 net. Van Nostrand.
Technical chemists' handbook. '09(My1) 12°, leath., *$3.50 net. Van Nostrand.

LUNGS.
Nash, E. B. Leaders in respiratory organs. $1.50. Boericke & T.
Neusser, E. v. Clinical treatises on symptomatology and diagnosis of disorders of respiration and circulation. $1.50. Treat.
See also Breathing;—Hygiene;—Thorax;—Tuberculosis.

Lunn, Arth. Constant.
The differential equations of dynamics. '09 (O) 26 p. 4°. (Add. author for price.) A. C. Lunn.

Lunt, Ernest Miller.
Golden opportunity; address. '10(Ja22) c. por. O. bds. (Priv. pr.) Towle Mfg.

Lupton, J. H., D.D.
Life of John Colet, D.D., Dean of St. Paul's School; with an appendix on some of his English writings. New ed. '09 (Mr13) por. O. *$2.75 net. Macmillan.

Luquer, Lea McIlvaine.
Minerals in rock sections: pract. methods of identifying minerals in rock sections with the microscope. 3d rev. ed. '08 (Ag1) c. il. tab., 8°, **$1.50 net. Van Nostrand.

Luquiens, F: Bliss.
Introd. to old French phonology and morphology. '09(D11) c. O. *$1.50 net. Yale Univ.

Lure of Eve. Moore, E. M. $1.50. Cassell.

Lure of inadequate rates; reproduced from the Fraternal Monitor. '10(N) c. 8 p. 8°, 10 c. Fraternal Monitor.

Lure of life. Opp-Dyke, O. $1 net. Sherman, F.

Lure of the antique. Dyer, W. A. $2.40 net. Century Co.

Lure of the Book. Miller, M. F. $1. Winona.

Lure of the city. Burrell, D: J. **$1 net. Funk.

Lure of the Indian country. Littleheart, O. $1; 25 c. A. Abbott.

Lure of the land. Fullerton, E. L. Long Island R. R.

Lure of the mask. MacGrath, H. †$1.50. Bobbs-M.

Lurie, L: Aryah.
Effect of a constant stimulus upon touch localization. '09(F6) il. tabs., O. (University studies.) pap., 50 c. Univ. of Cin.

Lusby, Ja. W:
County examiner. 2d ed. '09(Je5) 12°, bds., $1. Teachers' Supply.
Stocks and bonds made easy; with a supplement on mensuration; arranged for the assistance of teachers and pupils in high, normal and common schools. '09 (My) c. '08. 53 p. 16°, 50 c. Teachers' Supply.

Lusk, Mrs. Alice Freeman.
Woman's answer to Roosevelt: story on race suicide. '08(Ap4) c. D. 75 c. Commercial Pr. Ho.

Lusk, Graham, M.D.
Elements of the science of nutrition. 2d ed., rev. and enl. '09(D) 13-402 p. il. 8°, *$3 net. Saunders.

Lusk, W: Thompson.
War letters of William Thompson Lusk, Captain, Assistant Adjutant General U. S. Volunteers, 1861-1863; afterward M.D., LL.D. '10(Jl) il. cr. 8°. (Priv. pr.) F. F. Sherman.

Lussy, Mathis.
Short treatise on musical rhythms, from "Le rhythme musical"; abr., with the author's sanction, by his pupil, Ernest Dutoit; the Eng. rendering, notes, questions and exercises prep. by Ernest Fowler. '09 (Jl) c. 11+82 p. 16° $1. T: J. Donlan.

Luster, Lewis.
See Missouri. *St. Louis, etc., cts.*

Lustgarten, J.
See Zeidler, J.

LUSTRES.
See Ceramics.

Lute of jade. Cranmer-Byng, L. A., *comp.* *60 c. net. Dutton.

LUTEN BRIDGES.
See Bridges.

Luther, D. Dana.
Geology of the Geneva-Ovid quadrangles. '09(Ag) 5-41 p. 8°, (New York State Museum bull.) (Add. pubs. for price.) N. Y. State Educ.
See also Clarke, J: Mason.

Luther, Martin.
Kinderlehre; die fünf hauptstücke des kleinen katechismus dr. Martin Luther's in fortlaufenden lektionen erklärt von dr. Wa. Eickmann; vollständige ausg. (deutsch-englisch) für die sonntagschule, das haus und den konfirmandenunterricht. '10(D) c. various p. 8°, 50 c. W. Eickmann.
Letters; sel. and tr. by Marg. A. Currie. '08(Ap4) 8°, *$3.75 net. Macmillan.
[Sermons;] tr. with the help of others by Prof. J: N: Lenker. v. 1, Luther's Christmas sermons; Epistles; v. 2, Luther's Epistle sermons, Epiphany, Easter and Pentecost. '09(My1); v. 3 Trinity Sunday to Advent (Jl10) c. O. (Christtian educational ser.) v. 1, 50 c.; v. 2, 3, ea., $1.65. Luther Press.
Small catechism: God's call to repentance, faith and prayer; tr., with the help of others, by J: N. Lenker; pt. 1 of Luther's catechetical writings. [Also] Luther's large catechism; tr., with the help of others, by J: N. Lenker; pt. 2 of Luther's catechetical writings. '08(D5) c. D. (Christian educational ser.) 50 c. Luther Press.
Small catechism, with Hints and helps to the way of salvation. Rev. 3d ed.; prep. by Rev. P. G: Sieger. [1910.] (F) c. '09. 74 p. 16°, 25 c. P. G: Sieger.
Two catechisms explained by himself in six classic writings; tr., with the help of others, by J: N. Lenker; pt. 3 of Luther's catechetical writings. '08(D5) c. D. (Christian educational ser.) 50 c. Luther Press.

LUTHER, Martin.
Luther-album; precursor of the fourth centennial celebration in memory of the nailing of the 95 theses upon the door of the castle church at Wittenberg on Oct. 31st, 1517, by Dr. Martin Luther; submitted by Martin S. Sommer. '10 (Ag) 4+149 p. por. il. 8°, $1. Lange.
Published also in German.
Stumpf, J. Explanation of Luther's small catechism. 35 c.; 50 c. Gen. Council.
Tilly, F: E., *comp.* Stories from the life of Dr. Martin Luther. 25 c. E. Kaufmann.
Waring, L. H. Political theories of Martin Luther. $1.50. Putnam.

LUTHERAN CHURCH.
Gerberding, G. H. Vägen till frälsnig enlight der Lutherska kyrkans uppfattning af Guds ords lära. $1. Augustana.
Lohe, W. Three books concerning the church, offered to friends of the Lutheran Church for consideration and discussion. $1. Pilger.
Richard, J. W: Confessional hist. of the Lutheran church. $3. Lutheran Pub.
Sure word of prophecy; sermons and addresses on the Reformation and the Lutheran church. *85 c. net. Germ. Lit. Bd.
Wedel, C. H. Meditationen zu den fragen und antworten unseres katechismus. $1.25. C. H. Wedel.

LUTHERAN CHURCH.—*Continued.*
Williams, G. M. Church of Sweden, and the Anglican communion. 50 c. Young Churchman.
See also Catechisms;—Community of true inspiration;—*also* First English Evangelical Church, Pittsburgh.
Lutheran handbook ser. il. 16°. Lutheran Pub.
—Monroe. Hist. of the life of Gustavus Adolphus II.
Lutheran teacher-training ser. for the Sunday school. 8°. Lutheran Pub.
—Alleman *and* Dunbar. Book and the message. 50 c.
Lutkin, P: Christian.
Music in the church; Hale lecture, 1908-9. '10(Ag20) c. D. $1 net. Young Churchman.
Lutz, Fk. Eug.
Variation and correlations of certain taxonomic characters of *Gryllus.* '08(Ag8) tabs., figs. O. (Carnegie Inst. of Wash. pub.) pap., 40 c. Carnegie.
Lutz, F:
Elementary German reader. '09(N20) c. 12°, (Silver series of modern language text-books.) $1. Silver.
Lutz, Mrs. Grace Livingston Hill-.
Girl from Montana. '09(Ja30) c. il. D. $1. Golden Rule.
Marcia Schuyler. '08(Ap4) c. il. D. †$1.50. Lippincott.
Phœbe Deane. '09(O9) c. il. D. †$1.50. Lippincott.
Lützow, Franz Heinrich Hieronymus Valentin, Graf v.
Bohemia. '10(Ap23) 16°, (Everyman's lib.) 35 c. net; leath., 70 c. net. Dutton.
Life and times of Master John Hus. '09 (Je19) il. 8°, *$4 net. Dutton.
Luxembourg illustrated lib. il. O. $1.50, boxed. Crowell.
—Kingsley. Hereward, the Wake.
Luxury of children. Martin, E: S. $1.50. Harper.
Luyckx, Francis.
See Paul, *of Moll, Father.*
Luzac's Oriental religious ser. 8°. Bloch.
—Thompson. Semitic magic. *$4 net.
Lyal ser. 12°, 50 c. Lyal Bk.
—Atkinson. Practical mental influence.—Practical psychomancy.
Lyall, Sir Arth.
Poems. '08(F22) 12°, (New universal lib.) 50 c.; leath., 75 c. Dutton.
Lyall, Sophie.
See Silberrad, Una Lucy.
Lybarger, Lee Fs.
Tariff, what it is, how it works, whom it benefits; protection, revenue, free trade. '09(Ag) 180 p. por. 8°, 25 c. Beaver Pr.
Lybrand, W: M., MacPherson, F. H., and Dickinson, Arth. Lowes.
Accounting for modern corporations. '09 (D4) c. 8°, (American School of Correspondence pubs.) 50 c. Am. Sch. Corr.
Lyde, Lionel W.
Man in many lands; introd. to the study of geographic control. '10(Je4) il. 12°, 65 c. net. Macmillan.
School text-book of geography. '08(S19) 12°. *$1 net. Macmillan.

Lydekker, R:
Hertfordshire. [1910.] (My) 10+174 p. 8°, (Cambridge county geographies.) 45 c. Putnam.
See also Johnston, *Sir* Harry Hamilton.

Lydston, G. Fk.
Poker Jim, gentleman, and other tales and sketches. '08(O) 12+396 p. il. 12°, $1. Walter.

Lyell, Sir C:
Travels in North America in the years 1841-2; abridged and ed. by J: P: Cushing. '09(D) c. 172 p. 16°, (Maynard's English classic ser.) 30 c. C: E. Merrill.

Lyle, Eug. P., jr.
Blaze Derringer. '10(Je25) c. il. D. $1.20 fixed. Doubleday, P.

Lyle, S: Hartley, jr.
Leaves of life: [poems.] '10(Jl16) por. 12°, $1.25. McGregor Co.

LYLY, John.
Feuilerat, A. John Lyly; contribution à l'histoire de la Renaissance en Angleterre. $4 net. Putnam.

Lyman, Alb. Josiah, D.D.
Christian pastor in the new age; comrade, sponsor, social mediator; lectures for 1909 on the George Shepard Foundation, Bangor Theological Seminary. '10(Ja15) c. D. **$1 net. Crowell.
Underneath are the Everlasting Arms. '10 (N5) c. D. bds., 50 c. net. Pilgrim Press.

Lyman, B: Smith.
The Philippines. '07, [1908.] 20 p. il. 8°, (Ag) pap. (Add. author for price.) B: S. Lyman.

Lyman, Edna.
Story telling; what to tell and how to tell it. '10(O8) c. S. 75 c. net. McClurg.

Lyman, Mrs. Eliz. Hills.
If I were you, and other things. '09(D) c. 8+158 p. 12°, $1.12. Miss Hills' Sch.

Lyman, Elmer Adelbert.
Plane and solid geometry. '08(O3) c. figs. D. $1.25. Am. Bk.
Plane geometry. '08(Jl18) c. il. D. 75 c. Am. Bk.
Solid geometry. '08(S12) il. por. D. hf. leath., 75 c. Am. Bk.

Lyman, Eug. W:, D.D.
Theology and human problems; comparative study of absolute idealism and pragmatism as interpreters of religion; the Nathaniel William Taylor lectures for 1909-10; given before the Divinity School of Yale University. '10(O1) c. D. $1 net. Scribner.

Lyman, Maria Bruce.
Only a dog; or, our pet. '10(N5) c. il. 12°, 25 c. Am. Humane.

Lyman, Olin Linus.
The lash. '09(N20) c. front. D. $1.50. Badger.

Lyman, Rollo Lu Verne.
Principles of effective debating. [Rev. ed.] '09(Je12) D. (Univ. of Wis. bull.) pap., 15 c Univ. of Wis.

Lyman, W: Denison.
Columbia River. '09(Je26) c. il. map, O. (American waterways.) **$3.50 net, boxed. Putnam.

Lyman Beecher lectures. *See* Beecher (Lyman) lectures.

Lynch, Abigail, comp.
Classified index of the material contained in the different series of school readers; comp. by a normal training teacher and her students. '10(Jl30) c. 8°, 50 c. Dulfer Pr.

Lynch, C:
American Red Cross text-book on first aid and relief columns. '08(N7) c. il. T. *$1 net. Blakiston.

—, and Shields, M. J.
American Red Cross abr. text-book on first aid. Industrial ed.; manual of instruction; prep. for and endorsed by the American Red Cross. '10(O15) c. il. T. General ed. (N) 13+183 p. ea., pap., 30 c. net. Blakiston.

Lynch, Harriet Powe, comp.
Year book of southern poets. '09(Ag21) c. 12°, $1.25. Dodge.

Lynch, J. S. M., D.D.
Essentials of the Five Scapulars. New and rev. ed. '09(Je) 25 c. Cathedral Lib.

Lynch, Lawrence L., pseud.
See Van Deventer, E. M.

Lynch, M. Antonia.
Old district of Southwark in the county of Philadelphia. '09(D) 87-126 p. il. plan, 8°, (City Hist. Society of Philadelphia pub.) 50 c. (Sold to members only.) City Hist., Phil.

Lynch's daughter. Merrick, L. †$1.50. McClure.

Lynd, Rob.
Home life in Ireland. '10(S17) il. O. $2.50 net. McClurg.

Lynde, Fs.
King of Arcadia. '09(Mr6) c. il. D. †$1.50. Scribner.
Taming of Red Butte Western. '10(Ap16) c. il. D. $1.50. Scribner.

Lynde, Lester E:
See Newton, F: Edn.

Lyndon, Lamar.
Development and electrical distribution of water power. '08(Ap25) c. figs. 8°, **$3 net. Wiley.

Lynn, Mass. First Church of Christ. Celebration of the 275th anniversary of the First Church of Christ, organized June, 8, 1632. '07, [1908.] (Mr.) 16-154 p. il. 8°, subs., $1.25. T: P Nichols.

LYNN, Mass.
Sanderson, H. K., *comp.* Lynn in the Revolution. 2 v. $10. W: B. Clarke.
See also Genealogies: Lewis, G. H.

LYNNFIELD, Mass.
Vital records of Lynnfield, Mass., to the end of the year 1849. *$1.05 net. Essex Inst.

Lyon, D. Everett.
How to keep bees for profit. '10(My14) c. il. D. $1 net. Macmillan.

Lyon, Fk. D., comp.
See New York [State.] Highway code.

Lyon, Harris Merton.
Sardonics: sixteen sketches. '09(Je) 225 p. D. $1.25. Stuyvesant Press.

Lyon, Ida Luella Rettinghouse.
The wonders of life. '10(My7) c. D. $1. Fenno.

Lyon, Marcus Ward, and Osgood, Wilfred Hudson.
Catalogue of the type-specimens of mammals in the United States National Museum; incl. the Biological Survey collection. '09(F27) O. pap. (Add. Superintendent for price.) U. S., Supt. of Docs.

LYON, Mary.
Gilchrist, B. B. Life of Mary Lyon. $1.50 net. Houghton M.

Lyon, Milford Hall.
For the life that now is; present worth of Christian faith. '09(Je5) c. 12°, 75 c. Revell.

Lyon, Ralph Aberdein, comp.
Pocketful of limericks. '08(Je13) c. D. 50 c. Mayhew.

Lyon, T: Lyttleton, and Fippin, Elmer O.
Principles of soil management. '01(Ja1) c. il. tabs., D. (Rural text-book ser.) **$1.75 net. Macmillan.

Lyon, Waldo Vinton.
Problems in electrical engineering. '08, [1909.] (F) c. 8+209 p. il. 8°, *$1.50 net. McGraw.

Lyon campaign in Missouri. Ware, E. F. $1. Crane.

Lyon Hart's heroism. Adams, W: T. $1. Lothrop, L. & S.

Lyons, A. Neil.
Arthur's. '08(N7) 12°, $1.50. Lane.
Cottage pie; country spread. '10(D3) D. $1.50. Lane.
Robert Blatchford; the sketch of a personality: an estimate of some achievements. '10(Jl30) pors. facsim. D. bds., 75 c. net. Lane.
Sixpenny pieces. '09(Ag21) D. $1.50. Lane.

Lyons, And. W.
Grammar of lettering: hdbk. of alphabets systematically arranged for the use of art students, architects, decorators, sign-writers, and all classes of craftsmen. '09 (Mr13) O. *$2.50 net. Lippincott.

Lyons, Ja. A.
Modern corporation accounting. '08(N) c. 80 p. il. 8°, (Accounting ser.) $1.25. Powers.

Lyre (La) française. Masson, G. J. G., *ed.* $1. Macmillan.

Lyric garland. *See* Mosher's.

Lyric love. *See* Browning, Rob.

LYRIC POETRY.
See Poetry.

Lyrics and idyls. Herbert, *Mrs.* N. C. T. $1.25. Badger.

Lyrics and landscapes. Morris, H. S. **$1 net. Century Co.

Lyrics from cotton land. McNeill, J: C: $1.50. Stone & B.

Lyrics from the hills. McGinnis, H. P., $1. Marshall Print.

Lyrics of childhood. Mayhew, E. **$1 net. Grafton Press.

Lyrics of fir and foam. Coe, A. R. $2. A. Harriman.

Lyrics of life. Coates, F. E. $1.25. Houghton M.

Lyrics of lowly life. Dunbar, P. L. **$1.60 net. Dodd.

Lyrics of New England. Flagg, J: H: $1. W: J. Taylor.

Lyrics of the field. Davis, S: I. $1. S: I. Davis.

Lyrics, pathetic and humorous, from A to Z. Dulac, E. **$2 net. Warne.

Lys, Christian, pseud.
See Brebner, Percy Ja.

Lyster, Gertrude, [Mrs. J: Lyster,] ed.
Family chronicle; derived from notes and letters sel. by Barbarina, the Hon. Lady Grey. '08(Ag1) il. pors. 8°, *$5 net. Dutton.

Lyte, Rev. H: Fs.
Poetical works; ed., with a biographical sketch, by J: Appleyard. '08(Je13) 8°, *$2 net. Young Churchman.

Lytle, H. M.
Tragedies of the white slaves. '10(S) c. 3-193 p. 12°, 25 c. C. C. Thompson.

Lyttleton, Rev. E:
Schoolboys and school work. '09(O23) O. $1.25. Longmans.

Lytton, Lord.
See Bulwer-Lytton, *Sir* E: G: Earle Lytton.

M., A. D., comp.
Friendship tried is ever true; passages sel. from the writings of great teachers, writers and poets. '10(O29) c. Tt. bds., 30 c. Stokes.

M. C., pseud.
Light on the path: treatise written for the use of those who are ignorant of Eastern wisdom. '08(Ja4) T. leath., 75 c. Theo. Pub. Co.

M. E. M., pseud.
See Mixer, *Mrs.* Mary Eliz. Knowlton.

M., G.
With the beloved: book of private devotion in verse. '09(Ap10) *60 c. net. Young Churchman.

M. P. for Russia. Novikoff, *Mme.* O. K. *$7.50 net. Putnam.

"M. Y. T. H. Myth," pseud.
See Nicolovius, Ludwig.

Maartens, Maarten, pseud.
See Schwartz, Joost Marius Willem Van der Poorten.

Maas, Rev. Anthony J.
Day in the temple: an account of the sacrificial services and the temple-rites in the time of our Blessed Lord, in the form of a story. '08(Ag8) 8°, *50 c. net. Herder.

Mabie, Hamilton Wright.
Christmas to-day. '08(N14) c. nar. D. **75 c. net. Dodd.
Introductions to notable poems. '01(Ja1) c. pors. 8°, $2. Dodd.
—, comp. Stories new and old: typical American and English tales; sel., with introds. '08(Je27) c. pors. D. †$1.50. Macmillan.

Mabie, Hamilton Wright, ed.
Essays that every child should know. '08 (Mr14) c. front. D. (Every child should know ser.) **90 c. net; hf. leath., **$1.50 net. Doubleday, P.
Folk tales every child should know; selection of the popular traditions of various nations, for young people. '10(N5) c. D. (Every child should know ser.) 90 c. net. Doubleday, P.
Young folks' treasury; E: Everett Hale, associate ed. 12 v. [1910.] (N) c. il. pors., map, 8°. Univ. Soc.
"List of best books" at end of each volume.

—, and Stephens, Kate, eds.
Heroines that every child should know. '08(Mr14) c. front. D. (Every child should know ser.) **90 c. net; hf. leath., **$1.50 net. Doubleday, P.

Mabie, H: Clay, D.D.
Divine right of missions; or, Christianity the world-religion and the right of the church to propagate it. '08(My23) D. **50 c. net Am. Bapt.
How does the death of Christ save us? '08(Ap25) c. D. **50 c. net. Am. Bapt.
Task worth while; or, the divine philosophy of missions. Seminary lectures, 1909-1910. '10(D17) c. D. $1.25 net. Griffith.

MABINOGION.
See Legends.

Mac; his book. Leigh, F. $1.50. Stokes.

McAdam, D:
Rights, duties, remedies and incidents belonging and growing out of the relation of landlord, and tenant. 3 v. 4th ed. by T: F. Keogh. '10(N) c. O. $19.50. Baker, V. & Co.

McAdie, Alex. G:
Infra nubem, The lights outside, La Bocana. '09, [1910.] c. 7-42 p. il. 12°, (Philopolis ser.) $1.50. A. M. Robertson.

McAfee, Cleland Boyd, D.D.
Growing church. '09, [1910.] (F) 131 p. 12°, *50 c. net. Northfield Press.
Studies in the Sermon on the Mount. '10 (N5) c. 12°, $1 net. Revell.
Worth of a man. '09, [1910.] (F) 35 p. 12°, bds., 30 c. Northfield Press.

McAfee, Jos. Ernest.
Missions striking home. '08(Ap11) c. 12°, 75c. Revell.

McAleer, G:, M.D., comp.
Study in the origin and signification of the surname McAleer and a contribution to McAleer genealogy. '09(Je19) c. pors. fold. tab., (in pocket,) 8°, $1.50. G: McAleer.

MCALEER FAMILY.
See Genealogies.

MacAlister, Donald A.
See Thomas, Herbert H.

McAllister, Addams Stratton.
Alternating current motors. 3d ed., rev. and enl. '09(N6) c. il. 8°, $3. McGraw-H.

McAllister, Earle Cabot.
Island secret. '09(O2) c. il. O. †$1.50. Estes.

McAllister, Jos. Thompson.
Historical sketches of Virginia Hot Springs, Warm Sulphur Springs and Bath County, Va. '08(S) c. 51 p. 12°. (Add. author for price.) J. T. McAllister.

McAndrew, W:
College influence on public high schools. '10(D17) D. bds., 30 c. Bardeen.

McArdle, Fred.
Every-thing behind the engine for conductors and brakemen: complete treatise on the duties of conductors and brakemen, questions and answers on train rules and train orders, standard signals, block signal rules, train heating, air brake instructions, questions and answers on air brake operation (car equipment). '10 (Ap9) c. il. (partly col.) 12°, $2. F. McArdle.

—, and Helmholtz, H:, eds.
Air brake text for engineers and firemen: treatise on the Westinghouse and New York air brake and signal systems. '09 (Ap24) c. il. figs. O. $2.50. McArdle & H.
Locomotive text for engineers and firemen. '09(Ap24) c. figs. O. $2.50. McArdle & H.
Westinghouse diagramatic and sectional views; air-brake and air-signal instruction charts. '09(Ap24) c. F. pap., $2. McArdle & H.

McArthur, Alex.
The leveller. '08(O24) c. D. $1.50. Doscher.

MacArthur, Douglas.
Military demolitions. [1910.] (N) 34 p. il. 12°. Staff Coll.

MacArthur, Ja.
Contented rivals, and other poems. '08, [1909.] (F) c. 112 p. 8°, 75 c. Mich. Chr. Herald.

McArthur, N. J.
Pen pictures of standard cotton grades. '10(D31) c. por. 8°, $1. Mutual Pub. Co.

MacArthur, Rob. Stuart, D.D.
Advent, Christmas, New Year, Easter, and other sermons. '08(Ap25) c. 12°, $1. Am. Bapt.
Christic reign, and other sermons. '09 (Jl10) c. O. $1.25. Am. Bapt.

—, and others.
Royal messages of cheer and comfort; ed. by Sarah Conger Robinson; with an introd. by Rev. D. C. Hughes, D.D. '09 (N20) c. pors. O. *$2 net, boxed. Treat.

MCARTHUR, Robert Stuart, *D.D.*
Randolph, H. S. F., *comp.* Fortieth anniversary of Rev. Robert Stuart MacArthur. 50 c.; $2. H. S. Randolph.
Robinson, S. C., *ed.* Precepts and prayers; souvenirs for 40th anniversary of the pastorate of Robert Stuart MacArthur. 50 c. Treat.

MACARTNEY, George, *Earl of.*
Robbins, *Mrs.* H. H. M., *ed.* George, Earl of Macartney, first British ambassador to China. *$5 net. Dutton.

MACARTNEY, *Sir* Halliday.
Boulger, D. C. de K. Life of Sir Halliday Macartney. *$6 net. Lane.

Macartney, Mervyn Edm.
English houses and gardens in the 17th and 18th centuries; with descriptive notes by Mervyn Macartney. '09(Jl3) obl. O. bds., *$6 net. Scribner.
Recent English domestic architecture: L'architecture domestique Anglaise de nos jours; Neueste beispiele des modernen wohnhauses in England; being a special issue of *The Architectural Review.* '09(S11) il. F. *$3.50 net. Scribner.

MacAtamey, Hugh Entwistle, comp.
Cradle days of New York. '09(N) 11-230 p. il. 8°, pap., 50 c. Drew & L.

McAulay, Allen.
Eagle's nest. '09(S18) D. $1.50. Lane.

Macaulay, G: Campbell.
James Thomson. '08(F8) 12°, (English men of letters ser.) **75 c. net. Macmillan.

Macaulay, T: Babington, Lord.
Essay and speech on Jewish disabilities; ed., with introd. and notes, by Israel Abrahams and Rev. S. Levy. '10(Ap23) por. 12°, $1 net. Bloch.
Essay on Lord Clive; ed., with notes and introd., by Preston C. Farrar. '10(Jl2) c. map. D. (Longmans' English classics.) 25 c. net. Longmans.
Essay on Warren Hastings; ed. by Jos. Villiers Denney. '08(F1) c. front. map, 12°, (Academy ser. of Eng. classics.) 40 c. Allyn & B.
Essay on Warren Hastings; ed. by Allan Abbott. '10(D10) c. map, 16°, (Riverside literature ser.) 15 c. Houghton M.
Essay on Warren Hastings; ed., with notes and introd., by S: M. Tucker. '10(Jl2) c. map, D. (Longmans' English classics.) 25 c. net. Longmans.
Essays. '08(O10) 2 v., 12°, ("Best books" ser.) leath., ea., *$1 net. Dutton.
Essays. 3 v. New imperial lib. ed. '10 (D) il. 8°, ea., $1.25; hf. cf., $2.25; New il. sterling ed., ea., $1. (Sets only.) Estes.
Essays on Clive and Hastings; ed., with introd. and notes, by C: Rob. Gaston. '10(D31) c. il. map, S. (English classics.) 35 c. Ginn.
Essays on Lord Clive and Warren Hastings; ed. by Allan Abbott. '10(O8) c. D. (Riverside literature ser.) 40 c. Houghton M.
Essays on Lord Clive and Warren Hastings; ed., with an introd. and notes, by Cornelia Beare. '10(Ap23) c. il. por. map, 12°, (Merrill's English texts.) 40 c. C: E. Merrill.
Essays on Clive and Hastings; ed. for school use by Alphonso G. Newcomer. '09(D11) c. S. (Lake English classics.) 35 c. Scott, F. & Co.
History of England. 3 v. '08(O17) 16°, (Best books ser.) leath., ea., *$1 net. Dutton.
Hist. of England from the accession of James II. 3 v. [1910.] (My) 16°, (Everyman's lib.) ea., 35 c. net; leath., 70 c. net. Dutton.
Bibliography (1 p.).

Macaulay, T: Babington, Lord.—*Continued.*
Hist. of England; chapter III.: with introd. and statistical notes by A. L. Bowley. '09(D4) map, S. 50 c. Oxford Univ.
Life and writings of Addison; Samuel Johnson; ed., with introd. and notes, by Cecil Fairfield Lavell. '08(D5) c. por. 16°, (English classics.) **25 c. net. Scribner.
Lord Macaulay's speeches on politics and literature; introd. by Rt. Hon. W. E. Gladstone. '09(O30) 12°, (Everyman's lib.) *35 c. net; leath., *70 c. net. Dutton.
Miscellaneous essays; [and] Lays of ancient Rome; ed. by T. P. Ellis. '10 (Ap16) 16°, (Everyman's lib.) 35 c. net; leath., 70 c. net. Dutton.
See also Carlyle, T:

—, and Arnold, Matthew.
Lays of ancient Rome; Horatius, The battle of Lake Regillus, Virginia, The prophecy of Capys; ed., with an introd. and notes, by Cornelia Beare; [with this is bound Sohrab and Rustum, by Matthew Arnold.] '09(D) c. 175 p. por. 16°, (Merrill's English texts.) 30 c. C: E. Merrill.

MACAULAY, Thomas Babington, *Lord.*
Courthope, W: J: Consideration of Macaulay's comparison of Dante and Milton. 40 c. Oxford Univ.
Trevelyan, *Sir* G: O. Life and letters of Lord Macaulay. In 2 v. $2. Harper.

Macauley, Mrs. Fanny Caldwell.
See Little, Frances, *pseud.*

McAuley, Jerry.
Jerry McAuley: apostle to the lost; introd. by the Rev. S. Irenaeus Prime, D.D.; personal recollections by A. S. Hatch, Ja. Talcott, [and others.] 5th ed., rev. and enl. '08(Ja4) il. pors. D. *$1 net. Am. Tr.

Macauliffe, Max. Arth.
Sikh religion; its Gurus, sacred writings and authors. In 6 v. '09(Ag14) il. 8°, *$19.25 net. Oxford Univ.

McBain, Howard Lee.
How we are governed in Virginia and the nation. '08(My16) c. il. 12°, 55 c. H. L. McBain.

—, and Hill, I: W:
How we are governed in Alabama and the nation. '08(O3) il. 12°, 65 c. Bell Bk.

—, and Mynders, Seymour Allen.
How we are governed in Tennessee and the nation. '09(N) 256 p. il. 12°, 55 c. Southern Sch. Supply.

McBee, Silas.
South and Mr. Taft: [reprinted from the *Sewanee Review* for October, 1908.] '09 (Mr20) 8°, 50 c. Univ. Press (Sewanee).

McBeth, Kate C.
Nez Percés Indians since Lewis and Clark. '08(Ap25) c. 12°, *$1.50 net. Revell.

Macbeth, Madge.
Winning game. '10(Jl2) 12°, $1.50. B'way Pub.

MacBrayne, Lewis E:
Men we marry. '10(D3) il. 12°, $1.50. C. M. Clark.

McBridge, Rev. R. E., tr.
See Euripides.

McCABE, *Bp.* Charles Cardwell.
Bristol, F. M. Life of Chaplain McCabe. *$1.50 net. Revell.

McCabe, Jos.
Decay of the Church of Rome. '09(D18) 8°, *$2.50 net. Dutton.
Evolution; general sketch from nebula to man. '10(Mr26) il. D. (Twentieth century science ser.) *50 c. net. Stokes.
Evolution of mind. '10(N12) 8°, $2 net. Macmillan.
Iron cardinal; being the romance of Richelieu. '09, [1910.] (D) 320 p. il. 8°, *$3.50 net. J: McBride.
Prehistoric man. '10(D17) il. D. (Twentieth century science ser.) 50 c. net. Stokes.

McCabe, Rob. Lorenzo.
Central bank of issue for the United States. '08(D) 23 p. 8°, 10 c. R. L. McCabe.

MACCABEES (Knights of the).
See Freemasonry.

McCahan, Mrs. Belle T.
Preshus child. '08(D12) 12°, $1.50. Cochrane.

McCain, C: C.
Diminishing purchasing power of railway earnings. '09, [1910.] (D) 111 p. 50 c. C: C. McCain.

McCall, Arth. Gillett.
Physical properties of soils. '09(Ap3) il. 8°, *50 c. net. Judd.

McCall, Hugh.
Hist. of Georgia; cont. brief sketches of the most remarkable events up to the present day, (1784.) '10(Ja15) por. O. $5. (700 copies.) A. B. Caldwell.

McCall, S: Walker.
Payne tariff law; article '09, [1910.] (Mr) 8 p. 8°, pap. Gov. Pr. Off.

McCall, Sidney, [pseud. for Mrs. Mary McNeil Fenollosa.]
Red Horse Hill. '09(My22) c. D. †$1.50. Little, B. & Co.
Truth Dexter. New popular ed. '08(Je13) c. front. D. †$1. Little, B. & Co.

McCallen, Rob. Seth, [Col. Dick Maple.]
Master and slave. '08(Ja11) il. por. 8°, $1.50. Nat. Bk.

McCallie, S: Washington.
Preliminary report on the marbles of Georgia. 2d ed., rev. and enl. '08(Je20) il. maps, 4°, (Georgia Geological Survey bull.) pap., 13 c. S: W. McCallie.

McCallum, Arth. Newell, and Horn, Paul Whitfield.
New century spelling book. In 2 pts. '08 (Ag15) c. 12°, 24 c. Silver.

MacCallum, Mungo W.
Shakespeare's Roman plays and their background. '10(Ap16) O. $3 net. Macmillan.

McCallum, Percival D.
Rivulets of song. '08(D) c. 3+57 p. 12°, $1. B'way Pub.

McCampbell, Eugene Franklin.
Lab'y methods for the experimental study of immunity. '09(N) c. 197 p. 8°, $1.25. Heer.
See also Frost, W: Dodge.

McCann, Mary Agnes, Sister.
Little blossoms of love, kindness, and obedience, scattered during a lifetime in honor of Our Immaculate Mother. '10 (D) il. 8°, $1.50. M. A. McCann.
Mother Seton, foundress of the Sisters of Charity. '09, [1910.] (Mr) c. 5-74 p. il. 8°, $1. Sisters of Charity.

McCants, Elliott Crayton.
One of the grayjackets, and other stories. '09(O2) c. D. $1. State Co.

McCarter, Mrs. Marg. Hill.
Cuddy, and other stories. 4th ed. '09 (Mr13) c. 8°, Library ed., 50 c. Crane.
Cuddy's baby. '08(Ja11) il. 8°, 50 c. Crane.
In old Quivira. '08, [1909.] c. 139 p. il. 8°, 50 c. Crane.
Price of the prairie; story of Kansas. '10 (O29) c. col. il. O. $1.35 net. McClurg.

McCarthy, Dennis Aloysius.
Round of rimes. 2d ed., rev. and enl. '09 (O2) c. D. **$1 net. Little, B. & Co.
Voices from Erin, and other poems. New ed., rev. and enl. '10(N5) c. D. $1 net. Little, B. & Co.

MacCarthy, Fs. Hamilton, M.D.
Hygiene for mother and child. '10(O1) c. D. $1.25 net. Harper.

McCarthy, Justin Huntly.
Duke's motto: a melodrama. '08(Ag29) c. D. †$1.50. Harper.
God of love. '09(N6) c. D. †$1.50. Harper.
Gorgeous Borgia: a romance. '09(Mr6) c. front. D. †$1.50. Harper.
The O'Flynn; novel. '10(My21) front. O. $1.50. Harper.
Seraphica: a romance. '08(F15) c. D. †$1.50. Harper.
Short history of our own times from the accession of Queen Victoria to the accession of Edward VII. New ed., rev. and enl. '08(M7) 12°. $1.50. Harper.

McCarthy, Myles.
Advance agent; first experience ahead of a show told in amusing anecdote and yarn. '09(F20) c. il. por. O. 75 c.; pap., 25 c. Excelsior.

McCarty, Dwight G.
Territorial governors of the Old Northwest; study in territorial administration. '10(D17) O. $2. State Hist., Ia.

McCarty, L: Philippe.
Great pyramid of Jeezeh. '08(Ja4) il. tabs., 8°, $5; leath., $6. McCarty.

McCasland, C: Orville.
Right and riches: being a scientific study of wealth and its relations to producer, consumer and society. '08(Je27) c. por. O. *$1.50 net. Wilbur Pub.

MacChesney, Nathan W:, ed.
Abraham Lincoln; the tribute of a century, 1809-1909; commemorative of the Lincoln centenary and cont. principal speeches made in connection therewith. '10(Je4) c. il. pors. O. $2.75 net. McClurg.

McClain, Emlin.
Constitutional law in the United States. 2d ed. '10(O15) c. D. (American citizen ser.; ed. by Alb. Bushnell Hart.) price increased from $2 to $2.25. Longmans.
Selection of cases on constitutional law; [to accompany The general principles of constitutional law, by T: M. Cooley.] 2d ed. '09(N) 41+1297 p. Q. $5. Little, B. & Co.
—, **comp.** *See* Iowa. *Sup. ct.* Digest.

McClellan, Elisabeth.
Historic dress in America, 1800-1870; being a continuation of Historic dress in America, 1607-1800. '10(D17) il. 4°, $6 net. Jacobs.

McClelland, T. Calvin, D.D.
Mind of Christ; an attempt to answer the question what did Jesus believe? '09 (Ag14) c. D. **$1.25 net. Crowell.

McClendon, J. F.
Ophiurans of the San Diego region. '09 (Ag7) il. O. (Univ. of Cal. pubs.; Zoology; Contributions from the laboratory of the Marine Biological Association of San Diego.) pap., 30 c. Univ. of Cal.

McClendon, W: A:
Recollections of war times, by an old veteran, while under Stonewall Jackson and Lieut.-General James Longstreet; how I got in and how I got out. '09(S) c. 238 p. por. 8°. $1.25. W: A: McClendon.

McClintock, Wa.
Old North Trail; or, life, legends and religion of the Blackfeet Indians. '10(D10) col. il. fold. map, O. $4 net. Macmillan.

McCloskey, Fs. A.
Appellate papers in New York state: synoptical analysis of the mode of preparing papers on appeal in the cts. of this state, and of incidental practice rel. to appeals before and after the determination thereof, entitled the case and points. '08(Mr) c. 49 p. Q. pap. (Add. author for price.) F. A. McCloskey.

McCloskey, Marg. Orvis.
Primer. '09(Je5) il. D. 30 c. Ginn.

McClung, Mrs. Nellie Letitia Mooney.
Second chance. '10(O22) c. il. D. $1.20, fixed. Doubleday, P.
Sowing seeds in Danny. '08(Ag8) c. D. †$1. Doubleday, P.

McClung, Rob. Kenning.
Conduction of electricity through gases and radio-activity; text-book with experiments. '09(D4) c. il. O. (Blakiston's science ser.) *$1.50 net. Blakiston.

McClure, Edm.
British place names in their historical setting. '10(N12) 8°, $2. Gorham.

McClure, Harry B.
Conditions affecting the value of market hay. '09(S) 29 p. il. 8°, (U. S., Dept. of Agriculture, farmers' bull.) pap. (Add. Superintendent for price.)

McClure, Ja. Gore King, D.D.
Supreme things: [sermons.] '08(Ja18) 12°, *75 c. net. Revell.

McClure's lib of children's classics. Now Children's crimson classics.

McClymonds, J: W:, and Jones, D. R.
Essentials of arithmetic. '08(F8) c. D. 60 c. Am. Bk.

MacColl, Alex.
Working theology. '09(Mr6) c. D. **75 c. net. Scribner.

McColl, Florence Linder.
Helps for skat players. 2d ed. '08(Ag8) c. 12°, pap., 35 c. W: R. Jenkins.

McCollom, M. L., comp.
German verb form: [blank-book.] '08 (Ag22) c. obl. 8°, parchment, 30 c. Am. Bk.

McCollum, And. J.
New Arkansas form book: pleadings and practice. '08(Jl) c. 425 p. 8°, $3.50. A. J. McCollum.

McComb, S:, D.D.
Christianity and the modern mind. '10 (D24) c. D. $1.50 net. Dodd.
Healing ministry of the church. '08(D12) c. 12°, (Religion and medicine publications.) pap., **25 c. net. Moffat.
Making of the English Bible; with an introductory essay on the influence of the English Bible on English literature. '09 (Ag28) c. D. **$1 net. Moffat.
Power of self-suggestion. '09(Jl3) c. D. **50 c. net. Moffat.
See also Worcester, Elwood, *D.D.*

Macomber, W:
History of the Emmanuel movement from the standpoint of a patient. '08(D12) c. D. (Religion and medicine publications.) pap., **25 c. net. Moffat.

McConaughy, J. W.
Madame X. '10(N12) c. il. D. $1.50. H. K. Fly.

McConaughy, Ja.
Great events in the life of Christ. '09 (Je12) c. il. maps, 8°, 75 c.; pap., 50 c. Y. M. C. A.

McConnel, G: Murray.
Presidential campaigns, from Washington to Roosevelt. '08(N14) c. il. pors. D. $1.25. Rand, McN. & Co.

McConnell, Fs. J., D.D.
Christmas sermons. '09(D18) c. 12°, (Christian festival ser.) $1. Eaton & M.; Jennings.
Diviner immanence. '10(My14) c. 12°, 75 c. Eaton & M.
Edward Gayer Andrews, bishop of the Methodist Episcopal Church. '09(Ag14) c. por. O. *$1.50 net. Eaton & M.
Religious certainty. '10(Ag27) c. D. $1 net. Eaton & M.

McConnell, Jos. Moore, ed.
Southern orators; speeches and orations. '10(My14) 24°, (Pocket Am. and Eng. classics.) 25 c. Macmillan.

McConnell, Marie Florence.
Some essentials in musical definitions for music students. Rev. ed. '09(Je19) c. O. (Music students lib.) $1. Ditson.
Standard songs and choruses for high schools. '09(Ja23) c. O. 75 c. Am. Bk.

McConnell, Miriam.
See Lewis, W: Draper.

McConnell, Primrose.
Complete farmer. '10(O1) il. 8°, $1.50 net. Cassell.
Farm equipment. '10(S) il. 8°, (Complete farmer.) 60 c. net. Cassell.
Live stock; breeding and management. '09 (Jl3) il. D. (Complete farmer.) *60 c. net. Cassell.
Soils: their nature and management. '08 (My16) il. D. (Complete farmer.) *60 c. net. Cassell.

McConnell, Ray Madding.
Duty of altruism. '10(Ap2) c. D. $1.50 net. Macmillan.

McCook, H: Christopher, D.D.
Ant communities and how they are governed; study in natural civics. '09(N6) c. il. O. **$2 net. Harper.

McCord, P: B.
Wolf: the memories of a cave-dweller. '08 (N14) c. il. D. $1. B. W. Dodge.

MacCorkle, W: Alex.
An address: [patriotism in the South;] del. before the Literary Societies of Washington and Lee University, Lexington, Va. '08(D12) c. 12°. (Add. pubs. for price.) Putnam.
Some southern questions. '08(D19) O. **$1.75 net. Putnam.

McCormack, Mary Anna.
Spool knitting. '09(Jl17) c. il. D. *$1 net. Barnes.

McCormick, C: N.
Amy, the stolen wife; true love story; combined with medical facts of importance mentally and physiologically; proofs of the domination over a non-resistant by positive malevolent people. '10(N) 184 p. il. pors. 12°, $2. McCormick Med.

McCormick, Cyrus Hall.
Casson, H. N. Cyrus Hall McCormick, his life and work. $1.50. McClurg.
Thwaites, R. G. Cyrus Hall McCormick and the reaper. 50 c. State Hist., Wis.

McCormick, F:
Tragedy of Russia in Pacific Asia. '08(Ja4) 2 v., il. maps, O. *$6 net. Outing.

McCormick, J: N:, M.D.
Bible holiness. '10(S) c. 170 p. 8°, 50 c. Pub. Assoc. Friends.
Way of life. '10(D3) c. S. pap., 35 c. J: N: McCormick.

MacCoun, Townsend.
Early New York; [5 maps.] '10(Ap23) c. 4°, half moon ed., in portfolio, $5. T. MacCoun.

McCourt, Rob. Shepard.
Hist. of the old Sibley house; incl. brief hist. of the lives of Gen. Henry H. Sibley, his wife and mother, and some reminiscences by our old pioneers. Official D. A. R. souvenir, 1910. '10(Ag) c. 3-42 p. il. 8°, 25 c. R. S. McCourt.

McCourt, W. E.
Fire-resisting qualities of some New Jersey building stones. '08(Je13) il. O. (New Jersey, Geological survey.) pap. (Add. author for price.) W. E. McCourt.

McCoy, G: W.
Evidence of plague infection among ground squirrels. '10(Ag) 8 p. 8°. Gov. Pr. Off.
—, and Mitzmain, Maurice B.
Experimental investigation of biting of man by fleas from rats and squirrels '09(Je) 9 p. 8°. (Add. Superintendent for price.) U. S., Supt. of Docs.

McCoy, J. H.
South Dakota digest. '09(S) 236 p. 8°, flex. leath., $10. News Print.

McCrackan, W: Denison.
Christian science: eine religion des fortschritts; ein vortrag; aus dem englischen übertragen. '10(Je) c. 46 p. 16°, pap., 6 c. Chr. Sci. Pub.

MacCracken, H: Mitchell.
Tercentenary announcements, 1609-1909: "Three epochs in education in New York City." [1910.] (Jl) 40 p. 12°, (N. Y. Univ. bull.) gratis. N. Y. Univ.

MacCracken, H: Noble.
See Canby, H: Seidel.
—, Pierce, F: Erastus, and Durham, Willard Higley.
Introd. to Shakespeare. '10(O1) c. il. pors. D. 90 c. net. Macmillan.

McCrae, T:, ed.
See Osler, W:

McCrary and Johnson's general rules and instructions for grading cotton. '08(D) c. 11 p. 8°, pap. (Add. pubs. for price.) Standard Cotton.

McCrea, Roswell Cheney.
Humane movement. '10(Je4) 8°, $2 net. Lemcke.

McCrimmon, Abraham Lincoln.
Child in the normal home; pub. for the Social Service Commission of the Northern Baptist Convention. '10(Je4) c. 8°, (Social service ser.) 15 c. Am. Bapt.

McCrossan, G: E., comp.
See Canada Digest.

McCullough, Annie Willis, and Titus, Ida Maude.
Chimes of childhood; singable songs. '09 (Ja30) c. Q. pap., $1. Ditson.

McCullough, Ernest.
Engineering contractor's pocket book. '08 (D26) (Add. pubs. for price.) M. C. Clark.
Engineering work in towns and cities. 2d ed. '08(N21) c. il. tabs., 8°, *$3 net. M. C. Clark.
Reinforced concrete. '08(N21) c. il. tabs., 12°, *$1.50 net. M. C. Clark.

McCullough, Fs. Michael.
Tests on the permeability of concrete. '09. [1910.] (O) 36 p. il. tabs., 8°, (Univ. of Wis. bull., Engineering ser.) 25 c. Univ. of Wis.

McCullough, Mrs. Myrtle Reed.
See Reed, Myrtle.

McCune, Fk. H:
Spokane rate case: epitome of the case; sequel of the rate case, story of a great moral crime: [railroad rates.] '08(S) c. 37 p. O. pap., 25 c. F. H: McCune.

McCune, W: G:
Fire insurance agency for profit. '07, [1908.] (Ap.) c. 77 p. S. leath., $1. Northern Pub.

MacCunn, Florence A.
Sir Walter Scott's friends. '10(Ag27) il. pors. O. $3 net. Lane.

MacCunn, J:
Six radical thinkers: Bentham, J. S. Mill, Cobden, Carlyle, Mazzini, T. H. Green. '10(O1) D. $1 net. Longmans.

McCurdy, Stewart Le Roy.
Arthrosteopedic surgery (extremities and skeleton). '09(D) c. 210 p. 16°, $1. Medical Abstract.

McCurry, J: H:
Book of pract. points gathered from various sources, gleaned from many minds, with chapters on hook-worm and pellagra. '10(O) c. 199 p. 12°, $1. J: H: McCurry.

Careful study and presentation of malaria and its manifestations, with the most thorough and exhaustive methods of treatment of any work of its kind on the subject. '10(D) c. 8-170 p. 16°, $1.50. J: H: McCurry.

McCutcheon, G: Barr.
The alternative. '09(Ap17) c. il. D. †$1.25. Dodd.

Brood house; play in four acts. '10(D3) c. 8°, $5. (75 copies.) G: B. McCutcheon.

Butterfly man. '10(My7) c. il. D. $1.25. Dodd.

Husbands of Edith. '08(My2) il. D. †$1.25. Dodd.

Man from Brodney's. '08(S26) c. D. †$1.50. Dodd.

Purple parasol. '10(D) 75 c. Burt.

Rose in the ring. '10(S24) c. il. D. $1.50. Dodd.

Truxton King; a story of Graustark. '09 (S18) c. il. D. †$1.50. Dodd.

McCutcheon, J: Tinney.
In Africa; hunting adventures. '10(D31) c. il. map, O. $3. Bobbs-M.

T. R. in cartoons. '10(Jl2) c. il. Q. pap., 75 c. net. McClurg.

—, and Jones, Jenkin Lloyd.
What does Christmas really mean?: sermon. [New ed.] '09(O16) c. front. D. bds., 50 c. Forbes.

What does Christmas really mean?; a sermon published for Santa Claus. '08(N21) c. il. D. bds., *50 c. net. Unity.

McDaniel, C: Foster.
See La Tourette, Clara.

McDermott, C: Hubert.
Gospel of greed. '08(Je27) c. D. $1. Chapple Pub.

McDermott, Rev. D. I.
Preachers' protests. In 3 v. v. 1, Protests against President Roosevelt's denunciation of religious bigotry in politics: a lecture del. in St. Mary's Church, Philadelphia, Dec. 6, 1908. '08(D); v. 2, A reply to a criticism of lecture one, by Rev. S. M. Vernon, D.D.; del. in St. Mary's Church, Phil., Dec. 20, 1908; v. 3, Reply to last attack of Rev. S. M. Vernon, D.D., on the Catholic Church; del. in St. Mary's Church, Phil., Jan. 3, 1909. '09 (Je12) D. pap., ea., 10 c.; 3 v. in 1, 25 c. P: Reilly.

MacDermott, Rev. G. M.
Gospel according to St. Luke. '10(Ag13) S. (Plain commentaries.) 35 c. net. Young Churchman.

Gospel according to St. Mark. '10(F19) S. (Plain commentaries.) 35 c. Young Churchman.

Gospel according to St. Matthew. '10(F19) S. (Plain commentaries.) 35 c. Young Churchman.

McDermott, Laura Frances.
Illustrated key to the North American species of trifolium. '10(Jl2) il. 8°, $4. Cunninngham, C. & W.

MacDonald, Alex.
Invisible island; tale of the Gulf of Carpentaria. '10(D10) il. 12°, $1.25. Caldwell.

Island traders. '08(D26) c. il. D. $1.25. Caldwell.

Through the heart of Tibet. '09, [1910.] (D) 12°, $1.25. Caldwell.

White trail: story of the early days of Klondike. '08(O31) c. il. D. $1.25. Caldwell.

MacDonald, Arth., M.D.
Criminal statistics in Germany, France and England. [1910.] (S) 12 p. tabs., 4°, 25 c. A. MacDonald.

Juvenile crime and reformation, including stigmata of degeneration: hearing on the bill to establish a laboratory for the study of the criminal pauper, and defective classes. '08(Ag15) il. 8°, pap., 50 c. U. S., Supt. of Docs.

Reform of wayward youth. '08(Je) 24 p. 8°, pap. (Add. pubs. for price.) Univ. Press, (Sewanee.)

Studies of juvenile criminals. '07, [1908.] (Je.) 8 p. 12°. (Add. author for price.) A. MacDonald.

Study of the criminal, pauper, and defective classes; statement [Feb. 21, 1908,] before the Committee on Education and Labor, United States Senate. '08(Je6) 8°, pap., 25 c. U. S., Supt. of Docs.

McDonald, C: Middleton, comp.
Kentucky forms; cont. all legal forms under the Kentucky code of practice and Kentucky statutes. '08(Je) c. 11-591 p. 8°, $4.50. J. E. Hughes.

McDonald, Dan.
Twentieth century hist. of Marshall Co., Ind. 2 v. '08, [1909.] (Mr) il. pors. 4°, $18. Lewis Pub.

McDonald, D:
Treatise on the laws of Indiana pertaining to the powers and duties, [etc.,] of justices of the peace. [etc.;] rev. by B: F. Watson. 3d ed. '10(Mr) c. O. $7.50. W. H. Anderson.

Macdonald, Donald, M.D.
Oceanic languages: their grammatical structure, vocabulary and origin. '08(Ja18) maps, D. $4.20. Oxford Univ.

McDonald, Donald W:
What we are and what we will be; positive proof of identity; individuality and immortality of man; Biblictic, scientific, with witnesses; and we will know each other there—spirits made perfect; family circles eternal in the heavens. '09(N) 224 p. por. 12°, $1.50. D. W: McDonald.

Macdonald, Duncan Black.
Religious attitude and life in Islam: being the Haskell lectures on comparative religion del. before the University of Chicago in 1906. '09(Mr6) c. D. *$1.75 net. Univ. of Chic.

McDonald, E: R:
See McDonald, Raymond, *pseud.*

McDonald, Mrs. Etta Austin Blaisdell, and Dalrymple, Julia.
Betty in Canada. '10(S10) c. col. front. D. (Little people everywhere.) 60 c. Little, B. & Co.
Boris in Russia. '10(S10) c. col. front. il. D. (Little people everywhere.) 60 c. Little, B. & Co.
Fritz in Germany. '10(S10) c. col. front. il. D. (Little people everywhere.) 60 c. Little, B. & Co.
Gerda in Sweden. '10(S10) c. col. front. il. D. (Little people everywhere.) 60 c. Little, B. & Co.
Kathleen in Ireland. '09(S18) c. il. D. (Little people everywhere.) 60 c. Little, B. & Co.
Manuel in Mexico. '09(S18) c. il. D. (Little people everywhere.) 60 c. Little, B. & Co.
Rafael in Italy. '09(S18) c. il. (Little people everywhere.) 60 c. Little, B. & Co.
Umé San in Japan. '09(S18) c. il. D. (Little people everywhere.) 60 c. Little, B. & Co.

MACDONALD, *Mrs.* Flora.
MacLean, J: P. Flora Macdonald in America. $1. A. W. McLean.

Macdonald, Mrs. Frederika Richardson, comp.
Iliad of the East: selection of legends drawn from Valmiki's Sanscrit poem the Ramayana. '08(Je13) D. *$1.50 net. Lane.

MacDonald, G. W.
See MacDonald, H. L.

MacDonald, G:
At the back of the North Wind. '09(O9) c. il. in col. O. $1.50. Lippincott.
Light princess. '08(S19) c. front. D. (Bimbi ser.) bds., **40 c. net. Crowell.
Princess and Curdie. '08(N7) c. il. O. †$1.50. Lippincott.

MacDonald, G: A.
Light side of the law. '10(D10) $1.75 net. Cassell.

MacDonald, H. L. and G. W.
New Testament alphabet in rhyme for little people. '10(D24) obl. 12°, $1 net. Pott.

McDonald, Ja. J.
Life in old Virginia; ed. by J. A. C. Chandler. '08(F1) c. il. por. O. $1.50. Old Virginia.

McDonald, Jasper Newton, comp.
Chicago as a medical center. '09, [1910.] (Mr) c. 17+186 p. il. 12°, $2. Stromberg, A. & Co.

MacDonald, Katharine Isabel.
Magazines for the small library. [New ed.] '08, [1909.] (My) 29 p. 12°. (Add. pubs. for price.) League Lib. Com.

Macdonald, Lucretia S.
Checkerberry. '08(N21) il. 12°, $1.50. Cochrane.

MacDonald, Mary E.
See Sisk, B: F.

McDonald, Raymond, [pseud. for E: R: McDonald and Raymond Alfr. Leger.]
Mad scientist: a tale of the future; with which is incorporated a secret cipher for the best solution of which the publishers offer $1000. '08(Jl4) c. D. $1.60. Cochrane.

MacDonald, Rob.
Mind, religion and health; with an appreciation of the Emmanuel movement. '08 (O24) c. D. **$1.30 net. Funk.

Macdonald, Rob. Maclauchlan.
Chillacoe Charlie: book for boys. '09(Jl31) il. 12°, $1.50. Brentano's.
Secret of the Saragasso: book for boys. '09(Jl31) il. 12°, $1.50. Brentano's.

Macdonald, W:
Dry-farming: its principles and practice. '09(O9) c. il. D. **$1.20 net. Century Co.

MacDonald, W:, ed., 1863-.
Documentary source book of American history, 1606-1898; ed., with notes. '08(S19) *$1.75 net. Macmillan.

McDONALD, William Jesse.
Paine, A. B. Captain Bill McDonald, Texas ranger. $2; $2.50; $3. W: J. McDonald.

McDonald, W: Naylor.
Hist. of the Laurel brigade, orig. the Ashby cavalry of the Army of No. Va. and Chew's battery; ed. by Bushrod C. Washington. '08(Ja11) il. pors. 8°, $3. K. S. McDonald.

Macdonell, Anne.
In the Abruzzi. '09(O2) il. maps, O. *$2 net. Stokes.

Macdonough, Michael.
Irish life and character. '09(D) 12°, *$1.50 net. Whittaker.

McDonough, Michael Vincent.
Chief sources of sin; seven discourses on pride, covetousness, lust, anger, gluttony, envy, sloth. '10(Ap23) c. 12°, 75 c. Murphy.

Macdonough, Rodney.
Life of Commodore Thomas Macdonough, U. S. Navy. '09(Ap17) c. il. facsim., pors. maps, O. $2. R. Macdonough.
See also Pennewill, Ja.

MACDONOUGH, *Commodore* Thomas.
Macdonough, R. Life of Commodore Thomas Macdonough, U. S. Navy. $2. R. Macdonough.
Pennewill, J., *and* Macdonough, R. Addresses del. at the unveiling of a memorial tablet to Commodore Thomas Macdonough. 50 c. Delaware Hist. Soc.

Macdougal, Dan. Trembly.
Across Papagueria. '09(S) 21 p. il. maps, 8°, pap., 50 c. Am. Geog. Soc.
Botanical features of North American deserts. '08(O10) il. maps, Q. pap., $1.75. Carnegie.

MacDougall, August, ed.
See MacDougall, Duncan.

MacDougall, Duncan and August, eds.
Bond of music: an anthology. '08(O3) front. D. $1.25; lambskin, $2. Stokes.

McDougall, W:
Introduction to social psychology. '09 (Mr20) D. *$1.50 net. J: W. Luce.

McDowell, E: Alex.
Verses. '08(N21) c. por. D. 75 c. A. P: Schmidt.

MacDowell, Edward Alexander.
Gilman, L. Edward MacDowell: a study. **$1.50 net. Lane.
Page, *Mrs.* E. F. P. Edward MacDowell. $1 net; $1.50 net. Dodge.

MacDowell, Thdr. L.
Outline of a plan for utilizing the salary schedule as a means for improving the efficiency of teachers in the public elementary schools. '09(O9) 8°. pap., 10 c. T. L. MacDowell.

McDowell, Bp. W: Fraser.
In the school of Christ; Cole Lecture for 1910. '10(S17) c. 12°, $1.25 net. Revell.
Right sort of men for the ministry. '09 (Mr) c. 19 p. 12°, (Claims and opportunities of the Christian ministry.) 10 c.; per 100, $8. Y. M. C. A.

McDowell family.
See Genealogies: Boyd, L., *comp.*

McDuffie, David Gee.
Guthrie, W: A. McDuffie's discovery of the natural causes for the variations of the magnetic needle of the compass. 50 c. W: A. Guthrie.

Macé, Jean.
Contes du petit château; le petit ravageot et Mademoiselle Sans-Soin; ed. by J. E. Mansion. '10(Ja29) (Crowell's shorter French texts.) *25 c. net. Crowell

Mace, W: Harrison.
Primary history; stories of heroism. '09 (Mr27) c. il. maps, 12°, *65 c. net. Rand, McN. & Co.

McElfresh, Rev. Franklin.
Teacher-training class; the plan, the organization, the results. '09(My) c. 48 p. 16°, pap., 10 c. Presb. Bd.

McElrath, Frances.
See Adventures with Indians.

MacElree, Wilmer W.
Along the western Brandywine. '10(F5) c. il. pors. maps, facsims., 4°, $5. F. S. Hickman.

McElroy, G: W., ed.
See New York [State.] Transfer tax.

McElroy, J:
Economic functions of vice. '08(My23) c. D. bds., 50 c. Nat. Tribune.
Si Klegg, his transformation from a raw recruit to a veteran. [2d ed., rev. and enl.] '10(Mr) c. 13-15-268 p. il. 8°, $1. pap., 50 c. Nat. Tribune.

McElroy, J:—*Continued.*
Si Klegg thru the Stone River campaign and in winter quarters at Murfreesboro. 2d ed., enl. and rev. '10(Je) c. 16+271 p. il. 12°, $1. Nat. Tribune.
Soul growth of Abraham Lincoln. '10 (N19) c. pors. 8°, 10 c. J: McElroy.
Struggle for Missouri. '09(O16) c. O. $2. Nat. Tribune.

McElroy, Rob. McNutt.
Kentucky in the nation's hist. '09(D11) c. il. pors. map, O. **$5 net. Moffat.

MacElroy family.
See Genealogies: Boyd, L., *comp.*

McEvoy, T: Jefferson.
Methods in education. '08(N) 13+446 p. 12°, $1.50. T: J. McEvoy.

Macewen, Rev. Alex. Robertson.
Antoinette Bourignon, quietist; her life and doctrines. '10(D10) 12°, $1.25 net. Doran.

McEwen, G: Fs.
Preliminary rept. on the hydrographic work carried on by the Marine Biological Station of San Diego. '10(Je) 189-204 p. map, Q. (Univ. of Cal. pubs.; Geology; contribs. from the Lab'y of the Marine Biological Soc. of San Diego.) pap., 15 c. Univ. of Cal.

Macewen, Hugh A.
Food inspection. '10(Jl9) 12°, $2.50 net. Van Nostrand.

Macewen, J: A.
Surgical anatomy. '09(D) 492 p. il. 8°, *$3 net. Wood.

McFadden, Effie Belle.
Course of study in language for elem. schools and hdbk. to accompany the California State Series text. '10(Ap16) 8°, (San Francisco, State Normal School bull.) 55 c.; pap., 30 c. San F. St. Normal.
Course of study in primary language and hdbk. to the state ser. text. '09(Mr) 4°, (San Francisco State Normal School bulls.; new ser.) pap., 30 c. San F. St. Normal.
Course of study in language for grammar grades. '09(O) 4°, (San Francisco State Normal School bulls.; new ser.) pap., 30 c. San F. St. Normal.
See also Burk, Frederic.

McFadden, Eliz. Apthorp, and Davis, Lilian E., comps.
Sel. list of plays for amateurs and students of dramatic expression; with an introd. by Ludella L. Peck. '08(F1) c. O. $2. McFadden.

McFadden, G:
Blocking and hitting. '10(Ja8) c. il. 12°, (Fox's athletic lib.) pap., 10 c. R: K. Fox.

McFadyen, Allan.
Cell as the unit of life, and other lectures; ed. by R. Tanner Hewlett. '09(Ja16) *$3 net. Blakiston.

McFadyen, J: Edg., D.D.
City with foundations. '09(D11) D. *$1.25 net. Armstrong.
Way of prayer. '10(O1) c. D. bds., 50 c. net. Pilgrim Press.
See also Abbott, Lyman.

McFadyen, J: Edg., D.D., and Votaw, Clyde Webster, comps.
Best books for Old and New Testament study; reprinted from *The Methodist Review,* Oct., 1908, Jan., 1909; with an introd. by Gross Alexander, ed. '09 (Ap3) c. D. pap., 20 c. Pub. Ho. of M. E. Ch., So.

McFall, C. Haldane.
Beautiful children immortalized by the masters; ed. by T: Leman Hare. '09 (D4) c. col. il. Q. **$5 net, boxed. Dodd.
Fragonard. '09(O9) il. O. (Masterpieces in colour.) bds., *65 c. net; limp leath., *$1.50 net. Stokes.
French pastellists of the eighteenth century; ed. by T. Leman Hare. '09(D11) il. Q. *$10.50 net. Macmillan.
Vigée Le Brun. '09(Je26) il. O. (Masterpieces in colour.) bds., *65 c. net. Stokes.

McFalls, Mrs. Cornelia A. Pierce.
Forget-me-nots, and other poems. '10 (Jl9) c. por. 12°, $1.50. Badger.

Macfarland, Rev. C: Stedman, ed.
Christian ministry and the social order: lectures del. at Yale Divinity School, 1908-1909. '09(Je12) c. O. *$1.25 uet. Yale Univ.

MacFarland, Fk. Mace.
Opisthobranchiate mollusca of the Branner-Agassiz expedition to Brazil. '09 (Ag7) il. (Leland Stanford Junior University pubs., University ser., no. 2.) pap., $1. Stanford Univ.
Bibliography (5 p.).

McFarland, J: T., D.D.
Book and the child: some vital principles for a Sunday school platform. '08(Ja4) D. pap., *5 c. net. Eaton & M.
Etchings of the Master. '10(Ja1) c. O. *$1.25 net. Eaton & M.
Golden Text book, 1909: book of ready reference rel. to the International Sunday School lessons. '08(N7); 1910. '09 (N13) c. Tt. pap., ea., *30 c. net, per doz; *$2 net, per 100. Eaton & M.

McFarland, Jos., M.D.
Biology, general and medical. '10(N) 13-440 p. il. 8°, $1.75. Saunders.
References at end of most of the chapters.
Text-book of pathology, for practitioners and students. 2d ed., thoroughly rev. '10(Ap) c. 9-856 p. il. 8°, $5 net. Saunders.
Text-book upon the pathogenic bacteria. 6th ed., thoroughly rev. '09(N) c. 709 p. il. fold. tab., 8°, $3.50. Saunders.

McFarlane, Arth. Emerson.
Redney McGaw. '09(O23) c. il. D. †$1.50. Little, B. & Co.

Macfarlane, Catharine, M.D.
Reference hdbk. of gynecology for nurses. '08(D) c. 150 p. il. 32°, flex. leath., *$1.25 net. Saunders.

Macfarlane, C: Albert.
Letitia; thrilling novel of western life. '09(Mr) c. '08. 287 p. il. 12°, $1.50. C. M. Clark.

Macfarlane, P: Clark.
Centurion's story. '10(Mr19) c. D. (Idyll envelope ser.) pap., *25 c. net. Revell.
Quest of the yellow pearl. '09(Ag7) c. il. D. (Idyll envelope ser.) pap., *25 c. net. Revell.

Macfarlane, Wa.
Laboratory notes on iron and steel analyses. '09(O23) D. *$2.50 net. Longmans.

McFee, W:
Letters from an ocean tramp. '08(D12) front. D. *$1.50 net. Cassell.

McFerrin, C: Betteys.
Mother's part in her child's musical education. '10(Ag13) c. il. pors. 12°, $2. Alert Pub.

MacFie, Ronald.
Air and health. '09(N) 8+346 p. 8°, (Hygiene lib.) *$2.50 net. Dutton.

McGaffey, Kenneth.
Sorrows of a show girl; a story of the great "white way." '08(N) c. 243 p. 12°, $1.50. J. I. Austen.

McGarvey, J: W:
Short essay in Biblical criticism; repr. from the *Christian Standard.* '10(Ap9) c. 12°, $1.50. Standard Pub.

McGavick, Bp. Alex. Jos.
Some incentives to right living. '09(Je12) 12°, *$1 net. Wiltzius.

McGavick, Rev. Ja. E:
Catholic belief and practice. 4th ed., rev. and enl. '10(Je18) c. 16°, 25 c. Wiltzius.

McGaw, Virginia.
Construction work for rural and elementary schools. '09(Ag14) c. il. figs. D. 60 c. Flanagan.

MacGeary, J: S:
Free Methodist church; brief outline history of its origin and development. '08, [1909.] (F) c. 224 p. 12°, 50 c. W: B. Rose.

McGee, Guy C.
McGee's tables; hdbk. of excavation and embankment tables, a simple, rapid and accurate method for obtaining quantities, in cubic yards, for 100 foot sections, and containing descriptive data for their use. 1st ed. '10(My) c. 48 p. 8°, $2.50. G. C. McGee.

McGeeney, Patrick Sylvester.
Down at Cross Timbers. '09, [1910.] (F) c. 66 p. por. 12°, $1. Angel Press.
Down at Stein's Pass; romance of New Mexico. '09, [1910.] (F) 114 p. c. por. 12°, $1. Angel Press.

McGhee, Zach.
Dark corner. '08, [1909.] (Ja) c. 212 p. 16°, $1. Grafton Press.

McGiffert, Ja.
Mathematical short cuts. '10(S) 31 p. S. pap., 25 c. A. M. Allen.

McGill, Mary Robson.
You and your friends. '06, [1908.] (D) c. 12+380 p. il. pors. 4°, $3. M. R. McGill.

McGillicuddy, Cornelius, ["Connie Mack."]
How to play base-ball. '08, [1909.] (F) c. various paging, il. pors. 12°, pap., 25 c. Barse & H.

McGinnis, Herbert P., and Maddox, Hoadly Foster.
Lyrics from the hills; little book of West Virginia verse; designed by Oloe-Marie Myers. '09, [1910.] (Ja) c. 107 p. pors. 12°, $1. Marshall Print.

McGlauflin, Idabelle.
Handicraft for girls; tentative course in needlework, basketry, designing, paper and cardboard construction, textile fibers and fabrics; and home decoration and care. '10(N5) c. il. O. $1. Manual Arts.

McGlothlin, W: J., D.D.
Guide to the study of church history. '08 (D5) c. O. *$1.50 net. Bapt. World.

McGLYNN, *Father* Edward.
Preuss, A. Fundamental fallacies of socialism: exposition of the question of landownership; authentic account of the famous McGlynn case. *$1 net. Herder.

McGovern, J:
Hospitality; mine host, from the time of Babylon to the age of the aeroplane. '10 (D3) c. 12°, $1. Hotel Monthly.

MacGowan, Alice.
Judith of the Cumberlands. '08(O10) c. il. D. †$1.50. Putnam.
Sword in the mountains. '10(O29) c. il. map, D. $1.35 net. Putnam.
Wiving of Lance Cleaverage. '09(O9) c. il. in col. D. **$1.35 net. Putnam.

McGowan, Fs. Xavier.
Two series of lenten sermons on, I, Sin and its remedies; II, The seven deadly sins. 2d ed. '10(Mr5) c. 12°, 75 c. Pustet.

Macgowan, Rev. J.
Sidelights on Chinese life. '08(O17) il. Q. *$3.75 net. Lippincott.

MacGrath, Harold.
Enchanted hat. '08(D5) c. il. O. †$1.50. Bobbs-M.
Goose girl. '09(Ag21) c. D. †$1.50. Bobbs-M.
Lure of the mask. '08(Je13) c. D. †$1.50. Bobbs-M.
Splendid hazard. '10(Je4) c. il. D. $1.50. Bobbs-M.

McGrath, J: Jos.
Operative surgery, for students and practitioners. 3d rev. ed. '09(N) c. il. 16+653 p. il. 8°. $5. Davis.

McGraw, Donald, comp.
See Jenkins, Floyd, *comp.*

McGraw, J: J.
Scientific baseball; also the official rules for 1908 and schedule of games to be played. '08(My16); 1909. '09(Jl31); 1910. '10 (Ap) c. il. pors. 16°, (Fox's athletic library.) pap., ea., 10 c. R: K. Fox.

MacGregor, Ford H.
City government by commission; address del. before the League of Wisconsin Municipalities at Marinette, Wis., July 23, 1909. [1910.] (Ja) 12 p. 4°, pap., 10 c. Univ. of Wis.
Tenement house legislation, state and local. '09(Mr6) D. (Comparative legislation bull.) pap., 25 c. Wisconsin Free Lib.

McGregor, Malcolm.
See Michigan corporation law.

MacGregor, Mary.
The Netherlands. '08(S5) O. (Romance of history ser.) *$2 net. Stokes.
Stories from Dante. '09(N) 12+160 p. 24°, (Told to the children ser.) 50 c. Dutton.
Stories from the ballads; told to the children. '10(Ja22) il. 24°, (Told to the children ser.; ed. by Louey Chisholm.) 50 c. Dutton.
Stories of Siegfried. '09(F13) 24°, (Told to the children ser.) 50 c. Dutton.
Stories of the Vikings. '08(N21) il. T. (Stories from history.) 50 c. Dutton.
Stories of three saints: [St. Francis, St. Columba, St. Cuthbert.] '08(D12) il. 16°, (Told to the children ser.) 50 c. Dutton.
See also Dante Alighieri. Stories from Dante.
—, ed. Undine. '08(Ag15) 24°, (Told to the children ser.) 50 c. Dutton.

McGregor, R: C.
Manual of Philippine birds; published by the Bureau of Science, Government of the Philippine Islands. In 2 pts. '09(D) $4. Macmillan.

MacGregor, Thdr. Douglas.
Pushing your business: a book of pract. advice on advertising for banks, trust companies, investment brokers, real estate dealers. '08(My23); 3d ed., rev. and enl. '09(D18) c. il. facsims., 12°, ea., *$1 net. Bankers Pub.

McGregory, Jos. Fk.
Manual of qualitative chemical analysis. Rev. ed. '09(N6) c. O. $1. Ginn.

McGrew, T: Fletcher, and Howard, G: Ellsworth.
Perfected poultry of America. '08(F1) c. O. $2.50. Howard Pub. Co.

McGroarty, J: S.
Wander songs '08, [1909.] (Je) c. 197 p. por. $2. Grafton Press.

McGuire, Hunter Holmes, and Christian, G: L.
Confederate cause and conduct in the war between the states, as set forth in the reports of the History Committee of the Grand Camp, C. V. of Virginia. '07, [1908.] (Mr.) c. 11+229 p. pors., 12°, (Add. pub. for price.) L. H. Jenkins.

McGuire, Stuart.
Lectures on principles of surgery. '08(D) c. 480 p. 8°, $4; mor., $5.25. Southern Med.

Mach, Edm. Rob. Otto v.
Art of painting in the nineteenth century. '09(Ja9) c. il. O. *$1.25 net. Ginn.

MacHarg, W:
See Balmer, Edn.

Machen, Arth. Webster, jr.
Treatise on the federal corporation tax law of 1909. '10(F) c. D. $1.50. Little, B. & Co.
Treatise on the modern law of corporations. '08(N21) c. 2 v., 8°, **$12 net. Little, B. & Co.

Machiavelli, Niccolo.
History of Florence; tr., with an introd., by Marriott. '09(Ap3) 16°, (Everyman's lib.) *35 c. net; leath., *70 c. net. Dutton.
History of Florence; with introd. by C: W. Colby. '08(Je27) c. il. 8°, $1.75; hf. mor., $3.50. Lamb Pub.
The prince; special tr. and introd. by W. K. Marriott. '08(F22) 16°, (Everyman's lib.) *35 c. net; leath., *70 c. net. Dutton.

MACHIGANGA INDIANS.
See Indians.

Machinations of the American Medical Association. Strong, H: R. pap., 25 c. Nat. Druggist.
Machine (The). Lucier, A. J. $1. Mahew.
Machine blacksmithing. Cran, J. 25 c. Indust. Press.

MACHINE DESIGN.
See Machinery.

Machine shop arithmetic. Colvin, F. H. 50 c. Henley.
Machine shop calculations. Colvin, F. H. $1. Hill Pub.

MACHINE-SHOP PRACTICE
See Machinery.

Machine tool drives. '08(N21) c. diagrs., 8°, (Machinery's reference ser.) pap., 25 c. Indust. Press.

MACHINE TOOLS.
See Machinery.

MACHINERY.
Adams, J. H: Harper's machinery book for boys. $1.75. Harper.
Anthony, G. C. Machine drawing. $1.50. Heath.
Bearings. 25 c. Indust. Press.
Blake, C. F. Mathematics of machine design. 25 c. Indust. Press.
Blanking dies. 25 c. Indust. Press.
Calculations of elements of machine design. 25 c. Indust. Press.
Carden, G. L. Machine-tool trade in Belgium. (Add. Superintendent for price.) U. S., Supt. of Docs.
Collins, H. E. Erecting work.—Knocks and kinks. ea., $1. Hill Pub.
Colvin, F. H. Machine shop calculations. $1. Hill Pub.
Colvin, F. H., *and* Stanley, F. A., *comps.* American machinists' hdbk. and dictionary of shop terms. $3.—Hill kink books. 10 v. ea., 50 c. Hill Pub.
Cramp, W: Continuous current machine design. $2.50. Van Nostrand.
Cyclopedia of modern shop practice. Raymond, H. M., *ed.* 4 v. $12.80. Am. Sch. Corr.
Deep hole drilling. 25 c. Indust. Press.
Details of machine tool design. 25 c. Indust. Press.
Dictionary of chemical and metallurgical machinery, appliances and material manufactured or sold by advertisers in *Electrical and Metallurgical Industry.* 50 c. Electrochemical Pub.
Directory of manufacturers of and dealers in engineers' and contractors' machinery and supplies. gratis. McGraw.
Drill jigs. 25 c. Indust. Press.
Examples of calculating designs. 25 c. Indust. Press.

MACHINERY.—*Continued.*
Fairchild. H. P. Examples of machine shop practice. 25 c. Indust. Press.
Files and filing. 25 c. Indust Press.
Flather, J: J. Transmission of power by leather belting, fibrous ropes and toothed gearing. *$1.35 net. H. W. Wilson.
Fly-wheels. 25 c. Indust. Press.
Golding, H: A. Engineers' and machinists' hdbk. $1.50 net. Fenno.
Goodrich, C. L., *and* Stanley, F. A. Automatic screw machines and their tools. *$2 net. Hill Pub.
Griffin, C: L. Machine design. $1.50. Am. Sch. Corr.
Grimshaw, R. Modern workshop hints; machine shop practice. $2. McKay.
Hartness, J. Machine building for profit and the Hartness flat turret lathe. gratis. Jones & Lamson.
Heck, R. C. H. Notes on the graphics of machine forces. $1. Van Nostrand.
Hecox, C. W. Students' manual for machine shop practice. $2. C. W. Hecox.
Hiscox, G. D. Mechanical appliances, mechanical movements and novelties of construction. In 2 v. v. 2.—Mechanical movements, powers and devices. ea., $2.50. Henley.
Hoffman, J. D: Course of instruction in elementary machine design. *$2.50 net. J. D: Hoffman.
Horner, J. G. Principles of fitting. *$1.75 net. Macmillan.
"Hunt" coal and ore handling machinery. gratis. C. W. Hunt.
Jones, F. R. Machine design. pt. 1, Kinematics of machinery. $1.50. Wiley.
Kimball, D. S., *and* Barr, J: H: Elements of machine design. *$3 net. Wiley.
Leonard, W: S: Machine shop tools and methods. $4. Wiley.
Machine tool drives. 25 c. Indust. Press.
Machinery's shop receipts and formulas. $1. Indust. Press.
Marshall, A. W. Winshurst machine: how to make and use it. 25 c. Spon.
Milling fixtures. 25 c. Indust. Press.
Modern punch and die construction. 25 c. Indust. Press.
Morin, E. Jigs and fixtures. pts. 2-3. ea., 25 c. Indust. Press.
Nagel, O. Mechanical appliances of the chemical and metallurgical industries. $2 net. O. Nagel.
Oberg, E. V. Shop arithmetic for the machinist.—Tables and formulas for shop and drafting-room. ea., 25 c. Indust. Press.
Portland (Ore.) Library Association. List of practical books on machine shop practice, foundry work and electricity. gratis. Portland (Ore.) L. A.
Principles and practice of assembling machine tools. pt. 1. 25 c. Indust. Press.
Punch and die work. 25 c. Indust. Press.
Reid, J: Text book of mechanical drawing and machine design. $3. Wiley.
Sheldon, S:, *and* Hausmann, E. Dynamo electric machinery. $2.50. Van Nostrand.

MACHINERY.—*Continued.*
Smith, A. W:, *and* Marx, G. H. Machine design. $3. Wiley.
Smith, R. H: Text-book of the principles of machine work. $3.—Text-book of the elements of machine work. $2. Indust. Educ. Co.
Spooner, H: J: Machine design, construction and drawing. $3.50.—Machine drawing and design for beginners. $1.25. Longmans.
Sylvester, F. L., *and* Oberg, E. Self-taught mechanical drawing and elem. machine design. $2. Henley.
United States. *Dept. of Commerce and Labor. Bureau of Manufactures.* Machine tool trade in Germany, France, Switzerland, Italy and United Kingdom by Capt. Godfrey L. Carden. '09(My) 246 p. il. 8°, pap. (Add. Superintendent for price.) U. S., Supt. of Docs.
United States. *Naval Academy.* Notes on machine design. $2.50. U. S. Naval Inst.
Unwin, W: C. Elements of machine design. $2.50. Longmans.
Weston, E. M. Rock drills. $4. McGraw-H.
Williams, A. Wonders of mechanical ingenuity. 75 c. Lippincott.
Working drawings and drafting-room kinks. 25 c. Indust. Press.
Worm gearing. 25 c. Indust. Press.
See also Agricultural machinery; — Air-brake; — Alternating currents; — Arithmetic; — Automobiles; — Chains; — Compressed air; — Dynamos and motors;—Electrical engineering;—Electricity; — Elevators; — Engineering;—Engines; — Gages;—Gears and gearing;—Grinding;—Hoisting machinery;—Hydraulic engineering;—Inventions; — Knitting;—Locomotives;—Lumber; — Manufactures; — Marine engineering; — Mathematics; — Mechanical drawing; — Mechanics;— Mines and mining;—Patents;—Pattern-making; —Pumps;—Railroads;—Refrigeration;—Screws; — Sewing machines; — Shaft governors; — Springs; — Steam engine; — Steel; — Sugar; — Technical education; — Tools; — Turbines; — Turning;—Valves;—Ventilation;—Windmills.

Machinery's reference ser. il. 8°, pap., 25 c. Indust. Press.

—Bearings.
—Blake. Mathematics of machine design.
—Blanking dies.
—Branston. Girders for electric overhead cranes.
—Calculations of Elements of machine design.
—Care and repair of dynamos and motors.
—Cran. Machine blacksmithing.
—Deep hole drilling.
—Design of electric overhead cranes.—Files and filing.
—Designing and cutting cams.
—Details of machine tool design.
—Drafting-room practice.
—Drill jigs.
—Drop forging.
—Examples of calculating designs.
—Fairchild. Examples of machine shop practice.
—Flanders. Bevel gearing.
—Fly wheels.
—Fowler *and* Mellin. Locomotive design.
—French. First principles of theoretical mechanics.—Milling fixtures.
—Grinding and lapping.
—Hardening and tempering.

Machinery's reference ser.—Continued.
—Hubbard. Fans, ventilation and heating.
—Lathe and planer tools.
—Machine tool drives.
—Machines, tools and methods of automobile manufacture.
—Measuring tools.
—Modern punch and die construction.
—Morin. Jigs and fixtures. pts. 2, 3.
—Oberg. Shop arithmetic for the machinist. —Tables and formulas for shop and drafting-room.
—Principles and practice of assembling machine tools.
—Punch and die work.
—Screw thread cutting.
—Screw thread tools and gages.
—Solution of triangles. 2 v.
—Spiral gearing.
—Spur gearing.
—Strength of cylinders.
—Systems and practice of the drafting-room.
—Theory of crane design.
—Use of logarithms and logarithmic tables.
—Working drawings and drafting-room kinks.
—Worm gearing.

Machinery's shop receipts and formulas; 412 shop receipts and formulas sel. from *Machinery;* classified and rev. '10(Je4) c. 8°, $1. Indust. Press.

Machines, tools and methods of automobile manufacture. '10(My21) c. il. 8°, (Machinery's reference ser.) pap., 25 c. Indust. Press.

Machray, Rev. Rob.
Life of Robert Machray, D.D., LL.D., D.C.L., archbishop of Rupert's Land, primate of all Canada, prelate of the Order of St. Michael and St. George. '10(Ja8) il. 8°. *$6.50 net. Macmillan.

MACHRAY, *Archbp.* Robert.
Machray, R. Life of Robert Machray. *$6.50 net. Macmillan.

McHugh, Hugh, pseud.
See Hobart, G: Vere.

McIlhany, E: Washington.
Recollections of a 49er. '08(N) c. 212 p. il. pors. 8°, $1. Hailman.

McIlwain, C: Howard.
High Court of Parliament and its supremacy; historical essay on the boundaries between legislation and adjudication in England. '10(N12) c. O. $2.50 net. Yale Univ.

McIlwaine, R:, D.D.
Addresses and papers bearing chiefly on education. '08(N) c. 184 p. 8°, $1. R: McIlwaine.
Memoirs of three score years and ten. '08(Jl4) c. pors. O. *$3 net. Neale.

McInnes, Tom.
In amber lands; poems. '10(My21) c. por. 12°, $1. B'way Pub.

McIntosh, Atwell Campbell.
Selected cases on the law of contracts; with annots. '08(N) c. 29+615 p. O. shp. (Add. pubs. for price.) Edwards.
See also Mordecai, S: F.

McIntosh, Herbert.
Pract. hdbk. of medical electricity for students and practitioners. '09, [1910.] (F) c. 510 p. il. 8°, $3. Therapeutic.

M'Intyre, Rev. D: M.
Life in His name. '10(Ja22) D. $1.25. Armstrong.

McIntyre, Canon J:
See Rickaby, Jos.

McIntyre, J: T:
Ashton-Kirk, investigator. '10(D3) c. D. $1.20 net. Penn Pub. Co.
In the dead of night. '08(My9) c. D. †$1.50. Lippincott.
Street singer. '08(O3) c. il. D. †$1.25. Penn Pub. Co.
Young Continentals at Bunker Hill. '10 (D3) c. il. map, D. $1.25. Penn Pub. Co.
Young Continentals at Lexington. '09 (N13) c. il. D. †$1.25. Penn Pub. Co.

McIntyre, Mrs. Louise Leverenz.
How's your health?: series of scientific lectures and exercises for the proper care of the body. '09(My1) c. il. por. O. $1.25. L. L. McIntyre.

MacIntyre, W: Irwin.
Legislative reminiscences. '09(N) c. 22 p. 8°, pap., 25 c. W: I. MacIntyre.

McIsaac, Isabel.
Bacteriology for nurses. '09(D) c. 12+179 p. il. 12°, *$1.25 net. Macmillan.
Hygiene for nurses. '08(S26) il. 12°, *$1.25 net. Macmillan.
—, **comp.** Elements of hygiene for schools. '09(Je5) c. figs. D. **60 c. net. Macmillan.

McIver, C: Duncan.
Charles Duncan McIver, 1860-1906: memorial volume prepared under direction of William C. Smith, Viola Boddie, Mary S. Sharpe, of the Faculty of No. Carolina State Normal and Industrial College. '07. [1908.] (Mr.) 12+286 p. por. 8°, (Add. pubs. for price.) J. J. Stone.

McIvor, Ivor Ben, pseud.
See Welsh, C:

Mack, Arth. Carlyle.
Palisades of the Hudson; their formation, tradition, romance, historical associations, natural wonders and preservation. '09 (S18) c. il. maps, O. *75 c. net. Palisades Press.

Mack, Connie, pseud.
See McGillicuddy, Cornelius.

Mack, Louise.
Theodora's husband. '10(Mr12) D. $1.50. Lane.

Mack, Newton H.
See Kiefer, W: R.

Mack, W:, ed.
Cyclopedia of law and procedure. Popular ed. Bks. 1-5. '09(Je); bk. 6 (Jl); bk. 7 (Ag); bks. 8, 9 (N); bk. 10 (D) c. O. ea., $7.50. (Sold in sets of 12 v.) Am. Law Bk.
—, **and Blashfield, De Witt C., eds.**
Cyclop. of law and procedure; cyc.. annots., 1-34 cyc. Canadian cases; ed. by J: King. '10(Mr) c. O. $6.60. Am. Law Bk.
Cyc. annots. to Cyclopedia of law and procedure, 1-27 cyc.; annot. with all cases decided since the original articles were written and with omitted cases; errata corrected; new principles announced, etc. '08(F) c. O. subs., $4.60. Am. Law Bk.
Cyc. annots. to Cyclopedia of law and procedure, 1-30 cyc.; annot. with all cases decided since the original articles were written and with omitted cases; errata corrected; new principles announced, etc. Canadian cases ed. by J: King. '09(Mr) c. O. subs., $6. Am. Law Bk.
—, **[and others,] eds.**
Cyclopedia of law and procedure. v. 28. '08(Je); v. 29 (Ag8); v. 30 (D); v. 31. '09(Je); v. 32 (Jl); v. 33 (N); v. 34. '10(F); v. 35 (Jl); v. 36 (N) c. O. shp., subs., ea., $7.50. (Sold only in sets of 40 v.) Am. Law Bk.

MACK, W:
Grattan, R. Glossary of technical words, phrases, maxims and abbreviations found in the text of the popular or students' ed. of the Cyclopedia of law and procedure [by W: Mack and others.] $1.50. Am. Law Bk.

McKaig, Rob. Newton, D.D.
Life and times of the Holy Spirit. v. 1. '08(Ap.) c. por. 12°, 50 c. Chr. Witness.

Mackail, J: W:
Henry Birkhead and the foundation of the Oxford chair of poetry: lecture. '08 (D19) O. pap., 35 c. Oxford Univ.
Lectures on Greek poetry. '10(N12) O. $3 net. Longmans.
Springs of Helicon: study in the progress of English poetry from Chaucer to Milton. '09(Ap3) c. O. **$1.25 net. Longmans.
Swinburne: a lecture delivered before the University on April 30, 1909. '09(Ag14) pap., *35 c. net. Oxford Univ.
William Morris; address del. in the town hall, Birmingham, at the annual meeting of the National Home Reading Union, 28th October, 1910. '10(D24) O. pap., 30 c. net. Longmans.
—, **ed.** Select epigrams from the Greek anthology. '08(N7) S. *75 c. net; leath., *$1 net. Longmans.

Mackay, Constance D'Arcy.
The house of the heart, and other plays for children; designed for use in the schools. '09(D11) c. S. **$1.10 net. Holt.
Silver thread, and other folk plays for young people. '10(D31) c. S. $1.10 net. Holt.

Mackay, Donald Sage.
Religion of the threshold, and other sermons; introd. by Hugh Black. '08(D26) c. por. *$1.50 net. Armstrong.

MacKay, Elsie M.
Loveland stories in verse. '07, [1908.] (Ap) c. 39 p. il. 8°, $1.25. L. Washington.

McKay, G:
Commentary on the law of community; property for Arizona, California, Idaho, Louisiana, Nevada, New Mexico, Texas and Washington. '10(O) c. 748 p. O. $7.50. Courtright.

McKay, G: Lewis, and Larsen, Christian.
Principles and practice of butter-making. 2d ed., rev. and enl. '08(Ag29) c. il. 8°, **$1.50 net. Wiley.

Mackay, Mrs. Helen Gansevoort Edward.
Houses of glass: stories of Paris. '09 (Mr20) c. il. D. pap., **$1 net. Duffield.

Mackay, Ja. Alex. Kenneth.
Across Papua; being an account of a voyage round and a march across, the territory of Papua, with the Royal Commission. '09(D11) il. fold. map, O. *$2.50 net. Scribner.

Mackay, J: S., comp.
See New Jersey. Digest.

McKay, W. J. Stewart.
Operations upon the uterus, perineum and round ligaments; final revision by Arth. Giles. '09(Ap) 472 p. il. *$6 net. Wood.

McKay, Winsor.
Little Nemo in Slumberland. '09(D18) il. 4°, bds., 60 c. Cupples & L.

Mackaye, Percy Wallace.
Anti-matrimony; satirical comedy. '10 (D10) c. front. D. $1.25 net. Stokes.
Garland to Sylvia: dramatic reverie; with a prologue. '10(Je11) c. D. $1.25 net. Macmillan.
Mater: an American study in comedy: [a play.] '08(O17) c. D. **$1.25 net. Macmillan.
Ode on the centenary of Abraham Lincoln. '09(F13) c. D. *75 c. net. Macmillan.
Playhouse and the play, and other addresses concerning the theatre and democracy in America. '09(My8) c. D. **$1.25 net. Macmillan.
Poems. '09(D18) c. D. **$1.25 net. Macmillan.
The scarecrow; or, the glass of truth: a tragedy of the ludicrous. '08(Mr14) c. D. **$1.25 net. Macmillan.

McKean, T:
Master influence. '08(My9) c. D. †$1.50. Lippincott.
Mercy of fate. '10(O8) c. D. $1.20 net. Wessels & B.

McKee, Barclay.
See Stevens, W: O.

McKee, Brainerd.
Shakespeare in limerick. '10(Mr12) c. D. 75 c. Morton.

McKeehan, C: L., comp.
See Negotiable instruments law.

McKeever, W: Archibald.
Assisting the boy in the choice of a vocation. '10(O) c. no paging, O. (Home training bull.) pap., gratis. W: A. McKeever.
Better crop of boys and girls. '10(O) c. no paging, O. (Home training bull.) pap., gratis. W: A. McKeever.
Cigarette smoking boy. '10(O) c. '09. no paging, fig. O. (Home training bull.) pap., gratis. W: A. McKeever.
Psychologic method in teaching. '09(Ap10) c. D. $1. Flanagan.
Psychology and higher life. Rev., enl. ed. '08(Ap11) c. il. 12°, $1. Crane.
Psychology and higher life. 3d ed. '09 (Ag14) c. figs. D. $1. Flanagan.
Teaching the boy to save. '10(O) no paging, O. (Home training bull.) pap., gratis. W: A. McKeever.

McKeever, W: Archibald.—*Continued.*
Training the girl to help at home. '10(O) c. '09. no paging, O. (Home training bull.) pap., gratis. W: A. McKeever.

McKelway, A. J.
Child labor in the Carolinas. '09(Je19) il. 8°, (National Child Labor Committee pubs.) pap., gratis. Nat. Child Labor.

McKenna, Rev. C: Hyacinthe, comp.
Dominican tertiaries' guide; for the use of private tertiaries of St. Dominic's third order of penance. '09(D) c. 8+17-426 p. front. 16°, 75 c.; mor., $1.25. Rosary.

McKennan, Fk. B.
Man's incarnation; key to life eternal. Bk. 1, Man's elements, attributes, and religion; the book, or canonical, and the bookless, or illiterate, religions; summaries of the books of the English Bible; the story of the Old Testament part, and the prophetically declared sins of the people represented in the Old Testament part of the English Bible. '09(Mr27) c. O. $1. McKennan.

McKenney, Mrs. Marie M.
Studies of Shakespeare's women. '09 (Mr20) c. pors. 8°, leath., $2, boxed. M. M. McKenney.

McKenny, C:
Personality of the teacher. '10(D17) c. 12°, $1. Row, P. & Co.

McKenzie, Fayette Avery.
Indian in relation to the white population of the U. S. '08(S19) c. 117 p. 8°, $1; pap., 50 c. F. A. McKenzie.
Tragedy of Korea. '08(Jl18) 12°, *$2 net. Dutton.

MACKENZIE, *Sir* George.
Lang, A. Sir George Mackenzie, king's advocate of Rosehaugh: his life and times. *$4.20 net. Longmans.

MCKENZIE, Mae.
Williams, *Mrs.* C. G. Morning glory: [life of Mae McKenzie.] 75 c. net. Pub. Ho. M. E. Ch., So.

Mackenzie, Millicent.
Hegel's educational theory and practice; with an introd. note by J. S. Mackenzie. '09(O16) D. $1. Bardeen.

McKenzie, Rob. Tait, M.D.
Exercise in education and medicine. '09 (Ag) *$3.50 net; mor., *$5 net. Saunders.

Mackenzie, W. M.
Outline of Scottish history; from Roman times to the disruption. '08(Ap18) il. maps, plans, 12°, $1.25. Macmillan.
Pompeii. '10(Jl16) col. il. 8°, (Color book ser.) $2.50 net. Macmillan.

Mackenzie, W: Douglas, D.D.
Final faith; statement of the nature and authority of Christianity as the religion of the world. '10(D10) O. $1.75 net. Macmillan.

McKenzie, W: Patrick.
Christian science (La science chrétienne); ou la délivrance du mal. '09(S) c. 31 p. 16°, pap., 6 c. Chr. Sci.

Mackereth, Ja. A.
Son of Cain: [poems.] '10(Jl9) D. $1.25 net. Longmans.

Mackey, Alb. Gallatin.
Lexicon and hist. of freemasonry; cont. definitions of all its communicable terms, notices of its traditions and antiquities; together with an acct. of all the rites and mysteries of the ancient world. '09, [1910.] (Je) c. 10+11-532 p. il. pors. facsims., 4°, $6. T. A. McClure.

Mackey, Rev. W. M.
Man in the street, and other Bible types of modern men. '10(D) 12°, $1.50 net. Doran.

McKilliam, A. E.
Hist. of England for elem. and secondary schools. '10(D24) il. 12°, 60 c. Macmillan.
Makers of history. '10(S) il. 8°, 60 c. net. Cassell.

McKim, Randolph Harrison.
Soldier's recollections; leaves from the diary of a young Confederate. '10(O22) c. il. pors. O. $2 net. Longmans.

MACKINAC, Mich.
Bailey, J: R. Mackinac, formerly Michilimackinac. $1. Tradesman.

MACKINAC ISLAND, Mich.
Newton, S. Mackinac Island and Sault Ste. Marie. 50 c. Sault.

Mackinder, Halford J:
The Rhine. '08(N14) c. il. maps, O. **$3.50 net. Dodd.

Mackinlay, Malcolm Sterling.
Manuel Garcia: a biography. '08(D5) il. 8°, *$4 special net. Appleton.
Singing voice and its training. '10(Je4) 8°, $1.25 net. Dutton.

McKinley, Carlyle E.
Appeal to Pharaoh: the negro problem, and its radical solution. 3d ed.; ed., with introd., by Gustavus M. Pinckney. '08 (Ja18) 12°, $1. State Co.

McKinley, Edna M.
Pupil's notebook and study outline in Roman hist. '10(Ja22) O. pap., 25 c. Am. Bk.

McKINLEY, William.
Snow, J. E. Life of William McKinley. 75 c. J. E. Snow.

McKinley Memorial Association, Philadelphia, Pa. McKinley memorial in Philadelphia; hist. of the movement and account of the dedication exercises, incl. the oration by Ja. M. Beck. '09(Je) 48 pors. 4°, pap., gratis L. W. Miller.

McKinney, Alex. Harris.
Our big boys and the Sunday school. '10 (D3) c. 12°, 50 c. net. Revell.
Sunday school graded: why? what? how? '08(F8) c. S. pap., 10 c. Presb. Bd.

McKinney, Fk. C.
See Denney, Jos. Villiers.

McKinney, Ida Scott Taylor, [Mrs. W: E. McKinney.]
Year book of English authors. New ed. '09, [1910.] (Ja) il. 12°, $1.50; leath., $3. Caldwell.

McKinney, Mrs. W: E.
See McKinney, Ida Scott Taylor.

McKinney, W: M., comp.
Supplement to Encyclopedia of pleading and practice. v. 4. '09(Ap) c. O. shp., $6. E: Thompson.
See also United States. Federal statutes.

—, ed. *See* Am. and Eng. annot. cases.—Digest.

—, and Garland, D. S., eds.
American and English encyclopædia of law and practice. v. 1, 1909. '09(Jl); v. 2, 1910. (F); v. 3 (Jl); v. 4, 5 (D) c. O. shp., ea., $7.50. E: Thompson.

Mackinnon, Albert G.
Truths of to-day; young man's creed. '09 (D4) D. *75 c. net. Eaton & M.

Mackinnon, Ja.
History of modern liberty. In 8 v. v. 3, The struggle with the Stuarts, 1603-1647. '08(Mr28) O. *$5 net. Longmans.

McKinsey, Folger, ["Bentztown Bard."]
Rose of the old regime, and other poems. '09(Ap24) c. D. **$1 net. Eichelberger.
Formerly pub. by Doxey Bk. Shop Co.

Mackintosh, Rev. Hugh Ross.
Life on God's plan: sermons. '10(D) 12°, $1.50 net. Doran.

Mackintosh, R.
Thessalonians and Corinthians. '09(Jl31) 18°, (Westminster New Testament.) *75 c. net. Revell.

McKishnie, Archie P.
Love of the wild. '10(N19) c. col. front. 12°, $1.20. FitzGerald.

McKitrick, Reuben.
Accident insurance for workingmen. '09 (Ag28) D. (Comparative legislation bull.) pap., 25 c. Wisconsin Free Lib.

Macklin, Alys Eyre.
Greuze. '08(F22) il. O. (Masterpieces in colour.) bds., *65 c. net. Stokes.

MacKnight, F: Elijah.
Fertilizer and acid plants. '10(Ja8) c. il. plans, 8°, (Insurance engineering ser.) 50 c. Insurance Press.

McKnight, Ja. D.
Design of marine multiannular boilers. '10 (D) 8°, $1.50. Van Nostrand.

McKnight, Levi Adolphus.
Indiana: a drama of progress; history of Indiana in a play of four acts. '09(F20) c. por. Q. pap., 50 c. L. A. McKnight.

McKone, W: Ja.
Michigan state and local government. 6th ed. '10(Jl) c. 226 p. il. 12°, 60 c. Hammond Pub.

McLachlan, J:, M.D.
Applied anatomy: surgical, medical and operative. In 2 v., rev. and largely rewritten, by A. A. Scott-Skirving. 4th ed. '08(Jl18) il. 12°, *$6 net. Wood.

MacLafferty, Ja. H:
City loved around the world; toast to San Francisco. '10(D) 24°, pap., 10 c. net. P. Elder.
Light through the valley. '10(D) 50 c. net. P. Elder.
My soul's cathedral: [poems.] '10(O22) c. O. bds., 90 c. net. P. Elder.

Maclaren, Alex., D.D.
Expositions of Holy Scriptures. In 30 v. 3d ser. In 6 v. v. I, The Acts of the apostles: chapter XIII. to end; v. 2, 3, 4, The gospel according to St. John: chapters I. to VIII.; IX. to XIV.; XV. to XXI.; v. 5, The second book of Kings from chap. VIII. and the books of Chronicles, Ezra, and Nehemiah; v. 6, The books of Esther, Job, Proverbs, and Ecclesiastes. '08(Ap4) O. per set, *$7.50 net; 4th ser.; in 6 v. v. I, The book of Psalms, I. to XLIX.; v. 2, The book of Psalms, LI. to CXLV.; v. 3, The books of Ezekiel, Daniel and the minor prophets; v. 4, The Gospel according to St. Luke, chapters I. to XII.; v. 5, The Gospel according to St. Luke, chapters XIII. to XXIV.; v. 6, St. Paul's Epistle to the Romans. '09(Ap3) O. per set, *$7.50 net; 5th ser., in 8 v. v. I, St. Paul's epistles to the Corinthians (to II. Corinthians, chapter V.); v. 2, St. Paul's epistle to the Ephesians; v. 3, II. Corinthians, Galatians and Philippians; v. 4, Philippians, Colossians, I. and II. Thessalonians and I. Timothy; v. 5, II. Timothy, Titus, Philemon and Hebrews; v. 6, The epistle to the Hebrews (chapters VII to XIII), the general epistle of James; v. 7, The epistles general of I. and II. Peter and I. John; v. 8, The epistles of John, Jude and the Book of Revelation. '10(D10) O. $10. (Sold in series only.) Armstrong.
Similes and figures of Alexander Maclaren; comp. by Fs. E: Clark. '10(O8) c. 12°, $1 net. Revell.

"Maclaren, Ian," pseud.
See Watson, J:

McLaren, J:
Gardening in California, landscape and flower. '09(F13) c. il. 8°, *$3.75 net. A. M. Robertson.

McLaren, R. S.
Mechanical engineering for beginners. '08 (My23) D. *$1.75 net. Lippincott.

McLaughlin, And. Cunningham.
History of the American nation. [20th ed.] '09(Je19) c. il. por. maps, facsims., 12°, (Twentieth century text-books.) *$1.40 net. Appleton.

McLaughlin, Rev. G: A.
Commentary on the Gospel according to St. Matthew. '09(Jl) c. 8+9-392 p. 12°, $1.50. Chr. Witness.

McLaughlin, J. Candor.
Abridgment of practical medicine and allied sciences, arranged in alphabetical order with definitions of principal medical terms. 2d ed., rearranged, rev. and enl. '09(Ag) c. 677 p. 32°, $2. J. C. McLaughlin.

McLaughlin, Ja.
My friend the Indian. '10(Ap16) c. il. pors. O. $2.50 net Houghton M.

McLaughlin, Ja. M., and Gilchrist, W: Wallace.
Song reader; graded course in school music in one book based on the new educational music course. '10(Ag20) c. O. 45 c. Ginn.

McLaughlin, Wa. Wesley.
Irrigation of grain. '10(Jl) 23 p. il. 8°, (U. S. Dept. of Agriculture; farmers' bull.)

McLaughlin, Wendell, comp.
"Little perfect hour": [poems.] '07, [1908.] (Ap) c. 48 p. O. pap., 75 c. W. McLaughlin.

Maclaurin, R: Cockburn.
Light. '10(Ja8) c. il. tabs., por. 8°, (Columbia Univ. lectures; Jesup lectures, 1908-1909.) **$1.50 net. Lemcke.
Theory of light: treatise on physical optics. '08(O10) diagrs., 8°, *$2.75 net. Putnam.

Maclay, Edg. Stanton.
Youthful man-o'-warsman, from the diary of an English lad who served in the British frigate "Macedonian" during her memorable action with the American frigate "United States." '10(N5) c. il. 12°, $1.50. Navy Blue.

MacLean, Annie Marion.
Wage-earning women; introd. by Grace H. Dodge. '10(Jl2) c. tab. D. (Citizens lib.) $1.25 net. Macmillan.

McLean, Archibald.
Alexander Campbell as a preacher. '09 (F13) c. por. 12°, *30 c. net. Revell.

MacLean, Grace Edith.
"Uncle Tom's cabin" in Germany. '10 (Jl16) c. O. (Americana Germanica.) $1.50. Univ. of Penn.; [Appleton.]

Maclean, J. Kennedy.
Heroes of the Polar seas. '10(D31) il. 8°, $1.50. Lippincott.

Maclean, J:
Winning the front place: book of ideals and illustrations from real life on working for the best, and winning the first places in the world. '08(Ag1) D. 75 c. Am. S. S.

MacLean, J: Patterson.
Flora Macdonald in America; with brief sketch of her life and adventures. '10 (Ap9) c. il. pors. 8°, $1. A. W. McLean.

Maclean, Rev. Norman.
Can the world be won for Christ?; record of the World's Missionary Conference. '10(D) $1.25 net. Doran.

McLean, Ridley.
Bluejackets manual, U. S. navy, 1908. 5th ed. '08(D) c. il. 24°, $1.25. U. S. Naval Inst.

Maclean, Salmon.
Leisure moments: [poetry.] '08(D) $1. B'way Pub.

MacLear, Anne Bush.
Early New England towns: [Massachusetts.] '08(My23) c. front. O. (Columbian Univ. studies in hist., economics and public law.) pap., $1.50. Longmans.

McLennan, J:
Manual of pract. farming. '10(Ap30) c. il. D. $1.50 net. Macmillan.

McLeod, C. H.
Elem. descriptive geometry. 2d ed., rev. '08(Ag1) c. diagrs., 8°, $1.50. Wiley.

McLeod, Christian.
Heart of the stranger. '08(D5) c. il. 12°, $1.25. Revell.

Macleod, Fiona, [pseud. for W: Sharp.]
Writings of "Fiona Macleod"; ed. by Mrs. W: Sharp. Uniform ed. In 7 v. v. 1, Pharais and The mountain lovers; v. 2, The dominion of dreams [and] Under the dark star; v. 3, The sin-eater, The washer of the ford, and other legendary moralities. '10(Je18); v. 4, The divine adventure, Iona, Studies in spiritual history; v. 5, The winged destiny, Studies in the spiritual, History of the Gael (Ag20); v. 6, The silence of Amor, Where the forest murmurs (N5); v. 7, Poems and dramas (D3) c. por. O. ea., $1.50 net. Duffield.
Little book of nature thoughts sel. by Mrs. W: Sharp and Roselle Lathrop Shields. '08(N21) c. 24°, 40 c.; leath., 75 c.; pap., 25 c. T: B. Mosher.
Songs and poems. '09(O16) 12°, *$1.50 net. Duffield.

MACLEOD, Fiona.
Sharp, E. A. S., *comp.* William Sharp (Fiona Macleod). $3.75 net. Duffield.

McLeod, Malcolm Ja.
Comfortable faith. '08(O24) c. 12°, *$1 net. Revell.

Macleod, Mary, comp.
Red Cross knight and Sir Guyon from Spenser's Faery queen. '09(Ag) 123 p. il. 16°, (Children's bookshelf.) 60 c. Dodge.
Story of King Arthur, from Malory's Morte d'Arthur. '09(Ag) 123 p. il. 16°, (Children's bookshelf.) 60 c. Dodge.
—, **comp. and ed.** Robin Hood and his merry men. '10(D17) col. il. 16°, (Children's bookshelf.) bds., 50 c. Dodge.
Tiny true tales of animals. '10(S10) il. S. 50 c. Stokes.

McMahan, Mrs. Anne Benneson.
Shakespeare's love story, 1580-1609. '09 (O16) c. O. vellum, $2.50. boxed; hf. cf. or hf. mor., $5.50, boxed. McClurg.

McMahon, A. Philip.
See Noll, Arth. Howard.

McMahon, Anna M.
See McMahon, Helen A.

McMahon, Helen A., Marie M. and Anna M.
Rhyme and story primer. '08(O3) c. il. D. 30 c. Heath.

McMahon, Maria M.
See McMahon, Helen A.

McManus, Blanche, [Mrs. M. F. Mansfield.]
Our little Egyptian cousin. '08(O3) c. map, D. (Little cousin ser.) 60 c. L. C. Page.

McMaster, Ja. Smith.
Commercial digest and business forms. '09 (Mr) c. O. shp., $6. Weed-Parsons.

McMaster, J: Bach.
Brief hist. of the United States; rev. by the State Text-Book Committee, and approved by the State Board of Education. [1910.] (N) c. '09. 435+30 p. il. pors. maps, 12°, (Cal. state ser.) Cal. Dept. Pub. Instruction.
Hist. of the people of the United States from the Revolution to the Civil War. In 8 v. v. 7, 1841-1850. '10(Mr26) c. O. **$2.50 net. Appleton.

McMasters, Carlos Lenox.
See Wilson, Victor Tyson.

MACMILLAN, Alexander.
Graves, C: L. Life and letters of Alexander Macmillan. $3.50 net. Macmillan.

McMillan, Archibald Harold.
Telephone law: organization and operation of telephone companies. '08(Ag) c. 14+331 p. O. *$3 net. McGraw.

McMillan, Hamilton.
Sir Walter Raleigh's lost colony: sketch of the attempts made to establish a colony in Virginia, with traditions of an Indian tribe in North Carolina, indicating the fate of the colony of Englishmen left on Roanoke Island in 1587. Rev. ed. '08 (Jl4) c. O. pap., 50 c. H. McMillan.

MacMillan, Ja. Alex.
Chronic constipation and allied conditions. '08(My.) c. 257 p. 8°, $2. Burton Co.

Macmillan, Wa.
Electro-metallurgy. 3d ed.; rev. by W. R. Cooper, and enl. '10(S) 449 p. il. 8°, $4 net. Lippincott.

Macmillan standard agricultural library. 9 v. '10(D17) per set, $10 net, boxed. Macmillan.
Contents: Bailey, L. H., Principles of agriculture, $1.25 net; Principles of fruit growing, $1.50 net; Lyon, T. L., *and* Fippin, E. O., Principles of soil management, $1.75 net; Jordan, W. H., Feeding of animals, $1.50 net; Roberts, I. P., The horse, $1.25 net; Valentine, C. S., How to keep hens for a profit, $1.50 net; Mayo, N. S., Diseases of animals, $1.50 net; Voorhees, E. B., Fertilizers, $1.25 net; Wing, H. H., Milk and its producers, $1.50 net.

Macmillan's animal autobiographies. il. 8°, *$2 net. Macmillan.
—Hurst. Life story of a fowl.

Macmillan's animal behavior ser. il. 12°. Macmillan.
—Washburn. Animal mind. *$1.60 net.

Macmillan's biological studies and addresses. il. 8°. Macmillan.
—Osborn. Evolution of mammalian molar teeth. *$2 net.

Macmillan's classical ser. for colleges and schools. 16°. Macmillan.
—Plato. Apology of Plato. *50 c. net.

Macmillan's color book ser. il. 12°, 8°. Macmillan.
—Austen. Haunts of ancient peace. *$2 net.
—Baillie-Grohman. Tyrol. *$2 net.
—Bonhote. Birds of Britain. *$6 net.
—Bradley. Rivers and streams of England. *$6 net.—Worcestershire. *$3 net.—The Wye. $3 net.
—Butler. From sketch-book and diary. (Miscellaneous.) *$2.50 net.
—Calvert. Southern Spain. *$6 net.
—Cane. Isle of Man. *$2 net.
—Calthrop. Charm of gardens. $2.50 net.
—Conway. The Alps. $1.50 net.
—Cook. Gardens of England. *$2.50 net.
—Dobson. St. Petersburg. (Travel and description.) $2.50 net.
—Du Cane. Flowers and gardens of Madeira. *$2 net.—Flowers and gardens of Japan. *$6 net.
—Duckworth. The Cotswolds. *$2.50 net.
—Felton. British floral decoration. $2.50 net.

Macmillan's color book ser.—Continued.
—Fox. Australia. $6 net.—Ramparts of empire (Miscellaneous). $2.25 net.
—Gribble. Geneva. *$2 net.—Lake of Geneva. **$6 net.—Lausanne. *$3 net.—Montreux. *$2.50 net.
—Hardie. John Pettie. *$6 net.
—Headlam. Inns of Court. *$2 net.
—Holmes. Windsor. *$3 net.
—Home. Motor routes of France. $2 net; $2.25 net.—Romance of London. (Travel and description.) $1 net.—Yorkshire vales and wolds. *$3 net.
—Huish. Happy England. *$6 net.
—Kelman. From Damascus to Palmyra. *$6 net.
—Mackenzie. Pompeii. $2.50 net.
—Malcolm *and* Maxwell. Grouse and grouse moors. $2.75 net.
—Moncrieff. Adventures in America. (Miscellaneous.) $1.75.—Beasts of business. (Miscellaneous.) $1.50.—Essex. *$6 net.—Heart of Scotland. *$3 net.—Isle of Wight. *$2.50 net.—Kew Gardens. *$2.50 net.—London. $2.50 net.—Peak country. *$2.50 net.
—Munro. The Clyde. *$6 net.
—Musson. Upper Engadine. *$2.50 net.
—Omond. Liège and the Ardennes. *$3 net.
—Belgium. *$6 net.
—Ponting. In Lotus-land: Japan. $6 net.
—Poyser. Tower of London. *$2.50 net.
—Rawnsley. Country sketches for city dwellers. *$3 net.
—Reeves. New Zealand. *$6 net.
—Ryan. Malta. $3 net.
—Sloan. Galloway. *$2 net.
—Smith. Ancient tales and folk lore of Japan. *$6 net.
—Stone. Eton. *$2 net.
—Stokes. Hungary. *$6 net.
—Swinburne. Royal navy. *$6 net.
—Varley. Winchester. (Travel and description.) $3 net.
—Younghusband. Kashmir. *$6 net.

Macmillan's color books for boys and girls. il. 8°. Macmillan.
—Finnemore. Story of Robinhood. *$1.50 net.
—Grierson. Children's book of Celtic stories. —Children's tales of English minsters. ea., *$2 net.
—Kidd. Bull of the Kraal and the heavenly maidens. *$2 net.
—Mitton. Book of the railway. *$2 net.
—Senior. King who never died. $1.50.
—Wyss. Child's world in pictures. 75 c. net.

Macmillan's English classics. 16°. Macmillan.
—Chaucer. Canterbury tales; Nun's priest's tale. *40 c. net.

Macmillan's garden-craft ser. 12°. Macmillan.
—Bailey. Horticulturists' rule-book. 75 c.

Macmillan's guides. 12°. Macmillan.
—Guide to Greece. *$2.75 net.

Macmillan's handbooks of Am. government; ed. by L. B. Evans. 12°, *90 c. net. Macmillan.
—McVey. Government of Minnesota.

Macmillan's handbooks of archæology and antiquities. il. O. Macmillan.
—Frothingham. Monuments of Christian Rome. **$2.25 net.
—Gardiner. Greek athletic sports and festivals. $2 net.
—Marquand. Greek architecture. **$2.25 net.

Macmillan's how to ser. il. 8°, $2. Macmillan.
—Wylde. How to collect continental china.

Macmillan's illustrated pocket classics. il. 12°, $1; leath., $1.50. Macmillan.
—Dickens. Our mutual friend.

Macmillan's language reader ser. il. 12°. Macmillan.
—Baker., *and others.* Primer. **25 c. net.

Macmillan's Latin classics; ed. by Ja. C. Egbert. 12° and 16°. Macmillan.
—Cicero. Letters. 60 c. net.
—Livy. [Works:] book 1 and selections from books 2-10. *60 c. net.
—Plautus. The Trinummus. *60 c. net.
—Seneca. Selected essays of Seneca and The satire on the deification of Claudius. —Three tragedies. ea., *60 c. net.
—Tacitus. The Agricola. **40 c. net.—Histories. bks. 1 and 2. 60 c. net.

Macmillan's Latin ser.; ed. by J. C. Kirtland, jr. il. 12°. Macmillan.
—Cæsar. Gallic War. bks. I-VII. **$1.25 net; text ed., 35 c. net.

Macmillan's library of philosophy; ed. by J. H. Muirhead. 8°. Macmillan.
—Bergson. Time and free will. $2.75 net.
—Bradley. Appearance and reality. *$3 net.
—Hegel. Phenomenology of mind. $5.50 net.
—Pillsbury. Attention. *$2.75 net.
—Urban. Valuation. *$2.75 net.

Macmillan's new classical lib.; ed. by Emil Reich. 12°, *$1 net. Macmillan.
—Gaius. Institutes.
—Seyffert. Dictionary of classical antiquities.

Macmillan's new ser. of French texts; ed. by Otto Siepmann. 16°, 35 c. net. Macmillan.
—Bernard. L'anneau d'argent.
—Biart. Monsieur Pinson.
—Bourget. Un saint.
—Coppée. Contes choisis.
—Corneille. Nicomiède.
—Daudet. Jack. pt. 1.—Lettres de mon moulin.—La Tour des Maures.
—Lamy. Voyage du novice Jean-Paul à travers la France d' Amerique.
—Laurie, *pseud.* Une année de collège à Paris.
—Marivaux. Le jeu de l'amour et du hasard.
—Pascal *and* Vauvenargues. Pensées Maximes et reflections.
—Sandeau. Sacs et Parchensins.

Macmillan's new ser. of German texts. 16°, 35 c. net. Macmillan.
—Goebel. Rübezahl.
—Schrader. Friedrich der Grosse und Der Siebenjährige Krieg.

Macmillan's new ser. of German texts.—Cont.
—Wachenhusen. Vom ersten bis zum letzten schuss; Kriegserinnerungen.
—Zastro. Wilhelm der Siegreiche.

Macmillan's old world travels. il. O. Macmillan.
—Headlam. Venetia and northern Italy. *$2.50 net.
—Home. Along the rivieras of France and Italy. *$3 net.

Macmillan's pocket Am. and Eng. classics. 24°, *25 c. net. Macmillan.
—Austen. Pride and prejudice.
—Bible. O. T. Selections.
—Bulwer-Lytton. Last days of Pompeii.
—Burns. Selected poems.
—Cooper. The spy.
—Dana. Two years before the mast.
—Defoe. Robinson Crusoe. pt. 1.
—Emerson. Earlier poems.
—Fuess *and* Sanborn, *eds.* English narrative poems.
—Gray *and* Cowper. Elegy written in a country church yard; and John Gilpin.
—Hale. Man without a country.
—Hawthorne. Mosses from an old manse.
—Hughes. Tom Brown's school days.
—Huxley. Selected essays and addresses.
—Irving. Knickerbocker's history of New York.—Selected tales from Tales of a traveller.
—Lincoln. Selections.
—McConnell, *ed.* Southern orator.
—Parkman. Oregon trail.
—Ruskin. Crown of wild olive.
—Shakespeare. Midsummer night's dream.—Tragedy of Richard II.
—Stevenson. Kidnapped.—Travels with a donkey, and An inland voyage.
—Swiggett, *ed.* Selections from Le Morte d'Arthur.
—Thackeray. English humorists.
—Thomas à Kempis. Imitation of Christ.
—Thoreau. Walden.
—Virgil. Aeneid.
—Whittier. Snow-bound.

Macmillan's pocket classics. 16°, 80 c.; leath., $1.25. Macmillan.
—Irving. The Alhambra.—Rip Van Winkle.
—Sheridan. School for scandal, and The rivals.
—Swift. Travels into several remote nations.

Macmillan's queen's treasure ser. 12°, $1. Macmillan.
—Eliot. Silas Marner.
—Ewing. Brownies.—Flatiron for a farthing.—Jan of the Windmill.—Lob Lie-by-the-Fire.—Mrs. Overtheway's remembrances.—We and the world.
—Gaskell. Cousin Phillis.—Cranford.

Macmillan's rural science ser.; ed. by L. H. Bailey. il. 12°. Macmillan.
—Bailey. Forcing book. **$1.25 net.—Garden making. **$1.50 net.—Principles of agriculture. **$1.25 net.—Principles of fruit-growing.—Principles of vegetable gardening. ea., **$1.50 net.
—Card. Bush-fruits. **$1.50 net.
—Jordan. Feeding of animals. **$1.50 net.

Macmillan's rural science ser.—Continued.
—King. Irrigation and drainage. **$1.50 net.
—Lipman. Bacteria and country life. *$1.50 net.
—Lodeman. Spraying of plants. **$1.25 net.
—Watson. Farm poultry. **$1.25 net.

Macmillan's rural text-books ser.; ed. by L. H. Bailey. D. Macmillan.
—Lyon *and* Fippin. Principles of soil management. **$1.75 net.

Macmillan's special campaign ser. 12°, *$1.60 net. Macmillan.
—Maude. Jena campaign.—Leipzig campaign.
—Redway. War of the Secession, 1861-1862.
—Sawyer. Grant's campaign in Virginia.
—Sedgwick. Russo-Japanese war.

Macmillan's York lib. 12°, 80 c.; leath., $1.25. Macmillan.
—Brontë. Jane Eyre.
—Fielding. History of Tom Jones. 2 v.
—Jameson. Shakespeare's heroines.
—Ranke. History of the popes. In 3 v.
—Theocritus *and* Virgil. Idylls of Theocritus and Eclogues of Virgil.

MacMillar, Jude, pseud.
See Miller, Ja. Marion.

MacMunn, Norman, comp.
Dictionary of quotations. '08(S5) c. S. 50 c. Jacobs.

MacMurray, Arth.
Pract. lessons in public speaking. '10 (Jl) c. 95 p. 8°, 75 c. A. MacMurray.

Macmurray, T: Ja.
Highways of success. '10(F5) c. 12°, $1. Progress Co.

McMurry, C: Alex.
The Alps. '09(N13) c. S. (Central topics in geography.) pap., 10 c. Flanagan.
The Rhine. '09(N13) c. S. (Central topics in geography.) pap., 10 c. Flanagan.
Special method in reading the grades. '08 (D5) D. *$1.25 net. Macmillan.

McMurry, Fk. Morton.
How to study and teaching how to study. '09(O2) c. D. **$1.25 net. Houghton M.
See also Tarr, Ralph Stockman.
—, **ed.** *See* Beach, Chandler B., *ed.*

McNally, Augustin Fs.
Catholic centenary, 1808-1908. '08(Je27) c. il. pors. D. **$1.25 net. Moffat.

Macnamara, N. C.
Evolution and function of living purposive matter. '10(Je25) figs. D. (International scientific ser.) $1.75 net. Appleton.
Human speech: its physical basis. '09 (Ap17) il. D. (International scientific ser.) *$1.75 net. Appleton.

Macnaughtan, S.
Expensive Miss du Cane. '08(O10) 12°, $1.50. Dutton.
Three Miss Graemes. '09(Ja30) D. $1.50. Dutton.

McNaughton, Mrs. Allan.
See Kelly, Myra.

McNeal-Sweeney, Mildred I.
See Sweeney, Mildred I. McNeal-.

McNeil, Everett.
Boy forty-niners. '08(O3) c. il. D. †$1.50. McClure.
Fighting with Fremont. '10(O8) c. il. 12°, $1.50. Dutton.
In Texas with Davy Crockett. '08(Ag15) 8°, $1.50. Dutton.
With Kit Carson in the Rockies. '09(S11) il. 12°, $1.50. Dutton.
See also Mosher, Maude Bayliss.

McNeill, G: Edn.
Eight hour primer: the fact, theory and the argument. 3d ed. '07, [1908.] (Mr.) 19 p. 12°, (Am. Federation of Labor Eight hour ser.) (Add. author for price.) G: E. McNeill.

McNeill, J: C:
Lyrics from cotton land. '08(My16) c. il. por. 12°, $1.50. Stone & B.

McNeill, T:
Minnecotah, an Indian legend of Lake Kampeska. '08(Mr) c. 16 p. pl. S. pap., gratis. Saturday News.

McNicholas, J: T.
New legislation on engagements and marriage in [Catholic church]: commentary on the decree "Ne temere"; repr., with additions and new illustrations, from the *Ecclesiastical Review.* '08(Ap18) c. 8°, pap., 10 c. Dolphin.

McNichols, J: Patrick.
Fundamental English. '08, [1909.] (Mr) c. 272 p. 12°, 80 c. Schwartz, K. & F.
Teachers' hdbk. to accompany Fundamental English. '09(Ap) c. 20+447 p. 12°, $1.50. Schwartz, K. & F.

McNIEL, John William Thomas.
Merritt, M. C. **Rev. J. W. T. McNiel; brief biography. 75 c. J. F. Elwell.**

MacNutt, Barry.
See Franklin, W: Suddards.

MacNutt, Fs. A:
Bartholomew de Las Casas: his life, his apostolate, and his writings. '09(Ja30) c. pors. maps, O. **$3.50 net. Putnam.
Fernando Cortes and the conquest of Mexico, 1485-1547. '09(S25) c. pors. maps, D. (Heroes of the nations ser.) **$1.35 net; hf. leath., **$1.60 net. Putnam.

Macomber, W:
Fixed law of patents, as established by the supreme court of the U. S., and the nine circuit courts of appeals. '09(N) c. 145+925 p. O. $7.50. Little, B. & Co.

MACOMBER COLLECTION.
See Ceramics.

MACOMBER FAMILY.
See Genealogies, Stackpole, E. S.

Macon cook book; a collection of recipes tested principally by members of Benson-Cobb Chapter, Wesleyan College Alumnæ, Macon, Ga. '09(Ag) 284 p. 8°, $1. J. W. Burke.

MACON COUNTY, Mo.
General hist. of Macon County, Missouri. $15. H. Taylor & Co.

Macphail, And.
Essays in fallacy. '10(Je25) c. D. $1.50 net. Longmans.
Essays in politics. '09(Ag14) D. *$1.80 net. Longmans.

MacPhail, Malcolm Leod.
Magnetism of the Bible. '09(D4) c. D. (Green Fund ser.) *75 c. net. Am. S. S.

McPhail, W. M.
Presbyterian church; its creed, worship, and polity. '09(D) 12°, *$1.50 net. Doran.

Macpherson, Mrs. A. H.
See Henderson, Anna Wilson.

Macpherson, C: Stewart.
Form in music with special reference to the designs of instrumental music. '08 (D26) c. 8°, $2.25. Schirmer.

MacPherson, F. H.
See Lybrand, W: M.

MacPherson, Hector, jr.
Romance of modern astronomy. '10(D31) 12°, (Romance ser.) $1.50 net. Lippincott.

McPherson, J: Ambrose.
Waterworks distribution: guide to the laying out of systems of distributing mains for the supply of water to cities and towns. 2d ed., rev. and enl. '08(Ap25) il. 8°, *$2.50 net. Van Nostrand.

McPherson, Logan Grant.
Railroad freight rates in relation to the industry and commerce of the United States. '09(Je5) c. maps, tabs., O. **$2.25 net. Holt.
Transportation in Europe. '10(Ag27) c. map, D. $1.50 net. Holt.

Macpherson, W:
Principles and method in the study of English literature. '08(O17) D. 60 c. Putnam.

McPike, Eug. Fairfield.
Extracts from British archives on the families of Halley, Hawley, Parry, Pyke, etc. (third series); repr. from the *Magazine of History.* '10(S) 28 p. coat of arms, 8°. (Priv. pr.) E. F. McPike.

MacQueen, P:
In wildest Africa; record of a hunting and exploration trip through Uganda, Victoria Nyanza, the Kilimanjaro Region, and British East Africa. '09(N20) c. il. fold. map, O. $3, boxed. L. C. Page.

McQuillin, Eug., and Campbell, W: S.
Forms of code pleading for Missouri and Arkansas; fully annotated. '09(Mr) c. 53+1073 p. O. $7.50. F. H. Thomas.

Macquoid, Percy.
History of English furniture. In 4 v. v. 4, The age of satinwood. '09(Mr6) il. f°, $15. Putnam.
Plate collector's **guide; arranged from Cripps's "Old English plate." '09(F13)** il. tabs., O. ***$2 net. Scribner.**

McRae, Anna Mont.
See Leland, Claude G.

McSorley, Father Jos.
Sacrament of duty and other essays. '10 (Je11) c. 8°, $1. Columbus.

McSpadden, Jos. Walker.
Land of Nod and what Tinkie and Tess found there. '09(S11) c. il. O. †$1.50. Crowell.
—, **ed.** Waverley synopses: a guide to the plots and characters of Scott's Waverley novels. '09(S11) c. T. 50 c. Crowell.

McTurnan, Lawrence.
Personal equation: with introd. by Ja. L. Hughes. '10(O22) c. D. $1.25 net. Moffat.

Macvane, Edith.
Black flier. '09(Je26) c. front. D. †$1.50. Moffat.
Duchess of dreams. '08(My9) c. D. †$1.50. Lippincott.
The thoroughbred. '09(Mr20) c. il. D. †$1.50. G: W. Dillingham.

MacVeagh, Franklin.
Interview, concerning the proposed changes in design and size of paper money, of the Honorable Franklin MacVeagh, Secretary of the Treasury, September 10, 1910. [1910.] (N) 4 p. 8°. Gov. Pr. Off.

McVey, Fk. Le Rond.
Government of Minnesota. '08(My2) c. map, 12°, (Hdbks. of Am. government.) *90 c. net. Macmillan.
Railroad transportation; some phases of its history, operation and regulation. '10 (S17) c. il. 8°, (Business, commerce and finance.) $5. Cree.
Taxation of mineral properties. '09(D) 411-430 p. 8°, pap., 5 c. Int. Tax.

McWillie, T. A., rep.
See Mississippi. *Sup. ct.* Repts.

Macy, Albert W:
Short-cut philosophy, home-made and hand-turned. '09(D4) c. il. S. bds., 75 c. Sturgis & W.

Macy, J: Albert.
Guide to reading for young and old. '10 (Ja1) c. pors. D. (Guide ser.) **$1.25 net. Baker & T.
Edgar Allan Poe. '08(My16) c. T. (Beacon biographies of eminent Americans.) 50 c. net. Small.

Macy, S. B.
From slavery to freedom. '10(O22) il. O. $1.25 net. Longmans.
In the beginning; being the book of Genesis told to children; with introd. by the Bp. of London. '10(Jl30) c. il. O. $1.25 net. Longmans.
Formerly pub. by Dodge Pub. Co.

Mad Anthony's young scout. Tomlinson, E. T. †$1.50. Houghton M.

Mad Barbara. Deeping, G: W. †$1.50. Cassell.

Mad majesties. Rappoport, A. S. $4 net. Brentano's.

Mad scientist. McDonald, R., *pseud.* $1.60. Cochrane.

Mad shepherds. Jacks, L. P. $1.20 net. Holt.

Mad? which? neither. Mason, E. L. $2. E. L. Mason

Madách, Imre.
Tragedy of man: dramatic poem tr. from the orig. Hungarian by W: H. Loew. '09(Ja9) D. *$1.50 net, boxed. Arcadia.

Madame, mother of the Regent. Vincens, C. **$3 net. Putnam.

Madame Thérèse. Erckmann, E. 40 c. Heath.

Madame X. McConaughy, J. W. $1.50. H. K. Fly.

Madan, A. C.
Lala-Lamba handbook: a short introd. to the south-western division of the Wisa-Lala dialect of Northern Rhodesia; with stories and vocabulary. '08(N21) S. $1.15. Oxford Univ.
Lenje handbook: short introd. to the Lenje dialect spoken in northwest Rhodesia. '08(N21) S. $1.15. Oxford Univ.

Madan, Falconer.
Brief account of the University Press at Oxford, together with a chart of Oxford printing. '09(Mr6) il. pors. facsims., 8°, pap., *60 c. net. Oxford Univ.

Madden, Dodgson Hamilton.
Some passages in the early history of classical learning in Ireland: address del. at the inaugural meeting of the Trinity College Classical Society; rev., with notes and appendix. '08(Ag1) D. $1. Longmans.

Madden, Edn. C:
U. S. government's shame: story of the great Lewis case. '08(My) c. 324 p. il. 16°, pap., 50 c. Nat. Bk. Co.

Maddocks, Mildred, ed.
Good housekeeping family cook book. '09 (D) c. 28+31-320 p. il. 8°, (Good housekeeping lib.) 50 c. Phelps.

Maddox, Rev. Finis Ewing.
Passing of medievalism in religion. '08 (S5) c. O. pap., 60 c. Texarkanian.

Maddox, Hoadly Foster.
See McGinnis, Herbert P.

Maddren, Alfr. G.
See Moffitt, Fred Howard.

Madeira, Percy Child.
Hunting in British East Africa; with foreword by F: Courteney Selous. '09(D18) c. il. O. **$5 net. Lippincott.

MADEIRA ISLANDS.
Du Cane, F. Flowers and gardens of Madeira. *$2 net. Macmillan.
Thomas-Stanford, C: Leaves from a Madeira garden. $1.50. Lane.

Madeley, Dora Ford.
Heroic life and exploits of Siegfried the dragon-slayer; old story of the north retold by Dora Ford Madeley. '10(S3) il. D. $1.50. Crowell.

Mademoiselle Celeste. Knight, A. F. $1.50. Jacobs.

Madge-make-the-best-of-it. Blundell, M. E. S. *80 c. net. Benziger.

Madison, Ja.
Writings of James Madison; comprising his public papers and his private correspondence; ed. by Gaillard Hunt. In 9 v. v. 7, 1803-1807. '08(Ag29); v. 8, 1808-1819. '09(F20); v. 9, 1819-1836. '10 (O8) 8°, hf. leath., subs., per v., $5 net. Putnam.
—, **comp.** Journal of the debates in the convention which framed the constitution of the U. S., May-September, 1787; ed. by Gaillard Hunt. In 2 v. '08(My2) facsim., O. *$4.50 net. Putnam.
See also Federalist (The).

Madison, Ja. Otis.
Madison's complete grading system, improved and extended; coats, vests and trousers from one model. [1910.] (O) c. 71 p. il. 48°, $10. J. J. Mitchell.

Madison, Janet, comp.
Toasts you ought to know. '08(S19) c. D. 75 c.; Persian ooze, $1.50; under title "Twentieth century toasts," pap., 25 c. Reilly & B.

Madison, Mrs. Lucy Foster.
Peggy Owen, patriot; story for girls. '10 (D3) c. il. D. $1.25. Penn Pub. Co.
Peggy Owen: story for girls. '08(O3) c. il. D. $1.25. Penn Pub. Co.

MADISON COUNTY, Va.
See Hebron Lutheran church.

Madison's direct shoulder measure coat system. '08(D) $10. J: J. Mitchell.

Madison's direct shoulder measure vest system. '08(D) $10. J: J. Mitchell.

Madison's self-balancing trousers and breeches systems. '08(D) $10. J: J. Mitchell.

MADNESS.
See Insanity.

MADONNA, The.
See Mary, *Virgin*.

Madonna [in art.] Hale, P. L. $1. Bates & G.

MADRID, Spain.
Calvert, A. F: Madrid. *$1.50 net. Lane.
See also Painters and paintings.

Maennel, Bruno.
Auxiliary education, the training of backward children; tr. from the German by Emma Sylvester. '10(Ja22) O. $1.50. Doubleday, P.

Maestro, S.
New grammar for Italians to speedily learn the English language, (*Nuovissima grammatica accelerata Italiana-Inglese corso completo per imparare a scrivere, parlare en comprendere la lingua Inglese in breve tempo.*) '08(Ap18) 12°, bds., *$1 net. Caspar.

Maeterlinck, Maurice.
Blue bird: fairy play in five acts; tr. by Alex. Teixeira de Mattos. '09(Ap10) c. D. **$1.20 net; New theatre ed. '10(D3) c. por. O. $2 net, boxed. Dodd.
Mary Magdalene; play in 3 acts; tr. by Alex. Teixeira de Mattos. '10(O15) c. D. $1.20 net. Dodd.
Pélléas and Mélisande; tr. by Erving Winslow, with an introd. by Montrose J. Moses. '08(O10) c. il. O. **$1.50 net, boxed. Crowell.
Plays; tr. by R: Hovey. 1st and 2d ser. '09(D) 16°, ea., $1.25. Duffield.

Magada (The). Ardagh, W. M. $1.50. Lane.

Magazine subject-index. v. 1, A subject-index to seventy-nine American and English periodicals; forty-four indexed from their first issues to December 31, 1907; thirty-five indexed for the year 1907; comp. by F: Winthrop Faxon. '08(S19) O. *$3 net; hf. mor., *$4 net. Boston Bk.

Magazine writing and the new literature. Alden, H: M. **$2 net. Harper.

MAGAZINES.
See Periodicals.

MAGDALENA RIVER.
Mozans, H. J., *pseud.* Up the Orinoco and down the Magdalena. $3 net. Appleton.

Magdalene of France. Fitzpatrick, E. H. (Add. pubs. for price.) Sentinel Pub.

MAGENDIE, François.
Dawson, P. M. Biography of François Magendie. *$1.25 net. A. T. Huntington.

Maggie McLanehan. Zollinger, G., *pseud.* $1.50. McClurg.

MAGI (The).
See Persia.

MAGIC AND MAGICIANS.
Abbott, D: P. Marvelous creations of Joseffy. 15 c. Open Court.
Clymer, R. S. Imperial ritual of magic. $1. Philosophical.
Constant, A. L: Transcendental magic. $3.75. De Laurence, S.
Devant, D: Magic made easy. 50 c. net. Cassell.
Downs, T. N. Art of magic. $5. Martinka.
Evans, H: R. Old and new magic. $2. Open Court.
Kirsch, W: Scientific magical experiments. 50 c. W: Kirsch.
See also Conjuring;—Hinduism;—Magic squares;—Occultism;—*also* Houdin, Robert.

Magic casement. Noyes, A., *ed.* *$2 net. Dutton.

Magic image from India. Baker, *Mrs.* C. M. $1.25. Stern.

MAGIC LANTERN.
See Stereopticon.

Magic map book. '09(D) *50 c. net. Doran.

Magic squares and cubes. Andrews, W. S. *$1.50 net. Open Court.

Magic wand. Hamer, S. H. $1. Estes.

Magical man of mirth. Sabin, E. H. $1.25. Jacobs.

Magical message according to Iôannês. *See* Bible. N. T. John.

Magician (The). Maugham, W: S. †$1.50. Duffield.

Magician's tricks. Hatton, H: $1.60 net. Century Co.

Magie, D:, D.D.
Life of Garret Augustus Hobart, twenty-fourth Vice-President of the United States. '10(F19) c. il. pors. O. **$2.50 net. Putnam.

Magill, Harry Byron, ["Ben Boston."]
Little journeys to ancient sanctuaries [in Colorado.] '08, [1909.] (Ap) 128 p. il. 8°, *$1 net. Little Journeys.
Time, the place and the girl: [a play.] '08 (Je6) c. il. 12°, pap., 25 c. Yellowstone.

Magister moritur. Hammond, J. *$2 net. Whittaker.

Magistrate's own case. Rosenkrantz, P. A. V., *Baron.* †$1.50. McClure.

MAGISTRATES.
Campbell, J. H., *comp.* Magistrate's manual. $1. Popp.
See also Justices of the peace.

Magnate (The). Elson, R. †$1.50. Brentano's.

Magner, D.
A B C guide to sensible horse shoeing. '09 (Ap3) il. 8°, $1. Saalfield.

MAGNESITE.
Hess, F. L. Magnesite deposits of California. 15 c. U. S., Supt. of Docs.

Magnet (The). Crozier, A. O. †$1.50. Funk.

MAGNETIC HEALING.
See Medical electricity.

MAGNETIC INDUCTION.
See Magnetism.

MAGNETISM.
Berkeland, K. Norwegian Aurora Polaris Expedition, 1902-1903. v. 1, On the cause of magnetic storms and the origin of terrestrial magnetism. 1st section, $7. Longmans.

Burrows, C: W: Best method of demagnetizing iron. (Add. Superintendent for price.) U. S., Supt. of Docs.

Cummings, G: W. Electricity and magnetism in telephone maintenance. $1.50. McGraw.

Foster, G: C., *and* Porter, A. W. Elem. treatise on electricity and magnetism. $3.50. Longmans.

Franklin, W: S., *and* MacNutt, B. Elements of electricity and magnetism. *$1.60 net. Macmillan.

Jeans, J. H. Mathematical theory of electricity and magnetism. *$4.50 net. Putnam.

Lloyd, M. G. Errors in magnetic testing with ring specimens. (Add. Superintendent for price.) U. S., Supt. of Docs.

Marshall, A. W: Magnets and magnetism simply explained. 25 c. Spon.

Richardson, S. S. Magnetism and electricity and the principles of electrical measurement. *$2 net. Van Nostrand.

Steel, R. E. Pract. electricity and magnetism. 50 c. net. Macmillan.

United States. *Dept. of Commerce and Labor. Coast and Geodetic Survey.* Principal facts of the earth's magnetism and methods of determining the true meridian and the magnetic declination. '09 (My) 99 p. il. tabs., charts, f°, pap., gratis. U. S., Supt. of Docs.

United States. *Dept. of Commerce and Labor. Coast and Geodetic Survey.* Results of observations made at the Coast and Geodetic Survey Magnetic Observatory at Baldwin, Kan., 1901-04; by Dan. L. Hazard. '09(Je) 138 p. il. tabs., f°. 25 c. U. S., Supt. of Docs.

United States. *Dept. of Commerce and Labor. Coast and Geodetic Survey.* Results of observations made at the Coast and Geodetic Survey Magnetic Observatory at Baldwin, Kansas, 1905 and 1906.

United States. *Dept. of Commerce and Labor. Coast and Geodetic Survey.* Results of observations made at the Coast and Geodetic Survey Magnetic Observatory at Vieques, Porto Rico, 1903-1904, by Dan. L. Hazard. '09(Je) 70 p. il. plan, tabs., f°, pap., 15 c.

United States. *Dept. of Commerce and Labor. Coast and Geodetic Survey.* Results of observations made at the Coast and Geodetic Survey Magnetic Observatory at Vieques, Porto Rico, 1905 and 1906.

MAGNETISM.—*Continued.*
United States. *Dept. of Commerce and Labor. Coast and Geodetic Survey.* Results of observations made at the Coast and Geodetic Survey Magnetic Observatory near Honolulu, Hawaii, 1902-1904, by Dan. L. Hazard. '09(Je) 130 p. il. tabs., f°, pap., 25 c. U. S., Supt. of Docs.

United States. *Dept. of Commerce and Labor. Coast and Geodetic Survey.* Results of observations made at the magnetic observatory at Sitka, Alaska, 1905-1906.

Wonder book of magnetism. Houston, E. J. **$1.50 net. Stokes.

See also Compass;—Electricity;—Petroleum;—Telephone.

MAGNETISM (*personal*).
See Mental science;—Personality;—Sex;—Vibration.

Magnetism of the Bible. MacPhail, M. L. *75 c. net. Am. S. S.

MAGNETITE DEPOSITS.
See Iron.

MAGNETO-OPTICS.
See Optics.

Magnetos for automobiles. Bottone, S. R. *$1 net. Van Nostrand.

Magnolia lib. 12°, 50 c. Hurst.
—Collins. Moonstone.
—Dumas. Man in the iron mask.
—Ebers. Emperor.
—Gaboriau. File no. 113.
—Hungerford. Airy fairy Lilian.—Dick's sweetheart.
—James. House on the marsh.
—La Ramée. Moths.
—Russell. Sailor's sweetheart.
—Stevenson. Dynamiter.

Magnus, Lady.
Picture stories from the Bible. '09(N13) col. il. F. $2; bds., $1.75. Tuck.

Magnus, Laurie.
English literature in the nineteenth century. '09(Jl3) O. *$2 net. Putnam.

Magnus, Sir Philip.
Educational aims and efforts, 1880-1910. '10(D10) por. O. $2.25 net. Longmans.

Magoffin, Ralph Van Deman.
Study of the topography and municipal history of Praeneste: [Palestina, Italy.] '08 (S5) c. O. pap., 50 c. Johns Hopkins.

Magoun, Herbert W.
Glacial epoch and the Noachian deluge. Special ed. for Y. M. C. A. '10(O29) O. pap., 25 c. H. W. Magoun.

Magruder, Harriet.
Hist. of Louisiana. '09(D18) c. il. map, 12°, 65 c. Heath.

Magruder, W: E:
Claims arising from results of personal injuries; the relation injury bears to disease and disease to injury; treatise showing how personal injuries may affect various diseases, and how certain diseases may add to claims for accidents by protracting recovery. '10(Ap) c. 266 p. 12°, $2.50. Spectator.
Bibliographies at end of chapters.

Maguire, Emma M.
Story plays for little ones; hdbk. for teachers. [1910.] (D) c. 128 p. il. 12°, 50 c. Educ. Pub.
Two little Indians. '08(O24) c. il. 12°, 30 c. Flanagan.

Mahabharata.
Bhagavad gītā. "The songs of the Master;" tr. with introd. and commentary by C: Johnston. '08(Jl) c. 62+61 p. 8°, $1. C: Johnston.
See also Sanskrit literature.

Mahaffy, Mrs. Amanda Mae Yoho, ed.
Priscilla drawn work book; collection of beautiful designs, with lessons and stitches. '09(D) c. 48 p. il. 4°, 25 c. Priscilla.

Mahaffy, J: Pentland, D.D.
What have the Greeks done for modern civilization?; Lewell lectures of 1908-09. '09(O16) c. O. **$2.50 net. Putnam.

Mahan, Captain Alfr. Thayer.
Harvest within: thoughts on the life of the Christian. '09(Je12) c. D. **$1.50 net. Little, B. & Co.
Interest of America in international conditions. '10(N5) c. D. $1.50 net. Little, B. & Co.
Naval administration and warfare. '08 (N14) c. map, D. *$1.50 net. Little, B. & Co.

Mahany, Rowland B.
Tuscany, and other poems. '09(My) $1. W: A. King.

MAHASKA COUNTY.
See Iowa.

Mahin advertising data book: list of the representative publications, their circulation, rates, etc.; population, street car and bill posting facilities of the important cities and towns in the United States and Canada. '08(O3) c. 24°, leath., $2. Mahin Adv.

Mahood, J: Wilmot, D.D.
Make Jesus king. '08(S5) c. S. *25 c. net. Eaton & M.
Master workman. '10(My21) c. D. 25 c. Praise Pub.

Maid and a man. Dorrance, *Mrs.* E. A. S. **$1.50 net. Moffat.

Maid of Bar Harbor. Rowe, H. G. †75 c. Little, B. & Co.

Maid of France. Lang, A. *$3.50 net. Longmans.

Maid of moods. Shepard, E. W. $1.50. C. M. Clark.

Maida's little shop. Gillmore, *Mrs.* I. H. $1.25. B: W. Huebsch.

Maiden of the mist. Barlow, J: R: 25 c. J: R: Barlow.

Maiden up to date. Irons, G. *$1.60 net. Herder.

Maid's forgiveness. Chapman, J: J. **75 c. net. Moffat.

MAIL.
See Post-office.

MAIL ORDER BUSINESS.
See Business.

MAIL STEAMERS.
See Ship subsidies.

MAILLES, Jacques de.
Andrews, A. G., *ed.* Story of Bayard; [founded on the Histoire du bon Chevalier Bayard, by the Loyal Serviteur.] $1.50 net. Lane.

Main, Arth. Elwin, D.D.
Bible studies on the Sabbath question for the use of pastors, Sabbath schools, young people's classes, home study, etc. '10(Ap2) O. 25 c.; pap., 7 copies for $1. A. E. Main.

Main, Josiah.
Manual for high schools, with special reference to science and agriculture. '08, [1909.] (Mr) c. 34 p. il. 8°, gratis. J. Main.

MAINE, *Duchesse* du.
See Condé, Louise Adélaide de Bourbon, *Princesse* de.

Maine. Railroad laws of the state, comp. by E. C. Farrington. '09(Jl) c. 137 p. Q. bds., $2; shp., $3. Kennebec Journ.

Maine. Superintendence of Maine schools through the union of towns: the law and the explanation, 1907. '08(Mr) 14 p. 8°, (Not for sale.) P. Smith.

Maine. *Supreme judicial ct.* Repts. v. 102-103; (G: H. Smith.) '08(D) O. shp., ea., $4. W: W. Roberts.

Maine. *Supreme judicial ct.* Supp. index-digest of the repts. of cases. v. 89-103, by Albert R. Savage. '09(N) 400 p. O. shp., $4. Loring, S. & H.

MAINE.
Barton, L., *comp.* Maine official index and court directory. $1. Smith & S.
Bastin, E. S., *and* Davis, C: A. Peat deposits of Maine. 20 c. U. S., Supt. of Docs.
Clapp, F: G. Underground waters of southern Maine. 55 c. U. S., Supt. of Docs.
Kaler, J. O. Geography of Maine. (Priv. pr.) J. O. Kaler.
Knight, O. W. Birds of Maine. subs., $3.50. Glass.
Little, G: T:, *ed.* Genealogical and family history of the state of Maine. 4 v. $25. Lewis Pub.
Nason, E. H. Old colonial houses in Maine. (Add. author for price.) E. H. Nason.
Norton, O. W. Strong Vincent and his brigade at Gettysburg, July 2, 1863. (Not for sale.) O. W. Norton.
Pope, C: H: Pioneers of Maine and New Hampshire. $5. C: H: Pope.
Smith, J: D. Hist. of the 19th regiment of Maine volunteer infantry, 1862-1865. $3. Great Western Pr.
Sylvester, H. M. Maine pioneer settlements; [formerly Maine coast romances.] In 5 v. v. 4, 5. per set, $20. W: B. Clarke.
Thoreau, H: D. Maine woods. **$2 net. Crowell.
Verrill, H. M., *and* Booth, C: D. Maine civil officer: guide and hdbk. for attorneys, trial justices, justices of the peace. $6. Loring, S. & H.

MAINE.—*Continued.*
Whitin, E. S. Factory legislation in Maine. $1. Longmans.
Woodward, J. T. Historic record and complete biographic roster, 21st Maine Volunteers. $2; $2.50. J. T. Woodward.
See also Farmingdale;—Hallowell; — Jefferson;— Lincoln Park; — Narraguagus Valley; — Penobscot Expedition;—Popham colony;—Portland;— Pownal;—Randolph;—Waterville.

"MAINE" (Battle-ship).
United States. *Navy Department.* Proposed removal of wreck of battleship "Maine" in harbor of Habana, Cuba. 15 c. U. S., Supt. of Docs.

Maine corporation law; statutes rel. to business corporations, except banking, railroad and insurance companies, with notes of decisions and blank forms; comp. by I: W. Dyer. 6th ed., with an appendix cont. the legislation of 1909. '09(Je) c. 21+274 p. O. $3.50. Loring, S. & H.

Maine Historical Society. Tercentenary of the landing of the Popham colony at the mouth of the Kennebec river, August 29, 1607. '07, [1908.] (My.) 58 p. por. plan, 8°, pap., 50 c. Me Hist.

Mains, G: Preston.
Francis Asbury; with an introd. by Bp. Dan. A. Goodsell. '09(Je19) c. nar. S. *25 c. net. Eaton & M.

MAINTENON, Francoise d' Aubigné, *Marquise* de.
Dyson, C. C. Madame de Maintenon; her life and times. *$4 net. Lane.

"Maintop," pseud.
See Forbes, W. B.

Maiocchi, Rodolfo, D.D.
See Ffoulkes, Constance Jocelyn.

Maiollo, Vesconte de.
Vesconte de Maiollo conposuy hanc cartan, in Janua anno dny. 1527; die xx Decembris. [facsim.] '07, [1909.] (N) $35. Hispanic Soc.

Maire, F:
Colors, what they are and what to expect of them; ser. of pract. treatises on development of the color making industry. '10(D17) c. il. 16°, (Red book ser. of trade school manuals.) 60 c. Drake.
Exterior painting; ser. of pract, treatises. '10(D17) c. il. 16°, (Red book ser. of trade school manuals.) 60 c. Drake.
Interior painting; ser. of pract. treatises. '10(D17) c. il. 16°, (Red book ser. of trade school manuals.) 60 c. Drake.
Modern painter's cyclopedia. '10(Je11) c. il. D. $1.50. Drake.
Modern pigments and their vehicles: their properties and uses. '08(Ja18) 12°, $2. Wiley.

Mairet, Jeanne.
See Bigot, Marie Healy.

Maisies' music. Henius, J. $1.25 net. Schirmer.

Maison de Shine. Green, H. $1. B. W. Dodge.

Maisonneuve, Paul, M.D.
Experimental prophylaxis of syphilis; cont. the results of the experiments on the subject carried out at the Pasteur Institute, by Professors Metchnikoff and Roux; tr. and with an introd. by Fernand S. de Vertenil. '08(My16) c. 12°, *$1.50 net. Wood.

Maistre, Xavier de.
Les prisonniers du Caucase; ed., with introd., notes, vocab. and French and English exercises, by C: Wesley Robson. '08 (F1) c. S. (Internat. modern lang. ser.) 30 c. Ginn.

Maitland, E:
See Kingsford, Anna Bonus.

Maitland, F: W:
Constitutional history of England: a course of lectures. '08(Ag15) O. **$3.50 net. Putnam.

MAITLAND, Frederic William.
Fisher, H. A. L. Frederic William Maitland, Downing professor in the laws of England. $1.65 net. Putnam.
Smith, A. L. Frederic William Maitland. *85 c. net. Oxford Univ.

Maitland, J. W.
Equity; also, The forms of action at common law; two courses of lectures. '09 (O) 7+412 p. 8°, *$4 net. Putnam.

Maître (Le) des forges. *See* Ohnet, Georges.

Mâitres (Les) sonneurs. *See* Sand, G., *pseud.*

MAIZE.
Collins, G. N. Apogamy in the maize plants. (Add. Superintendent for price.) U. S., Supt. of Docs.
See also Corn.

Majestic art ser. 12 v. '10(D) ea., 25 c. Cupples & L.

MAJOLICA.
See Ceramics.

Major, C:, ["Edn. Caskoden."]
Gentle knight of Old Brandenburg. '09 (N6) il. D. $1.50. Macmillan.
Little king; story of the childhood of Louis XIV., King of France. '10(N19) c. il. D. $1.50. Macmillan.
Uncle Tom Andy Bill: story of bears and Indian treasure. '08(N7) il. 12°. $1.50. Macmillan.

Major, Mrs. Gertrude.
Revelation in the mountain. '08(D12) il. 12°, $1.50. Cochrane.

Make-believe boys. Dalrymple, J. †$1. Little, B. & Co.

"Make believe grammar." Buck, G. (Priv. pr.) Univ. of Chic.

Make Jesus king. Mahood, J: W. *25 c. net. Eaton & M.

Makers and defenders of America. Foote, A. E. 60 c. Am. Bk.

Makers of America; historical and biographical work. 3 v. '10(Ja22) c. il. (partly col.) pors. 8°, per set, $50. A. B. Caldwell.

Makers of American literature. Bowen, E. W. *$2.50 net. Neale.

Makers of British art. See Scribner's.

Makers of electricity. O'Reilly, M. F. *$2 net. Fordham Univ.

Makers of Hebrew books in Italy. Amram, D: W. *$3 net. J. H. Greenstone.

Makers of history. McKilliam, A. E. 60 c. net. Cassell.

Makers of Methodism. il. S. *25 c. net. Eaton & M.
—Tipple. Freeborn Garrettson.
—Upham. Thomas Coke.
—Watters. Peter Cartwright.
Makers of sorrow and makers of joy. Melegari, D. $1.25 net. Funk.
Making a soldier. Sharpe, A. C. 25 c. Acme Pub.
Making and unmaking of a dullard. Shields, T: E: *$1 net. Cath. Educ.
Making bread dear: controversy between "Wheelbarrow" and "Sympathizer" upon corners and the board of trade, with reference to the labor question. '10(My14) 12°, 50 c. Open Court.
Making faces. Williams, H. 50 c. net. McClurg.
Making good; stories of golf and other outdoor sports by F. H. Spearman, Van Tassel Sutphin, Poultney Bigelow and others. '10(My21) c. il. D. (Harper's athletic ser.) 60 c. Harper.
Making him buy. Lawrence, H: C. $2. Consol. Pub.
Making him pay. Lawrence, H: C. $2. Consol. Pub.
Making horticulture pay. Kains, M. G., *comp.* $1.50. Judd.
Making life worth while. Fisher, H. W. $1.20 net. Doubleday, P.
Making of a churchman. Shayler, E. V. 25 c. E. V. Shaylor.
Making of a king. Taylor, I. A. $3.50 net. Dodd.
Making of a millennium. Rosewater, F. $1; 30 c. Centry.
Making of a motor car. Leechman, D. 50 c. Spon.
Making of a sermon. Pierson, A. T. *$1.50 net. Gospel Pub.
Making of a state. Whitney, O. F. $1. Deseret News.
Making of a teacher. Colgrove, C. P: 75 c. C. P: Colgrove.
Making of a trade school. Woolman, *Mrs.* M. S. 50 c. net. Whitcomb.
Making of Bobby Burnit. Chester, G: R. †$1.50. Bobbs-M.
Making of Canada. Bradley, A. G. *$3 net. Dutton.
Making of Carlyle. Craig, R. S. *$4 net. Lane.
Making of Colorado. Parsons, E. 60 c. Flanagan.
Making of ice cream. Gratz, H. $5. H. Gratz.
Making of Ireland and its undoing. Green, *Mrs.* A. S. *$2.50 net. Macmillan.
Making of Jim O'Neill. F., M. J. 35 c. net. Herder.
Making of Mortlake. Copus, J: E. 85 c. Benziger.
Making of personality. Carman, W: B. $1.50; $3.50. L. C. Page.
Making of religion. Crowthers, S: M. *40 c. net. Am. Unitarian.
Making of religion. Lang, A. $2. Longmans.
Making of species. Dewar, D. *$2.50 net. Lane.
Making of the Balkan states. Murray, W: S. $1.50. Longmans.
Making of the English Bible. McComb, S: **$1 net. Moffat.
Making of the English constitution. White, A. B. **$2 net. Putnam.
Making of Wisconsin. Smith, C. J. 60 c. Flanagan.
Making the best of both worlds. Horton, R. F. 25 c. net. Union Press.
Making the best of our children. Allen, *Mrs.* M. W-. 1st and 2d ser. ea., *$1 net. McClurg.
Making the best of things ser. See Fallows, Alice Katharine.
Making the business pay. Bean, B. C. $1. Domestic Engineering.
Making the most of ourselves. Wilson, C. D. *$1 net. McClurg.
Making the up-grade. Ellett, F. G. $1. F. G. Ellett.
Making wireless outfits. Harrison, N. 50 c.; 25 c. Spon.
Makin's of a girl. Meguire, *Mrs.* E. E. $1.50. Badger.

Makower, Stanley Victor.
Perdita: romance in biography. '08(O10) il. O. *$4 special net. Appleton.

Makower, Wa.
Radioactive substances, their properties and their behavior. '08(D5) il. 12°. (International scientific ser.) *$1.75 special net. Appleton.

Malanotte, Mario, pseud.
See Gibson, P:

MALARIA.
Craig, C: F. Malarial fevers, hæmoglobinuric fever and blood protozoa of man. *$4.50 net. Wood.
Darling, S: T. Studies in relation to malaria. Gov. Pr. Off.
Deaderick, W: H. Pract. study of malaria. $4.50. Saunders.
Jones, W: H: S: Malaria: a neglected factor in the history of Greece and Rome. *80 c. net. Macmillan.
McCurry, J: H: Careful study and presentation of malaria. $1.50. J: H: McCurry.
Ross, R. Prevention of malaria. $5 net. Dutton.
See also India;—Mosquitoes.

MALAYSIA.
Daniel, J. F. Animal life of Malaysia. **$1.20 net. Bobbs-M.
See also Basketry.

Malcolm, C: Wesley.
Text-book on graphic statics. '09(D18) c. il. 8°, $3. M. C. Clark.

Malcolm, G:, and Maxwell, Aymer.
Grouse and grouse moors. '10(N19) col. il. 8°, (Color books; miscellaneous.) $2.75 net. Macmillan.

Malden, R. H.
Foreign missions; study of some principles and methods in the expansion of the Christian church. '10(Ap9) O. $1.25 net. Longmans.

Malefactors of great wealth. Benedict, R. A. $2. Am. Business.

Maler, Teobert.
Exploration in the Department of Peten, Guatemala and adjacent region. '09 (F13) c. il. map, 4°, (Memoirs of Peabody Museum.) pap., $4. Peabody Museum.

"Malet, Lucas," pseud.
See Harrison, *Mrs.* Mary St. Leger Kingsley.

Malkiel, Theresa Serber.
Diary of a shirtwaist striker; story of the shirtwaist makers' strike in New York. '10(N5) c. 8°, 50 c. Co-operative Press.

Malkmus, Bernard.
Outlines of clinical diagnostics of the internal diseases of domestic animals. 2d ed., rev. and enl.; tr. by D: S. White and Dr. Paul Fisher. '08(Ag) c. 11-244 p. il. 8°, $3. A. Eger.

Mall, Franklin Paine.
See Keibel, Franz.

Mallet, Bernard.
Thomas George, Earl of Northbrook, G. C. S. I.: a memoir. '08(N21) il pors. O. $5. Longmans.

Mallet's masterpiece. Peple, E: H: **75 c. net. Moffat.

Mallette, Gertrude Ethel.
Elsewhere land. '10(Ap16) 16°, 50 c. Univ. Bk. Store.

Malloch, P. D.
Life hist. of the salmon, sea trout and other fresh-water fish. '10(Ap9) 4°, $3.50 net. Macmillan.

Mallock, W: Hurrell.
Doctrine and doctrinal disruption: examination of the intellectual position of the Church of England. '08(O10) 12°, *$1.50 net. Macmillan.
Immortal soul: a novel. '08(N14) c. D. †$1.50. Harper.
Nation as a business firm; attempt to cut a path through jungle. '10(D10) tabs., O. $1 net. Macmillan.

Mallory, Fk. Burr, and Wright, Ja. Homer.
Pathological technique manual of pathological histology and bacteriology. 4th ed., rev. and enl. '08(D) c. 9-480 p. il. 8°, *$3 net. Saunders.

Mallory, Herbert S:
Tempered steel: a romance. '09(Je26) c. front. D. $1.50. Fenno.

Mallory, J: A., comp.
See United States. Compiled statutes.

Mally, F: W.
Panhandle and Llano Estacado of Texas. '10(D) 177 p. 8°, (Texas, Dept. of Agriculture bull.) Texas.

Malone, Paul Bernard.
West Point cadet. '08(O3) c. il. D. (West Point ser.) †$1.25. Penn Pub. Co.

Malone, P: Jehu.
Poems. '10(Ja15) c. por. D. *$1.25 net. Neale.

Malone cook book; comp. from receipts contributed by ladies of Malone and others, and published by the Woman's Aid Society of the First Congregational Church, Malone, N. Y. '08(O) c. 325-350 p. front. 12°, $1.25. Tuttle Co.

Malory, Sir T:
Boy's King Arthur; ed. for boys, with an introd. by Sidney Lanier. '08(D5) c. il. 8°, (Boys' lib of legend and chivalry.) $2. Scribner.
King Arthur stories from Malory; done from the text of Sir Thomas Malory's Morte d'Arthur by Lillian O. Stevens and E: Fk. Allen. '08(N14) c. il. D. (Riverside literature ser.) **40 c. net. Houghton M.
Le Morte d'Arthur. Limited ed. '09(O30) il. 4°, *$7.50 net. Dutton.
Le Morte d'Arthur. '08(D) 2 v., 16°, (Best books ser.) leath., ea., *$1 net. Dutton.
Selections from Le Morte d'Arthur; ed. by Douglas Swiggett. '09(S4) 24°, (Pocket Am. and Eng. classics.) *25 c. net. Macmillan.

MALORY, *Sir* Thomas.
Macleod, M., *comp.* Story of King Arthur, from Malory's Morte d'Arthur. 60 c. Dodge.

Malsbary, G: Elmer.
Diagnosis of syphilis. '11, [1910.] (O) 18+422 p. 4°, $5. Harvey Pub.
Bibliography (117 p.).

MALT.
LeClerc, J. A., *and* Wahl, R. Chemical studies of American barleys and malts. 20 c. U. S., Supt. of Docs.

MALTA.
Hardman, W: Hist. of Malta during the period of the French and British occupations. *$6.50 net. Longmans.
Ryan, F: W. Malta. $3 net. Macmillan.

Maltbie, Birdsey L.
Practical pharmacy for pharmacists and physicians; text book for students in medicine and pharmacy. [1910.] 7+434 p. 8°, $3. Physicians' Drug.

Maltbie, Milo R.
Report on the indeterminate franchise for public utilities, submitted Dec. 29, 1908. '09(Ap24) O. pap. (Add. author for price.) M. R. Maltby.

Maltby, Albert Elias.
American citizen in Pennsylvania; the government of the state and of the nation. '10(Mr12) c. front. D. $1. Am. Bk.

MALTING.
See Brewing.

Maltzahn, Kurt Leopold Wilhelm, Baron v.
Naval warfare: its historical development; tr. from the German by J: Combe Miller. '09(Ja9) D. 75 c. Longmans.

Malzbender, Mathew.
Praktischer ratgeber für conditoren, cakebäcker und brotbäcker. '10(Ag20) c. front. por. 8°, 2. Volksfreund Press.

Mamma Nelly and I. Gregory, L. F. $1.25. Stern.

MAMMALIA.
Davison, A. Mammalian anatomy, with special reference to the cat. *$1.50 net. Blakiston.
Gregory, W: K. Orders of mammals. $5. Am. Museum.

MAMMALIA.—*Continued.*
Heller, E., *and* Grinnell, J. Mammals of the 1908 Alexander Alaska expedition. $1. Univ. of Cal.
Hollister, N. Mammals collected by John Jay White in British East Africa. Smith. Inst.
Lyon, M. W., *and* Osgood, W. H. Catalogue of the type-specimens of mammals in the United States National Museum. U. S., Supt. of Docs.
Merriam, J: C. New mammalia from Rancho La Brea. 5 c. Univ. of Cal.
Miller, G. S., *jr.* Descriptions of two new genera and sixteen new species of mammals from the Philippine Islands. Gov. Pr. Off.
Osborn, H: F. Age of mammals in Europe, Asia and North America. $4.50 net. Macmillan.
Osgood, W. H. Diagnosis of new East African mammals.—Further new mammals from British East Africa.—Mammals from the coast and islands of northern South America. ea., 50 c. Field Museum.
Warren, E: R. Mammals of Colorado. $3.50 net Putnam.
Westell, W: P. Book on the animal kingdom; mammals. $4. Dutton.
See also Animals;—Domestic animals;—Embryology; — Man; — Paleontology; —Teeth;—Vertebrates;—Zoology;—*also* Alaska;—*also* names of animals.

Mammon in verseland. Nims, G: W. (Add. pubs. for price.) E. L. Grimes.

MAMMOTH CAVE, Ky.
Hovey, H. C. Hdbk. of the Mammoth Cave of Kentucky. 25 c. Morton.
Thompson, J: Mammoth Cave, Kentucky. 15 c. J: Thompson.

Mamreov, Anna F.
Day with the Good Shepherd. '10(N12) c. il. D. 50 c. net. Eaton & M.

MAN.
Atkinson, W: W. Human nature, its inner states and outer forms. $1. Progress Co.
Beary, H. R. Individual development of man; discussion of the influence of labor on the evolution of the individual. $1. Hartman Pub.
Conder, C. R. Rise of man. *$3 net. Dutton.
Denifle, H: Humanity; its destiny and the means to attain it. *$1.25 net. Pustet.
Halfyard, S: F. Spiritual basis of man and nature. $1. Jennings.
Heineman, T. W: Physical basis of civilization. $1.25. Forbes.
Hopf, L. Human species. *$3 net. Longmans.
Jastro, J. Qualities of men. $1 net. Houghton M.
McAfee, C. B. Worth of a man. 30 c. Northfield Press.
Osborn, S. O. Nature and man. 75 c. S. O. Osborn.
Rommel, J: Natural philosophy. $1. Cataract.
Tyler, J: M. Man in the light of evolution. **$1.25 net. Appleton.

MAN.—*Continued.*
Wheelock, E. M. Proteus, a rhapsody on man. $1. Open Court.
See also Anatomy;—Archæology;—Biology;—Ethics; — Ethnology; — Etiquette; — Eugenics; — Evolution;—Family;—Folk-lore; — Future life; — Heredity;—History; — Hygiene;—Longevity; —Manners and customs;—Paleontology;—Philosophy;—Phrenology; — Physiology;—Population;—Psychology;—Religion; — Salvation;—Sex;—Social science;—Woman;—Young men.

Man and his mate. Jennings, N. I., *comp.* 50 c.; $1.50. Lone Star.
Man and his neighbors. Fuller, A. F. 35 c. Solar Lit.
Man and master. Van Deventer, E. M. $1; 25 c. Laird.
Man and the Bible. Picton, J. A. **$2 net. Holt.
Man and the dragon. Otis, A. $1.50. Little, B. & Co.
Man-eaters of Tsavo. Patterson, J: H: *$2 net. Macmillan.
Man forbid (The). Davidson, J. $1.25 net. Ball Pub.
Man from Brodney's. McCutcheon, G: B. †$1.50. Dodd.
Man from home. Tarkington, N. B. $1.25. Harper.
Man from Mars. Dowding, H: W. $1.50. Cochrane.
Man from the moon. Carmichael, P. †$1.50. Stokes.
Man (The) from the moon; or, the reign of self; story in rhyme for good old boys and girls, by P. Q. '10(Mr12) c. il. 12°, 75 c. Conkey.
Man higher up. Miller, H: R. $1.50. Bobbs-M.
Man in lower ten. Rinehart, *Mrs.* M. R. †$1.50. Bobbs-M.
Man in many lands. Lyde, L. W. 65 c. net. Macmillan.
Man in the basement. Rosenkrantz, *Baron* P. A. V. 75 c. Cupples & L.
Man in the corner. Orczy, E. M. R. M. J. B., *Baroness.* †$1.50. Dodd.
Man in the iron mask. Dumas, A. 50 c. Hurst.
Man in the mirror. Aitken, R. $1.50. W. J. Watt.
Man in the street. Mackey, W. M. $1.50 net. Doran.
Man in the tower. Holland, R. S. †$1.50. Lippincott.
Man next door. Morris, E. B. 15 c. Penn Pub. Co.
Man of destiny. Frost, T: G. $1.50. Gramercy.
Man of destiny. Staples, E. L. $1; $2; 75 c. Lincoln.
Man of Galilee. Wendling, G: R. *$3 net; *$1 net. Olcott.
Man of genius. Willcocks, M. P. †$1.50. Lane.
Man of Sorrows. Hubbard, E. $2. Roycrofters.
Man of two countries. Harriman, *Mrs.* A. $1.50. A. Harriman.
Man of valor. Spaulding, A. W. 75 c. Review and Herald Pub.
Man of yesterday. Kinkaid, *Mrs.* M. H. M. †$1.50. Stokes.

Man outside. Martyn, W. †$1.50. Dodd.
Man remade. Roman, C: $1. Reilly & B.
Man Shakespeare and his tragic life story. Harris, F. *$2.50 net. M. Kennerley.
Man-song. Neihart, J: G. *$1 net. M. Kennerley.
Man who ended war. Godfrey, H. †$1.50. Little, B. & Co.
Man who was dead. Marchmont, A. W. †$1.50. Stokes.
Man who was Thursday. Chesterton, G. K. †$1.50. Dodd.
Man without a county. *See* Hale, E: Everett.
Man without a head. De Saix, T. **$1.50 net. Moffat.
Man without a shadow. Cabot, O. C. †$1.50. Appleton.
Man without principle. Broyles, L. E. $1.08. Hocking.
Man, woman, know thyself! Bartholomew, E. J. $2. E. J. Bartholomew.

MANABI, Ecuador.
Saville, M. H. Antiquities of Manabi. $25. F. P. Harper.

Management and feeding of cattle. Shaw, T: *$2 net. Judd.
Management of a city school. Perry, A. C., *jr.* *$1.25 net. Macmillan.
Management of dynamos. Lummis-Paterson, G. W. $1.50. Henley.
Management of private affairs. King, J. 85 c. Oxford Univ.

Manchester, Arth. Livingston.
Twelve lessons in the fundamentals of voice production. '08(O3) c. il. O. (Music students' lib.) $1. Ditson.

MANDALAY, Burma.
See Burma.

Mandamet der keyserlijcker maiesteit; vuytghegeue int Iaer xlvi; met Dintitulatie ende declaratie vande gereprobeerde boecken, gheschiet bijden Doctoren inde Faculteyte van Theologie in Duniuersiteyt van Loeuen; Duer dordonnantie ende beuel der seluer K. M. Ghedruckt Te Loeuen by Seruaes van Sassen. [facsim.]. '96, [1909.] (N) no paging, $5.50. (100 copies.) Hispanic Soc.

MANDAN INDIANS.
See Indians.

MANET, Edouard.
Duret, T. Manet and the French impressionists. *$3.75 net. Lippincott.

MANGANESE.
Harder, E. C. Manganese deposits of the United States with sections on foreign deposits. Gov. Pr. Off.
Watson, T: L. Preliminary rept. on manganese deposits of Georgia. 12 c. S: W. McCallie.

Mangasarian, Mangasar M.
Bryan on religion; del. before the Independent Religious Society, Orchestra Hall, Chicago. '08(D) 21 p. 8°, pap., 10 c. Independent Religious.
Lectures. '10(Ap) $1.50. Independent Religious.
New catechism. 5th ed., rev. and enl. '10(Ap) por. $1. Independent Religious.

Mangasarian, Mangasar M.—*Continued.*
Pearls; brave thoughts from brave minds. New ed. '10(Ap) 25 c.; limp leath., $1. Independent Religious.
Religion of Washington, Jefferson and Franklin; lecture del. before the Independent Religious Society, Orchestra Hall, Chicago. '07, [1910.] (Ap) 23 p. 8°, pap., 10 c. Independent Religious.
Story of my mind; or, how I became a rationalist. [1910.] (Ap) c. '09 125 p. 16°, 50 c. Independent Religious.
Truth about Jesus: is he a myth? '09 (Ap10) c. il. 8°, $1; pap., 50 c. Independent Religious.
What was the religion of Shakespeare?; lecture del. before the Independent Religious Society, Orchestra Hall, Chicago. '07, [1910.] (Ap) 22 p. 8°, pap., 10 c. Independent Religious.

—, and Crapsey, Algernon Sidney, D.D.
Mangasarian-Crapsey debate: Resolved that the Jesus of the New Testament is an historical personage. Affirmative, Algernon Sidney Crapsey, D.D. Negative, Mangasar M. Mangasarian. '08(My9) c. 16°. (Add. pub. for price.) T. Brentano.

MANGOES.
See Fruit.

Mangold, G: B:
Child problems. '10(N5) c. D. (Citizens' lib. of economics, politics and sociology.) $1.25 net. Macmillan.
Labor arguments in the American protective tariff discussion. '09(F6) O. (Univ. of Wis. bull.; Economics and political science ser.) pap., 35 c. Univ. of Wis.

Manguse, W: P., comp.
See Schultze, Arth., *comp.*

MANHATTAN.
See New York City.

Manhattan; [ode.] Clarke, J. I. C. $2. Roycrofters.
Manhattan; [poems.] Towne, C: H. *$1 net. M. Kennerley.
Manhattan classics. S. 25 c.; pap., 10 c. Manhattan Bk.
—Coleridge. Rime of the ancient mariner.
Manhattan English classics. S. Manhattan Bk.
—Shakespeare. Julius Cæsar. 10 c.

MANHATTAN TRADE SCHOOL.
See Technical education.

MANHATTANVILLE.
See New York City.

Manhood. Smith, O. E. $4. Sentinel Pr.
Manifests of the communist party. Marx, K. 50 c. Kerr.
Manikin chart of the human system. '08 (Ap25) O. $1.50. Funk.

MANILA, P. I.
O'Connell, D. Manila, the pearl of the Orient. (Add. pubs. for price.) Manila Merchants.

MANITOBA, Canada.
Bryce, G: Romantic settlement of Lord Selkirk's colonists [pioneers of Manitoba.] $1.50 net. Barse & H.
Seton, E. T. Life-histories of northern animals; account of the mammals of Manitoba. *$18 net. Scribner.

Manitou cliff dwellers' ruins: historical facts of the ancient cliff dwellers and a glimpse of the ruins and cañon at Manitou. '08 (Mr14) c. il. oblong D. pap., 25 c. Manitou.

MANLEY, *Captain* John.
Peabody, R. E. Naval career of Captain John Manley of Marblehead. (Not for sale.) Essex Inst.

Manley, W. D., comp. and ed.
Georgia country banker. '08(Jl) c. 2-75 p. 12°, $1.25. Mutual Pub. Co.

Manly, J: Matthews.
See Bailey, Eliza R.
—, comp. and ed. English prose, (1137-1890.) '09(Jl3) c. O. $1.50. Ginn.

Mann, C: Riborg, and Twiss, G: Ransom.
Physics. Rev. ed. '10(O15) c. D. figs. $1.25. Scott, F. & Co.

Mann, Chester.
Jester men. '09, [1910.] (Mr) c. 292 p. il. 12°, $1.50. Weed-Parsons.

Mann, Franklin Weston.
The bullet's flight from powder to target; the internal and external ballistics of small arms; study of rifle shooting with the personal element excluded, disclosing the cause of the error at target. '09(N) c. 8+384 p. il. por. 8°, $4. Munn.

MANN, Horace.
Hubbell, G: A. Horace Mann, educator, patriot and reformer. $1.50. Fell.

Mann, Rev. Horace K.
Lives of the Popes in the early Middle Ages. v. 2, Popes during the Carolingian Empire: Leo III. to Formosus (795-853); v. 3, Popes during the Carolingian Empire (858-891); v. 4, Popes in the days of feudal anarchy, Formosus to Damascus II. (891-999); v. 5, Popes in the days of feudal anarchy (999-1048). [1910.] (Jl) il. map, plan. 8°, ea., $3 net. Herder.

Mann, J. Dixon, M.D.
Physiology and pathology of the urine, with methods for its examination. New ed., rev. and enl. '09, [1910.] (F) il. 8°, *$3.25 net. Lippincott.

Mann, J. S., ed.
See Traill, H: D., *ed.*

Mann, Mina.
See Avery-Stuttle, *Mrs.* Lilla Dale.

Mann, Newton M.
Import and outlook of socialism. '10(D24) c. O. $1.50 net. J. H. West

Mannaseh. Cozart, W. F. 25 c. W. F. Cozart.

MANNERS AND CUSTOMS.
Fischel, O., *and* Von Boehm, M. Modes and manners of the XIXth century. 3 v. **$7 net. Dutton.
Knowlson, T: S. Origins of popular superstitions and customs. $1.75 net. Pott.
Morris, C: Home life in all lands; bk. 2, Manners and customs of uncivilized people. **$1 net. Lippincott.
See also Archæology;—Etiquette; — Folk-lore; — Toasts.

Manners for the metropolis. Crowninshield, F. W. **$1 net. Appleton.

Mannheim and multiplex slide rules. Rosenthal, L. W. 50 c. E: Dietzgen.

Mannierre, L:
Business law: ready reference desk manual. '08(Jl) 169 p. 12°. (Not for sale.) Am. Business Man.

Manning, Anne, [later Mrs. Rathbone.]
Household of Sir T: More. '08(N21) 16°, (Best books ser.) leath., *$1 net. Dutton.
Mary Powell and Deborah's diary. '08 (S19) 16°, (Everyman's lib.) *35 c. net; leath., *70 c. net. Dutton.

Manning, Frederic.
Scenes and portraits. '09, [1910.] (F) *$1.75 net. Putnam.

Manning, Gloria.
Improper Prue. '09(Mr) il. $1.50. B. W. Dodge.

MANNING, *Cardinal* Henry Edward.
Taylor, I. A. Cardinal Democrat: Henry Edward Manning. *$1.25 net. Herder.

Manning, H: Parker, ed.
Fourth dimension simply explained; collection of essays selected from those submitted in the *Scientific American's* prize competition; with introd. and editorial notes. '10(Mr5) c. il. 8°, *$1.50 net. Munn.

Mannix, Mary Ellen.
Cupa revisited. '09(Ap3) c. front. S. 45 c. Benziger.
See also Nixon-Roulet, Mary F.

Manns, W. H.
Erecting and operating engineer's guide; giving proper methods of receiving, checking, unloading, distribution of parts, erection of machines, compression sides, [etc.;] also testing of apparatus and general operation of an ice-making or refrigerating plant as manufactured by Frick Co., Waynesboro, Pa., which will apply to any modern apparatus of a similar character. '10(Jl16) c. tabs., 12°, $1. W. H. Manns.

Manor houses of England. Ditchfield, P. H. $3 net. Scribner.

Manors of Virginia in Colonial times. Sale, E. T. *$5 net. Lippincott.

Manquat, Alfr.
Principles of therapeutics; tr. by M. Simbad Gabriel. '10(D) c. 6+298 p. 8°, $3. Appleton.

Manrrique, Jorge.
Jorge Manrrique; coplas por la muerte de su padre; primera edición crítica publícala R. Foulché-Delbosc. '07, [1909.] (N) 8+43 p. (Bibliotheca hispanica.) $1. Hispanic Soc.

Man's faith. Grenfell, W. T. *50 c. net. Pilgrim Press.

Man's great charter. Goggin, T. E. *$1.75 net. Gorham.

Man's helpers. Grenfell, *Sir* W. T. 50 c. net. Pilgrim Press.

Man's incarnation. McKennan, F. B. $1. McKennan.

Man's influence with God. Wilt, D. W. 75 c. D. W. Wilt.

Man's man. Hay, I., *pseud.* $1.20 net. Houghton M.

Man's need of God. Smith, D: $1.50 net. Doran.

Man's partnership with Divine Providence. Telford, J: *$1.25 net. Eaton & M.

Mansfield, Howard.
Descriptive catalogue of the etchings and dry-points of James Abbott McNeill Whistler. '09(Je12) c. por. 4°. (Add. pubs. for price.) Caxton Club.

Mansfield, Milburg Francisco.
See Miltoun, Fs., *pseud.*

Mansfield, Mrs. Milburg Francisco.
See McManus, Blanche.

MANSFIELD, Richard.
Wilstach, P. Richard Mansfield. **$3.50 net. Scribner.
Winter, W: Life and art of Richard Mansfield. **$6 net. Moffat.

Mansfield College essays; testimonial volume presented to Principal Fairbairn upon the occasion of his 70th birthday. '09(D) 8°, *$3 net. Doran.

Mansfield Park. *See* Austen, Jane.

Mansion, Jean Edmond, comp.
Easy French selections for sight translation. '09(N13) S. (Heath's modern language ser.) pap., 15 c. Heath.

Manson, Sir Patrick.
Tropical diseases; manual of the diseases of warm climates. 4th ed., thoroughly rev. and enl. '09, [1910.] (Ap) 20+876 p. il. 12°, $4.50 net. Wood.

MANTELS.
Modern mantels. $1. Knoxville Furniture.

Manthey-Zorn, Carl.
See Zorn, Carl Manthey-.

Mantzius, Karl.
History of theatrical art in ancient and modern times; author. tr. by Louise von Cossel. In 5 v. v. 4, 5. '09(Ap24) il. pors. O. ea., *$3.50 net. Lippincott.

Manual art with the scissors. Moran, M. L. 75 c. M. Bradley.

Manual of otology. Bacon, G. *$2.25 net. Lea.

Manual of spiritual fortification. Willcox, *Mrs.* L. C., *comp.* $1.25 net. Harper.

Manual of statistics: Stock Exchange handbook, 1909; 31st annual issue; railroad securities, industrial securities, government securities, Stock Exchange quotations, mining, grain and provisions, cotton, money, bank and trust companies. '09(Je26); 1910, 32d annual issue. '10(Jl2) maps, O. ea., $5. Manual of Statistics.

Manual of style; compilation of the typographical rules in force at the University of Chicago Press, with specimens of types in use. '10(Ap30) D. pap., 75 c. net. Univ. of Chic.

MANUAL TRAINING.
Burnham, F. L. Supervision and teaching of the manual arts in the high school. gratis. G: H. Martin.
Eppendorff, L. Handwork construction. $1.58. L. Eppendorff.
Graves, E. M. Year of primary occupation work. 50 c. Educ. Pub.
Hammock, C. S. *and* A. G. Manual arts for elem. schools. vs. 1-3, ea., per doz., $1.50; vs. 4-8, ea., per doz., $2.25.—Manual arts for elem. schools; drawing, design, construction, shop work. per doz., $3.—Teachers' manual, to accompany The manual arts for elem. schools. gratis. Heath.

MANUAL TRAINING.—*Continued.*
Henderson, A. W., *and* Palen, H. O. What and how: systematized course of hand work for primary grades. $2. M. Bradley.
Jensen, G: H. Elem. industrial work. $1. G: H. Jensen.
Johnson, A. Education by doing; occupations and busy work for primary classes. 50 c. net. Barnes.
Kent, E. B. Constructive interests of children. 50 c. Teachers' Coll.
Littlefield, M. S. Hand-work in the Sunday-school. *$1 net. S. S. Times.
McGaw, V. Construction work for rural and elementary schools. 60 c. Flanagan.
McGlauflin, I. Handicraft for girls. $1. Manual Arts.
Mount, C. S. Seat work and sense training. 50 c. Educ. Pub.
Rathman, C. G. Mission of manual training. Manual Training Sch.
Rouillion, L: Economics of manual training. $2. Van Nostrand.
Row, R. K. Educational meaning of manual arts and industries. $1.25. Row, P., & Co.
Seaton, G: A. Selected shop problems. 75 c. Manual Arts.
Sexton, L., *comp.* Manual work for use in Sunday schools. 75 c. Young Churchman.
Walker, M. C. Tales come true. $1.25 net. Baker & T.
See also Basketry; — Boys; — Carpentry;—Furniture; — Kindergarten; — Kites; — Knitting;—Modelling; — Needlework; — Paper work; — Sloyd;—Technical education;—Turning;—Useful arts;—Wood-carving;—Woodwork.

Manual training reprints. il. O. pap., 20 c. Manual Arts.
—Johnson. Coping saw work.
—Miller. Construction and flying of kites.
—Seaton. Selected shop problems.

Manuals for the people. Anchor.
—Stansfield. Symbolism. 10 c.

Manucci Niccolao.
Storia do Mogor; or, Mogul India, 1653-1708; tr., with introd. and notes, by W: Irvine. v. 3. '08(My9); v. 4. '09(F13) 8°, (Indian texts ser.) ea., *$3.50 net. Dutton.

Manuel, Earle Vincent.
See Levi, L: Emanuel.

Manuel Alanus. Wyneken, L. E. $2. Cochrane.

Manuel in Mexico. McDonald, *Mrs.* E. A. B. 60 c. Little, B. & Co.

Manufacture of explosives. Guttmann, O. *$1.10 net. Macmillan.

Manufacture of leather. Bennett, H. G. $4.50 net. Van Nostrand.

Manufacture of rubber goods Heil, A. *$3.50 net. Lippincott.

MANUFACTURES.
Gibson, C: R. Romance of modern manufacture. *$1.50 net. Lippincott.
Putney, A. H., *and others.* Manufactures; mining, irrigation, real estate. $4. Cree.
Scientific American index of manufactures: "who's who" among American manufacturers. (Add. pubs. for price.) Scientific American.

MANUFACTURES.—*Continued.*
Spon's workshop receipts for manufacturers. v. 2, 3, Mechanics and others. ea., $1.50 net. Spon.
See also Commerce;—Corporations;—Knitting;—Textile fabrics;—Useful arts;—*also* Kansas.
MANURES.
See Fertilizers.
MANUSCRIPTS.
Book of Fate; now tr. into English from the German of an ancient Egyptian ms. found in 1801 in one of the royal tombs near Mount Libysus in upper Egypt. $1; 50 c. Anglo-Am. Authors.
Bradley, J: W. Illuminated manuscripts. *$1 net. McClurg.
Chevalerie Vivien; facsimile phototypes of the Sancti Bertini manuscript of the Bibliothèque Municipale of Boulogne-sur-mer. $1.25. Univ. of Mo.
Deissmann, G. A. Light from the ancient East; New Testament and new and recently discovered manuscripts of the Græco-Roman world. $4 net. Doran.
Gregory, C. R. Das Freer logion. 65 c. Lemcke.
Hellenica Oxyrhynchia cum Theopompi et Cratippi fragmentis. $1.10. Oxford Univ.
International manuscripts. $1.50 net. Brentano's.
Keidel, G: C: Hist. of French fable manuscripts. $1. Modern Lang. Assoc.
Keith, A. B., *ed.* Aitareya Aranyaka. $7.75. Oxford Univ.
Rawlinson, B. 502; collection of pieces in prose and verse in the Irish language; compiled during the eleventh and twelfth centuries. $40.50. Oxford Univ.
See also Arabic literature;—French and Indian War;—Lettering;—Papyri.
Many gods. Rice, C. Y. **$1.25 net. Doubleday, P.
Many inventions. *See* Kipling, Rudyard.
Many kingdoms. Jordon, E. G. †$1.50. Harper.
Map maneuvers. Sayre, F. 60 c.; 75 c. Staff Coll.
Mapes, Victor.
The gilded way; novel. '10(D3) c. D. $1.50. Neale.
Partners three. '09(Ap10) c. D. †$1.25. Stokes.
Maple, Col. Dick, pseud.
See McCallen, Rob. Seth.
MAPLE SYRUP.
Bryan, A. H. Methods for the analysis of maple products and the detection of adulterants. 5 c. U. S., Supt. of Docs.
MAPLES.
Mosher, E. R. Studies of our oaks and maples. $2. Bardeen.
MAPS.
Stevenson, E: L. Early Spanish cartography of the New World. 50 c. Davis Press.
See also Atlases;—Automobiles;—Military art and science;—Surveying;—Topographical drawings;—*also* names of places.
Maps of old London: atlas, with descriptions by Geraldine Edith Mitton. '08(S19) 4°, *$1.75 net. Macmillan.
Mar, Graham.
Little tin soldier. '10(D31) il. 12°, $1. Lippincott.

Marathon running. Sullivan, J. E: 10 c. Am. Sports.
Marble, T: Littlefield.
The Hessian: a revolutionary drama. '08 (N7) c. D. pap., 15 c. Penn Pub. Co.
MARBLE.
Renwick, W. G. Marble and marble working. *$5 net. Van Nostrand.
Marble faun. *See* Hawthorne, Nathaniel.
MARBLES.
See Georgia.
Marbot, Jean Baptiste Marcellin de, Baron.
Memoirs of Baron de Marbot, late lieutenant-general in the French army; tr. from the French by Arth. J: Butler. '08(Ja4) 2 v., por. D. (Silver lib.) $2.50. Longmans.
Marburg, Thdr.
Do we want an asset currency? '08(Je6) T. pap., 10 c. Dulany.
Panic and the present depression: address del. before the Am. Academy of Political and Social Science, Philadelphia, Apr. 10, 1908. '08(D) 23 p. 16°. (Add. pubs. for price.) Am. Acad. Pol. Sci.
Marbut, Curtis Fletcher.
Geology of Morgan Co., [Mo.] '08, [1909.] (Mr) 14+97 p. il. fold. map, 4°. (Missouri Bureau of Geology and Mines, repts.) pap., 20 c. Missouri Bu. Geol.
Marcasson, I: F:
See Turnour, Jules.
March, Fs. A.
Thesaurus dict. of the Eng. language. '02, [1909.] (D) il. 4°. (Add. pubs. for price.) Stanley & W.
March, G: Otis, comp., ["Archibald Humboldt."]
School plays for festive days. [1910.] (F) c. '09. 144 p. 12°, 30 c. March.
March, J: Lewis.
Theory of mind. '08(D19) c. O. **$2 net. Scribner.
March of Portola. Eldredge, Z. S. 50 c. Cal. Promotion Co.
March of the intellect. Brooks, T. J. $1. B'way Pub.
Marchand, C: M.
Elem. course in practical French for beginners; rational method with mutual aids. '08(Ap11) c. 12°, **60 c. net. Brentano's.
Marchant, Arth. W:
Phrasing, as applied to pianoforte playing. '09(Ap3) c. 12°, 40 c. Ditson.
Marching with Morgan. Lane, J: V. $1.50. L. C. Page.
Marchmont, Arth. Williams.
An imperial marriage. '10(Je4) c. il. 12°, $1.20 net. Dodge.
Case of Lady Broadstone. '09(Ja30) c. front. D. $1.50. Empire Bk.
Man who was dead. '08(F22) c. il. D. †$1.50. Stokes.
My lost self. '08(Ap25) c. il. 12°, 75 c. Cupples & L.
Mystery of Mortimer Strange. '08(F1) c. D. (Popular copyright fiction.) 75 c. Rand, McN. & Co.
Sir Jaffray's wife. '08(F1) c. D. (Popular copyright fiction.) 75 c. Rand, McN. & Co.

Marcia and the major. Harbour, J. L. **40 c. net. Crowell.
Marcia Schuyler. Lutz, *Mrs.* G. L. H.- †$1.50. Lippincott.
Marcin, Max.
Are you my wife? '10(D3) c. D. $1.25 net. Moffat.
Marcus Aurelius.
See Antoninus, Marcus Aurelius.
Marcus and Miriam. **Springer, *Mrs.* R. R.** 25 c. Cook.
Marcy, Mrs. Mary Edna Tobias.
Out of the dump: [story of the poor of Chicago.] '09(Ja16) il. 12°, 50 c. Kerr.
Marczali, Henry.
See Temperley, Harold W: Vazeille.
Marden, Orison Swett.
Be good to yourself. '10(D3) c. por. D. $1 net. Crowell.
Getting on. '10(D3) c. por. D. $1 net. Crowell.
He can who thinks he can, and other papers on success. '08(O31) c. D. *$1 net. Crowell.
Miracle of right thought. '10(D24) c. D. $1 net. Crowell.
Not the salary but the opportunity. '09 (My15) c. D. pap., *10 c. net. Crowell.
Peace, power and plenty. '09(Ja23) c. por. D. **$1 net. Crowell.
Why grow old? '09(S18) c. D. (What is worth while ser.) leatherette, **30 c. net. Crowell.
—, and Connolly, Margaret.
Do it to a finish. '10(Ja15) c. D. (What is worth while ser.) leatherette, *30 c. net. Crowell.
Marden, Philip Sanford.
Travels in Spain. '09(N20) c. il. O. **$3 net, boxed. Houghton M.
Mare (La) au diable. Sand, G:, *pseud.* *$1.40 net Macmillan.
Marett, R. R.
Birth of humility; inaugural lecture del. before the University of Oxford 27 October, 1910. '10(D24) O. pap., 35 c. Oxford Univ.
—, ed. Anthropology and the classics: six lectures del. before the University of Oxford, by Arth. J: Evans, And. Lang, Gilbert Murray, Fk. Byron Jevons, J: Linton Myres, W: Warde Fowler. '08(D19) figs. O. $2. Oxford Univ.
MARGARET OF AUSTRIA, *Regent of the Netherlands.*
Tremayne, *Mrs.* E. E. First governess of the Netherlands, Margaret of Austria. *$3 net. Putnam.
Margaret's influence. Geiermann, P: $1. Herder.
Margarita's soul. Bacon, *Mrs.* J. D. D. †$1.50. Lane.
Margery Redford and her friends. Spielmann, *Mrs.* M. H. $1.50. Stokes.
Margetson, G: Reginald.
Songs of life. '10(Jl16) c. 12°, $1. Sherman, F.
Margolis, Max L.
Manual of the Aramaic language of the Babylonian Talmud; grammar, chrestomathy and glossaries. '10(Ap30) D. $3 net. Stechert.
Margraff, Anthony W:
International exchange, its terms, parts, operations and scope: pract. work on the foreign banking department. 3d ed. '08 (Ag1) c. por. Q. $5. Int. Exchange.
Marguerite de Valois. *See* Dumas, Alexandre.
MARIA CHRISTINA, *Queen Regent of Spain.*
Auvergne, E. B. d'. Queen at bay. $5 net. Lane.
MARIA CORONEL DE JESUS DE AGREDA.
Pandolfi, U., *tr.* Life of Venerable Sister Mary of Jesus, D. Agreda, Poor Clare nun. 50 c. Keller-C.
MARIA LUISA, *Infanta of Spain.*
Bearne, *Mrs.* C. M. C. Royal quartette: [Maria Luisa of Spain, Marie Adelaide of Burgundy, Marie Adelaide of France, Marie Amelie Therese of Naples.] *$3 net. Brentano's.
Maria Stuart. *See* Schiller, Johann Christoph Friedrich v.
Mariage (Un) d' amour. Halévy, L. 25 c. Heath.
MARIE ADELAIDE, *Duchess of Burgundy.*
Bearne, *Mrs.* C. M. C. Royal quartette: [Maria Luisa of Spain, Marie Adelaide of Burgundy, Marie Adelaide of France Marie Amelie Therese of Naples.] *$3 net. Brentano's.
MARIE ADELAIDE, *of France.*
Bearne, *Mrs.* C. M. C. Royal quartette: [Maria Luisa of Spain, Marie Adelaide of Burgundy, Marie Adelaide of France, Marie Amelie Therese of Naples.] *$3 net. Brentano's.
MARIE AMELIE THERESE, *of Naples.*
Bearne, *Mrs.* C. M. C. Royal quartette: [Maria Luisa of Spain, Marie Adelaide of Burgundy, Marie Adelaide of France, Marie Amelie Therese of Naples] *$3 net. Brentano's.
MARIE AMELIE, *Queen of France.*
Dyson, C. C. Life of Marie Amélie, last queen of the French, 1782-1866. $3.50 special net. Appleton.
Küchler, C. G. F. Queen Maria Sophia of Naples. 50 c. net. McClurg.
MARIE ANTOINETTE, *Queen of France.*
Belloc, J. H. P. Marie Antoinette. **$2.75 net. Doubleday, P.
Haggard, A. C: P. Louis XVI. and Marie Antoinette. *$6 special net. Appleton.
Lenk, H. v. Marie Antoniette's youth. *60 c. net. McClurg.
***See also* Louis XVI.**
MARIE DE MEDICIS, *Queen of France.*
Batiffol, L. Marie de Medicis and the French court. *$2 net. Scribner.
MARIE LOUISE, *Empress of France.*
Billard, M. Marriage ventures of Marie Louise. $3.50 net. Pott.
Marie, Armand.
Pellagra; with a preface by Prof. Lombroso; authorized tr. from the French by C. H. Lavinder, M.D., and J. W. Babcock, M.D. '09(N) $2.50. State Co.
Marie of Arcady. Lancaster, F. H. †$1.25. Small.
Marignan. *See* Sismondi, Jean Charles Léonard de.
Marigold garden. *See* Greenaway, K.

Marigold's winter. Foster, E. F. †$1.25. Estes.

MARINE ALGAE.
See **Seaweeds.**

MARINE BIOLOGICAL ASSOCIATION OF SAN DIEGO.
Ritter, W: E. Marine Biological Station of San Diego. Marine Biol.
See also **Hydrography.**

MARINE BIOLOGY.
See Biology;—Marine zoology.

MARINE ENGINEERING.
Dinger, H: C. Hdbk. for the care and operation of naval machinery. *$2 net. Van Nostrand.
Linch, C: S. Marine engine indicating. $2. Am. Steam Gauge.
McKnight, J. D. Design of marine multi-annular boilers. $1.50. Van Nostrand.
Peabody, C. H. Computations for marine engines. (For private distribution.) C. H. Peabody.
Reed's engineers' hdbk. to examinations for marine engineers. *$5 net.—Reed's useful hints to sea going engineers. $1.50. Spon.
Sennett, R:, *and* Oram, H: J. Marine steam engine. $6. Longmans.
Sothern, J. W. Verbal notes and sketches for marine engineers. *$2.60 net. Macmillan.
Tompkins, A. E. Marine engineering: (a text-book.) *$4.50 net. Macmillan.
Ware, B. R., *jr.* Handy book for the aid and instruction of the enlisted men in the Engineer Dept., U. S. N. 50 c. U. S. Naval Inst.
See also Boilers:—Naval art and science;—Ships and shipbuilding;—Submarines;—Turbines.

MARINE INSURANCE.
See **Insurance.**

MARINE LAW.
See **Admiralty.**

Marine propellers. Barnaby, S. W. $4.50. Spon.

Marine steam engine. Sennett, R. $6. Longmans.

Marine steam turbine. Sothern, J. W. *$5 net. Van Nostrand.

MARINE SURVEYING.
See **Nautical surveying.**

MARINE ZOOLOGY.
Carnegie Institution of Washington. Papers from the Tortugas Laboratory. v. 1, 2, 4, [Marine biology.] v. 1, $2; v. 2, $3; v. 4, $4. Carnegie.
Duncan, F. M. Denizens of the deep. *$1.75 net. Cassell.
Johnson, M. E. Quantitative study of the development of the salpa chain in *salpa fusiformis runcinata.* 35 c. Univ. of Cal.
Johnstone, J. Conditions of life in the sea. $3. Putnam.
Ritter, W: E. Halocynthia Johnsoni n. sp. 50 c. Univ. of Cal.
Torrey, H. B., *and* Kleeberger, F. L. Three specimens of cerianthus [anemone] from Southern California. 10 c. Univ. of Cal.
See also **Amphibia;—Crustaceans;—Echinoderms;—Fish;—Jellyfish;—Mollusks.**

Marinoni, Antonio, comp. and ed.
Italian reader. '09(Ap3) 12°, 90 c.; pap., 75 c. W: R. Jenkins.

Mario, Auguste.
Easy French cookery. '09, [1910.] (Ja) il. **60 c. net. Cassell.

Mario, Signora Jessie White.
Birth of modern Italy; posthumous papers; ed., with introd., notes and epilogue, by the Duke Litta Visconti-Arene. '09(D11) il. pors. O. *$3.50 net. Scribner.

Marion. Haseldon, F. T. $1. B'way Pub.

MARION COUNTY, Ill.
Brinkerhoff, J. Hist. of Marion Co., Ill. B. F. Bower.

"Marion Harland," pseud.
See Terhune, *Mrs.* Mary Virginia Hawes.

Mariposa (La) blanca. Selgas y Carrasco, J. 60 c. Holt.

Mariposa grove of big trees. Leitch, B. M. 50 c. B. M. Leitch.

Marique, Pierre Joseph, and Gilson, H: Brockway.
Exercises in French composition; introd. to original work in composition. '09 (Ja23) c. S. (Internat. modern lang. ser.) 40 c. Ginn.

Maris, Clarence.
Dangers and chemistry of fire; for grammar schools '08, [1909.] (Jl) 8°. (Add. pubs. for price.) Ohio State Fire Marshal.

Maris, Ja. and W:
Masterpieces; reproductions from their most renowned pictures. '08(O24) T. (Dutch painters.) leath., *75 c. net; pap., *25 c. net. Stokes.

Marison, Fiscar, pseud.
See Blatter, G: J:

Marital messenger. Gibson, W. E. $1.50. Neale.

Mariti, Giovanni.
Travels in the Island of Cyprus; tr. from the Italian by Claude Delaval Cobham; with contemporary accounts of the sieges of Nicosia and Famagusta. '09(Mr) 7+199 p. 12°, *$1.25 net. Putnam.

MARITIME LAW.
See **Fish and fishing.**

Marius, G. Hermine.
Dutch art in the nineteenth century; tr. by A. Teixeira de Mattos. '09(O9) 8°, *$3.75 net. Lippincott.

Marius the epicurean. *See* Pater, Wa.

Marivaux, Pierre Carlet de Chamberlain de.
Le jeu de l'amour et du hasard; ed. by Eugene Pellissier. '10(D24) 16°, (Macmillan's new ser. of French texts.) 35 c. net. Macmillan.

Marjery. Benson, E: F. $1.20. Doubleday, P.

Marjorie Daw. *See* Aldrich, T: Bailey.

Marjorie in command. Wells, C. $1.25. Dodd.

Marjorie Moxie. Huey, M. M. $1.25. Rand, McN. & Co.

Marjorie's busy days. Wells, C. †$1.25. Dodd.

Marjorie's new friend. Wells, C. †$1.25. Dodd.

Mark Enderby. Hoffman, R. $1.50. McClurg.

Markens, I:
Abraham Lincoln and the Jews. '09(Ap17) c. 8°, $1. I: Markens.

Market dairying. Michels, J: $1. J. Michels.

Market for souls. Goodnow, E. *$1.25 net. M. Kennerley.

MARKET GARDENING.
See **Gardens and gardening.**

MARKETS.
United States. *Dept. of Commerce and Labor. Bu. of Manufactures.* **Municipal markets and slaughterhouses in Europe.** '10(Jl) 117 p. il. 8°.

Markham, C: Edn., ed.
Real American in romance. Art ed. 13 v. '09, [1910.] (F) il. pors. 8°, $47.50; ¾ mor., $54.50; mor., $64.50. W. H. Wise.

Markham, Sir Clement Rob.
Incas of Peru. '10(D10) il. 8°, $3 net. Dutton.
King Edward VI.: an appreciation. '08 (Je20) il. 8°, *$3 net. Dutton.

Markino, Yoshio.
Japanese artist in London; written and il. by Yoshio Markino. '10(S17) c. il. (partly col.) O. $2 net. Jacobs.

Markoe, Ralston Joshua.
Impressions of a layman. '09(N) c. 271 p il. por. 12°, $1.50. Willwerscheid.
Startling statements; or, the downfall of a great republic. '10(D31) c. por. D. $1.50. R. J. Markoe.

Marks, Mrs.
See Hoppus, Mary A. M.

Marks, E: C: Rob.
Notes on the construction and working of pumps. 2d and enl. ed. '08(Ap25) il. 12°, $1.50. Van Nostrand.

Marks, G: Croydon.
Inventions, patents and designs; with notes and the full text of the New British Patents and Designs Act, 1907. '09(My) 116 p. 12°, *$1 net. Van Nostrand.

Marks, Jeannette Augustus.
English pastoral drama from the Restoration to the date of the publication of the "Lyrical ballads," (1660-1798.) '08(D5) D. *$1.50 net. Stechert.
Through Welsh doorways. '09(Ap3) c. il. D. **$1.10 net. Houghton M.

—, and Moody, Julia.
Holiday with the birds. '10(Ap2) c. il. D. (Story-told science.) 75 c. Harper.
Little busybodies: life of crickets, ants, bees, beetles, and other busy bodies. '09 (Ap24) c. il. D. (Story-told science.) 75 c. Harper.

Marks, Lionel Simeon, and Davis, Harvey Nathaniel.
Marks and Davis diagrams; reproduced from tables and diagrams of the thermal properties of saturated and superheated steam. no. 1, Total heatentropy diagram; no. 2, Total heat-pressure diagram. '10(Mr26) c. D. **40 c. net, in envelope. Longmans.
Tables and diagrams of the thermal properties of saturated and superheated steam. '09(Jl17) c. fold. tab. in pocket, O. **$1 net. Longmans.

Marks, Mrs. Lionel Simeon.
See Peabody, Josephine Preston.

Marks of the bear claws. Spalding, H: S. 85 c. Benziger.

MARLBOROUGH, Mass.
Bigelow, *Mrs.* E. A. F. Historical reminiscences of the early times in Marlborough, Mass., from 1860 to 1910. $3. Marlborough.
First records of Marlborough, Mass. $1. F. P. Rice.
Grand Army of the Republic. *Dept. of Massachusetts. John A. Rawlins Post, no.* 43. Story of the John Brown bell. 25 c. J: A. Rawlins Post.
Rice, F. P., *comp.* Marlborough, Mass., burial ground inscriptions. $3. F. P. Rice.
Vital records of Marborough, Mass., to the end of the year 1849. (Add. pub. for price.) F. P. Rice.

MARLBOROUGH, N. Y.
Woolsey, C. M. Hist. of the town of Marlborough. $4. C. M. Woolsey.

Marley, F. E.
Sunny side of life. '08, [1909.] (Ap) 5-94 p. il. 12°, 25 c. F. E. Marley.

Marlitt, E., pseud.
See John, Eugenia.

Marlowe, Christopher.
Works of Christopher Marlowe; ed. by C. F: Tucker Brooke. '10(My14) D. (Oxford English texts.) $1.75; thin pap., $2.50. Oxford Univ.
Dr. Faustus (with Goethe's Faust); introd. by Adolphus W: Ward. '09(My15) 16°, (World's classics.) 40 c.; leath., 75 c. Oxford Univ.
Plays and poems; introd. by E: Thomas. '09(Ap3) 16°, (Everyman's lib.) *35 c. net; leath., *70 c. net. Dutton.
Tragical history of Doctor Faustus; with an introd. and notes. '09(My15) S. (Swan dramatists.) 45 c. Sturgis & W.

—, and Chapman, G:
Hero and Leander; poem begun by Christopher Marlowe and finished by G: Chapman. Limited ed. '09(N) 8+104 p. 8°, mor. and vel., *$5 net. Dutton.

Marlowe, Fs.
Secret of the sandhills. '08(N7) O. $2. Lippincott.

MARLOWE, Julia.
Barry, J: D. Julia Marlowe. $1. E. H. Bacon.

"Marmaduke," pseud.
See Jerningham, C: E: Wynne.

Marmaduke maxims. Jerningham, C: E: W. *$1.25 net. Brentano's.

Marmier, Xavier.
Les fiancés du Spitzberg; ed. by A. A. Hentsch. '08(Ja18) D. (Oxford modern French ser.) 75 c. Oxford Univ.

Marmon, Mrs. Willie Fain.
Daughter of the hills. '09(Ja23) c. D. $1.50. Neale.

Marohnic, Josip.
English-Croatian letter-writer for the Croatian and Servian people in the United States. '09(F13) il. O. $1. J. Marohnic.

Maroon tales. Cuppy, W. J. $1.25. Forbes.

Marooner (The). Holder, C: F: $1.50. B. W. Dodge.

Marotz. Ayscough, J:, *pseud.* †$1.50. Putnam.

Marpessa. *See* Phillips, Stephen.

MARPRELATE CONTROVERSY.
See England.

Marquand, Allan.
Greek architecture. '09(Ap10) c. il. figs. O. (Handbooks of archæology and antiquities.) **$2.25 net. Macmillan.

Marquis, Albert Nelson, ed.
Book of Detroiters: biographical dictionary of living men of Detroit. '08(O3) c. O. $10. Marquis.

Marquis and Pamela. Cooper, E: H. †$1.50. Duffield.

Marquis of Murray Hill. Ronzone, B: A. $1.25. Roxburgh.

Marr, J: E:
Westmorland. '10(My) 10+152 p. 8°, (Cambridge county geographies.) 45 c. Putnam.

MARRIAGE.
Arner, G: B. L. Consanguineous marriages in the American population. 75 c. Longmans.
Baughman, *Mrs.* N. R. B. True way of life: [talks on true marriage.] $1. N. R. B. Baughman.
Biddle, C. S. Principles, pleading and practice obtaining in the court of chancery of New Jersey in divorce and other causes matrimonial. $3. Soney.
Brady, N. C. Modern marriage and how to bear it. $1.25. M. Kennerley.
Clark, J. W., *ed.* Weddings and wedding anniversaries. 25 c. Butterick.
Didier, E. L. Way to keep him.—Way to win him. ea., 10 c. Am. Press.
Donovan, J M. Law of marriage, annulment, domicile, divorce. $1. J. M. Donovan.
Flory, J. S. Love's sweet dream fully realized through holy matrimony and a sanctified home. 50 c. Higher Life.
Hamilton, C. Marriage as a trade. **$1.25 net. Moffat.
Hoffmann, *Mrs.* A. L. R. Before marriage: a mother's parting counsel to her son on the eve of his marriage. **35 c. net. Vir Pub.
Honeymoon confidences, by the bride herself. $1.25. Hudson Press.
Jordan, W: G: Little problems of married life. $1 net. Revell.
Keith, M. C. Marriage bed; medical and philosophical treatise on the marital habits of the human race. $3.50. Keith & G.
Lombard, L: Observations of a bachelor. $1. Estes.
MacBrayne, L. Men we marry. $1.50. C. M. Clark.
O'Reilly, J. J: E:, *comp.* Marriage law and church regulations. 50 c. Chief.
Post, *Mrs.* A. T. Marriage as a present-day problem. 5 c. Public.
Price, G: B. Problem of happy marriage. $1. Chelston Press.
Robertson, E. Marriage. 10 c. E. H. Riddell-Huston.
Rogers, *Mrs.* A. A. Why American marriages fail. $1.25. Houghton M.
Senator, H., *and* Kaminer, S., *eds.* Marriage and disease. $2.50. Hoeber.

MARRIAGE.—*Continued.*
Smart, G: T:, *ed.* Golden bond. *35 c. net. Pilgrim Press.
Stone, D. Law of Christian marriage. 10 c. Longmans.
Thomas, N. W. Kinship organizations and group marriage in Australia. *$2 net. Putnam.
Tyson, S. L. Teaching of Our Lord as to the indissolubility of marriage. 50 c. Univ. Press, (Sewanee.)
United States. *Bu. of the Census.* Marriage and divorce, 1867-1906. 2 v. (Add. Superintendent for price.)
Verland, F. Affinities who never meet. 25 c. Homingwood.
White, F: A. Laws on marriage, divorce and property rights of married women. $5. Baumgardt.
See also Catholic church;—Celibacy;—Divorce;—Domestic relations; — Family; — Generative organs; — Heredity; — Sex; — Spiritualism; — Woman.

Marriage (A) à la hell, by the woman concerned. '09(D) $1. B'way Pub.

Marriage à la mode. Ward, *Mrs.* M. A. A. †$1.20. Doubleday, P.

Marriage à la mode. *See* Hogarth, W:

Marriage of Theodore. Seawell, M. E. $1.50. Dodd.

Marriage under the terror. Wentworth, P. $1.35 net. Putnam.

Marriage ventures of Marie Louise. Billard, M. $3.50 net. Pott.

Married life of the Frederic Carrolls. Williams, J. L. $1.50. Scribner.

Married priest. Houtin, A. *70 c. net. Sherman. F.

Marriner, Harry Lee.
Joyous days, then and now; selected verses. '10(D) 60 p. il. 8°. 50 c. Western Press.

Marriott, C:
Intruding angel. '10(Mr19) D. $1.50. Lane.
Kiss of Helen. '08(D26) D. $1.50. Lane.
"Now!" '10(Ag13) D. $1.50. Lane.
Spanish holiday. '08(N14) il. 8°, *$2.50 net. Lane.
When a woman woos. '09(O9) D. $1.50. Lane.

Marriott, Crittenden.
How Americans are governed in nation, state and city; with an introd. by Dr. Ja. Sullivan. '10(Ap2) c. D. $1.75. Harper.
Isle of dead ships. '09(O23) c. il. D. **$1 net. Lippincott.
Uncle Sam's business told to young Americans. '08(O3) c. D. $1.25. Harper.

Marriott, J: Arth. Ransome.
English political institutions; introductory study. '10(D24) D. $1.10. Oxford Univ.
Second chambers; inductive study in political science. '10(My14) O. $1.75. Oxford Univ.

Marriott, L. M.
Mother and child; being letters from an old nurse to a young mother. '10(D) 9+126 p. 16°, 40 c. Simmons.

Marrs, S. M. N.
Educational miscellany. '10(Je18) O. pap., 15 c. S. M. N. Marrs.

Marrs, W: Taylor.
Confessions of a neurasthenic. '09(Mr) c. 7+114 p. il. 8°, *$1 net. Davis.

Marryat, Captain F:
Works. 12 v. New imperial lib. ed. '10 (D) il. 8°, ea., $1.25; hf. cf., $2.25; New il. sterling ed., ea., $1. (Sets only.) Estes.
Jacob Faithful. '08(Jl4) 12°, (Young America lib.) 50 c. Hurst.
Japhet in search of a father. '08(Jl11) 12°, (Young America lib.) 50 c. Hurst.
Masterman Ready; or, the wreck of the "Pacific." '10(Mr26) il. 8°, (Bowman's illustrated lib. of world famous books.) $1. Bowman
Masterman Ready. '08(Ag1) 12°, (Young America lib.) 50 c. Hurst.
Mr. Midshipman Easy. '08(Ag8) 12°, (Young America lib.) 50 c. Hurst.
Percival Keene. '09(Ap3) 16°, (Everyman's lib.) *35 c. net; leath., *70 c. net. Dutton.
Rattlin, the reefer. '08(Jl4) 12°, (Young America lib.) 50 c. Hurst.
Settlers in Canada. '09(Ap3) 16°, (Everyman's lib.) *35 c. net; leath., *70 c. net. Dutton.

Marrying and giving in marriage. Molesworth, *Mrs.* M. L. S. 50 c. Hurst.

Marrying of Brian. Dease, A. 50 c. net. Herder.

Mars, Gerhardt Cornell.
Interpretation of life; in which is shown the relation of modern culture to Christian Science. '08(Je13) c. O. **$3 net. Appleton.

MARS (planet).
Lowell, P. Mars, as the abode of life. **$2.50 net. Macmillan.
Wallace, A. R. Is Mars habitable?: critical exam. of Prof. Lowell's "Mars and its canals." *60 c. net. Macmillan.

Mars via the moon. Wicks, M. $1.50. Lippincott.

Marsden, Rufus E.
See Binns, C: L.—Burns, Cecil Lawrence.

Marsh, Arth. Merwin.
See Haight, C: Sherman.

Marsh, B: Clarke, and Ford, G: B.
Introd. to city planning; democracy's challenge to the American city; with a chapter on the technical phases of city planning, by G: B. Ford. '09(Ag28) c. il. plans, 8°, $1. B: C. Marsh.

Marsh, C: Dwight.
Loco-weed disease of the plains. '09(Ag) 130 p. il. maps, 8°, (U. S., Dept. of Agriculture, Bu. of Animal Industry bull.) pap., 35 c. U. S., Supt. of Docs.

Marsh, C: Fleming.
Concise treatise on reinforced concrete: companion volume to "The manual of reinforced concrete and concrete block construction." '10(Jl30) il. 12°, $2.50 net. Van Nostrand.

—, and Dunn, W:
Manual of reinforced concrete and concrete block construction. '08(D26) il. *$2.50 net. Engineering News.
Manual of reinforced concrete and concrete block construction. 2d ed. '10(Jl30) tabs., 16°, limp leath., $2.50 net. **Van Nostrand.**

Marsh, C: W.
Recollections, 1837-1910. '10(D31) c. il. 8°, $1.50. Farm Impl. News.

Marsh, F: E:
Pearls, points and parables. '08, [1909.] (Ap) c. 28+269 p. 8°, $1.50. Gospel Pub.

MARSH, *Captain* Grant Prince.
Hanson, J. M. Conquest of the Missouri; being the story of the life and exploits of Captain Grant Marsh. *$2 net. McClurg.

Marsh, Harriet Anne.
Grammar in a nutshell; or, English without rules; abr. and easy grammar and letter writer for business men, offices, business colleges, etc. '10(Je) c. 5-63 p. 16°, 35 c. Hammond Pub.

Marsh, R:
The beetle: a mystery. '09(Je) 12°, $1.50. Brentano's.
Interrupted kiss. '09(Jl3) front. D. $1.50. Cassell.
Lovely Mrs. Blake. '10(D10) front. 12°, $1.20 net. Cassell.

Marshall, Alfr. W:
Alternating currents simply explained. '09 (Mr13) c. il. 12°, pap., 25 c. Spon.
Magnets and magnetism simply explained. '10(N5) 12°, 50 c.; pap., 25 c. Spon.
Wimhurst machine: how to make and use it. '08(Jl18) il. 12°, pap., 25 c. Spon.

Marshall, Archibald.
Exton Manor. '08(F15) c. D. †$1.50. Dodd.

Marshall, Bernard.
Gentleman from East Blueberry: sketch of the Vermont legislature; State vs. Burton: a drama of the court room. '09 (S11) c. D. pap., 50 c. Capital City Press.

Marshall, Carl Coran.
Business speller and technical word book. '08(My16) c. 8°, 90 c. Goodyear-M.
—, comp. Technical word list. '08(My16) c. 8°, 30 c. Goodyear-M.

Marshall, Davis E:, and Dazey, C: Turner.
In old Kentucky; founded on C: T. Dazey's play. '10(Ap2) c. il. D. $1.50. G: W. Dillingham.
Old flute-player; romance of to-day. '10 (O8) il. D. $1.50. G: W: Dillingham.

Marshall, E:
Writing on the wall; novel founded on Olga Nethersole's play, by W: J. Hurlbut. '09(N20) c. il. D. †$1.50. G: W. Dillingham.

Marshall, E: A.
Christianity and non-Christian religions compared; cont. 800 library references to facilitate further study. '10(D17) c. il. 8°, 50 c. Bible Inst.

Marshall, Francesca, pseud.
See Chadwick, *Mrs.* Mara Louise Pratt.

Marshall, Captain Fs. Cutler.
Elements of hippology; prepared for the Dept. of Tactics, U. S. Military Acad. 2d and rev. ed. '08(Mr7) c. il. 12°, $1.25. Hudson.

Marshall, Fs. Hugh Adam.
Physiology of reproduction; with preface by A. E. Schäfer, and contribs. by W: Cramer and Ja. Lochhead. '10(N12) il. O. $6 net. Longmans.

Marshall, G: Catlett, jr.
See Sherrill, Clarence Osborne.

Marshall, H. E.
An empire story; stories of India and the greater colonies; told to children. '09 (O9) il. maps, O. *$2.50 net. Stokes.
An island story; child's hist. of England. '10(Jl30) il. O. $2.75 net. Stokes.
Child's English literature. '10(F19) col. il. O. *$2.50 net. Stokes.
Scotland's story; child's hist. of Scotland. '10(Jl30) il. O. $2.75 net. Stokes.
Stories of Beowulf; told to the children. '09(F13) il. 24°, (Told to the children ser.) 50 c. Dutton.
Stories of Guy of Warwick, told to the children; with pictures by L. D. Luard. '08(Ap4) il. 16°, (Told to the children ser.) 50 c. Dutton.
Story of Cromwell. '08(Ag15) 24°, (Children's heroes ser.) 50 c. Dutton.
Story of Napoleon. '08(Ag15) 24°, (Children's heroes ser.) 50 c. Dutton.
— **comp.** Stories of Roland. '08(Ag15) 24°, (Told to the children ser.) 50 c. Dutton.

Marshall, H: Rutgers.
Consciousness. '09(D18) 8°, *$4 net. Macmillan.

Marshall, J:
Kansas druggist's intoxicating liquor law. '08(My.) c. 91 p. O. $1.25; pap., 50 c. State Temperance.

MARSHALL, John.
Platt, H. G. John Marshall, and other addresses. $1.50. Argonaut.

Marshall, J: Sayre.
Manual of the injuries and surgical diseases of the face, mouth and jaws. 3d ed., rev. and enl. '09(Ag) 16+717 p. il. 4°, $5.50; shp., $6.50. White Dental.
Principles and practice of operative dentistry. 3d ed. '09(Ag) c. 25+654 p. il. 8°, **$5 net; shp., **$6 net. Lippincott.

Marshall, Leonard B., comp.
Halcyon song-book. '09(N13) c. O. 75 c. Silver.

Marshall, Levi.
Rivets for truth; with introd. by J. H. Garrison. '10(Ap9) c. 12°, 60 c. Chr. Pub. Co.

Marshall, Park.
Life of William B. Bate, citizen, soldier and statesman; with memorial addresses. '08(N) 363 p. por. 12°, $1.25. P. Marshall.

Marshall, Percival.
Workshop wrinkles and recipes; collection of useful workshop hints in mechanics and electricity. '10(D17) 12°, bds., 50 c. Spon.

Marshall, Roy, comp.
See Boynton, Wa. Channing, *comp.*

Marshall, Ruth.
Ferns of the Dells of the Wisconsin River. '10(Jl) c. 61 p. il. obl. 24°, 25 c. R. Marshall.

Marshall, Stewart McCulloch.
See Spangler, H: Wilson.

Marshall, W: Crosby.
Elem. machine drawing. '10(Mr5) c. tabs., 24°, $1.50. Yale Co-op.

Marshall, W: L.
See Clark, W: Laurence, *jr.*

Marshall, W: Vickroy.
Curb to predatory wealth. '09(D4) c. D. $1. Fenno.

MARSHALL COUNTY, Indiana.
McDonald, D. Twentieth century hist. of Marshall County. 2 v. $19. Lewis Pub.

Marshall's handy automobile record. '10 (D3) 16°, $1 net. Winston.

Marsland, Agnes Eliz.
First principles of esoterism; text-book for students of the first degree of the Oriental Esotoeric Society in the United States of America and elsewhere. '10 (Jl16) c. il. S. $1 net; leath., $1.50 net. Oriental Esoteric.
What esoterism is. '10(O15) c. S. 50 c.; pap., 35 c. Oriental Esoteric.

Marsten, Fs. E:, D.D.
Mask of Christian Science. '10(Ja1) c. pors. D. $1. Am. Tr.

Marston, Anson.
Sewers and drains. '09(F20) c. il. 8°, (American School of Correspondence pubs.) $1. Am. Sch. Corr.

Marston, E:, ["The Amateur Angler."]
How does it feel to be old?; repr. fr. the [London] *Monthly Review,* with much additional matter. '08(Ag15) por. 16°, $1. Scribner.
Thomas Ken and Izaak Walton: sketch of their lives and family connection. '08 (O10) il. D. *$2 net. Longmans.

MARTHA'S VINEYARD, Mass.
Hine, C: G. Story of Martha's Vineyard. $1.50. Hine Bros.

Martial, [Martialus Marcus Valerius.]
Select epigrams. Spectaculorum liber and books I-VI.; ed. from the text of Professor Lindsay by R: T. Bridge and E. D. C. Lake. '08(N21) D. 90 c. Oxford Univ.
Selected epigrams; ed., with introd. and notes, by Edw. Post. '08(N21) c. D. (College ser. of Latin authors.) $1.50. Ginn.

MARTIAL LAW.
See **Habeas corpus.**

Martin, —.
See Brown, —.

Martin, C. F.
French verb, its conjugation and idiomatic use. '10(Ja29) c. O. $1.25. Am. Bk.

Martin, Rev. C: Alfr.
Catholic religion; statement of Christian teaching and hist. '10(N5) il. pors. 12°, $1. Apostolate.

Martin, Deborah Beaumont.
Local history story hour; rept. of an experiment in the Kellogg Public Library at Green Bay. '08(D) 47-51 p. 8°, (State Hist. Society of Wis. bull.) 10 c. State Hist. Wis.

Martin, E. M.
Wayside wisdom: book for quiet people. '09(N20) D. *$1.50 net. Longmans.

Martin, E:, M.D.
Surgical diagnosis: text book for students and practitioners. '09(O) 764 p. il. 8°, *$5.50 net. Lea.
See also White, Ja. W:

Martin, E: Sandford.
In a new century: [essays.] '08(O24) c. D. **$1.50 net. Scribner.
Luxury of children and other luxuries. New ed. '10(N19) c. il. O. $1.50. Harper.

Martin, Farrel J. G.
Divorce. '09, [1910.] (Mr) c. 38 p. S. pap., 25 c. Jackson Print.

Martin, Fk. A.
Under the absolute Amir. '08(Ag8) il. *$2.25 net. Harper.

Martin, G: E.
See Searson, Ja. W:

Martin, G: H:
Industrial education and the public schools; address before the Massachusetts Teachers' Association, Boston, Nov. 27, 1908. '08, [1909.] (Ap) 20 p. 8°. (Add. pubs. for price.) Wright & P.
School hygiene in Massachusetts [cont. a statement rel. to the present condition of medical inspection in the schools of Massachusetts; disclosures by school inspection; limitations on school work; the teeth; also tuberculosis; suggestions to teachers regarding tuberculosis and its prevention; printed rules of health; outdoor class in Boston.] '09(Jl) 27 p. 8°, pap., gratis. G: H: Martin.

Martin, G: Washington.
Boundary lines of Kansas; address before the Old Settlers' Association at Alma, Sept. 28, Independence, Oct. 16, and at the banquet at Kansas City, Kan., Oct. 18, 1909, in honor of the Wyandotte convention. [1910.] (D) 28 p. il. pors. map, 8°, gratis. State Hist., Kan.
First two years of Kansas. '07, [1908.] (Ag) 30 p. O. pap., gratis. G: W. Martin.

Martin, Harold.
See Adventures in field and forest.

Martin, Mrs. Helen Reimensnyder.
The crossways. '10(F26) c. D. †$1.50. Century Co.
Revolt of Anne Royle. '08(O3) c. D. †$1.50. Century Co.

Martin, H:
Notes on the syntax of the Latin inscriptions found in Spain. '09(Ag) 49 p. 8°, $1. Furst.

Martin, H: Desires.
Progress and profit for mill men [cotton manufacture]. '09(O) c. 7-212 p. il. por. 8°, $1. H: D. Martin.

Martin, H: Newell.
Human body. 8th ed., rev. '09(Je19); 9th ed. '10(Ag) c. il. 8°, (American science ser., Advanced course.) ea., **$2.50 net. Holt.

Martin, Mrs. Ida Shaw.
Sorority hdbk. 3d ed. '09(D) 164 p. il. 12°, $1.50. I. S. Martin.

Martin, Isemena Teresa.
Voice from the West; a few sketches written in various moods—culled from the pages of a western journal. '08(D) c. 256 p. 12°, $1. Becktold.

Martin, J. A., rep.
See Texas. *Cts. of civil appeals.* Repts.

Martin, Ja.
Jason Jones; life story of an American politician; autobiog. sketch found among the papers of a capitalist and political boss, recently deceased. '10(F26) c. 8°, $2. Chronicle Pub.

Martin, Ja. Lee.
Delmarree, a story of love and war. '08 (Mr) c. 84 p. il. por. S. pap. (Add. author for prce.) J. L. Martin.

Martin, J:
Public benefits derived from water power developments in California. '10 (Ap30) O. pap., gratis. J: Martin.

Martin, J: And.
The Jayhawker. '08(O10) c. il. D. $1.50. C. M. Clark.

Martin, J: F.
Gypsy moth; novel. '10(D31) c. D. B'way Pub.

Martin, Julius.
See Walling, Burns Tracy.

Martin, Mrs. Nettie Parrish.
Pilgrim's progress in other worlds, recounting the wonderful adventures of Ulysum Storries and his discovery of the last star "Eden." '08(N) c. 482 p. por. 12°, $1. Mayhew.

Martin, Prestonia Mann, [Mrs. J: Martin.]
Is mankind advancing? '10(D31) il. 12°, $2 net. Baker & T.

Martin, R: Allen, comp.
Castor family, Holmesburg, [Pa.,] branch. '09(Ag21) chart, O. pap., *$2 net. Martin & A.

Martin, Rev. S., ed.
See Garbett, *Canon.*

Martin, Thdr.
Mining law and land-office procedure with decisions of the courts; rules, regulations, and decisions of the general land-office, and of the Department of the Interior; federal, state, territorial, and insular mining statutes; with statutes and forms. '08 (Ag1) 8°, shp., $7.50. Bender-M.

Martin, T: Commerford.
See Dyer, Fk. Lewis.

Martin, Violet.
See Ross, Martin, *pseud.*

Martin, Wa. Drane.
Lenora, and other poems. '09(N) c. 87 p. il. 8°, 75 c. Pub. Ho. of M. E. Ch., So.

Martin, Sir W:
See Conway, Agnes Ethel.

Martin, W: Alex.
Treatise on the law of labor unions. '10 (Je) O. $6. Byrne.

Martin, W: Frank.
Sir Henry Vane: a drama. '08(Ja11) por. O. $1.25. Roxburgh.

Martin Eden. London, J. †$1.50. Macmillan.

Martin Hyde. Masefield, J: $1.50. Little, B. & Co.

Martin Merryvale, his x mark. *See* Trowbridge, J: T.

Martindale, C. C., ed.
Lectures on the history of religions. '10 (O8) 12°, ea., 60 c. net; per set, $2.40 net. Herder.

Martindale, Ja. Boyd.
Am. law directory (annual). Jan., 1908. '08(Ja4); Jan., 1909. '08(D); Jan., 1910. '10(Ja) c. O. shp., subs., ea., $15.50. Martindale.

Martindale, T:
Sport indeed. New ed. '09, [1910.] (Ja) c. **$1.50 net. Jacobs.
With gun and guide. '10(S17) c. il. O. $2 net. Jacobs.

Martineau, G:
Sugar, cane and beet; object lesson. '10 (Je18) il. diagr., D. (Common commodities of commerce.) 75 c. Pitman.

Martineau, Harriet.
Feats on the Fiord. '10(Ap2) il. 16°, (Everyman's lib.) 35 c. net; 70 c. net. Dutton.

Martinengo-Cesaresco, Contessa.
See Cesaresco Evelyn Lilian Hazeldine Carrington *Contessa* Martinengo.

MARTINIQUE.
See Mt. Pelée.

Martique, L. F.
Scarlet mother on the Tiber; or, trials and travels of Evangelist L. J. King, twenty-five years a Roman Catholic, 15 years a Protestant preacher and reformer. v. 1. '08(O) c. il. pors. 12°, $1. L. J. King.

Marton, Violet.
See Ross, Martin, *pseud.*

Martyn, Wyndham.
Man outside. '10(Ja29) c. il. D. †$1.50. Dodd.

Martyrdom of man. Reade, W: W. $1.50 net. Lane.

MARTYRS.
Allen, W: Briefe historie of the glorious martyrdom of twelve reverend priests: Father Edmund Campion and his companions. *$1.25 net. Herder.
Foxe, J: Christian martyrs of the world. $1.50. C: Foster.
See also Saints.

"Marvel, Ik," pseud.
See Mitchell, Donald Grant.

Marvel, T: Littlefield.
Giuseppina: drama in one act. '09(N) 16°, pap., 25 c. Dramatic.

MARVELLOUS (The).
See Folk-lore.

Marvellous adventures of Pinocchio. *See* Lorenzini, Carlo.

Marvellous (The) year; introd. by Edn. Markham; drawings by Gertrude Huebsch. '09(D18) c. Q. bds., *$1.25 net. B: W. Huebsch.

Marvelous career of Theodore Roosevelt. Morris, C: $1.50. Winston.

Marvelous creations of Joseffy. Abbott, D: P. 15 c. Open Court.

Marvels beyond science. Grasset, J. $1.75 net. Funk.

Marvin, Mrs. A. I., comp.
Mrs. Marvin's cook book. '10(S17) 12°, 50 c. Cochrane.

Marvin, C: F:
Barometers and the measurement of atmospheric pressure: pamphlet of information respecting the theory and construction of barometers in general, with summary of instructions for the care and use of the standard Weather Bureau instruments. '09(Ag) 110 p. il. 8°, (U. S., Dept. of Agriculture; Weather Bu., Instrument Division circular.) pap. (Add. Superintendent for price.) U. S., Supt. of Docs.

Marvin, Dwight Edwards.
The Christman. '08(My9) c. front. D. $1.50. B'way Pub.
Church and her prophets. '09(S) c. 7-94 p. 12°, 50 c. B'way Pub.
Prof. Slagg, of London. '08(D12) c. il. 8°. (Add. pubs. for price.) B'way Pub.

Marvin, Rev. Frederic Rowland.
Book of quatrains, original and translated. '09(N6) c. 12°, $1. Sherman, F.
Christ among the cattle: a sermon. 5th ed. '08, [1909.] (Ja) 58 p. 16°, 50 c. Pafraets.
Excursions of a booklover; being papers on literary themes. '10(Je25) c. O. $1.50 net. Sherman, F.
Poems and translations. '08(Ja18) O. *$1 net. Pafraets.

Marvin, Winthrop Lippitt.
American merchant marine; remarks before the Senate Committee on Commerce, March 3, 1910. '10(Ap) 6 p. 8°, pap. Gov. Pr. Off.

Marx, Guido Hugo.
See Smith, Albert W:

Marx, Karl.
Capital. In 3 v. v. 3. '09(Jl31) 8°, $2; per set, $6, boxed. Kerr.
Poverty of philosophy; being a tr. of the Misere de la philosophie; (a reply to La philosophie de la misère of M. Prudhon); with preface by Friedrich Engels; tr. by H. Quelch. '10(My21) D. (International lib. of social science.) $1. Kerr.
Value, price and profit; ed. by his daughter, Eleanor Marx Aveling. '08(Jl11) S. 50 c. Kerr.

—, **and Engels, F:**
Manifests of the communist party; authorized Eng. translation, ed. and annot. by F: Engels; [text in English and Esperanto.] '08(Ja11) S. (Standard socialist ser.) 50 c. Kerr.

MARX, Karl.
Liebknecht, W. Karl Marx biographical memoirs. 50 c. Kerr.
Spargo, J: Karl Marx. $2.50 net. B: W. Huebsch.
Spargo, J: The Marx he knew. 50 c. Kerr.

Marx, Simon.
See Grandin, Egbert H:

MARY, *Virgin.*
Catholic church. Office of the Blessed Virgin Mary and office of the dead: Latin and English. '08(Ag8) 45 c.; leath., 75 c. Herder.
Hale, P. I. Madonna [in art.] $1. Bates & G.
Hammer, B., *comp.* Mary, help of Christians, and the fourteen saints invoked as holy helpers. *$2 net. Benziger.
Jameson, *Mrs.* A. B. M. Legends of the Madonna as represented in the fine arts. $1.25. Bowman.
Jenner, *Mrs.* K. L. R. Our Lady in art. $1 net. McClurg.
Opitz, H. Sodality of Our Lady. 25 c. Kenedy.

MARY, *Queen of England.*
Froude, J. A. Mary Tudor. 35 c. net; 70 c. net. Dutton.
Hume, M. A. S. Two English queens and Philip. $4.50 net. Putnam.
Mary, Queen of Scots.
Queen Mary's book: collection of poems and essays; ed. by Mrs. P. Stewart-Mackenzie Arbuthnot. '08(Ja25) por. 8°, *$3.50 net. Macmillan.
MARY, *Queen of Scots.*
Stoddart, J. T. Girlhood of Mary, Queen of Scots. $3.50. Clode.
Mary. Björnson, B. $1.25. Macmillan.
Mary Cary. Bosher, *Mrs.* K. L. L. **$1 net. Harper.
Mary Derwent. Stephens, *Mrs.* A. S. $1. Burt.
Mary Gray. Hinkson, *Mrs.* K. T. $1.50. Cassell.
Mary Jane's pa. Way, N. $1.50. H. K. Fly.
Mary Josephine, Sister.
Story of our Lord's life told for children, by a Carmelite nun. '10(D10) c. il. 8°, $1. Cathedral Lib.
Mary Lawson. Swigart, F. $1.25. Roxburgh.
Mary Magdalene. Maeterlinck, M. $1.20 net. Dodd.
Mary of Magdala. Robertson, *Mrs.* H. G. $1.50. Saalfield.
Mary of Plymouth. Kaler, J. O. 35 c. Am. Bk.
Mary Powell. Manning, A. *35 c. net; *70 c. net. Dutton.
Mary Ware. Johnston, *Mrs.* A. F. $1.50. L. C. Page.
Mary Ware in Texas. Johnston, *Mrs.* A. F. $1.50. L. C. Page.
Maryland. Corporation law; ed. by H: W. Williams. '08(Je) c. 32+350 p. O. cl., $2.50. G: W. King.
Maryland. *Ct. of appeals.* Repts.; (W: T. Brantly.) v. 105. '08(My); v. 106 (N); v. 107. '09(Mr); v. 108 (Jl) ea., $5; v. 109, 110. '09(D); v. 111. '10(Jl) c. O. shp., ea., 95 c. King Bros.
Maryland. Law of domestic relations; by H: D: Harlan. '09(D) O. $3. Balto. Pr.
Maryland. Public school law, [etc.] '10(Jl) c. O. pap., 15 c. Meyer & T.
MARYLAND.
Buchholz, H. E. Governors of Maryland from the Revolution to the year 1908. $2.50. Williams & W.
Hall, C. C., *ed.* Narratives of early Maryland, 1633-1684. $3 net. Scribner.
Hanna, H. S. Financial history of Maryland, (1789-1848.) 75 c. Johns Hopkins.
Myers, W: S. Self-reconstruction of Maryland. 50 c. Johns Hopkins
Noble, E: N., *and* Tubbs, E: T., *comps.* Maryland in prose and poetry. 75 c. Lehmen.
Payment of certain moneys advanced by Maryland and Virginia; adverse report. '09(My) 15 p. 8°, pap. (Add. Superintendent for price.) U. S., Supt. of Docs.
Ridgeley, H. W., *ed.* Hist. graves of Maryland and the District of Columbia. **$2 net. Grafton Press.

MARYLAND.—*Continued.*
Russell, W: T: Maryland. $1.75. Furst.
Williams, T: J: C., *comp.* State of Maryland. gratis. Sun Pr.
See also Annapolis;—Antietam River;—Baltimore;—Bushey cavern;—Civil War.
Maryland, my Maryland. Randall, J. R. *$1.50 net. Murphy.
Maryland (The) Original Research Society of Baltimore. Bull. no. 2; [ed. by] Alb. Levin Richardson. '10(Jl) c. 105 p. Q. pap., $1. J: H. Saumenig.
Maryland Weather Service, Special pub. il. 4°, pap., *$2.50 net. Maryland Geol.
—Fassig. Climate and weather of Baltimore.
Mary's adventures on the moon. Worth, A. S. †$1. Badger.
Marzio's crucifix. *See* Crawford, Fs. Marion. Zoroaster.
Marzo, Eduardo, comp. and ed.
Art of vocalization. [In 6 pts., for soprano, mezzo-soprano, alto, tenor, baritone, bass; ea. pt. in 3 bks., containing 100 vocalizes.] '08(F22) c. Q. pap., ea. bk., 75 c. Ditson.
Coloratura album for soprano. '09(O9) c. 4°, pap., $1. Ditson.
Masaccio, Tommaso Guidi, Called.
Masterpieces. '10(D17) il. 24°, (Painters' ser.) leath., 75 c. net; pap., 25 c. net. Stokes.
Mascot of Sweet Brier Gulch. Phillips, H: W. †$1.50. Bobbs-M.
Masefield, J:
Captain Margaret. '08(D19) D. *$1.50 net. Lippincott.
Martin Hyde; the Duke's messenger. '10 (O22) c. '09. il. D. $1.50. Little, B. & Co.
Tarpaulin muster. '08(Mr28) D. $1. B. W. Dodge.
Tragedy of Nan, and other plays. '09, [1910.] (Je) 114 p. 12°, $1 net. M. Kennerley.
—, **comp.** Chronicles of the pilgrim fathers; set of the vivid contemporary tracts and narratives of the sailing of the "Mayflower" and the founding of New England; with introd. and bibliography by J: Masefeld. '10(D10) 16°, (Everyman's lib.) 35 c. net; leath., 70 c. net. Dutton.
Mask of Christian Science. Marsten, F. E: $1. Am. Tr.
Masliansky, Harris.
Yiddish sermons. '08(Jl) c. 11+276 p. por. 16°, $1. Turberg.
Mason, Alfr. E: Woodley.
At the Villa Rose. '10(S17) c. il. D. $1.50. Scribner.
Mason, Arth. Ja., D.D.
Memoir of George Howard Wilkinson, Bishop of St. Andrews, Dunkeld and Dunblane and Primus of the Scottish Church, formerly Bishop of Truro. '09 (My8) 2 v., il. pors. O. *$8 net; Shorter ed. (in 1 v.) '10(N12) pors. D. $2 net. Longmans.
Mason, Mrs. Auguste Francke Hermann.
See Mason, Eveleen Laura.
Mason, A: Lynch.
Corporations and social changes: an address. '09(My15) c. 8°. (Priv. pr.) A: L. Mason.

Mason, B: F.
Village mystery, and Through war to peace. '10(D31) c. por. D. B'way Pub.

Mason, Mrs. Caroline Atwater.
Binding of the strong: love story. '08 (S12) c. 12°, $1.50. Revell.
Mystery of Miss Motte. '09(My8) c. front. D. $1.25. L. C. Page.
Spell of Italy. '09(Ap10) c. il. pors. map, D. $2.50, boxed. L. C. Page.

Mason, C: Field.
Complete hdbk. for the hospital corps of the U. S. army and navy and state military forces. 2d rev. ed. '09(Ag) 590 p. il. 8°, *$4 net. Wood.

Mason, Dan. Gregory.
Guide to music. '09(N6) c. pors. D. (Guide ser.) **$1.25 net. Baker & T.
Orchestral instruments and what they do. '09(Je12 c. il. D. **$1.25 net. Baker & T.
See also Surette, T: Whitney.

Mason, Edith Huntington.
The politician. '10(Ap16) c. col. il. O. $1.50. McClurg.

Mason, Enoch M.
Pellagra; its etiology, diagnosis, and treatment. [1910.] (Je) 4 p. 8°. Gulf States Med.

Mason, Eveleen Laura, [Mrs. Auguste Francke Hermann Mason.]
Discovery of discoveries, climaxingly collated in the month of Una-and-her-lion (1908), inclusive of August; and fulfilling "the message of Ishtar." '09(Je) c. 119 p. il. 12°, $1.25. E. L. Mason.
Episode in the doings of the dualized. '09 (Jl) 50 c. E. L. Mason.
Heiro-Salem: the vision of peace; fiction founded in ideals. 2d ed. '09(Je) c. 11+508 p. il. 12°, $2. E. L. Mason.
Mad? which? neither. '09(Je) 12°, $2. E. L. Mason.
Twelve outputs selected from among lectures and articles put out from 1879 to summer tide of 1907. '09(Je) c. 105 p. il. 12°, $1.25. E. L. Mason.
Who builds?; romance dedicated to brother builders of the 32° and 33° of Ancient Scottish rites and to builders yet more ancient the world throughout. '09(Je) c. 11+351 p. il. 12°, $2. E. L. Mason.

Mason, Fk. Richardson.
Business principles and organization. '10 (Ja1) c. 8°, $4.80. Cree.

Mason, Freeman Clark.
Hist. of the Borton and Mason families in Europe and America. '08(D) c. 264 p. il. pors. facsim., 4°, leath., $3.25. Rep. Pr. Co.

Mason, Mrs. Grace Sartwell.
The god-parents. '10(Mr26) c. il. D. **$1.10 net. Houghton M.
See also Megargel, Percy F.

Mason, Harry Beckwith.
How to get registered; outlining a systematic, graded course of home study for pharmaceutical students who are unable to avail themselves of the superior advantages of education in a school or college of pharmacy. 4th ed., rev. and largely rewritten by Wilbur L. Scoville. '09 (S18) c. O. pap., 50 c. C: L. Mason.
—, ed. 350 dollar ideas for druggists; valuable compilation of dispensing, manufacturing, advertising, book-keeping, window-display and business-bringing methods, devised by druggists themselves and paid for at the rate of one dollar each. '10(Ap) c. 186 p. il. 12°, $1. E. G. Swift.
Window displays for druggists; comprising for the most part engravings and descriptions of over a hundred attractive displays which have been designed and used with successe by druggists throughout the country, together with some useful suggestions on the subject of window dressing in general. 2d ed., containing 22 new displays. '10(Ap) c. 182 p. il. 12°, $1. E. G. Swift.

Mason, Herbert Delevan.
On highways law, [etc.,] annotated. 7th ed., by C: G. Blakeslee. '09(D) c. O. $3.50. Banks & Co.
See also Ivins, W: M.

Mason, Isabel S.
Songs by the way. '09(N) 23 p. por. 8°. (Add. pubs. for price.) Herald Pub., (Md.)

Mason, Ja.
Art of chess. 3d ed., rev. and enl. '10 (Jl30) figs. D. $1.25. McKay.
Principles of chess in theory and practice. 4th ed., rev. and enl. '10(Jl) figs. D. $1.25. McKay.

Mason, Ja.
Bernardino Luini. '08(D19) il. O. (Masterpieces in colour.) il. bds., *65 c. net. Stokes.
Fra Angelico. '08(F22) il. O. (Masterpieces in colour.) bds., *65 c. net. Stokes.

Mason, Max.
See Moore, Eliakim Hastings.

Mason, Otis Tufton.
Anyam gila (mad weave); Malayasian type of basket work. '09(Je12) O. pap. Gov. Pr. Off.
Vocabulary of Malaysian basket-work: study in the W. L. Abbott collections. '08, [1909.] (My) 51 p. il. figs. O. pap. Gov. Pr. Off.

Mason, Redfern.
Song lore of Ireland; Erin's story in music and verse. '10(O29) c. O. $2 net. Wessels & B.

Mason, Rosalind Fay, ed.
See Branham, Grace Bagnall, ed.

Mason, Roswell H.
Military Order of the Loyal Legion of the United States: address before the Arche Club of Chicago, Ill., Feb. 21, 1908. '09 (Mr) 5 p. 8°, pap. (Add. pubs. for price.) M. O. L. L., (Ill.)

Mason, Roy.
When I am rich: a novel. '09(Jl31) c. D. $1.50. G: W. Dillingham.

Mason, Rufus Dodd.
Office treatment of rectal diseases explained and simplified: exposition of the treatment of all diseases of the rectum, etc., the cure of which may be accomplished without surgical anæsthesia. 4th ed. '08(Ag15) il. 12°, $2.50. Burton Co.

Mason, Ruth Little.
The trailers. '09(F27) c. D. **$1.20 net. Revell.

Mason, Thdr. West.
Family record in our line of descent from Major John Mason of Norwich, Ct. '09, [1910.] (My) 59+8 p. front. 8°. (Priv. pr.) Grafton Press.

Mason, W. L.
See Hammond, H. W.
—, comp. How to become a law stenographer. '09(Je26) O. $1; 75 c. Pitman.

Mason, Wa.
Uncle Walt [Walt Mason], the poet philosopher. '10(D17) c. il. por. 12°, $1.25. G: M. Adams.

Mason, W: Pitt.
Examination of water; chemical and bacteriological. 4th ed., rev. '09(D) 5+167 p. 12°, $1.25. Wiley.
Notes on qualitative analysis; arranged for the use of students of the Rensselaer Polytechnic Institute. 5th ed. '08(D) 57 p. tabs., 12°, 80 c. Chemical.

Mason, Winfield Scott.
Frozen Northland; life with the Esquimo in his own country. '10(D17) c. il. maps, 12°, $1. Jennings.

MASON FAMILY.
See **Genealogies.**

Masonic (The) chronicler catechism rel. to masonic law and usage, together with suggestions to masters, secretaries and members. '10(Je) c. 5-121 p. 12°, 75 c.; pap., 50 c. Masonic Chronicler.

MASONRY.
Baker, J. O. Treatise on masonry construction. $5. Wiley.
Bragdon, C., *and* Fiske, J. P. B. Tapestry brick work. 20 c. Fiske & Co., (Bost.)
Chatley, H. Stresses in masonry. *$1.25 net. Lippincott.
Hodgson, F: T: Practical stonemasonry self-taught. $1. Drake.
Webb, W. L., *and* Gibson, W. H. Masonry and reinforced concrete. $3. Am. Sch. Corr.
See also Arches; — Bricklaying; — Bricks; — Concrete;—Stone.

MASONS.
See Freemasonry.

Maspero, Gaston Camille Charles.
New light on ancient Egypt; tr. from the French by Eliz. Lee. [2d ed.] '09 (My22) il. 8°, *$4 net. Appleton.
See also Davis, Thdr. M.

Masque of sibyls. Converse, F. $1 net. Houghton M.

Masqueraders (The). Jones, H: A. 50 c. S: French.

Masquerading of Margaret. Welty, C. G. $1.50. C. M. Clark.

MASS.
See Catholic church;—Lord's supper.

Mass of Christ. *See* Adams, Fs. Songs of the army of the night.

Massachusetts. *Bd. of Education.* List of principals of high schools and principals of some private schools which supply the place of high schools in towns where they are located. '10(D) 11 p. T. pap., gratis. Mass. Bd. Educ.

Massachusetts. Business corporation law of 1903; (Prescott Farnsworth Hall.) 2d ed. '08(Je) c. 95+631 p. 8°, $5. W: J. Nagel.

Massachusetts. *Commission for the Blind.* Bulletin; no. 1, Needlessly blind for life. Ophthalmia neonatorum, commonly called infantile ophthalmia, or inflammation of the eyes in the new-born, or "babies' sore eyes." '09, [1910.] (Ap) 19 p. il. O. pap., gratis; per 1000, $30. Mass. Com. Blind.

Massachusetts. *Commission on High Cost of Living.* Wages and prices of commodities; Rept. '10(Jl) 13 p. 8°. Gov. Pr. Off.

Massachusetts. *Commission on the Cost of Living.* Rept. of the Commission on the Cost of Living. '10(S3) fold. tabs., O. gratis. Wright & P.

Massachusetts. *Commissioners on Inland Fisheries and Game.* Report upon the mollusk fisheries of Massachusetts. '09(Jl3) il. charts, O. pap., gratis. Mass. Com. Inland Fisheries.

Massachusetts. *Committee for International Congress on Tuberculosis, 6th, Washington,* 1908. Tuberculosis in Massachusetts; ed. by Edn. Allen Locke. '08(D) 13+223 p. il. fold. map, facsim., 4°. (Add. pubs. for price.) Wright & P.

Massachusetts. Draft of an act designed to simplify and improve transfers of land and titles to land, and to enlarge the jurisdiction of the land court, by C: S. Rackemann. '08(D) c. 35 p. O. pap. (Add. pubs. for price.) Mudge.

Massachusetts. Forest laws. (F. W: Rane.) '07, [1908.] (Ag.) 10+39 p. il. 24°, pap. (Add. pub. for price.) F. W: Rane.

Massachusetts. Hdbk. on forest mensuration of the white pine in Mass.; how to estimate standing timber; log scales; volume tablets; yield tables; financial rotations; growth tables; thinnings, etc., by Harold O. Cook, under the direction of F. W. Rane. '08, [1909.] (F) 50 p. il. tabs., S. gratis. Wright & P.

Massachusetts. Law of landlord and tenant, incl. the cases of v. 195 of the repts., and the legislation of 1907; by Prescott F. Hall. 2d ed., rev. and enl. '08(O) c. 62+619 p. O. (Add. pubs. for price.) Little, B. & Co.

Massachusetts. Law of Massachusetts rel. to the sale of goods; chapter 237, acts of 1908; an act to make uniform the law relating to the sale of goods. '09(F20) O. pap., 25 c. G. A. Jackson.

Massachusetts. Law rel. to money and negotiable instruments, annot., [repr. of Chap. 73, Rev. Laws.] '09(N) 32 p. O. pap., *25 c. net. G. A. Jackson.

Massachusetts. Laws of the commonwealth of Mass. rel. to qualifications and registration of voters, polit. committees, caucuses, etc. Summary of legislation, 1908; comp. by R: L. Gay. '08(Ag); 1909. '09 (S); 1910. '10(S) c. 16°, pap., ea., 35 c. R: L. Gay

Massachusetts. Legacy and succession tax, by E. H. Brewster. '10(My) $2 net. Little, B. & Co.

Massachusetts. New motor vehicle law; arr. for the use of owners, dealers, garages, operators, and chauffeurs, [etc.,] by C: J. Babbitt. '09(O) c. 52 p. O. **$1 net. Little, B. & Co.

Massachusetts. Regulations for the uniform of the Massachusetts volunteer militia: general orders, no. 27, Dec. 2, 1907. '08 (D5) 8°, pap., gratis. Adjutant General, Mass.

Massachusetts. Rept. of the Joint Special Committee on Taxation. '08(Ja11) O. pap., gratis. Wright & P.

Massachusetts. *Supreme judicial ct.* Repts., v. 194; (H: Walton Swift.) '08(Mr); v. 195 (Ag); v. 196 (O); v. 197 (D); v. 198. '09(F); v. 199 (Mr); v. 200 (Je); v. 201 (N); v. 202. '09, [1910.] (Ja); v. 203 (Ap); v. 204 (Jl); v. 205 (D) c. O. shp., ea., **$2 net. Little, B. & Co.

Massachusetts. Uniform sales act of 1908, with annots. by Fs. M. Burdick. '08(O) c. 69 p. O. pap. (Add. pubs. for price.) Little, B. & Co.

MASSACHUSETTS.

Bailey, H. R. Attorneys and their admission to the bar of Massachusetts. $2.50. W: J. Nagel.

Billings, J: D. Hist. of the 10th Mass. Battery of Light Artillery in the War of the Rebellion. $2. Arakelyan.

Bradford, W: Hist. of Plymouth plantation, 1606-1646. **$3 net. Scribner.

Clarke, D. A. Commercial forest trees of Massachusetts. (Add. pubs. for price.) Wright & P.

Cutter, W: R., *ed.* Genealogical and personal memoirs rel. to the families of the state of Massachusetts. $15.—Genealogical and personal memoirs rel. to the families of Boston and eastern Mass. 4 v. Lewis Pub.

Dale, T: N. Chief commercial granites of Massachusetts, New Hampshire and Rhode Island. (Add. Superintendent for price.) U. S., Supt. of Docs.

French, C: S. Worship of the golden calf: a study of wage-slavery in Massachusetts. $1. C: S. French.

Gardner, J. B. Massachusetts memorial to her soldiers and sailors who died in the department of No. Carolina, 1861-1865. $3.25. Gardner & T.

Gates, B. N. Miscellaneous papers on apiculture; bee keeping in Mass. 5 c. U. S., Supt. of Docs.

Green, S: A. Early mile-stones leading from Boston; and mile-stones at Groton. 25 c. S: A. Green.

Hasse, A. R. Index of economic material in documents of the states of the U. S.: Massachusetts. $2.25. Carnegie.

Hilkey, C: J. Legal development in colonial Mass., 1630-1686. $1.25. Longmans.

Jackson, G: L. Development of school support in colonial Mass., $1; pap., 75 c. Teachers' Coll.

Johnson, E: Wonder-working providence, 1628-1651. $3 net. Scribner.

MacLear, A. B. Early New England towns. *$1.50 net. Longmans.

MASSACHUSETTS.—*Continued.*

Martin, G: H: School hygiene in Massachusetts. gratis. G: H: Martin.

Maxwell, H. Study of the Mass. wood-using industries. F. W. Rane.

Morse, A. E. Federalist party in Massachusetts to the year 1800. *$2 net. Princeton Univ.

Paul, F. Notes on Massachusetts practice. (Add. pubs. for price.) Little, B. & Co.

Ramsay, J. P. Massachusetts probation system. (Add. author for price.) J. P. Ramsay.

Stark, J. H: Loyalists of Mass. and the other side of the American Revolution. $5. W: B. Clarke.

Stevens, W: B. History of the 50th Reg. of Infantry, Mass. vol. militia. $2. Griffith-S.

Updegraff, H. Origin of the moving school in Massachusetts. $1.50. Teachers' Coll.

Webber, H. E. Twelve months with the 8th Massachusetts Infantry in the service of the United States. $2. H. E. Webber.

Who's who along the north shore of Massachusetts. $2.50. Salem Press.

See also Acushnet;—Ashburnham;—Athol;—Andover;—Berkshire Hills;—Blandford;—Bolton;—Boston; — Bridgewater; — Brimfield; — Brookfield;—Bunker Hill; — Cambridge;—Cambridge Bridge;—Cohasset; — Danvers;—Dedham;—Dover;— Dudley;—Duxbury;—Education;—Essex;—Essex Co.;—Fall River;—Forests and forestry; — Gas and gas-fitting; — Genealogies; — Groton;—Hamilton;—Hatfield; — Haverhill; — Hingham;—Hygiene;—Ipswich;—King George's War;—Lincoln;—Lynn;—Lynnfield;— Marlborough;—Martha's Vineyard;—Medford;—Methuen;—Middlesex Co.;—Milton; — Nantucket; — Nantucket Island;—Natick;—New England;— Northampton;—Northfield;—Paint;—Plymouth; Plymouth Co.;—Quincy;—Salem;—Scituate;— Sharon;—Spencer; — Springfield;—Tisbury; — Tuberculosis;—Warren; — Watertown; — Wayland;—Westminster; — Weymouth;—Winchendon;—Worcester;—Worcester Co.;—Wrentham; —*also* Andros, *Sir* Edmund;—Quincy, John; —Shepard, Thomas;—Vane, *Sir* Henry, *jr.*

Massachusetts Agricultural College, Amherst. List of books on agriculture and related subjects; prepared by Short Course Dept., Mass. Agricultural College. '10(Ag) 15 p. 8°, gratis. W. D. Hind.

Massachusetts Association of Plumbing Inspectors. Official hdbk., 1910. '10(S) c. 216 p. O. $1.50. Mass. Assoc. Plumbing.

MASSACHUSETTS BAY COLONY.

Cawein, M. J. Ode: read August 15, 1907, at the dedication of the monument erected at Gloucester, Mass., in commemoration of the founding of the Massachusetts Bay Colony. 25 c. Morton.

Ford, W. C., *and* Mathews, A. Bibliography of the laws of the Massachusetts Bay, 1641-1776. (Priv. pr.) Univ. Press, (Camb.)

See also Pownall, Thomas.

Massachusetts Historical Society, Boston. Proceedings of the Massachusetts Historical Society in commemoration of the tercentenary of the birth of John Milton, 9 Dec., 1908. '09, [1910.] (Ap) 20 p. 8°. (Add. pubs. for price.) Mass. Hist. Soc.

Massachusetts Institute of Technology. Concerning the Massachusetts Institute of Technology; pub. by undergraduates. '09, [1910.] (Mr) 154 p. por. 12°, $1. G. James.

Massachusetts land court decisions, 1898-1908, by C: Thornton Davis. '09(Je) c. 21+327 p. O. $4. Little, B. & Co.

Massachusetts lawyers' diary, for 1908. '08 (Mr); for 1909. '08, [1909.] (Ja); for 1910. '10(F) c. sq. D. ea., $1.50; hf. leath., *$2 net; full rus., *$2.50 net. Standard Diary.

Massachusetts series. il. O. pap. Soc. Americana.

—Weeks *and* Bacon, *comps. and eds.* Historical digest of the provincial press. subs., per v., $7.50; per set, $150.

Massachusetts town law: digest of statutes and decisions concerning towns and town officers, by Ja. S. Garland. '08, [1909.] (Mr) c. O. $2.50. Boston Bk.

Massachusetts year book; daily court record, 1910. [1910.] (F) c. $1.50. F. S. Blanchard.

MASSAGE.

Abbott, G: K., *comp.* Technique of hydrotherapy and Swedish massage. 25 c. Loma Linda Coll.

Bennett, *Sir* W: H: Lectures on the use of massage and early movements in recent fractures. *$1.75 net. Longmans.

Hale, A. Art of massage. $2. W: R. Jenkins.

Masseck, Fk. Lincoln.

See Forbush, W: Byron.

Massee, G:

Diseases of cultivated plants and trees. '10(Jl16) il. 8°, $2.25 net. Macmillan.

MASSENET, Jules Émile Frédéric.

Finck, H: T. Massenet and his operas. $1.50 net. Lane.

Massey, G: Betton.

Conservative gynecology and electro-therapeutics; pract. treatise on the diseases of women and their treatment by electricity. 6th rev. ed. '09(My) 16+462 p. il. 8°, *$4 net. Davis.

Ionic surgery in the treatment of cancer, with a chapter on ionization in surgical tuberculosis and in hemorrhoids. '10 (Ap) c. 15+243 p. il. 8°, $3. Chatterton.

Massey, Rev. J: E:

Autobiography of John E. Massey; ed. by Eliz. H. Hancock. '09(S18) c. por. *$2 net. Neale.

Massie, Jos.

Essay on the governing causes of the natural rate of interest; wherein the sentiments of Sir William Petty and Mr. Locke, on that head, are considered; London, 1750. '08(F22) 8°, (Reprint of economic tracts.) subs., per set of 4 tracts, pap., *$2 net. Johns Hopkins.

Massie, Wa. W., and Underhill, C: R.

Wireless telegraphy and telephony popularly explained with special article by Nikola Tesla. '08(S19) c. il. D. **$1 net. Van Nostrand.

Masson, George Joseph Gustave, ed.

La lyre française. '08(D12) 12°, (Golden treasury ser.) $1. Macmillan.

Masson, J:

Lucretius, epicurean and poet. [v. 2, supplementary.] '09(Jl17) 8°, **$2 net. Dutton.

Masson, Rosaline.

Edinburgh. '10(D24) c. col. il. 12°, (Peeps at many lands ser.) 75 c. net. Macmillan.

Masson, T: Lansing.

New Plato; or, Socrates redivivus. '08 (Ap11) c. D. **75 c. net. Moffat.

Massys, Quinten.

Masterpieces. '09(Mr13) il. T. (Painters' ser.) parchment; *25 c. net; leath., *75 c. net, boxed. Stokes.

Masten, Vincent Myron.

Crime problem; what to do about it, how to do it. '09(Je12) c. 12°, $1.50. Star-Gazette.

Master (The). Bacheller, I. A. **$1.20. fixed. Doubleday, P.

Master and man. *See* Tolstoi, *Count* L. N.

Master and slave. McCallen, R. S $1.50. Nat. Bk.

Master (The) as I saw him. Noble, M. E. $1.50 net. Longmans.

Master Bob Robin. Stannard, H: 50 c. Warne.

Master builders. Dunning, J. E. †$1.50. Appleton.

Master Car Builders' Association. Car builders' dictionary. '10(F5) c. il. f°, $6. Railway Age Gazette.

Master code. '09(Ap17) 8°, $12. Business Code.

Master criminal. Paternoster, G: S. 75 c. Cupples & L.

Master-girl. Hilliers, A. $1.25 net. Putnam.

Master influence. McKean, T: †$1.50. Lippincott.

Master-knot. Birkhead, A. †$1.50. Lane.

Master minds at their commonwealth's heart. Epler, P. H. $2. F. S. Blanchard.

Master motive. Conan, L., *pseud.* $1. Herder.

Master musicians. Hadden, J. C. $1.75. Barse & H.

Master of game. York, E: P., *Duke* of. *$4 net. Duffield.

Master of life. Lighthall, W: D. $1.50. McClurg.

Master of the heart. Speer, R. E. *$1 net. Revell.

Master of the inn. Herrick, R. **50 c. net. Scribner.

Master of the vineyard. Reed, M. $1.50 net-$3.50 net. Putnam.

Master painters of Britain. White, G., *ed.* *$3 net. Lane.

Master preacher. Bond, A. R. $1 net. Am. Tr.

Master profession. Baker, S. 50 c. Franklin-T.

Master road. Eastwood, C. A. Harriman.

Master St. Elmo. Senour, C. *$1 net. Juvenile Bk.

Master singers of Japan; tr. by Clara A. Walsh. '10(Ap16) 16°, (Wisdom of the East ser.) 60 c. net. Dutton.

Master spirit. Kleber, J: C. **$1.50. Cochrane.**

Master workman. Mahood, J: W. 25 c. Praise Pub.

Masterman, Ernest W: Gurney.
Studies in Galilee; with a preface by G: Adam Smith. '09(N6) c. O. *$1 net. Univ. of Chic.

Masterman, Rev. J: Howard Bertram.
Rights and responsibilities of national churches. '08(D12) 12°, (Hulsean lectures.) *75 c. net. Putnam.

Masterman and Son. Dawson, W: J. *$1.20 net. Revell.

Masterman Ready. *See* Marryat, *Captain* F:

Masterpieces from Swedish literature in English form. Foss, C. W., *ed.* 75 c. Augustana.

Masterpieces in color; ed. by T. Leman Hare. il. O. bds., *65 c. net; leath., *$1.50 net. Stokes.

—Baldry. Burne-Jones.—Leighton.
—Bensusan. Holbein.—Lawrence.—Murillo.—Rubens.—Tintoretto.—Titian.
—Binns. Botticelli.
—Brockwell. Leonardo da Vinci.
—Caw. Raeburn.
—Coleridge. Holman Hunt.
—Finberg. Ingres.
—Furst. Dürer.
—Hare. Watts.
—Hay. Bellini.—Carlo Dolci.
—Hind. Constable.—Hogarth.—Watteau.
—Israels. Rembrandt.
—Konody. Chardin.—Raphael.
—Macfall. Fragonard.—Vigée Le Brun.
—Macklin. Greuze.
—Mason. Bernardino Luini.
—Pissaro. Fra Angelico.—Rossetti.
—Rothschild. Gainsborough.
—Staley. Franz Hals.
—Turner. Millet.—Van Dyck.
—Weale. Memlinc.
—Wood. Sargent.—Whistler.

Masterpieces of fiction. [1910.] (D) 8°, per v., $1 net; hf. mor., $1.50 net; hf. cf., $2 net. Little, B. & Co.
Contents: Dumas, Three musketeers, 2 v.; Twenty years after, 2 v.; Hugo, Les miserables, 4 v.; Lever, Charles O'Malley, 2 v.; Austen, Pride and prejudice; Dumas, Count of Monte Cristo, 4 v.; Daudet, Sappho; Eliot, *pseud.*, Romola; Lover, Handy Andy; Bulwer-Lytton, Last days of Pompeii.

Masterpieces of handicraft; ed. by T. Leman Hare. '09(D25) il. 16°, ea., *75 c. net. Dodd.
Contents: Chinese porcelains; Dresden porcelains; Japanese porcelains; Old Bow porcelains; Sèvres porcelains; Wedgewood porcelains.

Masterpieces of Moorish architecture. '09 (D25) 16°, (Parchment booklets.) pap., 25 c. Stokes.

Masterpieces of Spanish architecture. '09 (D25) 16°, (Parchment booklets.) pap., 25 c. Stokes.

Masterpieces of the Ohio mound builders. Randall, E. O. $1. Ohio Archæolog.

Masterpieces of the world's best literature. Gilder, J. L., *ed.* 8 v. $3. O. T. Harris.

Master's call to service. Houtz, A. 60 c. Ref. Ch. Pub.

Master's carpet. Ronayne, E. 75 c. T. B. Arnold.

Master's friendships. Miller, J. R. **30 c. net; 50 c. net. Crowell.

Masters, Ellen T.
One hundred useful things. '08(D5) *75 c. net. Cassell.

Masters of achievement. Ruoff, H: W., *ed.* $5.50; $6.25; $7.50. Frontier Press.

Masters of literature. il. 12°, *$1.10 net. Macmillan.

—Carlyle. Selections.
—Defoe. Selections.
—Fielding. Selections.
—Scott. Selections.
—Thackeray. Selections.

Masters of the English novel. Burton, R: $1.25. Holt.

Masters of the wheatlands. Bindloss, H. $1.30 net. Stokes.

Masters of the wilderness. Reed, C: B. 50 c. Chic. Hist.

Mastersinger. Rix, F. R. 65 c. Am. Bk.

Mastery of death. Eaves, A. O. *$1 net. Badger.

Mastery of destiny. Allen, J. **$1 net. Putnam.

Mastery of mind. Frank, H: $1. Fenno.

Mastery of self. Larson, C: D. 50 c. Eternal Progress.

Maston, Ray T:
Poems. [1910.] (Ap) c. '09. 13-25 p. 12°. (Priv. pr.) R. T: Maston.

"Matasiso," pseud.
See Bates, Fk. Amasa.

Mater. Mackaye, P. W. **$1.25 net. Macmillan.

MATERIA MEDICA.
Beasley, H: Book of prescriptions; with an index of diseases and remedies. *$2 net. Blakiston.
Bruce, J: M. Materia medica and therapeutics. $2 net. Funk.
Butler, G: F. Text book of materica medica, pharmacology and therapeutics. *$4 net; *$5.50 net. Saunders.
Butler, G: F., *and others, eds.* Materia medica and therapeutics. $1.50. Year Bk.
Coblentz, V. Newer remedies. $1. Apothecary.
Cowperthwaite, A. C. Text-book of materia medica and therapeutics. $5. Boericke & T.
Culbreth, D: M. R. Manual of materia medica and pharmacology. $4.75 net. Lea.
Dawborn, R. H. M. Aid to materia medica. **$1.75 net. Macmillan.
Desjardins, A. U. Manual of materia medica for students. $1.50. A. U. Desjardins.
Dose book of specific medicines. (Add. pubs. for price.) Lloyd Bros.
Farrington, E. A. Clinical materia medica. $6; $7. Boericke & T.
Foote, J: A. Essentials of materia medica and therapeutics for nurses. $1.25. Lippincott.
Greenish, H: G: Microscopical examination of foods and drugs. $3. Blakiston.
Groff, J: E. Materia medica for nurses. *$1.25 net. Blakiston.
Lloyd, J: U. Electric alkaloids, resins, resinoids, oleo resins and concentrated principles. $1. Lloyd Lib.

MATERIA MEDICA.—*Continued.*
Nash, E. B. Regional leaders. $1.50. Boericke & T.
Nelson, B. E. Introd. to the analysis of drugs and medicines. $3 net. Wiley.
Potter, S. O. L. Therapeutics, materia medica, and pharmacy. $5. Blakiston.
Shoemaker, J: V. Pract. treatise on materia medica and therapeutics. *$6 net. Davis.
Stevens, A. A. Modern materia medica and therapeutics. $3.50. Saunders.
Stimson, J. C. Nurses hdbk. of drugs and solutions. $1 net. Whitcomb.
See also Homœopathy;—Medical chemistry;—Medical jurisprudence;—Medicine; — Pharmacy; — Pinkroot;—Poisons;—Teeth;—Veterinary medicine and surgery.

Material culture of the Klamath Lake and Modoc Indians. Barrett, S: A. 75 c. Univ. of Cal.

MATERIALISM.
Wayland-Smith, F. Materialism and Christianity. 25 c. Wayland-Smith.

Materialized apparitions. Brackett, E: A. $1.25. Badger.

MATERIALS (Strength of).
See Strength of materials.

Materials and methods of fiction. Hamilton, C. M. **$1.50 net. Baker & T.

Materials for a bibliography of the public archives of the thirteen original states. Hasse, A. R. (Add. Superintendent for price.) U. S., Supt. of Docs.

MATERNITY.
See Midwifery;—Mothers.

Maternity: play. Brieux, E. (Add. pub. for price.) B: R. Tucker.

MATHEMATICAL DRAWING.
See Mechanical drawing.

Mathematical ser. of college text-books. O. Holt.
—Hall *and* Frink. Trigonometry. $1.25.

Mathematical text. See Ginn's.

Mathematical theory of electricity and magnetism. Jeans, J. H. *$4.50 net. Putnam.

MATHEMATICS.
Agnew, P. G. Approximate experimental method for the analysis of E. M. F. waves. Gov. Pr. Off.
American Mathematical Society, New York. Catalogue of the library, January, 1910. gratis. Am. Math.
Andrews, W. S. Magic squares and cubes. *$1.50 net. Open Court.
Berkeley, H. Mysticism in modern mathematics. $3.20. Oxford Univ.
Branford, B. Study of mathematical education. $1.10. Oxford Univ.
Breckenridge, W: E., *and others.* Shop problems in mathematics. $1. Ginn.
Butts, W: H. Elliptic cylinder function of class K, synthetic treatment and computation of tables. 50 c. Lord Balto Pr.
Coffin, J. G: Vector analysis. *$2.50 net. Wiley.
Columbia University. Teachers' College. Educational Museum. Exhibition of material illustrating the historical development of mathematics from the collection of D: Eug. Smith. gratis. D: E. Smith.

MATHEMATICS.—*Continued.*
De Morgan, A: On the study of mathematics. *$1.25 net. Open Court.
Fink, K. Brief history of mathematics. *$1.50 net. Open Court.
Finkel, B: F. Mathematical solution book. $2. Kibler.
Fuller, R. Circle and square; the ancient problem arranged in four parts. $1. R. Fuller.
Hardy. G. H. Course in pure mathematics. *$4 net. Putnam.
Hilton, H. Introd. to the theory of groups of finite order. *$4.75 net. Oxford Univ.
Holton, E: E. Shop mathematics. $1.25. Taylor-H.
International Correspondence Schools, *Scranton, Pa.* Tratado elemental de matemâticas y mecânica. (Priv. pr.) Int. Correspondence.
Kelvin, W: T., *Lord.* Mathematical and physical papers. v. 4. $6.40 net. Putnam.
Keyser, C. J. Mathematics. 25 c. Macmillan.
Lagrange, J. L. Lectures on elementary mathematics. *$1 net. Open Court.
Lehmer, D. N. Factor tables for the first ten millions. $20. Carnegie.
McGiffert, J. Mathematical short cuts. 25 c. A. M. Allen.
Manning, H: P., *ed.* Fourth dimension simply explained. *$1.50 net. Munn.
Mellor, J. W: Higher mathematics for students of chemistry and physics. $4.50. Longmans.
Moore, E. H., *and others.* New Haven mathematical colloquium. *$3 net. Yale Univ.
Myers, G: W:, *and others.* Second-year mathematics for secondary schools. $1.50 net. Univ. of Chic.
Phillips, E: C: On the pentacardioid. 35 c. Johns Hopkins.
Saxelby, F. M. Introd. to practical mathematics. 80 c. Longmans.
Schubert, H. Mathematical essays and recreations. *75 c. net. Open Court.
Short, R. L:, *and* Elson, W: H. Secondary-school mathematics. $1. Heath.
Sylvester, J. J. Collected mathematical papers. *$6 net. Putnam.
Symposium on mathematics for engineering students. gratis. H. E. Slaught.
Waterbury, L. A. A vest-pocket hdbk. of mathematics for engineers. **$1 net. Wiley.
White, W: F. Scrap-book of elem. mathematics. $1. Open Court.
See also Algebra;—Arithmetic;—Astronomy;—Calculus;—Engineering; — Equations;—Geodesy;—Geometry;—Graphics;—Interest; — Logarithms;—Longitude; — Mechanical engineering; — Mechanics;—Mensuration;—Nautical surveying;—Navigation;—Numerals;—Percentage;—Physics;—Projection;—Slide rule; — Squares;—Surveying;—Trigonometry.

Mathematics of machine design. Blake, C. F. 25 c. Indust. Press.

Mather, Rev. Cotton.
Elegy on the much-to-be-deplored death of that never-to-be-forgotten person, the Reverend Nathaniel Collins, who after he had been many years a faithful pastor to the church at Middletown of Ct., New England, about the 43d third year of his age, expired on 28th 10. moneth 1684; [ed. by Holdridge O. Collins.] '10(F12) 12°, leath., $3. (300 copies.) Baumgardt.

Mather, Rob.
Commemoration address on the seventieth anniversary of the founding of Knox College and the city of Galesburg, del. at Galesburg, Ill., Wednesday, June 12, 1907. '07, [1908.] (Mr.) 35 p. front., 8°. (Priv. pr.) R. G. Cooke.

Mather, Sedgwick.
Anatomy and physiology of the nervous system. '10(F12) c. il. D. *$1.50 net. McVey.

Matheson, Ewing.
Depreciation of factories, mines and industrial undertakings and their valuation. 4th ed., rev. and enl. '10(S) 12+230 p. tabs., diagr., 8°, $4. Spon.

Matheson, G:, D.D.
Day unto day: brief prayer for every day. '08(S12) 16°, *50 c. net. Revell.
Messages of hope. '08(D12) D. *$1.25 net. Armstrong.
Spiritual development of St. Paul. New ed. '09(O) 12°, *80 c. net. Whittaker.
Thoughts for life's journey. '08(Mr28) D. *$1.25 net. Armstrong.

Mathews, Albert.
See Ford, Worthington Chauncey.

Mathews, Byron Collins.
Our irrational distribution of wealth. '08 (O17) c. D. **$1.25 net. Putnam.

Mathews, Catharine Van Cortlandt.
Andrew Ellicott: his life and letters. '08 (My9) c. il. pors. map, facsims., O. **$2.50 net. Grafton Press.

Mathews, Frances Aymar.
Flame dancer. '08(S19) c. il. D. †$1.50. G: W. Dillingham.
If David knew. '10(O8) c. D. $1.50. G: W: Dillingham.

Mathews, J: Lathrop.
Conservation of water. '10(D10) c. il. O. $2 net. Small.
Remaking the Mississippi. '09(My22) c. il. O. **$1.75 net. Houghton M.

Mathews, J: Mabry.
Legislative and judicial history of the Fifteenth Amendment. [Negro vote.] '09 (Je12) O. (Johns Hopkins Univ. studies in history and political science.) pap. $1. Johns Hopkins.

Mathews, Lois Kimball.
Expansion of New England; spread of New England settlement and institutions to the Mississippi River, 1620-1865. '09 (N20) maps, O. **$2.50 net. Houghton M.

Mathews, Rob. Valentine.
Lost legion. '10(F19) c. O. $1. E. C. Hill.

Mathews, Shailer, D.D.
Gospel and the modern man. '10(My14) c. D. $1.50 net. Macmillan.
Hist. of New Testament times in Palestine, 175 B.C.-70 A.D. Rev. ed. '10(O1) c. map, D. $1 net. Macmillan.
Social gospel. '10(F19) c. D **50 c. net. Griffith.
Social gospel. '10(D31) c. (Pilgrim advanced Sunday-school lessons.) bds., 50 c. net. Pilgrim Press.
See also Burton, Ernest Dewitt.
—, **ed.** *See* Bible.—Bible for home and school

Mathewson, Champion Herbert.
First principles of chemical theory. '09 (F6) c. il. 8°, $1. Wiley.

Mathewson, Christopher.
Won in the ninth; ed. by W. W. Aulick. '10(My7) c. il. 12°, (Matty books.) $1. Bodmer.

Mathewson, Fk. Elliott.
Perspective sketching from working drawings. '08(N) 77 p. diagrs. 4°, $1. Taylor-H.
Supplementary notes for mechanical drawing, ser. 1. '07, '08(Je) il. obl. 16°, pap., 40 c. Taylor-H.

Mathewson, H: S., M.D.
Prophylactic value of vaccination. '09 (My15) 8°. (Add. Superintendent for price.) U. S., Supt. of Docs.

MATILDA, *Countess of Tuscany.*
Duff, N. Matilda of Tuscany. *$3.50 net. Dutton.

Matinée idol. Wills, A. E. 15 c. Dick.

Matlock, G. A., comp.
See Oklahoma. Laws and legal forms.

Matlock, S: Dreher.
See Pepper, G: Wharton.
—, **comp.** *See* Pennsylvania. Table of cases.

MATRIMONY.
See Marriage.

Matson, E., ed.
Nature year book. '10(D) 12°, (Day by day ser.) 60 c.; ooze, $1. Crowell.

Matson, G: Charlton.
Water resources of the Blue Grass region, Kentucky; with a chap. on the quality of the waters, by Chase Palmer. '09, [1910.] (F) 223 p. il. fold. map, 8°, (U. S., Dept. of the Interior, U. S. Geolog. Survey; water-supply paper.) pap.

Matt of the water-front. Eastland, F. M. *60 c. net. Jennings.

Mattack, S: Dreher.
See Pennsylvania. Index.

Mätter, J:
Once. '10(O15) c. D. $1.20 net. Holt.

MATTER.
Farrar, L. B. Eternity of matter. $2. N. E. Stevens.

Matter and some of its dimensions. '10 (Mr12) c. figs. D. *$1 net. Woodward & L.

Matter with nervousness. Sawyer, H. C. $1. Cunningham, C. & W.

Matteson, D: Maydole, comp.
Analytic index. *See* Hart, A. B., *ed.* American nation. v. 27.

MATTHEW (*Gospel of*).
See Bible.

Matthew Porter. Bradford, G., *jr.* $1.50. L. C. Page.

Matthew Strong. Francis, *Mrs.* $2. Lippincott.

Matthews, A.
Retail liquor dealers' manual of United States internal revenue laws; rev. to date, Apr. 2, 1908. '08(My.) c. 52 p. O. pap., 75 c. J. M. Wolfe.

Matthews, Albert.
Snake devices, 1754-1776, and the Constitutional courant, 1765. '08, [1909.] (Ap) 409-452 p. il. facsims., 8°. (Priv. pr.) A. Matthews.
Uncle Sam. '08(N) 21-65 p. 8°. (Not for sale.) Davis Press.

Matthews, Albert Franklin.
Back to Hampton Roads; cruise of the U. S. Atlantic fleet from San Francisco to Hampton Roads, Jl. 7, 1908-Feb. 22, 1909; supplementary to With the battle fleet. '09(O23) c. il. D. $1.50. B: W. Huebsch.
With the battle fleet; cruise of the 16 battleships of the United States Atlantic fleet from Hampton Roads to the Golden Gate. '08(O24) c. il. D. $1.50. B: W. Huebsch.

Matthews, C. H. S.
Parson in the Australian Bush. '08(N7) il. D. $2. Longmans.

Matthews, Mrs. Frances Eliz. Morgan.
Dreams of yesterdays (in the Orient.) '08 (Ag1) c. il. D. $1. Cochrane.

Matthews, Fs. E., ed.
See Illinois. *Courts.* Repts.

Matthews, Ja. Brander.
American of the future, and other essays. '09(O16) c. D. **$1.25 net. Scribner.
Molière. '10(O22) c. pors. O. $3 net. Scribner.
Study of the drama. '10(Mr19) c. il. plans. D. **$1.50 net. Houghton M.
—, ed. The short-story: specimens illustrating its development; with introd. and notes. '08(Ja11) D. $1. Am. Bk.

Matthews, Jos. Merritt.
Laboratory manual of dyeing and textile chemistry. '09(Ap3) c. 8°, $3.50. Wiley.

Matthews, Schuyler Colfax.
How to keep well and live long. 3d ed. '09(O23) c. il. 8°, $1. Matthews.

Matthews, W: Dennis.
Manual of inspectors: reference book for use of fire underwriters. '08(S) c. 304 p. il. map, 16°, flex. leath., $3. Insurance Field.

Matty books. il. 12°. Bodmer.
—Mathewson. Won in the ninth. $1.

Mature man's difficulties with his Bible. Faunce, D. W. **75 c. net. Am. Bapt.

Mauchline, Rob.
Mine foreman's handbook of pract. and theoretical instruction on the opening, ventilating, and working of collieries. 3d ed., thoroughly rev. and enl. '10 (O15) il. 8°, $3.75. Baird.

Maud, Constance.
Tales of Wagner's heroes; Lohengrin, Hans Sachs, Tannhäuser, Parsifal. '09 (N13) il. O. 50 c. McLoughlin.

Maud, Constance Elisabeth.
Daughter of France. '09(Mr20) front. D. $1.50. Lane.

Maud. *See* Tennyson, Alfr., *Lord.* Enoch Arden.

Maud Muller's ministry. Smiley, J. L. 50 c. J. L. Smiley.

Maud the mirthful mule. Opper, F: B. 60 c. Stokes.

Maude, Aylmer.
Life of Tolstoy. In 2 v. [v. 1,] First fifty years; [v. 2,] Later years. '10(D3) pors. O. $6 net, boxed. Dodd.

Maude, E.
Oriental campaigns and European furloughs. '08(eJ6) por. O. *$2.50 net. Wessels.

Maude, Col. Frederic Natusch.
Jena campaign, 1806. '09(Je26) fold. tabs., fold. maps in pocket, D. (Special campaign ser.) *$1.60 net. Macmillan.
Leipzig campaign, 1813. '08(Ag22) maps, plans, 12°, (Special campaign ser.) *$1.60 net Macmillan.

Maude, Sophie.
Child countess; with a foreword by Rob. Hugh Benson. '08(D) 232 p. 12°, *75 c. net. Benziger.

Maugham, W: Somerset.
The explorer. '09(F13) c. front. D. †$1.50. Baker & T.
The magician. '09(F6) c. D. †$1.50. Duffield.

Maule, Fs. I.
El dorado "29"; along with other weird Alaskan tales, done into verse. '10(S10) c. il. D. $1 net. Winston.

Maule, G: Edm.
Life and law; or, way to a bigger life. '08(Je6) c. por. D. $1.25. G: E. Maule.

Maule, Mrs. Mary K.
Little knight of the X Bar B. '10(Ap23) c. il. D. $1.50. Lothrop, L. & S.

MAULSBY FAMILY.
See Genealogies, Barnard E. K.

MAUNA LOA, Hawaii.
Brigham, W: T. Volcanoes of Kilauea and Mauna Loa. $3.50: $4.50. Bishop Museum.

Maunder, E: Walter.
Astronomy of the Bible; elem. commentary on the astronomical references of Holy Scripture. 3d ed. '09(N20) il. D. *$1.25 net. Doran.
Astronomy of the Bible. '08(N21) il. 8°. *$2 net. M. Kennerley.

Maupassant, Guy de.
Works. [Edition de luxe.] '09(N20) c. 10 v., il. por. 8°. subs., $35. (1000 sets.) Bigelow, S.
[Works.] In 8 v. '10(My14) fronts. 16°, $3, with subs. to *Pearson's Magazine.* Pearson Pub. Co.
Complete works; translations and critical and interpretive essays by Alfred de Sumichrast, Adolphe Cohn, Henri C. Olinger, and others; verses by Percy Fitzhugh. 9 v. [Ed. de luxe.] '10 (Ap9) c. il. 8°, ea., $1.10. Brainard.

Maupassant, Guy de.—*Continued.*
Miromesnil edition of Guy de Maupassant; tr. by A. E. Henderson, B.A., Mme. Quesada, and others. 8 v. '10(Je18) c. fronts. 8°, $5.60. Collier.

Pierre and Jean; with preface by the author; tr. by Hugh Craig. '09(D4) c. il. S. (Wayside lib.) leath., $1. Brentano's.

Maupin, B: Franklin, comp.
Publisher's calculator; covering billing, royalty statements and inventories. '08 (D26) obl. f°, $10. B: F. Maupin.

Publisher's calculator. In 3 v. v. 1, Inventory tables; v. 2, Billing tables; v. 3, Royalty tables. '09(Ap3) v. 1, nar. F.; v. 2, Q.; v. 3, obl. O. ¾ leath., ea., $3; 2 vs., $5.40; 3 vs., $6.75; additional vs., ea., $2.25. B: F. Maupin.

MAUPIN FAMILY.
See Genealogies: Miller, W: H.

Maurer, E: Rose.
See Turneaure, F: Eug.

Maurer, Mrs. Ruth D. Johnson, ["Emily Lloyd."]
Prismatic ray in the treatment of face and scalp. '10(Ag) 108 p. il. 12°, $1.50. New Med.

Skin, its care and treatment. 3d ed., rewritten and greatly enl. '08(F1) c. il. D. $2. McIntosh.

Maurice, W:
Electric blasting apparatus and explosives; with special reference to colliery practice. [1910.] (Ag) 10+166 p. il. 8°, ("Electrician" ser.) $3.50. Van Nostrand.

Maurice Guest. Richardson, H: H., *pseud.* †$1.50. Duffield.

Maurin. Aicard, J. F. V. $1.50. Lane.

Mauro, Philip.
Life in the Word. '09(Mr6) c. 12°, *50 c. net. Revell.

Number of man: the climax of civilization. '09(D11) c. D. *$1.25 net. Revell.

Maury, J. C.
See Harris, Gilbert Dennison.

Maury, Matthew Fontaine, and Simonds, Frederic W:
Physical geography; rev. and largely rewritten by Frederic W: Simonds. '08 (My2) c. il. maps, O. $1.20. Am. Bk.

Maury, Mrs. Sarah Webb.
The beech. '10(My14) T. bds., 25 c. net. Lane.

Ginko tree. '10(D) 10 p. pap., 25 c. net. Lane.

The holly. '09, [1910.] (Ap) 10 l. col. il. 24°, 25 c. Lane.

Mauve, Anton.
Masterpieces; reproductions from his most renowned pictures. '08(O24) T. (Dutch painters.) leath., *75 c. net; pap., *25 c. net. Stokes.

Maver, W:, jr.
American telegraphy and encyclopedia of the telegraph. '09(Ja23) c. il. 8°, $5. Maver

Wireless telegraphy and telephony. [4th ed.] '10(F5) c. 8°, $3. Maver.

Maw, Jessy Maud.
Whims and visions. '09, [1910.] (Ja) c. 75 p. 8°, $1. J. M. Maw.

Maw, Percival Trentham.
Practice of forestry. '10(Ag13) $7. Scribner.

Max, Jos., M.D.
Hdbk. of cosmetics; auth. English tr., rev. from the 3d German ed. '10(Jl) 87 p. 12°, $1 net. Treat.

Max. Thurston, *Mrs.* K. C. $1.50. Harper.

Maxim, Sir Hiram Stevens.
Artificial and natural flight. '09(Ja16) il. O. *$1.75 net. Macmillan.

Maxim, Hudson.
Science of poetry and philosophy of language. '10(S3) c. il. por. O. $2.50 net. Funk.

Maxim, Ja. L.
Apprentices' course in experimental physics and mechanics for preliminary technical students and secondary school pupils; with recent examination questions. '10(Ap2) il. S. 50 c. Longmans.

Experimental applied mechanics for technical students. '10(O1) il. S. 60 c. Longmans.

Maximes et reflections. *See* Pascal, Blaise La Rochefoucauld.

MAXIMS.
Balzac, H. de. Maxims. *75 c. net. Putnam.
Dodsley, R. Economy of human life. $1.50. C. C. Owens.
Jerningham, C: E. W. Marmaduke maxims. *$1.25 net. Brentano's.
Penn, W: Reflections and maxims. $3; $15. Seymour.
Swetchine, *Mme.* A. S. S. Maxims. **55 c. net. Herder.
Watson, M. L., *comp.* Our breakfast book. $1. Volland.
See also Aphorisms;—Epigrams;—Proverbs;—Quotations.

Maxson, Harold R.
Practical up-to-date guide to Mexico City and vicinity. '07, [1908.] (Mr.) c. 239 p. il. map, S. (Add. pub. for price.) Am. Bk. and Pr.

Maxson, L: W., comp.
Spalding official archery guide. New ed.; rev. by E: B. Weston. '10(S) c. 130 p. il. pors. 16°, (Spalding's athletic lib.) pap., 10 c. Am. Sports.

Maxwell, Anna Caroline, and Pope, Amy Eliz.
Pract. nursing; text-book for nurses and a handbook for all who care for the sick. 2d ed., rev. and enl. '10(S) c. 13+571 p. il. 12°, $1.75 net. Putnam.

Maxwell, Aymer.
See Malcolm, G:

Maxwell, Sir Herbert Eustace.
Century of empire, 1801-1900. In 3 v. v. 1, 1801-1832. '09(N20); v. 2, 1833-1863. '10(Ap23) pors. O. ea., $4 net. Longmans.

Memories of the months; fifth ser. '09 (D11) il. O. $2.50. Longmans.

Scottish gardens. '08(D19) il. Q. *$6 net, boxed. Longmans.

Maxwell, Hu.
Study of the Massachusetts wood-using industries; by Hu Maxwell, under the direction of F. W: Rane and H. S. Sackett. '10(My) 38 p. O. pap. F. W: Rane.
See also Hall, W: Logan.

Maxwell, Ja. L.
See Jefferys, W. Hamilton.

Maxwell, S: Steen.
Experiments on the functions of the internal ear. '10(S) 4 p. O. (Univ. of Cal. pubs.; Physiology.) pap. Univ. of Cal.

Maxwell, W: Babington.
Hill Rise. '08(F15) c. D. 75 c. Cupples & L.
Rest cure; novel. '10(O22) c. D. $1.50. Appleton.
Seymour Charlton; a novel. '09(O9) c. il. †$1.50. Appleton.

Maxwell, W: Grey, comp.
Message of song; with illustrative poems selected by the author. '10(F26) c. D. **$1.50 net. Lippincott.

Maxwell, W: H:, Johnston, Emma L., and Barnum, Madalene D.
Speaking and writing; bk. 1, (for use in third year classes.) '10(Ap9) 20 c.; bk. 2 for use in fourth year classes.) (O1) c. il. S. 23 c. Am. Bk.

Maxwell, Sir W: Stirling-.
See Stirling-Maxwell, *Sir* W:

Maxwell-Scott, Mrs. Mary Monica.
See Scott, *Mrs.* Mary Monica Maxwell-.

MAXWELL FAMILY.
See Genealogies: Boyd, L., *comp.*

May, C: Fremont.
The devil rebellion and the reason why. [1910.] (N) c. 227 p. por. 12°, $1.25. M. L. & I.

May, C: H:, M.D.
Manual of the diseases of the eye for students and general practitioners. 6th ed., rev. '09(Ag) 397 p. il. figs. *$2 net. Wood.

May, Clarence Earl.
Oxygen ethers of the type—N: C. (O R), derived from certain nitrogen heterocycles. '08, [1909.] (Mr) 51 p. 8°. (Add. author for price.) C. E. May.

May, Florence Land.
Broken wheel. '10(Ap23) c. il. D. $1.50. C. M. Clark.

May, J: Wilder.
Law of crimes. 3d ed.; ed. by Harry A: Bigelow. '08(D) c. 54+366 p. O. shp., $3.50. Little, B. & Co.

May, Phil.
See Humorous masterpieces.

May, Seton.
Little Perkie. '10(D) il. (12 in col.) sq. 12°, 30 c. Jacobs.

May, Sophie, pseud.
See Clarke, Rebecca Sophia.

Mayall, G.
Cows, cowhouses and milk. '10(D) $1. A. Eger.

MAYAS (The).
Bowditch, C: P. Numeration, calendar systems and astronomical knowledge of the Mayas. (Priv. pr.) Univ. Press.

MAYAS (The).—*Continued.*
Diven, T: J. Aztecs and Mayas. In 2 v. v. 1. $1. Antiquarian.
Tozzer, A. M., *and* Allen, G. M. Animal figures in the Maya codices. $1. Peabody Museum.

Maybank, T:
Alice's adventures in Wonderland; in words of one syllable. '10(D10) il. bds., 50 c. Dutton.

Mayberry, Ja. Willard.
Physiology and hygiene. '10(N) 6+350 p. il. 12°, 60 c. Southern Pub. (Tex).

Maybloom and myrtle. Peck, S: M. $1. Estes.

Maycock, W: Perren.
Electric lighting and power distribution. In 2 v. v. 1. 7th ed., thoroughly rev. and mostly rewritten. '08(S19) il. 12°, *$1.90 net. Macmillan.

Mayer, Alfr. Goldsborough.
Medusae of the world. In 3 v. v. 1, The hydromedusae; v. 2, The hydromedusae; v. 3, The sychomedusae. '10(S17) Q. pap., ea., $6; per set, $18. Carnegie.

Mayer, C.
See Zerr, G:

Mayer, Clarence.
Telephone construction; methods and cost; with additional data by J. C. Slippy and others. '08(Ag22) c. il. tabs., 12°, *$3 net. M. C. Clark.

Mayer, Rabbi Eli.
Joshua to Ruth: a Sabbath-school book. '08(Ag15) il. S. pap., 30 c. E. Mayer.

Mayer, Fk.
Song of the wolf. '10(My14) c. D. $1.50. Moffat.

Mayer, Hy, [i.e., Henry.]
Jumbo and his family. '08(N7) il. obl. Tt. (Little mother ser.) bds., 50 c. Dutton

Mayer, Lucius W.
Mining methods in Europe. '09(Je12) c. il. 8°, $2.50. Hill Pub.

Mayer, Otto S.
End of the game, and other plays and stories. '09, [1910.] (F) 125 p. 12°, $1. Moods.

Mayes, E:
Ribs of the law; being a series of concise statements of the outlines of legal study for the service of law students. '09(O) c. 180 p. O. (Add. pubs. for price.) Lex.

Mayes, Josie S.
Breezes from the Southland. '09(D4) c. 12°, $1. B'way Pub.

Mayfield, Ja. J.
See Alabama. Code.

"MAYFLOWER" descendants.
See Rhode Island.

Mayflower to mistletoe. Day, S. J. **$1.25 net. Putnam.

Mayhew, E:
Lyrics of childhood. '08, [1909.] (Jl) c. 9+76 p. il. por. 8°, **$1 net. Grafton Press.

Mayhew, Thdr., comp.
See Coyle, H:

Maylard, Alfr. Ernest.
Abdominal tuberculosis. '08(D) 57 p. il. 8°, *$4 net. Blakiston.

Maynadier, Emily W., comp.
Perfect strength: sequence of verses by various authors forming an ideal love history. '08(D5) c. D. *75 c. net. J: W. Luce.

Maynard, C: Johnson.
Directory to the birds of eastern North America. '08(Je6) c. il. 16°, $2; flex. leath., $2.50; $6. C: J. Maynard.

Maynard, S: Taylor.
Small country place. '08(Je6) c. O. **$1.50 net. Lippincott.

Maynard's English classic ser. 12°. C: E. Merrill.
—Lyell. Travels in North America. 2 v. 30 c.

Mayne, Ethel Colburn.
Enchanters of men; 24 studies of fascinating women. '09, [1910.] (Ja) il. 8°, *$3.50 net. Jacobs.
Romance of Monaco and its rulers. '10 (O15) il. O. $5 net. Lane.

Mayne, J:
Journal during a tour on the continent upon its reopening after fall of Napoleon, 1814; ed. by his grandson, J: Mayne Colles. '09(Ap24) il. O. *$4 net. Lane.

Mayo, Marg.
Polly of the circus. '08(S26) c. il. S. †$1. Dodd.

MAYO, *Mrs.* Mary Anne Bryant.
Buell, J. One woman's work for farm women: story of Mary A. Mayo's part in rural social movements. 50 c.; 25 c. Whitcomb.

Mayor of Casterbridge. *See* Hardy T:

Mayor of New York. Gratacap, L: P. $1.50. G: W: Dillingham.

Mayor of Romanstown. Rees, W: G. 75 c. Cochrane.

Mayow, J:, M.D.
Medico-physical works: being a translation of Tractatus quinque medico-physici. '08 (Je20) il. por. 12°, (Alembic Club reprints.) *$1.25 net. Univ. of Chic.

MAYOW, John.
Gotch, F. Two Oxford physiologists: Richard Lower, 1631 to 1691; John Mayow, 1643 to 1679. 35 c. Oxford Univ.

Mazdaznan encyclopedia of dietetics and home cook book. Hanish, O. Z.-A-. $1.25. Mazdaznan.

Mazeppa. *See* Byron, *Lord* G: G. N. Childe Harold.

MAZZINI, Giuseppe.
Lloyd, H: D. Mazzini and other essays. $1.50 net. Putnam.

Mead, Dan. Webster.
Relations of experimental results to the theory of the tangential water wheel. '09, [1910.] (O) 104 p. il. tabs., diagrs., 8°, (Univ. of Wis. bull.; Engineering ser.) 40 c. Univ. of Wis.
Bibliography (3 p.).
Water power engineering. '08(N7) c. il. maps, tabs., O. *$6 net. McGraw.

Mead, Edn. Doak.
Literature of the peace movement. '10 (Ap2) O. (Int. Sch. of Peace pamphlets.) pap., gratis. Int. Sch. of Peace.
Results of the two Hague conferences and the demands upon the third conference. '10(D) 14 p O. (International School of Peace pamphlets.) pap., per 100, $3. Int. Sch. of Peace.

Mead, Herman Ralph, comp.
Bibliography of George Berkeley, Bishop of Cloyne. '10(Jl16) O. (Univ. of Cal. Lib., bull.) pap. Univ. of Cal.

Mead, Mrs. Lucia True Ames.
Educational organizations promoting international friendship. '10(D) 19 p. O. (International School of Peace pamphlets.) pap., per 100, $3. Int. Sch. of Peace.

Mead, Marion.
See Pearl (The).

Mead, W: Leon.
How words grow. '08(D12) c. 12°, (Handy information ser.) 50 c. Crowell.

Mead, Willis Waldo.
Apocalypse of Jesus Christ: an exposition. '09(Jl3) D. **$1 net. W. W. Mead.

Meade, E: Sherwood.
Corporation finance. '10(N5) c. D. (Appleton's business ser.) $2 net. Appleton.
Economics; pract. exposition of the science of business. '10(Ja8) c. 12°, (Modern business.) $3.50. De Bower-E.
Story of gold. '08(N14) c. il. D. **75 c. net. Appleton.

Meade, L. T.
See Smith, *Mrs.* Eliz. Thomasina.

Meade, Norman Gardner.
Electric motors. '08(D5) c. il. tabs., D. *$1 net. McGraw.

Meade, Mrs. Rebecca Paulding.
Life of Hiram Paulding, rear-admiral, U. S. N. '10(D10) c. pors. D. $1.50 net. Baker & T.

Meade, R: Kidder.
Chemists' pocket manual; pract. hdbk. cont. tables, formulas, calculations, information, physical and analyt. methods for use of chemists, chemical engineers, assayers, metallurgists, manufacturers and students. 2d ed. '10(Ag) 12+443 p. il. (incl. tabs.,) 16°., $3. Chemical.
Contains references.
Design and equipment of small chemical laboratories. '09(Ap24) il. 8°, *$2 net. Chemical Engineer.

MEADE, *Bp.* William.
Wise, J. C., *comp.* Digested index and genealogical guide to Bp. Meade's "Old churches, ministers and families of Virginia." $2 net. Bell Bk.

Meader, Clarence Linton.
Usage of idem, ipse and words of related meaning. '10(My7) 8°, (Univ. of Mich. studies; Humanistic ser.) pap., 50 c. net. Macmillan.

Meader, Herman Lee.
Cupid the surgeon. '08(D5) c. il. D. †$1. Altemus.

Meadon, Jos., ed.
Graphic arts and crafts year book. 3d year. '09(Jl10) il. 8°, $5. Oswald.

Meadow sprite. Schottenfels, G. R. 50 c. Educ. Pub.

Meagher, Rev. Ja. Luke.
Wonders of the universe; what science says of God. '10(Mr5) 12°, $1. Chr. Press.

Meakin, F:
Function, feeling, and conduct; attempt to find a natural basis for ethical law. '10(Mr26) c. D. **$1.50 net. Putnam.

Meakin, J: Phillips.
Leaves of truth; Utah and the Mormons; papers, poems and letters: appeal for a nobler manhood. '09(My) 8+274 p. il. por. 12°, $1.50. J: P. Meakin.

Meaning and value of life. Eucken, R. C. *$1.40 net. Macmillan.

Meaning of friendship. *See* Stevenson, Rob. L:

Meaning of infancy. Fiske, J: **35 c. net. Houghton M.

Meaning of life. Cook, S. A. 35 c. Jennings.

Meaning of money. Withers, H. $1.50 net. Dutton.

Meaning of social science. Small, A. W. $1.50 net. Univ. of Chic.

Meaning of the times. Beveridge, A. J. **$1.50 net. Bobbs-M.

Meaning of truth. James, W: **$1.25 net. Longmans.

Means, D: MacGregor.
Methods of taxation compared with the established principles of justice. '09 (Ap24) c. O. **$2.50 net. Dodd.

Means of education and self-culture. Buffalo Public Library. gratis. Buffalo Pub. Lib.

Meany, Edm. Stephen, comp.
Hist. of the state of Washington. '10 (O8) c. il. 12°, $1.25 net. Macmillan.
Indian geographic names of Washington. '08(Ag) c. 20 p. Tt. pap., 25 c. Hyatt-F.

Mears, Brainerd.
Osmotic pressure of cane sugar solutions at 15° centigrade. '09(S) 36 p. 8°, pap., 40 c. Johns Hopkins.

Mears, Mary Martha.
Bird in the box. '10(D3) c. D. $1.20 net. Stokes.
Rosamond the second; being the true record of the unparalleled romance of one Claudius Fuller. '10(My7) c. S. 80 c. net. Stokes.

Measure of our youth. Herbert, A. $1.50. Lane.

Measure of the rule. Barr, R. †$1.50. Appleton.

Measurements.
See Weights and measures.

Measuring tools. '09(Ap3) il. 8°, (Machinery's reference ser.) pap., 25 c. Indust. Press.

Meat.
Armsby, H: P. Feeding for meat production. 10 c. U. S., Supt. of Docs.
Bigelow, W. D., *and* Cook, F. C. Meat extracts and similar preparations. 10 c. U. S., Supt. of Docs.
Cook, F. C. Comparison of beef and yeast extracts of known origin. Gov. Pr. Off.

Meat.—*Continued.*
Edelmann, R: Text-book of meat hygiene. $4.50. G: E. Howard.
Farrington, A. M. Need of state and municipal meat inspection to supplement federal inspection. Gov. Pr. Off.
Langworthy, C: F., *and* Hunt, C. L. Economical use of meat in the home. Gov. Pr. Off.
Leffingwell, A. American meat. $1.25 net. Schulte.
Robertson, W:, *and* Herzog, M. J. Meat and food inspection. *$3.50 net. Chic. Med. Bk.
Secrets of meat curing and sausage making, and how to comply with all pure food laws. gratis. B. Heller & Co.
Wagner, E. Recipes for preserving of fruit, vegetables and meat. *$2.50 net. Van Nostrand.

See also Abattoirs.

Meat versus rice. Gompers, S: (Add. pubs. for price.) Asiatic Exclusion.

Mechanical appliances.
See Machinery.

Mechanical drawing.
Anthony, G. C. Machine drawing. $1.50. Heath.
Bennett, C: A. Problems in mechanical drawing. $1.20; $1. Manual Arts.
Colvin, F. H. Machine shop drawings. $1. McGraw.
Curtis, N. C. Elements of graphics, orthographic projections, shades, shadows and perspective. $1.50. N. C. Curtis.
Drafting-room practice. 25 c. Indust. Press.
Drawing standards and conventions. 25 c. Wahr.
Giesecke, F: E. Mechanical drawing. pts. 1 and 2. ea., $1. E. Dietzgen.
Hanstein, H. Constructive drawing: a text-book for home instruction, high-schools, etc. $1. Keuffel.
Jagger, J: E. Elem. text book on mechanical drawing. $3.50 net. Lippincott.
Jepson, G: Elem. principles of industrial drawing. 50 c. G. Jepson.
Kenison, E. Mechanical drawing. 50 c. Am. Sch. Corr.
Leeds, C: C. Mechanical drawing for trade schools. High-school ed., **$1.25 net; Machinery trades ed., *$1.50 net. Van Nostrand.
Marshall, W: C. Elem. machine drawing. $1.50. Yale Co-op.
Mathewson, F. E. Supplementary notes for mechanical drawing. ser. 1. 60 c.; 40 c. Taylor-H.
Reid, J: S. Mechanical drawing. $2 net. Wiley.
Reid, J: S. *and* D. Text book of mechanical drawing and machine design. $3. Wiley.
Spink, B. E., *and others.* Mechanical drawing for high schools. 2 v. $1.45. Atkinson, M. & G.
Spinney, R: D. Drawings for medium-sized repetition work. $1.50. Spon.
Starbuck, R. M. Mechanical drawing for plumbers. $1.50. Henley.

MECHANICAL DRAWING.—*Continued.*
Starkey, L. C. Notes on mechanical drawing, graphic statics, machine design and kinematics. $1.50. L. C. Starkey.
Stephens, W. G: Drawing instruments. *$1 net. McGraw.
Sylvester, F. L., *and* Oberg, E. V. Self-taught mechanical drawing and elem. machine design. $2. Henley.
Systems and practice of the drafting room. 25 c. Indust. Press.
Treleaven, J. T. Preliminary mechanical drawing. 50 c. Longmans.
Willard, W: F. Pract. course in mechanical drawing. 50 c. Popular Mechanics.
Wilson, V. T., *and* McMaster, C. L. Notes on pract. mechanical drawing. $1.50. Wilson & M.
See also Architectural drawing;—Graphics;—Pattern-making; — Perspective;—Plumbing; —Projection;—Slide rule;—Tailoring.

MECHANICAL ENGINEERING.
Lobben, P. Machinists' and draftsmen's handbook. $2.50. Van Nostrand.
See also Engineering;—Machinery;—Mechanics; —Steam engine.

Mechanical movements. Hiscox, G. D. $2.50. Henley.
Mechanical production of cold. Erving, J. A. *$3.25 net. Putnam.

MECHANICS.
Barr, J: H: Kinematics of machinery. $2.50. Wiley.
Bedford, E: J. Introd. mechanics. 50 c. Longmans.
Bond, A. R., *comp. and ed.* Handy man's workshop and laboratory. $2. Munn.
Breckenridge, W: E., *and others.* Shop problems in mathematics. $1. Ginn.
Collins, H. E. Shafting, pulleys, belting and rope transmission. $1. Hill Pub.
Crew, H: Principles of mechanics. $1.50. Longmans.
Cross, C: R. Notes on mechanics. (Not for sale.) C: R. Cross.
Franklin, W: S., *and* Macnutt, B. Mechanics and heat. $1.75 net. Macmillan.
French, L. G. First principles of theoretical mechanics. 25 c. Indust. Press.
Hancock, E: L. Applied mechanics for engineers. **$2 net. Macmillan.
Hartmann, F. M. Elem. mechanics for engineering students. $1.25 net. Wiley.
Hasluck, P. N., *ed.* Cassell's cyclopedia of mechanics. 5 v. ea., *$2.50 net. Cassell.
Hawkins, N. Mechanical dictionary. $3.50. Audel.
Heck, R. C. H. Notes on elem. kinematics. $1. Van Nostrand.
Hedrick, E. R., *and* Kellogg, O. D. Applications of the calculus to mechanics. $1.25. Ginn.
Hoskins, L. M. Theoretical mechanics. $3. Stanford Univ. Bkstore.
Houghton, C: E. Elements of mechanics of materials. **$2 net. Van Nostrand.
International Correspondence Schools, Scranton, Pa. Tratado elemental de matemáticas y mecánica. (Priv. pr.) Int. Correspondence.
Jameson, J. M. Elem. pract. mechanics. $1.60. Longmans.

MECHANICS.—*Continued.*
Jones, A. C., *and* Blomfield, C. H. Elem. mechanics of solids and fluids. $1.30. Longmans.
Kent, W: Mechanical engineer's pocket-book. $5 net. Wiley.
Lester, O. C. Integrals of mechanics. 80 c. Ginn.
Low, D: A. Applied mechanics. $2.75. Longmans.
Marshall, P. Workshop wrinkles and recipes. 50 c. Spon.
Maxim, J. L. Apprentices' course in experimental physics and mechanics.—Experimental applied mechanics for technical students. 60 c. Longmans.
Popular Mechanics. Amateur mechanics. 25 c. Popular Mechanics.
Sanborn, F. B. Mechanics: problems for engineering students. 50 c. Engineering News.
Smith, P. F., *and* Longley, W: R. Theoretical mechanics. $2.50. Ginn.
Spon's mechanics own book. $2.50. Spon.
United States. *Superintendent of Documents.* Engineering: mechanics; government documents. gratis.
Use of formulas in mechanics. 25 c. Indust. Press.
See also Aerial navigation;—Cams;—Dynamos and motors;—Engineering; — Fans;—Gases; — Hydraulic engineering; — Hydrostatics; — Inventions;—Machinery; — Pattern-making; — Physics; — Pumps; — Statics; — Steam engine; — Strength of materials.

Mechanics for young America; book for old and young who like to make things; repr. from *Popular Mechanics.* '10(Jl16) c. il. 8°, 25 c. Popular Mechanics.

MECHANICS' LIENS.
Alexander, H: A. Mechanics' and materialmen's lien laws of the southeastern states. *$6 net. Harrison Co.
Bloom, S. Treatise on the law of mechanics' liens and building contracts. $7.50. Bender-M.
Kerr, J. M. Treatise on the law of mechanics' liens. (Add. pubs. for price.) Bender-M.
New Jersey. Mechanics lien law. $3.50. Soney.
New York. Treatise on the mechanics' lien law of the state. $3.50. Trow Press.
Rockel, W: M. Treatise on the law of mechanics' liens. *$6 net. Bobbs-M.
See also names of states.

Mechanics of engineering. Church, I. P. $6. Wiley.
Mechanics of internal work. Church, I. P. $1.50 net. Wiley.
Mechanics of piano technic. Grabill, E. W. $1.25. A. W. Hunt.
Mechanics of pumping machinery. Weisbach, J. *$4 net. Macmillan.
Mechanics of the earth's atmosphere. Abbe, C. Smith. Inst.
Mechanics of writing. Woolley, E. C. $1. Heath.

MECHANISM.
See Machinery;—Mechanics.

Mechanism of speech. Bell, A. G. **$1.20 net. Funk.
Mechanism of the linotype. Thompson, J: S. $2. Inland Pr.

Mechem, Floyd Russell, and Gilbert, Barry.
Cases on damages, selected from decisions of English and American courts. '09 (My) c. 23+626 p. Q. (Am. casebook ser.) $4. West Pub.

Mecklenburg-Strelitz, Adolph Friedrich, Duke of.
In the heart of Africa; tr. by G. E. Maberly-Oppler. '10(D10) il. (4 in col.) maps, 8°, $5 net. Cassell.

MECKLENBURG DECLARATION OF INDEPENDENCE.
Moore, J. H. Defence of Mecklenburg declaration of independence. *$1.50 net. Stone & B.

Médaille, Pierre.
Meditations on the Gospels for every day in the year: tr. from the French by the Rev. W: H. Eyre. New ed. '09(My) c. 41+542 p. 12°, *$1.50 net. Herder.

Medal and cross of St. Benedict. Veth, M. 5 c. Abbey Student.

MEDALS.
See Coins and medals;—Hudson-Fulton celebration.

Medbury, C: S.
From Eden to the Jordan: series of lessons in the Pentateuch. '09(Mr27) c. 16°, (Training for service ser.) 50 c.; pap., 30 c. Standard Pub.
From the Jordan to the throne of Saul; for advanced teacher-training classes, adult Bible classes, etc. '10(My14) c. S. (Training for service ser.) pap., 25 c. Standard Pub.

Meddlings of Eve. Hopkins, W: J: $1 net. Houghton M.

Médecin (Le) de campagne. *See* Balzac, Honoré de.

Médecin (Le) malgré lui. Molière, J. B. P. de. *25 c. net. Crowell.

MEDFORD, Mass.
Wild, H. T. Old Royall House. 50 c. Salem Press.

MEDIAEVAL HISTORY.
See History;—Middle Ages.

Mediaeval towns ser. il. 12°. Dutton.
—Foligus. Padua. $1.75 net; $2.25 net.
—Noyes. Story of Milan. $1.75 net; $2.25 net.
—Ross *and* Erichsen. Story of Pisa. $1.75 net; $2.25 net.

Mediaevalism. Tyrrell, G: *$1.25 net. Longmans.

Medical chaos and crime. Barnesby, N. $1.50 net. M. Kennerley.

MEDICAL CHEMISTRY.
French, H. Medical laboratory methods and tests. *$1.75 net. Chic. Med. Bk.
Holland, J. W: Urine and clinical chemistry of the gastric contents. *$1 net. Blakiston.
Wolff, L. Essentials of medical chemistry. $1. Saunders.
See also Poisons.

MEDICAL DIAGNOSIS.
See Diagnosis.

MEDICAL ELECTRICITY.
Bennett, H. C. Electro-therapeutic guide. $2. Nat. Coll. Electro-Therapeutics.
Burdick, G. G. X-ray and high frequency in medicine. $2.75. Physical Therapy.

MEDICAL ELECTRICITY.—*Continued.*
Clymer, R. S. International system of magnetic (alchemic) therapeutics. gratis. C. R. Clymer.
Crook, H. E. High frequency currents, their production, physical properties, physiological effects and therapeutical uses. *$2 net. Wood.
Dugan, W: J. Manual of electro-therapeutics. $2. Davis.
Eberhart, N. M. Brief guide to vibratory technique. $1. New Med.
Goodson, G: A. Electrical activities in the human body. 75 c. G: A. Goodson.
Harris, W. Electrical treatment. $2 net. Funk.
Kassabian, M. K. Röntgen rays and electro-therapeutics. $3.50. Lippincott.
Leduc, S. Electric ions and their use in medicine. *$1 net. Hoeber.
McIntosh, H. Pract. hdbk. of medical electricity for students and practitioners. $3. Therapeutics.
Massey, G: B. Conservative gynecology and electro-therapeutics. *$4 net. Davis.
Mauer, *Mrs.* R. D. J. Prismatic ray in treatment of face and scalp. $1.50. New Med.
Monell, S: H. Elements of correct technique; clinics from the N. Y. School of Special Electro-therapeutics. *$2.50 net. —High frequency electric currents in medicine and dentistry. *$4 net.—Hot air, vibration and high frequency currents. *$15 net.—Rudiments of modern medical electricity. *$1 net.—Thirty chapters on static electricity. *$2 net.—Treatment of disease by electric currents. *$6 net. W: R. Jenkins.
Morton, E: R. Essentials of medical electricity and radiography. $1.75. Chic. Med. Bk
Neiswanger, C: S. Electro-therapeutical practice. $2.50. Ritchie.
Rice, M. C. Electricity in gynecology. $1. Laing.
Strong, F: F. Essentials of modern electro-therapeutics. $1.—High-frequency currents. *$3 net. Rebman.
Tibbles, W: Theory of ions: consideration of its place in biology and therapeutics. *$1 net. Hoeber.
Tousey, S. Medical electricity and Röntgen rays. $7 net; $8.50 net. Saunders.
See also Radiography;—Roentgen rays.

Medical epitome ser.; ed. by V. C. Pedersen. 12°. Lea.
—Price. Hygiene and public health. $1.
—Schalek. Diseases of the skin. $1.

Medical Greek. Rose, A. $1. Stechert.

Medical guide and monograph ser. 8°. Mosby.
—Benedict. Golden rules of dietetics. $3.

Medical gynecology. Bandler, S: W. *$5 net; *$6.50 net. Saunders.

Medical inspection of schools. Gulick, L. H. $1. Charities Pub.

MEDICAL JURISPRUDENCE.
American Medical Assoc. Laws (abstract) regulating the practice of medicine in U. S. and elsewhere. 30 c. Am. Medical.

MEDICAL JURISPRUDENCE.—*Continued.*
Emerson, R. L. Legal medicine and toxicology. $5. Appleton.
Ewell, M. D. Manual of medical jurisprudence. $2.50. Little, B. & Co.
Purrington, W. A. Review of recent legal decisions affecting physicians, dentists, druggists and the public health. $1. Treat.
Stewart, G. H. Legal medicine. $5. Bobbs-M.
Wade, M. J. Selection of cases on malpractice of physicians, surgeons and dentists. (Add. pubs. for price.) Medico-Legal Pub.
Witthaus, R. A., *and* Becker, T. C. Medical jurisprudence, forensic medicine and toxicology. In 4 v. v. 3. per v., *$6 net; *$7 net. Wood.
See also Pharmacy;—Poisons.

Medical language. Zimmerer, H. *25 c. net. Stechert.

Medical men in the time of Christ. Willson, R. W. 60 c. net. S. S. Times.

Medical milk commissions. Lane, C. B. 15 c. U. S., Supt. of Docs.

Medical Record. State board examination questions and answers of thirty-four states; a valuable guide to the medical student, giving accurate answers that will prove helpful in passing state board examinations; ed. of 1908. '08(D) c. 479 p. 12°, *$2 net. Wood.

Medical Record visiting list for 1909. '08 (D); for 1910. '09(D); for 1911. '10(D) 12°, mor., for 30 patients a week, ea., $1.25; for 60 patients, ea., $1.50; for 90 patients, ea., $2. Wood.

MEDICI, Catherine de.
Balzac, H. de. Catherine de Medici. 35 c. net; 70 c. net. Dutton.

MEDICI, Giovanni de, [Giovanni delle Bande Nere.]
Hare, C. Romance of a Medici warrior. $2.50 net. Scribner.

MEDICI, Lorenzo de, (*called the Magnificent.*)
Horsburgh, E. L. S. Lorenzo the Magnificant and Florence in her golden age. *$4.50 net. Putnam.

MEDICI (The).
Ross, *Mrs.* J. A. D: G., *ed. and tr.* Lives of the early Medici. $4 net. Badger.
Staley, E. Tragedies of the Medici. *$3.50 net. Scribner.
Vaughan, H. M. Medici popes (Leo x. and Clement VII). *$4 net. Putnam.
Young, G: F: The Medici. In 2 v. per set, *$8 net. Dutton.

Medici viola. Gibson, P: $1. P: Gibson

MEDICINAL PLANTS.
See Medicine.

MEDICINE.
Abrams, A. Diagnostic therapeutics. $5. Rebman.
Allbutt, *Sir* T: C., *and others, eds.* System of medicine and gynæcology. In 12 v. v. 4, pts. 1, 2; v. 5, 6, 7, 8. ea., $6; $7; $8. (Subs. only.) Macmillan.
American Medical Association. New and non-official remedies. *50 c. net. Am. Medical.
Anders, J. M. Text-book of the practice of medicine. $5.50. Saunders.

MEDICINE.—*Continued.*
Anshutz, E: P. Guide to the twelve tissue remedies of biochemistry. 75 c. Boericke & T.
Barnesby, N. Medical chaos and crime. $1.50 net. M. Kennerley.
Barrett, E. Family doctor. $1.25 net. Dutton.
Bartlett, C. Text-book of clinical medicine: treatment. $8; $10. Boericke & T.
Bass, F. H. Outlines of the hist. of medicine. *$6 net. W: R. Jenkins.
Beck, E. G. Bismuth paste in chronic suppurations. $2. Mosby.
Billings, F., *and* Salisbury, J. H., *eds.* General medicine. $1.25. Year Bk.
Black's medical dict. $2.25 net. Macmillan.
Brand, A. T., *and* Keith, J: R. Clinical memoranda for general practitioners. *$1.50 net. Wood.
Brooke, G. E. Aids to tropical medicine. *$1 net. Wood.
Brown, W. L. Physiological principles in treatment. *$2 net. Wood.
Butler, G: F., *and others, eds.* Materia medica and therapeutics. $1.50. Year Bk.
Calwell, W: Text-book of medical treatment. *$4.50 net. Longmans.
Camac, C: N. B., *comp.* Epoch-making contributions to medicine, surgery and allied sciences. *$4 net. Saunders.
Camp, E. J. Nature's law of health and disease and the ladies' toilet. $1. Winkelman.
Campbell, W. B. Hdbk. of modern treatment and medical formulary. *$2.50 net. Davis.
Cattell, H: W., *ed.* Lippincott's new medical dict. $5 net. Lippincott.
Chittick, A., *comp.* Medicine; 1000 questions and answers for state board examinations. $2. Crescent Pub.
Colwell, N. P. Need, methods and value of medical college inspection. gratis. Am. Medical.
Councilman, W: T: Methods and the object of state examinations. gratis. Am. Medical.
Cowperthwaite, A. C. Text-book of materia medica and therapeutics. $5. Boericke & T.
Crawford, M. M., *and* Welton, T. S. Before the doctor comes. $1. Chr. Herald.
Croftan, A. C. Clinical therapeutics. $5. Cleveland Press.
Cushny, A. R. Text book of pharmacology and therapeutics. $3.75. Lea.
Darier, A. Therapeutics. $4. Blakiston.
Davis, A. P. Neuropathy. $5. F: L: Rowe.
Deutsch, S. Medical German. *$2 net. W: R. Jenkins.
Dobson, W: H. Modern medicine in China. (Not for sale.) George Washington Univ.
Doctor says: book of advice for the household. **$1 net. Jacobs.
Dorland, W: A. N., *ed.* American il. medical dict. *$4.50 net; *$5 net.—American pocket medical dict. *$1 net; with thumb index, *$1.25 net. Saunders.

MEDICINE.—*Continued.*

Drewry, W: F. Correlation of the physician and the layman. (Priv. pr.) Williams Pr.

Edwards, A. R. Treatise on the principles and practice of medicine. *$5.50 net. Lea.

Ehrlich, P. Experimental researches on specific therapeutics. *$1 net. Hoeber.

Emerson, C: P. Essentials of medicine. **$2 net. Lippincott.

Emery, W. D'E. Immunity and specific therapy. *$3.50 net. Hoeber.

Ency. and dict. of medicine, surgery and the specialties. In 10 v. v. 6, 7. ea., *$5 net. Chic. Med. Bk.

Fischer-Dueckelmann, A. Wife as the family physician. $5. Int. Medical.

Flexner, A. Medical education in the United States and Canada. Carnegie Found.

Foote, J: A. Essentials of materia medica and therapeutics for nurses. $1.25. Lippincott.

Forchheimer, F: Prophylaxis and treatment of internal diseases. subs., $5. Appleton.

Fortescue-Brickdale, J. M. Pract. guide to the newer remedies. $2 net. Wood.

Franz, S. I. Psychology and the medical school. (Not for sale.) George Washington Univ

French, J. M. Text-book of the practice of medicine for students and practitioners. $5.50 net; leath., $6.50 net. Wood.

Goepp, R. M. State Board questions and answers: [examinations in medicine.] (Add. pubs. for price.) Saunders.

Gorgas, F. J. S: Dental medicine; manual of dental materia medica and therapeutics. $4 Blakiston.

Gould, G: M. Borderland studies. v. 2, Miscellaneous addresses and essays pertaining to medicine, [etc.] $2.—Illustrated dict. of medicine biology and allied sciences. $14.—Pocket medical dict. *$1 net; *$1.25 net.—Practitioner's medical dict. $4; $4.50. Blakiston.

Griffiths, T: M. Non-secret formulas. $5. Interstate Pr.

Harding, A. R. Ginseng and other medicinal plants. $1. A. R. Harding.

Hare, H. A., *and* Beardsley, E: J: G. Medical complications, accidents and sequels of typhoid fever and other exanthemata. *$3.25 net.—Text-book of practical therapeutics. *$4 net; *$5 net; *$5.50 net. Lea.

Harvery Society, New York. Harvey lectures, 1906-'07.—1908-'09: [medical lectures.] ea., **$2 net. Lippincott.

Henkel, A. American medicinal barks. 15 c. U. S., Supt. of Docs.

Henry, J: N. Nurse's handbook of medicine. **$1.50 net. Lippincott.

Herter, C. A. Imagination and idealism in the medical sciences. (Not for sale.) Am. Medical.

Hoblyn, R: D. Dict. of terms used in medicine and collateral sciences. *$3 net. Macmillan.

Household physician; twentieth century medica. $8. Woodruff Pub.

MEDICINE.—*Continued.*

Hoxie, G: H. Symptomatic and regional therapeutics. $4. Appleton.

Hoyt, D. M. Practical therapeutics and prescription writing. $3.50. Dolbey.

Hudson, B. Aids to medicine. *$1.25 net. Wood.

Hutchison, R., *and* Collier, H. S., *eds.* Index of treatment. *$6 net; *$7.50 net. Wood.

Hutchison, R., *and* Rainy, H. Clinical methods: guide to pract. study of medicine. $2.50 net. Funk.

International medical annual. *$3.50 net. Treat.

Jacobi, A. Dr. Jacobi's works, essays, addresses, scientific papers and miscellaneous writings. 8 v. $15. Critic & G.

John Crerar Library, Chic. List of current medical periodicals and allied serials. 10 c. John Crerar Lib.

Kelly, A. O. J. Practice of medicine. $4.75 net. Lea.

Keyes, T: B. Renewal of life: arguments for subcutaneous injections of oil in the cure and prevention of senility and disease. $2. Tubercle Press.

Latham, A. Dict. of treatment. *$2 net. Blakiston.

Lewis, B. Medical vademecum in German and English. $5 net. Blakiston.

Littlefield, C: W. Twelve vitalized tissue remedies for private and domestic use. $2.50. C: W. Littlefield.

Ludy, R. B., *ed.* Answers to questions prescribed by medical state boards. $1.50. McVey.

Luke, T: D. Manual of natural therapy. *$2.50 net. Wood.

McCurry, J. H. Book of pract. points gathered from various sources, gleaned from many minds with chapters on hook-worm and pellagra. $1. J. H. McCurry.

McDonald, J. N., *comp.* Chicago as a medical center. $2. Stromberg, A. & Co.

McLaughlin, J. C. Abridgment of pract. medicine and allied sciences. $2. J. C. McLaughlin.

Manquat, A. Principles of therapeutics. $3. Appleton.

Mayow, J: Medico-physical works. *$1.25 net. Univ. of Chic.

Medical Record. State board examination questions and answers of thirty-four states. *$2 net. Wood.

Medical Record visiting list for 1909; 1910; 1911. ea., $1.25; $1.50; $2. Wood.

Meyer, W., *and* Schmieden, V. Bier's hyperemic treatment in surgery, medicine and specialties. *$3 net. Saunders.

Moody, C: S. Backwoods surgery and medicine. 75 c. net. Outing.

Moon, R. O. Relation of medicine to philosophy. *$1.50 net. Longmans.

Moore, N. History of the study of medicine in the British Isles. $3.40. Oxford Univ.

Mother's remedies. $3.85. Foote.

New York. State Library, Albany. Medical serials. 25 c. N. Y. State Educ.

Ortner, N. Treatment of internal diseases. *$5 net. Lippincott.

MEDICINE.—*Continued.*

Osler, W: Principles and practice of medicine. $5.50. Appleton.

Osler, W: Treatment of disease. 40 c. Oxford Univ.

Osler, W:, *and* McCrae, T: Modern medicine. In 7 v. v. 2, 3, 4. ea., *$6 net; *$7 net; *$7.50 net. Lea.

Paget, S. Confessio medici. **$1.25 net. Macmillan.

Parke, Davis & Co. Manual of therapeutics, referring especially to the products of the pharmaceutical and biological laboratories of Parke, Davis & Company. '09(O) c. 643 p. il. 12°. (Add. pubs. for price.) Parke, D. & Co.

People's home library; people's home medical book; people's home recipe book; people's home stock book. $4.50. R. C. Barnum.

Pierce, R. V. People's common sense medical adviser in plain English. 31 c. World's Dispensary.

Potter, S. O. L. Therapeutics, materia medica, and pharmacy. $5. Blakiston.

Powell, T: Fundamentals and requirements of health and disease. $5. Powell Pub.

Powell, W: M. Saunders' pocket medical formulary. *$1.75 net. Saunders.

Redfield, H. H. Compend of the active principles, with symptomatic indications for their therapeutic use. (Alkaloids.) 75 c. Clinic.

Reissig, C., Jelliffe, S. E., *and others, comps.* Standard family physician. 3 v. $15. Funk.

Richardson, J. G. Health and longevity. $12. Stanley Inst.

Richardson, J. G., *and others.* Medicology; home encyclopedia of health. $8; $9. University Med.

Ritter, T: J. People's home medical book. $3. R. C. Barnum.

Rose, A. Medical Greek. $1. Stechert.

Sajous, C. E. de M., *ed.* Analyt. cyclop. of pract. medicine. $30. Davis.

Savill, T: D. System of clinical medicine dealing with diagnosis, prognosis, and treatment of disease. *$7 net. Longmans.

Scheffer, T. H. Loose leaf system of laboratory notes. *75 c. net. Blakiston.

Seufert, E: C., *and* Stuart, J: Vademecum of treatment. $2.50. Chic. Med. Bk.

Shaw, H. B. Organotherapy. $1.75 net. Funk.

Smith, E. Some common remedies and their use in practice. *$1.25 net. Hoeber.

Stedman, T: L. Appendix to the reference hdbk. of the medical sciences. subs., $5; $6; $7. Wood.

Stevens, A. A. Modern materia medica and therapeutics. $3.50. Saunders.

Stewart, M., *jr.* Pocket therapeutics and dose-book. $1. Saunders.

Taber, C. W., *and* Senn, N:, *eds.* Pocket encyclopedic medical dictionary. $1.50. Laird.

Thomas, J. Lippincott's new medical dict. $5 net. Lippincott.

Thompson, R. L. Glimpses of medical Europe. **$2 net. Lippincott.

MEDICINE.—*Continued.*

Thornton, E: Q. Medical pocket formulary. *$1.50 net. Lea.

Tucker, W. G. On the character of the state board examinations and the competency of state medical examining boards. gratis. W. G. Tucker.

Tyson, J. Practice of medicine. *$5.50 net; *$6.50 net; *$7 net. Blakiston.

Vorbeck, J. C. First aid to the sick by the use of domestic remedies. $1. J. C. Vorbeck.

Walsh, R. Desk book of facts for physicians and pharmacists. $1.50. R. Walsh.

Warbasse, J. P: Medical sociology. $2. Appleton.

Welsh, L. Outlines of lecture notes. *$1.75 net. L. Welsh.

Wheeler, A., *and* Jack, W: R. Hdbk. of medicine and therapeutics. *$3 net. Wood.

Wilcox, R. W. Treatment of disease. $6; $7.50. Blakiston.

Williams, L. Minor maladies and their treatment. *$3.50 net. Wood.

Wood, H. C. Therapeutics. *$5 net; *$6 net. Lippincott.

Wooton, E. Toilet medicine. *$1 net. W: R. Jenkins.

Wynter, W. E. Minor medicine. $2. (Subs. only.) Appleton.

Yeo, I. B., *and others.* Manual of medical treatment. 2 v. *$6 net. Wood.

Young, D. H. First aid to the sick. $1.25 net. Dutton.

Zimmerer. Medical language. *25 c. net. Stechert.

See also Abdomen;—Accidents;—American Medical Association; — Anatomy; — Anæsthetics;—Antiseptics;—Appendicitis; — Bacteria; —Bladder;—Blood;—Bones; — Breathing;—Cancer;—Chemistry;—Children; — Chiropractic;—Cholera infantum;—Christian science;—Climate;—Contagion;—Diagnosis; — Digestion;—Divine healing;—Ear; — Embryology; — Examinations;—Eye;—Faith cure;—Fasting—Food;—Fractures;—Generative organs;—Glands;—Gynecology;—Head;—Heredity;—Hernia; — Histology;—Homeopathy; — Hospitals; — Hydrotherapy;—Hygiene; — Hypnotism; — Idiocy;—Infectious diseases;—Kidneys; — Knee;—Liver; — Lungs;—Malaria; — Massage; — Materia medica; —Medical chemistry; — Medical electricity; —Medical jurisprudence;—Medicine and religion;—Mental science;—Metabolism;—Midwifery;—Milk;—Mind and body;—Mineral waters;—Nervous system;—Neurasthenia;—New thought;—Nose;—Nurses and nursing;—Osteopathy;—Pathology;—Pharmacy;—Physicians;—Physiology; Poisons; — Pregnancy; — Psychotherapy; —Quacks and quackery; — Radium; — Roentgen rays; — Serum; — Skin; — Stimulants and narcotics; — Stomach; — Suggestion (Mental); —Surgery; — Teeth; — Temperance;—Throat; —Tropical diseases;—Tuberculosis; — Tumors; —Typhoid fever;—Urine and urinary organs;—Vaccination; — Venereal diseases; — Veterinary medicine and surgery; — Vibration;—Vivisection; — Water-cure; — Woman;—Worry;—*also* Thomson, Samuel.

MEDICINE AND RELIGION.

Boughton, L. G. Religion and health. *25 c. net. Revell.

Huckel, O. Mental medicine. **$1 net. Crowell.

James, W: Energies of men. **25 c. net. Moffat.

McComb, S: Healing ministry of the church. **25 c. net. Moffat.

MEDICINE AND RELIGION.—*Continued.*
MacDonald, R. Mind, religion and health. **$1.30 net. Funk.
Wenzlick, W: Greatest good of mankind. 75 c. W: Wenzlick.
White, E. G. H. Ministry of healing. $3. Pacific Press.
Worcester, E., *and others.* Religion and medicine : [Emanuel Church movement.] **$1.50 net. Moffat.
See also **Christian Science;—Emmanuel church;—Faith cure;—Mind and body;—Nervous system;—Psychotherapy.**

Medico-chirurgical ser.; ed. by Ja. Cantlie. il. 12°. Wood.
—Bosanquet *and* Clogg. Stomach, intestines and pancreas. $4 net.

Medicology. Richardson, J. G. $8; $9. University Med.

Medieval architecture. 2 v. Porter, A. K. $15. Baker & T.

Meditationen zu den fragen und antworten unseres katechismus. Wedel, C. H. $1.25. C. H. Wedel.

Meditationes de praecipiis fidei nostrae mysteriis. pt. 1. Ponte, P. L. de. *$1.10 net. Herder.

MEDITATIONS.
See **Devotional exercises and meditations.**

Meditations. *See* Antoninus, Marcus Aurelius.

Meditations on the Gospels. Médaille, P. *$1.50 net. Herder.

Meditations on the office and work of the Holy Spirit. Barry, J. G. H. *$1.50 net. Young Churchman.

Meditations on the passion of Our Lord Jesus Christ. Philip, *Brother.* $1. La Salle Bureau.

MEDITERRANEAN FLOUR MOTH.
See **Moths.**

MEDITERRANEAN SEA.
Bayne, S: G. Fantasy of Mediterranean travel. **$1.25 net. Harper.
Bureau of University Travel, Boston. Cruises of the "Athena" in Greece and the eastern Mediterranean, 1910. gratis. Bu. Univ. Travel.
Cook, J. Mediterranean Sea and its borderlands. In 2 v. $5; $10. Winston.
Millard, B., *comp.* Mediterranean cruise. $2.25 net. Putnam.

MEDIUMS.
See **Spiritualism.**

Mediumship. Erwood, W: J. 50 c. W: J. Erwood.

Medley, Dudley Julius.
Church and the Empire; being an outline of the church from A.D. 1003 to A.D. 1304. '10(D24) 12°, (Church universal.) $1.40 net. Macmillan.

Medley, W.
Interpretations of Horace; ed. by J. G. Skemp and G. W. Macaulpine. '10(Ag20) c. 8°, $3. Oxford Univ.

MEDUSAE.
See **Jellyfish.**

Meehan, Michael.
Mrs. Eddy and the late suit in equity. Authorized ed. '08(Mr) pors. 8°. $2.50; leath., $3.50. M. Meehan.

Meek, G:
George Meek, bath chairman, by himself; with introd. by H. G. Wells. '10(Ag) 31+291 p. 12°, $1.50. Dutton.

Meek, Seth Eug.
Batrachians and reptiles from British East Africa. '10(D10) 8°, (Field Museum of Natural Hist pubs.; Zoölogical ser.) pap., 50 c. Field Museum.
New species of fishes from tropical America. '09(S) 207-211 p. 8°, (Field Museum of Natural History pubs.; Zoölogical ser.) 50 c. Field Museum.
Notes on batrachians and reptiles from the islands north of Venezuela. '10(D10) 8°, (Field Museum of Natural Hist. pubs.; Zoölogical ser.) pap., 50 c. Field Museum.
Notes on fresh-water fishes from Mexico and Central America. '07, [1908.] (Jl.) 133-157 p. 8°, (Field Columbian Museum pubs., Zoölogical ser.) pap., 50 c. Field Museum.
Zoölogy of lakes Amatitlan and Atitlan, Guatemala, with special reference to ichtyology. '08(Jl18) il. maps, 8°, (Field Columbian Museum pub, Zoölogical ser.) pap., 50 c. Field Museum.

—, and Hildebrand, S. F.
Synoptic list of the fishes known to occur within fifty miles of Chicago. '10(Jl) 116 p. il. 8°, (Field Museum of Nat. Hist. pubs.; Zoological ser.) $1. Field Museum.

Mees, C: E: Kenneth.
Atlas of absorption spectra. '09(N20) il. O. *$2 net. Longmans.
Photography of coloured objects. '09(Je5) il. O. *50 c. net. Tennant.

Meese, W: A:
Abraham Lincoln: incidents in his life relating to waterways. '08(Ap18) por. 8°, pap., 40 c. W: A. Meese.

Megargel, Percy Freeman, and Mason, Grace Sartwell.
The car and the lady. '08(Ag22) c. D. †$1.50. Baker & T.

Megraw, Herbert Ashton.
Pract. data for the cyanide plant. '10 (O8) c. il. 16°, $2. McGraw-H.

Meguire, Emma Elise Geiselman.
Makin's of a girl. '10(D31) c. D. $1.50. Badger.

Mehl, B. Max.
Star coin book; encyclop. of rare American and foreign coins. 4th ed. '10(Je4) c. 12°, pap., 50 c. net. Caspar.

Mehrtens, August Christian.
Gas engine theory and design. '09(My8) c. figs. 12°, $2.50. Wiley.

Meier, Mrs. Lina Wachtelborn.
Aechte deutsche kochkunst; the art of German cooking and baking. '09(Ag7) por. O. $2.50. L. W. Meier.

Meier, W: Herman Dietrich.
Animal study, with directions for lab'y and field work. '10(Ag20) c. Q. bds., 75 c. (portfolio.) Ginn.
Plant study and plant description; [portfolio.] '09(Ap3) Q. 75 c. Ginn.

Meier-Graefe, Julius A.
Modern art; [tr.] from the German by Florence Simmonds and G: W. Chrystal. '08 (N14) 2 v., il. Q. *$10.50 net, boxed. Putnam.

Meiklejohn, Rob.
See French, T: Ewing.

Meine lieder. Ruyter, C. *$1 net. Caspar

Meinert, F.
Biochemical treatment of domestic animals; tr. from the 2d German ed. and provided with a glossary by F. A. Pritschau. '08, [1910.] (F) c. 5-130 p. 12°, $2. J: H. Meinert.

Meinhardt, T: F.
Practical lettering for beginners, draftsmen, architects, engineers, engravers, sign-painters, stone-cutters, lithographers, etc.; with original system for spacing. 2d enl. ed. '09(Ap17) c. figs. obl. O. pap., 60 c. Stechert.

Meissner, Mme. de.
Words of our Lord and Savior Jesus Christ spoken from the cross: a meditation. '09(My) 26 p. 16°, 25 c. Woodward & L.

Meissner, Carl.
See Watteyne, Victor.

Meistersingers. Hadden, J. C., *comp.* 50 c.; $1. Stokes.

MELANESIA.
Abbott, J. H. M. South seas (Melanesia). *75 c. net. Macmillan.
Brown, G: Melanesians and Polynesians. $3 net. Macmillan.

Melanesians of British New Guinea. Seligmann, C: G. $7 net. Putnam.

MELBA, [*Mrs.* Helen Porter Mitchell Armstrong.]
Murphy, A. G. Melba. $2.75. Doubleday, P.

Melberg, P: L.
How to sell real estate; or, the realty business. '09(Jl) c. 272 p. por. 12°, $2.50. P: L. Melberg.

Melchior of Boston. Earls, M. $1. Benziger.

Melchisedec. Benson, P. R. †$1.50. Harper.

Melegari, Dora.
Makers of sorrow and makers of joy, Deo favente; auth. tr. from the orig. French by Marian Lindsay. '10(Je4) c. D. $1.25 net. Funk.

Melibea. *See* Allen, H. Warner, *ed.* Celestina.

Melick, C: W.
Some phases of the negro question. '08 (N14) c. il. por. O. $1. C: W. Melick.

Melitz, Leo Leopold.
Opera goer's complete guide, plots with musical numbers and casts; tr. by R. Salinger. '09(Ja9) c. D. **$1.20 net. Dodd.

Mell, Clayton Dissinger.
Basket willow culture. '08(Je) c. 19 p. O. pap., 25 c. C. D. Mell.

Meller, Josef, M.D.
Ophthalmic surgery: as practiced at the clinic of Prof. Hofrat Fuchs. '08(Ag15) c. il. 8°, *$3 net. Blakiston.

Melliar, Rev. A. Foster-.
Book of the rose; ed. by Rev. F. Page-Roberts and Herbert E. Molyneux. 4th ed. '10(Je18) il. 12°, $2 net. Macmillan.

Mellin, Carl J.
See Fowler. G: Little.

Mellor, Jos. W:
Higher mathematics for students of chemistry and physics, with special reference to practical work. 3d ed., enl. '09(S11) figs. O. $4.50. Longmans.

Melodia. Cole. S: W. $1.50. Ditson.

Melodies of English verse. Morse, L. K., *comp.* 80 c. net. Houghton M.

MELODY.
See Music.

Melting-pot (The). Zangwill, I. $1.25. Macmillan.

Melton, Frances Jones.
Daughter of the Highlanders. '10(Jl30) c. por. D. $1.50. Roxburgh.

Melville, Helen and Lewis.
Full fathom five; sea-anthology in prose and verse. '10(Jl16) 16°, $1.50 net. Macmillan.
London's lure: anthology in prose and verse. '09(Je5) S. *$1.25 net. Macmillan.

Melville, Herman.
Works. 4 v. New imperial lib. ed. '10 (D) il. 8°, ea., $1.25; hf. cf., $2.25; New il. sterling ed., ea., $1. (Sets only.) Estes.
Omoo; introd. by Ernest Rhys. '08(Mr7) 16°, (Everyman's lib.) *35 c. net; leath., *70 c. net. Dutton.

Melville, Irving B., rep.
See Colorado. *Sup. ct.* Repts.

Melville, Lewis.
Farmer George: study of the life and character of George III. '08(Ap11) 2 v., pors. demy 8°, *$7.50 net. Brentano's.
The first George, in Hanover and England. '09(D4) O. *$6 net. Scribner.
Life and letters of William Beckford of Fonthill (author of "Vathek"). '10 (Ag20) il. pors. Q. $3.50 net. Duffield.
See also Melville, Helen.

MELVILLE BELL SYMBOLS.
See Deaf and dumb.

Melvin memorial. Roe, A. S., *ed.* (Priv. pr.) J. C. Melvin.

Mementos and sea pictures. Farnsworth, E: C. $1.50. Smith & S.

Meminger, Mrs. Laura Stewart.
"The little man from Chicago"; the life story of Wilbur F. Meminger, by his wife. '10(O15) c. il. pors. 12°, $1. Alliance Press.

MEMINGER, Wilbur Fiske.
Meminger, *Mrs.* L. S. "Little man from Chicago." $1. Alliance Press.

MEMLING, Hans.
Weale, W. H. J. *and* J. C. Memlinc. *$1.50 net. Stokes.

Memminger, Allard.
Diagnosis by the urine; or, the practical examination of urine with special reference to diagnosis. 3d ed., rev. and enl. '08(D) c. 11+116 p. il. 12°, *$1 net. Blakiston.

Memoir of the Right Hon. William Hartpole Lecky. Lecky, E. Van D. *$2.50 net. Longmans.

Memoir ser. *See* Putnam's

Memoirs of a cavalier. *See* Defoe, Dan.

Memoirs of a failure. Kittredge, D. W. *$1.25 net. U. P. James.

Memoirs of a Russian governor. Urussov, *Prince,* S. D. **$1.50 net. Harper.

Memoirs of a senate page. Eckloff, C. F: $1. B'way Pub.

Memoirs of a vanished generation. Blake, *Mrs.* W., *ed.* *$5 net. Lane.

Memoirs of an American citizen. Herrick, R. $1.50. Macmillan.

Memoirs of an American lady. Grant, *Mrs.* A. M. *$2.50 net. Dodd.

Memoirs of the Bernice Pauahi Bishop Museum. F. pap. Bishop Museum.

—Brigham. Volcanoes of Kilauea and Mauna Loa on the Island of Hawaii. $3.50; $4.50.

Memoirs of the Graham family. Walker, A. K. $2. T. A. Wright.

Memorabilia. Xenophon. *See* Plato. Apology of Socrates.

Memorable American speeches. Cheney, J: V., *comp.* v. 1. *$1.50 net. Reilly & B.

Memorandum and anecdotes of the Civil War. Robinson, A. J. 25 c. A. J. Robinson.

Memorial address on the battlefield of Gettysburg. Knox, P. C. (Add. author for price.) P. C. Knox.

MEMORIAL DAY.

Revell, E. I., *comp.* Memorial day exercises for the school-room. 25 c. Educ. Pub.

Rice, O. S., *comp.* Wisconsin Memorial Day annual. C: P. Cary.

Memorial of Choctaw Indians; against reopening the Choctaw and Chickasee rolls. '09(My8) 8°. (Add. Superintendent for price.) U. S., Supt. of Docs.

Memorial prayers and meditations. Selikovitsch, G: G. 50 c. Hebrew Pub.

Memorials of Canterbury. *See* Stanley, Arth. Penrhyn.

Memories of a musical life. Haweis, H. R. (Add. pubs. for price.) Fischer.

Memories of Brown. Brown, R. P., *ed.* $2.50; $5. Brown Alumni.

Memories of Cuba. Ewyn, J. $1. Badger.

Memories of eight parliaments. Lucy, H: W. *$2.50 net. Putnam.

Memories of fifty years. St. Helier, M. S. M. J., *Lady.* *$4.20 net. Longmans.

Memories of half a century. Lehmann, R. C. (Add. pubs. for price.) Scribner.

Memories of my life. Galton, F *$3.50 net. Dutton.

Memories of sixty years. Browning, O. $5 net. Lane.

Memories of the months. 5th ser. Maxwell, *Sir* H. E. $2.50. Longmans.

Memories of the Twilight Club. Benton, J. $1; $1.50. B'way Pub

Memories of three score years and ten. McIlwaine, R. *$3 net. Neale.

MEMORY.

Arnold, L. E., *ed.* Graded memory work for schools. (Add. pub. for price.) T. Pillot.

Atkinson, W: W. Memory: how to develop, train and use it. $1. Progress Co.

Evans, W: How to memorize. *50 c. net. Bible Inst.

Gamble, E. A. M. Study in memorizing various materials by the reconstruction method. $2.25. Psychological Review.

Peterson, H. A. On the influence of complexity and dissimilarity on memory. $1. Psychological Review.

Watt, H: J. Economy and training of the memory. 50 c. Longmans.

Memory days. Paxton, A. S. $1.50. Neale.

MEMPHIS, Tenn.

Hamilton, G. P. Bright side of Memphis: compendium of information concerning the colored people of Memphis. $2.50. G. P. Hamilton.

Men and manners of old Florence. Biagi, G. *$3.50 net; *$6.50 net. McClurg.

Men and missions. Ellis, W: T. 60 c. net. S. S. Times.

Men and mules. Ries, W. F. 10 c. W. F. Ries.

Men and women. *See* Browning, Rob. Pippa passes.

Men and women of America; biographical dict. of contemporaries. '10(F5) c. pors. 8°, $10. Hamersly.

Men in the making. Shepherd, A. $1.25 net. Jennings; Doran.

Men of America: a biographical dict. of contemporaries; ed. by J. W. Leonard. '08 (F1) c. O. hf. mor., $10. Hamersly.

Men of mark in Connecticut. *See* Osborn, Norris Galpin, *ed.*

Men of mark in Georgia. Northen, W: J., *ed.* In 6 v. v. 2. $50; $100. A. B. Caldwell.

Men of mark in South Carolina. Hemphill, J. C., *ed.* v. 1. $10. Men of Mark.

Men of Sapio Ranch. Du Bose, H. M. $1. Pub. Ho. of M. E. Ch., So.

Men of the kingdom. D. *$1 net. Jennings.

—Faulkner. Erasmus.

—Smith. Hildebrand.

Men of the mountain. Crockett, S: R. †$1.50. Harper.

Men, the workers. Lloyd, H: D. **$1.50 net. Doubleday, P.

Men *versus* the man. La Monte, R. R. **$1.35 net. Holt.

Men we marry. MacBrayne, L. E: $1.50. C. M. Clark.

Men who dared. Trumbull, C: G. (Add. pubs. for price.) Y. M. C. A.

Men who dared. Veatch, B. E. $1.50. Harisun.

Men who found America. Hutchinson, F: W. $1.50. Stern.

Men, women and mirth. '09(S4) c. il. 4°, $2. Life Pub.

Menace of socialism. Wilson, W. L. **$1.50 net. Jacobs.

Menace to business of Sherman anti-trust act; from *Leslie's Weekly,* July 7, 14, 21, and Oct. 20, 1910, and *American Banker,* May 28, 1910. '10(D24) O. pap., 20 c. Am. Banker.

Menander, of Athens.
Four plays: The hero, Epitrepontes, Periceiromene and Samia; ed., with introds., explanatory notes, critical appendix, and bibliography, by E: Capps. '10(N12) c. front. 8°, (College ser. of Greek authors.) $2.50. Ginn.

Menardos, Simos.
Value of Byzantine and modern Greek in Hellenic studies: lecture. '09(Ap3) O. pap., 35 c. Oxford Univ.

Mencken, H: L:
Philosophy of Friedrich Nietzsche. '08 (F8) c. por. O. *$2 net. J: W. Luce.
See also La Monte, Rob. Rives.

MENDELISM.
See Heredity.

Mendelsohn, C: Jastrow.
Studies in the word-play in Plautus: I. The name-play; II. The use of single words in a double meaning. '08(F8) c. 8°, (Pubs. of the Univ. of Penn., Ser. in philology and literature.) bds., $1.25. Univ. of Penn.; [Appleton.]

Mendelsohn, J.
Complete method of musical composition, according to the system of A. B. Marx. v. 1. '10(Je) 231 p. 8°, $2. Fischer.

MENDELSSOHN, Moses.
Isaacs, A. S: Step by step; story of the early days of Moses Mendelssohn; [fiction for children.] 75 c. Jewish Pub.

Mendelssohn Club, Rockford, Ill. Mendelssohn Club cook book; this book contains 1394 valuable receipts with instructions for cooking and serving them, also menus for social functions. '09, [1910.] (Ja) c. 32+369 p. 8°, $1.50. Mendelssohn Club.

Mendenhall, Wa. Curran.
Ground waters and irrigation enterprises in the foothill belt, southern California. '09 (F6) il. tabs., maps, O. (Dept. of the Interior, U. S. Geolog. Survey bull.) pap. 50 c. U. S., Supt. of Docs.
Ground waters of the Indo region, Cal.; with a sketch of the Colorado desert. '09(My) 56 p. pls. O. (U. S., Dept. of the Interior, Geol. Survey, water-supply paper.) pap. (Add. Superintendent for price.) U. S., Supt. of Docs.
Preliminary report on the ground waters of San Joaquin Valley, Cal. '09(F6) fold. map, O. (Dept. of the Interior, U. S. Geolog. Survey bull.) pap., 10 c. U. S., Supt. of Docs.
Some desert watering places in southeastern California and southwestern Nevada. '09(Ag7) il. fold. maps, in pocket, O. (U. S., Dept. of the Interior, Geol. Survey bull.; Water supply paper.) pap.

MENDING.
See Repairing.

Mending and repair of books. Brown, M. W., *comp.* 15 c. A. L. A.

Mendoza, Diego Hurtado de.
La vida de Lazarillo de Tormes, y de sus fortunas y aduersidades; Restitución de la edición príncipe por R. Foulché-Delbosc. '00, [1909.] (N) 67 p. 8°, (Bibliotheca hispanica.) $1. Hispanic Soc.
Life of Lazarillo de Tormes; tr. fr. the ed. of 1554 by Sir Clements Markham; with notice of the Mendoza family and a short life of the author. '08(Ag22) il. map, 8°, *$1.25 net. Macmillan.

MENDOZA FAMILY.
See Mendoza, Diego, Hurtado de.

MENEHUNES (The).
See Hawaiian Islands.

Menken, H:, ed.
Bungalowcraft; book on bungalow and cottage building in its latest development. '08, [1909.] (Ap) c. 120 p. il. plans, 4°, $1. Bungalowcraft.
California bungalow homes. 2d ed. of Bungalowcraft. '10(Ap16) c. il. 12°, $1 net. Bungalowcraft.

Menken, Percival S., rep.
See New York [State.] Civil procedure. Repts.

MENNONITES.
Smith, C. H: Mennonites of America. $2. Mennonite Pub. Ho.

Menotomy. Sears, M. L. $1.50. Badger.

Menpes crown ser. il. Q. Macmillan.
—Blake. China. *$1.50 net.

MEN'S GARMENTS.
See Tailoring.

Mensch, L. J.
Reinforced concrete pocket book. '10(Jl16) il. tabs., 12°, leath., $4. M. C. Clark.
Reinforced concrete pocket book; containing useful tables, rules and il. for the convenient design, rational construction and ready computation of cost of reinforced concrete girders, slabs, footings. '09(O) c. il. tabs., 16°, $10. Engineering News.

MENSTRUATION.
See Gynecology.

MENSURATION.
Furst, S: W. Mensuration, with special application of the prismoidal formula. 50 c. Sower.
Murray, D. A. Essentials of trigonometry and mensuration. 80 c. Longmans.
Neubecker, W: Mensuration for sheet metal workers. 50 c. D: Williams.
See also Graphics;—Surveying.

Mental and spiritual health. Schofield, A. T. 50 c. Fenno.

MENTAL ARITHMETIC.
See Arithmetic.

Mental assassination. Haldeman, I: M. 10 c. C: C. Cook.

Mental deficiency. Tredgold, A. F. *$4 net. Wood.

MENTAL DEVELOPMENT.
See Psychology.

Mental discipline and educational value. Heck, W. H. **$1 net. Lane.

MENTAL DISEASES.
See Insanity.

MENTAL HEALING.
See Mental science;—Psychotherapy.

Mental hygiene in everyday living. Fallows, A. K. *35 c. net. McClurg.

Mental man. Wenzlaff, G. G. $1.10. C: E. Merrill.

Mental medicine. Huckel, O. **$1 net. Crowell

Mental mouth wash. Conover, J. F. 25 c. Roycrofters.

Mental nursing. Harding, W: 50 c. W: R. Jenkins.

Mental ontogeny. Harvey, N. A. N. A. Harvey.

Mental pathology in its relation to normal psychology. Storring, G. *$2.75 net. Macmillan.

MENTAL PHILOSOPHY.
See Philosophy;—Psychology.

MENTAL SCIENCE.
Atkinson, W: W. Practical mental influence. 50 c. Loyal Bk.
Atkinson, W: W. Science of psychic healing. $1. Yogi Pub.
Atkinson, W: W. Thought culture. $1. Progress Co.
Brown, C: R. Gospel of good health. *75 c. net; *35 c. net. Pilgrim Press.
Bruce, H: A. B. Riddle of personality. **$1.50 net. Moffat.
Cheney, *Mrs.* V. What it is that heals. $1. R. G. Cooke.
Dresser, H. W. Message to the well. **$1.25 net. Putnam.
Granger, I. P. Law of liberty. 20 c. I. P. Granger.
Leavitt, S. "As ye will": [mental healing.] $1.50. Magnum Bonum.
Lindsay, A. A. Mind the builder. $1.—New psychology. $1.50; $1. Lindsay Pub. Co.
Maule, G: E. Life and law; or, way to a bigger life. $1.25. G: E. Maule.
Militz, A. R. Spiritual housekeeping; study in concentration. 50 c. Absolute Press.
Munro, H: S. Hdbk. of suggestive therapeutics; applied hypnotism and psychic science. $3. Mosby.
Patterson, C: B. Dominion and power. $1.20 net. Funk.
Rayon, M. Fads or facts?: [healing power.] 15 c. Open Court.
Starrett, D. W: Discoveries which make mental therapeutics and the transmission of mental communications an exact science.—Mental therapeutics. ea., $1.75. D. W: Starrett.
Wattles, W. D. New science of living and healing. 50 c.—Science of being well. $1. E. J. Towne.
Westall, *Mrs.* L. M. H. Common sense view of the mind-cure. **75 c. net. Funk.
Whipple, L. E. Mental healing. $1.50. Metaphysical.
Willman, R. Errors of mind healing compared with the miracles of Christ. $1. Advocate Pub.
Witmer, L. Mental healing and the Emmanuel Movement. 25 c. Psychological Clinic.
Womer, P. P. Relation of healing to law. $1.25. Magnum Bonum.

MENTAL SCIENCE.—*Continued.*
Wood, *Mrs.* A. E. Revival of the gifts of healing. $1.25. Judd & D.
See also Medicine and religion;—Mind and body;—Nervous system;—New thought;—Nurses and nursing;—Personality;—Suggestion (Mental);—Telepathy;—Vibration.

MENTAL SUGGESTION.
See Hypnotism;—Suggestion (Mental);—Telepathy;—Vibration.

MENTAL THERAPEUTICS.
See Mental science.

Mentally deficient children. Shuttleworth, W. A. $2. Blakiston.

MENTONE, France.
Müller, G: F. Mentone and its neighborhood. $4 net. Doran.

Menu (The) book; what to eat to-day. '09 (D) il. $1.25, boxed. Reilly & B.

MENUS.
See Cookery.

Méras, Baptiste and Emile Jules.
French verbs and verbal idioms in speech. '09(O2) c. D. *60 c. net. Sturgis & W.

Méras, Emile Jules.
See Méras, Baptiste.

MERCANTILE LAW.
See Commercial law.

Mercantile speller. '10(My7) 4°, $2.50 net. Franklin Press (Pa.)

Mercer, G: E., and Bonsall, Mabel.
Complete arithmetic. pt. 1. Rev. ed. '09 (D4) il. 8°, (Philippine education ser.) 54 c. World Bk.

Mercer, J. W.
Calculus for beginners. '10(O29) figs. D. $2 net. Putnam.

Mercer, Ja. Kazerta.
Representative men of Ohio, 1904-1908; administration of Myron T. Herrick, governor of Ohio, 1904-5. '09(F20) c. pors. 8°, $25. J. K Mercer.

Mercer, Bp. J: E:
Science of life and the larger hope. '10 (My21) D. $1.20 net. Longmans.

Mercer, S. C.
Poems. '08(D) c. 6+113 p. il. pors. facsim., 12°, $1. Morton.

MERCER COUNTY, N. J.
Lee, F. B., *ed.* Genealogical and personal memorial of Mercer County, N. J. 2 v. $18. Lewis Pub.

MERCER COUNTY, Pa.
White, J: G., *ed.* Twentieth century hist. of Mercer County, Pennsylvania. 2 v. $18. Lewis Pub.

MERCHANT MARINE.
See Commerce;—Ships and shipbuilding.

MERCHANTS.
See Business;—Commerce.

Merchants' Association of New York. Against construction of more reservoirs in the Croton valley; rept. by Committee on Water Supply, May 2, 1909. '09(N) 13 p. O. pap., gratis. Merchants' Assoc.

Merchants' Association of New York. House-fly at the bar: indictment; guilty or not guilty?; evidence:— in the matter of the people *against* the common house fly. '09 (My22) il. tab., charts, Q. pap., gratis. Merchants' Assoc.

Merchants' Association of New York. Investigation of the Fire Department of New York: report by Greely S. Curtis. '09 (My8) tabs., O. pap., gratis. Merchants' Assoc.

Merchants' Association of New York. Plan for reforming the accounts, records and reports of New York City; report to the Merchants' Association of New York by its Committee on Taxation and Finance, January 19, 1909. '09(O) 10 p. 8°. (Add. pubs. for price.) Merchants' Assoc.

Merchants' Association of New York. Subsidy for American ships only; argument of the Merchants' Association of New York by its Committee on Foreign and Colonial Commerce, at the hearing by the House Committee on Merchant Marine and Fisheries, Feb. 3, 1910. '10(Ap9) O. pap., gratis. Merchants' Assoc.

Merchants' friend stock calculator tables. Dean, E: P., *comp.* $5. Merchants' Friend.

MERCURY.
Hillebrand, W: F., *and* Schaller, W. T. Mercury minerals from Terlingua, Texas. (Add. Superintendent for price.) U. S., Supt. of Docs.

MERCURY TREATMENT.
See Tuberculosis.

Mercy of fate. McKean, T: $1.20 net. Wessels & B.

Mère (La) de la marquise. About, E. F. V. 25 c. W: R. Jenkins.

Mere hints, moral and social. Graham, J: E. $1. Mercy.

Meredith, G:
Works. Memorial ed. In 27 v. v. 1, The shaving of Shagpat; v. 2, Ordeal of Richard Feverel; v. 3, Sandro Belloni, v. 1; v. 4, Sandro Belloni, v. 2. '10(F5); v. 5, Rhoda Fleming; v. 6, Evan Harrington (My14); v. 7-8, Vittoria; v. 9-10, Harry Richmond (Je4); v. 11, 12, Beauchamp's career; v. 13, 14, The egoist (Jl9); v. 15, The tragic comedians; v. 16, Diana of the Crossways; v. 17, One of our conquerors; v. 18, Lord Ormont and his Aminta; v. 19, The amazing marriage; v. 20, Celt and Saxon. '10(D10) c. il. 8°, subs., ea., $2. (Sold in sets only.) Scribner.
Celt and Saxon. '10(Ag6) c. D. $1.50. Scribner.
Last poems. '09(O23) c. D. **$1.25 net. Scribner.
Love in the valley. '10(Jl16) 4°, pap., 40 c.; bds., 60 c.; Japan vellum, $1. T: B. Mosher.
Love in the valley and two songs. '09(D) $1.25. (300 copies.) Seymour.
Modern love; introd. by R: Le Gallienne. '09, [1910.] (Je) c. 50 p. por. 8°, $5. M. Kennerley.
Poems written in early youth (published 1851); Poems from modern love (1st ed.,) and Scattered poems. '10(Ja1) D. *$1.50 net. Scribner.

—, Ward, Adolphus W:, and Bridge, Sir F:
Tercentenary of Milton's birth inaugural meeting at the theatre, Burlington Gardens, Tuesday, Dec. 8, 1908, (the eve of the tercentenary;) lines by G: Meredith; orations by Dr. A. W. Ward; summary of addresses on Milton and music by Sir F: Bridge. '09(N13) O. pap., 35 c. Oxford Univ.

MEREDITH, George.
Barrie, J. M. Neither Dorking nor the Abbey. 50 c. Browne's Bookstore.
Curle, R: H. P. Aspects of George Meredith. *$1.75 net. Dutton.
Hammerton, J: A. George Meredith in anecdote and criticism. *$4 net. M. Kennerley.
Moffatt, J. George Meredith; introd. to his novels. *$1.25 net. Doran.
Sclater, J. R. P. Sons of strength; [study of poems of Meredith.] 35 c. net. Revell.

Meredith, H. O.
Outlines of the economic history of England. '08(D26) charts, O. $2. Pitman.

Meredith, W: H:
Jesse Lee, a Methodist apostle. '09(D25) c. nar. S. *25 c. net. Eaton & M.

Merely players. Tracy, V. †$1.50. Century Co.

Mérimée, Prosper.
Carmen. '09(Ap10) front. 32°, (Ariel booklets.) leath., 75 c., boxed. Putnam.
Colomba; ed. by Theodora de Sélincourt. '10(N19) map, D. (Oxford modern French ser.) 50 c. Oxford Univ.
Contes et nouvelles; ed. by J. E. Michell. '08(Ja18) por. S. (Oxford higher French ser.) 70 c. Oxford Univ.
La chronique du règne de Charles IX.; ed. by A. T. Baker. '10(Ag20) c. 8°, (Oxford higher French ser.) $1. Oxford Univ.
Stories by Mérimée. '09(F13) 16°, (World's story tellers ser.) *40 c. net. Dutton.
Writings; tr. fr. the French; with essays on author by G: Saintsbury. In 8 v. '08 (Je27) c. $14. Lamb Pub.

Merington, Marguerite.
Holiday plays; 5 one-act pieces for Washington's birthday, Lincoln's birthday, Memorial day, Fourth of July, and Thanksgiving. '10(N19) c. front. O. $1.25. Duffield.
Vicar of Wakefield: play founded on Oliver Goldsmith's novel. '09(D18) c. col. front. 12°, $1.25. Duffield.

Merino, Hernando.
Las Julianas de Hernando Merino español [facsim.] '02, [1909.] (N) no paging 4°, $3.50. Hispanic Soc.

Merit system: letter. Goodwin, E. H. 25 c. Civic League.

Merit system in appointment to office. Civic League of St. Louis. gratis. Civic League.

Merivale, C:
History of Rome; ed. by O. Smeaton. '10(Ap2) 16°, (Everyman's lib.) 35 c. net; leath., 70 c. net. Dutton.

Meriwether, Mrs. Eliz. Avery, ed.
Sowing of swords; or, the soul of the 'sixties. '10(D31) c. D. $1.50. Neale.

Mermaid of the magic city. Heyser, O. E. 75 c. Cochrane.

Mermaid ser. 16°, *$1 net. Scribner.
—Greene. Plays.

Mero, Everett Bird, ed.
See American playgrounds.

Merrell, E: Huntington, D.D.
Person of Christ; being a consideration of the homiletic value of the Biblical view of the nature of that person. '10(Jl2) c. 12°, 90 c. net. Bibliotheca Sacra Co.

Merrell, Lewis C.
Preparation and use of sweet whey in powder form. '07, [1908.] c. 10 p. 8°, gratis. Merrill-S.

Merriam, C: E:
Primary elections. '08(D5) c. D. *$1.25 net. Univ. of Chic.

Merriam, Clinton Hart.
See Wiley, Harvey Washington.
—, **ed.** Dawn of the world; myths and weird tales told by the Mewan Indians of California. '10(Ag6) c. il. map, 8°, $3.50. A. H. Clark.

Merriam, J: Campbell.
New mammalia from Rancho La Brea. '10 (F) 391-395 p. Q. (University of California pubs.; Geology.) pap., 5 c. Univ. of Cal.
Notes on the osteology of the *Thalattosaurium* genus *Nectosaurus.* '08(Je20) il. Q. (Univ. of Cal. pubs., Geology,) pap., 10 c. Univ. of Cal.
Occurrence of strepsicerine antelopes in the tertiary of northwestern Nevada. '09, [1910.] (Ja) 319-330 p. O. (Univ. of California pubs.; Geology.) pap., 10 c. Univ. of Cal.
Skull and dentition of a primitive ichthyosaurian from the middle Triassic. '10 (F) 381-390 p. Q. (Univ. of Cal. pubs.; Geology.) pap., 10 c. Univ. of Cal.
Skull and dentition of an extinct cat closely allied to *felix atrox* Leidy. '09(N) 291-304 p. il. Q. (Univ. of Cal. pubs.; Geology.) pap., 15 c. Univ. of Cal.
Tertiary mammal beds of Virgin Valley and Thousand Creek in northwestern Nevada. pt. 1, Geologic hist. '10(D) 21-53 p. il. O. (Univ. of Cal. pubs.; Geology.) pap., 50 c. Univ. of Cal.
Triassic *ichthyosauria;* with special reference to the American forms. '08(D5) il. figs. F. (Memoirs of the Univ. of Cal.) pap., $3. Univ. of Cal.

Merriam, Lillie Fuller.
Jenny's bird house. '10(Jl2) il. $1. C. M. Clark.

Merriam ser. *See* Webster's new international dictionary.

Merrick, G: Byron.
Old times on the upper Mississippi: recollections of a steamboat pilot from 1854 to 1863. '09(Ja2) c. il. pors. maps, facsim., 8°, *$3.50 net. A. H. Clark.

Merrick, Howard B.
See Davis, Jos. Baker.

Merrick, Leonard.
Lynch's daughter. '08(O10) c. il. D. †$1.50. McClure.

Merrick, Mary Virginia.
Life of Christ; course of lectures; foreword by His Eminence Ja. Cardinal Gibbons. '09(O) 11+67 p. maps, 8°, *50 c. net. Herder.

Merrick lectures. *See* Stelzle, C:

Merrie England. Lippincott, *Mrs.* S. J. C. 40 c. Ginn.

Merrie tales of Jacques Tournebroche. *See* France, Anatole, *pseud.*

Merrill, G: Perkins.
Non-metallic minerals: their occurrence and uses. '10(D17) c. il. figs. 8°, $4. Wiley.

Merrill, Ja. Milford.
American sovereign. '10(F19) c. il. 12°, $1.50. C. M. Clark.

Merrill, Lilburn, M.D.
Winning the boy. '08(Ap4) c. 12°, *75 c. net. Revell.

Merrill, S: Pearce.
My loves and my lovers; [incl. Merrill and Wilcox genealogies.] '09(D) c. 11+149 p. por. 12°, $1. Marion Press.

Merrill, Selah, D.D.
Ancient Jerusalem. '08(Ap4) c. 8°, *$6 net. Revell

Merrill, W: A:
Cicero's knowledge of Lucretius's poem. '09(N) 35-42 p. Q. (Univ. of Cal. pubs.; Classical philology.) pap., 10 c. Univ. of Cal.
On the contracted genetive in I in Latin. '10(Ap) 57-798 p. Q. (University of California pubs.; Classical philology.) pap., 25 c. Univ. of Cal.

MERRILL FAMILY.
See Genealogies.

Merrill's English texts. 12° and 16°. C: E. Merrill.
—Bunyan. Pilgrim's progress. pt. 1. 40 c.
—Carlyle. Essay on Burns. 25 c.
—Dickens. Tale of two cities. 50 c.
—Eliot. Silas Marner. **40 c. net.
—Emerson. Essays. 30 c.
—Gray. Elegy in a country churchyard. 30 c.
—Hawthorne. House of the seven gables. 40 c.
—Lamb. Essays of Elia. 50 c.
—Lincoln. Selections from the writings and addresses. 25 c.
—Lowell. Vision of Sir Launfal. 25 c.
—Macaulay. Essays on Lord Clive and Warren Hastings. 40 c.
—Macaulay *and* Arnold. Lays of ancient Rome, and Sohrab and Rustum. 30 c.
—Poe, Longfellow, *and* Whittier. Raven; Courtship of Miles Standish; Snowbound. 25 c.
—Shakespeare. Julius Cæsar.—Twelfth night. ea., 25 c.
—Stevenson. Inland voyage and Travels with a donkey.—Treasure Island. ea., 40 c.
—Thoreau. Walden. 50 c.

Merrill's German texts. il. 12°. C: E. Merrill.
—Goethe. Hermann und Dorothea. 60 c.
—Hillern. Höher als die kirche. 50 c.

Merrill's graded supplementary reading ser. il. 12°. C: E. Merrill.
—Dinman. Stories from Greek history for children. 40 c.
—Judson. Young American. *60 c. net.
—Turpin. English history stories. *50 c. net.

Merrill's story books. *See* Howard, Fk. Ward, *comp.*

Merritt, Mrs. Magdalene Isadora La Grange.
Helderberg harmonies; ed. by M. G. Kains. '09, [1910.] (F) c. 13-96 p. il. 12°, $1.25. M. I. L. Merritt.

Merritt, Mary Carr, comp.
Rev. J. W. T. McNiel; brief biography. [1910.] (F) c. '09. 13-130 p. facsim., por. 8°, 75 c. J. F. Elwell.

Merritt, Wa. Gordon.
Strikes and public utilities; a remedy. '10 (My7) 8°, gratis. Am. Anti-Boycott.

Merry, W: Wa., D.D.
Orationes tvm creweianae tvm gratvlatoriae in Theatro Sheldoniano plervmqve habitatæ. '09(My15) O. $2. Oxford Univ.

Merry old maids. Bugbee, W. N. 25 c. Dick

Merry past. Nevill, R. $3 net. Brentano's.

Merry tales of the wise men of Gotham. Darton, F. J. H. $1. Stokes.

Merry widow: novel, founded on Franz Lehar's Viennese opera, "Die lustige witwe," as produced by H: W. Savage. '09(My1) c. il. D. †$1.50. G: W. Dillingham.

Merry Xmas! Kellogg, E. 50 c. U. P. James.

Mersereau, S: Foster.
See Breckenridge, W: Edn.

Merton, Holmes Whittier, ["Yarmo Vedra."]
Heliocentric astrology; or, essentials of astronomy and solar mentality. '10(F19) c. il. 8°, $1.50. McKay.

Merwin, H: Bannister.
Girl and the bill. '09(Ap10) c. il. D. †$1.50. Dodd.

Merwin, H: Childs.
Dogs and men. '10(Je4) c. il. D. 60 c. net. Houghton M.

Merwin, Pearl.
American system of dressmaking. '10 (Ag6) c. il. 8°, $20. Am. Coll. Dressmaking.

Merwin, S:
Drugging a nation: story of China and the opium curse. '08(D12) c. D. *$1 net. Revell.

Merwine, Wellington Lee.
Judicial conveyance of real estate, [etc.;] with forms. '10(Ag) c. O. $6. W. H. Anderson.

Meryl. Eldridge, W: T. †$1.50. Dodd.

Merz, Heinrich.
Louise, Queen of Prussia; tr. from the German by G: P. Upton. '09(S11) c. pors. S. (Life stories for young people.) *60 c. net. McClurg.

MESA VERDE NATIONAL PARK, Colo.
See Cliff dwellers.

Mésaventures (Les) de Jean-Paul Choppart. *See* Desnoyers, L. C. J. F.

Meschler, Moritz.
Life of Our Lord Jesus Christ, the son of God in meditation; tr. from the 4th ed. of the German orig. 2 v. '09(N) map, 8°, *$4.75 net. Herder.
Sublimity of the holy eucharist, also A visit to the seven churches in Rome on the occasion of the jubilee; five essays; auth. tr. by A. C. Clarke. '10(My) 6+173 p. 8°, 75 c. net. Herder.

Meslier, Jean.
Superstition in all ages; dying confession by Jean Meslier, a Roman Catholic priest, who at his death left as his "Last will and testament" this now famous manuscript as contained herein, entitled Common sense; tr. from the French by Anna Knoop; same to now serve as "text-book" number five, for "The congress of ancient, divine, mental and Christian masters." '10(S17) c. por. 12°, $2.25. De Laurence, S.

MESMERISM.
See Hypnotism.

Message (The). Crosbee, M. F. 50 c. Tudor Press.

Message (The). Tracy, L: $1.50. Clode.

Message for you. Telfer, W: $1. Pentecostal.

Message of Philo Judæus of Alexandria. Guthrie, K. S. $1. Open Court.

Message of song. Maxwell, W: G., *comp.* **$1.50 net. Lippincott.

Message of the church in collect, epistle and gospel. *See* Sanders, H: Martyn.

Message of the cross: notes for the use of clergy taking the three hours' service and for private devotion. '09(Ap10) pap., *60 c. net. Young Churchman.

Message of the modern minister. Jackson F: E. *50 c. net. Revell.

Message of the Son of Man. Abbott, E. *$1.75 net. Macmillan.

Message ser. D. 50 c. Am. Bapt.
—Peters. Sermons that have won the masses.

Message to the well. Dresser, H. W. **$1.25 net. Putnam.

Messages for home and life. Young, D. T. *$1.25 net. Jennings.

Messages for new comers to the United States from the North American Civic League for Immigrants. '10(O) no paging, S. pap., Teachers' ed., 1st ser., $2.30 per 100; Teachers' ed., 2d ser., $5 per 100. North Am. Civic.
Also printed in Spanish and Hebrew.

Messages from the epistle to the Hebrews. Moule, H. C. G. *60 c. net. Doran.

Messages of hope. Matheson, G: *$1.25 net. Armstrong.

Messages to mothers. Partsch, H. **$1.50 net. P. Elder.

Messenger, Fk. Mortimer.
Catacombs of worldly success; or, history of Coarsellor Dell; glimpse of the interior workings of a large industrial concern, showing its social and religious sides with relation to its business policies. '10(Jl16) c. il. 12°, 50 c. Metropolitan Ch. Assoc.

Messenger (The). Brown, K. H. **50 c. net. Scribner.

Messersmith, G: Straussser.
Government of Delaware. '08(Ap18) c. D. $1. Am. Bk.
See also Sypherd, W. Owen.

MESSIAH.
Jacob, son of Aaron, High priest of the Samaritans. Messianic hope of the Samaritans. 25 c. Open Court.
See also Jesus Christ.

MESSINA DISASTER.
Belknap, R. R. American house building in Messina and Reggio. $2 net. Putnam.
Miller, J. M. World's greatest disaster: the complete story of the Italian earthquake horror. $1.50. Monarch.

MESSINA DISASTER.—*Continued.*
Morris, C:, *ed.* Story of the great earthquake disaster of 1908. $1.50. Winston.
Mowbray, J. H:, *comp.* Italy's great horror of earthquake and tidal wave. $1. Nat. Pub. Co.

Messmer, Archbp. Sebastian Gebhard.
Outlines of Bible knowledge. '10(O) 12+298 p. il. maps, 8°, $1.80 net. Herder.

Messum, Stuart Victor Semour Craigie.
Hydrographic surveying; elementary, for beginners; seamen, and others. '10(Je4) il. figs. D. $3.75 net. Lippincott.

METABOLISM.
Benedict, F. G., *and* Carpenter, T. M. Influence of muscular and mental work on metabolism and the efficiency of the human body. 15 c. U. S., Supt. of Docs.
Benedict, F. G., *and* Carpenter, T. M. Metabolism and energy transformations of healthy man during rest. $1.75. Carnegie.
Benedict, F. G., *and* Joslin, E. P. Metabolism in diabetes mellitus. $2. Carnegie.
Cabot, R: C., *ed.* Diseases of metabolism and of the blood. $5. Appleton.
Noorden, C. H. v. Clinical treatises on the pathology and therapy of disorders of metabolism and nutrition. pt. 8, Inanition and fattening cures; pt. 9, Technique of reduction cures and gout. ea., $1.50 net. Treat.
See also Breathing.

Metal plate printing. Browne, W. C. $2. Nat. Lithographer.

METAL SPINNING.
See Turning.

METAL WORK.
Atkins, E. A. Practical sheet and plate metal work. *$2 net. Macmillan.
Chandler, F. A. Art crafting in metal for amateurs. $1.50. Fort Hill.
Perry, J. T. Dinanderie; hist. and description of mediæval art work in copper, brass and bronze. $5.50 net. Macmillan.
See also Brasses.

Metallic alloys. Brannt, W: T., *ed.* *$5 net. Baird.
Metallic alloys. Gulliver, G. H: *$2 net. Lippincott.

METALLOGRAPHY.
See Metals and metallurgy.

Metallurgy. Wysor, H: $3. Chemical.
Metallurgy of cast iron. West, T: D. $3. Gardner Pr.
Metallurgy of iron. Turner, T: *$1.25 net. Lippincott.

METALS AND METALLURGY.
Austin, L. S. Metallurgy of common metals. $4. Mining and Scientific.
Barr, J. A. Testing for metallurgical processes. $2. Mining and Scientific.
Bernier, L: L. Autogenous welding of metals. $1. Boiler Maker.
Brannt, W: T., *ed.* Metallic alloys: guide to the manufacture of all kinds of alloys, amalgams, and solders. *$5 net. Baird.
Coblentz, W: W. Radiation constants of metals. (Add. superintendent for price.) U. S., Supt. of Docs.
Desch, C. H: Metallography. $3 net. Longmans.

METALS AND METALLURGY.—*Continued.*
Dictionary of chemical and metallurgical machinery, appliances and material manufactured or sold by advertsers in *Electrochemical and Metallurgical Industry.* 50 c. Electrochemical Pub.
Dict. of metallurgical and chemical machinery. 50 c. Metallurgical.
Fulton, C: H. Principles of metallurgy. $5. McGraw-H.
Goerens, P. Introd. to metallography. *$2.50 net. Longmans.
Groth, L. A. Welding and cutting of metals by aid of gases or electricity. **$3 net. Van Nostrand.
Gulliver, G. H: Metallic alloys. *$2 net. Lippincott.
Gunther, C: G. Electro-magnetic ore separation. *$3 net. Hill Pub.
Johnson, J. P. Ore deposits of South Africa. $2. Henley.
Langbein, G. Complete treatise on the electro-deposition of metals. *$4 net. Baird.
Louis, H: Dressing of minerals. *$8.50 net. Longmans.
Low, A. H. Technical methods of ore analysis. $3. Wiley.
Nagel, O. Mechanical appliances of the chemical and metallurgical industries. *$2 net. O. Nagel.
Richards, J. W: Metallurgical calculations. pts. 1-3. ea., *$2 net. McGraw.
Richards, R. H. Text-book of ore dressing. *$5 net. McGraw.
Roberts-Austen, *Sir* W: C. Introd. to the study of metallurgy. $6 net. Lippincott.
Ruer, R. Elem. of metallography. *$3 net. Wiley.
Sauveur, A., *and* Boylston, H. M. Laboratory experiments in metallurgy. $1.25. A. Sauveur.
Thomas, H. H., *and* MacAlister, D. A. Geology of ore deposits. $2.50. Longmans.
Turner, T. Practical metallurgy. *$1.25 net. Lippincott.
Wysor, H. Metallurgy. $3. Chemical.
See also Alloys;—Antimony;—Assaying;—Bronze;—Copper;—Cyanide process;—Electro-metallurgy;—Electro-plating;—Enamel;—Forge;—Foundries;—Gold;—Iron;—Lead;—Machinery;—Mercury;—Meteorites;—Mineralogy;—Mines and mining;—Pattern-making;—Platinum;—Silver;—Soldering;—Steel;—Teeth;—Tin;—Turning;—Useful arts;—Zinc.

Metamorphoseon. *See* Ovid.
Metamorphoses (The). *See* Apuleius, Lucius.
Metaphysica Fratris Rogeri. *See* Bacon, Roger.

METAPHYSICS.
Bacon, R. Metaphysica Fratris Rogeri ordinis fratrum minorum de viciis contractis in studio theologie. $1.75. Oxford Univ.
Fawcett, E: D. Individual and reality; essay touching the first principles of metaphysics. *$4.25 net. Longmans.

METAPHYSICS.—*Continued.*

Gould, G. M. Infinite Presence. $1.50 net. Moffat.

Proclus. **Metaphysical elements.** $2. T: M. Johnson.

Snowden, J. H: World a spiritual system; outline of metaphysics. $1.50 net. Macmillan.

Woodbridge, F: J. E. Metaphysics: [a lecture.] (Add. pubs. for price.) Columbia Univ.

See also Ethics; — Logic; — Mind; — Mind and body;—New thought; — Philosophy;—Psychology;—Soul;—Will.

Metcalf, Edn. Styles.

Talien, a Spanish princess. '10(S3) c. front. 16°, 50 c. L'Ora Queta.

Metcalf, Haven.

Immunity of the Japanese chestnut to the bark disease. '08(Ag1) 8°, (U. S., Dept. of Agriculture, Bureau of Plant Industry, bull.) pap., 5 c. U. S., Supt. of Docs.

Metcalf, H: Harrison.

Memorial of Hon. Harry Bingham, LL.D., lawyer, legislator, author; ed. by H: Harrison Metcalf, under the direction of Edg. Aldrich, Alb. S. Batchellor, J: M. Mitchell, literary executors. '10(N) 14+505 p. por. 8°. (Not for sale.) H: H. Metcalf.

Metcalf, M. A.

Knitting; manual of pract. instruction in the mechanical details of all types of knitting machinery. '09(My1) c. il. 8°, (American School of Correspondence pubs.) $3. Am. Sch. Corr.

—, **comp.** Knit goods finishing; instruction paper. '09(N) c. 68 p. front. il. 8°, (American School of Correspondence pubs.) $3. Am. Sch. Corr.

Metcalf, Rob. C., and Rafter, Augustine L.

Language series. Bk. 1. '10(Je18) c. D. 40 c.—Bk. 2. '10(S17) c. D. 60 c. Am. Bk.

Metcalfe, Ja. Stetson.

Another three weeks; not by El-n-r Gl-n. '08(F1) c. D. pap., 25 c. Life Pub. Co.

Diary of a district messenger. '09(Jl10) c. S. pap., 25 c Life Pub. Co.

Metcalfe, R: J., comp.

See Bryan, W: Jennings.

Metcalfe, R: Lee.

"Bishop Sunbeams" and other stories of service. '09(O16) front. D. $1. R: L. Metcalfe.

"Of such is the kingdom": school reader. '09(Jl) c. 288 p. il. 8°, $1. Woodruff-C.

Metchnikoff, Elie.

Nature of man; or, studies in optimistic philosophy; Eng. tr.; ed. by P. Chalmers Mitchell. '08(D19) c. il. por. figs. O. (Science ser.) **$2 net. Putnam.

Prolongation of life; the English translation ed. by P. Chalmers Mitchell. '08 (F1) il. O. (Science ser.) *$2.50 net; Popular ed.; with introd. by C: S. Minot. '10(Mr26) c. O. **$1.75 net. Putnam.

METEORITES.

Farrington, O. C. Meteorite studies, II. 50 c. Field Museum.

METEOROLOGY.

Bailey, S. I. Peruvian meteorology. $1.50. Harvard Univ.

Bartlett, J. L. Frosts in Wisconsin. 25 c. Univ. of Wis.

Bigelow, F. H. Manual for observers in climatology and evaporation. (Add. Superintendent for price.) U. S., Supt. of Docs.

Bjerknes, V. F. K., *and others.* Dynamic meteorology and hydrography. Carnegie.

Fassig, O. L. Climate and weather of Baltimore. *$2.50 net. Maryland Geol.

Hepworth, M. W. C. Notes on maritime meteorology. *$1.25 net. Van Nostrand.

Marvin, C: F: Barometers and the measurement of atmospheric pressure. (Add. Superintendent for price.) U. S., Supt. of Docs.

Moore, W. L. Descriptive meteorology. $3 net. Appleton.

Newcomb, S. Search for fluctuations in the sun's thermal radiation through their influence on terrestial temperanture. (Add. pubs. for price.) Am. Philosophical Soc.

Taylor Instrument Companies. Weather and weather instruments. '09(N) c. '08. 175 p. il. 12°, $1; pap., 50 c. Taylor-Instrument.

United States. *Dept. of Agriculture. Weather Bureau.* Brief list of meteorological text-books and reference books; selection of works suitable for general, scientific and university libraries in the U. S.; prep. by C: Fitzhugh Talman. '09(Je) 16 p. 8°. (Add. Superintendent for price.) U. S., Supt. of Docs.

United States. *Dept. of Agriculture. Weather Bu.* Bulletins, circulars, maps, and monthly weather review. gratis.

United States. *Dept. of Agriculture. Weather Bu.* Psychrometric tables for obtaining the vapor pressure, relative humidity and temperature of the dew-point; from readings of the wet and dry bulb thermometers; by C. F. Marvin. '10(Ag) 87 p. il. 8°. Gov. Pr. Off.

United States. *Dept. of Agriculture. Weather Bu.* Studies on the vortices in the atmosphere of the earth; by Fk. Hagar Bigelow. '10(Jl) 4+46 p. tabs., f°.

United States. *Dept. of Agriculture. Weather Bu. Library.* Brief list of meteorological text-books and reference books.

United States. Weather Bureau: bulletins, circulars, maps, and Monthly Weather Review; Agriculture Dept., U. S. A.; for sale by the Superintendent of Documents, Washington. '09(N) 10 p. 12°, pap., gratis. U. S., Supt. of Docs.

Weather and weather instruments. *$1 net. Taylor Instrument.

Weather and weather instruments. $1.50; 50 c. Van Nostrand.

See also Air;—Altitudes; — Climate; — Ocean; — Physical geography.

Method for the identification of pure organic compounds. Mulliken, S: P. v. 3. $5. Wiley.

Method of deducting liability rates. Law, F. E. $1. Spectator.

Méthode (La) Tournier. Talbot-Tournier, E. $1.25. Belisle Pr.

Methodist Episcopal Church. Doctrines and discipline of the Methodist Episcopal church, 1908; ed. by Bishop Dan. A. Goodsell. '08(N7) c. 16°, *25 c. net. Eaton & M.

Methodist Episcopal Church. Reprint of the disciplines of the Methodist Episcopal Church of the years 1789 and 1792; with introd. and comments by the owner of the originals, [A. H. Ege.] '09(Mr) c. '08. 22 p. 8°, pap., 25 c. A. H. Ege.

Methodist Episcopal Church. The ritual. '08 (D19) c. 12°. (Add. pubs. for price.) Eaton & M.

METHODIST EPISCOPAL CHURCH.

Alexander, G., *ed.* Doctrine and discipline of the Methodist Episcopal Church, South, 1910. 40 c. net. Pub. Ho. M. E. Ch., So.

Anderson, J. F. Methodist dictionary. 50 c.; 25 c. net. Eaton & M.

Brodhead, *Mrs.* C. A. S., *ed.* Our free Methodist missions in Africa. $1. Aldine Pr.

Burt, W: Europe and Methodism. 35 c. Jennings.

Dorris, C: E. W. Interesting correspondence; discussion bet. C: E. W. Dorris and Miss Nora Yount (Christians), and A. E. Clement, W. H. Lovell, [etc.] (Methodists). $1. C: E. W. Dorris.

Edwards, R. T: Short Methodist stories. *$1 net. Cochrane.

Fowler, C: H: Addresses on notable occasions. *$1.50 net. Jennings.

Goodsell, D. A., *and others.* Doctrines and discipline of the Methodist-Episcopal church. 30 c. Jennings.

Harrison, J: E. Parliamentary usage of the general conference, M. E. church, South. 25 c. Pub. Ho. of M. E. Ch., So.

Koons, W: G: Junior history of Methodism. 25 c. Eaton & M.

Lewis, T: H. Fraternal address to the General Conference of the M. E. Church, South. Pub. Ho. M. E. Ch., So.

MacGeary, J: S: Free Methodist church. 50 c. W: B. Rose.

Platt, W., *ed.* Methodism and the Republic. 50 c.; 35 c. Bd. Home Miss.

Smith, R. E. Methodist Episcopalians. 5 c. Eaton & M.

Southern Methodist handbook, 1909; 1910. ea., 25 c. Pub. Ho. of M. E. Ch., So.

Thomas, W: H. Some educational history of Alabama Methodism. (Add. author for price.) W: H. Thomas.

Townsend, W. J., *ed., and others.* New hist. of Methodism. *$7.50 net. Doran.

Vaughan, D: D. Lessons for Methodists. $1. Jennings.

Wheeler, H: History and exposition of the twenty-five Articles of religion of the Methodist Episcopal church. *$2 net.—One thousand questions and answers concerning the Methodist Episcopal church. 75 c. Eaton & M.

METHODIST EPISCOPAL CHURCH.—*Continued.*

Williams, S: W. Pictures of early Methodism in Ohio. $1. Jennings.

See also Catechisms;—*also* African M. E. church;—Epworth League;—Makers of Methodism ser.;—*also* Asbury, *Bp.* Francis;—Lee, Jesse;—Wesley, J:

METHODIST EPISCOPAL CHURCH, New Bedford, Mass.

Howland, F. Centennial history of the first Methodist Episcopal Church of New Bedford, Fairhaven and Acushnet, Mass. $2. E. H. Howland.

Methodist founders' ser. il. D. Pub. Ho. of M. E. Ch., So.

—Du Bose. Francis Asbury. $1.

Methodist year book, 1908; ed. by Stephen V. R. Ford. '08(Ja4); 1909. '09(Ja2); 1910. '10(Ja1) il. D. pap., ea., *25 c. net; 1911, ed. by Oliver S. Baketel. '10(D31) pors. tabs., D. pap., 20 c. net. Eaton & M.

METHODOLOGY.

See Teachers and teaching.

Methods and devices for bacterial treatment of sewage. Venable, W: M. $3. Wiley.

Methods for the analysis of maple products. Bryan, A. H. 5 c. U. S., Supt. of Docs.

Methods in education. McEvoy, T: J. $1.50. T: J. McEvoy.

Methods of assessment as applied to different classes of subjects. Boyle, J. E. 7 c.; per 100, $5. Nat. Tax Assoc.

Methods of attracting birds. Trafton, G. H. $1.25 net. Houghton M.

Methods of Mr. Ames: [a novel.] Carrel, F. $1.50. M. Kennerley.

Methods of teaching. Charters, W. W. $1.10. Row, P. & Co.

Methods of textile chemistry. Dannerth, F: $2. Wiley.

Methods of the Santa Fe; economy in the manufacture of transportation. Going, C: B. $1. Engineering Mag.

Methods used in the examination of milk and dairy products. Barthel, C. $1.90 net. Macmillan.

METHUEN, Mass.

Vital records of Methuen, Mass., to the end of the year 1849. *$3.65 net. Topsfield Hist. Soc.

Metour, Eug. Paul.

In the wake of the green banner. '09 (My15) c. il. D. †$1.50. Scribner.

METRE.

See Prosody.

METRIC SYSTEM.

Molesworth, *Sir* G. L. Metric tables. 80 c. Spon.

Williamson, H. Metric tables for setting out curves in metres. 80 c. Spon.

METROLOGY.

See Numerals.

Metropolis (The). Sinclair, U. B., *jr.* †$1.50. Moffat.

Metropolitan automobile guide; series of one- and two-day trips from New York to near-by shore, hill and lake resorts, to which is added sight-seeing tours covering the boroughs of Greater New York; comp. by H: McNair. '10(N5) c. map, fold. map, 8°, $2.50. Automobile Blue Book.

Metropolitan Museum of Art, New York. Exhibition of contemporary German art; list of books and periodicals relating to modern German art and artists in the library of the Museum. '09(Mr13) O. pap., gratis. Metropolitan Museum.

Metropolitan Museum of Art, New York. Paintings in oil and pastel by James A. McNeill Whistler, New York, March 15 to May 31, 1910. [1910.] (D) 25+44 p. por. 8°, 25 c. net. Metropolitan Museum.

METROPOLITAN MUSEUM OF ART, New York City.
Preyer, D: C. Art of the Metropolitan Museum of New York. $3; $7. L. C. Page.

Metsu, Gabriel.
Masterpieces of Gabriel Metsu. '10(S10) il. T. (Dutch painters' ser.) leath., 75 c. net; pap., 25 c. net. Stokes.

Mettler, Arth. J.
See Sherman, H: Clapp.

Metzgar, C: Marine.
Home-made ice cream and candy. '08 (Jc) c. 108 p. 12°, $1; pap., 50 c. Metzgar.

Metzler, Reed.
See Ohio. Outline of law of evidence.

Metzler, W: H:, Roe, E: Drake, jr., and Bullard, Warren G.
College algebra. '08(My23); [New ed., enl.] '10(D24) c. diagrs., 8°, ea., $1.50. Longmans.

Meunier (Le) d'Angibault. *See* Sand, George, *pseud.*

MEWAN INDIANS.
See **Indians.**

Mews and musings. Gardner, A. P. 75 c. Cochrane.

MEXICAN COTTON BOLL WEEVIL.
See **Weevil.**

MEXICAN LANGUAGE.
Denison, T: S. Mexican-Aryan comparative vocab. $2.—Morphology of the Mexican verb. pap., 75 c.—Primitive Aryans of America. $3.25; $2.50. T: S. Denison.
See also Aryans.

Mexican trails. Kirkham, S. D. **$1.75 net. Putnam.

MEXICAN WAR.
Owen, C: H: Justice of the Mexican war. **$1.25 net. Putnam.
Perry, O., *comp.* Indiana in the Mexican war. (Add. author for price.) O. Perry.
Taylor, Z. Letters of Zachary Taylor from the battle-fields of the Mexican war. (Priv. pr.) W: K. Bixby.

Mexican war ser. *See* Stratemeyer, E:

Mexican year book, 1908; comprising historical, statistical and fiscal information; comp. from official and other records; 1st year of publication; issued under the auspices of the Dept. of Finance. '09(My22) il. fold. maps, 8°, *$6 net. Brentano's.

Mexican year book, 1909-10. '10(S) 700 p. tabs., maps, 8°, mor., $6. Mexican Year Bk.

Mexico. Business corporations under the laws; comparative advantages of domestic and foreign corporations, [etc.] '08, [1909.] (F) c. 24 p. S. pap., gratis. Corp Trust Co.

Mexico. Compendium of the laws, [etc.,] by Jos. Wheless. 2 v. '10(N) c. O. $10. F. H. Thomas.

Mexico. Corporations in Mexico; synopsis of the laws of Mexico rel. to the formation of Mexican corporations; registration of foreign corporations; conveyance of real estate; creation of bond issues; management through powers of attorney; prep. by Johnson and Galston. '09, [1910.] (Mr) c. 15 p. 8°, gratis. Johnson & G.

Mexico. Richardson's manual of Mexican law; by D. A. Richardson and Frank W. Doan, [etc.,] full annot. '10(O) c. 382 p. T. $3. Courtright.

MEXICO.
Across America; article entitled "Across America: Mexico's new inter-ocean route, rival to Panama canal," from the *South American Journal* (London), Aug. 15, 1908. '09, (My) 5 p. 8°. (Add. Superintendent for price.) U. S., Supt. of Docs.
Barber, E. A. Maiolica of Mexico. $2.10. Penn. Mus. and Sch. of Ind. Art.
Barca, *Mme.* C. de la. Life in Mexico during a residence of two years in that country. $2.25. Am. News.
Brandegee, T. S. Plantae Mexicanae Purpusianae. 15 c.—Plantae Mexicanae Purpusianae, II. 10 c. Univ. of Cal.
Campbell, R. New rev. complete guide and descriptive book of Mexico. $1.50. Rogers & S.
Carson, W: E. Mexico, the wonderland of the south. **$2.25 net. Macmillan.
Cornyn, J. H. Mexican topics prep. for The new students' reference work. With New students' reference work. $25. Compton.
Cortes, F. Letters; [written to Charles v., describing the Mexican conquest.] 2 v. **$10 net. Putnam.
Coxhead, M. D. Mexico. **$2 net. Stokes.
Dale, J. G. Mexico and our mission. $1. J. G. Dale.
Edwards, W. S. On the Mexican highlands. $1.50. Jennings.
Enock, C. R. Mexico; its ancient and modern civilization. $3. Scribner.
Flandrau, C: M. Viva Mexico. **$1.25 net. Appleton.
Fornaro, C. de. Mexico tal cual es. $2.50; $1. C. de Fornaro.
Gadow, H. F. Through southern Mexico. *$6 net. Scribner.
Harper, H: H. Journey in southeastern Mexico [Vera Cruz and Tuxpan.] (Priv. pr.) H: H. Harper.
Hornaday, W: T. Camp-fires on desert and lava. **$3 net. Scribner.
International Bureau of American Republics. Mexico; general descriptive data. Int. Bu. Am. Republics.
Kerr, R. J. Hdbk. of Mexican law. $3.50. —Translation of the mining law of Mexico. $1.50. Pan-Am. Law.
Kirkham, S. D. Mexican trails. **$1.75 net. Putnam.
Macdougal, D. T. Across Papagueria. 50 c. Am. Geog. Soc.

MEXICO.—*Continued.*

Meek, S. E. Notes on fresh-water fishes from Mexico and Central America. 50 c. Field Museum.

North, A. W. Camp and camino in lower California. $3 net. Baker & T.

Plain facts about Mexico. (Add. pubs. for price.) Davis Bros.

Prescott, W: H. Conquest of Mexico. 2 v. ea., *35 c. net; *70 c. net. Dutton.

Shaw, G: R. Pines of Mexico. *$25 net. C. S. Sargent.

Smith, E. S. Truth about Mexico. (Add. pubs. for price.) Bankers' Pub.

Standley, P. C. *Allioniaceae* of the U. S. with notes on Mexican species. (Add. Superintendent for price.) U. S., Supt. of Docs.

Starr, F. In Indian Mexico. *$5 net. Forbes.

Terry, T. P. Mexico: hdbk. for travellers. **$2.50 net. Houghton M.

Turner, J: K. Barbarous Mexico. $1.50. Kerr.

United States. *Dept. of Commerce and Labor. Bu. of Manufactures.* Zinc industry in Mexico. (Add. Superintendent for price.) U. S., Supt. of Docs.

United States. *Dept. of the Interior.* Petroleum fields of Mexico; message from the president of the U. S., transmitting a communication from the Secretary of the Interior inclosing a statement by Dr. C. W. Hayes respecting the petroleum fields of Mexico. '09(Ag) 3 p. 8°. (Add. Superintendent for price.)

Wallace, D. Beyond the Mexican Sierras. $2 net. McClurg.

See also Aztecs;—Banks and banking;—Chihuahua; — Guanajuato; — Indians;—Irrigation; — Lower California;—Mexican language;—Mexico City;—Monroe doctrine;—Yucatan;—*also* Cortes, Fernando;—Diaz, Porfirio;—Hidalgo y Costillo, Miguel.

MEXICO CITY, Mexico.

Janvier, T: A., *comp.* Legends of the City of Mexico. **$1.30 net. Harper.

Maxson, H. R. Practical up-to-date guide to Mexico City. (Add. pub. for price.) Am. Bk. and Pr

Meycliar, Leo.
English-Russian and Russian-English dictionary. '09(Je19) 16°, $1. Spon.

Meyer, Arnold.
Jesus or Paul. '10(Ja29) 12°, (Harper's lib. of living thought.) *75 c. net. Harper.

Meyer, F. W.
Rock and water gardens; their making and planting; with chapters on wall and health gardening; ed. by E. T. Cook. '10(Jl2) 8°, (Country Life lib.) $2. Scribner.

Meyer, F: Brotherton.
See King, *Rev.* Elisha Alonzo.

Meyer, G: von Longerke.
Our unelastic currency: article from the *Atlantic Monthly* of July, 1906. '08 (Ap11) 8°, pap., 10 c. U. S., Supt. of Docs.

Meyer, Hans.
Determination of radicles in carbon compounds authorized tr. by J. Bishop Tingle. 3d American ed., rev. and enl. '08(Je20) c. il. 12°, **$1.25 net. Wiley.

Meyer, H: Herman.
Graded Sunday-school in principle and practice. '10(My14) c. D. (Modern Sunday-school manuals.) 75 c. net. Eaton & M.

Lesson hdbk., 1910; concise commentary on the International Sunday School Lessons for the entire year based on the text of the American standard Bible; with an introd. by C: F. Sitterly. '09(N13); 1911, with an introd. by J: T. McFarland. '10(N19) c. T. (Berean ser.) leath., ea., *25 c. net. Eaton & M.

Meyer, Hermann H: Bernard, comp.
Library of Congress. List of works rel. to the Sup. ct. of the U. S. '09(Jl) 124 p. 4°, 20 c. U. S., Supt. of Docs.

Library of Congress. Select list of references on inland waterways of Europe. '10(Je) 75 p. 8°, (Occasional papers, Engineer School, U. S. army.) pap. Engineer Sch.

Library of Congress. Select list of references on sugar, chiefly in its economic aspects. '10(F12) Q. pap., 25 c. Gov. Pr. Off.

Library of Congress. Select list of references on the cost of living and prices. '10(Je25) O. pap., 15 c. Gov. Pr. Off.

Library of Congress. Select list of references on the valuation and capitalization of railroads. '09(Je12) Q. pap., 10 c. U. S., Supt. of Docs.

MEYER, Konrad Ferdinand.

Taylor, M. L. Study of the technique in Konrad Ferdinand Meyer's novellen. 75 c. Univ. of Chic.

Meyer, Lucy Rider.
Some little prayers. '08(F29) c. S. bds., *35 c. net. Jennings.

—, comp. Jesus; selections. '10(Ja) c. 24 p. Ff. pap., *10 c. net. Jennings.

Meyer, Martin H.
Treatise on commercial starters in butter and cheese making. [1910.] (F) c. '09. 29 p. D. pap., gratis. M. H. Meyer.

Meyer, Max.
Sinlessness of Jesus. '08(Ja4) c. S. (Foreign religious ser.) *40 c. net. Eaton & M.

Meyer, Max Friedrich.
Introduction to the mechanics of the inner ear. '08(F1) c. 4°, (Univ. of Mo. studies, Science ser.) pap., *$1 net. Univ. of Mo.

Meyer, Rudolph J.
World in which we live: [intended as a second part to the author's "First lessons in the science of the saints."] '08(Ag8) c. 12°, *$1.50 net. Herder.

Meyer, Virginia May Keller.
Enlarged small talks on bridge. '09(Mr6) c. S. 50 c. Ruledge.

Enlarged small talks on skat; small talks on solo. '09(Mr6) c. S. 75 c. Ruledge.

Small talks on auction bridge. '10(My7) c. D. pap., 50 c.; Score book to accompany above, pap., 25 c. P. Elder.

Meyer, Willy, M.D., and Schmieden, Victor.
Bier's hyperemic treatment in surgery, medicine and specialties. '08(My2); 2d rev. and enl. ed. '09(O) 280 p. il. 8°, ea., *$3 net. Saunders.

Meyer & Son. Tilton, D., *pseud.* $1.50. C. M. Clark.

Meyers, Rob. C. V.
Cousin Tom: a comedietta. '08(N7) c. D. pap., 15 c. Penn Pub. Co.

Meynell, Mrs. Alice Christina Thompson, [Mrs. Wilfrid Meynell.]
Ceres' runaway, and other essays. '09(D4) D. *$1.25 net. Lane.
Flower of the mind; choice among the best poems. '10(S) 12°, $1.50 net. Lane.

Meynell, Everard.
Corot and his friends. '09(O2) il. O. **$3.25 net. Wessels.

Meynell, Mrs. Wilfrid.
See Meynell, *Mrs.* Alice Christina Thompson.

Meyrick, Rev. F.
Doctrine of the church of England on the Holy Communion; with a preface by E: Harold Browne. 4th ed. '08(Je13) D. $1. Longmans.
Scriptural and Catholic truth and worship; or, the faith and worship of the primitive, the mediæval and the reformed Anglican churches. New ed. '08(Jl11) D. $1. Longmans.

MIAMI Co., O.
Harbaugh, T: C., *ed. and comp.* Centennial hist.; Troy, Piqua and Miami Co., O., and representative citizens. $16. Richmond-A.

MIAMI UNIVERSITY, Oxford, O.
Bradford, J: E. James McBride manuscripts; selections relating to the Miami University. (Not for sale.) Hist. and Phil. Soc., O.
Upham, A. H. Old Miami. $1. Rep. Pub.

MICE.
Dixon, J. New harvest mouse from Petaluma, Cal. 5 c. Univ. of Cal.
Hagedoorn, A. L. Origin of two new retrogressive varieties by one mutation in mice. (Add. pubs. for price.) Univ. of Cal.
Piper, S. E: Nevada mouse plague of 1907-8. (Add. Superintendent for price.) U. S., Supt. of Docs.

Michael Thwaites's wife. Michelson, M. †$1.50. Doubleday, P.

Michaelis, Adolf Theodor Friedrich.
Century of archæological discoveries; tr. by Bettina Kahnweiler. '08(D12) 8°, $4. Dutton.

Michaels, H. Sargent.
Principal automobile routes of the United States and Canada, 1910. '09(D18) c. 16°, $2. Henneberry.

Michaud, Régis, comp.
See Vreeland, Williamson Updike, *comp.*

Michel, François Emile.
Great masters of landscape painting. '10 (D3) il. 4°, $7.50 net. Lippincott.

Michel Perrin. Bawr, S. de C. *Baroness* de. *25 c. net. Crowell.

Michelet, Jules.
Histoire de France; selections; ed., with introd., notes and vocab., by Douglas Labaree Buffum. '10(Ja29) c. map, S. $1. Holt.
Jeanne D'Arc; ed. by J. H. Sacret. '09 (N13) fold. maps, D. (Oxford modern French ser.) 50 c. Oxford Univ.
L'oiseau; ed. by Louis Cazamian. '09(Mr6) 16°, (Oxford higher French ser.) 70 c. Oxford Univ.
Modern history. *See* Hallam, H: History of Europe during the Middle Ages. v. 3.

Michell, Sir Lewis.
Life and times of the Right Honorable Cecil John Rhodes, 1853-1902. 2 v. '10 (D17) c. il. 8°, $7.50 net. M. Kennerley.

Michels, J:
Creamery butter-making. 5th ed., rev. and enl. '09(N) 11-327 p. il. 12°, $1.50. J: Michels.
Market dairying. '09(Ag7) il. D. $1. J: Michels.

Michelson, Miriam.
Awakening of Zojas. '10(Mr26) c. D. $1, fixed. Doubleday, P.
Michael Thwaites's wife. '09(Je12) c. il. D. †$1.50. Doubleday, P.

Michie, T: Johnson, ed.
See Georgia. Encyclop. digest.—Railroad repts.—Tennessee. Encyclopedic digest. —United States. *Sup. ct.* Encyclop. of repts.—Virginia and West Virginia. Encyclop. digest.

Michigan. Law of negotiable paper; with index and review questions by Rob. J. Bennett. 2d ed. '08. c. 61 p. O. pap., 60 c. Detroit Bus. Univ.

Michigan. Law of personal injuries, by Willis Baldwin. 2d ed. '09(Je) c. 99+779 p. O. *$4 net. Callaghan.

Michigan. Law of taxation; incl. general taxation, drain taxes, special assessments, pleading, practice, forms; by Willis Baldwin. '09(O) c. O. $6.50. Drake Law Bk.

Michigan. Modern law of general business corporations, [etc.;] by Burritt Hamilton. 2d ed., rev. '09(D) c. O. $4. Drake Law Bk.

Michigan. *Supreme ct.* Repts.; (Herschel Bouton Lazell.) v. 149. '08(Ja25); v. 150 (My); v. 151 (Ag); v. 152 (N); v. 153. '08, [1909.] (Mr); v. 154 (Je) c. O. shp., ea., $3.50; v. 155 (O); v. 156 (D) ea., $2.50; (Ja. M. Reasoner.) v. 157. '10 (F); v. 158 (My); v. 159 (Je); v. 160 (S); v. 161 (D) c. O. shp., ea., $1.30. Callaghan.

MICHIGAN.
Beecher, F. A. Law of contracts in Michigan. Drake Law Bk.
Dooling, J: C. Equitable remedies of creditors in Michigan. $4. Drake Law Bk.
Etzenhouser, R. Engravings of prehistoric specimens from Michigan. R. Etzenhouser.
Fairlie, J: A. Some changes in the constitution of Michigan. 25 c. J: A. Fairlie.
King, J. A. Government of the people of the state of Michigan. 50 c. Hinds.
McGregor, M. Michigan corporation law. *$4 net. Callaghan.

MICHIGAN.—*Continued.*
McKone, W: J. Michigan state and local government. 60 c. Hammond Pub.
Potter, W. W. Law of interest [in Michigan]. $2.50. Drake Law Bk.
See also Detroit;—Holland, Mich.;—Isle Royal;—Mackinac Island;—University of Michigan.

Michigan Agricultural College bulletin. O. pap. Michigan Agricultural Coll.
—Snyder. Agriculture and democracy. (Add. pubs. for price.)

Michigan corporation law and limited partnership associations, organization, management, [etc.;] by Malcolm McGregor and Howard B. Bloomer. '09(N) c. 28+574 p. O. $4. Callaghan.

Michigan, Dept. of Public Instruction bull. 8°. Mich. Supt. Pub. Instruction.
—Warriner. Industrial and vocational training in the public schools.

Michigan digest: digest of the reported decisions of all the cts. of Mich. down to Oct., 1907. In 6 v. v. 1. '08(Jl); v. 2 (O); v. 3 (N); v. 4 (D); v. 5, 6. '09(Mr) c. O. (Am. digest system, state ser.) ea., $7.50; per set, $37.50. West Pub.

Michigan Normal College bull. Q. pap. Mich. State Normal Coll.
—Public school libraries. gratis.

Michigan State Normal College, Ypsilanti. Suggestive outlines of the courses of study as followed in the kindergarten and elem. grades, 1908-1909. '09, [1910.] (F) c. 167 p. il. 4°, 50 c. Mich. State Normal Coll.

Micou, Mrs. Mary Dunnica, comp.
Reflected lights from Paradise; comfort-thoughts for those who grieve. '08(D19) c. S. *50 c. net. Young Churchman.

Micou, R: Wilde.
Manual of fundamental theology and Christian apologetics. '07, [1908.] c. 15+164 p. 8°. (Add. author for price.) R: W. Micou.

MICROBES.
See Bacteria.

MICRONESIA.
Bliss, *Mrs.* E. T. C. Micronesia: fifty years in the island world. 30 c. J: G. Hosmer.

MICROSCOPE.
Gage, S. H: Microscope. $1.50. Comstock Pub.
Scales, F. S. Pract. microscopy. $1.50. A. Eger.
Zsigmondy, R. A. Colloids and the ultramicroscope: manual of colloid chemistry. $3. Wiley.
See also Food.

Microscopical examination of foods and drugs. Greenish, H: G: $3. Blakiston.

Mid-channel. Pinero, A. W. 50 c. W. H. Baker.

'Mid pines and heather. Carmichael, J. 60 c. net. Herder.

MIDDLE AGES.
Munro, D. C., *and* Sellery, G: C. Syllabus of medieval history. $1. Longmans.
Ogg, F. A., *ed.* Source book of mediæval history. $1.50. Am. Bk.
Stories of the Middle Ages. **65 c. net. Century Co.
Vinogradoff, P. G. Roman law in mediæval Europe. *75 c. net. Harper.

MIDDLE AGES.—*Continued.*
Walsh, J. J. Thirteenth greatest of centuries. $2.50. Cath. Summer Sch.
See also Architecture;—Crusades;—Frankpledge;—Inquisition;—Monasticism;—Renaissance;—*also* names of countries.

MIDDLE STATES.
Griffis, W: E. Story of New Netherland. **$1.25 net. Houghton M.
Penn-Jersey automobile road guide, covering principal points in Pennsylvania, New Jersey and Delaware. $1. Nuneviller.

MIDDLEBOROUGH, Mass.
See Plymouth County, Mass.

Middlebrook, L: Fk.
Register of the Middlebrook family, descendants of Joseph Middlebrook of Fairfield, Conn. '09(Ag) 7-411 p. il. plan, 4°, $6. L: F. Middlebrook.

MIDDLEBROOK FAMILY.
See Genealogies.

Middlemore, J: T.
Navy in the House of Commons. '10(F5) D. 50 c.; leath., 30 c. Longmans.

MIDDLESEX, Eng.
Jerrold, W. C. Highways and byways of Middlesex. *$2 net. Macmillan.

MIDDLESEX COUNTY, Mass.
Cutter, W: R:, *ed.* Historic homes and places and genealogical and personal memoirs relating to the families of Middlesex Co., Mass. (Add. pubs. for price.) Lewis Pub.

Middleton, Cornelia Scribner.
Flower family; drawings by Isabella Morton. '10(Ap) 31 p. 8°, 60 c. Aberdeen.
Happy Child Town; drawings by Isabella Morton. '10(Ap) 22 p. 8°, 60 c. Aberdeen.
The one little girl; drawings by Isabella Morton. '10(Ap) 31 p. 8°, 60 c. Aberdeen.
Polly for short; drawings by Isabella Morton. '09, [1910.] (Ap) c. 31 p. il. 8°, 50 c. Aberdeen.

Middleton, G: Alex. T:
Elements of reinforced concrete building. '10(Je4) il. 12°, $1.50. Spon.

Middleton, Gustavus Memminger.
Sketches of South Carolina. '08(S12) c. O. pap., 25 c. G. M. Middleton.

Middleton, J. A.
Love songs and lyrics. '08(D5) c. D. *75 c. net. J: W. Luce.

Middleton, May, comp.
Recipes from old Mexico. '09(Mr) c. 36 p. 16°, 25 c. J. C. Middleton.

Middleton, T:, and Rowley, W:
Spanish gipsie, and All's lost by lust; ed. by Edg. Coit Morris. '08(N21) por. 12°, (Belles-lettres ser.; Section III., The English drama.) 60 c. Heath.

Middleton, Rev. T: Cooke.
Catholic periodicals published in the United States from the earliest in 1809 to the close of the year 1892. '08, [1909.] (F) 24 p. 8°, pap. (Priv. pr.) T: C. Middleton.

MIDDLETOWN, Ct.
Adams, C: C. Middletown Upper Houses. **$10 net. Grafton Press.

Middling, Theophilus, pseud.
See Snider, Denton Jaques.

Middy of the "Blunderbore." Gleig, C: $1.50. Lippincott.

Midgley, W.
See Lilley, A. E. V.

MIDRASH RABBOTH.
See Bible;—Talmud.

Midshipman Ralph Osborn at sea. Beach, E: L. $1.50. Wilde.

Midsummer in Whittier's country. Armes, E. 75 c. E. Armes.

Midsummer memory. Burton, R: $1.25. E. D. Brooks.

Midsummer night's dream. *See* Sidgwick, Fk., *ed.*—Shakespeare, W:

Midsummer nights with a great dreamer. Willey, J: H. *$1 net. Eaton & M.

MIDWIFERY.
Andrews, H: R. Midwifery for nurses. *$1.25 net. Longmans.
Bishop, H. D. Motherhood. $1.50. Rose.
Cadwallader, R. Hdbk. of obstetrics. *$2 net. Davis.
Cheadle, C. M. Care of mother and child. $2; $2.50. C. M. Cheadle.
Cooke, J. B. Nurse's hdbk. of obstetrics. $2.—Obstetrical technique. **$1.50 net. Lippincott.
Davis, E: P. Obstetric and gynecologic nursing. *$1.75 net. Saunders.
De Lee, J. B. Obstetrics for nurses. *$2.50 net. Saunders.
De Lee, J. B., *and* Stowe, H. M., *eds.* Obstetrics. $1.25. Year Bk.
Eden, T: W. Manual of midwifery. *$3.50 net. Chic. Med. Bk.
Evans, D: J. Obstetrics. *$2.25 net. Lea.
Galabin, A. L., *and* Blacker, G: Practice of midwifery. $6 net. Macmillan.
Grandin, E. H:, *and others.* Text book on practical obstetrics. $4. Davis.
Hamlin, F: W: Manual of practical obstetrics. $2.50. Boericke & R.
Herman, G: E. Difficult labor. $2.50 net. Wood.
Hirst, B. C. Text-book of obstetrics. $5. Saunders.
Jardine, R. Clinical obstetrics. *$6.50 net; *$7.50 net. Wood.
Jellett, H. Manual of midwifery. $6 net; $7 net. Wood.
Kerr, J. M. M. Operative midwifery. *$6 net. Wood.
King, A. F. A. Manual of obstetrics. $2.75 net. Lea.
Nall, S: Aids to obstetrics. *$1 net. Wood.
New tocology; science of sex and life. 60 c. Laird.
Spaeth, L: A. Coming motherhood. *$1 net. P: Reilly.
Tuley, H: E. Obstetrical nursing. $1.50. Morton.
Tweedy, E. H., *and* Wrench, G. T. Rotunda practical midwifery. $6. Oxford Univ.
Williams, J: W. Obstetrics. $6. Appleton.
See also Embryology;—Gynecology;—Pregnancy.

Mieir, W: O.
Possible method of reclamation for the arid West. '09(Je12) c. D. 25 c. W: O. Mieir.

Mifflin, Lloyd.
Flower and thorn; later poems. '10(Ja1) O. $1. Oxford Univ.
Toward the uplands: later poems. '09 (Ja16) c. O. $1.25. Oxford Univ.

Mig Robin, his story. Crummer, *Mrs.* E. C. C. $1. W. F. Crummer.

Migeon, Gaston.
In Japan: pilgrimages to the shrines of art; tr. from the French by Florence Simmonds. '09(D11) il. map, 12°, *$1.50 net. Lippincott.

Mighels, Ella Sterling, [Mrs. Philip Verrill Mighels, formerly Mrs. Ella Sterling Cummings.]
Full glory of Diantha. '09(My15) c. D. $1.50. Forbes.

Mighels, Philip Verrill.
Furnace of gold. '10(F19) c. il. D. $1.20. FitzGerald.
Pillars of Eden: a novel. '09(O9) c. D. $1.50. FitzGerald.
See also Adventures with Indians.

Mighels, Mrs. Philip Verrill.
See Mighels, Ella Sterling.

Might is right. "Redbeard, R.," *pseud.* 50 c. G: Engelke.

Mighty hunters. Russan, A. **$1.35 net. Longmans.

Mighty hunters in Toyland. Gordon, E. M. $1. Dodd.

Miglon, Gaston.
In Japan; pilgrimages to the shrines of art; tr. by Florence Simmonds. '10(Ja1) 12°, *$1.50 net. Lippincott.

Mike. Wodehouse, P. G. $1.50. Macmillan.

Mike Flannery on duty and off. Butler, E. P. 50 c. Doubleday, P.

Mikell, W: Ephraim.
Cases on criminal law; sel. from decisions of English and American cts. '08(D) c. 20+610 p. O. (Am. casebook ser.) $4. West Pub.

Mikkelsen, Ejnar.
Conquering the arctic ice. '09, [1910.] (Ja) 18+470 p. il. pors. maps, 8°, *$3.50 net. Jacobs.

MILAN, Italy.
Noyes, E. Story of Milan. $1.75 net; $2.25 net. Dutton.

Milbank, Jane Hungerford.
Florence Gardiner sings; some thoughts and some bridges. '10(N5) c. il. D. $1.50. Goerck.

Milbourne, J. S.
Heraldry for amateurs; incl. concise instructions regarding the tracing of pedigrees. '09(My) 232 p. il. 12°, $1.40. Scribner.

Milburg, Francisco Mansfield.
See Miltoun, Fs., *pseud.*

MILDEW.
See Fungi.

Mildews of the cereals. Reed, G: M. (Not for sale.) G: M. Reed.

Mildmay, Herbert, ed.
See Mildmay, *Mrs.* S. St. J. M., *ed.*

Mildmay, Mrs. Susan St. John Motley and Herbert, eds.
John Lothrop Motley and his family; further letters and records; ed. by his daughter and Herbert St. John Mildmay. '10(My21) il. O. $5 net. Lane.

Mildren, Nan Langdon.
Seat work for primary grades. '10(Mr5) c. 8°, 35 c. N. L. Mildren.

MILE-STONES.
See Roads.

Milecete, Helen.
Detached pirate. '08(My) c. 12°, (Popular ed. of recent fiction.) †75 c. Little, B. & Co.

Miles, Alfr. H:, ed.
Poets and poetry of the XIXth century (humor). In 12 v. v. 8, Crabbe to Christian. '08(F22); v. 12, E. H. Plumptre to Selwyn Image. (Ap4) 16°, ea., *50 c. net; leath., *$1 net. Dutton.

Milham, Willis Isbister.
How to identify the stars. '09(Jl17) c. il. D. **75 c. net. Macmillan.

MILITARY ART AND SCIENCE.
Alten, G. K. F. V. v. Studies in applied tactics. $2. Hudson.
Buckey, M. C. Manual for the instruction of gunners of mine companies. 50 c. M. C. Buckey.
Buddecke, A. Tactical decisions and orders: study in troop-leading. no. 1. $1.25; no 2, $1.50. Hudson.
Bush, H. M. Diary of an enlisted man. 50 c.; 25 c. E: T. Miller.
Eames, H: E. Military maps explained. $1. Hudson.
Fitch, R. S. Estimating tactical situations and composing field orders. (Priv. pr.) Staff Coll.
Hanna, M. E. Tactical principles and problems. $2.50. M. E. Hanna.
MacArthur, D. Military demolitions. Staff Coll.
Morrison, J: F., *and* Munson, E. L. Lectures on patrols, advance guards and outposts. (Not for sale.) Army Service.
Morrison, J: F., *and* Munson, E. L. Study in troop leading and management of the sanitary service in war. $1.25. J: F. Morrison.
Norwood, J: W. Instructions for the noncommissioned officer. (Add. pubs. for price.) E: T. Miller.
Sayre, F. Map maneuvers: [war game.] 60 c.; 75 c. Staff Coll.
Selkirk, W. O. Catechism of manual of guard duty, United States Army. 50 c. net. Wiley.
Sharpe, A. C. Making a soldier. 25 c. Acme Pub.
Sherrill, C. O. Military map reading. 40 c.; 30 c.—Military topography for the mobile forces, including map reading, surveying and sketching. $2.50. Army Service.
Sherrill, C. O. Military sketching. (Priv. pr.) C. O. Sherrill.
Summer night's dream; tr. from German by Capt. Gawne. [Also] Defence of Duffer's drift, by Capt. E. D. Swinton. $1. Hudson.

MILITARY ART AND SCIENCE.—*Continued.*
Verdy du Vernois, J. von. Studies in the leading of troops. $1.50. Hudson.
Wagner, A. L. Catechism of outpost duty, including reconnaissance, independent cavalry, [etc.] 50 c. Hudson.
Willcox, C. De W. French-English military technical dict. Gov. Pr. Off.
Winslow, E. E. Lectures on seacoast defense. (Not for sale.) Engineer Sch.
See also Aerial navigation;—Artillery;—Battles;—Cavalry;—Chancellorsville (Campaign of);—Courts martial;—Examinations;—Explosives;—Fortification;—Infantry;—Leipzig campaign;—Military hygiene;—Naval art and science;—Peace;—Rifle;—Signals and signalling;—Submarines;—War;—*also* Germany;—United States Army.

Military consul in Turkey. Townshend, A. F. *$3.50 net. Lippincott.

Military Historical Society of Massachusetts. v. 3, Campaigns in Virginia, Maryland, Pennsylvania, 1862-1863. '08, [1909.] (F) (Add. pubs. for price); v. 7, [Kentucky and Tennessee campaigns and their battles.] '09(Ja16) $2.50; v. 11, Naval actions and operations against Cuba and Porto Rico, 1593-1815. '01, [1909.] (F) 8°, (Papers of the Hist. Soc. of Mass.) (Add. pubs. for price.) Military Hist. Soc.

MILITARY HYGIENE.
Ashburn, P. M. Elements of military hygiene. **$2 net. Houghton M.
Harvard, V. Manual of military hygiene. *$4 net. Wood.
Morrison, J: F. Study in troop leading and management of the sanitary service in war. $1.25. J: F. Morrison.
Munson, E: L., *and* Eltinge, Le R. Study in camp sanitation. (Not for sale.) Army Service.
Straub, P. F: Medical service in campaign. $1.50. Blakiston.
Wanheill, C. F., *and* Beveridge, W. W: O. Sanitary officer's handbook of practical hygiene. *$1.40 net. Longmans.
Woodhull, A. A. Military hygiene for officers of the line. **$1.50 net. Wiley.

MILITARY LAW.
See Courts-martial.

MILITARY ORDER OF THE LOYAL LEGION.
Mason, R. H. Military Order of the Loyal Legion of the United States: an address. (Add. pubs. for price.) M. O. L. L., (Ill.)

Military Order of the Loyal Legion of the United States. *New York Commandery.* Addresses del. before the Commandery of the State of New York at the regular meeting held Feb. 3, 1909, at Delmonico's, in observatory of the 100th anniversary of the birth of President Abraham Lincoln. '09(Ag) 5-31 p. 8°. (Add. pubs. for price.) M. O. L. L. (N. Y.)

Military Order of the Loyal Legion of the United States. *Pennsylvania Commandery.* Abraham Lincoln: memorial meeting, February 12, 1908. '08(D5) O. 15 c. M. O. L. L., (Pa.)

Military Order of the Loyal Legion of the United States. *Pennsylvania Commandery.* Abraham Lincoln memorial meeting, Feb. 3, 1909. '09(Jl) 19 p. 8°. (Add. pubs. for price.) **M. O. L. L., (Pa.)**

MILITARY TOPOGRAPHY.
See Military art and science.

Militz, Annie Rix.
Spiritual housekeeping; study in concentration in the busy life. '10(D17) c. 12°, 50 c. Absolute Press.

Miliukov, Pavel Nikolaevich.
Constitutional government for Russia: address del. before the Civic Forum. '08 (D5) pors. 12°, (Civic Forum addresses.) pap., 10 c. Civic Forum.

MILK.
American Association of Medical Milk Commissions. Manual of working methods and standards. gratis. Milk Com. Assoc.
Ayers, S: H:, *and* Johnson, W: T., *jr.* Bacteriology of commercially pasteurized and raw market milk. Gov. Pr. Off.
Campbell, H. C. Leucocytes in milk. (Add. Superintendent for price.) U. S., Supt. of Docs.
Coit, H: L. Clean milk in its economic and medical relations. (Add. pubs. for price.) Jefferson Co. Med. Soc.
Farrington, E: H., *and* Woll, F. W. Testing milk and its products. $1. Mendota.
Herschell, G: A. Soured milk and pure cultures of lactic acid bacilli in the treatment of disease [auto intoxication]. *50 c. net. Chic. Med. Bk.
Jensen, C. O. Essentials of milk hygiene. **$2 net. Lippincott.
Kerr, J: W. Hist. development, and statistics of milk charities in the United States. Gov. Pr. Off.
Lane, C. B. Medical milk commissions. 15 c. U. S., Supt. of Docs.
Lane, C. B., *and* Parks, K. E. Improved methods for the production of market milk by ordinary dairies. Gov. Pr. Off.
Lane, C, B., *and* Weld, I. C. Competitive exhibitions of milk and cream. (Add. Superintendent for price.) U. S., Supt. of Docs.
Merrill, L. C. Preparation and use of sweet whey in powder form. gratis. Merrill-S.
Milk and its relation to the public health. '08, [1909.] (My) 758 p. il. 8°, (U. S., Treasury Dept., Public Health and Marine Hospital Service of the U. S., Hygienic Laboratory bull.) pap., 75 c. U. S., Supt. of Docs.
Milner, R. D. Use of milk as food. 5 c. U. S., Supt. of Docs.
Porter, C: S. Milk diet as a remedy for chronic diseases. *$1.25 net. Stechert.
Publow, C: A. Questions and answers on milk and milk-testing. 50 c. Judd.
Rogers, L. A. Bacteria in milk. 5 c.—Directions for the home pasteurization of milk. (Add. Superintendent for price.) U. S., Supt. of Docs.
Shaw, R. H., *and* Eckles, C. H. Chemical and physical study of the large and small fat globules in cows' milk. 5 c. U. S., Supt. of Docs.
Spargo, J: Common sense of the milk question. **$1.50 net. Macmillan.

MILK.—*Continued.*
United States. Milk and its relation to the public health; rev. and enl. ed. of bulletin no. 41, (by various authors.) '09, [1910.] (Je) 834 p. il. tabs., 8°, (U. S., Treasury Dept., Public Health and Marine Hospital Service; Hygienic Laboratory, bull.)
Ward, A. R., *and* Jaffa, M. E: Pure milk and the public health. *$2 net. Taylor & C.
Whitaker, G: M., *and others.* Care of milk and its use in the home. Gov. Pr. Off.
Winslow, K. Production and handling of clean milk. $2.50. W: R. Jenkins.
Winslow, K., *and* Hill, H. W. Production and handling of clean milk. $3.25. W: R. Jenkins.
See also Butter;—Children;—Cow;—Dairy.

Mill, Hugh Rob., ed.
International geography, by seventy authors; [chap. 37-42,] North America, Central America, and the West Indies. '08(D12) c. O. **90 c. net. Appleton.

Mill, J: Stuart.
Auguste Comte and positivism. '08(Je6) 16°, (New universal lib.) 50 c.; leath., 75 c. Dutton.
Autobiography. New ed. '08(D5) D. 50 c. Longmans.
Letters; ed., with introd, by Hugh S. R. Elliott, with a note on Mill's private life by Mary Taylor. In 2 v. '10(My21) pors. O. $6.50 net. Longmans.
On liberty. '10(D) front.. 32°, (Ariel booklets.) 75 c. Putnam.
Principles of political economy, with some of their applications to social philosophy; ed., with an introd., by W. J. Ashley. '09 (D25) D. *$1.50 net. Longmans.
Principles of political economy with special introd. by Arth. T. Hadley. '08(Je27) c. 2 v., il. 8°, $3.50; hf. mor., $7.50. Lamb Pub.
Utilitarianism. '08(Ap4) 12°, (New universal lib.) 50 c.; leath., 75 c. Dutton.
Utilitarianism, liberty, representative government; with introd. by A. D. Lindsay. '10(D10) c. 16°, (Everyman's lib.) 35 c. net; leath., 70 c. net. Dutton.

MILL, John Stuart.
Tawney, G. A. J. S. Mill's theory of inductive logic. In 2 pts. 50 c. Univ. of Cin.
Whittaker, T: W. Comte and Mill. *50 c. net. Dodge.

MILL CREEK INDIANS.
See Indians.

Mill on the Floss. *See* Eliot, G:

MILLAIS, *Sir* John Everett.
Reid, J. E. Sir J. E. Millais. $1.25. Scribner.

Millais, J: Guille.
Natural hist. of British game birds. '10 (F19) col. il. 4°, *$60 net. (550 copies.) Longmans.

Millar, Adam Veuse.
See Phillips, Ja. D:

Millard, Bailey, ["Fk. Bailey."]
Jack Morning's treasure. '09(N20) il. 12°, *$1 net. Clode.

Millard, Bruce, comp.
Mediterranean cruise; describing all Mediterranean points usually visited in a winter's cruise in Europe, Asia and Africa. '10(Ap2) c. il. D. $2.25 net. Putnam.

Millard, Columbus Norman.
Building and care of the body; elem. text-book in pract. physiology and hygiene. '10(My7) il. 12°, 40 c. net. Macmillan.
Wonderful house that Jack has: reader in practical physiology and hygiene. '08 (Jl11) il. 12°, *50 c. net. Macmillan.

Millard, Fk. Bailey, ["Fk. Bailey."]
Sea hawk. '10(O22) c. D. $1 net. Wessels & B.

Millard, Junius W:, D.D.
Life's to-morrows: [seven sermons.] '08 (F29) c. D. **75 c. net. Am. Bapt.

Millard, T: Franklin Fairfax.
America and the Far Eastern question. '09(Ap24) c. O. **$4 net. Moffat.

Mille et une nuits. *See* Blanchaud, R. de, *ed.*

Millenium. *See* More, *Sir* T:

MILLENNIAL DAWN (*sect*).
See Creeds.

Millennial essays. Severance, H. S. $1.50. H. S. Severance.

Miller, A. V.
Sermons on modern spiritualism. '08(D5) 8°, *75 c. net. Herder.

Miller, Adam Marion, M.D.
See Bailey, F: Randolph.

Miller, Mrs. Alice Duer.
Blue arch. '10(O29) c. D. $1.20 net. Scribner.
Less than kin. '09(Je12) c. D. †$1.25. Holt.

Miller, Andrew.
Problem of theology in modern life and thought. '09(N20) O. *$1.25 net. Doran.

Miller, Mrs. Anne Archbold.
Little old outlaws. '10(S17) c. O. bds., 75 c. net. McClurg.

Miller, Mrs. Annie Jenness.
Triune development, the road to self-mastery. '10(Ja8) c. 8°, (Triune development ser.) 60 c. Triune Order.

Miller, Barnette.
Leigh Hunt's relations with Byron, Shelley and Keats. '10(Je18) 8°, (Columbia Univ. studies in English.) $1.25 net. Lemcke.

Miller, Celeste J.
Newest way round the world. '08(Ag15) il. 8°, *$2.50 net. C. J. Miller.

Miller, Chall Charlesmayne.
Zigzag-lightning shorthand. '07, [1908.] (Ap.) c. 32 p. S. (Add. pubs. for price.) Zigzag.

Miller, C: C., M.D.
Cure of rupture by paraffin injections. '08 (O3) c. D. $1. C: C. Miller.

Miller, C: M.
Construction and flying of kites. '09(O2) c. il. (Manual training reprints.) pap., 20 c. Manual Arts.
Kite craft. [1910.] (Je) 23 p. il. 12°. (Not for sale.) Davis Press.

Miller, C: Winthrop.
Experiment in colonization of the house martin. '09(Ap3) il. O. (Worthington Society for the Study of Bird Life, bulletin.) pap., gratis. Worthington Soc.
Occurrence of the larvæ of a parasitic fly, *Protocalliphora chrystorrhœa,* Meigen, in bird nests in the vicinity of Shawnee, Pa. '09(Ap3) il. O. (Worthington Society for the Study of Bird Life, bulletin.) pap., gratis. Worthington Soc.

Miller, Cincinnatus Heine, ["Joaquin Miller."]
Poems. 6 v. '09(D) ea., *$1.25 net; De luxe ed., subs., ea., mor., *$5 net. De Witt & S.
Poems. [Bear ed.] In 6 v. v. 1-5. '09 (My22); v. 6. '10(Jl2) c. pors. D. bds., ea., $1.25 net; de luxe ed., ea., $5 net. Whitaker & R.

Miller, Clara Huston.
Scent of sandal wood. '10(Mr5) il. 8°, $2.50. (300 copies.) C. H. Miller.

Miller, Claude H.
The new hollow-tile construction. [1910] (My) 16 p. il. S. pap., gratis. Nat. Fire Proofing.
—, comp. Garden and farm almanac for 1909. '08(D26) c. il. O. pap., 25 c. Doubleday, P.

Miller, Delavan S.
Drum's story and other tales. '09(N20) c. D. $1. Hungerford-H.

Miller, Donald Herbert.
Miller system book of poultry culture. '10 (Ap16) c. il. O. pap., $1.50. Miller System.

Miller, Edith Abercrombie-.
Rosemary: book of verse. '09(My22) c. D. *$1 net. F. F. Sherman.

Miller, Edm. Howd.
Calculations of analyt. chemistry. 3d ed., rev. and enl. '09, [1910.] (My) 10+201 p. tabs., 8°, $1.50 net. Macmillan.

Miller, Edm. W., comp.
Sail and steam; historical sketch showing New Jersey's connection with the events commemorated by the Hudson-Fulton Celebration, Sept. 25-Oct. 9, 1909. [2d ed.] '09(O30) c. il. O. pap., gratis. Jersey City Lib.

Miller, E: Furber.
See Peabody, Cecil Hobart.

Miller, Eliz. Jane.
City of delight. '08(Mr21) c. il. D. †$1.50. Bobbs-M.

Miller, Mrs. Eliz. Kumler.
Poems; with a tribute by her sister, Mrs. G. A. Funkhouser. '09(N) c. 14+28 p. il. 12°, 55 c. Un. B. Pub.

Miller, Elmer I.
Legislature of the province of Virginia: its internal development. '08(Ja25) 8°, (Columbia Univ. studies in hist., economics and public law.) *$2 net; pap., *$1.50 net. Lemcke.

Miller, Fs. Trevelyan.
Hero tales from American life. '09(D25) c. il. por. 8°, $1. Chr. Herald.
Portrait life of Lincoln. '10(D17) c. il. pors. 4°, $2. Patriot.

Miller, Fk. Ebenezer.
The voice; its production, care and preservation; with a note by Gustav Kobbé. '10(F5) c. front. S. *$1.25 net. Schirmer.

Miller, Fk. Justus, tr.
See Virgil, Maro Publius.

Miller, Fred Robinson.
Progressive problems in physics. '08(O10) c. tabs., figs. D. 60 c. Heath.

Miller, G: Washington.
Mine examiner's and prospector's companion. 6th ed. '10(Ag20) c. 8°, flex. leath., $3. Hall & W.

Miller, Gerrit Smith, jr.
Description of a new species of hippopotamus. '10(Ap) 3 p. O. (Smithsonian miscellaneous collections.) pap., 10 c. Smith. Inst.
Descriptions of two new genera and sixteen new species of mammals from the Philippine Islands. '10(S) 391-404 p. il. O. pap. Gov. Pr. Off.
New carnivore from China. '10(S) 385-386 p. il. O. pap. Gov. Pr. Off.
New rodent of the genus Saccostomus from British East Africa. '10(Mr19) il. O. (Smithsonian misc. collections.) pap. Smith. Inst.

Miller, Mrs. Harriet Mann, ["Olive Thorne Miller."]
Bird our brother. '08(My16) c. D. **$1.25 net. Houghton M.
See also In American fields and forests.

Miller, H: Russell.
Man higher up; story of the fight, which is life, and the force, which is love. '10 (My21) c. il. D. $1.50. Bobbs-M.

Miller, Irving Elger.
Psychology of thinking. '09(My1) c. D. **$1.25 net. Macmillan.

Miller, Ja. H:
History of Summers County, [W. Va.,] from the earliest settlement to the present time '08(Je) c. 15+838 p. il. pors. 8°, $3.50. J. H: Miller.

Miller, Ja. Marion, [Jude Macmillar.]
Random shaft. '08(Je6) c. il. D. $1.50. C. M. Clark.

Miller, Ja. Martin.
Hunting big game in the wilds of Africa; cont. thrilling adventures of the famous Roosevelt expedition. '10(F26) c. il. pors. maps, 8°, $1.50. Nat. Pub. Co.
World's greatest disaster: story of the Italian earthquake horror; cont. also a history of Italy and Sicily; other great disasters of the world, both by earthquakes, volcanoes and tidal waves. '09(F13) c. il. O. $1.50. [Published also in Italian.] Monarch.

Miller, Ja. Russell, D.D.
Beauty of every day. '10(O15) c. S. bds., 65 c. net. Crowell.
Bethlehem to Olivet: the life of Jesus Christ il. by modern painters. '09(Ag14) il. O. **$1.50 net. Crowell.
Cure for care. '08(O10) c. D. (What is worth while ser.) bds., **30 c. net. Crowell.

Miller, Ja. Russell, D.D.—*Continued.*
Devotional hours with the Bible. In 8 v. [v. 1,] From the creation to the crossing of the Red Sea. '09(N20); v. 2, From the crossing of the Red Sea to the close of the life of David; v. 3, The Gospel by Matthew (D11); v. 4, Historical books from Solomon to Malachi. '10(D) c. D. ea., *$1.25 net. Doran.
Devotional hours with the Sunday-school lessons for 1911. '10(D) $1.25 net. Doran.
Evening thoughts for every day in the year. '08(O17) c. S. bds., **65 c. net; gilt top, **85 c. net. Crowell.
Gate beautiful. '09(S25) c. S. **85 c. net. Crowell.
Glimpses of the heavenly life. '08(O17) c. il. D. (Chiswick ser.) **50 c. net. Crowell.
Go forward. '09(S11) c. il. D. **50 c. net. Crowell.
Master's friendships. '09(S18) c. D. (What is worth while ser.) leatherette, **30 c. net. Crowell.
Master's friendships. '10(S10) c. col. il. 12°, 50 c. net. Crowell.
Turning northward. '08(O10) c. D. (What is worth while ser.) bds., **30 c. net. Crowell.
Wider life. '08(O17) c. S. bds., **65 c. net; gilt top, **85 c. net. Crowell.

Miller, Ja. W:
English composition and essay-writing. '10 (D31) D. 60 c. Longmans.

Miller, Joaquin, pseud.
See Miller, Cincinnatus Heine.

Miller, J:
Twentieth century hist. of Erie County, Pa.; narrative acct. of its historical progress, its people, and its principal interests. 2 v. '10(Ap) c. il. pors. 4°, $18. Lewis Pub.

Miller, J: Calvin.
Power gas and the gas producer. '10(N5) c. il. 8°, $1. Popular Mechanics.

Miller, Kelly.
Race adjustment: essays on the negro in America. '08(S19) c. O. *$2 net. Neale.

Miller, Lewis B.
Crooked trail: story of a 1000 mile saddle trip up and down the Texas frontier in pursuit of a runaway ox. '08(My9) c. D. (Stockman ser.) 50 c.; pap., 25 c. Axtell-R.
White River raft. '10(N5) c. il. O. $1.50. Estes.

Miller, Loye Holmes.
Condor-like vultures of Rancho La Brea. '10(D) 19 p. O. (Univ. of Cal. pubs.; Geology.) pap., 15 c. Univ. of Cal.
Pavo Californicus, a fossil peacock from the quaternary asphalt beds of Rancho La Brea. '09(S11) il. O. (Univ. of Cal. pubs.; Geology.) pap., 5 c. Univ. of Cal.
Teratornis; new avian genus from Rancho La Brea. '09(O) 305-317 p. il. Q. (University of California pubs.; Geology.) pap., 10 c. Univ. of Cal.
Wading birds and the quaternary asphalt beds of Rancho La Brea. '10(O) 439-448 p. Q. (Univ. of Cal. pubs.: Geology.) pap., 10 c. Univ. of Cal.

Miller, Metta Frazee.
Lure of the Book. '08(D5) c. D. $1. Winona.

Miller, Millicent Welles.
Helps for young mothers; in the physical and moral training of infants and young children. '08(Ag29) c. D. bds., 50 c. Jacobs.

Miller, Mills.
See Murray, J:

Miller, Olive Thorne, pseud.
See Miller, *Mrs.* Harriet Mann.

Miller, Peyton Farrell.
Story of Robert Fulton. '08(D19) c. front. D. $1. P. F. Miller.

Miller, Raymond Durbin.
See Bright, Ja. Wilson.

Miller, Rob. Clinton.
Historic views of Gettysburg. '09(Jl) c. 68 p. il. f°, 50 c. J. I. Mumper.

Miller, Roman J:
Around the world with the battleships; with an introd. note by Ja. B. Connolly. '09(N6) c. il. D. $1.25. McClurg.
Pictorial log of the battle fleet cruise around the world. '09(Je19) c. il. obl. O. *$3 net. McClurg.

Miller, Russell B:
See Walker, Rollin Hough.

MILLER, Samuel Freeman.
Gregory, C: N. Samuel Freeman Miller. *$2 net. State Hist., Ia.; Torch Press.

Miller, T: Southworth.
American cotton system historically treated, showing operations of the cotton exchanges, also cotton classification; with numerous pract. domestic and foreign commercial calculations; tells what you want to know. '10(My14) c. por. D. $1.50. T: S. Miller.

Miller, Vallentine.
Standard recipes for ice cream makers, wholesale and retail. '09(Jl17) c. il. D. $1; $1.50. Laird.

Miller, W:, 1864-.
The Balkans: Roumania, Bulgaria, Servia and Montenegro; with new chapter cont. their hist. from 1896 to 1908. 2d ed. '08 [1909.] (N) 19+476 p. il. por. maps, 8°, (Story of the nations.) $1.50; hf. leath., $1.75. Putnam.

Miller, Rev. W:, 1838-.
Latins in the Levant: hist. of Frankish Greece, 1204-1566. '08(N21) maps, 8°, *$5 net. Dutton.

Miller, W: D.
See Spaulding, Fk. Ellsworth.

Miller, W: Harris.
History and genealogies of the families of Miller, Woods, Harris, Wallace, Maupin, Oldham, Kavanaugh, and Brown, with interspersions of notes of the families of Dabney, Reid, [etc.] '07, [1908.] (Mr.) c. '06. 6-728+127 p .pors., 8°, $5. W: H. Miller.

Miller, W: J:
Geology of the Remsen quadrangle. incl. Trenton Falls and vicinity in Oneida and Herkimer Counties. '09(Ap) 51 p. il. fold. map, 8°, (N. Y. State Museum bull.) pap., 25 c. N. Y. State Educ.

Miller and the toad. Clifton, R: *$1.20 net. Sherman, F.

MILLER FAMILY.
See Genealogies.

Millerd, Clara Eliz.
On the interpretation of Empedocles. '08 (O24) c. 8°, pap., 75 c. Univ. of Chic.

Millers and their new home. Pierson, C. D. $1. Dutton.

MILLET, Jean François.
Turner, P. M. Millet. 65 c. net; $1.50 net. Stokes.

Milligan, G:, D.D.
St. Paul's Epistle to the Thessalonians: Greek text; with introd. and notes. '08 (F22) 8°, *$2.60 net. Macmillan.
—, **ed.** Selections from the Greek papyri; ed., with trs. and notes. '10(O1) D. $1.50 net. Putnam.

Milligan, Rob. H.
Jungle folk of Africa. '08(S12) c. 8°, *$1.50 net. Revell.

Millikan, Rob. Andrews, and Mills, J:
Short university course in electricity, sound and light. '08(O31) c. diagrs., O. $2. Ginn.

Milliken, J. A.
Narraguagus Valley; some acct. of its early settlement and settlers; covers towns of Steuben, Milbridge, Harrington and Cherryfield. '10(D) 30 p. O. pap., $2. A. J. Huston.

MILLINERY.
Ben Yûsuf, *Mme.* A. Art of millinery. $2. Millinery Trade.

Milling fixtures. '08(M14) c. il. 8°, (Machinery's reference ser.) pap., 25 c. Indust. Press.

Million a minute. Aitken, R. $1.50. W. J. Watt.

Millionaire and the policeman's wife. Harper, O. 25 c. J. S. Ogilvie.

Mills, Ja. Franklin.
See Stone, J: C:

Millner, Wa. D.
Bill of lading. '09. [1910.] (F) 59 p. 24°, 50 c. Stone Pr.

Mills, C: Fs. H:
Voice, and vocal exercises. '09(Je12) c. O. pap., $1. Univ. of Neb.
Voice and vocalism; incl. subjects of illustrated, descriptive and applied vocal anatomy. '10(My7) c. il. 8°, $1.50. Hawk-Eye.

Mills, C: H., rep.
See New York [State.] Criminal reports.

Mills, Enos Abijah.
Wild life on the Rockies. '09(Ap3) c. il. Q. **$1.75 net. Houghton M.

Mills, Herbert Elmer.
Outlines of economics; syllabus for introductory study. 2d ed. '09(N20) 8°, $1. H. E. Mills.

Mills, Ja. Cooke.
Our inland seas; their shipping and commerce for three centuries. '10(N5) c. il. O. $1.75 net. McClurg.

Mills, Ja. Porter, M.D.
Health: omnipresence, omniscience, infinite. abstract and concrete. '08(Ag15) c. 12°, $2. Brentano's.

Mills, Jessie.
See Mills, *Mrs.* Lusina Strong.

Mills, Job Smith, Funk, W. R., and Hough, S: Strickler.
Our foreign missionary enterprise. '08(D) c. 16+282 p. il. 12°, (United Brethren mission study course.) *50 c. net; pap., *35 c. net. Un. B. Pub.

Mills, J:
Introd. to thermodynamics, for engineering students. '10(D3) c. tabs., O. $2. Ginn.
See also Millikan, Rob. Andrews.

Mills, Lawrence Heyworth, D.D.
Avesta eschatology compared with the books of Daniel and Revelations. '08 (Mr7) c. por. O. bds., 50 c.; Strathmore pap., 75 c. Open Court.

Mills, Mrs. Lusina Strong and Jessie.
Verses. '08(N21) c. por. D. $1.25. Badger.

Mills, Mary Wilda.
See Rossman, Mary Blanche.

Mills, Wesley, M.D.
How to keep a dog in the city. '10(D) 40 p. 8°, pap., 25 c. W: R. Jenkins.

Mills, Weymer Jay.
Girl I left behind me. '10(O22) c. col. il. Q. bds., $2 net, boxed. Dodd.

Mills-Young, F. G.
See Young, F. G. Mills-.

MILLS.
Hobart, J. F. Millwrighting. *$3 net. Hill Pub.
Ketchum, M. S. Design of steel mill buildings and the calculation of stresses in framed structures. $3. Engineering News.
Puppe, J. Experimental investigation on the power required to drive rolling mills. $4.50 net. Lippincott.
Swingle, C. F. Pract. hdbk. for millwrights. $2. Drake.
See also Cotton;—Factories;—Flour;—Gold;—Knitting;—Lumber;—Paper;—Useful arts.

Mills of mammon. Brower, J. H. $1.50. P. H. Murray.
Mills of man. Payne, P. 75 c. Rand, McN. & Co.
Mills of the gods. Robins, E. †$1. Moffat.

Millspaugh, C: F:
Prænunciæ Bahamenses—[pt.] 2, Contribs. to a flora of the Bahamian Archipelago. '09, [1910.] (F) 289-321 p. map, 8°, (Field Columbian Museum pub., Botanical ser.) 50 c. Field Museum.

Milman, H: Hart.
Hist. of the Jews. '08(Ag8) 8°, $1.50. Bloch.
History of the Jews; introd. by Dr. Hartwell Jones. 2 v. '09(Ap3) 16°, (Everyman's lib.) *35 c. net; leath., *70 c. net. Dutton.

Milman, Lena.
Sir Christopher Wren. '08(D5) il. 8°, (Library of art.) *$2 net. Scribner.

Milmine, Georgine.
Life of Mary Baker G. Eddy and the hist. of Christian science. '09(D18) c. il. pors. O. **$2 net. Doubleday, P.

Milne, Ja.
My summer in London. '10(Jl30) il. 8°, $1.50 net. Dutton.

Milne, Rob., M.D.
Plea for the home treatment and prevention of scarlet fever. [1910.] (Je) 12°, $1 net. Wood.

Milne, W: Ja.
Key to Standard algebra. '09(Jl3) c. D. $1. Am. Bk.
Standard algebra. '08(O3) c. il. D. $1. Am. Bk.

Milner, Byron A.
See Barnes, H. Edg.

Milner, Rob. Denniston.
Use of milk as food. '09(S) 44 p. il. 8°, (U. S., Dept. of Agriculture, farmers' bull.) pap., 5 c. U. S., Supt. of Docs.

MILO.
Ball, C. R., *and* Leidigh, A. H. Milo as a dry-land grain crop. 5 c. U. S., Supt. of Docs.

Milton, G: F.
Compulsory education in the South. '09 (S) 10+2 p. 8°, (National child labor committee pubs.) pap., gratis. Nat. Child Labor.

Milton, J:
Catalogue of an exhibition commemorative of the tercentenary of the birth of John Milton, 1608-1908; incl. original editions of his poetical and prose works, together with three hundred and twenty-seven engraved portraits; held at the Grolier Club, December 3, 1908, to January 9, 1909. '09(Ja30) facsims., 12°. (Priv. pr.) Grolier Club.
Comus; being the Bridgewater manuscript; with notes and short family memoir, by the Lady Alix Egerton. '10(D24) il. 8°, parchment, $5 special net. Dodd.
Comus, L'allegro, Il penseroso, and Lycidas, with other of Milton's shorter poems; ed., with introd. and notes by Clarence Griffin Child. '10(Je4) c. por. 12°, (Scribner English classics.) 25 c. Scribner.
Ode on the morning of Christ's nativity. '10(D) 16°, (Abbey classics.) pap., 25 c., boxed; bds., 50 c., boxed; limp leath., $1, boxed. Abbey Co.
Formerly published by Paul Elder.
Ode on the morning of Christ's nativity. '09(D) pap., *40 c. net; bds., *60 c. net; Japan vellum, *$1 net. T: B. Mosher.
Paradise lost; ed. by A. W. Verity. '10 (Ap16) D. $2.50 net. Putnam.
Poems; introd. by H. H. D. Rouse. '09 (Ap3) 16°, (Everyman's lib.) *35 c. net; *70 c. net. Dutton.
Treatise on education. '09(Ja16) (Old South leaflets) pap., 5 c. Old South Work.

—, and Wordsworth, W:
Sonnets; sel. and arr. by A. T. Quiller-Couch. '08(D19) S. (Select English classics.) 10 c. Oxford Univ.

MILTON, John.
Ames, P. W., *ed.* Milton memorial lectures, 1908. $2. Oxford Univ.
Beers, H: A. Milton's tercentenary. 50 c. Yale Univ.
Firth, C: H. Milton as a historian. 40 c. Oxford Univ.

MILTON, John.—*Continued.*

Leach, A. F. Milton as a schoolboy and schoolmaster. 40 c. Oxford Univ.

Little, C: John Milton. (Priv. pr.) Chic. Lit. Club.

Massachusetts Historical Society, Boston. Proceedings of the Massachusetts Historical Society in commemoration of the tercentenary of the birth of John Milton. Mass. Hist. Soc.

Meredith, G:, *and others.* Tercentenary of Milton's birth inaugural meeting at the theatre, Burlington Gardens. 35 c. Oxford Univ.

Robertson, J: G. Milton's fame on the continent. 35 c. Oxford Univ.

Milton, W: H., D.D.

Cure of souls; or, Christ's treatment of the individual. '08(N7) c. D. *$1 net. Whittaker.

MILTON, Mass.

Tucker, J: A. First four meeting houses of Milton, Mass. 75 c. J: A. Tucker.

Miltoun, Fs., [pseud. for Milburg Francisco Mansfield.]

Castles and chateaux of old Burgundy and the border provinces. '09(D4) c. col. il. fold. maps, O. $3, boxed. L. C. Page.

In the land of the mosques and minarets. '08(My16) c. maps, O. $3; leath., $7. L. C. Page.

Italian highways and byways from a motor car. '09(My22) c. il. O. $3, boxed. L. C. Page.

Royal palaces and parks of France. '10 (D3) c. il. O. $3. L. C. Page.

MILWAUKEE, Wis.

Caspar's guide and map of the city of Milwaukee. 25 c. Caspar.

Larson, L. M. Financial and administrative hist. of Wisconsin. 50 c. Univ. of Wis.

Poetsch, C: J., *and* Leidel, E: F. Official quarter sectional atlas of city of Milwaukee. *$40 net; *$60 net; in 2 v., *$65 net; *$75 net. Caspar.

See also South Side Library.

Mimma-Bella. *See* Lee-Hamilton, E.

Mims, Edn., and Payne, Bruce Ryburn.

Southern prose and poetry for schools. '10(My21) 12°, 80 c. Scribner.

MIND.

Atkinson, W: W. Inner consciousness 50 c. Advanced Thought.

Atkinson, W: W. Mind-power; or, the law of dynamic mentation. $2. Progress Co.

Burke, R: M. Cosmic consciousness: study in the evolution of the human mind. $4.25. Progress Co.

Du Bois, P. Self-control and how to secure it. **$1.50 net. Funk.

Godlover, H. B. Science of minds. $1. H. B. Godlover.

Hegel, G. W. F. Phenomenology of mind. In 2 v. $5.50 net. Macmillan.

Locke, J: Essay on the human understanding. *$1.50 net. Dutton.

March, J: L. Theory of mind. **$2 net. Scribner.

MIND.—*Continued.*

Stoddart, W: H: B. Mind and its disorders. Blakiston.

See also Brain;—Culture;—Hypnotism;—Insanity;—Memory;—Mental science;—Mind and body; Nervous system;—New thought;—Nurses and nursing;—Personality; — Phrenology; — Psychology;—Vibration;—Worry.

MIND AND BODY.

Achorn, J. W. Some physical disorders having mental origin. **25 c. net. Moffat.

Ash, E: Mind and health; mental factor and suggestion in treatment, with special reference to neurasthenia and other common nervous disorders. $1.50 net. Wood.

Atkinson, W: W. Mind and body. $1. Progress Co.

Bainbridge, W: S. Life's day: guide-posts and danger-signals in health. **$1.35 net. Stokes.

Bartholomew, E. J. Man, woman, know thyself! $2. E. J. Bartholomew.

De Voe, W: Doors of life; or, studies in self-healing. $1. Funk.

Fallows, A. K. Mental hygiene in every day living.—Point of view: [health and happiness through a correct mental attitude.] ea., *35 c. net. McClurg.

Fitch, M. H. Physical basis of mind and morals. $1. Kerr.

Frank, H: Mastery of mind in the making of man. $1. Fenno.

Gulick, L. H. Mind and work. **$1.20 net. Doubleday, P.

Hawkins, C. J. Quest for health and happiness. *50 c. net. Pilgrim Press.

Jewett, *Mrs.* F. G. Control of body and mind. 50 c. Ginn.

Jones, E. E. Influence of bodily posture on mental activities. 50 c. Science Pr. (N. Y.)

Kirkman, S. D. Philosophy of self-help. **$1.25 net. Putnam.

Pearson, P. Psycho-harmonical philosophy. $3.50. P. Pearson.

Tuttle, C. R. New idea; methods of thinking for self-life unfoldment. (Not for sale.) Metropolitan Press.

See also Brain;—Divine healing;—Hypnotism;—Hysteria;—Insanity;—Medicine and religion;—Mental science; — Nervous system; — New thought;—Nurses and nursing;—Personality;—Psychology;—Telepathy;—Vibration;—Worry.

Mind and health. Ash, E: $1.50 net. Wood.

Mind and voice. Curry, S: S. $1.50. Expression.

Mind and work. Gulick, L. H. **$1.20 net. Doubleday. P.

MIND CURE.

See Mental science.

Mind in the making. Swift, E. J. **$1.50 net. Scribner.

Mind of Christ. McClelland, T. C. **$1.25 net. Crowell.

Mind of Christ in St. Paul. Greenhough, J. G. $1.50 net. Doran.

Mind of Christ Jesus in the church of the living God. Brent, C: H: **50 c. net. Longmans.

Mind over body: letters to a friend—a Christian scientist. '09(Je12) c. D. $1. J. H. West.

Mind, religion and health. MacDonald, R. **$1.30 net. Funk.

Mind that found itself. Beers, C. W. $1.50 net. Longmans.

MINDANAO.
See **Philippine Islands.**

Mine investor's guide. Davis, F. $1.50. Western Corr. Sch.

Mine of faults. Bain, F. W: **$1.25 net. Putnam.

MINE SURVEYING.
See **Mines and mining;—Surveying.**

Miner, H: Clay.
"Get the hook": [explanation of the origin of this popular slang phrase.] '08(Jl4) c. il. D. pap., gratis. H: C. Miner.

Miner, W. H.
Dickens ball. '08(O10) $2. W. H. Miner.

Mineral industry: vol. xvi. for 1907. '08 (S19) il. 8°, $10. Hill Pub.

Mineral kingdom. Brauns, R. $16.50 net. Lippincott.

Mineral land surveying. Underhill, J. $3. Mining Science.

Mineral location. Reynolds, C: L., *comp.* $1.50; $1. Dettner-Travers.

MINERAL WATERS.
United States. Tansan mineral water; letter from E: Bedloe, inclosing petition asking that the duty be removed on certain mineral water imported from Japan. '09(S) 6 p. 8°. (Add. Superintendent for price.) U. S., Supt. of Docs.
Yeo, I. B. Therapeutics of mineral springs and climates. $3.50 net. Funk.
See also Water.

MINERALOGY.
Beck, C. R: Nature of ore deposits. $6. Hill Pub.
Benson, H. T. Compendium on mines, mining, minerals, ores, rocks. $2. Hall & W.
Brauns, R. Mineral kingdom. $16.50 net. Lippincott.
Butler, G. M. Pocket hdbk. of minerals. $3. Wiley.
Dana, E: S., *and* Ford, W: E. Second appendix to the 6th ed. of Dana's System of mineralogy. $1.50. Wiley.
Dana, J. D. System of mineralogy. $12.50. Wiley.
Erni, H: Chemical determinative mineralogy and physical determinative mineralogy. (Add. pubs. for price.)—Mineralogy simplified. *$2.50 net. Baird.
Farrington, O. C., *and* Tillotson, E. W. Notes on various minerals in the museum collection. (Add. pubs. for price.) Field Museum.
Frazer, P., *and* Brown, A. P. Tables for the determination of minerals by physical properties ascertainable with the aid of new field instruments. $2.50. Lippincott.
Imhaus, N: E: Hdbk. on some minerals and rocks. 50 c. Ryder Bros.
Johannsen, A. Determination of rock-forming minerals. $4. Wiley.
Luquer, L. M. Minerals in rock sections. **$1.50 net. Van Nostrand.
Merrill, G: P. Non-metallic minerals. $4. Wiley.

MINERALOGY.—*Continued.*
Moses, A. J. Elements of mineralogy, crystallography and blowpipe analysis. $2.50 net. Van Nostrand.
Osborn, H: S. Prospector's field book and guide in search for and the easy determination of ores and other useful minerals. $1.50. Baird.
Papers on the conservation of mineral resources. '09(N) 214 p. pls. fold. maps, diagrs., O. (U. S., Dept. of the Interior; U. S. Geolog. Survey Bull.) pap. (Add. Superintendent for price.)
Phillips, W: B. Mineral resources of Texas. Texas.
Pirsson, L: V. Rocks and rock minerals. **$2.50 net. Wiley.
Tillman, S: E. Text-book of important minerals and rocks. **$2 net. Wiley.
Winchell, N. H. *and* A. N. Elements of optical mineralogy. *$3.50 net. Van Nostrand.
See also Assaying;—Coal;—Copper;—Crystallography;—Diamonds;—Fluorspar; — Geology; — Gold;—Iron;—Lead; — Manganese; — Mercury;—Metals and metallurgy;—Mines and mining;—Rocks;—Silver; — Steel; — Thallium;—*also* California;—Philippine Islands.

Miner's geology. Corder, G: A. $2. Spon.

Miners and smelters code; (adopted by American Smelting and Refining Co.) '09 (Ap24) 8°, $12. Business Code.

Miners' pocketbook. Lock, C: G. W. *$4 net. Spon.

MINES AND MINING.
American Institute of Mining Engineers. General alphabetical and analytical index: Transactions. v. 1-35. $5; $6. Am. Inst. Mining Eng.
Bailes, G: M. Modern mining practice. 5 v. ea., $3. Van Nostrand.
Beard, J. T. Mine gases and explosions. *$3 net. Wiley.
Benson, H. T. Compendium on mines, mining, minerals, ores, rocks. $2. Hall & W.
Brownell, M. G. Information from *Mining Science.* v. 1. $1. Mining Science.
Cantwell, H. J. Importance of the mining industry to the industrial and commercial life of a nation. gratis. H. J. Cantwell.
Chamberlin, R. T: Notes on explosive mine gases and dusts, with special reference to explosions in the Monongah, Darr and Naomi coal mines. 10 c. U. S., Supt. of Docs.
Clifford, H: B. Rocks in the road to fortune: unsound side of mining. $1.50. Gotham Press.
Corder, G: A. Miner's geology and prospector's guide. $2. Spon.
Costigan, G: P. Hdbk. on American mining law. $3.75. West Pub.
Crane, W. R: Ore mining methods. $3 net. Wiley.
Davis, F. Mine investor's guide. $1.50. Western Corr. Sch.
Depreciation of factories, mines and industrial undertakings and their valuation. $4 net. Spon.
Donaldson, F. Pract. shaft sinking. $2. McGraw-H.

MINES AND MINING.—*Continued.*
Emmons, W: H. Some ore deposits in Maine and the Milan mine. Gov. Pr. Off.
Finlay, J. R. Cost of mining. *$5 net. McGraw-H.
Garforth, W: E: Suggested rules for recovering coal mines after explosions and fires. *$1.50 net. Van Nostrand.
Halse, E. Dict. of Spanish and Spanish American mining, metallurgical and allied terms. *$3.50 net. Lippincott.
Hancock, E. T: Notes accompanying the lectures on geology applied to mining. $1. New Era Print.
Hatch, F. H., *and* Vallentine, E. J. Mining tables. *$1.90 net. Macmillan.
Hoover, H. C. Principles of mining. $2.50. Hill Pub.
Howell, E: B. Lode and placer claims. $1. Keefe.
Johnson, J. P. Ore deposits of South Africa, with a chapter on hints to prospectors. $2. Henley.
Kerr, R. J. Translation of the mining law of Mexico. $1.50. Pan Am. Law.
Lock, C: G. W. Miners' pocketbook. *$4 net. Spon.
McVey, F. L. Taxation of mineral properties. 5 c. Int. Tax.
Martin, T. Mining law and land-office procedure. $7.50. Bender-M.
Mayer, L. W. Mining methods in Europe. $2.50. Hill Pub.
Miller, G: W. Mine examiner's and prospector's companion. $3. Hall & W.
Mineral industry: vol. XVI. for 1907. $10. Hill Pub.
Morrison, R. S. Mining rights on the public domain. $3.50. Courtright.
Morrison, R. S., *and* De Soto, E. D. Mining rights on the public domain. $3. Smith-B.
Munroe, C: E., *and* Hall, C. Primer on explosives for coal miners. Gov. Pr. Off.
Nicholas, F. C. Mining investments and how to judge them. $1. Moody's Mag.
Peele, R. Compressed air plant for mines. $3. Wiley.
Putney, A. H., *and others.* Manufactures, mining, irrigation, real estate. $4. Cree.
Redmayne, R: A. S. Modern practice in mining. v. 1, Coal: its occurrence, value, etc.; v. 2, The sinking of shafts. v. 1, $2 net; v. 2, *$2.25 net. Longmans.
Reynolds, C: L., *comp.* Mineral location, annot. $1.50; $1. Dettner-Travers.
Rice, G: S. Explosibility of coal dust. Gov. Pr. Off.
Rickard, T: A. Journeys of observation. $3.50. Dewey Pub.
Ritter, E. A. From prospect to mine. $2.
—Origin of ore deposits. 50 c. Mining Science.
Scholz, C. Settlement of dust in mines and prevention of explosion by the increase of humidity. (Add. pub. for price.) Hodgart.

MINES AND MINING.—*Continued.*
Stokes, R. S. G. Mines and minerals of the British Empire. *$4.20 net. Longmans.
Storms, W: H. Timbering and mining. *$2 net. McGraw-H.
Trumbull, L. W. Manual of underground surveying. $3. McGraw-H.
United States. *Dept. of the Interior.* Disasters in mines; letters from the Secretary of the Interior, in response to Senate resolution no. 101, of Dec. 16, 1909, requesting information with reference to disasters in mines. '09, [1910.] (Mr) 4 p. 8°, pap.
United States. *Geological Survey.* Papers on the conservation of mineral resources; repr. from rept. of the National Conservation Commission, Feb., 1909. '09 (S) 214 p. il. 8°, (U. S., Geological Survey bull.) pap. (Add. Superintendent for price.) U. S., Supt. of Docs.
United States mining laws and regulations thereunder. '09 (Je) 66 p. 8°, pap. (Add. Superintendent for price.) U. S., Supt. of Docs.
Vermont. *Geological Survey.* Rept. of the state geologist on the mineral industries and geology of certain areas of Vermont. 15 c. G: H. Perkins.
Vigouroux, G: E., *ed.* Diary of a mining investor. $1. Quick News.
Walker, S. F. Electricity in mining. $3.50. Van Nostrand.
Wallace, D: Simple mine accounting. $1. Hill Pub.
Wallace, J. P. Study of ore deposits for the practical miner. *$3 net. Hill Pub.
Watson, T: L: Mineral resources of Virginia. gratis. C. A. Swanson.
Watteyne, V., *and others.* Prevention of mine explosions. (Add. Superintendent for price.) U. S., Supt. of Docs.
Young, G: J. Ventilating system at the Comstock mines, Nevada. gratis. Univ. of Neb.
See also Coal;—Copper;—Cyanide process;—Diamonds;—Explosives; — Fluorspar; — Gold; — Iron;—Lead;—Metals and metallurgy;—Mineralogy; — Silver; — Surveying; — Taxation; — Tin;—Useful arts;—Water;—Zinc;—*also* Alaska;—Humboldt Co., Nev.;—*also* names of states.

Mines (The) directory. v. 1; cont. accurate information on listed and unlisted mining properties in the western states; mining laws of various states and a list of principal mining districts, by counties. [1910.] (S) c. 8°, $10. Mines Directory.

Ming, Rev. J: Jos.
Characteristics and the religion of modern socialism. '08 (My23) c. D. $1.50. Benziger.
Morality of modern socialism. '09 (N20) c. D. *$1.50 net. Benziger.

Mingled wine. Bunston, A. *$1.20 net. Longmans.

Miniature dictionary of literary terms. Vivian, P. 50 c. Dutton.

Miniature reference lib. *See* Dutton's.

Miniatures (The). 6 v. '08(N21) il. 24°, ea., 35 c. Pott.
Contents: 1, Sir Roger de Coverley, Addison; 2, Notes of a week's holiday, Thackeray; 3, The Rubaiyat of Omar Kháyyám; 4, The seven poor travellers, Dickens; 5, Tam O'Shanter and other poems, Burns; 6, Coaches and coaching, Hunt.

MINIATURES.
Davenport, C. Miniatures, ancient and modern. *$1 net. McClurg.
Foster, J. J. Chats on old miniatures. $2. Stokes.
Heath, D. Miniatures. *$7.50 net. Putnam.
Holme, C:, *ed.* Portrait miniatures. $3 net; $2.50 net. Lane.

MINING.
See Mines and mining.

MINING ENGINEERING.
See Engineering.

MINISTERS (*of the Gospel*).
Absente reo; [reflections on parish work of a clergyman.] $1.60 net. Macmillan.
Baker, S:, *and* Jenkins, F. E. Master profession. 50 c. Franklin-T.
Bosworth, E: I. Modern interpretation of the call to the ministry. 10 c.—Weak church and the strong man. 5 c. Y. M. C. A.
Confessions of a clergyman. 90 c. net. Macmillan.
Davis, J. L. Mountain preacher: being some experiences told in the language of the people among whom he so successfully labored. 50 c. F: L: Rowe.
Ede, W: M. Clergy and social service. 90 c. Longmans.
Faunce, W: H. P. Educational ideal of the ministry. **$1.25 net. Macmillan.
Garrison, S. O. Probationers' handbook. $1.25. Jennings.
George, E: A: Seventeenth century men of latitude; forerunners of the new theology. **$1.25 net. Scribner.
Gordon, G: A. Claims of the ministry on strong men. 10 c, Y. M. C. A.
Herbert, G: Priest of the temple. 75 c. Whittaker.
Hill, D: S. Education and problems of the Protestant ministry. $1. Stechert.
Hodges, G: Independence of the ministry. 10 c. Y. M. C. A.
How, F: D. Clerical humour of olden time; sketches of some clerical humorists between 12th and 18th centuries. $2. Pitman.
Hoyt, A. S. Call of the country church. 5 c.; per 100, $4. Y. M. C. A.
Jackson, H: E. Message of the modern minister. *50 c. net. Revell.
Jefferson, C: E: Minister as preacher. 5 c.: per 100, $4. Y. M. C. A.
Johnson, H. Ideal ministry. *$1.75 net. Revell.
Joynt, R. C. Pastoral work. *40 c. net. Longmans.
Kernodle, P: J. Lives of Christian ministers. $2. P: J. Kernodle.
King, E: Requirements for the ministry. 15 c. Oxford Univ.
Lyman, A. J. Christian pastor in the new age. **$1 net. Crowell.

MINISTERS (*of the Gospel*).—*Continued.*
McDowell, W: F. Right sort of men for the ministry. 10 c.; per 100, $8. Y. M. C. A.
Macfarland, C: S., *ed.* Christian ministry and the social order. *$1.25 net. Yale Univ.
Mahood, J: W. Master workman. 25 c. Praise Pub.
Moore, W. W: Preparation of the modern minister. 10 c.; per 100, $8. Y. M. C. A.
Mott, J: R. Future leadership of the church: [training of candidates for the ministry.] $1. Y. M. C. A.
Nichols, W: F. Apt and meet: councils to candidates for holy orders. *$1 net. Whittaker.
Pittman, R: H., *ed.* Biograph. hist. of primitive or old school Baptist ministers of the United States. $2. R: H. Pittman.
Richmond, E. Picture talks for pastors, Sunday-schools, [etc.] 10 c. E. Richmond.
Skrine, J: H. Pastor ovium: day book of a country parson. *$1.60 net. Longmans.
Webb, W: W. Cure of souls; manual for the clergy. $1.50 net. Young Churchman.
Whallon, E: P. Pastoral memories. (Add. pubs. for price.) Montfort.
Wilson, W. Minister and the community. 10 c.; per 100, $8. Y. M. C. A.
See also Anglican orders;—Apostolic succession;—Christian work;—Church (The);—"H. & S." lib.;—Missions and missionaries;—Negroes;—Preaching; — Priests; — *also* Paul, *St.;* — *also* names of ministers.

Ministry of daily communion. Zulueta, F. M. de. 60 c. Herder.
Ministry of healing. White, E. G. H. $3. Pacific Press.

Minkler, Mrs. Carrie Ruth Stillwell.
Day dreams: [poems.] [1910.] (Ja) c. '09. 11-95 p. por. 12°, $1. C. R. S. Minkler.

MINKS.
Elfer, W: A. Breeding minks in Louisiana for their fur. 75 c. Gessner.

Minna von Barnhelm. *See* Lessing, Gotthold Ephraim.

MINNEAPOLIS, Minn.
Hudson, H. B. Half century of Minneapolis. $15. Hudson Pub.

Minnecotah, an Indian legend. McNeill, T: gratis. Saturday News.

MINNESINGERS.
See German poetry.

Minnesota. Digest; covering Minn. repts., 1-109, northwestern reporter, 1-125; by Mark B. Dunnell. 3 v. '10(D) c. O. $10 (Sold only in sets.) Minn. Law.

Minnesota. Drainage of certain lands held in trust for the Chippewa Indians in Minnesota. '08, [1909.] (Je) 20 p. 8°, pap. (Add. Superintendent for price.) U. S., Supt. of Docs.

Minnesota. *Forestry Commissioner.* Plan of reforestration: (extract from thirteenth annual report of the Forestry Commissioner of Minnesota.) '09(Ap) 17 p. 8°. (Add. Commission for price.) Minn. Forestry Com.

Minnesota. Justice's manual for the state; complete guide for justices of the peace and constables, [etc.;] by Wa. S. Booth. 15th ed. '09(N) c. 534 p. O. shp. (Add. pubs. for price.) Booth.

Minnesota. 1909. Annotations for rev. laws of 1905, and session laws of 1905 and 1907, also for all previous compilations and session laws specifically amended by laws 1909, together with sup. ct. decisions and references to current law citations subsequent to 1907 annots. '09(Je) c. 50 p. T. $1. Keefe-D.

Minnesota. Rev. laws; supp. 1909; comp. and annot. by Fs. B. Tiffany. '10(F) c. O. $5. West Pub.

Minnesota. *Supreme ct.* Repts. v. 102; (H: Burleigh Wenzell.) '08(My); v. 103 (S); v. 104 (N) ea., $2.75; v. 105. '09 (Ap); v. 106 (Jl) ea., $2.25; v. 107 (N); v. 108. '10(Mr); v. 109 (Je); v. 110 (N) c. O. shp., ea., $2. Lawyers' Co-op.

Minnesota. Tax laws; comp. and published by the Minnesota Tax Commission. '08 (Je) 184 p. O. (Add. pubs. for price.) Minn. Tax Commission.

Minnesota. Township manual: complete guide for township officers; by Wa. S. Booth. 19th ed. '08(Ja4); 20th ed. '09(Jl) c. D. pap., ea., $1. Booth.

Minnesota. Village manual for the state; complete guide for village officers in their various duties under the revised laws, 1905, and general laws, 1905, 1907 and 1909; by Wa. S. Booth. 4th ed. '09(Jl) 315 p. D. pap., $1. Booth.

MINNESOTA.
 Baker, J. H. Lives of the governors of Minnesota. $2.50. Minn. Hist. Soc.
 Cronk, V. D. Selection of business forms, incl. local precedents and official forms under the laws of Wisconsin and Minnesota. Flood.
 Folwell, W: W. Minnesota. **$1.25 net. Houghton M.
 Kellerman, K. F., *and* Whittaker, H. A. Farm water supplies of Minn. Gov. Pr. Off.
 McVey, F. Le R. Government of Minnesota. *90 c. net. Macmillan.
 See also Day, John Albert;—Lichens;—Mines and mining;—Minneapolis;—Norman Co.:—Seaweed.

Minnesota Historical Society collections. 8°. Minn. Hist. Soc.
—Baker. Lives of the governors of Minnesota. $2.50.

Minnesota in three centuries, 1655-1908; board of editors: Lucius F. Hubbard, W: P. Murray, Ja. H. Baker, Warren Upham. Semi-centennial ed. '09(Mr13) c. 4 v., il. pors. maps, 8°, per set, $20. Minn. Pub. Soc.

Minnesota State Board of Immigration. Minnesota's fiftieth anniversary, St. Paul, Minn., State Board of Immigration. '08 (O) 196 p. il. O. pap. (Add. pubs. for price.) Minn. State Bd. Immigration.

Minnesota State Board of Immigration. Minnesota's timber lands. '09(Jl3) il. tab. O. pap. (Add. pubs. for price.) Minn. State Bd. Immigration.

MINNESOTA STATE PRISON, Stillwater, Minn.
 Heilbron, W: C. Convict life at the Minnesota State Prison. 25 c. H. L. Taylor.

Minns, E: R.
 Barnyard manure, its value and uses. [1910.] (F) c. '09. 28 p. 8°, gratis. Sears, Roebuck.

Minor, Raleigh Colston.
 Law of real property, (based on Minor's institutes.) In 2 v. v. 1. '08(O); v. 2. '08, [1909.] (Ja) c. O. shp. (Add. pubs. for price.) Anderson.

—, and Wurts, J:
 Law of real property, (based on Minor's institute.) '10(F) c. O. $5. West Pub.

Minor Elizabethan drama. Thorndike, A. H., *comp.* 2 v. ea., 35 c. net; 70 c. net. Dutton.

Minor maladies and their treatment. Williams, L. *$3.50 net. Wood.

Minor tactics of the chalk stream. Skues, G. E. M. $2. Macmillan.

Minority report of the Poor Law Commission. *See* Webb, Sidney, *ed.*

Minot, C: Sedgwick.
 Lab'y text-book of embryology. 2d ed., rev. '10(O) c. 12+402 p. il. 4°, $3.50. Blakiston.
 Problem of age, growth, and death: a study of *cytomorphosis* based on lectures at the Lowell Institute. '08(S5) c. il. figs. tabs., O. (Science ser.) **$2.50 net. Putnam.

MINSTERS.
 See Cathedrals.

Minstrel with the self-same song. Fisher, C: G. $1. F. Fisher.

Mint Julep. Doyle, *Mrs.* M. C. M. $2.50. W. D. Lane.

Mintage (The). *See* Hubbard, Elbert.

Minter, Luther.
 Compendium of everyday wants; or, practical information for the millions; with an introd. by H. A. Davis. '08(N) c. 17+5-626 p. por. il. 8°, $1.90; mor., $2.75. Minter.

Minton, Orlena Mariana.
 Rag weed rhymes of rural folks. '10(N19) c. D. $1. Aberdeen.

Mintz, Frances Sankstone.
 First reader for new American citizens. '10(N19) il. 12°, 50 c. net. Macmillan.
 New American citizen: reader for foreigners. '09(Jl31) c. il. map, D. **50 c. net. Macmillan.
 Pract. speller for evening schools. '10 (N19) 12°, 25 c. net. Macmillan.

Minute boys of Boston. Kaler, J. O. $1.25. Estes.

Minute boys of Long Island. Kaler, J. O. †$1.25. Estes.

Minute boys of New York City. Kaler, J. O. †$1.25. Estes.

MIRABEAU, Gabriel Honoré Riquetti, *Comte* de.
 Fling, F. M. Mirabeau and the French revolution. In 3 v. v. 1. **$3.50 net. Putnam.
 Tallentyre, S. G. Life of Mirabeau. *$3 net. Moffat.
 Trowbridge, W: R. Mirabeau, the demigod. *$3.75 net. Scribner.

Miracle of life. Kellogg, J: H. $1.50. Modern Medicine.
Miracle of right thought. Marden, O. S. $1 net. Crowell.
MIRACLES.
Best, N. R. Beyond the natural order: essays on prayer miracles and the incarnation. *75 c. net. Revell.
Beth, K. Miracles of Jesus. *40 c. net. Eaton & M.
Boissarie, P. G. Heaven's recent wonders; or, the work of Lourdes. $1.50. Pustet.
Gordon, G. A. Religion and miracle. **$1.30 net. Houghton M.
Lamb, F. J. Miracle and science. *$1.50 net. Bibliotheca Sacra.
Of the tumbler of Our Lady, and other miracles. *$2.50 net. Duffield.
Trench, R: C. Notes on the miracles of our Lord. *$1 net. Dutton.
Whitney, L. H. Question of miracles; parallels in the lines of Buddha and Jesus. $1. Lib. Shelf.
Willman, R. Errors of mind healing compared with the miracles of Christ. $1. Advocate Pub.
See also Divine healing; — Faith cure; — Jesus Christ;—Psychical research;—Saints.
Miracles of anti-Christ. Lagerlöf, S. O. L. †$1.50. Little, B. & Co.
Miracles of grace in Japan. Smelser, F. L. (Add. pubs. for price.) Hudson.
Miracles of St. Cuthbert. Gibson, R. E: L. $1. Morton.
Mirage. Thurston, E. T. $1.50. Dodd.
Mirage of the many. Walsh, W: T: $1.50. Holt.
Miraglia-Gullotti, Paolo Vescovo.
Vera scienza e vera religione; poema didascalico di teologia popolare. 1. ed. ad. uso esclusivo degl' Italiani di America. '10(My) c. 128 p. 12°, (Biblioteca poplare "Gerolamo Savonarola.") 30 c. P. V. Miraglia-Gullotti.
Miriam's tower. Knapp, H. L. $1.25. Wichita.
Mirror of perfection. *See* Francis of Assisi, *St.*, and Bonaventura, *St.*
Misadventures of a hack cruiser. Kempson. F. C. $1.75 net. Longmans.
Misadventures of Marjory. Naylor, J. B. $1.50. C. M. Clark.
Misawa, Tadasu.
Modern educators and their ideals. '09 (Mr20) c. D. **$1.25 net. Appleton.
Miscellaneous correspondence commercial and legal forms. Browne, T: R. pt. 1. 50 c. Browne's Business Coll.
Mischief love hath done. North, J. $1. Evolution Pub.
Misconceptions of life insurance policy holders. Bonham, A. N. $3. A. N. Bonham.
Misèrables (Les). *See* Hugo, Victor.
Miser's daughter. Ainsworth, W: H. 50 c.; 75 c. Dutton.
Misery and its causes. Devine, E: T: **$1.25 net. Macmillan.
Miss Betty of New York. Deland, E. D. †$1.25. Harper.
Miss Bobbie. Turner, E. †75 c. McKay.
Miss Eagle: the suffragette. Dale, M. 50 c. Aberdeen.
Miss Esperance and Mr. Wycherly. Harker, *Mrs.* L. A. †$1.50. Scribner.
Miss Fallowfield's fortune. Fowler, E. T. †$1.50. Dodd.
Miss Marshall's boys. Bass, E: C. $1. Badger.
Miss Minerva and William Green Hill. Calhoun, F. B. $1. Reilly & B.
Miss Peackle. Bessier, F. 15 c. Penn Pub. Co.
Miss Robinson Crusoe. '09(D) col. il. 32°, bds., 25 c. Doran.
Miss Selina Lue and the soap-box babies. Daviess, M. T. †$1. Bobbs-M.
Miss Susan's fortune. *See* Thompson, Alice C. Her scarlet slippers.
Missing empire. Gher, A. M. 35 c. A. M. Gher.
Mission and expansion of Christianity. Harnack, C. G. A. *$7 net. Putnam.
Mission and ministration of the Holy Spirit. Downer, A. C. $3 net. Scribner.
MISSION FURNITURE.
See Furniture.
Mission, history and times of the Farmers' Union Barrett, C: S. (Add. author for price.) C: S. Barrett.
Mission inn. Benton, A. B. $2; $4. M. E. L. Allen.
MISSION MOUNTAINS, Montana.
See Flathead Co., Montana.
Mission of a liberal church. Bigelow, H. S. 5 c. Public.
Mission of manual training. Rathmann, C. G. Manual Training Sch.
Mission of the Christian college. Reed, E. E. gratis. Lenox Coll.
Mission of the United States in the cause of peace. Brewer, D: J. gratis. Int. Sch. of Peace.
Mission of woman. Johnston, R. E. 40 c. Longmans.
Mission preaching for a year: 80 original mission sermons by well-known authors; ed. by Rev. W: H: Hunt. In 4 pts. pt. 2. '08(Jl); pt. 3. '09(D) 12°, pap., ea., *$1 net. Whittaker.
Mission record of the California Indians. Kroeber, A. L: 25 c. Univ. of Cal.
Mission remembrance of the Redemptorist fathers. Geiermann, P: 50 c. Benziger.
Mission tales in the days of the dons. Forbes, H. R. P. S. $1.50. McClurg.
Mission to hell. Eells, E: *80 c. net. Sherman, F.
Missionary achievement. Whitley, W. T. *$1 net. Revell.
Missionary heroes in Asia. Lambert, J: C. *75 c. net. Lippincott.
Missionary's notebook. Gallagher, A. M. $1. Cath. Standard and Times.
Missioner (The). Oppenheim, E: P. †$1.50. Little, B. & Co.
MISSIONS AND MISSIONARIES.
Barton, J. L. Unfinished task of the Christian church: studies in the problem of the world's evangelization. 50 c.; 35 c. Student Vol.
Bliss, E. M. The missionary enterprise. *$1.25 net. Revell.

MISSIONS AND MISSIONARIES.—*Continued*.

Bone, F. Brownie's box: story for little missionary workers at home. $1. Am. Tr.

Brewster, W: N. Cost of Christian conquest. *35 c. net. Jennings

Brodhead, *Mrs.* C. A. S., *ed.* Our free Methodist missions in Africa. $1. Aldine Pr.

Brown, A. J. Why and how of foreign missions. 50 c.; 35 c.; Leaders' helps, 10 c. Dom. and For. Mission.

Brown, A. J. Why and how of foreign missions. *50 c. net. Young People's Miss.

Campbell, T: J. Pioneer priests of North America, 1642-1710. *$1.60 net. Fordham Univ.

Carver, W: O. Missions and modern thought. $1.50 net. Macmillan.

Carver, W: O. Missions in the plan of the ages. *$1.25 net. Revell.

Centenary Missionary Conference records: report of the great Shanghai conference, 1907. *$2.50 net. Am. Tr.

Clark, F. E:, *and* Abbott, H. E. Gospel in Latin lands. **50 c. net. Macmillan.

Cook, C: A: Stewardship and missions. **50 c. net. Am. Bapt.

Crawford, W: H: Church and the slum. 75 c. Eaton & M.

Dawson, E. C. Heroines of missionary adventure. *$1.50 net. Lippincott.

Dennis, J. S. New horoscope of missions. *$1 net. Revell.

Douglass, H. P. Christian reconstruction in the South. *$1.50 net. Pilgrim Press.

Ellis, W: T. Men and missions. 60 c. net. S. S. Times.

Engelhardt, Z. Missions and missionaries of Lower California. v. 1. *$2.50 net. Z. Engelhardt.

Forsyth, P: T. Missions in state and church. *$1.75 net. Armstrong.

Forward Movement Mission studies. Bks. 1-6. ea., **15 c. net. Am. Bapt.

Freeman, J: H. Oriental land of the free. 50 c. Westminster.

Gardner, M. T., *and* W: E: Winners of the world during twenty centuries. 60 c. net; 30 c. net. Revell.

Gladden, W. Nation and the kingdom. gratis. Am. Bd. For Miss.

Goddard, O. E. Manual of missions for laymen. (Add. author for price.) O. E. Goddard.

Harris, M. C. Christianity in Japan. *35 c. net. Jennings.

Haywood, K. H. Torchbearers on the King's highway. 20 c. Young Churchman.

Helm, M. Upward path: the evolution of a race. 50 c.; 35 c. Young People's Miss.

Houtz, A. Master's call to service. 60 c. Ref. Ch. Pub.

Hughson, W., *comp.* Church's mission to the mountaineers of the south. 75 c.; 50 c. Church Missions.

Johnson, T: C. Introduction to Christian missions. 75 c. Presb. Pub.

Jones, J: P: Modern missionary challenge. $1 50 net. Revell.

MISSIONS AND MISSIONARIES.—*Continued.*

Kirk, J. W. Brotherhood. $1. J. W. Kirk.

Lambert, J: C. Missionary heroes in Oceanica. 75 c. Lippincott.

Mabie, H: C. Task worth while. $1.25 net. Griffith.

McAfee, J. E. Missions striking home. 75 c. Revell.

Maclean, N. Can the world be won for Christ $1 net. Doran.

Malden, R. H. Foreign missions. $1.25 net. Longmans.

Mills, J. S., *and others.* Our foreign missionary enterprise. *50 c. net; *35 c. net. Un. B. Pub.

Moninger, H. N. Fifty lessons in training for service. *40 c. net; *25 c. net. Standard Pub.

Montgomery, H. B. Western women in eastern lands. $1.50 net. Macmillan.

Montgomery, H: H. Service abroad. 90 c. net. Longmans.

Morgan, G: C. Missionary manifesto. *75 c. net. Revell.

Mott, J: R. Decisive hour of Christian missions. $1. Student Vol.

Murray, J. L. Apologetic of modern missions. 15 c. Student Vol.

Mylne, L: G: Missions to Hindus. *$1.20 net. Longmans.

Osgood, E. I. Breaking down Chinese walls. *$1 net. Revell

Pfeiffer, E: Mission studies. *75 c. net. Lutheran Bk.

Platt, W. The frontier. 50 c.; 35 c. Young People's Miss..

Ray, T. B., *ed* Highway of mission thought. 75 c. S. S. Bd. So. Bapt.

Ray, T. B., *and others.* Southern Baptist foreign missions. 50 c. S. S. Bd. So. Bapt.

Richter, J. Hist. of Protestant mission in the near east. $2.50. Revell.

Robinson, C: H: Interpretation of the character of Christ to non-Christian races; an apology for Christian missions. *$1.20 net. Longmans.

Robson, J: Resurrection gospel: [study of New Testament warrant for missionary enterprise.] *$1.25 net. Jennings.

Speer, R. E. Christianity and the nations. $2 net. Revell.

Speer, R. E. Servants of the King. 50 c.; 35 c. Young People's Miss.

Students and the present missionary crisis. $1.50. Student Vol.

Vedder, H: C. Christian epoch-makers. **$1.20 net. Am. Bapt.

Watson, T: E: Foreign missions exposed. 25 c. T: E: Watson.

Weekly, W: M., *and* Fout, H. H. Our heroes; or, United Brethren home missionaries. 50 c.; 35 c. Un. B. Pub.

Whitley, W. T. Missionary achievement. *$1 net. Revell.

Williams, H: F. In four continents; sketch of the foreign missions of the Presbyterian Church, U. S. 50 c. Presb. Pub.

World-call to men of to-day. $1. Presb. Bd.

MISSIONS AND MISSIONARIES.—*Continued.*

World Missionary Conference; rept. of the Ecumenical Conference held in Edinburgh in 1910. 9 v. ea., 75 c. net; per set, $5 net. Revell.

Young People's Missionary Movement. Church and missionary education. $1.25. Young People's Miss.

Zorn, C. M. Dies und das aus dem leben eines ostindischen missionars. $1.25. Concordia Pub.

See also American Board of Commissioners for Foreign Missions;—Armenia;—Martyrs; — Old San Gabriel Mission;—Turkey;—Water Street Mission;—*also* names of missionaries and churches, countries and places.

Mississippi. *Courts.* Repts. of cases. Annot. ed. In 31 v. Bks. 22-20; cont. a verbatim repr. v. 45-42 of the Miss. repts. '07, [1908.] (My); Bk. 19; repr. v. 41-38. '08(Je); Bk. 18; repr. v. 37-36. '08(O); Bk. 17; repr. v. 35-34. '08(D); Bks. 16-15; repr. of v. 33-29. '08, [1909.] (My); Bk. 14, repr. of v. 28-27 (Jl); Bk. 13, repr. of v. 26-25 (N); Bks. 12-10. '09, [1910.] (F) c. '10. Bk. 9 (Mr); Bk. 8 (Ap); Bks. 6, 7 (Je); Bk. 5 (Jl); Bk. 4 (Ag); Bks. 3-1 (D) O. ea., $6. (Sold only in complete sets. Repr. backwards.) West Pub.

Mississippi. *Supreme ct.* Repts. v. 90; (T. A. McWillie.) '07, [1908.] (Ag) c. O. shp., $4. Flood.

MISSISSIPPI (*State*).

Ellett, A. H. Federal Union and Mississippi. 75 c. B. F. Johnson.

Logan, W: N. Clays of Mississippi. pt. 1. (Add. pubs. for price.) Brandon Pr.

Logan, W: N. Pottery clays of Miss. 50 c. Miss. Geol. Survey.

Rowland, D., *ed.* Encyclop. of Mississippi history. In 2 v. $12. Brant.

See also Forests and forestry; — Natchez; — Pike Co.;—Jackson.

MISSISSIPPI MARINE BRIGADE.

Crandall, W. D. History of the ram fleet and the Mississippi marine brigade in the war for the Union. $2.50. W. D. Crandall.

MISSISSIPPI RIVER.

Chambers, J. Mississippi River and its wonderful valley. $3.50 net. Putnam.

Mathews, J: L. Remaking the Mississippi. **$1.75 net. Houghton M.

Merrick, G: B. Old times on the upper Mississippi. *$3.50 net. A. H. Clark.

Short, P. Brief accts. of journeys in the western country, 1809-1812. Hist. and Phil. Soc., O.

Mississippi State Geological Survey. bulletin. il. 8°, pap. Brandon Pr.

—Brown. Lignite of Mississippi. (Add. pubs. for price.)

—Crider. Cement and Portland cement materials of Mississippi. (Add. pubs. for price.)

—Holmes *and* Foster. Study of forest conditions of southwestern Miss., Jan., 1908. 25 c.

—Logan. Clays of Mississippi. pt. 1. (Add. pubs. for price.)

MISSISSIPPI VALLEY.

Carman, J. E. Mississippi Valley between Savanna and Davenport. 8 c. Univ. of Ill.

Thwaites, R. G. Romance of the Mississippi Valley history. 75 c. State Hist., Ia.

Missouri. *Courts.* Digest of the decisions. v. 12, 13. '09(Je) c. O. ea., $6. West Pub.

Missouri. *Dept. of Education.* State course of study for the rural and graded schools and for approved high schools in the state of Missouri, 1909; rev. and enl. by Howard A. Gass, state supt. public schools; appended: List of library books from which schools libraries must be selected. '09, [1910.] (F) 210 p. il. 8°. Missouri Dept. Educ.

Missouri. Index to the rev. statutes for 1899 and the session acts of 1901-1907; comp. by D. E. Adams. '08(Ja4) 8°, $1.25. Vernon Law Bk.

Missouri. Law governing manufacturing and business corporations, [etc.;] by I: H. Lionberger. '10(D) c. 220 p. D. shp., $4.50. Nixon-J.

Missouri. *St. Louis, Kansas City and Springfield cts. of appeals.* Cases; (J: Turner White and Ben Eli Guthrie.) v. 125-126. '08(My); v. 127 (Je); v. 128. '08(Ag); v. 129. '08(O); v. 130. '08(N); v. 131, 132. '08, [1909.] (Mr); v. 133 (Je); v. 134 (Ag) c. ea., $5; v. 135 (O); v. 136, 137, 138 (Je); v. 139, 140 (S); v. 141 (N); v. 142, 143 (D) c. O. ea., shp., $3. Stephens.

Missouri. *State Board of Agriculture.* Boys' corn growing contest. [1910.] (Ja) 12 p. il. 8°, gratis. Missouri State Bd.

Missouri. Supp. to Pattison's digest of Missouri repts., v. 7, 8; (Everett W. Pattison.) '08(Mr); v. 9. '10(Ap) c. O. shp., ea., $7.50. Gilbert Bk.

Missouri. *Supreme ct.* Repts.; (Perry S. Rader.) v. 203, 204. '08(Ja1); v. 205, 206. '08(Mr); v. 207. '08(My); v. 208. '08 (Jl); v. 209. '08(S); v. 210. '08(N); v. 211-212. '08, [1909.] (Ja); v. 213 (Ap); v. 214 (Je); v. 215 (Jl); v. 216 (Ag); v. 217 (O) ea., $4; v. 218-221. '09, [1910.] (Ja); v. 222 (My); v. 223 (Jl); v. 224, 225 (N); v. 226 (D) c. O. ea., shp., $3. **Stephens.**

MISSOURI (*State*).

Barnard, J. U. Missouri. *20 c. net. Macmillan

Buckley, E. R. Geology of the disseminated lead deposits of St. Francois and Washington counties, [Mo.] (Add. pubs. for price.) Missouri Bu. Geol.

Buehler, H: A. Lime and cement resources of Missouri. 25 c. Missouri Bu. Geol.

Crane, H. S., *comp.* Lawyer's guide; cont. a complete table of Missouri cases, overruled, reversed, modified and distinguished by the U. S. court, etc. $1. F. T. Riley.

Fowke, G. Antiquities of central and southeastern Missouri. 40 c. Smith. Inst.

Houck, L: History of Missouri. In 3 v. $18. Donnelley.

MISSOURI (*State*).—*Continued.*
Houck, L:, *ed.* Spanish régime in Missouri [formerly upper Louisiana.] In 3 v. $18, boxed. Donnelley.
McElroy, J: **Struggle for Missouri. $2. Nat. Tribune.**
McQuillin, E., *and* Campbell, W: S. Forms of code pleading for Missouri and Arkansas. $7.50. F. H. Thomas.
See also Kansas City;—Marion Co.;—Morgan Co.;—Pike Co.;—St. Louis;—*also* Marsh, *Capt.* Grant Prince;—Porter, Joseph Chrisman.

Missouri Baptist Sanitarium, St. Louis. Saint Louis cook book. '08(Ag) c. 241 p. 8°, $1. Missouri Bapt. San.

Missouri Bureau of Geology and Mines repts. il. maps, 4°, pap. Missouri Bu. Geol.
—Buckley. Geology of the disseminated lead deposits.—Public roads. (Add. pub. for price.)
—Buehler. Lime and cement resources of Missouri. 25 c.
—Marbut. Geology of Morgan county. 20 c.
—Rowley. Geology of Pike county. 20 c.

MISSOURI COMPROMISE.
Ray, P. O. Repeal of the Missouri compromise. *$3.50 net. A. H. Clark.

MISSOURI RIVER.
Neihardt, J: G. River and I. $2 net. Putnam.

Missouri state automobile blue book; comp. by Nelson T. Gutelius. '08(Jl18) c. il. maps, 8°, $3. Auto Review.

Mistaken marriage. Young, F. E. M. †$1.50. Lane.

Mistaken signs. Watkinson, W: L. *50 c. net. Revell.

Mistakes and disputed points in music. Elson, L: C: $1.25. T. Presser.

Mr. and Mrs. Villiars. Wales, H. $1.50. Stuyvesant Press.

Mr. Brown, the tariff teacher. Nesbitt, P. 25 c. Brown & Co.

Mr. Carteret and others. Gray, D: **$1 net. Century Co.

Mr. Crewe's career. Churchill, W. †$1.50. Macmillan.

Mr. Dooley says. Dunne, F. P: $1 net. Scribner.

Mr. Ingleside. Lucas, E: V. $1.35 net. Macmillan.

Mr. Jackson. Green, H. $1.25. B. W. Dodge.

Mr. Jorrocks' lectors. Surtees, R. S. $4.50 net. Doran.

Mr. Justice Raffles. Hornung, E. W. **†$1.50. Scribner.**

Mr. Midshipman Easy. Marryat, F: 50 c. Hurst.

Mr. Opp. Rice, *Mrs.* A. C. H. †$1. Century Co.

Mr. Pickwick. *See* Dickens, C:

Mr. Whistler and the Wimples. Lea, J: 35 c. Stokes.

Mr. Wind and Madam Rain. Musset, P. E. de. 60 c. Harper.

MISTLETOE.
United States. *Dept. of Agriculture. Bu. of Plant Industry.* **Mistletoe pest in the** Southwest.
York, H. H. Anatomy and some of the biological aspects of the "American mistletoe." 50 c. Univ. of Tex.

Mistress art. Bloomfield, R. *$1.40 net. Longmans.

Mrs. Bailey's debts. Eddy, C: $1.50. Cassell.

Mistress Brent. Thurston. *Mrs.* L. M. †75 c. Little, B. & Co.

Mrs. De Brie says. Saunders, F. W. 75 c. C. M. Clark.

Mrs. Featherweight's musical moments. *See* Brady, J:

Mrs. Fitz. Snaith, J: C. $1.35 net. Moffat.

Mrs. Forrester's crusade. Dalrymple, C. L. 15 c. Dick.

Mrs. Gorringe's necklace. Davis, H. H: 50 c. W. H. Baker.

Mrs. Gramercy-Park. Goring-Thomas, A. R. $1.50. Lane.

Mrs. John Vernon. Addison, *Mrs.* J. D. G. $1.50. Badger.

Mistress of Brae farm. Carey, R. N. 75 c. Burt.

Mistress of Langdale Hall. Kettle, R. M. †$1.25. Estes.

Mistress of Shenstone. Barclay, *Mrs.* F. L. C. $1.35 net. Putnam.

Mrs. Overtheway's remembrances. Ewing, *Mrs.* J. H. G. $1. Macmillan.

Mrs. Temple's telegram. Wyatt, F. (Add. pubs. for price.) S. French.

Misunderstood children. Harrison, E. $1. Central Pub. Co.

Mit ränzel und wanderstab. Frommel, E. 35 c. Heath.

Mitchel, Ja. S.
Weight throwing. '10(Jl2) c. il. 12°, (Spalding's athletic lib.) pap., 10 c. Am. Sports.

Mitchell, C: Ainsworth.
Oil, animal, vegetable, essential, and mineral. '10(Jl16) il. D. (Common commodities of commerce.) 75 c. Pitman.

Mitchell, Dan. Holmes.
God's country. '10(O22) c. il. por. 4°, $6. Ebbert & R.

Mitchell, Donald Grant, ["Ik Marvel."]
Reveries of a bachelor. '10(D31) c. col. il. O. $1.50, boxed; leath., $2, boxed. Bobbs-M.

Mitchell, Edm.
Her sacrifice; drama. '09(Jl17) c. O. pap., 50 c. Grafton Pub.

Mitchell, E: Bedinger.
Shadow of the crescent. '09(Je26) c. D. †$1.25. Stokes.

Mitchell, G: W.
Latin composition based on Cæsar. '09 (Ap24) 12°, *60 c. net. Macmillan.

Mitchell, H: Bedinger, comp.
Talks on religion. '08(My16) c. O. **$1.50 net. Longmans.

Mitchell, Hinckley G., ed.
See Bible. **Bible for home and school.** Genesis.

Mitchell, Rev. Ja. Clayton.
Character: some talks to young men. '09 (Ja2) 12°, **75 c. net. Jacobs.

Mitchell, J: Ames.
Dr. Thorne's idea; originally published as "Gloria Victis." '10(Jl2) c. il. D. $1 net. Doran.
Villa Claudia. 3d ed. '08(F8) c. il. 12°. bds., 50 c. Life Pub.

Mitchell, J: Kearsley, M.D.
Self help for nervous women: familiar talks on economy in nervous expenditure. '09(F20) c. D. **$1 net. Lippincott.

Mitchell, Jos. D.
See Hunter, Wa. D.

Mitchell, Langdon Elwyn.
New York idea: a comedy in four acts. '08(N) c. 12+175 p. 12°, 50 c. W: H. Baker.

Mitchell, Marg. Johnes.
Fireless cook book. '09(Je5) c. D. $1.25. Doubleday, P.

Mitchell, Silas Weir, M.D.
Comfort of the hills and other poems. '10 (Mr15) c. D. **$1 net. Century Co.
Privately printed in 1909 by S. W. Mitchell.
Guillotine Club, and other stories. '10(O8) c. il. D. $1.50. Century Co.
Red city: a novel of the second administration of President Washington. '08 (N7) c. il. D. †$1.50. Century Co.
Venture in 1777. '08(O17) c. il. D. †$1.25. Jacobs.
See also Pearl (The).

Mitchell, Wesley Clair.
Gold, prices, and wages under the greenback standard. '08(My9) charts, 8°, (Univ. of Cal. pubs., Economics.) pap., $5. Univ. of Cal.

Mitchell, Wilmot Brookings.
Abraham Lincoln: the man and the crisis. '10(Jl9 c. por. 8°, 50 c. Smith & S.

Mitchell & Co.'s hdbk. of the Great Lakes. Green, F. W:, *comp.* $1.50. Mitchell & Co.

MITES.
Ewing, H: E. Systematic and biological study of the *Acarina* of Illinois. $1. Univ. of Ill.

Mitford, Mary Russell.
Our village; with introd. by Anne Thackeray Ritchie. '10(D10) il. (partly col.) Q. $3.50 net. Macmillan.
Studies of English life and character. '10 (O1) il. D. $1.75 net. McClurg.

Mittelstaedt, Otto.
Technical calculations for sugar works; contrib. to the chemical control of sugar manufacture; tr. from the 3d German ed. by C. J. Bourbakis. '10(My7) c. 12°, $1.50 net. Wiley.

Mitton, G: E:, ed.
Animal autobiography ser. New ed. v. 1-6. '10(O22); v. 7 (N19) il. in col. 8°, ea., $1.40 net. Macmillan.

Mitton, Geraldine Edith.
Book of the railway. '09(D25) col. il. 12°, (Color books for boys and girls.) *$2 net. Macmillan.
Hackney and Stoke Newington; ed. by Sir Wa. Besant. '08(N21) il. map, 16°, (Fascination of London ser.) *90 c. net. Macmillan.

Mitton, Geraldine Edith.—*Continued.*
The Thames. '10(Jl30) col. il. O. (Beautiful England ser. bds., $1.25, boxed. Estes.
See also Maps of old London.

Mitzmain, Maurice B.
See McCoy, G: W.

MIWOK INDIANS.
See Indians.

Mix, C: L:, M.D.
See Patrick, Hugh Talbot.

Mixer, Mrs. Mary Eliz. Knowlton, [M. E. M.]
Mosaics, book of poems. '09(F20) il. D. $1.25. M. E. K. Mixer.

Mixson, Fk. M.
Reminiscences of a private. '10(D17) c. pors. 12°, $1. State Co.

Mixter, Marg.
Health and beauty hints. '10(S17) c. il. 12°, $1. Cupples & L.

Miyakawa, Masuji.
Life of Japan; preface by the Prince of Nijo; introd. by Viscount Kentaro Kaneko. 2d ed., completely rev. '10 (O22) c. '07. por. D. $1.50 net. Neale.
Powers of the American people, Congress, Presidents, and courts. 2d ed., completely rev. throughout with extensive additions. '08(D5) c. 8°, **$2.50 net. Baker & T.

Miyatovic, Chedomil.
Servia and the Servians. '08(D19) 8°, *$3 net. L. C. Page.

Mizner, Addison.
See Herford, Oliver;—Mumford, Ethel Watts-.

MOBILE, Ala.
Hamilton, P: J. Colonial Mobile. $3.50 net. Houghton M.

Moccasin Ranch. Garland, H. †$1. Harper.
Mock trial. Wall, W. C. $1. W. C. Wall.
Mocking-bird. Harrison, E. O. *50 c. net. McClurg.

Mockler-Ferryman, A: Ferryman.
Golden girdle: [a story.] '08(N7) il. 12°, $1.50. Macmillan.
Norway. '09(Ag14) il. map, 12°, (Peeps at many lands ser.) *75 c. net. Macmillan.

Model balloons and flying machines. Alexander, J. H. $1.50. Henley.
Model book of engines. '10(D) il. in col. 4°, 50 c. Dutton.
Model book of games. '10(D) il. in col. 4°, 50 c. Dutton.
Model lib. 12°, pap. Spon.
—Harrison. Making wireless outfits. 50 c.; 25 c.—Wireless telephone. 25 c.
—Morgan. How to build a 20 ft. bi-plane glider. 25 c.
—Schneider. Model vaudeville theatre. 25 c.
Model menagerie. Weeden, L. L. $2.50. Dutton.
Model prayer. Jones, J: D. *75 c. net. Doran.
Model puzzle book. '10(D) il. in col. 4°, 50 c. Dutton.
Model steam engine. Vignier, R. M. de. 25 c. Spon.
Model steam turbines. Harrison, H. H. 25 c. Spon.

Model tenement house law. Veiller, L. $1.25. Charities Pub.

MODELLING.
Carter, L. Modelling from nature. 35 c. net. Cassell.
Ganz, H: F. W. Practical hints on modelling, design and mural decoration. *$1 net. Lippincott.
Lester, K. M. Clay work: hdbk. for teachers. $1.25. Manual Arts.
Sargent, W. Modelling in public schools. 60 c. J. L. Hammett.
Toft, A. Modelling and sculpture. $1.75 net. Lippincott.
See also Decoration and ornament.

Modern accounting. Hatfield, H: R. **$1.75 net. Appleton.
Modern achievement. Hale, E: E. 10 v. $9. Westminster, (Chic.)
Modern American library economy. *See* Dana, J: Cotton.
Modern American railway practice. Swingle, C. F., *ed.* In 10 v. $60. Drake.
Modern Arabic literature. Green, A. O., *comp.* In 2 pts. pt. 1, $1.75; pt. 2, $1.50. Oxford Univ.
Modern art. Meier-Graefe, J. A. 2 v. *$10.50 net. Putnam.
Modern art at Venice. G., A. E. $2 net. Bowles.
Modern artists. Brinton, C. $6. Baker & T.
Modern asphalt pavement. Richardson, C. $3. Wiley.
Modern assaying. Smith, J. R. $1.50 net. Lippincott.
Modern authors' ser. bds., 25 c. Brown Bros.
—Andreiyeff. Silence.
Modern baths and bath houses. Gerhard, W: P. *$3 net. Wiley.
Modern belief in immortality. Smyth, N. **75 c. net. Scribner
Modern billiards. Garmo, B: $1. Brunswick.
Modern billiards; with diagrams showing various shots, and with complete record of all principal amateur and professional matches and tournaments played in the U. S. '08 (Ap18) c. 12°, $1. Brunswick.
Modern British locomotives. Taylor, A. T. $2. Spon.
Modern business. 12°. De Bower-E.
—Meade. Economics. $3.50.
Modern business arithmetic. Sweet, J. S. $1.25. Sweet.
Modern business ser. In 12 v. '10(Ap) c. 8°, with Institute course, $78. Alexander Hamilton.
Contents: v. 1, Economics of business, by E: Sherwood Meade; v. 2, Organization, correspondence and transportation, by Lee Galloway, Ja. Mavor, G. B. Hotchkiss; v. 3, Accounting theory and practice, by Leo Greendlinger; v. 4, Corporation finance, by W: H. Lough, jr.; v. 5, Money and banking, by Jos. French Johnson; v. 6, Banking practice and foreign exchange, by H. M. Jefferson; v. 7, Investment and speculation, by T: Conway; v. 8, Insurance and real estate, by E: R. Hardy; v. 9, Buying, selling and advertising, by Lee Galloway; v. 10, Accounting systems, by E: P. Moxey; v. 11, Auditing and cost accounts, by Leon Brummer and Stephen W. Gilman; v. 12, Commercial law, by T: W. Hughes.
Modern cabinet work. Wells, P. A. $5 net. Lane.
Modern card manipulation. Neil, C. L. 50 c. Lippincott.
Modern Christianity. Peters, J: P. **$1.50 net. Putnam.
Modern chronicle. Churchill, W. $1.50. Macmillan.
Modern Cinderella. Alcott, L. M. 50 c. Hurst.
Modern city. Kirk, W:, *ed.* *$2.50 net. Univ. of Chic.
Modern city. Warner, A. D. 25 c. Baumgardt.
Modern classical philosophy. Rand, B., *comp.* **$2.50 net. Houghton M.
Modern clinical medicine ser. See Appleton's.
Modern clinics ser. il. 12°. Wood.
—Sherren. Injuries of nerves. *$2 net.
Modern coking practice. Byrom, T. H. *$3.50 net. Henley.
Modern constitutions. Alston, L. 90 c. Longmans.
Modern commentary. *See* Bacon, B: Wisner.
Modern constitutions. Dodd, W. F., *comp.* *$5 net. Univ. of Chic.
Modern corporation. Conyngton, T: $2. Ronald Press.
Modern corporation accounting. Lyons, J. A. $1.25. Powers.
Modern dances. Satori, J. A. 25 c.; 15 c. V. H. Krull.
Modern dental **materia medica.** Buckley, J. P. *$2.50 net. Blakiston.
Modern dict. of the English language. '10 (N5) D. 60 c. net. Macmillan.
Modern domestic science. il. 12°. Assoc. Schs. Dom. Sci.
—Seely. Fireless cookery. 25 c.
Modern educators and their ideals. Misawa, T. **$1.25 net. Appleton.
Modern electric railway practice. 4 v. '09 (S11) c. il. 8°, $22.50 W. V. Wheat.
Modern engineering practice. Gunsaulus, F. W., *ed.* 12 v. $29.80. Am. Sch. Corr.
Modern English. Krapp, G: P. **$1.25 net. Scribner.
Modern English grammar. Jesperson, O. pt. 1. *$3 net. Stechert.
Modern farming. Gas Traction Co. gratis. Gas Traction.
Modern formulary. Cummings, W: L. $2.50. W: L. Cummings.
Modern foundry practice. Sharp, J: $8. Spon.
Modern French literature. Wells, B: W. **$1 net. Little, B. & Co.
Modern gas and oil engines. Grover, F: $2. Spon.
Modern gas engine. Levin, G. M. $4. Wiley.
Modern German prose. Nichols, A. B., *comp.* $1. Holt.
Modern German sculpture. Schulz, A., *comp. and ed.* $14. Hessling.
Modern Germany. Barker, J. E. *$3 net. Dutton.
Modern golf. Vaile, P: A. *$2.25 net. Macmillan.
Modern Greek folklore. Lawson, J: C. $4 net. Putnam.
Modern guide for fruit and truck shippers. Thomas, T. G: $2. Thomas-W.

MODERN HISTORY.
See History.
Modern homes. Davison, T. R. *$5.25 net. Macmillan.
Modern hospitals. Holmes, C. R. gratis. Univ. of Cin.
Modern illustrative bookkeeping. Neal, E. V. $1. Am. Bk.
Modern inductive bookkeeping. Goodyear, S: H. 2 v. $3.75. Goodyear-M.
Modern industrialism and the negroes of the United States. Grimké, A. H: 15 c. Am. Negro Acad.
Modern interpretation of the call to the ministry. Bosworth, E: I. 10 c. Y. M. C. A.
Modern Jewish history. Harris, M. H: 30 c. net. Bloch.
MODERN LANGUAGE.
See Language.
Modern language ser. *See* Crowell's.—Heath's.
Modern lettering. Heyny, W: $2. W: T. Comstock.
Modern light on immortality. Frank, H: *$1.85 net. Sherman, F.
Modern love. *See* Meredith, G:
Modern mantels; hdbk. for the discriminating buyer of wooden mantels for the home. '10(Je18) c. il. (partly col.) O. pap., $1. Knoxville Furniture.
Modern manuals of commerce. 8°. *$1 net. Macmillan.
—Hooper *and* Graham. Import and export trade.
Modern marriage and how to bear it. Brady, N. C. $1.25. M. Kennerley.
Modern materia medica and therapeutics. Stevens, A. A. $3.50. Saunders.
Modern medicine. Osler, W: *$6 net; *$7 net; *$7.50 net. Lea.
Modern methods for teachers. Boyer, C: C. $1.50. Lippincott.
Modern methods of street cleaning. Soper, G: A. $3. Engineering News.
Modern methods of treatment ser. il. 12°. *$1.50 net. Funk.
—Harris. Electrical treatment. $2.25.
—Morris *and* Dore. Light and X-ray treatment of skin diseases.
Modern mining practice. Bailes, G: M. 5 v. ea., $3. Van Nostrand.
Modern missionary challenge. Jones, J: P: $1.50 net. Revell.
Modern model school house on the unit plan. Corwin, R. W. 10 c. R. W. Corwin.
Modern mother. Gordon, H. L. $2. Fenno.
Modern organ accompaniment. Richardson. A. M. $2.50. Longmans.
Modern organic chemistry. Keane, C: A. *$1.50 net. Scribner.
Modern painter's encyclopedia. Maire, F: $1.50. Drake.
Modern painters. *See* Ruskin, J:
Modern pigments. Maire, F. $2. Wiley.
Modern power gas producer. Allen, H. *$2.50 net. Van Nostrand.
Modern practical joinery. Ellis, G: *$6 net. Scribner.
Modern practice in mining. *See* Redmayne, R: Augustine Studdert.
Modern presswork. Gage, F. W: $2. Inland Pr.
Modern Prometheus. Dickinson, M. G. †$1.50. Duffield.
Modern punch and die construction. '09(F13) c. diagrs., 8°, (Machinery's reference ser.) pap., 25 c. Indust. Press.
Modern religious problems; ed. by Ambrose White Vernon. S. **50 c. net. Houghton M.
—Bacon. Founding of the church.
—Burkitt. Earliest sources for the life of Jesus.
—Hyde. Sin and its forgiveness.
—Knox. Gospel of Jesus.
—Moffatt. Paul and Paulinism.
—Paton. Early religion of Israel. 50 c. net.
—Scott. Historical and religious value of the fourth Gospel.
—Stelzle. Church and labor.
Modern research as illustrating the Bible. Driver, S: R. $1.20. Oxford Univ.
Modern revolt from Rome. Berkeley, J:, *pseud.* $1.25 net. Jennings.
Modern school houses; being a ser. of authoritative articles on planning, sanitation, heating and ventilation, by A. D. F. Hamlin, C. B. J. Snyder and others. '10(N19) c. il. plans, f°, $7.50. Swetland.
Modern seamanship. Knight, A. M. $7.50. Van Nostrand.
Modern sermons by world scholars. Scott, R., *ed.* 10 v. $7.50. Funk.
Modern silage methods; feeding, and a treatise on rations, feeders' and dairymen's guide. 7th rev. ed. '08(Mr7) c. tabs., D. pap., 10 c. Silver Manufacturing.
Modern Spanish painting. Temple, A. G. *$20 net. Lippincott.
Modern speech New Testament. *See* Bible, N. T.
Modern substitutes for Christianity. Muir, P. M. *$1.50 net. Doran.
Modern Sunday-school manuals; ed. by C: Foster Kent in collaboration with J: T. McFarland. D. Eaton & M.
—Hurlbut. Organizing and building-up the Sunday school. 65 c. net.
—Meyer. Graded Sunday-school in principle and practice. 75 c. net.
Modern surgery. Da Costa, J: C. *$5.50 net. Saunders.
Modern thought and the crisis in belief. Wenley, R. M. **$1.50 net. Macmillan.
Modern turnout formulas. Raymond, W: G. *50 c. net. A. M. Allen.
Modern Valkyrie. Svenson, E. $1. Cochrane.
Modern way. *See* Clifford, *Mrs.* W. K. Three plays.
Modern woman and how to manage her. Gallichan, W. M. $1.50 net. Lane.
Modern Woodmen of America. Official floor work manual of the Modern Woodmen of America, prepared for use in connection with the latest ritual, and providing foresters team drill work before beneficial and fraternal degrees; with directions as to funeral honors; approved 1910. '10(My) c. 59 p. il. diagrs., 8°, 50 c. Modern Woodmen.

Modern Woodmen of America. Official ritual (third revision) of the Modern Woodmen of America, 1909; containing the opening and closing ceremonies, ceremony of adoption, installation, Memorial day, and funeral services, prescribed by the Head camp. '09, [1910.] (Ap) 109 p. il. por. 12°, 50 c. Modern Woodmen.

MODERNISM.
B., C. S. Modernism : what it is and why it was condemned. *10 c. net. Herder.
De Bary, R: Franciscan days of vigil. $1.50 net. Longmans.
Doan, F. C. Religion and the modern mind, and other essays on modernism. *$1.10 net. Sherman, F.
Godrycz, J: A. Doctrine of modernism. *75 c. net. McVey.
Jordan, L. H. Modernism in Italy. 50 c. Oxford Univ.
Letters to His Holiness Pope Pius x, by a Modernist. $1.25. Open Court.
Lilley, A. L. Modernism. *$1.75 net. Scribner.
Loisy, A. Gospel and the Church: [criticism of the Roman Catholic church and denial of the Pope's supremacy.] *$1 net. Scribner.
Palmer, W: S. Diary of a Modernist. $1.40 net. Longmans.
Programme of modernism: reply to the encyclical of Pius x., *Pascendi Dominici Gregis*. *$1.50 net. Putnam.
Sabatier, P. Modernism. $1.50. Scribner.
Torrey, D: C. Protestant modernism. $1. D: C. Torrey.
Tyrrell, G: Christianity at the cross-roads. *$1.50 net.—Medievalism: reply to Cardinal Mercier. *$1.25 net.—Much-abused letter. 90 c. net. Longmans.
Wright, A. L. Modernism to the law of sensual impression and historical inspiration. J. McDonough.
See also Catholic church.

Modernism and romance. Scott-James, R. A. *$2.50 net. Lane.
Modernity and the churches. Gardner, P. $1.50 net. Putnam.
Modes and manners of the XIXth century. Fischel, O. 3 v. **$7 net. Dutton.

MODESTY.
See Sex.

Modification of Illinois coal by low temperature distillation. Parr, S: W. gratis. Univ. of Ill.

Modjeska, Helena, [Countess Bozenta Chlapowski.]
Memories and impressions of Helena Modjeska; autobiography. '10(N12) c. il. pors. O. $4 net, boxed. Macmillan.

MODOC INDIANS.
See Indians.

Moffat, Ja., D.D.
George Meredith; introduction to his novels. '10(Ja15) O. *$1.25 net. Doran.
Paul and Paulinism. '10(F26) c. S. (Modern religious problems.) **50 c. net. Houghton M.

Moffat, Reuben Burnham.
Moffat genealogies: descent from Rev. John Moffat of Ulster County, New York. '09, [1910.] (F) c. 13-158 p. il. map, 8°. (Priv. pr.) R. B. Moffat.

MOFFATT FAMILY.
See Genealogies.

Moffett, Cleveland.
The battle. '09(My22) c. il. D. †$1.50. G: W. Dillingham.
Through the wall. '09(O23) c. il. D. †$1.50. Appleton.

Moffett, L: Burdelle.
Manual of bookkeeping and accounting. 8th ed. '08(S12) c. forms. O. $1.25. Peirce Sch.

Moffett, S: Erasmus.
Americanization of Canada. '07, [1908.] (Jl) 126 p. 8°, pap. (Priv. pr.) S: E. Moffett.

Moffit, Fred Howard, Knopf, Adolph, and Capps, S. R.
Mineral resources of the Nabesna-White River district, Alaska, by F. H. Moffit and Adolph Knopf, with a section on the quaternary by S. R. Capps. '10(Jl) 64 p. O. (U. S., Dept. of the Interior, U. S. Geolog. Survey, bull.) pap. Gov. Pr. Off.

—, and Maddren, Alfr. G.
Mineral resources of the Kotsina-Chitina region, Alaska. '09(Jl) 103 p. il. maps, 8°, (U. S. Geological Survey bull.) (Add. Superintendent for price.)

Moffitt, B. L.
French pronoun drill. '08(Ag8) c. 12°, bds., *25 c. net. W: R. Jenkins.
Drill in French pronunciation. '08(Ag8) c. 12°, bds., *15 c. net. W: R. Jenkins.

MOHAMMED AND MOHAMMEDANISM.
Becker, C. H. Christianity and Islam. *75 c. net. Harper.
Macdonald, D. B. Religious attitude and life in Islam. *$1.75 net. Univ. of Chic.
Zwemer, S: M. Islam: a challenge to faith. $1; 35 c. Student Vol.
See also Babism.

MOHAWK VALLEY, N. Y.
Diefendorf, M. R. Historic Mohawk. $2 net. Putnam.

MOHEGAN INDIANS.
See Indians.

Mohler, J: Robbins.
Infectious anemia, or swamp fever of horses. '09(Ap) 4 p. 8°, (U. S. Dept. of Agriculture; Bureau of Animal Industry circular.) pap., 5 c.
Tuberculin test of cattle for tuberculosis. '09(My) 8 p. 8°, (U. S., Dept. of Agriculture; farmers' bull.) pap. (Add. Superintendent for price.)

—, and Eichhorn, Adolph.
Need of controlling and standardizing the manufacture of veterinary tetanus antitoxin. '09, [1910.] (Mr) 22 p. tabs., 8°, (U. S., Dept. of Agriculture, Bu. of Animal Industry, bull.) pap.

—, and Rosenau, Milton Jos.
Origin of the recent outbreak of foot-and-mouth disease in the U. S. '09(Ag) 29 p. il. 8°, (U. S., Dept. of Agriculture; Bu. of Animal Industry, bull.) pap., 5 c.

Mohn, Earl J:
Advisability of electing United States senators by popular ballot. '09(N) 18 p. 8°. (Priv. pr.) Georgetown Univ.

Mohonk addresses. Hale, E: E. 90 c. Int. Sch. of Peace.

Moisseiff, Leon Solomon.
Review of the literature of reinforced concrete; to which is added a list of current books on cement, concrete, limes and allied subjects, with descriptive notes. '09(Ag28) 8°, pap., 5 c. Engineering News.

Moisture content and physical condition of soils. Cameron, F. K. 15 c. U. S., Supt. of Docs

Molé, A.
See James, W.

Mole, Marion.
Vera of the strong heart. '10(Jl2) c. D. $1.25. Putnam.

Molera, Eusabius J.
See Eldredge, Zoeth Skinner.

Molesworth, Sir Guilford Lindsey.
Economic and fiscal facts and fallacies. '10 (F5) D. $1.50. Longmans.
Metric tables. 4th ed., rev. and enl. '09 (D18) 24°, 80 c. Spon.
Pocket-book of useful formulæ and memoranda for civil, mechanical and electrical engineers. 26th ed., rev. and enl. '09 (Ap3) 32°, leath., $2. Spon.

Molesworth, Mrs. Mary Louise Stewart, ["Ennis Graham."]
Fairies-of-sorts. '08(N7) il. 12°, (Golden ser. of illustrated juvenile books.) $1.50. Macmillan.
February boys. '09(O2) il. 16°, $1.50. Dutton.
Marrying and giving in marriage. '08(Ag8) 12°, (Home ser.) 50 c. Hurst.
Old pincushion. '10(D31) col. il. 16°, $1.50. Dutton.
Story of a year. '10(N19) il. 12°, $1.50. Macmillan.
Us. '08(Je27) 12°, (Home ser.) 50 c. Hurst.

Molière, Jean Baptiste Poquelin de.
Eight plays; new tr. by Curtis Hidden Page; with introd. by Brander Matthews. '08(Ag15) 2 v., photogravure por. 8°, (French classics for English readers.) *$5 net. Putnam.
L'avare; arr. and ed., with introd., notes, exercises, by Marc Ceppi. '09(O16) S. (Crowell's shorter French texts.) *25 c. net. Crowell.
L'avare: comédie; ed. by O. H. Fynes-Clinton. '08(Je13) 16°, (Siepmann's classical French texts.) *50 c. net. Macmillan.
L'avare. '08(Ag) 115 p. por. il. 12°, 50 c. Wahr.
Le bourgeois gentilhomme; abgd. and ed., with introd., notes, grammatical and retranslation exercises and vocab. '09 (O16) S. (Crowell's shorter French texts.) *25 c. net. Crowell.
Le bourgeois gentilhomme; comédie-ballet; ed., with introd. and notes, by M. Levi. '10(O1) c. por. S. 35 c. Holt.
Le médecin malgré lui; abgd. and ed., with introd., notes, grammatical and retranslation exercises and vocab., by Marc Ceppi. '09(O16) S. (Crowell's shorter French texts.) *25 c. net. Crowell.

MOLIÈRE, Jean Baptiste Poquelin de.
Matthews, J. B. Molière; his life and works. $3 net. Scribner.

Molitor, D: Albert.
Geodetic surveying for the use of students in the College of Civil Engineering, Cornell University. '10(Ap) c. 29 p. diagrs., 8°, 30 c. D: A. Molitor.
Hydraulics of rivers, weirs and sluices. '08(Je20) c. figs. 8°, **$2 net. Wiley.

Moll, Albert.
Hypnotism; tr. from the 4th enl. [German] ed. by Arth. F. Hopkirk. '09(Je26) D. $1.50. Scribner.

Moll, Theophilus J:
Treatise on the law of independent contractors and their liability, [etc.] '10 (F) c. O. $3.75. W. H. Anderson.

Mollie and the Unwiseman abroad. Bangs, J: K. $1.50. Lippincott.

Mollie Deverill. Yorke, C., *pseud.* $1.50. Estes.

Molloy, Jos. Fitzgerald.
Victoria Regina: her court and her subjects, from her accession to the death of the prince-consort. '08(N14) il. O. *$6 net, boxed. Dodd.

MOLLUSKS.
Baker, F. C. Ecology of the Skokie Marsh area, with special reference to the mollusca. 60 c. Ill. Lab'y Nat. Hist.
Dall, W: H. Description of two new pulmonate mollusks, with list of other species from the Solomon Islands. 50 c. Field Museum.
Dall, W: H., *and* Bartsch, P. Monograph of West American pyramidellid mollusks. 35 c. U. S., Supt. of Docs.
Kellogg, J. L. Shell-fish industries. **$1.75 net. Holt.
MacFarland, F. M. *Opisthobranchiate mollusca* of the Branner-Agassiz expedition to Brazil. $1. Stanford Univ.
Massachusetts. *Commissioners on Inland Fisheries and Game.* Report upon the mollusk fisheries of Massachusetts. gratis. Mass. Com. Inland Fisheries.
Rogers, J. E. Shell book: guide to knowledge of the families of living mollusks: aid to the identification of shells. **$4 net. Doubleday, P.
See also Bryozoa.

Molly Make-Believe. Abbott, E. H. $1 net. Century Co.

Molmenti, Pompeo Gherardo.
Venice, its individual growth from the earliest beginnings to the fall of the republic; tr. by Horatio F. Brown. In 3 pts. of 2 v. each. pt. 3 in 2 v., The decadence. '08 (O17) c. il. pors. O. per 2 v., *$5 net, boxed; hf. mor., *$10 net. (Sold only in 2 v. sections.) McClurg.

Molnar, Ferenc.
The devil; adapted by Oliver Herford. '08 (S12) c. il. D. *$1 net. M. Kennerley.
The devil. '08(S26) il. 12°, *50 c. net; pap., *25 c. net. J. S. Ogilvie.
See also Westrum, Adrian Schade van.

Moloch. Johnson, *Mrs.* M. K. 50 c. net. W: B. Clarke.

Molsberger, E. C. Godée-, comp.
See Godée-Molsbergen, E. C.

Moltke, Count Helmuth Karl Bernhard von.
Die beiden freunde; with introd., notes and vocab. by Karl Detlef Jessen. '08(Ja25) front. S. *35 c. net. Holt.

Moment diagrams and typical live loads. Derleth, C:, *jr.* 10 c. Univ. of Cal.

Momyer, G: Rob.
Normal institute manual of Colorado school law, Dec., 1909. '10(Ap) c. 72 p. S. pap., 25 c. Herrick.

Mon étoile. *See* Scribe, Augustin Eugène.

Mon livre de petites histoires. Gay, A. G. $1. W: R. Jenkins.

Monachesi, Mrs. Hannah Davis, [Mrs. Nicola di Rienzi Monachesi.]
Manual for china painters. Rev. and enl. ed. '09(Je5) c. il. D. $1.25, boxed. Lothrop, L. & S.

MONACO.
Mayne, E. C. Romance of Monaco and its rulers. $5 net. Lane.

Monaghan, Ja., ed.
See Pennsylvania. Monaghan's cumulative annual digest.

Monaghan, Ja. P.
Complete legal advertising, form book for lawyers, administrators, assignees, receivers, trustees, state, county, city and village officials, [etc.] '07, [1908.] (My.) c. 335 p. D. shp. (Add. pubs. for price.) Legal.

Monahan, M., ed. and comp.
Text-book of true temperance. '09(D4) D. 40 c. U. S. Brewers' Assoc.

Monahan, Michael.
Palms of papyrus; being forthright studies of men and books; with some pages from a man's inner life. 2d ed., rev., with new matter. '09. [1910.] (D) c. 240 p. 8°, $2.50 net. M. Kennerley.

Monarchs of Merry England. Carse, R. $1.50. Stokes.

MONASTICISM.
Gueranger, P. L. P. Religious and monastic life explained. *50 c. net. Herder.
Harnack, C. G. A. Monasticism. $1.50 net. Putnam.
See also France;—Mt. Athos;—Nunneries;—*also* Vinogradoff, P., *ed.* Oxford studies in social and legal hist. v. 1.

Monckton, C. C. F.
Radio-telegraphy. '08(D5) il. 8°, (Westminster ser.) *$2 net. Van Nostrand.

Moncrief, J: Wildman.
Short history of the Christian church. 3d ed., rev. '08(O24) c. 8°, *$1.50 net. Revell.

Moncrieff, Ascott Rob. Hope, ["Ascott Rob. Hope."]
Adventurers in America. '09(N6) col. il. 8°, (Color books, Miscellaneous.) $1.75. Macmillan.
Beasts of business. '09(N6) col. il. 8°, (Color books, Miscellaneous.) $1.50. Macmillan.
Essex. '09(Jl3) col. il. map, 8°, (Color books.) *$6 net. Macmillan.
Heart of Scotland. '09(My15) map, 8°, (Color books.) *$3 net. Macmillan.
Isle of Wight. '08(O3) il. map, 8°, (Color books.) *$2.50 net. Macmillan.
Kew gardens. '08(Ag8) il. 12°, (Color books.) *$2.50 net. Macmillan.

Moncrieff, Ascott Rob. Hope, ["Ascott Rob. Hope."]—*Continued.*
London. '10(N19) col. il. 8°, (Color books.) $2.50 net. Macmillan.
Peak country: [highlands of Derbyshire, Eng.] '08(Je13) il. 12°, (Color books.) *$2.50 net. Macmillan.
The world. '08(O10) il. map, 12°, (Peeps at many lands ser.) *$1.50 net. Macmillan.

Monday Club sermons on the International Sunday school lessons; new series for 1911. '10(D31) c. 12°, $1.25. Pilgrim Press.

Monday morning. Oppenheim, J. *$1.25 net. Sturgis & W.

Monell, S: Howard, M.D.
Elements of correct technique: clinics from the N. Y. School of Special Electrotherapeutics. '10(Mr) 8°, *$2.50 net. W: R. Jenkins.
Formerly published by E. R. Pelton.
High frequency electric currents in medicine and dentistry, their nature and actions and simplified uses in external treatments. '10(Mr) c. 465 p. il. 8°, *$4 net. W: R. Jenkins.
Hot air, vibration and high frequency currents. '10(Mr) *$15 net. W: R. Jenkins.
Formerly published by E. R. Pelton.
Rudiments of modern electrical chemistry. '10(Mr) *$1 net. W: R. Jenkins.
Formerly published by E. R. Pelton.
Thirty chapters on static electricity. '10 (Mr) *$2 net. W: R. Jenkins.
Formerly published by E. R. Pelton.
Treatment of disease by electric currents. '10(Mr) *$6 net. W: R. Jenkins.
Formerly published by E. R. Pelton.

Money, Hernando De Soto.
Tariff schedules: statement of the labor cost and value of products under each schedule and the total of all schedules of the Senate bill and cost of indirect taxation. '09(Jl) 3 p. 8°, pap. (Add. Superintendent for price.) U. S., Supt. of Docs.

MONEY.
Adams, J. T. Some notes on the currency problem. gratis. Broun-G.
American Bankers' Association. Rept. of the Currency Commission to the American Banker's Association. (Add. Association for price.) Am. Bankers' Assoc.
Balch, T: W. Free coinage and a self-adjusting ratio. (Not for sale.) T: W. Balch.
Balch, T: W. Law of Oresme, Copernicus, Gresham. $1. Allen, L. & S.
Blake, G: H. United States paper money. $1. G: H. Blake.
Crane, W: H. Scientific currency. $1. B'way Pub.
Davies, A. E. Money and the stock and share markets. 50 c. Pitman.
Davis, A. M. Two forgotten pamphleteers in the Massachusetts currency controversy, 1720-1740. (Priv. pr.) A. M. Davis.
Depreciated currency and diminished railway rates. (Add. pubs. for price.) Railway World.

MONEY.—*Continued.*

Doll, W: F: Money and democracy. 25 c. W: F: Doll.

Fry, R: Scheme for a paper currency. $3.75. Club for Colonial Reprs.

Fulton, J. A. Other side of the money question. 25 c. Hutchinson & B.

Gardner, J. P: Moneys of the world. 50 c. Bankers' Pub.

Gilbert, E: H., *and* Elder, T: L. Varieties of the United States cents of 1796. $1. T: L. Elder.

Hurlbut, E. What was nominated on the bond?: gold standard in the crucible of facts. (Add. pubs. for price.) Baur.

Jevons, W: S. Investigations in currency and finance. *$3 net. Macmillan.

Kinnaird, P. Evolution of money. $1; 50 c. P. Kinnaird.

Libby, C: T. Cash, panics and industrial depressions. gratis. C: T. Libby.

Long, C: A. Solution of interests dependent upon money, subsidiary money, currency, emergency currency and banking for every nation. $1. Aberdeen.

MacVeagh, F. Interview concerning the proposed changes in design and size of paper money. Gov. Pr. Off.

Marburg, T. Do we want an asset currency? 10 c. Dulany.

Massachusetts. Law rel. to money and negotiable instruments. *25 c. net. G. A. Jackson.

Meyer, G: v. L. Our unelastic currency. 10 c. U. S., Supt. of Docs.

Mitchell, W. C. Gold, prices, and wages under the greenback standard. $5. Univ. of Cal.

Morawetz, V. Banking and currency problems in the United States. *$1 net. North American.

Morgan, A. T., *and* Ridpath, J: C. Bank of the beast. 25 c. Ware & Co.

Muhleman, M. L: Monetary and banking systems, 1908. *$2 net. Monetary.

Noyes, A. D. Hist. of the national-bank currency. Gov. Pr. Off.

O'Sullivan, D. Cold-storage baby: textbook on honest money and irredeemable paper. 25 c. Ontario Pub.

Putney, A. H. Currency, banking and exchange. $4.80. Cree.

Rawic H: Quantity of money from distribution. 15 c. Distribution League.

Ripley, A. L. Recent plans for currency reform. (Add. pub. for price.) Ellis.

Roberts, J: G. Currency reform. 25 c. J: G. Roberts.

Rollins, M. Money and investments. $2 net. Estes.

Scott, W: A. Money and banking. $2. Holt.

Stone, G: H. World money. $1.25. G: H. Stone

United States. Clean money, Committee on Banking and Currency, House of Representatives: [hearings] Jan. 20, 29 [and Feb. 10] 1904 [and Mar. 12, 1910]. [1910.] (Jl) 22 p. 8°. Gov. Pr. Off.

United States. *Congress. House. Committee on Ways and Means.* Transportation of moneys by express. 25 c.

United States. Currency association law. gratis. Nat. City Bank.

United States. *National Monetary Commission.* List of conferences in London, Paris and Berlin, held by representatives of the National Monetary Commission.

United States. *Treasury Dept.* Information respecting bonds, paper currency, coin, production of precious metals.

Vallette, J. C. Financial gatling gun: [currency question.] 50 c. J. C. Vallette.

White, H. Money and banking; illustrated by American history. *$1.80 net; *$1.50 net. Ginn.

Wichelman, F: A: Dangerous currency system of the U. S. 10 c. F: A: Wichelman.

Widney, R. M. National currency and banks. (Add. author for price.) R. M. Widney.

Withers, H. Meaning of money. $1.50 net. Dutton.

See also **Banks and banking;—Bonds;—Business;—Capital and labor;—Coins and medals;—Commerce; — Credit; — Exchange; — Finance; — Gold (*as money*);—Interest;—Investments;—Panics;—Prices;—Wealth.**

Money and Stamp Brokerage Company. Money and stamp manual; compendium of the coins of the United States of America, as well as of the earlier American governments; also of rare coins (ancient and modern) of other governments and their dependencies; also of the rare varieties of fractional, continental and Confederate paper currency; also, a schedule of many postage stamps of the United States and other countries, with market values. '09 (Mr6) c. il. 16°, $1. Money and Stamp.

Money answers all things. *See* Vanderlint, Jacob.

Money changers. Sinclair, U. B., *jr.* $1.50. B. W. Dodge.

Money god. Van Dyke, J: C: **$1 net Scribner.

Money hunger. Wood, H: A. W. **$1 net. Putnam.

Money value of good health. Robertson, G. 10 c. G. Robertson

MONGOLIA.

Hedley, J: Tramps in dark Mongolia. $3.50 net. Scribner.

MONGOLS (The).

Curtin, J. Mongols in Russia. **$3 net. Little, B. & Co.

'Mongst the hills of Kentucky. Arnett, L. $1: 50 c. L. Arnett.

Moninger, Herbert H.

Fifty lessons in training for service. Rev. ed., for use in teacher-training classes, young people's societies, mid-week prayer-meetings, adult Bible classes, etc. '08 (Apil) c. il. 12°, *40 c. net; manilla, *25 c. net. Standard Pub.

New Testament church, for advanced teacher-training classes, adult Bible classes, etc. '08(D) c. 158 p. 16°. (Training for service ser.) 50 c.; pap., 30 c. Standard Pub.

Moninger, Herbert H.—*Continued.*
Standard commentary on the International Sunday-school lessons: geographical notes by J: W. McGarvey. '08(Mr21) c. il. maps, 8°, 75 c. Standard Pub.
Studies in the Gospel and Acts for advanced teacher-training classes, adult Bible classes, etc. '08(D) c. 154 p. il. maps, 16°. (Add. pubs. for price.) Standard Pub.

MONITORIAL SYSTEM OF EDUCATION.
See **Education.**

Monk of Cruta. Oppenheim, E: P. 75 c. J. S. Ogilvie.

Monkey shines of Marseleen. Jennett, N. E. 60 c. Cupples & L.

MONKEYS.
Peterson, O. A. Revision of the Entelodontidæ. $2.50. Carnegie Museum.

Monkeys and monkeyettes. Ries, W. F. 10 c. W. F. Ries.

MONKS.
See Monasticism.

Monksglade mystery. Grainger, F. E: $1.50. Fenno.

Monmouth Baptist ladies' cook book. Sexton, M. B., *comp.* 60 c.; 85 c. M. B. Sexton.

Monnier, Philippe.
Venice in the eighteenth century; [tr.] from the French. '10(D24) front. O. $3 net, boxed. Badger.

MONOGRAMS.
See **Lettering.**

Monographs on American book-plate designers. il. 8°. Goodspeed.
—Hapgood. Bookplates. 12 brochures, per set, $18; $30.

Monographs on biochemistry; ed. by R. H. Anders Plimmer and F. J. Hopkins. il. O. bds. Longmans.
—Armstrong. Simple carbohydrates and the glucosides. *$1.20 net.
—Bayliss. Nature of enzyme action. *$1 net.
—Leathes. The fats. $1.25 net.
—Osborne. Vegetable proteins. *$1.20 net.
—Plimmer. Chemical constitution of the proteins. In 2 pts. pt. 1. *$1 net; pt. 2, *80 c. net.
—Schryver. General character of proteins. *80 c. net.

Monographs on education. 12°, 25 c. Palmer Co.
—Leonard. Moral training in public schools.

MONOLOGUES.
Cooke, M. B. More modern monologues. $1.25. Dramatic.
Gettner, F. I. Joan of Arc; monologue. 40 c. M. I. Gettner.
Hartmann, J. F., *comp.* Monologues and parodies. 75 c. T: J. Carey.
Herford, B. B. Monologues. $1.25. Scribner.
Saunders, F. W. Mrs. De Brie says. 75 c. C. M. Clark.
Wood, L. Lennawood's monologues. $1. Holliswood.
See also Plays:—Recitations.

MONOPLANES.
See **Aerial navigation.**

MONOPOLIES.
Brooks, J: G. Conflict between private monopoly and good citizenship. **50 c. net. Houghton M.
Cooke, F: H. Law of combinations, monopolies and labor unions. $6. Callaghan.
Davidson, J:, *and* Gray, A. Scottish staple at Veere. *$4.50 net. Longmans.
Jenckes, A. L. Origin, the organization and the location of the staple of England. (Add. pubs. for price.) Univ. of Penn.
See also Capital and labor;—Trusts.

MONOPOLY.
See **Business.**

MONOTHEISM.
Ballard, F. True God. *$1 net. Eaton & M.
See also God.

MONOTYPE.
See **Printers and printing.**

Monroe, Mrs. Harriet Earhart.
Hist. of the life of Gustavus Adolphus II., the hero-general of the Reformation. '10 (D10) c. pors. map, 16°, (Lutheran handbook ser.) 40 c. Lutheran Pub.
Washington: its sights and insights. New and rev. ed. '09(D) c. 8+184 p. il. pors. 12°, **$1 net. Funk.

Monroe, Paul.
Syllabus of a course of study on the history and principles of education. '08 (S5) c. 8°, (Columbia Univ., Extension syllabi, Ser. A.) pap., 20 c. Teachers' Coll.

Monroe, Will Seymour.
Bohemia and the Czechs. '10(S17) c. il. pors. fold. map, O. $3, boxed. L. C. Page.
Norway: its peoples, its fjords and its fjelds. '08(N14) c. il. pors. map, O. $3, boxed. L. C. Page.
Sicily, the garden of the Mediterranean. '09(Ag14) c. il. fold. map, D. (Travel lovers' ser.) $3, boxed. L. C. Page.

MONROE COUNTY, N. Y.
Peck, W: F. Hist. of Rochester and Monroe Co., N. Y. 2 v. $18. Pioneer Pub. Co.

MONROE DOCTRINE.
Crichfield, G: W. American supremacy: the rise and progress of the Latin American republics and their relation to the United States under the Monroe doctrine. 2 v. **$6 net. Brentano's.

Monsieur D'Or. Haney, J: L: $1.20 net. Egerton Press.

Monsieur Pinson. Biart, L. 35 c. net. Macmillan.

Monster-land. Quiz, R. $2.50. Putnam.

Montagu, Gordon.
Glen Ellyn, paint maker; original paint novel. [1910.] (S) c. 5+342 p. 12°, $1.50. G. Montagu.

Montagu, Lord J: Scott.
Motor cars and how to drive them. In 2 pts. '08(Ag1) il. 8°, ea., $1.50. Spon.

Montagu, Lady Mary Pierrepont Wortley.
Selected letters. '10(Ag20) por. T. (Remarque ser. of literary masterpieces.) 40 c., boxed; limp leath., 75 c., boxed. Caldwell.

Montagu, Rear-Admiral Victor Alex.
Reminiscences of Admiral Montagu. '10 (N19) il. pors. O. $4.20 net. Longmans.

Montague, Marg. Prescott.
In Calvert's valley. '08(N14) c. il. D. †$1.50. Baker & T.

MONTAGUE, Mass.
See Communities.

Montaigne, Michel Eyquem de.
Essayes; tr. by J: Florio; ed. by A. R. Waller. In 3 v. '10(Ap16) 16°, (Everyman's lib.) ea., 35 c. net; 70 c. net. Dutton.
Essayes; tr. by J: Florio; with an introd. by T: Seccombe. 3 v. [Limited ed.] '09(Mr13) il. 8°, hf. mor., *$10 net. Dutton.

MONTAIGNE, Michel Eyquem de.
Compayré, J. G. Montaigne, and education of the judgment. **90 c. net. Crowell.
Norton, G., *comp.* Montaigne: personal relations to some of his contemporaries.—Spirit of Montaigne. ea., *$1.25 net. Houghton M.
Robertson, J. M. Montaigne and Shakespeare. *$2 net. Macmillan.

Montana. *Supreme ct.* Repts. v. 35. '08 (Ja18); v. 36 (S); v. 37. '09(Ap); v. 38 (O); v. 39. '10(Ap); v. 40 (Ag) c. O. shp., ea., $4. Bancroft-W.

MONTANA.
Fisher, C. A. Geology of the Great Falls coal field, Mont. 20 c. U. S., Supt. of Docs.
Judson, K. B. Montana. *75 c. net. McClurg.
Rowe, J. P. Some economic geology of Montana. (Add. University for price.) Univ. of Mont.
United States. *Dept. of the Interior. U. S. Geolog. Survey.* Geology of the Lewistown coal field, Montana. 35 c.
See also Flathead County;—Yellowstone Valley.

Montana. Thorne, G. E. 25 c. J. S. Ogilvie.

MONTCLAIR, N. J.
Doremus, P. Reminiscences of Montclair. $1. P. Doremus.
Nolen, J: Montclair: the preservation of its natural beauty, and its improvement as a residence town. $1 net. J: Nolen.

Montefiore, Rabbi Claude Jos. Goldsmid-.
Bible for home reading. pt. 1. '10(D) price changed from $1.25 net to $1.50 net. pt. 2. '10(F5) price changed from *$1.25 net to *$1.75 net. Macmillan.
Some elements of the religious teaching of Jesus according to the synoptic gospels; being the Jowett Lectures for 1910. '10(Jl16) 12°, 75 c. net. Macmillan.
—, ed. *See* Bible. N. T. Gospels.

Montenegro, Carlota Maria.
Alcestis: drama. '09(N6) c. D. $1.25. Badger.
Two travelers: book of fables. '09(F20) c. D. $1.25. Badger.

Montes the matador. Harris, F. $1 net. M. Kennerley.

Monteser, F.
See Kayser, C. F.

MONTESPAN, *Marquise* de, (Françoise Athénaïs de Rochechouart.)
Williams, H. N. Madame de Montespan and Louis XIV. $2. Scribner.

Montesquieu, Charles Louis de Secondat, Baron de Montesquieu et de la Brède.
Spirit of laws; including d'Alembert's analysis of the work; tr. fr. the French by T: Nugent; with introd. by Frederic R. Coudert. '08(Je27) c. 2 v., il. 8°, $3.50; hf. mor., $7. Lamb Pub.

Monteverde, R. D.
Commercial and technical terms in the English and Spanish languages; together with weights and measures. '09(F6) 12°, *70 c. net. Macmillan.
Spanish idioms with their English equivalents. '09(F6) 12°, 80 c. Macmillan.

MONTEZ, Lola.
See Gilbert, Marie Dolores Eliza Rosanna.

Montezuma and the conquest of Mexico. Eggleston, E: †$1.25. Dodd.

Montgomery, C: Alex.
Discoveries which "prove," authoritatively, ye "secret parentage of ye works of "Shake-speare." I, Ye prefatorie verse in ye first folio, 1623; II, Ye verse to ye memorie of W. Shaxpere; III, Le "Latine" inscription on ye monument, 1616-1623; IV, Ye English inscription on ye monument, 1616-1623; V, Ye "epitaph" on ye tombstone, 1616. '09(Jl10) il. F. in portfolio, $1. C: A. Montgomery.
Shake-speare's anagrams: epitaphic, no. 1; att laste!—1616-1909, ye "Shake-speare epitaph" deciphered. '10(Je25) c. obl. Tt. pap., 25 c., in envelope. C: A. Montgomery.

Montgomery, D: H:
Leading facts of American hist. Rev. ed. '10(F19) c. il. maps, tabs., D. (Leading facts of hist. ser.) $1. Ginn.

Montgomery, Mrs. Frances Trego.
Billy Whiskers' grandchildren. '09(N13) c. il. O. bds., $1. Saalfield.
Billy Whiskers kidnapped. '10(D3) c. il. O. bds., $1. Saalfield.
Billy Whiskers' vacation. '08(N14) c. il. O. bds., $1. Saalfield.
Cats and kitts. '08(N21) c. il. O. 50 c. Brewer, B.

Montgomery, G: Redington.
The unexplored self; introd. to Christian doctrine. '10(O1) c. D. $1.25. Putnam.

Montgomery, Harry Earl.
Vital American problems: attempt to solve the "trust," "labor," and "negro" problems. '08(S12) c. D. (Questions of the day.) **$1.50 net. Putnam.

Montgomery, Helen Barrett.
Empire of the East: simple account of Japan as it was, is, and will be. '09 (Ap10) il. O. *$2.50 net. McClurg.
Western women in eastern lands; outline study of fifty years of woman's work in foreign missions. '10(My7) c. il. pors. fold. tab., D. (United study of missions ser.) $1.50 net. Macmillan.

Montgomery, Bp. H: Hutchinson.
Service abroad; lectures del. in the Divinity School of the University of Cambridge. '10(Je11) S. 90 c. net. Longmans.

Montgomery, J. H.
Specifications for electrical construction. '09(Je5) c. 12°, $1. Wahr.

Montgomery, K. L.
The cardinal's pawn; how Florence set, how Venice checked, and how the game fell out. '10(Mr12) front. D. 75 c. McClurg.

Montgomery, Lucy Maud.
Anne of Avonlea. '09(S4) c. D. $1.50. L. C. Page.
Anne of Green Gables. '08(Je20) c. D. †$1.50. L. C. Page.
Kilmeny of the orchard. '10(My14) c. col. il. D. $1.25. L. C. Page.

Montgomery, Rob. Hiester.
Auditing. 3 v. '09(D25) c. 8°, (American School of Correspondence pubs.) ea., 50 c. Am. Sch. Corr.

Montgomery, Winfield S.
Historical sketch of education for the colored race in the District of Columbia, 1807-1905. '08(My9) 8°, pap., 25 c. Smith Bros.

MONTGOMERY COUNTY, Md.
See Cabin John Bridge.

Month of solitaires. Preble, H: *50 c. net. Brentano's.

Monthly sonata. Evans, M. A. B. $1.25. Putnam.

Months (The). Blake, J. V. *75 c. net. J. H. West.

MONTIGNOSO, *Countess.*
See Anna Monica Pia, *Duchess of Saxony.*

Montolieu, J. I. P. de B., Baronne de.
See Wyss, Johann Rudolf.

MONTREUX, Switzerland.
Gribble, F. Montreux. *$2.50 net. Macmillan.

MONUMENTS.
Breasted, J. H. Monuments of Sudanese Nubia. *50 c. net. Univ. of Chic.
Capart, J. Une rue de tombeaux à Saggarah. [Egypt.] In 2 v. $15. Stechert
Carus, P., *ed.* Nestorian monument: ancient record of Christianity in China. 40 c. Open Court.
Frothingham, A. L. Monuments of Christian Rome. **$2.25 net. Macmillan.

Monypenny, W: Flavelle.
Life of Benjamin Disraeli, Earl of Beaconsfield. [In 4 v.] v. 1, 1804-1837; with portraits and illustrations. '10(N19) c. O. $3 net. Macmillan.

Mood, Ja. Raider.
Some figurative usages of *venire* and *ire.* '08(S5) 8°, pap., gratis. Johns Hopkins.

Moody, A. Penderel, and Tompkins, A. E.
Devon pillow lace: its history and how to make it. '08, [1909.] (S) 160 p. il. 8°, *$1.50 net. Cassell.

Moody, C: Stuart, M.D.
Backwoods surgery and medicine. '10(Ag6) c. D. 75 c. net. Outing.

Moody, Dwight Lyman.
Fulness of the gospel. '08(Je27) c. 12°, *50 c. net. Revell.

Moody, J:
Analysis of railroad investments. 1st annual number, 1909. '09(F20) c. tabs., Q. *$12 net. Analyses.
Investors' primer. '08(Ja11) D. (Investors' lib.) *$1.50 net. Moody Corporation.

Moody, Julia.
See Marks, Jeannette Augustus.

Moody, Paul Dwight.
First Easter sermon; address. '10(Ap2) c. S. bds., 30 c. Northfield Press.

Moody, Rob. Neill.
Eunice Loyd; or, the struggle and triumph of an honest heart. '10(F19) c. 12°, $1.50. F: L: Rowe.

Moody, W: Vaughn.
The faith healer; play in three acts. '10 (Mr12) c. D. *$1.25 net. Macmillan.
Formerly published by Houghton Mifflin Co.
Great Divide: a play. '09(O16) c. D. **$1.25 net. Macmillan.

—, Lovett, Rob. Morss, and Boynton, Percy H.
First view of English and American literature. '09, [1910.] c. 11+488 p. il. pors. 12°, $1.25 net. Scribner.

Moody's investors' lib. D. *$1.50 net. Moody Corporation.
—Moody. Investors' primer.
—Nicholas. Mining investments.

Moody's manual of railroads and corporation securities. 9th annual number, 1908. '08 (S19) c. 8°, $10; leath., $12. Moody Corporation.

Moomaw, B. C.
Tank line unlimited; being an acct. of the wonderful travels of Dr. Seethings. '10(Mr26) c. 12°, 75 c. Editor Co.

Moon, Edg. Lafayette.
Contents of the boy. '09, [1910.] (Mr) c. 303 p. 12°, $1. Jennings.

Moon, Ja. H.
Why Friends (Quakers) do not baptize with water. '09(D) c. 70 p. 12°, 25 c. J. H. Moon.

Moon, Rob. C., M.D.
Morris family of Philadelphia. Supplement. v. 4, 5. '08, [1910.] (F) 196; 197-483 p. il. 8°, $20. R. C. Moon.
For former volumes *see* American Catalog, 1895-1900.

Moon, Rob. Oswald.
Relation of medicine to philosophy. '09 (N20) D. *$1.50 net. Longmans.

MOON.
Brown, E. W: Inequalities in the motion of the moon. *$2 net. Putnam.
Fauth, P. Moon in modern astronomy. *$2 net. Van Nostrand.

Moon madness. Gouraud, A. C. $1. B'way Pub.

Mooney, H: J:
How to train your own dogs; arranged by E: Fraser Carson. '09(Jl3) c. il. 16°, 50 c. Saalfield.

Moonlight banquet. Puterbaugh, L. P. $1. L. P. Puterbaugh.

Moons of Balbanca. Davis, M. E. M. †$1. Houghton M.

Moonstone. Collins, W. 50 c. Hurst.

Moore, Addison.
Heir of the ages and his inheritances; series of lectures del. to the Young Men's Bible Class of the Fifth Ave. Baptist Church, New York. '10(Jl30) c. 12°, 75 c. Doran.

Moore, Addison Webster.
Pragmatism and its critics. '10(D3) c. D. $1.25 net. Univ. of Chic.

Moore, Anne.
Physiology of man and other animals. '09 (D18) c. il. D. 80 c. Holt.

Moore, Arth. Russell.
Biochemical conception of dominance. '10 (O) 9-15 p. O. (Univ. of Cal. pubs.: Physiology.) pap. Univ. of Cal.

Moore, Blaine F.
History of cumulative voting and minority representation in Illinois, 1870-1908; with a preface by Ja. Wilford Garner. '09 (Jl17) c. O. (Univ. of Ill. bull.; University studies.) pap., 50 c. Univ. of Ill.

Moore, C: Chilton.
Tamám. '08(O24) c. D. $1.50. Neale.

Moore, C: Church.
Treatise on facts or the weight and value of evidence. v. 1, 2. '08(O) c. O. $12. E: Thompson.

Moore, C: Forrest.
Hist. of the states, united and otherwise. '10(Ja15) c. D. *$1.50 net. Neale
See also Breckenridge, W: Edn.

Moore, Clarence Bloomfield.
Antiquities of the Ouachita Valley; by Clarence B. Moore; rept. on an additional collection of skeletal remains, from Arkansas and Louisiana (made and presented to the National Museum, in 1909, by Clarence B. Moore), by Dr. Ales Hrdlicka. '09, [1910.] (Ap) 7-252 p. il. maps, f°, $3.75. C. B. Moore.

Moore, Clement Clarke.
Night before Christmas [by C. C. Moore], and Cinderella; or, the little glass slipper. '10(D17) c. D. (Turnover books.) 60 c. Reilly & B.

Moore, Dewitt Clinton.
Treatise on fraudulent conveyances and creditors' remedies at law and in equity. '08(Jl) 2 v., 267+515; 26+516-1302 p. O. $12. M. Bender.
See also United States. Law of interestate commerce.

Moore, Dorothea.
Sydney Lisle; the heiress of St. Quentin. '10(Je4) front. D. (Girls' own lib.) 75 c. McKay.

Moore, Edith Mary.
Lure of Eve. '09(O30) front. D. $1.50. **Cassell.**

Moore, E: Crozier Sibbald.
Sanitary engineering. 3d ed., rev. and in part rewritten by E. J. Silcock. In 2 v. '09(Je5) il. tabs., figs. O. *$14 net. Lippincott.

Moore, Eliakim Hastings, Wilczynski, Ernest Julius, and Mason, Max.
New Haven mathematical colloquium; lectures del. before members of the American Mathematical Society in connection with the summer meeting, held Sept. 5th to 8th, 1906, under the auspices of Yale University. '10(Mr26) Q. *$3 net. Yale Univ.

Moore, F. J.
Outlines of organic chemistry; book designed especially for the general student. '10(Je4) c. 12°, $1.50 net. Wiley.

Moore, Fs. Marion.
"Ghosts or devils," I'm done; the startling adventure of two officers of the 62nd Ohio Infantry on Polly Island, S. C., during General Gilmore's siege of Fort Sumpter in the war of the rebellion. '09 (Jl31) c. O. pap., $1. F. M. Moore.

Moore, Fk. Frankfort.
Georgian pageant: [stories of Goldsmith, Boswell, etc.] '09(My8) 8°, $3.50. Dutton.

Moore, F:
Passing of Morocco. '08(My16) D. **$1.50 net. Houghton M.

Moore, G: Foot, D.D., ed.
See Harper, Rob. Fs.

Moore, H. Fk.
Commercial sponges and the sponge fisheries. '10(Je) 399-511 p. il. 8°. U. S., Supt. of Docs.
Bibliography (1 p.).
Pract. method of sponge culture. '10(Je) 545-585 p. il. 8°. U. S., Supt. of Docs.

Moore, Irving.
See Robinson, L. E.

Moore, Ja. Hall.
Defence of the Mecklenburg declaration of independence. '08(Jl4) c. 8°. *$1.50 net. Stone & B.

Moore, Ja. Vernon.
Truth about tuberculosis and its only cure: plain book for plain people by one of them. [1910.] (O) c. 64 p. 12°, 25 c. J. V. Moore.

Moore, J: Bassett, ed.
See Buchanan, Ja.

Moore, J: Howard.
New ethics. Rev. ed. '09(Je5) c. D. *$1 net. S: A. Bloch.
Universal kinship. '08, [1909.] (D) 10+329 p. il. 12°, $1. Kerr.

Moore, J: Monroe, D.D.
Etchings of the East. '09(Ag7) c. il. D. *$1 net. Pub. Ho. M. E. Ch., So.

Moore, J: Trotwood.
Old cotton-gin: [poem.] '10(My21) c. il. 8°, $1. Winston.
Ole Mistis, and other songs and stories of Tennessee. '09(Je) c. 7+358 p. por. 12°, 75 c. Winston.
Uncle Wash, his stories. '10(Je4) c. il. D. $1.50. Winston.

Moore, Jos. Hampton.
Our national beginnings; address at Independence Hall, Phila., Monday, July 5, 1909. '09, [1910.] (F) 7 p. 8°, pap. (Add. author for price.) J. H. Moore.
With Speaker Cannon through the Tropics: voyage to West Indies, Venezuela and Panama. '08(F) c. il. 8°, $2. Book Pr.

Moore, Lewis Eug.
See Goodenough, G: Alfr.

Moore, Mabel.
Days in Hellas; rambles through present-day Greece. '09, [1910] (Ja) c. il. 12°, **$2 net. Jacobs.

Moore, Mrs. N. Hudson.
Delftware Dutch and English. '08(O3) c. il. O. (Collector's handbooks.) **$1 net. Stokes.
Wedgwood and his imitators. '09(O2) c. O. (Collectors' hdbks.) **$1 net. Stokes.

Moore, Norman, M.D.
History of the study of medicine in the British Isles: Fitz-Patrick lectures for 1905-6, del. before the Royal College of Physicians of London. '08(My23) facsims., O. $3.40. Oxford Univ.

Moore, R: Bishop.
See Schlundt, Herman.

Moore, Rob. Webber.
Weimar, the Athens of Germany. '08(F1) il. pors. O. pap., *75 c. net. Stechert.

Moore, Roy Lewis.
Hist. of Woodford County. '10(Ap) c. 8+9-248 p. il. pors. 8°, $1. R. L. Moore.

Moore, Sarah Wool.
Libro illustrato di lingua inglese; illustrated English-Italian language book and reader. Rev. ed. '08, [1909.] (F) c. 31+150 p. il. 16°, 35 c. Heath.

Moore, Stanley Holmes.
Mechanical engineering and machine shop practice. '08(Ag1) il. 8°, *$4 net. Hill Pub.

Moore, T:
Irish melodies and songs. '08(Je6) 16°, (Muses' lib.) 50 c.; leath., 75 c. Dutton.

MOORE, Thomas.
Clark, J: C. L. Tom Moore in Bermuda. *$2 net. Smith & McCance.

Moore, T: Emmett.
Haunted king. '10(N19) il. 12°, $1.50. C. M. Clark.

Moore, T: Verner, D.D.
Honoring God with our substance. '08 (Je20) T. pap., *5 c. net. Presb. Bd.
Process of abstraction; experimental study. '10(D) 73-197 p. figs. Q. (Univ. of Cal. pubs.; Psychology.) pap., $1. Univ. of Cal.

Moore, Veranus Alva.
Pathology and differential diagnosis of infectious diseases of animals; with an introd. by Dan. Elmer Salmon. 3d ed., rev. and enl. '08(Je6) c. 8°, *$4 net. Taylor & C.

Moore, Wa. W:, D.D.
The indispensable book. '10(D10) c. 12°, 75 c. net. Revell.
Preparation of the modern minister. '09 (Mr) c. 28 p. 12°, (Claims and opportunities of the Christian ministry.) 10c.; per 100, $8. Y. M. C. A.

Moore, Will H.
"If I had known" about Gary in 1909. '09 (Jl) c. 118 p. il. pors. fold. map, 4°, $1. P. E. Moore.

Moore, Rev. W: T:
Comprehensive hist. of the Disciples of Christ. '09(D) c. 830 p. 8°, *$3.50 net; hf. mor., *$4.50 net; mor., *$6 net. Revell.
Supremacy of the heart life: plea for the regnancy of love. '08(O10) c. 12°, *$1.25 net. Revell.

Moore, W: Underhill.
See Smith, Howard L.

Moore, W: V.
Legal secretary; series of articles on commercial law; prepared especially for business men and students of business practice. '09(Je) c. 312 p. O. $3. Boger.

Moore, W: Walker.
Christianity in the light of reason and revelation. '09(Jl3) c. D. $1.50. W: W. Moore.

Moore, Willis Luther.
Descriptive meteorology. '10(Ap16) c. il. O. $3 net. Appleton.

Moore-Smith, G: C.
Hymenaeus: comedy acted at St. John's College, Cambridge, now first printed, with an introd. and notes. '09(Mr) 16+84 p. 16°, *$1.10 net. Putnam.

Moore-Willson, Mrs. Minnie.
See Willson, *Mrs.* Minnie Moore-.

Moorehead, Warren King.
See Peabody, C:
—, comp. Prehistoric relics: catalogue describing some 850 specimens. '08(Mr) 12°, pap., $1. Andover.

Moorehead, W: Gallogly, D.D.
Outline studies in the New Testament; Catholic epistles: James I. and II., Peter I., II., III., John, and Jude. '10(Ap9) c. D. 75 c. net. Un. Presb. Bd.
Studies in the Book of Revelation. '08 (Ap18) c. D. *75 c. net. Un. Presb. Bd.

Moores, C: Washington.
Life of Abraham Lincoln, for boys and girls. '09(F13) c. il. pors. D. **60 c. net; *Same* in (Riverside literature ser.) **25 c. net; pap., **15 c. net. Houghton M.

Moorhouse, E. Hallam.
Nelson's Lady Hamilton. '08(Ag15) il. pors. O. *$3 net. Brentano's.
Samuel Pepys, administrator, observer, gossip. '09(My22) il. 8°, $3. Dutton.

Moorland, Jesse E.
Demand and the supply of increased efficiency in the negro ministry. '09, [1910.] (Ja) 14 p. O. (American Negro Academy, Occasional papers.) pap., 15 c. D. 75 c. net. Un. Presb. Bd.

Moorman, Frederic W:
Robert Herrick; biographical and critical study. '10(Ap30) il. O. $5 net. Lane.

Moors, H. J.
With Stevenson in Samoa. '10(S17) c. il. D. $1.50 net. Small.

Mopsa, the fairy. Ingelow, J. $1.50. Lippincott.

MOQUELUMNAN INDIANS.
See Indians.

MOQUI INDIANS.
See Indians.

Moral conditions in intellectual attainment. Buckham, M. H: gratis. M. H: Buckham.

Moral damage of war. Walsh, W. *90 c. net. Ginn.

Moral (Die) des hotels. Vehling, P. $1. Didion.

Moral discourses. *See* Epictetus.

MORAL EDUCATION.
See Ethics;—Religious education.

Moral instruction and training in schools. Sadler, M. E. 2 v. ea., **$1.50 net. Longmans.

Moral life. Davies, A. E. *$2 net. Psychological Review.

MORAL PHILOSOPHY.
See Ethics.

Moral principles in education. Dewey, J: **35 c. net. Houghton M.

Moral system of Dante's Inferno. Reade, W: H: V. $4.15. Oxford Univ.
Moral theology for English speaking countries. Slater, T: *$2.75 net. Benziger.
Moral training in public schools. Leonard, M. H. 25 c. Palmer Co.
Moral training in the public schools. Brownlee, J. 10 c. Holden Pat. Bk.
MORALITY.
See Ethics.
Morality of modern socialism. Ming, J: J. **$1.50 net. Benziger.
Morality of social pleasures. Fowler, M. $1.25 net. Longmans.
MORALITY PLAYS.
See Plays.
MORALS.
See Ethics.
Morals and dogma. *See* Pike, Albert.

Morals in modern business; address del. in the Page lecture series, 1908, before the senior class of the Sheffield Scientific School, Yale University. '09(My8) c. D. (Page lecture ser.) *$1.25 net. Yale Univ.

Moran, Mary L.
Manual art with the scissors. '08(Ja11) il. obl. D. bds., 75 c. M. Bradley.

Moran, Pearl Van Antwerp.
In a monk's cassock. '10(D17) c. por. 12°, $1. Conkey.

Moran, T: Fs.
Theory and practice of the English government. New ed. '08(Ag22) c. D. **$1.20 net. Longmans.
See also Woodburn, Ja. Alb.

Moras, Edmond Raymond.
Autology (study thyself) and autopathy (cure thyself). [6th ed.] '10(Ag) 250 p. il. por. 12°, $2. E. R. Moras.

MORAVIAN CHURCH.
Brief hist. of the Moravian church; prep. by teachers and friends of the Salem Home Sunday School, Winston-Salem, N. C., Jan., 1909. '09(My) 146+23 p. 8°, *75 c. net; pap., *35 c. net. F. H. Bahnson.

MORAVIAN CHURCH, New Dorp, S. I.
See New York City.

Morawetz, Victor.
Banking and currency problem in the United States. '09(F6) c. D. *$1 net. North American.

Moray, J:
Brief acct. of last century's inventive steam pirate; [James Rumsey.] '10(Je4) c. 8°, 10 c. J: Moray.

Morbules (The). Page, J. $1. Ferris.

Mord, W.
Babes in the wood, and the three bears. '09(S) col. il. Q. bds., 35 c. Stokes.
Captives of Israel. '09(S) col. il. Q. bds., 35 c. Stokes.
Children of Israel: sixteen Bible stories. '09(S) Q. bds., $1.50. Stokes.
Chosen people. '09(S) col. il. Q. bds., $1. Stokes.
Friends from the Book of books: twelve Bible stories. '08(S5) Q. bds., $1.50. Stokes.
Kings of Israel. '09(S) col. il. Q. bds., 35 c. Stokes.

Mord, W.—*Continued.*
Old tales retold; Red Riding Hood, The three bears, Aladdin, The babes in the woods. '09(S) col. il. Q. bds., $1. Stokes.
Red Riding Hood and Aladdin. '09(S) col. il. Q. bds., 35 c. Stokes.
Return to Jerusalem. '09(S) col. il. Q. bds., $1. Stokes.
Shepherds of Israel. '09(S) col. il. Q. bds., 35 c. Stokes.
Wanderings of Israel. '09(S) col. il. Q. bds., 35 c. Stokes.
See also Campbell, A. M.

—, and Robinson, C:
Four champions of Great Britain and Ireland. '09(S) col. il. Q. bds., $1.50. Stokes.
St. Andrew of bonny Scotland. '09(S) col. il. Q. bds., 35 c. Stokes.
St. David of gallant Wales. '09(S) col. il. Q. bds., 35 c. Stokes.
St. George of merry England. '09(S) col. il. Q. bds., 35 c. Stokes.
St. Patrick of the Emerald Isle. '09(S) col. il. Q. bds., 35 c. Stokes.
Stories of St. Andrew and St. Patrick. '09 (S) col. il. Q. bds., $1. Stokes.
Stories of St. George and St. David. '09 (S) col. il. Q. bds., $1. Stokes.

Mordecai, Marg.
Flower of destiny; old days of the Serail. '10(Je4) c. D. $1.50 net. Putnam.

Mordecai, S: Fox.
Domestic relations; condensed summary of the more important principles of common law governing the topics of husband and wife, parent and child, infancy and coverture. '08(D) 39 p. 8°. (Add. author for price.) S: F. Mordecai.
Law lectures: treatise from a North Carolina standpoint on those portions of the 1st and 2d books of the commentaries of Sir W: Blackstone which have not become obsolete in the U. S. '08(Ja11) O. shp., $10. Edwards.
See also North Carolina. Notes on code of civil procedure.

—, and McIntosh, Atwell C.
Remedies by selected cases, annot. '10(N) c. O. $6. State Journ. Co.

Morden, Gilbert Walworth.
Determination of thallium in the electrolytic way. '08, [1910.] (Ap) 14 p. il. 8°. (Add. pubs. for price.) Univ. of Penn.

Morden Training School. Complete course of instructions in real estate business. '10 (My14) c. 10 v., 8°, $15. R. O. Morden.

More, Gertrude.
Holy practises of a divine lover; or, the saintly Ideot's devotions; ed., with introd., by Dom H. Lane Fox. '09(Jl) 20+216 p. 12°, *75 c. net. Herder.

More, Paul Elmer.
Shelburne essays. 5th ser. '08(My2); 6th ser. '09(Mr20); 7th ser. '10(D3) c. D. ea., **$1.25 net. Putnam.

More, Sir T:
More's Millenium: being the Utopia of Sir T: More rendered into modern English by Valerian Paget. '08(N21) c. D. $1.50. J: McBride.
Utopia and the Dialogue of comfort against tribulations; with introd. by J: O'Hagan. '10(D10) c. 16°, (Everyman's lib.) 35 c. net; leath., 70 c. net. Dutton.
Utopia; Ralph Robinson's tr.; with Roper's life of More and some of his letters; ed. by G: Sampson; with an introd. and bibliography by A. Guthkelch, to which is added the Latin text of the Utopia reprinted from the first edition. '10(N19) por. 12°, $1.75 net. Macmillan.
Utopia; tr. by Ralph Robinson; with introd. and notes by H. B. Cotterill. '08(Ap4) 16°, *50 c. net. Macmillan.

MORE, *Sir* Thomas.
Manning, A. Household of Sir Thomas More. *$1 net. Dutton.

More: a study of financial conditions. Draper, G: O. **$1 net. Little, B. & Co.

More charades. Bellamy, W: **$1 net. Houghton M

More modern monologues. Cooke, M. B. $1.25. Dramatic.

More recent cyanide practice. Bain, H. F., *ed.* $2. Mining and Scientific.

More stories from Shakespeare. Lang, J. 50 c. net. Dutton.

More tricks and illusions. Goldston, W. 50 c. Dutton.

Moreau, Hégésippe.
Contes à ma sœur; la souris blanche et les petits souliers; ed. by L. Lailavoix. '09 (O16) S. (Crowell's shorter French texts.) *25 c. net. Crowell.

Morehead, Jos. M.
Battle of Guilford Court House, North Carolina, and the preservation of that historic field. [1910.] (Ap) 8 p. 8°, gratis. J. M. Morehead.

Morehouse, G: Pierson.
Kansa, or Kaw Indians, and their history, and the story of Padilla. '09(Jl) 52 p. il. por. 8°. (Add. pubs. for price.) G: Martin.

Moreland, G: Matthew.
Idle songs of an idle soldier. '09(D) c. 7-50 p. 12°, 50 c. G: M. Moreland.

Moreland, Sinclair.
Noblest Roman: story of political debauchery and prostituted allegiance. [1910.] (O) c. 384 p. il. por. 12°, $1.50. Noblest Roman.

Moretto da Brescia, Alessandro Bonvincino.
Masterpieces; 60 reproductions of photographs from the original paintings, affording examples of the different characteristics of the artist's work. '10(N5) T. (Painters' ser.) pap., 25 c.; leath., 75 c. Stokes.

Morgan, Albert Talmon.
On our way to the Orient; or, Mr. Bryan, don't you know. '09(My) c. 5-82 p. 12°, 25 c. Denver Int. Corr. Sch.
Passing of gold; or, what is lawful money. '08(N7) c. por. D. $1. J: A. Anderson.

Morgan, Alb. Talmon, and Ridpath, J: Clark.
Bank of the beast; cont. The bond and the dollar, by J: Clark Ridpath, and The bank of the beast, by Col. Alb. Talmon Morgan. [1910.] (D) c. 80 p. O. pap., 25 c. Ware & Co.

Morgan, Alfr. Powell.
How to build a 20 ft. bi-plane glider. '10 (Je4) il. 12°, price changed from 25 c. to 50 c. Spon.
Wireless telegraph construction for amateurs. '10(N5) c. il. 12°, $1.50. Van Nostrand.
See also Laughter, Victor Hugo.

Morgan, Anna.
Art of speech and deportment. '09(Je12) c. D. *$1.50 net. McClurg.
—, comp. Selected readings. '09(Je12) c. D. *$1.50 net. McClurg.

—, and Bailey, Mrs. Alice Ward, [Mrs. A. G. Bailey, "A. B. Ward."]
Great experiment: Shakespeare fantasy. '09(D) pap., 50 c. (300 copies.) Seymour.

Morgan, Arth. E.
Preliminary rept. on the St. Francis Valley drainage project in northeastern Arkansas. '09, [1910.] (Mr) 31 p. fold. maps, fold. plan. 8°, (U. S., Dept. of Agriculture, Office of Experiment Stations, circular.) pap.

Morgan, C: Carroll.
Lawyer's brief on the atonement. '10 (My) c. 14+136 p. 12°, 75 c. C: C. Morgan.

Morgan, C: Herbert, Taylor, T: Eddy and S. Earl.
Studies in the early church; introd. by Marcus D. Buell. [Rev. ed.] '08(Ja4) maps, O. 75 c. Jennings.

Morgan, Conroy Lloyd.
Animal behaviour. 2d ed. '08(My23) il. D. $2.50. Longmans.

Morgan, Erlaine, [pseud. for Mrs. Teda Morgan Earle.]
Jack Frost jingles. '10(D3) il. 75 c. C. M. Clark.

Morgan, F. P.
See Kebler, Lyman Frederic.

Morgan, G: Campbell, D.D.
Analyzed Bible. v. 2, The Old Testament, Job to Malachi. '08(Mr21); v. 3, The New Testament introduction, Matthew to Revelation (Ap18); v. 4, The Gospel according to John. '09(Ap3); v. 5, The book of Job (Je19); v. 6, Romans (O23); v. 7, The prophecy of Isaiah, v. 1; v. 8, The prophecy of Isaiah, v. 2. '10(Ag20) c. 12°, ea., *$1 net. Revell.
Bible and the cross. '10(F12) c. 16°, *50 c. net. Revell.
Christian principles. '08(Ap11) c. 12°, *50 c. net. Revell.
Missionary manifesto. '09(O2) c. 12°, *75 c. net. Revell.
Mountains and valleys in the ministry of Jesus. '09(F13) c. 16°, *25 c. net. Revell.
Study and teaching of the English Bible. '10(S17) c. 16°, 50 c. net. Revell.
Teaching of the lesson; commentary on the International Sunday School Lessons for the year 1910. '09(D4); 1911. '10(D) c. T. leath., ea., 25 c. Doran.

Morgan, Ike.
See Boylan, *Mrs.* Grace Duffie.

Morgan, J. Ja.
Blast furnace practice. '10(F19) 12°, *75 c. net. Lippincott.

Morgan, Jacque Lloyd, ["John Lloyd."]
Captain's wife. '08(My9) c. 12°, $1.50. M. Kennerley.
The invaders; story of the "Hole-in-the-Wall" country. '10(N12) c. il. D. $1.50. Fenno.

Morgan, Ja.
Abraham Lincoln, the boy and the man. '08(O17) c. il. pors. D. **$1.50 net. Macmillan.

Morgan, J: Livingston Rutgers.
Elements of physical chemistry. 4th ed., rev. and enl. '08(N14) c. figs. 12°, $3. Wiley.
Physical chemistry for electrical engineers. 2d ed., rev. '09(D11) c. il. 12°, $1.50. Wiley.

Morgan, J: Pierpont.
Cylinders and other ancient oriental seals in the library of J: Pierpont Morgan; catalogued by W: Hayes Ward. '09 (Je5) il. f°. (Priv. pr.) J: P. Morgan.

MORGAN. John Pierpont.
Bonum Meritum, *pseud.* War of words between President Roosevelt and J: Pierpont Morgan concerning railroad, tariff and trust questions. $1; 25 c. Donohue.

Morgan, K. K.
Gleanings gathered from many sources. [1910.] (Ap) 80 c. Book & Art.

Morgan, Mrs. Mary Ella Hughes.
How to dress a doll. '08(Ag15) c. il. diagrs., S. bds., 50 c. Altemus.

Morgan, Morris Hicky.
Addresses and essays. '10(Mr26) c. D. $1.50. Am. Bk.
Bibliography of Persius, by Morris H. Morgan; incl. the catalogue of a collection made by him and by Dan. B. Fearing. '09, [1910.] 5+90 p. facsims. 8°, (Bibliographical contributions of the Library of Harvard University.) 75 c. Harvard Univ.

Morgan, W: Sacheus.
Nuggets of gold: [sermons.] '09, [1910.] (Je) 3-56 p. 16°, 50 c. W: S. Morgan.

MORGAN COUNTY, Mo.
Marbut, C. F. Geology of Morgan County. 20 c. Missouri Bu. Geol.

MORGAN HORSE.
See Horse.

Morhart, C: Christian.
Voice training for speakers; objective and subjective voice. '09(D) c. 193 p. 8°, $1.50. Am. Luth.

Moriarty, Bp. of Kerry.
Sermons. '07, [1908.] (Mr.) 502 p. 12°, *$2 net. Benziger.

Morin, Einar.
Jigs and fixtures. pts. 2-3. '09(O16) c. il. 8°, (Machinery's reference ser.) ea., pap., 25 c. Indust. Press.

Morison, J. H. S.
Rules of pleading as adapt. to cts. of law in Tennessee, together with numerous annot. forms. '08(F) c. '07. 19+554 p. O. shp., $5.50. F. H. Thomas.

Morituri. Sudermann, H. $1.25 net. Scribner.

MORLAND, George.
Gilbey, *Sir* W., *and* Cuming, E: W: D. George Morland. *$6 net. Macmillan.

Morley, Arth.
Strength of materials. '08(D5) il. O. *$2.50 net. Longmans.

Morley, C:
London at prayer. '10(F19) 8°, *$2.50 net. Dutton.

Morley, H:
First sketch of English literature. [New and rev. ed.] '09(O23) D. $2.50 net. Cassell.
Library of English literature. 5 v. New ed. [1910.] (Ap) ea., $2.50 net. Cassell.

Morley, J:
Critical miscellanies. '08(J14) D. **$1.50 net. Macmillan.
Indian speeches, (1907-1909.) '10(F12) O. *$1 net. Macmillan.
Life of Richard Cobden. In 2 v. '08(My9) 12°, (Eversley ser.) $3. Macmillan.

Morley, Marg. Warner.
Donkey John of the toy valley. '09(O9) c. il. D. $1.25. McClurg.

"Morley, Ralph," pseud.
See Hinton, Howard.

MORMONISM.
Bonsall, M. Tragedy of the Mormon woman. 35 c. Housekeeper Corp.
Evans, J: H: Birth of Mormonism in picture. 75 c.—One hundred years of Mormonism. $1.25. Deseret S. S. Un.
Freece, H. P. Letters of an apostate Mormon to his son. 50 c. H. P. Freece.
Gibbs, J. F. Lights and shadows of Mormonism. $1.25. Salt Lake Trib.
Meakin, J: P. Leaves of truth; Utah and the Mormons. $1.50. J: P. Meakin.
Peterson, E. Redemption. 25 c. E. Peterson.
Roberts, B. H: Defense of the faith and the saints. v. 1. $1.50. Deseret News.
Sanders, P: J. Key to succession in the presidency of the church. 80 c.; leath., $1.30. P: J. Saunders.
Smith, J. F. Origin of the "reorganized" church, and the question of succession. 50 c. Deseret News.
Talmage, J. E: Great apostasy. 60 c. Deseret News.
Talmage, J. E: Story of "Mormonism." 15 c. Bu. Information Salt Lake.
Traum, S: W. Mormonism against itself. $1. Standard Pub.
Ursenbach, O. F. Why I am a "Mormon." $1. O. F. Ursenbach.
See also Woodruff, Wilford.

MORNING GLORY.
See Bindweed.

Morning glory. Williams, *Mrs.* C. G. 75 c. net. Pub. Ho. M. E. Ch., So.

Morning star. Haggard, H: R. $1.50. Longmans.

MOROCCO, Africa.
Ashmead-Bartlett, E. Passing of the Shereefian Empire. $4 net. Dodd.
Finnemore, J. Morocco. *75 c. net. Macmillan.

MOROCCO, Africa.—*Continued.*
Moore, F: Passing of Morocco. **$1.50 net. Houghton M.
Rankin, J. R. L. In Morocco with General D'Amade. *$2.50 net. Longmans.
Sternberg, *Count.* Barbarians of Morocco. **$2 net. Duffield.
See also Hafid, Mulai.

Morphia habit and its voluntary renunciation. Jennings, O., *ed.* *$2 net. Wood.

Morphological variation and its causes in *Amblystoma tigrinum.* Powers, J. H. $1. Univ. of Neb.

MORPHOLOGY.
Davenport, C: B. Experimental morphology. *$3.50 net. Macmillan.
Keith, A. Human embryology and morphology. $3.50 net. Longmans.
See also Anatomy;—French language;—Histology.

Morphology of gymnosperms. Coulter, J: M. $4 net. Univ. of Chic.

Morphology of the Mexican verb. Denison, T: S. pap., 75 c. T: S. Denison.

Morris, Agnes.
Studies in the civil government of the state of Louisiana and the Constitution of the United States. '10(Mr5) c. 8°, 50 c. Natchitoches Times.

Morris, C:
Historical tales, the romance of reality. [Angelus ed.] 15 v. '08(N) c. il. pors. 8°, (Text-books of the Angelus Univ. course in the hist. of the world's greatest nation.) (Sold by subs. only.) Angelus Univ.
Home life in all lands; bk. 2, manners and customs of uncivilized peoples. '09(Jl31) c. il. D. **$1 net. Lippincott.
Industrial and commercial geography for use in schools. '10(D17) c. il. maps, 12°, $1.10 net. Lippincott.
King Arthur and the knights of the Round Table: a modernized version of the "Morte D'Arthur." '08(D5) c. il. D. (Thin paper ser. of popular classics.) limp leath., ea., $1.25. Lippincott.
Marvelous career of Theodore Roosevelt, incl. what he has done and stands for; his early life and public services; the story of his African trip; his memorable journey through Europe; and his enthusiastic welcome home. '10(D17) c. il. pors. map, 8°, $1.50. Winston.
Also published under title "Battling for the right."
School hist. of the United States of America. '09(O9) c. il. 12°, **90 c. net. Lippincott.

—, **ed.** Cyclopedia, dictionary and atlas of the world. '09(Je19) c. il. maps, 8°, $3.50; hf. mor., $4.50; mor., $5.50. Hampden Pub.
Story of the great earthquake of 1908, and other historic disasters. '09(Mr20) c. il. maps, pors. 8°, $1.50. Winston.

—, and others, eds.
Imperial reference lib. 6 v. '10(Ap9) il. pors. fold. maps, tabs., 4°, $55. Syndicate Pub.

Morris, Clara, [Mrs. Harriott.]
New "East Lynne." '08(Jl4) c. front. D. *$1 net. Doscher.

Morris, Clyde T.
Designing and detailing of simple steel structures. 2d ed. '10(O15) c. il. diagrs., 8°, (Ohio State Univ.: Civil engineering pubs.) $2.25. Hann.

Morris, Dan. H:
As the gods decree; novel. '10(D31) c. D. B'way Pub.

Morris, E. W.
Hist. of the London Hospital. '10(Ap2) il. pors. O. $1.75 net. Longmans.

Morris, Edn. Bateman.
Man next door: a comedy. '08(N7) c. D. pap., 15 c. Penn Pub. Co.

Morris, Gouverneur.
The footprint, and other stories. '08(Mr7) D. †$1.50. Scribner.
Putting on the screws. '09(N13) c. D. **50 c. net. Doubleday, P.
Spread eagle, and other stories. '10(O8) c. D. $1.20 net. Scribner.
Voice in the rice. '10(Ap2) c. il. D. $1.25. Dodd.

Morris, Hannah Perot.
Glimpses of the life of Samuel Morris: [modern apostle of Philadelphia Quakerism;] by his daughter. '07, [1908.] (Mr.) c. 206 p. il. por. D. 75 c. S: N. Rhoads.

Morris, Harrison Smith.
Lyrics and landscapes. '08(Ap18) c. D. **$1 net. Century Co.
Tales from Shakespeare. 2 v. in 1. '08 (D5) c. il. por. D. (Thin paper ser. of popular classics.) limp leath., $1.25. Lippincott.

Morris, H: C.
History of colonization, from the earliest times to the present day. In 2 v. '08 (Ap11) 12°, *$4 net. Macmillan.

Morris, Ja. Cheston.
Kosmos; poem from the proverbs of Solomon, son of David, who ruled in Israel; tr. from the Van Ess ed. of the Septuagint version, and compared with American revised version of Proverbs of Solomon I-IX. '09, [1910.] (Ag) 32 p. 8°, 50 c. MacCalla.

Morris, J:
Organic history of English words. pt. 1, Old English. '09(Mr6) O. pap., $1.25. Stechert.

Morris, M.
Reign of William and Mary. (Dog and cat story.) '10(D) 26 p. il. 8°, $1.50. Dutton.

Morris, Rev. M. C. F.
Nunburnholme [Yorkshire, Eng.]: its history and antiquities. '08(Ja18) il. map, O. $5. Oxford Univ.

Morris, Sir Malcolm.
Diseases of the skin. New and enl. ed. '09(Mr27) il. 12°, *$3.50 net. Wood.

—, and Dore, S. Ernest.
Light and X-ray treatment of skin diseases. '08(Mr28) il. 12°, (Modern methods of treatment ser.) *$1.50 net. Funk.

Morris, Martin Ferdinand.
Introduction to the history of the development of law. '09(Jl) c. 315 p. O. $2. Byrne.

Morris, Ray.
Railroad administration. '10(O15) c. tabs.. fold. charts, O. (Appleton's railway ser.) $2 net. Appleton.

Morris, Rob. Tuttle.
Dawn of the fourth era in surgery, and other short articles previously published. '10(S) 5-145 p. il. 12°, $1.25 net. Saunders.

MORRIS, Samuel.
Morris, H. P. Glimpses of the life of Samuel Morris. 75 c. S. N. Rhoads.

Morris, Seymour.
Hale family of Connecticut. '07, [1909.] (Mr) 12 p. 8°. (Priv. pr.) Clapp.

Morris, W:
Collected works; ed. by May Morris. In 24 v. v. 1, The defense of Guenevere, The Hollow Land, and other contributions to *The Oxford and Cambridge Magazine;* v. 2, The life and death of Jason; v. 3, The earthly Paradise, v. 1; v. 4, The earthly Paradise, v. 2. '10 (D31) il. 8°, $78. (Sold in sets only.) Longmans.
Poems by the way. New ed. '10(N19) S. (Longmans' pocket lib.) 75 c. net; leath., $1 net. Longmans.
Story of Sigurd the Volsung; written in verse by W: Morris with portions condensed into prose by Winifred Turner and Helen Scott. '10(Je11) D. (Longmans' class-books of English literature.) 50 c. Longmans.
See also Wyatt, Fk.

—, and Bax, Ernest Belfort.
Socialism: its growth and outcome. '09 (Ap3) S. 50 c. Kerr.

MORRIS, William.
Hubbard, E. This then is a William Morris book. $2. Roycrofters.
Mackail, J: W: William Morris; address del. in the town hall, Birmingham. 30 c. net. Longmans.
Noyes, A. William Morris. *75 c. net. Macmillan.

Morris, W: Alfr.
Frankpledge system. '10(O1) c. O. (Harvard historical studies.) $1.75. Longmans.

Morris, W: Lorenzo.
Steam power plant piping systems: their design, installation, and maintenance. '09 (Ag7) c. il. O. *$5 net. McGraw-H.

Morris and Morgan's Latin ser.; ed. by E: P. Morris and Morris H. Morgan. D. Am. Bk.
—Horace. Satires. $1.

MORRIS DANCE.
See Dancing.

MORRIS FAMILY.
See Genealogies: Moon, R. C.

MORRIS MANSION, New York City.
Smith, E. A. F. Hist. sketch of Washington's headquarters; prep. under the auspices of the Washington Headquarters Association. 25 c. E. A. F. Smith.

Morrison, Adelbert Harland.
See Ewart, Jos. Archibald.

Morrison, Alfr. Ja.
District [of Columbia] in the XVIIIth century; history, site-strategy, real estate market, landscape, etc., as described by the earliest travellers: Henry Wansey, Francis Baily, Isaac Weld, Duke of La Rochefoucauld-Liancourt, John Davis of Salisbury. '09(Mr) c. 53 p. 8°, 50 c. Lowdermilk.

Morrison, Arth.
Green ginger. '09(S4) c. O. †$1.50. Stokes.

Morrison, C: E:
Highway engineering. '08(O3) c. figs. 8°, $2.50. Wiley.

—, and Brodie, Orrin Lawrence.
High masonry dam design. '10(My21) c. il. 8°, $1.50. Wiley.

Morrison, Deborah.
Open door of the soul. '08, [1909.] (My) 132 p. 12°, $1. C. M. Clark.

Morrison, Egbert R:
Spring tables; hdbk. for engineers, students and draughtsmen. '08, [1909.] (F) 84 p. 8°, $2. Morrison & M.

Morrison, Rev. G. H.
Addresses from a Glasgow pulpit: The wings of the morning. '08(F1) O. *$1.50 net. Armstrong.
Return of the angels; Sunday evenings in a Glasgow pulpit. 2d ed. '10(Ag20) O. $1.35 net. Doran.
Sunday evening sermons. '10(D) 12°, $1.35 net. Doran.

Morrison, Gilbert Burnet.
Scope and content of the district high school. '09(F) 29 p. 8°, 25 c. G. B. Morrison.

Morrison, J: Fk.
Lectures on patrol, advance guards, and outposts. '10(Je) 46 p. il. 8°. (Not for sale.) Army Service.

—, and Munson, E: Lyman.
Study in troop leading and management of the sanitary service in war. '10(D) c. 245 p. fold. map, 12°, $1.25. J: F. Morrison.

Morrison, J: Harrison.
History of New York shipyards. '09(Jl31) 8°, $2. Sametz.

Morrison, Rob. Stewart, and De Soto, Emilio Dominguez.
Corporation manual. 2d ed., rev. and enl.; compilation of the statute laws of Colorado, as rev. in 1908. '10(Je) c. T. $3. Courtright.
Mining rights on the public domain. 14th ed., enl. and rev. to date. '10(Ag) c. D. buckram, $3.50. Courtright.
Mining rights on the public domain, lode and placer claims, tunnels, mill sites and water rights, statutes decisions, forms and land office procedure for prospectors, attorneys, surveyors and mining companies. 13th ed., rev. and enl. '08 (Je) c. 578 p. T. shp., $3. Smith-B.
See also Colorado code.

Morrison, Sarah Graham.
From lotos to cherry blossom. '10(F19) c. il. D. $1.50. Cochrane.

Morrison, W: Douglas.
Crime and its causes. [New and rev. ed.] '09(Mr13) D. (Social science ser.) $1. Scribner.

Morrow, Jackson.
Hist. of Howard County, Indiana. 2 v. [1910.] (My) il. pors. 4°, $18. B. F. Bowen.

Morrow, Rob. G.
See Oregon. *Sup. ct.* Repts.

Morrow, W: C.
Lentala of the south seas: the romantic tale of a lost colony. '08(Ag22) c. il. O. †$1.50. Stokes.

Mörsch, Emil.
Concrete-steel construction (Der eisenbetonbau); auth. tr. from the 3d (1908) German ed., rev. and enl., by E. P. Goodrich. '10(F5) c. il. tabs., 8°, $5 net. Engineering News.

Morse, Anson Ely.
Federalist party in Massachusetts to the year 1800. '09(O9) O. *$2 net. Princeton Univ.

Morse, C: H., and Vernon, Ambrose White, eds.
Songs for the chapel; arranged for male voices, for use in colleges, academies, schools, and societies; with an introd. by W: Jewett Tucker, D.D. '09(S4) c. O. **$1.50 net. Scribner.

Morse, Harmon Vail.
Osmotic pressure of cane sugar solutions at 10° '08, [1909.] (S) 41 p. 8°, pap., 40 c. Johns Hopkins.

Morse, Harriet Clara.
Cowboy cavalier. '08(Je20) c. D. $1.50. C. M. Clark.

Morse, Harry W.
See Ostwald, Wilhelm.

Morse, Herbert W:
See Kelley, A: Hill.

Morse, Hosea Ballou.
Gilds of China, with an account of the gild merchant or co-hong of Canton. '09 (Jl17) O. *$1.20 net. Longmans.
International relations of the Chinese Empire: the period of conflict, 1834-1860. '10(D31) il. maps, O. $6 net. Longmans.
Trade and administration of the Chinese Empire. '08(Ap25) il. maps, facsims., O. *$2.50 net. Longmans.

Morse, Howard Holdridge.
Historic old Rhinebeck, N. Y. '09(Ja23) c. il. pors. map, 12°, *$3 net. H. H. Morse.

Morse, Leighton B.
Selective reflection of salts of carbonic and other oxygen acids. '07, [1909.] (Jl) 225-243 p. 8°, (Phœnix Physical Laboratory contributions.) pap. (Add. pubs. for price.) Astrophysical.

Morse, Lewis Kennedy, comp.
Melodies of English verse; selections for memorizing. '10(D10) c. 12°, 80 c. net. Houghton M.

Morse, Marg. Fessenden.
On the road to Arden. '09(Ap3) c. il. D. **$1 net. Houghton M.
Scottie and his lady. '10(D10) c. il. D. $1.10 net. Houghton M.

Morse, Sidney Levi.
Household discoveries; encyclopedia of practical recipes and processes. '08, [1909.] (Ja) c. 21-536 p. il. tabs., 8°, subs., $1.90; $2.25. Success.
Same bound with Mrs. Curtis's cook book by Isabel Gordon Curtis. $2.70; oil cl., $2.90; im. leath., $3.25.

Morse, W: Fs.
Collection and disposal of municipal waste. '09(Mr27) il. tabs., $5. Municipal Journ.

Morshead, Edm. Doidge Anderson.
See Æschylus.

Mortality.
See Children;—Insurance;—Statistics.

Morte (Le) d'Arthur. *See* **Malory, *Sir* T:**

Mortensen, Arthon Christian.
Law of transformation in nature of natural bodies. '09(My8) c. O. pap., 50 c. A. C. Mortensen.

Mortensen, Theodor.
On some West Indian echinoids. '10(D) 5+31 p. il. f°, (Smithsonian Institution, U. S. National Museum, bull.) Gov. Pr. Off.

Mortgages.
Campbell, R. A. Mortgage taxation. 25 c. Wisconsin Free Lib.
Jones, L. A: Treatise on the law of mortgages on personal property. (Add. pubs. for price.) Bobbs-M.
Marsh, John P., & Co., Chicago. Real estate mortgage investments; discussion of real estate mortgage investments in Chicago; ed. by J: P. Marsh & Co. '09, [1910.] (F) c. 31 p. il. plan, 12°, $1. J: P. Marsh.
Sharp, R. W. Chattel mortgage loan business. 75 c. R. W. Sharp.

Mortimer, Alfr. Garnett, D.D.
In the light of the cross; addresses on the seven last words. '10(F26) 12°, *80 c. net. Whittaker.
Shadows of the valley. '10(D17) 12°, $1.50 net. Jacobs.

Mortimer, Fk. C.
Investment of trust funds. '09(S) 11-46 p. 12°, 75 c.; mor., $2. R. C. Ayres.

Mortimer, Ja. Howard.
Sprig of Plantagenet; or, the national debt of England. '09(Ap) c. 461 p. por. 12°, $1.50. Independent Pub.

Mortimer, Mrs. M., [Mrs. Favell Lee Mortimer.]
New peep of day: volume of religious instruction for little children; new and rev. issue of "The peep of day"; ed. by J: E. Hodder Williams; with a preface by the Bishop of Durham. '09(D) 216 p. il. (in color) S. bds., 50 c. Doran.

Mortimer, Mrs. Favell Lee.
See Mortimer, *Mrs.* M.

Morton, Cavendish.
Art of theatrical make-up. '09(D11) il. O. *$2.50 net. Macmillan.

Morton, E: Reginald, M.D.
Essentials of medical electricity and radiography. '10(Mr) 349 p. 12°, $1.75. Chic. Med. Bk.

Morton, Francis T.
Roman Catholic Church and its relation to the federal government. '09(N20) c. O. $2. Badger.

Morton, J. W.
How to run 100 yards. [1910.] (S) c. 44 p. il. por. 16°, (Spalding's athletic lib.) pap., 10 c. Am. Sports.

Morton, J: Watson.
Artillery of Nathan Bedford Forrest's cavalry, "the wizard of the saddle." '10 (F5) c. il. pors. 8°, $2.50. Pub. Ho. of M. E. Ch., So.

Morton, Julius Sterling.
White cow and other tales; being some anecdotes about Indian orators of the territorial period of Nebraska. '08, [1909.] (S) 20 p. il. 16°. (Priv. pr.) P. Morton.

Morton, Nelson Glazier.
Silver lining, and other poems. '09(D4) c. D. bds., $1. Badger.

Morton, Oren Frederic.
Hist. of Pendleton County, W. Va.; [incl. family-group histories.] '10(Je) c. 8+493 p. il. fold. map, 8°, $3.50. O. F. Morton.

Morton Eichman Co.
Town promotion and municipal advertising. '09(Jl) 29 p. 12°. (Add. pubs. for price.) Morton Eichman Co.

MORTON FAMILY.
See Genealogies: Allen, J: K.

Moryson, Fynes.
Itinerary of Fynes Moryson: his ten yeeres travell through the twelve dominions of Germany, Bohmerland, Sweitzerland, Netherland, Denmarke, Poland, Italy, Turky, France, England, Scotland and Ireland. In 4 v. vs. 3 and 4. '08(My2) 8°, ea., *$3.25 net. Macmillan.

Mosaics. Mixer, *Mrs.* M. E. K. $1.25. M. E. K. Mixer.

Mosby, Colonel J: Singleton.
Stuart's cavalry in the Gettysburg campaign. '08(Mr21) c. pors. map, O. **$2 net. Moffat.

MOSBY'S RANGERS.
Williamson, J. J. Mosby's Rangers: operations of the 43d battalion of Virginia cavalry. *$2.50 net. Sturgis & W.

Mosenthal, Salomon Hermann von.
Stories of Jewish home life; tr. from the German. '08(Ja4) D. $1.25. Jewish Pub.

Moser, Gustav von.
Der bibliothekar, schwank in vier akten; ed., with notes and vocab. by Hollon A. Farr. '08(O10) c. D. 40 c. Holt.
Ultimo, lustpiel in fünf akten; ed., with introd., notes and glossary, by C: Langley Crow. '08(N21) c. S. 35 c. Holt.

Moses, Alfr. Jos., and Parsons, C: Lathrop.
Elements of mineralogy, crystallography and blowpipe analysis from a pract. standpoint. 4th ed. '10(Ag) 448 p. il. 8°, $2.50 net Van Nostrand.

Moses, Belle.
Lewis Carroll in Wonderland and at home. '10(N12) c. por. D. $1.25 net. Appleton.
Louisa May Alcott, dreamer and worker. '09(O16) c. por. D. **$1.25 net. Appleton.

Moses, Bernard.
South America on the eve of emancipation: southern Spanish colonies in the last half-century of their dependence. '08(Je6) c. D. **$1.50 net. Putnam.

Moses, Mrs. Bernard.
See Moses, Edith Briggs.

Moses, Edith Briggs, [Mrs. Bernard Moses.]
Unofficial letters of an official's wife. '08 (O17) c. D. **$1.50 net Appleton.

MOSES, *Mrs.* Helen Elizabeth Turney.
Moses, J. T., *ed.* Helen E. Moses of the Christian Woman's Board of Missions. $1. Revell.

Moses, Jasper T., ed.
Helen E. Moses, of the Christian Woman's Board of Missions; biographical sketch, memorial tributes, missionary addresses by Mrs. Moses, sonnets and other verses. '09(N) c. 192 p. pors. 12°, $1. Revell.

Moses, Montrose Jonas.
Henrik Ibsen: the man and his plays. '08 (D12) c. cr. O. *$1.50 net. M. Kennerley.
The literature of the South. '10(O1) c. pors. O. $2.50 net. Crowell.
—, **ed.** *See* Everyman.
—, **tr.** *See* Passion play of Oberammergau.

Moses, Rob., and Thurston, Carl Hammond Philander, comps.
Yale verse. '09(Ap) 12+191 p. 12°, *$1.25 net. Yale Pub.

Moses, W: J: Barr.
Dreaming river. '09(Ja23) c. D. $1. Stokes.

Moses, Zebina.
Colonial war services of Colonel Ninian Beall, 1625-1717; Colonel George Beall, 1695-1780; Colonel George Beall, 1729-1807; owners of the "Rock of Dumbarton" estate of 2,175 acres, on which Georgetown, D. C., was located. '08 (Ag15) 12°, pap. (Add. author for price.) Z. Moses.

Mosher, Edith R.
Studies of fruit and nut bearing trees. '08 (S5) c. il. obl. Q. $2. Bardeen.
Studies of our cone-bearing trees. '10(F5) c. obl. O. $2. Bardeen.
Studies of our oaks and maples. '10(F5) c. obl. Q. $2. Bardeen.

Mosher, Maude Bayliss, McNeil, Everett, Byrne, Mary A., and others.
School days and play days. '09, [1910.] (Ja) c. 67 p. il. 8°, $1. Saalfield.

Mosher's ideal ser. of little masterpieces. 32°, *50 c. net; *$1 net. T: B. Mosher.
—Baudelaire. Poems in prose.
—Hinkson. Little book for John O'Mahony's friends.

Mosher's lyric garland. 4°, 50 c.; Japan vellum, *$1 net. T: B. Mosher.
—Bottomley. Riding to Lithend.
—Dobson. Proverbs in porcelain.
—Henley. London voluntaries.—Rhymes and rhythms and Arabian nights' entertainment.
—Reese. Branch of may.
—Shelley. Lyrical poems.

Mosher's old world ser. 12°, vellum, *$1 net; bds., *$1.25 net; leath., *$1.50 net; Japan vellum ed., *$2.50 net. T: B. Mosher.
—Pearl (The).
—Swinburne. Felise.
—**Symons. Silhouettes.**

Mosher's vest pocket ser. 32°, *25 c. net; *50 c. net; leath., *75 c. net; Japan vellum, *$1 net. T: B. Mosher.
—Ingersoll. Toward humanity.
—Pater. Child in the house.
—Schreiner. Lost joy and other dreams.

MOSLEM.
See Mohammed and Mohammedanism.

MOSQUITOES.
Boyce, *Sir* H. Mosquito or man. *$3.50 net. Dutton.
Craig, C: F. Importance to the army of diseases transmitted by mosquitoes. gratis. Assoc. Military Surgeons.
Levy, E. C. Extermination of mosquitoes. gratis. Richmond Dept. of Health.
Seal, W: P. Fishes in their relation to the mosquito problem; from Bulletin of the Bureau of Fisheries, volume XXVIII, 1908. '10(Jl) 831-838 p. 4°. Gov. Pr. Off.
See also Malaria.

Moss, Catherine Winspear.
Thousand leggers. '09(D) c. 92 p. por. 12°, 75 c. C. M. Clark.

Moss, Ja. Alfr.
Noncommissioned officers' manual. '09 (D4) c. il. facsim., fold. map, D. $1.50; Supplement, published annually, S. pap., 40 c. U. S. Infantry.
Privates' manual. '09(D4) il. D. bds., 50 c. U. S. Infantry.
Story of a troop mess. '09(D4) c. il. D. pap., 75 c. U. S. Infantry.

MOSSES.
Evans, A. W:, *and* Nichols, G: E. Bryophytes of Connecticut: [mosses.] 30 c. Conn. Lib.
Williams, R. S. Mosses from tropical America: [Colombia, Guatemala and Cuba.] 25 c. N. Y. Botanical.

Mosses from an old manse. *See* Hawthorne, Nathaniel.

Mosso, Angelo.
Palaces of Crete and their builders. '08 (Ja25) il. plans, O. *$2.25 net. Putnam.

Most beautiful thing in the world. Swift, F. H. 30 c. net. Dutton.

Most popular hymns. Noble, G. C., *ed.* 50 c. Hinds.

Most popular piano instructor. Gallico, P., *comp. and ed.* 75 c. Hinds.

Mother and the father. Howells, W: D. **$1.20 net. Harper.

Mother animal stories: book of the best animal stories that mothers can tell their children. '09(D18) c. 8°, (Mother stories ser.) †50 c. Altemus.

Mother Goose.
Complete Mother Goose. '09(N13) c. col. il. O. $1.50. Stokes.
Favorite rhymes of Mother Goose. '10 (N5) il. O. $1.50. Cupples & L.
Old Mother Goose nursery rhymes; ed. by Wa. Jerrold. '10(D) il. 12°, (Children's classics.) $1.25. Dutton.

MOTHER GOOSE.
Barnes, B. Scissors Mother Goose. 75 c. Dodd.

Mother Goose and what happened next. Smith, A. M. $1.25. Dutton.

Mother Goose nursery tales; ed. by Wa. Jerrold. '10(D) il. 12°, (Children's classics.) $1.25. Dutton.

Mother Goose on bridge. Avery, M. A. $1. Lyman Bros.

Mother Goose; or, the old nursery rhymes. New ed.; il. in colors by Kate Greenaway. '10(D31) col. il. 16°, bds., 60 c. net. Warne.

Mother Goose primer. Wiley, B. 32 c. C: E: Merrill.

Mother Goose's nursery rhymes. Jerrold, W. C. *$1.50 net. Dodge.

Mother Goose's nursery rhymes. il. S. bds., 50 c. Stokes.
—Curly-Locks, and other nursery rhymes.
—Wee Willie Winkie.

Mother-heart. Barber, M. L., *comp.* 50 c. net. G: W. Parker.

Mother of California. North, A. W. **$2 net. P. Elder.

Mother of pearl. *See* France, Anatole.

Mother of the man. Phillpotts, E. †$1.50 Dodd.

Mother Santa Claus stories. O'Donnell, W: F. †50 c. Altemus.

Mother the child's first Bible teacher. Foster, *Mrs.* M. J. C. *25 c. net. Jennings.

Mother tongue. *See* Arnold, Sarah Louise.

Mother Tucker's seven. Wray, A. W. †$1.25. Lothrop, L. & S.

Motherhood. Bishop, H. D. $1.50. Rose.

Mother's book. Burrell, C. B., *ed.* Univ. Soc.

Mother's day poems. Van Galder, F. O., *comp.* 30 c. Modern Woodmen.

Mother's hero. Dow, E. C. $1.25. Stern.

Mother's list of books for children. Arnold, G. W. $1. McClurg.

Mother's love songs. Toldridge, E. $1. Badger.

Mother's part in her child's musical education. McFerrin, C: B. $2. Alert Pub.

Mother's remedies: over one thousand tried and tested remedies from mothers of the United States and Canada; also symptoms, causes, prevention, diet, nursing, treatment, etc., of every known disease, by Dr. T. J. Ritter: Manners and social customs, by Mrs. Elizabeth Johnstone, and various other departments. [1910.] (O) c. 10+951 p. por. il. pl. (partly col.) 8°, $3.85. Foote.

Mother's year-book. Washburne, *Mrs.* M. F. **$1.25 net. Macmillan.

MOTHERS.
Barton, *Mrs.* C. J. W. Mother of the living. $1.50; 50 c. C. J. W. Barton.
Campbell, H. Y. Pract. motherhood. $2.50. Longmans.
Chance, M. S. B. Mother and daughter. $1 net. Century Co.
Gordon, H. I. Modern mother. $2. Fenno.
Hoffman, *Mrs.* A. L. R. Social duty of our daughters: talk with mothers and their grown daughters. **35 c. net. Vir Pub.
Marriott, L. M. Mother and child. 40 c. Simmons.
Miller, M. W. Helps for young mothers; in the physical and moral training of infants and young children. 50 c. Jacobs.

MOTHERS.—*Continued.*
National Congress of Mothers. How to organize parents' associations or mothers' circles in public schools. 10 c. Nat. Congress Mothers.
Woolard, S. F., *comp.* Glorious mother. *50 c. net; *$1.25 net. Goldsmith-W.
See also Children;—Generative organs;—Hygiene;—Midwifery;—Pregnancy;—Woman.
Mothers and fathers. Tompkins, J. W. $1.50. Baker & T.
Mothers in Israel. Fletcher, J. S. †$1.50. Moffat.
Mothers' verses and home songs. '08(D26) c. D. 75 c. Caldwell.
MOTHS.
Chittenden, F. H. Control of the Mediterranean flour moth. (Add. Superintendent for price.) U. S., Supt. of Docs.
Fernald, C: H: Genera of the *tortricidæ* and their types. 75 c. C: H: Fernald.
Jackson, A. D. Study of Ohio forms of the genus *Lepidocyrtus.* gratis. Ohio State Univ.
Jenne, E. L. Papers on deciduous fruit insects and insecticides; the codling moth in the Ozarks. (Add. Superintendent for price.) U. S., Supt. of Docs.
South, R: Moths of the British Isles, first series; second series. ea., *$3 net. Warne.
Moths. La Ramée, L. de. 50 c. Hurst.
Motion picture, its making and its theatre. Hulfish, D: S. 50 c. Elec. Mag.
Motives and results of the social settlement movement. Cole, W: I. (Add. pubs. for price.) Harvard Univ.
Motley, Ja.
Importers ready reference tables. '10(F19) c. 8°, $1.25. Motley Press.
Motley, Ja. Marvin.
Apprenticeship in American trade unions. '08(Mr7) c. O. (Johns Hopkins Univ. studies in hist. and pol. science.) pap., 50 c. Johns Hopkins.
Motley, J: Lothrop.
Dutch nation: being "The rise of the Dutch Republic, 1555-1584"; condensed, with introd., notes and a brief history of the Dutch people to 1908, by W: Elliot Griffis. New ed. '08(Ap11) c. il. pors. O. $1.75. Harper.
History of the United Netherlands. 2 v. '09(Je5) O. $3. Harper.
Rise of the Dutch Republic. 2 v. '10(D) il. $2.50, boxed. Crowell.
Rise of the Dutch Republic. 3 v. '08(O17) 16°, (Best books ser.) leath., ea., *$1 net. Dutton.
MOTLEY, John Lothrop.
Mildmay, *Mrs.* S. S. J. M. *and* H. *eds.* John Lothrop Motley and his family. $5 net. Lane.
Motley (A). Galsworthy, J: $1.20 net. Scribner.
Motley jest. Adams, O. F. *$1 net. Sherman, F.
MOTOR BICYCLES.
See Bicycles.
Motor Boat Club and the wireless. Hancock, H. I. $1. Altemus.
Motor Boat Club at Nantucket. Hancock, H. I. $1. Altemus.
Motor Boat Club at the Golden Gate. Hancock, H. I. †$1. Altemus.
Motor Boat Club in Florida. Hancock, H. I. †$1. Altemus.
Motor Boat Club of the Kennebec. Hancock, H. I. $1. Altemus.
Motor Boat Club off Long Island. Hancock, H. I. $1. Altemus.
MOTOR-BOATS.
See Boats.
Motor boys in strange waters. Young, C. 60 c. Cupples & L.
Motor boys in the clouds. Young, C. 60 c. Cupples & L.
Motor boys on the Atlantic. Young, C. 60 c. Cupples & L.
Motor boys on the Pacific. Young, C. 60 c. Cupples & L.
Motor car model book: [juvenile.] '08(D19) il. f°, pap., 50 c. Dutton.
Motor car Peter. Williams, A. $1.25. Jacobs.
MOTOR CARS.
See Automobiles.
Motor days in England. Dillon, J: M. **$3 net. Putnam.
Motor-flight through France. Wharton, *Mrs.* E. N. J. **$2 net. Scribner.
Motor girls ser. See Penrose, Marg.
Motor maid. Williamson, C: N. $1.20, fixed. Doubleday, P.
Motor routes of England. Home, G. C. $1.50; $2.25. Macmillan.
Motor routes of France. Home, G. C. $2 net; $2.25 net. Macmillan.
Motor that went to court. Penfield, F. C. (Priv. pr.) F. C. Penfield.
Motor tours in the west country. Stawell, *Mrs.* R. $1.75 net. Doran.
Motor tours in Wales. Stawell, *Mrs.* R. $2.50. L. C. Page.
Motor tours in Yorkshire. Stawell, *Mrs.* R. $1.75 net. Doran.
Motorboat handbook. '09(Mr27) c. il. 8°, *$1 net. Motor Boat Pub.
Motoring. Hearne, R. P. 50 c. Dutton.
Motoring abroad. Presbrey, F. *$2 net. Outing.
Motoring in tthe Balkans. Hutchinson, F. K. *$2.75 net. McClurg.
Motorman and his duties. Gutmann, L. *$1 net. McGraw.
Motorman's practical air brake instructor. Denehie, G: R. $1.50. Drake.
MOTORMEN.
See Street railroads.
MOTORS.
See Automobiles;—Dynamos and motors;—Electricity;—Engines;—Machinery.
Mott, E: Harold.
Lincoln; brief biographical sketch, fitting appreciations of his character, and a compilation of selections from his state papers, addresses and letters; prep. under the direction of Lincoln Centenary Committee of the City of New York appointed by His Honor George Brinton McClellan, mayor, 1908. '09(Mr20) c. il. por. 8°. (Not for sale.) M. B. Brown.
Mott, F: Walker, M.D.
Brain and the voice in speech and song. '10(N12) S. (Harper's lib. of living thought.) 75 c. net. Harper.

Mott, Hopper Striker.
New York of yesterday: narrative of old Bloomingdale. '08(Je6) il. map, O. **$10 net. Putnam.

Mott, J: Raleigh.
Chinese student migration to Tokyo. '09 (Jl31) il. fold. map, 24°, pap., 5 c. Y. M. C. A.
Decisive hour of Christian missions. '10 (N12) il. pors. fold. map, 8°, $1. Student Vol.
Future leadership of the church: [discovering, enlisting and training of candidates for the ministry.] '09(Mr13) $1. Y. M. C. A.

MOTTOES.
Hubbard, E. Motto book. 10 c. Roycrofters.

Moulder, Martha, comp.
Left hand autograph book; scientific pastime. '09(O2) S. (Thumb-o-graph ser.) *50 c. net. Stokes.

Moule, Bp. Handley Carr Glyn.
Faith: its nature and its work. '09(Ap24) por. D. *$1.25 net. Cassell.
Messages from the Epistle to the Hebrews. '09(N13) D. *60 c. net. Doran.

—, Drury, Bp. T: Wortley, and Girdlestone, Rev. Rob. Baker.
English Church teaching on faith, life and order. '08(D12) D. *40 c. net. Longmans.

Moull, J:
Auditing for accountant students. '08(D) c. 140 p. forms, 8°. (Add. pubs. for price.) Universal Business.

Moulton, Arth. Wheelock.
Memoirs of Augustine Heard Amory. '09, [1910.] (Mr) c. 205 p. por. 8°. $1.25. A. W. Moulton.

Moulton, C: Wells, ed.
Library of literary criticism. New ed. 8 v. '10(S) c. pors. per set, $40. Malkan.

Moulton, Forest Ray.
See Chamberlin, T: Chrowder.

Moulton, Mrs. Louise Chandler.
New bedtime stories. '08(D19) c. il. 12°, †$1.25. Little, B. & Co.
Poems and sonnets. '09(Ja16) c. por. 12°, $1.50. Little, B. & Co.

MOULTON, *Mrs.* Louise Chandler.
Whiting, L. Louise Chandler Moulton; poet and friend. $1.50 net. Little, B. & Co.
See also Boston Public Library.

MOUND BUILDERS.
Randall, E. O. Masterpieces of the Ohio mound builders; the hill top fortifications, incl. Fort Ancient. $1. Ohio Archæolog.
Young, B. H. Prehistoric men of Kentucky. $4.50. Morton.
See also Fort Ancient.

Mount, Christiana Stagg.
Seat work and sense training. '10(N19) c. il. 12°, 50 c. Educ. Pub.

MT. ATHOS, Turkey.
Lake, K. Early days of monasticism on Mount Athos. $2.90. Oxford Univ.

MOUNT HOLYOKE COLLEGE, South Hadley, Mass.
Kinney, A. S. Views of Mount Holyoke College. 50 c. A. S. Kinney.
See also Lyon, Mary.

MT. MCKINLEY, Alaska.
Cook, F: A. To the top of the continent: discovery, exploration and adventure in sub-arctic Alaska. **$2.50 net. Doubleday, P.

MT. PELÉE, Martinique.
Heilprin, A. Eruption of Pelée. $4. Geographical Soc.

MOUNT PLEASANT ACADEMY, N. Y.
Hinton, H. My comrades; or, school-days at Mt. Pleasant: story of the Hudson. $1.25. C. F. Brusie.

MT. RANIER, Wash.
Williams, J: H. Mountain that was "God." $1 net; 50 c. net. J: H. Williams.

MT. VERNON, Va.
Hudson, *Mrs.* S. E. J. Washington's home, [Mount Vernon.] (Add. pubs. for price.) Hanzsche.
Inventory of the contents of Mount Vernon. (Priv. pr.) Univ. Pr.
Page, T: N. Mount Vernon and its preservation, 1858-1910. 75 c. Mount Vernon Ladies' Assoc.

MT. WILSON, Cal.
Hale, G: E. Tower telescope of Mount Wilson solar observatory. (Not for sale.) Carnegie.
Ritchey, G: W. 60-inch reflector of the Mount Wilson solar observatory. (Not for sale.) Carnegie.

Mt. Wilson Solar Observatory contributions. il. 4°, pap. Carnegie.
—Hale. Preliminary note on rotation of the sun. (Not for sale.)
—King. Electric furnace for spectroscopic investigations. (Add. Institution for price.)

Mountain preacher. Davis, J. L. 50 c. F: L: Rowe.

Mountain that was "God." Williams, J: H. $1 net; 50 c. net. J: H. Williams.

MOUNTAINEERING.
Abraham, G: D. Complete mountaineer. *$4.80 net.—Mountain adventures. $3.80 net. Doubleday, P.
Harrison, F. My Alpine jubilee. *$1.25 net. Dutton.
Larden, W. Recollections of an old mountaineer. $4 net. Longmans.
Le Blond, E. A. F. H.-W. Mountaineering in the land of the midnight sun. *$3.50 net. Lippincott.
See also Alps (The);—Mt. McKinley;—Mustagh Range;—Ruwenzori.

Mountains and valleys in the ministry of Jesus. Morgan, G: C. *25 c. net. Revell.

Moure, Jean Gabriel Emile, M.D., and Bouyer, Achille, jr.
Abuse of the singing and speaking voice. '10(D24) il. 12°, $1 net. Scribner.

Mourey, Gabriel.
See Utrillo, *Don* Miguel.

Mourning for **Lincoln.** Barrett, F. W. Z. **$1 net. Winston.

MOUTH.
Broomell, I: N., *and* Fischelis, P. Anatomy and histology of the mouth and teeth. *$3 net. Blakiston.
Brown, W. C. Sprue and its treatment. *$2.50 net. Wood.
Bruck, A. Diseases of the nose, mouth and larynx. $5. **Rebman.**
Marshall, J: S. Manual of the injuries and surgical diseases of the face, mouth and jaws. $6.50. White Dental.
See also Speech;—Taste;—Teeth.
Movable kidney. Wilson, H. W. *$1.25 net. Longmans.
MOVEMENT.
See Psychology.
Movements and men of Christian history. Billings, C: T. 45 c.; 35 c.; 65 c. Unitarian S. S.
Moving loads on railway underbridges. Bamford, H. *$1.25 net. Macmillan.
Moving of the waters. Cady, J. $1.50. J: McBride.
MOVING PICTURES.
See Cinematograph.
Mowbray, Jay H:
Conquest of the air by air-ships and other flying machines; marvellous achievements of the bird men; how to build and sail an aeroplane. '10(D10) c. il. 8°, $1.50. Nat. Pub. Co.
Discovery of North pole by Cook and Peary, including the marvelous wonders of the polar world. [1910.] (Mr) c. '09, 17-432 p. il. pors., maps, 8°, $1.50. G: W. Bertron.
Roosevelt's marvellous exploits in the wilds of Africa, cont. thrilling accounts of his killing lions, rhinoceri and other ferocious beasts of the jungle. [1910.] (Mr) c. '09, 1 p. l., 19-256 p. il. pors., 8°, $1. G: W. Bertron.
—, comp. Italy's great horror of earthquake and tidal wave. '09(Ap3) c. il. 8°, $1. Nat. Pub. Co.
Mowry, Don Ensminger.
See Walden, C: O.
Mowry, Duane.
Appreciation of James Rood Doolittle; from the proceedings of the State Historical Society of Wisconsin, for 1909. '10(Ap) 281-293 p. por. O. pap., 15 c. State Hist., Wis.
Mowry, W: A:
Descendants of John Mowry of Rhode Island. '09(N) $3. Preston.
Elements of civil government, local, state, and national; brief course for ungraded, grammar, and high schools. '09, [1910.] (Mr) il. 12°, Illinois ed.; Minnesota ed.; Vermont ed.; Michigan ed.; Massachusetts ed.; Pennsylvania ed., ea., 72 c. Silver.
Recollections of a New England educator, 1838-1908. '08(D26) c. pors. O. *$1.50 net. Silver.
Talks with my boys. 5th ed., rev. and enl. '09(N6) c. por. D. $1. Silver.
MOWRY FAMILY.
See Genealogies.
Moyer, Harold N:, M.D., ed.
See Baum, W: L.

Moyer, Ja. Ambrose.
Steam turbine. '08(D19) c. figs. 8°, **$4 net. **Wiley.**
MOYER AND HAYWOOD CASE.
Langdon, *Mrs.* E. F. **Labor's greatest conflicts [Moyer, Haywood and Pettibone case.]** 50 c. **E. F. Langdon.**
See also **Orchard, Harry.**
MOYER FAMILY.
See **Genealogies: Fretz, A. J.**
Moyes, Canon Ja.
Aspects of Anglicanism. '09(Je5) D. *$1 net. **Longmans.**
MOYLAN, *General* Stephen.
Griffin, M. I. J. General Stephen **Moylan.** $1.50. **M. I. J. Griffin.**
Moynihan, Berkeley G: Andrew, M.D.
Pathology of the living, and other essays. '10(Je) c. 260 p. 12°, $2 net. Saunders.
Mozans, H. J., pseud.
Up the Orinoco and down the Magdalena following the conquistadores '10(My21) c. il. O. $3 net. Appleton.
MOZART, Johann Chrysostom Wolfgang Amadeus.
Wilder, V. Mozart. 2 v. *$3.50 net. Scribner.
MOZART REGIMENT.
See New York State.
Mozley, J. B., D.D.
Lectures and other theological papers. New ed. '08(Jl11) O. *$1.25 net. Longmans.
Review of the baptismal controversy. New ed. '08(Jl18) D. $1.25. Longmans.
Ruling ideas in early ages and their relation to Old Testament faith: lectures del. to graduates of the University of Oxford. New and cheaper ed. '08(Jl11) O. *$1.25 net. Longmans.
Much-abused letter. Tyrrell, G: 90 c. net. Longmans.
Much ado about Peter. Webster, A. J. †$1.50. Doubleday, P.
Much ado about something. Lawrence, C. E. *$2.40 net. Scribner.
Muckenstrum, L: Jaques.
Louis' every woman's cook book. '10(S3) c. front. Q. $1.50. Caldwell.
Mudd, Jos. Aloysius.
With Porter in north Missouri: chapter in the hist. of the war between the states. '09, [1910.] (Ap) 452 p. il. pors. 8°, $2.70. J. A. Mudd.
Mudge, Isadore Gilbert, and Sears, M. Earl.
Thackeray dict.; characters and scenes of the novels and short stories alphabetically arranged. '10(D10) 8°, $3.. Dutton.
Mudge, Ja., D.D.
Riches of His grace; a portion for every Sunday. Ephesians 1.7. '09(S18) c. D. *$1 net. Eaton & M.
Mueller, Eug. F.
See Dickinson, Hobert C.
Mueller, Max.
See Müller, Max.
Mueller, W: C:
New manual of natural trigonometrical functions to seven places of decimals of sines and cosines of the angles from 0 to 10000 seconds. '08(My23) c. 4°, leath.. $9. W: C: Mueller.
Muffin shop. Garnett, L. A. $1.50. Rand, McN. & Co.

Mugan, Esther Laurentine.
Side lights K. of C. as viewed from without. [1910.] (S) 111 p. il. pors. 8°. Donohue.

Mugby Junction. *See* Dickens, C:

Mugen. Poole, F. R. $1. Niles Pub.

Mügge, M. A.
Friedrich Nietzsche: his life and work. '09 (Jl17) por. 8°, *$3 net. Brentano's.

Muhleman, Maurice L:
Monetary and banking systems, 1908. '08 (Jl11) 8°, *$2 net. Monetary.

Muir, J:
Our national parks. New and enl. ed. '09(N13) c. il. O. *$3 net, boxed. Houghton M.
Stickeen. '09(Ap3) c. D. **60 c. net. Houghton M.
See also In American fields and forests.

Muir, Pearson M'Adam, D.D.
Modern substitutes for Christianity: the Baird lecture for 1908. '09(D); for 1909. [1910.] (My) 8°, ea., $1.50 net. Doran.

Muir, Rob., Browning, Carl Hamilton, and others.
Studies in immunity. '09(D) 11+216 p. 8°, (Oxford medical pubs.) *$3 net. Oxford Univ.

Muir, W: Carpenter Pendleton.
Treatise on navigation and nautical astronomy. 2d ed. '08(O) c. 16+763 p. il. 12°, $5. U. S. Naval Inst.

Muirheid, Wa. Gregory, ed.
Jersey City of to-day; its history, people, trades, commerce, institutions and industries. '10(Jl) c. 109 p. il. pors. f°, $10. F. Stevens.

Mulertt, Hugo.
Goldfish and its systematic culture; thorough guide for goldfish keeping and goldfish breeding. 6th ed. '10(My) c. 10+3-155 p. il. por. 8°, $2. H. Mulertt.

Mulford, Clarence E:
Bar—20. 5th ed. '07, [1910.] (F) il. 12°, $1.50. McClurg.
Formerly published by Outing Publishing Co.
Hopalong Cassidy. '10(Mr26) c. col. il. O. $1.50. McClurg.
The orphan. '08(Mr21) c. il. D. $1.50. Outing.

Mulhall, Mrs. Marion McMurrough.
Explorers in the New World before and after Columbus; and the story of the Jesuit missions of Paraguay. '09(Jl17) por. maps. D. *$2.25 net. Longmans.

Mulholland, Clara.
In a roundabout way. '09(Je19) 12°, *75 c. net. Benziger.

Mullany, J: Fs.
Bible studies. '08, [1909.] (Mr) c. 10+3-251+187 p. 12°, $1.25. Mason-H.

Müller, Ernest Friedrich Karl, D.D.
Our Lord: belief in the deity of Christ. '08(Mr14) c. S. (Foreign religious ser.) *40 c. net. Eaton & M.

Müller, Georg, and Glass, Alex.
Diseases of the dog and their treatment. New il. ed., rev. and enl. '08(My23) c. Q. *$5 net. Franklin Press, (Pa.)

Müller, G: F.
Mentone and its neighborhood: past and present; ed. by Rev. J. E. Somerville. '10 (S) il. 8°, $4 net. Doran.

Muller, Gustav.
Ecce homo: eine erzählung aus Jesu Christi tagen. '08(D19) c. 8°, $2. Lemcke.

Müller, Hermann.
See Knuth, Paul.

Müller, Johannes.
Hindrances of life; tr. by F. F. Strecker. '09(D25) c. 8°, *$1.50 net. M. Kennerley.

Müller, Jörgen Peter.
Fresh-air book. '10(F19) c. il. D. **85 c. net. Stokes.

Muller, Julius Washington.
Rulers of the surf; story of the mysteries and perils of the sea. '10(O29) c. il. D. $1.50. Appleton.
—, and Knowlson, Arth.
Fishing around New York; where to find them, how to rig, how to catch them; chart of hooks showing the exact sizes to use, etc. '09(My) c. 64 p. il. 16°, leath., 50 c.; pap., 25 c. Knowlson & M.

Müller, Margarethe.
Carla Wenckebach, pioneer. '08(N7) c. pors. D. **$1.25 net. Ginn.

Müller, Max, i.e., Friedrich Max.
Comparative mythology. '09(N) 48+184 p. 16°, (New universal lib.) *50 c. net; leath., *75 c. net. Dutton.
Persona. '08(Ag15) 8°, pap., 25 c. Open Court.
—, ed. Sacred books of the East; tr. by various Oriental scholars. v. 1, The Upanishaps; tr. by F. Max Müller; pt. 1, The Khandogva-Upanishad, The Talavakâra-Upanishad, The Aitereya-Aranyaka, The Kaushitaki-Brâhmana-Upanishad, and The Vâgasaneyi-Samhitâ-Upanishad. v. 3, The sacred books of China: the texts of Confucianism; tr. by Ja. Legge; pt. 1, The Shû King, The religious portions of the Shih King, and The Hsiâo King. 2d ed. v. 4, The Zend-Avesta, pt. 1, The Venidad; tr. by Ja. Darmesteter. 2d ed. v. 6, The Qur'ân [Koran], pt. 1, Chapters 1-16; tr. by E. H. Palmer. '08(N21) tabs., O. v. 1, pt. 1, $4.75; v. 3, pt. 1, $5; v. 4, pt. 1, $5.25; v. 6, pt. 1, $4. Oxford Univ.

Müller, Wilhelm.
Diary and letters [in German]; with explanatory notes and a biographical index; ed. by Philip Schuyler Allen and Ja. Taft Hatfield. '09(My22) por. O. price reduced from $1.25 to 30 c. Stechert.

Müller, Wilhelm Max.
Egyptological researches. v. 2, Results of a journeying in 1906. '10(S17) il. Q. pap., $9. Carnegie.

Mulliken, Clara A.
Reading list on modern dramatists: D'Annunzio, Hauptmann, Ibsen, Maeterlinck, Phillips, Rostand, Shaw and Sudermann. '08(Ap18) 12°, (Bulletin of Bibliography pamphlets.) pap., 20 c. Boston Bk.

Mulliken, Mrs. G. E.
Giant of the treasure caves. '10(Ag20) il. O. $1.50. Estes.

Mulliken, S: Parsons.
Method for the identification of pure organic compounds, by a systematic analyt. procedure, based on physical properties and chemical reactions. v. 3, Identification of the commercial dyestuffs. '10 (Je18) c. 8°, $5. Wiley.

Mulliner, Gabrielle Stewart.
New York laws of interest to women: [paper read before N. Y. State Federation of Women's Clubs.] Federation ed. '08, [1909.] (Mr) c. 31 p. D. pap., 25 c. G. S. Mulliner.

Mullins, Edg. Young, D.D.
Axioms of religion: new interpretation of the Baptist faith. '08(Mr7) c. D. **$1 net. Am. Bapt.

Mulock, Miss.
See Craik, *Mrs.* Dinah Maria Mulock.

Mulready, Edn.
Probation; address at a conference of probation officers held by the New York State Probation Commission in Albany, Nov. 16 and 17, 1909. '10(S) 8 p. O. pap., gratis. N. Y. State Probation.

Mumby, Fk. Arth., comp.
Girlhood of Queen Elizabeth; narrative in contemporary letters; with an introd. by R. S. Rait. '09(N13) il. O. **$3 net. Houghton M.

Mumford, Eben.
Origins of leadership; doctor's dissertation. '09(Ap10) 8°, pap., *50 c. net. Univ. of Chic.

Mumford, Edith E. Read.
Dawn of character; study of child life. '10 (D3) D. $1.20 net. Longmans.

Mumford, Ethel Watts-, [now Mrs. Grant.]
See Herford, Oliver.

—, Mizner, Addison, and Herford, Oliver.
Perfectly good cynic's calendar [1909]; with astronomical attachment. '08(O10) c. T. bds., **75 c. net. P. Elder.

Mumford, Ja. Gregory, M.D.
Practice of surgery. '10(O) 1015 p. il. 8°, $7. Saunders.
Some end-results of surgery. '09(Ja30) c. 12°, (Religion and medicine publications.) pap., **25 c. net. Moffat.
Surgical memoirs, and other essays. '08 (D19) c. pors. O. **$2.50 net. Moffat.

Mumm, Arnold L:
Five months in the Himalaya. '09(Je) il. fold. maps, Q. *$6 net. Longmans.

Mumma, Rosa Meyers.
Fallina: tale of modern American social life. '08(D) 146 p. 12°, $1. Roxburgh.

Mummery, P. Lockhart.
After-treatment of operations; manual for practitioners and house surgeons. 3d ed., rev. '10(F) 260 p. il. 12°, *$2.25 net. Wood.
Diseases of the colon and their surgical treatment. '10(Jl) il. 8°, $3.25 net. Wood.

Mumper, W: Norris.
Teachers' manual to accompany "A text-book in physics." '09(Ap3) c. D. pap., 25 c. Am. Bk.

Munby, Alan E:
Introd. to the chemistry and physics of building materials. '09(Je19) (Westminster ser.) *$2 net. Van Nostrand.

Muncie, Mrs. Eliz. Hamilton, M.D.
Four epochs of life. '10(S17) c. il. por. D. $1.50 net. Greaves.

Mundy, Floyd Woodruff, comp. and ed.
Earning power of railroads, 1908; mileage—capitalization, [etc.] '08(My9) c. D. $2. Metropolitan Adv.
Earning power of railroads, 1909. '09 (Je5) c. D. $2.—1910. '10(My14) c. D. $2.50. J. H. Oliphant.

Mundy, W: Nelson, M.D.
Eclectic practice in diseases of children. 2d ed., rev., rewritten and enl. '08(O3) c. il. O. $3. Scudder.

Munford, Beverley Bland.
Virginia's attitude toward slavery and secession. '09(N13); New ed. '10(Je11) O. ea., $2 net. Longmans.

Munger, Thdr. Thornton.
On the threshold. Rev. and enl. ed. '08 (D) c. 14+246 p. 12°, $1. Houghton M.

MUNICH, Germany.
Ansell, F. J., *and* Fraprie, F. R. Art of the Munich galleries. $2 net; $5 net. L. C. Page.
Wadleigh, H: R. Munich. $2 net. Stokes.

Municipal Art Society of Hartford. Street name plates; investigation by the Committee on Street Fixtures and Advertising Signs. '09(D18) il. 8°, (Publications of the Municipal Art Society of Hartford, Ct., bull.) pap., gratis. Municipal Art Soc.

MUNICIPAL BONDS.
See Bonds.

MUNICIPAL GOVERNMENT.
Bradford, E. S. Commission government in American cities. $4. Nat. Municipal.
Cleveland, F: A. Chapters on municipal administration and accounting. **$2 net. Longmans.
Deming, H. E: Government of American cities. **$1.50 net. Putnam.
Fairlie, J: A. Essays in municipal administration. **$2.50 net. Macmillan.
Goodnow, F. J. Municipal government. **$3 net. Century Co.
Hamilton, J: J. Dethronement of the city boss. $1.20 net. Funk.
International Bureau of American Republics, Washington, D. C. Municipal organizations in Latin America. (Add. pubs. for price.) Int. Bu. Am. Republics.
League of American Municipalities. Book of American municipalities; summary of civic progress and achievements. $3.50. Municipal Information.
MacGregor, F. H. City government by commission. 10 c. Univ. of Wis.
Municipal betterment bibliography. 4°, gratis. Kansas City Pub. Lib.
Munroe, W: B. Government of European cities. **$2.50 net. Macmillan.
Robbins, E. C., *comp.* Selected articles on the commission plan of municipal government. H. W. Wilson.
Rowe, L. S. Problems of city governments. **$1.50 net. Appleton.

MUNICIPAL GOVERNMENT.—*Continued.*
Shaffner, M. A. Municipal home rule charters. 25 c. Wisconsin Free Lib.
Warner, A. D. Modern city. 25 c. Baumgardt.
Wilcox, D. F. Great cities in America. $1.25 net. Macmillan.
Wilcox, D. F. Municipal franchises. 2 v. ea., $5. Gervaise Press; [Engineering News.]
See also Cities; — Corporations; — Local government;—Municipal ownership; — Police; — Public utilities;—Roads;—Town Officers;—Towns; —Villages; — *also* Kansas City; — New York City.

MUNICIPAL LAW.
Chicago. Municipal court, with marginal notes. $2.50. Callaghan.

MUNICIPAL OWNERSHIP.
American Academy of Political and Social Science. Control of municipal public service corporations. $1. Am. Acad. Pol. Sci.
Darwin, L. Municipal ownership. *$1.25 net. Dutton.
Grant, A. H., *comp.* List of defunct municipal lighting plants. 40 c. Municipal Ownership.
See also Collectivism;—Fine arts;—Markets;—Public utilities;—Socialism.

MUNICIPAL TRADING.
See Socialism.

Municipal water supplies of Illinois. Bartow, E: (Add. Univ. for price.) Univ. of Ill.

Munk, Jos. Amasa, M.D.
Arizona bibliography. 2d ed. '09(Ap17) O. pap., gratis. J. A. Munk.

Munn, C: Allen.
Three types of Washington portraits: John Trumbull, Charles Willson Peale, Gilbert Stuart. '08(Ap18) c. il. pors. facsims., 8°. (Priv. pr.) Gillis Press.

Munn, C: Clark.
Castle builders. '10(Ag20) c. il. D. $1.50. Lothrop, L. & S.
Myrtle Baldwin. '08(S5) c. il. D. †$1.50. Lothrop, L. & S.
Some "thinks"; also a few "sparks" from other wires. '10(N) c. 32 p. S. pap., 10 c. C: C. Munn.

Munn, Mrs. Marg. Crosby.
Will Shakespeare of Stratford and London; drama in four acts. '10(Je4) c. D. $1.20 net. Dodd.

Munn & Co. *Scientific American* handbook relating to patents, caveats, designs, trademarks, copyrights, etc. '08, [1909.] (Ap) c. 64 p. il. 24°, gratis. Munn.

Munro, Dana Carleton, and Sellery, G: Clarke.
Syllabus of medieval history, 395-1500; published by the Department of History of the University of Pennsylvania. [5th ed.] '09(O30) O. bds., $1. Longmans.

Munro, H: S., M.D.
Hdbk. of suggestive therapeutics, applied hypnotism, and psychic science. 2d ed. '09. [1910.] (O) 367 p. 8°, $3. Mosby.

Munro, J. J., ed.
Shakespeare allusion book; cont. reprints of all known references to Shakespeare from 1591 to 1700; orig. coll. by Dr. Ingleby, Miss Toulmin Smith, Dr. Furnival and other helpers and now for the first time arr. in chronological order and suppl. with new material. '09(O16) 2 v., 8°, (Shakespeare lib.) *$7 net. Duffield.

Munro, J:
Story of electricity. '10(F5) c. il. 12°, (Lib. of valuable knowledge.) 92 c. S. S. McClure.

Munro, J:
See Furnivall, F: Ja.

Munro, Neil.
The Clyde: river and firth. '08(Ja11) il. map, 8°, (Color book ser.) *$6 net. Macmillan.

Munroe, C: E:
Detonation of gun cotton. [1910.] (Ag) 71 p. 8°. (Priv. pr.) Am. Philosophical.

—, and Hall, Clarence.
Primer on explosives for coal miners. '09, (1910.] (Mr) 61 p. il. diagrs. 8°, (U. S., Dept. of the Interior, U. S. Geological Survey, bull.) pap.

Munroe, Ja. Phinney.
Educational ideal; an outline of its growth in modern times. '09(S) 8+262 p. 12°, (Heath's pedagogical lib.) $1. Heath.
Specialist blight on American education. '09(Ap3) O. (Add. author for price.) J. P. Munroe.

Munroe, Kirk.
Cab and caboose; story of a railroad boy. '10(D17) il. 12°, (Knickerbocker ser.) $1.25. Putnam.
Under the Great Bear. '08(N14) c. il. D. †$1.25. Harper.
See also Stevens, Rowan.

Munroe, W: Bennett.
Government of European cities. '09(Ap3) c. O. **$2.50 net. Macmillan.

Munson, E: Lyman.
See Morrison, J: Fk.

—, and Eltinge, Le Roy.
Study in camp sanitation. '10(Je) 15 p. il. maps, 8°. (Not for sale.) Army Service.

Munson, Ja. Eug.
Pocket phonographic dictionary; containing 12,000 words. '08(N14) c. nar. S. (Munson system of phonography.) leath., $1. Am. Bk.

Munson, T: Volney.
Foundations of American grape culture. '09(O16) c. il. por. Q. $3. Judd.

Munson shorthand dictionary. Van Sant, E., *ed.* $1. J. A. Lyons.

Munson's system of phonography. *See* Munson, Ja. Eug.

Münsterberg, Hugo.
American problems from the point of view of a psychologist. '10(My14) c. O. $1.60 net. Moffat.
Eternal values. '09(Je12) c. O. **$2.50 net. Houghton M.
On the witness stand: essays on psychology and crime. '08(Ap18) c. D. **$2.50 net. McClure.
Psychology and the teacher. '09(O23) c. D. **$1.50 net. Appleton.
Psychotherapy. '09(My1) c. O. **$2 net. Moffat.

—, and others.
Subconscious phenomena. '10(D31) 12°, $1.20 net. Badger.

MURAL DECORATION.
See Wall decoration.

MURAT, Caroline Bonaparte, *Grand Duchess of Berg and Cleves.*
See Bonaparte family.

Murat, Princess Caroline Laetitia.
My memoirs. '10(N5) il. pors. O. $3.50 net. Putnam.

Murder Point. Dawson, W: C. $1.50. Doran.

Murdoch, G: H:
Building a law business; how to advertise in proper ways. '10(F) c. 76 p. nar. D. flex. leath., $10. Murdoch Law, (N. J.)

Murdoch, W. G. Burn-.
See Burn-Murdoch, W. G.

Murdock, Harold, ed.
1872: letters written by a gentleman in Boston to his friend in Paris, describing the great fire; with introductory chapters and notes by Harold Murdock. '09 (Ag21) il. 8°, *$5 net. Houghton M.

Murdock, W: G.
Brady family reunion and fragments of Brady history and biography. '09, [1910.] c. 124 p. il. pors. facsims., 8°, $1.25. W: G. Murdock.

Murfree, Mary Noailles, ["Charles Egbert Craddock."]
Fair Mississippian. '08(O24) c. front. O. †$1.50. Houghton M.

MURIDAE.
See Rodents.

Muriel and her Aunt Lee. Baldwin, M. $1.50. Lippincott.

MURILLO, Bartolome Esteban.
Bensusan, S: L. Murillo. 65 c. net. Stokes.

Murison, W:
English composition; with chapters on précis writing, prosody and style. '10 (O22) D. $1.10 net. Putnam.

Murnane, Timothy H.
How to play baseball. New ed. '10 (Mr26) c. il. por. 16°, (Spalding's athletic lib.) pap., 10 c. Am. Sports.

Murphy, Agnes G.
Melba; a biography; with chapters by Madame Melba on the selection of music as a profession and on the science of singing. '10(Ja22) il. O. $2.75. Doubleday, P.

Murphy, Dawsey Cope.
Popular patriotic poems explained: supplementary reader. '09(My8) c. il. pors. 12°, 65 c. Hinds.

Recreations in history and geography. '08. [1909.] (Jl) 109 p. 12°, pap., *30 c. net. Educ. Pub

Turning points in teaching; or, law making and law breaking in the schoolroom. '09(Ag) c. 7-208 p. 12°, 60 c. Flanagan.

Murphy, Edg. Gardner.
Basis of ascendancy: discussion of certain principles of public policy involved in the development of the southern states. '09 (Jl17) c. D. **$1.50 net. Longmans.

Problems of the present South. '09(Je12) c. D. **$1.50 net. Longmans.

Murphy, Rev. E: Josephy.
Latin pronounced for altar boys; or, the right way to pronounce the Latin for serving mass. '09(Je) c. 10 p. 8°, *50 c. net. Chr. Press.

Latin pronounced for church services. 2d ed. '09(My) 60 p. 12°, *75 c. net. Chr. Press.

Murphy, Ethel Allen.
Angel of thought, and other poems. '09 (Ja16) c. O. $1. Badger.

Murphy, H: Cruse.
Henry Hudson in Holland: an inquiry into the origin and objects of the voyage which led to the discovery of the Hudson River. '09(Ag28) 8°, *$2.50 net. Tice & L.

Murphy, J: B:, ed.
General surgery. [1910.] (Jl) c. 615 p. il. pls. 12°, (Pract. medicine ser.) $2. Year Bk.

Murphy, Rev. Patrick, comp.
St. Patrick, apostle of Ireland, who he was, whence he came, what he did; the shamrock; the green; snakes; from the most authentic sources. '09(Je12) c. O. pap., 25 c. Patrick Murphy.

Murphy, T: Dowler.
British highways and byways from a motor car: record of a five thousand mile tour in England, Wales and Scotland. '08 (Ap4) il. maps, D. $3, boxed; levant mor., $7, boxed. L. C. Page.

In unfamiliar England; record of a seven thousand mile tour by motor; with incursions into Scotland and Ireland. '10 (F19) c. col. il. O. $3, boxed; ¾ levant mor., $7, boxed. L. C. Page.

Murphy, T: E:
Popular errors about classical studies. [1910.] (N) 24 p. 8°, (St. Mary's College bull.) St. Mary's Coll.

Murray, A. J.
Diseases of the stomach and bowels of cattle; rev. in 1904 by Leonard Pearson, and in 1908 by R. W. Hickman. '09, [1910.] (F) 14 p. 8°, (U. S., Dept. of Agriculture, Bu. of Animal Industry, circular.) pap.

Murray, Ada Foster.
Flower o' the grass. '10(Ap9) c. D. $1.25 net. Harper.

Murray, Aitken.
Tommy Brown: a bad boy's memoirs. '08 (My9) c. D. 75 c. Fenno.

Murray, Alfr. N:
Minor ophthalmic and aural technique; short treatise dealing with minor procedures about the eye and ear. '09(N) c. 14+17-247 p. il. 8°, $3. Cleveland Press.

Murray, And., D.D.
Full blessing of Pentecost: the one thing needful. '08(My23) c. 12°, *75 c. net. Revell.

Murray, C: H:
Practice of osteopathy, its practical application to the various diseases of the human body. '09(N) c. 338 p. il. 8°, $3.50. C: H: Murray.

Murray, Clara.
Story book friends. New ed '08(S19) c. il. sq. 12°, †50 c. Little, B. & Co.
Wide awake second reader. '08(F22) c. il. 12°, *35 c. net. Little, B. & Co.
—, comp. Story Land. '09(S18) c. il. D. (Playtime ser.) 50 c. Little, B. & Co.

Murray, Dan. Alex.
Differential and integral calculus. '08(S19) c. O. $2. Longmans.
Essentials of trigonometry and mensuration, with four-place tables. New ed. '09 (Ag14) c. il O. 80 c. Longmans.

Murray, G: Gilbert Aimé.
Interpretation of ancient Greek literature. '09(Ap3) O. pap., 35 c. Oxford Univ.
—, tr. *See* Euripides.

Murray, H:
Stepson of fortune; memoirs, confessions and opinions of Henry Murray. '10(Ap9) por. O. $2.75 net. Baker & T.

Murray, J. Alan.
Soils and manures. '10(Jl30) il. 8°, (Westminister ser.) $2 net. Van Nostrand.

Murray, J. Lovell.
Apologetic of modern missions; eight outline studies. '09(D4) c. D. pap., 15 c. Student Volunteer.

Murray, Ja. A: H:, [and others,] eds.
New English dictionary on historical principles. [Reissue in quarterly parts.] [Jan. pt. of v. 7.] '08(Ja18) $1.90; [Ap. pt. of v. 6.] (My23) $1.25; [July pt. of v. 8.] (Ag1) $1.25; [Oct. pt. of v. 6.] (O31) 60 c.; [Jan. pt. of v. 7.] '09(Ja23) $1.43; [Oct. pt. of v. 7,] (O23) $1.43; [Apr. pt. of v. 8.] (Ap24) 94 c.; [July pt. of v. 8.] (Je31) 94 c.; [January pt. of v. 8.] '10(Ja22): [April pt. of v. 8.] (My14) F. pap., ea., pt. 60 c.; [July pt. of v. 8.] (Jl16) $1.25; [October pt. of v. 8.] (N5) 94 c. Oxford Univ.

Murray, Ja. D. Erskine-.
See Erskine-Murray, Ja. D.

Murray, J:, 1851-.
Handbook for Rome and the Campagna; ed. by Norwood Young. New, enl. and rev. ed., (17th.) '08(D5) maps, plans, 12°, *$4 net. Scribner.
Hdbk. of travel talk. '10(Ag27) 24°, $1.25 net. Scribner.

Murray, J:, and Miller, Mills.
The round-up; novelized from Edmund Day's melodrama. '08(Mr28) c. il. D †$1.50. G: W. Dillingham.

Murray, J: Clark.
Hand-book of Christian ethics. '08(D19) 12°, *$2.25 net. Scribner.

Murray, J: Tucker.
English dramatic companies, 1558-1642. In 2 v. v. 1, London companies, 1558-1642; v. 2, Provincial companies, 1558-1642; appendices. '10(N19) fold. tabs., O. $7.50 net. Houghton M.

Murray, Lawrence O.
Co-operation as a factor in effective bank supervision; address del. at the ninth annual convention of the National Association of Supervisors of State Banks, held in Washington, D. C., Sept. 12th, 13th and 14th, 1910. '10(D) 32 p. 12°. (Priv. pr.) Nat. City Bank.

Murray, Mrs. Louise Welles.
History of old Tioga Point and early Athens, Pa. '08(D) c. '07. 14+656 p. il. pors. maps, facsims., 8°, *$5 net. L. W. Murray.

Murray, R. W.
Hernia; its cause and treatment. 2d ed. '10(N) 7+184 p. il. 8°, $1.75. Blakiston.

Murray, Sara Van Alen.
Christian science versus personal opinion as found in "Science and health with key to the scriptures," by Mary Baker G. Eddy; a criticism. '09(Ja30) c. D. pap., 50 c. S. V. Murray.
Flesh and matter: Scriptures vs. Christian science. '09(Ja16) c. D. pap., 50 c. S. V. Murray.

Murray, T. Douglas, ed.
Jeanne D'Arc, maid of Orleans, deliverer of France. New and rev. ed. '08(D12) il. 8°, *$3.50 net. McClure.

Murray, T: E:
Electric power plants; description of a number of power stations; designed by T: E: Murray. '10(My7) c. il. plans, O. (Priv. pr.) T: E: Murray.

Murray, T: Holt.
Speeches of T: Holt Murray of Clearfield, Penn. v. 1. '08(D) c. il. pors. 8°, $1. Eaton & M.

Murray, W: D.
Bible stories to tell children. '10(O8) c. front. D. $1 net. Revell.
Principles and organization of the Young Men's Christian Association. '10(S) 127 p. il. 12°, 60 c. net. Y. M. C. A.
Bibliography (2 p.).

Murray, W: Smith.
Making of the Balkan states. '10(S17) c. O. (Columbia Univ. studies in history, economics and public law.) pap., $1.50. Longmans.

Murray-Aaron, Eug.
Heart of our country: graphic presentation from official sources of the history, development and methods of the United States federal government in all its departments, bureaus, divisions, offices and special commissions throughout the legislative. executive and judicial branches of our national administration; with the assistance of numerous federal authorities. '09(Ag7) c. il. maps, f°, $11; hf. mor., $12.50; ¾ mor., $15. G: F. Cram.

MURRAY BAY, Canada.
See Canada.

Muschler, Reno.
Manual flora of Egypt; with preface by Georg Schweinfurth. '10(Jl16) 8°, $6. Lemcke.

MUSCLES.
See Eye.

Muse in motley. Carrick, H. *$1.10 net. Macmillan.

Musenblüten. Wienand, P. $1. Central.

Muses' lib.; ed. by A. H. Bullen. 16°, 50 c.; leath., 75 c.; lambskin, $1. Dutton.
—Darley. Complete poetical works.
—Moore. Irish melodies.
—Ruskin. Poems.

MUSEUM OF DECORATIVE ART, Paris.
Hessling, E., *ed.* Louis xv. furniture in the Museum of Decorative Arts, Paris. $12. Hessling.
See also Paris.
Museums of education. Andrews, B: R: 30 c. Teachers' Coll.
Mushroom fairies. Sutton, A. L. $1.25. Saalfield.
MUSHROOMS.
Burlingham, G. S. Study of the *Lactariae* of the United States: [mushrooms.] $1.25. Torrey.
Cole, E. T. Guide to the mushrooms. $1.50 net. Doubleday, P.
Hard, M. E. Mushroom, edible and otherwise. $4.75; $6; $7.50. Mushroom Pub.
How to grow mushrooms for market. 50 c. U. S. Mushroom.
MUSIC.
Abbott, A. J. Music manual for teachers of rural schools. 15 c. Am. Bk.
Aiken, W. H. Melody studies for primary grades. 15 c.—Music course. 50 c. Am. Bk.
Bigelow, M. E. New way to write music. (Add. author for price.) M. E. Bigelow.
Bingham, W: V. D. Studies in melody. $1. Psychological Review.
Bloomfield, D. Important events in musical history. 25 c. Presser.
Bowen, G: O. Teacher's manual of music for elem. schools. $1.75 net. G: O. Bowen.
Burrowes, K. Burrowes course of music study. $3. K. Burrowes.
Combarieu, J. L. J. Music; its laws and evolution. Appleton.
Cooke, J. F. Standard hist. of music. $1.25. T. Presser.
Cornill, C. H. Music in the Old Testament. 50 c. Open Court.
Crane, J. E. Music teacher's manual. 75 c. J. E. Crane.
De Bekker, L. J. Stokes' encyclopedia of music and musicians. **$3 net. Stokes.
Dickinson, E: Study of the history of music. **$2.50 net. Scribner.
Edwards, J: H. God and music. **$1.25 net. Baker & T.
Elson, A. Music club programs from all nations. $1.25. Ditson.
Elson, L: C: Curiosities of music: facts not generally known, regarding the music of ancient and savage nations. $1.—Pocket music dict. 35 c. Ditson.
Elson, L: C: Mistakes and disputed points in music and music teaching. $1.25. T. Presser.
Engel, C. Music of the most ancient nations. $3.50 net. Scribner.
Evans, E. How to compose within the lyric form. *$1 net. Scribner.
Evans, M. G., *comp.* Questions and answers on the elements of music. 80 c. M. G. Evans.
Farnsworth, C: H. Education through music. $1. Am. Bk.
Feininger, K. Experiential psychology of music. $2. A. Gemunder.

MUSIC.—*Continued.*
Feininger, K. First ser. of four essays on the experimental psychology of reproductive music. (Add. pubs. for price.) Business Press.
Finck, H: T. Success in music and how it is won. **$2 net. Scribner.
Fowles, E. Key to the questions and exercises in "Studies in musical graces." 75 c. Boston Music.
Galloway, W: J. Musical England. $1.50 net. Lane.
Gardner, M. A. Scale and chord helps. 20 c. M. A. Gardner.
Gaynor, J. L. Elements of musical expression. $1.25. C. F. Summy Co.
Gehring, A. Basis of musical pleasure. $1.50. Putnam.
Giddings, T. P. School music teaching. $1. C. H. Congdon.
Glyn, M. H. Analysis of the evolution of musical form. *$3.50 net. Longmans.
Goddard, J. Rise of music. *$2.50 net. Scribner.
Goodrich, A. J: Music as a language. $1. Schirmer.
Goodsell, A. T. Vocalist's and pianist's companion. 50 c. A. T. Goodsell.
Grau, R. Forty years' observation of music and the drama. $5. B'way Pub.
Grosvenor Lib., Buffalo, N. Y. Catalogue of the books rel. to music in the Grosvenor Library, Buffalo. gratis. Grosvenor Lib.
Grove, *Sir* G:, *ed.* Dict. of music and musicians. In 5 v. ea., **$5 net. Macmillan.
Hackney, *Mrs.* A. J. H., *comp.* Cullings of forty years, from musical lanes and hedges. $1. Bapt. Bk.
Hamilton, C. G. Outlines of music history. $1.50. Ditson
Hofer, M. R. Music for the child world. v. 1, Characteristic scenes and sketches; v. 2, Rhythms, marches and games. v. 1, $1.25; v. 2, $1.50. C. F. Summy Co.
Hoffman, R: Some musical recollections of fifty years. $1.50 net. Scribner.
Hooper, L. M. Selected list of music and books about music for public libraries. 25 c. A. L. A.
Hubbard, W: L., *ed.* American history and encyclopedia of music. In 10 v. ea., $3.50; $4.50; $6. Squire-C.
Jewett, A. D. Idiomatic ear training: [teaches music in the same way as reading.] $1. A. D. Jewett.
Kitson, C: H. Studies in fugue. $1.50. Oxford Univ.
Klauser, J. Nature of music. $2.50. Houghton M.
Klein, H. Unmusical New York. $1.50 net. Lane.
Kreymborg, A. Apostrophes; book of tributes to masters of music. 50 c. Grafton Press.
Lane, L. P. Tone, silence and time. $1.75. L. P. Lane.
Logan, M. S. Musicology. $1.25. Hinds.
Lucas, C. Story of musical form. *$1.25 net. Scribner.

MUSIC.—*Continued.*

Lussy, M. Short treatise on musical rhythms. $1. T: J. Donlan.

McConnell, M. F., *comp. and ed.* Some essentials in musical definitions for music students. $1. Ditson.

MacDougall, D. *and* A., *eds.* Bond of music. $1.25; $2. Stokes.

Macpherson, C: S. Form in music with special reference to the designs of instrumental music. $2.25. Schirmer.

Mason, D. G. Child's guide to music. **$1.25 net. Baker & T.

Mendelsohn, J. Complete method of musical composition. $2. Fischer.

New York Public Library. Selected list of works in the N. Y. Public Library rel. to the hist. of music. gratis. N. Y. Pub. Lib.

Newman, E. Musical studies. $1.50 net. Lane.

Newton, E. W. Music in the public schools. $1. Ginn.

O'Neill, F. Irish folk music. $2. Lyon & H.; McClurg; Regan.

Pauer, E. Musical forms. 75 c. Ditson.

Pratt, W. S. Class notes in music history. *30 c. net. Schirmer.

Princeton Univ. Lib. Finding list for the music library. 1909. $1.25 net. Princeton Univ.

Prout, E. Instrumentation. 75 c. Ditson.

Rix, F. R. Manual of school music in elementary grades. *60 c. net. Macmillan.

San Francisco Public Library. Music catalogue. gratis. San Francisco Lib.

Seymour, H. A. How to think music. $1. H. W. Gray.

Smith, E. Eleanor Smith music course. Bk. 1, 25 c.; Bk. 2, 30 c.; Bk. 3, 40 c.; Bk. 4, 50 c.—Music course; manual. 50 c. Am. Bk.

Studies in musical education hist. and æsthetics. $1.60. Music Teachers' Nat. Assoc.

Surette, T: W., *and* Mason, D. G. Appreciation of music. **$1.50 net. Baker & T.

Symons, A. Plays, acting and music. **$2 net. Dutton.

Upton, G: P. Standard concert guide.—Standard concert repertory. ea., $1.75. McClurg.

Van Dyke, H: J. Music lover. *50 c. net. Moffat.

Wagner, W. R. Judaism in music. $1.25 net. Scribner.

Wallace, W: Threshold of music. *$1.50 net; *$2.25 net. Macmillan.

Wead, C: K. Music and science. 10 c. Philosophical Soc.

Whitcomb, I. P. Young people's story of music. $2. Dodd.

Williams, C: F. A. Rhythm of modern music. *$1.50 net. Macmillan.

Winsett, R. E. Standard rudiments, a self-instructor: [music.] 15 c. R. E. Winsett.

MUSIC.—*Continued.*

Zuchtmann, F. New American music reader; no. 2; introductory—4. no. 2, *45 c. net; introductory—4, *32 c. net. Macmillan

See also Bibliographies;—Cantatas;—Church music;—Counterpoint; — Ear;—Flute;—Hand;—Harmony; — Hymns and hymn writers; — Indians;—Musicians;—Operas;—Orchestral music;—Organs and organists;—Pianoforte;—Singing;—Songs;—Violin; —Violoncello;—Voice;—*also* Library of Congress;—*also* names of musicians.

Music lovers' lib. pors. D. Lippincott.
—Davidson. Stories from the operas. *$1.25 net.
—Racster. Chats on violoncellos. *$1.25 net.

Music master. Klein, C: †$1.50. Dodd.

Music of the masters ser.; ed. by Wakeling Dry. 12°, $1. Brentano's.
—Colles. Brahms.

Music of the wild. Porter, *Mrs.* G. S-. $2.50. Jennings.

Music story ser. See Scribner's.

Music students' lib. O. Ditson.
—Chase. Natural laws in piano technic. $1.25.
—Elson. Music club programs. $1.25.
—Hamilton. Outlines of music history. $1.50.
—McConnell. Some essentials in musical definitions. $1.
—Manchester. Twelve lessons in the fundamentals of voice production. $1.
—Panseron. A B C of vocalization. $1.
—York. Text-book in simple strict counterpoint. $1.25.

Music trade directory of United States and Canada. '07, [1908.] (Mr.) c. 8°, $5. Thompson

MUSICAL INSTRUMENTS.

Engel, C. Musical instruments. $1.25 net. Scribner.

See also Flute;—Orchestral music;—Organs and organists;—Pianoforte;—Violin;—Violoncello.

Musical memories. Upton, G: P. *$2.75 net. McClurg

MUSICAL NOTATION.
See Music.

Musical poems. Field, E. $1. Scribner.

MUSICIANS.

Crawford, R., *and* Tousey, E. Great musicians' art and glory told in picture and in story. $2.50. D. W. Newton.

De Bekker, L. J. Stokes' encyclop. of music and musicians. *$3 net. Stokes.

Garbett, A. S., *comp.* Gallery of musical celebrities. 75 c. T. Presser.

Hadden, J. C. Master musicians. $1.75. Barse & H.

New York church and musical directory of New York and Brooklyn and other adjacent suburbs. 50 c. W: A. James.

Oldmeadow, E. Great musicians. $1.50. Jacobs.

Polko, *Frau* E. V. Musical sketches; [episodes from lives of great musicians.] *$1.25 net. Sturgis & W.

Rowbotham, F. J. Story-lives of great musicians. $1.50. Stokes.

Upton, G: P. Musical memories. *$2.75 net.—Standard musical biographies. $1.75. McClurg.

See also Music;—Opera;—*also* Days with great musicians;—*also* names of musicians.

Musicians' lib. Q. $2.50; pap., $1.50. Ditson.
—Bach. Piano composition.
—Beethoven. Piano compositions.
—Brahms. Selected piano compositions.
—Chopin. Greater Chopin.
—**Grieg. Fifty songs.—Larger piano compo**sitions.—Piano lyrics and shorter compositions.
—Krehbiel, *ed.* Songs from the operas for alto.—Songs from the operas for mezzo soprano.—Songs from the operas for tenor.
—Wolf. Fifty songs.

Musick, J: Roy.
Real America in romance; with reading courses, complete and authentic history of America from time of Columbus to the present day. In 14 v. '08(Ap4) c. 8°, complete work, $43.50; hf. mor., $51.50; mor., $62.50. W. H. Wise.

Musicology. Logan, M. S. $1.25. Hinds.

Musings of a Chinese mystic. Chuang Tzu. *60 c. net. Dutton.

Musket boys of old Boston. Warren, C: E. Cupples & L.

Musket boys on the Delaware. Warren, G: A. $1. Cupples & L.

Musket boys under Washington. Warren, C: E. $1. Cupples & L.

MUSLIM.
See Mohammed and Mohammedanism.

Musselman, De Lafayette.
Bookkeeping for business colleges, schools, and private instructions. '09(D) c. 73 p. forms, 4°, $2. D. L. Musselman.

Musselman, Rev. Hugh T:, ed.
National Teacher-Training Institute textbooks. Introductory bk., Baptist teacher training manual, by H. T. Musselman. '09(N6) **30 c. net; **50 c. net.—Bk. 2, The Sunday-school teacher's pupils. '08 (F15); Bk. 3, The Sunday-school teacher's pedagogy. (Je6) c. S. ea., **40 c. net; pap., **25 c. net; Bk. 4, The Sunday-school teacher's school; pt. 1, by H. T. Musselman; pt. 2, by H. E. Tralle. '09(Ap17) c. D. *40 c. net; pap., *25 c. net; Bk. 5, Child-study for Sunday-school teachers. '08, [1909.] (Mr) c. S. bds., **40 c. net; pap., **25 c. net; Bk. 6, The early church-history and doctrine, by J: Wesley Conley, D.D. '09(Mr13) 16°, *50 c. net. Am. Bapt.

Musset, Louis Charles Alfr. de.
Complete writings; tr. into English. In 10 v. '08(Je27) c. ed. de luxe, $12.50. Lamb Pub.
Croisilles; ed. by S. Tindall. '10(Ja29) S. (Crowell's shorter French texts.) *25 c. net. Crowell.

Musset, Paul Edme de.
Mr. Wind and Madam Rain; tr., with permission of the author, by Emily Makepeace. '08(S19) il. D. (Harper's young people ser.) 60 c. Harper.

Musson, Mrs. Louise Walbridge.
Frau von Colson's Christmas eve. '08 (Je27) c. S. pap., 75 c. Rust-Graft.

Musson, Spencer C.
Upper Engadine. '08(Ap11) il. map. 8°, (Color books.) *$2.50 net. Macmillan.

Must women suffer everlastingly? Hegyessy, J. $2.50. J. Hegyessy.

MUSTAGH RANGE, Kashmir.
Workman, F. B. *and* W: H. Ice-bound heights of Mustagh: [Kashmir.] *$5 net. Scribner.

Mutation theory. **De Vries, H.** In 2 v. ea., $4 net. Open Court.

Muther, R:
Rembrandt; tr. by Fs. Cox. '10(N5) il. (Belgravia art monographs.) limp leath., $1.50 net, boxed; Persian cf., $1.75 net, boxed. Caldwell.

Muthu, C., M.D.
Pulmonary tuberculosis and sanatorium treatment; record of ten years' observation and work in open-air sanatoria. '10(Je) il. 8°, $2 net. Wood.

Mutt and Jeff cartoons. Fisher, H. C. 50 c. net. Ball Pub.

Muzzey, D: Saville.
Spiritual Franciscans: Herbert Baxter Adams prize essay, awarded December, 1905. '08(My16) 8°, pap., gratis. D: S. Muzzey.

My advice book. Williams, H. 50 c. net. McClurg.

My African journey. Churchill, W. G. *$1.50 net. Doran.

My Alma Mater; **designed by Clara Powers Wilson.** '10(My) 8°, **$1.50; lev., $6.** Reilly & B.

My Alpine jubilee. Harrison, F. *$1.25 net. Dutton.

My auto book. Pulitzer, W. $1. Outing.

My belief. Horton, R. F. *$1.25 net. Revell.

My boy. Pell, E: L. 10 c. Harding.

My brother. Bradford, A. H. $1.25 net. Pilgrim Press.

My brother the king. Cooper, E: H. $1.50. Lane.

My brother's keeper. Jackson, C: T. $1.50. Bobbs-M.

My bunkie and others. Schreyvogle, C: **$4 net. Moffat.

My busy days. Sturgis, *Mrs.* E. B. **$2 net. Appleton.

My chums in caricature. Williams, H. *50 c. net. McClurg.

My college days: record. '10(S10) front. O. $2.50, boxed. Stokes.

My commencement. New ed. '10(My14) col. front. 12°, $1.50, boxed; limp leath., $3 special net, boxed. Dodd.

My country. Smith, S: F. *$3 net. Tandy-T.

My Cranford. Gilman, A. **$1.25 net. Houghton M.

My day. Pryor, *Mrs.* S. A. R. **$2.25 net. Macmillan.

My day and generation. Carr, C. E. *$3 net. McClurg.

My days and nights on the battlefield. Coffin, C: C. 50 c. Hurst.

My enemy the motor. Street, J. L. †$1. Lane.

My experiences in Cyprus. Stewart, B. *$2 net. Dutton.

My Father's business. Fisher, M. H. 60 c. China Inland.

My Father's business. Jefferson, C: E: **$1.25 net. Crowell.

My favorite novelist: entertaining papers by Frank R: Stockton, Mrs. Burton Harrison, and Paul Bourget. '08(Ag8) c. sq. 16°, (Bookish books.) bds., *55 c. net. Burrows.

My first cousin or myself. Barnard, A. E. 75 c. Cochrane.

My fraternity; designed by J. O. Smith. [1910.] (My) 8°, $1.50; mor., $3. Reilly & B.

My friend the Indian. McLaughlin, J. $2.50 net. Houghton M.

My friend the partridge. Hammond, S. T. $1. Forest.

My friends. Strong, H. P., *comp.* 50 c.; $1.25. Caldwell.

My gift to thee. Potts, J. H: $1. Jennings.

My grandfather's best brand. Hays, M. D. $1. M. D. Hays.

My grandmother's garden. Bray, *Mrs.* M. M. $1. Badger.

My heart and Stephanie. Kauffman, R. W. $1.50. L. C. Page.

My high school days. Bridgman, L. J. $1.50; $2.50; $3; $5. Caldwell.

My inner life. Crozier, J: B. 2 v. *$2.50 net. Longmans.

My Lady Beatrice. Cooke, F. $1.25. Benziger.

My Lady of Cleeve. Hartley, P. J. †$1.50. Dodd.

My lady of the fog. Barbour, R. H. †$2. Lippincott.

My lady of the South. Parrish, R. $1.50. McClurg.

My Lady Vaudeville. Golden, G: F. $1. White Rats.

My lady's fortune hunt. Kinkade, F: $1.50. C. M. Clark.

My lady's kiss. Innes, N. $1.50. Rand, McN. & Co.

My lady's toilet. Nolan, G. V., *comp.* $1. Peoples News.

My life. Flynt, J., *pseud.* *$2 net. Outing.

My life and my lectures. Fontaine, L. $3. Neale.

My life as a disassociated personality. Prince, M., *ed.* 50 c. Badger.

My life in China and America. Yung Wing. **$2 net. Holt.

My little German travelling companion. Kettner, L. 25 c. net. Cassell.

My Lord and Savior Jesus Christ. Hanly, J. F. 85 c. Hollenbeck Press.

My lost duchess. Williams, J. L. †$1.50. Century Co.

My lost self. Marchmont, A. W. 75 c. Cupples & L.

My loves and my lovers. Merrill, S: P. $1. Marion Press.

My Mark Twain. Howells, W: D. $1.40 net. Harper.

My memoirs. *See* Dumas, Alexandre.

My own name ser. '10(Ag20) 25 v., il. Tf., ea., 40 c.; cf., $1, boxed. Caldwell.
Contents: Alice, Annie, Bertha, Charlotte, Dorothy, Elizabeth, Eleanor, Edith, Fanny, Gertrude, Gladys, Helen, Isabel, Jane, Katharine, Lucy, Marjorie, Margaret, Mary, Mildred, Marion, Nellie, Ruth, Sarah, Winifred.

My own philosophy. Eggerth, W. $1.50. W. Eggerth.

My pedagogic creed. Dewey, J: 15 c. Flanagan.

My personal experience with tuberculosis. Ross, W: M. 50 c. W. M. Ross.

My pets. Saunders, M. M. $1.25. Am. Bapt.

My pets. *See* Dumas, Alexandre.

My place in the world. Faithfull, R. C. $1.40 net. Whittaker.

My playtime book. Gale, N. B. C. 50 c. Tuck.

My policies in Jungleland. Ransom, F. C: $1. Barse & H.

My prayer book. Lasance, F. X. $1.25. Benziger.

My Quaker maid. Ryan, *Mrs.* M. E. 75 c. Rand, McN. & Co.

My quest of the Arab horse. Davenport, H. C. **$2 net. B. W. Dodge.

My recollections. *See* Cardigan and Lancastre, Adeline Louise Maria de Horsey, *Countess* of.

My religion in every-day life. Strong, J. 50 c. Baker & T.

My school and my gospel. Herkomer, *Sir* H. v. *$7.50 net. Doubleday, P.

My school days. '10(S10) front. O. $2.50, boxed. Stokes.

My school life. Iorio, A. J., *comp.* $1; $2.50. Caldwell.

My soldier lady. Durley, E. H. $1.50. C. M. Clark.

My sorority; designed by Louise Perrett. [1910.] (My) 8°, $1.50; mor., $3. Reilly & B.

My soul's cathedral. MacLafferty, J. H: 90 c. net. P. Elder.

My story. Caine, T: H: H. **$2 net. Appleton.

My summer in London. Milne, J. $1.50 net. Dutton.

My three days in Gilead. Hoenshel, E. U. 50 c.; 30 c. E. U. Hoenshel.

My three years at Andover. Perrin, L. J. $1. Mayhew.

My two gardens. Sprague, A. 50 c.; $1. Manas Press.

My Uncle Toby. Sterne, L. 50 c. Dutton.

My voice and I. Rogers, *Mrs.* C. K. B. $1.50 net. McClurg.

My wonder book. Harvey, *Mrs.* E. M. B. $1. Chapple Pub.

MYCOLOGY.
See Bacteria.

Myers, A. Wallis.
Complete lawn tennis player. '08(Ag1) il. pors. 8°, *$3 net. Jacobs.

Myers, Allen O.
Alfalfa, "the grass," in Ohio; where, how and why to grow it. '08(Ja11) il. 12°, $1. Heer.

Myers, C: S:
Text-book of experimental psychology. '09 (Ap3) il. D. *$2.40 net. Longmans.
Vivisection problem: controversy between Charles S. Myers and Albert Leffingwell. '09(F20) 8°, pap. (Add. pubs. for price.) S. R. Taber.

Myers, Cora Bosworth Glacier, [**"Mrs. P. M. Myers."**]
City of dreams (Guanajuato), [Mexico.] '08, [1909.] (F) c. 7-33 p. il. 8°, 50 c. P. M. Myers.

Myers, Cortland, D.D.
Boy Jesus. '08(F29) c. il. D. bds., **60 c. net. Am. Bapt.
Real Holy Spirit. '09(Ap10) c. *50 c. net. Revell.

Myers, Eliab.
Champion text-book on embalming. 5th ed., greatly enl. and almost entirely rewritten. '08(Je6) c. 8°, $5; hf. russia, $5.50; russia, $6. Champion Chemical.

Myers, Fk. A.
Apologies for love. '09(N6) c. D. †$1.50. Badger.

Myers, Frederic W: H:
Saint Paul. '09(S18) 32°, *35 c. net. Macmillan.

Myers, G: W:
Arithmetic, grammar school. '09(Mr) c. 470 p. il. 12°, 60 c. Scott, F. & Co.
—, and others.
Second-year mathematics for secondary schools. '10(Jl2) c. il. D. (Univ. of Chicago mathematical ser.) $1.50 net. Univ. of Chic.

Myers, Gustavus.
Beyond the borderline of life. '09, [1910.] (F) *$1 net. Ball Pub.
Hist. of the great American fortunes. In 3 v. v. 1, pt. 1, Conditions in settlement and Colonial times; pt. 2, The great land fortunes. '09(D18); v. 2, Great fortunes from the railroads. '10(Ap9); v. 3, Great fortunes from the railroads (continued). (Jl2) c. pors. D. ea., $1.50. Kerr.

Myers, Jack M.
Jewish story book. '10(Je4) 8°, 30 c. Bloch.
Story of the Jewish people. In 2 v. v. 1. '09(My22) il. maps, 8°, *60 c. net. Bloch.

Myers, Leopold H.
Arvat: a dramatic poem. '08(N7) D. *$1.25 net. Longmans.

Myers, Minard C.
Different types of modern engines and their valve setting, in a condensed form. '10(Ap23) c. il. 8°, $1. M. C. Myers.

Myers, Mrs. P. M.
See Myers, Cora Bosworth Glasier.

Myers, Stella Evelyn.
Heroes and happenings of Egypt, Assyria, Greece; continuous acct. from papyri, inscriptions, and modern authors; with adaptations from the Green historians. '10(N5) c. 12°, 80 c. S. E. Myers.

Myers, W: Starr.
Self-reconstruction of Maryland, 1864-1867. '09(Mr13) c. O. (Johns Hopkins Univ. studies in hist. and pol. science.) pap., 50 c. Johns Hopkins.

Mygatt, J: Tracy.
What I do not know of farming. '08(N21) c. 8°, 75 c. B'way Pub.

Myhrman, D: Wilhelm.
Sumerain administrative documents, dated in the reigns of the kings of the second dynasty of Ur, from the temple archives of Nippur, preserved in Philadelphia. '10 (O15) F. (Babylonian Expedition of the Univ. of Pennsyivania, series A: Cuneiform texts; ed. by H. V. Hilprecht.) pap., $6. Univ. of Penn.

Myland, Rev. D: Wesley.
Latter rain covenant and pentecostal power; with testimony of healings and baptism. '10(Je) c. 215 p. il. 16°, 50 c. Evangel.

Mylne, Bp. L: G:
Missions to Hindus. '08(Ja25) D. *$1.20 net. Longmans.

Mynders, Seymour Allen.
See McBain, Howard Lee.

Myomata of the uterus. Kelly, H. A. *$7.50 net; *$9 net. Saunders.

Myra of the pines. Viele, H. K. †$1.50. Duffield.

MYRIAPODA.
See Insects.

Myrtle Baldwin. Munn, C: C. †$1.50. Lothrop, L. & S.

Mysteries of God. Ingram, A. F. W. $1. Young Churchman.

Mysteries of life revealed. Patterson, C: E. $1. C: E. Patterson.

Mysteries of Paris. Sue, M. J. E. 2 v. $2.50, boxed. Crowell.

Mysteries of the people ser. See Sue, Marie Joseph Eugène.

Mysterious discovery of nature. Pooley, P: $1. P: Pooley.

Mystery of Ashton Hall. Austin, B: F. $1.25. Austin.

Mystery of education. Wendell, B. **$1.25 net. Scribner.

Mystery of Evangeline Fairfax. Kunst, E. $1. Metropolitan Press, (N. Y.)

Mystery of existence. Armstrong, C: W. *90 c. net. Longmans.

Mystery of golf. *See* Haultain, T. A.

Mystery of Hamlet, Prince of Denmark. Benedict, R. R. $1 net. Lippincott.

Mystery of life. Ruskin, J: 50 c. Rand, McN. & Co.

Mystery of love scientifically and philosophically considered. Anderson, L. H. $2. L. H. Anderson.

Mystery of Miss Motte. Mason, *Mrs.* C. A. $1.25. L. C. Page.

Mystery of Mr. Bernard Brown. Oppenheim, E: P. $1.50. Little, B. & Co.

Mystery of Monastery Farm. Naylor, H: R. 75 c. Eaton & M.

Mystery of Mortimer Strange. Marchmont, A. W. 75 c. Rand, Mc.N. & Co.

Mystery of Naples. Graham, E: A. P. $1.50. Herder.

Mystery of Osiris. Clymer, R. S. $5. Philosophical.

Mystery of pain. *See* Henton, Ja.

Mystery (The) of sex; or, sex polarity. '09, [1910.] (F) 110 p. 12°, $1. Arcane.

Mystery of the four fingers. White, F. M. $1.50. W. J. Watt.

Mystery of the green heart. Pemberton, M. $1.30 net. Dodd.

Mystery of the miniature. Edwards, R: K. $1.50. C. M. Clark.

Mystery of the Pinckney draught. Nott, C: C. **$2 net. Century Co.

Mystery of the sandal-wood box. Barnard, M. C. $1. Mayhew.
Mystery of the yellow room. Leroux, G. †$1.50. Brentano's.
Mystery play in honour of the nativity of our Lord. Benson, R. H. 20 c.; 90 c. Longmans.
Mystic Christianity. Ramacharaka, *Yogi*. $1. Yogi Pub.
Mystic ride of the somnial bride. Harriman, J: E., *jr.* $1. Cycle Press.
Mystic spring. Higgins, D: W. $1.50. B'way Pub.
Mystic test book of "The Hindu occult chambers." De Laurence, L. W: $2. De Laurence, S.
Mystic will. Leland, C: G. 50 c. Progress Co.
Mystical element in Hegel's early theological writings. Adams, G: P. 35 c. Univ. of Cal.
Mystical element in religion. Hügel, *Baron* F. v. 2 v. *$6 net. Dutton.
MYSTICISM.
Atkinson, W: W. Mystic Christianity. $1. Yogi Pub.
Berkeley, H. Mysticism in modern mathematics. $3.20. Oxford Univ.
Cell of self-knowledge. $2 net. Duffield.
Gardner, E. G. Cell of self-knowledge; seven early English mystical treatises. *$2 net. Duffield.
Iliowizi, H: Revelation: world's mystic and realistic. $2 net. Dutton.
Jones, R. M. Studies in mystical religion. *$3.50 net. Macmillan.
Oppenheimer, F. J. Reign of the negative; studies in mysticism and skepticism. $2 net. Moods Pub.
Remensnyder, J. B: Mysticism. 25 c. Germ. Lit. Bd.
See also Occultism;—Soul.
Myth, M. Y. T. H., pseud.
See Nicolovius, Ludwig.
Myth, magic and morals. Conybeare, F: C. $2.50 net. Am. Unitarian.
Myth of a free press. Reedy, W: M. (Add. author for price.) W: M. Reedy.
Myth of Hercules at Rome. Winter, J: G. 50 c. Macmillan.
MYTHOLOGY.
Cartwright, T: One for Wod and one for Lok. 50 c. Dutton.
Cartwright, T:, *ed.* Old, old myths of Greece and Rome. 50 c. Dutton.
Clarke, H. A. Ancient myths and modern poets. $2 net.—Child's guide to mythology. **$1.25 net. Baker & T.
Clymer, R. S. Mystery of Osiris: Egyptian mythology. $5. Philosophical.
Ebbutt, M. I. Hero-myths and legends of the British race. $2 net. Crowell.
Edmison, J: P. Stories from the Norseland. †$1.25. Penn Pub. Co.
Farmer, F. V. Nature myths of many lands. 45 c. Am. Bk.
Farnell, L. R: Cults of the Greek states. In 5 v. v. 5. $6. Oxford Univ.
Farrar, F. A. Old Greek nature stories. $1.50 net. Crowell.
MYTHOLOGY.—*Continued.*
Frazer, J. G: Adonis, Attis, Osiris: [studies in mythology.] *$3.25 net. Macmillan.
Goddard, P. E. Kato texts. 50 c. Univ. of Cal.
Harrison, J. E. Prolegomena to the study of Greek religion. *$6 net. Putnam.
Hartley, C. G. Stories from the Greek legends. *$1.25 net. Lippincott.
Hawthorne, N. Stories of classical fables: wonder book for boys and girls. 35 c. McLoughlin.
Hutchinson, W. M. L. Orpheus with his lute; stories of the world's springtime. *$1.40 net. Longmans.
Little stories for boys and girls, [Greek heroes and heroines.] $1.50. Seymour.
Macgregor, M. Stories from Siegfried. 50 c. Dutton.
Müller, M. Comparative mythology. *50 c. net; *75 c. net. Dutton.
Niebuhr, B. G. Greek heroes. 50 c. Cassell.
Riis, J. A. Hero tales of the far North. $1.35 net. Macmillan.
Stories of classic myths. **65 c. net. Century Co.
Wilmot-Buxton, E. M. Stories of Norse heroes. $1.50. Crowell.
Woodhouse, S. C. Dictionary of classical mythology. 50 c. Dutton.
Woolsey, J: M. Original Garden of Eden discovered and the final solution of the mystery of the woman. $1.50. J: M. Woolsey.
Zimmern, A. Gods and heroes of the north. *36 c. net; *60 c. net. Longmans.
See also Archæology; — Fables; — Fairy tales; — Folk-lore;—Hercules; — Heroes; — Indians;— Ireland;—Legends; — Orpheus;—Religions; — Totemism;—*also* Santa Claus.
Myths about monarchs. Watt, H. **$1 net. Dodd.
Myths and facts of the American Revolution. Johnston, A. $1.50 net. W: B. Clarke.
Myths and legends of the New York State Iroquois. Converse, *Mrs.* H. M. C. 75 c.; 50 c. N. Y. State Educ.
Myths and legends of the Pacific northwest. Judson, K. B., *comp.* $1.50 net. McClurg.
"N., Will," pseud.
See Harben, W: Nathaniel.
N. W. Harris lectures. *See* Harris, (N. W.)
Nabuco, Joaquim.
Place of Camoens in literature; address del. before the students of Yale University, May 14, 1908. '08(D) 26 p. 8°. (Add. author for price.) J. Nabuco.
Spirit of nationality in the history of Brazil: address del. before the Spanish Club of Yale University on the 15th May, 1908. '08(O) 14 p. 8°. (Not for sale.) J. Nabuco.
Nachette. Nye, E: $1.50. J. H. Remick.
Nadaud, Gustave, and Dorr, Julia C. R.
Carcassonne, by Gustave Nadaud; tr. by J: R. Thompson; and To one who went to Carcassonne, by Julia C. R. Dorr; with introd. by C: Mason Fairbanks. '09 (My) (Priv. pr.) T: N. Fairbanks.
Nadia Grey. Collins, H. C. $1.50. H. C. Collins.

NADIR, *Shah of Persia.*
Durand, *Sir* H: M. Nadir Shah. *$3 net. Dutton.

Na Gael, Shane, pseud.
See Welsh, C:

Nagel, Oskar.
Die Welt als arbeit. 2d ed. '09(N) c. 208 p. 12°, 80 c. O. Nagel.
Mechanical appliances of the chemical and metallurgical industries. '09(F20); 2d ed. '09, [1910.] (My) c. il. 8°, ea., $2 net. O. Nagel.
Producer gas fired furnaces; of the chemical, metal, metallurgical, iron, steel, lime, cement, glass, brick and ceramic industries; hdbk. for engineers, chemists, manufacturers, superintendents and students. '10(Ja1) c. il. O. *$2 net. O. Nagel.
The transportation of gases, liquids and solids by means of steam, compressed air and pressure water; complete description of the theory, construction, operation and application of jet machines, montejus, spray nozzles, etc. '09(D11) c. il. D. *$2 net. O. Nagel.

Nahum (Book of). *See* Bible. O. T.

Nainfa, Rev. J: Abel Felix Prosper.
Costume of prelates of the Catholic church according to Roman etiquette. '09 (My22) c. il. D. *$1.50 net. Murphy.

Najac, Emily de.
See Sardou, Victorien.

Nakamura, Kaju.
Prince Ito; the man and statesman; brief hist. of his life. '10(My14) c. front. D. $1. Anraku.

Nall, S:, M.D.
Aids to obstetrics. 7th ed. '09, [1910.] (F) 193 p. 16°, (Students' aid ser.) *$1 net. Wood.

Nameless woman. Jackson, L. $2.50. L. Jackson.

NAMES (*geographical*).
Douglas-Lithgow, R. A. Dict. of American-Indian place and proper names in New England. $7. Salem Press.
Long, C: M. Virginia county names. *$1.50 net. Neale.
McClure, E. British place-names in their historical setting. $2. Gorham.
Meany, E. S., *comp.* Indian geographical names of Washington. 25 c. Hyatt-F.

NAMES (*personal*).
Baring-Gould, S. Family names and their story. *$3 net. Lippincott.
Douglas-Lithgow, R. A. Dict. of American-Indian place and proper names in New England. $7. Salem Press.
Hargrave, B. Origins and meanings of popular phrases and names. $1.50 net. Lippincott.
Key to noted names in hist., science, mythology, literature, art, and fiction. 25 c. Funk.
Oliphant, S: G. Clan of fire and forge; or, the ancient and honorable Smiths. 60 c. S: G. Oliphant.
See also Nicknames;—Pseudonyms.

Nancy Clark. Freear, R. L. $1.50. C. M. Clark.

Nancy MacIntyre. Parker, L. S. $1. Badger.

NANDI (African race).
Hollis, A. C. Nandi; their language and folk-lore. $5.25. Oxford Univ.

Nannie Walters. Sloper, *Mrs.* A. 25 c. J. S. Ogilvie.

NANTUCKET ISLAND, Mass.
Turner, H. B. Story of the island steamers [Nantucket]. 65 c. Inquirer.
Wilson, A. Boggy solitudes of Nantucket. $1.25. Neale.

NAPLES, Italy.
Favilli, M. Echoes of Naples; (thirty Neopolitan songs.) $1.25. Ditson.
Graham, E: A. P. Mystery of Naples. $1.50. Herder.

Napoleon I., Emperor of the French.
The Corsican; diary of Napoleon's life in his own words. '10(D3) c. O. $1.75 net. Houghton M.

NAPOLEON I., *Emperor of the French.*
Andrews, E: L. Napoleon and America. *$2 net. M. Kennerley.
Baring-Gould, S. The life of Napoleon Bonaparte. *$3.50 net. Stokes.
Bourrienne, L. A. F. de. Memoirs of Napoleon. 2 v. $2.50. Crowell.
Broadley, A. M. Napoleon in caricature, 1785-1821. $12.50 net. Lane.
Frémeaux, P. Drama of Saint Helena. $3 net. Appleton.
Gonnard, P. Exile of St. Helena. *$3.50 net. Lippincott.
Hathaway, E. V. Little Corsican, Napoleon Bonaparte. $1. Rand, McN. & Co.
Hopkins, T. Women Napoleon loved. $4.50 net. Little, B. & Co.
Johnston, R. M. Napoleon. **$1.25 net. Holt.
Marshall, H. E. Story of Napoleon. 50 c. Dutton.
Petre, F. L: Napoleon and the Archduke Charles: hist. of the Franco-Austrian campaign. *$4 net. Lane.
Rose, J. H. Dumouriez and the defense of England against Napoleon. *$5 net. Lane.
Shorter, C. K. Napoleon and his fellow travellers.—Napoleon in his own defense. ea., *$4 net. Cassell.
Sloane, W: M. Life of Napoleon Bonaparte. In 4 v. $10 net. Century Co.
Thibaudeau, A. C., *Comte.* Bonaparte and the consulate. *$3.25 net. Macmillan.
Turquan, J. Love affairs of Napoleon. *$5 net. Lane.
Warwick, C: F. Napoleon and the end of the French Revolution. $2.50 net. Jacobs.
Wheeler, H. F. B. Boy's Napoleon. $1.50. Crowell.
See also France;—Leipzig campaign;—Peninsular war;—*also* Bonaparte family.

NAPOLEON II., *titular Emperor of the French.*
See Reichstadt, *Duc* de.

NAPOLEON III., *Emperor of the French.*
Cheetam, F. H. Louis Napoleon and the genesis of the Second Empire. *$5 net. Lane.
Simpson, F: A. Rise of Louis Napoleon. *$3.50 net. Putnam.
See also France.

Napoleonic wars.
Arndt, E. M. Deutsche patrioten in Ruszland zur zeit Napoleons. 30 c. Heath.
Dunn-Pattison, R. P. Napoleon's marshals. *$3 net. Little, B. & Co.
Stanley, E: Before and after Waterloo. *$3.75 special net. Appleton.
See also Franco-Austrian campaign;—Jena campaign;—Leipzig campaign; — Waterloo (Battle of);—*also* Napoleon I.

Napoleon's brothers. Atteridge, A. H. *$5 net. Brentano's.

Napoleon's marshals. Dunn-Pattison, R. P. *$3 net. Little, B. & Co.

Narcissus. Litchfield, G. D. **$1 net. Putnam.

Narcoochee. Worrill, I. G. $1. Neale.

Narcotics.
See Stimulants and narcotics.

Nareen. Pitblado, C: B. $1. Pitblado.

Narodny, Ivan.
Echoes of myself; romantic studies of the human soul. '10(Ja22) O. $2. (999 copies.) Liberty Pub.

Narraguagus Valley, Me.
Milliken, J. A. Narraguagus Valley; some acct. of its early settlement and settlers. $2. A.. J. Huston.

Narrative and lyric poems, for students. Seward, S: S., *jr., ed.* **$1 net. Holt.

Narrative art.
See Poetry.

Narrative lyrics. White, E: L. **$1.25 net. Putnam.

Narrative of a journey to the shores of the Polar Seas. Franklin, *Sir* J: 35 c. net; 70 c. net. Dutton.

Narrative of Indian history. Allen, J. C. 90 c. Longmans.

Narratives of New Netherland. Jameson, J: F., *ed.* **$3 net. Scribner.

Narrowing of the cotton market. Thompson, W: B. gratis. W: B. Thompson.

Nascher, Ignatz Leo, M.D.
Wretches of Povertyville: sociological study of the Bowery. '09(Je26) c. il. D. $1.50. J. J. Lanzit.

Nash, Abner.
Hamilton, J. G. de R. Presentation of portrait of Governor Abner Nash to the state of North Carolina. (Not for sale.) J. G. R. Hamilton.

Nash, C: Sumner.
Congregational administration; Carew lectures before the Hartford Theological Seminary, 1908-1909. '10(Mr5) c. D. *75 c. net. Pilgrim Press.

Nash, Clarissa Hosmer Hapgood.
Verses; selections from poems published from time to time in various periodicals. '09, [1910.] (F) c. 8+98 p. por. 8°, $1. C. H. H. Nash.

Nash, Eug. Beauharnais.
Leaders in respiratory organs. '09(Je) c. 6+188 p. 12°, $1.50. Boericke & T.
Regional leaders. 2d ed., rev. and enl. '08 (Ag) c. 315 p. 12°, flex., $1.50. Boericke & T.

Nash, H: Sylvester, D.D.
Atoning life. '08(My2) c. D. **$1 net. Macmillan.
History of the higher criticism of the New Testament. '09(Ap3) 12°, (New Testament handbooks.) Price raised from *75 c. net to *$1 net. Macmillan.

Nash, L. L., D.D.
Early morning scenes in the Bible. '10 (Ag27) c. 12°, $1 net. Revell.

Nason, Arth. Huntington.
Short themes; a freshman manual for the first semester. '09(O9) c. D. *$1 net; 2d ed. '10(Ag27) c. D. $1.25 net. A. H. Nason.

Nason, Mrs. Emma Huntington.
Old colonial houses in Maine built prior to 1776. '08(Jl4) c. il. 8°. (Add. author for price.) E. H. Nason.
Old Hallowell on the Kennebec. '09, [1910.] (Mr) 359 p. il. pors. 8°, $3.50. E. H. Nason.

Natal, South Africa.
See Green, James, *D.D.*

Natchez, Miss.
Reber, T: "Proud old Natchez." 50 c. T: Reber.

Nathan, Sir Nathaniel.
Economic heresies. '09(My22) O. *$3 net. Houghton M.

Nathan Burke. Watts, *Mrs.* M. S. $1.50. Macmillan.

Nathan Hale of '73. Cushing, C. C. S. *$1 net. Yale Pub.

Nathaniel ibn al-Fayyumi.
Bustan al-ukul; ed. and tr. from an unique manuscript in the library of Columbia Univ. by David Levine. '08(Mr7) c. 8°, (Columbia Univ. oriental studies.) *$2.50 net. Lemcke.

Nathaniel William Taylor lectures. *See* Taylor (Nathaniel William) lectures.

Natick, Mass.
Vital records of Natick, Mass. $2.75. T: W. Baldwin.

Nation, Mrs. Carrie A. Moore.
Use and need of the life of Carry A. Nation, written by herself. Rev. ed. '08 (N) 17-396 p. il. por. 12°, $1. F. H. Breyfogle.

Nation and the kingdom. Gladden, W. gratis. Am. Bd. For. Miss.

Nation as a business firm. Mallock, W: H. $1 net. Macmillan.

National Amateur Playground Ball Association of the United States. Official hdbk. '08(Je6) c. il. por. S. (Spalding's athletic lib.) pap., 10 c. Am. Sports.

National and social problems. Harrison, F. **$1.75 net. Macmillan.

National Association of Engine and Boat Manufacturers. Foreign trade and yacht club directory. '08(Je) c. 8°. (Not for sale.) Nat. Assoc. Engine and Boat Manufact.

National Association of Manufacturers of the United States of America. Arguments for a permanent non-partisan expert tariff commission. '08(D) 118 p. 8°. (Add. pubs. for price.) Lumbermen's Pr.

National Association of Railway Commissioners. Proceedings of sub-committee on car service and demurrage, Washington, D. C., June 4-5, 1909. '09(Ag) 162 p. 8°, pap. (Add. Superintendent for price.) U. S., Supt. of Docs.

National Association of Railway Commissioners. Rept. of the Committee on grade crossings and trespassing on railroads. '09 (D11) 8°, pap. (Add. Superintendent for price.) U. S., Supt. of Docs.

National Association of Railway Commissioners. Rept. of the Committee on railroad taxes and plans for ascertaining the fair valuation of railroad property. '09 (D11) 8°, pap. (Add. Superintendent for price.) U. S., Supt. of Docs.

National Association of Railway Commissioners. Rept. of the Committee on safety appliances; [with supplemental report.] '09 (D18) 8°. (Add. Superintendent for price.) U. S., Supt. of Docs.

National Association of Stationary Engineers of America. Five years questions and answers. 2 v. in 1. '08(O) c. il. diagrs., 8°, $2. Nat. Assoc. Stationary Engineers.

National Association of Tanners. Free hide text book. '08, [1909.] (Mr) c. 45 p. tabs., 8°. (Add. pubs. for price.) Nat. Assoc. Tanners.

NATIONAL BANK NOTES.
See Money.

NATIONAL BANK OF THE NORTHERN LIBERTIES OF PHILADELPHIA, Pa.
Simon, L. C. Century of the National Bank of Northern Liberties of Philadelphia. (Priv. pr.) L. C. Simon.

NATIONAL BANKS.
See Banks and banking.

National Baptist Sunday school lesson commentary of the International lessons. *See* Boyd, R. H., *ed.*

National bird and mammal reservations in Alaska in charge of the U. S. Department of Agriculture. '10(Je) 15 p. maps, 8°, (U. S., Dept. of Agriculture; Bureau of Biological Survey, circular.)

National Board of Fire Underwriters. Building code recommended by the National Board of Fire Underwriters, providing for all matters concerning, affecting or rel. to the construction, alteration, equipment, repair or removal of buildings or structures erected or to be erected. 3d ed. '09(S) 268 p. 8°. (Add. pubs. for price.) Nat. Bd. Fire.

National Board of Fire Underwriters. Fire engine tests and fire stream tables. [1910.] (Je) c. 3-47 p. il. 16°, gratis. Nat. Bd. Fire.

National Brick Manufacturers' Assoc. of U. S. Study of the chemical status of the carbon, iron and sulphur in clays during the various stages of burning. '08(Mr) c. 108 p. il. tabs., 8°, $1. Randall.

National Bridge Company. Reinforced concrete bridges, Luten patents. '08(Jl) c. 146 p. il. 8°, pap., gratis. Nat. Bridge.

National Business League of America. American universities, American foreign service and an adequate consular law. [2d ed., amplified.] '10(Ja8) 8°. (Add. pubs. for price.) Nat. Business.

National Business League of America. Banking, by Leslie M. Shaw; The cotton industry, by Colonel Rob. J. Lowry; Ship building, by W. Irving Babcock; The iron horse, by Jacob M. Dickinson; The interurban railway, by Hugh J. McGowan: addresses del. at the annual banquet. '09(F6) 8°, pap. (Add. pubs. for price.) Nat. Business.

National Business League of America. Practical suggestions for the development of American export trade; with directories of the chief cities of Brazil, South America, by G: E. Anderson; Chile, South America, by Alfr. A. Winslow; Panama, by Arnold Shanklin; Southeast Africa, by W. Stanley Hollis. '09(My8) O. pap. (Add. pubs. for price.) Nat. Business.

National Business League of America. Pract. suggestions for the development of American export trade; with directories of the chief cities of European and Asiatic Turkey, by E: F. Ozmun; Russia, by W: Dawson; Argentina, South America, by Alban G. Snyder. '08(D) 71 p. O. pap. (Add. pubs. for price.) Nat. Business.

National Business League of America. Pract. suggestions for the development of American export trade; with directories of the chief cities of Switzerland by Silas C. McFarland; Haiti, West Indies, by J: B. Terres; Ecuador, South America, by Herman R. Dietrich. '08(D) 78 p. O. pap. (Add. pubs. for price.) Nat. Business.

National Business League of America. Schedule of inquiries concerning the lands, waters, forests, minerals and other resources of America. 4th ed. '09(My15) O. pap. (Add. pubs. for price.) Nat. Business.

National Canners' Association. Canners' directory and allied industries of the U. S., 1909. '09(Ag) c. 8°, $2. T. E. Gorrill.

National Child Labor Committee pubs. il. 8°, 16°, pap. Nat. Child Labor.
—Clopper. Child labor in Indiana. gratis.
—Hall. Scholarships for working children.
—Lord. Child labor and the public schools.
—Lovejoy. Children in the glass industry in Pennsylvania.
—McKelway. Child labor in the Carolinas. gratis.

National church. Henson, H. H. *$1.50 net. Macmillan.

National Congress of Mothers. How to organize parents' associations or mothers' circles in public schools, with suggestions for programs. '09(O9) T. pap., 10 c. Nat. Congress Mothers.

National Conservation Commission, Washington, D. C. Rept., Feb., 1909; special message from the President of the U. S. transmitting a rept. of the National Conservation Commission, with accompanying papers; ed. under the direction of the executive committee by H: Gannett. '09(Ag) 3 v., il. maps, 8°, pap. (Add. Superintendent for price.) U. S., Supt. of Docs.

NATIONAL CONSUMERS' LEAGUE.
American Academy of Political and Social Science. Consumers' control of production: work of National Consumers' League. 75 c. Am. Acad. Pol. Sci.

National Correspondence School of Railroading. Air brake text for engineers and firemen; a complete treatise on the Westinghouse and New York air brake and signal systems, air brake practice and train handling. '08(N) c. 4+330 p. il. (Not for sale.) Nat. Corr. Sch. R. R.

National Correspondence School of Railroading. Locomotive text for engineers and firemen; treatise on the engine, electric head-light and standard code of train rules. '08, [1909.] (F) c. 420 p. il. 8°. (Add. pubs. for price.) Nat. Corr Sch. R.R.

National currency and banks. Widney, R. M. (Add. author for price.) R. M. Widney.

National Electric Light Association. Electrical solicitors' hdbk. '09(S) c. 4+236 p. 16°. (Not for sale.) Nat. Electric.

National Federation of Religious Liberals. Unity of the spirit; proceedings and papers of the first congress of the National Federation of Religious Liberals; ed. by C: W. Wendte, D.D. '10(Ja22) 8°, 75 c. Nat. Fed. of Rel. Liberals.

National flag. Curry, F. E., *comp.* gratis. Cal. Sec'y State.

National Fraternal Congress. International Congress on Tuberculosis; rept. of the delegation from the National Fraternal Congress, by the chairman, Ira W. Porter; 23d annual meeting, Boston, Aug. 16, 1909. '09 (D18) il. por. 8°, $1; pap., 50 c. I. W. Porter.

National Gallery [London]; ed. by Maurice W. Brockwell, Paul G. Konody and F. W. Lippman. In 17 pts. '09(Ag28) il. in col. f°, bds., ea., *60 c. net; complete in 2 v., *$8 net. Dodge.

NATIONAL GALLERY OF ART, Washington, D. C.
Rathbun, R: National Gallery of Art, Department of Fine Arts of the National Museum. U. S., Supt. of Docs.

National game. Spink, A. H: $1.50. Nat. Game.

National highway route book. New York Herald. N. Y. Herald.

National holiday ser. il O. Appleton.
—Hill. On the trail of Washington. **$1.50 net.

National land system. Treat, P. J. $2.50. Treat.

National Lumber Exporters Association. Car service, storage, switching, and other terminal rules and charges at principal ports of the United States and Montreal, Canada; also dock rules and charges at foreign ports; comp. from special consular reports to the National Lumber Exporters Association; issued under authority of annual meeting held at Cincinnati, 1909, for the information of the membership only. '09, [1910.] (Ap) c. 127 p. 8°. (Priv. pr.) Nat. Lumber.

NATIONAL MONETARY COMMISSION.
See **Banks and banking.**

NATIONAL OWNERSHIP.
See **Government ownership.**

National perils and hopes. Crafts, W. F. 50 c. net. F. M. Barton.

National reporter system; state ser. O. West Pub.
—Atlantic reporter. v. 68-76. ea., $4.
—New York [State] supplement. v. 106-116. ea., $4.—v. 117-123. ea., $3.
—New York [State] supp. and New York [State] reporter. Digest. In 2 v. $5.
—Northeastern reporter. v. 82-91. ea., $4.
—Northwestern reporter. v. 113-126. ea., $4.
—Pacific reporter. v. 91-110. ea., $4.—Digest. v. 5. $6.
—Southeastern reporter. v. 58-68. ea., $4.
—Southern reporter. v. 44-51. ea., $4.
—Southwestern reporter. v. 105-129. ea., $4. —Penn ed. v. 51. $4.—Digest of vs. 90-106; 106-120. ea., $6.
—United States. Federal reporter. v. 156-178. ea., $3.50.—Digest. v. 7. $7.50.
—United States. Supreme court reporter. v. 28. $4; v. 29. $5.

National Rivers and Harbors Congress. Proceedings, third annual convention, Washington, D. C., 1907. '08(O24) O. gratis. Ebbert & R.

National Society for the Promotion of Industrial Education. Circular of information: constitution, state branches, officers and members. '09(Ap3) 8°, (National Society for the Promotion of Industrial Education.) pap., 10 c. Nat. Soc. Promotion Indust. Educ.

National Society for the Promotion of Industrial Education. Industrial education; communication from C. R. Richards, president of the Society, transmitting repts. by a Committee of the Society on the subject, together with resolutions urging upon Congress an appropriation to enable the Department of Education to develop schools for industrial training. [1910.] (Jl) 8 p. 8°. Gov. Pr. Off.

National Society for the Promotion of Industrial Education. Rept. of the Committee of Ten on the relation of industrial training to the general system of education in the United States. [1910.] (S) 16 p. 8°. (Not for sale.) Nat. Soc. Promotion Indust. Educ.

National Society for the Promotion of Industrial Education bull. 8°, pap., 10 c. Nat. Soc. Promotion Indust. Educ.
—Dean. Education of workers. in the shoe industry.

National Society for the Scientific Study of Education. Eighth yearbook; by C: Richmond Henderson. In 2 pts. pt. 1, Education with reference to sex: pathological, economic and social aspects; pt. 2, Education with reference to sex: agencies and methods; with a paper on sex instruction in high schools, by Helen C. Putnam. '09 (Je26); Ninth yearbook. pt. 1, Health and education, by T: Denison Wood. '10 (Ap23) c. O. pap., per pt., *75 c. net. **Univ. of Chic.**

National Society of the Fine Arts. Tapestries, textiles and embroideries: a loan exhibition given in the Corcoran Gallery of Art, February 14th to 29th, 1908. '08(Je27) il. O. pap. (Add. pubs. for price.) Nat. Soc. of Fine Arts.

NATIONAL SOLDIERS' HOME, South Branch, Va.
Cobb, E: L. Optic views and impressions of the National Soldiers' Home, South Branch, N. H. D. V. S., near Hampton, Va., as seen and described by one of its members. [1910.] (N) 156 p. il. 8°. E. L. Cobb.

National standard dispensatory. Hare, H. A $8. Lea

National standard squab book. Rice, E. C 50 c. Plymouth Rock

National Tax Associaton. State and local taxation: first national conference under the auspices of the National Tax Association, Columbus, Ohio, November 12-15, 1907. '08(Mr28) c. O. $4. Macmillan.

National Teacher-training Institute textbooks. *See* Musselman, *Rev.* Hugh T:, *ed.*

National University Committee of Four Hundred. Appeal in behalf of proposed University of United States. '08(Ap18) 12°. U. S., Supt. of Docs.

NATIONALISM.
See Socialism.

Nation's crime. Lowenberg, *Mrs.* I. $1.50. Neale.

Native born. Wylie, I. A. R. $1.50. Bobbs-M.

Native life in East Africa. Weule, J. K. K. *$4.50 special net. Appleton.

NATIVITY PLAYS.
See Plays.

NATURAL HISTORY.
Hancock, J. L. Nature sketches in temperate America. $2.75 net. McClurg.
Harmer, S. F:, *and* Shipley, A. E., *eds.* Cambridge natural history. In 10 v. v. 3, 4, 6, 10. v. 3, *$3.25 net; v. 4, *$4.25 net; v. 6, *$3.50 net; v. 10, *$4 net. Macmillan.
Nicoll, M. J. Three voyages of a naturalist. *$2.50 net. Scribner.
Pierson, C. D. Among the meadow people. 40 c. Dutton.
Frothero, E. Handy natural hist. $4 net. Badger.
Smith, G. W. Naturalist in Tasmania. $2.50. Oxford Univ.
United States. *Dept. of Agriculture. Bu of Biolog. Survey.* Biolog. Survey; bulletins, circulars, [etc.] gratis.
See also Agriculture;—Animals;—Biology;—Birds;—Botany;—Chemistry;—Domestic animals;—Evolution;—Fish and fishing;—Flowers;—Geology;—Hunting;—Man;—Marine zoology;—Mineralogy;—Nature;—Ocean;—Paleontology;—Physical geography;—Physics;—Physiology;—Reptiles;—Rocks;—Science;—Trees;—Water;—Zoology.

Natural History Survey of Illinois; State Laboratory of Natural History. f°. Ill. Lab'y Nat. Hist.
—Forbes *and* Richardson. Fishes of Illinois. Exchange or gratis.

Natural laws in piano technic. Chase, M. W. $1.25. Ditson.

Natural life in the human world. Watkins, L. B. 10 c. L. B. Watkins.

Natural method of physical training. Checkley, E. **$1.25 net. Baker & T.

Natural music course leaflets; ed. by Frederic H. Ripley and T: Tapper; nos. 559, 560, 561, 562, 563, 564, 565, 566. '08(My2) c. O. pap., ea., 2 c.-3 c. Am. Bk.

NATURAL PHILOSOPHY.
See Man;—Physics.

NATURAL RESOURCES.
American Academy of Political and Social Science. Conservation of natural resources. $1; $1.50. Am. Acad. Pol. Sci.
California. *Dept. of Public Instruction.* Conservation of natural resources. Cal. Dept. Pub. Inst.
Fletcher, H: F. Ethics of conservation. 10 c. H: F. Fletcher.
Holman, M. L. Conservation idea as applied to the American Society of Mechanical Engineers. 30 c. Am. Soc. Mech. Engineers.
Hyatt, E:, *comp.* Conservation of natural resources. Cal. Dept. Pub. Inst.
National Conservation Commission. Rept., Feb., 1909. 3 v. (Add. Superintendent for price.) U. S., Supt. of Docs.
Pinchot, G. Conservation of natural resources. 10 c. Gov. Pr. Off.
Pinchot, G. Fight for conservation. 60 c. net. Doubleday, P.
Sharpe-Patterson, *Mrs.* V. Lady of the green scarf; entertainment embodying need of conserving our country's national resources; suitable for Arbor day. 35 c. Flanagan.
Taft, W: H. Address of President Taft before the National Conservation Congress at St. Paul, Minnesota.—Conservation of natural resources. Gov. Pr. Off.
Van Hise, C: R: Conservation of natural resources in the United States. $2 net. Macmillan.
See also Mineralogy;—Mines and mining;—Water;—Water-supply;—*also* names of countries.

Natural salvation. Stephens, C: A. $1.75. Laboratory Co.

NATURAL SCIENCE.
See Natural history;—Physics;—Science.

Natural sources of power. Ball, R. S. *$2 net. Van Nostrand.

Natural speller. Kelly, A: H. **25 c. net. Scribner

NATURALISM.
See Philosophy.

Naturalist in Tasmania. Smith, G. W. $2.50. Oxford Univ.

Naturalist in the Bahamas. Northrop, J: I. $2.50 net. Macmillan.

Naturalist on the Amazon. *See* Bates, H. W.

NATURALIZATION.
Caracciolo, J. F., *comp.* Guida dell' operaio italiano in America. 50 c. Italian Am.
How to become a citizen of the U. S. gratis. Y. M. C. A.
O'Neil, R. K., *and* Estes, G. K. Naturalization made easy. 50 c. Carlisle.

NATURALIZATION.—*Continued.*

United States. *Dept. of Commerce and Labor. Bureau of Immigration and Naturalization.* Naturalization of aliens in the United States; how to become citizens, what is required, rights and duties; prep. by the National Society of the Sons of the American Revolution. '09(My) 8 p. 12°, pap. (Add. Superintendent for price.) U. S., Supt. of Docs.

United States. *Dept. of Commerce and Labor.* Naturalization laws and regulations, Aug. 17, 1909; this ed. supersedes all previous eds. '09(D) 28 p. 8°. (Add. Superintendent for price.)

See also Citizenship.

Naturalization of the supernatural. Podmore, F. **$2 net. Putnam.

NATURE.

Bailey, L. H. Nature-study idea. *$1.25 net. Macmillan.

Baker, E. A. Voices of nature: [anthology.] *$1 net. Dutton.

Bascomb, E. L. Selected books on nature study for schools and libraries. gratis. N. Y. State Educ.

Bigelow, A. W. Relation of nature study and science teaching. (Add. author for price.) M. A. Bigelow.

Blake, J. V. The months. *75 c. net. J. H. West.

Burroughs, J: Leaf and tendril: [essays.] **$1 net. Houghton M.

Cady, M. E. Bible nature series no. 1; natural development of geography, physiology, and the other elem. sciences. $1.20. Pacific Press.

Capps-Oliver, M., *comp.* Round the year with the poets: compilation of nature poems. $1.50; $3. Caldwell.

Conwentz, H. Care of natural monuments. *$1 net. Putnam.

Coulter, J: M., *and others.* Pract. nature study and elem. agriculture. $1.35. Appleton.

Cummings, H. H. Nature study by grades. $1.—Nature study by grades; for lower grammar grades, 60 c.; for higher grammar grades. 75 c. Am. Bk.

Emerson, R. W. Nature, and The conduct of life. *35 c. net; *70 c. net. Dutton.

Ewald, C. Queen bee, and other nature stories. $1.25. Nelson.

Gatty, M. S. Parables from nature. $2 net. Macmillan.

Halfyard, S: F. Spiritual basis of man and nature. $1. Jennings.

Holtz, F: L. Nature-study. **$1.50 net. Scribner.

Howes, E. Sun's babies: nature study. $1.25 net. Cassell.

In American fields and forests. **$1.50 net. Houghton M.

Jeffries, R: Life of the fields.—Nature near London.—The open air. ea., *$1.50 net. Lippincott.

Kearton, R: Fairy-land of living things. *$1.25 net. Cassell.

Kirkham, S. D. In the open. **$1.75 net. P. Elder.

Lazell, F: J: Isaiah as a nature-lover. 60 c. Torch Press.

NATURE.—*Continued.*

Mcleod, Fiona, *pseud.* Little book of nature thoughts. 40 c.; 75 c.; 25 c. T: B. Mosher.

Maxwell, *Sir* H. E. Memories of the months; 5th ser. $2.50. Longmans.

Packard, W. Wild pastures.—Wildwood ways.—Wood wanderings.—Woodland paths. ea., **$1.20 net. Small.

Rankine, W. F. Nature study and brush drawing. *$1.25 net. Cassell.

Reed, C. A. Nature study guides. 2 v. v. 1, Flower guide; v. 2, Bird guide; pt. 1, Water and game birds, birds of prey; pt. 2, Land and song birds. ea. pt., 50 c.; 75 c. Denholm.

Reynolds, M. Treatment of nature in English poetry. *$2.50 net. Univ. of Chic.

Rogers, J. E. Key to The nature library. $1.50. Doubleday, P.

St. Paul. Public Library. Select list of books on birds, insects and nature study. gratis. St. Paul Pub. Lib.

Schmucker, S: C. Study of nature. $1.25. —Under the open sky. $1.50 net. Lippincott.

Serl, E. W. Swaying tree tops. $1. Neale.

Sharp, D. L. Lay of the land. **$1.25 net. Houghton M.

Shaylor, J., *comp.* In nature's garden. $1.25; $2. Stokes.

Smith, A. Dreamthorp. 50 c.; 75 c. Dutton.

Thomson, J: A. Bible of nature. **$1 net. Scribner.

Todd, *Mrs.* M. L. Cycle of sunsets. $1.20 net. Small.

United States. *Dept. of Agriculture. Office of Experiment Stations.* Forestry in nature study.

Van Dyke, H: J., *comp.* Poetry of nature. *$2 net. Doubleday, P.

Westell, W. P. Fifty-two nature rambles. $1.50. Dodge.

Whittemore, H: W. Blueberry pasture, and other outdoor sketches made in New Hampshire. 75 c. Tufts Coll.

See also Country life;—Outdoor life;—Science;—*also* references under Natural history.

Nature [verse]. Crum, *Mrs.* E. T. $1; 50 c. E. J. Goodrich.

Nature. *See* Emerson, Ralph Waldo.

Nature and man. Osborn, S. O. 75 c. S. O. Osborn.

Nature and ornament. *See* Day, Lewis Foreman.

Nature and sources of the law. Gray, J: C. *$1.50 net. Macmillan.

Nature book: popular description by pen and camera of the delights and beauties of the open air. '09(Jl3) 2 v., il. col. Q. ea., *$5 net. Cassell.

Nature drawing from various points of view. Bailey, H: T., *ed.* $1.50. David Press.

Nature myths of many lands. Farmer, F. V. 45 c. Am. Bk.

Nature of enzyme action. Bayliss, W: M. *$1 net. Longmans.

Nature of God. Hall, J: A. $1.25. Lutheran Pub.

Nature of man. Metchnikoff, E. **$2 net. Putnam.

Nature of music. Klauser, J. $2.50. Houghton M.
Nature of ore deposits. Beck, R: $6. Hill Pub.
Nature round the house. Wilson, P. $1. Longmans.
Nature study made easy. Shallow, E: B. *40 c. net. Macmillan.
Nature year book. Matson, E., *ed.* 60 c.; $1. Crowell.
Nature's help to happiness. Achorn, J: W. **50 c. net. Moffat.
Nature's message. Carmel, J: P. $1. Dodge.

NAUATL LANGUAGE.
See Aryans.

NAUHEIM-SCHOTT TREATMENT.
See Blood.

Naulahka (The). *See* Kipling, Rudyard.

Naundorff, Karl Wilhelm.
See Eckard, Jean.

NAUTICAL ASTRONOMY.
See Navigation.

Nautical charts. Putnam, G. R. $2. Wiley.

NAUTICAL SURVEYING.
Logan, G: W. Elements of hydrographic surveying. (Add. pubs. for price.) U. S. Naval Inst.
Messum, S. V. S. C. Hydrographic surveying. $3.75 net. Lippincott.
See also Hydrography;—Navigation;—Surveying.

Navaho-English catechism of Christian doctrine for the use of Navaho children. '10 (D3) c. S. pap., $1. Franciscan Fathers.

NAVAJO INDIANS.
See Indians.

Naval Annual, 1909. Brassey, T: A., *ed.* *$6 net. Scribner.

NAVAL ARCHITECTURE.
See Ships and shipbuilding.

NAVAL ART AND SCIENCE.
Armor and ships. 50 c. Journ. U. S. Artillery.
Attwood, E: L: War-ships; text-book on the construction, protection, stability, turning, etc., of war vessels. $3 net. Longmans.
Brassey, T: A., *ed.* Naval Annual, 1909. *$6 net. Scribner.
Brittain, C. B., *comp.* Elements of naval warfare. U. S., Naval Inst.
Darrieus, P. J. G. G. War on the sea. $2. U. S. Naval Inst.
De Leon, P. M. Navies in war and the Confederate Navy in the war between the states. 25 c. H. T. Graves.
Fraser, E: "Londons" of the British fleet. **$1.50 net. Lane.
Hackett, F. W. Deck and field. *$1.25 net. Lowdermilk.
Hislam, P. A. Admiralty of the Atlantic: enquiry into the development of German sea power. *$2 net. Longmans.
Howden, J. R. Boy's book of warships. $2. Stokes.
Mahan, A. T. Naval administration and warfare. **$1.50 net. Little, B. & Co.
Maltzahn, K. L. W., *Baron* v. Naval warfare. 75 c. Longmans.
Paasch, H. Vom kiel zum flaggenknopf, (From keel to truck:) marine-wörterbuch. English-Französisch-Deutsch-Spanisch-Italienisch. *$10 net. Lemcke.

NAVAL ART AND SCIENCE.—*Continued.*
Swinburne, H. L. Royal navy. *$6 net. Macmillan.
United States. *Office of Naval Intelligence.* Information concerning some of the principal navies of the world. (Add. Superintendent for price.)
See also Artillery;—Battles;—Marine engineering;—Navigation;—Sailors;—Ships and shipbuilding;—Signals and signalling;—Submarines;—*also* "Bellerophon," The;—United States Navy.

NAVAL BIOGRAPHY.
See Sailors.

Naval career of Captain John Manley of Marblehead. Peabody, R. E. (Not for sale.) Essex Inst.
Naval electrician's text book. Bullard, W: H. G. $6.50. U. S. Naval Inst.

NAVAL ENGINEERING.
See Marine engineering.

NAVAL HYGIENE.
See Hygiene.

Nave, Orville Ja.
Theology for young people, for instruction in religious doctrines and history. '10 (Mr26) c. il. 8°, (Home school ser.) $1.25. College Assoc. Pub.

Nave of Westminster. Rackham, R. B. $2. Oxford Univ.

NAVIGATION.
Bowditch, N. Extracts from American pract. navigator; epitome of navigation and nautical astronomy. Gov. Pr. Off.
Dunraven, *Earl of.* Self-instruction in the practice and theory of navigation. 3 v. *$8 net. Macmillan.
Groves-Showell, P. Definitions in navigation and nautical astronomy. *$1.25 net. Lippincott.
Hewlett, G. Sea terms and phrases; English-Spanish: Spanish-English. *$1.25 net. Lippincott.
Hosmer, G. L. Azimuth. $1. Wiley.
International lib. of technology. (Navigation lib.) 8 v. ea., $5. Int. Text-Bk.
Knight, A: M. Modern seamanship. $7.50. Van Nostrand.
Lecky, S. T. S. Wrinkles in practical navigation. *$8 net. Van Nostrand.
Muir, W: C. P. Treatise on navigation and nautical astronomy. $5. U. S. Naval Inst.
Poor, C: L. Nautical science in its relation to pract. navigation. $2 net. Putnam.
Pugsley, R: M. New York pilot and guide to the U. S. local inspectors' examination of masters and pilots for N. Y. Bay, [etc.] $1. R: M. Pugsley.
Putnam, G. R. Nautical charts. $2. Wiley.
Rudder (The). Handy Jack book of navigation tables. $1. Rudder.
Rust, A. Ex-meridian altitude, azimuth and star-finding tables. $5. Wiley.
Searle, G: M. "Sumner's method" for finding a ship's position. 50 c. Van Nostrand.
United States. *Dept. of Commerce and Labor. Bu. of Statistics.* Foreign commerce and navigation of the U. S. for the year ending June 30, 1909.

NAVIGATION.—*Continued.*

United States. Description of azimuth instrument. (Add. Superintendent for price.) U. S., Supt. of Docs.

United States. Newfoundland and the Labrador coast. 3d ed., 1909; pub. by the Hydrographic Office under the authority of the Secretary of the Navy. '09(O) 816 p. charts, 8°. (Add. Superintendent for price.) U. S., Supt. of Docs.

See also Aërial navigation;—Astronomy;—Boats;—Canoeing;—Compass; — Inland navigation; — Nautical surveying;—Naval art and science;—Ocean;—Rivers; — Rowing; — Sailors;—Ships and shipbuilding; — Signals and signalling; — Voyages and travels;—Yachts and yachting;—*also* Pacific coast.

Naville, Edouard Henri.

Old Egyptian faith; tr. by Colin Campbell, D.D. '10(Je4) 8°, (Crown theological lib.) $1.50 net. Putnam.

NAVY.

See Naval art and science;—United States navy;—*also* names of countries.

Navy in the House of Commons. Middlemore, T: D. 50 c.; 30 c. Longmans.

Navy mail service. United States. *Post-Office Dept.* (Add. Superintendent for price.) U. S., Supt. of Docs.

Navy of Venice. Weil, A. $5 net. Dutton.

Naya. Egleston-Hinman, *Mrs.* E. T. $1.50. Rand, McN. & Co.

Naylor, H: Rodley.

Mystery of Monastery Farm. '08(Jl4) c. D. 75 c. Eaton & M.

Naylor, Ja. Ball.

Dicky Delightful in Rainbow Land. '09 (N13) c. il. [partly in col.] O. (Billy Whiskers ser.) bds., $1. Saalfield.

Misadventures of Marjory. '08(N14) c. front. D. $1.50. C. M. Clark.

The scalawags. '08(Ap11) c. 12°, (Popular priced copyrights.) 50 c. B. W. Dodge.

Songs from the heart of things. '07, [1908.] (Mr.) c. 44-207 p. por. il. 4°, Orig. ed., buckram, $4.75; mor., $7.50; Ant. ed., buckram, $7.50; mor., $10. Ohio Lib. Co.

"Ne temere." *See* Pius x.

Nead, B: Matthias.

Some hidden sources of fiction: paper read before the Historical Society of Dauphin County, Pa. '09(Jl31) (Priv. pr.) Jacobs.

Neal, E. Virgil, and Cragin, C. T.

Modern illustrative bookkeeping; introductory course; rev. and enl. by D. D. Mueller. '09(O2) il. O. (Williams & Rogers ser.) $1. Am. Bk.

Neale, J: Mason, D.D.

Letters of John Mason Neale; sel. and ed. by his daughter. '10(F19) por. O. *$3 net. Longmans.

Neale, Wa.

Sovereignty of the states; an oration; address to the survivors of the Eighth Virginia Regiment, while they were gathered about the graves of their fallen comrades, on the battleground of Manassas, July 21, 1910. '10(Jl30) c. D. $1 net. Neale.

Neale, Wa., and Hancock, Eliz. Hazelwood.

The betrayal: a novel. '10(Jl30) c. D. $1.50. Neale.

Neall, Fk. L., and Pierson, Ward W.

Before the Interstate Commerce Commission; cement; informal presentation in the matter of discrimination against the city and port of Philadelphia, in railroad freight rates for transportation of Portland cement. '10(Ja22) fold. map, 4°, gratis. F. L. Neal.

Neall, Wa. H.

Before the war: a musical comedy. '08 (N7) c. pap., 15 c. Penn Pub. Co.

NEAR EAST.

See Ceramics;—Europe.

Nearer and farther East. Zwemer, S: M. 50 c. Macmillan.

Nearing, Scott, and Watson, Fk. D.

Economics. '08(O17) 12°, *$1.90 net. Macmillan.

'Neath Austral skies. Becke, G: L: $1.50. Lippincott.

Nebraska. Cobbey's annot. statutes, ed. 1907; prep. by J. E. Cobbey. '08(F) c. 2 v., 1008+246; 1505-3904+246 p. O. shp., $12; ed. 1909. '09(N) c. 3685+256 p. O. $15; in 2 v., $12. J. E. Cobbey.

Nebraska. Cobbey's compiled statutes. Ed. 1909; by J. E. Cobbey. '09(Jl) c. 2239+256 p. O. *$6 net. J. E. Cobbey.

Nebraska. Liquor laws; cont. the liquor laws in force July 1, 1909; also, internal revenue laws and taxes and U. S. postal regulations affecting Neb. liquors; comp. by Trenmor Cone. '09(Jl) 64 p. O. pap. (Add. pubs. for price.) Klopp.

Nebraska. Supp. to the law of probate and administration, [etc.;] by Arth. K. Dame. '09(D) c. O. $2. Keefe-D.

Nebraska. *Supreme ct.* Repts. v. 73. (H. C. Lindsay;) ed. by H: P. Stoddart. '08 (Ap); v. 74 (My); v. 75 (Je); v. 76 (O); v. 77 (N); v. 78, 79. '09(Mr); v. 80 (Je); v. 81 (O); v. 82 (N) ea., $3; v. 83. '09, [1910.] (Ja); v. 84 (Ap); v. 85 (My); v. 86 (O) c. O. shp., ea., $2. State Journ. Co.

NEBRASKA.

Fulmer, C. A. State and local government of Neb. 50 c. Ginn.

Sheldon, A. E. Poems and sketches of Nebraska. $1.50. A. E. Sheldon.

Stevens, J: C. Surface water-supply of Nebraska. 35 c. U. S., Supt of Docs.

Warren, J. A. Notes on the number and distribution of native legumes in Nebraska and Kansas. (Add. Superintendent for price.) U. S., Supt. of Docs.

Wilson, E. P. Local and state government in Nebraska. 20 c. Univ. Pub.

Nebraska synoptical digest; digest of the decisions of the supreme ct. 3 v.; J. H. Broady, jr., ed., D. A. Haggard, ass't ed. '10(O) c. O. shp., $30. State Journ. Co.

NEBULAR HYPOTHESIS.

See Solar system.

Necessity for individual engineering libraries. Harrington, J: L. 10 c. J: L. Harrington.

Necessity for new standards of hop valuation. Stockberger, W. W. (Add. Superintendent for price.) U. S., Supt. of Docs.

Necessity of religion. Stiege, P. 40 c. Wagner.

NECK.
Cunningham, D. J., *and others.* Imperial stereoscopic anatomy of the head and neck. $10. Imperial Pub.

Ne Collins, J. E.
Institute songs. [1910.] (S) 80 p. O. (Standard musical lib.) pap., 15 c. Am. Bk.

Necromancers (The). Benson, R. H. $1.50. Herder.

Ned Rieder. Wehs, J: A. 85 c. Benziger.

Need of change. Street, J. L: 50 c. Lane.

Needham, Ja. G:
General biology; book of outline and pract. studies for general student. '10(Je4) c. il. pors. 8°, $2 net. Comstock Pub.

NEEDLEWORK.
Goodwin, E. E. Course in sewing. 3 v. $1.50. Beattys.
Hoare, *Lady* K. L. Art of tatting. $7 net. Longmans.
Huish, M. B. Samplers and tapestry embroideries. $17. Longmans.
Johnson, F. K. How shall the little ones sew? 10 c. People's Univ.
Lowes, *Mrs.* E. L. Chats on old lace and needlework. $2. Stokes.
Mahaffy, *Mrs.* A. M. Y., *ed.* Priscilla drawn work book. 25 c. Priscilla.
Morgan, *Mrs.* M. E. H. How to dress a doll. 50 c. Altemus.
Ralston, *Mrs.* V. When mother lets us sew. **75 c. net. Moffat.
Townend, *Mrs.* F. B. Plain needlework and cutting out. 75 c. net. Cassell.
Woolman, *Mrs.* M. S. Sewing course. *$1.50 net; *$3.50 net. Fernald.
See also Crocheting;—Dressmaking; — Embroidery;—Knitting; — Lace; — Manual training;—Tailoring;—Tatting.

Needs of the South. Griggs, S. E. 10 c. Orion Pub.

Neef, F: Emil.
Practical points in anesthesia. '08(D) c. 46 p. 16°, 60 c.; ed. de luxe, $1.50. Surgery.

Neely, Flora.
Hand-book for the kitchen and housekeeper's guide; containing household recipes of every description, as well as hints for the management of the storeroom, laundry, housekeeper's department, the nursery, sick-room, the toilet; family dyes. 3d ed., rev. '10(Ap) c. 364 p. il. 12°, $1.50. F. Neely.

Neely, Bp. T: B:
South America: its missionary problems. '09(Ag) 10+312 p. il. fold. maps, fold. tab., 12°, (Foreign mission study courses.) 50 c.; pap., 35 c. Young People's Miss.

Neeser, Rob. Wilden.
Statistical and chronological history of the United States Navy, 1775-1907. '09 (Mr20) c. 2 v., tabs., F. **$12 net, boxed. Macmillan

NEESIMA, Joseph Hardy.
Takahira, K. Address on the life and works of the late Dr. Joe Neesima. (Add. author for price.) K. Takahira.

Neet, G: Wallace.
Practical methodology. '09(My) 6+9-495 p. 8°, $1.25. Bogarte.

Neff, Eliz.
Altars to mammon. '08(F22) c. il. D. †$1.50. Stokes.

Neff, G: Oliver.
The check-figure: [new system for checking accounts.] '08(Ap18) c. D. 60 c. G: O. Neff.

Neffe (Der) als onkel. Picard, L. B. **35 c. net. Holt.

Neglected neighbors. *See* Weller, C: F:

Neglected period of anti-slavery in America. Adams, A. D. **$1.50 net. Ginn.

Neglected point in connection with crises. Johannsen, N: A. L. J. $1.50. Bankers Pub.

NEGLIGENCE.
Abbott, T. O. Primer of the law of negligence for conductors and motormen. (Add. author for price.) T. O. Abbott.
American negligence digest. $8.50. Remick.
Eastman, C. Work-accidents and the law. $1.50. Charities' Pub.
Hard, W:, *and others.* Injured in the course of duty. gratis. Ridgway.
Thornton, W. W. Treatise on the federal employers' liability and safety appliance acts. $4.50. W. H. Anderson.
Washington. Adams' briefs on negligence law. $7.50. E. L. Boardman.
See also Salaries;—*also* names of states.

NEGOTIABLE INSTRUMENTS.
Crawford, J: J. Negotiable instruments law. $2.50. Baker, V. & Co.
Huffcut, E. W., *ed.* Law of negotiable instruments. $4.50. Baker, V. & Co.
Laws, C. R. Manual for the collection of commercial paper. 50 c. C. R. Laws.
Massachusetts. Law rel. to money and negotiable instruments. *25 c. net. G. A. Jackson.
Ogden, J. M. Negotiable instruments. *$4 net. Callaghan.
Selover, A. W. Negotiable instruments law. $5. Keefe-D.
Smith, H. L., *and* Moore, W: U. Cases on the law of bills and notes. $4.50. West Pub.
See also Bonds;—Commercial law;—Exchange;—Interest;—Investments; — Mortgages;—Stocks;—*also* names of states.

Negotiable instruments law; with comments and criticisms by J. B. Ames, L. D. Brewster and C: L. McKeehan; annot. with references to the English Bills of exchange act and with cases under the negotiable instruments law and the bills of exchange act by Jos. Doddridge Brannan. '08(O) 16+250 p. O. (Add. pubs. for price.) Harvard Law.

Negro mystic lore. Sims, *Mrs.* M. H. $1. M. H. Sims.

NEGRO REGIMENTS.
See United States army.

NEGROES.

Adams, C: F., *jr.* "The Solid South" and the Afro-American race problem. (Priv. pr.) C: F. Adams.

Adriaans, J: H: Has a negro the right to vote? (Add. author for price.) J: H. Adriaans.

Baker, R. S. Following the color line. **$2 net. Doubleday, P.

Boyd, R. H. Separate, or "Jim crow" car laws. 25 c. Nat. Bapt. Pub.

Brawley, B: G. Negro in literature and art. 50 c. B: G. Brawley.

Brown, W: M. Crucial race question. Arkansas Churchman.

Bruce, J: E:, *comp.* Short biograph. sketches of eminent negro men and women. In 4 v. v. 1. $1. J: E: Bruce.

Chavers, P. W: Conditions that confront the colored race. (Add. author for price.) P. W: Chavers.

Du Bois, W: E: B., *ed.* Economic co-operation among negro Americans. $1.—Efforts for social betterment among negro Americans. 75 c. Atlanta Univ.

Edwards, R: H:, *ed.* Negro problem. 10 c. R: H: Edwards.

Flack, H. E. Adoption of the fourteenth amendment. $2. Johns Hopkins.

Fleming, W. L. Jefferson Davis, the negroes and the negro problem. gratis. W. L. Fleming.

Griggs, S. E. Race question in a new light. 15 c. Orion Pub.

Grimké, A. H: Modern industrialism and the negroes of the United States. 15 c. Am. Negro Acad.

Grimke, F. J. Christianity and race prejudice. 15 c.—Equality of rights for all citizens black and white alike. 5 c.—Progress and development of the colored people of our nation. 10 c. F. J. Grimke.

Hamilton, G. P. Bright side of Memphis: compendium of information concerning the colored people of Memphis. $2.50. G. P. Hamilton.

Hartshorn, W: N., *and* Penniman, G: W., *eds.* An era of progress and promise, 1863-1910; development of the American negro. $5.75. Priscilla.

Hayen, E. Negro question. 25 c. E. Hayen.

Hayne, J. E. Ham and his immediate descendants. Weltz Press.

Hayne, J. E. President Taft measured by his most remarkable speech on the Hamitic race question. 35 c. J. E. Hayne.

Helm, M. From darkness to light: story of negro progress. *50 c. net; *30 c. net. Revell.

Johnston, *Sir* H. H. Negro in the New World. $6 net. Macmillan.

Leiding H. K. "Street cries of an old southern city." 25 c. H. K. Leiding.

McKinley, C. E. Appeal to Pharaoh: the negro problem. $1. State Co.

Mathews, J: M. Legislative and judicial history of the Fifteenth amendment: [negro vote.] $1. Johns Hopkins.

NEGROES.—*Continued.*

Melick, C: W. Some phases of the negro question. $1. C: W. Melick.

Miller, K. Race adjustment: essays on the negro in America. *$2 net. Neale.

Mr. Taft's new trust. (Priv. pr.) Hampton Inst.

Montgomery, W. S. Historical sketch of education of the colored race in the District of Columbia, 1807-1905. 25 c. Smith Bros.

Moorland, J. E. Demand and the supply of increased efficiency in the negro ministry. 15 c. Am. Negro.

Odum, H. W. Social and mental traits of the negro. $2 net. Longmans.

Pickett, W: P. Negro problem: Abraham Lincoln's solution. **$2.50 net. Putnam.

Randle, E. H. Characteristics of the southern negro. $1 net. Neale.

Reed, W: B. Echoes of the Emancipation Proclamation. 15 c. W: B. Reed.

Riley, B: F. White man's burden. $1.25. B: F. Riley.

Shackelford, O. M. Seeking the best; dedicated to the negro youth. $1. Hudson.

Sieg, V., *comp.* Negro problem: a bibliography. 25 c. Wisconsin Free Lib.

Stephenson, G. T: Race distinctions in American law. $1.50 net. Appleton.

Stone, A. H. Studies in the American race problem. **$2 net. Doubleday, P.

Waddell, C: W. Race problem. 25 c. C: W. Waddell.

Walker, J. G. Presbyterianism and the negro. 50 c. J. G. Walker.

Waring, R. L. As we see it. $1.50. R. L. Waring.

Washington, B. T. Story of the negro. In 2 v. **$3 net. Doubleday, P.

Weatherford, W. D. Negro life in the South. 75 c. Y. M. C. A.

Webb, J. M. Black man, the father of civilization. 75 c. J. M. Webb.

Withers, J. Our inheritance: [argument for rights of negro people.] 50 c. Z. Withers.

Woods, C. A. "Intelligent labor": address at Industrial Conference. State Co.

See also Congo Free State; — Co-operation; — Hookworm disease;—Jews; — Slavery;—Social science;—South (The);—*also* Levington, William.

Neher, Bertha Miller.

Among the giants; story introducing six common failings. 9th ed. '10(Mr5) c. il. D. 40 c. Flanagan.

Neid. Wildenbruch, E. von. 35 c. Heath.

Neighborhood entertainments. Stern, R. B. 75 c. net. Sturgis & W.

Neighbors and friends. Loane, M. $2. Longmans.

Neihardt, J: Gneisenau.

Bundle of myrrh: [poems.] '08(F8) c. D. bds., *$1 net. Outing.

Dawn-builder. '10(D17) c. 12°, $1.50. M. Kennerley.

Man-song. '09(O2) c. 8°, *$1 net. M. Kennerley.

The river and I. '10(D3) c. il. O. $2 net. Putnam.

Neil, C. Lang.
After-dinner sleights and pocket tricks: explaining and illustrating tricks by T. Nelson Downs, H. de Manche, C: Bertram, G: Stillwell, C: O. Williams and Mdlle. Patrice. '09(O2) il. D. bds., 50 c. Lippincott.
Modern card manipulation. '09(O2) il. D. bds., 50 c. Lippincott.
Neil, G. Lang, ed.
Rambles in Bible land. '10(Ja1) il. 8°, *$1.75 special net. Appleton.
Neil, H:, ["Marshall Everett."]
Columbia encyclopedia of useful knowledge; showing the newest and most wonderful inventions. '08(Ja11) il. 8°, $2.50. Columbia Pub.
Roosevelt's thrilling experiences in the wilds of Africa hunting big game. '09 (D) 400 p. il. $2. Bible House.
True story of the Cook and Peary discovery of the North Pole, incl. account of all other polar expeditions and stories of life among the Eskimos. '09(N20) c. il. pors. 8°, $1.50. Educ. Co.
Neil, Marion Harris, comp.
Alcono cook-book. '09(D4) c. O. pap., 50 c. J. M. Pitkin.
NEIL FAMILY.
See Genealogies, Crandall, *Mrs.* R. R. N.
Neill, C: P.
See Stelzle, C:
Neill gift book ser. il. D. $1.25, boxed. Reilly & B.
—Longfellow. Evangeline.—Hiawatha.
—Poe. Raven.
—Whittier. Snowbound.
Neilson, Rob. Morrison.
Steam turbine. 4th ed., rev. and enl. '08 (Mr28) il. O. *$4.20 net. Longmans.
Neiswanger, C: Sherwood.
Electro-therapeutical practice. 15th ed., rev. and enl. '08(My); 16th ed., rev. '09(N) c. il. 12°, flex. leath., ea., *$2.50 net. Ritchie.
Neither do I. Redford, E. A. $1.50. B'way Pub.
Neither Dorking nor the Abbey. Barrie, J. M. 50 c. Browne's Bookstore.
Nell Beverly, farmer. Brown, *Mrs.* E. D. J. 50 c. Rural.
Nellie's memories. Carey, R. N. 50 c. Hurst.
Nelligan, R: Fs.
See Hitchcock, E:
Nelly's silver mine. *See* Jackson, *Mrs.* Helen M. F. Hunt.
Nelson, Battling.
See Nelson, Oscar Battling Matthew.
Nelson, Burt Everette.
Introd. to the analysis of drugs and medicines; elem. hdbk. for the beginner. '10 (Je18) 12°, $3 net. Wiley.
Nelson, Mrs. Dora, and Henderschott, F. C.
Her strange marriage. '08(D) 192 p. 12°, pap., 25 c. J. S. Ogilvie.
Nelson, E: W:
Rabbits of North America. '09(D) 314 p. il. 8°, (U. S., Dept. of Agriculture, Bu. of Biological Survey, North American fauna.) pap. (Add. Superintendent for price.) U. S., Supt. of Docs.
Nelson, Hector W:
Weaving; guide to the mechanical construction, operation, and care of weaving machinery. '09(My8) c. il. 8°, (American School of Correspondence pubs.) $3. Am. Sch. Corr.
—, **comp.** Jacquard machines; instruction paper. '09(N) c. 32 p. front. il. 8°, (American School of Correspondence pubs.) pap., 50 c. Am. Sch. Corr.
NELSON, Horatio, *Lord.*
Thursfield, J. R. Nelson and other naval studies. *$4 net. Dutton.
Nelson, J: Horatio.
Law rel. to the interstate commerce commission, the Sherman anti-trust act, and the bureau of corporations. '08(N) c. 22+430 p. O. $5. Banks.
Nelson, J: Maurice.
Some compounds derived from the ethyl-*p*-diiminosuc-cinylosuccinate. '07, [1908.] (Je.) 42+2 p. 8°, pap. (Add. author for price.) J: M. Nelson.
Nelson, Knute.
Brief and memorandum rel. to riparian and water rights of the federal government and of the various states. '10(Ap) 14 p. 8°. Gov. Pr. Off.
Nelson, Nels Christian.
Ellis Landing shellmound. '10(My) 357-426 p. il. Q. (Univ. of Cal. pubs.; American archæology and ethnology.) pap., 75 c. Univ. of Cal.
Shellmounds of the San Francisco Bay region. '09, [1910.] (F) 309-356 p. il. fold. map, Q. (Univ. of Cal. pubs.; Am. archæology and ethnology.) pap., 50 c. Univ. of Cal.
Nelson, Oscar Battling Matthew.
Life, battles and career of Battling Nelson, lightweight champion of the world, by himself. '09, [1910.] (Ap) 3+7-265 p. il. por. 12°, $1; pap., 50 c. O. B. M. Nelson.
Nelson, P: W:
Calciminer's handy book. '08(Ja11) il. por. charts, 12°. (Add. pubs. for price.) Muralo.
Nelson, R: Ja.
New book-keeping. '08(F) c. 4+330 p. il. 8°, $3. Cincinnati & S.
Nelson, T:
Home, health and success. '08(O17) c. por. 12°, $1. Gospel Trumpet Co.
Nelson, W:
Controversy over the proposition for an American episcopate, 1767-1774; bibliography of the subject. '09, [1910.] (F) 19 p. 8°, $2.50. (100 copies.) Paterson Hist.
See also New Jersey. Law and practice concerning wills.
—, **ed.** *See* New Jersey. Archives.
Nelson's Lady Hamilton. Moorhouse, E. H. *$3 net. Brentano's.
Neoplatonism in relation to Christianity. Elsee, C: *75 c. net. Putnam.
Nephilim. Bohannon, W: J: H. $1.50. R. A. Silk.

Nernst, Wa.
Theoretical chemistry; fr. the standpoint of Avogadro's rule in thermodynamics; rev. in accordance with the 4th German ed. '08(Ag15) 8°, *$4.50 net. Macmillan.
Nerves and common sense. Call, A. P. **$1.25 net. Little, B. & Co.
Nervous and mental disease monograph ser. il. 8°. Journal Nervous Disease.
—Gierlich *and* Friedmann. Studies in paranoia. $1.
—White. Outlines of psychiatry. $2.
NERVOUS DISEASES.
See Nervous system.
NERVOUS PROSTRATION.
See Neurasthenia.
NERVOUS SYSTEM.
Bailey, P. Diseases of the nervous system resulting from accident or injury. $5; $6. Appleton.
Call, A. P. Nerves and common sense. **$1.25 net. Little, B. & Co.
Campbell-Thomson, H: Diseases of the nervous system. $2.75 net. Funk.
Church, A., *ed.* Diseases of the nervous system. $7 net; $8 net. Appleton.
Church, A., *and* Peterson, F: Nervous and mental diseases. *$6.50 net. Saunders.
Clark, L. P., *and* Diefendorf, A. R. Neurological and mental diagnosis. *$1.25 net. Macmillan.
Collins, J. Letters to a neurologist. *$1 net. Wood.
Coriat, I. H. Some familiar forms of nervousness. **25 c. net. Moffat.
Dana, C: L. Text-book of nervous diseases and psychiatry. *$5 net; *$6 net. Wood.
Du Bois, P. Nervous states, their nature and causes. 75 c. net.—Psychic treatment of nervous disorders. **$3 net. Funk.
Gordon, A. Diseases of the nervous system. $2.50. Blakiston.
Krause, F. Surgery of the brain and spinal cord. $6. Rebman.
McComb, S: Healing ministry of the church. 25 c. S: McComb.
Mather, S. Anatomy and physiology of the nervous system. *$1.50 net. McVey.
Mitchell, J: K. Self-help for nervous women. **$1 net. Lippincott.
Patrick, H. T., *and* Mix, C: L., *eds.* Nervous and mental diseases. $1.25. Year Bk.
Potts, C: S. Nervous and mental diseases. *$2.50 net. Lea.
Purves, S. Diagnosis of nervous diseases. *$4.20 net. Longmans.
Sawyer, H. C. Matter with nervousness. $1. Cunningham, C. & W.
Schofield, A. T. Functional nerve diseases. *$2.50 net. Dutton.
Schofield, A. T. Mental and spiritual health. 50 c. Fenno.
Schofield, A. T. Nervousness. **50 c. net. Moffat.
Sherren, J. Injuries of nerves and their treatment. *$2 net. Wood.
Shute, D. K. Reflex neuroses with particular reference to eyestrain. (Not for sale.) George Washington Univ.

NERVOUS SYSTEM.—*Continued.*
Skillern, P., *jr.* Anatomy of the central nervous system, eye and ear, cranial nerves (deep). *$1 net. Dolbey.
Starr, M. A. Organic and functional nervous diseases. *$6 net; *$7 net. Lea.
Stewart, P. Diagnosis of nervous diseases. *$4.20 net. Longmans.
Thomson, H. C. Diseases of the nervous system. *$2.75 net. Chic. Med. Bk.
Turner, W: A., *and* Stewart, T: G. Text-book of nervous diseases. *$6 net. Blakiston.
Walton, G: L. Those nerves. **$1 net. Lippincott.
Worcester, E., *and others.* Religion and medicine. **$1.50 net. Moffat.
See also Anatomy;—Brain;—Hysteria;—Insanity;—Mind and body;—Neurasthenia;—Psychology;—Psychotherapy;—Sleep;—Spine;—Worry.

Nesbit, Edith.
See Bland, *Mrs.* **Edith Nesbit.**

Nesbit, W. H.
Sweetheart dreams of yesterday. '09(N20) col. il. 8°, $2, boxed. C: C. Thompson.

Nesbit, Wilbur Dick, comp. and ed.
Baby; little book of big thoughts about little ones. '10(Ap9) c. obl. 16°, 50 c. Volland.
—, **ed.** The loving cup; original toasts by original folks. '09(D25) c. S. pap., 50 c., boxed. Volland.

Nesbitt, Paul.
Mr. Brown, the tariff teacher. '10(Je4) c. 12°, 25 c. Brown & Co.
Nest of the sparrowhawk. Orczy, E. M. R. M. J. B., *Baroness.* †$1.50. Stokes.
Nest of vipers. Jones, M. D. B'way Pub.
Nestorian monument. Carus, P., *ed.* 40 c. Open Court.
NESTS.
See Birds.
Netherland Chamber of Commerce in America, New York City. 1609-1909; the Dutch in New Netherland and the United States. '09(D11) c. 12°, 75 c. Netherland Chamber of Com.
NETHERLANDS.
Babson, R. W. Printed bankers' directory for Holland. $3.50. R. W. Babson.
Baedeker, K. Belgium and Holland. $1.80 net. Scribner.
Conventions between the U. S. and the Netherlands; arbitration. (Add. Superintendent for price.) U. S., Supt. of Docs.
De Mont, P., *comp.* Stories of the Flemish artists from Van Eyck to the XVIIIth century. *$3 net. Duffield.
Edwards, G: W. Holland of to-day. **$6 net. Moffat.
Guide to Holland. $1 net. Platt & P.
Higinbotham, J: U. Three weeks in Holland and Belgium. $1.50. Reilly & B.
Lucas, E: V. Wanderer in Holland. $2.50 net. Macmillan.
Motley, J: L. Dutch nation: being "The rise of the Dutch Republic" condensed. $1.75.—History of the United Netherlands. 2 v. $3. Harper.
Motley, J: L. Rise of the Dutch Republic. 2 v. $2.50. Crowell.

NETHERLANDS.—*Continued.*
Motley, J: L. Rise of the Dutch republic. 3 v. ea., *$1 net. Dutton.
People of Holland. $1.75 net. Macmillan.
Roche, C: E. Things seen in Holland. *75 c. net; leath., *$1 net. Dutton.
Silberrad, U. L., *and* Lyall, S. Dutch bulbs and gardens. *$2 net. Macmillan.
Singleton, E. Holland: [descriptions of pictures in Dutch galleries.] *$1 net. McClurg.
Waller, M. E. Through the gates of the Netherlands. **$1.50 net. Little, B. & Co.
See also Dutch in the United States;—Haar, Chateau of;—*also* Margaret of Austria;—William *the Silent.*

Nettleship, J: Trivett.
Robert Browning: essays and thoughts. [4th ed.] '09(Mr13) D. *$2.25 net. Scribner.

Neubecker, W:
Mensuration for sheet metal workers. '08 (F22) figs. 12°, 50 c. D: Williams.
Sheet-metal work. '09(F20) c. il. 8°, (American School of Correspondence pubs.) $3. Am. Sch. Corr.

Neuer englischer lehrgang. Dommasch, O. 50 c. Stechert.

Neuhausen, Simon A.
Tables of declension and conjugation. '10 (Ag) 33 p. 8°, 15 c. Druckerman.

Neumann, Angelo.
Personal recollections of Wagner; tr. from the 4th German ed. by Edith Livermore. '08(O10) c. pors. facsim., O. **$2.50 net. Holt.

Neumann, Arnold Johannes Rob., comp.
Sacrament of the altar; testimony of Scripture and the confessions on the last supper of our Lord Jesus Christ; with quotations from the writings of noted men in the Lutheran church. '10(Ap23) c. front. 12°, 30 c. Germ. Lit. Bd.

NEURASTHENIA.
Ballet, G. Neurasthenia. *$2.50 net. Hoeber.
Cleaves, M. A. Autobiography of a neurasthene. $1.50. Badger.
Gardiner, M. D. Universal neurasthenia. *$1 net. F. F. Sherman.
Marrs, W: T. Confessions of a neurasthenic. *$1 net. Davis.
Savill, T: D. Clinical lectures on neurasthenia. *$2 net. Wood.
See also Hysteria; — Mind and body; — Nervous system.

NEUROLOGY.
See Medicine;—Nervous system.

Neus, Englebert.
General instructions in drawing. '09(D) c. 39 p. il. 8°, 50 c. Sch. Liberal Arts.

Neusser, Edm. von.
Clinical treatises on the symptomatology and diagnosis of disorders of respiration and circulation; authorized Eng. tr. by And. MacFarlane. pt. 1, Dyspnea and cyanosis. '08(Ja11) 8°, $1.50; pt. 2, Bradycardia and tachycardia. '08, [1909.] (Ap) 8°, *$1.25 net; pt. 3, Angina pectoris. (Ag) $1. Treat.

Neutral line. Towne, H: R. gratis. Merchants' Assoc.

Neutral rights and obligations in the Anglo-Boer war. Campbell, R. G. 75 c. Johns Hopkins.

NEUTRALITY.
Holland, T. E. Letters to *The Times* upon war and neutrality. *$1.75 net. Longmans.

Nevada. School law, 1907; comp. by the superintendent of public instruction. '08(F) 8°, gratis. Nev. State Educ.

NEVADA.
California and Nevada. Attorneys and bankers directory, 1908-09. $2. C. A. Murdock.
Emmons, W: H. Reconnaissance of some mining camps in Elko, Lander and Eureka counties, Nev. U. S., Supt. of Docs.
Mendenhall, W. C. Some desert watering places in southeastern California and southwestern Nevada. (Add. Superintendent for price.) U. S., Supt. of Docs.
See also Paleontology;—Rodents;—*also* Goldfield; —Humboldt Co.; — Virginia Valley; — Washoe Co.;—West (The).

Nevada mouse plague. Piper, S. E: (Add. Superintendent for price.) U. S., Supt. of Docs.

Never-old stories ser. *See* Bell, Lettice.

Never-told tales. Robinson, W: J. $1. Altrurians.

Nevill, Lady Dorothy Fanny Walpole.
Leaves from the note-books of Lady Dorothy Nevill; ed. by Ralph Nevill. '08 (D12) pors. 8°, *$3.75 net; New ed. '10 (D24) 16°, 50 c. net. Macmillan.
Under five reigns, by Lady Dorothy Nevill; ed. by her son. '10(N19) il. O. $5 net. Lane.

Nevill, Ralph.
French prints of the eighteenth century. '08(D26) il. 8°, $5. Macmillan.
Light come, light go; gambling gamesters, wagers, the turf. '10(F19) il. in col. O. *$4.50 net. Macmillan.
Merry past. '10(D31) 8°, $3 net. Brentano's.
Sporting days and sporting ways. '10 (D10) front. 8°, $3.50 net. Brentano's.

—, and Jerningham, C: E: Wynne, ["**Marmaduke.**"]
Piccadilly to Pall Mall: morals, manners and men. '09(Mr13) il. 8°, *$3.50 net. Dutton.

Nevill, Bp. S: Tarratt.
Spiritual philosophy: lectures. '09(Je5) D. *50 c. net. Longmans.

Neville, Florence.
What dreams may come; study in failure; with a preface by T. K. Cheyne. '10 (O22) c. D. 75 c. net. Sherman, F.

Nevin, Thdr. Williamson.
Ralph Ranscomb, banker. '08(D5) c. D. $1.50. Neale.

Nevin, W. Scott, comp.
Manual for undertakers. '10(Je) 3-62 p. 12°, $1. Manual Pub.
Contents: **Order of burial services;—Hymns and poems.**

New agriculture. Collins, T. B. $2. Munn.

New America and the Far East. Browne, G: W. $36.25; $49.75. M. Jones.

New American citizen. Mintz, F. S. **50 c. net. Macmillan.

New American music reader. *See* Zuchtmann, Friedrich.
New American type. Sedgwick, H: D. **$1.50 net. Houghton M.
New Amphion classics. 16°, pap., 50 c. Somerville.
—Case. There is no unbelief.
New and non-official remedies. *See* American Medical Association.
New art lib. *See* Lippincott's.
New baby's biography. Kaplan, A. O. $2.50. Brentano's.
New Baedeker. Peck, H. T. $1.50 net. Dodd.
New bed-time stories. Moulton, *Mrs.* L. C. †$1.25. Little, B. & Co.
NEW BEDFORD, Mass.
See Methodist Episcopal church.
New Bible country. Day, T; F. 30 c. Crowell.
New book of the cat. Simpson, F. *$5 net. Cassell.
New boundary stone of Nebuchadrezzar I. from Nippur. Hinke, W: J: $3.50. Univ. of Penn.
New boy. Pier, A. S. †$1.50. Houghton M.
New boy at Hilltop. Barbour, R. H: $1.50. Appleton.
NEW BRUNSWICK, N. J.
City of New Brunswick; its hist., its homes and its industries; presented as a New Year's greeting by the *New Brunswick Times*, Jan. 1, 1909. '08, [1909.] (Je) 163 p. il. pors. 8°, 50 c. Times Pub. Co.
Lawrence, J: Hist. of the Grand Army of the Republic and New Brunswick's representation in the Civil War. (Not for sale.) Times Pub. Co.
Wall, J: P. New Brunswick, [N. J.,] in the critical period of the Revolution. (Priv. pr.) J: P. Wall.
New building estimator. Arthur, W: $2.50. D: Williams.
New business code. '09(D) 324 p. 12°, $7.50. Business Code.
New century arithmetics. Nihart, B: F. 2 v. (Add. pubs. for price.) Silver.
New century book of facts. Wright, C. D., *ed.* $4.50; $7.50. King-R.
New century geographical ser. *See* Tolman, *Mrs.* S. W. C.
New century lib. 16°, limp leath., $1.25. Nelson.
—Dumas. Works. In 15 v. v. 1.
—Hugo. Novels. 8 v.
—Irving. Sketch book and Bracebridge Hall.
—Kingsley. Alton Locke.—Hereward the Wake.—Two years ago.
—Longfellow. Poetical works.
—Palgrave. Golden treasury of the best songs.
New century spelling book. McCallum, A. N. In 2 pts. (Add. pubs. for price.) Silver.
New Christmas book. Sindelar, J. C: 30 c. Flanagan.
NEW CHURCH.
See Swedenborgian church.
New classical library. *See* Macmillan's.
New classification of the motor anomalies of the eye. *$1.25 net. W: R. Jenkins.
New Columbia. Phelps, G: H. $1; 50 c. New Columbia.
New commandment. Long, M. B. 75 c. M. B. Long.
New commandment. Verrall, A. *$1 net. Clode.
New complete accountant; designed for the use of schools and for private study. '08 (Ag22) c. O. $1.10. Powers.
New complete condensed encyclopedia. Chandler, W: H:, *ed.* $3.75; $5. Collier.
New cookery books. S. 50 c. McKay.
—Douglas. Cake and biscuit-book.—Pudding and pastry book.—Soup and sauce book.
New dancing as it should be. Scott, E: 50 c. Dutton.
New democracy. Downes, L. $2. Sherman, F.
New dictionary of Americanisms. Clapin, S. $1. Weiss.
New "East Lynne." Morris, C. *$1 net. Doscher.
New echinoids from the Ripley group of Mississippi. Slocum, A. W. 50 c. Field Museum.
New electoral law for the Russian Duma. Harper, S: N. *25 c. net. Univ. of Chic.
New elementary arithmetic. Wentworth, G: A. 35 c. Ginn.
NEW ENGLAND.
Automobile laws of the New England states, New York, New Jersey and Pennsylvania. (Add. pub. for price.) Rhode Island Lib.
Boston & Maine Railroad. Outdoors in New England. Boston & Maine.
Clarke, J: M. Early Devonic hist. of New York and eastern North America. pt. 1. $2.50. N. Y. State Educ.
Collins, J. F., *and* Preston, H. W. Key to New England trees. 40 c. Preston.
Douglas-Lithgow, R. A. Dict. of American-Indian place and proper names in New England. $7. Salem Press.
Drake, S: A. Book of New England legends and folk lore in prose and poetry. $1.50 net. Little, B. & Co.
Fire insurance in New England for ten years, 1899-1908. $3.50. Standard Pub. Co.
Higginson, F. New England's plantation, with the Sea Journal and other writings. (Not for sale.) Essex Bk.
Ideal tour. gratis. Pierce.
Lampton, W: J. Trolley car and the lady: a trolley trip from Manhattan to Maine. 25 c. Badger.
"Pilot" sectional road maps of New England and the Hudson River District. $5. F. S. Blanchard.
"Red book" interstate automobile guide, 1909; [New England.] $2.50. F. S. Blanchard.
Skelton, E: O. Story of New England. 50 c. E: O. Skelton.
Sylvester, H. M. Indian wars of New England. In 3 v. $50; $15 net; $1000. W. B. Clarke.
Thoreau, H: D: Notes on New England birds. $1.75 net. Houghton M.

NEW ENGLAND.—*Continued.*

Trolley trips through New England and Hudson River Valley. 15 c. Trolley Press.

Weeks, L. H., *and* Bacon, E. M., *comps. and eds.* Historical digest of the provincial press: [New England.] subs., per v., $7.50; per set, $150. Soc. Americana.

Who's who in New England. $5. Marquis.

Winthrop, J: Journal, "History of New England." 2 v. **$6 net. Scribner.

See also Coal;—Pilgrims;—West (The); —*also* Harvard, John;—*also* names of states.

New England Association of School Superintendents. Rept. on the physical welfare of the public school child, May, 1909. '09, [1910.] (F) 43 p. 8°, gratis. N. E. Assoc. Sch. Supts.

Bibliography (1 p.).

New England cook book. Goold, M. 75 c. M. G. Buckley.

New England Historic Genealogical Society, vital records of the towns of Massachusetts. 8°. N. E. Hist.

—Vital records of Tisbury. $3.25.

—Vital records of Wayland. $2.25.

—Vital records of Weymouth. 2 v. $9.25.

New England tax rates, 1907-8; giving the tax rates of all cities and towns in New England, with counties and population and revised building laws of Boston. '08(Je) c. 3-158 p. 16°, pap., 35 c. L. W. Lee.

New England year ser. S. Small.

—Packard. Wood wanderings. $1.20 net.

New English dictionary on historical principles. *See* Murray, *Sir* J. A: H:, *ed.*

New era in natural philosophy. Schumaker, E: E. $1. E: Schumaker.

New ethics. Moore, J: H. *$1 net. Bloch.

New Eureka art ser. 18 v. '10(D) 32°, ea., 25 c. Cupples & L.

New examples of American Indian skulls with low forehead. Hrdlicka, A. (Add. Superintendent for price.) U. S., Supt. of Docs.

New faces. Kelly, M. $1.50. G: W. Dillingham.

New facts concerning John Robinson. Burrage, C. 60 c. Oxford Univ.

New friends in storyland. Spaulding, F. E. 60 c. Newson.

New golfer's almanac. Stoddard, W. L., *comp.* **90 c. net. Houghton M.

New gospel. Persona, *pseud.* 75 c. Brentano's.

New Greece. Ithomites, A. 75 c. A. Ithomites.

NEW GUINEA.

See Papua.

New Hampshire. *Supreme ct.* Repts.; (J: H. Riedell.) v. 72-74. '08(N) c. O. shp., ea., $3.50. Rumford Pr.

NEW HAMPSHIRE.

Blaisdell, F. One hundred years of New Hampshire surgery. (Add. author for price.) F. Blaisdell.

Cram, J. Journal of a missionary tour through the new settlements of northern New Hampshire and Vermont. $1.50. G: P. Humphrey.

NEW HAMPSHIRE.—*Continued.*

Dale, T: N. Chief commercial granites of Massachusetts, New Hampshire and Rhode Island. (Add. Superintendent for price.) U. S., Supt. of Docs.

Fry, W: H: **New Hampshire as a Royal Province.** $3. **Longmans.**

Lucier, A. J. The machine: political satire. [New Hampshire.] $1. Mahew.

Pope, C: H: Pioneers of Maine and New Hampshire. $5. C: H: Pope.

Stearns, E. S., *ed.* Genealogical and family history of the state of New Hampshire. 4 v. (Add. pubs. for price.) Lewis Pub.

Whittemore, H: W. Blueberry pasture, and other outdoor sketches made in New Hampshire. 75 c. Tufts Coll.

See also Andover;—Concord;—Newport;—Portsmouth; — Salem; — Sandwich; — White Mountains.

New harvest mouse from Petaluma, California. Dixon, J. 5 c. Univ. of Cal.

NEW HAVEN, Ct.

See Yale University.

New Haven mathematical colloquium. Moore, E. H. *$3 net. Yale Univ.

New health science. Walgren, J: A. $1. Rand, McN. & Co.

New heaven and a new earth. Patterson, C: B. **$1.25 net. Crowell.

New horoscope of missions. Dennis, J. S. *$1 net. Revell.

New Hudson Shakespeare. *See* Shakespeare, W:

New idea. Tuttle, C: R. $5. C: R: Tuttle.

New ideals in healing. Baker, R. S. **85 c. net. Stokes.

New Inferno. Phillips, S. $1.25 net. Lane.

New instruction book on ocean bathing. Doyle, W: S. 25 c. W: S. Doyle.

New international year book: a compendium of the world's progress for the year 1907; ed. by Fk. Moore Colby and Allen Leon Churchill. '08(O10); 1908. '09(Je12); 1909. '10(My7) c. il. pors. maps, 4°, ea., $5; buckram, $6; hf. russia, $7; hf. mor., $8; full russia, $9; full mor., $12.50. Dodd.

New Italy. Gifford, *Mrs.* A. H. **$1.20 net. Lothrop, L. & S.

New Jersey. Act concerning corporations. 14th ed.; (W: H. Corbin.) '08(O) c. 32+192 p. O. (Add. pubs. for price.) Soney.

New Jersey. Archives; ed. by W: Nelson. 1st ser., Documents rel. to the colonial history of the state. In 27 v.; 2d ser., Documents rel. to the Revolutionary history of the state. In 3 v. '08(D) 8°, ea., $3. W: Nelson.

New Jersey. Borough law; cont. the revision of 1897, and all supplements and amendments thereto; with notes of decisions and a collection of forms. 3d ed.; Alfr. F. Skinner. '08(O) c. 10+140 p. O. $2.50. Soney.

New Jersey. Criminal law and procedure; including the subjects of disorderly persons and bastardy; statutes, decisions and forms; by Clifford Lee Newman. '09(Mr) c. 23+575 p. O. (Add. pubs. for price.) **Soney.**

New Jersey. Digest of the decisions of the courts of law and equity, from 1898 to 1907; by J: S. Mackay and Clifford L. Newman. '07, [1908.] (My.) c. 1101 p. 4°, $7.50. News Pr. Co., (N. J.)

New Jersey. *Forest Park Reservation Commission.* Planting and care of shade trees; extract from the Fourth annual report of the Forest Park Reservation Commission of New Jersey, 1908. '09, [1910.] (Je) 61-120, 139-142 p. il. 8°. N. J. Forest.

New Jersey. Index-analysis of the statutes, 1896-1909; by A. Van Doren Honeyman. '10(Ap) c. O. $5.35. Law Journ.

New Jersey. Law and the practice from the earliest times concerning the probate of wills, [etc.;] by W: Nelson. '09, [1910.] (F) c. O. pap., $1.50. Paterson Hist.

New Jersey. Laws rel. to business companies, an act concerning corporations (revision of 1896 and the various acts amendatory thereof and supplemental thereto. Annotations and forms. '08(My.) c. 12+227 p. O. pap. (Add. pubs. for price.) Sinnickson.

New Jersey. Laws rel. to the regulation and traffic in intoxicating liquors, including statutes and decisions; (P: Backes.) '10 (Ag) c. O. $2. Soney.

New Jersey. Mechanics lien law. 2d ed.; by E: J. Luce. '10(N) c. O. $3.50. Soney.

New Jersey. Official souvenir, the New Jersey Commission to the Jamestown Tercentennial Exposition. '07, [1908.] (Jl) 5-32+42 p. il. f°, gratis. E. M. Jackson.

New Jersey. Sales act; complete text, [etc.,] by J: Elliott. '09, [1910.] (F) c. O. $6. Dissell.

New Jersey. Statute and case law of the state rel. to business companies, [etc.;] with annots. and forms by Ja. B. Dill. Ed. of 1910. '10(F) c. O. $2. Sinnickson.

New Jersey.
- Abbott, C: C. Archæologia nova Cæsarea: [New Jersey.] 2 v. (Add. author for price.) C: C. Abbott.
- Automobile laws of the New England states, New York, New Jersey and Pennsylvania. (Add. pub. for price.) Rhode Island Lib.
- Biddle, C. S. Principles, pleading and practice obtaining in the court of chancery of New Jersey in divorce and other causes matrimonial. $3. Soney.
- Ellis, E: S., and Snyder, H: Brief hist. of New Jersey. 60 c. Am. Bk.
- Honeyman, A. Van D. Justice of the peace: practice and forms in New Jersey. $6. Honeyman.
- Industrial directory of New Jersey; cities towns and villages having a population of one hundred and over, with their respective populations, railroad, banking, express and postal facilities; also alphabetically arranged list of articles manufactured in New Jersey, with names of firms and location of factories, cities and towns offering special industrial opportunities. '09, [1910.] (Je) 40+620 p. fold. map, 8°. (Not for sale.) **W. C. Garrison.**

New Jersey.—*Continued.*
- Kümmel, H: B., *and* Gage, R. B. Glass-sand industry of New Jersey. (Add. author for price.) H: B. Kümmel.
- Lee, F. B., *ed.* Genealogical and memorial hist. of the state of New Jersey. 4 v. Lewis Pub.
- Lewis, J. V. Origin and relations of the Newark rocks. (Add. author for price.) J. V. Lewis.
- Records of officers and men of New Jersey in wars, 1791-1815; comp. in the office of the Adjutant-General; pub. by authority of the legislature, 1898-1903. '09, [1910.] (N) 411 p. f°. N. J. Adj.-Gen.
- Tanner, E. P. Province of New Jersey, 1664-1738. $4.50; $4. Longmans.
- *See also* Corporations;—Genealogies;—Sewage and sewerage; — *also* Camden; — Fairton; — Glen Ridge;—Greenwich; — Hudson River;—Jersey City; — Mercer County; — Montclair; — New Brunswick; — Newark; — Old Mine Road; — Princeton; — Salem; — Salem County; — Sussex County.

New Jersey digest: a digest of the reported decisions of the cts. of New Jersey; (C: W. Parker, comp.) In 7 v. v. 1. '08(Mr); v. 2-3 (My); v. 4-5 (Je); v. 6 (Ag); v. 7 (O) O. ea., shp., $6. Soney.

New Jersey, Geological survey. See Kümmel, H: B.;—Lewis, J. V.;—McCourt, W. E.

New Jersey lawyers' diary and bar directory. 1908; cont. also schedule of time for service of notices, county and district court rules, etc.; comp. by J: A. Hartpence. '08 (F) $1; 1909. '09(F); 1910. '10(F) c. D. ea., $1.50. Soney.

New June. Newbolt, H: J: *$1.35 net. Dutton.

New laboratory manual of physics. Coleman, S. E. 80 c. Am. Bk.

New Laokoön. Babbitt, I. $1.25 net. Houghton M.

New lib. of medicine. See **Dutton's.**

New library of music; ed. by Ernest Newman. il. O. Lane.
—Newman, *ed.* Hugo Wolf. *$2.50 net.
—Streatfeild. Handel. **$2.50 net.

New life. *See* Fair, J:

New light on ancient Egypt. Maspero, G. C. C: *$4 net. Appleton.

New light on immortality. Albe, E. E: F. d'. *$1.75 net. Longmans.

New light on the Renaissance. Bayley, H. *$4 net. Dutton.

New little Americans. Wade, *Mrs.* M. H. B. †$1. Wilde.

New manual of botany. Gray, A. $2.50. Am. Bk.

New Marcion. Sanday, W. *36 c. net. Longmans.

New mayor. Terhune, A. P. 50 c.; 25 c. J. S. Ogilvie.

New medical ser. See **Lippincott's.**

New medieval lib. 12°, 16°, pigskin, *$2.50 net. Duffield.
—Ancient English Christmas carols, 1400-1700. *$3.25 net.
—Babees' book.
—Book of the divine consolation of Saint Angela Da Foligno.
—Cell of self-knowledge. $2 net.

New medieval lib.—Continued.
—Chatelaine of Vergi.
—Christine *de Pisan.* Book of the Duke of True Lovers.
—**Early English romance in verse. 2 v. ea., *$2 net.**
—Gardner. Cell of self-knowledge. *$2 net.
—Legend of the Holy Fina.
—Of the tumbler of Our Lady.
—Rickert, *comp.* Ancient English Christmas carols, MCCCC to MDCC. $3.25 net.

New message in the teaching of Jesus. Bachmann, P. *40 c. net. Eaton & M.

New method for Cæsar. *See* Potter, Franklin Hazen. Elementary Latin course.

New Mexico [Territory.] *Bureau of Immigration.* Ho! to the land of sunshine: guide to New Mexico for the homeseeker; public lands and the laws and regulations under which they can be obtained. 7th rev. ed. '07, [1908] (O) 70 p. map, 12°. (Not for sale.) N. M. Bu. of Immigration.

New Mexico [Territory.] *Cattle Sanitary Board.* Brand book of the territory of New Mexico; showing all the brands on cattle, horses, mules and asses, re-recorded under the provisions of the act, approved February 16th, 1899, and other brands recorded since May 1st, 1899, up to December 31st, 1906. '08(O3) O. $1.50. N. M. Cattle.

New Mexico Territory. Kanen's corporation laws; by C: F. Kanen. '10(O) c. O. $7. Morning Journ.

New Mexico Territory. *Supreme ct.* Digest. vs. 1 to 14; by Ja. Derden. '10(Je) c. O. $10. Courtright.

New Mexico Territory. *Supreme ct.* Repts.; (A. J. Abbott.) v. 13. '08(My.) c. O. shp., $3.50. Stephens.

New Mexico. Territory. *Supreme ct.* Repts.; (Paul A. F. Walter.) v. 14. '09, [1910.] (F) c. O. shp., $2.70. N. M. Pr.

NEW MEXICO TERRITORY.
Lindgren, W., *and others.* Ore deposits of New Mexico. Gov. Pr. Off.
Sullivan, V. L. Irrigation in New Mexico. U. S., Supt. of Docs.
Twitchell, R. E. Hist. of the military occupation of the Territory of New Mexico from 1846 to 1851. (Add. author for price.) R. E. Twitchell.
United States. *Congress. House. Committee on the Judiciary.* Establishing boundary line between Colorado and New Mexico and Oklahoma. 5 c. U. S., Supt. of Docs.
See also Guadaloupe mountains;—Santa Fé County.

New monologues. Parker, M. M. $1. Drake.

New movement leaflets. 7 v. '09(Je19) T. pap. Am. S. S.
Contents: Harris, Rev. Hugh H:; Grading the country Sunday-school, 5 c.; Landis, W: C. What a country Bible class did, 3 c.; Rice, Edwin Wilbur, D.D., Boys: organization for them, 6 c., New Bible-class movement, 6 c., Self-activity of child mind, 5 c., Working adult Bible class. 6 c.; Wilson, Florence A., Primary work in country Sunday-schools, 5 c.

New musical education. Dickinson, E: $1. Aeolian Co.

New New York. Van Dyke, J: C: **$3.50 net. Macmillan.

New north. Cameron, A. D. **$3 net. Appleton.

New old healing. Wood, H: **$1.20 net. Lothrop, L. & S.

NEW ORLEANS, La.
Architectural New Orleans. (Add. pubs. for price.) Contractors and Dealers.
See also St. Louis Cathedral.

NEW ORLEANS COTTON EXCHANGE, New Orleans.
Thompson, W: B. New future rules of the New Orleans Cotton Exchange. W: B. Thompson.
See also Cotton.

New peep of day. Mortimer, *Mrs.* M. 50 c. Doran.

New philosophy of life ser. See Randall, J: Herman.

New physics. Baker, T: R. $1. Stradling.

New physics. Battell, J. $1.25. Am. Pub. Co., (Vt.)

New Plato. Masson, T: L. **75 c. net. Moffat.

New poems. Le Gallienne, R. *$1.50 net. Lane.

New price fiction ser. il. 12°, 75 c. Cupples & L.
—Vachell. Turn of the tide.

New primary methods. Block, J. E. 2 v. $7. Interstate Sch. Corr.

New psychology. Lindsay, A. A. $1.50; $1. Lindsay Pub. Co.

New psychology ser. $1. Progress Co.
—Atkinson. Memory.—New psychology.—Suggestion and auto-suggestion.

New reading of evolution. Thompson, H: C. *$1.60 net. New Reading.

New regime, A.D. 2202. Brant, J: I. $1. Cochrane.

New religion. Haldeman, I: M. 10 c. C: C. Cook.

New rosemary series. 62 v. '09(O2) front. S. limp Thibet mor., ea., $1.25, boxed. Caldwell.

New salesmanship. Lindgren, C: $1.50; $2. Laird.

New Schaff-Herzog encyclop. of religious knowledge; embracing Biblical, historical, doctrinal and pract. theology, and Biblical, theological and ecclesiastical biography, from the earliest times to the present day; based on the 3d ed. of the Realencyklopadie [für protestantische theologie und kirche] by Johann Jakob Herzog; ed. by Albert Hauck and now in course of publication; prepared by more than 600 scholars and specialists under the supervision of S: Macauley Jackson, D.D., editor-in-chief, C: Colebrook Sherman and G: W: Gilmore. Complete in 12 v. v. 1. '08(Jl4); v. 2. '09 (Mr6); v. 3 (My22); v. 4 (Ag28); v. 5 (N13); v. 6. '10(F19); v. 7 (Je11); v. 8 (O22) c. Q. ea., $5; per set, $60; shp., $84; hf. mor., $96; full mor., $108. Funk.

New scholar at St. Anne's. Browne, M. J. 85 c. Benziger.

New self-help. Bryant, E. A. $1.50. Cassell.

New series of homilies for the whole year. Bonomelli, J. In 4 v. $5. Benziger.

New socialism. Stoddart, J. T. *$1.75 net. Doran.

New songs for old. White, H. 50 c. H. White.

New sophomore. Hamilton, J. S. †$1.50. Appleton.

New South. American Academy of Political and Social Science. $1. Am. Acad. Pol. Sci.

New South. Thomas, W: H., gratis. W: H. Thomas.

NEW SOUTH WALES, Australia.
Bean, C. E. W. On the wool track. $1.50 net. Lane.

New standard trousers and breeches system. '08(D) 104 p. diagrs., f°, $10. J: J. Mitchell.

New students' reference work. Beach, C. B. $16.50. Compton.

New studies in Acts. Bosworth, E: I. 75 c.; 50 c. Y. M. C. A.

New tariff bill. United States. 10 c. C. S. Hammond.

New teacher of ladies' home tailoring. Hurwitz, G: $10. G: Hurwitz.

New teachers' and pupils' cyclopædia. Holst, B. P. 5 v., $18.75. Holst.

NEW TESTAMENT.
See Bible.

New Testament church. Srygley, F. D. $1. F. D. Srygley.

New Testament handbooks; ed. by Shailer Mathews. 12°, *$1 net. Macmillan.
—Bacon. Introduction to the New Testament.
—Gould. Biblical theology of the New Testament.
—King. Ethics of Jesus. **1.50 net.
—Mathews. History of the New Testament times in Palestine.
—Nash. History of the higher criticism of the New Testament.
—Stevens. Teaching of Jesus.
—Vincent. History of the textual criticism of the New Testament.

New Testament ser. il. 12°. Doran.
—Cragin. Kindergarten stories for the Sunday-school and home. *$1.25 net.

NEW THEATRE, New York City.
See Theatre.

New theology. White, H. $1.25. B'way Pub.

New theology and the old religion. Gore, C: *$2 net. Dutton.

New theory of vision. Berkeley, G: 35 c. net; 70 c. net. Dutton.

New things of God. Stimson, H: A. *$1.25 net. Revell.

NEW THOUGHT.
Allen, J. Mastery of destiny. **$1 net. Putnam.
Atkinson, W: W. Secret of success. 50 c. Advanced Thought.
Baum, *Mrs.* M. E. D. Studies in divine science. *$1 net. C. L. Baum.
Colville, W: W. J. Glints of wisdom. 40 c. Macoy Pub.
Colville, W: W. J. Life and power from within. $1 net. Fenno.
Fair, J:, *ed.* The new life. In 4 v. v. 1, 2, 3, ea., $2; $5; v. 4, 25 c.; per set, $6.25; $15.25. Fair Pub.
Fletcher, H. Optimism, a real remedy. 75 c. McClurg.

NEW THOUGHT.—*Continued.*
Haddock, F. C. Business power.—Culture of courage. ea., $3.—Personal atmosphere: studies in poise and power. $1.—Power for success through culture of vibrant magnetism. $10. Power-Bk.
Hatch, D: P. Straight goods in philosophy. $1. Roger Bros.
Hatch, D: P. Twentieth century Christ. $1. Fenno.
Larson, C. D. The great within.—Mastery of self. ea., 50 c. Eternal Progress.
Larson, C. D. Ideal made real. (Not for sale.) Progress Co.
Lyon, I. L. R. Wonders of life. $1. Fenno.
Marden, O. S. Miracle of right thought. $1 net. Crowell.
Miller, *Mrs.* A. J. Triune development, the road to self-mastery. 60 c. Triune Order.
Newcomb, C: B: Principles of psychic philosophy. **$1.40 net. Lothrop, L. & S.
Norton, C. Woman's cause. 50 c.; $1. Caldwell.
Patterson, C: B. New heaven and a new earth. **$1.25 net. Crowell.
Patterson, C: B. New way to happiness.—New way to health.—New way to self control. ea., 25 c. Roger Bros.
Pearce, *Mrs.* M. H. B. New thought school, Avenel system. 50 c. P. Avenel.
Sears, J. S. Key to health, wealth and love. 25 c. Sears Invest.
Sears, J. S. Shells from life—love—God. $1 net. New Thought.
Towne, *Mrs.* E. J. Lessons in living. $1. E. J. Towne.
Towne, W: E. Health and wealth from within; how to apply New Thought. $1. E. J. Towne.
Troward, T: Doré lectures; Sunday addresses at the Doré Gallery, London. 50 c.—Edinburgh lectures and mental science. 75 c. Roger Bros.
True, H. B., *ed.* How to obtain our own. $1 Roger Bros.
Warnack, H: C. Life's new psalms. $1; 30 c. Roger Bros.
Warner, *Mrs.* F. L. Our invisible supply: how to obtain. pts. 1 and 2. ea., *$1 net. Roger Bros.
Wilcox, *Mrs.* E. W. New thought common sense. $1.25. Conkey.
Wood, H: New-old healing. **$1.20 net. Lothrop, L. & S.
Young, J. Subconscious mind and its illuminating light; an interpretation. *$1 net. Whitaker & R.
See also Divine healing;—Medicine and religion;—Mental science;—Will.

New Thought pastels. *See* Wilcox, *Mrs.* Ella Wheeler. Poems of progress.

New tocology: science of sex and life. '08 (D19) il. 12°, 60 c. Laird.

New universal lib. *See* Dutton's.

New views on old subjects. Wilson, J. $1.50. Lemcke.

New way of life. Strachey, J: St. L. *50 c. net. Macmillan.

New way ser. D. pap., 25 c. Roger Bros.
—Patterson. New way to happiness.—New way to health.—New way to self control.

New way to educate children. Patterson, C: B. 25 c. New Way.

New way to happiness. Patterson, C: B. 25 c. Roger Bros.

New way to health. Patterson, C: B. 25 c. Roger Bros.

New way to self control. Patterson, C: B. 25 c. Roger Bros.

New way to write music. Bigelow, M. E. (Add. author for price.) M. E. Bigelow.

New word. Upward, A. $1.50. M. Kennerley.

NEW WORLD.
See **Explorers.**

New world. Hauskins, J. E. (Add. author for price.) J. E. Hauskins.

New-World science ser. il. 12°. World Bk.
—Ritchie. Human physiology. 80 c.—Primer of sanitation. 60 c.—Sanitation and physiology. $1.20.
—Ritchie *and* Caldwell. Primer of hygiene. 40 c.
—Ritchie *and* Purcell. Primer of sanitation for the tropics. 60 c.

New-world speller. Wohlfarth, J. H. 35 c. World Bk.

New world text book. il. D. World Bk.
—Tuttle. Principles of public health. 50 c.
—Wolfarth *and* Rogers. New world speller. 25 c.

New worlds for old. Wells, H. G: **$1.50 net. Macmillan.

New York [City.] *Advisory Commission on Taxation and Finance.* Final rept., Oct., 1908. '08, [1909.] (Je) 162 p. 8°. (Add. pubs. for price.) E. J. Levey.

New York [City.] *Board of Health.* What you should know about tuberculosis. '10 (Ag27) il. 12°, gratis. N. Y. Dept. Health.

New York [City.] *Bureau of Municipal Research.* Business methods of New York City's Police Deparament; critical study and constructive suggestions pertaining to administrative and accounting methods of the Bureau of Repairs and Supplies. '10 (Je) 212 p. fold. tabs., 8°, $1; abr. ed., 10 c. Bu. Municipal.

New York [City.] *Bureau of Municipal Research.* How should public budgets be made?; how budgets have been made, how budgets are made, how budgets should be made; fourteen stages in budget making. '09, [1910.] (Ja) 19 p. il. O. pap., 10 c. Bu. Municipal.

New York [City.] *Bureau of Municipal Research.* Illustrated guide to school subjects of interest. '09, [1910.] (Ja) 88 p. il. O. pap., 25 c. Bu. Municipal.

New York [City.] *Bureau of Municipal Research.* Memorandum of matters rel. to New York City debt that suggest the necessity either for judicial ruling or for legislation. '08, [1909.] (My) 31 p. tabs., 8°, (Add. pubs. for price.) Bu. Municipal.

New York [City.] *Bureau of Municipal Research.* Municipal reform through revision of business methods, New York City. '10 (S) 58 p. 8°, pap., 10 c. Bu. Municipal.

New York [City.] *Bureau of Municipal Research.* New York City's debt; facts and law rel. to the constitutional limitation of New York's indebtedness; brief of the evidence taken by Hon. B: F. Tracy, referee in Levy vs. the Board of Estimate and Apportionment; submitted by Bureau of Municipal Research. '09(My) 83 p. fold. tabs., 8°. (Add. pubs. for price.) Bu. Municipal.

New York [City.] *Bureau of Municipal Research.* Park question. 2 v. '09(My22) il. tabs., 8°, pt. 1, $1; pt. 2, 50 c. Bu. Municipal.

New York [City.] *Bureau of Municipal Research.* Questions answered by school repts. as they are; submitted to the Conference of State Superintendents., Chic., Feb. 22, 1909; based upon analysis of 72 city repts. by the Bureau of Municipal Research. 09(Jl) 18 p. 8°, pap. (Add. pubs. for price.) Bu. Municipal.

New York [City.] *Bureau of Municipal Research.* School progress and school facts; are you interested in school problems; school needs; school results; school facts? school reports as they are? '09, [1910.] (Ja) 73 p. O. pap., 25 c. Bu. Municipal.

New York [City.] *Bureau of Municipal Research.* Steps taken to locate and to solve problems of enforcing tenement house laws. '10(Ap9) 16°, 50 c. Bu. Municipal.

New York [City.] *Bureau of Municipal Research.* Tenement house administration; steps taken to locate and to solve problems of enforcing the tenement house law. '09(N) 175 p. il. fold. tab., 8°. (Add. pubs. for price.) Bu. Municipal.

New York [City.] *Bureau of Municipal Research.* Tuition for non-resident pupils. [1910.] (D) 12 p. 8°, pap., gratis. Bu. Municipal.

New York [City.] *Bureau of Municipal Research.* What should New York's next comptroller do?; the business issue of the next administration. '09, [1910.] (Ja) 15 p. O. pap., 5 c. Bu. Municipal.

New York [City.] *Bureau of Municipal Research.* What should New York's next mayor do?; specific evils to avoid, specific conditions to correct, specific steps to take, specific opportunities to realize. '09, [1910.] (Ja) 19 p. O. pap., 10 c. Bu. Municipal.

New York [City] charities directory, 1909. '09(F) 813 p. $1. Charity Organ.

New York [City.] Code of ordinances. Approved Nov. 8, 1906; the sanitary code, the building code, and the park regulations; together with all ordinances and amendments passed from Jan. 1, 1906, to Jan. 1, 1910; comp. and annot. by Arth. F. Cosby. '10(Mr) c. S. flex. leath., $3. Banks.

New York [City.] Code of ordinances, 1908. **'08(My.) c. S. $1.50.** Chief.

New York [City.] *Dept. of Finance.* Manual of accounting and business procedure of the city of New York; issued by the Department of Finance, Herman A. Metz, comptroller. '10(Ap23) il. forms, 4°. (Priv. pr.) M. B. Brown.

New York [City.] *Dept. of Health.* **Brief history of the campaign against tuberculosis in New York City; catalogue of the tuberculosis exhibit, 1908. '09(F13) diagr., 8°, pap., gratis. N. Y. Dept. Health.**

New York [City.] *Dept. of Health.* Bureau of child hygiene; co-operative studies and experiments by the Department of Health and the Bureau of Municipal Research. '08 (D) 40 p. tabs., forms, 8°, 35 c. Bu. Municipal.

New York [City.] *Dept. of Health.* **Consumption is a preventable and curable disease; information for consumptives and those living with them: [in English and Hebrew.] '09(F13) 4°, pap., gratis. N. Y. Dept. Health.**

New York [City.] *Dept. of Health.* **Do not spit; tuberculosis (consumption) catechism and primer for school children. '09(F13) diagr., 16°, pap., gratis. N. Y. Dept. Health.**

New York [City.] *Dept. of Health.* Hand book of help for persons suffering from pulmonary tuberculosis. '08(D) 64 p. (Add. pubs. for price.) J. W. Pratt.

New York [City.] Greater New York City charter of 1901. 3d ed. of 1906. Supplement, no. 2, 1908; arr. by Mark and W: Ash. '08(S); no. 3, 1909; no. 4, 1910. '10 (S) c. O. pap., ea., 75 c. Baker, V. & Co.

New York [City.] Metropolitan Museum of Art. Hudson-Fulton celebration: catalogue of an exhibition held in the Metropolitan Museum of Art commemorative of the tercentenary of the discovery of the Hudson river by Henry Hudson in the year 1609, and the centenary of the first use of steam in navigation of said river by Robert Fulton in the year 1807, New York, Sept. to Nov., 1909. 2 v. '09(D18) c. il. pors. 4°, pap., 50 c.; bds., $5. Metropolitan Museum.

New York [City.] *Metropolitan Sewerage Commission.* Digest of data collected before the year 1908, **rel. to the sanitary condition of New York harbor. '09, [1910.]** (F) 87 p. 8°, gratis. Metropolitan Sewerage.

New York [City.] *Municipal ct.* Law and practice; with the boundaries of boroughs, [etc.;] index by G: F. and J. C. Julius Langbein. 6th ed. '08(O) c. 31+790 p. 8°, shp., $5. Baker, V. & Co.

New York [City.] *Municipal ct.* Supplement to the 6th ed. of Langbein's Law and practice of the municipal court of the city of New York; by G: F. Langbein. '10 (Ap) c. 100 p. O. pap., $1. Baker, V. & Co.

New York [City] Public Library. Selected list of works in the N. Y. Public Library rel. to the hist. of music. '09(Mr) 36 p. 4°, pap., gratis. N. Y. Pub. Lib.

NEW YORK CITY.

Bennett, W: H. Catholic footsteps in old New York. $2.50. Schwartz, K. & F.

NEW YORK CITY.—*Continued.*

Bromley, G: W. *and* W. S. Owners' names of the city of New York, borough of Manhattan. $30. G: W. Bromley.

Brooks, Brothers, *New York.* Chronicles, 1818-1909; being a record of sundry happenings which have had place since A.D. 1818 in the part of Greater New York which at present is distinguished as the borough of Manhattan. '09, [1910.] (Ja) c. 39 p. il. 32°, gratis. Brooks Bros.

Devine, E: T: Report on the desirability of establishing an employment bureau in the City of New York. (Priv. pr.) Charities Pub.

Directory of directors in the city of New York, [1909.] $5. Audit Co.

Disposal of West Side railroad tracks. gratis. Merchants' Assoc.

Evening Post. Real estate values. 25 c. N. Y. Eve. Post.

Export commission houses, New York City. Directory. $2. Am. Exporter.

Gould, W: R. Greater New York and state lawyers' diary, 1908; 1909; 1910. ea., $1. W: R. Gould.

Gratacap, L: P. Geology of the city of New York. $2.50. Holt.

Hall, E: H. Brief hist. of the City Hall Park of New York City. gratis. Am. Scenic.

Hamilton, I. Palatial homes in the city of New York. 15 c.; 25 c. I. Hamilton.

Hammond's atlas of New York City and the metropolitan district. 25 c.—Guide map of Brooklyn Borough. 15 c.—Road map of the country around New York. 25 c. C. S. Hammond.

Jameson, J: F., *ed.* Narratives of New Netherlands. **$3 net. Scribner.

Japan in New York. 50 c. Anraku.

Kelley, F. B., *comp.* Historical guide to the city of New York. **$1.50 net. Stokes.

Klein, H. Unmusical New York. $1.50 net. Lane.

Leonard, J: W: Hist. of the city of New York, 1609-1909. $15. Journal of Commerce.

Little old New York. 10 c. Oxford Pub.

MacAtamey, H. E., *comp.* Cradle days of New York. 50 c. Drew & L.

MacCoun, T. Early New York. [5 maps.] $5. T. MacCoun.

McNally A. F. Catholic centenary, 1808-1908. **$1.25 net. Moffat.

Merchants' Association of New York. Plan for reforming the accounts, records and reports of New York City. (Add. pubs. for price.) Merchants' Assoc.

Morrison, J: H. History of New York shipyards. $2. Sametz.

Mott, H. S. New York of yesterday: descriptive narrative of old Bloomingdale. **$10 net. Putnam.

Nascher, I. L. Wretches of Povertyville: [study of the Bowery.] $1.50. J. J. Lanzit.

New York [State.] **Public Service Commission.** Hist. and description of rapid transit routes in New York City. **N. Y. Pub. Service Com.**

NEW YORK CITY.—*Continued.*

Old buildings of New York City. **$2 net. Brentano's.

Public Utility Commission of New York City. (Add. pubs. for price.) City Club, Chicago.

Ramsey, W: V., *ed.* Story of the Church Street Terminal buildings of the Hudson & Manhattan Railroad Company. Wynkoop, H.

Robinson, E., *and* Pidgeon, R. H., *comp.* Atlas of the borough of Richmond, city of New York. $30. E. Robinson.

Seckerson, F: C. Manual of civics: textbook of municipal government for city of New York. $1. Chief.

Singleton, E. Dutch New York. *$3.50 net. Dodd.

Skal, G. v. Illustrated hist. of the borough of Queens, N. Y. City. $5. F. T. Smiley.

Staten Island and Staten Islanders; comp. by the Richmond Borough Association of Women Teachers; ed. by Marg. Louise Lynd. '09(S) 76 p. il. por. map, D. pap., *50 c. net. Grafton Press.

Strachan, G. C. Equal pay for equal work; story of struggle made by women teachers of New York City. $1 net. B: F. Buck.

Strong, T: M. Hist. of the town of Flatbush in Kings County, Long Island. (Add. pubs. for price.) F: Loeser.

Vanderbilt, G. L. Social history of Flatbush. $1.50. F: Loeser.

Van Dyke, J: C: New New York. **$3.50 net. Macmillan.

Van Rensselaer, M. G. History of the city of New York in the seventeenth century. In 2 v. **$5 net. Macmillan.

Wayfarer in New York. **$1.25 net. Macmillan.

Who's who in New York City and State. $5. Hamersly.

Wilgus, W: J: Proposed new railway system for the transportation and distribution of freight by improved methods in the city and port of New York. (Add. author for price.) W: J: Wilgus.

Woolston, H. B. Study of the population of Manhattanville. $1.25. Longmans.

Wright, T. A., *ed.* Records of the Dutch Reformed Church of Port Richmond, S. I.; United Brethren Congregation, commonly called Moravian Church, S. I.; St. Andrew's Church, Richmond, S. I. $15. T. A. Wright.

See also Ashokan Reservoir;—Brick Presbyterian Church — Education; — Elgin Botanic Garden; —Fifth Avenue Presbyterian Church;—Finance; —Fire Department; — Hudson River; — Insurance;—Jews;—Labor and laboring classes;—Loans;—Morris mansion;—People's Institutes; —Police;—Rockefeller Institute for Medical Research;—Schools;—Sewage and sewerage;—Singer building; — Society of Iconophiles; — Usury;—Wall Street;—*also* New York [City] *Bureau of Municipal Research.*

New York [State.] Abbott's cyclopedic digest. 2d supp. (in 2 v.). Vs. 3, 4 of supp.—vs. 17, 18, of the set. '10(Jl) c. O. ea., $7.50. N. Y. Law.

New York [State.] Annotated code of civil procedure of the state, 1910; ed. by F. B. Gilbert, assisted by Austin B. Griffin. 2d ed. '10(N) c. 13+1428 p. O. $10. M. Bender.

New York [State.] Annot. codes of civil procedure. Supp. (1902-1907). '08(Ja4); Supp. (1907-1910); Supp. (1908). '08, [1909.] (Ja); (A. J. Parker, jr.) '10(Ag); Supp. (1902-1907); (1907-1910) c. O. ea., $6.50; Supp. (1908) $3.50. Banks.

New York [State.] Annotated consolidated laws as amended to Jan. 1, 1910; ed. by Clarence F. Birdseye, Rob. C. Cumming and Frank B. Gilbert. v. 1, 2. '09(N); v. 3, 4. '09(D); v. 5, 6. '10(F) c. O. ea., $6. Banks; Baker, V. & Co.; M. Bender.

New York [State.] Automobile law, [etc.] '10(Ag) c. T. pap., $1. Sturtevant.

New York [State.] Banking law; includ. all amendments of 1908; (Amasa J. Parker, jr.) '08(Je) $2.50; 1909. '09(Jl) $3.50; 1910. '10(Jl) c. O. $3. Banks.

New York [State.] Banking law; being chapter 2 of the consolidated laws as prepared by the board of statutory consolidation, (chap. 6 of the laws of 1909,) [etc.;] by C: J. Hailes. '09(Jl) $3.50; 1910. '10(Jl) c. O. $2.50. Banks & Co.

New York [State.] Bender's health officers' manual and public health law, [etc.;] by C: J. Hailes. '10(O) c. O. $2. M. Bender.

New York [State.] Bender's justices' manual of civil and criminal law and practice, [etc.;] comp. and ed. by Edn. Baylies. '09 (D) c. O. $7.50. M. Bender.

New York [State.] Bender's selected statutes of the state of New York. '08(S) c. 258 p. O. pap., $1; 6th ed. '09(N) c. 5+457 p. O. $3. M. Bender.

New York [State.] Bender's supervisors', county and town officers' manual of the state; by Fk. B. Gilbert. 5th ed. '10(D) c. O. $7.50. M. Bender.

New York [State.] Bender's village laws of the state, as amended through 1910; by Rob. Grattan. '10(O) c. O. $5. M. Bender.

New York [State.] Business corporations, [etc.] 3d ed., rev. and enl. by Jos. A. Arnold. '09(N) c. 25+400 p. O. $2.25. Baker, V. & Co.

New York [State.] Certain laws rel. to savings banks, trust companies, banks of discount and safe deposit companies. '08(S) 53 p. 8°, $2. Lyon.

New York [State.] Civil procedure repts. New ser., v. 1; by W. Byrnes. '09(D) c. 450 p. 8°, $4. Peloubet.

New York [State.] Civil procedure repts.; (Percival S. Menken.) v. 37. '08(Ap); v. 38. '08(My); v. 39. '09(Mr) c. 8°, ea., $4. Peloubet.

New York [State.] Code of civil procedure as amended, 1908; (G: Chase.) '08(Je); 1909. '09(Jl); 1910. '10(Jl) c. D. (Chase's pocket code.) flex. skiver, ea., $3.50. Banks.

New York [State.] Code of civil procedure; cont. all amendments of 1908; (Amasa J. Parker, jr.) 8th ed., rev. by C: J. Hailes. '08(Je); 1909, 9th ed., rev. by C: J. Hailes. '09(Jl); 1910, 10th ed., rev. by C: F. Bridge. '10(Jl) c. D. (Parker's pocket code of civil procedure.) flex. skiver, ea., $3.50. [Bound with Code of civil procedure as amended, 1910, by W: Hazlitt Smith.] Banks & Co.

New York [State.] Code of civil procedure; cont. all amendments of 1908; with topical index; (J: C. Thomson.) 33d ed. '08 (Je); 1909, 34th ed., '09(Je); 1910, 35th ed. '10(Jl) c. S. (Parsons' complete annot. pocket code.) flex. skiver, 33d, 34th eds., ea., $3.50; 35th ed., $4.
Baker, V. & Co.; M. Bender.

New York [State.] Code of criminal procedure; chapter 442, as amended; ed. by Lewis Rathbone Parker, jr. 10th ed.; by Amasa J. Parker, jr. '09(Jl) c. D. flex. skiver, $2.50; 11th ed. by Amasa J. Parker, jr. '10(Ag) c. D. flex. leath., $3. Banks.

New York [State.] Code of criminal procedure: chapter 442, as amended; ed. by Lewis R. Parker. '08(Jl) c. 467 p. S. flex. im. mor., *$2 net. Banks.

New York [State.] Code of criminal procedure as amended, incl. 1882-1908; a full index 27th, 28th rev. eds. '07, '08(Jl) ea., $2; 29th rev. ed. '09(Jl) c. D. $2.50.
Banks & Co.

New York [State.] Code of criminal procedure; (C: D. Rust.) 22d ed. '08(Je) c. D. flex. im. alligator, $3.50. (Bound with penal code of New York.) M. Bender.

New York [State.] Code of criminal procedure and penal code, as amended 1908; (J: T. Cook.) 20th ed. '08(Jl) c. O. $5.
M. Bender.

New York [State.] *Commissioners for Detecting and Defeating Conspiracies.* Minutes of the Commissioners for Detecting and Defeating Conspiracies in the state of New York; Albany county sessions, 1778-1781; ed. by Victor Hugo Paltsits. In 3 v. v. 1, 1778-1779; v. 2, 1780-1781. '09(N13); v. 3, Analytical index. '10(S10) facsims., O. (Distributed officially and by exchange.)
New York.

New York [State.] Consolidated laws, 1909: prep. under the direction and control of the Board of Statutory Consolidation; ed. by F: E. Wadhams. In 7 v. v. 1-4. '09(Jl); v. 5-7 (N) c. O. subs., ea., $3.—Amendments to Consol. laws. $3. Am. Law Bk.

New York [State.] *Ct. of appeals.* Repts.; rev. ed. with notes; ed. by J: T. Cook. bk. 38, comprising v. 186-190, incl. of Bedell's repts, v. 24-28. '09(Mr) c. O. shp., shp., $5. M. Bender.

New York [State.] *Ct. of appeals.* Repts.; (Edwin A. Bedell.) v. 189. '08(Mr); v. 190. '08(My); v. 191 (Ag) ea., $2.50; (Alvah S. Newcomb.) v. 192. '09(Mr); v. 193, 194; (J. Newton Fiero.) (Je) ea., $2.50; v. 195 (S) $2; v. 196. '10(Ap); v. 197 (Je) c. O. shp., ea., 65 c. Lyon.

New York [State.] *Ct. of appeals.* Rules of practice, annot.: by Edm. H. Smith. 9th ed.; by C: J. Hailes. '10(N) c. O. $2.
M. Bender; Baker, V. & Co.

New York [State.] Court rules of the state, and bankruptcy rules and orders, [etc.] 3d ed.; prep. by Rob. C. Cumming and Fk. B. Gilbert. '10(N) c. O. $4.50. Banks.

New York [State.] *Courts.* Current court decisions; comp. by F. W. Noble. v. 1, pt. 1. '08(F) 8°, pap., 25 c. Peloubet.

New York [State.] *Cts. of record.* General rules of practice; with annots., notes and references. 10th ed.; by Marcus T. Hun. '10(N) c. O. $4.50.
M. Bender; Baker, V. & Co.

New York [State.] *Cts. of record.* Miscellaneous repts.; (C: C. Lester.) v. 55. '07, [1908.] (Ap); v. 56 (My); v. 57 (Ag); v. 58 (N); v. 59. '09(Ja); v. 60, 61 (Je); v. 62 (Ag); v. 63 (D) ea., $2; v. 64. '10 (Ap); v. 65 (Jl) c. O. shp., ea., 75 c. Lyon.

New York [State.] *Cts. of record.* Practice in special actions in the cts. of record of the state of New York, under the code of civil procedure and statutes; with forms by J. A. Newton Fiero. 2 v. 3d ed. '08(O) c. 9+1096; 4+1097-2169 p. 8°, $13. M. Bender.

New York [State.] Criminal repts.; by C: H. Mills. v. 20. '08(F); v. 21 (O); v. 22. '09, [1910.] (F); v. 23 (Jl) c. O. shp., ea., $5.50. W. C. Little.

New York [State.] Current court decisions; being reports of cases decided at trial term, special term and chambers of the New York supreme ct., 1st and 2d departments, the city court of New York, and surrogate's court of New York and Kings Co., involving points of practice; ed. by F: W. Noble. v. 1. '08, [1909.] (Ja) 275 p. O. $3.
F. C. Hill.

New York [State.] *Dept. of Agriculture.* Agricultural advantages of New York state. '09(S18) il. obl. S. pap., gratis.
N. Y. State, Dept. of Agri.

New York [State.] *Dept. of Agriculture. Bureau of Statistics.* List of farms occupied and unoccupied for sale or rent, in New York state; comp. by R. R. Riddell. '09(S18) il. map, O. (N. Y. State, Dept. of Agriculture, Bu. of Statistics; Farm bull.) pap. (Add. pubs. for price.)
N. Y. State. Dept. of Agri.

New York [State.] Digest of statutes and repts. fr. Jan 1, 1907, to Jan. 1, 1908; continuation of Abbott's N. Y. digest by Ja. MacGregor Smith. '08(Mr); fr. Jan. 1, 1908, to Jan. 1, 1909. '09(Mr) ea., $5; fr. Jan. 1, 1909, to Jan. 1, 1910. '10(Ap) c. O. $4.25. Baker, V. & Co.

New York [State.] Digested treatise and compendium of law applicable to titles to real estate; by Ja. Watson Gerard. 5th ed., rev. and enl. by Rob. Ludlow Fowler and Ja. H. Hickey. '09(Mr) c. O. $8.50 net.
Baker, V. & Co.

New York [State.] *Education Dept.* Course of study and syllabus for elem. schools. '10 (D) 3-256 p. il. (partly col.) 8°.
N. Y. State Educ.
Contains bibliographies.

New York [State.] *Education Dept.* Professional examination papers for the academic year 1908-9. '09(O23) D. pap. (Add. pubs. for price.) N. Y. State Educ.

New York [State.] *Education Dept.* Twenty-fifth rept. of the state entomologist on injurious and other insects of the state of New York. '10(S) 178 p. il. O. (N. Y. State Educ. Dept., bull.) pap., 35 c. N. Y. State Educ.

New York [State.] Education law, 1909. '09, [1910.] (Ap) 3-402 p. 8°, (Education Dept. bull.) N. Y. State Educ.

New York [State.] Forest, fish and game laws. '08, [1909.] (Mr) 50 c. M. Bender.

New York [State.] Highway code; with explanatory notes of cases and forms; contains highway law of 1908 as revised; motor vehicle law of 1904, etc.; (Fk. Bixby Gilbert and Fk. D. Lyon.) '08(O) c. 14+567 p. O. $3.50. Lyon.

New York [State.] Insurance law; incl. all amendments of 1908; with notes and annots., by Amasa J. Parker, jr. '08(Je); 1909. '09(Jl) ea., $2.50; 1910. '10(Jl) c. O. $3. Banks.

New York [State.] Insurance law; with all amendments to and incl. 1908; by And. Hamilton. (Neile F. Towner.) '08(Je) c. O. pap., $1.50; 1909, with amendments by the legislature of 1910; [by] Andrew Hamilton; rev. by N. F. Towner. '10(Ag) c. O. $2.50. Banks & Co.

New York [State.] Judiciary law as consolidated by the board of statutory consolidation, as amended to Jan. 1, 1910; full annotations to date by Albert J. Danaher. '09 (O) c. 226 p. O. $3. Banks & Co.

New York [State.] Kreidler's analyzed citations (cumulative plan) of all decisions Feb., 1910; ed. by C: R. Kreidler. '10 (Mr) c. issued 3 times a year; 1st year $7.50; succeeding years, ea., $5. M. Bender; Baker, V. & Co.

New York [State.] Labor laws and decisions; comp. by J: A. Cipperly; rev., with all amendments to Dec., 1907. '08(Mr) c. 25+462 p. O. $2.50; pap., $2. Banks & Co.,

New York [State.] Land title registration law: chapter 444, laws of 1908; completely indexed: [Torrens system.] c. 61 p. O. pap., 50 c. M. Bender.

New York [State.] Land title registration law fully cross-indexed. '08(Ag) c. 38+23 p. 8°, 50 c.; bds., $1. Hall & McC.

New York [State.] Law and practice of surrogates' courts in the state; by Amasa A. Redfield. 7th ed., rev. and enl., by Rob. L. Redfield. '10(Mr) c. O. $9. Baker, V. & Co.

New York [State] law finder, from the earliest issue of the N. Y. repts. '10(My) c. S. $5. Law Stamp.

New York [State.] Law of domestic relations in the state; by Fletcher W. Battershall '10(N) c. O. $5. M. Bender.

New York [State.] Laws of the state rel. to banks, banking, trust companies, [etc.;] annot. by Willis S. Paine. 6th ed. '10 (F) c. O. $6. M. Bender.

New York [State.] Laws rel. to general religious and non-business corporations, taxation and exemption, [etc.;] (Cumming and Gilbert;) comp. for clergymen, [etc.,] by Rev. H. E. Waugh. 14th ed. '08(Ag) c. O. buck., $2. Banks & Co.

New York [State.] Lien law; chapter 33 of the consolidated laws, [etc.,] by W: L. Snyder. 5th ed. '09(Ag) c. 36+613 p. O. $5. Baker, V. & Co.

New York [State.] Manual of corporation law; cont. the important statutes regulating business incorporations, a digest of the statutes and the principal forms used by corporations operating in the state of New York. Interleaved ed.; by R: Compton Harrison. '09(Mr) c. O. $3.50. Ronald Press.

New York [State.] New automobile law, enacted by the legislature of 1910, as article 11 of the highway law. '10(Je) c. O. pap. Banks & Co.

New York [State.] New index to the code of civil procedure as amended 1909, [etc.,] by W: Hazlitt Smith. '09(N) c. 255 p. O. $3. Banks & Co.

New York [State.] Notes on the law of wills, for use in connection with "Chaplin on wills," by Stewart Chaplin. '09(N) c. 64 p. O. pap., 75 c. Baker, V. & Co.

New York [State.] Penal code and code of criminal procedure as amended to close of 132d sess. of legislature, 1909. 21st ed., annot. by J: T. Cook. '09(S) c. 550 p. Q. $7.50. M. Bender.

New York [State.] Penal code, as amended 1882-1908. 27th rev. ed. '08(Jl) c. D. $2. Banks & Co.

New York [State.] Penal code: being chapter 676, as amended; ed. by Amasa J. Parker, jr. '08(Jl) c. 349 p. S. flex. im. mor., *$2 net. Banks.

New York [State.] Penal code, incl. amendments 1908; (C: D. Rust.) 22d ed. '08 (Je) c. D. flex. im. alligator, $3.50. M. Bender

New York [State.] Penal law. 2d ed., 1910; ed. by Amasa J. Parker, jr. '10(Ag) c. D. flex. skiver, $3. Banks.

New York [State.] Penal law and amendments of code of criminal procedure, as enacted by the legislature of 1909, with index and tables; prepared by Harry M. Ingram. '09(Ap) c. 4+511 p. O. $3.50. Am. Law Bk.

New York [State.] Penal law and code of criminal procedure, with all amendments passed at the legislative session of 1909. '09 (Jl); 1910. '10(Jl) [Bender's ed.] c. O. ea., $4. M. Bender.

New York [State.] Penal law and code of criminal procedure, as amended at the close of the 133d session of the legislature, 1910. 22d ed.; annot. by J: T. Cook. '10(N) c. O. $7.50. M. Bender.

New York [State.] Penal law; being chapter 40 of the consolidated law as prepared by the Board of Statutory Consolidation, [etc.;] with all amendments made by the legislature of 1909; with complete annots. to May 1, 1909; new and thorough index by C: J. Hailes. '09(Jl) c. 483 p. O. $3.50. Banks & Co.

New York [State.] Penal law of the state; with complete annots. to May 1, 1910. New and thorough index; by C: J. Hailes. '10(Ag) c. O. $2.50. Banks & Co.

New York [State.] Penal law of the state, with amendments. '09(N) O. shp., $1.50 Chief.

New York [State.] Personal property law; chapter 41 of the consolidated laws; together with all amendments, [etc.] 2d ed.; by Rob. Ludlow Fowler. '09(Jl) c. 44+351 p. O. $5. Baker, V. & Co.

New York [State.] *Probation Commission.* County probation officers; the new law, what probation is, illustrative cases, advantages of probation, organization on the county plan. '10(S) 12 p. O. pap., gratis. N. Y. State Probation.

New York [State.] *Probation Commission.* Forms for juvenile and adult probation work, with suggestions as to their use. '09 (Je5) 4°. (Add. pubs. for price.) Lyon.

New York [State.] Public health law, [etc.;] together with a manual for boards of health and health officers, by Lewis Balch; rev. by C: J. Hailes. '09(N) c. 270 p. D. $2.50. Banks & Co.

New York [State.] *Public Service Commission.* History and description of rapid transit routes in New York City, adopted under the Rapid transit act; embracing routes constructed, under construction and validated for construction, together with a map of each route and a combination map showing all such routes. '10(Je) 108 p. maps, (fold.,) 8°. N. Y. Pub. Service Com.

New York State. *Public Service Commission, 2d District.* In the matter of fire prevention along the lines of the railroads in the Adirondacks forest preserve. '09(Ag14) tab., O. pap. (Add. pubs. for price.) N. Y. Pub. Service Com.

New York [State.] *Public Service Commission.* Supervision of street railways in England and Prussia; repr. from Annual rept. of the Public Service Commission for the first district of the state of New York for the year ending December 31, 1908. '09(D25) 8°. (Add. pubs. for price.) Lyon.

New York [State.] Public service commissions law; C: J. Hailes. '10(Jl) c. O. pap., $1. Banks & Co.

New York [State.] Public service commissions law as enacted in 1907, affecting all railroads, common carriers, [etc.;] prepared by Neile F. Towner. 4th ed. '07, [1908.] (Jl) c. 136 p. O. pap., $1. Banks & Co.

New York [State.] Real property law of the state, [etc.,] by Rob. Ludlow Fowler. 3d ed., rev. and enl. '09(N) c. O. $8.50. Baker, V. & Co.

New York [State.] State of New York; messages from the governors, comprising executive communications to the Legislature and other papers rel. to legislation from the organization of the first colonial Assembly in 1683 to and including the year 1906, with notes; ed. by C: Z. Lincoln. 11 v. '09, [1910.] (F) c. por. 8°. (Add. pubs for price.) New York.

New York [State.] Statutory revision of the laws affecting banks, banking and trust companies as amended, 1908; (And. Hamilton.) New ed. by C: J. Hailes. '08(Je) c. 169+8 p. O. $2; pap., $1.50. Banks & Co.

New York [State.] Statutory revision of the laws affecting miscellaneous corporations, enacted in 1892, [etc.;] indexed, with amendments of 1908; prepared by And. Hamilton. '08(N) c. various paging, O. $2. Banks & Co.

New York [State.] Statutory revision of the laws affecting railroads, enacted in 1892, and amended in 1893-1908, [etc.] '08(N) c. various paging, O. $2. Banks & Co.

New York [State] supplement, v. 106. Permanent ed. v. 107. '08(Ap); v. 108 (My); v. 109 (Jl); v. 110 (O); v. 111 (N); v. 112, 113. '09(Mr); v. 114 (Je); v. 115 (Jl); v. 116 (S); v. 117 (N); ea., $4; v. 118. '09, [1910.] (F); v. 119 (Ap); v. 120 (My); v. 121 (Jl); v. 122 (Ag); v. 123 (O) c. O. (National reporter system, N. Y. supp. and state reporter.) ea., $3.—Digest. 2 v. $5. West Pub.

New York [State.] *Supreme ct.* Repts.; (Jerome B. Fisher.) v. 121. '07, [1908.] (Ap); v. 122. '08(My); v. 123 (Jl); v. 124 (O); v. 125 (D); v. 126. '09(Ja); v. 127 (Mr); v. 128 (Ap); v. 129 (Je); v. 130 (Ag) ea., *$3 net; v. 131-132. '09, [1910.] (F); v. 133 (Mr); v. 134 (My); v. 135 (Jl); v. 136 (Ag) c. O. shp., ea., $1. Lyon.

New York [State.] *Surrogates' cts.* Procedure and law. 2 v.; by Willis E. Heaton. 1909 revision. '09(N) c. 106+715; 716-1548 p. O. *$12 net. M. Bender.

New York [State.] *Surrogates' cts.* Repts.; with annots.; (Willard S. Gibbons.) v. 2. '08, [1909.] (Ja) c. O. shp., $5.50. W. C. Little.

V. 1, published in 1905, *see* American Catalog, 1905-'07, v. 2.

New York [State.] Tax law; completely indexed. '08(Je) c. O. pap., $1. Baker, V. & Co.; M. Bender.

New York [State.] Tax law, incl. the consolidated tax law of 1909, as amended Jan. 1, 1910, [etc.;] together with annots., decisions, tables and forms; ed. by Rob. C. Cumming and G: W. Webster. 5th ed. '09 (Ag) c. 25+509 p. O. $5. Baker, V. & Co.

New York [State.] Tax law; with all amendments to 1910; completely indexed, 1910. '10(Ag.) c. O. pap., $1. Baker, V. & Co.

New York [State.] Tax law; being chapter 60 of the consolidated laws (Chapter 62, laws of 1909), [etc.;] hdbk. for assessors, collectors and lawyers; by J: N. Drake. New ed., by C: F. Bridge. '09(O) c. O. $2.50. Banks & Co.

New York [State.] Tax law, incl. 1908 amendments to the article on taxable transfers. '08(O) c. O. (Add. pubs. for price.) (Bound with Cumming and Gilbert's membership and religious corporations of New York.) Banks & Co.

New York [State.] Tax law of 1896, with all amendments to date, [etc.;] cont. amendments and decisions to June 1, 1908; by J: N. Drake; rev. by C: J. Hailes. '08(N) c. 9+5-364+31 p. O. $2. Banks & Co.

New York [State.] Text bk. on school law; by T: E. Finegan. 6th ed., rev. '10(D) c. D. $1.25. M. Bender.

New York [State.] Transfer tax law of the state, [etc.;] annots. and references and a complete table of cases and forms, [etc.;] by G: W. McElroy. 2d ed. '09(Jl) c. 42+765 p. O. $6. M. Bender.

New York [State.] Treatise on the mechanics' lien law of the state; by Carl Arth. Jensen. '10(O) c. D. $3.50. Trow Press.

New York [State.] Village law of the state, [etc.,] by Amasa J. Parker, jr. 8th ed., rev. by C: J. Hailes. '08(Ag) $2; 9th ed. by C: G. Blakeslee. '09(N) c. O. $3. Banks & Co.

New York [State.] Village law, [etc.;] with explanatory notes, cross references, decisions and forms; (Cumming and Gilbert.) 4th rev. ed. '08(Ag) c. O. $3. M. Bender.

New York [State.] Village laws; as amended to Jan. 1, 1908; (Fk. S. Becker and Edn. D. Howe.) 3d ed. '07, [1908.] (O) c. O $2.50. Williamson Law Bk.

New York State.

Alexander, De A. S. Political history of the state of New York. v. 3, 1861-1882. **$2.50 net. Holt.

Arnold, J. A. Guide for business corporations in the state of New York. $1.50; $1.25. Baker, V. & Co.

Automobile laws of the New England states, New York, New Jersey and Pennsylvania. (Add. pub. for price.) Rhode Island Lib.

Banks' New York state lawyers' diary, 1908, 1909, 1910. ea., $2. Banks & Co.

Becker, C. L. Hist. of the political parties in the province of New York, 1760-1776. 75 c. Univ. of Wis.

Bender's national lawyers' diary and directory for the state of New York, 1908, 1909, 1910. ea., $2. M. Bender.

Cardozo, B: N. Jurisdiction of the court of claims of the state of New York. $3. Banks & Co.

Clarke, J: M. Early Devonic hist. of New York and eastern North America. pt. 1. $2.50. N. Y. State Educ.

Clarke, J: M., *and others.* Geologic map and descriptions of the Portage and Nunda quadrangles, incl. map of Letchworth Park; accompanied by rept. on Pleistocene hist. of Genesee Valley. 20 c. N. Y. State Educ.

Danaher, F. M. Bar examinations (N. Y.) $4. Lyon.

Eastman, C: R. Devonic fishes of the New York formations. $1.25. N. Y. State Educ.

Eaton, E. H. Birds of New York. In 2 v. v. 1. $3. N. Y. State Educ.

Fairchild, H. L. Glacial waters in central New York. 40 c. N. Y. State Educ.

Finegan, T: E: Textbook on New York school law. $1. M. Bender.

Floyd, F: C. History of the Fortieth [Mozart] regiment, New York Volunteers. $3. F: C. Floyd.

New York State.—*Continued.*

Foote, A. R. Speech del. before Wis. legislature: [public utilities bills of Wis. N. Y.] (Add. author for price.) A R. Foote.

Ford's travelers' and shippers' guide book "A" of New York State. $1.50. H. M. Ford.

Forsythe, M. I. Beginnings of New York: old Kingston, the first capital. 25 c. Badger.

Fullerton, A. R., *comp.* Life insurance law chart, 1908-1909; summary of [N. Y.] state laws applicable to life insurance companies of other states. (Add. pubs. for price.) Spectator.

Gould, W: R. Greater New York and state lawyers' diary, 1908, 1909, 1910. ea., $1. W: R. Gould.

Hall, H. A. Hist. of the Sixth New York Cavalry. $5. F. A. Eaton.

Hamlin, L. B., *ed.* Select. from the Follett papers. Hist. and Phil. Soc., O.

Harrison, R: C. Manual of New York corporation law. $4.25. Ronald Press.

Hasse, A. R. Index of economic material in documents of the states of U. S.: New York. $3.75. Carnegie.

Hedrick, U. P., *and others.* Grapes of New York. (Not for sale.) Lyon.

Hill, H: W. Historical review of waterways and canal construction in New York State. $5; $4. Buffalo Hist. Soc.

Ivins, W: M., *and* Mason, H. D. Control of public utilities in the form of an annotation of the public service commissions law of the state of N. Y., and covering all important Am. cases. *$7 net. Baker, V. & Co.

Jewett, F. G. Manual for elections officers and voters. $2.50; $2. M. Bender.

Joyce, J. A. Treatise on franchises, especially those of public service corporations; cont. also in an appendix the public service commissions law of New York and the public utility law of Wisconsin. $6.50. Banks.

Kemp, J. F., *and* Ruedemann, R. Geology of the Elizabethtown and Port Henry quadrangles. 40 c. N. Y. State Educ.

Luther, D. D. Geology of the Geneva-Ovid quadrangles. (Add. pubs. for price.) N. Y. State Educ.

McCloskey, F. A. Appellate papers in New York state. (Add. author for price.) F. A. McCloskey.

Miller, W: J: Geology of the Remsen quadrangle, [N. Y.] 25 c. N. Y. State Educ.

Mulliner, G. S. New York laws of interest to women. 25 c. G. S. Mulliner.

New York State Library. Translation and publication of the manuscript Dutch records of New Netherland. (Add. pubs. for price.) N. Y. State Educ.

Newland, D: H., *and* Hartnagel, C. G. Iron ores of the Clinton formation in New York. 35 c. N. Y. State Educ.

NEW YORK STATE.—*Continued.*

Noble, W: N. Disposition of a decedent's real property for the payment of debts and funeral expenses under the code of civil procedure of the state of N. Y. $3.50. Banks & Co.

Odell, B: B., *jr.* Public papers: [while governor of New York,] 1901-1904. 4 v. $2.50. Lyon.

Paltsits, V. H. Function of state historian of New York. gratis. N. Y. State Hist.

Pelletreau, W: S. Historic homes and institutions and genealogical and familiar hist. of New York. 4 v. (Add. pubs. for price.) Lewis Pub.

"Pilot" sectional road maps of New England and Hudson river district. $5. F. S. Blanchard.

Scott, H: W. Courts of the state of New York: their history, development and jurisdiction. $5. Wilson Pub. Co.

Standard road-book of New York State. $1.50. W. L. Chase.

Van Rensselaer, K. Van Rensselaer Bowier manuscripts: letters and documents rel. to the colony of Rensselaerswyck. $1.25. N. Y. State Educ.

Who's who in New York City and state. $5. Hamersly.

Zwierlein, F: G. Religion in New Netherland. $2 net. Stechert.

See also Adirondack mountains;—Agriculture;—Albany County;—Ballston Spa;—Buffalo;—Canals;—Catskill mountains;—Champlain Valley;—Claverack;—Courts;—Dutchess County;—Erie canal;—Fredericksburgh; —Genealogy;—George Junior Republic;—Glen Falls;—Hudson;—Hudson river;—Hudson River Valley;—Hygiene;—Kinderhook; — Kings Co.; — Kreischerville; — Lake Champlain;—Lake George;—Long Island; — Marlborough; — Mohawk Valley; — Monroe County;—Niagara Falls;—Old Mine Road;—Oneida County; — Orange County; — Otsego County;—Port Jervis;—Quaker Hill;—Rhinebeck;—Ripley;—Saranac;—Saratoga Springs;—Schenectady;—Staten Island; — Stocks;—Westchester;—West Point;—Wheatland.

New York Association for the Blind. *Special Committee on Prevention of Blindness.* Prevention of blindness. no. 1, no. 2, Children who need not have been blind: prevention a public duty. 3d ed., rev., no. 3. Special committee on the prevention of blindness. '09(My15) il. pap., gratis. N. Y. Assoc. for Blind.

New York Association for the Blind. The first report, from its formation, November 25, 1905, to November 1, 1907: light through work. '08(Je13) il. pors. Q. pap., gratis. N. Y. Assoc. for Blind.

NEW YORK BIBLE AND COMMON PRAYER BOOK SOCIETY.

Lowndes, A. Century of achievement: hist. of the New York Bible and Common Prayer Book Society. $5. Gorham.

New York Botanical Garden contributions. 4° and 8°, pap., 25 c. N. Y. Botanical.

—Britton. Genus *Ernodea.*—Taxonomic aspect of the species question.

—House. Studies in North American convolvulaceae.

—Howe. Physiological studies III.

—Pond. Further studies of solution tension and toxicity in lipolysis.

—Robinson. *Alabastra philippinensia.*

—Williams. Mosses from tropical America.

New York Botanical Garden memoirs. il. 4°, $2. N. Y. Botanical.

—Gager. Effects of the rays of radium on plants.

—Hollick *and* Jeffrey. Studies of cretaceous coniferous remains from Kreischerville, N. Y.

New York, Brockton and Boston Canal: its importance to Massachusetts industries and great value to the nation. [2d ed.] '08, [1909.] (My) 82 p. il. maps, 4°. (Add. pub. for price.) E. B. Mellen.

New York cake book; fifty recipes by a famous New York chef. '09(F6) c. T. 50 c. Stokes.

New York church and musical directory of New York and Brooklyn and other adjacent suburbs; ed. by W: G. James. '08 (Jl) c. il. pors. 12°, pap., 50 c. W: G. James.

New York City Art Commission. Catalogue of the works of art belonging to the City of New York. '09(N20) c. il. pors. Q. pap., gratis, boxed. Art. Com. N. Y.

NEW YORK [CITY] HARBOR.

Soper, G: A. Pollution of New York harbor. $2.50. G: A. Soper.

See also Navigation.

New York Herald. National highways route book, N. Y. City to Atlanta. '10(Mr5) c. il. maps, 8°. (Add. pubs. for price.) N. Y. Herald.

New York idea. Mitchell, L. E. 50 c. W. H. Baker.

New York Institution for the Instruction of the Deaf and Dumb. 100th anniversary of the birth of Abraham Lincoln; commemorative exercises; prize essays in the N. Y. *Times* Lincoln Composition Contest. '10 (Ap2) il. por. O. pap. (Add. pubs. for price.) N. Y. Inst. Deaf and Dumb.

NEW YORK PUBLIC LIBRARY, New York City.

Helbig, R: E. German American researches: growth of the collection of the N. Y. Public Library, 1906-07. gratis. N. Y. Pub. Lib.

NEW YORK SOCIETY LIBRARY, New York City.

Keep, A. B. History of New York Society Library, with an introductory chapter on libraries in colonial New York. $7.50. Scribner.

New York society on parade. Pulitzer, R. **$1.20 net. Harper.

New York State College of Agriculture bull. pap. Cornell Univ.

—Taylor. Street trees. (Experiment station.) gratis.

New York State Education Dept. bull. O. pap. N. Y. State Educ.

—Bascom. Selected books on nature study for schools and libraries. gratis.

—Education law, 1909. (Add. pubs. for price.)

—Felt. Control of flies and other household insects. 15 c.

—New York [State.] Education law, 1909.

—New York State Library, Albany. Medical serials. 25 c.—Translations and publication of the manuscript Dutch records of New Netherland.

—New York State University. Course of study and syllabus for guidance of nurse training schools. (Add. pubs. for price.)

New York State Library, Albany. Calendar of the Sir William Johnson manuscripts in the New York State Library; comp. by R: E. Dey. '09(N20) 8°, $1. N. Y. State Educ.

New York State Library, Albany. Catalogue of the Duncan Campbell collection. '08 (Ag15) O. gratis. N. Y. State Library.

New York State Library, Albany. Medical serials; comp. by Ada Bunnell, with bibliography of medical jurisprudence by W. Burt Cook, jr. [2d ed. rev. and corr.] '10(Je) 5-153 p. 8°, (N. Y. State Educ. Dept., bull.) 25 c. N. Y. State Educ.

New York State Library, Albany. Translation and publication of the manuscript Dutch records of New Netherland; with acct. of previous attempts at translation. '10(F) 28 p. O. (N. Y. State Education Dept. bull.) pap. N. Y. State Educ.

New York State Museum bulletins. 8°, pap. N. Y. State Educ.

—Clarke, *and others.* Geologic map and descriptions of the Portage and Nunda quadrangles. (Paleontology.) 20 c.

—Converse. Myths and legends of the New York State Iroquois. 75 c.; 50 c.

—Felt. Control of household insects. (Add. pubs. for price.)

—Luther. Geology of the Geneva-Ovid quadrangles. (Add. pubs. for price.)

—Miller. Geology of the Remsen quadrangle. 25 c.

—Newland *and* Hartnagel. Iron ores of the Clinton formation in New York State. 35 c.

—Parker. Excavations in an Erie Indian village. (Archæology.) 30 c.

—Shufeldt. Osteology of birds. (Add. pubs. for price.)

New York State Museum memoirs. il. 4°. N. Y. State Educ.

—Clarke. Early Devonic hist. of N. Y. and eastern North America. $2.50.

—Eastman. Devonic fishes of N. Y. formations. $1.25.

—Eaton. Birds of New York. In 2 v. v. 1. $3.

New York State University. Course of study and syllabus for guidance of nurse training schools in preparing their students for examination before the State Board. '09(N) 3-32 p. 8°, (New York State Educ. Dept. bull.) (Add. pubs. for price.) N. Y. State Educ.

New York University. School of Commerce, Accounts and Finance. Graded accounting problems; comp., arranged and classified by W: H. Dennis and Leo Greendlinger. 3 v. '09(N) 8°, $2. L. Greendlinger.

New York University bull. 12°. N. Y. Univ.

—MacCracken. Tercentenary announcements, 1609-1909: "Three epochs in education in New York City."

New York Zoological Park. Popular official guide to the New York Zoological Park, by W: T. Hornaday. 10th ed. '09(D4) il. front. maps, plans, 12°, pap., 25 c. N. Y. Zoological.

NEW ZEALAND.

Douglas, *Sir* A. P. Dominion of New Zealand. *$3 net. Little, B. & Co.

Gorst, *Sir* J: E. New Zealand revisited. *$4 net. Pitman.

Horsley, R. New Zealand. *$2 net. Stokes.

Le Rossignol, J. E., *and* Stewart, W: D. State socialism in New Zealand. $1.50 net. Crowell.

Le Rossignol, J. E:, *and* Stewart, W: D. Taxation in New Zealand. 75 c. Univ. of Neb.

Loughan, R. A. New Zealand at home. *$1.75 net. Scribner.

Reeves, W: P. New Zealand. *$6 net. Macmillan.

Scholefield, G. H. New Zealand in evolution. *$3 net. Scribner.

Vaile, P. A. New Zealand. *75 c. net. Macmillan.

Zeagler, J: W. Trip through New Zealand. 40 c. J: W. Zeagler.

See also Civil service.

Newall, Hugh Fk.

Spectroscope and its work. '10(D) 160 p. 16°, 85 c. net. Gorham.

NEWARK, N. J.

Urquart, F: J. Short history of Newark. *75 c. net. Baker Pr.

See also St. John's Church.

NEWARK, N. J., FREE PUBLIC LIBRARY.

Dana, J: C. Modern American library economy, as illustrated by the Newark Free Public Library. pt. 1, Lending department; section 1, Work of the registration desk. 25 c.; pt. 5, The school department; section 2, Course of study for normal school pupils on the use of a library. 75 c. Elm Tree Press.

NEWBAKER FAMILY.

See Genealogies: Genealogical record.

Newbegin, Marion I.

Tillers of the ground. '10(Je4) il. 12°, (Readable books in natural knowledge.) 50 c. net. Macmillan.

Newberry, Arth. St. John.

Caught on the fly: fugitive notes of sport and other things. '08(D) c. 3-306 p. il. (Priv. pr.) A. S. Newberry.

Newberry, Percy E:

See Davis, Thdr. M.

Newbolt, H: J:

New June. '10(Ja22) 12°, *$1.35 net. Dutton.

Newbolt, Canon W: C: Edm.

Sacrament of the altar. '08(Ap4) D. (Oxford lib. of practical theology.) *$1.40 net. Longmans.

NEWCASTLE, William Cavendish, *Duke* of, and Margaret, *Duchess* of.

Longueville, T: First Duke and Duchess of Newcastle-upon-Tyne. $3.50 net. Longmans.

NEWCASTLE.

See Wyoming.

Newcomb, Alvah S., rep.

See New York State. *Ct. of appeals.* Repts.

Newcomb, C: B:
Principles of psychic philosophy. '08 (Ap11) c. D. **$1.40 net. Lothrop, L. & S.

Newcomb, G: T:
Simple method of translating Hebrew. '09 (Ag) c. 30 p. 8°. (Not for sale.) G: T: Newcomb.

Newcomb, Harry Turner.
Diminished dollar and railway rates. [1910.] (Ap) c. '09. 14 p. 8°, 35 c. North American.
Some recent phases of federal railway control; address del. before the 16th annual convention of the Commercial Law League of America, at Narragansett Pier, R. I., July 20, 1910. '10(D) 24 p. 8°, (Priv. pr.) H. T. Newcomb.

Newcomb, Mrs. Katharine Hinchman.
Steps along the path. '09(Mr13) c. D. **$1.40 net. Lothrop, L. & S.

Newcomb, Simon.
Search for fluctuations in the sun's thermal radiation through their influence on terrestrial temperature. '08(Mr) 309-387 p. tabs., diagrs., 4°. (Add. pubs. for price.) Am. Philosophical Soc.

Newcomer, Alphonso Gerald, and Andrews, Alice Ebba.
Twelve centuries of English poetry and prose. '10(S10) c. O. $1.75. Scott, F. & Co.

Newcomes. *See* Thackeray, W: M.

Newell, F: Haynes.
Hawaii, its natural resources and opportunities for home-making. '09(My) 51 p. il. 8°, pap. 10 c. U. S., Supt. of Docs.

Newell, Lyman Churchill.
Course in inorganic chemistry for colleges. '09(My) c. 10+594 p. il. pors. 12°, *$2 net. Heath.
Descriptive chemistry. Rev. '09(Ag21) il. pors. 12°, (Science text-books.) $1.20. Heath.

Newell, P:
Hole book: [verses.] '08(O24) c. il. O. $1.25. Harper.
Jungle-jangle. '09(S) pap., 15 c. Harper.
Slant book. '10(N12) c. il. O. bds., $1.25. Harper.

Newell, W: S., and Dow, Carl Stephen.
Steam boilers. pt. 1, Construction of boilers; pt. 2, Types of boilers. '09(F20) c. il. 8°, (American School of Correspondence pubs.) $1. Am. Sch. Corr.

Newer remedies. Coblentz, V. $1. Apothecary.

Newest way round the world. Miller, C. J. *$2.50 net. C. J. Miller.

NEWFOUNDLAND.
See Navigation.

Newhall, Roberts De Saussure.
Discourses of Jimmy. '08(Je) c. 128 p. 16°, 50 c. Circular Adv.

Newhall, W: B., M.D.
English ball drill. '09(Ap24) il. O. (Hygiene and physical education ser.) pap., 10 c. Bassette.

NEWINGTON, Ct.
Willard, J. Census of Newington, Ct., in 1776. *$1.75 net. Hartranft.

Newkirk, Clyde, ["Newton Newkirk."]
Cynical kids or the stork book. '09(O2) c. S. 75 c. Caldwell.

Newkirk, Newton, pseud.
See Newkirk, Clyde.

Newland, D: Hale, and Hartnagel, C. A.
Iron ores of the Clinton formation in New York State. '08, [1909.] (Mr) 5-76 p. il. fold maps, 8°, (New York State Museum bull.) 35 c. N. Y. State Educ.

Newlands, B: E. R.
See Newlands, J: A. R.

Newlands, J: A. R. and B: E. R.
Sugar: hdbk. for planters and refiners. '09 (Ap3) il. 8°, $10. Spon.

Newman, Arth.
Writing on the clouds. '10(Ag6) c. D. 90 c. net. Sherman, F.

Newman, Carrie Sophia.
Kindergarten in the home. '09(Jl31) c. il. D. $1.50. L. C. Page.

Newman, Clifford Lee, ed.
See New Jersey. Criminal law and procedure.—Digest.

Newman, Ernest.
Hugo Wolf. '09(S4) il. O. (New lib. of music.) *$2.50 net. Lane.
Musical studies. New ed. '10(S) 9+319 p. 12°, $1.50 net. Lane.
Richard Strauss; with a personal note by Alfr. Kalisch. '08(O31) il. pors. (Living masters of music.) *$1 net. Lane.

Newman, G:, M.D.
See Whitelegge, B: Arth., *M.D.*

Newman, J:
Scamping tricks and odd knowledge; occasionally practiced on public works. '08 (Jl4) 12°, $1. Spon.

Newman, Cardinal J: H:
Church of the fathers: (repr. from *Historical Sketches,* v. 2.) '08(Je13) S. (Longmans' pocket lib.) *75 c. net. Longmans.
Dream of Gerontius; with facsims. of the original fair copy; with a biog. sketch of the Rev. J: Gordon, to whom the poem is inscribed; cont. appreciation by Cardinal Newman. '10(Ja22) f°, vellum, *$10 net, boxed. Longmans.
Meditations and devotions. In 3 pts. pt. 1, The month of May; pt. 2, Stations of the cross; pt. 3, Meditations on Christian doctrine. '08(M14) S. ea., *40 c. et. Longmans.
University teaching: being the first part of "The idea of a university, defined and illustrated." '08(Je13) S. (Longmans' pocket lib.) *75 c. net. Longmans.

NEWMAN, *Cardinal* John Henry.
O'Dwyer, E: T: Cardinal Newman and the Encyclical *Pascendi Dominici Gregis.* *36 c. net. Longmans.
Sarolea, C: Cardinal Newman and his influence on religious life and thought. *$1 net. Scribner.

Newman, R: Brinsley.
Belle Islers: a novel. '08(Ap4) c. il. D. †$1.50. Lothrop, L. & S.

NEWMAN MEMORIAL CHURCH.
Rickaby, J., *and* McIntyre, *Canon.* Newman memorial sermons. 36 c. net. Longmans.

Newmarch, Rosa.
Tchaikovsky: his life and works; ed. with a complete classific account of works, copious analyses of important works, analytical and other indices; also, supplement dealing with "the relation of Tchaikovsky to art questions of the day," by Edn. Evans. [New ed.] '08(Je20) por. facsim., D. *$2.50 net. Scribner.

Newnes Art lib. il. 8°, bds. Warne.
—Clouston. Sir Thomas Lawrence. *$1.25 net.

Newnham-Davis, Nathaniel.
Gourmet's guide to Europe. 2d ed. '08 (Ag15) S. limp leath., *$1.50 net. Brentano's.
Gourmet's guide to London. '09(Jl3) 12°, limp leath., *$1.50 net. Brentano's.

NEWPORT, N. H.
Edes, M. J. *and* S: H., *comps.* Book of old Newport. $1. M. J. Edes.

Newport (R. I.) social index, season of 1909; cont. a full and accurate list of the summer residents, with their winter addresses; junior members of families, diplomatic corps, officers of the army and navy. '09(Ag) 12°, $2. Social Index.

NEWPORT, R. I.
Chandler, A. D. Local self-government, and the recent charter of the city of Newport, R. I. (Priv. pr.) A. D. Chandler.
See also Jews.

NEWPORT NEWS, Va.
Green, B. W. How Newport's News got its name. gratis. W. E. Jones.

Newsboy partners. Webster, F. V. 35 c. Cupples & L.

NEWSDEALERS.
See Booksellers.

Newsholme, Arth., M.D.
Prevention of tuberculosis. '08(S19) 4°, *$3 net. Dutton.

Newson, J: H:
Homes of character. '10(Je4) c. il. plans, 4°, $1. J: H: Newson.

Newson's standard literature ser. il. 12°. Newson.
—Carlyle *and* Macaulay. Robert Burns, and Samuel Johnson. 30 c.; 20 c.
—Parkman. Oregon trail. 40 c.
—Scott. Ivanhoe. 40 c.; 30 c.

NEWSPAPERS.
American Assoc. of Foreign Language Newspapers. Unreached millions. (Add. pubs. for price.) L. N. Hammerling.
American newspaper annual, 1908, 1909. ea., *$5 net. Ayer.
Ayer, M: F., *comp.* Checklist of Boston newspapers. $3.50. Colonial Soc. of Mass.
Century Club of American Newspapers. (Not for sale.) St. L. Republic.
Current events index: cumulative guide to material in newspapers. subs., $3. Wis. Free Lib.
Hyamson, A. M. Newspaper reader's companion. 50 c. Dutton.
Lord & Thomas' pocket directory of the American press for 1910. $2. Lord.
Rogers, J. E: American newspaper. *$1 net. Univ. of Chic.

NEWSPAPERS.—*Continued.*
Rosewater, V. Combat with ignorance, with special reference to the part of the modern newspaper. (Priv. pr.) V. Rosewater.
Street, A. I., *ed. and comp.* Pandex of the news; cumulative index and digest of the newspapers of the United States. $10. Pandex.
Thwaites, R. G. Ohio Valley press before the War of 1812-15. (Not for sale.) Davis Press.
United States. *Library of Congress.* Want list of American 18th century newspapers. U. S., Supt. of Docs.
Winship, G: P. Early South American newspapers. Am. Antiquarian.
See also Journalism;—Liberty of the press;—Periodicals;—Spectator (The).

Newte, Horace W. C.
Lonely lovers; love-story. [1910.] (My) c. '09. 368 p. 12°, $1.50. M. Kennerley.
Sparrows; story of an unprotected girl. '09(N20) c. 8°, $1.50. M. Kennerley.

Newton, Alex. Herritage.
Out of the briars; autobiography and sketch of the 29th regiment, Connecticut volunteers; with introd. by Rev. J. P. Sampson. '10(D) c. 15+19-269 p. il. pors. 8°, $1.25. A. H. Newton.

Newton, C: Bertram, and Treat, Edn. Bryant.
Outline for review: American history. '08 (Mr21) c. S. 25 c. Am. Bk.

Newton, Elbridge Ward.
Music in the public schools; manual of suggestions for teachers. '09(N6) c. O. $1. Ginn.

Newton, F: Edn., and Lynde, Lester E:
Syllabus of plane geometry, with exercises; course designed for a second reading of the subject. '09(Ap) c. 73 p. 8°. $1. Andover.

Newton, Jos. Fort.
Abraham Lincoln; essay. '10(D17) c. por. 16°, (Torch ser.) 60 c. Torch Press.
Address on Albert Pike, 33°, master genius of masonry; del. before Iowa Consistory, no. 2, A. A. rite, at banquet, Montrose Hotel, Cedar Rapids, Iowa, Oct. 29, 1909. [1910.] (Je) 8 p. por. 8°, 75 c. Torch Press.
David Swing, poet-preacher. '08(D) 8°, $2. Torch Press.
Lincoln and Herndon. '10(D17) c. il. pors. 8°, $3. Torch Press.

Newton, Marion Bromley.
Graded games and rhythmic exercises; ed. by Ada Van Stone Harris. '08(My9) c. il. D. **$1.25 net. Barnes.

Newton, Stanley.
Mackinac Island and Sault Ste. Marie. '09 (S) c. 137 p. il. 8°, pap., 50 c. Sault.

Next life. Howatt, J. R. *$1 net. Revell.

Next of kin, heirs at law, legatees. International Claim Agency, Pittsburgh, Pa. $1. Int. Claim.

Next step. Jefferson, C: E: 35 c.; condensed, 5 c. Y. M. C. A.

Next step in agricultural education. Davenport, E. gratis. E. Davenport.

Next step in evolution. Funk, I: K. **50 c. net. Funk.

Next street but one. Loane, M. $1.25. Longmans.

Neymarck, Alfr.
See Patron, Maurice.

NEZ PERCÉS INDIANS.
See Indians.

Ng Poon Chew.
Treatment of the exempt classes of Chinese in the United States: statement from the Chinese in America. '08(O17) 8°, 5 c. Ng Poon Chew.

NIAGARA FALLS, N. Y.
Fernald, F. A. Index guide to Buffalo and Niagara Falls. 25 c. Fernald.
Greene, F. V. Niagara Falls in 1907. Ontario Power.
Hulbert, A. B. Niagara River. **$3.50 net. Putnam.
United States. *War Dept.* National Park at Niagara Falls; letter from the Secretary of War, submitting with copy of a rept. of a special committee, a recommendation for the establishment of a national park at Niagara Falls. '09, [1910.] (Mr) 10 p. il. 8°, pap.

NIAGARA, FORT, N. Y.
See **French and Indian war.**

NIBELUNGEN RING.
Layton, K. A. W. Nibelungen of Wagner. 75 c. Univ. of Ill.
Schuler, J: Language of Richard Wagner's Ring des Nibelungen. (Priv. pr.) Steinman & F.
Shaw, G: B. Perfect Wagnerite: commentary on the ring of the Niblungs. $1.25. Brentano's.

Nibelungenlied (The). Fall of the Nibelungs; tr. by Marg. Armour; introd. by Ernest Rhys. '08(Mr7) 16°, (Everyman's lib.) *35 c. net; leath., *70 c. net. Dutton.

Nibelungenlied; tr. from the middle high German; with an introd. sketch and notes by Dan. Bussier Shumway. '09(O30) c. O. $2. Houghton M.

Nibelungenlied (The); tr. by W: Nanson Lettsom; with special introd. by W: H. Carpenter. '08(Je27) c. il. 8°, $1.75; hf. mor., $3.50. Lamb Pub.

NIBELUNGENLIED.
Wagner, W. R. Song of the Nibelungen; Rheingold and Valkyrie. $5 net; $15 net. Doubleday, P.

Niblack, W: Caldwell.
Abstracters and title insurance, 1908. '08 (Jl) 8°, *$2 net. Callaghan.
Abstracters of title; their rights and duties. '08(Ag) c. 8°, *$2 net. Callaghan.

Niblick, pseud.
See Hanks, C: Stedman.

NICARAGUA, Central America.
International Bureau of American Republics. Nicaragua; general descriptive data. Int. Bu. Am. Republics.
See also Walker, *General* William.

NICENE CREED.
Lias, J. J. Nicene creed. $1.75 net. Macmillan.
See also **Creeds.**

Nichol, J:
Tables of European history, literature, science and art; from A.D. 200 to 1909; and of American history, literature and art; rev. and brought down to date by W: R. Jack. 5th ed. '09(D25) 8°. *$2.25 net. Macmillan.

Nicholas, Fs. Child.
Across Panama and around the Caribbean. 3d ed. of "Around the Caribbean and across Panama." '09(Je19) c. il. maps, O. $1.50. Caldwell.
Mining investments and how to judge them. '09(O9) c. 12°, (Investors' lib.) $1. Moody's Mag.
Power supreme: a novel of church and state in South America. '08(Jl18) c. il. D. $1.50. R. E. Lee.

Nicholls, Mrs. Charlotte B.
See Brontë, Charlotte.

Nicholls, Wa.
Sergeant Francis Nicholls of Stratford, Ct., 1639, and the descendants of his son, Caleb Nicholls. '09, [1910.] (F) c. 101 p. col. front. 8°, $5. Grafton Press.

Nichols, Alfr. Bull, comp.
Easy German reader; with vocabulary. '10 (Jl2) c. D. 40 c. Holt.
Modern German prose; comp. and annot. '09(Ja23) c. D. $1. Holt.

Nichols, Clark A.
Treatise on pleading and practice in the courts of New York; superseding v. 5 of the set. '10(F) O. shp., $5. Keefe-D.

Nichols, Clinton G., comp.
Automobilists' ready legal advisor: latest automobile laws enacted by states and territories of the U. S. '08(F) c. '07. S. mor., 50 c. Glennick.

Nichols, E:
Building superintendence: working guide to the requirements of modern American building practice and the systematic supervision of building operations. '08 (Ap11) c. il. plans, 8°, (American School of Correspondence pubs.) $1.50. Am. Sch. Corr.
Estimating: guide to systematic methods in taking off quantities and making up estimates of cost in building operation, with quotations of current prices for materials and labor. '08(Ap11) c. il. plans, 8°, (American School of Correspondence pubs.) $1. Am. Sch. Corr.

Nichols, E: West.
Analytic geometry. Rev. ed. '08(N21) diagrs., 12°, $1.25. Heath.

Nichols, Ernest Fox.
Physics. '08(F29) c. 8°, pap., 25 c. Macmillan.

Nichols, G: Elwood.
See Evans, Alex. W:

Nichols, Gideon Parsons, D.D.
Preciousness of God's thoughts. '10(F12) c. 12°, *$1.25 net. Revell.

Nichols, Irvin Eug.
Rhymes of the road, written for the entertainment of brother knights of the gripsack and other friends. '09(Ag) 111 p. 12°, 75 c. Stilwell & R.

Nichols, J. L., and Goodrich, H. H.
Robinson's business points: compendium of legal and business forms. '08(O) c. 8+9-252 p. il. tabs., 12°, $1. J. L. Nichols.

Nichols, Ja. T:
Lands of sacred story; sketch of travel and personal experiences which apeared in the [Des Moines] *Christian Union* during 1908-1909; introd. by C: S. Medbury. '10 (Ap9) c. por. 8°, $1.25. Chr. Un.

Nichols, J: H.
The golden candlestick. '10(O1) D. pap., 10 c.; per doz., $1. Smith & L.

Nichols, Mrs. Josephine Genung.
See Abbe, Cleveland.

Nichols, Lucy Adda.
Sonnets. [1910.] (D) 53 p. D. pap., 25 c. L. A. Nichols.

Nichols, Maurice Barstow.
Contributions to the knowledge of the California species of *crustaceous corallines.* [pt. I.] '08(D19); [pt. II.] '09(My15) il. Q. (Univ. of Cal. pubs., Botany.) pt. 1, pap., 10 c.; pt. 2, 15 c. Univ. of Cal.

Nichols, Philip.
Power of eminent domain; treatise on the constitutional principles which affect the taking of property for public use. '09 (Jl) 21+560 p. 8°, $5. Boston Bk.

Nichols, Starr Hoyt.
Breath of the world: [sonnets.] '08(D19) c. O. **$1.50 net. Putnam.

Nichols, W:
Rule four (of the Standard train rules) change of time table; thorough explanation thereof, together with plates and charts illustrating pract. conditions, with applied questions and answers. '10(O15) c. tabs. (partly col.) 12°, $1. Los Angeles Pr.

Nichols, Bp. W: Ford.
Apt and meet: councils to candidates for holy orders. '09(F13) c. D. *$1 net. Whittaker.

Nichols, W: G.
Cost finding; instruction paper. '09(N20) c. il. 8°, (American School of Correspondence pubs.) pap., 50 c. Am. Sch. Corr.

NICHOLS FAMILY.
See **Genealogies: Nicholls, W.**

Nicholson, Anne M.
Concept standard; historical survey of what men have conceived as constituting or determining life values. '10(Jl16) c. 8°, (Teachers' Coll., Contrib. to education.) $1.50. Teachers' Coll.

Nicholson, Ja. W.
Elem. arithmetic. '10(Je18) c. D. 34 c. Am. Bk.
Grammar school arithmetic. '09(F20) c. figs. D. 45 c. Am. Bk.
School algebra; [with answers.] '09(N20) c. il. 12°, $1. Am. Bk.

Nicholson, Jerome Lee.
Factory organization and costs. '09(Je12) c. il. forms, f°, $12.50. Kohl Technical.

Nicholson, Jos. Shield.
Project of empire; critical study of economics of imperialism, with special reference to the ideas of Adam Smith. '10 (F19) 8°, *$2.25 net. Macmillan.

NICHOLSON, June.
White, M. C. Days of June: life story of June Nicholson. *50 c. net. Revell.

Nicholson, Mrs. Malcolm.
See Hope, Laurence, *pseud.*

Nicholson, Meredith.
Little brown jug at Kildare. '08(O3) c. il. D. †$1.50. Bobbs-M.
Lords of high decision. '09(N13) c. col. il. D. †$1.50. Doubleday, P.
Siege of the seven suitors. '10(N5) c. il. D. $1.20 net. Houghton M.

Nicholson, Reynold Alleyne.
Elem. Arabic second reading-book. '09 (D25) D. (Thornton's Arabic ser.) $2. Putnam.

"Nick, Uncle," pseud.
See Wilson, Elijah N.

Nickles, J: Milton.
Bibliography of North American geology for 1908; with subject index. '09, [1910.] (Mr) 8°, (U. S., Dept. of the Interior, Geological Survey, bull.) pap.
Continuation of Bibliography of North American geology for 1906 and 1907, by F. B. Weeks and J. M. Nickles.
See also Weeks, Fred. Boughton.

Nicklin, W:
See Porritt, H. W.

NICKNAMES.
Dawson, L. H. Nicknames and pseudonyms. 50 c. Dutton.

Nicolay, Helen.
Boys' life of Ulysses S. Grant. '09(O2) c. il. pors. facsims., D. $1.50. Century Co.

Nicoll, M. J.
Three voyages of a naturalist: an account of many little-known islands in three oceans visited by the "Valhalla," R. Y. S.; with an introd. by the Earl of Crawford. '08(D5) il. maps, 8°, *$2.50 net. Scribner.

Nicoll, Sir W: Robertson, ["Claudius Clear."]
"Ian Maclaren," the life of the Rev. John Watson. '08(D5) c. por. O. **$2 net. Dodd.
Round the clock: ser. of essays. '10(D) 12°, $1.25 net. Doran.
Sunday evening; 52 short sermons for home reading. '10(D) $1.50 net. Doran.
Ten minute sermons. '10(D) 16°, leath., $1 net. Doran.
—, ed. Expositor's Greek Testament. v. 3. '10(D17); v. 4. '09(D25) O. ea., $7.50. Dodd.

Nicolls, W: Jasper.
Brunhilda of Orr's Island. '08(Je13) c. front. D. †$1.50. Jacobs.
Daughters of Suffolk. '10(My14) c. il. D. $1.50. Lippincott.

Nicolovius, Ludwig, ["M. Y. T. H. Myth."]
Dorothy of Angelwood. '09(S) 46 p. 12°, 75 c. B'way Pub.
Eastern lion in the West; or, marvelous find of an ideal. '09(S) c. 118 p. il. 12°, 75 c. B'way Pub.

Nicolovius, Ludwig.—*Continued.*
Eugenius, the star-child. '08, [1909.] (S) 45 p. 12°, 75 c. B'way Pub.
Great world mystery: poem. '09(D) $1. B'way Pub.
Tale confided by the woods. In 5 acts. '09 (Ja16) $1. B'way Pub.
Tales of enchantment. '09(Ja16) $1.25. B'way Pub.

Nicolson, J: T:, and Smith, Dempster.
Lathe design for high- and low-speed steels: treatise on the kinematical and dynamical principles governing the construction of metal turning lathes. '08 (Ag22) il. O. $6. Longmans.

Nicolson, Mrs. Malcolm.
See Hope, Laurence, *pseud.*

Nicomachean ethics. *See* Aristotle.

Nicomède. *See* Corneille, Pierre.

Nida, August.
Doktor Kritikus; schwank in 3 akten. '10 (Ag6) c. 12°, $1. A. Nida.

Nida, W: Lewis.
Story of Illinois and its people. '10(D31) c. il. pors. maps, 8°, 80 c. O. P. Barnes.

NIEBELUNGENLIED.
See Nibelungenlied.

Niebuhr, Barthold Georg.
Greek heroes; stories tr. from Niebuhr, with additions; with four col. pls. and numerous other il. by Arth. Rackham. '10(D) 96 p. 12°, 50 c. Cassell.

Niedieck, Paul.
Cruises in Bering Sea; tr. from the orig. German by R. A. Ploetz. '10(Mr26) il. O. *$5 net. Scribner.
With rifle in five continents; tr. from the orig. German. '09(F13) il. O. *$5 net. Scribner.

Nietzsche, Friedrich Wilhelm.
[Works; ed. by Oscar Levy.] In 18 v. v. 1-6, [v. 1,] The birth of tragedy; or, Hellenism and pessimism; tr. by W: A. Houssmann; [v. 2,] Human all too human; book for free spirits; pt. 1; tr. by Helen Zimmern; with introd. by J. M. Kennedy; [v. 3,] Thoughts out of season; pt. 1, David Strauss, the confessor and the writer; Richard Wagner in Bayreuth; tr. by Anthony M. Ludovici; [v. 4,] Thoughts out of season; pt. 2, The use and abuse of history; Schopenhauer as educator; tr. by Adrian Collins; [v. 5,] The will to power; attempted transvaluation of all values; tr. by Anthony M. Ludovici; v. 1, bks. 1-2, [v. 6,] On the future of our education: Homer and classical philology; tr., with introd., by J. M. Kennedy; v. 7, Genealogy of morals, a polemic; Peoples and countries (fragment). '10(D17) 12°, v. 1, 3, 4, 6, ea., $1.25 net; v. 2, 5, ea., $1.75 net; v. 7, $1.50 net. Macmillan.
Ecce homo: wie man wird—was man ist. '09(Jl3) 8°, $6.20. Brentano's.
Gist of Nietzsche; arranged by H: L. Mencken. '10(Ap23) c. D. 60 c. net. J: W. Luce.
Human, all too human: book for free spirits; tr. by Alex. Harvey. '08(Ap11) c. S. (Lib. of science for the workers.) 50 c. Kerr.

NIETZSCHE, Friedrich Wilhelm.
Becker, W: C. Nietzsche-kultus. 75 c. W. C. Becker.
Common, T: Nietzsche as philosopher, critic, poet, prophet. *$2 net. Dutton.
Ellis, E. M. O. L. Three modern seers.—James Hinton, Nietzsche, Edward Carpenter. $1.25 net. M. Kennerley.
Kennedy, J. M. Quintessence of Nietzsche. $1.50 net. Duffield.
Ludovici, A. M. Nietzsche, his life and works. 50 c. net. Dodge.
Mencken, H: L: Philosophy of Friedrich Nietzsche. *$2 net. J: W. Luce.
Mugge, M. A. Friedrich Nietzsche; his life and work. *$3 net. Brentano's.
Orage, A. R: Nietzsche in outline and aphorism. 75 c. McClurg.

NIGER RIVER, Africa.
Dennett, R. E. Nigerian studies. $2.75 net. Macmillan.

NIGERIA, Africa.
Dayrell, E. Folk stories from Southern Nigeria. $1.50. Longmans.

"Nigger" (The). Sheldon, E: $1.25 net. Macmillan.

Night before Christmas. *See* Moore, Clement Clarke.

Night in Alexandria. Lewisohn, L. 50 c. Moods.

Night out. Peple, E: H: 50 c. Moffat.

Night riders. *See* Dumont, Fk. Girl from "L Triangle" Ranch.

Night riders. Wood, H: C. 75 c.; 25 c. Laird.

Night thoughts for the sick and desolate. Eaton, R. *45 c. net. Herder.

NIGHTINGALE, Florence.
Richards, *Mrs.* L. E. H. Florence Nightingale, the angel of the Crimea. **$1.25 net. Appleton.

Nightless city. De Becker, J. E. *$10 net. Wessels.

Nightmare Abbey. *See* Peacock, T: Love. Headlong Hall.

Nightshade. Gwynne, P. $1.35 net. Brentano's.

Nihart, B: Franklin, and Stryker, W:
New century arithmetics. 2 v. '10(M) c. il. 12°. (Add. pubs. for price.) Silver.

Nikaido, Yasujuro.
Beet-sugar making and its chemical control. '09, [1910.] (Ja) c. 12+354 p. tabs., il. 8°, $3. Chemical.

Niles, Lorenzo.
See Fowler, Orson Squire.

Nimmo, D: Chalmers.
Selections from "Songs." '09(O23) c. S. pap., 15 c. D: C. Nimmo.
Songs: collection of church, home, nature, soul and miscellaneous songs. '08(Je13) c. 12°. (Add. author for price.) D. C. Nimmo.
Songs and tales; collection of songs and tales from life and imagination. [1910.] (Je) c. 9-289 p. 12°. D: C. Nimmo.

Nimrod, pseud.
See Apperley, C: Ja.

Nims, G: Washington.
Mammon in verseland; or, the power of money. '08, [1909.] (F) c. 70 p. 12°. (Add. pubs. for price.) E. L. Grimes.

Nims, Harry Dwight.
Law of unfair business competition, incl. chapters on trade secrets and confidential business relations; unfair interference with contracts, libel and slander of articles of merchandise, trade names, and business credit and reputation. '09(My) c. 46+581 p. O. $6.50. Baker, V. & Co.

Nimsgern, E: Gray.
Illustrated and descriptive account of the main dams and dikes of the Ashokan reservoir, Brown Station, N. Y.; photos by W. W. Wright. [1910.] (Mr) c. '09. 63 p. il map, diagr. 4°, 50 c. E: G. Nimsgern.

Nine days queen. Davey, R: *$3.50 net. Putnam.

999 points in law. Keppel, W: H. 25 c. Keppel Pub.

Nine motorboats and how to build them; book of complete building plans and instruction, which contains all necessary information for the amateur who wants to build his own boat. '10(D3) c. il. 4°, $1. Motor Boat.

Nine Spanish poems. Arteaga y Pereira, F. de, *comp.* *40 c. net. Oxford Univ.

"9009." Hopper, J. M. †$1.25. McClure.

1909 single tax catechism. Fillebrown, C: B. 5 c. C: B. Fillebrown.

1909 year book (motor cyclopædia). '09 (Ag) c. 643, 112, 306 p. il. 4°, $6. Automobile Topics.

Nineteenth century English prose. Dickinson, T: H., *ed.* $1. Am. Bk.

Nineteenth century teachers and other essays. Wedgwood, J. *$3 net. Doran.

NIPPUR, Babylonia.
See Babylonia.

Nirdlinger, C: Frederic.
World and his wife: [a play;] after the verse of Jose Echegaray's El Gran Galeoto. '08(D26) c. il. D. bds., $1. M. Kennerley.

Nirdlinger, Daisy Ella.
Althea. '08(Ap18) c. D. 60 c. Benziger.
Dear friends: sequel to "Althea." '08(My2) c. front. D. 60 c. Benziger.

Nirvana days. Rice, C. Y. **$1.25 net. Doubleday, P.

NISBET, Charles.
Parkinson, S. W. Charles Nisbet, first president of Dickinson College; his book, 1736-1804. gratis. S. W. Parkinson.

Nissen, Hartvig.
Fifteen lessons on the stall bars. '09(Ap24) S. pap., 30 c. Bassette.
Twenty gymnastic lessons on the boom. '09(Ap24) S. pap., 30 c. Bassette.

Nitchie, E: Bartlett.
Lessons in lip-reading for self-instruction. Rev. ed. '09(S18) c. O. *$1.25 net. Surdus.

Nitram, Nocta W., pseud.
See Acton, Martin W:

NITRIFICATION
See Agricultural chemistry.

NITROGEN.
Sidgwick, N. V. Organic chemistry of nitrogen. $4.75. Oxford Univ.
See also Agricultural chemistry.

NITROQUINAZOLONES.
See Chemistry.

Nitsua, B:, pseud.
See Austin, B: Fish.

Nitti, Francesco S.
Catholic socialism; tr. from the 2d Italian ed. by Mary Mackintosh; with an introd. by D: G. Ritchie. '08(D5) 8°, *$2.75 net. Macmillan.

Nivedita, Sister.
See Noble, Marg. E.

Niven, F:
Island providence. '10(Ap30) D. $1.50. Lane.
Lost cabin mine. '09(Mr6) c. D. †$1.50. Lane.

Niver, Harmon B., and Farrell, E: D.
Geographies: 6A and 6B grades. '10(D31) 12°, 80 c.; 6A separate, 160 p. 55 c.; 6B separate, 177 p. 55 c. Hinds.

Nixie well. Marshall, F. *30 c. net. Educ. Pub.

Nixon, Alfr.
See Holland, Rob. W.

Nixon-Roulet, Mary F.
Japanese folk stories and fairy tales. '08 (Je6) c. il. D. 40 c. Am. Bk.
Our little Australian cousin. '08(O3) c. il. D. (Little cousin ser.) 60 c. L. C. Page.
Our little Grecian cousin. '08(O3) c. il. D. (Little cousin ser.) 60 c. L. C. Page.
Our little Hungarian cousin. '09(D25) c. il. D. (Little cousin ser.) 60 c. L. C. Page.
Seven little Marshalls. '10(Ja8) c. front. S. 45 c. Benziger.
Spaniard at home. '10(N5) c. il. O. $1.75 net. McClurg.

—, Waggaman, Mrs. Mary Teresa, Mannix, Mary Ellen, and others.
Bit of old ivory and other stories. '10 (My14) c. D. $1.25. Benziger.

Nizra, the flower of the Parsa. Klarmann, A. F. *$1 net. Herder.

No and yes. Eddy, *Mrs.* M. M. B. G. (Add. pubs. for price.) A. V. Stewart.

No government guarantee of bank deposits. Clews, H: (Add. author for price.) H: Clews.

No Man's Land. Vance, L: J. $1.50. Dodd.

No refuge but in truth. Smith, G. **$1 net. Putnam.

No room in the inn. Knight, W: A. 50 c. Pilgrim Press.

Nobility of boyhood. Willson, R. N. 50 c. Winston.

Noble, C: Percy, M.D., ed.
See Kelly, Howard Atwood.

Noble, E: M., and Tubbs, E: T., comps.
Maryland in prose and poetry: recitations and readings pertaining to the state; with notes. '09(Ap) c. 250 p. 12°, 75 c. Lehmen.

Noble, Frances.
Not for this world only, and The trial of Mabel Dering. '09(My) 4+173 p. 8°, *75 c. net. Herder.

Noble, F: W., ed.
See New York [State.] *Courts.*—Current court decisions.

Noble, Gilbert Clifford, ed.
Most popular hymns. '09(Ap24) c. 8°, pap., 50 c. Hinds.

Noble, I: Clegg.
Cotton spinners' companion. '10(Ja) c. 32°, $1. I. C. Noble.

Noble, Marg. E., ["Sister Nivedita."]
Indian study of love and death. '09(Ja9) S. 75 c. Longmans.
The master as I saw him; being pages from the life of the Swami Vivekanada. '10(Je4) D. $1.50 net. Longmans.
Web of Indian life. [New ed.] '08(Ja25) D. *$1.75 net. Holt.

Noble, W: Nelson.
Disposition of a decedent's real property for the payment of debts and funeral expenses under the code of civil procedure of the state of New York. '08(O) c. 44+340 p. O. $3.50. Banks & Co.

Noble company of adventurers. Wilson, R. R. $1. B. W. Dodge.

Noble friendship. Nonnen, E. 25 c. E. Kaufmann.

Noble lives of a noble race. St. Mary's Industrial School. $2. St. Mary's Indust.

Noble numbers. *See* Herrick, Rob. Hesperides.

Noble thoughts ser.; ed. by Dana Estes. S. por. hf. parchment, $1.50; parchment, $5, boxed. Estes.
—Antoninus. Thoughts.
—Epictetus. Noble thoughts.
—Ruskin. Thoughts from John Ruskin.

Noble (William Belden) lectures. *See* Brent, *Bp.* C: H:—King, H: Churchill.

Noble womanhood. Dole, C: F. $1. Caldwell.

Noblest Roman. Moreland, S. $1.50. Noblest Roman.

Nobody's cousin. Van Ogle, A. 50 c. Cochrane.

Nodaway, Max.
Rollo in Hawaii. '09(Ja16) c. il. D. $1. Thompson & T.

Noellets (Les). *See* Bazin, René.

Noguchi, Hideyo, M.D.
Serum diagnosis of syphilis and the butyric acid test for syphilis. '10(F) c. 7+173 p. il. tabs., O. **$2 net. Lippincott.
Bibliography (19 p.).
Snake venoms; an investigation of venomous snakes, with special reference to the phenomena of their venoms. '09(S18) il. Q. (Carnegie Institution of Washington pubs.) pap., $10. Carnegie.

Noguchi, Yone.
From the Eastern Sea. '10(Jl2) c. 8°, pap., $1 net. M. Kennerley.

Nojine, E. K.
Truth about Port Arthur; tr. by Captain A. B. Lindsay; ed. by Major Ernest Dunlop Swinton. '08(Je13) il. 8°, *$5 net. Dutton.

Nolan, Aretas Wilbur.
One hundred lessons in elementary agriculture: manual and text of elem. agriculture for rural schools. '08, [1909.] (Mr) c. 15+280 p. il. 12°, 65 c. Acme.

Nolan, E: Ja.
Biography of Dr. Henry Cadwalader Chapman; [repr. from Proceedings of the Academy of Natural Sciences of Philadelphia.] '10(D) c. 16 p. 8°, por. pap. Acad. Nat. Sci., Phil.

Nolan, G. V., comp.
My lady's toilet; complete, up-to-date treatise on the toilet; also a systematic course of physical culture instruction. '08(O) c. 223 p. front. 8°, $1. Peoples News.

Nolen, J:
Montclair: preservation of its natural beauty and its improvement as a residence town. '10(Ap) il. bds., $1 net. J: Nolen.
Plan for the borough of Glen Ridge. '10 (Ap) bds., $1 net. J: Nolen.
Remodeling Roanoke. '07, [1910.] (Ap) 97 p. il. bds., $1 net. J: Nolen.
Replanning Reading, industrial city of a hundred thousand. '10(Ap16) il. fold. plans, O. bds., $1 net. J: Nolen.
Repton's art of landscape gardening. '10 (Ap) 275 p. il. bds., $3 net. J: Nolen.
San Diego, [Cal.:] a comprehensive plan for its improvement. '08(D26) il. plans, maps, O. bds., 50 c. J: Nolen.
State parks for Wisconsin. '09, [1910.] (Ap) 94 p. il. $1 net. J: Nolen.

Nolhac, Annet Mariet Pierre Giraud de.
Petrarch and the ancient world, [with special account of his library.] '08(Ja18) O. (Humanists' lib.) bds., $6. Merrymount.

Noll, Arth. Howard.
General Kirby-Smith. '08(F1) c. por. O. $1.50. Univ. Press, (Sewanee.)

—, and McMahon, A. Philip.
Life and times of Miguel Hidalgo y Costilla. '10(O1) c. D. $1 net. McClurg.

Nolloth, C: F:
Person of our Lord and recent thought. '08(D12) 12°, *$1.25 net. Macmillan.

Non-Catholic denominations. Benson, R. H. $1.20 net. Longmans.

Noncommissioned officers' manual. Moss, J. A. $1.50. U. S. Infantry.

"None so blind." Deane, E. $1.50. Reid Pub.

Non-metallic minerals. Merrill, G: P. $4. Wiley.

Nonnen, Emily.
Fortunes of life; or, struggles of the Ornshield family, [tr.] from the Swedish by Ernst Wilhelm Olson. '09(My) c. 170 p. il. 12°, 50 c. Engberg-H.
Noble friendship; tr. '09(N20) il. S. bds., 25 c. E. Kaufmann.
Ruby ring: or, truth will prevail; tr. from the Swedish by E. W. Olson. '08, [1909.] (F) c. 160 p. il. 16°, 50 c. Engberg-H.

Non-secret formulas. Griffiths, T: M. $5. Interstate Pr.

Non-sectarian peacemaker. Dunlap, C: E. 50 c. C: E. Dunlap.

Non-sporting dogs. Barton, F. T. $1.75. W: R. Jenkins.

NONSUCH EUCHRE.
See Euchre.

Nonnen, Emily.
The fugitives; or, the motto above the door; from the Swedish by E. W. Olson. '10(Ap23) c. il. 16°, 50 c. Engberg-H.

Nooks and corners of old London. Hemstreet, C: $1. Pott.

Noonday addresses. Watkinson, W: L. *50 c. net. Revell.

Noorden, Carl Harko v.
Clinical treatises on the pathology and therapy of disorders of metabolism and nutrition; ed. by Boardman Reed, M.D. pt. 7, Diabetes mellitus. '09(Ag); pt. 8, Inanition and fattening cures; pt. 9, Technique of reduction cures and gout. '10(Je) 212; 112; 112 p. 12°, ea., $1.50 net. Treat.

Noot, Judith.
Lady Dean's daughter. '09(Ap17) c. D. $1.50. Cochrane.

Nor all your tears. Yardley, *Mrs.* M. H. $1.50. Fenno.

Norah Conough. Henderson, W: G: $1.50. Outing.

Nordell, Philip A., D.D.
Studies in Old Testament history. '08(Ja4) maps, O. (Bible studies for adult classes.) pap., *20 c. net. Am. Bapt.
Studies in the apostolic age. '08(Ja4) maps, O. (Bible studies for adult classes.) pap., *20 c. net. Am. Bapt.
Studies in the life of Christ. '08(Ja4) maps, O. (Bible studies for adult classes.) pap., *20 c. net. Am. Bapt.

NORFOLK, Eng.
Dutt, W: A. Norfolk. *45 c. net. Putnam.
Dutt, W: A. Norfolk and Suffolk coast. $2.25 net. Stokes.

Norma Lane. Cook, S: N. $1.25. S: N. Cook.

Normal class manual of Old Testament history. Goodrich, A. S. *50 c. net. Revell.

Normal evangelism. Green, O. O. $1 net. Revell.

Normal school instruction in agriculture. Abbey, M. J. U. S., Supt. of Docs.

NORMALISM.
See Happiness.

Norman, Sir H:
Real Japan: studies of contemporary Japanese manners, morals, administration and politics. '09(Mr13) il. O. *$1.50 net. Scribner.

Norman Carver ser. *See* Burleigh, Clarence Blendon.

NORMAN CONQUEST.
See England.

NORMAN COUNTY, Minn.
Hintze, L: Atlas of Norman County, Minnesota. $10. L: Hintze.

Norman Wait Harris lecture. *See* Harris (Norman Wait) lecture.

Normands (Les) en Angleterre et en France. *See* Thierry, Jacques Nicholas Augustin.

Normandy, Fk.
Sea water distillation. '10(F19) 8°, *$2 net. Lippincott.

NORMANDY, France.
Dodd, *Mrs.* A. B. B. In and out of three Normandy inns. $2.50 net. Little, B. & Co.

Norrie, H. S., pseud.
See Schneider, Norman Hugh.

Norris, Fk.
Third circle; introd. by Will Irwin. '09 (Je5) c. D. †$1.50. Lane.

Norris, H: Hutchinson.
Introd. to the study of electrical engineerin. 2d ed., rev. '08(Ag15) c. il. tabs., chart, 8°, **$2.50 net. Wiley.

Norris, Mary Harriott.
The veil: a fantasy. '08(F1) c. D. $1.50. Badger.

Norris, W: E:
Not guilty. '10(N5) D. $1.50. Brentano's.
Pauline. '10(D31) 12°, $1.50. Brentano's.
The perjurer. '10(Je4) D. $1.50. Brentano's.

Norse fairy tales. Dasent, *Sir* G: W., *ed.* $1.75. Lippincott.

Norsworthy, Naomi.
Psychology of mentally deficient children. '06, [1909.] (Ap) 3+111 p. tabs., (Archives of psychology.) $1. Science Pr., (N. Y.)

North, Arth. Walbridge.
Camp and camino in lower California; record of the adventures of the author while exploring peninsular California, Mexico; with foreword by Admiral Robley D. Evans. '10(Je11) c. O. $3 net. Baker & T.
Mother of California: hist. sketch of the little known land of Baja California, from the days of Cortez to the present time, depicting the ancient missions therein established, the mines there found, and the physical, social and political aspects of the country: together with an extensive bibliography relative to the same; with an introd. by Cyrus C. Adams. '08(Ap4) c. il. map, O. **$2 net. P. Elder.

North, Ja.
Mischief love hath done, and other poems; ed. by Mary Eliza North. '09(F) c. '08. 11-145 p. 12°, $1. Evolution Pub.

North, Lawrence.
Syrinx. '09(Ap17) c. front. 12°, †$1.50. Duffield.

"North, Leigh," pseud.
See Phelps, *Mrs.* Eliz. Stewart.

North, Luke.
The white flame; play. '10(Mr19) c. S. bds., $1. (240 copies.) Golden Press.

NORTH AFRICA.
See Africa.

NORTH AMERICA.
Baxter, J. S. America: her grandeur and her beauty. $12.50. Union Bk.
Durrett, R. T: Traditions of the earliest visits of foreigners to North America. $4. Morton.
Hulbert, A. B., *comp. and ed.* Crown collection of photographs of American maps. In 5 v. v. 4, 5. $100. A. H. Clark.
Jepson, W. L. Synopsis of the North American godetias. 40 c. Univ. of Cal.
Lyell, *Sir* C: Travels in North America in the years 1841-2. 30 c. C: E. Merrill.
MacDougal, D. T. Botanical features of North American deserts. $1.75. Carnegie.
Markham, C: E., *ed.* Real American in romance. per v., $3.50. W. H. Wise.

NORTH AMERICA.—*Continued.*

Ridgway, R. Manual of North American birds. $5 net. Lippincott.

Roberts, P: Immigrant races in North America. 50 c. Y. M. C. A.

Stevenson, E: L. Facsimile reproduction in ten sheets of the map of 1502 of Nicolo de Canerio. $20. Hispanic Soc.

United States. *Dept. of Commerce and Labor. Bu. of Statistics.* Commercial America; showing commerce, productions, etc., of North, South and Central America and West Indies. (Add. Superintendent for price.)

Van Hise, C: R:, *and* Leith, C: K. Pre-Cambrian geology of North America. U. S., Supt. of Docs.

Wade, *Mrs.* M. H. B. Little folks of North America. †$1. Wilde.

Waldseemüller, M. Cosmographiae introductio; followed by The four voyages of Amerigo Vespucci. $5. U. S. Cath.

Weeks, F. B., *and* Nickles, J. M. Bibliography of North American geology for 1906-'07. (Add. Superintendent for price.) U. S., Supt. of Docs.

See also **Alaska;—Animals;—Aryans;—Canada;—Caribbean Sea;—Central America;—Explorers;—Geology;—Gulf of Mexico;—Maps;—Mexico; Natural history;—Pacific coast;—Panama;—Priests;—United States.**

North American, Philadelphia. Confessions of a newspaper; published for the information of its friends and enemies. '09(Ap) c. 28 p. 12°, gratis. North American, Phil.

North American index fossils. Grabau, A. W. In 2 v. v. 2. $6 net. Seiler.

North American Indian. Curtis, E: S. (Add. author for price per v. or set.) E: S. Curtis.

North American trees. Britton, N. L. **$7 net. Holt.

North and South. *See* **Gaskell,** *Mrs.* **Eliz.** Cleghorn Stevenson.

North and the South at Antietam and Gettysburg. Spear, W: E. $1. W: E. Spear.

North Atlantic coast fisheries arbitration. Borchardt, E. M., *comp.* Gov. Pr. Off.

North Carolina. *Dept. of Public Instruction.* Approved list of books for rural libraries, 1909. [1910.] (N) 44 p. il. 8°. N. C. Dept. Pub. Instruct.

North Carolina. Notes on the code of civil procedure; notes on constitutional law; by S: F. Mordecai. '10(D) c. 43+75 p. O. pap. (Priv. pr.) Seeman.

NORTH CAROLINA.

Ashe, S: A'C. History of North Carolina. In 2 v. v. 1. $5; $6. Van Noppen.

Ashe, W: W. Shade trees for North Carolina. 8 c. Uzzell.

Connor, R: D. W. North Carolina's priority in the demand for a Declaration of Independence. 50 c. R. D. W. Connor.

Coon, C: L. Significant educational progress in N. C., 1900-1906. (Not for sale.) N. C. Dept. Pub. Instruct.

Dockery, A. V. Black bass and other fishing in North Carolina. 75 c. Commercial Pr. Co.

NORTH CAROLINA.—*Continued.*

Gardner, J. B. Massachusetts memorial to her soldiers and sailors who died in the Department of No. Carolina, 1861-1865. $3.25. Gardner & T.

Haywood, M. De L. Lives of the bishops of North Carolina from the establishment of the episcopate in that state down to the division of the diocese. $1.50. A. Williams.

Kunz, G: F: Hist. of gems found in North Carolina. (Add. pubs. for price.) Uzzell.

Laney, F. B. Gold Hill mining district of North Carolina. N. C. Geolog. Survey.

Laney, F. B., *and* Wood, K. H. Bibliography of North Carolina geology, mineralogy and geography, with list of maps. 25 c. N. C. Geolog. Survey.

McKelway, A. J. Child labor in the Carolinas. gratis. Nat. Child Labor.

Mordecai, S: F. Law lectures: treatise from North Carolina standpoint on those portions of 1st and 2d books of the commentaries of Sir W: Blackstone which have not become obsolete. $10. Edwards.

Reformed Church in the United States. *Classics of North Carolina.* Hist. sketch of the Reformed Church in North Carolina. $1. Ref. Ch. Pub.

Whitaker, B. L. Provincial council and committees of safety in North Carolina. (Add. Univ. for price.) Univ. of N. C.

See also **Edgecombe Co.;—Guilford Court House;—Mecklenberg declaration of independence;—Roanoke Island;—*also* Harnett, Cornelius;—Nash, Abner.**

North Carolina, Dept. of Public Instruction, education bull. 8°. N. C., Dept. Pub. Instruct.

—Barwick. Manual of physiology and hygiene. gratis.—Opening exercises for public schools.

—Coon. How to teach reading. gratis.

North Carolina Geological and Economic Survey bull. il. 8°, 4°. Uzzell.

—Ashe. Shade trees of North Carolina. 8 c.

—Terracing of farm lands. pap., 6 c.

—Coker. Experiments in oyster culture.

—Kunz. History of gems found in North Carolina.

—Laney *and* Wood. Bibliography of North Carolina geology, mineralogy and geography, with list of maps. 25 c.

North Carolina Historical Commission pubs. 8°. Edwards.

—Worth. Correspondence of Jonathan Worth. 2 v. gratis.

North Carolina manual of law and forms for justices of the peace, county officers, executors and administrators, [etc.;] by Rob. N. Simms. 6th ed. '08(Ja11) O. $3. Edwards.

North Dakota. *Supreme ct.* Repts.; (F. W. Ames.) v. 15. '07, [1908.] (Mr); v. 16 (O); v. 17. '09(D) c. O. shp., ea., $4.25. Tribune Pr. Co., (N. Dak.)

NORTH DAKOTA.

Atkinson, T. R. Irrigation in North Dakota. (Add. Superintendent for price.) U. S., Supt. of Docs.

Boyle, J. E. Government of North Dakota. $1. Am. Bk.

NORTH DAKOTA.—*Continued.*
Cram, G: F. Superior reference atlas of North and South Dakota. (Add. pubs. for price.) G: F. Cram.
See also Barnes Co.;—Indians;—Red River Valley.
NORTH DEVON.
See Devonshire.
North Italian folk. Carr, *Mrs.* C. 50 c. net. Macmillan.
North Pacific coast country. Chicago, Milwaukee & St. Paul Railway. (Add. pubs. for price.) Chic., Milwaukee & St. P.
NORTH POLE.
See Arctic regions.
North-West Mills Company. Saccharine feeds and feeding. '08(Jl4) c. il. D. gratis. North-West Mills.
NORTHAMPTON, Mass.
Powell, L. P. Emmanuel Movement in a New England town, [Northampton, Mass.] **$1.25 net. Putnam.
Northanger Abbey. *See* Austen, Jane.
NORTHBROOK, Thomas George, *Earl of.*
Mallet, B. Thomas George, Earl of Northbrook. $5. Longmans.
Northcote, Philip M.
Sunlight and shadow. '09(Ja16) 12°, *$1 net. Herder.
Northeastern reporter, v. 82. Permanent ed. '08(Mr); v. 83 (Je); v. 84 (Ag); v. 85. '09(Mr); v. 86 (Je); v. 87 (S); v. 88 (N); v. 89. '10(Mr); v. 90 (Je); v. 91 (S) c. O. (National reporter system, state ser.) shp., ea., $4. West Pub.
Northen, W: J., ed.
Men of mark in Georgia; historical introductory by J: Temple Graves, ed. In 6 v. v. 2. '09(N) pors. 8°, per set, ¾ mor., $50; full mor., $100. A. B. Caldwell.
Northern France. Baedeker, K. *$2.25 net. Scribner.
Northern lights. Parker, *Sir* G. †$1.50. Harper.
NORTHERN ORATORICAL LEAGUE.
See Orators and oratory.
NORTHERN PACIFIC RAILWAY.
See Railroads.
Northern trails. Long, W: J. Bks. 1, 2. ea., 45 c. Ginn.
NORTHFIELD, Mass.
Fitt, A. P. All about Northfield. $1. Northfield Press.
Northrop, Cyrus.
Addresses, educational and patriotic. '10 (Jl9) 8°, $1.80 net. Univ. of Minn.
Northrop, H: Davenport.
Model speaker and reciter; being a standard work on composition and oratory; together with a peerless collection of readings and recitations. '10(Jl2) c. il. 4°. $1. G: W. Bertron.
Northrop, J: I.
Naturalist in the Bahamas; ed. by H: F. Osborn. '10(O15) $2.50 net. Lemcke.
Northrup, Ansel Judd.
Northrup-Northrop genealogy. '08(D) c. 10+461 p. pors. 8°, **$10 net. Grafton Press.
NORTHRUP FAMILY.
See Genealogies.
NORTHUMBERLAND. Eng.
Bradley, A. G. Romance of Northumberland. *$2.75 net. McClurg

NORTHWEST (The).
See Canada;—West.
NORTHWEST PASSAGE.
Amundsen, R. E. G. Northwest passage. 2 v. *$8 net. Dutton.
Burpee, L. J. Search for the northwest passage. *$5 special net. Appleton.
Northwestern reporter, v. 113. Permanent ed. '08(F); v. 114 (My); v. 115 (Jl); v. 116 (O); v. 117 (D); v. 118. '09(Mr); v. 119 (Je); v. 120 (S); v. 121 (N) ea., $4; v. 122. '10(F); v. 123 (Ap); v. 124 (Je) ea., $6; v. 125 (Jl); v. 126 (O) c. O. (National reporter system, state ser.) ea., $4. West Pub.
Northwestern Univ. Law School bull., Gary Library of Law. 8°. Northwestern Univ.
—Wigmore. Preliminary bibliography of modern criminal law. 65 c.
Norton, Mrs. Alice Peloubet.
Food and dietetics. [Text book ed.] '10 (N5) c. il. tabs., 12°, $1.25. Home Economics.
Norton, Arth. Orlo.
Readings in the hist. of education: mediæval universities. '09(My) c. 10+155 p. 8°. 85 c. Harvard Univ.
Norton, B:
Biography of youthful Willie and Wall Street Bill. '09(D18) c. col. il. 12°, bds., 60 c Cupples & L.
Norton, Carol.
Woman's cause. '10(N) 16°, (Caldwell's character and wisdom ser.) 50 c.; $1. Caldwell.
Woman's cause. '08(Ap25) c. D. **bds.**, **75 c. net. Estes.
NORTON, *Mrs.* Caroline Elizabeth Sarah Sheridan.
Perkins, J. G. Life of the Honorable Mrs. Norton. *$3.50 net. Holt.
Norton, Dora Miriam.
Freehand perspective and sketching. '09 (Ap17) c. figs. Q. $3. D. M. Norton.
Norton, E: Quincy.
Construction, tuning and care of the pianoforte. [1910.] (My) c. '87. 6+7-117 p. il. 12°, $1. Ditson.
Norton, Eliot.
On "short sales" of securities through a stock broker. '08(Ja18) D. *$1 net. J: McBride.
Norton, F: Owen.
Lexicographical and historical study of Diatheke. '08(Ag29) c. O. pap., *75 c. net. Univ. of Chic.
Norton, Grace, comp.
Montaigne: his personal relations to some of his contemporaries, and his literary relations to some later writers. '08 (My23) c. D. *$1.25 net. Houghton M.
Spirit of Montaigne: some thoughts and expressions similar to those in his essays. '08(My23) c. D. *$1.25 net. Houghton M.
Norton, Oliver Willcox.
Strong Vincent and his brigade at Gettysburg. July 2, 1863. '09. [1910.] (Ap) 57 p. il. por. 8°. (Not for sale.) O. W. Norton.

Norton, Roy.
Garden of fate. '10(S24) c. il. D. $1.50. W. J. Watt.
Toll of the sea. '09(Je19) c. il. D. †$1.50. Appleton.
Vanishing fleets. '08(F1) c. il. D. †$1.50. Appleton.

Norton, Stephen A.
Call of the heights; echoes from the letter to the Philippians. '10(N5) D. bds., 50 c. net. Pilgrim Press.

Norton, Wa. Whittlesey.
Some descendants of John Norton of Branford, 1622-1709; with notes and dates of other emigrant Nortons, etc. '09(Ag14) front. O. pap. (Add. pubs. for price.) Journal Press, (Ct.)

Norton, W: Harrison.
The ideal Christian life. '09, [1910.] (F) c. 13-263 p. 12°, $1. W: H. Norton.

Norton-Thomson, Mrs. L.
Not to have and to hold. '09(D) il. $1.50. B'way Pub.

NORTON FAMILY.
See Genealogies.

Norvell, Rev. Jos. Elgon.
Lost guide. '10(O8) c. il. por. 12°, $1. Chr. Witness.

NORWAY.
Baedeker, K. Norway, Sweden and Denmark, with excursions into Iceland and Spitzbergen. $2.40. Scribner.
Bumpus, T. F. Cathedrals and churches of Norway, Sweden, and Denmark. *$4 net; *$7.50 net. Pott.
Le Blond, E. A. F. H.-W. Mountaineering in the land of the midnight sun. *$3.50 net. Lippincott.
Mockler-Ferryman, A: F. Norway. *75 c. net. Macmillan.
Monroe, W. S. Norway: its peoples, its fjords and its fjelds. $3. L. C. Page.
Willson, T: B. Norway at home. *$1.75 net. Scribner.
Wood, M. B. Trip to the Land of the Midnight Sun. $2 net. Brandu's.
See also Legends;—Norwegian language;—Norwegians in the United States.

Norwegian Aurora Polaris Expedition, 1902-1903. *See* Birkeland, Kr.

NORWEGIAN LANGUAGE.
Hanson, H. J., *comp.* English-Norwegian-Danish dict. 50 c. J: Anderson.
Holvik, J. A. Beginner's book in Norse. $1.25. Augsburg.
Ibsen, H. Brand, et dramatisk digt. $1.50. J: Anderson.

NORWEGIAN LITERATURE.
Kildal, A., *comp.* Selected list of Norwegian and Danish books. 25 c. A. L. A.

NORWEGIANS IN THE UNITED STATES.
Flom, G: T. Norwegian immigration to the United States. (Priv. pr.) G: T. Flom.

Norwell, Alexandra.
Elem. applied mechanics (statics); introducing the unitary system. '08(O3) il. 90 c. Longmans.

Norwood, J: Wall.
Instructions for the infantry private of the National Guard. 3d ed. '08(Je) c. 95 p. il. 24°, pap., 25 c. Arms and the Man.
Instructions for the non-commissioned officer. '09(Ag28) c. nar. S. pap. (Add. pubs. for price.) E: T. Miller.

NOSE.
Ballenger, W: L. Treatise on medical and surgical diseases of the nose, throat and ear. *$5.50 net. Lea.
Beck, E. G. Bismuth paste in chronic suppurations, with chapter on its application in sinuses and diseases of the nose. $2. Mosby.
Bishop, S. C. Diseases of the nose, throat and ear. $4.50; $6. Davis.
Bruck, A. Diseases of the nose, mouth, pharynx and larynx. $5. Rebman.
Burnham, W: H: Hygiene of the nose. W: H: Burnham.
Coakley, C. G. Laryngology: manual of diseases of the nose and throat. $2.75. Lea.
Gleason, E: B. Manual of diseases of the nose, throat, and ear. $2.50. Saunders.
Knight, C: H., *and* Bryant, W. S. Diseases of the nose, throat and ear. *$4.50 net; *$6 net. Blakiston.
Kyle, D: B. Diseases of the nose and throat. *$4 net; *$5.50 net. Saunders.
Lamb, W: Pract. guide to the diseases of the nose, throat and ear. *$3 net. Wood.
Packard, F. R. Text-book of diseases of the nose, throat and ear. subs., **$3.50 net; **$4 net. Lippincott.
Williams, P. W. Rhinology: book of diseases of the nose and nasal accessory sinuses. *$4.20 net. Longmans.
Wood, C. A., *and others, eds.* Eye, ear, nose and throat. $1.50. Year Bk.
See also Ear;—Nurses and nursing;—Tuberculosis.

NOSODES.
See Homeopathy.

NOSOLOGY.
See Pathology.

Not for this world only. Noble, F. *75 c. net. Herder.

Not guilty. Norris, W: E: $1.50. Brentano's.

Not of her race. Foster, N. K. $1.50. Badger.

Not the salary but the opportunity. Marsden, O. S. **10 c. net. Crowell.

Not to have and to hold. Norton-Thomson, *Mrs.* L. $1.50. B'way Pub.

Notable men of Chicago and their city. '10 (D31) pors. Q. Chic. Daily Journ.

NOTARIES.
Snyder, W: L. Notaries' and commissioners' manual. $1.75. Baker, V. & Co.
White, H. H. Notarial guide and book of forms for the use of notaries, clerks of court and lawyers. $10. Hansell.
See also names of states.

Note-taking. Seward, S: S., *jr.* 50 c. Allyn & B.

NOTES.
See Negotiable instruments.

Notes accompanying the lectures on geology applied to mining. Hancock, E. T: $1. New Era Print.

Notes and documents relating to Westminster Abbey. No. 1, The manuscripts of Westminster Abbey, by J. Armitage Robinson, D.D., and Montague Rhodes James; No. 2, The history of Westminster Abbey, by J: Flete; ed. by J. Armitage Robinson, D.D. '09(Je12) Q. *$1.60 net. Putnam.
Notes of a botanist on the Amazon and Andes. Spruce, R: 2 v. $6.50. Macmillan.
Notes of sermons for the year. pt. 1. Buxton, H. J: W. *$1 net. Whittaker.
Notes on bookbinding for libraries. Dana, J: C. $1. Lib. Bu.
Notes on non-metals. Pond, F. J. $1.50. F. J. Pond.
Notes on sermons for a year. Buxton, H. J: W. pt. 2. *$1 net. Whittaker.
Notes on Shoshonean dialects of southern California. Kroeber, A. L. 35 c. Univ. of Cal.
Notes on soils. Whitson, A. R. 90 c. A. R. Whitson.
Notes on the rebel invasion of Maryland. Jacobs, M. $1; 25 c. G. E. Jacobs.
Notes on the syntax of the Latin inscriptions found in Spain. Martin, H: $1. Furst.
Nothing without labor. George Junior Republic. gratis. George Jr. Repub.
Nothnagel's practice. il. 8°, *$5 net; hf. mor., ***$6 net.** Saunders.
—Dock, *ed.* Diseases of the heart.
Notions of a Yankee parson. Clark, G: L. $1 net. Sherman, F.
Notitia venatica. Vyner, R. 2 v. $10 net. Dutton.
Notre-Dame de Paris. *See* Hugo, Victor.
Nott, C: Cooper.
Mystery of the Pinckney draught. '08 (D12) c. O. **$2 net. Century Co.
Notter, J. Lane, M.D.
Theory and practice of hygiene. 3d ed. '08, [1909.] (Mr) 16+993 p. il. *$7 net. Blakiston.
Nourse, E: Everett, D.D., ed.
See Jacobus, Melancthon Williams.
Nourse, Edn. Griswold.
Brokerage. '10(Jl) c. 7-331 p. tabs., forms, 8°. (Priv. pr.) Universal Business.
Nourse, Harold Alvah, and others.
Turkeys, ducks and geese; book of the latest, most complete and reliable information on breeding, hatching, rearing, fattening, developing, showing and selling for pleasure and profit. '09, [1910.] (F) c. 128 p. il. 8°, 50 c. Webb.
Nova Scotia.
Paine, A. B. Tent dwellers: [camping in Nova Scotia.] $1.50. Outing.
Silver, A. P. Farm, cottage, camp and canoe in maritime Canada. *$2 net. Dutton.
See also Kings County.
"Novalis," pseud.
See Hardenberg, Friedrich Leopold. *Freiherr* von.
Novatian, [Lat. Novatianus.]
Novatiani Romanae urbis presbyteri, De Trinitate liber; Novatian's treatise on the Trinity; ed. by W. Yorke Fausset. '09 (Je5) 12°, (Cambridge patristic texts.) *$2 net. Putnam.
Novelists.
See Authors;—French literature.
Novello, Clara Anastasia, Countess Gigliucci.
Clara Novello's reminiscences; comp. by her daughter, Countess Valeria Gigliucci; with memoir by Arth. D. Coleridge. '10(N19) pors. O. $3 net. Longmans.
Novels.
See Fiction.
Novikoff, Mme. Olga Kireef.
M. P. for Russia: reminiscences and correspondence; ed. by W: T: Stead. '09 (Ap10) 2 v., pors. O. *$7.50 net, boxed. Putnam.
Novveav (Le) Cynée. *See* Crucé, Émeric.
"Now!" Marriott, C: $1.50. Lane.
Nowell, Rev. W: Cullen.
Lectures on the Book of Revelation; with brief sketch of the author's life and six choice sermons. '10(N5) c. por. 12°, $1. Edwards.
Noyes, Alex. Dana.
Forty years of American finance; being the 2d and extended ed. of "Thirty years of American finance." '09(My22) 8°, *$1.50 net. Putnam.
History of the national-bank currency. '10 (O) 20 p. 8°. Gov. Pr. Off.
Noyes, Alfr.
Drake: an English epic. Bks. 1-12. '09 (S11) c. por. O. **$1.50 net. Stokes.
Enchanted island and other poems. '10 (Ap16) c. D. $1.25 net. Stokes.
The "Golden Hynde," and other poems. '08(F29) c. D. **$1.25 net. Macmillan.
William Morris. '09(Ja16) 12°, (English men of letters ser.) *75 c. net. Macmillan.
—, ed. Magic casement: anthology of fairy poetry; ed., with an introd. '09(F6) il. D. *$2 net. Dutton.
Noyes, Carleton Eldredge.
Approach to Walt Whitman. '10(My21) c. D. $1.25. Houghton M.
Noyes, Ella.
Story of Milan. '08(My9) map, 16°, (Mediæval towns ser.) $1.75 net; leath., $2.25 net. Dutton.
Noyes, I: Pitman.
Ode on Lincoln. '07, [1908.] (O.) 7 p. 12°, 10 c. I: P. Noyes.
Ode to the Union.—Ode on anæsthetics.—Ode on finance.—Ode on McClellan.—The corporations. '08(Ap.) 8°, pap. (Add. author for price.) I: P. Noyes.
Noyes, Mrs. Marion Ingalls Osgood, and Ray, Blanche H.
Little plays for little people. '10(Ag27) c. il. D. 35 c. Ginn.
Noyes, Parker Jewitt.
Why Dr. Dobson became a quack. '10 (Jl2) 12°, $1.50. Cochrane.
Noyes, Wa. Chadwick.
Treatise on the law of intercorporate relations. 2d ed., rev. and enl. '09(Ja) c. 60+924 p. O. $6. Little, B. & Co.
Noyes, W:
Handwork in wood. '10(O1) c. O. $2. Manual Arts.
Nubia.
Breasted, J. H. Monuments of Sudanese Nubia. *50 c. net. Univ. of Chic.

Nuelsen, J: L:, D.D.
Some recent phases of German theology. '08(M7) c. O. *75 c. net. Jennings.

Nuesse, G: C.
Founding the South Side Library, [Milwaukee, Wis.] '09(Jl17) T. leath., 50 c. Enterprise Pr.

Nuggets from King Solomon's Mine. Schmalz, J: B. $2. Schmalz.

Nuggets of gold. Morgan, W: S. 50 c. W: S. Morgan.

NUISANCE.
Woodruff, C. R., *ed.* Billboard nuisance. gratis. Am. Civic League.
See also Smoke.

Number by development. Gray, J: C. **$1 net. Lippincott.

Number of man. Mauro. P. *$1.25 net. Revell.

Number primer. Bailey, M. A. 30 c. Am. Bk.

NUMBERS.
See Numerals.

NUMERALS.
Goudy, H: Trichotomy in Roman law. $1.35. Oxford Univ.
Peeke, *Mrs.* M. B. Numbers and letters; or, the thirty-two paths of wisdom. $2. B'way Pub.
Wood, H. G. Ideal metrology in nature, art, religion and history. $1.50. H. G. Wood.

NUMISMATICS.
See Coins and medals;—Seals.

Nun (The). Bazin, R. $1. Scribner.

NUN KUN.
See Himalaya Mts.

NUNBURNHOLME, England.
Morris, M. C. F. Nunburnholme. $5. Oxford Univ.

Nunc dimittis. Gurney, T: A. *60 c. net. Longmans.

NUNDA QUADRANGLE.
See New York State.

Nungasser, Ida Morell Newcomb.
Israel Lo Ammi: twentieth century martyr. '10(O) 75 c. B'way Pub.

NUNNERIES.
Lanslots, D. I. Hdbk. of canon law for congregations of women under simple vows. *$1.25 net. Pustet.
Life of an enclosed nun; by a Mother Superior. $1 net. Lane.
See also Port Royalists.

Nun's priest's tale. *See* Chaucer, Geoffrey.

Nuns of Port Royal. Lowndes, M. E. $4.15. Oxford Univ.

Nürnberg stove. *See* La Ramée, Louisa de. Dog of Flanders.

Nurse Lee. Spencer, *Mrs.* K. S. 50 c. K. S. Spencer.

Nursery fire. Richards, R. $1.25. Little, B. & Co.

NURSERY GARDENS.
See Trees.

Nursery manual. Benson, R. A. *$1 net. Boericke & T.

NURSERY RHYMES.
See Children's poetry.

Nursery tales. Steedman, A. 50 c. Dutton.

Nurse's handbook of obstetrics. Cooke, J. B. $2. Lippincott.

NURSES AND NURSING.
Aikens, C. A. Clinical studies for nurses. $2.—Primary studies for nurses. *$1.75. net. Saunders.
Barus, C. Nursing the insane. **$2 net. Macmillan.
Beck, A. K. Reference hand-book for nurses. *$1.25 net. Saunders.
Bishop, E. S. Lectures on surgical nursing. $1 net. Wood.
Childe, C: P. Operative nursing and technique. *$2 net. Wood.
Donahoe, M. F. Manual of nursing. $2.—Text-book of nursing. $1.75 net. Appleton.
Education of nurses. 30 c. Teachers' Coll.
Friedenwald, J., *and* Ruhräh, J: Dietetics for nurses. *$1.50 net. Saunders.
Giles, J. E: Nursing in diseases of the eye, ear, nose and throat. $1.50. Saunders.
Harding, W: Mental nursing. 50 c. W: R. Jenkins.
Hawes, A. T. Care of the patient. $1 net. Blakiston.
Henry, J: N. Nurses' handbook of medicine. **$1.50 net. Lippincott.
Hoxie, G: H. Practice of medicine for nurses. *$1.50 net. Saunders.
Hufton-Windust, F. Home nursing and hygiene. *50 c. net. Macmillan.
McIsaac, I. Bacteriology for nurses. —Hygiene for nurses. ea., *$1.25 net. Macmillan.
Maxwell, A. C., *and* Pope, A. E. Pract. nursing. $1.75 net. Putnam.
New York State University. Course of study and syllabus for guidance of nurse training schools in preparing their students for examination before the State board. (Add. pubs. for price.) N. Y. State Educ.
Pope, A. E. *and* T. A. Quiz book of nursing for teachers and students. *$1.75 net. Putnam.
Robb, I. A. H. Educational standards, with other papers on nursing subjects. $1.25. —Hampton's nursing. $2 net.—Nursing ethics for hospital and private use. $1.50. Koeckert.
Science and art of nursing. 4 v. per set, *$7.50 net. Cassell.
Stimson, J. C. Nurses' hdbk. of drugs and solutions. $1 net. Whitcomb.
Stoney, E. M. A. Bacteriology and surgical technic for nurses. $1.50.—Pract. points in nursing. $1.75. Saunders.
Tracy, S. E. Studies in invalid occupation. $1.50 net. Whitcomb.
Ward, A. S. Lessons in surgical technique. (Not for sale.) A. S. Ward.
Waters, Y. Visiting nursing in the United States. $1.25. Charities Pub.
Wilcox, R. W. Manual of fever nursing. $1. Blakiston.
Wilson, J. C. Fever nursing. $1 net. Lippincott.
See also Accidents;—Anatomy;—Children;—Cookery;—Food;—Gynecology; — Materia medica;—Midwifery;—Physiology;—Surgery.

Nursey, Wa. R.
Story of Isaac Brock; hero. defender and savior of upper Canada, 1812. '09(O9) c. il. (partly in col.) D. (Canadian heroes ser.) *$1.50 net. McClurg.

NUTRITION.
See Food.

NUTS.
Jaffa, M. E: Nuts and their uses as food. U. S., Supt. of Docs.
See also Peanuts;—Pecans;—Trees.

Nutshells of truth. Popham, W: L. $1. B'way Pub.

Nuttall, G: H: Falkiner, and Graham-Smith, G: Stuart, eds.
Bacteriology of diphtheria. '09(Je19) il. por. 4°, *$7 net. Putnam.

—, and Shipley, Arth. Everett, eds.
Parasitology: supp. to the Journal of Hygiene. '08(Je6) il. Q. pap., *$1.50 net. Putnam.

Nutting, Herbert Chester.
Conspiracy at Rome in 66-65 B.C. '10(F) 43-55 p. Q. (Univ. of Cal. pubs.; Classical philology.) pap., 10 c. Univ. of Cal.

Nutting, Rev. J: Keep.
Nutting genealogy: record of the descendants of John Nutting, of Groton, Mass. '09(F13) il. pors. O. $5. Bardeen.

Nutting, Perley Gilman.
Method for constructing the natural scale of pure color; [April 27, 1909.] '09, [1910.] (Mr) 89-93 p. il. 4°, pap. Gov. Pr. Off.
Resolving power of objectives. '09 [1910] (Mr) 121-124 p. il. 4°, pap. Gov. Pr. Off.

NUTTING FAMILY.
See Genealogies.

Nutt's conversation dictionaries; comp. by R: Jäschke. Tt. Lemcke.
—English-Arabic dictionary. $1.50.

Nweeya, S. Kasha.
Persia, the land of the magi, or, the home of the wise man; historical and descriptive acct., incl. Afghanistan and Beloochistan. 4th ed., rev. '10(S17) c. il. pors. map, 8°, $2. S. K. Nweeya.

Nyaishes or Zoroastrian litanies. Dhalla, M. N. **$2 net. Lemcke.

Nyblom, Helena.
Little maid who danced to every mood. '09, [1910.] (F) col. il. 12°, †75 c. Estes.

Nye, Edg. Wilson, ["Bill Nye."]
See Stories of humor.

Nye, E:, and Wason, Rob. A.
Nachette. '09(O9) il. D. $1.50. J. H. Remick.

Nye, G: Hyatt, and Best, Fk. Eug., comps.
Genealogy of the Nye family; ed. by D: Fisher Nye. '07, [1909.] (F) 704 p. il. pors. 8°. (Add. pubs. for price.) Nye.

Nye, Stephen Girard.
Addresses and letters of travel; with a biographical sketch by Alfr. Bourne Nye. '08(Jl4) c. il. pors. 8°. (Add. pubs. for price.) Stanley-T.

NYE FAMILY.
See Genealogies.

Nygaard, Andreas Christian.
Toleration: a novel. '09(Je12) c. front. 12°, $1.50. Badger.

O-Heart-San. Haskell, H. E. †$1. L. C. Page.

OAK.
See White oak.

Oak among the pines. Henderson, J. D. M. $1.50. Badger.

Oak flooring. Gibson, H: H. 50 c. Hardwood Record.

Oakenfull, J. C.
Brazil in 1910. 2d ed. '10(Ag20) il. fold. map, D. gratis. Com. Brazil.

Oakleaf, Jos. B., comp.
Analysis of the Gettysburg address [of Lincoln.] '08(Ap18) il. por. 12°, pap., gratis. J. B. Oakleaf.

Oakleaf ser. 12 v. [1910.] (D) nar. 12°, ea., vellum, 50 c. net; leath., 75 c. net; cf., $1.25 net. Jacobs.

Oakley, E. Clarence.
Dyke's Corners. '09(Je12) c. 12°, $1.50. Badger.

Oakley, Russell Arth.
Canada bluegrass: its culture and uses. '10 (Ag) 20 p. il. 8°, (U. S., Dept. of Agriculture; Farmer's bull.) Gov. Pr. Off.

OAKS.
Mosher, E. R. Studies of our oaks and maples. $2. Bardeen.

Oaten reeds. Childress, R. J. 60 c. R. J. Childress.

Oath of allegiance. Ward, *Mrs.* E. S. P. **$1.25 net. Houghton M.

OATS.
Clark, C: C., *comp.* Oat crops of the United States. 5 c. U. S.. Supt. of Docs.
Warburton, C. W. Improvement of the oat crop. (Add. Superintendent for price.) U. S., Supt. of Docs.

OBADIAH.
See Bible. O. T.

Obenchain, Mrs. Eliza Caroline Calvert.
See Hall, Eliza Calvert, *pseud.*

Ober, F: Albion.
Guide to the West Indies and Bermudas. '08(Mr14) c. il. maps, S. **$2.25 net. Dodd.
John and Sebastian Cabot. '08(Ap11) c. il. pors. maps, D. (Heroes of American history ser.) **$1 net. Harper.
Juan Ponce de Leon. '08(Mr21) c. il. por. D. (Heroes of American history.) **$1 net. Harper.
Sir Walter Raleigh. '09(F13) c. pors. D. (Heroes of American history.) **$1 net. Harper.
With Osceola in Florida: adventures of two boys in the Seminole war in 1835. '08 (Ap4) c. il. 12°, †$1. Burt.

OBERAMMERGAU, Germany.
Day, E. H. Ober-Ammergau and the Passion Play. 45 c. net. Young Churchman.
Passion Play of Oberammergau. *$1.25 net. Duffield.
Schroeder, J. Oberammergau and its Passion Play. 75 c. net. Lemcke.
Short, J. H. Oberammergau. $1 net. Crowell.

Oberg, Erik Valdemar.
Handbook of small tools; comprising threading tools, taps, dies, cutters, drills, and reamers. '09(Ja2) c. figs. 12°, $3. Wiley.

Oberg, Erik Valdemar.—*Continued.*
Shop arithmetic for the machinist. '08 (Ap18) c. il. tabs., 12°, (*Machinery's* reference ser.) 25 c. Indust. Press.
Tables and formulas for shop and drafting-room. '09 (My8) c. diagrs., 8°, (Machinery's reference ser.) pap., 25 c. Indust. Press.
See also Sylvester, F. L.
Oberholtzer, Ellis Paxson.
Book of the pageant, Philadelphia, October 9th, 1908. '08 (D19) c. il. 8°. (Add. pubs. for price.) Jacobs.
Oberland chalet. Wood, *Mrs.* E. E. $2 net. Wessels & B.
OBERLIN, Johann Friedrich.
Beard, A: F. Story of John Frederick Oberlin. *$1.25 net. Pilgrim Press.
OBERLIN COLLEGE, Oberlin, O.
General catalogue of Oberlin College, 1833-1908; incl. an acct. of the principal events in the hist. of the college, with il. of the college buildings. '09, [1910.] (N) 5-184+1187 p. il. maps, 8°. Oberlin Coll.
Songs of Oberlin. 2d ed. '09 (N) 3-104 p. 12°, 75 c. C. A. Pickett.
Obil. Bell, L. C. 50 c. P. Elder.
OBJECTIVES.
See Lenses.
Obligation of hearing mass on Sundays and holy days. Roche, J. T. 10 c. net; per doz., 75 c. net; per 100, $5 net. Wiltzius.
O'Brien, Fk. G: and Mrs. Lizzie E. Bostwick.
Chimes of cheer: [poems.] '08 (D12) c. pors. O. $2. F. G. O'Brien.
O'Brien, J: Emmet, M.D.
Telegraphing in battle; reminiscences of the Civil War. '10 (Ap16) il. pors. maps, 8°, $2 net. J. E. O'Brien.
O'Brien, Sara Redempta.
English for foreigners. '09 (Ap10) il. map, D. 50 c. Houghton M.
O'Brien, Mrs. Sibyl Wilbur.
Life of Mary Baker Eddy. '08 (D5) c. il. por. 8°, $3. Concord Pub.
O'Brien, W:
Olive branch in Ireland and its history. '10 (D10) pors. O. $3.25 net. Macmillan.
O'Brien, W: L.
Aaron Burr; a play. '09 (Ap10) c 8°. (Add. pubs. for price.) Review Pub.
Observation of symptoms. Hawes, A. T. *$1 net. Whitcomb.
Observations. *See* Browne, *Sir* T:, *and* Digby, *Sir* Kenelm. Religio medici.
Observations in Asia. Grant, P. S. **$1.25 net. Brentano's.
Observations of a bachelor. Lombard, L. $1. Estes.
Observations of an Illinois boy. Eby, H: H. $1. H: H. Eby.
OBSTETRICS.
See Midwifery.
O'Byrnes, The.
See Idyls of Lakeside.
Occasional sermons and addresses comprising discourses suitable for: burials of lay people, priests and religious gatherings of Catholics and non-Catholics; conventions, etc. '10 (Ap) c. 380 p. 8°, $1.50 net. Wagner.
Occluded gases in coal. Parr, S: W. gratis. Univ. of Ill.
OCCULTISM.
Abbott, D: P. Hist. of a strange case: a study in occultism. (Add. pubs. for price.) Open Court.
Atkinson, W: W. Arcane teaching. $1. Arcane.
Atkinson, W: W. Hindu-Yogi science of breath. 75 c.; 50 c. Yogi Pub.
Butler, H. E. Goal of life; or, science and revelation. $2. Esoteric.
Clement, L. Ancient science of numbers: [its] application in the attainment of health, success and happiness. $1. Roger Bros.
Goetia; or, the lesser key of Solomon the king. $1. Occult Pub.
Heindel, M. Rosicrucian cosmo-conception; or Christian occult science. $1. M. Heindel.
Reichel, W. Occultist's travels. $1. Fenno.
Rogers, L: W: Hints to young students of occultism.—Occultism in the Shakespeare plays. ea., 25 c. Theosophical Bk.
See also Astrology;—Crystal gazing;—Esoterism;—Hypnotism;—Hinduism;—Magic and magicians;—Mysticism;—Personality;—Spiritualism;—Telepathy;—Theosophy.
Occultist's travels. Reichel, W. $1. Fenno.
OCCUPATIONAL DISEASES.
See Pathology.
OCCUPATIONS.
See Success.
Occurrence of the larvæ of a parasitic fly, *Protocalliphora chryssorrhoea,* Meigen, in bird nests. Miller, C: W. gratis. Worthington Soc.
OCEAN.
Bullen, F. T: Call of the deep. $1.50. Dutton.
McFee, W: Letters from an ocean tramp. *$1.50 net. Cassell.
Shaw, F. H., *and* Robinson, E. H. Sea and its story. $3.50 net. Cassell.
Stead, R: Adventures on the high seas. *$1.50 net. Lippincott.
Melville, H. *and* L. Full fathom five; sea anthology. $1.50 net. Macmillan.
Whidden, J: D. Ocean life in the old sailing ship days. **$1.50 net. Little, B. & Co.
See also Biology;—Commerce;—Fish and fishing;—Hydrography:—Marine zoology;—Naval art and science;—Navigation;—Physical geography;—Seaweed;—Ships and shipbuilding;—Tides;—Voyages and travels;—Water.
Ocean carrier. Smith, J. R. **$1.50 net. Putnam.
OCEAN COMMERCE.
See Commerce.
Ocean mail service between United States and foreign ports; rept. '09 (My) 14+5 p. 8°, pap. (Add. Superintendent for price.) U. S., Supt. of Docs.
Ocean mail service between United States and foreign ports. United States. *Congress. Senate. Committee on Commerce.* 10 c. U. S., Supt. of Docs.
Ocean waifs. Reid, M. †$1. Dutton.

OCEANIC LANGUAGES.
Macdonald, D. Oceanic languages: their grammatical structure, vocabulary and origin. $4.20. Oxford Univ

OCEANICA.
Alexander, J: M. Islands of the Pacific. $1.50. Am. Tr.
Grimshaw, B. E. In the strange south seas. *$3.50 net. Lippincott.
Lambert, J: C. Missionary heroes in Oceanica. 75 c. Lippincott.
Stevenson, R. L: In the South Seas. *$1 net; *$1.25 net. Scribner.
Wheeler, W: W. Glimpse of the isles of the Pacific. (Not for sale.) Hardman.
Wilcox, *Mrs.* E. W. Sailing sunny seas. $1.50. Conkey.
See also Borneo;—Gilbert Islands;—New Zealand;—Papua;—Philippine Islands.

Ochsenford, Solomon Erb, D.D.
Passion story as recorded by the four evangelists; together with psalms and prayers suitable for the services of Holy Week. 2d rev. and enl. ed. '08(Ap18) c. D. 75 c. Gen. Council.

Ochsner, Albert J:, and Thompson, Ralph Leroy.
Surgery and pathology of the thyroid and parathyroid glands. '10(My) c. 391 p. il. 8°, $6 net. Mosby.
Parathyroid literature (7 p.).

Ocklye cookery book. Jenkinson, E. L. 60 c. net. Cassell.

O'Connell, Rev. Cornelius Jos.
Holy Eucharist and frequent daily communion. '09(Je5) c. D. *60 c. net. Benziger.

O'Connell, Dan.
Manila, the Pearl of the Orient; guide book to the intending visitor; pub. by the Manila Merchants' Association. '09(N) 59 p. il. map, plans, 12°. (Add. pubs. for price.) Manila Merchants'.

O'Connor, J: Bartholomew.
Chapters in the history of actors and acting in ancient Greece. '08(O24) c. 8°, pap., $1. Univ. of Chic.

O'Connor, V. C. Scott.
Mandalay, and other cities of the past in Burma. '08(O10) il. plans, maps, O. *$5 special net. Appleton.

October vagabonds. *See* Le Gallienne, R:

Octopus (The). Jenner, W: A. gratis. W: A. Jenner.

Odd bits of travel with brush and camera. Taylor, C: M. *$1.25 net. Jacobs.

ODD-FELLOWS.
See Freemasonry.

Odd man. Holcombe, A. $1.50. Lane.

Odd moments. Boyden, E. 75 c.; 50 c. Cochrane.

Odd prices and bargains in retail trade. Brooks, R. C. 50 c. Univ. of Cin.

Odd soldiery. Fuller, A. F. 25 c. Solar Lit.

Odds and ends. Tabor, R. M. $1.75. Longmans.

Odds and the ends. Smith, *Mrs.* E. T. $1. Burt.

Ode on Lincoln. Noyes, I: P. 10 c. I: P. Noyes.

Ode on the morning of Christ's nativity. *See* Milton, J:

Ode to memory of our country's Father. Alloway, C: R. 25 c. C: R. Alloway.

Ode to prophesy. Dilworth, H. P. 25 c. H. P. Dilworth.

Ode to the Union. Noyes, I: P. (Add. author for price.) I: P. Noyes.

Odell, B: Barker, jr.
Public papers of Benjamin B. Odell, jr., governor of [New York State] for 1901-1904. 4 v. '07, [1908.] (My.) 8°, per set, $2.50. Lyon.

Odell, Fk. Iglehart.
Larry Burke, freshman. '10(Ag20) c. il. D. $1.25. Lothrop, L. & S.

Odes on the generations of man. Alexander, H. B. **$1 net. Baker & T.

O'Donnell, C: Ja.
Causes of present discontent in India. '08 (Jl4) c. 8°, **85 c. net. Wessels

O'Donnell, Fk. Hugh Macdonald.
History of the Irish parliamentary party. In 2 v. v. 1, Butt and Parnell: nationhood and anarchy, the curse of American money; v. 2, Parnell and the lieutenants; complicity and betrayal; with an epilogue to the present day. '10(Ap30) il. pors. O. $5 net. Longmans.

O'Donnell, W: C:, jr.
Around the Emerald Isle; record of impressions. '10(O1) c. D. $1. Roxburgh.

O'Donnell, W: F.
Mother Santa Claus stories. '09(D18) c. il. 8°, (Altemus mother stories ser.) †50 c. Altemus.

O'Donovan, Michael Jos.
See Donovan, Mike.

Odum, Howard Washington.
Social and mental traits of the negro; research into the conditions of the negro race in southern towns; study in race traits, tendencies and prospects. '10(Jl9) c. O. (Columbia Univ. studies in hist., economics and public law.) pap., $2 net. Longmans.

O'Dwyer, Bp. E: T:
Cardinal Newman and the Encyclical *Pascendi Dominici Gregis.* '08(F29) O. pap., *36 c. net. Longmans.

Odysseus, pseud.
See Eliot, *Sir* C: Norton Edgecumbe.

Odyssey. *See* Homer.

OECOLOGY.
See Botany;—Zoology.

ŒDEMA.
See Edema.

Oehlschlaeger, Rev. Christian Jonathan.
Song of faith. '08(D12) il. 12°, $2. Cochrane.

Oeland, P: Jos.
Around town boys. '10(Je4) c. O. $1.25. Walker, E. & C.

O'er oceans and continents. *See* Blatter, G: J:

Oesterley, W: Oscar Emil, D.D.
Evolution of the Messianic idea: study in comparative religion. '08(S19) 8°, *$1.25 net. Dutton.

—, and Box, G: Herbert.
Religion and worship of the Synagogue. '08(Je20) il. O. *$3 net. Scribner.

"Of such is the kingdom." Metcalfe, R: L. $1. Woodruff-C.

Of the tumbler of Our Lady and other miracles; now first tr. from the middle French MSS., anonymous and by Gautier de Coinci [preserved at Soissons]; with notes and introd. by Alice Kemp Welch. '08(O17) 16°, (New medieval lib.) pigskin, with clasps, *$2.50 net. Duffield.

Off the reservation. Ellis, E: S. †$1. Winston.

Office of the Blessed Virgin Mary and office of the dead. Catholic church. 45 c.; 75 c. Herder.

Office treatment of rectal diseases explained and simplified. Mason, R. D. $2.50. Burton Co.

Official athletic rules and official hdbk. of the Amateur Athletic Union of the United States; constitution, by-laws, general and athletic rules; also the rules of gymnastics, swimming, wrestling, boxing, water polo. '10(D10) S. (Spalding's athletic lib.) pap., 10 c. Am. Sports.

Official Catholic directory and clergy list for 1908, U. S. and Canada ed. '08(Mr7) il. por. maps, pap., $1.75; leath., $2.50; complete ed., pap., $2.50; leath., $3; for 1909, U. S., Alaska, Philippine Islands, Cuba, Porto Rico, Hawaiian Islands, Canada, Newfoundland, England, Ireland, Scotland and Wales. v. 24. '09(Ap3) il. fold. map, pors. D. abridged ed., pap., $1.75; leath., $2.50; complete ed., pap., $2.50; leath., $3; for 1910, U. S. Alaska, Philippine Islands, Cuba, Porto Rico, Hawaiian Islands, Canada, Newfoundland, England, Ireland, Scotland and Wales. v. 25. '10(Mr19) il. fold. map, pors. D. abrdg. ed., pap., $1.75; leath., $2.50; complete ed., pap., $2.50; leath.. $3. Wiltzius.

Official horse show blue book. '07, [1908.] c. il. 8°, $5; leath., $6.50. J. W. Waring.

Official motor guide. Chicago Automobile Club. $1.50; $2. Chic. Automobile.

Official Pythian lodge directory; cont. full and valuable information regarding the supreme, grand, and subordinate lodges of the order of Knights of Pythias, [etc.] '08(Jl) c. 256 p. por. O. $2. H. H. Richardson.

Official theatrical guide. Cahn, J. $1. J. Cahn.

Official year book and directory of golf and automobiling, 1909. [11th yr.] '10(Ja8) c. Q. $5. Stettiner.

O'Flynn, T: F.
Story of Worcester, Mass. '10(O1) c. il. pors. map, D. $1.50 net. Little, B. & Co.

O'Flynn (The). McCarthy, J. H. $1.50. Harper.

Ogden, C: Jones.
De infinitivi finalis vel consecutivi constructione apud priscos poetas Græcos. '09 (S4) 8°, (Columbia Univ. studies in classical philology.) *$1.25 net. Lemcke.

Ogden, H: Neely.
Sewer construction. '08(N7) figs. 8°, $3. Wiley.

Ogden, Ja. Matlock.
Law of negotiable instruments; incl. promissory notes, bills of exchange, bank checks, [etc.] '09(N) 9-69+550 p. Q. *$4 net. Callaghan.

Ogden, Jay Bergen.
Clinical examination of the urine and urinary diagnosis; clinical guide for the use of practitioners and students of medicine and surgery. 3d ed., rev. '09(N) c. 7-427 p. il. 8°, $3. Saunders.

OGDEN FAMILY.
See Genealogies: Wheeler, W: O., *comp.*

Ogg, Fréderic Austin, ed.
Source book of mediæval history. '08 (Ap25) c. O. $1.50. Am. Bk.

Ogilvie, G: W.
See Vest pocket reference book ser.

Ogilvy, C:
See Taylor, H: Ling.

Ogilvy, Ja. S.
Relics and memorials of London City. '10 (D10) c. col. il. 4°, $5 net. Dutton.

Ogle, Ponsonby.
Selections from the writings. '08(D5) c. 12°. (Priv. pr.) Brentano's.

Oh! Christina! Bell, J: J. *60 c. net. Revell.

Oh, to be rich and young. Sunderland, J. T: $1. Am. Unitarian.

O'Hara, Barratt.
From Figg to Johnson; complete hist. of the heavyweight championship, cont. dates and accurate descriptions of every contest for the world's boxing title from the time of the first champion down to the present day. [1910] (F) c. '09. 179 p. pors. 12°, $1. Blossom Bk.

O'Hara, J: Myers.
Poems of Sappho; interpretative rendition into English. '10(Ag27) front. 8°, $2. Smith & S.
Songs of the open. '09(Ag) c. 64 p. por. 8°, $1. Smith & S.

O'Higgins, Harvey Jerrold.
Grand Army man; founded on the play by D: Belasco, Pauline Phelps, and Marion Short. '08(S19) c. il. D. †$1.50. Century Co.
Old Clinkers: story of the New York Fire Department. '09(O2) c. il. D. †$1.50. Small, M.
See Lindsay, B: Barr.

Ohio. Annot. probate code; by W: H: Whittaker. 3d rev. ed. '08(O) c. 9+ 1190 p. 12°, $4. W. H. Anderson.

Ohio. *Circuit ct.* Repts. v. 28-30. '09(Ap) c. O. shp., ea., $2.50. Laning.

Ohio. *Circuit ct.* Repts. New ser., v. 10; (Vinton R. Shepard.) '08(D); v. 11. '09 (Jl); v. 12. '10(My) c. O. shp., ea., $2.50. Ohio Law.

Ohio. *Circuit cts.* Annots. to all the decisions, alphabetically arranged; syllabi revised, [etc.;] a brief with every case. '08 (D) c. 1182 p. O. (Add. pubs. for price.) Laning.

Ohio. Complete guide for township officers, cont. all the sections of the revised statutes of O. applicable to township officers, [etc.;] by W: M. Rockel. 11th ed. '09(Jl) c. 2+ 961 p. O. $4. W. H. Anderson.

Ohio. *Cts. of record.* Repts. v. 13-19. '08, [1909.] (Ap) c. O. shp., ea., $2.50. Laning.

Ohio. *Federal cts.* Repts. v. 15. '08(N) c. O. shp., $2.50. Laning.

Ohio. Municipal code, [etc.;] by Wade H. Ellis. 4th ed., by Challen B. Ellis. '09(D) c. O. $6. W. H. Anderson.

Ohio. Nisi prius reports. New ser., v. 5, 6; ed. by Vinton R. Shepard. '08(D); v. 7. '09(Ap); v. 8 (D); v. 9. '10(O) c. O. shp., ea., $2.50. Ohio Law.

Ohio. Outline of the law of evidence, with Illustrative cases; by Reed Metzler. '10 (Mr) c. S. $1. R. Metzler.

Ohio. *State Bd. of Health.* Rept. of an investigation of water and sewage purification plants in Ohio, made under authority of an act of legislature passed Feb. 23, 1906. '08, [1909.] (My) 888 p. il. plans, tabs. (Add. pubs. for price.) Heer.

Ohio. Supplement, (1908,) to the encyclopedic digest of repts., [etc.] '08(D) c. O. shp. (Add. pubs. for price.) Michie.

Ohio. *Supreme ct.* Repts.; (Emilius O. Randall.) New ser. v. 77. '08(My); v. 78 (O); v. 79. '09(Je); v. 80 (N); v. 81. '10 (Jl); v. 82 (N) c. O. shp., ea., $2.50. W. H. Anderson.

Ohio. *Supreme ct.* Repts. reduced to questions and answers: being the leading principles of the Ohio law as laid down by the supreme court of Ohio, beginning with the 1st Ohio and ending with the 77th Ohio state court, by F: L. Hoffman. '08(My.) c. 350 p. O. $2.50. W. H. Anderson.

Ohio. Treatise on the laws pertaining to the powers and duties of and practice [etc.,] before justices of the peace; by Jos. R. Swan. 22d ed., by Jos. R. Swan, 3d. '10 (D) c. O. $6.50. W. H. Anderson.

OHIO.

Ashburn, J. N. Hist. of 86th regiment, Ohio volunteer infantry. $1.50. J. N. Ashburn.

Bownocker, J: A., *and others.* Coal [in Ohio.] 50 c. Ohio Geol.

Chadock, R. E. Ohio before 1850. $1.50. Longmans.

Galbreath, C: B., *comp.* Ohio emblems and monuments. gratis. C: B. Galbreath.

Keeler, L. E. Old Fort Sandoski of 1745 and the Sandusky country. 25 c. L. E. Keeler.

Mercer, J. K. Representative men of Ohio. $25. J. K. Mercer.

Rockel, W: M. Guide for administrators and executors in the settlement of estates of deceased persons in Ohio. $1.50. W. H. Anderson.

Schaffner, J: H: Trees of Ohio. 50 c. Ohio State Acad.

Slocum, C: E. Ohio country between 1783 and 1815. $2 net. Putnam.

Smith, C: H. Hist. of Fuller's Ohio Brigade, 1861-1865. $3. C. H. Smith.

Society of Colonial Wars, Ohio. Register of the Society in the state of Ohio, Oct. 1, 1909. (Not for sale.) Soc. Colon. Wars, (O.)

Stauffer, C. R. Middle Devonian of Ohio. 25 c. Ohio Geolog. Survey.

Thomas, T: E. Correspondence, mainly relating to the anti-slavery conflict in Ohio. *$1 net. Clarke.

OHIO.—*Continued.*

Upton, *Mrs.* H. T., *and others.* Hist. of the Western Reserve. In 3 v. $21. Lewis Pub.

Venable, E., *ed.* Poets of Ohio. **$1.50 net. Clarke.

See also Cincinnati;—Cleveland;—Clarksfield;—Dayton;—Fort Ancient;—Green County;—Greenville (*Treaty of*);—Methodist Episcopal church;—Miami County;—Sandusky Bay;—Schools;—Town officers;—Trumbull County;—Tuscarawas County;—*also* Hall, James.

Ohio cumulative digest; issue of Oct., 1910. '10(D) c. O. pap., $3.75 per year. Ohio Law.

Ohio farm laws (latest rev. ed.) with business forms and business letters; by W: K. Williams. '10(Jl) c. O. 25 c. Rural Pub.

Ohio Geological Survey bull. 8°. Ohio Geolog. Survey.

—Bownocker, *and others.* Coals of the Monongahela formation. 50 c.

—Stauffer. Middle Devonian of Ohio. 25 c.

Ohio law note and brief finder from the earliest issue of the O. reports to the year 1910; comp. by W. G. Pilkington. '10 (My) c. S. $3. Law Stamp.

Ohio law stamps, from the earliest issue of the O. reports to the year 1910; comp. by W. G. Pilkington. '10(My) c. S. pap., $3. Law Stamp.

OHIO RIVER.

Thwaites, R. G., *and* Kellogg, L. P., *eds.* Revolution on the upper Ohio, 1775-1777. $1.50. State Hist., Wis.

Ohio State Academy proceedings. 8°, pap. Ohio State Acad.

—Schaffner. Trees of Ohio. 50 c.

Ohio State Univ. Agricultural College extension bull. 8°, pap. Ohio State Univ.; A. B. Graham.

—Graham. Centralized schools in Ohio. gratis.—County school of Ohio.

Ohio State University; Civil engineering pubs. il. 8°. Hann.

—Morris. Designing and detailing of simple steel structures. $2.25.

Ohio State University. Contributions from the Department of Zoology and Entomology. il. 8°. Ohio State Univ.

—Hine. Robberflies of the genus *Asilus* 50 c.

—Jackson. Study of Ohio forms of the genus *Lepidocyrtus.* gratis.

OHIO VALLEY.

Saugrain de Vigni, A. F. Dr. Saugrain's note-books, 1788. 50 c. Davis Press.

See also Newspapers.

OHIO WESLEYAN UNIVERSITY, Delaware, O

Crook, I: Great five: first faculty of the Ohio Wesleyan University. *25 c. net. Jennings.

"Ohiyesa," pseud.

See Eastman, C: Alexander.

Ohl, Mrs. J. Kingsley.

See Andrews, Annulet.

Ohlander, Marcus, comp.

Little Rock and Pulaski County, Arkansas, illustrated. '07, [1908.] (Ap.) c. 90 p. f°, pap., 50 c. M. Ohlander.

Ohnet, Georges.
The ironmaster; [Le maitre des forges;] tr. fr. the 146th French ed. '08(Je6) 12°, 50 c. Warne.
Red flag. '10(Ap30) c. D. $1.50. G: W. Dillingham.

OIL ENGINE.
See Engines.

Oil tank tables. Squier, E. 50 c. E. Squier.

OILS AND FATS.
Brodé, J. L. Oil-seed products and feed stuffs. Gov. Pr. Off.
Ennis, W: D. Linseed oil and other seed oils. $4. Van Nostrand.
Gill, A: H. Short hand-book of oil analysis. **$2 net. Lippincott.
Harris, G. D., *and others.* Oil and gas in northwestern Louisiana. La. Geol. Survey.
Leathes, J: B. The fats. $1.25 net. Longmans.
Lewkowitsch, J. I. Chemical technology of oils, fats and waxes. 3 v. *$15 net. Macmillan.
Mitchell, C: A. Oil, animal, vegetable, essential, and mineral. 75 c. Pitman.
See also Chemistry;—Cottonseed products;—Petroleum.

Oiseau (L'). *See* Michelet, Jules.

OJIBWAY INDIANS.
See Songs.

Okabe-Kakuya.
Museum of Fine Arts, Boston: Japanese sword guards, by Okabe-Kakuya, in cooperation with the Department of Chinese and Japanese Art. '08(Jl18) il. 8°, $1.25. Boston Museum.

Okakura, Kakuzo.
Ideals of the East: with ref. to the art of Japan. New ed. '08(Mr21) 12°, *$1.50 net. Dutton.

Okey, T:
Venice and its story. '10(N5) il. 8°, $4 net. Dutton.

Oklahoma. Codes of civil and criminal procedure, [etc.;] by Clinton Orrin Bunn. Pocket ed. '10(D) c. S, flex. im. mor., $3.50. Bunn.

Oklahoma. Compiled laws, 1909; comp. by H: G. Snyder. '09(N) c. 20+2063 p. O. $6. Pipes-R.

Oklahoma. Constitution and enabling act of the state, annot. and indexed, [etc.;] comp. by Clinton O. Bunn and W: C. Bunn. '08 (Ja11) O. shp., $3. Bunn.

Oklahoma. Constitution, with copious notes referring to and digesting decisions construing and applying identical and similar provisions of the constitutions and statutes of other states and of the U. S.; by H: G. Snyder. '08(D) c. 4+521 p. O. $5. Pipes-R.

Oklahoma. *Criminal ct. of appeals.* Repts. v. 1, 2; (Howard Parker.) '10(Je); v. 3 (N) c. O. shp., ea., $1.50. State Cap.

Oklahoma. *Dept. of Education.* Some suggestions in school gardening as an aid to the teachers in teaching of agriculture in the public schools as required by law. '09 (N) 10 p. il. 8°, gratis. Oklahoma Dept. Educ.

Oklahoma. Form book, pleading and practice annot., by R. A. Kleinschmidt and Mont Frederic Highley. 2d ed., rev. and enl. '08(My.) c. 12+699 p. O. shp., $6. Democrat Pr. and Litho.

Oklahoma. General statutes, 1908; a comp. of all the laws of a general nature, incl. the session laws of 1907; annot. to v. 18 Okla. repts.; 96, Pacific reporter; 76, Kan. repts., and 150, Cal. repts.; (Benedict Elder.) '08, [1909.] (Ja) c. 1774 p. O. (Add. pubs. for price.) Pipes-R.

Oklahoma. Laws and legal forms. Business manual; comp. by G: A. Matlack. '09(O) c. 102 p. O. pap., $1. Warden-E.

Oklahoma. *Supreme ct.* Repts. v. 19; (R. L. Williams and Howard Parker.) '09 (Ap); v. 20 (Je); v. 21 (S) ea., $3.50; v. 22. '10(Mr); v. 23 (Jl); v. 24 (S); v. 25 (D) c. O. shp., ea., $1.50. State Cap.

Oklahoma. *Supreme ct. and Ct. of appeals.* Criminal repts. v. 1; (Howard Parker.) '09(N) c. O. shp., $1.50. Leader Print.

OKLAHOMA.
Abbott, L. J. Hist. and civics of Oklahoma. $1 net. Ginn.
Evans, C:, *and* Bunn, C. O. Study of civil government, incl. Oklahoma. 55 c. Bunn.
Girty, G: H. Fauna of the Caney shale of Oklahoma. 25 c. U. S., Supt. of Docs.
Gould. C. N. Geography of Oklahoma. 75 c. Bunn.
Hill, L. B. History of the state of Oklahoma. 2 v. $20. Lewis Pub.
Honnold, A. B. Powers and duties of justices of the peace in civil, criminal and special cases in the state of Oklahoma. $6. Flood.
Rader, P. S. Civil government of the United States and the state of Oklahoma. 75 c. H. Stephens.
Thoburn, J. B., *and* Holcomb I: M. Hist. of Oklahoma. $1.10. Doub.
Townes, J: C: Civil government in the United States and in the state of Oklahoma. (Add. pubs. for price.) Austin Pr.
United States. *Congress. House. Committee on the Judiciary.* Establishing boundary line between Colorado and New Mexico and Oklahoma. 5 c. U. S., Supt. of Docs.
See also Coal;—Indians;—Kay Co.

Oklahoma and Indian Territory. Digest of the reported decisions of all the courts down to 1908; comp. under the Am. digest classification. In 2 v. '08(O) c. O. (Am. digest system, state ser.) $15. West Pub.

Oklahoma laws made plain; for the use of farmers, [etc.;] comp. by W: C. Reeves. '09(N) c. 100 p. D. pap., $1. Combe.

Oklahoman almanac and industrial record, 1908. '08(Je13) il. 12°, 50 c. Daily Oklahoman.

Okuma, Count Shigenobu, comp.
Fifty years of new Japan (Kikoku gojunen shi); English version ed. by Marcus Bourne Huish. In 2 v. v. 1. '09 (D); v. 2. '10(Ap23) 4°, ea., $7.50 net. Dutton.

O'Laughlin, J: Callan.
From the jungle through Europe with Roosevelt. '10(Jl16) c. il. por. 12°, 25 c. Chapple Pub.

Olcott, C: Sumner.
George Eliot; scenes and people in her novels. '10(S10) c. il. pors. O. $2 net. Crowell.

Olcott, W: Tyler.
In Starland with a three-inch telescope. '09 (O16) c. il. S. **$1 net. Putnam.

OLD AGE.
See Longevity.

Old age deferred. Lorand, A. $2.50. Davis.

Old-age pensions. Lecky, W: E: 25 c. Longmans.

Old allegiance. Wales, H., *pseud.* $1.50. M. Kennerley.

Old and new magic. Evans, H: R. $2. Open Court.

Old and new Peru. Wright, *Mrs.* M. R. *$10 net. Barrie.

Old and odd memories. Tollemache, L. A. *$3.50 net. Longmans.

Old Andover days. Robbins, *Mrs.* S. S. *$1 net. Pilgrim Press.

Old Andy. Gielow, M. S. 50 c. W. F. Roberts.

Old ballads. Sidgewick, F., *ed.* *50 c. net. Putnam.

Old Bay road. Waters, T: F. 25 c. Ipswich Hist.

Old beliefs and new knowledge. Drawbridge, C. L. 25 c. Longmans.

Old Boston boys and the games they played. Lovett, J. DeW. **$1.50 net. Little, B. & Co.

Old Boston days and ways. Crawford, M. C. **$2.50 net. Little, B. & Co.

Old Boston taverns and tavern clubs. Drake, S: A. 50 c. W. A. Butterfield.

Old buildings of New York City; with notes regarding their origin and occupants. '08 (F8) c. O. **$2 net. Brentano's.

Old cannon foundry above Georgetown, D. C. Davis, M. (Add. pubs. for price.) New Era Print.

Old Christianity vs. new paganism. Otten, B. J. 25 c. Herder.

Old Christmas. *See* Irving, Washington.

Old churches, ministers and families of Virginia. *See* Indexes.

Old Clinkers. O'Higgins, H. J. †$1.50. Small.

Old colonial houses in Maine. Nason, E. H. (Add. author for price.) E. H. Nason.

Old continental towns. Gallichan, W. M. $2 net. Pott.

Old cottages and farm-houses in Surrey. Green, W. C. $8.40. Helburn.

Old cotton-gin. Moore, J: T. $1. Winston.

Old court life in France. Elliott, F. B. $1.50 net. Brentano's.

Old court life in Spain. Elliott, F. B. $1.50 net. Brentano's.

Old criticism and new pragmatism. O'Sullivan, J. M. $3. Longmans.

Old Deerfield ser. *See* Smith, *Mrs.* Mary Prudence Wells.

Old Dominion. Page, T: N. **$1.50 net. Scribner.

OLD EAGLE SCHOOL.
See Tredyffrin, Pa.

Old Edinburgh. Watkeys, F: W: 2 v. $3. L. C. Page.

Old Egyptian faith. Naville, E. $1.50 net. Putnam.

Old England. Sparrow, W. S. *$6 net; *$10 net. Pott.

Old England ser. il. Tt. 60 c.; leath., $1. Stokes.
—Lang. Some old English abbeys.

Old English Bible. Gasquet, F. A. *$2.25 net. Macmillan.

Old English Christian epic. Smithson, G: A. $1. Univ. of Cal.

Old English Christmas. Irving, W. $1.25 net. Jacobs.

Old English colour-prints. Holme, C:, *ed.* *$3 net. Lane.

Old English furniture. Wheeler, G. O. $3. Scribner.

Old English grammar. Wright, J. $2. Oxford Univ.

Old English stories. Darton, F. J. H., *comp.* 50 c. Dodge.

Old English towns. Andrews, W: *$2 net. Pott.

Old events and modern meanings. Aked, C: F. *$1.25 net. Revell.

Old farm story box. Bennett, V. 4 v. per set, $1. Dutton.

Old fashioned Christmas day. *See* Irving, Washington.

Old fashioned fairy tales. Washburne, *Mrs.* M. F. †$1.25. Rand, McN. & Co.

Old-fashioned senator. Coolidge, L: A. $3 net. Putnam.

Old favorites ser. 7 v. '09, [1910.] (F) sq. 16°, ea., $1.25. Putnam.
Contents: Prentiss, E. P., Fred, Maria and me; Fuller, A., Literary courtships; De Quincey, Essays; Johnson, S:, Rasselas; Kinglake, Eothen; Hazlitt, W:, Spirit of the age; Randolph, A. D. F., Changed Cross.

Old flute player. Marshall, D. E: $1.50. G: W: Dillingham.

Old Fort Sandoski of 1745. Keeler, L. E. 25 c. L. E. Keeler.

Old friends. Winter, W: **$3 net. Moffat.

Old friends. '09(O2) il. O. (Playtime ser. of toy books.) bds., 40 c.; pap., 25 c. Warne.

Old friends are best. Brooks, R., *comp.* $1.25; $2. Dodge.

Old Greek nature stories. Farrar, F. A. $1.50 net. Crowell.

Old Hallowell. Nason, *Mrs.* E. H. $3.50. E. H. Nason.

Old Harbor. Hopkins, W: J: *$1.35 net. Houghton M.

Old homestead. Coryell, J: R. 75 c. G: W. Dillingham.

Old houses of Rouen of the 17th and 18th century; published under the direction of MM. E. Delabarre and M. Boulanger; series 1-36; with descriptive text in French. [portfolio.] '09(Je19) il. f°, $15. Hessling.

"Old International," pseud.
How to play rugby. '10(S) 150 p. il. pors. plans, 16°, (Spalding's athletic lib.) pap., 10 c. Am. Sports.

Old Irish folk music and songs. Joyce, P. W., *ed.* *$3.50 net. Longmans.

Old Ironsides. De Morgan, J: 75 c. McLoughlin.
Old Jim Case of South Hollow. Rice, E: I. †$1. Doubleday, P.
Old Kensington Palace. Dobson, H: A. $1.50 net. Stokes.
Old Kentucky. Cook, J. F. *$3 net. Neale.
Old lace. Jourdain, M. $4.50. Scribner.
Old lace manual. '10(Je4) 12°, $1. A. M. Kohlsaat.
Old lady number 31. Waddell, *Mrs.* C. C. $1. Century Co.
Old librarian's almanack. *See* Pearson, Edm. Lester.
Old log cabin. Watkins, L. B. 15 c. L. B. Watkins.
Old man Coyote. Bayliss, *Mrs.* C. K. †$1. Crowell.
Old man's beard. Faulding, G. M. $2. Dutton.
Old masters; examples of their work reproduced in color; with notes on pictures and painters. '08(D) 2 v., 8+94; 6+94 p. f°, *$8 net. Dutton.
Old meeting houses. Hayes, J: R. $1. Biddle Press.
Old Miami. Upham, A. H. $1. Rep. Pub.
Old mill on the Withrose. Spalding, H: S. 85 c. Benziger.
OLD MINE ROAD, N. Y. and N. J.
Hine, C: G. Hist. and legend, fact, fancy and romance of the Old Mine Road, Kingston, N. Y., to the mine holes of Pahaquarry. $1. Hine Bros.
Old Mr. Davenant's money. Case, F. S. †$1.50. Scribner.
Old Mother West Wind. Burgess, T. W. $1. Little, B. & Co.
Old New England church. Child, F. S. $1. Fairfield Hist.
Old New Hampshire home. *See* Dumont, Fk. Girl from "L Triangle" Ranch.
Old ninety-nine's cave. Gray, E. H. $1.50. C. M. Clark.
Old North Trail. McClintock, W. $4 net. Macmillan.
Old, old myths of Greece and Rome; ed. by T: Cartwright. '08(Ag15) 16°, (Every child's lib.) 50 c. Dutton.
"Old, old story." Wishard, S: E., 50 c. Montfort.
Old, old story-book. Tappan, E. M., *comp.* $1.50. Houghton M.
Old order changeth. White, W. A. $1.25 net. Macmillan.
Old people. Paine, H. E. $1.25 net. Houghton M.
Old pin-cushion. Molesworth, *Mrs.* M. L. S. $1.50. Dutton.
Old plantation. Gordon, J. $1.25. J. Gordon.
Old plantation days. De Saussure, *Mrs.* N. B. $1. Duffield.
Old rhymes pictured [in col.] by Mabel Lucie Attwell. '09(N13) F. bds., $1.50. Tuck.
Old riddle and the newest answer. Gerard, J: 20 c. Longmans.
Old road. Buxton, H. J: W. *$2 net. Whittaker.
Old room. Ewald, C. †$1.25. Scribner.
Old rose and silver. *See* Reed, Myrtle.
Old Royall House. Wild, H. T. 50 c. Salem Press.
Old San Gabriel mission. Sugranes, E. 50 c. E. Sugranes.
Old school day romances. Riley, J. W. $1.50. Bobbs-M.
OLD SOUTH CHURCH, Boston.
25th anniversary; record of the celebration by the Old South Church and Society of the 25th anniversary of the installation as minister of the Old South Church of Rev. George A. Gordon, D.D., April, 1909. [1910.] (N) 144 p. por. 8°. Old South Ch.
Old South leaflets. Wells, R. W., *comp.* 5 c. McKinley Pub.
Old South leaflets. pap., 5 c. Old South Work.
—Milton. Treatise on education.
Old sweethearts. Crossley, R., *comp.* $2. Platt & P.
Old tales retold. Mord, W. $1. Stokes.
OLD TESTAMENT.
See Bible.
Old-time favorites. West, E. E., *comp.* 35 c. Werner.
Old-time parson. Ditchfield, P: H. *$2.50 net. Dutton.
Old time recipes for home made wines. Wright, H. S., *comp.* $1.50. Estes.
Old time wall papers. Sanborn, K. *$5 net. Dutton.
Old times in oildom. Brown, G: W. $1. G: W. Brown.
Old times on the upper Mississippi. Merrick, G: B. *$3.50 net. A. H. Clark.
Old town. Riis, J. A. **$2 net. Macmillan.
"Old town by the sea." Fuller, W: O. 5 c. W. O. Fuller.
Old Virginia cooking. Retail Grocers' Assoc. of Richmond. gratis. Richmond Press.
Old Virginia gentleman. Bagby, G: W: $1.50 net. Scribner.
OLD WEST (The).
See United States.
Old wives for new. Phillips, D: G. †$1.50. Appleton.
Old wives' tale. Bennett, A. *$1.50 net. Doran.
Old wood engravings, views and buildings in the county of Essex. Dow, G: F. (Priv. pr.) G: F. Dow.
Old world favorites. 2 v. '10(D) 16°, ea., ooze, 75 c. net; pap., 50 c. net. Dodge.
Contents: Stevenson on friendship;—Sonnets from the Portuguese.
Old world ser. *See* Mosher's.
Old world travels. *See* Macmillan's.
Old yellow book. Hodell, C: W. $7. Carnegie.
Oldest English epic: Beowulf, Finnsburg, Waldere, Deor, Widsith, and the German Hildebrand; tr. into the original metres with introds. and notes by Frances B. Gummere. '09(Ap24) c. D. **$1.10 net. Macmillan.
Oldest paint shops in Massachusetts. Wall, W: E. 25 c. W: E. Wall.
Oldham, Bethenia McLemore.
Pract. plans for primary teachers in public or private schools. '10(S3) c. il. 12°, 30 c. C. J. Bell.

OLDHAM FAMILY.
See Genealogies: Miller, W: H.

Oldmeadow, Ernest Ja.
Antonio. '09(Jl3) c. front. D. **$1.30 net. Century Co.
Aunt Maud. '08(Ag8) c. D. †$1.50. McClure.
Great musicians. '08(Ag15) 12°, $1.50. Jacobs.
Portugal. '10(D10) il. 8°, $3.50 net. Lippincott.
Virginie. '08(F8) c. front. D. †$1.50. McClure.

Oldroyd, Osborn Hamiline, comp.
Centenary of the birth of Abraham Lincoln; program of exercises. [2d ed.] '09 (F13) c. il. 8°. (Add. author for price.) O. H. Oldroyd.

Oldys, H:
Pheasant raising in the United States; with a chapter on diseases of pheasants, by G: Byron Morse. '10(Je) 40 p. il. 8°, (U. S., Dept. of Agriculture, farmers' bull.) U. S., Supt of Docs.

Ole Mistis. Moore, J: T. 75 c. Winston.

O'Leary, Agnes Marie.
Beyond these voices. '09(N20) c. il. 12°, $1.25. B'way Pub.

Olin, C: H:
Phrenology; how to tell your own and your friend's character from the shape of the head. '10(D3) c. il. T. 50 c. Penn Pub. Co.

Olin, Mrs. Helen Remington.
Women of a state university; illustration of the working of co-education in the Middle West. '09(O16) c. D. **$1.50 net. Putnam.

Oliphant, S: Grant.
Clan of fire and forge; or, the ancient and honorable Smiths; popular disquisition upon the origin and history of this ubiquitous and sempiternal family and a philological account of the origin and meaning of the name and its variants in many lands. '10(Ag) c. 36 p. 8°, 60 c. S: G. Oliphant.

Olive branch in Ireland. O'Brien, W: $3.25 net. Macmillan.

Oliver, C: Alex.
Helps for leaders of teacher training classes using "Preparation for teaching." '10 (Jl2) c. S. pap., 10 c. Westminster.
Preparation for teaching [Sunday-school.] '09(Je19) c. il. maps, 12°, pap., 25 c. Westminster.

Oliver, Edn. Austin.
Holiday tales. '08(F1) D. 75 c. Yonkers Pub.

Oliver, F: Scott.
Alexander Hamilton; essay on American union. Popular ed. '09, [1910.] (F) por. 16°, *75 c. net; limp leath., *$1.25 net; Lib. ed., with pors. and map, 8°, *$2.50 net. Putnam.

Oliver, Rev. French Earl.
Cain's wife, and other addresses. '09(N) c. 253 p. 8°, $1.50. F. E. Oliver.

Oliver, G: A. S.
See Graham, Ja.

Oliver, G: Fletcher, ed.
Out of doors with God: [results of several camp meetings.] '08, [1909.] (Mr) c. 3-227 p. 12°, 50 c. Chr. Witness.

Oliver, G: W.
Plant culture; working hdbk. of every day practice, for all who grow flowering and ornamental plants in the garden and greenhouse. [2d ed.] '09(N) 308 p. il. 12°, $1.50. De La Mare.
Production of Easter lily bulbs in the U. S. '08(Ap18) il. 8°, (U. S. Dept. of Agriculture, Bureau of Plant Industry, bull.) pap., 15 c. U. S., Supt. of Docs.

Oliver, J:
Salvation of the little child. '09(Je) c. 96 p. 12°. (Add. author for price.) J: Oliver.

Oliver, Martha Capps-.
See Capps-Oliver, Martha.

Oliver, T:, M.D.
Diseases of occupation. '08(Ap4) 8°, (New lib. of medicine.) *$2.50 net. Dutton.

Oliveros de Castilla.
La historia de los nobles caualleros Oliueros de Castilla y artus dalgarbe. [facsim.] '02. [1909.] (N) 4°, $10. (200 copies.) Hispanic Soc.

Olivia L. Carew. Syrett, N. $1.50. Lane.

Ollivant, Alfr.
The gentleman: a romance of the sea. '08 (O17) c. D. **$1.50 net. Macmillan.

Olmstead, Albert Ten Eyck.
Western Asia in the days of Sargon of Assyria, B.C. 722-705. '08(My23) c. O. (Cornell studies in history and political science.) **$1.25 net. Holt.

Olmstead, Rev. W: Backus.
Hdbk. for Sunday-school workers; introd. by Rev. J. T. Logan. 2d ed., rev. '08 (Ja18) il. tabs., maps, D. 50 c. W: B. Rose.

—, **and Warner, Rev. D. S., eds.**
Arnold's practical Sabbath-school commentary on the International lessons, 1909. '08(O3); 1910. '09(O23) c. 8°, ea., *50 c. net. Revell.

Olmsted, Franklin H:
Father Crow and his crew: story for children. '08(N21) c. il. D. †$1. B. W. Dodge.

Olmsted, F: Law.
See Arnold, Bion Jos.

—, **Kelsey, Harlan Page, and others.**
Smoke nuisance. '08, [1909.] 32 p. il. 12°, (American Civic Association; Dept. of Nuisance publications.) pap., gratis. Am. Civic League.

Olmsted, Millicent.
Land of Never Was: adventures of Great-A, Little-A and Bouncing-B. '08(O3) c. il. O. $1. Jacobs.
Land of Really True; being the everyday life of Great-A, Little-A, and Bouncing-B; pictured by Elenore Plaisted Abbott and Helen Alden Knipe. '09, [1910.] (Ja) 187 p. il. 8°, †$1. Jacobs.

Olmsted, Stanley.
The emotionalist. '08(N14) c. D. †$1.50. Appleton.

Olney, L: Atwell.
Textile chemistry and dyeing. '09(My1) c. il. por. 8°, (American School of Correspondence pubs.) $3. Am. Sch. Corr.

Olsen, J: C:
Text-book of quantitative chemical analysis by gravimetric, electrolytic, volumetric and gasometric methods. 3d ed., rev. '08(D12) c. il. tabs., 8°, $4. Van Nostrand.

Olsen, Mahlon Ellsworth.
Out-of-doors; or, the open-air spirit in relation to modern life; with introd. by Jacob Riis. '10(Jl30) c. front. 12°, 60 c. Pacific Press.

Olsen, O. T.
International regulations of the fisheries on the high seas; from bulletin of the Bureau of Fisheries, volume XXVIII, 1908; proceedings of the Fourth International Fishery Congress: Washington, 1908. '10 (Mr) 8°, (United States, Bu. of Fisheries, bull.)

Olson, Ernest Wilhelm, ed.
History of the Swedes of Illinois. In 2 v. '09(F13) c. il. pors. 4°, *$20 net; mor., *$25 net. Engberg-H.

Olsson, Andrew.
Motor control as used in connection with turret turning and gun elevating (the Ward Leonard system). '09(O23) c. il. 12°, (U. S. Navy electrical ser.) 50 c. Van Nostrand.

Olympe de Cleves. *See* Dumas, Alexandre.

Olympic victory. Connolly, J. B. †$1.25. Scribner.

O'Mahony, Nora Tynan.
See Taggart, Marion Ames.

Oman, C: W: Chadwick.
Column and line in the Peninsular War. '10(Ag27) c. 8°, pap., 40 c. Oxford Univ.
History of the Peninsular war. v. 3, Sept., 1809-Dec., 1810: Oceana, Cadiz, Bussaco, Torres Vedras. '08(O3) il. maps, 8°, *$4.75 net. Oxford Univ.
—, ed. Hist. of England. In 7 v. v. 1, England before the Norman conquest; being a hist. of the Celtic, Roman and Anglo-Saxon periods down to the year A.D. 1066, by C: W: Chadwick Oman. '10(Je11) O. $3 net. Putnam.

Oman, J: Campbell.
Cults, customs and superstitions of India: rev. and enl. ed. of India life, religious and social. '09, [1910.] (F) c. 329 p. il. 8°, **$3.50 net. Jacobs.

Omar and the Rabbi: Fitzgerald's translation of the Rubáiyát of Omar Khayyám, and Browning's Rabbi Ben Ezra; arranged in dramatic form by F: Le Roy Sargent. '09(F20) c. S. pap., *25 c. net. Harvard Co-op.

Omar Khayyám.
Edward Fitzgerald's Rubáiyát of Omar Khayyám with a Persian text, a transliteration and a close prose and verse translation, by Eben Fs. Thompson. '08(F1) c. pors. 8°, $15; hf. bds., $5. (Priv. pr.) Commonwealth Press.

Omar Khayyám.—*Continued.*
Omar sonnets and the Lefra lyrics; ed. and tr. by Oliver Opp Dyke. '09(O) c. 88 p. 16°, hf. vel. bds., *$2 net. Gorham.
Rose garden of Omar Khayyám, founded on the Persian, by Eben Fs. Thompson. '10(Ap) c. 8+27 p. 8°, $3. E. F. Thompson.
Rubáiyát of Omar Khayyám; tr. by I: Dorman. '10(D31) c. D. $1 net. Badger.
Rubáiyát; tr. by E: Fitzgerald. '09(Jl) c. 105 p. 16°, bds., 60 c.; leath., $1.25. Barse & H.
Rubaiyat; tr. by E: Fitzgerald; quatrains tr. into prose by Justin Huntly McCarthy. '09(Je) 12°, (Wayside lib.) limp leath., $1. Brentano's.
Rubáiyát; tr. into English verse by E: Fitzgerald. '10(O1) D. $2.50 net, boxed; cf., $5 net, boxed. Caldwell.
Rubaiyat of Omar Khayyam; [tr. into Gaelic by J: J. Carroll, and in English by E: Fitzgerald.] [1910.] (Je) 35 p. 12°, pap., 50 c. J: J. Carroll.
Rubáiyát; presented by Willy Pogany. [Fitzgerald centenary ed.] '09(O16) il. Q. $5; illuminated sides, $5; ooze cf., *$10 net, boxed. Crowell.
Rubáiyát; rendered into English by E: Fitzgerald. '09(D18) il. 4°, $5. Doran.
Rubáiyát of Omar Khayyám; tr. by E: Fitzgerald. '08(Ag15) 16°, (English masterpieces ser.) 50 c.; pap., 25 c. Dutton.
Rubaiyat; [tr.] by E: Fitzgerald; (authors' final revision;) with the literal Omar; being a version of those quatrains of the orig. upon which Fitzgerald's poem was based; ed. by Arthur Guiterman. '09 (D18) il. 8°, Naishapur ed., Oriental bds., *$1.50 net, boxed; Tentmaker's ed., flex. Italian bds., *$3 net; Wilderness ed., Persian lamb, *$2 net, boxed. P. Elder.
Rubáiyát; tr. by E: Fitzgerald; introd. by Jos Jacobs. '09(O9) front. 12°, *$1.50 net. Lippincott.
Rubáiyát; [tr. by] E: FitzGerald; with an introd. by Wallace Rice. '09(O16) c. S. bds., *50 c. net. McClurg.
Rubáiyát; tr. into English verse by E: Fitzgerald; with introd. by A. C. Benson; reproduced from a manuscript written and illuminated by F. Sangorski and G. Sutcliffe. '10(O15) f°, $6 net, boxed; 2500 copies large paper ed., 100 copies vellum, $12 net, boxed. McKay.
Rubáiyát; tr. by E: FitzGerald; ed., with introd. and notes, by Reynold Alleyne Nicholson. '09(O30) il. in col. O. $2.50, boxed. Macmillan.
Rubáiyát. '08(D) c. various paging, 8°. (Add. pubs. for price.) Roycrofters.

OMAR KHAYYAM.
Hazeldine, N. F. W. Sufism of the Rubáiyát. $1. N. F. W. Hazeldine.

Omar repentant. Le Gallienne, R: *75 c. net. M. Kennerley.

Omond, G: W: Thomson.
Belgium. '08(S19) il. sq. 8°, (Color books.) *$6 net. Macmillan.
Belgium. '09(S18) map, 12°, (Peeps at many lands ser.) *75 c. net. Macmillan.
Liège and the Ardennes. '08(Jl11) 12°, (Color books.) *$3 net. Macmillan.
Omoo. Melville, H. *35 c. net; *70 c. net. Dutton.
On a margin. Chambers, J. $1.50. M. Kennerley.
On Aaron's neck. Smith, W: C. 25 c. W: C. Smith.
On anything. Belloc, J. H. P. $1.25 net. Dutton.
On Christmas day in the evening. Richmond, *Mrs.* G. L. S. 50 c., fixed. Doubleday, P.
On Christmas day in the morning. Richmond, *Mrs.* G. L. S. **75 c. net. Doubleday, P.
On diseases of children. Koplik, H: $5 net. Lea.
On everything. Belloc, J. H. P. $1.25 net. Dutton.
On fads and feeding. Read, C. S. *$1 net. Dutton.
On holy ground. Worcester, W: L. 2 v. ea., **$1.50 net. Lippincott.
On nothing and kindred subjects. Belloc, J. H. P. *$1.25 net. Dutton.
On our way to the Orient. Morgan, A. T. 25 c. Denver Int. Corr. Sch.
On Plymouth Rock. Riley, A. C. D. 60 c. C. F. Summy Co.
On retreats. Liguori, *St.* A. *6 c. net. Herder.
On safari. Chapman, A. *$4.50 net. Longmans.
On self-culture. Blackie, J: S. 75 c. Funk.
On "short sales" of securities. Norton, E. *$1 net. J: McBride.
On the branch. Favre de Coulevain, *Mlle.* $1.25. Dutton.
On the calculation of thermo-chemical constants. Redgrove, H. S. *$1.70 net. Longmans.
On the canal zone. Grier, T: G. $1. Wagner & H.
On the grammar of rowing. Warre, E. 85 c. Oxford Univ.
On the gridiron and other stories of outdoor sport by Jesse Lynch Williams, S. Scoville, jr., J. Conover, W. J. Henderson and Paul Hull. '09(O9) c. il. D. (Harper's athletic ser.) †60 c. Harper.
On the heights. Ibsen, H. 25 c. Univ. Extension Dept.
On the heights. Larson, C. D. 50 c. Progress Co.
On the history of the ballads. Ker, W: P. 4 v. 60 c. Oxford Univ.
On the knees of the gods. Dodd, *Mrs.* A. B. B. †$1.50. Dodd.
On the light-ship. Vielé, H. K. **$1.50 net. Duffield.
On the Mexican highlands. Edwards, W. S. $1.50. Jennings.
On the nature of things. Lucretius, C. T. *$1.50 net Macmillan.
On the old "Kearsarge." Brady, C. T. **$1.35 net. Scribner.
On the open road. Trine, R. W. **50 c. net. Crowell.
On the Pacific with our navy. '08(My9) c. il. 4°, pap., 25 c.; Atlantic coast, pap., 10 c. L. H. Nelson.
On the rate of formation of carbon monoxide in gas producers. Clement, J. K. (Add. Univ. for price.) Univ. of Ill.
On the road to Arden. Morse, M. F. **$1 net. Houghton M.
"On the rock." Guiness, H: G. *$1 net. Revell.
On the school team. Earl, J: P. †$1.25. Penn Pub. Co.
On the Spanish Main. Strang, H. †$1.50. Bobbs-M.
On the stature of the Indians. Hrdlicka, A. 50 c. Torch Press.
On the study of Celtic literature. Arnold, M. 35 c. net; 70 c. net. Dutton.
On the threshold. Munger, T. T. $1. Houghton M.
On the tracks of life. Sera, L. G. *$2.50 net. Lane.
On the trail of Washington. Hill, F: T. **$1.50 net. Appleton.
On the training of parents. Abbott, E. H. **$1 net. Houghton M.
On the weight of developing eggs. Ritter, W: E. 10 c. Univ. of Cal.
On the witness stand. Münsterberg, H. **$2.50 net. McClure.
On the wool track. Bean, C. E. W. $1.50 net. Lane.
On track and diamond. '09(Ap10) c. il. D. (Harper's athletic ser.) 60 c. Harper.
On trail and rapid. Cody, H. A. $1 net. Lippincott.
On trial for his life. Harper, O. 25 c. J. S. Ogilvie.
Onar. Osborn, E. F. $1.50. Sylvan Press.
Once. Mätter, J: $1.20 net. Holt.
Once aboard the lugger. Hutchinson, A. S. M. $1.50. M. Kennerley.
Once upon a time. Davis, R: H. $1.50. Scribner.
Once upon a time. Holliday, C. 75 c. B'way Pub.
ONCKEN, Johann Gerhard.
Cooke, J: H. Johann Gerhard Oncken: his life and work. **50 c. net. Am. Bapt.
Onderdonk, Elmer, comp.
Genealogy of the Onderdonk family in America; with revisions, addenda and appendix. '10(My) 374 p. il. 8°, $6. A. J. Onderdonk.
ONDERDONK FAMILY.
See Genealogies.
One and all reciter. Steele, M., *comp.* *$1 net. Lane.
One and I. Freemantle, E. †$1.50. Jacobs.
One braver thing. Dehan, R: $1.40. Duffield.
One Christmas eve at Roxbury Crossing. Wallace, C. 75 c. Pustet.
One day: sequel to Three weeks. '09(Jl) c. 301 p. front. D. $1.50. Macaulay.
One day and another. Lucas, E: V. *$1.25 net. Macmillan.

One fair daughter. Ladd, F. P. $1.50. M. Kennerley.
One family ser. *See* Lefferts, Sara Tawney.
One for Wod and one for Lok. Cartwright, T: 50 c. Dutton.
150 years of unparalleled thrift. White, E:, *ed.* 25 c. E: White.
One hundred and one entrees. Southworth, M. E., *comp.* **$1 net; **$2 net; **50 c. net. P. Elder.
101 epicurean thrills ser. *See* Southworth, May E.
One hundred and one layer cakes. Southworth, M. E., *comp.* **$1 net; **$2 net; **50 c. net. P. Elder.
One hundred choice selections. Shoemaker, J. W. 30 c. Penn Pub. Co.
One hundred country houses. Embury, A., 2d. **$3 net. Century Co.
One hundred lessons in elementary agriculture. Nolan, A. W. 65 c. Acme.
One hundred masterpieces of painting; with introd. by R. C. Witt. '10(D3) O. $4 net. Lane.
One hundred masterpieces of sculpture. Hill, G. F. $4 net. Lane.
One hundred popular pictures. In 25 portfolios. '10(D31) 4°, $4 net. Cassell.
One hundred responsive readings from the Scriptures. Aked, C: F., *comp.* *75 c. net. Revell.
100 stories in black. Smith, B. 25 c. J. S. Ogilvie.
$100,000 per year from poultry. Boyer, M. K. 25 c. W. Atkinson.
One hundred useful things. Masters, E. T. *75 c. net. Cassell.
One hundred years of masonry in the Oranges. Davis, G: H. $2. Chronicle Pub.
One hundred years of Mormonism. Evans, J: H: $1.25. Deseret S. S. Un.
One hundred years of New Hampshire surgery. Blaisdell, F. (Add. author for price.) F. Blaisdell.
One immortality. Hall, H: F. †$1.50. Macmillan.
One Irish summer. Curtis, W: E. **$3.50 net. Duffield.
One little girl. Middleton, C. S. 60 c. Aberdeen.
One man. Aldrich, *Mrs.* F. L. S. $1.25. Roxburgh.
One man power, plus. Phelps, G: O. $1. Roxburgh.
One night in Bethlehem. Dawson, W: J. 75 c. Doran.
One of our conquerors. *See* Meredith, G:
"One of the Craft," pseud.
See Schofield, R. J.
One of the gray-jackets. McCants, E. C. $1. State Co.
One session a day, or two in the public schools? Burnham, W: H: 10 c. Bassette.
"1001" questions and answers on Philippine history. Jernegan, P. F. (Add. pub. for price.) Philippine Educ.
One thousand common French words. Blanchaud, R. de, *comp. and ed.* *25 c. net. Crowell.
One thousand questions. Wheeler, H: 75 c. Eaton & M.
One thousand salads. Reed, M. **$1 net. Putnam.
One thousand ways to make money. Fox, P. 50 c. B'way Pub.
One who saw. Grainger, F. E. 50 c. B. W. Dodge.
One woman's work for farm women. Buell, J. 50 c.; 25 c. Whitcomb.
One year course in English and American literature. Heydrick, B: A. $1. Hinds.
One year of Sunday school lessons. Palmer, F. U. *$1.25 net. Macmillan.

Oneal, Ja.
Workers in American history. '10(Ag27) c. 12°, 25 c. J. Oneal.

ONEIDA COUNTY, New York.
Canfield, W. W., *and* Clark, J. E. Things worth knowing about Oneida county. *$1 net. T: J. Griffiths.
Century Map Co. New century atlas, Oneida county, N. Y. $16.50; $25. Century Map.

ONEIDA INDIANS.
See Indians.

O'Neil, Arth. W:
Travelling school of seven abroad. '10 (O15) il. 12°, $1.50. C. M. Clark.

O'Neil, Rob. Kingsley, and Estes, Gustavus Kendall.
Naturalization made easy, what to do and what to know; book of instruction for aliens wishing to become citizens of the United States. 2d ed. '10(Ap) c. 111 p. 16°, 50 c. Carlisle.
Naturalization made easy: a book of instruction for aliens wishing to become citizens of the U. S. '08(Ag8) c. 16°, pap., $1. R. K. O'Neil.

O'Neill, Anna Theodora Lee, comp.
Recitations for assembly and class-room. '09(Je5) c. D. **$1.10 net. Macmillan.

O'Neill, D. J. Scannell, comp.
Life's little day; book of seriousness from Catholic sources. '10(Mr26) T 25 c. Soc. Divine World.

O'Neill, Rev. Felix J.
Does Christ say go to church? '09(My) 14 p. 16°, pap., 5 c. F. J. O'Neill.

O'Neill, Fs.
Irish folk music; fascinating hobby, with some acct. of allied subjects, incl. O'Farrell's treatise on the Irish or union pipes and Touhey's hints to amateur pipers. '10 (D17) il. por. $2. Lyon & H.; McClurg; Regan.

O'Neill, Rose Cecil, [Mrs. H. L. Wilson.]
Lady in the white veil. '09(My22) c. il. D. †$1.50. Harper.

O'NEILL, *Captain* William Owen.
Hartmann, H: A. G: Tales of Aztlan: romance of a hero of our late Spanish-American war. $1. B'way Pub.

Oneness with God. Cady, E. H. 15 c. Roger Bros.
Onesimus, the runaway slave. Brumbaugh, H: B. 75 c. Brethren Pub. Ho.

ONIONS.
Beattie, W: R. Onion culture. (Add. Superintendent for price.) U. S., Supt. of Docs.

Onken, W: H:, jr., and Baker, Jos. Black.
Harper's how to understand electrical work; with a dictionary of electrical terms prepared by Jos. H. Adams. '08(N21) c. il. D. (Harper's practical books for boys.) $1.75. Harper.

Only a boy. Johnson, *Mrs.* A. L. (Not for sale.) A. L. Johnson.

Only a dog. Lyman, M. B. 25 c. Am. Humane.

Only a farm boy. Webster. F. V. 35 c. Cupples & L.

Only a mask? Schaad, J. A. 25 c. J. A. Schaad.

Only Betty. Yorke, C., *pseud.* $1.50. Estes.

Onodi, A.
Optic nerve and the accessory sinuses of the nose; contribution to canalicular neuritis and atrophy of the optic nerve of nasal origin; auth. tr. by J. Lückhoff. '10 (Ap) c. il. 8°, $3.50 net. Wood.

Onomatopoeia: [poems.] Henderson, J. M. 50 c. Enterprise Pub.

Ontario, Canada. Drainage acts: annotation of the Municipal drainage act, R. S. O. 1897, C. 26, and of the Ditches and watercourses act, R. S. O. 1897, C. 285, and amending acts. '09(Ja23) O. ¾ leath., $5. A. Poole.

Opal. Hoover, B. R. $1.20 net. Harper.

Opal fire. Praed, R. C. M.-P. $1.20 net. Cassell.

Open air. Jeffries, R: *$1.50 net. Lippincott.

Open-air or sanatorium treatment of pulmonary tuberculosis. Walters, F. R. *$2.25 net. Wood.

Open air schools. Ayres, L. P. $1.20 net. Doubleday, P.

Open air treatment of pulmonary tuberculosis. Burton-Fanning, F. W. *$1.50 net. Hoeber.

Open country. Hewlett, M. H: †$1.50. Scribner.

Open Court Publishing Co., Chicago. Work of the Open Court Publishing Co.; illustrated catalogue of its publications covering a period of 21 years, (1887-1907,) consisting of a complete book list, with brief characterization of authors and contents, incl. also a selection of noteworthy articles from the *Monist* and the *Open Court;* with complete index of subjects systematically arranged, and alphabetical reference index. '09(Ag) 208 p. il. pors. 8.° (Add. pubs. for price.) Open Court.

Open door. Wolcott, E. A. $1.25 net. Dodd.

Open door of the soul. Morrison, D. $1. C M. Clark.

OPEN-HEARTH PROCESS.
See Furnaces.

Open house. Tompkins, J. W. †$1.50. Baker & T.

Open letter to His Eminence, Cardinal Gibbons. Sabatier, P. *60 c. net. Sherman, F.

Open road. Woodman, H. R. $1.25 net. H. R. Woodman.

Open road lib. of juvenile literature. See Lansing, Marion Florence.

OPEN SHOP.
See **Trade-unions.**

Open water. Connolly, J. B. $1.20 net. Scribner.

Open window. Wright, *Mrs.* M. O. †$1.50. Macmillan.

Opening exercises for public schools in North Carolina. Barwick, A. J. gratis. N. C., Dept. of Pub. Instruct.

Opening of Indian reservations. United States. *Dept. of the Interior. General Land Office.* (Add. Superintendent for price.) U. S., Supt. of Docs.

OPERA.
Annesley, C:, *pseud.* Standard opera glass. $1.50 net; $2.50 net. Brentano's.
Davidson, G. Stories from the operas. *$1.25 net. Lippincott.
Gilbert, *Sir* W: S. Savoy operas. 1st and 2d ser. ea., $5 net. Macmillan.
Gilman, L. Aspects of modern opera. **$1.25 net. Lane.
Hadden, J. C. Favorite operas from Mozart to Mascagni. $2.25. Stokes.
Jenkins, F., *and others.* Dolls and toy balloons: musical comedy. $1. B'way Pub.
Krehbiel, H: E: Book of operas. **$1.75 net. Macmillan.
Krehbiel, H: E: Chapters of opera. **$3.50 net. Holt.
Krehbiel, H: E:, *ed.* Songs from the operas for alto.—Songs from the operas for mezzo soprano.—Songs from the operas for soprano.—Songs from the operas for tenor. ea., $2.50; $1.50. Ditson.
Law, F. S. Operatic tales. $1.50. Hatch.
Lee, E. M. Story of opera. $1.25 net. Scribner.
Melitz, L. L. Opera goer's complete guide. **$1.20 net. Dodd.
Prendergast, J: Great operas told for children. $1.50. Stokes.
Reynolds, R. G: King of U-Kan. $1.50. R. G: Reynolds.
Riley, A. C. D., *and* Gaynor, J. L. On Plymouth rock: operetta. 60 c. C. F. Summy Co.
Singleton, E. Guide to modern opera. **$1.50 net. Dodd.
Sonneck, O. G: T., *comp.* Library of Congress dramatic music catalogue of full scores. 40 c. U. S., Supt. of Docs.
Towers, J:, *comp.* Dictionary-catalogue of operas and operettas which have been performed on the public stage. $25. Acme.
Zell, F., *and* Genée, F. F. R. Boccaccio: comic opera; [with music.] $2. Ditson.
See also Boston Opera House;—Electra;—Nibelungen ring;—Songs;—*also* Eugene Onégin;—Wagner, Wilhelm Richard.

Operation of trains and station work. Prior, F: J:, *comp.* $1.50. Drake.

OPERATIONS.
See Nurses and nursing;—Surgery;—Teeth.

Operations of the other mind. Edgerly. W. $25. Ralston Univ.

Operative midwifery. Kerr, J. M. M. *$6 net. Wood.

Operative nursing and technique Childe. C: P. *$2 net. Wood.

Operator's wireless telegraph and wireless telephone handbook. Laughter, V. H. $1. **Drake.**

OPHIURANS.
See Echinoderms.

Ophthalmic and cutaneous diagnosis of tuberculosis. Wolf-Eisner, A. *$2.75 net. Wood.

Ophthalmic surgery. Meller, J. *$3 net. Blakiston.

OPHTHALMOLOGY.
See Eye.

OPHTHALMOSCOPY.
See Eye.

Opie, Eug. Lindsay.
Disease of the pancreas, its cause and nature. 2d ed., rewritten. '10(N) 12+387 p. il. 8°, $3. Lippincott.

Opinion journalistic. Trouvillon, H. W. gratis. H. W. Trouvillon.

OPISTHOBRANCHIATA.
See Mollusks.

Opisthophorus; or, the man who walked backwards. Jones, C. $1.25. Conkey.

Opitz, Heinrich.
Sodality of Our Lady: under the banner of Mary; tr. by a sodalist of Our Lady; ed. by Father Elder Mullen. '09(Mr) c. 206 p. 16°, 25 c. Kenedy.

OPIUM.
International Opium Commission. Opium problem; message from the President of the United States, transmitting from the Secretary of State a rept. on the International Opium Commission and on the opium problem as seen within the United States and its possessions; prep. by Hamilton Wright on behalf of the American delegates to the said commission, held at Shanghai in Feb., 1909. '10(Ap) 83 p. 8°, pap. Gov. Pr. Off.
Merwin, S: Drugging a nation: story of China and the opium curse. *$1 net. Revell.

Opium smugglers of 'Frisco. Harper, O. 25 c. J. S. Ogilvie.

Opp, Fs., pseud.
See Oppenheimer, Fs. J.

Opp-Dyke, Oliver.
Lure of life; lyrics of the "zeitgeist." '10 (D17) c. D. bds., $1 net. Sherman, F.
Unfathomable sorrow; sonnet sequence from The Passion and other scriptural sonnets. '10(Ap2) c. S. $1 net. Revell.

Oppenheim, E: Phillips.
As man lives; or, the mystery of the yellow house. '08(D19) c. il. 12°, †$1.50. Little, B. & Co.
The avenger. '08(My16) c. D. †$1.50 Little, B. & Co.
Daughter of the Marionis. New ed. '10 (S24) il. D. $1.50. Little, B. & Co.
The governors. '09(Je12) c. il. D. †$1.50. Little, B. & Co.
Great secret. '08(Ja18) il. D. †$1.50. Little, B. & Co.
Illustrious prince. '10(My14) c. il. D. $1.50. Little, B. & Co.
Jeanne of the marshes. '09(N13) c. il. D. †$1.50. Little, B. & Co.
Long arm of Mannister. '08(O17) c. il. D. †$1.50. Little, B. & Co.
Lost ambassador; or, the search for the missing Delora. '10(O1) c. col. il. O. $1.50. Little, B. & Co.

Oppenheim, E: Phillips.—*Continued.*
The missioner. '09(Ja16) c. il. D. †$1.50. Little, B. & Co.
Monk of Cruta. '09(Ap) 340 p. 12°, 75 c. J. S. Ogilvie.
Mystery of Mr. Bernard Brown. New ed. '10(S24) il. D. $1.50. Little, B. & Co.
Peer and the woman. [Popular ed.] '08 (F15) c. D. 75 c. Fenno.
Peer and the woman. '09(Ap) 260 p. 12°, 75 c. J. S. Ogilvie.
Yellow house. '08(D5) c. 12°, 50 c. Doscher.

Oppenheim, Ja.
Doctor Rast. '09(O9) c. D. $1.50. Sturgis & W.
Monday morning and other poems. '09 (D25) c. S. *$1.25 net. Sturgis & W.
The pioneers; poetic drama in two scenes. '10(D10) c. D. bds., 50 c. net. B: W. Huebsch.
Wild oats; with a foreword by E: Bok. '10(Jl30) c. D. $1.20 net. B: W. Huebsch.
See also Viereck, G: Sylvester.

Oppenheim, Lassa.
International incidents for discussion in conversation classes. '09, [1910.] (F) 5-11+129 p. 12°, *$1 net. Putnam.

Oppenheim, S:
Early hist. of the Jews in New York, 1654-1664; some new matter on the subject. '10(O1) c. O. pap., $1. S: Oppenheim.
Jews and masonry in the United States before 1810. '10(D24) c. O. pap., 50 c. S: Oppenheim.

Oppenheimer, Fs. J., ["Francis Opp."]
Reign of the negative; studies in mysticism and skepticism; with introd. by Edn. Markham. '10(Ap30) c. 16°, hf. leath., $2 net. Moods.

Opper, F: Burr.
Handy Happy Hooligan. '08(Ag8) c. il. obl. Q. (Stokes' comic juveniles.) bds., 60 c. Stokes.
Maud the mirthful mule. '08(Ag8) c. il. obl. Q. (Stokes' comic juveniles.) bds., 60 c. Stokes.

OPSONIC TREATMENT.
See Vaccination.

"Optic, Oliver," pseud.
See Adams, W: Taylor.

OPTICAL INSTRUMENTS.
See Eye.

Optical instruments simply explained. '10 (D) 12°, pap., 25 c. Spon.

OPTICS.
King, A. S. Correspondence between Zeeman effect and pressure displacement for the spectra of iron, chromium and titanium.—Zeeman effect for titanium. Carnegie.
Morse, L. B. Selective reflection of salts of carbonic and other oxygen acids. (Add. pubs for price.) Astrophysical.
Whittaker, E. T. Theory of optical instruments. *25 c. net. Putnam.
See also Eye;—Light;—Stereoscope.

OPTIMISM.
Fletcher, H. Optimism, a real remedy. 75 c. McClurg.
Ludlow, J. M. Judge West's opinion: [optimistic views of life.] *$1 net. Revell.

OPTIMISM.—*Continued.*
Skinner, C: R., *comp.* Bright side; little excursions into the field of optimism. 50 c. Beattys.
Optimistic voices. Hoffman, O. S., *ed.* *35 c. net. O. S. Hoffman.
Optimist's good night. Perin, F. P., *comp.* $1 net. Little, B. & Co.
Optimos. Traubel, H. $1.50 net. B: W. Huebsch.
Optimus, Gertrude D.
Yankee Doodle book for young Americans. '10(D3) c. col. il. Q. 75 c. J. B. Best.
Options. Henry, O., *pseud.* †$1.50. Harper.
Opvs epistolarum des Erasmi Roterdami. *See* Erasmus, Desiderius.
Orage, Alfr. R:
Nietzsche in outline and aphorism. '10 (Mr5) O. bds., 75 c. McClurg.
Oraisons funèbres. Bossuet, J. B. *$1 net. Putnam.

ORAL ARITHMETIC.
See Arithmetic.
Oram, H: J.
See Sennett, R:
Oram of the forest. Staley, B. E. $1. Tower.
ORANGE, N. J.
See Freemasonry.
ORANGE COUNTY, N. Y.
Headley, R., *ed.* History of Orange County, New York. $15. Van Deusen & E.
ORANGES.
Canada, J: W: How to plant and cultivate an orange orchard. 50 c. J: W: Canada.
Powell, G: H. Decay of oranges while in transit from California. 15 c. U. S., Supt. of Docs.
See also Cookery.
ORANGIA, South Africa.
Johnson, J. P. Geological and archæological notes on Orangia. $3 net. Longmans.
Orationes et epistolae Cantabrigienses. Sandys, J: E. $3 net. Macmillan.
Orations of American orators; incl. biographical and critical sketches [of S: Adams, Washington, Jefferson, Webster, Sumner, H: Ward Beecher and others.] '08(Je27) c. 2 v., il. 8°, $3.50; hf. mor., $7. Lamb Pub.
Orations of British orators: incl. biographical and critical sketches [of Latimer, J: Knox, Cromwell, J: Bunyan, Burke, Erskine, Rob. Emmet, W: Pitt, J: Bright and others.] '08(Je27) c. 2 v., il. 8°, $3.50; hf. mor., $7. Lamb Pub.
Oratorio Society, New York. Historical sketch of thirty-seven seasons of the Oratorio Society of New York, 1873-1874, 1908-1909. '10(Mr5) tab. O. pap., 50 c. Oratorio Soc.

ORATORS AND ORATORY.
Beveridge, A. J. Meaning of the times, and other speeches. **$1.50 net. Bobbs-M.
Brewer, D: J., *and others, eds.* Crowned masterpieces of eloquence that have advanced civilization. 10 v. (Add. pubs. for price.) Kaiser.
Bryan, W: J. Real Bryan: being extracts from the speeches and writings of "a well-rounded man." $1.25. Personal Help.

ORATORS AND ORATORY.—*Continued.*
Cheney, J: V., *comp.* Memorable American speeches. v. 1. *$1.50 net. Reilly & B.
Daggy, M. L. Principles of public speaking. $1.50. M. L. Daggy.
Denney, J. V., *ed.* American public addresses. $1. Scott, F. & Co.
Erasmus, D. Ciceronianus; or, a dialogue on the best style of speaking. $1. Teachers' Coll.
Fiske, J: Unpublished orations: "The discovery of the Columbia River, and the Whitman controversy; "The Crispus Attucks memorial," and "Columbus memorial." (Priv. pr.) Bibliophile.
Fowler, C: H: Patriotic orations. *$1.50 net. Eaton & M.
Fulton, R. I., *and* Trueblood, T: C. Essentials of public speaking. $1. Ginn.
Graves, J: T., *and others, eds.* Eloquent sons of the South; hdbk. of southern oratory. $2. Chapple Pub.
Harding, S: B., *comp. and ed.* Select orations illustrating American political history. **$1.25 net. Macmillan.
Howard, J: R., *comp. and ed.* Best American orations. 35 c. Crowell.
Hunt, S: F. Orations and historical addresses. **$2.50 net. Clarke.
Jebb, *Sir* R: C. Attic orators from Antiphon to Isaeus. 2 v. now *$5.50 net. Macmillan.
Jeffords, S. G., *ed.* Series of notable debates by men of the hour. 50 c. S. G. Jeffords
Lawrence, E. G. Power of speech and how to acquire it. $1.25. Hinds.
Lee, G. C., *and others, eds.* World's orations. In 10 v. ea., $1.50. Putnam.
McConnell, J. M., *ed.* Southern orators. 25 c. Macmillan.
MacMurray, A. Pract. lessons in public speaking. 75 c. A. MacMurray.
Merry, W: W. Orationes tum creweianae tum gratvlatoriae in Theatro Sheldoniano plervomqve habitae. $2. Oxford Univ.
Philips, A. E: Effective speaking. *$1.50 net. Newton Co.
Prather, C: E., *comp. and ed.* Winning orations of the inter-state oratorical contests. 2 v. v. 1, $1.25; v. 2, $1.75. Crane.
Schleininger, N. Principles of eloquence. *$2 net. Herder.
Seymour, C: Speaking in public. *$1.25 net. Dutton.
Shurter, E. Du B. Extempore speaking. $1. Ginn.
Shurter, E. Du B. Representative college orations. **$1.25 net.—Rhetoric of oratory. **$1.10 net. Macmillan.
Shurter, E. Du B., *ed.* American oratory of to-day. $1.65. South-West Pub.
Shurter, E. Du B., *ed.* Oratory of the South, from the Civil War to the present time. *$1.25 net. Neale.
Speer, R. E. How to speak effectively without notes. 10 c. Nat. Bible.
Taft, W: H. Present day problems: addresses. **$1.50 net. Dodd.

ORATORS AND ORATORY.—*Continued.*
Trinity College, Dublin. Speeches [in Latin.] of public orators delivered at the comitia held for conferring honorary degrees. $1.75. Longmans.
Trueblood, T: C., *and others, eds.* Winning speeches in the contests of the Northern Oratorical League. $1. Am. Bk.
West, E. E., *comp.* Famous modern orations. 35 c. Werner.
Young, B. H., *ed.* Kentucky eloquence, past and present. $5. B: La Bree.
See also Debating; — Elocution; — Lecturing; — Preaching;—Recitations; —Rhetoric;—Toasts;—*also* Leland Powers School, Boston.

Orbförster (Der). Ludwig, O. 35 c. net. Holt.

Orcagna, Andrea.
Masterpieces. '10(D17) 24°, (Painters' ser.) leath., 75 c net; pap., 25 c. net. Stokes.

Orchard, Harry, [alias for Albert E. Horsley.]
Confessions and autobiography. '08(F8) c. il. pors. D. **$1 net. McClure.

ORCHARD GRASS.
See Seed.

ORCHARDS.
See Apples;—Fruits.

ORCHESTRAL MUSIC.
Coerne, L: A. Evolution of modern orchestration. *$3 net. Macmillan.
Mason, D. G. Orchestral instruments and what they do. **$1.25 net. Baker & T.
Schlesinger, K. Instruments of the modern orchestra. 2 v. $6 net. Scribner.

ORCHIDACEAE.
See Botany.

ORCHIDS.
Curtis, C: H. Orchids for every one. $6 net. Dutton.

Orcutt, Emma Louise.
Divine seal. '10(Ja1) c. il. D. $1.50. C. M. Clark.

Orcutt, W: Dana.
The spell. '09(Ja30) c. il. D. †$1.50. Harper.

Orcutt girls. Vaile, *Mrs.* C. M. †$1.50. Wilde.

Orczy, Emma Magdalena Rosalia Maria Josefa Barbara, Baroness, [Mrs. Montagu Barstow.]
Elusive pimpernel. '08(D5) c. D. †$1.50. Dodd.
Emperor's candlesticks. '08(D) c. 7-283 p. 12°, 50 c. Doscher.
In Mary's reign. '08(Ap4) c. il. D. 75 c. Cupples & L.
Man in the corner. '09(O9) c. il. D. †$1.50. Dodd.
Nest of the Sparrowhawk; romance of the XVIIth century. '09(N20) c. D. †$1.50. Stokes.
Petticoat rule. '10(S3) c. D. $1.20 net. Doran.

Ordahl, G:
College curricula: study of required and elective courses in American colleges and universities. [1910.] (Jl) gratis. Univ. of Nev.

Order of salvation. Richter, A. 20 c. E. Kaufmann.

Order of the Eastern Star. Auth. standard ritual of the Order of Eastern Star in the state of New York; system of forms and ceremonies, with necessary instructions for chapters, as rev. by a committee. [15th ed.] '10(Jl) c. 5-235 p. il. 16°, 75 c. Order Eastern Star.

ORDER OF THE GARTER.
Payne-Gallwey, *Sir* R. W: History of the George worn on the scaffold by Charles I. $2.50. Longmans.

Orders and unity. Gore, C: *$1.35 net. Dutton.

ORDERS OF KNIGHTHOOD AND CHIVALRY.
Gore, J. H., *comp.* American members of foreign orders. $2. W. F. Roberts.

ORDNANCE.
See Artillery.

ORE.
See Metals and metallurgy.

Ore mining methods. Crane, W. R: $3 net. Wiley.

Oregon. Mining laws; cont. a synopsis of all the Oregon mining laws and a digest of all the federal statutes pertaining to the mining industry, [etc.] 3d ed. '08(Jl) c. 60 p. D. pap., 40 c. A. Conklin.

Oregon. *Supreme ct.* Repts.; (Rob. G. Morrow.) v. 48, 49. '08(S) c. O. shp., ea., $5. J. R. Whitney.

OREGON.
Brandeis, L: D., *and* Goldmark, J. Women in industry: decision of U. S. Sup. Ct. in Curt Muller vs. State of Oregon, upholding the constutionality of the ten hour law for women. gratis. L: D. Brandeis.
Brereton, R. M. Question: Did Sir Francis Drake land on any part of the Oregon coast? 25 c. Gill.
Chapman, C: H. Story of Oregon and its people. 60 c. O. P. Barnes.
Fiske, J: Unpublished orations: "The discovery of the Columbia River, and the Whitman controversy;" "The Crispus Attucks memorial," and "Columbus memorial." (Priv. pr.) Bibliophile.
Gaines, F. W. Oregon and her politicians vs. honest politics. 25 c. F. W. Gaines.
Goulder, W: A. Reminiscences: incidents in the life of a pioneer in Oregon and Idaho. $3. T. Regan.
Hunter, B. Clover seed production in the Willamette Valley, Ore. (Add. Superintendent for price.) U. S., Supt. of Docs.
Lewis, J: H., *and* Cupper, P A. Irrigation in Oregon. 15 c. U. S., Supt. of Docs.
Parkman, F. Oregon trail. 25 c. net. Longmans.
Parkman, F. Oregon trail. **25 c. net. Macmillan.
Parkman, F. Oregon trail. 40 c. Newson.
Schafer, J. Acquisition of Oregon territory. pt. I. gratis. Univ. of Ore.
Shaw, W: T. China or Denny pheasant in Oregon. *$1.50 net. Lippincott.
Waring, G. A. Geology and water resources of the Harney Basin region, Oregon. (Add. Superintendent for price.) U. S., Supt. of Docs.

OREGON.—*Continued.*
Watson, C. B. Prehistoric Siskiyou Island and marble halls of Oregon. (Priv. pr.) C. B. Watson.
See also Columbia river.

O'Reilly, Eliz. Boyle.
Heroic Spain. '10(N19) c. il. pors. O. $2.50 net. Duffield.

O'REILLY, John Boyle.
Roche, J. J. Life of John Boyle O'Reilly. *$2 net. McVey.

O'Reilly, Jos. J: E:
How to become a fireman. 4th ed. '09 (Ap3) c. il. S. 75 c. Chief.
How to become a patrolman: [New York City.] 4th ed. '08(O) c. 149 p. 16°, 50 c. Chief.
—, comp. Marriage law and church regulations. '08(Ag) c. 23 p. O. pap., 50 c. Chief.

O'Reilly, Michael Fs., [Brother Potamian,] and Walsh, Ja. Jos., M.D.
Makers of electricity. '09(O2) c. O. (Fordham Univ. Press ser.) *$2 net. Fordham Univ.

Orelli, Hans Conrad von.
Peculiarity of the religion of the Bible. '08(Mr14) c. S. (Foreign religious ser.) *40 c. net. Eaton & M.

Orem, Leonora.
Story of Julius Cæsar; ed. by W: Fs. Rocheleau. '09(D) c. 30 p. 8°, 5 c. O. Brewer.
Story of The tempest; ed. by W: Fs. Rocheleau. '10(Mr) c. 48 p. 8°, pap., 8 c. O. Brewer.

ORES.
See Coal;—Metals and metallurgy;—Mineralogy;—Mines and mining.

ORESME.
See Money.

Orestes. Le Gallienne, R: $1 net. M. Kennerley.

Orestes. *See* Leconte de Lisle, Charles Marie René.

Orgain, Kate Alma.
Southern authors in poetry and prose. '08 (S19) c. O. *$2 net. Neale.

ORGAN AND ORGANISTS.
Benjamin, W: H. Biographies of celebrated organists of America. subs., $25. W: H. Benjamin.
Demarest, C. Hints on organ accompaniment. 50 c. H. W. Gray.
Eddy, C. Twenty-five organ recital programmes. gratis. Schuberth.
Richardson, A. M. Modern organ accompaniment. $2.50. Longmans.
Stainer, *Sir* J: The organ; principles of playing. $1 net. Ditson.
Statham, H. H. Organ and its position in musical art. $2. Scribner.
See also Church music.

Organic and functional nervous diseases. Starr, M. A. *$6 net; *$7 net. Lea.

ORGANIC CHEMISTRY.
See Chemistry.

Organic history of English words. Morris, J: pt. 1. $1.25. Stechert.

ORGANIC SENSATION.
See Psychology.

Organismic theories of the state. Coker, F. W. $1.50. Longmans.

Organization among the farmers of the United States. Coulter, J: L. 10 c. Yale Pub.

Organization of certain *coenobic* plants. Harper, R. A. 40 c. Univ. of Wis.

Organization work, and publication of the Agricultural Education Service; corrected to Dec. 1, 1909. '10(Mr5) 8°, (U. S., Dept. of Agriculture, Office of Experiment Stations, circular.)

Organization, work, and publications of food and nutrition investigations. '09(D18) 8°, (U. S., Dept. of Agriculture, Office of Experiment Stations, circular.) pap., gratis. U. S., Supt. of Docs.

Organizations for boys. Gelston, W. L. 10 c. Presb. Bd.

Organized adult Bible class. Bryan, J. H. 50 c. Chr. Pub. Co.

Organized Christianity. Ketcham, K. P. 75 c. K. P. Ketcham.

Organized Sunday-school work in America, 1905-1908; official report of the 12th International Sunday-school Convention held at Louisville, June, 1908. '09(Mr) $1. Int. S. S. Assoc.

Organizing a shoe factory. Small, F. L. $5. Weekly Bulletin.

Organizing and building up the Sunday school. Hurlbut, J. L. 65 c. net. Eaton & M.

Organotherapy. Shaw, H. B. $1.75 net. Funk.

ORIBATOIDEA.
See Antelopes.

ORIENT (The).
Austin, H. H. Scamper through the Far East. $5. Longmans.
Gibson, C: C. In the golden East. *60 c. net. Little, B. & Co.
Hogarth, D: G: Ionia and the East. $1.15. Oxford Univ.
Lambuth, W. R. Side lights on the Orient. *75 c. net. Pub. Ho. of M. E. Ch., So.
Lewis, L. B. Pupils' notebook and study outline in Oriental and Greek history. 25 c. Am. Bk.
Literature of the Orient. 10 v. $20; $50. Lamb Pub.
Matthews, *Mrs.* F. E. M. Dreams of yesterdays (in the Orient.) $1. Cochrane.
Miller, C. H. Scent of sandal wood. $2.50. C. H. Miller.
Nichols, J. T: Lands of sacred story. $1.25. Chr. Un.
Paine, A. B. Ship dwellers. $1.50 net. Harper.
Rice, E. W. Orientalisms in Bible lands. $1 net. Am. S. S.
Rothfeld, O. Indian dust; studies of the Orient. *$1.50 net. Lane.
See also Armenia;—Mediterranean Sea;—Missions and missionaries;—Turkey.

Oriental campaigns. Maude, E. *$2.50 net. Wessels.

Oriental carpets, runners and rugs. Humphries, S. $10.50 net. Macmillan.

ORIENTAL LITERATURE.
See Fables.

ORIENTAL RELIGIONS.
Degroot, J. J. M. Religion of the Chinese. **$1.25 net. Macmillan.
Hall, C: C. Christ and the eastern soul. **$1.25 net. Univ. of Chic.
Müller, F: M., *ed.* Sacred books of the East. v. 1, pt. 1, $4.75; v. 3, pt. 1, $5; v. 4, pt. 1, $5.25; v. 6, pt. 1, $4. Oxford Univ.
Underwood, H. G. Religions of eastern Asia. **$1.50 net. Macmillan.
Wigam, W. A. Hist. of the Assyrian church, or the Church of the Sassanid Persian Empire. $2 net. Gorham.
Winternitz, M. Index to the names and subject matter of the sacred books of the East. $5.75. Oxford Univ.
See also Assyria;—Babylonia;—Buddha and Buddhism; — Hinduism; — Jews; — Mohammed and Mohammedans;—Semitic religion; — Shintoism; —Sikh religion;—Zoroaster.
Oriental rugs. Dilley, A. U. 50 c. Dilley.
Oriental rugs and carpets. 2d and enl. ed. '10(Mr5) c. il. map, 8°, $1.50. Review Pub.
Oriental tale in England. Conant, M. P. **$2 net. Lemcke.
ORIFICIAL SURGERY.
See Surgery
Origin and character of the Bible. Sunderland, J. T: *$1.20 net. Am. Unitarian.
Origin and deeds of the Goths. Jordanes. 50 c. C: C. Mierow.
Origin and development of the moral ideas. In 2 v. v. 2. Westermarck, E: *$3.50 net. Macmillan.
Origin and early development of the English universities. Vaugn, E. V. $1. Univ. of Mo.
Origin of land flora. Bower, F: O. *$5.50 net. Macmillan.
Origin of ore deposits. Ritter, E. A. 50 c. Mining Science.
Origin of terms in human relationship. Lang, A. 40 c. Oxford Univ.
Origin of the Easter festival. Kent, A. 25 c. C. E. Kent.
Origin of the moving school in Massachusetts. Updegraff, H. $1.50. Teachers' Coll.
Origin of the New Testament. Wrede, W: *75 c. net. Harper.
Origin of the Pentateuch. Wiener, H. M. 35 c. Bibliotheca Sacra.
Origin of the recent outbreak of foot-and-mouth disease. Mohler, J: R. 5 c. U. S., Supt. of Docs.
Origin of the "reorganized" church. Smith, J. F. 50 c. Deseret News.
Origin of the werewolf superstition. Stewart, C. T. 50 c. Univ. of Mo.
Origin of two new retrogressive varieties by one mutation in mice. Hagedoorn, A. L. (Add. pubs. for price.) Univ. of Cal.
Origin of vertebrates. Gaskell, W. H. *$6 net. Longmans.
Origin, structure and function of the polar caps in *smilacina amplexicaulis,* Nutt. Densmore, H. D. 35 c. Univ. of Cal.
Origin, the organization and the location of the staple of England. Jenckes, A. L. (Add. pubs. for price.) Univ. of Penn.
Original Garden of Eden. Woolsey, J: M. $1.50. J: M. Woolsey.
Original gentleman. Warner, A. †$1.50. Little, B. & Co.
Original narratives of early American history; ed. by J. Franklin Jameson. il. O. *$3 net. Scribner.
—Bradford. History of Plymouth plantation.
—Hall, *ed.* Narratives of early Maryland, 1633-1684.
—Jameson, *ed.* Narratives of New Netherland.
—Johnson. Wonder-working providence.
—Winthrop. Journal. 2 v.
Original portrait of Dr. Franklin. Hart, C: H: *$2.50 net. C: H: Hart.
Original religion of China. Ross, J: *$1.25 net. Eaton & M.
Original year. Jefferson, C: E: 50 c. net. Pilgrim Press.
Origines eucharisticæ. Alston, E. A. *35 c. net. Whittaker.
Origins and faith. Rickett, *Sir* J. C. *$1.50 net. Revell.
Origins of Christianity. Bigg, C: $4.15. Oxford Univ.
Origins of leadership. Mumford, E. *50 c. net. Univ. of Chic.
Origins of popular superstitions and customs. Knowlson, T: S. $1.75 net. Pott.
Origins of the British Colonial system. Beer, G: L: **$3 net. Macmillan.
ORINOCO RIVER, South America.
Mozans, H. J., *pseud.* Up the Orinoco and down the Magdalena. $3 net. Appleton.
ORLEANS, Elizabeth Charlotte, *Duchess* of.
Henderson, E. F. Lady of the old régime. **$2.50 net. Macmillan.
Vincens, C. Madame, mother of the Regent. **$3 net, boxed. Putnam.
Ormond, Frederic.
Three keys. '09(Je26) c. il. D. $1.50. W. J. Watt.
ORNAMENT.
See Decoration and ornament.
Ornamental concrete without molds. Houghton, A. A. $2. Henley.
Ornamental shrubs of the United States. Apgar, A. C. $1.50. Am. Bk.
Ornamental turning. Evans, J. H. $1. McKay.
Ornamental window glass work. Duthie, A. L. *$2 net. Van Nostrand.
ORNITHOLOGY.
See Birds.
O'Rourke, Stephen G.
See Harrington, W.
Orphan (The). *See* Mulford, C. E:—Otway, T:
ORPHANS.
Reeder, R. R. How two hundred children live and learn. $1.25. Charities Pub.
Orphant Annie book. *See* Riley, Ja. Whitcomb.
ORPHEUS.
Schuré, E. Orpheus and Krishna. *$1.25 net. Badger.
Sir Orfeo; adapted from the middle English. '10(F) c. 16°, 50 c. Harvard Co-op.
Orpheus. Reinach, S. **$3 net. Putnam.**
Orpheus. Vittum, W. H. $1.50 net. Badger.
Orpheus with his lute. Hutchinson, W. M. L. *$1.40 net. Longmans.

Orr, Alexandra Leighton, [Mrs. Sutherland Orr.]
Life and letters of Robert Browning. New ed., rev. and in part rewritten by Frederic G. Kenyon. '08(My2) pors. O. *$2 net. Houghton M.

Orr, C: Ebert.
Hidden life; or, walks with God. '08 (My16) c. 12°, 60 c. Gospel Trumpet Co.

Orr, Ja., D.D.
Faith of a modern Christian. '10(D) 12°, $1.50 net. Doran.
Resurrection of Jesus. '08(D19) O. *$1.50 net. Jennings.
Revelation and inspiration. '10(Mr26) D. (Studies in theology.) *75 c. net. Scribner.
Sidelights on Christian doctrine. '09(My1) O. *$1.50 net. Armstrong.
Sin as a problem of to-day. '10(D) $1.50 net. Doran.

Orrock, J: Wilson.
Railroad structures and estimates. '09 (My1) c. figs. 8°, **$3 net. Wiley.

ORSAY, *Comte* Alfred Guillaume Gabriel d'.
Shore, W: T. D'Orsay; or, the complete dandy. $3.50 net. Brentano's.

Orth, S: P:
Industrial education; address [del.] at the dedication of the Cleveland Technical High School, April 15th, 1909. [1910.] (Jl) 6 p. 8°, gratis. Technical High Sch.

ORTHODONTIA.
See Teeth.

Orthodoxy. Chesterton, G. K. **$1.50 net. Lane.

ORTHOËPY.
See Phonetics;—Pronunciation.

ORTHOGRAPHY.
See Spelling.

ORTHOPEDIA.
See Teeth.

ORTHOPEDICS.
See Surgery.

Orthwein, Edith Hall.
Love in the weaving. '10(Ag) front. $1.50. B'way Pub.
Songs of the beloved. '09(Ag) 90 p. front. 12°, $1.50; ooze, $2. Dodge.

Ortiz, Alonso.
Cvrioso tratado de tres romances nueuos a lo diuino. [facsim.] '03, [1909.] (N) no paging, 4°, $3.50. (200 copies.) Hispanic Soc.

Ortner, Norbert, M.D.
Treatment of internal diseases; ed. by Nathaniel Bowditch Potter, and tr. by F: H. Bartlett from the 4th German ed. '08 (Mr7) c. 8°, *$5 net. Lippincott.

Orton, C. W. Previté-.
See Previté-Orton, C. W.

Orton, G: W., ed.
Athletic training for school boys. '10(Jl2) c. il. por. 12°, (Spalding's athletic lib.) pap., 10 c. Am. Sports.

O'Ryan, W: Patrick.
Plough and the cross; story of new Ireland. '10(O) 378 p. il. 12°, $1. Aryan.

OSAGE INDIANS.
See Indians.

Osborn, Albert Sherman.
Questioned documents. '10(O) c. 501 p. il. O. $5.25. Lawyers' Co-op.
Bibliography (8 p.).
Typewriting as evidence. '08(Je27) c. il. O. pap. (Add. pubs. for price.) Genesee.

Osborn, Chase Salmon.
Andean land, (South America.) In 2 v. '09(Je12) c. il. maps, O. *$5 net, boxed. McClurg.

Osborn, Edn. Faxon.
Onar. '09(N) c. 12+15-345 p. front. 8°, $1.50. Sylvan Press.

Osborn, G.
See French, C. H.

Osborn, H: Fairfield.
Age of mammals in Europe, Asia, and North America. '10(N12) c. il. maps, O. $4.50 net. Macmillan.
Evolution of mammalian molar teeth, to and from the triangular type; ed. by W. K. Gregory. '08(F22) il. 8°, (Biological studies and addresses.) *$2 net. Macmillan.

Osborn, H: Stafford.
Prospector's field book and guide in the search for and the easy determination of ores and other useful minerals. 8th ed. '10(Jl30) c. il. 12°, $1.50. Baird.

Osborn, Herbert.
Economic zoology. '08(O24) il. 12°, *$2 net. Macmillan.

Osborn, Max.
Joshua Reynolds. [German text.] '08 (Ap11) 8°, bds., $1.35. Lemcke.

Osborn, Norris Galpin, ed.
Men of mark in Connecticut; introd. chapter, "What Connecticut stands for in the history of the nation," by S: Hart. '08 (Je6) c. 4 v., pors. 8°, $30; hf. mor., $50; mor., $60. W. R. Goodspeed.

Osborn, Solomon Oliver.
Nature and man. '10(Ag) c. 215 p. 12°, 75 c. S. O. Osborn.

Osborne, Albert E.
Stereograph and the stereoscope; with special maps and books forming a travel system. '09(Jl3) c. il. D. $1. Underwood.

Osborne, C: Fs., ed.
Historic houses and their gardens: palaces, castles, country places and gardens of the old and new worlds described by several writers; introd. by Fk. Miles Day. '08 (Ag8) c. F. $6. Winston.

Osborne, Harold Allen.
See Bailey, S: Willson.

Osborne, Maitland Le Roy, ["A. Vagrant."]
Pipe dreams. '08(S5) c. O. 75 c. Ellis.

Osborne, T: Burr.
Vegetable proteins. '09(O23) O. (Monographs on biochemistry.) bds., *$1.20 net. Longmans.

Osborne, T: Mott.
Adventures of a green dragon, [European travel.] '08, [1909.] (Mr) c. 15-179 p. 12°. (Priv. pr.) Auburn Pub.

Osborne, W. F:
Faith of a layman. '10(My14) 12°, $1.25. Cassell.

Osborne, W: Hamilton.
Red mouse. '09(Ja9) c. il. D. †$1.50. Dodd.
Running fight. '10(My7) c. il. D. $1.50. Dodd.

Osbornes (The). Benson, E: F. $1.20. Doubleday, P.

Osbourne, Lloyd.
Infatuation. '09(Mr13) c. il. D. †$1.50. Bobbs-M.

Osgar und Adolf. Schaefer, F. W. 50 c.; 25 c. Laird.

Osgood, Eliz.
See Davenport, G: Lyman.

Osgood, Elliott I., M.D.
Breaking down Chinese walls. '08(F15) c. 12°, *$1 net. Revell.

Osgood, Grace Rose.
At the sign of the Blue Anchor: tale of 1776. '09(O23) c. il. 12°, $1.50. C. M. Clark.

Osgood, Irene, [Mrs. Rob. Harborough Sherard.]
Servitude. '09(Ap10) c. D. †$1.50. Estes.
To a nun confess'd. '09(Ap10) D. $1.50. Estes.

Osgood, Phillips Endicott.
Temple of Solomon: study of Semitic culture. '10(S3) c. il. O. pap., 30 c. Open Court.

Osgood, Rob. Bayley, M.D.
See Goldthwait, Joel Ernest, *M.D.*

Osgood, Wilfred Hudson.
Biological investigations in Alaska and Yukon territory. I. East Central Alaska; II. Ogilvie range, Yukon; III. Macmillan River, Yukon. '09(D) 96 p. il. maps, 8°, (U. S., Dept. of Agriculture, Bu. of Biological Survey, North American fauna.) Gov. Pr. Off.
Diagnosis of new East African mammals, incl. a new genus of *Muridæ*. '10(Ap) 5-13 p. 8°, (Field Museum of Natural History pubs.; Zoölogical ser.) 50 c. Field Museum.
Further new mammals from British East Africa. '10(Jl) 9 p. 8°, (Field Museum of Nat. Hist. pubs.; Zoological ser.) 50 c. Field Museum.
Mammals from the coast and islands of northern South America. '10(D10) il. 8°, (Field Museum of Natural Hist. pubs.; Zoölogical ser.) pap., 50 c. Field Museum.
Peculiar bear from Alaska. '09, [1910.] (F) 3 p. front. 8°, (Field Museum of Natural History pubs.; Zoological ser.) 50 c. Field Museum.

Osgood, W: Fogg.
Differential and integral calculus: first course. [Rev. ed.] '09(Mr27) 12°, *$2 net. Macmillan.

Osgood, W: Newton.
Law points for business men. '08(My.) c. 64 p. 12°. (Add. pubs. for price.) Tudor Press.

O'Shea, Michael Vincent.
Social development and education. '09 (S25) c. O. $2. Houghton M.

O'Sheridan, Mary Grant.
Gaelic folk tales; designed as supplementary school reading. '09(Je26) c. D. 60 c. M. G. O'Sheridan.

OSIER.
See Willows.

Osler, W:, M.D.
Alabama student, and other biographical essays. '08(O17) front. facsims., O. *$2 net. Oxford Univ.
Michael Servetus. '10(Mr26) il. por. O. pap., 40 c. Oxford Univ.
Principles and practice of medicine; designed for the use of practitioners and students of medicine. 7th ed., thoroughly rev. '09(Jl) 17+1143 p. il. charts, 8°, $5.50. Appleton.
Thomas Linacre: Linacre lecture, 1908, St. John's College, Cambridge. '08(N7) 8°, *75 c. net. Putnam.
Treatment of disease; address in medicine before the Ontario Medical Association, Toronto, June 3, 1909. '09(N) 26 p. O. pap., 40 c. Oxford Univ.

—, and McCrae, T:, M.D., eds.
Modern medicine; its theory and practice; by American and foreign authors. In 7 v. v. 2, 3, 4. '08(Ag29) c. il. per v., *$6 net; leath., *$7 net; hf. mor., *$7.50 net. Lea.

Oslin, Stephen Jesse.
Eureka harmony method; plain and pract. course in harmony and composition designed for self-instruction, private teaching, normal schools and conservatories. '10(N19) c. il. pors. 8°, 60 c. Eureka.

Osman, Eaton Goodell.
Cleaning and renovating at home; household manual. '10(Ap9) c. D. bds., 75 c. net. McClurg.

OSMOSIS.
See Chemistry.

Osru. Sterns, J. $1.25. Lenox Pub.

Ostade, Adriaen van.
Masterpieces of Adriaen van Ostade. '10 (S10) il. T. (Dutch painters' ser.) leath., 75 c. net; pap., 25 c. net. Stokes.

OSTEOLOGY.
See Bones.

Osteology of birds. Shufeldt, R. W. (Add. pubs. for price.) N. Y. State Educ.

OSTEOPATHY.
American College of Mechano-Therapy, Chicago, Ill. Text book of osteopathy. $2. Amer. Coll. Mechano-Therapy.
American Osteopathic Association. Osteopathic directory and year book of the A. O. A. $1. Journal of Osteopathy.
Bartholomew, E. J. Man, woman, know thyself. $2. E. J. Bartholomew.
Murray, C: H: Practice of osteopathy. $3.50. C. H. Murray.
Still, A. T. Osteopathy. $6; $8. A. T. Still.
See also Quacks and quackery.

Osterfestberechnung in der abendländischen kirche. Schmid, J. *80 c. net. Herder.

Osterhout, W. J. V.
Value of sodium to plants by reason of its protective action; [also] On the effects of certain poisonous gases of plants. '08 (Jl11) O. (Univ. of Cal. pubs.) pap., 10 c. Univ. of Cal.
See also Hilgarde, Eugene Woldemar.

Osthaus, Carl Wilhelm Ferdinand, and Biermann, Ernest H., eds.
German prose composition; with notes and vocabularies. '09(Ap24) c. D. 65 c. Am. Bk.
Key to German prose composition. '10 (Ap30) c. D. 65 c. Am. Bk.

Ostrander, Fannie E.
Baby Goose book. Rev. and separated into a ser. of 3 v. v. 1, Baby Goose goes to town; v. 2, The gosling's trip with a dog and a cat; v. 3, Piggy and the kittens. '08(D19) il. in col. ea., 50 c. Laird.
Boy who won; or, more about the little white Indians. '10(O29) c. il. D. $1.25. L. C. Page.

Ostrogorski, Moisei IAkovlevich.
Democracy and the party system in the United States; study in extra-constitutional government. '10(O1) c. O. $1.75 net. Macmillan.

Ostrom, H:, D.D.
"All His benefits": [talks on praise and thanksgiving.] '08(O17) c. D. 30 c. Praise Pub.
Crisis in church work. '08(O17) c. D. *50 c. net. Jennings.
Law of prayer. '10(O) c. 154 p. 12°, 50 c. Praise Pub.
Rich in yesterdays; message to the aged. '09(O9) c. il. D. 75 c. Praise Pub.

Ostrovsky, Alex.
The storm; tr. by Constance Garnett. '08 (Mr21) D. (Modern plays.) *$1 net. J: W. Luce.

Ostrup, J: Christian.
Standard specifications for structural steel —timber—concrete and reinforced concrete. '10(N12) c. il. 8°, $1. McGraw-H.

Ostwald, Wilhelm.
Fundamental principles of chemistry; author. tr. by Harry W. Morse. '09(Je26) c. O. $2.25. Longmans.
Natural philosophy; tr. by T: Seltzer. '10 (D10) 12°, $1.25 net. Holt.
Principles of inorganic chemistry; tr. by Alex. Findlay. 3d ed. '09(F20) il. figs. 8°, *$6 net. Macmillan.
Scientific foundations of analytical chemistry; tr. with the author's sanction by G: McGowan. 3d English ed. '08(Jl11) il. 12°, *$2 net. Macmillan.

—, and Morse, Harry Wheeler.
Elem. modern chemistry. '09(Jl17) c. il. D. $1. Ginn.

O'Sullivan, Denis.
Cold-storage baby: lawyer's text-book on honest money and irredeemable paper currency. '08(My9) c. 16°, pap., 25 c. Ontario Pub.

O'Sullivan, J. M.
Old criticism and new pragmatism. '10 (F) O. $3. Longmans.

Osuna, Andrés.
Elementos de psicologia pedagógica. '10 (Jl9) c. 12°, $1.25. Smith & L.

Oswald, Michael Fs.
See Bible. N. T.

Oswell, G. D.
Sketches of rulers of India. v. 1, The mutiny era and after; v. 2, The company's governors. '08(D19); v. 3, The governors-general and Dupleix; v. 4, The princes of India and Albuquerque. '09(Ja23) D. ea., 70 c. Oxford Univ.

Other Americans. Ruhl, A. B. **$2 net. Scribner.
Other days. Winter, W: **$3 net. Moffat.
Other main-travelled roads. Garland, H. $1.50. Harper.
Other man's wife. Richardson, F. $1.50. M. Kennerley.
Other people's houses. Dewing, E. B. †$1.50. Macmillan.
Other Sara. Yorke, C., *pseud.* †$1.50. Estes.
Other side. Vachell, H. A. $1.20 net. Doran.
Other side of psychotherapy. Parker, G: L. 25 c. G: L. Parker.
Other side of the door. Chamberlain, L. †$1.50. Bobbs-M.
Other side of the lantern. Treves, *Sir* F: $2.75 net. Cassell.
Other side of the money question. Fulton, J. A. 25 c. Hutchinson & B.
Other side of the rainbow. Bone, F. 85 c. net. Eaton & M.
Other Sylvia. Rhoades, N. $1. Lothrop, L. & S.

Otis, Alex.
Hearts are trumps. '09(My8) c. front. D. $1.50. J: McBride.
The man and the dragon. '10(O1) c. il. D. $1.50. Little, B. & Co.

Otis, E: Osgood, M.D.
Great white plague; tuberculosis. '09(O2) c. D. **$1 net. Crowell.

Otis, Ja., pseud.
See Kaler, Ja. Otis.

Otis, W: Bradley.
American verse, 1625-1807. '09(Ap3) c. D. **$1.75 net. Moffat.

Otis Hamilton's quest. Huck, O. $1 net. Am. S. S.

OTOLOGY.
See Ear.

OTSEGO COUNTY, N. Y.
Blakely, S. B. History of Otsego. (Add. author for price.) S. B. Blakely.

Ott, E: Amherst.
"Sour grapes"; or, heredity and marriage. '09(N) c. 124 p. por. 8°, $1. Lyceumite.

Ott, I:
Text-book of physiology. 3d ed., rev. and enl. '09(N) c. 16+891 p. il. 4°, $3.50. Davis.

Otten, Rev. Bernard J:
Old Christianity vs. new paganism. '10(D) 199 p. 16°, 25 c. Herder.
What think you of Christ?; historical inquiry into Christ's Godhead. '09(N) 8+167 p. 16°, 25 c. Herder.

OTTER.
See Sea-otter.

Otterbein cook book: published by Ladies' Aid Society of the United Brethren Church, Honey Creek, Ind. '08(N) c. 160 p. il. 8°, 50 c. B. R. Inman.

Otterbrook people. Ireland, *Mrs.* M. E. H. 35 c. Un. B. Pub.

Ottley, Rev. Rob. Lawrence.
Christian ideas and ideals; outline of Christian ethical theory. '09(O9) O. $2.50. Longmans.

Otto, Rudolph.
Life and ministry of Jesus, according to the historical method; tr. from the 3d unaltered ed. by W. J. Whitby. '08 (Ag1) bds., 50 c. Open Court.

OTTOMAN EMPIRE.
See Turkey.

Otway, T:
The orphan, and Venice preserved; ed. by C: F. McClumpha. '09(Ja23) c. por. 16°, (Belles-lettres ser., Section 3, The English drama.) *60 c. net. Heath.

OUACHITA VALLEY, La.
Moore, C. B. Antiquities of the Ouachita Valley. $3.75. C. B. Moore.

"Ouida," pseud.
See La Ramée, Louise de.

"Oulot, B.," pseud.
See Suttner, B. F. S. K. *Freifrau* von.

Oulton, Leonard, and Wilson, Norman J.
Pract. testing of electrical machines. '10 (Ja1) il. S. (Whittaker's pract. hdbks.) *$1.40 net. Macmillan.

Our American Barclays. Barclay, C. B. (Priv. pr.) Grafton Press.

Our American holidays.* See Schauffler, Rob. Haven, *ed.

Our baby's record. Smith, S. K. $1; $2; $2.50. Dodge.

Our Benny. Waller, M. E. **$1 net. Little, B. & Co.

Our best mutual friend. Johnson, E. C. 75 c. E. C. Johnson.

Our big boys and the Sunday school. McKinney, A. H. 50 c. net. Revell.

Our bird comrades. Keyser, L. S. $1.25; $1.75. Rand, McN. & Co.

Our bird friends. Burba, G: F. $1. Outing.

Our blessed dead. Jowett, J. H: 25 c. net. Revell.

Our boys and girls. Kennedy, *Mrs.* M. G. 75 c. Wilde.

Our boys lib. 3 v. '10(D) il. 12°, ea., $1. Estes.
Coffin, Boys of '61; Kaler, Boys of Fort Schuyler; Boys of '98; Fighting for the empire.

Our breakfast book. Watson, M. L., *comp.* $1. Volland.

Our brother in red. Williams, J: L. 25 c. Pub. Ho. of M. E. Ch., So.

Our brother's child. Reynolds, W: H. 50 c. Mayhew.

Our children. Felix, M. 50 c. Phœnix.

Our children for Christ. Scudder, D. *15 c. net. Revell.

Our children, our schools, and our industries. Draper, A. S. 50 c. Bardeen.

Our church. Coyle, H:, *comp.* 3 v. $8. Angel Press.

Our church life. Frost, J. M. 90 c. S. S. Bd. So. Bapt.

Our city schools. Chancellor, W: E. *$1.25 net. Heath.

Our colonial history. Gerson, O. 50 c. Hinds.

Our daily bread. Viebig, C. $1.50. Lane.

Our darlings. '10(Je) 300 p. il. Q. $1.50 Fenno.

Our debt to antiquity. Zillinski, *Prof.* *75 c. net. Dutton.

Our defective American banking system. Gookin, F: W: (Priv. pr.) Chic. Lit. Club.

Our dogs. Brown, J: 50 c. Altemus.

Our first ambassador to China. Robbins, *Mrs.* H. H. M. *$5 net. Dutton.

Our flag. Bowron, E. M. B. 50 c. H: S. Bowron.

Our flag. Champion, S. E. B. $1. Tuttle, M. & T.

Our flag. Key, F. S., *3rd.* 25 c. H. C. Brown.

Our flag, our rose and our country. Leavitt, J: M. $1.50. Bible League.

Our foreign missionary enterprise. Mills, J. S. *50 c. net; *35 c. net. Un. B. Pub.

Our foreign service. Van Dyne, F: $2.50. Lawyers' Co-op.

Our free Methodist missions in Africa. Brodhead, *Mrs.* C. A. S., *ed.* $1. Aldine Pr.

Our garden flowers. Keeler, H. L. $2 net. Scribner.

Our heroes. Weekley, W: M. 50 c.; 35 c. Un. B. Pub.

Our holidays. Blair, M., *comp.* 50 c. McLoughlin.

Our home and country; pictured by W: Ladd Taylor. '08(N14) c. O. **$3 net, boxed. Moffat.

Our home railways. 2 v. Gordon, W. J. $4.50 net; $7.50 net. Warne.

Our homes and how to make the best of them. Sparrow, W. S., *ed.* $3.50 net. Doran.

Our homes and our children. Klykken, O. 75 c. Lutheran Pub.

Our house and the people in it. Pennell, *Mrs.* E. R. $1.25 net. Houghton M.

Our inheritance. Withers, Z. 50 c. Z. Withers.

Our inland sea. Lambourne, A. $2.50. A. Lambourne.

Our inland seas. Mills, J. C. $1.75 net. McClurg.

Our insect friends and enemies. Smith, J: B. **$1.50 net. Lippincott.

Our invisible supply. 2 v. Warner, *Mrs.* F. L. ea., *$1 net. Roger Bros.

Our irrational distribution of wealth. Mathews, B. C. **$1.25 net. Putnam.

Our jungle friends. '08(Ag22) c. il. obl. 4°, (Saalfield's cut-out picture books.) pap., 20 c. Saalfield.

Our Lady in art. Jenner, *Mrs.* K. L. R. $1 net. McClurg.

Our Lady of Darkness. Dorrington, A. $1.50. Macaulay.

Our lady of the sunshine and her international visitors. Aberdeen, I. M., *Countess* of. 50 c. net. Dutton.

Our Lady's lutenist. Bearne, D: 65 c. Benziger.

Our leader. Cole, W. V. $2. Anglo-Am. Authors.

Our little Australian cousin. Nixon-Roulet, M. F. 60 c. L. C. Page.

Our little Egyptian cousin. McManus, B. 60 c. L. C. Page.

Our little Grecian cousin. Nixon-Roulet, M. F. 60 c. L. C. Page.
Our little Hungarian cousin. Nixon-Roulet, M. F. 60 c. L. C. Page.
Our little Persian cousin. Shedd, E. C. 60 c. L. C. Page.
Our Lord: belief in the deity of Christ. Muller, E. F. K. *40 c. net. Eaton & M.
Our military rifle. Bowman, G: T. 10 c. Arms and the Man.
Our misunderstanding concerning the Jews. Cooke, P. (Add. author for price.) P. Cooke.
Our mutual friend. *See* Dickens, C:
Our national beginnings. Moore, J. H. (Add. author for price.) J. H. Moore.
Our national government. Willhauck, G. P. 35 c. Monarch Pr.
Our national government. Logan, M. S. C., *ed.* $3.25; $3.75; $4.25. Baldwin.
Our national parks. Muir, J: *$3 net. Houghton M.
Our nation's altar. Coolidge, A. C. 25 c. A. C. Coolidge.
Our native trees and their uses. Secord, L. M. 60 c. L. M. Secord.
Our naval war with France. Allen, G. W. **$1.50 net. Houghton M.
Our New Testament; how did we get it? Vedder, H: C. **$1 net. Am. Bapt.
Our northern domain: Alaska, picturesque, historic and commercial. '10(D17) c. Q. $2. Estes.
Our old ships and their commanders. il. O. 75 c. McLoughlin.
—De Morgan. Old Ironsides.—Taming the Barbary pirates.
—Yankee ship and a Yankee crew.
Our one Priest on high. Dimock, N. 50 c. net. Longmans.
Our own Columbia. Brown, L. $2. E. T. Meredith.
Our own land ser. *See* Tomlinson, Everett Titsworth.
Our own story book; by E. Nesbit, Sheila Braine, L. L. Weedon, [and others.] '08 (O31) il. Q. bds., $1.25. Dutton.
Our periodic earth. Taber, C: A. M. 75 c.; 50 c. G. H. Ellis.
Our Plymouth forefathers. Hanks, C: S. $1.50. Estes.
Our present needs. Webster, W: F. (Priv. pr.) W: F. Webster.
Our rich inheritance. Jenness, J. F. **30 c. net. Crowell.
Our search for a wilderness. Beebe, *Mrs.* M. B. R. $2.75 net. Holt.
Our silent partner. Hobart, A. S. *75 c. net. Revell.
Our sisters' recipes. Kaufman, N. M., *comp.* $1. J. A. Perley.
Our Slavic fellow citizens. Balch, E. G. $2.50. Charities Pub.
Our Southern quintette. Rosser, J: L. $1.25. Neale.
Our story reader. Ketchum, I. A. *35 c. special net. Scribner.
Our trees. Emerson, A. L. $3. Lippincott.
Our unelastic currency. Meyer, G. v. L. 10 c. U. S., Supt. of Docs.
Our village. *See* Lincoln, J. C.—Mitford, Mary Russell.
Our visit to France. Fricero, K. $1. Dodge.
Our wasteful nation. Cronau, R. $1. M. Kennerley.
Our world. Hemiup, *Mrs.* M. R. $2. Hemiup.
Out in the open. *See* Ruskin, J:
Out of door studies in geography. Fultz, F. M. In 2 pts. ea., 60 c. Pub. Sch. Pub.
Out-of-doors. Olsen, M. E. 60 c. Pacific Press.
Out of doors in the Holy Land. Van Dyke, H: J. **$1.50 net. Scribner.
Out of doors with God. Oliver, G: H., *ed.* 50 c. Chr. Witness.
Out of Drowning Valley. Jones, S. C. $1.50. Holt.
Out of the blue grass. Dunlap, L. $1. Transylvania.
Out of the briars. Newton, A. H. $1.25. A. H. Newton.
Out of the darkness. Grant, J: W. $1.10. Nat. Bapt. Pub.
Out of the depths. Parker, G: A: $1.25. Reid Pub.
Out of the depths. Varney, G: R. **$1.25 net. Am. Bapt.
Out of the depths. Vaughan, C. B. $1.25. Badger.
Out of the ditch. Lewis, J. V. $1.50. Jos. Vance Lewis.
Out of the dump. Marcy, M. E. T. 50 c. Kerr
Out of the night. Reynolds, *Mrs.* L: B. $1.20 net. Doran.
Out of the Ozarks. Ruggles, W: N. $1.50. Neale.
Out of the silence. Long, J. S. $1.25. J. S. Long.
Out of the way places. Frizell, W: G. *$1.20 net. Un. B. Pub.
Out with gun and camera. Stratemeyer, E: 60 c. Cupples & L.
Outcast manufacturers. Fort, C: $1.50. B. W. Dodge.

Outcault, R: Felton.
Buster Brown, the busy body. '09(D18) il. 8°, bds., 60 c. Cupples & L.
Buster Brown up to date. '10(Jl16) c. Q. bds., 60 c. Stokes.
Buster, Mary-Jane and Tige. '08(Ag8) c. col. il. obl. Q. (Stokes' comic juveniles.) bds., 60 c. Stokes.
Real Buster and the only Mary Jane. '09 (D25) il. obl. Q. bds., 60 c. Stokes.

OUTDOOR LIFE.
Olsen, M. E. Out-of-doors. 60 c. Pacific Press.
Whitney, F. Two years in a tent. 50 c. net. Moffat.
See also Camping.

Outdoor music. Ives, E. G. $1. Arakelyan.
Outdoor pastimes of an American hunter. Roosevelt, T. **$3 net. Scribner.
Outdoor world ser. il. D. Longmans.
—Farneaux. Field and woodland plants.
Outdoors in New England. Boston & Maine Railroad. (Add. pubs. for price.) Boston & Maine.

Outline for the study of American civil government, with special reference to training for citizenship, for use in secondary schools; prep. for the New England History Teachers' Association by its committee: Ray Greene Huling, Wilson Ryder Butler, and others. '10(D10) c. il. 8°, 50 c. net. Macmillan.

Outline of lecture notes. Welsh, L. *$1.75 net. L. Welsh.

Outline of practical sociology. **Wright, C: D.** $2. **Longmans.**

Outline studies in the New Testament. Moorehead, W: G. 75 c. net. Un. Presb. Bd.

Outlines for review. *See* Newton, C: B.

Outlines of economics; prep. by members of the Department of Political Economy of the University of Chicago. '10(N12) c. 12°, bds., $1.25 net. Univ. of Chic.

Outlines of music history. Hamilton, C. G. $1.50. Ditson.

Outlines of the life of Christ. Sanday, W: **$1.25 net. Scribner.

Outlines of the literary history of colonial Pennsylvania. Jackson, M. K. *$1.25 net. Lemcke.

OUTLINING.
See **Rhetoric.**

OUTLOOK MAGAZINE.
Roosevelt, T. **Outlook editorials. (Priv. pr.)** Outlook.

OUTRAM, *General Sir* James.
Trotter, L. Bayard of India: life of General Sir James Outram. *35 c. net; *70 c. net. Dutton.

Outwitted. Bob O'Link, *pseud.* 15 c. Dick.

Oval ser. See Dutton's.

Over against Green Peak. Humphrey, H. Z. †$1.25. Holt.

Over against the treasury. Fenn, C. H. 50 c. Westminster.

Over Bemerton's. Lucas, E: V. †$1.50. Macmillan.

Over the dead-line. Bullard, K. C., *comp.* *$1 net. Neale.

Over the Nonsense Road. Gulliver, L. $1.50 net. Appleton.

Over the quicksands. Ray, A. C. †$1.50. Little, B. & Co.

Over the sea. Pendergast, *Mrs.* E. W. $1. E. W. Pendergast.

Over the waters to Edinburgh town. Batten, J: M. $2. J: M. Batten.

Overheard in Fairyland. Bigham, M. A. †$1.50. Little, B. & Co.

Overland, Martha Uboe.
Manual of corporation law; classified corporation laws of all the states, cont. a digest of the general corporation laws of every state and territory of the U. S. arranged uniformly. Interleaved ed. of 1909. '09(Ap) c. 508 p. O. shp., $4. Ronald Press.
Manual of the statutory corporation law: classified corporation laws of all the states. Ed. of 1908-9. '08(Jl18) c. 8°, $4, incl. 1909 supplement. Ronald Press.

OVERLAND AUTOMOBILE.
See **Automobiles.**

Overland Route to the road of a thousand wonders [Union Pacific and Southern Pacific R.R.] '09(Mr) pap., 12 c. U. P. & S. P. R.R.

Overland ser. **il. 12°.** Winston.
—Ellis. **Alden among the Indians. $1.—Alden, the pony express rider. $1; per set, $2.**

Overland to India. Hedin, S. A. 2 v. $7.50 net. Macmillan.

Overland trek from India by side-saddle, camel and rail. Benn, E. A. F. P. *$5 net. Longmans.

Overlock, Melvin G:
Working people; their health and how to protect it. '10(Ap23) c. por. 8°, $2. M. G: Overlock.

Overman, D: R.
Womanhood; or, the physical life of maiden, wife and mother. '10(Mr26) c. il. por. 8°, $2. N. D. Thompson.

Overman, Neal, and Whitaker, Oliver Barr.
Public discussion on the question: Does the church of Christ offer a scriptural basis for the union of all Christians?; held at Lincoln, Kan., Jan. 8-11, '06, reported by W: M. Day. '06, [1909.] (F) c. 200 p. 12°. (Add. pubs. for price.) Donohue.

Overstreet, Harry Allen.
Dialectic of Plotinus. '09(Je12) Q. (Univ. of Cal. pubs.; Philosophy.) pap., 25 c. Univ. of Cal.

Overtones. Gordon, B. F. 25 c. McClurg.

Ovid [Lat. Ovidius] Naso, Publius.
Metamorphoseon; Liber 3; ed., with introd. and notes, by M. Cartwright. '09(D4) D. 50 c. Oxford Univ.
Phaëthon and other stories from Ovid; ed., with notes and vocab., by G. M. Edwards. '10(Je4) 16°, (Pitt Press ser.) 50 c. net. **Putnam.**

OVIEDO, Spain.
See **Spain.**

Ovitz, F. K.
See Porter, Horace Chamberlain.

Owen, Alice.
Root of all evil. '09(N20) c. por. 12°, $1.25. B'way Pub.

Owen, C: H:
Justice of the Mexican war: a review of the causes and results of the war. '08 (Ag15) c. D. **$1.25 net. Putnam.

Owen, Fk. Allen, and Standage, H. C.
Dyeing and cleaning of textile fabrics; by F. A. Owen; based partly on notes of H. C. Standage. '09(F20) c. 12°, $2. Wiley.

Owen, Marg. Cunliffe, ["Mme. la Marquise de Fontenoy," née Marguerite du Plantz.]
Cradle of the Rose. '08(N7) c. il. O. **$1.50 net. Harper.
Snow-fire; story of the Russian court. '10 (Ap23) c. il. O. $1.50 net. Harper.

Owen, Mrs. Nellie Huggins.
Short stories and poems. '09(N) 129 p. 12°, $1. N. H. Owen.

Owen, Rob. Latham.
Establishment of the probation system in United States courts; brief in support of the bill (S. 3798) for the establishment of a probation system in the United States courts, except in the District of Columbia. '09, [1910.] (Mr) 3 p. 8°, pap. Gov. Pr. Off.
—, **comp.** Code of the people's rule; compilation of various statutes, etc., rel. to the people's rule system of government and for terminating the abuses of machine politics, viz., an adequate registration system; secret ballot; direct primaries; publicity of campaign contributions; corrupt practices act, etc. '10(O) 169 p. 8°. Gov. Pr. Off.

Owl and the bee. '08(Ag22) c. il. obl. 4°, (Saalfield's cut-out picture books.) pap., 20 c. Saalfield.

OWLS.
Swarth, H. S. Two new owls from Arizona. 10 c. Univ. of Cal.

Owls of St. Ursula's. Reid, J. B. $1.25. Baker & T.

Owners names of the City of New York. Bromley, G: W. $30. G: W. Bromley.

Oxford, A. W.
Ruins of Fountains Abbey. '10(D3) il. 8°, $1.40 net. Oxford Univ.

OXFORD, Eng.
How, F: D. Oxford. $1.25. Estes.

OXFORD, Ohio.
See Miami University.

Oxford and Cambridge; delineated by Hanslip Fletcher; with introd. by J. Willis Clark, and notes by various writers. '10(O8) Q. $6 net. Wessels & B.

Oxford and working-class education: being the report of a joint committee of university and working-class representatives on the relation of the university to the higher education of work people. '09(Ja23) O. pap., 35 c. Oxford Univ.

Oxford book of ballads. *See* Couch, *Sir* Arth. T: Quiller-.

Oxford book of French verse. Lucas, S. W. L., *comp.* *$1.75 net; *$2.40 net; *$3 net. Oxford Univ.

Oxford book of Italian verse. Lucas, S. W. L., *comp.* $2 net; $2.50 net. Oxford Univ.

Oxford classical texts. D. Oxford Univ.
—Antoninus. Imperata ad se ipsum. 75 c.
—Apollonius *of Rhodes.* Argonavtica. $1.
—Herodotus. Historiæ. v. 1, 2. ea., $1.10.
—Theophrastus. Characteres. 90 c.; pap., 75 c.
—Xenophon. Opera omnia. 4 v. v. 1, 75 c.; v. 2, 90 c.; v. 3, 75 c.; v. 4, 90 c.; 75 c.

Oxford ed. of standard authors. 30 v. [1910.] (D) il. 8°, ea., 50 c. net; (formerly 75 c.) Oxford Univ.

Oxford geographies; ed. by A. J. Herbertson. il. maps, D. Oxford Univ.
—Herbertson, A. J. Physiographical introd. to geography. 40 c.—Senior geography. 75 c.
—Herbertson, F. L. D. R. Elem. geography. v. 1, 2, 3, ea., 30 c.; v. 4, 40 c.; v. 7, 60 c.
—Kirk. Senior geography questions. 25 c.
—Unstead. Practical geography. pts. 1, 2, ea., 40 c.: pts. 1-2, together, 60 c.

Oxford German ser.; ed. by Julius Goebel. D. Oxford Univ.
—Droste-Hülshof. Die Judenbuche. 60 c.
—Lessing. Minna von Barnhelm. 60 c.

Oxford higher French ser.; ed. by Leon Delbos. S. Oxford Univ.
—Angellier. Pages choisies. $1.15.
—Balzac. Eugênie Grandet. 85 c.
—Béranger. Chansons choisis. $1.15.
—Campan. Mémoires. 85 c.
—Cousin. La société française au XVIIe siècle. $1.15.
—Flaubert. Salammbô. $1.15.
—Gautier. España, and Emaux.—Trois grotesques. ea., 70 c.
—Hugo. Notre Dame de Paris. $1.15.—Preface du Cromwell. 85 c.
—Lamartine. Jocelyn. $1.
—Mérimée. Contes et nouvelles. 70 c.—La chronique du règne de Charles IX. $1.
—Michelet. L'oiseau. 70 c.
—Quinnet. France et Allemagne. $1.15.
—Sainte-Beuve. Trois portraits litteraires. $1.
—Sand, *pseud.* Francois le champi. 85 c.—Les maîtres sonneurs. $1.15.
—Staël-Holbein. De l'Allemagne. 85 c.
—Vigny. Chatterton. $1.

Oxford hymn book. '08(D19) Tt. 30 c.; D. 50 c.; with music, $1.15. Oxford Univ.

Oxford lectures on poetry. Bradley, A. C. *$3 net. Macmillan.

Oxford lib. 106 v. [1910.] (Jl) 12°, ea., 75 c. Simmons.

Oxford lib. of practical theology; ed. by W: C: Edmond Newbolt and Rev. Darwell Stone. D. *$1.40 net. Longmans.
—Gibson. Three creeds.
—Holmes. Immortality.
—Newbolt. Sacrament of the altar.

Oxford lib. of prose and poetry. S. 90 c.; lambskin, $1.15. Oxford Univ.
—Barnes. Selected poems.
—Barrett. The heroine.
—Browning. Men and women.
—Clare. Poems.
—Coleridge. Literary criticism.
—De Quincey. Literary criticism.
—Echoes from the *Oxford Magazine.*
—Fujiwara, *comp.* Hundred verses from Old Japan.
—Galt. Annals of a parish.
—Gray. Poems.
—Inchbald. Simple story.
—Keats. Poems.
—Lowell. Fireside travels.
—Lucas Hambledon men.
—Peacock. Memoirs of Shelley.
—Praed. Select poems.
—Shelley. Literary and philosophical criticism.
—Stone, *ed.* War songs.

Oxford library of translations. 8°, *$1 net. Oxford Univ.
—Dante Alighieri. Convivio.

OXFORD MAGAZINE, Oxford, Eng.
Echoes from the *Oxford Magazine.* 90 c. Oxford Univ.

Oxford medical pubs. il. 8°. Oxford Univ.
—Bardswell. Expectation of life of the consumptive after sanatorium treatment. $1.50 net.
—Muir, *and others.* Studies in immunity. *$3 net.
—Sutherland, *ed.* System of diet and dietetics. *$9.25 net.
—Thomson. Consumption, its prevention and home treatment. $1 net.
—Tweedy *and* Wrench. Rotunda practical midwifery. $6.

Oxford modern French ser.; ed. by Leon Delbos and W. Robertson. D. Oxford Univ.
—Balzac. César Birotteau.—Une ténébreuse affaire. ea., 60 c.
—Bellot. Journal d'un voyage aux mers polaires. 60 c.
—Berthet. Le douanier de mer. 60 c.
—Bouët-Willaumez. Batailles de terre et de mer. 60 c.
—David. Le serment. 40 c.
—Gautier. Voyage en Espagne. 50 c.
—Lamartine. Le tailleur de pierres de Saint-Point. 60 c.
—Landelle. Une haine a bord. 75 c.
—Marmier. Les fiancés du Spitzberg. 75 c.
—Mérimée. Colomba. 50 c.
—Michelet. Jeanne D'Arc. 50 c.
—Sand, *pseud.* La petite Fadette. 60 c.
—Sandeau. Un heritage. 60 c.
—Sismondi. Marignan.—Pavie et le sac de Rome. ea., 50 c.
—Taine. Voyage aux Pyrénées. 60 c.
—Thierry. Les Normands en Angleterre et en France. 60 c.
—Vigny. Servitude et grandeur militaires. 60 c.

Oxford moment ser. por. Ff. 40 c. net. Oxford Univ.
—Brown. Rab and his friends.
—Dickens. Christmas carol.
—Longfellow. Longfellow.

Oxford Museum, Oxford, Eng.
Vernon, H. M. *and Mrs.* K. Dorothea Ewart. Hist. of the Oxford Museum. 50 c. Oxford Univ.

Oxford plain texts. 6 v. '09(Ap3); 7 v. (N13) S.; 4 v. '10(Mr26); (My14) S.; 3 v. (Ag27); 4 v. (D17) 8°. Oxford Univ.
Contents: Matthew Arnold's Sohrab and Rustum, 10 c.; Byron's Childe Harold's pilgrimage, Canto 3, Canto 4, ea., 10 c.; Coleridge's Rime of the ancient mariner and Christabel, 10 c.; Gray's Elegy and odes, 10 c.; Keats's Isabella and The eve of St. Agnes, 10 c.; Byron, Prisoner of Chillon, Mazeppa, 10 c.; Lament of Tasso, 10 c.; De Quincey, Spanish military nun, and Revolt of the Tartars, 25 c.; Macaulay, History of England, chapter III., 25 c.; Milton, Paradise lost, bks. 1, 2, ea., 10 c.; Shelley, Adonais. Alastor and other poems, 10 c.; Spenser, Faerie Queene, bk. 1, 25 c.; John Milton's Comus, 10 c.; pap., 7 c.; Minor poems and sonnets, 10 c.; pap., 7 c.; Paradise lost, Bks. III., IV., 10 c.; pap., 7 c.; Cowper, The task, 10 c.; pap., 7 c.; Dryden, Preface to the fables, 10 c.; pap., 7 c.; Pope, Essay on criticism, 10 c.; pap., 7 c.; Wordsworth, The excursion, Bk. 1, 10 c.; pap., 7 c.; Carlyle, T., Essay on Burns, 15 c.; pap., 10 c.; Macaulay, Essay on Bacon, 25 c.; pap., 20 c.; Macaulay, Lays of ancient Rome, 20 c.; pap., 15 c.; Macaulay's essay on Addison, 20 c.; pap., 15 c.; Macaulay's essay on Warren Hastings, 25 c.; pap., 20 c.; Macaulay's essay on Milton, 15 c.; pap., 10 c.; Macaulay's essay on Johnson, 15 c.; pap., 10 c.; Milton, Minor poems and sonnets, 7 c.

Oxford poets. 12°. $1.25; Oxford India pap., $1.75. Oxford Univ.
—Crabbe. Poetical works.
—Pageant of English poetry.
—Poe. Poetical works.
—Thomson. Poetical works.
—Scott. Poetical works.
—Southey. Poetical works.

Oxford student's history of India. Smith, V. A. 60 c. Oxford Univ.

Oxford studies in social and legal history. *See* Vinogradoff, P., *ed.*

Oxford translations. 8°. Oxford Univ.
—Deeds of Beowulf. $1.

Oxford treasury of English literature. Hadow, G. E. v. 3. 90 c. Oxford Univ.

Oxford Tudor and Stuart lib. D. Oxford Univ.
—Shakespeare. Merry wives of Windsor. —Sonnets; and A lover's complaint. ea., $1.75.
—Turberville. Booke of hunting, 1576. $2.50.
—Wilson. Arte of rhetorique. $1.75.

Oxford University, England.
Durand, R. Oxford. $5 net. Duffield.
Godley, A. D. Oxford in the eighteenth century. *$2.25 net. Putnam.
Lang, E. M. Oxford colleges. 90 c. net. Jacobs.
Sélincourt, H. de. Oxford from within. $3 net. Jacobs.
Tuckwell, W: Reminiscences of Oxford. *$2 net. Dutton.
Vaughan, E. V. Origin and early development of the English universities to the close of the XIII century. $1. Univ. of Mo.
See also Bodleian Library;—*also* Birkhead, Henry; —Lower, Richard;—Mayow, John.

Oxford University calendar for the year 1911. '10(D24) D. $1.75. Oxford Univ.

Oxford University Extension Summer Meeting. il. 8°, pap., 35 c. Oxford Univ.
—Gotch. Two Oxford physiologists.

Oxford University Press, Oxford, Eng.
Madan, F. Brief account of the University Press at Oxford. *60 c. net. Oxford Univ.

Oxygen.
See Coal.

Oxyrhynchus gospel. *See* Egypt Exploration Fund.

Oyster Bay, L. I.
See Reformed church.

Oysters.
Coker, R. E. Experiments in oyster culture in Pamlico Sound, North Carolina. (Add. pubs. for price.) Uzzell.
Rowe, H: C. Wholesomeness of oysters as food. Gov. Pr. Off.
United States. *Dept. of Commerce and Labor; Bureau of Fisheries.* Condition and extent of the oyster beds of James River, Virginia. '10(F) 3-83 p. charts, 8°, pap.

Ozaki, Yei Theodora.
Warriors of old Japan, and other stories. '09(D4) c. il. D. **$1.25 net. Houghton M.

P. & O. pocket book. Peninsular and Oriental Steam Navigation Co. *$1 net. Macmillan.

P., G. H.
See Putnam, G: Haven.

"P. L.," pseud.
See Pope, Paulina Saxton.
P. Q. & G. (The). Ellis, E: Sylvester. †$1.25. Estes.
P. W.-M., pseud.
See Sloper, *Mrs.* Allie.
Pa Flickinger's folks. Hoover, B. R. †$1. Harper.
Paasch, Captain H.
Vom kiel zum flaggenknopf, (From keel to truck:) marine-worterbuch, English-Französisch - Deutsch - Spanisch - Italienisch. 5th auflage, verbessert und vermehrt. '08(Ap25) il. tabs., obl. O. hf. leath., *$10 net. Lemcke.
Pace, E: A., ed.
See Catholic encyclopedia.
—, and Shields, T: E:
Religion; first book. '09(Ap17) c. D. *40 c. net. Cath. Educ.
Pacific blockade. Hogan, A. E. $2. Oxford Univ.
PACIFIC COAST.
Aflalo, F: G: Sunset playgrounds: fishing days and others in California and Canada. *$2.25 net. Scribner.
Dall, W: H. Contributions to the Tertiary paleontology of the Pacific coast; 1, Miocene of Astoria and Coos Bay, Ore. U. S., Supt. of Docs.
Enock, C. R. Great Pacific coast. $4 net. Scribner.
Holder, C: F: Recreations of a sportsman on the Pacific coast. $2 net. Putnam.
Johnson, C. Highways and byways of the Pacific coast. **$2 net. Macmillan.
United States. *Coast and Geodetic Survey.* United States coast pilot; Pacific coast; California, Oregon and Washington. 2d ed. '09(S) 251 p. il. f°. (Add. Superintendent for price.)
Woods, S. D. Lights and shadows of life on the Pacific coast. $1.20 net. Funk.
See also Birds;—Columbia River Valley;—*also* names of states.
PACIFIC ISLANDS.
See Melanesia;—Micronesia;—Oceanica.
PACIFIC OCEAN.
See Birds.
Pacific railroads. Paxson, F: L. Gov. Pr. Off.
Pacific reporter, v. 91. Permanent ed. '08 (Ja11); v. 92. '08(Mr); v. 93 (My); v. 94 (Je); v. 95 (Ag); v. 96 (O); v. 97. '08, [1909.] (F): v. 98 (Ap); v. 99 (Je); v. 100 (S); v. 101. '09(N); v. 102, 103, 104. '10 (F); v. 105 (Ap); v. 106 (Je); v. 107 (Jl); v. 108 (S); v. 109 (N); v. 110 (D) O. (National reporter system, state ser.) ea., $4.—Digest of v. 81-85; with table of cases digested, [etc.] v. 5. '09(S) c. O. (National reporter system.) $6. West Pub.
Pacific Scientific Institution pubs. 8°. W: A. Bryan.
—Bryan. Pacific Scientific Institution. gratis.
Pacific ser. See Houston, Edn. Ja.
Pack, R. W.
Notes on *echinoids* from the tertiary of California. '09(Ag7) il. Q. (Univ. of Cal. pubs.; Geology.) pap., 10 c. Univ. of Cal.

Packard, Charlotte Mellen.
From the foothills of song. '08(Jl) c. 7-62 p. 12°, $1. Badger.
Packard, Fs. Randolph.
Text-book of diseases of the nose, throat and ear for the use of students and general practitioners. '09(F) c. 384 p. 8°, (New medical ser.) subs., **$3.50 net; leath., **$4 net. Lippincott.
Packard, Mrs. Lottie Hill.
How to make a living, arranged for learners of Munson phonography. '08, [1909.] (Mr) c. 136 p. 12°, 75 c. S. S. Packard.
Practical phonography; a revision of Lessons in Munson phonography. '08(N) c. 233 p. 12°, $1. S. S. Packard.
Packard, Winthrop.
Florida trails as seen from Jacksonville to Key West and from November to April, inclusive. '10(D3) c. il. O. $3 net, boxed. Small.
Wild pastures. '09(Je19) c. D. **$1.20 net. Small.
Wildwood ways. '09(D18) c. front. S. **$1.20 net. Small.
Wood wanderings. '10(S17) c. il. S. (New England year ser.) $1.20 net. Small.
Woodland paths. '10(Je4) il. 12°, $1.20 net. Small.
Paddock, Munson.
Angelic Angelina. '09(D18) il. 4°, bds., 60 c. Cupples & L.
Paddock, Wendell, and Whipple, Orville B.
Fruit-growing in arid regions; acct. of approved fruit-growing practices in the inter-mountain country of the western United States, comprising the states of Colorado, Montana, Idaho, Utah, Nevada, and in Northern Arizona and New Mexico, with applications to adjacent regions. '10(Je11) c. D. $1.50 net. Macmillan.
Paddock lectures. *See* Du Bose, W: Porcher. —Hall, Fs. Jos.
Padelford, F: Morgan, and Benham, Allen Rogers, eds.
Songs of Rawlinson ms. C813. '09(My) 89 p. 8°, (Univ. of Wash bull., University studies.) pap. (Add. University for price.) Univ. of Wash.
Padovani, P.
Laird & Lee's standard vest pocket English-Italian (Inglese-Italiano), Italian-English (Italiano-Onglese) dictionary (dizionario). '09(N20) c. T. double index, 50 c.; leath., double index, 75 c. Laird.
PADUA, Italy.
Foligus, C. Padua. $1.75 net; $2.25 net. Dutton.
Paestum. Thaw, A. B. *$1 net. Brentano's.
Paetow, L: J:
Arts course at medieval universities with special reference to grammar and rhetoric. '10(My) 134 p. Q. (Univ. of Ill. bull., University studies.) pap., $1. Univ. of Ill.
Bibliography (21 p.).
PAGANINI, Nicolo.
Stratton, S. S: Nicolo Paganini. *$2 net. Scribner.

Page, Curtis Hidden, ed.
Golden treasury of American songs and lyrics. '08(D12) 16°, (Golden treasury ser.) $1. Macmillan.

Page, E: C., ed.
See Sparks, Edn. Erle.

Page, Mrs. Eliz. Fry.
Edward MacDowell, his work and ideals. '10(Ag6) c. por. O. $1 net; leath., $1.50 net. Dodge.
Vagabond Victor; or, the downfall of a dog: a true story. '08, [1909.] (Ja) c. 105 p. il. 16°, 50 c. Pub. Ho. of M. E. Ch., So.

Page, Frederic Ja. M.
Elements of physics. [1910] (My) 288 p. il. $1.50 net. Funk.

Page, Howard L.
Dual mind. [1910.] (Ja) c. '09. 7-194 p. 12°, $1. Green Leaf.

Page, Ja. Madison, and Haley, M. J.
True story of Andersonville prison: a defense of Major Henry Wirz. '08(Ap4) c. por. O. $2. Neale.

Page, Jane.
The morbules: [rhymes.] '10(D) 62 p. 8°, $1. Ferris.

Page, Jesse.
Black bishop: Samuel Adjar Crowther. '09(Je19) 8°, *$2 net. Revell.

Page, Ralph Barlow.
Letters of Alcuin. '09(Jl) c. 102 p. 8°, bds., $1; pap., 50 c. Forest Press.
Bibliography (2 p.).

Page, T: Nelson.
John Marvel, assistant. '09(O16) c. il. D. †$1.50. Scribner.
Mount Vernon and its preservation, 1858-1910; acquisition, restoration, and care of the home of Washington by the Mount Vernon Ladies' Association of the Union for over half a century. [1910.] (D) c. 11+84 p. pls. pors. (partly col.) 12°, 75 c. Mount Vernon Ladies' Assoc.
Old Dominion: her making and her manners. '08(Ap4) D. **$1.50 net. Scribner.
Robert E. Lee, the southerner. '08(D19) c. por. D. *$1.25 net. Scribner.
Tommy Trot's visit to Santa Claus. '08 (O24) c. il. O. †$1. Scribner.

Page, Villa Faulkner.
Christmas message to you [and] With the new year. [1910] (F) c. '09. 3-49 p. 16°, 50 c. V. F. Page.
Prayer. [1910] (F) c. '09. 44 p. 16°, 50 c. V. F. Page.

Page, W: Herbert, and Jones, Paul.
Treatise on taxation by local and special assessments, incl. assessments for streets, sidewalks, alleys, sewers, and all other city improvements, as well as assessments for all rural improvements, [etc.] '09(Mr) c. 2 v., 1248+1110; 1111-2497 p. O. $12. W. H. Anderson.

Page and the prince. Chipman, C: P. $1.25. Ball Pub. Co.

Page, esquire and knight. Lansing, M. F., *comp.* 35 c. Ginn.

Page lecture ser. D. Yale Univ.
—Morals in modern business. *$1.25 net.

Pageant of English poetry; being 1150 poems and extracts by 300 authors, covering a period of upwards of 600 years; [comp. by R. M. Leonard.] '09(D18) front. 12°, (Oxford poets.) $1.25; Oxford India pap., $1.75. Oxford Univ.

PAGEANTS.
See Italy;—Philadelphia.

Pages from the book of Paris. Washburn, C. C. $3 net. Houghton M.

Paget, Bp. Fs.
Introduction to the fifth book of Hooker's treatise of the laws of ecclesiastical polity. '08(My23) O. $1.75. Oxford Univ.

Paget, Bp. H: Luke.
Home life in England. '10(S24) D. 75 c. net Longmans.

Paget, Stephen, M.D.
Case against Christian Science. '10(S) pap., 10 c. Cassell.
Confessio medici. '08(F15) c. D. **$1.25 net. Macmillan.
Faith and works of Christian Science. '09 (My1) c. O. *$1.25 net. Macmillan.

Paget, Violet.
See Lee, Vernon, *pseud.*

Paid in full. Harding, J: W: †$1.50. G: W. Dillingham.

PAIN.
See Suffering.

Paine, Albert Bigelow.
Captain Bill McDonald, Texas ranger; story of frontier reform; with introd. letter by Thdr. Roosevelt. Special subscription ed. '09(Ap) c. 448 p. por. il. facsim., 8°, $2; $2.50; ¾ leath., $3. W: J. McDonald.
Elsie and the Arkansaw bear. '09(D4) c. col. il. D. $1. Altemus.
Hollow tree snowed-in book. '10(O22) c. il. O. $1.50. Harper.
Ship dwellers: story of a happy cruise. '10(My21) il. O. $1.50 net. Harper.
Tent dwellers. '08, [1909.] (N) c. il. O. $1.50. Harper.
Formerly published by Outing Publishing Co.

Paine, Dorothy Charlotte.
Hilda of the hippodrome. '10(O15) c. col. front. il. D. $1 net. Reilly & B.

Paine, Harriet Eliza, ["Eliza Chester."]
Old people; with introd. by Alice Brown. '10(N5) c. D. $1.25 net. Houghton M.

Paine, Ralph Delahaye.
Cadet of the Black Star Line. '10(S17) c. il. D. $1.25. Scribner.
College years. '09(S11) c. †$1.50. Scribner.
Fugitive freshman. '10(O1) c. il. D. $1.50. Scribner.
Greater America. '07, [1910.] (F) il. 8°, *$1.50 net. McClurg.
Formerly published by Outing Publishing Co.
Head coach. '10(Ap2) c. il. O. $1.50. Scribner.
Ships and sailors of old Salem. '09(O16) c. il. pors. facsims., O. *$3.50 net. McClurg.
Stroke oar. '08, [1910.] (F) c. il. 12°, $1.50. McClurg.
Formerly published by Outing Publishing Co.

Paine, T:
Life and writings; containing a biography by Thomas Clio Rickman and appreciations by Leslie Stephen, Lord Erkskine, Paul Desjardins, Rob. G. Ingersoll, Elbert Hubbard and Marilla M. Ricker; ed. and annot. by Dan. Edn. Wheeler. 10 v. [Independent ed.] '09(My8) c. il. pors. facsims., 8°, per set, $39.50; $65; $75; $100; $250; $500; $1000. Parke.

PAINE, Thomas.
Randall, J. A. Paper on the life and character of Mr. Thomas Paine. 10 c. J. A. Randall
Sherman, A. O. Thomas Paine the patriot. 20 c. Paine Nat. Hist. Assoc.

Paine, Willis Seaver.
See New York State. Laws rel. to banking.

PAINT.
Friend, J. A. N. Introd. to the chemistry of paints. $1.20 net. Longmans.
Holley, C. D. Lead and zinc pigments. **$3 net. Wiley.
Holley, C. D., *and* Ladd, E. F. Analysis of mixed paints, color pigments and varnishes. $2.50. Wiley.
Lowe, H. Paints for steel structures. $1. Wiley.
Maire, F: Colors, what they are and what to expect of them. 60 c. Drake.
Maire, F: Modern pigments and their vehicles. $2. Wiley.
Toch Brothers. "R. I. W." book: dampproofing and protection of modern building construction of every type. (Not for sale.) Toch.
Wall, W: E. Oldest paint shops in Massachusetts. 25 c. W: E. Wall.
Zerr, G:, *and* Rübencamp, R. Treatise on color manufacture. (Add. pubs. for price.) Lippincott.
See also Chemistry;—Painting (*mechanical*).

Painted shadows. Le Gallienne, R: †75 c. Little, B. & Co.

Painter, C: Fairbank, M.D.
See Goldthwait, Joel Ernest, *M.D.*

Painter, Rev. Franklin Verzelius Newton.
See Richard, Ja. W:

Painter of Madonnas. Stebbins, C: M. 50 c. English Leaflets.

Painter's progress. Low, W: H. $1.50 net. Scribner.

PAINTERS AND PAINTINGS.
Abbey, E. A. Quest of the Holy Grail: portfolio of paintings. $5; subjects sold separately, ea., 50 c. Curtis & C.
Allen, G. Evolution of Italian art. *$3.50 net. Wessels.
Art prices current, 1908-9. $3.25 net. Dodd.
Atkins, G. Extracts from the letters with notes on painting and landscapes. *$1.25 net. A. M. Robertson
Bacon, *Mrs.* D. M., *pseud.* Pictures that every child should know. **$1.20 net. Doubleday, P.
Behrens, C. Louis XVI. painting. $8. Hessling
Berenson, B. Florentine painters of the Renaissance. **$1.50 net. Putnam.
Beruete y Moset, A. de. School of Madrid. *$2 net. Scribner.

PAINTERS AND PAINTINGS.—*Continued.*
Binyon, L. Painting in the Far East. *$6 net. Longmans.
Bode, W. Great masters of Dutch and Flemish painting. *$2 net. Scribner.
Brinton, S. Renaissance in Italian art. (Add. pubs. for price.) Scribner.
Bryant, *Mrs.* L. M. Pictures and their painters. $2.50 net.—What pictures to see in Europe in one summer. $1.50 net. Lane.
Burckhardt, J. C. The cicerone: art guide to painting in Italy. $1.50. Scribner.
Buxton, H. J: W., *and* Koehler, S. R. Painting: English and American.—Painting: German, Flemish and Dutch. ea., $1.25. Gorham.
Caffin, C: H: Child's guide to pictures. **$1.25 net. Baker & T.
Caffin, C: H: Story of Dutch painting. —Story of Spanish painting. ea., **$1.20 net. Century Co.
Caw, J. L. Scottish painting, past and present. *$8 net. Stokes.
Copley prints: reproductions of notable paintings publicly and privately owned in America. ea., 25 c. Curtis & C.
Cosmo collection; duotone hand-colored reproductions of the most famous paintings. 10 v. ea., $3.75; $5; $10. Cosmo.
Crowe, *Sir* J. A., and Cavalcaselle, G. B. History of painting in Italy. In 6 v. v. 1-3. ea., *$6 net. Scribner.
Crowe, *Sir* J. A., *and* Cavalcaselle, G. B. New hist. of painting in Italy from the 2d to the 16th century. 3 v. ea., *$5 net. Dutton.
Cundall, H. M. History of British watercolor painting. *$6 net. Dutton.
De Groot, C. H. Catalogue raisonné of the most eminent Dutch painters of the seventeenth century. In 10 v. v. 1, 2, 3. ea., *$7.50 net. Macmillan.
Dow, A. W. Composition; standard treatise for art teachers and students. $2.50 net. Baker & T.
Dowman, F. Great English painters. **$1.50 net. Jacobs.
Duret, T. Manet and the French impressionists. *$3.75 net. Lippincott.
Eaton, D. C. Hdbk. of modern French painting. **$2 net. Dodd.
Glasgow gallery. 35 c.; $1. Caldwell.
Great English portrait painters of the 18th century; ed. by T. Leman Hare. *$2 net. Stokes.
Havell, E. B. Indian sculpture and painting. *$25 net. Scribner.
Herkomer, *Sir* H. v. My school and my gospel. *$7.50 net. Doubleday, P.
Holme, C:, *ed.* Sketching grounds. *$3 net. Lane.
Holmes, C: J: Notes on the science of picture-making. $3 net. Appleton.
Huneker, J. G. Promenades of an impressionist. $1.50 net. Scribner.
Hyamson, A. M. Dictionary of artists and art terms. 50 c. Dutton.
Ideal collection of the world's great art. In 12 pts. subs. Doubleday, P.

PAINTERS AND PAINTINGS.—*Continued.*

Inglis, J. S. Illustrated catalogue of oil and water color paintings belonging to the estate of the late James S. Inglis. $1; $5. Am. Art Assoc.

Jackson, H: E. Great pictures as moral teachers. $1.50. Winston.

Jewett, L. R. History of Italian painting. 60 c. Mt. Holyoke Coll.

Knight, W: Six lectures on some nineteenth century artists. $2. Seymour.

Lasar, C: A. Pract. hints for art students. **$1 net. Duffield.

Laurie, A. P. Greek and Roman methods of painting. 75 c. net. Putnam.

Leaders of the English Pre-Raphaelites; ed. by T. Leman Hare. *$2 net. Stokes.

Library Association of California. *Committee on Pictures for Libraries.* Picture list. 25 c. Cal. L. A.

Low, W: H. Painter's progress. $1.50. Scribner.

Macfall, H. French pastellists of the eighteenth century. *$10.50 net. Macmillan.

Mach, E. R. O. v. Art of painting in the nineteenth century. *$1.25 net. Ginn.

Marius, G. H. Dutch art in the nineteenth century. *$3.75 net. Lippincott.

Meier-Graefe, J. A. Modern art. 2 v. *$10.50 net. Putnam.

Metropolitan Museum of Art. Exhibition of contemporary German art: list of books and periodicals on modern German art in the library of the Museum. gratis. Metropolitan Museum.

Michel, F. E. Great masters of landscape painting. $7.50 net. Lippincott.

Moretto da Brescia, A. B. Masterpieces, 1489-1554. 25 c.; 75 c. Stokes.

New York. Metropolitan Museum of Art. Hudson-Fulton celebration; catalogue of an exhibition held in the Metropolitan Museum of Art. 2 v. 50 c.; $5. Metropolitan Museum.

Old masters: examples of their work reproduced in color; with notes on pictures and paintings. 2 v. *$8 net. Dutton.

One hundred masterpieces of painting. $4 net. Lane.

One hundred popular pictures. $4 net. Cassell.

Patterson, J. W. Painters since Leonardo. *$4 net. Duffield.

Phythian, J: E. Fifty years of modern painting. *$3.50 net. Dutton.

Poynter, *Sir* E: J: Painting: classic and Italian. $1.25. Gorham.

Preyer, D: C., Art of the Netherland galleries. *$2 net. L. C. Page.

Rose, G: B. Renaissance masters. **$1 net. Putnam.

Royal Academy pictures and sculpture, 1909, 1910. ea., *$1.75 net. Cassell.

Ruskin, J: Modern painters. 5 v. ea., *$1 net.—Pre-Raphaelitism. *$1 net. Dutton.

Schreyvogle, C: My bunkie and others. **$4 net. Moffat.

Singleton, E. Art of the Belgian galleries. **$2 net. L. C. Page.

PAINTERS AND PAINTINGS.—*Continued.*

Singleton, E. Holland: [descriptions of pictures in Dutch galleries.] *$1 net. McClurg.

Smith, G. Painting: Spanish and French. $1.25. Gorham.

Smith, J. Catalogue raisonné of the works of the most eminent Dutch, Flemish and French painters. In 9 v. $25 net. Dutton.

Solomon, S. J. Practice of oil painting and of drawing as associated with it. $1.75 net. Lippincott.

Sterling-Maxwell, *Sir* W: Stories of the Spanish artists until Goya. $3 net. Duffield.

Tabor, M. E. Saints in art. *$1.20 net. Stokes.

Temple, A. G: Modern Spanish painting. *$20 net. Lippincott.

Thieme, W., *and others, eds.* Allgemeines lexikon der bildenden künstler. [In 20 v.] v. 2. *$8.75 net. Stechert.

Thirty favorite paintings, by leading American artists. $1.50. Collier.

Three great Florentine painters; ed. by T. Leman Hare.—Three great modern painters. ea., *$2 net. Stokes.

Turner, P. M., *and* Baker, C. H. C., *eds.* Stories of the French artists. *$3 net. Duffield.

Van Dyke, J: C: What is art?; studies in the technique and criticism of painting. $1 net. Scribner.

Wertz, A. P. Outlines in picture study to harmonize with the Illinois state course of study. 30 c. Flanagan.

What is a picture? *60 c. net McClurg.

White, G., *ed.* Master painters of Britain. *$3 net. Lane.

Wilson, *Mrs.* L. L. W., *ed.* Picture study in elementary schools. 2 v. in 1. *$1.25 net. Macmillan.

World's great pictures. *$3.50. net. Cassell.

Yerkes, C: T. Catalogue de luxe of ancient and modern paintings belonging to estate of Charles T. Yerkes. $30. Am. Art Assoc.

See also Æsthetics;—Anatomy for artists;—Artists;—Barbizon school;—British Institution;—Children;—China painting;—Color;—Cupid and Psyche;—Decoration and ornament;—Drawing;—Fine arts;—Florence;—Jesus Christ;—Landscape painting;—Louvre (The);—Madonna;—Mary (*Virgin*);—Miniatures;—Paint;—Painting books;—Perspective;—Portraits;—Wall decoration;—Water-color painting;—Woman;—*also* Boston Museum of Fine Arts;—Brentano's international art ser.;—Frances, *St.*;—Great galleries of Europe ser.;—National Gallery of Art, Washington;—Wallace collection;—*also* names of various painters.

Painters' ser. il. T. leath., 75 c. net; pap., 25 c. net. Stokes.

—Angelico. Masterpieces.

—Botticelli. Masterpieces.

—Bronzino. Masterpieces.

—Buonarotti. Masterpieces of Michaelangelo.

—Carpaccio *and* Giorgione. Masterpieces.

—Constable. Masterpieces.

—Correggio. Masterpieces.

—Dürer. Masterpieces.

—Gainsborough. Masterpieces.

—Gerard. Masterpieces.

—Giotti. Masterpieces.

Painters' ser.—Continued.
—Goya y Lucientes. Masterpieces.
—Greuze. Masterpieces.
—Hogarth. Masterpieces.
—Holbein. Masterpieces.
—Luini. Masterpieces.
—Masaccio. Masterpieces.
—Massys. Masterpieces.
—Moretto da Brescia. Masterpieces.
—Orcagna. Masterpieces.
—Ostade. Masterpieces.
—Perugino. Masterpieces.
—Poussin. Masterpieces.
—Raeburn. Masterpieces.
—Romney. Masterpieces.
—Sarto. Masterpieces.
—Tintoretto. Masterpieces.
—Veronese. Masterpieces.
—Watteau. Masterpieces.

PAINTING (*mechanical*).
Harn, O. C. How to protect structural metal; pract. hdbk. upon mixing and application of paint to iron and steel, tin, and galvanized iron. gratis. Nat. Lead.
Maire, F: Exterior painting.—Interior painting. ea., 60 c.—Modern painters' encyclopedia. $1.50. Drake.
Nelson, P: W: Calciminer's handy book. (Add. pubs. for price.) Muralo.
Schriber, F. Complete carriage and wagon painter. $1. M. T. Richardson.
See also Color;—Enamel;—Lettering;—Paint.

PAINTING BOOKS.
Kellogg, E., *and* Keller, H: G. Thirteen good animals: [pictures to color and rhymes.] 75 c. Davis Press.
Schaeffer, A. J. Happy hour paint book. 50 c. Saalfield.

PAINTINGS.
See Painters and paintings.

Pair of blue eyes. *See* Hardy, T:

Pair of madcaps. Trowbridge, J: T. †$1.50. Lothrop, L. & S.

Pais, Ettore.
Ancient Italy: hist. and geograph. investigations in central Italy, Magna Græcia, Sicily, and Sardinia; tr. from the Italian by C. Densmore Curtis. '08(F1) c. il. map, O. *$5 net. Univ. of Chic.

Palace made by music. Alden, R. M. 50 c. net. Bobbs-M.

Palace of danger. Wagnalls, M. †$1.50. Funk.

Palace of death. Fogle, H. M. $1. Fogle.

PALACES.
Miltoun, F., *pseud.* Royal palaces and parks of France. $3. L. C. Page.
Rait, R. S., *ed.* English episcopal palaces: Canterbury. $2.50 net. Pott.
See also Architecture.

Palaces of Crete. Mosso, A. *$5.25 net. Putnam.

Palacio Valdés, Armando.
José; ed., with introd. and notes, by F. J. A. Davidson, and with a vocab. by Alice P. F. Hubbard. '09(D18) (Modern language ser.) 90 c. Heath.

Paladin (The). Vachell, H. A. †$1.50. Dodd.

Palaprat, Jean.
See Brueys, David Auguste de.

Palatial homes in the city of New York. Hamilton, I. 15 c.; 25 c. I. Hamilton.

PALEOBOTANY.
See Paleontology.

PALEONTOLOGY.
Brown, B. Conard fissure, a *pleistocene* bone deposit in northern Arkansas. $2.50. Am. Museum.
Dall, W: H. Contributions to the Tertiary paleontology of the Pacific coast; 1, Miocene of Astoria and Coos Bay, Ore. 50 c. U. S., Supt. of Docs.
Gilbert, J. Z. Evesthes Jordani; primitive flounder from the Miocene of California. 15 c. Univ. of Cal.
Gilmore, C: W. Smithsonian exploration in Alaska in 1907 in search of *pleistocene* fossil vertebrates. (Add. Institution for price.) Smith Inst.
Grabau, A. W:, *and* Hervey, W. S. North American index fossils, invertebrates. $6. Seiler.
Grabau, A. W:, *and* Shimer, H. W. North American index fossils; invertebrates. In 2 v. v. 2. $6 net. Seiler.
Hollick, C: A. Studies of Cretaceous coniferous remains from Kreischerville, N. Y. $2. N. Y. Botanical.
Kindle, E: M. Devonian fauna of the Ouray limestone. Gov. Pr. Off.
Kofoid, C: A. Revision of the genus *ceratocorys,* based on skeletal morphology. 10 c. Univ. of Cal.
Merriam, J: C. Occurrence of strepsicerine antelopes in the tertiary of northwestern Nevada. 10 c.—Tertiary mammal beds of Virgin Valley and Thousand Creek in northwestern Nevada. pt. 1. 50 c. Univ. of Cal.
Miller, L. H. Teratornis, a new avian genus from Rancho la Brea. 10 c. Univ. of Cal.
Moorehead, W. K., *comp.* Prehistoric relics. $1. Andover.
Scott, D. H: Studies in fossil botany. v. 1, *$2 net; v. 2, *$4 net. Macmillan.
Seward, A. C. Fossil plants. $5 net. Putnam.
Walcott, C: D. Cambrian geology and paleontology; no. 6, Olenellus and other genus mesonacidæ; no. 7, Pre-cambrian rocks of the Bow River Valley, Alberta, Canada. No. 6, 70 c.; no. 7, 10 c. Smith. Inst.
Zittel, K. A. v. Text-book of palæntology. v. 1. *$7.40 net. Macmillan.
See also Birds;—Cat;—Echinoderms;—Fossils;—Geology; — Ichthyosauria; — Mammalia; —Peacock;—Rodents;—Turtle;—Vultures;—*also* California;—New York;—Oklahoma;—Virgin Valley.

PALESTINA, Italy.
Magoffin, R. Van D. Study of the topography and municipal history of Praeneste. 50 c. Johns Hopkins.

PALESTINE.
Eva Mary, *Sister.* Little pilgrimage to holy places. Order Transfiguration.
Finnemore, J: Holy Land. *75 c. Macmillan.
Haggard, H: R. Winter pilgrimage: travels through Palestine, Italy, and the island of Cyprus. $1.50. Longmans.

PALESTINE.—*Continued.*
Hazard, C. Brief pilgrimage in the Holy Land. **$1.25 net. Houghton M.
Hichens, R. S. Holy Land. $6 net. Century Co.
Hoenshel, E. U. My three days in Gilead. 50 c.; 30 c. E. U. Hoenshel.
Kelman, J: Holy Land. *$1.75 net. Macmillan.
Knight, W: A. No room in the inn. 50 c. Pilgrim Press.
Lees, G; R. Life and adventure beyond Jordan. **$1.75 net. Appleton.
Masterman, E. W: G. Studies in Galilee. *$1 net. Univ. of Chic.
Mathews, S. History of the New Testament times in Palestine. *$1 net. Macmillan.
Neil, G. L., *ed.* Rambles in Bible lands. *$1.75 special net. Appleton.
Schofield, A. T. With Christ in Palestine. $1.25. Fenno.
Scott, J. Pilgrimage to Canaan. $1.75. Jennie Scott.
Tarbell, M. In the Master's country. 50 c. net. Doran.
Thomson, W: M. The Land and the Book. 3 v. $7.50; $12. Harper.
Van Dyke, H: J. Out of doors in the Holy Land. **$1.50 net. Scribner.
Wilson, T: W. Knight Templar's pilgrimage to the Holy Land. $1.50; $2. T: W. Wilson.
Worcester, W: L. On holy ground: [Palestine.] 2 v. ea., **$1.50 net. Lippincott.
See also Agriculture; — Apostles; — Bedouins; — Bethlehem; — Jerusalem; —Jews;—Samaritans; —Syria.

Palestrina. Avellanus, A. 25 c. A. Avellanus.

Palgrave, Fs. Turner, comp.
Golden treasury of songs and lyrics. '08 (O10) 12°, (Best books ser.) leath., *$1 net. Dutton.
Golden treasury; sel. from the best songs and lyrical poems in the English language and arr. with notes; rev. and enl. 2 v. in 1. '09(O2) S. (Golden treasury ser.) $1.50. Macmillan.
Golden treasury. Rev. and enl. '08(Je6) 16°, *50 c. net. Macmillan.
Golden treasury of the best songs and lyrical poems in the English language. '08 (Mr21) S. (New century lib.) $1; limp leath., $1.25. Nelson.
Golden treasury of songs and lyrics, with notes; with an introd. on the study of poetry by Alphonso Gerald Newcomer. '08(Ag15) c. 16°, (Lake English classics.) 50 c. Scott, F. & Co.
—, **ed.** Latin anthology. '09(D25) 16°, (Golden treasury ser.) *$1 net. Macmillan.

Palgrave, Rob. Harry Inglis, ed.
Dict. of political economy. 3 v. [Rev. ed.] (Je18) 8°, $15. Macmillan.

PALISADES (The), N. J.
See Hudson River.

Palisades cook book; pub. by the Ladies' Aid Society of the Tenafly Presbyterian Church. [1910.] c. 5-265 p. 8°. Tenafly Presb. Ch.

PALL MALL.
See London.

PALLADINO, Eusapia.
Carrington, H. Eusapia Palladino. *$2 net. B. W. Dodge.

Palliser, C:
Modern cement sidewalk construction. '09 (F6) il. 12°, 50 c. Indust.
Practical concrete block making. '09(F6) il. 12°, 50 c. Indust.

Palm, Baroness Louise von.
Rainy day pastimes for children. '10(S10) c. il. Q. $1. Estes.

Palm Tree Island. Strang, H. $1.25 net. Doran.

Palmedo, D. Petri-.
See Petri-Palmedo, D.

Palmer, Abram Smyth, D.D.
Ideal of a gentleman; or, a mirror for gentle folks; portrayal in literature from the earliest times. '08(O17) 12°, *$1.50 net. Dutton.

Palmer, Mrs. Alice Elvira Freeman.
See Palmer, G: Herbert.

PALMER, *Mrs.* Alice Elvira Freeman.
Palmer, G: H. Life of Alice Freeman Palmer. **$1.50 net. Houghton M.

Palmer, Clarence A.
Compendium of parliamentary rules concerning motions, debate and decorum in business meetings. '07, [1908.] (My.) c. 56 p. 24°, 35 c.; pap., 15 c. C. A. Palmer.

Palmer, Clarence S.
Index to Kansas City charter, 1908. '08 (O) c. 60 p. O. pap. (Add. pub. for price.) Pipes-R.

Palmer, Clayton F.
Elem. horticulture for California schools; manual for teachers and amateur gardeners. [1910.] (Jl) c. 11-76 p. il. 8°, (Los Angeles Normal School bull.) 50 c. C. F. Palmer.

Palmer, Dan. D:, and Bartlett, J.
The science of chiropractic. v. 3, 4, 5. '08 (N) 8°, v. 3, $8; v. 4, $2; v. 5, $2; per set, $15. Palmer Sch.

Palmer, Mrs. Fanny Purdy.
California and other sonnets. '09(D18) 12°, bds., *$1.50 net. (250 copies.) P. Elder.

Palmer, Florence Ursula, [Mrs. Florence Palmer King.]
One year of Sunday school lessons for young children. New ed. '08(D12) il. 12°, *$1.25 net. Macmillan.
Second year of Sunday school lessons for young children. '09(Mr13) c. il. O. **$1.25 net. Macmillan.

Palmer, Fs. Sterne.
See Adventures in field and forest.

Palmer, Fk. Herb., ed.
See Sawin, Rosa L.

Palmer, Rev. Frederic.
Winning of immortality. '10(Ap30) c. D. $1 net. Crowell.

Palmer, F:
Big fellow. '08(S12) c. il. D. †$1.50. Moffat.
Central America and its problems; acct. of a journey from the Rio Grande to Panama; with introd. chapters on Mexico and her relations to her neighbors. '10(F19) c. il. fold. map, O. **$2.50 net. Moffat.
Danbury Rodd, aviator. '10(My7) c. D. $1.50. Scribner.

Palmer, G: Herbert.
Ethical and moral instruction in schools. '09(O16) c. D. (Riverside educational monographs.) **35 c. net. Houghton M.
The ideal teacher. '10(Ag20) c. D. (Riverside educational monographs.) 35 c. Houghton M.
Life of Alice Freeman Palmer. '08(My2) c. il. pors. O. **$1.50 net. Houghton M.
Self-cultivation in English. '09(Je5) c. D. pap., **10 c. net. Crowell.
Self-cultivation in English. '09(S18) 12°, (Riverside educational monographs.) **35 c. net. Houghton M.

Palmer, H: Robinson, ed.
See Brown, Rob. Perkins.

—, and Mrs. Alice Elvira Freeman.
The teacher. '08(N21) c. O. **$1.50 net. Houghton M.

Palmer, Lois Sedgwick, and Pease, G: W:
Lesson stories for the kindergarten grades of the Bible school; general subject; God the workman, the creator and His works. '08(Ag1) 16°, *75 c. net. Macmillan.

Palmer, Mary Eliz. Blake.
Guide to hotel housekeeping. '08(My23) c. 12°, $1. M. E. Palmer.

Palmer, Thdr. Sherman.
Private game preserves and their future in the United States. '10(Jl) 11 p. il. 8°, (U. S., Dept. of Agri., Bu. of Biological Survey, cir.)

Palmer, Truman G.
Beet sugar; letter and data concerning the beet sugar industry of Europe and the U. S. '09(S) 20 p. 8°. (Add. Superintendent for price.) U. S., Supt. of Docs.

Palmer, Wa.
Young switch tender. '08(N14) D. 50 c, McLoughlin.

Palmer, W: C.
Farm bacteriology. '08(My23) c. D. pap., 15 c. W: C. Palmer.

Palmer, W: Scott.
The church and modern men. '08(Ja4) D. *$1.20 net. Longmans.
Diary of a Modernist. '10(O22) D. $1.40 net. Longmans.
Studies in the teaching of religion. '09 (Je5) D. bds., *40 c. net. Longmans.

PALMISTRY.
Gratz, T: D. Palmistry made easy. **25 c. net. Winston.
Heron-Allen, E: Manual of cheirosophy. $1.75 Putnam.
René, E. Hands and how to read them. 50 c. Fenno.
Stevens, A. L. Palmistry made easy. 50 c. A. L. Stevens.

Palms of papyrus. *See* Monahan, M.

PALMYRA.
See Syria.

Paltsits, Victor Hugo.
First Presbyterian Church founded in 1763, Albany, New York; commemorative discourses on the occasion of the twenty-fifth anniversary of the dedication of the present edifice; corner State and Willett Streets, 23 May, 1909. '09(O23) front. O. pap., gratis. Albany First Presb. Ch.
Function of state historian of New York; read before the New York State Historical Association at its annual meeting held in Albany, Oct. 13, 1908. '09(Mr13) Q. pap., gratis. N. Y. Hist.

—, ed. *See* New York [State.] *Commissioners for Detecting and Defeating Conspiracies.*

Pam, Max.
Place of religion in good government. [1910.] (N) 37 p. 12°, 50 c. Univ. Press (Notre Dame).

Pammel, L: Hermann.
Manual of poisonous plants, chiefly of eastern North America; with brief notes on economic and medicinal plants. '10(D10) c. il. 8°, $2.50. Torch Press.
Talk on weeds; address del. before the county road school, Clinton County, Iowa, 1910; with appendix describing a few weeds. '10(D3) c. il. 12°, 50 c. L. H. Pammel.

Pan. *See* Wilde, Oscar.

PANAMA.
Ambard, E. M. Tourist guide to the West Indies, Venezuela and Isthmus of Panama. (gratis to passengers.) Hamburg-American Line.
Byford, H: T. To Panama and back. (Add. pubs. for price.) Conkey.
Hall, A. B., *and* Chester, C. L. Panama and the canal. 60 c. Newson.
International Bureau of American Republics. Panama. (Add. pubs. for price.) Int. Bu. Am. Republics.
Moore, J. H. With Speaker Cannon through the Tropics: voyage to West Indies, Venezuela and Panama. $2. Book Pr.
Nicholas, F. C. Across Panama and around the Caribbean. $1.50. Caldwell.
Randall, W. W., *and* Bartels, J: M., *comps.* Check list of the postage stamps of Panama. 50 c. Bartels.
Stevens, W. B. Trip to Panama. gratis. Lesan-G.
United States. *War Dept.* Payment of certain claims in Panama. (Add. Superintendent for price.)

PANAMA CANAL.
Bates, L. W. Retrieval at Panama. $5. Technical Lit.
Best type of canal for Panama. (Add. Superintendent for price.) U. S., Supt. of Docs.
Bigelow, J: Panama canal and the Daughters of Danaus. *50 c. net. Baker & T.
Campbell, D: N. E. Searchlight on the Panama canal. $1.25. Baltimore Bk.
Chatfield, M. A. Light on dark places at Panama. $1.50. B'way Pub.

PANAMA CANAL.—*Continued.*
Cornish, V. Panama canal and its makers. *$1.50 net. Little, B. & Co.
Freeman, J: R. Lock canal at Panama. U. S., Supt. of Docs.
Goethals, G: W. Isthmian canal. (Add. Superintendent for price.) U. S., Supt. of Docs.
Gorgas, W: C. Annual rept. of the Dept. of Sanitation of the Isthmian Canal Commission, 1907. 15 c. U. S., Supt. of Docs.
Grier, T: G. On the canal zone, Panama. $1. Wagner & H.
Hall, A. B., *and* Chester, C. L. Panama and the canal. 60 c. Newson.
Hart, A. B., *ed.* Extracts from official papers rel. to the Isthmian canal. 10 c. Simmons.
Increasing cost of construction of Panama canal. Rept. '09(My) 3 p. 8°, pap. U. S., Supt. of Docs.
Isthmian Canal: message of the President [Roosevelt.] (Add. Superintendent for price.) U. S., Supt. of Docs.
Lindsay, F. Panama and the canal to-day. $3. L. C. Page.
Papers rel. to the construction of the Panama canal. '09(My) 42 p. 8°, pap. U. S., Supt. of Docs.
Roosevelt Panama libel case against the New York *World* and Indianapolis *News*. gratis. N. Y. World.
Rousseau, Harry H. Isthmian canal; presented at the 20th annual session of the Trans-Mississippi Commercial Congress, Denver, Colo., Aug. 16-21, 1909. '10(Jl) 54 p. 8°. Gov. Pr. Off.
Stevens, J: F. Sketch of the Panama Canal. (Priv. pr.) J: F. Stevens.
United States. *War Dept.* Defenses of the Panama Canal; message from the President, transmitting letter from the Secretary of War inclosing the rept. of a board of officers of the army and the navy appointed by him to consider the defenses of the Panama Canal. [1910.] (Jl) 5 p. 8°.
Weir, H. C. Conquest of the Isthmus. **$2 net. Putnam.
Weir, H. C. With the flag in Panama; story of the construction of the Panama canal. $1.50. Wilde.
See also Dams;—Inland navigation.

Pañchatantra (The): collection of ancient Hindu tales in the recension, called Panchakhyanaka, and dated 1199 A.D., of the Jaina monk, Purnabhadra, critically ed. in the orig. Sanskrit by Dr. Johannes Hertel. '08, [1909.] (Je) 48+298 p. facsim. 4°. (Harvard Oriental ser.; ed. by C: Rockwell Lanman.) $1.50. Ginn.

Pancoast, H: Spackman.
Study lists, chronological tables and maps to accompany "An introduction to English literature." '08(O10) c. maps, 12°, 50 c. Holt.

—, and Shelly, Percy Van Dyke.
First book in English literature. '10(D10) c. il. pors. map, D. $1.25. Holt.

PANCREAS.
Bosanquet, W. C., *and* Clogg, H. S. Stomach, intestines and pancreas. $4 net. Wood.
Opie, E. L. Disease of the pancreas. $3. Lippincott.

Panders and their white slaves. Roe, C. G. $1 net. Revell.
Pandex of news. *See* Street, Arth. Irwin.

Pandolfi, Ubaldus de, tr.
Life of Venerable Sister Mary of Jesus—D. Agreda, Poor Clare nun; tr. from the original Spanish by Very Rev. Fr. Ubaldus de Pandolfi. '10(O) c. 17-193 p. 16°, 50 c. Keller-C.

Pandosto; or, Dorastus and Fawnia. *See* Greene, Rob.
Panel books; specially imported editions of great works. 20 v. '08(D12) front. ea., lambskin, *$1.25 net, boxed; leath., *$1.40 net, boxed. P. Elder.
Panel ser. 2 v. '10(D) bds., 40 c. Cassell.

PANICS.
Albert, J: C. Roosevelt and the money power: responsibility of dishonest high fianance for the panic of 1907. 10 c. Sudwarth Co.
American Academy of Political and Social Science. Lessons of the financial crisis. $1. Am. Acad. Pol. Sci.
Andrew, A. P. Substitute for cash in the panic of 1907. (Add. pub. for price.) Ellis.
Boss, W: L. Hist. of the panic of 1907. $1. Boss.
Clews, H: Financial and trade situation, past, present, and to come. (Add. pubs. for price.) H: Clews.
Conant, C: A. Hist. of modern banks of issue; with account of economic crises of the nineteenth century. $3. Putnam.
Disbrow, C: W. Analysis of the banking and currency system of the United States indicating the cause of periodic panics. gratis. U. S. Fidelity.
Fourtner, S: Cause of our financial panics. 50 c. S: Fourtner.
Johannsen, N: A. L. J. How to relieve the depression: suggestion to railroad men and bankers. (Add. author for price.) N: Johannsen.
Johannsen, N: A. L. J. Neglected point in connection with crises. $1.50. Bankers' Pub.
Kinnear, P: Wrecking the nation: crime of 1907-8. (Add. pubs. for price.) Co-operative Pub. Co.
Kohler, J. P. About panics. 15 c. Outing.
Libby, C: T. Cash, panics and industrial depressions. gratis. C: T. Libby.
Marburg, T. Panic and present depression. [1908.] (Add. pubs. for price.) Am. Acad. Pol. Sci.
Sprague, O. M. W. Hist. of crises under the national banking system. Gov. Pr. Off.

Panmure papers. Ramsay, F. M. $6. Clode.
Panorama of creation. Holbrook, D: L. *50 c. net. S. S. Times.
Pan's mountain. Rives, A. $1.50. Harper.
Pan's pipes. *See* Stevenson, Rob. L:

Panseron, Auguste Mathieu.
A B C of music: primer of vocalization; rev. and extended by N. Clifford Page. '08(O10) c. O. (Music students' lib.) $1. Ditson.

Pansies and rosemary. Rexford, E. E. $1.50 net. Lippincott.

"Pansy," pseud.
See Alden, *Mrs.* Isabella Macdonald.

PANSY.
Crane, H. H. Book of the pansy, viola and violet. *$1 net. Lane.
Cuthbertson, W: Pansies, violas and violets. 65 c. net. Stokes.

Pansy wedding. Lefferts, S. T. 60 c. Cupples & L.

Pantheistic idealism. Barrett, H. D. $1. H. D. Barrett.

Panther (The). Warner, A. †$1.25. Small.

Panting, J. Harwood.
Two runaways. '08(O10) il. D. †$1.25. Warne

PANTOMIME.
Irish, M. Favorite song pantomimes. 30 c. Flanagan.
Schell, S., *comp.* Werner's book of pantomimes. 60 c.; 35 c. Werner.

Panton, Mrs. Jane Ellen Frith.
Fresh leaves and green pastures. '09(Jl10) O. *$3.50 net. Brentano's.
Leaves from a life. '08(Ag15) O. *$3.50 net. Brentano's.

PAPACY.
See Catholic church;—Popes.

PAPER.
Andés, L: E. Treatment of paper for special purposes. (Add. pubs. for price.) Van Nostrand.
Clapperton, G: Practical paper-making. $2.50. Van Nostrand.
Cross, C. F., *and* Bevan, E: J: Text-book on paper making. $5. Spon.
Lawson, P. V. Paper-making in Wisconsin. State Hist., Wis.
Sindall, R. W. Manufacture of paper. *$2 net. Van Nostrand.
Stevens, H: P. Paper mill chemist. **$2.50 net. Van Nostrand.
United States. *Congress House. Committee on Agriculture.* Substitute for wood in the manufacture of paper pulp; report. '09(My) 8 p. 8°. (Add. Superintendent for price.) U. S., Supt. of Docs.
Watt, A. Art of paper-making. $3. Van Nostrand
Wiley, H. W., *and others.* Durability and economy in papers for permanent records. pap., 15 c. U. S., Supt. of Docs.
See also Stationers and stationery.

Paper birch. '08, [1909.] (My) 7 p. 8°, (U. S., Dept. of Agriculture; Forest Service, silvical leaflet.) pap. (Add. Superintendent for price.) U. S., Supt. of Docs.

PAPER MONEY.
See Money.

PAPER TRADE.
Post, L. D. Watermarks and brands used in the American paper trade. $1. L. D. Post.

PAPER WORK.
Beckwith, M. H. Story telling with the scissors. 50 c. M. Bradley.
Kunou, C: A. Manual of cardboard construction for third, fourth and fifth grades. 35 c. Jones' Bk. Store.
Leonard, R. J. Manual of cardboard construction. (Add. pubs. for price.) Bd. of Educ., Berkeley, (Cal.)
Moran, M. L. Manual art with the scissors. 75 c. M. Bradley.

Papers of the Historical Society of Delaware. 4°. Delaware Hist. Soc.
—Smith. Brief acct. of the services rendered by the Second Regiment Delaware Volunteers in the War of the Rebellion. 50 c.

PAPUA.
Grimshaw, B. E. New New Guinea. $3.50 net. Lippincott.
Ker, A. Papuan fairy tales. $1.50 net. Macmillan.
Mackay, J. A. K. Across Papua. *$2.50 net. Scribner.
Seligmann, C: G. Melanesian of British New Guinea. $7 net. Putnam.

PAPYRI.
Davis, T. M. Excavations: Biban el Moluk; funeral papyrus of Iouiya. *$12.50 net. Dutton.
Goodspeed, E. J. Chicago literary papyri. *50 c. net. Univ. of Chic.
Milligan, G: Selections from the Greek papyri. $1.50 net. Putnam.

Paquin, S: Savil.
Garden fairies. '08(N21) c. il. O. **$1 net. Moffat.

"Parabellum," pseud.
See Grautoff, Ferdinand Heinrich.

Parable of the rose. Allen, L. W. **$1.25 net. Putnam.

PARABLES.
Bell, L. C. Obil, keeper of camels; being the parable of the man whom the disciple saw casting out devils. 50 c. P. Elder.
Broughton, L. G. Kingdom parables and their teaching. 75 c. net. Revell.
Calkins, W. Parables for our times. 50 c. Pilgrim Press.
Finlayson, T. C. Ship engines: a parable. **15 c. net. Eaton & M.
Linn, S: Seven parables of the kingdom. 40 c. S: Linn.
Russell, E. Parables of Jesus. 20 c. Y. M. C. A.
Wilberforce, S: Agathos; The rocky island, and other Sunday stories and parables. *45 c. net. Putnam.

Parables from nature. Gatty, M. S. $2 net. Macmillan.

PARACELSUS, Philippus Aureolus, [Theophrastus Bombastus von Hohenheim.]
Hartmann, F. Life and doctrines of Philippus Theophrastus Bombast of Hohenheim. $2.50. Theo. Pub. Co.

Paradise, Rev. Fk. Ilsley.
Church and the individual. '10(O22) c. D. $1.50 net. Moffat.

Paradise lost. *See* Milton, J:

Paradise of childhood. *See* Wiebé, E: Golden jubilee ed.

Paradise or gardens of the **holy fathers.** Budge, E. W. A., *ed.* *$4 net. Duffield.

Paradise, the city and throne. Scott, E. 80 c.; 50 c. E. Scott.

PARADISO (*by Dante*).
Vernon, W: W. **Readings on the Paradiso.** 2 v. *$4 net. **Macmillan.**
See also Dante Alighieri.

Paragraph-writing. Scott, F. N. $1.25. Allyn & B.

PARAGUAY, South America.
International Bureau of American Republics. Paraguay; general descriptive data. Int. Bu. Am. Republics.

Paralipomena. *See* Bible. N. T.

Parallel bar exercises. Cromie, W: J. 10 c. Spalding.

PARALLELISM.
See **History.**

Paramânanda, Swami.
Principles and purposes of Vedanta. '10 (My) c. 37 p. 16°, 25 c. Paramananda.
True spirit of **religion is universal. '08,** [1909.] (F) c. 40 p. 12°. (Add. pubs. for price.) **Vedanta.**
Vedanta in practice. '09(Ap3) c. por. S. **$1 net. Baker & T.

PARANOIA.
See **Insanity.**

PARASITES.
Braun, M. G., *and* Lühe, M. Hdbk. of pract. parasitology. $3.50 net. Wood.
Campbell, D. M., *and* Lacroix, J. V. Essentials of parasitology. $1.25. E. Herbert.
Hindle, E: Life hist. of *trypanosoma dimorphon,* Dutton & Todd. 50 c. Univ. of Cal.
Hunter, S: J:, *and* Glenn, P. A. Green bug and its enemies; study in insect parasitism. gratis. S: J: Hunter.
Kaupp, B: F. Animal parasites and parasitic diseases. $2.25. A. Eger.
Nuttall, G: H. F., *and* Shipley, A. E., *eds.* Parasitotogy. *$1.50 net. Putnam.
Stitt, E. R. Practical bacteriology, blood work and animal parasitology. *$1.50 net. Blakiston.
Ward, H: B. Iconographia parasitorum hominis: **parasites of man. 50 c.** Univ. of Neb.
Wilson, H. L. Gracilariophila, a new parasite on gracilaria confervoides. 10 c. Univ. of Cal.
See also **Bacteria;—Fungi;—Mistletoe.**

PARASITOLOGY.
See **Parasites.**

PARATHYROID GLANDS.
Ochsner, A. J:, *and* Thompson, R. L. Surgery and pathology of the thyroid and parathyroid glands. $6 net. Mosby.

PARCELS-POST.
See **Post-Office.**

Parchment (The). Wade, R. A. S. $1. Cochrane.

Parcimony in nutrition. Browne, *Sir* J. C-. **75 c. net. Funk.

Pardee, Laura Peckham, and Smith, Carrie J.
The primer. '08(Ag22) c. il. D. (Nature and life readers.) 28 c. Powers.

Pardoned lifer. Contant, G: C. $1.25. G: C. Contant.

Parent and child. Lodge, *Sir* O. J. 50 c. net. Funk.

Parenthood and race culture. Saleeby, C. W. **$2.50 net. **Moffat.**

Parent's mistake. *See* Hays, Milton D. My grandfather's best brand.

PARENTS.
See Family.

Parerga. Sheehan, P. A. **$1.60 net. **Longmans.**

Paret, Anna Parmly, ed.
Harper's handy book for girls. '10(F19) c. il. D. $1.75. **Harper.**

Paret, Jahial Parmly.
How to play lawn-tennis; cont. pract. instruction from an expert on making lawn tennis strokes; brief description and history of the game, and other useful information. '10(S3) c. il. 12°, (Spalding's athletic lib.) pap., 10 c. Am. Sports.

Parham, Eug. Chilton, and Shedd, J: Cutler.
Miscellaneous tests of electric car equipment. '10(Je4) c. figs. D. $1 net. McGraw-H.
Shop tests on electric car equipment for inspectors and foremen. '09(Mr13) c. D. $1. McGraw.

Paris, Burt Jay.
Care of automobiles. '08(Je20) c. D. $1. Doubleday, P.

PARIS, France.
Baedeker, K. Paris and its environs. 90 c. net. Scribner.
Cain, G. Walks in Paris. $2. Macmillan.
Descaves, L., *ed.* Color of Paris. ***$6 net. Dodd.**
Dickens, C: Parisian scenes from A tale of two cities. 30 c. net. Putnam.
Guide to Paris and its environs. $1 net. Platt & P.
Hessling, E. *and* W. **Louis XIV. furniture in the Louvre and the Museum of Decorative Arts (Paris). $13.40. Hessling.**
Ivimy, A. M. Woman's guide to Paris. $1.25 net. Brentano's.
Lucas, E: V. Wanderer in Paris. $2.50 net; *$1.75 net. Macmillan.
Raphael, J: N. P. Pictures of Paris and some Parisians. *$1.50 net. Macmillan.
Rutter, F. Path to Paris. *$5 net. Lane.
Savidge, E. C. American in Paris; biographical novel of Franco-Prussian war. $1.50. Lippincott.
Society recollections in Paris and Vienna, 1879-1904. $3. Appleton.
Washburn, C. C. Pages from the book of Paris. $3 net. Houghton M.
Whiting, L. Paris the beautiful. **$2 net. Little, B. & Co.
Williams, L. **Vest pocket guide to Paris.** *50 c. net. **Doubleday, P.**
Williams, M. Paris. 75 c. net. Macmillan.
See also **French Academy;—French Revolution;—Louvre;—Museum of Decorative Art.**

PARIS BOURSE.
Vidal, E. Hist. and methods of the Paris Bourse. Gov. Pr. Off.

PARIS GREEN.
Fuller, F: D. Analysis of Paris green. —Preliminary report on results of analysis of Paris green. **Penn. Dept. of Agriculture.**

Parish, J: Carl.
John Chambers. '09, [1910.] (Jl) 11+279 p. pors. 8°, (Iowa biographical ser.) $2. State Hist. Ia.
"Notes and references" (6 p.).

PARISHES.
See Church of England.

Parisian scenes from a Tale of Two Cities. Dickens, C: 30 c. net. Putnam.

Park, C: Edwards.
Jesus of Nazareth. '09(N) c. 72 p. 8°, (Beacon ser.) 40 c.; pap., 30 c.; Teachers' ed., 65 c. Unitarian S. S.

Park, Ja.
Text-book of theodolite surveying and levelling. '08(D19) il. 12°, *$2 net. Lippincott.

Park, J: Edg.
Wonder of His gracious works; exposition of the Sermon on the Mount. '09(D25) c. D. *$1 net. Pilgrim Press.

Park, Jos. C.
Educational woodworking for home and school. '08(Ap4) c. il. 12°, *$1 net. Macmillan.

Park, W: Hallock, M.D., and Williams, Anna W., M.D.
Pathogenic micro-organisms, including bacteria and protozoa. 3d ed., rev. and enl. '08(Ag29); 4th ed. '10(N) il. 8°, ea., *$3.75 net. Lea.

Park-Street papers. Perry, B. **$1.25 net. Houghton M.

Parke, Jos. Richardson, M.D.
Human sexuality; medico-literary treatise on the hist. and pathology of the sex instinct, for the use of physicians and jurists. 4th rev. ed. '09, [1910.] (Jl) c. 16+476 p. 8°, $3. Professional.
Bibliography (10 p.).
Wizard of Damavant; tale of the crusades. '10(D3) c. il. D. $1.20 net. Professional.

PARKE FAMILY.
See Genealogies: Parks, F. S.

Parker, Amasa Junius, jr., ed.
See New York [State.] Annot. codes.—Banking law.—Code of civil procedure.—Code of criminal procedure.—Insurance law.—Penal code.—Penal law.—Village law.

Parker, Arth. C.
Excavations in an Erie Indian village and burial site at Ripley, Chautauqua Co., N. Y. '08(Je13) il. 8°, (New York State Museum bulletin, Archeology.) pap., 30 c. N. Y. State Educ.

Parker, B.
Last of the Grays: verses. '09(O9) il. obl. O. bds., $1.50. Stokes.

Parker, C. I., comp.
See Flanigan, D: W.

Parker, C: W., comp. and ed.
See New Jersey digest.

Parker, Clara Hathaway Stetson, [Mrs. H. C. Parker.]
Stories from the Old Testament '09(N) c. 122 p. 8°, (Beacon ser.) 35 c.; pap., 25 c.; Teachers' ed., 65 c. Unitarian S. S.

Parker, E: Harper.
Ancient China simplified. '08(D12) 4°, *$3 net. Dutton.
John Chinaman and a few others. New and rev. ed. '09(My22) 12°, *$1.25 net. Dutton.
Studies in Chinese religion. '10(D10) il. 8°, $3 net. Dutton.

Parker, Rev. Edn. Pond.
Appreciation of Calvin Chapin, D.D., of Rocky Hill, Conn. '08, [1909.] (My) 12 p. il. por. 8°, (Chapin Family Association pubs.) (Priv. pr.) G. W. Chapin.

Parker, Eric.
Highways and byways in Surrey. '08(D26) il. map, 12°, (Highways and byways ser.) $2. Macmillan.

Parker, Frances.
Winding waters. '09(N20) c. il. D. $1.50. C. M. Clark.

Parker, Mrs. G. R.
See Robins, Eliz.

Parker, G: A:
Out of the depths. '09(Ja16) c. il. D. $1.25. Reid Pub.

Parker, G: F.
Recollections of Grover Cleveland. '09(O9) c. pors. facsim., O. **$3 net. Century Co.

Parker, Rev. G: Lawrence.
Other side of psycho-therapy. '09(Ja23) c. 12°, 25 c. G: L. Parker.

Parker, G: Warren.
Poems. '09(My) 62 p. il. 12°, 35 c. G: W. Parker.

Parker, Sir Gilbert.
Adventurer of the North. [1910.] (F) $1.25. Harper.
Formerly published by Macmillan.
Battle of the strong. [1910.] (F) $1.50. Harper.
Formerly published by Houghton Mifflin Co.
Lane that had no turning. [1910.] (F) $1.50. Harper.
Formerly published by Doubleday, Page & Co.
Lover's diary. [1910.] (F) $1.25. Harper.
Northern lights. '09(O2) c. il. D. †$1.50. Harper.
Pierre and his people. [1910.] (F) $1.25. Harper.
Formerly published by Macmillan.
Romany of the snows. [1910.] (F) $1.25. Harper.
Formerly published by Macmillan.
When Valmond came to Pontiac. [1910.] (F) $1.25. Harper.
Formerly published by Macmillan.

Parker, Mrs. H. C.
See Parker, Clara Hathaway Stetson.

Parker, Harry Caldwell.
Hdbk. of diseases of the eye; text-book for students and practitioners. '10(O) c. 11+303 p. il. 8°, $2. Davis.

Parker, Sir Horatio Gilbert.
Cumner's son, and other South Sea folk. '10(O1) c. D. $1.20 net. Harper.

Parker, Howard, rep.
See Oklahoma. *Criminal ct. of appeals.* Repts.—*Sup. ct.* Criminal repts.—Repts.

Parker, Ja.
Rear-Admirals Schley, Sampson and Cervera; review of the naval campaign of 1898 in pursuit and destruction of the Spanish fleet. '10(F5) c. il. pors. O. **$3 net. Neale.

Parker, J: H:
Indoor target practice with sub-target gun machine. '10(Mr) 28 p. il. 16°, $1. Arms and the Man.

Parker, J: Scott.
Draft of by-laws for a New Jersey corporation. '10(Ap) c. 11 p. O. pap., 50 c. Broun-G.
Draft of by-laws for a New York corporation. '10(My) c. 14 p. O. pap., 50 c. Broun-G.
Where and how: hdbk. of incorporation, a digest and comparison of the corporation laws of Arizona, Delaware, Maine, Massachusetts, New Jersey, New York, Pennsylvania, South Dakota and West Virginia. 3d ed., rev. 1907, with the addition of a chapter of hints, comp. by C: F. Bostwick. '08(Ja25); 4th ed., rev. 1910. '10(O) c. O. ea., $1; pap., 50 c. Broun-G.
—, **ed.** Corporation manual, [etc.] 16th ed. '10(Ap) c. O. $6.50. Corp. Manual.
See also Corporation legal manual.

Parker, Lester Shepard.
Nancy MacIntyre: tale of the prairies. '08 (D19) c. il. D. $1. Badger.

Parker, Lewis Rathbone, ed.
See New York [State.] Code of criminal procedure.

Parker, Lottie Blair.
Homespun. '09(Je19) c. D. †$1.50. Holt.

Parker, L: Napoleon.
See Jacobs, W: Wymark.

Parker, Mary Moncure.
New monologues and dialect stories. '09 (Ja23) c. por. 12°, $1. Drake.

Parker, Mary Saltonstall, [Mrs. W. P. Parker.]
Small things antique [in verse]. '09(Jl) c. 24 p. il. 16°, 50 c. W. P. Parker.

Parker, Prescott Alphonso.
Tom and Kitty, story of Mobile Bay. '09 (F6) c. il. D. pap., 25 c. P. A. Parker.

Parker, T. Jeffery.
An element. course of practical zoology. 2d ed. '08(Ap18) il. 12°, *$2.60 net. Macmillan.

Parker, Rev. Thdr.
Works. Centenary ed. In 14 v. v. 4-6. '08(D19); v. 7-9. '09(N20); v. 10-14. '10(D) pors. 8°, ea., $1 net; per set, $10 net. Am. Unitarian.

Parker, W. B., ed.
Psychotherapy: course of reading in sound medicine, sound psychology and sound religion. 12 nos. '08(O3) c. il. 8°, (Course of reading.) pap., $10. Centre Pub.

Parker, Mrs. W. P.
See Parker, Mary Saltonstall.

Parker, W: Ruston Percival, and Clark, G: M.
Canadian company law. '08(D) 32+683 p. 8°, $6.50. Cromarty.

Parkes, Mrs. G. R.
See Robins, Eliz.

Parkes, L: Coltman, and Kenwood, H: R:
Hygiene and the public health. 3d ed. '08, [1909.] (Mr) 11+620 p. il. 8°, *$3 net. Blakiston.

Parkhurst, C: H:, D.D.
Little lower than the angels. '08(D26) c. O. *$1.25 net. Revell.

Parkhurst, Howard Elmore.
Complete system of harmony. '08(N21) c. por. 8°, $2. Fischer.

Parkhurst, Lucia F.
Good-night stories. '08(N21) c. il. D. 50 c. Eaton & M.

Parkinson, E: Kneeland.
Guide to the country home. '09(S18) c. il. D. *$1 net. Outing.

Parkinson, Ethel, and Chapman, Wa.
Dutchie doings. '09(Ag) 50 p. il. in col. f°, $1. Dodge.

Parkinson, J:
A reformer by proxy. '09(S18) D. $1.50. Lane.

Parkinson, R:
George Washington. '09(Ap10) c. 12°, 50 c. Lord Balt. Pr.

Parkinson, Sarah Woods.
Charles Nisbet, first president of Dickinson College; his book, 1736-1804. '08(Ag22) c. il. 12°, pap., gratis. S. W. Parkinson.

Parkman, Fs.
Works. New library ed. In 13 v. '10 (O15) il. 8°, ea., $2; per set, $26; hf. cf., $58.50; hf. mor., $58.50; hf. levant, $78. Little, B. & Co.
Conspiracy of Pontiac: introd. by T: Seccombe. '08(Mr7) 2 v., 16°. (Everyman's lib.) ea., *35 c. net; leath., *70 c. net. Dutton.
Oregon trail; ed., with notes and introd., by Ottis B. Sperlin. '10(Jl2) c. D. (Longmans' English classics.) 25 c. net. Longmans.
Oregon trail; sketches of prairie and Rocky Mountain life; ed. by C: H. J. Douglas. '10(F12) c. por. map. T. (Macmillan's pocket Am. and Eng. classics.) **25 c. net. Macmillan.
Oregon trail; ed. for use in schools; with an introd. and explanatory notes by E: E. Hale, jr. '10(S17) c. map. 12°. (Standard literature ser.) 40 c. Newson.

Parks, Fk. Sylvester, comp.
Genealogy of the Parke families of Massachusetts; including Richard Parke of Cambridge, William Park, of Groton, and others. '09(Ap24) il. pors. 8°, $5.20. F. S. Parks.

Parks, Karl E.
See Lane, Clarence Bronson.

PARKS.
American Academy of Political and Social Science. Public recreation facilities. $1.50; $1. Am. Acad. Pol. Sci.
Bashore, H. B. Sanitation of recreation camps and parks. $1. Wiley.
Blackmar, F. W. Playgrounds and parks. gratis. Univ. of Kan.
Miltoun, F., *pseud.* Royal palaces and parks of France. $3. L. C. Page.

PARKS.—*Continued.*
Muir, J: Our national parks. *$3 net. **Houghton M.**
New York [City.] Bureau of Municipal Research. Park question. 2 v. pt. 1, $1; pt. 2, 50 c. Bu. Municipal.
See also Birds;—Gardens and gardening;—Playgrounds;—Trees;—Wisconsin.

Parkyn, Herbert Arth., M.D.
Auto-suggestion; what it is and how to use it for health, happiness and success. 6th ed. '09(S) c. 190 p. 16°, $1. **Suggestion.**

Parler (Le) populaire des Canadiens français. Dionne, N-E., *ed.* *$3 net. Stechert.

PARLIAMENT (*English*).
Firth, C: H. House of Lords during the Civil War. $2.60. Longmans.
Lucy, H: W. Memories of eight parliaments. *$2.50 net. Putnam.
McIlwain, C: H. High Court of Parliament and its supremacy. $2.50 net. Yale Univ.
O'Donnell, F. H. M. Hist. of the Irish parliamentary party. 2 v. $5 net. **Longmans.**

PARLIAMENTARY LAW.
Coggins, P. H. Parliamentary law. 50 c. Penn Pub. Co.
Crocker, G: G. Principles of procedure in deliberative bodies. 75 c. net. Putnam.
Gregg, F. M. Hdbk. of parliamentary law. 50 c. Ginn.
Longan, *Mrs.* E. L. Parliamentary rules made easy. Hudson.
Palmer, C. A. Compendium of parliamentary rules. 35 c.; 15 c. C. A. Palmer.
Paul, N. B. Parliamentary law. 75 c. Century Co.
Rogers, A. E. Manual of the essentials of parliamentary law. 25 c. A. E. Rogers.
Scanlan, C: M. Rules of order for societies, conventions, public meetings and legislative bodies. 50 c. net. Caspar.
Sherman, *Mrs.* M. B. K. Parliamentary law and rules of procedure. 75 c. J: D. Sherman.
Strong-Tracy, *Mrs.* E. Club woman's friend. $1. Dealy.

Parliamentary usage of the general conference, M. E. church, South. Harrison, J: E. 25 c. Pub. Ho. of M. E. Ch., So.

Parlin, C: C.
Twentieth century high school. [1910.] (Je) 15 p. D. pap., gratis. A. B. O'Neil.

Parloa, Maria.
New cook book and marketing guide. Rev. ed. of 1908, with up-to-date treatise on food, working appliances and sanitation. '09(Je19) c. il. D. $1.50. Estes.

—, and Hill, Mrs. Janet McKenzie.
Chocolate and cocoa recipes, by Miss Parloa, and home made candy recipes, by Mrs. Janet McKenzie Hill. '09, [1910.] (Ap) c. 63 p. il. 16°, gratis. W. Baker.

Parmele, Mrs. Mary Platt.
Short history of Rome and Italy. New and enl. ed. '08(D5) c. 12°, $1. Scribner.

Parmelee, Maurice.
Principles of anthropology and sociology in their relation to criminal procedure. '08 (S26) 12°, (Citizens' library.) *$1.25 net. Macmillan.

PAROCHIAL DUTIES.
See Ministers (*of the Gospel*).

PAROCHIAL SCHOOLS.
See Schools.

PARODY.
Bangs, J: K. Potted fiction. †50 c.; †25 c. Doubleday, P.
Hartman, J. F., *comp.* Monologues and parodies. 75 c. T: J. Carey.
McKee, B. Shakespeare in limerick. 75 c. Morton.
Metcalfe, J. S. Another three weeks. 25 c. Life Pub. Co.

Parr, Olive Katharine.
A red-handed saint. '10(My14) 12°, $1.10 net. Benziger.

Parr, S: Wilson, jr., and Barker, Perry.
Occluded gases in coal. [1910.] (Mr) 28 p. il. tabs., 8°, (Univ. of Ill. bull.; Engineering Experiment Station.) pap., gratis. Univ. of Ill.
Bibliography: [footnotes] (7 p.).

—, and Hamilton, Nain Delf.
The weathering of coal. '08(Mr) pap., gratis. Univ. of Ill.

—, and Kenworthy, Fs. C:
Modification of Illinois coal by low temperature distillation. '08(N) c. 48 p. il. 8°, (Univ. of Illinois bull.) gratis. Univ. of Ill.

—, and Wheeler, Wilfred Forrest.
Unit coal and the composition of coal ash. [1910.] (Je) 67 p. il. tabs., 8°, (Univ. of Ill. Engineering Experiment Station bull.) gratis. Univ. of Ill.
Weathering of coal; ser. of 1909. [1910.] (Jl) 43 p. il. 8°, (Univ. of Ill., Engineering Experiment Station, bull.) pap., gratis. Univ. of Ill.

Parrish, Randall.
Don MacGrath. '10(O22) c. il. O. $1.50. McClurg.
Keith of the border. '10(O8) c. col. il. O. $1.35 net. McClurg.
Last voyage of the "Donna Isabel." '08 (Ag29) c. il. D. $1.50. McClurg.
My lady of the South: a story of the Civil War. '09(O9) c. il. O. $1.50. McClurg.
Prisoners of chance. '08(Ap4) c. il. O. $1.50. McClurg.

Parrock, H. P.
"Grades of steel." '10(S3) c. il. 16°, $1. H. P. Parrock.

Parry, Sir C: Hubert Hastings.
Johann Sebastian Bach; story of the development of a great personality. '09 (N6) c. il. por. O. **$3.50 net. Putnam.

Parry, Oliver Randolph.
Betsy Ross and the United States flag; Philadelphia woman maker of the first standard: paper read before the Bucks County Historical Society, at Doylestown, Pa., Jan. 19, 1909. '09(N) 34 p. 12°, 20 c.; pap., 10 c. T. W. Worrall.

Parry, T:, D.D.
Riches of grace. '10(Je25) c. D. 50 c. **Westminster.**

Parry, T: Wood.
When daddy was a boy. '08(Ja11) il. 12°, $1. Hudson.

PARRY FAMILY.
See Genealogies: McPike, E. F.

PARSEES.
See Zoroaster.

PARSIFAL.
Schottenfels, G. R. Parzifal, and other stories from the German. 50 c. Educ. Pub.

Parson, Kirk.
Fast game. '10(Ag6) c. il. D. $1.25. Roxburgh.

Parson Gay's three sermons. Edes, R. T. $1.50. Cochrane.

Parson in the Australian bush. Mathews, C. H. S. $2. Longmans.

Parsonage between two manors. Gebhard, E. L. $1.50. E. L. Gebhard.

Parsons, Belle Ragnar.
Plays and games for indoors and out; rhythmic activities correlated with the studies of the school program. '09 (My15) c. il. O. $1.50. Barnes.

Parsons, Carl C.
Business administration; principles of business organization and system, and the actual methods of business operation and management. '09(N) c. 232 p. figs. $3. System.

Parsons, C: Lathrop.
Chemistry and literature of beryllium. '09 (Ap10) c. 8°, $2. Chemical.
See also Moses, Alfr. Jos.

Parsons, Mrs. Clement.
See Parsons, Florence Mary.

Parsons, Eugene.
Making of Colorado. '08(My16) c. il. pors. S. 60 c. Flanagan.

Parsons, Florence Mary, [Mrs. Clement Parsons.]
Incomparable Siddons. '09(N20) il. O. *$3.50 net. Putnam.

Parsons, Fk.
Choosing a vocation. '09(Je12) c. tabs., O. **$1 net Houghton M.

Parsons, Harry de Berkeley.
See Soper, G: Alb.

Parsons, Henrietta Grace.
Jimpy stories. '08(O10) c. il. 12°, †$1.25. Dutton.

Parsons, H: Griscom.
Children's gardens for pleasure, health and education. '10(My14) c. il. D. $1 net. Sturgis & W.

Parsons, Ja. G.
Protection's favor to foreigners. '09(Jl3) O. pap. (Add. pubs. for price.) Reform Club.

Parsons, J:, D.D.
Each for all and all for each: the individual in his relation to the social system. '10 (Ja8) c. D. *$1.50 net. Sturgis & W.

Parsons, Lillian Belle, comp.
Found in friendship's fields. '09, [1910.] (F) c. 128 p. 12°, $1.25. L. B. Parsons.

Parsons, Philip A.
Responsibility for crime. '09(Jl17) c. O. (Columbia Univ. studies in history, economics and public law.) pap., $1.50. Longmans.

Parsons, Rev. Reuben.
Sermons; ed. by Rev. J. H. Cronenberger. '08(D) c. 14+462 p. 12°, $1.50. McVey.

Parsons, S:
Landscape gardening. '10(O8) c. il. O. bds., $2 net. Lane.

Parsons, Theophilus.
Laws for business for all the states and territories of the Union and the Dominion of Canada, with forms and direction for all transactions, [etc.] New enl. ed., rev. to date, with valuable fresh chapters on recent business legislation. '08(F); New and enl. ed., rev. to date. '09(N) c. O. shp., ea., $4. Scranton.

Parsons, W: Franklin.
Parsons' hdbk. of forms; compendium of business and social rules and a complete work of reference and self-instruction. 14th ed., rev. and enl. '10(F19) c. il. por. 8°, $4. Nashville Bk.

Parsons' complete annot. pocket code. See New York [State.] Code of civil procedure.

Particeps criminis. Chapman, E. S. 75 c. net. Revell.

Participle in Plautus, Petronius, and Apuleius. Sidey, T: K. *50 c. net. Univ. of Chic.

Participle in the book of Acts. Williams, C: B. *50 c. net. Univ. of Chic.

PARTIES.
See Entertainments.

PARTIES (*political*).
Bacon, A: O. Democrats and the tariff. U. S., Supt. of Docs.
Fess, S. D. History of political theory and party organization in the U. S. $1.50. World's Events.
Griffin, A. P. C., *comp.* Lib. of Congress list of works rel. to political parties in U. S. 10 c. U. S., Supt. of Docs.
Ostrogorski, M. I. Democracy and the party system in the United States. $1.75 net. Macmillan.
Salt, M. H., *ed.* Candidates and the issues; official hist. of the campaign of 1908. $1.50. Vansant.
Smith, C: E., *comp.* From Lincoln to Taft, 1854-1908; why I am a Republican. (Add. pubs. for price.) Hammerling.
Tweedy, J: Hist. of the Republican National Conventions from 1856 to 1908. $2. J: Tweedy.
See also Democratic party:—Republican party;—Socialism.

Partners three. Mapes, V. †$1.25. Stokes.

PARTNERSHIP.
Gilmore, E. A. Cases on the law of partnership. $3.75. West Pub.
Pepper, G: W., *and* Lewis, W: D. Cases on the law of association. pt. 1, 60 c.; pt. 2, 55 c.; pt. 3, 55 c. W: D. Lewis.
See also Contracts;—Corporations.

Partridge, Anthony.
The distributors. '08(N14) c. D. †$1.50. McClure.
Kingdom of earth. '09(My22) c. il. D. †$1.50. Little, B. & Co.
Passers-by. '10(Ja8) c. il. D. †$1.50. Little, B. & Co.

Partridge, Bernard.
See Guthrie, T: Anstey.

Partridge, C: Sumner.
Electrotyping. 2d ed. '09(My22) c. il. 12°, $2. Inland Pr.
Stereotyping: a practical treatise of all known methods of stereotyping. 2d ed., rev. and enl. '09(Ag7) c. il. 12°, $2. Inland Pr.

Partridge, G: Everett.
Outline of individual study. '10(Ap23) c. D. $1.25 net. Sturgis & W.

PARTRIDGE.
See Birds.

Partsch, Herman, M.D.
Messages to mothers: presenting a simple, practical and natural scheme for the right diet, care and treatment of mother and child. '08(My2) c. front. D. **$1.50 net. P. Elder.

Pa's picnic. Wyeth, A. H. Dramatic.

Pascal, Blaise.
Thoughts; sel. and tr. by Moritz Kaufmann. '08(N7) 16°, (Cambridge devotional ser.) *45 c. net; *60 c. net; leath., *75 c. net. Putnam.

—, **La Rochefoucauld, François, [6th Duc de, Prince de Marsillac,] and Vauvenargues, Luc de Clapier, Marquis de.**
Pensees, Maximes et Réflexions; ed. by Alfr. T. Baker. '08(Je6) 16°, *40 c. net; '10(D24) 16°, (Macmillan's new ser. of French texts.) 35 c. net. Macmillan.

PASCAL, Blaise.
St. Cyres, *Viscount.* Pascal. *$3 net. Dutton.

Pass (The). White, S. E: **$1.25 net. Doubleday, P.

Passages from the past. Argyll, J. D. S. C., *Duke* of. 2 v. *$6.50 net. Dodd.

Passer-by (The). Troubetzkoy, *Prince* P. †$1.50. Doubleday, P.

"Passerby" in London. Campbell, W. S. *$1.75 net. Scribner.

Passers-by. Partridge, A. †$1.50. Little, B. & Co.

Passing English of the Victorian era. Ware, J. R. *$3 net. Dutton.

Passing of gold. Morgan, A. T. $1. J: A. Anderson.

Passing of medievalism in religion. Maddox, F. E. 60 c. Texarkanian.

Passing of Morocco. Moore, F: **$1.50 net. Houghton M.

Passing of the saloon. **Hammell, G: M.,** ***ed.*** $2; $2.75; $3.50. Tower Press.

Passing of the Shereefian Empire. Ashmead-Bartlett, E. $4 net. Dodd.

Passing of the Tariff. **Bridgman, R. L.** **$1.25 net. Sherman, F.

Passing of the third floor back. Jerome, J. K. †$1. Dodd.

Passing of the word. Henshaw, H. H. $1.50. Torch Press.

Passing of time. Thomson, W: de F. *$1 net. R. G. Cooke.

Passing Protestantism and coming Catholicism. Smyth, N. **$1 net. Scribner.

Passing voice: [poems.] '07. [1908.] 89 p. D. bds., $1. Badger.

PASSION (The).
See Good Friday;—Holy week;—Jesus Christ;—Lent.

Passion for men. Hallenbeck, E. F. 40 c. net. Revell.

Passion for reality. Scudder, D. 50 c. net. Revell.

Passion in the desert. *See* Balzac, Honoré de.

PASSION PLAY, Oberammergau.
See Oberammergau.

Passion (The) play of Oberammergau; tr. from the German text, with an historical introd., by Montrose J. Moses. '09(D18) por. O. $1.50. Duffield.

PASSION WEEK.
See Holy Week.

Passions of the French romantics. Gribble, F. H: $3.75 net. Scribner.

Passiontide and Easter. **Lennard, V. R. 80 c. Whittaker.**

Passmore, Herbert Jefferson.
See Texas. Instructions to juries.

Passover (The). Howard, C. $1 net. Fenno.

Passy, Jean, and Rambeau, Adolphe.
Chrestomathie française: morceaux choisis de prose et de poésie avec pronunciation figurée a l'usage des etrangers; précédés d'une introduction sur la methode phonetique. 3d ed., rev. and corr. '08(O17) c. O. (Association phonétique internationale.) *$1.25 net. Stechert.

Past and present. *See* **Carlyle, T:**

Past, present and future. White, J. E. $1.50; $2; $3. Southern Pub.

Past-times. Pegram, W: M. *$1 net. J: H. Saumenig.

Pasteboard proclivities. Hubbard, E. 10 c. Roycrofters.

Paston, G:, [pseud. for Emily Morse Symonds.]
Mr. Pope, his life and times. In 2 v. '09 (N20) il. O. *$6.50 net, boxed. Putnam.

Paston letters: selections; ed. by M. D. Jones. '10(Ag13) 12°, 40 c. net. Putnam.

Pastor ovium. Skrine, J: H. *$1.60 net. Longmans.

Pastor-preacher. Quayle, W: A. *$1.50 net. Jennings.

PASTORAL DRAMA.
See Drama and dramatists.

Pastoral homilies. **Grier, J. A.** $1. Un. Presb. Bd.

Pastoral memories. Whallon, E: P. (Add. pubs. for price.) Montfort.

Pastoral teaching of St Paul. Chadwick, W. E: $2.50. Scribner.

Pastoral work. Joynt, R. C. *40 c. net. Longmans.

Pastorate of Martin Wentz. Landis, D: R. *$1 net. Elmcroft.

PASTORIUS, Francis Daniel.
Learned, M. D. The life of Francis Daniel Pastorius. *$5 net. W: J. Campbell.

Pastor's ideal funeral book. De Long, A. $1. Jennings.

PASTORS.
See Ministers (*of the Gospel*);—Priests.

PASTRY.
See Cookery.

Pasture, Mrs. Eliz. Bonham de la.
See De la Pasture, *Mrs.* Eliz. Bonham.

PASTURES.
See Farms and farming.

Patch, Fk. Wallace.
Individual responsibility. '10(Ja22) c. D. bds., **50 c. net. Moffat.

Patch, Mrs. Kate Whiting.
Sensitive child, as revealed in some talks with a little boy. '10(Ja22) c. D. bds., **75 c. net. Moffat.

Patchel, G:
Eureka rate tables, calculated for any given number of pounds at any given gross tonnage rate. '09, [1910.] (Ap) c. 211 p. f°, $50. G: Patchel.

Patchin, Fk. Gee.
Pony rider boys in Montana; or, the mystery of the old Custer trail. '10(D) il. 12°, (Pony rider ser.) $1. Altemus.
Pony rider boys in New Mexico; or, the end of the Silver Trail. '10(D) il. 12°, (Pony rider ser.) $1. Altemus.
Pony rider boys in Texas; or, the veiled riddle of the plains. '10(D) il. 12°, (Pony rider boys ser.) $1. Altemus.
Pony rider boys in the Alkali; or, finding a key to the desert maze. '10(D) il. 12°, (Pony rider ser.) $1. Altemus.
Pony rider boys in the Ozarks; or, the secret of Ruby Mountain. '10(D) il. 12°, (Pony rider ser.) $1. Altemus.
Pony rider boys in the Rockies; or, the secret of the lost claim. '10(D) il. 12°, (Pony rider ser.) $1. Altemus.

Pate, McCall, comp.
Hdbk. of general information for men under instruction in the Artificer School, Dept. of C. & R. Navy Yard, Norfolk, Va. '08, [1909.] (Mr) c. 88 p. diagrs., 16°, $1. U. S. Naval Inst.

Paten, Hasbrouck Osterhoudt.
See Henderson, Anna Wilson.

PATENTS.
Gladney, F. Y. Restraints of trade in patented articles. $3.50. Mazda.
Macomber, W: Fixed law of patents. $7.50. Little, B. & Co.
Marks, G: C. Inventions, patents and designs. *$1 net. Van Nostrand.
Munn & Co. *Scientific American* handbook relating to patents, designs, trade marks, copyrights, etc. gratis. Munn.
Patent laws, with annotations. '09(My) 55 p. 8°, pap. (Add. Superintendent for price.) U. S., Supt. of Docs.
Pontius, A. W., *comp.* Protection extended to patents, designs, trade-marks and copyrights in China, Japan and Korea. (Add. Superintendent for price.) U. S., Supt. of Docs.
Prindle, E. J. Patents as a factor in manufacturing. $2. Engineering Mag.
Protect your ideas: handbook of the laws rel. to patents. gratis. M. B. Stevens.
Stoddard, E. J. Interlocutory motions in the United States Patent Office. $1. E. J. Stoddard.
Stoddard, E. J. Patent citator. $1.65. Drake Law Bk.
Swan, K. R. Law and commercial usage of patents, designs and trade marks. *$2 net. Van Nostrand.
Thomas, E: Digest of process and composition decisions: [patent law.] **$1.50 net. Winston.

PATENTS.—*Continued.*
Thornton, —. British and foreign patents. $6. Callaghan.
Torbert, W: S., *comp.* Digest of patent and trade-mark cases. $4.50. Byrne.
United States. *Patent Office.* Price list of publications of the United States Patent Office. with schedule of fees of the office; ed. of April, 1910. '10(Jl) 10 p. 12°, gratis. Gov. Pr. Off.
See also **Inventions;—Trade-marks.**

Pater, Wa.
[Works.] In 10 v. v. 1, The Renaissance; studies in art and poetry; v. 2, 3, Marius the epicurean. '10(Jl16); v. 4, Imaginary portraits; v. 5, Appreciations with an essay on style; v. 6, Plato and Platonism; v. 7, Essays from *The Guardian* (N19); v. 8, Greek studies; v. 9, Gaston de Latour; unfinished romance; v. 10, Appreciations, with essay on style (D10) 8°, ea., $2 net. Macmillan.
Child in the house. '09(D) 32°, (Vest pocket ser.) *25 c. net; *50 c. net; leath., *75 c. net; Japan vellum, *$1 net. T: B. Mosher.

Paternoster, G: Sidney.
Master criminal. '08(Ap4) c. il. D. 75 c. Cupples & L.

Paternoster ruby. Walk, C: E. $1.35 net. McClurg.

Paterson, G. W. Lummis-.
See Lummis-Paterson, G. W.

Paterson, W. E.
School algebra. In 2 pts. '09(Ap3) D. ea., 60 c.; complete, $1; with answers, ea., 75 c.; complete, $1.25. Oxford Univ.

Paterson-Smyth, J:
Gospel of the hereafter. '10(S17) c. 12°, $1 net. Revell.

Patet, François Joseph.
Prĕcis d'histoire de France (avec de nombreuses illustrations, une carte de France, un questionnaire et des notes.) '10 (Ap) c. 242 p. il. fold. map, 8°, $1.50. F. J. Patet.

Path of honor. Stevenson, B. E. $1.50. Lippincott.

Path of light: rendered for the first time into English from the Bodicharyavatara of Santi Deva: a manual of Mahâ-Yâna Buddhism by L. D. Barnett. '09(D) 108 p. 16°, (Wisdom of the East ser.) *60 c. net. Dutton.

Path to Paris. Rutter, F. *$5 net. Lane.
Path to peace. *See* Carnegie, And.
Path which led a Protestant lawyer to the Catholic church. Burnett, P: H. *$1.50 net. Herder.
Pathfinder (The). *See* Cooper, Ja. Fennimore.
Pathfinder to Greylock Mountain. Phillips, W: H. $1. W: H. Phillips.
Pathogenic micro-organisms, including bacteria and protozoa. Park, W: H. *$3.75 net. Lea.

PATHOLOGY.
Adami, J: G: Principles of pathology. 2 v. ea., *$6 net. Lea.
Beattie, J. M., *and* Dickson, W. E. C. Text-book of pathology. 2 v. ea., *$5 net. Blakiston.

PATHOLOGY.—*Continued.*

Bertillon, J. International classification of causes of sickness and death. Gov. Pr. Off.

Clarke, J. J. Protozoa and disease. pt. 2. *$2.50 net. Wood.

Coplin, W: M. L. Manual of pathology. $4. Blakiston.

Dunham, W: R. Science of human life. $1. Badger.

Governor's special message transmitting the report of the Commission on Occupational Diseases. gratis. Ill. State Journ.

Gruner, O. C. Studies in puncture fluids. *$3 net. Blakiston.

Hutchinson, W. Preventable diseases. **$1.50 net. Houghton M.

Iowa University. College of Medicine. Contributions from the Dept. of Pathology and Bacteriology. v. 1. 25 c. Univ. of Ia.

Jefferys, W. H., *and* Maxwell, J. L. Diseases of China, incl. Formosa and Korea. $6. Blakiston.

Kleinschrod, F. Inherent law of life. $1.25 net. Macmillan.

McFarland, J. Textbook of pathology. $5 net. Saunders.

Mallory, F. B., *and* Wright, J. H. Pathological technique. *$3 net. Saunders.

Moynihan, B. G: A. Pathway of the living. $2 net. Saunders.

Oliver, T: Diseases of occupation. *$2.50 net. Dutton.

Park, W: H., *and* Williams, A. W. Pathogenic microörganisms. $3.75 net. Lea.

Sajous, C: E. de M. Internal secretions and the principles of medicine. *$6 net. Davis.

Senator, H., *and* Kaminer, S., *eds.* Marriage and disease. $2.50. Hoeber.

Ziegler, E. Text book of general pathology. *$5.50 net; *$6.50 net. Wood.

See also Abdomen;—Anatomy;—Anemia;—Anus and rectum;—Auto-intoxication;—Appendicitis;—Bacteria; — Bladder; — Blood; — Bones; — Brain;—Breast;—Breathing;—Bright's disease;—Cancer; — Children; — Colds;—Constipation;—Contagion;—Diagnosis; — Diathesis; — Digestion;—Diphtheria; — Dyspepsia;—Ear;—Eye;—Fasting;—Fleas;—Generative organs;—Gout;—Gynecology;—Hair; — Head;—Heart;—Heredity;—Hernia;—Histology; — Hookworm disease;—Hygiene;—Hysteria;—Idiocy;—Infectious diseases;—Inflammation; — Insanity; — Insects;—Intestines; — Kidneys; — Knee; — Leprosy; — Liver;—Longevity; — Lungs;—Malaria;—Medicine; — Metabolism; — Midwifery; — Mind and body;—Nervous system;—Neurasthenia;—Nose;—Parasites; — Pellagra;—Plague;—Poisons;—Prostate gland;—Psychology;—Radium;—Scarlet fever;—Serum;—Sex;—Skin;—Smallpox;—Spine; — Stomach; — Straw itch;—Surgery;—Syphilis;—Teeth;—Throat;—Tropical diseases;—Tuberculosis;—Uric acid;—Urine and urinary organs; — Vaccination; — Venereal diseases; — Woman;—Yellow fever.

Paths crossing. Gay, *Mrs.* M. C. $1.50. C. M. Clark.

Paths of the righteous. Dougall, L. $1.50. Macmillan.

Paths to the heights. Leavitt, S. **$1 net. Crowell.

Pathway of the cross. Shettle, G. T. 40 c. Whittaker.

Pathway of the pioneer. Wyllarde, D. †$1.50. Lane.

Pathway to happiness. Hutton, W. S. 50 c. net. Dutton.

Pathway to western literature. Gaines, *Mrs.* N. V. S., *comp.* 75 c. N. S. Gaines.

PATIENCE (*card game*).
See **Solitaire.**

Patience and her garden. Decker, I. S. 35 c., in envelope. P. Elder.

Patience of John Morland. Dillon, *Mrs.* M. C. J. †$1.50. L. C. Page.

Patience Sparhawk. Atherton, *Mrs.* G. F. H. †$1.50. Macmillan.

Patmore, K. A.
Court of Louis XIII. '09(Jl31) il. 8°, *$3.50 net. Brentano's.

Patmore, W: J., pseud.
See Clarke, W: Ja. Patmore.

Paton, Lewis Bayles, D.D.
Early religion of Israel. '10(O8) S. (Modern religious problems.) 50 c. net. Houghton M.
Jerusalem in Bible times. '08(S26) c. il. plans, maps, O. $1. Univ. of Chic.
See also International critical commentary.
—, ed. Recent Christian progress; studies in Christian thought and work during the last seventy-five years; by professors and alumni of Hartford Theological Seminary, in celebration of its seventy-fifth anniversary, May 24-26, 1909. '09(O9) c. O. **$3 net. Macmillan.

Patriarche, Valance.
Tag, or the chien boule dog. '09(O23) c. il. D. †$1. L. C. Page.

Patricia. Jacobs, C. E. $1. Jacobs.

Patricia at the inn. Snaith, J: C. 50 c. B. W. Dodge.

Patrician and plebeian in Virginia. Wertenbaker, T: J. $1.50. Wertenbaker.

PATRICK, *St.*
Murphy, P., *comp.* St. Patrick, apostle of Ireland. 25 c. Patrick Murphy.
Skinner, H. M. Saint Patrick. 20 c. T: Scholes.

Patrick, Hugh Talbot, M.D., and Mix, C: L:, M.D., eds.
Nervous and mental diseases. '08(F) c. 240 p. il. 12°, (Practical medicine ser.) $1.25. Year Bk.

Patrick, Lewis Seaman.
Washington's headquarters and the Revolutionary army at Fredericksburgh in the state of New York. '08(Ja18) il. facsim., D. (Quaker Hill local history ser.) pap., 10 c. Quaker Hill.

Patriot (The). Stubbins, T: A. $1. Donohue.

Patriotic classics. por. 12°. Reilly & B.
—Cheney, *comp.* Memorable American speeches. v. 1. *$1.50 net.

Patriotic jubilee. Lefferts, S. T. 60 c. Cupples & L.

Patriotic orations. Fowler, C: H. *$1.50 net. Eaton & M.

Patriotic poems of New Jersey. Armstrong, W: C. $1.50. S. A. R., N. J. Soc.

Patriotic studies for men's leagues. International Reform Bureau. 75 c.; 35 c. Int. Ref. Bu.

PATRIOTISM.
Ammerman, A. Pro patria: patriotic recitation with lesson talk. 35 c. Werner.
Davis, J: W., *ed.* Young America's manual: child's guide to patriotism. 25 c. Educ. Pub.
Ferree, J. B. Sentiment as a national asset. gratis. B. Ferree.
Rice, W. de G. C., *comp.* Catchwords of patriotism. *$1 net. McClurg.
Strachey, J: St. L. New way of life. *50 c. net. Macmillan.
Patris. Allen, F. E. $1. H. Carr.
PATRISTIC LITERATURE.
See Texts and studies, ed. by J. A. Robinson.
PATROLMEN.
See Police.
Patrology. Bardenhewer, O. *$3.75 net. Herder.
PATROLS.
See Military art and science.
Patron, Maurice, and Neymarck, Alfr.
Bank of France in its relation to national and international credit, by Maurice Patron, and an article upon French savings, by Alfred Neymarck. '10(Ag) 181 p. fold. diagr. 8°. Gov. Pr. Off.
Bibliography (1 p.).
Pattee, Alida Frances.
Pract. dietetics with ref. to diet in disease. 6th ed. [1910.] (Je) 420 p. 12°, $1.50 net. A. F. Pattee.
Pattee, Fred Lewis.
Elements of religious pedagogy; course in Sunday-school teacher-training. '09(O23) c. D. *75 c. net. Eaton & M.
Hist. of American literature; with a view to the fundamental principles underlying its development; text-book for schools and colleges. New ed., rev. and enl. '10 (Jl30) c. 12°, $1.20 net. Silver.
Pattee, G: Kynett.
Practical argumentation. '09(Ag21) c. D. **$1.10 net. Century Co.
Pattee, W: Sullivan.
Essential nature of law; or, the ethical basis of jurisprudence. '09(D) c. O. $2.50. Callaghan.
—, comp. *See* Illustrative cases in equity.
Patten, Gilbert.
See Standish, Burt L., *pseud.*
Patten, Harrison Eastman.
Heat transference in soils. '09(D) 54 p. il. tabs., 8°, (U. S., Dept. of Agriculture, Bu. of Soils, bull.) pap. (Add. Superintendent for price.) U. S., Supt. of Docs.
Town and the trust; novel. '10(D1) $1.25. Neale.
Patten, Simon Nelson.
Product and climax. '09(Je5) c. D. (Art of life ser.) *50 c. net. B: W. Huebsch.
Patten, W:, ed.
Great short stories; new collection of famous examples from the literature of France, England and America. '09(Ap) c. pors. 8°, $2.25. Collier.
International short stories; new collection of famous examples from the literatures of England, France and America. In 3 v. '10(My7) c. pors. 12°, $2.10. Collier.
—, comp. Among the humorists and after-dinner speakers; new collections of humorous stories and anecdotes. 3 v. '09(Je) c. pors. 8°, $2.25. Collier.
Patten, W:, and Homans, J. E., eds.
New encyclopedic atlas and gazetteer of the world; cont. an entirely new ser. of colored maps, showing every country and all political or civil divisions; also an index gazetteer of the world, and a complete physical and commercial analysis of the United States. 3d ed., rev. [1910.] (D) c. 348 p. il. col. maps, f°. Collier.
PATTEN FAMILY.
See Genealogies: Baldwin, T: W.
PATTERN-MAKING.
Horner, J. G. Principles of pattern making. *90 c. net. Macmillan.
Ritchey, J. Pattern making. $1. Am. Sch. Corr.
Willard, G. H., *and* Crawshaw, F. D. Pattern-making. $1. Popular Mechanics.
Patterson, Alice Jean.
See Coulter, J: Merle.
Patterson, Alma Mary.
Course of study for the teaching of reading to beginners, and hdbk. to the State ser. Primer and First reader. '09(Mr); 2d and 3d grades. (O) 4°, (San Francisco State Normal School bulls; new ser.) pap., ea., 30 c. San F. St. Normal.
Patterson, Burd Shippen.
Head of Iron: romance of colonial Pennsylvania. '08(N21) c. il. O. *$1.20 net. T. M. Walker.
Patterson, C: Brodie.
Dominion and power; or, the science of life and living. 7th ed., rev. and enl. '10(My21) c. O. $1.20 net. Funk.
New heaven and a new earth; or, the way to life eternal; (thought studies of the fourth dimensions.) '10(Ja22) c. 8°, **$1.25 net. Crowell.
New way to educate children; with practical suggestions for mental and physical development. '09(S) 81-105 p. pap., 25 c. New Way.
New way to happiness; with practical suggestions for mental and physical development. '08(N7) c. D. (The new way.) pap., 25 c. Roger Bros.
New way to health. '08(D5) c. D. (New way.) pap., 25 c. Roger Bros.
New way to self control. '10(O) 12°, pap., 25 c. Roger Bros.
Patterson, C: Edn.
Mysteries of life revealed; truth in verse, as came through spiritual consciousness. '08, [1909.] (Mr) c. 193 p. front. 8°, $1. C: E. Patterson.
Patterson, Eliz.
Judy, pioneer girl. '08(N14) il. D. 50 c. McLoughlin.
Patterson, Mrs. Flora Wambaugh, Charles, Vera Katharine, and Veihmeyer, Fk. J.
Some fungous diseases of economic importance: I, Miscellaneous diseases, by Flora W. Patterson and Vera K. Charles; II, Pineapple rot caused by *Thielaviopsis paradoxa,* by Flora W. Patterson and Vera K. Charles and Fk. J. Veihmeyer. '10(Ag) 41 p. il. 8°, (U. S., Dept. of Agriculture, Bu. of Plant Industry; bull.)

Patterson, Ja. W.
Painters since Leonardo. '09(D) il. 8°, *$4 net. Duffield.

Patterson, J: And.
Breaking dawn; or, how long may we live in the body; survey of the doctrines of renewed youth and the perpetuation of life in physical embodiment. '10(Jl16) c. por. 8°, $1. Chronicle Pub.

Patterson, J: H:
In the grip of the nyika; further adventures in British East Africa. '09(D18) c. il. maps, O. **$2 net. Macmillan.
Man-eaters of Tsavo, and other East African adventures; with a foreword by F: Courteney Selous. '09(F13) il. map, O. *$2 net. Macmillan.

Patterson, Jos. Medill.
Little brother of the rich. '09(N) 75 c. Grosset.
Little brother of the rich. '08(S12) c. il. D. $1.50. Reilly & B.
—, comp. Socialist campaign book. '08(D) 160 p. 8°, 25 c. Socialist.

Patterson, Rev. Melville Watson.
Hist. of the Church of England. '09(My22) maps, O. *$2 net. Longmans.

Patterson, Raymond Albert.
Taft's training for the presidency. '09 (Mr6) 8°, pap., 15 c. Chapple Pub.

Patterson, Mrs. Virginia Sharpe-.
See Sharpe-Patterson, *Mrs.* Virginia.

Patterson, W: Seeds.
Sixty years of Uppingham cricket. '09 (Jl17) pors. O. *$2 net. Longmans.

PATTERSON, N. Y.
See Fredericksburgh.

Patteson, Mrs. Susanna Louise.
Kitty Kat Kimmie. '09(O16) c. 211 p. il. 8°, $1.25. Jacobs.

Pattillo, H:
Geographical catechism; ed. by N. W. Walker and M. C. S. Noble. '10(Mr5) c. 8°, (University reprints.) 75 c. Univ. of N. C.

Pattison, Everett W., comp.
See Missouri. Supp. to Pattison's digest.

Pattison, Mark.
Essays. '08(Ag15) 2 v., 16°, (New universal lib.) ea., 50 c.; leath., 75 c. Dutton.

Pattison, Reginald Philipson Dunn-.
See Dunn-Pattison, Reginald Philipson.

Patton, I: Wesley.
New universal system of touch or sight typewriting. 3d ed., completely rev. '08 (Ja4) Q. pap., 60 c. Pitman.

Patton, Jacob Harris, and others.
Hist. of the American people; introductory article on "True Americanism," by Thdr. Roosevelt; other material. 4 v. '10(D3) c. 12°, $6.50. Walter.

Patton, J:, and Rosecrans, J. H.
Gospel hymns. '09(Ja30) c. 12°, vellum, 35 c.; per doz., $4; per 25, $8. Showalter-P.

Patton, J: Shelton, ed.
See Kent, C: W:

Patton, J: Woodbridge.
New replevin in Pennsylvania, with forms of procedure. '09(S) 104 p. $1. Welsh.
See also Pennsylvania. Foreign attachment.

Pattou, Ange Albert.
Art of voice production established on a true scientific basis. [1910.] (Ja) c. '09. 7-30 p. por. 12°, 50 c. A. A. Pattou.

Patty of the circus. Griffith, H. S. 60 c. Penn Pub. Co.
Patty's friends. Wells, C. †$1.25. Dodd.
Patty's pleasure trip. Wells, C. †$1.25. Dodd.
Patty's success. Wells, C. $1.25. Dodd.

Pau, Charlotte.
Sunbeams and shadows: [poems.] '10(O) 32 p. 12°, 55 c. Cochrane.

Pauer, Ernst.
Musical forms. '08(D) 75 c. Ditson.

PAUL, *of Moll, Father,* (*originally* Francis Luyckx).
Van Speybrouck, E. Very Rev. Father Paul of Moll. $1.25. Benedictine.

PAUL, *St.*
Alexander, A. B. D. Ethics of St. Paul. $2 net. Macmillan.
Atkinson, L. W. Story of Paul of Tarsus; home work book. *25 c. net.—Story of Paul of Tarsus; manual for teachers. *$1 net. Univ. of Chic.
Campbell, J. M. Paul the mystic. *$1.50 net. Putnam.
Chadwick, W. E: Pastoral teaching of St. Paul. $2.50. Scribner.
Feine, K. E. St. Paul as a theologian. In 2 pts. ea., *40 c. net. Eaton & M.
Frost, J. M., *ed.* Experience of grace, three notable instances: Saul of Tarsus, John Jasper, Edward Everett Hale, jr. 40 c. S. S. Bd. So. Bapt.
Greenhough, J. G. Mind of Christ in St. Paul. $1.50 net. Doran.
Johnston, C. N. St. Paul and his mission to the Roman Empire. *75 c. net. Revell.
Jones, M. St. Paul the orator. $1.50 net. Doran.
Matheson, G. Spiritual development of St. Paul. *80 c. net. Whittaker.
Meyer, A. Jesus or Paul? *75 c. net. Harper.
Moffat, J. Paul and Paulinism. **50 c. net. Houghton M.
Myers, F. W: H: Saint Paul. *35 c. net. Macmillan.
Ramsay, W: M. Cities of St. Paul. *$3 net. Armstrong.
Robertson, A. T: Epochs in the life of Paul. **$1.25 net. Scribner.
Speer, R. E. Paul, the all round man. *50 c. net. Revell.
Stevenson, J. G. Children's Paul. 85 c. net. Eaton & M.
Weiss, J. Paul and Jesus. *75 c. net. Harper.
Wrede, W. Paul. *$1 net. Am. Unitarian.
See also Bible. N. T. Thessalonians.

Paul, Mrs. Dan.
See Paul, Nanette B.

Paul, Fk.
Notes on Massachusetts practice, with reference to proceedings before masters and auditors, and their reports. '09(O) c. 26+234 p. O. (Add. pubs. for price.) Little, B. & Co.

Paul, Rev. H. A. C.
Immorality and foolishness of prohibition. '08(Ap4) c. O. pap., 20 c. H. A. C. Paul.

Paul, Harry G., ed.
See Baldwin, E: Chauncey.

Paul, J: Haywood.
The hereafter. '10(Ap23) c. 12°, 50 c. Pentecostal.

Paul, Nanette B., [Mrs. Dan. Paul.]
Parliamentary law; with forms and diagram of motions. New ed. '10(Je25) c. D. 75 c. Century Co.

Paul, Nendick.
Child in the midst; South African story. '10(Ap2) front. D. $1. Longmans.

Paul-Dubois, Louis François Alphonse.
Contemporary Ireland; with an introd. by T. M. Kettle. '08(D19) O. *$2 net. Baker & T.

Paul Anthony, Christian. Hayes, H. W. $1.50. Reid Pub.

Paul Douglas—journalist. Sheldon, C: M. $1. Advance Pub. Co., (Chic.)

Paul Merritt. Jones, A. M. $1. Washington Bk.

Paul Prescott's charge. Alger, H., *jr.* 50 c. Hurst.

Paula. Cory, V. 75 c. Fenno.

PAULDING, Hiram.
Meade, *Mrs.* R. P. Life of Hiram Paulding, rear admiral U. S. N. $1.50 net. Baker & T.

Pauline, Eliz. Ottilie Louise, Queen of Roumania, ["Carmen Sylva."]
Golden thoughts of Carmen Sylva, Queen of Roumania; tr. by permission by H. Sutherland Edwards. '10(N12) por. T. (Lib. of golden thoughts.) 50 c. net. Lane.

Pauline. Norris, W: E: $1.50. Brentano's.

PAULINE EPISTLES.
See Bible.

Paullin, C: Oscar.
Commodore John Rodgers, captain, commodore, and senior officer of the American navy, 1773-1838; biography. '10 (F19) c. il. pors. facsims., 8°, *$4 net. A. H. Clark.
Services of Commodore John Rodgers in our wars with the Barbary corsairs, (1802-1806.) '08, [1909.] (S) 114-1188 p. 8°, $1. U. S. Naval Inst.

Paulsen, Friedrich.
German education past and present; tr. by T. Lorenz. '09(My22) 12°, *$1.25 net. Scribner.

Pauper of Park Lane. Le Queux, W: 75 c. Cupples & L.

PAUPERISM.
See Poor.

Pausanias.
Attica of Pausanias: ed. by Mitchell Carroll. '08(S19) c. O. (College ser. of Greek authors.) $1.65. Ginn.

PAVEMENTS.
Barber, A. L. Best road and the right way to make it. (Not for sale.) Barber Asphalt.
Judson, W: P. City roads and pavements. *$2 net. Engineering News.

PAVEMENTS.—*Continued.*
Peckham, S. F. Solid bitumens, together with a treatise on the chemical technology of bituminous pavements. $5. M. C. Clark.
Richardson, C. Modern asphalt pavement. $3. Wiley.
Spalding, F: P. Text book on roads and pavements. $2. Wiley.
Wheeler, H. A. Vitrified paving brick. $2. T. A. Randall.
See also Asphalt;—Cement;—Roads.

Pavie et le sac de Rome. *See* Sismondi, Jean Charles Leonard Sismonde de.

Paving brick and paving brick clays of Illinois. Rolfe, C: W. (Add. pubs. for price.) Univ of Ill.

Pawlie, E:
Practical hdbk. of garment dyeing and cleaning. '09(My8) c. il. 8°, $3.75. M. M. Frank.

Pawn in the game. Fitchett, W: H: $1.25. Eaton & M.

Paxon, Frederic Logan.
Last American frontier. '10(F19) c. il. maps, D. **$1.50 net. Macmillan.
Pacific railroads and the disappearance of the frontier in America. '10(Ja8) 8°. U. S., Supt. of Docs.

Paxton, Alex. Sterret.
Memory days: in which the Shenandoah Valley is seen in retrospection. '08 (My23) c. D. $1.50. Neale.

Paying the piper. Bates, *Mrs.* M. H. E. $1.50. B'way Pub.

Payne, A. G.
Choice dishes at small cost. New and enl. ed. '10(S) 380 p. il. 8°, $1.25 net. Cassell.

Payne, Bruce Ryburn.
Common words commonly misspelled. '10 (N19) c. 12°, 28 c. Johnson.
See also Mims, Edn.

Payne, Eli Lawrence.
Pract. arithmetic for advanced grades. '10 (Je) c. 10+322 p. il. 12°, 65 c. Inland.

Payne, F. M., pseud.
See Carey, T: J.

Payne, Irene.
Baby Bunting & Co. '07, [1909.] (Jl) il. in col. 16°, 50 c. Jacobs.

Payne, Philip.
Mills of man. '08(F1) c. D. (Popular copyright fiction.) 75 c. Rand, McN. & Co.

Payne, Will.
Automatic capitalists. '09(O23) c. il. D. †$1. Badger.
Losing game. '10(F26) c. il. D. †$1.50. G: W. Dillingham.

PAYNE, *General* William Henry.
Robinson, L. Address del. before R. E. Lee Camp, C. V., at Richmond, Va., in the acceptance of the portrait of General William H. Payne. (Priv. pr.) Leigh Robinson.

Payne, W: Morton.
Björnstjerne Björnson, 1832-1910. '10(Je4) c. por. D. bds., 50 c. net. McClurg.
Leading American essayists. '10(My21) c. pors. O. (Biographies of leading Americans.) $1.75 net. Holt.

Payne, W: Morton.—*Continued.*
Quarter-century of Eng. literature, 1880-1905. '08(Ag15) c. 16°, (Club papers.) [priv. pr.] Chic. Lit. Club.

Payne, W: Wallace, comp.
General index to *Sidereal Messenger.* v. 1-10, March, 1882-December, 1891; *Astronomy and Gastro-Physics,* v. 1-3, January, 1892-December, 1894; *Popular Astronomy,* v. 1-16, begun, September, 1893; by authors and subjects; comp. under the supervision of the editor. '09, [1910.] (Ap) 148 p. 8°, $1.50. Popular Astronomy.

Payne-Gallwey, Sir Ralph W:
History of the [St.] George worn on the scaffold by Charles I. '08(D5) il. pors. O. $2.50. Longmans.

Paynter, Mrs.
See Sidgwick, *Mrs.* Cecily Ullman.

Payot, Jules.
Education of the will; theory and practice of self-culture; authorized tr. by Smith Ely Jelliffe from the 13th French ed. '09(N6) c. D. **$1.50 net. Funk.

Payson, Howard.
Boy scouts. '10(Ag13) c. 12°, 60 c. Hurst.

Payson, W: Farquhar.
Barry Gordon. '08(O10) c. il. D. †$1.50. McClure.
Periwinkle; idyl of the dunes. '10(O15) c. il. D. $1.25 net. Sturgis & W.

Peabody, Cecil Hobart.
Computations for marine engines. '08(F15) c. tabs., diagrs., 8°. (For private distribution.) C. H. Peabody.
Tables of the properties of steam and other vapors, and temperature-entropy table. 8th ed. '09(My1) c. 8°, $1. Wiley.
Thermodynamics of the steam-engine and other heat-engines. 6th ed., rev. '09, [1910.] (Je) c. 543 p. il. tabs., 8°, $5. Wiley.

—, and Miller, E: Furber.
Steam-boilers. '08(N14) c. il. figs. 8°, $4. Wiley.

Peabody, C:, and Moorehead, Warren King.
Exploration of Bushey cavern near Cavetown, Md., by C: Peabody; pt. 1, Fort Ancient, the great prehistoric earthwork of Warren Co., Ohio, by Warren K. Moorehead; pt. 2, '08(O) c. 166 p. il. 8°, (Phillips Acad., Dept. of Archæology, bull.) pap., 75 c. Andover.

Peabody, Fs. Greenwood, D.D.
Approach to the social question; introd. to the study of social ethics. '09(D11) c. D. **$1.25 net. Macmillan.
Social museum as an instrument of university teaching; a classified list of the collections in the Social Museum of Harvard University to Jan., 1908. '08(D) 34 p. O. (Harvard Univ., Dept. of Social Ethics pubs.) gratis. F. G. Peabody.
See also King, H: Churchill.

Peabody, F: W:
Religio-medical masquerade; complete exposure of Christian Science. '10(Je11) c. D. $1. Hancock Press.

Peabody, Josephine Preston, [Mrs. L. S. Marks.]
Book of the little past: [verses for children.] '08(O10) c. il. Q. bds., $1.50. Houghton M.
Fortune and men's eyes; new poems. '09 (N20) c. D. bds., $1.25. Houghton M.
The piper: a play. '09(N20) c. O. **$1.10 net. Houghton M.

Peabody, Rob. E.
Derbys of Salem, Massachusetts. '08(Ag8) (Hist. collections of the Essex Inst.) pap. [priv. pr.] Essex Inst.
Naval career of Captain John Manley of Marblehead. '09(Ap) (Not for sale.) Essex Inst.

Peabody, Rob. Swain.
Holiday study of cities and ports: notes of travel offered to the Commission on the Improvement of Metropolitan Boston. '08 (Jl4) il. map, plans, tabs., F. pap., $1. Boston Soc. Architects.

Peabody, Susan Wade.
Historical study of legislation regarding public health in the states of New York and Massachusetts. '09, [1910.] (Ja) c. 4-158 p. 8°, $1. Journal Infectious Diseases.

Peabody Academy of Science. Whaling industry: exhibition of objects illustrating the whaling industry and the natural history of whales; list of Essex County whaling vessels; list of pictures of whaling vessels in the marine room; list of log-books of whaling vessels in the library of the Essex Institute; list of books on whales and whaling in the Salem Public Library. '08(O3) il. 8°, gratis. Salem Pub. Lib.

Peabody Museum memoirs. *See* Harvard University.

Peabody Museum papers. il. 8°. Peabody Museum.
—Tozzer *and* Allen. Animal figures in the Maya codices. $1.

Peace, Darius.
Have Congregationalists abandoned the Bible? '08(O) c. 96 p. 8°, $1; pap., 50 c. S. D. Towne.

PEACE.
Bigelow, J: Folly of building temples of peace with untempered mortar. $1 net. B: W. Huebsch.
Brewer, D: J. Mission of the United States in the cause of peace. gratis. Int. Sch. of Peace.
Brooklyn Public Library. International peace: list of books with references to periodicals in the Library. gratis. Brooklyn Lib.
Carnegie, A. Path to peace; [also] Supplement to same. (Add. pubs. for price.) Peace Soc.
Crucé, E. Novveav Cynée; [plan proposed 1623 for international peace conference.] $2. Allen, L. & S.
Duras, V. H. Universal peace. $2. B'way Pub.
Mead, E. D. Literature of the peace movement. gratis. Int. Sch. of Peace.

PEACE.—*Continued.*
Mead, *Mrs.* L. T. A. Educational organizations promoting international friendship. per 100, $3. Int. Sch. of Peace.
Wylie, F. L. Cecil Rhodes and his scholars as factors in international conciliation. gratis. Am. Assoc. Int. Conciliation.
See also **Arbitration;—Hague peace conference;—War;—***also* **Cremer,** ***Sir*** **William Randal.**

Peace and happiness. Lubbock, *Sir* J: **$1.50 net. Macmillan.

Peace of Mad Anthony. Wilson, F. E. $1.25. F. E. Wilson.

Peace, power and plenty. Marden, O. S. **$1 net. Crowell.

Peacemakers (The). Hayes, H. W. †$1.50. Reid Pub.

Peacock, T: Love.
Headlong Hall, and Nightmare Abbey. '08 (S19) 16°, (Everyman's lib.) *35 c. net; leath., *70 c. net. Dutton.
Memoirs of Shelley; with Shelley's letters to Peacock; ed., with introd., by H. F. B. Brett Smith. '09, [1910.] (F) 16°, (Oxford lib. of prose and poetry.) 90 c. Oxford Univ.

Peacock, W., comp.
Selected English essays. '08, [1910.] (F) 12+543 p. 16°, (World's classics.) *40 c. net; leath., *75 c. net. Oxford Univ.

PEACOCK.
Miller, L. H. Pavo Califonicus, fossil peacock from the quaternary asphalt beds of Rancho La Brea. 5 c. Univ. of Cal.

Peacock of jewels. Hume, F. W. $1.25. G: W. Dillingham.

Peacock's pleasaunce. B., E. V. *$1.50 net. Lane.

Peadro, Rob. Mandiville.
Idle hours of a busy lawyer. '10(Mr26) c. 12°, $1. Shelby Co. Leader.

Peak country. Moncrieff, A. R. H. *$2.50 net. Macmillan.

Peake, Arth. S:, D.D.
Bible in the 20th century. '10(D) $1.25 net. Doran.
Christianity, its nature and its truth. '09 (Jl31) D. *$1.25 net. Crowell.
Critical introd. to the New Testament. '10 (F5) D. (Studies in theology.) *75 c. net. Scribner.
Heroes and martyrs of faith: exposition of the 11th chapter of the Epistle to the Hebrews. '10(D) 12°, $1.50 net. Doran.

Peake, R. J.
Cotton from the raw material to the finished product. '10(Ap9) il. map, D. (Common commodities of commerce.) 50 c. Pitman.

Peaks and glaciers **of Nun** Kun. Workman, *Mrs.* F. B. *$4.50 net. Scribner.

PEANUTS.
Beattie, W: R. Peanuts. (Add. Superintendent for price.) U. S., Supt. of Docs

Pearce, Mrs. Mary Haines Bunting.
New thought school, Avenel system, for the development of mind, the preservation of health, and the evolution of character. '10(N19) c. 8°, 50 c. P. Avenel.

Pearce, W. B.
Practical bookbinding. '08(Jl4) il. 12°, bds., 50 c. Spon.

Pearce, W: Cliff.
Adult Bible class; its organization and work. '09(F6) c. charts, facsim., D. 25 c. Westminster.

Pearce, W: Houghton Sprague.
See Vox, Carol, *pseud.*

Pearl, Raymond, comp.
Methods of poultry management at the Maine agricultural experiment station. '09(Jl) 39 p. il. 8°, (U. S., Dept. of Agriculture; Farmers' bull.) pap. (Add. Superintendent for price.)

—, and Surface, Fk. Macy.
Biometrical study of egg production in the domestic fowl. '09(Jl) 8°, (U. S., Dept. of Agriculture; Bu. of Animal Industry bull.) pap., 15 c.

Pearl (The): middle English poem; modern version in the metre of the original by Sophie Jewett. '08(O10) c. S. front. **$1 net; Students' ed., **40 c. net. Crowell.

Pearl (The): an English vision-poem of the fourteenth century, done into modern verse by Marian Mead. '08(N21) c. 12°, (Old world ser.) *$1 net; bds., *$1.25 net; flex. leath., *$1.50 net; Japan vellum ed., *$2.50 net. T: B. Mosher.

Pearl (The); rendered into modern English verse by Silas Weir Mitchell. '08(Ag1) c. 16°. (Not for sale.) T: B. Mosher.

Pearl (The): anonymous English poem of the fourteenth century; rendered in prose by C: G. Osgood, jr. '08(Ja18) S. vellum, *$1 net. C: G. Osgood, Jr.

PEARL.
Kunz, G: F:, *and* Stevenson, C: H. Book of the pearl. **$12.50 net. Century Co.
Washburn, H. E. American pearls. 50 c. H. E. Washburn.

Pearls. Mangasarian, M. M. 25 c.; $1. Independent Religious.

Pearls at random strung. Piggott, C: H: $1. C: H: Piggott.

Pearls of comfort. Zimmerman, L. M. (Add. author for price.) L. M. Zimmerman.

Pearls, points and parables. Marsh, F: E: $1.50. Gospel Pub.

Pears, C:
From the Thames to the Seine: narrative of a sketching cruise along the north coast of France. '10(D10) il. (partly in col.) 8°, $4 net, boxed. Jacobs.

Pearse, Rev. Mark Guy.
Bridgetstow: some chronicles of a Cornish parish. '08(Mr7) c. D. *$1 net. Jennings.
Prophet's raven: [a story.] '08(O24) c. D. *75 c. net. Eaton & M.

Pearson, Rev. Arth. Cyril, ed.
Pictured puzzles and word play: a companion to the "20th century standard puzzle book." '08(D) 6+382 p. 12°, $1.50. Dutton.

Pearson, C: W:
Literary and biographical essays. '08(Jl4) c. O. *$1.25 net. Sherman, F.
Search after truth: sermons and addresses. '08(Jl4) c. O. *$1.25 net. Sherman, F.
Threefold cord: poems. '08(Jl4) c. O. *$1.25 net. Sherman, F.
All three of these books may also be had as a uniform set, at *$3 net per set.

Pearson, Edm. Lester, ["Philobiblos."]
Library and the librarian; selection of articles from the Boston *Evening Transcript* and other sources. '10(My21) c. 8°, (Librarian's ser.) $1.50. Elm Tree Press.
Old librarian's almanack, by Philobiblos; very rare pamphlet first pub. in New Haven, Ct., in 1773, and now repr. for the first time. '10(Ja15) c. O. (Librarians' ser.) sold by subs. only, per set of 6 v., bds., $5. Elm Tree Press.

Pearson, Gustaf Adolph.
Reproduction of western yellow pine in the Southwest. '10(Mr) 16 p. 8°, (U. S., Dept. of Agriculture, Forest Service, circular.) pap. (Add. Superintendent for price.) U. S., Supt. of Docs.

Pearson, H: Carr.
Key to Essentials of Latin for beginners. '09(D18) c. D. pap., 25 c. Am. Bk.
Latin prose composition; based on Cæsar. '08(My2) c. D. 50 c. Am. Bk.

Pearson, H: Clemens.
Crude rubber and compounding ingredients. 2d ed. '09(Je19) c. tabs., 8°, $10. India Rubber.
—, comp. Rubber trade directory for 1908. '08(N) 260 p. 8°, $3. India Rubber.

Pearson, Ja. Larkin.
Castle gates: [a book of poems.] '08(N) c. 108 p. 12°, $1. J. L. Pearson.

Pearson, P.
Psycho-harmonical philosophy. '10(N5) c. col. il. por. O. $3.50. P. Pearson.

Pearson, Paul Martin, ed.
Intercollegiate debates; being briefs and repts. of many intercollegiate debates; Harvard-Yale-Princeton, Brown-Dartmouth-Williams, Michigan-Northwestern-Chicago, Indiana-Illinois-Ohio, and many others; ed., with an introd. '10(Ja15) c. D. $1.50. Hinds.
The speaker. 16 nos. '09(My) ea., 60 c.; pap., 40 c.; complete in 4 v., ea., $1.50; nos. 17, 18 19. '10(D) ea., 60 c.; pap., 40 c. Hinds.
Formerly pub. by Pearson Bros.
—, comp. Humorous speaker; book of humorous selections for reading and speaking. '10(Ja29) c. 12°, $1.25. Hinds.

Pearson, P: H:
Questions for interpretative and literary study. 16 v. '09(Ja23) D. ea., 7 c. P: H: Pearson.

Pearson, Rob. Hooper.
Book of garden pests. '08(F1) il. D. (Handbooks of practical gardening.) *$1 net. Lane.

Peary, Rob. Edn.
North Pole: its discovery in 1909 under the auspices of the Peary Arctic Club; with introd. by Thdr. Roosevelt, and foreword by Gilbert H. Grosvenor. '10(O8) c. il. (some in col.) O. $4.80; Library ed., $5 net; Autographed ed., $15 net. Stokes.

PEARY, Robert Edwin.
Ingersoll, E. Conquest of the North; authentic account of the finding of the North Pole by Dr. Frederick A. Cook, Com. R. E. Peary, U. S. N., together with biographies of the explorers and a brief hist. of Arctic discovery. 10 c. C. S. Hammond.
See also Arctic regions.

PEAS.
See Preserving.

Peasant art in Sweden, Lapland and Iceland. Holme, C:, *ed.* $3 net. Lane.

Pease, C: Schermerhorn.
Freight transportation on trolley lines. '10 (My7) c. il. 12°, $1. McGraw-H.

Pease, G: W:
See Palmer, Lois Sedgwick.

Pease, Leonora.
The child you used to be. '09(O2) c. il. O. $1.50. McClurg.

Pease, Martin A.
Candy making secrets. '08(Ag) c. 94 p. 8°, $3. Pease & D.

PEAT.
Davis, C: A. Peat, essays on its origin, etc. $1. Mich. Geol. Survey.
Gissing, F: T. Commercial peat, its uses and its possibilities. *$2 net. Lippincott.
See also Maine.

PECANS.
Dygert, H. A. Crops that pay: pecans, mangoes, avocados, pineapples. 10 c. Am. Fruit & Nut Co.
Hume, H. H. Pecan and its culture. $1.50. H. H. Hume.

Peck, Ellen Mary Hayes, [Mrs. Ja. Sidney Peck.]
Travels in the Far East. '09(Mr27) c. il. O. $3, boxed. J. S. Peck.

Peck, Harry Thurston.
Literature: [a lecture.] '08(N21) c. 8°, pap. (Add. pubs. for price.) Lemcke.
New Baedeker; being casual notes of an irresponsible traveller. '10(My7) c. il. D. $1.50 net. Dodd.
Studies in several literatures. '09(My15) c. D. **$1.20 net. Dodd.

Peck, Mrs. Ja. Sidney.
See Peck, Ellen Mary Hayes.

Peck, S: Minturn.
Maybloom and myrtle: [poems.] '10 (Ag27) c. por. D. $1. Estes.

Peck, Theodora.
Sword of Dundee. '08(O17) c. il 12°, †$1.50. Duffield.

Peck, T: Bellows.
William Slade of Windsor, Conn., and his descendants. '10(S) c. 7+197 p. il. pors. 8°, $3.50. Sentinel, (N. H.)

Peck, W: Farley.
History of Rochester and Monroe Co., N. Y., from the earliest historic times to the beginning of 1907. '08(Ag) 2 v., 8+5-706; 11+711-1433 p. il. pors. maps, f°, $18. Pioneer Pub. Co.

Peckham, G: A.
Introd. to the study of Obadiah; dissertation. '10(Ap16) c. 8°, pap., 25 c. net. Univ. of Chic.

Peckham, Stephen Farnum.
Solid bitumens, their physical and chemical properties and chemical analysis; together with a treatise on the chemical technology of bituminous pavements, by S. F. Peckham. '09(D18) c. il. 8°, $5. M. C. Clark.

Pecorini, Alberto.
Gli Americani nella vita moderna osservati da un Italiano. '09(Ag) 12°, pap., $1.25. F. Tocci.

Peculiar bear from Alaska. Osgood, W. H. 50 c. Field Museum.

Peculiarity of the religion of the Bible. Orelli, H. C. v. *40 c. net. Eaton & M.

PEDAGOGY.
See Teachers and teaching.

PEDDICORD, Kelion Franklin.
Logan, *Mrs.* I. W. P. Kelion Franklin Peddicord of Quirk's Scouts. *$2 net. Neale.

Peddie, J: Bailey.
Construction of graphical charts. '10(N5) c. il. diagrs., 8°, $1.50. McGraw-H.

PEDIATRICS.
See Surgery.

Pedley, G. F.
Motor car mechanics for beginners. 3d ed. '10(D) 12°, 50 c. Spon.

Pedro Sánchez. Pereda, J. M. de. $1. Ginn.

Peebles, Ja. Martin, M.D.
Five journeys around the world. '10(D31) c. il. pors. 8°, $1.75. Peebles.
Immortality and our employment hereafter. '09(D) $1.25; pap., 75 c. Austin.
Spirit mates, their origin and destiny, sex-life, marriage, divorce, by J. M. Peebles; also, a symposium, by forty noted writers, spirit mates—their pre-existence, earth pilgrimages, reunions in spirit-life; ed. and arranged by Robert Sudall. '09(D) c. 23+318 p. $1.25. Peebles.
What is spiritualism? 5th ed., rev. and enl. '10(D31) c. por. 8°, 75 c. Peebles.

Peeke, Mrs. Margaret Bloodgood.
Numbers and letters; or, the thirty-two paths of wisdom. De luxe ed. '09(S) c. '08. 191 p. por. 12°, $2. B'way Pub.

Peele, Rob.
Compressed air plant; production, transmission and use of compressed air. '08 (Ag29) $3; 2d ed., rev. and enl. '10 (N5) c. il. tabs., 8°, $3.50 net. Wiley.

Peep-Bo. '09(D) col. il. 32°, bds., 25 c. Doran.

Peep-in-the-world. Crichton, F. E. $1.25. Longmans.

Peeps at many lands ser. il. 12°, *75 c. net. Macmillan.
—Abbott. South seas.
—Bealby. Canada.
—Browne. Greece.—Spain.
—Clark. Ceylon.
—Coulson. Korea.
—Finnemore. England.—Holy Land.—Morocco.—Switzerland.
—Goodall. Portugal.
—Henderson. Jamaica.

Peeps at many lands ser.—Continued.
—Hinkson Ireland.
—Johnston. China.
—Kelly. Burma.—Egypt.
—Kidd. South Africa.
—Leith. Iceland.
—Masson. Edinburgh.
—Mockler-Ferryman. Norway.
—Moncrieff. The world.
—Omond. Belgium.
—Sidgwick. Germany.
—Thomson. Denmark.—Finland.
—Vaile. New Zealand.
—Walter. Russia.
—Williams. Paris.
—Young. Corsica.—Siam.

Peer, Fk. Sherman.
Hunting field with horse and hound in America, the British Isles and France. '10(My14) c. il. pors. 4°, $5. M. Kennerley.

Peer and the woman. *See* Oppenheim, E: P.

PEERAGE.
Burke, *Sir* J: B. *and* A. P. Genealogical and heraldic history of the peerage and baronetage. *$2 net. Putnam.

Peerless Alaska. Hallock, C: $1.25. B'way Pub.

Peerless orator. Wood, E. M. $1.50. Pittsburgh.

Peers, Mrs. C. R.
Saints in story. '10(N19) il. 8°, $1.50. Macmillan.

Peet, T. Eric.
Stone and bronze ages in Italy and Sicily. '09(N13) il. O. $5.25. Oxford Univ.

Peffley, D. Fk.
Verses. '08(O) c. 120 p. pors. 24°. (Not for sale.) D. F. Peffley.

Peg Woffington. Reade, C: *35 c. net; *70 c. net. Dutton.

Peggy-Alone. Byrne, M. A. $1.25. Saalfield.

Peggy Owen. Madison, *Mrs.* L. F. $1.25. Penn Pub. Co.

Peggy, the daughter. Hinkson, *Mrs.* K. T. $1.50. Cassell.

Peggy the millionaire. Costello, M. 35 c. net. Herder.

Pegram, H:
Land title registration, (Torrens and other systems.) '08(Je) 112 p. 8°, pap. (Not for sale.) H: Pegram.

Pegram, W: Meade.
Past-times: [poems.] '09(D11) c. D. *$1 net. J: H. Saumenig.

Peile, Rev. Ja. Hamilton Fs.
Ecclesia discens: the church's lesson from the age. '09(Mr20) D. *$1.60 net. Longmans.

Peirce, E: Beauchamp.
Digest of decisions of the cts. and interstate commerce commission under the act to regulate commerce from 1887 to 1908; with a copy of act to regulate commerce as amended to date. '08(N) c. 8+1205 p. O. *$6 net. Callaghan.

Peirce, Grace Howard.
Elizabeth's story. '10(N19) c. front. 12°, 50 c. G. H. Peirce.

Peirce ser. 4°. Peirce Sch.
—Luman, *ed.* Comprehensive arithmetic. $1.50.

Peixotto, Ernest Clifford.
Romantic California. '10(O15) c. il. O. $2.50 net. Scribner.
Through the French provinces. '09(O16) c. il. O. **$2.50 net. Scribner.

Peker, C: Godfrey, ["Albert Fair."]
Hints for carpenters; collection of useful hints that will lessen the work of the carpenter and joiner. '09(O9) il. 12°, 50 c. Indust. Bk.
How to read plans: a simple practical explanation of the meaning of the various lines, marks, symbols and devices used on working drawings. '08(F1) il. plans, D. 50 c. Indust.
Practical house framing: simple explanation of the best methods of laying out and erecting balloon and braced frames. '09 (O9) il. 12°, 50 c. Indust. Bk.
Short cuts in carpentry. '09(F6) c. il. 12°, 50 c. Indust.

Pell, Albert.
Reminiscences; ed., with introd., by T: MacKay; with an appreciation by Ambassador Ja. Bryce. '08(My9) il. pors. 8°, *$5 net. Dutton.

Pell, E: Leigh, D.D.
My boy. '10(D) 16 p. pap., 10 c. Harding.
Prayer for each day in the week. '10(D) 16 p. pap., 10 c. Harding.
Prayers. '10(D17) 25 c. Harding.
Secrets of true success. Vest pocket ed. '10(My14) 10 c. Harding Press.
—, **comp.** Prayers we love to pray; incl. the world's greatest prayers suitable for private devotion. '10(Ja15) c. 12°, $1. Harding.

PELLA, Ia.
Huizinga, G: F. What the Dutch have done in the west of the United States. (Priv. pr.) E: Bok.

PELLAGRA.
Lavinder, C. H. Prophylaxis of pellagra. U. S., Supt. of Docs.
Lavinder, C. H., *and others.* Prevalence of pellagra in the U. S. (Add. Superintendent for price.) U. S., Supt. of Docs.
Marie, A. Pellagra. $2.50. State Co.
Mason, E. M. Pellagra. Gulf States Med.
See also Medicine.

Pélléas and Mélisande. Maeterlinck, M. **$1.50 net. Crowell.

Pelletreau, W: Smith.
Historic homes and institutions and genealogical and family history of New York. 4 v. '07, [1909.] (N) il. pors. map, facsims., 4°. (Add. pubs. for price.) Lewis Pub.

Pellissier, Georges Jacques Maurice, comp.
Anthologie des prosateurs francais contemporains. v. 1, Les romanciers (1850 à nos jours). '10(Ag6) facsims., S. leath., $1.20 net. Lemcke.
Anthologie du théatre français contemporain (prose et vers) (1850 à nos jours). '10(D24) facsims., S. leath., $1.25. Lemcke.

PELOPONNESIAN WAR.
Thucydides. Hist. of the Peloponnesian war. 35 c. net; 70 c. net. Dutton.

Peloubet, Fs. Nathan, D.D., and Wells, Amos Russel.
Select notes on the International lessons for 1909. '08(O10); for 1910. '09(O9); for 1911. '10(N5) c. il. maps, O. ea., $1.25; limp mor., $2; interleaved ed., $2. Wilde.

Peloubet, Seymour S.
Students' law dictionary of words and phrases in law Latin, law French and Anglo-Saxon. 3d ed., rev. and corrected. '08(Ja4) $1.50; shp., $2. Peloubet.

Peloubet's legal maxims: a collection of legal maxims in law and equity, with English translations. '08(Ja18) 12°, $1.50; shp., $2. Peloubet.

Pelzer, L:
Augustus Cæsar Dodge. '08, [1909.] (Ap) 12+369 p. por. 8°, (Iowa biographical ser.) $2. State Hist., Ia.

Pemberton, Rev. Jos. Hardwick.
Roses: their history, development and cultivation. '08(F22) il. O. $3.50. Longmans.

Pemberton, Max.
Amateur motorist. '09(Jl17) c. il. pors. **$3.75 net. McClurg.
Fortunate prisoner. '09(O23) c. il. D. †$1.50. G: W. Dillingham.
Mystery of the green heart. '10(S24) c. front. D. $1.30 net. Dodd.
Show girl. '09(Je26) c. front. il. in col. D. †$1.50. Winston.
Sir Richard Escombe. '08(Je20) c. front. D. †$1.50. Harper.

Pemberton, Morton Hord.
Reuben, his book. '10(Ja) 305 p. 12°, $1.15. B'way Pub.
Formerly published by M. H. Pemberton.

PEMBROKE, Mass.
See First Church.

Pen pictures of standard cotton grades. McArthur, N. J. $1. Mutual Pub. Co.

PENAL CODE.
See Criminal law.

PENAL LAW.
See Criminal law.

PENANCE.
McKenna, C: H., *comp.* Dominican tertiaries' guide. 75 c.; $1.25. Rosary.
See also Confession;—Repentance.

Pendennis. *See* Thackeray, W: Makepeace.

Pendergast, Mrs. Ella Worth.
Over the sea; travel letters. '09(Ja16) c. il. D. hf. leath., $1. E. W. Pendergast.

Pendleton, And. L., jr., ["Billy Bilger."]
Silly syclopedia; containing "daffynishuns" of the words of the slang language spoken by midshipmen of the U. S. Naval Academy. '08(O) c. 72 p. il. 16°, 50 c. C: G. Feldmeyer.

Pendleton, Fk., pseud.
Tim and Roy in camp. '10(Ag20) c. il. O. $1.50. Lothrop, L. & S.

Pendleton, L: Beauregard.
Alexander H. Stephens. '08(Ap4) c. por. D. (American crisis biographies.) **$1.25 net. Jacobs.

PENDLETON COUNTY, W. Va.
Morton, O. F. Hist. of Pendleton Co., W. Va. $3.50. O. F. Morton.

Pendleton twins. Jameson, E. M. $1.25. Jennings.

Pendred, Vaughan.
Railway locomotive. '09(My22) il. tabs., 8°, (Westminster ser.) *$2 net. Van Nostrand.

Pendulum (The). Troop, *Mrs.* E. W. S. $1.25. Duffield.

Penfield, Frederic Courtland.
Motor that went to court; fact-story, with random illustrations. '09, [1910.] (F) c. 5-91 p. il. pors. 8°. (Priv. pr.) F. C. Penfield.

Penguin Island. *See* France, Anatole, *pseud.*

Peninsular and Oriental Steam Navigation Company. P. & O. pocket book; 16 pages il. maps, plans. '08(Ag15) 16°, *$1 net. Macmillan.

PENINSULAR WAR.
Oman, C: W: C. Column and line in the Peninsular War. 40 c.—History of the Peninsular war. v. 3. *$4.75 net. Oxford Univ.

PENITENTIARIES.
See Prisons.

PENMANSHIP.
Bennett, M. E. Method in teaching writing. $1.25. Bennett Pub.
Clark, A. W. Public school penmanship. 75 c. Ginn.
Downey, J. E. Control processes in modified handwriting. $1.50. Psychological Review.
Hdbk. of penmanship. 25 c. net. Macmillan.
Harman, G. W. Twenty lessons in free-arm movement writing. 25 c. Macmillan.
Healey, H. G. System of free arm movement writing. 10 nos. 10 c. Am. Bk.
Lavay, J. B. Disputed handwriting. $3. Harvard Bk.
Smith, L. D., *and* H. P: Hdbk. of penmanship. *25 c. net.—Practice books 3-4 for preparatory writing. per doz., 55 c. Macmillan.
See also Handwriting;—Lettering.

Penn, W:
Charter of liberties, from William Penn to the freemen of the province of Pennsylvania. '09(Ap17) por. 8°, pap., 50 c. Henkels.
Reflections and maxims. '09(D) $3 (300 copies); vellum, $15 (6 copies). Seymour.
Some fruits of solitude. New ed.; ed., with an introd., by Edm. Gosse. '10(Ja8) il. por. 32°, $1; leatherette, $1.25. Lane.

PENN, William.
Grant, *Mrs.* C. Quaker and courtier. *$3.50 net. Dutton.
Hewitt, C: E: Spirit of Penn. $1. J. S. Ogilvie.

Penn-Jersey (The) automobile road guide and route list; cont. road maps and descriptive routes covering the principle points in Pennsylvania, New Jersey and Delaware. '09(S) c. il. maps, 4°, $1. Nuneviller.

Penn Publishing Co. plays. 19 v. D. pap. Penn Pub. Co.
Contents: Chambers, T. B., Kentucky belle, 15 c.; Demark, H. van, The ranchman, 25 c.; Dumont, F., Gunner in the navy, 25 c.; Gould, E. M., On the sight-seeing car, 15 c.; Griffith, H. S., Reflected glory, 15 c.; Harris, E: M., Fatal blow, 15 c.; Locke, B. M., Hiartville Shakespeare Club, 15 c.; Mathews, F. A., Finished coquette, 15 c.; Macauley, W., Wanted, a companion, Graduation day at Wood Hill School, ea., 15 c.; Marble, T: L., Won by wireless; Meyers, R. C. V., Ze moderne English, 15 c.; Morris, E. B., The freshman, 25 c.; Millions in it, 15 c.; Murphy, L. B., A frat initiation, 15 c.; Sanford, A., Commanding position, 15 c.; Thompson, A. C., Return of Letty; Tubbs, A. L., Farm folks; Van Denmark, Along the Missouri, 25 c.; Young, L. D., The iceman.

Pennell, Mrs. Eliz. Robins.
French cathedrals, monasteries and abbeys and sacred sites of France. '09(N13) c. il. plans, O. **$5 net, boxed. Century Co.
Our house and the people in it. '10(N12) c. D. $1.25 net. Houghton M.
— and Jos.
Life of James McNeill Whistler. '08(N7) [New printing, with revisions.] '09 (Mr20) 2 v., il. pors. Q. ea., *$10 net. Lippincott.

Pennell, Jos.
See Pennell, *Mrs.* Eliz. Robins.

Pennell, Orrin H:, comp.
Religious views of Abraham Lincoln. '10 (F12) c. por. O. 75 c.; pap., 25 c. Timby.

Pennell, Thdr. Leighton, M.D.
Among the wild tribes of the Afghan frontier; with an introd. by Field-Marshal Earl Roberts. 2d ed. '09(Mr13) il. map, O. *$3.50 net. Lippincott.

Pennell, Vane.
Auction bridge. '08(Je6) T. *$1 net. Lippincott.

Pennewill, Ja., and Macdonough, Rodney.
Addresses del. at the unveiling of a memorial tablet to Commodore Thomas Macdonough at Dover, Del., Nov. 10, 1908. '08, [1909.] (My) 20 p. por. 8°, (Papers of the Historical Soc. of Del.) pap., 50 c. Delaware Hist. Soc.

Penniman, G: W., ed.
See Hartshorn, W. N., *ed.*

Pennington, A. Stuart.
Argentine Republic; its physical features, hist., fauna, flora, geology, literature and commerce. '10(D17) il. map, O. $3 net. Stokes.

Pennington, Jeanne Gillespie, ed.
All is well; [selections from poems.] '09 (My1) c. T. (Don't fret ser.) 50 c. Dodge.
Be strong. '09(Jl10) c. 32°, (Don't fret ser.) 50 c. Dodge.

PENNSVILLE, N. J.
See St. George's Church.

Pennsylvania. Acts of the General Assembly of the commonwealth of Pennsylvania rel. to corporations coming under the supervision of the banking department, passed during the session of 1907. '08(O) 17 p 8°. (Add. pubs. for price.) Harrisburg Pub.

Pennsylvania. *Antietam Battlefield Memorial Commission.* Second brigade of the Pennsylvania reserves at Antietam; rept. of Antietam Battlefield Memorial Commission of Pa. and ceremonies at dedication of the monuments erected by the Commonwealth of Pa. to mark the position of four regiments of the Pa. reserves engaged in the battle. '08, [1909.] (My) 110 p. il. pors. 8°, o. p. Harrisburg Pub.

Pennsylvania. Constables' guide; the law of constables; by W: F. Dill. 2d ed. by D. Clare Good. '10(F) c. 13+267 p. S. (Add. pubs. for price.) T. & J. W. Johnson.

Pennsylvania. *County cts.* Repts. v. 33. '07, '08(Je); v. 34 (N); v. 35. '09(Jl); v. 36. '10(Je) c. O. shp., ea., $5 (subs. only).—Digest. v. 1-35; by Alb. B. Weimer. (D) Q. $7.50. T. & J. W. Johnson.

Pennsylvania. *Dept. of Health.* Descriptive catalogue of the exhibits of the State Dept. of Health of Penn. at the International Congress on Tuberculosis, Washington, D. C., September 21 to October 12, 1908; Samuel G. Dixon, Commissioner of Health. '09(Jl17) 8°. (Add. pubs. for price.) Penn. Dept. Health.

Pennsylvania. Digest of the decisions of the courts of the commonwealth, from 1754 to 1907; (Ruby R. and T: E. Vale.) v. 1-2. '08(Ag); v. 3 (D); v. 4. '09(Je); v. 5. '09, [1910.] (F) c. Q. ea., $8. Bisel.

Pennsylvania. Digest of the statute law of the state; from 1700 to 1903, originally comp. in 1811 by J: Purdon. 13th ed.; comp., annot., and rev. by Ardemus Stewart. v. 4. '10(Je) c. O. (Stewart's Purdon's digest.) shp., $6. Bisel.

Pennsylvania. Digest of the statute law of state, 1905 to 1909; comp. and annot. by Ernest Watts; supp. to Stewart's Purdon's digest. [v. 5.] '10(N) c. O. shp., $6. Bisel.

Pennsylvania. *District ct.* Repts.; cases decided in all the judicial districts of the state, 1906-1907. v. 15, 16. '07, [1908.] (My.) c. O. shp., ea., $5.25. H. W. Page.

Pennsylvania. Foreign attachment; by J: W. Patton. '09(Je) c. 128 p. O. (Add. pubs. for price.) Welsh.

Pennsylvania. Index and concordance to Pepper and Lewis's digest of decisions and encyclopædia of Penna. law. vs. 1 to 23, and vs. 1 and 2 cross-reference annuals, 1682-1906; together with tables of acts of assembly, acts of Congress and British statutes construed and applied in the Penn. cases, and an alphabetical index to the acts; by S: Dreher Matlack and Lawrence J. Bur. '08(N) c. 3+863 p. O. $10. Welsh.

Pennsylvania. Index to cases construing the statutes, 1664 to 1908; the constitution of Pa., and the British statutes. 2d ed., by D. Clare Good. '08(N) c. 9+705 p. O. *$8 net. T. & J. W. Johnson.

Pennsylvania. Law of crimes including criminal evidence; by W: Trickett. In 2 v. '08 (F) c. 56+566; 13+567-1183 p. O. $11. T. & J. W. Johnson.

Pennsylvania. Law of taxation; by Fk. M. Eastman. v. 1, 2. '09(N) c. O. $12. Soney.

Pennsylvania. Legislation on associations; arr. by G: Wharton Pepper and W: Draper Lewis. '09(Je) c. 79 p. O. pap. (Add. pubs. for price.) Int. Pr.

Pennsylvania. Luzerne [Co.] legal register repts.; (Jos. D. Coons and W. E. Woodruff.) v. 13. '08(My.) c. O. shp. (Add. pubs. for price.) Yordy.

Pennsylvania. Mechanics' liens, under the act of June 4, 1901, P. L. 431, and supps. thereto, with forms and decisions to date, by Fs. Chapman. '09(Je) c. 9+136 p. O. (Add. pubs. for price.) Bisel.

Pennsylvania. Monaghan's cumulative annual digest of decisions, 1907; (Ja. Monaghan, G: M. Henry and G: H. Smith.) '08(Ap); 1908. '09(Ap); 1909. '10(Ap) c. O. ea., $6. Soney.

Pennsylvania. Practice; actions at law, [etc.;] with forms. In 4 v., by W: J. Johnson. v. 1. '10(F) c. O. $6. Welsh.

Pennsylvania. Rules and regulations of the Department of Health. '07, [1908.] (S) 14 p. 8°. (Add. pubs. for price.) Penn. Dept. of Health.

Pennsylvania. *Superior ct.* Repts., v. 34; (W: I. Schaeffer and Albert B. Weimer.) '08(Mr); v. 35 (Ag); v. 36 (D); v. 37. '09(Je); v. 38 (O) ea., $2; v. 39, 40. '09, [1910.] (Ja); v. 41 (Jl); v. 42 (D) c. O. shp., ea., $1.08. Banks.

Pennsylvania. *Supreme ct.* Repts. v. 218; (W: I. Schaffer.) v. 219 (Je); v. 220 (S); v. 221. '08, [1909.] (Ja); v. 222 (Jl); v. 223, 224 (N) ea., $3.50; v. 225. '10(F); v. 226 (Je); v. 227 (S) c. O. shp., ea., 89 c. Banks.

Pennsylvania. Table of cases, alphabetically arranged; cont. all the reported cases in the sup., superior and county cts., 1682 to 1906; with references to the vs. and pp. of the repts. and to the vs. and columns of Pepper and Lewis's digest of decisions, vs. 1 to 23, and vs. 1 and 2 cross-reference annuals where all the related, parallel and analogous cases will be found, showing all reversed and affirmed cases; comp. under the supervision of S: Dreher Matlack. '09(Mr) c. 1050 p. O. $10. Welsh.

Pennsylvania. *Topographic and Geologic Survey.* Topographic and geologic survey of Pennsylvania, 1906-1908. '08, [1909.] (Jl) 375 p. il. maps, 8°. (Add. pubs. for price.) Harrisburg Pub.

Pennsylvania. Treatise on executive clemency, by W: W. Smithers; with statistics, record data and forms by G: D. Thorn. '09(O) c. 289 p. O. $3. Int. Pr.

Pennsylvania. Treatise on the rules against perpetuities, restraints on alienation and restraints on enjoyment as applicable to gifts of property, [etc.,] by Roland R. Foulke. '09(O) c. O. $5. Bisel.

PENNSYLVANIA.
Automobile laws of the New England States, New York, New Jersey and Pennsylvania. (Add. pub. for price.) Rhode Island Lib.

PENNSYLVANIA.—*Continued.*

Clark, W:, *comp.* Hist. of Hampton battery F, independent Pennsylvania light artillery. $2. W. Clark.

Clarke, W: P. Official history of the militia and the National Guard of the State of Pennsylvania. 3 v. $50. C. J. Hendler.

Dickey, L. S: Hist. of the 103d Regiment, Pennsylvania Volunteer Infantry, 1861-1865. $5. L. S: Dickey.

Eastman, F. M. Supp. to 2d ed. of Eastman on private corporations [in Pennsylvania.] $1.50.—Treatise on the law rel. to private corporations [in Pennsylvania.] 2 v. (Add. pubs. for price.) Bisel.

Gould, J. Story of the 48th; record of campaigns of the 48th Regiment, Pa. Veteran Volunteer Infantry. $4. J. Gould.

Gruber, C. L. Government of the state of Pennsylvania. $1.50. C. L. Gruber.

Halberstadt, B. General map of bituminous coal fields of Pennsylvania, 1907. $6. B. Halberstadt.

Hays, G. A., *comp.* Under the red patch; story of 63d Regiment, Pa. Volunteers, 1861-1864. $2. G. A. Hays.

Higby, C. D. Government of Pennsylvania and the nation. 70 c. Heath.

Jackson, M. K. Outlines of the literary history of colonial Pennsylvania. *$1.25 net. Lemcke.

Kiefer, W: R., *and* Mack, N. H. Hist. of the 153d Regiment Pa. Volunteers Infantry. $2. Chemical.

Leonard, J: W. Who's who in Pennsylvania. $5. Hamersly.

Lovejoy, O. R. Children in the glass industry in Pennsylvania. (Add. pubs. for price.) Nat. Child Labor.

Loyd, W: H. Early courts of Pennsylvania. $3.50. Boston Bk.

Maltby, A. E. American citizen in Pennsylvania $1. Am. Bk.

Patton, J: W. New replevin in Pennsylvania. $1. Welsh.

Penn, W: Charter of liberties from William Penn to the freemen of the province of Pennsylvania. 50 c. Henkels.

Pennypacker, S: W. Pennsylvania in American hist. $4 net. W: J. Campbell.

Pepper, G: W., *and others.* Cross-reference annual ser., "C.R.A.": digest of Penn. decisions. v. 2. $10. Welsh.

Reed, J: A. Hist. of the 101st regiment, Pennsylvania Veteran Volunteer Infantry, 1861-1865. $5. Dickey.

Saugrain de Vigni, A. F. Dr. Saugrain's note-books, 1788. 50 c. Davis Press.

Shimmell, L. S. Government of Pennsylvania. *90 c. net.—Short hist. of Pennsylvania. 75 c. C: E. Merrill.

Smiley, A. W. Few scraps, oily and otherwise. $1. A. W. Smiley.

Smithers, W: W. Treatise on executive clemency in Pennsylvania. $3.25. Int. Pr.

Spencer, A. C. Magnetite deposits of the Cornwall type in Pennsylvania. (Add. Superintendent for price.) U. S., Supt. of Docs.

PENNSYLVANIA.—*Continued.*

Sullivan, J: J. Pennsylvania business law. $4. Winston.

Swank, J. M. Progressive Pennsylvania. $5. J. M. Swank.

Who's who in Pennsylvania. $5 Hamersley.

Yetter, J: M. Educational system of Pennsylvania. $1. Cochrane.

See also Athens;—Chester County;— Civil War;—Cumberland County;— Delaware river;—Education;—Erie County;—Freemasonry;—Germantown;— Gettysburg;—Indians;—Inland navigation; — Lebanon County; — Mercer County; — Ohio; — Philadelphia; — Philipsburg; — Pittsburgh;—Reading;—Tredyffrin; —Valley Forge; —Whitemarsh; — Wilkesbarre; —Williamsport; —Wills;—Wissahickon river.

Pennsylvania Cavalry. Hist. of the Eighteenth regiment of cavalry, Pennsylvania volunteers (163d regiment of the line), 1862-1865. '09, [1910.] (Ja) 299 p. il. pors. maps, 8°, $1. Wynkoop, H.

Pennsylvania Dept. of Agriculture, bull. 8°. Penn. Dept. of Agriculture.
—Fuller. Analysis of Paris green.
—Gay. Timely hints to horse breeders.

Pennsylvania Institution for the Instruction of the Blind, Overbrook, Philadelphia. About a school for children and youth who have bad eyesight or who are blind. '09 (S18) il. O. pap., gratis. Penn. Inst. Blind.

Pennsylvania law stamps from the earliest issue of the Penn. repts. to the year 1910. [1910] (My) c. S. pap., $3. Law Stamp.

Pennsylvania mountain stories. Shoemaker, H: W. (Priv. pr.) Bradford Record.

Pennsylvania Museum and School of Industrial Art, Art handbooks. il. 8°. Penn. Mus. and Sch. of Ind. Art.
—Barber. Maiolica of Mexico. $2.10.

Pennsylvania notaries public and commissioners manual; by L: Richards. '08(O) c. 77 p. O. (Add. pub. for price.) Soney.

Pennsylvania Society. Year book of the Pennsylvania Society, 1908; ed. by Barr Ferree. '08(Ap11) $2.50; 1910. '10(Jl30) c. il. pors. maps, facsims., O. $2. Penn. Soc., N. Y.

Pennsylvania State College bulletin, Dept. of Chemistry. 8°. Penn. State Coll.
—Pond. Calcium, carbide and acetylene. gratis.

Pennsylvania University. Wistar Institute of Anatomy and Biology. List of biological serials, exclusive of botany, in the libraries of Philadelphia. '09, [1910.] 61 p. 8°, (Bull. of the Wistar Institute of Anatomy and Biology.) pap., gratis. Wistar.

Pennsylvania University Library. Calendar of the papers of Benjamin Franklin in the library of the University of Pennsylvania; being the appendix to the "Calendar of the papers of Benjamin Franklin in the library of the American Philosophical Society," ed. by I. Minis Hays. '08, [1909.] (N) 399-546 p. 4°, (University of Pennsylvania pubs.; ser. in History.) $1.50. Univ. of Penn.; [Appleton.]

Pennybacker, Mrs. Anna J. Hardwicke.
History of Texas for schools. Rev. (1908) ed. '08(Mr) c. 412 p. il. pors., 12°, 65 c. P. V. Pennybacker.

Pennypacker, S: Whitaker.
Anthony Wayne; [address del. at Valley Forge, June 20, 1908, at the dedication of the equestrian statue of Major General Anthony Wayne, erected by the Commonwealth.] '08, [1909.] (Ap) 45 p. por. 4°. (Not for sale.) S: W. Pennypacker.
Pennsylvania in American hist. '10(D17) c. 8°, $4 net. W: J. Campbell.
PENOBSCOT EXPEDITION.
Calef, J: Siege of Penobscot by the rebels. $2.75. Abbatt.
PENOLOGY.
See Crime and criminals;—Prisons.
Penrose, C: Bingham.
Text-book of diseases of women. 6th ed., rev. '08(D) c. 9-550 p. il. 8°, *$3.75 net. Saunders.
Penrose, Marg.
Dorothy Dale. '08(D5) c. il. 12°, (Dorothy Dale ser.) 60 c. Cupples & L.
Dorothy Dale and her chums. '09(D18) c. il. 12°, (Dorothy Dale ser.) 60 c. Cupples & L.
Dorothy Dale at Glenwood school. '08 (D5) c. il. 12°, (Dorothy Dale ser.) 60 c. Cupples & L.
Dorothy Dale's great secret. '09(D18) c. il. 12°, (Dorothy Dale ser.) 60 c. Cupples & L.
Dorothy Dale's queer holidays. [1910.] (Jl) c. 250 p. il. 12°, (Dorothy Dale ser.) 60 c. Cupples & L.
Motor girls on a tour; or, keeping a strange promise. '10(D10) il. 12°, (Motor girls ser.) 60 c. Cupples & L.
Motor girls; or, a mystery of the road. '10 (D) il. 12°, (Motor girls ser.) 60 c. Cupples & L.
Penrose's process yearbook for 1908: [comprehensive survey of the progress of graphic arts.] '09(Mr) 300 p. il. 4°, $2.50. Tennant.
Pensées et réflections de La Bruyère et autres auteurs français. Crowther, C. S., *comp.* $1. W: R. Jenkins.
Pensées, maximes et réflexions. Pascal, B. *40 c. net. Macmillan.
PENSIONS.
Lecky, W: E: Old-age pensions. 25 c. Longmans.
United States. *Dept. of Commerce and Labor. Bu. of Labor.* Pension funds for municipal employees and railroad pension systems in the United States; prep. under the direction of C: P. Neill. '10(Jl) 89 p. 8°.
See also Civil service;—Insurance;—Slavery;—Teachers and teaching.
PENTACARDIOID.
See Mathematics.
PENTATEUCH.
See Bible.
Pentecostal experience. Ruth, C. W. 25 c. Chr. Witness.
PENTECOSTAL UNION.
White, *Mrs.* A. Demons and tongues. 30 c. Pentecostal Union.
Penton's foundry list, 1908: directory of the foundries of the United States and Canada. '08(S5) c. 12°, $10. Penton.

PEONIES.
Coit, J: E. Peony check-list. $5. Am. Peony Soc.
People and problems. Franklin, F. **$1.50 net. Holt.
People and questions. Street, G: S. $1.50 net. M. Kennerley.
People and their property. Jennings, E. B. $1. B'way Pub.
People at play. Hartt, R. L. **$1.50 net. Houghton M.
People I have met. Carradine, B. $1. Chr. Witness.
People (The) I meet: record of friendships. '10(S10) nar. S. (Thumb-o-graph ser.) 50 c. net. Stokes.
People of Egypt; with an introd. '10(D24) col. il. 8°, (Peoples of many lands ser.) $1.75 net. Macmillan.
People of Holland; introd. by Gordon Home. '10(D24) col. il. 8°, (Peoples of many lands ser.) $1.75 net. Macmillan.
People of India; introd. by G. E. Mitton. '10 (D24) col. il. 8°, (Peoples of many lands ser.) $1.75. Macmillan.
People of position. Hyatt, S. P. $1.20 net. Wessels & B.
People of the polar north. Rasmussen, K. *$5 net. Lippincott.
People (The), the railroads and the national authority. Knox, P. C. (Add. author for price.) P. C. Knox.
People's Biblical encyclopedia. Barnes, C: R., *ed.* 2 v. $9. People's Pub.
People's commonsense medical adviser in plain English. Pierce, R. V. 31 c. World's Dispensary.
People's co-operative banks. Devine, H: C. *35 c. net. Cassell.
People's hand-book of the Bible. Ayars, J: E. 85 c. Meth. Episcopal.
People's home library; library of three practical books: The people's home medical book, by T. J. Ritter, M.D.; The people's home recipe book, by Mrs. Alice G. Kirk; The people's home stock book, by W. C. Fair. '10(D3) c. front. pors. 4°, $4.50. R. C. Barnum.
People's home lib. por. il. 4°. R. C. Barnum.
—Fair. People's home stock book. $3.
—Kirk, *Mrs.* People's home recipe book. $3.
—Ritter. People's home medical book. $3.
People's hour and other themes. Gibson, G: H: $1. Englewood Pub.
People's Institute, New York. Memorial to Henry Codman Potter by the People's Institute, Cooper Union, Sunday, December 20, 1908. '09(N) 7+67 p. por. (Not for sale.) Cheltenham Press.
People's king. Holt-White, W: E: B. $1.25 net. Lane.
People's law. Lobingier, C: S. **$4 net. Macmillan.
People's lib. *See* Cassell's.
Peoples of many lands ser. il. 8°. $1.75 net. Macmillan.
—People of Egypt.
—People of Holland.
—People of India.
Pepita Jiménez. *See* Valera y Alcalà Galiano, J.

Peple, E: H:
Mallet's masterpieces. '08(D5) c. il. D. **75 c. net, boxed. Moffat.
A night out. '09(D11) c. front. S. bds., 50 c. Moffat.
The spitfire. '08(O3) il. D. †$1.50. Moffat.

Pepper, C: M.
See United States. *Dept. of Commerce and Labor.*

Pepper, G: Hubbard, and Wilson, Rev. Gilbert Livingstone.
Hidatsa shrine and the beliefs respecting it. '09(Ap10) il. O. (Memoirs of the American Anthropological Association.) pap., 50 c. Am. Anthropological.

Pepper, G: Wharton.
The way: devotional book for boys. '09 (Mr6) c. S. *40 c. net; leath., $1. Longmans.

—, comp. *See* Pennsylvania legislation on associations.

—, and Lewis, W: Draper.
Cases on the law of association. pts. 1, 2, 3. '08(D) c. 8°, pt. 1, 60 c.; pt. 2, 55 c.; pt. 3, 55 c. W: D. Lewis.
Cross reference annual series; being a digest of Pa. decisions, 1906-1908. v. 3, 4. '10(Ag) c. Q. ea., $10. Welsh.

—, Lewis, W: Draper, and Matlock, S: Dreher.
Cross-reference annual series, "C.R.A.": digest of Penn. decisions, 1898-1906. v. 2. '08(Je) c. O. $10. Welsh.

Pepper, J: R.
Thirty years at the superintendent's desk: lessons learned and noted. '10(Je4) 16°, bds., 25 c. Revell.

Pepperrell, Sir W:
Journal of Sir William Pepperrell kept during the expedition against Louisbourg Mar. 24-Aug. 22, 1745; ed. from the orig. in the library of the Society, by C: H: Lincoln; [repr. from the Proceedings of the American Antiquarian Society, Oct., 1909.] '10(Jl) 51 p. facsim., 4°, $1. Am. Antiquarian.
"Bibliographical notes" (7 p.).

Pepys, S:
Diary. '08(O10) 2 v., 12°, ("Best books" ser.) leath.., ea., *$1 net. Dutton.
Red-letter days of Samuel Pepys; ed. by E: Fk. Allen; with an introd. by H: B. Wheatley. '10(D24) c. pors. D. $1.25 net. Sturgis & W.

PEPYS, Samuel.
Lubbock, P. Samuel Pepys. *$1 net. Scribner.
Moorehouse, E. H. Samuel Pepys, administrator, observer and gossip. $3. Dutton.

PERCENTAGE.
Davison, L. A. Percentage and its applications. 30 c. Bardeen.

PERCEPTION.
See Psychology.

Perceptual factors in reading. Hamilton, F. M. 50 c. Science Pr., (N. Y.).

Perceval le Gallois.
See High history of the Holy Graal.

Percival, Archibald Stanley.
Practical integration; for the use of engineers, etc. '08(Ja11) 12°, *80 c. net. Macmillan.
Prescribing of spectacles. '10(N) il. 12°, $2 net. Wood.

Percival, Milton, and Jelliffe, Rob. Archibald, comps.
Specimens of exposition and argument. '08(N21) 12°, *90 c. net. Macmillan.

Percival Keene. *See* Marryat, F:

Percy, T:, Bp. of Dromore, ed.
Reliques of ancient English poetry; ed., with general introd., additional prefaces, notes, glossary, etc., by H: B. Wheatley. In 3 v. '10(F19) 8°, *$3 net. Macmillan.

PERDITA.
See Robinson, *Mrs.* Mary Darby.

Perdue, H. Avis, comp.
See Allison, S: B.

Père Raphael. *See* Cable, G: Washington. "Posson Jone."

Pereat Rochus. Fogazzaro, A. 40 c. Heath.

Pereda, José Maria de.
Pedro Sánchez; with introd., notes and vocab. by Ralph Emerson Bassett. '08 (D19) c. por. facsim., D. (International modern language ser.) $1. Ginn.

Perez, Luis M.
Bibliografia de la Revolucion de Yara; folletos y libros im presos de 1868 a 1908. In 3 pts. pt. 1. '08(D5) $1.25. Stechert.

Perfect French possible. Knowles, M. H. 35 c. Heath.

Perfect garden. Wright, W. P. *$2 net. Lippincott.

Perfect Man. Smith, J. T. S. *10 c. net. Revell.

Perfect strength. Maynadier, E. W., *comp.* *75 c. net. J: W. Luce.

Perfect through suffering. Villiers, H: M. *$1.50 net. Longmans.

Perfect tribute. Andrews, *Mrs.* M. R. S. †$1. Scribner.

Perfect Wagnerite. *See* Shaw, G: Bernard.

Perfect way. Kingsford, A. B. $2.50. Theo. Pub. Co.

Perfected poultry. McGrew, T: F. $2.50. Howard Pub. Co.

Perfectly good cynics' calendar, 1909. Mumford, E. W: **75 c. net. P. Elder.

Perfume holder. Betts, C. L. 50 c. C. L. Betts.

Perfume of the lady in black. Leroux, G. †$1.50. Brentano's.

Périgord, Dorothée von Biron, Duchesse de Talleyrand-.
See Talleyrand-Périgord, D. von B., *Duchesse* de.

Perin, Florence Perin, comp.
Optimist's good night. '10(N5) c. S. $1 net. Little, B. & Co.

Perine, E: Ten Broeck.
American trust companies; their growth and present wealth; two addresses. '10 (Ja22) c. fold. tabs., 8°, gratis. Audit Co.

Perine, Howland Delano, comp.
Daniel Perrin, "The Huguenot," and his descendants in America, of the surnames, Perrine, Perine, and Prine, 1665-1910. '10 (D) 547 p. il. pors. maps, (partly fold.,) facsims., 4°, $10 net. H. D. Perrine.

Periodic law. Garrett, A. E. *$1.75 net. Appleton.

Periodic law and the hydrogen spectrum. Kemble, W: F. 50 c. Van Nostrand.

PERIODICAL PUBLISHERS' ASSOCIATION.
See Post-office.

PERIODICALS.
Annual magazine subject-index, 1909. $5.50 net; Boston Bk.
Brief manual of leading periodicals in the United States and Canada. gratis. Chesman.
Catholic University of America Library. Periodicals and serials in the library of the Catholic University of America. (Priv. pr.) Cath. Univ.
Faxon, F: W., *comp.* Check-list of Am. and Eng. periodicals. (Not for sale.) Boston Bk.
Goodnight, S. H. German literature in American magazines prior to 1846. 50 c. Univ. of Wis.
Jones' Index to legal periodicals. 2 v. $20. Boston Bk.
Lord and Thomas' pocket dict. of the American press for 1910; complete list of newspapers, magazines and periodicals. $2. Lord.
MacDonald, K. I. Magazines for the small library. (Add. pubs. for price.) League Lib. Com.
Severance, H: O., *and* Walsh, C: H., *comps.* Guide to the current periodicals and serials of the United States. *$2 net. —Supplement, 1910, 50 c. Wahr.
United States. *Superintendent of Documents.* Periodicals issued by United States government with foreign and domestic subscription prices. gratis. Gov. Pr. Off.
Weeks, L. H., *and* Bacon, E. M., *comps. and eds.*. Historical digest of the provincial press: [New England.] subs., per v., $7.50; per set, $150. Soc. Americana.
See also Agriculture;—Biology;—Catholic church;—German literature;—Indexes;—Newspapers.

Periwinkle. Payson, W: F. $1.25 net. Sturgis & W.

Perjurer (The). Norris, W: E: $1.50. Brentano's.

Perkins, Agnes F., ed.
See Woman's Educational and Industrial Union.

Perkins, Charlton Bristow.
Travels from the grandeurs of the West to the mysteries of the East; or, from Occident to Orient and around the world. '09(S25) c. il. map, 4°, $3. C. B. Perkins.

Perkins, Clara Crawford.
Builders of Spain. '09(My8) c. 2 v., il. O. $5, boxed. Holt.
French cathedrals and chateaux. 2 v. [New ed.] '09(My8) il. 8°, *$5 net. Holt.

Perkins, Jane Gray.
Life of the Honorable Mrs. Norton. '09 (D4) pors. O. *$3.50 net. Holt.

Perkins, Marg., comp.
Echoes of Pawnee Rock. '08(N21) c. D. pap., 50 c. Goldsmith-W.

Perkins Institution and Massachusetts School for the Blind. A brief summary of the history of the Perkins Institution and Massachusetts School for the Blind; prepared for use in connection with House bill no. 285, asking the State legislature to have certain land in South Boston reconveyed to the Institution. '09(S18) 8°, pap., gratis. Perkins Inst.

Perkins Institution and Massachusetts School for the Blind. Circulating library; catalog of embossed books. '08(Je6); '09(Je19) 8°, pap. (Add. Institution for price.) Perkins Inst.

Perkins Institution and Massachusetts School for the Blind. List of embossed books, maps, appliances and tangible apparatus for the use of the blind. '09(Je19) il. 8°, pap., gratis. Perkins Inst.

Permanent way diagrams. Frere, F. H. $1.25. Spon.

PERRAUD, *Abbé* Charles Alexis.
Houtin, A. A married priest. *70 c. net. Sherman, F.

Perrault, Charles.
Fairy tales; told in easy French by Kathleen Fitzgerald. '10(D) il. sq. 16°, (Children's favorites.) 50 c. net. Jacobs.

Perrett, Louise, comp.
See Smith, Sarah K., *comp.*

Perrier, Jos. L:
Revival of scholastic philosophy in the nineteenth century. '09(My22) c. 8°, *$1.75 net. Lemcke.

Perrigo, C: Oscar Eug.
Change gear devices. '10(My21) $1. Henley.

Perrin, Alice Robinson, [Mrs. C: Perrin.]
Idolatry. '09(Mr13) c. D. †$1.50. Duffield.
Stronger claim. '10(F19) c. D. †$1.50. Duffield.

Perrin, Mrs. C:
See Perrin, Alice Robinson.

Perrin, Lee Ja., ["Ewer Struly."]
My three years at Andover. '08(O17) c. 12°, $1. Mayhew.

PERRIN FAMILY.
See Genealogies.

Perrine, C: Dillon, and others.
Determination of the solar parallax from photographs of Eros made with the Crossley reflector of the Lick Observatory, University of California. '10(O8) front. Q. (Carnegie Institution pubs.) pap., $2.50. Carnegie.

Perrine, Howland Delano, comp.
Daniel Perrin, "The Huguenot," and his descendants in America, of the surnames Perrine, Perine, and Prine, 1665-1910. '10 (D) 547 p. il. pors. maps (partly fold.), facsims., 4°, $10 net. H. D. Perrine.

Perrine, I.
See Harris, Gilbert Dennison.

Perrine, W:
See Edmonds, Franklin Spencer.

Perris, G: Herb.
How protection grows. '10(O) 28 p. D. pap., 10 c. Cassell.
Protection and corruption. '10(O) 19 p. D. pap., 10 c. Cassell.

Perrot, Emile G:
See Ballinger, Wa. F.

Perry, Arth. Cecil, jr.
Management of a city school. '08(Ap11) c. 12°, *$1.25 net. Macmillan.
Problems of the elementary school. '10 (Je18) c. D. $1.25 net. Appleton.

Perry, Bliss.
Park-Street papers. '08(O17) c. D. **$1.25 net. Houghton M.
Walt Whitman: his life and work. 2d ed., rev. '08(Ap11) c. il. pors. D. **$1.50 net. Houghton M.

Perry, Clarence Arth.
Wider use of the school plant; introd. by Luther Halsey Gulick. '10(D31) il. O. (Russell Sage Foundation pubs.) $1.25. Charities Pub. Comm.

Perry, E: Baxter.
Stories of standard teaching pieces. '10 (D31) c. 8°, $1.50. Presser.

Perry, Frances Foster.
Their hearts' desire '09(D4) c. col. il. O. *$2 net, boxed. Dodd.

Perry, Frances M.
Introductory course in exposition. '08(F8) c. D. $1. Am. Bk.
Punctuation primer; with notes on the preparation of manuscript. '08(O3) c. S. 30 c. Am. Bk.

Perry, F: Albertus.
Cressy, maid of Japan; story of the conversion of a high class girl to Christianity, setting forth religious and social conditions in Japan. '10(N12) c. il. por. 12°, $1.25. Hammond Pub.

Perry, G: Powell.
Wealth from waste: [manufacturing from by-products.] '09(F13) c. 12°, *50 c. net. Revell.

Perry, Jennette Barbour.
See Lee, Jennette.

Perry, J: Tavenor-.
Dinanderie; hist. and description of mediæval art work in copper, brass and bronze. '10(O8) il. 4°, $5.50 net. Macmillan.

Perry, Lawrence.
Dan Merrithew. '10(Ap2) c. il. O. $1.50. McClurg.

Perry, Adjutant-General Oran, comp.
Indiana in the Mexican war. '08, [1909.] (Mr) 496 p. pors. 8°. (Add. author for price.) O. Perry.

Perry, Ralph Barton.
Moral economy. '09(Je) c. D. **$1.25 net. Scribner.

Perry, S. Payson.
Tariff and the farmer. '09(Je19) 12°, 50 c. F. S. Blanchard.

Perry, Wa. Copland.
Boys' Iliad. '08(Ag15) il. 12°, $1.50. Macmillan.
Boys' Odyssey. '08(Ag15) il. 12°, $1.50. Macmillan.
Sicily in fable, history, art and song. '08 (Ag1) map, 12°, *$1.50 net. Macmillan.

PERSECUTION.
See Jews;—Martyrs.

Persecution of Stephen Strong. Babcock, C: E. $1. B'way Pub.

PERSIA.
Anet, C. Through Persia in a motor car. *$4.50 special net. Appleton.
Bradley-Birt, F. B. Through Persia from the Gulf to the Caspian. *$3.50 net. Dutton.
Buxton, E. M. W. Stories of Persian heroes: [fiction.] †$1.50. Crowell.
Cresson, W: P. Persia: the awakening East. **$3.50 net. Lippincott.
Hume-Griffith, *Mrs.* M. E. *and* A. Behind the veil in Persia and Turkish Arabia. *$3.50 net. Lippincott.
Jewett, M. Reminiscences of my life in Persia. $1. Torch Press.
Nweeya, S: K. Persia, the land of the magi. $2. S. K. Nweeya.
Renninger, E. D., *comp.* Story of Rustem and other Persian hero tales from Firdusi. **$1.50 net. Scribner.
Shedd, E. C. Our little Persian cousin. 60 c. L. C. Page.
Sykes, E. C. Persia and its people. $2.50 net. Macmillan.
Sykes, P. M., *tr. and ed.* Glory of the Shia World. $3.50 net. Macmillan.
Tolman, H. C. Cuneiform supplement (autographed) to the author's Ancient Persian lexicon and texts. $1.25. Am. Bk.
Wishard, J: G. Twenty years in Persia. *$1.50 net. Revell.
See also Artaxerxes III.

PERSIAN LANGUAGE.
Tolman, H. C. Ancient Persian lexicon and the texts of the Achaemenidan inscriptions transliterated and translated. $1.25. Am. Bk.

Persian literature: comprising The Shâh Nâmeh; The Rubâiyât; The Divan; and The Gulistan; with introd. by B: Gottheil. [Also] Japanese literature: incl. selections from Genji Monogatari; and classical poetry and drama of Japan; with critical and biographical sketches by Epiphanius Wilson. '08(Je27) c. 2 v., il. 8°, $3.50; hf. mor., $7. Lamb Pub.

Persian mystics; Jálala 'd-Din-Rumî; tr. by F. Hadland Davis. '08(Je6) 16°, (Wisdom of the East.) *60 c. net. Dutton.

Persian mystics: Jami; tr. by F. Hadland Davis. '08(Ag15) 16°, (Wisdom of the East; ed. by L. Cranmer-Bying and S. A. Kapadia.) *60 c. net. Dutton.

Persians (The). *See* Æschylus. Suppliant maidens.

Persinger, Clark Edm.
See Caldwell, Howard Wa.

Persis Putnam's treasure. Hamlin, M. S. †$1.25. Little, B. & Co.

Persistent problems of philosophy. Calkins, M. W. *$2.50 net. Macmillan.

PERSIUS FLACCUS, Aulus.
Morgan, M. H. Bibliography of Persius. 75 c. Harvard Univ.

Person and place of Jesus Christ. Forsyth, P: T. *$1.50 net. Pilgrim Press.

Person and work of the Holy Spirit. Torrey, R. A. $1 net. Revell.

Person of Christ. Merrell, E: H. 90 c. net. Bibliotheca Sacra.

Person of our Lord and recent thought. Nolloth, C: F: *$1.25 net. Macmillan.

Persona, [pseud. for Adolphe Fassler.]
New gospel. '08(F22) c. 12°, 75 c. Brentano's.

Persona. Müller, M. 25 c. Open Court.

Personal and party government. Winstanley, D. A. $1.50 net. Putnam.

Personal atmosphere. **Haddock, F. C.** $1. Power-Bk.

Personal conduct of Belinda. Brainerd, E. H. $1.20, fixed. Doubleday, P.

Personal contagion. Eddy, *Mrs.* M. M. B. G. 10 c. Chr. Sci.

Personal equation. McTurnan, L. $1.25 net. Moffat.

Personal help lib. 12°. Personal Help.
—Knox. Leadership. $1.40; $2.80.

Personal hygiene. Brewer, I: W. *$1 net. Davis.

Personal information for boys. Edwards, E. 50 c. Fenno.

Personal information for young men. Edwards, E. 50 c. Fenno.

Personal information for young women. Edwards, E. 50 c. Fenno.

Personal injuries. Wilkinson, J. D. $7. Hansell.

PERSONAL MAGNETISM.
See Personality.

Personal power. Tucker, W: J. **$1.50 net. Houghton M.

PERSONAL PROPERTY.
Erwin, F. A. Cases on sales of personal property. $3.50. Banks.
Smith, H. E. Treatise on the law of personal property. $4. Flood.
See also Mortgages;—Property;—Sale;—Taxation; *also* names of states.

***Personal purity publications.* D. Fenno.**
—Edwards. Personal information for boys.
—Personal information for young women. ea., 50 c.

Personal recollections. Abbott, L. A. (Add. author for price.) L. A. Abbott.

Personal recollections of a cavalryman. Kidd, J. H. $2. J. H. Kidd.

Personal recollections of Wagner. Neumann, A. **$2.50 net. Holt.

Personal religion in Egypt. Petrie, W: M. F. **75 c. net. Harper.

Personalism. Bowne, B. P. **$1.50 net. Houghton M.

PERSONALITY.
Bruce, H: A. B. Riddle of personality. **$1.50 net. Moffat.
Buckham, J: W. Personality and the Christian ideal. *$1.50 net. Pilgrim Press.
Carman, W: B. Making of personality. $1.50; $3.50. L. C. Page.
Prince, M. Dissociation of a personality. **$2.80 net. Longmans.
Ribot, T. A. Diseases of the personality. $1. Boericke & T.
See also Character;—Future life;—Mental science; —New thought;—Psychical research;—Psychology; — Spiritualism; — Suggestion (mental); — Vibration.

Personality in education. Conover, J. P. **$1.25 net. Moffat.

Personality of the teacher. McKenny, C: $1. Row, P. & Co.

PERSPECTIVE.
Dymond, C: W. Key to the theory and methods of linear perspective. 75 c. Spon.
Frederick, F. F. Simplified mechanical perspective. 75 c. Manual Arts.
Hicks, I. P. Simple treatise on architectural perspective. 50 c. Indust.
Matthewson, H. E. Perspective sketching from working drawings. $1. Taylor-H.
Norton, D. M. Freehand perspective and sketching. $3. D. M. Norton.
Richards, J. W., *and* Colvin, F. H. Pract. perspective. 50 c. Henley.
Storey, G: A. Theory and practice of perspective. $3.75. Oxford Univ.
Turrill, S. M. Elem. course in perspective. **$1.25 net. Van Nostrand.
See also Architectural drawing;—Drawing;—Projection.

Perspective history chart. Lamborn, E. A. G. $2.90. Oxford Univ.

Persuasion. ***See* Austen, Jane.**

Pertinent penetrating pen points. Fosdick, M. A. $1. Neuner.

Pertuch, Albert Richard.
German schlagball (German bat-ball); game of ball described in four grades of difficulty; tr. by Hans Ballin. '09(My8) O. pap., 15 c. McVey.

PERU.
Bailey, S. I. Peruvian meteorology. $1.50. Harvard Univ.
Clairmont, A. de. Guide to modern Peru. (Add. pub. for price.) A. de Clairmont.
Eberhardt, C: C. Indians of Peru. (Add. Inst. for price.) Smith. Inst.
Enock, C. R. Andes and the Amazon. $1.50 net.—Peru; its former and present civilization. *$3 net. Scribner.
Guinness, G. Peru: its story, people and religion. *$2.50 net. Revell.
Prescott, W: H. Conquest of Peru. *35 c. net; *70 c. net; *$1 net. Dutton.
Wright, *Mrs.* M. R. Old and new Peru. *$10 net. Barrie.
See also Incas.

PERUGIA, Italy.
Heywood, W: Hist. of Perugia. $3.50 net. Putnam.

Perugino, Pietro Vannucci.
Masterpieces. '09(Je26) il. T. (Painters ser.) leath., *75 c. net; pap., *25 c. net. Stokes.

PERUVIAN LITERATURE.
Brown University. Books printed in Lima and elsewhere in South America after 1800. 50 c. Brown Univ.

Pesch, Tilman.
Christian philosophy of life; reflections on the truths of religion; tr. from the German by M. C. M'Laren. '09(N) 14+637 p. 8°, *$4.50 net. Herder.

Pesel, Louisa F.
See Townsend, W. G. Paulson.

Pest (The). Shore, W: T. $1.50. Doscher.

PESTALOZZI, Johann Heinrich.
Holman, H: Pestalozzi: an account of his life and work. *$1.10 net. Longmans.

Pet Marjorie and **Sir Walter Scott. Wiley. K.** *$1 net; *75 c. net. Cochrane.

Petalesharoo. **Sanders, H. F.** $1.50; 50 c. H. F. Sanders.

Pete, cow-puncher. Ames, J. B. †$1.50. Holt.

PETEN, Guatemala.
Maler, T. Explorations in the Department of Peten, Guatemala, and adjacent region. $4. Peabody Museum.

Peter. Smith, F. H. †$1.50. Scribner.

PETER, *St.*
Smyth-Vaudry, T. Peter's name. $1. Soc. Divine Word.

"Peter Homunculus." Cannan, G. †$1.50. Duffield.

Peter Moor's journey to southwest Africa. Frenssen, G. †$1.25. Houghton M.

Peter of New Amsterdam. Kaler, J. O. 35 c. Am. Bk.

Peter Pan in Kensington Gardens. Barrie, J. M. $1.50 net. Scribner.

Peter-Peter. Warren, M. L. R. †$1.50. Harper.

Peter Pink-eye. Hamer. S. H. 75 c. Estes.

Peter Pumpkin in Wonderland. Huntington, I. M. $1.25. Rand, McN. & Co.

Peter Rabbit, pseud.
See Long, W: Jos.

Peter Rabbit ser. il. T. †50 c. Warne.
—Potter. Tale of Jemima Puddle-Duck.

Peters, C. H. F.
Heliographic positions of sun-spots observed at Hamilton College from 1860 to 1870; ed. for publication by Edn. B. Frost. '08(J24) F. (Carnegie Institution of Washington pub.) pap., $2.50. Carnegie

Peters, Fredus Nelson.
Key to Modern chemistry, with its pract. applications. '09(D) c. 20 p. 12°, 60 c. C: E. Merrill.

Peters, Ja. W. S.
Franchise facts. '10(F19) c. 8°, $1. J. W. S. Peters.

Peters, J: Punnett, D.D.
Hilprecht's answer: [analysis of Hilprecht's "So-called Peters-Hilprecht controversy."] '08, [1909.] (F) 15 p. 8°, pap. (Priv. pr.) J: P. Peters.
Modern Christianity; or, the plain Gospel modernly expounded. '10(F5) c. D. (Crown theological lib.) **$1.50 net. Putnam.

See Hilprecht, Herman Volrath.

Peters, Madison Clinton, D.D.
Abraham Lincoln's religion. '09(F13) c. D. bds., 75 c. Badger.
How to make things go, (the strenuous career:) advice to young people. '09(F13) c. il. D. pap., 25 c. Laird.
Justice to the Jew: story of what he has done for the world. New and rev. ed.; [with an introd., "The influence of the Hebrew commonwealth upon the origin of republican government in the United States," by Oscar S. Straus.] '08(M21) c. D. **75 c. net. McClure.
Justice to the Jew. New and rev. ed. '10 (D31) 12°, $1. Trow Press.
Sermons that have won the masses. '08 (N7) c. D. (Message ser.) 50 c. Am. Bapt.
Strenuous career; or, short steps to success. '08(Je6) il. D. $1.25. Laird.

Peters, W: H., M.D.
Appeal to the boy. '09, [1910.] (Ja) 14 p. nar. O. pap., 10 c.; per 100, $5. Archive.

Petersen, Jens Christian.
"Cream of a thousand plans." '10(Ap) c. 63 p. il. plans, obl. 12°, 25 c. J. C. Petersen.

Peterson, Arth.
Sigurd; poem. '10(N5) c. il. $1.50 net. Jacobs.

Peterson, Ephraim.
Redemption. '09(D18) c. 12°, pap., 25 c. E. Peterson.

Peterson, F:
See Church, Archibald.

Peterson, Hans Christian.
First steps in English composition. New ed., rev. and enl. '08(My16) c. il. S. 40 c. Flanagan.

Peterson, Harvey Andrew.
On the influence of complexity and dissimilarity on memory. [1910.] (Jl) 87 p. il. tabs., 4°, (Psychological monographs.) $1. Psychological Review.

Peterson, Jos.
Combination tones and other related auditory phenomena. '09(Ja16) 8°, (Psychological monograph supplements.) $1.50. Psychological Review.

Peterson, Olof August.
A revision of the *Entelodontidae*. '09(N) 41-158 p. fold. plan, 8°, (Carnegie Museum pubs.) $2.50. Carnegie Museum.

Peterson, W:
See Widtsoe, J:

Petit, Rob.
How to build an aeroplane; tr. from the French by T. O'B. Hubbard and J. H. Lederboer. '10(Je18) il. 8°, $1.50 net. Van Nostrand.

Petit (Le) bon-homme, Pierre. King, L. 50 c. Longmans.

Petit (Le) chaperon rouge. *See* Reichenbach, M. Deux comédies enfantines.

"Petit (Le) Homme Rouge," pseud.
Favorites of Henry of Navarre. '10(D24) por. O. (Favorites of the French court ser.) $3 net. Badger.

PETIT TRIANON, Versailles.
Arnott, J. A., *and* Wilson, J: Petit Trianon-Versailles. In 3 pts. pt. 2. per set, *$27 net. Scribner.

Petite (La) Fadette. *See* Sand, George, *pseud.*

Petite (La) princesse. Bigot, M. H. 35 c. Am. Bk.

Petites (Les) ignorances de la conversation. *See* Rozan, Charles.

Petrarch, Francesco.
Letters to classical authors; tr. from the Latin, with a commentary, by Mario Emilio Cosenza. '10(Mr26) c. D. **$1 net. Univ. of Chic.

PETRARCH, Francesco.
Jerrold, M. F. Francesco Petrarca. **$4 net. Dutton.
Nolhac, A. M. P. G. de. Petrarch and the ancient world. $6. Merrymount.

Petre, Fs. Loraine.
Napoleon and the Archduke Charles: hist. of the Franco-Austrian campaign in the valley of the Danube in 1809. '08(O24) il. maps, plan, O. *$4 net. Lane.
Simon Bolivar, "El Libertador"; life of the chief leader in the revolt against Spain in Venezuela, New Granada and Peru. '10(Ap2) front. map, O. $4 net. Lane.

Petre, M. D.
Catholicism and independence: studies in spiritual liberty. '08(Ja25) D. *$1.20 net. Longmans.

Petri-Palmedo, D.
How to use slide rules. '08(My23); 2d rev. ed. '09(Je19) c. il. 16°, ea., pap., 50 c. Kloesch & Co.

Petrie, G: Laurens, D.D.
Jacob's sons. '10(D3) c. 12°, $1.25. Neale.

Petrie, Graham.
Tunis, Kairouan and Carthage. '09(Mr13) il. O. *$4.80 net. Doubleday, P.

Petrie, W: Matthew Flinders.
Ancient Egypt. '07, [1909.] (Ap) 8°, (Religions ancient and modern.) *40 c. net. Open Court.
Arts and crafts of ancient Egypt. '10(O1) c. D. (World of art ser.) $1.75 net. McClurg.
Growth of the Gospels as shown by structural criticism. '10(D3) tabs., D. 90 c. net. Baker & T.
Personal religion in Egypt before Christianity. '09(My15) c. 16°, (Lib. of living thought.) *75 c. net. Harper.

PETROL ENGINES.
See Engines.

PETROL MOTORS.
See Automobiles.

PETROLEUM.
Becker, G: F. Relations between local magnetic disturbances and the genesis of petroleum. (Add. Superintendent for price.) U. S., Supt. of Docs.
Brown, G: W. Old times in oildom. $1. G: W. Brown.
Cram, M. P. Fractionation of crude petroleum by capillary filtration. 50 c. Johns Hopkins.
Duty on oil; rept. of the Conference of the Independent Oil Producers and Independent Oil Refiners favoring a duty on petroleum and its products. '09(Ag) 50 p. 8°. (Add. Superintendent for price.) U. S., Supt. of Docs.
Gilpin, J. E., *and* Cram, M. P. Fractionation of crude petroleum by capillary diffusion. 10 c. U. S., Supt. of Docs.
Harris, G. D. Oil and gas in Louisiana. Gov. Pr. Off.
Smiley, A. W. Few scraps, oily and otherwise. $1. A. W. Smiley.
Squier, E. Oil tank tables; how to calculate them. 50 c. E. Squier.
Stone, N. I:, *comp.* Foreign tariffs on petroleum and petroleum products. (Add. Superintendent for price.) U. S., Supt. of Docs.
Thompson, A. B. Petroleum mining and oilfield development. $5 net. Van Nostrand.

PETROLEUM.—*Continued.*
Tower, W. S. Story of oil. **$1 net. Appleton.
United States. *Dept. of the Interior. U. S. Geological Survey.* Known productive oil and gas fields of the United States in 1908; comp. by David T. Day, 1909. 2d ed. '09, [1910.] (Mr) map, f°, pap.
See also Mexico.

PETROLOGY.
See Mineralogy;—Rocks.

Petronella. Smith, *Mrs.* E. T. $1. Burt.

Pettey, Katherine Fall.
Songs from the sage brush. '10(Ag13) c. 12°, $1.25. State Consol.

Petticoat rule. Orczy, E. M. R. M. J. B., *Baroness.* $1.20 net. Doran.

PETTIE, John.
Hardie, C: M. John Pettie. *$6 net. Macmillan.

Pettigrew, Ja. Bell, M.D.
Design in nature; illustrated by spiral and other arrangements in the inorganic and organic kingdoms, as exemplified in matter, force, life, growth, rhythms, etc., especially in crystals, plants, and animals. '08(D26) 3 v., il. pors. F. *$16 net. Longmans.

Pettingill, W: Leroy.
Simple studies in Daniel. '10(Ja22) c. 16°. (Not for sale.) F. Kelker.

Pettit, Mrs. Augusta Austin.
Old church of St. George's in Penn's Neck; paper read before Salem Co. Historical Society, Sept. 8, 1908. '08, [1909.] (Ag) 7 p. 12°, pap., 10 c. Salem Co. Hist. Soc.

PEWTER.
Gale, E. J. Pewter and the amateur collector. **$2.50 net. Scribner.

Peyton, J: Howe.
American transportation problem. '09 (Ja16) il. fold. maps, O. pap., 50 c. Courier Journ.

Pfarrherr (Der) von Silberburg. Berner, G. *$1.50 net. Ulbrich.

Pfättisch, Joannes Maria.
Die rede Konstantins des Grossen an die versammlung der heiligen auf ihre echtheit untersucht. '08(S12) 8°, (Strassburger theologische studien.) pap., *$1 net. Herder.

Pfaundler, M., M.D.
See Diseases of children.

Pfeiffer, E:
Mission studies; outlines of missionary principles and practice. '08(O) *75 c. net. Lutheran Bk.

Pfizenmayer, Paul.
Evolution of printing; [address] del. before the Technical Publicity Assoc.; published by resolution of the Technical Assoc. '08 (O10) c. O. pap., gratis. J. C. Powers.

Pfleiderer, Otto, D.D.
Development of Christianity; tr. from the German by Dan. A. Huebsch. Auth. ed. '10(My14) c. D. $1.50 net. B: W. Huebsch.
Development of theology in Germany since Kant. '09(D25) 8°, *$2.75 net. Macmillan.

Pfleiderer, Otto, D.D.—*Continued.*
Primitive Christianity: its writings and teaching in their historical connections; tr. by W. Montgomery. In 4 v. v. 2. '09(Ag21); v. 3. '10(D31) 8°, (Theological translation lib.) ea., *$3 net. Putnam.

Phædrus. *See* Plato. Apology of Socrates.
Phaëthon. *See* Ovid.

Phalen, W: Clifton.
Economic geology of the Kenova quadrangle, Kentucky, Ohio, and West Virginia. '08, [1909.] (Ja) 158 p. il. figs., fold maps, O. (Dept. of the Interior; U. S. Geolog. Survey bull.) pap., 25 c..

PHALLOIDEAE.
See Fungi.

PHANEROGAMS.
See Botany.

Phantom auto. Ellis, E: S. †75 c. Winston.
Phantom battleship. Chesterton, R. $1.50. Lippincott.
Pharais. *See* Macleod, Fiona, *pseud.*

PHARAOHS. (The).
See Egypt.

Pharisee and the publican. Bosanketh, E: B'way Pub.

PHARMACEUTICAL CHEMISTRY.
See Chemistry.

Pharmaceutical science ser.; ed. by E: Kremers, Monographs. il. 8°, 50 c. Pharmaceutical Review.
—Stockberger. Pinkroot.

Pharmaceutical syllabus; recommended by the national committee representing the boards and schools of pharmacy of the United States for the first syllabus period August 1, 1910, to July 31, 1915. '10(Ap) c. 146 p. il. 8°, $1. N. Y., State Pharmacy.

PHARMACOGNOSY.
See Pharmacy.

PHARMACOLOGY.
See Pharmacy.

PHARMACOPOEIA.
See Pharmacy.

PHARMACY.
Arny, H: V. Principles of pharmacy. *$5 net. Saunders.
Beal, J. H. Prescription practice and general dispensing. $1.50. J. H. Beal.
Berkwitz, W: L. $500.000 course in mixing. (Add. pubs. for price.) Mail Order.
Caspari, C:, *jr.* Treatise on pharmacy. $4.25. Lea.
Culbreth, D: M. R. Manual of materia medica and pharmacology. $4.75 net. Lea.
Cushny, A. R. Text-book of pharmacology and therapeutics. $3.75 net. Lea.
De Lorme, M. F. Manual of pharmacy for physicians. $1.25 net. Blakiston.
Francis, F., *and* Fortescue-Brickdale, J. M. Chemical basis of pharmacology. *$4 net. Longmans.
Greene, C: W. Experimental pharmacology. *$1 net. Blakiston.
Hallberg, C. S. N., *and* Salisbury, J. H:, *comp.* Physicians' manual of the Pharmacopeia and the national formulary. 40 c. Am. Medical.
Hare, H. A., *and others.* National standard dispensatory. $8. Lea.

PHARMACY.—*Continued.*
Hatcher, R. A., *and* Wilbert, M. I. Pharmacopeia and the physician. $1. Am. Medical.
Kebler, L. F. Drug legislation in the United States. (Add. Superintendent for price.) U. S., Supt. of Docs.
Kraemer, H: Text-book of botany and pharmacognosy. $5. Lippincott.
Maltbie, B. L. Pract. pharmacy. $3. Physicians' Drug.
Mason, H. B. How to get registered: course of study for pharmaceutical students. 50 c. C: L. Mason.
Mason, H. B., *ed.* 350 dollar ideas for druggists. $1. E. G. Swift.
Pharmaceutical syllabus. $1. N. Y., State Pharmacy.
Potter, S. O. L. Therapeutics, materia medica, and pharmacy. $5. Blakiston.
Rhode Island pure food and drug act. (Add. pub. for price.) E. L. Freeman.
Ruddiman, E. A. Incompatibilities in prescriptions. $2. Wiley.
Stevens, A. B. Manual of pharmacy and dispensing. *$2.50 net. Lea.
Stewart, F. E. Compend of pharmacy. *$1 net; *$1.25 net. Blakiston.
Sturmer, J. W: Rudiments of Latin, with special reference to the nomenclature of the U. S. pharmacopœia. $1. J. W: Sturmer.
Swan, J: M. Prescription writing and formulary. *$1.25 net. Saunders.
Tyrode, M. V. Pharmacology, the action and uses of drugs. *$1.50 net. Blakiston.
Wootton, A. C. Chronicles of pharmacy. 2 v. $6.50. Macmillan.
See also Chemistry; — Homeopathy; — Latin language;—Materia medica;—Medicine;—Poisons; —Teeth:—Veterinary medicine and surgery.

PHARAOHS.
See Egypt.

Phases of the sacred passion. Graham, W: *40 c. net. Wagner.

PHEASANTS.
Oldys, H: Pheasant raising in the United States. U. S., Supt. of Docs.
Simpson, E. M. Pheasant farming. 25 c. W. E. Smith.
Sudow, F. J. Reliable pheasant standard. 75 c. Haight.
See also Birds.

Phèdre. *See* Racine, Jean Baptiste.

Phelan, Raymond Vincent.
Financial history of Wisconsin. '08(Je6) O. (Univ. of Wis. bull., Economics and political science ser.) pap., 50 c. Univ. of Wis.

Phelps, Earle Bernard.
Disinfection of sewage and sewage filter effluents; with a chapter on putrescibility and stability of sewage effluents. '09(Jl) 91 p. fold. il. 8°, (U. S., Dept. of the Interior; U. S Geol. Survey bull., Water-supply paper.) pap., 15 c. U. S., Supt. of Docs.
Pollution of streams by sulphite pulp waste; study of possible remedies. '09 (My8) tabs., O. (U. S., Dept. of the Interior; Geol. Survey water-supply paper.) pap., 10 c. U. S. Supt. of Docs.

Phelps, Edith M., comp.
Selected articles on the income tax, with special reference to graduation and exemption. '10(Ap9) 12°, (Debater's handbook ser.) $1 net. H. W. Wilson.
Selected articles on the initiative and referendum. '09(D18) 12°, (Debater's hdbk. ser.) $1. H. W. Wilson.
Sel. articles on woman suffrage. '10(D10) 12°, (Debaters' hbdk. ser.) $1 net. H. W. Wilson.

Phelps, E: Bunnell.
Statistical study of infant mortality. '09 (Ja30) diagrs., O. pap. (Add. author for price.) E: B. Phelps.

Phelps, Eliz. Stuart, [now Mrs. Herbert D. Ward.]
Chariot of fire. '10(O15) c. il. D. 50 c. net. Harper.
Empty house, and other stories. '10(O29) c. il. D. $1.20 net. Houghton M.

Phelps, G: Hamilton, ["Patrick Quinn Tangent."]
New Columbia; or, the re-United States. '09(Jl17) c. D. $1; pap., 50 c. New Columbia.

Phelps, G: Olcott.
One man power, plus. '09(D25) c. il 12°, $1. Roxburgh.

Phelps, Rev. Guy F.
Ethel Vale, the white slave. '10(O) c. 7+9-217 p. il. 12°, $1. Chr. Witness.

Phelps, Ja. Ralph.
Birthday horoscopes; character reading. '08(N21) c. D. pap., 50 c. Brewer, B.

Phelps, Pauline.
See O'Higgins, Harvey Jerrold.

Phelps, Rear Admiral T: Stowell.
Reminiscences of Seattle, Washington Territory and the U. S. sloop-of-war "Decatur" during the Indian war of 1855-1856. '08(Ap11) c. 12°, (Puget Sound historical ser.) subs., *$2 net; pap., *60 c. net. A. Harriman.

Phelps, W: Lyon.
Dash at the pole. '09(D18) c. il. D. 75 c. Ball Pub.
Essays on modern novelists. '10(Ja22) c. D. **$1.50 net. Macmillan.

Phenomenology of mind. Hegel, G. W. In 2 v. $5.50 net. Macmillan.

Philadelphia. Free Library. Bulletin no. 8: list of serials in the principal libraries of Philadelphia and its vicinity; prepared by J: P. Lamberton. '08(Jl4) O. $2. Phila. Free Lib.

Philadelphia. Supp. to digest of laws and ordinances, with notes of decisions and city solicitor's opinions relating thereto, 1905-1910; comp. by W: Findlay Brown, assisted by G: Austin Welsh. '10(D) c. O. $2.50. W: F. Brown.

Philadelphia, County of. Probate cases; being cases heard and decided by the register of wills, Jacob Singer, 1901-1904. '09(Jl) c. 351 p. O. (Add. pubs. for price.) J. Singer.

PHILADELPHIA, Pa.
Campbell, J. Sixteen excursions to places of historic interest in Philadelphia. 25 c. J. Campbell.
Coxe, R. D. Legal Philadelphia. $2. W: J. Campbell.

PHILADELPHIA, Pa.—*Continued.*
Edmunds, A. J. Quaker literature in the libraries of Philadelphia. (Add. author for price.) A. J. Edmunds.
Founders' week memorial volume, cont. an acct. of the 225th anniversary of the founding of the city of Philadelphia, and histories of its principal scientific institutions, medical colleges, hospitals, etc.; ed. by F: P. Henry; pub. by the city of Philadelphia in commemoration of the 225th anniversary of its founding. '09, [1910.] 6+912 p. il. pors. 8°, o. p. Davis.
Gummere, A. M. City of Penn: history of Philadelphia. 20 c. Biddle Press.
Heyl, F. Battle of Germantown. 25 c. (Sold to members only.) City Hist., Phil.
Kirlin, J. L. J. Catholicity in Philadelphia. $3.50. McVey.
Leffmann, H: Consolidation of Philadelphia.—Philadelphia celebrations. ea., 25 c. (Sold to members only.) City Hist., Phil.
Lynch, M. A. Southwark. 50 c. (Sold to members only.) City Hist., Phil.
Oberholtzer, E. P. Book of the pageant, Philadelphia, Oct. 9, 1908. (Add. pubs. for price.) Jacobs.
Zimmerling, C: B., *comp.* Directory of members of Philadelphia bar. gratis. Guarantee.
See also American Philosophical Society;—Congregation Mikve Israel;—Education;—Fairmount Park; — Germantown; — Physicians;—*also* City Hist. Soc. of Phil. pubs.

PHILANTHROPY.
See Charities.

Philanthropy and public education. Brumbaugh, M. G. gratis. Phil. Trades School.

PHILATELY.
See Postage-stamps.

Philbrook, H: B.
The Bible; interpretation of its parables; discourse. '09(D4) O. pap., 20 c. H: B. Philbrook.

Phileas Fox. Sadlier, *Mrs.* A. T. $1.50. Ave Maria.

Philemon, pseud.
Philemon's verses; never before imprinted. '09(D18) c. D. pap., 25 c. Evergreen Press.

PHILIP II., *King of Spain.*
Hume, M. A. S. Two English queens and Philip. *$4.50 net. Putnam.

Philip, Brother.
Meditations on the passion of Our Lord Jesus Christ. New and rev. ed.; author. English version. '09, [1910.] (Ap) 10+387 p. 12°, $1. La Salle Bureau.

Philip, Ja. C.
Physical chemistry; its bearing on biology and medicine. '10(Ag6) figs. D. $2.10 net. Longmans.
Romance of modern chemistry; description in non-technical language of the diverse and wonderful ways in which chemical forces are at work, and of their manifold application in modern life. '09(O9) il. D. (Romance ser.) *$1.50 net. Lippincott.

Philip the forester. Kennedy, D. E. $4.50. Queen's Shop.

Philipp, E. L.
Political reform in Wisconsin; historical review of the primary election, taxation and railway regulation. '10(Ap9) c. 8°, pap., 50 c. net. Caspar.

Philippa at Halcyon. Brown, K. H. $1.50. Scribner.

Philippians. *See* Bible.

Philippics. *See* Demosthenes.

Philippine education ser. il. sq. 8°. World Bk.
—Copeland. Elements of Philippine agriculture. 96 c.
—Mercer *and* Bonsall. Complete arithmetic. pt. 1. 54 c.

Philippine Islands. '09(Ja16) fold. map, D. pap., gratis. Int. Banking.

Philippine Islands. *Bureau of Justice.* Criminality in the Philippine Islands, 1903-1908; by Ignacio Villamor. '10(Ap23) tabs., 4°. Bu. Public Pr.

Philippine Islands. *Bureau of Printing.* Price list of public documents for sale by the Bureau of Printing, Manila, P. I. Lista de precios de documentos públicos de venta en la oficina de la imprenta, Manila, I. F.; corrected to May 15, 1910. '10(D) 13 p. 8°. Bu. Public Pr.

Philippine Islands. *Bureau of Science.* Mineral resources of the Philippine Islands; with a statement of the production of commercial mineral products during the year 1907. '09(Mr6) il. maps, 4°. (Add. pubs. for price.) Bu. Public Pr.

Philippine Islands. *Weather Bu.* Return to Halley's comet and popular apprehensions; by G: M. Zwack. '10(Ag) 22 p. 8°. Bu. Public Pr.

PHILIPPINE ISLANDS.
Barrows, D: P. History of the Philippines. $1. Bobbs-M.
Bean, R. B. Racial anatomy of the Philippine Islanders. $2 net. Lippincott.
Blair, E. H., *and* Robertson, J. A., *eds. and trs.* Philippine Islands. In 55 v. v. 53-55. per v., *$4 net. A. H. Clark.
Bobbitt, J: F. Growth of Philippine children. (Add. author for price.) J: F. Bobbitt.
Christie, E. B. Mindanao the Subanuns of Sindangan Bay. $1.25. Bu. Public Pr.
Copeland, E. B. Elements of Philippine agriculture. 96 c. World Bk.
Fee, M. H. Woman's impressions of the Philippines. $1.50 net. McClurg.
Jernegan, P. F. "1001" questions and answers on Philippine history and civil government. (Add. pub. for price.) Philippine Educ.
Johnston, M. G. Plain American talk in the Philippines. $1.25. J: R. Edgar.
Lyman, B: S. Philippines. (Add. author for price.) B: S. Lyman.
McGregor, R: C. Manual of Philippine birds. $4. Macmillan.
Moses, E. B. Unofficial letters of an official's wife. **$1.50 net. Appleton.
Philippine civil service; revised act and rules, Jan., 1909. '09(My) 26 p. 8°, pap. U. S., Supt. of Docs.

PHILIPPINE ISLANDS.—*Continued.*
Robertson, J. A. Bibliography of the Philippine Islands. *$10 net. A. H. Clark.
Robinson, C: B. *Alabastra philippinensia.* 25 c. N. Y. Botanical.
Seidenadel, C. W. First grammar of the language, spoken by the Bontoc Igorot. —First written grammar of the Bontoc Igorot language. ea., $5. Open Court.
United States. *Congress. House. Committee on Insular Affairs.* Claims of friars in the Philippine Islands. '09 (My) 76 p. 8°, pap. (Add. Superintendent for price.) U. S., Supt. of Docs
United States. *Congress. Senate. Committee on the Philippines.* Catholic church claims in Philippine Islands. 15 c. U. S., Supt. of Docs.
Walker, H. W. Wanderings among South Sea savages, and in Borneo and the Philippines. $2.50 net. Scribner.
Winslow, E. Conditions and future of the Philippines. (Add. Superintendent for price.) U. S., Supt. of Docs.
Wooten, W: P. Provisional battalion of engineers in the Philippines. (Priv. pr.) Engineer Sch.
Worcester, D. C. Philippine Islands and their people. *$2 net. Macmillan.
See also Baler (Siege of);—Crime and criminals;—Mammalia;—Riddles.

Philippine question books. S. Philippine Educ.
—Jernegan. "1001" questions and answers on Philippine history and civil government.

Philippine studies. 24°. World Bk.
—Starr, *ed.* Little book of Filipino riddles. 50 c.

Philipps, Rev. Martin, comp.
Sunday school instructions for every Sunday of the year; with a short sketch of eminent saints, followed by prayers of the mass and hymns. '10(N19) 8°, $1. M. Philipps.

Philips, Alb. Edn.
Romance of the 10,000 islands. '09(D) $1.50. B'way Pub.

Philips, Arth. E:
Effective speaking: exposition of the laws of effectiveness in the choice of material in speech, with examples and exercises. '08, [1909.] (Mr) 314 p. 12°, *$1.50 net. Newton Co.

Natural drills in expression, with selections; series of exercises, colloquial and classical, based upon the principles of reference to experience and comparison, and chosen for their practical worth in developing power and naturalness in reading and speaking, with illustrative selections for practice. '09(D) 12+367 p. 12°, $1.25. Newton Co.

Philips, G: Morris.
See Sharpless, I: Philips.

PHILIPSBURG, Pa.
Row, S. B. Hist. of Philipsburg from pioneer days to present time. 35 c. S. B. Row.

Philipson, Rabbi D:
Jew in America. '09(O) 16 p. 8°, (Jewish tracts issued by the Central Conference of American Rabbis.) pap., gratis. J. Morgenstern.
Tone system in public speaking and reading. Rev. ed.; discussion of the sources of effectiveness in oral expression and in the teaching of oral expression, with illustrations and suggestions. '10(Jl) c. 4+116 p. 12°, $1. Newton Co.

Phillipic orations. *See* Cicero, Marcus Tullius.

Phillips, Alfr. E:
Surveying: manual of practical instruction in the art of plane surveying, including plotting, leveling, triangulation, line running, cross-sectioning, traversing, and other details of field work. '08(Ap11) c. il. 8°, (American School of Correspondence pubs.) $1.50. Am. Sch. Corr.
See also Byrne, Austin T.

Phillips, Barnet, comp.
Standard Hoyle: complete guide and reliable authority upon all games of chance or skill. '09(Je12) c. il. 16°, $1; bds., 75 c.; pap., 50 c. Excelsior.

Phillips, D: Graham.
Fashionable adventures of Joshua Craig. '09(Ja30) c. il. D. †$1.50. Appleton.
Hungry heart. '09(Ag21) c. D. †$1.50. Appleton.
Husband's story; a novel. '10(S24) c. D. $1.50. Appleton.
Light-fingered gentry. [1910.] (F) 75 c. Grosset.
Old wives for new. '08(Mr14) c. D. †$1.50. Appleton.
White magic. '10(Ap2) c. D. $1.50. Appleton.
Worth of a woman: a play in four acts; followed by A point of law: a dramatic incident. '08(S26) c. D. **$1.25 net. Appleton.

Phillips, E: C:
On the pentacardioid. '09, [1910.] (F) c. 24 p. diagrs., 4°, pap., 35 c. Johns Hopkins.

Phillips, Mrs. Fannie Frank, and Levy, Reeva Huson, comps.
Universal cook book; collection of tried and tested home receipts. '09(Mr) c. 162 p. 12°, leatherette, $1; pap., 50 c. F. F. Phillips.

Phillips, H: Wallace.
Mascot of Sweet Briar Gulch. '08(N7) c. il. O. †$1.50. Bobbs-M.
Trolley folly. '09(Ap3) il. D. $1.25. Bobbs-M.

Phillips, I: Newton.
Lincoln. '10(Mr5) c. por. D. bds., $1, boxed. McClurg.
—, rep. *See* Illinois. *Sup. ct.* Repts.

Phillips, Ja. D:, and Millar, Adam Vause.
Essentials of descriptive geometry. '09 (Mr6) c. figs. D. $1. Tracy, G. & Co.
Notes on descriptive geometry. '08(O) c. 100 p. diagrs., 12°, $1. A. V. Millar.

Phillips, J: Burton.
Freight rates and manufactures in Colorado. '10(Ja22) O. 75 c.; pap., 50 c. J: B. Phillips.
Increase of divorce. '07, [1909.] (Mr) 203-216 p. 4°, 25 c. Univ. of Col.

Phillips, J: Goddard, ed.
Memorial of Eugene Tappan, Esq., late corresponding secretary. '10(Ap) c. 70 p. por. 12°, (Publications of the Sharon Historical Society.) (Priv. pr.) Sharon Hist. Soc.

Phillips, J: Lewis.
See Allen, Bernard Melzar.

Phillips, L. March.
In the desert; the hinterland of Algiers. New ed. '09(N13) il. D. $2. Longmans.

Phillips, L: C:
See Virginia. Law of instructions to juries.

Phillips, M. J.
In our country's service. '09(Ag28) c. D. $1. E: T. Miller.

Phillips, Mary Eliz.
Handbook of German literature; rev., with an introd., by A. Weiss. 2d ed., rev. '08 (D5) 12°, *$1 net. Macmillan.
Laureled leaders for little folk; with introd. by E: Everett Hale, D.D. '08(Ap4) c. il. pors. O. $2, boxed. Lothrop, L. & S.

Phillips, Philip Lee.
First map of Kentucky, by J: Filson: a bibliographical account with facsimile reproduction from the copy in the Library of Congress. '08(Jl18) 4°, *$2.50 net. Torch Press.

Phillips, R: Jones.
Spectacles and eyeglasses. 4th ed., rev. '08 (My16) c. il. 8°, *$1 net. Blakiston.

Phillips, Ryland, W.
With other photographers. '10(Ag) 7-67 p. il. pors. f°, $2.50. Eastman Kodak.

Phillips, Stephen.
Works. Uniform set. In 4 v. '08(Je27) 12°, *$5 net; hf. mor., *$15 net. Lane.
Marpessa. '10(D) il. 16°, (Flowers of Parnassus.) 50 c. net; leath., 75 c. net. Lane.
New Inferno. '10(N12) D. $1.25 net. Lane.
Pietro of Siena; drama. '10(O22) c. D. $1 net. Macmillan.
—, and Carr, Jos. W: Comyns.
Faust; freely adapted from Goethe's dramatic poem. '08(S19) c. D. **$1.25 net. Macmillan.

Phillips, T: Whitefield, ["A Lumberjack."]
Story of John F. Deitz, the defender of Cameron Dam, (Thornapple River.) '08 (Ap18) c. il. pors. plan, 12°, 27 c. Phillips & E.

Phillips, Ulrich Bonnell.
Hist. of transportation in the eastern cotton belt to 1860. '08(F1) 12°, *$2.75 net. Lemcke.

PHILLIPS, Wendell.
Sears, L. Wendell Phillips, orator and agitator. **$1.50 net. Doubleday, P.

Phillips, W: Battle.
Mineral resources of Texas. '10(D) 5 p. pls. f°, (Texas, Dept. of Agriculture; bull.) Texas.

Phillips, W: Hamilton.
Pathfinder to Greylock Mountain, the Berkshire Hills and historic Bennington; maps showing roads, street railways and Greylock summit. '10(Jl2) c. il. por. fold. maps, O. pap., 50 c.; $1. W: H. Phillips.

Phillips Academy, Dept. of Archæology, bulletin. 8°, pap. Andover.
—Peabody *and* Moorehead. Exploration of Bushey cavern, and Fort Ancient.

Phillips Exeter ser. See also Dudley, Albertus True.

Phillpotts, Eden.
Flint heart; fairy story. '10(N5) il. 12°, $1.50. Dutton.
The haven. '09(N6) c. D. †$1.50. Lane.
Mother of the man. '08(F8) c. front. D. †$1.50. Dodd.
Tales of the tenements; [stories of Dartmoor farms.] '10(N12) D. $1.50. Lane.
Thief of virtue. '10(Mr26) c. D. $1.50. Lane.
Three brothers. '09(F13) c. D. †$1.50 Macmillan.
Virgin in judgment. '08(N14) c. D. †$1.50. Moffat.
Wild fruit: [poems.] '10(D3) D. $1.50 net. Lane.

—, and Bennett, Enoch Arnold.
The statue: story of international intrigue and mystery. '08(Ag29) c. D. †$1.50. Moffat.

Philo, E. W.
Philo system of progressive poultry keeping. '07, [1908.] (Mr.) c. 56 p. il. 8°. $1. Poultry Review.

"Philobiblos," pseud.
See Pearson, Edm. Lester.

PHILO JUDAEUS *of Alexandria.*
Bentwich, N. D. Philo-Judæus of Alexandria. $1.25. Jewish Pub.
Guthrie, K. S. Message of Philo Judæus of Alexandria. $1. Open Court.

PHILOLOGY.
See Classical Philology;—Language.

Philopolis ser. 12°. A. M. Robertson.
—McAdie. Infra nubem, The lights outside.

Philo's daughter. Robinson, N. G. $1. Jennings.

Philosopher's martyrdom: a satire. Carus, P. *$1 net. Open Court.

Philosophic studies issued under the direction of the Dept. of Philosophy of the University of Chicago; ed. by Ja. Hayden Tufts. 8°. pap. Univ. of Chic.
—Talbert. Dualism of fact and idea in its social implications. 50 c. net.

Philosophical basis of religion. Watson, J: *$3 net. Macmillan.

Philosophical foundations of charlatanry in medicine. Shute, D. K. (Not for sale.) George Washington Univ.

Philosophical Society of Washington bull. 8°. Philosophical Soc.
—Wead. Music and science. 10 c.

Philosophies ancient and modern from Pythagoras to Spencer. 12°, *50 c. net. Dodge.
—Alexander. Locke.
—Benn. Early Greek philosophy
—Fraser. Berkeley.
—Hudson. Herbert Spencer.

Philosophies ancient and modern from Pythagoras to Spencer.—Continued.
—Ludovici. Nietzsche, his life and works.
—Rickaby. Scholasticism.
—Sewall. Swedenborg and the "Sapientia angelica."
—Stock. Stoicism.
—Taylor Hobbes.—Plato.
—Whittaker. Comte and Mill.

PHILOSOPHY.
Alexander, A. B. D. Short hist. of philosophy. $2.75 net. Macmillan.
Armstrong, C: W. Mystery of existence in the light of an optimistic philosophy. *90 c. net. Longmans.
Atkinson, W: W. Inner teachings of the philosophies and religions of India. *$1 net. Yogi Pub.
Bakewell, C: M. Source book in ancient philosophy. **$1 net. Scribner.
Bax, E. B. Roots of reality: suggestions for a philosophical reconstruction. *$2 net. B. W. Dodge.
Benn, A. W: Early Greek philosophy. *50 c. net. Dodge.
Bonar, J. Philosophy and political economy in some of their historical relations. *$2.75 net. Macmillan.
Bourne, G: Ascending effort. $1.50 net. Dutton.
Bowne, B. P. Personalism. **$1.50 net. Houghton M.
Bradley, F. H. Appearance and reality. *$3 net. Macmillan.
Brainard, A. Study of God, man and destiny. $1. Cochrane.
Burnet, J: Early Greek philosophy. *$3 net. Macmillan.
Butler, A. Dictionary (miniature) of philosophical terms. 50 c. Dutton.
Butler, N: M: Philosophy: [a lecture.] (Add. pub. for price.) Columbia Univ.
Calkins, M. W. Persistent problems of philosophy. *$2.50 net. Macmillan.
Carus, P. Philosophy as a science; synopsis of the writings of Dr. Paul Carus. 50 c. Open Court.
Columbia University lectures on science, philosophy and art, 1907-1908. *$5 net. Lemcke.
Collier, A. Clavis universalis. $1.50. Open Court.
Coppens, C: Brief hist. of philosophy. $1. Schwartz, K. & F.
Crane, A. M. Search after ultimate truth. $1.50 net. Lothrop, L. & S.
Cushman, H. E. Beginner's hist. of philosophy. v. 1. $1.60 net. Houghton M.
Davis, C: G. Philosophy of life. $1.25. D. D. Pub.
Dewey, J: Influence of Darwin on philosophy, and other essays in contemporaneous thought. $1.40 net. Holt.
Dewey, J:, *and others.* Essays philosophical and psychological in honor of William James. **$3 net. Longmans.
Dewing, A. S. Life as reality. $1.25 net. Longmans.
De Wulf, M. C. J. Hist. of medieval philosophy. *$3 net. Longmans.
Dresser, H. W. Philosophy of the spirit. **$2.50 net. Putnam.

PHILOSOPHY.—*Continued.*
Eucken, R. C. Life of the spirit; introd. to philosophy. *$1.50 net. Putnam.
Eucken, R. C. Meaning and value of life. *$1.40 net. Macmillan.
Eucken, R. C. Problem of human life. **$3 net. Scribner.
Fichte, J. G. Vocation of man. 30 c. Open Court.
Fleetwood, H: Secret of life, death and immortality. $1. H: Fleetwood.
Floyd, A. H: Will to doubt. *$1.25 net. Macmillan.
Forsyth, T: M. English philosophy. $1.75 net. Macmillan.
Frick, C. Cursus philosophicus; in usum scholarum. *$1.10 net. Herder.
Goodsell, W. Conflict of naturalism and humanism. $1.50. Teachers' Coll.
Gredt, J. Elementa philosophiæ Aristotelico-Thomisticae. v. 1, Logica. *$2.45 net. Herder.
Harwood, H: H. Prohibition victorious: then—what? H: H. Harwood.
Hauptmann, C. F. M. Das geheimnis der gestalt, (The secret form.) (Add. pubs. for price.) R. Tombo.
Hibben, J: G. Philosophy of the enlightenment. **$1.50 net. Scribner.
Hicks, R. D. Stoic and Epicurean. **$1.50 net. Scribner.
Höddfing, H. History of modern philosophy. 2 v. *$9 net. Macmillan.
Hodge, W: H: Intuitive perception. $1.50. Wickersham.
James, W: Pluralistic universe. **$1.50 net. Longmans.
Kant, I. Critique of pure reason. $1.75; $3.50. Lamb Pub.
Kant, I. Philosophy of Kant: extracts from his own writings. *$1.75 net. Macmillan.
Kenilworth, W. W. Psychic control through self-knowledge. $2. Fenno.
Kybalion (The): study of the hermetic philosophy of ancient Egypt and Greece, by three initiates. $1.08. Yogi Pub.
Ladd, G: T. Knowledge, life and reality. $3.50. Dodd.
Landsberg, G. F. A B C of philosophy. 75 c. Fenno.
Leibnitz, G. W. v. Philosophical works of Leibnitz. $2.50. Tuttle, M. & T.
Levi. Aquarian philosophy. $1. E. S. Dowling.
Lucretius, C. T. On the nature of things. *$1.50 net. Macmillan.
MacCunn, J: Six radical thinkers. $1 net. Longmans.
Morrison, D. Open door of the soul. $1. C. M. Clark.
Muir, P. M. Modern substitutes for Christianity. *$1.50 net. Doran.
Münsterberg, H. Eternal values. **$2.50 net. Houghton M.
O'Sullivan, J. M. Old criticism and new pragmatism. $3. Longmans.
Perrier, J. L: Revival of scholastic philosophy in the nineteenth century. *$1.75 net. Lemcke.

PHILOSOPHY.—*Continued.*
Rand, B:, *comp.* Modern classical philosophy: selections illustrating philosophy from Bruno to Spencer. **$2.50 net. Houghton M.
Rashdall, H. Philosophy and religion. *75 c. net. Scribner.
Rhoades, D. P. Philosophy of change. **$2 net. Macmillan.
Rickaby, *Father.* Scholasticism. *50 c. net. Dodge.
Russell, B. A. W: Philosophical essays. $2 net. Longmans.
Schiller, F. C. S. Riddles of the sphinx. $3. Macmillan.
Schwegler, F. K. A. History of philosophy in epitome. $2. Appleton.
Shelley, P. B. Literary and philosophical criticism. 90 c. Oxford Univ.
Smith, G. No refuge but in truth. **$1 net. Putnam.
Spinoza, B. de. Short treatise on God, man and his well-being. $3 net. Macmillan.
Spinoza, B. de. Short treatise on God, man and human welfare. $1.25; 50 c. Open Court.
Stettheimer, E. Will to believe as a basis for the defense of religious faith. $1. Science Pr., (N. Y.)
Stock, S. Stoicism. *50 c. net. Dodge.
Talbert, E. L. Dualism of fact and idea in its social implications. 50 c. net. Univ. of Chic.
Urban, W. M. Valuation: its nature and laws. *$2.75 net. Macmillan.
Walker, L. J. Theories of knowledge, absolutism, pragmatism, realism. $2.75. Longmans.
Wardell, R. J. First lessons in philosophy. $1.25 net. Eaton & M.
Watson, J: Outline of philosophy. *$2.25 net. Macmillan.
Wilson, A. M. Principle of the ego in philosophy. *50 c. net. Stechert.
Windle, B. C. A. What is life?: study of vitalism and neovitalism. $1. Herder.
Wulf, M. M. C. J. de. Scholasticism old and new. $2.85. Benziger.
See also Æsthetics;—Agnosticism; — Biology; — Brain;—Christianity; — Consciousness;—Ethics; —Evolution;—Fine arts;—Future life;—God;—Hinduism;—History; —Idealism;—Imagination; —Individualism; — Liberty; — Logic;—Man;—Matter;—Medicine;—Memory;—Mental science; —Metaphysics;—Mind and body; — Mysticism; — Occultism; — Physics; — Pragmatism;—Psychology;—Religion;—Religion and science;—Science; — Skepticism; —Spiritualism;—Theology; —Transcendentalism; — Truth; — Universe; — — Utilitarianism; — Will; — *also* Aristotle; — Browne, Borden Parker;—Eucken, R. C.;— Gassendi, Pierre; — Kant, Immanuel; — Nietzsche, F. W.;—Plotinus; — Pythagoras; — Spencer, H.;—Pomponazzi, Pietro.
Philosophy and methods of operation of the analytic system for the measurements of relative fire hazard. Hess, H. M. gratis. H. M. Hess.
Philosophy and psychology of Pietro Pomponazzi. Douglas, A. H. $2.50 net. Putnam.
Philosophy of accounts. Sprague, C: E. $3. C: E. Sprague.
Philosophy of Christian Science. Downe, B. P. *10 c. net. Eaton & M.

Philosophy of Christianity. Hill, D: R. $1.50. Tribune Pr. Co., (W. Va.)
Philosophy of composition. *See* Poe, Edg. Allan The raven.
Philosophy of Friedrich Nietzsche. Mencken, H: L: *$2 net. J: W. Luce.
Philosophy of happiness. Joslyn, R. W. $1. Normalist.
Philosophy of history. *See* Hegel, G. W. F.
Philosophy of hope. Jordan, D: S. *75 c. net. Am. Unitarian.
Philosophy of life. Davis, C: G. 75 c.; 25 c. D. D. Pub.
Philosophy of life, mortal and immortal. Bull, C. E. $1.60. C. E. Bull.
Philosophy of living. Pogue, J: F. $1. Krehbiel.
Philosophy of long life. Finot, J. *$2.50 net. Lane.
Philosophy of loyalty. Royce, J. **$1.50 net. Macmillan.
Philosophy of numbers. Balliett, S. J. D. $1.50. L. D. Balliett.
Philosophy of revelation. Bavinck, H. **$2 net. Longmans.
Philosophy of self-help. Kirkham, S. D. **$1.25 net. Putnam.
Philosophy of the federal constitution. Hughes, H: C. *$1.50 net. Neale.
Philosophy of the great unconscious. Stevens, S: E. *$1.50 net. Old Corner.
Phil's happy girlhood. Blanchard, G. $1.50. Wilde.
Phin, J:
Evolution of the atmosphere as a proof of design and purpose in the creation and of the existence of a personal God: simple and rigorously scientific reply to modern materialistic atheism. '08(D5) il. 8°, *$1.25 net. Indust.
Phoebe and Ernest. Gillmore, *Mrs.* I. H. $1.50. Holt.
Phœbe Deane. Lutz, *Mrs.* G. L. H. †$1.50. Lippincott.
Phoenix Physical Laboratory contributions. 8°. Astrophysical.
—Morse. Selective reflection of salts of carbonic and other oxygen acids. (Add. pubs. for price.)
Phoenissae. *See* Euripides.
PHONETICS.
Haliburton, M. W. Phonics in reading. 40 c. B. F. Johnson.
Ives, M. I. **Illustrated phonics. 40 c. Longmans.**
Jones, D. Chart of English speech sounds. 15 c. Oxford Univ.
Jones, D. Pronunciation of English; phonetics and phonetic transcriptions. 90 c. Putnam.
Salisbury, A. Phonology and orthoëpy. 50 c. Row, P. & Co.
Seiler's phonanagrams for hygienic busy work in phonics, spelling and word-building: [cards.] set in 95 envelopes, *$12 net. Seiler.
Sweet, H: Sounds of English: phonetics. 60 c. Oxford Univ.
See also Spelling (Simplified).
PHONICS.
See Phonetics.
PHONOGRAPHY.
See Stenography.
PHONOLOGY.
See French language;—Phonetics.
PHONO-STENOGRAPHY.
See Stenography.
Phormio. *See* Terence Afer, Publius.
Photo-auto maps; photographs of every turn, together with topographical outline of road showing railroad crossings, bridges, [etc.,] with accurate distances bet. Chicago and N. Y., N. Y. to Chicago, South Bend to Indianapolis, Indianapolis to South Bend, Toledo to Detroit, Detroit to Toledo, Albany to Saratoga Springs, Saratoga Springs to Albany. '10(Ja1) c. O. limp leath., $5. Rand, McN. & Co.
PHOTO-ENGRAVING.
Amstutz, N. S. Hand-book of photo-engraving. $3. Inland Pr.
Photographer's Almanac; Daily Companion. *See* Brown, G: E., *ed.* British Journal.
Photographic optics and color photography. Johnson, G. L. *$3 net. Van Nostrand.
Photographing in old England. Adams, W. I. L. $2.50 net. Baker & T.
PHOTOGRAPHY.
American annual of photography, 1908. v. 22; 1909. v. 23; 1910. v. 24; 1911. v. 25. ea., $1.25; 75 c. G: Murphy; Tennant.
Baker, T. T. Telegraphic transmission of photographs. $1.25 net. Van Nostrand.
British Journal photographic almanac, 1908, 1909. ea., $1; 50 c. G: Murphy.
Brown, G: E., *ed.* British Journal, Photographic Almanac, Photographer's Daily Companion, "Year Book of Photography and Amateur's Guide." 1910. $1; 50 c. G: Murphy.
Buchanan, J. B. **Carbon print. 50 c. J. B. Buchanan.**
Cole, R. J. **Photography in a nutshell. 25 c. Tennant.**
Hanks, A. K. **Pract. suggestions regarding the selection and use of a photographic equipment. $1. A. K. Hanks.**
Harrison, C:, *and* Douglas, J: C. **Photographer's hdbk. **$1 net. Lane.**
Hartmann, S. Composition in portraiture: [photography.] $3. E: L. Wilson.
Hartmann, S. Landscape and figure composition. $3 net. Baker & T.
Holland, C. How to use a camera. 50 c. Dutton.
Holme, C:, *ed.* Colour photography, and other recent developments of the art of the camera. *$3 net. Lane.
Hulfish, D: S. Motion picture, its making and its theatre. 50 c. Elec. Mag.
Jenks, T. Photography for young people. **$1.50 net. Stokes.
Johnson, G. L. Photographic optics and color photography. *$3 net. Van Nostrand.
Mees, C: E: K. **Photography of colored objects. *50 c. net. Tennant.**
Phillips, R. W. **With other photographers. $2.50. Eastman Kodak.**

PHOTOGRAPHY.—*Continued.*

Schriever, J. B., *and* Cummings, T: H., *eds.* Complete self-instructing library of practical photography. 8 v. $32; $40; $48.—Popular ed. 10 v. $35; $50; $65. Am. Sch. Art.

Wall, E. J., *ed.* Photographic annual, 1910-11. $1 net; 50 c. net. Tennant.

Wallington, W. Chats on photography. $1.25 net. Lippincott.

Ward, H: S., *ed.* Photographic annual. $1; 50 c. Tennant.

Wellcome's photographic exposure record and diary, 1908, 1909, 1910. ea., 50 c. Burroughs, W. & Co.

See also Roentgen rays;—Spectrum;—Stereopticon.

Photometric observations. Wendell, O. C. $1. Harvard Univ.

Photometric observations of double stars. Stebbins, J. 75 c. Univ. of Ill.

PHOTOMETRY.

See Electric light;—Light;—Stars.

PHOTOTHERAPY.

See Radiotherapy.

Phrasing as applied to pianoforte playing. Marchant, A. W: 40 c. Ditson.

PHRENOLOGY.

Fowler, J. A. Brain roofs and porticos: psychological study of mind and character. $1. Fowler & W.

Olin, C: H: Phrenology. 50 c. Penn Pub. Co.

Spurzheim, J. G. Phrenology. *$3 net. Lippincott.

PHTHISIS.

See Tuberculosis.

Phucher, Itothe, pseud.

Puget Sound and Inland Empire Railway "Cascade Tunnel Route." '09(O2) c. front. fold. map, O. pap., 50 c. A. Harriman.

Phyfe, W: H: P.

Twelve thousand words often mispronounced: rev. and enl. ed. of "10,000 words often mispronounced," with supplement of 2000 add. words. '08(Ag22) c. S. **$1.25 net. Putnam.

Phyllanthography. Binion, S: A: $3. Fenno.

Physical and electrical engineering laboratory manuals. See Longmans'.

Physical basis of civilization. Heineman, T. W: $1.25. Forbes.

Physical basis of mind and morals. Fitch, M. H. $1. Kerr.

PHYSICAL CHEMISTRY.

See Chemistry.

PHYSICAL CULTURE.

See Athletics;—Gymnastics and physical culture;—Hygiene.

Physical development in relation to perfect voice production. Adams, H. T. *75 c. net. Scribner.

Physical diagnosis. Cabot, R: C. *$3 net. Wood.

Physical director as a hygienist. Hastings, W: W. 10 c. Bassette.

PHYSICAL GEOGRAPHY.

Babbitt, J. B. Physical history of the earth in outline. $1.50. E. E. Sherman.

Davis, W: M. Pract. exercises in physical geography. 50 c.; atlas to accompany above. 30 c. Ginn.

PHYSICAL GEOGRAPHY.—*Continued.*

Emerson, F: V. Manual of physical geography. **$1.40 net. Macmillan.

Everly, L. L., *and others.* Laboratory lessons in physical geography. 56 c. Am. Bk.

Gilbert, G. K. Introd. to physical geography. **$1.25 net. Appleton.

Gregory, H. E., *and others.* Physical and commercial geography. $3. Ginn.

Hopkins, T: C. Elements of physical geography. $1.35. B: H. Sanborn.

Hopkins, T. C., *and* Clark, B. W. Laboratory manual in physical geography. 50 c. B: H. Sanborn.

Kimm, S. C. Questions in physical geography given at examinations held by the Regents of the University of the State of New York. with key, $1. Bardeen.

Maury, M. F., *and* Simonds, F. W: Physical geography. $1.20. Am. Bk.

Redway, J. W. Elem. physical geography. $1.25. Scribner.

Salisbury, R. D. Elem. physiography. $3.50.—Physiography for high schools. $1.50. Holt.

Tarr, R. S., *and* Engeln, O. D. v. Lab'y manual of physical geography. $1.25 net. Macmillan.

See also Altitudes; — Climate; — Earth; — Earthquakes; — Geography; — Geology;—Glaciers;—Latitude;—Longitude; —Meteorology;—Nature;—Ocean; — Tides; — Tropics; — Volcanoes;—Water.

Physical history of the earth in outline. Babbit, J. B. $1.50. E. E. Sherman.

Physical laboratory manual. Adams, C: F. 60 c. Am. Bk.

PHYSICAL MEASUREMENTS.

See Physics.

Physical perfection. Simon, S. J. $3; $5. MacGerald.

Physical properties of soils. McCall, A. G. *50 c. net. Judd.

PHYSICAL SCIENCE.

See Physics;—Science.

Physical science in the time of Nero. *See* Seneca, Lucius Annæus.

Physical signs of diseases of thorax and abdomen. Sawyer, J. E. H. *$2 net. Wood.

PHYSICAL TRAINING.

See Athletics;—Gymnastics and physical culture.

Physician to the soul. Dresser, H. W. **$1 net. Putnam.

PHYSICIANS.

Blaisdell, F. One hundred years of New Hampshire surgery. (Add. author for price.) F. Blaisdell.

Medical record visiting list for 1911; for 30 patients a week, $1.25; for 60, $1.50; for 90, $2. Wood.

McDonald, J. N., *comp.* Chicago as a medical center. $2. Stromberg, A. & Co.

Mumford, J. G. Surgical memoirs. **$2.50 net. Moffat.

Osler, W: Alabama student, and other biographical essays. *$2 net. Oxford Univ.

Post graduate guide. $1. Wood.

PHYSICIANS.—*Continued.*

Roberts, J: B. Doctor's duty to the state. (Not for sale.) Am. Medical.

Trust, E:, *comp.* Professional directory of doctors and druggists of Philadelphia, incl. Atlantic City, N. J., and Camden, N. J., also, doctors in 80 nearby towns. E: Trust.

Webb, S. *and Mrs.* B. P. State and the doctor. $2 net. Longmans.

Willson, R. W. Medical men in the time of Christ. 60 c. net. S. S. Times.

See also Medical jurisprudence;—Medicine;—Osteopathy;—Quacks and quackery;—*also* Germantown, Pa.

Physicians' manual of the Pharmacopeia. Hallberg, C. S. N., *comp.* 40 c. Am. Medical.

Physicians' visiting list for 1909. '08, [1909.] (Mr) Regular ed., leath., for 25 patients weekly, *$1 net; 50 patients weekly, *$1.25 net; 2 v., *$2 net; 75 patients weekly, 2 v., *$2 net; 100 patients weekly, 2 v., *$2.25 net; Perpetual ed., without dates, space for 1300 names, leath., *$1.25 net; for 2600 names, leath., *$1.50 net; Monthly ed., without dates, *75 c. net; leath., *$1 net. Blakiston.

PHYSICS.

Adams, C: F. Physical laboratory manual for secondary schools. 60 c.—Physics for secondary schools. $1.20. — Teacher's manual to accompany Physics for secondary schools. 25 c. Am. Bk.

Adams, M. P. Simple physics in every-day life. (Add. author for price.) M. P. Adams.

Bacon, R. Liber primus Communium naturalium Fratris Rogeri. $3.40. Oxford Univ.

Baker, T: R. New physics. $1. Stradling.

Balderston, L. Elem. physics. $1.22. Sower.

Bardeen, C: W:, *ed.* Fundamental facts of elementary physics. $1. Bardeen.

Barnes, C. L. Lessons in elementary practical physics. v. 3, pt. 1, Practical acoustics. *$1.10 net. Macmillan.

Benton, J: R. Problems in physics to accompany Ames's Text-bk. of general physics. Am. Bk.

Blaker, E., *and* Fisher, W. J. Experiments in physics. *$1.25 net. Taylor & C.

Carhart, H: S. Physics for college students. $2.25. Allyn & B.

Coleman, S. E. New laboratory manual of physics. 80 c. Am. Bk.

Crabtree, H. Elem. treatment of the theory of spinning tops and gyroscopic motion. *$1.50 net. Longmans.

Crew, H: General physics. $2.75 net. Macmillan.

Crew, H:, *and* Jones, F. T. Elements of physics. *$1.10 net. Macmillan.

Culler, J. A. Text-book of general physics. **for colleges. $1.80. Lippincott.**

Duff, A. W., *ed.* Text-book of physics. *$2.75 net. Blakiston.

Duff, A. W., *and* Elwell, A. W. Physical measurements. $1.50 net. Blakiston.

PHYSICS.—*Continued.*

Duff, A. W., *and* Guthe, K. E. Mechanics and the properties of matter, and Heat. $1.60. Blakiston.

Duff, A. W., *and others.* Text-book of physics. *$2.75 net. Blakiston.

Ferry, E. S., *and* Jones, A. T. Manual of practical measurements. In 3 v. v. 1. $1.75. Longmans.

Franklin, W: S., *and others.* Practical physics. In 3 v. v. 1-2, ea., *$1.25 net; v. 3, *90 c. net. Macmillan.

Gibbs, W: E. Textbook of physics. pt. 1. $1.50. Van Nostrand.

Goodwin, H. M. Elements of the precision of measurements and graphical methods. 85 c. Maclachlan.

Gorton, F: R. High school course in physics. $1.25. Appleton.

Gregory, R: A., *and* Hadley, H: E. Class book of physics. *$1 net. Macmillan.

Hall, E. E., *and* Elston, T: S. Physical measurements in properties of matter and heat. $1. E. E. Hall.

Harrison, E: P. Course of pract. physics. $1.50 net. Longmans.

Higgins, L. D. Simple experiments in physics. 35 c. Ginn.

Hoadley, G: A. Elements of physics. $1.20. —Teacher's manual to accompany Elements of physics. 25 c.—Physical laboratory handbook. 50 c. Am. Bk.

Hurst, H. E., *and* Lattey, R. T. Text-bk. of physics. $3. Van Nostrand.

Jones, L. M. Practical physics. $1. Longmans.

Knott, C. G. Physics of earthquake phenomena. $4.75. Oxford Univ.

Le Bon, G. Evolution of forces. *$1.75 net. Appleton.

Linebarger, C: E. Text-bk. of physics. $1.25. Heath.

Mann, C: R., *and* Twiss, G: R. Physics. $1.25. Scott, F. & Co.

Maxim, J. L. Apprentices' course in experimental physics and mechanics for preliminary technical students and secondary school pupils. 50 c. Longmans.

Miller, F. R. Progressive problems in physics. 60 c. Heath.

Mumper, W: N. Teachers' manual to accompany "A text-book in physics." 25 c. Am. Bk.

Nichols, E. F. Physics: [lecture.] 25 c. Lemcke.

Ostwald, W. Natural philosophy. $1.25 net. Holt.

Page, F. J. M. Elements of physics. $1.50 net. Funk.

Poincaré, L. New physics and its evolution. *$1.75 net. Appleton.

Schumaker, E: E. New era in natural philosophy. $1.—Supplementary lecture, no. 1, to "The new era in natural philosophy." 50 c. E: Schumaker.

Searle, G: F: C: Experimental elasticity. $1.50. Putnam.

Sharpless, I: P., *and others.* Natural philosophy. $1. Lippincott.

Smithsonian physical tables. $1.20. Smith. Inst.

PHYSICS.—*Continued.*

Stewart, R. W. Elem. text-book of physics. pt. 2-4. ea., *$1.50 net. Lippincott.

Worthington, A. M. Study of splashes. *$2 net. Longmans.

See also Air;—Astronomy;—Chemistry; — Dynamics;—Electricity;—Gases;—Heat; — Hydraulic engineering;—Hydrogen; — Hydrostatics; — Light;—Magnetism; — Mathematics;— Matter; —Mechanics; — Meteorology;—Optics;—Physical geography;—Radio-activity;—Radium;—Science; —Sound; — Spectrum;—Statics;—Steam; —Water.

PHYSIOGNOMY.

See Face.

PHYSIOGRAPHY.

See Physical geography.

Physiological and medical observation among the Indians. Hrdlicka, A. (Add. Superintendent for price.) U. S., Supt. of Docs.

PHYSIOLOGICAL CHEMISTRY.

See Chemistry.

Physiological principles in treatment. Brown, W. L. *$2 net. Wood.

PHYSIOLOGY.

Alcock, N. H., *and* Ellison, F. O'B. Text-book of experimental physiology. *$1.50 net. Blakiston.

Ashby, H: Notes on physiology. $1.50. Longmans.

Barwick, A. J. Manual of physiology and hygiene, in primary grades. gratis. N. C. Dept. Pub. Instruct.

Beddard, A. P., *and others.* Pract. physiology. $4 net. Longmans.

Bishop, I. P. Methods and outlines for teaching physiology. 50 c. I. P. Bishop.

Blaisdell, A. F. How to keep well; text-book of physiology and hygiene. 45 c. Ginn.

Brubaker, A. P. Text-book of human physiology. *$3 net; leath., *$4 net. Blakiston.

Budgett, S. P. Essentials of physiology. $1. Saunders.

Coleman, W. M. Lessons in hygienic physiology. *60 c. net.—Physiology for beginners. *40 c. net. Macmillan

Conn, H. W: Elementary physiology and hygiene. *60 c. net.—Introd. physiology and hygiene. 36 c. Silver.

Conn, H. W:, *and* Budington. R. A. Advanced physiology and hygiene. $1.10. Silver.

Davison, A. Human body and health. 50 c. Am. Bk.

Dearborn, G: V. N. Text-book of physiology for students and practitioners. *$3.75 net. Lea.

Dunglison, R: J. New school physiology and hygiene. *$1 net. Am. Bk.

Eadie, R. *and* A. Physiology and hygiene for young people. 65 c. Scribner.

Eddy, W. H. Text-book in general physiology and anatomy. $1.20. Am. Bk.

Fitz, G: W. Principles of physiology and hygiene. $1.12. Holt.

Greenwood, M., *jr.* Physiology of the special senses. $2.40 net. Longmans.

Halliburton, W: D. Essentials of chemical physiology. $1.50. Longmans.

Hallock, E. B., *and* Gilbert, C: B. Some living things: primary lessons in physiology. 36 c. Barnes.

PHYSIOLOGY.—*Continued.*

Hill, A. Body at work: treatise on physiology. *$4.50 net. Longmans.

Hill, L., *ed.* Further advances in physiology. *$4.20 net.—Recent advances in physiology and biochemistry. *$5 net. Longmans.

Hoag, E. B. Health studies; applied physiology and hygiene. 75 c. Heath.

Howell, W: H: Text-book of physiology for medical students and physicians. $4. Saunders.

Hutchinson, R. Applied physiology. *$2 net. Longmans.

Jewett, *Mrs.* F. G. Body at work. 50 c. Ginn.

Jones, E: G., *and* Stephens, R. G. Outlines of physiology. *$1.50 net. Blakiston.

Kellogg, J: H. Miracle of life: [the body, its structure, functions and care.] $1.50. Modern Medicine.

Kimber, D. C. Text-book of anatomy and physiology for nurses. *$2.50 net. Macmillan.

Kirkes, W: S. Hdbk. of physiology. *$3.75 net. Blakiston.

Kirkes, W: S. Hdbk. of physiology. $3. Wood.

Krohn, W: O. Graded lessons in physiology and hygiene. *60 c. net. Appleton.

Lee, F. S. Physiology: [lecture.] 25 c. Lemcke.

Lewis, L. Anatomy and physiology for nurses. *$1.75 net. Saunders.

Manikin chart of the human system. $1.50. Funk.

Martin, H: N. Human body. $2.50. Holt.

Mayberry, J. W. Physiology and hygiene. 60 c. Southern Pub., (Tex.)

Metchnikoff, E. Nature of man. **$2 net. Putnam.

Millard, C. N. Building and care of the body. 40 c. net.—Wonderful house that Jack has: reader in practical physiology and hygiene. *50 c. net. Macmillan.

Moore, A. Physiology of man and other animals. 80 c. Holt.

Ott, I: Text-book of physiology. $3.50. Davis.

Ritchie, J: W. Human physiology. 80 c.—Sanitation and physiology. $1.20. World Bk.

Sherrington, C: S. Physiology. 50 c. net. Appleton.

Starling, E. H: Elem. of human physiology. *$3.75 net. Chic. Med. Bk.

Sterling, W: Outlines of practical physiology. *$2 net. Blakiston.

Stewart, G: N. Manual of physiology. $5 net; $6 net. Wood.

Walters, F. M. Physiology and hygiene for secondary schools. $1.20. Heath.

Wiggins, C. J: Brief text of physiology for dental, pre-medical and college students. $1.50. Wahr.

Wilson, A. Physiology. *50 c. net. Stokes.

See also Alcohol;—Anatomy;—Biology;—Blood;—Boys; — Brain; — Digestion; — Embryology;—Girls; — Heredity; — Hygiene;—Longevity; —Man; — Medicine; — Metabolism; — Mind and body:—Morphology;—Nervous system;—Nurses and nursing; — Pathology; —Phrenology;—Proteids;—Sex;—Temperance;—Woman.

Physiology and pathology of the semicircular canals. Bárány, R. $1. Hoeber.
Physiology and psychology of education. Brown, G: P. pt. 1. 25 c. Public Sch. Pub.
Physiology of reproduction. Marshall, F. H. A. $6 net. Longmans.
Physiology of stomata. Lloyd, F. E. $1.50. Carnegie.
Physiology of the blind. Kunz, M. 50 c. Volta.
Physique. Boeckmann, P. v. $1. P. v. Boeckmann.

Phythian, J: Ernest.
Fifty years of modern painting. '08(Ap4) il. 8°, *$3.50 net. Dutton.
Trees in nature, myth and art. '08(D19) 12°, *$1.50 net. Jacobs.

Piano lyrics. Grieg, E. H. $2.50; $1.50. Ditson.
Piano playing. Hofmann, J. **75 c. net. McClure.

PIANOFORTE.
Bach, J. S. Piano composition. $2.50; $1.50. Ditson.
Beethoven, L. v. Piano compositions. $2.50; $1.50. Ditson.
Brahms. J. Hungarian dances, for piano, four hands. Bk. 1, 2. ea., $1.50.—Sel. piano compositions. $1.50. Ditson.
Chase, M. W. Natural laws in piano technic. $1.25. Ditson.
Chopin, F. F. Greater Chopin: [contains 28 of his compositions.] $2 50; $1.50. Ditson.
Faelten, R., *comp.* Catechism of the Faelten system. 50 c. A. P: Schmidt.
Gallico, P., *comp. and ed.* Most popular piano instructor. 75 c. Hinds.
Gottschalk, L. M. Piano compositions. In 2 v. v. 1. $1. Ditson.
Grabeil, E W. Mechanics of piano technic. $1.25. A. W. Hunt.
Grieg, E. H. Larger piano compositions.—Piano lyrics and shorter compositions. ea., $2.50; $1.50. Ditson.
Hamilton, C. G. Piano teaching. $1.25. Ditson.
Henius, J. Maisie's music [piano pieces.] $1.25 net. Schirmer.
Hofmann, J. Piano playing. **75 c. net. McClure.
Hofmann, J. Piano questions answered. **75 c. net. Doubleday, P.
Johns, C. Essentials of pianoforte playing. $1.50. Ditson.
Johnstone, J. A. Touch, phrasing and inpretation. *$1.40 net. Scribner.
Köhler, C. L. H. Little School of velocity without octaves. 50 c. Ditson.
McFerrin, C: B. Mother's part in her child's musical education. $2. Alert Pub.
Marchant, A. W: Phrasing as applied to pianoforte playing. 40 c. Ditson.
Norton, E: Q. Construction, tuning and care of the pianoforte. $1. Ditson.
Perry, E: B. Stories of standard teaching pieces. $1.50. T. Presser.
Pirani, E. High school of piano-playing. *$2 net. Schirmer.

PIANOFORTE.—*Continued.*
Smeltzer, J. R., *comp.* Outlines and grades for the use of piano teachers. $2.50. J. R. Smeltzer.
White, W: B. Regulation and repair of piano and player mechanism, together with tuning as science and art.—Technical treatise on piano player mechanism. ea., $1.50. E: L. Bill.
Wilkinson, C: W. Well-known piano solos. *40 c. net. Scribner.

Pianoforte telegraphy. Griffin, R. B. $1. Morse Art.

Picard, Louis Benoit.
Der neffe als onkel; lustspiel in drei aufzügen, von Friedrich von Schiller, aus dem französischen des Picard; with notes and vocab. by F: B. Sturm. '09 (Je19) c. 12°, **35 c. net. Holt.

PICCADILLY.
See London.

Pick, Bernhard, D.D.
The Apocryphal acts. '09(O23) $1.25. Open Court.
—, comp. Hymns and poetry of the Eastern church. '08(Mr14) c. D. *$1 net. Eaton & M.
See also Bible. N. T.

Pickens, W:
Abraham Lincoln, man and statesman (abridged). '10(Ag) 12 p. 8°, 15 c. W: Pickens.

Pickering, E: C:
Future of astronomy. [1910.] (F) 105-116 p. 8°, pap. E: C: Pickering.

Pickering, W: H:
Researches of the Boyden department. '08 (D) 103 p. il. (Harvard Univ. Astronomical Observatory annals.) $1. Harvard Univ.
Search for a planet beyond Neptune. '09 (Jl10) 4°, (Annals of Astronomical Observatory of Harvard Univ.) pap., $1. Harvard Univ.

Pickett, W: Passmore.
Negro problem: Abraham Lincoln's solution. '09(Je5) c. por. O. **$2.50 net. Putnam.

Pickle, G: W., rep.
See Tennessee. *Sup. ct.* Repts.

Pickles. Aldin, C. C: W. *$2 net. Doran.

Picksford, A. G.
Elem. projective geometry. '10(Ag13) 8°, (Cambridge physical ser.) $1.25 net. Putnam.

Pickwick papers. *See* Dickens, C:
Picnic and other verses. Lauck, B. M. 50 c. Cochrane.

Picton, Ja. Allason.
Man and the Bible; review of the place of the Bible in human history. '09, [1910.] (F) c. 8°, **$2 net. Holt.
Pantheism. '07, [1909.] (Ap) 8°, (Religions ancient and modern.) *40 c. net. Open Court.

Pictorial and descriptive guide to London and its environs; with four section plans, showing every street within an area of about five miles east and west of St. Paul's Cathedral, and 3½ miles north and south. '10(Ag27) il. maps, plans, S. (Slip-in-the-pocket guide books.) $1 net. Platt & P.

Pictorial and descriptive guide to Stratford-upon-Avon, the home of Shakespeare; with excursions into the neighborhood, map of the district, plans of Stratford-upon-Avon, Warwick Castle, and Kenilworth Castle. 4th ed., rev. and re-illustrated. '10 (Ag27) S. (Slip-in-the-pocket guide books.) $1 net. Platt & P.

Pictorial log of the battle fleet cruise around the world. Miller, R. J: *$3 net. McClurg.

Pictorial Spanish course. Rees, J. D. *65 c. net. Little, B. & Co.

Picture primer. Beebe, E. M. 25 c. Am. Bk.

Picture stories from the Bible. Magnus, *Lady*. $2; $1.75. Tuck.

Picture study in elementary schools. Wilson, *Mrs.* L. L. W., *ed.* 2 v. in 1. *$1.25 net. Macmillan.

Picture talks for pastors. Richmond, E. 10 c. E. Richmond.

Picture work. Hervey, W. L. *30 c. net. Revell.

Pictured puzzles and word play. Pearson, A. C., *ed.* $1.50. Dutton.

PICTURES.
See Drawings; — Engravers and engravings; — Painters and paintings; — Portraits.

Pictures and their painters. Bryant, L. M. $2.50 net. Lane.

Pictures of early Methodism in Ohio. Williams, S: W. $1. Jennings.

Pictures of memory. Woolard, S: F., *comp.* *50 c. net; leath., *$1.25 net. Goldsmith-W.

Pictures of Old Chinatown. Irwin, W. H: **$1 net. Moffat.

Pictures of Paris. Raphael, J: N. P. *$1.50 net. Macmillan.

Pictures of the Apostolic church. Ramsay, *Sir* W: M. $1.50 net. S. S. Times.

Picturesque Asia and Africa. Stratton, C. R. $1. Nat. Pub. Co.

Picturesque camps, cabins and shacks. Holman, E. E. $2. E. E. Holman.

Picturesque China. Stratton, C. R. $1. Nat. Pub. Co.

Picturesque Europe. Stratton, C. R. $1. Nat. Pub. Co.

Picturesque Japan. Stratton, C. R. $1. Nat. Pub. Co.

Picturesque river ser. il. S. Macmillan.
—Johnson. Picturesque Hudson.—Picturesque St. Lawrence. ea., **$1.25 net.

Picturesque suburban houses. Holman, E. E. $2. E. E. Holman.

Pidal, Ramón Menéndez.
El romancero Español; conferencias dadas en la Columbia University de New York, los dias 5 v 7 de Abril de 1909; bajo los auspicios de The Hispanic Society of America. '10(O8) c. O. $1.25 net. Hispanic Soc.

Pidgeon, R. H., comp.
See Robinson, E.

Pidgin, C: Felton.
Further adventures of Quincy Adams Sawyer and Mason Corner folks. '09(Je19) c. il. O. $1.50. L. C. Page.

Pidgin, C: Felton.—*Continued.*
Labor or the money god! which?: a story. '08(My16) c. D. $1.50. Mayhew.
Theodosia, the first gentlewoman of her time: [Mrs. Theodosia Burr Alston.] '08(F1) c. il. pors. O. (Great triumvirate: Jefferson, Hamilton, Aaron Burr.) *$2.50 net; Library ed., *$3 net. C. M. Clark.

Pie and the pirate. Lee, A. 50 c. Collier.

Pieces people ask for. Baker, G: M., *ed.* 25 c. W. H. Baker.

Pied piper of Hamelin. *See* Browning, R.

Piedra (La) pintada. Angel, M. $1.25. Grafton Pub.

Piépape, General de.
Princess of strategy; the life of Anne Louise Bénédicte de Bourbon-Conde, Duchesse du Maine; tr. from the French by J. Lewis May. '10(D3) il. O. $4 net. Lane.

Pier, Arth. Stanwood.
Crashaw brothers. '10(O15) c. front. D. $1.50. Houghton M.
New boy. '08(O3) c. il. D. †$1.50. Houghton M.

Pier, Garrett Chatfield.
Inscriptions of the Nile monuments. '08 (D12) c. il. map, 8°, **$5 net. Putnam.
Pottery of the Near East. '09(N20) c. il. O. **$3.50 net. Putnam.

Pierce, C: Campbell, D.D.
Humor of the heart for faith, and other sermons del. at the Cathedral open air services, Washington, D. C.; with an introd. by the Bishop of Washington. 2d ed. '08(Je13) c. por. D. *$1 net. Young Churchman.

Pierce, Clarence A.
See Bedell, F:

Pierce, Rev. D: Rand.
Heavenly pilgrim, and other poems. 40th anniversary ed. '09, [1910.] (F) c. 114 p. il. por. 12°, $1. D: R. Pierce.

Pierce, Ella A.
Hartley House cook book and household economist; enl. and rev. by Martha B. Noyes. '10(O24) c. D. 60 c. net. Wessels & B.

Pierce, Fk., comp.
See United States. Pierce's federal code.

Pierce, Franklin.
Federal usurpation. '08(Ap18) c. D. **$1.50 net. Appleton.

Pierce, F: Erastus.
Collaboration of Webster and Dekker. '09 (Ap17) O. (Yale studies in English.) pap., $1. Holt.
See also Canby, H: Seidel;—MacCracken, H: Noble.

Pierce, G: Washington.
Principles of wireless telegraphy. '10(N5) c. il. 8°, $3. McGraw-H.

Pierce, J: Alfr.
Why the secrets of Freemasonry are withheld from members. '08(Jl) c. 24 p. por. 24°, pap., 10 c. J: A. Pierce.

PIERCE, *Capt.* Michael.
See King Philip's War.

Pierce, Percy.
Monoplane: drawing with descriptive matter. '10(D) 15 c. Spon.

Pierce, Ray Vaughn.
People's commonsense medical adviser in plain English; or, medicine simplified. 72d ed. [1910.] (Mr) c. '09. 16+11-1008 p. il. (4 col.) por. 8°, 31 c. World's Dispensary.

Pierce, Rob. Morris, ed.
Dict. of hard words. '10(D3) c. S. $1.20 net. Dodd.

Pierce, Ulysses Grant Baker.
Religion of the Spirit: five sermons. '10 (My7) c. 12°, 25 c. Unitarian Club.

Pierce, W:
Historical introd. to the Marprelate tracts: chapter in the evolution of religious and civil liberty in England. '09(Je19) 8°, *$3 net. Dutton.

Pierce, W: Dwight.
Monographic revision of the twisted winged insects comprising the order *Strepsiptera* Kirby. '09, [1910.] (Mr) 12+232 p. il. 8°, (Smithsonian Institution, United States National Museum, bull.) pap. Gov. Pr. Off.
Bibliography (15 p.).
On the biologies of the *rhynchophora* of North America. '07, [1909.] (Mr) 247-320 p. il. map. 8°, (Univ. of Neb. studies from the zoological laboratory.) (Not for sale.) Univ. of Neb.
Studies of parasites of the [Mexican] cotton boll weevil. '08(Ap18) il. 8°, (U. S. Dept. of Agriculture, Bureau of Entomology, bull.) pap., 25 c. U. S., Supt. of Docs.

Piercy, W: C., ed.
Illustrated Bible dictionary. '08(D19) il. 8°, *$5 net. Dutton.

Piercy, Willis Duff.
Death and its sorrow. '08(Je27) c. D. $1. Neale.

Pierille. Claretie, A. A. 40 c. Holt.

PIERPONT, John.
Ford, A. A. John Pierpont. (Priv. pr.) J. A. Crosby.

Pierre and his people. Parker, *Sir* G. $1.25. Harper.

Pierre and Jean. *See* Maupassant, Guy de.

Piersol, G: Arth.
Normal histology, with special reference to the structure of the human body. 8th ed., (rewritten.) [1910.] (O) c. 8+418 p. il. 4°, $3.50. Lippincott.
—, ed. Human anatomy, incl. structure and development and practical considerations by T: Dwight, J. Playfair McMurrich, Carl A. Hamann, G: A. Piersol, and J. W: White. In 2 v. '08(D) c. il. 8°, $15. Lippincott.

Pierson, Alb. Halsey.
Consumption of firewood in the United States. '10(O) 7 p. tabs., diagr., 8°, (U. S., Dept. of Agriculture, Forest Service, circular.)

Pierson, Arth. Tappan, D.D.
Bible and spiritual life. '08(Ap4) c. il. tabs., 8°, $1.50. Gospel Pub.
Godly self-control. '09(O30) T. *50 c. net. Armstrong.
Making of a sermon. [2d ed., rev. and enl.] '08(F1) c. D. *$1.50 net. Gospel Pub.

Pierson, Clara Dillingham.
Among the meadow people. School ed. '08 (D12) il. 40 c. Dutton.
Millers and their new home. '08(Ag15) 12°, $1. Dutton.

Pierson, Ward W.
See Neall, Fk. L.

Pies and the pirates. Rae, J: 75 c. net. Duffield.

Pietro of Siena. Phillips, S. $1 net. Macmillan.

PIG.
See **Hog.**

Pig brother. Richards, *Mrs.* L. E. H. **40 c. net. Little, B. & Co.

Pigeon Camp ser. *See* Doyle, *Mrs.* Martha Claire MacGowan.

PIGEONS.
De Lancey, F. W. A to Z of pigeons and bantams. 50 c. Item Pub.
Jones, M. O. Guide to successful squab raising. 50 c. M. O. Jones.
Rice, E. C. National standard squab book. 50 c. Plymouth Rock.
Sotter, F: A. Breeding for squabs. 50 c. Douglassville.

Piggott, C: H:
Pearls at random strung; or, life's tragedy from wedding to tomb, including the scientific causes of all diseases, poverty, premature death and longevity. '08 (My.) c. 11-110 p. por. 8°, $1. C: H: Piggott.

PIGMENTS.
See **Paints.**

Pigott, C., comp.
Exporters' encyclopædia, 1908. 4th ed. '08 (F); 1909. 5th ed. '09(My22); 1910. 6th ed. '10(Mr) ea., 8°, ea., $5. Exporters' Enc.

Pigou, Arth. Cecil.
Problem of theism, and other essays. '08 (O24) 12°, *$1 net. Macmillan.

PIKE, Albert.
Hugo, T. W. Digest-index of "Morals and dogma" of Albert Pike. $1. T. W. Hugo.
Newton, J. Address on Albert Pike, 33°, master genius of masonry. 75 c. Torch Press.

Pike, J:
Practical induction coil construction. '08 (Jl4) il. 12°, bds., 50 c. Spon.

Pike, Lillian.
See Hayford, J: Fillmore.

PIKE COUNTY, Miss.
Cornerly, L. W. Pike County, Mississippi. $2. Brandon Pr.

PIKE COUNTY, Mo.
Rowley, R. R. Geology of Pike County. 20 c. Missouri Bu. Geol.

PIKE FAMILY.
See **Genealogies: McPike, E. F.**

Pilgrim advanced Sunday-school lessons. Pilgrim Press.
—Matthews. Social gospel. 50 c. net.
Pilgrim church. Ainsworth, P. C. $1.25 net. Revell.
Pilgrim from Ireland. Carnot, M. 45 c. Benziger.
Pilgrim walks in Franciscan Italy. Jörgensen, J. *75 c. net. Herder.
Pilgrimage to Canaan. Scott, J. $1.75. Jennie Scott.
Pilgrim's march. Bashford, H: H. †$1.50. Holt.
Pilgrim's progress. *See* Bunyan, J:
Pilgrim's progress in other worlds. Martin, *Mrs.* N. P. $1. Mayhew.
Pilgrim's shell. *See* Sue, Marie Joseph Eugène.
Pilgrim's tales. Darton, F. J. H., *comp.* 60 c. Dodge.
PILGRIMS.
Cockshott, W. Pilgrim fathers. *$2.50 net. Putnam.
Hanks, C: S. Our Plymouth forefathers. $1.50. Estes.
Masefield, J:, *comp.* Chronicles of the Pilgrim fathers. 35 c. net; 70 c. net. Dutton.
See also Robinson, John.
Pilgrims (The). Dole, N. H. (Priv. pr.) N. H. Dole.
Pilgrims (The). Ketler, I: C. $1.50 net. Revell.
Pilgrims of the Rhine. *See* Bulwer-Lytton, *Sir* E: G: Earle Lytton, [*Lord* Lytton.]
Pilkerton's peerage. Hawkins, A. H. 50 c. S: French.
Pilkington, Woodford.
Co-ordinate geometry applied to land surveying. '09(D18) il. 16°, 60 c. Spon.
Pilkinton, W. G., comp.
See Indiana law stamps.—Ohio law note and brief finder.—Ohio law stamps.
Pillars of Eden. **Mighels, P. V. $1.50.** FitzGerald.
Pillsbury, Wa. Bowers.
Attention. '08(Mr14) 8°, (Lib. of philosophy.) *$2.75 net. Macmillan.
Psychology of reasoning. '10(My21) c. D. $1.50 net. Appleton.
Pilot of the Skylark. Russell, I: $1.50. Wilde.
"Pilot" sectional road maps of New England and Hudson River District; covering 53,000 square miles. '09(Ja23) c. maps, obl. O. limp leath., $5, boxed. F. S. Blanchard.
PILOTS AND PILOTAGE.
See Navigation.
PILPAI.
See Bidpai.
Pimbley, Arth. Fs.
Baltimore Conference of Grand Masters, together with acct. of dedication week; a description of the new Masonic temple and a story of the loss of the old home. '10(Ag) 94 p. pors. 8°, $2.50. A. F. Pimbley.
Dictionary of heraldry. '08(N21) c. il. O. $2. A. F. Pimbley.
Pin-wheel book. Williams, C. A. 75 c. Stokes.

Pinafore picture book. Gilbert, *Sir* W: S. *$2 net. Macmillan.
Pinanski, A. E.
Street railway system of metropolitan Boston. '08(D) 58 p. *$1 net. McGraw.
Pinches, Theophilus Goldridge.
Babylonia and Assyria. '07, [1909.] (Ap) 8°, (Religions ancient and modern.) *40 c. net. Open Court.
Pinchot, Gifford.
Conservation of natural resources. '08 (Ag1) 8°, (U. S., Dept. of Agriculture, Farmers' bull.) pap., 10 c. U. S., Supt. of Docs.
Fight for conservation. '10(S10) c. D. (Conservation primers.) 60 c. net. Doubleday, P.
PINCKNEY, Charles.
Nott, C: C. Mystery of the Pinckney draught. [U. S. Constitution.] **$2 net. Century Co.
PINE TREES.
Betts, H. S. **Properties and uses of the southern pines. (Add. Superintendent for price.) U. S., Supt. of Docs.**
Massachusetts. Hdbk. on forest mensuration of the white pine in Massachusetts. gratis. Wright & P.
Pearson, G. A. Reproduction of western yellow pine in the Southwest. Gov. Pr. Off.
Piñon pine. (Add. Superintendent for price.) U. S., Supt. of Docs.
Red or Norway pine; *Pinus resinosa* Ait. '09(O) 4 p. 8°, (U. S., Dept. of Agriculture; Forest Service; silvical leaflet.) pap. (Add. Superintendent for price.) **U. S., Supt. of Docs.**
Shaw, G: R. Pines of Mexico. *$25 net. C. S. Sargent.
Spaulding, P. **European currant rust on the white pine in America.—Present status of the white-pine blights. (Add.** Superintendent for price.) **U. S., Supt. of Docs.**
United States. *Congress House. Committee on Public Lands.* To create the Calaveras bigtree national forest. 5 c. U. S., Supt. of Docs.
PINEAPPLES.
See Fruit.
Pinero, Arth. Wing.
Mid-channel; a play. '10(D24) c. D. pap., 50 c. W. H. Baker
The thunderbolt; episode in the history of a provincial family; in four acts. '09 (Mr6) c. 12°, pap., 50 c. W. H. Baker.
Pinger, Wilhelm Robert Richard.
Der junge Goethe und das publikum. '09 (Je12) Q. (Univ. of Cal. pubs.; Modern philology.) pap., 50 c. Univ. of Cal.
Pinkham, Edn. G:
Fate's a fiddler. '08(Jl11) c. D. †$1.50. Small.
PINKHAM FAMILY.
See Genealogies: Sinnett, C: N.
PINKROOT.
Stockberger, W. W. Pinkroot and its substitutions. 50 c. Pharmaceutical Review.
Pinnix, Mrs. Hannah Courtney.
Chaney's stratagem. '10(Ja1) il. D. $1.50. C. M. Clark.

Pinocchio. *See* Lorenzini, Carlo.

Piñon pine; *pinus edulis.* '09(N) 4 p. 8°, (U. S., Dept. of Agriculture; forest service, silvical leaflet.) pap. (Add. Superintendent for price.) U. S., Supt. of Docs.

Pinto de Morales, Jorge.
Maravillas del parnaso y flor de los meiores romances graves, burlescos, y satiricos que hasta oy sean cantado en la Corte. [facsim.] '02, [1909.] (N) 96 p. 8°, $8. (200 copies.) Hispanic Soc.

Pioneer (The). *See* Cooper, Ja. Fenimore.

Pioneer days in the Southwest from 1850 to 1879. '09(N20) c. il. pors. 8°, $1.50. State Cap.

Pioneer days on Puget Sound. Denny, A. A. subs., *$2 net; *60 c. net. A. Harriman.

Pioneer in international arbitration. Rodeffer, J: D: 40 c. J: D: Rodeffer.

Pioneer priests of North America. *See* Campbell, T: J.

Pioneer sermons. Rowe, F: L:, *comp.* $1.25. F: L: Rowe.

Pioneer voyage to California. Coffin, G: $1.50. G. B. Coffin.

Pioneering for engineers. Shelford, F. $1.25. Spon.

PIONEERS.
See **Explorers.**

Pioneers (The). Oppenheim, J. 50 c. net. B: W. Huebsch.

Pioneers and makers of Arkansas. Shinn, J. H. (Add. pubs. for price.) Genealog. and Hist.

Pioneers in education ser. See Compayré, Jules Gabriel.

Pioneers of Maine and New Hampshire. Pope, C: H: $5. C: H: Pope.

PIOZZI, *Mrs.* Hester Lynch Salisbury Thrale.
See **Johnson, Samuel.**

Pipe dreams. Osborne, M. LeR. 75 c. Ellis.

Piper, F: S.
Lexington, birthplace of American liberty; hdbk. cont. acct. of the battle of Lexington, Paul Revere's narrative of his famous ride, a sketch of the town and the places of historic interest. 3d ed. '10 (Ag) 7-42 p. il. map, 8°, 25 c. Lexington Hist. Soc.

"Piper, Paul," pseud.
See Eaton, Seymour.

Piper, Stanley E:
Nevada mouse plague of 1907-8. '09(My) 23 p. il. 8°. (Add. Superintendent for price.) U. S., Supt. of Docs.

Piper (The). Peabody, J. P. **$1.10 net. Houghton M.

PIPES AND PIPING.
Bjorling, P. R. Pipes and tubes. *$1.25 net. Macmillan.
Browning, W: D. Dimensions of pipe, fittings and valves. 75 c. Nat. Bk.
Collins, H. E. Pipes and piping. $1. Hill Pub.
See also **Cement.**

Pippa passes. *See* Browning, Rob.

Pippins and peaches. Jameson, *Mrs.* H. F. $1. Reilly & B.

PIQUA, O.
See **Miami Co.**

Pirani, Eugenio.
High school of piano-playing, (Die hochschule des klavierspiels.) '08(O3) F. *$2 net. Schirmer.

Pirie, P.
Kashmir, the land of streams and solitudes. '08(O31) il. Q. *$5 net. Lane.

Pirscher, Johanna.
Variations on an old theme. '09(Je12) c. 12°, bds., $1. Badger.

Pirsson, L: Valentine.
Rocks and rock minerals: manual of the elements of petrology without the use of the microscope. '08(Ag1) c. il. 12°, **$2.50 net. Wiley.

PISA, Italy.
Ross, *Mrs.* J. A. D.-G., *and* Erichsen, N. Story of Pisa. $1.75 net; $2.25 net. Dutton.

PISCATOLOGY.
See **Fish and fishing.**

Pisek, Godfrey, R.
See Chapin, H: Dwight.

Pissarro, Lucien.
Rossetti. '08(F22) il. O. (Masterpieces in colour.) bds., *65 c. net. Stokes.

PISTOL.
See **Shooting.**

Pitblado, Rev. C: Bruce and Rev. Edwy Guthrie.
Nareen. '08(Ag29) c. D. $1. Pitblado.

Pite, Arth. Beresford, and others.
Building construction. In 2 v. v. 1. '10 (D24) il. O. (Architects' lib.) $5 net. Longmans.

Pitman, Benn.
New pract. shorthand manual; complete and comprehensive exposition of Pitman shorthand adapted for use in public and private schools, academies and colleges. 10th rev. ed. '10(Ag) 6+192 p. por. 12°, $1.25. Carnell.

—, and Howard, Jerome B.
Business letters. No. 4, Insurance correspondence, in the amanuensis style of phonography. '08(Je13) c.; No. 5, Classified correspondence in the amanuensis style of phonography; No. 6, Classified correspondence in the amanuensis style of phonography. '10(D) 52; 51 p. S. pap., ea., 25 c. Pitman.
Legal forms: in the amanuensis style of phonography. '08(Ap4) c. S. (American system of shorthand.) pap. (Add. pubs. for price.) Phonograph.

Pitman, Sir I:
Abr. shorthand dict.; with complete list of grammalogues and contractions. Twentieth century ed. '010(F19) Tt. 75 c. Pitman.
Course in Isaac Pitman shorthand. Special ed. in the form of lesson sheets. '08 (Ap25); New ed. '10(N12) c. S. pap., ea., $1.50, boxed. Pitman.
International mercantile letters: actual letters, arranged in groups, illustrating modern mercantile methods: English-French. '08(My2) D. 85 c. Pitman.
International mercantile letters: actual letters, arranged in groups, illustrating modern mercantile methods: English-German. '08(F1) D. 85 c. Pitman.

Pitman, Sir I:—*Continued.*
International mercantile letters: actual letters, arranged in groups, illustrating modern mercantile methods: English-Italian. '08(My2) D. $1. Pitman.
International mercantile letters: actual letters arranged in groups illustrating modern mercantile methods: English-Portuguese. '08(Je13) D. $1.25. Pitman.
Key to Pitman's shorthand writing exercises and examination tests. 20th century ed. '09(Ag28) D. $1.25. Pitman.
Key to Spanish shorthand. '08(Mr7) S. $1. Pitman.
Shorthand dictionary. 9th (twentieth century) ed. '10(Ja1) D. $1.50. Pitman.
PITMAN, *Sir* Isaac.
Baker, A. Life of Sir Isaac Pitman. *$2 net. Pitman.
Pitman, Norman Hinsdale.
Chinese fairy stories. '10(Ag6) c. col. il. D. $1. Crowell.
Pitmanic guide. Walton, D. W. 20 c. Pitman.
Pitman's banking phrase book; an adaptation of Pitman's shorthand to the requirements of banking business and correspondence. 20th century ed. '10(Mr12) S. pap., 25 c. Pitman.
Pitman's business man's guide. Slater, J: A. $1.25. Pitman.
Pitman's commercial dict. of the English language; with an appendix cont. forms of addresses, chemical elements, coinage systems, common foreign phrases, mensuration notes, metric system, correction of printers' proofs, notes on punctuation, signs and symbols. '09(N6) Tt. bds., 25 c. Pitman.
Pitman's common commodities of commerce il. D. Pitman.
—Ibbetson. Tea from grower to consumer. 75 c.
—Keable. Coffee from grower to consumer. 75 c.
—Martineau. Sugar, cane and beet. 75 c.
—Mitchell. Oil, animal, vegetable, essential, and mineral. 75 c.
—Peake. Cotton from the raw material to the finished product. 50 c.
Pitman's companies and company law. Connell, A. C. $2. Pitman.
Pitman's guide for the company secretary. Coles, A. $2. Pitman.
Pitman's mercantile law. Slater, J: A. $2. Pitman.
Pitman's practical primers of business. il. D. 50 c. Pitman.
—Bridgewater. Advertising.
—Davies. Money and the stock and share markets.
—Douglas. Elements of commercial law.
—Eke. Elements of insurance.
—Gandy. Elements of banking.
—Hall *and* Heywood. Shipping.
—Porritt *and* Nicklin. Bookkeeping for retailers.
Pitman's progressive dictator. Hammond, H. W. 85 c. Pitman.
Pitman's public man's guide. Slater, J. A., *ed.* $1.25. Pitman.
Pitman's secretary's handbook. Blain, H. E., *ed.* $2. Pitman.

Pitman's tourists' vade mecums. S. Pitman.
—Valgimigli. Tourists' vade mecum of Italian colloquial conversation. 40 c.
Pitman's traders' handbooks. D. $1. Pitman.
—Beynon. Drapery and drapers' accounts.
—Tupman. Grocery.
Pitman's where to look; easy guide to books of reference. 3d ed., rev. and augmented. '10(F19) D. 85 c. Pitman.
"Pitt, Mrs. G. L."
See Pitt, Sammie Wall.
Pitt, Sammie Wall, ["Mrs. G. L. Pitt."]
Poems dear to the heart. '09, [1910.] c. 126 p. il. 12°, $1.50. S. W. Pitt.
PITT, William, *Earl* of Chatham.
Rosebery, A. P. P., *Earl.* Lord Chatham, his early life and connections. $3 net. Harper.
Pitt Press ser. S. Putnam.
—Balzac. Le médecin de campagne. *90 c. net.
—Chaucer. Clerkes tale.—The prologue. ea., *75 c. net.
—Erasmus. Altera colloquia Latina. *40 c. net.
—Euripides. Phoenissae. *$1.25 net.
—Hugo. Selected poems. *50 c. net.
—Livy. Book IX. *75 c. net.
—Ovid. Phaëton. 50 c. net.
—Sidgwick, *ed.* Old ballads.
—Tennyson. Fifty poems. 75 c. net.
Pittenger, W:
Toasts and forms of public address for those who wish to say the right thing in the right way. '09, [1910.] (My) 6+7-174 p. 16°, (Popular hdbks.) 50 c. Penn Pub. Co.
Pittier de Fábrega, Henri François.
New or noteworthy plants from Colombia and Central America. '09(My) 5+171-181 p. il. 8°, (Smithsonian Inst. contributions from the U. S. National Herbarium.) pap. (Add. Superintendent for price.) U. S., Supt. of Docs.
Pittman, Mrs. Hannah Daviess.
Go forth and find. '10(F12) c. 12°, $1.50. Badger.
Heart of Kentucky. '08(D5) c. D. $1.50. Neale.
Pittman, Reden Herbert, ed.
Biographical hist. of primitive or old school Baptist ministers of the United States; incl. brief treatise on the subject of deacons, their duties, etc., with some personal mention of these officers. '09, [1910.] (F) c. 7-406 p. il. pors. 8°, $2. R. H. Pittman.
Pittsburgh. Chamber of Commerce, *comp.* Shippers' guide schedule of package car service from Pittsburgh. '09, [1910.] (F) c. 12°, $1. Pittsburgh Chamber of Com.
PITTSBURGH, Pa.
Arnold, B. J., *and others.* City planning for Pittsburgh. gratis. Pittsburgh Civic.
Boucher, J: N., *ed.* Century and a half of Pittsburg and her people. 4 v. ea., 25 c. Lewis Pub.
Church, S: H. Short history of Pittsburgh. *$1.25 net. De Vinne.
Fleming, G: T. Flem's views of old Pittsburgh. 25 c. Flem Pub.

PITTSBURGH, Pa.—*Continued.*
White, E:, *ed.* 150 years of unparalleled thrift; Pittsburgh sesquicentennial. 25 c. E: White.
White, E:, *ed.* Pittsburgh the powerful. $1.12. Industry.
See also Calvary Church;—First English Evangelical Church.

PIUS X., *Pope.*
Creagh, J: T: Commentary on the decree "Ne temere." $1.25. Furst.
O'Dwyer, E: T: Cardinal Newman and the Encyclical *Pascendi Dominici Gregis.* *36 c. net. Longmans.
Programme of modernism: reply to the encyclical of Pius x., *Pascendi Dominici Gregis.* *$1.50 net. Putnam.
Schmitz, *Canon* E. Life of Pope Pius x. $5. Amer. Cath. Pub.

Pixie (A) in petticoats. Trevena, J: †$1.50. Moffat.

Pixley, Fs. W.
Accountancy. '08(Je13) O. $2. Pitman.

Pixy's holiday journey. Lang, G: $1. Saalfield.

Piyadasi.
See Asoka.

PLACE, Francis.
Wallas, G. Life of Francis Place. *$1 net. Longmans.

Place of animals in human thought. Cesaresco, *Countess* E. M. *$3 net. Scribner.

Place of religion in good government. Pam, M. 50 c. Univ. Press, (Notre Dame.)

PLACER COUNTY, **California.**
Map of Placer County, California, showing boundaries of the national forests; comp. from data furnished by the U. S. Forest Service. '09(O) f°, map, pap., 20 c. **Cal. State Mining.**

Plagiarism (The) of The Merchant Prince of Cornville by Cyrano de Bergerac; demonstration that the celebrated French play, known as "Cyrano de Bergerac," was taken from The merchant prince of Cornville, a published play, in English, by Samuel Eberly Gross, U. S. A. '10(Ag) 7-220 p. pors. 12°. (Not for sale.) Rand, McN. & Co.

PLAGUE.
Gasquet, F. A Black death of 1348 and 1349. *$2 net. Macmillan
Simpson, W: J: R. Treatise on plagues. *$5 net. Putnam
See also Fleas;—Ground-squirrels;—San Francisco.

Plain American in England. Whitefield, C: T. 50 c. Doubleday, P.

Plain American talk in the Philippines. Johnston, M. G. $1.25. J: R. Edgar

Plain analysis of socialism. Eccles, L. F. 25 c. L. F. Eccles.

Plain and faithful narrative of the original design, rise, progress and present state of the Indian Charity School at Lebanon in Connecticut. Wheelock, E. $2.50. G: P. Humphrey.

Plain answers to religious questions. Black, S: C: 75 c. Presb. Bd.

Plain commentaries. S. 35 c. Young Churchman.
—MacDermott. Gospel according to St. Luke.—Gospel according to St. Mark.—Gospel according to St. Matthew.

Plain economic facts for all people. Thomas, A. M. $3. Cochrane.

Plain facts about Mexico. '08, [1909.] (Ag) c. 43 p. il. 4°. (Add. pubs. for price.) Davis Bros.

Plain facts on sex hygiene. Howard, W: L. $1 net. Clode.

Plain gold ring. Kane, R. 90 c. net. Longmans.

Plain man and his Bible. Boughton, L. G. **60 c. net. Am. Bapt.

Plain tales from the hills. *See* Kipling, Rudyard.

Plains of silence. Askew, *Mrs.* J. de C. L. †$1.50. Cassell.

Plaisted, Laura L.
Early education of children. '09(My22) il. fold. facsim., D. $1.50. Oxford Univ.

Plan for a direct election law. Ingram, T: D. 15 c. T: D. Ingram.

Plan for reforming the accounts, records and repts. of New York City. Merchants' Association of New York. (Add. pubs. for price.) Merchants' Assoc.

PLANE (*tool*).
See Woodwork.

Plane curves of the eighth order. Cowley, E. B. (Not for sale.) New Era Print.

PLANE GEOMETRY.
See Geometry.

PLANE TABLE.
See Surveying.

PLANE TRIGONOMETRY.
See Trigonomerty.

PLANERS.
Lathe and planer tools. 25 c. Indust. Press.

PLANS.
See **Architecture.**

Plans and specifications for playground construction. Leland, A. 25 c. Bassette.

Plans for suburban concrete dwellings. Association of American Portland Cement Manufacturers. **$1.** Assoc. Am. Portland Cement.

Plant, J: C., and Zapf, Alfr. E., eds.
Contracts and specifications; working manual of correct forms covering the relations of architect, contractor, and owner, methods of awarding and executing public and private contracts, and instruction in the art of specification writing. pt. 1, by Ja. C. Plant; pt. 2, ed. by Alfr. E. Zapf. '10(D17) c. il. plan, 8°, (Amer. Sch. of Corr. pubs.) $1. Am. Sch. Corr.

Plant babies and their cradles. Chase, A. 40 c. Educ. Pub.

Plant book for schools. Darbishire, O. V. *$1 net. Macmillan.

Plant cell. Haig, H. A. $2 net. Lippincott.

Plant culture. Oliver, G: W. $1.50. De La Mare.

PLANT DISEASES.
***See* Fungi.**

Plantæ Mexicanæ purpusianæ. Brandegee, T. S. [pt. 1,] 15 c.; [pt. 2,] 10 c. Univ. of Cal.

Plantation poems. Sherman, E. L. $1.25 net. F. F. Sherman.

Planter (The). **Whitaker, H.** †$1.50. **Harper.**

PLANTS.
See Botany, and references under that subject;—Decoration and ornament;—Radium.

Plantz, Marguriette du.
See Owen, Marg. Cunliffe.

PLASTER.
See Cement.

PLASTERING.
Bankart, G: P. Art of the plasterer. *$10 net. Scribner.
Richey, H. G. Building mechanics' ready reference. Cement workers' and plasterers' ed. **$1.50 net. Wiley.

Plate, Adrian.
See Hatton, H:

PLATE.
See Silver.

PLATES (iron and steel).
See Strength of materials.

PLATINUM.
Rose, T: K. Precious metals: gold, silver, and platinum. **$2 net. Van Nostrand.

Plato.
Apology of Socrates; ed., with introd. and notes, by Harold Williamson. '08(S19) 16°, (Classical ser.) *50 c. net. Macmillan.
Apology of Socrates and Crito; with extracts from the Phaedo and Symposium and from Xenophon's Memorabilia; ed. by L: Dyer; rev. by T: Day Seymour; with a vocab. '08(N21) c. O. (College ser. of Greek authors.) $1.40. Ginn.
Apology of Socrates and Crito, with a part of his Phaedo; tr. from the Greek by B: Jowett. '10(D) 12°, bds., $1 net (900 copies); Japan vel., $3 net (25 copies). T: B. Mosher.
The banquet, [The symposium;] tr. from the Greek by Percy Bysshe Shelley. Riverside Press ed. '08(D26) limp bds., **$5 net. Houghton M.
Dialogues with introd. by translator, B: Jowett, and special introd. by Maurice Fs. Egan. [Also] Aristotle, Politics of Aristotle; tr. by B: Jowett; with introd. by Maurice Fs. Egan. '08(Je27) c. il. 8°, $1.75; hf. mor., $3.50. Lamb Pub.
The Euthyphro of Plato; with introd. and notes by St. George Stock. '09(My15) S. 60 c. Oxford Univ.
The ion; with introd. and notes by St. George Stock. '09(D4) D. 60 c. Oxford Univ.
Opera; recognovit brevique adnotatione critica instruxit Ioannes Burnet, Apologia-Meno. '10(N19) D. pap., 50 c. Oxford Univ.
Republic: tr. by T: M. Lindsay. '08(S19) 12°, *$1.25 net. Dutton.
Republic; tr. by H. Speers. '08(O17) 16°, (Best books ser.) leath., *$1 net. Dutton.
Republic of Plato: an ideal commonwealth; tr. by B: Jowett; with introd. by W: Cranston Lawton. '08(Je27) c. il. 8°, $1.75; hf. mor., $3.50. Lamb Pub.
Republic; tr. into Eng. by B: Jowett. 3d ed. vs. 1, 2. '08(D19) ea., $1; in 1 v. '09(Ap3) $2.50. Oxford Univ.

Plato and Xenophon.
Socratic discourses; tr. by F. N. Stawell and others; with introd. by F. N. Stawell. '10(N5) 16°, (Everyman's lib.) 35 c. net; leath., 70 c. net. Dutton.

PLATO.
Cavenagh, F. A. Ethical end of Plato's theory of ideas. 50 c. Oxford Univ.
Stewart, J: A. Plato's doctrine of ideas. $2. Oxford Univ.
Taylor, A. E: Plato. *50 c. net. Dodge.
Williams, M. V. Six essays on the Platonic theory of knowledge as expounded in the late dialogues and reviewed by Aristotle. *$1 net. Putnam.

Plato and Platonism. *See* Pater, Wa.

Platt, Horace G.
John Marshall, and other addresses. '08 (D) c. 282 p. O. $1.50. Argonaut.

PLATT, Orville Hitchcock.
Coolidge, L: A. Old-fashioned senator. $3 net. Putnam.

Platt, S., comp.
Stories from the Old Testament. '09 (Ag21) 16°, (Told through the ages ser.) $1.50. Dodge.

Platt, T: Collier.
Autobiography of Thomas Collier Platt; comp. and ed. by L: J. Lang, with addenda. '10(D17) c. il pors. 8°, $5; leath., $10 net. (1000 copies.) B. W. Dodge.

Platt, Ward.
The frontier. '08(D) 12+292 p. 12°, (Forward mission study course.) 50 c.; pap., 35 c. Young People's Miss.
—, ed. Methodism and the Republic; view of the home field, present conditions, needs and possibilities. '10(Jl16) il. pors. 12°, 50 c.; pap., 35 c. Bd. Home Miss.

Platters and pipkins. Krout, M. H. 75 c. net. McClurg.

PLAUTUS, Titus Maccius.
Mendelsohn, C: J. Studies in the word-play in Plautus. $1.25. Univ. of Penn.; [Appleton.]
The Trinummus; with introd. and notes by H. R. Fairclough. '09(O9) 12°, (Macmillan Latin classics.) *60 c. net. Macmillan.

PLAY.
See Children.

Play. Angell, E. D. $1.50 net. Little, B. & Co.
Play book ser. 12°, pap., 25 c. J. S. Ogilvie.
—La Croix. Lucky Jim.
Play box. '09(D) il. 50 c. Doran.
Play days. Hoyt, E., *ed.* †50 c. Wilde.
Playbox (The) annual for 1910. '10(O) il. 4°, bds., $1.25. Fenno.

Player, Preston.
Notes on hydro-electric developments. '08 (Ag8) c. D. *$1 net. McGraw.

Player's Ibsen. 16°, *75 c. net. J: W. Luce.
—Doll's house.
—Little Eyolf.

PLAYERS.
See Actors and actresses.

Players o' London. Chancellor, *Mrs.* L. B. *$1.75 net. B. W. Dodge.

PLAYGROUND BALL.
See Baseball.

Playground of Europe. Stephen, *Sir* L. *$1.75 net. Putnam.

PLAYGROUNDS.

American Academy of Political and Social Science. Public recreation facilities. $1.50; $1. Am. Acad. Pol. Sci.

American playgrounds. $2 net. Baker & T.

Blackmar, F. W. Playgrounds and parks. gratis. Univ. of Kan.

Hanmer, L. F. First steps in organizing playgrounds. pap., 10 c. Charities Pub.

Johnson, G: E. What to do at recess. 25 c. Ginn.

Leland, A. *and* L. H. Plans and specifications for playground construction and playground apparatus. 25 c. Bassette.

Leland, A. *and* L. H., *eds.* Playground technique and playcraft. v. 1. $2.50. Bassette.

Playhouse and the play. Mackaye, P. W. **$1.25 net. Macmillan.

Playing house in kindergarten. Ayres, M. M. 50 c. M. M. Ayres.

Playing the game. Weiman, R. $1.50. Cupples & L.

Playmate (The). Tulley, C: $1.50. Dutton.

Playmate Polly. Blanchard, A. E. $1. Jacobs.

PLAYS.

Adams, O. F. Motley jest. *$1 net. Sherman, F.

Æschylus. Plays. *$1 net. Macmillan.

Andreyev, L. N. Anathema; tragedy in 7 scenes. $1.25 net. Macmillan.

Aristophanes. Plays: metrical version. 50 c.; 75 c. Dutton.

Avellaneda, G. G. de. Baltasar: a biblical drama in verse. 65 c. Am. Bk.

Bagg, H. F. His model wife. 15 c.—Untangling Tony. 25 c. Penn Pub. Co.

Bangs, J: K. Real thing, and three other farces. $1. Harper.

Barney, L. C. God's heroes; drama. $3 net. Lippincott.

Bates, E. W. Engaging Janet. 15 c. Penn Pub. Co.

Beaumont, F., *and* Fletcher, J: Knight of the burning pestle. $2.50; $2. Holt.

Beaumont, F., *and* Fletcher, J: Works. In 12 v. v. 3. *$3.50 net. Macmillan.

Beaumont, F., *and* Fletcher, J: Works. In 10 v. v. 5. *$1.50 net. Putnam.

Bell, *Lady* F. E. O. Fairy tale plays and how to act them. $1.50. Longmans.

Benedix, R. J. Eigensinn. 15 c. Oxford Univ.

Bennett, E. A. What the public wants; a play. $1 net. Doran.

Benson, R. H. Cost of a crown. $1 net.—Mystery play in honour of the nativity of our Lord. 20 c.; 90 c. Longmans.

Berlage, H. J. Incognito: a Greek tragedy in four acts. (Add. author for price.) H. J. Berlage.

Besier, R. Don; a comedy. $1 net. Duffield.

Bessier, F. Miss Peackle. 15 c. Penn Pub. Co.

Bjornson, B. Lesson in marriage. 50 c. net. Brandu's.

Björnson, B. Sigurd Slembe; dramatic trilogy. $1.50 net. Sergel.

PLAYS.—*Continued.*

Blake, J. V. So like her father. (Not for sale.) J. V. Blake.

Block, L: J. World's triumph. **$1.25 net. Lippincott.

Bob O'Link, *pseud.* Outwitted. 15 c. Dick.

Booth, E. G. Sorrowful princess. $1. Longmans.

Boucicault, D. London assurance. 50 c.; 25 c. P. Roberts.

Brandreth, P. Plays and poems. $1. B'way Pub.

Brieux, E. Maternity: play in three acts. (Add. pub. for price.) B: R. Tucker.

Briscoe, M. S., *and others.* Harper's book of little plays. $1. Harper.

Browne, H. B., *comp.* Short plays from Dickens. *$1 net. Scribner.

Browning, R. Poems and plays, 1833-1844—1844-1864. ea., *$1 net. Dutton.

Calderon de la Barca, P. La vida es sveño. Univ. of Toronto.

Callaway, E. H. Widow's wiles: comedy. 25 c. Dick.

Cawein, M. J. Shadow garden, and other plays. $1.50 net. Putnam.

Chambers, C: H., Sir Anthony; comedy. 50 c. S: French.

Chapin, H. L. Adoption, and other sketches, poems and plays. $1.25. H. L. Chapin.

Chapman, G: Tragedies. $2 net. Dutton.

Chapman, J: J. Four plays for children. **$1 net.—Maid's forgiveness. **75 c. net.—Sausage from Bologna. *75 c. net. Moffat.

Checkhov, A. P. Cherry garden: comedy. 40 c. Yale Courant.

Child, C. G., *ed.* Second shepherds' play, Everyman, and other early plays. 40 c. Houghton M.

Clark, F. A. Jack the Giant Killer. 40 c. Ditson.

Clark, S: N. Delegates from Denver. 25 c. Dick.

Classic drama: plays by Greek, Spanish, French, German and English dramatists. 2 v. $3.50; $7. Lamb Pub.

Clifford, L. L. Plays; Hamilton's second marriage; Thomas and the princess; The modern way. $1.50. M. Kennerley.

Converse, F. Masque of sibyls. $1 net. Houghton M.

Corbin, A. Adam's dream, and two other miracle plays for children. 75 c. Scribner.

Corbin, J: Husband and The forbidden guests; two plays. $1.25 net. Houghton M.

Cram, R. A. Excalibur, an Arthurian drama. $2; $10. Badger.

Crane, E. M. Rainbow kimona. 25 c. Dick.

Craw, G: R. Roxana. 75 c. Sterling.

Cushing, C. C. S. Nathan Hale of '73. *$1 net. Yale Pub.

Dalkeith, L. Little plays. 50 c. Dutton.

Dalrymple, C. L. Mrs. Forrester's crusade.—Surprises. ea., 15 c. Dick.

PLAYS.—*Continued.*

Dargan, O. T. Lords and lovers and other dramas. **$1.50 net. Scribner.

D'Avenant, *Sir* W: Love and honor and The siege of Rhodes. 60 c. Heath.

Davies, H. H: Cousin Kate: comedy.—Mrs. Gorringe's necklace. ea., 50 c. W. H. Baker.

Dale, M. Miss Eagle: the suffragette. 50 c. Aberdeen.

Dargan, *Mrs.* O. T. Semiramis and other plays. *$1 net. Scribner.

Davis, A. Promised land. $1. Harvard Dramatic.

Deutsch, G. Israel Bruna: historical tragedy. $1.25. Badger.

Devereux, W: Henry of Navarre. 50 c. Knickerbocker Press.

Dick & Fitzgerald plays. 16 v. ea., 25 c. Dick.

Dix, B. M. Allison's lad, and other martial interludes; being six one-act dramas. **$1.35 net. Holt.

Dix, B. M. Rose o' Plymouth-town. $1.25. Dramatic.

Doyle, E: The count. $1.25. Badger.

Drummond, *Mrs.* S. K. W. Dante and Beatrice. **$1.25 net. Macmillan.

Dryden, J:, *and* Villiers, G:, *Duke* of Buckingham. Select dramas of John Dryden, with the rehearsal by G: Villiers, Duke of Buckingham. $2. Scott, F. & Co.

Du Maurier, G. L: B. Englishman's home. $1.25. Harper.

Dumont, F. Caught with the goods.—The district convention.—The half breed. ea., 15 c.—Girl from "L Triangle" Ranch. —The night riders.—The old New Hampshire home. ea., 25 c. Penn Pub. Co.

Dunning, R. C. Hyllus; drama. $1.25 net. Lane.

Dyar, R. E. Hicks at college. 25 c. Dramatic.

Earls, M. Chorister's Christmas eve. 25 c. Herder.

Eeden, F. W. v. Ysbrand; tragicomedy. 25 c. Lawrence Journ.

Esque, J. L: de. Flight of a soul. $1.50. Connoisseurs' Press.

Euripides. Plays. v. 2. *35 c. net; *70 c. net. Dutton.

Euripides; tr. into English rhyming verse by G: G. A. Murray. $2. Longmans.

Evans, F. C. Rose of Eden. 25 c. Penn Pub. Co.

Everyman: a morality play. *$1 net. M. Kennerley.

Everyman: a morality play. 10 c. Oxford Univ.

Everyman, and other mystery prayers. *35 c. net; *70 c. net. Dutton.

Fagan, J. B. The earth. $1 net. Duffield.

Felix, M. Our children. 50 c. Phœnix.

Ficke, A. D. Breaking of bonds. $1 net. Sherman, F.

Fitch, W: C. Beau Brummel. **$1.50 net. Lane.

Fitzpatrick, E. H. Magdalene of France. (Add. pubs. for price.) Sentinel Pub.

PLAYS.—*Continued.*

Fitzpatrick, F. W. Fall of Babylon; scenario of a spectacular drama. gratis. Shaw Bros.

Freytag, G. Die journalisten. 35 c. Holt.

Galsworthy, J: Justice; a tragedy. 60 c. net. Scribner.

Galsworthy, J: Plays: The silver fox; Joy; Strife. *$1.35 net. Putnam.

Gardner, M. D. House of rest. *$1 net. F. F. Sherman.

Gerstenberg, A. Little world. $1.25. Dramatic.

Gogol, N. V. Revizór. $1; 50 c. C. P. Franchot.

Goldsmith, O. Good-natured man.—She stoops to conquer. ea., $2.50 net. Putnam.

Gray, E. T. Winning of Fuji: Japanese play. 25 c. Dramatic.

Greene, R. Plays. *$1 net. Scribner.

Gregg, A. E. Quest of the Holy Grail. 25 c. F. L. Masseck.

Griffith, H. S. Help wanted. 15 c. Penn Pub. Co.

Gruse, E: Spirit of the woods. $1. B'way Pub.

Hagedorn, H., *jr.* Horse thieves; comedy in one act. 60 c. net.—Silver blade. *$1.10 net. Harvard Co-op.

Hale, H. G., *and* Hall, N. M., *comps.* Biblical dramas for use especially in young people's meetings and the evening services of the church. 12 v. ea., 15 c. Pilgrim Press.

Haney, J: L: Monsieur D' Or; dramatic fantasy. $1.20 net. Egerton Press.

Hardy, T: The dynasts. pt. 3. *$1.50 net. Macmillan.

Harper, J: M. Champlain: a drama. **$1.75 net. Lane.

Harris, F. H. Plays for young people. $1. Cassell.

Harris, *Mrs.* J. Y. Thoroughly tested. 25 c. J. Y. Harris.

Hauptmann, G. Fuhrmann Henshel; play in five acts. $1.25. Dramatic.

Hauptmann, G. Hennele. **$1 net. Doubleday, P.

Hawkins, A. H. Adventure of Lady Ursula; comedy in four acts.—Pilkerton's peerage. ea., 50 c. S: French.

Hawtrey, C: Private secretary. 25 c. S: French.

Higgins, A. C. Thekla. $1. Badger.

Hill, J. S. Ways of an aristocrat. (Add. author for price.) J. S. Hill.

Heminway, S: B., *ed.* English nativity plays. $2.50; $2. Holt.

Hoffmannstal, H. H. v. Electra. **$1.25 net. Brentano's.

Hooker, W: B. Two burglars. 25 c. Dick.

Housman, L. Chinese lantern. (Priv. pr.) Brentano's.

Ibsen, H. Coll. works. In 11 v. v. 1. Scribner.

Ibsen, H. Doll's house, Wild duck, Lady from the sea. 35 c. net; 70 c. net. Dutton.

Ibsen, H. Doll's house.—Little Eyolf. ea., *75 c. net. J: W. Luce.

PLAYS.—*Continued.*

Ibsen, H. John Gabriel Borkman.—Little Eyolf.—When we dead awaken. ea., $1. Duffield.

Ibsen, H. On the heights. 25 c. Univ. Extension Dept.

Irish, M., *and others.* Thirty new Christmas dialogues and plays. 30 c. Flanagan.

Jacobs, W: W., *and* Parker, L: N. Beauty and the barge; farce. 50 c. S: French.

James, G: P. R. Richelieu. *35 c. net; *70 c. net. Dutton.

Jasper, W. Susanna. (priv. pr.) Meyhew.

Johnson, A. S. Six short French plays. 50 c. Longmans.

Johnston, A. F. Rescue of Princess Winsome. 50 c.; 35 c. Winston.

Jones, H: A. Case of rebellious Susan. 75 c.; 50 c.—Dolly reforming herself; comedy.—The hypocrites. 75 c.; 50 c.—The masqueraders. 50 c. S: French.

Jonson, B. Complete plays. 2 v. ea., 35 c. net; 70 c. net. Dutton.

Kaenders, P. Lucius Flavus. *25 c. net. Herder.

Kellogg, E. Merry Xmas!; farce comedy. 50 c. U. P. James.

Kennedy, C: R. The winterfeast. $1.25. Harper.

Lasalle, F, J. G. Franz von Sickingen; tragedy in five acts. $1. N. Y. Labor News.

Ledoux, L: V. Yzdra: a tragedy. **$1.25 net. Putnam.

Lee, S. L., *ed.* Play of King Leir and his three daughters. *$1 net; *$1.60 net; *$1.70 net. Duffield.

Le Gallienne, R: Orestes; tragedy. $1 net. M. Kennerley.

Levi, R. King's choice; Purim sketch. 15 c. Bloch.

Little plays and exercises. 35 c. F. A. Owen.

Lodge, G: C. Herakles. **$1.25 net. Houghton M.

London, J. Theft; play. $1.25 net. Macmillan.

Long, M. B. New commandment: comedy. 75 c. M. B. Long.

McCutcheon, G: B. Brood house; play. $5. G: B. McCutcheon.

McFadden, E. A., *and* Davis, L. E., *comp.* Sel. list of plays for amateurs and students. $2. McFadden.

Mackay, C. D. House of the heart, and other plays for children.—Silver thread, and other folk plays. ea., $1.10 net. Holt.

Mackaye, P. W. Anti-matrimony; satirical comedy. $1.25 net. Stokes.

Mackaye, P. W. Garland to Sylvia: dramatic reverie.—Mater.—The scarecrow; or, the glass of truth. ea., **$1.25 net. Macmillan.

McKnight, L. A. Indiana: drama. 50 c. L. A. McKnight.

Madach, I. Tragedy of man: dramatic poem. *$1.50 net. Arcadia.

Maeterlinck, M. Blue bird; fairy play. **$1.20 net; $2 net.—Mary Magdalene; a play. $1.20 net. Dodd.

PLAYS.—*Continued.*

Maeterlinck, M. Pélléas and Mélisande. **$1.50, boxed. Crowell.

Maeterlinck, M. Plays. 1st and 2d ser. ea., $1.25. Duffield.

Magill, H. B. Time, the place and the girl. 25 c. Yellowstone.

Maguire, E. M. Story plays for little ones. 50 c. Educ. Pub.

Marble, T. L. The Hessian. 15 c. Penn Pub. Co.

March, G: O., *comp.* School plays for festive days. 30 c. March.

Marlowe, C. Dr. Faustus. 40 c.; 75 c. Oxford Univ.

Marlowe, C. Plays and poems. *35 c. net; *70 c. net. Dutton.

Marlowe, C. Tragical history of Dr. Faustus. 45 c. Sturgis & W.

Martin, W: F. Sir Henry Vane. $1.25. Roxburgh.

Marvel, T: L. Giuseppina. 25 c. Dramatic.

Masefield, J. Tragedy of Nan. $1 net. M. Kennerley.

Menander, *of Athens.* Four plays: The hero, Epitrepontes, Periceiromene and Samia. $2.50. Ginn.

Merington, M. Holiday plays; 5 one-act pieces.—Vicar of Wakefield; play founded on Oliver Goldsmith's novel. ea., $1.25. Duffield.

Meyers, R. C. V. Cousin Tom. 25 c. Penn Pub. Co.

Middleton, T:, *and* Rowley, W: Spanish gipsie, and All's lost by lust. 60 c. Heath.

Mitchell, E. Her sacrifice. 50 c. Grafton Pub.

Mitchell, L. E. New York idea. 50 c. W. H. Baker.

Molière, J. B. P. de. Eight plays. 2 v. *$5 net. Putnam.

Molière, J. B. P. de. L'avare. 50 c. Wahr.

Molnar, F. The devil: (Fiske version.) *50 c. net; *25 c. net. J. S. Ogilvie.

Molnar, F. The devil: (Savage version.) *$1 net. M. Kennerley.

Montenegro, C. Alcestis. $1.25. Badger.

Moody, W: V. Faith healer.—Great Divide. ea., **$1.25 net. Macmillan.

Moore Smith, G: C. Hymenæus: comedy *$1.10 net. Putnam.

Morris, E. B. Man next door. 15 c. Penn Pub. Co.

Munn, *Mrs.* M. C. Will Shakespeare of Stratford and London; drama. $1.20 net. Dodd.

Myers, L. H. Arvat: dramatic poem. *$1.25 net. Longmans.

Neal, W. H. Before the war. 15 c. Penn Pub. Co.

Nida, A. Doktor Kritikus. $1. A. Nida.

Nirdlinger, C: F. World and his wife. $1. M. Kennerley.

North, L. White flame. $1. Golden Press.

Noyes, *Mrs.* M. I. O., *and* Ray, B. H. Little plays for little people. 25 c. Ginn.

O'Brien, W: L. Aaron Burr. (Add. pubs. for price.) Review Pub. Co.

PLAYS.—*Continued.*

Omar and the Rabbi: Fitzgerald's translation of the Rubáiyát of Omar Khayyâm, and Browning's Rabbi Ben Ezra. *25 c. net. Harvard Co-op.

Oppenheim, J. The pioneers; poetic drama. 50 c. net. B: W. Huebsch.

Ostrovsky, A. The storm. $1 net. J: W. Luce.

Otway, T: The orphan and Venice preserved. *60 c. net. Heath.

Peabody, J. P. Fortune and men's eyes. $1.25.—The piper. *$1.10 net. Houghton M.

Pellissier, G., comp. Anthologie du théatre français contemporain (prose et verse). $1.25. Lemcke.

Penn Publishing Co. plays. 18 v. Penn Pub. Co.

Phillips, D: G. Worth of a woman [and] A point of law. **$1.25 net. Appleton.

Phillips, S. Pietro of Siena; a drama. $1 net. Macmillan.

Phillips, S., *and* Carr, J. W: C. Faust. **$1.25 net. Macmillan.

Pinero, A. W. Mid-channel.—The thunderbolt. ea., 50 c. W. H. Baker.

Porter, H. Edward Garrett, a story of Mars; [drama in blank verse.] $1.25. Lincoln Pub. Co.

Raymond, G: L. The suffragettes. (Add. pubs. for price.) B. S. Adams.

Rees, A. D. Give up your gods. **$1 net. Lippincott.

Rees, A. D. Give up your gods. **$1 net. —William Tell. (Priv. pr.) Lippincott.

Rees, W: G. Mayor of Romanstown; drama in three acts. 75 c. Cochrane.

Rice, C. Y. Yolanda of Cyprus. **$1.25 net. McClure.

Rojas, F. de. The Celestina. [In Spanish.] (Add. pubs. for price.) Hispanic Soc.

Rollow, J. S. Trend. (Add. pub. for price.) Guide Pr. and Pub.

Rosenfeld, S. Children of destiny; in four acts. 50 c. G: W. Dillingham.

Ross, C. Lady of the Blackfriars. $2 net. C. Ross.

Rostand, E. Chantecler. $1.20 net. Duffield.

Rostand, E. Chantecler [in French]. $1; $1.75. Lemcke.

Sanders, H. F. Petalesharoo and The Star brave; poetic dramas. $1.50; 50 c. H. F. Sanders.

Sardou, V., *and* Najac, E. de. Divorcons. $1.25. Dramatic.

Sauter, E. Death of Gracchus. (Not for sale.) E. Sauter.

Schmidt, E. Wie man sich bildet. 15 c. Oxford Univ.

Schütze, M. Hero and Leander.—Judith; tragedy. ea., **$1.25 net. Holt.

Shaw, G: B. Admirable Bashville. *50 c. net. Brentano's.

Sheldon, E: "The nigger"; American play. $1.25 net. Macmillan.

Shelland, H: E. Fun in the school-room. 15 c. Dick.

Sheridan, R: B. B. The critic. 50 c.; 25 c. Tuttle, M. & T.

PLAYS.—*Continued.*

Sheridan, R: B. B. Plays. *$1 net. Dutton.

Sheridan, R: B. B. The rivals. 25 c. Houghton M.

Smith, G. C. M., *ed.* Laelia; a comedy. $1.10 net. Putnam.

Sophocles. Electra. *$1.10 net. Putnam.

Sophocles. Tragedies. 50 c.; 75 c. Dutton.

Spofford, *Mrs.* H. E. P. Fairy changeling. $1 net. Badger.

Stein, J. J. It's great to be crazy. 15 c. Penn Pub. Co.

Stevenson, A. Children's classics in dramatic form. Bk. 2. **35 c. net. Houghton M.

Strindberg, J. A. The father. *$1 net. J: W. Luce.

Strindberg, J. A. Swanwhite: fairy drama. $1. Brown Bros.

Sudermann, H. John the Baptist. *$1.50 net. Lane.

Sudermann, H. Morituri; three one act plays.—Roses; four one-act plays. ea., **$1.25 net. Scribner.

Sutro, A. John Glayde's honor. 50 c. S: French.

Swinburne, A. C: Dramas. **$1.50 net. Crowell.

Swinburne, A. C: Duke of Gandia. **$1.25 net. Harper.

Thompson, A. C. Her scarlet slippers.—Miss Susan's fortune. ea., 15 c. Penn Pub. Co.

Thompson, C. Awakening of Helena Ritchie. (Add. pub. for price.) Kauser.

Tiffany, E. B. The tocsin; drama of the renaissance. *$2 net. P. Elder.

Timayenis, T. T: Hevor, the Gaul. 50 c. T. T: Timayenis.

Townsend, C: Isabel, the pearl of Cuba. 25 c. Dick.

Trask, *Mrs.* K. N. King Alfred's jewel. *$1.25 net. Lane.

Travis, J: C. Simple life. (priv. pr.) J: C. Travis.

Trevelyan, R. C. Sisyphus: operatic tale. *$1.50 net. Longmans.

Van Dyke, H: J. House of Rimmon. **$1 net. Scribner.

Virgil, M. P. Two dramatizations: 1, Dido; 2, The fall of Troy. *$1 net. Univ. of Chic.

Wall, W. C. Mock trial for amateurs. $1. W. C. Wall.

Ward, R. Fucus histriomastix; comedy $1.10 net. Putnam.

Warren, M. J. Twig of thorn; Irish fairy play in two acts. W. H. Baker.

Webster, J: Duchess of Malfi. 45 c. Sturgis & W.

Wedekind, F. Awakening of spring; a tragedy of childhood. *$1.25 net. Brown Bros.

Whitney, A. C. Pontiac; drama of old Detroit. $1.50. Badger.

Wilde, O. Florentine tragedy. *$1.25 net. J: W. Luce.

Wilde, O. Salomé. $1 net; $2.50 net. T: B. Mosher.

Wills, A. E. Matinée idol. 15 c. Dick.

PLAYS.—*Continued.*
Wilson, C. N. Through the buhrs. $1.50. C. M. Clark.
World and his wife. *$1 net. M. Kennerley.
Wyatt, F., *and* Morris, W: Mrs. Temple's telegram. (Add. pubs. for price.) S. French.
Wyeth, A. H. Pa's picnic; in two scenes. 25 c. Dramatic.
Yeats, W: B. Land of hearts' desire. *$1.50 net. T: B. Mosher.
Yeats, W: B., *and* Gregory, *Lady* A. Unicorn from the stars. *$1.50 net. Macmillan.
Young, O. E. Little red mare. 15 c. Dick.
Zamacoïs, M. The jesters. **$1 net. Brentano's.
Zangwill, I. The melting-pot. $1.25. Macmillan.
See also Actors and actresses; — Dialogues; — Drama and dramatists; — Entertainments; — Games; — Monologues; — Oberammergau, Germany;—Pantomime; — Recitations;—Theatre:— —*also* plays in foreign languages;—*also* Dick & Fitzgerald's plays;—Shakespeare, W.

Plays, acting and music. Symons, A. **$2 net. Dutton.

Plays and games for indoors and out. Parsons, B. R. $1.50. Barnes.

Plays in the market-place. Burr, A. J. $3. Hillside.

Plays of to-day and to-morrow. por. D. $1 net. Duffield.
—Besier. Don; comedy.
—Fagan. The earth.

Playtime ser. il. D. Little, B. & Co.
—Murray, *comp.* Story Land. 50 c.

Playtime ser. of toy books. **il. Q bds., 40 c.; pap., 25 c.** Warne
—Around the farm.
—Old friends.
—Sleeping beauty.

Plaza ser. [masterpieces by the world's great authors]. 15 v. [1910.] (D) 12°, limp bds., ea., $1.50. Barse & H.

Plea for the home treatment and prevention of scarlet fever. Milne, R. $1 net. Wood.

Plea for the old faith of the old church. Danner, T: J. 25 c. T. J. Danner.

Plea for voluntaryism. *See* Herbert, Auberon. Voluntaryist creed.

Plea of the negro soldier. White, C: F. $1.25. C: F. White.

PLEADING AND PRACTICE.
Bates, C. Pleading, practice, and forms under the code. 3 v. per set, $18. W. H. Anderson.
Bradbury, H. B. Forms of pleading in legal and equitable actions adapted to codes of procedure. In 2 v. $13. Banks.
Foster, R. Treatise on federal practice, civil and criminal. In 3 v. v. 1. $6.50; per set, $19.50. Callaghan.
Gould, J. Treatise on the principles of pleading. $6.50. Banks & Co.
Hogg, C: E. Pleading and form. $6. Clarke.
Keigwin, C: A. Precedents of pleading at common law. $5. Byrne.

PLEADING AND PRACTICE.—*Continued.*
McKinney, W: M., *comp.* Supplement to Encyclopædia of pleading and practice. v. 4. $6. E: Thompson.
Morison, J. H. S. Rules of pleading as adapt. to cts. of law in Tennessee, together with numerous annot. forms. $5.50. F. H. Thomas.
Nichols, C. A. Treatise on pleading and practice. $5. Keefe-D.
Sutherland, W: A. Treatise on code pleading and practice. In 4 v. ea., $6.50. Bancroft-W.
United States Commissioners' manual of practice. $2. W. H. Anderson.
Wellman, F. L. Day in court; art of great advocates. **$2 net. Macmillan.
***See also* Actions at law;—Courts;—Forms (*in law*); — Law; — Negligence; — Trials;—*also* names of states.**

Pleasant day diversions. Wells, C. **$1 net. Moffat.

Pleasant land of France. *See* Prothero, R. E.

Pleasant thought year book. Du Bois, M. R. J., *comp.* **$1 net. Holt.

Pleasants, H:
Hist. of the Old Eagle School, Tredyffrin, in Chester County, Pa., with alphabetical lists of interments in the graveyard and of German settlers in Chester County, and a poem presenting the suggestive features of the place. '10(Je4) c. il. facsim., 8°, $2. Winston.

Pleasants, Mary Minta.
Which one?, and other ante bellum days. '10(Ag13) c. il. 12°, $1. Earle.

Pleasure and problem in South Africa. Harmsworth, C. B. *$1.50 net. Lane.

Pleasure and progress. *See* Lorentz, A. M. Individual sovereignty.

Pleasure of reading. Scott, T. *$1.25 net. M. Kennerley.

Pleasure of reading the Bible. Scott, T. 50 c.; $1. M. Kennerley.

Pleasures of sin. Talbert, D. H. $1. D. H. Talbert.

Plehn, Carl Copping.
Introduction to public finance. 3d ed., completely rev. and enl. '09(O16) c. D. **$1.75 net. Macmillan.
San Francisco clearing house certificates of 1907-1908. '09(N) c. '08. 14 p. front. tabs., O. (Publications of the Academy of Pacific Coast Hist.) pap., 10 c. Univ. of Cal.

Pleistocene geology of the Leadville quadrangle. United States. *Dept. of the Interior. U. S. Geolog. Survey.* 30 c.

Pleroma (The). Carus, P. $1. Open Court.

Pleydell, A. C. and Robb, W., Spence, F. S., and others.
Municipal taxation: address before the League of American Municipalities, Montreal, 1909, by A. C. Pleydell; [and] Canadian systems of local taxation: extracts from addresses by W. Robb, F. S. Spence, Theo. A. Hunt, [and others.] '09(D18) c. O. pap., 10 c. Tax Reform.

Plimmer, Rob. H: Aders.
Chemical constitution of the proteins. In 2 pts. '08(D19) O. (Monographs on biochemistry.) bds., pt. 1, *$1 net; pt. 2, *80 c. net. Longmans.
Pract. physiological chemistry. '10(N5) c. col. il. O. $1.80 net. Longmans.

PLIMPTON (GEORGE ARTHUR) LIBRARY.
See Arithmetic.

Plimpton Press. Specimen pages of printing types from the Plimpton Press. '08(N) c. 114 p. front. 12°. (Not for sale.) Plimpton.

PLOTINUS.
Guthrie, K. S. Philosophy of Plotinos. $1. Prophet Pub.
Guthrie, K. S. Plotinus, his life, times and philosophy. 50 c. Open Court.
Overstreet, H. A. Dialectic of Plotinus. 25 c. Univ. of Cal.

Plotting of Frances Ware. Locke, J. †$1.50. Moffat.

Plough and the cross. O'Ryan, W: P. $1. Aryan.

PLOWING.
United States. *Dept. of Agriculture. Bu. of Plant Industry.* Traction plowing.

Plumbe, G: E:
Chicago; its natural advantages as an industrial and commercial center and market. '10(Je) 71 p. il. maps, plan, 8°, 15 c. Chic. Assoc. Commerce.

PLUMBING.
Ainge, T: S. Sanitary sewerage of buildings. $1.50. Domestic Engineering.
Allen, J: K., *ed.* Hot water for domestic use.—Roughing-in house drains. ea., 50 c. Domestic Engineering.
American School of Correspondence. Cyclopedia of heating, plumbing and sanitation. $12. Am. Sch. Corr.
Ball, C: B., *and* Sherriff, H. T. Plumbing catechism. $1. Domestic Engineering.
Bean, B. C. Making the business pay: [plumbing.] $1. Domestic Engineering.
Bjorling, P. R. Pipes and tubes. *$1.25 net. Macmillan.
Cosgrove, J: J. Plumbing estimates and contracts.—Plumbing plans and specifications. ea., $3.—Wrought-pipe drainage systems. $2. Standard Sanitary Mfg.
Gray, W: B., *and* Ball, C: B. Plumbing. $1.50. Am. Sch. Corr.
Massachusetts Association of Plumbing Inspectors. Official hdbk., 1910. Mass. Assoc. Plumbing.
Richey, H. G. Building mechanics' ready reference. Plumbers', steam-fitters' and tinners' ed. **$1.50 net. Wiley.
Ryan, G: W. Bookkeeping for the plumber. 25 c. Standard Sanitary Mfg.
Starbuck, R. M. Mechanical drawing for plumbers. $1.50.—Modern plumbing. $4. —Standard pract. plumbing. $3. Henley.
Starbuck, R. M. Questions and answers on the practice and theory of sanitary plumbing. 2 v. ea., $1. R. M. Starbuck.
Tower, F. W. Plumbers' manual and textbook. $1. F. W. Tower.
See also Metal work;—Sanitary engineering.
See also Pipes and piping.

Plummer, Alfr., D.D.
Exegetical commentary on the Gospel according to St. Matthew. '09(D11) O. *$3 net. Scribner.

Plummer, C:
Vitae sanctorum Hiberniae; partim hactenus ineditae ad fidem codicum manuscriptorum recognovit prolegomenis notis indicibus instruxit. In 2 v. '10(My14) O. $9.75. Oxford Univ.

Plummer, Mary Wright.
Roy and Ray in Canada. '08(O10) c. il. map, O. **$1.75 net. Holt.
—, **comp.** Stories from the Chronicles of the Cid. '10(D3) il. D. 90 c. net. Holt.

Plunket, Ierne L.
Fall of the old order: a textbook of European history, 1763-1815. '09(S11) maps, D. $1.10. Oxford Univ.

Plunkett, Sir Horace Curzon.
Ireland in the new century. New and popular ed., rev. '08(Mr21) 8°, *40 c. net. Dutton.
Rural life problems of the United States; notes of an Irish observer. '10(Je11) c. D. $1.25 net. Macmillan.

"Plupy." Shute, H: A: $1.50. Badger.

Pluralistic universe. James, W: **$1.50 net. Longmans.

Plus (Les) jolis contes de fées. Lazare, J., ed. 35 c. Ginn.

Plutarch [Lat. Plutarchus.]
Complete works. 6 v. '09(My22) c. il. 8°, $7.50. Crowell.
Works. De luxe ed. 6 v. '10(D) $18. Crowell.
Children's Plutarch; tales of the Greeks; by F. J. Gould; with introd. by W: D. Howells: Plutarch's lives told in simple language with a special topical index; il. by Wa. Crane. '10(Jl30) c. D. 75 c. Harper.
Children's Plutarch, tales of the Romans; tr. by F. J. Gould; with introd. by W: D. Howells: Plutarch's lives told in simple language with a special topical index; il. by Wa. Crane. '10(Jl30) c. D. 75 c. Harper.
Cimon and Pericles, with the funeral oration of Pericles (Thucydides II., 35-46); newly tr., with introd. and notes, by Bernadotte Perrin. '10(D10) c. front. O. $2 net. Scribner.
Lives. 2 v. '10(D) il. $2.50, boxed. Crowell.
Lives; ed. by Arth. H. Clough. In 3 v. '10(Ap23) 16°, (Everyman's lib.) ea., 35 c. net; leath., 70 c. net. Dutton.
Lives of illustrious men; John Dryden's translation corrected from the Greek and rev. and annot. by Arth. Hugh Clough; introd. by Hamilton Wright Mabie. 4 v. '08, [1909.] (Mr) c. 12°, (Ideal classics.) $5. Winston.
Shakespeare's Plutarch; ed. by C. F. Tucker Brooke. In 2 v. '09(D4) facsims., S. (Shakespeare lib.; ed. by I. Gollancz: Shakespeare classics.) ea., bds., *$1 net; Persian, *$1.60 net; Lib. ed., *$1.70 net. Duffield.

PLYMOUTH, Mass.
Bradford, W: Hist. of the Plymouth Settlement, 1608-1650. *$1.50 net. J: McBride.
Burbank, A. S. Guide to historic Plymouth. 10 c. A. S. Burbank.

PLYMOUTH BRETHREN.
Church of the Brethren. Two centuries of the Church of the Brethren. $1.50; $2.50. Brethren Pub. Ho.
Heckewelder, J: G. E. Narrative of the mission of the United Brethren among the Delaware and Mohegan Indians. *$30 net. Burrows.
Ziegler, D. H. History of the Brethren in Virginia. $1.50. Brethren Pub. Ho.

PLYMOUTH COUNTY, Mass.
Kinnicutt, L. N. Indian names of places in Plymouth, Middleborough, Lakeville and Carver, Plymouth County, Massachusetts. $2. N. J. Bartlett.

PLYMOUTH PLANTATION.
See Massachusetts.

Plympton, G: Washington.
Aneroid barometer, its construction and use. 11th ed., rev. and enl. '09, [1910.] 126 p. il. tabs., 16°, (Van Nostrand's science ser.) 50 c. Van Nostrand.

PNEUMATIC-TUBE SERVICE.
See Post-office.

PNEUMATICS.
See Compressed air;—Gases.

Pocket American and English classics. See Macmillan's.

Pocket Bible; or, Christian the printer. Sue, M. J. E. $2. N. Y. Labor News.

Pocket-book of useful formulæ. Molesworth, *Sir* G. L. $2. Spon.

Pocket classics. See Macmillan's.

Pocket dictionary ser. 32°, 50 c. Dutton.
—Wesseley *and* Allen. Spanish-English dictionary.
—Wesseley *and* Gray. Italian-English dictionary.—Spanish-English dictionary.

Pocket Kipling. See Kipling, Rudyard.

Pocket optical dictionary. Lewis, J. J: $1.25. J. J: Lewis.

Pocket-railroad dict. and vade mecum. Colvin, F. H. $1. Henley.

Pocket reference lib. 5 v. '10(D) 16°, 25 c.; leath., 35 c. Cassell.
Contents: English dict; Pocket doctor; Proverbs and maxims; Mythology; Poetical quotations.

Pocket therapeutics. Stewart, M. $1 net. Saunders.

Pocket tokens. Wagar, V. W. $1. Badger.

Pocketbook of refrigeration and ice making. Wallis-Taylor, A. J. $1.50. Henley.

Pocketful of limericks. Lyon, R. A., *comp.* 50 c. Mayhew.

Podmore, Fk.
Mesmerism and Christian Science: a short history of mental healing. '09(S18) O. *$1.50 net. Jacobs.
Naturalization of the supernatural. '08 (Ag15) c. O. **$2 net. Putnam.
Telepathic hallucinations. '10(Mr26) il. D. (Twentieth century science ser.) *50 c. net. Stokes.

Poe, Edg. Allan.
Complete works; with memoir, critical introds., notes and variorum texts, by Edm. Clarence Stedman and G: E: Woodberry. In 10 v. '08(D5) pors. facsims., per set, *$15 net, boxed; hf. leath., *$40 net, boxed. Duffield.
Complete poetical works; with three essays on poetry; ed., with memoir, notes and bibliography, by R. Brimley Johnson. '09 (My15) por. 12°, *75 c. net. Oxford Univ.
Complete works; with biography and introd. by Nathan Haskell Dole. [Centenary ed.] In 10 v. '08(D26) c. il. pors. 8°, $18; ¾ Persian mor., $30. Werner.
Works. [Raven ed.] '08(O10) 5 v., front. 8°, $3.75. Collier.
Works. De luxe ed. 11 v. '10(N) il. levant, $33. Crowell.
Works. 6 v. New imperial lib. ed. '10 (D) il. 8°, ea., $1.25; hf. cf., $2.25. New il. sterling ed., ea., $1. (Sets only.) Estes.
Works. In 8 v. Centenary ed. '09 (Ja9) hf. leath., per set, $12. (Sold by sub. only.) Lippincott.
Works; with introds., recollections of Poe, by R: H: Stoddard; biography, contemporary estimates, by Lowell and Willis; notes. India paper ed. 4 v. [in 2 v.] '08(D5) c. il. 24°, flex. mor., per set, *$1.75 net. Newold.
Complete poems. Centennial ed.; with a critical introd. by C: F. Richardson. '08 (S5) c. il. por. O. **$1.75 net; leath., **$3 net; cf., **$3.50 net. Putnam.
Edgar Allan Poe; centenary tribute, by W: P. Trent, Oliver Huckel, J: Prentiss Poe, Lizette Woodworth Reese and Mrs. J: C. Wrenshall; ed. by Heinrich Ewald Buchholz. '10(S3) c. il. pors. 12°, $2.50. E. A. Poe Memorial.
Last letters of Edgar Allan Poe to Sarah Helen Whitman; ed. by Ja. A. Harrison; in commemoration of the hundredth anniversary of Poe's birth, Jan. 19, 1909; published under the auspices of the University of Virginia. '09(F27) c. O. **$2.50 net. Putnam.
Material by and about Edgar Allan Poe to be found in the library of Columbia University; prepared by Clara W. Bragg. '09(Mr13) S. pap. (Add. University for price.) Columbia Univ.
The raven; prefaced by The philosophy of composition. '08(D12) bds., *$6 net, boxed; Fordham ed., suede, *$10 net, boxed. P. Elder.
The raven. [1910.] (My) il. 12°, (Neill gift book ser.) $1.25, boxed. Reilly & B.
Selected tales of mystery; il. in colour by Byam Shaw. '09(N20) O. *$3 net, boxed. Lippincott.
Selections from critical writings; ed., with introd. and notes, by F. C. Prescott. '09 (O30) c. S. (English readings.) **75 c. net. Holt.
Stories by Poe. '08(Ag15) 16°, (World's story-tellers' ser. *40 c. net. Dutton.

Poe, Edg. Allan.—*Continued.*
Tales. Centenary ed. '09(D) col. il. 8°, *$2.50 net. Duffield.
Tales. [Centennial ed.] '09(O2) c. il. O. †$1.50; leath., †$2.50. Putnam.
Tales of mystery and imagination. '08 (O10) il. D. (Bowman's illustrated lib. of world-favorite books.) $1. Bowman.
Tales of mystery and imagination. '08 (S19) 16°, (Everyman's lib.) *35 c. net; leath., *70 c. net. Dutton.
Tales of the grotesque and arabesque; with other stories. '09(My15) por. S. (Caxton thin paper classics.) limp lambskin, *$1.25 net. Scribner.
See also Good stories;—*also* Coleridge, S: Taylor.

—, Longfellow, H: Wadsworth, and Whittier, J: Greenleaf.
The raven, by Edg. Allan Poe; The courtship of Miles Standish, by H: Wadsworth Longfellow; Snowbound, by J: Greenleaf Whittier; ed., with an introd. and notes, by C: Robert Gaston. [1910.] (Mr) c. 196 p. il. pors. 16°, (Merrill's English texts.) 25 c. C: E. Merrill.
Three American poems: The raven, Edg. Allan Poe; The courtship of Miles Standish, H: Wadsworth Longfellow; Snow-bound, J: Greenleaf Whittier; ed. for school use by Garland Greever. '10 (My21) c. S. (Lake English classics.) 25 c. Scott, F. & Co.

POE, Edgar Allan.
Didier, E. L. Poe cult and other Poe papers. $1.50. B'way Pub.
Hazelton, G: C., *jr.* Raven: the love story of Edgar Allan Poe. †$1.50. Appleton.
Kent, C: W:, *and* Patton, J: S., *eds.* Book of the Poe centenary. $1. J: S. Patton.
Macy, J: A. Edgar Allan Poe. **50 c. net. Small.
Ransome, A. Edgar Allan Poe. $2.50 net. M. Kennerley.
Stanard, *Mrs.* M. M. P. N. The dreamer: romantic rendering of the life story of Edgar Allan Poe. *$1.50 net. Bell Bk.
Stedman, E. C. Edgar Allan Poe. $2.50. Torch Press.
Stewart, R. A. Case of Edgar Allan Poe. 25 c. R. A. Stewart.
Woodberry, G: E: Life of Edgar Allan Poe. 2 v. **$5 net; **$7 net. Houghton M.

Poe, Clarence H.
Southerner in Europe. '09(F) 75 c. Mutual Pub. Co.

Poebel, Arno.
Babylonian legal and business documents from the time of the 1st dynasty of Babylon, chiefly from Nippur. '09(Jl17) il. (Babylonian expedition of the Univ. of Penn.) pap., $6. Univ. of Penn.

Poem of the Cid. *See* Cid.
Poem of the olden time. Storrow, A. G. (Priv. pr.) Rosemary.
Poem outlines. Lanier, S. **$1 net. Scribner.
Poemes Napoléoniens. Auzas, A., *ed.* *25 c. net. Crowell.
POEMS.
See Poetry.

Poems and essays for the workers. Robb, D: B. 30 c. D: B. Robb.
Poems by the way. Morris, W: 75 c. net; $1 net. Longmans.
Poems dear to the heart. Pitt, S. W. $1.50. S. W. Pitt.
Poems for travelers. Du Bois, M. R. J., *comp.* **$1.50 net. Holt.
Poems from *Punch.* Burnand, *Sir* F. C., *ed.* 40 c.; 75 c.; $1.25. Caldwell.
Poems, in memoriam. Strong, L. C. [priv. pr.] Riverside Press.
Poems of belief. Williams, T. C. $1 net. Houghton M.
Poems of inspiration. Copeland, C: F. $1.50. Union Bk.
Poems of life. Wilkins, T. $1; $1.50. T. Wilkins.
Poems of New England. *See* Longfellow, H: Wadsworth, *ed.*
Poems of personality. 2d ser. Robbins, R. C. (Not for sale.) Riverside Press.
Poems of progress. Wilcox, *Mrs.* E. W. $1.25. Conkey.
Poems of soldier, sailor and civilian life. Stanyan, J: M. $1. E: M. Stanyan.
Poems of the nineteenth century. Fletcher, J. W. 50 c. J. W. Fletcher.
Poems of truth, love and power. Popham, W: L. $1. B'way Pub.
Poems that every child should know. Burt, M. E., *ed.* 3 v. $1.50. Doubleday, P.
Poems that heal the sick. Cole, W. V. 75 c.; $2. Universal-Good.
Poems written on the journey from sense to soul. Stetson, A. E. $2. A. E. Stetson.
Poésies diverses. *See* Furetière, Antoine.
Poésies et nouvelles. Shoenfeld, *Mrs.* G. 50 c. G. Shoenfeld.
Poet and other animals. Richardson, H. $2. Dutton.
Poet in exile. Hay, J: $5. Houghton M.
Poet of Galilee. Leonard, W: E. C. *$1 net. B: W. Huebsch.
Poetic classics. 15 v. [1910.] (D) nar. 16°, vel., 30 c.; leath., 75 c. net. Jacobs.
Poetic new-world. Humphrey, L. H., *comp.* $1.50 net; $2.50 net. Holt.
Poetic old-world. Humphrey, L. H., *comp.* **$1.50 net; **$2.50 net. Holt.
Poetic plural of Greek tragedy in the light of Homeric usage. Jones, H. L. 80 c. Longmans.
Poetical and prose quotations. Ward, A. L., *comp.* 2 v. $2.50. Crowell.
Poetische auslese. Andriessen, H. 50 c. H. Andriessen.

POETRY.
Alden, R. M. Introduction to poetry. $1.25. Holt.
Aristotle. On the art of poetry. $5.25. Oxford Univ.
Association of Collegiate Alumnæ. *Washington Branch, comp.* List of poems chosen from standard English poets, suitable to be learned by children between the ages of five and fourteen. 25 c. L. Madeira.
Austin, A. Bridling of Pegasus; prose papers on poetry. $2.40 net. Macmillan.

POETRY.—*Continued.*

Baker, E. A., *ed.* Praise of a simple life. *$1 net. Dutton.

Baldwin, E: C., *and* Paul, H. G. English poems. $1. Am. Bk.

Bang, O., *ed.* Good-luck book. $1. Brandu's.

Barbe, W. Famous poems explained. $1. Hinds.

Bradley, A. C. Oxford lectures on poetry. *$3 net. Macmillan.

Braithwaite, W: S., *comp.* Book of Georgian verse. **$2 net; **$3.50 net. Brentano's.

Braithwaite, W: S., *ed.* Book of Restoration verse. *$2 net; *$3 net. Brentano's.

Brett, G. S., *comp.* Representative English poems. *75 c. net. Macmillan.

Bronson, W. C., *comp. and ed.* English poems. [In 4 v. v. 1-3.] ea., *$1.50 net; *$1 net. Univ. of Chic.

Burt, M. E., *ed.* Poems that every child should know. 3 v. $1.50. Doubleday, P.

Capps-Oliver, M., *comp.* Round the year with the poets. $1.50; $3. Caldwell.

Clarke, H. A. Ancient myths and modern poets. $2 net. Baker & T.

Coates, H: T., *comp.* Fireside encyclopedia of poetry. $2-$7.50. Winston.

Copeland, C: T., *and* Rideout, H: M., *eds.*

Courthope, W: J: Hist. of English poetry. In 6 v. v. 5, 6. ea., $3.25 net. Macmillan.

Day with the poets ser. 6 v. ea., 50 c. Doran.

Dixon, W: M., *and* Grierson, H. J: C., *comps.* English Parnassus. $1.50. Oxford Univ.

Du Bois, M. R. J., *comp.* Poems for travelers. **$1.50 net. Holt.

Early English lyrics. 10 c. Oxford Univ.

Fletcher, J. W. Poems of the nineteenth century. 50 c. J. W. Fletcher.

French, D. G. Points about poetry. 60 c. Editor Co.

Fuess, C. M., *and* Sanborn, H. N., *eds.* English narrative poems. *25 c. net. Macmillan.

Hart, W. M. Ballad and epic: study in the development of the narrative art. $2.50. Ginn.

Hazlitt, W: Lectures on English poets, and the spirit of the age. 35 c. net; 70 c. net. Dutton.

Hoe, R. Catalogue of books of emblems. (Priv. pr.) R. Hoe.

Holliday, C., *comp.* Three centuries of southern poetry. *$1 net. Pub. Ho. of M. E. Ch., So.

Housley, W. H. All kinds of gems of prose and verse; by a farmer. B'way Pub.

Humphrey, L. H., *comp.* Poetic new-world.—Poetic old-world. ea., $1.50 net; $2.50 net. Holt.

Hyatt, A. H., *ed.* Winds of heaven: an anthology. *$1 net. Dutton.

Jeffers, L. R. List of editions selected for economy in book buying. 25 c. A. L. A.

Krans, H. S., *ed.* English love poems. **$1.25 net. Putnam.

POETRY.—*Continued.*

Lear, E: Book of limericks. $1.50. Little, B. & Co.

Love poems XVIII century. *$2.50 net. Stokes.

Lucas, St. J., *comp.* Rose-winged hours: English love lyrics. *$1.40 net. Longmans.

Lynch, H. P., *comp.* Year book of southern poets. $1.25. Dodge.

Mabie, H. W. Introductions to notable poems. $2. Dodd.

Mackail, J: W: Springs of Helicon: study in the progress of English poetry. **$1.25 net. Longmans.

Maxim, H. Science of poetry and philosophy of language. $2.50 net. Funk.

Miles, A. H:, *ed.* Poets and poetry of the XIXth century. In 12 v. v. 8, Crabbe to Christian (humor).—v. 12, E. H. Plumptre to Selwyn Image. ea., *50 c. net; *$1 net. Dutton.

Morse, L. K., *comp.* Melodies of English verse. 80 c. net. Houghton M.

Murphy, D. C. Popular patriotic poems explained. 65 c. Hinds.

Noyes, A., *ed.* Magic casement: anthology of fairy poetry. *$2 net. Dutton.

Oldest English epic: Beowulf, Finnsburg, Waldere, Deor, [etc.] **$1.10 net. Macmillan.

Otis, W: B. American verse, 1625-1807. **$1.75 net. Moffat.

Pageant of English poetry. *75 c. net; *$1.50 net. Oxford Univ.

Palgrave, F. T., *comp.* Golden treasury. *50 c. net. Macmillan.

Palgrave, F. T., *comp.* Golden treasury of songs and lyrics. *$1 net. Dutton.

Palgrave, F. T., *comp.* Golden treasury of the best songs and lyrical poems. $1; $1.25. Nelson.

Percy, T:, *ed.* Reliques of ancient English poetry. In 3 v. *$3 net. Macmillan.

Reynolds, M. Treatment of nature in English poetry bet. Pope and Wordsworth. *$2.50 net. Univ. of Chic.

Rice, W. de G. C. *and* V., *comps.* Humbler poets. $1.50 net. McClurg.

Richardson, C: F. Study of English rhyme. $1.25. E. P. Storrs.

Rickert, M. E., *comp.* American lyrics. $1.50 net. Baker & T.

Schauffler, R. H., *comp.* Through Italy with the poets. **$2 net. Moffat.

Selections from Byron, Wordsworth, Shelley, Keats and Browning. 40 c. Am. Bk.

Seward, S: S., *jr., ed.* Narrative and lyric poems, for students. **$1 net. Holt.

Shelley, P. B. Defence of poetry. 50 c.; 25 c.; 75 c. T: B. Mosher.

Sidney, *Sir* P. Apologie for poetrie. *35 c. Macmillan.

Sidney, *Sir* P. Apologie for poetrie. 60 c. Oxford Univ.

Smile on the face of the tiger; a collection of limericks. *50 c. net. Bacon & B.

Smithson, G: A. Old English Christian epic. $1. Univ. of Cal.

POETRY.—*Continued.*

Springfield, Mass. City Library. Some modern verse: partial list of recent poetry in the City Library. 5 c. City Lib. Assoc.

Stevenson, B. E., *comp.* Poems of American history. **$3 net. Houghton M.

Symons, A. Romantic movement in English poetry. *$2.50 net. Dutton.

Time of the singing of birds; anthology. $1 net. Oxford Univ.

Vail, B. Little book of too familiar family verse. $2. J: B. Ryan.

Varney, G: L., *ed.* Favorite poems of famous people. $1.50. Vaughan Pub.

Venable, E., *ed.* Poets of Ohio. **$1.50 net. Clarke.

Vest pocket limericks. *50 c. net. Ball Pub. Co.

Viereck, G: S., *and others.* "Younger choir"; book of poems from younger writers of poetry in America. $1 net; $2.50 net. Moods.

Vox, C., *pseud.* Sphinx and the mummy: limericks. 50 c. Caldwell.

Walker, R. J. Anti mias; essay in isometry. $6.50 net. Macmillan.

Warren, T: H. Essays of poets and poetry, ancient and modern. $3. Dutton.

Wegelin, O., *comp.* Early American poetry, 1800-1820. $3. O. Wegelin.

Willcox, *Mrs.* L. C., *comp.* Manual of spiritual fortification. $1.25 net. Harper.

Woodberry, G: E: Inspiration of poetry. *$1.25 net. Macmillan.

See also Accent;—Ballads;—Children's poetry;—Drama and dramatists;—Epigrams;—Essays;—Hymns;—Love;—National literature;—National poetry; — Nature; — Poets;—Prosody;—Quotations;—Satire;—Songs; — Versification;— *also* national literatures;—*also* Arthur, *King.*

Poetry and truth of my own life. Goethe, J. W. v. 2 v. ea., 80 c.; $1.25. Macmillan.

Poetry in song, and some other studies in literature. Dewey, T: E. $1.50. C: M. Harger.

Poetry of eating. Wilson, E: S. 50 c. E: S. Wilson.

Poetry of nature. Van Dyke, H: J., *comp.* *$2 net. Doubleday, P.

Poet's May. Capes, H. M. 50 c. net. Herder.

Poet's vision. Gairy, R. A. 25 c. N. Y. Age.

POETS.

Brooke, S. A: Four Victorian poets: study of Clough, Arnold, Rossetti, Morris. **$1.75 net. Putnam.

Hazlitt, W: Lectures on the English poets. 50 c.; 75 c. Dutton.

Hill, J. Great English poets. $1.50. Jacobs.

Jerrold, W. C., *ed.* Book of living poets. *$2.50 net. Lane.

Stebbing, W: The Poets: Geoffrey Chaucer to Alfred Tennyson. In 2 v. $3.20. Oxford Univ.

See also Authors;—French poetry;—*also* names of poets;—*also* Days with the poets ser.

Poets and poetry of the XIXth century. *See* Miles, Alfred H:, *ed.*

Poets on Christmas. Knight, W: A., *ed.* *$1 net. Gorham.

Poetsch, C: J., and Leidel, E: F.

Official quarter sectional atlas of city of Milwaukee. '08(F8) c. hf. rus., *$40 net; mounted on cl., *$60 net; 2 v., *$65 net; in cl., *$75 net. Caspar.

Poffenbarger, Mrs. Livia Nye Simpson-.

Battle of Point Pleasant; battle of the revolution, Oct. 10th, 1774; biog. sketches of the men who participated. '09(N) c. 141 p. il. por. 8°, 50 c. State Gazette.

Pogue, J: F.

Philosophy of living, which is loving. '08 (D26) por. sq. D. $1. Krehbiel.

Poincaré, Jules Henri.

Value of science; authorized tr., with an introd., by G: Bruce Halsted; with a special prefatory essay. '08(Ap11) 12°, (Archives of psychology.) *$1.25 net. Science Pr., (N. Y.)

Poincaré, Lucien.

New physics and its evolution; being the authorized tr. of "La physique moderne, son evolution." '08(S26) D. (International scientific ser.) *$1.75 net. Appleton.

Poindexter, Mrs. Charlotte Mason, comp.

Jane Hamilton's recipes. '09(Je5) c. D. $1. McClurg.

Poinsettia. Small, C: W. gratis. C: W. Small.

Point of contact in teaching. Du Bois, P. 75 c. Dodd.

Point of honor. Conrad, J. †$1.25. McClure.

Point of law. *See* Phillips, D: Graham. Worth of a woman.

Point of view. Fallows, A. K. *35 c. net. McClurg.

POINT PLEASANT, W. Va., (Battle of.)

Lewis, V. A. Hist. of the battle of Point Pleasant. $1.50. Tribune Pr. Co.

Poffenbarger, *Mrs.* L. N. S. Battle of Point Pleasant 50 c. State Gazette.

Pointing the way. Griggs, S. E. $1. Orion Pub.

Points about poetry. French, D. G. 50 c. Westminster.

POISON IVY.

See Sumach.

Poisoned lake. Hartpence, A. $1. B'way Pub.

POISONOUS PLANTS.

See Botany.

POISONS.

Bosanquet, W: C. Serums, vaccines and toxins. $2 net. Funk.

Brundage, A. H. Manual of toxicology. $1.50; Illustrated ed., $2. H: Harrison.

Calmette, A. Venoms: venomous animals and antivenomous serum-therapeutics. *$5 net. Wood.

Emerson, R. L. Legal medicine and toxicology. $5. Appleton.

Fayrer, C: Venomous snakes: poison and the methods of preventing death from their bite. *75 c. net. Macmillan.

Holland, J. W: Text-book of medical chemistry and toxicology. *$3 net. Saunders.

Noguchi, H. Snake venoms. (Add. Institution for price.) Carnegie.

POISONS.—*Continued.*
Witthaus, R. A., *and* Becker, T. C. Medical jurisprudence, forensic medicine and toxicology. In 4 v. v. 3. per v., *$6 net; *$7 net. Wood.
See also Arsenic;—Autointoxication;—Bacteria;—Medical jurisprudence;—Opium;—Serum.
Poker Jim, gentleman. Lydston, G. F. $1. Walter.
Poker patience. "Trumps, *jr.*," *pseud.* 15 c. Dick.
Poland, Addison B.
See Haaren, J: H:
POLAND.
Bain, R. N. Slavonic Europe: political hist. of Poland and Russia, 1447-1796. *$2 net. Putnam.
See Stanislaus II., Augustus Poniatowski.
POLAR REGIONS.
See Arctic regions.
Polar star. Harrison, E. O. *50 c. net. McClurg.
POLE, Reginald.
Haile, M. Life of Reginald Pole. $5.25 net. Longmans.
Pole Baker. Harben, W: N. 75 c. Burt.
POLES IN THE UNITED STATES.
Sanford, A. H. Polish people of Portage County, [Wis.] 35 c. State Hist., Wis.
POLICE.
Fuld, L. F. Police administration. **$3 net. Putnam.
How to get on the police force. 50 c. Police Chronicle.
New York City. *Bu. Municipal Research.* Business methods of New York City's Police Dept. $1; abr. ed., 10 c. Bu. Municipal.
O'Reilly, J: E: How to become a patrolman. 50 c. Chief.
See also Constables;—Detectives;—Justices of the peace.
Police captains' and lieutenants' catechism: previous questions answered: questions heretofore asked by the Civil Service Commission for inspector, captain and lieutenant are answered. '08(Jl4) c. S. pap., 75 c. Democracy and Civil Service.
POLICE DOGS.
See Dog.
Police sergeant's catechism: previous questions asked and answered. '08(Jl4) c. S. pap., 75 c. Democracy and Civil Service.
Polish people of Portage County. Sanford, A. H. 35 c. State Hist., Wis.
Political development of Japan, 1867-1909. Uyehara, G. E. $3 net. Dutton.
POLITICAL ECONOMY.
American Academy of Political and Social Science. American business conditions. $1. Am. Acad. Pol. Sci.
American Academy of Political and Social Science. Consumer's control of production. 75 c. Am. Acad. Pol. Sci.
Arner, E. E. Truth: [government, trusts, prosperity, panics.] 25 c. Faribault Pilot.
Berkeley, G: The querist. (Reprints of economic tracts.) subs., per set of 4 tracts, pap., *$2 net. Johns Hopkins.
Bibliography of economics for 1909; [from] *Journal of Political Economy.* $2.50 net. Univ. of Chic.

POLITICAL ECONOMY.—*Continued.*
Bigelow, J: Reply of J: Bigelow in answer to an invitation by the Civic Forum of New York City to attend its annual municipal dinner. Gov. Pr. Off.
Bonar, J. Philosophy and political economy in some of their historical relations. *$2.75 net. Macmillan.
Bower, F. Dictionary of economic terms. 50 c. Dutton.
Bullock, C: J. Introd. to study of economics. $1.28. Silver.
Clark, I. C. Automatic system: treating of the doctrine of triple tax. $1; 50 c. D. S. Clark
Daniels, J: Outline of economics. 40 c. Ginn.
Davenport, H. J. Value and distribution. *$3.50 net. Univ. of Chic.
Dewe, J. A. History of economics. $1.50. Benziger.
Dore, P. E: Theory of human progression. 25 c. Blanchard.
Draper, G: O. More: study of financial conditions. **$1 net. Little, B. & Co.
Ely, R: T. Outlines of economics. *$2 net. Macmillan.
Fauquier, F. Essay on ways and means for raising money for the support of the present war without increasing the public debts: [Seven Years' War.] (Reprints of economic tracts.) subs., per set of 4 tracts. *$2 net. Johns Hopkins.
Fawcett, H: Manual of political economy. *$2.60 net. Macmillan.
Flürscheim, M. Economic and social problem. 25 c. Jefferson.
Gibson, A. H. Human economics. *$3.50 net. Longmans.
Hasse, A. R. Index of economic material in documents of the states of the U. S.: California, 1849-1904. $2.25.—Delaware. $1.50.—Illinois, 1809-1904. $5.—Kentucky. $5.—Massachusetts. $2.25.—New York. $3.75.—Rhode Island. 75 c. Carnegie.
Hillier, A. P: The commonweal. *$1.50 net. Longmans.
Hobson, J: A. Industrial system. *$2.50 net. Longmans.
Johnson, A. S. Introduction to economics. $1.50. Heath.
Johnson, A. S. Introductory economics. $1.50. Sch. of Liberal Arts.
Lloyd, H: D. Lords of industry. $1.50 net. Putnam.
McCasland, C: O. Right and riches. $1.50. Wilbur Pub.
McDermott, C: H. Gospel of greed. $1. Chapple Pub.
Making bread dear. 50 c. Open Court.
Mallock, W: H. Nation as a business firm. $1 net. Macmillan.
Marx, K. Capital. In 3 v. v. 3. $2; per set, $6.—Value, price and profit. 50 c. Kerr.
Massie, J. Essay on the governing causes of the natural rate of interest. (Reprint of economic tracts.) subs., per set of 4 tracts, *$2 net. Johns Hopkins.
Meade, E: S. Economics. $3.50. De Bower-E.

POLITICAL ECONOMY.—*Continued.*

Mill, J: S. Principles of political economy. 2 v. $3.50; $7.50. Lamb Pub.

Mill, J: S. Principles of political economy. *$1.50 net. Longmans.

Mills, H. E. Outlines of economics. $1. H. E. Mills.

Mitchell, W. C. Gold, prices, and wages under the greenback standard. $5. Univ. of Cal.

Molesworth, *Sir* G. L. Economic and fiscal facts and fallacies. $1.50. Longmans.

Nathan, *Sir* N. Economic heresies. *$3 net. Houghton M.

Nearing, S., *and* Watson, F. D. Economics. *$1.90 net. Macmillan.

Outlines of economics. $1.25 net. Univ. of Chic.

Palgrave, R. H. I., *ed.* Dict. of political economy. 3 v. $15. Macmillan.

Price, L. L. F. R. Position and prospects of the study of economic history: a lecture. 35 c. Oxford Univ.

Putney, A. H., *and* Skinner, H. M. Principles of political economy. $4.80. Cree.

Rawie, H: Problem stated of distribution. Distribution League.

Richardson, B. J. Woman who spends. *$1 net. Whitcomb.

Schrijvers, J. Hdbk. of pract. economics. $1.35 net. Herder.

Seager, H: R. Economics: briefer course. $1.75. Holt.

Seager, H: R. Economics: [lecture.] 25 c. Lemcke.

Seager, H: R. Social insurance. $1. Macmillan.

Seligman, E. R. A. Principles of economics. $2.50. Longmans.

Smart, W: Economic annals of the nineteenth century, 1801-1820. $6.50 net. Macmillan.

Small, A. W. The Cameralists; pioneers of German social polity. *$3 net. Univ. of Chic.

Stanton, R. Essay on distribution of livelihood. *$1.50 net. Farwell.

Stone, D. C. From the evidence presented: [discussion of economic questions.] 25 c. Saginaw.

Thomas, A. M. Plain economic facts for all people. $3. Cochrane.

Trine, R. W. Land of living men. $1.25. Crowell.

Underwood, J. H. Distribution of ownership. *$2 net; *$1.50 net. Macmillan.

Vanderlint, J. Money answers all things. (Reprints of economic tracts.) subs., per set of 4 tracts, *$2 net. Johns Hopkins.

Watson, T: E: Political and economic handbook. $1. Watson.

Wicksteed, P. H: Common sense of political economy. $4.25 net. Macmillan.

Winsor, T: Standard intrinsic unit. $1. Winsor.

See also Banks and banking;—Capital and labor;—Charities; — Commerce;—Communism;—Co-operation;—Corporations; — Cost;—Credit;—Democracy; —Education;—Finance;—Gold;—Government ownership; — Guilds; — Individualism; — Insurance; — Interest;—Investments;—Labor and laboring classes;—Labor colonies;—Lotteries; — Money; — Monopolies; —Municipal government;—Municipal ownership;—Panics;—Poor;—Population; — Prices;—Prisons;—Property;—Social science;—Socialism;—Statistics;—Stocks;—Strikes;—Tariff; —Taxation;—Trades-unions; — Trusts; — Wages; — Wealth; — *also* names of countries.

Political history of England. *See* Hunt, W:

Political history of the state of New York. *See* Alexander, De Alva Stanwood.

Political issues and outlooks. Taft, W: H. **$1.25 net. Doubleday, P.

Political problems of American development. Shaw, A. *$1.50 net. Columbia Univ.

Political reform in Wisconsin. Philipp, E. L. 50 c. net. Caspar.

Political satire in English poetry. Previté-Orton, C: W: $1.50 net. Putnam.

POLITICAL SCIENCE.

Acton, J: E. E: D.-A., *Lord.* History of freedom and other essays. *$3 net. Macmillan.

Balfour, A. J. Decadence. *50 c. Putnam.

Batten, S: G. Christian state. *$1.50 net. Am. Bapt.

Beard, C: A. Politics: [a lecture.] Columbia Univ.

Bentley, A. F. Process of government: study of social pressures. *$3 net. Univ. of Chic.

Browne, J: H. B. Some further letters to an elector and some political fables. 25 c. Longmans.

Bryan, W: J. Thou shalt not steal: [address on political ethics.] 10 c. Civic Forum.

Carlyle, R. W. *and* A. J. Hist. of mediæval political theory in the West. In 3 v. v. 1, 2. ea., *$3.50 net. Putnam.

Carlyle, T: Past and present. 35 c.; 65 c. Oxford Univ.

Chandler, A. D. Local self government. [priv. pr.] A. D. Chandler.

Chapman, J: J. Causes and consequences. —Practical agitation. ea., $1.25. Moffat.

Chester, *Lord, pseud.* Great red dragon; or, the flaming devil of the Orient. [Utopia.] 75 c.; 35 c. Guiding Star.

Civic reader for new Americans. 38 c. Am. Bk.

Clairmont, R. de. Reform: essay on the political, financial, and social condition of the United States. $1. Roxburgh.

Clark, E. J. Outlines of civil government. 75 c. Palmer Co.

Coker, F. W. Organismic theories of the state. $1.50. Longmans.

Davis, C: G. Why not now?; [plea for reform.] $1. Badger.

Dealey, J. Q. Development of the state. $1.50. Silver.

Dealey, J. Q. Ethical and religious significance of the state. **10 c. net. Am. Bapt.

Dunn, A. W: Civics, the community and the citizen. 50 c. Cal. Dept. Pub. Instruction.

Dye, J: T. Ideals of democracy. **90 c. net. Bobbs-M.

Eliot, C: W: Conflict between individualism and collectivism in a democracy. 90 c. net. Scribner.

Ellett, A. H. Federal Union and Mississippi. 75 c. B. F. Johnson.

POLITICAL SCIENCE.—*Continued.*

Fleming, W: H: Tariff, civil service, income tax, imperialism, the race problem and other speeches. *$2.50 net. A. B. Caldwell.

Folk, J. W. Era of conscience. 10 c. Civic Forum.

Forman, S: E. Essentials of civil government. 60 c. Am. Bk.

Foster, E. Cyclopedia of civil government. $2.50. College Pub. Co.

Gettell, R. G. Introd. to political science. Gettell, R. G. $2. Ginn.

Gillette, K. C. World corporation. $1. World Corporation.

Hughes, C: E., *and* Brewer, D: J: Idea of public office: address by C. E. Hughes, [and] Public office in relation to public opinion: address by D. J. Brewer. 10 c. Civic Forum.

John *of Salisbury*. Episcopi Carnotensis Policratici sive de nugis cvrialivm et vestigiis philosophorvm, libri VIII. 2 v. $11. Oxford Univ.

Kaye, P. L. Readings in civil government. $1.20 net. Century Co.

Laughlin, J. L. Latter-day problems. **$1.50 net. Scribner.

Lecky, W: E: H. Historical and political essays. $1.60 net; *$3.50 net. Longmans.

McBain, H. L., *and* Hill, I: W: How we are governed in Alabama and the nation. 65 c. Bell Bk.

Machiavelli, N. The prince. *35 c. net; *70 c. net. Dutton.

Marriott, J: A. R. Second chambers; inductive study in political science. $1.75. Oxford Univ.

Marx, K. Poverty of philosophy: being a tr. of the Misère de la philosophie (a reply to La philosophie de la misère of M. Prudhon). $1. Kerr.

Mill, J: S. Utilitarianism, liberty, representative government. 35 c. net; 70 c. net. Dutton.

More, *Sir* T: Utopia. $1.75 net. Macmillan.

Reid, D: C. Effective industrial reform. $1.35. D. C. Reid.

Reinsch, P. S: Young citizen's reader. 60 c. B: H. Sanborn.

Savay, N. L. Emancipation; introd. to the system of progressive government. [priv. pr.] Knickerbocker Press.

Schenck, F. J. Washington party; "shall the people rule?" $1. F. J. Schenck.

Shaw, L. M. Current issues. **$2 net. Appleton.

Slater, J. A., *ed.* Public man's guide. $1.25. Pitman.

Waterman, S. D. Pract. aids to the teaching of civics. 60 c. Whitaker & R.

Webb, S. *and Mrs.* B. P. State and the doctor. $2 net. Longmans.

Wendell, B. Privileged classes. **$1.25 net. Scribner.

Wilson, W. Civic problems. (Add. pubs. for price.) Civic League.

Woerner, W: F. Evolution of the state universal from an American standpoint. gratis. W: F. Woerner.

POLITICAL SCIENCE.—*Continued.*

Zueblin, C: Democracy and the overman. $1 net. B: W. Huebsch.

See also Agriculture;—Boycotting;—Capital and labor; — Christian science; — Church (The); — Cities;—Citizenship; — Colonial government; — Communism;—Constitution;—Crime and criminals;—Declaration of Independence;—Democracy; — Diplomacy; — Elections; — Finance; — Frankpledge systems;—Government ownership; —Immigration; — Imperialism;—Individualism; —Labor and laboring classes;—Law;—Liberty; —Liquors;—Local government;—Magistrates;— Monroe doctrine;—Municipal government;—Municipal ownership; — Naturalization; — Negligence;—Negroes;—Parliament; — Parties (*political*); — Patriotism; — Police; — Political economy;—Politics; — Primaries; — Prisons;— Property; — Prostitution;—Railroads; — Referendum;—Representation;—Slavery;—Social science; — Socialism; — Statistics; — Suffrage;— Taxation;—Town officers;—Towns;—Trusts;— Villages;—War;—*also* Plato;—*also* names of states and countries.

Political socialism. Crawford, J. S. 25 c. J. S. Crawford.

Political theories of Martin Luther. Waring, L. H. $1.50. Putnam.

Politician (The). Fogazzaro, A. $1.50. J: W. Luce.

Politician (The). Mason, E. H. $1.50. McClurg.

POLITICS.

Dewe, J. A. Psychology of politics and history. $1.75 net. Longmans.

Hedges, J. E. Common sense in politics. $1.25. Moffat.

Jenks, J. W. Principles of politics from the viewpoint of the American citizen. *$1.50 net. Columbia Univ.

Jordan, D: S. Call of the nation. $1. Am. Unitarian.

Lieber, F. Manual of political ethics. 2 v. $5.50 net. Lippincott.

Macphail, A. Essays in politics: [England.] *$1.80 net. Longmans.

Owen, R. L., *comp.* Code of the people's rule. Gov. Pr. Off.

Sidgwick, H: Elem. of politics. *$4.25 net. Macmillan.

Wallas, G. Human nature in politics. *$1.50 net. Houghton M.

See also United States.

Politzer, Adam.

Text-bk. of the diseases of the ear; for students and practitioners; tr. and ed. by Milton J. Ballin, M.D., and Clarence L. Heller, M.D. 5th ed., rev. '09(Je) 892 p. il. 8°, *$8 net. Lea.

Polk, J. M.

Confederate soldier; and Ten years in South America. '10(Ap) c. 57 p. il. 8°, 35 c. Von Boeckmann-J.

First pub. 1905 under title: Memories of the lost cause.

Polk, Ja. Knox.

Diary of James K. Polk, during his presidency, 1845 to 1849; ed. and annotated by Milo Milton Quaife; with introd. by And. Cunningham McLaughlin. In 4 v. '10 (Ag13) pors. O. $20 net, boxed. McClurg.

Polko, Frau Elise Vogel.

Musical sketches; tr. from the 15th German ed. '09(D18) c. pors. D. *$1.25 net. Sturgis & W.

Polk's architects', engineers', builders' and contractors' directory (cities and towns of 5000 population and over) of Ohio. '08 (F15) c. 2 v., 4°, $5. Polk.
Polk's vest pocket street directory and car line guide of Baltimore. '08(Ag) c. 160 p. nar. 16°, pap., 25 c. Polk.
Pollak, Gustav.
Hygiene of the soul; memoir of a physician and a philosopher; [synopsis of Baron von Feuchtersleben's book of the same title.] '10(Ap2) c. D. $1.20 net. Dodd.
Pollard, Eliza F.
Liberty or death; a story of the Green Mountain Boys in the American Revolution. '09(S18) c. il. D. †$1.50. Dodd.
Pollard, J: Garland, ed.
See Virginia. Pollard's supp.
Pollard, Percival.
Their day in court. '10(Ja15) c. O. *$3 net. Neale.
Pollard, Rob. N., comp.
See Virginia. Business man's code.
Pollen, M. M., [Mrs. J: Hungerford Pollen.]
Seven centuries of lace; with a preface by Alan Cole. '08(Ag1) il. 4°, *$9 net. Macmillan.
Polley, G: H:, comp.
Gothic architecture, furniture and ornament of England from the 11th to the 16th century; introd. by Langford H. Warren. '08(Ag8) c. 2 v. in 1, por. pls. F. $40. Polley.
Polley, Jos. B:
Hood's Texas Brigade: its marches, its battles, its archives. '10(Ap2) c. pors. O. $3.50 net. Neale.
Soldier's letters to charming Nellie. '08 (F15) c. pors. O. *$2 net. Neale.
POLLINATION.
See Botany.
Pollitt, Arth. W., and Bryson, Ernest.
The unison chant choir-book: a collection of original chants designed to encourage congregational singing. '09(Ag14) c. Q. $1. Oxford Univ.
Pollitt, S.
See Baily, Ja. T:
Pollock, Fk. Lillie.
Frozen fortune. '10(N12) c. D. $1.20 net. Macaulay.
Pollock, Horatio M., and Rowell, G: Clarence.
American examination and reviewer book: [arithmetic, grammar, geography, spelling.] '08, [1909.] (Mr) c. 6+372 p. 12°, $1.50. N. Y. Educ. Co.
Pollock, Ja. B., ed.
Lab'y directions for general biology; botanical pt.; rev. '09(N) c. 50 p. O. pap., 40 c. Wahr.
Pollock, M. I., ["Emery West."]
Country sketches. '10(My21) c. 12°, 50 c. Cochrane.
Pollock, Simon Oscar.
Russian Bastille: [Schlussenburg Fortress.] '08(Je20) c. pors. S. 50 c. Kerr.
Pollock, Walter Herries.
Impressions of Henry Irving; with a preface by H. B. Irving. '08(Ag22) D. **$1 net. Longmans.

Pollution of New York harbor. Soper, G: A. $2.50. G: A. Soper.
Pollution of streams by sulphite pulp waste. Phelps, E. B. 10 c. U. S., Supt. of Docs.
Polly, Lady, pseud.
See Lucas, Paula Easby-Smith.
Polly and Dolly. Blaisdell, M. F. 60 c. Little, B. & Co.
Polly for short. Middleton, C. S. 50 c. Aberdeen.
Polly of the circus. Mayo, M. †$1. Dodd.
Polly Page Yacht Club. Forrester, I. L. $1.25. Jacobs.
Polly Winford. Hussey, E. $1.50. Longmans.
Polo, Marco.
Travels: introd. by J: Masefield. '08(Mr7) 16°, (Everyman's lib.) *35 c. net; leath., *70 c. net. Dutton.
POLO.
FitzPatrick, H. L. Equestrian polo. 10 c. Am. Sports.
Polygeneric theory. Rinaldo, J. $1.50. J. Rinaldo.
Polyglot phrases. Worthington, L. N: *$1.10 net. Macmillan.
POLYNESIA.
Brown, G: Melanesians and Polynesians. $3 net. Macmillan.
POLYNESIAN LANGUAGES.
Churchill, W: Weather words of Polynesia. 80 c. Am. Anthropological.
POLYZOA.
See Bryoza.
Pomegranite. Beckingsale, J. $1. Northfield Press.
Pomeroy, C. P., rep.
See California. *District cts. of appeals.* Repts.—*Sup. ct.* Repts.
Pomeroy, Sarah Gertrude.
Christmas in Spain; or, Marquita's day of rejoicing. New ed. '10(Ag27) c. il. D. (Christmas in many lands ser.) 50 c. Estes.
A loyal little subject; Christmas in Holland. '08(N7) c. il. D. 50 c. Estes.
Saburo's reward; Christmas in Japan. '09 (O23) c. il. D. †50 c. Estes.
Pomeroy Family Association. Pomeroy; romance and history of Eltweed Pomeroy's ancestors in Normandy and England. '09 (O) c. 7+9-81 p. il. facsim., 8°, $1.25. Franklin Pr. and Eng.
POMO INDIANS.
See Indians.
Pomp and circumstance. Gerard, D. $1.50. B. W. Dodge.
POMPADOUR, Jeanne Antoinette Poisson le Normant d' Etioles, *Marquise* de.
Williams, H. N. Madame de Pompadour. *$2 net. Scribner.
POMPEII, Italy.
Mackenzie, W. M. Pompeii. $2.50 net. Macmillan.
POMPONAZZI, Pietro.
Douglas, A. H. Philosophy and psychology of Pietro Pomponazzi. $2.50 net. Putnam.
Pomroy, G:
Hesperides; poems and songs. '09(My) c. 94 p. 12°, 80 c. G: Pomroy.

PONCE DE LEON, Juan.
Ober, F: A. Juan Ponce de Leon. **$1 net. Harper.

Pond, Edg. Le Roy.
Tories of Chippeny Hill, Conn.; brief account of the Loyalists of Bristol, Plymouth and Harwinton, who founded St. Matthew's Church in East Plymouth in 1791. '09(D4) il. por. map, D. **$1 net. Grafton Press.

Pond, Fs. Jones.
Notes on non-metals. 2d ed. '08(N) c. 11+211 p. 8°, $1.50. F. J. Pond.

Pond, G: Gilbert.
Calcium carbide and acetylene. '08, [1909.] (Ja) 118 p. 8°, (Penn. State College, Dept. of Chemistry bull.) gratis. Penn. State Coll.

Pond, Raymond Haines.
Further studies of solution tension and toxicity in lipolysis [effects of chemicals on plants]. '08, [1909.] (Mr) 232-253 p. 8°, (Contributions from the New York Botanical Garden.) pap., 25 c. N. Y. Botanical.

Poniard's hilt. Sue, M. J. E. 75 c. N. Y. Labor News.

Ponte, P. Ludovici de.
Meditationes de praecipiis fidei nostrae mysteriis. pt. 1. '08(Ag8) 12°, (Bibliotheca ascetica mystica.) *$1.10 net. Herder.

Pontiac. Whitney, A. C. $1.50. Badger.

PONTIAC'S WAR.
See Indians.

Pontificial services. v. 1 and 2, [published in England, 1901;] cont. descriptive notes and a liturgical introd. by Rev. Wa. Howard Frere; v. 3, with descriptive notes by F. C. Eeles. '08(Ja18); v. 4; with descriptive notes by Athelstan Riley. '08(O3) il. Q. (Alcuin Club collections.) ea., bds., *$6 net. Longmans.

Ponting, Herbert G.
In Lotus-land: Japan. '10(Jl16) col. il. 8°, (Color book ser.) $6 net. Macmillan.

Pontius, Albert W., comp.
Protection extended to patents, designs, trademarks and copyrights in China, Japan and Korea. '09(My) 15 p. 8°, pap. (Add. Superintendent for price.) U. S., Supt. of Docs.

PONY.
White, O. A. Childhood and ponyhood blended; [hist. of Shetland pony.] 35 c. Dunlap Pony Co.

PONY EXPRESS.
See Express.

Pony rider ser. *See* Patchin, Fk. Gee.

Pool, Bettie Freshwater.
Carolina: [song in honor of North Carolina.] '09(F) 50 c. B. F. Pool.
Under Brazilian skies: [short stories.] '08, [1909.] (F) c. 60 p. 8°, $1. B. F. Pool.

Pool, Maria Louise.
See Adventures at sea.

POOL (*game*).
Hood, J. G. Trick and fancy pool shots exposed. 50 c. Exposé.
See also Billiards;—Games.

Pool of flame. Vance, L: J. †$1.50. Dodd.

Poole, Cecil Percy.
Gas engine. '09(Mr27) 8°, *$1 net. Hill Pub.

Poole, Fanny Runnells.
Mugen: a book of verse. '08(O17) c. il. S. $1. Niles Pub.

Poole, Jos.
Pract. telephone hdbk. and guide to the telephone exchange. 4th ed., rev. and enl. '10(Ag13) il. 12°, $1.75 net. Macmillan.

Poole, Mary, comp.
See Fletcher, W: I:

Poole, Murray E:
History of Jan Van Cleef of New Utrecht, L. I., N. Y., (1659,) and some of his descendants. '09(Ap24) O. pap. (Add. pubs. for price.) Ithaca Journ.

Poole, Reginald Lane, ed.
See Hunt, W:, *ed.*

Poole's index. *See* Fletcher, W: I:

Pooley, P:
Mysterious discovery of nature, shown in a dream to Dr. P. Polack, and relating directly to the question of the discovery of the North Pole; facts governing the movements of the earth, and many important secrets of nature that have never been given to the world up to this day are shown to him. '10(Ag) c. 9-131 p. il. por. 12°, $1. P. Pooley.

Pooley, W: Vipond.
Settlement of Illinois from 1830 to 1850. '09(F6) O. (Univ. of Wis. bull., History ser.) pap., 75 c. Univ. of Wis.

Pools of silence. Stacpoole, H: D. $1.50. Duffield.

Poor, C: Lane.
Nautical science in its relation to pract. navigation, together with a study of the tides and tidal currents. '10(Je4) c. il. por. diagrs., 8°, $2 net. Putnam.
Solar system: study of recent observations. '08(F15) c. il. diagrs., O. (Science ser.) **$2 net. Putnam.

POOR (The).
Conyngton, M. How to help. *$1.50 net. Macmillan.
Crawford, W: H: Church and the slum. 75 c. Eaton & M.
Devine, E: T: Misery and its causes. **$1.25 net. Macmillan.
Edwards, R: H:, *ed.* Poverty. 10 c. R: H: Edwards.
Help to self-help. gratis. People's Univ.
Holmes, T: Known to the police. *$3 net. Longmans.
Kolb, C: B. Helping the man who is down. 25 c. C: B. Kolb.
Loane, M. Englishman's castle: [papers on the English poor.]—Neighbors and friends. ea., $2.—Next street but one: [studies of the Eng. poor.]—The queen's poor [in England]. ea., $1.25.—From their point of view: [studies among the poor in England.] $2. Longmans.
Lyons, A. N. Sixpenny pieces: [a doctor's experiences in London's slums.] $1.50. Lane.
Marcy, *Mrs.* M. E. T. Out of the dump: [story of the poor of Chicago.] 50 c. Kerr.

POOR (The).—*Continued.*
Nascher, I. L. Wretches of Povertyville. $1.50. J. J. Lanzit.
Wallace, G: The disinherited: observations in travel: [studies of poverty and its causes.] $1. J. S. Ogilvie.
Webb, S. *and* B. English poor law policies. *$2.50 net.—Minority report of the Poor Law Commission. In 2 pts. pt. 1, *$2.50 net; pt. 2, *$1.75 net. Longmans.
Weller, C: F: Neglected neighbors: [stories of Washington, D. C., poor.] **$1.50 net. Winston; Charities Pub.
See also Capital and labor;—Charities;—Children;—Immigration;— Labor and laboring classes;—Salvation army;—Social science; — Tramps;—*also* Washington, D. C.

Poor dear dollies. '09(D) *50 c. net. Doran.

Poor man's house. Reynolds, S. $1.50. Lane.

Poor Richard's almanac. *See* Franklin, B:

Poor Uncle Harry. Jacberns, R. $1.50. Lippincott.

Poor's handbook of investors' holdings; showing ownership of securities by savings banks, trust companies, insurance companies and other institutions. '09(Ja16) c. 8°, $15. Poor's.

Pope, Alex.
Essay on criticism; ed., with introd. and notes, by J: Sargeaunt. '10(Mr26) D. 50 c. Oxford Univ.
Rape of the lock; ed. by G: Holden. '09 (Ap3) D. 50 c. Oxford Univ.

POPE, Alexander.
Lefferts, M. C. Alexander Pope; notes toward a bibliography of early editions of his writings. $2.50; without facsims., gratis. Dodd.
Paston, G: Mr. Pope, his life and times. *$6.50 net. Putnam.

Pope, Amy Eliz., and Carpenter, Mary Lovina.
Essentials of dietetics in health and disease: a text-book for nurses and a practical dietary guide for the household. '08 (Ag8) c. il. tabs., D. *$1 net. Putnam.

—, and Thirza A.
Quiz book of nursing for teachers and students: together with chapters on visiting nursing, by Marg. A. Bewley; hospital planning, construction and equipment by Bertrand E. Taylor; and hospital bookkeeping and statistics by Frederick B. Morlok. '09, [1910.] (F) 8+469 p. il. plan, 12°, *$1.75 net. Putnam.

Pope, C: H:
Pioneers of Maine and New Hampshire, 1623 to 1660: descriptive list, drawn from records of the colonies, towns, churches, courts, [etc.;] with foreword by Ja. Phinney Baxter. '08(S5) c. 8°, $5. C: H: Pope.

—, and Hooper, T: comps.
The Hooper genealogy. '08(O10) il. pors. 8°, *$7 net. C: H: Pope.

Pope, Curran.
Practical hydrotherapy; manual for students and practitioners. '09(D) c. 15+646 p. il. plans, 4°, $6. Cin. Medical.

Pope, Franklin.
Stranger's visit: [Christian Science.] '09 (Je) 61 p. 8°, 60 c Zuriel.

Pope, Jessie.
Babes and birds. '10(Ag27) col. il. D. 75 c. Caldwell.
Bunny book. '10(D) col. il. 4°, bds., 60 c. Dodge.

Pope, Paul Russel.
German composition; with notes and vocab. '08(Mr7) c. D. 90 c. Holt.

Pope, Paulina Saxton, ["L. P."]
White flame of sculpture. '09(Mr) c. 42 p. 12°, 75 c. Torch Press.

Pope, Thirza A.
See Pope, Amy Eliz.

POPES.
Kruger, G. The Papacy; the idea and its exponents. $1.50. Putnam.
Mann, H. K. Lives of the Popes in the early Middle Ages. v. 2, 3, 4, 5. ea., $3 net. Herder.
Ranke, L. v. History of the popes. 3 v. $5.25; $10.50. Lamb Pub.
Ranke, L. v. Hist. of the popes. In 3 v. ea., 80 c.; $1.25. Macmillan.
Vaughan, H. M. Medici popes, (Leo X. and Clement VII.) *$4 net. Putnam.
Walsh, Ja. J. Popes and science. $2. Fordham Univ.
See also Apostolic succession; — Infallibility — Rome;—Vatican;—*also* Pius X.

Popham, W: Lee.
Love poems and the boyhood of Kentucky's poet; being the life-story of William Lee Popham, by Maude Miller Estes. '10(O) 92 p. por. 12°, $1. World Supply.
Love's rainbow dream. [1910.] (S) c. 62 p. 16°, 50 c. W: L. Popham.
Nutshells of truth; cont. short sayings and toasts. '10(D31) c. por. D. $1. B'way Pub.
Poems of truth, love and power, original and complete. '10(O) c. 7-15-192 p. por. 12°, $1. B'way Pub.
She dared to win. [1910.] (N) c. 76 p. 16°, 50 c. W: L. Popham.
Tramp's love. [1910.] (Jl) c. 79 p. 16°, 50 c. W: L. Popham.
Valley of love. [1910.] (N) c. 60 p. 16°, 50 c. W: L. Popham.
Village by the sea. [1910.] (N) c. 5-56 p. il. 16°, 50 c. W: L. Popham.

POPHAM COLONY, Maine.
Maine Historical Society. Tercentenary of the landing of the Popham colony at the mouth of the Kennebec river. 50 c. Me. Hist.

Poplars (The). Taulman, F. A. $1.50. Cochrane.

Poppea of the post-office. Wright, *Mrs.* M. O. †$1.50. Macmillan.

Popper, W:, ed.
See Yûsuf ibn Taghri-Birdî.

Popplewell, W: C:
Strength of materials. '08(Ja11) il. O. *$2 net. Van Nostrand.

Poppy. Stockley, C. *$1.35 net. Putnam.

"POPULAR ASTRONOMY."
See Indexes.

Popular copyright fiction. D. 75 c. Rand, McN. & Co.
—Marchmont. Mystery of Mortimer Strange. —Sir Jaffray's wife.
—Payne. Mills of man.
—Russell. Country sweetheart.
—Ryan. My Quaker maid;—Told in the hills.

Popular edition of recent fiction. 12°, †75 c. Little, B. & Co.
—Agnus. Sarah Tuldon.
—Bailey. Sage brush parson.
—Carling. Shadow of the czar.—Viking's skull.
—Charles. In the country God forgot.—Siege of youth.
—Crowley. Daughter of New France.—Heroine of the strait.—Love thrives in war.
—Daudet. Sappho.
—Devereux. From kingdom to colony.—Up and down the sands of gold.
—Embree. Dream of a throne.
—Erskine. When the gates lift up their heads.
—Fletcher. Kismet.
—Gillman. Hassan.
—Goodwin. White aprons.
—Johnson. King's henchman.
—Lawrence. The Wolverine.
—Le Gallienne. Love-letters of the king.—Painted shadows.
—Milecete. Detached pirate.
—Ray. By the good Sainte Anne.
—Rowe. Maid of Bar Harbor.
—Sienkiewicz. With fire and sword.—Without dogma.
—Thruston. Girl of Virginia.—Mistress Brent.
—Whitson. Barbara.
—Wilson. Rose of Normandy.

Popular election of senators. '09(My22) D. (Univ. of Wis. bull.) pap., gratis. Univ. of Wis.

Popular electricity. Hibbert, W. *$1.25 net. Cassell.

Popular fallacies. Ackerman, A. S. E. *$1.50 net. Lippincott.

Popular fruit growing. Green, S: B. $1. Webb.

Popular garden flowers. Wright, W. P. $2 net. Clode.

Popular hdbk. for cement and concrete users. Lewis, M. H: $2.50. Henley.

Popular handbooks. il. S. 50 c. Penn Pub. Co.
—Flemming. Receipts and remedies.
—Hapgood. Solitaire.
—Lindsay. Bridge.
—Pittenger. Toasts.
—Xanto. Dream books.—Fortune telling.

Popular history of astronomy. *See* Clerke, A. M.

Popular hymns. Duncan, J. $2 net. Whittaker.

Popular lectures of Sam P. Jones. Jones, S: P. *75 c. net. Revell.

Popular lib. of art. *See* Dutton's.

Popular Mechanics. Amateur mechanics. '07, [1908.] (Mr.) c. 93 p. il. 8°, pap., 25 c. Popular Mechanics.

Popular Mechanics 25-cent handbook ser. il. 16°. Popular Mechanics.
—Crawshaw. Metal spinning.
—Windsor. Mission furniture.
—Windsor, *ed.* Mission furniture. pt. 2.

Popular patriotic poems explained. Murphy, D. C. 65 c. Hinds.

Popular priced copyrights. il. 12°, 50 c. B. W. Dodge.
—Belloc-Lowndes. Barbara Rebell.
—Burgin. Shutters of silence.
—Grainger. The avengers.—One who saw.
—Hudson. J. P. Dunbar.
—Hutten. Araby.
—Le Queux. Closed book.
—Ludlow. Hasheesh eater.
—Naylor. The scalawags.
—Russell. Greatest trust in the world.
—Snaith. Patricia at the inn.
—Williamson. House by the lock.

Popular recitations and how to recite them. Faxon, G. B. $1. F. A. Owen.

Popular scientific ser. D. *$1.50 net. Lippincott.
—Dolmage. Astronomy of to-day.
—Gibson. Scientific ideas of to-day.

Popular use of the Athanasian creed. Legg, J. W. *60 c. net; *40 c. net. Longmans.

POPULATION.
Woodruff, C: E: Expansion of races. $4. Rebman.
See also Census;—Statistics.

PORCELAIN.
See Ceramics.

PORK.
See Pig.

Porritt, E:
Sixty years of protection in Canada, 1846-1907. '08(F22) 12°, *$1.50 net. Macmillan.

Porritt, H. W., and Nicklin, W:
Bookkeeping for retailers; with chapters on insurances and income tax returns. '09 (Ag7) tabs., D. (Practical primers of business.) 50 c. Pitman.

PORT ARTHUR, Manchuria.
Nojine, E. K. Truth about Port Arthur. *$5 net. Dutton.
See also Russo-Japanese war.

PORT JERVIS, N. Y.
Fritts, J: P. Port Jervis. 25 c. E. L. Parks.

Port o' dreams. Dickens, *Mrs.* E. P. **$1 net. Putnam.

PORT ROYALISTS.
Lowndes, M. E. Nuns of Port Royal. $4.15. Oxford Univ.
See also Pascal, Blaise.

Porta linguarum Orientalium. O. Lemcke.
—Brockelmann. Kurzgefasste vergleichende grammatik der semitischen sprachen. $3.

PORTABLE HOUSES.
See Architecture.

PORTAGE COUNTY, Wis.
Sanford, A. H. Polish people of Portage County, [Wis.] 35 c. State Hist., Wis.

PORTAGE QUADRANGLES.
See New York State.

Porter, Alfr. W.
See Foster, G: Carey.

Porter, Mrs. Arina Louelah Abbott, and Ball, Mrs. Eva Blanche Allen, comps.
Crumbs from everybody's table: [cookery.] 3d ed. '07, '08(Je) c. 11-362+9 p. front. 12°, $1. Monterey.

Porter, Arth. Kingsley.
Medieval architecture: its origins and development; with lists of monuments and bibliographies. [In 2 v.] '09(F13) c. il. plans, Q. $15, boxed. Baker & T.

Porter, C:, M.D.
Sanitary law, in question and answer. for the use of students of public health. '10 (O1) D. 90 c. net. Longmans.

Porter, Mrs. C: Darwin.
See Porter, Gene Stratton-.

Porter, C: Sanford, M.D.
Milk diet as a remedy for chronic diseases. 2d ed. '09(D4) c. S. *$1.25 net. Stechert.

Porter, C: Talbot.
Engineering reminiscences contributed to *Power* and *American Machinist*. Rev. and enl. '08(Mr28) il. pors. 8°, *$3 net. Wiley.

Porter, Charlotte.
Lips of music: [poems.] '10(O8) c. il. D. $1.25. Crowell.

Porter, Mrs. Delia Lyman, comp.
Year of ideals for every-day living. '09 (D25) c. D. bds., *75 c. net, boxed. Pilgrim Press.

Porter, Dwight.
Notes on hydraulic measurements, prepared for use of students in civil and sanitary engineering at the Mass. Institute of Technology. '09, [1910.] (F) 78 p. il. 4°, $1.50. D. Porter

Porter, Mrs. Eleanor Hodgman.
Turn of the tide: story of how Margaret solved her problem. '08(O17) c. il. D. †$1.25. Wilde.

Porter, Gene Stratton-, [Mrs. C: Darwin Porter].
At the foot of the rainbow. '10(D) 12°, $1.50. Doubleday, P.
Formerly published by Outing Co.
Birds of the Bible. '10(F12) c. il. map, 8°, $2. Jennings.
Girl of the Limberlost. '09(Ag28) c. il. O. †$1.50. Doubleday, P.
Music of the wild; with reproductions of the performers, their instruments and festival halls. '10(D3) c. il. 8°, $2.50. Jennings.

Porter, Harry.
Edward Garrett, story of Mars; [drama in blank verse.] '10(Mr5) c. por. D. $1.25. Lincoln Pub.

Porter, Harry Franklin.
Concrete, its composition and use. '10 (My7) c. il. tabs., 8°, (Structural concrete ser.) $2. Concrete Engineering.

Porter, H: Dwight.
Henry Dickinson Smith: a biography. '08 (O24) por. 8°. (Add. pubs. for price.) Revell.

Porter, H: H.
How to provide for Chicago's growth. '09 (Ag28) O. pap. (Priv. pr.) G: F. Porter.

Porter, Horace Chamberlain, and Ovitz, F. K.
Volatile matter of coal. '10(D) 56 p. il. tabs., diagrs., 8°, (U. S., Dept. of the Interior, Bu. of Mines, bull.) Gov. Pr. Off.

Porter, Jermain Gildersleeve.
Variations of latitude, 1899 to 1906. '08(D) 31 p. front. 4°, (Univ. of Cincinnati pubs.) $1. Univ. of Cin.

PORTER, *Col.* Joseph C.
Mudd, J. A. With Porter in north Missouri. $2.70. G. A. Mudd.

Porter, Sarah Harvey.
Life and times of Anne Royall. '08(N21) 12°, *$1.50 net. Torch Press.

Porter, W: Harley.
Shield reversed. '09, [1910.] (F) c. 22 p. 12°, *50 c. net. Gorham.

Porter, W: Sydney.
See Henry, O., *pseud.*

Porterfield, C:, ed.
See American and Eng. ency. of law.

PORTLAND, Me.
Lowell, *Mrs.* C. T., *comp.* Impressions in and about Portland, Me. 50 c. A. W. Lowell.
See also Lincoln Park.

Portland, Ore. Library Association. List of books on agriculture. '10(My7) 24°, gratis. Portland (Ore.) L. A.

Portland (Ore.) Library Association. List of practical books on machine shop practice, foundry work and electricity. '09(Je) 33 p. 24°, pap., gratis. Portland (Ore.) L. A.

PORTLAND CEMENT.
See Cement;—Ceramics.

Portland cement industry in the United States; directory of manufacturers having plants in operation. '08, [1909.] (Mr) c. fold. maps, 24°. (Add. pubs. for price.) Asoc. Am. Portland Cement.

Porto Rico. *Supreme ct.* Decisions, 1906, '07. v. 1 and 2. '08(Mr) c. O. shp., ea., $6. Lawyers' Co-op.

Porto Rico. *Supreme ct.* Decision of the Supreme court of Porto Rico and dissenting opinion in the case of the Roman Catholic Apostolic Church vs. the people of Porto Rico. '09(My) 45 p. 8°, pap. (Add. Superintendent for price.) U. S., Supt. of Docs.

Porto Rico. *United States district ct.* Federal repts., C: F. McKenna and Bernard S. Rodney, judges; (H: F. Hord.) v. 2. '08 (Mr) *$5 net; v. 3, 4. '09(O) $6; v. 5. '10(S) c. O. shp., $5. Lawyers' Co-op.

PORTO RICO.
Affairs in Porto Rico: message from the President inviting the attention of the Congress to the legislative difficulties in Porto Rico, with accompanying papers, and recommending an amendment to the Foraker Act. '09(Je) 17 p. pap., 5 c. U. S., Supt. of Docs.
Fowles, G: M. Down in Porto Rico. 75 c. Eaton & M.
Government of Porto Rico; rept. '09(Jl) 12 p. 8°. (Add. Superintendent for price.) U. S.. Supt. of Docs.

PORTO RICO.—*Continued.*
Military Historical Society of Massachusetts. v. 11, Naval actions and operations against Cuba and Porto Rico, 1593-1815. $2.50. Military Hist. Soc.
United States. Affairs in Porto Rico; message from the President inviting the attention of the Congress to the affairs of the Island of Porto Rico, and recommending legislation amending the act under which the island is governed. '09 (Ag) 6 p. 8°, pap. (Add. Superintendent for price.) U. S., Supt. of Docs.
United States. *Dept. of Commerce and Labor. Bu. of the Census.* Electrical industries of Porto Rico, 1907. (Add. Superintendent for price.)

PORTOLA, Gaspar de.
Costanso, M. Narrative of the Portola expedition. 50 c. Univ. of Cal.
Eldredge, Z. S., *and* Molera, E. J. March of Portola and discovery of the Bay of San Francisco. and The log of the "San Carlos." 50 c. Cal. Promotion Co.
Smith, D. E., *and* Teggart, F: J., *eds.* Diary of Gaspar de Portola during the California expedition of 1769-1770. 50 c. Univ. of Cal.
Teggart, F: J., *ed.* Official account of the Portola expedition of 1769-1770. 10 c. Univ. of Cal.

Portrait life of Lincoln. Miller, F. T. $2. Patriot.

Portrait miniatures. Holme, C:, *ed.* $3 net; $2.50 net. Lane.

PORTRAITS.
British historical portraits. v. 1. $2.90. Oxford Univ.
Hale, P. L. Great portraits: children.—Great portraits: women. ea., $1.50. Bates & G.
See also Engravers and engravings;—Miniatures;—Photography.

Portraits of the presidents of the United States and views of the Capitol and White House. '08(Ja18) 4°, $2. Lee & Co.

PORTS.
See Harbors.

PORTSMOUTH, N. H.
"Old town by the sea." 5 c. W: O. Fuller.

PORTSMOUTH, Louise Renée de Keroualle, *Duchess* of.
Grant, *Mrs.* C. Louise Renée de Keroualle, Duchess of Portsmouth. *$4 special net. Appleton.

PORTUGAL.
Baedeker, K. Spain and Portugal. *$4.80 net. Scribner.
Goodall, A. M. Portugal. *75 c. net. Macmillan.
Inchbold, *Mrs.* A. Lisbon and Cintra. *$3.50 net. Duffield.
Koebel, W. H. Portugal, its land and people. *$4 net. Dodd.
Oldmeadow, E. J. Portugal. $3.50 net. Lippincott.
See also Madeira Islands.

PORTUGUESE LANGUAGE.
Branner, J: C. Brief grammar of the Portuguese language. $1.25. Holt.
Pitman, *Sir* I: International mercantile letters: English-Portuguese. $1.25. Pitman.

Posey, Alex. Lawrence.
Alex. Posey, the Creek Indian poet; poems collected and arr. by Mrs. Minnie H. Posey; with memoir by W: Elsey Connelley. '10(N12) c. il. pors. 8°, $1. Crane.

POSITIVISM.
Comte, A. General view of positivism. 75 c.; 50 c. Dutton.

Positivo (Lo). Tamayo y Baus, *Don* M. 45 c. Heath.

POSSENTI, Gabriel.
Hage, H. Life of Blessed Gabriel of Our Lady of Sorrows. 50 c.; 25 c. Kilner.

Possible method of reclamation for the arid West. Mieir, W: O. 25 c. W: O. Mieir.

"Posson Jone." Cable, G: W. †$1.50. Scribner.

Post, Mrs. Alice Thacher.
Marriage as a present-day problem: an address del. before the N. Y. Association of the New Church, Feb. 22, 1909. '09 (S) 15 p. pap., 5 c. Public.

Post, Mrs. C. A.
See Post, Marie Caroline De Trobriand.

Post, Mrs. Caroline Lathrop.
Aunt Carrie's poems. '09(N) c. 157 p. por. 8°, $1. C. W. Post.

Post, Mrs. Emily Price.
Eagle's feather. '10(D10) c. il. D. $1.50. Dodd.
Title market. '09(O9) c. il. D. †$1.50. Dodd.
Woven in the tapestry. '08(Mr21) c. D. vellum, **$1 net. Moffat.

Post, L: Freeland.
Social service. '09(D11) c. O. *$1 net. Wessels.

Post, Lyman D.
Watermarks and brands used in the American paper trade; extracted from Post's paper mill directory for 1910. '10(My14) c. 8°, $1. L. D. Post.

Post, Marie Caroline De Trobriand, [Mrs. C. A. Post.]
Life and memoirs of Comte Régis de Trobriand, Major General U. S. A. '10(Ja8) 8°, **$5 net. Dutton.

Post, Mary A.
My little French book. '10(D) 84 p. il. 12°, 50 c. Dutton.

Post, Melville Davisson.
Corrector of destinies. '08(O10) c. 12°, $1.50. Clode.
Gilded chair. '10(My21) c. il. D. $1.50. Appleton.

Post, Van Zo.
Retz: a novel. '08(My9) c. D. †$1.50. McClure.

Post-apostolic age and current religious problems. Remensynder, J. B: $1.25. Lutheran Pub.

Post-Augustan poetry. Butler, H. E. $2.90. Oxford Univ.

Post-girl (The). Booth, E: C. †$1.50. Century Co.

Post graduate guide; what to do after you graduate; how to secure salaried positions and appointments after you graduate; repr. from the *Medical Record.* '09(N) c. 244 p. 12°, $1. Wood.

POST-OFFICE.

Allen, G: H. "I am reminded." [Parcels post.] 5 c. G: H. Allen.

Carr, C. E. Railway mail service. *50 c. net. McClurg.

Committee on Railway Mail Pay. Railway mail pay primer. Com. Railway.

Hecht, S. How to become a letter carrier or postal clerk. 50 c. Police Chronicle.

Lachaussee, C: A. How to become a letter carrier or post office clerk. 25 c.—How to enter the postal service. 50 c. Chief.

Madden, E. C: U. S. government's shame: the great Lewis case. 50 c. Nat. Bk. Co.

Ocean mail service between U. S. and foreign ports. (Add. Superintendent for price.) U. S., Supt. of Docs.

United States. *Congress. House. Committee on Expenditures in Post-Office Dept.* Expenditures in the Post-Office Dept.: rept. '09(My) 13 p. 8°, pap. (Add. Superintendent for price.)

United States. *Congress. Senate. Committee on Commerce.* Development of the American ocean mail service and American commerce. 25 c.

United States. *Congress. Senate. Committee on Commerce.* Ocean mail service between United States and foreign ports. 10 c. U. S., Supt. of Docs.

United States. *Post-office Dept.* Domestic and foreign mail; classification; conditions; rates of postage. (Add. Superintendent for price.)

United States. *Post Office Dept.* Information issued by the second assistant postmaster-general relative to the transportation of mails by railroad. '09(Jl) 22 p. 8°. (Add. Superintendent for price.)

United States. *Post-Office Dept.* Investigations as to pneumatic-tube service for mails. (Add. Superintendent for price.)

United States. *Post-office Dept.* Letter from the office of the third assistant postmaster-general; containing a discussion of the policy of the Post-office Department regarding fraternal and other publications issued by societies entered, or for which entry is sought, under the act of March 3, 1879. '09, [1910.] (Mr) 7 p. 8°, pap.

United States. *Post-Office Dept.* Navy mail service. (Add. Superintendent for price.) U. S., Supt. of Docs.

United States. *Post-office Dept.* The postal laws and regulations pertaining to the second class of mail matter corr. to July 1, 1909); promulgated by authority of the postmaster-general. '09(Ag) 54 p. 8°, pap. (Add. Superintendent for price.)

United States. *Post-Office Dept.* Rural delivery service. 15 c.

POST-OFFICE.—*Continued.*

United States. *Post Office Dept.* Summary of the department's reply to the Periodical Publishers' Association of America regarding second-class mail.

Votaw, C. E. Jasper Hunicutt of Jimpsonhurst: [railway mail service.] $1.50. Union Bk.

Williams, N. B. American post-office; discussion of its hist., development, and present-day relation to express companies. '10(Jl) 49 p. 8°. Gov. Pr. Off.

POSTAGE STAMPS.

Bellows, W. C. Campeche; some notes on the most remarkable postage stamp ever issued [Mexican]. $3.50. W. C. Bellows.

Burroughs, W: D. Wonderland of stamps. $1.50. Stokes.

Money and Stamps Brokerage Co. Money and stamp manual. $1. Money and Stamp.

Power, E. B. Le P. General issues of United States stamps, their shades and varieties. $1. S. Gibbons.

Randall, W. W., *and* Bartels, J: M., *comps.* Check-list of the postage stamps of Panama. 50 c. Bartels.

POSTAL SAVINGS BANKS.
See Banks and banking.

Postal savings banks. '09(My22) D. (Univ. of Wis. bull.) pap., gratis. Univ. of Wis.

POSTAL SERVICE.
See Post-office.

Postance, W:
See Bragdon, Guy F.

Postell, Jehu Glenn, ["Uncle Dudley."]
All about poultry. '10(Ag27) il. por. 8°, 50 c. J. W. Burke.

POSTER ADVERTISING.
See Advertising.

Postgate, J: Percival.
Flaws in classical research; from the Proceedings of the British Academy. v. 3. '09(D) 51 p. 8°, *$1.40 net. Oxford Univ.

Postscript (The). Childs, *Mrs.* E. S. †$1.25. McClure.

Posty ser. 2 v. '10(D) ea., bds., 40 c. Cassell.

Posty ser. 8 v. '10(D) ea., bds., 25 c. Cassell.

Potamian, Brother.
See O'Reilly, Michael Francis.

Potash & Perlmutter. Glass, M. $1.50. Doubleday, P.

POTATO.

Clark, C: C., *comp.* Potato crops of the United States, 1866-1906. 5 c. U. S., Supt. of Docs.

Dodge, L. G. Farm management in northern potato-growing sections. (Add. Superintendent for price.) U. S., Supt. of Docs.

Wente, A. O., *and* Tolman, L. M. Potato culls as a source of industrial alcohol. Gov. Pr. Off.

Potato child. Woodbury, L. P. H. 25 c. P. Elder.

POTOMAC RIVER, Va.

Farley, J. P. Three rivers, the James, the Potomac, the Hudson; a retrospect of peace and war. *$2 net. Neale.

Potted fiction. Bangs, J: K. †50 c.; †25 c. Doubleday, P.

Pottenger, Fs. Morton, M.D.
Diagnosis and treatment of pulmonary tuberculosis. '08(Mr7) il. 8°, *$3.50 net. Wood.

Potter, Alex.
Rept. upon joint outlet sewer in Essex and Union counties, N. J. 2d ed. '10(O) 110 p. il. map, 4°, pap. A. Potter.

Potter, Beatrix.
Ginger and Pickles. '09(D18) c. il. (partly in col.) D. bds., 50 c. Warne.
Roly-poly pudding. '09(F13) c. il. 8°, **$1 net. Warne.
Tale of Jemima Puddle-Duck. '08(O10) c. il. T. (Peter Rabbit ser.) bds., †50 c. Warne.
Tale of Mrs. Tittlemouse. '10(O15) c. il. in col. T. bds., 50 c. Warne.
Tale of the Flopsy Bunnies. '09(O2) c. col. il. T. bds., 50 c. Warne.

—, and Bannerman, Helen.
Story of Peter Rabbit [by Beatrix Potter]; and The story of little black Sambo, [by Helen Bannerman]. '10(D17) c. col. il. D. (Turnover books.) 60 c. Reilly & B.

Potter, C: N., rep.
See Wyoming. *Sup. ct.* Repts.

Potter, Mrs. Cora Urquhart, [Mrs. James Brown Potter.]
Secrets of beauty and mysteries of health: practical suggestions for the right care of the person. '08(Ap11) c. pors. O. satin-finish linen, **$1.75 net. P. Elder.

Potter, D:
Eleventh hour. '01(Mr26) c. col. front. D. †$1.50. Dodd.
Lady of the spur. '10(O1) c. front. D. $1.50. Lippincott.

Potter, Franklin Hazen.
Elem. Latin course. [Also] A new method for Cæsar. '08(My9) c. il. maps, D. (Students' ser. of Latin classics.) $1.12. B: H. Sanborn.

POTTER, *Bp.* Henry Codman.
Henry Codman Potter: memorial addresses del. before the Century Association, Dec. 12, 1908. '08, [1909.] (My) 34 p. por. 8°, pap., gratis. Century Assoc.
Keyser, H. A. Bishop Potter, the people's friend. $1 net. Whittaker.
People's Institute. Memorial to Henry Codman Potter. (Not for sale.) Cheltenham Press.

Potter, Mrs. Ja. Brown.
See Potter, *Mrs.* Cora Urquhart.

Potter, Marg. Horton, [now Mrs. J. D. Black.]
Golden ladder: a novel. '08(Ap18) c. D. †$1.50. Harper.

Potter, Marion E., Tannehill, Bertha, and Teich, Emma L., comps.
Children's catalog; guide to the best reading for young people, based on 22 selected library lists. pt. 1, Author, title and subject catalog of 3000 books; [pt. 2, Author and subject index to *St. Nicholas,* v. 28-36, and analytical subject reference to over 500 books cataloged in pt. 1.] '10(Ap16) Q. (Standard catalog ser.) $6 net. H. W. Wilson.

Potter, Mary Knight.
How Richard won out. '08(O24) c. front. D. †75 c. Wilde.
Richard in camp: story. '09(O9) c. front. D. †75 c. Wilde.

Potter, Olave Muriel.
Colour of Rome; historical, personal and local; introd. by Douglas Sladen and an essay by the artist. '09(N20) il. 8°, *$5 net. Jacobs.

Potter, S: L.
Bible stories as they are recorded in the Bible. '10(Ag13) c. 12°, $1.50. S. L. Potter.

Potter, S: Otway Lewis.
Therapeutics, materia medica, and pharmacy. 11th ed., rev. and enl. '09(O) 13+937 p. 8°, $5. Blakiston.

Potter, T. Chalmers.
Bee-keeping for sedentary folk. '08, [1909.] (F) 20 p. nar. T. il. pap., gratis. A. I. Root.

Potter, T. F.
Don't kill the laying hen; book describing and explaining the Potter system of selecting laying and non-laying hens. '09 (Ap1c) c. il. por. 16°, $1. T. F. Potter.

Potter, T:
Concrete: its use in building from foundations to finish. '09(Ja16) *$3 net. Van Nostrand.

Potter, W: W.
Law of interest [in Michigan]; commentary. '10(F) c. O. $2.50. Drake Law Bk.

Potter's craft. Binns, C: F. $2. Van Nostrand.

POTTERY.
See Ceramics.

Pottery clays of Mississippi. Logan, W: N. 50 c. Miss. Geol. Survey.

Pottier, Edmond.
Douris and the painters of Greek vases; tr. by Bettina Kahnweiler, with preface by Jane Ellen Harrison. '09(Ag21) il. 8°, $2.50. Dutton.

Pottle, Emery Bemsley.
Handicapped. '08(Je6) c. D. †$1.50. Lane.

Potts, C: Shirley.
Crime and the treatment of the criminal. '10(Jl9) O. (Univ. of Texas bull., humanistic ser.) pap., gratis. Univ. of Tex.
Railroad transportation in Texas. '09 (N) 214 p. fold. maps, O. (Univ. of Texas bulletin; Humanistic ser.) pap. Univ. of Tex.

Potts, C: Sower, M.D.
Nervous and mental diseases. 2d ed., enl. and thoroughly rev. '08(My2) il. 12°, *$2.50 net. Lea.

Potts, Ja. H:
My gift to thee; present time verses. '10 (D17) c. il. 12°, $1. Jennings.

Potts, J: Vinton.
Secret lodge system: unique, comprehensive and impartial study and discussion of this important subject in all its phases: [argument against secret societies.] '09 (Mr27) c. O. $1.25. Germ. Lit. Bd.

Potts, W. A., M.D.
See Shuttleworth, G. E., *M.D.*

Poucher, Mrs. Florence Holbrook.
Boy and the books. '09(Mr) c. 28 p. 12°, 75 c. Kimball Press.

POUGHKEEPSIE, N. Y.
See Vassar College.

Poulton, E: Bagnall.
Charles Darwin and The origin of species; addresses, etc., in America and England in the year of the two anniversaries. '09 (D25) O. $3. Longmans.
Essays on evolution, 1889-1907. '08(S26) 8°, *$4 net. Oxford Univ.

POULTRY.
Banks, E. E. Twentieth century poultry buildings and how to build them. 50 c. E. E. Banks.
Basley, *Mrs.* A. Poultry book.—Western poultry book. ea., $1. A. Basley.
Bickel, M. V. Poultry packers' guide. $2. Pool.
Biggle, J. Poultry book. 50 c. W. Atkinson.
Boyer, M. K. $100,000 per year from poultry.—Poultry secrets. ea., 25 c. W. Atkinson.
Boyer, M. K., *ed.* $6.41 per hen per year; Corning egg-book. 25 c. W. Atkinson.
Briggs, E. Profits in poultry keeping solved. $1. Hosterman.
Brigham, A. A. Progressive poultry culture. $1.50. Torch Press.
Columbia School of Poultry Culture text-books. Course A. In 12 sections. $2. Columbia Sch. Poultry.
Davenport, C: B. Inheritance of characteristics in domestic fowl. $4.50. Carnegie.
De Lancey, F. W. A to Z of pigeons and bantams. 50 c. Item Pub.
Dryden, J. Syllabus of illustrated lecture on the production and marketing of eggs and fowls. (Add. Superintendent for price.) U. S., Supt. of Docs.
Hadley, L. D. How to get eggs from your own hens during the winter months. $1. L. D. Hadley.
Hastings, M. M. Dollar hen. $1. Arcadia Press.
Hawks, E. B. Incubation and brooding. 50 c.—Science and art of poultry culture. $2.75. E. B. Hawks.
Heck, F. Secrets of expert exhibitors and easy lessons in judging. $2. F. Heck.
Hicks, R. V., *comp. and ed.* Tricks of the poultry trade. 50 c. Poultry Culture.
Hurst, J. W. Life story of a fowl. *$2 net. Macmillan.
Husselman, C. Southern poultry guide. $1. Southern Planter.
Johnson, A. T Chickens and how to raise them. 25 c.; 50 c. Penn Pub. Co.
Kains, M. G. Profitable poultry production. $1.50. Judd.
Kellerstrass, E. Kellerstrass way of raising poultry. $1. E. Kellerstrass.
Lehman, H: H. Poultry doctor. 75 c. H: H. Lehman.
Lewis, H. R. Poultry lab'y guide. 65 c. net. Macmillan.

POULTRY.—*Continued.*
McGrew, T: F., *and* Howard, G: E. Perfected poultry of America. $2.50. Howard Pub. Co.
Miller, D. H. Miller system book of poultry culture. $1.50. Miller System.
Pearl, R. Methods of poultry management. U. S., Supt. of Docs.
Philo, E. W. Philo system of progressive poultry keeping. $1. Poultry Review.
Postell, J. G. All about poultry. 50 c. J. W. Burke.
Potter, T. F. Don't kill the laying hen. $1. T. F. Potter.
Poultry houses and fixtures. 7th ed. '10 (Je) c. 95 p. il. 4°, 50 c. Reliable Poultry Journ.
Purvis, M. Poultry breeding. $1.50. Sanders Pub.
Reliable Incubator and Brooder Co. Success with poultry. $1. Reliable Incubator.
Reliable Poultry Journal Publishing Co. Chicken book. 50 c. Reliable Poultry Journ.
Robinson, J: H. Common-sense poultry doctor. 50 c. Farm-Poultry.
Sando, R. B. American poultry culture. *$1.50 net. McClurg.
Savage, H. B. Poultry culture in Texas. Texas.
Sevenich, J. M. Des landmann's gefügelbuch. 40 c. Excelsior Pub.
Simple poultry remedies; book which describes in simple language the symptoms of the leading diseases of poultry and tells how they may be cured and prevented by simple methods; by competent authorities. '09, [1910.] (F) c. 79 p. 8°, 25 c. Webb.
Sperle, C: H. Correct chicken culture. gratis. C: H. Sperle.
Spillman, W: J. Successful poultry and dairy farm. (Add. Superintendent for price.) U. S., Supt. of Docs.
Standard-bred wyandottes, silver, golden, white, buff, partridge, black, silver penciled and Columbian; their practical qualities; the standard requirements; how to judge them; how to mate and breed for best results, with a chapter on new non-standard varieties; J. H. Drevenstedt, editor; contributed to by the best known and most expert breeders and judges in America; text and il. are based on the requirements of the 1910 ed. of the American standard of perfection. [1910.] (S) c. 160 p. il. pors. 4°, $1. Reliable Poultry Journ.
Trafford, H:, *ed.* Smith method of poultry keeping. $1. Hosterman.
Two years with poultry. 50 c. Poultry Trib.
United States. *Superintendent of Documents.* Poultry: U. S. public documents. '09(My) 7 p. 12°, pap., gratis.
Valentine, C. S. How to keep hens for profit. $1.50 net. Macmillan.
Van Arsdale, L. F: How to build up a heavy laying strain: [treatise on egg production.] 50 c. Poultry Monthly.
Warren, E. Two dollars a day from poultry and eggs. 50 c. De Puy.

POULTRY.—*Continued.*
Watson, G: C. Farm poultry. **$1.25 net. Macmillan.
Weir, H. W: Poultry book. 3 v. in 1. $5 net. Doubleday, P.
Wiley, H. W., *and others.* Preliminary study of the effects of cold storage on eggs, quail, and chicken. (Add. Superintendent for price.) U. S., Supt. of Docs.
Wittman, W. T. Twelve months' work in the poultry yard. 25 c. Item Pub.
Woods, P. T. Facts about white diarrhœa; how to stop losses and reduce the mortality in small chicks.—Poultryman's formulary: recipes for ready-mixed grain foods. ea., $1. P. T. Woods.
See also Ducks;—Embryology;—Geese;—Pigeons:—Turkeys.

Pound, Ezra.
Provença; poems sel. from Personae, Exultations, and Canzoniere. '10(D17) c. D. bds., $1 net. Small.
Spirit of romance; attempt to define somewhat the charm of the pre-Renaissance literature of Latin Europe. '10(O8) 12°, $2.50 net. Dutton.

Pound, Louise, ed.
See Clapp, Anne Barr.

Pound of brains. Fadner, G: M. $1. G: M. Fadner.

Pour la couronne. *See* Coppée, François.

Pourrat, Rev. P.
Teaching of the fathers on the real presence of Christ in the holy eucharist. '08(S19) pap., 15 c. Cathedral Lib.
Theology of the sacraments; study in positive theology; auth. tr. from the 3d French ed. '10(My) c. 15+417 p. 8°, $1.50. net. Herder.

Poussin, Nicolas.
Masterpieces. '09(Je26) il. T. (Painters ser.) leath., *75 c. net; pap., *25 c. net. Stokes.

POVERTY.
See **Poor (The).**

Poverty of philosophy. Marx, K. $1. Kerr.

POWDER.
See Gunpowder.

Powder and Jam. Bisgood, M. $1. Stokes.

Powder puff. Blei, F. *$1.25 net. Duffield.

Powe, Ja. Harrington.
Reminiscences and sketches of Confederate times by one who lived through them; ed. by Harriet Powe Lynch. '09, [1910.] (Mr) c. 44 p. 8°. H. P. Lynch.

Powe, Louise M.
See Powers, Harry Huntington.

Powell, Addison Monroe.
Echoes from the frontier: verses. '09 (Ag7) c. il. D. **$1 net. Wessels.
Trailing and camping in Alaska. '09(D18) il. O. *$2 net Wessels.

Powell, Edg., ed.
Suffolk hundred in the year 1283: the assessment of the hundred of Blackbourne for a tax of one-thirtieth and a return showing the land tenure there. '10(O29) fold. tabs., Q. $3.50 net. Putnam.

Powell, Ellis T:
Essentials of self-government, (England and Wales.) '09(Mr13) O. *$1.50 net. Longmans.

Powell, Ernest.
Poems. '10(F12) 12°, $1.25. Badger.

Powell, F. E.
Small dynamos and motors; how to make, test, and repair them; pract. hdbk. for electrical amateurs and students. 8th ed. '10(Je4) 12°, pap., 25 c. Spon.

Powell, Frances, pseud.
See Case, Frances Powell.

Powell, Fred. Wilbur.
See Cleveland, F: Albert.

Powell, G: Harold, and Chace, E: Mackay.
Italian lemons and their by-product. I. Italian lemon industry, by G: Harold Powell; II. By-products of the lemon in Italy, by E: M. Chace. '09(D) 57 p. il. 8°, (U. S., Dept. of Agriculture, Bu. of Plant Industry, bull.) pap. (Add. Superintendent for price.)

—, [and others.]
Decay of oranges while in transit from California. '08(Je) 79 p. il. 8°, (U. S. Dept. of Agriculture, Bureau of plant industry bull.) pap., 15 c.

Powell, Rev. Lyman Pierson.
Art of natural sleep; with definite directions for the wholesome cure of sleeplessness, illustrated by cases treated in Northampton and elsewhere. '08(N21) c. D. bds., **90 c. net. Putnam.
Credentials of the church. '10(My14) c. D. pap., 20 c. Whittaker.
Emmanuel Movement in a New England town, [Northampton, Mass.] '09(Ap10) c. il. D. **$1.25 net. Putnam.
Heavenly heretics. '09(D4) c. pors. D. **$1.25 net. Putnam.

Powell, Sir Rob. Stephenson Smythe Baden-.
See Baden-Powell, *Sir* Rob. Stephenson Smythe.

Powell, T:
Fundamentals and requirements of health and disease. In 3 pts. '10(F) c. 7-602 p. il. por. 8°, $5. Powell Pub.

Powell, W: M.
Saunders' pocket medical formulary. 9th ed., thoroughly rev., enl. and adapted to the eighth revision, (1905,) of the U. S. pharmacopœia. '09(Jl) c. 7+308 p. il. 16°, flex. mor., *$1.75 net. Saunders.

Power, Effie L., comp.
Selected list of children's books for school libraries of Michigan. '09(My) 72 p. 12°, pap., gratis. L. L. Wright.

Power, Eustace Bertram Le Poer.
General issues of United States stamps, their shades and varieties; to which is affixed a hist. of the private perforating machines and their products. '10(Mr5) c. il. 8°, $1. Gibbons.

Power, J. Clyde.
See Price, C: R.

Power, M.
At the root of Socialism; study of a Glasgow manifesto; lecture del. before the Social Democratic Federation. '09 (N) 36 p. 8°, pap., *10 c. net. Herder.
True rationalism: lecture del. in the Univ. of Glasgow before St. Miriam's Society. '08(Ag8) 8°, pap., 10 c. Herder.

POWER.
See Dynamos and motors;—Electricity;—Heating;—Machinery;—Mechanics.
Power and its transmission. Smith, T: A. $1. Spon.
Power and the glory. Cooke, *Mrs.* G. M. $1.20, fixed. Doubleday, P.
Power and weakness of trade unions. Collins, J: M. 10 c. J: M. Collins.
POWER BOATS.
See Boats.
Power for service. Lawrence, J: B. $1.15. C: O. Chalmers.
Power gas producers. Robson, P. W. *$3 net. Longmans.
Power handbooks. See Collins, Hubert Edn.
Power, heating and ventilation. Hubbard, C: L. 3 v. $5 net. Technical Press.
Power of a lie. Bojer, J. $1.25. M. Kennerley.
Power of eminent domain. Nichols, P. $5. Boston Bk.
Power of gold. Sangster, U. N. $2. U. N. Sangster.
Power of innocence. Westermayr, A. J. $1.50. Fenno.
Power of purpose. Jordan, W: G. 35 c. net. Revell.
Power of self-suggestion. McComb, S: **50 c. net. Moffat.
Power of speech and how to acquire it. Lawrence, E. G. $1.25. Hinds.
Power of will. Haddock, F. C. $3. Power-B.
POWER PLANTS.
See Gas and gas-fitting.
Power; Success; and Greatness. *See* Emerson, Ralph Waldo.
Power supreme. Nichols, F. C. $1.50. R. E. Lee.
Powers, Mrs. Carol Hoyt.
See Powers, Leland Todd.
Powers, Harry Huntington and Mrs. Mary Montague, and Powe, Louise M.
Outlines for the study of art. '07, [1908.] (S.) c. 2 v., fronts., 12°, ea., $1.50. Bu. Univ. Travel.
Powers, Rev. J. D. O.
Love never faileth: [a sermon.] '09(My8) c. nar. O. (Puget Sound friendship ser.) pap., 50 c., in envelope. A. Harriman.
Powers, Ja. Knox.
See Colaw J: Marvin.
Powers, Jos. Horace.
Morphological variation and its causes in *Amblystoma tigrinum.* '08(Ja4) il. 8°, (Univ. studies.) pap., $1. Univ. of Neb.
Powers, Leland Todd and Mrs. Carol Hoyt.
Talks on some fundamentals of expression. '09, [1910.] (Ap) 61 p. 12°, $1.25. L. Powers Sch.
POWERS, LELAND, SCHOOL, Boston.
Powers, L. T. Practice book; Leland Powers School. '09, [1910.] (Ja) c. 111 p. 12°, 75 c. L. Powers Sch.
Powers, Mrs. Mary Montague.
See Powers, Harry Huntington.
Powers and duties of justices of the peace in civil, criminal and special cases in the state of Oklahoma. Honnold, A. B. $6. Flood.
Powers of the American people. Miyakawa, M. **$2.50 net. Baker & T.

POWNAL, Maine.
Latham, *Mrs.* E. J. Hist. of the town of Pownal. 30 c. Lewiston Journ.
Pownall, C: Assheton Whately.
Thomas Pownall, M.P., F.R.S., governor of Massachusetts Bay, author of The letters of Junius; with a supplement comparing the colonies of Kings George III. and Edward VII. '09(Ja30) por. maps, fold. facsims., chart. Q. *$5 net. Abbatt.
POWNALL, Thomas.
Pownall, C: A. W. **Thomas Pownall, M.P. F.R.S., governor of Massachusetts Bay, author of The letters of Junius.** *$5 net. Abbatt.
Poynter, Sir E: J:
Painting: classic and Italian. '10(D) 12°, (Hdbks. of art hist.) hf. leath., $1.25. Gorham.
Poynting, J: H:
Pressure of light. '10(D) 103 p. 16°, 75 c. net. Gorham.
Poyser, Arth.
Tower of London. '08(Ag1) il. plan, 8°, (Color books.) *$2.50 net. Macmillan.
Practical aids to literature. front. map, 12°. Whitaker & R.
—Whittier. Whittier in the schools. 25 c.
Practical agitation. Chapman, J: J. $1.25. Moffat.
Practical and perplexing questions. Torrey, R. A. *50 c. net. Revell.
Practical argumentation. Pattee, G: K. **$1.10 net. Century Co.
Practical assistance to owners of forest land and to tree planters. '09(Ag14) 8°, (U. S., Dept. of Agriculture; Forest service, circular.) pap. (Add. Superintendent for price.) U. S., Supt. of Docs.
Practical citizenship. Roeder, A. *$1.50 net. Blanchard.
Practical communism. Eeden, F. van. 10 c. Civic Forum.
Practical designing. White, G. *$1.25 net. Macmillan.
Practical geography. *See* Unstead, J. F.
Practical guide ser. 16°, **$1 net. Small.
—Frazar. Pract. guide to Great Britain and Ireland.
—Hale. Pract. guide to Latin America.
Practical guide to embossing and die stamping, together with explanatory text on copperplate engraving and printing, chapters on the theory and practice of color printing. '08(O17) c. il. O. $1.50. Inland Pr.
Practical house framing. Peker, C: G. 50 c. Indust. Bk.
Practical integration. Percival, A. S. *80 c. net. Macmillan.
Practical lessons in nursing. il. diagrs., 12°. Lippincott.
—Wilson. Fever-nursing. $1 net.
Practical medicine ser. of yearbooks; ed. by G. P. Head. il. 12°. Year Bk.
—Abt *and* Ridlon, *eds.* Pediatrics. $1.25.
—Baum *and* Moyer. Skin and venereal diseases. $1.25.
—Billings *and* Salisbury, *eds.* General medicine. $1.25.
—Butler. Materia medica and therapeutics. $1.50.

Practical medicine ser. of yearbooks.—Cont.
—De Lee *and* Stowe. Obstetrics. $1.25.
—Dudley *and* Bachellé, *eds.* Gynecology. $1.25.
—Murphy. General surgery. $2.
—Patrick *and* Mix, *eds.* Nervous and mental diseases. $1.25.
—Wood. Eye, ear, nose and throat. $1.50.
Practical papers. il. 8°. Henley.
—Pratt. Wiring a house. 25 c.
Practical primers of business. See Pitman's.
Practical real estate methods. 3d ed. '10 (S3) 12°, $2. Doubleday, P.
Practical reinforced concrete standards. Andrews, H. B. $2. Simpson.
Practical service. Safford, J. H. 15 c. Y. M. C. A.
Practical suggestions for drawing wills and the settlement of estates in Pennsylvania. *$2 net. T. & J. W. Johnson.
Practical upholstery; methods of stuffing and covering various styles of furniture clearly explained, with hints on repairing, renovating. '10(Je4) il. 12°, (Wood worker ser.) pap., 25 c. Spon.
Practice and theory of the injector. Kneass, S. L. $1.50. Wiley.
Practice of anæsthetics. Collum, R. W. *$3 net. Wood.
Practice of forestry. Maw, P. T. $7. Scribner.
Practice of medicine. Tyson, J. *$5.50 net; *$6.50 net; *$7 net. Blakiston.
Practice of oil painting and of drawing. Solomon, S. J. $1.75 net. Lippincott.
Practitioner's handbooks; ed. by Harry Roberts. D. Lane.
—Jones. Short practice of aural surgery. *$1.75 net.
Praed, Mrs. Campbell Mackworth.
See Praed, Rosa Caroline Murray-Prior.
Praed, Rosa Caroline Murray-Prior, [Mrs. Campbell Mackworth Praed.]
By their fruits: a novel. '08(D12) front. D. $1.50. Cassell.
Opal fire. '10(D31) $1.20 net. Cassell.
Praed, Winthrop Mackworth.
Poems; selected and arranged, with introd., by Ferris Greenslet. '10(F19) c. por. 12°, $5. Houghton M.
Select poems; ed., with an introd., by A. D. Godley. '10(Ja22) por. S. (Oxford lib. of prose and poetry.) 90 c. Oxford Univ.
Praeger, S. Rosamond.
How they went to the seaside. '10(S10) col. il. O. $1. Stokes.
PRAENESTE, Italy.
See Palestina.
Prag, E:
Course in dyeing for garment dyers. '09 (N20) c. il. 8°, $5. Modern Dyer.
PRAGMATISM.
Bawden, H: H. Principles of pragmatism. **$1.50 net. Houghton M.
James, W: Meaning of truth. **$1.25 net. Longmans.
Laguna, T. de L. *and* G. A. de. Dogmatism and evolution. $1.75 net. Macmillan.
Lyman, E. W: Theology and human problems. $1 net. Scribner.

PRAGMATISM.—*Continued.*
Moore, A. W. Pragmatism and its critics. $1.25 net. Univ. of Chic.
Pratt, J. B. What is pragmatism? **$1.25 net. Macmillan.
Schinz, A. Anti-pragmatism. $1.50. Small.
See also Philosophy.
Prairie. Bush, B. E. $1.50. Little, B. & Co.
Prairie (The). *See* Cooper, Ja. Fenimore.
PRAIRIES.
See West (The).
Praise of a simple life. Baker, E. A., *ed.* *$1 net. Dutton.
Prather, C: Edg.
Spiritual healing. '10(Mr5) c. obl. 32°, $1.25. Power Pub.
—, comp. and ed. Winning orations of the inter-state oratorical contests. '07, [1908.] (My) c. 2 v., 241; 300 p. pors. 8°, v. 1, $1.25; v. 2, $1.75. Crane.
Prather, Rev. C: H:
Hdbk. of classics; or, a volume of illustrations from classical literature and current life. '10(N5) c. D. $1. Pub. Ho. M. E. Ch., So.
Pratt, Ambrose.
Living mummy. '19(F19) c. col. il. D. †$1.50. Stokes.
Vigorous Daunt: billionaire. '08(Jl4) c. D. *$1 net. Fenno.
Pratt, Edn. Hartley.
Synthetic clinic, incl. a three days' course in orificial surgery, Sept. 27-Oct. 2, 1909; 22d annual session of the American Association of Orificial Surgeons, Chicago, Ill., Sept. 29-30, 1909. [1910.] c. 6+343 p. 8°, $5. N. L. McCall.
Pratt, Ella Farman.
Little cave-dwellers. '08(S19) c. front. D. (Bimbi ser.) bds., **40 c. net. Crowell.
Pratt, Florence Evelyn, [Mrs. Clarence Herbert Youngs.]
Songs of many days. '08(F1) c. D. $1. Badger.
Pratt, Gilbert H.
See Stabler, Herman.
Pratt, Grace Tyler.
Bainbridge mystery: the housekeeper's story. '10(D17) c. O. $1.20 net. Sherman, F.
Pratt, Helen Marshall.
Cathedral churches of England; their architecture, hist and antiquities. '10(Je18) c. il. D. $2.50 net. Duffield.
Pratt, Herbert.
Wiring a house. 4th ed. '09(Je5) c. il. 8°, (Practical papers.) pap., 25 c. Henley.
Pratt, Ja. Bissett.
What is pragmatism? '09(Mr6) c. D. **$1.25 net. Macmillan.
Pratt, Ja. Randall.
Satan: lectures. '08(O) c. 96 p. 12°, 35 c. J. R. Pratt.
Pratt, Lucy.
Ezekiel. '09(Je12) c. il. D. †$1. Doubleday, P.
Pratt, Rob. Winthrop.
See Kinnicutt, Leonard Parker.

Pratt, S: Wheeler, D.D.
Deity of Jesus Christ according to the gospel of St. John. '08(F8) c. D. *50 c. net. S. S. Times.

Pratt, Waldo Selden.
Class notes in music history; to accompany "History of music." '08(O17) c. O. pap., *30 c. net. Schirmer.

Pratt, Wa. Merriam.
Burning of Chelsea. '08(Jl18) c. il. O. $1.50. Sampson.

Pratt, W: Knight.
Advertising manual. '09(My8) c. il. 12°, (American artisan manuals.) $3.50. D. Stern.

Pratt-Chadwick, Mrs. Mara Louise.
See Chadwick, *Mrs.* Mara Louise Pratt-.

Pratt Institute, Brooklyn. *Free Library.* Books for Christmas for the children. '09, [1910.] (Mr) 16 p. 12°, pap., gratis. Pratt Inst.

Pratt Institute, Brooklyn. *Free Library.* Technical books of 1908: a selection. '09 (Jl31) 12°. (Add. Institute for price.) Pratt Inst.

Pratt's digest: laws rel. to national banks; with notes, digest, [etc.] Ed. of 1908. '08, [1909.] c. (Mr) 26+401 p. O. $2. A. S. Pratt.

Pratz, C. de.
French dishes for English tables. '08(O31) D. $1. McKay.

Prayer.
Bayley, F. T. Can the modern man pray? 10 c. Y. M. C. A.
Best, N. R. Beyond the natural order; essays on prayer, miracles and the incarnation. *75 c. net. Revell.
Biederwolf, W: E: How can God answer prayer? *75 net. Revell.
Broadhurst, C. N. Wireless messages; possibilities through prayer. $1 net. Revell.
Brooks, F. L. Prevailing prayer: sermons. 60 c. F. L. Brooks.
Egger, J. S. J. Are our prayers heard. 15 c. Herder.
Faris, W: W. How to talk with God. *50 c. net. S. S. Times.
Gamertsfelder, S. J. Bible study on prayer. 40 c. Pub. Ho. of Evangelical Assoc.
Huntley, *Mrs.* F. C., *ed.* Who answers prayer? 50 c. Indo-Am. Bk.
McFayden, J: E. Way of prayer. 50 c. net. Pilgrim Press.
Ostrom, H: Law of prayer. 50 c. Praise Pub.
Page, V. F. Prayer. 50 c. V. F. Page.
Soulsby, L. H. M. Suggestions on prayer. 35 c. Longmans.
See also Lord's prayer;—Lord's supper;—Prayer meetings;—Prayers;—Worship.

Prayer-book.
See Book of common prayer.

Prayer book of the Protestant Episcipal church simplified and arranged. [1910.] (D) c. 3-25+329-508 p. 16°, 30 c. Ritzmann, B. & Co.

Prayer-meeting talks: one hundred selections from Scripture with explanations. '10 (Mr5) c. 12°, $1.25. Pub. Ho. of Evangelical Assoc.

Prayer-meetings.
Benjamin, R. Echoes from Oak Street; or, the twentieth century prayer meeting. 50 c. Donohue.
Richardson, N. E., *ed.* Present-day prayer-meeting helps for laymen and ministers. 50 c. net. Eaton & M.
Union prayer-meeting helper for 1909. 25 c.; per doz., $2.50; per 25, $4.75; per 50, $9; per 100, $15. Funk.
See also Devotional exercises and meditations.

Prayers.
Ames, C: G. Book of prayers. *$1.50 net; *$2.50 net. Am. Unitarian.
Building the walls; book of prayer and thanksgiving. *65 c. net. Macmillan.
Frere, W. H., *and* Illingworth, A. L., *eds.* Sursum corda: hdbk. of intercession and thanksgiving. *55 c. net; *75 c. net. Young Churchman.
Garbett, *Canon, and* Martin, S., *eds.* Family prayer-book. *$1.50 net. Cassell.
Hyde, W: De W. Abba Father: [prayers for each day.] *50 c. net. Revell.
Matheson, G: Day unto day: brief prayer for every day. *50 c. net. Revell.
Meyer, L. R. Some little prayers. *35 c. net. Jennings.
Pell, E: L. Prayer for each day in the week. 10 c.—Prayers. 25 c. Harding.
Pell, E: L., *comp. and ed.* Prayers we love to pray; incl. the world's greatest prayers suitable for private devotion. $1. Harding.
Rankin, I: O. Closet and altar; book of prayers for every day of the month. 25 c. net. Pilgrim Press.
Rauschenbusch, W. For God and the people; prayers of the social awakening. $1 net. Pilgrim Press.
Reisner, C. F. Week-day prayers. *35 c. net. Jennings.
Selikovitsch, G: G. Memorial prayers and meditations. 50 c. Hebrew Pub.
Sommer, M. S., *comp.* Prayers. 25 c.; 50 c. Volkening.
Soulsby, L. H. M., *comp.* Week by week; ms. of private prayers. 30 c. Longmans.
Strong, A. L. Psychology of prayer. *$1.75 net. Univ. of Chic.
Thomas, A. Prayers and instructions with forms. (Add. pub. for price.) Lord Balto. Pr.
Tipple, S: A. Sunday mornings at Norwood; being twenty-two sermons and twenty-two prayers. *$1.25 net. Eaton & M.
Tobie, W. N. Two beautiful prayers from the lips of Jesus. *50 c. net. Jennings.
Tomkins, F. W. Prayers for the quiet hour. $1. Un. Soc. C. E.
See also Book of common prayer;—Burial;—Devotional exercises and meditations;—Jews;—Lent:—Lord's prayer;—Lord's supper;—*also* names of churches;—*also* MacArthur, Robert Stuart.

Preacher (The). Hoyt, A. S. **$1.50 net. Macmillan.

Preacher's protests. *See* McDermott, D. I.

PREACHERS.
Reisner, C. F. Preacher-persuader. 50 c. Jennings.
See also Ministers (*of the Gospel*);—Missions and missionaries;—Priests.

PREACHING.
Carter, F. E. Preaching. *90 c. net. Longmans.
Corbett, F: S. J. Thousand thoughts for pract. preachers. $2 net. Whittaker.
Culler, D: D. Problems of pulpit and platform. 75 c. Brethren Pub. Ho.
Edwards, J: Primer of homiletics. *75 c. net. Jennings.
Henson, H. H. Liberty of prophesying. *$1.50 net. Yale Univ.
Hoyt, A. S. Preacher: his person, message and methods. **$1.50 net. Macmillan.
Quayle, W: A. Pastor-preacher. *$1.50 net. Jennings.
Simpson, *Canon* J. G. Preachers and teachers. $1.40 net. Longmans.
Slattery, C: L. Present-day preaching. **$1 net. Longmans.
Young, W: H: How to preach with power. $1. How Pub.
See also Illustrations (*religious*);—Sermons.

Preble, G: H:, comp.
Did your child say this?; collection of 500 bright, wise and witty sayings by the little ones. '09(N13) c. S. 50 c. J: W. Luce.

Preble, H:
Month of solitaires. '09(Je) 16°, *50 c. net. Brentano's.

Pre-Cambrian geology of North America. Van Hise, C: R. (Add. Superintendent for price.) U. S., Supt. of Docs.
Pre-Cambrian volcanic and intrusive rocks of the Fox River valley, Wisconsin. Hobbs, W: H. 25 c. Univ. of Wis.
Precedents of pleading at common law. Keigwin, C: A. $5. Byrne.
Precepts and prayers. Robinson, S. C., *ed.* 50 c. Treat.
Precinct of religion in the culture of humanity. Shaw, C: G. *$2 net. Macmillan.
Precious blood of Christ. Randolph, B. W: *75 c. net. Longmans.
Precious blood the price of our redemption. Walz, M. F. 15 c. St. Joseph's Pr.
Precious metals. Rose, T: K. **$2 net. Van Nostrand.

PRECIOUS STONES.
Goodchild, W. Precious stones. *$2 net. Van Nostrand.
Wodiska, J. Book of precious stones. **$2.50 net. Putnam.
See also Diamonds; — Jewelry; — Pearls; — *also* North Carolina.

Preciousness of God's thoughts. Nichols, G. P. *$1.25 net. Revell.

PRECIPITATION.
See Temperature.

Précis d'histoire de France. Patet, F. J. $1.50. F. J. Patet.
Predestined. Whitman, S. F. †$1.50. Scribner.
Pre-eminent Lord, and other sermons. Holden, J. S. *$1.25 net. Doran.

Preetorius, Carl.
Tone placed and developed. '08(Ja11) facsim., O. $1.50. C. Preetorius.

Préface du Cromwell. *See* Hugo, Victor.

PREGNANCY.
Kraft, M. J. Suggestions to the expectant mother. $2. M. J. Kraft.
Witkowski's atlas of gestation. *$3 net. W: R. Jenkins.
See also Midwifery.

Pre-historic archæology. Astley, H. J: D. *$2 net. Scribner.
Prehistoric man. McCabe, J. 50 c. net. Stokes.
Pre-historic man. Tanner, H: S: 25 c. H: S: Tanner.
Prehistoric men of Kentucky. Young, B. H. $4.50. Morton.
Prehistoric Rhodesia. Hall, R: N. $3.50 net. Jacobs.
Prehistoric Siskiyou Island. Watson, C. B. (Priv. pr.) C. B. Watson.
Prejudice. Krauskopf, J. 75 c.; 35 c. Bloch.

PRELATES.
See Catholic church;—Priests.

Preliminary bibliography of modern criminal law. Wigmore, J. H: 65 c. Northwestern Univ.
Preliminary note on rotation of sun. Hale, G: E. (Not for sale.) Carnegie.

Prelini, C:
Graphical determination of earth slopes, retaining walls and dams. '08(N7) c. diagrs., tabs., Q. **$2 net. Van Nostrand.
Tunneling; exhaustive treatise; with additions by C: S. Hill. 3d ed., rev. '10(My14) il. 8°, $3 net. Van Nostrand.

Premature cheapening of copyright books. Spurgeon, A. (Priv. pr.) Cassell.

Prendergast, J:
Great operas told for children; tales from the great operas retold. '09(O30) c. col. il. O. $1.50. Stokes.

Prentice, And. N.
Spanish renaissance: architecture and ornament. '08(Ag8) il. por. F. $22.50. Polley.

Prentice, W: Kelly.
Greek and Latin inscriptions. '08(D) c. 14+352 p. f°, (Am. archeological expedition to Syria pubs.) **$10 net. Century Co.

Prentis, Noble Lovely.
Hist. of Kansas; ed. and rev. by Henrietta V. Race. '09(S) c. 403 p. il. pors. 12°, 60 c. C. Prentis.

Prentys, Elsie Pym.
French for daily use; comprising conversations for journeying and for daily use in town and country; French rev. by L: Ferdinand Richard. '10(Je18) c. T. 50 c. W: R. Jenkins.

Preparation and use of sweet whey in powder form. Merrill, L. C. gratis. Merrill-S.
Preparation for teaching. Oliver, C: A. 25 c. Westminster Press.
Preparation for United States civil service examination. Goff, R. R. $3. Clerk Agency.
Preparation of the modern minister. Moore, W. W: 10 c.; per 100, $8. Y. M. C. A.

Preparatory school question. Baker, T: S. Tome Sch.

Prepare to meet thy God. Long, S. P: 35 c. S. P: Long.

Pre-Raphaelitism. *See* Ruskin, J:

Presbrey, Fk.
Information guide for transatlantic travellers. 6th ed. '09(N) c. 128 p. col. il. maps, 8°, 25 c.; ed. de luxe, $1. Presbrey.
Motoring abroad. '08(Je27) c. il. maps, O. *$2 net. Outing.

Presbyterian book of common worship. '08 (D19) 75 c.; leath., $1.50; smaller type, 35 c. Presb. Bd.

Presbyterian Brotherhood of America. The Brotherhood and the church; rept. of the third convention at Pittsburgh, Feb. 23-25, 1909. '09(S) c. 328 p. il. 12°, 50 c.; pap., 35 c. Presb. Bd.

Presbyterian Brotherhood of America. Report of the second convention held at Cincinnati, November 14th-16th, 1907. '08, (Mr28) c. por. 12°, 50 c.; pap., 35 c. Presb. Bd.

PRESBYTERIAN CHURCH.
Jolly, A. H. Ruling elder's hdbk. 50 c. Presb. Pub.
Lukens, V. H., *and* Russell, J. E. Presbyterian church membership. (Add. pubs. for price.) Westminster.
McPhail, W. M. Presbyterian church. *$1.50 net. Doran.
Stephens, J: V. Presbyterian churches, divisions and unions in Scotland, Ireland, Canada and America. 75 c. Presb. Bd.
Walker, J. G. Presbyterianism and the negro. 50 c. J. G. Walker.
See also Calvinism.

Presbyterian hdbk., 1910. '10(F) 84 p. Tt. pap., 5 c. Presb. Bd.

Presbyterian pulpit. 10 v. '08(D19) por. D. ea., *50 c. net; per set, *$4 net. Presb. Bd.

PRESBYTERIAN THEOLOGICAL SEMINARY, San Francisco.
Curry, J. Hist. of the San Francisco Theological Seminary of the Presbyterian church. $1.50. J. Curry.

Prescott, De Witt Clinton.
Early day railroading from Chicago; narration with some observations. '10(Je11) c. il. pors. D. $1.50. D: B. Clarkson.
Evolution of modern band saw mills for sawing logs. [1910.] (S) c. 49 p. il. pors. O. pap., gratis. Prescott.

Prescott, S: Cate, and Winslow, C: E:
Elements of water bacteriology. 2d ed., rewritten. '08(Mr.14) c. 12°, $1.50. Wiley.

PRESCOTT, William.
Green, S: A. Colonel William Prescott and Groton soldiers in the battle of Bunker Hill. 35 c. S: A. Green.

Prescott, W: Hickling.
Works. De luxe ed. 12 v. '10(D) $36. Crowell.
Conquest of Mexico. 2 v. '09(O30) 12°, (Everyman's lib.) ea., *35 c. net; leath., *70 c. net. Dutton.
Conquest of Peru. '08(O10) 12°, (Best books ser.) leath., *$1 net.—*Same*. Introd. by T: Seccombe. '08(Mr7) 16°, (Everyman's lib.) *35 c. net; *70 c. net. Dutton.

PRESCRIPTIONS.
See Materia medica;—Pharmacy.

Present and future of the cement block. Smith, J. A. 25 c. J. A. Smith.

Present-day conditions in China. Broomhall, M. *50 c. net. Revell.

Present-day Japan. Davidson, A. M. C. *$1.50 net. Scribner.

Present-day prayer-meeting helps. Richardson, N. E., *ed.* 50 c. net. Eaton & M.

Present-day preaching. Slattery, C: L. **$1 net. Longmans.

Present day primers. il. D. Moffat.
—Kennelly. Wireless telegraphy and wireless telephony. **$1 net.

Present day problems. Taft, W: H. **$1.50 net. Dodd.

Present status of military aeronautics. Squier, G: O. 80 c. Am. Soc. Mech. Engineers.

Presentation of reality. Wodehouse, H. $1 net. Putnam.

Preservation of iron and steel. Cushman, A. S. 10 c. U. S., Supt. of Docs.

PRESERVING.
Bitting, A. W. Canning of peas. 10 c. U. S., Supt. of Docs.
Breazeale, J. F. Canning vegetables in the home. (Add. Superintendent for price.) U. S., Supt. of Docs.
National Canners' Association. Canners' directory and allied industries. $2. T. E. Gorrill.
Wagner, E. Recipes for preserving of fruit, vegetables and meat. *$2.50 net. Van Nostrand.
See also Food.

Preshus child. McCahan, *Mrs.* B. T. $1.50. Cochrane.

PRESIDENTIAL CAMPAIGNS.
See United States.

PRESIDENTS.
See United States;—White House.

PRESS.
See Journalism;—Liberty of the press;—Newspapers;—Periodicals.

Pressure of Asia. Coleman, W: M. (Add. author for price.) W: M. Coleman.

Pressure of light. Poynting, J: H: 75 c. net. Gorham.

PRESSWORK.
See Printers and printing.

Pressy, E: Pearson.
Vision of new Clairvaux; [introducing experiences of Montague, Mass., colony of idealists.] '09(O) 8°, *$1.25 net. Sherman, F.

Preston, De Forest A., and Stevens, E: Lawrence.
Preston-Stevens ser. of arithmetics. bk. 1, Elem. arithmetic; bk. 2, Standard arithmetic. '10(D17) 12°, bk. 1, 35 c. net; bk. 2, 50 c. net. Macmillan.

Preston, Howard Willis.
See Collins, Ja. Franklin.

Preston, P. J.
See Beach, C: Worth.

Pretty-girl and others. Smith, *Mrs.* E. T. $1.50. Dutton.

Pretty girl papers. Walker, E. E. $1.25 net. Little, B. & Co.

Preuss, Arth.
Fundamental fallacies of socialism: exposition of the question of landownership; authentic account of the famous McGlynn case. '08(F22) 8°, *$1 net. Herder.
—, **ed.** Study in American freemasonry; based upon Pike's "Morals and dogma of the ancient and accepted Scottish rite," and other American masonic standard works. '07(Ag8) c. 8°, *$1.50 net. Herder.

Prevailing prayer. Brooks, F. L. 60 c. F. L. Brooks.

Preventable diseases. Hutchinson, W. **$1.50 net. Houghton M.

Prevention and treatment of abortion. Taussig, F: J. $2. Mosby.

Prevention of accidents. Johnson, F: W: 25 c. McGraw-H.

Prevention of industrial accidents. Fidelity and Casualty Company, New York. 25 c. Fidelity and Casualty.

Prevention of malaria. Ross, R. $5 net. Dutton.

Prevention of mine explosions. Watteyne, V. (Add. Superintendent for price.) U. S., Supt. of Docs.

Prevention of tuberculosis. Newsholme, A. *$3 net. Dutton.

Previté-Orton, C: W:
Political satire in English poetry; being the Members' prize essay for 1908. '10 (Ap16) D. $1.50 net. Putnam.

Prévost, Marcel.
Simply women; selections from the works of Marcel Prévost; tr. by R. I. Brandun-Vauvillez. '10(N12) c. D. $1 net. Macaulay.

Preyer, D: C.
Art of the Metropolitan Museum of New York; giving a descriptive and critical account of its treasures. '09(D14) c. il. pors. maps, O. $3, boxed; ¾ mor., $7, boxed. L. C. Page.
Art of the Netherland galleries. '08(N7) c. il. D. (Art galleries of Europe.) *$2 net, boxed; ¾ mor., *$5 net, boxed. L. C. Page.

Price, A. C.
Leeds and its neighborhood; illustration of English hist. '09(N13) fold. map, D. 90 c. Oxford Univ.

Price, B: Lincoln, and Stow, Arth. W:
Wills and how to make them: a brief outline of the law of wills with suggestions and forms. '08(My.) c. 24 p. T. pap. (Add. author for price.) B: L. Price.

Price, Carl F.
Babe of Bethlehem; Christmas service, [with music.] '09(N6) c. O. pap., per 100, $2.50. Eaton & M.

Price, C: R.
Irrigated lands of United States, Canada and Mexico. '08, [1909.] (Ap) c. 71 p. il. tab., 8°, 30 c. Scenic America.
—, **and Power, J. Clyde.**
Irrigated lands of United States, Canada and Mexico, by C: R. Price; supplemented by Irrigated lands of the west coast of Mexico, by J. Clyde Power. '10 (Ap9) il. maps, tabs., 8°, 50 c. Pan-Pacific.

Price, E. D.
Letters of Mildred's mother to Mildred. '09(D) 160 p. 12°, pap., 25 c. J. S. Ogilvie.

Price, G: Bacon.
Problem of happy marriage. '09(Mr6) c. S. $1. Chelston Press.

Price, G: Moses, M.D.
Hygiene and public health. [1910.] (N) c. 10+17-255 p. 12°, (Medical epitome ser.; ed. by V. C. Pedersen.) $1 net. Lea.
Tenement-house inspector. 2d ed., rev. and improved. '10(D17) c. 16°, $1.50. Chief.

Price, Langford Lovell Frederic Rice.
Position and prospects of the study of economic history: lecture del. in the examination schools [Oxford.] '08(O24) O. pap., 35 c. Oxford Univ.

Price, Overton Westfeldt, Kellogg, Royal Shaw, and Cox, W: T.
Forests of the United States: their use. '09, [1910.] (F) 25 p. 8°, (U. S., Dept. of Agriculture; Forest Service, circular.) pap.

Price, W: Hyde.
Life insurance reform in New York. '10 (Ja8) c. O. (Am. Economic Assoc. quarterly.) pap., 75 c. Am. Economic Assoc.

Price, W: Thompson.
Analysis of play construction and dramatic principle. '08(O3) c. O. $5. W: I. Price.

Price inevitable. Sidner, A. I. 50 c. J. S. Ogilvie.

Price of blood. Semenoff, V. I. $1.50 net. Dutton.

Price of Lis Doris. Schwartz, J. M. W. V. der P. Appleton.

Price of power. Holden, J. S. *50 c. net. Revell.

Price of the prairie. McCarter, *Mrs.* M. H. $1.35 net. McClurg.

PRICES.
Adiassewich, A. English prices with Russian equivalents. 50 c. Spon.
Brooks, R. C. Odd prices and bargains in retail trade. 50 c. Univ. of Cin.
Kempthorne, W. O. Railway stories' price-book. $4. Spon.
Massachusetts. *Commission on High Cost of Living.* Wages and prices of commodities. Gov. Pr. Off.
Meyer, H. H: B., *comp.* Library of Congress select list of references on the cost of living and prices. 15 c.
Prices of food products; comparison of prices of food products in Detroit, Mich., and Windsor, Ontario, taken from the advertisements in the *Evening Record*, of Windsor, and the *Detroit News* for Feb. 25, 1910. '10(Jl) facsim. 8°. Gov. Pr. Off.
St. Koczorowski, —. English prices with German rates of exchange. 50 c. Spon.
United States. Comparison of wholesale prices in Buffalo and Ottawa, 1907. '10 (Ag) 4 p. 8°. Gov. Pr. Off.

PRICES.—*Continued.*

United States. *Dept. of Agriculture.* Prices of farm products; letter from the Secretary of Agriculture, transmitting series of tables showing the average farm price on Dec. 1 of each year from 1900 to 1909, inclusive, of important crops, and averages of the monthly range of prices of important crops in certain cities from 1900 to 1909. '10(Jl) 9 p. 8°.

United States. *Dept. of Commerce and Labor. Bu. of Labor.* Increase in cost of food and other products.

United States. *Dept. of Commerce and Labor. Bu. of Labor.* Price of food products; letter from the Commissioner of Labor. '10(Jl) 47 p. 8°.

United States. *Dept. of Commerce and Labor. Bu. of Labor.* Retail prices of food in the U. S., 1900 to 1907.

United States. *Dept. of Commerce and Labor. Bu. of Labor.* Wages and prices of commodities; rept. of the United States Bureau of Labor, giving the monthly prices of commodities from Jan., 1909, to March, 1910. '10(Jl) 26 p. 8°.

United States. *Dept. of Commerce and Labor. Bureau of Labor.* Wholesale prices, 1890-1908. (Add. Superintendent for price.) U. S., Supt. of Docs.

See also Canada;—Cost;—Cost of living;—Money;—Political economy;—Wages.

Prichard, Harold Arth.
Kant's theory of knowledge. '09(Ap3) O. $2.15. Oxford Univ.

Prichard, Hesketh Vernon Hesketh-.
Hunting camps in wood and wilderness; with foreword by F: Courteney Selous. '10(N12) il. O. $4 net. Sturgis & W.

Prichard, Sarah Johnson.
Shawnie Wade. '09(N6) c. D. †$1. Badger.
Wonderful Christmas in Pumpkin Delight Lane. '08(D) c. 185 p. 8°, $1.25. Tuttle, M. & T.

Pride and prejudice. *See* Austen, Jane.

Pride of the Graftons. Craven, P. †$1.50. Appleton.

Pride of the rancho. Smith, H: E. $1. J. S. Ogilvie.

Priest, G: Madison.
Brief hist. of German literature; based on Gotthold Klee's Grundzüge der deutschen literaturgeschichte. '09(N20) c. O. **$1.50 net. Scribner.

Priest and pagan. Hopkins, H. M. †$1.50. Houghton M.

Priest and parson. Fogarty, J. H: *$1.25 net. Chr. Press.

Priest of the temple. Herbert, G: 75 c. Whittaker.

Priest or pretender. Cunningham, F. B. $1.50. C. M. Clark.

Priest, the woman and the confessional. Chinique, —. $1. L. J. Jones.

Priestly vocations and tonsure. Bacuez, L. *$1 net. Cathedral Lib.

Priestman, Dorothy Tuke.
Home decoration. '09(N13) c. il. D. (Family books.) *$1 net. Penn Pub. Co.

Priestman, Howard.
Principles of woollen spinning. '08(Jl18) O. $2.50. Longmans.

Priestman, Mabel Tuke.
Art and economy in home decoration. '08 (S26) c. il. D. **$1.50 net. Lane.
Artistic homes. '10(D3) c. il. O. $2 net. McClurg.
Handicrafts in the home. '10(D3) c. il. O. $2 net. McClurg.

PRIESTS.

Bacuez, N. L: Priestly vocations and tonsure. *$1 net. Cathedral Lib.

Campbell, T: J. Pioneer priests of North America, 1642-1710. v. 2. $2. Am. Press, (N. Y.)

Dimock, N. Christian doctrine of sacerdotium. 75 c. net. Longmans.

Lelen, J. M. Towards the altar; papers on vocations to the priesthood.—Towards the eternal priesthood. ea., 15 c. Herder.

Rules of life for the pastor of souls. $1.25. Benziger.

Scannell, T: B. Priest's studies. *$1.20 net. Longmans.

Sheldon, H: C. Sacerdotalism in the nineteenth century. *$2 net. Eaton & M.

Smith, J: T. Training of a priest. **$1.50 net. Longmans.

See also Catholic church;—Celibacy;—Ministers (*of the Gospel*).

Priests of progress. Weaver, G. R. $1.50. B. W. Dodge.

Primadonna (The). Crawford, F. M. †$1.50. Macmillan.

PRIMARIES.

Merriman, C: E: Primary elections. *$1.25 net. Univ. of Chic.

Schaffner, M. A. Primary elections, the test of party affiliation. 25 c. Wisconsin Free Lib.

See also Elections.

PRIMARY.

See Schools;—Sunday-school.

Primary cause of anti-semitism. Schomer, A. S. $1. A. S. Schomer.

PRIMARY EDUCATION.

See Education.

Primary history. Mace, W: H. *65 c. net. Rand, McN. & Co.

Primary studies for nurses. Aikens, C. A. *$1.75 net. Saunders.

Primer of American literature. Howes, A. W. **50 c. net. Heath.

Primer of architectural drawing. Dana, W: S: B. $1.25. W: T. Comstock.

Primer of English for foreign students. Thorley, W. C. 60 c. net. Macmillan.

Primer of eye diseases. Albrecht, J. F. E. (Add. pubs. for price.) Ware.

Primer of Hebrew history. Stearns, W. N. *40 c. net. Eaton & M.

Primer of homiletics. Edwards, J: *75 c. net. Jennings.

Primer of hygiene. Ritchie, J: W. 40 c. World Bk.

Primer of sanitation. Ritchie, J: W. 60 c. World Bk.

Primer of socialism. Kirkup, T: *40 c. net. Macmillan.

Primer of statistics. Elderton, W. P. *60 c. net. Macmillan.

Primer of the government of Texas. Kittrell, N. G. 40 c. Southern Pub., (Tex.)
Primer of theosophy. Theosophical Society in America. 15 c. Theosophical Soc.
Primer of wood preservation. Sherfesse, W: F. 5 c. U. S., Supt. of Docs.
PRIMERS.
Baker, F. T:, *and others.* Primer. **25 c. net. Macmillan.
Baum, M. Little helper: supplementary primer to accompany "The rational method in reading." 28 c.; bk. 2. 32 c. Silver.
Beebe, E. M. Picture primer. 25 c. Am. Bk.
Beginner's primer. *25 c. net. Houghton M.
Bentley, A. E., *and* Johnston, G. R. Child's world primer. 30 c. Barnes.
Hervey, W. L., *and* Hix, M. Primer. 30 c. Longmans.
Howell, L. D. Howell primer. 25 c. Hinds.
Hyde, A. A primer. 25 c. Am. Bk.
McCloskey, M. O. Primer. 30 c. Ginn.
McMahon, H. A., M. M. *and* A. M. Rhyme and story primer. 30 c. Heath.
Pardee, L. P., *and* Smith, C. J. The primer. 28 c. Powers.
Ruskin, J: Dame Wiggins and her seven wonderful cats. *30 c. net. Educ. Pub.
Swem, L., *and* Sherwood, R. Primer of nursery rhymes. 30 c. Houghton M.
See also Readers.
Primers of art. il. O. **90 c. net. Doubleday, P.
—Barber. Lead glazed pottery. pt. 1.
Primitive Aryans of America. Denison T: S. $3.25; $2.50. T: S. Denison.
Primitive Christianity. *See* Pfleiderer, Otto.
Primitive church and the primacy of Rome. Bartoli, G. $1.50 net. Doran.
Primitive psychotherapy and quackery. Lawrence, R. M. $2 net. Houghton M.
Primitive secret societies. Webster, H. **$2 net. Macmillan.
Prince, J: Dyneley.
Assyrian primer. '09(Jl3) 8°, pap., *$1 net. Lemcke.
Prince, J: Tilden.
Pract. English grammar for upper grades. '10(Je25) c. D. 60 c. Ginn.
Prince, Morton, M.D.
Dissociation of a personality: biographical study in abnormal psychology. 2d ed. '08 (O24) c. O. **$2.80 net. Longmans.
—, ed. My life as a dissociated personality, by B. C. A.; with an introd. by Morton Prince. '09(Ap17) c. O. pap., 50 c. Badger.
—, **Gerrish, F: H., M.D., Putnam, Ja. J., M.D., and others.**
Psychotherapeutics: symposium. '09(N6) c. D. *$1.50 net. Badger.
Prince (The). Machiavelli, N. *35 c. net; *70 c. net. Dutton.
Prince and his ants. Bertelli, L. $1.35 net. Holt.
Prince Bohoo and little Smuts. Jones, H. $1.50. Stokes.
Prince Charlie. Delannoy, B. *$1 net. Fenno.
Prince Domino and "Muffles." Eaton, S. $1.25. Stern.
Prince Hagen. Sinclair, U. B. $1; 25 c. Kerr.
Prince Izon. Kelly, J. P. $1.50. McClurg.
Prince of dreamers. Steel, *Mrs.* F. A. W. †$1.25. Doubleday, P.
Prince of peace. Bryan, W: J. 35 c. Reilly & B.
Prince of spendthrifts. Jackman, A. S. 25 c. J. S. Ogilvie.
Prince of the apostles. Francis, P. J. *75 c. net. Lamp Pub.
Prince Pimpernel. Rix, H. $1. Estes.
PRINCE WILLIAM COUNTY, Va.
See Truro Parish.
Prince's pranks. Lowe, C: $1.50. Lane.
Princess (The). *See* Tennyson, Alfr., *Lord.*
Princess and another. Jenkins, S. $1.50. B: W. Huebsch.
Princess and Curdie. Macdonald, G: †$1.50. Lippincott.
Princess and the dragon. Hamer, S. H. $1. Estes.
Princess Dehra. *See* Scott, J: Reed.
Princess Flower Hat. Wright, *Mrs.* M. O. $1.50. Macmillan.
Princess Nadine. Tiernan, *Mrs.* F. C. F. **$1.50 net. Putnam.
Princess of Forge. Shedd, G: C. $1.50. Macaulay.
Princess of Hackney. Compton, C. G. $1.25. Lane.
Princess of intrigue. Williams, H. N. 2 v. *$6.50 net. Putnam.
Princess of strategy. Piépape, *General* de. $4 net. Lane.
Princess of the Old World. Price, E. C. *$3 net. Putnam.
Princess of the revels. Smith, *Mrs.* E. T. †$1.50. Dutton.
Princess Polly ser. *See* Brooks, Amy.
Princess Sayrane. Harrison, E. O. $1.35 net. McClurg.
Princess Wisla. Swett, S. M. †$1.50. Little, B. & Co.
Princess Zara. Beeckman, R. $1.50. W. J. Watt.
Princesse (La) Lointaine. *See* Rostand, Edmond.
Princeton, Ind. First Presbyterian Church. Princeton cook book; selection of tested recipes collected in the interest of the First Presbyterian Church of Princeton, Indiana. 2d ed., rev. and enl. [1910] (F) c. '09. 9-205 p. 8°, $1. A. J. Paxton.
PRINCETON, N. J.
Collins, V. L. Continental Congress at Princeton, [1783.] *$3 net. Princeton Univ.
Princeton University. Class of 1863. Autumnal sprays, wreathing the forty-fifth year, Princeton, sixty-three; tablet to the faculty of our college days, gathered by the class historian June 6, 1908. '09(N) 15 p. 8°. (Add. pubs. for price.) H: U. Swinnerton.
Princeton University. Library. Finding list for the music library, 1909. '09, [1910.] (Je) 93 p. 8°, $1.25 net. Princeton Univ.
PRINCIPAL AND AGENT.
Steele, S. Students' text on the law of principal and agent. (Add. pubs. for price.) Flood.

PRINCIPALS (*of schools*).
See Schools.

Principles and practice of assembling machine tools. pt. 1. '10(My7) c. il. 8°, (Machinery's reference ser.) pap., 25 c. Indust. Press.

Principles of American statesmanship; ed. by Fs. Newton Thorpe. O. Tandy-T.
—Jackson. Statesmanship of Andrew Jackson. $2.50.

Principles of the ego in philosophy. Wilson, A. M. *50 c. net. Stechert.

Prindle, Edn. Jay.
Patents as a factor in manufacturing. '08 (D5) c. 12°, (Works management lib.) $2. Engineering Mag.

Prindle, L: Marcus.
Forty mile quadrangle, Yukon-Tanana region, Alaska. '09(Jl) 52 p. il. maps, 8°, (U. S. Geological Survey bull.) pap. U. S., Supt. of Docs.

Pringle, W: Ja., comp.
Cases on the law of torts. '10(O) buckram, $1.50. Thompson & Co.

PRINTERS AND PRINTING.
Amram, D: W. Makers of Hebrew books in Italy. *$3 net. J. H. Greenstone.
Barnett, G: E. The printers: study in American trade unionism. $2; $1. Am. Economic Assoc.
Barr, J: W: Inductive method of learning stonework; simplified system for acquiring the art of preparing forms for letterpress printing. $3.50. J: W: Barr.
Book of monotype success, wherein we talk about ourselves, our factory and the men whose genius—the infinite capacity for taking pains—has made and is making still better "the versatile machine that keeps itself busy." '10(Je) 35 p. il. nar. F. pap., gratis. Lanston.
Carroll, E:, *comp.* Law printing laws. $1. E: Carroll.
Collins, F: H. Authors' and printers' dictionary. 35 c. Oxford Univ.
Davis, W. B. Specimen faces, linotype composition; borders, rules and dashes. gratis. W. B. Davis.
De Vinne, T. L. Notable printers of Italy during the 15th century. $15. Grolier Club.
Dodge, O. Experiments in producing printing surfaces. (Add. pubs. for price.) De Vinne.
Gage, F. W: Modern presswork. $2. Inland Pr.
Gress, E. G. Art and practice of typography. $5. Oswald.
Hansen, H. C., Type Foundry. Book of types, borders, ornaments, brass rule, printing materials and the like for printerdom. (Not for sale.) H. C. Hansen.
Kahn, A. N: Printers' vade mecum: calculations as to cost of paper, press work, [etc.] $5. A. N: Kahn.
Lennox, P. J. Early printing in Ireland. (Add. pubs. for price.) Cath. Univ.
Manual of style. 75 c. Univ. of Chic.
Meadon, J., *ed.* Graphic arts and crafts year book, [1909.] $5. Oswald.

PRINTERS AND PRINTING.—*Continued.*
Pfizenmayer, P. Evolution of printing. P. Pfizenmayer; J. C. Powers.
Plimpton Press. Specimen pages of printing types. (Not for sale.) Plimpton.
Practical guide to embossing and die stamping, together with explanatory text on copperplate engraving and printing. $1.50. Inland Pr.
Ruxton, P., Inc. Printing inks. $2. Ruxton.
Schott, C: J. Theory and practice of book imposition. $3.50. C: J. Schott.
Specimens of monotype book faces. [1910.] (N) 80 p. 8°. (Priv. pr.) Scientific Press.
Style and general format for the publications of the Arthur H. Clark Co. '10 (Ap) c. 48 p. 8°, $5. A. H. Clark.
Sweetland, C: A: Publishers' and printers' accounts. 50 c. Am. Sch. Corr.
Thezise, F: J. Design and color in printing. $1. Inland Pr.
United States. *Government Printing Office.* Manual of style for use of copy editors, proofreaders, operators, and compositors engaged in the production of executive, congressional and departmental publications. 2d ed. Nov., 1909; prep. under direction of the public printer. '09, [1910.] (Mr) 91 p. 8°.
United States. *Government Printing Office.* Monotype manual.
See also Authorship;—Bookbinders and bookbinding;—Electrotyping; — Incunabula;—Lettering; —Linotype machine;—Lithography; — Paper; — — Proof-reading; — Stereotyping;—*also* Oxford University Press.

Printers and printing in Providence, 1762-1907; prepared by a committee of Providence Typographical Union, No. 33, as a souvenir of the 50th anniversary of its institution. '08(Ap11) il. pors. O. $2. W: Carroll.

PRINTS.
See Engravers and engravings.

Prinz, Hermann.
Dental materia medica and therapeutics, with special reference to the rational application of remedial measures to dental diseases; text-book for students and practitioners. '09(N) c. 595 p. il. 8°, $5. Mosby.

Prior, F: J:
Construction and maintenance of railway roadbed and track. '08(S12) c. il. tabs., 16°, $2. Drake.
—, **comp.** Operation of trains and station work. '08(S12) c. il. 16°, leath. $1.50. Drake.

Prior, Ja.
Walking gentleman. '08(Mr28) D. †$1.50. Dutton.

Priscilla crochet book. Hettich, L. B., *ed.* 25 c. Priscilla.
Priscilla Hardanger book. Brown, N. C., *ed.* 25 c. Priscilla.
Priscilla Irish crochet-book. Harvey, L. M. 25 c. Priscilla.
Priscilla knitting book. Keys, G., *ed.* 25 c. Priscilla.
Priscilla of the Good Intent. Sutcliffe, H. $1.50. Little, B. & Co.

Priscilla Publishing Company. Wallachian embroidery. '08(Je27) c. il. 4°, pap., 15 c. Priscilla.
Prison diary. Dougherty, M. (Not for sale.) C: A. Dougherty.
Prison ships. Walsh, T: *$1 net. Sherman, F.
Prisoner at the bar. Train, A. C. $1.50. Scribner.
Prisoner in holy orders. Alexander, J. (Add. pubs. for price.) Dutton.
Prisoner of Chillon. *See* Byron, G: Gordon Noel, *Lord.*
Prisoner of the sea. Hotchkiss, C. C. $1.50. J: McBride.
Prisoners of chance. Parrish, R. $1.50. McClurg.
Prisonniers (Les) du Caucase. Maistre, X. de. 30 c. Ginn.
PRISONS.
Crime and criminals. $1. Prison Reform.
Hopper, J. M., *and* Becholt, F: R. "9009": [story of a convict.] †$1.25. McClure.
Keeler, *Mrs.* C. O. American bastiles. 25 c. C. O. Keeler.
Masten, V. M. Crime problem: [study of our prison system.] $1.25. Star-Gazette.
Wines, F: H. Punishment and reformation; study of the penitentiary system. *$1.75 net. Crowell.
See also Andersonville;—Crime and criminals;—Police;—Probation system;—*also* Minnesota State Prison.

Pritchett, H: Smith.
Relations of Christian denominations to colleges: an address before the Conference on Education of the Methodist Episcopal Church, South, at Atlanta, Ga., May 20, 1908. '08(N21) Q. pap., gratis. Carnegie Found.

Privat, Edm.
Esperanto at a glance. '08(Jl) D. pap., *15 c. net. Revell.
Esperanto in fifty lessons. '08(Jl) D. *50 c. net. Revell.
Private freight cars. Weld, L: D. H. *$1.50 net. Longmans.
Private house electric lighting. Taylor, F. H. 50 c. Spon.
Private lessons in the cultivation of sex magnetism. Edgerly, W. $25. Ralston Univ.
Private palaces of London. Chancellor, E. B. *$5 net. Lippincott.
Private retreat for religious. Geirmann, P: *$1.50 net. Benziger.
Private secretary. Hawtry, C: 25 c. S: French.
PRIVATEERS.
See Ships and shipbuilding.
Privates' manual. Moss, J. A. 50 c. U. S. Infantry.
Privilege and democracy in America. Howe, F. C. **$1.50 net. Scribner.
Privileged classes. Wendell, B. **$1.25 net. Scribner.
Prize articles on promoting and conducting the affairs of college and high school annuals. '10(Je4) c. 8°, $1. Stafford Engraving.
Pro patria. Ammerman, A. 35 c. Werner.

PROBATE.
See Wills.
Probate repts. annot.; recent cases decided in the courts of the several states; with notes and ref. by W: Lawrence Clark, jr. v. 12. '08(Jl); v. 13. '09(Jl) c. O. shp., ea., *$5.50 net. Baker, V. & Co.
PROBATION LAW.
See names of states.
PROBATION SYSTEM.
Mulready, E. Probation. gratis. N. Y. State Probation.
New York [State.] *Probation Commission.* Advantages of probation; brief description and some illustrations. '09, [1910.] (S) 16 p. S. pap., gratis.—County probation officers. gratis. N. Y. State Probation.
New York [State.] *Probation Commission.* Forms for juvenile and adult probation. (Add. pubs. for price.) Lyon.
See also Courts.
Probationer's hdbk. Garrison, S. O. $1.25. Jennings.
Problem of age, growth and death. Minot, C: S. **$2.50 net. Putnam.
Problem of city government. Rowe, L. S. **$1.50 net. Appleton.
Problem of evil. Burton, M. Le R. $1.25. Open Court.
Problem of happy marriage. Price, G: B. $1. Chelston Press.
Problem of logic. Gibson, W. R. B. *$4.50 net. Macmillan.
Problem of method. Sandison, H. $1.25. H. Sandison.
Problem of religious instruction in the state universities. Kelsey, F. W. (Add. author for price.) F. W. Kelsey.
Problem of theism. Pigou, A. C. *$1 net. Macmillan.
Problem of vocational education. Snedden, D: S: 35 c. Houghton M.
Problems and perils of socialism. Strachey, J. St. L. *25 c. net. Macmillan.
Problems in the Prometheus. Harry, J. E: 50 c. Univ. of Cin.
Problems in wood-turning. Crawshaw, F. D. 80 c. Manual Arts.
Problems of adapting history to children in the elementatry school. Johnson, H: 30 c. Teachers' Coll.
Problems of discipleship. Bisseker, H. *50 c. net. Eaton & M.
Problems of international practice and diplomacy. Barclay, *Sir* T: $6.50. Boston Bk.
Problems of pulpit and platform. Culler, D: D. 75 c. Brethren Pub. Ho.
Problems of the elementary school. Perry, A. C., *jr.* $1.25 net. Appleton.
Problems of the present South. Murphy, E. G. **$1.50 net. Longmans.
Problems of the spiritual. Chambers, A. **$1 net. Jacobs.
Problems of theology in modern life and thought. Miller, A. *$1.25 net. Doran.
Problems of to-day. Carnegie, A. $1.40. Doubleday, P.
Problems of your generation. Dewey, D. $1. Arden.

Problems of youth. Banks, L: A. **$1.30 net. Funk.

Probyn-Williams, Rob. Ja., M.D.
Pract. guide to the administration of anæsthetics. 2d ed. '09, [1910.] (F) 228 p. il. D. *$1.60 net. Longmans.

PROCEDURE.
See Actions at law;—Parliamentary law;—Sale.

Procedure of the House of Commons. Redlich, J. $10 net. Dutton.
Process of abstraction. Moore, T: V. $1. Univ. of Cal.
Process of government. Bentley, A. F. *$3 net. Univ. of Chic.

Proclus.
Metaphysical elements, (Stoicheiōsis Theologikē;) tr. from the orig. Greek by T: M. Johnson. '10(Mr12) O. pap., $2. T: M. Johnson.

Procter, H: Richardson.
Leather industries laboratory book of analytical and experimental methods. '08 (Jl4); 2d ed., rev. and enl. '09(Ja16) il. tabs., 8°, ea., $7.50. Spon.

Prodigal daughter. Culter, *Mrs.* M. N. M. 50 c. Monfort.
Prodigal father. Clouston, J. S. †$1.50. Century Co.
Prodigal pro tem. Bartlett, F: O. $1.50. Small.
Prodigal son. Shaw, C. $1.50. Fenno.
Prodigious Hickey. Johnson, O. M. $1.50. Baker & T.

PRODUCER GAS.
See Gas and gas-fitting.

Producer gas fired furnaces. Nagel, O. *$2 net. O. Nagel.
Product and climax. Patten, S. N. *50 c. net. B: W. Huebsch.
Production and handling of clean milk. Winslow, K. $3.25. W: R. Jenkins.
Production of Easter lily bulbs. Oliver, G: W. 15 c. U. S., Supt. of Docs.
Professional aunt. Wemyss, *Mrs.* M. C. E. L. **$1 net. Houghton M.
Professional wrestling. Smith, E: W. 10 c. Am. Sports.

PROFESSIONS.
See Vocations.

Professor (The). *See* Brontē, Charlotte.
Professor at the breakfast table. *See* Holmes, Oliver Wendell.
Prof. Slagg, of London. Marvin, D. E. (Add. pubs. for price.) B'way Pub.
Professor's son. Adams, W: T. $1. Lothrop, L. & S.
Profit and loss in man. Hopkins, A. A. **$1.20 net. Funk.
Profit making in shop and factory. Carpenter, C: U. $2. Engineering Mag.
Profitable authorship. Hadlock, E. H. $3. Un. Press.
Profitable dairying. Benkendorf, G. H: W: gratis. Babsom.
Profitable poultry production. Kains, M. G. $1.50. Judd.
Profits in poultry keeping solved. Briggs, E. $1. Hosterman.
Profligate (The). Hornblow, A. †$1.50. G: W. Dillingham.
Program book. Denton, C. J., *comp.* 40 c. J. Fischer.

Programme (The) of modernism: a reply to the encyclical of Pius x., *Pascendi Dominici Gregis;* with the text of the encyclical in an English version; tr. from the Italian by Rev. Father G: Tyrrell; with an introd. by A. Leslie Lilley. '08(Ap11) D. (Crown theological lib.) *$1.50 net. Putnam.

PROGRESS.
See Social science.

Progress after entire sanctification. Zepp, A. C. 50 c. Chr. Witness.
Progress and development of the colored people of our nation. Grimke, F. J. 10 c. F. J. Grimke.
Progress from experience. Hyde, E: S. $1.25. Cochrane.
Progress in religious and moral education. Coe, G: A. 25 c. Rel. Educ.
Progress in the life to come. Gray, J. 25 c. net. Revell.
Progress reports of experiments in dust prevention, road preservation, and road construction. '09(Ag) 23 p. 8°, (U. S., Dept. of Agriculture; Office of Public Roads circular.) (Add Superintendent for price.) U. S., Supt. of Docs.

Progress ser. 16°. Progress Co.
—Larson. How great men succeed. 50 c.

Progress series. 10 v. '09(Ap24) ea., 50 c.; per set, $5, boxed. Progress Co.
Contents. Allen, Ja., As a man thinketh; Drummond, H:, The greatest thing in the world; Edgeworth, Maria, Murad the unlucky; Hawthorne, Nathaniel, The great stone face; Larson, Christian Daa, The great within, The hidden secret, Mystery of fate, Mastery of self, On the heights, Poise and power.

Progressive age of reason. Hotchkiss, S: $1.75. S: Hotchkiss.
Progressive business accounting. Goodyear, L. E. $2. Waterloo.
Progressive course in English. *See* Stebbins, C: M.
Progressive French idioms. Blanchaud, R. de, *comp.* 60 c. Heath.
Progressive melodies for sight singing. Baldwin, R. L. 35 c. Ginn.
Progressive Pennsylvania. Swank, J. M. $5. J. M. Swank.
Progressive problems in general chemistry. Baskerville, C: 90 c. Heath.
Progressive problems in physics. Miller, F. R. 60 c. Heath.
Progressive road to reading. *See* Burchill, Georgine.
Progressive taxation. Seligman, E. R. A. $1.75; $1.25. Am. Economic Assoc.

PROHIBITED BOOKS.
See Index expurgatorius;—Liberty of the press.

PROHIBITION.
See Liquors;—Parties (*political*);—Temperance.

Prohibition: its relation to temperance, good morals and sound government; selections from the writings of men who have given thought and study to this question. '10 (Ag27) O. 50 c. J. Debar.
Prohibition victorious: then—what? Harwood, H: H. H: H. Harwood
Project of empire. Nicholson, J. S. *$2.25 net. Macmillan

PROJECTILES.
See Artillery.

PROJECTION.
Brown, J. S. Trigonomerty and stereographic projections. (Not for sale.) Lord Balto. Pr.
See also Perspective.

Prokosch, Eduard.
See Evans, M. Blakeman.

Prolegomena to history of Italico-Romanic rhythm. Fitzhugh, T: 25 c. Anderson.

Prolegomena to study of Greek religion. Harrison, J. E. *$6 net. Putnam.

Prolegomena to systematic theology. Davies, E. O. *$1.25 net. Doran.

Prolegomena to theism. "Justus," *pseud.* $2. A. H. Kellogg.

Prologue (The). *See* Chaucer, Geoffrey.

Prolongation of life. Metchnikoff, E. *$2.50 net; **$1.75 net. Putnam.

Promenades of an impressionist. Huneker, J. G. $1.50 net. Scribner.

Prometheus bound. *See* Æschylus. Suppliant maidens.

Promise of American life. Croly, H. **$2 net. Macmillan.

Promised land. Davis, A. $1. Harvard Dramatic.

PROMISSORY NOTES.
See Negotiable instruments.

Promoter's assistant. Carney, W: A. $3. Carlisle.

Promotion exercises for the beginners' and primary grades of the Sunday-school. Thomas, M., *ed.* 5 c. Presb. Bd.

PRONUNCIATION.
Chase, F. D. Speaker's manual of pronunciation. 25 c. Review and Herald Pub.
Jones, D. Pronunciation of English. 90 c. Putnam.
Phyfe, W: H: P. Twelve thousand words often mispronounced. **$1.25 net. Putnam.
Read, W: A. Southern R. (Add. pubs. for price.) Louisiana State Univ.
See also Phonetics;—Words.

Proof of design in creation. Kavanagh, M. A. 10 c. Flanagan.

PROOF-READING.
United States. Manual of style for use of copy editors, proof-readers, operators, and compositors engaged in the production of the executive, congressional, and departmental publications. Gov. Pr. Off.

PROPELLERS.
Barnaby, S. W. Marine propellers. $4.50. Spon.

Proper distribution of expense burden. Church, A. H. $1. Engineering Mag.

PROPERTY.
Gray, J: C., *comp.* Select cases and other authorities on the law of property. v. 5, 6. ea., $3.50. G: H. Kent.
Lafargue, P. Evolution of property from savagery to civilization. 50 c. Kerr.
McKay, G: Commentary on the law of community property for Arizona, California, Idaho, Louisiana, Nevada, New Mexico, Texas and Washington. $7.50. Courtright.

PROPERTY.—*Continued.*
Terry, E: S. Laws of the various states concerning aliens, estates, descent and distribution, powers of attorney, wills, etc. (Add. author for price.) E: S. Terry.
See also Communism;—Copyright;—Damages;—Executors and administrators; — Family;—Insurance; — Land; — Mechanics' liens; — Mortgages;—Personal property;—Real property;—Sale;—Socialism;—Taxation;—Titles; — Trademarks;—Wealth;—Wills.

PROPHECIES.
Joyce, G. C. Inspiration of prophecy. $1.40. Oxford Univ.

Prophecy and poetry. Rogers, A. **$1.25 net. Longmans.

Prophecy of Yah-Ma-Sun. Rich, O. V. 50 c. A. Harriman.

Prophet of peace. Coolidge, A. C. $1. Hungerford-H.

Prophetic romancer. *See* Slosson, *Mrs.* Annie Trumbull. Dissatisfied soul.

Prophet's raven. Pearse, M. G. *75 c. net. Eaton & M.

PROPHETS (*Hebrew*).
Bennett, W: H:, *ed.* Religion of the post-exilic prophets, 586-300 B.C. *$2 net. Scribner.
Eiselen, F: C. Prophecy and the prophets in their historical relations. *$1.50 net. Eaton & M.
Kaplan, J. H. Psychology of prophecy; a study of the prophetic mind as manifested by the ancient Hebrew prophets. *$1.50 net. J. H. Greenstone.
Westphal, A. Law and the prophets. $2.75 net. Macmillan.
Zollars, E. V. Hebrew prophecy. $1. Standard Pub.
See also Bible.

Prophylactic value of vaccination. Mathewson, H: S. (Add. Superintendent for price.) U. S., Supt. of Docs.

Prophylaxis and treatment of internal diseases. Forchheimer, F: subs., $5. Appleton.

Prophylaxis of pellagra. Lavinder, C. H. U. S., Supt. of Docs.

Proportional representation. Curtis, R. E. 25 c. Wisconsin Free Lib.

Proposals to Kathleen. Clifford, *Mrs.* L. L. †$1.50. Barnes.

Propper, Albert Herschel.
Tears and smiles. '09(N20) c. 12°, $1. B'way Pub.

Prosch, T: Wickham.
Conkling-Prosch family with some references to the Dotter, Roe, Reynolds, Brooks, Mapes, Elder, McCarver and other connections. '09(N) 141 p. il. pors. 8°. (Priv. pr.) T: W. Prosch.

PROSCH FAMILY.
See Genealogies.

PROSE.
See Rhetoric;—*also* names of national literatures.

Prose that every child should know. Burt, M. E., *ed.* **90 c. net; **$1.50 net. Doubleday, P.

Proselytes of the Ghetto. Dushaw, A. T: 75 c. J. Heidingsfeld.

Prosit! Spinners' Club. *$1.25 net; *$3 net; *$6 net. P. Elder.

PROSKE, Karl.
Weinmann, K. Karl Proske. 30 c. Pustet.

PROSODY.
Saintsbury, G: E: B. Hist. of English prosody. 3 v. ea., $3.75 net. Macmillan.
See also Accent; — Poetry;—Rhetoric;—Versification.

PROSPECTING.
See **Mines and mining.**

Prospector's field book. Osborn, H: S. $1.50. Baird.

PROSTATE.
See **Urine and urinary organs.**

PROSTITUTION.
Agreement between the U. S. and other powers for the repression of the trade in white women. '08, [1909.] (My) 9 p. 8°, pap. (Add. Superintendent for price.) U. S., Supt. of Docs.
Bell, E. A., *ed.* War on the white slave trade. $1.50. C: C. Thompson.
Chrysler, C: B. White slavery. $1. C. B. Chrysler.
De Becker, J. E. Nightless city, or, the hist. of the Yoshiwara Yukwaku. *$10 net. Wessels.
Goodnow, E. Market for souls. *$1.25 net. M. Kennerley.
Greer, J. H. Social evil; its cause, effect and cure. 50 c. J. H. Greer.
Hatch, D: P. Under world and its women. 15 c. Roger Bros.
Law, E. N. Shame of a great nation. $1. E. N. Law.
Lehman, F: M. White slave hell. $1.50. Chr. Witness.
Lytle, H. M. Tragedies of the white slaves. 25 c. C. C. Thompson.
Roe, C. G. Panders and their white slaves. $1 net. Revell.
United States. *Dept. of Commerce and Labor. Immigration Commission.* Importing women for immoral purposes; rept. from the Immigration Commission transmitting, in response to Senate Resolution no. 86, by Senator Lodge, a partial rtp. to Congress on the importation and harboring of women for immoral purposes. '09, [1910.] (F) 3+61 p. 8°, pap.
United States. *Dept. of State.* Suppression of the white-slave traffic.
United States. Memorandum in re white-slave trade; printed by order of Committee on Interstate and Foreign Commerce. '09, [1910.] (F) 28 p. 8°.
United States. White-slave traffic: rept. '10(Ag) 32 p. 8°. Gov. Pr. Off.
Washburn, J. Under-world sewer. $1.50. Washburn.

See also. **Syphilis.**

Protect your ideas: hand-book of the laws and rules of practice relative to patents, trade-marks, copyrights, labels, etc.; prepared by Milo B. Stevens & Co., attorneys. '08(My23) c. il. 12°, gratis. M. B. Stevens.

PROTECTION.
See Tariff.

Protection of railroads from overhead transmission line crossing. Fowle, F. F. *$1.50 net. Van Nostrand.

PROTECTIVE MIMICRY.
See **Animals;—Butterflies.**

PROTEIDS.
Osborne, T: B. Vegetable proteins. *$1.20 net. Longmans.
Plimmer, R. H: A. Chemical constitution of the proteins. In 2 pts. pt. 1, *$1 net; pt. 2, *80 c. net. Longmans.
Robertson, T. B. Proteins. $1. Univ. of Cal.
Rosenbloom, J. Contrib. to study of nature and origin of Bunce Jones protein. (Add. author for price.) J. Rosenbloom.
Schryver, S: B. General character of the proteins. *80 c. net. Longmans.

PROTEINS.
See **Proteids.**

PROTESTANT EPISCOPAL CHURCH.
Alcock, D. Romance of Protestantism. $1.25 net. Eaton & M.
Brent, C: H: Mind of Christ Jesus in the church of the living God. **50 c. net. Longmans.
Cooke, R: J. Questions for High-Churchmen. **25 c. net. Eaton & M.
Grafton, C: C. Catholic atlas; or, digest of Catholic theology. **$2.50 net. Longmans.
Gwynne, W: Gospel in the church manual of instruction according to the church catechism. 40 c. Gorham.
Haverstick, A. C. Churchman's ready reference. $1. Young Churchman.
Johnson, G: B. How to take part in the services of the [Protestant] Episcopal church. per 100, $3. Young Churchman.
Living Church annual and Whittaker's churchman's almanac; a church, cyclopedia and almanac, 1911. 75 c.; 50 c. Young Churchman.
Powell, L. P. Credentials of the church. 20 c. Whittaker.
Richmond, A. B. American Episcopal church in China. 75 c.; 50 c. Dom. and For. Mission.
Virginia State Library. Separation of church and state in Virginia. $1. Virginia State Lib.
Who's who in the General Convention of 1910, held at Cincinnati. 50 c. Young Churchman.
Wilson, H. Why and wherefore; [simple explanations of the ornaments, vestments and ritual of the church.] 25 c. Young Churchman.
See also Anglican orders;—Apostles' creed; — Apostolic succession;—Athanasian creed;—Baptism;—Book of common prayer;—Catechisms;—Charities;—Christian unity;—Church history;—Church music;—Church of England;—Church polity;—Church unity;—Confirmation;—Creeds;—Good Friday;—Holy week;—Lent; — Lord's supper;—Ministers (*of the Gospel*); — Sacraments;—Sunday-school;—Worship.

Protestant Episcopal Church Congress of the United States. Papers and speeeches of the Church Congress, held in Boston, May, '09. '09(D25) 8°, pap., *$1 net. Whittaker.

PROTESTANTISM.
Benson, R. H. Non-Catholic denominations. $1.20 net. Longmans.
Bousset, W. Faith of a modern Protestant. **75 c. net. Scribner.
Good, J. I. Famous places of the reformed churches. $1.50. Heidelberg.

PROTESTANTISM.—*Continued.*
Lobstein, P. Introd. to Protestant dogmatics $1.50 net. Univ. of Chic.
Smyth, N. Passing Protestantism and coming Catholicism. **$1 net. Scribner.
Torrey, D: C. Protestant modernism. $1.50. Putnam.
See also Calvinism;—Catholic church;—Ministers (*of the Gospel*);—Reformation.
Proteus. Wheelock, E. M. $1. Open Court.
Prothero, Ernest.
Handy natural history. '10(D24) col. il. O. $4 net, boxed. Badger.
Prothero, G: Wa., ed.
See Acton, J: E. E: D.-A., *Lord.*
Prothero, Rowland Edm.
Pleasant land of France. '08(Mr21) 12°, *$2 net; '08(My9) *$3.50 net. Dutton.
Psalms in human life. '08(Je6) 16°, (Everyman's lib.) *35 c. net; leath., *70 c. net. Dutton.
PROTOCALLIPHORA CHRYSORRHOEA.
See Flies.
PROTOZOA.
Calkins, G. N. Text-book of protozoölogy. *$3.25 net. Lea.
Clarke, J. J. Protozoa and disease. pt. 2. *$2.50 net. Wood.
Herzog, M. J. Text-bk. on disease-producing micro-örganisms. $4.75. Lea.
Landacre, F. L. Protozoa of Sandusky Bay and vicinity. 35 c. Ohio Acad. of Sci.
Park, W: H., *and* Williams, A. W. Pathogenic microörganisms, incl. bacteria and protozoa. $3.75 net. Lea.
See also Tropical medicine.
"Proud old Natchez." Reber, T: 50 c. T: Reber.
Proud Roxana. Dow, E. C. $1.25. Stern.
Prout, Ebenezer.
Instrumentation. '08(D) 75 c. Ditson.
Provença. Pound, E. $1 net. Small.
PROVENCE, France.
Wilkinson, M. Last phase of the League in Provence. *$1.50 net. Longmans.
Proverb stories. Alcott, L. M. †$1.50. Little, B. & Co.
PROVERBS.
Skeat, W. W:, *comp.* Early English proverbs chiefly of the thirteenth and fourteenth centuries. $1.15. Oxford Univ.
Walker, J., *comp.* Handy book of proverbs. 50 c. Crowell.
See also Aphorisms;—Epigrams;—Maxims;—Mottoes;—Quotations.
Proverbs in porcelain. *See* Dobson, H: Austin.
PROVIDENCE, R. I.
Hodges, A. D., *ed.* Almon Danforth Hodges and his neighbors. A. D. Hodges.
Kirk, W:, *ed.* Modern city: Providence, Rhode Island. *$2.50 net. Univ. of Chic.
Printers and printing in Providence, 1762-1907. $2. W: Carroll.
Weeden, W: B. Early commercial Providence. 50 c. Davis Press.
See also Brown University;—First Baptist Church.
Providence and calamity. Heisley, C: W. *$1.10 net. Sherman, F.

Provincial council and committees of safety in North Carolina. Whitaker. B. L. (Add. Univ. for price.) Univ. of N. C.
Prudden, Theophil Mitchell.
Dust and its dangers. 2d ed. '10(D) c. 113 p. il. 16°, 75 c. Putnam.
Story of the bacteria and their relations to health and disease. 2d ed., rev. and enl. '10(D) c. 10+232 p. il. pls. 12°, 75 c. Putnam.
Prude, Alfr. Marion.
Soliloquy of Birmingham Bob of Rainbow Glen. '08(O) c. 6+119 p. pors. 12°, $1. A. M. Prude.
Prudentius, Aurelius Clemens.
Glossemata de Prudentio; ed. by J: M. Burnam. '08, [1909.] (Mr) 102 p. pap., $1. Univ. of Cin.
Prue and I. *See* Curtis, G: W:
Prue at school. Brooks, A. †$1. Lothrop, L. & S.
Prue books. See Brooks, Amy.
PRUSSIA.
Supervision of street railway in England and Prussia. (Add. pubs. for price.) Lyon.
See also Germany;—Jena campaign;—Street railroads;—*also* Louise, *Queen of Prussia.*
Prussian cadet. Szczepanski, P. v. $1 net. Dutton.
Pryor, Mrs. Roger A.
See Pryor, Sara Agnes Rice.
Pryor, Sarah Agnes Rice, [Mrs. Roger A. Pryor.]
My day reminiscences of a long life. '09 (N6) c. il. pors. O. **$2.25 net, boxed. Macmillan.
Przibram, Hans.
Embryogeny: account of the laws governing the development of the animal egg as ascertained through experiment. '08(N7) 8°, *$2.50 net. Putnam.
Psalmody question. Bonner, D: F. *50 c. net. Hanford & H.
PSALMS.
See Bible.
Psalms of the early Buddhists. Davids, *Mrs.* C. A., *tr. and ed.* v. 1. $2. Oxford Univ.
PSALTER.
See Bible.
PSEIRA, Crete.
Seagar, R: B. Excavations on the Island of Pseira. $5. Univ. of Penn.
Pseudo church doctrine of anti-Pedo-Baptists defined and refuted. Collinsworth, J. R. $2.50. Hudson.
Pseudo-Ciceronian Consolatio. Sage, E. T. 50 c. Univ. of Chic.
PSEUDONYMS.
Dawson, L. H. Nicknames and pseudonyms. 50 c. Dutton.
Psmith in the city. Wodehouse, P. G. $1.50 net. Macmillan.
PSYCHE.
See Cupid.
Psyche [treatise on insanity] Talmey, M. $2.50. Medico-Legal.
Psyche sleeps. Emmet, A. C. $1. Moffat.
Psyche's task. Frazer, J. G: *80 c. net. Macmillan.
PSYCHIATRY.
See Insanity;—Nervous system.

Psychic control through self-knowledge. Kenilworth, W. W. $2. Fenno.
Psychic lib. 12°, cl. Badger.
—Eaves. Mastery of death. *$1 net.
—Lâo-Tsze. Book of the simple way. *$1.25 net.
—Lees. Through the mists. $1.50.
—Schuré. Jesus, the last great initiate. *$1.25 net.—Orpheus and Krishna. *$1.25 net.—Pythagoras and his system of philosophy. *$1.25 net.
—Wilmshurst. Christianity and science. *$1 net.
Psychic phenomena. Bennett, E: T. *75 c. net. Brentano's.
Psychic science ser. D. McClurg.
—Warman. Hypnotism. 50 c. net.
Psychic solution of the problem of cure. Leavitt, S. $3. Magnum Bonum.
Psychic treatment of nervous disorders. Dubois, P. **$3 net. Funk.
PSYCHICAL RESEARCH.
Bates, E. K. Psychical science and Christianity. $1.50. Dodge.
Bennett, E: T. Psychic phenomena. *75 c. net. Brentano's.
Björnson, B. Wise-Knut. *$1 net. Brandu's.
Bruce, H: A. B. Riddle of personality. **$1.50 net. Moffat.
Carleton, G. M. Autobiography of a disembodied soul. $1.50. Vreeland.
Carrington, H. Coming science. **$1.50 net. Small.
Carson, R. M. Through the valley of the shadow. $3. Hudson.
Edgerly, W. Book of the Psychic Society. $2.—Operations of the other mind. $25. Ralston Univ.
Garland, H. Shadow world. $1.35. Harper.
Grasset, J. Marvels beyond science. $1.75 net. Funk.
Heysinger, I: W. Spirit and matter before the bar of modern science. $3.75 net. Lippincott.
Hyslop, J. H. Psychial research and the resurrection. **$1.50 net. Small.
Jones, A. T. Psychic autobiography. $2. Alden Bros.
Lodge, *Sir* O. J. Survival of man. **$2 net. Moffat.
Myers, G. Beyond the borderline of life. *$1 net. Ball Pub.
Page, H. L. Dual mind. $1. Green Leaf.
Podmore, F. Naturalization of the supernatural. **$2 net. Putnam.
Rider, A. F. Are the dead alive? $1.75, fixed. B. W. Dodge.
Warman, E: B. Psychic science ser. v. 1-4. v. 1, Psychology; v. 2, Personal magnetism; v. 3, Telepathy; v. 4, Hypnotism; v. 5, Suggestion; v. 6, Spiritism; v. 7, Clairvoyance; v. 8, Hindu philosophy. ea., 50 c. net McClurg.
See also Crystal gazing;—Future life;—Ghosts;—Hypnotism;—Mental science;—New Thought;—Spiritualism;—Suggestion; — Telepathy; —*also* Swedenborg, Emanuel.
Psychical science and Christianity. Bates, E. K. $1.50. Dodge.
Psycho-harmonical philosophy. Pearson, P. $3.50. P. Pearson.
Psychologic method in teaching. McKeever, W: A. $1. Flanagan.
Psychological interpretation of society. Davis, M. M. $2. Longmans.
Psychological Review, monograph supplements. 4°. Psychological Review.
—American Psychological Assoc. *Committee on the Teaching of Psychology.* Rept. $1.
—Bingham. Studies in melody. $1.
—Fernald. Effect of achromatic conditions on the color phenomena of peripheral vision. (Studies from the Psychological Lab'y of the University of Chicago.) $1.
—Gamble. Study in memorizing various materials by the reconstruction method. (Wellesley College studies in psychology.) $2.25.
—Gatewood. Experimental study of dementia præcox. (Ohio State Univ., Psychological studies.) 75 c.
—Hayden. Social will. $1.
—Johns Hopkins University. *Psychological Laboratory.* Studies. $1.
—Peterson. Combination tones and other related auditory phenomena. $1.50.—On the influence of complexity and dissimilarity on memory. $1.
—Richardson. Study of sensory control in the rat. (Studies from the Psychological Lab'y of the Univ. of Chicago.) $1.25.
—Rowland. Psychological experiences connected with different parts of speech. (Add. pubs. for price.)
—University of Illinois. Studies from the psychological laboratories of the University of Illinois. v. 1. $1.75.
—Urban. Application of statistical methods to the problems of psychophysics. $2.50.
—Yoakum. Experimental study of fatigue. $1.35.
Psychological origin and nature of religion. Leuba, J. H. *40 c. net. Open Court.
Psychological phenomena of Christianity. Cutten, G: B. **$2.50 net. Scribner.
PSYCHOLOGY.
American Psychological Association. *Committee on the Teaching of Psychology.* Report. $1, Psychological Review.
Ames, E: S. Psychology of religious experience. $2.50 net. Houghton M.
Angell, J. R. Psychology. $1.60. Holt.
Arnold, F. Attention and interest. **$1 net. Macmillan.
Atkinson, W: W. New psychology: its principles and practice. $1. Progress Co.
Bennett, C: J. C. Formal discipline. 50 c. Teachers' Coll.
Betts, G: H. Distribution and functions of mental imagery. $1; 75 c. Teachers' Coll.
Bligh, S. M. Direction of desire. 70 c. net; $1. Oxford Univ.
Brown, W. Judgment of difference with special reference to the doctrine of the threshold in the case of lifted weights. 50 c. Univ. of Cal.
Burrow, N. T. Determination of the position of a momentary impression in the temporal course of a moving visual impression. 65 c. Psychological Review.
Calkins, M. W. First book in psychology. $1.90 net. Macmillan.

PSYCHOLOGY.—*Continued.*

Coriat, I. Abnormal psychology. $2 net. Moffat.

Crawley, A. E. Idea of the soul. *$2.25 net. Macmillan.

Cutten, G: B. Psychological phenomena of Christianity. **$2.50 net. Scribner.

Dewey, J: How we think. $1. Heath.

Dewey, J:, *and others.* Essays philosophical and psychological in honor of William James. **$3 net. Longmans.

Dorland, W: A. W. Age of mental virility. **$1 net. Century Co.

Ebbinghaus, H. Psychology. $1.20. Heath.

Elkus, S. A. Concept of control. 40 c. Science Pr., (N. Y.)

Froeberg, S. Relation between magnitude of stimulus and the time of reaction. 35 c. Science Pr., (N. Y.)

Hamilton, F. M. Perceptual factors in reading; quantitative study of the psychological processes involved in word perception. 50 c. Science Pr., (N. Y.)

Hannahs, E. H. Lessons in psychology. $1. E. H. Hannahs.

Harvey, N. A. Mental ontogeny.—Thinking process. 50 c. N. A. Harvey.

Hollingworth, H. L. Inaccuracy of movement. rhythm. 60 c. Science Pr., (N. Y.)

Ithomites, A. New Greece; pedagogic and instructive psychology. 75 c. A. Ithomites.

Jastro, J. Qualities of men. $1 net. Houghton M.

Johns Hopkins University. *Psychological Laboratory.* Studies. $1. Psychological Review.

Judd, C: H. Psychology. In 3 v. v. 2, 3. v. 2, *75 c. special net; v. 3, *$1.50 special net. Scribner.

Jung, C. Psychology of dementia præcox. $2. Journal Nervous Disease.

Kirkpatrick, E. A. Genetic psychology. **$1.25 net. Macmillan.

McCabe, J. Evolution of mind. $2 net. Macmillan.

McDougall, W: Introd. to social psychology. *$1.50 net. J: W. Luce.

McKeever, W: A. Psychologic method in teaching.—Psychology and higher life. ea., $1. Flanagan.

Marshall, H: R. Consciousness. *$4 net. Macmillan.

Miller, J. E. Psychology of thinking. *$1.25 net. Macmillan.

Moore, T: V. Process of abstraction. $1. Univ. of Cal.

Münsterberg, H. American problems from the point of view of a psychologist. $1.60 net. Moffat.

Munsterberg, H. On the witness stand: essays on psychology and crime. **$2.50 net. McClure.

Münsterberg, H. Psychology and the teacher. **$1.50 net. Appleton.

Münsterberg, H., *and others.* Subconscious phenomena. $1.20 net. Badger.

Myers, C: S: Text-book of experimental psychology. *$2.40 net. Longmans.

PSYCHOLOGY.—*Continued.*

Osuna, A. Elementos de psicologia pedagógica. $1.25. Smith & L.

Pillsbury, W. B. Attention. *$2.75 net. Macmillan.

Pillsbury, W. B. Psychology of reasoning. $1.50 net. Appleton.

Poincaré, J. H. Value of science. $1.25. Science Pr., (N. Y.)

Ritchey, J. A. Psychology of the will. $1.50. B'way Pub.

Ross, E. A. Social psychology. **$1.50 net. Macmillan.

Rowland, E. H. Psychological experiences connected with the different parts of speech. (Add. pubs. for price.) Psychological Review.

Ruger, H: A. Psychology of efficiency. Science Pr.

Savage, G: H: Harveian oration on experimental psychology and hypnotism. 40 c. Oxford Univ.

Scott, W. D. Psychology of advertising. **$2 net. Small.

Seashore, C. E. Elem. experiments in psychology. $1. Holt.

Sinclair, S: B., *and* Tracy, F: Introductory educational psychology. 90 c. Macmillan.

Stewart, J: A. Plato's doctrine of ideas. $2. Oxford Univ.

Storring, G. Mental pathology in its relation to normal psychology. *$2.75 net. Macmillan.

Swift, E. J. Mind in the making. **$1.50 net. Scribner.

Talmey, M. Psyche; concise and easily comprehensible treatise on the elements of psychiatry and psychology. $2.50. Medico-Legal.

Thorndike, E: L. Educational psychology. $1.50. Teachers' Coll.

Titchener, E: B. Lectures on the elem. psychology of feeling and attention. *$1.40 net.—Lectures on the experimental psychology of the thought-process. **$1.25 net.—Text-book of psychology. pts. 1, 2. ea., $1.30 net; complete in 1 v., $2 net. Macmillan.

University of Illinois. Studies from the psychological lab'y of the Univ. of Ill. v. 1. $1.75. Psychological Review.

Ware, E. F. Autobiography of Ithuriel, (a chapter in psychology.) (Not for sale.) E. F. Ware.

Washburn, M. F. Animal mind. *$1.60 net. Macmillan.

Watson, J: B. Kinæsthetic and organic sensations: their role in the reactions of the white rat to the maze. (Add. pubs. for price.) Psychological Review.

Wenzlaff, G. G. Mental man: outline of the fundamentals of psychology. $1.10. C: E. Merrill.

Whipple, G. M. Manual of mental and physical tests. $2.50 net. Warwick-Y.

Whipple, G. M. Questions in general and educational psychology. 75 c. Bardeen.

Wodehouse, H. Presentation of reality. $1 net. Putnam.

Woodrow, H. Quantitative study of rhythm. 60 c. Science Pr., (N. Y.)

PSYCHOLOGY.—*Continued.*

Woodworth, R. S. Psychology: [a lecture.] (Add. pubs. for price.) Columbia Univ.

See also Æsthetics;—Animal psychology;—Animals;—Brain;—Character; — Children; — Consciousness;—Education;—Ethics; — Ethnology; —Faith;—Fatigue; — Future life;—Hearing;—Heredity;—History;—Humility; — Hypnotism; —Hysteria;—Imagination; — Immortality;—Insanity;—Logic; — Love; — Memory; — Mental science;—Mind;—Mind and body; — Music; — Personality; — Philosophy; — Phrenology; — Politics;—Psychical research;—Psychotherapy; —Rat;—Sex; — Soul; — Speech; — Suggestion (Mental);—Teachers and teaching;—Telepathy; —Touch;—Will;—*also* Pomponazzi, Pietro.

Psychology and pedagogy of reading. Huey, E. B. *$1.40 net. Macmillan.

Psychology and the medical school. Franz, S. I. (Not for sale.) George Washington Univ.

Psychology of Christ. Wright, E. D. *$1 net. Cochrane.

Psychology of inspiration. Raymond, G: L. **$1.40 net. Funk.

Psychology of Jesus. Hitchcock, A. W. *$1.25 net. Pilgrim Press.

Psychology of prayer. Strong, A. L. *$1.75 net. Univ. of Chic.

Psychology of prophecy. Kaplan, J. H. *$1.50 net. J. H. Greenstone.

Psychology of singing. Taylor, D: C. *$1.50 net. Macmillan.

Psychology of skill. Book, F: W: $1. Univ. of Mont.

Psychology of success. Atkinson, W: W. $1. Progress Co.

Psychology of success. Riddell, N. N. $1.50. Riddell Pub.

Psychoma, (soul-sleep.) Rhodes, H. $1. E. J. Towne.

PSYCHOMANCY.
See **Crystal gazing.**

PSYCHOPATHOLOGY.
See Insanity.

PSYCHOPHYSICS.
See Suggestion (Mental).

Psychoprophylaxis in childhood. Williams, T. A. T. A. Williams.

Psycho-therapeutics. Prince, M. *$1.50 net. Badger.

PSYCHOTHERAPY.

Boyd, T: P. How and why of the Emmanuel movement. $1. Whitaker & R.

Brown, C: R. Faith and health. **$1 net. Crowell.

Cabot, R: C. Psychotherapy in its relation to religion. **25 c. net.—Social service and the art of healing. **$1 net. Moffat.

Colville, W: W. J. Health from knowledge; or, the law of correspondence as related to psycho-therapy. 50 c. Macoy.

Coriat, I. H. New psychology in medicine. $2 net. Moffat.

Dick, S: M. Psychotherapy. 25 c. S: M. Dick.

Dubois, P. Psychic treatment of nervous disorders. **$3 net. Funk.

Fallows, S. Health and happiness. *$1.50 net. McClurg.

Feuchtersleben, E. v. Health and suggestion. $1 net. B: W. Huebsch.

Harlow, W. E. Mental and moral therapeutics. $1.50. W. E. Harlow.

PSYCHOTHERAPY.—*Continued.*

Lawrence, R. M. Primitive psychotherapy and quackery. $2 net. Houghton M.

Leavitt, S. Psychic solution of the problem of cure. $3. Magnum Bonum.

Münsterberg, H. Psychotherapy. **$2 net. Moffat.

Parker, G: L. Other side of psychotherapy. 25 c. G: L. Parker.

Parker, W. B., *ed.* Psychotherapy. (Add. pubs. for price.) Centre Pub.

Pollak, G. Hygiene of the soul. $1.20 net. Dodd.

Prince, M., *and others.* Psycho-therapeutics. *$1.50 net. Badger.

Walgren, J: A. New health science. $1. Rand, McN. & Co.

Williams, T. A. Psychoprophylaxis in childhood. T. A. Williams.

See also Divine healing;—Emanuel Church, Boston—Faith cure; — Hypnotism; — Insanity;— Medicine and religion;—Mental science;—Mind and body;—Nervous system;—New thought;— Personality;—Sleep;—Suggestion (Mental).

PTOMAINE POISONING.
See Bacteria.

Public abattoirs. Ayling, R. S. $3.50. Spon.

Public benefits derived from water power developments in California. Martin, J: gratis. J: Martin.

PUBLIC DOCUMENTS.
See **United States.**

Public domain and democracy. Hill, R. T. $2. Longmans.

PUBLIC HEALTH.
See **Hygiene.**

PUBLIC INSTITUTIONS.
See **Charities;—Prisons;—Schools.**

PUBLIC LANDS.
See **Lands.**

Public mindedness. Tucker, W: J. $2. Rumford Press.

Public office in relation to public opinion. Brewer, D: J. *See* Hughes, C: Evans.

Public recreation facilities. American Academy of Political and Social Science. $1.50; $1. Am. Acad. Pol. Sci.

Public roads. Buckley, E. R. (Add. pub. for price.) Missouri Bu. Geol.

Public school agriculture, 1909; rept. of committee appointed at the Conference on Agricultural Science at Amherst, Mass., 1908. '09(Je19) 8°, pap., gratis. R. J. Watts.

Public Schools Athletic League. Official handbook; ed. by Dr. Luther Halsey Gulick and Emanuel Haug. '08(N21) c. il. por. 16°, (Spalding's athletic lib.) pap., 10 c. Am. Sports.

Public school libraries; 500 books and how to buy them. '09(Jl10) Q. (Mich. Normal Coll. bull.) gratis. Mich. State Normal Coll.

Public school methods; the teacher's professional library. 4 v. '09(D) c. il. pls. 8°, $13.50 per set. Sch. Methods.

Public school penmanship. Clarke, A. W. 75 c. Ginn.

Public school physiology. Herrick, *Mrs.* S. M. B. gratis. U. S. Brewers' Assoc.

PUBLIC SCHOOLS.
See Schools.

Public Schools Athletic League. Official. hdbk.; ed. by C. Ward Crampton, M.D., and Emanuel Haug. '09(D4) c. il. pors. 12°, (Spalding's athletic lib.) pap., 10 c. Am. Sports.

PUBLIC UTILITIES.
Joyce, J. A. Treatise on franchises, especially of public service corporations. $6.50. Banks.
Maltbie, M. R. Report on the indeterminate franchise for public utilities. (Add. author for price.) M. R. Maltbie.
Merritt, W. G. Strikes and public utilities. gratis. Am. Anti-Boycott.
New York State. Public service commissions law. $1. Banks & Co.
Skinner, H. M., *and* Putney, A. H. Government revenue; public utilities. $4.80. Cree.
Sullivan, J. W. Municipal and private operation of public utilities. (Priv. pr.) J. W. Sullivan.
Wyman, B. Cases on public service companies, public carriers, public works, and other public utilities. (Add. pubs. for price.) Harvard Law.
See also Baltimore;—Railroads;—*also* names of states.

Public Utility Commission of New York City. '09(Jl) 235-250 p. (City Club bull.) pap. (Add. pubs. for price.) City Club, Chicago.

Public water-supplies. Turneaure, F: E. $5. Wiley.

PUBLICITY.
See Advertising.

Publisher against the people. Jenner, W: A. gratis. W: A. Jenner.

PUBLISHERS AND PUBLISHING.
Directory of publishers, 1905-1907. $1. Pub. Weekly.
Jenner, W: A. Publisher against the people: examination of new copyright law. gratis. W: A. Jenner.
Jones, A. H. Strange adventures of an author in search of a publisher. 10 c. Am. Press.
Maupin, B: F., *comp.* Publisher's calculator. 3 v. ¾ leath., ea., $3; 2 v., $5.40; 3 v., $6.75; additional v., ea., $2.25. B: F. Maupin.
Open Court Publishing Co. Work of the Open Court Publishing Co. (Add. pubs. for price.) Open Court.
Spurgeon, A. Premature cheapening of copyright books. (Priv. pr.) Cassell.
Sweetland, C: A: Publishers' and printers' accounts. 50 c. Am. Sch. Corr.
Thayer, J: A. Astir: publisher's life-story. $1.20 net. Small.
See also Authorship;—Copyright;—Printers and printing;—*also* Shearman, Abraham.

Publishers' (The) trade list annual, 1908. 36th year. '08(Ag22); 1909. 37th year. '09(Ag28); 1910. 38th year. '10(Ag27) Q. ea., $2. Pub. Weekly.

Publishers' Weekly (The). American Educational list, 1908. '08(Ag22); 1909. '09 (Ag21); 1910. '10(Ag27) c. O. leatherette, ea., 50 c. Pub. Weekly.

Publow, C: Alb.
Fancy cheese in America, from the milk of cows, sheep and goats. '10(D) 96 p. il. 12°, 75 c. Am. Sheep.
Questions and answers on buttermaking. '09, [1910.] (Ja.) 75 p. 12°. 50 c. Judd.
See also Van Slyke, Lucius Lincoln.

Publow, C: Alb., and Troy, Hugh' C.
Questions and answers on milk and milk-testing. '09, [1910.] (F) c. 97 p. front. 12°. 50 c. Judd.

Puck of Pook's Hill. *See* **Kipling, Rudyard.**

Pucker, pseud.
See Rogers, W: Osgood.

Puddicombe, Mrs. Beyon, [**"Allen Raine."**]
Under the thatch. '10(S24) D. $1.50. Dodd.

PUDDINGS.
See Cookery.

Pudgy. Hughes, D. 50 c. Dutton.

PUEBLO INDIANS.
See Indians.

PUGET SOUND, Washington.
Denny, A. A. Pioneer days on Puget Sound. subs., *$2 net; *60 c. net. A. Harriman.
Phucher, I., *pseud.* Puget Sound and Inland Empire Railway "Cascade Tunnel Route." 50 c. A. Harriman.

Puget Sound friendship ser. nar. O. pap., 50 c., in envelope. A. Harriman.
—Powers. Love never faileth.

Puget Sound historical ser. D. subs., *$2 net; pap., *60 c. net. A. Harriman.
—Denny. Pioneer days on Puget Sound.
—Phelps. Reminiscences of Seattle.

Puget Sound Indian ser. nar. D. 50 c., in envelope. A. Harriman.
—Rich. Prophecy of Yah-Ma-Sun.

Pugh, Mabel Feger, ed.
Typewriting manual. 3d ed. of Peirce manual for the typist. '08(O) c. 200 p. 4°, $1.25. Peirce Sch.

Pugsley, R: Marriotte.
New York pilot and guide to the United States local inspectors examination of masters and pilots for New York Bay and Harbor to Yonkers and Great Captain Island, and a complete New York pilot cont. all useful information. '10 (My14) c. 12°, $1. R: M. Pugsley.

PULASKI, Kazimierz.
Clarke, J:, *and* Bentalou, P. Impartial and authentic narrative of battle fought on the 17th of June on Bunker's Hill, [and] Pulaski vindicated from an unsupported charge introduced in Judge Johnson's Sketches of the life and correspondence of Major Gen. Nathaniel Greene. to subscribers. $1.65. Abbatt.

Pulaski Co., Va. Historic and descriptive sketch designed to show forth the natural advantages, resources and general adaptability of the banner county of southwest Virginia. '07, [1908.] (D) 96 p. il. 8°, 15 c. Southwest Pub.

Pulitzer, Ralph.
New York society on parade. '10(F19) c. D. *$1.20 net. Harper.

Pulitzer, Wa.
Cupid's pack of cards. '08(Mr28) c. il. O. bds., $1. J: W. Luce.
My auto book. '08(O10) c. il. D. $1. Outing.

Pullan, Rev. Leighton.
New Testament criticism during the past century. '08(Ja4) O. pap., *30 c. net. Longmans.

Pulling, F: Sanders, ed.
See Low, Sidney, Ja. Mark, *ed.*

PULMONARY DISEASE.
See Consumption;—Lungs;—Tuberculosis.
Pulmonary hemorrhage in the tuberculous at high altitude. Smith, F: C. Gov. Pr. Off.
PULMONARY TUBERCULOSIS.
See Tuberculosis
Pulpit commentary on Catholic teaching: exposition of Catholic doctrine, discipline and cult in original discourses by pulpit preachers of our own day. v. 1. '08(Mr21) c. 8°, $2. Wagner.
Pulpit year book: storehouse of sound teaching, containing two outline sermons for each Sunday of the liturgical year, sermons for Saints' Days, Holy Week and the Three Hours, and a set of sermons for special occasions. '09(Mr27) 12°, *$1 net. Gorham.
PULPITS.
See Church architecture.
Pulsating exophthalmos. Schweinitz, G: E. de. *$2 net. Saunders.
Pulse of life. Belloc-Lowndes, *Mrs.* M. A. †$1.50. Dodd.
Pumpelly, Raphael, ed.
Explorations in Turkestan, expedition of 1904; prehistoric civiliations of Anau. In 2 v. '09(Ja9) il. fold. maps, Q. $10. Carnegie.
Pumping machinery. Barr, W: M. $5. Lippincott.
PUMPS.
Collins, H. E. Pumps. $1. Hill Pub.
Gregory, W: B: Selection and installation of machinery for small pumping plants. Gov. Pr. Off.
Marks, E: C: R. Notes on the construction and working of pumps. $1.50. Van Nostrand.
Nagel, O. Transportation of gases, liquids and solids by means of steam, compressed air and pressure water. $2. O. Nagel.
Stewart, C. B. Investigation of centrifugal pumps. pt. 1. 50 c. Univ. of Wis.
Weisbach, J., *and* Herrmann, G. Mechanics of pumping machinery. *$4 net. Macmillan.
See also Hydraulic engineering;—Water-supply.
Punch, Rosalind Mae Guggenheim.
See Burr, Jane, *pseud.*
"PUNCH" (*English weekly*).
Walsh, W: S. Abraham Lincoln and the London *Punch:* cartoons, comments and poems. **$1 net. Moffat.
See also Burnand, *Sir* F. C.;—Jerrold, Douglas William.
Punch and die work. '08(My23) c. il. 8°, (Machinery's reference ser.) pap., 25 c. Indust. Press.
PUNCHES.
See Machinery.
Punchinellos. Davis, K. W. 40 c. Flanagan.
PUNCTUATION.
Baldwin, C: S. Summary of punctuation. 5 c. Longmans.
Chase, F. N. Punctuation and paragraphing. 15 c. F. N. Chase.
Guthrie, J. D. Byrne duplex English punctuation and correspondence. $1. Byrne Pub.
Perry, F. M. Punctuation primer; with notes on the preparation of manuscript. 30 c. Am. Bk.

PUNCTUATION.—*Continued.*
Ramsay, R. L. Principles of modern punctuation. gratis. R. L. Ramsay.
Winchell, S: R. Orthography, etymology, and punctuation. 60 c. Flanagan.
Punishment and reformation. Wines, F: H. *$1.75 net. Crowell.
Punnett, Reginald Crundall.
Mendelism. American ed., with preface by Gaylord Wilshire. '09(Je19) c. il. 12°, 50 c. Wiltshire Bk.
Pupil and how to teach him. Burritt, E. G. 60 c. W: B. Rose.
Pupils' arithmetic. *See* Byrnes, Ja. C.
Pupils' notebook and study outline in Oriental and Greek history. Lewis, L. B. 25 c. Am. Bk.
Puppe, J.
Experimental investigation on the power required to drive rolling mills. '10(Jl30) 4°, $4.50 net. Lippincott.
PURBECK, *Lady* Frances Coke.
Longueville, T: Curious case of Lady Purbeck. $2. Longmans.
PURCELL, Henry.
Runciman, J: F. Purcell. *50 c. net; *$1 net. Macmillan.
Purcell, Marg. Anna.
See Ritchie, J: Woodside.
Purchase of coal. Randall, D. T. 15 c. U. S., Supt. of Docs.
Purchase price. Hough, E. $1.50. Bobbs-M.
Purchasing agents' buying list and railway supply index. v. 1, no. 1. '10(Ap) c. f°, $6. Buyers' Index.
Purchasing and stores department. Griffith, J. B. 50 c. Am. Sch. Corr.
Purdon, J:
See Penn. Digest.
Purdue, Albert Homer, and Branner, J: Casper.
Slates of Arkansas, by A. H. Purdue; with a bibliography of the geology of Arkansas, by J. C. Branner. [1910.] (Mr) 170 p. il. maps, fold. tab., 8°, (Geological Survey of Arkansas pubs.) gratis. Arkansas Geol. Survey.
Pure milk. Ward, A. R. *$2 net. Taylor & C.
PURGATORIO (*by Dante*).
Vernon, W: W. Readings on Purgatorio of Dante. *$4 net. Macmillan.
Purification of public water supplies. Bridge, J. H. (Add. pubs. for price.) Aldine Bk.
Purification of some textile and other factory wastes. Stabler, H. (Add. Superintendent for price.) U. S., Supt. of Docs.
Purification of water for boiler feeding. Harrison Safety Boiler Works, Philadelphia. (Priv. pr.) Harrison.
Puritan captain. Charlton, E. C. $1. Chr. Pub.
Puritanism and art. Crouch, J. $3.75 net. Cassell.
PURITANS.
Heron, J. Short history of Puritanism. *50 c. net. Scribner.
Kirbye, J. E: Puritanism in the South. 75 c. Pilgrim Press.
See also Church of England; — Congregational church;—England; — Friends (*Society of*);—Presbyterian church.

Purity and truth. Rupp, F: A. 50 c. Vir

Purity, birth and sexual problems. Evans, *Mrs.* F. (Add. pubs. for price.) Purity Pub.

Purple and homespun. Gardenhire, S: M. †$1.50. Harper.

Purple parasol. McCutcheon, G: B. 75 c. Burt.

PURPOSE.
See Conduct of life.

Purrington, W. A.
Review of recent legal decisions affecting physicians, dentists, druggists and the public health. '08(Ja4) D. bds., $1. Treat.

Pursuit (The). Saville, F. M. $1.50. Little, B. & Co.

Purves, Stewart.
Diagnosis of nervous diseases. 2d ed., rev. and enl. '08(D19) figs. O. *$4.20 net. Longmans.

Purvis, J: Bremner.
Through Uganda to Mount Elgon. '09 (N6) il. map, O. $1.50. Am. Tract.

Purvis, Miller.
Poultry breeding; complete guide for keepers of poultry. '10(Je25) c. il. por. 8°, $1.50. Sanders Pub.

Pusey House occasional papers. D. Longmans.
—Stone. Episcopacy and valid orders in the primitive church. 40 c.—Law of Christian marriage. 10 c.

Pushing your business. MacGregor, T. D. *$1 net. Bankers Pub.

Puter, Stephen A. Douglas, and Stevens, Horace.
Looters of the public domain: complete exposure of the fraudulent system of acquiring titles to the public lands of the United States. '08(Ag1) c. il. pors. 8°, $3. Portland.

Puterbaugh, Lewis Prather.
The moonlight banquet; comedy. '10(S) c. 113 p. 12°, $1. L. P. Puterbaugh.

Putnam, Arth. Alwyn.
Selection from the addresses, lectures and papers, with a biographic sketch, of Arthur A. Putnam. '10(N5) c. 8°, $1.50. Riverside Press.

Putnam, Bertha Haven.
Enforcement of the statutes of labourers during the first decade after the Black Death, 1347-1359. '08(D5) c. O. (Columbia Univ. studies in history, economics and public law.) pap., $4. Longmans.

Putnam, Eben.
Putnam lineage; historical-genealogical notes concerning the Puttenham family in England. '07, [1908.] (Mr.) c. 152+341+27 p. il. pors. map, geneal. tabs., 8°, $15. Salem Press.

Putnam, E: Kirby.
Spelling reform and authority in language; paper read before the Contemporary Club, Davenport, Ia., Dec. 26, 1907. '08, [1909.] (F) 20 p. 8°. (Add. pubs. for price.) Contemporary Club.

Putnam, Mrs. Emily James Smith.
The lady; studies of certain significant phases of her hist. '10(D3) c. il. O. $2.50 net. Sturgis & W.

Putnam, F: Ward.
See Putnam anniversary volume.

Putnam, G: Haven.
Abraham Lincoln, the people's leader in the struggle for national existence; with the above is incl. the speech del. by Lincoln in New York, Feb. 27, 1860; with an introd. by C: C. Nott. '09(D4) c. por. O. **$1.25 net. Putnam.
Little gingerbread man. '10(N12) c. il. O. $1.25, boxed. Putnam.

Putnam, G: Rockwell.
Nautical charts. '08(N7) figs. 8°, $2. Wiley.

Putnam, Ja. J., M.D.
See Prince, Morton, *M.D.*

Putnam, Ruth.
Charles the Bold, last Duke of Burgundy, 1433-1477. '08(F29) c. il. pors. maps, D. (Heroes of the nations.) **$1.35 net; **$1.60 net. Putnam.

Putnam anniversary volume; anthropological essays; presented to F: Ward Putnam in honor of his seventieth birthday, April 16, 1909, by his friends and associates. '10 (Ap16) il. por. Q. pap., $8 net. Stechert.

PUTNAM FAMILY.
See Genealogies: Putnam, E.;—Wyand, E. C.

Putnam Hall champions. Stratemeyer, E: 60 c. Grosset.

Putnam Hall rebellion. Stratemeyer, E: 60 c. Grosset.

Putnam's English literature for schools; ed. by J. H. Lobban. S. Putnam.
—Goldsmith. Selected essays. 40 c. net.

Putnam's French classics for English readers; ed. by Adolphe Cohn and Curtis Hidden Page. 8°, **$2 net. Putnam.
—Molière. Eight plays.

Putnam's home maker ser. *See* Reed, Myrtle.

Putnam's memoir ser. il. O. Putnam.
—Lair. Louise de La Vallière and the early life of Louis XIV. *$3.50 net.
—Sélincourt. Great Ralegh [*sic.*] *$3.50 net.

Putnam's science ser.; ed. by E: Lee Thorndike and F. E. Beddard. il. O. Putnam.
—Launay. World's gold. **$1.75 net.
—Metchnikoff. Nature of man. **$2 net.—Prolongation of life. *$2.50 net.
—Minot. Problem of age, growth and death. **$2.50 net.
—Poor. Solar system. **$2 net.
—Soddy. Interpretation of radium. *$1.75 net.
—Thomson. Heredity. *$3.50 net.
—Ward. Climate considered especially in relation to man. **$2 net.

Putney, Alb. Hutchinson.
Bar examination review. '10(O) 491 p. 8°, $4. Ill. Bk.
Commercial law. '09(D25) c. 8°, $4.80. Cree.
Corporations; organization, financing, management. '09(D25) c. 8°, $4.80. Cree.
Currency, banking and exchange. '09(D25) c. 8°, $4.80. Cree.

Putney, Alb. Hutchinson.—*Continued.*
Foreign laws. '10(Mr) c. O. (Business, commerce and finance.) hf. im. mor., $5. Cree.
Law library. '08(Jl) c. 12 v., 8°, hf. shp., subs., per set, $57. Cree.
United States constitutional history and law. '08(O10) c. 8°, *$3.50 net. Ill. Bk.
—, **ed.** Popular law library. 12 v. 2d ed. '10(S) c. O. ea., shp., $5. Cree.
—, **and Skinner, Hubert Marshall.**
Principles of political economy, by Albert H. Putney; Sociology, by Hubert M. Skinner. '09(D25) c. 8°, $4.80. Cree.
—, **Skinner, Hubert Marshall, and Kirkman, G: Wycherly.**
Manufactures, mining, by Albert H. Putney; Irrigation, by Hubert M. Skinner; Real estate, by G: W. Kirkman. '10 (Ap9) c. il. 8°, (Business, commerce and finance.) $4. Cree.
See also Skinner, Hubert Marshall.
PUTTENHAM FAMILY.
See Genealogies: Putnam, E.;—Wyand, E. C.
PUTTING GREENS.
See Lawns.
Putting on the screws. Morris, G. **50 c. net. Doubleday, P.
Putzel, C:, and Bähr, H. A., comps.
Commercial precedents sel. from the column of Replies and decisions of the N. Y. *Journal of Commerce and Commercial Bulletin.* '07, [1908.] (Mr.) 21+776 p. 8°. (Add. pubs. for price.) Am. Pub.
Puzzle pictures of animals to cut up and glue. Williams, C. A. $1. Stokes.
Puzzle pictures of farmyard friends. Williams, C. A. $1. Stokes.
PUZZLES.
Dudeney, H: E. Canterbury puzzles. *$1.25 net. Dutton.
Model puzzle book. 50 c. Dutton.
Pearson, A. C. Pictured puzzles and word play. $1.50. Dutton.
Pycraft, W. P.
Animal why book. '10(S10) col. il. Q. $2. Stokes.
Pyeschkoff, Alexéi Maximovitch.
See Górky, Maxim, *pseud.*
PYKE FAMILY.
See **Genealogies: McPike, E. F.**
Pyle, Rev. C: Bertram.
Philosophy of Borden Parker Bowne and its application to the religious problem. '10(D31) c. 12°, $1 net. S. F. Harriman.
Pyle, Howard.
Ruby of Kishmoor. '08(N14) c. il. O. †$1. Harper.
Story of the Grail and The passing of Arthur. '10(O1) c. il. O. $2.50 net. Scribner.
See also Adventures of pirates.
Pyle, Katharine.
Where the wind blows. '10(N5) il. 8°, $2. Dutton.
Pyle, Wa. L., M.D., ed.
Manual of personal hygiene; proper living upon a psychologic basis; by American authors. 4th ed., rev. and enl. '10(O) 14+472 p. il. 8°, $1.50 net. Saunders.
Pyramid building. Cromie, W: J. 10 c. **Spalding.**

PYRAMIDELLIDAE.
See **Mollusks.**
PYRAMIDS.
McCarty, L: P. Great pyramid of Jeezeh. $5; $6. McCarty.
Schmalz, J: B. Nuggets from King Solomon's Mine. $2. Schmalz.
Pyre, Ja. Fs. Augustine, Dickinson, T: Herbert, and Young, Karl, comps.
Century outlines for a course in English literature. '10(D24) c. O. 75 c. net. Century Co.
—, **ed.** *See* Cunliffe, J: W:
"Pythagoras, 38," pseud.
See Clymer, Reuben Swinburne.
PYTHAGORAS.
Schuré, E. Pythagoras and his system of philosophy. *$1.25 net. Badger.
"Q," pseud.
See Couch, *Sir* Arth. T: Quiller-.
QUACK GRASS.
See **Quitch-grass.**
Quackenbos, J: Duncan, M.D.
Enemies and evidences of Christianity; thoughts on questions of the hour. Rev. ed. '09(Je) c. 9-355 p. 8°, $1.50. Eaton & M.
Hypnotic therapeutics in theory and practice. '08(F15) O. **$2 net. Harper.
Quacks and grafters, by Ex-osteopath: being an exposé of the state of therapeutics at the present time, with some reasons why such grafters flourish, and suggestion to remedy the deplorable muddle. '08, [1909.] (Mr) c. 126 p. 12°, $1.25. Cin. Medical.
QUACKS AND QUACKERY.
Quack and grafters, by Ex-osteopath. $1.25. Cin. Medical.
Shute, D. K. Philosophical foundations of charlatanry in medicine. (Not for sale.) George Washington Univ.
Quaestio de aqua et terra. *See* Dante Alighieri.
Quaestiones naturales. *See* Seneca, Lucius Annæus.
QUAIL.
Wiley, H. W., *and others.* Preliminary study of the effects of cold storage on eggs, quail and chickens. (Add. Superintendent for price.) U. S., Supt. of Docs.
Quain, Jones and Sir R:
Elements of anatomy; ed. by E: Albert Schäfer, Johnson Symington, T: Hastie Bryce. In 4 v. v. 1, Embryology. '08 (Jl11) $3; v. 2, pt. 1, Osteology, arthrology, pt. 2, Myology, angeiology; v. 3, Neurology, pt. 1, Containing the general structure of the nervous system and the structure of the brain and spinal cord. 11th ed. '08(N21); pt. 2, cont. the descriptive anatomy of the peripheral nerves and of the organs of special sense. '09(N13) il. figs. Q. v. 2, pt. 1, $3.50; pt. 2, $4.50; v. 3, pt. 1, $4.50; pt. 2, $4.50. Longmans.
Quain, Sir R:
See Quain, Jones.
Quaint ser. Tt. bds., 25 c. Stokes.
—Byron. Just for a change.—Little wee bear and Golden Hair.—Toysy-Turvy Land.

Quaint subjects of the King. Fraser, J: F. *$1.25 net. Cassell.

Quaintance, Altus Lacy.
Fumigation of apples for the San Jose scale. '09(D) 43 p. il. tabs., 8°, (U. S., Dept. of Agriculture, Bu. of Entomology, bull.) (Add. Superintendent for price.) U. S., Supt. of Docs.

Quaker and courtier. Grant, *Mrs.* C. *$3.50 net. Dutton.

Quaker boy. Foulke, W: D. $1.50. Cochrane.

Quaker boy on the farm. Sharpless, I: $1. Biddle Press.

QUAKER HILL, N. Y.
Wilson, W. H. Quaker Hill in the 19th century. 10 c. Quaker Hill.

Quaker Hill local history ser. D. pap., 10 c. Quaker Hill.
—Patrick. Washington's headquarters. 10 c.
—Rogers. Historical landmarks in the town of Sherman, Ct.
—Wilson. Quaker Hill in the nineteenth century.

Quaker idyls. Gardner, S. M. H. **$1 net. Holt.

Quaker Jim. Kelty, R: A. $1.50. B'way Pub.

QUAKERS.
See Friends (*Society of*).

QUALITATIVE ANALYSIS.
See Chemistry.

Qualities of a good superior. Champagnat, J. B. M. *$1.25 net. Herder.

Qualities of men. Jastro, J. $1 net. Houghton M.

Quality folks. Hovis, W: F. *$1 net. Jennings.

QUANTITATIVE ANALYSIS.
See Chemistry.

Quantitative experiments in general chemistry. Stoddard, J: T. $1. Longmans.

Quantitative study of rhythm. Woodrow, H. 60 c. Science Pr., (N. Y.)

Quantity of money from distribution. Rawie, H: 15 c. Distribution League.

QUANTRELL, W: C.
Connelley, W: E. Quantrill and the border wars. $3.50. Torch Press.

QUARANTINE.
Sanitary convention between the United States and other powers. '09(My) 27 p. 8°. (Add. Superintendent for price.) U. S., Supt. of Docs.
See also Hygiene.

Quarter-back's pluck. Chadwick, L. $1. Cupples & L.

Quarter-century of English literature. Payne, W: M. [priv. pr.] Chic. Lit. Club.

Quarter to four. Cook, W: W. †$1.50. G: W. Dillingham.

Quatrains of Christ. Creel, G: 50 c. net; **75 c. net. P. Elder.

Quatre contes des Mille et une nuits. *See* Blanchaud, R. de, *ed.*

Quayle, Bp. W: Alfr.
Book of Ruth. '09(Ag) 160 p. il. 8°, *$1.50 net; ooze, *$2.50 net. Dodge.
The pastor-preacher. '10(Mr12) c. O. *$1.50 net. Jennings.
Songs of songs. '10(O15) c. nar. D. pap., 35 c. net. Eaton & M.

Queen at bay. Auvergne, E. B. d'. $5 net. Lane.

Queen bee. Ewald, C. $1.25. Nelson.

Queen of flowers and her maids of honor. Gregory, *Sister, comp.* 50 c. Sisters of St. Joseph.

Queen of the outlaw's camp. Harper, O. 25 c. J. S. Ogilvie.

Queen of the secret seven. Harper, O. 25 c. J. S. Ogilvie.

Queen Sheba's ring. Haggard, H: R. $1.50. Doubleday, P.

Queen's Gate mystery. Curties, H: †$1.50. Estes.

Queen's poor. Loane, M. $1.25. Longmans.

Queen's treasure ser. See Macmillan's.

QUEENS (Borough).
See New York City.

Queens of Egypt. Buttles, J. R. *$3 net. Appleton.

QUEENSLAND, Australia.
Banfield, E. J. Confessions of a beach comber. $4 special net. Appleton.

Queer things about Egypt. Sladen, D. B. W. $5 net. Lippincott.

Quentin Durward. *See* Scott, *Sir* Wa.

QUERCUS ALBA.
See White oak.

Querido, I.
Toil of men. '09(O16) D. *$1.35 net. Putnam.

Queries and answers. Lipscomb, D: $1.50. J. W. Shepherd.

Querist (The). *See* Berkeley, G:

Querists' drawer. Errett, I: $1.50. Standard Pub.

"Quest" (The). Stoddard, T: A. $1.50. Cochrane.

Quest eternal. Lillibridge, W: O. †$1.50. Dodd.

Quest flower. Burnham, *Mrs.* C. L. R. †$1. Houghton M.

Quest for health and happiness Hawkins, C. J *50 c. net. Pilgrim Press.

Quest for the rose of Sharon. Stevenson, B. E. $1.25. L. C. Page.

Quest of Douglas Holms. Inman, H. E. $1.50. Warne.

Quest of the absolute. Balzac, H. de. *35 c. net; *70 c. net. Dutton.

Quest of the ages. Dean, O. S. 50 c. Cochrane.

Quest of the Christ in New York City. Boyle, *Mrs.* M. M. R. $1.25. B'way Pub.

Quest of the historical Jesus. Schweitzer, A. $3.50 net. Macmillan.

Quest of the Holy Grail. *See* Abbey, Edn. Austin.—Gregg, A. E.

Quest of the simple life. Dawson, W: J. $1.50. Dutton.

Quest of the white merle. Gask, L. $1.50. Crowell.

Quest of the yellow pearl. McFarlane, P. C. *25 c. net. Revell.

Question (The). Ramsay, F. P. *$1 net. Neale.

Question: did Sir Francis Drake land on any part of the Oregon coast? Brereton, R. M. 25 c. Gill.

Question (La) des pêcheries de l'Atlantique. Balch, T: W. $1.25. Allyn, L. & S.

Question of divination, (Medea 240.) Harry, J. E: (Add. Univ. for price.) Univ. of Cin.
Question of miracles. Whitney, L. H. $1. Lib. Shelf.
Question of Romanism. Bruner, J. W. $1.50. J. W. Bruner.
Question of the hour. Conway, J. P. *$1.25 net. J: McBride.
Questioned documents. Osborn, A. S. $5.25. Lawyers' Co-op.
Questionings on criticism and beauty. Balfour, A. J. 70 c. Oxford Univ.
Questions and answers for bar-examination review. Haight, C: S. $4. Baker, V. & Co.
Questions and answers in the use of coal and oil fuels and locomotive operation. Rhodes, J: C., *comp.* $2. J: C. Rhodes.
Questions and answers on contracts. Tyler, F: S., *comp.* 50 c. Byrne.
Questions and answers on real property. Tyler, F: S., *comp.* 50 c. Byrne.
Questions and answers on the elements of music. Evans, M. G., *comp.* 80 c. M. G. Evans.
Questions and answers on the practice and theory of sanitary plumbing. Starbuck, R. M. In 2 v. v. 2. $1. R. M. Starbuck.
Questions at issue in our English speech. Bowen, E. W. $1. B'way Pub.
Questions for High-Churchmen. Cooke, R: J. **25 c. net. Eaton & M.
Questions for interpretive and literary study. 16 v. Pearson, P: H: ea., 7 c. P: H: Pearson.
Questions in general and educational psychology. Whipple, G. M. 75 c. Bardeen.
Questions in school hygiene. Whipple, G. M. 60 c. Bardeen.
Questions of the day ser. D. Putnam.
—Crosby. Strikes. $1.25.
—Kelly. Elimination of the tramp.
—Montgomery. Vital American problems. **$1.50 net.
—Rankin. American transportation system. **$1.50 net.
—Taussig. Tariff hist. of the United States. $1.50.
Quests of Paul Beck. Bodkin, M. $1.50. Little, B. & Co.
QUÉTELET, Lambert Adolphe Jacques.
Hankins, F. H. Adolphe Quetelet as statistician. *$1.25 net. Longmans.
Qui etes-vous?, [Who are you?;] annuaire des contemporains, 1908. '08(Ap4) 12°, leath., *$2 net. Lemcke.
Qui etes-vous?, [Who are you?]: annuaire des contemporains, 1909-1910. '09(Je19) D. leath., $2. Stechert.
Qui Vive, Madam, pseud.
See Jameson, *Mrs.* Helen Follett.
Quick, J: Herbert.
American inland waterways; their relation to railway transportation and to the national welfare: their creation, restoration, and maintenance. '09(D4) c. il. map, O. (American waterways.) **$3.50 net, boxed. Putnam.
Virginia of the air lanes. '09(O16) c. il. D. †$1.50. Bobbs-M.

Quick and dead; to teachers, by two of them. '09(Je12) S. pap., 50 c. Longmans.
Quick helps to the injured: [chart.] '08, [1909.] (Mr) 25 c. W: R. Jenkins.
Quickened. Ray, A. C. †$1.50. Little, B. & Co.
Quicksteps through Scandinavia. Bayne, S: G. **$1.25 net. Harper.
Quiet days in Spain. Luffmann, C. B. $2 net. Dutton.
Quiet hour ser. S. Stokes.
—E., J., *and* S., H., *comps.* Golden threads of life. 50 c.
Quiet singer. Towne, C. H. *$1 net. B. W. Dodge.
Quiet talks about the tempter. Gordon, S. D. 75 c. net. Revell.
Quiet talks on home ideals. Gordon, S: D. *75 c. net. Revell.
Quiet talks with world winners. Gordon, S: D. **75 c. net. Armstrong.
Quietest talk. Gordon, S: D. 10 c. net. Revell.
QUIETISM.
See **Bourignon, Antoinette.**
Quiller-Couch, Sir Arth. T:
See Couch, *Sir* Arth. T: Quiller-.
Quin, F. Oliver, comp. and ed.
How to be a good salesman, and pointers for retail clerks. '09(O) c. 128 p. pap., 50 c. Harper-Adams.
Quin, Rev. G: E:
Boy-saver's guide: society work for lads in their teens. '08(D26) c. front. D. *$1.35 net. Benziger.
QUINCY, John.
Wilson, D. M. John Quincy, master of Mount Wollaston. (Priv. pr.) C: F. Adams, Jr.
QUINCY, Mass.
Branch, E. W. Atlas of the city of Quincy. $15. E. W. Branch.
Quinn, Dan.
Helladian vistas: [essays on Greece.] '08 (N21) c. D. $1.50. D. Quinn.
Quinn, Silvanus Jackson.
Hist. of the city of Fredericksburg, Va.; prep. and printed by authority of the Common Council thereof, under the direction of its committee on publication. '08, [1909.] (Mr) c. 349 p. il. pors. 8°, $1.50. R. L. Knox.
Quinnet, Edg.
France et Allemagne; ed. by C. Cestre. '08 (O24) por. S. (Oxford higher French ser.) $1.15. Oxford Univ.
Quint, Wilder Dwight.
See Tilton, Dwight, *pseud.*
Quintessence of Ibsenism. Shaw, G: B. $1. Brentano's.
Quintessence of Nietzsche. Kennedy, J. $1.50 net. Duffield.
Quinton, R: Frith, M.D.
Crime and criminals. '10(O22) D. $1.50 net. Longmans.
Quirt and the spur. Rye, E. ($1.50. Conkey.
Quish, Agnes E.
See Jones, Olivia Mary.
QUITCH-GRASS.
Crane, P: B. Quack grass eradication. $1. Webb Pub. Co.

Quitters (The). Beyerle, L. H. $1.50. Conkey.

Quiver of arrows. Weitzel, L. A. $1. L. A. Weitzel.

Quiz, Roland.
Giant-land; or, the wonderful adventures of Tim Pippin. '09(O16) il. in col. O. *$2 net. Putnam.
Monster-land; or, the further adventures of King Pippin. '10(O29) col. il. O. $2.50. Putnam.

Quiz book of nursing for teachers and students. Pope, A. E. *and* T. A. *$1.75 net. Putnam.

Quiz book on Clark's Elementary law. Clark, W: L. (Add. pubs. for price.) Am. Law Bk.

Quizzer (The). *See* Stoner, Gordon.

Quizzer ser. O. Sprague.
—Snyder. Questions and answers on domestic relations. 50 c.
—Sprague. Questions and answers on sales of personal property. 50 c.

QUOITS.
Deshong, M. W. Quoits. 10 c. Am. Sports.

QUOTATIONS.
Grover, E. O., *ed.* Book of good cheer. $1. Volland.
Harbottle, T: B., *and* Dalbaic, P. H. Dictionary of quotations, (Italian.) *$1.25 net. Macmillan.
Hickman, S. H., *comp.* Golden treasury from gifted minds. $1. B'way Pub.
Lewis, J: H:, *comp.* Gathered fragments. 50 c. Lewis & W.
MacMunn, N., *comp.* Dict. of quotations. 50 c. Jacobs.
Mangasarian, M. M. Pearls; brave thoughts from brave minds. 25 c.; $1. Independent Religious.
Pennington, J. G., *ed.* All is well. 50 c. Dodge.
Rowe, F: L: Duties and beauties of life; a book for the home of selected prose and poetry. $2.50; $3.50. F: L: Rowe.
Simpson, K. D., *comp.* From a book lover's notes. 60 c. Cloister.
Walsh, W: S., *comp.* International encyclopedia of prose and poetical quotations. **$5 net. Winston.
Ward, A. L., *comp.* Dictionary of quotations from English and American poets. $1.25; $1.75.—Poetical and prose quotations. 2 v. $2.50. Crowell.
Woolard, S: F., *comp.* Good fellowship. *$1 net. Goldsmith-W.
See also Almanacs;—Birthday books;—Calendars and year-books;—Devotional exercises and meditations;—Epigrams;—Latin literature; — Maxims;—Proverbs.

R., J. G.
Father Jim; some pages from my note book. '09(Jl) pap., 10 c. Ave Maria.

R. J.'s mother. Deland, *Mrs.* M. W. C. †$1.50. Harper.

R. S. D. guide. Tilson, J. P. 25 c. Harrison Pr.

Rab and his friends. *See* Brown, J:, *M.D.*

Rabb, Kate Milner.
Boer boy of the Transvaal; from the German of August Niemann. '07, [1910.] (My) 348 p. il. 12°, $1.25. Penn Pub. Co.

Rabbi Ben Ezra. *See* Browning, Rob.

RABBINIC THEOLOGY.
See Jews.

Rabbino, Bernhard.
Domestic relations court; plea for the preservation of the home; arguments in favor of its establishment. '10(Mr12) c.. il. por. 8°, 25 c. Hebrew Standard.

RABBIT.
Bensley, B: A. Pract. anatomy of the rabbit. *$2 net. Blakiston.
Castle, W: E., *and others.* Studies of inheritance in rabbits. (Add. Institution for price.) Carnegie.
Chapman, E. S. Particeps criminis; story of the California rabbit drive. 75 c. net. Revell.
Nelson, E: W: Rabbits of North America. U. S., Supt. of Docs.

Raber, B: F:
See Hoffman, J. D:

RABIES.
Hart, G: H. Rabies and its increasing prevalence. 15 c. U. S., Supt. of Docs.
Keirle, N. G. Studies in rabies. (Add. pubs. for price.) Lord Balto. Pr.
Kerr, J: W., *and* Stimson, A. M. Prevalence of rabies in the United States; prep. by direction of the surgeon-general. '09, [1910.] (Ap) 16 p. il. 8°, pap., 5 c. Gov. Pr. Off.
Prevalence of rabies in the United States; by J: W. Kerr and Arth. M. Stimson; prep. by direction of the surgeon-general. '09, [1910.] (F) 16 p. il. 8°, pap. Gov. Pr. Off.

Race adjustment. Miller, K. *$2 net. Neale.

Race distinction in American law. Stephenson, G. T: $1.50 net. Appleton.

RACE IMPROVEMENT.
See Eugenics.

RACE LEGISLATION.
See Law.

Race or mongrel. Schultz, A. P. $2.50. L. C. Page.

Race problem. Waddell, C: W. 25 c. C: W. Waddell.

Race question in a new light. Griggs, S. E. 15 c. Orion Pub.

Race questions. Royce, J. **$1.25 net. Macmillan.

RACE SUICIDE.
Lusk, *Mrs.* A. F. Woman's answer to Roosevelt: [stories.] 75 c. Commercial Pr. Ho.

RACES OF MEN.
See Ethnology.

Rachel Lorain. Dudeney, *Mrs.* H: E. †$1.50. Duffield.

Racial contrasts. Gehring, A. **$1.50 net. Putnam.

RACIAL DESCENT.
See Jews.

Racine, Jean Baptiste.
Andromaque; ed., with an introd., remarks and notes, by F. M. Warren. '09(Jl10) c. S. 35 c. Holt.
Britannicus; ed., with introd., remarks and notes, by F. M. Warren. '09(Jl10) c. S. 35 c. Holt.
Phèdre; ed., with introd. and notes, by Irving Babbitt. '10(F19) c. por. S. (Modern language ser.) 30 c. Heath.

Rackermann, C: S.
See Massachusetts. Draft of an act.

Rackham, Bernard.
Book of porcelain. '10(D31) col. il. sq. 8°, $4 net. Macmillan.

Rackham, Rev. R. B.
Nave of Westminster; [from The proceedings of the British Academy, v. 4.] '09 (D4) il. fold. map, O. pap., $2. Oxford Univ.

Racowitza, Princess Helene von Dönniges.
An autobiography; auth. tr. from the German by Cecil Mar. '10(Jl16) por. 8°, $3.50 net. Macmillan.

RACQUETS.
See Tennis.

Racster, Olga.
Chats on violoncellos. '08(Mr7) il. D. (Music lovers' lib.) *$1.25 net. Lippincott.

Radasch, H: Erdmann.
Compend of histology, 2d ed., rev. and enl. '09(N) c. 15+350 p. il. 12°, (Blakiston's quiz-compends.) $1. Blakiston.

Radau, Hugo.
Bel, the Christ of ancient times. '08(Ag1) bds., *75 c. net. Open Court.
—, ed. and tr. Letters to Cassite kings from the Temple archives of Nippur. '08, [1909.] (Ja) 15+174 p. il. facsims., f°, (Babylonian expedition of the Univ. of Penn.) $6. Univ. of Penn.

Radcliffe, W: Hiram, and Cushing, Harry Cooke, jr.
Telephone construction, installation, wiring, operation and maintenance. '08 (Mr28) c. 12°, $1. Henley.

RADCLIFFE COLLEGE, Cambridge, Mass.
Book of Radcliffe College songs. $1. Boston Music.
Radcliffe College monographs. 8°. Ginn.
—Adams. Neglected period of anti-slavery in America. **$1.50 net.
—Studies in English and comparative literature by former and present students of Radcliffe College, 1894-1909. $1.50.

Rademacher, Johann Gottfried Wilhelm.
Universal and organ remedies (Erfahrungsheillehre): abr. and tr. by A. A. Ramseyer. '09(My) c. 11+104 p. 12°, $1. Boericke & T.

Rader, Perry Scott.
Civil government of the United States and the state of Oklahoma. '08(Ag) c. 377+22+6 p. il. maps, 12°, 75 c. H. Stephens.
—, rep. *See* Missouri. *Sup. ct.* Repts.

Radford, Ernest.
Dante Gabriel Rossetti. '09(D) various paging, il. Q. (Great artist ser.) *$2 net. Doran.

Radford, W: A.
Artistic bungalows; unique collections of 208 designs. '09(Ap10) c. il. 4°, $1. Radford Architectural.
Artistic homes; 250 designs. '09(N) c. '08. 261 p. il. plans, 4°. Radford Architectural.
Cement houses and how to build them. '09 (Mr27) c. il. plans, 4°, 50 c. Radford Architectural.
Cyclopedia of construction; carpentry, building and architecture; based on the pract. experience of a large staff of experts in actual construction work. 12 v. '09(D11) c. il. plans, 8°, ea., $2. Radford Architectural.
Modern homes; 200 house plans. '09(Jl) c. 215 p. il. plans, 8°, $1. Radford Architectural.
—, comp. Garages and how to build them. '10(Ap9) il. 4°, $1. Radford Architectural.
Portfolio of plans; standard collection of new and orig. designs for houses, bungalows, store and flat buildings, apartment houses, banks, churches, schoolhouses, barns, outbuildings, etc., together with estimates of cost. '09(D) 316 p. il. plans, 4°, $2. Radford Architectural.
—, ed. Cement and how to use it. '10(Ap9) c. il. tabs., 8°, $1. Radford Architectural.
Combined house and barn plan book; being a complete collection of practical, economical and common sense plans of houses, barns, outbuildings, stock sheds, etc. '09(Mr) c. '08. 287 p. il. plans, 4°, $1. Radford Architectural.
Pract. barn plans. '10(Ja15) c. il. plans, 4°, $1. Radford Architectural.
—, Johnson, Alfr. Sidney, and Bernard L., eds. Framing; practical manual of approved up-to-date methods of house framing and construction. '09(N6) c. il. 8°, $1. Radford Architectural.

RADIATION.
Coblentz, W: W. Selective radiation from various solids. Gov. Pr. Off.
Steinmetz, C: P. Radiation, light and illumination. *$3 net. McGraw-H.
See also Metals and metallurgy;—Sun.

Radical cure for the swarming of bees. Jones, H: 25 c. H: Jones.

RADIO-ACTIVITY.
Ashman, G: C. Studies in radio-activity. (Add. author for price.) G: C. Ashman.
Joly, J: Radioactivity and geology. *$3 net. Van Nostrand.
McClung, R. K. Conductivity of electricity through gases and radio-activity. *$1.50 net. Blakiston.
Makower, W. Radio-active substances, their properties and their behavior. *$1.75 special net. Appleton.
Raffety, C: W. Introd. to the science of radio-activity. *$1.25 net. Longmans.
Schlundt, H., *and* Moore, R: B. Radio-activity of the thermal waters of Yellowstone National Park. (Add. Superintendent for price.) U. S., Supt. of Docs.

Radio communication; rept. '10(Jl) 9 p. 8°, pap., 5 c. Gov. Pr. Off.

RADIO-TELEGRAPHY.
See Wireless telegraphy.

RADIOGRAPHY.
See Radiotherapy.

RADIOTHERAPY.
Judd, A. Practical points in the use of X-ray and high frequency currents. $1.50. Rebman.
Kellogg, J: H. Light therapeutics. $2.50. Good Health.
Morris, *Sir* M. Light and X-ray treatment of skin diseases. $1.50 net. Funk.
Morton, E: R. Essentials of medical electricity and radiography. $1.75. Chic. Med. Bk.
Rogers, C. E. Textbook on the therapeutic action of light. $3.50. C. E. Rogers.
Snow, W: B. Therapeutics of radiant light and heat and convective heat. $2. Sci. Authors.

RADIUM.
Gager, C: S. Effects of the rays of radium on plants. pap., $2. N. Y. Botanical.
Robarts, H. Practical radium: uses of radium in the treatment of disease. $1. H. Robarts.
Soddy, F: Interpretation of radium. *$1.75 net. Putnam.
Wickham, L., *and* Degrais, —. Radium therapy. $5 net. Funk.

Rae, J:
Pies and the pirates; shadow show; with scissors supplement. '10(N5) c. il. O. bds., 75 c. net. Duffield.
Why; reflections for children; verses and pictures. '10(O15) c. O. $1.25. Dodd.

Raeburn, D:
Hoodman Grey, Christian. '09(Ap24) front. D. $1.50. Cassell.

Raeburn, Sir H:
Masterpieces of Raeburn: sixty reproductions of photographs from the orig. paintings by T. and R. Annan & Sons. '08 (Ag8) T. (Painters' ser.) pap., *25 c. net; leath., *75 c. net, boxed. Stokes.

RAEBURN, *Sir* Henry.
Caw, J. L. Raeburn. 65 c. net; $1.50 net. Scribner.

Rafael in Italy. McDonald, *Mrs.* E. A. B. 60 c. Little, B. & Co.

Raff, L. Edson.
Landsman. '09(O) c. '08. 104 p. 16°, 50 c. Rudder.

Raffety, C: W.
Introd. to the science of radio-activity. '09 (Mr13) D. *$1.25 net. Longmans.

Rafter, Augustine L.
See Metcalf, Rob. C.

Raftery, J: H:, comp.
Historical and descriptive sketch of Yellowstone National Park; letter from Lieut.-Gen. S. B. M. Young to the President of the United States, with sketch of the Yellowstone National Park. '09 (My) 23 p. 8°, pap. (Add. Superintendent for price.) U. S., Supt. of Docs.

Rag weed rhymes. Minton, O. M. $1. Aberdeen.

Ragan, Rob. A.
Escape from East Tennessee to the federal lines; the history given as nearly as possible, by Captain R. A. Ragan, of his individual experiences during the War of the Rebellion. '10(O8) c. il. pors. 12°, $1. Dony.

Ragg, Rev. Lonsdale.
Book of Books; story of the Bible. '10 (D3) D. $1.40 net. Longmans.
Church of the Apostles; being an outline of the history of the Apostolic age. '09 (S18) 12°, *$1.40 net. Macmillan.

Ragna. Costantini, *Mme.* A. $1.50. Sturgis & W.

Raible, Marie.
Deutsch-Amerika; gedichte. '10(Ag13) c. il. por. 12°, $1. M. Raible.

Raile, Arthur Lyon.
Wild rose: volume of poems. '09(N13) D. $1.50. Publishers' Pr.

Railroad repts., v. 48.; (T: J. Michie.) '08 (My); v. 49-50 (D); v. 51. '08, [1909.] (Ja); v. 52 (Ap); v. 53 (Jl); v. 54 (N) ea., $5; v. 55. '10(F); v. 56 (My); v. 57 (Jl); v. 58 (O) c. O. shp., ea., $4.50. Michie.

Railroad ser. *See* Chapman, Allen.

RAILROADS.
Acworth, W: M. Relation of railroads to the state. gratis. Allen, L. & S.
Allen, W: F: Railway operating associations. (Priv. pr.) W: F: Allen.
American Institute of Architects. Relation of railways to city development. Glenn Brown.
American Railway Engineering and Maintenance of Way Association. Manual of recommended practice for railway engineering. $3.50. Am. Railway.
Ardrey, R. L. **Railway capitalization: review of the corporate history of ten leading western railroads. $10. R. L. Ardrey.**
Baker, G: H: Brakeman's preparatory instruction. 3 v. $20.—Fireman's preparatory instruction. 3 v. $20. Railway Educ.
Beahan, W. Field practice of railway location. $3. Engineering News.
Bell, C: E., *comp.* Everyday freight rules and tariff manual applicable to interstate traffic. $1. C: E. Bell.
Bender, C. W. Electric train lighting hdbk. for railway electrical engineers. (Not for sale.) Nat. Elec. Lamp.
Bonum Meritum, *pseud.* War of words between President Roosevelt and J. Pierpont Morgan concerning railroad, tariff and trust questions. $1; 25 c. Donohue.
Byers, M. L. Economics of railway operation. *$5 net. Engineering News.
Car interchange manual, 1908: [information for master car builders and car inspectors.] 25 c. J. D. McAlpine.
Carter, C: F: **When railroads were new. **$2 net. Holt.**
Case, G: A. Giant American causeway: outline of plan for industrial development.—[Railroads.] 15 c. G: A. Case.

RAILROADS.—*Continued.*

Chicago. *City Council. Committee on Local Transportation.* Electrification of railway terminals as a cure for the locomotive smoke evil in Chicago. (Add. pubs. for price.) Donnelley.

Clark, J: M. Standards of reasonableness in local freight discriminations. $1.25 net. Longmans.

Cleveland, F: A., *and* Powell, F. W. Railroad promotion and capitalization in the United States. **$2 net. Longmans.

Clews, H: No government guarantee of bank deposits and no ownership of railroads by the government. (Add. author for price.) H: Clews.

Collingwood, G: E., *ed.* Standard train rule examination. $1.50; $2. Train Despatcher's.

Colvin, F. H. Pocket-railroad dict. and vade mecum. $1. Henley.

Cram, G: F. Standard American railway system atlas of the world. $12.50. G: F. Cram.

Crandall, C: L., *and* Barnes, F. A. Field book for railroad surveying. $2. Wiley.

Cuénot, G. Deformations of railroad tracks. $2. Railroad Gazette.

Daggett, S. Railroad reorganization. **$2 net. Houghton M.

Depreciated currency and diminished railway rates. (Add. pubs. for price.) Railway World.

Eastman, H. B: Experiments with railway cross-ties. 15 c. U. S., Supt. of Docs.

Eaton, J. S. Education for efficiency in railroad service. Gov. Pr. Off.

Education and railroad men: [list of books applying to railroad work.] 25 c. Y. M. C. A.

Elliott, B. K. *and* W: F. Law of railroads. 5 v. $27. Bobbs-M.

Encyclopedia of railroading. 6 v. $36.50. Nat. Textbk.

Fagan, J. O. Confessions of a railroad signalman.—Labor and the railroads. ea., *$1 net. Houghton M.

Fish, S. Address: Under what conditions will the railroads of the United States best serve the public. gratis. S. Fish.

Fowle, F. F. Protection of railroads from overhead transmission line crossing. *$1.50 net. Van Nostrand.

Fuller, A. W: Manual for 1908 of questions and answers for exams. on the standard code of railroad rules, etc. A. W. Fuller.

Going, C: B. Methods of the Santa Fe; economy in the manufacture of transportation. $1. Engineering Mag.

Gordon, W. J. Our home railways [English.] 2 v. $4.50 net; hf. mor., $7.50 net. Warne.

Hadley, E: S. Railway working and appliances. *50 c. net. Longmans.

Halden, G: M. Setting out of tube railways. *$4 net. Spon.

Haney, L. H: Congressional hist. of railways in the United States to 1850.—1850-1887. ea., 50 c. Univ. of Wis.

RAILROADS.—*Continued.*

Hanks, C: S. Benefit of the Hepburn law to the banker, broker, shipper and the public. 50 c. Authors' Pub.

Harden, E: W. Cost of living to railways. E: W. Harden.

Hines, E: W. Abstracts of cases decided by the federal cts. rel. to the 14th amendment upon the power of states to regulate rates of railroads. $5. Morton.

Hoile, J. T., *and* Brown, W: C. Correspondence on railway freight rates. Manufacturers' Assoc.

Howden, J. R. The boys' book of railways. $2. Stokes.

Huebner, G. G. Five years of railroad regulation by the states. 25 c. Am. Acad. Pol. Sci.

Iowa. Statistical abstract of Iowa railroads. gratis. A. H. Davison.

Ivatts, E. B. Railway management at stations. $2.50. Van Nostrand.

Jacobs, H: W: Betterment briefs: papers on organized industrial efficiency: [railroads.] $3.50. Wiley.

Jaros, S: How the public can own and control new railroads. (Add. pubs. for price.) Jaros Co.

Johnson, E. R: American railway transportation. **$1.50 net. Appleton.

Johnson, E. R: Trend of governmental regulation of railroads. 15 c. Am. Acad. Pol. Sci.

Kempthorne, W. O. Principles of railway stores management.—Railway stores price-book. ea., *$4 net. Spon.

Ketchum, E. S. Beginning and development of American railroads.—Construction of classifications and tariffs. ea., 25 c. La Salle Extension.

Kirkman, M. M. Science of railways. 10 v. per set, $36. C. Phillips.

Knox, P. C. People (The), the railroads and the national authority. pap., 10 c. Civic Forum.

Larimer, J. M. Bucyrus, the railroad wrecker. 25 c. Muskogee.

Lee, I. L. Railroad valuation. (Not for sale.) Bankers Pub.

McArdle, F. Everything behind the engine for conductors and brakemen. $2. F. McArdle.

McCain, C: C. Diminishing purchasing power of railway earnings. 50 c. C: C. McCain.

McCune, F. H: Spokane rate case. 25 c. F. H: McCune.

McPherson, L. G. Railroad freight rates. **$2.25 net. Holt.

McVey, F. L. Railroad transportation. $5. Cree.

Master Car Builders' Association. Car builders' dict. $6. Railway Age Gazette.

Meyer, H. H: B., *comp.* Select list of references on the valuation and capitalization of railroads. 10 c. U. S., Supt. of Docs.

Mitton, G. E. Book of the railway. *$2 net. Macmillan.

Moody, J: Analysis of railroad investments. *$12 net. Analyses.

RAILROADS.—*Continued.*

Moody's manual of railroads and corporation securities, 1908. $10; $12. Moody Corporation.

Morris, R. Railroad administration. $2 net. Appleton.

Mundy, F. W., *comp. and ed.* Earning power of railroads, 1908. $2. Metropolitan Adv.

Mundy, F. W., *comp. and ed.* Earning power of railroads, 1909. $2; 1910. $2.50. J. H. Oliphant.

National Association of Railway Commissioners. Proceedings of the sub-committee on car service and demurrage.—Rept of Committee on delays attendant upon enforcing orders of railroad commissions. '09(D) 2 p. 8°.—Rept. of the Committee on grade crossings and trespassing on railroads.—Rept. of the Committee on railroad taxes.—Rept. of the Committee on safety appliances. (Add. Superintendent for price.) Gov. Pr. Off.

Neall, F. L., *and* Pierson, W. W. Before the Interstate Commerce Commission; cement informal presentation in the matter of discrimination against the city and port of Philadalphia, in railroad freight rates for transportation of Portland cement. gratis. F. L. Neall.

New York [State.] Public Service Commissions law, 1907. $1. Banks & Co.

Newcomb, H. T. Diminished dollar and railway rates. 35 c. North American.

Newcomb, H. T. Some recent phases of federal railway control. (Priv. pr.) H. T. Newcomb.

Nichols, W: Rule four (of the Standard train rules) change of time table. $1. Los Angeles Pr.

Orrock, J: W. Railroad structures and estimates. **$3 net. Wiley.

Paxson, F: L. Pacific railroads and the disappearance of the frontier in America. U. S., Supt. of Docs.

Phillips, J: B. Freight rates and manufactures in Colorado. 75 c.; 50 c. J: B. Phillips.

Prescott, D. W. C. Early day railroading from Chicago. $1.50. D: B. Clarkson.

Prior, F: J: Construction and maintenance of railway roadbeds and tracks. $2. Drake.

Prior, F: J:, *comp.* Operation of trains and station work. $1.50. Drake.

Purchasing agents' buying list and railway supply index. v. 1, no. 1. $6. Buyers' Index.

Raymond, W: G. Elements of railroad engineering. $3.50.—Railroad field geometry. $2. Wiley.

Raymond, W: G. Modern turnout formulas: [railroad tracks.] *50 c. net. A. M. Allen.

Reeder, R. P. Rate regulation as affected by the distribution of governmental powers in the constitutions. $1. T. & J. W. Johnson.

Roberts, S. S. Track formulæ and tables. $3. Wiley.

RAILROADS.—*Continued.*

Ross, G: W: Railways and international fellowship [Canada and U. S.] gratis. Am. Railway.

Shorter, R. G. How to successfully keep railroad accounts. $2.50. R. G. Shorter.

Silsbee, W. E., *and* Blood, P. E. Railway special work. $2. McGraw-H.

Southern Schools of Railway Science. Pract. studies adopted by the Southern Schools of Railway Science as a standard text book. 6 v. $24. Southern Sch. R'way Sci.

Spokane, Wash. City of Spokane et al. v. Northern Pacific railway et al.: brief for complainants. (Add. pub. for price.) B. Adams.

Stewart, B. Hdbk. for railway surveying. *$1 net. Spon.

Stilwell, A. E: Confidence, or national suicide? $1. Bankers' Pub.

Swingle, C. F., [*and others,*] *eds.* Modern American railway practice. In 10 v. $60. Drake.

Taft, W: H. Address of President Taft at the joint meeting of brotherhoods in train service. Gov. Pr. Off.

Taylor, C. W. Railroad a public servant. 50 c. C. W. Taylor.

Thompson, S. Cost, capitalization and estimated value of American railways. 50 c. S. Thompson.

Thompson, S., *comp. and ed.* Railway library, 1909. 75 c. S. Thompson.

Tilson, J. P. R. S. D. guide, railroad short distances. 25 c. Harrison Pr.

Tratman, E. E. R. Railway track and trackwork. *$3.50 net. Engineering News.

United States. *General Land Office.* Regulations concerning railroad right of way over the public lands, and forfeiture acts. '09(Ag) 13 p. 8°, pap. (Add. Superintendent for price.) U. S., Supt. of Docs.

United States. *Interstate Commerce Commission.* Freight rates on commodities of life; letter from the Secretary of the Interstate Commerce Commission to the Hon. H. C. Lodge, transmitting tables showing comparisons of rates from and incl. 1900 between various points on necessary commodities of life, etc. [1910.] (Jl) 18 p. 8°.

United States. *Interstate Commerce Commission.* Hours of service of railway employees; state statutes and related court decisions, Feb., 1909. '09(My) 39 p. 8°, pap. (Add. Superintendent for price.)

United States. *Interstate Commerce Commission.* Safety appliance, railway accidents, Block signal and train control board, and hours of service reports. '10 (Je) 25 p. 8°.

United States. New railroad law $1. Baker, V. & Co.

Van Wagenen, A. Government ownership of railways considered as the next great step in American progress. $1.25. Putnam.

Vrooman, C. S. American railway problems in the light of European experience. $2. Oxford Univ.

RAILROADS.—*Continued.*
Walsh, J: W. Hepburn rate law. 25 c. La Salle Extension.
Washington, W: D'H. Answer to the charge of railroad robbery. (Priv. pr.) W: D. Washington.
Washington [State.] General laws and constitutional provisions of the state of Washington rel. to railroads. 75 c. C. W. Gorham.
Washington (State) Railroad Commission. Findings of facts relative to the value of railroads in the state of Washington. gratis. Wash. R. R. Com.
Webb, W. L. Railroad construction, theory and practice. $5. Wiley.
White, E: J. Law of personal injuries on railroads. In 2 v. $13. **F. H. Thomas.**
Whitehead, J. B. Electric operation of steam railways. (Add. author for price.) **J. B. Whitehead.**
Williams, A. Wonders of the modern railway. 75 c. Lippincott.
Williams, S. C: Economics of railway transport. *$1.25 net. Macmillan.
Wilson, W. L. Elements of railroad track and construction. $2. Wiley.
Y. M. C. A. Educ. Dept. Education and railroad men; hints, suggestions and outlines for conducting educational privileges in the R. R. Y. M. C. Assoc. 25 c. Y. M. C. A.
See also Air-brake;—Atlases;—Bridges;—Carriers;—Concrete; — Cotton; — Cross-ties; — Culverts; — Curves; — Earthwork; — Electric railroads;—Electric switchboards;—Express;—Fire;—Freight; — Locomotives; — Negroes; — Pensions;—Post-office; — Signals and signalling; — Steam engines;—Street railroads;—Transportation;—Tunnels and tunnelling;—Useful arts;—Wealth;—*also* Erie Railroad;—New York City;—Union Pacific Railway;—*also* names of states.

Railroads and railroaders. '09(S18) 8°, pap., 25 c. Y. M. C. A.
Railway accounting. Goodyear, S: H. 30 c. Goodyear-M.
RAILWAY MAIL SERVICE.
See Post-office.
Railway signaling; written by a staff of expert signal engineers. '08(Ag15) c., il. 8°. (Add. pub. for price.) Elec. Journ.
Railway that glue built. Williams, C. A. $1. Stokes.
Railway through the Word. *See* Bible. [Selections.]
Railway track and trackwork. Tratman, E. E. R. *$3.50 net. Engineering News.
RAILWAYS.
See Railroads.
Raiment of the soul. Howard, H: *$1.25 net. Eaton & M.
Raimond, C. E., pseud.
See Robins, Eliz.
Rainbow and the pot of gold. Burdette, *Mrs.* C. B. $1. Clara Vista.
Rainbow book. Spielmann, *Mrs.* M. H. *$1.50 net. Warne.
Rainbow kimona. Crane, E. M. 25 c. Dick.
Rainbow ser. 8 v. '10(D) il. 42°, ea., 15 c. Doran.
Raindrop (The); collection of entertaining stories for young people. '10(S3) c. il. 4°, $2.50. Volta.

"Raine, Allen," pseud.
See Puddicombe, *Mrs.* Beynon.
Raine, W: MacLeod.
Bucky O'Connor; tale of the unfenced border. '10(Ag20) c. il. D. $1.50. G: W. Dillingham.
Ridgway of Montana. '09(My1) c. il. D. †$1.50. G: W. Dillingham.
Wyoming: a story of the outdoor West. '08(Ag29) c. D. †$1.50. G: W. Dillingham.
Rainsford, W: Stephen, D.D.
Land of the lion. '09(N13) c. il. fold. map, O. **$3.80 net. **Doubleday, P.**
RAINY, Adam Roland.
Simpson, P. C. Life of Principal Rainy. *$6 net. Doran.
Rainy, Harry, M.D.
See Hutchison, Rob., *M.D.*
Rainy day pastimes for children. Palm, *Baroness* Louise von. $1. Estes.
Rainy day scrap book. Schuman, E. L. $1.25. Reilly & B.
Rait, Rob. S., ed.
English episcopal palaces; Province of Canterbury. '10(N19) il. 8°, $2.50 net. Pott.
Five Stuart princesses: Margaret of Scotland, Elizabeth of Bohemia, Mary of Orange, Henrietta of Orleans, Sophia of Hanover. New ed. '08(Mr7) 8°, *$3.50 net. Dutton.
Rajan Iyengar, Tirumangalum Chrishna.
Hindu-Aryan theory on evolution and involution; or, the science of raja-yoga. '08 (D) c. 20+77 p. por. 8°, **$1.50 net. Funk.
Raleigh, Cecil, [pseud. for J. F. Rowlands.]
Sins of society; novel. '10(Ja29) D. $1.50. G: W. Dillingham.
Raleigh, Sir Wa.
Selections from the writings of Sir Walter Ralegh; ed. by Fk. W. C. Hersey. '09, [1910.] (My) c. 57 p. 12°, 35 c. net. Sherman, F.
RALEIGH, *Sir* Walter.
McMillan, H. Sir Walter Raleigh's lost colony. 50 c. H. McMillan.
Ober, F: A. Sir Walter Raleigh. **$1 net. Harper.
Sélincourt, H. de. Great Ralegh [*sic.*] *$3.50 net. Putnam.
Raleigh, Wa. Alex.
English voyages of the sixteenth century. 3d ed. '10(Je11) front. D. $1.25 net. Macmillan.
Samuel Johnson; the Leslie Stephen lecture, delivered in the Senate house, Cambridge, 22 February, 1907. '09(Mr6) 8°, *35 c. net. Oxford Univ.
Six essays on Johnson. '10(N19) O. $1.75. Oxford Univ.
Raleigh. Devereux, W: $1. Lippincott.
Ralph Connor, pseud.
See Gordon, C: W:
Ralph Fabian's mistakes. Dickson, S. O. $1. B'way Pub.
Ralph on the engine. Chapman, A. 60 c. Grosset.
Ralph Osborn—midshipman at Annapolis. Beach, E: L. †$1.50. Wilde.

Ralph Ranscomb, banker. Nevin, T. W. $1.50. Neale.

Ralston, Jackson Harvey.
International arbitral law and procedure; being a resumé of the procedure and practice of international commissions, and incl. the views of arbitrators upon questions arising under the law of nations. '10(D) 19+352 p. O. $2. Ginn.
Some supposed just causes of war. '10(D) O. (International School of Peace pamphlets.) pap., per 100, $3. Int. Sch. of Peace.

Ralston, Mrs. Virginia.
When mother lets us sew. '10(F12) c. il. O. (When mother lets us ser.) **75 c. net. Moffat.

Ralston Health Club. Personal book of the Ralston Health Club, introducing its "personal system." [1910.] (N) 158 p. 8°, $1.25. Ralston Univ.

Ralston Health Club. Universal system of the Ralston Health Club. '09(N) c. 342 p. il. 8°, $2.50. Ralston Health.

Ramacharaka, Yogi, pseud.
See Atkinson, W: Walker.

Ramakrishna.
Gospel of Râmâkrishna; [ed. by Swâmi Abhedânanda.] Authorized ed. '08 (Mr7) c. il. S. $1.50; leath., $3. Vedanta.

Ramaley, Fs.
Wild flowers and trees of Colorado. '09 (Je12) c. figs. O. $1.25; pap., $1. A. A. Greenman.

Ramayana (The), and The Mahabharata; tr. by Romesh Dutt. '10(Ap23) 16°, (Everyman's lib.) 35 c. net; leath., 70 c. net. Dutton.

RAMAYANA.
See Sanskrit literature.

Rambeau, Adolphe.
See Passy, Jean.

Rambler Club ser. *See* Sheppard, W: H: Crispin.

Rambles in Bible lands. Neil, G. L., *ed.* *$1.75 special net. Appleton.

Rambles in Spain. FitzGerald, J: D., *2d.* $3 net. Crowell.

Rambles with an American. Tearle, C. $2.50 net. Duffield.

Rambling recollections. Wolff, *Sir* H: D. 2 v. *$7.50 net. Macmillan.

Rambuteau, Comte Claude Philibert Barthelot de.
Memoirs; ed. by his grandson; tr. from the French by J. C. Brogan; with an introd. and notes by M. Georges Sequin. '08 (N21) pors. O. *$3.50 net. Putnam.

Ramparts of empire. Fox, F. $2.25 net. Macmillan.

Ramrodders. Day, H. F. $1.50. Harper.

RAMS (*machinery*).
See Hydraulic engineering.

Ramsay, A.
Revelation and the Johannine epistles. '10 (D17) 16°, (Westminster New Testament.) 75 c. net. Revell.

Ramsay, Andrew Maitland, M.D.
Diathesis and ocular diseases. '10(Ap) 192 p. il. 12°, $2 net. Wood.

Ramsay, E: Bannerman Burnett, D.D.
Reminiscences of Scottish life and character. '08(D12) il. D. *$2.75 net. McClurg.

Ramsay, Fox Maule, Baron Panmure, Earl of Dalhousie.
Panmure papers: being a selection from the correspondence of Foxmaule, second Baron Panmure, eleventh Earl of Dalhousie; ed. by Sir A: Douglas and Sir G: Dalhousie Ramsay. 2 v. '08(D) 8°, $6. Clode.

Ramsay, Franklin Pierce.
The question: a novel. '09(Jl17) c. D. *$1 net. Neale.

Ramsay, Sir Ja. H:
Dawn of the constitution; or, the reigns of Henry III. and Edward I., (A.D. 1216-1307.) '08(Ap4) il. maps, 8°, *$2.75 net. Macmillan.

Ramsay, Ja. P.
Massachusetts probation system: the law and its results. '08(My.) c. 54 p. O. pap. (Add. author for price.) J. P. Ramsay.

Ramsay, Sir J:
See Virginia Colony. *General ct.*

Ramsay, Rina.
The straw. '09(F20) c. D. †$1.50. Macmillan.

Ramsay, Rob. Lee.
Principles of modern punctuation. '08, [1909.] (F) 15 p. 8°, gratis. R. L. Ramsay.

Ramsay, Sir W:
Essays, biographical and chemical. '09 (Ap17) 8°, *$2.50 net. Dutton.

Ramsay, Sir W: Mitchell, D.D.
Cities of St. Paul: their influence on his life and thought: the cities of eastern Asia Minor. '08(F8) il. O. (Dale memorial lectures in Mansfield College, Oxford.) *$3 net. Armstrong.
Luke the physician, and other studies in the history of religion. '09(Ja16) il. O. *$3 net. Armstrong.
Pictures of the Apostolic Church; its life and thought. '10(D17) c. D. $1.50 net. S. S. Times.
Revolution in Constantinople and Turkey; diary, by Sir W. M. Ramsay; with episodes and photographs by Lady Ramsay. '09, [1910.] (S) 15+323 p. il. 8°, $3.75 net. Doran.

—, **and Bell, Gertrude Lowthian.**
The thousand and one churches. '10(Je4) il. 8°, $5 net. Doran.

Ramsdell, C: W:
Reconstruction in Texas. '10(Jl9) c. O. (Columbia Univ. studies in hist., economics and public law.) $4 net; (Ap) pap., $2.50 net. Longmans.

Ramsey, Murray Elliott, M.D.
Practical life insurance examinations. '08 (Ap18) c. D. **$1.25 net. Lippincott.

Ramsey, W: V., ed.
Story of the Church Street Terminal buildings of the Hudson & Manhattan Railroad Company (Hudson River terminal system) Church, Cortlandt, Dey and Fulton Streets, New York City, [1910.] (N) c. 32 p. il. map, 4°. Wynkoop, H.

Rand, B:, comp.
Classical moralists; selections illustrating ethics from Socrates to Martineau. '09 (D11) c. O. **$3 net. Houghton M.
Modern classical philosophy: selections illustrating philosophy from Bruno to Spencer. '08(Ap18) c. 8°, **$2.50 net. Houghton M.

Rand, G: Hart.
Sherman Hale, the Harvard half-back. '10 (O29) c. col. il. O. $1.50. Fenno.

Rand, Ja. L.
Systematic supplementary Bible studies. In 3 pts. pt. 1, Primary department; pt. 2, Junior department; pt. 3, Intermediate and senior department. '08(Jl11) c. D. pap., pt. 1, **5 c. net; pts. 2 and 3, ea., **10 c. net. Am. Bapt.

Rand, McNally & Co.'s enlarged business atlas and shipper's guide; containing large-scale maps of all states and territories, in the U. S., Canada, Mexico, Central America, the West Indies, Cuba, Porto Rico, Hawaii, the Philippines, Japan and China. 39th ed. '08(D19) c. f°, $10.50; hf. mor., $12.50. Rand, McN. & Co.

Rand, McNally & Co.'s guide to California via the Santa Fe. '08(D19) c. il. map, 12°. (Add. pubs. for price.) Rand, McN. & Co.

Rand-McNally guide to the great Northwest; cont. information regarding the states of Montana, Idaho, Wash., Ore., Minn., N. D., Alaska, also western Canada and British Columbia, with description of the route along the Great Northern Railway; gives early hist., topography, climate, resources, and valuable statistics on the states comprising the great Northwest; by S. H. Soulé. Alaska-Yukon exposition ed. '09, [1910.] (Ja) c. 16+365 p. il. fold. map, 12°, 50 c. Rand, McN. & Co.

Rand, McNally & Co.'s new ideal state and county survey and atlas: cont. a large county and railway map of Indiana printed in colors, also a new, complete and ready reference index to the state of Indiana. '08, [1909.] (Mr) c. 104 p. il. maps, f°. (Subs. only.) Rand, McN. & Co.

Rand-McNally photo-auto guides. 28 v. [1910.] (D) Rand, McN. & Co.
Contents: Chicago to New York and New York to Chicago, $5; New York to Chicago and Chicago to New York, $5; Chicago to New York, $3; New York to Chicago, $3; Chicago to South Bend and South Bend to Chicago, $1.50; Chicago to Toledo and Toledo to Chicago, $2; Chicago to Detroit and Detroit to Chicago, $2.50; Chicago to Cleveland and Cleveland to Chicago, $2.50; Chicago to Buffalo and Buffalo to Chicago, $3; Chicago to Albany and Albany to Chicago, $4; South Bend to Toledo and Toledo to South Bend, $1.50; Toledo to Cleveland and Cleveland to Toledo, $1.50; Toledo to New York and New York to Toledo, $4 Detroit to New York and New York to Detroit, $4; Detroit to Cleveland and Cleveland to Detroit, $1.50; Detroit to Buffalo and Buffalo to Detroit, $2; Cleveland to New York and New York to Cleveland, $4; Cleveland to Buffalo and Buffalo to Cleveland, $1.50; Buffalo to New York and New York to Buffalo, $2; Buffalo to Albany and Albany to Buffalo, $2; Buffalo to Saratoga and Saratoga to Buffalo, $2.50; Syracuse to New York and New York to Syracuse, $2.50; New York to Albany and Saratoga and Saratoga to Albany and New York, $2; Chicago to Milwaukee and return (Kilbourn route), $1.25; Chicago to Milwaukee—one way (shore route), $1.25; Chicago to Lake Geneva, Delevan and Beloit, returning via Antioch, $1.25; Chicago to Rockford, Beloit, Delavan and Lake Geneva, $1.

Rand, McNally & Co.'s political atlas; a compendium of facts and figures, platforms, biographies, and portraits; the men and the issues of the presidential campaign of 1908. '08(D19) c. il. f°. (Add. pubs. for price.) Rand, McN. & Co.

Randall, Dwight T.
Purchase of coal under government and commercial specifications on the basis of its heating value. '08(My23) O. (Dept. of the Interior, U. S. Geolog. Survey bull.) pap., 15 c. U. S., Supt. of Docs.
Tests of coal and briquets as fuel for house-heating boilers. '09(Mr6) il. 8°, (U. S. Dept. of the Interior, Geolog. Survey, bull.) (Add. Superintendent for price.) U. S., Supt. of Docs.

—, and Weeks, H. W.
Smokeless combustion of coal in boiler plants, with a chapter on central heating plants. '09(N) 188 p. il. tabs., O. (U. S., Dept. of the Interior, U. S. Geolog. Survey bull.) pap., 20 c.

Randall, E: Caleb.
Future of man, metapsychic. '09(Ja23) c. 12°, *$1.50 net. Ulbrich.

Randall, Emilius Oviatt.
Masterpieces of the Ohio mound builders; the hill top fortifications, incl. Fort Ancient. '08(O) 126 p. il. 12°, $1. Ohio Archæolog.

—, rep. *See* Ohio. *Sup. ct.* Repts.

Randall, F. J.
Love and the ironmonger. '08(Ap25) D. †$1.50. Lane.

Randall, Ja. A.
Paper on the life and character of Mr. Thomas Paine; read before the Society of the Psychic Band of Research, Detroit, Mich. '09(Je19) D. pap., 10 c. J. A. Randall.

Randall, Ja. Ryder.
Maryland, my Maryland, and other poems. '08(Ap18) c. por. D. *$1.50 net. Murphy.
Poems; ed., with introd. and notes, by Matthew Page Andrews. '10(Ap23) c. por. facsim., il. D. $1 net. Tandy-T.

Randall, J: Herman.
New philosophy of life series. 7 v. The real God; The subconscious mind; The power of suggestion: Mind and body; Man's undeveloped powers; The supreme victory; The rebirth of religion. '09 (O2) c. D. bds., ea., 60 c.; limp leath., ea., $1.25. Caldwell.
The real God: the universal mind, and the divinity of man. '09(Jl3) c. D. (New philosophy of life ser.) bds., 60 c.; leath., $1.25. Caldwell.

—, and Smith, J. Gardner, M.D., eds.
Unity of religions; popular discussion of ancient and modern beliefs. '10(O8) c. O. $2 net. Crowell.

Randall, W. W., and Bartels, J: Murray, comps.
Bartels' check list of the postage stamps of Panama, 1907. '07, [1908.] (Mr.) 56 p. il. 16°, 50 c. Bartels.

Randall, Wainwright, ed.
Angler's guide; manual for campers and anglers, cont. descriptions of all popular fresh-water and salt-water fishes; tackle and baits, etc.; summary of fishing resorts of the U. S. and Canada. 5th annual ed. '09(Ag) c. 242 p. il. 12°, 60 c.; bds., 50 c. Field and Stream.

Randall, W: H:
Golden rule republic no Utopia: [socialism.] '08(My.) c. 181 p. 12°, pap., 25 c. Co-operative Pr. Co.

RANDALL FAMILY.
See **Genealogies: Chaffin, W: L.**

Randle, Edn. Henderson.
Characteristics of the southern negro. '10 (Ap2) c. D. $1 net. Neale.

Randleson, Mrs. Sara A.
Just one blue bonnet: life story of Ada Florence Kinton, [of the Salvation Army.] '09(My) $1. A. N. Ingersoll.

Randolph, Althea.
Bouquet of rhymes; [children's nature verse.] '09(N6) col. il. 16°, *$1.50 net. Silver.
Jeannie's journal. '08(N14) c. il. D. $1. Bonnell, S.

Randolph, Berkeley W:, D.D.
Precious blood of Christ; being thoughts on the doctrine of the atonement. '09 (Mr13) D. *75 c. net. Longmans.

Randolph, Corliss Fitz.
Rept. of a visit to European schools, incl. England, Wales, Scotland, Holland and Germany, Jan.-Mar., 1909. '10(My7) il. por. 4°, 75 c. C. F. Randolph.

Randolph, Edg. Fritz.
Inter-ocean hunting tales. '08(O10) c. il. D. $1. Forest.

Randolph, Edm.
Letters, etc., of Edmund Randolph; ed. by Rev. A. T. S. Goodrich. v. 1-7. '09(N) c. pors. 8°, pap. (Add. pubs. for price.) Prince Soc.

Randolph, Howard Stelle Fitz, comp.
Fortieth anniversary of Rev. Robert Stuart MacArthur, D.D., LL.D., as pastor of Calvary Baptist Church, New York City, May 15-20, 1910, 1870-1910. '10 (Jl) c. 11+114 p. pls. pors. front. 12°, 50 c. H. S. F. Randolph.

Randolph, Mary.
Love letters from the Nile. '10(D31) c. il. 12°, $1.50. Knickerbocker Press.

Randolph, Vern Curtis.
Air brake catechism and instruction book on the construction and operation of the Westinghouse and New York air brakes. 1908 ed. 08'(O10) c. il. tab., T. $1. V. C. Randolph.

RANDOLPH, Me.
Vital records of Randolph, Maine, to the year 1892. $1.25. Reporter-Journal.

Random reminiscences. Rockefeller, J: D. $1. Doubleday, P.

Random shaft. Miller, J. M. $1.50. C. M. Clark.

Random shots. Sinclair, E. M. *$1 net. Badger.

Rane, Fk. W:
Forestry from a commercial standpoint; address del. before the Mass. Horticulture Society, Feb. 23, 1907. '09(Mr) 16 p. 8°, pap. (Add. author for price.) F. W: Rane.
We must stop forest fires in Massachusetts. '09(Ag21) il. O. pap. (Add. author for price.) F. W. Rane.

Range and trail. Sabin, E. L. $1.50. Crowell.

Ranger, Wa. Eug., comp.
Nineteenth annual program for the observation of Arbor Day in the schools of Rhode Island, May 13, 1910. '10(My14) il. O. (Rhode Island education circulars.) pap., gratis. W. E. Ranger.

RANGES.
See **Arizona.**

Ranke, Leopold von.
History of the popes: their church and state; tr. by E. Fowler; with introd. by W: Clark. '08(Je27) c. 3 v., il. 8°, $5.25; hf. mor., $10.50. Lamb Pub.
Hist. of the popes during the last four centuries. In 3 v. '08(Mr21) 16°, (York lib.) ea., 80 c.; leath., $1.25. Macmillan.

Rankin, Mrs. Carroll Watson.
Adopting of Rosa Marie: (a sequel to "Dandelion cottage.") '08(S12) c. il. D. (Dandelion ser.) †$1.50. Holt.

Rankin, G: A.
An American transportation system; criticism of the past and the present and a plan for the future. '09(O16) c. D. (Questions of the day ser.) **$1.50 net. Putnam.

Rankin, I: Ogden.
Closet and altar; book of prayers for everyday in the month for private devotion and family worship. '10(N5) c. D. pap., 25 c. net, in envelope. Pilgrim Press.

Rankin, J. C.
See Symington, Johnson.

Rankin, Ja. Reginald Lea.
In Morocco with General D'Amade. '08 (N21) il. map, O. *$2.50 net. Longmans.

Rankine, W. Fs.
Nature study and brush drawing. '08 (My16) il. Q. *$1.25 net. Cassell.

Ranlett, Susan Alice.
Shepherd who did not go to Bethelehem. '09(Je5) c. 12°, $1. Badger.

Ranney, D: J.
Dave Ranney; or, thirty years on the Bowery; an autobiography; introd. by Rev. A. F. Schauffler, D.D. '10(O15) c. il. por. 12°, 75 c. Am. Tr.

RANNEY FAMILY.
Adams, C: C. Middletown Upper Houses; with a full genealogy of the Ranney family. **$10 net. Grafton Press.

Ransom, Fletcher C:
My policies in Jungleland. '10(My7) c. il. Q. bds., $1. Barse & H.

Ransom, Ja. Harvey.
Experimental general chemistry. '09(N) c. 136 p. il. 12°, 60 c. J. H. Ransom.

Ransome, Arth.
Edgar Allan Poe: critical study. '10(D17) por. 12°, $2.50 net. M. Kennerley.
Hist. of story-telling; studies in the development of narrative. '10(S10) pors. O. $3 net. Stokes.
—, **comp.** Book of friendship: essays, poems, maxims and prose passages. '10(S10) front. O. $2.50 net. Stokes.

Ransome, F: Leslie.
Geology and ore deposits of Goldfield, Nevada, by F: Leslie Ransome, assisted in the field by W. H. Emmons and G. H. Garrey. '09(N) 258 p. il. fold. maps, Q. (U. S., Dept. of the Interior U. S. Geol. Survey; Professional papers.) (Add. Superintendent for price.) U. S., Supt. of Docs.
Notes on some mining districts in Humboldt County, Nevada. '09, [1910.] 75 p. il. fold. map, 8°, (U. S., Dept. of the Interior; Geological Survey, bull.)
"Literature" (2 p.).

Rantoul, Rob. S:
Abraham Lincoln; an address delivered before the Essex Institute and the city government of Salem, at the Tabernacle Church, Feb. 12, 1909. '09(S4) por. 8°, 50 c. Essex Inst.

Ranum, Mrs. Louise Cann.
Dreams. '10(Je25) c. 12°, $1. Badger,

Rapaport, Rev. S:, and Deutsch, Emanuel.
Tales and maxims from the Talmud; with an essay on the Talmud by Emanuel Deusch. '10(O8) 12°, (Semitic ser.) $1.75 net. Dutton.

Rape of the lock. *See* Pope, Alex.

Raphael, Alice P.
The fulfillment. '10(Jl2) c. front. D. $1.50. Sturgis & W.

Raphael, J: N. Percival.
Pictures of Paris and some Parisians. '08 (S19) il. 12°, *$1.50 net. Macmillan.

RAPHAEL, Sanzio di Urbino.
Konody, P. G. Raphael. *65 c. net. Stokes.
Staley, E. Raphael. *$2 net. Doran.

Rapid methods for the chemical analysis of special steels. Johnson, C: M. $3. Wiley.

RAPID TRANSIT.
See **Transportation.**

Rappoport, Angelo S.
Leopold the Second: King of the Belgians. '10(N12) il. O. $3 net. Sturgis & W.
Mad majesties; or, raving rulers and submissive subjects. '10(D10) il. 8°, $4 net. Brentano's.
Royal lovers and their favorites. '09(Jl3) il. 8°, *$4 net. Brentano's.

Rara arithmetica. *See* Smith, D: E.

Rare days in Japan. Ladd, G: T. $2.25 net. Dodd.

Rashdall, Rev. Hastings.
Philosophy and religion; six lectures del. at Cambridge. '10(Ja29) D. (Studies in theology.) *75 c. net. Scribner.

Rasmussen, Knud.
People of the Polar North; comp. from the Danish originals and ed. by G. Herring. '08(O3) il. map, Q. *$5 net. Lippincott.

Rasmussen, Wa.
Graded dictation. '10(Mr5) c. 4°, $1. Gregg Pub.

Rasplata. Semenoff, V. I. $3.50. Dutton.

Rastall, B: McKie.
Labor history of the Cripple Creek district. '08(Je6) il. O. (Univ. of Wis. bull., Economics and political science ser.) pap., 50 c. Univ. of Wis.

Rastall, R. H.
See Lake, Philip.

RAT.
Lantz, D: E. Brown rat in the U. S. —How to destroy rats. (Add. Superintendent for price.) U. S., Supt. of Docs.
Richardson, F. E. Study of sensory control in the rat. $1.25. Psychological Review.
U. S. *Treasury Dept. Public Health and Marine Service.* Rat and its relation to the public health.

Ratcliffe, Rev. Fs. Asbury, and Smith, Rev. H. Turner.
Baptism; or, the controversy. '08, [1909.] (Mr) c. 219 p. por. 12°, 30 c. F. A. Ratcliffe.

RATE-MAKING.
See **Railroads.**

Rath, E. J.
The sixth speed. '08(M21) c. il. D. †$1.50. Moffat.

Rathbone, Mrs.
See Manning, Anne.

Rathbone, R. L. B.
Simple jewelry; pract. hdbk. dealing with certain elem. methods of design and construction. '10(Je18) il. 12°, $2 net. Van Nostrand.

Rathbun, R:
National Gallery of Art, Department of Fine Arts of the National Museum. '09, [1910.] (Je) 140 p. il. plan, 4°, (Smithsonian Institution, U. S. National Museum, bull.) U. S., Supt. of Docs.

Rathmann, Carl Gustav.
Mission of manual training; address before the graduating class of the Manual Training School of Washington University, June 23, 1909. '10(Mr12) 8°. (Add. pubs. for price.) Manual Training Sch.

RATINGS.
See **Business.**

Rational immunization in the treatment of pulmonary tuberculosis. Hort, E. C. *$1.50 net. Wood.

Rational life. Erwood, W: J. $1. W: J. Erwood.

Rational test. Keyser, L. S. 75 c.; 60 c. Lutheran Pub.

Rationale of investment in zinc mining. Ruhl, O. 25 c. Mining News.

RATIONALISM.
Mangasarian, M. M. Story of my mind; or, how I became a rationalist. 50 c. Independent Religious.
Power, M. True rationalism. 10 c. Herder.

Ratner, H: Wolf.
Up-to-date method of designing: school of designing, cutting, grading and fitting, for ladies', gentlemen's and children's garments. '08(My23) c. il. por. (Add. author for price.) H: W. Ratner.

Ratsmädelgeschichten. Böhlau, H. 40 c. Heath.

Ratti, Aurel de.
Simple scientific experiments. 2d ed. '09 (D18) c. pap., 25 c. Spon.

Rattlin, the reefer. Marryat, F: 50 c. Hurst.

Rau, Heribert.
Beethoven: a biographical romance; tr. by S. E. Randolph, from the German of H. Rau. '08(N21) c. 12°, $1.50. Ditson.

Raub, Adams Danforth.
World an educational unit with centralized education as the controlling force; plea from the poor for the same educational home environments as the rich enjoy, and a plea from the rich for better thought. '10(Ap9) c. 4°, 25 c. A. D. Raub.

Raub, Alb. Newton.
Studies in English and American literature, from Chaucer to the present time. '08 (S) c. 477 p. 12°, $1.50. Stradling.

Raudabaugh, Israel Franklin.
Latitude and departure calculations of land made easy and self-proving. '08(N) c. 119 p. il. tabs., $1.25; $1.50; $2. I. F. Raudabaugh.

Raum, Harry Angle.
Affinity: [a story.] '08(O17) c. D. $1.50. H. A. Raum.

Raupert, J: Godfrey Ferdinand.
Supreme problem; examination of historical Christianity from the standpoint of human life and experience, and in the light of psychical phenomena. '10(F5) c. D. $1.50. Paul.

Rauschenbusch, Wa.
For God and the people; prayers of the social awakening. '10(D3) c. O. $1 net. Pilgrim Press.

Rausenberger, F.
Theory of the recoil of guns with recoil cylinders; tr. by Alfr. Slater. '09(Ag14) il. 8°, *$4.50 net. Van Nostrand.

Rauser, Friedrich Ch.
"Siegfried Bergmann." '08(My.) c. 142 p. por. 12°, pap., 25 c. Schaefer & K.

Raven (The). *See* Poe, Edg. Allan.

Raven: the love story of Edgar Allan Poe. Hazelton, G: C., *jr.* †$1.50. Appleton.

Ravenbyrne, Ervie Mary.
Good health and good manners; with suggestive questions and notes. '10(Jl16) c. il. 12°, 25 c. Ainsworth.
Good health; with suggestive questions and notes. '10(Jl16) c. il. 12°, 30 c. Ainsworth.

Ravenswood. Gilliam, E: W. $1.25. Neale.

Raw gold. *See* Sinclair, B. W.

Rawie, H:
In quest of prosperity. '10(My21) c. D. (Science of value.) pap., 25 c. H: Rawie.
Problem stated of distribution. 2d ed., rev. and enl. '09(S) 44 p. 12°, (Science of value.) pap. (Add. pubs. for price.) Distribution League.
Quantity of money from distribution. 2d ed. '09(Ag21) c. D. pap., 15 c. Distribution League.
Wages and the price of land. '10(Ap16) c. 12°, (Science of value.) 25 c. H: Rawie.

Rawl, Bernard H., Stuart, Duncan, and Whitaker, G: M.
Dairy industry in the South. '09(My) 37+2 p. il. 8°, (U. S., Dept. of Agriculture, farmers' bull.) pap. (Add. Superintendent for price.) U. S., Supt. of Docs.

Rawley, Jos. Pierce.
Character reading dict. gleaned from the books of all ages. '10(Ap23) c. 16°, $1. J. P. Rawley.

Rawlings, Gertrude Burford.
Coins, and how to know them. '08(D19) il. D. *$1.50 net. Stokes.

Rawlinson, B.
502; collection of pieces in prose and verse in the Irish language comp. during the eleventh and twelfth centuries, now published in facsimile from the original manuscript in the Bodleian Library; with an introd. and indexes by Kuno Meyer. '09(N13) F. bds., $40.50. Oxford Univ.

Rawlinson, G:
Ancient history; fr. the earliest times to the fall of the Western Empire; with introd. by W: F. McDowell. '08(Je27) c. il. 8°, $1.75; hf. mor., $3.50. Lamb Pub.

Rawlinson, W. G.
Engraved work of J. M. W. Turner. v. 1, Line engravings on copper, 1794-1839. '08(D19) por. 8°, *$6 net. Macmillan.

RAWLINSON MANUSCRIPT.
See Bodleian Library, Oxford, Eng.

Rawnsley, Rev. Hardwicke.
Round the Lake Country. '09(Jl17) il. 12°, *$1.50 net. Macmillan.

Rawnsley, Mrs. Willingham.
Country sketches for city dwellers. '08 (Ag8) il. (Color books.) *$3 net. Macmillan.

Rawson, Christopher.
See Knecht, Edm.

Rawson, Maud Poona, [Mrs. Stepney Rawson.]
Bess of Hardwick and her circle. '10 (O22) il. O. $5 net. Lane.

Rawson, Mrs. Stepney.
See Rawson, Maud Poona.

Rawson, W. W.
Manual of drawing. pt. 1. '10(O1) il. O. 90 c. net. Longmans.
Success in market gardening; new vegetable grower's manual; [rev. by his son, Herbert Rawson.] Rev. and enl. ed. '10(Ap23) c. il. D. $1.10 net. Doubleday, P.

Ray, Anna Chapin, ["Sidney Howard."]
Bridge builders. '09(F20) c. D. †$1.50. Little, B. & Co.
By the good Sainte Anne. '08(Ap4) c. front. D. (Popular eds. of recent fiction.) †75 c. Little, B. & Co.
Janet at odds. '09(S25) c. il. D. (Sidney books.) †$1.50. Little, B. & Co.
Over the quicksands. '10(Mr5) c. front. D. †$1.50. Little, B. & Co.
Quickened. '08(Mr21) c. D. †$1.50. Little, B. & Co.
Sidney at college. New ed. '08(S19) c. il. D. †$1.50. Little, B. & Co.
Sidney: her senior year. '10(O15) c. il. D. (Sidney books.) $1.50. Little, B. & Co.

Ray, Blanche H.
See Noyes, *Mrs.* Marion Ingalls Osgood.

Ray, Ethelbert Sheb.
Song of the pines. '10(Ja8) c. il. 12°, $1.50. C. M. Clark.

Ray, F: A:
Devil worshipper. '08(N14) c. front. D. $1.50. C. M. Clark.

Ray, Mary Katherine.
Immigration problem: bibliography. '09, [1910.] (F) 21 p. 12°, (Wisconsin Free Library Commission; American social questions.) pap., 25 c. Wis. Free Lib.

Ray, Perley Orman.
Repeal of the Missouri compromise: its origin and authorship. '09(Ap3) 8°, *$3.50 net. A. H. Clark.

Ray, T. Bronson, ed.
Highway of mission thought: eight of the greatest discourses on missions. '07. [1908.] (F) c. 270 p. 12°, 75 c. S. S. Bd. So. Bapt.

—, and others.
Southern Baptist foreign missions. [1910.] (S) c. 277 p. il. maps, pors. 12°, 50 c. S. S. Bd. So. Bapt.
Bibliography (2 p.).

Ray, Wa. T., and Kreisinger, H:
Comparative tests of run-of-mine and briquetted coal on the torpedo boat "Biddle," made with the collaboration of Kenneth McAlpine and J. W. Hayward. '09(D) 49 p. il. 8°, (U. S., Dept. of the Interior, U. S. Geological Survey, bull.) pap. (Add. Superintendent for price.) U. S., Supt. of Docs.

Raymer's dictionary of Greater Seattle. Rev. 1908 ed. '08(Ag22) c. il. D. pap., 25 c. C. D. Raymer.

Raymer's dict. of Tacoma; encyclop. dict. of city and its environs. '09(N) 126 p. map, 12,° 25 c. C. D. Raymer.

Raymond, C: Fraser.
Cheer up. '09(My1) c. S. 75 c.; leath., $1.25. Dodge.
The happy life. '10(D17) 16°, bds., 75 c.; ooze, $1.25. Dodge.

Raymond, E: Brackett.
Tracing of direct-current and alternating-current motor troubles. '08(Ap18) c. il. 12°, $1.50. Hill Pub.

Raymond, Mrs. Evelyn Hunt, [Mrs. J: Bradford Raymond.]
Carlota of the rancho. '09(N13) c. il. D. †60 c. Penn Pub. Co.
Dorothy at Oak Knowe. '10(Jl2) c. il. D. 60 c. Chatterton-P.
Dorothy in California. '09(D) c. 9-252 p. pls. 12°, 60 c. Chatterton-P.
Dorothy on a house boat. '09(Ag14) c. il. 12°, 60 c. Chatterton-P.
Dorothy on a ranch. '09(Ag14) c. il. 12°, 60 c. Chatterton-P.
Dorothy's schooling. '08(Je13) c. D. 60 c. Chatterton-P.
Dorothy's travels. '08(Ag1) c. D. 60 c. Chatterton-P.

Raymond, Mrs. Evelyn Hunt.—*Continued.*
Jessica Trent's inheritance. '08(My23) c. il. 12°, 75 c. McKay.
Little Miss Evangeline. '08(O3) c. il. D. †$1.25. Penn Pub. Co.

Raymond, G: Lansing.
Dante and collected verse. '09(S11) c. S. **$1.25 net. Putnam.
Fundamentals in education, art and criticism. '10(D31) 12°, $1.40 net. Funk.
Psychology of inspiration: attempt to distinguish religious from scientific truth and to harmonize Christianity with modern thought. '08(Mr21) c. D. **$1.40 net. Funk.
The suffragettes: play. '08, [1909.] (Jl) c. 53 p. 12°. (Add. pubs. for price.) B. S. Adams.

Raymond, H: Warren.
Story of Saranac, [New York.] '09(Ap10) c. il. sq. D. *$1 net; limp leath., *$2 net, boxed. Grafton Press.

Raymond, Mrs. J: Bradford.
See Raymond, *Mrs.* Evelyn Hunt.

Raymond, Rossiter Worthington.
Story of Gaspar. '10(N12) c. D. pap., 25 c. net, in envelope. Pilgrim Press.

Raymond, W: Gait.
Elements of railroad engineering. '08 (My16) c. il. maps, 8°, $3.50. Wiley.
Modern turnout formulas. [Railroad tracks.] '08(N7) diagrs., D. pap., *50 c. net. A. M. Allen.
Railroad field geometry. '10(O22) figs. 16°, mor., $2. Wiley.

Raynes, F. W.
Domestic sanitary engineering and plumbing. '09(O2) il. O. *$3 net. Longmans.

Rayon, Mesha.
Fads or facts? '08(Ag1) c. front. S. 75 c. M. S. Pub.

Rea, Lilian.
Life and times of Marie Madeleine, Countess of La Fayette. '09(Je) il. 8°, *$3.50 net. Brentano's.

Rea, Russell.
Imports and employment; economic note. '10(O) 20 p. O. pap., 10 c. Cassell.

Reaching the boys of an entire community. Horton, C. B., *ed.* $1. Y. M. C. A.

Read, C. Stanford.
On fads and feeding. '08(D) 8+164 p. 12°, *$1 net. Dutton.

Read, Carveth.
Natural and social morals. '09(D25) 8°, *$2.75 net. Macmillan.

Read, D. H. Moutray.
Highways and byways in Hampshire. '08 (My9) il. map, (Highways and byways ser.) $2. Macmillan.

Read, Harlan Eugene.
Alarm talks. '08(Je) c. 5-61 p. 12°, 30 c. Business Monthly.
A beggar or a king, and other essays. '09 (N) c. 3-62 p. 12°, 30 c. Business Pub.
Lessons in salesmanship. '10(N12) c. 12°, 85 c. J. A. Lyons.

Read, Harmon Pumpelly.
Rossiana: papers and documents relating to the history and genealogy of the ancient and noble house of Ross, of Ross-shire, Scotland, and its descent from the ancient earls of Ross, together with the descent of the ancient and historic family of Read, from Rede of Troughend, Reade of Barton Court, Berks, and Read of Delaware; also some account of the related families; being a compilation of original documents found in the archives of the late General J: Meredith Read. '09(Ap3) c il. pors. charts, 8°, $10. H. P. Read.

Read, Opie Percival.
Tom and the squatter's son; stirring tale of adventures in the pioneer days for boys from 7 to 60. '10(My7) c. il. 12°, 50 c.; pap., 25 c. Laird.

Read, W: Alex.
Southern R. '10(My7) O. (La. State Univ. bull.) pap. La. State Univ.

READ FAMILY.
See Genealogies: Wright, *Mrs.* E. F. R.

Readable books in natural knowledge. il. 12°, 50 c. net. Macmillan.
—Albe. Wonders of physical science.
—Newbegin. Tillers of the ground.
—Thomson *and* Thomson. Threads in the web of life

Reade, C:
Works. Illustrated cabinet ed. In 16 v. '08(D5) D. ea., $1.50; per set, $24; hf. cf. or mor., $48. (Sold only in sets.) Estes.

Works. 12 v. New imperial lib. ed. '10 (D) il. 8°, ea., $1.25; hf. cf., $2.25; New il. sterling ed., ea., $1. (Sets only.) Estes.

Cloister and the hearth. '08(O17) 16°, (Best books ser.) leath., *$1 net. Dutton.

Cloister and the hearth. '09(D25) il. (partly color.) 8°. *$3.50 net. Stokes.

Love me little, love me long. '08(Mr21) c. O. (Large print lib.) †$1.50. Doubleday, P.

Peg Woffington; and Christie Johnson. '08 (Mr7) 16°, (Everyman's lib.) *35 c. net; leath., *70 c. net. Dutton.

Reade, Philip Hildreth, comp.
First generation of the name of Hildreth in Middlesex County in Massachusetts, 1643-1693; Richard Hildreth, Sergeant of Militia of Cambridge and Chelmsford, Middlesex Co., Mass.; born in England or Scotland, 1605, died, Chelmsford, 23rd Feb., 1693. '09, [1910.] (Ap) 38 p. por. il. facsims., 8°, $1.25. P. Reade.
Bibliography.

Reade, W: H: Vincent.
Moral system of Dante's Inferno. '09(Ap3) O. $4.15. Oxford Univ.

Reade, W: Winwood.
Martyrdom of man. 18th ed.; with introd. by F. Legge. '10(Jl30) por. D. $1.50 net. Lane.

Reade, Willoughby.
Notes on the Arthurian epic and the Idylls of the king. '08(My9) c. 12°, pap., 50 c. W. Reade.

Reader, Ethel.
Story of the little merman. '09(D11) il. D. *$1.25 net. Macmillan.

Reader's basis. Carey, A. P. $1. Echo Press.

Reader's guide to Irish fiction. Brown, S. J. $1.25 net. Longmans.

READERS.
Alcott, L. M. Louisa Alcott reader. *50 c. net. Little, B. & Co.

Alderman, E. A. Classics old and new. 1st reader. 25 c.; 5th reader. 40 c. Am. Bk.

Alexander, G. *and* G. Child classics. Primer; 1st-5th readers. primer, 30 c.; 1st reader, 35 c.; 2d reader, 40 c.; 3d reader, 50 c.; 4th reader, 55 c.; 5th reader, 60 c. Bobbs-M.

Allison, S: B., *and* Perdue, H. A., *comp.* Sixteen stories. 25 c. Flanagan.

Baldwin, J. Another fairy reader. 35 c. Am. Bk.

Blodgett, F. E. *and* A. B. Blodgett readers by grades. Bk. 1, 30 c.; Bk. 2, 35 c.; Bk. 3, 40 c.—Fifth reader. 75 c.—Fourth reader. 65 c. Ginn.

Bryce, C. T., *comp.* Child-lore dramatic reader. (Add. pubs. for price.) Scribner.

Buckwalter, G. Fourth reader. pt. 1. 42 c. Simmons.

Buffington, B. E., *and others.* Circus book for children. 50 c. B: H. Sanborn.

Burchill, G., *and others.* Progressive road to reading. bks. 1, 2. bk. 1, 32 c.; bk. 2, 40 c.; bk. 3, 48 c. Silver.

Burt, M. E., *ed.* Prose that every child should know. **90 c. net; **$1.50 net. Doubleday, P.

Carpenter, F. G: How the world is clothed. 60 c. Am. Bk.

Chamberlain, J. F. How we travel: geographical reader. *40 c. net. Macmillan.

Civic reader for new Americans. 38 c. Am. Bk.

Clemens, S: L. Travels at home.—Travels in history; arr. for supp. reading in sixth, seventh and eighth grades. ea., 50 c. Harper.

Coe, F. E. School reader. Third grade; Fourth grade. Third grade, 40 c.; Fourth grade, 50 c. Am. Bk.

Cooper, C: H., *ed.* Responsive readings for schools. (Add. pubs. for price.) Barnes.

Curry, C: M. New reading note-book; designed for use in connection with the Howe readers. $1. Inland Pub.

Cyr, *Mrs.* E. M. Story of three great artists. 50 c. Ginn.

Daffan, K. Texas hero stories. 50 c. B: H. Sanborn.

Davis, J: W., *and* Julien, F. Finger play readers. pts. 1 and 2. ea., 35 c.; teachers' ed., ea., 50 c. Heath.

Deutsch-englische lesebücher für katholische schulen. In 3 v. v. 1, 13½ c.; v. 2, 16⅔ c.; v. 3, 25 c. Benziger.

READERS.—*Continued.*

Doyle, M. E. Standard Catholic readers; first, second, third, fourth, and fifth readers. 1st reader, 20 c.; 2d reader, 30 c.; 3d reader, 40 c.; 4th reader, 50 c.; 5th reader, 60 c. Am. Bk.

Dunton, L. School-children the world over. $1.50. Stokes.

Eginton, L. J. First practice reader. 30 c. Silver.

Elson, H: W:, *and* Keck, C. Elson grammar school reader. Bks. 2, 3, 4. Bk. 2, 50 c.; Bks. 3, 4, ea., 60 c. Scott, F. & Co.

Farmer, F. V. Nature myths of many lands. 45 c. Am. Bk.

Faustine, M., *and* Wagner, M. E. New reader for evening schools. 50 c. Hinds.

Gardner, M. Work that is play: dramatic reader based on Æsop's fables. 35 c. Flanagan.

Gibson, C. C. In the golden East. *60 c. net. Little, B. & Co.

Gordy, W. F. Colonial days: historical reader. *50 c. net. Scribner.

Haliburton, M. W. Drill book. 18 c. B. F. Johnson.

Harvey, M. L. American normal readers. Bk. 3. 50 c. Silver.

Hervey, W. L., *and* Hix, M. First reader. 30 c.—Second reader. 40 c.—Third reader. 48 c. Longmans.

Howells, W: D. Boy life. 50 c. Harper.

Hülshof, J: L. Reading made easy for foreigners. 1st reader, 30 c.; 2d reader, 40 c.; 3d reader, 50 c. Hinds.

Jenks, T. When America became a nation. $1.25. Crowell.

Judson, H. P. Young American; civic reader. *60 c. net. C: E. Merrill.

Judson, K. B. Montana: [historical reader.] *75 c. net. McClurg.

Kahn, A. Barnes' first year book; silhouette reader. 30 c. net. Barnes.

Kaler, J. O. Calvert of Maryland. 35 c. Am. Bk.

Kenyon-Warner, *Mrs.* E. E. Character building readers. 8 v. 1st reader, pt. 1 and 2, ea., 25 c.; 35 c.; 2d reader, pt. 1, 30 c.; pt. 2, 35 c.; 3d and 4th years, ea., 45 c.; 5th, 6th and 7th years, ea., 50 c. Hinds.

Ketchum, I. A. Our story reader. *35 c. special net. Scribner.

Knight, M. Dramatic reader for grammar grades. 50 c. Am. Bk.

Lansing, M. F., *comp. and ed.* Fairy tales. 2 v. 35 c—Tales of old England in prose and verse. 35 c. Ginn.

Lucia, R. Stories of American discoverers for little Americans. 40 c. Am. Bk.

Lynch, A., *comp.* Classified index to the material contained in the different series of school readers. 50 c. Dulfer Pr.

Metcalfe, R: L. "Of such is the kingdom": school reader. $1. Woodruff-C.

Millard, C. N. Wonderful house that Jack has: reader in practical physiology and hygiene. *50 c. net. Macmillan.

READERS.—*Continued.*

Mintz, F. S. First reader for new American citizens.—New American citizen; reader for foreigners. ea., **50 c. net. Macmillan.

Murphy, D. C. Popular patriotic poems explained: [reader.] 65 c. Hinds.

Murray, C. Wide awake second reader. *35 c. net. Little, B. & Co.

Richards, *Mrs.* L. E. H. Pig brother, and other fables. **40 c. net. Little, B. & Co.

Richman, J., *and* Wallach, I. R. Good citizenship. 45 c. Am. Bk.

Roberts, P: Reader for coming Americans. 50 c. Y. M. C. A.

Sheldock, M. L. Collection of Eastern stories and legends for narration and reading in schools. 50 c. net. Dutton.

Smith, L. R. Hawk Eye. 30 c. Flanagan.

Spaulding, F. E., *and* Bryce, C. T. Fourth reader. 65 c.—Fifth reader. 75 c. Newson.

Stevenson, A. Children's classics in dramatic form: reader for the fourth grade. **40 c. net. Houghton M.

Tolman, *Mrs.* S. W. C. Around the world Bk. 1, 36 c.; Bk. 2, 42 c.; Bk. 3, 48 c.; Bk. 4, 54 c.; Bk. 5, 60 c. Silver.

Tucker, L. E. Universal school reader, 4th year. *45 c. Macmillan

Wade, J. H., *and* Sylvester, E. Fifth reader. 65 c. Ginn.

Webster, H. H., *ed.* American classics for seventh and eighth grade reading. **80 c. net. Houghton M.

Winslow, I: O. Geography readers. 5 v. ea., 50 c. net. Heath.

See also Arabic language;—Books and reading;—Christmas;—Dialogues; — Monologues; — Poetry;—Primers;—Reading;—Recitations.

Readers' lib. *See* Dawson, W: Ja. *and* Coningsby W:, *eds.*

Readers' library of illustrated handy pocket editions. 97 v. 16°, ea., *$1 net. Winston.

New volumes: Antoninus, Marcus Aurelius, Meditations; Austen, J., Pride and prejudice; Brontë, C. Agnes Gray, Professor, Poems; Craik, *Mrs.*, Noble life; Eliot, G:, Felix Holt; Emerson, R. W., Essays; Goldsmith, O., Vicar of Wakefield; Holmes, O. W., Professor at the breakfast table; Irving, W., Sketch book; Kingsley, C:, Hypatia; Lover, S:, Handy Andy; Lytton, *Lord,* Harold; Marryat, *Capt.*, Mr. Midshipman Easy;—Melville, W., Gladiators; Oliphant, *Mrs.*, Marjorie Banks; Scott, *Sir* W., Old Mortality, Poetical works; Thackeray, W. M., The Virginians; Trollope, A., Framley Parsonage; Yonge, C. M., Heir of Redclyffe.

Readers on commerce and industry. il. D. Am. Bk.

—Carpenter. How the world is clothed. 60 c.

Reading, Adda Sproul, comp.

My bridge scores. '10(Ja8) nar. D. bds., $1, boxed. Daly.

READING.

Briggs, T: H:, *and* Coffman, L. D. Reading in public schools. $1.25. Row, P. & Co.

Clark, S. H: How to teach reading in the public schools. $1. Scott, F. & Co.

Coon, C: L. How to teach reading. gratis. N. C., Dept. Pub. Instruct.

Hamilton, F. M. Perceptual factors in reading. 50 c. Science Pr., (N. Y.)

Huey, E. B. Psychology and pedagogy of reading. *$1.40 net. Macmillan.

READING.—*Continued.*
Hughes, J. L. Teaching to read. 50 c. Barnes.
Laing, M. E. Reading; manual for teachers. $1. Heath.
McMurry, C: A. Special methods in reading in the grades. *$1.25 net. Macmillan.
Patterson, A. M. Course of study for the teaching of reading to beginners.—Course of study in the teaching of reading. ea., 30 c. San F. St. Normal.
Searson, J. W., *and* Martin, G: E. Studies in reading. 80 c. Univ. Pub. Co.
Sherman, E. B., *and* Reed, A. A. Essentials of teaching reading. $1.12. Univ. Pub.
See also Books and reading;—Phonetics;—Recitations.
READING, Pa.
Nolen, J: Replanning Reading. $1 net. J: Nolen.
See also St. Stephen's Reformed Church.
READING COMPANY.
See Coal.
Readings from Latin verse. Bushnell, C. C. 75c. Allyn & B.
Readings in American government and politics. Beard, C: A., *comp.* **$1.90 net. Macmillan.
Readings in English history. Cheyney, E: P. $1.80. Ginn.
Readings in modern European history. Robinson, J. H. v. 1. $1.40; v. 2, $1.50; 2 v. in 1, abridged ed., $1.50. Ginn.
Readings in the history of education. Norton, A. O. 85 c. Harvard Univ.
Readings on American federal government. Reinsch, P. S:, *ed.* $2.75. Ginn.
Readings on the Paridiso of Dante. Vernon, W: W. *$4 net. Macmillan.
Readjustment. Irwin, W: H: $1.20 net. B: W. Huebsch.
READY RECKONERS.
See Arithmetic.
Ready reference of menu terms. Gancel, J. $1. J. Gancel.
Real America in romance. *See* Markham, E. C:—Musick, J: R.
Real Bryan. Bryan, W: J. $1.25. Personal Help.
Real Buster Brown and the only Mary Jane. Outcault, R: F. 60 c. Stokes.
Real Chinaman. Holcombe, C. *$2 net. Dodd.
Real college. Benton, G. P. *75 c. net. Jennings.
REAL ESTATE.
See Land;—Real property.
Real France. Jerrold, L. $1.50 net. Lane.
Real Francis Joseph. Weindel, H. de. $4 special net. Appleton.
Real (The) God. Randall, J: H. $1.25. Caldwell.
Real Holy Spirit. Myers, C. *50 c. net. Revell.
Real issue. White, W: A. **$1.25 net. Macmillan.
Real Japan. Norman, *Sir* H: *$1.50 net. Scribner.
Real letters to a real girl. Garity, M. E. $1.25. C. M. Clark.
Real letters to real boys. Taylor, C: K. *50 c. net. Revell.
Real power back of James J. Hill. Reeve, B. 50 c. B. Reeve.
REAL PROPERTY.
American School of Correspondence. Insurance and real estate accounts. $1.50. Am. Sch. Corr.
Ballard, E. E., *ed.* Index digest of Ballard's Law of real property. v. 1-12. $4. —Law of real property. v. 12.—Complete index to Ballard's Law of real property. v. 1-12. ea., $6.50. Flood.
Bromley, G: W. *and* W. S. Owners' names of the city of N. Y. $30. G: W. Bromley.
Carey, T: J. Real estate educator. *$2 net. Carey.
Central real estate directory of Iowa, Kentucky and Texas. $5. Cen. Real Estate.
Evening Post. Real estate values. 25 c. N. Y. Eve. Post.
Gross, F. L. Law of real estate brokers. $4. Ronald Press.
How to sell real estate at a profit; proved methods for starting and conducting a real estate business—publicity campaigns that bring results—tried and tested plans for building up a clientele—specific systems for executing sales and rentals, as used successfully by thirty-two real estates concerns. 5th rev. ed. '09, [1910.] (N) c. 128 p. il. forms, 12°, (System "how-books.") System.
Lewis, J: Eminent domain. *$13 net. Callaghan.
Melberg, P: L. How to sell real estate. $2.50. P: L. Melberg.
Merwine, W. L. Judicial conveyance of real estate. $6. W. H. Anderson.
Minor, R. C. Law of real property. In 2 v. (Add. pubs. for price.) Anderson.
Minor, R. C., *and* Wurts, J: Law of real property. $5. West Pub.
Morden Training School. Complete course of instructions in real estate business. 10 v. $15. R. O. Morden.
New York [State.] Real property law of the state. $8.50. Baker, V. & Co.
Nichols, P. Power of eminent domain. $5. Boston Bk.
Noble, W: N. Disposition of a decedent's real property for the payment of debts and funeral expenses. $3.50. Banks & Co.
Practical real estate methods. $2. Doubleday, P.
Practical real estate methods for broker, operator and owner. '09(O) c. 416 p. 12°, $2. Y. M. C. A.
Putney, A. H., *and others.* Manufactures, mining, irrigation, real estate. $4. Cree.
Reeves, A. G. Treatise on the law of real real property. 2 v. $13. Little, B. & Co.
Rood, J: R. Decisions, statutes, etc., concerning the law of estates in land. (Add. pubs. for price.) Callaghan.

REAL PROPERTY.—*Continued.*
System Company. How to sell real estate at a profit; proved methods as used successfully by 32 real estate concerns. Rev. ed. '09(S) c. 128 p. il. 12°. (Not for sale.) System.
Tyler, F: S., *comp.* Questions and answers on real property. 50 c. Byrne.
Walker, W: S. American law of real estate agency. $6. W. H. Anderson.
Warvelle, G: W: Practical treatise on abstracts and examinations of title to real property. *$4 net.—Principles of the American law of real property for the use of students. $4. Callaghan.
Washington [State.] Reality law for owners, agents and tenants. $5. Vancouver.
See also Land;—Landlord and tenant;—Mechanics' liens;—Mortgages;—Property;—Sale;—Taxation;—Titles;—Trespass;—*also* Chicago;—New York City.
Real religion. Bridgman, H. A. 75 c. net. Pilgrim Press.
Real Roosevelt. Roosevelt, T. $1. Putnam.
Real Roosevelt. Smith, E: G. $1.50. States Pub.
Real thing. Bangs, J: K. $1. Harper.
Real Wall Street. Black, W: H. $1.25; $1. Corporations.
REALISM.
See Philosophy.
Realities and ideals. Harrison, F: **$1.75 net. Macmillan.
REALITY.
See Psychology.
Realization. Weltmer, E. $1. Weltmer.
Really babies. Brownell, E. B. $1.25. Rand, McN. & Co.
Realm of light: a novel. Hatfield, F., *pseud.* $1.50. Reid Pub.
REAPERS.
See Agricultural machinery.
Reaping (A). Benson, E: F. $1.25, fixed. Doubleday, P.
Reaping (The). Taylor, M. I. †$1.50. Little, B. & Co.
Reappear (The). Laughlin, A., *ed.* 60 c. A. Laughlin.
Rear-Admirals Schley, Sampson and Cervera. Parker, J. **$3 net. Neale.
REASON.
Kant, I. Critique of practical reason. $4.50. Longmans.
Reason and belief. *See* Lodge, *Sir* Oliver.
Reasonable life. Bennett, E. A. 50 c. net. Doran.
Reasonable social policy for Christian people. Henderson, C: R. 10 c. Am. Bapt.
Reasonableness of Catholic ceremonies. Burke, J. J. *25 c. net; *13 c. net. Benziger.
Reasoner, Ja. M., rep.
See Michigan. *Sup. ct.* Repts.
REASONING.
See Logic.
REBATES.
See Railroads.
Rebecca of Sunnybrook farm. *See* Wiggin, Kate Douglas Smith.
Rebel private, front and rear. Fletcher, W: A. $1. Greer Pr.
Rebel woman. Sharp, E. $1 net. Lane.
Reber, T:, comp.
"Proud old Natchez"; hist. and romance; comp. from ancient chronicles and modern histories. '09, [1910.] (F) c. 71 p. pl. pors. plan, 8°, 50 c. T: Reber.
Rebuilding of King Solomon's temple. Franklin, J: H. $1.50. J: H. Franklin.
RECALL.
See Elections.
Recall of love. Gordon, C: W: 50 c. net. Doran.
Receipts and remedies. Flemming, L: A. 50 c. Penn Pub. Co.
RECEIVERS.
High, J. L. Treatise on the law of receivers. $7.50. Callaghan.
Recent advances in physical and inorganic chemistry. Stewart, A. W. *$2.50 net. Longmans.
Recent advances in physiology. Hill, L., *ed.* *$5 net. Longmans.
Recent Christian progress. Paton, L. B., *ed.* **$3 net. Macmillan.
Recent English domestic architecture. Macartney, M. E., *ed.* *$3.50 net. Scribner.
Recent plans for currency reform. Ripley, A. L. (Add. pub. for price.) Ellis.
Recent progress in the study of variation, heredity and evolution. Lock, R. H. $2 net. Dutton.
Recent progress of the socialist and labor movement in the United States. Hillquit, M. 10 c. Kerr.
Reception of Goethe's Faust in England. Hauhart, W: F. *$1 net. Lemcke.
RECESS (*school*).
See Games;—Schools.
RECIPES.
See Cookery;—Useful arts.
RECIPROCITY.
Kirwan, T: Reciprocity (social and economic) in the thirtieth century. *$1 net. Cochrane.
Library of Congress list of references on reciprocity. 15 c. Gov. Pr. Off.
Wilson, J. H. Free trade with Cuba. U. S., Supt. of Docs.
See also Commerce;—Tariff.
RECITATIONS.
Avery-Stuttle, *Mrs.* L. D., *and others, comps.* Selections for our little folk. 60 c. Pacific Press.
Baker, G: M. Pieces people ask for. 25 c. W. H. Baker.
Baum, L. F., *comp.* Juvenile speaker. $1.25 Reilly & B.
Blair, M., *comp.* Our holidays: recitations and exercises. 50 c. McLoughlin.
Bugbee, W. N. Jolly bachelors: motion song or recitation.—Merry old maids: motion song or recitation. ea., 25 c. Dick.
Burke, M. C. School room echoes. Bk. 1. $1.50. Badger.
Children's speakers. 2 bks. ea., 25 c.; 15 c. Penn Pub. Co.
Denton, C. J., *comp.* Program book; recitations, dialogues, etc. 40 c. J. Fischer.
Faxon, G. B. Popular recitations and how to recite them. $1. F. A. Owen.
Irish, M. Patriotic celebrations. 25 c. T. S. Denison.

RECITATIONS.—*Continued.*
Kleiser, G. Humorous hits, and How to hold an audience. **$1 net. Funk.
Little people's recitation series. 4 v. ea., 75 c. Caldwell.
Morgan, A., *comp.* Selected readings [prose and poetry.] *$1.50 net. McClurg.
Northrop, H: D. Model speaker and reciter. $1. G: W. Bertron.
O'Neill, A. T. L., *comp.* Recitations for assembly and classroom. **$1.10 net. Macmillan.
Parker, M. M. New monologues and dialect stories. $1. Drake.
Pearson, P. M., *comp. and ed.* Humorous speaker. $1.25. Hinds.
Pearson, P. M., *ed.* The speaker. 19 nos. ea., 60 c.; 40 c.; nos. 1-16 complete in 4 v., ea., $1.50. Hinds.
Redington, M. E., *comp.* Strong selections for public reading. $1.50.. Cen. Me.
Schell, S. Platform and all-round. Werner.
Shoemaker, C: C., *comp.* One hundred choice selections. 30 c. Penn Pub. Co.
Shoemaker, J. W. Best selections. v. 1-9. ea., $1.50; per set, $9. Penn Pub. Co.
Steele, M., *comp.* One and all reciter. *$1 net. Lane.
West, E. E., *comp.* All-round recitations.—Old-time favorites. ea., 35 c. Werner.
Workman, *Mrs.* H. C., *comp.* Recitations for children. 35 c. H. C. Workman.
See also Dialogues; — Monologues; — Readers; — *also* Lincoln, Abraham.

Récits tirés des Impressions de voyage. Dumas, A. *25 c. net. Crowell.
Reclaimed. Gray, J. J. $1.50. B'way Pub.
Reclamation of alluvial lands in southern Louisiana. 2d ed. '09(O9) c. il. O. pap., gratis. La. Meadow.
RECLAMATION OF LAND.
See Land.
Reclamation of the Florida everglades. Smith, S: R. gratis. Miami Pr.
Recognition of our friends in heaven. Anstadt, P: $1; $1.50. Anstadt.
Recollections. Frénilly, F. A. de. *$3 net. Putnam.
Recollections. Gladden, W. **$2 net. Houghton M.
Recollections of a fire insurance man. Critchell, R. S. $1.25. R. S. Critchell.
Recollections of a 49er. McIhany, E: W. $1. Hailman.
Recollections of a long life. Broughton, J: C. H., *Lord.* In 2 v. *$6 net. Scribner.
Recollections of a New England educator. Mowry, W: A: *$1.50 net. Silver.
Recollections of a Scottish novelist. Walford, *Mrs.* L. B. C. $3 net. Longmans.
Recollections of a spinster aunt. Beale-Demy, S. S., *ed.* (Add. pubs. for price.) P. R. Reynolds.
Recollections of a varied career. Draper, W: F. **$3 net. Little, B. & Co.
Recollections of a varied life. Eggleston, G: C. $2.75 net. Holt.
Recollections of an old mountaineer. Larden, W. $4 net. Longmans.
Recollections of Grover Cleveland. Parker, G: F. **$3 net. Century Co.
Recollections of seventy years. Sanborn, F. B: 2 v. *$5 net. Badger.
Recompense. '10(D) 32°, (Selections from great authors.) pap., 30 c. Stokes.
Reconstructed marriage. Barr, *Mrs.* A. E. H. $1.25 net. Dodd.
Reconstructing Eden. Conard, H. L: 50 c.; 25 c. New Eden.
Reconstruction of the English church. Usher, R. G. 2 v. 6 net. Appleton.
RECONSTRUCTION PERIOD (*United States*).
See Georgia;—Louisiana;—Maryland;—Texas.
Record of a year's reading. Soulsby, L. M., *comp.* 30 c. Longmans.
Record of letters. '10(O24) nar. O. pap., 75 c., boxed. Reilly & B.
Records of labor and manufacturing orders. Griffith, J. B. 50 c. Am. Sch. Corr.
Recovery (The). Altstheler, J. A. $1.50. Lovell.
Recovery of a lost Roman tragedy. Wright, H: B. $1.50. Yale Univ.
RECREATION CAMPS.
See Parks.
Recreations in history and geography. Murphy, D. C. *30 c. net. Educ. Pub.
Recreations of a sportsman on the Pacific Coast. Holder, C: F: $2 net. Putnam.
Recruiting for Christ. Stone, J: T. $1 net. Revell.
RECTUM.
See Anus and rectum.
Red-blooded (The). Bronson, E. B. $1.50. McClurg.
"Red book": interstate automobile guide; cont. detailed descriptions of the best routes between all the leading centers and coast and mountain resorts; gazetteer of cities, towns, villages; street maps of principal cities and towns, and a diagrammatic map of popular tours in New England. 1908. 2d ed. '08(Je6); 1909. '09(Je) c. il. nar. O. leath., with map, ea., $2.50. F. S. Blanchard.
Red book of heroes. Lang, L. B. *$1.60 net. Longmans.
Red book ser. of trade school manuals. il. 16°. Drake.
—Maire. Colors.—Exterior painting.—Interior painting. ea., 60 c.
Red Cap adventures. Crockett, S: R. †$1.75. Macmillan.
Red Cap tales from Sir Walter Scott. *See* Crockett, S: Rutherford.
Red Caps of Lyons. Hayens, H. †$1.50. Appleton.
Red city. Mitchell, W. S. †$1.50. Century Co.
RED CLOVER.
See Seed.
Red Cross knight and Sir Guyon. Macleod, M., *comp.* 60 c. Dodge.
RED CROSS SOCIETY.
Lynch, C. American National Red Cross text-book on first aid and relief columns. *$1 net. Blakiston.
Red flag. Ohnet, G. $1.50. G: W. Dillingham.
Red hair from a cock of hay. Sexton, M. H: G: W: Browning.

Red-handed saint. Parr, O. K. $1.10 net. Benziger.
Red Horse Hill. McCall, S., *pseud.* †$1.50. Little, B. & Co.
Red House on Rowan Street. Doubleday, R. †$1.50. Little, B. & Co.
Red-letter days of Samuel Pepys. Pepys, S: $1.25 net. Sturgis & W.
Red letter ser. il. S. Penn Pub. Co.
—Johnson. Chickens and how to raise them. 25 c.
Red lily. *See* France, Anatole.
Red magic book. Knipe, A. A. $1.25 net. Doubleday, P.
Red-man (The); or, the destruction of a race. Waddell, W: 85 c. W: Waddell.
Red moon. Bacon, *Mrs.* E. J. $1.25. Neale.
Red mouse. Osborne, W: H. †$1.50. Dodd.
Red oak (*quercus rubra*). '09(Je) 3 p. 8°, (U. S., Dept. of Agriculture, forest service; forest planting leaflet.) pap. (Add. Superintendent for price.) U. S., Supt. of Docs.
Red Pepper Burns. Richmond, *Mrs.* G. L. S. $1.20, fixed. Doubleday, P.
Red Riding Hood and Aladdin. Mord, W. 35 c. Stokes.
RED RIVER VALLEY, N. D.
Hist. of the Red River Valley. 2 v. $15. Herald Pr. (N. Dak.)
Red Saint. Deeping, G: W. $1.50. Cassell.
Red scull. Hume, F. W. $1.50. Dodge.
Red symbol. Ironside, J: $1.50. Little, B. & Co.
Red year. Tracy, L: $1.50. Clode.
"Redbeard, Ragnar," pseud.
Might is right; or, the survival of the fittest. '10(Jl) 165 p. D. pap., 50 c. G: Engelke.
Redcloud of the lakes. Burton, F: R. $1.50. G: W. Dillingham.
Reddale, Frederic, pseud.
See Reddall, H: Frederic.
Reddall, H: Frederic, ["Frederic Reddale."]
Wit and humor of business. '08(S5) c. por. S. (Wit and humor ser.) **50 c. net; leath., **80 c. net. Jacobs.
—, **comp.** Climbing the ladder of fame. '08 (D) 10-291 p. 12°, (Young people's lib.) 75 c. Educ. Pub.
See also Wit and humor of stage.
REDDINGTON FAMILY.
See **Genealogies, Carter,** ***Mrs.*** **C. M. R.**
Rede (Die) Konstantins des Grossen an die versammlung der heiligen auf ihre echt heit untersucht. Pfättisch, J. M. *$1 net. Herder.
Rede lecture. *See* Satow, *Sir* Ernest Mason.
Redeemed captive. Williams, J. $2.50; $5. Hunttíng.
Redeeming vision. Holden, J: S. *$1.25 net. Revell.
REDEMPTION.
See **Salvation.**
Redemption. Bazin, R. †$1.50. Scribner.
Redemption. Peterson, E. 25 c. E. Peterson.
Redemption (The). Stollnitz, H: S. (Add. pubs. for price.) H: S. Stollnitz.
Redemption of Arthur True. Bratten, A. 75 c. Stafford.
Redemption of Kenneth Galt. Harben, W: N. †$1.50. Harper.

Redemption of Paradise Pond. Root, E: T. 75 c. E: T. Root.
REDEMPTORIST FATHERS.
See **Catholic church.**
Redesdale, Algernon Bertram Freeman-Mitford, Lord.
Tales of old Japan. '10(D24) il. 16°, 50 c. net. Macmillan.
Redfield, Amasa A.
See New York. Law and practice of surrogates' courts in the state.
Redfield, Harold Hamilton.
Compend of the active principles, with symptomatic indications for their therapeutic use. '10(N) 115 p. 12°, 75 c. Clinic.
Redford, Eliz. Adamson.
Neither do I. '10(Jl30) c. il. por. 12°, $1.50. B'way Pub.
Redford, G:
Sculpture: Egyptian, Assyrian, Greek and Roman. '10(D) 12°, (Hdbks. of art hist.) hf. leath., $1.25. Gorham.
Redgrave, Gilbert R:
Water-color painting in England. '10(D) 12°, (Hdbks. of art hist.) hf. leath., $1.25. Gorham.
Redgrove, H. Stanley.
On the calculation of thermo-chemical constants. '09(My22) O. *$1.70 net. Longmans.
Redi, Francesco, of Arezzo.
Experiments on the generation of insects; tr. from the Italian ed. of 1688 by Mab Bigelow. '09(N6) il. $2. Open Court.
Redic, Marg.
Trixey, the manicure girl. '08(Je) c. 192 p. D. cl., $1. B'way Pub.
Redington, Mary Emily, comp.
Strong selections for public reading; ed. by Herbert Carlyle Libby for the use of students in fitting schools and colleges. '08, [1909.] (Ag) 328 p. 12°, $1.50. Cen. Me.
Redlich, Josef.
Procedure of the House of Commons; study of its hist. and present form; tr. from the German by A. Ernst Steinhal; an introd. and supp. chapter by Sir Courtenay Boyle. '10(Je4) 4°, $10 net. Dutton.
Redmayne, R: Augustine Studdert.
Modern practice in mining. v. 1, Coal. '08(S5) *$2 net; v. 2, Sinking of shafts. '09(O30) il. figs. O. *$2.25 net. Longmans.
Redmond, J: E:
Home rule speeches of John Redmond, M.P.; ed., with introd. by R. Barry O'Brien. '10(O29) por. O. $2.50 net. Stokes.
Redmond, J: W., rep.
See Vermont. *Sup. ct.* Repts.
Redney McGaw. McFarlane, A. E. †$1.50. Little, B. & Co.
Redway, Major G: W:
War of the Secession, 1861-1862. '10 (My21) maps, 12°, (Special campaign ser.) $1.60. Macmillan.

Redway, Jacques Wardlaw.
All around Asia. '10(Jl2) c. il. maps, 12°, (Redway's geographical readers.) 60 c. Scribner.
Elem. physical geography. New ed. '08 (Je27) c. il. maps, 12°, $1.25. Scribner.
Redway school hist.; outlining the making of the American nation. '10(D3) c. il. maps, por. D. $1 net. Silver.

REDWOODS.
See Calaveras Grove.

Reed, Albert A.
See Sherman, Eug. Buren

Reed, Alonzo.
Word lessons for intermediate and grammar grades. [New ed.] '09(N) c. 192 p. 12°, 25 c. C: E. Merrill.

—, and Kellogg, Brainerd.
Higher lessons in English; work on English grammar and composition, in which the science of the language is made tributary to the art of expression. [New ed., 1909.] '09(D) c. 442 p. 12°, 70 c. C: E. Merrill.

Reed, C: Bert, M.D.
First great Canadian; story of Pierre Le Moyne, Sieur D'Iberville. '10(Ap9) c. il. maps, por. O. $2 net. McClurg.
Masters of the wilderness; study of the Hudson's Bay Company from its origin to modern times. '10(My14) fold. map, O. pap., 50 c. Chic. Hist.

Reed, C: K. and Chester Albert.
Guide to taxidermy. New ed., enl. and rewritten. '08(Ag1) c. 12°, *$1.50 net. C: K. Reed.

Reed, Chester Albert.
Bird guide. Rev. ed. pt. 1, Water birds, game birds and birds of prey east of the Rockies; pt. 2, Land birds east of the Rockies. '10(D10) c. obl. 48°, il. in col. ea., $1 net, boxed; pts. 1 and 2, bound in 1 v., limp leath., $2.25 net. Doubleday, P.
Flower guide: wild flowers east of the Rockies. '10(D3) il. 24°, limp leath., $1 net. Doubleday, P.
Nature study guides. 2 v. v. 1, Flower guide: wild flowers east of the Rockies; v. 2, Bird guide. pt. 1, Water and game birds; birds of prey. pt. 2, Land and song birds. '08(D) 24°, ea. pt., 50 c.; flex. leath., 75 c. Denholm.
Wild flowers. '10(D17) col. il. $2.50 net. Doubleday, P.
See also Bowman, Isaiah.—Reed, C: K.

Reed, E. E., D.D.
Mission of the Christian college: inaugural address del. by president of Lenox College, Hopkinton, Iowa, June 9, 1907. '08 (Ap18) 12°, gratis. Lenox Coll.

Reed, E: Bliss, ed.
See Yale University, Class of 1894.

Reed, Fk. A.
Textbk. used in the Reed School for the Correction of the Stammering Habit. '10 (N12) 8°, $1. F. A. Reed.

Reed, G:
Poems. '09, [1910.] (Ja) c. 76 p. il. por. 12°. 50 c. V. B. Reed.

Reed, G: Matthew.
Infection experiments with *erysiphe cichoracearum* DC: [study of mildews.] '09 (F6) O. (Univ. of Wis. bull.; Science ser.) pap., 35 c. Univ. of Wis.
Mildews of the cereals. '10(Jl16) tabs., 8°, (Contribs. from the Dept. of Botany of the Univ. of Mo.) (Not for sale.) G: M. Reed.

Reed, Helen Leah.
Irma in Italy. '08(N14) c. D. (Irma ser.) †$1.25. Little, B. & Co.

Reed, Rev. Ja., and Hay, Rev. H: Clinton.
Essential needs of the soul: [ten discourses.] '09(Je5) 12°, 75 c. Badger.

Reed, J: A.
Hist. of the 101st regiment, Pennsylvania Veteran Volunteer Infantry, 1861-1865; with Luther S. Dickey as collaborator. '10(Je) 285 p. il. pors., maps, plan. 4°, subs., $5. Dickey.

Reed, Jos. F.
See Tracy, J: Edwards Woodbridge.

Reed, Milton.
A-roving he would go; from the Southern Cross to the Arctic Circle. '09(D11) c. D. *$1.25 net. Sherman, F.
Sea of faith. '08(N14) D. *80 c. net. Am. Unitarian.

Reed, Myrtle, [now Mrs. Myrtle Reed McCullough, "Olive Green."]
Flower of the dusk. '08(S12) c. front. O. **$1.50 net; full leath., **$2 net; ant. cf., **$2.50 net; lavender silk, **$3.50 net, boxed. Putnam.
How to cook fish. '08(Ag15) c. 16°, (Putnam's home maker ser.) **$1 net. Putnam.
How to cook meat and poultry. '08(S19) c. S. (Putnam's home maker ser.) **$1 net. Putnam.
How to cook vegetables. '09(Jl3) c. 16°, (Putnam's home maker ser.) **$1 net. Putnam.
Master of the vineyard. '10(S24) front. [in col.] O. $1.50 net, boxed; leath., $2 net, boxed; antique cf., $2.50 net, boxed; lavender silk, $3.50 net, boxed. Putnam.
Old Rose and Silver. '09(O2) c. front. in col. O. **$1.50 net, boxed; leath., **$2 net, boxed; cf., **$2.50 net, boxed; silk, **$3.50 net, boxed. Putnam.
One thousand salads. '09(D4) c. S. (Home maker ser.) **$1 net. Putnam.
Sonnets to a lover. '10(O15) c. D. $1.25, boxed. Putnam.

Reed, Sarah Ann.
Romance of Arlington House. '08(Mr7) c. il. por. D. $1. Chapple Pub.

Reed, W: B.
Echoes of the Emancipation Proclamation. '09(Mr) c. 8°, 15 c. W: B. Reed.

REED FAMILY.
See Genealogies: Wright, *Mrs.* E. F. R.

Reeder, Rob. Patterson.
Rate regulation as affected by the distribution of governmental powers in the constitutions. '09(Ja2) c. O. $1. T. & J. W. Johnson.

Reeder, Rudolph Rex.
How two hundred children live and learn. '09(D25) c. il. D. $1.25. Charities Pub.

Reed's engineers' hdbk. to examinations for marine engineers. 18th ed., rev. and enl.; with supp. and plates. '08(Ag1); 19th ed., rev. and enl. '09(D18) il. 8°, ea., *$5 net. Spon.

Reed's useful hints to sea going engineers. '08(Ag1) il. 12°, $1.50. Spon.

Reedy, W: Marion.
The myth of a free press; address del. before the Missouri Press Association at Excelsior Springs, Mo., May 28, 1908. '08, [1910.] (Mr) 31 p. 16°. W: M. Reedy.

Reeks, Marg.
Hints for crystal drawing; with a preface by J: W. Evans. '08(S5) O. *$1.10 net. Longmans.

Reepen, H. v. Buttel-.
See Buttel-Reepen, H. v.

Rees, Arth. Dougherty.
Give up your gods; drama of pagan and Christian Russia. '09(F6) c. 12°, **$1 net. Lippincott.
William Tell: a drama. '08(D19) c. 12°. (Priv. pr.) Lippincott.

Rees, Frances Byrne.
Adventures of Little Knight Brave. '09 (O16) c. il. D. †$1.50. Appleton.

Rees, J. D.
Pictorial Spanish course. '09, [1910.] (F) il. 12°, *65 c. net. Little, B. & Co.

Rees, Janet E. Ruutz-.
See Ruutz-Rees, Janet E.

Rees, Kelley.
Rule of three actors in the classical Greek drama. '08(Mr28) c. 8°, pap., *75 c. net. Univ. of Chic.

Rees, T:
Sixty days in Europe and what we saw there. '08(Ag1) c. il. pors. 8°, $1.25. State Register.

Rees, T: H:
Topographical surveying and sketching. '09(Ja23) il. c. tabs., O. $2.50. Staff Coll.

Rees, W: Geulph.
Mayor of Romanstown; drama in three acts. '10(My14) c. 12°, 75 c. Cochrane.

Reese, Albert Moore.
Development of the American alligator: (*A. mississippiensis.*) '08(Ap4) O. (Smithsonian miscellaneous collections.) pap., 50 c. Smith. Inst.
Development of the brain of the American alligator; the paraphysics and hypophysics. '10(Mr19) il. O. (Smithsonian misc. collections.) pap. (Add. Inst. for price.) Smith. Inst.
Introd. to vertebrate embryology based on the study of the frog, chick, and mammal. 2d ed., rev. and enl. '09, [1910.] (My) c. 21+340 p. il. 12°, $1.50 net. Putnam.

Reese, Lizette Woodworth.
Branch of may: poems. '09(Ap24) c. S. (Mosher's lyric garland.) vellum, *$1 net, boxed; bds., *50 c. net, boxed. T: B. Mosher.
Wayside lute. '09(D) bds., *$1.50 net; Japan vellum, *$3 net. T: B. Mosher.

Reese, R. A.
Complete digest of Texas decisions. 3 v. '10(Ag) c. Q. $25. Flood.

Reeve, Budd.
Jerome; or, the real power back of James J. Hill. v. 1; written under impressions received from the book of Moses. '08 (N) c. 284 p. D. pap., 50 c. B. Reeve.

Reeve, J. Stanley.
Rhubarb; diary of a gentleman's hunter. '09(Ja23) $1. J. S. Reeve.

Reeve, Ja. Knapp.
Pract. authorship; work designed to afford writers an insight into certain technical, commercial, and financial aspects of the profession of letters as followed by the general writer for current publication. '10(Je11) c. 8°, $1.50. Editor Co.

Reeve, Katharine Roosevelt.
Covert-side courtship. '10(F19) c. il. D. $1.50. Lippincott.

Reeve, Sidney Armor.
Energy, work, heat and transformations. '09(D4) c. figs. O. *$2 net. McGraw-H.

Reeves, Alfr. Gandy.
Treatise on the law of real property. In 2 v. v. 1. '09(Ap); v. 2 (My) c. O. ea., $6.50; per set, $13. Little, B. & Co.

Reeves, W: C., comp.
See Oklahoma laws.

Reeves, W: Pember.
New Zealand. '08(N7) il. map, 8°, (Color books.) *$6 net. Macmillan.

Reference book. Baker, J. W: $1. Southwestern Co., (Nashville.)

REFERENCE BOOKS.
See Books and reading;—Encyclopedias.

REFERENDUM.
Schaffner, M. A. Initiative and referendum. 5 c. Wisconsin Free Lib.
White, J: Z. Direct legislation: the initiative and referendum. 5 c.; per doz., 40 c.; per 100, $2. Timby.
See also Debating.

Reflected lights from Paradise. Micou, *Mrs.* M. D., *comp.* *50 c. net. Young Churchman.

REFLECTION.
See Optics.

Reflections. Lichtenberg, G. C. $1. Scribner.

Reflections of a bachelor. '08(N14) c. S. bds., 75 c.; Novelty ed. '08(Je20) $1, boxed. Dodge.

Reflections of a bachelor girl. Rowland, H. 75 c. Dodge.

Reflections of Ambrosine. Glyn, *Mrs.* E. S. †$1.50. Duffield.

Reflections of nature with affection taught. Gibson, C. B. 60 c. C. B. Gibson.

Reflections on the French Revolution. *See* Burke, Edm.

Reflections on the Psalms. Ruutz-Rees, J. E. 50 c. Newson.

Reflex neuroses. Shute, D. K. (Not for sale.) George Washington Univ.

REFORESTATION.
See Forests and forestry;—Pine trees.

Reform. Clairmont, R. de. $1. Roxburgh.

Reform in life insurance taxation; insurance journals of two countries indorse conference held in New York, December 4th and 5th, 1908, and point out necessity for continued activity in this campaign for the policyholders. '09(O2) O. pap., gratis. Assoc. Life.

Reform of wayward youth. MacDonald, A. Univ. Press, (Sewanee.)

REFORM SCHOOLS.
MacDonald, A. Reform of wayward youth. Univ. Press, (Sewanee.)

REFORMATION.
Calvin and the Reformation. *$1.25 net. Revell.
Fleming, D: H. The Reformation in Scotland; causes, characteristics and consequences. $3 net. Doran
Gairdner, J. Lollardy and the Reformation in England. 2 v. *$6.50 net. Macmillan.
Hurlbert, E. B. English Reformation and Puritanism. *$2.50 net. Univ. of Chic.
Littell, J: S. Historians and the English Reformation. $2.50 net. Young Churchman.
Lumsden, C. B. Dawn of modern England; being hist. of the Reformation in England, 1509-1525. $3 net. Longmans.
Schapiro, J. S. Social reform and the Reformation. $1.25. Longmans.
Sure word of prophecy; sermons and addresses on the Reformation and the Lutheran church. *85 c. net. Germ. Lit. Bd.
Tanner, E. M. Renaissance and the Reformation. 90 c. Oxford Univ.
See also Church history;—Protestantism;—Renaissance;—*also* Luther, M.;—*also* names of countries and churches.

REFORMED CHURCH.
Stoutenburgh, H. A. Documentary hist. of the Dutch congregation of Oyster Bay. [10 pamphlets.] $5.50. H: A. Stoutenburgh.
See also St. Stephen's Reformed Church.

Reformed Church in the United States. *Classis of North Carolina.* Historic sketch of the Reformed Church in North Carolina; with an introd. by the late G: W: Welker, D.D. '08(Ap25) c. il. pors. 12°, $1. Ref. Ch. Pub.

Reformed Episcopal Church. Book of common praise; hymnal companion to the prayer book; with accompanying tunes, comp. and harmonies rev. by W: J. Boehm. '07, [1908.] (D) 22+538 p. 8°, 90 c. Armstrong-K.

Reformer by proxy. Parkinson, J: $1.50. Lane.

REFRACTION.
See Eye.

REFRACTION INDEX.
See Light.

Refractive and motor mechanism of the eye. Souter, W: N. $2. Keystone Pub.

REFRACTORIES.
See Harbison-Walker Refractories Co.

REFRIGERATION.
Anderson, J. W. Refrigeration. **$2.25 net. Longmans.
Armstrong Cork Co., Pittsburg. Nonpareil corkboard insulation for cold storage warehouses, abattoirs, breweries, ice plants, etc. gratis. Armstrong Cork.
Dickerman, C:, *and* Boyer, F. H. Refrigeration. $1. Am. Sch. Corr.

REFRIGERATION.—*Continued.*
Ewing, J: A. Mechanical production of cold. *$3.25 net. Putnam.
Gueth, O. Refrigerating engineer's pocket manual. $1.50. O. Gueth.
Hastings. Cold-storage evaporimeter. (Add. Superintendent for price.) U. S., Supt. of Docs.
Levey, J: Refrigeration memoranda. 75 c. Nickerson & C.
Manns, W. H. Erecting and operating engineer's guide; testing of apparatus and general operation of an ice-making or refrigerating plant. $1. W. H. Manns.
Schmidt, L: M. Principles and practice of artificial ice making and refrigeration. *$3 net. Phila. Bk.
Selfe, N. Machinery for refrigeration. $3.50; *$4.50 net. Nickerson & C.
Taylor, A. J. W-. Pocketbook of refrigeration and ice making. $1.50. Henley.
United States. *Bu. of Chemistry.* Use of cold storage; letter from the Secretary of Agriculture transmitting certain data on cold storage and cold storage products, by Dr. H. W. Wiley. '10(Jl) 23 p. 2 pl. 8°.
Voorhees, G. T. Indicating the refrigerating machine. $1; $1.50. Nickerson & C.
See also Dairy.

Refugee (The). Gilson, C: J. L: $1.25 net. Century Co.

REFUSE AND REFUSE DISPOSAL.
Morse, W: F. Collection and disposal of municipal waste. $5. Municipal Journ.
Springborn, W: J. Cleveland garbage disposal plant. gratis. W: J: Springborn.

REGENERATION.
See Salvation.

REGGIO, Sicily.
See Messina disaster.

REGIMENTAL HISTORIES.
See under names of countries and states.

REGINA CAELI.
See Easter.

Regional leaders. Nash, E. B. $1.50. Boericke & T.

REGISTRATION DESK.
See Librarians and libraries.

Registration of city school children. Haney, J: D. $1.50. Teachers' Coll.

Regulation and repair of piano and player mechanism. White, W: B. $1.50. E. L. Bill.

Regulation of the liquor traffic. American Academy of Political and Social Science. $1. Am. Acad. Pol. Sci.

Reich, Emil.
Atlas antiquus; with elaborate text to each map, and full index. '09(Je19) maps, 8°, *$3 net. Macmillan.
Foundations of modern Europe: 12 lectures del. in the University of London. 2d rev. ed. '08(Ap25) c. D. **$1.50 net. Macmillan.
General history of western nations from 5000 B.C. to 1900 A.D. pt. 1, Antiquity, 2 v. '08(My2) 8°, *$4 net. Macmillan.
Woman through the ages. '09(My22) 2 v., il. *$7 net. Dutton.
See also Seyffert, Oscar.

Reichel, Willy.
Occultist's travels. '08(O10) c. por. D. $1. Fenno.

Reichenbach, Mathilde.
Das Rothkäppchen: spiel in fünf scenen. '09(Je19) S. (Modern lang. ser.) *25 c. net. Crowell.
Deux comédies enfantines, (Le petit chaperon rouge; Jean et Marguerite;) ed. by J. E. Mansion. '10(Ja29) S. (Crowell's shorter French texts.) *25 c. net. Crowell.

Reichert, E: Tyson, M.D., and Brown, Amos Peaslee.
Differentiation and specificity of corresponding proteins and other vital substances in relation to biological classification and organic evolution: the crystallography of hemoglobins. '10(F5) il. Q. $9. Carnegie.

Reichsbank (The), 1876-1900. '10(Je) 362 p. 8°. U. S., Supt. of Docs.

REICHSTADT, *Duc* de.
Kubinyi, V. v. King of Rome: [Napoleon II.] (For private circulation.) Knickerbocker Press.

Reid, Christian, pseud.
See Tiernan, *Mrs.* Frances Christine Fisher.

Reid, D:
See Reid, J: Simpson.

Reid, Rev. D: Collins.
Effective industrial reform. '10(Ja22) c. il. D. $1.35. D. C. Reid.

Reid, G: Archdall O'Brien.
Laws of heredity. '10(Jl9) 8°, $5.50 net. Macmillan.

Reid, Harvey.
Thomas Cox. '09, [1910.] (Jl) 8+257 p. por. 8°, (Iowa bibliographical ser.) $2. State Hist., Ia.
"Notes and references" (42 p.).

Reid, J. Eadie.
Sir J. E. Millais. '10(Je4) il. pors., 12°, (Makers of British art.) $1.25. Scribner.

Reid, Jane Brewster.
Owls of St. Ursula's; story for girls. '10 (Ap2) c. il. D. $1.25. Baker & T.

Reid, J: Simpson.
Mechanical drawing, elem. and advanced. '10(O22) c. figs. 8°, $2 net. Wiley.
— **and D:**
Text-book of mechanical drawing and elem. machine design. 2d ed., rev. and enl. '08(N14) c. il. tabs., 8°, $3. Wiley.

Reid, Legh Wilber.
Elements of the theory of algebraic numbers; with introd. and notes by D: Hilbert. '10(N19) 8°, $3.50 net. Macmillan.

Reid, Captain Mayne.
Afloat in the forest. '08(Je27) 12°, (Young America lib.) 50 c. Hurst.
Child wife. '08(Jl18) 12°, †$1. Dutton.
Desert home. '08(Ag15) 12°, †$1. Dutton.
Guerilla chief, and other tales. '08(D12) 12°, $1. Dutton.
Gwen Wynn. '08(Ag15) 12°, †$1. Dutton.
Lone ranch. '08(O17) 12°, †$1. Dutton.
Lost Lenore. '08(Jl18) 12°, †$1. Dutton.
Ocean waifs. '08(Ap4) 12°, †$1. Dutton.

Reid, Captain Mayne.—*Continued.*
The scalp-hunters; romance of New Mexico. '10(Mr26) il. 8°, (Bowman's illustrated lib. of world famous books.) $1. Bowman.

Reid, W: Maxwell.
Lake George and Lake Champlain; the war trail of the Mohawk and the battleground of France and England in their contest for the control of North America. '10(Je11) c. il. O. $3.50 net. Putnam.

Reign of the negative. Oppenheimer, F. J. $2 net. Moods.

Reiley, Katharine Campbell.
Studies in the philosophical terminology of Lucretius and Cicero. '09(S) c. 9+133 p. 12°, (Columbia Univ. studies in classical philology.) *$1.25 net. Columbia Univ.

Reilly, F: Jos.
"Right-dress!": a manual of simple drill regulations for schools. '09(My) c. 96 p. il. 12°, 50 c. Educ. Pub.

Reilly, Ja. M.
Veldt, the lion hunter; comic opera whirl. '10(O8) c. il. front. 12°, $1.25. B'way Pub.

Reilly, T. S.
Locomotive firing. '09(Je5) c. il. 8°, 50 c. Crandall Pub.

Reimensnyder, Rev. J: Milton.
Ancient history and the Bible: review of important chronological data. '09(Ap10) c. 12°, 35 c.; pap., 20 c. Lutheran Pub.

Reinach, Salomon.
Orpheus; general hist. of religions; [tr.] from the French by Florence Simmonds; rev. by the author. '10(F12) front. O. *$3 net. Putnam.

Reincarnated: [poem.] Beede, C: G. $1.25. Newport Pub.

REINCARNATION.
Atkinson, W: W. Reincarnation and the law of Karma. $1.10. Advanced Thought.
Bertholet, A. Transmigration of souls. *75 c. net. Harper.
Ingalese, R: *and* I. From incarnation to re-incarnation. Rev. ed. $2. Occult Bk.
Rogers, L. W. Logic of Reincarnation.—Reincarnation from the scientific viewpoint. ea., 10 c. Theosophical Bk.
See also Buddha and Buddhism;—Hinduism;—Theosophy.

Reinecke, L.
See Harris, Gilbert Dennison.

Reinertsen, Emma May Alexander, ["Mrs. R. C. Reinertsen;" "Gale Forest."]
Five cousins in California; sunny picture of a sunny land. '09(D25) c. il. pors. 12°, $1.50. C. M. Clark.

Reinertsen, Mrs. R. C.
See Reinertsen, Emma May Alexander.

REINFORCED CONCRETE.
See Concrete;—Earthwork.

Reinhard, Ph.
See Banderet, P.

Reinhardt, L., ed.
See Hills, Clarence Elijah.

Reinhardt, Victor.
Drummer boy of Shiloh. '10(Je4) c. 8°, 25 c. V. Reinhardt.

Reinsch, Paul S:, ed.
Readings on American federal government. '09(Je5) c. O. $2.75. Ginn.
Young citizen's reader. '09(Mr6) c. il. D. 60 c. B: H. Sanborn.
Reisner, Christian Fichthorne, D.D.
The preacher-persuader. '10(D17) c. 16°, 50 c. Jennings.
Social plans for young people. '08(Je6) D. *75 c. net. Jennings.
Week-day prayers. '09(Mr6) c. nar. T. *35 c. net. Jennings.
Reissig, Carl, Jelliffe, Smith Ely, and others, comps.
Standard family physician; practical international encyclopedia of medicine and hygiene especially prep. for the household; with the assistance of many American, British, Canadian and German specialists in the treatment of diseases and experts in medicine and surgery. 3 v. '09(My) il. 4°, $15. Funk.
Reiter, Harriet G.
Story of Lincoln. [1910.] (Je) c. 31 p. il. por. 12°, (School classic ser.) 5 c. Paine.
Relation between the magnitude of stimulus and the time of reaction. Froeberg, S. 35 c. Science Pr., (N. Y.)
Relation of healing to law. Womer, P. P. $1.25. Magnum Bonum.
Relation of medicine to philosophy. Moon, R. O. *$1.50 net. Longmans.
Relation of nature study and science teaching. Bigelow, M. A. (Add. author for price.) M. A. Bigelow.
Relation of railroads to the state. Acworth, W: M. gratis. Allen, L. & S.
Relation of speculation to business. Armstrong, C. gratis. C. Armstrong.
Relation of the trade school to the trade. Sayward, W: H: gratis. S: F. Hubbard.
Relations between chemical constitution and some physical properties. Smiles, S: $4 net. Longmans.
Relations of Christian denominations to colleges. Pritchett, H: S. gratis. Carnegie Found.
Relations of the United States and Spain. Chadwick, F. E. **$4 net. Scribner.
RELAXATION.
See Hygiene.
Released. Eagan, A. L. 75 c. B'way Pub.
Reliable candy teacher. Rigby, W. O. $2. W. O. Rigby.
Reliable Incubator and Brooder Company. Success with poultry. 6th ed. '08(Jl11) c. il. F. pap., $1. Reliable Incubator.
Reliable Poultry Journal Publishing Co. Chick book, from the breeding pen through the shell to maturity. '09(Ap3) c. il. 4°, 50 c. Reliable Poultry Journ.
Relics and memorials of London City. Ogilvy, J. S. $5 net. Dutton.
Religio-medical masquerade. Peabody, F: W: $1. Hancock Press.
Religio medici. *See* Browne, *Sir* T.
RELIGION.
Ames, E: S. Psychology of religious experience. $2.50 net. Houghton M.
Antrim, E. M. Greatest things in religion. 75 c. Jennings.

RELIGION.—*Continued.*
Baker, R. S. Spiritual unrest. $1.35 net. Stokes.
Best, N. R. Beyond the natural order: essays on prayer, miracles and the incarnation. *75 c. net. Revell.
Black, S: C: Plain answers to religious questions modern men are asking. 75 c. Presb. Bd.
Bowne, B. P. Essence of religion. $1.50 net. Houghton M.
Bridgman, H. A. Real religion. 75 c. net. Pilgrim Press.
Brierley, J. Aspects of the spiritual.—Side lights on religion. ea., *$1.40 net. Whittaker.
Cabot, R: C. Psychotherapy in its relation to religion. **25 c. net. Moffat.
Chamberlin, G. L., *and* Kern, M. R. Child religion in song and story. [v. 2,] Walks with Jesus in His home country. $1.38. Univ. of Chic.
Chapman, E: M. English literature in account with religion, 1800-1900. **$2 net. Houghton M.
Church, S: H. Religious progress in America. 25 c. R. P. Morris.
Coke, H: J: Domain of belief. $2.50 net. Macmillan.
Colville, W: W. J. Ancient mysteries and modern revelation. $1 net. Fenno.
Crowthers, S: M. Making of religion. *40 c. net. Am. Unitarian.
Curtis, C: N. Epoch in the spiritual life. *$1.25 net. Eaton & M.
Dawson, G: E. **Child and his religion. *75 c. net. Univ. of Chic.**
Dole, C: F. Coming religion. $1 net. Small.
Drawbridge, C. L. Is religion undermined? 50 c. Longmans.
Eliot, C: W: Religion of the future. *50 c. net. Ball Pub. Co.; Stokes.
Eliot, C: W: Religion of the future. 75 c. J: W. Luce.
Elwang, W: W. Social function of religious belief. $1. Univ. of Mo.
Foster, G: B. Function of religion in man's struggle for existence. *$1 net. Univ of Chic.
Galloway, G: Principles of religious development. *$3 net. Macmillan.
Gordon, G. A. **Religion and miracle. **$1.30 net. Houghton M.**
Guiness, H: G. **"On the rock"; the certainties of religion contrasted with the speculations of philosophy. *$1 net. Revell.**
Guthrie, K. S. **Spiritual message of literature. $1. Open Court.**
Harris, T. Banker's views on religious and other important subjects. (Add. pub for price.) W. P. Harvey.
Hastings, J., *ed.* Encyclopedia of religion and ethics. In 10 or 12 v. v. 1, 2. ea., $7; $9. (Sold in sets only.) Scribner.
Hinckle, W: A. Evolution of religion. 80 c. net. Sherman, F.
Hoffman, F. S. Sphere of religion. **$1.75 net. Putnam.
Holden, J: S. Supposition and certainty. *75 c. net. Revell.

RELIGION.—*Continued.*

Holley, C: D. Great discovery of four worlds and their inhabitants: external world, world of mind within us, world of eternity, world of everlasting punishment. 75 c. C: D. Holley.

Horton, R. F. My belief: answers to certain religious difficulties. *$1.25 net. Revell.

Jevons, F. B. Introd. to the study of comparative religion. **$1.50 net. Macmillan.

Johnston, H. A. Famine and the bread. (Add. pubs. for price.) Y. M. C. A.

Jones, A. T. Divine right of individuality in religion. 25 c. A. T. Jones.

Jordan, D: S. Religion of a sensible American. *80 c. net. Am. Unitarian.

Kelman, J. Courts of the temple. 35 c. net. Revell.

King, I. Development of religion. **$1.75 net. Macmillan.

Lang, A. Making of religion. $2. Longmans.

Law, W: Liberal and mystical writings. *$1 net. Longmans.

Leckie, J. H. Authority in religion. *$2 net. Scribner.

Leuba, J. H. Psychological origin and nature of religion. *40 c. net. Open Court.

Lodge, *Sir* O. Reason and belief. $1.25 net. Moffat.

McConnell, F. J. Religious certainty. $1 net. Eaton & M.

M'Fadyen, J: E. City with foundations. *$1.25 net. Armstrong.

Maddox, F. E. Passing of medievalism in religion. 60 c. Texarkanian.

Mitchell, H: B., *comp.* Talks on religion. **$1.50 net. Longmans.

National Federation of Religious Liberals. Unity of the spirit. 75 c. Nat. Fed. Rel. Liberals.

New Schaff-Herzog encyclopedia of religious knowledge. In 12 v. v. 1-8. ea., $5: per set, $60; shp., $84; hf. mor., $96; full mor., $108. Funk.

Orelli, H. C. v. Peculiarity of the religion of the Bible. *40 c. net. Eaton & M.

Paramânanda, *Swami.* True spirit of religion is universal. (Add. pubs. for price.) Vedanta.

Ramsay, *Sir* W: M. Luke the physician, and other studies in the history of religion. *$3 net. Armstrong.

Rashdall, H. Philosophy and religion. *75 c. net. Scribner.

Reinach, S. Orpheus; general hist. of religions. *$3 net. Putnam.

Remensnyder, J. B: Post-apostolic age and current religious problems. $1.25. Lutheran Pub.

Richardson, E. C., *comp. and ed.* Alphabetical subject index and index encyclopædia to periodical articles on religion, 1890-1899. $10. Hartford Sem., [Scribner.]

Roche, J. T: Business side of religion. *15 c. net. Wiltzius.

Roosevelt, T. Americanism in religion. 35 c. E. E. Swadener.

RELIGION.—*Continued.*

Ross, G: A. J., *and others.* Religion and the modern mind. *$1.50 net. Armstrong.

Rumball, E. A. Jesus and modern religion. *75 c. net. Open Court.

St. John, C: E. Religion of the dawn. 60 c. Am. Unitarian.

Shaw, C: G. Precinct of religion in the culture of humanity. *$2 net. Macmillan.

Sihler, E. G. Testimonium animae or Greek and Roman before Jesus Christ. **$2.25 net. Stechert.

Smith, M. R. Common-sense in religion. $1. Longmans.

Stelzle, C:, *and others.* Social application of religion. *75 c. net. Jennings.

Stimson, H: A. Behind the world and beyond. $1.25 net. Eaton & M.

Strong, J. My religion in everyday life. 50 c. net. Baker & T.

Tisdall, W. St. C. Comparative religion. *40 c. net. Longmans.

Torrey, R. A. Practical and perplexing questions. *50 c. net. Revell.

Tyler, W. F. Dimensional idea as an aid to religion. 50 c. Fenno.

Van Ormer, A. B. B. Studies in religious nurture. $1. Lutheran Pub.

Vrooman, H. Religion rationalized. v. 1. 75 c. Nunc Licet.

Wagner, C: Home of the Soul. **$1.20 net. Funk.

Watson, J: Philosophical basis of religion. *$3 net. Macmillan.

Wenley, R. M. Modern thought and the crisis in belief. **$1.50 net. Macmillan.

What shall I believe? **$1 net. Presb. Bd.

Whiton, J. M. Interludes, ethical, social and theological. *$1.40 net. Whittaker.

Womer, P. P. Valid religion for the times. $1. B'way Pub.

Wrixon, *Sir* H: J: Religion of the common man. *$1 net. Macmillan.

See also Agnosticism; — Bible; — Catechism; — Christian life;—Christianity;—Church history; — Colleges and universities; — Conscience; — Consolation;—Devotional exercises;—Ethics;—Evil;—Faith;—Fine arts;—Future life;—God; — Holy Spirit;—Hymns; — Immortality; — Indians;—Jesus Christ;—Medicine and religion; —Miracles;—Missions and missionaries;—Modernism;—Monasticism; — Mysticism;— Mythology;—Philosophy;—Prayer;—Religion and science;—Religions;—Religious education;—Religious orders; — Revivals;—Sacraments;—Saints; —Sermons;—Sin;—Skepticism;—Social science; —Souls; — Suggestion (Mental); — Sunday;— Theology;—Theosophy; — Totemism;— Truth; —Worship;—*also* names of churches and countries;—*also* Little books on religion.

Religion and art in ancient Greece. Gardner, E. A. 75 c. net. Harper.

Religion and life: chapel addresses by members of the faculty of the Meadville Theological School. '09(Je26) c. D. *$1.10 net. Sherman, F.

RELIGION AND MEDICINE.

See Medicine and religion.

Religion and medicine. Worcester, E. **$1.50 net. Moffat.

Religion and medicine publications. D. pap., **25 c. net. Moffat.

—Achorn. Some physical disorders having mental origin.

Religion and medicine publications.—Cont.
—Cabot. Psychotherapy and its relation to religion.
—Coriat. Some familiar forms of nervousness.
—James. Energies of men.
—McComb. Healing ministry of the church.
—Macomber. History of the Emmanuel movement.
—Mumford. Some end-results of surgery.
Religion and miracle. Gordon, G: A. $1.30 net. Houghton M.
RELIGION AND SCIENCE.
Bohannan, W: J: H. Nephilim. $1.50. R. A. Silk.
Butler, H. E. Goal of life; or, science and revelation. $2. Esoteric.
Ladd, H. O. Trend of scientific thought away from religious beliefs. 75 c. Badger.
Nevill, S: T. Spiritual philosophy. *50 c. net. Longmans.
Palmer, W: S. Studies in the teaching of religion. *40 c. net. Longmans.
Phinn, J: Evolution of the atmosphere as a proof of design and purpose in the creation and of the existence of a personal God. *$1.25 net. Indust.
Randall, J: H. New philosophy of life series. 7 v. ea., 60 c.; $1.25. Caldwell.
Raymond, G: L. Psychology of inspiration: attempt to distinguish religious from scientific truth. **$1.40 net. Funk.
Towne, E: C. Headlights of new knowledge, new science, new religion, new education. 50 c. E: C. Towne.
Tyndall, C: H. Electricity and its similitudes: analogy of phenomena, natural and spiritual. *$1 net. Revell.
See also Evolution; — Medicine and religion; — Scientists.
Religion and worship of the Synagogue. Oesterley, W: O. E. *$3 net. Scribner
Religion in New Netherland. Zwierlein, F: G. $2 net. J: P. Smith Pr.
Religion of a democrat. Zueblin, C: *$1 net. B: W. Huebsch.
Religion of ancient Palestine. Cook, S. A. *40 c. net. Open Court.
Religion of Evelyn Hastings. Cory, V. $1.50. M. Kennerley.
Religion of Israel. Loisy, A. $1.50. Putnam.
Religion of Ruskin. Burgess, W: *$2 net. Revell.
Religion of science lib. 62 v. v. 46, Enquiry concerning the principles of morals, by D: Hume; v. 48, Treatise concerning the principles of human knowledge, by G: Berkeley. [1910.] (Je) 12°, pap., ea., 30 c. Open Court.
Religion of science lib. 12°. Open Court.
—Aristotle. Aristotle on his predecessors. 40 c.
—Fichte. Vocation of man. 30 c.
Religion of the civilized world and Judaism. Kisch, H. J. 40 c. Bloch.
Religion of the dawn. St. John, C: E. 60 c. net. Am. Unitarian.
Religion of the Luiseño Indians. Du Bois, C. G. $1.25. Univ. of Cal.
Religion of the post-exilic prophets. Bennett, W: H:, *ed.* *$2 net. Scribner.
Religion of the spirit. Pierce, U. G. B. 25 c. Unitarian Club.
Religion of the threshold. Mackay, D. S. *$1.50 net. Armstrong.
Religion of Washington, Jefferson and Franklin. Mangasarian, M. M. 10 c. Independent Religious.
RELIGIONS.
International Congress for the History of Religions. Transactions of the third International Congress. $6.75. Oxford Univ.
Lloyd, A. S. Christianity and religions. **75 c. net. Dutton.
Marshall, E: A. Christianity and non-Christian religions compared. 50 c. Bible Inst.
Martindale, C. C., *ed.* Lectures on the hist. of religions. ea., 60 c. net; per set, $2.40 net. Herder.
Randall, J: H., *and* Smith, J. G., *eds.* Unity of religions. $2 net. Crowell.
Sanday, W: Address del. at the opening of the Christian section of the Third International Congress of the History of Religions. 27 c. Oxford Univ.
Ward, D. J. H. Classifications of religion. 75 c. Open Court.
See also Buddha and Buddhism;—China;—Christianity;— Egypt; — Hinduism; — Jews; — Mohammed and Mohammedanism;—Mormonism;—Oriental religions;—Rosary;—Semitic religioins;—Sikh religion;—Spiritualism; — Theosophy;—Zoroaster;—*also* Babylonia;—*also* Schwenckfeld von Ossig, C:
Religions ancient and modern. 8°, *40 c. net. Open Court.
—Abrahams. Judaism.
—Ali. Islam.
—Anwyl. Celtic religion.
—Ashton. Shinto: the ancient religion of Japan.
—Bailey. Religion of ancient Rome.
—Barnett. Hindusim.
—Clodd. Animism.
—Cook. Religion of ancient Palestine.
—Craigie. Scandinavian religion.
—Davids. Early Buddhism.
—Giles. Ancient China.
—Haddon. Magic and fetishism.
—Harrison. Ancient Greece.
—Leuba. Psychological origin and nature of religion.
—Petrie. Ancient Egypt.
—Picton. Pantheism.
—Pinches. Babylonia and Assyria.
—Slack. Early Christianity.
—Spence. Religion of ancient Mexico and Peru.
—Squier. Mythology of ancient Britain and Ireland.
Religious and hospitable rite of feet washing. Fleming, W. L. gratis. W. L. Fleming.
Religious and monastic life explained. Gueranger, P. L. P. *50 c. net. Herder.
Religious attitude and life in Islam. Macdonald, D. B. *$1.75 net. Univ. of Chic.
RELIGIOUS CEREMONIAL.
See Worship.
Religious certainty. McConnell, F. J. $1 net. Eaton & M.
RELIGIOUS CORPORATIONS.
See names of states.

RELIGIOUS EDUCATION.
Coe, G: A. Progress in religious and moral education. 25 c. Rel. Educ.
Drane, A. T. Christian schools and scholars. $6 net. Stechert.
Drawbridge, C. L. Religious education. *90 c. net; *50 c. net. Longmans.
Fountain of life, to Catholic teachers by one. *35 c. net. Longmans.
Gailor, T: F. Christian church and education. $1 net. Whittaker.
Halpin, P. A. Christian pedagogy. $1.50. J. F. Wagner.
Kelsey, F. W. Problem of religious instruction in state universities. (Add. author for price.) F. W. Kelsey.
St. John, E: P. Stories and story-telling in moral and religious education. *60 c. net. Pilgrim Press.
Scannell, T: B. Priest's studies. *$1.20 net. Longmans.
Semple, H: C. What times! What morals! Where on earth are we? 35 c. Benziger.
Smith, J: T. Training of a priest. **$1.50 net. Longmans.
Smith, W: W. Religious education. *$2 net. Young Churchman.
Snow, A. B. Movement for reform in teaching of religion in the public schools of Saxony. Gov. Pr. Off.
See also Bible; — Children; — Priests; — Sunday-school.

RELIGIOUS HISTORY.
See Church history.

RELIGIOUS LIBERTY.
James, C: F. Struggle for religious liberty in Virginia. $1.25. Review and Herald Pub
See also Calvinism;—Modernism;—Pilgrims.

RELIGIOUS MANIA.
See Insanity.

RELIGIOUS ORDERS.
Champagnat, J. B. M. Qualities of a good superior. *$1.25 net. Herder.
Lacey, T: J. Beginning at Jerusalem; studies in historic communions of Christendom. 60 c. Gorham.
See also Monasticism.

Religious practices of the Diegneño Indians. Waterman, T. T. 80 c. Univ. of Cal.
Religious progress in America. Church, S: H. 25 c. R. P. Morris.
Religious spirits of the American Indian. Alexander, H. B. 30 c. Open Court.
Religious teachers of Greece. Adam, J. *$4 net. Scribner.
Religious teaching of Jesus. Montefiore, C. G. 75 c. net. Macmillan.
Religious views of Abraham Lincoln. Pennell, O. H:, *comp.* 75 c.; 25 c. Timby.
Religious work for boys. '08(Ja4) D. pap., 15 c. Y. M. C. A.
Reliques of ancient English poetry. *See* Percy, T:, *ed.*
Relyea classics. 30 v. '10(N) fronts. 16°, ooze, ea., 75 c. Barse & H.
Remaking the Mississippi. Mathews, J: L. **$1.75 net. Houghton M.
Remarkable fertilizer. Leavens, G. D. (Add. pubs. for price.) Coe-M.
Remarque ser. of literary masterpieces. T. 40 c.; 75 c. Caldwell.
—Burnand, *ed.* Poems from *Punch.*
—Lubbock. Duty of happiness.—Value of time.
—Montagu. Selected letters.
—Ruskin. Sesame and lilies.—Unto this last.

Rembrandt van Rhyn, Paul.
Etchings; with introduction by A. M. Hind. '08(Mr14) il. 4°, (Great etchers ser.) *$2.50 net. Scribner.

REMBRANDT VAN RHYN, Paul.
Bell, M. Drawings of Rembrandt. *$2.50 net. Scribner.
Israels, J. Rembrandt. *65 c. net. Stokes.
Muther, R: Rembrandt. $1.50 net; $1.75 net. Caldwell.

Remedies by selected cases. Mordecai, S: F. $6. State Journ. Co.

Remensnyder, Junius B:, D.D.
Heavenward: a guide for youth. New rev. ed. '08(My16) c. 12°, 50 c. Lutheran Pub.
Mysticism: psychology, history and relation to Scripture, church and Christian life. '09(My8) c. D. pap., 25 c. Germ. Lit. Bd.
Post-apostolic age and current religious problems. '10(Ja29) c. 12°, $1.25. Lutheran Pub.

Remick, Grace May.
Glenloch girls. '09(N13) c. il. D. †$1.25. Penn Pub. Co.
Glenloch girls abroad. '10(D3) c. il. D. $1.25. Penn Pub. Co.

Reminders of Walks with Jesus in His home country. Chamberlin, G. L. 45 c. Univ. of Chic.

Remington, Arth.
See Washington. Remington & Ballinger's annot. codes.
—, **rep.** *See* Washington [State.] *Sup. ct. Repts.*

Remington, Harold.
Treatise on the bankruptcy law of the United States. v. 1. '08(Mr): v. 2 (My); v. 3, Supp. '10(D) c. O. ea., *$6 net. Michie.

Reminiscences. Pell, A. *$5 net. Dutton.
Reminiscences. Beckwitz, W: L. $1. Mail Order.
Reminiscences and sketches. Smith, C: F. *$1.25 net. Pub. Ho. of M. E. Ch., So.
Reminiscences and sketches of Confederate times. Powe, J. H. H. P. Lynch.
Reminiscences of a K. C. Crispe, T: E: $3.50 net. Little, B. & Co.
Reminiscences of a pioneer in the Rock River country. Coe, E. D. 35 c. State Hist., Wis.
Reminiscences of a ranchman. Bronson, E. B. $1.50. McClurg.
Reminiscences of Ennius in Silius Italicus. Woodruff, L. B. 40 c. net. Macmillan.
Reminiscences of Oxford. Tuckwell, W: *$2 net. Dutton.
Reminiscences of my life in Persia. Jewett, M. $1. Torch Press.
Reminiscences of Scottish life and character. Ramsay, E: B. B. *$2.75 net. McClurg.
Reminiscences of Seattle. Phelps, T: S. *$2 net; *60 c. net. A Harriman.

Reminiscences of the past sixty years. Alexander, J: B. $2. J: B. Alexander, (N. C.)
Remodeling Roanoke. Nolen, J: $1 net. J: Nolen.
Removal of the Cherokee Indians from Georgia. Lumpkin, W. 2 v. (Add. pubs. for price.) Dodd.
Remsen, Dan. Smith.
On the preparation and contest of wills. '08(O) 880 p. 8°, **$6 net. Baker, V. & Co.
Remsen, Ira.
College text-book of chemistry. 2d ed., rev. '08(O10) c. il. 8°, (American science ser.) $2.25. Holt.
Introd. to the study of chemistry. 8th ed., rev. and enl. '09(D) c. 26+574 p. il. 12°, (American science ser., briefer course.) $1.25. Holt.
Introd to the study of the compounds of carbon; or, organic chemistry 5th revision. '09(D25) c. 12°, $1.20. Heath.
REMSEN QUADRANGLE.
See New York State.
Remy, Alfr., comp. and ed.
Spanish composition; comp. and ed., with notes and vocab. '08(Ap18) c. S. (Modern lang. ser.) 60 c. Heath.
Remy, Jean S.
Bible stories for little children in words of one syllable. '09(S) c. 13-132 p. il. 12°, (Altemus' one syllable ser.) 50 c. Altemus.
Story of Jesus told for little children in words of one syllable. '09(S) c. 8+9-96 p. il. 12°, (Altemus' one syllable ser.) 50 c. Altemus.
RENAISSANCE.
Bayley, H. New light on the Renaissance. *$4 net. Dutton.
Brinton, S. Renaissance in Italian art; sculpture and painting. 9 pts. $9 net. Scribner.
Goodyear, W: H: Renaissance and modern art. *$1 net. Macmillan.
Lee, V., *pseud.* Renaissance fancies and studies. *$1.50 net. Lane.
Leo, S. L. French Renaissance in England. $2.50 net. Scribner.
Tanner, E. M. Renaissance and the Reformation. 90 c. Oxford Univ.
See also Architecture;—Ceramics; — Criticism; — Furniture;—Middle Ages.
Renaissance, The. *See* Pater, Wa.
Renaissance furniture. Hessling, E., *ed.* $21. Hessling.
Renaissance in Italian art. Brinton, S. (Add. pubs. for price.) Scribner.
Renaissance masters. Rose, G: B. **$1 net. Putnam.
Renaissance of Hebrew literature. Slouschz, N. $1.25. Jewish Pub.
RENAL DISEASES.
See Kidneys.
Renard, Paul.
Dr. Morgan. '10(Jl30) 12°, 1.50. C. M. Clark.
Rendall, Rev. Gerald H:
Epistle of St. Paul to the Corinthians. '09 (D25) 12°, *$1 net. Macmillan.
René, E.
Hands and how to read them. '10(O) 12°, 50 c. Fenno.

Renegade poet. Thompson, F. $1.25 net. Ball Pub.
Renn, G: Benton.
Practical auditing. 2d ed., rev. and enl. '08(F1) c. por. O. $3. G: B. Renn.
Rennert, Hugo Albert.
Spanish stage in the time of Lope de Vega. '10(F5) c. O. *$3 net. Hispanic Soc.
Renninger, Eliz. D., comp.
Story of Rustem and other Persian hero tales from Firdusi. '09(O9) c. il. D. **$1.50 net. Scribner.
Renouf, V. A.
Outlines of general history. '09(Jl17) il. maps, 8°, *$1.30 net. Macmillan.
Renshaw, Raemer Rex.
4-aminophthalic acid and some of its derivatives. '07, [1908.] (My.) 29+3 p. 8°. (Add. author for price.) R. R. Renshaw.
RENSSELAERSWYCK, N. Y.
See New York State.
Rentschler, Harvey Clayton.
New method for measuring the index of refraction of a gas for different light-waves and the results obtained for several gases. '08, [1910.] (F) 345-359 p. diagrs., 8°, pap., 20 c. Johns Hopkins.
Renwick, G:
Romantic Corsica; wanderings in Napoleon's isle; with a chapter on climbing by T. G. Ouston. '10(Mr26) il. map O. *$3 net. Scribner.
Renwick, W. G.
Marble and marble working: hdbk. for architects, sculptors, marble quarry owners and workers, and all engaged in the building and decorative industries. '09, [1910.] (F) 13+226 p. il. 8°, *$5 net. Van Nostrand.
Reorganization of our colleges. Birdseye, C. F. **$1.75 net. Baker & T.
REPAIRING.
Hasluck, P. N., *ed.* Domestic jobbing 50 c. McKay.
Repeal of the Missouri compromise. Ray, P. O. *$3.50 net. A. H. Clark.
REPENTANCE.
Hall, A. C. A. Forgiveness of sins. **$1 net. Longmans.
Kinsey, R. B. Serious question, what is true repentance? $1. R. B. Kinsey.
Long, S. P. Prepare to meet thy God. 35 c. S. P: Long.
See also Confession;—Conversion;—Penance.
Repertory theatre. Howe, P. P. $1 net. M. Kennerley.
Replanning Reading. Nolen, J: $1 net. J: Nolen.
Report of the Industrial Insurance Commission to the Governor of Illinois. '10(Ap9) O. pap., gratis. J. A. Rose.
Report on the indeterminate franchise for public utilities. Maltbie, M. R. (Add. author for price.) M. R. Maltbie.
REPORTING.
See Journalism;—Stenography.
Repplier, Agnes.
Happy half-century, and other essays. '08 (O3) c. D. **$1.10 net. Houghton M.

REPRESENTATION.
Curtis, R. E. Proportional representation. 25 c. Wisconsin Free Lib.
Representative biographies of English men of letters. Copeland, C. T., *comp. and ed.* **$1.25 net. Macmillan.
Representative cement houses. '10(Ap16) c. il. 8°, 50 c. Universal Portland Cement.
Representative college orations. Shurter, E. D., *ed.* **$1.25 net. Macmillan.
Representative English poems. Brett, G. S., *comp.* *75 c. net. Macmillan.
Representative men. Emerson, R. W. *35 c. net; *70 c. net. Dutton.
Representative men of Ohio. Mercer, J. K. $25. J. K. Mercer.
Reprints of economic tracts; 3d ser.; ed. by Jacob H. Hollander. 8°, pap., subs., per set of 4 tracts, *$2 net. Johns Hopkins.
—Berkeley. The querist.
—Fauquier. Essay on ways and means for raising money for the support of the present war.
—Massie. Essay on the governing causes of the natural rate of interest.
—Vanderlint. Money answers all things.
REPRODUCTION.
See Embryology;—Generative organs;—Heredity.
REPTILES.
Ditmars, R. L. Reptiles of the world. $5 net. Sturgis & W.
Grinnell, J. *and* H. W. Reptiles of Los Angeles County, Cal. gratis. Throop Poly. Inst.
Meek, S. E. Batrachians and reptiles from British East Africa.—Notes on batrachians and reptiles from the islands north of Venezuela. ea., 50 c. Field Museum.
See also Alligator;—Amphibia.
Republic (The). *Sec* Plato.
REPUBLICAN PARTY.
See Parties (*political*).
Requests to charge in civil and criminal cases. Cann, G: T. $6.25. Harrison Co.
Requirements for the ministry. King, E: 15 c. Oxford Univ.
Rescue of Cuba. Draper, A. S. $1. Silver.
Rescue of the Princess Winsome. Johnston, *Mrs.* A. F. 50 c.; 35 c. L. C. Page.
Rescuer. White, P. †$1.50. G: W. Dillingham.
Rescuers (The). Trace, G. $1. Sentinel.
Research in China. *See* Willis, Bailey.
Research lib. 12°. Dutton.
—Abram. Social England in the xvth century. *$1 net.
Researches and experiments in aerial navigation. Langley, S: P. (Add. pubs. for price.) U. S., Supt. of Docs.
Researches concerning Jean Grolier. Le Roux de Lincy, A. J. V. (Add. Club for price.) Grolier Club.
Researches in Assyrian and Babylonian geography. Toffteen, O. A. pt. 1. *$1 net. Univ. of Chic.
Researches in Biblical archæology. *See* Toffteen, Olaf A.
Researches of the Boyden department. Pickering, W: H: $1. Harvard Univ.
Researches on fungi. Buller, A. H. R. *$4 net. Longmans.
Researches on the performance of the screw propeller. Durand, W: F: 75 c. Carnegie.
Resemblance (A). Benedict, C. †$1.50. Putnam.
Reser, Alva O., comp.
Tippecanoe battlefield monument; history of the association formed to promote the enterprise, the action of Congress and the Indiana legislature, work of the commission and the ceremonies at the dedication of the monument. '09(Jl17) il. pors. facsim., 8°, 60 c. A. O. Reser.
Reservation (The). Brooks, A. P. 50 c. A. P. Brooks.
RESERVOIRS.
Merchants' Association of New York. Against construction of more reservoirs in the Croton valley. gratis. Merchants' Assoc.
Schuyler, J. D. Reservoirs: for irrigation, water-power, and domestic water supply. $6. Wiley.
See also Ashokan Reservoir.
Resistance and propulsion of ships. Durand, W: F: $5. Wiley.
Resistance of ships and screw propulsion. Taylor, D: W. *$2.25 net. Macmillan.
Resolving power of objectives. Nutting, P. G. Gov. Pr. Off.
Resources. Kirkham, S. D. **$1.25 net. Putnam.
Respectable sins. Watson, J: $1.25 net. Doran.
RESPIRATION.
See Breathing.
RESPIRATORY ORGANS.
See Lungs.
Responsibility for crime. Parsons, P. A. $1.50. Longmans.
REST.
See Metabolism.
Rest and unrest. Thomas, E: $1 net. Dutton.
Rest cure; a novel. Maxwell, W: B. $1.50. Appleton.
Rest harrow. Hewlett, M. H: $1.50. Scribner.
Restatement of Baptist principles. Jones, P. L. **50 c. net. Am. Bapt.
Restraint of domestic animals. White, G: R. $3.75. G: R. White.
Restraints of trade in patented articles. Gladney, F. Y. $3.50. Mazda.
Restricted diet made palatable. Caro, M. T. $1 net. Ball Pub.
Restriction of immigration. (Rev. ed.) '09, [1910.] 10 p. 12°, (Univ. of Wis. bull.) Univ. of Wis.
Resurgam. Elliot, J: **$1 net. Lane
RESURRECTION.
See Easter;—Future life;—Jesus Christ.
Resurrection: short cantata. Stanford, C: V. 30 c. Ditson.
Resuscitation of subjects in a condition of apparent death. Robinovitch, L. G. $1. Journ. Mental.
Retail advertising. Farrington, F. $1. Byxbee Pub.
RETAIL BUSINESS.
See Business.
Retail Grocers' Association of Richmond. Old Virginia cooking. '10(Mr5) c. O. pap., gratis. Richmond Press.

RETAINING WALLS.
Cain, W: Pract. designing of retaining walls. 50 c. Van Nostrand.
Coleman, T: E. Retaining walls in theory and practice. $2. Spon.
See also Earthwork.

Retardation. Falkner, R. P. (Add. pubs. for price.) Educ. Review.

RETINA.
See Eye.

RETINITIS PIGMENTOSA.
See Eye.

Retreat from Pulaski. Scofield, L. T. (Add. pubs. for price.) Burrows.

RETREATS (*religious*).
See Catholic church.

Retrieval at Panama. Bates, L. W. $5. Technical Lit.

Retrospection. Little, *Mrs.* M. W. $1. B'way Pub.

Retrospections of an active life. Bigelow, J: 3 v. **$12 net. Baker & T.

Retrospective reviews. *See* Le Gallienne, R:

Return of the angels. Morrison, G. H. $1.35 net. Doran.

Return of the "Half Moon." Bruce, K. $1. B'way Pub.

Return of the native. *See* Hardy, T:

Return to Jerusalem. Mord, W. $1. Stokes.

Retz. Post, Van Z. †$1.50. McClure.

Reuben, his book. Pemberton, M. H. $1.15. B'way Pub.

Reuterdahl, Arvid.
Theory and design of reinforced concrete arches. '08(N21) c. il. tabs., 8°, $2. M. C. Clark.

Revealed translation of John's Revelation. Inger, A. J. 50 c. A. J. Inger.

Revel of the toys. Ingalls, H. A. $1.25. Ball Pub.

REVELATION.
See God.

REVELATION (Book of).
See Bible, N. T.

Revelation. Iliowizi, H: $2 net. Dutton.

Revelation and inspiration. Orr, J. *75 c. net. Scribner.

Revelation and inspiration. Seeberg, R. *75 c. net. Harper.

Revelation of "the things that are." Gowen, H. H: *50 c. net. Whittaker.

Revelation to the monk of Evesham Abbey in the year of our Lord eleven hundred ninety-six concerning the places of Purgatory and Paradise; rendered into modern English by Valerian Paget. '09(Ap17) c. D. *$1.50 net. J: McBride.

Revelations in the mountain. Major, *Mrs.* G. $1.50. Cochrane.

Revelations of the life beautiful. Davis, *Mrs.* M. E. C. $1. Baumgardt.

Revell, Alex. Hamilton.
Guaranty of bank deposits: outline of a plan of deposit insurance. '08(O10) (Add. author for price.) A. H. Revell.

Revell, Ellen Isabel.
Lincoln's birthday; exercises for the school-room. '09(Ja9) c. por. 12°, (Teachers' help ser.) 25 c. Educ. Pub.
—, comp. Arbor day exercises for the school-room. '09(Jl10) c. D. (Teachers' help ser.) pap., 25 c. Educ. Pub.
Memorial day exercises for the school-room. '09(Jl10) c. D. (Teachers' help ser.) pap., 25 c. Educ. Pub.

Revellers (The). *See* Euripides.

Revell's idyll envelope ser. D. 25 c. net. Revell.
—Duncan. Christmas eve at Topmast Tickle.
—Gatty. Life beyond.
—Gordon. Crowding out the Christ-child.
—Macfarlane. Centurion's story.—Quest of the yellow pearl.
—Steiner. Cup of Elijah.

Revenge of Gilbert Strange. Wood, W. $1.50. Cassell.

REVENUE.
See Tariff;—Taxation.

Reveries. Hult, G. E. **$1.25 net. Putnam.

Reveries of a bachelor. *See* Mitchell, Donald Grant.

Review of historical publications relating to Canada. *See* Wrong, G: McKinnon.

Review of the baptismal controversy. Mozley, J. B. $1.25. Longmans.

Revision and amendment of state constitutions. Dodd, W. F. $2. Johns Hopkins.

Revision of the *Entelodontidae.* Peterson, O. A. $2.50. Carnegie Museum.

Revival of scholastic philosophy. Perrier, J. L. *$1.75 net. Columbia Univ.

Revival of the gifts of healing. Wood, *Mrs.* A. E. $1.25. Judd & D.

Revival sermons. Johnson, S: D. *$1 net. Revell.

REVIVALS.
Oliver, G: F., *ed.* Out of doors with God: [results of several camp meetings.] 50 c. Chr. Witness.
Swift, P. H. Gospel cheer messages. *$1.25 net. Jennings.
See also Church history;—Conversion;—Pentecostal Union;—*also* Alexander, Charles McCallon;—Sunday, W: A.

Revizór. Gogol, N. V. $1; 50 c. C. P. Franchot.

Revolt of Anne Royle. Martin, *Mrs.* H. R. †$1.50. Century Co.

Revolt of the Tartars. *See* De Quincey, T: Spanish military nun.

Revolution. *See* London, Jack.

Revolutionary ser. *See* Warren, G: A.

REVOLUTIONARY TRIBUNAL.
See French Revolution.

REVOLUTIONARY WAR.
See American Revolution.

REVOLVER.
See Shooting.

Reward of capital. Franklin, M. 25 c. M. Franklin.

Rewards and fairies. Kipling, R. $1.50. Doubleday, P.

Rexford, Eben Eug.
Home garden: book on vegetable and small-fruit growing. '09(Mr13) c. il. D. **$1.25 net. Lippincott.
Indoor gardening. '10(Mr5) c. il. O. **$1.50 net. Lippincott.
Pansies and rosemary: [poems.] '10(N19) c. D. $1.50 net. Lippincott.

Rexford, Edg. Adelbert.
Tables and diagrams for obtaining the resisting moments of eccentric riveted connections. '09(Jl17) c. il. 4°, *$1 net. Engineering News.

Reynard the fox; ed. by T: Cartwright. '08 (Ag15) 16°, (Every child's lib.) 50 c. Dutton.

Reynolds, C: Bingham.
Standard guide to Cuba; with maps, il., routes of travel, history, and an Eng.-Spanish phrase book. '08(Ag15) il. maps, 12°, pap., 50 c. Foster & R.

Reynolds, C: L., comp.
Mineral location, annot. United States, California, Oregon, Nevada, Arizona; syllabi of leading decisions. '08(N) c. 70 p. O. $1.50; pap., $1. Dettner-Travers.

Reynolds, J. B.
Ireland: elem. rational geography, Ireland and Great Britain in outline. '10(Je18) maps, 12°, 50 c. net. Macmillan.

Reynolds, J: Hugh, and Thomas, D: Yancey.
Hist. of the University of Arkansas. '10 (Ag27) c. il. pors. 8°, $2. Univ. of Ark.

Reynolds, J: Phillips.
The cruise of the "Golden Eagle," by one of the party: [yachting story of the Kiel regatta, 1907.] '07, [1908.] c. 87 p. pls. O. pap.. (Not for sale.) J: P. Reynolds.

Reynolds, Sir Joshua.
Discourses, to which are added his letters to *The Idler;* with an introd. by Austin Dobson. Pocket ed. '09(Mr6) por. S. (World's classics.) 35 c. Oxford Univ.

REYNOLDS, *Sir* Joshua.
Baldry, A. L. Sir Joshua Reynolds. *$2 net. Doran.
Osborn, M. Joshua Reynolds. [German text.] $1.35. Lemcke.

Reynolds, Kate Beatty.
Outline lessons in English hist. '09(D18) c. O. 75 c. Putnam.

Reynolds, Mrs. L. Baillie, [formerly Gertrude M. Robins.]
False position. '09(Je5) D. $1.50. Brentano's.
Out of the night. '10(Jl2) c. D. $1.20 net. Doran.
Supreme test. '08(N21) c. D. †$1.50. Brentano's.

Reynolds, M. H., and Beebe, W. L.
Dissemination of tuberculosis by the manure of infected cattle. '08(D) 38-62 p. il. 8°, (Univ. of Minn., Agricultural Experiment Station.) pap., gratis. Univ. of Minn.

Reynolds, Marcus Mathias.
Investor's catechism. 2d ed., rev. and enl. '09(S4) c. 12°, $1. Moody's Mag.

Reynolds, Myra.
Treatment of nature in English poetry bet. Pope and Wordsworth. [2d ed.] '10 (Ja8) c. O. *$2.50 net. Univ. of Chic.

Reynolds, Rollo G:, and Libby, C: Otis, jr.
King of U-Kan; musical comedy, with music by W. H. Golde; presented at junior promenade and commencement, Dartmouth College, 1909; [Libretto only.] '09(Je) c. 50 p. 8°, $1.50. R. G. Reynolds.

Reynolds, Stephen.
Alongshore. '10(O22) c. il. D. $1.50. Macmillan.
The Holy Mountain: satire on English life. '09(O16) D. $1.50. Lane.
Poor man's house. '08(D5) D. $1.50. Lane.

Reynolds, Victor.
Stories of the Flemish artists from the Van Eycke to the end of the XVIIth century. '08(O17) cr. 8°, (Art and letters lib.) *$3 net. Duffield.

Reynolds, Wa. Doty.
Chimes of Swarthmore. '10(N) 5-46 p. il. 8°, 45 c. Clarion.

Reynolds, W: Hampton.
Our brother's child, and other stories. 2d rev. ed. '08, [1909.] (F) c. 121 p. 12°, 50 c. Mayhew.

Reynolds-Ball, Eustace Alfr.
Rome: pract. guide. 2d ed. '08(My2) il. 16°, *$1.10 net. Macmillan.
Tourist's India: [guide to principal cities; with notes on the topographical, archæological, historic and social aspects of modern India.] '08(Ap11) il. map, 12°, *$2 net. Brentano's.

Reynolds Library, Rochester, N. Y. Catalogue of works on engineering and allied subjects in the Reynolds Library, Rochester, N. Y. '10(Ja22) S. limp leath. (Add. Library for price.) Reynolds Lib.

Rhead, G: Woolliscroft.
Hist. of the fan. '10(Ja1) *25 net. Lippincott.

Rhead, L: J:
Book of fish and fishing. '08(Je6) c. il. D. **$1.50 net. Scribner.

RHETORIC.
Aristotle. Rhetoric. *$1.75 net. Putnam.
Ashmun, M. Composition in the high school. 10 c. Univ. of Wis.
Ashmun, M. Prose literature for secondary schools. 80 c. Houghton M.
Atkinson, W: W. Art of expression and principles of discourse. $1. Progress Co.
Baker, F. T:, *and* Abbott, H. V. English composition. 80 c. Holt.
Baldwin, C: S. Composition, oral and written.—Writing and speaking: textbook of rhetoric. ea., $1.20. Longmans.
Ball, M. Principles of outlining for colleges and advanced classes in secondary schools. 65 c. B: H. Sanborn.
Berkeley, F. C., *ed.* College course in writing from models. $1.25. Holt.
Brubacher, A. R., *and* Snyder, D. E. High school English. $1. C: E. Merrill.
Cairns, W: B. Forms of discourse; with an introductory chapter on style. $1.15. Ginn.
Canby, H: S., Pierce, F: E., *and others.* English composition in theory and practice. **$1.25 net. Macmillan.
College entrance requirements in English, 1909-1915. 90 c. Am. Bk.
Erskine, J: *and* H. Written English. 40 c. net. Century Co.
Gass, S. B. English composition. $1. Scott, F. & Co.

RHETORIC.—*Continued.*
Hitchcock, A. M. Enlarged practice-book in English composition. $1.—Theme-book in English composition. 50 c. Holt.
Miller, J. W: English composition and easy writing. 60 c. Longmans.
Murison, W: English composition; with chapters on précis writing, prosody and style. $1.10 net. Putnam.
Nason, A. H. Short themes. $1.25 net. A. H. Nason.
Perry, F. M. Introductory course in exposition. $1. Am. Bk.
Reed, A., *and* Kellogg, B. Higher lessons in English. 70 c. C: E. Merrill.
Scott, F. N., *and* Denney, J. V. Paragraph-writing. $1.25. Allyn & B.
Sykes, F: H: English composition.—Grammar-school composition. ea., *65 c. net. Scribner.
Taylor, J. R. Composition in narration. 75 c. Holt.
Thomas, C: S., *and* Howe, W. D. Composition and rhetoric. $1.20. Longmans.
Wilbur, W: A. Exposition in English rhetoric.—Syllable in English rhetoric. ea., 50 c. Collins, H. & Co.
Wilson, *Sir* T: Arte of rhetorique, 1560. $1.75. Oxford Univ.
Woolley, E. C. Mechanics of writing. $1. Heath.
See also Authorship; — Criticism; — Debating;—Drama;—Elocution; — English language; — Fiction;—Letter-writing;—Orators and oratory;—Parody;—Poetry;—Preaching; — Punctuation; —Satire;—Translation.

RHEUMATISM.
See Gout;—Uric acid.

Rhine, Abraham Benedict.
Leon Gordon; an appreciation. '10(D17) c. por. D. 75 c. Jewish Pub.

RHINE RIVER.
Baedeker, K. The Rhine. $1.10 net. Scribner.
Mackinder, H. J: The Rhine. **$3.50 net. Dodd.
McMurry, C: A. The Rhine. 10 c. Flanagan.

RHINEBECK, N. Y.
Morse, H. H. Historic old Rhinebeck. *$3 net. H. H. Morse.

RHINOLOGY.
See Nose.

Rhoades, Ja.
Training of the imagination. '08(Je27) 16°, (Bibliophiles lib.) *50 c. net; leath., *75 c. net. Lane.

Rhoades, Lewis Addison.
See Becker, Henrietta Katherine.

Rhoades, Nina, [pseud. for Cornelia Harsen Rhoades.]
Brave little Peggy. '08(O17) c. il. D. (Brick House books.) †$1. Lothrop, L. & S.
Dorothy Brown: a story for girls. '09 (S11) c. il. D. $1.50. Lothrop, L. & S.
The other Sylvia. '10(Ag20) c. il. D. (Brick house books.) $1. Lothrop, L. & S.

Rhoda of the Underground. Kelly, *Mrs.* F. F. $1.50. Sturgis & W.

Rhoda Roland. Sutton, H. S. $1.50. Madison.

Rhode Island. Check list of Rhode Island nesting birds, with data; pub. by the Commissioners of birds. '08(O17) c. il. 12°. (Not for sale.) C: H. Remington.

Rhode Island. Manual for voters in the state, 1909. '09 (O) c. 20 p. O. pap. (Add. pubs. for price.) Green, H. & A.

RHODE ISLAND.
Bicknell, T: W. Sowams; with ancient records of Sowams and parts adjacent. $3. Assoc. Pub.
Brigham, C. S., *comp.* List of books upon Rhode Island history. gratis. R. I. Dept. Educ.
Dale, T: N. Chief commercial granites of Massachusetts, New Hampshire and Rhode Island. (Add. Superintendent for price.) U. S., Supt. of Docs.
Hasse, A. R. Index of economic material in documents of the states of the U. S.: Rhode Island, 1789-1904. 75 c. Carnegie.
Society of Mayflower Descendants (Rhode Island and Providence). Second record book. (Add. pubs. for price.) Standard Pr. Co.
Towles, J: K. Factory legislation of Rhode Island. $1. Macmillan.
Weeden, W: B. Early Rhode Island. $2.50. Grafton Press.
See also Centerdale;—Genealogies (Mowry, W: A.):—King Philip's War;—Newport; — Providence;—*also* "Gaspee (The)";—*also* Vane, *Sir* Henry, *jr.*;—Williams, Roger.

Rhode Island Citizens' Historical Association. Address and poems at the one hundred and thirty-second anniversary of the independence of Rhode Island and the twenty-fifth anniversary of the Rhode Island Citizens' Historical Association at Providence, 1909; ed. by T: W. Bicknell for the Association. '09(O) 8°, pap., 75 c. R. I. Hist.

Rhode Island College of Agriculture and Mechanic Arts; joint bulletin of the State Board of Agriculture and Extension Dept. il. O. R. I. Coll.
—Stene. San José scale. gratis.

Rhode Island education circulars. il. O. pap. W. Ranger.
—Ranger, W. E., *comp.* Nineteenth annual program for the observation of Arbor Day. gratis.

Rhode Island educational circular; historical ser. O. pap., gratis. R. I. Dept. Educ.
—Brigham. List of books upon Rhode Island history.
—Eaton *and* Craig. Roger Williams, the founder of Providence.
—Knox. Destruction of the "Gaspee."

Rhode Island Normal School bull. 8°. R. I. Normal.
—Jones. Syllabus for the study of the hist. of education. 25 c.

Rhode Island pure food and drug act, passed by the General Assembly May 26, 1908; together with standards of purity for food products; also rules and regulations for the enforcement of the act in force Jan. 1, 1908. '09(Je) 70 p. 8°. (Add. pubs. for price.) E. L. Freeman.

Rhode Island State Library, Legislative reference bulletin. R. I. State Lib.
—Automobile laws of the New England states, New York, New Jersey and Pennsylvania. (Add. pub. for price.)
—Veto power in the several states. (Add. pub. for price.)

RHODES, Cecil John.
Fuller, *Sir* T: E. Right Hon. Cecil John Rhodes. $1.60 net. Longmans.
Michell, *Sir* L. Life and times of the Right Honorable Cecil John Rhodes. 2 v. $7.50 net. M. Kennerley.
Wylie, F. L. Cecil Rhodes and his scholars as factors in international conciliation. gratis. Am. Assoc. Int. Conciliation.

Rhodes, Dan. P.
Philosophy of change. '09(O2) c. figs. O. **$2 net. Macmillan.

Rhodes, Edn. S., comp.
First centennial history and atlas of Tuscarawas Co., Ohio. '08, [1909.] (Mr) c. 236 p. il. maps, f°, $10; $15. E. S. Rhodes.

Rhodes, Eug. Manlove.
Good men and true. '10(S3) c. il. D. $1 net. Holt.

Rhodes, Mrs. H. H:
Where men have walked: study of the Lucayos: [fiction.] '09, [1910.] (Jl) 294 p. il. 12°, $1.50. C. M. Clark.

Rhodes, Harrison Garfield.
Adventures of Charles Edward. '08(My9) c. D. †$1.50. Little, B. & Co.
See also Wise, T: A.

Rhodes, Helen.
Psychocoma (soul-sleep); with introd. by Eliz. J. Towne. '08(D5) c. por. D. $1. E. J. Towne.

Rhodes, Ja. Ford.
Historical essays. '09(D18) c. O. **$2.25 net. Macmillan.

Rhodes, J: Chester, comp.
Questions and answers in the use of coal and oil fuel and locomotive operation. '10(Ja15) c. 16°, $2. J: C. Rhodes.

Rhodes, Jos.
English-Esperanto dictionary. '08(S12) c. 8°, *$2 net. Revell.

Rhodes, Kathlyn.
Will of Allah. '09(Mr13) c. 12°, †$1.50. Estes.

Rhodes, Ledru Rollin.
Circumstantial evidence: the brief of a lawyer using the revealed truths of the infinite as a basis from which to demonstrate the existence of a God of design. '09(Ap3) c. por. D. pap., 75 c. L. R. Rhodes.

RHODES (*Island of*).
Belabre, *Baron* de. Rhodes of the knights; [describes the monuments of the Knights of St. John that still stand in Rhodes.] $9.75. Oxford Univ.

RHODESIA, South Africa.
Hall, R: N. Prehistoric Rhodesia. $3.50 net. Jacobs.
Hone, P. F. Southern Rhodesia. *$3.50 net. Macmillan.
Madan, A. C. Lala-Lamba hdbk.; introd. to the southwestern division of the Wisa-Lala dialect of Northern Rhodesia.—Lenje hdbk.; introd. to the Lenje dialect spoken in northwest Rhodesia. ea., $1.15. Oxford Univ.

Rhodian sea-law. Ashburner, W. $5.75. Oxford Univ.

RHORER FAMILY.
See Genealogies: Houser, W: W.

"Rhoscomyl, Owen," pseud.
See Vaughan, Owen.

Rhubarb; the diary of a gentleman's hunter. Reeve, J. S. $1. J. S. Reeve.

Rhyme and story primer. McMahon, H. A. 30 c. Heath.

Rhyme of a run. Harrison, F. $2. Caldwell.

Rhymes and jingles. Bass, W: W. 50 c. W: W. Bass.

Rhymes from the Cumberland. Waller, E. 75 c. B'way Pub.

Rhymes of happy childhood. Fillebrown, *Mrs.* R. H. M. **$2 net. Winston.

Rhymes of home. Johnson, B. $1 net. Crowell.

Rhymes of the golden age. Brill, G: R. $1.50. Stern.

Rhymes of the road. Nichols, I. E. 75 c. Stilwell & R.

Rhymes of the stream and forest. Buckland, F. M. $1.25. Forest.

Rhymes of ye olde sign boards. Lewin, F. G. $1.50. Stokes.

Rhyming ring. Garnett, L. A. $1.25. Rand, McN. & Co.

RHYNCHOPHORA.
See Beetles.

Rhys, Sir J:
Notes on the Coligny calendar; together with an ed. of the reconstructed calendar, from the Proceedings of the British Academy. v. 4. '10(O1) O. pap., $4.20. Oxford Univ.

RHYTHM.
See Psychology.

Rhythm of modern music. Williams, C. F. A. *$1.50 net. Macmillan.

Ribbon roads. Wood, A. T. $2.50 net. Putnam.

RIBE, Denmark.
Riis, J. A. Old town. **$2 net. Macmillan.

Ribot, Théodule Armand.
Diseases of the personality; tr. (with homœotherapeutic annotations) by P. W. Shedd. '09(N) c. 31+142 p. 12°, $1. Boericke & T.

Ribs of the law. Mayes, E: (Add. pubs. for price.) Lex.

Ricci, Corrado.
Art of northern Italy. '10(D24) il. 12°, (Ars una: species mille; general history of art.) $1.50 net. Scribner.

Rice, Mrs. Alice Caldwell Hegan, [formerly Alice Caldwell Hegan.]
Mr. Opp. '09(My1) c. il. D. †$1. Century Co.

Rice, Allen Thorndike, comp. and ed.
Reminiscences of Abraham Lincoln by distinguished men of his time. New and rev. ed. '09(Ja30) c. por. facsim., O. **$2 net. Harper.

Rice, Alonzo Leora.
Sun-ways of song; with introd. by C: Major and an epilogue by Fk. L. Stanton. '10(S10) c. D. $1 net. Sherman, F.

Rice, Cale Young.
Charles di Tocca. '08, [1910.] (F) c. 3-134 p. 12°. (Add. pubs. for price.) Doubleday, P.
David. '09(S11) c. D. bds., **$1.25 net. Doubleday, P.
Many gods. '10(Mr26) c. D. bds., *$1.25 net. Doubleday, P.
Nirvana days: [poems.] '09(Mr13) c. D. **$1.25 net. Doubleday, P.
Song-surf. '10(O8) c. D. bds., $1.25 net. Doubleday, P.
Yolanda of Cyprus: [play.] '08(Ap18) D. **$1.25 net. McClure.

Rice, E: Baldwin, ed.
See Held, R. Johnson.

Rice, E: Irving.
Old Jim Case of South Hollow. '09(F20) c. front. D. †$1. Doubleday, P.

Rice, Edn. Wilbur, D.D.
Commentary on the Acts; giving the common version, 1611, the revised version, 1881, with critical, exegetical and applicative notes and illustrations from life and history in the East. 4th ed. '09(S) 4+5-371 p. il. maps, 8°, *$1.25 net. Am. S. S.
Commentary on the Gospel according to Matthew. 6th ed., newly rev. '10(Ja29) c. il. 8°, (Green fund book.) $1.25. Am. S. S.
Orientalisms in Bible lands; Green fund book. '10(D24) c. il. D. $1 net. Am. S. S.
Sunday-school: how to start and keep it; rev. by the committee. '09(Jl3) c. S. *25 c. net; pap., *10 c. net. Am. S. S.

Rice, Elmer Cook.
National standard squab book: pract. manual giving complete and precise directions for the installation and management of a successful squab plant. '09(Mr) c. 11-303 p. il. por. 8°, 50 c. Plymouth Rock.

Rice, Fannie Bond.
Saint of the twentieth century. '10(My21) c. D. $1.50. Badger.

Rice, Frances.
See Rice, Wallace de Groot Cecil.

Rice, Franklin Pierce, comp.
Marlborough, Mass., burial ground inscriptions copied by G: Maynard: Old Common, Spring Hill, and Brigham cemeteries. '08(Ag22) il. 8°, (Systematic hist. fund, auxiliary pubs.) pap., $3. F. P. Rice.

Rice, G: S.
Explosibility of coal dust; with chapters by J. C. W. Frazer and others. '10(N) 186 p. il. diagrs., 8°, (U. S., Geological Survey; bull.)
Bibliography (15 p.).

Rice, Grantland.
Base-ball ballads. [1910.] (Je) c. 128 p. il. 8°, $1. G. Rice.

Rice, Harry E.
Eve and the evangelist: romance of A.D. 2108. '08(O10) c. il. D. $1.25. Roxburgh.

Rice, May Cushman, M.D.
Electricity in gynecology; the practical uses of electricity in diseases of women. '09 (O) 159 p. il. D. $1. Laing.

Rice, O. S., comp.
Wisconsin Memorial Day annual, 1910. '10 (F) 90 p. il. por. O. pap. C: P. Cary.

Rice, Pat.
Tangles untangled. '10(Je4) c. D. 75 c.; pap., 25 c. J. S. Ogilvie.

Rice, Viola, comp.
See Rice, Wallace de Groot Cecil, *comp.*

Rice, Wallace de Groot Cecil, comp.
Catchwords of patriotism. '08(O10) c. front. O. *$1 net. McClurg.
For the gaiety of nations; fun and philosophy from the American newspaper humorists. '09(Ag28) c. 12°, *50 c. net. Dodge.
Little book of school-days; comp and ed., with an introd., by Wallace and Frances Rice. '10(D3) c. col. front. 12°, 60 c. Reilly & B.
Toasts and table sentiments; collection to gladden dinners and aid the good work of digestion. '09(O16) c. S. bds., *50 c. net; ooze cf., *$1.25 net, boxed. McClurg.
See also Little book ser.

— and Frances, comps.
Little book of friendship; ed., with introd., by Wallace and Frances Rice. '10(N5) D. front. bds., 35 c.; Booklovers' ed., 60 c.; limp leath., $1. Reilly & B.
Wealth of friendship; with a homily on friendship by the Rev. F. W. Gunsaulus. '09(N20) c. O. $1.25, boxed; ooze, $2, boxed. Barse & H.

— and Viola, comps.
The humbler poets; second ser.: collection of newspaper and periodical verse, 1885 to 1910. '10(D17) 8°, $1.50 net. McClurg.

Rice gambit. Keidanz, H., *comp. and ed.* 17 c. Am. Chess.

Rich, Burdett A., ed.
See Lawyers' repts. annot.

Rich, Olive Verne.
Prophecy of Yah-Ma-Sun. '09(My8) c. il. nar. D. (Puget Sound Indian ser.) pap., 50 c. A. Harriman.

Rich, W: Watson, comp. and ed.
Hand book of the United States tariffi containing the Tariff act of 1897, revised to July 1, 1902. [3d ed.] '09(Mr6) c. por. 12°, $2.50. Vandegrift.
Hdbk. of the U. S. tariff; cont. tariff act 1909. '10(Ja8) c. por. D. $2.50. Vandegrift.
See also United States. Pocket ed. of the tariff act.

Rich in yesterdays. Ostrom, H: 75 c. Praise Pub.

Richard, Ja. W:
Confessional hist. of the Lutheran church. '09(S) c. 8+637 p. 8°, $3. Lutheran Pub.

Richard, Rev. Ja. W:, and Painter, Rev. Franklin Verzelius Newton.
Christian worship: its principles and forms. 2d ed. '08(O) c. 8+9-368 p. 8°, $1.50. Lutheran Pub.

Richard in camp. Potter, M. K. †75 c. Wilde.

RICHARD, the Fearless, *Duke* of Normandy.
Yonge, C. M. Little duke, or, Richard the Fearless. 35 c. net; 70 c. net. Dutton.

Richard of Jamestown. Kaler, J. O. 35 c. Am. Bk.

Richards, C. H.
See Davison, C:

Richards, Caroline Cowles.
Diary, 1852-1872. '10(Ja22) il. pors. D. $1.25. E. C. Clarke.

Richards, C: Russell.
Industrial training. '09(D25) 8°. (New York Bureau of Labor Statistics.) (Add. pubs. for price.) N. Y. Dept. Labor.

Richards, Edn. Gilmore.
Nationalism according to Richards. '10 (Mr5) c. por. 16°, 60 c. E. G. Richards.

Richards, Mrs. Ellen Henrietta Swallow, [Mrs. R. H. Richards.]
Cost of cleanness. '08(N7) 12°, $1. Wiley.
Cost of food: study in dietaries. 2d ed. '08(Ag1) c. 12°, $1. Wiley.
Euthenics; the science of controllable environment; plea for better living conditions as a first step toward higher human efficiency. '10(Jl30) c. D. $1 net. Whitcomb & B.
Laboratory notes on industrial water analysis. '08(D19); 2d ed., rev. '10(Ap) c. 8°, ea., **50 c. net. Wiley.

—, and Woodman, Alpheus G.
Air, water, and food from a sanitary standpoint. 3d ed., rev. and enl. '09(D18) c. il. fold. map, 8°, $2. Wiley.

Richards, G:
Selection of cases on the law of insurance, [etc.;] with appendix of forms, etc. '10 (O) c. 19+380 p. O. cl., $3.50. Banks.
Treatise on the law of insurance in all its branches, especially fire, life, accident, marine, title, fidelity, credit, and employers' liability, with an appendix of statutes affecting the insurance contract and a collection of forms. 3d ed., enl. and rewritten. '09(Je) c. 27+959 p. O. $6.75. Banks.

Richards, G: W., D.D., and Good, Ja. I:, D.D.
Life pictures of Calvin for young and old. '09(My22) il. 25 c. Heidelberg.

Richards, Herbert Maule.
Botany. '08(F29) c. 8°, pap., 25 c. Lemcke.

Richards, Jos. W:
Metallurgical calculations. 2d ed., rev. and corr. pt. 1, Introd., chemical and thermal principles, problems in combustion. '08(Je13); pt. 2, Iron and steel; pt. 3, The metals other than iron. '09(Mr27) c. 8°, ea., *$2 net. McGraw.

—, and Colvin, F: Herbert.
Pract. perspective. '09(D) c. 64 p. il. 8°, 50 c. Henley.

Richards, Mrs. Laura Eliz. Howe.
Florence Nightingale, the angel of the Crimea: story for young people. '09(O9) c. il. D. **$1.25 net. Appleton.
Happy little time; partly-true story, for children of Betty's age. '10(N5) c. il. (partly in col.) O. $1.25. Estes.
Pig brother, and other fables and stories. '08(Je20) c. il. 12°, **40 c. net. Little, B. & Co.
"Up to Calvins." '10(N5) c. D. $1.25. Estes.
Wooing of Calvin Parks. '08(S12) c. il. D. †$1.25. Estes.

Richards, L:
See Pennsylvania notaries public.

Richards, Luther Adolph.
Comets. '09, [1910.] c. 16 p. 12°, pap. Eddy Press.

Richards, Marian Edwards.
Zandrie. '09(S18) c. front. D. †$1.50. Century Co.

Richards, Mrs. R. H.
See Richards, *Mrs.* Ellen Henrietta Swallow.

Richards, Ralph Coffin.
Conservation of men; address to the operating men of the Chicago & North Western Railway on the prevention of accidents. '10(N5) c. 12°, 50 c.. R. C. Richards.

Richards, Rob. Hallowell.
Text book of ore dressing. '09(N20) c. il. 8°, *$5 net. McGraw-H.

Richards, Rosalind.
The nursery fire. New ed. '10(O1) c. D. $1.25. Little, B. & Co.

Richards, Thdr. W:, and Willard, Hobart Hurd.
Determination of atomic weights; Further investigation concerning the atomic weights of silver, lithium and chlorine, by T. W. Richards and H. H. Willard; Harvard determination of atomic weights bet. 1870 and 1910, by T. W. Richards; Methods used in precise chemical investigation, by T. W. Richards. '10(Je) 113 p. tabs., Q. pap. Carnegie.

Richards, Theodore W:, Wilson, J. Hunt, and Garrod-Thomas, R. N.
Electrochemical investigation of liquid amalgams of thallium, indium, tin, zinc, cadmium, lead, copper, and lithium. '09 (Ag28) figs. Q. pap. (Add. Institution for price.) Carnegie.

Richards, W: Allyn.
Text-book of elem. foundry practice for the use of students in colleges and secondary schools. '10(D10) c. il. O. $1.25 net. Macmillan.

Richards, Rev. W: Rogers.
Study of the Lord's prayer. '10(Ja29) c. D. 75 c. Presb. Bd.

Richardson, Albert Lewis, comp.
See Rowell, B: Winslow.

Richardson, Alfr. Madeley.
Modern organ accompaniment. '08(Mr28) 12°, $2.50. Longmans.

Richardson, Anna Steese.
Girl who earns her own living. '10(Ja1) c. il. 12°, *$1 net. B. W. Dodge.

Richardson, Mrs. Aubrey.
Lover of Queen Elizabeth: being the life and character of Robert Dudley, Earl of Leicester. '08(O10) il. O. *$3.50 special net. Appleton.

Richardson, Bertha June, [Mrs. Lucas.]
Woman who spends; study of her economic function; with introd. by Ellen H. Richards. 2d ed., rev. '10(Mr26) c. D. *$1 net. Whitcomb.

Richardson, C:
New book of the horse. 2 v. '10(D) il. (partly col.) 8°. (Subs only.) Cassell.

Richardson, C: Fs.
Study of English rhyme; printed for classroom use. '09(D11) c. 8°, pap., $1.25. E. P. Storrs.

Richardson, C: J.
Fragments and details of architecture, decoration and furniture of the Elizabethan period; sel. from "Studies from old English mansions," published in 1841. '08 (F22) f°, pap., $12; hf. leath., $15. Helburn.

Richardson, Clifford.
Modern asphalt pavement. 2d ed., rev. and enl. '08(N21) c. figs. 8°, $3. Wiley.

Richardson, D: Argyle.
See Mexico. Richardson's manual.

Richardson, Dan. Sidney.
Trail dust: western verse. '09(Ja23) c. D. *$1.25 net. A. M. Robertson.

Richardson, Delmer Dalton.
Treatise on diseases of the rectum, prostate and associate organs. 2d ed., rev. '08, [1909.] (N) 111 p. il. (partly col.) 4°. (Add. pubs. for price.) Campbell Co.

Richardson, E.
Artist songs. '08(Jl11) 16°, *$1.15 net. Wessels.

Richardson, Ernest Cushing, comp. and ed.
Alphabetical subject index and index encyclopædia to periodical articles on religion, 1890-1899. '08(F22) c. 4°, $10. Hartford Sem., [Scribner.]

Richardson, Florence Ella.
Study of sensory control in the rat. [1910.] (Jl) 4+124 p. il. tabs., 4°, (Psychological monographs; studies from the Psychological laboratory of the University of Chicago.) $1.25. Psychological Review.

Richardson, Fk.
Love; and all about it: [satirical essays.] '08(Ja18) 8°, *75 c. net. M. Kennerley.
Other man's wife. '08(O3) c. 8°, $1.50. M. Kennerley.

Richardson, G. B.
Reconnaissance of the Book Cliffs Coal Fields between Grand River, Colo., and Sunnyside, Utah. '09(My) 54 p. il. map, O. pap., 20 c. U. S., Supt. of Docs.

Richardson, Rev. G. Lynde.
Travail of His soul: three hours' devotion for Good Friday. '09(Ap10) bds., *60 c. net. Young Churchman.

Richardson, G: Tilton.
See Tilton, Dwight, *pseud.*

Richardson, Harold, and Thompson, G. H.
The poet and other animals. '09(D18) il. 4°, $2. Dutton.

Richardson, H: Handel, pseud.
Getting of wisdom. '10(O15) c. D. $1.50. Duffield.
Maurice Guest. '09(F6) c. D. †$1.50. Duffield.

Richardson, J:
Practical treatise on the theory, construction and use of the modern steam engine. '09(My) 380 p. il. 8°, *$3 net. Van Nostrand.

Richardson, Jos. Gibbons.
Health and longevity; by Jos. G. Richardson, assisted by B. F. Scholl, W: H. Ford, C. C. Vanderbeck, etc. '09, [1910.] (F) c. 33-1382+34 p. il. (partly col.) 4°, $12. Stanley Inst.

Richardson, Jos. Gibbons, M.D., and others.
Medicology; or, home encyclopedia of health. '08(My9) c. front. il. pors. 4°, $8; leath., $9. University Med.

Richardson, N. A.
Industrial problems. '09(N6) c. D. $1. Kerr.

Richardson, Norman Egbert, ed.
Present-day prayer-meeting helps for layman and minister, by Alumni of Boston University School of Theology. '10 (Jl30) c. S. 50 c. net. Eaton & M.

Richardson, Norval.
Lead of honour. '10(N12) c. col. front. il. D. $1.50. L. C. Page.

Richardson, Rob. Earl.
See Jordan, D: Starr.

Richardson, S. S.
Magnetism and electricity and the principles of electrical measurement. '09(My) 604 p. il. 12°, *$2 net. Van Nostrand.

RICHELIEU, *Cardinal* and *Duc* de, [Armand Jean du Plessis.]
McCabe, J. Iron cardinal; being the romance of Richelieu. *$3.50 net. J: McBride.

RICHELIEU, Louis François Armand Du Plessis, *Duc* de.
Williams, H. N. Fascinating Duc de Richelieu, Louis François, Armand Du Plessis, (1696-1788.) $4 net. Scribner.

Richelieu. *See* James, G: Payne Rainsford.

RICHES.
See Wealth.

Riches of grace. Parry, T: 50 c. Westminster.

Riches of His grace. Mudge, Ja. *$1 net. Eaton & M.

Richey, Harry Grant.
Building mechanics' ready reference. Cement workers' and plasterers' ed. Plumbers', steam-fitters' and tinners' ed. '08 (Ag29) c. il. 16°, mor., ea., **$1.50 net. Wiley.
Building mechanics' ready reference; The building foreman's pocketbook and ready reference. '09(My1) c. figs. 16°, mor., $5. Wiley.

Richman, Julia.
See Byrnes, Ja. C.

Richman, Julia, and Wallach, Isabel Richman.
Good citizenship. '08(Ag22) c. il. D. 45 c. Am. Bk.

Richmond, Mrs.
In my lady's garden. '09, [1910.] (D) 457 p. il. 8°, **$3.50 net. Jacobs.

Richmond, Annette B.
American Episcopal church in China. '07, [1908.] (Jl) c. 11+170 p. il. pors. 12°, 75 c.; pap., 50 c. Dom. and For. Mission.
Bibliography.

Richmond, E.
Picture talks for pastors, Sunday schools, young people's societies, etc.; introd. by Rev. C: Roads. '08, [1909.] (F) c. 23 p. il. T. pap., 10 c. E. Richmond.

Richmond, Mrs. Grace Louise Smith.
Court of inquiry. '09(O16) c. il. D. $1, fixed. Doubleday, P.
On Christmas day in the evening. '10 (N12) c. il. in col. D. bds., 50 c., fixed. Doubleday, P.
On Christmas day in the morning. '08 (O24) c. il. D. bds., **75c. net. Doubleday, P.
Red Pepper Burns. '10(O29) c. D. $1.20, fixed. Doubleday, P.
Round the corner in Gay Street. '08 (Ag29) c. D. †$1.50. Doubleday, P.

Richmond, J. L.
Game of draughts; over 150 games and variations on the "single corner" and "alma" openings. 2d ed., with corrections. '09 (Ap) figs. S. 50 c. Warne.

RICHMOND (Borough of).
See New York City.

RICHMOND, Va.
Burgess, M. A. Richmond guide book. 25 c. Burgess.

Richter, A.
Order of salvation; tr. from the 5th German ed. '08(N14) S. 20 c. E. Kaufmann.

Richter, Julius, D.D.
History of missions in India. '08(D5) 8°, *$2.50 net. Revell.
Hist. of Protestant missions in the near east. '10(Je4) 8°, $2.50. Revell.

Rickaby, Rev. Jos.
Four-square; or, the cardinal virtues; addresses to young men. '09(Ja23) c. 8°, *60 c. net. Wagner.
Scholasticism. '09(Jl31) 12°, (Philosophies ancient and modern from Pythagoras to Spencer.) *50 c. net. Dodge.

—, and McIntyre, Canon J:
Newman memorial sermons. '10(My21) O. pap., 36 c. net. Longmans.

Rickard, T: Arth.
Guide to technical writing. '08(Ag22) c. 12°, $1. Mining and Scientific.
Journeys of observation. '08(F29) c. il. maps, 8°, $3.50. Dewey Pub.
Through the Yukon and Alaska. '09(Jl17) c. il. maps, O. $2.50. Mining and Scientific.

Ricker, Nathan Clifford.
Study of base and bearing plates for columns and beams. [1910] (My) 36 p. 8°, (Univ. of Ill., Engineering Experimental, bull.) gratis. Univ. of Ill.
Study of roof trusses. '08(Ap4) il. 8°, (Univ. of Ill., Engineering experiment station, bull.) pap., gratis. Univ. of Ill.

Rickert, Martha Edith.
Beggar in the heart. '09(O23) c. D. †$1.50. Moffat.
—, comp. American lyrics. '10(O) 300 p. 12°, $1.50 net. Baker & T.
Ancient English Christmas carols MCCCC to MDCC. '10(D17) il. 16°, (New medieval lib.) leath., $3.25 net, boxed. Duffield.
See also Early English romances.

Rickett, Arth. Compton.
London life of yesterday. '09(D) 19+400 p. 8°, *$2.50 net. Dutton.

Rickett, Sir Jos. Compton.
Origins and faith: essay on reconciliation. '09(D) c. 276 p. 12°, *$1.50 net. Revell.

Ricketts, T. F., M.D.
Diagnosis of small-pox. [1910] (My) il. 8°, $6 net. Funk.

Rickmers, W. Rickmer.
Ski-ing, for beginners and mountaineers. '10(Je4) il. 12°, $1.50 net. Scribner.

RICKS FAMILY.
See Genealogies: Rix, G. S.

Riddell, Newton N.
Psychology of success and human nature studies; with one hundred suggestions for business and professional men. '09(D18) v. 12°, $1.50. Riddell Pub.

RIDDING, *Bp.* George.
Ridding, *Lady* L. E. George Ridding, schoolmaster and bishop. $5. Longmans.

Ridding, Lady Laura Eliz.
George Ridding, schoolmaster and bishop, forty-third head master of Winchester, 1866-1884; first bishop of Southwell, 1884-1904. '08(My2) il. pors. plans, O. $5. Longmans.

Riddle, Matthew Brown.
Story of the Revised New Testament, American standard ed. '08(Jl18) c. por. 12°, *75 c. net. S. S. Times.

Riddle and puzzle books. 12°. Caldwell.
—Jerrold. Babes and blossoms. 75 c.
—Pope. Babes and birds. 75 c.

RIDDLES.
Starr, F:, *ed.* Little book of Filipino riddles. 50 c. World Bk.

Riddles of the Exeter book; ed., with introd., notes and glossary, by F: Tupper, jr. '10 (Je4) (Albion ser. of Anglo-Saxon and Middle English poetry.) $2.50. Ginn.

Riddles of the Sphinx. Schiller, F. C. S. $3. Macmillan.

Rideout, H: Milner.
Dragon's blood. '09(Ap24) c. il. D. **$1.20 net. Houghton M.
Twisted foot. '10(My14) c. il. D. $1.20 net. Houghton M.
—, ed. *See* Copeland, C: Townsend.

Rider, Arth. Fremont.
Are the dead alive?: the problem of physical research; with statements of their personal belief by Sir Oliver Lodge, Count Leo Tolstoi, Dr. Cesare Lombroso, And. Lang, Prof. W: James, [and others.] '09(Je5) c. il. O. $1.75, fixed. B. W. Dodge.

Riders of the plains. Haydon, A. L. $2.75 net. McClurg.

Ridgefield tavern. Enright, M. $1.25; 75 c. Brooklyn Eagle.

Ridgely, Albert Newton.
By law of might; or, the campaign in Sunset. '08(S12) c. il. D. $1.50. H. A. Simmons.

Ridgely, Helen West, ed.
Historic graves of Maryland and the District of Columbia, with the inscriptions appearing on the tombstones; ed. under the auspices of the Maryland Society of the Colonial Dames of America. '08 (Ag1) c. il. por. 12°, (Grafton historical ser.) **$2 net. Grafton Press.

Ridgeway, Dean C: J:
Social life. '08(My23) D. (Christian life ser.) *60 c. net. Cassell.

Ridgeway, W:
Early age of Greece. v. 1. '08(F8) il. 8°, *$5 net. Putnam.

Ridgway, Rob.
Manual of North American birds. Popular ed. '10(D31) il. 8°, $5 net. Lippincott.

Ridgway, W: H.
Ridgway's religion, for folks who don't have any; being some notes on John as taught to the Iron Rose Bible Class. '09(Jl31) c. D. **50 c. net. Griffith & R.

Ridgway of Montana. Raine, W: M. †$1.50. G: W. Dillingham.

Riding.
See Horsemanship

Riding to Lithend. *See* Bottomley, Gordon.

Ridpath, J: Clark.
Hist. of the world. 9 v. '10(Ap16) c il. pors. maps, 4°, $65. Jones Bros.
See also Morgan, A. T.

Riedell, J: H., rep.
See New Hampshire. *Sup. ct.* Repts.

Riedinger, Mrs. Laura Rhodes.
Fireless cookery with the hay box. '09 (Je26) c. 8°, pap., 10 c. L. R. Riedinger.

Riegler, Gideon.
Amateur astronomer; tr. by G: Aubourne Clarke. '10(S24) il. S. $1.25 net. Dodd.

Riehl, Wilhelm Heinrich v.
Der fluch der schönheit: novelle; ed., with introd., notes, exercises and vocab., by Arth. N. Leonard. '09(Ap17) c. map, S. (International modern language ser.) 40 c. Ginn.

Rienzi. *See* Bulwer-Lytton, *Sir* E: G: E. L.

Ries, C. E.
Easy German stories: ed., with notes, exercises and vocab., by Ernest H. Bierman. '10(Ja22) c. S. 35 c. Am. Bk.

Ries, Heinrich.
Clays of Texas. '08(D19) il. tabs., O. (Univ. of Tex. bull., scientific ser.) pap., $2. Univ. of Tex.

Clays, their occurrences, properties, and uses; with especial reference to those of the United States. 2d ed., rev. '09(F20) c. il. maps. tabs., 8°, **$5 net. Wiley.

Economic geology, with special reference to the United States. New and rev. ed. '10(O8) c. il. maps, 8°, $3.50 net. Macmillan.

History of the clay-working industry in the United States. '09(Jl31) c il. 8°, **$2.50 net. Wiley.

Ries, W. F.
Men and mules: [blames present competitive system for condition of society.] 37th ed. '09(Ap17) il. S. pap., 10 c. W. F. Ries.

Monkeys and monkeyettes: reply to ex President Roosevelt: [cure for economic ills.] '09(My8) c. T. pap., 10 c. W. F. Ries.

Rietz, H: Lewis, and Crathorne, Arth. Rob.
College algebra. '09(O30) c. il. O. **$1.40 net. Holt.

—, and Shade, Imogene.
Correlation of efficiency in mathematics and efficiency in other subjects. '09(Ap3) O. (Univ. of Ill. bulletin; University studies.) pap., 35 c. Univ. of Ill.

Rifle.
Bowman, G: T: Our military rifle and how to use it. 10 c. Arms and the Man.
Eames, H: E. Rifle in war. $2. U. S. Cavalry.
Greener, W: W. Gun and its development. $4 net. Scribner.
Hinkle, F: W. Army rifles. (Not for sale.) F: W. Hinkle.
Mann, F. W. Bullet's flight from powder to target; the internal and external ballistics of small arms; a study of rifle shooting. $4. Munn.
Parker, J: H: Indoor target practice. $1. Arms and the Man.
Rifle shooting in educational institutions; college and university rifle clubs, schoolboy rifle clubs; National Board for Promotion of Rifle Practice. [1910.] (D) 48 p. il. pors., fold. diagr., 8°. Gov. Pr. Off.
Whelen, T. Suggestions to military riflemen. (Add. pubs. for price.) Hudson.
Wilson, H. C., *and* Casey, K. K. V. Rifle range construction. $1. Du Pont de Nemours.
Winans, W. Sporting rifle. **$5 net. Putnam.
Wingate, G: W. Why should boys be taught to shoot? (Add. pubs. for price.) Sub-Target.
See also Gun.

Rifle range.
See Rifle.

Riflemen of the Ohio. Altsheler, J. A. $1.50. Appleton.

Rigby, Lilian M.
See Russell, C: E: B.

Rigby, Will O.
Reliable candy teacher and soda and ice cream formulas. [10th ed., rev. and enl.] '09(Ap17) c. por. D. pap., $2. W. O. Rigby.

Riggenbach, Eduard.
Resurrection of Jesus. '08(Ja4) S. (Foreign religious ser.) *40 c. net. Eaton & M.

Riggs, Mrs. G:
See Wiggin, Kate Douglas Smith.

Riggs, J: Franklin.
Next step in school legislation; annual address del. before the Iowa State Teachers' Assoc., Dec. 3, 1908. '08, [1909.] (My) 12 p. 12°. (Add. author for price.) J: F. Riggs.

Riggs, Norman Colman.
Analytic geometry. '10(O8) c. D. $1.60 net. Macmillan.

Right and riches. McCasland, C: O. *$1.50 net. Wilbur Pub.

Right-at-hand stories. Sawin, R. L., *ed.* 80 c. Palmer Co.

"Right-dress!" Reilly, F: J. 50 c. Educ. Pub.

Right living ser. 16°. Revell.
—Babcock. Joy of work. 35 c. net.
—Cope Friendly life. 35 c.
—Jordan. Power of purpose. 35 c. net.
—Ludlow. Discovery of self. 35 c. net.

Right man. Hooker, B. †$1.50. Bobbs-M.

Right-Motive Club. Jefferson, E. P. *$1 net; *$2 net. Washington Bk.

Right sort of men for the ministry. McDowell, W: F. 10 c.; per 100, $8. Y. M. C. A.

Right stuff. Hay, I., *pseud.* $1.25 net. Houghton M.

Right to believe. Rowland, E. H. **$1.25 net. Houghton M.

RIGHTHANDEDNESS.
See Hand.

Rights and responsibilities of national churches. Masterman, J: H. B. *75 c. net. Putnam.

Rights of the minority stockholders. Harvey, R: S. $2. Baker, V. & Co.

Riis, Jacob August.
Hero tales of the far North. '10(O1) c. il. D. $1.35 net. Macmillan.

The old town. '09(O23) c. il. O. **$2 net. Macmillan.

Riley, Alice C. D., and Gaynor, Jessie L.
Lilts and lyrics for the school room. '08 (O) 104 p. $1. C. F. Summy Co.

On Plymouth Rock: operetta for amateur production; book and lyrics by Alice C. D. Riley; music by Jessie L. Gaynor. '09(F20) Q. pap., 60 c. C. F. Summy Co.

Welcome spring!: spring or Easter program for Sunday or day schools; lyrics and program by Alice C. D. Riley; music by Jessie L. Gaynor. '09(F20) c. Q. pap., 25 c. C. F. Summy Co.

Riley, B: Franklin.
History of the Baptists of Texas. '07, [1908.] (Ag) c. 509 p. il. pors. 8°, **$1.50 net. Am. Bapt.

White man's burden; discussion of the interracial question with special reference to the responsibility of the white race to the negro problem. '10(Ag27) c. 12°, $1.25. B. F. Riley.

Riley, Franklin Lafayette, Chandler, Julian Alvin Carroll, and Hamilton, Jos. Grégoire de Roulhac.
Our republic; hist. of the United States for grammar grades. '10(O15) c. il. pors. maps, 12°, 65 c. Riley & C.

Riley, Ja. Whitcomb.
Boys of the old glee club. '08(Ja18) il. 8°, **$1.50 net. Bobbs-M.

Girl I loved. '10(D31) c. il. O. $2, boxed; leath., $3, boxed. Bobbs-M.

Home again with me. '08(O24) c. il. O. $2, boxed; red leath., $3. Bobbs-M.

Hoosier romance, 1868; Squire Hawkin's story. '10(O15) c. il. $1.50 net, boxed. Century Co.

Old school day romances. '09(D) 38 p. il. 8°, $1.50. Bobbs-M.

Orphant Annie book. '08(O24) c. il. Q. bds., **$1.50 net. Bobbs-M.

Riley child verse. 1st ser.; 2d ser., Runaway boy. '08, [1909.] (Mr) 17-58; 61-110 p. il. 8°, ea., $1.25. Bobbs-M.

Riley roses. '09(D) 30 p. il. 8°, $2. Bobbs-M.

Riley songs of home. '10(D31) c. il. D. $1.25; leath., $2. Bobbs-M.

Songs of summer. '08(D12) c. il. D. $1.25; leath., $2. Bobbs-M.

See also Stories of humor.

RILEY, James Whitcomb.
Daggett, M. P. In Lockerbie Street; little appreciation of James Whitcomb Riley. 50 c. B. W. Dodge.

Kendall, E. F. Vinegar buyer; sharp sayings of sharp people, founded on James Whitcomb Riley's poem, "Jap Miller." 50 c. Cleveland News.

Riley, J: Lawrence.
Springfield tests, 1846-1905-6: study in the three R's. '08(Ag22) c. O. pap., 25 c. Holden.

Riley, W: Bell, D.D.
Finality of the higher criticism; or, the theory of evolution and false theology. '10(Mr12) c. D. $1. W: B. Riley.

Rimas (The). Becquer, G. A. D. $1.25. Badger.

Rime of the ancient mariner. *See* Coleridge, S: Taylor.

Rinaldo, Joel.
Polygeneric theory; treatise on the beginning and end of life. '10(S3) c. il. map, 12°, $1.50. J. Rinaldo.

Rine, G: W.
Essentials of English: a textbook. '08(O) c. 4+7-308 p. 12°, 75 c. Pacific Press.

Rinehart, Mrs. Mary Roberts.
Circular staircase. '08(Ag15) c. il. D. †$1.50. Bobbs-M.
Man in lower ten. '09(Mr20) c. il. D. †$1.50. Bobbs-M.
When a man marries. '09(D4) c. il. D. †$1.50. Bobbs-M.
Window at the White Cat. '10(Ag20) c. il. D. $1.50. Bobbs-M.
Ring and the book. *See* Hornbrooke, Francis Bickford.
Ring and the man. Brady, C. T. †$1.50. Moffat.
Ring of the Nibelung. Hadden, J. C., *comp.* 50 c.; $1. Stokes.
Ringhoffer, Karl.
Bernstorff papers: life of Count Albrecht von Bernstorff; tr. by Mrs. C: E: Barrett-Lennard and M. W. Hoper; with an introd. by Sir Rowland Blennerhassett. '08(D12) 2 v., O. *$6 net. Longmans.
Ringrose, Hyacinthe.
Inns of Court. '09(Jl) 200 p. il. *$2 net. Lawyers' Co-op.
Rings, F:
Reinforced concrete: theory and practice. '10(Jl9) 12°, $2.50 net. Van Nostrand.
RIO DE JANEIRO, Brazil.
See International Bureau of American Republics, Washington, D. C. Municipal organizations.
Rion, Hanna.
See Ver Beck, *Mrs.* Hannah Rion.
Rip Van Winkle. *See* Irving, Washington.
RIPARIAN RIGHTS.
See Water-rights.
Ripley, Alfr. Lawrence.
Recent plans for currency reform. '07, [1908.] (Ag) 22 p. 12°, pap. (Add. pub. for price.) Ellis.
Ripley, Frederic H., ed.
See Natural music course leaflets.
Ripley, Lillie Rosalie.
Poems. '10(D31) c. D. $1. Badger.
RIPLEY, N. Y.
Parker, A. C. Excavations in an Erie Indian village and burial site at Ripley, N. Y. 30 c. N. Y. State Educ.
Ripper, W:.
Heat engines: (being a new ed. of "Steam.") '10(Ap2) il. D. 90 c. net. Longmans.
Rise and progress of the British explosives industry; pub. under the auspices of the International Congress of Applied Chemistry by its Explosive Section. '09(Jl3) il. pors. figs., facsims., O. *$5.25 net. Macmillan.
Rise of Louis Napoleon. Simpson, F: A. *$3.50 net. Putnam.
Rise of man. Conder, C. R. *$2.50 net. Dutton.
Rise of music. Goddard, J. *$3 net. Scribner.
Rise of Silas Lapham. *See* Howells, W: Dean.
Rise of South Africa. Cory, G: E: $5. Longmans.
Rise of the Dutch Republic. *See* Motley, J: Lothrop.
Rise of the mediæval church. Flick, A. C. **$3.50 net. Putnam.
Rise of the republic of the United States. Frothingham, R: $2. Little, B. & Co.
RISING FAMILY.
See Genealogies: Dewey, L: M.
Risley, Edn. Hills.
Risley family hist., incl. records of some of the early English Risleys; genealogy of the descendants of Richard Risley, of Newtown (Cambridge), Massachusetts (1633), and of Hartford, Connecticut (1636); acct. of the family reunion at Hartford, Aug. 3, 1904, and a list of the founders of the commonwealth of Connecticut. '09, [1910.] (F) c. 3-306 p. il. map, 8°, $5. Grafton Press.
RISLEY FAMILY.
See Genealogies.
Ristine, Fk. Humphrey.
English tragicomedy; its origin and history. '10(D24) c. 8°, (Columbia Univ. studies in English.) $1.50. Columbia Univ.
Ritchey, G: Willis.
60-inch reflector of Mt. Wilson Solar Observatory. '09(My) 12 p. il. 4°, (Contributions from Mount Wilson Solar Observatory.) pap. (Not for sale.) Carnegie.
Ritchey, Ja.
Pattern making: manual of practical instruction in the use of woodworking tools and machinery. '08(Ja18) il. diagrs., 8°, $1. Am. Sch. Corr.
Ritchey, Ja. A.
Psychology of the will. '08(D19) c. O. $1.50. B'way Pub.
Ritchie, Anne Isabella Thackeray, Lady.
Blackstick papers. '08(D5) c. por. O. **$1.75 net. Putnam.
Ritchie, Fs.
First steps in Latin; ed. by F: C. Staples. '09(Jl3) c. D. 60 c. Longmans.
Second steps in Latin; ed. by F: C. Staples. '10(O1) D. 75 c. Longmans.
Ritchie, J: Woodside.
Human physiology: elem. text-book. '09 (My15) c. il. figs. D. (New world science ser.) 80 c. World Bk.
Primer of sanitation; being a simple work on disease germs and how to fight them. '09(D4) c. il. D. (New-world science ser.) 60 c. World Bk.
Sanitation and physiology; being primer of sanitation and human physiology in 1 v. '10(D) c. il. 12°, (New-World science ser.) $1.20. World Bk.
Each part also issued separately.
—, and Caldwell, Jos. Stuart.
Primer of hygiene. '10(Jl16) c. 12°, (New-world science ser.) 40 c. World Bk.
—, and Purcell, Marg. Anna.
Primer of sanitation for the tropics; with an introd. by D: P. Barrows, and a chapter on opium by the Rt. Rev. C: H. Brent. '10(D) c. 10+182 p. il. 12°, (New-World science ser.) 60 c. World Bk.
RITES AND CEREMONIES.
Fleming, W. L. Religious and hospitable rite of feet washing. gratis. W. L. Fleming.
See also Baptism;—Lord's supper;—Marriage;—Worship.

Ritsch, J:, Esq., pseud.
See Steppes, J: P.

RITSCHLIANISM.
See Theology.

Ritter, Etienne Alphonse.
From prospect to mine. '10(Je4) c. il. 12°, $2. Mining Science.
Origin of ore deposits. 3d ed. '08(O17) c. il. 16°, 50 c. Mining Science.

Ritter, T: Jefferson.
People's home medical book. '10(N) 4+478 p. por. il. (partly col.) 4°, (People's home lib.) $3. R. C. Barnum.

Ritter, W: Emerson.
Halocynthia Johnsoni n. sp.; comprehensive inquiry as to the extent of law and order that prevails in a single animal species. '09(N) 65-114 p. il. 4°, (Univ. of Cal. pubs.; Zoology; Contribs. from the lab'y of the Marine Biological Association of San Diego.) pap., 50 c. Univ. of Cal.
Marine Biological Station of San Diego; sketch of its hist. and purposes, and what the station is, with an example popularly told, of the investigations being carried on. '10(D) 40 p. il. 8°. Marine Biol.

—, and Bailey, S: E.
On the weight of developing eggs. pt. 1, The possible significance of such investigations by W: E. Ritter; pt. 2, Practicability of the determinations by S: E. Bailey. '08(D) 10 p. (Univ. of Cal. pubs.; Zoology.) pap., 10 c. Univ. of Cal.

RITUAL.
See Odd-Fellows;—Worship.

Ritual "reason why." Walker, C:, *ed.* *$1 net. Young Churchman.

Rival campers ser. *See* Smith, Ruel Perley.

Rival pitchers. Chadwick, L. $1. Cupples & L.

Rivals (The). *See* Sheridan, R: Brinsley Butler. School for scandal.

Rivals and chums. Carr, K. $1.25. Lippincott.

River and I. Neihardt, J: G. $2 net. Putnam.

River pirates. Harper, O. 25 c. J. S. Ogilvie.

Riverman. White, S. E: †$1.50. McClure.

Rivers, W. H. R.
Influence of alcohol and other drugs on fatigue: the Croonian lectures del. at the Royal College of Physicians in 1906. '08 (Ap18) O. *$1.70 net. Longmans.

RIVERS.
Abbot, H: L. Regulation of rivers in the interest of navigation. $1.25. "Professional Memoirs."
Singleton, E., *comp. and ed.* Great rivers of the world. **$1.60 net. Dodd.
United States. *Engineer School.* On the amelioration of rivers with unstable beds by the system Audouin. (Not for sale.) Engineer Sch.
United States. *Treasury Dept.* Balance of appropriations for river and harbor improvements. (Add. Superintendent for price.) U. S., Supt. of Docs.
See also Floods;—Inland navigation;—*also* names of rivers.

Rivers and streams of England. Bradley, A. G. *$6 net. Macmillan.

RIVERSIDE, Cal.
Benton, A. B. Mission inn. $2; $4. M. E. L. Allen.

Riverside educational monographs; ed. by H: Suzzallo. D. **35 c. net. Houghton M.
—Cubberley. Changing conceptions of education.
—Dewey. Moral principles in education.
—Earhart. Teaching children to study. 60 c.
—Eliot. Education for efficiency.
—Emerson. Education.
—Fiske. Meaning of infancy.
—Hyde. Teacher's philosophy in and out of school.
—Palmer. Ethical and moral instruction in schools.—Ideal teacher.—Self-cultivation in English.
—Snedden. Problem of vocational education.

Riverside literature ser. il. D. Houghton M.
—Bacon. Essays. *40 c. net; *30 c. net.
—Byron. Childe Harold, canto 4, Prisoner of Chillon and Mazeppa. ea., 25 c.
—Child, *ed.* Second shepherds' play, Everyman, and other early plays. 40 c.
—Gaskell. Cranford. 40 c.
—Goldsmith. Good natured man; [and] She stoops to conquer. 40 c.—Separately. ea., 15 c.
—Harris. Little Mr. Thimblefinger stories. 40 c.
—Homer. Odyssey. *75 c. net.
—Howells. Rise of Silas Lapham. 40 c.
—Huxley. Autobiography. 40 c.
—Irving. Selections from Bracebridge Hall. 25 c.
—Macaulay, *Lord.* Essay on Warren Hastings. 15 c.—Essays on Lord Clive and Warren Hastings. 40 c.
—Malory. King Arthur stories. **40 c. net.
—Moores. Life of Abraham Lincoln. **25 c. net; **15 c. net.
—Ruskin. Selections. **50 c. net.
—Shakespeare. King Lear. 25 c.
—Sheridan. The rivals. 25 c.
—Thomas. How to teach English classics.
—Thoreau. Katahdin and Chesuncook. 25 c.
—Virgil. Æneid of Virgil. 75 c.
—Witham. English and Scottish ballads. 40 c.

Rives, Amélie, (Princess Troubetzkoy.)
Golden Rose. '08(My16) c. D. †$1.25. Harper.
Pan's mountain. '10(O8) c. D. $1.50. Harper.
Trix and Over-the-moon. '09(O23) c. il. O. hf. cl., †$1. Harper.

Rives, Hallie Erminie, [Mrs. Post Wheeler.]
Kingdom of slender swords; with foreword by His Excellency Baron Makino. '10 (F5) c. col. il. D. †$1.50. Bobbs-M.

Rivets for truth. Marshall, L. 60 c. Chr. Pub. Co.

RIVIERA (The), France.
Home, G. C. Along the rivieras of France and Italy. *$3 net. Macmillan.

Rivoira, G. Teresio.
Lombardic architecture, its origin and derivation; tr. by G. McN. Rushparth. In 2 v. '10(O15) il. $20. Helburn.

Rivot, Charles Gaston.
Souvenirs d' Algérie et nouveaux pastels, prose et poésie. '09(Ap3) c. D. *$1 net. Neale.

Rivulets of song. McCallum, P. D. $1. B'way Pub.

Rix, Fk. Reader.
Assembly song book. New ed. '09 (My15) 8°, bds., *50 c. net. Barnes.
Manual of school music in elementary grades. '09(Ap24) c. il. D. *60 c. net. Macmillan.
The mastersinger; collection of choruses and part songs arr. and adapt. for the classroom and for large and small assemblies. '10(D10) c. Q. 65 c. Am. Bk.
Songs of school and flag. New ed. '10 (O8) 8°, 75 c. net. Macmillan.
Voice training for school children. '10 (Jl30) c. D. 50 c. net. Barnes.

Rix, Guy Scoby.
Hist. and genealogy of the Ricks family in America. '08(N) 184 p. il. pors. $5. J. Ricks.

Rix, Herb.
Prince Pimpernel; or, Kitty's adventures in Fairyland and the regions adjoining; fairy story. '10(S17) O. $1. Estes.

Ro (*a universal language*).
Foster, E: P. Ro. $1. Ro Co.

Roach, Arno L.
Graphic history: correlated and illustrated history: [United States.] '08(D) c. 160 p. 8°, $3. Dixon.

Road of life. Smith, M. C. $1. A. Harriman.

Road rights of motorists. Abbott, T. O. $1.50 net. Outing.

Road to Oz. Baum, L. F. $1.25. Reilly & B.

Road to power. Kautsky, K. 50 c. S: A. Bloch.

Road to Providence. Daviess, M. T. $1.50. Bobbs-M.

Roads, C:, D.D.
Rural christendom; or, the problems of Christianizing country communities; prize book. '09(N6) c. D. (Green Fund book.) *90 c. net. Am. S. S.

ROADS.
Baker, F: A. Duration of municipal street grants. $2.50. Record Pr. (Mich.)
Barrett Manufacturing Co. Tarvia and pitch filler. (Not for sale.) Barrett Mfg. Co.
Becker, N. D. Road rules and the law of automobiles. $1. E. W. Whitfield.
Brandt, C: E. Road locating and building simplified. $1. C. E. Brandt.
Buckley, E. R. Public roads, their improvement and maintenance. (Add. pub. for price.) Missouri Bu. Geol.
Byrne, A. T., *and* Phillips, A. E. Highway construction. $1. Am. Sch. Corr.
Eno, W: P. Street traffic regulations. $2. Rider & D.
Frost, H. Art of roadmaking. $3. H. Frost.

ROADS.—*Continued.*
Good Roads Party from states of Arkansas, Oklahoma, Louisiana, Texas, on tour of inspection through eastern states. St. Louis and San Francisco R.R.
Green, S: A. Early mile-stones leading from Boston; and mile-stones at Groton. 25 c. S: A. Green.
Hubbard, P. Dust preventives and road binders. $3 net. Wiley.
Judson, W: P. City roads and pavements. *$2 net.—Road preservation and dust prevention. *$1.50 net. Engineering News.
Mason, H. D. On highways law. $3.50. Banks & Co.
Morrison, C: E: Highway engineering. $2.50. Wiley.
Municipal Art Society of Hartford. Street name plates. gratis. Municipal Art Soc.
Progress repts. of experiments in dust prevention and road preservation. [1910.] '10(Ag) 32 p. 8°, (U. S., Dept. of Agriculture, Office of Public Roads, circular.)
Progress reports of experiments in dust prevention, road preservation, and road construction. [1909.] U. S., Supt. of Docs.
Smith, J. W. Dustless roads. *$3.50 net. Lippincott.
Spalding, F: P. Text book on roads and pavements. $2. Wiley.
Spoon, W: L. Sand-clay and earth roads in the Middle West. U. S., Supt. of Docs.
United States. *Dept. of Agriculture. Office of Public Roads.* Publications of the Office of Public Roads.
United States. Exhibit of the Office of Public Roads; Alaska-Yukon-Pacific exposition. '09(N) 23 p. il. 8°. (Add. Superintendent for price.)
United States. Public Roads Office. Bulletins and circulars relating to the improvement of roads; Agricultural Department, U. S. A.; for sale by the Superintendent of Documents. '09(O) 9 p. 8°. (Add. Superintendent for price.)
United States. *Superintendent of Documents.* Public Roads Office; bulls. and circulars. gratis.
United States. *Treasury Dept.* Roads and canals; letter from the Secretary of the Treasury, transmitting rept. respecting roads and canals. '10(Jl) 42 p. 8°.
Whinery, S: Specifications for street roadway pavements. *50 c. net. Engineering News.
Wilcox, D. F. Municipal franchises; description of the terms and conditions upon which private corporations enjoy special privileges in the streets of American cities. In 2 v. ea., $5. Gervaise Press.
See also Automobiles;—Bridges;—Concrete;—Culverts;—Electric railroads;—Railroads;—Street cleaning;—Street railroads;—*also* Chicago;—*also* names of states:—*also* Old Mine Road.

Roads of destiny. Henry, O., *pseud.* †$1.50. Doubleday, P.

Roadtown. Chambless, E. $1.25 net; $1.35 net. Roadtown.

ROANOKE, Va.
Nolen, J: Remodeling Roanoke. **$1 net. J: Nolen.**

ROANOKE ISLAND, N. C.
Connor, R. D. W. Beginnings of English America: Sir Walter Raleigh's settlements on Roanoke Island, 1584-1587. gratis. N. C. Hist.
McMillan, H. Sir Walter Raleigh's lost colony: Roanoke Island. 50 c. H. McMillan.

Roark, Ruric Nevel, ed.
See Holst, Bernhart Paul, *ed.*

Rob Roy. *See* Scctt, *Sir* Wa.

Robarts, Edith.
True stories from history. '10(D24) il. (partly in col.) 4°, bds., 60 c. Dodge.

Robarts, Heber, M.D.
Practical radium: practical uses of radium in the treatment of obstinate forms of disease. '09(Ap24) c. il. pors. D. $1. H. Robarts.

Robb, D: Broadfoot.
Poems and essays for the workers. '07, [1908.] (Mr.) c. 57 p. por. D. pap., 30 c. **D: B. Robb.**

Robb, Mrs. Isabel Adams Hampton.
Educational standards with other papers on nursing subjects. '10(D) 268 p. 12°, $1.25. Koeckert.
Hampton's nursing: its principles and practice for hospital and private use. 3d ed., rev. and enl. '10(D) 565 p. il. 8°, $2 net. Koeckert.
Nursing ethics for hospital and private use. '10(D) 273 p. 12°, $1.50. Koeckert.

Robb, W.
See Pleydell, A. C.

Robberflies of the genus *Asilus.* Hine, J. S. 50 c. J. S. Hine.

Robbins, Anne Manning.
Both sides of the veil; personal experience. '09, [1910.] (F) various paging, por. facsim., 12°, *$1.25 net. Sherman, F.

Robbins, E: Rutledge.
Key to Plane and solid geometry. '08 (Ja11) O. $1. Am. Bk.
Plane trigonometry. '10(Ja15) c. il. 8°, 60 c. Am. Bk.

Robbins, Edn. Clyde, comp.
Selected articles on a central bank of the United States. '10(O15) 12°, (Debaters' hdbk. ser.) $1 net. H. W. Wilson.
Selected articles on the commission plan of municipal government. '10(Ja8) 12°, (Debaters' hdbk. ser.) $1 net. H. W. Wilson.

Robbins, Mrs. Helen Henrietta, ed.
George, Earl of Macartney, first British ambassador to China: personal narrative and extracts from letters and narrative of his experiences in China as told by himself, 1737-1806. '08(Mr14) il. pors. 8°, *$5 net. Dutton.

Robbins, Leonard H.
Jersey jingles. '08(Ja11) il. O. $1. Vance.

Robbins, Reginald Chauncey.
Love poems. 3d series. '10(Jl) 3-148 p. 12°. R. C. Robbins.
Poems of personality. 2d ser. '09(Jl) 4+229 p. 12°. (Not for sale.) Riverside Press.

Robbins, Mrs. Sarah Stuart.
Old Andover days. '08(O3) c. il. D. bds., *$1 net. Pilgrim Press.

Roberson, Mrs. Harriette Gunn.
Mary of Magdala. '09(My22) c. D. $1.50. Saalfield.

ROBERT COLLEGE, Constantinople, Turkey.
Washburn, G: Fifty years in Constantinople: [hist. of Robert College.] **$3 net. **Houghton M.**

Robert Emmet. Gwynn, S. L. *$1.50 net. Macmillan.

Robert Emmet's wooing. Blum, E. C. $1. Cochrane.

Roberts, Brigham H:
Defense of the faith and the saints. v. 1. '08(Ap18) c. 12°, $1.50. Deseret News.
—, comp. Seventy's course in theology. First year. '07, [1908.] (Ag) c. 12+168 p. 8°. (Add. pub. for price.) Deseret News.

Roberts, Rev. Cassius Marcus.
Last salute, and other poems. '08(My.) c. 75 p. por. 8°, $1.50; $1. C. M. Roberts.

Roberts, C: G: Douglas.
The backwoodsmen. '09(N6) c. il. D. †$1.50. Macmillan.
House in the water: book of animal stories. '08(Je20) c. D. $1.50. L. C. Page.
Kings in exile. '10(F26) c. il. D. †$1.50. Macmillan.

Roberts, C: Rhoads, and Schindel, Rev. Jacob D.
Hist. of Egypt Church; read before the Lehigh County, [Pa.] Historical Society. '08, [1909.] (F) 72 p. il. pors. 8°, 55 c.; pap., 27 c. Lehigh Co. Hist. Soc.

Roberts, F: Sleigh, Earl.
Forty-one years in India, from subaltern to commander-in-chief. [Cheaper ed.] '09 (F20) 2 v. in 1, il. pors. fold. maps, D. $2. Longmans.

Roberts, G: E: Thdr.
Captain Love. '08(My16) c. D. †$1.50. L. C. Page.
Cavalier of Virginia; romance. '10(Ap23) c. il. D. $1.50. L. C. Page.
Comrades of the trails. '10(Ag13) c. D. $1.50. L. C. Page.
Flying Plover, his stories; told him by Squat-by-the-fire. '09(Jl17) c. il. O. $1. L. C. Page.

Roberts, G: Evan, and Sprague, Oliver Mitchell Wentworth.
Central bank of issue. '10(Jl2) c. 24°, (Bankers handy ser.) 50 c. Bankers Pub.

Roberts, J: Bingham.
Doctor's duty to the state. '08(O) 9-108 p. 12°. (Not for sale.) Am. Medical.

Roberts, J: Gray.
Currency reform: issue of legal tender Treasury notes, elastic currency, guaranteeing bank deposits, emergency currency, restoration of silver 16 to 1, illegal coinage. '09(Mr6) c. 16°, pap., 25 c. J: G. Roberts.

Roberts, J: S.
See Byrnes, Ja. C.

Roberts, Morley.
"Blue Peter": sea yarns. '08(Ag1) c. D. $1.50. L. C. Page.
Captain Spink, and other sea comedies. '08 (Je27) D. †$1.50. Lippincott.
David Bran. '09(F6) c. front. D. $1.50. L. C. Page.

Roberts, Osseannah.
Son of the North. '08, [1909.] (Mr) c. il. 12°, $1.50. C. M. Clark.

Roberts, P:
English for coming Americans: rational system for teaching English to foreigners. '09(Mr27) c. 8°, Teachers' manual, 50 c.; pap., 35 c. Students' lesson leaves, 4 series, ea. 10 lessons. 1, Domestic; 2, Industrial; 3, Commercial; 4, Textile subjects. per series, 5 c. Y. M. C. A.
Immigrant races in North America. '10 (D10) c. il. pors. maps, 12°, 50 c. Y. M. C. A.
Reader for coming Americans; readings and language lessons in history, industries and government. '10(Ap9) c. il. 8°, 50 c. Y. M. C. A.

Roberts, R. Ellis.
Samuel Rogers and his circle. '10(N5) il. 8°, $3.50 net. Dutton.

Roberts, Rob.
See Vermont digest.

Roberts, Shelley Saufley.
Track formulæ and tables. '10(D17) c. figs. tabs., 16°, mor., $3. Wiley.

Roberts, T: G.
Merchant marine and the navy. '10(Je) 27 p. 8°. U. S., Supt. of Docs.

Roberts, W. J.
Love story of Empress Josephine. '08 (O10) 8°. *$3.50 net; ¾ levant, *$7 net. Pott.

Roberts-Austen, Sir W: Chandler.
Introd. to the study of metallurgy. 6th ed.; rev. by F. W. Harbord. '10(D17) il. 8°, $6 net. Lippincott.

Roberts and Rolfe Latin ser. il. map, 12°. Scribner.
—Cæsar. Gallic war; books I-II and selections from V-VII. $1.25.

Roberts home builder. '10(Ap) c. 96 p. il. plans, obl. 16°, $1. Roberts & R.

Robertson, Alice.
Incrusting *Chilostomatous bryozoa* of the west coast of North America. '08(Je27) il. Q. (Univ. of Cal. pubs., Zoology.) pap., $1. Univ. of Cal.

Robertson, Alice Alberthe.
See St. Luz, Berthe, *pseud.*

Robertson, Archibald T:, D.D.
Epochs in the life of Paul. '09(Ap24) c. D. **$1.25 net. Scribner.
Short grammar of the Greek New Testament. '08(O17); 2d ed., rev. '09(N) c. 12°, ea., $1.50. Armstrong.

Robertson, Duncan Maclaren.
Hist. of the French Academy, 1635[4]-1910; with an outline sketch of the Institute of France. '10(D24) c. por. O. $3 net. G: W. Dillingham.

Robertson, Elbertine, ["Alberta."]
Marriage: [true meaning of marriage.] '07, [1908.] (Je.) c. 36 p. T. pap., 10 c. E. H. Riddell-Huston.

Robertson, F: W:
Sermons on Bible subjects. '08(O17) 16°, (Best books ser.) leath., *$1 net. Dutton.
Sermons on Christian doctrine. '08(O17) 16°, (Best books ser.) leath., *$1 net. Dutton.
Sermons on religion and life. '08(O17) 16°, (Best books ser.) leath., *$1 net. Dutton.

Robertson, Georgia, comp.
Common sense recipes for everyday use. '07, [1908.] (My.) c. 66 p. O. pap., 25 c. G. Robertson.
Money value of good health. '08(My.) c. 40 p. O. pap., 10 c. G. Robertson.

Robertson, J: G.
Milton's fame on the continent. '09, [1910.] (F) pap., 35 c. Oxford Univ.

ROBERTSON, James.
Gordon, C: W: Life of James Robertson, missionary superintendent in the Northwest. *$1.50 net. Revell.

Robertson, Ja. Alex.
Bibliography of the Philippine Islands. '08 (Je20) c. 8°, $10. A. H. Clark.
List of documents in Spanish archives rel. to the hist. of the U. S., which have been printed or of which transcripts are preserved in American libraries. '10(Ag27) Q. pap., $2.25. Carnegie.
—, ed. and tr. *See* Blair, Emma Helen.

Robertson, J: Mackinnon.
Montaigne and Shakespeare. '09(O9) 8°, *$2 net. Macmillan.
Trade and tariffs. '08(N7) 12°, *$1.50 net. Macmillan.
See also Ross, G: Alex. Johnston.

Robertson, S: L.
Gulf songs. '09(My22) por. O. (Add. author for price.) S: L. Robertson.

Robertson, T. Brailsford.
On the synthesis of paranuclein through the agency of pepsin and the chemical mechanics of the hydrolysis and synthesis of proteins through the agency of enzymes, (preliminary communication.) '08(D) 4°, (Univ. of Cal. pubs.; Physiology.) pap. (Add. Univ. for price.) Univ. of Cal.
The proteins. '09(N13) O. (Univ. of Cal. pubs.; Physiology.) pap., $1. Univ. of Cal.

Robertson, W:, and Herzog, Maximilian.
Meat and food inspection. '08(My16) c. il. 8°, *$3.50 net. Chic. Med. Bk.

Robertson-Scott, J. W., ["Home Counties."]
The case for the goat, with the practical experience of twenty-four experts. '08 (My9) il. 12°, *$1.25 net. Dutton.

ROBESPIERRE, Maximilien Marie Isidore.
Warwick, C: F. Robespierre and the French Revolution. **$2.50 net. Jacobs

Robichez, E.
See Williams-White, H.

Robin, Albert.
See Rohé, G: H:

Robin Aroon. Gordon, A. C. *$1.25 net. Neale.

ROBIN HOOD.
Clawson, W: H. Gest of Robin Hood. $1. Univ. of Toronto.
Finnemore, J: Story of Robinhood. *$1.50 net. Macmillan.
Lansing, M. F. Life in the greenwood: [tales of Robin Hood and his "merrie men."] 35 c. Ginn.
Macleod, M., *comp.* Robin Hood and his merry men. 50 c. Dodge.

Robin Hood; ed. by Clifton Johnson. '10 (N19) c. il. D. (Golden books for children.) $1 net. Baker & T.

Robinovitch, Louise G.
I. Resuscitation of subjects in a condition of apparent death, caused by chloroform, electrocution, etc. II. Electric anesthesia in lab'y surgery successfully applied during a period of three years. III. Resuscitation of a woman in profound syncope caused by chronic morphine poisoning. IV. Different effects of various electric currents. Choice of current for resuscitation. V. Presentation of instruments for electric anesthesia and resuscitation. VI. Jolyet's cannula modified by Dr. Robinovitch. [1910.] (O) 40 p. il. 4°, $1. Journ. Mental.

Robin's love story. Bray, B. 50 c. Cochrane.

Robins, E:
Romances of early America. New ed. '08 (D19) c. il. cr. 8°, $1.50. Jacobs.

Robins, Eliz., [Mrs. G. R. Parkes; "C. E. Raimond."]
Come and find me. '08(F29) c. il. D. †$1.50. Century Co.
Florentine frame. '09(N20) c. D. †$1.50. Moffat.
Mills of the gods. '08(O17) c. D. †$1. Moffat.

Robins, Gertrude M.
See Reynolds, *Mrs.* L: Baillie.

Robins, Herbert W. H.
See Cope, E: A.

Robinson, A. M.
Heaven: what and where? '09(Mr27) c. D. 50 c.; pap., 25 c. Pub. Ho. of M. E. Ch., So.

Robinson, Arth. J.
Memorandum and anecdotes of the Civil War, 1862-1865. '10(Ag6) c. il. 12°, 25 c. A. J. Robinson.

Robinson, Arth. W., D.D.
Co-operation with God. '08(D12) D. *60 c. net. Cassell.

"Robinson, Bud."
See Robinson, Reuben.

Robinson, C:
See Jerrold. Wa. Copeland;—Mord, W.

Robinson, C: Asbury.
This book contains one hundred reasons why I am a Red man and some nuggets of gold. [1910] (Mr) c. '09. 192 p. il. pors. 8°, 50 c. C: A. Robinson.

Robinson, C: Budd.
Alabastra philippinensia. '08, [1909.] (Mr) 63-75 p. 8°, (Contributions from the New York Botanical Garden.) 25 c. N. Y. Botanical.

Robinson, C: H:, D.D.
Human nature a revelation of the divine: argument for the inspiration of the Old Testament; sequel to "Studies in the character of Christ." New ed. '08(Je13) D. pap., 25 c.; New ed. '10(D24) D. 40 c. Longmans.
Interpretation of the character of Christ to non-Christian races; apology for Christian missions. '10(Mr26) D. *$1.20 net. Longmans.
Studies in Christian worship. 2d ed. '09 (F6) D. 50 c.; pap., 25 c. Longmans.
Studies in the resurrection of Christ: an argument. '09(Mr13) D. *$1.25 net. Longmans.

Robinson, C: Mulford.
Call of the city. '08(O3) c. front. D. bds., **$1.25 net. P. Elder.
The city beautiful; suggestions, together with plans and pictures. '10(Mr5) 4°, $1. Municipal Art Com. (Los A.)

Robinson, C: Napier.
British tar in fact and fiction; poetry, pathos and humor of the sailor's life; with an introd. chapter on the place of the sea officer and seaman in naval history and historical literature by J: Leyland. '09(Je26) il. 8°, *$4 net. Harper.

Robinson, Doane, [pseud. for Jonah Leroy Robinson.]
Sioux Indians. '08(Ag1) il. pors. maps, 8°, $2. Torch Press.

Robinson, E., and Pidgeon, R. H., comps.
Atlas of the borough of Richmond, city of New York. 2d and rev. ed. '07, [1908.] (Jl.) c. maps, f°, $30. E. Robinson.

Robinson, Edn. Arlington.
Town down the river; book of poems. '10 (O15) c. S. $1.25 net. Scribner.

Robinson, Ella M.
See Avery-Stuttle, *Mrs.* Lilla Dale.

Robinson, Emma Amelia.
Short studies of Christ, the ideal hero. '09 (N20) c. D. 50 c. Eaton & M.
Short studies of the heroes of the early church. '08(Jl18) c. maps, plans, D. *50 c. net. Jennings.

Robinson, Ernest H.
See Shaw, Fk. H.

Robinson, Rev. Forbes.
Letters to his friends; ed. with an introductory notice by his brother Charles. '08 (Ap4) pors. D. *$1 net. Longmans.

Robinson, G: Livingstone.
Book of Isaiah, in fifteen studies. '10 (My) 175 p. tab. 12°, 75 c. Y. M. C. A.
Selected literature (2 p.).

Robinson, Harry Perry.
Twentieth century American: comparative study of the peoples of the two great Anglo-Saxon nations. '08(Jl4) c. map, O. **$1.75 net. Putnam.

Robinson, H: Hollister.
See Gregory, Herbert Ernest.

Robinson, Humphrey.
Simple explanation of modern banking customs; ed. from a legal standpoint by W. Overton Harris. '09(S) c. 9-54 p. 8°. (Add. author for price.) H. Robinson.
Simple explanation of modern banking customs; ed. from a legal standpoint by W. Overton Harris. [1910.] (Je) 111 p. c. 16°, 25 c. net. Small.

Robinson, J. Armitage, D.D.
Vision of unity: [sermons.] '08(O10) D. 50 c.; pap., 25 c. Longmans.

Robinson, Mrs. J. Enders, ed.
Restoration of the name of Jefferson Davis to the Cabin John Bridge, Washington, D. C.; being the official correspondence leading to this restoration. '09, [1910.] (Ja) c. 95 p. il. pors. 8°, 75 c. Confederated Southern.

Robinson, Ja. Harvey.
History: [a lecture.] '08(N21) c. 8°, pap. (Add. pubs. for price.) Columbia Univ.

—, and Beard, C: Austin.
Development of modern Europe. '08(Ap4) c. 2 v., il. pors. maps, D. v. 1, $1.50; v. 2, $1.60. Ginn.
Readings in modern European history. In 2 v. v. 1. '08(D19) $1.40; v. 2. '09 (Je5) c. D. $1.50; 2 v. in 1, abrg. ed., $1.50. Ginn.

Robinson, Ja. Watts.
Robinsonian bond and investment tables. [3d ed.] '10(Je4) c. 8°, $5. J. W. Robinson.
Robinsonian building-loan interest tables; complete reference book for the use of building-loan and co-operative bank and other accountants and agents. 6th ed., with supplement. [1910.] (F) c. '09. 218 p. 8°, $5. J. W. Robinson.

Robinson, John.
Burrage, C. New facts concerning John Robinson. 60 c. Oxford Univ.

Robinson, J: Beverley.
Architectural composition. '08(F8) il. 8°, *$2.50 net. Van Nostrand.

Robinson, J: H.
Common-sense poultry doctor. '08(Ja11) 12°, (Farm-poultry ser.) 50 c.. Farm-Poultry.

Robinson, Jonah Leroy Doane, comp.
History of South Dakota from earliest times; rev. by Rob. Floyd Kerr. '07, [1908.] (My.) c. 124 p. il. 8°, (Educator ser.) 75 c. Educator.

Robinson, Dean Jos. Armitage, D.D
Historical character of St. John's gospel: three lectures del. in Westminster Abbey in Advent, 1907. '08(My23) D. pap., 25 c. Longmans.

—, ed. *See* Texts and studies.

Robinson, L. E., and Moore, Irving.
History of Illinois. '09(Ap17) c. map, D. *60 c. net. Am. Bk.

Robinson, Leigh.
Address del. before R. E. Lee Camp, C. V., at Richmond, Va., Dec. 18th, 1908, in the acceptance of the portrait of General William H. Payne. '09(N) 64 p. 8°. (Priv. pr.) Leigh Robinson.

Robinson, Leonard Browning, comp.
See Iowa. Reference work on justice practice.

Robinson, Rev. Leonidas.
Gates and keys to Matthew, incl. short survey of the years between the Testaments. [1910.] (Jl) c. 111 p. 12°, 50 c. Pentecostal.

Robinson, *Mrs.* Mary Darby.
Makower, S. V. Perdita: [biography of Mary Robinson.] *$4 special net. Appleton.

Robinson, Nellie Grace.
Philo's daughter: story of the daughter of the thief with whom Christ was crucified. '09(Ja2) c. D. $1. Jennings.

Robinson, Nina Hill.
That boy o' mine. '08(N) c. 143 p. il. 12°, *75 c. net. Pub. Ho. of M. E. Ch., So.

Robinson, Reuben, ["Bud Robinson."]
Story of Lazarus. '09(D) c. 111 p. por. 50 c. Pentecostal.

Robinson, R: Hallett Meredith.
Naval construction; prepared for the use of the midshipmen of the United States Naval Academy; rev. and enl. '09(N) c. 6+376 p. il. 8°. (Add. pubs. for price.) U. S. Naval Inst.

Robinson, Sarah Conger, ed.
Precepts and prayers; souvenir for the 40th anniversary of the pastorate of Robert Stuart MacArthur, minister of Calvary Baptist Church, New York, since May 15, 1870. '10(Ap23) c. nar. O. 50 c. Treat.
Royal messages of cheer and comfort beautifully told, by Rob. Stewart MacArthur and 230 well-chosen authors; with an introd. by D. C. Hughes, D.D. '09(My) c. 14+384 p. por. 8°, *$1 net; de luxe, *$2 net. Treat.

Robinson, T.
Baldness and grayness. [1910.] (Mr) *$1 net. W: R. Jenkins.
Formerly published by E. R. Pelton.

Robinson, T: Ralph.
Seed sterilization and its effect upon seed inoculation. '10(O) 11 p. tabs., 8°, (U. S., Dept. of Agriculture, Bureau of Plant Industry, circular.)

Robinson, Victor.
Comrad Kropotkin. '09(Mr) 16°, (Lives of great Altrurians.) $1. Altrurians.

Robinson, W: Callyhan.
Elementary law. New ed., rev. '10(F) c. O. *$3.50 net. Little, B. & Co.

Robinson, W: Josephus, M.D.
Never-told tales: [stories of the disastrous results of sexual ignorance.] '09(F13) c. D. $1. Altrurians.
See also Holt, W: Leland.

Robinson, Wilton Howarth.
Dermatology in abstract; guide to the clinical study of diseases of the skin. '09(N) c. 175 p. 24°, $1. Medical Abstract.

Robinson Crusoe. *See* Defoe, Dan.

Robinson Crusoe Library. 3 v. '10(D17) S. leath., per set, $4 net, boxed. Outing.

Robinson's business points. Nichols, J. S. $1. J. L. Nichols.

Robson, Isabel Suart.
Evan Grayle's daughters. '10(Je4) front. D. (Girls' own lib.) 75 c. McKay.
Fortunes of eight; or, the house in Hartford Place. '10(Je4) D. (Girls' own lib.) 75 c. McKay.

Robson, J:, D.D.
Resurrection gospel: study of Christ's great commission. '08(D26) O. *$1.25 net. Jennings.

Robson, Philip W.
Power gas producers. '08(My2) il. O. *$3 net. Longmans.

Roche, C: E.
Things seen in Holland. '09(O2) il. 16°, *75 c. net; leath., *$1 net. Dutton.

Roche, Ja. Jeffrey.
Life of John Boyle O'Reilly; together with his complete poems and speeches; ed. by Mrs. J: Boyle O'Reilly; introd. by Cardinal Gibbons. '10(F12) c. il. por. facsims., O. *$2 net. McVey.

Roche, Rev. Jos. T.
Business side of religion. '08(N) c. 96 p. S. pap., *15 c. net; per 100, *$10 net. Wiltzius.
Die geschæftliche seite der religion. '09 (Je12) c. S. pap., *10 c. net; per 100, $6.50. Wiltzius.
Obligation of hearing mass on Sundays and holy days. New ed. '10(O1) T. pap., 10 c. net; per doz., 75 c. net; per 100 $5 net. Wiltzius.

Rocheleau, W: Fs.
Geography of commerce and industry. Rev. ed. '08(My9) il. maps, 4°, $1. Educ. Pub.
Great American industries. Bk. 4, Transportation. '10(D24) c. il. D. (Home and school ser. for young folks.) 60 c. Flanagan.
Intermediate and grammar methods; series of pract. home studies in pedagogy. 2 v. '09(Jl) c. il. 8°, $6.50. Interstate Sch. Corr.
—, ed. Pract. hist. of the world; acct. of the progress of civilization; prep. with the assistance of eminent educators from the leading colleges and universities. 8 v. '10 (Jl9) c. il. maps, tabs., 8°, (Historians' home study ser.) $26.75. Dixon.

Rochester, N. Y. Chamber of Commerce. Waterways development: Rochester, Pittsburg and New Orleans waterway; the middle line from Lake Ontario to Gulf of Mexico. '08(Jl4) map, 8°, pap., gratis. Wegman.

ROCHESTER, N. Y.
See Monroe Co., N. Y.

Rochester reprints. In 10 v. vs. 1-9. [1910.] (S) 8°, $20. 125 sets. (Sold in sets only.) G. P. Humphrey.
Contents: v. 1, Wheelock, Eleazer, Plain and faithful narrative of the original design, rise, progress and present state of the Indian Charity School at Lebanon, in Conn., Boston, 1763; v. 2, Continuation of the narrative, Boston, 1765; v. 3, Brief narrative of the Indian School [by Nathaniel Whitaker], London, 1766; v. 4, Brief narrative, etc., 2d ed., London, 1767; v. 5, Continuation of the narrative, etc., with appendix, London, 1769; v. 6, Continuation of the narrative, 1771; v. 7, Continuation of the narrative, New Hampshire, 1773; v. 8, Continuation of the narrative, Hartford, 1773; v. 9, Continuation of the narrative, Hartford, 1775; v. 10, Colonel Thomas Blood: crown stealer.

Rock, Ja.
Thro' space. '09(D11) D. bds., 60 c. N. E. Druggist.

Rock and water gardens. Meyer, F. W. $2. Scribner.

Rock-climbing in Skye. Abraham, A. P. *$7 net. Longmans.

ROCK DRILLS.
See Machinery.

ROCK RIVER VALLEY, Wis.
Coe, E. D. Reminiscences of a pioneer in the Rock River country. 35 c. State Hist., Wis.

ROCK SALT.
See Salts.

Rockefeller, J: Davison.
Random reminiscences of men and events. '09(Ap17) c. O. $1. Doubleday, P.

Rockefeller Institute for Medical Research, New York City. Rockefeller Institute for Medical Research; description of the buildings; addresses del. at the opening of the laboratories, in New York City, May 11, 1906. '07, [1909.] (Je) 50 p. Q. (Add. pubs. for price.) Rockefeller Inst.

Rockel, W: Mahlon.
Complete guide for township officers, cont. all the sections of the revised statutes of Ohio applicable to township affairs, with forms and citations for the guidance of township officers. 12th ed. '10 (D) 2+1032 p. 8°, $4. W. H. Anderson.
Guide for administrators and executors in the settlement of estates of deceased persons in the state of Ohio. '08(My.) c. 8+209 p. 12°, $1.50. W. H. Anderson.
Treatise on the law of mechanics' liens, incl. the procedure for perfecting and enforcing such liens, together with complete forms. '09(Jl) c. 82+801 p. O. *$6 net. Bobbs-M.
—, comp. *See* Ohio. Complete guide for township officers.

ROCKINGHAM, Vt.
Vital records to Jan. 1, 1845. $3.50. Littlefield.

ROCKS.
Bowles, O. Tables for the determination of common rocks. 50 c. Van Nostrand.
Clarke, F. W. Analysis of rocks and minerals from the lab'y of the U. S. Geolog. Survey. U. S., Supt. of Docs.
Harker, A. Natural history of igneous rocks. *$3 net. Macmillan.
Harker, A. Petrology for students. *$2 net. Putnam.
Hatch, F: H. Text books of petrology. *$1.90 net. Macmillan.
Hillebrand, W: F. Analysis of silicate and carbonate rocks. Gov. Pr. Off.
Iddings, J Igneous rocks. v. 1. $5. Wiley.
Lewis, J. V. Origin and relations of the Newark rocks. (Add. author for price.) J. V. Lewis.
Pirsson, L: V. Rocks and rock minerals. **$2.50 net. Wiley.
Tillman, S: E. Text-book of important minerals and rocks. **$2 net. Wiley.
Washington, H: S. Manual of the chemical analysis of rocks. $2. Wiley.
See also Chemistry; — Diamonds; — Geology; — Granite;—Mineralogy;—Stone;—Water.

Rocks in the road to fortune. Clifford, H: B. $1.50. • Gotham Press.

Rockwood, Elbert W:
Introd. to chemical analysis; for students of medicine, pharmacy, and dentistry. 3d rev. ed. '10, [1909.] (N) c. 13+247 p. il. 8°, *$1.50 net. Blakiston.

Rockwood, Roy, pseud.
Adrift on the Pacific. '08(Je6) c. il. 12°, (Deep sea ser.) 60 c. Grosset.
Five thousand miles underground. '08 (D12) c. il. 12°, (Great marvel ser.) 60 c. Cupples & L.
Through space to Mars; or, the longest journey on record. [1910.] (Jl) c. 248 p. il. 12°, (Great marvel ser.) 60 c. Cupples & L.

ROCKY MOUNTAINS.
Coulter, J: M. New manual of botany of the central Rocky Mountains. $2.50. Am. Bk.
Johnson, C. Highways and byways of the Rocky Mountains. $2 net. Macmillan.
Longyear, B. O. Rocky Mountain wild flower studies. $1. Merchants Pub.
Mills, E. A. Wild life on the Rockies. **$1.75 net. Houghton M.
Sherzer, W: H. Glaciers of the Canadian Rockies and Selkirks. Smith. Inst.
Wilcox, W. D. Guide-book to the Lake Louise region, incl. Paradise Valley, Valley of the Ten Peaks and neighborhood of Lake O'Hara. $1. Judd & D.
Wilcox, W. D. Rockies of Canada. **$5 net. Putnam.

Rod of justice. Askew, *Mrs.* A. J. de C. L. $1.50. Brentano's.

Rodeffer, J: D:
Pioneer in international arbitration; reprinted from the *Sewanee Review* for April, 1907. '07, [1909.] 6 p. 8°, pap., 40c. J: D: Rodeffer.

RODENTS.
Hagerdoorn, A. L. Inheritance of yellow color in rodents. 5 c. Univ. of Cal.
Heller, E. Five new rodents, from British East Africa. Smith. Inst.
Kellogg, L. Rodent fauna of the late tertiary beds at Virgin Valley and Thousand Creek, Nev. 15 c. Univ. of Cal.
Miller, G. S. New rodent of the genus Saccestomus from British East Africa. Smith. Inst.
Osgood, W. H. Diagnosis of new East African mammals, incl. new genus of *Muridae.* 50 c. Field Museum.
Taylor, W. P., *and* Dixon, J. Two new rodents from Nevada. 20 c. Univ. of Cal.
See also Mice;—Rats;—Squirrels.

RODGERS, John.
Paullin, C: O. Commodore John Rodgers. *$4 net. A. H. Clark.
Paullin, C: O. Services of Commodore John Rodgers in our wars with the Barbary corsairs. $1. U. S. Naval Inst.

RODIN, François-Auguste.
Lawton, F: François Auguste Rodin. *$1 net. M. Kennerley.

Rodmaking for beginners. Frazar, P. D. $1. Forest.

Rodman, W: L:, M.D.
Diseases of the breast, with special reference to cancer. '08(Ap4) c. il. 8°, *$4 net. Blakiston.

Rodman, Willoughby.
Hist. of the bench and bar of southern California; introd. by W. J. Hunsaker. '09(My) 262 p. pors. 4°, $17.50. W. J. Porter.

Rodney, Mary.
Girl from Dixie. '10(O8) c. 12°, $1. Cochrane.
In the mountain's shadow. '08(S5) il. 12°, $1.50. C. M. Clark.

Roe, A. S.
China as I saw it; woman's letters from the Celestial Empire. '10(Je11) il. O. $3 net. Macmillan.

Roe, Alfr. Seelye, ed.
Melvin memorial; Sleepy Hollow Cemetery, Concord, Mass., a brother's tribute; exercises at dedication, June 16, 1909. '10 (N) 12+148 p. pors. fold. facsim. 8°. (Priv. pr.) J. C. Melvin.

Roe, Clifford Griffith.
Panders and their white slaves. '10(Je18) c. D. $1 net. Revell.

Roe, E: Drake, jr.
See Metzler, W: H:

Roe, Rev. E: Payson.
Day of fate. '08(N21) c. front. 12°, (Ajax ser.) †$1.25. Dodd.

Roe, E: Reynolds.
Rum and ruin; plea for temperance. '09 (D4) c. front. D. $1; pap., 25 c. Laird.

Roe, E: T:
Business and law; or, the careful man's guide. '08(Ap.) c. 698 p. $2.75; hf. mor., $3; mor., $3.50. J: A. Hertel.
700 lessons in business; complete compendium of how to do business by the latest and safest methods. [9th ed.] '10(Jl16) c. il. 12°, $1. J: A. Hertel.

Roe, Mrs. Frances Marie Antoinette Mack.
Army letters from an officer's wife, 1871-1888. '09(O16) c. D. il. **$2 net. Appleton.

Roe, F: W:
Thomas Carlyle as a critic of literature. '10(Ap9) c. 8°, $1.25 net. Lemcke.
—, ed. *See* Dickinson, T: H.

Roe, G:
Ibiis in Paradise: a story of the temptation. '09(Mr6) c. front. S. leath., $1.25, boxed. Altemus.

Roeder, Rev. Adolph.
Practical citizenship. '08(Jl11) c. D. *$1.50 net. Blanchard.
Symbol stories for children of all ages. '10(Ja15) D. $1; bds., 75 c.; mor., $1.50. New Church.

Roeding, F: W.
Irrigation of sugar beets. '10(Je) 52 p. il. 8°, (U. S., Dept. of Agriculture, farmers' bull.) U. S., Supt. of Docs.

ROENTGEN RAYS.
Burdick, G. G. X-ray and high frequency in medicine. $2.75. Physical Therapy.
Eberhart, N. M. Pract. X-ray therapy. $1.50. New Med.
Kassabian, M. K. Röntgen rays and electro-therapeutics. $3.50. Lippincott.

ROENTGEN RAYS.—*Continued.*
Morris, M., *and* Dore, S. E. Light and X-ray treatment of skin diseases. $1.50 net. Funk.
Rotch, T: M. Living anatomy and pathology; diagnosis of diseases in early life by the Roentgen method. $6 net. Lippincott.
Tousey, S. Medical electricity and röntgen rays. $7 net; $8.50 net. Saunders.
Tousey, S. X-ray in dentistry. (Priv. pr.) S. Tousey.
See also Electrotherapeutics;—Radiotherapy.

Rogers, Allen.
Laboratory guide of industrial chemistry. '09(My) 175 p. il. 8°, *$1.50 net. Van Nostrand.

Rogers, Allen E.
Manual of the essentials of parliamentary law. '09(Ap3) T. 25 c. A. E. Rogers.

Rogers, Mrs. Anna Alexander.
Why American marriages fail. '10(Ja8) c. 12°, $1.25. Houghton M.

Rogers, Arth.
Prophecy and poetry; studies in Isaiah and Browning; the Bohlen lectures for 1909. '09(Ap10) c. D. **$1.25 net. Longmans.

Rogers, Arth. D.
House of brick for ten thousand dollars; plea for the greater use of brick in our domestic architecture. [2d ed.] '10 (S17) c. il. plans, 4°, 25 c. Rogers & M.

Rogers, Arth. W., and Du Toit, A. L.
Introd. to the geology of Cape Colony; with a chapter on the fossil reptiles of the Karroo formation. 2d ed. '09(D11) il. map, D. (South African science ser.) *$3.50 net. Longmans.

Rogers, Mrs. Clara Kathleen Barnett, ["Clara Doria."]
My voice and I; or, the relation of the singer to the song. '10(N5) c. por. D. $1.50 net. McClurg.

Rogers, Corydon Eug.
Textbook on the therapeutic action of light, incl. the rho rays, solar and violet rays, electric arc light, the light cabinet. [1910.] (S) c. 12+323 p. il. col. front. 8°, $3.50. C. E. Rogers.

Rogers, Euclid Beauclerc, D.D., comp.
The topical excerpt library. '08(Je) c. 8°, $10. Springfield Lib. Pub.

Rogers, Fernando E.
See Williams, L: L.

Rogers, Ja. E:
American newspaper. '09(S18) c. D. *$1 net. Univ. of Chic.

Rogers, Ja. Edn. Thorold.
Economic interpretation of history. New and cheaper ed. '09, [1910.] (F) 8°, *$1.50 net. Putnam.

Rogers, Ja. F:, M.D.
Life and health. '10(My14) c. D. $1 net. Lippincott.

Rogers, Jessie.
Living fire, the soul power of the universe. 2d and enl. ed. '08(S12) c. 12°, $1.50. Occult Pub. Co.

Rogers, Julia Ellen.
Earth and sky every child should know; easy studies of the earth and the stars for any time and place. '10(N19) c. il. D. (Every child should know ser.) $1.20 net. Doubleday, P.
Key to The nature library; with pract. suggestions on the every-day use of the volumes. '09(Je19) c. il. 8°, $1.50. Doubleday, P.
Shell book: guide to a knowledge of the families of living mollusks; aid to the identification of shells, native and foreign. '08(Ap18) c. il. O. **$4 net. Doubleday, P.
Trees that every child should know. '09 (D25) il. D. (Every child should know ser.) **$1.20 net. Doubleday, P.

Rogers, L. W.
Beyond the border; lecture on the reasonableness of clairvoyance, premonitions. materializations and other occult phenomena, and the unreasoning prejudice against them. '09(N) 16 p. S. pap., 10 c. Theosophical Bk.
Hidden side of evolution; lecture on the reasonableness of the existence of a spiritual heirarchy and the guidance of human evolution. '09(N) 16 p. S. pap., 10 c. Theosophical Bk.
Hints to young students of occultism. '09 (D4) c. S. 25 c. Theosophical Bk.
Invisible world about us; lecture on the unseen regions beyond the grasp of the physical senses and the life we live after bodily death. '09(N) 16 p. S. pap., 10 c. Theosophical Bk.
Karma: nature's law of justice; lecture on the law of cause and effect as operating in some of the affairs of daily life. '09 (N) 16 p. S. pap., 10 c. Theosophical Bk.
Life sublime; lecture on the application of the higher principles to the conduct of daily life. '09(N) 16 p. S. pap., 10 c. Theosophical Bk.
Logic of reincarnation; lecture on reincarnation as a method of human evolution that develops the inherent qualities of the soul. '09(N) 16 p. S. pap., 10 c. Theosophical Bk.
Reincarnation from the scientific viewpoint; lecture on some of the natural laws and facts of life that show reincarnation to be a logical and necessary part of human evolution. '09(N) 16 p. S. pap., 10 c. Theosophical Bk.
Scientific evidence of future life: lecture on some of the scientific and historic facts that indicate the existence of an unseen world and a future life. '09(N) 24 p. S. pap., 10 c. Theosophical Bk.
Soul powers and possibilities; lecture on methods of nature in evolving latent power and faculties in human beings. '09 (N) 14 p. S. pap., 10 c. Theosophical Bk.
Theosophical questions answered. 2d ed.; cont. elem. questions and answers on reincarnation, Karma, the astral plane, and misc. occult subjects. '09(N) 32 p. S. pap., 15 c. Theosophical Bk.

Rogers, L. W.—*Continued.*
Universal brotherhood; lecture on the fundamental relationship of human beings to each other and to the animal kingdom. '09(N) 16 p. S. pap., 10 c. Theosophical Bk.
What theosophy is. '09(N) 15 p. T. pap., 5 c. Theosophical Bk.

Rogers, Lillian Emily.
See Wohlfarth, Julia Helen.

Rogers, Lore Alford.
Bacteria in milk. '09(My) 24 p. il. 8°, (U. S., Dept. of Agriculture; Farmers' bull.) pap., 5 c. U. S., Supt. of Docs.
Directions for the home pasteurization of milk. '09(D18) 8°, (U. S., Dept. of Agriculture; Bu. of Animal Industry, circular.) pap. (Add. Superintendent for price.) U. S., Supt. of Docs.
Paraffining butter tubs. '08, [1909.] (My) 6 p. il. 8°, (U. S., Dept. of Agriculture; Bu. of Animal Industry circular.) pap. 5 c. U. S., Supt. of Docs.
See also Whitaker, G: M.

—, and Gray, C. Earl.
Influence of acidity of cream on the flavor of butter. '09(Ag) 22 p. 8° (U. S., Dept. of Agriculture; Bu. of Animal Industry bull.) pap., 10 c. U. S., Supt. of Docs.

Rogers, L: W:
Occultism in the Shakespeare plays. '10 (F19) c. 12°, 25 c. Theosophical Bk.

Rogers, Rob. W:
Religion of Babylonia and Assyria, especially in its relation to Israel; five lectures del. at Harvard University. '09 (Ja2) c. il. facsim., O. *$2 net. Eaton & M.

Rogers, Ruth.
Historical landmarks in the town of Sherman, Ct. '07, [1908.] (Mr.) 26 p. D. (Quaker Hill local history ser.) pap., 10 c. Quaker Hill.

Rogers, S:
Autobiography of Elder S: Rogers; ed. by his son, Elder J: I. Rogers. 4th ed. '09 (D) c. 13+208 p. il. pors. 12°, $1. Standard Pub.

ROGERS, Samuel.
Roberts, R. E. Samuel Rogers and his circle. $3.50 net. Dutton.

Rogers, Shober J.
See Scofield, Carl Schurz.

ROGERS, *Rev.* Timothy Foster.
Kellogg. *Mrs.* L. J. C. Memoirs of Rev. Timothy Foster Rogers. (Priv. pr.) W. H. Pierce.

Rogers, W:, pseud.
See Hawkins, Nehemiah.

Rogers, W: Osgood, ["Pucker."]
Boy's-eye view of the Sunday-school. '09 (Ja23) c. il. D. *60 c. net. S. S. Times.

Roget, P: Mark, M.D.
Thesaurus of English words and phrases; enl. and improved, and with a full index by J: Lewis Roget. '09(F27) O. *$1.60 net. Longmans.

ROGUERY.
See Crime and criminals.

Rogues de Fursac, Marie Henri Joseph Pierre Etienne, M.D.
Manual of psychiatry. 2d Amer. fr. 2d Fr. ed., rev. and enl. '08(Ag29) c. 8°, $2.50. Wiley.

Rogues (The) and vagabonds of Shakespeare's youth: Awdeley's "Fraternitye of vacabondes" and Harman's "Caveat"; ed., with an introd. by E: Viles and F. J. Furnivall. '08(Ja18) il. O. (Shakespeare lib.: Shakespeare's England.) *$1.75 net. Duffield.

Rohé, G: H:, and Robin, Albert.
Text-book of hygiene; a comprehensive treatise on the principles and practice of preventive medicine from an American standpoint. 4th rev. and enl. ed. '08(N) c. 8+582 p. il. 8°, *$3.50 net. Davis.

Rohlfs, Mrs. Anna Katharine Green, [formerly Anna Katharine Green.]
House of the Whispering Pines. '10(Ap2) c. front. D. $1.50. Putnam.
Three thousand dollars. '09(O30) c. il. D. $1. Badger.

Rohrer, Caleb Wyand Geeting.
Contribution to the comparative anatomy of the prostate gland. '09, [1910.] 32+124 p. por. 12°, gratis. C. W. G. Rohrer.

Roiné, Jules Edouard.
See Lincoln centennial medal.

Rojas, Fernando de.
Celestina; or, the tragi-comedy of Calisto and Melibea; tr. from the Spanish by Ja. Mabbe, 1631; also, An interlude of Calisto and Melebea; ed. by H. Warner Allen. '08(O10) 12°, (Library of early novelists; Picaresque section.) $2. Dutton.
La Celestina comedia de Calisto y Melibea. [facsim.] '02. [1909.] (N) 179 p. 8°, $2.50. Hispanic Soc.
La Celestina de Calisto y Melibea (unico texto auténtico de La Celestina). '00, [1909.] (N) 180 p. 8°, (Bibliotheca hispanica.) $2. Hispanic Soc.
The Celestina; facsimile of the first known ed. Burgo, 1499; argumento del primer auto defta comedia. '09(N20) il. 8°. (Add. pubs. for price.) (200 copies.) Hispanic Soc.

ROLAND.
Marshall, H. E., *comp.* Stories of Roland. 50 c. Dutton.

Rolfe, C: Wesley, Talbot, Arth. Newell, and Baker, Ira Osborn.
Paving brick and paving brick clays of Illinois. '08, [1909.] (Jl) 13+316 p. il. diagrs., 8°, (Illinois State Geol. Survey bull.) pap. (Add. pubs. for price.) Univ. of Ill.

Rolfe, W: Ja., comp. and ed.
Hist. of the Cambridge Public Library, 1858-1908: with the addresses at the celebration of its fiftieth anniversary. '08(O) 906 p. il. 8°. (Not for sale.) Cambridge Pub. Lib.
See also Satchel guide.

Rolland, Romain.
Jean-Christophe: dawn, morning, youth, revolt; tr. by Gilbert Cannan. '10(D10) c. D. $1.50 net. Holt.

ROLLER SKATING.
See Skating.

Rolleston, Humphry Davy, M.D., ed.
See Allbutt, *Sir* T: Clifford, *M.D., ed.*

"Rollingstone, A," pseud.
See Hood, C: Newton.

Rollins, Montgomery.
Convertible securities: tables showing the prices of the various convertible issues which are equivalent to the market quotations of the securities exchangeable therefor; also tables for accumulated dividends and accrued interest. '09(My22) c. 12°, $3. M. Rollins.
Money and investments; reference book for the use of those desiring information in the handling of money or the investment thereof. 2d ed. '10(My14) c. 8°, $2 net. Estes.
Municipal and corporation bonds, terms, customs and usages; reference book for the investor and banker. '10(D3) c. 32°, 60 c. Estes.
Tables showing the net returns from serial and instalment bonds. '10(Ja8) c. 12°, $5. M. Rollins.

Rollo at work. Abbott, J. *35 c. net; *70 c. net. Dutton.

Rollo in Hawaii. Nodaway, M. $1. Thompson & T.

Rollow, Ja. Smith.
The trend. '07, [1908.] (Ag.) c. 142 p. 8°, $1. Guide Pr. and Pub.

Rolt-Wheeler, Fs.
Boy with the U. S. Survey. '09(S11) c. il. D. (U. S. service ser.) †$1.50. Lothrop, L. & S.
—, ed. Boy with the U. S. Foresters. '10 (N12) c. il. O. (U. S. service ser.) $1.50. Lothrop, L. & S.
Science-history of the universe. '10(Ja8) 10 v., il. 12°, $6. Current Lit.

Roly Poly book. Smith, L. R. 35 c. Flanagan.

Roly-poly pudding. Potter, B. **$1 net. Warne.

Roma. Donnelly, C: F. (Priv. pr.) J. T. White & Co.

Roman, C:
A man remade; or, out of delirium's wonderland. '09(D18) $1. Reilly & B.

Roman breviary. Baudot, J. *$ net. Herder.

ROMAN CAMPAGNA.
See Italy.

Roman Catholic and Protestant Bibles compared. Jacobus, M. W., *ed.* **$1.25 net. Scribner.

ROMAN CATHOLIC CHURCH.
See Catholic church;—*also* Syracuse.

Roman church before Constantine. Duchesne, L. M. O. 10 c. Cathedral Lib.

Roman cities in Italy and Dalmatia. Frothingham, A. L. $1.75 net. Sturgis & W.

Roman diary. Lacey, T. A. $3.50 net. Longmans.

ROMAN EMPIRE.
See Rome.

Roman forum. Lanciani, R. $1.50 net. Stechert.

ROMAN HISTORY.
See Rome.

Roman holidays. Howells, W: D. **$3 net. Harper.

ROMAN INDEX.
See Index expurgatorius.

Roman index and its latest historian. Hilgers, J. *10 c. net. Herder.

ROMAN LAW.
See Civil law.

Roman law in mediæval Europe. Vinogradoff, P. G. *75 c. net. Harper.

Roman law studies in Livy. Evans, A. E. 40 c. net. Macmillan.

Roman lawyer in Jerusalem. *See* Story, W: Wetmore.

Roman life and manners. *See* Friedländer, Ludwig.

Roman Republic. Heitland, W: E. In 3 v. per set, *$10 net. Putnam.

Romance of a friar and a nun. Anderson, A. J. *$2.50 net. Dodd.

Romance of a Medici warrior. Hare, C. $2.50 net. Scribner.

Romance of a monk. King, A. $1.20 net. Metropolitan Press (N. Y.)

Romance of a nun. King, A. $1.50. Kearney.

Romance of a plain man. Glasgow, E. A. G. †$1.50. Macmillan.

Romance of Alexander and Roxana. Kirkman, M. M. $1.50. C. Phillips.

Romance of Alexander the king. Kirkman, M. M. $1.50. C. Phillips.

Romance of Alexander the prince. Kirkman, M. M. $1.50. C. Phillips.

Romance of American expansion. Bruce, H: A. B. **$1.75 net. Moffat.

Romance of Arlington House. Reed, S. A. $1. Chapple Pub.

Romance of Barnstable. Bray, M. M. $1.50. Badger.

Romance of bird life. Lea, J: *$1.50 net. Lippincott.

Romance of empire ser.; ed. by J: Lang. il. O. Stokes.
—Willson. Canada. *$2 net.

Romance of George Villiers. Gibbs, P. H. *$3.50 net. Putnam.

Romance of history ser.; ed. by J: Lang. il. O. *$2 net. Stokes.
—Colvin. South Africa.
—Coxhead. Mexico.
—Horsley. New Zealand.
—Lang. Australia.—Gibraltar and the West Indies.—Land of the golden trade (West Africa).
—Macgregor. Netherlands.
—Surridge. India.

Romance of life insurance. Graham, W: J. $1.50. World To-day.

Romance of London. Home, G. C. $1 net. Macmillan.

Romance of modern astronomy. MacPherson, H., *jr.* $1.50 net. Lippincott.

Romance of modern chemistry. Philip, J. C. *$1.50 net. Lippincott.

Romance of modern geology. Grew, E. S. *$1.50 net. Lippincott.

Romance of modern manufacture. Gibson, C. R. *$1.50 net. Lippincott.

Romance of Monaco and its rulers. Mayne, E. C. $5 net. Lane.

Romance of Northumberland. Bradley, A. G. *$2.75 net. McClurg.
Romance of Protestantism. Alcock, D. $1.25 net. Eaton & M.
Romance of Roman villas. Champney, *Mrs.* E. W. **$3.50 net. Putnam.
Romance of the American navy. Hill, F. S. **$2.50 net. Putnam.
Romance of the East ser.; ed. by L. Cranmer-Byng. 12°, *$1 net. Dutton.
—Barnett, *comp.* Golden town.
—Field. Tales of the caliphs.
—Wollaston. Tales within tales.
Romance of the Mississippi valley history. Thwaites, R. G. 75 c. State Hist., Ia.
Romance of the nursery. Harker, *Mrs.* L. A. $1.25. Scribner.
Romance of the railroad. Hubbard, E. 10 c. Roycrofters.
Romance of the reaper. Casson, H. N. **$1 net. Doubleday, P.
Romance of the ship. Chatterton, E: K. $1.50 net. Lippincott.
Romance of the silver shoon. Bearne, D. 85 c. Benziger.
Romance of the 10,000 islands. Philips, A. E. $1.50. B'way Pub.
Romance ser. il. D. *$1.50 net. Lippincott.
—Chatterton. Romance of the ship. $1.50 net.
—Gibson. Romance of modern manufacture.
—Philip. Romance of modern chemistry.
—Grew. Romance of modern geology.
—Lea. Romance of bird life.
—MacPherson, *jr.* Romance of modern astronomy. $1.50 net.
Romancero (El) Español. Pidal, R. M. $1.25 net. Hispanic Soc.
Romancero general, en qve se contiennen todos los romances que andan impressos en las nueue partes de Romanceros. 2 v. [facsim.] '04, [1909.] (N) 8°, ea., $15. Hispanic Soc.

ROMANCES.
See Fairy tales;—Fiction;—Legends.

Romances of early America. Robins, E: $1.50. Jacobs.
Romances of Imperial Rome. Champney, *Mrs.* E. W. $3.50. Putnam.
Romances of royalty; dramas and tragedies of chivalric France. 12 v. '09(My22) fronts. Marie Antoinette ed., $3.75; Fleur-de-Lis ed., ¾ levant mor., $6.25; Imperial ed., ¾ crushed French levant mor., $15. Millet.
Romances of the French Revolution. Gosselin, L. L. T. 2 v. *$6 net. Brentano's.

Romanes, Ethel Duncan.
An appreciation: Charlotte Mary Yonge. '09(Ap10) $1.65. Young Churchman.

Romanes lectures. O. pap. Oxford Univ.
—Balfour. Questionings on criticism and beauty. 70 c.
—Curzon. Frontiers. 50 c.
—Holland. Optimism of Butler's "Analogy." 70 c.
—Roosevelt. Biological analogies in history. 60 c.; 35 c.
Romanesque architecture. Browne, E. A. $1.75 net. Macmillan.

ROMANISM.
See Catholic church.

Romantic California. Peixotto, E. C. $2.50 net. Scribner.
Romantic Corsica. Renwick, G: *$3 net. Scribner.
Romantic days in old Boston. Crawford, M. C. $2.50 net. Little, B. & Co.
Romantic Germany. Schauffler, R. H. *$3.50 net. Century Co.
Romantic history ser.; ed. by Martin Hume. il. O. Putnam.
—Davey. Nine days queen. *$3.50 net.
—Tremayne. First governess of the Netherlands. *$3 net.
Romantic legends of Spain. Becquer, G. A. D. **$1.50 net. Crowell.
Romantic movement in English poetry. Symons, A. *$2.50 net. Dutton.
Romantic stories of famous families: an account of certain noted English families, concerning the love stories and lives of bygone celebrities. '08(N21) pap., 40 c. Scribner.

ROMANTICISM.
See German literature;—Literature;—*also* Grillparzer, Franz.

Romany of the snows. Parker, *Sir* G. $1.25. Harper.

Rombauer, Rob. Julius.
Union cause in St. Louis in 1861; historical sketch. '09(N) 14+475 p. il. 8°, $2. Nixon-Jones.

ROME.
Abbott, F. F. Society and politics in ancient Rome. **$1.25 net. Scribner.
Anderson, W: J., *and* Spiers, R. P. Architecture of Greece and Rome. *$7.50 net. Scribner.
Baedeker, K. Central Italy and Rome. $2.25. Scribner.
Botsford, G: W. Roman assemblies, from their origin to the end of the Republic. **$4 net. Macmillan.
Buckland, W: W. Roman law of slavery. *$5.75 net. Putnam.
Bury, J: B. Constitution of the later Roman Empire. 50 c. net. Putnam.
Bussell, F: W: The Roman Empire. 2 v. $9 net. Longmans.
Champney, *Mrs.* E. W. Romance of imperial Rome. $3.50. Putnam.
Champney, *Mrs.* E. W. Romance of Roman villas: (the Renaissance.) **$3.50 net. Holt.
Dalkeith, L. Stories from Roman history. 50 c. Dutton.
Davis, W: S. Influence of wealth in imperial Rome. $2 net.—Outline history of the Roman Empire. *65 c. net. Macmillan.
De Cesare, R. Last days of Papal Rome. *$3.50 net. Houghton M.
Ferrero, G. Characters and events of Roman history from Cæsar to Nero. **$2.50 net.—Greatness and decline of Rome. v. 3-5. ea., *$2.50 net. Putnam.
Fowler, W: W. Social life at Rome in the age of Cicero. **$2.25 net. Macmillan.
Friedländer, L. Roman life and manners under the early empire. v. 1-3. ea., *$1.50 net. Dutton.

ROME.—*Continued.*
Frothingham, A. L. Monuments of Christian Rome, from Constantine to the Renaissance. **$2.25 net. Macmillan.
Gibbon, E: Decline and fall of the Roman Empire. 6 v. ea., 35 c. net; 70 c. net. Dutton.
Hamilton, M. A. Junior hist. of Rome. $1.10. Oxford Univ.
Hayes, C. H. Introduction to the sources relating to the Germanic invasions. $1.50. Longmans.
Heitland, W: E. Roman republic. 3 v. per set, *$10 net. Putnam.
Henderson, B. W: Civil war and rebellion in the Roman empire, A.D. 69-70. *$2.60 net. Macmillan.
Howe, M. Roma beata. **$1.50 net. Little, B. & Co.
Howells, W: D. Roman holidays. **$3 net. Harper.
Hutton, E: Rome. *$2 net. Macmillan.
Jones, H: S. Roman Empire, B.C. 29-A.D. 476. **$1.35 net; **$1.60 net. Putnam.
Jones, W: H: S: Malaria: a neglected factor in the history of Greece and Rome. *80 c. net. Macmillan.
Launspach, C: W. L. State and family in early Rome. *$2.50 net. Macmillan.
McKinley, E. M. Pupil's notebook and study outline in Roman hist. 25 c. Am. Bk.
Merivale, C: Hist. of Rome. 35 c. net; 70 c. net. Dutton.
Murray, J: Hdbk. for Rome and the Campagna. *$4 net. Scribner.
Nutting, H. C. Conspiracy at Rome in 66-65 B.C. 10 c. Univ. of Cal.
Parmele, *Mrs.* M. P. Short history of Rome and Italy. $1. Scribner.
Potter, O. M. Colour of Rome. *$5 net. Jacobs.
Reynolds-Ball, E. A. Rome: pract. guide. *$1.10 net. Macmillan.
Sanders, H: A., *ed.* Roman hist. and mythology. $2.25. Macmillan.
Sands, P. C. Client princes of the Roman Empire under the Republic. *$1.50 net. Putnam.
Stories of Greece and Rome. **65 c. net. Century Co.
Tucker, T: G: Life in the Roman world of Nero and St. Paul. $2.50 net. Macmillan.
Watson, T: E: Sketches from Roman history. 50 c. T: E: Watson.
See also American college;—Atrium of the Vestals; Catacombs;—Church history;—Forum;—Heliogabalus;—International Institute of Agriculture;—Painters and painting.

Romeus and Juliet. *See* Brooke, Arth.

Rominger, Cornelius A:, D.D.
Coming kingdom. '08(Ag15) c. por. D. $1. C. A. Rominger.

Rommel, G: McCullough.
Regeneration of the Morgan horse. '10 (O) 14 p. il. 8°, (U. S., Dept. of Agriculture, Bu. of Animal Industry, circular.)

Rommel, J:
Natural philosophy; or, man from anterior to posterior. '10(N5) c. 12°, $1. Cataract.

Romney, G:
Masterpieces. '10(D17) il. 12°, (Painters' ser.) leath., 75 c. net; pap., 25 c. net. Stokes.

ROMNEY, George.
Chamberlain, A. B. George Romney. $5. Scribner.

Romola. *See* Eliot, George.

Ronald, Mary, [pseud. for Mrs. Augusta Foote Arnold.]
Century cook book. New il. ed. '10(My14) $2. Century Co.

Ronaldshay, Lawrence J: Lumley Dundas, Earl of.
Wandering student in the Far East. In 2 v. '09(Mr13) il. map, O. *$8.40 net. Scribner.

Ronayne, Edmond.
Master's carpet; or, masonry and Baal worship identical; reviewing the similarity between masonry, Romanism and the mysteries, and comparing the whole with the Bible. '07, [1909.] (Ap) c. 5+10-406 p. il. por. 12°, 75 c. T. B. Arnold.

Ronsard, Pierre de.
Selected poems; chosen by St. John Lucas. [In French.] '08(D19) S. $1.75. Oxford Univ.

RÖNTGEN RAYS.
See Roentgen rays.

Ronzone, B: Anthony, ["The Baron."]
The Marquis of Murray Hill. '09(D) c. 360 p. 8°, $1.25. Roxburgh.

Rood, Mrs. Emma.
See Tuttle, Hudson.

Rood, J: Romaine.
Leading and illustrative cases; with notes on the law of judgments, attachments, garnishments and executions. 2d ed. '09 (N) 8+426 p. 8°, $3. Wahr.
—, **comp.** Decisions, statutes, etc., concerning the law of estates in land. 2d ed. '09, [1910.] (Mr) c. O. $4. Callaghan.

ROOFS.
Burr, W: H., *and* Falk, M. S: Graphic method by influence lines for bridge and roof computations. $3. Wiley.
Hearne, H. C. Tables of stresses in roof trusses. *$4 net. Hill Pub.
Thomson, W: C. Bridge and structural design. $2. Engineering News.
See also Trusses.

Rook, Clarence.
London side-lights. '08(N7) front. D. *$1.70 net. Longmans.

Roose, T: Wa., ["Bayard de Saumara."]
Souls of fire: [poems.] '09(Mr) 10+114 p. 8°, $1. T: W. Roose.

Rooses, Max.
Jacob Jordaens, his life and work; tr. from the Dutch by Eliz. C. Broers. '08(D12) il. f°, *$12.50 net. Dutton.

Roosevelt, Thdr.
Addresses and papers; ed. by Willis Fletcher Johnson. '09(Je) c. 510 p. por. 12°. (Add. pubs. for price.) Sun Dial.

Roosevelt, Thdr.—*Continued.*

African and European addresses; with introd. presenting a description of the conditions under which the addresses were given during Mr. Roosevelt's journey in 1910 from Khartoum through Europe to New York, by Lawrence F. Abbott. '10 (D3) c. D. $1.50 net. Putnam.

African game trails; acct. of the African wanderings of an American hunter-naturalist; with il. from photographs by Kermit Roosevelt and other members of the expedition, and drawings by Philip R. Goodwin. '10(Ag27) c. map, O. $4 net. Scribner.

Americanism in religion. '08(D19) c. D. 35 c. E. E. Swadener.

Biological analogies in history; del. before the University of Oxford, June 7th, 1910. '10(Je18) c. O. (Romanes lecture.) 60 c.; pap., 35 c. Oxford Univ.

Outlook editorials. '09, [1910.] (F) 3-125 p. por. 12°. (Priv. pr.) Outlook.

Outdoor pastimes of an American hunter. New and enl. ed., [cont. 2 additional chapters, "In the Louisiana canebrakes" and "Small country neighbors."] '08 (F22) c. il. O. **$3 net. Scribner.

Real Roosevelt; his forceful and fearless utterances on various subjects; sel. and arr. by Alan Warner; with foreword by Lyman Abbott. '10(Jl9) c. pors. D. $1. Putnam.

Roosevelt policy: speeches, letters and state papers, rel. to corporate wealth and closely allied topics; with introd. by And. Carnegie. '08(Ag1) c. 2 v., pors. facsims., 12°. (Not for sale.) Current Lit.

Stories of the great West. '09(Jl3) c. il. D. **60 c. net. Century Co.

ROOSEVELT, Theodore.

Albert, J: C. Roosevelt and the money power. 10 c. Sudwarth Co.

Albrecht, F: C. "World movement"; extracts from Mr. Theodore Roosevelt's address del. at Berlin, May 12, 1910. 50 c. F: C. Albrecht.

Bennett, J: W: Roosevelt and the republic. $1.50. B'way Pub.

Bonum Meritum, *pseud.* War of words between President Roosevelt and J. Pierpont Morgan concerning railroad, tariff and trust questions. $1; 25 c. Donohue.

Chase, L. Rooseveltiana: [articles antagonistic to Mr. Roosevelt reprinted from newspapers.] 50 c. Grafton Press.

Donovan, M. Roosevelt that I know; ten years of boxing with the President. *$1 net. B. W. Dodge.

Gros, R., *ed.* T. R. in cartoon. $1. Saalfield.

Hale, *Mrs.* A. R. Rooseveltian fact and fable. $1. A. R. Hale.

Hale, W: B. Week in the White House with Theodore Roosevelt. **$1.25 net. Putnam.

Lundeberg, A., *and* Seymour, F: Great Roosevelt African hunt and the wild animals of Africa. $1.75. D. B. McCurdy.

McCutcheon, J: T. T. R. in cartoons. 75 c. net. McClurg.

Roosevelt, Thdr.—*Continued.*

McDermott, D. I. Preachers' protests [against President Roosevelt's denunciation of religious bigotry in politics.] In 3 v. ea., 10 c.; 3 v. in 1, 25 c. P: Reilly.

Morris, C: Marvelous career of Theodore Rosevelt. $1.50. Winston.

Mowbray, J. H: Roosevelt's marvelous exploits in the wilds of Africa. $1. G: W. Bertron.

Neil, H: Roosevelt's thrilling experiences in the wilds of Africa hunting big game. $2. Bible House.

O'Laughlin, J: C. From the jungle through Europe with Roosevelt. 25 c. Chapple Pub.

Ransom, F. C: My policies in Jungleland: [verse.] $1. Barse & H.

Roosevelt album, consisting of portraits of Theodore Roosevelt. gratis. Cole.

Seymour, F: Roosevelt in Africa. $2; $2.75. Educ. Co.

Shaw, A. Cartoon hist. of Roosevelt's career. Review of Reviews.

Smith, E: G. Real Roosevelt. $1.50. States Pub.

Spaulding, W. When Theodore is king. 25 c. W. Spaulding.

Thomas, A. C: Roosevelt among the people. $1. Walter.

Vrooman, F. B. Theodore Roosevelt, dynamic geographer. $1; 75 c. Oxford Univ.

Wilcoxon, M. H. Roosevelt steam rolled by the Bible. $1. M. H. Wilcoxon.

Wilhelm, D. Theodore Roosevelt as an undergraduate. 75 c. net. J: W. Luce.

See also Africa;—Catholic church.

Roosevelt, Captain Wyn.

Frontier boys in Colorado. '08(D5) il. 60 c. Chatterton P.

Frontier boys in Hawaii; or, the mystery of the Hollow Mountain. '09(Ag14) c. il. 12°, 60 c. Chatterton-P.

Frontier boys in the Rockies; or, a winter in the big canyon. '09(D) c. 9-245 p. il. 12°, 60 c. Chatterton-P.

Frontier boys in the saddle. '10(Jl2) c. il. D. 60 c. Chatterton.

Frontier boys in the Sierras; or, the lost mine. '09(Ag14) c. il. 12°, 60 c. Chatterton-P.

Frontier boys on the coast; or, in the pirate's power. '09(D) c. 9-252 p. il. 12°, 60 c. Chatterton-P.

Frontier boys on the overland trail. '08 (My23) c. il. D. (The frontier boys ser.) 60 c. Chatterton-P.

Roosevelt album, consisting of a collection of portraits of Theodore Roosevelt, president of the United States, made at different periods in his career. '07, [1908.] (N) 32 p. il. 24°, gratis. Cole.

Roosevelt bears ser. *See* Eaton, Seymour.

Roosevelt bears visit Llanerch. Husband, A. P. (Add. author for price.) A. P. Husband.

Roosevelt in the jungle. '10(D) col. il. $1.25. Saalfield.

Roosevelt (The) Panama libel case against the New York *World* and Indianapolis *News;* decision of Hon. C: M. Hough, judge of the United States court for the southern district of New York, and Hon. Alb. B. Anderson, judge of the United States court for the district of Indiana; together with acct. of the circumstances that led to these unprecedented prosecutions on the part of the United States government, and a stenographic rept. of the trial of the New York *World.* '10(D17) 4°, pap., gratis. N. Y. World.

Rooseveltian fact and fable. Hale, *Mrs.* A. R. $1. B'way Pub.

Root, A. I. and Ernest R.
A B C and X Y Z of bee culture; cyclopedia of everything pertaining to the care of the honey-bee; bees, hives, honey, implements, honey-plants, etc. '10(S) 576 p. il. 8°, $1.50; hf. leath., $2.25; leath., $2.50. A. I. Root.

Root, C: P.
Automobile troubles and how to remedy them. '09(O2) il. D. (Thompson ser. of home study books.) $1; flex. leath., $1.50. C: C. Thompson.

Root, Rev. E: Tallmadge.
Redemption of Paradise Pond, Barbara: stories of Rhode Island life. '09(My8) front. D. 75 c. E: T. Root.

Root, Elihu.
Proposed income-tax amendment; letter from to Hon. Frederick M. Davenport on the subject of the scope and effect of the proposed income-tax amendment. '10(Ap) 5 p. 8°, pap. Gov. Pr. Off.

Root, Ernest R.
See Root, A. I.

Root of all evil. Owen, A. $1.25. B'way Pub.

Roots of reality. Bax, E. B. *$2 net. B. W. Dodge.

ROPES.
Sherrill, C. O., *and* Marshall, G: C., *jr.* Notes on cordage and tackle. (Priv. pr.) Staff Coll.

Ropes of sand. Clendening, L. K. $1.50. Badger.

Ropke, Otto.
See Bandelier, —.

ROQUE.
***See* Croquet.**

Rorer, Mrs. Sarah Tyson Heston.
Vegetable cookery and meat substitutes. '09(Ap10) c. D. **$1.50 net. Arnold.

Rorke, T. Scott.
Government positions; how to get a government job and courses of study for civil service examinations. '10(D3) c. il. 8°, $1.25. T. S. Rorke.

Rosa Regina. *See* Smith, *Mrs.* Eliz. Thomasina.

Rosaline. Beshshure, B. M. 26 c. Beshshure.

Rosalynde. *See* Lodge, T:

Rosamond the second. Mears, M. M. 80 c. net. Stokes.

ROSARY.
Casanowicz, I. M. Collection of rosaries in the United States National Museum. (Add. Superintendent for price.) U. S., Supt. of Docs.

Rosary (The). *See* Barclay, *Mrs.* Florence Louise Charlesworth.—Rose, E: Everett.

Roscoe, Sir H: Enfield, and Schorlemmer, C.
Treatise on chemistry. In 2 v. v. 2, The metals. New ed., completely rev. by Sir H: E. Roscoe and Dr. A. Harden. '08 (F15) il. 8°, *$7.50 net. Macmillan.

Rose, Achilles, M.D.
Christian Greece and living Greek. '09 (My1) c. D. $1. Stechert
Medical Greek: collection of papers on medical onomatology and a grammatical guide to learn modern Greek. '08(S5) c. D. $1. Stechert.

Rose, Dorothy.
See Haymes, Rob.

Rose, E: Everett.
Father Kelly of the Rosary; novelized from his beautiful play, "The rosary." '10(N19) c. il. 16°, 50 c. Rosary.

Rose, Elsie Whitlock.
Cathedrals and cloisters of the Isle de France (incl. Bourges, Troyes, Reims and Rouen). 2 v. '10(D3) c. il. O. $5 net, boxed. Putnam.

Rose, G: B.
Renaissance masters: art of Raphael, Michelangelo, Leonardo da Vinci, Titian, Correggio, Botticelli and Rubens. 3d ed., to which is added a study of the art of Claude Lorraine. '08(F1) c. D. **$1 net. Putnam.

Rose, Mrs. Héloise Durant.
Dante: dramatic poem. '10(D17) front. 12°, $2 net. M. Kennerley.

Rose, J: Holland.
Dumouriez, and the defence of England against Napoleon. '08(N14) il. maps, facsims., por. O. *$5 net. Lane.

Rose, T: Kirke.
Precious metals; comprising gold, silver, and platinum. '09(Ag14) il. 8°, (Westminster ser.) *$2 net. Van Nostrand.

Rose, Wa. Malins.
See Texas. Notes on repts.

Rose, W:, and Carless, Albert.
Manual of surgery, for students and practitioners. 7th ed. '08(N7) c. il. 8°, *$5.50 net; leath., *$6.50 net. Wood.

Rose and the ring. *See* Thackeray, W: Makepeace.

Rose-colored world. Brodie, E. M. $1.25 net. Metropolitan Press (N. Y.)

Rose garden of Omar Khayyam. Omar Khayyam. $3. E. F. Thompson.

Rose-garden of Sa'di. *See* Sadi *the Persian.*

Rose Goddess. Russell, *Lady* C. $7 net. Longmans.

Rose in the ring. McCutcheon, G: B. $1.50. Dodd.

Rose-jar. Jones, T: S:, *jr.* *$1 net; $3.50. G: W. Browning.

Rose MacLeod. Brown, A. †$1.50. Houghton M.

Rose of Eden. Evans, F. C. 25 c. Penn Pub. Co.

Rose of Normandy. Wilson, W: R. A. †75 c. Little, B. & Co.

Rose o' Plymouth-town. Dix, B. M. $1.25. Dramatic.

Rose of Savoy. Williams, H. N. *$3.50 net. Scribner.

Rose of Sharon. Sheffield, A.. $1.50. C. M. Clark.

Rose of the old regime. *See* McKinsey, F.

Rose of the wind. Branch, A. H. $1.25 net. Houghton M.

Rose-white youth. Wyllarde, D. †$1.50. Lane.

Rose-winged hours. Lucas, St. J., *comp.* *$1.40 net. Longmans.

Rosebery, Archibald Philip Primrose, Earl of.
Lord Chatham, his early life and connections. '10(D3) c. O. $3 net. Harper.

Rosecrans, J. H.
See Patton, J:

Rosemary. Miller, E. A. *$1 net. F. F. Sherman.

Rosemary booklets. 5 v. '09(D25) S. pap.. ea., 25 c. Stokes.

Rosemary of pansies. Smith, E. $1. Badger.

Rosenau, Milton Jos.
See Mohler, J: Robbins.

Rosenberg, Albert von.
Pocketbook of veterinary medical practice. '09, [1910.] (F) c. 126 p. 16°, 75 c. Boericke & T.

Rosenbloom, Jacob.
Contribution to the study of the nature and origin of the Bunce Jones protein. '09, [1910.] (Ap) 64 p. 8°. (Add. author for price.) J. Rosenbloom.
Bibliography (15 p.).

Rosenblum, Abraham.
Advanced course in Isaac Pitman phonography. '10(Ag6) c. 12°, $1. Blythebourne Pub.
Intermediate course in Isaac Pitman phonography. '08, [1909.] (F) c. 12°, 75 c. Blythebourne Pub.

Rosenfeld, Sydney.
Children of destiny; play in four acts. '10(Ap30) c. D. pap., 50 c. G: W. Dillingham.

Rosengarten, Jos. G:
American Philosophical Society. [1910.] (N) 19 p. 8°, 25 c. Am. Philosophical Soc.
German archives as sources of German-American history. '08(Je6) 4°, pap. (Not for sale.) J. G: Rosengarten.

Rosenhain, Wa.
Glass manufacture. '08(D5) il. 8°, (Westminster ser.) *$2 net. Van Nostrand.

Rosenkrantz, Palle Adam Vilhelm, Baron.
Magistrate's own case. '08(F8) c. D. †$1.50. McClure.
Man in the basement. '08(F15) c. il. D. 75 c. Cupples & L.

Rosenthal, Alter.
Differences between the Socialist party and the Socialist Labor party, also between socialism, anarchism and anti-political industrialism. '08(D) c. 44 p. 8°, pap., 10 c. Grayzel.

Rosenthal, D: F., ed.
See Illinois. *Courts.* Repts.

Rosenthal, Leon Wa.
Mannheim and multiplex slide rules: theory and practical application. 2d ed., rev. '08(Mr) c. 12-60 p. il. tabs., 12°, 50 c. E. Dietzgen.

Rosenthal, Leon Wa.—*Continued.*
Practical calculation of transmission lines, for distribution of direct and alternating currents by means of overhead, underground, and interior wires. '09(Mr13) c. il. tabs., 8°, *$2 net. McGraw.

ROSES.
Kingsley, R. G. Roses and rose growing. *$2 net. Macmillan.
Melliar, A. F-. Book of the rose. $2 net. Macmillan.
Pemberton, J. H. Roses. $3.50. Longmans.

Roses. Sudermann, H. **$1.25 net. Scribner.

Roses and rue. Crawford, A. M. $1.50. Badger.

Roses of St. Elizabeth ser. il. D. $1. L. C. Page.
—Fox. Carlota.—Seven Christmas candles.—Seven little wise men.
—Haskell. O-Heart-San.

Rosewater, Fk.
Making of a millennium. '08(F) c. D. $1; pap., 30 c. Centry.

Rosewater, Victor.
Combat with ignorance, with special reference to the part of the modern newspaper; Charter Day address del. to the Univ. of Nebraska, at Lincoln, Neb., Tuesday, Feb. 15, 1910. '10(My) 15 p. 8°. (Priv. pr.) V. Rosewater.

ROSICRUCIANS.
Clymer, R. S. Rosicrucians, their teachings and mysteries. $3. Philosophical.
Heindel, M. Rosicrucian cosmo-conception. $1. Donohue.
Heindel, M. Rosicrusian philosophy. $1. Rosicrucian.

Rosnah. Kelley, M. †$1.50. Appleton.

Ross, Betsy.
See Claypool, *Mrs.* Elizabeth Griscom Ross Ashburn.

Ross, Clinton.
Lady of the Blackfriars; or, the old play. '09(O) c. 34 p. pap., $5 (200 copies); New ed. '10(D24) c. O. $2 net. C. Ross.
Tale of a Capitolene Venus. 4th ed. '10 (D24) c. O. $1 net. C. Ross.

Ross, Mrs. D. H: J.
See Ross, *Mrs.* Janet Ann Duff-Gordon.

Ross, E: Alsworth.
Latter day sinners and saints. '10(My14) c. S. (Art of life ser.) 50 c. net. B: W. Huebsch.
Social psychology. '08(Je13) c. 12°, **$1.50 net. Macmillan.

Ross, G: Alex.
Wood turning; prepared for the use of students in manual training high schools, technical schools and colleges. '09(O9) c. D. figs. $1. Ginn.

Ross, Rev. G: Alex. Johnston, Crofton, Rev. W. J., Robertson, J: Mackinnon, [and others.]
Religion and the modern mind: lectures del. before the Glasgow Society of St. Ninian; with an introd. by Donald Macalister. '08(D5) O. *$1.50 net. Armstrong.

Ross, G: W:
Railways and international fellowship; address del. at the 10th annual dinner of the Am. Railway Engineering and Maintenance of Way Association, Chicago, Mar. 17, 1909. '10(Ja8) 8°, pap., gratis. Am. Railway.

Ross, Harold Ellis.
Dairy lab'y guide. '10(D17) c. front. 12°, 50 c. Judd.

Ross, Mrs. H: J.
See Ross, *Mrs.* Janet Ann Duff-Gordon.

Ross, H: M.
Test of courage. '08(Ap11) c. D. $1.25. Benziger.

Ross, James.
Brownson, J. I. Life and times of Senator James Ross. gratis. Wash. Co. Hist. Soc.

Ross, Mrs. Janet Ann Duff-Gordon, [Mrs. H: J. Ross,] ed. and tr.
Lives of the early Medici, as told in their correspondence. '10(D24) pors. O. $4 net. Badger.

—, and Erichsen, Nelly.
Story of Pisa. '09(Mr6) il. fold. plan, S. (Mediæval town ser.) $1.75 net; leath., $2.25 net. Dutton.

Ross, J:, D.D.
Original religion of China. '09(N20) il. D. *$1.25 net. Eaton & M.

Ross, J: Asa.
South Dakota civil government, with brief treatise on the Constitution of the United States. Rev. ed. '10(D) c. 7-219 p. 8°, (Educator ser.) 75 c. Educator.

Ross, Martin, pseud.
See Somerville, Edith Anne Œnone.

Ross, P: V.
Probate law and practice: a treatise on wills, administration and guardianship, with forms. In 2 v. '08(N) c. 43+870; 877-1669 p. O. $13. Bancroft-W.
Supp. to Ross on probate law and practice, [etc.] '09, [1910.] (Ja) c. O. pap. (Add. pubs. for price.) Bancroft-W.

Ross, Riley R.
Abraham Lincoln. '10(S3) c. 12°, 50 c. R. R. Ross.

Ross, Rob.
Aubrey Beardsley; with a revised iconography by Aymer Vallance. '09(F13) D. *$1.25 net. Lane.

Ross, Ronald.
Prevention of malaria; with contributions by Prof. L. O. Howard, Col. C. W. Gorges, J. A. Le Prince, and others. '10 (D10) il. 8°, $5 net. Dutton.

Ross, S: Holcomb.
Suggested modification of the Winton lead number, especially as applied to mixtures of maple and cane sugar sirups. '10(Je) 9 p. 8°, (U. S., Dept. of Agriculture, Bu. of Chemistry, circular.)

Ross, W: Monroe.
My personal experience with tuberculosis. '10(Je11) c. S. pap., 50 c. W. M. Ross.

Ross FAMILY.
See **Genealogies, Read, H. P.**

Ross' BRIGADE.
See **Civil War.**

Rosser, J: Leonidas.
Our Southern quintette, and other poems. '08(Ag1) c. D. $1.25. Neale.

Rossetti, Christina Georgina.
Family letters of Christina Georgina Rossetti, with some supplementary letters and appendices; ed. by W: Michael Rossetti. '08(D12) O. $3.50. Scribner.
Poems; introd. by Alice Meynell. '10 (Ag27) il. (partly col.) Q. $6 net, boxed. Estes.
Sing-song: nursery rhyme book. '08 (Ja11) il. 16°, (Pocket classics for the young.) 80 c.; leath., $1.25. Macmillan.

Rossetti, Dante Gabriel.
Dante at Verona. '10(D) 16°, (Venetian ser.) pap., 50 c. net; Japan vel., $1 net. T: B. Mosher.
Poems. New ed. 2 v. '09(Je) por. 4°, *$5 net. Brentano's.
See also Coleridge, S: Taylor.

ROSSETTI, Dante Gabriel.
Pissaro, L. Rossetti. *65 c. net. Stokes.
Radford, C. Dante Gabriel Rossetti. *$2 net. Doran.
Rutter, F. Rossetti. $1 net. M. Kennerley.

Rossiter, F: Magee.
Practical guide to health. '09(F6) il. O. subs., $3; mor., $5. Review and Herald.

Rossman, Mary Blanche, and Mills, Mary Wilda.
Graded sentences for analysis. 2d ed. '09, [1910.] (Ap) c. 86 p. 8°, bds., 30 c. M. W. Mills.

Rostand, Edmond.
Chantecler: play in four acts; tr. by Gertrude Hall. '10(Ag20) c. D. $1.20 net. Duffield.
Chantecler; pièce en quatre actes, en vers; representée pour la première fois au Théatre de la Porte-Saint-Martin, le 7 fevrier, 1910. '10(Je4) O. pap., $1; hf. mor., $1.75. Lemcke.
La Princesse Lointaine; ed. by Jos. Leopold Borgerhoff. '09(My22) 12°, (Modern lang ser.) 40 c. Heath.

ROSTAND, Edmond.
Liberma, M. F. Story of Chantecler. 75 c. net. Moffat.
Plagiarism of The merchant prince of Cornville, by Cyrano de Bergerac. (Not for sale.) Rand, McN. & Co.

Rotation period of the sun. Hale, G: E. 40 c. Carnegie.

Rotch, Abbott Lawrence.
Benjamin Franklin and the first balloons. '07, [1908.] (Mr.) 18 p., 8°, pap. (Not for sale.) A. L. Rotch.
Conquest of the air; or, the advent of aërial navigation. '09(O16) c. il. D. **$1 net. Moffat.

Rotch, T: Morgan.
Living anatomy and pathology; the diagnosis of diseases in early life by the Roentgen method. '10(My) 25+225 p. il. 8°, $6 net. Lippincott.

Roth, E:
Conversationaliste (Le) Français. '08, [1909.] (Mr) 10 lessons, 25 c.; 50 lessons, $1. E: Roth.

Roth, Richard.
Ein nordischer held; ein bild aus der geschichte; ed., with introd., a brief outline of Scandinavian hist., notes, exercises and vocab., by Helene H. Boll. '10 (F19) c. S. 35 c. Am. Bk.

Roth, W. A.
Exercises in physical chemistry; authorized tr. by A. T. Cameron. '09(S11) il. 8°, *$2 net. Van Nostrand.

ROTHENBURG, Germany.
Uhde-Bernays, H. Rothenburg on the Tauber. *$1.50 net. Scribner.

Rothfeld, Otto.
Indian dust; studies of the Orient; incl. a biograph. appreciation of Laurence Hope. '10(Mr12) D. *$1.50 net. Lane.

Rothkäppchen (Das). Reichenbach, M. *25 c. net. Crowell.

Rothrock, D: And.
Elements of plane and spherical trigonometry. '10(O8) c. tabs., O. $1.40 net. Macmillan.

Rothschild, Alonzo.
Lincoln, master of men. Anniversary ed. '08(O24) c. por. O. **$1.50 net. Houghton M.

Rothschild, Max.
Gainsborough. '08(O3) il. O. (Masterpieces in colour.) bds., *65 c. net. Stokes.

Rotunda practical midwifery. Tweedy, E. H. $6. Oxford Univ.

ROUEN, France.
Old houses of Rouen of the 17th and 18th century. $15. Hessling.

Rough rider. Carman, W: B. $1. M. Kennerley.

Roughing-in house drains. Allen, J: K., *ed.* 50 c. Domestic Engineering.

Roughriders of the Pampas. Brereton, F: S. $1.25. Caldwell.

Rouillion, L:
Economics of manual training; study of the cost of equipping and maintaining hand work in the elementary and secondary schools. '10(Jl9) il. 8°, $2. Van Nostrand.

Roulet, Mary F. Nixon-.
See Nixon-Roulet, Mary F.

Round about Chicago. Chapin, L. *$1.50 net. Unity.

Round of rimes. McCarthy, D. A. **$1 net. Little, B. & Co.

ROUND TABLE (The).
See **Arthur, *King*.**

Round the clock. Nicoll, *Sir* W: R. $1.25 net. Doran.

Round the corner in Gay Street. Richmond, *Mrs.* G. L. S. †$1.50. Doubleday, P.

Round the fire stories. Doyle, *Sir* A. C. †$1.50. McClure.

Round the Lake Country. Rawnsley, H. D. *$1.50 net. Macmillan.

Round the world for the American Bible Society. Fox, J: gratis. Am. Bible.

Round the world in a motor car. Scarfoglio, A. *$5 net. M. Kennerley.

Round the world in seven days. Strang, H. $1.25 net. Doran.

Round the world: series of interesting il. articles on a great variety of subjects. v. 4, 5. '08(N14); v. 6. '09(Ap10); v. 7 (D18); v. 8. '10(N5) c. il. D. (Round the world ser.) ea., $1. Benziger.

Round the world with our navy. '09(Mr27) il. obl. 8°, pap., 25 c. L. H. Nelson.

Round the year with the poets. Capps-Oliver, M., *comp.* $1.50; $3. Caldwell.

Round the year with the stars. Serviss, G. P. $1 net. Putnam.

Round-up (The). Murray, J: †$1.50. G: W. Dillingham.

Round-up (The). Ellis, E: S. †$1. Winston.

Rousseau, Jean Jacques.
Julie; ou, la nouvelle Heloïse. Edition abrégee; avec préface de Fk. A. Hedgcock. '09(Je5) por. S. (Les classiques français.) limp leath., *$1 net. Putnam.

ROUSSEAU, Jean Jacques.
Gribble, F. H. Rousseau and the women he loved. *$3.75 net. Scribner.

Rout of the foreigners. Zollinger, G. $1.50. McClurg.

Routhier, Adolphe Basile.
The centurion; romance of the time of the Messiah; tr. from the French by Lucille P. Borden. '10(N19) c. 8°, $1.50. Herder.

Routledge rides alone. Comfort, W. L. $1.50. Lippincott.

Routledge's everyman's encyclopædia. Villiers, A., *ed.* $1.50 net. Dutton.

Roux, L: A.
Lessons in [French] grammar and composition based on Mérimée's Colomba. '09(Ap24) c. S. (Modern lang. ser.) pap., 18 c. Heath.

Rover boys' ser. for young Americans. See Stratemeyer, E:

Rover the farm dog. Wesselhoeft, *Mrs.* E. F. P. †$1.50. Little, B. & Co.

Row, Rob. Keable.
Educational meaning of manual arts and industries. '10(F19) c. il. 12°. $1.25. Row, P. & Co.

Row, S. B.
Hist. of Phillipsburg from pioneer days to present time. '09, [1910.] (Ap) c. 5-31 p. map, 4°, 35 c. S. B. Row.

ROWAN, Stephen Clegg.
Ayres, S. C. Sketch of the life and services of Vice Admiral Stephen C. Rowan, U. S. Navy. gratis. W. R. Thrall.

Rowbotham, Fs. Jameson.
Story-lives of great authors. '09(O2) il. pors. O. $1.50. Stokes.
Story-lives of great musicians. '08(S5) il. pors. O. $1.50. Stokes.

Rowe, F: L:, and Chadwick, Mary Alice, comps.
Pioneer sermons and addresses. '08(Je) c. 295 p. 12°, $1.25. F: L: Rowe.
——, eds. Duties and beauties of life; book for the home; selected prose and poetry. '08, [1909.] (F) c. 339 il. 8°, $2.50; $3.50. F: L: Rowe.

Rowe, Harry M.
Bookkeeping and accountancy; presenting the art of bookkeeping in accordance with the principles of modern accountancy. '10(Ag6) c. forms, 8°, $1.50. Sadler-R.

Rowe, Henrietta Gould.
Maid of Bar Harbor. '08(My.) c. 12°, (Popular ed. of recent fiction.) †75 c. Little, B. & Co.

Rowe, H: C.
Wholesomeness of oysters as food; paper presented before the Fourth International Fishery Congress, held in Washington, Sept. 22 to 26, 1908. '10(Mr) 259-267 p. 4°, pap. Gov. Pr. Off.

Rowe, Jesse Perry.
Some economic geology of Montana. '08, [1909.] (My) 3-70 p. il. tabs., 8°, (Univ. of Mont. bull.; Geological ser.) pap. Univ. of Mont.

Rowe, Leo Stanton.
Problem of city government. '08(O17) c. D. **$1.50 net. Appleton.

Rowe, S: McMath.
Hdbk. of timber preservation. Souvenir ed. rev. 1909. '09(My) c. 330+331-402 p. il. pors. tabs., 16°, $5. S: M. Rowe.

Rowe, Stuart H:
Habit-formation and the science of teaching. '09(N6) c. O. **$1.50 net. Longmans.

Rowe, W: H., jr.
Verse and toast. 2 v. '09(Je26) c. 12°, $1. W: H. Rowe.

Rowell, B: Winlow, and Richardson, Albert Lewis, comps.
Massachusetts consistory of sublime princes of the royal secret, thirty-second degree of the ancient and accepted Scottish rite for the northern jurisdiction of the United States, Boston, Mass. '08, [1909.] (Mr) c. 15+142 p. il. pors. 8°. (Priv. pr.) B: W. Rowell.

Rowell, Harvey.
Allan, son of a gunmaker. '09(S4) c. D. $1.50. Cochrane.

ROWING.
Lehmann, R. C. Complete oarsman. *$3 net. Jacobs.
Warre, E. On the grammar of rowing. 85 c. Oxford Univ.

Rowland, Arth. J:, and Creagmile, W: B.
Experiments in applied electricity. 2d ed., rev. and corrected. '10(N12) c. il. 8°, $1.25. McGraw-H.

Rowland, Dunbar, ed.
Encyclopedia of Mississippi hist. 2d ed. In 2 v. '08(Ag22) c. 8°, hf. mor., $12. Brant.

Rowland, Eleanor Harris.
Psychological experiences connected with the different parts of speech. '07. [1909.] (F) 42 p. 4°, (Monograph supplements; Psychological Review.) (Add. pubs. for price.) Psychological Review.
Right to believe. '09(O2) c. D. **$1.25 net. Houghton M.

Rowland, Helen.
Reflections of a bachelor girl. '09(My1) c. il. D. 75 c. Dodge.
The widow; [to say nothing of the man.] '08(Je20) c. D. $1. Dodge.

Rowland, H: Cottrell.
Across Europe in a motor boat. '08(O10) c. il. D. **$2 net. Appleton.
Countess Diane. '08(N14) c. il. D. †$1.25. Dodd.
Germaine. '09(O9) D. $1.50. Lane.
In the service of the princess. '10(Ap2) c. front. D. $1.50. Dodd.

Rowlands, J. F.
See Raleigh, Cecil, *pseud.*

Rowley, Anthony, pseud.
See Guthrie, Arth.

Rowley, R. R.
Geology of Pike Co. '08, [1909.] (Mr) 14+122 p. il. fold. map., diagr. 4°, (Missouri; Bureau of Geology and Mines.) pap., 20 c. Missouri Bu. Geol.

Rowley, W:
See Middleton, T:

Rowntree, B. Seebohm.
Land and labor; lessons from Belgium. '10(Ag13) map, 8°, $3.50 net. Macmillan.

Rowsell, Mary Catharine.
Ninon de l'Enclos and her century. '10 (D10) 8°, $3.75 net. Brentano's.

Roxana. Craw, G: R. 75 c. Sterling.

Roy, And.
History of the coal miners of U. S. from the development of the mines to the close of the anthracite strike of 1902. 3d ed., rev. and enl. '07, [1908.] (Mr.) c. 16+465 p. il. pors. 8°, $1.75. Trauger.

Roy, Mrs. Lillian Eliz. Becker.
Little Indian tales. '08, [1909.] (F) c. 38 p. 8°, wood venire, $1. E: S. Whaples.
Seedling's harvest. '10(O29) c. il. D. $1.25. Wessels & B.

Roy and Ray in Canada. Plummer, M. W. **$1.75 net. Holt.

Royal Academy pictures and sculpture, 1909; 22d year of issue. '09(Jl3); 1910; 23d year of issue. '10(Jl9) il. f°, ea., *$1.75 net. Cassell.

Royal Americans. Foote, *Mrs.* M. H. $1.25 net. Houghton M.

Royal Baking Powder Co., New York. My favorite receipt. 9th ed. '09(N) 10+123 p. 8°, 50 c. Royal Baking.

Royal cavalier. Erskine, *Mrs.* B. $3.75 net. Appleton.

Royal end. Harland, H: †$1.50. Dodd.

Royal family in the Temple Prison. Cléry, J. B. C.-H. $1.50 Sturgis & W.

Royal good fellow. Hayes, H. W. 75 c. net. Howerton.

Royal lovers. Vacaresco, H. $1.50. Lane.

Royal lovers and their favorites. Rappoport, A. S. *$4 net. Brentano's.

Royal message of cheer and comfort. MacArthur, R. S. *$1 net; *$2 net. Treat.

Royal navy. Swinburne, H. L. *$6 net. Macmillan.

ROYAL NORTHWEST MOUNTED POLICE.
Haydon, A. L. Riders of the plains. $2.75 net. McClurg.

Royal palaces and parks of France. Miltoun, F., *pseud.* $3. L. C. Page.

Royal palaces of Spain. Calvert, A. F: *$1.50 net. Lane.

Royal quartette. Bearne, *Mrs.* C. M. C. *$3 net. Brentano's.

Royal road to health. Strohecker, C. $1. C. Strohecker.

Royal road to health. Tyrrell, C: A. (Not for sale.) Tyrrell's Hygienic Inst.

Royal Society of London. Catalogue of scientific papers, 1800-1900; subject-index. v. 1. '08(D5) royal 8°, $6.50; hf. pigskin, $8; v. 2. '10(Ja22) 8°, buckram, *$5 net; hf. pigskin, *$6.50 net. Putnam.

Royal Tarr's pluck. Adams, W: T. $1. Lothrop, L. & S.

Royal ward. Brebner, P. J. †$1.50. Little, B. & Co.

ROYALE, *Mme.*
See Angoulême, Marie Thérèse Charlotte.

ROYALL, *Mrs.* Anne Newport.
Porter, S. H. Life and times of Anne Royall. *$1.50 net. Torch Press.

Royall, W: Lawrence.
Some reminiscences. '09(Ap24) c. D. *$1.50 net. Neale.

ROYALL FAMILY.
See Medford, Mass.

Royce, Mrs. Caroline Halstead Barton.
First century of Lake Champlain. '09, [1910.] (Ap) 26 p. front. 8°, 25 c. C. H. B. Royce.

Royce, Josiah.
Philosophy of loyalty. '08(Ap18) c. D. **$1.50 net. Macmillan.
Race questions, provincialism and other American problems. '08(N7) c. D. **$1.25 net. Macmillan.

Roycroft leather-book; being a catalog of beautiful leathern things made Roycroftie by hand by Roycrofter artists. [1910.] (F) c. '09. 9-46 p. il. 12°, 10 c. Roycrofters.

ROYER FAMILY.
See Genealogies, Gift, A. K., *comp.*

Royle, E: Milton.
Silent call. '10(Je4) c. il. D. $1.50. Scribner.

Royle, Harold M.
Chemistry of gas manufacture: pract. manual for the use of gas engineers, gas managers and students. '08(Ag8) c. il. 8°. $4.50. Henley.

Roys, Cyrus D.
Captain Jack, a story of Vermont. '10 (Ja22) il. D. $1.50.. C. D. Roys.

Rozan, Charles.
Les petites ignorances de la conversation; ed. by R. de Blanchaud. '10(Ja29) S. (Crowell's shorter French texts.) *25 c. net. Crowell.

Rozant, Ina.
Life's understudies. '09(Jl10) O. $1.50. M. Kennerley.

Rubáiyát. *See* Hafiz, Shams ed-din Muhammad.—Omar Khayyám.

Rubaiyat of a huffy husband. Little, M. W. B. $1. Badger.

Rubaiyat of bridge. Wells, C. $1. Harper.

RUBBER.
See India rubber.

Rubber-neck (The). Clivette, the Man in Black, *pseud.* 15 c. L. Sweet.

Rubencamp, R.
See Zerr, G:

RUBENS, *Sir* Peter Paul.
Bensusan, S: L. Rubens. *65 c. net. Stokes.
Stevenson, R. A. M. Peter Paul Rubens. *75 c. net; *$1 net. Dutton.

Rube's twenty years' adventures. Kinder, T: S: 50 c.; 25 c. Laird.

Rübezahl. *See* Goebel, Ferdinand.

Rubinow, I: M.
Russian wheat and wheat flour in European markets. '08(O3) il. (U. S. Dept. of Agriculture, Bu. of Statistics bull.) pap. (Add. pubs. for price.) U. S., Supt. of Docs.

Rubric ser. 12°, **60 c. net. Duffield.
—Bible. N. T. Sermon on the Mount.
—Browning, E. B. Sonnets from the Portuguese.
—Browning, R. Pippa passes.
—Dickens. Christmas carol.
—Emerson. Nature.
—Franklin. Poor Richard's almanac.
—Wilde. Ballad of Reading Gaol.

Rubrical revision. Bishop, W. C. 36 c. net. Longmans.

Ruby of Kishmoor. Pyle, H. †$1. Harper.

Ruby ring. Nonnen, E. 50 c. Engberg-H.

Rucker, W. C.
Plague among ground squirrels in Contra Costa County, California. '09(N) 18 p. 8°, pap. (Add. Superintendent for price.) U. S., Supt. of Docs.

Rudaux, Lucien.
How to study the stars; astronomy with small telescopes and the naked eye and notes on celestial photography; tr. by A. H. Keane. '10(F12) il. O. *$2 net. Stokes.

Rudd, E: Huntting.
Dedham's ancient landmarks and their national significance. '08(D26) large 8°, $1. Dedham Transcript.

Rudder (The). Handy Jack book of navigation tables, especially prepared for use with "Navigation simplified." '09(Ja16) c. tabs., 16°, (Rudder "on" ser.) $1. Rudder.

Rudder (The). How to build an 18-inch racing cat [boat.] '08(N) c. 23 p. front., diagrs., 4°, $1. Rudder.

Rudder "on" ser. il. 16°, $1. Rudder.
—Rudder. Handy Jack book of navigation.

Ruddiman, Edsel Alex., M.D.
Incompatibilities in prescriptions, for students in pharmacy and medicine, and practising pharmacists and physicians. 3d ed. '08(Ag29) c. $2. Wiley.

Rude, C: Burr.
The A. D. Rude "great modern system" for designing and cutting men's garments as taught at the New York Cutting School, New York City. [6th ed.] '09 (O16) c. il. por. F. $12.50. A. D. Rude.

Rudiments of Latin. Sturmer, J. W: $1. J. W: Sturmer.

Rudiments of modern medical electricity. Monell, S. H. *$1 net. W: R. Jenkins.

Rudolph, Johannes F. S., D.D.
Luise; aus dem leben einer emanzipierten. '09(Ap) c. '08. 85 p. 16°, 30 c. J. F. S. Rudolph.

Rue (Une) de tombeaux à Saggarah. Capart, J. In 2 v. $15. Stechert.

Ruedemann, Rudolf.
See Kemp, Ja. Furman.

Ruediger, W: Carl.
Principles of education. '10(Mr5) c. D. **$1.25 net. Houghton M.

Ruel Durkee. Browne, G: W. $1.50. Badger.

Ruen, H: C.
See United States statute citer-digest.

Ruer, Rudolf.
Elements of metallography; authorized tr. by C. H. Mathewson. '09(N20) c. figs. 8°, **$3 net. Wiley.

RUGBY.
See Foot-ball.

Ruge, Carl.
See Winter, Georg.

Ruger, H: Alford.
Psychology of efficiency; experimental study of the processes involved in the solution of mechanical puzzles and in the acquisition of skill in their manipulation. '10 (Jl2) Q. (Archives of psychology.) pap. Science Press, (N. Y.)

Ruggles, Fk. A.
Massachusetts gas companies: properties, capitalization, income, growth, statistics. '10(Je) c. 8 p. fold. tab., 12°. (Priv. pr.) F. A. Ruggles.

Ruggles, W: Nelson.
Out of the Ozarks. '09(Mr27) 12°, $1.50. Neale.

RUGS.
Claflin, H. B., Co. Rugs and carpets from the Orient. gratis. Claflin.
Dilley, A. U. Oriental rugs. 50 c. Dilley.
Dunn, E. Rugs in their native land. $2.50 net. Dodd.
Holt, R. B. Rugs: oriental and occidental. *$5 net. McClurg.
Humphries, S. Oriental carpets, runners and rugs, and some Jacquard reproductions. $10.50 net. Macmillan.
Oriental rugs and carpets. $1.50. Review Pub.

Ruhl, Arth. Brown.
Athletics in accountancy: account of the organization and exploits of the Haskins & Sells Athletic Association, 1907. '08 (Jl) c. 4+12 p. il. pors. F. cl. (Not for sale.) Haskins & S.
Other Americans: cities, the countries, and especially the people of South America. '08(O3) c. il. map, O. **$2 net. Scribner.

Ruhl, Otto.
Rationale of investment in zinc mining. '10(Mr26) c. il. map, 8°, 25 c. Mining News.

Ruhmer, Ernst.
Wireless telephony in theory and practice; tr. fr. the German by Ja. Erskine-Murray. '08(Ap25) il. 8°, *$3.50 net. Van Nostrand.

Ruhräh, J:
Manual of the diseases of infants and children. 2d ed., thoroughly rev. '08(Mr14) c. il. chart, diagrs., 12°, *$2 net. Saunders.
See also Friedenwald, Julius.

Ruinous face. Hewlett, M. H: †$1. Harper.

Ruins of Fountains Abbey. Oxford, A. W. $1.40 net. Oxford Univ.

Rule, U. Z.
Old Testament institutions: their origin and development; with preface by Rev. Prof. Sayce. '10(D) 8°, $2 net. Gorham.

Rule of "not too much." Heinemann, H. E. O. 25 c. H. E. O. Heinemann.

Rule of three. Estabrook, A. M. †$1.25. Small.

Rule of three actors in the classical drama. Rees, K. *75 c. net. Univ. of Chic.

Rulers of India ser.; ed. by Sir W: Wilson Hunter. il. D. Oxford Univ.
—Smith. Asoka. $1.15.

Rulers of the surf. Muller, J. W. $1.50. Appleton.

Rules and instructions for a holy life. Leighton, R. *60 c. net. Longmans.

Rules of life for the pastor of souls; from the German by Rev. T: Slater and Rev. A. Rauch. '09(My15) c. $1.25. Benziger.

Rules of the game. White, S. E. $1.40, fixed. Doubleday, P.

Ruley, Clara North.
Confessions of Linda Poindexter. '10 (Ag27) c. il. D. $1. B'way Pub.

Ruling elders' handbook. Jolly, A. H. 50 c. Presb. Bd.

Ruling ideas in early ages. Mozley, J. B. *$1.25 net. Longmans.

Rum and ruin. Roe, E: R. $1; 25 c. Laird.

Rum Bellow, H: Albert.
Factory glazes for ceramic engineers. A. of the series. '09(Ja16) c. charts, f°, *$10 net. Spon.

Rumball, Edn. Alfr.
Jesus and modern religion. '08(Ag1) bds., *75 c. net. Open Court.

Rumbaugh, Jacob.
Reminiscences of Jacob Rumbaugh. '10(D) 103 p. il. pors. 12°, $1. Hudson.

Rumbo rhymes. Calmour, A. C. $2 net. Harper.

Rumbold, Sir Horace.
Francis Joseph and his times. '09(N6) c. il. O. **$4 net. Appleton.

Rumpel, Oskar.
Cystoscopy as adjuvant in surgery; with an atlas of cystoscopic views and concimitant text for physicians and students; only authorized English tr. by P. W. Shedd. '10(Ag) c. 6+131 p. il. 4°, $8.50 net. Rebman.

Rumsey, Frances.
Leonora; a novel. '10(O) 311 p. D. $1.50. Appleton.

RUMSEY, James.
Moray, J: Brief account of last century's inventive steam pirate. 10 c. J: Moray.

Rumsey, Judson Smith.
Rumsey on corporations, [etc.] '08, [1910.] (F) c. O. $6.30. Banks & Co.

Runaway boy. *See* Riley, Ja. Whitcomb.
Runaway (The) flying-machine, and other stories of outdoor adventures by R: Barry and others. '10(O29) c. D. (Harper's athletic ser.) 60 c. Harper.
Runaway place. Eaton, W. P. †$1.25. Holt.
Runciman, J: F.
Haydn. '08(Ag29) il. por. 16°, (Bell's miniature ser. of musicians.) 50 c.; limp leath., *$1 net. Macmillan.
Purcell. '09(D4) il. 16°, (Bell's miniature ser. of musicians.) *50 c. net; leath., *$1 net. Macmillan.
RUNNERS.
See **Rugs.**
RUNNING.
Duffey, A. F., *ed.* How to sprint. 10 c. Am. Sports.
Morton, J. W. How to run 100 yards. 10 c. Am. Sports.
Sullivan, J. E: Marathon running. 10 c. Am. Sports.
Running fight. Osborne, W: H. $1.50. Dodd.
Runnymede, Edgar J: G: *35 c. net; *70 c. net. Dutton.
Runyon, S. D.
Baby's history. '08(N7) il Q. $3; gilt top, with line guards, $4; moire silk, $7.50; with only 4 color pls., $2, boxed. Stokes.
Ruoff, H: Woldmar, ed.
Masters of achievement. '10(My14) c. il pors. $5.50; extra cl., $6.25; leath., $7.50. Frontier Press.
Standard dictionary of facts. '09(Jl3) il. pors. 8°, $4.90; $5.50; $6.25: $6.75. Frontier Press.
RUPERT, *Prince* of the Palatinate.
Erskine, *Mrs.* B. Royal cavalier; romance of Rupert, Prince Palatine. $3.75 special net. Appleton.
Rupp, F: Augustine, M.D.
Purity and truth; letters of a physician to his daughters on the great black plague. '10(Ap30) c. S. bds., 50 c. Vir.
Rupp, F: A:
John Montcalm, heretic; tale of the Maryland hills. '08, [1909.] (F) c. 272 p. il. 12°, $1. I. M. Beaver.
Rupp, Philip.
See Kebler, Lyman Frederic.
RUPTURE.
See **Hernia.**
Rural christendom. Roads, C: *90 c. net. Am. S. S.
RURAL DELIVERY SERVICE.
See Post-Office.
Rural hygiene. Brewer, T: W. **$1.25 net. Lippincott.
RURAL LIFE.
See Social science.
Rural life problem of the United States. Plunkett, *Sir* H. C. $1.25 net. Macmillan.
Rural rides. Cobbett, W: *40 c. net. Putnam.
Rural school Agriculture. Bull, C. P. 60 c. C. P. Bull.
Rural school-teacher. White, B. $1. B'way Pub.
RURAL SCHOOLS.
See **Schools.**
Rural science ser. *See* Macmillan's.
Rural text-book ser. *See* Macmillan's.

Ruscom, Russ, pseud.
See Whitcomb, Russell.
Rush, Elmer Ellsworth.
Constitution of the United States in outline, with questions and answers. '10 (Ag13) c. 12°, 75 c. Hudson.
Rush, G: F:
Manual of equity pleading, state and federal, with illustrative forms, and incl. the federal equity rules of court, special attention given to modern practice in relation to the master's office. '09(Je) c. 11+219 p. O. (Add. pubs. for price.) Chic. Legal News.
Rushing waters and deep sea pearls. Young. W. M. 10 c. Ulbrich.
Ruskin, J:
Works. De luxe ed. 15 v. '10(N) il. levant. $45. Crowell.
Works. 13 v. New imperial lib. ed. '10 (D) il. 8°, ea., $1.25; hf. cf., $2.25; New il. sterling ed., ea., $1. (Sets only.) Estes.
Beautiful thoughts from J: Ruskin. '08 (Ag29) c. 16°, $1. Pott.
Crown of wild olive. '08(Je20) 16°, (New universal lib.) 50 c.; leath., 75 c.—*Same*, [and] The cestus of Aglaia. '08(S19) 16°, (Everyman's lib.) *35 c. net; leath., *70 c. net. Dutton.
Crown of wild olive, and The queen of the air; ed., with notes and an introd., by Wightman F. Melton. '10(Ap9) c. T. (Pocket Am. and Eng. classics.) 25 c. Macmillan.
Dame Wiggins and her seven wonderful cats; made into a primer by Francesca Marshall. '08, [1909.] (Mr) il. 12°, (Folk lore ser.) *30 c. net. Educ. Pub.
Elements of drawing. '08(O17) 16°, (Best books ser.) leath., *$1 net. Dutton.
Ethics of the dust. '08(O17) 16°, (Best books ser.) leath., *$1 net.—*Same*. Introd. by Grace Rhys. '08(F22) 16°, (Everyman's lib.) *35 c. net; leath., *70 c. net.—*Same*. With notes and a new index. '08(F22) 12°, (New universal lib.) 50 c.; leath., 75 c. Dutton.
King of the Golden River; or, the black brothers; legend of Stiria. [1910.] (Ap) c. '09. 75 p. il. por. 12°, (Golden classics.) 50 c. Rand, McN. & Co.
"A reading list" (2 p.)
Modern painters. 5 v. '08(O17) 16°, (Best books ser.) leath., ea., *$1 net. Dutton.
Mystery of life. [1910.] (Ap) c. '09. 9-80 p. por. 12°, (Golden classics.) 50 c. Rand, McN. & Co.
Out in the open: extracts; comp. by Ruth Merriam Lawton. '08(D5) c. por. O. $1. Bassette.
Poems; with an essay on the author by Gilbert Keith Chesterton. '08(S19) 12°, (Muses' lib.) 50 c.; leath., 75 c. Dutton.
Pre-Raphaelitism. '08(O17) 16°, (Best books ser.) leath., *$1 net. Dutton.
Ruskin calendar; ed. by Rev. Albert E. Simms. '08(O3) por. D. (Chiswick ser.) **50 c. net. Crowell.

Ruskin, J:—*Continued.*
Ruskin day by day; ed. by A. E. Sims. '10 (D) 12°, (Day by day ser.) 60 c.; ooze, $1. Crowell.
Selections; ed., with introd. and notes, by Chauncey B. Tinker. '08(N14) c. il. por. D. (Riverside literature ser.) **50 c. net. Houghton M
Selections; ed., with notes, by H. Hampshire. '10(D24) c. 12°, 30 c. net. Macmillan.
Sesame and lilies. '10(D) limp leath., $1.50, boxed. Barse & H.
Sesame and lilies. '08(D26) front. T. (Remarque ed. of literary masterpieces.) 40 c.; limp leath., 75 c., boxed; chamois, $1.25, boxed. Caldwell.
Sesame and lilies. '08(O17) 16°, (Best books ser.) leath., *$1 net. Dutton.
Sesame and lilies; ed. by C: Rob. Gaston. '09(Ag21) c. por. 16°, 35 c. Heath.
Seven lamps of architecture. '08(O17) 16°, (Best books ser.) leath., *$1 net. Dutton.
Stones of Venice. 3 v. '08(O17) 16°, (Best books ser.) leath., ea., *$1 net. Dutton.
Thoughts of John Ruskin; ed. by Dana Estes. '08(N7) c. por. S. (Noble thoughts of the world's greatest minds.) hf. parchment, $1.50, boxed; parchment, $5, boxed. Estes.
Time and tide; notes on the construction of sheepfolds; lecture to the Cambridge School of Art, and Picture galleries, their function and formation; with introd. by "A Ruskin Student." '10(D10) c. 16°, (Everyman's lib.) 35 c. net; leath., 70 c. net. Dutton.
Unto this last. '08(O17) 16°, (Best books ser.) leath., *$1 net. Dutton.

RUSKIN, John.
Burgess, W: Religion of Ruskin. *$2 net. Revell.
Earland, A. Ruskin and his circle. $1.75 net. Putnam.
Wyngate, A. Life of John Ruskin. $1. Scribner.

Russan, Ashmore.
Mighty hunters; being an account of some of the adventures of Richard and Helen Carson in the forests and plains of Chiapas in Mexico. '09(N20) c. il. D. **$1.35 net. Longmans.

Russel, Edgar.
Wireless telegraphy, Signal Corps, U. S. Army, principles—field and station equipment. '10(Jl) 44 p. pl. diagrs., 12°. (Priv. pr.) E. Russel.

Russel, Mrs. Florence Kimball.
In West Point gray as plebe and yearling. '08(D5) c. il. O. (Boys' story of the army ser.) $1.50. L. C. Page.

Russell, Alex.
Theory of electric cables and networks. '09(Ap24) il. 8°, *$3 net. Van Nostrand.

Russell, Anna Virginia.
Story told by pins. '08(Ap18) c. il. D. $1. Neale.

Russell, Bertrand Arth. W:
Philosophical essays. '10(D10) O. $2 net. Longmans.

Russell, C: E:
Greatest trust in the world, [the beef trust.] '08(Ap11) c. 12°, (Popular priced copyrights.) 50 c. B. W. Dodge.
Lawless wealth: origin of some great American families. '08(Je6) c. D. $1.50. B. W. Dodge.
Songs of democracy and other themes. '09(N20) c. D. **$1.25 net. Moffat.
Thomas Chatterton, the marvelous boy. '08 (Ap11) c. il. pors. facsims., O. **$2.50 net. Moffat.

Russell, C: E: B., and Rigby, Lilian M.
Why I am a Socialist. '10(Jl30) 12°, $1.50 net. Doran.
Working lad's clubs. '08(N21) il. 12°, *$1.50 net. Macmillan.

Russell, C: Russell, Baron.
Diary of a visit to the United States of America in the year 1883; with introd. by the Rev. Matthew Russell, and appendix by T: Fs. Meehan; ed. by C: G: Herbermann. '10(Ag13) c. il. pors. 8°, $3. Benziger.

Russell, C: Taze, and White, Lloyd S.
Russell-White debate: a public discussion between Pastor Charles T. Russell (Millennial Dawn) of Allegheny, Pa., and Lloyd S. White (Christian) of Dallas, Tex. '08 (My9) c. il. pors. 8°, $1.10; pap., 60 c. F: L: Rowe.

Russell, Lady Constance.
Rose Goddess and other sketches of mystery and romance. '10(O15) il. pors. O. $7 net. Longmans.

Russell, Dora.
Country sweetheart. '08(F1) c. D. (Popular copyright fiction.) 75 c. Rand, McN. & Co.

Russell, Elbert.
Jesus of Nazareth in the light of to-day. '10(F19) c. D. **60 c. net. Winston.
Parables of Jesus; a course of ten lessons arranged for daily study. '09(S18) c. D. pap., 20 c. Y. W. C. A.

Russell, G: Besore.
Four score and more. '08(Jl) c. 18+383 p. il. pors. 8°, $1.25. Ref. Ch., S. S. Bd.

Russell, G: E.
Text-book on hydraulics. '09(D18) c. il. 8°, $2.50. Holt.

Russell, G: W: Erskine.
Sketches and snapshots. '10(Ag27) front. O. $2.50 net. Duffield.

Russell, Gurdon Wadsworth.
Acct. of some of the descendants of John Russell, the emigrant from Ipswich, England, who came to Boston, New England, Oct. 3, 1635; together with some sketches of the allied families of Wadsworth, Tuttle, and Beresford; ed. by Edn. Stanley Welles. '10(D) 318 p. il. por. pls. facsim., geneal. tab., 8°, $4. Conn. Hist.

Russell, Harry Luman.
See Turneaure, F: Eug.
—, and Hastings, Edn. G:
Agricultural bacteriology. '10(Mr5) c. il. 12°, $1.25. H. L. Russell.
Experimental dairy bacteriology. '09(Jl17) c. il. D. $1. Ginn.
Outlines of dairy bacteriology. 9th ed., wholly rewritten. '10(D31) c. il. 12°, $1. H. L. Russell.

Russell, Mrs. Hattie Sanford.
What Christmas brought to Tom and Nell; holiday entertainment in five parts. '09 (D) c. 27 p. 12°, 50 c. Cochrane.

Russell, I:
Pilot of the Skylark: story of how an enterprising boy became a master air man in the U. S. army. '10(D) 348 p. 12°, $1.50. Wilde.

Russell, I: Franklin, comp.
Cases on measure of damage. '09(N) c. 29+714 p. O. $4. Callaghan.

Russell, Ja. Elmer.
See Lukens, Victor Herbert.

Russell, L. E.
Abraham Lincoln; contribution toward a bibliography. '10(O15) S. bds., 50 c. Torch Press.

Russell, Lev.
Statute law and how to find it; treating of the origin, growth and philosophy of statute law, [etc.]: lecture. '09(Jl) c. 18 p. O. pap. (Add. pub. for price.) J. E. Hughes.
See also Kentucky. Statutes.

Russell, Rev. Matthew.
At home with God; priedieu papers on spiritual subjects. '10(N19) D. $1.25 net. Longmans.

Russell, T. Baron.
Science at home; simple experiments for young people. '09(Jl3) il. D. 75 c. Fenno.

Russell, T: H.
Faulty diction; or, errors in use of English language. '08. (Vest pocket size.) 25 c.; 50 c. McKay.

Russell, T: Herbert.
Automobile driving self taught. '10(Ja15) c. figs. D. (Thompson ser. of home study books.) $1; leath., $1.50. C: C. Thompson.
Automobile motors and mechanism; pract. treatise on power plant and motive parts of the modern motor car. '10(F12) c. il. figs. D. (Thompson ser. of home study books.) $1; limp leath., $1.50. C: C. Thompson.
Ignition, timing and valve setting. '10 (Ja22) c. il. D. $1; limp leath., $1.50. C: C. Thompson.
Motor boats; construction and operation. '10(F19) c. il. D. (Thompson ser. of home study books.) $1; limp leath., $1.50. C: C. Thompson.
See also Jackman, W. J.
—, and others, eds.
International business lib. v. 1, Business principles and methods; v. 2, Salesmanship; v. 3, Advertising methods and mediums; v. 4, Banking and finance; v. 5, Business correspondence and forms. [1910.] (N) 8°, (International business lib.) Int. Law.

Russell, Waterman S. C., and Kelly, Howard Clinton.
Lab'y manual of first year science for secondary schools. '09(D4) c. Q. pap., 75 c. Holt.

Russell, W:
On scientific horseshoeing, for levelling and balancing the action and gait of horses. 10th ed., rev. and enl. '08(Ja11) il. por. 8°, $4. Krehbiel.

Russell, W: Clark.
Sailor's sweetheart. '08(Je27) 12°, (Magnolia lib.) 50 c. Hurst.
Wreck of the "Grosvenor." '09(My15) c. il. D. (Deep-water ser.: popular tales of the sea.) $1.25. Sturgis & W.

Russell, Rev. W: T:
Maryland; the land of sanctuary: a hist. of religious toleration in Maryland. '08 (Ja11) il. por. O. $1.75. Furst.

Russell family.
See Genealogies.

Russell Sage Foundation pubs. *See* Sage (Russell) Foundation pubs.

Russia.
Andreiyeff, L. Seven who were hanged: [fiction.] $1. J. S. Ogilvie.
Bain, R. N. Slavonic Europe: political hist. of Poland and Russia, 1447-1796. *$2 net. Putnam.
Callahan, J. M. Russo-American relations during the American Civil War. 30 c. Univ. of W. Va.
Curtin, J. Mongols in Russia. **$3 net. Little, B. & Co.
Gasiorowski, W. Tragic Russia. *$2.50 net. Cassell.
Harper, S: N. New electoral law for the Russian Duma. *25 c. net. Univ. of Chic.
Hodgetts, E: A. B. Court of Russia in the nineteenth century. 2 v. *$6 net. Scribner.
Kennard, H. P. Russian peasant. *$1.50 net. Lippincott.
Latimer, R. S. Liberty of conscience under three Tsars. *$1.50 net. Revell.
Miliukov, P. N. Constitutional government. 10 c. Civic Forum.
Rubinow, I: M. Russia's wheat trade. 15 c. **U. S., Supt. of Docs.**
Walling, W: E. Russia's message: true world import of the revolution. **$3 net. Doubleday, P.
Walter, L. E. Russia. 75 c. net. Macmillan.
See also Caucasus;—Corea;—Lithuanian language;—Russian language;—Russo-Japanese war;—St. Petersburg;—Schlussenburg Fortress;—Siberia;—Slavs in the United States;—*also* Alexander III.

Russian army and the Japanese war. Kuropatkin, A. N. 2 v. *$7.50 net. Dutton.
Russian Bastille. Pollock, S. O. 50 c. Kerr.

Russian church.
See Greek church.

Russian conquest of the Caucasus. Baddely, J: F. *$5 net. Longmans.

Russian language.
Lowe, W: H: Systemization of the Russian verb. *$1.50 net. Putnam.
Meycliar, L. English-Russian and Russian-English dictionary. $1. Spon.
See also **Tauchnitz manuals of conversation.**

RUSSIAN LITERATURE.
Baring, M. Landmarks in Russian literature. $1.75 net. Macmillan.
Brückner, A. Literary history of Russia. $4. Scribner.
Wolfe, A. J: Aspects of recent Russian literature. (Not for sale.) A. J: Wolfe.
Russian lyrics. Bianchi, *Mrs.* M. G. D., *comp.* $1.25 net. Duffield.
Russian road to China. Bates, L. W., *jr.* $3 net. Houghton M.
Russian wheat. Rubinow, I. M. (Add. pubs. for price.) U. S., Supt. of Docs.
RUSSO-JAPANESE WAR.
Kuropatkin, A. N. Russian army and the Japanese war. 2 v. *$7.50 net. Dutton.
McCormick, F: Tragedy of Russia in Pacific Asia. 2 v. *$6 net. Outing.
Sedgwick, F. R. Russo-Japanese war. *$1.60 net. Macmillan.
Semenoff, V. I. Price of blood. $1.50 net.
—Rasplata (the reckoning); diary kept during the blockade of Port Arthur, etc. $3.50. Dutton.
Takahashi, S. International law applied to the Russo-Japanese war. *$8 net. Banks.
See also Corea;—Port Arthur.

Rust, Armistead.
Ex-meridian altitude, azimuth and star-finding tables; with diagrams for finding the latitude and facilitating plotting lines of position, and giving new and practical methods for identifying stars in cloudy weather; latitudes 0°-65°; declinations 0°-71° north and south. '08(O3) c. il. figs. 8°, $5. Wiley.

Rust, C: D., ed.
See New York [State.] Code of criminal procedure.—Penal code.

Rust, C: Herbert.
Church on wheels: ten years on a chapel car. 2d ed. '08(F8) por. 12°, 50 c. Am. Bapt.
Rust of Rome. Deeping, G: W. $1.20 net. Cassell.

Ruston, J: E:
Decedents' estates. [1910.] (S) c. 58 p. $2. E. W. Whitfield.

Ruth, Christian Wismer.
Pentecostal experience. '09(Jl) 75 p. 12°, 25 c. Chr. Witness.
Ruth, Book of. *See* Bible.
Ruth of Boston. Kaler, J. O. 35 c. Am. Bk.

Ruther, F:
Long Island to-day; consisting of sketches on the political, industrial, topographical and geological hist. of Long Island, but more particularly of general views illustrating Long Island scenes of to-day. '10(F5) c. il. 4°, $2. F: Ruther.

Rutherford, Fk. Emory.
Private lessons on diseases of the horse and cow. [Rev. ed.] [1910.] (Jl) c. 7-116 p. il. por. 12°, $5. F. E. Rutherford.

Rutherford, H. W., comp.
Catalogue of the library of C: Darwin, now in the Botany School, Cambridge; with an introd. by Fs. Darwin. '08(N7) 8°, *30 c. net. Putnam.

"Rutherford, Mark," pseud.
See White, W: Hale.

Rutherford, W. R.
Cheeriness. '10(Ja1) 16°, (Cheerful life ser.) bds., 75 c.; leath., $1.25. Dodge.
Look on the brighter side. '10(Ja1) 16°, (Cheerful life ser.) bds., 75 c.; leath., $1.25. Dodge.

Rutledge, Archibald Hamilton.
Banners of the coast: [poems.] '08(Je13) 8°, $1. State Co., (S. C.)

Rutter, Fk.
Path to Paris. '08(Ag8) il. Q. *$5 net. Lane.
Rossetti. '10(D) il. $1 net. M. Kennerley.

Ruutz-Rees, Janet E.
Reflections on the Psalms. '08(Ap4) 16°, 50 c. Newson.
RUWENZORI (*mountains*), Africa.
Filippi, F. de. Ruwenzori: [account of the Duke of Abruzzi's expedition to the snow ranges of central Africa.] *$8 net. Dutton.

Ruxton, Philip, Inc.
Printing inks by Ruxton: a handbook for the printer. '07, [1908.] (Mr.) c. 120 p. il. f°, $2. Ruxton.
Ruy Blas. *See* Hugo, Victor.

Ruyl, Beatrice Baxter.
Little Indian maidens at work and play. '09, [1910.] (Ja) c. 40 p. 4°, †$1. Dutton.
Zodiac birthday book. '10(N19) c. O. $1 net. Baker & T.

Ruyter, Claus.
Meine lieder. '08(Mr21) c. 12°, pap., *$1 net. Caspar.

Ryan, F: W.
Malta. '10(D24) il. map, 8°, (Color books of travel and description.) $3 net. Macmillan.

Ryan, G: Weiser.
Bookkeeping for the plumber. 2d ed. '09, [1910.] (F) 5-58 p. il. por. 12°, 25 c. Standard Sanitary Mfg.

Ryan, Mrs. Marah Ellis Martin, [Mrs. S. E. Ryan.]
Flute of the gods. '09(O9) c. il. O. **$1.50 net. Stokes.
My Quaker maid. '08(F1) c. D. (Popular copyright fiction.) 75 c. Rand, McN. & Co.
Told in the hills. '08(F1) c. D. (Popular copyright fiction.) 75 c. Rand, McN. & Co.

Ryan, Mrs. Millie.
What every singer should know. '10(D31) c. por. D. $1. Franklin Pub., (Neb.)

Ryan, P. F. W:
Queen Anne and her court. 2 v. '09 (Mr13) il. 8°, *$6 net. Dutton.

Ryan, Mrs. S. E.
See Ryan, *Mrs.* Marah Ellis Martin.

Rydberg, Per Axel.
Scandinavians who have contributed to the knowledge of the flora of North America. '08(My2) 4°, (Augustana library pubs.) pap., $1. Augustana.

Ryder, Arth. W:
Women's eyes; being verses tr. from the Sanskrit. '10(Je11) c. S. pap., $1 net, boxed. A. M. Robertson.

Ryder, Rob. O.
Young lady across the way. '08(F29) c. il. T. bd's., *50 c. net. Young Lady Across the Way.
—, and Westerman, Harry J.
Some further observations of the young lady across the way. '08, [1909.] (F) 50 c. Young Lady Across the Way.
Ryder-Taylor, H:
See Taylor, H: Ryder-.
Rye, Edg.
Quirt and the spur; vanishing shadows of the Texas frontier. '09(Je19) c. il. por. D. $1.50. Conkey.
RYE.
Clark, C: C., *comp.* Rye crops of the United States. 5 c. U. S., Supt. of Docs.
Ryer, Julian C.
Principles of commercial law. '08(O) c. 20+264 p. D. (Add. pubs. for price.) Cross Co.
Ryman, Dean Ernest.
Compilation of words and phrases judicially defined by the supreme court of Georgia and the court of appeals. '10(Ag) c. O. $6. Harrison Co.
Ryno, Wakeman, M.D.
Amen, the god of the Amonians. '10(D31) D. $1. B'way Pub.
Rythmic psalter. *See* Bible. O. T.: Psalms.
S., H., comp.
See E., J., *comp.*
Saalfield, Mrs. Arth. Ja.
See Sutton, Adah Louise.
Saalfeld, Edmund.
Lectures on cosmetic treatment: manual for practitioners; with introd. and notes by P. S. Abraham, M.D.; tr. by J. F. Halls Dally, M.D. '10(S) 201 p. il. 8°, $1.75 net. Hoeber.
Saalfield annual, 1910; picture book for boys and girls; ed. by H. Golding. '10(D10) il. col. 4°, $1.50; bds., $1.25. Saalfield.
Saalfield's cut-out picture books. il. 4°, pap., 20 c. Saalfield.
—Little froggie green. (In shape of frog.)
—Our jungle friends. (In shape of tiger.)
—Owl and the bee. (In shape of owl.)
—Topsy tabbykins. (In shape of cat.)
Sabatier, Paul.
An open letter to His Eminence, Cardinal Gibbons, apropos of his interview on the separation of church and state in France; tr. by J: R: Slattery. '08(My9) c. D. *60 c. net. Sherman, F.
Modernism. '08(D19) $1.50. Scribner.
Sabatini, Rafael.
Arms and the maid; or, Anthony Wilding. '10(Je4) c. D. $1.25 net. Putnam.
SABBATH.
See Sunday.
Sabin, Alvah Horton.
House painting, glazing, paper hanging, and white-washing. '08(Ag29) c. 12°, $1. Wiley.
Sabin, Edn. Legrand.
Bar B. boys; or, the young cow punchers. '09(D4) c. il. 12°, †$1.50. Crowell.
Range and trail; or, the Bar B's great drive. '10(S3) c. il. O. $1.50. Crowell.
Sabin, Elbridge Hosmer.
Magical man of mirth. '10(S17) c. il. O. $1.25. Jacobs.
Sabiston, Magnus.
Biblical account of the creation; shown to be in accordance with the discoveries of science. '10(Mr5) c. il. 12°, $1.50. Knickerbocker Press.
Sable and purple. Watson, W: $1.25 net. Lane.
Sabrina. Shoop, M. P. $1.25. M. P. Shoop.
Sabura's reward. Pomeroy, S. G. †50 c. Estes.
Saccharine feeds and feeding. gratis. North-West Mills.
SACERDOTALISM.
See Priests.
Sacerdotium of Christ as taught in the Holy Scriptures. Dimock, N. 75 c. net. Longmans.
Sachs, Julius.
Syllabus of general course on the theory and practice of teaching in the secondary school. '09, [1910.] (Jl) c. 31 p. 8°, (Columbia Univ., Teachers' College; extension syllabi ser.) 20 c. Teachers' Coll.
—, ed. Studies in secondary education. '09 (Ag27) il. 8°, (Teachers' College record.) pap., 30 c. Teachers' Coll.
Sachse, Helena Viola, [Mrs. S. S. Sadtler.]
How to cook for the sick and convalescent. 4th ed. '10(D31) c. 12°, $1.25. Lippincott.
Sachse, Julius Friedrich, comp.
See Barratt, Norris S.
Sackett on instruction to juries. *See* Brickwood, Albert W.
Sacrament of duty. McSorley, J. $1. Columbus.
Sacrament of the altar. Newbolt, W: C: E. *$1.40 net. Oxford Univ.
SACRAMENTO VALLEY, Cal.
See Irrigation.
SACRAMENTS.
Dimock, N. Doctrine of the sacraments. 60 c. Longmans.
Henry VIII. Assertio septem sacramentorum: defence of the seven sacraments. *$2 net. Benziger.
Hornyold, J: J. Commandments and sacraments. 75 c. Chr. Press.
Pourrat, P. Theology of the sacraments. $1.50 net. Herder.
See also Baptism;—Confirmation;—Lord's supper;—Marriage.
Sacred and profane love. Austin, A. *$1.40 net. Macmillan.
Sacred books of the East: incl. selections from the Vedic hymns; Zend-Avesta; Dhammapada; Upanishads; the Koran; and the Life of Buddha; with critical and biographical sketches by Epiphanius Wilson. '08(Je27) c. il. 8°, $1.75; hf. mor., $3.50. Lamb Pub.
See also Müller, F: Max, *ed.*
Sacred books of the East. 8°. Oxford Univ.
—Winternitz. Index to the names and subject matter of the sacred books of the East. $5.75.
SACRED HEART OF JESUS.
See Jesus Christ.
Sacred herb. Hume, F. W. †$1.25. G: W. Dillingham.

SACRED HISTORY.
See Bible;—Church history.

Sacred songs. '09(D4) c. 4°, pap., $1. Ditson.

Sacred tenth. Lansdell, H: 2 v. *$6 net. Gorham.

Sacred tripudium. Fitzhugh, T: 75 c. Anderson.

SACRIFICE.
See Jews.

Sacrifice (The). Campbell, *Mrs.* A. B. J. $1.25. Badger.

Sacrifice at Prato. Hewlett, M. H: $2.50. Hillside.

Sacs et Parchensins. *See* Sandeau, Léonard. Sylvan Jules.

Sadi the Persian, [pseud. for **Shaikh Muslim-'d-Din.**]
Rose-Garden of Sa'di; tr. by L. Cranmer Bying. '08(Je6) 16°, (Wisdom of the East.) *40 c. net. Dutton.
Sa'di's scroll of wisdom; tr. by Sir Arth. Naylor Wollaston. '08(Je6) 16°, (Wisdom of the East.) *40 c. net. Dutton.

Sadler, Michael Ernest, ed.
Moral instruction and training in schools: report of an international inquiry. In 2 v. '08(O3) D. ea., *$1.50 net. Longmans.

Sadler, S. H.
Infant feeding by artificial means. '09(N) 28+254 p. il. 12°, *$1.25 net. Dutton.

Sadler, Warren H., and Will, W: R.
New essentials of business arithmetic; rev. by H. M. and G: H. Rowe. '08(Jl) c. 299 p. il. 8°, 90 c. Sadler-R.

Sadler, W: S:, M.D.
Cause and cure of colds. '10(O15) c. il. D. $1 net. McClurg.
Science of living; or, the art of keeping well. '10(Ap9) c. il. D. $1.50 net. McClurg.

Sadlier, Mrs. Anna Theresa.
Phileas Fox, attorney. '10(Ja8) c. O. $1.50. Ave Maria.

Sadtler, Mrs. S. S.
See Sachse, Helena Viola.

Safe building construction. Bergh, L: de C. **$5 net. Macmillan.

Safeguard for the prevention of industrial accidents. Van Schaack, D:, *ed.* 50 c. Ætna Life.

SAFETY VALVE.
See Boilers.

Safford, J: H.
Practical service, by the Student Association: [suggestions for practical Christian service to enlist and hold college men.] '09(Mr13) pap., 15 c. Y. M. C. A.

Safford, W: Edn.
Chamorro language of Guam; grammar of the idiom spoken by the inhabitants of the Marianne, or Ladrones Islands. '09 (O) 10+289-319 p. por. 8°, *$1 net. Lowdermilk.

SAGARA.
See Egypt.

SAGAS.
See Legends.

Sage, Agnes Carr.
Boys and girls of the White House. '09 (S11) c. il. pors. O. $1.50. Stokes.

Sage, Evan Taylor.
Pseudo-Ciceronian Consolatio; dissertation. '10(Ap) 11+64 p. O. pap., 50 c. Univ. of Chic.
Bibliography (1 p.).

Sage brush parson. Bailey, *Mrs.* A. W. †75 c. Little, B. & Co.

Sage (Russell) Foundation. Dept. of Child Hygiene. Pamphlets. v. 1-18. '10(Ag27); v. 19-30 (O1); v. 31-37 (N12) 8°, $2 per 100. Charities Pub.
Contents: De Groot, E. B., Recent playground development; Gulick, Luther Halsey, Children of the century; Heller, Mrs. Harriet Hickox, The playground as a phase of social reform; Hibbard, G: Albee, The playground from the standpoint of the executive officer of the city; Holfer, Amalie, The significance of recent national festivals in Chicago; Hughes, C: Evans, Why we want playgrounds; Leland, Arth., Winter organization of playgrounds; Leland, Mrs. Lorna Isabel Higbee, Playground construction: an ideal development for a playground on an irregular tract of land between five and six acres in extent; Lord, Everett W:, The playground a necessary accompaniment to child labor restriction; Maxwell, W: H:, The city and the child; Perry, Clarence Arth., The wider use of the school plant; Playground Association of America, Committee on Athletics for Boys, Athletics for boys; Playground Association of America, Committee on Folk Dancing, Report of the committee on folk dancing; Public Schools Athletic League, Public schools athletic league of New York City; Robinson, C: Mulford, Landscape gardening for playgrounds; Roessing, Mrs. Fk. M., Athletics for girls; Russell Sage Foundation Backward Children Investigation, Retardation, some account of a study conducted in the New York public schools by the Backward Children Investigation; Wingate, G: Wood, Address of General George W. Wingate, president at the annual meeting of the Public Schools Athletic League, held December 7, 1909, New York City; Ayres, Leonard P., The effects of physical defects on school progress, Irregular attendance, a cause of retardation, The money cost of the repeater, Mortality and survival in the grades, Physical defects and school progress; Burchenal, Eliz., May day celebrations; Cline, Earle, Inter-high-school athletics, Gulick, Luther Halsey, The doctrine of "hands off" in play; Johnson, G: Ellsworth, The playground as a factor in school hygiene, Why teach a child to play?; Playground Association of America, How can a city celebrate Independence Day without loss of life or fire damage; Bradstreet, Howard, The need of a play organizer; Burns, Allen, The relation of playgrounds to juvenile delinquency; Hutchinson, Woods, Can the child survive civilization.; Johnson, G: Ellsworth, Games every boy and girl should know; Kennard, Beulah, What the playground can do for girls; Lee, Jos., The home playground.

Sage (*Russell*) *Foundation pubs.* il. D and O. Charities Pub.
—Ayres. Laggards in our schools. $1.50.
—Bureau of Social Research, New York. Chattel loan business. 25 c.
—Chapin. Standard of living among workingmen's families. $2.
—Devine. Report on the desirability of establishing an employment bureau in the city of New York. (Priv. pr.)
—Frankel *and* Dawson. Workingmen's insurance in Europe. $2.50.
—Greene. Among school gardens. $1.25.
—Gulick *and* Ayres. Medical inspection of schools. $1.
—Hanmer. First steps in organizing playgrounds. 10 c.
—Hart. Cottage and congregate institutions for children. $1; 50 c.
—Hart, *ed.* Juvenile court laws in the United States. $1.50.
—Jacobs, *comp.* Campaign against tuberculosis in the United States. $1.

Sage (Russell) Foundation pubs.—Continued.
—Perry. Wider use of the school plant. $1.25.
—Scudder. Field day and play picnic for country children. 10 c.
—Veiller. Housing reform.—Model tenement house law. ea., $1.25.
—Wassam. Salary loan business. 75 c.

Sage (Russell) Foundation pubs.; Pittsburg Survey findings; ed. by Paul Underwood Keller. il. O. Charities Pub.
—Butler. Women and the trades. *$1.50 net.
—Eastman. Work-accidents and the law. $1.50.

Sager, Lawrence K.
See Crocker, Fs. B.

SAHARA DESERT, Africa.
Furlong, C. W. **Gateway to the Sahara. **$2.50 net. Scribner.**
Leeder, S. H. Desert gateway: Biskra and thereabouts. $1.75 net. Cassell.
See also Algeria.

Sahler, Florence L.
Captain Kidd, and other charades. '08 (Ag15) c. sq. O. bds., $1. Stokes.

Sail and steam. Miller, E. W., *comp.* gratis. **Jersey City Lib.**

Sailing ships and their story. Chatterton, E: K. *$3.75 net. Lippincott.

Sailing sunny seas. Wilcox, E. W. $1.50. Conkey.

Sailor's sweetheart. *See* Russell, W: C.

SAILORS.
Callender, G. A. R. Sea kings of Britain. v. 1, 75 c.; v. 2, $1. Longmans.
Robinson, C: N. British tar in fact and fiction. *$4 net. Harper.
See also American Seamen's Friend Society;—United States Navy;—*also* Leech, Samuel.

Sailors' knots. Jacobs, W: W. †$1.50. Scribner.

Sainsbury, Ethel Bruce, comp.
Calendar of the court minutes, etc., of the East India Company, 1640-1643; with introd. and notes by W: Foster. '10(Ja1) O. $4.15. Oxford Univ.

Sainsbury, Harrington, M.D.
Drugs and the drug habit. '09(Ag21) il. 8°, *$2.50 net. Dutton.

St. Andrew of bonny Scotland. Mord, W. 35 c. Stokes.

ST. ANDREW'S CHURCH, Richmond, N. Y.
See New York City.

ST. AUGUSTINE, Fla.
Brooks, A. M., *comp.* Unwritten history of old St. Augustine. 75 c. Record Co.

ST. BARTHOLOMEW-THE-GREAT., **Smithfield,** London.
Worley, G: Priory church of St. Bartholomew-the-Great, **Smithfield.** *60 c. **Macmillan.**

St. Botolph's Town. Crawford, M. C. $2.50; $6. L. C. Page.

St. Clair, Victor, pseud.
See Browne, G: Waldo.

ST. CLAIR'S CAMPAIGN.
See Greenville (Treaty of).

ST. CLARE.
See Clare, *St.*

St. Cyres, Viscount.
Pascal. '10(F19) 8°, *$3 net. Dutton.

St. David of gallant Wales. 35 c. Stokes.

St. Dunstan ser. O. Lothrop, L. & S.
—Eldred. Crimson rambles. $1.50.

St. Elmo. *See* Wilson, *Mrs.* A. J. E.

Saint Francis and his friends; rendered into English from Franciscan chronicles by Horatio Grimley. '08(Je6) T. *45 c. net. Putnam.

ST. FRANCIS VALLEY, Ark.
Morgan, A. E. Preliminary rept. on the St. Francis Valley drainage project in northeastern Arkansas. (Add. Superintendent for price.) U. S., Supt. of Docs.

ST. FRANCOIS COUNTY, Mo.
See Missouri.

SAINT-GAUDENS, Augustus.
Art Assoc. of Indianapolis. Catalogue of sculptured works of Augustus Saint-Gaudens, with biographical sketch. Art Assoc. Indianapolis.
Chicago. Art Institute. Catalogue of sculptured works of Augustus Saint-Gaudens, with biographical sketch. o. p. Chic. Art.
Hind, C: L. Augustus Saint-Gaudens. **$5 net; **$2.50 net. Lane.
Johnson, R. U. Saint-Gaudens; an ode. **$1.20 net. Century Co.

St. George, H:
Fiddles; their selection, preservation, and betterment. '10(D24) il. 12°, (Strad lib.) $1. Scribner.

St. George of merry England. Mord, W. Stokes.

ST. GEORGE'S CHURCH, Pennsville, N. J.
Pettit, *Mrs.* A. A. Old church of St. George's in Penn's Neck. 10 c. Salem Co. Hist. Soc.

Saint Helena. Farnsworth, E: C. $1. Smith & S.

St. Helier, Susan Mary Eliz. Stewart-Mackenzie, Jeune, Baroness.
Memories of fifty years. '09(N20) il. pors. O. *$4.20 net. Longmans.

Saint-Hilaire, Marco de, [Emile Marc Hilaire.]
Anecdotes sur Napoléon; ed. by A. Auzas. '10(Ja29) (Crowell's shorter French texts.) *25 c. net. Crowell.

ST. IGNATIUS LOYOLA.
See **Loyola, Ignatius de.**

St. John, C: E:
Absolute wave-lengths of the H and K lines of calcium in some terrestrial sources. [1910.] (Je) 14 p. tabs., 4°, (Contribs. from the Mt. Wilson Solar Observatory.) pap., gratis. Carnegie.

St. John, Rev. C: Elliott.
Religion of the dawn. '10(D3) D. 60 c. Am. Unitarian.

St. John, E: Porter.
Stories and story-telling in moral and religious education. '10(F19) c. D. bds., *50 c. net. Pilgrim Press.

"St. John, J. Ferriss," pseud.
See **Whiteside, Guy Kenneth.**

St. John, T: Matthew.
Electrical handicraft; cont. complete directions for making and using nearly 150 pieces of electrical apparatus, incl. various devices and outfits for experimental purposes. '08(D) c. 10+11-252 p. il. 12°, $1. T: M. St. John.
Study of electric motors by experiment. '10(Ap23) c. il. 12°, 25 c. T: M. St. John.

ST. JOHN'S CHURCH, Newark, N. J.
Flynn, P. V. History of St. John's Church, Newark. $3. P. V. Flynn.

Saint Josephine. Blake, F. *$1.25 net. Jennings.

ST. JOSEPH'S COUNTY, Indiana.
Howard, T. E: Hist. of St. Joseph's Co., Indiana. $18. Lewis Pub.

St. Koczorowski, —.
English prices with German equivalents, calculated at seven rates of exchange. '09(Je19) 32°, leath., 50 c. Spon.

ST. LAWRENCE RIVER, Canada.
Johnson, C. Picturesque St. Lawrence. $1.25 net. Macmillan.
Smith, A. H. Tourists' guide of the wonderful St. Lawrence. 25 c. A. H. Smith.

St. Ledger, A.
Australian socialism; historical sketch of its origin and developments. '09(D18) 12°, *$1 50 net. Macmillan.

ST. LOUIS, Mo.
Anderson, G. Story of a border city during the Civil War. **$1.50 net. Little, B. & Co.
Civic League of St. Louis. *Housing Committee.* Housing conditions in St. Louis. (Add. pubs. for price.) Civic League.
Goodwin, E. H. Merit system: letter in defense of the Civic League's detailed provision for a new city charter. 25 c. Civic League.
Head, I. Historical and interesting places of Saint Louis. 25 c. Missouri Hist.
Rombauer, R. J. Union cause in St. Louis in 1861. $2. Nixon Jones.
Skrainka, P. St. Louis: its hist. and ideals. 50 c. P. Skrainka.
See also **Civic League.**

ST. LOUIS CATHEDRAL, New Orleans.
Chambon, C. M. In and around the old St. Louis Cathedral. 50 c. C. M. Chambon.

Saint Louis cook book. **Missouri Baptist** Sanitarium. $1. Missouri Bapt. San.

St. Louis labor and hotel directory. '08(Je) c. 8°, pap., gratis. H. W. Steinbiss.

St. Louis Municipal Commission on Tuberculosis. First rept., Feb., 1909. '09(Ag14) il. tabs., O. pap. (Add. pubs. for price.) St. L. Com. Tuberculosis.

St. Louis; one hundred years in a week, celebration of the centennial of incorporation, October 3d to 9th, 1909; ed. by Wa. B. Stevens. '10(O) 192 p. il. 12°, $1. St. Louis Centennial.

St. Louis Republic. One hundredth anniversary, July 12, 1808-1908. '08(D) 192 p. pors. f°, 16 c. St. L. Republic.

ST. LOUIS UNIVERSITY, St. Louis, Mo.
Fanning, W: H. W. **Hist. sketch** of St. Louis University. **gratis.** **St.** L. Univ.

St. Louis University; bulls. 8°, pap. St. Louis Univ.
—Borgmeyer. Halley's comet. (Priv. pr.)

St. Luz, Berthe, [pseud. for Alice Alberthe Robertson.]
Tamar Curze. '08(Ag15) c. D. *$1 net. Fenno.

Saint Mammon. Freeman, W: N. $1.50. B'way Pub.

St. Mary's College bull. 8°. St. Mary's Coll.
—Murphy. Popular errors about classical studies.

St. Mary's Industrial School, Odanah, Wis.
Noble lives of a noble race. '09(S) c. 283 p. il. pors. maps, 8°, $2. St. Mary's Indust.

Saint Maur, Mrs. Kate Vandenhoff.
Earth's bounty. '09(Ap10) c. D. **$1.75 net. Macmillan.

ST. MICHAEL'S CHURCH, Charleston, S. C.
Beesley, C: N. Illustrated guide to St. Michael's Church. 50 c. C: N. Beesley.

St. Morris, C:
Law of love. '08(D5) c. il. D. $1.50. C. M. Clark.

St. Nicholas ser. of beautiful books. il. 12°. Benziger.
—Blundell. Madge-make-the-best-of-it. *80 c. net.

St. Nicotine. Heward, E: V. *$1.50 net. Dutton.

St. Ninian lectures. '09(D) 8°, *$1.50 net. Doran.

Saint of the twentieth century. Rice, F. B. $1.50. Badger.

St. Patrick of the Emerald Isle. Mord, W. 35 c. Stokes.

ST. PATRICK'S CATHEDRAL, New York City.
Farley, J: M. History of St. Patrick's Cathedral, [New York City.] (Add. Society for price.) Soc. for Propagation of Faith.

St. Paul. Public Library. Select list of books on birds, insects and nature study; comp. January, 1910. '10(My) 25 p. 12°, gratis. St. Paul Pub. Lib.

ST. PAUL'S CATHEDRAL, London.
Sinclair, W: M. Memorials of St. Paul's Cathedral. *$4 net. Jacobs.

ST. PETER.
See **Peter, *St.***

Saint Peter. Greene, R: A. *75 c. net. Sherman, F.

ST. PETERSBURG, Russia.
Dobson, G. St. Petersburg. $2.50 net. Macmillan.

Saint Rita's prayer book. Ferina, C:, *comp.* (Add. pub. for price.) C: Ferina.

ST. STEPHEN'S COLLEGE, Annandale, N. Y.
Reminiscences of St. Stephen's College, Annandale, N. Y. '10(D) c. 8°, 60 c.; $1 net. Gorham.

ST. STEPHEN'S REFORMED CHURCH, Reading, Pa.
Dickert, T: W. Hist. of St. Stephen's Reformed Church. $1.25. T: W. Dickert.

ST. THOMAS CHURCH, New York City.
Stires, E. M. Plans and elevations for St. Thomas' church. (Add. pub. for price.) St. Thomas Church.

Saint (Un). Bourget, P. C. J. 35 c. net. Macmillan.

St. Winifred's. *See* Farrar, F: W:

Sainte-Beuve, Charles Augustin.
Causeries du lundi. v. 1; tr., with introd. and notes, by E. J. Trechmann. '09 (My22); v. 2 (O2); v. 3 (O2); v. 4. '10(Ja8); v. 5 (Je4); v. 6 (Jl30); v. 7 (D10) 16°, (New universal lib.) ea., 50 c.; leath., 75 c. Dutton.
Trois portraits littéraires; ed. by D. L. Savory. '09(Mr6) por. S. (Oxford higher French ser.) $1. Oxford Univ.

SAINTE-BEUVE, Charles Augustin.
Harper, G: M. Charles Augustin Sainte-Beuve. **$1.50 net. Lippincott.

SAINTS.
Baxter, R: Saints' everlasting rest. *$2.50 net. Lippincott.
Dawson, L. H. Book of the saints. 50 c. Dutton.
Hammer, B., *comp.* Mary, help of Christians, and the fourteen saints invoked as holy helpers. *$2 net. Benziger.
Macgregor, M. Stories of three saints: [Saints Francis, Columba and Cuthbert.] 50 c. Dutton.
Peers, *Mrs.* C. R. Saints in story. $1.50. Macmillan.
Stone, D. Invocation of saints. *40 c. net. Longmans.
Tabor, M. E. Saints in art. *$1.20 net. Stokes.
Taylor, J. A. Silver legend: saints for children. *$1.25 net. Herder.
See also Apostles:—Fathers of the church;—Martyrs;—*also* names of saints.

Saintsbury, G: E: Bateman.
Hist. of English prosody from the 12th century. In 3 v. v. 1. '10(D); v. 2. '08(O10); v. 3. '10(Je18) 8°, ea., *$3.75 net. Macmillan.

Sajous, C: Eucharisté de Medici.
Internal secretions and the principles of medicine. 3d ed. '09(N) 2 v., il. 8°, $12. Davis.
—, ed. Analyt. cyclop. of pract. medicine, by Charles E. de M. Sajous and 100 associate editors, assisted by corresponding editors, collaborators, and correspondents. 6th rev. ed. 6 v. '10(F) c. il. maps, 4°, $30. Davis.

Sal, the circus gal. Harper, O. 25 c. J. S. Ogilvie.

SALADS.
See Cookery.

Salaman, Malcolm C:
See Holme, C:, *ed.*—Vallance, Aymer.

SALAMANCA, Spain.
Calvert, A. F: Leon, Burgos and Salamanca. *$1.25 net. Lane.

Salammbo. *See* Flaubert, Gustave.

SALARIES.
United States. Pay of certain government employees injured while in the discharge of duty; rept. '10(Ag) 57 p. 8°. Gov. Pr. Off.

Salary loan business in New York City. Wassam, C. W. 75 c. Charities Pub.

Sale, Edith Tunis.
Manors of Virginia in Colonial times. '09 (O9) c. il. 8°, **$5 net Lippincott.

SALE.
Chapman, C. Law of advertising and sales. 2 v. $10. C. Chapman.

SALE.—*Continued.*
Haring, F. B. Manual of procedure; law of conditional sales. $5. Ronald Press.
Simkins, W: S. Contracts and sales. $6.50. Von Boeckmann-J.
Sprague, W: C. Questions and answers on sales of personal property. 50 c. Sprague.
Tiffany, F. B. Hdbk. of the law of sales. *$3.75 net. West Pub.
Williston, S: Law covering sales of goods at common law and under the uniform sales act. $7.50. Baker, V. & Co.
See also Commercial law;—*also* names of states.

Saleeby, Caleb Williams, M.D.
Health, strength and happiness. '08(N21) cr. 8°, *$1.50 net. M. Kennerley.
Parenthood and race culture: an outline of eugenics. '09(Ag28) c. O. **$2.50 net. Moffat.

SALEM, Mass.
Paine, R. D. Ships and sailors of old Salem. *$3.50 net. McClurg.

SALEM, N. H.
Gilbert, E. History of Salem, N. H. $4. Rumford Pr.

SALEM, N. J.
Sharpe, E. S. Craven's Choyce; [historical] paper read before Salem Co. Historical society. 10 c. Salem Co. Hist. Soc.

SALEM COUNTY, N. J.
Sharpe, E: S. An old deed, May 31, 1675. (Add. pubs for price.)—Descendants of the pioneers [Salem]. 10 c. Salem Co. Hist. Soc.
See also Woman's Christian Temperance Union.

SALESMAN.
See Business.

SALESMANSHIP.
See Business

Saley, Met Lawson.
Book of lumber shed construction for retail lumber yards, etc.; also lime houses, coal sheds, sash and door rooms, offices and shed and yard conveniences. '10 (Ja15) c. il. plans, 4°, $1.50. Am. Lumberman.

Salisbury, Albert.
Phonology and orthoëpy. Rev. ed. '08 (F) c. 77 p. il. 12°, 50 c. Row, P. & Co.

Salisbury, Jerome H:, M.D., comp. and ed.
See Billings, Fk.—Hallberg, Carl Svantè Nicanor.

Salisbury, Minnie E., comp.
Holiday and social happenings. '10(S) il. 8°, $1.25, boxed; paste grain, $2.50, boxed; velvet ooze, $2.50, boxed. Barse & H.

Salisbury, Rollin D.
Elem. physiography. '10(D3) c. il. maps, D. (American science ser.) $3.50. Holt.
Physiography for high schools. '08(Mr7) c. il. maps, D. (American science ser., briefer course.) $1.50. Holt.
See also Chamberlin, T: Chrowder.
—, ed. Outlines of geologic history, with especial reference to North America; series of essays involving a discussion of geologic correlation presented before section E of the American Association for the Advancement of Science in Baltimore, Dec., 1908; symposium organized by Bailey Willis. '10 (Jl30) c. maps, O. $1.50 net. Univ. of Chic.

Salisbury, Rollin D., ed., and Atwater, Wallace Wa.
Interpretation of topographic maps. '09 (Ap3) c. il. maps, Q. (U. S. Dept. of the Interior, Geol. Survey, professional papers.) pap., $2.75. U. S., Supt. of Docs.

Salisbury, W:
Career of a journalist. '08(Mr28) c. il. O. *$1.50 net. B. W. Dodge.

Salley, Alex. S:, jr., ed.
Documents rel. to the history of South Carolina during the Revolutionary War. '09 (My22) 8°, $2. S. C. Hist.

Sallust [Lat. Sallustius] Crispus, C.
C. Sallvsti Crispi Bellvm Catalinæ; ed., with introd., notes and vocabulary, by Dan. A. Penick. '08(N21) c. il. map, 12°, (Gildersleeve-Lodge Latin ser.) $1. Heath.
See also Cicero, Marcus Tullius.

Sally Ann's experience. Hall, E. C., *pseud.* 50 c. net. Little, B. & Co.

Sally Bishop. Thurston, E. T. $1.50. M. Kennerley.

Salmon, Arth. L.
Cornwall coast. '10(D17) il. O. (County coast ser.) $2.25 net. Stokes.
Dorset. '10(O22) il. maps, D. (Cambridge county geographies.) 45 c. net. Putnam.

SALMON.
Calderwood, W: L. Salmon rivers and lochs of Scotland. *$6 net. Longmans.
Chaytor, A. H: Letters to a salmon fisher's sons. $3 net. Houghton M.
Malloch, P. D. Life hist. of the salmon. $3.50 net. Macmillan.

Salomé. *See* Wilde, Oscar.

Salomy Jane. Harte, F. B. $1 net. Houghton M.

SALOONS.
See Liquors;—Temperance.

SALPA.
See Marine Zoology.

Salt, Mark H., ed.
Candidates and the issues; policies and platforms of all parties, with portraits and biographies of the leaders, incl. the lives of the presidential candidates; an official history of the campaign of 1908; with special chapters revealing the inside truths of the industrial, financial and business world by Herbert B. Mulford and Trumbull White. '08(D) c. 430 p. il. pors. 8°, $1.50. Vansant.

Salt and sincerity. Humphreys, A. L. $1. Dodge.

SALT LAKE CITY, Utah.
Fohlin, E. V. Salt Lake City, past and present. $1.25; 75 c. E. V. Fohlin.

Salthaven. Jacobs, W: W. †$1.50. Scribner.

SALTS.
Harris, G. D., *and others.* Rock salt, its origin, geological occurrences and economic importance in Louisiana. (Add. pubs. for price.) La. Geol. Survey.

Saltus, Edg. Evertson.
Daughters of the rich. '09(My) c. 259 p. front. D. $1.25. M. Kennerley.

Salud y hogar; un manual doméstico que contiene más del mil recetas y sugestiones muy útiles para el cuidado del hogar, en armonía con las leyes sanitarias; la preservación de la salud mediante una alimentación sencilla, el aseo y una vida confortable; y sobre el tratamiento casero de las enfermedades por medio de los recursos naturales y racionales que están á nuestro alcance. en sustitución de las drogas; preparado y ed. por un competente comité de medicos y expertos. '09(D) c. 10+11-438 p. il. 8°, $3. Pacific Press.

SALVADOR, Central America.
International Bureau of American Republics. Salvador. (Add. pubs. for price.) Int. Bu. Am. Republics.

Salvage. Seaman, O. *$1.25 net. Holt.

SALVATION.
Begbie, H. Twice-born men; clinic in regeneration. *$1.25 net. Revell.
Bishop, G: S. Doctrines of grace. $1.50. Gospel Pub.
Bowman, T: Great salvation. 50 c. Pub. Ho. of Evangelical Assoc.
Cook, C: C. Truth about grace, by a Berean. 25 c. C: C. Cook.
De Mill, R: M. Foundation and the superstructure; or, the faith of Christ and the works of man. **$3 net. Putnam.
Holden, J: S. Redeeming vision. *$1.25 net. Revell.
Jones, J: D. Gospel of grace. *$1.25 net. Doran.
Luther, M. Small catechism, with Hints and helps to the way of salvation. 25 c. P. G: Sieger.
McCormick, J: N: Way of life. 35 c. J: N: McCormick.
Parry, T: Riches of grace. 50 c. Westminster.
Searcy, W: E. Way to the kingdom of heaven and what to do to be saved in it. $1. Searcy.
Stephens, C: A. Natural salvation: immortal life on earth. $1.75. Laboratory Co.
Walz, M. F. Precious blood the price of our redemption. 15 c. St. Joseph's Pr.
Wilson, P. Great salvation. *$1.25 net. Jennings.
Zepp, A. C. Progress after entire sanctification. 50 c. Chr. Witness.
See also Conversion;—Future life.

Salvation and the old theology. Broughton, L. G. *75 c. net. Revell.

SALVATION ARMY.
Lamb, E. G. Social work of the Salvation Army. $1. E. G. Lamb.

Salvation of society. Straton, J: R. $1. Fleet-M.

Salvation of the little child. Oliver, J: (Add. author for price.) J: Oliver.

Salvator. Gibbon, P. †$1.50. Doubleday, P.

Salvatore, Camillo.
Italian architecture: interiors and furniture during the 14th, 15th, 16th and 17th centuries. '08(Ag8) il. por. F. $25. Polley.

Samantha on children's rights. Holley, M. †$1.50. G: W. Dillingham.

SAMARITANS.
Cowley, A. E., *ed.* Samaritan liturgy. In 2 v. $19.25. Oxford Univ.
Jacob, son of Aaron, High priest of the Samaritans. Messianic hope of the Samaritans. 25 c. Open Court.

Sames, C: MacCaughey.
Pocket-book of mechanical engineering. 3d ed., rev. and enl. '08(Ja11) il. tabs., 16°, leath., $2. C: M. Sames.

Samlede skrifter i udvalg. Sverdrup, G. $2.50. Free Church.
Sammie and Susie Littletail. Garis, H. R. 60 c. Fenno.
Sammlung göschen. S. Stechert.
—Kampmann. Die graphischen künste. 20 c.
Sammlung "Kirchenmusik" hrsg. von dr. Karl Weinmann. il. 16°. Pustet.
—Weinmann. Karl Proske. 30 c.

SAMOSET (*Indian chief*).
Sylvester, H. M. Samoset; an appreciation "Welcome, Englishman!" 60 c. W. B. Clarke.

Sampey, J: R:
Heart of the Old Testament; manual for Christian students. '09(D) c. 283 p. 16°, 50 c. S. S. Bd. So. Bapt.

Samplers and tapestry embroideries. Huish, M. B. $17. Longmans.

Sampson, Arth. W:
Natural revegetation of depleted mountain grazing lands; progress rept. '09(D) 28 p. il. tabs., 8°, (U. S., Dept. of Agriculture, Forest Service, circular.) pap. (Add. Superintendent for price.)

Sampson, Ralph Allen.
Discussion of the eclipses of Jupiter's satellites, 1878-1903. '10(My7) il. 4°, (Annals of the Astronomical Observatory of Harvard College.) $1. Harvard Univ.

Sampter, Jessie Ethel.
Great adventurer. '09(Ja23) c. obl. D. 75 c. R. Kerr.

Samson Agonistes and the Hellenic drama. Jebb, *Sir* R: C. 35 c. Oxford Univ.
Samuel the seeker. Sinclair, U. B. $1.50. B. W. Dodge.

SAN ANTONIO, Texas.
Taylor, H: R. Visitor's guide and history of San Antonio, Tex. 25 c. M. Tengg.

SAN ANTONIO CANYON, Cal.
Frankish, C: G. Beautiful San Antonio Canyon; from recent photographs. 50 c. C: G. Frankish.

SAN BERNARDINO MOUNTAINS, Cal.
Grinnell, J. *Biota* of the San Bernardino Mountains, [California.] $2. Univ. of Cal.

"SAN CARLOS."
See Portola, Gaspare de.

San Celestino. Ayscough, J:, *pseud.* †$1.50. Putnam.

SAN DIEGO, California.
Nolen, J: San Diego: a comprehensive plan for its improvement. 50 c. J: Nolen.
See also Marine Biological Association.

San Francisco. Public Library. Music catalogue. '09(Ag7) 8°, pap., gratis. San Francisco Lib.

SAN FRANCISCO, Cal.
Irwin, W: H: Pictures of Old Chinatown, [San Francisco.] **$1 net. Moffat.
Langdon, W: H:, *and* Markham, E: Struggle between graft and democracy, in San Francisco;] address by W: H: Langdon; [and] Vermin in the dark: poem by E. Markham. 10 c. Civic Forum.
McAdie, A. G: Infra nubem, The lights outside. A. M. Robertson.
MacLafferty, J. H: City loved around the world; toast to San Francisco. 10 c. net. P. Elder.
Plehm, C. C. San Francisco clearing house certificates. 10 c. Univ. of Cal.
San Francisco. *Citizens' Health Committee.* Eradicating plague from San Francisco; rept., with brief descriptions, of the measures taken, copies of ordinances in aid of sanitation, articles by sanitarians on the nature of plague and the best means of getting rid of it, facsimiles of circulars issued by the committee and a list of subscribers to the health fund, Mar. 31, 1909; prep. by Fk. Morton Todd. '09(S) 313 p. il. pors. 8°. (Add. pubs. for price.) C. A. Murdock.
Steel, R. City that is. *$1 net. A. M. Robertson.
Stellman, L: J. Vanished ruin era; San Francisco's classic artistry of ruin depicted in picture and song. $2.50. P. Elder.
See also Portola, Gaspar de.

San Francisco Committee of Vigilance of 1851. Papers of the San Francisco Committee of Vigilance of 1851; ed. by Porter Garnett. '10(S) 69 p. facsim., O. (Academy of Pacific Coast History pubs.,) pap., 50 c. Univ. of Cal.

San Francisco Motor Club tour book; covering the principal tours in California north of Los Angeles and extending to the Oregon line. [1910.] (Ap) il. maps, nar. 4°, $1.50. San F. Motor.

San Francisco State Normal School bull., new ser. 4°, pap., 30 c. San F. St. Normal.
—Anderson. Course of study in history.
—Burk *and* McFadden. Course of study in grammar.
—Jones. Course of study in primary arithmetic.
—McFadden. Course of study in language. 55 c.; 30 c.—Course of study in language for grammar grades.—Course of study in primary language.
—Patterson. Course of study for the teaching of reading to beginners.—Course of study in the teaching of reading.
—Ware. Course of study and teachers' hdbk. in the common literature of life. 40 c.—Course of study and teachers' manual in map geography.—Course of study in literature.—Plan of literature study for grammar grades.
—Wiebalk. Course of study in composition.

SAN FRANCISCO STOCK AND EXCHANGE BOARD, San Francisco.
King, J. L. Hist. of the San Francisco Stock and Exchange Board. $2. J. L. King.

SAN GABRIEL MISSION, Cal.
Sugranes, E. Old San Gabriel mission. 50 c. E. Sugranes.

SAN JOAQUIN VALLEY, Cal.
Mendenhall, W. C. Preliminary rept. on the ground waters of San Joaquin Valley, Cal. (Add. Superintendent for price.) U. S., Supt. of Docs.
See also Drainage.

SAN JOSÉ SCALE.
Quaintance, A. L. Fumigation of apples for the San José scale. (Add. Superintendent for price.) U. S., Supt. of Docs.
Stene, A. E: San José scale (*Aspidiotus perniciosus*, Comst): [injurious insect.] gratis. R. I. Coll.

SAN JUAN MOUNTAINS, Colo.
Howe, E. Landslides in the San Juan Mountains, Colo. (Add. Superintendent for price.) U. S., Supt. of Docs.

SAN LUIS, Obispo Co., Cal.
Angel, M. La piedra pintada, the painted rock of Cal.; a legend. $1.25. Grafton Pub.

SAN PABLO, Cal.
See California.

San Pedro, Diego de.
Diego de San Pedro; Carcel de amor. '04, [1909.] (N) 86 p. (Bibliotheca hispanic.) $1. Hispanic Soc.

San Rafael cook book. Jones, M. M. W., *ed.* $1. W. F. Jones.

Sanborn, Fk. Berry.
Mechanics: problems for engineering students. '08(Ag22) c. il. 12°, 50 c. Engineering News.

Sanborn, Franklin B:
Bronson Alcott at Alcott House, England, and Fruitlands, New England, (1842-1844.) '08, [1909.] (F) c. 103 p. il. pors. 8°, *$3 net. Torch Press.
Hawthorne and his friends; reminiscence and tribute. '08, [1909.] (Ja) c. 84 p. por. 8°, $3. Torch Press.
John Brown, liberator of Kansas and martyr of Virginia, life and letters; ed. by F. B. Sanborn. 4th ed. '10(N12) c. il. pors. facsims., 12°, $1.50 net. Torch Press.
Recollections of seventy years. '09(Je19) 2 v., il. pors. facsims., O. *$5 net, boxed. Badger.

Sanborn, H: N.
See Fuess, Claude Moore.

Sanborn, Kate.
Old time wall papers: pictorial papers of our grandfathers' walls, with a study of the hist. devel. of wall paper making and decoration. '08(F8) il. f°, bds., *$5 net. Dutton.

Sanborn, Mrs. Mary Farley Sanborn.
The canvas door. '09(D11) c. front. D. $1.50. B. W. Dodge.

Sánchez, Pedro.
Arrepentimiento qve el alma tiene de auer ofendido a su Criador [facsim.] '03 (N) no paging, 4°, $3.50 (200 copies.) Hispanic Soc.

SANCTI BERTINI MANUSCRIPT.
See Manuscripts.

Sanctuary of God. Whitworth, W: A. *$1.50 net. Macmillan.

Sand, George, [pseud. for Mme. A. L. A. Dudevant.]
François le champi. '09(Ja9) il. 12°, (Les classiques français illustrés.) *$1.40 net. Macmillan.
François le champi; ed. by Alfred Mercier. '10(Mr26) por. S. (Oxford higher French ser.) 85 c. Oxford Univ.
La mare au diable; notice analytique de C. A. Sainte-Beuve. '08(Mr7) il. 12°, (Les classiques français illustrées.) *$1.40 net. Macmillan.
La petite Fadette; ed. by Madeleine Delbos. '08(N21) D. (Oxford modern French ser.) 60 c. Oxford Univ.
Le meunier d'Angibault; ed.. with an introd., notes and vocab., by J. W. Kuhne. '09(D25) c. por. S. 40 c. Am. Bk.
Les maîtres sonneurs; préface d' Emile Faguet. '08(F22) il. 12°, (Les classiques français illustrées.) *$1.40 net. Macmillan.
Les maîtres sonneurs; ed. by Stéphanie Barlet. '10(Mr26) por. S. (Oxford higher French ser.) $1.15. Oxford Univ.

SAND, George, [*pseud.* for *Mme.* A. L. A. Dudevant.]
Doumic, R. George Sand. $3.50. Putnam.

Sandars, Mary Frances.
Duke of Lauzun: courtier and adventurer. 2 v. '09(Jl3) il. 8°, *$6 net. Brentano's.
Louis XVIII. '10(N19) il. pors. 8°, $4 net; ¾ mor., $7 net. Pott.

Sanday, W:, D.D.
Address delivered at the opening of the Christian section of the Third International Congress of the History of Religions. '08(D5) Q. pap., 27 c. Oxford Univ.
Christologies ancient and modern. '10 (Ag27) c. 8°, $1.75. Oxford Univ.
A new Marcion; being a criticism of Mr. F. C. Conybeare's "Myth, magic and morals." '09(D4) O. pap., *36 c. net. Longmans.
Outlines of the life of Christ. 2d ed., rev., with additions. '08(Mr28) c. 12°, **$1.25 net. Scribner.
See also Driver, S: Rolles.

Sandeau, Léonard Sylvain Jules.
Sacs et Parchensins. '10(D24) 16°, (Macmillan's new ser. of French texts.) 35 c. net. Macmillan.
Un heritage. '10(Ag27) c. O. (Oxford modern French ser.) 60 c. Oxford Univ.

Sandeman, G:
Uncle Gregory. '09(Mr20) c. D. †$1.50. Putnam.

Sanders, D: W.
Manual of civil government of Indiana; describes legislature at work, machinery of political parties, etc. Rev. ed. '08(F) c. 101 p. il. 12°, 50 c. Manual Pub. Co.

Sanders, Helen Fitzgerald.
Petalesharoo and The Star brave; poetic dramas. '10(Ap) c. 35 p. 8°, leath., $1.50; pap., 50 c. H. F. Sanders.
Trails through western woods. '10(Jl16) c. il. O. $2 net. A. Harriman.

Sanders, H: Arth., ed.
Roman history and mythology. '10(O15) 8°, (Univ. of Michigan studies: Humanistic ser.) $2.25. Macmillan.

Sanders, H: Martyn.
Message of the church in collect, epistle and gospel. v. 1. '08(O10); v. 2. '09(F6) D. ea., *$1.20 net. Longmans.

Sanders, Lloyd.
Holland House circle. '08(S26) il. O. *$3.50 net. Putnam.

Sanders, P: Ja.
Key to succession in the presidency of the church and a complete ready reference for the missionary. '09(O) 231 p. 12°, 80 c.; leath., $1.30. P: J. Sanders.

Sanders, T: E.
Twenty talks to teachers. '09(F) c. '08. 178 p. 12°, cl., 85 c. Teachers' Co-op.

Sanders Publishing Co., Chicago. Farm buildings. New and enl. ed. '09(D18) c. il. plans, 4°, $2. Sanders Pub.

Sanderson, Howard Kendall, comp.
Lynn in the Revolution. 2 v. '10(F19) c. il. pors. maps, facsims., 4°, $10. W: B. Clarke.

Sanderson, J: Franklin.
See Finley, J: Huston.

Sandiford, P:
Training of teachers in England and Wales. Teachers' Coll. '10(O15) c. 8°, (Teachers' College, Columbia Univ.; Contrib. to education.) $1.50. Teachers' Coll.

Sandison, Howard.
Problem of method. '09(S) 6+442 p. il. 12°, $1.25. H. Sandison.

Sandman: his sea stories. Hopkins, W: J: $1.50. L. C. Page.

Sando, Roscoe Briant.
American poultry culture. '09, [1910.] (F) c. 12°, *$1.50 net. McClurg.
Formerly published by Outing Publishing Co.

Sands, Beatrice.
Weepers in playtime. '08(Ag1) c. D. †$1.50. Lane.

Sands, Hayden.
Lights and shadows. '10(My21) c. 12°, $1.25. Cochrane.

Sands, Percy Cooper.
Client princes of the Roman Empire under the Republic; Thirlwald Prize, 1906. '09 (Mr) 12+242 p. 16°, (Cambridge historical ser.) *$1.50 net. Putnam.

SANDUSKY BAY, Ohio.
Landacre, F. L. Protozoa of Sandusky Bay and vicinity. 35 c. Ohio Acad. of Sci.

SANDWICH, N. H.
Armes, E. Midsummer in Whittier's country. 75 c. E. Armes.

SANDWICH.
See Cookery.

Sandwick, R: Lanning, and Bacon, Mrs. Anna Tilden.
High school word book, incl. in round numbers 5000 words. '08(S19) c. D. 40 c. Heath.

Sandy Carmichael. Hyne, C: J: C. W. †$2. Lippincott.

Sandys, J: Edn.
History of classical scholarship, from the sixth century B.C. to the end of the Middle Ages. 2d ed. '08(F8) il. 8°, *$3.50 net. Putnam.
History of classical scholarship; with chronological tables. In 3 v. v. 2, 3. '08 (D12) il. pors. cr. 8°, ea., *$2.75 net. Putnam.
Orationes et epistolae Cantabrigienses, (1876-1909.) '10(Je18) 4°, $3 net. Macmillan.
—, **ed.** *See* Aristotle.

Sane evangelism. Hamilton, W: W. **75 c. net. Am. Bapt.

Sanford, Albert Hart.
Polish people of Portage County, [Wis.] '08(O10) il. maps, 8°, 35 c. State Hist., Wis.
See also James, Ja. Alton.

Sanford, C: Thomas-.
See Thomas-Sanford, C:

Sanford, J: Ithiel.
Manual of color. '10(N5) c. front. O. 50 c. J: I. Sanford.

Sang, Alfr.
Corrosion of iron and steel. '10(My7) c. 12°, $1. McGraw-H.

SANGER, Ralph.
Smith, F. Ralph Sanger. o. p. F. Smith.

Sangster, Mrs. Marg. Eliz. Munson.
From my youth up: personal reminiscences. '09(S4) c. pors. O. *$1.50 net. Revell.
Good manners for all occasions. '10(D10) il. 12°, $1.25. Cupples & L.
Happy school days. '09(Ap3) c. D. $1.25, boxed. Forbes.

Sangster, Urania Nott.
Power of gold; romance of London. '10 (Ja22) c. por. O. $2. U. N. Sangster.

SANHEDRIM.
See **Jesus Christ.**

SANITARY CHEMISTRY.
See Air;—Domestic economy;—Food;—Water.

SANITARY ENGINEERING.
American School of Correspondence. Cyclopedia of heating, plumbing, and sanitation. $12. Am. Sch. Corr.
Bashore, H. B. Sanitation of recreation camps and parks. $1. Wiley.
Cosgrove, J: J. History of sanitation. $1.50. Standard Sanitary Mfg.
Ekin, T. C. Water pipe and sewer discharge. *$3 net. Van Nostrand.
Gerhard, W: P. Guide to sanitary inspections. $1.50.—Water supply, sewerage, and plumbing of modern city buildings. *$4 net. Wiley.
Gerhard, W: P. Sanitation and sanitary engineering. $1.50. W: P. Gerhard.
Gerhard, W: P. Sanitation, water supply and sewage disposal of country houses. $2. Van Nostrand.
Moore, E: C. S. Sanitary engineering. In 2 v. *$14 net. Lippincott.
Ogden, H: N. Sewer construction. $3. Wiley.
Price, G: M. Tenement-house inspector. $1.50. Chief.
Raynes, F. W. **Domestic sanitary engineering and plumbing. *$3 net. Longmans.**

SANITARY ENGINEERING.—*Continued.*
Smith, A. W., *comp.* Selected bibliography of sanitary science. *50 c. net. Stechert.
See also Heating;—Plumbing;—Refuse and refuse disposal;—Sewage and sewerage;—Street cleaning;—Ventilation;—Water-supply.

Sanitary officer's handbook of practical hygiene. Wanhill, C. F. *$1.40 net. Longmans.

SANITARY SCIENCE.
See Hygiene; — Military hygiene; — Plumbing;— Quarantine; — Sanitary engineering; — Sewage and sewerage;—Water-supply.

Sanitary sewerage of buildings. Ainge, T: S. $1.50. Domestic Engineering.

SANITATION.
See Sanitary engineering.

Sanitation and physiology. Ritchie, J: W. $1.25. World Bk.

Sanity of art. Shaw, G: B. 75 c. B: R. Tucker.

Sankey, Captain H. R.
Energy chart for reciprocating steam engines. '08(Jl4) il. 8°, $3. Spon.

SANSKRIT LITERATURE.
Hindu classics: literature of India. $1.75; $3.50. Lamb Pub.
Macdonald, *Mrs.* F. R.. *comp.* Iliad of the East. *$1.50 net. Lane.
Mahabharata. Bhagavad-gītā. $1. C: Johnston.
Pañchatantra; collection of ancient Hindu tales. $1.50. Ginn.
Path of light. *60 c. net. Dutton.
Ramayana and The Mahabharata. 35 c. net; 70 c. net. Dutton.
Ryder, A. W: Women's eyes; being verses tr. from the Sanskrit. $1 net. A. M. Robertson.
Sacred books of the East. $1.75; $3.50. Lamb Pub.
See also Mahabharata;—Upanishads.

SANTA BARBARA, Cal.
Hawley, W. A: Early days of Santa Barbara. $1. W. A: Hawley.
Steele, J. K. Hope Ranch, [Santa Barbara.] $1.25. Pacific Improvement.

SANTA CLARA, Cal.
See Catala, *Fr.* Magin.

SANTA CLAUS.
O'Donnell, W: F. Mother Santa Claus stories. †50 c. Altemus.
Smith, E. B. Santa Claus and all about him. $2; $2.25. Stokes.
Walsh, W: S. Story of Santa Klaus. **$1.50 net. Moffat.

SANTA FE COUNTY, N. M.
Santa Fe County, New Mexico; country rich in attractions for the sight seeker, the health seeker, the wealth seeker and home seeker; by Paul A. F. Walter; pub. by authority of the Bureau of Immigration of New Mexico, 1909. '09, [1910.] (Ap) 63 p. il. 8°. N. M. Pr.

SANTA FÉ TRAIL.
Vernon, J. S. Along the Old Trail. $1. Tucker-V.

Santa Lucia. Austin, *Mrs.* M. H. †$1.50. Harper.

Santayana, G:
Three philosophical poets: Lucretius, Dante, and Goethe. '10(Ag13) 8°, (Harvard studies in comparative literature; ed. by W: H: Schofield.) $2.25. Harvard Univ.

Santi-deva.
See Path of light.

SANTIAGO DE CHILE.
See International Bureau of American Republics, Washington, D. C. Municipal organizations.

Santillana Iñigo López de Mendoza, Marqués de.
Bias contra Fortua; hecho por coplar: por el Marques de Santillana endereçado al duque daluo [facsim.] '02 [1909.] (N) no paging, 4°, $5. Hispanic Soc.

Santleben, August.
Texas pioneer; early staging and overland freighting days on the frontiers of Texas and Mexico; ed. by I. D. Affleck. '10 (Ap2) c. O. $2 net. Neale.

Santley, Sir C:
Art of singing and vocal declamation. '08 (Je13) c. D. **$1.25 net. Macmillan.
Reminiscences of my life. '09(D4) pors. O. *$4 net. Brentano's.

Sapir, E:
Takelma texts. '10(Ag13) Q. (Univ. of Penn., Anthropological pubs.) pap., $2.50. Univ. of Penn.

—, and Dixon, Roland B.
Yana texts by E: Sapir, together with Yana myths collected by Roland B. Dixon. '10(Mr12) Q. (Univ. of Cal. pubs.; Am. archæology and ethnology.) pap., $2.50. Univ. of Cal.

Sapphics. Scollard, C. $1 net; 50 c. net. G: W. Browning.

Sapphire bracelet. Field, E: S. $1.25. W. J. Watt.

SAPPHO.
O'Hara, J: M. Poems of Sappho. $2. Smith & S.

Sappho. Daudet, A. †75 c. Little, B. & Co.

Sappho in Boston. Wood-Leys, R. A. †$1.50. Moffat.

Sappington, Joe.
Joe Sap's tales, by himself. '09(Mr13) c. il. pors. O. $1. Embree Pr.

"Sarah Jane" (The). Kaler, J. O. †$1.50. Estes.

Sarah Tuldon. Agnus, O. †75 c. Little, B. & Co.

Sarah's school friend. Baldwin, M. $1.50. Lippincott.

SARANAC, N. Y.
Raymond, H: W. Story of Saranac. *$1 net. Grafton Press

SARATOGA SPRINGS, N. Y.
Visitors' and automobilists' guide book of Saratoga Springs, N. Y., with map of village and vicinity map for automobilists; authentic hist. and information on all matters of interest to visitors or residents, complete to May, 1910. '10(Ag) c. 127 p. fold. maps, 16°, 25 c. Saratogian.

Sardi, Vincenzo.
Leben des seligen Kaspar del Bufalo, kanonikers des basilika S. Marco, gründers der Kongregation der Missionäre vom Kostbaren Blute Unseres Herrn Jesu Christi beschrieben nach den akten des seligsprachungeprozesser von Msgr. Vinzenz Sardi; Deutsch bearb. und hrsg. von "Konradi," [pseud.] und Gregor M. Jussel. '08, [1909.] (Ja) c. 220 p. il. 8°, *75 c. net. P. A. Gietl.

SARDINIA.
Pais, E. Ancient Italy: hist. and geograph. investigations in central Italy, Magna Græcia, Sicily, and Sardinia. *$5 net. Univ. of Chic.

Sardonics. Lyon, H. M. $1.25. Stuyvesant Press.

Sardou, Victorien, and Najac, Emily de.
Divorcons: comedy in three acts. '09(N) 12°, $1.25. Dramatic.

Sargent, C: Sprague, ed.
Trees and shrubs. v. 2, pt. 2. '08(My16) c. il. F. pap., **$5 net. Houghton M.

Sargent, F: Le Roy.
See Omar and the Rabbi.

SARGENT, John Singer.
Wood, T. M. Sargent. 65 c. net; $1.50 net. Stokes.

Sargent, Wa.
Modelling in public schools. '09(My) c. 31 p.. il. 8°, 60 c. J. L. Hammett.

SARGON, *King of Assyria.*
Olmstead, A. T. Western Asia in the days of Sargon of Assyria. **$1.25 net. Holt.

Sarolea, C:
Cardinal Newman and his influence on religious life and thought. '08(Je20) D. (World's epoch-makers.) *$1 net. Scribner.

Sarto, Andrea del.
Masterpieces of Andrea del Sarto sixty reprod. of photographs fr. the orig. paintings. '08(Ag8) T. (Painters' ser.) pap., *25 c. net; leath., *75 c. net, boxed. Stokes.

Sartor resartus. *See* Carlyle, T:

SASSETTA, Stefano.
Berenson, B. A Sienese painter of the Franciscan legend. *$2 net. Lane.

Satan. Chafer, L. S. 75 c. Gospel Pub.

Satan. Pratt, J. R. 35 c. J. R. Pratt.

Satan and the saint. Gray, J. M. 25 c. Bible Inst.

Satchel guide for the vacation tourist in Europe: itinerary of the British Isles, Belgium and Holland, Germany and the Rhine, Switzerland, France, Austria, and Italy; ed. by W: J. Rolfe; rev. annually; first edition for 1908. [37th ed.] '08(Mr7); first edition for 1909. [38th ed.] '09(Mr13); first edition for 1910. [39th ed.] '10(Mr5) c. maps, S. limp leath., ea., **$1.50 net. Houghton M.

SATIRE.
Busch, W. Edward's dream: the philosophy of a humorist. *$1 net. G: W. Dillingham.
Carus, P. Philosopher's martyrdom: a satire. *$1 net. Open Court.

SATIRE.—*Continued.*
Chaloner, J. A. Scorpio sonnets: [satires.] $1.50. Palmetto Press.
Conard, H. L: Reconstructing Eden. 50c.; 25 c. New Eden.
Previté-Orton, C: W: Political satire in English poetry. $1.50 net. Putnam.
Pulitzer, R. New York society on parade. **$1.20 net. Harper.
Seneca, L. A. Selected essays of Seneca and The satire on the deification of Claudius. *60 c. net. Macmillan.
Tucker, S: M. Verse satire in England before the Renaissance. *$1 net. Macmillan.
See also Caricature;—Epigrams;—Parody;—Wit and humor.

Satires (The). *See* Horace, Quintus Horatius Flaccus.

Satires épitres. Boileau, Despereaux, N. *$1 net. Putnam.

Satisfied at last. Sindell, M. $1.50. Reid Pub.

Satori, Jos. Aloysius.
Modern dances. '10(Mr12) c. il. por. 12°, 25 c.; pap., 15 c. V. H. Krull.

Satow, Sir Ernest Mason.
An Austrian diplomatist in the fifties: [Baron Joseph Alexander von Hübner]: the Rede lectures delivered in the Cambridge Senate House. '08(O17) D. 50 c. Putnam.

Satterthwaite, T: E:, M.D.
Diseases of the heart and aorta. '10(Mr) il. 8°, *$3 net. W: R. Jenkins.
Formerly published by E. R. Pelton.

Sattler, Otto.
Stille und sturm gedichte: [poems.] '10 (Ag27) D. pap., 75 c. Lemcke.

Saturarum. *See* Horace.

SAUCES.
See Cookery.

Saugrain de Vigni, Antoine François.
Dr. Saugrain's note-books, 1788; stay opposite Louisville, observations upon Post Vincennes, diary of journal from Louisville to Philadelphia, by Eug. F. Bliss; [repr. from Proceedings of the Amer. Antiquarian Soc. at the annual meeting, Oct., 1909.] '10(Jl16) 4°, 50 c. Davis Press.

SAUGUS, Mass.
Vital records of Saugus, Mass., to the end of the year 1849. *88 c. net. Essex Inst.

SAUL OF TARSUS.
See Paul, *St.*

Saumarez, Bayard de, pseud.
See Roose, T: Wa.

Saunders, Catharine.
Costume in Roman comedy. '09(S4) 12°, (Columbia Univ. studies in classical philology.) $1.25 net. Lemcke.

Saunders, E. D., ed.
See Louisiana. Rev. civil code.

Saunders, Florence Wenderoth.
Letters to a business girl. '09(F27) il. D. $1.25; pap., 25 c. Laird.
Mrs. De Brie says: monologues. '09(Jl3) c. D. 75 c. C. M. Clark.

Saunders, Marg. Marshall.
See Saunders, Marshall.

Saunders, Marshall, [Marg. Marshall Saunders.]
Girl from Vermont; the story of a vacation school teacher. '10(Mr12) c. il. D. *$1.25 net. Griffith.
My pets; real happenings in my aviary. '08 (N21) c. il. 8°, $1.25. Am. Bapt.
'Tilda Jane's orphans. '09(N20) c. il. D. †$1.50. L. C. Page.
Saunders' medical hand atlases. il. 12°. Saunders.
—Haab. Atlas and epitome of ophthalmoscopy.—Atlas of the external diseases of the eye. ea., $3.
—Wolff. Essentials of medical chemistry. $1.
Saunders' pocket medical formulary. Powell, W: M. *$1.75 net. Saunders.
***Saunders' question-compend ser.* il. 12° Saunders.**
—Ball. Essentials of bacteriology. *$1 net.
—Cragin. Essentials of gynecology. $1.
—Wilcox. Essentials of genito-urinary and venereal diseases. $1.
SAUNDERSON, *Colonel, M.P.*
Lucas, R. Colonel Saunderson, M.P.: memoir. *$4 net. Dutton.
Saurusaitis, Rev. Peter, comp.
Brief Lithuanian grammar; or, principal rules to learn the Lithuanian language. '10(Mr) c. 76 p 12°, 50 c. P: Saurusaitis.
Sausage from Bologna. Chapman, J: J. *75 c. net. Moffat.
SAUSAGES.
See Meat.
Sauter, B.
Sunday epistles; ed. by his monks; tr. by J. F. Scholfield. '09(Jl) 2+559 p. 8°, *$4.50 net. Herder.
Sauter, Edn.
Death of Gracchus: tragedy. Private ed. '08(S12) c. S. (Not for sale.) E. Sauter.
Sauveur, Albert, and Boylston, Herbert Melville.
Laboratory experiments in metallurgy. '09 (Ja9) c. il. tabs., forms, Q. $1.25. A. Sauveur.
Savage, Albert R.
See Maine. *Sup. judicial ct.*
Savage, C: Albert.
Athenian family: sociological and legal study based chiefly on the works of the Attic orators. '07, [1909.] (F) 13+137 p. 8°, *$1.50 net; pap., *$1.25 net. Lord Balto. Pr.
Savage, Ernest Albert.
Story of libraries and book-collecting. '09 (Mr13) 16°, *75 c. net. Dutton.
Savage, G: H:, M.D.
Harveian oration on experimental psychology and hypnotism; del. before the Royal College of Physicians of London, Oct. 18, 1909. '10(Mr26) O. pap., 40 c. Oxford Univ.
—**, and Goodall, Edn., M.D.** Insanity and allied neuroses, pract. and clinical. New and enl. ed. [1910.] (My) 674 p. il. $2.75 net. Funk.
Savage, H. B.
Poultry culture in Texas. '10(D) 27 p. il. 8°, (Texas, Dept. of Agriculture; bull.) Texas.
Savage, Dean H: E:
Gospel of the kingdom; or, the Sermon on the Mount considered in the light of contemporary Jewish thought and ideals. '10(Mr12) O. $3.50. Longmans.
Savallo, Teresa de, [Marquesa d' Alpens.]
House of the lost court. '08(Mr14) c. D. †$1.50. McClure.
Savay, Norbert Lafayette-.
Emancipation: introd. to the system of progressive government. Author's complimentary ed. '08(Je20) c. 12°. Knickerbocker Press.
Savidge, Eug. Coleman, M.D.
American in Paris; biograph. novel of the Franco-Prussian war; siege and commune of Paris from an American standpoint. 3d ed. '10(My14) c. O. $1.50. Lippincott.
Savile, Fk. Mackenzie.
The pursuit. '10(Je11) c. il. D. $1.50. Little, B. & Co.
Savill, T: Dixon, M.D.
Clinical lectures on neurasthenia. 4th ed. '09(Je) 242 p. 12°, *$2 net. Wood.
Lectures on hysteria and allied vaso-motor conditions. '09(Ag) 274 p. il. 8°, *$2.50 net. Wood.
System of clinical medicine dealing with the diagnosis, prognosis and treatment of disease for students and practitioners. 2d ed., rev. by the author assisted by F: S. Langmead and Agnes F. Caville. '09, [1910.] 27+963 p. il. O. *$7 net. Longmans.
Saville, Marshall Howard.
Antiquities of Manabi, Ecuador. '08(O10) il. (Contributions to South American archæology.) $25. [priv. pr.] F. P. Harper.
SAVINGS BANKS.
See Banks and banking.
Savinien, Francis Piedmont.
Bonbons: [poems.] '09(D) c. 64 p. 8°. (Add. pubs. for price.) B'way Pub.
SAVONAROLA, Girolamo Maria Francesco Matteo.
Baird, E. S. Angels of Savonarola. 50 c. Am. Tr.
Savory, D. L., comp.
Deutsches reformlesebuch, enthaltend dreiszig erzählungen aus der deutschen geschichte; mit fragen für sprechübungen mit grammatischen übungen und einem deutschen wörterverzeichnis. '08(D12) il. por. D. 60 c. Oxford Univ.
Savoy operas. Gilbert, *Sir* W: S. $5 net. Macmillan.
Savoy ser. 30 v. '10(N) fronts. 16°, ooze, ea., 75 c. Barse & H.
Saward, F: E:, comp.
Large coal consumers of New England; careful compilation of names, addresses and fuel requirements of leading consumers of the New England states who use 1,200 tons or more annually; prep. from authoritative information. '10(N) 75 p. il. maps, obl. 8°, $10. F: E: Saward.

Sawin, Rosa L., and Palmer, Fk. Herbert, eds.
Right-at-hand stories for dictation and reproduction in the school-room. '07, [1908.] (Jl) c. 210 p. 12°, 80 c. Palmer Co.

SAWMILLS.
See **Lumber.**

SAWS.
Johnson, C: L. Saw directory. $1. C: L. Johnson.
Treatise on the care of saws and knives. $2 net. Baldwin.

Sawyer, C: Winthrop.
Firearms in American history, 1600 to 1800. '10(F5) c. il. O. $2.60. C. W. Sawyer.

Sawyer, Edith Augusta.
Christmas Makers' Club. '08(O3) c. il. O. $1.50. L. C. Page.

Sawyer, G: H: Vaughan.
Grant's campaign in Virginia, 1864, (the Wilderness campaign.) '08(D12) maps, 12°, (Special campaign ser.) *$1.60 net. Macmillan.

Sawyer, H. C., M.D.
Matter with nervousness. '09(Ap24) c. D. $1. Cunningham, C. & W.

Sawyer, Ja. E. H., M.D.
Physical signs of diseases of the thorax and abdomen. '08(Jl4) 12°, *$2 net. Wood.

Sawyer, R. H.
Livery of heaven. '10(My14) il. 12°, $1.50. C. M. Clark.

Sawyer, Captain Vaughan-.
See Vaughan-Sawyer, *Captain.*

Sawyer, Wa. Leon.
See Standish, Winn, *pseud.*

Saxe, G: Alex. De Santos.
Examination of the urine; manual for students and practitioners. 2d ed., rev. '09 (N) c. 448 p. il. 12°, $1.75. Saunders.

SAXE, Maurice de, *Marshal of France.*
Trowbridge, W: R. H. Beau Sabreau: Maurice de Saxe, Marshal of France. *$4.50 net. Brentano's.

Saxelby, F. M.
Introd. to practical mathematics; with diagrams. '08(D26) D. 80 c. Longmans.

SAXONY.
See **Religious education.**

Saxton, Edm.
Logs for four-place work. '08, [1909.] (F) c. 200 p. 4°, $3. E. Saxton.

SAYINGS.
See Epigrams;—Quotations.

Sayings of grandmamma. Glyn, *Mrs.* E. S. $1.25. Duffield.

Sayler, H. L.
Airship boys adrift; or, saved by an aeroplane. '09(N6) c. il. D. (Airship boys' ser.) †$1. Reilly & B.
Airship boys due north; or, by balloon to the pole. '10(Ap9) il. 12°, (Airship boys ser.) $1. Reilly & B.
Airship boys in barren lands; or, the secret of the White Eskimos. '10(D17) c. il. D. (Airship boys ser.) $1. Reilly & B.
Airship boys; or, the quest of the Aztec treasure. '09(Jl3) c. il. chart, D. (Airship boys ser.) $1. Reilly & B.

Sayler, H. L.—*Continued.*
Johnny Hep, the soldier boy, sometimes bad, but mostly good. '08(O24) c. il. O. bds., 35 c. Reilly & B.
Terrible Teddy and Peaceful Bill. '08 (Je20) c. il. 12°, pap., 50 c. Reilly & B.

Sayles' annot. civil statutes. *See* Texas.

Saylor, H: H., ed.
Distinctive homes of moderate cost; being a collection of country and suburban homes in good taste, with some value in suggestion for the home-builder. '10 (Ag20) c. il. F. $2 net. McBride, W.

Sayre, Farrand.
Map maneuvers. Rev. ed. '08(My.) c. 144 p. il. map, tab., 8°, 60 c.; leath., 75 c. Staff Coll.

Sayward, W: H:
Relation of the trade school to the trade: address del. at the graduating exercises of the North End Union Plumbing School, Boston. 1908. '09(Je19) D. pap., gratis. S: F. Hubbard.

Scalawags (The). Naylor, J. B. 50 c. B. W. Dodge.

Scale and chord helps. Gardner, M. A. 20 c. M. A. Gardner.

Scales, F. S.
Practical microscopy. '10(D) $1.50. A. Eger.

Scales of justice. Knapp, G: L. $1.50. Lippincott.

Scales of justice. White, F. M. $1.50. Kearney.

Scallop shell of quiet. Hazard, C. **$1 net. Houghton M.

Scalp-hunters. *See* Reid, *Captain* Mayne.

Scamper through the Far East. Austin, H: H. $5. Longmans.

Scamping tricks and odd knowledge. Newman, J: $1. Spon.

SCANDINAVIA.
Bayne, S: G. Quicksteps through Scandinavia. **$1.25 net. Harper.
Roth, R. **Ein nordische held; ein bild aus der geschichte; brief outline of Scandinavian history.** 35 c. **Am. Bk.**
See also Denmark;—Mythology;—Norway;—Sweden.

SCANDINAVIAN LITERATURE.
Flom, G: T. **Hist. of Scandinavian studies in Am. universities.** 50 c. **Univ. of Ia.**

SCANDINAVIANS IN THE UNITED STATES.
Rydberg, P. A. Scandinavians who have contributed to the knowledge of the flora of North America. $1. Augustana.

Scanlan, C: Martin.
Law of church and grave; clergyman's hdbk. of law. '09(My) c. 26+13-265 p. 12°, $1.35. Benziger.
Rules of order for societies, conventions, public meetings and legislative bodies. 2d ed. [1910.] (Je) c. '07. 110 p. 24°, 50 c. net. Caspar.

Scannell, T: Bartholomew, D.D.
The priest's studies. '08(F8) D. (Westminster lib.) *$1.20 net. Longmans.

SCANSION.
See **Poetry.**

Scantlebury, Eliz. Ellis.
Homes of the world's babies. '10(Jl2) il. c. cbl. D. 50 c. Flanagan.
World babies. '10(Ja22) c. il. 8°, *35 c. net, in portfolio. Educ. Pub.

Scar (The). Dawson, F. W. $1.50. Small.

Scarecrow (The). Mackaye, P. W. **$1.25 net. Macmillan.

Scarfoglio, Antonio.
Round the world in a motor car; tr. by J. Parker Heyes. '09(N20) c. il. 8°, *$5 net. M. Kennerley.

Scarlet feather. Townley, H. $1.50. W. J. Watt.

SCARLET FEVER.
Geddings, H: D. Précis on the management of outbreaks of smallpox, diptheria and scarlet fever. (Add. Superintendent for price.) U. S., Supt. of Docs.
Milne, R. Plea for the home treatment and prevention of scarlet fever. $1 net. Wood.

Scarlet mother on the Tiber. $1. L. J. King.

Scarlet shadow. Hurt, W. $1.50. Appeal.

Scenes and portraits. Manning, F. *$1.75 net. Putnam.

Scenes from every land. Grosvenor, G. H., *ed.* $1; $2; $2.50. Nat. Geographic Soc.

Scenes of clerical life. *See* Eliot, G:, *pseud.*

Scenic treasures of California. Jones, T: W., *comp.* 50 c. F. Harvey.

Scent of sandal wood. Miller, C. H. $2.50. C. H. Miller.

Schaad, Rev. Julius A:
Only a mask?: comparison of the teachings of the Christ and of Christian Science; also the Apostles Creed and Christian Science paralleled. '09(Je26) c. nar. D. pap., 25 c. J. A. Schaad.

Schaaf, E:
20th century harmony text-book compend system; designed for students. '10(Ap9) c. Q. pap., $1. Schirmer.

Schaefer, F. W.
Diana's diary: flashes of wit. '08(Ap4) c. il. D. bds., 50 c.; pap., 25 c. Laird.
Osgar und Adolf; or, comic vaudeville stunts; also, "Rollo and his father." '08 (Ap4) c. il. D. bds., 50 c.; pap., 25 c. Laird.

Schaeffer, A. J.
Happy hour paint book. '09(N6) c. palette shaped, O. bds., 50 c. Saalfield.

Schaeffer, Casper.
Memoirs and reminiscences, together with sketches of the early history of Sussex County, New Jersey; with notes and genealogic record of the Schaeffer, Shaver or Shafer family; comp. by William Mindred Johnson. '07, [1908.] (Jl) 87 p. il. por. 8°. [priv. pr.] W: M. Johnson.

Schaeffer, E.
Sandro Botticelli; tr. by Fs. F. Cox. '10 (N5) il. S. (Belgravia art monographs.) limp leath., $1.50 net, boxed; Persian cf., $1.75 net, boxed. Caldwell.

SCHAEFFER FAMILY.
See Genealogies.

Schäfer, E: Alb.
Essentials of histology descriptive and practical. 8th ed., thoroughly rev. '10 (O) 571 p. il. 8°, $3.50 net. Lea.
—, ed. *See* Quain, Jones.

Schafer, Jos.
Acquisition of Oregon territory. pt. 1. '08, [1909.] (Ap) 8°, (University of Oregon bull.; new ser.) gratis. Univ. of Ore.

Schaff, Morris.
Battle of the Wilderness. '10(O22) c. maps, plans, O. $2 net. Houghton M.

Schaff, Philip, D.D.
Hist. of the Christian church. v. 5, pt. 2, The Middle Ages from Boniface VIII., 1294, to the Protestant Reformation, 1517, by D: S. Schaff, D.D. '10(Ap16) c. pors. O. $3.25 net. Scribner.

Schaff-Herzog encyclopedia of religious knowledge. *See* New Schaff-Herzog encyclopedia.

Schaffer, W: I., rep.
See Pennsylvania. *Superior ct.* Repts.

Schaffner, J: H:
Lab'y outlines for general botany; for the elem. study of plant structures and functions from the standpoint of evolution. 2d ed. '10(My7) c. il. 8°, 75 c. J: H. Schaffner.
Trees of Ohio and surrounding territory, incl. the area westward to the limits of the prairie and south to the thirty-seventh parallel. '09(S) 73-191 p. 8°, (Ohio State Academy of Science proceedings.) pap., 50 c. Ohio State Acad.

Schaffner, Lillyan.
Love and friendship. '10(D3) c. D. pap., 35 c. net, in envelope. P. Elder.

Schaffner, Marg. Anna.
Effect of the recent boycott decisions. '10 (N12) 8°, (Amer. Acad. of Political and Social Sci. pubs.) 25 c. Am. Acad. Pol. Sci.
Initiative and referendum: state legislation; prep. with the co-operation of the Political Science Department of the University of Wisconsin. '08(Ja25) D. (Comparative legislation bull.) pap., 5 c. Wisconsin Free Lib.
Labor contract from individual to collective bargaining. '08(My23) 8°, (Bulletin of the Univ. of Wis., Economics and pol. sci. ser.) pap., 50 c. Univ. of Wis.
Municipal home rule charters. '09(Mr6) D. (Comparative legislation bull.) pap., 25 c. Wisconsin Free Lib.
Primary elections, the test of party affiliation. '09(Mr6) D. (Comparative legislation bull.) pap., 25 c. Wisconsin Free Lib.
The recall; prep. with the co-operation of the Political Science Department of the University of Wisconsin. '08(Ja25) D. (Comparative legislation bull.) pap., 5 c. Wisconsin Free Lib.

Schalek, Alfr.
Diseases of the skin; manual for students and practitioners. 2d ed., thoroughly rev. '10(Ap) c. 7+255 p. il. 12°, (Medical epitome ser.) $1. Lea.

Schaller, Waldemar Thdr.
See Hillebrand, W: Fs.

Schamberg, Jay Fk.
Diseases of the skin, and the eruptive fevers. '08(D) c. 9-534 p. il. 8°, *$3 net. Saunders.
Grain itch (acaro-dermatitis urticarioides): study of a new disease in this country. [1910.] (D) 3 p. il. 8°. (Priv. pr.) Journal Cutaneous.

Schapiro, Jacob Salwyn.
Social reform and the Reformation. '09 (Jl3) O. (Studies in history, economics and public law.) pap., $1.25. Longmans.

Schapper, Heinrich.
Laboratory guide for students in physical sciences. '08(F8) c. 12°, $1. Wiley.

Scharnagl, Anton.
Das feierliche gelübe als ehehindernis in seiner geschichtlichen entwicklung dargestellt. '08(S12) 8°, (Strassburger theologische studien.) pap., *$1.50 net. Herder.

Schatz, W: Jackson.
Club swinging for physical exercise and recreation; with an introd. by W. G. Anderson; exercises progressively arranged. '08(D5) c. il. 12°, $1. Am. Gymnasia.

Schauffler, Rev. Adolphus F:, D.D.
Knowing and teaching the scholar. '10 (F5) c. il. 12°, ("Times" hdbks. for Sunday-school workers.) 50 c. S. S. Times.
Sparks from a superintendent's anvil; pract. helper for every Sunday-school worker. '09(N20) c. 12°, $1. Wilde.
—, **Lamoreaux, Mrs. Antoinette Abernethy, Brumbaugh, Martin Grove, and Laurence, Marion.**
Training the teacher; supp. chapters by C: A. Oliver. Ira Maurice Price; approved as a First Standard Course by the Committee on Education, International Sunday School Association. '08(N14) c. D. *50 c. net; pap., *30 c. net. S. S. Times.

Schauffler, Rob. Haven.
Romantic Germany. '09(N6) c. il. O. **$3.50 net, boxed. Century Co.
—, comp. Through Italy with the poets. '08 (F15) c. front. D. **$2 net. Moffat.
—, ed. Arbor Day: its history, observance, spirit and significance; with pract. selections on tree-planting and conservation, and a nature anthology. '09(D4) c. D. (Our American holidays.) **$1 net. Moffat.
Lincoln's birthday: essays, orations and poems and Lincoln's own writings. '09 (F13) c. por. D. (Our American holidays.) **$1 net. Moffat.
Washington's birthday; its **hist., observance, spirit, and significance; with selection from Washington's speeches and writings. '10(F19) c. D. (Our American holidays.)** **$1 net. Moffat.

Schechter, Solomon.
Abraham Lincoln: memorial address del. at Lincoln centennial celebration of the Jewish Theological Seminary of America. '09(My15) O. pap. (Add. author for price.) S. Schechter.
Some aspects of Rabbinic theology. '09 (Ja30) c. O. **$2.25 net. Macmillan.
Studies in Judaism, second series. '08 (My2) c. O. $2. Jewish Pub.

Scheffauer, Herman G:
Looms of life: poems. '08(Ag1) c. front. D. $1.25. Neale.

Scheffer, Thdr. H.
Loose leaf system of laboratory notes. '08 (N) c. 6+122 p. 8°, *75 c. net. Blakiston.

Scheffler, Johann, ["Angelus Silesius."]
Angelus Silesius; selection from the rhymes of a German mystic; tr. in the original meter by Paul Carus. '09(Jl17) il. 16°, *$1 net. Open Court.

Schell, Stanley.
Platform and all-round. '10(D) c. 192 p. 12°, (Werner's readings and recitations.) Werner.
—, comp. Werner's book of pantomimes written, arr. or adapt. by Stanley Schell. '08(Ag22) c. il. 12°, (Werner's readings and recitations.) 60 c.; pap., 35 c. Werner.
—, ed. Hiawatha entertainments; scene of "Hiawatha bids farewell to his people," "transformation scene." '07, [1909.] (Je) c. '09. 92 p. il. 12°, pap., 35 c. Werner.
See also Anderson, H: S.

Schelling, Felix Emanuel.
Elizabethan drama, 1558-1642: hist. of the drama in England from the accession of Queen Elizabeth to the closing of the theaters, to which is prefixed a résumé of the earlier drama from its beginnings. '08(Mr7) c. 2 v., O. **$7.50 net. Houghton M.
English literature during the lifetime of Shakespeare. '10(O15) c. O. $2.50. Holt.

Scheme and estimates for a national theatre. Archer, W: $2.50. Duffield.
Scheme for a paper currency. Fry, R: $3.75. Club for Colonial Reprs.
Scheme for the detection of the more common classes of carbon compounds. Weston, F. E. 90 c. Longmans.
Schemers (The). Torbett, D. 75 c. Doscher.

Schenck, Carl Alwin.
Forest finance: guide to lectures del. at the Biltmore forest school. '09(Je12) tabs., 8°, $1. C. A. Schenck.
Forest protection; guide to lectures del. at the Biltmore Forest School. '10(Jl16) tabs., 8°, $1.50. Inland Press.

Schenck, Ferdinand Schureman.
Christian evidences and ethics. '10(Jl2) c. il. 8°, 75 c. Y. M. C. A.
Sociology of the Bible. '09(My1) 8°, *$1.50 net. Reformed.

SCHENECTADY, N. Y.
Shafer, D. C. Stories of an old Dutch town; in verse. 50 c. Robson.

Schevill, Ferdinand.
Siena: story of a mediæval commune. '09 (Ap3) c. il. maps, O. **$2.50 net. Scribner.

Schiffini, S.
De vera religione seu de Christi ecclesia ejusque munere doctrinali. '08, [1909.] (Mr) 19+750 p. hf. mor., *$2.65 net. Herder.

Schildbürger (Die) ihre wisheit und grosze torheit. Betz, F:, *ed.* 35 c. net. Heath.

Schiller, Ferdinand Canning Scott.
Riddles of the Sphinx; study in the philosophy of humanism. New and rev. ed. '10(D24) 8°, $3. Macmillan.

Schiller, Johann Christoph Friedrich v.
Works. 5 v. New imperial lib. ed. '10 (D) il. 8°, ea., $1.25; hf. cf., $2.25. New il. sterling ed., ea., $1. (Sets only.) Estes.
Jungfrau von Orleans; ed., with introd., notes and vocab., by Warren Washburn Florer. '09(Ja9) c. S. 70 c. Am. Bk.
Jungfrau von Orleans; ed., with introd., notes, and vocab., by Philip Schuyler Allen and Steven Tracy Byington. '10 (F5) c. front. map, 8°, (International modern language ser.) 70 c. Ginn.
Maria Stuart; ed., with introd., repetitional exercises, notes and vocab., by J: Scholte Nollen. '09(Ap17) c. por. tabs., S. (International modern lang. ser.) 75 c. Ginn.
Selections from Schiller's ballads and lyrics; ed., with notes and vocab., by Lewis Addison Rhoades; with questions by Berthold Auerbach Eisenlohr. '08(Jl4) c. S. 60 c. Am. Bk.

SCHILLER, Johann Christoph Friedrich v.
Picard, L. B. Der neffe als onkel; lustspiel von Friedrich Schiller, aus dem französischen des Picard. **35 c. net. Holt.
See also Weimar.

Schilling, J.
Don Basilio: practical guide to Spanish conversation and correspondence; tr. and ed. by F: Zagel. '08(F1) D. *$1 net. Holt.

Schilling, W: Paul.
Upper tenor tones and how every tenor may acquire them without strain or effort. Pt. 1. '10(My7) c. 8°, $1. W: P. Schilling.

Schimer, Edg. Dubs.
See Burchill Georgine.

Schimmelreiter (Der). Storm, T. 70 c. Ginn.

Schimpf, H: W:
Manual of volumetric analysis, for the use of pharmacists, sanitary and food chemists. 5th ed., rewritten. '09(Ap3) c. figs. 8°, $5. Wiley.

Schindel, Rev. Jacob D.
See Roberts, C: R.

Schinz, Albert.
Anti-pragmatism; examination into the respective rights of intellectual aristocracy and social democracy. '10(Mr12) c. 12°, $1.50. Small, M.

Schipper, Jakob.
Hist. of English versification. '10(Ag27) c. 8°, $2.90. Oxford Univ.

Schirmer, R: C.
Philadelphia Fairmount park; general description; short historical sketch; life of Robert Morris; description of all the monuments, works of art, etc., and all the interesting and historical buildings in the park, with illustrations. [1910.] (S) c. 37 p. 12°, 50 c. R: C. Schirmer.

Schirmer's collection of operas. Q. Schirmer.
—Tschaikowsky. Eugene Onégin. $3.50; $2.50.

SCHLAGBALL.
See Bat-ball.

Schlapp, G:
Erzählende dichtungen, gedichte und aphorismen: bilder aus dem früheren ansiedlerleben des Westens. '08(D) c. 526 p. 12°, *$1.50 net. Caspar.

SCHLEGEL, August Wilhelm von.
Helmholtz, A. A. Indebtedness of Samuel Taylor Coleridge to August Wilhelm von Schlegel. 40 c. Univ. of Wis.

Schleif, Oscar.
Technique of English. '08(My23) c. 12°, 75 c. O. Schleif.

Schleininger, Nikolaus.
Principles of eloquence, together with examples selected from the works of the most famous orators of ancient and modern times; rev. and enl. by Karl Rache; tr. from the 6th German ed. by Jos. Skelton. [1910.] (Mr) 29+367 p. 8°, *$2 net. Herder.

Schleip, Karl Friedrich Wilhelm.
Hematological atlas, with a description of the technic of blood examination: Eng. adaptation of text, by Frederic E. Sondern. '08(Mr14) c. il. 4°, hf. leath., $10. Rebman.

Schleppey, Mrs. Blanche Bloor.
Soul of a mummy, and other stories. '09 (Ja16) c. O. $1.50. B. B. Schleppey.

Schlesinger, Alex.
Labor amendment our next great job; published under the auspices of the American Anti-Wage Slavery Society. '10(D3) c. D. $1.50. N. Y. Medical.

Schlesinger, Kathleen.
Instruments of the modern orchestra, and early records of the precursors of the violin family. 2 v. '10(Je4) il. 8°, $6 net. Scribner.

Schlossmann, A., M.D.
See Diseases of children.

Schlundt, Herman, and Moore, R: Bishop.
Radioactivity of the thermal waters of Yellowstone National Park. '09(D) 35 p. il. 8°, (U. S., Dept. of the Interior, Geological Survey, bull.) pap. (Add. Superintendent for price.) U. S., Supt. of Docs.

SCHLUSSENBURG FORTRESS, Russia.
Pollock, S. O. Russian Bastile: [Schlussenburg Fortress, near St. Petersburg.] 50 c. Kerr.

Schlüter, Hermann.
Brewing industry and the brewery workers' movement in America; [issued also in German.] '10(Jl16) D. $1; leath., $1.50. Int. Union United Brewery.

Schmalz, J: Barnes.
Nuggets from King Solomon's Mine. '09 (Jl10) c. il. 12°, $2. Schmalz.

Schmeer, L:
Flow of water; new theory of the motion of water under pressure and in open conduits and its pract. application. '10 (F19) c. tabs., il. 8°, **$3 net. Van Nostrand.

Schmeisser, W: C.
See Paugh, F:

Schmid, Christoph von.
Easter eggs; from the German. '08(My2) il. 8°, $1.25. Macmillan.

Schmid, Jos.
Die Osterfestberechnung in der abendländischen kirche vom I. allgemeinen konzil zu Nicäa bis zum ende des VIII. jahrhunderts. '08(S12) 8°, (Strassburger theologische studien.) pap., *80 c. net. Herder.

Schmidt, Adolf, M.D.
Examination of the function of the intestines by means of the test diet; its application in medical practice and its diagnostic and therapeutic value; authorized tr. from the 2d rev. and enl. German ed. by C: D. Aaron. '09(D) c. 7+126 p. 8°, *$1.50 net. Davis.

Schmidt, C. L. A.
Table of H+ and OH-concentrations corresponding to electromotive forces determined in gas-chain measurements. '09 (O16) Q. (Univ. of Cal. pubs.; Physiology.) pap., 10 c. Univ. of Cal.

Schmidt, Ernst.
Wie man sich bildet: [play.] '09(N13) pap., 15 c. Oxford Univ.

Schmidt, Ferdinand.
Charlemagne; tr. from the German by G: P. Upton. '10(O22) c. il. S. (Life stories for young people.) 50 c. net. McClurg.
Youth of the great Elector, [Frederick William of Brandenburg;] tr. from the German by G: P. Upton. '09(S11) c. il. por. S. (Life stories for young people.) *60 c. net. McClurg.

Schmidt, L: M.
Principles and practice of artificial ice making and refrigeration. 3d ed., rev. and enl. '08(F22) il. 8°, *$3 net. Phila. Bk.

Schmidt, Oscar Centennial, ed.
Pract. railroading; treatise on steam, electric and motor car operation. 6 v. '10 (Ja29) c. il. 8°, $20. Stanley Inst.
Pract. treatise on automobiles. '09(Je26) c. 2 v., il. fold. tab., form, 4°, $12. Am. Text-Bk.

Schmidt, Otto Ernest, ["Otto Ernest."]
Überwunden; ed., with introd. and notes, by Ja. Taft Hatfield. '08(Jl11) c. por. S. 30 c. Holt.

Schmidt, Rudolph.
Pain: its causation and diagnostic significance in internal diseases. '08(Ag8) c. figs. O. **$3 net. Lippincott.

Schmiedel, Paul Wilhelm.
Johannine writings; tr. by Maurice A. Canney. '08(O3) 12°, *$1.50 net. Macmillan.

Schmieden, Victor.
See Meyer, Willy.

Schmitter, Ferdinand.
Upper Yukon native customs and folklore. '10(Je11) O. (Smithsonian miscellaneous collections.) pap., 12 c. Smith. Inst.

Schmitz, Emil, [W: Emil Schmitz Didier.]
Life of Pius X. '07, [1908.] (Ag15) c. 15+443 p. il. pors. 8°, $5. Am. Cath. Pub.
Royalty from this work is to be presented to Pope Pius X. as Peter's pence.

Schmucker, S: Christian.
Columbia elem. geography. '09(D4) c. il. maps, 4°, 60 c. Hinds.
Study of nature. '08(D19) c. il. D. (Lippincott's educational ser.) $1.25. Lippincott.
Under the open sky; being a year with nature. '10(D3) c. O. $1.50 net, boxed. Lippincott.

Schneck, Fk. Jos.
The Washington party; "shall the people rule?"; if so parties must be destroyed. '09(D4) c. il. O. $1. F. J. Schneck.

Schneider, C: Conrad.
General specifications for structural work of buildings. '10(S3) c. il. tabs., 8°, 75 c. Engineering News.

Schneider, Norman Hugh, ["H. S. Norrie."]
Electrical circuits and diagrams. In 2 pts. '09(Mr13) c. figs. D. pap., ea., 25 c. Spon.
Model vaudeville theatre; how to construct and operate it. '09(D18) c. 12°, (Model lib.) pap., 25 c. Spon.

Schneider, Philip F.
Preliminary rept. on the Arkansas diamond field; issued by the Bureau of Mines, Manufacturers and Agriculture. '07, [1909.] (Mr) 16 p. O. pap. (Add. pubs. for price. Cen. Pr.

SCHNEIDER FAMILY.
See **Genealogies: Wyand, E. C.**

Schnell, Albert F:
Schnell astronomy; being a treatise on the origin of the planets and daylight by vibration. '09(My) c. 201 p. il. 12°, $1.50. A. F: Schnell.

Schock, Georg, pseud.
See Loose, Katherine Riegel.

Schoff, Wilfred Harvey, comp.
See Burk, Addison B., *comp.*

Schofield, Alfr. Taylor, M.D.
Christian sanity; with a preface by Dr. Handley Moule, [Bishop of Durham.] '08(Ap4) D. *$1 net. Armstrong.
Divine in man; four lectures given by request at the Alliance Club, London; with diagram. '09(N20) D. *75 c. net. Armstrong.
Fit for work; or, health in Christian service. '09(N20) O. *$1.25 net. Armstrong.
Functional nerve diseases. '08(My9) diagrs., 8°, (New lib. of medicine.) *$2.50 net. Dutton.
How to keep fit; unconventional manual. '10(S3) c. D. 75 c. Moffat.
Mental and spiritual health. '10(Ap2) D. 50 c. Fenno.
Nervousness: brief and popular review of the moral treatment of disordered nerves. '09(Mr13) c. D. **50 c. net. Moffat.
With Christ in Palestine: four addresses. '09(S18) il. O. $1.25, boxed. Fenno.

Schofield, Rob. J., ["One of the Craft."]
Drummer's yarns and funny jokes. 16th crop. '08(Je27) c. O. pap., 25 c. Excelsior.

Scholar gipsy. *See* Arnold, Matthew. Thyrsis.

SCHOLARSHIP.
See Education.

Scholarships for working children. Hall, F: S. (Add. pubs. for price.) Nat. Child Labor.

SCHOLASTICISM.
See Philosophy.

Scholefield, Guy H.
New Zealand in evolution, industrial, economic and political; with introd. by the Hon. W. Pember Reeves. '10(Mr26) il. fold. map, O. *$3 net. Scribner.

Scholia on hypokrisis in the Commentary of Donatus. Basore, J: W: gratis. Johns Hopkins.

Scholl, J: W:
Hesper-phosphor, and other poems. '10 (Jl30) c. D. pap., 75 c. (200 copies.) Wahr.

Scholz, Carl.
Settlement of dust in mines and prevention of explosions by the increase of humidity. '08(O10) c. il. 8°. (Add. pub. for price.) Hodgart.

Schomer, Abraham Shaikewitz.
Primary cause of antisemitism: answer to the Jewish question. '09(My8) c. D. $1. A. S. Schomer.

Schon, Hans August Evald Conrad von.
Hydro-electric practice: pract. manual of the development of water power, its conversion to electric energy, and its distant transmission. '08(Ag22) c. il. charts, O. **$6 net. Lippincott.

School algebra. Nicholson, J. W. $1. Am. Bk.

School arts booklet. il. 12°. Davis Press.
—Bowers. Dorothy and her ward-robe. 35 c.

School-children the world over. Dunton, L. $1.50. Stokes.

School classic ser. il. 12°. Paine.
—Reiter. Story of Lincoln. 5 c.

School-day memories; [Helen P. Strong, *ed.*] '09(Je19) il. sq. S. decorated bds., 50 c.; leath., $1.25, boxed. H. M. Caldwell.

School days and play days. Mosher, M. B. $1. Saalfield.

School economic atlas. Bartholomew, J: G: 85 c. Oxford Univ.

School favorite. *See* Smith, *Mrs.* E. T.

School-fellow days; designed by Clara Powers Wilson. [1910] (My) 8°, $1.25; Schoolmate ed., ooze, $2. Reilly & B.

School for scandal. *See* Sheridan, R: Brinsley Butler.

School four. Dudley, A. T. $1.25. Lothrop, L. & S.

School garden book. Weed, C. M. $1.25. Scribner.

School garden note book. Elford, P., *comp.* 25 c. Oxford Univ.

School-girl days; designed by Clara Powers Wilson. [1910] (My) 8°, $1.75; Classmate ed., ooze, $2. Reilly & B.

School history of Essex. Weston, W. H. 50 c. Oxford Univ.

School history of the County Palatine of Durham. Eden, F. S. 50 c. Oxford Univ.

School history of the United States of America. Morris, C: **90 c. net. Lippincott.

School hygiene in Massachusetts. Martin, G: H: gratis. G: H: Martin.

School music teaching. Giddings, T. P. $1. C. H. Congdon.

School of Calvary. Jowett, J. H. 50 c. net. Pilgrim Press.

School of Madrid. Beruete y Moret, A. de. *$2 net. Scribner.

School of Railway Signaling. Railway signaling. v. 1. '09(Mr13) c. il. 8°. (Add. pubs. for price.) Sch. of R'way Signaling.

School of Railway Signaling. Signal drawing. '10(Mr5) c. il. 8°, $15. Sch. of R'way Signaling.

SCHOOL READERS.
See Readers.

School room echoes. Burke, M. C. Bk. 1. $1.50. Badger.

School sermons. Coit, H: A. **$1.50 net. Moffat.

SCHOOL SONGS.
See Music;—Songs.

School team in camp. Earl, J: P. †$1.25. Penn Pub. Co.

School year books; ed. by Thdr. B. Moss. il. D. Flanagan.
—Lilley. Second school year. 60 c.

Schoolboys and school work. Lyttleton, E: $1.25. Longmans.

Schoolgirl's battlefield. Jacberns, R. $1.50. Dutton.

Schoolmaster (The). Benson, A. C. *$1.25 net. Putnam.

SCHOOLS.
Akron, O. Board of Education. Rules governing medical inspection in Akron public schools. (Add. pubs. for price.) Akron Bd. Educ.
American college and private school directory. $2. Educational Aid.
Ayres, L. P. Open air schools. $1.20 net. Doubleday, P.
Ayres, L. P. Some factors affecting grade distribution. 10 c. Psychological Clinic.
Baker, T: S. Preparatory school question. Tome Sch.
Baldwin, W: A. The high school. 5 c. N. E. Pub. Co.
Bard, H. E. City school district. $1. Teachers' Coll.
Bardeen, C: W: New York school officers' hdbk. *$1.50 net. Bardeen.
Barwick, A. J. Opening exercises for public schools in North Carolina. gratis. N. C., Dept. Pub. Instruct.
Bedichek, U., *and* Baskett, G: T. Consolidation of rural schools with and without transportation. 25 c. Univ. of Tex.
Brown, J: F. American high school. **$1.40 net. Macmillan.
Brownscombe, F. J. State control of courses of study. $1. Silver.
Bruce, W: G:, *and others, comps.* School architecture. 75 c. Am. Sch.
Burnham, W: H: One session a day or two in the public schools? 10 c. Bassette.
Burns, J. A. Catholic school system in the U. S. $1.25. Benziger.
Cary, C: P. Superintendent and superintendence; [school supervision.] (Add. author for price.) C: P. Cary.
Chancellor, W: E. Our city schools. *$1.25 net. Heath.

SCHOOLS.—*Continued.*

Conference for the Study of the Problems of Rural Life. 2d, Charlottesville, Va., 1909. Addresses del. at the Univ. of Va. summer school. (Add. pub. for price.) B. R. Payne.

Corwin, R. W. Modern model school house on the unit plan. 10 c. R. W. Corwin.

Curriculum of the elementary school. $2. Teachers' Coll.

Doerflinger, C: H. Prospectus of the People's New Education Advanced Common School. 25 c. C: H. Doerflinger.

Draper, A. S. Adaptation of the schools to industry and efficiency. gratis. A. S. Draper.

Earhart, L. B. Systematic study in elementary schools. $1. Teachers' Coll.

Evans, C. E. School buildings. gratis. C. E. Evans.

Falkner, R. P. Elimination of pupils from school. 10 c.—What can and do school reports show? 20 c. R. P. Falkner.

Farrington, F. E. French secondary schools. $2.50. Longmans.

Finegan, T: E: Textbook on New York school law. $1. M. Bender.

Foght, H. W. American rural school. $1.25 net. Macmillan.

Fowler. W: K., *ed.* Suggestive exercises for special day programs for the use of public schools. 25 c. Univ. Pub.

Graham, A. B. Centralized schools in Ohio. gratis. A. B. Graham.

Graham, A. B. Country schools of Ohio. Ohio State Univ.

Gulick, L. H., *and* Ayres, L. P. Medical inspection of schools. $1. Charities Pub.

Harris, W: T. Question of recess. 30 c. Bardeen.

Harvard University. Associated Harvard Clubs. *Committee on Public School Administration.* Reform in city school administration. Assoc. Harvard Clubs.

Hockenberry, J: C. Rural school in the United States. 75 c. J: C. Hockenberry.

Hollister, H. A. High school administration. $1.50. Heath.

Hollister, H. A. Public school buildings and their equipment; with special reference to high schools. gratis. Univ. of Ill.

Hugh, D: D. Bulletin concerning rural schools and their consolidation. Colo. State Normal.

Hyatt, E: School architecture and school improvement. Cal. Dept. Pub. Instruction.

Jones, E. A. Needed school legislation. (Add. author for price.) E. A. Jones.

Kelly, M. I. American public school as a factor in international conciliation. gratis. Am. Assoc. Int. Conciliation.

King, F: A. Suggestion note-book, prep. especially for teachers visiting foreign schools. $1. F. A. King.

Knorr, G: W. Consolidated rural schools and organization of a county system. Gov. Pr. Off.

Leland, C. G., *and others.* Library and the school. 50 c. Harper.

SCHOOLS.—*Continued.*

Leonard, M. H. Moral training in public schools. 25 c. Palmer Co.

Lewis, P., *comp.* Golden hour; stories and poems for opening exercises in the school-room. $1. Bobbs-M.

Lilley, H. M. Second school year. 60 c. Flanagan.

Lyttleton, E. Schoolboys and school work. $1.25. Longmans.

McAndrew, W: College influence on public high schools. 30 c. Bardeen.

Maryland. Public school law. 15 c. Meyer & T.

Massachusetts. *Bd. of Education.* List of principals of high schools and principals of some private schools which supply the place of high schools in towns where they are located. gratis. Mass. Bd. Educ.

Mildren, N. L. Seat work for primary grades. 35 c. N. L. Mildren.

Missouri. Dept. of Education. State course of study for the rural and graded schools and for approved high schools in the State of Missouri. (Add. pubs. for price.) Missouri Dept. Educ.

Modern school houses. $7.50. Swetland.

Momyer, G: R. Normal institute manual of Colorado school law, Dec., 1909. 25 c. Herrick.

Morrison, G. B. Scope and content of the district high school. 25 c. G. B. Morrison.

New England Association of School Superintendents. Rept. on the physical welfare of the public school child. gratis. N. E. Assoc. Sch. Supts.

New York City. *Bu. of Municipal Research.* Illustrated guide to school subjects of interest.—School progress and school facts. ea., 25 c. Bu. Municipal.

New York City. *Bu. of Municipal Research.* Questions answered by school reports. (Add. pubs. for price.) Bu. Municipal.

New York City. *Bu. of Municipal Research.* Tuition for non-resident pupils. gratis. Bu. Municipal.

New York [State.] Text-bk. of school law. $1.25. M. Bender.

Parlin, C: C. Twentieth century high school. gratis. A. B. O'Neil.

Perry, A. C., *jr.* Management of a city school. *$1.25 net. Macmillan

Perry, A. C., *jr.* Problems of the elem. school. $1.25 net. Appleton.

Perry, C. A. Wider use of the school plant. $1.25. Charities Pub.

Riggs, J: F. Next step in school legislation. (Add. author for price.) J: F. Riggs.

Sadler, M. E., *ed.* Moral instruction and training in schools. 2 v. ea., *$1.50 net. Longmans.

Sisson, E: O. High school's cure of souls. (Add. Univ. for price.) Univ. of Wash.

Snedden, D: S., *and* Allen, W: H. School reports and school efficiency. *$1.50 net. Macmillan.

SCHOOLS.—*Continued.*

Sneyd-Kynnersley, E. M. Some passages in the life of one of H. M. inspectors of schools. *$2.60 net. Macmillan

Snyder, E. R. Legal status of rural high schools in the U. S. $1.50. Teachers' Coll.

Sogard, J: Public school relationships. $1. Hinds.

Stewart, J. S., *ed.* Hdbk. for the secondary schools of Georgia. gratis. J. S. Stewart.

Stowe, M. A. English grammar schools in the reign of Queen Elizabeth. *$1.50 net. Teachers Coll.

Updegraff, H. Origin of the moving school in Massachusetts. $1.50. Teachers' Coll.

Watson, F. English grammar schools to 1660. *$2 net. Putnam.

Worcester, Mass. *School Committee.* Course of study. gratis. Worcester Sch. Com.

See also Agriculture;—Arbor Day;—Athletics;—Bible;—Children;—Colleges and universities;—Drawing;—Education;—English language;—Entertainments;—Games;—Gardens and gardening;—History;—Hygiene;—Indians; — Kindergarten; — Librarians and libraries; — Manual training;—Massachusetts; — Music; — Orators and oratory;—Painters and paintings;—Playgrounds;—Plays;—Readers; — Reform schools;—Rifles;—Songs;—Statistics; — Sunday-school;—Teachers and teaching;—Technical education;—Tuberculosis;—*also* names of states.

Schoolyard athletics. Sullivan, J. E: 10 c. Am. Sports.

Schoonmaker, Nancy Musselman.
The eternal fires. '10(Je4) c. 12°, $1.50. B'way Pub.

Schoonover, Draper Tolman.
Study of Cn. Domitius Corbulo as found in the "Annals of Tacitus." '09(Mr27) c. 8°, pap., *50 c. net. Univ. of Chic.

Schoonover, T. J.
Life and times of Gen. John A. Sutter. Rev. and enl. ed. '07, [1908.] (Mr.) c. 312+3 p. il. por. 8°, $1.50. A. N. Bullock.

Schopenhauer in the air. Hartmann, S. 50 c. S. Hartmann.

Schorer, Edn. H:
Vaccine and serum therapy; incl. also a study of infections, theories of immunity, opsonins and the opsonic index. '09(O) c. 131 p. il. 4°, $2. Mosby.

Schorlemmer, C.
See Roscoe, *Sir* H: Enfield.

Schott, C: Jos.
Theory and practice of book imposition. '10(D31) c. il. 16°, $3.50. C: J. Schott.

Schottenfels, Gertrude Ruth.
Meadow sprite, and other tales of modern Germany. '10(Je4) c. il. 12°, 50 c. Educ. Pub.

Parzival, and other stories from the German. '10(Ja29) c. il. por. 12°, 50 c. Educ. Pub.

Schouler, Ja.
Ideals of the republic. '08(N7) c. O. **$1.50 net. Little, B. & Co.

Law of wills and administration. '10(Je) c. O. $6. Bost. Bk.

Schrader, George Herman Ferdinand.
Friedrich der Grosse, und Der Siebenjährige Krieg; adptd. and ed. by R. H. Allpress. '10(D24) 16°, (Macmillan's new ser. of German texts.) 35 c. net. Macmillan.

Grüne sklaven: [poems.] '08(Je27) c. O. *$1 net. Stechert.

Schrakamp, Josefa, ed.
Ernstes und heiteres; tales by modern German writers; ed. for school use. '10(O1) c. S. 35 c. Am. Bk.

Schreiner, Mrs. Olive, ["Ralph Iron."]
Lost joy and other dreams. '09(D) 32°, (Vest pocket ser.) *25 c. net; *50 c. net; leath., *75 c. net; Japan vellum, *$1 net. T: B. Mosher.

Schreiner, Oswald, and Shorey, Edm. C.
Isolation of harmful organic substances from soils. '09(Je) 53 p. il. 8°, (U. S., Dept. of Agriculture, Bureau of Soils bull.) pap. (Add. Superintendent for price.) U. S., Supt. of Docs.

—, and Skinner, Joshua J:
Some effects of a harmful organic soil constituent. '10(N) 98 p. il. tabs., diagrs., 8°, (U. S., Dept. of Agriculture, Bu. of Soils bull.)

"Schreiner, Tin," pseud.
See Broderick, Therese.

Schreyvogle, C:
My bunkie and others; pictures of western frontier life. '09(N6) c. obl. Q. **$4 net, boxed. Moffat.

Schriber, Fritz.
Complete carriage and wagon painter. '08 (Je20) c. il. 12°, $1. M. T. Richardson.

Schriever, Ja. Boniface, ed.
Complete self-instructing lib. of pract. photography. In 10 v. Popular ed. '10 (My7) c. il. pors. 8°, $35; ¾ leath., $50; leath., $65. Am. Sch. Art.

—, and Cummings, T: Harrison, eds.
Complete self-instructing library of practical photography. 8 v. '08(O10) c. il. pors. 8°, $32; hf. leath., $40; ¾ mor., $48. Am. Sch. Art.

Schrijvers, J.
Hdbk. of pract. economics; tr. from the French by F. M. Capes. '10(Jl) 16+312 p. 8°, $1.35 net. Herder.

Schroeder, Ernest C:
Milk and its products as carriers of tuberculosis infection. '09(My) 3+183-199 p. 8°, (U. S., Dept. of Agriculture, Bu. of Animal Industry, circular.) pap., 5 c.

—, and Cotton, W: Edn.
Tests concerning tubercle bacilli in the circulating blood. '09(O) 23 p. 8°, (U. S., Dept. of Agriculture, Bu. of Animal Industry, bull.) pap. (Add. Superintendent for price.)

Tubercle bacilli in butter; their occurrence, vitality and significance. '08(Je6) 8°, (U. S. Dept. of Agriculture, Bureau of Animal Industry, circular.) pap., 15 c.

Schroeder, Mgr. Jos.
Oberammergau and its Passion Play. 2d rev. ed., from official sources; tr. from the German by Reginald Maxse. '10 (Je4) il. pors. D. pap., 75 c. net. Lemcke.

Schroeder, Reginald.
See Davis, Schroeder, *pseud.*

Schroeder, Thdr.
"Due process of law" in relation to statutory uncertainty and constructive offences. '08(Ag) c. 74 p. O. pap. (Add. pubs. for price.) Free Speech

—, comp. Free press anthology. '10(Mr12) c. 8°, $2. Free Speech; Truth Seeker.

Schrotter, L. von.
See Dock, G:

Schryver, S: Barnett.
General character of the proteins. '09 (Ap3) O. (Monographs on biochemistry.) *80 c. net. Longmans.

SCHUBERT, Franz Peter.
Antcliffe, H: Schubert. 50 c. net; $1 net. Macmillan.

Schubert, Hans von.
Outlines of church history; tr. from the 3d German ed., by Maurice A. Canney; with a supp. chapter by Alice Gardner. '08 (D12) 8°, (Theological translation lib.) *$3 net. Putnam.

Schubert, Hermann.
Mathematical essays and recreations; tr. from the German by T: J. McCormack. 2d ed. '09(Mr) 149 p. *75 c. net. Open Court.

Schuette, H. G:
Athonia; or, the original four hundred. '10(Ag13) c. il. 8°, $1.50. H. G. Schuette.

Schuh, Rev. L: Herman.
Two kings; or, talks for the young. '08(N) c. 129 p. il. 12°, 50 c. Lutheran Bk.

Schulder, Mrs. Irene Dickson.
Virginia Russell. '08(Ag29) c. il. D. $1.25. Cochrane.

Schuler, J:
Language of Richard Wagner's Ring des Nibelungen. '09, [1910.] (My) 97 p. 8°. (Priv. pr.) Steinman & F.

Schultz, Alfr. Paul.
Race or mongrel: brief history of the rise and fall of the ancient races of earth; a theory that the fall of nations is due to intermarriage with alien stocks; a demonstration that a nation's strength is due to racial purity; a prophecy that America will sink to early decay unless immigration is rigorously restricted. '08(O3) c. O. $2.50. L. C. Page.

Schultz, F: Wa., ["F: Walter."]
Sciota, an Indian romance: [poetry.] '08 (O24) c. O. $1. F: W. Schultz.

Solder, its production and application; with a brief history of tin and lead. '08(Ap4) c. D. $1.25. MacNeal; F: W. Schultz.

Schultz, Rob. W., Voysey, C. F. A., Dawber, E. Guy, and others.
Arts connected with building; lectures on craftsmanship and design delivered at Carpenter's Hall, London Wall, for the worshipful Company of Carpenters; ed. by T. Raffles Davison. '09(D11) il. O. *$2 net. Scribner.

Schultz, S: D., comp.
See Canada. Digest.

Schultze, Arth.
Elements of algebra. '10(Je11) c. D. 85 c. net. Macmillan.
Graphic algebra. '08(Mr7) c. il. 12°, *80 c. net. Macmillan.

—, and Manguse, W: P., comps.
Answers to Elements of algebra. '10(O22) 12°, pap., 20 c. net. Macmillan.

Schultze, Carl Emil, ["Bunny."]
Foxy Grandpa and his boys. '08(Ag8) c. il. obl. Q. (Stokes' comic juveniles.) bds., 60 c. Stokes.

Foxy Grandpa and Little Brother. '09 (D25) c. il. in color, obl. Q. bds., 60 c. Stokes.

Schulz, A., comp. and ed.
Modern German sculpture. '00, [1909.] (Ag) il. f°, 3 series, pap., $14, in portfolio. Hessling

Schumacher, Tony.
Tower angel; tr. from the German by Mary E. Ireland. '08(Ag1) c. D. $1. Saalfield.

Schumaker, E: Edg.
New era in natural philosophy. '08(My9) c. 12°, $2. E: Schumaker.

Supplementary lecture no. 1 to The new era in natural philosophy. '09(F6) c. D. pap., 50 c. E: Schumaker.

Schuré, Edouard.
Jesus: the last great initiate; tr. by F. Rothwell. '09(S) 148 p. 12°, (Psychic lib.) bds., *$1.25 net. Badger.

Orpheus and Krishna, the great initiates of the East and West. '09(S) 154 p. 12°, (Psychic lib.) bds., *$1.25 net. Badger.

Pythagoras and his system of philosophy. '09(S) 180 p. 12°, (Psychic lib.) bds., *$1.25 net. Badger.

Schurig, Richard.
Tabulae caelestes continentes stellas caeli borealis nec non australis nudis oculis conspicuas, (Himmels-atlas enthaltend alle mit blossen augen sichtbaren sterne beider hemisphaeren; in 2ter neubearbeiteter und ergänzter auflage, herausgegeben von De P. Götz.) '09(Je26) F. $1. Lemcke.

Schurz, Carl.
Reminiscences. v. 3; with a sketch of his life and public services from 1869 to 1906, by Frederic Bancroft and W: A. Dunning. '08(D12) c. il. pors. O. **$3 net. McClure.

Schuster, Arth.
Introd. to the theory of optics. 2d ed., rev. '10(Mr12) figs. O. $4. Longmans.

Schütze, Martin.
Hero and Leander: a tragedy. '08(O17) c. D. **$1.25 net. Holt.

Judith; tragedy in 5 acts. '10(N5) c. D. $1.25 net. Holt.

Schuyler, H: C.
Charity of Christ. '10(N19) c. il. 16°, (Virtues of Christ ser.) 50 c. net. P: Reilly.

Courage of Christ. '09(D18) c. il. 16°, (Virtues of Christ ser.) *50 c. net. P: Reilly.

Schuyler, Ja. Dix.
Reservoirs: for irrigation, water-power, and domestic water supply; with an account of various types of dams. 2d ed., rev. and enl. '08(D12) il. figs. 8°, $6. Wiley.

Schuyler, Rob. Livingston.
Transition in Illinois from British to American government. '09(Je5) c. 8°, *$1.25 net. Lemcke.

Schwann, C: Duncan.
Too many women; bachelor's story. '10 (S24) c. D. $1.25. Stokes.

Schwann, H.
German-French and French-German pocket dictionary. '09(Mr13) 32°, (Miniature reference lib.) leath., 50 c. Dutton.

Schwartz, G: Foss.
Catechism of harmony. '09(F20) c. S. pap., 50 c. White-S.

Schwartz, H: B.
In Togo's country: some studies in Satsuma and other little known parts of Japan. '08(O3) c. il. D. *$1.50 net. Jennings.

Schwartz, Joost Marius Willem Van der Poorten, ["Maarten Maartens."]
Brothers all. '09(Je19) D. †$1.50. Appleton.

Harmen Pols. '10(O22) c. D. $1.35 net. Lane.

Price of Lis Doris. '09(N13) c. D. †$1.50. Appleton.

Schwartz, Julia Augusta.
Wonderful little lives. '09(O23) c. il. D. $1.50. Little, B. & Co.

Schwarz, Amelia Grant.
See "Laurence, Hope," *pseud.*

Schwarz, Ernest Hubert Lewis.
Causal geology. '10(Ag6) 8°, $2.50 net. Van Nostrand.

Schwarz, J: Robley, comp.
Cumberland blue book: a compendium of information of lower Cumberland County, [Pa.] '08(Mr) c. 100 p. il. O. $1. J: R. Schwarz.

Schwegler, Friedrich Karl Albert.
History of philosophy in epitome; tr. from the 1st ed. of the orig. German by Julius H. Seelye; rev. from the 9th German ed., with an appendix, by B: E. Smith. '08 (D5) c. 8°, $2. Appleton.

Schweinitz, G: Edm. de, M.D.
Diseases of the eye. 6th rev. ed. '10(Je) 945 p. il. 8°, $5 net; hf. mor., $6.50 net. Saunders.

—, and Holloway, T: Beaver.
Pulsating exophthalmos; its etiology, symptomatology, pathogenesis, and treatment. '08(D) c. 9-124 p. tabs., 8°, *$2 net. Saunders.

Schweitzer, Albert.
Quest of the historical Jesus; critical study of its progress from Reimarus to Wrede; tr. by W. Montgomery, with a preface by F. C. Burkett. '10(Ap9) O. $3.50 net. Macmillan.

Schwenckfeld von Ossig, Caspar.
Corpus Schwenckfeldianorum; pub. under the auspices of the Schwenckfelder church, Pennsylvania, and the Hartford Theological Seminary, Hartford, Ct. v. 1, A study of the earliest letters of Caspar Schwenckfeld v. Ossig; ed. by Chester D: Hartranft, assisted by associate editors Otto Bernbam Schlutter and Elmer Elsworth Schultz Johnson. '08(Ap25) O. hf. leath., *$7.50 net. Lemcke.

SCHWENKFELDERIAN CHURCH.
See Hymns and hymn writers.

Schwiegersohn (Der). *See* Baumbach, R.

SCIENCE.
Ackerman, A. S. E. Popular fallacies. *$1.50 net. Lippincott.
Albe, E: E. F. d'. Wonders of physical science. 50 c. net. Macmillan.
Battell, J. Ellen; or, the whisperings of an old pine tree: [talks about science.] v. 2. $3; $4. Am. Pub. Co., (Vt.)
Bray, H: T. Living universe. $3.50. Truro.
Columbia University lectures on science, philosophy and art, 1907-1908. *$5 net. Lemcke.
Darwin, *Sir* G: H. Scientific papers. v. 1-3. ea., *$4.50. Putnam.
Getman, F: H. Introd. to physical science. **$1.50 net. Wiley.
Gibson, C: R. Scientific ideas of to-day. *$1.50 net. Lippincott.
Hodson, F., *ed.* Broad lines in science teaching. *$1.25 net. Macmillan.
Houllevigue, A. C. L. Evolution of the sciences. $2 net. Van Nostrand.
Lodge, *Sir* O. J. Science and immortality. *$2 net. Moffat.
Mortensen, A. C. Law of transformation in nature of natural bodies: [science applied to man's moral development.] 50 c. A. C. Mortensen.
Pettigrew, J. B. Design in nature. 3 v. *$16 net. Longmans.
Poincaré, J. H. Value of science. *$1.25 net. Science Pr., (N. Y.)
Pratt Institute, Brooklyn, N. Y. *Free Library.* Technical books of 1908. (Add. Institute for price.) Pratt Inst.
Ratti, A. de. Simple scientific experiments. 25 c. Spon.
Rolt-Wheeler, F., *ed.* Science-history of the universe. $6. Current Lit.
Royal Society of London. Catalogue of scientific papers, 1800-1900; subject index. v. 11, Mechanics. *$5 net; *$6.50 net. Putnam.
Russell, T. B. Science at home: simple experiments. 75 c. Fenno.
Russell, W. S. C., *and* Kelly, H. C. Lab'y manual of first year science. 75 c. Holt.
Schapper, H. Laboratory guide for students in physical sciences. $1. Wiley.
Seneca, L. A. Physical science in the time of Nero; tr. of Quaestiones naturales. $3.50 net. Macmillan.
Seward, A. C:, *ed.* Darwin and modern science. *$5 net. Putnam.
Sheehy, J. Heat and cold; or, the key to the universe. $1.75. J. Sheehy.

SCIENCE.—*Continued.*
Sihler, E. G. Testimonium animæ; or, Greek and Roman before Jesus Christ. **$2.25 net. Stechert.
Wilmshurst, W. L. Christianity and science. *$1 net. Badger.
Woodhull, J: F. How the public will solve our problems of science teaching. gratis. C: P. Cary.
Woollatt, G: H: Laboratory arts: teacher's hdbk. dealing with materials and tools used in construction, adjustment and repair of scientific instruments. $1 net. Longmans.
See also Astrology;—Astronomy;—Biology;—Botany;—Chemistry; — Crystallography;—Electricity;—Ethics;—Ethnology; — Evolution; — Geography; — Geology; — History; — Inventions; —Language;—Law;—Logic; — Man; — Mathematics;—Medicine;—Meteorclogy;—Military art and science; — Mineralogy; — Paleontology; — Philosophy;—Physical geography; — Physics;— Political economy;—Poltical science;—Psychical research;—Psychology;—Religion and science;—Scientists;—Social science; — Spectrum; —Surgery;—Theology;—Useful arts;—Zoology.

Science and art. Jones, C. M. (Add. author for price.) C. M. Jones.
Science and art of debate. Shurter, E. D. *$1.25 net. Neale.
Science and art of nursing: guide to the various branches of nursing, theoretical and practical, by medical and nursing authorities. In 4 v. '09(O23) col. il. figs. O. per set, *$7.50 net. Cassell.
Science and art of poultry culture. Hawks, E. B. $2.75. E. B. Hawks.
Science and art of writing life insurance. Young, M. $2. N. Y. Insurance.
Science and key of life. In 6 v. v. 4-6. Hodges, H: C. ea., $2. Astro Pub.
Science and philosophy of the organism. Driesch, H. In 2 v. v. 2. *$3 net. Macmillan.
Science and practice of cheese making. Van Slyke, L. L. *$1.75 net. Judd.
SCIENCE AND RELIGION.
See Religion and science.
Science and singing. White, E. G. $1.25. T: J. Donlan.
Science and suffrage. Brashere, O. M. 25c. O. M. Brashere.
Science lib. See Appleton's.
Science of accounts made clear and simple. Allen, G: $1. Edwards.
Science of advertising. *See* Balmer, E. *and* T.
Science of being well. Wattles, W. D. $1. E. J. Towne.
Science of commercial bookkeeping. Hirsch, A. $2. J. S. Ogilvie.
Science of diamonds. Chester, C. B. 50 c. Chester & B.
Science of getting rich. Wattles, W. D. $1. E. J. Towne.
Science of happiness. Williams, H: S. $2 net. Harper.
Science of human life. Dunham, W: R. $1. Badger.
Science of jurisprudence. Taylor, H. $3.50 Macmillan.
Science of life and the larger hope. Mercer, J: E: $1.20 net. Longmans.
Science of living. Sadler, W: S. $1.50 net. McClurg.
Science of minds. Godlover, H. B. $1. H. B. Godlover.
Science of poetry and philosophy of language. Maxim, H. $2.50 net. Funk.
Science of railways. *See* Kirkman, Marshall Monroe.
Science of skirt drafting. Williams, W. R. $10. Gazette Co.
Science of trapping. Kreps, E. H. 60 c. A. R. Harding.
Science of value. O. H: Rawie.
—Rawie. In quest of prosperity.—Wages and the price of land. ea., 25 c.
Science ser. See Blakiston's;—Putnam's.
Science text-books. See Heath's.
Science, the mind, revelation, the heart of God. Barwell, J. W. 25 c. Jacobs & H.
Scientific American hdbk. of travel. Hopkins, A. A., *comp. and ed.* $2 net; $2.50 net. Munn.
Scientific American handbook relating to patents, designs, trade-marks, copyrights, etc. Munn & Co. gratis. Munn.
Scientific American index of manufacturers: "who's who" among American manufacturers. '08(My23) c. 12°. (Add. pubs. for price.) Scientific American.
Scientific aspects of Luther Burbank's work. Jordan, D: S. *$1.75 net. A. M. Robertson.
Scientific baseball. McGraw, J: J. 10 c. R: K. Fox.
Scientific Christianity. Leighton, G. $1.25 net. Moffat.
Scientific education of dogs. H., H. $1.75. W: R. Jenkins.
Scientific feeding of animals. Kellner, O. $1.90 net. Macmillan.
Scientific foundations of analytical chemistry. Ostwald, W. *$2 net. Macmillan.
Scientific French reader. Dike, F. H., *comp.* $1. Silver.
Scientific ideas of to-day. Gibson, C: R. *$1.50 net. Lippincott.
Scientific living for prolonging the term of human life. Brown, *Mrs.* L. N. $1. Health-Culture.
Scientific magical experiments. Kirsch, W: 50 c. W: Kirsch.
Scientific nutrition simplified. Brown, G. *75 c. net. G. Brown.
Scientific tone production. James, *Mrs.* M. I. *$1.25 net. C: W. Thompson.
SCIENTISTS.
Cattell, J. M., *ed.* American men of science. $5. Science Pr. (N. Y.)
Jordan, D: S., *ed.* Leading American men of science. $1.75 net. Holt.
Walsh, J. J. Catholic churchmen in science: 1st ser.; 2d ser. ea., $1 net. Dolphin.
Sciota, an Indian romance. Schultz, F: W. $1. F: W. Schultz.
Scioto speculation. Belote, T. T: 75 c. Univ. of Cin.
Scissors book. Barnes, B. 75 c. Dodd.
Scissors Mother Goose. Barnes, B. 75 c. Dodd.
SCITUATE, Mass.
Vital records of Scituate, Mass., to the year 1850. 2 v. $11. N. E. Hist.

Scituate, Mass., Second Church. Scituate, Massachusetts: Second Church records (in abstract), 1645-1850. '09, [1910.] (F) 111 p. 8°, $2.50. W. J. Litchfield.

Sclater, J. R. P.
Sons of strength; [study of Meredith's poems.] '10(S17) c. 16°, bds., 35 c. net. Revell.

Scoble, And. Harvey.
Sun time and cloud time; verses, sketches, tales. '09(Ja9) c. D. $1. Fenno.

Scofield, Carl Schurz, and Rogers, Shober J.
Truckee-Carson experiment farm. '09(O) 38 p. il. map, 8°, (U. S., Dept. of Agriculture, Bu. of Plant Industry. bull.) pap.

Scofield, Rev. Cyrus Ingerson.
See Bible.

Scofield, Levi Tucker.
Retreat from Pulaski to Nashville, Tenn.; battle of Franklin, Tennessee, Nov. 30th, 1864; with maps, sketches, portraits and photographic views. '09(N) 7-67 p. il. 8°. (Add. pubs. for price.) Burrows.

Scofield, W: J.
Witness for Jesus Christ; eternity back; the present time; eternity forward as revealed by the Word of God. '08(Ja18) 8°, pap., 25 c. W: J. Scofield.

Scogin, Mrs. S: Martha Caldwell, and Howe, J: Dicks.
Down on the old plantation; original sketches of every-day life on a Mississippi cotton plantation. '09(Mr27) il. por. 12°, pap., 25 c. J: D. Howe.

Scollard, Clinton.
Chords of the zither. '10(N5) c. 8°, $1.25. G: W: Browning.
Knight of the highway. '08(D) c. 5+228 p. 12°, $1. G: W: Browning.
Song for the tercentenary of Lake Champlain. '09(S) 32 p. 12°, pap., 50 c. G: W: Browning.
Vicar of the marches. '10(D24) O. $1.20 net. Sherman, F.
Voices and visions. '08(My2) c. D. *$1 net. Sherman, F.

—, and Jones, T: S., jr.
From the heart of the hills: [poems.] '10(Mr5) c. 16°, bds., $1. G: W: Browning.
Sapphics: [poems.] '10(Ag6) O. bds., $1 net; pap., 50 c. net. (100 copies.) G: W. Browning.

Scoones, P., and Todd, L.
Eton algebra. pt. 1. '08(O24) diagrs., 12°, *50 c. net. Macmillan.

Scope and content of the district high school. Morrison, G. B. 25 c. G. B. Morrison.

Scope and content of the science of anthropology. Dieserud, J. *$2 net. Open Court.

Score (The). Harrison, *Mrs.* M. St. L. K. †$1.50. Dutton.

Scorpio. Chaloner, J. A. $1.50. Palmetto Press.

Scorso, Rob. Ryer.
Amateur taxidermist; complete course of instruction in mounting mammals, birds, snakes, fish and minor specimens. '10 (N5) c. il. 8°, 50 c. Fur News.

SCOTCH-IRISH IN THE UNITED STATES.
Bolton, C: K. Scotch Irish pioneers in Ulster and America. $2 net. Bacon & B.

SCOTLAND.
Adam, F. Clans, septs and regiments of the Scottish Highlands. *$6 net. Scribner.
Briggs, E. E: Angling and art in Scotland. *$4 net. Longmans.
Brown, P: H. History of Scotland. In 3 v. v. 3. $1.50. Putnam.
Calderwood, W: L. Salmon rivers and lochs of Scotland. *$6 net. Longmans.
Catholic Highlands of Scotland. v. 1. *$1.10 net. Herder.
Caw, J. L. Scottish painting. *$8 net. Stokes.
Crockett, S: R. Footsteps of Scott. *$1.25 net. Jacobs.
Davidson, J:, *and* Gray, A. Scottish staple at Veere. *$4.50 net. Longmans.
Graham, H. Group of Scottish women. *$3.50 net. Duffield.
Kerr, J: Scottish education. $2 net. Putnam.
Lang, J. Land of romance: the Border; its hist. and legend. $2.50 net. Dodge.
Leith, W: F. Memoirs of Scottish Catholics during the XVIIth and XVIIIth centuries. In 2 v. *$7 net. Longmans.
Mackenzie, W. M. Outline of Scottish history. $1.25. Macmillan.
Marshall, H. E. Scotland's story. $2.75 net. Stokes.
Maxwell, *Sir* H. E. Scottish gardens. *$6 net. Longmans.
Moncrieff, A. R. H. Heart of Scotland. *$3 net. Macmillan.
Ramsay, E: B. B. Reminiscences of Scottish life and character. *$2.75 net. McClurg.
Sloan, J. M. Galloway. *$2 net. Macmillan.
Strong, J: Hist. of secondary education in Scotland. $2.50. Oxford Univ.
Warrack, A. Scots' dialect dict. $3 net. Lippincott.
See also Clyde river;—Edinburgh;—Gowrie conspiracy;—Granton;—Reformation.

Scott, Rev. A. Boyd.
Branches of the cross. '09(D) 8+329 p. O. *$1.50 net. Doran.

Scott, A. Macallum.
Through Finland. '09(Mr13) 12°, *$1.25 net. Dutton.

Scott, Angelo Cyrus.
Practical English. '08(N) c. 208 p. 12°, 80 c. Row, P. & Co.

Scott, C. A. Dawson-.
See Dawson-Scott, C. A.

Scott, Charlotte Angas.
Introd. acct. of certain modern ideas and methods in plain analytical geometry. '10 (F5) price changed from *$2.50 net to *$3 net. Macmillan.

Scott, Colin Alex.
Social education. '08(S19) c. diagrs., D. $1.25. Ginn.

Scott, Dukinfield H:
Introduction to structural botany. 5th ed. 2 pts. pt. 1, Flowering plants; pt. 2, Flowerless plants. '08(Ap18) il. 12°, ea., *$1 net. Macmillan.
Studies in fossil botany. 2d ed. v. 1. '08 (Je13) 12°, *$2 net; v. 2. '09(Ag14) il. 8°, *$4 net. Macmillan.

Scott, E:
New dancing as it should be; pract. guide for the ballroom, the classroom and the stage. '10(D10) 12°, 50 c. Dutton.

Scott, Rev. Elwood.
Paradise, the city and throne. '09(N) 149 p. 12°, 80 c.; pap., 50 c. E. Scott.

Scott, Ernest Findlay, D.D.
Apologetic of the New Testament. '08 (F8) D. (Crown theological lib.) *$1.50 net. Putnam.
Historical and religious value of the fourth Gospel. '09(N13) c. S. (Modern religious problems.) 50 c. Houghton M.

Scott, Fred Newton.
Genesis of speech; repr. from the publications of the Modern language Association. '09(Mr6) O. pap. (Add. pubs. for price.) Modern Lang. Assoc.

—, and Denney, Jos. Villiers.
Elem. English composistion. New ed., rev. and rewritten. '08(S12) il. 12°, 80 c. Allyn & B.
Paragraph-writing; rhetoric for colleges. New ed., rewritten and much enl. '09 (N20) c. il. 12°, $1.25. Allyn & B.

Scott, H. Fletcher, and Van Tuyl, C: H.
Cæsar composition book. '10(Jl30) c. D. bds., 40 c. Scott, F. & Co.

Scott, H: Brownfield.
Lorelei and other poems with prose settings. '10(N5) c. il. O. $1. Werner Co.

Scott, H: Wilson.
Courts of the state of New York; their history, development and jurisdiction; embracing a complete history of all the courts and tribunals of justice, both colonial and state, established from the first settlement of Manhattan Island and incl. the status and jurisdiction of all the cts. of the state as now constituted. '09(Mr) c. 506 p. O. $5. Wilson Pub. Co.
Evolution of law; historical review, based upon the author's commentaries on the evolution of law, following the thread from the earliest known history of mankind to the present era and times; observations by the late Senator Ingalls on law, government and biography. 4th ed. '08, [1909.] (Mr) c. 25-165 p. 8°, $3; mor., $4. Wilson Pub. Co.

Scott, Hugh Lenox.
Testimony regarding trouble on Navajo Reservation; letter from the secretary of the interior, transmitting a copy of the correspondence and testimony taken by Col. H. L. Scott during the investigation of charges preferred by Rev. H. R. Antes, regarding the trouble on the Navajo Reservation two years ago. '09(My) 56 p. 8°. (Add. Superintendent for price.) U. S., Supt. of Docs.

Scott, Ja. Brown.
Hague Peace Conference of 1899 and 1907. In 2 v. '09(Je19) 8°, $5. Johns Hopkins.
Work of the second Hague Conference. '08(Mr14) D. pap., gratis. Assoc. Int. Conciliation.
See also Hill, D: Jayne.
—, ed. Texts of the Peace Conferences at the Hague, 1899 and 1907; with Eng. translation and appendix of rel. documents; ed., with an introd.; prefatory note by Elihu Root. '08(D5) c. O. $2. Ginn.

Scott, Ja. Foster.
Heredity and morals as affected by the use and abuse of the sexual instinct. 2d ed., rev. and enl. '08(F8) c. il. 12°, $2. Treat.

Scott, Jennie.
Pilgrimage to Canaan. '08(Ag1) c. il. pors. maps, 8°, $1.75. Jennie Scott.

Scott, J: Reed.
The impostor; tale of old Annapolis. '10(O8) c. col. il. D. $1.50. Lippincott.
Princess Dehra. '10(D) 75 c. Burt.
Princess Dehra. '08(Je27) c. il. D. †$1.50. Lippincott.
Woman in question. '09(My22) c. il. D. †$1.50. Lippincott.

Scott, J. W. Robertson-.
See Robertson-Scott, J. W.

Scott, Laura.
Telephones; interchange of service. '09 (Mr6) D. (Comparative legislation bull.) pap., 25 c. Wisconsin Free Lib.

Scott, Laurence Winfield.
Great crisis in the life of Christ; His trials and crucifixion. '09 (Ap) c. 235 p. por. 12°, $1. F: L: Rowe.

Scott, Leader.
Sculpture: Gothic, Renaissance and modern. '10(D) 12°, (Hdbks. of art hist.) hf. leath., $1.25. Gorham.

Scott, Leroy.
Shears of destiny. '10(O8) c. il. D. $1.20, boxed. Doubleday, P.

Scott, Mrs. Mary Monica Maxwell-.
Madame Elizabeth de France, 1764-1794. '08(D5) il. pors. O. *$3.50 net. Longmans.

Scott, Ralph.
Automatic block signals and signal circuits: American practice in the installation and maintenance of signals electrically controlled. '08(Ap18) c. il. 8°, *$2.50 net. McGraw.

Scott, Rob., D.D.
Pauline Epistles: critical study. '09(My15) O. (Literature of the New Testament.) *$2 net. Scribner.

—, and Stiles, W: Curtis, eds.
Modern sermons by world scholars; introd. by Newell Dwight Hillis. 10 v. '10 (Je4) c. 16°, $7.50. Funk.

Scott, S. R., tr. and ed.
Visigothic code; tr. from the orig. Latin. '10(Ag) c. O. $5. Boston Bk.

Scott, Sydney R.
See West, C: Ernest.

Scott, Temple.
Pleasure of reading. '09(N20) c. 8°, *$1.25 net. M. Kennerley.
Pleasure of reading the Bible. '09(O30) c. D. bds., 50 c.; flex. leath., $1. M. Kennerley.
—, comp. Christmas treasury of song and verse. '10(D31) c. S. front. D. $1.25 net. Baker & T.
In praise of gardens. '10(Ap23) c. front. S. $1.25. Baker & T.

SCOTT, Thomas A.
Smith, F. H. Capt. Thomas A. Scott, master diver. **60 c. net. Am. Unitarian.

Scott, Sir Wa.
Works. De luxe ed. 12 v. '10(N) il. levant, $36. Crowell.
Works. 12 v. New imperial lib. ed. '10 (D) il. 8°, ea., $1.25; hf. cf., $2.25. New il. sterling ed. ea., $1. (Sets only.) Estes.
Works. De luxe ed. 25 v. '10(D) 16°, ea., mor., $1.50 net. (Sets only.) Nelson.
Complete novels and tales. 24 v. '08(Je27) c. il. hf. mor., $30. Lamb Pub.
Novels. 12 v. '10(D) 16°, ea., mor., $2.50 net. (Sets only.) Nelson.
Complete poetical works. '08(D19) 12°, (Crowell's thin paper poets.) ooze leath., $1.75, boxed. Crowell.
Poetical works; ed. by J. Logie Robertson. '10(Jl30) 12°, (Oxford poets.) $1.50 net; pap., $1.75 net. Oxford Univ.
Black dwarf and Legend of Montrose. Oxford ed. '09, [1910.] (Mr) 50 c. Oxford Univ.
Bride of Lammermoor. Oxford ed. '09, [1910.] (Mr) 50 c. Oxford Univ.
Guy Mannering; or, the astrologer. Oxford ed. '10(Ap2) D. 50 c. Oxford Univ.
Ivanhoe; abr. by Herbert P. Williams. '10 (O15) c. col. il. D. $1.50. Appleton.
Ivanhoe. '08(O17) 16°, (Best books ser.) leath., *$1 net. Dutton.
Ivanhoe; with an introd. and notes by M. A. Eaton. '09(Jl1c) c. por. D. 50 c. Educ. Pub.
Ivanhoe; with a preface by the Hon. Mrs. Maxwell Scott of Abbottsford. '08(O24) il. O. $2.50. Lippincott.
Ivanhoe; with an introd. and explanatory notes. '08, [1909.] (Ja) c. 10+486 p. por. map, 12°, (Standard literature ser.) 40 c.; condensed, 30 c. Newson.
Ivanhoe; ed. by C. E. Theodosius. [1910.] (Mr) 8°, 50 c. Oxford Univ.
Kenilworth; with a preface by the Hon. Mrs. Maxwell Scott of Abbottsford. '08 (O24) il. O. $2.50. Lippincott.
Lady of the lake; ed. and comp., with an introd. and notes, by C: E. S. Fielden. '08(N) c. 42+166 p. map, 12°, (Lakeside ser. of English readings.) pap., 20 c. Ainsworth.
Lady of the lake; il. [in col.] by Howard Chandler Christy. '10(D31) Q. $3, boxed. Bobbs-M.
Lady of the lake; ed. by W. F. Rocheleau. '08, [1909.] (F) c. 135 p. map, 8°, 20 c. O. Brewer.
Lady of the lake; ed. with notes by W: J. Rolfe. '08(D19) il. 12°, 75 c. Houghton M.
Lady of the lake; ed. by Florus A. Barbour. '10(O29) c. por. il. (partly col.) 12°, (Canterbury classics.) 45 c. Rand, McN. & Co.
Lady of the lake; ed., with introd. and notes, by Ralph Hartt Bowles. '09(Ap17) c. por. 16°, (Scribner English classics.) **25 c. net. Scribner.

SCOTT, *Sir* Walter.—*Continued.*
Legend of Montrose; ed. by G. S. Gordon. [1910.] (Mr) map, 8°, 50 c. Oxford Univ.
Lives of the novelists; introd. by G: F. Bateman Saintsbury. '10(N5) 16°, (Everyman's lib.) 35 c. net; leath., 70 c. net. Dutton.
Quentin Durward; abr. by Herbert P. Williams. '10(O15) c. col. il. D. $1.50. Appleton.
Quentin Durward; ed., with notes and an introd., by Mary E. Adams. '10(Jl2) c. map, D. (Longmans' English classics.) 25 c. net. Longmans.
Quentin Durward; ed. for school use by W: E: Simonds. '10(Ap16) c. S. (Lake English classics.) 45 c. Scott, F. & Co.
Rob Roy; ed., with introd., notes and glossary, by Rob. S. Rait. '08(N14) il. D. 50 c. Oxford Univ.
Scott: [selections;] ed. by Arth. Ja. Grant. '09(N6) por. 12°, (Masters of literature.) *$1.10 net.. Macmillan.
Tales of a grandfather, being the history of Scotland from the earliest period to the Battle of Flodden, 1513; ed., with introd. and notes, by P. Giles. '09(My) 6+308 p. 16°, (Cambridge English literature for schools.) *40 c. net. Putnam.
Talisman; abr. by Herbert P. Williams. '10(O15) c. col. il. D. $1.50. Appleton.
Talisman; with a preface by the Hon. Mrs. Maxwell Scott of Abbottsford. '08 (O24) il. O. $2.50. Lippincott.
Talisman; ed. by H. B. George. [1910.] (Mr) 8°, 50 c. Oxford Univ.
Waverley; or, 'tis sixty years since; ed., with introd., notes, and glossary, by A. D. Innes. '09(D4) il. pors. D. 50 c. Oxford Univ.
Woodstock; or, the cavalier. '10(Ap2) 16°, (Everyman's lib.) 35 c. net; leath., 70 c. net. Dutton.
Woodstock; ed., with introd., notes and glossary, by J. S. C. Bridge. '08(N14) il. D. 50 c. Oxford Univ.

SCOTT, *Sir* Walter.
Ball, M. Sir Walter Scott as a critic of literature. *$1 net. Lemcke.
Canning, A. S. G: Sir Walter Scott studied in eight novels. $2.50 net. Wessels & B.
Crockett, S: R. Footsteps of Scott. *$1.25 net. Jacobs.
Crockett, S: R. Red cap tales from Sir Walter Scott. 7 v. ea., 75 c. net. Macmillan.
Grey, H: Key to the Waverley novels in chronological sequence. $1. Bowman.
Husband, M. F. A. Dict. of the characters in the Waverley novels of Sir Walter Scott. $3 net. Dutton.
Jackson, A. F., *ed.* Ivanhoe; retold.—The talisman. ea., 75 c. net. Jacobs.
Lang, A. Sir Walter Scott and the border minstrelsy. $1.50 net. Longmans.
Lockhart, J: G. Selections from Lockhart's life of Sir Walter Scott. 30 c. net. Macmillan.
MacCunn, F. S. Sir Walter Scott's friends. $3 net. Lane.

Scott, Sir Wa.—*Continued.*
McSpadden, J. W., *ed.* Waverley synopses: guide to plots and characters of Waverley novels. 50 c. Crowell.

Wiley, K. Pet Marjorie and Sir Walter Scott. *$1 net; *75 c. net. Cochrane.

Scott, Wa. Dill.
Psychology of advertising. '08(D26) c. il. O. **$2 net. Small.

Scott, Wa. L.
Threads of moss. '08(Ag) c. 56 p. 8°, $1. W. L. Scott.

Scott, W: Amasa.
Money and banking. 4th ed., rewritten, rearranged and enl.. '10(D) c. 9+377 p. 8°, $2. Holt.
"List of references" (14 p.).

Scott-James, R. A.
Englishman in Ireland; impressions of a journey in a canoe by lough, river and canal. '10(D10) il. 8°, $2 net. Dutton.

Modernism and romance. '08(Mr14) O. *$2.50 net. Lane.

SCOTT FAMILY.
See Genealogies: Cole, A. S., *comp.*

SCOTT TOWNSHIP, **Mahaska Co., Ia.**
See Iowa.

Scottie and his lady. Morse, M. F. $1.10 net. Houghton M.

Scottish education. Kerr, J: $2 net. Putnam.

Scottish fairy book. Grierson, E. W. $1.50 net. Stokes.

Scottish gardens. Maxwell, *Sir* H. E. *$6 net. Longmans.

Scottish men of letters. Graham, H: G. *$2 net. Macmillan.

Scottish painting. Caw, J. L. *$8 net. Stokes.

Scottish poems. *See* Bruce, Wallace.

Scottish staple at Veere. Davidson, J: *$4.50 net. Longmans.

Scottish toasts. Welsh, C. 50 c. Caldwell.

Scourge (The). Dawson, F. W. $1.50. Small.

Scout's story. Vaughan, O. $1.25. Estes.

SCOUTS.
See Biography.

Scoville, S., jr.
See On the gridiron.

Scrap-book of elementary mathematics. White, W: F. $1. Open Court.

Screen (The). Brown, V. $1.25 net. Dutton.

Screens and galleries in English churches. Bond, F. $2 Oxford Univ.

SCREW MACHINES.
See Machinery.

SCREW PROPELLER.
See Ships and shipbuilding.

Screw thread cutting. '09(Ap3) c. diagrs., 8°, (Machinery's reference ser.) pap., 25 c. Indust. Press.

Screw thread tools and gages. '09(Ap3) c. diagrs., 8°, (Machinery reference ser.) pap., 25 c. Indust. Press.

SCREWS.
De Vries, D. Calculation of change-wheels for screw-cutting on lathes. $1.25. Spon.

Goodrich, C. L., *and* Stanley, F. A. Automatic screw machines and their tools. $2. Hill Pub.

Scribe, Augustin Eugène.
Mon étoilè; ed. by Neil S. Snodgrass. '10 (Ja29) S. (Crowell's shorter French texts.) *25 c. net. Crowell.

—, and Legouvé, Gabriel Jean Baptiste Ernest Wilfrid.
Bataille de dames; ou, un duel en armour; comédie en trois actes; ed., with introd., notes and vocabulary, by C: A. Eggert. '08(D26) c. S. 30 c. Am. Bk.

SCRIBNER, Gilbert Hilton.
Gilbert Hilton Scribner; memorial addresses. '10(S) 83 p. por. 8°. (Not for sale.) Fortnightly Club Anthropology.

Scribner's classics in art ser. 8°. Scribner.
—Chamberlain. George Romney. $5.
—Finberg. Turner's sketches and drawings. $4 net.

Scribner's contemporary science ser.; ed. by H: Havelock Ellis. il. D. *$1.50 net. Scribner.
—Ellis. The criminal.
—Keane. Modern organic chemistry.

Scribner's English classics; ed. by F. H. Sykes. D and S. Scribner.
—Browning. Shorter poems.
—Burke. Speech on conciliation with the colonies.
—Carlyle. Essay on Burns.
—Coleridge. Ancient mariner.
—Eliot. Silas Marner.
—Gaskell. Cranford.
—Macaulay. Life and writings of Addison; Samuel Johnson.
—Milton. Comus, L'allegro, Il penseroso, and Lycidas, with other shorter poems.
—Scott. Lady of the lake.
—Shakespeare. Julius Cæsar.—Macbeth.
—Washington *and* Webster. Farewell address and Bunker Hill oration.

Scribner's great etchers ser. il. 4°, *$2.50 net. Scribner.
—Rembrandt van Rhyn. Etchings.

Scribner's lib. of art ser. il. 8°, *$2 net. Scribner.
—Beruete y Moret. School of Madrid.
—De Selincourt. William Blake.
—Millman. Sir Christopher Wren.

Scribner's lib. of literary history. 8°, $4. Scribner.
—Brückner. Literary history of Russia.

Scribner's makers of British art; ed. by Ja. Alex. Manson. il. pors. 12°, *$1.25 net. Scribner.
—Fletcher. Richard Wilson.
—Reid. Sir J. E. Millais.

Scribner's music story ser.; ed. by F. J. Crowest. 12°, *$1.25 net.
—Lee. Story of opera.
—Lucas. Story of musical form.

Scribner's social science ser. D. $1. Scribner.
—Morrison. Crime and its causes.

Scripta Minoa. Evans, A. J: v. 1. $12.75. Oxford Univ.

Scriptorum classicorum bibliotheca Oxoniensis. See Oxford classical texts.

Scriptural and Catholic truth and worship. Meyrick, F. $1. Longmans.

Scripture and song in worship. Shephardson, F. W., *ed.* *50 c. net. Univ. of Chic.

SCRIPTURES.
See Bible.

Scriva, Ludovico.
Veneris tribunal; Ludovico Scriva Cavallero Valenciano. [facsim.] '02, [1909.] (N) 67 p. 8°, $6 (200 copies). Hispanic Soc.

Scriven, G: P.
Transmission of military information: outline of the service of a corps of intelligence, or of a signal corps, under modern conditions affecting the transmission of military information to troops in the field, and to the coast defense. '08(O3) c. il. O. (Not for sale.) G: P. Scriven.

Scroll of wisdom. Sadi *the Persian.* *40 c. net. Dutton.

Scudder, Doremus.
Our children for Christ. New ed. '09 (O23) c. 16°, pap., *15 c. net. Revell.
Passion for reality. '10(Jl9) c. 12°, 50 c. net. Revell.

Scudder, Horace Elisha, ed.
Children's book; collection of the best and most famous stories and poems. [New holiday ed.] '10(O29) c. Q. $2.50. Houghton M.

Scudder, Myron Tracy.
Field day and play picnic for country children. '08(Jl11) il. D. (Russell Sage Foundation pub.) pap., 10 c. Charities Pub.

Scudder, Sam.
Counterfeit citizen. '08(Je20) c. D. $1.50. B'way Pub.

Scull, D:
Union with God in thought and faith. '08 (O3) il. pors. O. **$1 net. Winston.

Scullin, P. H.
Socialism means slavery for the working man. [1910.] (D) 32 p. O. pap., gratis. P. H. Scullin.

SCULPIN.
Jordan, D: S., *and* Thompson, W: F. Description of a new species of deep-water sculpin. U. S., Supt. of Docs.

SCULPTORS.
Gardner, E. A. Six Greek sculptors. $2 net. Scribner.

Sculptors of life. Yates, T: *$1 net. Armstrong.

SCULPTURE.
Balcarro, *Lord.* Evolution of Italian sculpture. *$6 net. Dutton.
Bode, W. Florentine sculptors of the Renaissance. *$4 net. Scribner.
Gronau, G., *comp.* Masterpieces of sculpture. In 2 v. ea., 25 c. net. Stokes.
Havell, E. B. Indian sculpture and painting. *$25 net. Scribner.
Hill, G. F. One hundred masterpieces of sculpture. $4 net. Lane.
Pope, P. S. White flame of sculpture. 75 c. Torch Press.

SCULPTURE.—*Continued.*
Redford, G: Sculpture: Egyptian, Assyrian, Greek and Roman. $1.25. Gorham.
Royal Academy pictures and sculpture, 1909, 1910. ea., *$1.75 net. Cassell.
Schulz, A., *comp. and ed.* Modern German sculpture. 3 series. $14. Hessling.
Scott, L. Sculpture: Gothic, Renaissance and modern. $1.25. Gorham.
Singleton, E., *comp. and ed.* Famous sculpture as seen and described by great writers. $1.60 net. Dodd.
Toft, A. Modelling and sculpture. $1.75 net. Lippincott.
See also Cupid and Psyche;—Fine arts;—Lead;—Modelling;—Renaissance;—Sculptors;—*also* St. Gaudens, Augustus.

"Se Arcy, Ann."
See Jett, Ann Searcy.

SEA.
See Ocean.

Sea and its story. Shaw, F. H. $3.50 net. Cassell.

Sea hawk. Millard, F. B. $1 net. Wessels & B.

Sea kings of Britain. Callender, G. A. R. v. 1, 75 c.; v. 2, $1. Longmans.

Sea-kings of Crete. Baikie, J. $2 net. Macmillan.

Sea of faith. Reed, M. *80 c. net. Am. Unitarian.

Sea of matrimony. Childs, *Mrs.* J. D. H. $1.50. B'way Pub.

SEA-OTTER.
Snow, H. J. In forbidden seas; recollections of sea-otter hunting in the Kurils. $3.50 net. Longmans.

SEA POWER.
See Naval art and science.

Sea-scamps. Handler, B. 50 c. Stokes.

Sea terms and phrases. Hewlett, G. *$1.25 net. Lippincott.

SEA-URCHINS.
See Echinoderms.

Sea water distillation. Normandy, F. *$2 net. Lippincott.

SEABURY, *Bishop* Samuel.
Seabury, W: J. Memoir of Bishop Seabury: (the first American bishop.) *$2 net. Gorham.

Seabury, W: Jones.
Memoir of Bishop Seabury: [first American bishop.] '09(Ja23) por. 12°, *$2 net. Gorham.

SEACOAST DEFENSE.
See Military art and science.

Seager, H: Rogers.
Economics; briefer course. '09(Mr6) c. 8°, $1.75. Holt.
Economics: lecture. '08(F29) c. 8°, pap., 25 c. Lemcke.
Social insurance; program of social reform; the Kennedy Lectures for 1910, in the School of Philanthropy, conducted by the Charity Organization Soc. of the City of New York. '10(Jl16) c. D. $1 net. Macmillan.

Seager, R: B.
Excavations on the Island of Pseira Crete. '10(Ag13) il. fold. map, Q. (Univ. of Penn., Anthropological pubs.) pap., $5. Univ. of Penn.
See also Hawes, *Mrs.* Harriet Boyd.

Sealed message. Hume, F. W. †$1.25. G: W. Dillingham.
Sealed verdict. Vandeventer, E. M. $1; 25 c. Laird.
SEALS (animals).
Jordan, D: S. Story of Matka. $1. Whitaker & R.
United States. *Dept. of Commerce and Labor. Bu. of Fisheries.* Fur seals and the seal fisheries.
SEALS (numismatics).
Birch, W. de G. Seals. *$7.50 net. Putnam.
Morgan, J: P. Cylinders and other ancient oriental seals. (Priv. pr.) J: P. Morgan.
Ward, W: H. Seal cylinders of western Asia. $7.50. Carnegie.
Seaman, Augusta Huiell.
Jacqueline of the carrier-pigeons. '10 (Mr26) c. D. *$1.25 net. Sturgis & W.
Seaman, Owen.
Salvage: [selections from *Punch.*] '09 (F13) 16°, *$1.25 net. Holt.
SEAMANSHIP.
See Navigation.
SEAMEN.
See Sailors.
Seamless robe. Carter, A. †$1.50. Wessels.
Seamon, W: H:
Manual for assayers and chemists. '10 (Ag27) c. 8°, $2.50 net. Wiley.
Search after truth. Pearson. C: W: *$1.25 net. Sherman, F.
Search after ultimate truth. Crane, A. M. $1.50 net. Lothrop, L. & S.
Search for a planet beyond Neptune. Pickering, W: H: $1. Harvard Univ.
Search for Basil Lyndhurst. Carey, R. N. 50 c. Hurst.
Search for God. Van Ness, T: 30 c. Unitarian S. S.
Search for the western sea. Burpee, L. J. *$5 special net. Appleton.
Search of Belisarius. Grant, P. S. **$1.50 net. Brentano's.
Searchers. Szymanowski, S. K. $2. S. K. Szymanowski.
Searchlight (The). Stinson, J. C. 25 c. J. C. Stinson.
Searchlight on the Panama canal. Campbell, D: N. E. $1.25. Baltimore Bk.
Searchlights. Coleman, G: W: 75 c. Golden Rule.
Searcy, W: Everard Hamilton.
Way to the kingdom of heaven and what to do to be saved in it. '08, [1909.] c. 166 p. il. 12°, $1. Searcy.
Seares, F: Hanley.
Practical astronomy for engineers. '09 (N) 9+134 p. il. 4°, *$2.25 net. F: H. Seares.
Searle, G: F: C:
Experimental elasticity. '08(O17) figs. O. (Cambridge physical ser.) $1.50. Putnam.
Searle, G: Mary.
"Sumner's method" for finding a ship's position; condensed and improved by Rev. G. M. Searle. '10(S17) c. 16°, (Van Nostrand science ser.) 50 c. Van Nostrand.
Searle, W: G:, ed.
Grace book; containing the records of the University of Cambridge for the years 1501-1542. '08(Je6) O. *$6 net. Putnam.
Sears, Mrs. Julia Seton, M.D.
Key to health, wealth and love. '08(Jl11) c. S. pap., 25 c. Sears Invest.
Shells from life—love—God. [1910.] (Jl) $1 net. New Thought.
Sears, Lorenzo.
Wendell Phillips, orator and agitator. '09 (S4) c. por. D. **$1.50 net. Doubleday, P.
Sears, M. Earl.
See Mudge, Isadore Gilbert.
Sears, Marg. L.
Menotomy: romance of 1776. '08(D12) c. D. $1.50. Badger.
Searson, Ja. W:, and Martin, G: E.
Studies in reading. '10(Je4) c. il. 12°, 80 c. Univ. Pub. Co.
Seashore, Carl Emil.
Elem. experiments in psychology. '08(Jl11) il. D. $1. Holt.
Seasoning and preservative treatment of hemlock and tamarack cross-ties. Sherfesse, W: F. 15 c. U. S., Supt. of Docs.
Seasons and other poems. Esque, J. L: de. $1. Connoisseurs' Press.
Seat work and sense training. Mount, C. S. 50 c. Educ. Pub.
Seat work for primary grades. Mildren, N. L. 35 c. N. L. Mildren.
Seaton, A. E.
Screw propeller, and other competing instruments for marine propulsion. '09 (Je5) il. O. *$4 net. Lippincott.
Seaton, G: Ambrose.
Selected shop problems. '10(Je18) c. il. O. (Manual training reprints.) pap., 20 c. Manual Arts.
SEATTLE, Wash.
Phelps, T. S. Reminiscences of Seattle, Washington Territory and the U. S. sloop-of-war "Decatur." *$2 net; *60 c. net. A. Harriman.
Raymer's dict. of Greater Seattle. 25 c. C. D. Raymer.
See also Alaska-Yukon-Pacific Exposition.
Seattle Public Library. List of books about birds in the Seattle Public Library. '09, [1910.] (My) 11 p. 16°, gratis. Seattle Pub. Lib.
Seattle Public Library. Municipal plans; list of books and references to periodicals in the Seattle Public Library. '10(O) 13 p. 12°, gratis. Seattle Pub. Lib.
Seattle Public Library reference list. 12°. Seattle Pub. Lib.
—Hess. List of books for teachers in the Seattle Public Library. gratis.
Seaver, Jay Webber.
Anthropometry and physical examination; book for pract. use in connection with gymnastic work and physical education. '10(Mr5) c. il. 8°, $1.50. J. W. Seaver.
Seaver, Rob.
Ye butcher, ye baker, ye candlestick-maker: being sundry amusing and instructive verses for both old and young. '08(O3) c. il. T. bds., **50 c. net. Houghton M.

SEAWEEDS.
Conn, H. W:, *and* Webster, L. W. H. Preliminary report on the algæ of the fresh waters of Conecticut. 35c. Conn. Lib.
Gardner, N. L. New *chlorophyceae* from California. 10 c.—Variations in nuclear extrusion among the Fucaceæ. 15 c. Univ. of Cal.
Harper, R. A. Organization of certain *coenobic* plants. 40 c. Univ. of Wis.
Howe, M. A. Phycological studies; III, Further notes on *Halimeda and Avrainvillea.* 25 c. N. Y. Botanical.
Nichols, M. B. Contributions to the knowledge of the California species of *crustaceous corallines.* 10 c.—II. 15 c. Univ. of Cal.

Seawell, Molly Elliot.
Imprisoned midshipmen. '08(O3) c. il. D. †$1.25. Appleton.
Last duchess of Belgrade. '08(Je6) c. il. D. †$1.25. Appleton.
Marriage of Theodora. '10(Ap2) c. front. D. $1.50. Dodd.
See also Boys on the railroad.

Sebastian. Danby, F. †$1.50. Macmillan.

Sébillot, Paul.
Choix de contes populaires de la Haute-Bretagne; ed. by E. K. Sheldon. '09 (O16) S. (Shorter French texts.) *25 c. net. Crowell.
Contes des marins de la Haute-Bretagne; adpt. and ed. by J. E. Mansion. '10 (Ag27) S. (Crowell's shorter French texts.) 25 c. Crowell.

SECESSION.
See Civil War.

Seckerson, F: Clinton.
Manual of civics: text book of municipal government for the City of New York; with an exposition of the principles of government in New York State and the United States. [3d ed.] '08(Jl4) c. 12°, $1. Chief.

SECOND ADVENT.
Fairbanks, A. D. Christ's second coming. $1. Roxburgh.
Funk, I: K. Next step in evolution. **50 c. net. Funk.
Speer, R. E. Second coming of Christ. 30 c. Northfield Press.
Whish, E. Until Shiloh come. 50 c. net. Longmans.

Second chambers. Marriott, J: A. R. $1.75. Oxford Univ.
Second chance. McClurg, *Mrs.* N. L. M. $1.20, fixed. Doubleday, P.

SECOND CONGREGATIONAL CHURCH, Leicester, Mass.
Chenoweth, *Mrs.* C. Van D. History of the Second Congregational church and Society in Leicester, Mass. $1.50. C. V. Chenoweth.

Second elopement. Flowerdew, H. $1.50. Brentano's.
Second mile. Fosdick, H. E. *40 c. net. Y. M. C. A.
Second post. Lucas, E: V., *comp.* $1.25; $1.75 net. Macmillan.
Second shepherd's play. Child, C. G., *ed.* 40 c. Houghton M.

SECOND SIGHT.
See Psychical research.

Second steps in Latin. Ritchie, F. 75 c. Longmans.
Second string. Hawkins, A. H. $1.50. Doubleday, P.

SECONDARY EDUCATION.
See Education.

Secondary stresses in bridge trusses. Grimm, C. R. $2.50. Wiley.

Secor, W: Lee.
Hdbk. of the principles and practices of modern hydro-therapy. [1910.] (Ag) c. 5-360 p. il. 12°, $1.50. Chic. Med. Bk.

Secord, Lauchlen McCallum.
Our native trees and their uses. '08(O10) c. il. 12°, 60 c. L. M. Secord.

Secret Bible history of Adamic innocence. Acton, M. W: $2. New Age.
Secret history of the court of Spain. Challice, R. *$4 special net. Appleton.
Secret lodge system. Potts, J: V. $1. Germ. Lit. Bd.
Secret of old Thunderhead. Irwin, L. G. †$1.50. Holt.
Secret of life, death and immortality. Fleetwood, H: $1. H: Fleetwood.
Secret of sex. Dawson, E: R. 50 c. Cochrane.
Secret of success. Atkinson, W: W. 50 c. Advanced Thought.
Secret of the ages. *See* Eccles, Lewis Franklin. Trumpet voice from the throne.
Secret of the island. *See* Verne, Jules.
Secret of the Lord. Clow, W. M. $1.50 net. Doran.
Secret of the sand-hills. Marlowe, F. $2. Lippincott.
Secret of the Saragasso. Macdonald, R. M. $1.50. Brentano's.
Secret paper. Wood, W. $1.50. Cassell.
Secret signatures of my friends. Fetherston, *Sir* G: R. 50 c. net. Stokes.

SECRET SOCIETIES.
Martin, *Mrs.* I. S. Sorority hdbk. $1.50. I. S. Martin.
Potts, J: V. Secret lodge system: [argument against secret societies.] $1. Germ. Lit. Bd.
Webster, H. Primitive secret societies. **$2 net. Macmillan.
See also Benefit societies;—Freemasonry.

SECRETIONS.
See Glands.

Secrets of beauty. Potter, *Mrs.* C. U. **$1.75 net. P. Elder.
Secrets of expert exhibitors. Heck, F. $2. F. Heck.
Secrets of meat curing and sausage making; how to cure hams, shoulders, bacon, corned beef, etc., and how to make all kinds of sausage, etc., and comply with all pure food laws. 2d ed. '08(N) c. 265-303 p. il. 16°. gratis. B. Heller & Co.
Secrets of the past. Upward, A. $1.50. Brentano's.
Secrets of the sword. Bazancourt, *Baron* de. *$1.25 net. Macmillan.
Secrets of true success. Pell, E: L. 10 c. Harding Press.

Secrist, H: T.
Comparative studies in religion; introd. to Unitarianism. '09(N) c. 72+46 p. 8°, (Beacon ser.) 45 c.; pap., 35 c.; Teachers' ed., 65 c. Unitarian S. S.

Sectionalism and some of its fruits. Grady, B: F. 25 c. B: F. Grady.

Sectionalism in Virginia. Ambler, C: H: $1.50 net. Univ. of Chic.

SECTS.
Pritchett, H: S. Relations of Christian denominations to colleges. gratis. Carnegie Found.
See also names of sects.

SECURITIES.
See Bonds;—Corporations;—Investments;—Mortgages;—Railroads;—Speculation;—Stocks.

Sedbury, Ja. Hamilton.
Under the flag of the cross: [story.] '08 (Mr) c. 5+472 p. il. 12°, $1.50. C. M. Clark.

Sedgwick, Adam.
Student's text-book of zoölogy. v. 3, Tunicata, enteropneusta echinodermata and arthropoda. '09(Ap3) il. 8°, *$5.50 net. Macmillan.

Sedgwick, Anne Douglas, [Mrs. Basil de Sélincourt.]
Amabel Channice. '08(O10) c. D. †$1.50. Century Co.
Franklin Winslow Kane. '10(Ap23) c. D. $1.50. Century Co.

Sedgwick, Arth. G:
Elements of the law of damages: hdbk. for the use of students and practitioners. 2d ed., rev. and enl. '09(My) c. 35+368 p. O. $3; shp., $3.50. Little, B. & Co.

Sedgwick, Captain Fs. Roger.
Russo-Japanese war. '09(Ap3) maps, 12°, (Special campaign ser.) *$1.60 net. Macmillan.

Sedgwick, H: Dwight.
New American type, and other essays. '08 (My2) c. D. **$1.50 net. Houghton M.

Sedlasky, Ferdinand Ja.
Defence of the truth. '10(S3) c. il. por. 8°, $1.25. F. J. Sedlasky.

SEE, Edwin Francis.
Warburton, G: A: Typical general secretary; life of Edwin F. See. 75 c. Y. M. C. A.

See, T: Jefferson Jackson.
Researches on the evolution of the stellar systems. v. 2, Capture of cosmical evolution. '10(D24) c. il. 4°, $10. T: P. Nichols.

See of Peter and the voice of antiquity. Dolan, T: S. *60 c. net. B. Herder.

Seebach, Marg. R.
That man Donaleitis: story of the coal regions. '09(N) 451 p. front. 12°, $1.25. Lutheran Pub.

Seeberg, Reinhold.
Fundamental truths of the Christian religion. '08(D12) cr. 8°, (Crown theological lib.) *$1.50 net. Putnam.
Revelation and inspiration. '10(Ja29) 12°, (Harper's lib. of living thought.) *75 c. net. Harper.

SEED.
Adulteration and misbranding of the seeds of alfalfa, red clover, orchard grass, and Kentucky blue-grass. '09(My) 5 p. 8°, (U. S., Dept. of Agriculture, circular.) pap. (Add. Superintendent for price.) U. S., Supt. of Docs.
Fultz, F. M. Fly-aways and other seed travelers. 60 c. Pub. Sch. Pub.
Robinson, T: R. Seed sterilization and its effect upon seed inoculation. Gov. Pr. Off.
Tracy, W: W. Production of vegetable seeds. Gov. Pr. Off.
See also Clover.

Seed of the righteous. Bullen, F: T. $1.25. Eaton & M.

SEED OILS.
See Oils and fats.

Seed that was sown in the colony of Georgia. Wylly, C: S. $1.25 net. Neale.

Seed, the soil and the sower. Slattery, M. 35 c. net. F. M. Barton.

Seeding and preservation of golf links. Thorburn, J. M. & Co. (Add. pubs. for price.) J. M. Thornburn.

Seedling's harvest. Roy, *Mrs.* L. E. B. $1.25. Wessels & B.

Seeds, Rob. S:
Lectures, "How God made the soil fertile." '08(My.) c. 44 p. il. 12°. (Add. author for price.) R. S. Seeds.

SEEDS.
See Gardens and gardening.

Seegmiller, Wilhelmina, ed.
Applied arts drawing books: autumn and winter series: drawing books for schools from third to eighth grades. 6 v. '08 (N) ea. 40 p. il. v. 1-2, ea., 10 c.; v. 3-6, ea., 15 c. Atkinson, M. & G.

Seeing England with Uncle John. Warner, A. †$1.50. Century Co.

Seekers in Sicily. Bisland, E. *$1.50 net. Lane.

Seeking after God. Abbott, L. $1. Crowell.

Seeking the best. Shackelford, O. M. $1. Hudson.

Seekings, Herbert S.
For joy's sake: studies in the teaching of St. John. '08(D26) S. *50 c. net. Jennings.

Seeley, E. L., comp.
Artists of the Italian Renaissance and their influence as set forth by Vasari, Ridolfi, Lanzi and the Chroniclers. '08(O17) cr. 8°, (Art and letters lib.) *$3 net. Duffield.
Stories of the Italian artists from Vasari. '08(O17) cr. 8°, (Art and letters lib.) *$3 net. Duffield.

Seeley, Sir J: Rob.
Ecce homo: a survey of the life and work of Jesus Christ; introd. by Sir Oliver Lodge. '08(Mr7) 16°, (Everyman's lib.) *35 c. net; leath., *70 c. net.—*Same.* '08 (F22) 12°, (New universal lib.) 50 c.; leath., 75 c. Dutton.

Seeligmann, Thdr., Torrillion, G. Lamy, and Falconnet, H.
Indiarubber and gutta percha; complete pract. treatise on indiarubber and gutta percha in their historical, botanical, arboricultural, mechanical, chemical and electrical aspects; tr. from the French by J: Geddes McIntosh. 2d English ed., rev. and enl. '10(D) 16+408 p. il. tabs., 8°, $5 net. Van Nostrand.

Seely, Mrs. Frances.
Fireless cookery. '10(F5) c. il. 12°, (Modern domestic science.) 25 c. Assoc. Dom. Sci.

Seely, F:
See Seely, Wa.

Seely, Wa. and F:
How to become an inspector on public works. '08(D26) (Add. pubs. for price.) M. C. Clark.

Seelye, Mrs. Lillie Eggleston.
See Eggleston, E:

Seeming unreality of spiritual life. King, H: C. **$1.50 net. Macmillan.

Seer (The). Johnson, H: $1.50. F. W. Chandler.

Segal, Josephine.
Wanderings of Christ. [In verse.] '08 (My9) c. il. 12°, $2.50. J. Segal.

Segerblom, Wilhelm.
First year chemistry; text in elem. chemistry for secondary schools. '09(N) c. 25+410 p. il. 8°, $1.50. Exeter Bk.
Laboratory manual of qualitative analysis. '08(Je13) c. tabs., O. $1.25. Longmans.
Tables of properties of over fifteen hundred common inorganic substances. '09(Jl3) c. O. $3. Exeter Bk.

Segno, A. Victor.
Cours scientifique de l'analyse du caractère, comprenant la physiognomonie, la phrénologie et la graphologie: le visage, la tête et l'écriture. '08, [1909.] (Ap) c. 103 p. il. 4°, $5.75. Chirological Coll.

SEGOVIA, Spain.
See Spain.

Seguin, E:, M.D.
Idiocy; its treatment by the physiological method. '08(F8) O. (Columbia Univ., Teachers' Coll., education reprints.) $2. Teachers' Coll.

Ségur, Sophie Rostochine, Comtesse de.
Life of Christ for children; as told by a grandmother; adapted from the French by Mary Virginia Merrick. '09(D4) c. il. 12°, $1. Herder.

Seibert, Venita.
Gossamer thread; being the chronicles of Velleda, who understood about "the Different World." '10(Jl9) c. il. D. $1 net. Small.

Seide, Jos. N.
Easy arrangement of the Spanish verb (Mexico's mastery method). '10(Je4) c. 8°, $2. J. N. Seide.

Seidel, Heinrich.
German Christmas Eve; tr. from the German by Jane Hutchins White. '10(N12) c. S. bds., 50 c., boxed; pap., 25 c., in envelope. Abbey Co.
See also Storm, Theodor.

Seidenadel, Carl Wilhelm.
First grammar of the language, spoken by the Bontoc Igorot; with a vocab. and texts. '10(Je4) 8°, $5 net. Open Court.

Seidlitz, Woldemar von.
Hist. of Japanese color-prints. '10(D3) il. (partly col.) 4°, $6.50 net. Lippincott.

Seignobos, Michel Jean Charles.
History of contemporary civilization. v. 3, [Modern civilization;] tr. ed. by Ja. Alton James. '09(F6) c. D. **$1.25 net. Scribner.

Seiler's phonanagrams for hygienic busy work in phonics, spelling and word-building; [cards.] '09(Ag14) set in 95 envelopes, *$12 net. Seiler.

Seilhamer, G: Overcash.
Bard family: hist. and genealogy of the Bards of "Carroll's Delight." '08(Jl) c. 9+507 p. il. pors. tabs., 8°, $10. Kittochtinny.

Seipt, Allen Anders.
Schwenkfelder hymnology and the sources of the first Schwenkfelder hymn-book printed in America. '09(N20) c. facsim., Q. (Americana Germanica new ser.) $2. Americana Germanica.

SEISMOLOGY.
See Earthquake.

Seitz, Don Carlos.
Elba and elsewhere. '10(S17) c. il. D. $1.25 net. Harper.
Writings by and about James Abbott M'Neill Whistler: bibliography. '10 (Jl30) c. 16°, $3. (350 copies.) E. D. North.

Selbie, W. B., D.D.
Aspects of Christ. '10(Je4) 8°, $1.50 net. Doran.

SELBORNE, England.
Shelley, H: C: Gilbert White and Selborne. *$1.50 net. Scribner.

Selby, Paul.
Abraham Lincoln: evolution of his emancipation policy: address del. before the Chicago Historical Society, Feb. 27, 1906. '09(My) 107-133 p. por. 8°, 50 c. Chic. Hist.

Selby, Rev. T: Gunn.
Divine Craftsman, and other sermons. '10 (Mr26) O. *$1.25 net. Eaton & M.

Selden, Fk. H:
Elem. cabinetwork for manual training classes. '09(D11) c. il. 12°, $1.25. Rand, McN. & Co.

Selecman, Edg. H.
Specialty salesman. '10(Ja8) c. 12°, $1. Progress Co.

Select English classics; sel. and arr. by A. T. Quiller-Couch. '09(Ja16); '10(D17) S. ea., 10 c.; pap., 8 c. Oxford Univ.
Contents: Poems, Matthew Arnold; Poems, W: Blake; Boswell's Johnson; Lyrical poems, Rob. Browning; Selections, John Bunyan; Lyrical poems, S: Taylor Coleridge; Poems, W: Cowper; Selections from poems, G: Crabbe; Selections, Daniel Defoe; Early English lyrics; Everyman: a morality play; Goldsmith's Traveller, and Deserted village; Selections, W: Hazlitt; Poems, T: Hood; Odes and lyrics, J: Keats; Essays, C: Lamb; Scenes from Marlowe's plays; Poems, Andrew Marvell; Minor poems, J: Milton; Sonnets, Milton and Wordsworth; Napier's Peninsular war; Old ballads; Robin Hood, old ballads; Seventeenth century characters; Shakespeare's songs and sonnets; Lyrical poems, Percy Bysshe Shelley; Poems, Lord Tennyson; Earlier letters, Horace Walpole; Selections, Izaak Walton; Lyrical poems, Wordsworth.

Select epigrams from the Greek anthology. Mackail, J: W:, *ed.* *75 c. net; *$1 net. Longmans.

Select essays in Anglo-American legal history, by various authors; comp. and ed. by a committee of the Association of American Law Schools. In 3 v. v. 2. '08(N); v. 3. '09 (O) c. O. per set, **$12 net. Little, B. & Co.

Select notes. *See* Peloubet, Fs. Nathan.

Selected articles on capital punishment. Fanning, C. E., *comp.* $1. H. W. Wilson.

Selected articles on the initiative and referendum. Phelps, E. M., *comp.* $1. H. W. Wilson.

Selected articles on woman suffrage. Phelps, E. M., *comp.* $1 net. H. W. Wilson.

Selected poems from the *Harvard Monthly,* 1885-1910. '10(Jl16) c. 8°, pap., $1. Harvard Monthly.

Selected tales of mystery. *See* Poe, Edg. Allan.

Selections for our little folks. Avery-Stuttle, *Mrs.* L. D., *comp.* 60 c. Pacific Press.

Selections from early German literature. Collitz, K. H., *comp.* $1. Am. Bk.

Selections from great authors. 32°, pap. Stokes.

—Recompense. 30 c.

Selections of harmony. Hadley, W. B: 75 c.; in 2 pts., ea., 25 c. R: Bylsma.

Selective reflection of salts of carbonic and other oxygen acids. Morse, L. B. (Add. pubs. for price.) Astrophysical.

Self, G: W., rep.

See Indiana. *Appellate ct.* Repts.—*Sup. ct.* Repts.

Self and sex ser. 16°, *$1 net. Vir Pub.

—Drake. What a woman of forty-five should know.—What a young wife ought to know.

—Stall. What a young boy ought to know.

—Wood-Allen. What a young girl ought to know.

SELF CONTROL.

See New thought.

Self-control and how to secure it. Du Bois, P. **$1.50 net. Funk.

Self cultivation in English. *See* Palmer, G: H.

SELF-CULTURE.

See Culture.

SELF-GOVERNMENT.

See Local government.

Self help for nervous women. Mitchell, J: K. **$1 net. Lippincott.

SELF-INSTRUCTION.

See Home-study.

Self-instruction in the practice and theory of navigation. Dunraven, *Earl of.* 3 v. *$8 net. Macmillan.

Self-interpreting Bible. *See* Bible.

Self-measurement. Hyde, W: D. *50 c. net. B: W. Huebsch.

Self-propelled vehicles. Homans, J. E: $2. Audel.

Self-reconstruction of Maryland. Myers, W: S. 50 c. Johns Hopkins.

Self-revelation of our Lord. Durell, J. C. $2 net. Scribner.

Selfe, Norman.

Machinery for refrigeration. '08(N21) il. $3.50; mor., $4.50. Nickerson & C.

Selgas y Carrasco, José.

La mariposa blanca; ed., with notes and vocabulary, by Herbert Alden Kenyon. '10(Mr26) c. S. 60 c. Holt.

Seligman, Edn. Rob. Anderson.

Principles of economics; with special reference to American conditions. 4th ed., rev. and enl. '09(O23) c. tabs., charts, O. (American citizen ser.) $2.50. Longmans.

Progressive taxation in theory and practice. 2d ed., completely rev. and enl. '09 (F6) c. O. (American Economic Assoc. Quarterly.) $1.75; pap., $1.25. Am. Economic Assoc.

Separation of state and local revenues. '08 (S.) (Add. pubs. for price.) Nat. Tax. Assoc.

The shifting and incidence of taxation. 3d ed., rev. and enl. '10(Je) 12+427 p. 8°, $3 Lemcke.

Bibliography (27 p.).

Seligmann, C: Gabriel.

Melanesians of British New Guinea. '10 (My7) c. il. 12°, $7 net. Putnam.

Sélikovitsch, G: Guetzel.

Memorial prayers and meditations; tr. with many orig. additions by Prof. G. Sélikovitsch. '10(N5) c. 12°, 50 c. Hebrew Pub.

"Selim," pseud.

See Henderson, Percy E.

Sélincourt, Mrs. Basil de.

See Sedgwick, Anne Douglas.

Sélincourt, Hugh de.

Great Ralegh [*sic.*] '08(S5) pors. O. (Memoir ser.) *$3.50 net. Putnam.

Oxford from within. '10(D10) col. il. 12°, $3 net. Jacobs.

SELKIRK, Dunbar James, *Earl* of.

See Manitoba, Canada.

Selkirk, Wyatt O.

Catechism of manual of guard duty, United States Army. '10(Jl30) c. 24°, 50 c. net. Wiley.

Sellers, Alvin V.

Classic of the bar; stories of the world's great jury trials and a compilation of forensic masterpieces. '09(N) c. 5-314 p. por. 12°, $2. Classic.

Sellers, D: Foote.

Unofficial telegraph and cable code prepared for the use of officers of the navy and marine corps and their families, 1909. '09(D) c. 134 p. 16°, $2.50. Navy Pub.

Sellers, Edn. Jaquett.

Genealogy of the De Carpentier family of Holland. '09(Je12) il. pors. 8°, $3. E. J. Sellers.

Genealogy of the Jaquett family. Rev. ed. '07, [1908.] (Mr.) 226 p. il. pors. 8°, $5. E. J. Sellers.

Sellers, J. F.

Elementary treatise on qualitative chemical analysis. [2d] rev. ed. '09(N6) c. D. $1. Ginn.

Sellery, G: Clarke.

Lincoln's suspension of habeas corpus as viewed by Congress. '08(F1) O. (Univ. of Wis. bull., History ser.) pap., 35 c. Univ. of Wis.

See also Munro, Dana Carleton.

Sells, Elijah Watt.
Corporate management compared with government control. 5th ed. '08(O) 11 p. O. pap., gratis. Haskins & S.

Sellstedt, Lars Gustaf.
Art in Buffalo. '10(Jl) c. 228 p. por. 8°, $1.50. L. G. Sellstedt.

Selous, Edm.
Wonders of the insect world. '10(D3) il. 8°, (Lippincott's wonder lib.) 75 c. Lippincott.

Selous, F: Courteney.
African nature notes and reminiscences; with a foreword by President Roosevelt. '08(Je6) 8°, *$3 net. Macmillan.

Selover, Arth. W:
Negotiable instruments law. 2d ed.; by W: H. Oppenheimer. '10(S) 473 p. c. O. $5. Keefe-D.

SELWYN, George.
Kerr, S. P. George Selwyn and the wits. *$3.50 net. Brentano's.

Semenoff, Vladimir Ivanovich.
Price of blood; sequel to "Rasplata" and "The battle of Tsushima." '10(Ap23) 8°, $1.50 net. Dutton.
Rasplata (the reckoning) by Commander Vladimir Semenoff, imperial Russian navy: his diary during the blockade of Port Arthur and the voyage of Admiral Rojestvensky's fleet; tr. by L. A. B. '09 (Ag21) 8°, $3.50. Dutton.

Semi-history of a boy-veteran. Hobart, E. L. $1.25. E. L. Hobart.

SEMICIRCULAR CANALS.
See Ear.

SEMINOLE INDIANS.
See Indians.

Semiramis. Dargan, *Mrs.* O. T. *$1 net. Scribner.

SEMITES.
See Jews.

SEMITIC LANGUAGE.
Armbruster, C. H. Initia Amharica. 2 pts. pt. 1, $3.50 net; pt. 2, $5 net. Putnam.
Brockelmann, C. Kurzgefasste vergleichende grammatik der semitischen sprachen; elemente der laut-und-formenlehre. $3. Lemcke.
Yusuf Ibn Taghrî Birdî. Annals, entitled An-nujum az-zâhiri fi muluk Misr wal-Kâhira. pts. 1, 2. ea., $1.50. Univ. of Cal.
See also Arabic language;—Aramaic language;—Languages.

SEMITIC LITERATURE.
Goodspeed, E. J. Chicago literary papyri. *50 c. net. Univ. of Chic.
Harper, R. F., *and others, eds.* Old Testament and Semitic studies. 2 v. $10. Univ. of Chic.

SEMITIC RELIGIONS.
Berry, G: R. Old Testament among the Semitic religions. *$1 net. Griffith.
Thompson, R. C. Semitic magic. *$4 net. Bloch.
See also Jews.

Semitic ser. 12°. Dutton.
—Rapaport. Tales and maxims from the Talmud. $1.75 net.

SEMITISM.
See Jews.

Semple, Rev. H: Churchill.
What times! What morals! Where on earth are we? '10(Ap9) c. S. 35 c. Benziger.

Semsch, Otto Fs., ed.
Hist. of the Singer building construction; its progress from foundation to flagpole. '08(D) c. 117 p. il. plans, f°. (Add. author for price.) 35 Wall St., N. Y. O. F. Semsch.

Senator, Professor Hermann, and Kaminer, Siegfried, M.D., eds.
Marriage and disease: being an abridged ed. of "Health and disease in relation to marriage and the married state"; tr. from the German by J. Dulberg. '09(Ja16) O. *$2.50 net. Hoeber.

SENATORS.
See Elections;—United States.

Seneca, Lucius Annaeus.
Physical science in the time of Nero; being a tr. of the Quaestiones naturales of Seneca by J: Clarke; together with notes on the treatise by Sir Archibald Geikie. '10(Ap9) O. $3.50 net. Macmillan.
Sel. essays of Seneca and The satire on the deification of Claudius; with introd. and notes by Allan P. Ball. '08(Ag8) c. 16°, (Latin classics.) *60 c. net. Macmillan.
Select letters; ed., with introd. and explanatory notes, by Wa. C. Summers. '10 (N19) 16°, $1.25 net. Macmillan.
Three tragedies: Hercules Furens, Troades, Medea; with an introd. and notes by Hugh Macmaster Kingery. '08(Mr7) c. 16°, (Latin ser.) *60 c. net. Macmillan.

Senior, Dorothy.
Caprice: her book. '10(My21) 12°, $1.50 net. Macmillan.
Clutch of circumstances. '08(N7) front. 12°, $1.50. Macmillan.
King who never died; tales of King Arthur. '10(N19) il. in col. 12°, (Color books for boys and girls.) $1.50. Macmillan.

Senior quarter-back. Hare, T: T. $1.25. Penn Pub. Co.

Senn, N:
Principles of surgery. 4th ed., thoroughly rev. by Emanuel J. Senn and Emanuel Friend. '09(D) c. 2+706 p. il. 8°, *$5 net; shp., *$6.50 net. Davis.
—, ed. *See* Taber, Clarence Wilbur.

Sennett, R:, and Oram, H: J.
Marine steam engine; treatise for engineering students, young engineers and officers of the Royal Navy and mercantile marine. 10th ed. '10(Ap2) il. O. $6. Longmans.

Senour, Mrs. Caro Smith.
Captain Kidd, jr., and Sinbad the sailor: a tale of two kittens. '08(Ap11) c. il. 12°, $1. C. S. Senour.
Master St. Elmo: the autobiography of a celebrated dog. '08(Ap18) c. il. 12°, vellum, *$1 net. Juvenile Bk.
See also Field, Eugene.

Sense and sensibility. *See* Austen, Jane.

Sense and sentiment. *See* Thackeray, W: Makepeace.

Sense of humor. Hamilton, C. $1.50. Brentano's.
Sense of the infinite. Kuhne, L. O. **$1.50 net. Holt.
SENSE ORGANS.
See **Physiology.**
Sensitive child. Patch, K. W. **75 c. net. Moffat.
Sentence improvement. Stebbins, C: M. 75 c. Sibley.
Sentiment and story. Gresham, R. J. $1.50. Neale.
Sentiment as a national asset. Ferree, J. B. gratis. B. Ferree.
Sentimental adventures of Jimmy Bulstrode. Van Vorst, M. †$1.50. Scribner.
Sentimental journey. *See* Sterne, Laurence.
Separate or "Jim crow" car laws. Boyd, R. H. 25 c. Nat. Bapt. Pub.
Separation of church and state in Virginia. Virginia State Library. $1. Virginia State Lib.
Separation of state and local revenues. Seligman, E. R. A. (Add. pubs. for price.) Nat. Tax Assoc.
Sepharial, pseud.
Astrology: how to make your own horoscope. '10(O) 12°, 50 c. Fenno.
SEPSIS.
See Antisepsis.
September roses. Evans, N. S. $1. D. Evans.
Septimus. Locke, W: J. †$1.50. Lane.
Sepúlveda, Lorenzo de.
Romances Nucuamente sacados de historias antiquas dela cronica de España compuestor por Lorenço de Sepulueda [facsim.] '03 [1909.] (N) 259 p. 8°, $10 (200 copies). Hispanic Soc.
SEQUOIA.
See **Pine trees.**
Sera, Leone Gioacchino.
On the tracks of life; the immorality of morality; tr. from the Italian by J. M. Kennedy; with an introd. by Dr. Oscar Levy. '09(S4) O. *$2.50 net. Lane.
Sérafon, Amélie.
See Colin, Henrietta Louise Thérèse.
Serao, Matilde.
After the pardon. '09(Je) c. 334 p. D. $1.50. Stuyvesant Press.
Seraphica. McCarthy, J. H. †$1.50. Harper.
Sergeant, Philip Walsingham.
Cleopatra of Egypt: antiquities' queen of romance. '10(O15) pors. map. O. $4 net. Dodd.
Empress Josephine. In 2 v. '09(D25) il. 8°, †$6.50 net, boxed. Dodd.
Sergio, Arturo.
Logical method to learn the Italian language. '10(Ag27) c. 12°, $1. Italian Sch.
Series of instruction books for schools and families; ed. by Bishop Doane. il. 16°. Gorham.
—Gwynne. Gospel in the church. 40 c.
Series of notable debates by men of the hour. Jeffords, S. G., *ed.* 50 c. S. G. Jeffords.
Serious question, what is true repentance? Kinsey, R. B. $1. R. B. Kinsey.
Serl, Elmer Willis.
Swaying tree tops. '08(Ja4) D. $1. Neale.

Serment (Le). *See* David, Jules.
Sermon (The). Greenbarry, H. 50 c. Good Thoughts.
Sermon lib. in the kingdom of grace. 8°. Germ. Lit. Bd.
—Sure word of prophecy. *85 c. net.
Sermon of the sea. Kane, R. *$1.50 net. Longmans.
SERMON ON THE MOUNT.
Cohn, J. B. Sermon on the Mount as viewed from the modern standpoint. $1.40. Whittaker.
Kaiser, P. The law in the light of the gospel: series of sermons on the precepts of Christ concerning the law in the Sermon on the Mount. 85 c. Germ. Lit. Bd.
McAfee, C. B. Studies in the Sermon on the Mount. $1 net. Revell.
Savage, H: E: Gospel of the kingdom; or, the Sermon on the Mount. $3.50. Longmans.
See also Bible. N. T.
SERMONS.
Adams, T: Sermons. 45 c. Putnam.
Adler, H. Anglo-Jewish memories and other sermons. *$1.50 net. Bloch.
Ainsworth, P. C. Pilgrim church, and other sermons. $1.25 net. Revell.
Aked, C: F. Old events and modern meaning, and other sermons. *$1.25 net. Revell.
Aked, C: F. Weils and palm trees. $1; $2. Dodge.
Albertson, C: C. College sermons. 75 c. Westminster.
Allan, W: T. Council sermon preached in the Church of the Advent, Birmingham, Alabama. 5 c. Clark Pub.
Atkins, G. G. Things that remain. $1.25. G. G. Atkins.
Banks, L: A. World's childhood; series of Sunday evening sermons. $1.30 net. Funk.
Bayley, F. T. "Little ten-minutes"; or, a pastor's talks with his children. *$1 net. Revell.
Belasco, G: S. God of our fathers. *$1.20 net. Bloch.
Black, H. Gift of influence. *$1.25 net. Revell.
Bonomelli, J. New series of homilies for the whole year. In 4 v. $5. Benziger.
Book, W: H: Columbus Tabernacle sermons. $1. Standard Pub.
Brady, C. T. Love test, and other sermons. *$1.25 net. Young Churchman.
Branch, J. O. Sermons. $1.25. J. Magath.
Brooks, P. Sermons. 10 v. per set, $6 net. Dutton.
Brown, C:, *and others.* God's garden. *$1 net. Eaton & M.
Burke, J: J. Great problem; sermon for every Sunday and feast day in the year. *$1 net Herder.
Buxton, H. J: W. Notes of sermons for a year. pts. 1, 2. ea., *$1 net.—Old road; thirty plain sermons. *$2 net. Whittaker.
Byington, E. H. Children's pulpit. 75 c. net. Pilgrim Press.

SERMONS.—*Continued.*

Campbell, R. J: Thursday mornings at the City Temple. *$1.50 net. Macmillan.

Candole, H. L. V. de. Confirmation, authority, confession: three sermons. *36 c. net. Longmans.

Chapman, J. W. Another mile and other addresses. *75 c. net; *25 c. net. Revell.

Clark, H. H. Sword of the nation and other sermons. $1. Severn River.

Clarke, J. F. Transfiguration of life. *$1 net. Am. Unitarian.

Coit, H: A: School sermons. **$1.50 net. Moffat.

Cole, S. W. R. Sermons outlined. 50 c. Nat. Baptist Pub.

Collyer, R. Where the light dwelleth. *$1.40 net. Am. Unitarian.

Dalton, L. M. Sermon outlines. 80 c. net. Whittaker.

Dodd, I. S. Brother and the brotherhood. **$1.50 net. Dodd.

Dresser, H. W. Greatest truth. 90 c. Progressive Lit.

Ely, S. Sermons, essays and outlines. $1. Standard Pub.

Evangelistic sermons. 75 c.; 35 c. P. E. Zartmann.

Faithfull, R. C. My place in the world and other sermons. $1.40 net. Whittaker.

Falconer, J. W. Three crosses. *75 c. net. Jennings.

Farrar, F: W: Bells and pomegranates. $1.50 net. Whittaker.

Farrar, J. M. Junior congregation.—Little talks to little people. ea., **$1.20 net. Funk.

Gibbons, J. Discourses and sermons for every Sunday and the principal festivals of the year. $1. Murphy.

Graham, W: S. Divine praises: addresses to Holy Name societies.—Fruits of the devotion to the Sacred Heart. ea., *75 c. net. Wagner.

Greenhough, J. G., *and others.* Great texts of the New Testament. *$1 net. Eaton & M.

Grier, J. A. Pastoral homilies. $1. Un. Presb. Bd.

Hall, C: C. Silver cup: simple messages to children. **$1.25 net. Houghton M.

Hall, F. O. Soul and body. *$1 net. Universalist.

Harris, W: S. Sermons by the devil. $1; $1.50; $2. Minter.

Hart, H: M. Tragedy of Hosea and other sermons. (Add. pubs. for price.) Whittaker.

Henson, C. H. H. Westminster sermons. $1.25 net. Doran.

Hodges, G: Baccalaureate sermon preached before the candidates for degrees in Columbia Univ. gratis. G: Hodges.

Hodges, G: Year of grace. $1.25 net. Whittaker.

Holden, J. S. Pre-eminent Lord and other sermons. *$1.25 net. Doran.

Horn, E: T. Summer sermons. *$1 net. Pilger.

SERMONS.—*Continued.*

Howard, H: Raiment of the soul.—Summits of the soul. ea., *$1.25 net. Eaton & M.

Hunter, J: De profundis clamavi. *$1.50 net. Macmillan.

Hurlbut, J. L., *ed.* Sunday half hours with great preachers. $1.50. Winston.

Huxley, T: H: Lectures and lay sermons. 35 c. net; 70 c. net. Dutton.

Ingram, A. F. W. Into the fighting line. $1.50 net. Whittaker.

Ingram, A. F. W. Mysteries of God. $1. Young Churchman.

Jefferson, C: E: My Father's business: sermons to children. **$1.25 net. Crowell.

Jellett, H: Sermons on special and festival occasions. *$1.20 net. Longmans.

Johnson, S: L. Revival sermons. *$1 net. Revell.

Jowett, J. H. School of Calvary. 50 c. net. Pilgrim Press.

Kane, R. Sermon of the sea, and other studies. *$1.50 net. Longmans.

Keesey, W. R. Six modern devils. *35 c. net. Jennings.

Keller, C: E. Eternal hills. 25 c. C: E. Keller.

King, E: Love and wisdom of God. $1.75 net. Longmans.

Kleiser, G., *comp.* World's greatest sermons. In 10 v. $7.50; $10. Funk.

Kleiser, G., *comp.* World's great sermons. In 10 v. per set, $2.75. Westminster (Chic.)

Knowles, D. C. Chapel talks. *$1 net. Eaton & M.

Lacey, T: J. Gospel of optimism, and other sermons. $1. Red Diamond.

Lambert, J: C., *and others.* Great texts of the Old Testament. *$1 net. Eaton & M.

Lennard, V. R: Passiontide and Easter: sermons. 80 c. Whittaker.

Long, S. P: Eternal epistle: sermons on the epistles for the church year. $2.50.—Way made plain. $1. S. P: Long.

Luce, F. W. King's conquest. $1. Jennings.

Luther, M. [Sermons.] v. 1, 2, 3.. v. 1, 50 c.; v. 2, 3, ea., $1.65. Luther Press.

MacArthur, R. S. Advent, Christmas, New Year, Easter, and other sermons. $1.—Christic reign, and other sermons. $1.25. Am. Bapt.

McClure, J. G. K. Supreme things. *75 c. net. Revell.

Mackay, D. S. Religion of the threshold, and other sermons. *$1.50 net. Armstrong.

Mackintosh, H. R. Life on God's plan. $1.50 net. Doran.

Masliansky, H. Yiddish sermons for Sabbaths and holy days. $1. Turberg.

Matheson, G: Messages of hope. *$1.25 net. Putnam.

Matheson, G: Thoughts for life's journey. *$1.25 net. Armstrong.

Millard, J. W: Life's tomorrows. **75 c. net. Jennings.

SERMONS.—*Continued.*

Miller, J. R. Evening thoughts for every day in the year. **65 c. net; **85 c. net. —Gate beautiful. **85 c. net.—Glimpses of the heavenly life. *50 c. net.—Wider life. **65 c. net; **85 c. net. Crowell.

Mission preaching for a year. In 4 pts. pts. 2, 3. ea., *$1 net. Whittaker.

Morgan, W: S. Nuggets of gold. 50 c. W: S. Morgan.

Moriarty, *Bp. of Kerry.* Sermons. *$2 net. Benziger.

Morrison, G. H. Addresses from a Glasgow pulpit: The wings of the morning. *$1.50 net. Armstrong.

Morrison, G. H. Return of the angels. —Sunday evening sermons. ea., $1.35 net. Doran.

Nicoll, *Sir* W: R. Sunday evening; 52 short sermons for home reading. $1.50 net.—Ten minute sermons. $1 net. Doran.

Occasional sermons and addresses suitable for burials, religious gatherings and conventions. $1.50 net. Wagner.

Parkhurst, C: H: Little lower than the angels. *$1.25 net. Revell.

Parsons, R. Sermons. $1.50. McVey.

Pearson, C: W: Search after truth. *$1.25 net. Sherman, F.

Peters, M. C. Sermons that won the masses. 50 c. Am. Bapt.

Pierce, C: C. Humor of the heart for faith: sermons. *$1 net. Young Churchman.

Pierson, A. T. Making of a sermon. *$1.50 net. Gospel Pub.

Powers, J. D. O. Love never faileth: [sermon.] 50 c. A. Harriman.

Presbyterian pulpit. 10 v. ea., *50 c. net; per set, *$4 net. Presb. Bd.

Pulpit year book: outline sermons. *$1 net. Gorham.

Robertson, F: W: Sermons on religion and life. *$1 net. Dutton.

Robinson, J. A., *D.D.* Vision of unity. 50 c.; 25 c. Longmans.

Rogers, E. B., *comp.* Topical excerpt library. $10. Springfield Lib. Pub.

Rowe, F: L:, *and* C., M. A., *comps.* Pioneer sermons and addresses. $1.25. F: L: Rowe.

Schuh, L. H. Talks for the young. 50 c. Lutheran Bk.

Scott, R., *and* Stiles, W: C., *eds.* Modern sermons by world scholars. $7.50. Funk.

Selby, T: G. Divine Craftsman, and other sermons. *$1.25 net. Eaton & M.

Singer, S. Literary remains. 3 v. *$1.25 net. Bloch.

Skrine, J: H. Sermons to pastors and masters. $1.50 net. Longmans.

Slattery, C: L. Historic ministry and the present Christ. **50 c. net. Longmans.

Smith, H: Sermons. 45 c.; 60 c.; 75 c. Putnam.

Smith, W. M. Giving a man another chance, and other sermons. *$1 net. Revell.

Steen, R. S. Strength of quietness, and other sermons. 75 c. Dodd.

SERMONS.—*Continued.*

Stewardson, L. C. Sermon preached at the dedication of St. Paul's chapel. (Add. pubs. for price.) Columbia Univ.

Stiegele, P. Necessity of religion: [Lenten sermons.] 40 c. Wagner.

Stimson, H: A. New things of God. *$1.25 net. Revell.

Stone, D. Witness of the spirit and the water and the blood; sermon. 20 c. net. Longmans.

Stone, H: M. Witness of the heart and other sermons. **$1.25 net. Longmans.

Straton, J: R. Salvation of society. $1. Fleet-M.

Strickler, G. B. Sermons. $1. Revell.

Thomas, R. Glad tidings. $1.25. Pilgrim Press.

Tipple, E. S., *ed.* Drew sermons on the golden texts for 1909, *$1.25 net; for 1910, *$1 net. Eaton & M.

Tipple, S: A: Sunday mornings at Norwood; being twenty-two sermons and twenty-two prayers. *$1.25 net. Eaton & M.

Van Buren, J. H. Sermons that have helped. *$1.25 net. Dutton.

Wakeford, J: Little sermons on the Sunday Gospels. $1.50 net. Longmans.

Wallace, W. Sermons for the Christian year. 3 v. $4 net. Herder.

Watkinson, W: L. Fatal barter, and other sermons. *$1 net. Revell.

Whitworth, W: A. Sanctuary of God, and other sermons. *$1.50 net. Macmillan.

Wilkinson, G: H. Invisible glory: selected sermons. *$2 net. Young Churchman.

Wilkinson, H. S. Alabaster box, and other sermons. 50 c. H. S. Wilkinson.

Wilmot-Buxton, H. J: Old road; thirty plain sermons. *$2 net. Whittaker.

Wright, L. Eighteen sermons on great themes. $1. Chr. Un.

Yates, T: Sculptors of life. *$1 net. Armstrong.

Young, D. T. Gospel of the left hand. *$1.25 net. Doran.

See also Atonement;—Bible;—Catholic church;—Children; —Christianity; — Christmas;—Cross; —Easter; — Holy week; — Hymns and hymn-writers; — Illustrations (*religious*); — Lent; — Lord's prayer;—Marriage;—Missions and missionaries; — Parables; — Preaching; — Repentance;—Revivals;—Sacraments;—Sin; —Sunday-school; — Thanksgiving Day; — Young men;— *also* Newman Memorial Church.

Sermons, epistles and apocalypses of Israel's prophets. Kent, C: F. $2.75 net. Scribner.

Sermons from Shakespeare. Vaughan, L. J. $1. Bartlett.

Sermons in syntax. Adams, J: *$1.50 net. Scribner.

Serpent's trail. Cullens, F. B. $1. F. B. Cullens.

SERRANIDAE.

See **Bass.**

SERUM.

Bolduan, C: F: Immune sera. $1.50. Wiley.

Bosanquet, W: C. Serums, vaccines and toxins in treatment and diagnosis. $2 net. Funk.

Schorer, E. H: Vaccine and serum therapy. $2. Mosby.

See also **Syphilis.**

Servant in the house. Kennedy, C: R. †$1.25 Harper.
SERVANTS.
Domestic employment. per 100, $4; per 300, $10; per 500, $16. Legal Aid.
See also Domestic economy.
Servants of the King. Speer, R. E. 50 c.; 35 c. Young People's Miss.
SERVETO, Miguel.
See Servetus, Michael.
SERVETUS, Michael.
Osler, W: Michael Servetus. 40 c. Oxford Univ.
SERVIA.
Lazarovich - Hrebelianovich, *Prince and Princess*. Servian people. 2 v. $5 net. Scribner.
Miyatovic, C: Servia and the Servians. *$3 net. L. C. Page.
Service, Rob. W.
Ballads of a Cheechako. '09(D4) 12°, $1. Stern.
Service abroad. Montgomery, H: H. 90 c. net. Longmans.
Service and sport in the Sudan. Comyn, D: C: E: $4 net. Lane.
Service of coast artillery. Hines, F. T: $3.50 net. Goodenough & W.
Service of the synagogue. Adler, H. M., *ed.* H. D. Buegeleisen.
SERVICES.
See Worship.
Serviss, Garrett Putnam.
Astronomy with the naked eye. '08(Ap25) c. charts, O. **$1.40 net. Harper.
Curiosities of the sky; popular presentation of the great riddles and mysteries of astronomy. '09(N20) c. il. O. **$1.40 net. Harper.
Round the year with the stars; the chief beauties of the starry heavens as seen with the naked eye. '10(S17) c. maps, O. $1 net. Harper.
Servitude. Osgood, I. †$1.50. Estes.
Servitude et grandeur militaires. Vigny, A. V., *Comte* de. 60 c. Oxford Univ.
Sesame and lilies. *See* Ruskin, J:
Sesame booklets. 21 v. '08(D5); v. 22-31. '09(O9) il. Tt. ea., 40 c.; leath., 75 c.—34 v. [New ed.] '10(N) fronts. 32°, ea., silk, 60 c., boxed. Crowell.
Set in silver. Williamson, C: N. †$1.50. Doubleday, P.
Setchell, W: Alb.
Genus Sphaerosoma. '10(Je) 107-120 p. il. Q. (Univ. of Cal. pubs.; Botany.) pap., 15 c. Univ. of Cal.
SETON, Elizabeth, *Mother*.
McCann, M. A., *Sister*. Mother Seton, foundress of the Sisters of Charity. $1. Sisters of Charity.
Seton, Ernest Thompson.
Biography of a silver-fox. '09(Ap3) c. il. D. †$1.50. Century Co.
Life-histories of northern animals; account of the mammals of Manitoba. In 2 v. '09(D25) c. il. maps, 4°, **$18 net. Scribner.
War dance and the fire-fly dance. '10 (Jl30) c. 12°, 10 c. Doubleday, P.
—, and Baden-Powell, Lieut. Gen. Sir Rob. Stephenson Smyth.
Boy scouts of America; handbook of woodcraft, scouting and life-craft; with which is incorporated by arrangement General Sir Rob. Baden-Powell's Scouting for boys. '10(Ag6) c. il. O. flex. linen, 25 c. Doubleday, P.
Setting out of tube railways. Halden, G: M. *$4 net. Spon.
"Settlement" (Jewish) cook book. Kander, *Mrs.* S. *$1 net. Caspar.
Settlement of dust in mines. Scholz, C. (Add. pub. for price.) Hodgart.
Settlement of Illinois. Boggess, A. C. $3. Chic. Hist.
Settlement of Illinois from 1830 to 1850. Pooley, W: V. 75 c. Univ. of Wis.
Settlement of labor disputes. American Academy of Political and Social Science. $1. Am. Acad. Pol. Sci.
SETTLEMENTS.
See Social science.
Settlers and scouts. Strang, H. $1.25 net. Doran.
Settlers in Canada. *See* Marryat, F:
Seufert, E: Constant, and Stuart, J:
Vademecum of treatment: for the use of medical students and practitioners. '08 (Ag15) c. 12°, $2.50. Keener.
Seven against Thebes. *See* Æschylus. Suppliant maidens.
Seven ages of childhood. Wells, C. **$2 net. Moffat.
Seven centuries of lace. Pollen, M. M. *$9 net. Macmillan.
Seven champions of Christendom; ed. by T: Cartwright. '08(Ag) 16°, (Every child's lib.) 50 c. Dutton.
Seven champions of Christendom; ed. by W. H. G. Kingston. '08(N7) il. T. (Books for the young.) 50 c. Stokes.
Seven Christmas candles. Fox, F. M. $1. L. C. Page.
Seven English cities. Howells, W: D. *$2 net. Harper.
Seven essentials to life and health. Ballou, G: D. $1.50 net. G: D. Ballou.
Seven great statesmen. White, A. D. $2.50 net. Century Co.
700 lessons in business. Roe, E: T: $1. J: A. Hertel.
Seven lamps of architecture. *See* Ruskin, J:
Seven little Australians. Turner, E. †75 c. McKay.
Seven little Marshalls. Nixon-Roulet, M. F. 45 c. Benziger.
Seven little wise men. Fox, F. M. $1. L. C. Page.
Seven little women. Twelvetrees, R. C. 75 c. Stokes.
Seven maids. Smith, *Mrs.* E. T. †$1. Burt.
Seven old ladies of Lavender Town. Bunner, H: C. 75 c. Harper.
Seven parables of the kingdom. Linn, S: 40 c. S: Linn.
Seven principals of successful salesmanship. Lenington, N. G. $1. Commercial Sci.
Seven seas. *See* Kipling, Rudyard.
Seven sonnets. Sharp, J. R. 85 c. J. R. Sharp.
Seven splendid sinners. Trowbridge, W. R. H. *$4.50. Brentano's.
Seven stages of golf. Simpson, H. *75 c. net. Lippincott.

Seven streams. Deeping, G: W. $1.50. Cassell.

Seven who were hanged. Andreiyeff, L. $1. J. S. Ogilvie.

Seven words from the cross. Watson, F: 81 c. Whittaker.

Sevenich, Jos. Mathew.
Des landmanns geflügel-buch; ein hand- und lehrbuch für den deutschen farmer. '10(D) c. 134 p. il. 12°, 40 c. Excelsior Pub.

Seventeen little bears. Smith, L. R. 30 c. Flanagan.

Seventeenth century men of latitude. George, E: A: **$1.25 net. Scribner.

SEVENTH DAY ADVENTISTS.
Lewis, A. H. Spiritual Sabbathism. $1.50. Am. Sabbath Tr. Soc.
Main, A. E. Bible studies on the Sabbath question for the use of pastors, Sabbath schools, etc. $1. A. E. Main.

Seventh day Baptists in Europe and America; series of historical papers written in commemoration of the 100th anniversary of the organization of the Seventh day Baptist General Conference; celebrated at Ashaway, Rhode Island, Aug. 20-25, 1902. 2 v. '10(O15) il. pors. facsims., 8°, $5. Am. Sabbath Tract Soc.

Seventh noon. Bartlett, F: O. †$1.50. Small.

Seventy's course in theology. Roberts, B. H:, *comp.* (Add. pub. for price.) Deseret News.

Severance, H: Ormal, and Walsh, C: Harper, comps.
Guide to the current periodicals and serials of the United States and Canada, 1909. '09(F6) c. Q. *$2 net.—Supplement, Sept. 1, 1910. '10(D3) c. Q. pap., 50 c. Wahr.

Severance, Howard S.
Millennial essays; rept. to my old friends and neighbors, covering the period of my absence from home; Philippine service, trip around the world and experiences and incidents of my travels and sojourn through foreign lands, and conclusions. '10(Ag27) front. O. $1.50. H. S. Severance.

Severed mantle. Lindsey, W: **$1.35 net. Houghton M.

Severest anæmias. Hunter, W: v. 1. *$3.25 net. Macmillan

Severy, Melvin Linwood.
Gillette's industrial solution; world corporation. '08(D19) c. il. O. *$1.50 net. Ball Pub.

SEVIER, John.
Turner, F. M. Life of General John Sevier. $1.50 net. Neale.

SEWAGE AND SEWERAGE.
Ashley, B. J: Cesspool and its dangers.—Principles of decay as applied to biologic sewage purification. ea., gratis. Ashley.
Battle of the microbes; [description of the methods of sewage disposal.] gratis. Merchants' Assoc.

SEWAGE AND SEWERAGE.—*Continued.*
Clark, H. W., *and* Gage, S. D. Review of 21 years' experiments upon the purification of sewage at the Lawrence Experiment Station. (Priv. pr.) Mass. Bd. Health.
Cosgrove, J: J. Sewage purification and disposal. $3. Standard Sanitary Mfg.
Davis, G: J., *jr., and* Bowles, J. T. B. Sewage purification with special reference to Wisconsin conditions. 30 c. Univ. of Wis.
Dunbar, W: P. Principles of sewage treatment. *$4.50 net. Lippincott.
Easdale, W. C. Sewage disposal works. $4. Spon.
Folwell, A. P. Sewerage; designing, construction, and maintenance of sewerage systems. $3. Wiley.
Kinnicutt, L. P., *and others.* Sewage disposal. $3 net. Wiley.
Marston, A. Sewers and drains. $1. Am. Sch. Corr.
New York [City.] *Metropolitan Sewerage Commission.* Digest of data collected before the year 1908, rel. to the sanitary condition of New York Harbor. gratis. Metropolitan Sewerage.
Phelps, E. B. Disinfection of sewage and sewage filter effluents. 15 c. U. S., Supt. of Docs.
Potter, A. Rept. upon joint outlet sewer in Essex and Union Counties, N. J. A. Potter.
Soper, G: A. Pollution of New York harbor. $2.50. G: A. Soper.
Soper, G: A., *and others.* Sewerage and sewage disposal in the metropolitan district of New York and New Jersey. gratis. N. Y. City.
Venable, W: M. Methods and devices for bacterial treatment of sewage. $3. Wiley.
See also Refuse and refuse disposal;—Sanitary engineering.

Sewall, C: H:
Lessons in telegraphy. '09(F6) c. il. 12°, $1. Van Nostrand.

Sewall, Fk., D.D.
Swedenborg and the "Sapientia angelica." '10(D17) 12°, (Philosophies ancient and modern from Pythagoras to Spencer.) 50 c. net. Dodge.
Swedenborg and the University; address on the commencement day of the schools of the Urbana University, July 19, 1908, '08 [1909.] (N) 16 p. 16°. (Add. University for price.) Urbana Univ.

Sewanee theological lib. 12°. Univ. Press, (Sewance.)
—Hart. Book of common prayer. $1.50.

Seward, Alb. C:
Fossil plants; text-book for students of botany and geology. '10(Je4) 4°, $5 net. Putnam.
—, **ed.** Darwin and modern science; essays in commemoration of the centenary of the birth of Charles Darwin and of the fifteenth anniversary of the publication of the Origin of species. '09(Je5) 8°, *$5 net. Putnam.

Seward, S: Swayze, jr.
Note-taking. '10(N5) c. 12°, 50 c. Allyn & B.
—, ed. Narrative and lyric poems, for students. '09(O30) c. D. **$1 net. Holt.

SEWARD, William Henry.
Callahan, J. M. Evolution of Seward's Mexican policy. 75 c. Univ. of W. Va.
Hale, E: E., *jr.* William H. Seward. $1.25 net. Jacobs.

SEWARD PENINSULA, Alaska.
See Alaska.

Sewell, Anna.
Black Beauty: autobiography of a horse. '10(D10) col. il. 12°, $1.25. Jacobs.

Sewell, Elisha Granville.
Gospel lessons and life history. '08(N) c. 8+338 p. por. 12°, *$1.15 net. McQuiddy.

SEWING.
See Embroidery;—Needlework;—Tailoring.

SEWING MACHINES.
Free Sewing Machine Co. Free family sewing machine; information on sewing machine construction. $1.50. Free Sewing.

SEX.
Alexander, J: L. Sex instruction for boys. 5 c. Westminster.
Aushutz, E: P. Sexual ills and diseases. $1 net. Boericke & T.
Brashere, O. M. Science and suffrage; inquiry into the causes of sex differences. 25 c. O. M. Brashere.
Cooper, A. Sexual disabilities of man and their treatment. *$1 net. Hoeber.
Crosbee, M. F. The message. 50 c. Tudor Press.
Dietrich, G. Biology of sex. 50 c. Educ. Press.
Dietrich, G. Biology of the sex problem. 50 c. S: A. Bloch.
Edgerly, W. Private lessons in the cultivation of sex magnetism. $25. Ralston Univ.
Edwards, E. Personal information for young women. 50 c. Fenno.
Ellis, H: H. Evolution of modesty. $2.—Studies in the psychology of sex. v. 6, Sex in relation to society. $3. Davis.
Erwood, W: J. Rational life. $1. W. J. Erwood.
Evans, *Mrs.* F. Purity, birth and sexual problems for mothers. (Add. pubs. for price.) Purity Pub.
Forel, A. Sexual question. *$5 net. Rebman.
Hoffmann, *Mrs.* A. L. R. Before marriage: a mother's parting counsel to her son on the eve of his marriage.—Social duty of our daughters: talks with mothers and their grown daughters. ea., **35 c. net. Vir Pub.
Howard, W: L. Plain facts on sex hygiene. $1 net. Clode.
Keith, M. C. Marriage bed; medical and philosophical treatise. $3.50. Keith & G.
King, E. A., *and* Meyer, F: B. Clean and strong; book for young men. $1. Un. Soc. C. E.

SEX.—*Continued.*
Kraft, F. Sex of offspring. $2. Barsuette.
Lowry, E. B. Confidences; talks with a young girl concerning herself. 50 c. net. Forbes.
Mystery of sex. $1. Arcane.
Parke, J. R. Human sexuality, medico literary treatise on the hist. and pathology of the sex instinct. $3. Professional.
Robinson, W: J. Never-told tales: [stories of the disastrous results of sexual ignorance.] $1. Altrurians.
Scott, J. F. Heredity and morals as affected by the use and abuse of the sexual instinct. $2. Treat.
Senator, H., *and* Kaminer, S., *eds.* Marriage and disease. $2.50. Hoeber.
Smith, O. E. Manhood; study of male vitality. $4. Sentinel Pr.
Stall, S. What a young boy ought to know. $1. Vir.
Talmey, B. S. Genesis; manual for the instruction of children in matters sexual. $1.50. Practitioner's Pub.
Walling, W:, *ed.* Sexology. $2. Puritan Pub.
Williams, *Mrs.* M. B. Sex problems. $1 net. Revell.
Zenner, P. Education in sexual physiology and hygiene. $1. Clarke.
See also Boys;—Education;—Eugenics;—Generative organs; — Girls; — Man; — Marriage; — Mothers;—Venereal diseases;—Woman.

Sexton, Alex. Humboldt.
Fuel and refractory materials. 2d ed. '10 (Ag6) 12°, $2.50 net. Van Nostrand.

Sexton, Ida, comp.
Manual work for use in Sunday schools; with a foreword by Rev. W: Walter Smith. '09(N20) c. il. D. 75 c. Young Churchman.

Sexton, Marian B., comp.
Monmouth Baptist ladies' cook book. 3d ed. '07, [1908.] (Je.) c. 7-298+14 p. il. 12°, 60 c.; 85 c. M. B. Sexton.

Sexton, Michael H:
Red hair from a cock of hay. '09(O) c. 5-71 p. il. por. 8°, $1. G: W: Browning.

Sexton, W: H:
Truth and near truth: poems. '08(My9) c. il. por. 12°, $1.50; hf. leath., $2. Winn & H.

Seyffert, Oscar.
Dictionary of classical antiquities; abr. by Dr. Emil Reich. '08(My9) 12°, (New classical lib.) *$1 net. Macmillan.

Seymour, C:
Speaking in public. '09(My22) 12°, *$1.25 net. Dutton.

Seymour, F:
Roosevelt in Africa; cont. also a complete hist. and study of wild animals of the world; with thrilling and exciting experiences of hunters of big game. '09(D18) c. front. il. maps, 8°, $2; hf. mor., $2.75. Educ. Co.
See also Lundeberg, Axel.

Seymour, F: H. A.
Up hill and down dale in ancient Etruria. '10(N5) il. map, O. $3 net. Appleton.

Seymour, H. Rippon.
Physical training. [1910.] (Mr) *$1 net. W: R. Jenkins.
Formerly published by E. R. Pelton.

Seymour, Harriet Ayer.
How to think music. '10(N19) c. D. $1. H. W. Gray.

Seymour, Ralph Fletcher.
Christ in Flanders. '10(D31) S. pap., $1.25; vellum., $5. (Six copies.) Seymour.

Seymour, Rob. Gillin, D.D.
Fresh water from old wells: being the wells of the Bible with their spiritual and moral lessons. '08(D26) c. O. **80 c. net. Am. Bapt.

SEYMOUR, Thomas Day.
White, J: W. Thomas Day Seymour, 1848-1907. gratis. B. Perrin.

Seymour, Wa.
Ups and downs of a wandering life. '10 (N12) por. O. $3 special net. Appleton.

Seymour Charlton. Maxwell, W: B. †$1.50. Appleton.

Seys, Roland Alex. Wood-.
See Wood-Seys, Roland Alex.

Shaad, G: C.
See Knox, C: E.

Shackelford, Otis M.
Seeking the best; dedicated to the negro youth. '09, [1910.] (F) c. 177 p. por. 12°, $1. Hudson.

Shackford, Martha Hale, and Judson, Marg.
Composition, rhetoric, literature. '08(S5) c. 12°, $1.12. B: H. Sanborn.

Shackleton, Mrs. Eliz. Fleming.
See Shackleton, Rob.

Shackleton, Shackleton, Sir Ernest H.
Heart of the Antarctic; being the story of the British Antartic Expedition, 1907-1909; with introd. by Hugh Rob. Mill; account of the first journey to the south magnetic pole by Professor T. W. Edgeworth David. In 2 v. '09(N20) c. il. por. diagrs., Q. **$10 net, boxed. Lippincott.

Shackleton, Rob. and Mrs. Eliz. Fleming.
Adventures in home making. '10(N12) c. il. O. $1.75. Lane.

SHACKS.
See Architecture.

Shade, Imogene.
See Rietz, H. L.

Shade trees for North Carolina. Ashe, W: W. 8 c. Uzzell.

"Shadow," pseud.
See Hammond, Stephen Tillinghast.

Shadow and shine. Doudney, S. $1.50. Jennings.

Shadow behind the throne. Harper, O. 25 c. J. S. Ogilvie.

Shadow between his shoulder blades. Harris, J. C. **50 c. net. Small.

Shadow garden. Cawein, M. J. $1.50 net. Putnam.

Shadow of a Titan. Wedgwood, A. F. $1.50. Lane.

Shadow of Christine. Vivian, E. C. H. $1.50. Fenno.

Shadow of Everleigh. Lansdowne, J. $1.25. Benziger.

Shadow of the cathedral. Ibanez, V. B. *$1.35 net. Dutton.

Shadow of the crescent. Mitchell, E: B. †$1.25. Stokes.

Shadow of the czar. Carling, J. R. †75 c. Little, B. & Co.

Shadow on the dial. Bierce, A. *$2 net. A. M. Robertson.

Shadow world. Garland, H. $1.35. Harper.

Shadowing wing. Krumreig, E: L. $1.50. E: L. Krumreig.

Shadowless man. Chamesso, A. v. $1 net. Warne.

Shadows of the old booksellers. Knight, C: 50 c.; 75 c. Dutton.

Shadows of the valley. Mortimer, A. G. $1.50 net. Jacobs.

Shadwell, Arth., M.D.
Industrial efficiency: comparative study of industrial life in England, Germany and America. New ed. '09(My22) O. *$2 net. Longmans.

Shaen, Marg. Josephine, ed.
Memorials of two sisters, Susanna and Catherine Winkworth; ed. by their niece, Marg. J. Shaen. '08(O31) pors. O. *$3.50 net. Longmans.

Shafer, Donald Cameron.
Stories of an old Dutch town [Schenectady, N. Y.] in verse. '09(Ap) c. 47 p. il. 8°, 50 c. Robson.

Shafer, J: Adolph.
See Britton, Nathaniel Lord.

Shafer, Mrs. Sara Andrew.
White-paper garden. '10(Je11) il. O. $2.50 net. McClurg.

Shaffner, Lillyan.
Love and friendship. '10(D) 12°, pap., 35 c. net. P. Elder.

SHAFT GOVERNORS.
Collins, H. E. Shaft governors. $1. Hill Pub.

Shafting, pulleys, belting and rope transmission. Collins, H. E. $1. Hill Pub.

"Shaftsbury, Edm.," pseud.
See Edgerly, Webster.

Shakelford, Ethel.
The life of me. '10(My14) il. 12°, $1.50. Dodge.

Shakespeare, W:, 1849.
Art of singing; based on the principles of the old Italian singing-masters, and dealing with breath-control and production of the voice, together with exercises; entirely rewritten. '10(N19) il. pors. O. $2. Ditson.

Shakespeare, W:, 1564-1616.
Works. In 12 v. Verona ed. '10(D) limp leath., $18, boxed. Barse & H.
Works of William Shakespeare, [Ed. de luxe.] 20 v. '09(D25) c. il. por. 8°, subs., $60. Bigelow, S.
Works. Dowden ed. vs. 13-25. '08(Jl11); v. 26-28. '10(O15) 8°, ea., $1.25. Bobbs-M.
[Works.] Century Shakespeare; introd. by F: Ja. Furnivall; with notes and glossary. In 40 v. '08(D19) fronts. 24°, ea., 35 c.; lambskin, 65 c. Caldwell.
Works. De luxe ed. 12 v. '10(N) il. levant, $36. Crowell.

SHAKESPEARE, William.—*Continued.*

[Works:] the old-spelling Shakespeare: being the works of Shakespeare in the spelling of the best quarto and folio texts; ed. by F. J. Furnivall and the late W. G. Boswell-Stone. In 40 v. [v. 1,] Love's labour's lost. '08(Ja18); [v. 2,] The taming of the shrew; ed. by W. G. Boswell-Stone. '08(F15); [v. 3,] The comedie of errors; [v. 4,] A midsommer nights dreame; [v. 5,] Twelfe night; or, what you will; [v. 6,] The two gentlemen of Verona. '07(Ap11); [v. 7,] The merry wives of Windsor. '08(S19); [v. 8,] Much adoe about nothing; [v. 9,] The winter's tale. '08(O31); [v. 10,] As you like it. '09(Ja16); [v. 11,] All's well that ends well. '09(F); [v. 12,] The Tempest; [v. 13,] The merchant of Venice. '09(F20); v. 14, The history of Henrie the Fourth. pt. 1; with introd. by F. W. Clarke. v. 15, The second part of Henrie the Fourth; with introd. by F. W. Clarke. (D4) 8°, (Shakespeare lib.: old-spelling Shakespeare.) ea., *$1 net; Persian, *$1.60 net; Lib. ed., *$1.70 net. (Sold in sets only.) Duffield.

Works. Stratford Town Shakespeare. In 10 v. Complete ed. printed in poet's native town from the Shakespeare Head Press. '08(My9) large 8°, $50. Duffield.

Works: the Temple Shakespeare; ed. by Israel Gollancz. In 40 v. '10(Ag27) 16°, ea., 35 c. net; leath., ea., 55 c. net; Pocket lexicon concordance, 60 c. net; 75 c. net. Dutton.

Works. 10 v. New imperial lib. ed. '10 (D) il. 8°, ea., $1.25; hf. cf., $2.25; New il. sterling ed., ea., $1. (Sets only.) Estes.

[Works.] New variorum ed.; ed. by Horace Howard Furness. v. 16, The tragedy of Richard the third; with the landing of Earle Richmond and the battell at Bosworth Field. '08(O10) c. O. **$4 net; ¾ levant, **$5 net. Lippincott.

[Works.] Longmans' school Shakespeare; consisting of twelve of the most suitable plays for school reading; ed., with glossary, by A. V. Houghton. '08(Ap18) D. *90 c. net. Longmans.

Works. De luxe ed. 6 v. '10(D) 16°, ea., mor., $1.75 net. (Sets only.) Nelson.

[Works.] Bankside-Restoration Shakespeare; plays of Mr. William Shakespeare as rewritten or rearranged by his successors of the Restoration period, as presented at the Dukes Theatre and elsewhere circa 1664-1669; being the text of these so-restored plays with the First Folio Shakespeare text with critical introd.; ed. by Appleton Morgan and Willis Vickery. Ed. de luxe. In 9 v. or more. v. 2, Hamlet and the Ur-Hamlet; v. 3, The tempest; with an introduction by F: W. Kilbourne. '08(F22); v. 4, Anthony and Cleopatra, by J: Dryden; v. 5, A law against lovers, (the rewriting of "Measure for measure," by Sir W: D'Avenant.) '08(D5) 8°, parchment, ea., $5; subs. for set, $35. Shakespeare Press.

SHAKESPEARE, William.—*Continued.*

All's well that ends well; ed., with notes, introd., glossary, list of variorum readings, and selected criticism by Charlotte Porter and Helen A. Clarke. [First folio ed.] '09(Ap3) c. front. S. 75 c.; limp leath., $1. Crowell.

Antonie and Cleopatra; ed., with notes, introd., glossary, list of variorum readings, and selected criticism, by Charlotte Porter and Helen A. Clarke. '09(N13) c. por. S. (First Folio ed.) 75 c.; leath., $1. Crowell.

Antony and Cleopatra; with introd. and notes by Margaret A. Eaton, B.A. '08, [1909.] c. 171 p. 16°, (Classic lib.) pap., 25 c. Educ. Pub.

As you like it. '09(D18) il. 4°, $4.50. Doran.

As you like it; with songs set to music. '08 (F22) D. (Shakespeare lib.:Lamb Shakespeare for the young.) *80 c.; net; limp lambskin, *$1 net. Duffield.

Children's Shakespeare. '10(D) il. 4°, bds., 75 c. Doran.

Comedies. '08(O10) 12°, ("Best books" ser.) leath., *$1 net. Dutton.

Coriolanus; ed., with notes, introd., glossary, list of variorum readings, and selected criticism by Charlotte Porter and Helen Archibald Clarke. [First folio ed.] '08(O24) c. front. S. 75 c.; limp leath., $1. Crowell.

Cymbeline; ed., with notes, introd., glossary, list of variorum readings, and selected criticism, by Charlotte Porter and Helen A. Clarke. [First folio ed.] '10 (Mr5) c. front. S. 75 c.; limp leath., $1. Crowell.

Cymbeline; with songs set to music by T. Maskell Hardy. '08(D5) 12°, (Shakespeare lib.: Lamb Shakespeare for the young.) *80 c. net; limp lambskin, *$1 net. Duffield.

Evening with Shakespeare; an entertainment of readings, tableaux and songs set to the old tunes; arranged by T. Maskell Hardy. '09(F20) 12°, (Shakespeare lib.: Lamb Shakespeare for the young.) *80 c. net; limp lambskin, *$1 net. Duffield.

Golden texts from the works of W: Shakespeare. '10(Ja29) c. por. 8°, $1. Werner Co.

Hamlet. '10(D10) col. il. 4°, $4.50 net; de luxe ed., vel., $15 net. Doran.

Hamlet; introd. and notes by H: Norman Hudson; ed. and rev. by Ebenezer Charlton Black; with the co-operation of Andrew Jackson George. School ed. '09 (N20) c. S. (New Hudson Shakespeare.) 50 c. Ginn.

Henry v.; with songs set to music by T. Maskell Hardy. '08(D5) 12°, (Shakespeare lib.: Lamb Shakespeare for the young.) *80 c. net; limp lambskin, *$1 net. Duffield.

Shakespeare, W:—*Continued.*

Henry v.; introd. and notes by H: N. Hudson; ed. and rev. by Ebenezer Charlton Black, with the co-operation of And. Jackson George. School ed. '08(O10) c. S. (New Hudson Shakespeare.) 50 c. Ginn.

Henry v.; ed. by W: Allan Neilson. '09 (D11) c. S. (Lake English classics.) 25 c. Scott, F. & Co.

Histories and poems. '08(O10) 12°, ("Best books" ser.) leath., *$1 net. Dutton.

Julius Cæsar. Verulam ed.; essay on envy; ed. by Edn. Reed. '10(Mr26) c. il. 16°, 75 c. Coburn Press.

Julius Cæsar; introd. and notes by H: N. Hudson; ed. and rev. by Ebenezer Charlton Black; with the co-operation of And. Jackson George. School ed. '08(O3) c. front. facsim., tab., S. (New Hudson Shakespeare.) 50 c. Ginn.

Julius Cæsar; ed., with introd., notes and regent's examination question, by J. B. Z. Raucher. '09(Mr6) c. por. S. (Manhattan English classics.) 25 c.; pap., 10 c. Manhattan Bk.

Julius Cæsar; ed., with an introd. and notes, by Brainerd Kellogg. '10(S3) c. il. front. 16°, (Merrill's English texts.) 25 c. C: E. Merrill.

Julius Cæsar; ed., with notes, outline study and examination questions, by Maud Elma Kingsley and Fk. Herbert Palmer. '08(Ag1) c. 16°, (Kingsley English texts.) 40 c.; pap., 25 c. Palmer Co.

Julius Cæsar; ed., with introd. and notes, by F: H: Sykes. '09(Ap17) c. front. 16°, (English classics.) **25 c. net. Scribner.

King John; ed., with notes, introd., glossary, list of variorum readings and selected criticism by Charlotte Porter. First folio ed. '10(O22) c. por. S. 75 c.; limp leath., $1. Crowell.

King Lear; from the Cambridge ed. by W: Allan Neilson; with an introd. and additional notes by Ashley H. Thorndike. '09 (Ap10) c. D. (Riverside literature ser.) 25 c. Houghton M.

Love poems; selected and arr. by Ethel Harris. [1910.] (Ap) 121 p. il. por. 8°, $1. Rand, McN. & Co.

Macbeth; with songs set to music. '09 (My8) il. 12°, (Shakespeare lib.: Lamb Shakespeare for the young.) *80 c. net; leath., *$1 net. Duffield.

Macbeth; introd. and notes by H: N. Hudson; ed. and rev. by Ebenezer Charlton Black, with the co-operation of And. Jackson George. School ed. '08(O10) c. S. (New Hudson Shakespeare.) 50 c. Ginn.

Macbeth; ed., with notes, outline study and examination questions by Maud Elma Kingsley and Fk. Herbert Palmer. '09 (S) 13+157 p. 16°, (Kingsley English texts.) pap., 25 c. Palmer Co.

Macbeth; ed., with introd. and notes, by F: H: Sykes. '10(Je4) c. front. 12°, (Scribner English classics.) 25 c. Scribner.

Macbeth; ed., with notes, by Homer B. Sprague; with critical comments, elocutionary analysis with suggestions for expressive reading, plans for the study of English literature, and specimens of examination papers. '09(D) c. 269 p. por. 12°, (Silver ser. of classics.) 40 c. Silver.

Measure for measure; ed., with notes, glossary, list of variorum readings, and selected criticism, by Charlotte Porter and Helen A. Clarke. [First folio ed.] '09 (Ap3) c. front. S. 75 c.; limp leath., $1. Crowell.

Merchant of Venice. '09(D18) il. 4°, $4.50, boxed. Doran.

Merchant of Venice; with songs set to music by T. Maskell Hardy. '08(S19) 12°, (Shakespeare lib.: Lamb Shakespeare for the young.) *80 c. net; limp leath., *$1 net. Duffield.

Merchant of Venice; with introd. and notes by Marg. A. Eaton. '09(Ag21) c. il. S. (Classic lib.) 25 c.; pap., 15 c. Educ. Pub.

Merry wives of Windsor; ed., with notes, introd., glossary, list of variorum readings and selected criticism, by Charlotte Porter and Helen A. Clarke. [First folio ed.] '09(Ap3) c. front. S. 75 c.; limp leath., $1. Crowell.

Merry wives of Windsor, 1602; ed. by W. W. Greg. New ed. '10(Jl2) 12°, (Tudor and Stuart lib.) $1.75 net. Oxford Univ.

Merry wives of Windsor. '10(O29) col. il. Q. $5 net, boxed. Stokes.

Midsummer-night's dream. '08(D19) Q. *$5 net, boxed. Doubleday, P.

Midsummer night's dream; with songs set to music. '08(Mr28) D. (Shakespeare lib.: Lamb Shakespeare for the young.) *80 c. net; leath., *$1 net. Duffield.

Midsummer night's dream; introd. and notes by the Rev. H: N. Hudson. '10 (D31) c. '80, '08. S. (Standard English classics.) 35 c. Ginn.

Midsummer night's dream; introd. and notes by H: Norman Hudson; ed. and rev. by Ebenezer Charlton Black, with the co-operation of Moses Grant Daniell. School ed. '10(D24) c. S. (New Hudson Shakespeare.) 50 c. Ginn.

Midsummer night's dream; ed., with an introd. and notes, by Ernest Clapp Noyes. '08(Ag15) c. 24°, (Pocket Am. and Eng. classics.) *25 c. net. Macmillan.

Midsummer-night's dream, As you like it, The tempest; ed., with introd. and notes, by G. S. Gordon. '10(D24) D. 60 c. Oxford Univ.

Midsummer night's dream; ed. by W: Allan Neilson.. '10(F12) c. S. (Lake English classics) 25 c. Scott.

Much ado about nothing. '10(D24) il. D. (Shakespeare lib.: Lamb Shakespeare for the young.) 80 c. net; lambskin, $1 net. Duffield.

Othello; biographical outlines and notes by Marg. Hill McCarter. '08, [1909.] (Je) c. 131 p. 12°. (Crane classics.) 25 c.; pap., 15 c. Crane.

Shakespeare, W:—*Continued.*

Othello; ed., with notes, introd., list of variorum readings, and sel. criticism, by Charlotte Porter and Helen Archibald Clarke. [First folio ed.] '08(F22) S. 75 c.; limp leath., $1. Crowell.

Pericles, Prince of Tyre; ed., with notes, introd., glossary, list of variorum readings and selected criticism, by Charlotte Porter and Helen A. Clarke. [First folio ed.] '10(Mr5) c. S. 75 c.; limp leath., $1. Crowell.

Richard II.; ed., with notes, introd., glossary, list of variorum readings and selected criticism, by Charlotte Porter. First folio ed. '10(O22) c. S. 75 c.; limp leath., $1. Crowell.

Richard II.; ed., with notes and introd., by Ja. Hugh Moffatt. '08(O10) por. 24°, (Pocket Am. and Eng. classics.) *25 c. net. Macmillan.

Richard II., Julius Cæsar and Macbeth; ed., with introd. and notes, by G. S. Gordon. '09(D4) D. 75 c. Oxford Univ.

Richard III.; ed., with notes, introd., glossary, list of variorum readings, and sel. criticism, by Charlotte Porter. [First folio ed. '10(O22) c. S. 75 c.; limp leath., $1. Crowell.

Romeo and Juliet; with songs set to music. '09(My8) il. 12°, (Shakespeare lib.: Lamb Shakespeare for the young.) *80 c. net; leath., *$1 net. Duffield.

Selections from six comedies and six tragedies. '10(D17) col. il. Q. bds., $2.50 net, boxed. Stokes.

Shakespeare calendar; ed. by Agnes Caldwell Way. '08(O3) c. por. D. (Chiswick ser.) **50 c. net. Crowell.

Shakespeare day by day; ed. by A. C. Way. '10(D) 12°, (Day by day ser.) 60 c.; ooze, $1. Crowell.

Shakespeare proverbs; or, the wise saws of our wisest poet collected into a modern instance, by Mary Cowden-Clarke; ed., with introd. and notes, by W: J. Rolfe. New ed. '08(S12) c. por. D. **$1.50 net. Putnam.

Sixty selections; comp. by Gerard Bridge. '08(Ja25) 8°, 60 c. G. Bridge.

Sonnets; and A lover's complaint: with an introd. by W. H. Hadow. '08(F22) D. (Oxford Tudor and Stuart lib.) pap., $1.75. Oxford Univ.

Taming of the shrew; ed., with notes, introd., glossary, list of variorum readings, and selected criticism by Charlotte Porter and Helen Archibald Clarke. [First folio ed.] '08(O24) c. front. S. 75 c.; limp leath., $1. Crowell.

Taming of the shrew; with introd. and notes by Marg. A. Eaton. '08(Je6) c. 16°, (Classic lib.) 25 c.; pap., 15 c. Educ. Pub.

Tempest. '08(D) il. 8°, $4.50. Clode.

Tempest. Verulam ed. The restoration of man's empire over nature; ed. by Edn. Reed. '10(Mr26) c. il. 16°, 75 c. Coburn Press.

Tempest; ed., with notes, introd. glossary, list of variorum readings, and sel. criticism, by Charlotte Porter and Helen Archibald Clarke. [First folio ed.] '08 (F22) S. 75 c.; limp leath., $1. Crowell.

Tempest; introd. story of the comedy by A. T. Quiller-Couch. '09(D) il. in col. 4°, *$4.50 net. Doran.

Tempest; with songs set to music by T. Maskell Hardy. '08(F22) D. (Shakespeare lib.: Lamb Shakespeare for the young.) *80 c. net; limp lambskin, *$1 net. Duffield.

Tempest; introd. and notes by H: Norman Hudson; ed. and rev. by Ebenezer Charlton Black; with the co-operation of Andrew Jackson George. School ed. '09 (N20) c. facsims., S. (New Hudson Shakespeare.) 50 c. Ginn.

Tempest; with songs by Jos. Moorat. '08(O10) il. *$4 net; ¾ levant, *$7.50 net. Pott.

Titus Andronicus; ed., with notes, introd., glossary, list of variorum readings, and selected criticism, by Charlotte Porter and Helen A. Clarke. '09(N13) c. por. S. (First Folio ed.) 75 c.; leath., $1. Crowell.

Tragedies. '08(O10) 12°, ("Best books" ser.) leath., *$1 net. Dutton.

Troylus and Cressida; ed., with notes, introd., glossary, list of variorum readings, and selected criticism, by Charlotte Porter and Helen A. Clarke. [First folio ed.] '10(Mr5) c. front. S. 75 c.; limp leath., $1. Crowell.

Twelfth night; introd. story of the comedy by A. T. Quiller-Couch. '09(D) il. in col. 4°, *$4.50 net. Doran.

Twelfth night; with songs set to music by T. Maskell Hardy. '08(S19) 12°, (Shakespeare lib.: Lamb Shakespeare for the young.) *80 c. net; limp lambskin, *$1 net. Duffield.

Twelfth night; or, what you will; ed., with introd. and notes, by Brainerd Kellogg. '10(D3) c. facsim., 16°, (Merrill's English texts.) 25 c. C: E. Merrill.

Twenty beautiful stories from Shakespeare; retold by E. Nesbit; ed. and arr. by E. T. Roe. '08(Ja11) il. 8°, $1.50; hf. mor., $2; mor., $2.50. Hertel.

Two gentlemen of Verona; ed., with notes, introd., glossary, list of variorum readings, and selected criticism by Charlotte Porter and Helen Archibald Clarke. [First folio ed.] '08(O24) c. front. S. 75 c.; limp leath., $1. Crowell.

Tymon of Athens; ed., with notes, introd., glossary, list of variorum readings, and selected criticsm, by Charlotte Porter and Helen A. Clarke. '09(N13) c. por. S. (First Folio ed.) 75 c.; limp leath., $1. Crowell.

Winter's tale; ed., with notes, introd., list of variorum readings, and sel. criticism, by Charlotte Porter and Helen A. Clarke. [First folio ed.] '08(F22) S. 75 c.; limp leath., $1. Crowell.

Shakespeare, W:—*Continued.*
Winter's tale; with songs set to music by T. Maskell Hardy. '08(Jl18) D. (Shakespeare lib.: Lamb Shakespeare for the young.) *80 c. net: limp lambskin, *$1 net. Duffield.
Wisdom of Shakespeare. '09, [1910.] (F) sq. 16°, (Wisdom ser.) *$1 net. **Brentano's.**
Worldly wisdom from Shakespeare. '08 (Je27) c. T. (Worldly wisdom ser.) leath., $1. Altemus.

SHAKESPEARE, William.
Adams, O. F. Motley jest: two plays modeled on Shakespeare and using Shakespearean characters. *$1 net. Sherman, F.
Albright, V. E. Shakespearean stage. $1.50 net. Lemcke.
Albright, V. E. Typical Shakespearean stage. [privately pr.] Putnam.
Beeching, H: C: William Shakespeare. *$1 net. Lane.
Benedict, R. R. Mystery of Hamlet, Prince of Denmark. $1 net. Lippincott.
Boardman, G: N. Shakespeare; five lectures. *$1 net. Revell.
Bradley, A. G. Avon and Shakespeare's country. $3.50 net. Dutton.
Brandes, G: William Shakespeare. *$2.50 net. Macmillan.
Brooke, C: F: T., *ed.* Shakespeare apocrypha. *$1.75 net; *$2.50 net. Oxford Univ.
Burgess, W: Bible in Shakespeare. *$1.50 net. Revell.
Carter, T: T. Stories from Shakespeare retold. $1.50 net. Crowell.
Chisholm, L. Stories from Shakespeare. 50 c. net. Dutton.
Clemens, S: L. Is Shakespeare dead? **$1.25 net. Harper.
Coleridge, S: T. Lectures and notes on Shakespeare, and other dramatists. 50 c.; 75 c. Dutton.
Cunliffe, R: J: New Shakespearean dict. $2.50 net. Scribner.
Davenport, A. Leadership of Shakespeare. 10 c. A. Davenport.
Davidson, *Mrs.* H. A. N. Study of King Henry Fourth. pt. 1-2.—King Henry Fifth.—King John.—King Richard the Second. ea., 25 c. H. A. Davidson.
Foster, J: Shakespeare word-book: glossary of archaic forms and varied usages of words employed by Shakespeare. *$3 net. Dutton.
Frank, H: Tragedy of Hamlet; psychological study. $1.50 net. Sherman, F.
Furnivall, F: J., *and* Munroe, J: Shakespeare, life and work. *35 c. net: *65 c. net. Cassell.
Gapen, J. K. Poems and plays of William Shakespeare, arranged in order of their first appearance. (Add. author for price.) J. K. Gapen.
Gateway to Shakespeare. $2. Nelson.
Gollancz, I. Pocket lexicon concordance to the Temple Shakespeare. 60 c. net; 75 c. net. Dutton.

Shakespeare, W:—*Continued.*
Greenwood, G. G: In re Shakespeare; Beeching v. Greenwood. *$1 net.—Shakespeare problem restated. *$5 net. Lane.
Greg, W. W., *comp.* Descriptive catalogue of the early editions of the works of Shakespeare preserved in the library of Eton College. $1.20. Oxford Univ.
Guerber, H. A. Stories of Shakespeare's comedies. $1.25 net. Dodd.
Harris, F. Man Shakespeare and his tragic life story. *$2.50 net. M. Kennerley.
Hazlitt, W: Characters of Shakespeare's plays. *40 c. net. Putnam.
Holinshead, R. Shakespeare's Holinshead: the Chronicle and the historical plays compared. *$3.50 net. Duffield.
Jameson, *Mrs.* A. Shakespeare's heroines. *80 c. net; *$1.25 net. Macmillan.
Jerrold, W. C. Shakespeare-land. $1.25. Estes.
Johnson, C: F: Shakespeare and his critics. **$1.50 net. Houghton M.
Johnson, S: On Shakespeare: essays and notes. 85 c. Oxford Univ.
Lamb, C: *and* M. Tales from Shakespeare. $1. Bowman.
Lamb, C: *and* M. Tales from Shakespeare. 35 c. net; 70 c. net; $1. Dutton.
Lamb, C: *and* M. Tales from Shakespeare. 2 v. $4. Lamb Pub.
Lamb, C: *and* M. Tales from Shakespeare. $1.25; $1.50. Lippincott.
Lang, J. More stories from Shakespeare. 50 c. net. Dutton.
Lanier, S. Shakespere and his forerunners. $1.60. Doubleday, P.
Lee, S. L. Life of William Shakespeare. **$2.25 net. Macmillan.
Lounsbury, T: R. Shakespeare as a dramatic artist. **$2 net. Scribner.
MacCallum, M. W. Shakespeare's Roman plays and their background. $3 net. Macmillan.
MacCracken, H: N., *and others.* Introd. to Shakespeare. 90 c. net. Macmillan.
McKenney, *Mrs.* M. M. Studies of Shakespeare's women. $2. M. M. McKenney.
McMahan, *Mrs.* A. B. Shakespeare's love story. $2.50; $5.50. McClurg.
Mangasarian, M. M. What was the religion of Shakespeare? 10 c. Independent Religious.
Morgan, A., *and* Bailey, A. W. Great experiment: Shakespearean fantasy. 50 c. Seymour.
Morris, H. S. Tales from Shakespeare. $1.25. Lippincott.
Munn, *Mrs.* M. C. Will Shakespeare of Stratford and London; drama. $1.20 net. Dodd.
Munro, J. J., *ed.* Shakespeare allusion book. 2 v. *$7 net. Duffield.
Orem, L. Story of Julius Cæsar. 5 c.—Story of the Tempest. 8 c. O. Brewer.
Robertson, J. M. Montaigne and Shakespeare. *$2 net. Macmillan.

Shakespeare, W:—*Continued.*
Rogers, L: W: Occultism in the Shakespeare plays. 25 c. Theosophical Bk.
Rogues and vagabonds of Shakespeare's youth. *$1.75 net. Duffield.
Stoddard, W: L. Life of William Shakespeare expurgated. $1.25. W. A. Butterfield.
Swinburne, A. C: Shakespeare. 80 c. Oxford Univ.
Swinburne, A. C: Three plays of Shakespeare. *75 c. net. Harper.
Tannenbaum, S: A. Was William Shakespeare a gentleman? 50 c. Tenny.
Tolman, A. H. Questions on Shakespeare. In 2 v. v. 1, 75 c. net; v. 2, $1 net. Univ. of Chic.
Vaughan, L. J. Sermons from Shakespeare. $1. Bartlett.
Ward, H: S., *and* Weed. C. Shakespeare's town and times. *$1.50 net. Lippincott.
Webb, M. P. Othello, an interpretation. *50 c. net. M. P. Webb.
Winter, W: Shakespeare's England. $3 net. Moffat.
Wislicenus, P. Shakespeare's totenmaske. $1.50. Lemcke.
Wood, A. I. P. Stage history of Shakespeare's King Richard the Third. *$1.25 net. Lemcke.
Wright, E. H. Authorship of Timon of Athens. $1.25 net. Lemcke.

SHAKESPEARE-BACON CONTROVERSY.
Booth, W: S. Some acrostic signatures of Francis Bacon. **$6 net. Houghton M.
Durning-Lawrence, *Sir* E. Bacon is Shakespeare. $1 net. McBride.
Harwood, H: H. Two of the most remarkable and interesting of the sonnets of Francis Bacon, the true Shakespeare. $1. H: H. Harwood.
Montgomery, C: A. Discoveries which prove authoritatively ye "secret parentage" of ye works of Shake-speare. $1.—Shake-speare's anagrams. 25 c. C: A. Montgomery.
Shakespeare, W: Shake-speare drama of The tempest.—Shake-speare tragedy of Julius Cæsar; [corrected and annot. from viewpoint of Fs. Bacon as author.] ea., 75 c. Coburn.

Shakespeare in limerick. McKee, B. 75 c. Morton.

Shakespeare lib.; ed. by Israel Gollancz: Lamb Shakespeare for the young. 12°. *80 c. net; leath., *$1 net. Duffield.
—As you like it.
—Cymbeline.—King Henry v.
—Evening with Shakespeare.
—Macbeth.
—Merchant of Venice.
—Midsummer night's dream.
—Much ado about nothing.
—Romeo and Juliet.
—Tempest.
—Twelfth night.
—Winter's tale.

Shakespeare lib.; ed. by Israel Gollancz: Old-spelling Shakespeare. 8°, bds., *$1 net; Persian, *$1.60 net; Lib. ed., *$1.70 net. Duffield.
—All's well that ends well.
—As you like it.
—Comedie of errors.
—Henrie the Fourth. pts. 1, 2.
—Love's labour's lost.
—Merchant of Venice.
—Merry wives of Windsor.
—Midsommer nights dream.
—Much adoe about nothing.
—Plutarch. Shakespeare's Plutarch. 2 v.
—Taming of the shrew.
—The tempest.
—Twelfe night.
—Two gentlemen of Verona.
—Winter's tale.

Shakespeare lib.; ed. by Israel Gollancz: Shakespeare classics. 16°, bds., *$1 net; Persian, *$1.60 net; Lib. ed., *$1.70 net. Duffield.
—Boas, *ed.* Taming of a shrew.
—Brooke. Romeus and Juliet.
—Greene. Pandosto.
—Lee, *ed.* Play of King Leir and his three daughters.
—Lodge. Rosalynde.
—Sidgwick, *ed.* Sources and analogues of "A midsummer night's dream."

Shakespeare lib.; ed. by Israel Gollancz: Shakespeare's England. O. Duffield.
—Holinshead. Shakespeare's Holinshead. *$3.50 net.
—Laneham. Letter. *$1.75 net.
—Rogues and vagabonds of Shakespeare's youth. *$1.75 net.

Shakespearean wars. See Lounsbury, T: Raynesford.

Shakespearian stage. Albright, V. E. *$1.50 net. Lemcke.

Shaler, Nathaniel Southgate.
Autobiography; with a supp. memoir by his wife. '09(Je26) c. il. pors. O. **$4 net. Houghton M.

Shall I go to confession? Hoare, E. *20 c. net. Am. S. S.

Shall we understand the Bible? Williams, T. R. *40 c. net. Macmillan.

Shallow, E: Byrne, and Cullen, Winifred T.
Nature study made easy. '08(Ap11) c. il. 12°, *40 c. net. Macmillan.

Shambaugh, B: Franklin.
Second report on the public archives, [Iowa.] '07, [1908.] (Mr.) c. 5+364 p. 8°. (For private distribution.) Hist. Dept. of Ia.

Shambaugh, Mrs. Bertha Maud Horack.
Amana: the community of true inspiration. '08(Jl4) c. il. facsims., O. $3. State Hist. Ia.

Shamburger, Julia Ida Jackson, ["Mrs. R. L. Shamburger."]
Select shorthand for general and verbatim reporting. [1910.] (N) c. 23 p. 12°, $1.50. R. L. Shamburger.

Shamburger, Mrs. R. L.
See Shamburger, Julia Ida Jackson.

Shame of a great nation. Law, E. N. $1. E. N. Law.

Shamrock land. Jones, P. F. **$2 net. Moffat.

"Shan"; bunch of girls and wayside flowers. [1910.] (My) 6+108 p. il. 12°, 50 c. net. Herder.

Shane, Na Gael, pseud.
See Welsh, C:

SHANKLIN, William Arnold.
Installation of William Arnold Shanklin, L.H.D.,LL.D., as ninth president of Wesleyan University, Middletown, Connecticut, November 12, 1909. [1910.] (N) 4+154 p. por. 8°, $1. Wesleyan Univ.

Shanks, Mrs. D. W.
See Cartmell, Fannie Sydnor.

Sharber, Kate Trimble.
Annals of Ann. '10(N5) c. il. D. $1.50. Bobbs-M.

Sharman, H: Burton.
Teaching of Jesus about the future, according to the synoptic Gospels. '09(Ap17) c. fold. documents in pocket, Q. *$3 net. Univ. of Chic.

Sharman, J: T:
Confirming the faith. '10(Jl16) c. 12°, $1.25. J: T: Sharman.

Sharon, Mass. First Congregational Church. Church records of Rev. Philip Curtis of Sharon, 1742-1797; ed. by J: G. Phillips. '08(Ag) c. 64 p. front. facsim., 8°, (Sharon Historical Society pub.) pap., 50 c. Kempton.

SHARON, Mass.
Vital records of Sharon, Mass., to the year 1850. $2 25. T: W. Baldwin.

Sharon Historical Society pubs. il. 12°. Sharon Hist. Soc.
--Phillips. Memorial of Eugene Tappan. (Priv. pr.)

Sharp, A. E.
Forms for analysis and parsing. '10(D17) obl. 8°, 75 c. W: R. Jenkins.

Sharp, Mrs. Abigail Gardner.
Hist. of the Spirit Lake massacre and captivity of Miss Abbie Gardner. 6th ed., rev. '10(Ag27) c. il. pors. D. $1.25. A. G. Sharp.

Sharp, Dallas Lore.
Lay of the land. '08(O3) c. il. D. **$1.25 net. Houghton M.
See also American fields and forests.

Sharp, Eliz. Amelia Sharp, [Mrs. W: Sharp,] comp.
William Sharp. (Fiona Macleod:) memoir; comp. by his wife. '10(N12) c. pors. facsims., O. $3.75 net. Duffield.

Sharp, Evelyn.
Child's Christmas. '08(D12) il. 4°, $2. Caldwell.
Rebel woman. '10(D3) c. D. $1 net. Lane.

Sharp. Fk. Chapman.
Study of the influence of custom on the moral judgment. '09(F6) O. (Univ. of Wis. bull.) pap., 30 c. Univ. of Wis.
Success: course in moral instruction for the high school. '09, [1910.] (F) c. 118 p. 12°, (Univ. of Wis. bull., High school ser.) pap. Univ. of Wis.

Sharp, G. E.
Fly-leaves from a fisherman's diary. '10 (N5) il. D. $1.40 net. Longmans.

Sharp, Gazelle Stevens.
Little patch o' blue, and other poems. '10 (D10) c. D. $1. Badger.

Sharp, Ja. Clement.
John Cotton Brooks. '09(S) 187 p. il. $1.50. Burgess, L. & Co.

Sharp, Ja. Rob.
Seven sonnets on scenes from the gospels and thirty hymns for sundry festivals and occasions. '09, [1910.] (F) c. 76 p. 8°, 85 c. J. R. Sharp.

Sharp, J:
Modern foundry practice. 2d ed., rev. '10 (Je4) c. il. 8°, $8. Spon.

Sharp, Katharine Lucinda.
Illinois libraries. pt. 3, College, institutional and special libraries, (excepting Chicago,) public school libraries by counties; pt. 4, Chicago libraries. '08(S19); pt. 5, Buildings: statement and table. '09, [1910.] (Je) Q. (Univ. of Ill. bull.) pap., ea., $1. Univ. of Ill.
5 pts. also pub. in 1 v.

"Sharp, Luke," pseud.
See Barr, Rob.

Sharp, Rob. W.
Chattel mortgage loan business: the disease and the remedy. '10(D3) c. fold. tab., 8°, pap., 75 c. R. W. Sharp.

Sharp, W:
See Macleod, Fiona, *pseud.*

Sharp, Mrs. W:, comp.
See Sharp, Eliz. Amelia Sharp.

Sharp & Alleman Co.'s lawyers' and bankers' directory for 1908. Jan. ed. '08(Ja); July ed. (Jl); for 1909. Jan. ed. '09(Ja) c. '08. July ed. (Jl); for 1910. Jan. ed. '10 (F); July ed. (Jl); for 1911. Jan. ed. (D) c. O. ea., $5. Sharp & A.

Sharpe, Rev. Alfr. Bowyer, and Aveling, Rev. Fs.
Spectrum of truth. '08(Ag8) 8°, 30 c. Herder.

Sharpe, Alfr. Clarence.
Making a soldier. '08, [1909.] (F) c. 71 p. por. 24°, pap., 25 c. Acme Pub.

Sharpe, E: S., M.D.
An old deed, May 31, 1675; Richard Guy John Fenwick, Thomas Pyle; read before the Salem County Historical Society on Dec. 8, 1908. '09(N) 12 p. il. 24°. (Add. pubs. for price.) Salem Co.. Hist. Soc.
Craven's Choyce; paper read before the Salem Co. Historical Society on June 9th, 1908. '08, [1909.] (Ag) 13 p. 12°, pap., 10 c. Salem Co. Hist. Soc.
Descendants of the pioneers; paper read before the Salem County Historical Society on March 10th, 1908. '09(N) 14 p. il. 12°, pap., 10 c. Salem Co. Hist. Soc.

Sharpe, Estelle Avery.
Foundation stones of success. 3 v. '10 (Ap) c. il. pors. 8°, $8; ¾ mor., $12. Howard-S.

Sharpe, Mrs. Maud Russell Lorraine.
Golden rule cook book; 600 recipes for meatless dishes. '09(D25) c. **$2.50 net; New ed. '10(O22) c. il. O. $2 net. Little, B. & Co.

Sharpe, Mrs. Maud Russell Lorraine, comp.
Golden rule cook book; 600 recipes for meatless dishes. '08(D) 4°, *$2.50 net. W. A. Butterfield.

Sharpe, T.
Modern foundry practice; incl. moulding, materials used, machinery and appliances. etc. 2d ed. '10(F19) il. 8°, $8. Spon.

Sharpe, W: Carvosso, comp.
Bethany sketches and records. '09(Ja16) il. O. $1.50. W: C. Sharpe.

Sharpe-Patterson, Mrs. Virginia.
Lady of the green scarf; entertainment exercise for schools embodying the need for conserving our country's natural resources; suitable for weekly rhetoricals, class exercises and Arbor Day. '10 (Mr12) c. front. O. pap., 35 c. Flanagan.

Sharpless, I:
Quaker boy on the farm and at school. '09 (My22) $1. Biddle Press.

—, Philips, G: Morris, and Balderston, Caleb Canby.
Natural philosophy. Rev. ed. '08(D19) c. il. 12°, hf. leath., $1. Lippincott.

Sharts, Jos. W:
Black sheep. '90(O2) il. 12°, $1.50. Duffield.

Shatzke, Jos. Shatz.
Unseen dangers behind humanity; or, the real causes why the Jew is hated the world over. '09(My15) c. 8°, $2.50. New Humanity.

Shaw, Adele Marie, and Beckwith, Carmelita.
Lady of the Dynamos. '09(Ap10) c. D. †$1.50. Holt.

Shaw, Albert.
Cartoon hist. of Roosevelt's career. '10 (O8) c. il. Q. $3.50; $5. Review of Reviews.
Political problems of American development. '08(N21) 12°, *$1.50 net. Columbia Univ.

Shaw (Albert) lectures on diplomatic history. O. Johns Hopkins.
—Benton. International law and diplomacy of the Spanish-American war. $1.50.

Shaw, Cathrine.
Good Shepherd. '10(N) il. (partly col.) 4°, $1.50. Fenno.
Prodigal son. '10(N) il. (partly col.) 4°, $1.50. Fenno.
Suffer little children; or, a child's life of Christ. '10(Ag13) col. il. 4°, $2.50. Fenno.

Shaw, C: Edg., jr.
"Lost"; trap-shooter's guide. '10(Jl) c. 9-55 p. il. (partly col.) 16°, 75 c. C: E. Shaw.

Shaw, C: Gray.
Precinct of religion in the culture of humanity. '08(D5) 8°, *$2 net. Macmillan.

Shaw, D. B.
Ten true secret service stories. '09(O30) pap., 25 c. J. S. Ogilvie.

Shaw, Elton Raymond, comp. and ed.
Stories of hell's commerce; or, the liquor traffic in its true light; introd. by S: Dickie. '09(D18) c. il. 8°, $1.50. Shaw Pub.

Shaw, Fk. H.
Daughter of the storm. '09, [1910.] (Ja) il. 12°, $1.50. Cassell.
First at the Pole. '10(S) il. $1.50. Cassell.

—, and Robinson, Ernest H.
Sea and its story. '10(D24) col. il. 8°, $3.50 net. Cassell.

Shaw, G: Bernard.
Admirable Bashville. '09(Je) 12°, bds., *50 c. net. Brentano's.
—, ed. Fabian essays in socialism; with a new preface. [Library ed.] '09(Ap10) c. D. *50 c. net. Ball Pub.
Perfect Wagnerite: commentary on the ring of the Nibelungs. New ed., with entirely new introd. '09(Je) 12°, $1.25. Brentano's.
Quintessence of Ibsenism. '06, [1910.] (D) 170 p. 12°, $1. Brentano's.
The sanity of art. '08(Ap11) c. 16°, 75 c. E: R. Tucker.
Socialism and superior brains: reply to Mr. Mallock. '10(S17) por. D. (Fabian socialist ser.) 75 c. net. Lane.

SHAW, George Bernard.
Chesterton, G. K. George Bernard Shaw. **$1.50 net. Lane.
Deacon, R. M. Bernard Shaw as an artist-philosopher. $1 net. Lane.

Shaw, G: Coombs.
Chinook jargon and how to use it. '09 (Ap10) c. O. pap. (Add. pubs. for price.) Rainier Pr.

Shaw, G: Russell.
Pines of Mexico. '09(My) c. 29 p. il. map, f°, (Publications of the Arnold arboretum.) *$25 net. C. S. Sargent.

Shaw, H. Batty.
Organotherapy or treatment by means of preparations of various organs. [1910.] (My) 256 p. 8°, $1.75 net. Funk.

Shaw, H: Wheeler, ["Josh Billings."]
See Stories of humor.

Shaw, Ja. Byrnie.
Synopsis of linear associative algebra. '08 (Ja25) O. (Carnegie Institution of Washington pub.) pap., $1.50. Carnegie.

Shaw, Jos. T.
Wool trade of the U. S.; hist. of a great industry; its rise and progress in Boston, now the second market of the world. '09 (Jl) 73 p. 8°. (Add. Superintendent for price.) U. S., Supt. of Docs.

Shaw, Jos. Thompson.
Spain of to-day. '09(Jl10) c. il. map, O. **$1.25 net. Grafton Press.

Shaw, Leslie Mortier.
Current issues. '08(Mr7) c. por. D. **$2 net. Appleton.

Shaw, Luella.
True hist. of some of the pioneers of Colorado. '09, [1910.] (F) c. 6+268 p. pls., pors. 8°, $1. L. Shaw.

Shaw, Rafael.
Spain from within. '10(D3) il. pors. O. $2.50 net. Stokes.

Shaw, Ralph H.
First Plymouth marriage, and other poems. '07, [1908.] c. 48 p. 8°, 35 c. R. H. Shaw.

Shaw, Roscoe Hart, and Eckles, C. H.
Chemical and physical study of the large and small fat globules in cows' milk. '09 (My) 16 p. il. 8°, (U. S., Dept. of Agriculture, Bureau of Animal Industry bull.) pap. (Add. Superintendent for price.)

Shaw, T:
Management and feeding of cattle. '10 (Mr5) il. 12°, *$2 net. Judd.

Shaw, Vero Kemball.
Encyclop. on the stable. '10(F19) 8°, hf. mor., *$2 net. Dutton.

Shaw, W: T.
China or Denny pheasant in Oregon. '07 (Mr28) c. il. obl. S. **$1.50 net. Lippincott.

Shawnie Wade. Prichard, S. J. †$1. Badger.

Shayler, Rev. Ernest Vincent.
Making of a churchman. '08(Ap18) c. plan, 12°, 25 c. E. V. Shayler.

Shaylor, Horace Woodbury.
Book of alphabets for use in schools. '08 (D12) il. O. pap., 10 c.; per doz., $1. Ginn.

Shaylor, Jos., comp.
In friendship's garden. '08(O3) D. $1.25; lambskin, $2. Stokes.
In nature's garden. '09(O9) D. $1.25; lambskin, $2. Stokes.

Shaylor, Sydney J., comp.
Joys of life. '10(D) 12°, limp leath., $2. Barse & H.

She dared to win. Popham, W: L. 50 c. W: L. Popham.

She-devil. Burke, M. H. $1.50. C. E. Apgar.

She stoops to conquer. *See* Goldsmith, Oliver. Good-natured man.

Shea, Christopher Ambrose, ["Billy Bachelor."]
Diary of a bachelor. [1910.] (N) c. 80 p. 8°, $1. Bachelor Pub.
Financial diary, 1908. 2d ed. '08(F) c. 12°, $3.50. Financial Calendar.

Shearer, J: Bunyan, D.D.
Hebrew institutions, social and civil. '10 (Je11) c. O. 60 c. net. Presb. Pub.
Scriptures, fundamental facts and features. '08(O10) c. O. 60 c. Presb. Pub.
Selected Old Testament studies. '10(Je11) O. 60 c. net. Presb. Pub.

SHEARMAN, Abraham.
Sherman, F. F. Old American publisher, (Abraham Shearman, jr.) (Priv. pr.) F. F. Sherman.

SHEARN CHURCH, Houston, Tex.
Blandin, *Mrs.* I. M. E. Hist. of Shearn Church, 1837-1907. $1. Dealy.

Shears of destiny. Scott, L. $1.20, fixed. Doubleday, P.

Shedd, Ephriam Cutler.
Our little Persian cousin. '09(Ag14) il. c. D. (Little cousin ser.) 60 c. L. C. Page.

Shedd, G: C.
Princess of Forge. '10(My14) c. il. D. $1.50. Macaulay.

Shedd, J: Cutler.
See Parham, Eug. Chilton.

Shedd, Percy W:
Clinic repertory; incl. a repertory of time modalities, by Dr. Ide; tr. from the Berliner Zeitschrift Homöopathischer Ærzte. '08(Je6) c. 12°, $1.50. Boericke & T.
See also Greeff, Richard.

SHEDS.
See Lumber.

Sheehan, Canon Patrick Augustine.
Blindness of Dr. Grey; or, the final law. '09(N20) c. D. $1.50. Longmans.
Parerga: a companion volume to "Under the cedars and the stars." '08(Mr28) c. O. **$1.60 net. Longmans.

Sheehy, Jerry.
Heat and cold; or, the key to the universe. '08(D26) c. O. $1.75. J. Sheehy.

SHEEP.
Bean, C. E. W. On the wool track. $1.50 net. Lane.
Immel, A. A. Scientific sheep and goat breeding. $1. E. E. Hahn.

SHEEPSHANKS, *Bp.* John.
Duthie, D. W., *ed.* Bishop in the rough: [Journal of Bishop Sheepshanks.] *$2 net. Dutton.

Sheer pluck. Bearne, D: 85 c. Benziger.

SHEET METAL.
Neubecker, W: Sheet-metal work. $3. Am. Sch. Corr.
See also Tin.

Sheffey, J: P., comp.
General resources and advantages of Smyth County, in the most attractive section of Appalachian Virginia. '07, [1909.] (F) 63 p. il. 16°, (Add. author for price.) J: P. Sheffey.

Sheffield, And.
Rose of Sharon. '08(N14) c. il. D. $1.50. C. M. Clark.

SHEFFIELD PLATE.
See Silver.

Shelburne essays. *See* More, Paul Elmer.

Sheldock, Marie L.
Collection of Eastern stories and legends for narration and readings in schools. '10(Je4) 8°, 50 c. net. Dutton.

Sheldon, Addison Erwin.
Poems and sketches of Nebraska. '08(D) 200 p. il. pors. 12°, $1.50. A. E. Sheldon.

Sheldon, C: Monroe.
A Charles M. Sheldon year book; arranged and comp. by C: D. Crane. '09(D18) c. por. S. $1, boxed. Crane.
Paul Douglas—journalist. '09(D) c. 305 p. 12°, $1. Advance Pub. Co., (Chic.)

Sheldon, E:
"The nigger"; American play in three acts. '10(S17) c. D. $1.25 net. Macmillan.

Sheldon, Mrs. Georgie, [Mrs. Sarah Elizabeth Forbush Downs.]
Gertrude Elliot's crucible. '08(Mr14) c. il. D. †$1.50. G: W. Dillingham.

Sheldon, H: Clay.
Sacerdotalism in the nineteenth century. '09(F20) c. O. *$2 net. Eaton & M.

Sheldon, J. P.
Farm and the dairy. 4th rev. ed. '08(Ag1) il. 12°, *$1 net. Macmillan.

Sheldon, Mary Boardman.
Coffee and a love affair: an American girl's romance on a coffee plantation. '08 (Ag22) c. S. †$1.50. Stokes.

Sheldon, Ruth Louise.
Social silhouettes. '08(Ja18) il. D. pap., 50 c. S. W. Anderson.

Sheldon, S:, and Hausmann, Erich.
Dynamo electric machinery; its construction, design, and operation. 8th ed., completely rewritten. '10(N5) c. il. 8°, **$2.50 net. Van Nostrand.

—, Mason, Hobart, and Hausmann, Erich.
Alternating-current machines; being the second volume of Dynamo electric machinery, its construction, design, and operation. 7th ed., completely rewritten. '08(D5) c. il. 12°, **$2.50 net. Van Nostrand.

Sheldon, Wa. Lorenzo.
Story of the Bible from the standpoint of modern scholarship. 2d ed. '10(Jl16) 12°, $1. S. B. Weston.

Shelford, Frederic.
Pioneering for engineers; incl. most suitable camp equipment, rations, medicines, clothing, etc. '10(Je4) il. 12°, $1.25. Spon.

SHELL BARK HICKORY.
See Trees.

SHELL-FISH.
See Mollusks.

Shelland, H: E.
Fun in a school-room farcical sketch. '08 (My16) c. 16°, pap., 15 c. Dick.

Shelley, H: C:
Gilbert White and Selborne. '09(D11) il. D. *$1.50 net. Scribner.
Inns and taverns of old London; setting forth the historical ancient hostelries, together with an account of the most notable coffee-houses, clubs, and pleasure gardens of the British metropolis. '09 (N6) c. il. O. $3, boxed. L. C. Page.
Literary by-paths in old England. [New popular ed.] '09(S18) c. il. O. **$1.50 net, boxed. Little, B. & Co.
Untrodden English ways. '08(O24) c. il. O. **$3 net; [New popular ed.] '10(S10) c. il. col. front. O. $1.50 net, boxed. Little, B. & Co.

Shelley, Percy Bysshe.
Complete poetical works. '08(D19) 12°, (Crowell's thin paper poets.) ooze leath., $1.75, boxed. Crowell.
Poetical works. '08(O10) 2 v., 12°, ("Best books" ser.) leath., ea., *$1 net. Dutton.
Poetical works. Cabinet ed. In 3 v. '08 (D19) 12°, (British poets ser.) ea., $1.50. Estes.
Poetical works; carefully rev., with notes and memoir by W: Michael Rossetti. In 3 v. '10(D24) 12°, $5 net. Scribner.
The Cenci; ed. by G: E: Woodberry. '09 (N6) c. front. 16°, (Belles-lettres ser.; Section III., The English drama.) 60 c. Heath.
Defence of poetry. '10(D) obl. 18°, (Vest pocket ser.) 50 c.; pap., 25 c.; flex. leath., 75 c., boxed. T: B. Mosher.
Letters; collected and ed. by Roger Ingpen. 2 v. '09(D11) il. pors. O. *$6 net. Scribner.
Letters from Percy Bysshe Shelley to Elizabeth Hitchener; with introd. and notes by Bertram Dobell. '08(Ap25) 12°, *$1.50 net. Dodd.

Shelley, Percy Bysshe.—*Continued.*
Literary and philosophical criticism; ed., with an introd., by J: Shawcross. '10 (Mr26) S. (Oxford lib. of prose and poetry.) 90 c. Oxford Univ.
Lyrical poems. '10(D) 16°, (Lyric garland.) pap., 50 c. net; Japan vel., $1 net. T: B. Mosher.
Select poems; ed., with introd. and notes, by G: E. Woodberry. '08, [1909.] (F) c. 31+316 p. 16°, (Belles-lettres ser.; Section 6: Nineteenth century poets.) *60 c. net. Heath.
Seven poems. '09(D) $3 (270 copies); vellum, $10 (8 copies). Seymour.
Shelley day by day; ed. by Edith L. Allen. '10(O8) c. por. D. (Day by day ser.) 60 c., boxed; leath., $1, boxed. Crowell.

SHELLEY, Percy Bysshe.
Bates, E. S. Study of Shelley's Drama "The Cenci." *$1 net. Lemcke.
Clutton-Brock, A. Shelley, the man and the poet. *$3.50 net. Putnam.
Peacock, T: L. Memoirs of Shelley. 90 c. Oxford Univ.
Thompson, F. Shelley. *$1 net; *$3 net. T: B. Mosher.
Thompson, F. Shelley. *$1 net. Scribner.
See also Hunt, James Henry Leigh.

SHELLMOUNDS.
See Ethnology.

SHELLS.
See Mollusks.

Shells from life. Sears, J. S. $1 net. New Thought.

Shelly, Percy Van Dyke.
See Pancoast, H: Spackman.

SHENANDOAH VALLEY, Va.
Cartmell, T: K. Shenandoah Valley pioneers and their descendants. $5. T: K. Cartmell.
Paxton, A. S. Memory days: in which the Shenandoah Valley is seen in retrospection. $1.50. Neale.
Wayland, J: W. Complete index to The German element in the Shenandoah Valley of Virginia. 30 c. J: W. Wayland.

Shepard, Edith Woodell.
Maid of moods; story of the great woods of Maine. '10(Jl2) $1.50. C. M. Clark.

Shepard, Fk. Hartson.
Key to "Harmony simplified," and a classroom manual. '08(O24) c. D. $1.25. Schirmer.

Shepard, Morgan.
Wags; philosophy of a peaceful pup. '09 (O23) c. il. D. bds., 50 c. Wessels.

SHEPARD, Thomas.
Davis, A. M. Hints of contemporary life on the writings of Thomas Shepard. (Priv. pr.) A. McF. Davis.

Shepard, Vinton R., ed.
See Ohio. *Circuit ct.* Repts.—Nisi prius repts.

Shepard, W:, pseud.
See Walsh, W: Shepard.

Shepard, W: Martin, and Jones, Allen Green.
The watt hour meter. '10(S17) c. il. 8°, $2. Technical Pub. Co.

SHEPARD FAMILY.
See Genealogies: Smyth, S: G.

Shepard's California citations. *See* California.

Shepard's northeastern reporter citations, Sept., 1909. '09(N) c. 631 p. D. flex. leath., $15. F. Shepard.

Shepard's Wisconsin citations. *See* Wisconsin.

Shepardson, Fs. Wayland, and Jones, Lester Bartlett, eds.
Scripture and song in worship: service book for the Sunday-school. '09(Je5) c. O. *50 c. net. Univ. of Chic.

Shepardson, G: Defrees.
Electrical catechism; introd. treatise on electricity and it uses. 2d ed., cor. and rev. '08, [1909.] (Mr) c. 14+417 p. il. 8°, *$2 net McGraw.

Shepherd, Ambrose, D.D.
Men in the making; addresses to young men. '10(D) 12°, $1.25 net. Doran; Jennings.

Shepherd, H: Elliot.
Commentary upon Tennyson's In memoriam. '08(Ag31) c. por. D. *$1.25 net. Neale

Shepherd, J. A., il.
See Cuming, E: W: Dirom.

Shepherd, W: Rob.
Guide to the materials for the hist. of U. S. in Spanish archives, (Simancas, the Archivo Historico Nacional, and Seville.) '08(Ja4) O. (Carnegie Institution of Washington pub.) pap., 50 c. Carnegie.

Shepherd of Jebel Nur. Knight, W: A. *50 c. net. Pilgrim Press.

Shepherd who did not go to Bethlehem. Ranlett, S. A. $1. Badger.

Shepherdess of to-day. De Barrios, A. $1. Aberdeen.

Shepherd's life impressions of the South Wiltshire Downs. Hudson, W. H. $2.50 net. Dutton.

Shepherds of Israel. Mord, W. 35 c. Stokes.

SHEPHERDSTOWN, W. Va.
Dandridge, *Mrs.* D. B. Historic Shepherdstown. $2. Michie.

Sheppard, Morris.
Abraham Lincoln; speech [at the] Republican Club banquet, New York, February 12, 1908. '08(D12) 8°, pap. (Add. author for price.) M. Sheppard.

Sheppard, W: H: Crispin.
Knight of the West Side. '09(N13) c. il. D. †60 c. Penn Pub. Co.
Rambler Club afloat. '09(N13) c. il. D. †60 c. Penn Pub. Co.
Rambler Club in the mountains. '10(D3) c. il. D. (Rambler Club ser.) 60 c. Penn Pub. Co.
Rambler Club's winter camp. '10(D3) c. il. D. (Rambler Club ser.) 60 c. Penn Pub. Co.

Shepperson, Alfr. B.
Cotton facts; compilation from official and reliable sources of the crops, receipts, exports, stocks, home and foreign consumption, visible supply, prices and acreage of cotton in the U. S. and other countries for a series of years; also cotton mill statistics of the U. S., Europe, India, [etc.] [33d year.] '10(Mr5) c. S. $1. A. B. Shepperson.

Sherard, Mrs.
See Osgood, Irene.

Sheraton, T:
Furniture designs of Thomas Sheraton; arranged by Ja. Munro Bell; with an introd. and critical estimate by Arth. Hayden. '10(D24) il. 4°, $6 net. Scribner.

Sherfesse, W: Forsythe.
Primer of wood preservation. '08(D) 15 p. O. (U. S. Dept. of Agriculture; forest service circular.) pap., 5 c.
Seasoning and preservative treatment of hemlock and tamarack cross-ties. '08 (Ag) 31 p. il. 8°, (U. S., Dept. of Agriculture, Forest service circular.) pap., 15 c. U. S., Supt. of Docs.
Wood preservation in the United States. '10(Ja29) map, 8°, (U. S., Dept. of Agriculture; Forest Service, bull.)

SHERIDAN, Philip Henry.
Sichel, W. S. Sheridan. 2 v. **$7.50 net. Houghton M.

Sheridan, R: Brinsley Butler.
The critic; acting version of the Yale University Dramatic Association; with a preface by W: Lyon Phelps, and an introd. by G: H: Nettleton. '09(Ja23) pors. O. 50 c.; pap., 25 c. Tuttle, M. & T.
Plays. '08(O17) 16°, (Best books ser.) leath., *$1 net. Dutton.
The rivals; comedy; with an introd. and notes by Jos. Quincy Adams, jr. '10 (O22) c. '10. por. D. (Riverside literature ser.) 25 c. Houghton M.
School for scandal, and The rivals; with introd. by Augustine Birrell. '08(O31) il. 16°, (Pocket classics.) 80 c.; leath., $1.25. Macmillan.

Sheriff of Angel Gulch. Blaney, C: E. 25 c. J. S. Ogilvie.

Sheriff of Dyke Hole. Cullum, R. $1.50. Jacobs.

Sherington, C: Scott.
Physiology. '10(S) il. 16°, (Appleton's scientific primers.) 50 c. net. Appleton.

Sherlock, Sophie M.
Eve, and other poems. '10(Jl9) D. 90 c. net. Longmans.

Sherman, A. Outram.
Thomas Paine the patriot; address del. before the Huguenot Society of New Rochelle, N. Y., at the opening of the Paine House, July 14, 1910. Special library ed. '10(O1) il. pors. O. pap., 20 c. Paine Nat. Hist. Assoc.
Westchester County and the town of Rye: an address. '09(Ap17) c. O. pap., 50 c. Westchester Press.

Sherman, Bryant Elihu.
Bell cow. '09(Ap3) c. front. D. $1.50. C. M. Clark.

Sherman, Edg. Jay.
Some recollections of a long life. '08(N) 322 p. il. pors. 8°. (Priv. pr.) E. J. Sherman.

Sherman, Eloise Lee.
Plantation poems. '10(Ap23) c. il. 8°, $1.25 net. F. F. Sherman.

Sherman, Eug. Buren, and Reed, Albert A.
Essentials of teaching reading. '09(Jl) 8+261 p. 8°, $1.12. Univ. Pub.

Sherman, Fk. Dempster.
Little folk lyrics. School ed. '10(D) 12°, 60 c. net. Houghton M.

Sherman, Frederic Fairchild.
Old American publisher (Abraham Shearman jun.). '10(Ap) c. 16 p. il. por. 8°. (Priv. pr.) F. F. Sherman.
Sonnets, suggested by books in the library of J. Pierpont Morgan. '09, [1910.] (F) c. 12°. (Priv. pr.) F. F. Sherman.

Sherman, H: Clapp, Metler, Arth. J., and Sinclair, J. Edn.
Calcium, magnesium, and phosphorus in food and nutrition. '10(O) 70 p. tabs., 8°, (U. S., Dept. of Agriculture; Office of Experiment Stations; bull.) Gov. Pr. Off.

SHERMAN, John.
Harn, G: W. John Sherman. (Add. pubs. for price.) P. J. Herr.
Kerr, W. S. John Sherman. 2 v. *$4 net. Sherman, F.

Sherman, Lucius Adelno.
Elements of literature and composition. '08 (My9) c. il. 12°, *$1.25 net. Univ. Pub.

Sherman, Mrs. Marg. Jane McMurphy.
Gleanings. '09, [1910.] (Ap) 151 p. pors. 12°, 85 c.; bds., 65 c. M. J. M. Sherman.

Sherman, Mrs. Mary Belle King.
Parliamentary law and rules of procedure; manual of practical information concerning deliberative bodies; motions and their purpose and relation; voting; elections; committees; officers and debates. 6th ed. '09(Ap) c. 180 p. tab., 16°, 75 c. J: D. Sherman.

Sherman, General W: Tecumseh.
Home letters of General Sherman; ed. by M. A. De Wolfe Howe. '09(O16) c. por. O. **$2 net. Scribner.

SHERMAN, *General* William Tecumseh.
Boyd, D: F. General W. T. Sherman as a college president. gratis. La. State Univ.

SHERMAN, Conn.
Rogers, R. Historical landmarks in the town of Sherman, Ct. 10 c. Quaker Hill.

Sherman Hale. Rand, G: H. $1.50. Fenno.

Sherren, Ja.
Injuries of nerves and their treatment. '08 (My2) il. 12°, **(Modern clinics ser.)** *$2 **net.** Wood.

Sherriff, H. T.
See Ball, C: Backus.

Sherrill, C: Hitchcock.
Stained glass tours in England. '09(Ag21) O. *$2.50 net. Lane.
Stained glass tours in France. '08(F1) c. il. maps, D. **$1.50 net. Lane.

Sherrill, Clarence Osborne.
Examination and repair of simple highway bridges, with principles relating to their design. '09(Ap24) c. diagrs., D. pap., 25 c. Staff Coll.
Military map reading; adopted by direction of the commandant for use in the service schools at Fort Leavenworth, Kansas. '09(D18) c. il. maps, O. 40 c.; bds., 30 c. Army Service.

Sherrill, Clarence Osborne.—*Continued.*
Military sketching. '10(Ag) c. 73 p. il. 8°. (Priv. pr.) C. O. Sherrill.
Military topography for the mobile forces, including map reading, surveying and sketching. [1910.] (O) c. 18+356 p. il. tabs., diagrs., fold. maps, 8°, $2.50. Army Service.

—, and Marshall, G: Catlett, jr.
Notes on cordage and tackle; adopted by direction of the commandant for use in the army service schools at Fort Leavenworth. '09, [1910.] (D) 2+25 p. il. 12°. (Priv. pr.) Staff Coll.

Sherrill, S: Wells.
Heroes in gray. '10(Ja22) 12°, 30 c. C. J. Bell.

Sherwood, Grace Mabel, comp.
Summary of the general banking laws of the commercial states. '08, [1909.] (Je) c. 334 p. 8°, (Legislative reference bull.) pap., gratis. R. I. State Lib.
See also Veto power in the several states.

Sherwood, Rowena.
See Swem, Leota.

Sherzer, W: Hittell.
Glaciers of the Canadian Rockies and Selkirks. '08(F1) pls. F. (Smithsonian contribs. to knowledge.) pap. Smith. Inst.

Shettle, G. T.
Pathway of the cross. '08(Jl) 12°, bds., 40 c. Whittaker.

Shiel, Roger R.
Twenty years in hell with the beef trust; "facts, not fiction." '09(Je12) pors. D. 60 c.; pap., 50 c. R. R. Shiel.

Shield, Alice.
Henry Stuart, Cardinal of York, and his times; with an introd. by And. Lang. '08 (D5) il. O. *$3.50 net. Longmans.

Shield reversed. Porter, W: H. *50 c. net. Gorham.

Shields, M. J.
See Lynch, C:

Shields, T: E:
Making and the unmaking of a dullard. '09(Ap10) c. D. *$1 net. Cath. Educ.
See also Pace, E: A.

Shifting and incidence of taxation. Seligman, E. R. A. $3. Lemcke.

"Shikári, A," pseud.
See Herbert, Agnes.

Shilling (The) Bermuda guide and history. '10(O8) c. S. pap., 25 c. S. Nelmes.

SHILOH (Battle of).
Reinhardt, V. Drummer boy of Shiloh. 25 c. V. Reinhardt.
United States. *Shiloh National Military Park Commission.* Battle of Shiloh and the organizations engaged; comp. from the official records by Major D. W. Reed under the authority of the Commission, 1902 (rev. 1909). '09, [1910.] (Ap) 122 p. fold. maps, 8°, pap. Gov. Pr. Off.

Shimer, Edg. Dubs.
See Burchill, Georgine.

Shimer, Hervey Woodburn.
See Grabau, Amadeus W:

Shimmell, Lewis Slifer.
Government of Pennsylvania; [also] The government of the United States. '08 (O3) c. il. 12°, *90 c. net. C: E. Merrill.
Short hist. of Pennsylvania. '10(Ag27) il. 12°, 75 c. C: E. Merrill.

Shinn, Josiah Hazen.
Pioneers and makers of Arkansas. '08(D) 10-423 p. 8°. (Add. pubs. for price.) Genealog. and Hist.

Shinn, Millicent Washburn.
Notes on the development of a child. 2, The development of the senses in the first three years of childhood. '08(Ag1) Q. (Univ. of Cal. pubs., Education.) pap., $2.50. Univ. of Cal.

SHINTOISM.
Terry, M. S. Shinto cult. 30 c. Jennings.

Ship dwellers. Paine, A. B. $1.50 net. Harper.

SHIP SUBSIDIES.
Merchants' Association of New York. Subsidy for American ships only. gratis. Merchants' Assoc.
United States. *Dept. of Commerce and Labor. Bu. of Navigation.* Ocean-mail systems and ship subsidies of the world. '10(Jl) 52 p. 8°.

SHIP-WORMS.
See Teredinidæ.

Shipley, Arth. Everett, ed.
See Harmer, Sidney F:—Nuttall, G: H. Falkiner.

Shipp, J. E. D.
Giant days; or, the life and times of William H. Crawford; embracing also excerpts from his diary, letters and speeches, together with a copious index to the whole. '09(Jl17) il. 8°, subs., $3. Americus.

Shipper's guide schedule of packing car service from Pittsburgh. Pittsburgh. *Chamber of Commerce.* $1. Pittsburg Chamber of Com.

Shippers and carriers of interstate freight. Watkins, E. $6. Flood.

SHIPPING.
See Commerce.

Shipping department. Griffith, J. B. (Priv. pr.) Am. Sch. Corr.

Shipping office organization. Calvert, A. $2. Pitman.

Ship's engines; a parable. Finlayson, T. C. **15 c. net. Eaton & M.

Ships and sailors of old Salem. Paine, R. D. *$3.50 net. McClurg.

SHIPS AND SHIPBUILDING.
Attwood, E: L. Text-book of theoretical naval architecture. $2.50.—War-ships: text-book on the construction, protection, stability, turning, etc., of war vessels. *$3 net. Longmans.
Biles, J: H. Design and construction of ships. v. 1. *$7.50 net. Lippincott.
Bowles, Fs. T. Construction of modern battle ships; letter from the President of the Fore River Shipbuilding Co., Quincy, Mass., addressed to Hon. William P. Frye, with reference to the underbidding of foreign competitors by the United States in the matter of the construction of modern battle ships. '10(Jl) 2 p. 8°. Gov. Pr. Off.

SHIPS AND SHIPBUILDING.—*Continued.*
Chatterton, E: K. Romance of the ship. $1.50 net.—Sailing ships and their story. *$3.75 net. Lippincott.
Chatterton, E. K. Steamships and their story. $5 net. Cassell.
Clark, A. H. Clipper ship era. $2 net. Putnam.
Curr, R. Lake ship yard methods of steel ship construction. $2. Penton.
Durand, W: F: Researches on the performance of the screw propeller. 75 c. Carnegie.
Durand, W: F: Resistance and propulsion of ships. $5. Wiley.
Fletcher, R. A. Steamships. $3.75 net. Lippincott.
Fyfe, C: A. Steamship coefficients, speeds and powers. $4. Spon.
Holms, A. C. Practical shipbuilding. 2 v. *$10 net. Longmans.
Howden, J. R. Boy's book of steamships. $2. McClure.
Marvin, W. L. American merchant marine. Gov. Pr. Off.
Morrison, J: H. History of New York shipyards. $2. Sametz.
Roberts, T: G. Merchant marine and the navy. U. S., Supt. of Docs.
Robinson, R: H. M. Naval construction. U. S. Naval Inst.
Seaton, A. E. Screw propeller. *$4 net. Lippincott.
Spears, J: R. Story of the American merchant marine. *$1.50 net. Macmillan.
Statham, E: P. Privateers and privateering. $2.50 net. Pott.
Taylor, D: W. Resistance of ships and screw propulsion. *$2.25 net. Macmillan.
Taylor, D: W. Speed and power of ships. In 2 v. $7.50 net. Wiley.
United States. *Dept. of Commerce and Labor. Steamboat Inspection Service.* General rules and regulations prescribed by the Board of Supervising Inspectors, as amended Jan., 1909. '09(Je) 144 p. diagrs. 8°, pap. (Add. Superintendent for price.) U. S., Supt. of Docs.
United States. Laws governing the Steamboat-inspection Service; ed. May 26, 1909. '09(Ag) 58 p. 8°. (Add. Superintendent for price.)
United States. *Navy Department.* Alleged structural defects in battle ships of U. S. navy. 15 c. U. S., Supt. of Docs.
United States. Preventing collisions of vessels, etc.; Committee on the Merchant Marine and Fisheries. [1910.] (Jl) 16 p 8°. Gov. Pr. Off.
United States. Steerage conditions; partial rept. on behalf of the Immigration Commission, on steerage conditions. '09, [1910.] (Mr) 46 p. 8°.
Urquhart, W. W. Reminiscences; merchant marine ocean travel in the sixties and now. 75 c. W. W. Urquhart.
See also **Boats;—Commerce;—Naval art and science;**—Navigation; — Propellers; — Sailors; — Ship subsidies; — Submarines; — Yachts and yachting;—*also* "Bellerophon," The.

Ships of desire. Horn, K. $1.50. Cassell.

Ships that glue sailed. Williams, C. A. 75 c. Stokes.

Shirley, J: B.
Part songs for girls' voices. '08(Je13) c. O. 75 c. Am. Bk.
Part songs for mixed voices. '09(Ap17) c. O. 75 c. Am. Bk.

Shirley. Brontë, C. *35 c. net; *70 c. net. Dutton.

Shirts, G:
See Indiana laws of negligence.

SHIRTWAIST MAKERS' STRIKE, New York City.
See Strikes.

Shive, R. J.
Handy digest (civil); key to the books that contain the law. '09(D) c. nar. O. $4.75. State Cap.

Shivell, Paul.
Stillwater Valley pastorals. '08(Ag) c. 11+13+48 p. front. 8°, 50 c. Rector.

Shobridge, Leonard.
Poems. '10(S) 12°, $1.50 net. Lane.

SHOE STORES.
See Business.

Shoemaker, C: Chalmers, comp.
One hundred choice selections; no. 39, a repository of reading, recitations and plays, comprising eloquence and sentiment, pathos and humor, dialect and impersonations, etc. '09(N13) c. D. 50 c.; pap., 30 c. Penn Pub. Co.

Shoemaker, H: Wharton.
Pennsylvania mountain stories. '08(My23) c. 12°. [priv. pr.] Bradford Record.

Shoemaker, Jacob W.
Practical elocution; for use in colleges and schools, and by private students; enl., with a wide variety of selections for practice. '08, [1909.] (Ap) c. 16+17-308 p. il. 12°, $1.25. Penn Pub. Co.
Shoemaker's best selections; best things from best authors. v. 1-9, comprising number 3 of Shoemaker's best selections. '09(N13) c. 12°, $1.50; per set, $9, boxed. Penn Pub. Co.

Shoemaker, J: Vietch, M.D.
Health and beauty. '08(Je20) c. 8°, *$3 net. Davis.
Pract. treatise on diseases of the skin. 5th ed., rev. and enl. '09(D) c. 11+1012 p. il. 8°, *$6 net; hf. mor., *$7.50 net. Davis.
Pract. treatise on materia medica and therapeutics; with especial reference to the clinical application of drugs. 7th ed. '08, [1909.] (Mr) c. 8+1255 p. 8°, *$6.50 net. Davis.

Shoemaker, L: Peirce.
Shall the government of the District of Columbia be American in form or un-American? '08(Je6) 8°, pap. (Add. pubs. for price.) Judd & D.

Shoemaker, Michael Myers.
Islam lands: Nubia, the Sudan, Tunisia, and Algeria. '10(D3) c. O. $2.50 net. Putnam.
Wanderings in Ireland. '08(Je6) c. il. O. **$2.50 net. Putnam.

Shoemaker, W: Toy, and Swan, J: Mumford.
Retinitis pigmentosa, with an analysis of seventeen cases occurring in deaf-mutes; being an essay for which was awarded the Abvarenga prize of the College of Physicians of Philadelphia, July, 1908; laboratory examinations of the blood and urine. '09(Mr) c. 4+106 p. il. 8°, *$2 net. Lippincott.

Shoenfeld, Mrs. Gabrielle.
Poésies et nouvelles. '10(Jl) c. 66 p. 12°, 50 c. G. Shoenfeld.

SHOES.
Dean, A. D. Education of workers in the shoe industry. 10 c. Nat. Soc. Promotion Indust. Educ.
Small, F. L. Organizing a shoe factory. $5. Weekly Bulletin.

Shoesmith, Vernon Morelle.
Study of corn. '10(My14) c. il. 12°, 50 c. Judd.

Shogun's daughter. Bennet, R. A. $1.35 net. McClurg.

Sholl, Anna McClure.
Greater love. '08(Je13) c. D. $1.50. Outing.

Shoobridge, Leonard.
See Waldstein, C:

Shoop, Max Pardoe.
Sabrina, the class goddess of Amherst College; a history. '10(Ag13) c. il. 12°, $1.25. M. P. Shoop.

SHOOTING.
Cloke, H. E: Gunners' examiner. $1.50. Wiley.
Himmelwright, A. L. Pistol and revolver. $1; $1.50; 60 c. U. S. Revolver.
Shaw, C: E., *jr.* "Lost"; trap-shooter's guide. 75 c. C: E. Shaw.
Winans, W. Hints on revolver shooting. **50 c. net. Putnam.
See also Artillery;—Ducks;—Hunting;—Rifle;—Sports and sportsmen;—Woodcock;—*also* Africa.

Shop arithmetic for the machinist. Oberg, E. 25 c. Indust. Press.

Shop problems in mathematics. Breckenridge, W: E. $1. Ginn.

Shop talks. Stafford, E: R. 75 c. Jennings.

Shop tests on electric car equipment. Parham, E. C. $1. McGraw.

Shops and shop practice. Kirkman, M. M. 2 v. ea., $5. C. Phillips.

Shore, Emily.
Land babies and sea babies at play. '09(S) col. il. Q. bds., $1. Stokes.

Shore, W: Teignmouth.
Charles Dickens and his friends. '09(N13) il. O. *$1.75 net. Cassell.
D'Orsay; or, the complete dandy. '10(D10) il. 8°, $3.50 net. Brentano's.
The pest. '09(Mr) D. $1.50. Doscher.

Shore, Mrs. W: Teignmouth, ["Priscilla Craven."]
Pride of the Graftons. '09(O9) c. D. †$1.50. Appleton.

SHOREBIRDS.
See Birds.

SHOREDITCH, London, Eng.
See London.

Shores, Rob. Ja.
At Molokai and other verse. '10(F) 16°, pap., 50 c. R. J. Shores.
Gay gods and merry mortals: verse. '10 (D31) c. D. B'way Pub.
Shores of the Adriatic. Jackson, F: H. *$6 net. Dutton.
Shorey, Edm. C.
See Schreiner, O.
Short, C: Wilkins, jr.
Digest of the foot ball rules for 1910 for officials and players. '10(D) c. 29 p. 16°, (Spalding's athletic lib.) pap., 10 c. Am. Sports.
Short, Floyd Truesdell.
See World's best books.
Short, Josephine Helena.
Oberammergau. '10(Je4) c. il. D. $1 net. Crowell.
Short, Marion.
See O'Higgins, Harvey Jerrold.
Short, Peyton.
Brief accounts of journeys in the western country, 1809-1812. [1910.] (S) 31 p. 8°, (Historical and Philosophical Society of Ohio, pubs.) Hist. and Phil. Soc., O.
Short, Rob. L., and Elson, W: H.
Secondary-school mathematics. '10(D3) 12°, hf. leath., $1. Heath.
Short and sweet. '09(D) 64 p. col. il. obl. 48°, 35 c. Doran.
Short biographical dict. of English literature. Cousin, J: W. 35 c. net; 70 c. net. Dutton.
Short biographical sketches of eminent negro men and women. Bruce, J: E., *comp.* In 4 v. v. 1. $1. J: E. Bruce.
Short cut. Flint, G: E. $1.50. Romance.
Short-cut philosophy. Macy, A. W: 75 c. Sturgis & W.
Short cut to India. Fraser, D: *$5 net. Scribner.
Short cuts in carpentry. Peker, C: G. 50 c. Indust.
Short essays in Biblical criticism. Malden, R. H. $1.25 net. Standard Pub.
Short grammar of the Greek New Testament. Robertson, A. T: $1.50. Armstrong.
Short histories of the literatures of the world; ed. by Edm. Gosse. D. Appleton.
—Thomas. History of German literature. **$1.50 net.
Short history of English literature. Baines, C. E. *$1 net. Longmans.
Short history of the Bible. Keeler, B. C. 75 c.: 50 c Farrell
Short history of the English people. *See* Green, J: R:
Short Methodist stories. Edwards, R. T: *$1 net. Cochrane.
Short plays from Dickens. Browne, H. B., *comp.* *$1 net. Scribner.
Short-stop. Grey, Z. $1.25. McClurg.
Short stories and poems, by American authors: Craven Langstroth Betts, Belle Travers McCahan, A. B. Woodworth, [etc.] '09(F13) c. D. $1. Cochrane.
Short stories for children. Curtman, W. J. G. 75 c. I. Curtman.
SHORT STORY.
See Fiction.
Short-story (The). Matthews, J. B., *ed.* $1. Am. Bk.
Short studies of Christ. Robinson, E. A. 50 c. Eaton & M.
Short studies on great subjects. Froude, J. A. 5 v. ea., *60 c. net. Scribner.
Short talks with young mothers. Kerley, C: G. *$1 net. Putnam.
Short themes. Nason, A. H. *$1 net. A. H. Nason.
Short treatise of musical rhythm. Lussy, M. $1. T: J. Donlan.
Short treatise on God, man and his wellbeing. *See* Spinoza, Barach.
Shorter, Clement King.
Highways and byways in Buckinghamshire. '10(O15) il. fold. map, 8°, (Highways and byways ser.) $2 net. Macmillan.
Immortal memories. '08(Ja4) 8°, $1.50. Harper.
Napoleon in his own defence. '10(O1) 8°, $4 net. Cassell.
—, comp. The Brontës: life and letters; being an attempt to present a full and final record of the lives of the three sisters, Charlotte, Emily, and Anne Brontë. 2 v. '08(D19) c. il. **$6 net. Scribner.
Napoleon and his fellow travellers. '08 (D12) il. 8°, *$4 net. Cassell.
Shorter, Dora Sigerson, [Mrs. Clement King Shorter.]
Collected poems. '08(Ja4) 8°, $1.50. Harper.
Shorter, Rob. Graves.
How to successfully keep railroad accounts. '09, [1910.] (Ja) c. 15 p. 12°, $2.50. R. G. Shorter.
Shorter French texts. *See* Crowell's.
SHORTHAND.
See Stenography.
SHORTSTOP.
See Baseball.
Shorty and Patrick. Whitman, S. F. $1. Collier.
SHOSHONEAN INDIANS.
See Indians.
SHOT-GUN.
See Gun.
Shotwell, Wa. G.
Life of Charles Sumner. '10(N5) c. front. O. $1.50 net. Crowell.
Should national bank deposits be guaranteed by the government. Forgan, J. B. (Add. author for price.) J. B. Forgan.
Shoulder knot. Dudeney, *Mrs.* H: E. $1.50. Cassell.
Shoulders of Atlas. Freeman, *Mrs.* M. E. W. †$1.50. Harper.
Shovelhorns; the biography of a moose. Hawkes, C. $1.50. Jacobs.
Show, Arley Barthlow.
Movement for reform in the teaching of religion in the public schools of Saxony. '10(Jl) 45 p. 8°, (U. S. Bu. of Education; bull.) Gov. Pr. Off.
"List of books, pamphlets, and periodicals used in this report" (3 p.).
SHOW CARDS.
See Lettering.
Show girl. Pemberton, M. †$1.50. Winston.
SHOW WINDOWS.
See Advertising;—Window dressing.

Showalter, Lewis Pendelton.
Jim Handy, the wandering preacher; or, life among the lowly. '09(Je) c. 223 p. il. por. 8°. (Add. author for price.) L. P. Showalter.

Showell, P. Groves-.
See Groves-Showell, P.

Showerman, Grant.
With the professor. '10(Mr12) c. D. **$1.50 net. Holt.

Showers of blessings. Eby, A. D. 15 c. A. D. Eby.

Shown to the children ser. 8 v. '10(D) col. il. ea., 90 c. net. Platt & P.
Contents: Beasts; Flowers; The farm; Butterflies; Birds; Sea-shore; Trees; Nests and eggs.

Shrady, G: F:, M.D.
General Grant's last days; with a short biographical sketch. '09(F6) c. il. pors. 4°. (Priv. pr.) De Vinne.

Shreve, W: P., comp.
Story of the Third Army Corps Union; comp. from the original records. '10 (Je) 96 p. por. 8°, $1.50. W: P. Shreve.

SHREWSBURY, Elizabeth Hardwick, *Countess* of.
Rawson, M. P. Bess of Hardwick, and her circle. $5 net. Lane.

SHRUBS.
See Trees.

Shufeldt, Rob. Wilson, M.D.
Osteology of birds. '09(Je12) il. figs. O. (N. Y. State Museum bull.) pap. (Add. pubs. for price.) N. Y. State Educ.

Shull, G: Harrison.
Bursa bursa-pastoris and *bursa heegeri* biotypes and hybrids. '09(Ag21) il. figs. O. pap., 50 c. Carnegie.

Shumaker, Elmer Ellsworth.
God and man; philosophy of the higher life. '00(D11) c. O. **$2 net. Putnam.

Shuman, E. L. and E. T.
Rainy day scrap book. '10(N5) c. O. (100 pictures in pocket.) $1.25. Reilly & B.

Shuman, Edn. Llewellyn.
How to judge a book; handy method of criticism for the general reader. '10 (O15) c. D. $1.25 net. Houghton M.

Shurter, Edn. Du Bois.
Extempore speaking, for school and college. '08(O3) c. D. $1. Ginn.
Rhetoric of oratory. '09(Ja30) c. D. **$1.10 net. Macmillan.
Science and art of debate. '08(D5) c. 12°, *$1.25 net. Neale.
—, **ed.** Oratory of the South, from the Civil American oratory of to-day. '10(Ap16) $1.65. South-West Pub.
Representative college orations. '09(N20) c. D. **$1.25 net. Macmillan.
War to the present time. '09(Ja2) c. 8°, *$1.25 net. Neale.

Shurts, J. Van der Veer.
Kedar Kross. '08(F8) c. D. $1.50. Badger.

Shute, Dan. Kerfoot.
Philosophical foundations of charlatanry in medicine. '08(Je6) 8°, (George Washington Univ. pubs., Medical science ser.) pap. (Not for sale.) George Washington Univ.

Shute, Dan. Kerfoot.—*Continued.*
Reflex neuroses with particular reference to eyestrain. '08(Je6) 8°, (George Washington Univ. pubs., Medical science ser.) pap. (Not for sale.) George Washington Univ.

Shute, H: A:
Country band. '08(D12) c. il. D. $1. Badger.
Farming it. '09(N20) c. il. D. **$1.20 net. Houghton M.
Plupy, "the real boy." '10(N5) c. il. D. $1.50. Badger.

Shutters of silence. Burgih, G: B. 50 c. B. W. Dodge.

Shuttleworth, G. E., M.D., and Potts, W. A., M.D.
Mentally deficient children; their treatment and training. 3d ed. [1910.] (Ag) il. 12°, $2. Blakiston.

Si Klegg. *See* McElroy, J:

SIAM.
Young, E. Siam. *75 c. net. Macmillan.
See also Far East.

Sibenmann, Friedrich.
See Bezold, Friedrich.

SIBERIA.
Curtin, J. Journey in Southern Siberia. **$3 net. Little, B. & Co.
De Packh, *Baroness* M. Twenty years in Siberia. $1.25. Guarantee Pub.
Kennan, G: Tent life in Siberia. $2.50 net. Putnam.

SIBLEY, Henry Hastings
McCourt, R. S. Hist. of the old Sibley house, incl. a brief hist. of the lives of General Henry H. Sibley, his wife and mother. 25 c. R. S. McCourt.

Sibley, M. W.
Criminal appeal and evidence. '08(Jl11) 8°, *$5 net. Wessels.

Sichel, Edith.
Later years of Catherine de Medici. '08 (Ag15) 8°, *$3 net. Dutton.

Sichel, Wa. Sydney.
Sheridan; from new and orig. material; incl. manuscript diary by Georgiana, Duchess of Devonshire. In 2 v. '09 (D18) c. pors. O. **$7.50 net, boxed. Houghton M.
Sterne; a study; to which is added the Journal to Eliza. '10(Je4) pors. O. $2.50. Lippincott.

Sicilian ways and days. Caico, *Mrs.* L. $3.50 special net. Appleton.

SICILY.
Baedeker, K. Southern Italy and Sicily. *$1.80 net. Scribner.
Bisland, E., *and* Hoyt, A. Seekers in Sicily. *$1.50 net. Lane.
Caico, *Mrs.* L. Sicilian ways and days. $3.50 special net. Appleton.
Howe, M. Sicily in shadow and in sun. $5.50 net. Little, B. & Co.
Jones, H: F. Diversions in Sicily. *$1.25 net. Scribner.
Monroe, W. S. Sicily. $3. L. C. Page.
Pais, E. Ancient Italy: hist. and geograph. investigations in central Italy, Magna Græcia, Sicily, and Sardinia. *$5 net. Univ. of Chic.

SICILY.—*Continued.*
Peet, T. E. Stone and bronze ages in Italy and Sicily. $5.25. Oxford Univ.
Perry, W. C. Sicily in fable, history, art and song. *$1.50 net. Macmillan.
Sullivan. T: R. Lands of summer: Italy, Sicily and Greece. **$1.50 net. Houghton M.
See also Agathocles;—Messina disaster.

Sickert, Bernhard.
Whistler. '08(Je6) 12°, (Popular lib. of art.) *75 c. net; leath., *$1 net. Dutton.

Siddons, A. W.
See Godfrey, C:

—, and Wassall, A.
Practical measurements. '10(O29) figs. O. bds., 45 c. net. Putnam.

SIDDONS, *Mrs.* Sarah Kemble.
Parsons, F. M. Incomparable Siddons. *$3.50 net. Putnam.

Side-stepping with Shorty. Ford, S. $1.50. M. Kennerley.

Sidelights on Chinese life. Macgowan, J. *$3.75 net. Lippincott.

Sidelights on Christian doctrine. Orr, J. *$1.50 net. Armstrong.

Sidelights on religion. Brierley, J. *$1.40 net. Whittaker.

Sidelights on the Bible. Lee, F. T. **$1 net. Winston.

Sidelights on the Orient. Lambuth, W. R. *75 c. net. Pub. Ho. of M. E. Ch., So.

"SIDEREAL MESSENGER."
See Indexes.

SIDEWALKS.
See Cement;—Concrete.

Sidey, T: K.
Participle in Plautus. Petronius and Apuleius; dissertation. '09(N20) c. 8°, pap., *50 c. net. Univ. of Chic.

Sidgwick, Mrs. Alfred.
See Sidgwick, *Mrs.* Cecily Ullman.

Sidgwick, Mrs. Cecily Ullman, [Mrs. Alfr. Sidgwick.]
Germany. '09(D25) il. 12°, (Peeps at many lands ser.) *75 c. net. Macmillan.
Home life in Germany. '08(Je13) il. 12°, *$1.75 net. Macmillan.

—, and Paynter, Mrs.
Children's book of gardening. '09(D4) col. il. O. *$2 net. Macmillan.

Sidgwick, Frank, ed.
Ballads and lyrics of love; il. after Byam Shaw. '08(Ag8) O. *$2 net. Stokes.
Legendary ballads; ed., with an introd. '08 (O3) il. O. *$2 net. Stokes.
Old ballads. '08(N7) 8°, (Pitt Press ser.) *50 c. net. Putnam.
Sources and analogues of "A midsummer night's dream." '08(O31) facsim., 16°, (Shakespeare lib.: Shakespeare classics.) bds., *$1 net; Persian, *$1.60 net; Lib. ed., hf. parchment, 12°, *$1.70 net. Duffield.

Sidgwick, H:
Elements of politics. '08(Ag15) 8°, *$4.25 net. Macmillan.

Sidgwick, Nevil Vincent.
Organic chemistry of nitrogen. '10(D3) O. $4.75. Oxford Univ.

Sidis, Boris, M.D.
Experimental study of sleep (from the physiological laboratory of the Harvard medical school and from Sidis' laboratory.) '09(Ap17) c. il. O. pap., *$1 net. Badger.
Psychopathological researches; studies in mental dissociation. '09(Je19) c. il. O. *$3 net. Badger.

Sidner, Aurelia I.
Price inevitable. '09(Je5) il. 12°, pap., 50 c. J. S. Ogilvie.

"Sidney, Marg.," pseud.
See Lothrop, *Mrs.* Harriet Mulford Stone.

Sidney, Sir Philip.
Apologie for poetrie, 1595; ed. by E: Arber. '08(Mr14) 16°, (Arber's Eng. reprints.) *35 c. net. Macmillan.
Apologie for poetrie; ed., with an introd. and notes, by J. Churton Collins. '08 (Ja18) D. 60 c. Oxford Univ.
Defence of poesie; A letter to Queen Elizabeth; A defence of Leicester; ed. by G. E. Woodberry. '08(Je27) c. O. (Humanists' lib.) bds., $6. Merrymount.

SIDNEY, *Sir* Philip.
Addleshaw, W: P. Sir Philip Sidney. $3.50 net. Putnam.
Hill, H. W. Sidney's Arcadia and the Elizabethan drama. (Add. Univ. for price.) Univ. of Nev.

Sidney at college. Ray, A. C. †$1.50. Little, B. & Co.

Sidney books. See Ray, Anna Chapin.

Siebenjährige (Der) Krieg. *See* Schrader, Ferdinand, Friedrich der Grosse.

Sieber, Ferdinand.
Art of singing, and vocal culture; tr. and adapt. from his "Katechismus der gesangs kunst," by A. W. Dohn. '08(D) c. 95 p. 12°, 50 c. Ditson.

Sieg, Vera, comp.
Negro problem: a bibliography. '09(Ja16) D. (American social questions.) pap. 25 c. Wisconsin Free Lib.

Siege of Rhodes. *See* D'Avenant, *Sir* W: Love and honour.

Siege of the seven suitors. Nicholson, M. $1.20 net. Houghton M.

Siege of youth. Charles, F. †75 c. Little, B. & Co.

Sieger, Rev. G: P.
See Luther, Martin.

SIEGES.
See Battles.

SIEGFRIED.
Madeley, D. F. Heroic life and exploits of Siegfried the dragon-slayer. $1.50. Crowell.
Peterson, A. Sigurd; poem. $1.50 net. Jacobs.
See also Wagner, Wilhelm Richard.

"Siegfried Bergmann." Rauser, F. C. 25 c. Schaefer & K.

SIENA, Italy.
Hutton, E: Siena and southern Tuscany. $2 net. Macmillan.
Schevill, F. Siena: story of a mediæval commune. **$2.50 net. Scribner.
Swinburne, A. C: Siena. 50 c. net; $1 net. T: B. Mosher.

Sienese painter of the Franciscan legend. Berenson, B. *$2 net. Lane.

Sienkiewicz, Henryk.

Whirlpools; novel of modern Poland; tr. from the Polish by Max A. Drezmal. '10 (Je11) c. D. $1.50. Little, B. & Co.

With fire and sword; tr. by Jeremiah Curtin. '08(My.) c. 12°. (Popular ed. of recent fiction.) †75 c. Little, B. & Co.

Without dogma. '08(My.) c. 12°, (Popular ed. of recent fiction.) †75 c. Little, B. & Co.

Siepmann, Otto.

Short French grammar; comprising essentials of accidence and syntax; with a chapter on French sounds. '08(F22) 12°, *60 c. net. Macmillan.

Siepmann's advanced French ser. 12°. Macmillan.

—Daudet. Lettres de mon moulin. *60 c. net.

Siepmann's classical French texts. 12°. Macmillan.

—Molière. L'Avare. *50 c. net.

Siepmann's primary French ser.; ed. by Otto Siepmann and Eugene Pellissier. 12°. Macmillan.

—La Bédollière. Histoire de la Mère Michel. *35 c. net.

—Töpffer, R. Le lac de Gers. *40 c. net.

Sierra Leone, Africa.

Alldridge, T: J. Transformed colony: Sierra Leone. *$3.50 net. Lippincott.

Sierra Nevada mountains, Cal.

Sinclair, W: J. Recent investigations bearing on the question of the occurrences of neocene man in the auriferous gravels of the Sierra Nevada. 35 c. Univ. of Cal.

Sifting of Philip. Tomlinson, E. T. †$1.25. Am. Bapt.

Sigerfoos, C: P.

Laboratory directions in general zoology; for use in the first course in zoology in the University of Minnesota. [4th ed.] '09(N20) c. il. 8°, 65 c. H. W. Wilson.

Natural history, organization and late development of the *Teredinidae.* '08(S12) 8°, pap., gratis. Johns Hopkins.

Sight.

See **Eye.**

Sign language.

See **Deaf and dumb.**

Sign painting.

Atkinson, F. H. Sign painting up to now. $3. Drake.

See also **Painting (*mechanical*).**

Signals and signalling.

Adams, B. B., *and* Hitt, R., *comps.* Railroad signal dictionary. $6. Railroad Gazette.

Block signals on the railroads of the United States, Jan. 1, 1909. '09(Je) 12 p. tabs., 4°, pap. (Add. Superintendent for price.) U. S., Supt. of Docs.

Elliott, W. H. A B C of railroad signaling. $1. Mackenzie-K.

Latimer, J. B. Railway signaling in theory and practice. $2.50. Mackenzie-K.

Lavarack, F: C: Locking: elem. treatise on the mechanics in interlocking lever machines. $2. F: C: Lavarack.

Signals and signalling.—*Continued.*

Railway signaling. (Add. pub. for price.) Elec. Journ.

School of Railway Signaling. Railway signaling. (Add. pubs. for price.) Sch. R'way Signaling.

School of Railway Signaling. Signal drawing. $15. Sch. R'way Signaling.

Scott, R. Automatic block signals and signal circuits. *$2.50 net. McGraw.

Scriven, G: P. Transmission of military information. (Not for sale.) G: P. Scriven.

Submarine signals; rept.; [to accompany S. 6603.] '10(Ap) 8 p. 8°, pap. Gov. Pr. Off.

United States. *Signal Office.* Visual signaling. Gov. Pr. Off.

Significance of hist. in a democracy. Smith, C: A. Guilford Battle.

Significance of the woman suffrage movement. American Academy of Political and Social Science. 50 c. Am. Acad. Pol. Sci.

Significant educational progress in North Carolina. Coon, C: L. (Not for sale.) N. C. Dept. Pub. Instruct.

Signs and symbols of the primordial man. Churchward, A. $8 net. Dutton.

Signs in the Christmas fire. Knight, W: A. *50 c. net; *35 c. net. Pilgrim Press.

Sigsbee, A. Eliz.

Heart poems. '09(F) 12°, 75 c. B'way Pub.

Sigurd. Peterson, A. $1.50 net. Jacobs.

Sigurd Slembe. *See* Björnson, B. $1.50 net. Sergel.

Sigurd the dragon-slayer; ed. by T: Cartwright. '08(Ag15) 16°. (Every child's lib.) 50 c. Dutton.

Sihler, Ernest Gottleib.

Annals of Cæsar; critical biography, with a survey of the sources for more advanced students. '10(D24) c. O. $1.75 net. Stechert.

Testimonium animae; or, Greek and Roman before Jesus Christ: a series of essays and sketches dealing with the spiritual elements in classical civilization. '08 (N14) c. O. *$2.25 net. Stechert.

Sikes, G: C.

Rept. on the Chicago dock problem; with special reference to the questions of municipal ownership and leasing policy; prep. for J: M. Ewing, Chicago Harbor Commissioner. '09(D) 81 p. O. pap. Chic. Harbor Com.

Sikh religion.

Macauliffe, M. A. Sikh religion; its Gurus, sacred writings and authors. In 6 v. *$19.25 net. Oxford Univ.

Sikhim, India.

White, J. C. Sikhim and Bhutan. *$6 net. Longmans.

Silage.

See **Ensilage.**

Silas Kinkendoron's sons. Bates, *Mrs.* M. H. E. $1.50. C. M. Clark.

Silas Marner. *See* Eliot, George, *pseud.*

Silber, Mendel.

Jewish achievement; with introd. by Abraham Rosenthal. '10(N) 122 p. il. 16°, $1. Modern View.

Silberrad, Una Lucy.
Desire. '08(D26) D. $1.50. Doubleday, P.
—, and Lyall, Sophie.
Dutch bulbs and gardens. '09(Jl31) il. in col. O. *$2 net. Macmillan.
Silburn, Percy Arth. Baxter.
Colonies and imperial defense. '09(Jl3) tabs., O. $2. Longmans.
Governance of empire. '10(Jl9) map. O. $3 net. Longmans.
Silence. Andreyve, L. 25 c. Brown Bros.
Silence. Stewart, —. $1.50. Connoisseurs' Press.
Silent battle. Williamson, *Mrs.* A. M. L. 75 c. Doscher.
Silent call. Royle, E: M. $1.50. Scribner.
Silent isle. Benson, A. C. $1.50 net. Putnam.
Silesius, Angelus, pseud.
See Scheffler, Johann.
Silhouettes. *See* Symons, Arth.
Silk, B.
See Goldin, H. E.
Silkwood, Rev. Barzillia.
Steps in the Christian life; together with life sketch, savings, and sermons. '10 (D17) c. por. diagr., 12°, 50 c. Jennings.
SILKWORMS.
Kellogg, V. L., *and* Smith, *Mrs.* R. G. Inheritance in silkworms. $1. Stanford Univ.
Sill, Mrs. G: Imbrie.
See Sill, Louise Morgan Smith.
Sill, Louise Morgan Smith, [Mrs. G: Imbrie Sill.]
Little adventures of Kitty Tipsy-Toe: verses. '08, [1910.] (D) c. il. 12°, 75 c. Harper.
Formerly published by B. W. Dodge.
Sunnyfield; adventures of Podsy and June. '09(Mr20) c. il. O. †$1.25. Harper.
Silly syclopedia. Pendleton, A. L., *jr.* 50 c. C: G. Feldmeyer.
SILOS.
See **Ensilage.**
Silsbee, Wa. Everett, and Blood, Percy Erford.
Railway special work. '10(Ag13) c. 16°, $2. McGraw-H.
Silvae (The). *See* Statius, Publius Papinius.
Silver, Arth. P.
Farm, cottage, camp and canoe in maritime Canada with an introduction by the Rt. Hon. Lord Strathcona and Mount Royal. '08(Je6) il. 12°, *$2 net. Dutton.
SILVER.
Crane, W. R: Gold and silver: economic history of mining. **$5 net. Wiley.
Lowes, *Mrs.* E. L. Chats on old silver. *$2 net; *$5 net. Stokes.
Macquoid, P. Plate collector's guide. *$2 net. Scribner.
Rose, T: K. Precious metals: gold, silver, and platinum. **$2 net. Van Nostrand.
Veith, H: N. Sheffield plate: its history, manufacture and art. *$8 net. Macmillan.
Silver blade. Hagedorn, H. *jr.* *$1.10 net. Harvard Co-op.
Silver blade: [novel.] Walk, C: E. $1.50. McClurg.
Silver box. *See* Galsworthy, J: Plays.
Silver butterfly. Woodrow, N. M. W. †$1.50. Bobbs-M.
Silver canoe. Hunting, H: G. $1.25. McClurg.
Silver cleek. Haywood, J: C. $1. M. Kennerley.
Silver cross. *See* Euwer, J: H.—Sue, Marie Joseph Eugène.
Silver cup. Hall, C: C. **$1.25 net. Houghton M.
Silver horde. Beach, R. E. †$1.50. Harper.
Silver legend. Taylor, J. A. *$1.25 net. Herder.
Silver lib. D. Longmans.
—Haggard. Farmer's year.—Winter pilgrimages. ea., $1.50.
—Marbot. Memoirs. 2 v. $2.50.
Silver lining. Morton, N. G. $1. Badger.
Silver pitchers. Alcott, L. M. †$1.50. Little, B. & Co.
Silver ser. of classics. 12°. Silver.
—Shakespeare. Macbeth. 40 c.
Silver ser. of modern language text books; ed. by Adolf Cohn. il. 12°. Silver.
—Dike, *comp.* Scientific French reader. $1.
—Lutz. Elem. German reader. $1.
Silver thread. Mackay, C. D. $1.10 net. Holt.
Silver wedding of the Bear. Abbott, H. (Priv. pr.) H. Abbott.
Silverwool. Jenkinson, E. $1.50. Baker & T.
Simeon Tetlow's shadow. Lee, J. †$1.50. Century Co.
Similes and figures. Maclaren, A. $1 net. Revell.
Simkins, W: Stewart.
Administration of estates in Texas. '08 (O) c. 6+674 p. 8°, $5.25. Von Boeckmann-J.
Contracts and sales. 2d ed. '10(D) c. 936 p. 8°, $6.50. Von Boeckmann-J.
"Simmie," pseud.
See Simon, Ferdinand P:
Simmons, Harold H.
Outlines of electrical engineering. '09(Ag) il. *$6 net. Cassell.
Simmons, J: B., rep.
See Wisconsin. ***Sup. ct.*** **Digest.**
Simmons, Laura.
Flights o' fancy: verses. '09(Ja16) c. por. O. $1; ooze leath., $1.75. Atlantis Press.
Simmons, Rob. Jasper Hogue.
Pract. English grammar for common schools. '08(Ag) c. 206 p. 12°, 50 c. R. J. H. Simmons.
Simms, Rob. N., comp.
See North Carolina manual.
Simon, Rabbi Abram.
Principle of Jewish education in the past; two essays. '09, [1910.] (Mr) 36 p. 8°, 25 c. A. Simon.
Simon, Ferdinand P:, ["Simmie."]
Antony and Hero. '09(My1) c. D. $1. F. P: Simon.
Simon, Lemuel C.
Century of the National Bank of the Northern Liberties of Philadelphia, Pa. '10(Ag) 53 p. pls. pors. 8°. (Priv. pr.) L. C. Simon.

Simon, Leon, ed.
Aspects of the Hebrew genius; volume of essays on Jewish literature and thought. '10(Je4) 8°, $1. Bloch.

Simon, Otto Torney.
Monograph on the art of singing. '07, [1909.] (F) 13 p. 16°. (Add. pubs. for price.) W. F. Roberts.

Simon, Sylvester Jacobi.
Physical perfection. '08(S12) c. il. por. O. $3; mor., $5. MacGerald.

Simon, W:
Manual of chemistry. 9th ed., rev. and enl. '09(S) 716 p. il. 8°, *$3 net. Lea.

Simon Peter: [fiction.] Upham, F. B. *75 c. net. Eaton & M.

Simon the jester. Locke, W: J: $1.50. Lane.

Simonds, Frederic W:
See Maury, Matthew, Fontaine.

Simonds, W: E:
Student's history of American literature. '09(S11) c. il. pors. D. $1.10. Houghton M.

Simons, Algie Martin.
Socialist program. '08(D) 32 p. 12°, pap., 5 c.; per 100, $2.50. Socialist.

Simons, C: C.
Commercial law simplified; being a simple and concise presentation of the subject of commercial law in question and answer form. '09(Je) c. 12+510 p. O. shp., $5. Business Man's Pub.

Simple carbohydrates and the glucosides. Armstrong, E. F. *$1.20 net. Longmans.

Simple case of Susan. Futrelle, J. †$1.25. Appleton.

Simple jewelry. Rathbone, R. L. B. $2 net. Van Nostrand.

Simple jography. Herford, O. $1. J: W. Luce.

Simple lessons in wood turning. '10(Je4) il. 12°, (Woodworker ser.) pap., 25 c. Spon.

Simple life. Travis, J: C. (priv. pr.) J: C. Travis

Simple physics. Adams, M. P. (Add. author for price.) M. P. Adams.

Simple single. Abbott, F. M. 50 c. Rumford Press.

Simple soldering. Thatcher, E: 50 c.; 25 c. Spon.

Simple story. *See* Inchbald, *Mrs.* Eliz. Simpson.

Simple Susan. Chisholm, L. 50 c. Dutton.

Simple treatise on architectural perspective. Hicks, I: I. 50 c. Indust.

Simples from the Master's garden. Slosson, *Mrs.* A. T. *$1 net. S. S. Times.

Simplicité. Tuckerman, J. 50 c. Am. Bk.

Simplified methods of calculating reinforced concrete beams. Twelvetrees, W. N. 20 c. Macmillan.

Simplified phonetic shorthand. Gaines, C. C., *ed.* $2. C. C. Gaines.

SIMPLIFIED SPELLING.
See Spelling (Simplified).

Simplified Spelling Board. Circulars. 23 nos. '09(Ap3) O. pap., gratis. Simplified Spell. Bd.

Simply women. Prévost, M. $1 net. Macaulay.

Simpson, Rev. Alb. B.
Cross of Christ. [1910.] (N) c. 9-157 p. 12°, 75 c. Alliance Press.
See also Wilson, Madèle.

Simpson, Bertram Lenox.
See Weale, B. L. Putnam, *pseud.*

Simpson, Eugene Milton.
Pheasant farming. '08(My9) c. il. 12°, 25 c. W. E. Smith.

Simpson, F. M.
History of architectural development. In 3 v. v. 2, Mediæval. '09(Ap17) il. O. (Architects' lib.) *$6 net. Longmans.

Simpson, Frances.
New book of the cat. '08(D12) il. 4°, *$5 net. Cassell.

Simpson, Fk. Leslie.
Case on torts to accompany "The law of torts," by Melville M. Bigelow. '08(D) c. 15+709 p. 8°, $4.50. Little, B. & Co.

Simpson, F: Arth.
Rise of Louis Napoleon; with unpublished documents and illustrations. '10(F12) O. *$3.50 net. Putnam.

Simpson, Harold.
Seven stages of golf, golf stories in picture and verse. '09(Je19) il F. bds., *75 c. net. Lippincott.

Simpson, Canon, Ja. Gilliland.
Christus crucifixus; or, Christ's crown and covenant. '10(S) 12°, $1.50 net. Doran.
Preachers and teachers. '10(D3) D. $1.40 net. Longmans.

SIMPSON, Jerry.
Diggs, *Mrs.* A. Le P. Story of Jerry Simpson. $1.10. J. Simpson.

Simpson, Katherine D., comp.
From a book lover's notes. '10(Je18) c. O. pap., 60 c., boxed. Cloister Press.

SIMPSON, *Bp.* Mathew.
Wood, E. M. Peerless orator, the Rev. Mathew Simpson. $1.50. Pittsburgh.

Simpson, Patrick Carnegie, D.D.
Life of Principal Rainy. 2 v. '09(D) pors. *$6 net. Doran.

Simpson, S: L.
Gold-gated West; songs and poems; ed., with introd. preface, by W. T. Burney. '10(O8) c. por. 8°, $2. Lippincott.

Simpson, T: Jefferson, M.D.
Book of facts, truths and reason. '08 (Ag) c. 231 p. por. 12°, $1. T: J. Simpson.

Simpson, W: J: Ritchie, M.D.
Principles of hygiene as applied to tropical and sub-tropical climates, and the principles of personal hygiene in them as applied to Europeans. '08(D19) il. plans, 8°, *$5 net. Wood.
Treatise on plagues. '08(F8) 8°, *$5 net. Putnam.

Simpson, Rev. W: J: Sparrow.
Roman Catholic opposition to papal infallibility. '10(Ap30) D. $2 net. Young Churchman.
St. Augustine and African church divisions. '10(N12) D. $1.25 net. Longmans.
Use of vestments in the English Church. '09(Je5) D. pap., *20 c. net. Longmans.

Sims, G: Rob.
Devil in London. '09(F13) c. il. D. $1. Dodge.

Sims, Mrs. Mamie Hunt.
Negro mystic lore: [stories.] '08(F) $1. M. H. Sims.

SIN.
Gray, J. M. Satan and the saint; or, the present darkness and the coming light. 25 c. Bible Inst.
Hall, F. J. Evolution and the fall. **$1.50 net. Longmans.
Hyde, W: D. Sin and its forgiveness. 50 c. Houghton M.
Jelfo, G: F: Commentaries on sin. $1 net. Sherman, F.
McDonough, M. V. Chief sources of sin; seven discourses on pride, covetousness, lust, anger, gluttony, envy, sloth. 75 c. Murphy.
McGowan, F. X. Two series of lenten sermons on, I., Sin and its remedies; II., The seven deadly sins. 75 c. Pustet.
Orr, J. Sin as a problem of to-day. $1.50 net. Doran.
Stroup, N. W. Fact of sin. *$1 net. Jennings.
Talbert, D. H. Pleasures of sin. $1. D. H. Talbert.
Watson, J: Respectable sins. $1.25 net. Doran.
See also Evil;—Repentance;—Salvation;—Temptation.

Sin-eater. *See* Macleod, Fiona, *pseud.*

Sinclair, Angus.
Locomotive engine running and management. 22d ed., enl. '08(Jl11) il. figs. 12°, $2. Wiley.

Sinclair, B. M.
See Bower, B. M., *pseud.*

Sinclair, Bertrand W:
Land of frozen suns; novel. '10(Ap23) c. il. D. $1.50. G: W: Dillingham.
Raw gold. '08(Ag29) D. †$1.50; '10(My) 50 c. G: W: Dillingham.

Sinclair, E. Marie.
Random shots: [poems.] '10(Mr26) por. D. *$1 net. Badger.

Sinclair, J. Edn.
See Sherman, H: Clapp.

Sinclair, May.
The creators; a comedy. '10(O8) c. il. D. $1.30 net. Century Co.
Immortal moment. '08(O10) c. il. D. †$1.50. Doubleday, P.
Judgment of Eve. '08(Mr21) c. il. D. †$1.25. Harper.

Sinclair, S: Bower, and Tracy, F:
Introductory educational psychology; book for teachers in training. '10(Jl16) 12°, 90 c. Macmillan.

Sinclair, Upton Beall, jr.
The metropolis. '08(Mr14) c. D. †$1.50. Moffat.
Money changers. '08(S19) c. D. $1.50. B. W. Dodge.
Prince Hagen; phantasy. '10(Ap9) c. D. $1; pap., 25 c. Kerr.
Samuel the seeker. '10(Ap2) c. D. $1.50. B. W. Dodge.
—, and Williams, Michael.
Good health, and how we won it. '09(F13) c. il. D. **$1.20 net. Stokes.

Sinclair, V: Macdonald.
Memorials of St. Paul's Cathedral. '09, [1910.] (D) 482 p. il. 8°, *$4 net. Jacobs.

Sinclair, W: J.
Recent investigations bearing on the question of the occurrence of neocene man in the auriferous gravels of the Sierra Nevada. '08(Mr7) Q. (Univ. of Cal. pubs., Am. archæology and ethnology.) pap., 35 c. Univ. of Cal.

Sindall, R. W.
Manufacture of paper. '09(Jl17) il. 8°, (Westminster ser.) *$2 net. Van Nostrand.

Sindelar, Jos. C:, ed.
Lincoln Day entertainments: recitations, plays, dialogues, drills. '09(Ja16) c. D. pap., 25 c. Flanagan.
New Christmas book: recitations, plays, dialogues, drills, tableaux, pantomimes, quotations, songs, facts and the novelty, A living Christmas magazine. '10(D17) c. il. 12°, 30 c. Flanagan.
Washington Day entertainments; recitations, plays, dialogues, drills, tableaux, pantomimes, quotations, songs, tributes, stories, facts. '10(Mr5) c. por. 12°, 30 c. Flanagan.

Sindell, Rev. Martin.
Satisfied at last. '09(Ja16) c. il. D. $1.50. Reid Pub.

Sing-song. Rossetti, C. G. 80 c.; $1.25. Macmillan.

Singer, Isidore, ed.
International insurance encyclopedia; descriptive record of the history, theory and practice of all branches of insurance throughout the world and from the earliest times to the present day. In 4 v. v. 1, The insurance men of the past and present; v. 2, Life insurance (fraternal insurance included): history, theory and practice; v. 3, Fire and marine insurance: history, theory and practice; v. 4, Casualty, surety and miscellaneous insurance: history, theory and practice. '10(O15) v. 1, $6; hf. mor., $8; mor., $10; v. 2, 3, 4, ea., $12; hf. mor., $15; mor., $18; per set in advance, $35; hf. mor., $45; mor., $55. Am. Encyclopedic.

Singer, Rev. Simeon.
Literary remains; sel. and ed. with a memoir by Israel Abrahams. In 3 v. v. 1, Sermons and memoir; v. 2, Lectures and addresses; v. 3, Sermons to children. '08(Je6) 8°, ea., *$1.25 net. Bloch.

SINGER BUILDING, New York City.
Semsch, O. F., *ed.* Hist. of the Singer Building construction. (Add. author for price.) O. F. Semsch.

SINGING.
Abbott, A. J. Individual singing exercises. 4th, 5th, 6th, 7th, 8th grades. ea., 10 c. Am. Bk.
Baldwin, R. L. Progressive melodies for sight singing. 35 c. Ginn.
Brouillet, G. A. Artistic tone production through natural breathing. $2. F. E. Bacon.

SINGING.—*Continued.*
Clare, H. N. Choir-boy's manual. *25 c. net.—Choirmaster's manual. *75 c. net. Schirmer.
Cole, S: W., *ed.* Exercises in sight singing. *60 c. net. Boston Music.
Cole, S: W., *and* Lewis, L. R. Melodia: course in sight-singing. $1.50. Ditson.
Curry, S: S. Mind and voice; principles and methods in vocal training. $1.50. Expression.
Delmarter, J. E. Elements of vocal music. 35 c. Delmarter Pub.
Girard, *Mrs.* M. A. G. B. Vocal art. $1. Cuneo.
Heinrich, M. Correct principles of classical singing. $1.50 net. Lothrop, L. & S.
James, *Mrs.* M. I. Scientific tone production. *$1.25 net. C: W. Thompson.
Kirkpatrick, H. Applied vocalization. 50 c. H. Kirkpatrick.
Mackinlay, M. S. Singing voice and its training. $1.25 net. Dutton.
Marzo, E., *comp. and ed.* Art of vocalization. In 6 pts., ea. pt. in 3 bks. ea. bk., 75 c.—Coloratura album for soprano. $1. Ditson.
Mills, C: F. H: Voice and vocalism. $1.50. Hawk-Eye.
Pattou, A. A. Art of voice production established on a true scientific basis. 50 c. A. A. Pattou.
Pauseron, A. M. A B C of vocalization. $1. Ditson.
Preetorius, C. Tone placed and developed. $1.50. C. Preetorius.
Rogers, *Mrs.* C. K. B. My voice and I; or, the relation of the singer to the song. $1.50 net. McClurg.
Ryan, *Mrs.* M. What every singer should know. $1. Franklin Pub., (Neb.)
Santley, *Sir* C: Art of singing and vocal declamation. **$1.25 net. Macmillan.
Schilling, W: P. Upper tenor tones and how every tenor may acquire them without strain or effort. $1. W: P. Schilling.
Shakespeare, W: Art of singing. $2. Ditson.
Sieber, F. Art of singing and vocal culture. 50 c. Ditson.
Simon, O. T. Monograph on the art of singing. (Add. pubs. for price.) W. F. Roberts.
Stubbs, G: E: Adult male alto or counter-tenor voice. 75 c. H. W. Gray.
Taylor, D: C. Psychology of singing. *$1.50 net. Macmillan.
Van Broeckhoven, J. True method of tone production. $1.50. H. W. Gray.
White, E. G. Science and singing. $1.25. T: J. Donlan.
See also Church music;—Hymns;—Music;—Songs;—Voice.

Singing caravan. Baerlein, H: 60 c. net. Dutton.
Singing mouse. Hough, E. $1. Bobbs-M.
Single proprietors' and partners' accounts. Griffiths, J. B. 50 c. Am. Sch. Corr.

Singleton, Esther.
Art of the Belgian galleries; being a hist. of the Flemish school of painting. '09 (N20) c. il. D. **$2 net, boxed. L. C. Page.
Dutch New-York. '09(S18) c. il. O. **$3.50 net, boxed. Dodd.
Furniture of our forefathers; with critical descriptions of plates by Russell Sturgis. [New ed.,] complete in 1 v. '08(D19) c. il. Q. **$5 net. Doubleday, P.
Guide to great cities, for young travellers and others; Northwestern Europe. '10 (Jl30) il. D. (Guide ser.) $1.25 net. Baker & T.
Guide to modern opera; description and interpretation of the words and music of famous modern operas. '09(D4) c. pors. D. **$1.50 net. Dodd.
Holland: [descriptions of pictures in Dutch galleries.] '08(O17) c. il. S. (Standard galleries.) *1 net. McClurg.
Wild flower fairy book. New ed. '10(D) col. il. 12°, $1.25. Dodd.
—, *comp. and ed.* Famous cathedrals, as seen and described by great writers. '09(O23) c. O. **$1.60 net. Dodd.
Famous sculpture as seen and described by great writers. '10(O22) c. O. $1.60 net. Dodd.
Florence as described by great writers. '10 (D3) c. il. O. $1.60 net. Dodd.
Great rivers of the world, as seen and described by famous writers. '08(D5) c. il O. **$1.60 net. Dodd.
Switzerland, as described by great writers. '08(D5) c. il. O. **$1.60 net. Dodd.
Turkey and the Balkan States, as described by great writers. '08(D19) c. il. O. **$1.60 net. Dodd.

Singleton, Terrell Wingfield.
Cotton-seed-buyer's book. '08(Ja4) 8°, leath., $3.50. T. W. Singleton.

Singmaster, Elsie.
When Sarah saved the day. '09(O16) c. il. D. †$1. Houghton M.
When Sarah went to school. '10(O22) c. D. $1. Dodd.

Sinking ship. Lathbury, E. †$1.50. Holt.
Sinlessness of Jesus. Meyer, M. *40 c. net. Eaton & M.

Sinnett, Rev. C: Nelson.
Richard Pinkham of old Dover, N. H., and his descendants. '08(Jl) 308 p. il. pors. 8°, $5. C: N. Sinnett.
Sinnett genealogy; Michael Sinnett of Harpswell, Maine, his ancestry and descendants; also records of other Sinnetts, Sinnotts, etc., in Ireland and America. '10(S) il. 137 p. pors. 8°, $4. C: N. Sinnett.

SINNETT FAMILY.
See Genealogies.

Sins of society. Raleigh, C., *pseud.* $1.50. G: W. Dillingham.
Sintram and his companions. *See* La Motte Fouqué, Friedrich Heinrich Karl, *Freiherr* de.

SIOUX COUNTY, Ia.
Anderson & Goodwin Company. Standard historical atlas of Sioux County, Iowa. $15. I. B. Goodwin.

SIOUX INDIANS.
See Indians.
Sir Anthony. Chambers, C: H. 50 c. S: French.
Sir Guy and Lady Rannard. Dickinson, H. N. $1.50. Duffield.
Sir Henry Vane. Martin, W: F. $1.25. Roxburgh.
Sir Jaffray's wife. Marchmont, A. W. 75 c. Rand, McN. & Co.
Sir Orfeo. *See* **Orpheus.**
Sir Richard Escombe. Pemberton, M. †$1.50. Harper.
Sir Roger de Coverley papers. *See* Addison, Jos.
SIRUP.
Ross, S. H. Suggested modification of the Winton lead number, especially as applied to mixtures of maple and cane sugar sirups. U. S., Supt. of Docs.
Sis. Coffey, W: H. 50 c. Burton Co.
Sisk, B: Franklin.
Elements of English grammar. '07, [1908.] (Mr.) c. 7+254 p. 12°, (Sisk's English course.) (Add. pubs. for price.) So. Sch. Bk.
Grammar as a science. '07. [1908.] (Mr.) c. 6+286 p. 12°, (Sisk's English course.) (Add. pubs. for price.) So. Sch. Bk.
—, and MacDonald, Mary E.
First steps in English grammar. '07, [1908.] (Mr.) c. 6+151 p. il. 12°, (Sisk's English course.) (Add. pubs. for price.) So. Sch. Bk.
Sismondi, Jean Charles Leonard Sismonde de.
History of the Italian republics. '08(O17) 16°, (Best books ser.) leath., *$1 net. Dutton.
Marignan: conquête et perte du Milanais; ed. by Arth. Wilson-Green. '09(Mr6) D. (Oxford modern French ser.) 50 c. Oxford Univ.
Pavie et le sac de Rome; ed. by Arth. Wilson-Green. '09(My15) D. (Oxford modern French ser.) 50 c. Oxford Univ.
Sisson, E: Octavius.
Essentials of character; pract. study of the aim of moral education. '10(D10) c. D. $1 net. Macmillan.
High school's cure of souls. '08, [1909.] (S) 359-372 p. 8°, (Univ. of Washington bull.) (Add. Univ. for price.) Univ. of Wash.
Sisson, Septimus.
Text-book of veterinary anatomy. '10(O) 11-826 p. il. (partly col.) 4°, $7. Saunders.
SISSON FAMILY.
See Genealogies: Wood, A. A.
Sister Clementia. Law, F: H. $1.50. Fenno.
Sister Nivedita, pseud.
See Noble, Marg. E.
Sister of Prince Rupert. Godfrey, E., *pseud.* *$4 net. Lane.
SISTERHOODS.
See **Nunneries.**
Sister's cake, and other stories. Field, E. 50 c. Hurst.
Sisters (The). Dearmer, M. W. †$1.50. McClure.
SISTERS OF CHARITY.
See **Vincent de Paul, *St.***
SISTERS OF CHARITY, Cincinnati, O.
See **Seton, Elizabeth, *Mother.***
Sisters of Napoleon. Turquan, J. *$3.75 net. Scribner.
Sisyphus. **Trevelyan, R. C. *$1.50 net. Longmans.**
Site and Relic Society of Germantown; historical addresses. 4°. Site and Relic.
—Willits. Early physicians of Germantown. (Not for sale.)
Situation at present. Klein, J. 10 c. J. Klein.
Situation in southeastern Europe. Crocker, H: G. (Add. pub. for price.) B. S. Adams.
Sittig, Mrs. Frank.
Good night stories. '08(D) il. 12°, $1.50. Crombie & Co.
Sivers, Arth. F:
See True, Rodney Howard.
Six ages of European history. Johnson, A. J., *ed.* 6 v. ea., *90 c. net. Macmillan.
Six essays on the Platonic theory of knowledge. Williams, M. V. *$1 net. Putnam.
Six girls and the seventh one. Taggart, M. A. †$1.50. Wilde.
Six girls growing older. Taggart, M. A. †1.50. Wilde.
Six girls ser. *See* Taggart, Marion Ames.
Six Greek sculptors. Gardner, E. A. $2 net. Scribner.
600 business law points. Ford, H: $3.50. H: Ford.
Six lectures on some nineteenth century artists. Knight, W: A. $2. Art Inst. of Chic.
Six masters in disillusion. Thorold, A. L. *$1.50 net. Dutton.
Six modern devils. Keesey, W. R. *35 c. net. Jennings.
Six radical thinkers. MacCunn, J: $1 net. Longmans.
Six to sixteen. Ewing, *Mrs.* J. H. G. $1. Macmillan.
Six to sixteen ser. il. D. Caldwell.
—Squires. Tom, Nadine and Snuffles. 60 c.
Six to sixteen series. 17 v. '09(O2) il. D. 60 c. Caldwell.
Sixpenny pieces. Lyons, A. N. $1.50. Lane.
Sixteen excursions to places of historic interest in Philadelphia. Campbell, J. 25 c. J. Campbell.
Sixteen stories. Allison, S: B. 25 c. Flanagan.
Sixth speed. Rath, E. J. †$1.50. Moffat.
Sixty days in Europe. Rees, T: $1.25. State Register.
Sixty-five on time. Baird, J. K. $1.25. Saalfield.
Sixty years in Texas. Jackson, G: $1.50. G: Jackson.
Sixty years in the wilderness. Lucy, *Sir* H: W. *$3 net. Dutton.
Sixty years of protection in Canada. Porritt, E: *$1.50 net. Macmillan.
Sixty years of Uppingham cricket. Patterson, W: S. *$2 net. Longmans.
Sixty years with the Bible. Clarke, W: N. **$1.25 net. Scribner.
Sixty years with the muse. Hager, L. L. 60 c. Un. B. Pub.

Sizes of flow and return steam mains. Allen, J: K. 50 c Domestic Engineering.

Skae, Hilda T.
Stories from English history. '08(Je6) il. 16°, (Stories from history ser.) 50 c. Dutton.

Skal, Georg von.
History of German immigration in the United States and successful German-Americans and their descendants. '08 (D5) c. pors. 4°, $10; mor., $15. G. v. Skal.
Hist. of German immigration in the U. S. and successful German-Americans and their descendants. '10(Mr12) c. pors. 8°, $10. F. T. Smiley.
Illustrated history of the borough of Queens, New York City. '08, [1910.] 167 p. il. front. pls., pors. 4°, F. T. Smiley.

Skarstrom, W:, M.D.
Gymnastic kinesiology; manual of the mechanism of gymnastic movements. '09 (D4) c. il. O. *$1.25 net. Bassette.

SKAT (*card game*).
Foster, R. F: Skat up to date. 25 c. Dick.
Granger, A. D. Skat and how to play it. $1. Brentano's.
Henry, A. Skat made easy. **50 c. net. Jacobs.
Liedtke, F. W. A B C des skat in Deutsch und English. 50 c. Schaefer & K.
McColl, F. L. Helps for skat players. 35 c. W: R. Jenkins.
Meyer, V. M. K. Enlarged small talks on skat. 75 c. Ruledge.
Wager-Smith, A. E. Skat: principles and illustrative games. $1.25 net. Lippincott.

SKATING.
Benson, E: F. English figure skating. *$2.50 net. Macmillan.
Brokaw, I. Art of skating. $5 net. Scribner.
Burchell, H. P., *ed.* Spalding's roller guide. 10 c. Am. Sports.

Skeat, Rev. Wa. W:
Etymological dict. of the English language. 4th ed., rev. and enl. '10(D17) 4°, $11.75. Oxford Univ.
—, comp. Early English proverbs chiefly of the thirteenth and fourteenth centuries, with illustrative quotations. '10(My14) front. D. $1.15. Oxford Univ.

SKEEING.
See Ski-ing.

Skeletal remains. Hrdlicka, A. 25 c. U. S., Supt. of Docs.

Skelton, E: Oliver.
Story of New England, illustrated, being a narrative of the principal events from the arrival of the Pilgrims in 1620 and of the Puritans in 1624 to the present. '10(Ap) c. 140 p. il. 12°, 50 c. E: O. Skelton.

SKEPTICISM.
Laforet, N. J. Causes and cure of unbelief. 60 c.; 30 c. Kilner.
Oppenheimer, F. J. Reign of the negative; studies in mysticism and skepticism. $2 net. Moods.
See also Agnosticism.

Sketch book. *See* Irving, Washington.

Sketch of the Panama Canal. Stevens, J: F. (Priv. pr.) J: F. Stevens.

Sketches and snapshots. Russell, G: W: E. $2.50 net. Duffield.

Sketches from life. Carpenter, E: $1.50. Macmillan.

Sketches from the Karen Hills. Bunker, A. $1 net. Revell.

Sketches of rulers of India. *See* Oswell, G. D.

Sketches of South Carolina. Middleton, G. M. 25 c. G. M. Middleton.

SKETCHING.
See Drawing;—Water-color painting.

Sketching grounds. Holme, C:, *ed.* *$3 net. Lane.

SKI-ING.
Rickmers, W. R. Ski-ing for beginners and mountaineers. $1.50 net. Scribner.

Skid Puffer; tale of the Kankakee Swamp. '10(Ap16) c. il. D. $1.50. Holt.

Skillern, Penn-Gaskell, jr.
Anatomy of the central nervous system, eye and ear, cranial nerves (deep). '09 (Jl) c. 107 p. 8°, *$1 net. Dolbey.
Descriptive anatomy; development; microscopic anatomy; bones. '10(Mr) c. 295 p. 8°, $2. Dolbey.

Skimming the skies. Whitcomb, R. $1.25. Badger.

SKIN.
Baum, W: L., *and* Moyer, H. N:, *eds.* Skin and venereal diseases. $1.25. Year Bk.
Dumesnil, A. H: O. Diseases of the skin. $4. Mosby.
Gilchrist, T: C. Outline of skin diseases. 75 c. Students Bk.
Hyde, J. N. Diseases of the skin. *$5 net; *$6 net.—Pract. treatise on diseases of the skin. $5. Lea.
Jackson, G: T: Diseases of the skin. *$3 net. Lea.
Jacobi, E. Portfolio of dermochromes. 3 v. $24. Rebman.
Maurer, *Mrs.* R. D. Skin, its care and treatment. $2. McIntosh.
Morris, *Sir* M. Diseases of the skin. *$3.50 net. Wood.
Morris, M., *and* Dore, S. E. Light and X-ray treatment of skin diseases. *$1.50 net. Funk.
Robinson, W. H. Dermatology in abstract. $1. Medical Abstract.
Schalek, A. Diseases of the skin. $1. Lea.
Schamberg, J. F. Diseases of the skin and the eruptive fevers. *$3 net. Saunders.
Shoemaker, J: V. Pract. treatise on diseases of the skin. *$6 net; *$7.50 net. Davis.
Stelwagon, H: W. Essentials of diseases of the skin. *$1 net.—Treatise on diseases of the skin. $6. Saunders.
Walker, N. Introd. to dermatology. *$3 net. Wood.
See also Cancer; — Medical electricity; — Radiotherapy;—Roentgen rays;—Tuberculosis.

Skinner, Alfr. F.
See New Jersey. Borough law.

Skinner, Avery Warner.
See Foote, Anna Eliz.

Skinner, C: Rufus, comp.
Bright side; little excursions into the field of optimism. '10(Ja22) c. D. 50 c. Beattys.

Skinner, Hubert Marshall.
Saint Patrick: a monograph in paragraphs. '08(Ap.) c. 48 p. por. 12°, pap., 20 c. T: Scholes.

—, ed. Collegiate course for home study. 12 v. '09(S) c. maps, 8°, $29.95; hf. mor., $39.95; ¾ mor., $57. Cree.

—, and Putney, Albert Hutchinson.
Government revenue, taxation, tariffs, by Hubert M. Skinner; Public utilities, by Albert H. Putney. '10(Ap9) c. 8°, (Business, commerce and finance.) $4.80. Cree.

See also Putney, Albert Hutchinson.

Skinner, Joshua J:
See Schreiner, Oswald.

SKIRTS.
See Dressmaking.

Skotheim, O. H.
See Washington [State] laws.

Skotlands rímur: Icelandic ballads on the Gowrie conspiracy; ed. by W: A. Craigie. '08(O24) D. hf. cl., $1.15. Oxford Univ.

Skrainka, Philip, M.D.
St. Louis: its hist. and ideals; prep. for the 61st annual session of the American Medical Association, June 7th, 8th, 9th and 10th, 1910. '10(Jl) c. 172 p. il. 12°, 50 c. P. Skrainka.

Skrine, Rev. J: Huntley.
Pastor ovium: day-book of a country parson. '09(Ap3) D. *$1.60 net. Longmans.

Sermons to pastors and masters. '10(O1) D. $1.50 net. Longmans.

Skues, G. E. M.
Minor tactics of the chalk stream, and kindred subjects. '10(Ap23) il. 4°, $2. Macmillan.

Skull and dentition of an extinct cat. Merriam, J: C. 15 c. Univ. of Cal.

Sky-man (The). Webster, H: K. $1.20 net. Century Co.

Sky pilot. *See* Gordon, C: W:

SKYE (*Island of*), Scotland.
Abraham, A. P. Rock-climbing in Skye. *$7 net. Longmans.

Slack, S. B.
Early Christianity. '09(Ap24) 8°, (Religions ancient and modern.) *40 c. net. Open Court.

Slade, C: Blount.
Physical examination and diagnostic anatomy. '10(O) c. 146 p. il. 8°, $1.25. Saunders.

SLADE FAMILY.
See Genealogies: Peck, T: B.

Sladen, Douglas Brooke Wheelton.
Queer things about Egypt. '10(D3) il. 8°, $5 net. Lippincott.

Secrets of the Vatican; palace of the Popes. New ed. '10(N) il. 8°, $2.50 net. Lippincott.

SLANG.
Miner, H. C. "Get the hook": [explanation of origin of the phrase.] gratis. H. C. Miner.
Sullivan, J. M., *comp.* Criminal slang. 15 c. Worcester Press.
See also Wit and humor.

Slant book. Newell, P: $1.25. Harper.

SLATE.
See Arkansas.

Slater, J:
See Smith, T. Roger.

Slater, J: Arth.
Pitman's business man's guide. 4th ed. '07, [1908.] (D) 7-482 p. 12°, $1.25. Pitman.

Pitman's mercantile law. 2d ed. '09(Jl31) O. $2. Pitman.

—, ed. Pitman's public man's guide. '10 (Ja22) D. $1.25. Pitman.

Slater, Rev. T:
Manual of moral theology; with notes on American legislation by Rev. Michael Martin. '08(Je27) c. 8°, pap., *$2.75 net. Benziger.

Short hist. of moral theology. '09(D4) c. O. *50 c. net. Benziger.

Slattery, C: Lewis, D.D.
Historic ministry and the present Christ: an appeal for unity. '08(N21) c. D. **50 c. net. Longmans.

Present-day preaching. '09(D11) c. D. **$1 net. Longmans.

Slattery, Marg.
Girl in her teens. '10(N5) c. D. 50 c. net. S. S. Times.

Living teachers. '09(Ag14) c. D. bds., *35 c. net. F. M. Barton.

Seed, the soil and the sower. '10(Jl2) c. S. bds., 35 c. net. F. M. Barton.

Teacher's candlestick. '09(Ag14) c. D. bds., *35 c. net. F. M. Barton.

Slaught, Herbert Ellsworth.
Key to High school algebra; elementary course [teachers only.] '08, [1909.] (F) 352 p. 12°, 75 c. Allyn & B.

Suggestions on the teaching of algebra with special reference to Slaught and Lennes' high school algebra. [1910] (F) c. '09. 30 p. 12°, pap., gratis. Allyn & B.

—, and Lennes, Nels Johann.
High school algebra: advanced course. '08 (My23) c. il. 12°, 65 c.—Complete course. '08, [1909.] (Ja) c. 510 p. diagrs., 12°, $1.20. Allyn & B.

Plane geometry, with problems and applications. '10(Ap16) c. il. 12°, $1. Allyn & B.

Slaughter, Philip, D.D.
History of Truro parish in Virginia; ed., with notes and addenda, by Rev. E: L. Goodwin. '08(Mr21) c. il. plan, facsim., D. **$1.50 net. Jacobs.

SLAUGHTER HOUSES.
See Abattoirs.

SLAVERY.
Adams, A. D. Neglected period of anti-slavery in America, (1808-1831.) **$1.50 net. Ginn.
Buckland, W: W. Roman law of slavery. *$5.75 net. Putnam.

SLAVERY.—*Continued.*
Fleming, W. L. Ex-slave pension frauds. La. State Univ.
Green, S: A. Slavery at Groton, Mass., in provincial times. 25 c. S: A. Green.
Lincoln, A. Emancipation proclamation. **$4 net. Houghton M.
Munford, B. B. Virginia's attitude toward slavery and secession. **$2 net. Longmans.
Oneal, J. Workers in American history. 25 c. J. Oneal.
Swan, C: A. Slavery of to-day; or, the present position of the open sore of Africa. 75 c. Gospel Pub.
Swann, A. J. Fighting the slave-hunters in Central Africa. *$3.50 net. Lippincott.
See also Congo Free State;—Missouri compromise;—Negroes;—Ohio;—Virginia;—*also* Dred Scott case.
Slavery of progress. Thomas, A. F. $1. Neale.
Slaves to the trust. Ingalls, J. S. 10 c. Social Justice.
Slavonic Europe. Bain, R. N. *$2 net. Putnam.
SLAVS.
See Croatian language.
SLAVS IN THE UNITED STATES.
Balch, E. G. Our Slavic fellow citizens. $2.50. Charities Pub.
SLEEP.
Powell, L. P. Art of natural sleep. **90 c. net. Putnam.
Sidis, B. Experimental study of sleep. *$1 net. Badger.
Upson, H: S. Insomnia and nerve strain. **$1.50 net. Putnam.
"Sleepin' at the foot." Brown, M. S. $1. J. M. Brown.
Sleeping Beauty (The). '09(O2)) il. Q. (Playtime ser. of toy books.) bds., 40 c.; pap., 25 c. Warne.
Sleeping beauty. *See* Couch, Arth. T: Quiller-.
SLEEPING SICKNESS.
Thimm, C. A., *comp.* Bibliography of trypanosomiasis. *$1.25 net. Stechert.
SLEIGHT OF HAND.
See Conjuring.
Sletzer, W: H:, comp.
Drill regulations, uniform rank, Knights of the Maccabees of the world: rev. by C: Sidney Haight. '08(My.) c. 183 p. il. 24°, *$1 net. Lilley.
Slicer, T: Roberts, D.D.
From poet to premier; centennial cycle, 1809-1909; Poe, Lincoln, Holmes, Darwin, Tennyson, Gladstone. '09(N20) c. il. O. hf. vellum, *$3 net. (1250 copies.) Grolier Club.
Way to happiness. '09(D25) c. S. *$1 net. Sturgis & W.
Slichter, C: Sumner.
Chamberlin, T: Chrowder.
SLIDE-RULE.
Blaine, R. G. Some quick and easy methods of calculating. $1. Spon.
Cajori, F. History of the logarithmic slide rule and allied instruments. $1. Engineering News.
Clark, J. J. Slide rule; elem. treatise. 60 c. Technical Supply.

SLIDE-RULE.—*Continued.*
Petri-Palmedo, D. How to use slide rules. 50 c. Kolesch.
Rosenthal, L. W. Mannheim and multiplex slide rules. 50 c. E. Dietzgen.
Thacher, E. Directions for using Thacher's calculating instrument. 75 c. Keuffel.
Sligh, J: Calhoun.
Christ's way of winning souls. '09(Mr6) c. D. 60 c. Pub. Ho. of M. E. Ch., So.
Slight indiscretion. Steinback, L. L. *$1.50 net. Cochrane.
Slip-in-the-pocket guide books. il S. $1 net. Platt & P.
—Guide to Belgium.
—Guide to Holland.
—Guide to Paris.
—Guide to Switzerland.
—Pictorial and descriptive guide to London.
—Pictorial and descriptive guide to Stratford-upon-Avon.
Sloan, Emily Eva.
Ballads of the plains. '08(Jl) c. 35 p. il. 8°, $1. E. E. Sloan.
Sloan, J. M.
Galloway. '08(Ag1) il. 8°, (Color books.) *$2 net. Macmillan.
Sloan, Rev. Patrick J.
Sunday-school director's guide to success. '09(Mr27) c. D. *$1 net. Benziger.
Sunday-school teacher's guide to success. '08(F8) c. D. *75 c. net. Benziger.
Sloane, Ja. Robinson, comp.
Golden gleanings to comfort the afflicted and help the toiler: poems. quotations, verses. '09(F6) c. 16°, bds., $1. J. R. Sloane.
Sloane, T: O'Conor.
Arithmetic of electricity. 20th ed. '09 (My8) c. il. tabs., D. $1. Henley.
Electric toy making for amateurs. '09 (Mr13) c. il. 12°, $1. Henley.
Electricians' handy book. '09(D) c. 768 p. il. 16°, leath., $3.50. Henley.
Elem. electrical calculations. '09(Jl3) c. il. 8°, $2. Van Nostrand.
Standard electrical dict. '10(My21) il. $3. Henley.
Sloane, W: Milligan.
Life of Napoleon Bonaparte; rev. and enl. with pors. 4 v. '10(N12) c. O. maps, $10 net, boxed. Century Co.
Slocum, Arth. Ware.
New crinoids from the Chicago area. '07, [1908.] (My.) 273-306 p. il. 8°, (Field Columbian Museum pub., Geological ser.) pap., 50 c. Field Museum.
New echinoids from the Ripley group of Mississippi. '09(Ag) 16 p. il. 8°, (Field Museum of Natural History pubs.; Geological ser.) 50 c. Field Museum.
Slocum, C: Elihu.
About tobacco and its deleterious effects; book for everybody, both users and nonusers. '09, [1910.] (Je) 70 p. 8°, $1. Slocum Pub.
Hist. of Frances Slocum, the captive; civilized heredity vs. a savage, and later barbarous environment. '08, [1909.] (N) 48 p. pors. 8°, $2.50. Slocum Pub.

Slocum, C: Elihu.—*Continued.*
Hist. of the Slocums, Slocumbs and Slocombs of America, genealogical and biographical; embracing twelve generations of the first-named family from A.D. 1637 to 1908, with their marriages and descendants in the female lines as far as ascertained. 2 v. '08. [1909.] (N) 15+543 p. il. pors. 8°. (Add. pubs. for price.) Tuttle Co.
Ohio country between the years 1783 and 1815, incl. military operations that twice saved to the United States the country west of the Allegheny mountains after the Revolutionary War. '10 (Ap30) c. O. $2 net. Putnam.

SLOCUM, Frances.
Slocum, C: E. Hist. of Frances Slocum, the captive. $2.50. Slocum Pub.

Slocum, G: Engs.
Wheatland, Monroe County, New York: sketch of its history. '09(Ja16) por. O. pap., $1. G: E. Slocum.

SLOCUM FAMILY.
See Genealogies.

Slocum lectures. *See* Holland, Rob. Afton.

Sloops of the Hudson. Verplanck, W: E: **$1.50 net. Putnam.

Sloper, Mrs. Allie, ["P. W.-M."]
Nannie Walters: a novel: a petition to the Order of the Eastern Star. '08(Ap11) c. il. D. pap., 25 c. J. S. Ogilvie.

Sloss, Rob. Thompson.
The automobile; its selection, care and use. '10(N5) c. D. $1.25 net. Outing.

Slosson, Mrs. Annie Trumbull.
Dissatisfied soul, and A prophetic romancer. '08(Jl18) c. il. D. *75 c. net. Bonnell.
Simples from the Master's garden. '08(F1) c. front. 12°, *$1 net. S. S. Times.

Slosson, Edn. Emery.
Great American universities. '10(N5) c. il. pors. O. $2.50 net. Macmillan.

Slouschz, Nahum.
Renaissance of Hebrew literature, (1743-1885;) tr. from the French. '09(D18) c. D. $1.25. Jewish Pub.

Slowcoach (The). Lucas, E: V. $1.50 net. Macmillan.

SLOYD.
Larsson, G. Sloyd for the three upper grammar grades. $1.25. Ellis.

Sluder, J. T.
See Texas municipal corporation laws.

Slumber Sea chanteys. Bell, L. C. $1. P. Elder.

SLUMS.
See Poor (The).

Sluss, J: W:, M.D.
Emergency surgery. '08(N); 2d ed., rev. '10(Mr) c. il. 12°, limp leath., ea., *$3.50 net. Blakiston.

Small, Albion Woodbury.
The Cameralists; the pioneers of German social polity. '09(O16) c. D. *$3 net. Univ. of Chic.
Meaning of social science. '10(D3) c. D. $1.50 net. Univ. of Chic.
See also Dewey, J:

Small, C: Sidney Aylmer-.
Electrical railroading. '08(Ap25) c. il. D. leath., $3.50. Drake.
Elem. electricity up-to-date. '09(Jl3) c. il. D. $1. Drake.
How to become a successful motorman. '08(Je20) c. il. 12°, $1.50. Drake.

Small, C: Wilder.
Poinsettia; [a story.] '07, [1908.] (Mr.) c. 106 p. pls. 12°, gratis. C: W. Small.

Small, Frederic Lincoln.
Organizing a shoe factory. '10(Mr12) c. il. tabs., 8°, $5. Weekly Bulletin.

Small, Herbert, comp.
Hdbk. of the Library of Congress. '09 (Ag) c. 112 p. il. 8°, 30 c. Curtis & C.

Small country place. Maynard, S: T. **$1.50 net. Lippincott.

Small family cook book. Davenport, *Mrs.* L., *comp.* $1.25. Reilly & B.

Small gardens for small gardeners. Flint, L. C. 50 c. Flanagan.

Small holding. Green, F. E. *$1 net. Lane.

Small house at Allington. *See* Trollope, Anthony.

SMALL-POX.
Geddings, H: D. Precis on the management of outbreaks of smallpox, diphtheria and scarlet fever. (Add. Superintendent for price.) U. S., Supt. of Docs.
Ricketts, T. F. Diagnosis of small-pox. $6 net. Funk.
Wertenbaker, C: P. Plan of organization for suppression of smallpox. (Add. Superintendent for price.) U. S., Supt. of Docs.
See also Vaccination.

Small talks on auction bridge. Meyer, V. M. K. 50 c. P. Elder.

Small things antique. Parker, M. S. 50 c. W. P. Parker.

Small yacht. Boardman, E. A: **$2 net. Little, B. & Co.

Smalley, G:
Life of Sir Sydney H. Waterlow, Bart.; London apprentice, Lord Mayor, captain of industry and philanthropist. '09(N20) por. O. *$3 net. Longmans.

Smallwood, W: Martin.
Syllabus of lectures on animal biology. '08 (N7) c. D. $1.35. W: M. Smallwood.

Smart, G: T:, D.D.
If I should meet the Master! '10(N5) c. D. bds., 50 c. net. Pilgrim Press.
—, **ed.** Golden bond. '09(D25) c. nar. D. pap., *35 c. net, in envelope. Pilgrim Press.

Smart, Janie Sawyer.
Vintage of Spain; story of Cuba. '10 (D31) il. 12°, $1.50. C. M. Clark.

Smart, W:
Economic annals of the nineteenth century, 1801-1820. '10(D10) O. $6.50 net. Macmillan.

Smedley, Anne Constance.
The daughter: a love story. '08(Ap11) c. D. †$1.50. Moffat.

Smeeth, Helen Marié.
Log of three across the sea. '10(N) 212 p. 12°, $1. Henneberry.

Smelser, Fred Lyndon and Mary Ellen Long, [Mrs. F. L. Smelser.]
Miracles of grace in Japan. '08(D) c. 192 p. il. pors. 12°. (Add. pubs. for price.) Hudson.

Smelser, Mary Ellen Long.
See Smelser, Fred Lyndon.

SMELTER WASTES.
Haywood, J. K. Injury to vegetation and animal life by smelter wastes. Gov. Pr. Off.

SMELTING.
See Copper;—Lead;—Metals and metallurgy.

Smeltzer, Jeannie Ringland, comp.
Outlines and grades for the use of piano teachers. '09(D) 7-219 p. 8°, $2.50. J. R. Smeltzer.

SMILACINA AMPLEXICAULIS.
See Botany.

Smile, don't worry. Lewis, E. C., *comp.* 50 c. Mutual Bk.

Smile on the face of the tiger; a collection of limericks. '08(D) c. 126 p. 16°, *50 c. net. Bacon & B.

Smiles, S:, jr.
Relations between chemical constitution and some physical properties. '10(Ag6) il. D. (Text-books of physical chemistry.) $4 net. Longmans.

Smiley, Alfr. Wilson.
A few scraps, oily and otherwise. '08(F1) c. il. pors. D. $1. A. W. Smiley.

Smiley, Amanda Jane.
Literary appreciations; little life stories. '08, [1909.] (Je) 96+4 p. il. pors. 8°, 60 c. A. J. Smiley.

Smiley, Rev. Ja. Lawrenson.
Maud Muller's ministry: [story.] '08(F1) c. D. pap., 50 c. J. L. Smiley.

Smiling road. Ver Beck, *Mrs.* H. R. $1 net. Clode.

Smiling 'round the world. Wilder, M. P. $1.50. Funk.

Smirnow, L:
Last days of St. Pierre. '10(N) il. 12°, $1.50. C. M. Clark.

Smith, A. Croxton.
Everyman's book of the dog. '10(My14) il. 12°, $1.50 net. Doran.

Smith, A. Eliz. Wager-.
See Wager-Smith, A. Eliz.

Smith, A. Georgette Bowden-.
See Bowden-Smith, A. Georgette.

Smith, Abbie N.
Bobtail Dixie: autobiography of a dog. '08(O10) il. 12°, 60 c. Educ. Pub.

Smith, Adam.
Wealth of nations. In 2 v. '10(Ap2) 16°, (Everyman's lib.) ea., 35 c. net; leath., 70 c. net. Dutton.

Smith, Adelaide.
See White, Rosamond Jane.

Smith, Albert Herman.
Tourists' guide of the wonderful St. Lawrence. '09(N) c. 61 p. il. 8°, 25 c. A. H. Smith.

Smith, Albert W:
Giant and other nonsense verse. '10(Jl2) c. O. pap., 75 c. Andrus.

—, and Marx, Guido Hugo.
Machine design. '08(Ja18); 3d ed., rev. and enl. '09(N20) c. il. 8°, ea., $3. Wiley.

Smith, Alex., 1830-1867.
Dreamthorp. '08(F22) 12°, (New universal lib.) 50 c.; leath., 75 c. Dutton.

Smith, Alex., 1856-.
General chemistry for colleges. '08(D) c. 13+529 p. 8°, **$2.15 net. Century Co.

Smith, Mrs. Andrew Heermance.
***See* Smith, Jane T. Sheldon.**

Smith, Anna Marion.
Mother Goose and what happened next. '09(Jl17) il. O. $1.25. Dutton.

Smith, Arth.
Game of Go, the national game of Japan. '08(Ag8) c. il. O. **$2.50 net. Moffat.

Smith, Arth. D. Howden.
Fighting the Turk in the Balkans. '08 (D19) c. il. pors. map, O. **$1.75 net. Putnam.

Smith, Arth. Lionel.
Frederic William Maitland; two lectures and a bibliography. '09(Mr6) 8°, *85 c. net. Oxford Univ.

Smith, Arth. Wells, comp.
Selected bibliography of sanitary science and allied subjects. '09(Mr13) 8°, pap., *50 c. net. Stechert.

Smith, Bridges.
100 stories in black; collection of bright, breezy, humorous stories of the colored race as seen in the sunny South. '10 (Jl16) c. il. D. pap., 25 c. J. S. Ogilvie.

Smith, C. Alfr.
Suction gas plants. '09(Mr13) il. figs. D. (Griffin's scientific text-books.) *$1.75 net. Lippincott.

Smith, C. D.
See Fernald, Rob. Heywood.

Smith, C. E.
Stories from Wagner. '09(N) 12+160 p. 24°, (Told to the children ser.) 50 c. Dutton.

Smith, C. H:
Mennonites of America. '09(Jl) 9-484 p. il. pors. plan, 8°, $2. Mennonite Pub. Ho.
Bibliography (22 p.).

Smith, Caroline Sprague.
Tarry with me, and other verses. '09(D24) c. O. $1.50. C. S. Smith.

Smith, Carrie Josephine.
Making of Wisconsin. '08(My16) c. il. pors. maps, S. 60 c. Flanagan.
Popular dict. for common use; cont. 25,000 words accurately pronounced and clearly defined, parts of speech and plurals. '08 (Ag22) c. T. leath., 50 c. Powers.
See also Pardee, Laura Peckham.

Smith, C: Alphonso.
Educational statesmanship in the South. '08 (My9) O. pap., gratis. C: A. Smith.
Significance of history in a democracy. '09, [1910.] (Ap) 10 p. front. 8°. (Add. pubs. for price.) Guilford Battle.

Smith, C: E:
Pract. course in touch typewriting. Oliver ed. '08(S19) c. O. 75 c. Pitman.
Practical course in touch typewriting: scientific method of mastering the keyboard by the sense of touch. Single keyboard ed. 7th ed., rev. '09(Ag7) c. chart, Q. pap., 50 c. Pitman.

Smith, C: E:, D.D.
Facts of faith. '10(Mr12) c. D. *80 c. net. Sherman, F.

Smith, C: Emory, comp.
From Lincoln to Taft, 1854-1908, why I am a Republican. '08(S19) c. pors. 32°. (Add. pubs. for price.) Hammerling.

Smith, C: Ernest, D.D.
Call to confirmation. Rev. ed. '08(N14) c. S. pap., 20 c. Longmans.
—, comp. Altar devotions: manual of self-examination, prayer and praise for the blessed sacrament. '08(O10) c. T. **50 c. net; [Cheaper ed.] '09(D4) c. T. **25 c. net. Longmans.

Smith, C: Forster.
Reminiscences and sketches. '09(My1) pors. D. *$1.25 net. Pub. Ho. M. E. Ch., So.

Smith, C: F:
See Cramp, W:

Smith, C: H.
Hist. of Fuller's Ohio Brigade, 1861-1865; its great march, with roster, portraits, battle maps and biographies. '09, [1910.] (F) c. 21-623 p. il. pors. 4°, $3. C: H. Smith.

Smith, C: Sprague.
Poems. '08(O3) c. D. **$1 net. Wessels.

Smith, C: Wesley.
Contribution toward a bibliography of Marcus Whitman. '09(Mr13) Q. (Univ. of Wash. bull.) pap. (Add. University for price.) Univ. of Wash.
—, comp. Check-list of books and pamphlets rel. to the hist. of the Pacific northwest to be found in representative libraries of that region; prepared co-operatively. '09(O) 191 p. 8°. (Add. Library for price.) Washington State Lib.

Smith, Charlotte Curtis.
Bob Knight's diary with the circus. '08 (D12) c. il. 8°, †$1.50. Dutton.

Smith, Clarence Beaman.
See Wilcox, Earley Vernon.
—, and Froley, J: W:
Replanning a farm for profit. '09(D) 36 p. 8°, (U. S., Dept. of Agriculture, farmers' bull.) pap. (Add. Superintendent for price.) U. S., Supt. of Docs.

Smith, D:, D.D.
Days of His flesh: earthly life of Our Lord and Savior Jesus Christ. New and cheaper ed. '10(D) 8°, $2 net. Doran.
Gospel of St. Matthew. '08(Je27) 16°, (Westminster New Testament.) *75 c. net. Revell.
Legend of Bethlehem. '09(N13) il. in col. D. 50 c. Doran.
Legend of Jerusalem. '10(D) col. il. 12°, 50 c. net. Doran.
Man's need of God. '10(D) $1.50 net. Doran.

Smith, D: Eug.
Rara arithmetica: catalogue of the arithmetics written before the year MDCI; with a description of those in the library of George Arthur Plimpton, of New York. '10(Mr5) c. il. facsims., O. *$5.50 net; 2 v. '09(Ja23) c. il. facsims., 8°, $20. Ginn.

Smith, D: Eug.—*Continued.*
Teaching of arithmetic. '09(Jl) 100 p. 8°, (Teachers' College Record.) 75 c.; pap., 30 c. Teachers' Coll.
See also Wentworth, G: Albert.

Smith, D: Nichol.
Function of criticism: a lecture. '09 (My15) O. pap., 35 c. Oxford Univ.

Smith, Dempster.
See Nicolson, J: T.

Smith, Donald Eug., and Teggart, F: J., eds.
Diary of Gaspar de Portola during the California expedition of 1769-1770. '09 (N) c. 59 p. facsim., O. (Publications of the Academy of Pacific Coast History.) pap., 50 c. Univ. of Cal.

Smith, E. S.
Truth about Mexico; [repr. from *The Bankers' Magazine.*] '09(D25) por. O. pap. (Add. pubs. for price.) Bankers' Pub.

Smith, Earl B.
Mechanical engineering lab'y manual. '09, [1910.] (Ja) c. 109 p. il. 8°, $2. E. B. Smith, (Pa.)

Smith, Edm. H.
See New York [State.] *Ct. of appeals.* Rules.

SMITH, *General* Edmund Kirby.
Noll, A. H. General Kirby-Smith. $1.50. Univ. Press, (Sewanee.)

Smith, Edm. Munroe.
Jurisprudence: [a lecture.] '08(D19) c. 8°, pap., 25 c. Columbia Univ.

Smith, Mrs. Edna Deran-.
See Deran-Smith, *Mrs.* Edna.

Smith, E: Garstin.
Real Roosevelt. '10(My7) c. il. por. 12°, $1.50. States Pub.

Smith, E: W.
Professional wrestling. '09(N) c. 95 p. il. por. 16°, (Spalding's athletic lib.) 10 c. Am. Sports.

Smith, Edn. Burritt.
Essays and addresses. '09(Jl10) c. por. 8°, *$2.50 net. McClurg.

Smith, Effie.
Rosemary and pansies. '09, [1910.] (F) 52 p. 12°, $1. Badger.

Smith, Egbert Bull.
Voyage of "The Two Sisters": cabin boy's story. '09(F20) c. il. por. 8°, $1.50. E. B. Smith.

Smith, Eleanor.
Eleanor Smith music course. Bk. 1. '08 (Ag1) c. O. 25 c.; bk. 2. '08(Ag8) c. O. 30 c.; bk. 3. '08(Ag29) c. O. 40 c.; bk. 4. '08(O3) c. O. 50 c.; Manual. '09(D11) c. O. 50 c. Am. Bk.

Smith, Mrs. Eliz. Thomasina, [formerly L. T. Meade.]
[Works.] v. 1, That brilliant Peggy; v. 2, The girl and her fortune; v. 3, The lady of delights; v. 4, Sarah's mother; v. 5, Hetty Beresford; v. 6, Loveday. [Cheaper ed.] '09(D) 12°, ea., 75 c. Doran.
Aylwin's friends. '09(D) 8+406 p. 12°, $1.50. Dutton.
Betty of the rectory. '08(Jl11) c. front. D. $1. Grosset.
Betty Vivian; story of Haddo Court school. '10(Ja1) 12°, $1.50. Lippincott.

Smith, Mrs. Eliz. Thomasina.—*Continued.*
Betty Vivian; story of Haddo Court school. '10(Je4) il. D. (Girls' own lib.) 75 c. McKay.
Court-Harmon girls. '08(D19) il. 12°, $1.50. Dutton.
Francis Kane's fortune. '08(Je13) 12°, (Home ser.) 50 c. Hurst.
Girls of the forest. '09(My) 325 p. il. 12°, †$1. Burt.
Heart of gold. '08(Ag1) 12°, (Home ser.) 50 c. Hurst.
How it all came about. '08(Je13) 12°, (Home ser.) 50 c. Hurst.
Odds and the ends. '09(Ap10) il. 12°, $1. Burt.
Petronella. '09(Ap10) il. 12°, $1. Burt.
Pretty-girl and others. '10(D10) il. 8°, $1.50. Dutton.
Princess of the revels. '09, [1910.] (F) 299 p. il. 12°, †$1.50. Dutton.
Rosa Regina. '10(D31) il. 12°, $1.50. Lippincott.
School favorite. '08(N7) il. D. $1.50. Lippincott.
School favorite. '09(Je5) il. D. (Girls' own lib.) †75 c. McKay.
Seven maids. '09(My) 290 p. il. 12°, †$1. Burt.
Sweet girl graduate. '10(Ag13) c. il. 12°, $1.25. Hurst.
Three girls from school. '09(My) 303 p. il. 12°, †$1. Burt.
A wild Irish girl. '10(O15) c. por. 12°, $1. Hurst.

Smith, Elmer Boyd.
Chicken world. '10(O22) c. il. in col. O. bds., $2, boxed. Putnam.
Circus and all about it. '09(O23) col. il. obl. O. bds., $2, boxed. Stokes.
Farm book: Bob and Betty visit Uncle John. '10(D10) c. col. il. obl. D. bds., $1.50 net. Houghton M.
Santa Claus and all about him. '08(N7) c. il. obl. O. bds., $2, boxed; Christmas ed., $2.25. Stokes.

Smith, Elsie Rhea.
Brother Luke. '09, [1910.] (Ap) 9-67 p. 16°, 50 c. E. R. Smith.

Smith, Emma A. F.
Historical sketch of Washington's headquarters; prep. under the auspices of the Washington Headquarters Association. Rev. ed. '10(Jl2) c. il. 8°, 25 c. E. A. F. Smith.

Smith, Ernest Ashton.
Hildebrand: the builder. '08(S5) c. D. (Men of the kingdom.) *$1 net. Jennings.

Smith, Eug. Randolph.
Plane geometry developed by the syllabus method. '09(D25) c. D. 75 c. Am. Bk.

Smith, Eustace, M.D.
Some common remedies and their use in practice. '10(Mr) 8°, *$1.25 net. Hoeber.

Smith, F. Dumont.
Blue waters and green and the Far East to-day. '08(My23) c. il. D. $1.50. Crane.
Book of a hundred bears. '09(Ap24) c. il. D. 75 c. Rand, McN. & Co.

Smith, Florence Ethel.
Woman, the eternal question. '09(S) c. 59 p. 16°, 35 c. Chr. Witness.

Smith, Frances M.
Colonial families of America. '09(N) c. il. 12°, $2. Allaben.

Smith, Fs. Hopkinson.
Captain Thomas A. Scott, master diver. '08(N14) c. D. (True American types ser.) *60 c. net. Am. Unitarian.
Forty minutes late, and other stories. '09 (O9) c. il. D. †$1.50. Scribner.
Peter. '08(S5) c. il. D. †$1.50. Scribner.

Smith, Fs. Wayland-.
See Wayland-Smith, Fs.

Smith, Fk.
Biographical sketch of the residents of that part of Dedham which is now Dover, who took part in King Philip's war, the last French and Indian war and the Revolution; together with the record of the services of those who represented Dover in the war of 1812; the war with Mexico; the Civil War, and the war with Spain. '09(Ag) 88+4 p. map, 8°. (Priv. pr.) F. Smith.
Founders of the First parish, Dover, Mass., with descriptions of all the houses now standing which were built before the Revolution. '08(N) 24 p. il. por. map, 8°, $1. J: H. Faulk.
Ralph Sanger, A.M., D.D.; paper read before the Dover Historical Society, Jan. 2, 1909. '09(Ag) 7 p. 4°, o. p. F. Smith.

Smith, Fk Berkeley.
Lady of Big Shanty. '09(O30) c. D. †$1.20. Doubleday, P.
Village of vagabonds. '10(My21) c. col. il. D. $1.50, fixed. Doubleday, P.

Smith, Fk. C:
Court to court procedure with forms. '10 (F) c. O. $5.50; shp., $5.75. Fiske & Co.

Smith, F: C.
Pulmonary hemorrhage in the tuberculous at high altitude (6,200 feet) report of 56 deaths; frequency of associated heart disease. '10(D) 9+3 p. 8°. Gov. Pr. Off.
Relations of climate to the treatment of pulmonary tuberculosis; prepared by direction of the surgeon-general. '10(S) 17 p. 8°, (U. S., Public Health and Marine Hospital Service; public health bull.)

Smith, F: G:
The Revelation explained. '08(Jl) c. 459 p. il. por. 12°, $1. Gospel Trumpet Co.

Smith, F: Miller.
Stolen signet. '09(N6) c. il. 12°, $1.50. Duffield.

Smith, F: Wa., M.D.
Essentials of practical hygiene. '07(Mr28) c. O. $2. G: K. Smith.

Smith, Geoffrey Watkins.
Naturalist in Tasmania. '09(Ap3) il. fold. map. O. $2.50. Oxford Univ.

Smith, G:
Life of William Carey, shoemaker and missionary. '09(O30) c. 12°, (Everyman's lib.) *35 c. net; leath., *70 c. net. Dutton.

Smith, G: Adam, D.D.
Jerusalem. '08(Je27) c. 2 v., il. maps, O. **$7.50 net. Armstrong.

Smith, G: C. Moore-.
Hymenaeus: comedy acted at St. John's College, Cambridge, now first printed, with an introd. and notes. '09(Mr) 16+84 p. 16°, *$1.10 net. Putnam.
See also Moore-Smith, G: C.
—, ed. Laelia; comedy acted at Queen's College, Cambridge, probably on March 1, 1595. '10(Ag6) c. $1.10 net. Putnam.
Smith, G: H.
See Pennsylvania. **Monaghan's cumulative** annual digest.
—, rep. *See* Maine. *Sup. judicial ct.* Repts.
Smith, G: Stuart Graham-.
See Graham-Smith, G: **Stuart.**
Smith, Gerald Birney.
See Burton, Ernest Dewitt.
Smith, Gerard.
Painting: Spanish and French. '10(D) 12°, (Hdbks. of art hist.) hf. leath., $1.25. Gorham.
Smith, Gertrude.
Delight: story of a little Christian Scientist. '08(F22) c. il. D. 50 c. Altemus.
Little Ned Happy and Flora. '08(O17) c. il. O. **$1.30 net. Harper.
When Roggie and **Reggie** were five. **'09** (O16) c. il. in col. O. *$1.30 net. Harper.
Smith, Goldwin.
No refuge but in truth. 2d ed., enl. '09 (Jl3) c. D. **$1 net. Putnam.
Reminiscences; ed. by Arnold Haultain. '10(D10) c. pors. O. $3 net. Macmillan.
Smith, Goodwin Brooke.
How to succeed as an inventor. '09(Je12) c. il. D. pap., 10 c. Inventors & Investors.
Smith, Grant H., comp.
See Utah. Compiled laws.
Smith, Gypsy.
See Smith, **Rodney.**
Smith, H. Clifford.
Jewellery. '08(Ag15) il. 8°, (Connoisseurs' lib.) *$7.50 net. Putnam.
Smith, Rev. H. Turner.
See Ratcliffe, Fs. Asbury.
Smith, Mrs. Hannah Whitall, [Mrs. Rob. Pearsall Smith.]
Christian secret of a happy life. New ed. '09(Ag7) 12°, *$1 net. Revell.
Smith, Harry Eaton.
Strength of material; elem. study prep. for the use of midshipmen at the U. S. Naval Academy. 2d ed., rev. '09(Ag14) c. 9+170 p. il. 12°, *$1.25 net. Wiley.
Smith, Harry Ja.
Amédée's son. '08(O3) c. D. †$1.50. Houghton M.
Smith, Harvey Leigh.
Christian race; course of twenty-four lessons for students' Bible classes. '08, [1909.] (Mr) c. 307 p. 12°, Students' ed., 20 c.; Teachers' ed., 75 c. Y. M. C. A.
Smith, Heman P.
Hdbk. of penmanship; to accompany the "Copy books" and "Practice books" of the "New intermedial system." '08(Je6) oblong 12°, pap., *25 c. net. Macmillan.
See also Smith, Lyman D.
Smith, Rev. H:
Sermons; a selection; ed. by J: Brown, D.D. '09(Mr) 8+254 p. 32°, (Cambridge devotional ser.) 45 c.; 60 c.; leath., 75 c. Putnam.

SMITH, Henry Dickinson.
Porter, H: D. Henry Dickinson Smith: biography and memorial. (Add. pubs. for price.) Revell.
Smith, H: E.
Pride of the rancho; novel founded on play. '10(Ja8) c. front. D. $1. J. S. Ogilvie.
Smith, Horace Edn.
Treatise on the law of personal property. 2d ed., rev. and enl., by G: Lawyer. '08 (O) c. 101+336 p. O. $4. Flood.
Smith, Howard Leslie, and Moore, W: Underhill.
Cases on the law of bills and notes. '10 (D) c. O. (Am. case book ser., Ja. Brown Scott, gen. ed.) $4.50. West Pub.
Smith, Hugh McCormick.
Japanese gold fish; their varieties and cultivation; pract. guide to the Japanese methods of gold fish culture. '10(My14) c. il. obl. D. $2. W. F. Roberts.
Smith, J. Augustine.
Present and future of the cement block, its manufacture, its availability, its cost; paper del. [at the] National Association Cement Users' Convention, Jan. 11th to 16th, 1909, Cleveland, O. '09(Ap3) c. il. 8°, pap., 25 c. J. A. Smith.
Smith, J. E. A., ["Godfrey Greylock."]
Taghconic: romance and beauty of the Berkshire Hills. '09(Ap10) por. O. $1.15. Eagle.
Smith, J. Gardner, ed.
See Randall, J: Herman, *ed.*
Smith, J. Reginald.
Modern assaying; concise treatise describing latest methods and appliances; ed. by F. W. Braun. '10(My14) c. il. D. $1.50 net. Lippincott.
Smith, Mrs. Jacqueline Harrison, [Mrs. W. Hinckle Smith,] comp.
Famous old receipts used a hundred years and more. 2d authorized ed. '09(My1) c. O. **$2 net. Winston.
Smith, Ja. Harry.
Enchanted ground; episode in the life of a young man. '10(Ag27) c. D. $1.50. Houghton M.
Smith, Ja. M.
See Dickson, D:
Smith, Ja. MacGregor, ed.
See New York [State.] Digest of statutes.
Smith, Ja. Stanislaus Easby-.
Georgetown University in the District of Columbia, 1789-1907; its founders, benefactors, officers, instructors and alumni. '08(My9) c. 2 v., il. pors. facsim., 8°, $30. Lewis Pub.
Smith, Ja. Washington.
Controversy between truth and falsehood, on the train of life. '10(S3) c. front. por. 8°, 75 c. J. W. Smith.
Smith, Jane T. Sheldon, [Mrs. Andrew Heermance Smith.]
The perfect man. '01(F12) 16°, pap., *10 c. net. Revell.
Smith, Jeremiah.
See Ames, **Ja. Barr.**

Smith, Jessie Willcox, comp. and il.
Child's book of old verses. '10(N5) c. col. il. O. $2.50. Duffield.

Smith, J:
Catalogue raisonné of the works of the most eminent Dutch, Flemish and French painters; with description of their principal pictures. New limited ed. In 9 v. '10(Ag13) il. $25 net. Dutton.

Smith, Captain J:
True travels, adventures and observations in Europe, Asia, Africa and America, and the general history of Virginia, New England, and the Summer Isles. Bks. 1, 2, 3; ed. with introd. and notes by E. A. Benians. '09(My) 12+247 p. 16°, (Cambridge English literature for schools.) *40 c. net. Putnam.

Smith, J: Bernhard.
Our insect friends and enemies; with a chapter on the war against insects. '09 (My22) c. il. O. **$1.50 net. Lippincott.

Smith, J: Day.
Hist. of the 19th regiment of Maine volunteer infantry, 1862-1865; with an introd. written by Brevet Major-General Alex. S. Webb. '09(N) 15+356 p. pls. pors. maps, 8°, $3. Great Western Pr.

Smith, J: H:
Official basket ball guide and Protective Association rules for 1908-'09. '08(D) c. 135+3 p. 16°, (Fox's athletic lib.) 10 c. R: K. Fox.

Smith, J: Merlin Powis.
Books for Old Testament study. '08(Mr28) c. 8°, pap., *50 c. net. Univ. of Chic.
See Burton, Ernest Dewitt.

Smith, J: Randolph.
Gladys, the angel of the good. '09(N20) il. 8°, $1. Jewel Pub.

Smith, Rev. J: Talbot.
Training of a priest: essay on clerical education. '08(My2) c. D. **$1.50 net. Longmans.

Smith, Jonah Walker.
Dustless roads, tar, macadam. '09(Je5) il. figs. tabs., O. *$3.50 net. Lippincott.

Smith, Jos. Fielding, jr.
Origin of the "reorganized" church, and the question of succession. '09(N20) c. 12°. 50 c. Deseret News.

Smith, Jos. Russell.
Ocean carrier: history and analysis of the service and a discussion of the rates of ocean transportation. '08(D12) c. il. maps, **$1.50 net. Putnam.
Story of iron and steel. '08(F15) c. front. D. (Appleton's lib. of useful stories.) **75 c. net. Appleton.

Smith, L. Bertrand.
Jesse Smith, his ancestors and descendants. '09(Je12) front. 8°, (Allaben genealogical ser.) $4; $6. Allaben.

Smith, Langdon.
Evolution; fantasy. '09(N13) c. il. O. hf. ooze, $1.25. Lane.

Smith, Laura Rountree.
Hawk Eye: Indian story; for first grade. '08(F1) c. il. D. 30 c. Flanagan.
Little Bear. '09(Jl3) c. il. 12°, 25 c. Flanagan.

Smith, Laura Rountree.—*Continued.*
Roly Poly book. '10(Mr26) c. il. S. 35 c. Flanagan.
Seventeen little bears. '10(Ja22) c. il. S. 30 c. Flanagan.
See also Irish, Marie.

Smith, Leonard Kingsley.
Songs east and west. '09(O9) c. O. pap., 50 c. L. K. Smith.

Smith, Logan Pearsall.
Life and letters of Sir Henry Wotton. '08 (My23) 2 v., pors. O. $7.75. Oxford Univ.

Smith, L: P.
Wanderings of a literary pilgrim: [little comments on the books most loved by the author. '07, [1908.] (Mr.) c. 72 p. D. pap., 25 c. L: P. Smith.

Smith, Mrs. Lucia Etta Loring.
By the bay. [1910] (F) c. '09. 60 p. front. 12°, *$1 net. P. Elder.

Smith, Lyman D. and Heman P.
Hdbk. of penmanship; manual for teachers and students of free-arm movement writing; arr. in 3 pts. '10(O8) il. obl. 12°, pap., 25 c. net. Macmillan.
Intermedial spelling blank, for pupil's work in written spelling with model alphabet in intermedial slant script. '08(Ag22) 8°, (Smith's educ. system.) pap., per doz., *60 c. net. Macmillan.
Practice books 3-4; for preparatory writing; with attached cover containing movement drills; intermedial penmanship. New and rev. ed. '08(D12) obl. 12°, pap., 55 c. per doz. Macmillan.

Smith, M. L. Stafford.
Supplementary exercises on "Ora maritima," by E. A. Sonnenschein. '10(Ag13) 16°, 35 c. net. Macmillan.

Smith, Mabell Shippie Clarke, ed.
Studies in Dickens. '10(Ag6) c. D. (Chautauqua home reading ser.) $1.25. Chautauqua Press.

Smith, Marion Courthouy.
Road of life, and other poems. '09(D25) c. 12°, $1. A. Harriman.

Smith, Martin Ridley.
Common-sense in religion. '08(My2) D. $1. Longmans.

Smith, Mrs. Mary Chapin.
Earth songs: [poems.] '10(Mr26) c. D. bds., $1.25. Badger.

Smith, Mrs. Mary Prudence Wells.
Boys and girls of seventy-seven. '09(S18) c. il. D. (Old Deerfield ser.) †$1.25. Little, B. & Co.

Smith, Middleton.
Agricultural graphics; United States and world crops and live stock. '10(N) 67 p. diagrs., 8°, (U. S., Dept. of Agriculture, Bu. of Statistics bull.)

Smith, Minnie Louise, and Laing, Gordon Jennings.
First Latin lessons. '08(Mr14) c. 12°, $1. Allyn & B.

Smith, Montraville Harrington.
Furnaceman's hdbk.; pract.-simplified rules and tables for warm air furnace heating. '09, [1910.] (Ja) 58 p. 12°, 50 c. Master Sheet Metal.

Smith, N:
Grant, the man of mystery. '09(Je12) c. pors. D. *$1.50 net. Young Churchman.

Smith, Norah Archibald, ed.
See Arabian nights;—*also* Wiggin, Kate Douglas Smith-, *ed.*

Smith, Olive A.
Sunflower stories and lullabies. '08, [1909.] (F) c. 96 p. il. 12°, 50 c. Brethren Pub. Ho.

Smith, Oliver Cromwell.
Vox musarum: rules and suggestions for developing the power, beauty, and sublimity of the English language by the proper application of the various sounds, signs, and other media for representing human thought. '08(Jl18) c. D. $1. O. C. Smith.

Smith, Orren Ernest.
Manhood; study of male vitality. '10 (Mr5) c. 8°, $4. Sentinel Pr.

Smith, Percey Franklyn, and Granville, W: Anthony.
Elem. analysis. '10(N19) c. il. D. $1.50. Ginn.

—, and Longley, W: Raymond.
Theoretical mechanics. '10(Je4) c. O. $2.50. Ginn.

Smith, Percy J.
Lettering and writing. '09(Ja2) il. 8°, $1.50. Scribner.

Smith, R: Gordon.
Ancient tales and folk lore of Japan. '08 (D12) il. 8°, (Color books.) *$6 net. Macmillan.

Smith, Rob. E.
Methodist Episcopalians. '09, [1910.] (Ap) c. 72 p. 24°, 5 c. Eaton & M.

Smith, Rob. G.
Brief account of the services rendered by the Second Regiment Delaware Volunteers in the War of the Rebellion. '09, [1910] (F) c. 32 p. por. il. 4°, (Papers of the Historical Society of Delaware.) 50 c. Delaware Hist. Soc.

Smith, Rob. H:
Text-book of the elements of machine work. '10(O8) c. il. tabs., 8°, $2. Indust. Educ. Co.
Text-book of the principles of machine work. '10(O8) c. il. tabs., 8°, $3. Indust. Educ. Co.

Smith, Mrs. Rob. Pearsall.
See Smith, *Mrs.* Hannah Whitall.

Smith, Rodney, ["Gypsy Smith."]
Lost Christ. '09(D) c. 22 p. il. (in color) D. pap., *25 c. net. Doran.

Smith, Rollin Edson.
Wheat fields and markets of the world. '08(S) c. 3-418 p. il. tabs., 8°, $2.15. Modern Miller.

Smith, Mrs. Ruby Green.
See Kellogg, Vernon Lyman.

Smith, Mrs. Ruel Perley, [formerly Ellen M. Cyr.]
Jack Harvey's adventures: or, the rival campers among the oyster pirates. '08 (O3) c. il. O. (Rival campers ser.) $1.50. L. C. Page.
Story of three great artists: Raphael, Michael Angelo, Leonardo Da Vinci. '09 (Je5) c. il. D. (Graded art readers.) 50 c. Ginn.

Smith, S: Fs.
My country; illustrated and illuminated version of the American national anthem, by Wa. Tittle. '09(Ag) c. il. 4°, *$3 net. Tandy-T.

Smith, S: G:
Religion in the making; study in Biblical sociology. '10(Ja29) c. D. **$1.25 net. Macmillan.

Smith, S: Rodmond.
Reclamation of the Florida everglades. '09, [1910.] (Ap) c. 43 p. il. fold. map, 8°, gratis. Miami Pr.

Smith, Sarah K., and Perrett, Louise, comps.
Our baby's record. '09(Ag) 30 p. il. 8°, $1; $2; ocze, $2.50. Dodge.

Smith, Sheila Kaye-.
See Kaye-Smith, Sheila.

Smith, Sophie Shilleto.
Dean Swift. '10(Mr26) il. O. *$3.50 net. Putnam.

Smith, T. Roger, and Slater, J:
Architecture: classic and early Christian. '10(D) 12°, (Hdbks. of art hist.) hf. leath., $1.25. Gorham.
Architecture: Gothic and Renaissance. '10 (D) 12°, (Hdbks. of art hist.) hf. leath., $1.25. Gorham.

Smith, T: A.
Power and transmission; pract. hdbk. for the factory works manager. '10(N5) 16°, $1. Spon.

Smith, Tunstall, ed.
Richard Snowden Andrews, lieutenant-colonel commanding the First Maryland Artillery (Andrews Battalion), Confederate States Army: a memoir. '10(O8) pors. facsims., O. $1.50 net. Eichelberger.

Smith, Vincent Arth.
Asoka: the Buddhist emperor of India. 2d ed., rev. and enl. '09(Ag14) front. fold. map, D. (Rulers of India ser.) $1.15. Oxford Univ.
Early history of India, from 600 B.C. to the Muhammedan conquest. 2d ed., rev. and enl. '08(D19) il. map, O. $4.75. Oxford Univ.
Oxford student's history of India. '08 (D26) il. maps, cr. 8°, 60 c. Oxford Univ.

Smith, W. Hazlitt.
See New York [State] New index.

Smith, Mrs. W. Hinckle.
See Smith, *Mrs.* Jacqueline Harrison.

Smith, W. Letterman.
William Updick: his philosophy. '08(Ag1) c. D. $1. Neale.

Smith, W. W.
Course in first year Latin. '10(D31) c. 365 p. 12°, $1. W: R. Jenkins.

Smith, Sir W:
Smaller classical dict.; rev. and ed. by E. H. Blakeney; with many important additions and corrections, also tables, bibliographies of classical literature. '10 (D10) il. 16°, (Everyman's lib.) 35 c. net; leath., 70 c. net. Dutton.

Smith, W: Cadid.
How to grow one hundred bushels of corn per acre on worn soils. '10(Ap30) c. il. 8°, $1. W. C. Smith.

Smith, W: Christopher.
On Aaron's Neck, and Amos Strong, legislator; two short stories. '10(Jl16) c. 12°, 25 c. W: C. Smith.

Smith, W: H:
Church and men. '10(D31) c. D. $1.50. B'way Pub.

Smith, W: Newton.
Pract. correspondence, for use in the Massey system of commercial colleges. '09 (D) c. 80 p. il. 8°, 75 c. Massey.

Smith, Rev. W: Wa.
Religious education; with foreword by C: W: Stoughton. '09(Ap17) c. O. *$2 net. Young Churchman.

Smith, Rev. Wilton Merle.
Giving a man another chance, and other sermons. '08(F15) c. 12°, *$1 net. Revell.

SMITH FAMILY.
See Genealogies;—*also* Names (*personal*).

Smith method of poultry keeping. Trafford, H:, *ed.* $1. Hostermann.

Smithers, W: West.
Treatise on executive clemency in Pennsylvania; with statistics, record data and forms, by G: D. Thorn. '09(Jl) 289 p. 8°, $3.25. Int. Pr.

—, rep. *See* Pennsylvania. Treatise on executive clemency.

SMITHFIELD, London, Eng.
See St. Bartholomew-the-Great.

Smith's educational system. *See* Smith, Lyman D.

Smithson, G: Arnold.
Old English Christian epic; study in the plot technique of the Juliana, the Elene, the Andreas, and the Christ, in comparison with Beowulf and with the Latin literature of the Middle Ages. '10(O) 303-400 p. O. (Univ. of Cal. pubs.; Modern philology.) pap., $1. Univ. of Cal.

Smithsonian contributions to knowledge. F. pap. Smith. Inst.
—Sherzer. Glaciers of the Canadian Rockies and Selkirks.

Smithsonian Institution. Classified list of Smithsonian publications available for distribution March, 1909. '09(My) 39 p. 8°, pap. (Add. Institution for price.) Smith. Inst.

Smithsonian Institution. Classified list of Smithsonian publications available for distribution, May, 1910. '10(Jl) 37 p. O. pap. Smith. Inst.

Smithsonian Institution. Exhibits of the Smithsonian Institution and United States National Museum at the Alaska-Yukon-Pacific Exposition, Seattle, Washington, 1909. '09, [1910.] (F) 114 p. il. 8°, 50 c. Smith. Inst.

SMITHSONIAN INSTITUTION, Washington, D. C.
Abbot, C: G., *and* Fowle, F. E., *jr.* Annals of the Astrophysical Observatory of the Smithsonian Institution. v. 2. gratis. U. S., Supt. of Docs.
Blackford, C: M., *jr.* Smithsonian Institution. (Add. Superintendent for price.) U. S., Supt. of Docs.

Smithsonian Institution bulletin. O. pap. U. S., Supt. of Docs.
—Clark. On a collection of feather stars, or *comatulids,* from Japan. 15 c.
—Langley. Researches and experiments in aerial navigation. (Add. Supt. for price.)

Smithsonian Institution, Bureau of American Ethnology bull. il. Q. U. S., Supt. of Docs.
—Bushnell. The Choctaw of Bayou Lacomb, St. Tammany Parish, Louisiana.
—Densmore. Chippewa music. 45 c.
—Emerson. Unwritten literature of Hawaii.
—Fewkes. Antiquities of the Mesa Verde National Park. (Add. Superintendent for price.)
—Fowke. Antiquities of central and southeastern Missouri. 40 c.
—Hrdlicka. Physiological and medical observation among the Indians of southwestern United States and northern Mexico. —Skeletal remains. 25 c.—Tuberculosis among certain Indian tribes.

Smithsonian Institution, United States National Museum bull. il. 8°. Gov. Pr. Off.
—Atwood. Catalogue of botanical lib. of J: Donnell Smith presented to Smithsonian Institution. 25 c.
—Banks. Directions for collecting and preserving insects. (Add. Superintendent for price.)
—Dall *and* Bartsch. Monograph of West American pyramidellid mollusks. 35 c.
—Fink. Lichens of Minnesota.
—Mortensen. On some West Indian echinoids.
—Pierce. Monographic revision of the twisted winged insects comprising the order *Strepsiptera* Kirby.
—Pittier de Fábrega. New or noteworthy plants from Colombia and Central America. (Add. Superintendent for price.) (Contribs. from U. S. National Herbarium.)
—Rathbun. National Gallery of Art, Department of Fine Arts of the National Museum.
—Standley. Allioniaceæ of the United States. (Add. Superintendent for price.) (Contribs. from U. S. National Herbarium.)

Smithsonian mathematical tables. O. Smith. Inst.
—Becker *and* Van Orstrand. Hyperbolic functions. $4.

Smithsonian miscellaneous collections. maps, O. pap. Smith. Inst.
—Becker. Age of the earth. 5 c.
—Clarke. Preliminary study of chemical denudation. 5 c.—Recalculation of the atomic weights.
—Gilmore. Smithsonian exploration in Alaska in 1907 in search of *Pleistocene* fossil vertebrates. (Add. Institution for price.)
—Green. Landmarks of botanical hist. 65 c.
—Hollister. Mammals collected by John Jay White in British East Africa.
—Miller. Description of a new species of hippopotamus. 10 c.—New rodent of the genus Saccestomus from British East Africa. (Add. Institution for price.)

Smithsonian miscellaneous collections.—Cont.
—Reese. Development of the American alligator. 50 c.—Development of the brain of the American alligator.
—Schmitter. Upper Yukon native customs and folk-lore. 12 c.
—Townsend. Taxonomy of the *Muscoidean* flies. 60 c.
—Walcott. Cambrian geology and paleontology. no. 1. 5 c.—no. 2. 25 c.—nos. 3, 4, 5. (Add. Institution for price.)—no. 6, 70 c.—no. 7, 10 c.

Smithsonian physical tables; prep. by T: Gray. 4th rev. ed. '08, [1909.] (Mr) 34+301 p. 8°, $1.20. Smith. Inst.

SMOKE.
Booth, W: H., *and* Kershaw, J. B. C. Smoke prevention and fuel economy. $2.50. Henley.
Olmsted, F: L., *and others.* **Smoke nuisance.** gratis. Am. Civic League.
Syracuse, N. Y. Chamber of Commerce. Rept. upon smoke abatement. gratis. Syracuse Chamber of Commerce.
See also Railroads.

Smokeless combustion of coal in boiler plants. Randall, D. T. (Add. Superintendent for price.) U. S., Supt. of Docs.

Smoker's reveries. Knight, J., *comp.* $1; $1.75. Caldwell.

Smokers' year book. Herford, O., *and* Collins, S. **$1 net. Moffat.

SMOKING.
See Cigarettes.

Smoky Day's wigwam evenings. Eastman, C: A. 60 c. Little, B. & Co.

Smoky god. Emerson, W. G: $1. Forbes.

Smoley, Constantine.
Tables containing parallel tables of logarithms and squares of feet, inches and fractions of interest. 4th ed. '08(Ag22) c. 12°, flex. leath., $2.50. Engineering News.
Fifth edition is just ready, at $3.

Smollett, Tobias G:
Works. 6 v. New imperial lib. ed. '10 (D) il. 8°, ea., $1.25; hf. cf., $2.25. New il. sterling ed. ea., $1. (Sets only.) Estes.
—, tr. *See* Lesage, Alain-René.

SMUGGLING.
See Tariff.

Smurr, Tom W.
Treatise on the law of farm drainage, founded on the laws and judicial decisions of the state of Illinois. '09(O) c. 24+496 p. O. **$5 net. Bobbs-M.

Smyth, J: Paterson-.
See Paterson-Smyth, J:

Smyth, Newman, D.D.
Modern belief in immortality. '10(Mr19) c. D. **75 c. net. Scribner.
Passing Protestantism and coming Catholicism. '08(Ap4) c. D. **$1 net. Scribner.

Smyth, P. G., comp.
Told out of court; personal experiences of members of the Chicago bench and bar. '10(Ja22) c. $1. P. G. Smyth.

Smyth, S: Gordon, comp. and ed.
Genealogy of the Duke-Shepherd-Van Metre family; from civil, military, church and family records and documents. '09 (D) 9+445 p. il. pors. facsim., 8°, $3. S: G. Smyth.

Smyth-Vaudry, Telesphor.
Peter's name; or, a divine credential in a name. '10(Je4) c. D. $1. Soc. Divine Word.

SMYTH COUNTY, Va.
Sheffey, J: P. **General resources and advantages of Smyth County.** (Add. author for price.) J. P. Sheffey.

Snaith, J: Collis.
Araminta. '09(F20) c. D. †$1.50. Moffat
Fortune. '10(Ap30) c. D. $1.50. Moffat.
Mrs. Fitz. '10(O22) c. D. $1.35 net. Moffat.
Patricia at the inn. '08(Ap11) c. il. 12°, (Popular priced copyrights.) 50 c. B. W. Dodge.
William Jordan, Junior. '08(Mr21) c. D. †$1.50. Moffat.

SNAKE DEVICES (American colonies).
See United States.

SNAKES.
Fayrer, C:, *ed.* Venomous snakes. *75 c. net. Macmillan.
Noguchi, H. Snake venoms. $10. Carnegie.
See also Reptiles.

Snapshots from sunny Africa. Springer, *Mrs.* J: M. *$1 net. Revell.

Snare of circumstance. Buckley, E. E. †$1.50. Little, B. & Co.

Snavely, Guy Everett.
Æsopic fables in the Mireoir Historical of Jehan de Vignay. '08(S5) 8°, pap., gratis. Johns Hopkins.

Snead, Georgie Tillman.
Joy-bells; lyrics of hope and other poems. '09(My) 32 p. 8°, *$1 net. Gorham.

Snead-Cox, F. G.
Life of Cardinal Vaughan. In 2 v. '10 (Ag27) il. facsim., 8°, $7 net. Herder.

Snedden, D: S:
Problem of vocational education. '10 (Ag20) D. (Riverside educational monographs.) 35 c. Houghton M.
See also Dutton, S: Train.
—, and Allen, W: Harvey.
School reports and school efficiency; for the New York Committee on Physical Welfare of School Children. '08(Ap4) c. tabs., O. *$1.50 net. Macmillan.

Snell, Florence M.
Essentials of English syntax. '09(O30) D. 50 c. Longmans.

Snell, F: J:
Hdbk. to the works of Dante. '09(N13) S. *$1.50 net. Macmillan.

Snelling, Wa. O.
See Hall, Clarence.

Sneyd-Kynnersley, E. M.
Some passages in the life of one of H. M. inspectors of schools. '08(Je6) 8°, *$2.60 net. Macmillan.

Snider, Denton Jaques, ["Theophilus Middling."]
Abraham Lincoln. '09(Ja16) c. O. $1.50. Sigma.
Cosmos and diacosmos; processes of nature physiologically treated. '09(N13) c. D. $1.50. Sigma.
European history: chiefly ancient in its processes. '08(F15) c. O. $1.50. Sigma.
Lincoln in the Black Hawk War; epoch of the Northwest. '10(O) O. $1.25. Sigma.
Writer of books in his genesis; written for and dedicated to his pupil-friends, reaching back in a line of 50 years. '10(Ap30) por. D. $1.50. Sigma; McClurg.

Snodgrass, J: McBeath.
Fuel tests with house-heating boilers. [1910.] (My) 108 p. il. 8°, (Univ. of Ill., Engineering Experiment Station bull.) gratis. Univ. of Ill.
Tests of two types of tile-roof furnaces under a water-tube boiler. '09, [1910.] (My) 20 p. il. diagrs., 8°, (Univ. of Ill., Engineering Experiment Station bull.) gratis. Univ. of Ill.

Snow, Bonnie E.
See Froehlich, Hugo B.

Snow, C: H:
Principal species of wood. 2d ed., rev., with additions. '08(Je20) il. figs. 8°, $3.50. Wiley.

Snow, Edn., comp.
See Idaho. *Sup. ct.* Digest.

Snow, Ellen.
Confession of Seymour Vane. '09(Ja9) c. D. bds., 50 c. Fenno.
Evolution of Rose: [a story.] '07(Ja25) D. bds., 50 c. Badger.

Snow, H. J.
In forbidden seas; recollections of sea-otter hunting in the Kurils. '10(N19) il. map, O. $3.50 net. Longmans.

Snow, Jane Elliott.
Life of William McKinley. '09(Ja16) c. por. D. 75 c. J. E. Snow.

Snow, Mrs. Julia F.
Afternoons. '10(D3) c. por. O. hf. cf., $1.20; $1.25, boxed. Ulbrich.
Early recollections of Buffalo. '08(D) il. bds., $1. Ulbrich.

Snow, Louise.
Leaflets; stories for children. '10(D31) c. D. $1.25. B'way Pub.

Snow, W: Benham.
Therapeutics of radiant light and heat and convective heat. '09(Ap) c. 13+15-119 p. il. 8°, $2. Sci. Authors'.

Snow, W: Gage.
Practical and comprehensive treatise on warming buildings with hot air; with appendices. 4th ed., corrected and enl. '09(My22) il. 8°, $1.75. D: Williams.

Snow-bound. *See* Whittier, J: Greenleaf.

Snow-fire. Owen, M. C. $1.50 net. Harper.

Snow-man's Christmas. *See* Bird, Mary Herrick.

Snowden, Clinton A.
Hist. of Washington; the rise and progress of an American state; advisory eds.: Cornelius H. Hanford, Miles C. Moore, W: D. Tyler, Stephen J. Chadwick. 4 v. '09 (D18) c. il. pors. maps, 8°, $25. Century Hist.

Snowden, Ja. H:, D.D.
Summer across the sea. '09(F13) c. il. por. 12°, *$1 net. Revell.
World a spiritual system; outline of metaphysics. '10(O8) c. D. $1.50 net. Macmillan

Snuff box full of trees and some apocryphal essays. Ellwanger, W: D. **$2 net. Dodd.

Snyder, Rev. Albert Whitcomb.
Through the forty days: addresses for Lenten and lay reading. '08(Mr14) c. D. *$1 net. Whittaker.

Snyder, C: McCoy.
Flaw in the sapphire. '09(N) 311 p. 12°, $1. Metropolitan Press, (N. Y.)

Snyder, Dorothy Ermina.
See Brubacher, Abraham Royer.

Snyder, Edn. Reagan.
Legal status of rural high schools in the U. S., with special reference to the methods employed in extending state aid to secondary education in rural communities. '09(Ag) 7-225 p. tabs., 8°, (Teachers' College, Columbia Univ. contributions to education.) $1.50. Teachers' Coll.

Snyder, Emil W:
Questions and answers on domestic relations, [etc.] [1910.] (D) c. O. (Quizzer ser.) pap., 50 c. Sprague.

Snyder, Harry.
Human foods and their nutritive value. '08 (D12) il. 12°, *$1.25 net. Macmillan.
Soils and fertilizers. 3d ed. '08(Jl11) il. 12°, *$1.25 net. Macmillan.

Snyder, H:
See Ellis, E: Sylvester.

Snyder, H: G.
See Oklahoma. Comp. laws.
—, comp. *See* Oklahoma. Constitution.

Snyder, J. J.
Texas school lands; millions of acres to be sold by the state; only one-fortieth cash, and forty years' time on the balance. '09(S) 119 p. 12°, 60 c. Von Boeckmann-J.

Snyder, Ja. U.
Cain, and other poems. '08(Ap11) c. S. 75 c. Missouri Pr.

Snyder, Jonathan Le Moyne.
Agriculture and democracy; an address. '09(My8) O. (Agricultural College bulletin.) pap. (Add. pubs. for price.) Mich. Agricultural Coll.

Snyder, Sherwood Percy, comp.
Treatise on foods and their effects upon health and the physical and moral life; also a complete list of recipes and instructions for the hygienic preparation of the common food products, with special lists of menus. 2d ed., rev. and enl. '10(D) 9+11-183 p. por. 12°, $1. Health.
Treatise on foods, and their effects upon health and the physical and moral life; also a complete list of recipes and instructions for the hygienic preparation of the common food products. '09(Ap10) c. 12°, 75 c. S. P. Snyder.

Snyder, W: L.
Notaries' and commissioners' manual, [etc.] 9th ed., rev. and enl. '10(Ap) c. O. $1.75. Baker, V. & Co.
See also New York [State.] Lien law.

SNYDER FAMILY.
See **Genealogies: Wyand, E. C.**

So as by fire. Connor, J. $1.25. Benziger.
So-called Peters-Hilprecht controversy. Hilprecht, H. V. **75 c. net. Holman.
So here cometh White hyacinths. Hubbard, E. $2. Roycrofters.
So like her father (a play.) Blake, J. V. (Not for sale.) J. V. Blake.

SOAP.
Gathman, H. American soaps: treatise on the manufacture of soap. $15. H. Gathman.

Sobotta, Johannes.
Atlas and text-book of human anatomy; ed., with additions, by J. Playfair McMurrich. In 3 v. v. 2, 3. '08(Ja4) il. 4°, ea., *$6 net; *$7.50 net. Saunders.

Social and industrial conditions in the North during the Civil War. Fite, E. D: **$2 net. Macmillan.
Social and mental traits of the negro. Odum, H. W. $2 net. Longmans.
Social application of religion. Stelzle, C: *75 c. net. Jennings.
Social aspects of religious institutions. Earp, E. L. *75 c. net. Eaton & M.
Social bucaneer. Isham, F. S. $1.50. Bobbs-M.
Social calendar, 1910. Adams, *Mrs.* H. $1.25. Macmillan.
Social contract. Dawbarn, C. Y. C. $1.25 net. Longmans.

SOCIAL DEMOCRACY.
See **Socialism.**

Social development and education. O'Shea, M. V. $2. Houghton M.
Social duties from the Christian point of view. Henderson, C: R. $1.25. Univ. of Chic.
Social duty of our daughters. Hoffmann, *Mrs.* A. L. R. **35 c. net. Vir Pub.
Social education. Scott, C. A. $1.25. Ginn.
Social engineering. Tolman, W: H. *$2 net. McGraw-H.
Social England. Traill, H: D., *ed.* 12 v. ea., $3 net; per set, $35 net. Putnam.
Social evil. Greer, J. H. 50 c. J. H. Greer.
Social forces. Devine, E: T: $1.25. Charities Pub.
Social function of religious belief. Elwang, W: W. $1. Univ. of Mo.
Social gospel. Mathews, S. *50 c. net. Griffith; Pilgrim Press.
Social history of Flatbush. Vanderbilt, G. L. $1.50. F: Loeser.
Social insurance. Seager, H: R. $1. Macmillan.
Social life. Ridgeway, C: J: *60 c. net. Cassell.
Social life at Rome. Fowler, W: W. **$2.25 net. Macmillan.
Social ministry. Ward, H. F., *ed.* $1 net. Eaton & M.
Social mirror. Jurgenson, G. M. $1.50. O. L. Panzer.
Social mission of the church. Wishart, A. W. 20 c. Am. Bapt.
Social museum as an instrument of unversity teaching. Peabody, F. G. gratis. F. G. Peabody.
Social organization. Cooley, C: H. **$1.50 net. Scribner.
Social plans for young people. Reisner, C. F. *75 c. net. Jennings.

SOCIAL PROBLEMS.
See **Social science.**

SOCIAL PSYCHOLOGY.
See **Social science.**

Social reform and the Reformation. Schapiro, J. S. $1.25. Longmans.
Social register, Cincinnati and Dayton, 1910 [*with* Social register, Cleveland]. '10(Ap) c. 16°, $2.50. Social Register.
Social relationships in the light of Christianity. Chadwick, W: E: *1.50 net. **Longmans.**

SOCIAL SCIENCE.
American Sociological Society. Papers and proceedings. 4 v. ea., $1.50 net. Univ. of Chic.
Bainbridge, O. Devil's note book; [comments on crimes and vices of several European rulers.] $1. Cochrane.
Beary, H. R. Individual development of man: discussion of the influence of labor on the evolution of the individual. $1. Hartman Pub.
Bell, G: M., *ed.* Social service: a handbook for workers and visitors in London and other large towns. 60 c. Longmans.
Bell, W. M. Social message of our Lord. *60 c. net. Otterbein.
Bliss, W: D. P., *and others, eds.* **Encyclopedia of social reform. **$7.50 net; **$9.50 net; **$12 net; **$14 net. Funk.**
Bradford, A. H. My brother. $1.25 net. Pilgrim Press.
Brown, E. E. Government by influence. $1.25 net. Longmans.
Butterfield, K. L. Chapters in rural progress. *$1 net. Univ. of Chic.
Carnegie, A. Problems of to-day. $1.40. Doubleday, P.
Chadwick, W: E: Social relationships in **the light of Christianity. *$1.50 net. Longmans.**
Chambless, E. Roadtown. $1.25 net; $1.35 net. Roadtown.
Chesterton, G. K. What's wrong with the world. $1.50. Dodd.
Church and life of to-day. $1.50 net. Doran.
Churchill, W. L. S. Liberalism and the social problem. *$1.50 net. Doran.
Cole, W. I. Motives and results of the social settlement movement. (Add. pubs. for price.) Harvard Univ.
Cole, W: M. American hope. $1.50 net. Appleton.
Coleman, G: W: Churches outside the church. 15 c. Am. Bapt.
Cooley, C: H. Social organization. **$1.50 net. Scribner.
Crafts, W. F. National perils and hopes. 50 c. net. F. M. Barton.
Cunningham, W. Christianity and social questions. 75 c. net. Scribner.

SOCIAL SCIENCE.—*Continued.*

Davey, J: Gloryville or Hellburg, which?: [study of present day social conditions.] 20 c. J: Davey.

Davis, M. M. Psychological interpretation of society. $2. Longmans.

Dawbarn, C. Y. C. Liberty and progress. *$3 net. Longmans.

Dealey, J. Q. Sociology. $1.50. Silver.

Devine, E: T: Social forces. $1.25. Charities Pub.

Dewey, J: *and* Small, A. W. My pedagogic creed by J: Dewey and The demands of sociology upon pedagogy by A. W. Small. 15 c. Flanagan.

Dickinson, G. L. Justice and liberty: political dialogue. **$1.20 net. McClure.

Dole, C: F. The coming people. 75 c. Crowell.

Downes, L. New democracy. $2. Sherman, F.

Earp, E. L. Social aspects of religious institutions. *75 c. net. Eaton & M.

Ede, W: M. Clergy and social service. 90 c. Longmans.

Ellwood, C: A. Sociology and modern social problems. $1. Am. Bk.

Fletcher, H: F. Ethics of conservation. 10 c. H: F. Fletcher.

Foster, R. O. Social game. 10 c. R. O. Foster.

Frazer, J. G: Psyche's task: [influence of superstition and growth of institutions.] *80 c. net. Macmillan.

Galsworthy, J: A commentary: [indictment of modern social conditions.] $1.50. Putnam.

Giddings, F. H: Sociology: [a lecture.] (Add. pubs. for price.) Columbia Univ.

Griggs, E: H. Human equipment, its use and abuse. *50 c. net. B: W. Huebsch.

Hall, T: C. Social solutions in the light of Christian ethics. *$1.50 net. Eaton & M.

Handy manual of social reform. 25 c. Funk.

Hapgood, H. Types from city streets. $1.50 net. Funk.

Hatfield, R., *ed.* Geyserland: empiricisms and social reform: [fiction.] $3. R: Hatfield.

Heineman, T. W: Physical basis of civilization. $1.25. Forbes.

Henderson, C: R. Reasonable social policy for Christian people. 10 c. Am. Bapt.

Henderson, C: R. Social duties from the Christian point of view. $1.25. Univ. of Chic.

Hodson, A. L. Letters from a settlement: [experiences in a settlement.] $1.50. Longmans.

Hubbard, H: L. Summing it up. 50 c. J. S. Ogilvie.

Hyde, E: S. Progress from experience. $1.25. Cochrane.

International Reform Bureau. Patriotic studies for men's leagues, young people's societies and civic clubs; incl. extracts from bills, acts and documents of U. S. Congress rel. to moral and social reforms, 1888-1908. 75 c.; 35 c. Int. Ref. Bu.

SOCIAL SCIENCE.—*Continued.*

Jenks, J. W. Governmental action for social welfare. $1 net. Macmillan.

Jones, H: Working faith of the social reformer. $2.40 net. Macmillan.

King, H. C., *and others.* Education and national character. *$1.50 net. Rel. Educ.

Le Bon, G. The crowd. $1.10 net. Macmillan.

Lewis, A. M. Vital problems in social evolution. 50 c. Kerr.

McDougall, W: Introd. to social psychology. *$1.50 net. J: W. Luce. Univ. of Chic.

McElroy, J: Economic functions of vice. 50 c. Nat. Tribune.

Martin, Mrs. J: Is mankind advancing? $2 net.. Baker & T.

Mathews, S. Social gospel. 50 c. net. Griffith; Pilgrim Press.

Mauro, P. Number of man. *$1.25 net. Revell.

Montesquieu, *Baron* de. Spirit of laws. 2 v. $3.50; $7. Lamb Pub.

Montgomery, H. E. Vital American problems. **$1.50 net. Putnam.

Paradise, F. I. Church and the individual. $1.50 net. Moffat.

Parsons, J: Each for all and all for each. *$1.50 net. Sturgis & W.

Patten, S. N. Product and climax. *50 c. net. B: W. Huebsch.

Peabody, F. G. Approach to the social question. **$1.25 net. Macmillan.

Pooley, P: Mysterious discovery of nature. $1. P. Pooley.

Rawie, H: In quest of prosperity. 25 c. H: Rawie.

Reeve, B. Jerome; or, the real power back of James J. Hill. v. 1. 50 c. B. Reeve.

Richards, *Mrs.* E. H. S. Euthenics; the science of controllable environment. $1 net. Whitcomb & B.

Robinson, H. P. Twentieth century American. *$7.50 net. Putnam.

Ross, E: A. Latter day sinners and saints. 50 c. net. B: W. Huebsch.

Ross, E. A. Social psychology. **$1.50 net. Macmillan.

Royce, J. Race questions. **$1.25 net. Macmillan.

Ruskin, J: Unto this last. 40 c.; 75 c. Caldwell.

Schenck, F. S. Sociology of the Bible. *$1.50 net. Reformed.

Severance, H. S. Millennial essays. $1.50. H. S. Severance.

Severy, M. L. Gillette's industrial solution: world corporation. *$1.50 net. Ball Pub.

Small, A. W. Meaning of social science. $1.50 net. Univ. of Chic.

Stelzle, C: Church and the labor movement. 10 c. Am. Bapt.

Stelzle, C:, *and others.* Social application of religion. *75 c. net. Jennings.

Strong, J., *ed.* Studies in the gospel of the kingdom. 75 c.; 60 c. Am. Inst. Social Service.

Tait, A. O. Heralds of the morning: the meaning of the social and political problems of to-day. $3.50. Pacific Press.

SOCIAL SCIENCE.—*Continued.*

Tenney, E: P. Contrasts in social progress. 85 c. E: P. Tenney.

Terry, S. B. Dynamics of organism. (Add. pubs. for price.) Terry.

Theodul, C. Let the nation arise; treatise on the subject of purification and the gathering of the purified. $1. Balance.

Tolman, W: H. Social engineering. *$2 net. McGraw-H.

Ulrich, J: Democratic foundations. 10 c. Co-operative Pr.

United States. *Superintendent of Documents.* Sociology; public documents of the U. S. gratis.

Warbasse, J. P: Medical sociology. $2. Appleton.

Ward, H. F., *ed.* Social ministry. $1 net. Eaton & M.

Ware, T: A. Story of the centuries: rise of the common people. $1. Cochrane.

Wright, C. D. Outline of practical sociology. $2. Longmans.

See also Capital and labor;—Capital punishment;—Character; — Charities;—Children;—Church; — Cities; — Communism; — Communities; — Consumer's League;—Co-operation; — Corporations;—Crime and criminals:—Democracy;—Divorce;—Education; Ethics; — Ethnology;—Etiquette; — Eugenics; — Factories; — Family;—Guilds; — History; — Immigration; — Individualism;—Labor and laboring classes;—Labor colonies; — Man; — Manners and customs; — Marriage;—Negroes;—Peace;—Political economy;—Political science;—Poor; — Population;—Prisons; — Property; — Religion; — Salvation Army; — Slavery; — Socialism;—Statistics; — Success; — Temperance; — Totemism;—Voluntaryism;—Wealth;—Woman;—Young people;—*also* Athens;—Rome;—United States.

Social science ser. See Scribner's.

Social service. Bell, G: M., *ed.* 60 c. Longmans.

Social service. Post, L: F. *$1 net. Wessels.

Social service and the art of healing. Cabot, R. C. **$1 net. Moffat.

Social service ser. 12° and 8°, pap. Am. Bapt.

—Batten. Working temperance programme. 15 c.

—Coleman. Churches outside the church. 15 c.

—Cope. Home as the school for social living. 15 c.

—Dealey. Ethical and religious significance of the state. **10 c. net.

—Henderson. Reasonable social policy for Christian people. **10 c. net.

—McCrimmon. Child in the normal home. 15 c.

—Stelzle. Church and the labor movement. 10 c.

—Wishart. Social mission of the church. 20 c.

—Woodruff. The city. 20 c.

Social silhouettes. Sheldon, R. L. 50 c. S. W. Anderson.

Social solutions in the light of Christian ethics. Hall, T: C. *$1.50 net. Eaton & M.

Social teaching of the Bible. Keeble, S. E:, *ed.* *$1 net. Eaton & M.

Social welfare and the liquor question. Warner, H. S. $1; 35 c. Intercollegiate Prohibition.

Social welfare and the liquor problem. Warner, H. S. $1. Intercoll. Prohibition.

Social will. Hayden, E. A. $1. Psychological Review.

Social work. Chadwick, W. E. *40 c. net. Longmans.

Social work of the Salvation Army. Lamb, E. G. $1. E. G. Lamb.

SOCIALISM.

Arnold-Forster, H. O. English socialism of to-day. *$1.25 net. Dutton.

Barker, J. E. British socialism. *$3 net. Scribner.

Barnett, S: A: *and Mrs.* H. R. Toward social reform. *$1.50 net. Macmillan.

Benson, A. L: What help can any workingman expect from Taft or Bryan? 5 c. Socialist.

Bernstein, E: Evolutionary socialism. *$1 net. B: W. Huebsch.

Clews, H: Individualism versus socialism. (Add. author for price.) H: Clews.

Coan, M. B. Coming peril: [socialism.] 50 c. Wilkie & C.

Cohen, J. E. Socialism for students. 50 c. Kerr.

Collins, J: M. Power and weakness of trade unions. 10 c. J. M. Collins.

Connolly, J. Socialism made easy. 10 c. Kerr.

Cooney, P. J. Roman Catholicism and socialism. 10 c. P. J. Cooney.

Crawford, J. S. Political socialism, would it fail in success? 25 c. J. S. Crawford.

Cullen, A. Adventures in socialism. $2 net. Macmillan.

Cullen, P: J. Socialism and the Christian religion. 35 c. Mirror.

Eccles, L. F. Plain analysis of socialism. 25 c. L. F. Eccles.

Ferri, E. Socialism and modern science, (Darwin, Spencer, Marx.) $1. Kerr.

Ghent, W: J. Socialism and success. $1 net. Lane.

Guyot, Y. Socialistic fallacies. $1.50 net. Macmillan.

Hanford, B. Fight for your life!: [socialism.] 25 c. Wiltshire Bk.

Harris, *Rev.* W. S. Hell before death. $1. Minter.

Hartman, E: R. Socialism versus Christianity. $1.50. Cochrane.

Hillquit, M. Hist. of socialism in the United States. **$1.50 net. Funk.

Hillquit, M. Recent progress of the socialist and labor movement in the United States. 10 c. Kerr.

Hillquit, M. Socialism in theory and practice. **$1.50 net. Macmillan.

Hofmeister, C. W., *and* Spencer, P. J. Acturi: synopsis of human progress. 25 c. C. W. Hofmeister.

Hugo, G: B., *and* Carey, J. F. Socialism, "the creed of despair." 75 c. G: B. Hugo.

Hunter, W. R. Socialists at work. **$1.50 net. Macmillan.

Hyde, E: S. Progress from experience. $1.25. Cochrane.

Kampffmeyer, P. Changes in the theory and tactics of the (German) social democracy. 50 c. Kerr.

SOCIALISM.—*Continued.*

Kauffman, R. W. What is socialism? **$1.25 net. Moffat.

Kautsky, K. Class struggle. 50 c.; 25 c. Kerr.

Kautsky, K. Road to power. 50 c.; 25 c. S: A. Bloch.

Kelly, E. Twentieth century socialism. $1.75 net. Longmans.

Kirkup, T: History of socialism. *$2.25 net.—Primer of socialism. *40 c. net. Macmillan.

Klein, J. Situation at present. 10 c. J. Klein.

Kutter, H. They must; or, God and the social democracy. $1. Co-operative Pr. Co.

La Monte, R. R., *and* Mencken, H: L: Men *versus* the man. **$1.35 net. Holt.

Lewis, A. M. Evolution: social and organic.—Vital problems in social evolution. ea., 50 c. Kerr.

London, J. Iron Heel: [fiction.]—Revolution and other essays. ea., $1.50 net. Macmillan.

London, J. Revolution. pap., 5 c.; 60 copies mailed for $1; 100, for $1.50; 1,000, for $10. Kerr.

London Municipal Society. Case against socialism. *$1.50 net. Macmillan.

Mann, N. M. Import and outlook of socialism. $1.50 net. J. H. West.

Ming, J: J. Characteristics and the religion of modern socialism.—Morality of modern socialism. ea., **$1.50 net. Benziger.

Morris, W:, *and* Bax, E. B. Socialism: its growth and outcome. 50 c. Kerr.

Nietzsche, F. W. Human, all too human. 50 c. Kerr.

Nitti, F. S. Catholic socialism. *$2.75 net. Macmillan.

Patterson, J. M., *comp.* Socialist campaign book. 25 c. Socialist.

Post, L: F. Social service. *$1 net. Wessels.

Power, M. At the root of Socialism. *10 c. net. Herder.

Preuss, A. Fundamental fallacies of socialism. *$1 net. Herder.

Randall, W: H: Golden rule republic no Utopia. 25 c. Co-operative Pr. Co.

Richards, E. G. Nationalism according to Richards. 60 c. E. G. Richards.

Richardson, N. A. Industrial problems. $1. Kerr.

Ries, W. F. Men and mules: [booklet on present conditions of society due to the competitive system.] 10 c. W. F. Ries.

Rosenthal, A. Differences between the Socialist party and the Socialist Labor party. 10 c. Grayzel.

Russell, C: E: Why I am a Socialist. $1.50 net. Doran.

St. Ledger, A. Australian socialism. *$1.50 net. Macmillan.

Scullin, P. H. Socialism means slavery for the working man. gratis. P. H. Scullin.

Shaw, G: B. Socialism and superior brains. 75 c. net. Lane.

SOCIALISM.—*Continued.*

Shaw, G: B., *ed.* Fabian essays in socialism. *50 c. net. Ball Pub. Co.

Simons, A. M. Socialist program. 5 c.; per 100, $2.50. Socialist.

Sinclair, U. B. Prince Hagen. $1; 25 c. Kerr.

Sombart, W. Socialism and the social movement. *$1.50 net. Dutton.

Spargo, J: Common sense of socialism. $1; 25 c. Kerr.

Spargo, J: Socialism: summary and interpretation. *$1.50 net. Macmillan.

Spargo, J: Socialist readings for children. $1. Woman's Nat. Prog. League.

Spargo, J: Spiritual significance of modern socialism. *50 c. net.—Substance of socialism. *$1 net. B: W. Huebsch.

Stoddart, J. T. New socialism. *$1.75 net. Doran.

Strachey, J: St. L. Problems and perils of socialism. *25 c. net. Macmillan.

Sullivan, J. W. Socialism as an incubus on the American labor movement. 50 c. Volunteer.

Taylor, G. R. S. Leaders of socialism, past and present. $1 net. Duffield.

Teitsworth, G: W., *ed.* Back to slavery. 75 c. Craven-D.

Towler, W. G. Socialism in local government. *$1.50 net. Macmillan.

Walsh, W: T: Mirage of the many [fiction]. $1.50. Holt.

Wells, H. G: New worlds for old. **$1.50 net.—War in the air: [fiction.] †$1.50. Macmillan.

Wells, H. G: Socialism and the family.—This misery of boots. ea., *50 c. net. Ball Pub.

Wilde, O. Soul of man under socialism. 60 c. net. J: W. Luce.

Wilson, W. L. Menace of socialism. **$1.50 net. Jacobs.

Ziv, R. L. Tree of modern life. 75 c.; 50 c. R. L. Ziv.

See also Anarchy and anarchism;—Collectivism;—Communism;—Communities; — Co-operation;—Individualism;—New Zealand;—Property;—*also* Marx, Karl.

Socialist (The). Thorne, G., *pseud.* **$1.35 net. Putnam.

Socialist lib.; ed. by J. Ramsay McDonald. D. Huebsch.

—Bernstein. Evolutionary socialism. *$1 net.

Socialist readings for children. Spargo, J: $1. Woman's Nat. Prog. League

Socialistic fallacies. Guyot, I. $1.50 net. Macmillan.

Socialized church. Tippy, W. M., *ed.* *$1 net. Eaton & M.

Société (La) française en XVIIe siècle. Cousin, V. $1.15. Oxford Univ.

SOCIETIES.

United States. *Library of Congress.* Want list of publications of societies. (Add. Superintendent for price.) U. S., Supt. of Docs

See also Benefit societies;—Boys;—Freemasonry;—Guilds;—Learned societies;—Secret societies;—Trade-unions.

Society and politics in ancient Rome. Abbott, F. F. **$1.25 net. Scribner.

Society for the Promotion of Social Service. Juvenile delinquent and the Young Men's Christian Association; addresses, papers and resolutions of the second annual conference, Chicago, February 12, 1909; with a bibliography on juvenile delinquency. '09 (D25) c. 8°, 50 c. Y. M. C. A.

Society of Colonial Wars. *District of Columbia.* Hist. address of Marcus Benjamin, with other papers rel. to the dedication of the Braddock boulder in the cathedral grounds, Mount St. Albans, Washington, D. C., Nov. 10, 1907. '09(My) 14 p. il. 4°, (Hist. papers of the Society of Colonial Wars in the District of Columbia.) pap., gratis. Soc. Colon. Wars., D. C.

Society of Colonial Wars, Ohio. Register of the Society of Colonial Wars in the state of Ohio, October 1, 1909. '09, [1910.] (Ap) 96 p. 8°. (Not for sale.) Soc. Colon. Wars (O.)

Society of Dofobs, Chicago. Second book of Dofobs. '09, [1910.] (Ap) c. o. p. Soc. Dofobs.

SOCIETY OF ICONOPHILES, New York City.
Lawrence, R: H., *comp.* Catalogue of the engravings issued by the Society of Iconophiles. (Priv. pr.) R: H. Lawrence.

Society of Mayflower Descendants (Rhode Island and Providence.) Second record book. '08(S) 154 p. 8°. (Add. pubs. for price.) Standard Pr. Co.

Society of the War of 1812. Constitution and register of membership of the General Society of the War of 1812, June 1, 1908. '08, [1909.] (Jl) c. il. 8°, $1.50. J. E. B. Buckenham.

Society recollections in Paris and Vienna, 1879-1904, by an English officer. '08(Ap25) il. 8°, $3. Appleton.

Society Wolf. Thrice, L. $1.50. Cupples & L.

SOCIOLOGY.
See Social science.

Sock and buskin biographies. il. D. $1. E. H. Bacon.
—Barry. Julia Marlowe.

Socratic discourses. *See* Plato *and* Xenophon.

SODA-WATER.
Dispenser soda water guide; collection of over 1300 formulas for the soda fountain, to which has been added numerous hints and suggestions for plant equipment and operation, refrigeration, the manufacture of ice cream, etc., etc.; comp. by the *Soda Fountain.* 2d ed. '09(Ag) 7-139 p. il. 8°, $1. Haynes.
Liquid Carbonic Co., Chicago. 1910 soda water guide and book of recipes. [Rev. ed.] [1910.] (Ap) c. '09. 192 p. il. 8°, $1. Liquid Carbonic.

Sodalist's Imitation of Christ. *See* Thomas à Kempis.

SODALITIES.
See Mary, *Virgin.*

Soddy, F:
Interpretation of radium. '09(My22) il. 8°, (Science ser.) *$1.75 net.. Putnam.

Soderholtz, E. E.
See Crane, E. A.

SODIUM BENZOATE.
See Food.

Soeur Alexandrine. *See* Champol, F.

Sogard, J:
Public school relationships; chapters on the interrelationships of the school officers, the teachers, the pupils and the community; with an introd. by Homer H. Seerley. '09(My) c. 24+197 p. 12°, $1. Hinds.

Sohrab and Rustum. *See* Macaulay, T: Babington, *Lord.* Lays of ancient Rome.

Soil pollution and its relation to hookworm disease and typhoid fever. Stiles, C. W. U. S., Supt. of Docs.

SOILS.
Cameron, F., *and* Gallagher, F. E. Moisture content and physical conditions of soils. pap., 15 c. U. S., Supt. of Docs.
Campbell, H. W. 1907 soil culture manual. $2.50. H. W. Campbell.
Carr, M. E. Preliminary rept. on the Valusia soils. (Add. Superintendent for price.) U. S., Supt. of Docs.
Gardner, F. D. Fertility of soils as affected by manures. 15 c. U. S., Supt. of Docs.
Hall, A. D. The soil: introd. to the scientific study of the growth of crops. *$1.50 net. Dutton.
Hopkins, C. G: Soil fertility and permanent agriculture. $2.75. Ginn.
Hopkins, C. G: Story of the soil: [fiction.] $1.50. Badger.
Hunt, E. W. Conserving and increasing the fertility of the soil. gratis. C. Hildreth.
Jeffrey, J. A. Elem. laboratory study in soils. gratis. Mich. Supt. Pub. Instruction.
Lyon, T: L., *and* Fippin, E. O. Principles of soil management. **$1.75 net. Macmillan.
McCall, A. G. Physical properties of soils. *50 c. net. Judd.
McConnell, P. Soils: their nature and management. *60 c. net. Cassell.
Murray, J. A. Soils and manures. $2 net. Van Nostrand.
Patten, H. E. Heat transference in soils. U. S., Supt. of Docs.
Schreiner, O., *and* Shorey, E. C. Isolation of harmful organic substances from soils. (Add. Superintendent for price.) U. S., Supt. of Docs.
Schreiner, O., *and* Skinner, J. J: Some effects of a harmful organic soil constituent. Gov. Pr. Off.
Snyder, H. Soils and fertilizers. *$1.25 net. Macmillan.
United States. Bulletins, circulars, and field operations of the Soils Bureau; Agriculture Dept., U. S. A.; for sale by the Superintendent of Documents. '09 (N) 8 p. 8°, gratis. U. S., Supt. of Docs.
United States. *Dept. of Agriculture. Bureau of Soils.* List of publications of the [United States] Bureau of Soils. '09 (My) 32 p. 8°, pap., gratis.

SOILS.—*Continued.*
United States. *Dept. of Agriculture. Bu. of Soils.* List of soil surveys. (Add. Superintendent for price.)
United States. *Superintendent of Documents.* Soils Bureau; bulletins, circulars, [etc.]
Vivian, A. First principles of soil fertility. *$1 net. Judd.
Whitney, M. Study of crop yields and soil composition in relation to soil productivity. (Add. Superintendent for price.) U. S., Supt. of Docs.
Whitson, A. R., *and* Walster, H. L. Notes on soils. 90 c. A. R. Whitson.
See also **Agricultural chemistry;—Agriculture;—Fertilizers;—Gardens and gardening.**
Sol: hwens?—hwither? Larisun, C. W. $1.50. Fonic.
Solar heat, non-solar. Elliott, J. 25 c. J. Elliott.
SOLAR SYSTEM.
Elliott, J. Nebular hypothesis untenable. 25 c. J. Elliott.
Poor, C: L. Solar system. **$2 net. Putnam.
See also Astronomy;—Sun
SOLDERING.
Schultz, F: W. Solder, its production and use. $1.25. MacNeal; F: W. Schultz.
Thatcher, E: Simple soldering. 50 c.; 25 c. Spon.
Soldier and servant ser. 12°. Church Missions.
—Andrews. Japan mission of the American church. $1; 50 c.
—Hughson, *comp.* Church's mission to the mountaineers of the south. 75 c.; 50 c.
Soldier of the future. Dawson, W: J. $1.50. Revell.
Soldier's letters to charming Nellie. Polley, J. B. *$2 net. Neale.
Soldier's recollections. McKim, R. M. $2 net. Longmans.
SOLDIERS.
Erckmann, E., *and* Chatrian, A. Hist. of a conscript of 1813. $1.50 net. Macmillan.
Johnston, C: H. L. Famous cavalry leaders. $1.50. L. C. Page.
Soldiers' score book. '09(Ag) $1.25. Hudson.
Vest-pocket diary and memorandum book for the soldier. 35 c. Hudson.
See also National Soldiers' Home.
Soldiers' home: [poetry.] Watkins, L. B. 15 c. L. B. Watkins.
SOLDIERS' HOME, Washington, D. C.
Flosser, F. Brief hist. of the U. S. Soldiers' Home, Washington, D. C. 25 c. H. B. Darling.
Soldiers of the light. Cone, H. G. $1 net. Badger.
Sclereder, Hans.
Systematic anatomy of the dicotyledons: hdbk. for laboratories of pure and applied botany; tr. by L. A. Boodle and F. E. Fritsch; rev. by D. H. Scott. In 2 v. '08(O24) O. ea., $8.75. Oxford Univ.
Solicitor's office organization. Cope, E: A. $2. Pitman.

Solid bitumens. Peckham, S. F. $5. M. C. Clark.
SOLID GEOMETRY.
See Geometry.
"Solid South." Adams, C: F., *jr.* (Priv. pr.) C: F. Adams.
Soliloquy of Birmingham Bob of Rainbow Glen. Prude, A. M. $1. A. M. Prude.
Solis-Cohen, Myer, M.D.
Family health. '10(F19) D. (Family bks.) **$1 net. Penn Pub. Co.
SOLITAIRE (*card game*).
Brock, C. C., *comp.* Solitaire; forty games. 25 c. C. C. Brock.
Dick, H. B., *ed.* Dick's games of patience; or, solitaire with cards. 75 c. Dick.
Hapgood, G: Solitaire and patience. 50 c. Penn Pub. Co.
Preble, H: Month of solitaires. *50 c. net. Brentano's.
"Trumps, *jr., pseud.* Poker patience. 15 c. Dick.
Solitary farm. Hume, F. W. †$1.25. G: W. Dillingham.
Sölling, A.
Improved and pract. method of packing fish for transportation; paper presented before the Fourth International Fishery Congress, held at Washington Sept. 22 to 26, 1908. '10(Mr) 295-301 p. 4°, pap. Gov. Pr. Off.
Solomon, Maurice.
Electric lamps. '09(Je19) il. tabs., 8°, (Westminster ser.) *$2 net. Van Nostrand.
Solomon, Simeon.
Vision of love revealed in sleep. '09(D) Japan vellum, *$3 net. T: B. Mosher.
SOLOMON, Simeon.
Ford, J. E. Simeon Solomon: an appreciation. *$3.50 net. F. F. Sherman.
Solomon, Solomon Jôs.
Practice of old painting and of drawing as associated with it. '10(Ap2) il. O. (New art lib.) $1.75 net. Lippincott.
SOLOMON ISLANDS.
See **Mollusks.**
SOLOMON'S TEMPLE.
See Temple (The).
Solon, L: Marc Emmanuel.
Ceramic literature. '10(S) 4°, hf. leath., $15 net. Lippincott.
Solution of interests dependent upon money. Long, C: A. $1. Aberdeen.
Solution of triangles. 2 v. '10(Jl9) c. 8°, (Machinery's reference ser.) ea., 25 c. Indust. Press.
Somadeva-Chatta of Kashmir.
See Barnett, L. D.
Sombart, Werner.
Socialism and the social movement; tr. from the 6th German ed. by M. Epstein. '09 (O30) 12°, *$1.50 net. Dutton.
Some acrostic signatures of Francis Bacon. Booth, W: S. **$6 net. Houghton M.
Some adventures of two vagabonds. York, W. A., *pseud.* $1. B'way Pub.
Some African highways. Kirkland, C. $1.50. Estes.
Some answered questions. Abdu 'l-Baha. *$1.50 net. Lippincott.
Some aspects of Rabbinic theology. Schechter, S. **$2.25 net. Macmillan.

Some assurances of immortality. Berry, J: B. $1. Fenno.
Some British birds. Thomas, E: *$2 net. Doran.
Some British butterflies and insects. Thomas, E: *$2 net. Doran.
Some common remedies. Smith, E. *$1.25 net. Hoeber.
Some customs of the Machenengas. Farabee, W: C. 50 c. Davis Press.
Some descendants of John Norton. Norton, W. W. (Add. pubs. for price.) Journal Press, (Ct.)
Some desert watering places. Mendenhall, W. C. (Add. Superintendent for price.) U. S., Supt. of Docs.
Some eminent Victorians. Carr, J. W: C. *$3.50 net. Scribner.
Some end-results of surgery. Mumford, J. G. **25 c. net. Moffat.
Some essentials in musical definitions. MacConnell, M. F., *comp. and ed.* $1. Ditson.
Some experiences and meditations of a jackass. Leonard, J. S. $1.25. Metropolitan Press, (Ore.)
Some experiences of an Irish R. M. Somerville, E. A. O. $1 net. Longmans.
Some factors affecting grade distribution. Ayres, L. P. 10 c. Psychological Clinic.
Some factors affecting the keeping qualities of American lemons. True, R. H. (Add. Superintendent for price.) U. S., Supt. of Docs.
Some familiar forms of nervousness. Coriat, I. H. **25 c. net. Moffat.
Some famous women. Creighton, *Mrs.* L. 50 c. Longmans.
Some figurative usages of *venire* and *ire.* Mood, J. R. gratis. Johns Hopkins.
Some forerunners of St. Francis of Assisi Davison, E. S. (Add. author for price.) E. S. Davison.
Some friends of mine. Lucas, E: V., *ed.* **$1.25 net. Macmillan.
Some fruits of solitude. *See* Penn, W:
Some fugitive verse. Buck, E: N. $1.75. E: N. Buck.
Some further letters to an elector. Brown, J: H. B. 25 c. Longmans.
Some further observations of the young lady across the way. Ryder, R. O. 50 c. Young Lady Across the Way.
Some Good Will boys. Hinckley, G W. 75 c. Good Will.
Some great stories. Wyche, R: T: $1. Newson.
Some hidden sources of fiction. Nead, B: M. (Priv. pr.) Jacobs.
Some incentives to right living. McGavick, A. J. *$1 net. Wiltzius.
Some insects injurious to truck crops. '10 (N) 10+108 p. il. 8°, (U. S., Dept. of Agriculture, Bureau of Entomology bull.)
Bibliographies interspersed.
Some Irish yesterdays. Somerville, E. A. O. $1 net. Longmans.
Some Jewish associates of John Brown. Hühner, L. o. p. L. Hühner.
Some ladies in haste. Chambers, R. W: †$1.50. Appleton.
Some little prayers. Meyer, L. R. *35 c. net. Jennings.
Some living things. Hallock, E. B. 36 c. Barnes.
Some memories. Collyer, R. *$1.25 net. Am. Unitarian.
Some minor chords. Jones, A. J. $1. Eaton & M.
Some musical recollections of fifty years. Hoffman, R: $1.50 net. Scribner.
Some new literary valuations. Wilkinson, W: C. **$1.30 net. Funk.
Some notable altars in the Church of England and the American Episcopal Church. Wright, J: *$6 net. Macmillan.
Some notes on catalog making. Graydon, S: $1. Trow Press.
Some notes on the currency problem. Adams, J. T. gratis. Broun-G.
Some of nature's antics. Balliet, M. R. $1. Roxburgh.
Some of the reasons why I cannot accept the results of the destructive criticism of the Old Testament. Hoyt, W. 10 c. Am. Bapt.
Some old Devon churches. Stabb, J: *$3 net. Scribner.
Some old English abbeys. Lang, E. M. 60 c.; $1. Stokes.
Some passages in the life of one of H. M. inspectors of schools. Sneyd-Kynnersley, E. M. *$2.60 net. Macmillan.
Some phases of the negro question. Melick, C: W. $1. C: W. Melick.
Some physical disorders having mental origin. Achorn, J. W. **25 c. net. Moffat.
Some plans and suggestions for housing consumptives. '10(My14) il. Q. pap. Nat. Assoc. Tuberculosis.
Some points in the surgery of the brain. Ballance, C: A. *$5 net. Macmillan.
Some purposes of paradise. Gwynne, W. *75 c. net. Gorham.
Some quick and easy methods of calculating. Blaine, R. G. $1. Spon.
Some recent phases of German theology. Nuelsen, J: L: *75 c. net. Jennings.
Some recollections of a long life. Sherman, E. J. (Priv. pr.) E. J. Sherman.
Some reminiscences. Royall, W: L. *$1.50 net. Neale.
Some roads to Rome in America. Curtis, G. P., *ed.* *$1.75 net. Herder.
Some southern questions. MacCorkle, W: A. **$1.75 net. Putnam.
Some spring days in Iowa. Lazell, F: J. $1.50. Torch Press.
Some stumbling blocks of the French language. Tricoche, G: N. 75 c. G: N. Tricoche.
Some summer days in Iowa. Lazell, F: J: $1.50. Torch Press.
Some "thinks." Munn, C: C. 10 c. C: C. Munn.
Some thoughts on speculation. Fayant, F. (Priv. pr.) Baruch.
Some uses of statistics in the supervision of schools. Falkner, R. P. (Add. author for price.) R. P. Falkner.
Some wander songs. Winslow, H. (Add. pubs. for price.) H. Winslow.

Some women, loving or luckless. Wyzewa, T. de. *$2.50 net. Lane.

Some wonders of biology. Thomson, W: H. **$1.20 net. Dodd.

Somehow good. De Morgan, W: F. †$1.75. Holt.

Someone pays. Barwell, N. $1.50. Lane.

Somermeier, E. E.
See Bownocker, J: Adams

SOMERSET, Eng.
Harper, C: G: Somerset coast. *$6 net. Scribner.
Knight, F. A. Somerset. 45 c. Putnam.

Somerville, C:
The wolf; founded on the play by Eug. Walter. '08(N14) c. il. D. †$1.50. G: W. Dillingham.
Woman's way; novel; from the play by Thompson Buchanan. '09(D4) c. il. D. $1.50. W. J. Watt.

—, and Thompson, Buchanan.
Woman's way. '10(D) 75 c. Grosset.

Somerville, Edith Anne Oenone, and Ross, Martin, [pseud. for Violet Martin.]
All on the Irish shore; Irish sketches. '10(D24) il. 12°, (Irish R. M. ser.) price reduced from $1.50 to $1 net. Longmans.
Further experiences of an Irish R. M. '10(D24) il. 12°, (Irish R. M. ser.) price reduced from $1.50 to $1 net. Longmans.
Some experiences of an Irish R. M. '10 (D24) il. 12°, (Irish R. M. ser.) price reduced from $1.50 to $1 net. Longmans.
Some Irish yesterdays. '10(D24) il. 12°, (Irish R. M. ser.) price reduced from $1.50 to $1 net. Longmans.

Somerville, F: Howland.
Elementary algebra. '08(F22) c. D. $1; Answers. '08(Mr7) D. pap., 10 c. Am. Bk.

Something about Singlefoot. Hicks, J: $1.50. Cochrane.

Something for you to look into. Fowler-Chumos, *Mrs.* O. S. 25 c. Fowler-Chumos.

Something of men I have known. Stevenson, A. E. *$2.75 net. McClurg

Something ser. v. 1-6. '09(D); v. 7, 8. '10 (D) il. in col. 8°, ea., 25 c. Doran.
Contents: Something to do; Something to make; Something to read; Something to paint; Something to play; Something to find; Something to pet; Something to draw.

Something to read for boys and girls. Brookline (Mass.) Public Library. o. p. Brookline Pub. Lib.

Somes House. Brooks, A. M. *$1.25 net. Dutton.

Sommer, H. J.
Index of 1180 post-mortems of the insane; State Hospital for the Insane, Norristown, Pa.; with an introd. by Allen J. Smith; pub. and distributed by authority of the Board of Trustees. '08, [1909.] (Mr) 316 p. il. 8°. (Add. pubs. for price.) State Hospital Insane.

Sommer, H. Oskar, ed.
Vulgate version of the Arthurian romances; ed. from mss. in the British Museum. In 2 v. v. 1, Lestoire del Saint Graal; v. 2, Lestoire de Merlin. '10(Ap2); v. 3, pt. 1, Le livre de Lancelot del Lac. '10(O8) Q. (Carnegie Institution pubs.) ea., pap., $5. Carnegie.

Sommer, Rev. Martin S., comp.
Prayers. 3d ed., rev. '10(D31) c. T. 25 c.; with gilt edges, 50 c. R. Volkening.

Son of Cain. Mackereth, J. A. $1.25 net. Longmans.

Son of Carolina. Stovall. G. O. $1.50. Neale.

Son of Mary Bethel. Barker, E. $1.50. Duffield.

Son of Siro. Copus, J: E. *$1.50 net. Benziger.

Son of the desert. Gilman, B. †$1.50. Century Co.

Son of the immortals. Tracy, L: $1.50. Clode.

Son of the north. Roberts, O. $1.50. C. M. Clark.

Son of the wind. Chamberlain, L. $1.50. Bobbs-M.

Song for the tercentenary of Lake Champlain. Scollard, C. 50 c. G: W: Browning.

Song of a stone wall. Keller, H. A. $1.20 net. Century Co.

Song of Demeter and Persephone. '09(D) $2. (400 copies.) Seymour.

Song of faith. Ochlschlaeger, C. J. $2. Cochrane.

Song of Hiawatha. *See* Longfellow, H: Wadsworth.

Song of sixpence picture book; containing Sing a song of sixpence, Princess Belle Etoile, An alphabet of old friends; with the original coloured designs by Walter Crane; including a preface and other embellishments. '09(N20) Q. $1.25. Lane.

Song of songs. Quayle, W: A. 35 c. net. Eaton & M.

Song of songs. Sudermann, H. *$1.40 net. B: W. Huebsch.

Song of the English. *See* Kipling, Rudyard.

Song of the Infinite. Crane, Fk. *50 c. net. Pilgrim Press.

Song of the Nibelungen. Wagner, W. R. $5 net; $15 net. Doubleday, P.

Song of the pines. Ray, E. S. $1.50. C. M. Clark.

Song of the Wahbeek. Bromwell, H: P. H. $1 $2. H. E. Bromwell.

Song of the wolf. Mayer, F. $1.50. Moffat.

Song-surf. Rice, C. Y. $1.25 net. Doubleday, P.

SONGS.
Aiken, W. H., *comp. and ed.* For high schools; part songs for mixed voices. 65 c. Am. Bk.
Banquet songs and ballads. 25 c. Reilly & B.
Bell, L. C., *and* James, R. B. Slumber Sea chanteys. $1. P. Elder.
Bell, R., *ed.* Songs of the great dramatists. $1.50. Estes.
Bentley, A. E. Song series: book one. 35 c.; book two, 40 c. Barnes.

SONGS.—*Continued.*

Birge, E: B. Choruses and part songs. 65 c. Am. Bk.

Book of Radcliffe, college songs. $1. Boston Music.

Brahms, J. [Songs:] collection of fifty songs with piano accompaniment. $2 net. Schirmer.

Bryant, L. Institute song book. 30 c. Barnes.

Burton, F: R. American primitive music; with especial attention to the songs of the Ojibways. **$5 net. Moffat.

Chapman, F: E., *and* Whiting, C: E., *comps. and eds.* Apollo song book for male voices. $1. Ginn.

Clough-Leighter, H: Youth and spring. *$1.25 net. Boston Music.

Earhart, W. Art songs for high schools. 80 c. Am. Bk.

Easter, A. M. Songs of sentiment and faith. $1.50 net. Eichelberger.

Ehrmann, M. B. Child's song garden. $1. —Child's song treasury. $2. W. H. Willis.

Favilli, M. Echoes of Naples; (thirty Neopolitan songs.) $1.25. Ditson.

Field, E., *and* Senour, C. S. Musical poems for school. $1. Scribner.

Gems of German songs. $1. Ditson.

Grieg, E. H. Fifty songs. $2.50; $1.50. Ditson.

Halsey, R. I. *and* H. A. One hundred new songs for primary schools. $1. Hinds.

Hamilton, W: W. Evangel; [song book.] *20 c. net; *15 c. net. Am. Bapt.

Hanson, J. M. Frontier ballads. $1. McClurg.

Hardenberg, F. L., *Freiherr* von. Devotional songs. $1. Open Court.

Heart songs; [collection of favorite songs voted on by 20,000 persons.] $2.50. Chapple Pub.

Hix, M., *comp.* Book of lullabies. 40 c. Educ. Pub.

Holmes, D. H: Under a fool's cap. $1. T: B. Mosher.

Howe, *Mrs.* J. W., *comp.* Original poems and other verse set to music as songs. $1.50; $5. Boston Music.

Hyatt, N. I. Twenty Father Goose melodies. 75 c. Ditson.

Jackson, V., *ed.* English melodies from the XIII to XVIII centuries; 100 songs. $3 net. Dutton.

Johnson, C., *ed.* Songs every one should know. 50 c. Am. Bk.

Jones, M. B. Songs of seasons. 25 c. Am. Bk.

Joyce, P. W., *ed.* Old Irish folk music and songs. *$3.50 net. Longmans.

Kaun, H., *comp.* Das deutsche lied. $1. Rohlfing.

Kingsley, H: R., *comp.* Patriotic and American songs. 10 c. H: R. Kingsley.

SONGS.—*Continued.*

Krehbiel, H: E:, *ed.* Songs from the operas for alto.—Songs from the operas for mezzo soprano.—Songs from the operas for soprano.—Songs from the operas for tenor. ea., $2.50; $1.50. Ditson.

Lent, E. M. Jolly ghost: pantomimed song. *$1 net. Werner.

Lomax, J: A., *comp.* Cowboy songs. $1.50 net. Sturgis & W.

McConnell, M. F. Standard songs and choruses for high schools. 75 c. Am. Bk.

McCullough, A. W., *and* Titus, I. M. Chimes of childhood. $1. Ditson.

McLaughlin, J. M., *and* Gilchrist, W: W. Song reader. 45 c. Ginn.

Marshall, L. B., *comp.* Halcyon songbook. 75 c. Silver.

Marzo, E. Coloratura album (for soprano). $1. Ditson.

Natural music course leaflets. nos. 559-566. ea., 2 c.-3 c. Am. Bk.

Ne Collins, J. E. Institute songs. 15 c. Am. Bk.

Nimmo, D: C. Songs: collection of church, home, nature, soul and miscellaneous songs. (Add. author for price.) D: C. Nimmo.

Riley, A. C. D., *and* Gaynor, J. L. Lilts and lyrics for the school room. $1. C. F. Summy Co.

Rix, F. R. Assembly song book. *50 c. net. Barnes.

Rix, F. R. Mastersinger; collection of choruses and part songs. 65 c. Am. Bk.

Rix, F. R. Song of school and flag. 75 c. net. Macmillan.

Shirley, J: B. Part songs for girls' voices. —Part songs for mixed voices. ea., 75 c. Am. Bk.

Songs of Oberlin. 75 c. C. A. Pickett.

Sonneck, O. G. T., *comp.* Rept. on "The star-spangled banner," "Hail Columbia," "America," "Yankee Doodle." (Add. Superintendent for price.) U. S., Supt. of Docs.

Speck, S: H:, *comp.* Song writers' guide. $1. J. H. Remick.

Steele, M., *and others.* Children's action songs. *35 c. net. Cassell.

Stone, C., *ed.* War songs. 90 c. Oxford Univ.

Tennyson, A. *Lord, and* Whelply, B: Songs from Tennyson's "Princess." *$1 net. Boston Music.

Terhune, A. Chinese child's day; words and music.—Colonial carols for children. —Dutch ditties for children. ea., $1.25 net. Schirmer.

Terry. H., *ed.* French songs and verse for children. 50 c. Longmans.

Tiersot, J., *comp.* Forty-four French folksongs and variants from Canada, Norway and Brittany. $2; $1. Schirmer.

University of Wisconsin. Germanistische Gesellschaft. Deutsches liederbuch. 75 c. Heath.

Withington, E., *comp.* Lullabies of many lands. 50 c. Caldwell.

Wolf, H. Fifty songs. $2.50; $1.50. Ditson.

SONGS.—*Continued.*
Zeiner, E: J. A., *comp.* High school song book. *85 c. net. Macmillan.
Zuchtmann, F. New American music reader; no. 3. *50 c. net. Macmillan.
See also Ballads;—Carols;—Church music;—Dartmouth College;—Games;—Hymns;—Kindergarten;—Music;—Singing;—*also* Ireland.

Songs and ballads. Basel, E. (Add. pubs. for price.) Nazareth Trade Sch.
Songs and sonnets. Colwell, E. *$2.50 net. F. F. Sherman.
Songs and tales. Nimmo, D: C. D: C. Nimmo.
Songs by the way. Mason, I. S. (Add. pubs. for price.) Herald Pub., (Md.)
Songs east and west. Smith, L. K. 50 c. L. K. Smith.
Songs from sky meadows. Crandall, C: H: *$1 net. Outing.
Songs from the garden of Kama. Hope, L., *pseud.* *$3 net. Lane.
Songs from the heart of things. *See* Naylor, J. B.
Songs from the sage brush. Pettey, K. F. $1.25. State Consol.
Songs from the silence. Hauenstein, M. F. $1.25. M. F. Hauenstein.
Songs from the wayside. Lowater, *Mrs.* N. M. $1. Sun Press.
Songs in the night. Durand, J. B. 50 c. S. H. Durand.
Songs of a cripple. Johnson, M. *$1 net. Grafton Press.
Songs of cheer. *See* Bangs, J: Kendrick.
Songs of Dartmouth College ser. Q. Grover & W.
—Grover *and* Wellman. Songs of Dartmouth College. *$1.20 net.
Songs of democracy. Russell, C: E: **$1.25 net. Moffat.
Songs of grief and gladness. Leavitt, E. (Add. pubs. for price.) Modern View.
Songs of home. Riley, J. W. $1.25; $2. Bobbs-M.
Songs of hope. Alden, L. C. $1. J. J. Metcalf.
Songs of innocence and of experience. '09 (D) $2. (300 copies.) Seymour.
Songs of life. Margetson, G: R. $1. Sherman, F.
Songs of many days. Pratt, F. E. $1. Badger.
Songs of Saint Bartholomew. Birchall, S. H. *$1 net. A. Bartlett.
Songs of sentiment; Christy gift book. '10 (N19) c. il. in col. D. $1.50 net, boxed. Moffat.
Songs of star and cloud. Burns, E: F. *$1.25 net. Ball Pub.
Songs of summer. Riley, J. W. $1.25; $2. Bobbs-M.
Songs of thankfulness and praise. '10(D) col. il. 50 c. net. Doran.
Songs of the Alps. Foster, L. N. $1.25. W. Y. Foote.
Songs of the army of the night. Adams, F. $1 net. M. Kennerley.
Songs of the beloved. Orthwein, E. H. $1.50. Dodge.
Songs o' the Olympics. Harriman, A. $1; $2; $2.50. A. Harriman.
Songs of the open. O'Hara, J: M. $1. Smith & S.
Songs of the people. O. Schirmer.
—Tiersot, *comp.* Forty-four French folksongs and variants from Canada, Norway and Brittany. $2; $1.
Songs of the times. Henney, W: F. $1. Cochrane.
Songs with silver linings. Foley, J. W: $2 net. Hoskins.

Sonneck, Oscar G: Thdr.
Music division of the Library of Congress; methods, policies and resources. '09(N) 30 p. 8°. (Add. author for price.) O. G: T. Sonneck.
—, **comp.** Library of Congress dramatic music, (Class M 1500, 1520:) catalogue of full scores. '08(Je20) Q. 40 c. U. S., Supt. of Docs.
Rept. on "The star-spangled banner," "Hail Columbia," "America," "Yankee Doodle." '09(D25) facsim., 4°. (Add. Superintendent for price.) U. S., Supt. of Docs.

SONNENSCHEIN, Edward Adolf.
Smith, M. L. S. Supplementary exercises on "Ora maritima," by E. A. Sonnenschein. 35 c. net. Macmillan.

Sonnenschein, W: Swann.
Best books; reader's guide to the choice of the best available books (about 100,000) in every department of science, art and literature, with the dates of the first and last editions, and the price, size, and publisher's name (both English and American) of each book; contribution toward systematic bibliography; with complete authors' and subjects index. 3d ed., (entirely rewritten.) In 3 pts. pt. 1. '10 (Je4) O. $3.50 net. Putnam.
Five thousand words frequently misspelt. '08(D19) 32°, (Miniature reference lib.) leath., 50 c. Dutton.

Sonnets. Huntington, A. M. (Not for sale.) De Vinne.
Sonnets. Shakespeare, W: $1 75. Oxford Univ.
Sonnets for choice. Aldrich, *Mrs.* M. C. $1 net. Moffat.
Sonnets from the Portuguese. *See* Browning, *Mrs.* Eliz. Barrett.
Sonnets of a chorus girl. Kiser, S: E. 50 c. Dodge.
Sonnets to a lover. Reed, M. $1.25. Putnam.

Sonnichsen, Albert.
Confessions of a Macedonian bandit. '09 (S4) 12°, $1.50. Duffield.

Sonny's father. Stuart, *Mrs.* R. M. $1 net. Century Co.
Sons of strength. Sclater, J. R. P. 35 c. net. Revell.
Sons of the Am. Revolution, Maine Society. Maine at Valley Forge; proceedings at the unveiling of the Maine marker, Oct. 17, 1907; also roll of Maine soldiers at Valley Forge. '08(N) 56 p. il. pors fold. map, 8°. (Not for sale.) S. A. R. Me. Soc.
Sons of the Puritans: a group of brief biographies. '08(N7) c. pors. D. *$1.50 net. Am. Unitarian.

Sooysmith, C:
See Soper, G: Albert.

Soper, G: Albert.
Air and ventilation of subways. '08(Ag1) c. diagrs., 12°, $2.50. Wiley.
Modern methods of street cleaning. '09 (Ag21) il. O. $3. Engineering News.
Pollution of New York harbor: paper read before the Boston Society of Civil Engineers. '08(O10) il. map, 8°, $2.50. G: A. Soper.

—, Sooysmith, C:, Parsons, Harry de Berkeley, Williams, Linsly R., and Fuertes, Ja. Hillhouse.
Sewerage and sewage disposal in the metropolitan district of New York and New Jersey. '10(Ag27) il. maps, 4°, gratis. N. Y. City.

Sophia Dorothea, *Electress of Hanover.*
Ward, A. W: Electress Sophia and the Hanoverian succession. *$2.75 net. Longmans.

Sophie May, pseud.
See Clarke, Rebecca Sophia.

Sophistries of Christian Science. Farnsworth, E: C. $1.25. Smith & S.

Sophocles.
Electra; with a commentary abridged from the larger ed. of Sir R: C. Jebb by Gilbert A. Davis. '09(Mr) 58+195 p. 16°, *$1.10 net. Putnam.
Sophocles; in English verse, by Arth. S. Way. '09(D25) 12°, *$1.10 net. Macmillan.
The trachiniæ; with a commentary abr. from the larger ed. of Sir R: C. Jebb, by Gilbert A. Davies. '08(D12) 8°, *$1 net. Putnam.
Tragedies; tr., with a biograph. essay, by E. H. Plumptre. '08(Ap4) 12°, (New universal lib.) 50 c.; leath., 75 c. Dutton.

Sophomore half-back. Hare, T: T. †$1.25. Penn Pub. Co.

So Relle, Rupert Pitt.
Expert shorthand speed course. '10(N5) c. il. pors. 12°, $1.25. Gregg Pub.
See also Cutler, Ida McLenan.

Sorenson, Grace.
Home made jingles. 2d ed. '08(Ag15) c. por. 12°, $1. Douglas Pr.

Sorghum.
Ball, C. R. Three much-misrepresented sorghums. U. S., Supt. of Docs.

"Sorin, Scota," pseud.
See Troop, *Mrs.* Edna Willa Sullivan.

Sorley, Lewis Stone.
Hist. of the Fourteenth U. S. Infantry, from Jan., 1890, to Dec., 1908. '09(Jl) 5-155 p. maps, 8°. (Priv. pr.) L. S. Sorley.

Sorley, W: Ritchie.
Interpretation of evolution; from the Proceedings of the British Academy. v. 4. '10(Mr26) O. pap., 60 c. Oxford Univ.

Sorolla y Bastida, Joaquin.
Hispanic Society of America. Catalogue of paintings by Joaquin Sorolla y Bastida. 25 c. Hispanic Soc.
Hispanic Society of America. Eight essays on Joaquin Sorrolla y Bastida, by Aureliano de Beruete [*and others*]. In 2 v. *$7.50 net. Hispanic Soc.

Sorority handbook. Martin, *Mrs.* I. S. $1.50. I. S. Martin.

Sorrow.
See Consolation.

Sorrowful princess. Booth, E. G-. $1. Longmans.

Sorrows of a show girl. McGaffey, K. $1.50. J. I. Austen.

Sothern, J. W.
Marine steam turbine; pract. description of the Parsons Marine Turbine as now constructed, fitted and run. 3d ed., rewritten and enl. '09, [1910.] (F) 352 p. il. 8°, *$5 net. Van Nostrand.
Verbal notes and sketches for marine engineers. 5th ed., rev. and enl. '08(Mr7) il. 8°. *$2.60 net. Macmillan.

Sotter, F: Alex.
Breeding for squabs. '08(F) c. 75 p. il. S. pap., 50 c. Douglassville.

Soudan, Africa.
Baedeker, K. Egypt and the Sudan. *$4.50 net. Scribner.
Comyn, D: C: E: ff. Service and sport in the Sudan. $4 net. Lane.
Tangye, H. L. In the torrid Sudan. $3 net. Badger.

Soul.
Alexander, J. B. Soul and its bearing. *$1 net. J. B. Alexander.
Awakening of the soul. *40 c. net. Dutton.
Clements, J. Metaphysics of the nature and in the conception of the soul. $1. Roxburgh.
Dorée, N. Is your soul progressing? $1. Am. News.
Erwood, W: J. Essentials of psychic development. 50 c. W: J. Erwood.
King, H: C. Seeming unreality of spiritual life. **$1.50 net. Macmillan.
Larisun, C. W. The sol: hwens?—hwither? $1.50. Fonic.
Matter and some of its dimensions. *$1 net. Woodward & L.
Reed, J., *and* Hay, H: C. Eessntial needs of the soul. 75 c. Badger.
Wilson, F. B. Discovery of the soul: out of mysticism, light and progress. $1. Fenno.
See also Future life;—Immortality;—Metaphysics;—Philosophy;—Psychicaal research;—Psychology;—Psychotherapy.

Soul and body. Hall, F. O. *$1 net. Universalist.

Soul and circumstance. Stanton, S. B. $1 net. Scribner.

Soul growth of Abraham Lincoln. McElroy, J: 10 c. J: McElroy.

Soul of a mummy. Schleppey, *Mrs.* B. B. $1.50. B. B. Schleppey.

Soul of a priest. Litta, D. †$1.50. Doubleday, P.

Soul of a serf. Ellis, J: B. $1.50. Laird.

Soul of a Turk. De Bunsen, V. *$3.50 net. Lane.

Soul of Crœsus. Stuart, G. V-. 75 c. Cupples & L.

Soul of man under socialism. Wilde, O. 60 c. net. J: W. Luce.

Soul of Spain. Ellis, H: H. *$2 net. Houghton M.

Soul of the singer. Du Bois, H. G. $1. Badger.

Soul of the world. Brokaw, *Mrs.* E. B. $1. Equitist.

Soul powers. Rogers, L. W. 10 c. Theosophical Bk.

Soul shadows. Beede, C: G. 75 c. C: G. Beede.

Soule, And. MacNairn.
Feeding of cotton seed meal and hulls. '08, [1909.] (My) 52 p. il. 8°. (Add. pubs. for price.) B. F. Taylor.

—, **and Turpin, Edna Henry Lee.**
Agriculture, its fundamental principles. '08 (F29) c. il. D. 75 c. B. F. Johnson.

Soul's inheritance. Lodge, G: C. **$1 net. Houghton M.

Souls of fire. Roose, T: W. $1. T: W. Roose.

Soulsby, Lucy H. M.
Suggestions on Bible reading.—Suggestions on prayer. '09(Ja9) T. prices reduced from 50 c. to 35 c. Longmans.
"The woman's kingdom." '10(S) 20 p. Tt. pap., 5 c. net. Longmans.
—, comp. Record of a year's reading. '10 (F19) S. 30 c. Longmans.
Week by week; ms. book of private prayer. New ed. '10(F19) S. 30 c. Longmans.
Year's Bible readings. '09(Ja9) T. 35 c. Longmans.

SOUND.
Barton, E. H: Text book on sound. *$3 net. Macmillan.
Battell, J. New physics; sound. $1.25. Am. Pub. Co., (Vt.)
Franklin, W: S., *and* McNutt, B. Light and sound. **$1.60 net. Macmillan.
Lamb, H. Dynamical theory of sound. *$3.50 net. Longmans.
Millikan, R. A., *and* Mills, J: Short university course in electricity, sound and light. $2. Ginn.

Sounds of English. Sweet, H: 60 c. Oxford Univ.

SOUPS.
Douglas, E. Soup and sauce book. 50 c. McKay.

Sour dough's Bible. Fair, A. T. 50 c. Trustee.

"Sour grapes." Ott, E: A. $1. Lyceumite.

Sour sonnets of a sorehead and other songs of the street. Haverson, J. P. 50 c. Caldwell.

Source book for social origins. Thomas, W: I: *$4.50 net. Univ. of Chic.

Source book in ancient philosophy. Bakewell, C: M. **$1 net Scribner.

Source book of mediæval history. Ogg, F. A., *ed.* $1.50. Am. Bk.

Source history of the United States. Caldwell, H. W. *$1.25 net. Ainsworth.

Source of "Jerusalem the golden." Bernard *of Cluny.* $1.25 net. Univ. of Chic.

Source studies on the French Revolution. Fling, F. M., *ed.* 50 c. F. M. Fling.

Sources and modes of infection. Chapin, C: V. $3 net. Wiley.

Soured milk and pure cultures of lactic acid bacilli in the treatment of disease. Herschell, G: A. *50 c. net. Chic. Med. Bk.

Sousa, J: Philip.
Through the year with Sousa; excerpts from operas, marches, miscellaneous compositions, novels, letters, magazine articles, songs, sayings, and rhymes. '10 (S24) c. por. D. $1 net. Crowell.

Souter, W: Norwood.
Refractive and motor mechanism of the eye. '10(D) il. 8°, $2. Keystone Pub.

South, R:
Moths of the British Isles: first series. '08 (Ap18); second ser. '09(Mr27) il. 16°, (Wayside and woodland ser.) ea., *$3 net. Warne.

South; results, [of 28 years,] resources, [for future work;] achievements the guaranty of future advance. '08(D19) O. pap., 25 c. Manufacturers' Record.

SOUTH (The).
Alderman, E. A. Growing South. 10 c. Civic Forum.
American Academy of Political and Social Science. The new South. $1. Am. Acad. Pol. Sci.
Archer, W: Through Afro-America. $3 net. Dutton.
Baird, H: C. The South: shall it ever become so far civilized as to be fit for a Republican form of government. gratis. Baird.
Blandin, *Mrs.* I. M. E. J. History of higher education of women in the South prior to 1860. *$3 net. Neale.
De Saussure, *Mrs.* N. B. Old plantation days; southern life before the Civil War. $1. Duffield.
Douglass, H. P. Christian reconstruction in the South. *$1.50 net. Pilgrim Press.
Gray, W: F. From Virginia to Texas. (Not for sale.) A. C. Gray.
Griggs, S. E. Needs of the South. 10 c. Orion Pub.
Harney, W: W. Spirit of the South. $1.50. Badger.
Hart, A. B. Southern South. $1.50 net. Appleton.
Hunter, A. Huntsman in the South. v. 1. *$1.50 net. Neale.
Jenkins, F. E., *and others.* Anglo-Saxon Congregationalism in the South. (Add. pubs. for price.) Franklin-T.
Johnson, J. G. Southern fiction prior to 1860. $2. Michie.
Kirbye, J. E: Puritanism in the South. 75 c. Pilgrim Press.
McBee, S. South and Mr. Taft. 50 c. Univ. Press, (Sewanee.)
MacCorkle, W: A. An address: [patriotism in the South.] (Add. pubs. for price.)—Some southern questions. **$1.75 net. Putnam.
Moses, M. J. Literature of the South. $2.50 net. Crowell.
Murphy, E. G. Basis of ascendancy: discussion of certain principles of public policy involved in the development of the southern states.—Problems of the present South. ea., **$1.50 net. Longmans.
Phillips, U. B. History of transportation in the eastern cotton belt to 1860. *$2.75 net. Macmillan.

SOUTH (The).—*Continued.*

Scogin, *Mrs.* S. M. C., *and* Howe, J: D. Down on the old plantation. 25 c. J: D. Howe.

Shurter, E. D., *ed.* Oratory of the South from the Civil War to the present time. *$1.25 net. Neale.

Smith, C: A. Educational statesmanship in the South. gratis. C: A. Smith.

South in the building of the nation. 12 v. $90. Southern Hist. Pub.

Stewart, W: H: Spirit of the South: orations, essays, and lectures. $2. Neale.

Thomas, W: H. New South. gratis. W: H. Thomas.

Thompson, S: H. Highlanders of the South. 50 c. net. Eaton & M.

See also American literature;—Civil War;—Education;—Negroes;—Orators and oratory;—Pronunciation;—Sante Fé Trail;—*also* names of Southern cities and states.

SOUTH AFRICA.

Brand, R. H: Union of South Africa. $2. Oxford Univ.

Bushman paintings copied [in color] by M. Helen Tongue. $19.25. Oxford Univ.

Campbell, R. G. Neutral rights and obligations in the Anglo-Boer war. 75 c. Johns Hopkins.

Colvin, I. D. South Africa. *$2 net. Stokes.

Cory, G: E: Rise of South Africa. $5. Longmans.

Frenssen, G. Peter Moor's journey to southwest Africa: narrative of the German campaign: [fiction.] †$1.25. Houghton M.

Fuller, R. H. South Africa at home. *$1.75 net. Scribner.

Godée-Molsbergen, E. C., *comp.* Hist. of South Africa. 90 c. net. Longmans.

Harmsworth, C. B. Pleasure and problem in South Africa. *$1.50 net. Lane.

Honey, J. A. South African folk-tales. $1 net. Baker & T.

Johnson, J. P. Ore deposits of South Africa. $2. Henley.

Johnson, J. P. Stone implements of South Africa. $3.25. Longmans.

Kidd, D. South Africa. *75 c. net. Macmillan.

White, R. J., *and* Smith, A. Little journey to South Africa. 50 c. Flanagan.

Wilson, *Lady* S. I. A. C. South African memories. *$4.20 net. Longmans.

See also Basutoland;—Cape Colony;—Kafirs;—Rhodesia.

South African natives: their progress and present condition; ed. by the South African Native Race Committee of Great Britain. '09(Mr13) 8°, *$2 net. Dutton.

South African science ser. il. D. Longmans.
—Rogers *and* Du Toit. Introd. to the geology of Cape Colony. *$3.50 net.

SOUTH AMERICA.

Brady, C. T. South American fights and fighters. $1.50. Doubleday, P.

Crichfield, G: W. American supremacy: rise and progress of the Latin American republics. 2 v. **$6 net. Brentano's.

Domville-Fife, C: W. Great states of South America. $4.50 net. Macmillan.

SOUTH AMERICA.—*Continued.*

Lowe, F. J. Around Africa and across the Andes. 50 c. F. J. Lowe.

Neely, T: B: South America: its missionary problems. 50 c.; 35 c. Young People's Miss.

Osborn, C. S. Andean land (South America). *$5 net. McClurg.

Polk, J. M. Confederate soldier; and Ten years in South America. 35 c. Von Boeckmann-J.

Ruhl, A. B. Other Americans: cities, countries, and people of South America. **$2 net. Scribner.

Spruce, R: Notes of a botanist on the Amazon and Andes. 2 v. $6.50. Macmillan.

United States. *Dept. of Commerce and Labor. Bureau of Statistics.* Commercial America, showing commerce, productions, etc., of North, South, and Central America, and West Indies. (Add. Superintendent for price.)

Waterton, C: Wanderings in South America, the northwest of the United States and the Antilles, in the years 1812, 1816, 1820 and 1824. $1.50. Macmillan.

Waterton, C: Wanderings in South America, the north-west of the U. S. and the Antilles in the years 1812, 1816, 1820 and 1824. *$2.50 net. Sturgis & W.

See also Amazon river;—Argentine Republic;—Bolivia;—Brazil;—British Guiana;—Chile;—Colombia;—Ecuador;—Indians;—Koati Island;—Magdalena river;—Mammalia;—Newspapers;—Orinoco river;—Paraguay;—Peru;—Spanish America;—Spanish colonies;—Spanish Main;—Titicaca Island;—Uruguay;—Venezuela;—*also* Bolivar, S.

South American ser.; ed. by Martin Hume. il. 8°. Scribner.
—Enock. Mexico. $3.
—Hirst. Argentina. $3 net.

South Carolina. *General Assembly,* 1776. Journal of the General Assembly of South Carolina, Sept. 17, 1776-Oct. 20, 1776; ed. by A. S. Salley, jr., secretary of the Historical Commission of South Carolina. '09, [1910.] (Mr) 174 p. 8°, $2. S. C. Hist.

South Carolina. State Board of Education. South Carolina list of library books, adopted Apr. 23, 1909, to continue till Je. 30, 1914. '09(D) 32 p. il. 8°, gratis. R. L. Bryan.

South Carolina. *Supreme ct.* Repts. v. 76-77; (C. M. Efird.) '08(My); v. 78, 79 (N); v. 80, 81. '09(Ap) ea., $5.75; v. 82-84. '10(S) c. O. ea., shp., $2. R. L. Bryan.

South Carolina. Trucking industry in South Carolina; repr. of extract from Annual report for 1906 of E. J. Watson, Commissioner, to the General Assembly. '07. [1908.] (Mr.) 8 p. il. 8°. gratis. State Co.

SOUTH CAROLINA.

Brooks, U. R. South Carolina bench and bar. *$1.50 net. State Co.

Crane, E. A., *and* Soderholtz, E. E. Examples of colonial architecture in South Carolina and Georgia. $16. Hessling.

Elzas, B. A. Leaves from my historical scrap book. (Hist. of S. C. with especial ref. to Jewish affairs.) $1. B. A. Elzas.

SOUTH CAROLINA.—*Continued.*
Hemphill, J. C., *ed.* Men of mark in South Carolina. v. 1. $10. Men of Mark.
McKelway, A. J. Child labor in the Carolinas. gratis. Nat. Child Labor.
Middleton, G. M. Sketches of South Carolina. 25 c. G. M. Middleton.
Salley, A. S:, *jr., ed.* Documents relating to the history of South Carolina during the Revolutionary War. $2. S. C. Hist.
Wauchope, G: A., *comp.* Writers of South Carolina. $2. State Co.
See also Charleston;—*also* Chamberlain, Daniel Henry.

South Dakota. *Supreme ct.* Repts.: (H: R. Horner.) v. 20. '08(Ag) c. O. shp., $3. Hipple.

SOUTH DAKOTA.
Cram, G: F. Superior reference atlas of North and South Dakota. (Add. pubs. for price.) G: F. Cram.
Darton, N. H. Geology and underground waters of South Dakota. Gov. Pr. Off.
Hare, W: H. Glimpses into the life of the Indian schools in South Dakota. (Add. author for price.) W. H. Hare.
Lea, S: H. Irrigation in South Dakota. U. S., Supt. of Docs.
McCoy, J. H. South Dakota digest. $10. News Print.
Robinson, J. L. D. Hist. of South Dakota. 75 c. Educator.
Ross, J: A. South Dakota civil government. 75 c. Educator.

SOUTH DEVON, Eng.
Heath, S. H. South Devon and Dorset coast. $2.25 net. Stokes.

SOUTH HADLEY, Mass.
See **Mount Holyoke College.**

South in the building of the nation: history of the southern states designed to record the South's part in the making of the American nation. 12 v. '09(Mr27) c. il. pors. map, facsim., 8°, subs., full mor., $90. Southern Hist. Pub.

SOUTH SEA ISLANDS.
See Borneo;—Oceanica;—Philippine Islands.

South seas. Abbott, J. H. M. *75 c. net. Macmillan.

SOUTH SIDE LIBRARY, Milwaukee, Wis.
Nuesse, G: C. Founding the South Side Library. 50 c. Enterprise Pr.

Southall, Ja. Powell Cocke.
Principles and methods of geometrical optics, especially as applied to the theory of optical instruments. '10(O8) c. il. 8°, $5.50 net. Macmillan.

SOUTHAMPTON, Eng.
Clarke, F., *ed.* Short hist. of Southampton. In 2 pts. 70 c. Oxford Univ.

Southeastern reporter, v. 58. Permanent ed. '08(Ja4); v. 59 (Ap); v. 60 (Je); v. 61 (N); v. 62. '09(Mr); v. 63 (Je); v. 64 (N); v. 65. '10(F); v. 66 (Je); v. 67 (Ag); v. 68 (O) c. O. (National reporter system, state ser.) ea., $4. West Pub.

Southern agriculture. Earle, F. S. **$1.25 net. Macmillan.

Southern authors in poetry and prose. Orgain, K A. *$2 net. Neale.

Southern fiction prior to 1860. Johnson, J. G. $2. Michie.

Southern Germany. Baedeker, K. $1.80 net. Scribner.

Southern Methodist handbook, 1909; ed. by T: N. Ivey. '09(Ap3); 1910. '10(Mr26) il. por. D. pap., ea., 25 c. Pub. Ho. of M. E. Ch., So.

Southern oratory. McConnell, J. M., *ed.* 25 c. Macmillan.

SOUTHERN POETRY.
See **Poetry.**

Southern poultry guide. Husselman, C. $1. Southern Planter.

Southern prose and poetry for schools. Morris, E. 80 c. Scribner.

Southern R. Read, W: A. La. State Univ.

Southern reporter, v. 44. Permanent ed. '08 (F); v. 45 (Je); v. 46 (O); v. 47. '09 (Ap); v. 48, 49 (N); v. 50. '10(Ap); v. 51 (Jl) c. O. (National reporter system, state ser.) ea., $4. West Pub.

Southern Schools of Railway Science. Pract. studies adopted by the Southern Schools of Railway Science as a standard text book; general course. 6 v., '10(N19) c. il. 12°, $24. Southern Sch. R'way Sci.

Southern South. Hart, A. B. $1.50. Appleton.

Southern Spain. Calvert, A. F: *$6 net. Macmillan.

Southerner (The). Worth, N:, *pseud.* **$1.20, fixed. Doubleday, P.

Southerner in Europe. Poe, C. H. 75 c. Mutual Pub. Co.

Southey, Rob.
Poems; cont. Thalaba, The curse of Kehama, Roderick, Madoc, A tale of Paraguay, and selected minor poems; ed. by Maurice H. FitzGerald. '10(Ap2) por. D. 75 c.; (Oxford poets) $1.25; Oxford India pap., $1.75. Oxford Univ.

Southwark. *See* Philadelphia.

SOUTHWEST (The).
See **West.**

Southwestern reporter, v. 105. Permanent ed. '08(F); v. 106-107 (My); v. 108, 109 (Ag); v. 110 (S); v. 111 (O); v. 112 (D); v. 113, 114. '09(Mr); v. 115 (Je); v. 116 (Jl); v. 117, 118 (S); v. 119, 120 (N); v. 121. '09, [1910.] (F); v. 122 (Mr); v. 123 (Ap); v. 124, 125 (Je); v. 126 (Jl); v. 127 (Ag); v. 128 (S); v. 129 (N) c. O. (National reporter system, state ser.) ea., $4.—Digest of vs. 90-106; 106-120. '10 (D) c. O. (National reporter system, digests, southwestern ser.) ea., $6. West Pub.

SOUTHWESTERN STATE NORMAL SCHOOL, California, Pa.
Ehrenfeld, C: L. Brief story of the founding of the Southwestern State Normal School at California, Pa. 75 c. New Era Print.

Southwick, Mrs. Jessie Eldridge.
Expressive voice culture. '08(S) c. 41 p. por. 12°, 60 c. J. E. Southwick.

Southworth, Gordon A:, and Stone, J: C:
Arithmetic. In 3 bks. '08(S5) c. il. 12°, Bk. 1, 42 c.; Bk. 2, 45 c.; Bk. 3, 50 c. B: H. Sanborn.

Southworth, May E., comp.
One hundred and one entrees. '08(D12) c. nar. 8°, (101 epicurean thrills ser.) **$1 net; pap., **50 c. net; flex. cf., **$2 net. P. Elder.
One hundred and one layer cakes. '08 (D12) c. nar. 8°, (101 epicurean thrills ser.) **$1 net; pap., **50 c. net; flex. cf., **$2 net. P. Elder.
Souvenir of the visit of the American fleet to Australia and New Zealand. '09(Ja23) obl. D. pap., 25 c. Am. News.
Souvenirs d'Algérie et nouveaux pastels. Rivot, C. G. *$1 net. Neale.
Sovereign good. Huntington, H. †$1.50. Putnam.
Sovereign in the street. Josaphare, L. *50 c. net. A. M. Robertson.
Sovereignty of the states. Neale, W. $1 net. Neale.
SOWAMS.
See Rhode Island.
Sower, J: W:
Compendium of facts, figures and formulas, for the home, the office, the farm, the shop. '09(D) c. 80 p. 8°, $1. J. W. Sower.
Sowerby, Githa.
Happy book; [verses.] '10(D31) 16°, 40 c. net. Doran.
Sowerby, Millicent and Githa.
Bumbletoes: fairy tale in verse. '08(O17) il. †75 c. Duffield.
Childhood. '08(O17) il. in new binding, $1.50. Duffield.
Yesterday's children: [verse.] '09(D) 47 p. col. il. 4°, bds., $1.50. Duffield.
See also Sowerby, Githa.
Sowing (The). Hough, E. $1.25. Vanderhoof-G.
Sowing of swords.. Meriwether, *Mrs.* E. A., *ed.* $1.50. Neale.
Sowing seeds in Danny. McClung, *Mrs.* N. L. M. †$1. Doubleday, P.
Spaeth, L: A., M.D.
Coming motherhood: pract. suggestions rel. to maternity and the care of infants and children. '08(My9) c. 16°, *$1 net. P: Reilly.
SPAIN.
Andújar, M. Spain of to-day from within. *$1.25 net. Revell.
Baedeker, K. Spain and Portugal. *$4.80 net. Scribner.
Becquer, G. A. D. Romantic legends of Spain. **$1.50 net. Crowell.
Bensusan, S: L. Home life in Spain. $1.75 net. Macmillan.
Browne, E. A. Spain. 75 c. net. Macmillan.
Calvert, A. F: Royal palaces of Spain. *$1.50 net.—Valladolid, Oviedo, Segovia, Zamora, Avila, and Zaragoza. *$1.25 net. Lane.
Calvert, A. F: Southern Spain. *$6 net. Macmillan.
Chadwick, F. E. Relations of the United States and Spain. **$4 net. Scribner.
Challice, R. Secret hist. of the court of Spain. *$4 special net. Appleton.
Collins, W. W. Cathedral cities of Spain. **$3.50 net. Dodd.

SPAIN.—*Continued.*
Elliott, F. B. Old court life in Spain. $1.50 net. Brentano's.
Ellis, H: H. Soul of Spain. *$2 net. Houghton M.
FitzGerald, J: D., *2d.* Rambles in Spain. $3 net. Crowell.
Froissart, *Sir* J: Chronicles of England, France and Spain. $2.50. Dutton.
Hartley, C. G. Things seen in Spain. 75 c. Dutton.
Howe, M. Sun and shadow in Spain. **$3 net. Little, B. & Co.
Irving, W. Conquest of Granada. 35 c. net; 70 c. net. Dutton.
Lomas, J: In Spain. *$2 net. Macmillan.
Luffmann, C. B. Quiet days in Spain. $2 net. Dutton.
Marden, P. S. Travels in Spain. **$3 net. Houghton M.
Marriott, C: Spanish holiday. *$2.50 net. Lane.
Nixon-Roulet, *Mrs.* M. F. Spaniard at home. $1.75 net. McClurg.
O'Reilly, E. B. Heroic Spain. $2.50 net. Duffield.
Penfield, F. C. Motor that went to court; fact story, with random illustrations. (Priv. pr.) F. C. Penfield.
Perkins, C. C. Builders of Spain. 2 v. $5. Holt.
Pomeroy, S. G. Christmas in Spain. 50 c. Estes.
Prentice, A. N. Spanish renaissance. $22.50. Polley.
Shaw, J. T. Spain of to-day. **$1.25 net. Grafton Press.
Shaw, R. Spain from within. $2.50 net. Stokes.
Shepherd, W: R. Guide to the materials for the history of U. S. in Spanish archives. 50 c. Carnegie.
Spanish colonial architecture. $30. Polley.
Tyler, R. Spain: study of her life and arts. *$3.50 net. M. Kennerley.
Villiers-Wardell, *Mrs.* J. Spain of the Spanish. *$1.50 net. Scribner.
Williams, L. Arts and crafts of older Spain. 3 v. *$4.50 net. McClurg.
See also Balearic Islands;—Burgos;—Catalina;—Galicia; — Granada; — Inquisition; — Leon;—Madrid;—Napoleonic wars;—Painters and paintings;—Peninsular war;—Salamanca; — Spanish dependencies;—Spanish-American war; — Theatre;—*also* Maria Christina, *Queen;*—Philip II.;—Servetus, Michael.
Spalding, F: Putnam.
Text-book on roads and pavements. 3d ed. '08(N7) figs. 12°, $2. Wiley.
Spalding, Rev. H: Stanislaus.
Marks of the bear claws. '08(Je6) c. D. 85 c. Benziger.
Old mill on the Withrose. '10(D3) c. il. D. 85 c. Benziger.
Spalding, J. Howard.
Spiritual world; as described in the writings of Emanuel Swedenborg. '09(O9) S. pap., *40 c. net; *60 c. net. Warne.
Spalding, Ja. Alfred, M.D.
Jeremiah Barker, M.D., Gorham and Falmouth, Maine, 1752-1835. '09(D) 24 p. 8°, pap. (Add. author for price.) J. A. Spalding.

Spalding, Volney Morgan.
Distribution and movements of desert plants. '09(N13) il. fold. map, Q. (Carnegie Inst. of Washington pubs.) pap., $2. Carnegie.

Spalding's athletic lib. il. pors. 16°, pap., 10 c. Am. Sports.
—Amateur Athletic Union of the United States. Official hdbk.
—Berenson. Spalding's official women's basket ball guide.
—Bojus. Dumb bell exercises.
—Borden. Physical training for the school and class room.
—Burchell, *ed.* Spalding's roller skating guide.
—Camp, *ed.* Spalding's how to play foot ball.—Spalding's official football guide, 1908; 1909.
—Canoes and canoeing.
—Chadwick, *ed.* Spalding's official base ball guide, 1908.—Spalding's official base ball record, 1908.
—Cromie. Parallel bar exercises.—Pyramid building.
—Deshong. Quoits.
—Duffey. How to sprint.
—Farrell. How to play ice hockey.
—FitzPatrick. Equestrian polo.
—Foster, *ed.* Spalding's official base ball guide.—Spalding's official base ball record, 1909.
—Games of drawing room hockey, [etc.]
—Greig. Game of bowling on the green.
—Gwathmey. Tumbling for amateurs.
—Handley. How to play water polo.
—Hitchcock *and* Nelligan. Wrestling.
—Inter-collegiate Association of Amateur Athletes of America. Constitution, by-laws and laws of athletics.
—Inter-collegiate Association of Amateur Gymnasts of America. Constitution, by-laws and records of the Association, 1899-1910.
—Inter-Scholastic Athletic Association of the Middle Atlantic States. Official hdbk., [1910.] gratis.
—Jacobus, *ed.* Croquet and its rules.
—Jiu-jitsu.
—Maxson, *comp.* Official archery guide.
—Mitchell. Weight throwing.
—Morton. How to run 100 yards.
—Murnane. How to play baseball.
—National Amateur Playground Ball Association of the United States. Official handbook. 10 c. Am. Sports.
—"Old International," *pseud.* How to play Rugby.
—Orton, *ed.* Athletic training for school boys.
—Paret. How to play lawn tennis.
—Public Schools Athletic League. Official hdbk. for the public schools.
—Roque guide.
—Short, *jr.* Digest of the foot ball rules for 1910 for officials and players.
—Smith. Professional wrestling. 10 c.
—Spalding's official athletic almanac, 1910.—Official lawn tennis annual, 1909.—Official Rugby foot-ball guide.

Spalding's athletic lib.—Continued.
—Sullivan, *comp.* Athletes' guide.—How to catch.—Marathon running.—Schoolyard athletics.—Spalding's official athletic almanac, 1909.
—Toombs. How to wrestle.
—United States Inter-Collegiate Lacrosse League. Constitution, by-laws and playing rules, 1909; 1910.
—Vaile. Strokes and science of lawn tennis.
—Walking for health.
—Warman. Health influenced by underwear. —Indian club exercises.—Twenty-minute exercises.
—White *and* Clark. All-around athletics.
—Worth. Ground tumbling.
—Wray, *ed.* How to play shortstop.—How to play first base.—How to play third base.

Spalding's official athletic almanac for 1908; comp. by Ja. E. Sullivan. '08(F15); 1910. '10(Ja29) c. il. por. S. (Spalding's athletic lib.) pap., ea., 10 c. Am. Sports.

Spalding's official foot ball guide, 1908; 1909. Camp, W. C., *ed.* ea., 10 c. Am. Sports.

Spalding's official lawn tennis annual, 1909; ed. by H. P. Burchell. '09(My15) c. il. S. (Spalding's athletic lib.) pap., 10 c. Am. Sports.

Spalding's official metropolitan base ball book and official inter-city base ball association guide. '09(Je19) c. il. pors. 16°, pap., 10 c. Spalding.

Spangenberg, Mrs. Fanny Ilgenfutz.
Forest land of Penn: [poems.] '09(S) c. 154 p. 12°, $1.50. Badger.

Spangler, H: Wilson.
Applied thermodynamics. '10(O15) c. il. O. $2.50. McVey.
Graphics. '10(O8) c. il. O. $1.50. McVey.
Notes on thermodynamics. 4th ed., rev. '08(O3) c. 12°, $1. Wiley.

—, Greene, Arth. Maurice, jr., and Marshall, Stewart McCulloch.
Elements of steam engineering. 3d ed., rev. and enl. '10(D3) c. figs. 8°, $3. Wiley.

Spangler, Martha.
See Aye, Olive.

Spanhoofd, Arnold Werner-.
See Werner-Spanhoofd, Arnold.

Spaninger, A: Abud.
Special sundries. '08(D) c. 78 p. 12°, 30 c. Morton.

SPANISH-AMERICA.
Barrett, J: Latin America, the land of opportunity. gratis.—United States and Latin America. gratis. Int. Bu. Am. Republics.
Fisher, H. N. Ethnography and commercial importance of Latin America and the West Indies in 1906. (Add. Superintendent for price.) U. S., Supt. of Docs.
Hale, A. B. Pract. guide to Latin America. **$1 net. Small.
International Bureau of the American Republics, Washington, D. C. List of Latin American hist. and description in the Columbus Memorial Library. gratis.—List of publications published or distributed by the International Bureau of American Republics. gratis. Int. Bu. Am. Republics.
See also Coal.

SPANISH-AMERICAN WAR.
Benton, E. J. International law and diplomacy of the Spanish-American war. $1.50. Johns Hopkins.
Grattan, F. W: With those that were: stories of two wars. $1.50. B'way Pub.
Parker, J. Rear-Admirals Schley, Sampson and Cervera. **$3 net. Neale.
Webber, H. E. Twelve months with the 8th Massachusetts Infantry. $2. H. E. Webber.

SPANISH ART.
See Painters and paintings.

Spanish colonial architecture: interiors and furniture, during the 17th, 18th and 19th centuries; ed. by W: Ralph Emerson. '08 (Ag8) il. por. F. $30. Polley.

SPANISH COLONIES.
Moses, B. South America on the eve of emancipation: southern Spanish colonies in the last half century. **$1.50 net. Putnam.
See also Cuba;—Mexico.

SPANISH DEPENDENCIES.
Lea, H: C: Inquisition in the Spanish dependencies. **$2.50 net. Macmillan.

Spanish documents; mss. in the British Museum; published in facsimile by Archer M. Huntington. '03, [1909.] (N) $30. (200 copies.) Hispanic Soc.

Spanish gipsie. Middleton, T: 60 c. Heath.

Spanish holiday. Marriott, C: *$2.50 net. Lane.

Spanish jade. Hewlett, M. H: **90 c. net. Doubleday, P.

Spanish journal. *See* Holland, Eliz. Vassall, *Lady.*

SPANISH LANGUAGE.
Arrom de Ayala, C. F. J. B. von F. y L. Un serviton y un liberalito ō tres almas de dios. 50 c. Heath.
Becquer, G. A. D. Legends, tales and poems. $1. Ginn.
Blasco Ibáñez, V. La barraca, novela. 90 c. Holt.
Braubach, A. L. Taquigrafia fonetica, Sloan-Duployan. $1.50. A. L. Braubach.
Brigham, F. H. Conjugation of Spanish verbs, complete. 60 c. F. H. Brigham.
Carrión, M. R., *and others.* Tres comedias modernas et un acto y en prosa. 60 c. Holt.
Cervantes Saavedra, M. de. Selections from Don Quixote. 80 c. Heath.
Chaytor, H. J. First Spanish book. 80 c. Longmans.
Cid, P. American in Spain; pocket interpreter and guide to Spain and its language. 50 c. McKay.
Course in Spanish prepared by the Department of Languages, for use in the Army Service Schools. '10(Je) c. 8+498 p. 8°. (Not for sale.) Army Service.
Crawford, J. P. W. Spanish composition. 75 c. Holt.
Cuentos modernos. 60 c. Am. Bk.
Dowling, M. C. Easy Spanish for beginners. 40 c. G: Dowling.

SPANISH LANGUAGE.—*Continued.*
Fernandez, J. M., *comp.* Lecturas escogidas, colleción de obras de autores eminentes. 90 c. Silver.
Giese, W: F., *and* Cook, C: D., *comps.* Spanish anecdotes. 60 c. Heath.
Gutierrez, A. G. El. trovador. 40 c. Heath.
Halse, E: Dict. of Spanish and Spanish-American mining, metallurgical and allied terms. *$3.50 net. Lippincott.
Hewlett, G. Sea terms and phrases; [English - Spanish; Spanish - English.] *$1.25 net. Lippincott.
Hill, R. G. English-Spanish manual. $1. Hudson.
Hills, E. C., *ed.* Spanish tales for beginners. $1.10. Holt.
Hills, E. C., *and* Reinhardt, L., *eds.* Spanish short stories. $1. Heath.
Huelin y Arssu, C. Technological dict. $4. Spon.
Monteverde, R. D. Commercial and technical terms in the English and Spanish languages. *70 c. net.—Spanish idioms with their English equivalents. 80 c. Macmillan.
Palacio Valdés, A. José. 90 c. Heath.
Pereda, J. M. de. Pedro Sánchez. $1. Ginn.
Pitman, *Sir* I: Key to Spanish shorthand. $1. Pitman.
Rees, J. D. Pictorial Spanish course. *65 c. net. Little, B. & Co.
Remy, A., *comp. and ed.* Spanish composition. 60 c. Heath.
Schilling, J. Don Bacilio: pract. guide to Spanish conversation and correspondence. *$1 net. Holt.
Seide, J. N. Easy arrangement of the Spanish verb. $2. J. N. Seide.
Selgas y Carrasco, J. La mariposa blanca. 60 c. Holt.
Tamayo y Baus, *Don* M. Lo positivo. 45 c. Heath.
Tornos, A. de. Combined Spanish method. $1.50. Appleton.
Turrell, C: A. Spanish reader. 80 c. Am. Bk.
Umphrey, G: W. Spanish prose composition. 75 c. Am. Bk.
Valera, J. Pepita Jimenez. 90 c. Am. Bk.; Heath.
Wagner, C: P. Spanish grammar. $1.25. C: P. Wagner.
Warren, J: Spanish grammar. $1. Longmans.
Wesseley, J. E., *and* Allan, H. W. Spanish-English dictionary. 50 c. Dutton.
See also Catechisms;—Handy pronouncing dictionaries;—Tauchnitz pocket dictionaries.

SPANISH LITERATURE.
Fitzmaurice-Kelly, J. Chapters on Spanish literature. $1.75. Hispanic Soc.

SPANISH MAIN, South America.
Hart, F. R. Attacks upon the Spanish Main by Admiral Vernon. 50 c. Assoc. Pub.

Spanish military nun. *See* De Quincey, T:

SPANISH MISSIONS.
See San Gabriel mission.

SPANISH PAINTING.
See Painters and painting.

SPANISH POETRY.
Arteaga y Pereira, F. de, *comp.* Nine Spanish poems. *40 c. net. Oxford Univ.
Pidal, R. M. El romancero español. $1.25 net. Hispanic Soc.

Spanish régime in Missouri. Houck, L:, *ed.* In 3 v. $18. Donnelley.

Spanish renaissance. Prentice, A. N. $22.50. Polley.

Spanish series. *See* Calvert, Albert F:

Spanish stage in the time of Lope de Vega. Reinert, H. A. *$3 net. Hispanic Soc.

Spare, Austin Osman.
Book of satyrs. '09(D18) il. F. bds., *$6 net. (300 copies.) Lane.

Spargo, J:
Common sense of socialism: series of letters addressed to Jonathan Edwards, of Pittsburg. '08(My23) D. $1; pap., 25 c. Kerr.
Common sense of the milk question. '08 (Ap25) c. D. **$1.50 net. Macmillan.
Karl Marx: his life and work. '10(Je4) c. pors. facsims., O. $2.50 net. B: W. Huebsch.
The Marx he knew. '09(N13) c. il. pors. S. bds., 50 c. Kerr.
Socialism. New and rev. ed. '09(My1) 12°, *$1.50 net. Macmillan.
Socialist readings for children. '09(Ag7) c. il. 8°, $1. Woman's Nat. Prog.
Spiritual significance of modern Socialism. '08(N21) c. D. *50 c. net. B: W. Huebsch.
Substance of socialism. '09(D4) c. D. *$1 net. B: W. Huebsch.

Sparhawk, Frances Campbell.
Dorothy Brooke's school days. '09(S11) c. il. O. †$1.50. Crowell.
Dorothy Brooke's vacation. '10(S3) c. il. O. $1.50. Crowell.

Sparkman, Philip Stedman.
Culture of the Luiseño Indians. '08(Ag22) Q. (Univ. of Cal. pubs., Amer. archæology and ethnology.) pap., 50 c. Univ. of Cal.

Sparks, Edn. Erle, ed.
English settlement in the Illinois; repr. of three rare tracts on the Illinois country. '08(My16) il. map, 8°, $2.50. Torch Press.

—, James, Ja. Alton, and Page, E: C., eds.
Semi-centennial of the Lincoln-Douglas debates in Illinois, 1858-1908. '08(S) 40 p. pors. map, 8°, (Illinois Dept. of Public Instruction circular.) pap., 35 c. Phillips Bros.

Sparks, Rev. S: Justin.
In the bend of the Estataue: [a poem.] '08 (My9) c. por. D. 75 c. B'way Pub.

Sparks from a superintendent's anvil. Schaffle, A. F: $1. Wilde.

Sparks of truth. Harris, W: S. $1. Minter.

Sparrow, Mrs. Maria Dunton.
Hereford: story. '10(Mr5) c. il. D. $1. Badger.

Sparrow, Rebecca E., comp.
Stories and rhymes in Melville Bell symbols; comp. and ed. at the Rochester School for the Deaf. '09(N) c. 156 p. por. il. 8°, $1. Volta.

Sparrow, Wa. Shaw.
English house; how to judge its periods and styles. '09(Je26) il. O. *$2.50 net. Lane.
Hints on house furnishing. '09(Je19) il. O. *$2.50 net. Lane.
Old England. '08(O10) il. Royal 8°, *$6 net; ¾ levant, *$10 net. Pott.

—, **ed.** Our homes and how to make the best of them. '10(Jl30) il. 4°, $3.50 net. Doran.

SPARROW.
Grinnell, J. Three new song sparrows from California. 5 c.—Two heretofore unnamed wrens; Cavannah sparrow of the Great Basin; spottled bat. 15 c. Univ. of Cal.
United States. *Dept. of Agriculture.* How to destroy English Sparrows.

Sparrows. Newte, H. W. C. $1.50. M. Kennerley.

Spaulding, Arth. W.
Man of valor: story of the life of Jonathan, son of Saul. '08(D26) c. il. D. 75 c. Review and Herald Pub.

Spaulding, Fk. Ellsworth, and Bryce, Catherine Turner.
Fourth reader; Fifth reader. '09(N) c. 7+376 p. il. 12°, (Aldine readers.) 4th reader, 65 c.; 5th reader, 75 c. Newson.
New friends in story land. '08, [1909.] (Ag) 7+288 p. il. 12°, 60 c. Newson.

—, and Miller, W: D.
Graded school speller. 7 bks. '08(O3) c. D. bks. 1-4, ea., 15 c.; bks. 5-7, ea., 18 c. Ginn.

Spaulding, Oliver Lyman, jr.
Notes on field artillery for officers of all arms. '08(N14) c. front. O. $1; with maps, $1.25. U. S. Cavalry.

Spaulding, Perley.
European currant rust on the white pine in America. '09(O) 4 p. 8°, (U. S., Dept. of Agriculture; Bureau of Plant Industry; circular.) pap. (Add. Superintendent for price.) U. S., Supt. of Docs.
Present status of the white-pine blights. '09(O) 12 p. 8°, (U. S., Dept. of Agriculture; Bureau of Plant Industry; circular.) pap. (Add. Superintendent for price.) U. S., Supt. of Docs.

Spaulding, Rev. Wayland, ["Viter Strikeshoulder."]
When Theodore is king: extracts taken from a complete account of the new declaration of the change from the United States of America to the United Kingdom of America and the establishing of Theodore on the throne. '08(Ja11) D. pap., 25 c. W. Spaulding.

Speaker (The). *See* Pearson, Paul Martin, *ed.*

Speaker's manual of pronunciation. Chase, F. D. 25 c. Review and Herald Pub.

SPEAKERS.
See Dialogues; — Monologues;—Readers;—Recitations.

Speakers of the House. Fuller, H. B. **$2 net. Little, B. & Co.

SPEAKING.
See Elocution;—Lecturing;—Orators and oratory;—Preaching;—Rhetoric.

Speaking voice. Cone, R: W. $1. Evans Music.
Speaking voice. Everts, K. J. **$1 net. Harper.

Spear, R. O.
Cerebration; is the science of the psychic, mental and physiological functions of the brain in the brain and body; vital supplants chemical physiology; rational vs. imaginary idealism; celluiar dynamics; by a cerebrationist. '08, [1909.] (F) c. 404 p. 12°, $2. Rational Cult.

Spear, Raymond Herbert, and others, eds.
Commercial World encyclopedia of accounting. In 2 v. v. 1. '09(Jl17) c. por. forms, Q. per set, leath., $15. Commercial World.

Spear, W: E.
North and the South at Antietam and Gettysburg. '08(S5) c. maps, D. $1. W: E. Spear.

Spearman, Fk. Hamilton.
See Adventures in field and forest.

Spears, J: Randolph.
Hist. of the United States navy. '08(F15) c. il. pors. map, O. **$1.50 net. Scribner.
Story of the American merchant marine. '10(Mr26) c. il. D. (Stories from American hist. ser.) *$1.50 net. Macmillan.
Story of the New England whalers. '08 (O10) c. il. D. $1.50. Macmillan.

Special agents and adjusters handbook. Steeb, G: V. $1.50. Spectator

Special campaign ser. *See* Macmillan's.

Special messenger. Chambers, R. W: †$1.50. Appleton.
Special sundries. Spaninger, A: A. 30 c. Morton.
Specialist blight on American education. Munroe, J. P. (Add. author for price.) J. P. Munroe.

SPECIALTY ADVERTISING.
See Advertising.

Specialty salesman. Selecman, E. H. $1. Progress Co.
Specific characters in the bee genus *Colletes.* Swenk, M. H. 50 c. M. H. Swenk.
Specifications and contracts. Waddell, J: A. L. *$1 net. Engineering News.
Specifications for electrical construction. Montgomery, J. H. $1. Wahr.
Specimen pages of printing types. Plimton Press. (Not for sale.) Plimpton.
Specimens of exposition and argument. Percival, M., *comp.* *90 c. net. Macmillan.

Speck, Fk. G.
Creek Indians of Taskigi Town, Oklahoma. '08(My9) il. map, diagr., 8°, (Memoirs of the Am. Anthropological Assoc.) pap., 55 c. Am. Anthropological.
Ethnology of the Yuchi Indians. '10(Ag13) il. Q. (Univ. of Penn., Anthropological pubs.) pap., $2.50. Univ. of Penn.

Speck, S: H:, comp.
Song writers' guide; treatise on how popular songs are written and made popular, and special articles on the subject by Jerome and Schwartz [and others]; contains also complete rhyming dict. and thesaurus of synonyms. '10(Mr26) c. il. pors. 8°, $1. J. H. Remick.

Speckled brook trout (*salvelinus fontinalis*); by various experts with rod and reel; ed. and il. by L: Rhead, with introd. by C: Hallock. [New ed.] '10(Jl16) c. O. $3 net. Stokes.

SPECTACLES.
Phillips, R: J. Spectacles and eyeglasses. *$1 net. Blakiston
See also Eye.

Spectator (The). *See* Addison, Jos.

SPECTATOR (The), *English periodical.*
Lewis, L. Advertisements of *The Spectator.* $2. Houghton M.

Spectator Company. Annual and deferred dividends, showing the dividends paid in 1907 and 1908 by life insurance companies on annual dividend policies issued in the years 1877 to 1906 and 1907, inclusive, on ordinary life, twenty-payment life and twenty-year endowment forms at ages 25, 35, 45 and 55. '08(Ag1) c. 8°, $1.50. Spectator.

SPECTROSCOPE.
See Spectrum.

Spectroscopic investigations of the rotation of the sun, 1908. Adams, W. S. (Not for sale.) Carnegie.

SPECTRUM.
Adams, W. S. Investigation of the displacements of the spectrum lines at the sun's limb. (Not for sale.) Carnegie.
Baker, T. T. Spectroscope: its use in general analytical chemistry. *$1.75 net. Wood.
Coblentz, W: W. Investigations of infrared spectra. pts. 5, 6, 7. (Add. pubs. for price.) Carnegie.
Coone, H: H. Draughon's pract. speller and dict. for use in commercial colleges and high schools. 60 c. Draughon's.
Hale, G: E., *and* Adams, W. S. Photography of the "flash" spectrum without an eclipse. Carnegie.
Jones, H. C., *and* Anderson, J: A: Absorption spectra of solutions of certain salts of cobalt, nickel, copper, [etc.] $3.50. Carnegie.
Jones, H. C., *and* Strong, W: W. Study of absorption spectra of solutions of certain salts of potassium, cobalt, nickel, copper chromium, erbium, praseodymium, neodymium and uranium, as affected by chemical agents and by temperature. $5. Carnegie.
Julius, W. H. Anomalous refraction phenomena investigated with the spectroheliograph. (Not for sale.) Carnegie.
King, A. S. Correspondence between Zeeman effect and pressure displacement for the spectra of iron, chromium and titanium.—Electric furnace for spectroscopic investigations. (Add. Institution for price.)—Further study of the H and K lines of calcium. (Add. Institution for price.)—Relative intensities of the yellow, orange and red lines of calcium in electric furnace spectra. (Not for sale.) Carnegie.
Mees, C: E: K. Atlas of absorption spectra. *$2 net. Longmans.
Mintz, F. S. Pract. speller for evening schools. 25 c. net. Macmillan.

SPECTRUM.—*Continued.*
Newall, H. F. Spectroscope and its work. 85 c. net. **Gorham.**
Payne, B. R. Common words commonly misspelled. B. F. Johnson.
See also **Calcium.** Sun.
Spectrum of truth. Sharpe, A. B. 30 c. Herder.
SPECULATION.
Campbell, D. Law rel. to securities carried on margin. 50 c. Dixie Bk.
Fayant, F. Some thoughts on speculation. (Priv. pr.) Baruch.
Gibson, T: Cycles of speculation. $1.50. Moody's Mag.
See also Gambling;—Investments;—Stocks.
Spedden, Ernest Radcliffe.
Trade union label. '10(O) 7+9-100 p. O. (Johns Hopkins Univ. studies in historical and political science.) $1; pap., 50 c. Johns Hopkins.
SPEECH.
Macnamara, N. C. Human speech. *$1.75 net. Appleton.
Witkowski's atlas of the mechanism of voice, speech and taste. *$2 net. W: R. Jenkins.
See also Deaf and dumb;—Elocution;—Phonetics;—Psychology;—Stammering and stuttering;—**Voice.**
SPEECHES.
See Orators and oratory.
Speed and power of ships. Taylor, D: W. 2 v. $7.50 net. Wiley.
Speer, Elwood B., comp.
See Bardwell, Fred Leslie, *comp.*
Speer, Emory.
Lincoln, Lee, Grant and other biographical addresses. '10(Ja15) c. por. O. *$2 net. Neale.
Speer, Rob. Elliott.
Christianity and the nations; Duff Lectures for 1910. '10(Jl16) c. 8°, $2 net. Revell.
Deity of Christ. '09(My1) c. 16°, bds., *25 c. net. Revell.
How to speak effectively without notes. '09 (Ap24) c. D. pap., 10 c. Nat. Bible.
Master of the heart. '08(Ag1) c. 12°, *$1 net. Revell.
Memorial of Alice Jackson. '08(D26) c. pors. D. 75 c. Revell.
Paul, the all round man. '09(Jl31) c. 18°, *50 c. net. Revell.
Second coming of Christ. '09, [1910.] (F) 46 p. 12°, 30 c. Northfield Press.
Servants of the King. '09(Ag) c. 8+216 p. il. fold. map, facsim. 12°, 50 c.; pap., 35 c. Young People's Miss.
Spell (The). Orcutt, W: D. †$1.50. Harper.
Spell Land. Kaye-Smith, S. $1.75 net. Macmillan.
Spell of Italy. Mason, *Mrs.* C. A. $2.50. L. C. Page.
SPELLERS.
Alexander, G. Spelling book. 25 c.; also in 2 pts., pt. 1, 14 c.; pt. 2, 18 c. Longmans.
Andrews, C. D., *pseud.* New standard speller. 25 c. Laird.
Bailey, E. R., *and* Manly, J: M. Spelling book. *30 c. net. Houghton M.
Chancellor, W: E., *and others.* Graded spelling lists. 16 c. net. Macmillan.

SPELLERS.—*Continued.*
Glen, F. A., *and* Byrne, H: E: Speller and dictionary. 25 c. Byrne Pub.
Hicks, W. E. Champion spelling book. 25 c.—In 2 pts. ea., 18 c. Am. Bk.
Hughes, A. A. Pract. dictation. 20 c.—Pract. spelling. 15 c. Longmans.
Kelley, A: H., *and* Morse, H. W. Natural speller. **25 c. net. Scribner.
King, G. G. Bryn Mawr spelling book. 25 c. G. G. King.
Lewis, M. H. Utility speller. 30 c. Educ. Pub.
McCallum, A. N., *and* Horn, P. W. New century spelling book. In 2 pts. (Add. pubs. for price.) Silver.
Marshall, C. C., *comp.* Business speller. 90 c.—Technical word list. 30 c. Goodyear-M.
Mercantile speller. $2.50 net. Franklin Press, (Pa.)
Sandwick, R: L., *and* Bacon, *Mrs.* A. T. High school word book. 40 c. Heath.
Smith, L. D. *and* H. P. Intermedial spelling blank. *60 c. net. Macmillan.
Sonnenschein, W. S. Five thousand words frequently misspelt. 50 c. Dutton.
Spaulding, F. E., *and* Miller, W: D. Graded school speller. 7 bks. Bks. 1-4, ea., 15 c.; bks 5-7, ea., 18 c. Ginn.
Winchell, S: R. Orthography, etymology and punctuation. 60 c. Flanagan.
Wolfarth, J. H., *and* Rogers, L. E. New world speller. 25 c. World Bk.
See also Primers;—Words.
SPELLING (Simplified).
Handlin, W: W. Speling book, gramar and reder ov the American language. $1. H: J. Brauer.
Lounsbury, T: R. English spelling and spelling reform. **$1.25 net. Harper.
Putnam, E. K. Spelling reform and authority in language. (Add. pubs. for price.) Contemporary Club.
See also Phonetics.
SPELMAN FAMILY.
See Genealogies: Barbour, *Mrs.* F. C. W.
Speltz, Alex.
Styles of ornament; designs arranged in historical order, with descriptive text; tr. from the German by D: O'Conor. '08 (F8) il. 8°, $6.70. Hessling.
Spence, F. S.
See Pleydell, A. C.
Spence, Fk.
Christian reunion; or, plea for the restoration of "The ecclesia of God." '09(N) 8°, *$1.50 net. Doran.
Spence, Lewis.
Religion of ancient Mexico and Peru. '08, [1909.] (Ap) 8°, (Religions ancient and modern.) *40 c. net. Open Court.
Spence, Wa.
Idylls of the king; spiritual interpretation. '09(N20) c. 8°, $1. Cochrane.
Spenceley, J. Winfred.
Check-list [chronologically arranged] J. Winfred Spenceley's book-plates. '09 (Ja30) c. S. pap., 35 c. Assoc. Bk.
SPENCELEY, Joseph Winford.
Anderson, J. M. J. Winford Spenceley; his etchings and engravings in the form of book plates. $4. Assoc. Bk.

Spencer, Arth. Coe.
Magnetite deposits of the Cornwall type in Pennsylvania. '09(Mr6) il. maps, plans, 8°, (U. S. Dept. of the Interior, Geol. Survey, bull.)

Spencer, C: Worthen.
Industrial and financial development of the United States. 6 pts. '10(S) c. 8°, ea., pap., 15 c.: per set, 90 c. La Salle Extension.

Spencer, Claudius B.
Easter reflections. [1910.] (F) c. 274 p. 12°, (Christian festivals ser.) $1. Jennings.

Spencer, Enos.
Art of modern bookkeeping and accounting. 3d ed. '09(Jl) c. 444 p. forms, 4°, $3. E. Spencer.

Spencer, Rev. F. Ernest.
Old Testament history. '09(N13) D. (Anglican Church hdbk.) *40 c. net. Longmans.

Spencer, H: Percival.
Haunted house: [poems.] '09(N6) c. D. bds., $1. Badger.
The lilies: [poems.] '08(Ag) c. 9-31 p. D. $1. Badger.

Spencer, Herbert.
Works. New uniform ed. 18 v. '10(Jl30) 12°, per set, $17.50. Appleton.
Passages from philosophy of Herbert Spencer; chosen by Clara Sherwood Stevens. '10(D24) 12°, $1.50 net; Japanese vellum, $3 net. T: B. Mosher.

SPENCER, Herbert.
Bourne, G. C: Herbert Spencer and animal evolution. 50 c. Oxford Univ.
Duncan, D: Life and letters of Herbert Spencer. 2 v. **$5 net. Appleton.
Hudson, W: H: Herbert Spencer. *50 c. net. Dodge.

Spencer, Jesse Ames.
Hist. of the United States of America; ed. by Edn. Wiley, with the assistance of Irving E. Rines. 6 v. '09(D18) c. il. pors. plan, facsims., 4°, ea., $10. Am. Educ. Alliance.

Spencer, Mrs. Katharine Smith.
Nurse Lee. '09(Je5) c. il. front. D. 50 c. K. S. Spencer.

Spencer, P. J.
See Hofmeister, Christopher W.

Spencer, T: G.
Deterioration of lead sheaths of aerial and underground telephone cables: paper read before the conference committee consisting of representatives of the leading independent telephone operating companies, Jan. 23, 1909. '09(My8) c. il. 8°, pap., gratis. Stromberg-C.

Spencer, Wa. G., and Gask, G: E.
Practice of surgery. '10(Mr) 16+1234 p. il. (partly col.) 8°, $6.50; hf. mor., $7. Blakiston.

SPENCER, Mass.
Vital records of Spencer, Massachusetts. (Add. pubs. for price.) F. P. Rice.

Spencer (Herbert) lecture. *See* Herbert, Auberon.—Kidd, B:

Spender, J: Alfr.
Comments of Bagshot. '08(Ap18) c. D. **$1.25 net. Holt.

Spendthrift (The). Ainsworth, W: H. 50 c.; 75 c. Dutton.
Spendthrift (The). Browne, P. E. $1.50. G: W: Dillingham.

Spenser, Edm.
[Works. In 3 v.] vs. 2, 3, Spenser's Faerie queene; ed. by J. C. Smith. In 2 v. v. 1, bks. 1-3; v. 2, bks. 4-7. '10 (Ja1) O. $5.75. Oxford Univ.
Complete poetical works; [ed. by R. E. Neil Dodge.] '08(Ap18) c. por. O. (Cambridge ed. of the poets.) $3; hf. cf., $5; hf. mor., $6; cf. or levant, $7.50. Houghton M.
Faerie Queene; ed. by J. W. Hales. In 2 v. '10(Ap2) 16°, (Everyman's lib.) 35 c. net; leath., 70 c. net. Dutton.
Fowre hymnes; ed. by Lilian Winstanley. '08(F1) 8°, *50 c. net. Putnam.
Stories from the Faerie Queene retold from Spenser by Lawrence H. Dawson. '09 (D4) col. il. O. *$1.50 net. Crowell.

SPENSER, Edmund.
Church, A. J: Faery Queen and her knights. $1.50. Macmillan.
Macleod, M., *comp.* Red Cross knight and Sir Guyon from Spenser's Faery Queen. 60 c. Dodge.

Sperle, C: H.
Correct chicken culture: license for a one-man plant, $100. '09(My15) c. il. double plan, O. pap., gratis. C: H. Sperle.

SPERMATOPHYTES.
See Botany.

SPHAEROSOMA.
See Fungi.

Sphere of religion. Hoffman, F. S. **$1.75 net. Putnam.
Spherical basis of astrology. Dalton, J. G. $2.50. Spenceley.

SPHERICAL PROJECTION.
See Projection.

SPHERICAL TRIGONOMETRY.
See Trigonometry.

Sphinx (The). Wilde, O. $1 net. Lane.
Sphinx and the mummy. Vox, C., *pseud.* 50 c. Caldwell.

SPICES.
Brooks, R. O. Federal spice standards, interpretations and possibilities of. 50 c. Spice Mill.
Gibbs, W. M. Spices and how to know them. $3.50. W. M. Gibbs.

Spielmann, Mrs. Mabel H.
Margery Redford and her friends. '09 (O2) il. D. $1.50. Stokes.
Rainbow book. '09(O2) il. D. *$1.50 net. Warne.

Spiers, Isidore H: Bowles.
Manual of elem. French. '10(My21) D. 50 c.—Exercises on Manual. 65 p. 50 c. Ginn.

Spiers, R. Phené.
See Anderson, W: J.

Spillane, E: P:
Life and letters of Henry Van Rensselaer, priest of the Society of Jesus. '08(D) c. 7+293 p. pors. 12°, $1.25. Fordham Univ.

Spiller, Gustav.
Faith in man: the religion of the twentieth century. '08(Je13) 16°, bds., *75 c. net. Macmillan.

Spillman, W: Jasper.
Application of some of the principles of heredity to plant breeding. '09, [1910.] (Mr) 74 p. 8°, (U. S., Dept. of Agriculture, Bureau of Plant Industry, bull.) pap.
Successful poultry and dairy farm. '09 (Je) 40 p. il. 8°, (U. S., Dept. of Agriculture, farmers' bull.) pap. (Add. Superintendent for price.)

Spinal adjustment. Gregory, A. A. $5. A. A. Gregory.

SPINAL CORD.
See Nervous system.

Spinden, Herbert Jos.
Nez Percé Indians. '08(D5) O. figs. (Memoirs of the American Anthropological Association.) pap., 95 c. Am. Anthropological.

SPINE.
Abrams, A. Spondylotherapy; spinal concussion and the application of other methods to the spine in the treatment of disease. $3.50. A. Abrams.
Gregory, A. A. Spinal adjustment. $5. A. A. Gregory.
See also Chiropractic.

Spingarn, Joel Elias.
History of literary criticism in the renaissance. 2d ed., rev. and augmented. '08 (N21) c. 8°, (Columbia Univ. studies in comparative literature.) *$1.50 net. Lemcke.
—, ed. Critical essays of the seventeenth century. In 3 v. v. 1, 1605-1650; v. 2, 1650-1685. '08(My23); v. 3, 1685-1700. '09 (D18) front. D. ea., $1.75. Oxford Univ.
See also Temple, *Sir* W:

Spink, Alfr. H:
National game; hist. of baseball. '10(N19) c. pors. 8°, $1.50. Nat. Game.

Spink, Berthe E., and others.
Mechanical drawing for high schools. In 2 v. '10(D31) c. il. plans, diagrs., obl. 12°, $1.45. Atkinson, M.

Spinners' Club, San Francisco. "Prosit!": book of toasts and sentiments for all occasions. '09(D18) *$1.25 net; Omarian ed., flex. leath., *$3 net; Craftsman ed., leath., *$6 net, boxed. P. Elder.

Spinney, R: D.
Drawings for medium-sized repetition work; with examples of drawings for motor car parts. '09(D18) 8°, $1.50. Spon.

SPINNING.
See Cotton;—Woolen spinning.

Spinning-wheel ser. *See* Alcott, Louisa May.

Spinoza, Barach, [or Benedict.]
Ethic demonstrated in geometrical order and divided into five parts, which treat (1) of God; (2) Of the nature and origin of the mind; (3) Of the nature and origin of the affects; (4) Of human bondage; or, of the strength of the affects; (5) Of the power of the intellect; or, of human liberty; tr. from the Latin by W. Hale White; tr. rev. by Amelia Hutchinson Stirling. 4th ed., rev. and corrected. '10(D3) O. $3. Oxford Univ.
Ethics, and de intellectus emendatione (treatise on the correction of the understanding); tr. by And. J. Boyle; with introd. by Prof. Santayana. '10(D10) c. 16°, (Everyman's lib.) 35 c. net; leath., 70 c. net. Dutton.
Short treatise on God, man and his well-being; tr. and ed., with an introd. and commentary and a life of Spinoza, by A. Wolf. '10(Ap9) il. 8°, $3 net. Macmillan.
"Short treatise" on God, man and human welfare; tr. from the Dutch by Lydia Gillingham Robinson. '09(My15) c. por. O. *$1.25 net; pap., 50 c. Open Court.

Spinster farm. Winslow, H. M. $2. L. C. Page.

Spiral course in English. Harris, T: G. 2 bks. bk. 1, 35 c.; 30 c.; bk. 2, 60 c.; 50 c. Heath.

Spiral gearing. '08(Ag1) c. il. 8°, (Machinery's reference ser.) pap., 25 c. Indust. Press.

Spiral tables. Sullivan, J: G. $1.50 net. McGraw-H.

Spirit and matter before the bar of modern science. Heysinger, I: W. $3.75 net. Lippincott.

Spirit in prison. Hichens, R. S. †$1.75. Harper.

Spirit in the New Testament. Winstanley, E: W: *$1.10 net. Putnam.

SPIRIT LAKE, Ia.
Sharp, *Mrs.* A. G. Hist. of the Spirit Lake massacre and captivity of Miss Abbie Gardner. A. G. Sharp.

SPIRIT LEVELING.
See Altitudes.

Spirit mates. Peebles, J. M. $1.25. Peebles.

Spirit of America. Van Dyke, H: J. **$1.50 net. Macmillan.

Spirit of Christ in common life. Bigg, C: *$2 net. Longmans.

Spirit of laws. *See* Montesquieu, C. L. de S., *Baron* de.

Spirit of Montaigne. Norton, G., *comp. and ed.* *$1.25 net. Houghton-M. Co.

Spirit of nationality in the history of Brazil. Nabuco, J. (Not for sale.) J. Nabuco.

Spirit of Penn. Hewitt, C: E: $1. J. S. Ogilvie.

Spirit of power. Edghill, E. A. $1.40 net. Longmans.

Spirit of romance. Pound, E. $2.50 net. Dutton.

Spirit of the Ghetto. Hapgood, H. *$1.25 net. Funk.

Spirit of the South. Harney, W: W. $1.50. Badger.

Spirit of the South. Stewart, W: H: $2. Neale.

Spirit of the woods. Gruse, E: $1. B'way Pub.

Spirit of youth in our city streets. Addams, J. **$1.25 net. Macmillan.

Spirit, soul and body. Ballard, J: H. $1. Alliance Press.

Spirit trail. Boyles, K. $1.50. McClurg.

SPIRITISM.
See Spiritualism.

Spiritmist. Trepoff, I., *pseud.* $1.50. D. W. Newton.

Spiritual adventures. Symons, A. *$2.50 net. Dutton.

Spiritual basis of man and nature. Halfyard, S: F. $1. Jennings.

Spiritual development of St. Paul. Matheson, G: *80 c. net. Whittaker.

Spiritual Franciscans. Muzzey, D: S. gratis. D: S. Muzzey.

SPIRITUAL HEALING.
See Divine healing.

Spiritual housekeeping. Militz, A. R. S. 50 c. Absolute Press.

SPIRITUAL LIFE.
See Soul.

Spiritual message of literature. Guthrie, K S. $1. Open Court.

Spiritual philosophy. Neville, S: T. *50 c. net. Longmans.

Spiritual Sabbathism. Lewis, A. H. $1.50. Am. Sabbath Tr. Soc.

Spiritual sense in sacred legends. Brailsford, E: J. $1.25 net. Eaton & M.

Spiritual significance of modern socialism. Spargo, J: *50 c. net. B: W. Huebsch.

Spiritual unrest. Baker, R. S. $1.35 net. Stokes.

Spiritual verses as aids to mental prayer. Johnson, J. B. 75 c. Longmans.

Spiritual world. Spalding, J. H. *40 c. net; *60 c. net. Warne.

SPIRITUALISM.

Aber, W: W. Dawn of another life. $1.50. W: W. Aber.

Bates, E. K. Do the dead depart? $1.50. Dodge.

Brackett, E: A. Materialized apparitions. $1.25.—World we live in: [study of materialized apparitions.] $1. Badger.

Bull, C. E. Philosophy of life mortal and immortal. $1.60. C. E. Bull.

Burke, *Mrs.* M. M-. Key to the laws of the occult psyche science. Titus Pub. Co.

Davis, A. J. Harmonial philosophy. 27 v. $30.—Principles of nature. $3.50. Austin.

Dewey, D. Problems of your generation. $1. Arden.

Edmonds, J. W. Spiritualism. $3.50. Austin.

Erwood, W: J. Mediumship; its use and abuse. 50 c. W: J. Erwood.

Francis, J: R. Home Circle Fraternity; evolution of a new religion. $1. Progressive Thinker.

Hotchkiss, S: Progressive age of reason. $1.75. S: Hotchkiss.

Lombroso, C. **After death—what? **$2.50 net. Small.**

Miller, A. V. Sermons on modern spiritualism. *75 c. net. Herder.

Peebles, J. M. Spirit mates, their origin and destiny. $1.25.—What is spiritualism? 75 c. Peebles.

Robbins, A. M. Both sides of the veil. $1.25 net. Sherman, F.

Stead, W: T: How I know that the dead return. *75 c. net. Ball Pub. Co.

Stevens, E. W. Watseka wonder; a narrative of startling phenomena, and authenticated instance of spirit manifestation. 60 c.; 35 c. Austin.

Tanner, A. D. Studies in spiritism. $2.50 net. Appleton.

SPIRITUALISM.—*Continued.*

Tiffany, J. Astral world. $2. De Laurence, S.

Tuttle, H. Acana of nature: [laws of creation revealed to the author through spiritualistic agency.] *$1.50 net. Stillman.

Wiltse, M. B. Theorem or teleology of spiritualism. 75 c. Eddy County Provost.

See also Personality;—Psychical research;—Telepathy;—Theosophy;—*also* Palladino, Eusapia.

Spitfire (The). Peple, E: H: †$1.50. Moffat.

Spivey, T: Sawyer.

Dr. Paul McKim. '08(F15) c. il. D. $1.50. Neale.

Hoosier widow. '08(Ap4) c. il. D. $1.50. Neale.

SPLASHES.
See Physics.

Splendid hazard. MacGrath, H. $1.50. Bobbs-M.

Splendor of God. Hammond. E., *comp.* *60 c. net. Dutton.

Spofford, Ainsworth Rand, 1825-1908: memorial meeting at the Library of Congress on Thursday, Nov. 12, 1908. '09(Je12) por. 8°, pap. (Add. pubs. for price.) D. C. L. A.

Spofford, Mrs. Harriet Eliz. Prescott.

Children of the valley. '08(S19) c. front. D. (Bimbi ser.) bds., **40 c. net. Crowell.

The fairy changeling; flower and fairy play. '10(O15) c. il. D. $1 net. Badger.

Spokane, Wash. City of Spokane et al. v. Northern Pacific railway et al.: brief for complainants. '07 [1908.] (S.) 127 p. 8°. (Add. pub. for price.) B. Adams.

SPOKANE, Wash.

McCune, F. H: Spokane rate case: [railroad rates.] 25 c. F. H: McCune.

SPONDYLOTHERAPY.
See Spine.

SPONGES.

Annandale, N. Fresh-water sponges collected in the Philippines by the Albatross expedition. (Add. Superintendent for price.) U. S., Supt. of Docs.

Cotte, J. Sponge culture. U. S., Supt. of Docs.

Moore, H. F. Commercial sponges and sponge fisheries.—Method of sponge culture. U. S., Supt. of Docs.

Spon's architects' and builders' pocket price book. Young, C. $1.50. Spon.

Spon's mechanics own book; manual for handicraftsmen and amateurs. 6th ed. '10 (N5) 8°, $2.50. Spon.

Spon's workshop receipts for manufacturers, mechanics, and others. New ed., rev. and partly rewritten; all the subjects being classified under one alphabet. v. 1. '09 (Ap3); v. 2, 3. '10(Je18) il. 12°, ea., $1.50 net. Spon.

Spool knitting. McCormack, M. A. *$1 net. Barnes.

Spoon, W: Luther.

Sand-clay and earth roads in the middle west. '10(Je) 31 p. il. 8°. (U. S., Dept. of Agriculture, Office of Public Roads circular.) U. S., Supt. of Docs.

Spooner, Cecil.
Fortunes of Betty; sweet and tender romance of an old soldier's daughter; novelized from the successful play of the same name. [1910.] (D) c. 5-218 p. il. 12°, 50 c. J. S. Ogilvie.

Spooner, H: J:
Machine design, construction, and drawing; text-book for the use of young engineers. '10(O15) O. $3.50. Longmans.
Machine drawing and design for beginners. '09(Mr27) tabs., figs. obl. S. $1.25. Longmans.
Notes on, and drawings of a four-cylinder petrol engine. '08(D19) il. obl. Q. bds., 75 c. Longmans.

Spooner, J: Coit.
Beeman versus Jackman: [suit in equity brought under the provisions of the prohibitory law of Iowa.] '08(My.) c. 2+131 p. 16°. (Add. author for price.) J: C. Spooner.

Sport and travel in the Far East. Grew, J. C. $3 net. Houghton M.

Sport indeed. Martindale, T: **$1.50 net. Jacobs.

Sporting deacon. Blaney, C: S: 25 c. J. S. Ogilvie.

Sporting dogs. Barton, F. T. $2.50. W: R. Jenkins.

Sporting rifle. Winans, W. **$5 net. Putnam.

SPORTS AND SPORTSMEN.
Andrews, T: S., *comp.* World's sporting annual record book, 1908; 1909. ea., 10 c. T: S. Andrews.
Armour, G. D. British sports past and present. *$6 net. Doran.
Breck, E: Way of the woods: manual for sportsmen. **$1.75 net. Putnam.
Cody, H. A. On trail and rapid. $1 net. Lippincott.
Hunter, A. Huntsman in the South. v. 1. *$1.50 net. Neale.
Nevill, R. Sporting days and sporting ways. $3.50 net. Brentano's.
Roosevelt, T. Outdoor pastimes of an American hunter. **$3 net. Scribner.
Syers, E. *and* M., *eds.* Book of winter sports. *$4.20 net. Longmans.
Ware, R: D. In the woods and on the shore: [fishing and shooting sketches.] $2. L. C. Page.
See also Amusements; — Archery; — Athletics; — Automobiles; — Baseball; — Batball; — Betting; — Boxing; — Bowling; — Camping; — Canoeing; — Cricket; — Fish and fishing; — Foot-ball; — Fox; — Game laws; — Game preserving; — Golf; — Gymnastics and physical culture; — Hockey; — Horsemanship; — Hunting; — Indian clubs; — Jiu-jitsu; — Lacrosse; — Lawn tennis; — Quoits; — Rowing; — Running; — Shooting; — Skating; — Ski-ing; — Swimming; — Tennis; — Walking; — Water polo; — Yachts and yachting.

Spoth, J: C:
Knight in homespun. '09(Ap3) c. il. D. $1.50. C. M. Clark.

Spots. Courvoisier, C. T. $2; $3 net. P. Elder.

Spouse of Christ and daily communion. Zulueta, F. M. de. 30 c. Herder.

Sprague, Alice, [Mrs. Carleton Sprague.]
My two gardens. '10(Mr12) D. pap., 50 c.: bds., $1. Manas Press.

Sprague, Mrs. Carleton.
See Sprague, Alice.

Sprague, C: Ezra.
Amortization; guide to the ready computation of the investment value of bonds by the use of the extended bond tables. '08 (N) c. 22 p. 8°, 50 c. C: E. Sprague.
Logarithms to 12 places and their use in interest calculations. '10(Je) c. 88 p. 8°, $3. C: E. Sprague.
Philosophy of accounts. '08(Ap.) 9+161 p. 8°, $3. C: E. Sprague.
Text-book of the accountancy of investment. '09, [1910.] (Ja.) c. 185 p. 8°, $4. C: E. Sprague.

Sprague, Oliver Mitchell Wentworth.
Hist. of crises under the national banking system. '10(Ag) 484 p. tabs., 8°. Gov. Pr. Off.
See also Roberts, G: Evan.

Sprague, W: C.
Questions and answers on sales of personal property, etc. 5th ed. [1910.] (D) c. O. (Quizzer ser.) pap., 50 c. Sprague.

SPRAYING.
Lodeman, E. G. Spraying of plants. **$1.25 net. Macmillan.

Spread eagle. Morris, G. $1.20 net. Scribner.

SPREW.
See Mouth.

Sprig of Plantagenet. Mortimer, J. H. $1.50. Independent Pub.

Spring, Helen Mary.
Individual recipes in use at Drexel Institute. 8th ed. '10(My7) c. 12°, 50 c Winston.

Spring, Herbert.
By the grey sea. '09(N) 297 p. 8°, $1. Herder.

Spring and summer school celebrations. Kellogg, A. M., *ed.* 50 c.; 30 c. Penn Pub. Co.

Spring cleaning. Burnett, *Mrs.* F. H. †60 c. Century Co.

Spring in London: poem on the nature of things, by E. A. '08(F8) 12°, 25 c. Dutton.

Spring flowers at Belvoir Castle. Divers, W. H. *$1.80 net. Longmans.

Springborn, W: J:
Cleveland garbage disposal plant. '08(O) c. 8 p. il. 8°, (Civil Engineers' Club of Cleveland, transactions.) gratis. W: J: Springborn.

Springer, Helen E.
See Springer, *Mrs.* J: McKendree.

Springer, J: McKendree.
Heart of Central Africa; with an introd. by Bishop J. C. Hartzell. '09(Ap3) c. il. map, D. *$1 net. Jennings.

Springer, Mrs. J: McKendree, [Helen E. Springer.]
Snap shots from sunny Africa. '09(Ag) c. il. por. D. *$1 net. Revell.

Springer, Max.
Art of accompanying plain chant. '08(D) c. 13+238 p. 8°, $1.50. J. Fischer.

Springer, Mrs. Rebecca Ruter.
Marcus and Miriam; story of Jesus. '08, [1909.] (F) c. 94 p. il. 8°, 25 c.; pap., 8 c. Cook.

SPRINGFIELD, Mass.
Barrows, C: H: History of Springfield in Massachusetts. 80 c. W. F. Adams.
Johnson, *Mrs.* G: P. Historical sketch. Museum of Natural History. 50 c.; 25 c. Springfield Lib. Assoc.
Springfield (Mass.) City Library. **Some modern verse: partial list of recent poetry in the City Library of Springfield.** '09 (F6) D. pap., 5 c. City Lib. Assoc.
Springfield Museum of Natural History bull. il. O. Springfield Mu. Nat. Hist.
—Stebbins. Insect galls. $1.50.
Springfield tests. Riley, J: L. 25 c. Holden.
Springhaven. *See* Blackmore, R: Doddridge.
SPRINGS FAMILY.
See Genealogies: Dinkins, J.
Springs of Helicon. Mackail, J: W: **$1.25 net. Longmans.
Springs, streams and spas of London hist. Foord, A. S. $3.50 net. Stokes.
SPRINTING.
See Running.
SPROAT, David.
Banks, J. L. David Sproat and naval prisoners in the War of the Revolution. (Priv. pr.) J. L. Banks.
Spruce, R:
Notes of a botanist on the Amazon and Andes; ed. and condensed by Alfr. Russel Wallace; with a biograpical introd. '09(Ja16) 2 v., il. maps, 8°, $6.50. Macmillan.
SPRUE.
See Sprew.
Sprunger, J: Abraham, and Dyck, Rev. H. J., comps.
Himmels-harfe für sonntag-schuler, jugendvereine und evangelisations-versammlungen. '07, [1909.] (Ja) 183 p. 12°, 35 c. Light and Hope.
Spulzberger, Mayer.
Am Ha-Aretz; the ancient Hebrew parliament; chapter in the constitutional hist. of ancient Israel. '10(My7) 12°, 75 c. net. J. H. Greenstone.
Spur gearing. '08(Jl4) c. il. 8°, (Machinery's reference ser.) pap., 25 c. Indust. Press.
Spurgeon, Arth.
Premature cheapening of copyright books: [a paper read at the International Publishers' Congress, Amsterdam, on July 19th, 1910.] '10(D) 16 p. 16°. (Priv. pr.) Cassell.
Spurzheim, J. G., M.D.
Phrenology; or, the doctrine of the mental phenomena; with an introd. by Cyrus Elder. Rev. ed. from the 2d American ed. in 2 v.; published in Boston in 1833. '08(D19) il. O. *$3 net. Lippincott.
Spy (The). *See* Cooper, Ja. Fenimore;—Górky, M.
Spyker, J: And., comp.
Human pilgrimage. '08(Je) c. 17+20+3 p. por. 12°, 75 c. Hammond Pr. Co.
Spyri, Mrs. Johanna Heusser.
Heidi. '09(D18) il. 12°, $2.50. Dutton.
Heidi. '10(Ap2) 16°, (Everyman's lib.) 35 c. net; leath., 70 c. net. Dutton.
Was der grosmutter lehre bewirkt: ed., with exercises, notes and vocab., by Sarah I. Barrows. '10(S17) c. S. (Heath's modern language ser.) Heath.

SQUABS.
See Pigeons.
Square look into eternity. **Jensen, J. C.** 25 c.; $1. J. C. Jensen.
SQUARES.
American School of Correspondence. **Stair-building and the steel square. $1. Am. Sch. Corr.**
Hodgson, F: T: A B C of the steel square and its uses. 50 c. Drake.
Inskip, G: D. New manual of squares and logarithms. $3. M. C. Clark.
Wakeham, R. Simplified applications of the steel square. $1.50. R. Wakeham.
SQUASH RACQUETS.
See Tennis.
Squaw (The) book. '10(Mr26) c. O. pap., 50 c. Free Dispensary.
Squaw man. Faversham, *Mrs.* J. O. 75 c. Grosset.
Squier, G: Owen.
Present status of military aeronautics. '09 (Ja23) pap., 80 c. Am. Soc. Mech. Engineers.
Squire, C:
Mythology of ancient Britain and Ireland. '07, [1909.] (Ap) 8°, (Religions ancient and modern.) *40 c. net. Open Court.
Squire, Edn.
Oil tank tables; how to calculate them. '09 (Ap) c. 29 p. 8°, 50 c. E. Squire.
Squire's tale. *See* Chaucer, Geoffrey. The Clerke's tale.
Squires, Grace.
Tom, Nadine and Snuffles. '10(S3) c. il. D. (Six to sixteen ser.) 60 c. Caldwell.
SQUIRRELS.
McCoy, G: W. Evidence of plague infection among ground squirrels. Gov. Pr. Off.
Rucker, W. **Plague among ground squirrels in Contra Costa County, California. U. S., Supt. of Docs.**
United States. *Public Health and Marine Hospital Service.* **Campaign against ground squirrels in Contra Costa County, California. by Rupert Blue. '09(S) 5 p. 8°. (Add. Superintendent for price.)**
Srygley, F. D.
New Testament church; editorials which appeared in the *Gospel Advocate* from 1889 to 1900; comp. and ed. by F. B. Srygley. '10(Jl2) pors. 12°, $1. F. B. Srygley.
Stabb, J:
Some old Devon churches; their rood screens, pulpits, fonts, etc. '09(My15) il. O. *$3 net. Scribner.
Stabler, Herman, and Pratt, Gilbert H.
Purification of some textile and other factory wastes; prep. in co-operation with Rhode Island State Board of Health. '09 (N) (U. S., Dept. of the Interior, Geolog. Survey bull.; Water Supply paper.) pap. (Add. Superintendent for price.)
Stables, W: Gordon, M.D.
Little gipsy lass. '08(N7) il. D. $1.25. Lippincott.
STABLES.
Shaw, V. Encyclop. of the stable. *$2 net. Dutton.

Stace, Fs. A.
Chancery forms and precedents; annot. with reference to the practice in Michigan. '08(D) c. 39+742 p. O. (Add. pubs. for price.) Drake Law Bk.

Stack, Frederic W:
Wild flowers every child should know; arranged according to color. '09(Je5) c. il. D. (Every child should know ser.) $1.20. Doubleday, P.

Stackpole, Everett Schermerhorn.
Macomber genealogy. '09(Je) 252 p. 8°, $5. E. S. Stackpole.

Stacpoole, H: De Vere.
Blue lagoon. '08(Je6) D. †$1.50. **Lippincott.**
The bourgeois. '10(Ag6) D. $1. Brentano's.
Crimson azaleas. '10(F5) c. D. †$1.50. Duffield.
Drums of war. '10(D17) c. D. $1.20 net. Duffield.
Fanny Lambert; novel. '10(Je25) D. $1.50. Fenno.
Garryowen. '10(My14) c. 8°, $1.50. Duffield.
Pools of silence. '10(Ag20) c. D. $1.50. Duffield.

Staël-Holstein, Anne Louise Germaine Necker, Baronne de, [Madame de Staël.]
De L'Allemagne; ed. by H: Weston Eve. '09(Mr6) por. S. (Oxford higher French ser.) 85 c. Oxford Univ.

Stafford, E: Russell.
Shop talks; series of addresses on Jesus Christ and His disciples delivered to working men; with introd. by the Rev. Levi Gilbert. '10(My14) c. 12°, 75 c. Jennings.

Stafford, J: R:
When cattle kingdom fell. '10(D17) c. D. $1.25 net. B. W. Dodge.

Stafford, Wendell Phillips.
Dorian days; poems. '09(D18) c. D. **$1.25 net. Macmillan.

STAGE.
See Actors and actresses; — Drama and dramatists;—Plays;—Theatre.

Stage days in Brimfield. Tarbell, M. A. $1. Bassette.

Stage door. Davis, C: B. †$1.50. Scribner.

Stage history of Shakespeare's King Richard the Third. Wood, A. I. P. *$1.25 net. Macmillan.

STAGING.
See Drama and dramatists.

STAINED GLASS.
Day, L. F. Windows; book about stained and painted glass. *$7.50 net. Scribner.
Duthie, A. L. Ornamental window glass work. *$2 net. Van Nostrand.
Sherrill, C. H. Stained glass tours in England. *$2.50 net.—Stained glass tours in France. **$1.50 net. Lane.

Stainer, C. L.
King Blackjack and his sword: strange tales for children. '09(D18) il. *$2.40 net. Oxford Univ.

Stainer, Sir J:
The organ; manual of the true principles of organ playing; ed. by Ja. H. Rogers. '10(My14) 8°, $1 net. Ditson.

STAIR-BUILDING.
American School of Correspondence. Stair-building and the steel square. $1. Am. Sch. Corr.

Staley, Byron E.
Oram of the forest. Author's ed. '08(F) c. '07. 104 p. 12°, (Wheel of progress, Primeval ser.) $1. Tower.

Staley, Edgcumbe.
Dogaressas of Venice. '10(Je4) il. 8°, $3.50 net. Scribner.
Famous women of Florence. '09(D11) il. O. $3.50. Scribner.
Franz Hals. '08(D19) il. O. (Masterpieces in colour.) bds., *65 c. net. Stokes.
Raphael. '09(D) various paging, il. Q. (Great artist ser.) *$2 net. Doran.
Tragedies of the Medici. '09(F13) il. pors. O. *$3.50 net. **Scribner.**

Stalker, Ja., D.D.
Ethic of Jesus according to the synoptic Gospels. '09(D11) O. *$1.75 net. Armstrong.
Life of Jesus Christ. New ed. '09(O23) 12°, *60 c. net. **Revell.**
The atonement. '09(F6) D. *$1 net. **Armstrong.**

Stalkey & Co. *See* Kipling, Rudyard.

Stalks abroad. Wallace, H. F. *$3.50 net. Longmans.

Stall, Sylvanus, M.D.
What a young boy ought to know. [New rev. ed.] '09(Je5) c. por. S. (Self and sex ser. for men.) $1. Vir Pub.

STALL BARS.
See Gymnastics and physical culture.

STALLIONS.
See Horse.

STAMMERING AND STUTTERING.
Bryant, F. A: George Watson, the trials and triumph of a stammer. 10 c. F. A: Bryant.
Hatfield, M. L. How to stop stammering. $1.50. M. L. Hatfield.
Reed, F. A. Textbook used in the Reed School for the Correction of the Stammering Habit. $1. F. A. Reed.

Stamper, Alva Walker.
Hist. of the teaching of elem. geometry. '09, [1910.] (Ap) 10+163 p. 8°, (Columbia University, Teachers' College, contribs. to education ser.) $1.50; pap., $1.15. Teachers' Coll.
Bibliography (8 p.).

STAMPS.
See Postage stamps;—Trade-marks.

Stanard, Mrs. Mary Mann Page Newton.
The dreamer: romantic rendering of the life-story of Edgar Allan Poe. '09(Jl3) c. D. *$1.50 net. Bell Bk.

Standage, H. C.
See Owen, F. A.
—, ed. Decoration of metal, wood, glass, etc.: book of recipes for all workmen in the fancy trades. '08(Mr14) c. 12°, $2. **Wiley.**

Standard against Uncle Sam. Tucker, H: H., *jr.* $1. H: H. Tucker, Jr.

Standard Biblical atlas; consisting of a series of nine maps depicting Bible lands. '09(F20) c. maps, 4°, 75 c. **Funk.**

Standard blue book of Texas, 1908-09. Ed. de luxe of Beaumont. '08. c. 216 p. il. pors. 4°, $5. A. J. Peeler.

Standard catalog ser. Q. H. W. Wilson.
—Potter. Children's catalog; guide to best reading. $6 net.

Standard Catholic readers. *See* Doyle, Mary E.

Standard concert guide. Upton, G: P. $1.75. McClung.

Standard concert repertory. Upton, G: P. $1.75. McClurg.

Standard dictionary of facts. Ruoff, H: W., *ed.* $4.90; $5.50; $6.25; $6.75. Frontier Press.

Standard dictionary of the English language. New ed., rev. and enl.; prep. under supervision of I: Kaufman Funk and others. '07, [1908.] (Jl) 2 v., 20+1060+21-140; 1061-2441 p. il. pors. maps, tabs., f°, shp., $12. Funk.

Standard domestic science cook book. Lee, W: H:, *comp.* $2.50; $1.75; $1.70. Laird.

Standard electrical dictionary. Sloane, T: O. $3. Henley.

Standard English classics. See Ginn's.

Standard every man's memo-book. '09 (My8) maps, T. mor., 50 c.; leath., 25 c. Laird.

Standard family physician. Reissig, C., *comp.* 3 v. $15. Funk.

Standard fiction. il. 12°, $1. Burt.
—Caruthers. Knights of the horse shoe.
—Stephens. Mary Derwent.

Standard galleries. il. S. *$1 net. McClurg.
—Singleton. Holland.

Standard guide for locomotive engineers. Turner, E., *pseud.* 75 c. Laird.

Standard hdbk. for electrical engineers; written and compiled by a staff of specialists. '08(Ja18); 2d ed. (Je6); 3d ed., fully rev. and enl. '10(O22) c. il. tabs., S. mor., ea., *$4 net. McGraw-H.

Standard handbook on wines and liquors. Hirschfeld, A. M. $1.50. Popper.

Standard home and school dictionary. Stevens, C: M., *ed.* $3. Judge.

Standard Hoyle. Phillips, B., *comp.* 50 c. Excelsior.

Standard intrinsic unit. Winsor, T: $1. Winsor.

Standard (The) library of natural history; embracing living animals of the world and living races of mankind; editors and special contributors: C: J: Cornish, F. C. Selous, Ernest Ingersoll, Sir Harry Johnston and others. '08(My23) c. 5 v., maps, 4°, $16.50; hf. mor., $19.50. Univ. Soc.

Standard literature ser. See Newson's.

Standard musical lib. O. Am. Bk.
—Abbott. Individual singing exercises; 4th-8th grade. ea., 10 c.
—Aiken. Melody studies for primary grades. 15 c.
—Barri. Flower Queen. 20 c.
—Ne Collins. Institute songs. 15 c.

Standard of living among workingmen's families in New York City. Chapin, R. C. $2. Charities Pub.

Standard of usage in English, Lounsbury, T: R. **$1.50 net. Harper.

STANDARD OIL COMPANY.
Hubbard, E. Standard Oil Company. 10 c. Roycrofters.
Tucker, H: H., *jr.* Standard against Uncle Sam. $1. H: H. Tucker, Jr.

Standard opera glass. Annesley, C:, *pseud.* $1.50 net; $2.50 net; $3. Brentano's.

Standard railway system atlas. Cram, G: F. $10.50. G: F. Cram.

Standard recipes for ice cream makers. Miller, V. $1; $1.50. Laird.

Standard road-book of New York state; complete road-maps, showing quality of the roads, together with the principal routes. '10(Je11) c. maps, 8°, $1.50. W. L. Chase.

Standard series of Esperanto. D. Revell.
—Privat. Esperanto at a glance. *15 c. net.

Standard socialist ser. S. 50 c. Kerr.
—Hitch. Goethe's Faust.
—Kautsky. Class struggle.
—Lafargue. Evolution of property.
—Lewis. Evolution: social and organic.
—Liebknecht. Karl Marx.
—Marx *and* Engels. Manifests of the communist party.

Standard songs and choruses. MacConnell, M. F. 75 c. Am. Bk.

Standard steel construction. Jones & Laughlins. (Add. pubs. for price.) Jones & Laughlins.

Standard train rule examination. Collingwood, G: E., *ed.* $1.50; $2. Train Dispatcher's.

Standard wiring for electric light and power. Cushing, H. C. $1. H. C. Cushing, Jr.

Standards in education. Chamberlain, A. H: $1. Am. Bk.

Standish, B. Hoskin.
Country life and agricultural education. In 3 v. '08(Jl18) c. 12°, $2.25; [also] sets of charts of colored il. from nature by Ada T. Landers and others, to accompany above, $10. Caspar.

Standish, Burt L., [pseud. for Gilbert Patten.]
Bill Bruce of Harvard. '10(O1) c. D. $1.25. Dodd.
Clif Stirling: captain of the nine. '10(O1) c. front. D. (Clif Stirling ser.) $1.25. McKay.
Frank Merriwell's champions. '08(N7) c. il. D. (Boys' own lib.) †75 c. McKay.
Frank Merriwell's courage. '08(N7) c. D. (Boys' own lib.) †75 c. McKay.
Frank Merriwell's daring. '08(N7) c. il. D. (Boys' own lib.) †75 c. McKay.
Frank Merriwell's faith. '10(Je4) c. D. (Boys' own lib.) 75 c. McKay.
Frank Merriwell's loyalty. '09(Je5) c. front. D. (Boys' own lib.) †75 c. McKay.
Frank Merriwell's return to Yale. '09 (Je5) front. D. (Boys' own lib.) †75 c. McKay.
Frank Merriwell's reward. '10(Je4) c. front. D. (Boys' own lib.) 75 c. McKay.
Frank Merriwell's secret. '09(Je5) c. front. D. (Boys' own lib.) †75 c. McKay.
Frank Merriwell's skill. '08(N7) c. il. D. (Boys' own lib.) †75 c. McKay.
Frank Merriwell's victories. '10(Je4) c. front. D. (Boys' own lib.) 75 c. McKay.

Standish, Winn, [pseud. for Wa. Leon Sawyer.]
Jack Lorimer's holidays. '08(O3) c. il. O. (Jack Lorimer ser.) $1.50. L. C. Page.
Jack Lorimer's substitute. '09(Jl31) c. il. O. $1.50. L. C. Page.

Standley, Paul C.
Allioniaceae of the United States, with notes on Mexican species. '09(Je) 303-389 p. il. 8°, (Smithsonian Inst., U. S. National Museum, contribs. from U. S. National Herbarium.) pap. (Add. Superintendent for price.)

Stanford, C: Villiers.
Resurrection: short cantata for Eastertide for tenor solo, chorus and organ, or orchestra: text by Friedrich G. Klopstock. '09(Mr13) 4°, pap., 30 c. Ditson.

Stanford, E:
Atlas of the Chinese Empire. '09(Mr13) f°, $4. China Inland.

Stanford (Leland) Junior University pubs. il. Stanford Univ.
—Kellogg *and* Smith. Inheritance in silkworms.
—MacFarland. *Opisthobranchiate mollusca* of the Branner-Agassiz expedition to Brazil. $1. (University ser.)

STANISLAUS II., **Augustus Poniatowski,** ***King of Poland.***
Bain, R. N. Last king of Poland, and his contemporaries. *$3 net. Putnam.

Stanislaus, Ignatius Valerius Stanley, M.D., and Kimberly, C: Hubbell.
Pharmaceutic chemistry. '09(Ja23) c. 12°, *$2.50 net. Blakiston.

Stanley, Dean Arth. Penrhyn.
Memorials of Canterbury. '08(O17) 16°, (Best books ser.) leath., *$1 net. Dutton.

Stanley, Bp. E:
Before and after Waterloo: letters; ed. by Jane H. Adeane and Maud Grenfell. '08 (O10) il. pors. *$3.75 special net. Appleton.

Stanley, Fk. Arth.
See Goodrich, Clarence Leon.
—, **comp.** *See* Colvin, Fred Herbert.

Stanley, Sir H: Morton.
Autobiography of Sir Henry Morton Stanley; ed. by his wife, Dorothy Stanley. '09(N6) c. il. pors. map, O. **$5 net. Houghton M.

Stanley universal plane, for moulding, matching, ploughing, etc.; by a practical woodworker. '09(Mr13) il. pap., 25 c. Spon.

Stannard, H:
Master Bob Robin '09(O2) c. il. in col. S. 50 c. Warne.

Stannus, Hugh.
Drawings of Alfred Stevens. '08(D5) 4°, (Drawings of the great masters.) *$2.50 net. Scribner.

Stansbie, J. H.
Iron and steel. '08(Mr7) il. O. (Westminster ser.) *$2 net. Van Nostrand.

Stansfield, Alfr.
Electric furnace: its evolution, theory and practice. '08(Ap11) il. 8°, $2. Hill Pub.

Stansfield, Rev. J. Attwood.
Symbolism. '09(O) il. 44 p. (Manuals for the people.) 10 c. Anchor.

Stanton, E. Brandon.
Grant Vernon. '09(Ap17) c. D. $1. Roxburgh.

Stanton, Gerrit Smith.
"When the wildwood was in flower": narrative covering the fifteen years' experiences of a stockman on the western plains, and his vacation days in the open. '09(F20) c. il. D. *$1 net. J. S. Ogilvie.

Stanton, Horace Coffin.
Starry universe, the Christian's future empire. '09(Je26) c. 12°, *$1.50 net. Revell.

Stanton, Mary, ed.
See Dickins, Lilian, *ed.*

Stanton, Rossington.
Essay on the distribution of livelihood. '08 (Jl4) c. S. *$1.50 net. Farwell.

Stanton, Stephen Berrien.
Essential life: essays on the philosophy of life. '08(My9) c. D. **$1 net. Scribner.
Soul and circumstance. '10(N5) c. D. $1 net. Scribner.

Stanton, Thdr., ed.
Manual of American literature. '09(Mr27) c. O. **$1.75 net. Putnam.
Reminiscences of Rosa Bonheur. '10(O22) il. O. $3 net, boxed. Appleton.

Stanton, Vincent H:
Gospels as historical documents. In 4 pts. pts. 1, 2. '09, [1910.] (F) 8°, pt. 1, *$2.50 net; pt. 2, *$3.25 net. Putnam.

Stanwood, E:
James Gillespie Blaine. [Large paper ed.] '09(Ap10) pors. 8°, (American statesman; second ser.) (Add. pubs. for price.) Houghton M.

Stanyan, J: Minot.
Poems of soldier, sailor and civilian life. '08(O) c. 18+98 p. por. 8°, $1. E: M. Stanyan.

STAPLE SYSTEM.
See Monopolies.

Staples, Abram.
Suit in bankruptcy. '09(My) c. 27+488 p. O. shp. (Add. pubs. for price.) Michie.

Staples, Ernest Linwood.
Man of destiny: story of Abraham Lincoln: epic poem. 3d ed. '09(Ja23) c. il. por. O. $1; art leath., $2; pap., 75 c. Lincoln.

Stapleton, Rev. Ammon.
Flashlights on evangelical history, illustrative of the evangelical work founded by Rev. Jacob Albright in A.D. 1800; [also] Evangelical daughters of song. '08 (Ag15) c. il. D. $1. A. Stapleton.

Stapp, Emilie Blackmore.
Trail of the Go-hawks. '08(D12) il. $1.25. C. M. Clark.

Star coin book. **Mehl, B. M.** 50 c. net. Caspar.

Star-gazer's handbook. Elson, H. W. *50 c. net. Sturgis & W.

Star-gazers. Goodloe, A. C. $1 net. Scribner.

Star-glow and song. Going, C: B. *$1.20 net. Harper.

Star maps and star facts. Kullmer, C. J. 15 c. net. C. J. Kullmer.

Star of love. Kingsley, *Mrs.* F. M. $2. Appleton.

Star of the salons. Jebb, C. *$3.50 net. Putnam.

Star people. Dewey, K. F. $1.50. Houghton M.

Starbrace. Kaye-Smith, S. *$1.50 net. Macmillan.

Starbuck, Rob. Macy.
Mechanical drawing for plumbers. '10 (D17) il. $1.50. Henley.
Modern plumbing. '09(D) c. 400 p. il. 4°, $4. Henley.
Questions and answers on the practice and theory of sanitary plumbing. In 2 v. v. 1, Drainage and venting. 9th ed., rev. and enl. '09(N20); v. 2, Range boiler work, hot water supply and circulation. '10(Mr5) c. il. S. bds., ea., $1. R. M. Starbuck.
Standard pract. plumbing: exhaustive treatise on all branches of plumbing construction, incl. drainage and venting, ventilation, hot and cold water supply and circulation. '10(D17) c. il. 8°, $3. Henley.

Starch, Dan.
Principles of advertising. '10(D31) c. 8°, $1. Univ. Co-op.

STARFISH.
See Echinoderms.

Stark, Gilbert Little.
Letters of Gilbert Little Stark, July 23, 1907--Mar. 12, 1908. '08, [1909.] (Mr) c. 509 p. por. 8°. (Priv. pr.) Riverside Press.

Stark, Ja. H:
Loyalists of Massachusetts and the other side of the American Revolution. '10 (Mr12) c. il. pors. map in pocket, O. $5. W: B. Clarke.

Stark, W: Weldon.
Guy Hunter. '08(Ag29) c. O. $1.50. Cochrane.

Starke, J.
Alcohol, the sanction for its use, scientifically established and popularly expounded by a physiologist, tr. from the German. '10(D) 20+317 p. 8°, $1.50 net. Putnam.
Bibliography (8 p.).

Starkey, L. Cheston.
Notes on mechanical drawing, graphic statics, machine design, and kinematics. '09, [1910.] (F) c. 6+117 p. il. 8°, $1.50. L. C. Starkey

Starkey, V. G.
See Berthon, H. E.

Starling, Ernest H:, M.D.
Elements of human physiology. 8th ed., rev. '08(O31) il. 8°, *$3.75 net. Chic. Med. Bk.

Starr, F:
Bibliography of Congo languages. '08(D5) c. il. royal 8°, pap., *$1 net. Univ. of Chic.
In Indian Mexico: a narrative of travel and labor. '08(Ap11) c. il. O. *$5 net. Forbes.
—, ed. Little book of Filipino riddles. '10 (Ja22) c. 24°, (Philippine studies.) 50 c. World Bk.

Starr. Laura B.
Doll book. '09(D25) c. col. il. O. *$2 net. Stokes.

Starr, Moses Allen, M.D.
Organic and functional nervous diseases. 3d ed., thoroughly rev. '09(O) 904 p. il., *$6 net; leath., *$7 net. Lea.

Starrett, Danvil W:
Discoveries which make mental therapeutics and the transmission of mental communications an exact science. '09(S4) c. D. leath., $1.75. D. W. Starrett.
Mental therapeutics; or, how to cure all diseases with the mind. '09(S4) c. D. leath., $1.75. D. W. Starrett.

Starry universe. Stanton, H. C. *$1.50 net. Revell.

STARS.
Boss, L. Preliminary general catalogue of 6188 stars for the epoch 1900. $7. Carnegie.
Campbell, L. Comparison stars for 252 variables of long period. (Add. University for price.) Harvard Univ.
Cannon, A. J. Maxima and minima of variable stars of long period. $1. Harvard Univ.
Doolittle, E. Catalogue and remeasurement of the 648 double stars discovered by Professor G. W. Hough. (Add. pubs. for price.) Univ. of Penn.; [Winston.]
Harvard University Astronomical Observatory; Catalogue of 36,682 stars fainter than the magnitude 6.50.—Revised Harvard Photometry. ea., $2. Harvard Univ.
Kapteyn, J. C. On certain statistical data which may be valuable in the classification of the stars. gratis. Carnegie.
Klein, H. J. Star atlas. $3.50 net. Gorham.
Milham, W. I. How to identify the stars. **75 c. net. Macmillan.
Stebbins, J. Photometric observations of double stars. 75 c. Univ. of Ill.
Wendell, O. C. Photometric observations made with the fifteen inch east equatorial during the years 1892 to 1902. $1. Harvard Univ.
Wisconsin University. *Washburn Observatory.* Determinations of proper motion, 1902-1907. '08, [1909.] (S) 317 p. 8°, $2. Univ. of Wis.
See also Astrology;—Astronomy.

Start your child right. Howard, W: L. 75 c. net. Revell.

STARTERS.
See Butter;—Cheese.

Starting in life. Fowler, N. C., *jr.* $2. Little, B. & Co.

Starting to teach. Foster, E. C. 40 c. Y. M. C. A.

Startling statements. Markoe, R. J. $1.50. R. J. Markoe.

Starving on a bed of gold. Hall, J. A: $1. J. A: Hall.

STATE (The).
See Political science.

State and family in early Rome. Launspach, C: W. L. *$2.50 net. Macmillan.

State and the farmer. Bailey, L. H. **$1.25 net. Macmillan.

State Board examination questions and answers. 3d ed., carefully rev. and greatly enl.; cont. questions and answers of 41 states and two Canadian provinces. '10(N) 800 p. 8°, $3 net. Wood.

State control of courses of study. Brownscombe, F. J. $1. Silver.

State Historical Society of Wisconsin. *See* Wisconsin State Historical Society.

State history ser. il. 12°. Am. Bk.
—Evans. History of Georgia. *$1 net.

State insurance. Lewis, F. W. **$1.25 net. Houghton M.

State Normal School, Chico, Cal., bull. il. 8°, C. A. Stebbins.
—Stebbins. Guide to the birds of the Pacific coast. 25 c.

STATE OWNERSHIP.
See Government ownership.

State publications. Bowker, R: R., *ed.* In 4 pts. pt. 4. $10 for complete work. Pub. Weekly.

State Socialism in New Zealand. Le Rossignol, J. E: $1.50 net. Crowell.

State Street Trust Company, Boston. Collection of interesting and historic prints; being a brief presentation of some of the originals and reproductions in the possession of the State Street Trust Company. '09(N) c. 46 p. il. 8°, gratis. State St. Trust Co.

STATEN ISLAND, N. Y.
See New York City.

Statesman's year-book, 1908; ed. by J. Scott Keltie, with the assistance of I. P. A. Renwick. 45th annual publication, rev. after official returns. '08(Je13); 1909. 46th annual publication. '09(Je26); 1910. 47th annual publication. '10(Jl30) tabs., fold. maps, 12°, ea., $3 net. Macmillan.

STATESMEN.
White, A. D. Seven great statesmen in the warfare of humanity with unreason. $2.50 net. Century Co.

Statesmen snowbound. Fitzgerald, R. *$1.25 net. Neale.

Statham, E: Phillips.
Privateers and privateering. '10(N19) il. 8°, $2.50 net. Pott.
See also Brenan, Gerald.

Statham, H. Heathcote.
Organ and its position in musical art; book for musicians and amateurs. '10(Je4) il. 12°, $2. Scribner.

STATIC ELECTRICITY.
See Medical electricity.

STATICS.
Johnson, L. J. Statics by algebraic and graphic methods. $2. Wiley.
Malcolm, C: W. Text book on graphic statics. $3. M. C. Clark.
Norwall, A. Elem. applied mechanics (statics). 90 c. Longmans.
See also Dynamics;—Graphics;—Mechanics.

Stationary engineering. Branch, J. G. 3 v. ea., $2.50. Rand, McN. & Co.

Stationary transformers. Taylor, W: T. *$1.50 net. McGraw.

STATIONERS AND STATIONERY.
Clark, J. W. Desk book on the etiquette of social stationery. $1. Eaton, C. & P.
Directory of booksellers, newsdealers and stationers in the U. S. and Canada. $5. H. W. Wilson.
See also Paper.

Statistical and chronological history of the United States Navy. Neeser, R. W. 2 v. **$12 net. Macmillan.

·Statistical study of infant mortality. Phelps, E: B. (Add. author for price.) E: B. Phelps.

Statistical study of literary merit. Wells, F. L. 30 c. Science Pr., (N. Y.)

STATISTICS.
Elderton, W. P. *and* E. M. Primer of statistics. *60 c. net. Macmillan.
Falkner, R. P. Some uses of statistics in the supervision of schools. (Add. author for price.) R. P. Falkner.
United States. *Dept. of Agriculture. Bu. of Statistics.* Statistics Bureau: bulletins, circulars, foreign markets, separates from yearbook, and crop reporter. gratis.
United States. *Dept. of Commerce and Labor. Bu. of the Census.* Mortality statistics. (Add. Superintendent for price.) U. S., Supt. of Docs.
United States. *Dept. of Commerce and Labor. Bu of Statistics.* Statistical abstract of the United States, 1909.
See also Agriculture;—Almanacs and annuals;—Census;—Crime and criminals;—Stocks.

Statius, Publius Papinius.
The Silvae; tr., with introd. and notes, by D: A. Slater. '09(Ja23) D. $1. Oxford Univ.

Statue. Phillpotts, E. †$1.50. Moffat.

STATUES.
See Sculpture;—*also* names of places.

Status of women under English law. Wallis-Chapman, A. B. *75 c. net. Dutton.

STATUTE LAW.
See Law.

STATUTES.
See names of places.

Staudt, Calvin Klopp.
Idea of the resurrection in the ante-Nicene period. '09(My8) c. 8°, pap., *50 c. net. Univ. of Chic.

Stauffer, Clinton R.
Middle Devonian of Ohio. '09, [1910.] (S) 8+204 p. il. maps, 8°, (Ohio Geological Survey, bull.) pap., 25 c. Ohio Geolog. Survey.

Stawell, F. Melian.
Homer and the Iliad; essay to determine the scope and character of the original poem. '10(Ja22) 8°, *$3 net. Dutton.

Stawell, Mrs. Rodolph.
Motor tours in the west country. '10(O15) il. 8°, $1.75 net. Doran.
Motor tours in Wales and the border counties. '09(Ap10) il. O. $2.50, boxed. L. C. Page.
Motor tours in Yorkshire. '10(O15) il. maps, 8°, $1.75 net. Doran.

Stay at home travels: book of fireside pictures of foreign lands. '09, [1910.] (F) 304 p. il. 4°, bds., $2. Nelson.

Stead, R:
Adventures on the high seas. '08(N7) il. D. (Adventure ser.) *$1.50 net. Lippincott.

Stead, W: T:
How I know that the dead return. '09 (My15) c. D. *75 c. net. Ball Pub. Co.

STEAM.
Marks, L. S., *and* Davis, H. N. Tables and diagrams of thermal properties of saturated and superheated steam. **$1 net. Longmans.
Peabody, C. H. Tables of the properties of steam and other vapors, and temperature-entrophy table. $1. Wiley.
See also Automobiles;—Boilers;—Engines:—Heat;—Locomotives;—Machinery;—Steam engine;—Steam pipes.

STEAM BOILERS.
See Boilers:—Engines.

Steam-electric power plants. Koester, F. **$5 net. Van Nostrand.

STEAM ENGINE.
Branch, J. G. Engineers' descriptive charts with explanatory text; showing development of the steam boiler, the steam engine and the electric generator. $1.—Stationary engineering. 3 v. ea., $2.50. Rand, McN. & Co.
Creighton, W: H: P. Steam-engines and other heat-motors. $5. Wiley.
Ewing, J. A. Steam engine and other heat engines. $3.75 net. Putnam.
Golden, D: W: **Steam engine science. $1. Sutton.**
Grimshaw, R. Engine runners' catechism. $2. Henley.
Hawkins, G: W. Economy factor in steam power plants. $3. Hill Pub.
Hawkins, N. Pract. treatise on the steam engine indicator $1. Audel.
Hutton, F: R. Mechanical engineering of steam power plants. $5. Wiley.
Lisk, J. P. A B C of the steam engine. 50 c. Spon.
Low, F: R. Steam engine indicator. $1.50. McGraw-H.
Richardson, J: Practical treatise on the theory, design, construction and use of the modern steam engine. *$3 net. Van Nostrand.
Sankey, H. R. Energy chart for reciprocating steam engines. $3. Spon.
Swingle, C. F. **Twentieth century hdbk. for steam engineers and electricians. $3. Drake.**
Trooien, O. N. **Current practice in steam engine design. 25 c. Univ. of Wis.**
Vignier, R. M. de. Model steam engine design. 25 c. Spon.
See also Air-brakes;—Boilers;—Engineering;—Engines;—Locomotives;—Marine engineering;—Railroads;—Steam;—Turbines;—Valves.

STEAM ENGINEERING.
See Engineering.

STEAM HEATING.
See Heating.

STEAM PIPES.
Allen, J: K., *ed.* Sizes of flow and return steam mains. 50 c. Domestic Engineering.
Collins, H. E. Pipes and piping. $1. Hill Pub.
Morris, W: L. Steam power plant piping. *$5 net. McGraw-H.

Steam power plant engineering. Gebhardt, G: F: *$6 net. Houghton M.; Wiley.

STEAM TURBINES.
See Turbines.

STEAMBOATS.
See Ships and shipbuilding.

STEAMSHIPS.
See Ships and shipbuilding.

Stearns, Amanda Akin.
Lady nurse of ward E. '09(N6) c. pors. S. **$1.20 net. Baker & T.

Stearns, B:
Diary kept at the siege of Louisburg, Mar. 11-Aug. 2, 1745, with notes and an introd. by S: A. Green. '09(Je) 12 p. 8°, 25 c. S: A. Green.

Stearns, Ezra Scollay, ed.
Genealogical and family history of the state of New Hampshire: record of the achievements of her people in the making of a commonwealth and the founding of a nation; comp. under the editorial supervision of Ezra S. Stearns; assisted by W: F. Whitcher and E: E. Parker. 4 v. '08 [1909.] (N) il. por. 4°. (Add. pubs. for price.) Lewis Pub.

Stearns, I: Newton.
Age of truth and right. '08(O3) c. O. por. 4°, $1.50. I: N. Stearns.

Stearns, Lyman Marshall, ed.
Draughts marvel and twentieth century checker compendium; comp. and ed. under the supervision of Lyman Marshall Stearns, assisted by Will H. Tyson, G: A. Pierce, Ivan Powers, Herbert L. Eddy, and the "silent author" of the Marvel manuscript. '09(Je19) c. il. pors. f°, $4. L. M. Stearns.

STEARNS, *Mrs.* Mary Emmeline (Kittredge.)
Todd, M. Mary E. Stearns. $1.75. D: Todd.

Stearns, Wallace Nelson.
Primer of Hebrew history; a manual for popular use. '09(S4) c. map, fold. tabs., D. *40 c. net. Eaton & M.
—, ed. Fragments from Græco-Jewish writers. '09(Ja16) c. 12°, *75 c. net. Univ. of Chic.

Stebbing, E: Percy.
Jungle by-ways in India; leaves from the note-book of a sportsman and a naturalist. '10(S24) il. O. $4 net. Lane.

Stebbing, W.
The poets: Geoffrey Chaucer to Alfred Tennyson, 1340-1892; impressions. In 2 v. '08(Ja18) D. $3.20. Oxford Univ.
Three essays. '10(D17) c. 8°, pap., 20 c. Oxford Univ.

Stebbins, C. A.
Guide to the birds of the Pacific coast. '10 (D17) il. 8°, (State Normal School, Chico, Cal., bull.) pap., 25 c. C. A. Stebbins.

Stebbins, C: Maurice.
Painter of Madonnas, and other poems. '09(Mr) c. 30 p. 8°, 50 c. English Leaflet.
Progressive course in English for secondary schools: third book for the third and fourth year. '09(Jl) 408 p. *85 c. net. Sibley.

Stebbins, C: Maurice.—*Continued.*
Progressive course in English; literature, composition. '08(Ap4) c. D. 60 c. Sibley.
Sentence improvement; practice book in applied grammar. [1910.] (Je) c. 10+208 p. 12°, 75 c. Sibley.
See also Frary, Marie Harriette.

Stebbins, Mrs. Edna Willett Hodgkins, and Saunderson, H: Hallam.
Old Testament narratives. pt. 1, Hebrew beginnings, by Edna H. Stebbins; pt. 2, Hebrew history, by Henry Hallam Saunderson. [1910.] (F) c. '09. 114; 149 p. 12°, (Beacon ser.) ea., 40 c.; pap., 30 c. Unitarian S. S.

Stebbins, Fannie A.
Insect galls of Springfield, Massachusetts, and vicinity. '10(Jl16) il. O. (Springfield Museum of Natural Hist. bull.) pap., $1.50. Springfield Mu. Nat. Hist.

Stebbins, Joel.
Photometric observations of double stars. '08(Ja25) tabs., O. (Univ. studies.) pap., 75 c. Univ. of Ill.

Stecher, W: A.
Handbook of graded lessons in physical training and games; for primary and grammar grades. In 2 pts. '08(Ag22) c. il. O. pap., ea., *35 c. net. McVey.

Stedman, Douglas C.
Story of Hereward: the champion of England. '09(O23) il. O. *$1.50 net. Crowell.

Stedman, Edm. Clarence.
Edgar Allan Poe. '09(D) pors. $2.50. Torch Press.
Poems. '08(D12) c. por. O. $1.50. Houghton M.

—and T: Lathrop, M.D., eds.
Complete pocket guide to Europe; rev. for 1908. '08, [1909.] (Mr); New ed., rev. '10(Ap23) c. maps, plans, 24°, leath., ea., $1.25 net. W: R. Jenkins.

STEDMAN, Edmund Clarence.
Stedman, L., *and* Gould, G. M. Life and letters of Edmund Clarence Stedman. $6.50 net. Moffat.

Stedman, J: Moore.
See Hamilton, J:

Stedman, Laura, and Gould, G: Milbry, M.D.
Life and letters of Edmund Clarence Stedman. '10(D3) c. il. pors. O. $6.50 net, boxed. Moffat.

Stedman, T: Lathrop, M.D., ed.
Appendix to the reference hdbk. of the medical sciences. Rev. to date. '08(Je13) il. 4°, subs., $5; leath., $6; hf. mor., $7. Wood.

—, ed. *See* Stedman, Edmund Clarence.

Steeb, G: Velten.
Special agents and adjusters handbook: [insurance.] '08(S12) c. il. tabs., 12°, $1.50. Spectator.

Steedman, Amy.
Legends and stories of Italy for children. '10(D31) col. il. 8°, $2.50 net. Putnam.
Little child's life of Jesus. '10(S10) col. il. O. bds., $1. Stokes.
Nursery tales. '08(Je6) il. 16°, (Told to the children ser.) 50 c. Dutton.
See also Steedman, C:

Steedman, C: and Amy.
Lazy John. '07, [1909.] (Jl) il. 4°, bds., $1.50. Jacobs.

Steel, Dan., D.D.
Love enthroned: essays on evangelical perfection. Rev. ed. '09(My22) c. 12°, $1.20. Eaton & M.

Steel, Estelle T:
Land of fortune. [1910.] (Ap) c. 102 p. il. 8°, 75 c. E. T. Steel.

Steel, Mrs. Flora Annie Webster.
India through the ages; popular and picturesque hist. of Hindustan. '10(Ap2) maps, 12°, $1.25 net. Dutton.
Prince of dreamers. '09(F27) c. D. †$1.25. Doubleday, P.

Steel, R. Elliot.
Pract. electricity and magnetism; first year course. '10(D24) c. 50 c. net. Macmillan.

Steel, Rufus.
The city that is: story of the re-building of San Francisco in three years. '09(N20) il. 8°, bds., *$1 net. A. M. Robertson.

STEEL.
American Iron and Steel Association. Directory to the iron and steel works of the U. S. $12.—Canadian supp. Am. Iron and Steel.
Becker, O. M. High-speed steel. $4. McGraw-H.
Cambria Steel Co. Cambria steel; hdbk. of information. $1. Cambria Steel.
Cole, M. Tempering steel; annealing and case hardening iron. 10 c. Sampson.
Collier, A. L. Steel. 35 c. A. L. Collier.
Cushman, A. S. Preservation of iron and steel. 10 c. U. S., Supt. of Docs.
Cushman, A. S., *and* Gardner, H: A. Corrosion and preservation of iron and steel. $4 net. McGraw-H.
Harbord, F. W., *and* Hall, J. W. Steel: its metallurgy and mechanical treatment. *$9 net. Lippincott.
Hardening and tempering. 25 c. Indust. Press.
Heess, J: K. Practical methods for the iron and steel works chemist. $1. Chemical.
Hodgson, F: T: Pract. steel construction. $1. Drake.
Johnson, C: M. Rapid methods for the chemical analysis of special steels, steel-making alloys, and graphite. $3. Wiley.
Jones & Laughlins. Standard steel construction. (Add. pubs. for price.) Jones & Laughlins.
Ketchum, M. S. Design of steel mill buildings and the calculation of stresses in framed structures. $3. Engineering News.
Lake, E. F. Composition and heat treatment of steel. $1.50. McGraw-H.
Macfarlane, W. Laboratory notes on iron and steel analyses. *$2.50 net. Longmans.
Parrock, H. P. "Grades of steel." $1. H. P. Parrock.
Sang, A. Corrosion of iron and steel. $1. McGraw-H.

STEEL.—*Continued.*
Smith, J. R. Story of iron and steel. **75 c. net. Appleton.
Stansbie, J. H. Iron and steel. *$2 net. Van Nostrand
Tariff on trust-made steel articles. gratis. Univ. of Wis.
Tucker, E: A. Steel construction. $1.50. Am. Sch. Corr.
United States. Iron and steel products; estimates of increases and reductions in duties of H. R. 1438. (Add. Superintendent for price.) U. S., Supt. of Docs.
Warren, W: H: Engineering construction in steel and timber. $5 net. Longmans.
Woodworth, J. V. Drop forging, die sinking, and machine forming of steel. $2.50. Henley.
See also Arches;—Bridges;—Concrete;—Furnaces;—Grinding;—Painting (*mechanical*); → United States Steel Corporation.

STEEL SQUARE.
See Squares.

Steele, Carol.
See Swift, Lance.

Steele, Francesca Maria Fanny, ["Darley Dale."]
Beautiful queen, Joanna I. of Naples. '10 (D3) il. 8°, $3.50 net. Dodd.

Steele, F: Morgan.
After hour idyls. '09, [1910.] (Mr) 11+3-126 p. por. 8°, $3. Smith & S.

Steele, Harold Brian.
Poems; with biog. introd. '09(N) c. 39 p. pors. 12°, $1.50. Lanthorne.

Steele, Jack.
Husband by proxy. '09(Je26) c. D. $1.50. FitzGerald.

Steele, Ja. King.
Hope Ranch, [Santa Barbara, Cal.] '09 (Ap3) c. il. map, F. bds., $1.25. Pacific Improvement.

Steele, Marshall, comp.
One and all reciter: serious, humorous and dramatic selections. '09(S18) S. *$1 net. Lane.
See also Arnold, Paul.

—, and others.
Children's action songs; actions by Marshall Steele; music by Paul Arnold, Valentine Hemery and Nora Reade. '08 (My16) il. F. pap., *35 c. net. Cassell.

Steele, Matthew Forney.
American campaigns. '09(D25) maps, 8°, (United States General Staff pub.) (Add. Superintendent for price.) U. S., Supt. of Docs.

Steele, Sir R:
See Addison, Jos.;—Irving, Washington.

Steele, Rob. Reynolds, comp.
Tudor and Stuart proclamations, 1485-1714; calendared by Rob. Steele under the direction of the Earl of Crawford. In 2 v. v. 1, England and Wales; v. 2, Scotland and Ireland. '10(D24) il. fold. map, F. $34. Oxford Univ.

Steele, Sherman.
Students' text on the law of principal and agent. '09(N) c. 15+347 p. O. (Add. pubs. for price.) Flood.

Steele, Zadock.
Indian captive; or, a narrative of the captivity and sufferings of Zadock Steele, related by himself, to which is prefixed an account of the burning of Royalton. '08(My23) facsim., map, S. (Indian captivities ser.) bds., $2.50; large pap. ed., $5. Huntting.

STEELMAN FAMILY.
See Genealogies: Hess, T:

Steen, Jan.
Masterpieces; reproductions from his most renowned pictures. '08(O24) T. (Dutch painters.) leath., *75 c. net; pap., *25 c. net. Stokes.

Steen, Rob. Service.
Strength of quietness, and other sermons. '08(D26) c. S. 75 c. Dodd.

STEENDAM, Jacob.
Andrews, W: L. Jacob Steendam. **$7.50 net. Lamb Pub.

STEERAGE.
***See* Ships and shipbuilding.**

Steere, C: Allen.
When things were doing. '08(Ja4) D. $1. Kerr.

Steering wheel. Wason, R. A. $1.50. Bobbs-M.

Steffens, Jos. Lincoln.
Upbuilders. '09(O16) c. il. D. **$1.20 net. Doubleday, P.

Steiger, Ernst.
Urheberrecht und nachdruck in Nord-Amerika: plaudereien zur berichtigung irriger anschauungen. Als manuskript gedruckt. '09(Ja9) S. pap., gratis. Steiger.

Stein, Evaleen.
Little shepherd of Provence. '10(N5) c. col. il. D. (Roses ser.) $1. L. C. Page.

Stein, Fs. Julius.
Improved Pitman shorthand; fastest and most accurate shorthand in the world. Standard system. '10(Ag27) c. 12°, $1. Stein Pub.

Stein, Gertrude.
Three lives; stories of the good Anna, Melanctha, and The gentle Lena. '09 (D4) c. D. **$1.50 net. Grafton Press.

Stein, Grace Maxine.
Glimpses around the world through the eyes of a young American. '10(My14) c. il. O. $2 net. Winston.

Stein, J. J.
It's great to be crazy: a farce. '08(N14) c. D. pap., 15 c. Penn Pub. Co.

Steiner, Rev. E: Alfr.
Against the current; simple chapters from complex life. '10(N5) c. O. $1.25 net. Revell.
Cup of Elijah. '10(Mr19) c. D. (Idyll envelope ser.) pap., *25 c. net. Revell.
Immigrant tide; its ebb and flow. '09(O23) c. il. O. *$1.50 net. Revell.
Tolstoy, the man and his message. Enl. ed. '09(F13) c. il. pors. D. *$1 net. Revell.

Steiner, Harry Lee.
How to keep farm accounts; pract. book for the pract. farmer and a text book for use in agricultural schools. [3d ed.] '09, [1910.] (F) c. 152 p. 8°, $1. Steiner & Co.

Steiner, Rudolf.
Initiation and its results; sequel to "The way of initiation"; tr. from the German by Clifford Bax. '10(F19) c 12°, $1.25. Macoy Pub.
Theosophy; introd. to the supersensible knowledge of the world and the destination of man; tr., with the permission of the author, from the 3d German ed. by E. D. S. '10(D24) c. D. $1. Rand, McN. & Co.
Way of initiation; or, how to attain knowledge of the higher worlds; from the German by Max Gysi, with some biographical notes of the author by Édouard Schuré. '10(Ap) c. 7-163 p. por. 12°, $1; 75 c. Macoy Pub.

Steinmetz, C: Proteus.
General lectures on electrical engineering; ed. by Jos. Le Roy Hayden. '08(Ag22); '10(My14) c. il. por. 12°, ea., $2 net. Robson.
Radiation, light and illumination; series of engineering lectures del. at Union College; comp. and ed. by Jos. Le Roy Hayden. '09(N6) c. il. O. *$3 net. McGraw-H.
Theoretical elements of electrical engineering. 3d ed., thoroughly rev. and greatly corrected. '09(N6) c. il. O. *$4 net. McGraw-H.
Theory and calculation of alternating current phenomena. 4th ed., thoroughly rev. and greatly enl. '08 [1909.] (F) c. 22+746 p. il. 8°, *$5 net. McGraw.
Theory and calculations of transient electric phenomena and oscillations. '09 (Mr27) c. O. fig. $5. McGraw.

Steinmetz, Estella Hartzler, ed.
Reminiscences; being a record of five and twenty years' progress in the Woman's Home and Foreign Missionary Society of the United Evangelical Church. '10 (Jl) c. 129 p. il. map, por. 8°, 60 c. Un. Evangelical.

Stellman, L: J.
Vanished ruin era; San Francisco's classic artistry of ruin depicted in picture and song. '10(O8) c. il. 4°, $2.50. P. Elder.

Stellwagen, Charlotte Fisher.
Beatrice; or, the princess with the wonderful hair. '10(O) c. 38 p. 8°. (Priv. pr.) W. F. Roberts.

Stelwagon, H: Weightman.
Essentials of diseases of the skin, incl. the syphilodermata, arr. in the form of questions and answers; prepared especially for students of medicine. 7th ed., thoroughly rev. '09(O) c. 11-291 p. il. 12°, (Saunders' question-compends.) *$1 net. Saunders.
Treatise on diseases of the skin, for the use of advanced students and practitioners. 6th ed., thoroughly rev. '10(O) c. 1195 p. il. 8°, $6. Saunders.

Stelzle, C:
The church and labor. '10(Mr5) c. S. (Modern religious problems.) **50 c. net. Houghton M.
Church and the labor movement. '10(D31) 12°, (Social service ser.) pap., 10 c. Am. Bapt.

Stelzle, C:—*Continued.*
Letters from a workingman. '08(O10) c. 16°, *$1 net. Revell.
Principles of successful church advertising. '09(Ja30) c. il. O. *$1.25 net. Revell.

—, Addams, Jane, Neill, C: P., and others.
Social application of religion: Merrick lectures for 1907-8, del. at Ohio Wesleyan University. '09(Ja16) c. D. *75 c. net. Jennings.

Stem of the crimson dahlia. Locke, J. †$1.50. Moffat.

STENCILING.
See Decoration and ornament.

Stene, And. E:
San José scale (*Aspidiotus perniciosus,* Comst) and methods of treatment. '09 (F20) il. figs. O. (Rhode Island College of Agriculture and Mechanics Arts; joint bulletin of the State Board of Agriculture and Extension Dept.) gratis. R. I. Coll.

Stenger, Gilbert.
Return of Louis XVIII.; [tr.] from the French by Mrs. Rodolph Stawell. '09 (D11) pors. O. *$3 net. Scribner.

Stenographer's and correspondent's hdbk.; reference work on stenographic and typewriting methods, business correspondence, diction, modern office practice, postal information, and allied subjects. '10(D3) c. T. $1.25; leath., $1.50. Int. Text-bk.

Stenographer's guide. Chase, F. N. 15 c. F. N. Chase.

STENOGRAPHY.
Abernethy, L. S: Shorthand. $1.50. Driggers.
Aldrich, T: B. Little violinist and other prose sketches in phonography. Phonograph.
Andersen, H. C. Ugly duckling, and other stories. [phonography.] 25 c. Phonograph.
Anderson, W: L. American phonography. $1.20.—Graded exercises to accompany the above. 50 c. Ginn.
Baillie, D: G. Swiftsure phonetic shorthand system. $1. Phillips Pr.
Barnes, L. E. Business letters in shorthand. $1.—Modern Graham shorthand. $1.25.—Practical course in shorthand. $1.25.—Shorthand dict. and phrasebook. $1.25; $1.40.—Shorthand lessons by the sentence method; American Pitman phonography. $1.25. A. J. Barnes.
Barnes, L. E. Heald's Pitman-Graham shorthand. $1.25. E: P. Heald.
Bellamy, W: W. Shorthand construction. 25 c. W: W. Bellamy.
Blodgett, H. T. Shorthand speed book. In 2 pts. ea., $1. Long Branch Press.
Bottome, W. B. Stenographic expert. $2. W. B. Bottome.
Brown, D: W. Factors of shorthand speed. 75 c. Gregg Pub.
Business correspondence in shorthand. no. 7. 25 c. Pitman.
Byrne, H. E: Simplified shorthand. $5. Byrne Pub.
Chartier, E: M. Dictation to reporting shorthand. $1.50. E: M. Chartier.

STENOGRAPHY.—*Continued.*

Chase, F. N. Stenographer and employer. $1.—Stenographer's guide for daily desk reference. 15 c. F. N. Chase.

Cope, E: A. Acquisition of speed in shorthand. 20 c. Pitman.

Curry, J. S: Euclid shorthand manual: Graham-Pitmanic. $1.50. Burrows.

Dement, I. S. Dement's Pitmanic shorthand. $2. Dement Pub.

Dettmann, E: O. Complete text-book of phono-stenography *$1 net. Stechert.

Dickens, C: Christmas carol; in amanuensis style of phonography. 35 c. Phonograph.

Dickens, C: Mugby Junction and other stories: printed in the corresponding style of Pitman's shorthand. 50 c. Pitman.

Eldridge, E: H. Shorthand dictation exercises. Edition without shorthand outlines; Graham ed.; Gregg ed.; Ben Pitan ed.; Isaac Pitman ed. ea., 65 c. Am. Bk.

Gaines, C. C., *ed.* Simplified phonetic shorthand. $2. C. C. Gaines.

Gardner, E. E. American Pitmanic shorthand. $1.25. Am. Pitmanic.

Glass, D: R. Lightning legible shorthand. (Add. author for price.) D: R. Glass.

Gregg, J: R. Gregg reporter. $1.50. Gregg Pub.

Guthrie, J. D. Sidelights on Byrne simplified shorthand. 75 c. Byrne Pub.

Hammond, H. W., *and others.* Pitman's progressive dictator. 85 c. Pitman.

Hardcastle, *Mrs.* M. A Word signs made easy, Graham phonography. $1. Word Sign.

Haven, C. Complete manual of practical phonography. $2. C. Haven.

Hayne, R. Y. Speech on Foote's resolution; in reporting style of phonography. (Add. pubs. for price.) Phonograph.

Hitlofi, I. Grafoni; new phonography. 50 c. I. Hitlofi.

Howard, J. B. Progressive dictation exercises, designed to accompany The phonographic amanuensis. 25 c. Phonograph.

Hurst, W: H. Silagraphy; new system of shorthand. $1.50. Hurst.

Kehoe, W: J. Manual of the Kehoe stenographic writer. $1. W. F. Roberts.

Kells, R. A. Stereopticon lecture on shorthand. 25 c. Pitman.

Kennedy, A. M. Essentials of phonography. 20 c. Pitman.

Lincoln, A. Selections from Lincoln's speeches and letters arr. for learners of Munson phonography. 75 c. S. S. Packard.

Mason, W. L., *comp.* How to become a law stenographer. $1: 75 c. Pitman.

Miller, C. C. Zigzag-lightning shorthand. (Add. pubs. for price.) Zigzag.

Munson, J. E. Pocket phonographic dictionary. $1. Am. Bk.

Packard, *Mrs.* L. H. How to make a living, arranged for learners of Munson phonography. 75 c.—Practical phonography. $1. S. S. Packard.

Pitman, B. New pract. shorthand manual. $1.25. Carnell.

Pitman, B., *and* Howard, J. B. Business letters. no. 4, 5, 6. ea., 25 c. Pitman.

Pitman, B., *and* Howard, J. B. Legal forms: in amanuensis style of phonography. (Add. pubs. for price.) Phonograph.

Pitman, *Sir* I: Abr. shorthand dict. 75 c. —Course in Isaac Pitman's shorthand. $1.50.—Key to Pitman's shorthand writing exercises and examination exercises. —$1.25.—Key to Spanish shorthand. $1. —Shorthand dict. $1.50. Pitman.

Rasmussen, W. Graded dictation. $1. Gregg Pub.

Rosenblum, A. Advanced course in Isaac Pitman phonography. $1.—Intermediate course in Isaac Pitman phonography. 75 c. Blythebourne Pub.

Shamburger, J. I. J. Select shorthand for general and verbatim reporting. $1.50. R. L. Shamburger.

So Relle, R. P. Expert shorthand speed course. $1.25. Gregg Pub.

Stein, F. J. Improved Pitman shorthand. $1. Stein Pub.

Stone, W. J. Shorthand for amanuensis, court and verbatim reporting. $2. W: J. Stone.

Tinus, W. I. Shorthand. $1.50. Tinus-H.

Van Sant, E., *ed.* Munson shorthand dict. $1. J. A. Lyons.

Wagner, W: H: Wagner phonography. $1. W: H: Wagner.

Walters, C. L. Presentation of Graham-Pitman phonographic shorthand. 80 c. C. L. Walters.

Walton, D. W. Pitmanic guide for students and teachers of Isaac Pitman shorthand. 20 c. Pitman.

Weichmann, L: J. Testimony of L: J. Weichmann, in reporting style of phonography. Phonograph.

See also Typewriting.

Stenstrand, August J.

Call of attention to the Behaists or Babists of America: [sect. of Mohammedans.] '08(My23) 12°, pap. (Add. pubs. for price.) A. J. Stenstrand.

Stenton, Fk. Merry.

William the Conqueror, and the rule of the Normans. '08(N7) c. il. maps, facsim., D. (Heroes of the nations.) **$1.35 net. Putnam.

Step, E.

Wayside and woodland ferns: guide to the British ferns, horse-tails and club-mosses. '09(Mr27) il. S. (Wayside woodland ser.) *$2.25 net. Warne.

Wayside and woodland trees: guide to British sylva. '07. [1908.] (F) 182 p. il. 12°, *$1.75 net. Warne.

Step by step. Isaacs, A. S: 75 c. Jewish Pub.

Step forward for the democracy of to-morrow. Thum, W: $1. Twentieth Century.

Stepanek, W. H.

Business methods in a hardware store. '09 (O2) c. il. Q. $1.50. W. H. Stepanek.

Stephan, Wa. G:

Drawing instruments: their use and abuse. '08(Ag1) c. il. D. *$1 net. McGraw.

Stephen, Caroline Emelia.
Light arising: thoughts on the central radiance. '08(O3) D. **90 c. net. Winston.

Stephen, Sir Leslie.
Playground of Europe. '09(My8) O. *$1.75 net. Putnam.

—, and Lee, Sidney Lazarus, eds.
Dictionary of national biography. New ed. in 22 v. v. 1. '08(Mr21); v. 2 (Ap); v. 3, 4 (Je); v. 5 (Ag1); v. 6 (Ag29); v. 7 (S19); v. 8 (O31); v. 9 (D5); v. 10 (D26); v. 11. '09(F6); v. 12 (F27); v. 13 (Ap3); v. 14 (My1); v. 15 (Je5); v. 16 (Jl3); v. 17 (Ag14); v. 18 (S18); v. 19 (O2); v. 20 (N6); v. 21, 22. '10(Ja15) 8°, ea., *$4.25 net. (Sold in sets only.) Macmillan.

Stephen (Leslie) lecture. *See* Raleigh, Wa. Alex.

Stephen of Philadelphia. Kaler, J. O. 35 c. Am. Bk.

Stephens, A. G.
See Dorrington, Alb.

Stephens, Alex. Hamilton.
Recollections of Alexander H. Stephens; his diary kept while a prisoner at Fort Warren, Boston Harbour, 1865. '10(N19) c. por. O. $2.50 net. Doubleday, P.

STEPHENS, Alexander Hamilton.
Pendleton, L: B. Alexander H. Stephens. **$1.25 net. Jacobs.

Stephens, Mrs. Ann S.
Mary Derwent. '09(Ap10) il. 12°, (Standard fiction.) $1. Burt.

Stephens, C: Asbury, M.D.
Natural salvation (salvation by science); immortal life on the earth from the growth of knowledge and the development of the human brain. 6th ed. '10 (Mr5) c. il 4°, $1.75. Laboratory Co.

Stephens, Edn. W:
Around the world; narrative in letter form of a trip around the world from Oct., 1907, to July, 1908. '10(Je4) c. il. 8°, $5. E. W. Stephens.

Stephens, Fk. Fletcher.
Transitional period, 1788-1789, in the government of the United States. '09(Ag21) Q. (Univ. of Mo. studies, Social science ser.) pap., $1. Univ. of Mo.

Stephens, J. E. R.
Law of carriage. '09(Jl31) O. $2. Pitman.

Stephens, Ja.
Insurrections: [poems.] '10(F19) S. *40 c. net. Macmillan.
Lonely God, and other poems. '09, [1910.] (My) 27 p. 12°, $1.50 net. Macmillan.

Stephens, J: Rittenhouse.
Principles of accounting. '09(D18) c. 8°, $1.25. J: R. Stephens.

Stephens, J: Vant, D.D.
Presbyterian churches, divisions and unions in Scotland, Ireland, Canada and America. '10(Je25) c. il. diagrs., D. 75 c. Presb. Bd.

Stephens, Kate, ed.
Stories from old chronicles; chosen and edited with brief introds. to the stories and a general introd. by Kate Stephens. '09(O9) c. D. $1.50. Sturgis & W.
See also Mabie, Hamilton Wright.

Stephens, Rob. Grier.
See Jones, E: Groves.

Stephens, Rob. Neilson.
Tales from Bohemia. '08(O3) c. il. D. D. $1.50. L. C. Page.

Stephens, Dean W: R: W., and Hunt, W:, eds.
New history of the English Church. In 8 v. v. 8, The nineteenth century, by F. W. W. Cournish. In 2 pts. '10(D31) 12°, per pt., $2 net. Macmillan.

Stephens, Winifred.
French novelists of to-day. '08(My2) por. D. $1.50. Lane.

Stephenson, Cora Bennett.
Hand of God: [novel.] '09(My1) c. front. D. $1.50. Ball Pub. Co.

Stephenson, Gilbert T:
Race distinctions in American law. '10 (S17) c. O. $1.50 net. Appleton.

Stephenson, H: Thew.
Elizabethan people. '10(F19) c. il. pors. D. **$2 net. Holt.

Stephenson, Ja., jr.
Irrigation in Idaho. '09(D) 59 p. fold. map, 8°, (U. S., Dept. of Agriculture, Office of Experiment Stations, bull.) pap.

Stephenson, Ja. H., and others.
Farm engines and how to run them. '10 (D31) c. il. 12°, $1. Drake.

Stephenson, J: W., comp.
Upholsterer vest pocket compendium of drapery styles, naming the fabrics, trimmings, period styles, and utility of each design. '09(O23) c. il. Tt. pap., 50 c. Clifford & L.

Steppes, J: P., ["John Ritsch, Esq."]
John Ritsch, Esq.: auslese aus den humoristischen briefen. '08(S19) c. D. pap., $1. J: P. Steppes.

Steps along the path. Newcomb, *Mrs.* K. H. **$1.40 net. Lothrop, L. & S.

Steps in the Christian life. Silkwood, B. 50 c. Jennings.

Steps to Christ. White, E. G. H. 60 c.; $1.25. Pacific Press.

Steps to Nowhere. Boylan, G. D. $1.50. Baker & T.

Steps unto heaven. Blaikie, W: G. $1.50. Northfield Press.

Stepson of fortune. Murray, H: $2.75 net. Baker & T.

STEREOGRAPH.
See Stereoscope.

STEREOPTICON.
Jenkins, C: F., *and* Depue, O. B. Hdbk. for motion picture and stereopticon operators. $2.50. Knega.

STEREOSCOPE.
Osborne, A. E. Stereograph and the stereoscope. $1. Underwood.

STEREOTYPING.
Partridge, C: S. Stereotyping; with special consideration of the papier maché process. $2. Inland Pr.

Sterling, Albert M.
Sterling genealogy. '10(Ja8) il. 8°, Sterling ed., *$50 net; Library ed., *$25 net. Grafton Press.

Sterling, G:
Wine of wizardry, and other poems. '09 (F27) c. D. *$1.25 net. A. M. Robertson.

STERLING, John.
Carlyle, T: Life of John Sterling. 35 c. Oxford Univ.

Sterling, Mary Blackwell, comp.
Story of Sir Galahad; retold from the Morte d'Arthur of Sir T: Malory and the original stories. '08(N21) il. 8°, $1.50. Dutton.

STERLING FAMILY.
See Genealogies.

Sternberg, Count.
Barbarians of Morocco; tr. from the German by Ethel Peck. '09(S11) il. 8°, **$2 net. Duffield.

Sternberg, C: Hazelius.
Life of a fossil hunter; with an introd. by H: Fairfield Osborn. '09(F27) c. il. por. facsim., O. (American nature ser.: group IV, Working with nature.) **$1.60 net. Holt.

Sternberg, G: Miller.
Rept. of committee on model houses. '08, [1909.] (My) 111 p. il. tabs., 8°. (Add. Superintendent for price.) U. S., Supt. of Docs.

Stern, Renée Bernd.
Neighborhood entertainments. '10(S10) c. il. D. (Young farmers' pract. lib.) 75 c. net. Sturgis & W.

Sterne, Laurence.
My Uncle Toby; ed. by T: Cartwright. '08(Ag15) 16°, (Every child's lib.) 50 c. Dutton.
Sentimental journey through France and Italy. '10(D) il. 16°, flex., leath., $1.25 net. Brentano's.
Sentimental journey through France and Italy. '08(O10) il. por. D. $1.50. Lippincott.
Sentimental journey through France and Italy. '10(D3) col. il. Q. $3. Putnam.

STERNE, Laurence.
Cross, W. L. Life and times of Laurence Sterne. *$2.50 net. Macmillan.
Sichel, W. S. Sterne; a study. $2.50. Lippincott.

Sterns, Justin.
Orsu; tale of many incarnations; hist. of a soul. '10(Je4) c. front. 12°, $1.25. Lenox Pub.

Stetson, Augusta Emma.
Poems written on the journey from sense to soul. 3d ed. '10(S17) il. $2. A. E. Stetson.

Stettheimer, Ettie.
Will to believe as a basis for the defense of religious faith. '08(Ap11) Q. (Archives of philosophy.) pap., $1. Science Pr., (N. Y.)

Stevens, Adeline T. Chapman.
See Stevens, *Mrs.* Fk. Lincoln.

Stevens, Agnes L.
Palmistry made easy. '09(My1) c. il. S. pap.. 50 c. A. L. Stevens.

STEVENS, Alfred.
Stannus, H: Drawings of Alfred Stevens. *$2.50 net. Scribner.

Stevens, Alviso Burdett.
Manual of pharmacy and dispensing. '09 (S) 421 p. il. 12°, *$2.50 net. Lea.

Stevens, Arth. Albert.
Modern materia medica and therapeutics. 5th ed., thoroughly rev. in conformity with the eighth revision (1905) of the United States Pharmacopœia. '09(N) c. 7-675 p. 8°, $3.50. Saunders.

Stevens, Beatrice.
See Boult, Ella M.

Stevens, C: McClellan, ed.
Standard home and school dictionary. '09 (My) c. 607 p. il. pors. 8°, $3. Judge.

Stevens, D: Kilburn.
Lays of a lazy dog, by Teddy; interpreted by D. K. Stevens. '09(D4) c. il. S. bds., 50 c. J: W. Luce.

Stevens, E. Ray, Keyes, Elisha, Williams, Holand, Hjalmar, Rued, and Burr, W. Jones.
John B. Cassoday, by E. Ray Stevens; Julius Taylor Clark, by Elisha W. Keyes; Nils Otto Tank, by Hjalmar Rued Holand; William Freeman Vilas, by Burr W. Jones: from the proceedings of the State Historical Society of Wisconsin for 1908. [1910.] (Ap) 136-164 p. O. pap., 20 c. State Hist., Wis.

Stevens, E. Winchester.
Watseka wonder: narrative of startling phenomena, and authenticated instance of spirit manifestation. '08(D) c. 72 p. pors. 12°, 60 c.; pap., 35 c. Austin.

Stevens, Edith, comp.
A-weaving for you. '10(O8) c. O. pap., 75 c., boxed; ooze, $1.50, boxed. Platt & P.
Lavender and rosemary; nature thoughts for nature lovers. '10(O8) c. O. pap., 75 c., boxed; ooze, $1.50, boxed. Platt & P.

Stevens, E: Laurence.
See De Forest, A. Preston.

Stevens, Ethel Stefana.
The veil: a romance of Tunis. '09(S18) c. D. †$1.50. Stokes.

Stevens, Fk. Lincoln, and Hall, J: G.
Diseases of economic plants. '10(O8) c. il. por. D. $2 net. Macmillan.

—, Butler, Tait, and Stevens, Adeline T. Chapman, [Mrs. Fk. Lincoln Stevens.]
Practical arithmetic. '09(Ap17) c. il. 12°, **65 c. net. Scribner.

Stevens, Mrs. Fk. Lincoln.
See Stevens, Adeline T. Chapman.

Stevens, G: B.
Teaching of Jesus. '09(Ap3) 12°, (New Testament handbooks.) Price raised from *75 c. net to *$1 net. Macmillan.

Stevens, G: T:, M.D.
Illustrated guide to flowering plants. '10 (D24) il. 8°, $2.50 net. Dodd.

Stevens, G: W., rep.
See Georgia. *Cts. of appeals.* Repts.—*Sup. ct.* Repts.

Stevens, Gorham Phillips.
See Fowler, Harold North.

Stevens, H: P.
Paper mill chemist. '08(Ag1) il. 12°, **$2.50 net. Van Nostrand.

Stevens, Horace.
See Puter, Stephen A. Douglas.

Stevens, Horace Jared, comp.
Copper handbook. v. 7, 1907. '08(Je27); v. 8, 1908. '09(My); v. 9. '09, [1910.] (Ag) c. 8°, ea., $5 net; mor., $7.50 net. H. J. Stevens.

Stevens, I: N.
The liberators. '08(Mr14) c. D. $1.50. B. W. Dodge.

Stevens, J: Cyprian.
Surface water supply of Nebraska. '09 (Jl) 25 p. il. 8°, (U. S. Geol. Survey, Water-supply paper.) pap. (Add. Superintendent for price.) U. S., Supt. of Docs.

Stevens, J: Fk.
Sketch of the Panama Canal. '09(Mr27) 8°. (Priv. pr.) J: F. Stevens.

Stevens, Nettie.
Tompkinsville folks; story of the central states' village life. '09(D18) c. il. 12°, $1.50. C. M. Clark.

Stevens, Plowdon.
Stephens-Stevens genealogy; lineage from Henry Stephens, or Stevens of Stonington, Connecticut, 1668. '09(O16) c. il. pors. facsim., 12°, (Allaben genealogical ser.) $5. Allaben.

Stevens, Rowan, Henderson, W: Ja., Munroe, Kirk, and others.
Battle for the Pacific, and other adventures at sea. '08(Ap18) c. il. D. †$1.25. Harper.

Stevens, S: Eug., M.D.
Philosophy of the great unconscious. '08 (N21) c. 12°, *$1.50 net. Old Corner.

Stevens, T: Holdup.
See Adventures at sea.

Stevens, T: Wood.
Book of words; pageant of the Italian renaissance; produced at the Art Institute, Chicago, January 26 and 27, 1909, under the auspices of the Antiquarian Society of the Art Institute. '09(Ap10) c. il. O. pap., 50 c. Antiquarian Soc.

Stevens, Wa. Barlow.
Trip to Panama: tour of observation through the canal zone, with some account of visits to Saint Thomas, Porto Rico, Jamaica and Cuba, by the Commercial Clubs of Boston, Chicago, Cincinnati and St. Louis. '08(My9) c. il. 4°, pap., gratis. Lesan-G.

Stevens, Wa. LeConte.
College standardization. '08, [1909.] (My) 528-539 p. 8°, pap. (Not for sale.) W. L. Stevens.

Stevens, W: Burnham.
Hist. of the Fiftieth Reg. of Infantry, Mass. vol. militia, in the late War of the Rebellion. '08(Ja4) il. pors. plan, 8°, $2. Griffith-S.

Stevens, W: Chase.
Plant anatomy from the standpoint of the development and functions of the tissues and hdbk. of microtechnic. 2d ed., rev. and enl. '10(N12) c. O. $2 net. Blakiston.

Stevens, W: Oliver.
Another Annapolis alphabet: limericks. '07. [1908.] (F) c. 57 p. il. 12°, bds., 50 c. Lord Balto. Pr.
See also Clark, G: Ramsey.

Stevens, W: Oliver, and McKee, Barclay.
Young privateersman. '10(O8) c. il. D. $1.50. Appleton.

STEVENS FAMILY.
See Genealogies.

Stevenson, Adlai Ewing.
Education and business leadership. '09 (N) 16 p. 8°. (Add. pubs. for price.) Univ. Extension.

Something of men I have known; with some papers of a general nature, political, historical and retrospective. '09 (N20) c. il. O. *$2.75 net. McClurg.

Stevenson, Augusta.
Children's classics in dramatic form: reader for the 4th grade. Bk. 1. '08(N14) **40 c. net; Bk. 2. '10(Mr5) c. il. 12°, **35 c. net. Houghton M.

Stevenson, Burton Egbert.
Guide to biography for young readers: American men of mind. '10(Jl30) c. pors. D. (Guide ser.) $1.25 net. Baker & T.

Path of honor; tale of the war in the Bocage. '10(N12) c. il. D. (Bastile ser.) $1.50. Lippincott.

Quest for the rose of Sharon. '09(My15) c. il. D. $1.25. L. C. Page.

Young train master. '09(O23) c. il. O. (Boys' story of the railroad ser.) †$1.50. L. C. Page.

—, comp. and ed. Poems of American history. '08(D12) c. O. **$3 net. Houghton M.

Stevenson, C: Hugh.
International regulations of the fisheries on the high seas; from bulletin of the Bureau of Fisheries, volume XXVIII, 1908; proceedings of the Fourth International Fishery Congress: Washington, 1908. '10(Mr26) maps, 8°, (U. S., Bu. of Fisheries, bull.)
See also Kunz, G: F:

Stevenson, E: Luther.
Early Spanish cartography of the New World; with special reference to the Wolfenbüttel-Spanish map and the work of Diego Ribero; [repr. from the Proseedings of the Amer. Antiquarian Society for April, 1909.] '10(Jl16) maps, 4°, 50 c. Davis Press.

Facsimile reproduction in ten sheets of the map of 1502 (?) of Nicolo de Canerio. '09(N20) 88 x 44 inches, with explanatory pamphlet, $20. Hispanic Soc.

Stevenson, Rev. J. G.
Children's Paul; life of St. Paul for young people. '10(S17) il. D. 85 c. net. Eaton & M.

Stevenson, Marion.
Studies in the books of the Bible; advanced standard teacher training course. '08(N) 12°, 75 c. Chr. Pub. Co.

Stevenson, R. A. M.
Peter Paul Rubens. [1910.] (F) 224 p. il. 12°, *75 c. net; leath., *$1 net. Dutton.

Stevenson, Rob. L:
Works; ed. by C: Curtis Bigelow and Temple Scott. In 10 v. '08(Je27) c. il. 8°, $15; ¾ Persian mor., $19.75. Lamb Pub.
Works. In 10 v. Popular ed. '10(D24) 12°, $6; hf. mor., $8. (Sold only in sets.) Scribner.
Child's garden of verses; sel. and arr. by Melvin Hix. '10(N12) c. 12°, (Golden hour ser.) 40 c. Educ. Pub.
Child's garden of verses. '09(Ap3) c. il. D. 40 c. Flanagan.
Child's garden of verses. '09(N13) c. col. il. Q. $1. McLoughlin.
Child's garden of verses; il. in col. by Millicent Sowerby. New ed. '09(My) o. p. Scribner.
Child's garden of verses. '09(O30) c. il. 12°, 50 c. Scribner.
Child's garden of verses; il. by Florence Edith Storer. '09(D4) c. il. (partly col.) O. $1.50. Scribner.
Dynamiter. '08(Ag8) 12°, (Magnolia lib.) 50 c. Hurst.
Edinburgh; picturesque notes. New ed. '09(Ap3) il. O. *$1.75 net. Scribner.
From day to day with Stevenson; comp. by Wallace and Frances Rice. '10(Ag27) c. front. por. 12°, 75 c. Barse & H.
In the South Seas: account of experiences and observations in the Marquesas, Paumotus and Gilbert Islands in the course of two cruises on the yacht "Casco" (1888) and the schooner "Equator" (1889). '08(D5) map, 12°, (Biographical ed. of the works of Robert Louis Stevenson.) *$1 net; leath., *$1.25 net. Scribner.
Inland voyage, and Travels with a donkey in the Cevennes; ed., with introd. and notes, by Allan Abbott. '10(My7) c. maps, por. 12°, (Merrill's English texts.) 40 c. C: E. Merrill.
Inland voyage and Travels with a donkey; ed. for school use by Arth. Willis Leonard. '10(O22) c. S. (Lake English classics.) 35 c. Scott, F. & Co.
Kidnapped. '08(Je6) 16°, (Everyman's lib.) *35 c. net; *70 c. net. Dutton.
Kidnapped: the adventures of David Balfour in the year 1751. '08(Ag22) c. il. sq. O. 35 c. McLoughlin.
Kidnapped; ed., with introd. and notes, by J: Thompson Brown. '09(Ja23) c. map, T. (Pocket Am. and Eng. classics.) 25 c. Macmillan.
Meaning of friendship; with an introd. note by Edn. Osgood Grover. '09(Je12) c. por. D. bds., 50 c. Canterbury Co.
Pan's pipes. [Riverside Press ed.] '10 (Jl30) S. leath., $1.50 net, boxed. (550 copies.) Houghton M.
Stevenson calendar; ed. by Florence L. Tucker. '09(Ag28) c. por. D. (Chiswick ser.) 60 c.; ooze, $1, boxed. Crowell.
Stevenson day by day; ed. by F. L. Tucker. '10(D) 12°, (Day by day ser.) 60 c.; ooze, $1. Crowell.

Stevenson, Rob. L:—*Continued.*
Travels with a donkey and An inland voyage; ed., with introd. and notes, by Wilbur L. Cross. '09(D4) 24°, (Pocket Am. and Eng. classics.) *25 c. net. Macmillan.
Treasure Island. '08(Je6) 16°, (Everyman's lib.) *35 c. net; leath., *70 c. net. Dutton.
Treasure Island; with an introd. by Marg. A. Eaton. '09(S4) c. 12°, 40 c. Educ. Pub.
Treasure Island; ed., with notes and introd., by Clayton Hamilton. '10(My21) c. map, D. (Longmans' English classics.) 25 c. Longmans.
Treasure Island; ed., with an introd. and notes, by Franklin T. Baker. '09(D18) c. front. por. map, 16°, (Merrill's English texts.) 40 c. C: E. Merrill.
Wisdom of Stevenson. '09(Je) c. 32°, leath., **$1 net. Brentano's.
See also Good stories.

STEVENSON, Robert Louis.
Hammerton, J: A. In the track of R. L. Stevenson and elsewhere in old France. *$1.50 net. Dutton.
Moors, H. J. With Stevenson in Samoa. $1.50 net. Small.
Stubbs, L. Stevenson's shrine. $2.50; $3. Barse & H.

Steve's woman. Ellis, E. M. O. $1.50. J. McBride.

Stewardship and missions. Cook, C: A: **50 c. net. Am. Bapt.

Stewardson, Langdon Cheeves.
Sermon preached at the dedication of St. Paul's chapel, February 3, 1907. '08 (N21) 8°. (Add. pubs. for price.) Columbia Univ.

Stewart, —, [pseud. for Jean Louis De Esque.
Silence: a compound problem novel. '08 (Jl18) c. il. D. $1.50. Connoisseurs' Press.

Stewart, Alfr. Wa.
Recent advances in organic chemistry; with an introd. by J. Norman Collie. '08(D5) O. *$2.50 net. Longmans.
Recent advances in physical and inorganic chemistry; with an introd. by Sir W: Ramsay. '09(D4) il. O. *$2.50 net. Longmans.

Stewart, Acheson.
Visceral surgery in abstract. '09(D) c. 176 p. 16°, $1. Medical Abstract.

Stewart, Ardemus.
See Penn. Digest.

Stewart, B.
Hdbk. for railway surveying. '08(Jl18) il. 12°, *$1 net. Spon.

Stewart, Basil.
My experiences in Cyprus: account of the people, mediæval cities, castles, antiquities and history; to which is added a chapter on the present economic problems. '09(Ap17) il. 8°, *$2 net. Dutton.

Stewart, Caroline Taylor.
Origin of the werewolf superstition. '09 (Je12) c. Q. (Univ. of Mo. studies; Social science ser.) pap., 50 c. Univ. of Mo.

Stewart, C: D:
Essays on the spot. '10(Ap30) c. D. $1.25 net. Houghton M.

Stewart, Clinton Brown.
Investigation of centrifugal pumps. pt. 1, Discussion of the theory of the centrifugal pump and tests of a six inch vertical centrifugal pump. '08(F1) il. tabs., O. (Univ. of Wis. bull., Engineering ser.) pap., 50 c. Univ. of Wis.
Investigation of flow through large submerged orifices and tubes. pt. 1. '09 (F13) il. tabs., O. (Univ. of Wis. bull., Engineering ser.; Researches in hydraulics.) pap., 25 c. Univ. of Wis.

Stewart, Fk. E., M.D.
Compend of pharmacy; based upon Prof. Jos. P. Remington's "Text-book of pharmacy and the U. S. P. eighth revision." 7th ed., rev. '08(D); 8th ed. '10(Je) 12°, (Blakiston's quiz-compend ser.) ea., *$1 net; *$1.25 net. Blakiston.

Stewart, G. Neil, M.D.
Manual of physiology. 6th ed. '10(O) 1084 p. il. 8°, $5 net; leath., $6 net. Wood.

Stewart, Gilbert Holland.
Legal medicine. '10(F) c. 16+506 p. 8°, $5. Bobbs-M.

STEWART, James, *D.D., M.D.*
Wells, J. Stewart of Lovedale. *$1.50 net. Revell.

Stewart, Jane Agnes.
Christmas book. '08(N14) c. il. O. *75 c. net. Am. Bapt.

Stewart, J: Alex.
Plato's doctrine of ideas. '09(Je19) O. $2. Oxford Univ.

Stewart, Jos. Spencer, ed.
Hdbk. for the secondary schools of Georgia. '09, [1910.] (Je) 60 p. 8°, (Univ. of Georgia., bull.) pap., gratis. J. S. Stewart.

Stewart, Manson A.
Latin abstract substantives. '10(O8) 8°, (Univ. of Michigan studies; Humanistic ser.) pap., 40 c. Macmillan.

Stewart, Mary, ed.
"Tell me a true story": tales of Bible heroes for children; with an introd. by A. F. Schauffler. '09(Je26) c. il. O. *$1.25 net. Revell.

Stewart, Merch Bradt.
Hdbk. for non-commissioned officers of infantry. [4th ed., rev. and enl.] '09 (N) c. 144 p. il. 16°, 50 c. Hudson.

—, and Davis, Rob. Courtney.
Notes and suggestions on the new infantry drill regulations. 4th ed., rev. '09(My) c. 158 p. 50 c.; leath., 75 c. Hudson.

Stewart, Morse, jr., M.D.
Pocket therapeutics and dose-book, with classification and explanation of the actions of medicine; index of diseases with remedies; useful hints to the prescriber. 4th ed., rewritten. '10(Ap) c. 5-263 p. 16°, $1 net. Saunders.

Stewart, Netta, and Young, Ja.
Prac. gynecology: manual for nurses and students. 2d enl. ed. of Gynecological nursing. '09(Mr) 343 p. il. 12°, *$2 net. Wood.

Stewart, Purves.
Diagnosis of nervous diseases. 2d ed., rev. and enl. '09(Ja) 8+451 p. 8°, *$4.20 net. Longmans.

Stewart, R. Wallace.
Elem. text-book of physics. pt. 2, Sound. '09(Je26); pt. 3, Light. '09(Ap17); pt. 4, Heat. '10(F19) il. D. (Griffin's scientific text-books.) ea., *$1.50 net. Lippincott.

Stewart, Rob. Armistead.
Case of Edgar Allan Poe; pathological study based on the investigations of Lauvrière. [1910.] (S) 29 p. 8°, 25 c. R. A. Stewart.
Knights of the golden horseshoe, and other lays. '09(O9) c. O. 50 c. R. A. Stewart.

Stewart, Rob. Laird, D.D.
Sheldon Jackson, pathfinder and prospector of the missionary vanguard in the Rocky Mountains and Alaska. '08(O24) c. il. pors. O. *$2 net. Revell.

Stewart, T: Grainger, M.D.
See Turner, W: Alden, *M.D.*

Stewart, W: Downie.
See Le Rossignol, Ja. E:

Stewart, W: H:
Spirit of the South; orations, essays, and lectures. '08(D12) c. 8°, $2. Neale.

Stewart, W: Morris.
Reminiscences; ed. by G: Rothwell Brown. '08(My16) c. por. O. $2. Neale.

Stewart and Gee ser. il. 12°. Macmillan.
—Barnes. Lessons in elementary practical physics. v. 3, pt. 1. *$1.10 net.

Stickeen. Muir, J: **60 c. net. Houghton M.

Stickley, Gustav.
Craftsman homes. '09(Ag7) c. 4°, $2. G. Stickley.

Stiegele, Paul.
Necessity of religion: [Lenton sermons.] '08(Mr) c. 57 p. 8°, 40 c. Wagner.

Stieler, Adolf.
Atlas of modern geography; pub by Justus Perthes' Geographical Institute, Gotha; adapt. for the use of the English-speaking public by B. V. Darbishire. 9th ed. '09(Ja16) F. ¾ leath., *$15 net. Lemcke.

Stienback, Leroy Lindley, ["N. Y. Homer."]
Slight indiscretion. '09(Ag14) c. D. *$1.50 net. Cochrane.

Stifler, Ja. Madison.
Fighting saint. '09(Je12) c. 12°, *75 c. net. Revell.

Stigand, C. H.
To Abyssinia through an unknown land. '10(D10) il. maps, 8°, $3.50 net. Lippincott.

Stil-lehre. Haebler, O. $8. Hessling.

Stiles, C: Wardell.
Hookworm disease in its relation to the negro. '09, [1910.] (Mr) 10 p. 8°. Gov. Pr. Off.
Soil pollution and its relation to hookworm disease and typhoid fever. '09(D) 10 p. il. 8°. (Add. Superintendent for price.)
Treatment of hookworm disease. '09, [1910.] (Mr) 5 p. 8°, pap. Gov. Pr. Off.

Stiles, W: Curtis, ed.
See Scott, Rob., *ed.*

Still, And. Taylor.
Osteopathy, research and practice. '10 (Jl) c. 13+543 p. 8°, $6; leath., $8. A. T. Still.

Still, G: Frederic, M.D.
See Goodhart, Ja. Frederic.

Stille und sturm gedichte. Sattler, O. 75 c. Lemcke.

Stillman, Liska.
City garden: [poems.] '08(D) (Add. pubs. for price.) Ulbrich.

Stillman, T: Bliss.
Engineering chemistry; manual of quantitative chemical analysis for use of students, chemists and engineers. 4th ed. '10(Ag27) c. il. 8°, $5. Chemical.

Stillwater Valley pastorals. Shivell, P. 50 c. Rector.

STILLWELL, Amos J.
Dawson, M. T. Stillwell murder. $2. M. T. Dawson.

Stilwell, Arth. E:
Confidence, or national suicide? 2d ed. '10(O1) c. D. $1. Bankers' Pub.

Stimpfl, Jos.
See Tracy, F:

Stimpson, W: C.
Foundry work: pract. guide to modern methods of moulding and casting in iron, bronze, steel and other metals. '08(N21) c. il. 8°, (American School of Correspondence pubs.) $1. Am. Sch. Corr.

Stimson, Frederic Jesup, ["J. S. of Dale," pseud.]
American constitution: the national powers, the rights of the states, the liberties of the people; Lowell Institute lectures, del. at Boston, October-November, 1907. '08(F1) c. diagr., D. **$1.25 net. Scribner.
Law of the federal and state constitutions of the United States. '08(My16) c. diagr., Q. *$3.50 net. Boston Bk.
Popular lawmaking; study of the origin, history, and present tendencies of lawmaking by statute. '10(O29) c. O. $2.50 net. Scribner.

Stimson, H: Alb.
Behind the world and beyond. '10(Ag27) c. D. $1.25 net. Eaton & M.
New things of God: [sermons.] '08(O10) c. 12°, *$1.25 net. Revell.

Stimson, Julia Catherine.
Nurses hdbk. of drugs and solutions. '10 (D) 5+82 p. D. $1 net. Whitcomb.

Stimson, Lewis Atterbury.
Pract. treatise on fractures and dislocations. 6th ed., rev. and enl. '10(Ap) 19-876 p. il. 8°, $5 net. Lea.

STIMULANTS AND NARCOTICS.
Jennings, O., *ed.* Morphia habit and its voluntary renunciation. *$2 net. Wood.
Kebler, L. F. Habit-forming agents. Gov. Pr. Off.
Sainsbury, H. Drugs and the drug habit. *$2.50 net. Dutton.
See also Alcohol.

Stine, Rev. Milton H:
Devil's bride; present day arraignment of formalism and doubt in the church and in society, in the light of the Holy Scriptures; given in the form of a pleasing story. [1910.] (N) c. 20+37-303 p. il. 8°, $1. Minter.

Stine, Wilbur Morris.
Crown of toil; book of sonnets. '10(Je11) c. 24°, $1.50. Acorn Press.

Stinson, Ja. Cyrus.
The searchlight; scientific review of Genesis; from whence came the different races of men? '09(N) c. 61 p. 8°, pap., 25 c. J. C. Stimson.

Stires, Ernest Milmore.
Plans and elevations for St. Thomas' church, made by Cram, Goodhue and Ferguson. '08(Je) c. 17+21 p. il. plans, 4°. (Add. pub. for price.) St. Thomas Church.

STIRLING, *Lord.*
See Alexander, *Sir* William.

Stirling, W:
Outlines of practical physiology. 3d ed., rev. and enl. '08(F29) il. 12°, *$2 net. Blakiston.

Stirling, Yates, jr.
United States midshipman afloat. '08(O3) c. il. D. (U. S. Navy ser.) †$1.25. Penn Pub. Co.
United States midshipman in China. '09 (N13) c. il. maps, D. †$1.25. Penn Pub. Co.
United States midshipman in the Philippines. '10(D31) c. il. D. $1.25. Penn Pub. Co.

Stirling-Maxwell, Sir W:
Stories of the Spanish artists until Goya; sel. and arr. by Luis Carreño; with introd. by E: Hutton. '10(O15) il. (partly col.) O. (Art and letters lib.) $3 net. Duffield.

Stitt, E: R., M.D.
Pract. bacteriology, blood work and animal parasitology. '09(Ja23); 2d ed. '10(D) il. 12°, ea., *$1.50 net. Blakiston.

Stock, Eug.
English church in the nineteenth century. '10(O1) D. (Anglican Church hdbk.) 40 c. net. Longmans.

Stock, St. George.
Stoicism. '09(Jl31) 12°, (Philosophies ancient and modern from Pythagoras to Spencer.) *50 c. net. Dodge.

STOCK.
See Cattle;—Domestic animals.

STOCK BROKERS.
Ball, C: E. Brokerage questions and problems (with course), $20. Universal Business.
Nourse, E. G. Brokerage. (Priv. pr.) Universal Business.
See also Bookkeeping.

STOCK COMPANIES.
See Corporations.

Stockberger, Warner W.
Necessity for new standards of hop valuation. '09(Ag) 11 p. 8°, (U. S., Dept. of Agriculture; Bu. of Plant Industry circular.) pap. (Add. Superintendent for price.) U. S., Supt. of Docs.
Pinkroot and its substitutions. '08(Ja18) il. 8°, (Pharmaceutical science ser., Monographs.) 50 c. Pharmaceutical Review.

Stockbridge, H:
Law of executors and administrators, with special reference to the state of Maryland; Gans' syllabus revised. '10(N) c. O. $1.25. C. A. Haskel.

Stockbridge, Horace E:
Land teaching; hdbk. of soils, plants, gardens and grounds, for teachers and cultivators. '10(Je18) c. il. 8°, $1. Southern Ruralist.

Stocking, Rev. Jay T.
Dearest spot on earth. [1910.] (N) 16°, (Caldwell's character and wisdom ser.) 50 c.; $1. Caldwell.

Stockley, Cynthia.
Poppy, the story of a South African girl. '10(Mr26) front. D. *$1.35 net. Putnam.

Stockman ser. D. 50 c.; pap., 25 c. Axtell-R.
—Miller. Crooked trail.

STOCKS.
American Academy of Political and Social Science. Stocks and the stock market. $1. Am. Acad. Pol. Sci.
Andrews, E: L. Stock Exchange and the public. 25 c. Bankers Mag.
Armstrong, C. Relation of speculation to business. gratis. C. Armstrong.
Babson, R. W. Miscellaneous stocks and how to find their market.—Stock brokers and bond dealers of London. ea., $5. R. W. Babson.
Black, W: H. Real Wall Street: understandable description of a purchase, a sale, a "short sale." $1.25; $1. Corporations.
Cowing, R. B. Speculative transactions as affected by recent New York legislation. gratis. Douring.
Davies, A. E. Money and the stock and share markets. 50 c. Pitman.
Gibson, T: Market letters for 1907. $1. T: Gibson.
Gibson, T: Special market letters, 1908. $1.—Weekly market letters. 2 v. ea., $1. Gibson Pub.
Harvey, R: S. Rights of the minority stockholders. $2. Baker, V. & Co.
Lusby, J. W. Stocks and bonds made easy. 50 c. Teachers' Supply.
Manual of statistics; Stock Exchange handbook, 1909; 1910. ea., $5. Manual of Statistics.
Norton, E. On "short sales" of securities through a stock broker. *$1 net. J: McBride.
Prevention of "dealing in futures" on boards of trade, etc. '09(My) 52 p. 8°, pap. (Add. Superintendent for price.) U. S., Supt. of Docs.
Rollins, M. Convertible securities. $3. M. Rollins.
Thompson, W: B. How can the economic features of the speculative exchanges be preserved and the ethical evils eliminated. W: B. Thompson.
Withers, H. Stocks and shares. $2 net. Dutton.
Wyckoff, R: D. Studies in tape reading. $3. Ticker Pub.
See also Bonds;—Corporations;—Investments;—Panics.

Stockton, Fk. R:
See My favorite novelist.

Stoddard, C: Coleman.
Kimona ballades. '08(Mr28) c. D. *50 c. net. Calkins & Co.

Stoddard, C: Warren.
Apostrophe to the skylark; selections; with an appreciation of Charles Warren Stoddard by G: Wharton James. '10(My7) facsims., 16°, (California classics ser.) bds., $1. Arroyo Guild.
Lepers of Molokai. New ed., enl. '09 (Ja16) c. D. 75 c. Ave Maria.

Stoddard, Elliot, Jos.
Interlocutory motions in the United States Patent Office; notes to rule 96-97, 109, 122, 123, 130 and 153. '08(O) $1. E. J. Stoddard.
Patent citator with practice notes in appeal cases. '09(My) c. 12+50 p. O. $1.65. Drake Law Bk.

Stoddard, Florence Jackson.
As old as the moon; Cuban legends; folklore of the Antilles. '09(O16) c. il. D. **$1 net. Doubleday, P.

Stoddard, J: Lawson, comp.
Stoddard library; thousand hours of entertainment with the world's great writers. 12 v. '10(N) c. fronts. 8°. Shuman.

Stoddard, J: Tappan.
Introd. to general chemistry. '10(N19) c. 12°, $1.60 net. Macmillan.
Quantitative experiments in general chemistry. '08(N21) c. figs. D. $1. Longmans.

Stoddard, T: A.
"The quest." '10(My14) c. il. por. 12°, $1.50. Cochrane.

Stoddard, W: Bliss.
Lovable degenerate. '08(N21) 12°, $1. Cochrane.

Stoddard, W: Leavitt.
Life of William Shakespeare expurgated. '10(Ap16) c. front. 8°, $1.25. W. A. Butterfield.
—, comp. New golfers' almanac. '09(O2) c. il. D. **90 c. net. Houghton M.

Stoddard, W: Osborn.
In the open: stories of outdoor life. '08 (N14) c. il. D. †60 c. Harper.
Longshore boys. '09(N13) c. il. D. †$1.50. Lippincott.
See also Adventures with Indians.
—, ed. *See* Lincoln, Abraham.

Stoddart, Anna M.
Life of Mrs. Isabella Bird Bishop. New cheaper ed. '08(My9) il. maps, 8°, *$2 net. Dutton.

Stoddart, H: P., rep.
See Nebraska. *Sup. ct.* Repts.

Stoddart, Jane T.
Girlhood of Mary, Queen of Scots. '08 (D) 8°, $3.50. Clode.
New socialism; impartial inquiry. '10 (Ja29) O. *$1.75 net. Doran.

Stoddart, W: H: Butter.
Mind and its disorders: moral psychology, psychology of the insane and mental diseases. '09(Mr) 16+488 p. il. 8°, *$4 net. Blakiston.

Stoffel, Rev. N. J.
See Bible. N. T.

STOICHIOMETRY.
See Chemistry.

STOICISM.
See Philosophy.

STOKE NEWINGTON, London, Eng.
See London.

Stoker, Bram.
Famous impostors. '10(D31) c. pors. O. $2 net. Sturgis & W.
Gates of life. '08(Jl11) c. D. 75 c. Cupples & L.
Lady Athlyne. '09(N) 12°, $1.50. Lovell.

Stokes, Adrian.
Hungary. '09(D25) fold. map, O. (Color books ser.) *$6 net. Macmillan.

Stokes, Anson Phelps, ed.
Historical prints of New Haven, Ct.; with special reference to Yale College and the Green. '10(Je) 33 p. facsim. 8°, pap., gratis. Tuttle, M. & T.

Stokes, Ralph S. G.
Mines and minerals of the British Empire. '08(My16) il. O. *$4.20 net. Longmans.

Stokes' comic juveniles. il. Q. Stokes.
—Dirks. Komical Katzenjammers.
—Opper. Handy Happy Hooligan.—Maud the mirthful mule.
—Outcault. Buster, Mary-Jane and Tige.
—Schultze. Foxy Grandpa and his boys.

Stokes' wonder book: picture annual for boys and girls; ed. by Harry Golding. '09(O2); '10(S10) col. il. Q. ea., $1.50. Stokes.

Stökl, Mrs. Helene Böckel.
Alle fünf!; ed., with exercises, notes and vocab., by Dr. Wilhelm Bernhardt. '09 (O2) c. S. (Heath's modern language ser.) 30 c. Heath.

Stolen aeroplane. Lamar, A. 60 c. Reilly & B.

Stolen signet. Smith, F: M. $1.50. Duffield.

Stoll, Albert, jr., comp.
Clever business sketches. '09(Je) c. 252 p. il. 8°, $1. Business Man's Pub.

Stollnitz, H: Sandé.
Glimpses of a strange world: [short stories of Ghetto life.] '08(N) c. 3-202 p. 12°, $1.50. H: S. Stollnitz.
The redemption: a double dream; [Jewish stories.] '08. c. 7-9+99 p. 12°. (Add. author for price.) H: S. Stollnitz.

STOMACH.
Bassler, A. Diseases of the stomach and upper alimentary tract. $6. Davis.
Bosanquet, W. C., *and* Clogg, H. S. Stomach, intestines and pancreas. *$4 net. Wood.
Deaver, J: B., *and* Ashhurst, A. P. C. Surgery of the upper abdomen: stomach and duodenum. v. 1. *$5 net. Blakiston.
Dienst, G: E. What to do for the stomach. $1. Boericke & T.
Habershon, S: H. Diseases of the stomach. $2.50. Chic. Med. Bk.
Holland, J. W: Urine and clinical chemistry of the gastric contents. *$1 net. Blakiston.
Kellogg, J: H. Stomach: its disorders and how to cure them. $1.50; $2. Modern Medicine.
Kemp, R. C. Diseases of the stomach and intestines. *$6 net. Saunders.
See also Digestion.

STOMATA.
See Botany.

Stone, Alfr. Holt.
Studies in the American race problem; with an introd. and three papers by Wa. F. Willcox. '08(O17) c. O. **$2 net Doubleday, P.

Stone, C: H: Howard.
Pract. testing of gas and gas meters. '09 (My8) c. figs. 8°, $3.50. Wiley.

Stone, C: J:
Advanced superlative coat and vest system based upon the proportions of the human form. '10(Ag27) c. il. por. 4°, $10. C: J. Stone.

Stone, Christopher.
Eton. '09(D4) col. il. map, 8°, (Color books.) *$2 net. Macmillan.
—, **ed.** War songs; with introd. by General Sir Ian Hamilton. '09(Je19) 16°, (Oxford lib. of prose and poetry.) 90 c. Oxford Univ.

Stone, Cliff Winfield.
Arithmetical abilities and some factors determining them. '08(Ag29) c. tabs., 8°, (Columbia Univ., Teachers' Coll., contribs. to education.) $1. Teachers' Coll.

Stone, Dan. Clifford.
From the evidence presented: [discussion of economic questions.] '08(Je) c. 86 p. por. 8°, 25 c. Saginaw.

Stone, Darwell, D.D.
Episcopacy and valid orders in the primitive church; statement of evidence. '10 (D17) D. (Pusey House occasional papers.) pap., 40 c. Longmans.
History of the doctrine of the holy eucharist. '09(Ap10) 2 v., O. *$8.50 net. Longmans.
Invocation of saints. New and enl. ed. '10 (Ja29) O. *60 c. net; pap., *40 c. net. Longmans.
Law of Christian marriage; especially in relation to the Deceased wife's sister's marriage act. '08(F8) D. (Pusey House occasional papers.) pap., 10 c. Longmans.
Witness of the spirit and the water and the blood: sermon preached at the festival of the Missionary College of St. Peter and St. Paul at Dorchester, on 7 June, 1910. '10(S) 16 p. O. pap., 20 c. net. Longmans.

Stone, Rev. E. D.
Gotham, and other stories: Latin reading book. '08(O31) 12°, *40 c. net. Macmillan.

Stone, G: Hapgood.
World money; study of the world problem of stable money. Abr. ed. '10 (Mr5) c. 8°, $1.25. G: H. Stone.

Stone, Rev. H: Morgan.
Witness of the heart, and other sermons. '09(Ap17) c. il. pors. D. **$1.25 net. Longmans.

Stone, J: C:
See Southworth, Gordon A:
—, **and Millis, Ja. Franklin.**
Elementary geometry, plane. '10(Ap9) c. il. 12°, 80 c. B: H. Sanborn.
Secondary arithmetic, commercial and industrial. '08(O24) c. il. 12°, *75 c. net. B: H. Sanborn.

Stone, J: Timothy, D.D.
Footsteps in a parish: appreciation of Maltbie Davenport Babcock as a pastor. '08 (O17) c. por. D. *75 c. net. Scribner.
Recruiting for Christ. '10(S17) c. 12°, $1 net. Revell.
Stone, Mary, comp.
Children's stories that never grow old: selection of the best children's classics. '08(S19) c. D. $1. Reilly & B.
Stone, Matilda Woods.
Every man his chance: [novel.] '09(Ja16) c. D. $1.50. Badger.
Stone, Melvil O.
See Tate, Ja. M.
Stone, Nahum I:, comp.
Export tariffs of foreign countries. '09 (My) 48 p. 8°, (U. S., Dept. of Commerce and Labor; Bu. of Manufactures, tariff ser.) pap. (Add. Superintendent for price.) U. S., Supt. of Docs.
Foreign tariffs on petroleum and petroleum products. '09(My) 16 p. 8°, (U. S., Dept. of Commerce and Labor; Bu. of Manufactures; tariff ser.) pap. (Add. Superintendent for price.)
Stone, W: Jasper.
Shorthand for amanuensis, court and verbatim reporting. '10(D31) c. 31 p. 12°, $2. W: J. Stone.
Stone & Webster.
Current literature references, [electrical engineering,] 1907. '08, [1909.] (Ja) 4°. (Add. pubs. for price.) Stone & W.
STONE.
Baker, I. O. Voids, settlement and weight of crushed stone. gratis. Univ. of Ill.
McCourt, W. E. Fire-resisting qualities of some New Jersey building stones. (Add. author for price.) W. E. McCourt.
See also Granite;—Masonry;—Rocks.
STONE AGE.
See Italy.
STONE-CUTTING.
Hodgson, F: T: Practical stonemasonry self-taught. $1. Drake.
Stone house at Gowanus. Fraser, G. $2.50. Witter & K.
Stone implements of South Africa. Johnson, J. P. $3.25. Longmans.
Stoner, Gordon.
Student's quiz book; cont. questions, answers and definitions on the law of criminal procedure. '10(Jl) c. O. (The quizzer, no. 13.) pap., 50 c. Callaghan.
Student's quiz book; cont. questions, answers and definitions on the law of torts. '10(Ag) c. O. (The quizzer, no. 9.) pap., 50 c. Callaghan.
Stoner, J. Rush.
Logic and imagination in perception of truth; the nature of pure activity in two series. bk. I. and II. '10(O15) 12°, $1.50. Cochrane.
Stoner, Winifred Sackville, jr.
Jingles; written for dear friends by Winifred Sackville Stoner, jr., (when five and six years of age.) '09(D) 52 p. il. pors. 8°, 60 c. Smith & B.
Stones in a life. Goldsmith, W: M. 65 c. W: M. Goldsmith.
Stones of Venice. *See* Ruskin, J:

Stoney, Emily Marjory Armstrong.
Bacteriology and surgical technic for nurses. 3d ed., thoroughly rev. and enl. by Frederic Richardson Griffith. '10(N) 311 p. il. 8°, $1.50. Saunders.
Pract. points in nursing, for nurses in private practice; with appendix cont. rules for feeding the sick; recipes for invalid foods and beverages; weights and measures; dose list; and a full glossary of medical terms and nursing treatment. 4th ed., thoroughly rev. '10(O) 9-495 p. il. 8°, $1.75. Saunders.
Stopes, Marie C.
Ancient plants. '10(Ag6) il. 8°, $2 net. Van Nostrand.
STORAGE BATTERIES.
See Electric batteries.
Storer, E:
Peter the Cruel; life of the notorious Don Pedro of Castile; together with acct. of his relations with the famous Maria de Padilla. '10(N19) il. O. $4 net. Lane.
Storey, G: Adolphus.
Theory and practice of perspective. '10 (My14) il. O. $3.75. Oxford Univ.
Storey, Moorfield.
Abraham Lincoln: address delivered at the Shawmut Congregational Church in Boston on Feb. 14, 1909. '09(N) 24 p. 8°. (Priv. pr.) M. Storey.
Storey, T: Andrew.
Department of physical instruction; repr. from the *City College Quarterly*. '09 (D) 67-80 p. il. 8°, 50 c. T: A. Storey.
Storia do Mogor. *See* Manucci, Niccolao.
STORIES.
See Fairy tales;—Fiction;—Legends;—Story-telling.
Stories about children of all nations. Hurlbut, J. L., *ed.* 75 c. Winston.
Stories and rhymes for a child. Bailey, C. S. $1. M. Bradley.
Stories and story telling. St. John, E. P. *50 c. net. Pilgrim Press.
Stories by the essayists. '09(Jl17) 12°, (World's story tellers ser.) 40 c. net. Dutton.
Stories children love. Welsh, C:, *ed.* $1.25; $2. Dodge.
Stories for children. Topelius, Z. Book 6, 7. ea., 25 c. Augustana.
Stories for the children ser. 12 v. '10 (O1) il. in col. S. ea., 50 c Platt & P.
Stories from American history. il. D. Macmillan.
—Bruce. Daniel Boone and the wilderness road. $1.50.
—Spears. Story of the American merchant marine. *$1.50 net.
Stories from beyond the Borderland. Tuttle, H. $1.25. Tuttle Pub.
Stories from Don Quixote. Havell, H. L., *comp.* $1.50. Dodge.
Stories from English history. Skae, H. T. 50 c. Dutton.
Stories from French history. Dalkeith, L. *50 c. net. Dutton.
Stories from history ser. *See* Dutton's.
Stories from old chronicles. Stephens, K., *ed.* $1.50. Sturgis & W.
Stories from old French romance. Wilmot-Buxton, E. M. 75 c. net. Stokes.

Stories from Roman history. Dalkeith, L. 50 c. Dutton.
Stories from Shakespeare. Lang, J. *50 c. net. Dutton.
Stories from the Æneid. Havell, H. L., *comp.* $1.50. Dodge.
Stories from the ballads. Macgregor, M. 50 c. Dutton.
Stories from the Crusades. Kelman, J. H. 50 c. Dutton.
Stories from the Faerie Queene. *See* Spenser, Edm.
Stories from the Greek legends. Hartley, C. G. *$1.25 net. Lippincott.
Stories from the Greek tragedy. Havell, H. L., *comp.* $1.50. Dodge.
Stories from the history of Berkshire. Lamborn, E. A. G. 25 c. Oxford Univ.
Stories from the Iliad. Havell, H. L., *comp.* $1.50. Dodge.
Stories from the Norseland. Edmison, J: P. †$1.25. Penn Pub. Co.
Stories from the Odyssey. Havell, H. L., *comp.* $1.50. Dodge.
Stories from the Old Testament. Platt, S., *comp.* $1.50. Dodge.
Stories from the operas. Davidson, G. *$1.25 net. Lippincott.
Stories from Wagner. Smith, C. E. 50 c. Dutton.
Stories new and old. Mabie, H. W., *comp.* †$1.50. Macmillan.
Stories of American discoverers for little Americans. Lucia, R. 40 c. Am. Bk.
Stories of an old Dutch town. Shafer, D. C. 50 c. Robson.
Stories of authors. Chubb, E. W. $1.25 net. Sturgis & W.
Stories of Beowulf. Marshall, H. E. 50 c. Dutton.
Stories of chivalry, retold from *St. Nicholas.* '09(Ag21) c. il. D. **65 c. net. Century Co.
Stories of classic myths, retold from *St. Nicholas.* '09(Ag21) c. il. D. **65 c. net. Century Co.
Stories of classical fables. Hawthorne, N. 35 c. McLoughlin.
Stories of colonial children. Chadwick, *Mrs.* M. L. P-. 60 c.; 40 c. Educ. Pub.
Stories of Don Quixote. Baldwin, J., *comp.* 50 c. Am. Bk.
Stories of English artists from Vandyck to Turner. Davies, R. *$3 net. Duffield.
Stories of great Americans. Hurlbut, J. L. *ed.* 75 c. Winston.
Stories of Greece and Rome, retold from *St. Nicholas.* '09(Ag21) c. il. D. **65 c. net. Century Co.
Stories of hell's commerce. Shaw, E. R., *comp. and ed.* $1.50. Shaw Pub.
Stories of humor by Oliver Wendell Holmes, Bill Nye, Mark Twain, Benjamin Franklin, Josh Billings, Bret Harte, James Whitcomb Riley, Eugene Field, and others. '08(D12) c. 2 pt. in 1 v., por. 12°, †75 c. Doubleday, P.
Stories of Jewish home life. Mosenthal, S. H. v. $1.25. Jewish Pub.
Stories of Norse heroes. Wilmot-Buxton, E. M. $1.50. Crowell.
Stories of our mother earth. Fairbanks, H. W. *25 c. net. Educ. Pub.
Stories of our naval heroes. Hurlbut, J. L., *ed.* 75 c. Winston.
Stories of Persian heroes. Wilmot-Buxton, E. M. †$1.50. Crowell.
Stories of Roland. Marshall, H. E., *comp.* 50 c. Dutton.
Stories of royal children, retold from *St. Nicholas.* '09(Ag21) c. il. D. **65 c. net. Century Co.
Stories of St. Andrew and St. Patrick. Mord, W. $1. Stokes.
Stories of St. George and St. David. Mord, W. $1. Stokes.
Stories of Siegfried. Macgregor, M. 50 c. Dutton.
Stories of standard teaching pieces. Perry, E: B. $1.50. T. Presser.
Stories of the ancient world, retold from *St. Nicholas.* '09(Ag21) c. il. D. **65 c. net. Century Co.
Stories of the ballads. Cameron, C. 50 c. Dutton.
Stories of the French artists. Turner, P. M. *$3 net. Duffield.
Stories of the great West. Roosevelt, T. **60 c. net. Century Co.
Stories of the Italian artists from Vasari. Seeley, E. L., *comp.* *$3 net. Duffield.
Stories of the king. Baldwin, J. 50 c. Am. Bk.
Stories of the Middle Ages, retold from *St. Nicholas.* '09(Ag21) c. il. D. **65 c. net. Century Co.
Stories of the red children. Brooks, D. 40 c.; 30 c. Educ. Pub.
Stories of the struggle. Winchevsky, M. 50 c. Kerr.
Stories of the Triangular League. *See* Dudley, Albertus True.
Stories of the United States. Davis, A. C. 40 c.; 30 c. Educ. Pub.
Stories of the Vikings. Macgregor, M. 50 c. Dutton.
Stories of three saints. Macgregor, M. 50 c. Dutton.
Stories of Wagner operas. Wheelock, E. M. $1.25. Bobbs-M.
Stories short and sweet. Wharton, H: M. $1 net. Neale.
Stories worth telling. Coggins, H. L., *comp.* 50 c. Penn Pub. Co.

Stork, C: Wharton.
Day dreams of Greece: [poems.] '09(F6) S. *75 c. net. Lippincott.

Storm, Theodor.
Auf der universität; with introd., notes and vocab. by Rob. N. Corwin. '10(D3) c. S. 35 c. Holt.
Der schimmelreiter: novelle; ed., with introd., exercises, notes and vocab., by J. Macgillivray and E: J. Williamson. '08 (My9) c. por. map, S. (Internat. modern lang. ser.) 70 c. Ginn.
Immensée. '10(D) front. 32°. (Ariel booklets.) leath., 75 c. Putnam.

—, Gerstäcker, Friedrich Wilhelm Christian, and Seidel, Heinrich.
Immensée, von Storm; Germelshausen, von Gerstäcker; Der lindenbaum, von Seidel; ed., with introd., notes and vocab., by F: Manley. '09(D18) c. D. (Lake German ser.) 50 c. Scott, F. & Co.

Storm (The). Ostrovsky, A. *$1 net. J: W. Luce.
Storm and treasure. Bailey, H: C. $1.50. Brentano's.
Storm birds. Davis, S. $1.50. Moffat.
Storm bound. Hutchinson, A. L. $1. Cochrane.
Storms, W: H.
Timbering and mining: treatise on practical American methods. '09(Ag7) c. il. O. *$2 net. McGraw-H.
Storr, Rayner.
Concordance to the Latin original of the four books known as De imitatione Christi given to the world A.D. 1441 by Thomas à Kempis; comp. with full contextual quotations by Rayner Storr. '10 (D17) $4.20 net. Oxford Univ.
Storring, Gustav.
Mental pathology in its relation to normal psychology; tr. by T: Loveday. '08(Ja11) 8°, *$2.75 net. Macmillan.
Storrow, Ann G.
Poem of the olden time, describing a ball at Cambridge, Mass., in the year 1840; read by Col. T: Wentworth Higginson at the annual meeting of the Omar Khayyám Club of America, Sat., Mar. 28, 1908, at the Algonquin Club, Boston, Mass. '09 (Je) c. 10 p. 4°. (Priv. pr.) Rosemary.
Story, Alfr. T:
American shrines in England. '08(Ag1) il. 12°, *$2 net. Macmillan.
Story, W: Wetmore.
Roman lawyer in Jerusalem. '09(Ap10) front. 32°, (Ariel booklets.) leath., 75 c., boxed. Putnam.
Story book friends. Murray, C. †50 c. Little, B. & Co.
Story Land. Murray, C., *comp.* 50 c. Little, B. & Co.
Story-lives of great authors. Rowbotham, F. J. $1.50. Stokes.
Story-lives of great musicians. Rowbotham, F. J. $1.50. Stokes.
Story of a beautiful childhood. Conway, K. E., *comp.* $1. C. M. Clark.
Story of a beautiful duchess. Bleakley, H. *$5 net. Dutton.
Story of a border city during the civil war. Anderson, G. **$1.50 net. Little, B. & Co.
Story of a century. Garrison, J. H. $1. Chr. Pub. Co.
Story of a red deer. Fortescue, J: W: **75 c. net. Macmillan.
Story of a scout. Finnemore, J: $1.50. Macmillan.
Story of a street. Hill, F: T. **$1.60 net. Harper.
Story of a troop mess. Moss, J. A. 75 c. U. S. Infantry.
Story of a wireless telegraph boy. Trowbridge, J: T. †$1.25. Houghton M.
Story of a year. Molesworth, *Mrs.* M. L. S. $1.50. Macmillan.
Story of coal and iron in Alabama. Armes, E. $5. Ala. Chamber of Com.
Story of Cromwell. Marshall, H. E. 50 c. Dutton.
Story of Daniel the prophet. Haskell, S. N. $1-$1.75. Bible Training.
Story of Dutch painting. Caffin, C: H: **$1.20 net. Century Co.
Story of electricity. Munro, J: 92 c. S. S. McClure.
Story of England. Harding, S: B. 60 c. Scott, F. & Co.
Story of Frederick the Great. Carpenter, *Mrs.* K. E. R. $1. Lothrop, L. & S.
Story of Gaspar. Raymond, R. W. 25 c. net. Pilgrim Press.
Story of Glencoe. Taylor, G: *$1 net. Caledonian Pub.
Story of gold. Meade, E: S. **75 c. net. Appleton.
Story of Gosta Berling. Lagerlöf, S. O. L. $2 net. Little, B. & Co.
Story of great inventions. Burns, E. E. $1.25. Harper.
Story of Grettir the Strong, by Allen French. '08(O10) c. 12°, †$1.25. Dutton.
Story of Hereward. Stedman, D. C. *$1.50 net. Crowell.
Story of iron and steel. Smith, J. R. **75 c. net. Appleton.
Story of Isaac Brock. Nursey, W. R. *$1.50 net. McClurg.
Story of Jesus. Hurlbut, J. L., *ed.* 75 c. Winston.
Story of Jonah. Boyd, J. S. *75 c. net. J. S. Boyd.
Story of Lazarus. Robinson, R. 50 c. Pentecostal.
Story of libraries and book-collecting. Savage, E. A. *75 c. net. Dutton.
Story of little black Bobtail. Bannerman, H. 50 c. Stokes.
Story of little black Quasha. Bannerman, H. †50 c. Stokes.
Story of little black Sambo. *See* Potter, Beatrix, *and* Bannerman, Helen.
Story of Matka. Jordan, D: S. $1. Whitaker & R.
Story of Moses. Gearhart, A. F. 10 c. Flanagan.
Story of musical form. Lucas, C. *$1.25 net. Scribner.
Story of my life. Terry, E. **$3.50 net. Doubleday, P.
Story of my mind. Mangasarian, M. M. 50 c. Independent Religious.
Story of Napoleon. Marshall, H. E. 50 c. Dutton.
Story of New Netherland. Griffis, W: E. **$1.25 net. Houghton M.
Story of oil. Tower, W. S. **$1 net. Appleton.
Story of old Boston town house. Benton, J. H: (Priv. pr.) Merrymount.
Story of old Japan. Longford, J. H. $1.75 net. Longmans.
Story of opera. Lee, E. M. $1.25 net. Scribner.
Story of Oregon and its people. Chapman, C: H. 60 c. Barnes.
Story of our country. Hurlbut, J. L. 75 c. Winston.
Story of Paul of Tarsus. *See* Atkinson, Louise Warren.
Story of Peter Rabbit. Potter, B. 60 c. Reilly & B.
Story of Puck. Hood, M. L. 35 c.; 50 c. Eaton & Co.

Story of rapid transit. Willson, H: B. 92 c. S. S. McClure.
Story of Red Feather. Ellis, E: S. 50 c. McLoughlin.
Story of Robert Fulton. Miller, P. F. $1. P. F. Miller.
Story of Robinhood. Finnemore, J: *$1.50 net. Macmillan.
Story of Rustem. Renninger, E. D., *comp.* **$1.50 net. Scribner.
Story of Santa Klaus. Walsh, W: S. **$1.50 net. Moffat.
Story of Saranac. Raymond, H: W. *$2 net. Grafton Press.
Story of Sigurd. Morris, W: 50 c. Longmans.
Story of Sir Galahad. Sterling, M. B., *comp.* $1.50. Dutton.
Story of sixty years. Hogan, W. F. 50 c. W. F. Hogan.
Story of the American merchant marine. Spears, J: R. *$1.50 net. Macmillan.
Story of the Bible. Foster, C: $1.50. C: Foster.
Story of the catacombs. Blake-Hedges, F. E. *$1 net. Jennings.
Story of the centuries. Ware, T: A. $1. Cochrane.
Story of the comets. Chambers, G: F: $2. Univ. of Chic.
Story of the Great Lakes. Channing, E: **$1.50 net. Macmillan.
Story of the Greek people. Tappan, E. M. **65 c. net; $1.50. Houghton M.
Story of the island steamers. Turner, H. B. 65 c. Inquirer.
Story of the Jewish people. Myers, J. M. In 2 v. v. 1. *60 c. net. Bloch.
Story of the little merman. Reader, E. *$1.25 net. Macmillan.
Story of the nations ser. il. D. **$1.35 net; hf. leath., **$1.60 net. Putnam.
—Jones. Roman empire, B.C. 29-A.D. 476.
—Miller. The Balkans.
Story of the negro. Washington, B. T. **$3 net. Doubleday, P.
Story of the New England whalers. Spears, J: R. $1.50. Macmillan.
Story of the outlaw. Hough, E. 75 c. Burt.
Story of the Pharaohs. Baikie, J. $2 net. Macmillan.
Story of the promise. Bell, C. C. *60 c. net. Young Churchman.
Story of the Revised New Testament. Riddle, M. B. *75 c. net. S. S. Times.
Story of the session of the California legislature of 1909. Hichborn, F. $1.25. Barry.
Story of the soil. Hopkins, C. G: $1.50. Badger.
Story of the submarine. Field, C. *$2 net. Lippincott.
Story of the violets. Laird, J. P. Knickerbocker Press.
Story of the Washington coachee. Beall, *Mrs.* M. S. (Priv. pr.) Neale.
Story of three great artists. Cyr, *Mrs.* E. M. 50 c. Ginn.
Story of Thyrza. Brown, A. **$1.35 net. Houghton M.
Story of twentieth century Christianity. Holmgren, C: J: A: (Add. pubs. for price.) Forum of Conscience.
Story plays for little ones. Maguire, E. M. 50 c. Educ. Pub.
STORY-TELLING.
Beckwith, M. H. Story telling with the scissors. 50 c. M. Bradley.
Burnham, M. Descriptive stories for all the year. 50 c. M. Bradley.
Lyman, E. Story telling. 75 c. net. McClurg.
Ransome, A. Hist. of story-telling. $3 net. Stokes.
St. John, E: P. Stories and story-telling in moral and religious education. *50 c. net. Pilgrim Press.
Wyche, R: T: Some great stories and how to tell them. $1. Newson.
See also Bible.
Story the crocus told. Hill, E. M. *$1 net. Uplook Pub.
Story-time ser. 6 v. '10(D) col. il. ea., bds., 60 c. Cassell.
Story told by pins. Russell, A. V. $1. Neale.
Story told science. il. D. 75 c. Harper.
—Marks *and* Moody. Holiday with the birds.
—Little busybodies.
STORY WRITING.
See Authorship.

Stott, W: Taylor.
Indiana Baptist history, 1798-1908. '08 (Jl18) c. il. pors. 12°, $2. W: T. Stott.

Stoutenburgh, H: A.
Documentary hist. of the Dutch congregation of Oyster Bay, Queens Co., Island of Nassau (now Long Island). '09(O) 966 p. 8°, [10 pamphlets.] $5.50. H: A. Stoutenburgh.

Stovall, Mrs. Eugenia Orchard.
Son of Carolina. '09(N13) c. D. $1.50. Neale.

Stow, Arth. W:
See Price, B: Lincoln.

Stow, J:
Survey of London; ed. by H: Morley. '08 (N21) 12°, *75 c. net. Dutton.
Survey of London; reprinted from the text of 1603; with introd. and notes by C: Lethbridge Kingsford. '08(O24) 2 v., il. pors. maps, O. $9.25. Oxford Univ.

Stow, Marion Cook.
Voices of the city. '09, [1910.] (Ja) c. various paging, il. 8°, $1. M. C. Stow.
Stowaway (The). Tracy, L: †$1.50. Clode.

Stowe, Mrs. Harriet Eliz. Beecher.
Uncle Tom's cabin. '08(O10) il. D. (Bowman's illustrated lib. of world-favorite books.) $1. Bowman.
Uncle Tom's cabin. '09(Ap3) il. 16°, (Everyman's lib.) *35 c. net; leath., *70 c. net. Dutton.
Uncle Tom's cabin, told to the children, by H. E. Marshall. '08(Je6) il. 16°. (Told to the children ser.) 50 c. Dutton.
Uncle Tom's cabin for children; designed by W. M. Rhoads; adapt. by Helen Ring Robinson. '08(O3) c. il. obl. O. (Sunbeam ser. for young people.) bds., †$1. Penn Pub. Co.
STOWE, *Mrs.* Harriet Eliz. Beecher.
MacLean, G. E. "Uncle Tom's cabin" in Germany. $1.50. Univ. of Penn.; [Appleton.]

Stowe, Herbert M., M.D., ed.
See De Lee, Jos. Boliver, *ed.*

Stowe, Monroe A.
English grammar schools in the reign of Queen Elizabeth. '09(Ap17) 8°, (Teachers' College ser.) *$1.50 net. Teachers' Coll.

Stowell, Ellery C.
Consular cases and opinions from the decisions of the Eng. and Am. courts and the opinions of the Attorneys General. 09(N) c. 36+811 p. O. $5. Byrne.

Stowell, J:
Don Coronado through Kansas, 1541. '08 (O17) c. front. $1.50. Don Coronado.

Strachan, Grace Charlotte.
Equal pay for equal work; story of the struggle for justice being made by the women teachers of the city of New York. '10(Ag13) c. pors. O. $1 net. B: F. Buck.

Strachan, Ja.
Captivity and pastoral epistles. '10(Ag27) 16°, (Westminster New Testament.) 75 c. net. Revell.

Strachey, J: St. Lce.
New way of life. '10(F19) 12°, *50 c. net. Macmillan.
Problems and perils of socialism. '08 (Je27) pap., *25 c. net. Macmillan.

Strachey, Lionel, ed.
Love letters of famous poets and novelists; prefaced with descriptive sketches by Wa. Littlefield. '09(Je5) c. O. *$2 net. J: McBride.
Love letters of famous royalties and commanders; prefaced with descriptive sketches by Walter Littlefield. '09(N20) c. O. *$2.50 net. J: McBride.

Strack, Heinrich.
Brick architecture of the Middle Ages and the Renaissance in Italy. '10(O15) c. f°, $11; in portfolio, $8. Helburn.

Strack, Herman Leberecht.
Jew and human sacrifice, (human blood and Jewish ritual;) tr. from the 8th ed., with corrections, new preface and additions by the author. '09(Je19) 8°, *$3 net. Bloch.

"Strad" lib. il. 12°. Scribner.
—St. George. Fiddles. $1.
—Stratton. Nicolo Paganini. *$2 net.

Stradella. Crawford, F. M. †$1.50. Macmillan.

STRADIVARI, Antonio.
Hill, W. H:, *and others.* Antonio Stradivari. *$2.50 net. Macmillan.

Straight goods in philosophy. *See* Hatch, D: P.

Strain of white. Woodruff, *Mrs.* A. W. †$1.50. Little, B. & Co.

STRAINS.
See Strength of materials.

Strand, Grace Browne, comp.
Faith, hope, love. '10(N5) c. D. 50 c. net. McClurg.
Love, friendship, and good cheer. '10 (N5) c. D. 50 c. net. McClurg.

Strang, Herbert.
Around the world in seven days. '10(D) col. il. 12°, $1.25 net. Doran.
Barclay of the guides; story of the Indian mutiny. '09(N13) col. il. D. *$1.25 net. Doran.
Humphrey Bold; story of the time of Benbow. '09(N13) c. il. D. †$1.50. Bobbs-M.
King of the air. '09(Ap3) c. il. O. †$1.50. Bobbs-M.
Lord of the sea: story of a submarine. '10 (D) col. il. 12°, $1 net. Doran.
On the Spanish Main. '09(Je26) c. il. O. †$1.50. Bobbs-M.
Palm Tree Island: story of a shipwreck. '10(D) col. il. 12°, $1.25 net. Doran.
Round the world in seven days. '10(D3) c. il. O. $1.25 net. Doran.
Settlers and scouts: tale of the African Highlands. '10(D) col. il. 12°, $1.25 net. Doran.
Swift and sure: story of a hydroplane. '10 (D) col. il. 12°, $1 net. Doran.

Strange adventures of an author in search of a publisher. Jones, A. H. 10 c. Am. Press.

Strange case of Eleanor Cuyler. Crosby, K. $1.20 net. Dodd.

Strange record. Houmas, M. $1.50. Neale.

Strange ways of God. Brown, C: R. *75 c. net. Pilgrim Press.

Stranger's visit. Pope, F. 60 c. Zuriel.

Strang's (Herbert) lib. 7 v. '10(D) col. il. 12°, ea., 50 c. Doran.
Contents same as Boys and girls ser.

Strasburger, Eduard.
Hdbk. of practical botany; tr. by W. Hillhouse. 6th ed., rev. '08(S19) il. *$2.50 net. Macmillan.

—, and others.
Text-book of botany. 3d Eng. ed., rev. with the 8th German ed. by W. H. Lang. '08(My9) il. 8°, *$5 net. Macmillan.

Strassburger theologische studien. 8°.
—Pfättisch. Die rede Konstantins des Grossen an die versammlung der heiligen auf ihre echtheit untersucht. *$1 net.
—Scharnagl. Das feirliche gelübe als ehehindernis in seiner geschichtlichen entwicklung dargestellt. *$1.50 net.
—Schmid. Die Osterfestberechnung in der abendlandishes kirche. *80 c. net.

Stratagems and spoils. White, W: A. **$1.25 net Macmillan.

STRATEGY.
See Military art and science.

Stratemeyer, E:, ["Captain Ralph Bonehill," "Arthur M. Winfield."]
Automobile boys of Lakeport; or, a run for fun and fame. '10(S10) c. il. D. (Lakeport ser.) $1.25. Lothrop, L. & S.
Baseball boys of Lakeport. '09(Ja23) c. il. 12°, (Lakeport ser.) †$1.25. Lothrop, L. & S.
Boat club boys of Lakeport. '08(S5) c. il. D. (Lakeport ser.) †$1.25. Lothrop, L. & S.
Dave Porter and his classmates. '09(Ap10) c. il. D. (Dave Porter ser.) †$1.25. Lothrop, L. & S.

Stratemeyer, E:—*Continued.*
Dave Porter at Star Ranch; or, the cowboy's secret. '10(Ag20) c. il. D. (Dave Porter ser.) $1.25. Lothrop, L. & S.
Dave Porter in the far North. '08(Ap4) c. il. D. (Dave Porter ser.) †$1.25. Lothrop, L. & S.
First at the north pole; or, two boys in the Arctic circle. '09(D11) c. il. D. $1.25. Lothrop, L. & S.
Foot-ball boys of Lakeport; or, more goals than one. '09(S11) c. il. (Lakeport ser.) †$1.25. Lothrop, L. & S.
For the liberty of Texas. '09(My15) c. il. 12°, (Mexican war ser.) †$1.25. Lothrop, L. & S.
Gun Club boys of Lakeport. '09(Ja23) c. il. 12°, (Lakeport ser.) †$1.25. Lothrop, L. & S.
Out with gun and camera; or, the boy hunters in the mountains. [1910.] (Jl) c. 6+258 p. il. 12°, (Boy hunters ser.) 60 c. Cupples & L.
Putnam Hall champions; or, bound to win out. '08, [1909.] (Ap) c. 6+277 p. il. 12°, (Putnam Hall ser.) 60 c. Grosset.
Putnam Hall rebellion. '09(Je5) c. il. 12°, (Putnam Hall ser.) 60 c. Grosset.
Rover boys at college. '10(D31) c. il. 12°, (Rover boys' ser. for young Americans.) 60 c. Grosset.
Rover boys at school. '08(O10) il. 12°, (Rover boys' ser. for young Americans.) 60 c. Grosset.
Rover boys on the farm. '08(Je6) c. il. D. (Rover boys' ser. for young Americans.) 60 c. Grosset.
Rover boys on Treasure Isle. '09(Je5) c. il. 12°, (Rover boys' ser. for young Americans.) 60 c. Grosset.
Under Scott in Mexico. '09(My15) c. il. 12°, (Mexican war ser.) †$1.25. Lothrop, L. & S.
With Taylor on the Rio Grande. '09 (My15) c. il. 12°, (Mexican war ser.) †$1.25. Lothrop, L. & S.

STRATFORD-ON-AVON, Eng.
Pictorial and descriptive guide to Stratford-on-Avon. $1 net. Platt & P.

Stratford Town Shakespeare. *See* Shakespeare, W:

Strathmore classics. 26 v. '10(D) pors. ea., ooze, $1.50, boxed. Crowell.

Stratigraphy and paleontology of the San Pablo formation in Middle California Weaver, C: E. 25 c. Univ. of Cal.

Straton, Rev. J: Roach.
Salvation of society, and other addresses. '09(F) 116 p. 12°, $1. Fleet-M.

Stratton, Arth.
See Garner, T:

Stratton, Chester R.
Picturesque Asia and Africa; together with strange sights in Zulu-land. '10(Je4) c. il. 8°, $1. Nat. Pub. Co.
Picturesque China; or, the flowery kingdom. '10(My21) c. il. 8°, $1. Nat. Pub. Co.

Stratton, Chester R.—*Continued.*
Picturesque Europe; cont. famous tours and scenes in the Old World; together with the wonders of astronomy. '10(Je4) c. il. 8°, $1. Nat. Pub. Co.
Asia and Europe bound together, $1.75.
Picturesque Japan; or, the land of the Mikado; cont. graphic accts. of the early hist. of Japan; Shintoism and Buddhism. '10(My21) c. il. 8°, $1. Nat. Pub. Co.

Stratton, Harriet Russell, comp.
Book of Strattons; collection of Stratton records from England and Scotland, and genealogical hist. of the early colonial Strattons in America. v. 1. '08(D5) c. il. facsims., charts, 8°, **$8 net. Grafton Press.

Stratton, Stephen S:
Nicolo Paganini: his life and work. '08 (D5) il. facsims., pors. 12°, ("Strad" lib.) *$2 net. Scribner.

Stratton, W: Alfr.
Letters from India; with a memoir by his wife, Anna Booth Stratton. '08(Je13) 8°, *$3.50 net. Dutton.

Stratton-Porter, Gene.
See Porter, Gene Stratton-.

STRATTON FAMILY.
See Genealogies.

Stratz, Rudolph.
Where snow is sovereign: romance of the glaciers; tr. from the German by Mary J. Safford. '09(O9) c. il. D. $1.50. Dodd.

Straub, Paul F:
Medical service in campaign; hdbk. for medical officers in the field; prepared under the direction of the surgeon-general, United States army. '10(Ag) 7+164 p. il. 12°, $1.50. Blakiston.
Bibliography (2 p.).

Straughn, M. N., and Church, Calvin Grant.
Influence of environment on the composition of sweet corn, 1905-1908. '09, [1910.] (F) 69 p. il. tabs., 8°, (U. S., Dept. of Agriculture, Bu. of Chemistry, bull.) pap.

Straus, Juliet Virginia, ["**Country Contributor.**"]
Ideas of a plain country woman. '08(Ap4) c. D. **$1 net. Doubleday, P.

Straus, Ralph.
Robert Dodsley, poet, publisher, and playwright. '10(My14) por. O. $6.50 net. Lane.

Strauss, Hermann.
Gout. '09(Ag) 70 p. 12°, $1. Treat.

STRAUSS, Richard.
Newman, E. Richard Strauss; with personal note by Alfred Kalisch. *$1 net. Lane.

Straw (The). Ramsay, R. †$1.50. Macmillan.

STRAW ITCH.
Goldberger, J. Straw itch; a disease new to American physicians. Gov. Pr. Off.
Schamberg, J. F. Grain itch. (Priv. pr.) Journal Cutaneous.

Strawberry handkerchief. Barr, *Mrs.* A. E. H. †$1.50. Dodd.

Streamer, Col. D., pseud.
See Graham, Harry.

Streatfeild, Rev. G: Sidney.
The incarnation. '10(Ja29) D. *40 c. net. Longmans.

Streatfeild, R: Alex.
Handel. '09(D4) il. 8°, (New lib. of music.) *$2.50 net. Lane.

Street, Arth. Irwin, ed. and comp.
Pandex of the news; cumulative index and digest of the newspapers of the United States; [monthly.] '09(Jl10) c. f°, per year, $10. Pandex.

Street, C: Stuart.
Outlines of auction bridge; being a concise statement of the rules of the game, together with an elucidation of the essential points a bridge player must know in order to play auction. '09, [1910.] (Mr) c. 29 p. 16°, 75 c. C: S. Street.

Street, G: Slythe.
People and questions. '10(D17) 12°, $1.50 net. M. Kennerley.

Street, Julian Leonard.
My enemy the motor. '08(Mr7) c. il. D. †$1. Lane.
Need of change. '09(Ag14) c. il. S. 50 c. Lane.

Street, T: Atkins.
Federal equity practice; treatise on the pleadings used and practice followed in courts of the United States in the exercises of their equity jurisdiction. In 3 v. '09(Ap) c. O. per set, shp., $19.50. E: Thompson.

STREET-CLEANING.
Soper, G: A. Modern methods of street cleaning. $3. Engineering News.

"Street cries of an old southern city." Leiding, H. K. 25 c. H. K. Leiding.

Street of adventure. Gibbs, P. $1.25 net. Dutton.

STREET RAILROADS.
Abbott, T. O. Primer of the law of negligence for conductors and motormen. (Add. author for price.) T. O. Abbott.
American street railway investments. $5. McGraw-H.
Forse, W: H., *jr.* Electric railway auditing and accounting. *$2 net. McGraw.
Johnson, F: W: Prevention of accidents. 25 c. McGraw-H.
New York [State.] *Public Service Commission.* Supervision of street railways in England and Prussia. (Add. pubs. for price.) Lyon.
Pinanski, A. E. Street railway system of metropolitan Boston. *$1 net. McGraw.
Supervision of street railways in England and Prussia. (Add. pubs. for price.) Lyon.
See also Electric railroads;—New York City.

Street railway reports, annot; ed. by Melvin Bender and Harold J. Hinman. v. 5-6. '10 (O) c. O. shp., ea., $5. M. Bender.

Street singer. McIntyre, J: T: †$1.25. Penn Pub. Co.

Street traffic regulation. Eno, W: P. $2. Rider & D.

Street trees. Taylor, A. D. gratis. Cornell Univ.

Streeter, G: L., M.D.
Lab'y guide in anatomy; outline of dissection designed for dental students. '09 (N) c. 34 p. figs. D. pap., 30 c. Wahr.
Lab'y guide in anatomy; outline of dissection designed for students of medicine at the University of Michigan. '09(N) c. 68 p. figs. D. 50 c. Wahr.

STREETS.
See Pavements;—Roads.

Strelitz, Adolph Friedrich.
See Mecklenburg-Strelitz, Adolph Friedrich, *Duke* of.

Strength and elasticity of structural members. Woods, R. J. *$3.50 net. Longmans.

Strength of being clean. Jordan, D: S. *50 c. net. Am. Unitarian.

Strength of being morally clean. Jordan, D: S. $1. Caldwell.

Strength of chain links. Goodenough, G: A. (Add. Univ. for price.) Univ. of Ill.

Strength of concrete beams. Humphrey, R: S. (Add. Supt. for price.) U. S., Supt. of Docs.

Strength of cylinders. '08(N21) c. il. 8°, (Machinery's reference ser.) pap., 25 c. Indust. Press.

Strength of England. Welsford, J. W. W. *$1.75 net. Longmans.

STRENGTH OF MATERIALS.
Bamford, H. Moving loads on railway underbridges. *$1.25 net. Macmillan.
Church, I. P. Mechanics of internal work (or work of deformation). $1.50 net. Wiley.
Derleth, C:, *jr.* Moment diagrams and typical live loads. 10 c. Univ. of Cal.
Diamant, S. Curves for calculating beams, channels and reactions. *$2 net. McGraw.
Heller, A. H: Stresses in structures and the accompanying deformations. $3. Wiley.
Morley, A. Strength of materials. *$2.50 net. Longmans.
Popplewell, W: C: Strength of materials. *$2 net. Van Nostrand.
Ricker, N. C. Study of base and bearing plates for columns and beams. gratis. Univ. of Ill.
Smith, H. E. Strength of material. *$1.25 net. Wiley.
Unwin, W: C. Testing of materials for construction. $5 net. Longmans.
Woods, R. J. Strength and elasticity of structural members. *$3.50 net. Longmans.
See also Architecture;—Bridges—Building materials; — Cement; — Concrete; — Earthwork;— Masonry;—Roofs;—Steel.

Strength of quietness. Steen, R. S. 75 c. Dodd.

Strength of the weak. Thacker, M. D. $1.50. B'way Pub.

Strength to yield. Bogue, V. $1.50. Cunningham, C. & W.

Strenuous career. Peters, M. C. $1.25. Laird.

STREPSICERINE ANTELOPE.
See Paleontology.

STREPSIPTERA.
See Insects.

STRESSES.
See Masonry;—Strength of materials.

Stretton, Hesba.
Christmas child. '09(S11) c. il. D. **50 c. net. Crowell.

Strickler, Givens Brown.
Sermons. '10(Ap23) c. 8°, $1. Revell.
Strictly business. Henry, O., *pseud.* $1.20, fixed. Doubleday, P.
Strife. *See* Galsworthy, J: Plays.
STRIKES.
Crosby, O. T. Strikes. $1.25. Putnam.
Malkiel, T. S. Diary of a shirtwaist striker; story of the shirtwaist makers' strike in New York. 50 c. Co-operative Press.
Merritt, W. G. Strikes and public utilities. gratis. Am. Anti-Boycott.
Strindberg, Johan August.
The father: (a tragedy;) tr. by N. Erichsen. '08(Mr28) D. *$1 net. J: W. Luce.
Swanwhite: fairy drama; tr. by Fs. J. Ziegler. '09(Mr17) c. O. $1. Brown Bros.
Stringer, Arth. J: Arbuthnott.
The gunrunner. '09(Ap17) c. D. $1.50. B. W. Dodge.
Under groove. '08(Ap25) c. il. D. †$1.50. McClure.
STRINGER, Thomas.
Wheeler, C. F. *and* J. R. Life of Scout Two Braids, (Thomas Stringer.) 25 c. Wood-B.
Stringham, Washington Irving.
In memoriam, Irving Stringham; [repr. from the Univ. of Cal. *Chronicle.*] '10 (Jl16) 8°, 25 c. Univ. of Cal.
Striving for his own. Adams, W: T. $1. Lothrop, L. & S.
Strobridge, Mrs. Idah Meacham.
Land of purple shadows. '09(D18) c. il. O. pap., $1.75; ¾ mor., $6.75; full mor., $10. Artemesia.
Loom of the desert. '08(Ja4) il. O. pap., $1.75. Artimisia.
Stroebe, Lilian Luise.
See Whitney, Marian P.
Strohecker, Clifford.
Royal road to health. '10(Ag13) c. S. $1.
Stroke oar. Paine, R. D. $1.50. McClurg.
Strokes and science of lawn tennis. Vaile, P. A. 10 c. Am. Sports.
Stromeyer, C: E.
Marine boiler management and construction. 3d ed. '08(Ja25) il. tabs., O. *$4 net. Longmans.
Strong, Anna Louise.
King's palace. '08, [1909.] (My) c. 59 p. il. 12°, 50 c. Oak Leaves.
Psychology of prayer. '09(S11) D. *$1.75 net. Univ. of Chic.
Strong, A: Hopkins, D.D.
Outlines of systematic theology. '08(S19) c. O. **$2.50 net. Am. Bapt.
Systematic theology. In 3 v. v. 2, The doctrine of man. '08(Ja4); v. 3, The doctrine of salvation. '09(Jl10) 8°, ea., **$2.50 net. Am. Bapt.
Strong, Forbes.
Echoes. [1910.] (N) c. il. 16°, 50 c. Werner Co.
Strong, F: Finch.
Essentials of modern electro-therapeutics. '08(F22) c. il. 12°, $1. Rebman.
High-frequency currents. '08(N) c. 19+289 p. il. 8°, *$3 net. Rebman.
Strong, Helen P., comp.
My friends. '09, [1910.] (Ja) 50 c.; limp leath., $1.25. Caldwell.
Strong, H: Rowland.
Machinations of the American Medical Association: exposure and a warning. '09 (Mr13) c. D. pap., 25 c. Nat. Druggist.
Strong, Rev. J. Selden.
Essential Calvinism. '09(D25) c. D. *75 c. net. Pilgrim Press.
Strong, J:
Hist. of secondary education in Scotland; from early times to education act of 1908. '10(Ja1) O. $2.50. Oxford Univ.
Strong, Josiah, D.D.
Challenge of the city. '08, [1909.] (Jl) c. il. 12°, (Forward mission study courses.) *$1 net; 50 c.; pap., 35 c. Young People's Miss.
My religion in everyday life. '10(S3) c. D. 50 c. net. Baker & T.
—, ed. Studies in the Gospel of the Kingdom; series no. 1; course of study on living social problems in the light of the Gospel of Jesus Christ. '10(Ap9) c. O. 75 c.; pap., 60 c. Am. Inst. Social Science.
Strong, Laura Coster.
Poems, in memoriam. '08(O) c. 10+343 p. il. pors. 8°. (Priv. pr.) Riverside Press.
Strong, Rob. M.
Commercial deductions from comparisons of gasoline and alcohol tests on internal-combustion engines. '09(D) 38 p. 8° (U. S., Dept. of the Interior, U. S. Geological Survey, bull.) pap. (Add. Superintendent for price.) U. S., Supt. of Docs.
Strong, T: Morris, D.D.
History of the town of Flatbush in Kings County, Long Island. Published by request. N. Y., Thomas R. Mercier, Jr., printer, 240 Pearl St., cor. Burling-slip, 1842. '08(D26) il. por. map, 12°. (Add. pub. for price.) F: Loeser.
Strong, W: Ellsworth.
Story of the American Board; acct. of the first hundred years of the American Board of Commissioners for Foreign Missions. '10(O15) c. il. map, O. $1.75 net. Pilgrim Press.
Strong, W: Walker.
Ionization in closed vessels. '08, [1909.] S. c. 39-60 p. il. 4°, 25 c. Johns Hopkins.
See Jones, Harry Clary.
Strong-Tracy, Mrs. Eliz.
Club woman's friend; analysis of parliamentary law; with explanations, clear and comprehensive. '10(F5) c. por. T. $1. Dealy.
Strong-hand Saxon. Beck, C. $1. Lippincott.
Strong selections for public reading. Redington, M. E., *comp.* $1.50. Cen. Me.
Stronger claim. Perrin, A. R. †$1.50. Duffield.
Strongheart. Burton, F: R. †$1.50. G: W. Dillingham.
Stronghold of hope. Tileston, *Mrs.* M. W. F., *comp.* $1 net. Little, B. & Co.
Stroup, Rev. Ner Wallace.
Fact of sin, viewed historically and doctrinally. '08(O17) c. D. *$1 net. Jennings.

Strouse, Mrs. G: H.
Asendi: a West African tale. '08(Mr7) c. il. 8°, $1.50. Chemical.

Strouse, Martyn W.
Judge Fritznoodle; a correct chronicle of the doings in the German-American settlement of Prairiestadt, Cabbage Township, Richsoil County; "Out West," during the free soil period. '09(Ag21) 12°, $1.25. Roxburgh.

Strout, C: H:
Plane geometry. '09, [1910.] (My) c. 106 p. il. 8°, $1. C: H: Strout.

Structural concrete ser. il. 8°. Concrete Engineering.
—Porter. Concrete, its composition and use. $2.

Structural details; or, elements of design in heavy framing. Jacoby, H: S. **$2.25 net. Wiley.

Structural drawing. Edminster, C. F. $2.50. D: Williams.

STRUCTURAL ENGINEERING.
See Engineering.

Structure and life-history of the hay-scented fern. Conard, H: S. 50 c. Carnegie.

Structure of the cotton fibre. Bowman, F. H. *$2.75 net. Macmillan.

Structure of the wool fibre. Bowman, F. H. *$2.60 net. Macmillan.

Struggle between graft and democracy. Langdon, W: H: 10 c. Civic Forum.

Struggle everlasting. Wessels, E: J. *$3 net. E: J. Wessels.

Struggle for a royal child. Kremer, *Mrs.* I. $1.50. M. Kennerley.

Struggle for American independence. Fisher, S. G: 2 v. **$4 net. Lippincott.

Struggle for freedom. Kaler, J. O. $1. Burt.

Struggle for imperial unity. Denison, G: T. *$2.25 net. Macmillan.

Struggle for Missouri. McElroy, J: $2. Nat. Tribune.

Struggle for religious liberty in Virginia. James, C: F. $1.25. Review and Herald Pub.

Struggles and triumph of the truth. Lowber, J. W: $2. Standard Pub.

Struly, Ewer, pseud.
See Perrin, Lee Ja.

Stryker, A. M.
Advertiser's hdbk. written and comp. according to the latest advertising knowledge. '09(N) c. 9-167 p. il. 16°, $1. Trade Journ.

Stryker, W:
See Nihart, B: Franklin.

Stuart, Mrs. Arth. T:, ed.
See Stuart, Nina.

Stuart, Donald Clive.
Stage decoration in France in the Middle Ages. '10(Je4) 12°, (Columbia Univ. studies in romance, philology and literature.) $1.50 net. Lemcke.

Stuart, Duncan.
See Rawl, Bernard H.

Stuart, Edn. R.
See Cole, Edn. Tuttle.

Stuart, Eleanor.
See Childs, *Mrs.* Eleanor Stuart.

Stuart, G: Rutledge.
Saloon under the searchlight. '08(Mr21) c. 12°, *35 c. net; pap., *20 c. net. Revell.
Stump digger on the saloon. '08(Je13) D. pap., 10 c. Pub. Ho. of M. E. Ch., So.

Stuart, Gerald Villiers-.
Soul of Croesus. '08(Ag1) c. D. 75 c. Cupples & L.

STUART, Henry, *Cardinal of York.*
Shield, A. Henry Stuart, Cardinal of York. *$3.50 net. Longmans.

Stuart, H: Longan.
Weeping cross: an unwordly story. '08 (Ag29) c. D. **$1.40 net. Doubleday, P.

Stuart, Ira Beal, jr.
Heart throbs: [poems.] '10(Mr5) c. D. 75 c. Charter Oak.

STUART, *Major-General* James Ewell Brown (*known as* J. E. B. Stuart).
Garnett, T. S. J. E. B. Stuart, (Major-General,) commander of the Cavalry Corps, Army of Northern Virginia, C. S. A. $1. Neale.
Mosby, J: S. Stuart's cavalry in the Gettysburg campaign. **$2 net. Moffat.

Stuart, J:
See Seufert, E: Constant.

Stuart, Nina, [Mrs. Arth. T: Stuart,] ed.
Chronicles of service life in Malta. '08 (N7) il. D. $2. Longmans.

Stuart, Mrs. Ruth McEnery.
Aunt Amity's silver wedding and other stories. '09(O9) c. il. D. †$1. Century Co.
Carlotta's intended. Forget-me-not ed. '09 '09(O16) c. il. D. †$1.25. Harper.
Sonny's father. '10(O29) c. il. D. $1 net. Century Co.
Unlived life of little Mary Ellen. '10(O17) c. D. $1. Bobbs-M.

STUARTS (The).
Rait, R. S., *ed.* Five Stuart princesses. *$3.50 net. Dutton.
See also Stuart, Henry, *Cardinal of York.*

Stub ends of thought and verse. Lewis, A. G. $1. Bohemian Soc.

STUB-TOOTH GEAR.
See Gears and gearing.

Stubbins, T: Alva.
The patriot. '08(Ap4) c. il. 12°, $1. Donohue.

Stubbs, G: E:
The adult male alto or counter-tenor voice. '08(F) c. 12°, 75 c. H. W. Gray.

Stubbs, Laura.
Stevenson's shrine; record of a pilgrimage. '10(D) 16°, limp leath., $2; ooze, $2.50; cf., $3. Barse & H.

Stubbs, Bp. W:
Germany in the early Middle Ages, 476-1250; ed. by Arth. Hassall. '08(My2) maps, O. *$2 net. Longmans.
Germany in the later Middle Ages, 1200-1500; ed. by Arth. Hassall. '09(My15) maps, 8°, *$2.25 net. Longmans.

Student cavalier. Forrest, J. R. *$1 net. Fenno.

Student's guide to accompany the Ellis tablet method of teaching bookkeeping and business practice; elem. course. '10(S3) c. forms, 4°, 55 c. Ellis Pub.

Student's history of American literature. Simonds, W: E: $1.10. Houghton M.

Student's Old Testament. *See* Kent, C: Foster.

Students and the present missionary crisis; addresses. '10(Ag6) c. O. $1.50. Student Volunteer.

Students' aids ser. 16°. Wood.
—Cunning. Aids to surgery. *$1.25 net.
—Hudson. Aids to medicine. *$1.25 net.
—Nall. Aids to obstetrics. *$1 net.
—Turner. Aids to osteology. *$1.25 net.

Student's edition of a Standard dict. of the English language; designed to give the orthography, pronunciation, meaning, and etymology of over 60,000 words and phrases. Thin paper ed., [ed. de luxe;] abr. from the Funk & Wagnalls Standard Dictionary of the English language by Ja. C. Fernald, Fs. A. March, J: W. Palmer, [and others.] '10(Mr19) c. O. limp leath., $5, boxed. Funk.

Students' ed. of a Standard dict. of the English language; cont. also an appendix of proper names, foreign phrases, faulty diction, disputed pronunciations, abbreviations, etc. '10, [1909.] (D) c. 8+917 p. il. 8°, $2.50. Funk.

Students' law dictionary. Peloubet, S. S. $1.50; $2. Peloubet.

Students' ser. 12°. Little, B. & Co.
—Ewell, *M.D.* Manual of medical jurisprudence. $2.50.

Students' ser. of English classics. S. Sibley.
—Goldsmith *and* Gray. Traveller and Deserted village, Elegy in a country churchyard. 25 c.

Students' ser. of hist. and comparative grammars; ed. by Jos. Wright. D. Oxford Univ.
—Wright. Old English grammar. $2.

Students' ser. of Latin classics. il. D. B: H. Sanborn.
—Elmore. Books of Latin prose composition. $1.
—Potter. Elementary Latin course. $1.12.
—Terence. Phormio. 50 c.—Havton timovrmenos. $1.
—Virgil. Æneid. bks. I.-IV. $1.40.

Students' text-book of zoölogy. v. 3. Sedgwick, A. *$5.50 net. Macmillan.

Studies from the geological department; Preliminary account of the geology of the Highlands in New Jersey, by W. S. Bayley; Some notes on river development in the vicinity of Danville, Ill., by Carroll H. Wegeman; Notes on the distribution of the mastodon in Illinois, by Rufus M. Bagg. '09(My8) il. map, 8°, (Univ. of Ill. bulletin; Universities studies.) pap., 75 c. Univ. of Ill.

Studies from the Psychological Laboratory of the University of Chicago. il. 4°. Psychological Review.
—Downey. Control processes in modified handwriting. $1.50.

Studies from the psychological laboratory of the University of Illinois. University of Illinois. v. 1. $1.75. Psychological Review.

Studies in American race problem. Stone, A. H. **$2 net. Doubleday, P.

Studies in American social conditions. See Edwards, R: H:, *ed.*

Studies in character building. Kellogg, *Mrs.* E. E. $1. Modern Medicine.

Studies in Chinese religion. Parker, E: H. $3 net. Dutton.

Studies in Christian worship. Robinson, C: H: 25 c. Longmans.

Studies in Christianity. Bowne, B. P. **$1.50 net. Houghton M.

Studies in development and learning. Kirkpatrick, E. A., *ed.* $1. Science Pr., (N. Y.)

Studies in economic relations of women. Woman's Educational and Industrial Union, Boston, Department of Research. v. 1. $1.20 net; pap., 60 c. net. Longmans.

Studies in English and American literature. Raub, A. N. $1.50. Stradling.

Studies in English and comparative literature by former and present students at Radcliffe College, presented to Agnes Irwin, Dean of Radcliffe College, 1894-1909. '10(Jl30) c. pors. 8°, (Radcliffe College monographs.) $1.50. Ginn.

Studies in eucalyptus. Graves, W: E., *comp. and ed.* $1. W: E. Graves.

Studies in French education. Hodgson, G. $1.10. Putnam.

Studies in Galilee. Masterman, E. W: G. *$1 net. Univ. of Chic.

Studies in heredity. Canno, W: A. (Add. Institution for price.) Carnegie.

Studies in history, economics, and public law; ed. by the Faculty of Political Science of Columbia University. O. Longmans.
—Ramsdell. Reconstruction in Texas. $2.50.

Studies in horse breeding. Carlson, G: L. $2. G: L. Carlson.

Studies in immunity. Bordet, J. $6. Wiley.

Studies in immunity. Ehrlich, P. $6. Wiley.

Studies in invalid occupation. Tracy, S. E. $1.50 net. Whitcomb.

Studies in Judaism. Schechter, S. 2d ser. $2. Jewish Pub.

Studies in musical education history and æsthetics; fourth ser.; papers and proceedings of the Music Teachers' National Association at its 31st annual meeting, Northwestern University, Evanston, Ill., Dec. 28-30, 1909. '10(Je11) O. $1.60. Music Teachers' Nat. Assoc.

Studies in mystical religion. Jones, R. M. *$3.50 net. Macmillan.

Studies in New England transcendentalism. Goddard, H. C. *$1 net. Lemcke.

Studies in ornamental trees and shrubs. Hall, H. M. 75 c. Univ. of Cal.

Studies in paranoia. Gierlich, N. $1. Journal Nervous Disease.

Studies in philology; pub. under the direction of the Philological Club; C. Alphonso Smith, editor; v. 2, Studies in the syntax of the King James version, by Ja. Moses Grainger. '08(F1); v. 3, Influence of E. T. A. Hoffman on the tales of Edgar Allan Poe, by Palmer Cobb. '08(Ag1); v. 4, Conjunction plus participle group in English, by Orestes Pearl Rhyne; [and] The dramatic monologue; its origin and development, by Claud Howard. '10(Mr); v. 5, Imprecation as a means of emphasis in old French *chansons de geste*, by Oliver Towles; Examples of secondary ablaut in the English weak verb, by Ja. Finch Royster; Hebbell's *Julia*, a forerunner of the modern drama, by Palmer Cobb. '10(Je) O. pap., ea., 50 c. Univ. of N. C.

Studies in puncture fluids. Gruner, O. C. *$3 net. Blakiston.

Studies in radio-activity. Ashman, G: C. (Add. author for price.) G: C. Ashman.

Studies in reading. Searson, J. W: 80 c. Univ. Pub. Co.

Studies in religion and theology. Fairbairn, A. M. *$3.50 net. Macmillan.

Studies in secondary education. Sachs, J., *ed.* 30 c. Teachers' Coll.

Studies in several literatures. Peck, H. T. **$1.20 net. Dodd.

Studies in tape reading. Wyckoff, R: D. $3. Ticker Pub.

Studies in the apostolic age. Nordell, P. A. *20 c. net. Am. Bapt.

Studies in the early church. Morgan, C: H. 75 c. Jennings.

Studies in the gospel of the kingdom. Strong, J., *ed.* 75 c.; 60 c. Am. Inst. Social Service.

Studies in the leading of troops. Verdy du Vernois, J. v. $1.50. Hudson.

Studies in the life and teachings of our Lord. $1.50. Bible Inst.

Studies in the marvellous. Kurtz, B: P. $2. Univ. of Cal.

Studies in the prophets of Israel. Walker, R. H. 25 c. Eaton & M.

Studies in the psychology of sex. *See* Ellis, H: H.

Studies in the resurrection of Christ. Robinson, C: H: *$1.25 net. Longmans.

Studies in the teaching of religion. Palmer, W: S. *40 c. net. Longmans.

Studies in theology. D. *75 c. net. Scribner.
—Inge. Faith and its psychology.
—Orr. Revelation and inspiration.
—Peake. Critical introd. to the New Testament.
—Rashdall. Philosophy and religion.

Studies in Victor Hugo's dramatic characters. Bruner, J. B. $1. Ginn.

Studies in wives. Belloc-Lowndes, *Mrs.* M. A. B. $1.50. M. Kennerley.

Studies of criminal responsibility. Folsom, C: F. (Priv. pr.) C: F. Folsom.

Studies of juvenile criminals. MacDonald, A. (Add. author for price.) A. MacDonald.

Studies of our cone-bearing trees. Mosher, E. R. $2. Bardeen.

Studies of our oaks and maples. Mosher, E. R. $2. Bardeen.

Studies of Shakespeare's women. McKenney, *Mrs.* M. M. $2. M. M. McKenney.

Studies of the eighteenth century in Italy. Lee, V., *pseud.* *$6 net. McClurg.

Studies of the historical plays of Shakespeare. *See* Davidson, *Mrs.* Hannah Amelia Noyes.

Studies of trees in winter. *See* Huntington, A. O.

Studies on immunization. Wright, *Sir* A. E: **$5 net. Wood.

Studio year book of decorative art, 1908. '08 (Je27) Q. *$5 net.—1909. '09(My22) *$3 net; pap., *$2.50 net.—1910. '10(Ap2) il. Q. pap., $3 net. Lane.

Studniczka, Henry.
Labor conditions and cost of living; rept. on British labor conditions and the cost of living as found in the wage scales secured from union organizations; also a statement of rates of wages and cost of living in Nova Scotia. [1910.] (Jl) 7 p. 8°. Gov. Pr. Off.

STUDY.
See Education.

Study-guide ser. *See* Davidson, *Mrs.* Hannah Amelia Noyes.

Study of electric motors by experiment. St. John, T: M. 25 c. T: M. St. John.

Study of God, man and destiny. Brainard, A. $1. Cochrane.

Study of nature. Schmucker, S: C. $1.25. Lippincott.

Study of religion in the Italian universities. Jordan, L: H: $2.40. Oxford Univ.

Study of Romola. Davidson, *Mrs.* H. A. N. 50 c. H. A. Davidson.

Study of Swedenborg's psychical states and experiences. Whitehead, J: gratis. Mass. New-Ch. Un.

Study of the Claisen condensation. Gorsline, E. E. 55 c. Johns Hopkins.

Study of the drama. Matthews, J. B. **$1.50 net. Houghton M.

Study of the Lord's prayer. Richards, W: R. 75 c. Presb. Bd.

Study of the open hearth. Harbison-Walker Refraction Co., Pittsburg. $1. R. S. Davis.

Study of the population of Manhattanville. Woolston, H. B. $1.25. Longmans.

Study of the technique in Konrad Ferdinand Meyer's novellen. Taylor, M. L. 75 c. Univ. of Chic.

Stuff of a man. Blake, K. E. †$1.50. Bobbs-M.

Stuff of dreams. Tupper, *Mrs.* E. S. $1.50. B. W. Dodge.

Stump digger on the saloon. Stuart, G: R. 10 c. Pub. Ho. of M. E. Ch., So.

Stumpf, Jos.
Explanation of Luther's small catechism. '08(F) c. '07. 16°, bds., 35 c.; interleaved, 50 c. Gen. Council.

Sturdy, W: A., ["Isaac Didwin."]
Economy of education. '09(My22) c. D. $1. J. D. Bonnell.

Sturge, M. Carta.
Truth and error of Christian Science. New ed. '09(Ap17) 8°, *$1 net. Dutton.

Sturge, Mary D., M.D.
See Horsley, *Sir* Victor Alex. Haden.

Sturgis, Mrs. Edith Barnes.
My busy days; verses. '08(N7) c. il. F. bds., **$2 net. Appleton.

Sturgis, Russell.
Artist's way of working in the various handicrafts and arts of design. '10(S24) c. il. O. $5 net, boxed. Dodd.
Hist. of architecture. In 3 v. v. 2, Romanesque and Oriental. '10(Ja15) c. il. Q. **$5 net; hf. mor., $7.50. Baker & T.
Short history of architecture: Europe. '08 (Mr7) c. il. 12°, **$2.50 net. Macmillan.

Sturmer, Julius W:
Rudiments of Latin: with special reference to the nomenclature of the U. S. pharmacopœia, the national formulary, and the text-books in materia medica and botany; incl. also prescription writing and notes on the nomenclature of the German pharmacopœia. '08, [1909.] (Mr) c. 92 p. 12°, $1. J. W. Sturmer.

Sturtevant, E. H.
Studies in Greek noun-formations based in part upon material collected by the late A. W. Stratton, and prepared under the supervision of Carl D. Buck. '10(O) 34 p. O. pap., 25 c. net. Univ. of Chic.

STUTTERING.
See Stammering.

Stuttle, Mrs. Lilla Dale Avery-.
See Avery-Stuttle, *Mrs.* Lilla Dale.

Stutzman, Mrs. Luella Walden.
Tribute to mother, and other poems. [1910.] (Je) c. 40 p. por. 8°, 35 c. L. W. Stutzman.

STYLE.
See Costume;—Rhetoric.

Style-book of business English. Hammond, H. W. 60 c.; 85 c. Pitman.

Styles of ornament. Speltz, A. $6.70. Hessling.

SUBCONSCIOUS (The).
See Consciousness.

Subconscious mind and its illuminating light. Young, J. *$1 net. Whitaker & R.

Subconscious phenomena. *See* Münsterberg, Hugo.

Subcutaneous hydrocarbon protheses. Kolle, F: S. **$2.50 net. Grafton Press.

Subject catalogs of the Library of Congress. Hanson, J. C. M. H. W. Wilson.

Sublimity of the holy eucharist. Meschler, M. 75 c. net. Herder.

Submarine boys ser. *See* Durham, Victor G., *pseud.*

Submarine cable-laying. Wilkinson, H. D. *$6 net. Van Nostrand.

SUBMARINES.
Field, C. Story of the submarine. *$2 net. Lippincott.
See also Signals and signalling.

SUBSIDIES.
See Ship subsidies.

Subsistence guide. Cook, F. A. $1. U. S. Military Pub.

Substance of socialism. Spargo, J: *$1 net. Huebsch.

Substantial prosperity. Kuhn, H. A. $2. Pittsburgh-W.

Substitute (The). Camp, W. C. †$1.50. Appleton.

Substitute for the tariff upon imports. Bigelow, J: (Priv. pr.) J: Bigelow.

Substitutes for cash in the panic of 1907. Andrew, A. P. (Add. pub. for price.) Ellis.

SUBURBAN HOMES.
See Architecture.

Suburbanite's hdbk. of dwarf fruit tree culture. Thornton, A: W. 50 c. A: W. Thornton.

SUBWAYS.
See Railroads;—Transportation;—Ventilation.

SUCCESS.
Atkinson, W: W. Psychology of success. $1. Progress Co.
Ayer, M. A., *ed.* Keep up your courage. **$1 net; **$2 net. Lothrop, L. & S.
Cushing, J: J. Law of success. $1. Jenckes.
Field, W. T. What is success? 25 c. net. Pilgrim Press.
Fowler, N. C., *jr.* Starting in life. $2. Little, B. & Co.
Hawthorne, J. Secret of Solomon. (Add. author for price.) J. Hawthorne.
James, L. Twelve steps to success. $1. A. Harriman.
Kaufman, H. Winning fight. $1.50. H. Kaufman.
Knox, G: H. Leadership: [success in business.] $1.40; $2.80. Personal Help.
Larson, C. D. How great men succeed. 50 c. Progress Co.
Maclean, J: Winning the front place. 75c. Am. S. S.
Macmurray, T: J. Highways of success. $1. Progress Co.
Marden, O. S. Getting on.—He can who thinks he can. ea., **$1 net. Crowell.
Pell, E: L. Secrets of true success. 10 c. Harding Press.
Riddell, N. N. Psychology of success and human nature studies. $1.50. Riddell Pub.
Sharp, F. C. Success; course in moral instruction for the high school. (Add. Univ. for price.) Univ. of Wis.
Sharpe, E. A. Foundation stones of success. 3 v. $8; $12. Howard-S.
Thayer, W: M. Tact, push and principle. 50 c. Hurst.
See also Business;—Conduct of life;—New thought;—Socialism;—Vocations.

Success in market gardening. Rawson, W. W. $1.10 net. Doubleday, P.

Success in music and how it is won. Finck, H: T. **$2 net. Scribner.

Success in retailing, the variety business; hdbk. for earnest beginners in merchandising. '10(My7) il. 8°, pap. Butler Bros.

Success with poultry. Reliable Incubator and Brooder Co. $1. Reliable Incubator.

Successful poultry and dairy farm. Spillman, W: J. (Add. Superintendent for price.) U. S., Supt. of Docs.

Successful wife. Dorset, G. $1.50. Harper.

Suckling, Sir J:
Works; ed. by A. Hamilton Thompson. '10(Ap23) 8°, $1.75 net. Dutton.

Suction gas plants. Smith, C. A. *$1.75 net. Lippincott.

SUDAN.
See Soudan.

Sudborough, J: Jos., and James, T. Campbell. Pract. organic chemistry. '09, [1910.] (F) 394 p. il. 12°, *$2 net. Van Nostrand.

Sudermann, Hermann.
Heimat; schauspiel in vier akten; ed., with an introd. and notes, by F. G. G. Schmidt. '09(D18) c. por. S. (Heath's modern language ser.) 35 c. Heath.
John the Baptist: a play; tr. by Beatrice Marshall. '08(O31) O. *$1.50 net. Lane.
Morituri; three one act plays: Teja, Fritzchen, The eternal masculine; tr. from the German by Archibald Alexander. '10(O15) c. D. $1.25 net. Scribner.
Roses; four one-act plays: Streaks of light; The last visit; Margot; The far away princess; tr. from the German by Grace Frank. '09(O9) c. D. bds., **$1.25 net. Scribner.
Song of songs [Das hohe lied]; tr. by T: Seltzer. '09(D4) c. D. *$1.40 net. B: W. Huebsch.

Sudlow, Mrs. Eliz. Williams.
All about the primary. '10(Mr5) c. 24°, 50 c. Hammond Pub.

Sudow, Ferdinand Jos.
Reliable pheasant standard; pract. guide on the culture, breeding, rearing, trapping, preserving of pheasants, game birds, ornamental land and water fowl, singing birds. 3d ed., enl. '10(Je) c. 13+94 p. il. 8°, 75 c. Haight.

Sue, Marie Joseph Eugène.
Abbatial crosier; tr. from the orig. French by Dan. De Leon. '09(Ja16) c. 12°, 50 c. N. Y. Labor News.
Blacksmith's hammer; or, the peasant code; tale of the Grand Monarch; tr. from the orig. French by Dan. De Leon. '10(N12) c. 12°, 75 c. N. Y. Labor News.
Branding needle; or, the monastery of Charolles; tr. from the orig. French by Dan. De Leon. '08(Jl18) c. D. (Mysteries of the people ser.) 50 c. N. Y. Labor News.
Carlovingian coins; or, the daughters of Charlemagne: tale of the 9th century; tr. from the orig. French by Daniel De Leon. '08. [1909.] (My) c. 160 p. 12°, (Mysteries of the people ser.) 50 c. N. Y. Labor News.
Casque's lark; or, Victoria, the mother of the camps; tr. from the original French by Daniel De Leon. '09(D18) c. 12°, 75 c. N. Y. Labor News.
Executioner's knife; or, Joan of Arc; tale of the inquisition; tr. by Dan. De Leon. '10(My) c. 9+382 p. 12°, (Mysteries of the people ser.) $1. N. Y. Labor News.
Iron arrow head; or, the buckler maiden: tale of the Northman invasion: tr. from the orig. French by Daniel De Leon. '08, [1909.] (My) c. 128 p. 12°, (Mysteries of the people ser.) 50 c. N. Y. Labor News.
Iron collar; or, Faustina and Syomara: tale of slavery under the Romans; tr. from the orig. French by Daniel De Leon. '09(My) 10+195 p. 12°, (Mysteries of the people ser.) 50 c. N. Y. Labor News.

Sue, Marie Joseph Eugène.—*Continued.*
Iron pincers; or, Mylio and Karvel; tale of the Albigensian crusades; tr. from the orig. French by Daniel De Leon. '09 (D) c. 5-193 p. 12°, 50 c. N. Y. Labor News.
Mysteries of Paris; repr. from the orig. Chapman and Hall ed. In 2 v. '10(S3) il. O. $2.50, boxed. Crowell.
Pilgrim's shell; or, Fergan the quarryman; tr. by Daniel de Leon. '09(Mr) 50 c. N. Y. Labor News.
Pocket Bible; or, Christian the printer; tale of the sixteenth century; tr. from the orig. French by Dan. De Leon. '10 (Ag27) c. 2 v., 12°, $2. N. Y. Labor News.
Poniard's hilt; or, Karadeucq and Ronan; tr. from the orig. French by Daniel De Leon. '08(My23) c. D. (Mysteries of the people ser.) 75 c. N. Y. Labor News.
Silver cross; or, the Carpenter of Nazareth. '09(Ag14) 12°, (Mysteries of the people ser.) 50 c. N. Y. Labor News.
Wandering Jew. 2 v. '08(D19) front. 12°, (Crowell's thin paper sets.) hf. mor., $3, boxed. Crowell.
Wandering Jew. 2 v. '10(D) il. $2.50, boxed. Crowell.

Sue Orcutt. Vaile, *Mrs.* C. M. †$1.50. Wilde.

Suess, Eduard.
Face of the earth (Das Antlitz der erde); tr. by Hertha B. C. Sollas under the direction of W. J. Sollas. v. 3. '09(O) $5.75; v. 4. '10(Mr26) maps, O. $7.75. Oxford Univ.

SUETONIUS, Tranquillius Caius.
Alexander, W: H. Some textual criticisms on the eighth book of the De vita Cæsarum of Suetonius. 30 c. Univ. of Cal.

Suffer little children. Shaw, C. $2.50. Fenno.

SUFFERING.
Hardy, T: J: Gospel of pain. *$1.25 net. Macmilan.
Schmidt, R. Pain. **$3 net. Lippincott.
See also Consolation.

Suffling, Ernest R.
English church brasses; from the 13th to the 17th centuries; manual for antiquaries, archæologists and collectors. 9th ed., rewritten. '10(D10) il. 8°, $4.20. Scribner.

SUFFOLK, Eng.
Dutt, W: A. Norfolk and Suffolk coast. $2.25 net. Stokes.
Dutt, W: A. Suffolk. *45 c. net. Putnam.
Powell, E., *ed.* Suffolk hundred in the year 1283. $3.50 net. Putnam.
See also Theberton.

SUFFRAGE.
American Academy of Political and Social Science. Significance of the woman suffrage movement. 50 c. Am. Acad. Pol. Sci.
Brashere, O. M. Science and suffrage. 25 c. O. M. Brashere.
Buckley, J. M. Wrong and peril of woman suffrage. *75 c. net. Revell.

SUFFRAGE.—*Continued.*
Crosby, J: F. Advisability of inserting the word sex before the word race in the fifteenth amendment of the Constitution of the United States. gratis. Georgetown Univ.
Dorr, *Mrs.* R. C. What eight million women want. $2 net. Small.
Harper, I. A. H. Woman suffrage throughout the world. (Add. author for price.) I. A. H. Harper.
Hecker, E. A. Short hist. of the progress of woman's rights from the days of Augustus to the present time. $1.50 net. Putnam.
Johnson, H. K. Woman and the Republic; survey of the woman-suffrage movement in the United States. 35 c. Nat. League.
Jurgenson, G. M. Social mirror. $1.50. O. L. Panzer.
Moore, B. F. Hist. of cumulative voting and minority representation in Illinois, 1870-1908. 50 c. Univ. of Ill.
Phelps, E. M., *comp.* Selected articles on woman suffrage. $1 net. H. W. Wilson.
Sharp, E. Rebel woman. $1 net. Lane.
Sumner, H. L. **Equal suffrage; results of an investigation in Colorado. **$2 net. Harper.**
United States. *Congress. House Committee on the Judiciary.* Hearing on Woman's suffrage, [March 3, 1908.]
See also Elections;—Negroes.

Suffragettes (The). Raymond, G: L. (Add. pubs. for price.) B. S. Adams.

Sufism of the Rubáiyát. Hazeldine, N. F. W. $1. N. F. W. Hazeldine.

SUGAR.
Albert, A. D., *jr.* Customs frauds in New York; article entitled The chase of the sugar smugglers. (Add. Superintendent for price.) U. S., Supt. of Docs.
Bass, W: L. **Dutch standard in the U. S. tariff law, H. R. 1438. (Add. Superintendent for price.) U. S., Supt. of Docs.**
Claassen, H. Beet sugar manufacture. $3 net. Wiley.
Martineau, G: Sugar, cane and beet. 75 c. Pitman.
Meyer, H. H: B., *comp.* **Library of Congress select list of references on sugar, chiefly in its economic aspects.** 25 c. U. S., Supt. of Docs.
Mittelslaedt, O. Technical calculations for sugar works. $1.50. Wiley.
Newlands, J: A. R. *and* B: E. R. Sugar: hdbk. for planters and refiners. $10. Spon.
Nikaido, Y. Beet-sugar making. $3. Chemical.
Palmer, T. G. Beet sugar: letter concerning the beet-sugar industry of Europe and the U. S. (Add. Superintendent for price.) U. S., Supt. of Docs.
Roeding, F: W. **Irrigation of sugar beets.** U. S., Supt. of Docs.
Sugar trust; article from the *New York Times* of June 13, 1909, giving further light on the transactions of the sugar trust in connection with the settlement of the $30,000,000 suit. '09(Ag) 19 p. 8°. U. S., Supt. of Docs.

SUGAR.—*Continued.*
Surface, G: T: Story of sugar. $1 net. Appleton.
Tayler, A. J. W. Sugar machinery. $2 net. Van Nostrand.
Tracy, J: E., *and* Reed, J. F. Comparative tests of sugar-beet varieties. (Add. Superintendent for price.) U. S., Supt. of Docs.
United States. *Dept. of Agriculture.* Beet-sugar industry in the United States; letter from the Secretary of Agriculture, transmitting, in response to a resolution of the Senate of April 8, 1909, information concerning the beet-sugar industry. '09(Jl) 32 p. fold. map, 8°, 15 c.
United States. *Treasury Dept.* Cane and beet sugars in the U. S.; letter from the Secretary of the Treasury transmitting, in response to Senate resolution of the first instant, information relative to cane and beet sugar. '09(Ag) 6 p. 8°, pap.
Vogt, P. L. Sugar refining industry in the U. S. $1.50. Univ. of Penn.; [Winston.]
See also Chemistry;—*also* American Sugar Refining Co.

Sugar and spice and all that's nice. Tileston, *Mrs.* M. W. F., *comp.* $1.50 net. Little, B. & Co.

Suggested rules for recovering coal mines after explosions and fires. Garforth, W. E. *$1.50 net. Van Nostrand.

SUGGESTION (Mental.)
Atkinson, W: W. Suggestion and auto-suggestion. $1. Progress Co.
Bramwell, J: M. Hypnotism and treatment by suggestion. $1.75 net. Funk.
Butterfield, C. d. Suggestion as applied to business. $1. Colonial Press, (Ct.)
Leavitt, S. Paths to the heights: [psychotherapy.] **$1 net. Crowell.
McComb, S: Power of self-suggestion. **50 c. net. Moffat.
Parkyn, H. A. Auto-suggestion. $1. Suggestion.
Urban, F. M. Application of statistical methods to the problems of psychophysics. $2.50. Psychological Clinic.
Winbigler, C: F. **Suggestion; its law and application. $2.50. S. A. Lewis.**
See also Hypnotism;—Psychology;—Psychotherapy.

Suggestion concerning the increased longevity of life insurance policyholders. Foster, B. gratis. Assoc. Life.

Suggestions on Bible reading. Soulsby, L. H. M. 35 c. Longmans.

Suggestions on prayer. Soulsby, L. H. M. 35 c. Longmans.

Suggestions to military riflemen. Whelan, T. (Add. pubs. for price.) Hudson.

Suggestions to the expectant mother. Kraft, M. J. $2. M. J. Kraft.

Sugranes, Rev. Eug.
Old San Gabriel mission; historical notes taken from old manuscripts and records, accurately compiled after diligent research. '10(Mr5) c. il. pors. 8°, 50 c. E. Sugranes.

SUICIDE.
Deans, J: Suicide. 15 c. H. Gregory.

Suitable child. Duncan, N. *60 c. net; *$1 net. Revell.

Sullivan, Ja. E:
How to catch. '09(Je) c. 52 p. por. il. 16°, (Spalding's athletic lib.) pap., 10 c. Am. Sports.
Marathon running; origin of Marathon running; how leading runners train; hints for novices; how to conduct a Marathon race; rules; records of leading Marathon races. '09(Ap3) il. por. S. (Spalding's athletic lib.) pap., 10 c. Am. Sports.
Schoolyard athletics. '09(D25) c. il. por. 12°, (Spalding's athletic lib.) pap., 10 c. Am. Sports.
—, **comp.** Athletes' guide; cont. full directions for learning how to sprint, jump, hurdle and throw weights; special chapters of advice to beginners and important A. A. U. rules and their explanations. '08 (Ag15); '10(S) c. il. por. 16°, (Spalding's athletic lib.) pap., ea., 10 c. Am. Sports. *See also* Spalding's official athletic almanac.

Sullivan, Ja. W:
Municipal and private operation of public utilities. '09(My22) 8°. (Priv. pr.) J. W. Sullivan.
Socialism as an incubus on the American labor movement. '09(Ag28) D. pap., 50 c. Volunteer.

Sullivan, J: G.
Spiral tables; prep. for the Canadian Pacific Railroad; repr. from the *Engineering Record.* '10(Ap30) il. tabs., 12°, $1.50 net. McGraw-H.

Sullivan, J: Ja.
American business law; with legal forms. '09(O16) c. D. *$1.50 net. Appleton.
American corporations; legal rules governing corporate organization and management. '10(N5) c. D. $2 net. Appleton.
Pennsylvania business law: a pract. hdbk. for business men and lawyers. 2d ed., rev. and enl. '08(N) c. 716 p. 8°, $4. Winston.

Sullivan, Jos. Matthew, comp.
Criminal slang. '09(Ap17) nar. T. pap.. 15 c. Worcester Press.

Sullivan, Mrs. May Kellogg.
Trail of a sourdough; life in Alaska. '10 (S3) c. il. D. $1.50. Badger.

Sullivan, T: Russell.
Lands of summer: sketches in Italy, Sicily and Greece. '08(My2) c. il. D. **$1.50 net. Houghton M.

Sullivan, Vernon L.
Irrigation in New Mexico. '09(Ag) 42 p. map, 8°. (U. S., Dept. of Agriculture; Office of Experiment Stations bull.) pap.

Sullivan, W. J: L.
Twelve years in the saddle for law and order on the frontier of Texas. '09(O) c. 3-284 p. il. pors. 8°, $1.50. Von Boeckmann-J.

SULLIVAN COUNTY, Ind.
Wolfe, T: J. Hist. of Sullivan Co., Ind. 2 v. Lewis Pub.

SULLIVAN COUNTY, Tenn.
Taylor, O. Historic Sullivan. $2.50. King Pr.

SULLIVAN'S INDIAN CAMPAIGN.
Hubley, A. Adm. Hubley, jr.; his journal. $1. Hist. Soc. Penn.

Sully, Duc de, [Maximilien de Béthune Baron de Rosny.]
Great design of Henry IV.; from the memoirs of the Duke of Sully; and The United States of Europe by E: Everett Hale; with introd. by Edwin D. Mead. '09(N20) c. D. (International peace lib.) **50 c. net. Ginn.

SULLY, Thomas.
Hart, C: H: Register of portraits painted by Thomas Sully. (Priv. pr.) C: H: Hart.

SULPHUR.
Brownlee, R. H. On precipitated sulphur. (Add. pub. for price.) Chemical.

SULPHURIC ACID.
Lunge, G: Manufacture of sulphuric acid and alkali. 3 v. v. 2, 3. ea., $15 net. Van Nostrand.
MacKnight, F: E. Fertilizer and acid plants. 50 c. Insurance Press.

Sulzberger, Mayer.
Am ha-aretz, the ancient Hebrew Parliament; chapter in the constitutional history of ancient Israel. '10(My7) 79 p. plan, 8°, 75 c. net. J. H: Greenstone.

SUMACH.
Huntington, A. O. Poison ivy and swamp sumach. 75 c. A. O. Huntington.

SUMERIA.
See Babylonia.

Sumerian administrative documents. Myhrman, D: W. $6. Univ. of Penn.

Sumerian hymns, from cuneiform texts in the British Museum; by F: A: Vanderburgh. '08(Ag29) 8°, (Contributions to oriental history and philology; Columbian Univ. Press.) pap., *$1 net. Lemcke.

SUMERIAN LANGUAGE.
Sumerian hymns, from cuneiform texts in the British Museum. *$1 net. Lemcke.

Sumichrast, F: Caesar J: Martin S: Roussy de.
Church and state in France: address del. before the Congregational Club, Worcester, Mass., March 18, 1907. '08(Ap18) c. 12°, pap., 25 c. F. H. Robson.

Summary of punctuation. Baldwin, C: S. 5 c. Longmans.
Summer across the sea. Snowden, J. H: *$1 net. Revell.
Summer diarrhea of infants. *$1 net. W: R. Jenkins.
Summer flowers on the high Alps. Hastings, S. $2.50 net. Dutton.
Summer garden of pleasure. Batson, *Mrs.* H. M. $3.50. McClurg.
Summer holiday. Tilney, R. 75 c. Biddle Press.
Summer in Touraine. Lees, F. *$2.75 net. McClurg.
Summer night's dream; tr. from the German by Capt. J: Moore Gawne. [Also] The defence of Duffer's drift by Capt. Ernest Dunlop Swinton. '08(Ag) 168 p. 12°, $1. Hudson.
Summer on the Canadian prairie. Binnie-Clark, G. $1.75 net. Longmans.

Summer reading for boys and girls; list of books sel. and arr. by classes. '10(O) 16 p. 12°, 15 c. net. Germantown Friends Sch.

Summer sermons. Horn, E: T. *$1 net. Pilger.

Summer tour in Finland. Waineman, P. *$2.50 net; *$5 net. Pott.

Summerbell, Jos. Ja., D.D.
Outline of church history of the first six centuries. '10(Je) 15-157 p. por. 12°, 75 c. Chr. Pub. Assoc.

Summerhayes, Mrs. Martha.
Vanished Arizona; recollections of my army life. '08(D19) c. il. pors. 12°, $1.60. M. Summerhayes.

SUMMERS COUNTY, W. Va.
Miller, J. H: Hist. of Summers County [W. Va.] from the earliest settlement. $3.50. J. H: Miller.

Summing it up. Hubbard, H: L. 50 c. J. S. Ogilvie.

Summits of the soul. Howard, H: $1.25 net. Eaton & M.

Sumner, C:
Addresses on war. [1910.] (My) 12°, (International lib.) 50 c. net. Ginn.

SUMNER, Charles.
Haynes, G: H: Charles Sumner. **$1.25 net. Jacobs.
Shotwell, W. G. Life of Charles Sumner. $1.50 net. Crowell.

Sumner, E: A.
Abraham Lincoln; address del. before the Men's League of the Broadway Tabernacle Church of New York, Feb. 10, 1902. '10(Mr19) O. 50 c.; pap., 25 c. Tandy-T.

Sumner, Helen Laura.
Equal suffrage; results of an investigation in Colorado made for the Collegiate Equal Suffrage League of New York State. '09(N13) c. O. **$2 net. Harper.

SUMNER COUNTY, Tenn.
Cisco, J. G. Historic Summer County, Tennessee. $2. J. G. Cisco.

"Sumner's method" for finding a ship's position. Searle, G: M. 50 c. Van Nostrand's.

SUN.
Adams, W. S. Spectroscopic investigations of the rotation of the sun during the year, 1908. (Not for sale.)—Summary of the results of a study of the Mount Wilson photographs of sun-spot spectra. (Add. Institution for price.) Carnegie.
Elliott, J. Sun spots, their cause and the cause of their periodicity. 25 c. J. Elliott.
Hale, G: E. Preliminary note on rotation of sun. (Not for sale.) Carnegie.
Hale, G: E., *and* Fox, P. Rotation period of the sun. 40 c. Carnegie.
King, A. S. On the separation in the magnetic field of some lines occurring as doublets and triplets in sun-spot spectra. (Not for sale.) Carnegie.
Peters, C. H. F. Heliographic positions of sun-spots. $2.50. Carnegie.
Willson, R. W. Times of sunrise and sunset in the United States. *$1 net. Harvard Co-op.
See also **Meteorology;—Solar system;—Spectrum.**

Sun and shadow in Spain. Howe, M. **$3 net. Little, B. & Co.

Sun and shield. Gottheil, G. *$1 net. Bloch.

Sun time and cloud time. Scoble, A. H. $1. Fenno.

Sun-ways of song. Rice, A. L. $1 net. Sherman, F.

Sunbeam ser. for young people. il. †$1. Penn Pub. Co.
—Curtis. Grandpa's little girls at school.
—Stowe. Uncle Tom's cabin for children.

Sunbeams and shadows. Pau, C. 55 c. Cochrane.

Suncooked food. Christian, E. $1. Christian's Sch.

Sunday, Rev. W: Ashley.
Life and labors of Rev. William A. [Billy] Sunday, the great modern evangelist; with sel. sermons. '08(Ag8) 12°, $1.50. Herman, P

SUNDAY.
Main, A. E. Bible studies on the Sabbath question. $1. A. E. Main.

Sunday epistles. Sauter, B. *$4.50 net. Herder.

Sunday evening. Nicoll, *Sir* W: R. $1.50 net. Doran.

Sunday evening sermons. Morrison, G: H $1.35 net. Doran.

Sunday half hours with great preachers. Hurlbut, J. L., *ed.* $1.50. Winston.

Sunday kindergarten. Ferris, C. S. *$1.25 net. Univ. of Chic.

Sunday mornings at Norwood. Tipple, S: A: *$1.25 net. Eaton & M.

SUNDAY-SCHOOL.
Alleman, H. C., *and* Dunbar, W. H. Book and the message. 50 c. Lutheran Pub.
Arnold, *Mrs.* T. B., *ed.* Pract. Sabbath school commentary on the International lessons. 50 c. net. Revell.
Axtell, J. W. Superintendent's hdbk. for 1909; 1910.—Teacher's hdbk. for 1909; 1910. ea., 35 c. Cumberland Press.
Baldwin, J. L. Record of credits; prep. for use in the junior department of the Sunday school. 35 c. net. Eaton & M.
Beauchamp, H. Graded Sunday school. 75 c. S. S. Bd. So. Bapt.
Boyd, R. H. Ancient and modern Sunday-school methods. 25 c. Nat. Bapt. Pub.
Boyd, R. H., *and* Ellington, W. S., *eds.* National Baptist Sunday school lesson commentary of the Internat. lessons for 1908; for 1909; for 1910. ea., 75 c.; $1. Nat. Bapt. Pub.
Bryan, J. H. Organized adult Bible class. 50 c. Chr. Pub. Co.
Chamberlin, G. L., *and* Kern, M. R. Reminders of Walks with Jesus in his home country. 45 c. Univ. of Chic.
Church Library Association. Catalogue of books recommended by the Church Library Association for Sunday-school and parish libraries. 25 c. Church Lib.
Convention normal manual for Sunday-school workers. 50 c.; 35 c. Bapt. S. S. Bd.
Coon, J. M. Self pronouncing lesson commentary on the International Sunday-school lessons, 1909. 50 c. G: W. Noble.

SUNDAY-SCHOOL.—*Continued.*

Cragin, L. E. Kindergarten stories for the Sunday school and home. $1.25 net. Doran.

Eiselen, F: C., *and* Barclay, W. C. Worker and his Bible. 55 c. Bd. S. S. M. E. Ch.

Evangel first standard teacher training course. 35 c. F. M. Barton.

Faris, J: T. Sunday school in the country. (Add. pubs. for price.) Westminster.

Fergusson, E. M. For home department workers: [Sunday school.] 10 c. Westminster.

Ferris, C. S. Sunday kindergarten. *$1.25 net. Univ. of Chic.

Foster, E. C. Conventions and how to care for them. *25 c. net. S. S. Times.

Foster, E. C. Starting to teach. 40 c. Y. M. C. A.

Groton, W: M., *and others, eds.* Sunday-school teacher's manual. **$1 net. Jacob.

Hamby, W: H. Getting and holding; for Sunday school teachers. 50 c. net. S. S. Times.

Howard, P. E. What a superintendent can do. (Add. pubs. for price.) Westminster.

Hurlbut, J. L. Organizing and building-up the Sunday school. 65 c. net.—Superintendent's helper for 1909; 1910; 1911. ea., 25 c. net.—Teacher-training lessons for the Sunday-school. *30 c. net; *50 c. net. Eaton & M.

International Sunday-school lesson. Lesson handbook, 1909. *20 c. net; *25 c. net. Eaton & M.

Lane, M. A. L. First book of religion. 35 c.; 25 c.; 65 c. Unitarian S. S.

Lawrance, M. Working manual of a successful Sunday-school. *25 c. net. Revell.

Lewis, D. E. Happy hours for the boys and girls; book for parents, junior leaders, Sunday-school teachers and pastors. 50 c. S. S. Times.

Littlefield, M. S. Handwork in the Sunday-school. *$1 net. S. S. Times.

McElfresh, F. Teacher-training class. 10 c. Presb. Bd.

McFarland, J: T. Golden text book, 1909; 1910. ea., *30 c. net, per doz.; *$2 net, per 100. Eaton & M.

McKinney, A. H. Our big boys and the Sunday school. 50 c. net. Revell.

McKinney, A. H. Sunday school graded: why? what? how? 10 c. Presb. Bd.

Meyer, H: H. Graded Sunday-school in principle and practice. 75 c. net.—Lesson hdbk., 1910; 1911. ea., 25 c. net. Eaton & M.

Miller, J. R. Devotional hours with the Sunday-school lessons for 1911. $1.25 net. Doran.

Monday Club sermons on the International Sunday-school lessons; new series for 1911. $1.25. Pilgrim Press.

Moninger, H. H. Standard commentary on the International Sunday-school lessons. 75 c. Standard Pub.

Morgan, G: C. Teaching of the lesson (1911). 25 c. net. Doran.

SUNDAY-SCHOOL.—*Continued.*

Musselman, H. T:, *ed.* National Teacher-Training Institute text-books. Introd. bk. **30 c. net; **50 c. net; Bk. 2, Sunday-school teachers' pupils. **40 c. net; **25 c. net; Bk. 3, Sunday school teacher's pedagogy. **40 c. net; **25 c. net; Bk. 4, Sunday-school teachers' school. **40 c. net; **25 c. net; Bk. 5, Child study for Sunday-school teachers. **40 c. net; **25 c. net; Bk. 6, Early church-history and doctrine. **50 c. net. Am. Bapt.

Oliver, C: A. Helps for leaders of teacher training classes using "Preparation for teaching." 10 c.—Preparation for teaching, [Sunday-schools.] 25 c. Westminster.

Olmstead, W: B. Hdbk. for Sunday-school workers. 50 c. W: B. Rose.

Olmstead, W: B., *and* Warner, D. S., *eds.* Arnold's practical Sabbath-school commentary on the International lessons, 1909; 1910. ea., *50 c. net. Revell.

Organized Sunday-school work in America. $1. Int. S. S. Assoc.

Palmer, F. U. One year of Sunday school lessons for young children.—Second year of Sunday-school lessons. ea., **$1.25 net. Macmillan.

Palmer, L. S., *and* Pease, G: W: Lesson stories for the kindergarten grades of the Bible school. *75 c. net. Macmillan.

Pearce, W. C. Adult Bible class; its organization and work. 25 c. Westminster.

Peloubet, F. N., *and* Wells, A. R. Peloubet's select notes on the International lessons for 1909; 1910; 1911. ea., $1.25; $2. Wilde.

Pepper, J: R. Thirty years at the superintendent's desk. 25 c. Revell.

Philipps, M., *comp.* Sunday school instructions for every Sunday of the year. $1. M. Philipps.

Rice, E. W. Sunday-school: how to start and keep it. *25 c. net; *10 c. net. Am. S. S.

Richmond, E. Picture talks for pastors, Sunday schools, young people's societies, etc. 10 c. E. Richmond.

Rogers, W: O. Boy's-eye view of the Sunday-school. *60 c. net. S. S. Times.

Schauffler, A. F: Knowing and teaching the scholar. 50 c.—Training the teacher. *50 c. net; *30 c. net. S. S. Times.

Schauffler, A. F: Sparks from a superintendent's anvil. $1. Wilde.

Sexton, L., *comp.* Manual work for use in Sunday schools. 75 c. Young Churchman.

Shephardson, F. W., *and* Jones, L. B., *eds.* Scripture and song in worship: service book for Sunday school. *50 c. net. Univ. of Chic.

Slattery, M. Living teacher.—Teacher's candlestick. ea., *35 c. net. F. M. Barton.

Sloan, P. J. Sunday-school director's guide to success. *$1 net.—Sunday-school teacher's guide to success. *75 c. net. Benziger.

SUNDAY-SCHOOL.—*Continued.*
Smith, H. L. Christian race; course of twenty-four lessons for students' Bible classes. 20 c.; 75 c. Y. M. C. A.
Stevenson, M. Studies in the books of the Bible; advanced standard teacher training course. 75 c. Chr. Pub. Co.
Sudlow, *Mrs.* E. W. All about the primary. 50 c. Hammond Pub.
Sutherland, A. Special days in the Sunday school. (Add. pubs. for price.) Westminster.
Tarbell, M. Teacher's guide to the International Sunday-school lessons, 1909; 1910. ea., *$1 net. Revell.
Thomas, M., *ed.* Promotion exercises for the beginners' and primary grades of the Sunday school. 5 c. Presb. Bd.
Torrey, R. A. Gist of the lesson, 1909; 1910; 1911. ea., *25 c. net; 50 c. net. Revell.
Trull, G: H. Manual of missionary methods for Sunday-school workers. *50 c. net. S. S. Times.
Welshimer, P. H. Bible-school vision, for use in teacher-training classes. 50 c.; 30 c. Standard Pub.
Westminster ideal class book. (Add. pubs. for price.) Westmister.
World-wide Sunday-school work. $1. W. N. Hartshorn.
World's Sunday-School Convention. Sunday-schools the world around. *$1 net. S. S. Times.
See also Bible;—Catechisms;—Jesus Christ;—Missions and missionaries;—Religious education;—Teachers and teaching;—*also* New movement leaflets; — Unitarian church: — Westminster course of supplementary education.

Sunday-school teacher's explanation of the Baltimore catechism. Urban, A. $1. Wagner

Sunday stories for a year. '09, [1910.] (F) 188 p. il. 4°, 75 c. Nelson.

Sunderland, Rev. Jabez T:
Bible and the Bible country. Teachers' ed., with helper. '10(D3) c. 8°, (Beacon ser.; graded study for the Sunday school.) 60 c. Unitarian S. S.
Oh, to be rich and young. '10(D24) c. D. $1. Am. Unitarian.
Origin and character of the Bible, and its place among sacred books: being a rev. and enl. ed. of "The Bible, its origin, growth and character"; brought up to date; with new introd., several new chapters, list of books for study, etc. '09 (Ja9) c. O. *$1.20 net. Am. Unitarian.

Sundial (The). White, F. M. $1.50. B. W. Dodge.
Sunflower stories. Smith, O. A. 50 c. Brethren Pub. Ho.
Sung in the shadow. France, A. $1. Sketch Bk.
Sunlight and shadow. Northcote, P. M. *$1 net. Herder.
Sunlit road. Horder, W. G., *ed.* $1.25. Dodge.
Sunny side of life. Marley, F. E. 25 c. F. E. Marley.
Sunny side of the hill. Carey, R. N. †$1.50. Lippincott.
Sunnyfield. Sill, L. M. S. †$1.25. Harper.
Sun's babies. Howes, E. $1.25 net. Cassell.
Sunset playgrounds. Aflalo, F: G: *$2.25 net. Scribner.

SUNSETS.
See Nature.

Sunshine and roses. Downes, C., *comp.* 75 c.; $1.50. Platt & P.
Sunshine and shadow. Jones, J: L. $1.50. Hudson.
Sunshine Annie. Gates, *Mrs.* J. S. $1.25. Bobbs-M.
Sunshine cook book. Underhill, *Mrs.* J. E., *comp.* 50 c. J. E. Underhill.
Sunshine of hope. Dawson, W: H: $1. Modern Woodmen.
Superheated steam in locomotive service. Goss, W: F. M. $1.25. Carnegie.
Superintendent (The). Grisson, I. W. $1.35 net. A. Harriman.
Superintendent and superitendence. Cary, C: P. (Add. author for price.) C: P. Cary.
Superintendent's hdbk., 1909; 1910. Axtell, J. W. ea., 35 c. Cumberland Press.
Superintendent's helper for 1909; 1910; 1911. Hurlbut, J. L. ea., *25 c. net. Eaton & M.

SUPERIOR, Wis.
Barnett, J: M. Annals of the early Protestant churches at Superior. 35 c. State Hist., Wis.

SUPERSTITIONS.
Frazer, J. G: Psyche's task: [influence of superstition on the growth of institutions.] *80 c. net. Macmillan.
Knowlson, T: S. Origins of popular superstitions and customs. $1.75 net. Pott.
Meslier, J. Superstition in all ages. $2.25. De Laurence S.
Stewart, C. T. Origin of the werewolf superstition. 50 c. Univ. of Mo.
See also Astrology;—Folk-lore;—India;—Legends;—Magic and magicians;—Mythology;—Occultism;—Palmistry; — Spiritualism; — Totemism;—Witchcraft.

Supervision of street railways in England and Prussia; reprint from annual rept. of the Public Service Commission for the first district of the state of New York. '09(Ag14) O. pap. (Add. pubs. for price.) Lyon.

SUPERVISORS.
Gilbert, F. B., *comp.* Manual for supervisors, county and town officers [in N. Y. state.] $6.30. M. Bender.

Suplee, H: Harrison.
Gas turbine; progress in the design and construction of turbines operated by gases of combustion. '10(F19) c. figs. O. **$3 net. Lippincott.

Supplemental harmonic ser. D. Indo-Am. Bk.
—Buck. Constructive psychology. $1.
—Crucifixion (The), by an eye-witness. $1.

Supplemental problems in arithmetic. Arnold, L. V. 25 c. L. V. Arnold.
Suppliant maidens. *See* Æschylus.
Suppositions and certainty. Holden, J: S. *75 c. net. Revell.
Suppressed plates. Layard, G: S. *$4 net. Macmillan.
Supremacy of the heart life. Moore, W: T: *$1.25 net. Revell.
Supreme gift. Litchfield, G. D. †$1.50. Little, B. & Co.

Supreme problem. Raupert, J: G. F. $1.50. Paul

Supreme test. Reynolds, *Mrs.* L. B. †$1.50. Brentano's.

Supreme things. McClure, J. G. K. *75 c. net. Revell.

Sure and living faith. Gordon, G: A. **30 c. net. Crowell.

Sure-dart. Costello, F. H. †$1.25. McClurg.

Sure possession. King, W: $1.50. A. B. Caldwell.

Sure word of prophecy; sermons and addresses on the Reformation and the Lutheran church, by pastors of the Lutheran church in America. '08(O) 163 p. 8°, (Sermon lib.) *85 c. net. Germ. Lit. Bd.

SURETIES.
See Guaranties and sureties.

Surette, T: Whitney, and Mason, Dan. Gregory.
Appreciation of music. '08(Ag8) c. il. pors. O. (Appreciation ser.) **$1.50 net. Baker & T.

Surev, pseud.
See True, C. E.

Surface, Fk. Macy.
See Pearl, Raymond.

Surface, G: T:
The story of sugar. '10(S17) c. il. map, D. $1 net. Appleton.

SURGEONS.
See Physicians.

SURGERY.
Abt, J: G., *and* Ridlon, J:, *eds*. Pediatrics [and] Orthopedic surgery. $1.25. Year Bk.
Belch, G. M. Pract. suggestions in borderland surgery. $1.50. Professional.
Bickham, W. S. Text-book of operative surgery. *$6.50 net. Saunders.
Binnie, J: F. Operative surgery. v. 1. *$3.50 net. Blakiston.
Bockenheimer, P. Atlas of clinical surgery. 3 v. $24. Rebman.
Brewer, G: E. Text book of surgery. *$5 net; *$6 net. Lea.
Bryant, J. D., *and* Buck, A. H., *eds*. American practice of surgery. 8 v. ea., $7; $8; $9. Wood.
Camac, C: N. B., *comp*. Epoch-making contribution to medicine, surgery and allied sciences. *$4 net. Saunders.
Collum, R. W., *and* Gray, H. M. W. Practice of anæsthetics; and General surgical technique. *$3 net. Wood.
Compton, A. T. Essentials of surgery. *$1.50 net. Chic. Med. Bk.
Crandon, L. R. G. Surgical after-treatment. $6 net; $7.50 net. Saunders.
Cunning, J. Aids to surgery. *$1.25 net. Wood.
Da Costa, J: C. Modern surgery. *$5.50 net. Saunders.
Eeles, W: M. Elem. anatomy and surgery. $1. W: R. Jenkins.
Ency. and dict. of medicine, surgery and the specialties. In 10 v. v. 6, 7. ea., *$5 net. Chic. Med. Bk.
Foote, E: M. Text-book of minor surgery. *$5 net. Appleton.
Gould, A. P. Elements of surgical diagnosis. $2 net. Funk.

SURGERY.—*Continued.*
Gray, H. M. W. General surgical technique. *$3 net. Wood.
Groves, E. W. H. Synopsis of surgery. *$3.25 net. Wood.
Johnson, A. B. Surgical diagnosis. 3 v. $18. Appleton.
Keen, W: W., *ed.* Surgery. 5 v. ea., *$7 net; *$8 net. Saunders.
Kolle, F: S. Subcutaneous hydrocarbon protheses: [paraffin in surgery.] **$2.50 net. Grafton Press.
Lamphear, E. Surgical therapeutics. $1. Clinic.
Lejars, F. Urgent surgery. 2 v. per set, *$14 net; *$16 net. Wood.
Lexer, E. General surgery. $6 net; $7 net. Appleton.
McCurdy, S. L. Arthrosteopedic surgery. $1. Medical Abstract.
McGrath, J: J. Operative surgery. $5. Davis.
McGuire, S. Lectures on principles of surgery. $4; $5.25. Southern Med.
Martin, E. Surgical diagnosis. *$5.50 net. Lea.
Meyer, W., *and* Schmieden, V. Bier's hyperemic treatment in surgery, medicine and specialties. *$3 net. Saunders.
Moody, C: S. Backwoods surgery and medicine. 75 c. net. Outing.
Morris, R. T. Dawn of the fourth era in surgery. $1.25 net. Saunders.
Mumford, J. G. Practice of surgery. $7. Saunders.
Mumford, J. G. Some end-results of surgery. **25 c. net.—Surgical memoirs. **$2.50 net. Moffat.
Mummery, P. L. After-treatment of operations. *$2.25 net. Wood.
Murphy, J: B: General surgery. $2. Year Bk.
Pratt, E. H. Synthetic clinic incl. a three-days' course in orificial surgery. $5. N. L. McCall.
Rose, W:, *and* Carless, A. Manual of surgery. *$5.50 net; *$6.50 net. Wood.
Senn, N: Principles of surgery. *$5 net; *$6.50 net. Davis.
Sluss, J: W: Emergency surgery. *$3.50 net. Blakiston.
Spencer, W. G., *and* Gask, G: E. Practice of surgery. $6.50; $7. Blakiston.
Stewart, A. Visceral surgery in abstract. $1. Medical Abstract.
Taylor, H: L., *and others.* Orthopedic surgery for practitioners. *$5 net. Appleton.
Treves, *Sir* F: Manual of operative surgery. *$13 net. Lea.
Treves, *Sir* F: Students' hdbk. of surgical operations. $2.50 net. Funk.
Wharton, H: R. Minor and operative surgery, incl. bandaging. *$3 net. Lea.
Whitman, R. Treatise on orthopedic surgery. $5.50. Lea.
Wilcox, S. F. Surgery of childhood. $3.50. Boericke & R.
Willard, De F. Surgery of childhood; incl. orthopædic surgery. $7. Lippincott.
Woolsey, G: Applied surgical anatomy. *$4.50 net. Lea.

SURGERY.—*Continued.*
Wyeth, J: A. Surgery. $7. M. S. Wyeth.
See also Abdomen;—Accidents;—Anæsthetics;—Anatomy;—Anus and rectum;—Appendicitis; Bacteria;—Blood; — Brain; — Cancer;—Children; — Diagnosis; — Digestion; —Ear;—Eye; —Face;—Fracture;—Generative organs;—Gynecology;—Hernia;—Intestines; — Knee;— Massage;—Medical electricity; — Medicine; — Midwifery; — Mouth; — Nervous system;—Nose;— Nurses and nursing;—Pathology;—Stomach;— Teeth;—Throat;—Tumor;—Urine and urinary organs;—Veterinary medicine and surgery.
Surgical anæsthesia. Gardner, H. B. *$2.25 net. Wood.
Surgical diagnosis. Johnson, A. B. 3 v. $18. Appleton.
Surgical diseases of children. Kelley, S: W. *$5 net. Treat.
Surgical memoirs. Mumford, J. G. **$2.50 net. Moffat.
Surprises. Dalrymple, C. L. 15 c. Dick.
SURREY, Eng.
Bosworth, G: F. Surrey. 45 c. Putnam.
Green, W. C. Old cottages and farm-houses in Surrey. $8.40. Helburn.
Parker, E. Highways and byways in Surrey. $2. Macmillan.
Surridge, Victor.
India. '09(O9) il. in col. map, O. (Romance of history ser.) *$2 net. Stokes.
SURROGATES' COURTS.
See Courts.
Sursum corda. Frere, W. H. *55 c. net; *75 c. net. Young Churchman.
Surtees, Rob. Smith.
Hunts with Jorrocks. Ed. de luxe. '10 (F19) col. il. 8°, *$5 net. Doubleday, P.
Hunts with Jorrocks: from Handley Cross. '10(D) col. il. 4°, $4.50 net. Doran.
Jorrocks on 'unting. '09(N) 32 p. il. 16°, 50 c. Dutton.
Mr. Jorrocks' lectors: from Handley Cross. '10(D) col. il. 4°, $4.50 net. Doran.
Survey of London. *See* Stow, J:
SURVEYING.
Berger, C. L: Hand-book and illustrated catalogue of the engineers' and surveyors' instruments made by C. L. Berger & Sons. 60 c. C. L. Berger.
Breed, C: B., *and* Hosmer, G: L. Principles and practice of surveying. v. 2. $3. Wiley.
Davis, J. B. Surveying for beginners. 90 c. Wahr.
Davis, J. B., *and* Merrick, H. B. Direction of a line. 75 c. Wahr.
Gurley's manual of the principal instruments used in American engineering and surveying. 50 c. W. & L. E. Gurley.
Hodgman, F. Surveyor's tables. $1.50; $1. Hodgman.
Johnson, J: B. Theory and practice of surveying. $3.50 net. Wiley.
Kagey, C: C. Land survey and land titles. 25 c. Douglas Co., Abs.
Kagey, C: C. Land survey and land titles. $1.12. C: C. Kagey.
Lovell, W: H. Plane table and its use in surveying. *$1 net. McGraw.
Park, J. Text book of theodolite surveying and levelling. *$2 net. Lippincott.
Phillips, A. E. Surveying. $1.50. Am. Sch. Corr.

SURVEYING.—*Continued.*
Pilkington, W. Co-ordinate geometry applied to land surveying. 60 c. Spon.
Raudabaugh, I. F. Latitude and departure calculations of land made easy and self-proving. $1.25; $1.50; $2. I. F. Raudabaugh.
Rees, T: H. Topographical surveying and sketching. $2.50. Staff Coll.
Stewart, B. Hdbk. for railway surveying. *$1 net. Spon.
Taylor, T: U. Surveyors' hand book. *$2 net. M. C. Clark.
Tracy, J: C. Exercises in surveying. **$1 net. Wiley.
Trumbull, L. W. Manual of underground surveying. *$3 net. Hill Pub.
Underhill, J. Mineral land surveying. $3. Mining Science.
United States. *Dept. of the Interior. General Land Office.* Manual of instructions for the survey of the mineral lands of the U. S. (Add. Superintendent for price.) U. S., Supt. of Docs.
United States. *General Land Office.* Restoration of lost or obliterated corners and subdivision of sections; rev. of June 1, 1909. '09(Ag) 23 p. 8°, pap. (Add. Superintendent for price.)
Wallace, J. Logarithmic land measurement. $2. Spon.
Wilson, H. M. Topographic surveying. $3.50. Spon.
See also Engineering;—Forests and forestry;—Geodesy;—Mensuration;—Mines and mining;—Nautical surveying;—Railroads;—Trigonometry.
Survival of man. Lodge, *Sir* O. J. **$2 net. Moffat.
Survivorship annuity tables. Dawson, M. M. $25. Chronicle Co.
Susan Clegg: her friend and her neighbors. Warner, A. $1.50. Little, B. & Co.
Susan in Sicily. Tozier, J. $2. L. C. Page.
Susanna. Jasper, W. (Priv. pr.) Mayhew.
Susanna and Sue. Wiggin, K. D. S. **$1.50 net. Houghton M.
Suspicions of Mrs. Allonby. Tuttiett, M. G. †$1.50. Appleton.
SUSQUEHANNA INDIANS.
See Indians.
SUSSEX, Eng.
Bosworth, G: F. Sussex. 45 c. Putnam.
SUSSEX COUNTY, Del.
Turner, C: H: B., *comp.* Some records of Sussex County, Delaware. $5 net. Allen, L. & S.
SUSSEX COUNTY, N. J.
Schaeffer, C. Memoirs and reminiscences, together with sketches of the early history of Sussex County, New Jersey. (Priv. pr.) W: M. Johnson.
Sutcliffe, Mrs. Alice Crary.
Homestead of a colonial dame; monograph. '10(Ap9) il. pors. facsims., O. pap., 50 c. A. C. Sutcliffe.
Robert Fulton and the "Clermont": the authoritative story of Robert Fulton's early experiments, persistent efforts, and historic achievements; containing many of Fulton's hitherto unpublished letters, drawings and pictures. '09(S18) c. il. facsim., D. **$1.20 net. Century Co.

Sutcliffe, Halliwell.
Priscilla of the Good Intent. '09(O2) c. D. †$1.50. Little, B. & Co.
Winter's comedy. '10(Ag27) D. $1.50. Lane.

Sutherland, Allan.
Famous hymns of the world, [their origin and romance.] '08(Ap11) c. 6 v., il. 12°, ea., floral ed., 50 c.; Florentine ed., 75 c. Stokes.
Special days in the Sunday school. '08(D) 48 p. S. pap. (Add. pubs. for price.) Westminster.

Sutherland, Dan. Fs.
Black plague of the American continent: [intemperance.] '08(Mr) c. 83+10 p. D. 50 c. D. F. Sutherland.

Sutherland, G. A., ed.
System of diet and dietetics. '08, [1909.] (D) 13+893 p. il. 8°, (Oxford medical pubs.) *$9.25 net. Oxford Univ.

Sutherland, G:
Powers of the national government. [1910.] (Je) 12 p. 8°. U. S., Supt. of Docs.

Sutherland, Howard Vigne.
Idylls of Greece. '08(N14) c. D. *$1 net. Sherman, F.
Idylls of Greece (second ser.). '10(N19) c. 12°, $1. FitzGerald.

Sutherland, Hugh.
Ireland yesterday and to-day; with introd. by J: E. Redmond. '10(F19) c. il. por. O. $1, boxed. North American, (Phil.)

Sutherland, W: Angus.
Treatise on code pleading and practice; also cont. 1900 forms adapted to practice in Cal., Alaska, Ariz., Id., Mont., Nev., N. M., [etc.] In 4 v. v. 1. '10(Mr); v. 2 (My); v. 3, 4 (Jl) c. O. ea., $6.50. Bancroft-W.

Sutherland, W: Ja.
Teaching of geography. '09(D18) il. D. $1.25. Scott, F. & Co.

Sutherland-Gower, Rowland, Lord.
Cleanliness versus corruption. '10(Ap23) il. D. pap., 25 c. Longmans.

Sutliff, S: Milton.
Hist. of the American and Puritanical family of Sutliff or Sutliffe, spelled Sutcliffe in England; the first American family (A.D. 1614) connected with New England, and amongst the first to be connected with the settlement of the original English possessions in the New World, and a genealogy of all the descendants through Nathaniel Sutliff, Jr. '09, [1910.] (F) 199 p. pors. 8°, $2. S: M. Sutliff.

SUTLIFF FAMILY.
See Genealogies.

Sutphen, Van Tassel.
See Harvey, G:

Sutro, Alfr.
John Glayde's honour: new and original play in four acts. '07, [1909] (Mr) c. 95 p. 12°, 50 c. S: French.

SUTTER, *General* John Augustus.
Schoonover, T. J. Life and times of Gen. John A. Sutter. $1.50. A. N. Bullock.

Suttner, Bertha Felicie Sophia Kinsky, Freifrau von, ["B. Oulot."]
Memoirs of Bertha von Suttner; records of an eventful life; auth. tr. 2 v. '10(D10) por. O. $5 net, boxed. Ginn.

Sutton, Adah Louise, [Mrs. Arth. Ja. Saalfield.]
Little maid in Toyland. '08(D12) c. il. O. bds., $1. Saalfield.
Mushroom fairies. '10(D3) c. col. il. obl. O. bds., $1.25. Saalfield.

Sutton, H. S.
Rhoda Roland. '08(Ag8) 12°, $1.50. Madison.

Sutton, Howard A., M.D., and Drinker, Cecil K.
Osteology and syndesmology. '10(O) 14+225 p. 8°, $1.50. Blakiston.

Sutton, J: Bland-, M.D.
See Bland-Sutton, J:, *M.D.*

Suzuki, Daisetz Teitaro.
Outlines of Mahayana Buddhism. '08 (Ag1) *$2.50 net. Open Court.

Suzzallo, H:
See Burnham, W: H:

Svenson, Emily Louisa, [now Mrs. Baker.]
Modern Valkyrie. '09(D) 150 p. $1. Cochrane.

Sverdrup, Georg.
Samlede skrifter i udvalg; udgivne ved Andreas Helland. '09, [1910.] (My) c. pors. 8°, $2.50. Free Church.

Swain, Clara A.
Glimpse of India: extracts from the letters of Dr. Clara A. Swain, first medical missionary to India of the Woman's Foreign Missionary Society of the Methodist Episcopal Church of America. '09(Jl) c. 9+366 p. il. pors. 12°, $1.25. Woman's For. Miss.

Swain, J: D.
A father to his son; letter to an undergraduate upon his entering college. '10 (Mr19) T. bds., *50 c. net. Yale Pub.

Swain, Rachel, M.D.
Cooking for health; or, plain cookery, with health hints. 3d ed., rev. '09(D11) c. 12°, $1. Health-Culture.

SWALLOWS.
See House martin.

SWAMP SUMACH.
See Sumach.

Swan, Almer U., comp.
See Iowa. Statistical abstract.

Swan, C: A.
Slavery of to-day; or, the present position of the open sore of Africa. '09(N6) c. il. 12°, 75 c. Gospel Pub.

Swan, F: Tyndall.
Use of the adjective as a substantive in the De rerum natura of Lucretius. '10(D) 179-214 p. 8°, (Univ. of Michigan studies; Humanistic ser.) pap., 40 c. Macmillan.

Swan, H.
In praise of books. '08(D) 12°, 50 c. Dutton.

Swan, J: Mumford, M.D.
Prescription writing and formulary. '10 (F) 185 p. flex. leath., *$1.25 net. Saunders.
See also Shoemaker, W: Toy.

Swan, Jos. Rockwell.
See Ohio. Treatise on laws.

Swan, Kenneth R.
Law and commercial usage of patents, designs and trade marks. '08(D5) il. 8°, (Westminster ser.) *$2 net. Van Nostrand.

Swan, Mrs. Laura.
Memoir of Robert Thaxter Swan. '08(N) 7 p. por. 8°. (Priv. pr.) L. P. Swan.

Swan, Mabel M., comp.
Her book; an engaged girl's record book arranged by Mabel M. Swan. '10(Je11) c. il. 8°, $2 net, boxed. Houghton M.

Swan, Mark E.
Top o' the world. '08(S19) c. il. O. †$1.50. Dutton.

SWAN, Robert Thaxter.
Swan, *Mrs.* L. P. C. Memoir of Robert Thaxter Swan. (Priv. pr.) L. P. Swan.

Swan dramatists. 16°. Sturgis & W.
—Marlowe. Tragical history of Dr. Faustus. 45 c.
—Webster. Duchess of Malfi. 45 c.

SWAN KNIGHT.
See Legends.

Swank, Ja. Moore.
Progressive Pennsylvania: a record of the remarkable industrial development of the Keystone state, with some account of its early and its later transportation systems, its early settlers, and its prominent men. '08(D) 360 p. 8°, $5. J. M. Swank.

Swann, Alf. Ja.
Fighting the slave-hunters in Central Africa; record of 26 years of travel and adventure round the Great Lakes, and of the overthrow of Tip-pu-tib, Rumaliza and other great slave-traders; with introd. by Sir H. H. Johnston. '10(Mr26) il. map, O. *$3.50 net. Lippincott.

Swanwhite. Strindberg, J. A. $1. Brown Bros.

Swarth, Harry Schelwaldt.
Two new owls from Arizona; with description of the juvenal plumage of *strix occidentalis* (Xantus). '10(Je) 8 p. Q. (Univ. of Cal. pubs.; Zoology.) pap., 10 c. Univ. of Cal.

Swarts, Gardner Taber, jr., comp.
Tuberculosis exhibitions; catalogue of necessaries for their outfitting and maintenance. August, 1909, supplied by the Educational Exhibition Co. '10(Mr5) il. 8°, pap., 25 c. Educ. Exhibit.

SWASTIKA.
See Symbols.

Swaying tree tops. Serl, E. W. $1. Neale.

Swazy folk and others. Wells, J: D. $1.25. Ulbrich.

SWEATING SYSTEM.
See Strikes.

SWEDEN.
Baedeker, K. Norway, Sweden and Denmark, with excursions to Iceland and Spitzbergen. $2.40. Scribner.

SWEDEN.—*Continued.*
Bergquist, N. W. Swedish folk dances. $1.50. Barnes.
Bumpus, T. F. Cathedrals and churches of Norway, Sweden, and Denmark. *$4 net; *$7.50 net. Pott.
Williams, G. M. Church of Sweden, and the Anglican communion. 50 c. Young Churchman.
See also Banks and banking;—Fine arts;—*also* Charles IX.

Swedenborg, Emanuel.
Arcana cœlestia; the heavenly arcana contained in the Holy Scriptures and Word of the Lord. In 12 v. v. 1-11. Lib. ed. '10(Je) per v., $1.25. Am. Swedenborg.
Commentary on the Gospel according to John; comp. from the theological works of Emanuel Swedenborg, by Rob. S: Fischer and L: G: Hoeck. '08(Mr) c. 7+368 p. 12°, $1.25. Mass. New-Ch. Un.
Delights of wisdom pertaining to conjugial love, after which follow the pleasures of insanity pertaining to scortatory love; first published in Latin, Amsterdam, 1768; tr. by S: M. Warren; tr. rev. by L: H. Tafel. Library ed. '10(Ap) 23+612 p. 8°, $1.25. Am. Swedenborg.
Heaven and hell. '09(Ap3) 16°, (Everyman's lib.) *35 c. net; leath., *70 c. net. Dutton.

SWEDENBORG, Emanuel.
Bible, O. T. Psalms. Commentary on the Psalms; comp. from the theological works of Emanuel Swedenborg. $1.25. Mass. New Ch. Un.
Haseltine, M. W. A great thinker; repr. of articles published in the New York *Sun,* on Emanuel Swedenborg. 3 c. Mass. New-Ch. Un.
Hyde, J. Bibliography of the works of Emanuel Swedenborg, original and translated. $10. New Church.
Sewall, F. Swedenborg and the "sapientia angelica." 50 c. net. Dodge.
Sewall, F. Swedenborg and the University. (Add. University for price.) Urbana Univ.
Spalding, J. H. Spiritual world; as described in the writings of Emanuel Swedenborg. *40 c. net; *60 c. net. Warne.
Whitehead, J: Study of Swedenborg's psychical states and experiences. gratis. Mass. New-Ch. Un.

SWEDENBORGIAN CHURCH.
General Church of the New Jerusalem. Liturgy. $2; $3.50. Acad. Bk. Room.
See also Future life;—Symbols.

SWEDES IN UNITED STATES.
Olson, E. W., *ed.* History of the Swedes of Illinois. In 2 v. *$20 net; *$25 net. Engberg-H.

Swedish banking system. Flux, A. W: Gov. Pr. Off.

Swedish folk dance, "Vafva Vadmal"; introd. and tr. by Jacob Bolin. '09(Ap24) obl. D. pap., 25 c. Bassette.

SWEDISH LITERATURE.
Foss, C. W., *ed.* Masterpieces from Swedish literature in English form. 2 v. 75 c. Augustana.

SWEDISH MASSAGE.
See Massage.

Sweeney, Mildred I. McNeal-.
When yesterday was young: poems. '09 (My22) c. D. $1.50. F. F. Sherman.

Sweet, Fk. Herbert.
Craig Cameron. '08(O17) c. 12°, 75 c. Standard Pub.
Illustrious boys of many lands. '09(N13) il. O. 50 c. McLoughlin.
Illustrious girls of many lands. '09(N13) il. O. 50 c. McLoughlin.

Sweet, H:
Sounds of English: an introd. to phonetics. '08(My23) D. 60 c. Oxford Univ.

Sweet, Ja. S.
Modern business arithmetic. '08(O) c. 260 p. O. $1.25. Sweet.

Sweet, Marvin P.
Theory of the universe; also a poem by the author. '08(Jl) c. 6+159 p. il. por. 12°, $1. M. P. Sweet.

Sweet girl graduate. Smith, *Mrs.* E. T. M. $1.25. Hurst.

Sweet Nancy. Taggart, M. A. $1.50. L. C. Page.

SWEET PEAS.
Crane, D. B. Book of the sweet pea. *$1 net. Lane.
Kerr, G: W., *comp.* Sweet peas up-to-date. 10 c. Burpee.
Thomas, H. H. Sweet peas and how to grow them. *50 c. net. Cassell.
Wright, H. J. Sweet peas. 65 c. net. Stokes.

SWEET POTATO.
Beattie, W: R. Sweet potatoes. 5 c. U. S., Supt. of Docs.

Sweetapple, H. D. S., D.D.
Earthly footprints of Jesus. '09(O16) 12°, *$2 net. Whittaker.

Sweetheart dreams of yesterday. Nesbit, W. H. $2. C: C. Thompson.

Sweetland, C: A:
Bank bookkeeping; instruction paper. '09 (D4) c. 2 v., forms, 8°, (American School of Correspondence pubs.) 50 c. Am. Sch. Corr.
Brewer's accounts; instruction paper. '09 (D4) c. forms, 8°, (American School of Correspondence pubs.) 50 c. Am. Sch. Corr.
Publishers' and printers' accounts; instruction paper. '09(D11) c. 8°, (American School of Correspondence pubs.) 50 c. Am. Sch. Corr.
See also Am. Sch. of Correspondence.

Sweetser, Kate Dickinson.
Ten boys from history. '10(N5) c. il. O. $2. Duffield.

Sweetshop. Copeland, W. 25 c. Dutton.

Swem, Leota, and Sherwood, Rowena.
Primer of nursery rhymes. '09(Ap10) c. il. D. 30 c. Houghton M.

Swenk, Myron Harmon.
Specific characters in the bee genus *colletes.* '08(D) 8°, pap., 50 c. M. H. Swenk.

Sweny, Harry Ray.
Big Stick and the Golf Stick. '09(S18) c. O. bds., 50 c. Lyon.
Symon Schermerhoorn's ride, February 8/9, 1690; [poem.] '10(Ag13) il. map, facsims., 8°, $3.50; full levant, $5; hand tooled, $10. (250 copies.) H. R. Sweny.

Swetchine, Mme. Anne Sophie Soymonoff.
Maxims of Madame Swetchine; selected and tr. with a biographical note by I. A. Taylor. '08(D) 64 p. front. 12°, **55 c. net. Herder.

Swete, H: Barclay, D.D.
Apocalypse of St. John. 3d ed. '09(S4) 8°, price raised from $3.50 net to *$3.75 net. Macmillan.
Appearances of our Lord after the Passion. '08(Ja25) 12°, *80 c. net. Macmillan.
Holy Spirit in the New Testament; study of primitive Christian teaching. '09(N20) O. *$2.60 net. Macmillan.
—, ed. Essays on some Biblical questions of the day; by members of the University of Cambridge. 09(N20) O. *$3.75 net. Macmillan.

Swett, Sophie Miriam.
Princess Wisla. New ed. '08(S19) il. D. †$1.50. Little, B. & Co.

Swift, Rev. Albert.
First principles of Christian citizenship. '08 (O3) 12°, *75 c. net. Revell.

Swift, Edg. Ja.
Mind in the making: study in mental development. '08(Je20) O. **$1.50 net. Scribner.

Swift, Fletcher Harper.
Most beautiful thing in the world. '10 (Ap23) 8°, 30 c. net. Dutton.

Swift, H: Walton, rep.
See Massachusetts. *Sup. judicial ct.* Repts.

Swift, Ivan.
Fagots of Cedar; Out of the North; and Blown by the winds; and Ashes and embers; with titles old and new not contained in the original limited ed. '09 (Jl10) c. front. O. $1.25; hf. leath., $2. Willows Shop.

Swift, Jonathan.
Prose works; ed. by Temple Scott. v. 12, Portraits of Swift and Stella, by Sir F: Falkiner; Relations between Swift and Stella, by Dr. Bernard, Dean of St. Patrick's; Bibliography; comp. by Spencer Jackson; Index. '08(N21) 12°, (Bohn's standard lib.) *$1 net. Macmillan.
Correspondence of Jonathan Swift. v. 1; ed. by F. Elrington Ball; with introd. by the Very Rev. J. H. Bernard. '10(D24) il. por. $3.50 net. Macmillan.
Gulliver's travels. '08(O10) il. D. (Bowman's illustrated lib. of world-favorite books.) $1. Bowman.
Gulliver's travels; il. by Arth. Rackham. '09(D18) f°, *$2.50 net; Large paper ed., *$7.50 net. Dutton.
Gulliver's travels into some remote countries; retold from Jonathan Swift and written anew for children by Ja. Baldwin. '08(Jl18) il. D. (Eclectic readings.) 35 c. Am. Bk.
Tale of a tub, etc.; introd. by Lewis Melville. '09(Ap3) 16°, (Everyman's lib.) *35 c. net; leath., *70 c. net. Dutton.
Travels into several remote nations of the world, by Lemuel Gulliver; with a preface by Sir H: Craik. '08(O31) il. 16°, (Pocket classics.) 80 c.; leath., $1.25. Macmillan.

SWIFT, Jonathan.
Smith, S. S. Dean Swift. *$3.50 net. Putnam.

Swift, Lance, and Steele, Carol.
Her caveman's letters and her's in reply. '09(F13) il. O. $1.25. Gillam's.

Swift, Lindsay.
Benjamin Franklin. '10(D17) c. T. (Beacon biographies.) 50 c. net. Small.

Swift, Polemus Hamilton, D.D.
Gospel cheer messages, del. in the Austin Methodist Episcopal Church, Chicago. '08 (D26) c. D. *$1.25 net. Jennings.

Swift and sure. Strang, H. $1 net. Doran.

Swiftsure phonetic shorthand system. Baillie, D: G. $1. Phillips Pr.

Swigart, Fk.
Mary Lawson. [1910] (F) c. '09. 280 p. 12°, $1.25. **Roxburgh.**

SWIMMING.
Brewster, E. T. Swimming. **$1 net. Houghton M.
Corsan, G: H. At home in the water; swimming, diving, life saving. 75 c.; 50 c. Y. M. C. A.
Doyle, W: S. New instruction book on ocean bathing, swimming and boating. 25 c. W: S. Doyle.

Swinburne, Algernon C:
Works. In 2 v. v. 1, Poems; v. 2, Tragedies. '10(Ap30) pors. O. ea., $1.50 net, boxed; ea., hf. cf., $4 net, boxed. McKay.
Age of Shakespeare. '08(O3) c. por. O. **$2 net. Harper.
Duke of Gandia: [drama.] '08(Ap11) c. D. **$1.25 net. Harper.
Félise: book of lyrics. '09(D) 12°, (Old world ser.) vellum, *$1 net; bds., *$1.25 net; leath., *$1.50 net; Japan vellum ed., *$2.50 net. T: B. Mosher.
List of the orig. manuscripts of Algernon C: Swinburne. '10(Je25) D. pap. W. M. Hill.
Shakespeare; written in 1905 and now first published. '10(Ja22) D. 80 c. Oxford Univ.
Siena. '10(D) 16°, (Venetian ser.) pap., 50 c. net; Japan vel., $1 net. T: B. Mosher.
Swinburne's dramas; selected and ed. by Arthur Beatty. '09(S11) c. por. D. **$1.50 net. Crowell.
Three plays of Shakespeare: [King Lear; Othello; King Richard II.] '09(My15) c. 16°, (Lib. of living thought.) *75 c. net. Harper.

SWINBURNE, Algernon Charles.
Mackail, J: W: Swinburne: lecture. *35 c. net. Oxford Univ.

Swinburne, H. Lawrence.
Royal navy; with some notes on the costume of the sailors of the past, by Commander C: N. Robinson. '08(Ja11) il. 8°, (Color book ser.) *$6 net. Macmillan.

SWINE.
See Hog.

SWING, David.
Newton, J. F. David Swing, poet-preacher. $2. Torch Press.

Swing, P: F.
What is life. '09(My15) c. S. pap. (Not for sale.) P: F. Swing.

Swingle, Calvin Franklin.
Catechism of steam, gas, and electric engineering; complete book of reference for the working engineer in the daily round of his duties. '10(Ag27) c. il. 16°, leath., $1.50. Drake.
Electric railway power stations. '09(Je12) c. il. tabs., 12°, $2. Drake.
Elevators, hydraulic and electric; complete hand book of a series of questions and answers follows; designed for the use of engineers and operators. '10(S17) c. il. 12°, $1. Drake.
Locomotive fireman's boiler instructor. '09 (Ap3) il. tabs., S. leath., $1.50. Drake.
Pract. hdbk. for millwrights, describing the pract. planning and arrangement of mill buildings; strength of materials and all subjects directly connected with the installation of mill machinery. '10(N5) c. il. 12°, $2. Drake.
Steam turbine engines; their construction, care and operation. '10(Ag27) c. il. 12°, $1. Drake.
Twentieth century hand-book for steam engineers and electricians, with questions and answers. '10(Je11) c. il. D. leath., $3. Drake.
Walschaert valve gear; breakdowns and how to adjust them. '08(O10) c. il. 12°, $1. Drake.

—, [and others,] eds.
Modern American railway practice. In 10 v. '08(D26) c. il. tabs., 8°, hf. mor., $60. Drake.

Swinnerton, Henry Ulyate.
See Princeton University. Class of 1863.

Swinton, Capt. Ernest Dunlop.
See Summer night's dream.

Swisher, C: Cummings, ed.
Twenty lessons in illustrating; compendium of the most modern ideas of the world's greatest authorities on illustrating and rendering drawings for reproduction. Autograph ed. '09(N) c. 176 p. il. 8°, $5. Art Pub.

Swiss family Robinson. *See* Wyss, Johann Rudolf.

SWITCHBOARDS.
See Electric switchboards.

SWITZERLAND.
Finnemore, J: Switzerland. *75 c. net. Dutton.
Guide to Switzerland. $1 net. Platt & P.
Hulme, F: E: Familiar Swiss flowers. *$3 net. Cassell.
Kuhns, L. O. Switzerland. $2 net. Crowell.
Landman, J. Swiss banking law. U. S., Supt. of Docs.
Little journey to Switzerland. 50 c. net. Cassell.
Musson, S. C. Upper Engadine. *$2.50 net. Macmillan.
Singleton, E., *comp. and ed.* Switzerland as described by great writers. **$1.60 net. Dodd.

SWITZERLAND.—*Continued.*
Webb, F. Switzerland of the Swiss. $1.50 net. Scribner.
Wood, *Mrs.* E. E. Oberland châlet. $2 net. Wessels & B.
See also Alps;—Geneva;—Lake Geneva;—Lausanne;—Montreux;—*also* Oberlin, John Frederic.
Swollen fortunes. Daniels, P. 15 c. P. Daniels.

Swoope, Coates Walton.
Lessons in practical electricity. 10th ed., rev. '09(Ja16); 11th ed., enl. with a chapter on alternating currents. '10(N) il. 12°, ea., $2 net. Van Nostrand.
Sword decides. Bowen, M., *pseud.* †$1.50. McClure.

SWORD GUARDS.
See Boston Museum.
Sword in the mountains. MacGowan, A. $1.35 net. Putnam.
Sword maker. Barr, R. $1.25. Stokes.
Sword of Dundee. Peck, T. †$1.50. Duffield.
Sword of the Lord. Hocking, J. $1.25. Dutton.
Sword of the nation. Clark, H. H. $1. Severn River.
Sword of the pyramids. Bill, E: L. 50 c. Fenno.
Sword of the spirit. Eades, J. A. $1.50. Skelton.
Sydney Carrington's contumacy. Lawson, X. $1.25. Pustet.
Sydney Lisle. Moore, D. 75 c. McKay.

Syers, Edg. and Madge, eds.
Book of winter sports; with an introd. by the Earl of Lytton. '08(N21) il. figs. plan, O. *$4.20 net. Longmans.

Syers, Madge, ed.
See Syers, Edg.

Sykes, Ella C.
Persia and its people. '10(D10) il. map, O. $2.50 net. Macmillan.

Sykes, F: H:
English composition for grammar schools. '08(D5) c. il. 12°, *65 c. net. Scribner.
Grammar school composition. '08(D5) *65 c. net. Scribner.

Sykes, Percy Molesworth, tr. and ed.
Glory of the Shia world; tale of a pilgrimage; tr. and ed. from a Persian manuscript by P. M. Sykes, assisted by Khan Bahadur Alnned Din Khan. '10(D10) il. O. $3.50 net. Macmillan.
Syllable in English rhetoric. Wilbur, W: A. 50 c. Collins, H. & Co.
Syllabus of a course on elementary bookmaking and bookbinding. Freeman, S. J. 30 c. Teachers' Coll.
Syllabus of European hist. Foster, H. D. 50 c. E. P. Storrs.
Syllabus of medieval history. Munro, D. C. $1. Longmans.
Syllabus of the history of education. Taylor, W: J. $1. Heath.

"Sylva, Carmen," pseud.
See Pauline, Eliz. Otillie Louise.

Sylvester, C: Herbert.
Journeys through Bookland. Library ed. In 10 v. '10(Jl2) c. il. 12°, $22.50; ¾ mor., $29.50. Thompson Pub. Co., (Chic.)

Sylvester, Emma.
See Wade, Jos. H.

Sylvester, F. L., and Oberg, Erik V.
Self-taught mechanical drawing and elem. machine design. '10(My21) il. $2. Henley.

Sylvester, Herbert Milton.
Indian wars of New England. In 3 v. '10 (D17) O. Colonial ed., hf. leath., $50; Library ed., $15 net; Special ed. de luxe, vel., $1000 (1 copy). W. B. Clarke.
Maine coast romances. In 5 v. v. 4, Ye romance of olde Pemaquid. '08(My23) c. il. plan, 8°, $3. H. M. Sylvester.
Maine pioneer settlements. [Author's ed.] 5 v. '10(F19) il. plan, 8°, $20. W. B. Clarke.
Samoset; an appreciation "Welcome, Englishmen!"; [repr. from Sylvester's "Indian wars of New England."] '10(D31) c. 16°, 60 c. W. B. Clarke.

Sylvester, Ja. Jos.
Collected mathematical papers. v. 2, (1854-1873.) '08(Je6); v. 3, 1874-1883.) '10 (Ap23) il. 8°, ea., $6 net. Putnam.

Sylvester, W. A.
Modern carpentry and building. 2d ed., enl. '07. [1908.] (F) c. 12-276 p. il. 8°, $1.50. D: Williams.
Sylvia's lovers. *See* **Gaskell, *Mrs.* Eliz. Cleghorn Stevenson.**
Symbolisms. Witmer, T: C. $1. Badger.
Symbolist movement in literature. Symons, A. *$2 net. Dutton.

SYMBOLS.
Butts, E: **Statement no. 1: the swastika.** $1; 25 c. E: Butts.
Jenner, *Mrs.* K. L. R. Christian symbolism. $1 net. McClurg.
Roeder, A. Symbol stories for children of all ages. $1; 75 c. New Church.
Stansfield, J. A. Symbolism. 10 c. Anchor.
Whitmer, T: C. Symbolisms. $1. Badger.
Wood, H. G. Ideal metrology in nature, art, religion and history: [symbolism of numbers.] $1.50. H. G. Wood.
See also Cross;—Freemasonry.

Symington, Johnson, M.D., and Rankin, J. C., M.D.
Atlas of skiagrams illustrating the development of the teeth; with explanatory note. '08(D5) Q. *$3.50 net. Longmans.
—, ed. *See* Quain, Jones.
Symon Schermerhoorn's ride. Sweny, H. R. $3.50; $5; $10. H. R. Sweny.

Symonds, Emily Morse.
See Paston, G:, *pseud.*

Symonds, Marg., [Mrs. W. W. Vaughan.]
Days spent on a Doge's farm; [life on the Pisani estate, Italy.] [2d ed.] '09(Ja16) il. por. O. *$2.50 net. Century Co.

Symons, Arth.
Cities of Italy. '08(Ja18) 12°, $2. Dutton.
Plays, acting and music. New ed. '09 (Je12) 8°, **$2 net. Dutton.
London; book of aspects. '08, [1910.] (Mr) 54 p. 8°. (Not for sale.) E. D. Brooks.
Romantic movement in English poetry. '09 (O23) c. 8°, *$2.50 net. Dutton.

Symons, Arth.—*Continued.*
Silhouettes: book of songs. '09(D) 12°, (Old world ser.) vellum, *$1 net; bds., *$1.25 net; leath., *$1.50 net; flex. leath., *$1.50 net; Japan vellum ed., *$2.50 net. T: B. Mosher.
Spiritual adventures. 2d ed. '08(My9) 8°, *$2.50 net. Dutton.
Symbolist movement in literature. [New and rev. ed.] '08(Mr21) 8°, *$2 net. Dutton.

SYMPATHY.
Knowlson, T: S. Art of sympathy. $1. Warne.

Symposium. *See* Plato. Apology of Socrates.

Symposium on mathematics for engineering students; being the proceedings of the joint sessions of the Chicago section of the American Mathematical Society and Section A, Mathematics, and Section D, Mechanical science and engineering of the American Association for the Advancement of Science, 1907. '09(Ap3) Q. pap., gratis. H. E. Slaught.

SYMPTOMS.
See Diagnosis.

Synagogue and the church. Goodman, P. $1.50. Dutton.

Synan, Arth.
Coming of the king; Jacobite romance. '10(Jl) 4+143 p. front. 12°, 35 c. net. Herder.

Synchronous commutation as a method for alternating current—direct-current transformation. Grondall, L. O. 20 c. Johns Hopkins.

SYNDESMOLOGY.
See Bones.

Synge, M. B.
Great Victorian age; record of achievement told for children. '09(D) il. maps, 12°, *$1 net. Doran.

Synopsis of draughts openings. Hill, J. 50 c. Warne.

Synopsis of surgery. Groves, E. W. H. *$3.25 net. Wood.

Synoptic text-book of zoölogy. Weysse, A. W. *$2.25 net. Macmillan.

SYNTAX.
See **English language.**

Syntax of the French verb. Armstrong, E: C. 90 c. Holt.

Syntax of the genitive case in the Lindisfarne Gospels. Bale, C. E. 50 c. Univ. of Ia.

Synthesis and analysis of the poetry of Sidney Lanier. Carroll, C: C. 25 c. C: C. Carroll.

Synthetic inorganic chemistry. Blanchard, A. A. *$1 net. Wiley.

Sypherd, W. Owen, and Messersmith, G: Strausser.
High school course in English. '08, [1909.] (Ag) 41 p. 8°, (Delaware College bull., new ser.) pap., gratis. Del. College.

SYPHILIS.
Baar, G. Modern view of syphilis and its treatment. $2. Appleton.
Ballenger, E. G. Genito-urinary diseases and syphilis. *$3 net. E. W. Allen.
Hutchinson, *Sir* J. Syphilis. $3 net. Funk.
Keyes, E: Syphilis. (Add. pubs. for price.) Appleton.

SYPHILIS.—*Continued.*
Maisonneuve, P. Experimental prophylaxis of syphilis. *$1.50 net. Wood.
Malsbary, G: E. Diagnosis of syphilis. $5. Harvey Pub.
Noguchi, H. Serum diagnosis of syphilis. **$2 net. Lippincott.
See also **Venereal diseases.**

Syracuse, N. Y. Chamber of Commerce. Rept. upon smoke abatement. 24 p. 8°, gratis. Syracuse Chamber of Commerce.

SYRACUSE, N. Y.
Hewitt, W: P. H., *ed.* Hist. of the diocese of Syracuse, established 1886. $2. W. P. H. Hewitt.

Syrett, Netta.
Anne Page. '09(O30) 12°, $1.50. Lane.
Castle of dreams. '09(Ag21) front. D. $1.25. McClurg.
Castle of four towers. '10(O) il. 8°, $1.50. Fenno.
Olivia L. Carew. '10(Ap30) D. $1.50. Lane.

SYRIA, Asia.
Bell, G. L. Desert and the sown. *$3 net. Dutton.
Cormack, G: Egypt in Asia. *$3 net. Macmillan.
Jessup, H: H. Fifty-three years in Syria. In 2 v. **$5 net, boxed. Revell.
Kelman, J: From Damascus to Palmyra. *$6 net. Macmillan.
See also **Palestine.**

Syrinx. North, L. †$1.50. Duffield.

System "how books." il. 12°. System.
—How to increase a bank's deposits.
—How to sell more fire insurance.
—How to sell real estate.

System of medicine. v. 5. Allbutt, *Sir* T: C., *ed.* $6; $7; $8. Macmillan.

System of mineralogy. Dana, J D. $12.50. Wiley.

Systematic history fund pubs. 8° F. P. Rice.
—First records of Marlborough, Mass. $1.
—Rice. Marlborough, Mass., burial ground inscriptions. $3
—Vital records of Ashburnham, Mass. $2.70.
—Vital records of Athol, Mass. $3.
—Vital records of Bolton, Mass. $3.
—Vital records of Brookfield, Mass. (Add. pub. for price.)
—Vital records of Dudley, Mass. (Add. pub. for price.)
—Vital records of Marlborough, Mass. (Add. pub. for price.)
—Vital records of Spencer, Mass. (Add. pubs. for price.)
—Vital records of Warren, Mass. $2.40.
—Vital records of Westminster, Mass. (Add. pub. for price.)
—Vital records of Winchendon, Mass. $2.80.

Systematic moral education. Clark, J: K. $1 net. Barnes.

Systematic relationship of the *coccoceæ.* Winslow, C: E: A. $2.50. Wiley.

Systematic study in elementary schools. Earhart, L. B. $1. Teachers' Coll.

Systematic supplementary Bible studies. *See* Rand, Ja. L.

Systematic theology. Strong, A: H. In 3 v. ea., **$2.50 net. Am. Bapt.

Systems and practice of the drafting-room. '09(Je) c. 40 p. diagrs. 8°, (Machinery's reference ser.) pap., 25 c. Indust. Press.

Szczepanski, Paul von, and Wildenbruch, Ernst von.
Prussian cadet, by Paul von Szczepanski, and A story of cadet life, by Ernest von Wildenbruch; tr. by W. D. Lowe. '10 (Je4) 8°, $1 net. Dutton.

Szymanowski, Stephen Korwin.
The searchers. '08(Jl4) c. il. D. $2. S. K. Szymanowski.

T., J., pseud.
See Benson, Arth. Christopher.

T., L. G.
Three years behind the guns. '08(S19) c. il. D. *$1.50 net. Century Co.

T. R. in cartoon. Gross, R., *ed.* $1. Saalfield.

T. R. in cartoons. McCutcheon, J: T. 75 c. net. McClurg.

Tabb, Rev. J: Banister.
Later lyrics. New ed. [1910.] (My) 24°, $1 net; hf. mor., $2.50 net. Lane.
Later poems. '10(D) 115 p. 16°, $1 net. M. Kennerley.
Selection from the verses, made by Alice Meynell. '07, [1908.] (Jl) 11+120 p. 16°, **$1 net. Small.

Taber, C: Austin Mendell.
Cause of geologic periods. '08(F1) c. O. 75 c. G. H. Ellis.
Our periodic earth. '10(S10) c. O. 75 c.; pap., 50 c. G. H. Ellis.
Our periodical world. '08, [1909.] (N) 47 p. 12°. (Add. author for price.) C: A. M. Taber.

Taber, Clarence Wilbur, and Senn, N:, eds.
Pocket encyclopedic medical dictionary for physicians. 3d ed., rev. '08(N7) c. nar. S. flex. leath., $1.50. Laird.

Table talk. *See* Hazlitt, W:;—Lincoln, Abraham.

TABLEAUX.
See Entertainments.

TABLES (Statistical).
See under subjects.

Tables of stone. Begbie, H. †$1.50. Doubleday, P.

Tables synoptiques de phonologie de l'ancien français. Berthon, H. E. 85 c. Oxford Univ.

Tabor, Grace, and Teall, Gardner.
Garden primer. '10(My21) c. il. D. $1. McBride, W.

Tabor, Marg. E.
Saints in art; with their attributes and symbols alphabetically arr. '08(Ag8) il. S. *$1.20 net. Stokes.

Tabor, R. Montagu.
Odds and ends. '10(F19) S. $1.75. Longmans.

Tabulæ caelestes. Schurig, R: $1. Lemcke.

Tacitus, Caius Cornelius.
[Selected works;] introds. by E. H. Blakeney. In 2 v. v. 1, Annals; v. 2, Agricola, and Germania. '08(Mr7) 16°, (Everyman's lib.) ea., *35 c. net; leath., *70 c. net. Dutton.
The Agricola; with introd. and notes by Duane Reed Stuart. '09(Ap17) c. D. (Latin classics.) **40 c. net. Macmillan.

Tacitus, Caius Cornelius.—*Continued.*
Agricola and Germania; Latin text rearr. to natural English order; with careful and exact interlinear translation. '10 (Ja15) c. D. $1.25. C. E. H. Whitlock.
Dialogus, Agricola, and Germania; tr., with introd. and notes, by W. Hamilton Fyfe. '08(O24) D. $1. Oxford Univ.
Histories; bks. 1 and 2; ed. by Fk. Gardner Moore. '10(D31) 16°, (Macmillan's Latin classics.) 60 c. net. Macmillan.

TACITUS, Caius Cornelius.
Schoonover, D. T. Study of Cn. Domitius Corbulo as found in the "Annals" of Tacitus. *50 c. net. Univ. of Chic.

TACKLE.
See Ropes.

TACOMA, Wash.
Raymer's dict. of Tacoma. 25 c. C. D. Raymer.

Tact, push and principle. Thayer, W: M. 50 c. Hurst.

TACTICS.
See Military art and science.

Taft, W: Howard.
Address at Winona, Minn., Sept. 17, 1909. '09(D) 93 p. 8°. (Add. Superintendent for price.) U. S., Supt. of Docs.
Address of President Taft at the joint meeting of brotherhoods in train service, at Mechanics Hall, Worcester, Mass., April 3, 1910. '10(Jl) 9 p. 8°. Gov. Pr. Off.
Address of President Taft before the National Conservation Congress at St. Paul, Minneapolis, September 5, 1910. '10 (N) 22 p. 8°. Gov. Pr. Off.
Conservation of natural resources; special message of the President transmitted to the two houses of Congress Jan. 14, 1910. '10(Mr5) 8°. Gov. Pr. Off.
Delays and defects in the enforcement of law in this country: address delivered before the Civic Forum. '08(D5) por. 12°, (Civic Forum addresses.) pap., 10 c. Civic Forum.
Labor and capital, their common interest, their necessary controversies, their lawful acts, and the legal remedies for their abuses. '08(My9) 8°, pap., gratis. W: H. Taft.
Mr. Taft's new trust. '09, [1910.] (Ag) 17 p. 16°. (Priv. pr) Hampton Inst.
Political issues and outlooks; speeches del. between August, 1908, and February, 1909. '09(N20) c. por. D. **$1.25 net. Doubleday, P.
Present day problems: a collection of addresses. '08(Jl4) c. por. D. **$1.50 net. Dodd.
Presidential addresses and state papers; from March 4, 1900, to March 4, 1910. '10(O8) c. D. $1.80 net. Doubleday, P.
Tariff speech: address of President Taft at Winona, Minn., Sept. 17, 1909. '09, [1910.] (Ap) 15 p. 8°, pap., 5 c. U. S., Supt. of Docs.

TAFT, William Howard.
Davis, O. K. William Howard Taft, the man of the hour. $1. Ziegler.
Dunn, R. L. William Howard Taft, American. $1. Chapple Pub.

TAFT, William Howard.—*Continued.*
Hayne, J. E. President Taft measured by his most remarkable speech on the Hamitic race question, and the duty of the American people to this race. 35 c. J. E. Hayne.
Judson F: N. Labor decisions of Judge Taft. (Add. author for price.) F: N. Judson.
McBee, S. South and Mr. Taft. 50 c. Univ. Press (Sewanee).
Patterson, R. A. Taft's training for the presidency. 15 c. Chapple Pub.

TAFT FAMILY.
See Genealogies: Washburn, M. T. R.

Tag. Patriarche, V. †$1. L. C. Page.

Taggart, Marion Ames.
Betty Gaston; the seventh girl. '10(N5) c. il. (Six girls ser.) $1.50. Wilde.
Six girls and the seventh one: story. '09 (O9) c. il. D. †$1.50. Wilde.
Six girls growing older. '08(O17) c. il. D. †$1.50. Wilde.
Sweet Nancy; or, more about the doctor's little girl. '09(N6) c. D. $1.50. L. C. Page.
See also Barton, G:

—, Cain, G: M. A., O'Mahony, Nora Tynan, and others.
The friendly little house and other stories. '10(O15) c. D. $1.25. Benziger.

Taghconic. Smith, J. E. A. $1.15. Eagle.

Tagliapietra, Marg. Townsend, [Mme. Giovanni Tagliapietra,] comp.
Townsend—Townshend, 1066-1909: the hist. genealogy and alliances of the English and American house of Townsend; comp. by Ja. C. Townsend, 1865; Hon. Martin I. Townsend, 1871; C: Hervey Townshend, 1875; a pamphlet by Hon. I: Townsend Smith, 1904; now newly comp., rev. and il. by Marg. Townsend. '09(D) c. 3-125 p. il. pors. 4°, $10. M. T. Tagliapietra.

Tagliapietra, Mme. Giovanni.
See Tagliapietra, Marg. Townsend.

Tailleur (Le) de pierres de Saint-Point. Lamartine A. M. L. 60 c. Oxford Univ.

TAILORING.
Gordon, S. S. "Standard" work on cutting ladies' tailor-made garments. $10. J: J. Mitchell.
Hurwitz, G: New teacher of ladies' home tailoring. $10. G: Hurwitz.
Madison, J. O. Complete grading system. —Direct shoulder measure coat system. —Direct shoulder measure vest system. —New standard trousers and breeches system.—Self balancing trousers and breeches system. ea., $10. J. J. Mitchell.
Ratner, H: W. Up-to-date method of designing: [tailoring.] (Add. author for price.) H: W. Ratner
Stone, C: J: Stone's advanced superlative coat and vest system based upon the propertions of the human form. $10. C: J: Stone.
Watkins, E: Secret of successful tailoring. $1. L'Art de la Mode.

TAILORING.—*Continued.*
Weidel, J. A. Instruction book for those using Weidel's combined tailor square and curves. $5. Weidel.
See also Garment cutting.

Taine, Herb. Greyson.
Bob Carleton, American. '10(N) il. 12°, $1.50. C. M. Clark.

Taine, Hippolyte Adolphe.
History of English literature: tr. from the French by H. Van Laun. [Standard ed.] '09(Je5) c. 4 v., pors. 12°, $6; hf. cf., $12. Altemus.
History of English literature; tr. fr. the French by H: Van Laun; with introd. by J. Scott Clark. '08(Je27) c. 3 v., il. 8°, $5.25; hf. mor., $10.50. Lamb Pub.
Life and letters; ed. by his wife. In 3 v.; tr. from the French by E. Sparvel-Bayly; with a prefatial note by T: Seccombe. '08(D19) cr. 8°, ea., *$2 net. Dutton.
Voyage aux Pyrénées; ed. by W: Robertson. '09(Mr6) map, S. (Oxford modern French ser.) 60 c. Oxford Univ.

Taintor, C: Wilson.
Brief analysis of the United States Steel Corporation, with chart of quarterly earnings since its organization. '10(Ap9) fold. sheet, fold. chart, 8°, $3. C: W. Taintor.

Tait, Rev. Arth. Ja.
Christ and the nations: examination of Old and New Testament teaching. '10 (D) 12°, $1.50 net. Doran.

Tait, Asa Oscar.
Heralds of the morning: the meaning of the social and political problems of today and the significance of the great phenomena in nature. Re-rev. '09(Jl31) c. il. 8°, $2; hf. leath., $3.50. Pacific Press.

Takahashi, Sakuyé.
International law applied to the Russo-Japanese war, with the decisions of the Japanese prize courts. Am. ed. '08(Je) c. 18+805 p. O. *$8 net. Banks.

Takahira, Kogoro.
Address on the life and works of the late Dr. Joe Neesima, at the unveiling of his portrait at Amherst College, Amherst, Mass., May 7, 1909. '09(D) 23 p. 8°. (Add. author for price.) K. Takahira.

TAKELMA INDIANS.
See Indians.

Taking men alive. Trumbull, C: G. 60 c. net; 40 c. net. Y. M. C. A.

Talbert, Dan. H.
Pleasures of sin. '10(Mr12) c. por. D. $1. D. H. Talbert.

Talbert, Ernest Lynn.
Dualism of fact and idea in its social implications. '10(Ap16) c. 8°, (Philosophic studies.) pap., 50 c. net. Univ. of Chic.

Talbot, Arth. Newell.
Test of three large reinforced concrete beams. '09(Je5) il. 8°, (Univ. of Ill.; Engineering experiment station bulletin.) pap., gratis. Univ. of Ill.
Tests of cast-iron and reinforced concrete culvert pipe. '08(Jl18) il. tabs., O. (Univ. of Ill., Engineering experiment station, bull.) pap., gratis. Univ. of Ill.

Talbot, Arth. Newell.—*Continued.*
Tests of reinforced concrete beams, series of 1906. '08(Ja25); series of 1907 and 1908. '09(Je19) il. tabs., O. (Univ. of Ill., Engineering experiment station bull.) pap., gratis. Univ. of Ill.
See also Rolfe, C: Wesley.

—, and Abrams, Duff, And.
Tests of brick columns and terra cotta block columns. '08, [1909.] (My) 50 p. il. 8°, (Univ. of Ill bull.; Engineering Experiment Station.) pap., gratis. Univ. of Ill.

Talbot, Clarence Weill.
Diseases of the eye and how recognized; series of articles on the more common diseases with which the optician meets in his every-day work—the causes, symptoms, diagnosis and outlines of treatment. '10(Ap) c. 68 p. il. 12°, $1. Boger.

Talbot, E: Stuart.
Fulness of Christ; three sermons preached before the University of Oxford, and other papers. '09(F27) 16°, *50 c. net. Macmillan.

Talbot, Fannie Sprague.
Poems. '10(Jl2) c. 12°, $1. Badger.

Talbot, H: Paul.
Introd. course of quantitative chemical analysis; with explanatory notes and stoichiometrical problems. 5th ed., rev. and rewritten. '08(Je6) 8°, *$1.50 net. Macmillan.

Talbot, Lester Raymond, ed.
See Josselyn, Freeman Marshall.

Talbot, Marion.
Education of women. '10(Ap30) c. D. $1.25 net. Univ. of Chic.

Talbot-Tournier, Eugène.
La méthode Tournier; easy graded reading book for beginners in the French language. '09(D25) c. 24°, $1.25. Belisle Pr.

Tale confided by the woods. Nicolovius, L. $1. B'way Pub.
Tale of a black cat. Johnson, C. 60 c. Dodge.
Tale of a Capitolene Venus. Ross, C. $1 net. C. Ross.
Tale of a tub. *See* Swift, Jonathan.
Tale of Jemima Puddle-Duck. Potter B. †50 c. Warne.
Tale of Mrs. Tittlemouse. Potter, B. 50 c. Warne.
Tale of six little travellers. Gaskin, *Mrs.* A. 50 c. Jacobs.
Tale of the Flopsy Bunnies. Potter, B. 50 c. Warne.
Tale of two cities. *See* Dickens, C:
Tale of two tailors. Hubbard, E. (Add. pubs. for price.) Stein, B.
Tales come true. Walker, M. C. $1.25 net. Baker & T.
Tales from Bohemia. Stephens, R. N. $1.50. L. C. Page.
Tales from British history. Aguilar, G. 2 v. ea., $1.50. Dutton.
Tales from Shakespere. *See* Lamb, C:—Morris, Harrison Smith.
Tales from the Alhambra. *See* Irving, Washington.
Tales from the Far North. Klugh, M. C. 60 c. Flanagan.
Tales from the Old French; tr. by Isabel Butler. '10(D10) c. D. $1.25 net. Houghton M.
Tales grotesque and arabesque. *See* Poe, Edg. Allan.
Tales of a grandfather. *See* Scott, *Sir* Wa.
Tales of a wayside inn. *See* Longfellow, H: Wadsworth.
Tales of Aztlan. Hartmann, G: H: $1. B'way Pub.
Tales of Bengal. Banerjea, S. B. $1 net. Longmans.
Tales of enchantment. Nicholovius, L. $1.25. B'way Pub.
Tales of English minsters. Grierson, *Mrs.* E. W. In 7 v. ea., 50 c. net. Macmillan.
Tales of Irish life and character. Hall, A. M. F. $1.75 net. McClurg.
Tales of King Arthur. Lang, A., *comp.* 30 c. Longmans.
Tales of laughter. Wiggin, K. D. S., *ed.* †$1.50. McClure.
Tales of men and ghosts. Wharton, *Mrs.* E. N. J. $1.50. Scribner.
Tales of mystery and imagination. *See* Poe, Edg. Allan.
Tales of old England. Lansing, M. F., *comp.* 35 c. Ginn.
Tales of old Japan. Redesdale, A. B. F.-M., *Lord.* 50 c. net. Macmillan.
Tales of the caliphs. Field, C. *$1 net. Dutton.
Tales of the Canterbury pilgrims. Darton, F. J. H., *comp.* $1.50. Stokes.
Tales of the Greeks. *See* Plutarch.
Tales of the Red Children. Brown, A. F. †$1. Appleton.
Tales of the Romans. *See* Plutarch.
Tales of the tenements. Phillpotts, E. $1.50. Lane.
Tales of travel. Taylor, H. A. *$1.50 net. Neale.
Tales of Wagner's heroes. Maud, C. 50 c. McLoughlin.
Tales of wonder. Wiggin, K. D. S., *ed.* †$1.50. Doubleday, P.
Tales out of school about naval officers. Hitchcock, M. E. $1. Gotham Press.
Tales that never die. *See* Edgeworth, Maria.
Tales within tales. Wollaston, *Sir* A. N., *comp.* *$1 net. Dutton.
Talien. Metcalf, E. S. 50 c. L'Ora Queta.
Talisman (The). *See* Scott, *Sir* Wa.
Talk on relaxation. Fallows, A. K. *35 c. net. McClurg.
Talk on weeds. Pammel, L: H. 50 c. L: H. Pammel.
Talking points and selling arguments. Holman, W. C. 2 v. $5. Salesmanship.
Talks on drawing. Colby, L. E. $1.50. Scott, F. & Co.
Talks on high themes. Jefferson C: E: *75 c. net. Pilgrim Press.
Talks on religion. Mitchell, H: B., *comp.* **$1.50 net. Longmans.
Talks on some fundamentals of expression. Powers, L. T. $1.25. L. Powers Sch.
Talks on successful gowning. Lee, E. B. $1.50. E. B. Lee.

Talks with my boys. Mowry, W: A: $1. Silver.

Tall, Lida Lee.
See Andrews, C: McLean.

Tallentyre, S. G., [pseud. for Miss E. V. Hall.]
Life of Mirabeau. '09(Ag28) pors. O. *$3 net. Moffat.
Life of Voltaire. New ed. '10(D31) il. 8°, $3.50 net. Putnam.

Talleyrand-Périgord, Dorothée von Biron, Duchesse de.
Memoirs of the Duchesse de Dino (afterwards Duchesse de Talleyrand et de Sagan), 1831-1835; ed., with notes and biographical index, by the Princesse Radziwill (née Castellane). In 3 v. v. 1. '10(Je4); v. 2, 3 (D24) 8°, ea., $2.50 net. Scribner.

Tallman, Myrtle Catherine.
Traveling trio. '08(O10) c. pors. D. $1. M. C. Tallman.

Talmadge, Arth. White.
Talmadge, Tallmade and Talmade genealogy; being the descendants of Thomas Talmadge of Lynn, Massachusetts; with an appendix incl. other families. '10 (Ja8) il. 8°, *$10 net. Grafton Press.

TALMADGE FAMILY.
See **Genealogies.**

Talmage, Ja. E:
Great apostasy, considered in the light of scriptural and secular history. '09(D) c. 7+176 p. 12°, 60 c. Deseret News.
Story of "Mormonism." 2d ed. '10(Je) 87 p. 16°, 15 c. Bu. Information Salt Lake.

Talmey, Bernard S., M.D.
Genesis; manual for the instruction of children in matters sexual. '10(Ag27) c. il. 12°, $1.50. Practitioners' Pub.
Woman: a treatise on the normal and pathological emotions of feminine love. 2d enl. and improved ed. '08(My); 5th ed. '09(O); 6th ed. '10(D) c. il. 8°, ea., $3. Practitioners' Pub.
Bibliography (5 p.).

Talmey, Max.
Psyche; concise and easily comprehensible treatment on the elements of psychiatry and psychology for students of medicine and law. '10(O) c. 8+282 p. diagrs., 8°. $2.50. Medico-Legal.

Talmud.
Talmudic sayings: sel. and arranged under appropriate headings, by Rabbi H: Cohen. 2d ed. '10(O15) c. 8+72 p. S. 50 c. net; leath., $1 net. Bloch.

TALMUD.
Babylonian Talmud. 10 v. $50-$100. New Talmud.
Fluegel, M. Humanity, benevolence and charity legislation of the Pentateuch and the Talmud. *$2 net. H. Fluegel.
Rapaport, S:, *and* Deutsch, E. Tales and maxims from the Talmud. $1.75 net. Dutton.
Wisdom of Israel: extracts from the Babylonian Talmud and the Midrash Rabboth. *40 c. net. Dutton.
See also Aramaic language;—Hebrew literature.

Talty, J: A.
See Jones, F. L.

Tam O'Shanter. *See* Burns, Rob.

Tama. Watanna, O., *pseud.* $1.60 net. Harper.

Tamám. Moore, C: C. $1.50. Neale.

Tamar Curze. St. Luz, B., *pseud.* *$1 net. Fenno.

Tamariz, Nicolás.
Cartilla, y lvz en la verdadera destreza. sacada de los escritos de D. Lvis Pacheco y Narvaez, y de los autores que refiere. [facsim.] '02, [1909.] (N) 205 p. 8°, $9. (200 copies.) Hispanic Soc.

Tamayo y Baus, Don Manuel, ["Don Joaquin Estébanez."]
Lo positivo; ed., with introd., notes and vocab. by Philip Harry and Alfonso de Salvio. '08(Ap4) c. S. (Modern lang. ser.) 45 c. Heath.

Tame bunnies and wild. Jewett, J: H. 50 c. Dutton.

Taming a vaquero. Chester, L. G. $1. Whitaker & R.

Taming of a shrew. *See* Boas, F: S:

Taming of Red Butte Western. Lynde, F. $1.50. Scribner.

Taming the Barbary pirates. De Morgan, J: 75 c. McLoughlin.

Tan and Teckle. Bryson, C: L. *$1.25 net. Revell.

Tangent, Patrick Quinn, pseud.
See Phelps, G: Hamilton.

Tangled wedlock. Jepson E. †$1.50. McClure.

Tangles untangled. Rice, P. 75 c.; 25 c. J. S. Ogilvie.

Tanglewood tales. *See* Hawthorne, Nathaniel. Wonder book.

Tangye, Harold Lincoln.
In the torrid Sudan. '10(D24) il. fold. map, O. $3 net. Badger.

Tank line unlimited. Moomaw, B. C. 75 c. Editor Co.

Tannehill, Bertha, comp.
See Potter, Marion E., *comp.*

Tannenbaum, S: A.
Was William Shakespere a gentleman?; some questions in Shakespere's biography determined. '09(S18) c. il. O. bds., 50 c. (250 copies.) Tenny Press.

Tannenforst, Ursula.
Heroines of a school-room: sequel to "The thistles of Mount Cedar." '08(O3) c. front. D. †$1.25. Winston.

Tanner, Amy Eliza.
Studies in spiritism: with introd. by G. Stanley Hall. '10(O8) c. O. $2.50 net. Appleton.

Tanner, Edn. Platt.
Province of New Jersey, 1664-1738. '08 (D5) c. O. (Columbia University, studies in history, economics and public law.) $4.50; pap., $4. Longmans.

Tanner, Emmeline Mary.
Renaissance and the Reformation. '08 (D12) maps, D. 90 c. Oxford Univ.

Tanner, H: S:, M.D.
Human body a volume of divine revelations, governed by laws of God's ordaining, equally with those written on "tables of stone" or in the Bible: [vegetarianism.] '08(Ag22) c. por. 8°, 35 c. H: S: Tanner.
Pre-historic man: the first settlers on the western continent Oriental free masons. '08(Ap11) c. il. por. 12°, pap., 25 c. H: S: Tanner.

Tanner, J: H:
Key to High school algebra. '08(Je13) c. O. 75 c. Am. Bk.

Tannhäuser, Minnesinger and Knight Templar. Wolff, J. $2 net. Badger.

TANNING.
See Chemistry;—Leather.

TANSAN MINERAL WATER.
See Mineral waters.

TANTALUM.
See Electricity.

Tantalus. Kimmell, M. F. $1.50. C. M. Clark.

"Tape, Rollo," pseud.
See Wyckoff, R: D.

TAPE READING.
See Stocks.

TAPESTRY.
Ffoulke, C: M. Monograph on the Judith and Holofernes series consisting of 8 Flemish tapestries. (Add. author for price.) C: M. Ffoulke.
National Society of Fine Arts. Tapestries, textiles and embroideries; loan exhibition. (Add. pubs. for price.) Nat. Soc. of Fine Arts.
See also Needlework.

Tapestry brick work. Bragdon, C. 20 c. Fiske & Co., (Bost.)

TAPPAN, Eugene.
Phillips, J: G., *ed.* Memorial of Eugene Tappan. (Priv. pr.) Sharon Hist. Soc.

Tappan, Eva March.
American hero stories, [1492-1865.] New ed. '08(S12) c. il. pors. O. $1.50. Houghton M.
Dixie Kitten. '10(S17) c. il. D. $1. Houghton M.
European hero stories. '10(Ja22) c. il. maps, D. **65 c. net. Houghton M.
Letters from Colonial children. '08(O3) c. il. pors. maps, O. $1.50. Houghton M.
Old ballads in prose; il. by Fanny Y. Cory. School ed. '10(D) 12°, 40 c. net. Houghton M.
Old, old story-book; comp. from the Old Testament. '10(N5) c. il. O. $1.50. Houghton M.
Story of the Greek people. '08(N14) c. il. map, D. **65 c. net; '09(N6) il. 8°, $1.50. Houghton M.
—, comp. Chaucer story book. '08(O17) c. il. O. $1.50. Houghton M.

Tapper, T:, ed.
See Natural music course leaflets.

Taquigrafia fonetica, Sloan-Duployan. Braubach, A. L. $1.50. A. L. Braubach.

TAR.
Lunge, G: Coal, tar and ammonia. 2 v. *$15 net. Van Nostrand.

Tarbell, Ida Minerva.
Father Abraham. '09(My1) c. il. pors. D. **50 c. net. Moffat.

Tarbell, Martha.
In the Master's country: geographical aid to the study of the life of Christ. '10 (D) il. col. maps, 8°, 50 c. net. Doran.
Teachers' guide to the International Sunday school lessons, 1909. '08(O3); 1910. '09(O2); 1911. '10(N5) c. 8°, ea., *$1 net. Revell.

Tarbell, Mary Anna.
Stage days in Brimfield. '09(D18) c. il. 8°, $1. Bassette.

Tardieu, André Pierre Gabriel Amédée.
France and the alliances: the struggle for the balance of power. '08(N7) c. O. **$1.50 net. Macmillan.

TARIFF.
Albert, A. D., *jr.* Customs frauds in New York; article entitled The chase of the sugar smugglers. (Add. Superintendent for price.) U. S., Supt. of Docs.
American Academy of Political and Social Science. Tariff revision. $1. Am. Acad. Pol. Sci.
Atkinson, E: Views on occupations in their relation to the tariff. (Add. Superintendent for price.) U. S., Supt. of Docs.
Atton, H. King's customs: account of maritime revenue and contraband traffic in England, Scotland and Ireland from earliest times to year 1800. *$3.50 net. Dutton.
Bacon, A: O. Democrats and the tariff. U. S., Supt. of Docs.
Barker, J. E. 101 points against free trade. U. S., Supt. of Docs.
Bastiat, F. Fallacies of protection. *$1 net. Putnam.
Benedict, R. A. Malefactors of great wealth! $2. Am. Business.
Bengough, J: W. Whole hog book: being George's thoro' going work "Protection or free trade?" rendered into words of one syllable. 25 c. Am. Free Trade.
Bigelow, J: Reply of J: Bigelow in answer to an invitation by the Civic Forum of New York City to attend its annual municipal dinner. Gov. Pr. Off.
Bigelow, J: Substitute for the tariff upon imports and a provision for the equitable distribution of the wealth of nations. (Priv. pr.) J: Bigelow.
Bridgman, R. L. Passing of the tariff. **$1.20 net. Sherman, F.
Clarke, A. Tariff made plain. 10 c. Home Market.
Cooke, E. C. Case against protection. 10 c. Cassell.
Farquhar, A. B. Tariff revision, from the manufacturer's standpoint. (Add. author for price.) A. B. Farquhar.
Giesecke, A. A. American commercial legislation before 1789. $1.50. Appleton.
Gratacap, L: P. Protection. 20 c. Twentieth Century Pub.
Jordan, D: S. Fate of Iciodorum: being the story of a city made rich by taxation: [allegory on free trade.] **90 c. net. Holt.

TARIFF.—*Continued.*

Justice, T. Tariff: wool and wool goods. U. S., Supt. of Docs.

Lybarger, L. F. Tariff, what it is, how it works, whom it benefits. 25 c. Beaver Pr., (Pa.)

McCall, S: W. Payne tariff law. Gov. Pr. Off.

Mangold, G: B: Labor argument in the American protective tariff discussion. 35 c. Univ. of Wis.

Money, H. D. Tariff schedules. (Add. Superintendent for price.) U. S., Supt. of Docs.

National Association of Manufacturers of the United States of America. Arguments for a permanent non-partisan expert tariff commission. (Add. pubs. for price.) Lumberman's Pr.

Nesbitt, P. Mr. Brown, the tariff teacher. 25 c. Brown & Co.

Parsons, J. G. Protection's favors to foreigners. (Add. pubs. for price.) Reform Club.

Perris, G: H. How protection grows. —Protection and corruption. ea., 10 c. Cassell.

Perry, S. P. Tariff and the farmer. 50 c. F. S. Blanchard.

Porritt, E: Sixty years of protection in Canada. *$1.50 net. Macmillan.

Rich, W: W., *comp. and ed.* Hand book of the United States tariff. $2.50. Vandegrift.

Robertson, J: M. Trade and tariffs. *$1.50 net. Macmillan.

Skinner, H. M., *and* Putney, A. H. Government revenue; public utilities. $4.80. Cree.

Stone, N. I. Export tariffs of foreign countries. (Add. Superintendent for price.) U. S., Supt. of Docs.

Taft, W: H. Address, Sept. 17, 1909. (Add. Superintendent for price.)—Tariff speech. 5 c. U. S., Supt. of Docs.

Tariff Act of 1909. '09(N) 8°, flex. leath. (Priv. pr.) Union Trust Co.

Taussig, F. W: Tariff hist. of the United States. $1.50. Putnam.

Theobald, W: H: Defrauding the government: tales of smuggling. $1.50. Myrtle.

Thompson, R. E. Harvard University lectures on protection to home industry. $1. Am. Protective.

Tichenor, H: D. Col. George C. Tichenor's views on revision of the tariff and customs laws. (Priv. pr.) H: D. Tichenor.

Towne, H: R. Neutral line: plea for scientific regulation of the tariff. gratis. Merchants' Assoc.

United States. Comparative statement of the conference rates of duty with the rates in the Dingley tariff law. (Add. Superintendent for price.) U. S., Supt. of Docs.

United States. Comparison of the tariffs of 1897 and 1909 in parallel columns. '10 (Ag) 254 p. 8°. Gov. Pr. Off.

United States. Compilation of customs laws and digest of decisions rendered by the courts and Board of U. S. General Appraisers. (Add. Superintendent for price.) U. S., Supt. of Docs.

United States. *Congress. House. Committee on Ways and Means.* To provide revenue, equalize duties, encourage the industries of the United States and for other purposes; rept. '09(My) 19+9 p. 8°, pap. (Add. Superintendent for price.) U. S., Supt. of Docs.

United States. Customs tariff act of Aug. 5. $2. Downing.

United States. *Dept. of Commerce and Labor.* Inheritance-tax laws; digest of the principal features of the laws of Great Britain, France, and Germany, together with an outline of inheritance taxation in the U. S., and a collection of judicial decisions rel. thereto. '09(Ag) 69 p. 8°, pap. (Add. Superintendent for price.)

United States. *Dept. of State.* Tariff negotiations bet. the U. S. and foreign governments. '10(Ag) 155 p. 8°.

United States. Iron and steel products; estimates of increases and reductions in duties of H. R. 1438, as reported from the Committee on Finance, compared with the present law and the House bill, showing percentages of increase and decrease. '09(Ag) 8 p. 8°. (Add. Superintendent for price.) U. S., Supt. of Docs.

United States. New tariff bill. 10 c. C. S. Hammond.

United States. Pocket ed. of the tariff act. 50 c. Vandegrift.

United States. ***Superintendent of Documents.*** Tariff; list of United States public documents rel. to the various tariff laws.

United States. Tariff act; Vandergrift's digest. 50 c. Vandergrift.

United States. Tariff act of 1909. (Add. Superintendent for price.) U. S., Supt. of Docs.

United States. Tariff acts, 1789-1909. Gov. Pr. Off.

United States. *Treasury Dept.* Customs regulations of the United States; prescribed for the instruction and guidance of customs officers. (Add. Superintendent for price.) U. S., Supt. of Docs.

United States. Votes on tariff bill; record of every yea-and-nay vote in the Senate on the tariff bill from May 5 to July 8, 1909, inclusive. '09(O) 92 p. 8°. (Add. Superintendent for price.) U. S., Supt. of Docs.

Webb, M. de P. India and the empire: consideration of the tariff problem. *$1.20 net. Longmans.

See also Hops;—Petroleum;—Political economy;—Reciprocity;—Sugar;—Taxation;—Wool.

Tariff on trust-made steel articles. '09 (My22) D. (Univ. of Wisconsin bull.) pap., gratis. Univ. of Wis.

Tarkington, J: Steventon.

Hermit of Capri. '10(Ap2) c. il. O. $1.25. Harper.

Tarkington, Newton Booth.
Beasley's Christmas party. '09(N13) c. col. il. D. †$1.25. Harper.
Guest of Quesnay. '08(O17) c. il. D. †$1.50. McClure.

—, and Wilson, Harry Leon.
Man from home. '08(N21) c. il. O. $1.25. Harper.

Tarpaulin muster. Masefield, J: $1. B. W. Dodge.

Tarr, Ralph Stockman, and Butler, Bert S.
Yakutat Bay region, Alaska; physiography and glacial geology; by Ralph S. Tarr; Areal geology; by Ralph S. Tarr and Bert S. Butler. '09(N) 183 p. il. maps, O. (U. S., Dept. of the Interior, Geological Survey; Professional papers.) pap.

—, and Engeln, O. D. v.
Lab'y manual of physical geography; for use in connection with a general course in physical geography in high and secondary schools and in colleges. '10(Je4) 8°, bds., $1.25 net. Macmillan.

—, and McMurry, Fk. Morton.
Advanced geography; rev. by the Text-book Committee and approved by the State Board of Education. '09(D) c. 20+649+10 p. il. maps, 8°, (California state ser.) $1. Cal. Supt. Pub. Instruction.
Geographies: five book ser. pt. 2, The earth as a whole. '09(D4) c. il. maps, 12°, price raised from *45 c. net to *55 c. net. Macmillan.
New geographies. In 2 bks. '10(O8) il. maps, 8°, Bk.1, complete, 65 c. net; Bk. 1, pt. 1, 40 c. net; pt. 2, 50 c. net; Bk. 2, complete, $1.10 net; Bk. 2, pt. 1, 65 c. net; pt. 2, 65 c. net. Macmillan.

Tarr and McMurry geographies. il. 8°. Macmillan.
—Barnard. Missouri. *20 c. net.
—Bender. Iowa. *20 c. net.

Tarry. Cope, F: J. $1. Pentecostal.
Tarry with me. Smith, C. S. $1.50. C. S. Smith.

TARTANS.
See Scotland.

Tartarin of Tarascon [and] Tartarin on the Alps. *See* Daudet, Alphonse.

Tarvia and pitch filler. Barrett Manufacturing Co. (Not for sale.) Barrett Mfg. Co.

Task worth while. Mabie, H: C. $1.25 net. Griffith.

Tasman. Brewster, M. K. 75 c. Everett Press.

TASMANIA.
Smith, G. W. Naturalist in Tasmania. $.50. Oxford Univ.

Tasso, Torquato.
Jerusalem delivered; tr. by E: Fairfax; ed. by H: Merley. '08(Je27) il. c. 8°, $1.75; hf. mor., $3.50. Lamb Pub.

TASTE (sense of).
Witkowski's atlas of the mechanism of voice, speech and taste. *$2 net. W: R. Jenkins.

Tate, G. P.
Frontiers of Baluchistan: travels on the borders of Persia and Afghanistan; with an introd. by Col. Sir H: McMahon. '09 (S4) pls. fold. maps, *$5 net. Scribner.

Tate, Ja. Murray, and Stone, Melvin Oscar.
Foundry practice: treatise on molding and casting in their various details; prepared for the use of students in the College of Engineering, University of Minnesota. '09(Ja30) figs. 12°, $2. Wiley.

Tate, W: Ramage.
Criminal commercialism; true story of the systematic frauds of a big corporation of interest to all and especially the clothing trade. '10(Jl2) c. por. 12°, 50 c. Nicoletti.

Tatham, H. F. W.
Footprints in the snow and other tales; with memoir by A. C. Benson. '10(D24) 8°, $1.50 net. Macmillan.

TATTING.
See Needlework.

Tatum, Edith.
When the bugle called. '08(Ap18) c. D. $1.25. Neale.

Tatum, Jos. W., comp.
Information of great value to newly married people; carefully comp. and ed. collection of such knowledge as is most needed in the home of the newly married, so indexed as to be readily found when needed. '09, [1910.] (Ap) c. 255 p. il. 8°, gratis. H. K. Palmer.

Tauchnitz manuals of conversations. 5 v. '09(O9) 16°, ea., *75 c. net. Macmillan.

Tauchnitz pocket dictionaries. 7 v. '09(O9) 16°, ea., *75 c. net. Macmillan.

Taulman, Fs. Asbury.
The poplars; or, the good results of an evil deed. '09(D) 376 p. 12°, $1.50. Cochrane.

Taussig, Fk. W:
Tariff hist. of the United States. 5th ed., rev. with additional material, incl. a consideration of the Aldrich-Payne act of 1909. '10(O15) c. D. (Questions of the day ser.) $1.50. Putnam.

Taussig, F: Jos.
Prevention and treatment of abortion. '10 (F) c. 10+180 p. il. 8°, $2. Mosby.

Tavenor-Perry, J.
See Perry, J. Tavenor-.

TAVERN CLUB, Boston, Mass.
Abbott, H. Silver wedding of the Bear; memorial of celebration of 25th anniversary of the Tavern Club. (Priv. pr.) H. Abbott.

TAVERNS.
See Inns.

Tawney, Guy Allan.
J. S. Mill's theory of inductive logic. In 2 pts. pt. 1, An expository outline; pt. 2, A discussion. '09(D4) O. (University studies.) pap., ea., 50 c. Univ. of Cin.

TAXATION.
Blow, B. E. Revenue law and the retail liquor dealer. $1. R. M. Wood.
Boyle, J. E. Methods of assessment as applied to different classes of subjects. 7 c.; per hundred, $5. Nat. Tax Assoc.
Dawbarn, C. Y. C. Social contract, more particularly in relation to taxation. $1.25 net. Longmans.
Edmunds, G: F. Income tax. Gov. Pr. Off.

TAXATION.—*Continued.*

Eliot, C: W: College taxation. gratis. Harvard Univ.

Fillebrown, C: B. A B C of taxation. $1.20. Doubleday, P.

Fillebrown, C: B. A 1909 single tax catechism, together with notices of the A B C of taxation. 5 c. C: B. Fillebrown.

Indiana. Laws concerning taxation. pap., 25 c. W: H. Scheiman.

International Conference on State and Local Taxation. State and local taxation; third international conference. $2. Int. Tax.

Kennan, K. K. Income taxation. $3.50. Burdick.

Lansdell, H: Sacred tenth; or, studies in tithe-giving, ancient and modern. 2 v. *$6 net. Gorham.

McVey, F. L. Taxation of mineral properties. (Add. pubs. for price.) Internal Tax. Assoc.

Means, D: M. Methods of taxation compared with established principles of justice. **$2.50 net. Dodd.

National Tax Association. State and local taxation. $4. Macmillan.

New England tax rates, 1907-8. 35 c. L. W. Lee.

New York [State.] Tax law. $1. Baker, V. & Co.

Page, W: H., *and* Jones, P. Treatise on taxation by local and special assessments. $12. W. H. Anderson.

Pennsylvania. Law of taxation. v. 1, 2. $12. Soney.

Phelps, E. M., *comp.* Select articles on the income tax. $1 net. H. W. Wilson.

Pleydell, A. C., *and others.* Municipal taxation. 10 c. Tax Reform.

Root, E. Proposed income-tax amendment. Gov. Pr. Off.

Seligman, E. R. A. Progressive taxation in theory and practice. $1.75; $1.25. Am. Economic Assoc.

Seligman, E. R. A. Separation of state and local revenues. (Add. pubs. for price.) Nat. Tax Assoc.

Seligman, E. R. A. Shifting and incidence of taxation. $3. Lemcke.

Skinner, H. M., *and* Putney, A. H. Governmental revenue; public utilities. $4.80. Cree.

Toof, M. D. Assessor's manual for Iowa. 25 c. M. D. Toof.

United States. *Dept. of Commerce and Labor.* Income and inheritance taxes; letter from the acting Secretary of Commerce and Labor, transmitting the rept. of special agent C: M. Pepper on the laws of Great Britain as to income and inheritance taxes. '09(Jl) 13 p. 8°. (Add. Superintendent for price.)

United States. Tax on net income of corporations: message from President [Taft]. (Add. Superintendent for price.) U. S., Supt. of Docs.

Walden, C: O., *and* Mowry, D. E. Revenue law informer. Dealers' ed. $1. Walden & M.

TAXATION.—*Continued.*

West, M. Inheritance tax. *$2.50 net; *$2 net. Macmillan.

See also Corporations;—Finance;—Insurance;—Liquors;—Mines and mining;—Mortgages;—Political economy;—Tariff;—*also* Indianapolis;—New Zealand;—Suffolk, Eng.;—*also* names of states.

TAXIDERMY.

Reed, C: K. *and* C. A. Guide to taxidermy. *$1.50 net. C: K. Reed.

Scorso, R. R. Amateur taxidermist. 50 c. Fur News.

Taxonomic aspect of the species question. Britton, N. L. 25 c. N. Y. Botanical.

Taxonomy of the *muscoidean* flies. Townsend, C: H: T. 60 c. Smith. Inst.

Taylor, A. T.

Modern British locomotives. '08(F8) c. il. obl. 8°, $2. Spon.

Taylor, Albert D.

Street trees: their care and preservation. '09(Mr6) (N. Y. State Coll. of Agriculture bull.; Experiment Station.) pap., gratis. Cornell Univ.

Tayler, Alex. Ja. Wallis-.

Pocketbook of refrigeration and ice making. 5th ed. '10(Je4) c. $1.50. Henley.

Sugar machinery; descriptive treatise devoted to the machinery and apparatus used in the manufacture of cane and beet sugars. 2d ed., enl. and extensively rev.; with 56 illustrations. '10 (Ap) 15+369 p. il. tabs., forms, 12°, (Rider's technical ser.) $2 net. Van Nostrand.

Bibliography (2 p.).

Taylor, Alfr. E:

Hobbes. '09(Jl31) 12°, (Philosophies ancient and modern from Pythagoras to Spencer.) *50 c. net. Dodge.

Plato. '09(Jl31) 12°, (Philosophies ancient and modern from Pythagoras to Spencer.) *50 c. net. Dodge.

TAYLOR, Bayard.

Haskell, *Mrs.* J. Bayard Taylor's translation of Goethe's "Faust." *$1 net. Lemcke.

Taylor, Carr White.

Railroad a public servant. '08(Ag) c. 112 p. por. D. pap., 50 c. C. W. Taylor.

Taylor, C: Keen.

Basic cause: discussion of modern morals. [1910.] (Je) 12 p. 12°, 25 c. net. Staton Bros.

Physical training for boys and a word or two for their parents. '10(Mr5) c. il. 8°, $1. Staton Bros.

Real letters to real boys. '08(Je27) c. 12°, *50 c. net. Revell.

Taylor, C: Maus, jr.

British Isles through an opera glass. New ed. '09, [1910.] (Ja) il. 12° *$1.25 net. Jacobs.

Odd bits of travel with brush and camera. New ed. '09, [1910.] (Ja) il. 12°, *$1.25 net. Jacobs.

Touring Alaska and the Yellowstone. New ed. '09, [1910.] (Ja) il. 12°, *$1.25 net. Jacobs.

Vacation days in Hawaii and Japan. New ed. '09, [1910.] (Ja) il. 12°, *$1.25 net. Jacobs.

Taylor, Mrs. C: Tracy.
See Taylor, Sophie C.

Taylor, D: Clark.
Psychology of singing. '08(D12) c. D. *$1.50 net. Macmillan.

Taylor, D: Watson.
Resistance of ships and screw propulsion. '08(Ja11) il. tabs., 8°, *$2.25 net. Macmillan.
Speed and power of ships; manual of marine propulsion. 2 v. '10(D3) c. il. tabs., 4°, $7.50 net. Wiley.

Taylor, E: Robeson.
Lavender and other verse. '10(N5) c. D. bds., $2. P. Elder.

Taylor, Frederic H.
Guide to the electrical examinations. '08 (Ag1) il. 12°, 75 c. Spon.
How to use electric light (with increased economy and efficiency), incl. chapter on electric heating; popular up-to-date hdbk. for the householder and every one using electric light or electric heating. '10 (D17) il. 12°, pap., 25 c. Spon.
Private house electric lighting; with a chapter on generating plants. 3d ed., rewritten. '09(Je19) il. 12°, bds., 50 c. Spon.

Taylor, F: Winslow, and Thompson, Sanford Eleazer.
Concrete, plain and reinforced. 2d ed. '09 (O30) c. il. 8°, $5. Wiley.
Extracts on reinforced concrete design. '10 (Ag13) il. 8°, $2 net. Wiley.

Taylor, G:
Story of Glencoe, and other poems. '09 (F20) c. il. por. *$1 net. Caledonian Pub.

TAYLOR, George Boardman.
Taylor, G: B. Life and letters of the Rev. George Boardman Taylor. *$1.50 net. J. P. Bell.

Taylor, G: Braxton.
Life and letters of Rev. George Boardman Taylor, D.D. '08, [1909.] (F) c. 413 p. pors. 8°, *$1.50 net. J. P. Bell.

Taylor, G: Rob. S.
Leaders of socialism, past and present. '10 (O15) D. $1 net. Duffield.

Taylor, H. Darnley.
Latin and English idiom: object lesson from Livy's preface. '09(My1) 8°, *60 c. net. Putnam.

Taylor, Hannis.
Science of jurisprudence. '08(O17) 8°, $3.50. Macmillan.
To the Congress of the United States. Memorial in behalf of the architect of our federal Constitution, Pelatiah Webster. '07, [1908.] (Mr.) 48 p. 8°. (Add. author for price.) H. Taylor.

Taylor, H: Ling, Ogilvy, C:, and Albee, Fred Houdlett.
Orthopedic surgery for practitioners. '09 (Ap) c. 24+503 p. il. 8°, *$5 net. Appleton.

Taylor, H: Ryder-.
Visitor's guide and history of San Antonio, Tex. 3d ed., rev. and enl. '08(Jl) c. 11-111 p. il. D. pap., 25 c. N. Tengg.

Taylor, Hobart Chatfield Chatfield-.
Fame's pathway. '09(Ap17) 12°, †$1.50. Duffield.

Taylor, Horace A.
Tales of travel all around the world. '09 (S18) c. por. O. *$1.50 net. Neale.

Taylor, I. E.
Essays on theosophy. '09(Ap3) 12°, *75 c. net. Macmillan.

Taylor, Ida Ashworth.
Cardinal Democrat: Henry Edward Manning. '08(D) 6+254 p. por. 12°, *$1.25 net. Herder.
Christina of Sweden. '10(Mr26) pors. O. *$4 special net. Appleton.
Lady Jane Grey and her times. '08(O10) il. O. *$4 special net. Appleton.
Making of a king. '10(D10) il. 8°, $3.50 net. Dodd.

Taylor, I:
Words and places; etymological illustrations of hist., ethnology and geography rev. by A. Smythe Palmer. '09(D18) map, 12°, *$1.50 net. Dutton.

Taylor, J. A.
Silver legend: saints for children. New ed. '08(D5) 8°, *$1.25 net. Herder.

Taylor, Jane, and Gilbert, Mrs. Ann Taylor.
Little Ann and other poems. '10(D31) col. il. 8°, bds., $1. Warne.

Taylor, Job.
Broken links; il. by J: Goss. '08(Mr14) c. D. $1.50. C. M. Clark.

Taylor, J: Edn.
Cy Hains's sermo-phone and other stories. '09(Je) c. 62 p. por. 12°, 50 c. J: E. Taylor.

TAYLOR, John Horton.
Taylor, *Mrs.* L. E. Life story of a college boy. $1. Chr. Witness.

Taylor, J: Metcalf.
Witchcraft delusion in colonial Connecticut, 1647-1697. '08(Jl4) c. il. (Grafton historical ser.) **$1.50 net. Grafton Press.

Taylor, J: T.
Cotton weaving and designing; rev. under the direction of F. Wilkinson and H. Nisbet. 6th ed. '10(N12) il. D. $2.50. Longmans.

Taylor, Jos. Russell.
Composition in narration. '10(Ap2) c. D. 75 c. Holt.

Taylor, Jos. Schimmel.
Word study in the elem. school. '10(Je4) c. il. 12°, $1. Educ. Pub.
Bibliography (1 p.).

Taylor, Mrs. Lillie Estella.
Life story of a college boy; real and happy Christian; or, memories of John Horton Taylor, by his mother. '09(N) c. 20+118 p. il. pls. pors. 12°, $1. Chr. Witness.

Taylor, Marion.
Life of Christ; also, a brief story or history of my life. '09(Jl) c. 190 p. pors. 8°, $1.25. Acme.

Taylor, Marion Lee.
Study of the technique in Konrad Ferdinand Meyer's novellen. '09(Jl31) c. 8°, pap., 75 c. Univ. of Chic.

Taylor, Mary Imlay.
Caleb Trench. '10(Mr26) c. front. D. †$1.50. Little, B. & Co.
Impersonator. [Popular ed.] '09(N) front. 12°, 75 c. Little, B. & Co.
The reaping. '08(F29) c. il. D. †$1.50. Little, B. & Co.

Taylor, Oliver.
Historic Sullivan; hist. of Sullivan County, Tenn.; with brief biographies of the makers of history. '09(N20) c. il. pors. maps, facsims., 8°, $2.50. King Pr.

Taylor, S. Earl.
See Morgan, C: Herbert.

Taylor, Sophie C., [Mrs. C: Tracy Taylor.]
Daughter of the manse. '10(Mr5) c. il. D. $1.50. Winston.

Taylor, T: Eddy.
See Morgan, C: Herbert.

Taylor, T: Ulvan.
Surveyor's hand book. '08(O17) c. il. tabs., 16°, *$2 net. M. C. Clark.

Taylor, W. B.
Studies in the Epistles and Revelation. '10(D31) c. 16°, 75 c. Standard Pub.

Taylor, Wa. P., and Dixon, Jos.
Two new rodents from Nevada, by Wa. P. Taylor; northern coast form of the California gray fox, by Jos. Dixon. '10 (Ap) 283-302 p. Q. (University of California pubs.; Zoology.) pap., 20 c. Univ. of Cal.

Taylor, W: G: Langworthy.
Financial legislation in principle and in history. [1910.] (Ag) 28 p. 8°, (Univ. of Nebraska studies.) $1. Univ. of Neb.
"References" (3 p.).

Taylor, W: H:, M.D.
De quibus: discourses and essays. '08 (Je6) c. O. $1.50. Bell Book.

Taylor, W: Ja.
Elem. logic, with special application to methods of teaching. '09(N6) c. il. 12°, $1.25. Scribner.
Syllabus of the history of education. '09 (N20) c. 12°, $1. Heath.

Taylor, W: M.
Taylor-Hamilton monitor of symbolic masonry; rev. by S: R. Hamilton. '08 (Ag) c. 294+5 p. il. 16°, 60 c,; mor., $1. Coyle.

Taylor, W: T.
Stationary transformers: theory, connections, operation and testing of constant-potential, constant-current, series and auto transformers, potential regulators, etc. '09(My22) c. figs. D. *$1.50 net. McGraw.

Taylor, Zachary.
Letters from the battle-fields of the Mexican war; repr. from the originals in the collection of Mr. William K. Bixby, of St. Louis, Mo.; with introd., biographical notes and appendix. '08(O10) c. pors. facsims., 4°. [priv. pr.] W: K. Bixby.

Taylor-Hamilton monitor of symbolic masonry. *See* Taylor, W: M.

Taylor (Nathaniel William) lectures. *See* King, H: Churchill.

TCHAIKOVSKY, Peter Ilich.
Newmarch, R. Tchaikovsky. *$2.50 net. Scribner.

Tchernychewsky, Nikolai.
What is to be done?; romance; tr. by B: R. Tucker. 4th ed. '10(Ja29) il. O. $1. Manhattan Bk.

TEA.
Ibbetson, A. Tea from grower to consumer. 75 c. Pitman.

Tea-burners of Cumberland county. Andrews, F. D. 30 c. F. D. Andrews.

TEA TAX.
See American Revolution.

Teacher, J: H.
See Bryce, T: H.

Teacher of Dante. Dole, N. H. **$1.75 net. Moffat.

Teacher-training class. McElfresh, F. 10 c. Presb. Bd.

Teacher-training lessons for the Sunday-school. Hurlburt, J. L. *30 c. net; 50 c. net. Eaton & M.

Teacher's candlestick. Slattery, M. *35 c. net. F. M. Barton.

TEACHERS AND TEACHING.
Adams, J: Exposition and illustration in teaching. **$1.25 net. Macmillan.
Armstrong, H: E: Teaching of scientific education. $1.75 net. Macmillan.
Arnold, F. Text-book of school and class management. In 2 v. v. 1, $1.25 net; v. 2, $1 net. Macmillan.
Bardeen, C: W: Fifty fables for teachers. $1. Bardeen.
Barret, S. M. Practical pedagogy. $1. Heath.
Beale, D. Addresses to teachers. 50 c. Longmans.
Bell, J., *comp.* "The Teacher" guide to certificate exams. of the Bd. of Educ., 1908-9 (England). *50 c. net. Pitman.
Best, L. A. Teachers' retirement fund. Gov. Pr. Off.
Black, J. E. New primary methods; series of pract. home studies in pedagogy. 2 v. $7. Interstate Sch. Corr.
Boyer, C: C. Modern methods for teachers. $1.50. Lippincott.
Brown, E. E. Distinctive functions of university, college and normal school in the preparation of teachers. (Add. author for price.) E. E. Brown.
Buck, E. C. Guide to the teachers mastery of texts. 85 c. E. C. Buck.
Burritt, E. G. Pupil and how to teach him. 60 c. W: B. Rose.
Calmerton, G. English; language; literature; ethics; reference.—Programs; public library; kindergarten; occupation.—Reading; phonics; spelling; penmanship. (Not for sale.) Fort Wayne Sch. Bd.
Carnegie Foundation for Advancement of Teaching. Financial status of the professor in . merica and in Germany.—Papers rel. to admission of state institutions to system of retiring allowances of Carnegie Foundation.—Plan for an exchange of teachers between Prussia and the U. S. gratis.—Rules for the admission of institutions for the granting of retiring allowances. gratis.—Third annual report of the president and treasurer. gratis. Carnegie Found.

TEACHERS AND TEACHING.—*Continued.*

Chancellor, W: E. Class teaching and management. $1. Harper.

Charters, W. W. Methods of teaching. $1.10. Row, P. & Co.

Colgrove, C. P: Making of a teacher. 75 c. C. P: Colgrove.

Colgrove, C. P: Teacher and the school. $1.25 net. Scribner.

Colvin, S. S. Some facts in partial justification of the so-called dogma of discipline. gratis. Univ. of Ill.

Dinsmore, J: W. Teaching a district school. $1. Am. Bk.

Du Bois, P. Point of contact in teaching. 75 c. Dodd.

Earhart, L. B. Teaching children to study. 60 c. Houghton M.

Harvey, N. A. Principles of teaching. $1.25. Row, P. & Co.

Hess, *Mrs.* G. F., *comp.* List of books for teachers in the Seattle Public Library. gratis. Seattle Pub. Lib.

Hildebrand, F. A. Dynamic school of tomorrow. $2. Aberdeen.

Hodson, F., *ed.* Broad lines in science teaching. *$1.25 net. Macmillan.

Holst, B. P., *and* Roark, R. N., *eds.* New Teachers' and pupils' encyclopædia. 5 v. $18.75. Holst.

Horn, P. W. Life of our schools. 15 c. Cargill.

Horne, H. H. Function of a school of pedagogy. gratis. Sch. Pedagogy.

Hyde, W: D. Teacher's philosophy in and out of school. 35 c. Houghton M.

Jones, O. M., *and others.* Teaching children to study. **80 c. net. Macmillan.

Kandel, I: L. Training of elem. school teachers in Germany. $1.50. Teachers' Coll.

Kilpatrick, V. Departmental teaching in elementary schools. *60 c. net. Macmillan.

Lincoln, E. B. Art of securing better teaching positions. 60 c. Progress Club.

Lomer, G. R: Concept of method. $1. Teachers' Coll.

MacDowell, T. L. Outline of a plan for utilizing the salary schedule as a means for improving the efficiency of teachers in the public elementary schools. 10 c. T. L. MacDowell.

McEvoy, T: J. Methods in education. $1.50. T: J. McEvoy.

McKeever, W: A. Psychologic method in teaching. $1. Flanagan.

McKenny, C: Personality of the teacher. $1. Row, P. & Co.

McMurry, F. M. How to study and teaching how to study. **$1.25 net. Houghton M.

Michigan. State Normal College. Suggestive outlines of the courses of study as followed in the kindergarten and elem. grades. 50 c. Mich. State Normal.

Misawa, T. Modern educators and their ideals. **$1.25 net. Appleton.

Murphy, D. C. Turning points in teaching. 60 c. Flanagan.

TEACHERS AND TEACHING.—*Continued.*

Neet, G: W. Practical methodology. $1.25. Bogarte.

Newman, J: H: University teaching. *75 c. net. Longmans.

Oldham, B. M. Pract. plans for primary teachers in public or private schools. 30 c. C. J. Bell.

Palmer, G: H. Ideal teacher. 35 c. Houghton M.

Palmer, G: H. *and Mrs.* A. E. F. The teacher. **$1.50 net. Houghton M.

Pattee, F. L: Elements of religious pedagogy. *75 c. net. Eaton & M.

Public school methods. 4 v. per set, $13.50. Sch. Methods.

Quick and dead; to teachers, by two of them. 50 c. Longmans.

Riley, J: L. Springfield tests, 1846-1905-6: a study in the three Rs. 25 c. Holden.

Rocheleau, W: F. Intermediate and grammar methods; series of pract. home studies in pedagogy. 2 v. $6.50. Interstate Sch. Corr.

Rowe, S. H: Habit-formation and the science of teaching. **$1.50 net. Longmans.

Sachs, J. Syllabus of general course on the theory and practice of teaching in the secondary school. 20 c. Teachers' Coll.

Sanders, T: E. Twenty talks to teachers. 85 c. Teachers' Co-op.

Sandiford, P: Training of teachers in England and Wales. $1.50. Columbia Univ.

Sandison, H. Problem of method. $1.25. H. Sandison.

Strachan, G. C. Equal pay for equal work; story of struggle made by women teachers of New York Cty. $1 net. B: F. Buck.

Thorndike, E: L. Teaching staff of secondary schools in the United States. (Add. Superintendent for price.) U. S. Supt. of Docs.

Ware, A. Course of study and teachers' hdbk. in the common literature of life. 40 c. San F. St. Normal.

Webb, L. T. Grading simplified: a teacher's aid. 75 c. Hackney.

Wedgwood, J Nineteenth century teacher and other essays. *$3 net. Doran.

Whipple, G. M. Guide to high school observation. 40 c. Bardeen.

Woodbury, S. E. Dramatization in the grammar grades. 30 c. S. E. Woodbury.

Youker, H. S., *comp.* Training of rural school teachers. (Not for sale.) Wisconsin Dept. Pub. Instruction.

See also Agriculture; — Arithmetic; — Civics; — Drawing; — Education; — Ethics; — Examinations; —Fine arts; —Geography; —Gymnastics and physical culture; —History; — Kindergarten; — Language; —Latin; —Literature; —Manual training; —Mathematics; — Memory; —Music; —Nature; —Penmanship; — Psychology; — Readers; —Reading; —Schools; —Story-telling; —Sunday-school; —Voice; —*also* Pestalozzi, Johann Heinrich.

Teachers of Emerson. Harrison, J: S. $1.50 net. Sturgis & W.

TEACHERS' COLLEGE.
See Columbia Univ.

Teachers' College contributions. See Columbia Univ. Teachers' Coll.

Teachers' College Record. See Columbia Univ. Teachers' Coll.

Teachers' College ser. See Columbia Univ. Teachers' Coll.

Teachers' College syllabi. See Columbia Univ. Teachers' Coll.

Teachers' guide. Tarbell, M. *$1 net. Revell.

Teachers' hdbk., 1909, 1910. Axtell, J. W. ea., 35 c. Cumberland Press.

Teachers' help ser. 12°, pap. Educ. Pub. —Revell. Arbor day exercises.—Lincoln's birthday: exercises.—Memorial day exercises. ea., 25 c.

Teachers' manuals. S. Flanagan. —Dewey *and* Small. My pedagogic creed. 15 c.

Teachers' outlines for studies in English. Blakely, G. S. 50 c. Am. Bk.

TEACHING.
See Teachers and teaching.

Teaching a district school. Dinsmore, J: W. $1. Am. Bk.

Teaching botanist. Ganong, W: F. $1.25 net. Macmillan.

Teaching of arithmetic. Smith, D: E. 30 c. Teachers' Coll.

Teaching of Christ in its present appeal. *$1 net. Scribner.

Teaching of citizenship. Hughes, E. H. $1.25. Wilde.

Teaching of Jesus. Stevens, G: B. *$1 net. Macmillan.

Teaching of Jesus about the future. Sherman, H: B. *$3 net. Univ. of Chic.

Teaching of Latin in secondary schools. Hecker, E. A. 80 c. Schoenhof.

Teaching of the fathers on the real presence of Christ in the holy eucharist. Pourrat, P. 15 c. Cathedral Lib.

Teaching of the holy Scriptures. Kemble, D. *40 c. net. Am. S. S.

Teaching the boy to save. McKeever, W: A. gratis. W: A. McKeever.

Teaching to read. Hughes, J. L. 50 c. Barnes.

Teagar, Michael Moores.
Altars of sacrifice: poem. '08(My16) c. por. D. $1.25. M. M. Teagar.

Teall, Gardner.
See Tabor, Grace.

Tear, Dan. Ambrose.
Logical basis of educational theory from the standpoint of the "instrumental" logic. '08, [1909.] (Mr) c. 58 p. 8°, pap., 50 c. Univ. of Chic.

Tearle, Christian.
Holborn Hill. '10(Jl30) 12°, $1.20. Clode.
Rambles with an American. '10(S3) il. pors. O. $2.50 net. Duffield.

Tears and smiles. Propper, A. H. $1. B'way Pub.

Technical chemists' handbook. Lunge, G: *$3.50 net. Van Nostrand.

Technical drawing ser. See Heath's.

TECHNICAL EDUCATION.

American Academy of Political and Social Science. Industrial education. $1. Am. Acad. Pol. Sci.

American Federation of Labor. Industrial education. 25 c. Am. Fed. Labor.

Baldwin, W: A., *and others.* Industrial-social education. $1.50. M. Bradley.

Carlton, F. T. Education and industrial evolution. *$1.25 net. Macmillan.

Chamberlain, A. H: Conditions of technical education in Germany. 50 c. Bardeen.

Chamberlain, A. H: Standards in education, with some consideration of their relation to industrial training. $1. Am. Bk.

Davenport, E. Education for efficiency. gratis.—Industrial education with special reference to high school. gratis. E. Davenport.

Dean, A. D. Industrial education and a state policy. o. p. N. Y. State Educ.

Dean, A. D. Industrial education considered in its relation to the high school problem. 30 c. Bardeen.

Dean, A. D. Worker and the state; study of education for industrial workers. $1.20 net. Century Co.

Draper, A. S. Industrial and trades schools. (Add. Dept. for price.) N. Y. State Educ.

Draper, A. S. Our children, our schools, and our industries. 50 c. Bardeen.

Haney, J. P. Vocational training and trade teaching in the public schools. 15 c. Am. Acad. Pol. Sci.

Hanus, P. H: Beginnings in industrial education. **$1 net. Houghton M.

Martin, G: H: Industrial education and the public schools. (Add. pubs. for price.) Wright & P.

National Society for the Promotion of Industrial Education. Circular of information. 10 c.—Rept. of the Committee of Ten on the relation of industrial training to the general system of education in the United States. (Not for sale.)

National Society for the Promotion of Industrial Education. Industrial education. Gov. Pr. Off.

New York State. *Education Dept.* Evening industrial improvement schools. '09 (S) 11 p. 8°. (Add. pubs. for price.)—General industrial and trades schools. '09 (S) 21 p. 8°. (Add. pubs. for price.) N. Y. State Educ.

Orth, S: P: Industrial education. gratis. Technical High Sch.

Richards, C: R. Industrial training. (Add. pubs. for price.) N. Y. Dept. Labor.

Row, R. K. Educational meaning of manual arts and industries. $1.25. Row, P. & Co.

Sayward, W: H: Relation of the trade school to the trade gratis. S: F. Hubbard.

Warriner, E. C. Industrial and vocational training in the public schools. Mich. Supt. Pub. Instruction.

TECHNICAL EDUCATION.—*Continued.*
Woolman, *Mrs.* M. S. Making of a trade school. 50 c. net. Whitcomb.
Woolman, *Mrs.* M. S. Trade schools and culture. 5 c. Manhattan Trade.
See also Boys;—Engineering;—Manual training;—Negroes; — Railroads; — Shoes;—Vocational education.

Technical instruction manuals. 12°, $1. McKay.
—Greenwood. Iron.

Technical method of ore analysis. Low, A. H. $3. Wiley.

Technical press index, Jan., 1908-June, 1909, (inclusive.) '09(N6) Q. *$3 net. Engineering News.

Technical word list. Marshall, C. C., *comp.* 30 c. Goodyear-M.

Technique of English. Schleif, O. 75 c. O. Schleif.

Technique of speech. Jones, D. D. **$1.25 net. Harper.

Technique of the novel. Horne, C: F. **$1.50 net. Harper.

Technological dict. Huelin y Arssu, C. $4. Spon.

TECHNOLOGY.
See Useful arts.

Teddie. Britton, F. H. $1. F: B: Dickerson.

Teddy-B and Teddy-G: the Roosevelt bears abroad. Eaton, S. $1.50. Stern.

Teddy bear book. '09(D) *50 c. net. Doran.

Teddy bears in fun and frolic. Towne, R. D. 35 c. Reilly & B.

Teddy Lester's chums. Finnemore, J: $1.50. Lippincott.

Teddysee (The). Irwin, W. A. 75 c. net. B: W. Huebsch.

TEETH.
Black, G. V. Work on operative dentistry. $10. Medico-Dental.
Broomell, I: N., *comp. and ed.* Practical dentistry. $2.50. Caulk.
Broomell, I: N., *and* Fischelis, P. Anatomy and histology of the mouth and teeth. *$3 net. Blakiston.
Buckley, J. P. Modern dental materia medica; pharmacology and therapeutics. *$2.50 net. Blakiston.
Burchard, H: H. Text-book of dental pathology and therapeutics for students and practitioners. *$5 net. Lea.
Case, C. S. Practical treatise on the technics and principles of dental orthopedia. $10. C. S. Case.
Colyer, J. F. Dental surgery and pathology. $7 net. Longmans.
Conover, J: F. Mental mouth wash. 25 c. Roycrofters.
Essig, C: J., *and* Koenig, A: Dental metallurgy. *$2 net. Lea.
Guerini, V. Hist. of dentistry from the most ancient times until the end of the 18th century. *$6 net. Lea.
Hepburn, W. B. Notes on dental metallurgy. $2 net. Wood.
Johnson, C: N., *ed.* Text-book of operative dentistry. *$6 net; *$7 net. Blakiston.
Johnson, H: H. **Teeth: their growth and preservation.** 75 c. H: H. Johnson.

TEETH.—*Continued.*
Kittredge, J: H. Method of impressions and bites: [for false teeth.] $3.50. J: H. Kittredge.
Lischer, B. E: Elem. of orthodontia. $1. Mosby.
Long, E. H. Text-book of dental materia medica, therapeutics and prescription writing. *$2.75 net. Lea.
Marshall, J: S. Principles and practice of operative dentistry. **$5 net; **$6 net. Lippincott.
Osborn, H: F. Evolution of mammalian molar teeth. *$2 net. Macmillan.
Prinz, H. Dental materia medica and therapeutics. $5. Mosby.
Streeter, G: L. Lab'y guide in anatomy; outline of dissection designed for dental students. 30 c. Wahr.
Symington, J., *and* Rankin, J. C. Atlas of skiagrams illustrating the development of the teeth. *$3.50 net. Longmans.
Trigger, T. C. Notes on methods of filling teeth with gold inlays. $2. T. C. Trigger.
See also Anesthetics;—Medical electricity;—Medical jurisprudence;—Medicine;—Roentgen rays.

Teggart, F: J., ed.
Official account of the Portola expedition of 1769-1770. '09(N) 15 p. facsim., O. (Publications of the Academy of Pacific Coast History.) pap., 10 c. Univ. of Cal.
See also Breen, Patrick;—Smith, Donald Eug., *ed.*

Tegnér, Esaias.
Axel; from the Swedish of Bishop Tegnér; adpt. by Magnus Bernhard. '10 (My21) c. 12°, $1. Cochrane.
Frithiof's saga; with introd., bibliography and explanatory notes by G: T. Flom, Ph.D., supplemented by Tegnér's own estimate of his work. '09(D) 24+202 p. il. 8°, *$2 net. Engberg-H.
Frithiof's saga; tr. from the Swedish in the original meters by Clement B. Shaw; with foreword, annotations, the 12 original songs of Crusell and other addenda. Private ed. '09(Ja16) c. il. O. $2. C. B. Shaw.

TEHUANTEPEC NATIONAL RAILWAY.
See Mexico.

Teich, Emma L., comp.
See Potter, Marion E., *comp.*

Teitsworth, G: Wilson, ed.
Back to slavery: [socialism.] '08(N) c. 132 p. 12°, 75 c. Craven-D.

Telegraph boy. Alger, H., *jr.* 50 c. Hurst.

Telegraphic transmission of photographs. Baker, T. T. $1.25 net. Van Nostrand.

Telegraphing in battle. O'Brien, J: E. $2 net. J: E. O'Brien.

TELEGRAPHY.
Crotch, A. Telegraphic systems. *$2 net. Lippincott.
Dodge, G: M. Telegraph instructor. $1. G: M. Dodge.
Gibson, C: R. How telegraphs and telephones work. *75 c. net. Lippincott.
Griffin, R. B. Pianoforte telegraphy (Morse telegraph code). $1. Morse Art.
Hitchcock, R. Automatic telegraphy. U. S., Supt. of Docs.

TELEGRAPHY.—*Continued.*

International cable directory of the world, 1908. $5. Int. Cable.

Jones, W. H. Telegraphy for beginners. 50 c.; 25 c. Spon.

Laughter, V. H. Operator's wireless telegraph and telephone hand-book. $1. Drake.

Maver, W:, *jr.* American telegraphy and encyclopedia of the telegraph. $5. Maver.

Sewall, C: H: Lessons in telegraphy. $1. Van Nostrand.

Thom, C:, *and* Collins, A. F: Electric telegraph. $1. Am. Sch. Corr.

United States. *Dept. of Commerce and Labor. Bu. of the Census.* Telegraph systems, 1907. '09(O) 47 p. il. f°. (Add. Superintendent for price.)

United States. *Signal Office.* Regulations for United States military telegraph lines, U. S. Signal Corps; prep. under the direction of Brigadier-General Ja. Allen. '09(Je) 94 p. 8°, pap. (Add. Superintendent for price.)

Wilkinson, H. D. Submarine cable-laying, repairing and testing. *$6 net. Van Nostrand.

See also Codes;—Electric wires;—Wireless telegraphy.

TELEOLOGY.

See Science.

TELEPATHY.

Grumbine, J. C: F. Telepathy. 50 c. Order of White Rose, (Mass.)

Podmore, F. Telepathic hallucinations. *50 c. net. Stokes.

See also Ghosts;—Psychical research.

TELEPHONE.

Ainsworth, J: H., *and* Gansey, R. J. Discussion of telephone competition. (Add. pubs. for price.) Columbus Citizens' Tel.

Allsop, F: C: Telephones, their construction and fitting. $1.25. Spon.

Bell Telephone Company of Pennsylvania. Specifications no. 3300. Bell Telephone.

Casson, H. N. Hist. of the telephone. $1.50 net. McClurg.

Collins, A. F: Manual of wireless telegraphy and telephony. **$1.50 net. Wiley.

Crotch, A. Elements of telephony. 60 c. Spon.

Cummings, G: W. Electricity and magnetism in telephone maintenance. $1.50. McGraw.

Erskine-Murray, J. D. Wireless telephones. $1. Henley.

Fleming, J: A. Elem. manual of radiotelegraphy and radiotelephony. *$2 net. Longmans.

Gernsback, H. Wireless telephone. 25 c. Modern Electrics.

Gibson, C: R. How telegraphs and telephones work. *75 c. net. Lippincott.

Harrison, N. Wireless telephone construction. 25 c. Spon.

Hyde, W: H: Telephone troubles and how to find them on both the magneto and central energy. 25 c. W: H: Hyde.

TELEPHONE.—*Continued.*

Johnston, G. R. Some comments on the 1907 Annual rept. of the Am. Telephone and Telegraph Co. 10 c. Int. Independent.

Kennelly, A. E. Wireless telegraphy and wireless telephony. **$1 net. Moffat.

Laughter, V. H. Operator's wireless telegraph and wireless telephone hand-book. $1. Drake.

Library Bureau. Decimal classification for filing telephone correspondence. 2 v. '09 (O) 8°. (Not for sale; leased only.) Lib. Bu.

McMillan, A. H. Telephone law: organization and operation of telephone companies. *$3 net. McGraw.

Maver, W: Wireless telegraphy and telephony. $3. Maver Pub.

Mayer, C. Telephone construction. *$3 net. M. C. Clark.

Poole J. Pract. telephone handbook. $1.75 net. Macmillan.

Radcliffe, W: H., *and* Cushing, H. C., *jr.* Telephone construction, installation, wiring, [etc.] $1. Henley.

Ruhmer, E. Wireless telephony in theory and practice. *$3.50 net. Van Nostrand.

Scott, L. Telephones; interchange of service. 25 c. Wisconsin Free Lib.

Spencer, T: G. Deterioration of lead sheaths of aerial and underground telephone cables. gratis. Stromberg-C.

Tutt, R. G. Telephone accounting. $1. R. G. Tutt.

United States. *Dept. of Commerce and Labor. Bu. of Labor.* Investigation of telephone companies; letter from the Secretary of Commerce and Labor transmitting rept. showing the results of an investigation made by the Bu. of Labor into telephone companies engaged in the conduct of interstate business. '10(Jl) 340 p. il. tabs., 8°.

Van Deventer, H. R. Telephonology. $4. McGraw-H.

Van Deventer, H. R., *comp.* Telephone hdbk. on the promotion, organization and construction of telephone lines. 50 c. H. R. Van Deventer.

See also Wireless telegraphy;—*also* Bell, Alexander Melville.

Telfer, W:

Message for you. '10(Jl2) c. front. por. 12°, $1. Pentecostal.

Telford, Emma Paddock, and Armington, M. A.
Evening Telegram cook book. '08(D5) c. 12°, 75 c.; pap., 35 c. Cupples & L.

Telford, J:

Man's partnership with Divine Providence. '08(D19) D. (Fernley lecture.) *$1.25 net. Eaton & M.

"Tell me a true story." Stewart, M., *ed.* *$1.25 net. Revell.

Telling Bible stories. Houghton, *Mrs.* L. S. **$1.25 net. Scribner.

TELLURIDES.

Tibbals, C: A., *jr.* Study of tellurides. 25 c. Univ. of Wis.

TELLURITES.

Wolesensky, E: Study of the metallic tellurites. 25 c. Univ. of Wis.

TEMPERANCE.

Alden, G: W. Fifteen reasons why no-license is better than license. 10 c. G: W. Alden.

American prohibition year book for 1910. 50 c.; 25 c. Nat. Prohibition.

Batten, S: Z. Working temperance program. 15 c. Am. Bapt.

Benton, J: C. Legal aspect of prohibition. 50 c. J: C. Benton.

Berry, C: W. Temperature-entrophy diagram. $2. Wiley.

Brown, G: G., *comp.* Holy Bible repudiates "prohibition." $1; 25 c. G: G. Brown.

Crafts, W. F. *and* S. J. World book of temperance. 75 c.; 35 c. Int. Ref. Bu.

Crafts, W. F., *and others.* Intoxicating drinks and drugs in all lands and times. 75 c. Int. Ref. Bu.

Durkee, J. H., *ed. and comp.* Hist. of World's Temperance Centennial Congress; and memorial of Dr. Billy J. Clark, held at Saratoga Springs, N. Y., June 14-23, 1908. $1. J. H. Durkee.

Erickson, M. Temperance torchlights. 50 c. Review and Herald Pub.

False science in the schools; how physiology is mistaught. gratis. U. S. Brewers' Assoc.

Gregory, C: L. Alcoholism and insanity. $1.50. Von Boeckmann-J.

Grimes, W. B. Water wagon and other poems. 15 c. W. B. Grimes.

Hammell, G: M., *ed.* Passing of the saloon. $2; $2.75; $3.50. Tower Press.

Hathaway, S., *comp.* Appeal to common sense and words that tell; guide to temperance on safe and sane lines. 50 c. Common Sense Pub.

Haynes, J. B. Economic aspects of prohibition. 15 c. J. B. Haynes.

Heinemann, H. E. O. Rule of "not too much." 25 c. H. E. O. Heinemann.

Herrick, *Mrs.* S. M. B. Public school physiology; perversion of truth and science in the name of temperance. gratis. U. S. Brewers' Assoc.

Homan, J. A. Prohibition the enemy of temperance. $1; 50 c. Christian Liberty.

Hopkins, A. A. Profit and loss in man: [plea for prohibition.] **$1.20 net. Funk.

Jeffords, S. G., *ed.* Series of notable debates by men of the hour. 50 c. S. G. Jeffords.

Jones, *Mrs.* C. E. H. Story of the wonderland under the stainless flag. 25 c. Kansas Prohibitionist.

Knott, H: Destroyer; man to demon, the devastation of a life by strong drink. 75 c. Vansant.

Monahan, M., *ed. and comp.* Text-book of true temperance. 40 c. U. S. Brewers' Assoc.

TEMPERANCE.—*Continued.*

Moomaw, B. C. Tank line unlimited. 75 c. Editor Co.

Paul, H. A. C. Immorality and foolishness of prohibition. 20 c. H. A. C. Paul.

Prohibition: its relation to temperance. 50 c. Debar.

Roe, E: R. Rum and ruin: [fiction.] $1; 25 c. Laird.

Shaw, E. R., *comp. and ed.* Stories of hell's commerce; or, the liquor traffic in its true light. $1.50. Shaw Pub.

Stuart, G: R. Saloon under the searchlight. *35 c. net; *20 c. net. Revell.

Stuart, G: R. Stump digger on the saloon. 10 c. Pub. Ho. of M. E. Ch., So.

Sutherland, D. F. Black plague of the American continent: [intemperance.] 50 c. D. F. Sutherland.

Vansant, W: R. Weaning the nation from strong drink. $1.50. Vansant.

Warner, H. S. Social welfare and the liquor problem. $1; 35 c. Intercollegiate Prohibition.

White, A. D., *jr.* Transgressor and other stories, showing the effects of liquor upon society. 50 c.; 75 c. Interstate Prohibition.

Winning orations in the national contests of the Intercollegiate Prohibition Association. 25 c. Intercollegiate Prohibition.

See also Alcohol;—Liquors;—Woman's Christian Temperance Union.

TEMPERATURE.

Bigelow, F. H. Daily normal temperature and the daily normal precipitation in the United States. $1.75.—Rept. on the temperature and vapor tensions of the United States reduced to a homogeneous system of 24 hourly observations for the 33-year interval, 1873-1905. (Add. Superintendent for price.) U. S., Supt. of Docs.

Burnett, T. C. On the rise of temperature in rabbits caused by the injection of salt solutions. Univ. of Cal.

See also Meteorology.

Tempered steel. Mallory, H. S: $1.50. Fenno.

Tempering steel. Cole, M. 10 c. Sampson.

Temperley, Harold W: Vazeille, and Marczali, H:

Hungary in the 18th century. '10(Je4) 4°, $2.50 net. Putnam.

Tempest (The). *See* Shakespeare, W:

Tempest and sunshine. Holmes, *Mrs.* M. J. H. $1. Rand, McN. & Co.

Templar tactics and manual. Chilcott, L. S. $1.50. L. S. Chilcott.

Temple, Alfr. G:

Modern Spanish painting. '08(D5) 8°, *$20 net. Lippincott.

Temple, Rev. W:

The faith and modern thought: six lectures. '10(Ap9) 12°, $1 net. Macmillan.

Temple, Sir W:

Essays on ancient and modern learning and on poetry; ed. by J. E. Spingarn. '10 (Ja1) D. 85 c. Oxford Univ.

TEMPLE (The).
Franklin, J: H. Rebuilding of King Solomon's temple. $1.50. J: H. Franklin.
Maas, A. J. Day in the temple: [fiction.] *50 c. net. Herder.
Osgood, P. E. Temple of Solomon. 30 c. Open Court.
Temple (The). Abbott, L. **$1.25 net. Macmillan.
Temple (The). Herbert, G: *35 c. net; 70 c. net. Dutton.
TEMPLE BAPTIST CHURCH, Los Angeles, Cal.
Burdette, *Mrs.* C. B. Rainbow and the pot of gold, [story of life of Temple Baptist Church, Los Angeles, Cal.] $1. Clara Vista.
Temple biographies. 12°. Dutton.
—Gibbon. Lawrences of the Punjaub. *$1.50 net.
Temple classics. 332 v. '10(Ag27) front. ea., 45 c. net; limp leath., ea., 65 c. net. Dutton.
Formerly published by Macmillan.
Temple classics for young people. 16 v. '10(Ag27) il. ea., 45 c.; lambskin, ea., 65 c. Dutton.
Formerly published by Macmillan.
Temple dict. of the Bible. Ewing, W. $4 net. Dutton.
Temple dramatists. 26 v. '10(Ag27) front. 16°, ea., 35 c.; limp leath., ea., 55 c. Dutton.
Formerly published by Macmillan.
Temple encyclopædic primers. 47 v. '10 (Ag27) 16°, ea., 35 c. net. Dutton.
Formerly published by Macmillan.
Temple Shakespeare, Pocket lexicon and concordance to the. '09(My8) c. il. T. 45 c.; roan, 65 c. Macmillan.
Temple treasury; Biblical diary; comp. with references. pt. 1. '09(N13) T. leath., $1.50, boxed. Am. Tr.
Templeton, Fk.
Idle moments; book for campfires, schools, societies, etc. '08(D) 52 p. 8°, 35 c. F. Templeton.
TEMPTATION.
Bogue, V. Strength to yield; psychology of a great temptation. $1.50. Cunningham, C. & W.
Gordon, S: D. Quiet talks about the tempter. 75 c. net. Revell.
Hughson, S. C. Warfare of the soul. **$1.20 net. Longmans.
Temptation of St. Anthony. Flaubert, G. $1.25. A. Harriman.
Tempting of Paul Chester. Askew, *Mrs.* A. J. de C. L. $1.50. Fenno.
Ten blind leaders of the blind. Lewis, A. M. 50 c. Kerr.
Ten books of the merrymakers. 10 v. Wilder, M. P. $6. Circle.
Ten boys from history. Sweetser, K. D. $2. Duffield.
TEN COMMANDMENTS.
See Commandments.
Ten days in Cuba. Whelan, N: J. 35 c. N. J. Whelan.
Ten great and good men. Butler, H: M. $2. Longmans.
Ten minute sermons. Nicoll, *Sir* W: R. $1 net. Doran.
"Ten o'clock." Whistler, J. A. M. *$1 net. E. D. North.
Ten personal studies. Ward, W. P. *$3 net. Longmans.
Ten to seventeen. Bacon, *Mrs.* J. D. D. †$1.50. Harper.
Ten true secret service stories. Shaw, D. B. 25 c. J. S. Ogilvie.
Ten weeks in arithmetic. Lee, A. S. $1. A. S. Lee.
Ten weeks in English grammar. Lee, A. S. 65 c. A. S. Lee.
Ten wise men. Visscher, W: L. (Not for sale.) W: L. Visscher.
Ten years of gamekeeping. Jones, O. *$3 net. Longmans.
TENANT.
See Landlord and tenant.
Tenant of Wildfell Hall. *See* Brontë, Anne.
Tenants (The). Watts, *Mrs.* M. S. †$1.50. McClure.
Tendency. Vance, J. I: $1.25 net. Revell.
Tenderfoot abroad. Grayson, J. $1. W. A. Butterfield.
Tenderfoot in California. Halsey, M. D. $1. M. D. Halsey.
Ténébreuse (Une) affaire. *See* Balzac, Honoré de.
TENEMENT HOUSE.
MacGregor, F. H. Tenement house legislation, state and local. 25 c. Wisconsin Free Lib.
New York [City.] Bureau of Municipal Research. Steps taken to locate and to solve problems of enforcing tenement house laws. 50 c. Bu. Municipal.
Price, G: M. Tenement-house inspector. $1.50. Chief.
Veiller, L. Housing reform.—Model tenement house law. ea., $1.25. Charities Pub.
TENEMENTS.
See Apartments;—Building laws.
Tennessee. Corporation laws, incl. counties as corporations, with powers, duties and jurisdiction of county cts.; notes of decisions of sup. ct. on pertinent cases; by Ja. L. Watts. '08(Ja11) O. $4.50. Marshall.
Tennessee. Encyclopedic digest of repts.: being a complete encyclopedia and digest of all the Tenn. case law up to and including v. 115 Tenn. repts., Cooper's chancery repts., Shannon's Tenn. cases, and the Tenn. chancery appeals repts.; under the ed. supervision of T: Johnson Michie. In 12 v. v. 6, '08(F); v. 7 (My); v. 8 (Je); v. 9 (Jl); v. 10 (Ag); v. 11, 12 (S) c. O. shp., ea., $7.50. Michie.
Tennessee. *Supreme ct.* Repts.; (G: W. Pickle.) v. 22. 2d ed. '08(O) c. O. shp., $3. Marshall.
Tennessee. *Supreme ct.* Repts.; (C: T. Cates, jr.) v. 10. '08(Ap); v. 11 (D); v. 12. '09(Jl); v. 13. '09, [1910.] (Ja); v. 14 (N) c. O. shp., ea., $3. Stephens.
TENNESSEE.
Albright, E: Early hist. of Middle Tenn. Brandon Pr.
McBain, H. L., *and* Mynders, S. A. How we are governed in Tennessee and the nation. 55 c. Southern Sch. Supply.

TENNESSEE.—*Continued.*
Moore, J: T. Ole Mistis, and other songs and stories from Tennessee. 75 c. Winston.
Morison, J. H. S. Rules of pleading adapt. to cts. of law in Tennessee, together with numerous annot. forms. $5.50. F. H. Thomas.
Wright, M. J., *comp.* Tennessee in the war, 1861-1865. $1.50. A. Lee.
See also Memphis;—Sullivan Co.;—Sumner Co.

TENNESSEE CAMPAIGN.
See Civil War.

Tennessee Tess. Blaney, C: E: 25 c. J. S. Ogilvie.

Tenney, E: Payson.
Contrasts in social progress. Rev. ed. '10 (Je18) O. 85 c. E: P. Tenney.

TENNIS.
Dewhurst, E: B. Science of lawn tennis. $2.50. Innes.
Myers, A. W. Complete lawn tennis player. *$3 net. Jacobs.
Paret, J. P. How to play lawn tennis. 10 c. Am. Sports.
Spalding's official lawn tennis annual, 1909. 10 c. Am. Sports.
Tompkins, F: C: Court tennis, with notes on racquets and squash-racquets. **$1 net. Lippincott.
Vaile, P. A. Strokes and science of lawn tennis. 10 c. Am. Sports.
See also Games.

Tennyson, Alfred, Lord.
Works; annot. by Alfr. Lord Tennyson; ed. by Hallam, Lord Tennyson. Eversley ed. In 6 v. v. 1. '08(F1); v. 2, 3 (My16); v. 4, 5, 6 (Jl4) c. por. 12°, ea., **$1.50 net. Macmillan.
Works; with preface by Elisabeth Luther Cary, together with various critical introds.; il. in photogravure from orig. designs by Frederick Simpson Coburn and Gustave Doré. 8 v. [Centenary ed.] '09, [1910.] (My) c. il. pors. 8°, $28. Putnam.
Complete poetical works. '08(D19) 12°, (Crowell's thin paper poets.) ooze leath., $1.75, boxed. Crowell.
Poetical works. 2 v. '10(D) il. $2.50, boxed. Crowell.
English idyls and other poems, 1842-1855; ed., with introd. and notes, by Beatrice C. Mulliner. '10(Ap2) D. 50 c. Oxford Univ.
Enid; ed., with introd. and notes, by C. B. Wheeler. '09(Ag14) 8°, 40 c. Oxford Univ.
Enoch Arden and Maud. '09(Ap10) front. 32°, (Ariel booklets.) leath., 75 c., boxed. Putnam.
From day to day with Tennyson; comp. by Leroy H. Westley. '10(Ag27) c. por. 12°, 75 c. Barse & H.
Idylls of the king. 2 v. v. 1, Enid and Vivien; v. 2, Elaine and Guinevere. '09 (Ap10) front. 32°, (Ariel booklets.) ea., leath., 75 c., boxed. Putnam.
In memoriam. '09(D18) c. il. O. *$2 net.—Centenary ed. de luxe. '10(F19) 4°, vellum, *$12.50 net, boxed. Sturgis & W.

Tennyson, Alfred, Lord.—*Continued.*
Love poems; sel. by Ethel Harris. '08 (D19) il. 8°, $1.25; ooze leath., $1.75. Rand, McN. & Co.
Poems, 1830-1863. '08(O17) 16°, (Best books ser.) leath., *$1 net. Dutton.
Poems. '10(D) 12°, (Autograph poets.) $1; hf. leath., $1.50. Houghton M.
Poems, 1830-1865; with introd. by T. Herbert Warren. New ed. '10(Jl2) 16°, (World's classics.) 35 c.; leath., 65 c. Oxford Univ.
Poems; sel. by A. T. Quiller-Couch. '08 (D19) S. (Select English classics.) 10 c. Oxford Univ.
The princess; medley; with notes by Rose Henderson. '10(Mr5) c. 16°. (Little classic ser.) 12 c. Flanagan.
The princess; medley; ed. by H: Allsopp. '10(N19) D. 50 c. Oxford Univ.
Select poems; ed. by Archibald MacMechan. '09(Ja23) c. 16°, (Belles-lettres ser.; Section 6, Nineteenth century poets.) *60 c. net. Heath.
Shorter poems and Lyrics, 1833-1842: ed., with introd. and notes, by Beatrice C. Mulliner. '09(D) 48+125 p. 8°, *80 c. net. Oxford Univ.
Tennyson; fifty poems, 1830-1864; ed. by J. H. Lobban. '10(O22) S. (Pitt Press ser.) 75 c. net. Putnam.
Tennyson day by day; ed. by A. R. Marble. '10(D) 12°, (Day by day ser.) 60 c.; ooze, $1. Crowell.

—, and Whelpley, B:
Songs from Tennyson's "Princess"; music by B: Whelpley. '08(O3) F. pap., *$1 net. Boston Music.

TENNYSON, Alfred, *Lord.*
Brooklyn Public Library. Alfred Tennyson, 1809-1892: list of books with references to periodicals in the Brooklyn Public Library. gratis. Brooklyn Lib.
Gordon, G: A. Crossing the bar; lyric of life everlasting. *50 c. net. Pilgrim Press.
Jones, H: Tennyson. 40 c. Oxford Univ.
Ker, W: P. Tennyson. 30 c. Putnam.
Lockyer, *Sir* J. N. *and* W. L., *comps.* Tennyson as a student and poet of nature. $1.50 net. Macmillan.
Reade, W. Notes on the Arthurian epic and the Idylls of the king. 50 c W. Reade.
Shepherd, H: E. Commentary upon Tennyson's In memoriam. *$1.25 net. Neale.
Spence, W Idylls of the king; spiritual interpretation. $1. Cochrane.
Warren, T: H. Centenary of Tennyson. 35 c. Oxford Univ.
Zimmerman, L. M. Pearls of comfort from Tennyson's "In Memoriam." (Add. author for price.) L. M. Zimmerman.

TENOR.
See Singing.

Tent dwellers. Paine, A. B. $1.50. Harper.

Tent life in Siberia. Kennan, G: $2.50 net. Putnam.

Tenters (The). Herr, H. D. *50 c. net. A. M. Adams.

TERATORNIS.
See Fossils.

86

Tercentenary history of Canada. Tracy, F. B. (Add. pub. for price.) Collier.

TEREDINIDAE.
Silberfoos, C: P. Natural history, organization and later development of the *Teredinidae.* gratis. Johns Hopkins.

Terence [Lat. Terentius] Afer, Publius.
Comedies; ed., with introd. and notes, by Sidney G. Ashmore. '08(Je27) c. D. **$1.50 net. Oxford Univ.
The Famulus, as it is performed at the Royal College of St. Peter, Westminster; ed. by J: Sargeaunt and the Rev. A. G. S. Raynor. '09(Ap3) S. 50 c. Oxford Univ.
Havton timorvmenos; ed., with introd. and notes, by F. G. Ballentine. '10(D31) c. 12°, (Students' ser. of Latin classics.) $1. B: H. Sanborn.
Phormio, simplified for the use of schools; tr. by H: R. Fairclough and Leon J. Richardson. [Teachers' ed.] '09(Ag) 52 p. 12°, (Students' ser. of Latin classics.) 50 c. B: H. Sanborn.
Phormio; ed. by Gordon J. Laing. '08(N) c. 18+97 p. 12°, 60 c. Scott, F. & Co.

TERESA, *of Spain, St.*
Colvill, M. H. Saint Teresa of Spain. *$2.50 net. Dutton.

Terhune, Albert Payson.
The fighter. '10(Ja22) c. D. $1.50. Lovell.
New mayor; founded upon G: Broadhurst's successful play, "The man of the hour." '08(F1) c. D. 50 c.; pap., 25 c. J. S. Ogilvie.
World's great events: [world's history from battle of Marathon to Chinese Gordon.] '08(O3) c. il. D. **$1.20 net. Dodd.

Terhune, Anice.
Barnyard ballads for children; fifteen songs. '10(D24) F. bds., $1.25 net. Schirmer.
Chinese child's day. '10(F12) bds., *$1.25 net. Schirmer.
Colonial carols for children; fifteen songs. '10(D24) F. bds., $1.25 net. Schirmer.
Dutch ditties for children; fifteen songs, with piano accompaniment. '09(D18) il. F. bds., $1.25. Schirmer.

Terhune, Mrs. Mary Virginia Hawes, ["Marion Harland."]
Housekeeper's week. '08(D26) c. il. O. **$1.50 net. Bobbs-M.
Marion Harland's autobiography; the story of a long life. '10(Ap30) c. O. $2 net. Harper.
Where ghosts walk; the haunts of familiar characters in history and literature. New series. '10(N19) c. il. pors. O. $2.50 net. Putnam.

TERLINGUA, Tex.
See **Mercury.**

Terms and themes of chess problems. Blackburne, S. S. *$1 net. Dutton.
Terracing of farm lands. Ashe, W: W. 6 c. Uzzell.

Terrell, Edn. Holland.
Further genealogical notes on the Tyrrell-Terrell family of Virginia and its English and Norman-French progenitors. 2d ed.; with addenda and corrigenda. '09, [1910.] (F) 41 p. O. pap. (Priv. pr.) E. H. Terrell.

Terreve, Retsel, pseud.
See Broyles, Lester Everret.

Terrible Teddy and Peaceful Bill. Sayler, H. L. 50 c. Reilly & B.

TERRIERS.
See **Dog.**

Territorial government of the Old Northwest. McCarty, D. G. $2. State Hist., Ia.

TERRITORIAL WATERS.
See **Fish and fishing.**

Terrors of the Tiny Tads. Verbeck, G. 60 c. Cupples & L.

Terry, E: S., comp.
Laws of the various states concerning aliens, estates, descent and distribution, powers of attorney, wills, etc. '08(My.) c. 278 p. O. (Add. author for price.) E: S. Terry.

Terry, Ellen, [Mrs. Ja. Carew.]
Story of my life. '08(D19) c. pors. O. **$3.50 net. Doubleday, P.

Terry, Helen, ed.
French song and verse for children; with an introd. by P. A. Barnett. '08(F15) il. D. 50 c. Longmans.

Terry, Howard Leslie.
Waters from an Ozark spring. '09(N20) c. front. D. bds., $1. Badger.

Terry, Hubert L.
India-rubber and its manufacture; with chapters on gutta-percha and balata. '08 (Mr7) il. O. (Westminster ser.) *$2 net. Van Nostrand.

Terry, Milton Spenser.
Shinto cult: Christian study of the ancient religion of Japan. '10(D17) c. 16°, 30 c. Jennings.

Terry, Stewart Bruce.
Dynamics of organism and physics. '08 (My16) c. 12°. (Add. pubs. for price.) Terry.

Terry, T: Philip.
Terry's Mexico; hdbk. for travellers. '09 (O25) c. maps, plans, S. **$2.50 net. Houghton M.

Terry, Thdr. Brainard.
How to keep well and live long. '10(Ja29) c. il. 8°, $1. Farmer Co.

Tertiary mammal beds. Merriam, J: C. 50 c. Univ. of Cal.
Tesla high frequency coil. Haller, G: F. $1.25. Van Nostrand.
Tess of the D'Urbervilles. *See* Hardy, T:
Tess of the storm country. White, *Mrs.* G. M. $1.50. W. J. Watt.
Test of courage. Ross, H: M. $1.25. Benziger.
Test of three large reinforced concrete beams. Talbot, A. N. gratis. Univ. of Ill.
Test questions for law students. Baylies, E. (Add. pubs. for price.) M. Bender.
Testaments of the twelve patriarchs. Charles, R. H., *ed.* *$5.25 net. Macmillan.
Testimonium animae. Sihler, E. G. *$2.25 net. Stechert.
Testimony. Askew, *Mrs.* A. J. de C. L. $1.50. Lane.
Testing of Diana Mallory. Ward, *Mrs.* M. A. A. †$1.50. Harper.
Testing of material for construction. Unwin, W: C. $5 net. Longmans.

Testing of Olive Vaughan. Brebner, P. J. $1.50. Doscher.

Tests of coal and briquets as fuel for house-heating boilers. Randall, D. T: (Add. Superintendent for price.) U. S., Supt. of Docs.

Tests of life. Law, R. *$3 net. Scribner.

Tests on plain and reinforced concrete. Withey, M. O. 25 c. Univ. of Wis.

TETANUS.

Mohler, J:, *and* Eichhorn, A. Need of controlling and standardizing the manufacture of veterinary tetanus antitoxin. U. S., Supt. of Docs.

Tether (The). Brudno, E. S. †$1.50. Lippincott.

TETHER BALL.

See **Games.**

Teubner's (B. G.) mathematische wissenschaften. O. Stechert.

—Lorentz. Theory of electrons. *$2.50 net.

Texas. *Ct. of civil appeals.* Repts.; (A. E. Wilkinson, B. R. Webb and J. A. Martin.) v. 37. '08(Jl); v. 38 (Ag); v. 39, 40, 41 (O); v. 42-44 (D); v. 45. '09(Je); v. 46 (O); v. 47 (D); v. 48. '08(Je) v. 49-50 (N) c. O. shp., ea., *$2 net. Flood.

Texas. *Ct. of criminal appeals.* Repts.; (Rudolph Kleberg.) v. 47-51. '08(Ag); v. 52 (N); v. 53. '08, [1909.] (—); v. 54 (Ag); v. 55 (D); v. 56. '09, [1910.] (Ap); v. 57 (N) c. O. shp., ea., *$2 net. Flood.

Texas. Encyclopedic digest of repts. (civil cases); ed. by T: Johnson Michie. v. 1. '10(N) c. O. $7.50. Michie Co.

Texas. Instructions to juries in civil cases, including forms and approved precedents; by H. J. Passmore. '09, [1910.] (F) c. O. shp., $6. Gilbert Bk.

Texas. Laws; compilation of the laws and legal forms for the convenience of farmers, mechanics, merchants, bankers and lawyers; comp. by J. W. Fisher. '10(Jl) c. D. pap., $1. J. L. Wilson.

Texas. Notes on repts.; by Wa. Malins Rose; rev. and brought down to date by C: L. Thompson. Bk. 1. '10(S); Bk. 2, 3 (D) c. O. shp., ea., $7.50. Bancroft-W.

Texas. Supp. to Sayles' annot. civil statutes; by W. W. Herron. '08(O); '10(F) c. O. shp., ea., $4. Gilbert Bk.

Texas. Supp. to Willson's annot criminal statutes, by W. W. Herron. '10(Je) c. O. $2. Gilbert Bk.

Texas. *Supreme ct.* **Repts.; (A. E. Wilkinson.)** v. 99. '08(Jl); v. 100, 101. '09, [1910.] (F); v. 102 (My) c. O. shp., ea., $2. Flood.

TEXAS.

Adams, E. D. British interests and activities in Texas, 1838-1846. $1.50. Johns Hopkins.

Alvord, C: H. Dairy industry in Texas. Von Boeckmann-J.

Clark, R. C. Beginnings of Texas. 1684-1718. 75 c. Univ. of Tex.

Daffan, K. Texas hero stories. 50 c. B: H. Sanborn.

TEXAS.—*Continued.*

Houk, R. W. Authentication, acknowledgment and proof of written instruments under the laws which have been in force in Texas. $5.50. Bancroft-W.

Jackson, G: Sixty years in Texas. $1.50. G: Jackson.

Kittrell, N. G. Primer of the government of Texas. 40 c. Southern Pub. (Tex.)

Mally, F: W. Panhandle and Llano Estacado of Texas. Texas.

Pennybacker, *Mrs.* A. J. H. History of Texas for schools. 65 c. P. V. Pennybacker.

Phillips, W: B. Mineral resources of Texas. Texas.

Pioneer days in the Southwest from 1850 to 1879. $1.50. State Cap.

Polley, J. B: Hood's Texas Brigade. $3.50 net. Neale.

Potts, C: S. Railroad transportation in Texas. (Add. University for price.) Univ. of Tex.

Ramsdell, C: W: Reconstruction in Texas. $4 net; $2.50 net. Longmans.

Reese, R. A. Complete digest of Texas decisions. $25. Flood.

Ries, H. Clays of Texas. $2. Univ. of Tex.

Riley, B: F. Hist. of Baptists of Texas. **$1.50 net. Am. Bapt.

Rye, E. Quirt and the spur; vanishing shadows of the Texas frontier. $1.50. Conkey.

Santleben, A. Texas pioneer. $2 net. Neale.

Simkins, W: S. Administration of estates in Texas. $5.25. Von Boeckmann-J.

Snyder, J. J. Texas school lands; millions of acres to be sold by the state. 60 c. Von Boeckmann-J.

Sullivan, W. J. L. Twelve years in the saddle for law and order on the frontiers of Texas. $1.50. Von Boeckmann-J.

Udden, J. A. Report on a geological survey of the lands belonging to the New York and Texas Land Co., Ltd., in the upper Rio Grande embayment in Texas. 50 c. Augustana.

United States. *Dept. of Agriculture. Office of Experiment Stations.* Irrigation in Texas.

Van Demark, H. Texas in a nutshell. 25 c. Nutshell.

See also Corporations;—*also* Beaumont;—Dallas;—San Antonio;—South (The);—Waters Pierce case;—Wise County;—*also* Bailey, Joseph Weldon;—McDonald, W: L.

Texas Blue Bonnet. Jacobs, C. E. $1.50. L. C. Page.

Texas; Dept. of Agriculture bull. 8°. Texas; Von Boeckmann-J.

—Alvord. Dairy industry in Texas.

—Mally. Panhandle and Llano Estacado of Texas.

—Phillips. Mineral resources of Texas.

—Savage. Poultry culture in Texas.

Texas Library and Historical Commission circular. 12°. Von Boeckmann-J.

—Texas. Law governing the Texas State Library and the Texas Library and Historical Commission. 35 c.

Texas municipal corporation laws, annot.; by J. T. Sluder. '09(D) c. O. $5.50. Von Boeckmann-J.

TEXAS STATE LIBRARY, Austin, Tex.
Law governing the Texas State Library and the Texas Library and Historical Commission. '09(S) 7 p. 12°, (Texas Library and Historical Commission circular.) 35 c. Von Boeckmann-J.

Text-books of physical chemistry. See Longmans'.

Textile chemistry and dyeing. Olney, L: A. $3. Am. Sch. Corr.

TEXTILE FABRICS.
Dooley, W: H: Textiles for commercial industrial, evening and domestic art schools. $1. Heath.
Emmons, G: T. Chilkat blankets. $2. Am. Museum.
Lowell, Mass. City Library. Textiles; list of books rel. to textiles in the Lowell City Library. gratis. Lowell Lib.
Textile processes. $1.50. F. P. Bennett.
Umpleby, F. Textile design. $2. Am. Sch. Corr.
Watson, K. H. Textiles and clothing. $1.25. Am. Sch. Home Economics.
Whitman, William, & Co. Brief outline of the business of William Whitman & Co. '10(Ap) c. 95 p. il. 8°. (Priv. pr.) W: Whitman.
See also Carpets;—Chemistry;—Cotton;—Dyeing; — Rugs; — Tapestry; — Weaving; — Wool; Woolen spinning.

Textile processes; collection of essays on processes in woolen, worsted and cotton manufacturing; from the *American Wool and Cotton Reporter.* '10(Je11) c. pors. O. $1.50. F. P. Bennett.

Textile World Record. Kinks for boss weavers, from the questions and answers dept. of the *Textile World Record;* comp. and ed. by Clarence Hutton. '10(Ag27) c. il. 16°, (*Textile World Record* kink books.) 75 c. Lord & N.

Textile World Record. Kinks for cotton superintendents; comp. from the questions and answers department of the *Textile World Record* for its subscribers only. [1910.] (Mr) c. '09. 88 p. 16°, (*Textile World Record* kink books.) (Sold to subscribers of *Textile World Record* only.] Lord & N.

Textile World Record. Kinks for wool and worsted finishers; comp. from the questions and answers department of the *Textile World Record* for its subscribers only. '10(Ja8) c. 16°, (*Textile World Record* kink bks.) 75 c. Lord & N.

Textile World Record. Kinks for wool and worsted superintendents; from questions and answers dept. of the *Textile World Record;* comp. and ed. by Clarence Hutton. '10(D17) c. 16°, (*Textile World Record* kink books.) 75 c. Lord & N.

Textile World Record. Kinks on cost finding in knitting mills; comp. from the questions and answers department of the *Textile World Record* for its subscribers only. [1910.] (Je) c. 94 p. il. 16°, (*Textile World Record* kink books.) 75 c. net. Lord & N.

Texts and studies; contributions to Biblical and patristic literature; ed. by Dean Jos. Armitage Robinson, D.D. '10(Ap) 8°. Putnam.
Contents: v. 1, no. 1, Apology of Aristides on behalf of the Christians, from a Syriac ms. preserved on Mount Sinai, ed. with an introd. and tr. by J. Rendel Harris, with appendix cont. the main portion of the orig. Greek text by J. Armitage Robinson, *D.D.*, 2d ed., $1.75; no. 2, Passion of S. Perpetua, newly ed. from mss. with introd. and notes, together with appendix cont. the orig. Latin text of the Scillitan martyrdom, by J. Armitage Robinson, *D.D.*, o. p.; no. 3, Lord's prayer in the early church, by F. H. Chase, *D.D.*, o. p.; no. 4, Fragments of Heracleon, newly ed. from mss. with introd. and notes by A. E. Brooke, $1.75; v. 2, no. 1, Codex Bezae: study of so-called Western text of the New Testament, by J. Rendel Harris, o. p.; no. 2, Testament of Abraham, Greek text now first ed. with introd. and notes by Montague Rhodes James, $1.75; no. 3, Apocrypha anecdota, collection of 13 Apocryphal books and fragments now first ed. from mss. by M. R. James, $2.60; v. 3, no. 1, Book of rules of Tyconius, newly ed. from the mss. with introd. and examination into the text of the Biblical quotations by F. C. Burkitt, $1.60; no. 2, Fourth book of Ezra, Latin version ed. from the mss. by Rob. L. Bensly, with introd. by M. R. James, $1.50; no. 3, Euthaliana: studies of the Euthalius, Codex H of the Pauline epistles and the Armenian version by J. Armitage Robinson, *D.D.*, $1.25; v. 4, no. 1, Athanasian Creed, and its early commentaries, by A. E. Burn, $1.75; no. 2, Coptic Apocryphal Gospels, translations together with the texts of some of them by Forbes Robinson, $3; no. 3, Old Latin and the Itala, with appendix cont. text of the S. Gallen Palimpsest of Jeremiah, by F. C. Burkitt, $1; v. 5, no. 1, Apocrypha anecdota: second ser., by M. R. James, $2.50; no. 2, Clement of Alexandria: "quis dives salvetur," re-edited by P. M. Barnard, $1; no. 3, Hymn of the soul, cont. in the Syriac acts of St. Thomas, re-edited with English tr. by Anthony Ashley Bevan, 60 c.; no. 4, Codex Purpureus Petropolitanus, text of Codex N of the Gospels, ed. with introd. and appendix by H. S. Cronin, *D.D.*, $1.60; no. 5, Biblical text of Clement of Alexandria in four Gospels and Acts of the Apostles, collected and ed. by P. M. Barnard, with introd. by F. C. Burkitt, $1.25; v. 6, no. 1, Lausiac hist. of Palladius, 1: critical discussion, together with notes on early Egyptian monachism, by Cuthbert Butler, $2.50; no. 2, Lausiac hist. of Palladius, II: Greek text, ed. with introd. and notes by Cuthbert Butler, $3: v. 7, no. 1, Meaning of Homoousios in the "Constantinople Creed," by J. F. Bethune-Baker, $1; no. 2, S. Epharim's quotations from the Gospels, collected and arr. by F. Crawford Burkitt, $1; no. 3, Codex I of the Gospels and its allies, by Kirsopp Lake, with front., $2.50; no. 4, Study of Ambrosiaster, by Alex. Souter, $2.25; v. 8, no. 1, Liturgical homilies of Narsai, by R. H. Connolly, tr. into English, $2.

Texts and studies of the Jewish Theological Seminary of America. 8°. (Add. pubs. for price.) Jewish Theological.
—Ginzberg. Geonica. 2 v.
—Yerushalmi fragments from the Genizah.

Thacher, Edn.
Directions for using Thacher's calculating instrument. '10(My) c. 74 p. 8°, 75 c. Keuffel.

Thacker, May Dixon.
Strength of the weak. '10(D31) c. D. $1.50. B'way Pub.

Thackeray, H: St. John.
Grammar of the Old Testament in Greek according to the Septuagint. v. 1, Introd., orthography and accidence. '09, [1910.] (F) 12°, *$2.75 net. Putnam.
Principal authorities (15 p.).

Thackeray, Lance.
Light side of Egypt. '08(N21) il. obl. 8°, *$2.50 net. Macmillan.

Thackeray, W: Makepeace.
Works. De luxe ed. 15 v. '10(N) il. levant, $45. Crowell.
Works. 10 v. New imperial lib. ed. '10 (D) il. 8°, ea., $1.25; hf. cf., $2.25; New il. sterling ed., ea., $1. (Sets only.) Estes.
Works. De luxe ed. 14 v. '10(D) 16°, ea., mor., $1.50 net. (Sets only.) Nelson.
[Works;] arranged and ed. by G: E: Bateman Saintsbury. In 20 v. v. 1-17. '08 (O3) il. 12°, (Oxford Thackeray). ea., 80 c.; limp leath., $1.25; lambskin, $1.50; per set, $16; limp leath., $25; lambskin, $30; India paper ed., in 17 v., lambskin, ea., $1.75; per set, $29.75; polished lambskin, $35 (sold only in sets); red rutland, $45 (sold only in sets). Oxford Univ.
Ballads. '10(D31) front. 32°, (Ariel booklets.) leath., 75 c., boxed. Putnam.
Christmas books; introd. by Wa. Jerrold. '09(Ap3) 16°, (Everyman's lib.) *35 c. net: leath., *70 c. net. Dutton.
Complete works. In 32 v. v. 1-12. [Bedford ed.] '09(N) il. 8°, ea., $3.50. 1000 copies.) Sproul.
English humorists; ed., with an introd. and notes, by J. C. Castleman. '10(F12) c. por. T. (Macmillan's pocket Am. and Eng. classics.) **25 c. net. Macmillan.
Four Georges; sketches of manners, morals, court and town life; with preface by Gordon Home. '10(D17) il. col. pors. 8°, $2 net. Macmillan.
Henry Esmond; ed. by Wa. L. Bissell. '08(Mr7) c. por. D. (Eclectic Eng. classics.) 60 c. Am. Bk.
History of Henry Esmond. '08(O10) il. D. (Bowman's illustrated lib. of world-favorite books.) $1. Bowman.
History of Henry Esmond. '08(O17) 16°, (Best books ser.) leath., *$1 net. Dutton.
History of Henry Esmond; ed., with introd. and notes, by T. C. Snow and W: Snow; with introd. by G: Saintsbury. '10 (Mr26) D. 90 c. Oxford Univ.
The Newcomes; with bibliographical note by Wa. Jerrold. 2 v. '10(D10) c. (Everyman's lib.) ea., 35 c. net; leath., 70 c. net. Dutton.
Pendennis; introd. by W. Jerrold. In 2 v. '10(Ap2) 16°, (Everyman's lib.) ea., 35 c. net; leath., 70 c. net. Dutton.
Rose and the ring; told by Amy Steedman. '08(D19) il. 16°, (Told to the children ser.) 50 c. Dutton.
Rose and the ring. '08(N21) il. 16°, *50 c. net. Macmillan.
Rose and the ring. '09(O9) il. O. $1.25. Stokes.
Sense and sentiment of Thackeray; comp. by Mrs. C: Mason Fairbanks. '09(O2) c. por. S. leath., **75 c. net, boxed. Harper.
Thackeray; [selections;] ed. by G. K. Chesterton. '10(Ap9) 12°, (Masters of literature.) $1.10 net. Macmillan.
Thackeray pocket book; comp. by Adelaide Rawnsley Fossard. '08(D19) limp leath., **75 c. net. Scribner.

Thackeray, W: Makepeace.—*Continued.*
Vanity fair; introd. by Whitelaw Reid. '08 (Mr7) 16°, (Everyman's lib.) *35 c. net; leath., *70 c. net. Dutton.
Wisdom of Thackeray. [1910.] (D) sq. 16°, (Wisdom ser.) $1 net. Brentano's.

THACKERAY, William Makepeace.
Mudge, I. G., *and* Sears, M. E. Thackeray dict. $3. Dutton.
Wilson, J. G. Thackeray in the United States. *$3.50 net. Dodd.

Thaïs. *See* France, Anatole, *pseud.*

THALATTOSAURIA.
Merriam, J: C. Notes on the osteology of the *Thalattosaurian* genus *Nectosaurus.* 10 c. Univ. of Cal.

THALLIUM.
Morden, G. W. Detemination of thallium in the electrolytic way. Univ. of Penn.

Thames (The) and its story from the Cotswolds to the Nore. New ed. In 2 v. '10 (Jl2) il. maps, $1.50 net. Cassell.

THAMES RIVER, England.
Mitton, G. E. The Thames. $1.25. Estes.

Thanatopsis. *See* Bryant, W: Cullen.

Thanet, Octave, [pseud. for Alice French.]
By inheritance. '10(Ap2) c. il. D. $1.50. Bobbs-M.

THANKSGIVING DAY.
Hughes, E. H. Thanksgiving sermons. *$1 net. Eaton & M.; Jennings.

That affair in Philadelphia. Darby, *Mrs.* S. $1. B'way Pub.
That boy o' mine. Robinson, N. H. *75 c. net. Pub. Ho. of M. E. Ch., So.
That freshman. Catrevas, C. $1.50. Appleton.
That gay prodigal: kiss in romance and history, by the author of some letters of Alfred Henry. '09(My) 60 c.; pap., 40 c.; limp leath., $1. Informant.
That girl. Turner, E. 75 c. McKay.
That man Donaleitis. Seebach, M. R. $1.25. Lutheran Pub.
That man from Wall Street. Everett, *Mrs.* R. $1.50. G: T. Long.
That other hand upon the helm. Goss, C: F. 75 c. Jennings.
That pup. Butler, E. P. †50 c. McClure.
That rock garden of ours. Hulme, F: E: **$3 net. Jacobs.
That same old lover. Abbott, S. W. 50 c. B. Castello.
"That they all may be one"; a plea for the reunion of Christians. '08(Ag22) c. D. *$1 net. Franklin Press Co.
That ye may know. Keppel, D: *35 c. net. Eaton & M.

Thatcher, E:
Simple soldering. '10(Ag6) c. il. 12°, 50 c.; pap., 25 c. Spon.

Thaw, Alex. Blair.
Paestum, and other poems. '09(D4) D. *$1 net. Brentano's.

Thaw, Mrs. Mary Copley.
Secret unveiled; [criticism of Thaw trial.] '09(N) c. 22 p. por. pap., 25 c. G. A. Thompson.

THAW CASE.
Thaw, *Mrs.* M. C. Secret unveiled; [criticism of Thaw trial.] 25 c. G. A. Thompson.

Thayer, Gerald Handerson.
Concealing-coloration in the animal kingdom; exposition of the laws of disguise through color and pattern; with an introd. essay by A. H. Thayer. '10(F19) il. 4°, $7. Macmillan.

Thayer, Ja. Bradley.
Legal essays. '08. il. O. *$3.50 net. Boston Bk.

Thayer, J: Adams.
Astir; publisher's life story. '10(Jl9) c. D. $1.20 net. Small.

Thayer, W: Makepeace.
From log cabin to the White House: life of James A. Garfield; with eulogy by Hon. Ja. G. Blaine. '09(Mr27) c. por. 12°, (Log cabin to White House ser.) 50 c. Hurst.
Tact, push, and principle. '09(Mr27) c. 12°, 50 c. Hurst.

Thayer, W: Roscoe.
Italica: studies in Italian life and letters. '08(My2) c. O. **$1.50 net. Houghton M.
Short history of Venice. '08(D12) maps, 12°, *$1.50 net. Houghton M.

—, and Warren, Winslow.
Commemorative exercises in connection with the erection of a memorial tablet to George Sewall Boutwell in Groton Cemetery, May 15, 1908; poem by W: Roscoe Thayer; address by Hon. Winslow Warren. '08(D5) O. pap., gratis. W. Warren.

THEATRE.
Albright, V. E. Shakesperian stage. *$1.50 net. Lemcke.
American stage of to-day. $2.50. Collier.
Amusement situation in the city of Boston. 10 c. Twentieth Century.
Archer, W:, *and* Barker, H. G. Scheme and estimates for a national theatre. $2.50. Duffield.
Cahn, J. Official theatrical guide. $1. J. Cahn.
Cashin's Theatre Ticket Office. Boston theatres and halls, with hist. notes. 25 c. W. B. Jones.
Eaton, W. P. At the New Theatre and others. $1.50 net. Small.
Faxon, F: W., *ed.* Dramatic index for 1909; covering articles and illustrations concerning the stage and its players in the periodicals of America and England. $3.50 net. Boston Bk.
Fleay, F: G. Chronicle hist. of the London stage, 1559-1642. *$6 net. Stechert.
Grau, R. Business man in the amusement world; volume of progress in the field of the theatre. $5. B'way Pub.
Hamilton, C. M. Theory of the theatre and other principles of dramatic criticism. $1.50 net. Holt.
Howe, P. P. Repertory theatre. $1 net. M. Kennerley.
Irving, *Sir* H: B. Theatre in relation to the state. 50 c. E. H. Bacon.
Mackaye, P. W. Playhouse and the play. **$1.25 net. Macmillan.

THEATRE.—*Continued.*
Morton, C. Art of theatrical make-up. *$2.50 net. Macmillan.
Rennert, H. A. **Spanish stage in the time of Lope de Vega. *$3 net. Hispanic Soc.**
Ross, C. Lady of the Blackfriars; or, the old play. $5. C. Ross.
Schneider, N. H. Model vaudeville theatre. 25 c. Spon.
Stuart, D. C. Stage decoration in France in the Middle Ages. $1.50 net. Macmillan.
See also Actors and actresses; — Drama and dramatists;—Opera; — Plays;—*also* Blackfriars Theatre;—Shakespeare, William.

THEBERTON, Suffolk, Eng.
Doughty, H. M. Chronicles of Theberton, a Suffolk village. $2.50 net. Macmillan.

Theft. London, J. $1.25 net. Macmillan.

Theiler, Rev. H:
Candle as a symbol and sacramental in the Catholic church; tr. from the German by Rev. J. F. Lang. '09(S4) c. S. 50 c. Pustet.
Holy water and its significance for Catholics tr. from the German by Rev. J. F. Lang; with a few scriptural and historical insertions by the translator. '09 (Je19) 50 c. Pustet.

Their day in court. Pollard, P. $3. Neale.
Their hearts' desire. Perry, F. F. *$2 net. Dodd.

THEISM.
See God.

Thekla. Higgins, A. C. $1. Badger.
Theme-book in English composition. Hitchcock, A. M. 50 c. Holt.

Theobald, W: H:
Defrauding the government; true tales of smuggling. '08(D5) c. por. 12°, $1.50. Myrtle.

"Theocratus," pseud.
Legacy of a man who wanted to do his duty. pt. 1. '09(My8) c. O. pap., 50 c. Corona Pub.

THEOCRITUS.
Kerlin, R. T: Theocritus in English literature. $1.50. J. P. Bell.
Leutner, W. G: The article in Theocritus. gratis. Johns Hopkins.

Theocritus and Virgil [Lat. Virgilius] Maro, Publius.
The idylls of Theocritus and the Eclogues of Virgil; tr. into Eng. verse by C. S. Calverley; with an introd. by R. Y. Tyrrell. '08(Jl11) 12°, (York lib.) *80 c. net; leath., *$1.25 net. Macmillan.

Theodora's husband. Mack, L. $1.50. Lane.
Theodosia Ernest. Dayton, A. C. *75 c. net. Bapt. Bk.
Theodosia, the first gentlewoman of her time. Pidgin, C: F. *$2.50 net; *$3 net. C. M. Clark.

Theodul, Carl.
Let the new nation arise; treatise on the subject of purification and the gathering of the purified. '08, [1909.] (My) c. 157 p. 12°, $1. Balance.

Theognis. Elegies of Theognis and other elegies included in the Theognidean Sylloge; rev. text based on a new collation of the Mutinensis MS.; with introd., commentary, and appendices by T. Hudson-Williams. '10(O8) 12°, $2.25 net. Macmillan.

Theological translation lib. O. Putnam.
—Haering. Ethics of Christian life. *$3 net.
—Harnack. Mission and expansion of Christianity in the first three centuries. *$7 net.
—Pfleiderer. Primitive Christianity. In 4 v. v. 2, 3. ea., $3 net.
—Schubert. Outlines of church history. *$3 net.

THEOLOGY.

Brooke, S. A: Theology in the English poets: Cowper, Coleridge, Wordsworth, Burns. 35 c. net; 70 c. net. Dutton.

Carter, S: T. Wanted—a theology. **75 c. net. Funk.

Chrysostom John, *Brother*. Manual of Christian doctrine. $1. McVey.

Classical Conference, Ann Arbor, Mich. Value of humanistic, particularly classical, studies as a preparation for the study of theology. Univ. of Mich.

Cunningham, W: Cure of souls; lectures on pastoral theology. *$1.10 net. Putnam.

Davies, E. O. Prolegomena to systematic theology. *$1.25 net. Doran.

De Laurence, L. W: God, the Bible, truth and Christian theology. $3.50. De Laurence, S.

Edghill, E. A. Faith and fact; study of Ritschlianism. $1.60 net. Macmillan.

Egerton, H. Liberal theology and the ground of faith. *$1.25 net. Dutton.

Fairbairn, A. M. Studies in religion and theology. *$3.50 net. Macmillan.

Gardner, P. Modernity and the churches. $1.50 net. Putnam.

Gore, C: New Theology and the old religion. *$2 net. Dutton.

Hall, F. J. Dogmatic theology. In 10 v. v. 2-4. ea., $1.50 net. Longmans.

Hauskins, J. E. New world: theological treatise. (Add. author for price.) J. E. Hauskins.

Lyman, E. W. Theology and human problems. $1 net. Scribner.

MacColl, A. Working theology. **75 c. net. Scribner.

Mallock, W: H. Doctrine and doctrinal disruption: examination of the intellectual position of the Church of England. *$1.50 net. Longmans.

Micou, R: W. Manual of fundamental theology. (Add. author for price.) R: W. Micou.

Miller, A. Problem of theology in modern life and thought. *$1.25 net. Doran.

Mozley, J. B. Lectures and other theological papers. *$1.25 net. Longmans.

Nave, O. J. Theology for young people. $1.25. College Assoc. Pub.

Nuelsen, J: L: Some recent phases of German theology. *75 c. net. Jennings.

Orr, J. Sidelights on Christian doctrine. *$1.50 net. Armstrong.

THEOLOGY.—*Continued.*

Pfleiderer, O. Development of theology in Germany since Kant. *$2.75 net. Macmillan.

Pourrat, P. Theology of the sacraments. $1.50 net. Herder.

Roberts, B. H:, *comp.* **Seventy's course in theology.** (Add. pub. for price.) **Deseret News.**

Slater, T: Short hist. of moral theology. *50 c. net. Benziger.

Strong, A: H. Outlines of systematic theology. **$2.50 net.—Systematic theology. 3 v. ea., **$2.50 net. Am. Bapt.

White, H. New theology. $1.25. B'way Pub.

Wolford, N. D. Popular manual of the-

See also Agnosticism;—Apostles;—Apostolic succession;—Atonement; — Baptism;—Bible;—Calvinism;—Catechisms;—Catholic church;—Christianity;— Church;—Church history;—Confirmation;—Conscience; — Conversion; — Creeds;—Death;—Ethics; — Evil;—Evolution;—Faith;—Fathers of the church;—Future life;—God;—Holy Spirit;—Jesus Christ; — Jews; — Lord's supper;—Miracles;—Missions and missionaries;—Mysticism;—Penance;—Philosophy ; Prayers; Protestantism; — Religion; — Religion and science;—Repentance; — Revivals; — Sacraments;—Salvation;—Sermons; — Sin;—Skepticism;—Spiritualism;—Sunday; — Temptation; —Trinity;—Worship.

Theophrastus.

Theophrasti Characteres; ed. by H. Diels. '09(Ag7) 8°, (Oxford classical texts.) 90 c.; pap., 75 c. Oxford Univ.

Characters. '09(Mr27) 8°, *$2.25 net. Macmillan.

Theorem or teleology of spiritualism. Wiltse, M. B. 75 c. Eddy County Provost.

Theoretical chemistry. Nernst, W. *$4.50 net. Macmillan.

Theoretical mechanics. Smith, P. F. $2.50. Ginn.

Theories of knowledge. Walker, L. J. $2.75. Longmans.

Theories of parallelism. Frankland, W: B. 90 c. net. Putnam.

Theory and practice of ancient education. Hobhouse, W. *$1 net. Stechert.

Theory and practice of infant feeding. Chapin, H: D. *$2.25 net. Wood.

Theory and practice of modern framed structure. Johnson, J: B. $3 net. Wiley.

Theory and practice of teaching art. Dow, A. W. $1. Teachers' Coll.

Theory and practice of the English government. Moran, T: F. **$1.20 net. **Longmans.**

Theory of crane design. '08(D5) c. diagrs., 8°, (Machinery's reference ser.) pap., 25 c. Indust.

Theory of human progression. Dove, P. E: Blanchard.

Theory of ions: consideration of its place in biology and therapeutics. Tibbles, W: *$1 net. Hoeber.

Theory of mind. March, J: L. **$2 net. Scribner.

Theory of the theatre. Hamilton, C. M. $1.50 net. Holt.

Theory of the universe. Sweet, M. P. $1. M. P. Sweet.

Theosophical Society in America. Primer of theosophy: very condensed outline issued by the American section of the Theosophical Society. '09, [1910.] (Ap) 128 p. il. pors. 16°, 15 c. Theosophical Soc.

THEOSOPHY.

Besant, *Mrs.* A. W. Karma, once more. 15 c. Manas Press.

Bjerregaard, C. H. A. Inner life. $2. Theo. Pub. Co.

Bragdon, C. Beautiful necessity; seven essays on theosophy and architecture. $2. —Theosophy and the Theosophical Society, 25 c. Manas Press.

Curtiss, F. H., *ed.* Letters from the teacher (of the Order of 15) transmitted by Rahmea, priestess of the flame. $1.10. Curtiss.

Kabbala denudata. Kabbalah unveiled. $3.50. Theo. Pub. Co.

Kingsford, A. B., *and* Maitland, E: Perfect way; or, the finding of Christ. $2.50. Theo. Pub. Co.

M. C., *pseud.* Light on the path: treatise written for the personal use of those who are ignorant of the Eastern wisdom. 75 c. Theo. Pub. Co.

Marsland, A. E. First principles of esoterism. $1 net; $1.50 net. Oriental Esoteric

Ramakrishna. Gospel. $1.50; $3. Vedanta.

Rogers, J. Living fire, the soul power of the universe. $1.50. Occult Pub. Co.

Rogers, L. W. Beyond the border, 10 c.—Invisible world about us, 10 c.—Karma: nature's law of justice, 10 c.—Soul powers, 10 c.—Theosophical questions answered, 15 c.—Universal brotherhood: lecture on fundamental relationship of human beings to each other and to the animal kingdom, 10 c.—What theosophy is, 5 c. Theosophical Bk.

Steiner, R. **Initiation and its results.** $1.25.—Way of initiation; or, how to attain knowledge of the higher worlds. $1; 75 c. Macoy Pub.

Steiner, R. Theosophy. $1. Rand, McN. & Co.

Taylor, I. E. Essays on theosophy. *75 c. net. Macmillan.

Theosophical Society in America. Primer of theosophy. 15 c. Theosophical Soc.

See also Conduct of life;—Evolution;—Future life;—Reincarnation;—*also* Blavatsky, *Mme.* H. P. H.H.

THEOTOCOPULI, Domenico.
See Greco, El.

Therapeutic dietetics. Hazeldine, N. F. W $1. N. F. W. Hazeldine.

THERAPEUTICS.
See Medicine;—Surgery.

Therapeutics of light vibration. Woodruff, W: L. *$1.50 net. J. F. Elwell.

Therapeutics of mineral springs and climates. Yeo, I. B. $3.50 net. Funk.

There is no unbelief. Case, *Mrs.* E. Y. 50 c. Somerville.

There she blows! Wheeler, J. C. **$1.20 net. Dutton.

THERMAL WATERS.
See Radio-activity.

THERMOCHEMISTRY.
See Chemistry.

THERMODYNAMICS.
See Heat.

Thermodynamics of the steam-engine. Peabody, C. H. $5. Wiley.

THERMO-ELECTRICITY.
See Electricity.

THERMOTHERAPY.
See Radiotherapy.

"Therold Archer Knowlton." Zeigen, F. $2. Conkey.

Thesaurus dictionary of the English language. March, F. A. (Add. pubs. for price.) Stanley & W.

Thesaurus of English words and phrases. Roget, P: M. *$1.60 net. Longmans.

THESSALONIANS, Epistle to.
See Bible.

They and I. Jerome, K. J. †$1.50. Dodd.

They must. Kutter. H. $1. Co-operative Pr. Co.

Thibaudeau, Antoine Claire, Comte.
Bonaparte and the Consulate; tr. and ed. by G. K. Fortescue. '08(Je13) il. 8°, *$3.25 net. Macmillan.

Thibault, Jaques Anatole.
See France, Anatole, *pseud.*

Thief of virtue. Phillpotts, E. †$1.50. Lane.

Thieme, Hugo P., and Effinger, J: R.
French grammar; with exercises and supp. reading. '08(Ag1) 12°, *$1.25 net. Macmillan.

Thieme, Ulrich, Becker, Felix, and others, eds.
Allgemeines lexikon der bildenden künstler, von der antike bis zur gegenwart. [In 20 v.] v. 2. '08(D5) Q. *$8.75 net. Stechert.

Thierry, Jacques Nicholas Augustin.
Les Normands en Angleterre et en France; from La conquête de l'Angleterre par les Normands; ed. by A. H. Smith. '09 (Mr6) D. (Oxford modern French ser.) 60 c. Oxford Univ.

Thimm, C. A., comp.
Bibliography of trypanosomiasis. '10(Ja22) O. pap., *$1.25 net. Stechert.

Thin paper ser. of popular classics. See Lippincott's.

Thin Santa Claus. Butler, E. P. †50 c. Doubleday, P.

Things Korean. Allen, H. N. *$1.25 net. Revell.

Things new and old. *See* Thomas Aquinas, *St.*

Things seen ser. 16° and 24°. *75 c. net; leath., *$1 net. Dutton.
—Chitty. Things seen in China.
—Hartley. Things seen in Spain.
—Holland. Things seen in Japan.
—Roche. Things seen in Holland.

Things that remain. Atkins, G. G. $1.25. G. G. Atkins.

Things worth knowing about Oneida County. Canfield, W. W. *$1 net. T: J. Griffiths.

Things worth while. Higginson, T: W. *50 c. net. B: W. Huebsch.

THINKING.
See Logic;—Philosophy;—Psychology.

Thinking above what is written. Haldeman, I: M. 10 c. C: C. Cook.

Thinking heavenward. De Waters, *Mrs.* L. S. 50 c. L. S. De Waters.
Thinking Machine on the case. Futrelle, J. †$1.50. Appleton.
Thinking process. Harvey, N. A. 40 c. N. A. Harvey.
THIRD ARMY CORPS UNION.
See Civil War (United States).
Third circle. Norris, F. †$1.50. Lane.
Third degree. Klein, C: †$1.50. G: W. Dillingham.
Third French Republic. Lawton, F: *$3.50 net. Lippincott.
Thirteen good animals. Kellogg, E. 75 c. Davis Press.
Thirteenth, greatest of centuries. Walsh, J. J. $2.50. Cath. Summer Sch.
Thirty chapters on static electricity. Monell, S: H. *$2 net. W: R. Jenkins.
Thirty favorite paintings, by leading American artists: Maxfield Parrish, Frederic Remington, H: Hunt, [and others.] '09 (Je5) c. il. f°, $1 50. Collier.
Thirty new Christmas dialogues and plays. Irish, M. 30 c. Flanagan.
Thirty years at the superintendent's desk. Pepper, J: R. 25 c. Revell.
Thirty years from home. Leech, S: $3.25. Abbatt.
Thirty years in hell. Fresenborg, —. $1. L. J. King.
This misery of boots. Wells, H. G: *50 c. net. Ball Pub. Co.
"This, my son." Bazin, R. †$1.25. Scribner.
This, that and the other. Ashmore, D: N. $1; 75 c. D: N. Ashmore.
This then is a William Morris book. Hubbard, E. $2. Roycrofters.
THOBURN, *Bp.* James Mills.
Crawford, W: H:, *ed.* Thoburn and India. *$1 net. Eaton & M.
Thoburn, Jos. Bradfield, and Holcomb, I: Mason.
Hist. of Oklahoma. '08(N) c. 11+266+13 p. il. 8°, $1.10. Doub.
Thom, C:
Camembert cheese problems in the United States. '09(D) 54 p. il. 8°, (U. S., Dept. of Agriculture, Bu. of Animal Industry, bull.) pap. (Add. Superintendent for price.)
—, and Collins, Archie F:
Electric telegraph: manual of complete instruction in the principles, mechanism, and practice of the art of sending and receiving telegraphic messages. pt. 1, The electric telegraph, by C: Thom; pt. 2, Wireless telegraphy, by A. F: Collins. '08(Ap11) c. il. por. dgrs., 8°, $1. Am. Sch. Corr.
Thomälen, Adolf.
Text-book of electrical engineering; tr. from the German by G. W. O. Howe. 2d ed. '09(N20) il. O. *$4.20 net. Longmans.
Thomann, Gallus.
American beer; glimpses of its hist. and description of its manufacture. '09, [1910.] (Mr) 104 p. 8°, 50 c. U. S. Brewers' Assoc.
Thomas, A. R. Goring-.
See Goring-Thomas, A. R.
Thomas, Addison C:
Roosevelt among the people; being an acct. of the fourteen thousand mile journey from ocean to ocean of Theodore Roosevelt. '10(Ag13) c. il. pors. D. $1. Walter.
Thomas, Alsen Franklin.
Slavery of progress; its causes and its cure. '10(My7) c. 12°, $1. Neale.
Thomas, Ambrose Milton.
Plain economic facts for all people. '09 (My8) c. 12°, $3. Cochrane Pub.
Thomas, Armstrong.
Prayers and instructions with forms. '08 (Jl) c. 42+539 p. 8°. (Add. pub. for price.) Lord Balto. Pr.
Procedure in justice cases, including forms with supplement. '09(Je) c. 41+160 p. O. (Add. pubs. for price.) Lord Balto. Pr.
Thomas, A:
Witching hour. '08(O24) c. il. O. †$1.50. Harper.
Thomas, Calvin.
Anthology of German literature. '09(D18) c. 8°, (Heath's modern language ser.) $2.25. Heath.
History of German literature. '09(Mr20) c. D. (Short histories of literatures of the world.) **$1.50 net. Appleton.
Thomas, Carl Clapp.
Steam turbines. 4th ed., rev. and enl. '10(O22) figs. il. 8°, $4. Wiley.
Thomas, C: Swain.
How to teach English classics; suggestions for study, questions, comments, and composition assignments on the books for careful study on the list of college entrance requirements. '10(D10) c. 16°, (Riverside literature ser.) 15 c. Houghton M.
—, and Howe, Will D:
Composition and rhetoric. '08(S19) O. $1.20. Longmans.
Thomas, D: Yancey.
See Reynolds, J: Hugh.
Thomas, Edith Matilda.
Guest at the gate. '09(N6) c. D. $1.50. Badger.
Thomas, E:
Digest of process and composition and allied decisions in patent cases. '08(N) c. blank interleaved, O. *$1.50 net. Winston.
Thomas, E:
Rest and unrest: [essays.] '10(Ap23) 12°, $1 net. Dutton.
Richard Jefferies; his life and work. '09 (O2) il. O. *$3 net. Little, B. & Co.
Windsor Castle. '10(Jl30) col. il. O. (Beautiful England ser.) bds., $1.25, boxed. Estes.
—, ed. British country life in autumn and winter. '09(D) il. in col. 8°, *$3.75 net. Doran.
British country life in spring and summer. '09(D) il. in col. *$3.75 net. Doran.
Some British birds. '09(D) il. in col. *$2 net. Doran.
Some British butterflies and insects. '09 (D) il. in col. 8°, *$2 net. Doran.

Thomas, Fk. W.
Cost accounting in a bank. '10(N19) c. por. 8°, $2. Bankers Pub. (O.)

Thomas, G: Clifford.
Autograph letters and autographs of the signers of the Declaration of Independence in the possession of George Clifford Thomas. '08(My9) c. pors. 8°. [priv. pr.] G: C. Thomas.

Thomas, Harry H.
Gardening difficulties solved. '10(O1) 8°, 60 c. net Cassell.
Gardening in town and suburb. '08(Ap4) il. 12°, $1. Longmans.
Ideal garden. '10(Je4) col. il. D. $2 net. Cassell.
Little gardens. '08(D5) il. *40 c. net. Cassell.
Sweet peas and how to grow them. '09 (Ap24) il. D. *50 c. net. Cassell.

Thomas, Herbert H., and MacAlister, Donald A.
Geology of ore deposits. '09(O2) figs. D. (Arnold's geological ser.) $2.50. Longmans.

Thomas, Isaiah.
Diary of Isaiah Thomas, 1805-1828; ed., with introd. and notes, by B: T: Hill. In 2 v. '10(Jl16) il. por. map, 4°, (Transactions and collections of the Amer. Antiquarian Society.) ea., $2.50. Am. Antiquarian.

Thomas, J. Evans.
Old Testament in the light of the religion of Babylonia and Assyria. '09(Jl17) 12°, *$1.40 net. Macmillan.

Thomas, J. Morriston.
Idylls of the beautiful. '08(O3) c. D. $1. J. M. Thomas.

Thomas, J: M., D.D.
Christian faith and the Old Testament. '08 (Ap18) c. D. **$1 net. Crowell.

Thomas, Jos.
Lippincott's new medical dictionary; ed. by H: Ware Cattell. '10(O8) il. 8°, limp leath., $5 net. Lippincott.

Thomas, Jos. Dawson, comp. and ed.
The Osages; their names, allotment, numbers, ages and sex. '10(Jl2) c. O. pap., with maps, 50 c. J. D. Thomas.

Thomas, M. M.
Captain Phil; boy's experience in the western army during the War of the Rebellion. '10(N5) c. il. D. $1.50. Holt.

Thomas, Marion, ed.
Promotion exercises for the beginners' and primary grades of the Sunday-school. '09(Je19) O. pap., 5 c. Presb. Bd.

Thomas, Northcote Whitridge.
Kinship organizations and group marriage in Australia. '08(F8) 8°, *$2 net. Putnam.
—, ed. *See* Joyce, T. Athol.

Thomas, Ralph Wlimer.
Manual of debate. '10(Ap30) c. D. 80 c. Am. Bk.

Thomas, Reuen.
Glad tidings: selection from the sermons. '08, [1909.] (F) c. 5+293 p. 8°, *$1.25 net. Pilgrim Press.

Thomas, Rowland.
Little gods: masque of the Far East. '09 (Mr27) c. il. D. †$1.50. Little, B. & Co.

Thomas, T. H.
French portrait engraving of the XVIIth and XVIIIth centuries. '10(D10) il. O. $5.50 net. Macmillan.

Thomas, Thdr. G:
First aid to shipping fruits, vegetables, butter, eggs and game for profit, to market; complete treatise on how to gather, prepare, pack and ship fruits, vegetables, and poultry to the markets, by express or carlots. '10(D) c. 98 p. il. 12°, $1. T. G: Thomas.
Modern guide for fruit and truck shippers and poultry raisers in the southern states. '08(Ja18) il. por. 8°, $2. Thomas-W.

Thomas, Rev. T: Ebenezer.
Correspondence; mainly relating to the anti-slavery conflict in Ohio, especially in the Presbyterian Church; published by his son. '09(Jl31) pors. O. *$1 net. Clarke.

Thomas, W. H. Griffith, D.D.
Christianity is Christ. '09(N13) D. (Anglican Church hdbks.) *40 c. net. Longmans.

Thomas, W. Jenkyn.
Welsh fairy-book. '08(Ag8) il. O. $1.50. Stokes.

Thomas, W: Holcombe.
Addresses and papers. 2 v. in 1. '09(D) 8°. (Add. author for price.) W: H. Thomas.
Contemporaneous pagan views of the early Christians; address del. before the Busy People's Bible Class, of Montgomery, Sunday, Nov. 7, 1909, also before the Mt. Meigs district S. S. convention held at Mathews, Ala., Nov. 21, 1909. '09, [1910.] (Mr) 15 p. 8°, 25 c. W: H. Thomas.
New South: address del. before the Congregational Club, Kingsley Hall, Boston. '08(Je13) O. pap., gratis. W: H. Thomas.
Some educational history of Alabama Methodism; addresses del. before centenary celebration of Methodist Church, Wetumpka, Ala., Ap. 13, 1908. '08(O) 14 p. 8°. (Add. author for price.) W: H. Thomas.

Thomas, W: I:
Source book for social origins; ethnological materials, psychological standpoint, classified, and annotated bibliographies for the interpretation of savage society. '09(N13) c. O. *$4.50 net. Univ. of Chic.

Thomas-Stanford, C:
Leaves from a Madeira garden. '09(S4) il. D. $1.50. Lane.

Thomas à Kempis.
Imitation of Christ; [recast by Principal Burrell of the earliest English translation (about 1440)]. '10(D10) 16°, 35 c. net; leath., 70 c. net. Dutton.
Imitation of Christ; ed., with introd. and notes, by Brother Leo. '10(O1) c. por. T. (Macmillan's pocket Am. and Eng. classics.) 25 c. net. Macmillan.
Imitation of Christ; Eng. translation ed. by J. H. Srawley. '08(Je6) T. *45 c. net. Putnam.

Thomas à Kempis.—*Continued.*
Of the imitation of Christ; tr. from the Latin by R: Whytford in 1556 ed.; tr. in modern English by Wilfred Raynol, and with a hist. introd. '09(N6) col. il. *$3.50 net. Duffield.
Sodalist's Imitation of Christ; an Eng. translation reproducing the rhythm of the orig. Rev., corr. and ed. by Elder Mullan. '09(My) c. '08. 25+568 p. 24°, 75 c.; flex. leath., $1.25. Kenedy.

THOMAS À KEMPIS.
Storr, R. Concordance to the Latin original of De imitatione Christi. $4.20 net. Oxford Univ.

Thomas and the princess. *See* Clifford. *Mrs.* W. K. Three plays.

Thomas Aquinas, St.
Things new and old in St. Thomas Aquinas: tr. of various writings and treatises of the angelic doctor; with an introd. by H. C. O'Neil. '09(Je19) 12°, *$1.50 net. Dutton.

Thomas of Celano, Brother.
Lives of St. Francis of Assisi; tr. by A. G. Ferrers Howell. '08(Ag1) D. *$2 net. Dutton.
See also Life of Saint Clare.

THOMAS OF ECCLESTON.
Cuthbert, *Father.* Chronicle of Thomas of Eccleston. *75 c. net. Herder.

THOMAS PHOSPHATE POWDER.
See Fertilizers.

Thompson, A. Beeby.
Petroleum mining and oil-field development. '10(O8) il. 8°, $5 net. Van Nostrand.

Thompson, A. M.
Japan for a week. '10(D3) il. D. $1.50 net. Lane.

Thompson, Adele Eugenia.
American Patty: a story of 1812. '09(S11) c. il. D. (Brave heart ser.) †$1.25. Lothrop, L. & S.

Thompson, Alice C.
Her scarlet slippers: a comedy; Miss Susan's fortune: a comedy. '08(N7) c. D. pap., ea., 15 c. Penn Pub. Co.

Thompson, Alonzo.
Gems of thought gathered along life's pathway. '10(Ap23) por. 12°, $1.50. A. Thompson.

Thompson, Buchanan.
See Somerville, C:

Thompson, C: L., ed.
See United States. *Sup. ct.* Notes.

Thompson, C: Miner.
Army mule. '10(Ap30) c. il. D. $1 net. Houghton M.
Calico cat. '08(N14) c. il. D. †$1.25. Houghton M.

Thompson, Charlotte.
Awakening of Helena Richie: a play in four acts from a novel of the same name, by Marg. Deland. '08(My16) c. 16° (Add. pubs. for price.) Kauser.

Thompson, Clarence Bertrand.
Churches and the wage earners: study of the cause and cure of their separation. '09(Mr6) c. D. **$1 net. Scribner.

Thompson, Denman.
See Coryell, J: Russell.

Thompson, Eben Fs., tr.
See Omar Khayyám.

Thompson, E: P.
See Chetwood, Edith.

Thompson, Effie Freeman.
Metanoeo and *metamelei* in Greek literature until 100 A.D., incl. discussion of their cognates and of their Hebrew equivalents. '08(Ap4) c. 4°, (Univ. of Chic., hist. and linguistic studies in lit. rel. to the New Testament, 2d ser.) pap., *25 c. net. Univ. of Chic.

Thompson, Ellen.
Book of hours. '09(My22) c. D. $1.50. Forest Press.

Thompson, Ernest Seton-.
See Seton, Ernest Thompson.

Thompson, Fs.
Works. '08(Je27) sq. 12°, *$1.75 net. Lane.
Hound of heaven: [poems.]. '08(F29) 16°, pap., *50 c. net. Lane.
Hound of heaven: [poems.] '08(Ap11) sm. 4°, *40 c. net; bds., *60 c. net; Japan vellum, *$1 net. T: B. Mosher.
Renegade poet and other essays; with introd. by E. J. O'Brien. '10(Je11) c. S. $1.25 net. Ball Pub. Co.
St. Ignatius Loyola; ed. by J: Hungerford Pollen. '10(F12) O. ***$3.25 net. Benziger.**
Select poems. '08(N7) por. S. *$1.50 net. Lane.
Shelley: essay. '09(D) 4°, *$1 net; Japan vellum, *$3 net. T: B. Mosher.
Shelley; with an introd. by Rt. Hon. G: Wyndham. '09(Je12) D. *$1 net. Scribner.

Thompson, Fk. C:, ed.
See Bible. Marginal chain reference Bible.

Thompson, G. H.
See Richardson, H.

Thompson, G: Fayette.
Angora goat; rev. (May, 1908,) by E: L. Shaw. '09(Mr6) il. 8°, (U. S., Dept. of Agriculture; farmers' bull.) pap., 5 c.

Thompson, Harry.
Cost of clearing logged-off land for farming in the Pacific northwest. '09(Je) 16 p. il. 8°, (U. S., Dept. of Agriculture; Bureau of Plant Industry circular.) pap.

Thompson, H: Clayton.
New reading of evolution: study-plan correlating the known facts of nature and forming a scientific basis for a synthetic philosophy of individual and social life. '08(Ap18) c. il. 12°, *$1.60 net. New Reading.

Thompson, H: Dallas.
See Fine, H: Burchard.

Thompson, Sir Herbert, ed.
See Bible. O. T.

Thompson, J. E. H.
See Ewing, W.

Thompson, J. M.
Jesus according to Saint Mark. '10(O8) 12, $1.50 net. Dutton.
—, comp. *See* Bible. N. T. Gospels.

Thompson, Ja. Westfall.
Wars of religion in France, 1559-1576; Huguenots, Catherine de Medici and Philip II. '09(My22) c. O. *$4.50 net. Univ. of Chic.

Thompson, J:
Mammoth Cave, Kentucky; hist. sketch, cont. a brief description of some of the principal places of interest in the cave; also a short description of Colossal Cavern. '09(Jl) c. 48 p. il. fold. map, 12°, pap., 15 c. J: Thompson.

Thompson, J: Smith.
Mechanism of the linotype. Rev. 3d ed. '08(My23) c. il. por. 16°, $2. Inland Pr.

Thompson, J: Wesley, comp.
See Indiana. *Supreme and appellate cts.* Second supp.

Thompson, Jos. Washington.
Alice Mansfield's sin. '08(Ag8) c. por. D. $1. Thompson Pub. Co.

Thompson, Lewis Nathan.
Lewis Craig, the pioneer Baptist preacher; his life, labors and character. '10(Je4) c. 12°, 35 c. Bapt. World.

Thompson, Priscilla Jane.
Gleanings of quiet hours: [poems.] '07, [1908.] (Mr.) c. 100 p. por. S. (Add. pubs. for price.) P. J. Thompson.

Thompson, R. Campbell.
Semitic magic: its origins and development. '09(Ja23) 8°, (Luzac's oriental religious ser.) *$4 net. Bloch.

Thompson, Ralph Leroy, M.D.
Glimpses of medical Europe. '08(Ap18) c. D. **$2 net. Lippincott.
See also Ochsner, Alb. J:

Thompson, Rob. Ellis.
Apostles as everyday men. '10(Ap30) c. S. 50 c. net. S. S. Times.
Harvard Univ. lectures on protection to home industry. '08(Ag8) c. $1. Am. Protective.
Historic episcopate. '10(Jl9) c. D. $1.50. Westminster.

Thompson, Rob. J:, comp.
Suggestions for the development of American export trade to Germany, with a directory of the chief cities of the empire, and a list of importers and dealers. '09(F6) O. pap., gratis. Nat. Business.

Thompson, S: Hunter.
Highlanders of the South. '10(D31) c. il. D. 50 c. net. Eaton & M.

Thompson, Sanford Eleazer.
Concrete in highway construction: textbook for highway engineers and supervisors. '09(O23) c. il. 8°. $1. Atlas Portland Cement.
See also Taylor, F: Winslow.

Thompson-Seton, Ernest.
See Seton, Ernest Thompson.

Thompson, Seymour Dwight.
Commentaries on the law of private corporations. 2d ed., thoroughly rev. and rewritten in the light of the latest authorities by Jos. W. Thompson. In 7 v. v. 1. '08(D); v. 2, 3. '09(F); v. 4 (N); v. 5-7. '10(S) c. O. ea., $6. Bobbs-M.

Thompson, Silvanus Phillips.
Life of William Thomson: Baron Kelvin of Largs. In 2 v. '10(Ap9) pors. O. $7.50 net, boxed. Macmillan.
Light, visible and invisible; ser. of lectures delivered at the Royal Institute of Great Britain at Christmas, 1806, with additional lectures. 2d ed., enl. '10(D24) c. il. 12°, $2 net. Macmillan.

Thompson, Slason.
Cost, capitalization and estimated value of American railways. 3d ed. '08(Je20) il. tabs., 12°, 50 c. S. Thompson.
—, **comp. and ed.** Railway library; 1909; collection of noteworthy chapters, addresses and papers rel. to railways, mostly published during the year. '10(S10) O. 75 c. S. Thompson.

Thompson, Waddy.
Primary hist. of the United States. '10 (D31) c. il. map, D. 60 c. **Heath.**

Thompson, Wa.
Commemoration of the faithful. '10(Ag) (Priv. pr.) Gorham.

Thompson, W: Alex.
Druggist and dispensers practical show card instructor. '09(Jl17) c. il. obl. T. pap., $1. W: A. Thompson.

Thompson, W: B.
American distributing markets for American cotton; address del. before the convention of the Texas Cotton Growers' Association at Waco, Texas, January 29, 1910. '10(Je) 16 p. O. pap. W: B. Thompson.
Analysis and exposition of the Scott Anti-Cotton-Future Bill (H. R. 24073), depressing the price of cotton by legislation. '10(Je) 14 p. O. pap. W: B. Thompson.
Central warehouse plan; address del. before a joint committee of the National Farmers' Union and the New Orleans Progressive Union at New Orleans, November 13, 1908. '10(Je) 15 p. O. pap. W: B. Thompson.
How can the economic features of the speculative exchanges be preserved and the ethical evils eliminated; discussion before the Republican Club of the city of New York, March 26, 1910. '10(Je) 21 p. O. pap. W: B. Thompson.
Narrowing of the cotton market; tendency toward trust control of prices. '10 (Mr26) O. pap., gratis. W: B. Thompson.
New future rules of the New Orleans Cotton Exchange. '09, [1910.] (Je) 13 p. O. pap. W: B. Thompson.

Thompson, W: Fs.
See Jordan, D: Starr.

Thompson, W: Gilman.
Practical dietetics, with special reference to diet in diseases. 4th ed., enl. and completely rewritten. '09(O) 26+928 p. il. 8°, $5. Appleton.

Thompson ser. of home study book. il. D. $1; leath., $1.50. C: C. Thompson.
—Jackman. A B C of the motor cycle.
—Jackman *and* Russell. Flying machines.
—Root. Automobile troubles.
—Russell. Automobile driving self taught.—Automobile motors and mechanism.—Ignition.—Motor boats.

Thomsen, Hans Peter Jorgen Julius.
Thermochemistry; tr. from the Danish by Katharine A. Burke. '08(Mr14) tabs., il. D. (Text-books of physical chemistry.) $2.50. Longmans.

Thomson, A. Landsborough.
Britain's birds and their eggs. '10(D17) col. il. 8°, $6.50 net. Lippincott.

Thomson, E: W:
When Lincoln died, and other poems. '09 (Je12) c. 12°, $1.25. Houghton M.

Thomson, H. Hyslop, M.D.
Consumption, its prevention and home treatment: guide for the use of patients. '10(D) 75 p. il. tabs., 12°, (Oxford medical pubs.) $1 net. Oxford Univ.

Thomson, H: Campbell-, M.D.
See Campbell-Thomson, H:, *M.D.*

Thomson, Ja.
Complete poetical works; ed., with notes, by J. Logie Robertson. Oxford ed. '09 (My15) por. D. 75 c.; (Oxford poets.) $1.25; Oxford India pap., $1.75. Oxford Univ.

THOMSON, James.
Macaulay, G: C. James Thomson. **75 c. net. Macmillan.

Thomson, J: Arth.
Bible of nature. '08(S19) c. D. (Bross lectures, 1907.) **$1 net. Scribner.

Darwinism and human life: South African lectures for 1909. '10(D31) 8°, por. $1.50 net. Holt.

Heredity. '08(My2) il. O. (Science ser.) *$3.50 net. Putnam.

See also Thomson, Marg. R.

Thomson, J: C., comp.
See New York [State] Code of civil procedure.

Thomson, J: Stuart.
The Chinese. '09(S25) c. il. O. *$2.50 net. Bobbs-M.

Thomson, Mrs. L. Norton-.
See Norton-Thomson, *Mrs.* L.

Thomson, M. Pearson.
Denmark. '10(N19) col. il. map, 12°, (Peeps at many lands ser.) 75 c. net. Macmillan.

Finland. '09(D25) il. map, 12°, (Peeps at many lands ser.) *75 c. net. Macmillan.

Thomson, Marg. R. and J. Arth.
Threads in the web of life. '10(O8) il. 16°, (Readable books in natural knowledge.) 50 c. net. Macmillan.

THOMSON, Samuel.
Life and medical discoveries of Samuel Thomson, and a hist. of the Thomsonian materia medica as shown in The new guide to health (1835) and the literature of that day, incl. the famous Letters of Professor Benjamin Waterhouse, M.D.; the celebrated Trial of Dr. Frost, and other features of a remarkable epoch in American medical history. '09(S) c. 139 p. Q. (Lloyd Lib. bull.; reproduction ser.) pap., $1. Lloyd Lib.

Thomson, Sir W:
See Kelvin, W: Thomson, *Lord.*

Thomson, W: Chase.
Bridge and structural design. [2d ed.] '10 (Mr5) c. il. 8°, ea., $2 net. Engineering News.

Design of typical steel railway bridges. '08 (My16) c. il. 8°, *$2 net. Engineering News.

Thomson, W: de Forest.
Passing of time. '08(Ja11) 16°, *$1 net. R. G. Cooke.

Thomson, W: Hanna, M.D.
Some wonders of biology. '09(D4) c. D. **$1.20 net. Dodd.

What is physical life? '09(Jl3) c. D. **$1.20 net. Dodd.

Thomson, W: McClure.
Land and the Book; or, Biblical illustrations drawn from the manners and customs, the scenes and scenery, of the Holy Land. 3 v. '08(D12) c. il. map, plans, 8°, Popular ed., $7.50; hf. leath., $12. Harper.

Thonger, C:
Book of the cottage garden. '09(Ap17) il. D. (Handbooks of practical gardening.) *$1 net. Lane.

THORAX.
Sawyer, J. E. H. Physical signs of diseases of thorax and abdomen. *$2 net. Wood.

See also Heart;—Lungs.

Thorburn, J. M. & Co.
Seeding and preservation of golf links. '08 (Je) c. 33 p. front. O. pap. (Add. pubs. for price.) J. M. Thorburn.

THOREAU, *Mrs.* Cynthia Dunbar.
Hill, E. B. Henry Thoreau's mother. 10 c. E. B. Hill.

Thoreau, H: D:
Cape Cod. '08(O3) c. il. por. O. **$2 net. Crowell.

Emerson's obituary. '08(D26) c. 24°, (Collectanea.) pap., 10 c. E. B. Hill.

Friendship. '10(D) front. 32°, (Ariel booklets.) leath., 75 c. Putnam.

Katahdin and Chesuncook; from The Maine woods; abrdg. and ed. by Clifton Johnson. '09(Ap10) c. (Riverside literature ser.) 25 c. Houghton M.

Maine woods. '09(S4) c. O. **$2 net, boxed. Crowell.

Notes on New England birds; arr. and ed. by Fs. H. Allen. '10(My21) c. il. maps, (fold.,) $1.75 net. Houghton M.

Thoreau calendar; ed. by Annie Russell Marble. '09(Ag28) c. por. D. (Chiswick ser.) 60 c.; ooze, $1, boxed. Crowell.

Thoreau day by day; ed. by A. R. Marble. '10(D) 12°, (Day by day ser.) 60 c.; ooze, $1. Crowell.

Walden; or, life in the woods. 2 v. '09 (S) c. il. facsims., 8°. (Priv. pr.) Bibliophile.

Walden. '10(S3) c. il. O. $2 net, boxed. Crowell.

Walden. '08(O17) 16°, (Best books ser.) leath., *$1 net. Dutton.

Walden; introd. by Wa. Raymond. '08 (F22) (Everyman's lib.) *35 c. net; leath., *70 c. net. Dutton.

Thoreau, H: D:—*Continued.*
Walden; or, life in the woods, with an introd. and notes by Fs. H. Allen, and with suggestive questions and comments. '10(D10) c. il. por. 12°, (Riverside literature ser.) 50 c. Houghton M.
Walden; ed., with notes and introd., by Raymond MacDonald Alden. '10(Jl2) c. map, D. (Longmans' English classics.) 25 c. net. Longmans.
Walden; or, life in the woods; ed., with an introd. and notes, by Byron Rees. '10(Ap9) por. T. (Pocket Am. and Eng. classics.) 25 c. net. Macmillan.
Walden; ed., with an introd. and notes, by J. Milnor Dorey. '10(Ap23) c. por. 12°, (Merrill's English texts.) 50 c. C: E. Merrill.
See also In American fields and forests.

THOREAU, Henry David.
Allen, F. H: Bibliography of Henry David Thoreau. **$5 net. Houghton M.

Thorington, Ja., M.D.
Refraction and how to refract, incl. sections on optics, retinoscopy, the fitting of spectacles and eye-glasses, etc. 4th ed. '09 (Ap); 5th ed. '10(Mr) c. il. 8°, ea., *$1.50 net. Blakiston.

Thorley, Wilfrid C.
Primer of English for foreign students. '10(Ap9) il. D. 60 c. net. Macmillan.

Thorndike, Ashley Horace.
Tragedy. '08(My16) c. D. (Types of English literature.) D. *$1.50 net. Houghton M.
—, comp. Minor Elizabethan drama; with introd. In 2 v. v. 1, Pre-Shakespearean tragedy; Norton and Sackville's Gorboduc, Kyd's Spanish tragedy, Peele's David and Bethsabe, and Arden of Feversham; v. 2, Pre-Shakespearean comedy; Udall's Ralph Roister-Doister, Lyly's Endimion, Peele's Old wives' tale, Green's Friar Bacon and Friar Bungay, and James the Fourth. '10 (D10) 16°, (Everyman's lib.) ea., 35 c. net; leath., 70 c. net. Dutton.

Thorndike, E: Lee.
Educational psychology. 2d ed., rev. and enl. '10(N) 248 p. il. 8°, (Columbia Univ. Teachers' College record.) $1.50. Teachers' Coll.
Handwriting. '10(Je18) facsims., 8°, (Teachers' College Record.) pap., 30 c. Teachers' Coll.
Teaching staff of secondary schools in the United States, amount of education, length of experience, salaries. '09(Ag) 60 p. 8°, (U. S., Dept. of the Interior, Bu. of Education bull.) (Add. Superintendent for price.)

Thorne, Grace Evelyn.
Montana. '09(O30) 12°, pap., 25 c. J. S. Ogilvie.

Thorne, Guy, [pseud. for Cyril Arth. E: Ranger Gull.]
The angel. '08(N14) c. D. †$1.50. G: W. Dillingham.
The socialist. '09(O2) c. D. **$1.35 net. Putnam.

Thorne, Marion, pseud.
See Thurston, *Mrs.* Ida T.

Thorne, W: Winter, ed.
See American business and accounting encyclopedia;—*also* Beach, Elmer H:, *ed.*

Thornton, —.
British and foreign patents. '10(Jl) $6. Callaghan.

Thornton, A: Willoughby.
Suburbanite's hdbk. of dwarf fruit tree culture, their training and management, with a discussion on their adaptability to the requirements of the commercial orchardist both in connection and in competition with standard trees. '09(Ag) 115 p. il. 8°, 50 c. A: W. Thornton.

THORNTON, D. M.
Gairdner, W. H. T. D. M. Thornton: study in missionary ideals. *$1.25 net. Revell.

Thornton, Mrs. Derck E:
See Hunt, Enid Leigh.

Thornton, E: Quin, M.D.
Medical pocket formulary: [medicine prescriptions.] 9th ed. '09(Je) 16°, *$1.50 net. Lea.

Thornton, W: Wheeler.
Indiana negligence: treatise on the law of negligence as administered in the courts of Indiana, including the law of accident insurance, common carriers, etc. v. 1, 2. '08(O) c. 73+898; 899-1936 p. O. $12. W. H. Anderson.
Law governing cities and towns in Indiana. 5th ed. '09(S) c. 979 p. O. (Add. pubs. for price.) W. H. Anderson.
Treatise on the federal employers' liability and safety appliance acts. '09(Jl) c. 47+410 p. O. $4.50. W. H. Anderson.
See Woollen, W: Watson.
—, comp. *See* Indiana. Complete guide for township officers.

Thornton's Arabic ser. D. Putnam.
—Nicholson. Elementary Arabic second reading-book. $2.

Thorold, Algar Labouchere.
Six masters in disillusion: [essays on Fontenelle, Prosper Mérimée, Ferdinand Fabre, Huysmans, Maeterlinck and Anatole France.] '09(Je19) 8°, *$1.50 net. Dutton.

Thoroughbred (The). Macvane, E. †$1.50. G: W. Dillingham.

Thoroughly tested. Harris, *Mrs.* J. Y. 25 c. J. Y. Harris.

Thorpe, Durrant.
Universal guide of standard routes and itineraries of tourist travel all over the world. '08(Ap11) c. il. S. leath., $1.25. D. Thorpe.

Thorpe, Sir E:
Hist. of chemistry. In 2 v. v. 1, From the earliest times to the middle of the nineteenth century. '09(D11) c. pors. S. (Hist. of the sciences.) **75 c. net. Putnam.

Thorpe, Fs. Newton, comp.
Federal and state constitutions, colonial charters, and other organic laws of the states, territories and colonies now or heretofore forming the United States of America. '09(My) 8°. (Add. Superintendent for price.) U. S., Supt. of Docs.
—, ed. *See* Jackson, Andrew.

Thorpe, Sir T: E:
Hist. of chemistry. In 2 v. v. 2, From 1850-1910. '10(O22) c. por. S. (Hist. of the sciences.) 75 c. net. Putnam.
Those Brewster children. Kingsley, *Mrs.* F. M. $1. Dodd.
Those nerves. Walton, G: L. **$1 net. Lippincott.
Those Preston twins. Forrester, I. L. $1.25. Wilde.
Those Smith boys. Garis, H. R. $1.25. Fenno.
Thou fool! Bell, J: J. †$1.50. Baker & T.
Thou shalt not steal. Bryan, W: J. 10 c. Civic Forum.
Though life do us part. Ward, *Mrs.* E. S. P. †$1.50. Houghton M.
THOUGHT.
See Brain; — Mind; — Logic;—Philosophy;—Psychology.
Thought and reality in Hegel's system. Cunningham, G. W. $1.25. Longmans.
Thought culture. Atkinson, W: W. $1. Progress Co.
THOUGHT TRANSFERENCE.
See Psychology;—Telepathy.
Thoughts and things. Baldwin, J. M. v. 2. *$2.75 net. Macmillan.
Thoughts at night-time. Elshemus, L: M. $1.25. Dreamers Press.
Thoughts for life's journey. Matheson, G: *$1.25 net. Armstrong.
Thoughts of a thinker. Josselyn, A. A. *75 c. net. Fowler & W.
Thoughts on business. 2d ser. Warren, W. P. $1.25. Forbes.
Thoughts on education. Watts, T: T. [priv. pr.] T: T. Watts.
Thoughts on modern church life and work. Wright, J: C: *$1 net. Longmans.
Thoughts on some questions relating to women. Davies, E. $1.25 net. Macmillan.
Thoughts on themes from Patmos. Downey, W: v. 1. $1.25. Downey.
Thousand and one churches. Ramsay, *Sir* W. M. $5 net. Doran.
Thousand leggers. Moss, C. W. 75 c. C. M. Clark.
Thousand thoughts for pract. preachers. Corbett, F: S. J. $2 net. Whittaker.
Thousand thoughts from Will Carleton. Carleton, W. 50 c. Everywhere.
Thousand years of Jewish hist. Harris, M. H: $1. Bloch.
THRALE, *Mrs.* Hester Lynch Salisbury.
See Johnson, Samuel.
Threads from three lives. Hollinger, L. I. $1. L. I. Hollinger.
Threads in the web of life. Thomson, M. R. 50 c. net. Macmillan.
Threads of gold. Curtis, H. G: $1. H. G: Curtis.
Threads of moss. Scott, W. L. $1. W. L. Scott.
Three amateur scouts. Jacberns, R. $1.50. Lippincott.
Three bold pirates. Hardy, E. S. 50 c. Dutton.
Three brothers. Phillpotts, E. †$1.50. Macmillan.
Three centuries of southern poetry. Holliday, C:, *comp.* *$1 net. Pub. Ho. of M. E. Ch., So.
Three chapters in Wisconsin local history. 1, Reminiscences of early Grant County, by Jonathan H: Evans; 2, Settlement of Arcadia, by Eben Douglas Pierce; 3, Settlement of Green Lake County, by R. Dart; from the proceedings of the State Historical Society of Wisconsin for 1909. '10(Ap) 232-272 p. O. pap., 25 c. State Hist., Wis.
Three clerks. *See* Trollope, Anthony.
Three creeds. Gibson, E. C: S. *$1.40 net. Longmans.
Three crosses. Falconer, J. W. *75 c. net. Jennings.
Three dwarfs. *See* Lang, Andrew, *ed.*
Three essays. Stebbing, W. 20 c. Oxford Univ.
Three-foot stool. Wright, P: *$1.50 net. Dutton.
Three generations of Northboro Davises. Estabrook, J: D. $3. J: D. Estabrook.
Three girls and a hermit. Conyers, D. $1.50. Dutton.
Three girls from school. Smith, *Mrs.* E. T. †$1. Burt.
Three great Florentine painters: Fra Angelico, Leonardo Da Vinci, and Botticelli; ed. by T. Leman Hare. '09(O) 237 p. col. il. O. *$2 net. Stokes.
Three great modern painters: Leighton, Burne-Jones, Whistler; ed. by T. Leman Hare. '09(O) 235 p. col. il. O. *$2 net. Stokes.
Three historical addresses at Groton, Mass. Green, S: A. $2.50. Littlefield.
350 dollar ideas for druggists. Mason, H. B., *ed.* E. G. Swift.
365 foreign dishes. '08(O10) c. S. (365 ser.) Gift ed., **50 c. net; bds., **40 c. net. Jacobs.
365 luncheon dishes. '08(D19) c. 16°, (365 ser.) Gift ed., **50 c. net; bds., **40 c. net. Jacobs.
365 orange recipes; an orange recipe for every day in the year; [compiled by Mrs. J. L. Lane.] '09(S11) c. D. bds., 50 c. Jacobs.
365 vegetable dishes; vegetable dish for every day in the year. '10(Je4) c. S. (365 ser.) bds., 50 c. net. Jacobs.
Three hundred games and pastimes. Lucas, E: V. $2 net. Macmillan.
Three hundred things a bright boy can do; by many hands. '10(D31) il. 8°, $2 net. Lippincott.
Three jovial puppies. Cuming, E: W: D. $2. Caldwell.
Three keys. Ormond, F. $1.50. Watt.
Three little bears. *See* Little Red Riding Hood.
Three little maids. Turner, E. 75 c. McKay.
Three little women. Jackson, *Mrs.* G. E. S. †$1. Winston.
Three little women at work. Jackson, *Mrs.* G. E. S. $1. Winston.
Three little women's success. Jackson, *Mrs.* G. E. S. $1. Winston.
Three lives. Stein, G. **$1.50 net. Grafton Press.

Three Miss Graemes. Macnaughtan, S. $1.50. Dutton.
Three modern seers. Ellis, E. M. O. L. $1.25 net. M. Kennerley.
Three musketeers. *See* Dumas, Alexandre.
Three of a kind. Burton, R: †$1.50. Little, B. & Co.
Three philosophical poets. Santayana, G: $2.25. Harvard Univ.
Three plays of Shakespeare. *See* Swinburne, Algernon C:
Three proclamations concerning the lottery for Virginia. Brown University. (Add. pubs. for price.) Brown Univ.
Three rivers. Farley, J. P. *$2 net. Neale.
Three senses. Countryman, C. C. 50 c.; 75 c.; 25 c. C. C. Countryman.
Three thousand dollars. Rohlfs, *Mrs.* A. K. G. $1. Badger.
Three thousand practical illustrations in religion and morals. Bomberger, J: H., *comp.* $2. Central.
Three vital problems. Delk, E. H. 50 c. Lutheran Pub.
Three voyages of a naturalist. Nicoll, M. J. *$2.50 net. Scribner.
Three weeks in Holland and Belgium. Higinbotham, J: U. $1.50. Reilly & B.
Three years behind the guns. T., L. G. *$1.50 net. Century Co.
Threefold cord. Pearson, C: W: *$1.25 net. Sherman, F.
Threshold of manhood. Dawson, W. J. *$1.25 net. Revell.
Threshold of music. Wallace, W: *$1.50 net; *$2.25 net. Macmillan.
Thrice, Luke.
Society wolf. '10(Ap16) c. il. D. $1.50. Cupples & L.
Thrice armed. Bindloss, H. †$1.50. Stokes.
Thrilling and truthful history of the pony express. Visscher, W: L. 75 c. Rand, McN. & Co.

Throat.
American Medical Association. Papers to be presented before the Section on Laryngology and Otology of the American Medical Association, 1908, $1.50; 1909. (Add. pubs. for price.) Am. Medical.
Ballenger, W: L. Treatise on medical and surgical diseases of the nose, throat and ear. *$5.50 net. Lea.
Bishop, S. C. Diseases of the nose, throat and ear. $4.50; $6. Davis.
Bruck, A. Diseases of the nose, mouth, pharynx and larynx. $5. Rebman.
Coakley, C. G. Laryngology: manual of diseases of the nose and throat. $2.75. Lea.
Downie, J. W. Clinical manual for the study of diseases of the throat. *$3.25 net. Macmillan.
Gleason, E: B. Manual of disease of the nose, throat and ear. $2.50. Saunders.
Knight, C: H., *and* Bryant, W. S. Diseases of the nose, throat and ear. *$4.50 net; *$6 net. Blakiston.
Kyle, D: B. Diseases of the nose and throat. *$4 net; *$5.50 net. Saunders.
Lamb, W: Pract. guide to the diseases of the nose, throat and ear. *$3 net. Wood.

Throat.—*Continued.*
Packard, F. R. Text-book of diseases of the nose, throat and ear. subs., **$3.50 net; **$4 net. Lippincott.
Wood, C. A., *and others, eds.* Eye, ear, nose and throat. $1.50. Year Bk.
See also Breathing;—Ear;—Mouth;—Nurses and nursing;—Tuberculosis;—Voice.

Throop Institute bull.; science ser. 8°. Throop Poly. Inst.
—Grinnell. Reptiles of Los Angeles Co. gratis.
Through Afro-America. Archer, W: $3 net. Dutton.
Through Death Valley. Harper, O. 25 c. J. S. Ogilvie.
Through Finland. Scott, A. M. *$1.25 net. Dutton.
Through five administrations. Crook, W: H: $1.80 net. Harper.
Through Italy with the poets. Schauffler, R. H., *comp.* *$2 net. Moffat.
Through library windows. Hubbard, F. C. $1.25. B'way Pub.
Through Persia from the Gulf to the Caspian. Bradley-Birt, F. B. B. *$3.50 net. Dutton.
Through Persia in a motor car. Anet, C. *$4.50 special net. Appleton.
Through Ramona's country. James, G: W. **$2 net. Little, B. & Co.
Through savage Europe. De Windt, H. $1.50 net. Lippincott.
Through southern Mexico. Gadow, H. F. *$6 net. Scribner.
Thro' space. Rock, J. 60 c. N. E. Druggist.
Through space to Mars. Rockwood, R., *pseud.* 60 c. Cupples & L.
Through the buhrs. Wilson, C: N. $1.50. C. M. Clark.
Through the forty days. Snyder, A. W. *$1 net. Whittaker.
Through the French provinces. Peixotto, E. C. **$2.50 net. Scribner.
Through the gates of the Netherlands. Waller, M. E. **$1.50 net. Little, B. & Co.
Through the heart of Tibet. MacDonald, A. $1.25. Caldwell.
Through the little green door. Donahey, *Mrs.* M. D. $1. Stern.
Through the looking-glass. *See* Dodgson, C: Lutwidge.
Through the magic door. Doyle, *Sir* A. C. **$1.25 net. McClure.
Through the mists. Lees, R. J. $1.50. Badger.
Through the valley of the shadow. Carson, R. M. $3. Hudson.
Through the wall. Moffett, C. †$1.50. Appleton.
Through the wilderness of Brazil. Cook, W: A. $1.50. Am. Tr.
Through the winter. Howell, M. H. 80 c. Am. S. S.
Through the year with Sousa. Sousa, J: P. $1 net. Crowell.
Through the Yukon and Alaska. Rickard, T: A. $2.50. Mining and Scientific.
Through Uganda to Mount Elgon. Purvis, J: B. $1.50. Am. Tr.

Through war to peace. *See* Mason, B: F. Village mystery.

Through Welsh doorways. Marks, J. A. **$1.10 net. Houghton M.

Thrum, T: G., comp.
Hawaii; almanac and annual for 1910. '10 (Ja22) c. il. O. pap., 75 c. T. G. Thrum.

—, and tr. Stories of the Menehunes; Hawaiian traditions (from "Hawaiian folk tales"). '10(O1) c. D. bds., 50 c. net. McClurg.

THRUSH.
See Mouth.

Thruston, Mrs. Lucy Meacham.
Girl of Virginia. '08(My.) c. 12°, (Popular ed. of recent fiction.) †75 c. Little, B. & Co.
Mistress Brent. '08(Ap4) c. il. D. (Popular eds. of recent fiction.) †75 c. Little, B. & Co.

Thucydides.
Histories, bk. 4; ed. by T. R. Mills; with a general introd. by H. Stuart Jones. '09(Je19) map, D. 90 c.; notes only, 60 c. Oxford Univ.
Hist. of the Peloponnesian war; done into English by R: Crawley. '10(D10) maps, 16°, (Everyman's lib.) 35 c. net; 70 c. net. Dutton.
History of Thucydides; tr. from the ancient Greek by B: Jowett. [Olympic ed.] '09(D25) il. c. 3 v., plan, 8°, (Historians of Greece.) $10.50. Tandy-T.

Thum, W:
Forward step for the democracy of tomorrow. '10(Jl9) c. 12°, $1.50. Twentieth Century.

Thumb nail ser. T. leath., $1, boxed. Century Co.
—Brainerd, *comp.* Great hymns of the middle ages.
—Emerson. Power, Success, and Greatness.
—Keats. Odes, sonnets, and lyrics.

Thumb-o-graph ser.; comp. by Martha Moulder. nar. S. *50 c. net; leath., *$1 net; *$1.50 net. Stokes.
—Fetherston. Secret signatures of my friends.
—Moulder, *comp.* Left hand autograph book.
—People I meet.
—Truth about my friends.

Thunderbolt (The). Pinero, A. W. 50 c. W. H. Baker.

Thurber, Orray E.
Venezuelan question; Castro and the asphalt trust from official records. '09(F6) por. 12°. (Add. author for price.) O. E. Thurber.

Thursday mornings at the City Temple. Campbell, R. J: *$1.50 net. Macmillan.

Thursfield, Ja. R.
Nelson and other naval studies. '09(Jl17) il. 8°, *$4 net. Dutton.

Thurston, Carl Hammond Philander.
See Moses, Rob.

Thurston, Clara Bell.
Discontented stuffed cat, and other moral tales. '10(D3) c. il. Q. bds., $1.25. Saalfield.

Thurston, Ernest Temple.
City of Beautiful Nonsense. '09(S18) c. D. †$1.50. Dodd.
Greatest wish in the world. '10(O1) c. D $1.50. M. Kennerley
Mirage. '08(D5) c. D. $1.50. Dodd.
Sally Bishop. [1910.] (Mr) c. '08. 424 p. D. $1.50. M. Kennerley.

Thurston, Mrs. Ida Treadwell, ["Marion Thorne."]
Big brother of Sabin Street; continuing the story of Theodore Bryan, The bishop's shadow. '09(S11) c. il. D. *$1 net. Revell.

THURSTON, John Lawrence.
Wright, H: B. Life with a purpose: memorial of John Lawrence Thurston. $1.50. Revell.

Thurston, Mrs. Katharine Cecil.
Fly on the wheel. '08(O10) c. front. D. †$1.50. Dodd.
Max; a novel. '10(O1) c. il. D. $1.50. Harper.

Thurston of Orchard Valley. Bindloss, H. **$1.30 net. Stokes.

Thwaites, Reuben Gold.
The colonies, 1492-1750; with numerous bibliographies. Rev. ed.. '10(D10) c. maps, S. (Epochs of American hist.) $1.25. Longmans.
Cyrus Hall McCormick and the reaper. '09 (Ap10) il. por. O. 50 c. State Hist., Wis.
Ohio Valley press before the war of 1812-15. '09, [1910.] (Je) 62 p. facsims., 4°. (Not for sale.) Davis Press.
"Files of the newspapers of the Ohio River Valley" (14 p.).
Romance of Mississippi Valley history. '08 (Je6) 8°, 75 c. State Hist., Ia.
Wisconsin. '08(D12) c. D. (American commonwealths.) **$1.25 net. Houghton M.

—, and Kellogg, Louise Phelps, eds.
Revolution on the upper Ohio, 1775-1777; comp. fr. the Draper manuscripts in the library of the Wisconsin Historical Society and pub. at the charge of the Wisconsin Society of the Sons of the American Revolution. '08(Ap4) c. pors. map, D. (Draper ser., v. 2.) $1.50. State Hist., Wis.

Thwing, C: Franklin.
Education in the Far East. '09(Je26) c. D. **$1.50 net. Houghton M.
Hist. of education in the United States since the Civil War. '10(D10) c. D. $1.25 net. Houghton M.

THYROID GLAND.
Ochsner, A. J., *and* Thompson, R. L. Surgery and pathology of the thyroid and parathyroid glands. $6 net. Mosby.

Thyrsis. *See* Arnold, Matthew.

Thyrza, Story of. Brown, A. **$1.35 net. Houghton M.

Thysia; an elegy. '10(Je4) c. leath., $1 net. M. Kennerley.

Tibbals, C: Austin, jr.
Study of tellurides. '09, [1910.] (Ap) 421-446 p. il. 8°, (Univ. of Wis. bull.; science ser.) 25 c. Univ. of Wis.

Tibbetts, F:
Word pictures; prose and verse. '09(N) c. 150 p. 12°, $1. Gift Bk.

Tibbles, W:
Theory of ions: consideration of its place in biology and therapeutics. '09(Mr) 131 p. *$1 net. Hoeber.

TIBERIUS, *Emperor of Rome.*
Beesly, E: S. Catiline, Clodius, and Tiberius. *$3 net. Stechert.

TIBET.
Hedin, S. A. Trans-Himalaya; discoveries and adventures in Tibet. **$7.50 net. Macmillan.
Landor, A. H: S. Explorer's adventures in Tibet. $1.50.—In the forbidden land. $3. Harper.
MacDonald, A. Through the heart of Tibet. $1.25. Caldwell.

TICHENOR, George Carter.
Col. George C. Tichenor's views on revision of the tariff and customs laws. '09(S) 3-68 p. por. 8°. (Priv. pr.) H: D. Tichenor.

TICHENOR, Isaac Taylor.
Dill, J. S. Isaac Taylor Tichenor, the home mission statesman. 50 c.; pap., 25 c. S. S. Bd. So. Bapt.

Ticknor, G:
Life, letters and journals of George Ticknor. '09(S25) c. 2 v., il. pors. facsim., O. $5. Houghton M.

Tidal and other problems. Chamberlin, T: C. $2; $1.50. Carnegie.

Tidball, V. J., comp. and ed.
See Wyoming. *Sup. ct.* Complete digest.

TIDES.
Chamberlin, T: C., *and others.* Tidal and other problems. $2; $1.50. Carnegie.
Harris, R. A. Manual of tides. (Add. Superintendent of Documents for price.) U. S., Supt. of Docs.
United States. Tidal observations and investigations by Commander Rob. E: Peary; adverse rept. [1910.] (Jl) 10 p. 8°. Gov. Pr. Off.

Tides of spring. Upson, A. W. $1. Small.

TIDONG LANGUAGE.
Beech, M. W. H. Tidong dialects of Borneo. $1.75. Oxford Univ.

TIEFLAND (*opera*).
Lothar, R. Tiefland (The lowland): music drama. Vocal score, Eng. and German, $5; piano score, $4; libretto, Eng. and German, 35 c. Boosey.

Tiernan, Mrs. Frances Christine Fisher, ["Christian Reid."]
Coin of sacrifice. '09(Mr27) nar. S. pap. 15 c. Ave Maria.
Princess Nadine. '08(Ja25) front. D. **$1.50 net. Putnam.
Vera's charge. '07, [1908.] (Mr.) c. 390 p. 8°, $1.50. Ave Maria.

Tiersot, Julien, comp.
Forty-four French folk-songs and variants from Canada, Normandy, and Brittany; collected and harmonized by Julien Tiersot; English tr. by H: Grafton Chapman. '10(Mr12) c. O. (Songs of the people.) $2; pap., $1. Schirmer.

Ties that bind. Houtz, A. 50 c. I. M. Beaver.

Tiffany, Esther Brown.
The tocsin; drama of the Renaissance. '09 (D18) front. bds., *$2 net. P. Elder.

Tiffany, Fs. B.
Hdbk. of the law of sales. 2d ed. rev. '08(My.) c. 10+534 p. O. (Hornbook ser.) *$3.75 net. West Pub.
See also Minnesota. Rev. laws.

Tiffany, Herbert Thorndike.
Law of landlord and tenant. In 2 v. '10 (My) c. O. ea., $6.50. Keefe-D.

Tiffany, Joel.
Astral world, higher occult powers; clairvoyance, spiritism, mediumship and spirit-healing fully explained; introd. by Phenix. 3d ed. '10(S3) c. front. 12°, $2. De Laurence, S.

Tiffany, Wa. C.
Hdbk. on the law of persons and domestic relations. 2d ed., by Roger W. Cooley. '09(Jl) 13+656 p. 8°, (Hornbook ser.) $3.75. West Pub.

'Tilda Jane's orphans. Saunders, M. †$1.50. L. C. Page.

Tilden, J: H:
Etiology of cholera infantum, typhoid fever and appendicitis, with the hygienic and dietetic treatment as applied by J: H. Tilden. '09(N) various paging, 12°. $5. Merchants' Pub.

Tilden, Josephine Eliz.
Minnesota *algae.* '10(D) il. 8°, ([Geological and Natural History Survey [of Minnesota]; Botanical ser.) $1. F: E. Clements.

Tilden, S: Jones.
Letters and literary memorials; ed. by J: Bigelow. '08(Mr7) c. 2 v., O. $6. Harper.

TILDEN, Samuel Jones.
See **Hayes-Tilden contest.**

Tilden, Sir W: A:
Chemistry. '10(S) 9+108 p. il. diagrs., 16°, (Appleton's scientific primers.) 50 c. net. Appleton.
The elements: speculations as to their nature and origin. '10(Ag13) 16°, (Harper's lib. of living thought.) 75 c. net. Harper.

TILES.
See Building materials;—Cement.

Tileston, Mrs. Mary Wilder Foote, comp.
Children's book of ballads. New ed. '10 (O1) c. il. D. $1.50. Little, B. & Co.
Child's harvest of verse. '10(O15) c. il. D. $1.50. Little, B. & Co
Stronghold of hope; collection of hymns of comfort. [New ed.] '10(O1) c. S. $1 net. Little, B. & Co.
Sugar and spice and all that's nice; book of nursery rhymes. New ed., enl. '10 (O1) c. il. D. $1.50. Little, B. & Co
—, ed. Children's treasure trove of pearls. '08(N14) c. il. O. †1.50. Little, B. & Co.

Till Eulenspiegels: lustige streiche; selected and enl., with notes, vocab. and exercises, by F: Betz. '09(Ap17) c. il. S. (Modern lang. ser.) 30 c. Heath.

Tillage of the heart. Hobart, A. S. 50 c. Am. Bapt.

Tillers of the ground. Newbegin, M. I. 50 c. net. Macmillan.

Tillinghast, J: Avery and F: Wheaton.
Little journey to the home of Elder Pardon Tillinghast. '08, [1909.] (Mr) 27 p. 8°. (Not for sale.) J: A. Tillinghast.

TILLINGHAST FAMILY.
See Genealogies.

Tillman, S: Escue.
Descriptive general chemistry. 4th ed., rev. '08(Ag1) c. 8°, **$3 net. Wiley.
Elem. lessons in heat. 4th ed., rev. and enl. '08(Ag1) c. diagrs., 8°, **$1.50 net. Wiley.
Text-book of important minerals and rocks. 3d ed., rev. '08(Ag1) c. diagrs., 8°, **$2 net. Wiley.

Tillotson, Edn. Ward.
See Farrington, Oliver Cummings.

Tilly, F: E., comp.
Stories from the life of Dr. Martin Luther. '09(N20) il. O. bds., 25 c. E. Kaufmann.
—, **ed.** God bless you; collection of Bible stories, narratives, and poetry. '09(N20) il. O. bds., 25 c. E. Kaufmann.

Tillyard, H: Julius Wetenhall.
Agathocles. '08(D19) 8°, (Cambridge historical essays.) *$1.50 net. Putnam.

Tilney, Rob.
Summer holiday, and other verses. '09 (D18) c. il. 16°, 75 c. Biddle Press.

Tilson, Jesse Paxon.
R. S. D. guide; railroad short distances, United States, Canada, Mexico, etc.; (from largest cities to all principal points of state and interstate;) geographical and miscellaneous references; mathematical tables, etc. '09(N) c. 5-70 p. 16°, 25 c. Harrison Pr.

Tilton, Dwight, [pseud. for Wilder Dwight Quint and G: Tilton Richardson.]
Meyer & Son; founded on the play by T: Addison. '08(D12) il. 12°, $1.50. C. M. Clark.

Tim. Coffey, W: H. 50 c. Burton Co.
Tim and Roy in camp. Pendleton, F., *pseud.* $1.50. Lothrop, L. & S.

Timayenis, Telemachus T:
Hevor, the Gaul: drama in five acts. '08 (O) c. 72 p. 8°, pap., 50 c. T: T. Timayenis

TIMBER.
See Forests and forestry;—Wood.

Timbering and mining. Storms, W: H. *$2 net. McGraw-H.

Timbie, W: H:
Elements of electricity for technical students. '10(D17) figs. 12°, $2 net. Wiley.

TIME.
Arthur, J. Time and its measurement. $1.50. Popular Mechanics.
See also **Almanacs and annuals;—Calendars and year-books;—Clocks and watches.**

Time and free will. Bergson, H. L. $2.75 net. Macmillan.
Time and tide. *See* Ruskin, J:
Time in English verse rhythm. Brown, W. 70 c. Science Pr., (N. Y.)
Time of roses. Cheney, J: V. *75 c. net; Japan vellum, *$1.50 net [50 copies]. T: B. Mosher.
Time of the singing of birds; an anthology. '10(D) 126 p. 8°, $1 net. Oxford Univ.
Time, the place and the girl. Harding, J: W: †$1. G: W. Dillingham.
Time, the place and the girl. Magill, H. B. 25 c. Yellowstone.
Time to strike. Bowes, A. M. 50 c. Pentecostal.
Timely aid. Horn, *Mrs.* D. H. $1.25. Austin.
Timely hints to horse breeders. Gay, C. W. Penn. Dept. of Agriculture.
Time's laughingstocks. Hardy, T: *$1.50 net. Macmillan.

"Times" handbooks for missionary workers. il. D. S. S. Times.
—Trull. Manual of missionary methods for Sunday-school workers. *50 c. net.

"Times" handbooks for Sunday-school workers. D. S. S. Times.
—Hamby. Getting and holding. 50 c. net.
—Schauffler. Knowing and teaching the scholar. 50 c.

Times of sunrise and sunset in the United States. Willson, P. W. *$1 net. Harvard Co-op.

Timlow, Eliz. Westyn.
April-fool twins; further adventures of Dorothy Dot. '08(O10) c. il. D. †$1.25. Dutton.

Timmermann, J: F.
Woolen and worsted finishing: pract. manual of instruction in the methods and machinery used in finishing woolen and worsted goods. '09(My8) c. il. 8°, (American School of Correspondence pubs.) $3. Am. Sch. Corr.
—, comp. Felt; instruction paper. '09(N) c. 21 p. front. il. 8°, (American School of Correspondence pubs.) pap., 50 c. Am. Sch. Corr.

Timoneda, Juan de.
Villete de Amor; cancionero-llamado Villete de Amor: copuesto por Baptista Montidea; en el qual se contienen Canciones, Villancicos, y otras obras diuersas; together with Villete de Amor; enfados de muy grandes avisos, y prouechosas sentencias, nunca impressos, ni vistos hasta agora; puestos a gesto por Montidea, grande amigo de Diamonte; and, Coplas en que se trata como Diego Moreno el qotro tiempo tuuo tanto defcuydo de su muger angora la mata de celos [facsim.] '03, [1909.] no paging, 8°. $5. (200 copies.) Hispanic Soc.

TIN.
Hasluck, P. N., *ed.* Tinplate work. 50 c. McKay.
Knopf, A. Geology of the Seward Peninsula tin deposits, Alaska. 15 c. U. S., Supt. of Docs.
See also Solder.

Tincker, Mary Agnes.
Grapes and thorns; or, a priest's sacrifice. '09. [1910.] (Ag13) 8°, $1. Chr. Press.

Tindall, W:
Origin and government of the District of Columbia; printed for use of the Committee on the District of Columbia, House of Representatives. '09(O) 228 p. 8°. U. S., Supt. of Docs.

Tinker, Chauncey Brewster, ed.
See Cook, Albert Stanburrough.

Tinkham, E. A.
How to play bridge; being full and complete instructions to the student, giving the leads and the best method of play to meet all situations; with illustrative hands. '09, [1910.] (F) c. 5-141 p. 16°, $1. E. A. Tinkham.
Tinsel and gold. Calthrop, D. C. $1.50. G: W: Dillingham.
Tintagel. Hinchman, W. S. $1. Groton Sch.
Tintoretto, Jacopo Robusti.
Masterpieces. '09(Je26) il. T. (Painters' ser.) leath., *75 c. net; pap., *25 c. net. Stokes.
TINTORETTO, Jacopo Robusti.
Bensusan, S: L. Tintoretto. *65 c. net. Stokes.
Tinus, Willard Ivory.
Shorthand; a logical system of modern phonography. '08(D19) c. S. $1.50. Tinus-H.
Tiny tots. Weiderseim, G. G. 70 c. Stokes.
Tiny true tales of animals. Macleod, M., *ed.* 50 c. Stokes.
TIOGA POINT, Pa.
See Athens, Pa.
TIPPECANOE (Battle of).
Reser, A. O., *comp.* Tippecanoe battlefield monument. 60 c. A. O. Reser.
TIPPECANOE COUNTY, Ind.
De Hart, R:, *ed.* Past and present of Tippecanoe Co. 2 v. B. F. Bowen.
Tipple, Ezra Squier, D.D., ed.
Drew sermons on the golden texts for 1909. '08(O24) *$1.25 net; for 1910. '09(D4) c. O. *$1 net. Eaton & M.
Freeborn Garrettson. '10(Mr12) c. por. S. *25 c. net. Eaton & M.
Tipple, Rev. S: A:
Sunday mornings at Norwood; being twenty-two sermons and twenty-two prayers. '09(N20) D. *$1.25 net. Eaton & M.
Tippy, Worth M., D.D., ed.
Socialized church: addresses before the First National Conference of the Social Workers of Methodism, St. Louis, November, 17-19, 1908. '09(Ag7) c. S. *$1 net. Eaton & M.
Tirant lo Blanc; reproduced in facsimile from the ed. of 1490. '04, [1909.] (N) no paging, 8°, $10. (200 copies.) Hispanic Soc.
TIRRELL FAMILY.
See **Genealogies: Terrell, E. H.**
TISBURY, Mass.
Vital records of Tisbury. $3.25. N. E. Hist.
Tisdall, W. St. Clair, D.D.
Comparative religion. '10(F19) D. (Anglican church hdbks.) *40 c. net. Longmans.
Titchener, E: Bradford.
Lectures on the elementary psychology of feeling and attention. '08(Ag15) *$1.40 net. Macmillan.
Lectures on the experimental psychology of the thought-process. '09(D18) c. D. **$1.25 net. Macmillan.
Text-book of psychology. pt. 1. '09(Jl17); pt. 2. '10(N19) c. 12°, ea., $1.30 net; pts. 1 and 2 complete in 1 v., $2 net. Macmillan.

TITHES.
See **Taxation.**
TITIAN (Tiziano Vecelli).
Bensusan, S: L. Titian. *65 c. net. Stokes.
TITICACA ISLAND.
Bandelier, A. F. A. Islands of Titicaca and Koati. $5. Hispanic Soc.
Title market. Post, *Mrs.* E. P. †$1.50. Dodd.
TITLES (*law*).
Kagey, C: C. **Land survey and land titles.** 25 c.; $1.12. Douglas Co. Abs.
Niblack, W: C. Abstracters of title. *$2 net. Callaghan.
See also Conveyancing;—Real property;—Sale;—Surveying;—*also* names of states.
Tittle, Wa., comp.
Colonial holidays; being a collection of contemporary accounts of holiday celebrations in colonial times. '10(O29) c. col. il. Q. $2.50 net. Doubleday, P.
Tittmann, Anna and C:
See Annesley, C:, *pseud.*
Titus, Ida Maud.
See McCullough, Annie Willis.
"Tivoli," pseud.
See Bleackley, Horace W:
Tjader, R:
Big game of Africa. '10(D3) c. il. O. $3 net. Appleton.
To a nun confess'd. Osgood, I. $1.50. Estes.
To Abyssinia through an unknown land. Stigand, C. H. $3.50 net. Lippincott.
To and fro. Warren, H: M. $1.50. Fell.
To auld acquaintance; toast book. '10(O1) c. Tt. bds., 35 c. net. Platt & P.
To-day: an age of opportunity. Young, J. B. *$1.25 net. Jennings.
To friendship. Foster, A. G. 35 c. P. Elder.
To have a friend, be one. Glasspool, R:, *comp.* $1; $2. Platt & P.
To know and believe. Foster, J: M. **90 c. net. Longmans.
To one who went to Carassonne. Dorr, J. C. R. *See* Nadaud, Gustave. Carcassonne.
To Panama and back. Byford, H: T. (Add. pubs. for price.) Conkey.
To ports beyond. Conway, E. E. 90 c. Editor Co.
To the end of the trail. Hovey, R: **$1.25 net. Duffield.
To the front. King, C: †$1.25. Harper.
To the poles by airship. Wright, A. K. $1. Baumgardt.
To the top of the continent. Cook, F: A. **$2.50 net. Doubleday, P.
To the unborn peoples. Gates, *Mrs.* E. M. H. $1. Baker & T.
To the zoo. Brewster, E. G. 50 c. Rust-Craft.
TOASTS.
Alderson, W: A., *comp.* Here's to you. $1.25; $2. Dodge.
Dwiggins, C. V., *comp.* Toasts. 35 c. Winston.
Grover, E. O., *ed.* Book of good fellowship: "a plate of toasts." $1. Volland.
Lowe, P. E., *ed.* Twentieth century book of toasts. 50 c. McKay.

TOASTS.—*Continued.*
Madison, J., comp. Toasts you ought to know. 75 c.; $1.50; under title "Twentieth century toasts," pap., 25 c. Reilly & B.
Nesbit, W. D., *ed.* Loving cup; original toasts; 50 c. Volland.
Pittenger, W. Toasts and forms of public address. 50 c. Penn Pub. Co.
Rice, W., *comp.* Toasts and table sentiments. *50 c. net; *$1.25 net. McClurg.
Rowe, W: H., *jr.* Verse and toast. 2 v. $1. W: H. Rowe.
Spinners' Club, San Francisco. "Prosit"!; book of toasts and sentiments for all occasions. *$1.25 net; *$3 net; *$6 net. P. Elder.
To auld acquaintance: [toasts.] 35 c. net. Platt & P.
Vest pocket toast book. 25 c.; leath., 50 c. Saalfield.
Waters, M., *comp.* Toasts. 50 c.; $1. Barse & H.
Welsh, C: Irish toasts.—Scottish toasts. ea., 50 c. Caldwell.

Toasts and maxims: book of humour to pass the time, collected from various sources. '08(O31) c. il. D. 75 c. Fenno.

TOBACCO.
Can it be defended?; by a lay member of the recent general conference. 10 c. Pub. Ho. of M. E. Ch., So.
Fowler-Chumos, *Mrs.* O. S. Something for you to look into. 25 c. Fowler-Chumos.
German Kali Works. Tobacco culture. gratis. Germ. Kali.
Gilbert, W: W. Root-rot of tobacco. (Add. Superintendent for price.) U. S., Supt. of Docs.
Heward, E: V. Saint Nicotine. $1.50 net. Dutton.
Killebrew, J. P. Tobacco districts and types. Gov. Pr. Off.
Slocum, C: E. About tobacco and its deleterious effects. $1. Slocum Pub.
Werner, C. Text-book on tobacco. $1. Tobacco Leaf.
See also **Cigarettes.**

Tobacco tiller. Hackley, S. B. $1.50. C. M. Clark.

Tobie, Willard Nathan.
Two beautiful prayers from the lips of Jesus. '10(Ja22) c. S. *50 c. net. Jennings.

"Toby, M. P.," pseud.
See Lucy, *Mrs.* H: W.

Toby Tyler. Kaler, J. O. 60 c. Harper.

Toch Brothers.
"R. I. W." book: damp-proofing and protection of modern building construction. '08(Jl) c. 132 p. il. 4°, bds. (Not for sale.) Toch.

TOCOLOGY.
See Midwifery;—Sex.

Tocqueville, Alexis Charles Henri Clerel de.
Voyage en Amérique; ed., with introd., notes and vocab., by R. Clyde Ford. '09 (Ap24) c. por. S. (Modern lang. ser.) 40 c. Heath.

Tocsin (The). Tiffany, E. B. *$2 net. P. Elder.

To-day, and other poems. Windolph, F. L. *$1 net. W: U. Hensell.

To-day's pictorial story of Alexander Campbell. Johnston, R. W. 75 c. R. W. Johnston.

Todd, D: Peck.
Halley's comet. '10(My21) il. O. pap., gratis. Am. Bk.

Todd, Ja. Campbell.
Manual of clinical diagnosis. '08(D) c. 11-319 p. il. 12°, *$2 net. Saunders.

Todd, Jeremy.
Looking forward; or, Bible studies into the future. '08(Ap18) c. S. bds., 50 c. Highlands.

Todd, L.
See Scoones, P.

Todd, Mrs. Mabel Loomis.
Cycle of sunsets. '10(Ap23) c. D. $1.20 net. Small.

Todd, Mrs. Mary Van Lennup Ives.
American madonna: a story of love. '08, [1909.] (Ja) c. 264 p. il. D. $1.25. Binghamton Bk.
Just friends. '08(My23) c. O. $1. M. I. Todd.

Todd, Millicent.
Mary E. Stearns, by one of her pupils. '09, [1910.] (Ap) 6+362 p. il. pors. 12°, $1.75. D: Todd.

Todd and his friends. Griffin, W: M. 25 c. Flanagan.

Toffteen, Olaf Alfr.
Researches in Assyrian and Babylonian geography. pt. 1. '08(Mr14) c. 8°. pap., *$1 net. Univ. of Chic.
Researches in Biblical archæology; pub. for the Oriental Society of the Western Theological Seminary. v. 1, Ancient chronology. pt. 1. '07, [1909.] (D); v. 2, The historic Exodus. '09(O23) map, facsims., tabs., O. ea., *$2.50 net. Univ. of Chic.

Toft, Alb.
Modelling and sculpture. '10(D10) il. 8°, (New art lib.) $1.75 net. Lippincott.

Together. Herrick, R. †$1.50. Macmillan.

Toil of men. Querido, I. *$1.35 net. Putnam.

Toilet medicine. Wooton, E. *$1 net. W: R. Jenkins.

Told in a little boy's pocket. Kennedy, *Mrs.* S. B. C. †75 c. Moffat.

Told in the hills. Ryan, *Mrs.* M. E. 75 c. Rand, McN. & Co.

Told in the smoker. Johnston, J. P. (Add. pubs. for price.) Thompson & T.

Told out of court. Smyth, P. G., *comp.* $1. P. G. Smyth.

Told through the ages. 16°, $1.50. Dodge.
—Havell, *comp.* Stories from Don Quixote. —Stories from the Æneid.—Stories from the Greek tragedy.—Stories from the Iliad. —Stories from the Odyssey.
—Platt, *comp.* Stories from the Old Testament.

Told to the children ser. *See* Dutton's.

Toldridge, Eliz.
Mother's love songs. '10(D31) c. D. $1. Badger.

Toleration. Nygaard, A. C. $1.50. Badger.

Tolhausen, Alex., ed.
Technological dictionary in French, English and German. New ed., rev. by L: Tolhausen. In 3 v. v. 1, [French;] v. 2, [English;] v. 3, [German.] '08(Ap18) 16°, per v., *$2.75 net. Macmillan.

Toll of the Arctic seas. Edwards, D. M. $2.50 net. Holt.

Toll of the sea. Norton, R. †$1.50. Appleton.

Tollemache, Lionel Arth.
Old and odd memories. '08(D5) il. pors. O. *$3.50 net. Longmans.

Tolman, Alb. Harris.
Questions on Shakespeare. In 2 v. v. 1, Introductory; v. 2, The first histories, poems and comedies. '10(Jl30) c. S. v. 1, 75 c. net; v. 2, $1 net. Univ. of Chic.

Tolman, Herbert Cushing.
Ancient Persian lexicon, and the texts of the Achaemenidan inscriptions transliterated and translated with special reference to their recent re-examination. '09 (Mr13) il. O. (Vanderbilt oriental ser.) $1.25. Am. Bk.
Cuneiform supplement (autographed) to the author's ancient Persian lexicon and texts; with brief historical synopsis of the language. '10(Jl9) c. O. (Vanderbilt Oriental ser.) $1.25. Am. Bk.

Tolman, Judson Allen, jr.
Study of the sepulchral inscriptions in Buechler's "Carmina Epigraphica Latina." '10(Je11) c. O. pap., 80 c. Univ. of Chic.

Tolman, Lucius Moody.
See Wente, Adam Oscar.

Tolman, Mrs Stella Webster Carroll.
Around the world. Bk. 1, For first and second grades; Bk. 2, For second and third grades; Bk. 3, For third and fourth grades; Bk. 4, For fourth and fifth grades. '09(N6); Bk. 5, for fifth and sixth grades. '10(O1) c. il. D. (New century geographical ser.) Bk. 1, 36 c.; Bk. 2, 42 c.; Bk. 3, 48 c.; Bk. 4, 54 c.; Bk. 5, 60 c. Silver.

Tolman, W: Howe.
Social engineering: record of things done by American industrialists employing upwards of one and one-half millions of people; with an introd. by And. Carnegie. '09(Ap3) il. por. 8°, *$2 net. McGraw.

Tolstoi, Count Lyoff Nikolaievich.
Works. De luxe ed. 12 v. '10(N) il. levant, $36. Crowell.
Kreutzer Sonata and other stories. '09 (Ap) 350 p. il. 12°, 75 c. J. S. Ogilvie.
Master and man and other parables and tales; new tr. by C. D. S. Hogarth and Constance Garnett. '10(D10) 16°, (Everyman's lib.) 35 c. net; leath., 70 c. net. Dutton.
Teaching of Jesus; tr. by L. and G. Maude. '09(My15) c. 16°, (Lib. of living thought.) **75 c. net. Harper.

TOLSTOI, *Count* Lyoff Nikolaievich.
Maude, A. Life of Tolstoy. 2 v. $6 net. Dodd.
Steiner, E: A. Tolstoy, the man and his message. *$1 net. Revell.

Tom and Kitty. Parker, P. A. 25 c. P. A. Parker.

Tom and the squatter's son. Read, O. P. 50 c.; 25 c. Laird.

Tom Brown's school days. *See* Hughes, T:

Tom Jones. *See* Fielding, H:

Tom, Nadine and Snuffles. Squires, G. 60 c. Caldwell.

Tom the telephone boy. Webster, F. V. 35 c. Cupples & L.

Tom Thumb ser. 8 v. '09(D) ea. 28 p. il. in col. 24°, ea., 15 c. Doran.
Contents: Tale of Tom Thumb; Noah's ark picnic; Goldilocks; Dolly pie; Dolly's diary; Red riding hood; Babes in the wood; Bad bunny book.

Tom Thumb's picture book. '09(D) il. *75 c. net. Doran.

Tomb of Iouiya and Touiyou. Davis, T. M. *$12.50 net. Dutton.

Tome School for Boys bull. O. pap. Tome Sch
—Baker. Preparatory school question.

Tomkins, Rev. Floyd Williams.
Faith and life of a Christian. '09(D11) c. D. (Green Fund book ser.) *75 c. net. Am. S. S.
Helps toward nobler living. '09(Ap3) c. nar. S. **50 c. net; **75 c. net. Jacobs.
Prayers for the quiet hour. [1910.] (N) c. 222 p. 16°, $1. Un. Soc. C. E.

Tomlinson, Everett Titsworth.
British Isles. '10(Ja22) c. il. map. D. **60 c. net. Houghton M.
Elder Boise: a novel. New ed. '08(F22) c. D. **50 c. net. Am. Bapt.
For the stars and stripes. '09(S11) c. D. (War for the Union ser.) †$1.50. Lothrop, L. & S.
Four boys and a fortune, why they went to England and what they found. '10 (Ap30) c. il. D. (Our own land ser.) $1.50. Lothrop, L. & S.
Four boys on the Mississippi. '08(O17) c. il. D. (Our own land ser.) †$1.50. Lothrop, L. & S.
Light Horse Harry's legion. '10(O1) c. il. D. $1.50. Houghton M.
Mad Anthony's young scout. '08(S12) c. il. D. †$1.50. Houghton M.
Sifting of Philip. '08(N7) c. il. D. (Home mission stories.) †$1.25. Am. Bapt.
Ward Hill—the teacher. '09(O23) c. front. 8°, †$1.25. Griffith.
Young Americans in the British Isles. '10 (Ag20) c. il. D. $1.50. Houghton M.
Young blockaders; story of the Civil War. '10(Ag20) c. il. D. (War for the Union ser.) $1.50. Lothrop, L. & S.

Tomlinson, Rev. Irving Clinton.
Christian science. '09(Ap3) c. 16°, pap., 6 c. Chr. Sci.

Tommy Brown. Murray, A. 75 c. Fenno.

Tommy Trot's visit to Santa Claus. Page, T: N. †$1. Scribner.

Tompkins, A. E.
Marine engineering: (a text-book.) 3d ed., with about 400 il. '08(Ag8) 8°, *$4.50 net. Macmillan.

Tompkins, Eug., and Kilby, Quincy, comps.
History of the Boston Theatre, 1854-1901. '08(D) **$5 net; Large pap. ed., $15. Houghton M.

Tompkins, F: C:
Court tennis; with notes on racquets and squash-racquets. '09(My22) c. il. por. S. **$1 net. Lippincott.

Tompkins, J. Calvin S.
Electricity explained in simple language. '09(D) il. $1. Cochrane.

Tompkins, Juliet Wilbor.
Dr. Ellen. '08(F1) c. il. D. †$1.50. Baker & T.
Mothers and fathers. '10(D3) c. col. front. D. $1.50. Baker & T.
Open house. '09(Ja30) c. front. D. †$1.50. Baker & T.
Top of the morning. '10(F19) c. D. †$1.50. Baker & T.

Tompkins, Leslie Jay.
Selection of cases on the law of private corporations. '08(O) c. 14+1148 p. O. $6. Baker, V. & Co.

Tompkinsville folks. Stevens, N. $1.50. C. M. Clark.

Tonalt Camembile. Fish, T. 25 c. House of Fun.

Tone and technique of the violin. Green, J: A. $1. J: A. Green.

Tone placed and developed. Preetorius, C. $1.50. C. Preetorius.

Tone silence and time. Lane, L. P. $1.75. L. P. Lane.

Tonge, Ja.
Coal. '08(Mr7) il. O. (Westminster ser.) *$2 net. Van Nostrand.

Tongue, Helen.
See Bushman paintings.

TONGUE.
See **Taste.**

Tono-Bungay. Wells, H. G: $1.50. Duffield.

Tony the bootblack. Harper, O. 25 c. J. S. Ogilvie.

Tony's wife. Gibbs, G: F. $1.50. Appleton.

Too many women. Schwann, C: D. $1.25. Stokes.

Toodles of Treasure Town and her snow man. Chapin, F. $1.50. Saalfield.

Toof, M. D.
Assessor's manual for Iowa. '07. [1908.] (F) c. 2+14 p. D. pap., 25 c. M. D. Toof.

Tooker, Rob. N.
All about the baby and preparations for its advent; together with the homeopathic treatment of its ordinary ailments. '08 (D19) c. il. 8°, *$1.50 net. Rand, McN. & Co.

TOOLS.
Becker, O. M. High-speed steel. $4. McGraw-H
Goodrich, C. L., *and* Stanley, F. A. Accurate tool work. *$2 net. Hill Pub.
Oberg, E. V. Hdbk. of small tools; together with a complete treatise on screw-thread systems. $3. Wiley.
See also Carpentry;—Machinery;—Saws;—Slide-rule.

Toombs, F: R., ed.
How to wrestle; poses by Hackenschmidt, Tom Jenkins, George Bothner. '10(Je25) c. il. por. 12°, (Spalding's athletic lib.) pap., 10 c. Am. Sports.

Top of the morning. **Tompkins, J. W.** $1.50. Baker & T.

Top o' the world. Swan, M. E. †$1.50. Dutton.

Top Soil, rich in wit and humor. Kendall, E. F. 50 c. Cleveland News.

Topelius, Zacharias.
Hertiginnan af Finland; berättelse fran 1700-talet, af Zach. Topelius; med. 6 planscher af Ben Blessum. '09, [1910.] (Ap) c. 272 p. il. 12°, $1; pap., 75 c. Engberg-H.
Stories for children; tr. from the Swedish by C. W. Foss. Book 6, 7. '08(D5) D. bds., ea., 25 c. Augustana.

Töpffer, Rodolphe.
Le lac de Gers; adapt. and ed. by F. Lutton Carter. '08(O24) 16°, (Siepmann's primary French ser.) *40 c. net. Macmillan.

Topographic surveying. Wilson, H. M. $3.50. Spon.

TOPOGRAPHICAL DRAWING.
Cole, E. T., *and* Stuart, E. R. Individual and combined military sketching. $1. U. S. Cavalry.
Salisbury, R. D., *and* Atwater, W. W. Interpretation of topographic maps. $2.75. U. S., Supt. of Docs.

Topographical surveying. Rees, T: H: $2.50. Staff Coll.

Topography of the chlorophyll apparatus in desert plants. Cannon, W. A. 75 c. Carnegie.

TOPSFIELD, Mass.
See **Congregational Church, Topsfield, Mass.**

Topsy tabbykins. '08(Ag22) c. il. obl. 4°, (Saalfield's cut-out picture books.) pap., 20 c. Saalfield.

Topsy-Turvy land. Byron, M. 25 c. Stokes.

Topsy Turvy tables. '09(D) col. il. *75 c. net. Doran.

Torbert, W: Sydenham, comp.
Digest of patent and trade-mark cases decided by the ct. of appeals of the District of Columbia on appeal from the commissioner of patents, and of copyright cases on appeal from the sup. ct. of the District of Columbia, [etc.] '09(Mr) c. 55+291 p. O. shp., $4.50. Byrne.
See also District of Columbia. Index digest.

Torbett, D.
The schemers. '08(Mr21) c. S. 75 c. Doscher.

Torch ser.; ed. by J. F. Newton. 16°. Torch Press.
—Lazell. Isaiah as a nature-lover. 60 c.
—Newton. Abraham Lincoln. 60 c.

Torchbearers on the King's highway. Haywood, K. H. 20 c. Young Churchman.

Torda, Thdr.
See Crocker, Fs. Bacon.

Tories of Chippeny Hill, Connecticut. Pond, E. L. **$1 net. Grafton Press.

Torn scrap book. Irons, G. $1. Longmans.

Tornos, Alberto de.
Combined Spanish method: pract. and theoretical system for learning the Spanish language. Rev. ed. '08(My2) c. 12°, hf. leath., $1.50. Appleton.

Torquato Tasso. Goethe, J. W. v. 80 c. Ginn.

Torre, Francisco de la.
Obras; dalas a la impression D. Francisco de Queuedo Villegas Cauallero de la orden de Santiago [facsim.] '03, [1909.] (N) 126 p. 8°, $6. (200 copies.) Hispanic Soc.

Torres, Jerónimo.
Conversion y arrepentimiento muy deuoto para el pecador, y para qualquiera que se quifieres entrar en religion [facsim.] '03, [1909.] (N) no paging, 4°, $3.50 (200 copies). Hispanic Soc.

Torrey, Bradford.
See In American fields and forests.

Torrey, C: Cutler.
Ezra studies. '10(Ja15) c. O. *$1.50 net. Univ. of Chic.

Torrey, Rev. D: Clarence.
Protestant modernism; or, religious thinking for thinking men. '10(N19) c. D. $1.50. Putnam.

Torrey, G: Arnold.
Lawyer's recollections in and out of court. '10(O1) c. D. $1.50 net. Little, B. & Co.

Torrey, Harry Beal.
Leptomedusae of the San Diego region. '09 (Ap24) figs. Q. (Univ. of Cal. pubs.; Zoology.) pap., 20 c. Univ. of Cal.

—, and Kleeberger, F. L.
Three specimens of cerianthus from Southern California. '09(D) 115-125 p. Q. (Univ. of California pubs.; Zoology.) pap., 10 c. Univ. of Cal.

Torrey, Jane Anne.
Alice in Sunderland. '09(D) $1. Cochrane.

Torrey, Reuben Archer, D.D.
Gist of the lesson, 1909. '08(N7); 1910. '09(D); 1911. '10(S17) c. 16°, leatherette, ea., *25 c. net; interleaved, *50 c. net. Revell.
Person and work of the Holy Spirit as revealed in the Scriptures and in personal experience. '10(Jl16) c. $1 net. Revell.
Practical and perplexing questions. '09 (My1) c. 12°, *50 c. net. Revell.
Studies in the life and teachings of our Lord. '09(N20) c. il. maps, 8°, $1.50. Bible Inst.

Torrey Botanical Club memoirs. 8°. Torrey.
—Burlingham. Studies of the *Lactariae* of the United States. $1.25.

Torrillion, G. Lamy.
See Seeligmann, Thdr.

Tortoise and the geese. Dutton, M. B., *comp.* $1. Houghton M

TORTRICIDAE.
See Moths.

TORTS.
Ames, J. B., *and* Smith, J. Selection of cases on the law of torts. v. 1, 2. ea., $6. Harvard Law.
Bigelow, M. M. Law of torts. *$4 net. Putnam.
Burdick, F. M. Law of torts. $3. Banks & Co.
Lewis, W: D., *and* McConnell, M. Equity jurisdiction torts. (Add. pubs. for price.) Int. Pr.
Pringle, W: J., *comp.* Cases on the law of torts. $1.50. Thompson & Co.

TORTS.—*Continued.*
Simpson, F. L. Cases on torts to accompany "The law of torts," by Melville M. Bigelow. $4.50. Little, B. & Co.
Stoner, G. Students quiz book; cont. questions, answers and definitions on the law of torts. 50 c. Callaghan.

TORY, Geofroy.
Bernard, A. Geofroy Tory. *$37.50 net. Houghton M.

TOTAL ABSTINENCE.
See **Temperance.**

TOTEMISM.
Frazer, J. G: Totemism and exogamy. 4 v. $16 net. Macmillan.

Totten, Mrs. Martha Barr.
Lew Ott. '09(My) c. 181 p. 8°, $1. M. B. Totten.

TOUCH.
Lurie. L: A. Effect of a constant stimulus upon touch localization. 50 c. Univ. of Cin.

Touch, phrasing and interpretation. Johnstone, J. A. *$1.40 net. Scribner.

TOUCH TYPEWRITING.
See **Typewriting.**

Touching second. Evers, J: J. $1.25. Reilly & B.

Tour (La) des Maures. Daudet, L. M. E. 35 c. net. Macmillan.

Tour in the Hebrides. *See* Boswell, Ja.

Tour through the West. Van Loan, I. A. $1. I. A. Van Loan.

TOURAINE, France.
Lees, F. Summer in Touraine. *$2.75 net. McClurg.

Tourgée, Albion Winegar.
Button's Inn: novel of stage-coach days and rise of Mormonism. New ed. '08 (S19) c. 12°, $1. E. K. Tourgée.

Touring Alaska and the Yellowstone. Taylor, C: M. *$1.25 net. Jacobs.

Tourist tales of California. Isaman, S. W. *$1 net. Reilly & B.

Tourist's India. Reynolds-Ball, E. A. *$2 net. Brentano's.

Tourists' guide of the wonderful St. Lawrence. Smith, A. H. 25 c. A. H. Smith.

Tourists' vade mecum of Italian colloquial conversation. Valgimigli, A. 40 c. Pitman.

Tournier, Eugène Talbot-.
See Talbot-Tournier, Eugène.

Tousey, Eliz.
See Crawford, Rebekah.

Tousey, Sinclair, M.D.
Medical electricity and Röntgen rays, with chapters on phototherapy and radium. '10 (Je) c. 11-1116 p. il. (partly col.) 8°, $7. Saunders.
X-ray in dentistry. '09(Ap10) c. 8°. (Priv. pr.) S. Tousey.

Tousley, Victor Hugo.
See Horstmann, H: C:

Toussaint-Langenscheidt methods. S. Lemcke.
--Feyerabend, *comp.* Complete Hebrew-English pocket-dictionary. 75 c.

Touton, Fk. C:
See Hawkes, Herbert Edn.

Toward humanity. Ingersoll, R. G. 40 c.; 75 c.; 25 c. T: B. Mosher.

Toward social reform. Barnett, S: A: *$1.50 net. Macmillan.

Toward the light. Karadja, *Princess* M. **50 c. net. Dodd.

Toward the uplands. Mifflin, L. $1.25. Oxford Univ.

Towards educational peace. Educational Settlement Committee, England. 36 c. net. Longmans.

Tower, Fk. Warren.
Plumbers' manual and text book, arranged. '09, [1910.] (Ap) 177 p. 24°, $1. F. W. Tower.

Tower, Olin Freeman.
Qualitative chemical analysis of inorganic substances. '09(My) 8°, *$1 net. Blakiston.

Tower, Wa. Sheldon.
Story of oil. '09(Je26) c. il. D. (Lib. of useful stories.) **$1 net. Appleton.

Tower angel. Schumacher, T. $1. Saalfield.

Tower of ivory. Atherton, *Mrs.* G. F. H. †$1.50. Macmillan.

TOWER OF LONDON.
Ainsworth, W: H. Tower of London. 35 c. net; 70 c. net. Dutton.
Davey, R: Tower of London. $3 net. Dutton.
Harper, C: G: Tower of London. *$2.50 net. Jacobs.
Poyser, A. Tower of London. *$2.50 net. Macmillan.

Tower telescope of the Mount Wilson solar observatory. Hale, G: E. (Not for sale.) Carnegie.

Towers, J:, comp.
Dictionary-catalogue of operas and operettas which have been performed on the public stage. '10(S3) c. front. 8°, $25. Acme.

Towers and tanks for water-works. Hazlehurst, J. N. $2.50. Wiley.

Towler, G: L., and Wood, W: W.
Locomotive breakdowns and their remedies. 6th rev. pocket ed. '09(D) c. 300 p. 16°, $1. Henley.

Towler, W. G.
Socialism in local government; with introd. by Captain H. M. Jessel. 2d ed. '09 (F20) D. *$1.50 net. Macmillan.

Towles, J: Ker.
Factory legislation of Rhode Island. '08 (D) c. 119 p. O. (American Economic Association quarterly.) pap., $1. Macmillan.

Town and the trust. Patten, H. E. $1.25. Neale.

Town child. Bray, R. A. *$2 net. Jacobs.

Town down the river. Robinson, E. A. $1.25 net. Scribner.

Town gas and its uses. Webber, W: H. Y. *$2 net. Van Nostrand.

TOWN OFFICERS.
Rockel, W: M. Complete guide for township officers [Ohio]. $4. W. H. Anderson.
See also names of states.

TOWN PLANNING.
United States. City planning; hearing before the Committee on the District of Columbia, United States Senate. '10(Jl) 105 p. 8°. Gov. Pr. Off.
Unwin, R. Town planning in practice. $6 net. Scribner.
See also Pittsburgh.

Towndrow, Grace Eleanore.
Career of Joy. '09, [1910.] (Ja) 231 p. front. 12°, $1.25. C. M. Clark.

Towne, C: Hanson.
Manhattan: [poems.] '09(N20) c. 4°, *$1 net. M. Kennerley.
Quiet singer and other poems. '08(D19) c. O. *$1 net. B. W. Dodge.

Towne, Rev. E: Cornelius.
Headlights of new knowledge, new science, new religion, new education. '10 (Ag) c. 32 p. 8°, 50 c. E. C. Towne.

Towne, Mrs. Eliz. Jones.
Lessons in living. '10(D31) c. por. 12°, $1. E. J. Towne.

—, and Twing, Catherine Struble, comps.
Character delineation and inspiration for those born under the sign of Capricorn December 21 to January 20. '09(D11) c. S. pap., 75 c., boxed. E. J. Towne.

Towne, H: Robinson.
Neutral line: plea for scientific regulation of the tariff; address to the National Tariff Commission convention at Indianapolis, Feb. 16, 17 and 18, 1909. '09(Ap3) O. pap., gratis, Merchants' Assoc.

Towne, Rob. D.
Teddy bears in fun and frolic. '08(O24) c. il. obl. O. pap., 35 c. Reilly & B.

Towne, W: E.
Health and wealth from within; how to apply New Thought to the attainment of health, success, and the solving of everyday problems. '09(Ap3) c. por. D. $1. E. J. Towne.
Way to perfect healing; the power of the Word in ancient and modern spiritual healing; how to apply this power in self-healing; how to train the mind to realize health. '10(Ag) c. 80 p. 12°, 50 c. W: E. Towne.

Townend, Mrs. F. B.
Plain needlework and cutting out. '10(S) il. 8°, 75 c. net. Cassell.

Towner, D. B., ed.
Ideal song and hymn book. '10(Jl16) 12°, church ed., 35 c. net; evangelistic ed., 30 c. net; pap., 15 c. net. Revell.

Towner, Neile F., comp. and ed.
See New York [State] insurance law.—Public Service Commissions law.

Townes, J: C:
Civil government in the United States and in the state of Oklahoma; a text-book on civics. '08(D) c. 347 p. 12°. (Add. pubs. for price.) Austin Pr.
Law books and how to use them. '10(F5) c. 8°, $2.50. Austin Pr.

Townesend, Mrs. Stephen.
See Burnett, *Mrs.* Frances Hodgson.

Townley, Houghton.
The bishop's emeralds. '08(Je27) c. il. D. $1.50. W. J. Watt.
Gay Lord Waring. '10(Je4) c. il. D. $1.50. W. J. Watt.
Scarlet feather. '09(Je26) c. il. D. $1.50. W. J. Watt.

TOWNS.
Morton Eichman Co. Town promotion and municipal advertising. (Add. pubs. for price.) Morton Eichman Co.
Triggs, H. I. Town planning. *$5 net. Scribner.
See also Cities;—Municipal government;—Town officers; — Town planning; — Villages; — *also* names of states.

Townsend, C:
Isabel, the pearl of Cuba: [a play.] '09 (F20) c. 12°, pap., 25 c. Dick.

Townsend, C: F.
Chemistry for launderers, also for cleaners and dyers. American ed. '10(S) 189 p. il. 8°, $1. Nat. Laundry.

Townsend, C: H: Tyler.
Taxonomy of the *Muscoidean* flies, including descriptions of new genera and species. '08(Je20) il. O. (Smithsonian miscellaneous collections.) pap., 60 c. Smith. Inst.

Townsend, C: Wendell, M.D.
Labrador spring. '10(Jl9) c. il. D. $1.50. Estes.

Townsend, Edg. Jerome, and Goodenough, G: Alfr.
Essentials of calculus. '10(D31) il. 8°, $2. Holt.
First course in calculus: [with answers.] '08(Mr7) c. il. O. (Mathematical ser.) $2.50. Holt.

Townsend, E: Waterman.
Climbing Courvatels. '09(F13) c. il. D. †$1.50. Stokes.

Townsend, J. A.
Hist. of Abingdon. '10(D3) il. 4°, $3 net. Oxford Univ.

Townsend, J: Wilson.
Life of James Francis Leonard, the first practical sound reader of the Morse alphabet. [Limited ed.] '09(Ap10) c. il. pors. f°, (Filson Club publications.) $4. Morton.

Townsend, Luther Tracy.
Bible inspiration; orthodox point of view; four lectures del. in Tremont Temple, Boston, under the auspices of the Evangelical Alliance. '09(My) c. 107 p. por. 12°, pap., 10 c. L. T. Townsend.

Townsend, T:
Home afloat; or, the boy trappers of the Hackensack. '09(O16) c. 12°, $1. Athenia Pub.

Townsend, W. G. Paulson, and Pesel, Louisa, F.
Embroidery, or the craft of the needle; with preface by Wa. Crane. '08(O3) il. D. *$1.50 net. Stokes.

Townsend, W. J., D.D., Workman, H. B., and Eays, G:, eds.
New hist. of Methodism. 2 v. '09(D) il. *$7.50 net. Doran.

TOWNSEND FAMILY.
See Genealogies: Abbe, C.;—Tagliapietra, *Mrs.* M. T.

Townshend, A. F.
Military consul in Turkey; experiences and impressions of a British representative in Asia Minor. '10(Ja1) il. 8°, *$3.50 net. Lippincott.

TOWNSHIP OFFICERS.
See Town officers.

TOXICOLOGY.
***See* Poisons.**

TOXINS AND ANTITOXINS.
***See* Poisons.**

TOXOPTERA GRAMINUM.
***See* Parasites.**

Toy dogs. Barton, F. T. $1. W: R. Jenkins.
Toy party. Bodger, J. 50 c. net. Warne.
Toyland. Hammers, E. (Add. pub. for price.) E. B. Holmes.
Toyland ser. of juvenile gift books. il. 8°, 40 c. Stern.
—Bird. How the Indian suit ran away.—Snow-man's Christmas.—Wreck of the nursery flyer. (In one box, $1.25.)

Toynbee, Arnold.
Lectures on the industrial revolution of the eighteenth century in England. New ed., together with a reminiscence by Lord Milner. '08(N21) D. $1. Longmans.

Toynbee, Paget Jackson.
Dante Alighieri; his life and works. '10 (D10) D. $1.50. Macmillan.
Dante in English literature; from Chaucer to Cary, (c. 1380-1844.) '09(Je5) 2 v., O. *$5 net. Macmillan.

TOYS.
Jackson, *Mrs.* E. N. Toys of other days. *$7.50 net. Scribner.
Sloane, T: O. Electric toy making for amateurs. $1. Henley.
See also Dolls.

Toyshop. Copeland, W: 25 c. Dutton.
Toyshop. Gerry, M. S. **50 c. net. Harper.

Tozier, Josephine.
Susan in Sicily. '10(Mr26) c. il. D. (Little pilgrimages ser.) $2, boxed. L. C. Page.

Tozzer, Alfr. Marston, and Allen, Glover Morrill.
Animal figures in the Maya codices. '10 (My14) il. 8°, (Peabody Museum papers.) pap. and cl., $1. Peabody Museum.

Trace, Granville.
The rescuers. '09(S) c. 137 p. 12°, $1. Sentinel.

Trachiniæ (The). *See* Sophocles.
Tracing and coloring book of animals. Williams, C: A. $1. Stokes.
Tracing of direct-current and alternating-current motor troubles. Raymond, E: B. $1.50. Hill Pub.

TRACKS.
See Railroads.

Tracks and tracking. Brunner, J. *$1.25 net. Outing.
Tract number 3377. Higgins, G: H: $1.50. C. M. Clark.

TRACTION.
See Electric railroads;—Railroads.

TRACTION PLOWING.
***See* Plowing.**

Tracy, C: A., comp.
Art of decorating show windows and interiors. '09(Jl31) c. il. 4°, $3.50. Merchants Record.

Tracy, Mrs. Eliz. Strong-.
See Strong-Tracy, *Mrs.* Eliz.

Tracy, Fk. Basil.
Tercentenary history of Canada, from Champlain to Laurier, 1608-1908. '08 (Ag8) c. v. 3, il. pors. maps, 8°. (Add. pubs. for price.) Collier.

Tracy, F:
See Sinclair, S: Bower.

—, and Stimpfl, Jos.
Psychology of childhood. 7th ed., rev. and enl. '09(O23) c. 12°, (Heath's pedagogical lib.) $1.20. Heath.

Tracy, J: Clayton.
Exercises in surveying for field work and office work; with questions for discussion; intended for use in connection with the author's book Plane surveying. '09 (Jl31) c. 12°, **$1 net. Wiley.

Tracy, J: Edwards Woodbridge, and Reed, Jos. F.
Comparative tests of sugar-beet varieties. '09(D) 21 p. il. tabs., 8°, (U. S., Dept. of Agriculture, Bu. of Plant Industry, circular.) pap. (Add. Superintendent for price.) U. S., Supt. of Docs.

Tracy, L:
Cynthia's chauffeur. '10(N12) c. D. $1.50. Clode.
The message. '09(F20) c. il. D. $1.50. Clode.
Red year: story of the Indian mutiny. '08 (Ja25) D. $1.50. Clode.
Son of the immortals. '09(D18) c. 12°, $1.50. Clode.
The stowaway. '09(O23) col. il. D. $1.50. Clode.
Wheel o' fortune. '08(O10) c. il. O. $1.50. Clode.

Tracy, Susan Edith.
Studies in invalid occupation. '10(D31) c. il. O. $1.50 net. Whitcomb.

Tracy, Suzanne.
Practical cook book. '08(Ag) c. 75 p. 8°, $1. S. Tracy.

Tracy, Virginia.
Merely players: stories of stage life. '09 (Ap24) c. D. †$1.50. Century Co.

Tracy, W: Warner.
Production of vegetable seeds: sweet corn and garden peas and beans. '10(S) 39 p. il. 8°, (U. S., Dept. of Agriculture, Bu. of Plant Industry, bull.)

TRADE.
See Business;—Commerce;—Tariff;—Trusts.

Trade and administration of the Chinese Empire. Morse, H. B. *$2.50 net. Longmans.

Trade and tariffs. Robertson, J: M. *$1.50 net. Macmillan.

Trade directory of lithographers; names and addresses of all the lithographing establishments in the United States and Canada; with a selected list from foreign countries. '09(Ja16) c. 12°, $5. Nat. Lithographer.

Trade follows the flag. Evans, H. A. 15 c. U. S., Supt. of Docs.

Trade list annual. *See* Publishers' trade list annual.

TRADE-MARKS.
Swan, K. R. Law and commercial usage of patents, designs and trade-marks. *$2 net. Van Nostrand.

TRADE-MARKS.—*Continued.*
Torbert, W: S., *comp.* Digest of patent and trade-mark cases. $4.50. Byrne.
United States. *Patent Office.* U. S. statutes concerning the registration of trade marks, with the rules of the Patent Office rel. thereto. '09(Je) 55 p. 8°, pap. (Add. Superintendent for price.)
See also Paper trade;—Patents.

TRADE RESTRAINT.
See Business.

TRADE SCHOOLS.
See Technical education.

TRADE-UNIONS.
Britton, W. White slavery; study of the present trades-union system. $1.50. Werner Co.
Collins, J: M. Power and weakness of trade unions. 10 c. J: M. Collins.
Cooke, F: H. Law of combinations, monopolies and labor unions. $6. Callaghan.
Darrow, C. S. "Open shop": arguments for trade-unions. 10 c. S: A. Bloch.
Eliot, C: W: Future of trades unionism and capitalism in democracy. $1 net. Putnam.
Hubbard, E. Closed or open shop? 10 c. Roycrofters.
Hunter, W. R. The crisis: the unions and the courts, the tyranny of injunctions. 10 c. S: A. Bloch.
Jackson, C. Unemployment and trade unions. 50 c. net. Longmans.
Judson, F: N. Labor decisions of Judge Taft. (Add. author for price.) F: N. Judson.
Kennedy, J. B. Beneficiary features of American trade unions. 50 c. Johns Hopkins.
Martin, W. A. Treatise on the law of labor unions. $6. Byrne.
Morse, H. B. Gilds of China. *$1.20 net. Longmans.
Motley, J. M. Apprenticeship in American trade unions. 50 c. Johns Hopkins.
St. Louis labor and label directory. gratis. H. W. Steinbiss.
Spedden, E. R. Trade union label. 50 c. Johns Hopkins.
Trant, W: Trade unions, their original objects. 10 c. Am. Federation of Labor.
See also Co-operation;—Guilds;—Injunctions;—Labor and laboring classes;—Printers and printing;—Strikes.

TRADES.
See Useful arts.

Trades for London boys, and how to enter them: comp. by the Apprenticeship and Skilled Employment Association. '08(O10) O. pap., *25 c. net. Longmans.

Trades for London girls, and how to enter them: companion book to Trades for London boys; comp. by the Apprenticeship and Skilled Employment Association. '09(Jl17) O. pap., *25 c. net. Longmans.

Tradition of scripture. Barry, W: **$1.20 net. Longmans.

Traditional methods of pattern designing. Christie, A. H. $2. Oxford Univ.

Traditions of the earliest visits of foreigners to North America. Durrett, R. T: $4. Morton.

TRAFALGAR CAMPAIGN.
Corbett, J. S. Campaign of Trafalgar. $4.50 net. Longmans.
TRAFFIC (street).
See Roads.
Traffic problems of interurban electric railroads. Conway, T:, *jr.* Univ. of Penn.
Trafford, H:, ed.
Smith method of poultry keeping; how one man made $2437.72 from a small lot, besides attending to his regular business, in 12 months; how to adapt the method to plants of any size or location. '10 (Jl16) c. il. 8°, $1. Hosterman.
Trafton, Gilbert Haven.
Methods of attracting birds. '10(O1) c. il. D. $1.25 net. Houghton M.
Tragedie of Othello. Shakespeare, W: 75 c.; $1. Crowell.
Tragedies of the Medici. Staley, E. *$3.50 net. Scribner.
Tragedies of the white slaves. Lytle, M. H. 25 c. C. C. Thompson.
TRAGEDY.
See Drama and dramatists.
Tragedy. Thorndike, A. H. **$1.50 net. Houghton M.
Tragedy of Hosea. Hart, H: M. (Add. pubs. for price.) Whittaker.
Tragedy of Korea. McKenzie, F. A. *$2 net. Dutton.
Tragedy of man. Madach, I. *$1.50 net. Arcadia.
Tragedy of Nan. Masefield, J: $1 net. M. Kennerley.
Tragedy of Russia in Pacific Asia. McCormick, F: 2 v. *$6 net Outing.
Tragedy of the deserted isle. Wood, W. $1.50. C. M. Clark.
Tragedy of the Mormon woman. Bonsall, M. 35 c. Housekeeper's Corp.
Tragedy queens of the Georgian era. Fyvie, J: *$4 net. Dutton.
Tragic comedians. *See* Meredith, G:
Tragic Russia. Gasiorowski, W. *$2.50 net. Cassell.
Tragical history of Dr. Faustus. *See* Marlowe, Christopher.
Traherne, T:
Poems of felicity; ed. from the ms. by H. J. Bell. '10(O24) facsim., D. bds., $1.75. Oxford Univ.
Trail dust. Richardson, D. S. *$1.25 net. A. M. Robertson.
Trail of a sourdough. Sullivan, M. K. $1.50. Badger.
Trail of the badger. Hamp, S. F: †$1.50. Wilde.
Trail of the Go-hawks. Stapp, E. B. $1.25. C. M. Clark.
Trail of the lonesome pine. Fox, J:, *jr.* †$1.50. Scribner.
Trailers (The). Little, R. M. **$1 net. Revell.
Trailing and camping in Alaska. Powell, A. M. **$2 net. Wessels.
Trailing Geromino. Ellis, E: S. †$1. Winston.
Traill, H: D., and Mann, J. S., eds.
Social England. New il. ed. 12 v. [1910.] (Ap) 8°, ea., $3 net; per set, $35 net. Putnam.
Trails through the western woods. Sanders, H. F. $2 net. A. Harriman.
Trails to peace. Gaut, H. L. 50 c. H. L. Stanton.
Train, Arth. Cheney.
Butler's story. '09(Mr20) c. il. D. †$1.25. Scribner.
Prisoner at the bar. 2d ed., rev. and enl. '08(D12) c. 8°, $1.50. Scribner.
True stories of crime. '08(My16) c. facsims., D. †$1.50. Scribner.
Training and treatment of the home. Hagerling, F: J. 50 c. F. J. Hagerling.
Training for debate. Davis, W: H. Univ. of Kan.
Training for service ser. 16°, 50 c.; pap., 30 c. Standard Pub.
—Medbury. From Eden to the Jordan.—From the Jordan to the throne of Saul.
—Moninger. New Testament church.
—Welshimer. Bible-school vision.
Training in church membership. Van Ness, I: J., *ed.* 50 c.; 30 c. S. S. Bd. So. Bapt.
Training of a priest. Smith, J: T. **$1.50 net. Longmans.
Training of children. Cradock, *Mrs.* H. C. $4. **Ronald Press.**
Training of elem. school teachers. Kandel, I: L. $1.50. Teachers' Coll.
Training of farmers. Bailey, L. H. *$1 net. Century Co.
Training of the chosen people. Horr, G: E. 75 c.; $1. Bible Study.
Training of the imagination. Rhoades, J. *75 c. net. Lane.
Training the bird dog. Whitford, C. B. *$1.25 net. Outing.
Training the girl to keep at home. McKeever, W: A. gratis. W: A. McKeever.
Training the teacher. Schauffler, A. F. *50 c. net; *30 c. net. S. S. Times.
Traitor's wooing. Grainger, F. E. $1.50. Kearney.
Trammelings. Curtis, G. P. $1.50. Herder.
Tramp machinist. Jones, J. (Add. author for price.) Ja. Jones.
Tramping Methodist. Kaye-Smith, S. $1.50. Macmillan.
Tramp's excuse. Lindsay, N: V. gratis. N: V. Lindsay.
Tramp's love. Popham, W: L. 50 c. W: L. Popham.
TRAMPS.
Kelly, E. Elimination of the tramp. **$1 net. Putnam.
Laws, W. Life of a tramp. 25 c. Donohue.
Livingston, L. R. Life and adventures of A-no. 1, America's most celebrated tramp. 25 c. Self Mastery.
Tramps in dark Mongolia. Hedley, J: $3.50 net. Scribner.
TRAMWAYS.
See Electric railroads;—Street railroads.
Transactions and collections of the American Antiquarian Soc. facsims., 4°. Am. Antiquarian.
—American Antiquarian Society. Manuscript records of the French and Indian War in the library of the Society. $2.50.
—Thomas. Diary of Isaiah Thomas, 1805-1828. 2 v. $2.50.

Transcendental magic. Constant, A. L: $3.75. De Laurence, S.

TRANSCENDENTALISM.

Goddard, H. C. Studies in New England transcendentalism. *$1 net. Lemcke.

Kuhns, L. O. Sense of the infinite: study of the transcendental element in literature, life and religion. **$1.50 net. Holt.

Transcontinental sketches. Chase, E. B. $1.50. Winston.

Transferred identity. Hudgins, C: D. 25 c. J. S. Ogilvie.

Transfiguration of life. Clarke, J. F. *$1 net. Am. Unitarian.

Transfigured. Hamilton, J. $1. Am. Tr.

Transfigured church. Jowett, J. H. $1.25 net. Revell.

Transformation of the animal world. Depéret, C: *$1.75 net. Appleton.

Transformation of the Truefitts. Hamer, S. H. 75 c.; 60 c. Cassell.

Transformed colony. Alldridge, T: J. *$3.50 net. Lippincott.

TRANSFORMERS.

See Alternating currents.

Transgressor. White, A. D., *jr.* 50 c.; 75 c. Interstate Prohibition.

Trans-Himalaya. Hedin, S. **$7.50 net. Macmillan.

Transient and permanent in Christianity. Parker, T. *$1 net. Am. Unitarian.

Transition (The). Hill, J: L. $1.50. B'way Pub.

Transition curve. Crandall, C: L. $2. Wiley.

Transition in Illinois from British to American government. Schuyler, R. L. *$1.25 net. Lemcke.

Transition in Virginia from colony to commonwealth. Lingley, C: R. $1.50 net. Longmans.

Transition of masonry. Kruse, C: H: $1. C: H: Kruse.

Transitional period, 1788-1789. Stephens, F. F. $1. Univ. of Mo.

Transitus in lucem. Chancellor, *Mrs.* L. B. 60 c. Fairfield.

TRANSLATION.

Harris, W: J., *comp.* First printed translation into English of the great foreign classics. *75 c. net. Dutton.

Translations from Hebrew and Aramaic. Gollancz, H. *$2 net. Bloch.

TRANSMIGRATION.

See Reincarnation;—Theosophy.

Transmission of military information. Scriven, G: P. (Not for sale.) G: P. Scriven.

Transmission of power. Flather, J: J. *$1.35 net. H. W. Wilson.

TRANSPORTATION.

Barnes, H. C. Interstate transportation. $6. Bobbs-M.

Barry, C: E. Lake and rail transportation. 25 c. La Salle Extension.

Bishop, A. L. State works of Pennsylvania. $1.50. Yale Univ.

Chicago. *City Council. Committee on Social Transportation.* Rept. on the transportation subway systems of Boston, New York, Philadelphia, Paris, London. Chic. City Council.

TRANSPORTATION.—*Continued.*

Gephart, W: F. Transportation and industrial development in the Middle West. $2. Longmans.

Hill, J. J. Future of rail and water transportation. (Add. author for price.) J. J. Hill.

Johnson, E. R: Elements of transportation. **$1.50 net. Appleton.

McPherson, L. G. Transportation in Europe. $1.50 net. Holt.

Peyton, J: H. American transportation conditions. 50 c. Courier-Journ.

Phillips, U. B. History of transportation in the eastern cotton belt to 1860. *$2.75 net. Lemcke.

Rankin, G: A. American transportation system. **$1.50 net. Putnam.

Rocheleau, W: F. Great American industries. Bk. 4, Transportation. 60 c. Flanagan.

Willson, H: B. Story of rapid transit. 92 c. S. S. McClure.

See also Carriers; — Commerce; — Explosives; — Express;—Farms and farming;—Railroads;—Roads.

Transportation of gases, liquids and solids. Nagel, O. *$2 net. O. Nagel.

TRANSUBSTANTIATION.

See Lord's supper.

Trant, W:

Trade unions, their origin and objects; with an appendix showing the hist. and aims of the American Federation of Labor. 14th ed. '08(F29) 8°, pap., 10 c. Am. Federation of Labor.

Trapper's companion; embracing everything a trapper should know. '10(O) c. 148 p. il. 16°, 50 c. Fur News.

TRAPPING.

Kreps, E. H. Science of trapping. 60 c. A. R. Harding.

See also Hunting;—Weasels;—Wolf.

Trask, Mrs. Katrina Nichols, [Mrs. Spencer Trask.]

King Alfred's jewel. '08(S19) front. D. *$1.25 net. Lane.

Tratman, E: Ernest Russell.

Railway track and trackwork. 3d ed. '08 (Ag29) c. il. tabs., 8°, *$3.50 net. Engineering News.

Traubel, Horace.

Optimos: [poetry.] '10(O) 12°, $1.50 net. B: W. Huebsch.

With Walt Whitman in Camden, (July 16. 1888-October 31, 1888.) v. 1 and 2. '08 (My2) c. pors. facsims., 8°, ea., *$3 net. Appleton.

Traum, S: Wegner.

Mormonism against itself. '10(Jl30) c. pors. facsims., 12°, $1. Standard Pub.

Träumereien an französischen kaminen. Volkmann-Leander, R v. 40 c. Ginn.

Trautwine, J: Cresson.

Civil engineer's pocket-book. 19th ed., rev. and enl. by J: C. Trautwine, jr., and J. C. Trautwine, 3d. 09(O2) mor., *$5 net. Wiley.

Trautwine, J: Cresson, jr., and J: Cresson, 3d.

Concrete, plain and reinforced; repr. from Trautwine's "Civil engineer's pocket-book." New (19th) ed. '09(O30) c. figs. **$2 net. Wiley.

Travail of His soul. Richardson, G. L. *60 c. net. Young Churchman.

Travel-adventure ser. il. D. Wilde.
—Knox. In wild Africa. †$1.50.

Travel and sport in Turkestan. Wood, J: N: P. *$3.50 special net. Appleton.

Travel lovers' lib. il. D. $3, boxed. L. C. Page.
—Monroe. Sicily.
—Watkeys. Old Edinburgh. 2 v.
—Winter. Guatemala and her people of to-day.

Travel studies on the apostolic heroes; guide-notes to accompany a journey to thirty places in Palestine, Macedonia, Greece and Italy, visited by the Apostles in their early work, according to the New Testament story; with schedule showing how these travel studies connect the International and Blakeslee courses. '09(Mr) c. 29 p. maps, 12°, pap., 20 c. Underwood.

Traveler and the grapes. Baird, J: C. $1.50. B'way Pub.

Travelers' railway guide; western section. '09 (Jl31) 12°, pap., 25 c. Railway Guide.

Traveller (The). *See* Goldsmith, Oliver.

TRAVELLERS.
See **Explorers;—Voyages and travels.**

Travelling companions. Guthrie, T: A. *$1 net. Dutton.

Travelling school of seven abroad. O'Neil, A. W: $1.50. C. M. Clark.

Travelling trio. Tallman, M. C. $1. M. C. Tallman.

TRAVELS.
See **Voyages and travels.**

Travels at home. Clemens, S: L. 50 c. Harper.

Travels in history. Clemens, S: L. 50 c. Harper.

Travels in Spain. Marden, P. S. **$3 net. Houghton M.

Travels in the Island of Cyprus. Mariti, G. *$1.25 net. Putnam.

Travels of a lady's maid. B., A. $1.50. L. C. Page.

Travels of four years and a half in the United States. Davis, J: *$2.50 net. Holt.

Travels of Phœbe Ann. Lawrence, A. L. $1.50. C. M. Clark.

Travels with a donkey. *See* Stevenson, Rob. L: Inland voyage.

Traver, Hope.
Four daughters of God: study of the versions of this allegory. '08(Je13) diagr., 8°, (Bryn Mawr College monographs.) pap., $1. Winston.

Travers, Mrs. Libbie Miller.
Honor of a Lee. '08(O3) c. D $1.50. Cochrane.

Travers. Dean, S. †$1.50. Stokes.

Travis, Elma Allen, M.D.
The cobbler. '08(Je13) c. D. $1.25. Outing.

Travis, J: Coleridge.
Simple life: an American play. '08(Ap18) 12°. (Priv. pr.) J: C. Travis.

Travis, T.
Young malefactor: study in juvenile delinquency, its causes and treatment; with an introd. by Judge Ben B. Lindsey. '08 (Ap25) c. D. **$1.50 net. Crowell.

Travis, Wa. J.
Practical golf. Rev. ed. '09(My22) il. 8°, *$2 net. Harper.

Treadwell, A:
Life thoughts in rhyme; volume of verse, no. 2. 09(D4) c. por. 8°, $1.50. A: Treadwell.

Treadwell, F: Pearson.
Analytical chemistry; tr. from the German by W: T. Hall. v. 2, Quantitative analysis. 2d ed., thoroughly rev. and enl. '10(Jl30) c. 8°, $4. Wiley.

Treasure (The). Eaton, P. W. $1.50. Fenno.

Treasure and the field. Hope, I. *$1 net. Herder.

Treasure Island. *See* Stevenson, Rob. L:

Treasure trove. Dawson-Scott, C. A. $1.50. Duffield.

Treasure valley, Keith, M. $1.50. Doran.

Treasures of truth. Butler, G: F. 75 c. S. D. Clough.

Treasures of two worlds. Imber, N. H. 50 c. Citizens Pr.

Treasury of English literature. Warren, K. M., *comp. and ed.* $2. Dodge.

Treasury of verse for little children. Edgar, M. G., *comp.* $2.50. Crowell.

Treasury ser. [anthologies]; ed. by Alb. Broadbent. 16 v. '10(N) col. fronts., ea., 35 c.; ooze, 75 c., boxed. Crowell.

Treasury ser. 6 v. '09(D) il. in col. 24° pap. ea., 25 c. Doran
Contents: As thy days so shall thy strength be; Love divine; O rest in the Lord; My hope is in thee; Stand fast in the faith; Tidings of great joy.

Treat, Edn. Bryant.
See Newton, C: Bertram.

Treat, Payson Jackson.
National land system, 1785-1820. '10(D17) c. il. maps, 8°, $2.50. Treat.

TREATIES.
Devlin, R. T: Treaty power under the Constitution of the United States. $6. Bancroft-W.
See also Prostitution;—*also* names of countries.

Treatise on care of saws and knives; book for mill managers, superintendents, foremen, and saw filers. '10(Ag) c. 208 p. il. 8°, $2 net. Baldwin, T. & B.

TREATMENT.
See Medicine, and references under that subject.

Treatment of disease. Ostler, W: 40 c. Oxford Univ.

Treatment of nature in English poetry. Reynolds, M. *$2.50 net. Univ. of Chic.

Treatment of the exempt classes of Chinese in the United States. Ng Poon Chew. 5 c. Ng Poon Chew.

Tredgold, A. F.
Mental deficiency. '08(N21) il. figs. charts, 8°, *$4 net. Wood.

TREDYFFRIN, Pa.
Pleasants, H: Hist. of the Old Eagle School, Tredyffrin, in Chester County, Pennsylvania. $2. Winston.

Tree, Sir Herbert Beerbohm.
Henry VIII. and his court. '10(D31) 16°, 50 c. net. Cassell.

TREE FAMILY.
See Genealogies: Leach, J. G., *ed.*

Tree of knowledge: a document by a woman: [a novel.] '08(Je) c. 6+306 p. 12°, $1.50. Stuyvesant Press.

Tree of modern life. Ziv, R. L. 75 c.; 50 c. R. L. Ziv.

TREES.
Apgar, A. C. Ornamental shrubs of the United States. $1.50. Am. Bk.
Ashe, W: W. Shade trees of North Carolina. 8 c. Uzzell.
Baily, W: L. Trees, plants, and flowers. 60 c. Lippincott.
Big shellbark: Ring-nut hickory. (Add. Superintendent for price.) U. S., Supt. of Docs.
Black walnut. (Add. Superintendent for price.) U. S., Supt. of Docs.
Britton, N. L., *and* Shafer, J: A. North American trees. **$7 net. Holt.
Burgess, A. F. Requirements to be complied with by nurserymen or others who make interstate shipments of nursery stock. (Add. pubs. for price.) U. S., Supt. of Docs.
Clarke, D. A. Commercial forest trees of Massachusetts. (Add. pubs. for price.) Wright & P.
Collins, J. F., *and* Preston, H. W. Key to New England trees. 40 c. Preston.
Cooper, C. S., *and* Westell, W. P. Trees and shrubs of the British Isles. 2 v. *$7 net. Dutton.
Emerson, A. I., *and* Weed, C. M. Our trees. $3. Lippincott.
European larch. (Add. Superintendent for price.) U. S., Supt. of Docs.
Fernow, B. C: Care of trees in lawn, street and park. $2 net. Holt.
Groom, P. Trees and their life histories. *$10 net. Cassell.
Hall, H. M. Studies in ornamental trees and shrubs. 75 c. Univ. of Cal.
Huntington, A. O. Studies of trees in winter. $2.50. Estes.
Irving, H: How to know the trees. $1.25 net. Cassell.
Jepson, W. L. Trees of California. *$2.25 net. Cunningham, C. & W.
Mosher, E. R. Studies of fruit and nut bearing trees.—Studies of our cone-bearing trees. ea., $2. Bardeen.
New Jersey. Forest Park Reservation Commission. Planting and care of shade trees. M. J. Forest.
Phythian, J. E. Trees in nature, myth and art. *$1.50 net. Jacobs.
Ramaley, F. Wild flowers and trees of Colorado. $1.25; $1. A. A. Greenman.
Rogers, J. E. Trees that every child should know. **$1.20 net. Doubleday, P.
Sargent, C: S., *ed.* Trees and shrubs. v. 2, pt. 2. **$5 net. Houghton M.
Schaffner, J: H. Trees of Ohio. 50 c. Ohio State Acad.
Secord, L. M. Our native trees and their uses. 60 c. L. M. Secord.
Step, E: Wayside and woodland trees. *$1.75 net. Warne.
Taylor, A. D. Street trees; their care and preservation. gratis. Cornell Univ.

TREES.—*Continued.*
Trees and plants for the world out of doors. '09(N) 100 p. il. (partly col.) plans, 4°, *$2 net. Brown Bros. Co.
Ward, H. M. Trees. v. 4-5. ea., *$1.50 net. Putnam.
See also Basswood;—Beech;—Boxelder;—Chestnuts;—Eucalyptus;—Evergreens; — Forests and forestry;—Fruits;—Ginko tree;—Insects;—Maples; — Oaks; — Paper-birch; — Pecans;—Pine oak;—Pine trees;—Red oak;—Shrubs;—White oak;—*also* California.

Trees in nature, myth and art. '08(Ap11) 12°, $1.50. Putnam.

Treleaven, Jos. T.
Preliminary mechanical drawing, for schools and evening classes. '10(Ap23) il. O. pap., 50 c. Longmans.

Tremain, H: Edn.
Fifty papers; addresses and writings. 09 (D11) 4 v., il. pors. 8°, $4. Bonnell.

Tremayne, Mrs. Eleanor E.
First governess of the Netherlands, Margaret of Austria. '08(O24) il. O. (Romantic history.) *$3 net. Putnam.

Tremendous trifles. Chesterton, G. K. *$1.20 net. Dodd.

Trench, Herbert.
Apollo and the seaman, The queen of Gothland, stanzas to Tolstoy and other lyrics. '08(S12) O. *$1.50 net. Holt.

Trench, Archbp. R: Chevenix.
Notes on the miracles of our Lord. '08 (Mr7) 8°, (London lib.) *$1 net. Dutton.

Trend. Rollow, J. S. $1. Guide Pr. and Pub.

Trend of governmental regulation of railroads. Johnson, E. R: 15 c. Am. Acad. Pol. Sci.

Trend of scientific thought away from religious beliefs. Ladd, H. O. 75 c. Badger.

Trendelenburg, Adolf.
Contribution to the hist. of the word person; with introd. by Rudolf Eucken. '10 (S3) O. pap., 40 c. Open Court.

Trenholme, Norman Maclaren.
Outline of English hist. for use in high schools and colleges; (based on Cheyney's Short hist. of England.) '10(My21) c. D. 50 c. Ginn.
Syllabus for the history of western Europe, with references and review questions, (based on "Robinson's Introduction to the history of western Europe.") In 2 pts. pt. 1, The middle ages; pt. 2, The modern age. '08(F1) c. D. ea., 40 c. Ginn.

Trent, W: Peterfield.
Longfellow, and other essays. '10(Ag13) c. D. $1.50. Crowell.
See also Adams, C: Kendall.

Trentham, Percival.
Practice of forestry. '10(Je4) 8°, $7 net. Scribner.

Trenton (N. J.) Free Public Library. City of Trenton, N. J.: bibliography. '09(Mr27) D. pap., gratis. Trenton Pub. Lib.

Trenton (N. J.) Free Public Library. List of entertaining autobiographies. '10(Jl16) 12°, gratis. Trenton Pub. Lib.

Trepoff, Ivan, [pseud. for G: Hatfield Dingley Gossip.]
The forsaken; argument in fiction for the morality of divorce. '10(Jl2) $1. Cochrane.
Spiritmist. '09(My) c. 288 p. D. $1.50. D.W. Newton.

Tres comedias modernas et un acto y en prosa. Carrión, M. R. 60 c. Holt.

Trésor (Le) du vieux seigneur. Erckmann, E. *25 c. net. Crowell.

TRESPASS.
Lewis, W: D., *and* McConnell, M. Equity jurisdiction, trespass to real property. $1. W: D. Lewis.

Trespass. Dudeney, *Mrs.* H: E. $1.25. Small.

Trevelyan, G: Macaulay.
England in the age of Wycliffe. New ed. '09(O2) O. **$2 net. Longmans.
Garibaldi and the thousand. '09(O30) il. maps, O. *$2.25 net. Longmans.

Trevelyan, Sir G: Otto.
Life and letters of Lord Macaulay. In 2 v. '09(Je19) 8°, $5; in 1 v., $2. Harper.

Trevelyan, R. C.
Sisyphus: operatic tale. '09(F20) sq. O. *$1.50 net. Longmans.

Trevena, J:
Arminel of the West. '09(Mr6) D. $1.50. Moffat.
Furze the cruel. '08(Mr14) D. †$1.50. Moffat.
Heather. '09(My15) D. $1.50. Moffat.
Pixie in petticoats. '09(D25) $1.50. Moffat.

"Trevert, E:," pseud.
See Bubier, E: Trevert.

Treves, Sir F:
Cradle of the deep: account of a voyage to the West Indies. '08(Ag15) 8°, *$4 net; New ed. '10(D31) il. maps, 8°, $2.50 net. Dutton.
Manual of operative surgery. 3d ed.; rev. by the author and Jonathan Hutchinson, jr. 2 v. '09(Jl) il. 8°, hf. mor., *$13 net. Lea.
Other side of the lantern. Cheaper ed. [1910.] (Ap) il. $2.25 net. Cassell.
Students' hdbk. of surgical operations. New ed., rev. [1910.] (My) 126 p. il. 12°, $2.50 net. Funk.
Uganda for a holiday. '10(D10) il. 8°, $3 net. Dutton.

Trevor, Jos. Ellis.
Lectures on thermodynamics. '09(O) 4+113 p. diagrs., 8°, $1. J. E. Trevor.

Trezise, F: Ja.
Design and color in printing. '09(My1) c. il. 8°. $1. Inland Pr.

Trial and crucifixion of Jesus Christ. Broderick, M. *$1.25 net. Longmans.

Trial by marriage. Jackson, W. S. $1.50. Lane.

Trial of Christ. Kaye, J: B. *$1 net. Sherman, F.

Trial of Mabel Dering. *See* Noble, Frances. Not for this world only.

TRIALS.
Deans, R. S. Trials of five queens. *$3.50 net. Brentano's.

TRIALS.—*Continued.*
Sellers, A. V. Classics of the bar. $2. Classic.
See also Actions at law;—Evidence;—Indictments;—Judges;—Jury;—Juvenile courts; — Pleading and practice;—*also* Dred Scott case;—Hayes-Tilden contest;—Moyer and Haywood case;—Thaw case;—Waters-Pierce case.

Trials and triumphs of a young preacher. Kilgore, E. G. *$1 net. Pub. Ho. of M. E. Ch., So.

Triassic *ichthyosauria.* Merriam, J: C. $3. Univ. of Cal.

TRIBUNAL OF THE TERROR.
See French Revolution.

Tribune almanac and political register, 1908. '08(Ja18); 1909. '09(Ja9); 1910. '10(Ja15) c. O. (Lib. of Tribune extras.) pap., ea., 25 c. Tribune Assoc.

Tribute to mother. Stutzman, *Mrs.* L. W. 35 c. L. W. Stutzman.

Trichotomy in Roman law. Goudy, H: $1.35. Oxford Univ.

Trick and fancy pool shots exposed. Hood, J. G. 50 c. Exposé.

Trickett, W:
See Pennsylvania. Law of crimes.

Tricks and illusions. Goldston, W. *$1.25 net. Dutton.

Tricks for every one. Devant, D: 50 c. Lippincott.

Tricoche, G: Nestler.
Some stumbling blocks of the French language and the way to avoid them. [3d ed., with a supplement.] [1910.] (My) c. '09. 114 p. 12°, 75 c. G: N. Tricoche.
Vade mecum du professeur de français; encyclopédie portative de connaissances et d'exercices utiles à ceux qui enseignent la langue et sa littérature. '09(S) c. 9+335 p. 12°, $1.50. G: N. Tricoche.

Tridon, André.
See Leconte de Lisle, Charles Marie René.

TRIFOLIUM.
See Clover.

Trigger, Thdr. Clark.
Notes on methods of filling teeth with gold inlays. '10(Mr) c. 111 p. il. 8°. $2. T. C. Trigger.

Triggs, H. Inigo.
Town planning, past, present, and possible. '09(D11) il. Q. *$5 net. Scribner.

TRIGONOMETRY.
Becker, G: F., *and* Van Orstrand, C. E. Hyperbolic functions. $4. Smith. Inst.
Brenke, W: C: Text-book on advanced algebra and trigonometry. $2 net. Century Co.
Brown, S. J. Trigonometry and stereographic projections. (Not for sale.) Lord Balto. Pr.
Carslaw, H. S. Plane trigonometry. *$1.10 net. Macmillan.
Conant, L. L. Five-place logarithmic and trigonometric tables. 50 c.—Plane and spherical trigonometry. 85 c.—With Five-place logarithmic and trigonometric tables. $1.20.—Plane trigonometry. 90 c. Am. Bk.
Davison, C: Class book of trigonometry. $1 net. Putnam.

TRIGONOMETRY.—*Continued.*
Durell, F. Logarithmic and trigonometric tables. 75 c—Plane trigonometry. $1; bound with Logarithmic and trigonometric tables, $1.25. C: E. Merrill.
Granville, W: A. Plane and spherical trigonometry. $1.25. Macmillan.
Hall, A. G., *and* Frink, F. G. Trigonometry. $1.25. Holt.
Keller, S: S. Mathematics for engineering students: algebra and trigonometry. *$1.75 net. Van Nostrand.
Mueller, W: C: New manual of natural trigonometrical functions to seven places of decimals. $9. W: C: Mueller.
Murray, D. A. Essentials of trigonometry and mensuration. 80 c. Longmans.
Robbins, E: R. Plane trigonometry. 60 c. Am. Bk.
Rothrock, D: A. Elem. of plane and spherical trigonometry. $1.40 net. Macmillan.
Solution of triangles. 2 v. ea., 25 c. Indust. Press.
See also Geodesy; — Geometry; — Logarithms; — Mensuration;—Navigation;—Surveying.

TRILOBITES.
See Paleontology.

Trimble, E. Dunlap.
Teachers' art manual. '10(D31) c. il. 8°, $1.25. Carnahan Press.

Trimming of Goosie. Hopper, J. M. **$1.10 net. Moffat.

Trine, Ralph Waldo.
Land of living men. '10(D3) c. O. $1.25. Crowell.
On the open road: being some thoughts and a little creed of wholesome living. '08(O31) c. D. *50 c. net. Crowell.

TRINITY (The).
Bishop, W: S: Development of trinitarian doctrine in the Nicene and Athanasian creeds. 75 c. net. Longmans.
Harvey, T. L. In antescript, two presidential nominees: [Unitarianism and Trinitarianism.] 25 c. T. L. Harvey.
Ingram, A. F. W. Love of the Trinity. *60 c. net. Whittaker.
Lanier, J: J. Kinship of God and man [trinitarian theology.] 3 v. ea., $1.50; per set, $3.50. J: J. Lanier.
Novatian. De Trinitate liber. *$2 net. Putnam.
See also God;—Holy Spirit;—Jesus Christ.

Trinity College, Dublin. Speeches [in Latin] of public orators del. at the comitia held for conferring honorary degrees. '10(Mr5) O. $1.75. Longmans.

Trinity College (Durham, N. C.) Dept. of Education bull. 8°. Trinity Coll.
—Brooks. Comparison of school systems.

TRINITY COUNTY, California.
Map of Trinity County, California, showing boundaries of the national forests; comp. from data furnished by the U. S. Forest Service. '09(N) f°, map, pap., 45 c. Cal. State Mining.

Trinummus (The). *See* Plautus, Titus Maccius.

Trip through New Zealand. Zeagler, J: W. 40 c. J: W. Zeagler.

Trip to Mars. Ash, F. $1.50. Lippincott.

Trip to Panama. Stevens, W. B. gratis. Lesan-G.

Trip to the Land of the Midnight Sun. Wood, M. P. $2 net. Brandu's.

Trip (A) to the North Pole. '10(D) col. il. bds., 75 c. Saalfield.

Trip to the unknown. Love, E. L. 75 c. Cochrane.

TRIPLE TAX.
See Political economy.

TRIPOLI, Africa.
Furlong, C. W. Gateway to the Sahara. **$2.50 net. Scribner.

Tripp, Howland.
In whaling days. '09(Je12) c. D. †$1.50. Little, B. & Co.

Tristan and Isolde. *See* Hadden, J. C.;—Wagner, Wilhelm Richard.

Tristram and Iseult. Bédier, J. $3.75 net. Lippincott.

Triumph of love. Allen, L. W. *$1.25 net. Putnam.

Triumphant life. Horton, R. F. 50 c. Revell.

Triune development ser. 8°. Triune Order.
—Miller. Triune development. 60 c.

Trix and Over-the-Moon. Rives, A. †$1. Harper.

Trixey, the manicure girl. Redic, M. $1. B'way Pub.

TROBRIAND, Philippe Regis de.
Post, M. C. D. Life and memoirs of Comte Régis de Trobriand, Major General U. S. A. **$5 net. Dutton.

Trois grotesques. *See* Gautier, Théophile.

Trois portraits littéraires. *See* Sainte-Beuve, Charles Augustin.

Trolley car and the lady. Lampton, W: J. 25 c. Badger.

Trolley folly. Phillips, H: W. $1.25. Bobbs-M.

Trolley trips through New England and Hudson River Valley. '09(Je12) il. maps, 16°, pap., 15 c. Trolley Press.

Trollope, Anthony.
Works. Uniform ed. In 16 v. '08(Je27) 24°, $8; flex. leath., $12. Lane.
Barchester novels. In 6 v. '09(D18) il. 8°, per set, $9. Dutton.
Barchester Towers. '08(O17) 16°, (Best books ser.) leath., *$1 net. Dutton.
Dr. Thorne. '09(Ap3) 16°, (Everyman's lib.) *35 c. net; leath., *70 c. net. Dutton.
Framley Parsonage. '08(O17) 16°, (Best books ser.) leath., *$1 net. Dutton.
Last chronicle of Barset. 2 v. '09(Ap3) 16°, (Everyman's lib.) ea., *35 c. net; leath., *70 c. net. Dutton.
Small house at Allington. '09(Ap3) 16°, (Everyman's lib.) *35 c. net; leath., *70 c. net. Dutton.
Three clerks; with an introd. by W. Teignmouth Shore. Pocket ed. '09(Mr6) por. S. (World's classics.) 35 c.; leath., 75 c. Oxford Univ.
The warden. '08(O17) 16°, (Best books ser.) leath., *$1 net. Dutton.

Trooien, Ole N.
Current practice in steam engine design; with foreword by Prof. H. J. Thorkelson: thesis submitted for the Degree oi Mechanical Engineer, University of Wisconsin. '09(F6) figs. O. (Univ. of Wis. bull.; Engineering ser.) pap., 25 c. Univ. of Wis.

Troop, Mrs. Edna Willa Sullivan, ["Scota Sorin."]
The pendulum; story. '01(D31) c. front. D. $1.25. Duffield.

Troop of the guard. Hagedorn, H., *jr.* **$1.10 net. Houghton M.

Trophées (Les). Heredia, J: M. de. $1.75. F. W. Chandler.

TROPICAL DISEASES.
Brooke, G. E. Aids to tropical medicine. *$1 net. Wood.
Castellani, A., *and* Chalmers, A. J. Manual of tropical medicine. $6 net. Wood.
Daniels, C: W., *and* Wilkinson, E. Tropical medicine and hygiene. In 3 pts. pt. 1, Diseases due to protozoa. **$3 net. Wood.
Manson, *Sir* P. Tropical diseases. $4.50 net. Wood.
See also Hygiene.

TROPICAL MEDICINE.
See Tropical diseases.

Tropical tales. Wyllarde, D., *pseud.* $1.50. Lane.

TROPICS.
Ritchie, J: W., *and* Purcell, M. A. Primer of sanitation for the tropics. 60 c. World Bk.
See also Agriculture.

Trotman, S. R.
Leather trades chemistry: analysis of materials and finished products. '08(My23) il. tabs., O. *$4.50 net. Lippincott.

Trotter, Lionel Ja.
The Bayard of India: life of General Sir James Outram. '09(O30) 12°, (Everyman's lib.) *35 c. net; leath., *70 c. net. Dutton.
Hodson of Hodson's Horse. '10(Ap23) 16°, (Everyman's lib.) 35 c. net; leath., 70 c. net. Dutton.
Life of Warren Hastings. '10(D17) 16°, (Everyman's lib.) 35 c. net; leath., 70 c. net. Dutton.

Trotter, Melvin E.
Jimmie Moore of Bucktown. [New rev. ed.] '09(D18) c. front. D. *75 c. net. Revell.

Troubetzkoy, Prince Pierre.
The passer-by. '08(D5) front. D. $1.50. Doubleday, P.

Troubetzkoy, Princess.
See Rives, Amélie.

Troubles, remedies and repairs of the automobile. Dyke, A. L. $2. A. L. Dyke.

TROUSERS.
See Tailoring.

TROUT.
Armistead, W. H. Trout waters: management and angling. *$1.75 net. Macmillan.
Skues, G. E. M. Minor tactics of the chalk stream and kindred subjects. $2. Macmillan.
Speckled brook trout. $3 net. Stokes.

Troutbeck, G. E.
Children's story of Westminster Abbey. '10 (S10) il. D. $1.35. Stokes.

Trouvillon, H. W.
Opinion journalistic. '10(Ag) gratis. H. W. Trouvillon.

Trovador (El). Gutiérrez, A. G. 40 c. Heath.

Trow, Harris C.
See Crocker, Fs. B.

Troward, T:
Doré lectures; Sunday addresses at the Doré Gallery, London, given in connection with the higher thought centre, 10 Chemiston Gardens, Kensington. '09 (N20) D. (Edinburgh lecture ser.) pap., 50 c. Roger Bros.
Edinburgh lectures on mental science. [Rev. and enl. ed.] '10(Mr5) c. 16°. 75 c. Roger Bros.

Trowbridge, Fs. Bacon.
Trowbridge genealogy; history of the Trowbridge family in America. '08, [1909.] (F) 848 p. il. pors. map, facsims., 4°, $15; hf. mor., $17.50. F. B. Trowbridge.

Trowbridge, J: Townsend, ["Paul Creyton."]
Coupon bonds. '08(Jl11) 12°, (Young America lib.) 50 c. Hurst.
Darius Green and his flying machine. '10 (N5) c. il. S. bds., 50 c. net. Houghton M.
Father Brighthopes. '08(Jl4) 12°, (Young America lib.) 50 c. Hurst.
Lucy Arlyn. '08(Jl18) 12°, (Young America lib.) 50 c. Hurst.
Martin Merryvale, his X mark. '08(Je27) 12°, (Young America lib.) 50 c. Hurst.
Pair of madcaps. '09(Ap10) c. il. D. †$1.50. Lothrop, L. & S.
Story of a wireless telegraph boy. '08(O17) c. front. †$1.25. Houghton M.
The vagabonds. '08(Je6) 12°. (Canterbury poets.) 75 c. Hurst.
The vagabonds, and other poems; a biographical sketch of the life of the author by Prof. H. L. Williams. '08(N21) c. il. 16°, 35 c. Hurst.

Trowbridge, W: Rutherford Hayes.
Beau Sabreur: Maurice de Saxe, Marshal of France; his loves, his laurels and his times, 1696-1750. '09(O23) il. O. *$4.50 net. Brentano's.
Cagliostro; splendor and misery of a master of magic. '10(D10) il. 8°, $3.50. Dutton.
Mirabeau, the demi-god. '08(Mr14) il. pors. 8°, *$3.75 net. Scribner.
Seven splendid sinners: [biographies of seven women.] '08(O31) por. O. *$4.50 net. Brentano's.

TROWBRIDGE FAMILY.
See Genealogies.

Troy, Hugh C.
See Publow, C: Albert.

TROY, O.
See Miami Co.

TRUCK FARMS.
See Farms and farming;—Gardens and gardening.

Truckee-Carson experiment farm. Scofield, C. S. (Add. Superintendent for price.) U. S., Supt. of Docs.

True, Alfr. C:
Notes on the history of agricultural pedagogy in the United States; del. at 28th annual meeting of the Society for the Promotion of Agricultural Science. '08 (Ap18) 8°, pap., gratis. T: F. Hunt.
Secondary education in agriculture in the United States. '10(Ja29) 8°, (U. S., Dept. of Agriculture, Office of Experimental Stations, circular.)
—, and Crosby, Dick Jay.
American system of agricultural education. '09(Jl31) il. 8°, (U. S., Dept. of Agriculture; Office of Experiment Stations, circular.) pap. (Add. pubs. for price.) U. S., Supt. of Docs.
True, C. E., ["Surev."]
Uncle Carl. '08(Je13) c. D. $1.50. Neale.
True, Ellen Isabel.
Labor problem; bibliography. '09, [1910.] (F) 37 p. 12°, (Wisconsin Free Library Commission; American social questions.) pap., 25 c. Wis. Free Lib.
True, Helen Belle, ed.
How to obtain our own. '10(Mr5) c. 12°, $1. Roger Bros.
True, Rodney Howard, and Sievers, Arth. F:
Some factors affecting the keeping qualities of American lemons. '09(Jl) 17 p. 8°, (U. S., Dept. of Agriculture, Bu. of Plant Industry circular.) (Add. Superintendent for price.) U. S., Supt. of Docs.
True aims of education. Goodspeed, F. L. 15 c. F. L. Goodspeed.
True American types ser. D. *60 c. net. Am. Unitarian.
—Kimball. Joshua James.
—Smith. Capt. Thomas A. Scott.
True Chatterton. Ingram, J: H. $3 net. Scribner.
True church. Dulles, A. M. *$1.25 net. Revell.
True constitution. Clayton, J. C. *$3 net. Assoc. Pub.
True detective stories. Drummond, A. L. $1.50. G: W. Dillingham.
True God. Ballard, F. *$1 net. Eaton & M.
True history of some of the pioneers of Colorado. Shaw, L. $1. L. Shaw.
True Indian stories. Dunn, J. P. $1. Sentinel Pub. Co.
True love. Adams, A. A: 75 c. A. A: Adams.
True manhood. Gibbons, J. 50 c. McClurg.
True method of tone production. Van Broekhoven, J. $1.50. H. W. Gray.
True rationalism. Power, M. 10 c. Herder.
True source of a happy life. Wayt, H. 50 c. Chr. Pub. Co.
True spirit of religion is universal. Paramânanda, *Swami.* (Add. pubs. for price.) Vedanta.
True stories about dogs. Gask, L. $1.50. Crowell.
True stories from history. Robarts, E. 60 c. Dodge.
True stories of crime. Train, A. C. †$1.50. Scribner.
True story of Andersonville prison. Page, J. M. $2. Neale.
True story of the American flag. Fow, J: H: 5 c. net. W: J. Campbell.
True story of the Cook and Peary discovery of the North Pole. Neil, H: $1.50. Educ. Co.
True tales of the plains. Cody, W: F. $1; 50 c. Cupples & L.
True Tilda. Couch, A. T: Q-. †$1.50. Scribner.
True way of life. Baughman, *Mrs.* N. R. B. $1. N. R. B. Baughman.
Trueblood, B: Franklin.
International arbitration at the opening of the twentieth century. '09, [1910.] (F) 23 p. 8°, pap., 5 c. B: F. Trueblood.
Trueblood, T: Clarkson.
See Fulton, Rob. Irving.
—, Caskey, W: G:, and Gordon, H: Evarts, eds.
Winning speeches in the contests of the Northern Oratorical League. '09(D11) c. por. D. $1. Am. Bk.
See also Fulton, Rob. Irving.
Truedson, Nils Peter.
Bibelns gudomlighet, eller, bibelns innehall bevisar dess gudomliga ursprung. '09, [1910.] (Ap) 5-305 p. 12°, $1. N. P. Truedson.
Truesdell, Amelia Woodward.
Francisca reina: [poems.] '08, [1909.] (Je) 44 p. il. 8°. (Priv. pr.) Badger.
Trull, G: Harvey.
Manual of missionary methods for Sunday-school workers. '08(Ag8) c. il. D. ("Times" handbooks for missionary workers.) bds., *50 c. net. S. S. Times.
Trumbull, C: Gallaudet.
Men who dared: studies in Old Testament manhood. Teachers' ed. '08(Ap18) c. maps, D. (Add. pubs. for price.) Y. M. C. A.
Taking men alive: studies in the principles and practice of individual soul-winning. '08(Ag1) c. pors. D. *60 c. net; pap., *40 c. net. Y. M. C. A.
Trumbull, Loyal Wingate.
Manual of underground surveying. '10 (O15) c. il. maps, 8°, $3 net. McGraw-H.
TRUMBULL COUNTY, Ohio.
Upton, *Mrs.* H. T. Twentieth century hist. of Trumbull County, O. $12 net. Lewis Pub.
Trumpet voice from the throne. Eccles, L. F 25 c. L. F. Eccles.
"Trumps," pseud.
See Dick, W: Brisbane.
"Trumps, jr," pseud.
Poker patience; cont. a thorough description of the game, with correct rules and useful hints. '09(N) 11p. S. pap., 15 c. Dick.
TRURO PARISH, Va.
Slaughter, P. History of Truro parish in Virginia. **$1.50 net. Jacobs.
TRUSSES (Architectural).
Dufour, F. O. Bridge engineering; roof trusses. $3. Am. Sch. Corr.
Ricker, N. C. Study of roof trusses. gratis. Univ. of Ill.
See also Bridges.

Trust, E:, comp.
Professional directory of doctors and druggists of Philadelphia, incl. Atlantic City, N. J., and Camden, N. J., also doctors in 80 nearby towns. '10(My7) c. D. $2. E: Trust.

TRUST COMPANIES.
See Banks and banking.

Trust companies of the United States, 1908 ed.; compilation of the statements of condition of trust companies of the United States as of June 30th, 1908, also of officers, directors, correspondents, dividend rates and stock quotations. '08(D19); 1909 ed.; compilation of the statements of condition of trust companies as of June 30th, 1909; also of officers, directors and correspondents, dividend rates and stock quotations: comp. by the Audit Company of N. Y. '10(Ja15) c. il. O. gratis. U. S. Mortgage.

Trusting and resting. Cady, E. H. 10 c. Roger Bros.

TRUSTS (*industrial*).
Abbott, N. T. Cases on the law of equity jurisprudence and trusts. (Add. pubs. for price.) Flood.
American Academy of Political and Social Science. Federal regulation of industry. pap., $1. Amer. Acad. Pol. Sci.
Bancroft, E. A. Destruction or regulation?: address [on trusts.] (Priv. pr.) E. A. Bancroft.
Batdorf, J: W. Why pay tribute. 25 c. Volunteer.
Benedict, R. A. Malefactors of great wealth! $2. Am. Business.
Bonum Meritum, *pseud.* War of words between President Roosevelt and J. Pierpont Morgan concerning railroad, tariff and trust questions. $1; 25 c. Donohue.
Cooke, F: H. Law of combinations, monopolies and labor unions. $6. Callaghan.
French, H: F. Federal control of trusts and combinations in restraint of trade under the commerce clause of the Constitution. (Add. pubs. for price.) Kohn & P.
Ingalls, J. S. Slaves to the trust. 10 c. Social Justice.
Jennings, E. B. People and their property. $1. B'way Pub.
Menace to business of Sherman anti-trust act. 20 c. Am. Banker.
Thomas, A. F. Slavery of progress; its causes and its cure. $1. Neale.
See also Capital and labor;—Commercial law;—Corporations;—Monopolies;—Social science;—Sugar;—*also* American Sugar Refining Co.;—Beef Trust;—Standard Oil Co.

TRUSTS AND TRUSTEES.
Woodman, A. S. Treatise on the law of trustees in bankruptcy. $6.50. Little, B. & Co.
See also Bookkeeping;—Executors and administrators.

TRUTH.
Ashenfelter, I. G. Truth: a message from the spirit. $1. I. G. Ashenfelter.
Dean, O. S. Quest of the ages; or, a search for the poles of truth. 50 c. Cochrane.
Sharpe, A. B., *and* Aveling, F. Spectrum of truth. 30 c. Herder.

TRUTH.—*Continued.*
Simpson, T: J. Book of facts, truths and reason. $1. T: J. Simpson.
Stoner, J. R. Logic and imagination in perception of truth. $1.50. Cochrane.
Zellars, E. V. Worth of truth. $1. Standard Pub.
See also Philosophy.

Truth. Arner, E. E. 25 c. Faribault-Pilot.
Truth. Joyce, J: A. $1. J: A. Joyce.
Truth about grace, by a Berean. Cook, C: C. 25 c. C: C. Cook.
Truth about Ireland. Corkey, A. 75 c. Shockley Bros.
Truth about Jesus. Mangasarian, M. M. $1; 50 c. Independent Religions.
Truth about Mexico. Smith, E. S. (Add. pubs. for price.) Bankers' Pub.
Truth (The) about my friends. '10(S10) S. (Thumb-o-graph ser.) 50 c. net. Stokes.
Truth about Port Arthur. Nojine, E. K. *$5 net. Dutton.
Truth and error of Christian Science. Sturge, M. C. *$1 net. Dutton.
Truth and near truth. Sexton, W: H: $1.50; $2. Winn & H.
Truth Dexter. McCall, S. †$1. Little, B. & Co.
Truth of Christianity. Turton, W. H., *comp.* $1.25. Putnam.
Truths of to-day. Mackinnon, A. G. *75 c. net. Eaton & M.
Truxton King. McCutcheon, G: B. $1.50. Dodd.

TRYPANOSOMA DIMORPHON.
See Parasites.

TRYPANOSOMIASIS.
See Sleeping sickness.

Tschaikowsky, Peter Iljitch.
Eugene Onégin: lyric scenes in three acts, after the Russian of Alex Sergeyvitch Pushkin; German translation by A. Bernhard; English version by H: Grafton Chapman; music by Tschaikowsky. Vocal score complete. '08(F1) c. 4°, (Schirmer's collection of operas.) $3.50; pap., $2.50. Schirmer.

Tscholl, Rev. J:
War on the white plague. '10(D10) c. il. por. O. pap., 60 c. net. Wiltzius.

Tschudi, Clara.
Ludwig, the second king of Bavaria; tr. from the Norwegian by Ethel Harriet Hearn. '08(F22) por. 8°, *$2.50 net. Dutton.
See also Holm, Eric, *pseud.*

Tubbs, E: T., comp.
See Noble, E: N.

TUBERCULOSIS.
Andrews, L: R. White peril; or, how I cured myself of consumption. $1. White Peril.
Bandelier, —, *and* Roepke, O. Tuberculin in diathesis and treatment. *$3 net. Wood.
Bardswell, N. D. Advice to consumptives. 75 c. net. Macmillan.
Bardswell, N. D. Expectation of life of the consumptive after sanatorium treatment. $1.50 net. Oxford Univ.

TUBERCULOSIS.—*Continued.*

Bonney, S. G. Pulmonary tuberculosis. $7 net; $8.50 net. Saunders.

Boston Association for the Relief and Control of Tuberculosis. Narrative of the work done in a year. 15 c. Bost. Assoc. Tuberculosis.

Boston School Committee. Rept. of the Commission appointed by the School Committee of the city of Boston to investigate the problem of tuberculosis among school children. (Not for sale.) Bost. Sch. Com.

Brewer, I: W. Treatment of tuberculosis in Arizona. gratis. Wood.

Burton-Fanning, F. W. Open air treatment of pulmonary tuberculosis. *$1.50 net. Hoeber.

California Association for the Study and Prevention of Tuberculosis. Warfare against tuberculosis. (Add. pubs. for price.) Cal. Assoc. Tuberculosis.

Colorado State Organization of the International Congress on Tuberculosis. Colorado souvenir book for the International Congress on Tuberculosis. (Add. pub. for price.) W: N. Beggs.

Connecticut. Commission to Investigate Tuberculosis. Rept. on factory conditions in Connecticut as related to tuberculosis. (Add. pubs. for price.) Conn. Com. Tuberculosis.

Connecticut. *Special Commission on Tuberculosis.* Rept. of special commission appointed to investigate tuberculosis. '08, [1909.] (Je) 86 p. il. chart, 8°. (Add. pubs. for price.) Connecticut.

Davis, C: H: S. Consumption: its prevention and cure without medicine. $1. Treat.

Davis, N. S., *jr.* Consumption: how to prevent it and how to live with it. *$1 net. Davis.

Flick, L. F. Tuberculosis, a curable and preventable disease. 10 c. Winston.

Henry Phipps Institute. Fourth annual rept. for the study, treatment, and prevention of tuberculosis. (Add. pubs. for price.) Henry Phipps Inst.

Hort, E. C. Rational immunization in the treatment of pulmonary tuberculosis and other diseases. *$1.50 net. Wood.

Hrdlicka, A. Tuberculosis among certain Indian tribes of the United States. (Add. Superintendent for price.) U. S., Supt. of Docs.

Hutchinson, W. Conquest of consumption. **$1 net. Houghton M.

Hutt, W: H. Evolution of the anti-tuberculosis crusade. gratis. W: H. Hutt.

International Congress on Tuberculosis. Transactions of the sixth International Congress on Tuberculosis. 8 v. per set, $10. Nat. Assoc. Tuberculosis.

Jacobs, P. P., *comp.* Campaign against tuberculosis in the United States. $1. Charities Pub.

Kaessman, F. G. Cure of consumption, coughs and colds. 10 c. Health-Wealth.

Kelynack, T. N., *ed.* Tuberculosis in infancy and childhood; its pathology, prevention and treatment. *$4 net. Wood.

TUBERCULOSIS.—*Continued.*

Keyes, T. B. Renewal of life: arguments for subcutaneous injections of oil. $2. Tubercle Press.

Klebs, A. C., *ed.* Tuberculosis. $6. Appleton.

Knopf, S. A. Kampen mod taering: [prevention of consumption.] 25 c. Amerika Pub.

Knopf, S. A. Tuberculosis, a preventable and curable disease. **$2 net. Moffat.

Lockhard, L. B., Tuberculosis of the nose and throat. *$5 net. Mosby.

Massachusetts. *Committee for International Congress on Tuberculosis, 6th Washington.* Tuberculosis in Massachusetts. (Add. pubs. for price.) Wright & P.

Maylard, A. E. Abdominal tuberculosis. *$4 net. Blakiston.

Mohler, J: R. Tuberculin test of cattle for tuberculosis. (Add. Superintendent for price.) U. S., Supt. of Docs.

Moore, J. V. Truth about tuberculosis and its only cure. 25 c. J. V. Moore.

Muthu, C. Pulmonary tuberculosis and sanatorium treatment. $2 net. Wood.

National Association for the Study and Prevention of Tuberculosis. Some plans and suggestions for housing consumptives. '09, [1910.] (Mr) 87 p. il. plans. 4°, 25 c. Nat. Assoc. Tuberculosis.

National Fraternal Congress. International Congress on Tuberculosis. $1; 50 c. I. W. Porter.

New York [City.] *Board of Health.* What you should know of tuberculosis. gratis. N. Y. Dept. Health.

New York [City.] *Dept. of Health.* Brief history of the campaign against tuberculosis in New York City; catalogue of the tuberculosis exhibit of Dept. of Health.—Consumption is a preventable and curable disease.—Do not spit; tuberculosis (consumption) catechism and primer. ea., gratis. N. Y. Dept. Health.

New York [City.] *Dept. of Health.* Hdbk. of help for persons suffering from pulmonary tuberculosis. (Add. pubs. for price.) J. W. Pratt.

Newsholme, A. Prevention of tuberculosis. *$3 net. Dutton.

Otis, E: O. Great white plague, tuberculosis. **$1 net. Crowell.

Pennsylvania. *Dept. of Health.* Descriptive catalogue of the exhibit of the State Dept. of Health of Penn. at the International Congress on Tuberculosis. (Add. pubs. for price.) Penn. Dept. Health.

Pottenger, F. M. Diagnosis and treatment of pulmonary tuberculosis. *$3.50 net. Wood.

Reynolds, M. H., *and* Beebe, W. L. Dissemination of tuberculosis by the manure of cattle. gratis. Univ. of Minn.

Ross, W: M. My personal experiences with tuberculosis. 50 c. W. M. Ross.

St. Louis Municipal Commission on Tuberculosis. First report. (Add. pubs. for price.) St. L. Com. Tuberculosis.

TUBERCULOSIS.—*Continued.*

Schroeder, E. C: Milk and its products as carriers of tuberculosis infection. 5 c. U. S., Supt. of Docs.

Schroeder, E. C:, *and* Cotton, W: E. Tests concerning tubercle bacilli in the circulating blood. (Add. Superintendent for price.)—Tubercle bacilli in butter. 15 c. U. S., Supt. of Docs.

Simple lessons on tuberculosis or consumption, with reference to its cause and prevention, by Dr. M. J. Rosenau, Dr. E. C. Schroeder and Emile Berliner, special committee. '08, [1909.] (My) c. 20 p. il. 12°. (Add. pubs. for price.) Assoc. Charities.

Smith, F: C. Pulmonary hemorrhage in the tuberculous at high altitude.—Relation of climate to the treatment of pulmonary tuberculosis. Gov. Pr. Off.

Some plans and suggestions for housing consumptives. Nat. Assoc. Tuberculosis.

Swarts, G. T., *jr., comp.* Tuberculosis exhibitions. 25 c. Educ. Exhibit.

Thomson, H. H. Consumption, its prevention and home treatment. $1 net. Oxford Univ.

Tscholl, J: War on the white plague. 60 c. net. Wiltzius.

United States. *Dept. of Agriculture. Bureau of Animal Industry.* Danger from products of tuberculous cattle. (Add. Superintendent for price.) U. S., Supt. of Docs.

United States. *Dept. of Agriculture. Bureau of Animal Industry.* Danger from tubercle bacilli in environment of tuberculous cattle. 5 c. U. S., Supt. of Docs.

United States. *Dept. of Agriculture. Bureau of Animal Industry.* Relation of tuberculosis lesions to mode of infection. 5 c. U. S., Supt. of Docs.

United States. *Dept. of Agriculture. Bureau of Animal Industry.* Susceptibility of tubercle bacilli to modification. 15 c. U. S., Supt. of Docs.

United States. *Dept. of Agriculture. Bureau of Animal Industry.* Unsuspected but dangerously tuberculous cow. 5 c. U. S., Supt. of Docs.

United States. *Dept. of Commerce and Labor. Bureau of Labor.* Mortality from consumption in dusty trades. (Add. Superintendent for price.) U. S., Supt. of Docs.

United States. *Office of Indian Affairs.* Manual on tuberculosis; its cause, prevention and treatment; by Jos. A. Murphy, M.D., medical supervisor, U. S. Indian Service. '10(Ap) 9 p. 8°, pap.

Walters, F. R. Open-air or sanitorium treatment of pulmonary tuberculosis. *$2.25 net. Wood.

Wilkinson, W. C. Treatment of consumption. *$3 net. Macmillan.

Wolf-Eisner, A. Ophthalmic and cutaneous diagnosis of tuberculosis. *$2.75 net. Wood.

Wright, B. L. Treatment of tuberculosis by the administration of mercury. 10 c. U. S., Supt. of Docs.

See also **Infectious diseases;—Lungs.**

Tuck, Clyde Edn.
Bald knobbers; romantic and historical novel. '10(N19) c. il. 12°, $1. B. F. Bowen.
For love of you. '09, [1910.] (Mr) 87 p. 8°, 75 c. B. F. Bowen.

Tucker, Bp. Alfr. Rob.
Eighteen years in Uganda and East Africa. '08(N21) 2 v., il map, O. *$8.50 net. Longmans.

Tucker, C: Cowles, rep.
See District of Columbia. *Ct. of appeals.* Repts.

Tucker, E: A.
Steel construction; pract. treatise on the modern use of steel in the erection of fireproof buildings, and its applications to structural work in general. '10(My21) c. il. 8°, (Amer. Sch. of Correspondence pubs.) $1.50. Am. Sch. Corr.

Tucker, G: Fox.
See United States. Federal penal code.—*also* Wilson, G: Grafton.

Tucker, Gilbert Milligan.
American agricultural periodicals; an historical sketch. '09(Ag14) il. 8°. (Priv. pr.) G. M. Tucker.

Tucker, H. B.
Book of anniversaries; 19th century and after. '09(O2) 32°, (Miniature reference lib.) mor., 50 c. Dutton.

Tucker, H: Harrison, jr.
Standard against Uncle Sam. '08(My9) c. il. 8°, pap., $1. H: H. Tucker, Jr.

Tucker, Ja. Irwin.
Contracts in engineering, the interpretation and writing of engineering-commercial agreements; elem. text-book for students in engineering, engineers, contractors and business men. '10(N5) c. 8°, $3. McGraw-H.

Tucker, J: Atherton.
First four meeting houses of Milton, Mass., covering a period of two and a half centuries. '08(N) 5 p. plans, f°, 75 c. J: A. Tucker.

Tucker, Louise Emery.
Universal school reader; 4th year. '09 (Je3) il. 12°, *45 c. net. Macmillan.

Tucker, S: Marion.
Verse satire in England before the Renaissance. '09(Ap24) 8°, (Columbia Univ. studies in English.) pap., *$1 net. Lemcke.

Tucker, T: G:
Life in the Roman world of Nero and St. Paul. '10(O29) c. il. O. $2.50 net. Macmillan.

Tucker, W: Jewett.
Personal power; counsels to college men. '10(Mr26) c. O. **$1.50 net. Houghton M.
Public mindedness; an aspect of citizenship considered in various addresses given while president of Dartmouth College. '10(Mr19) c. 8°, $2. Rumford Press.

Tucker, Willis Gaylor, M.D.
On the character of the state board examinations and the competency of state medical examining boards. '08, [1909.] (My) 4 p. 8°, gratis. W. G. Tucker.

Tucker & Vinton.
Reproductions from photographs of representative concrete structures built by Tucker & Vinton. '08, [1909.] (F) c. 63 p. of il. 12°. (Add. pubs. for price.) Tucker & V.

Tuckerman, Julius.
Am anfang; sprachgefühl-lesebuch für konversation, mit fragen und wörterbuch. '08(O10) c. D. 50 c. Holt.
Simplicité: reader of French pronunciation. '08(F22) c. D. 50 c. Am. Bk.

Tuckwell, Rev. W:
Reminiscences of Oxford. 2d ed., rev. and enl. '08(Mr21) il. 8°. *$2 net. Dutton.

Tudor and Stuart lib. See Oxford.

Tudor and Stuart proclamations, 1485-1714. Steele, R., *comp.* 2 v. $34. Oxford Univ.

Tufts, Ja. Hayden.
American college education and life; [an address given before the Section of Education at the Baltimore meeting of the American Association for the Advancement of Science.] '09(S) 17 p. 8°, pap. (Add. author for price.) J. H. Tufts.
See also Dewey, J:

Tulane University of Louisiana. Triangular debate bet. Tulane Univ. of La., Univ. of N. C. and Univ. of Va.: resolved, that postal savings banks, as described in the Carter bill as ordered repr. on January 6, 1909, should be established by the United States government. '10(Je11) 8°, $1. H. W. Kaiser.

Tuley, H: Enos.
Diseases of children. '09, [1910.] (O) c. '09. 9+653 p. il. diagrs., 8°, $5. Southern Med.
Obstetrical nursing, for nurses and students. [2d ed., rev. and rewritten.] '10(N) 9+246 p. il. 12°, $1.50. Morton.

Tulley, C:
The playmate. '08(F8) il. 12°, $1.50. Dutton.

Tully, Mrs. R: Walton.
See Gates, Eleanor.

Tumbleweed. Woodman, H. R. $1. H. R. Woodman.

TUMBLING.
See Acrobats and acrobatism.

TUMORS.
Bland-Sutton, J: Tumors, innocent and malignant. $5 net. Funk.
Cullen, T: S. Adenomyoma of the uterus. *$6.50 net. Saunders.
Kelly, H. A., *and* Cullen, T. S. Myomata of the uterus. *$7.50 net; *$9 net. Saunders.

TUNGSTEN.
See Electricity.

TUNGSTEN LAMP.
See Electric light.

TUNIS, Africa.
Milltoun, F., *pseud.* In the land of the mosques and minarets: [Algeria and Tunis.] $3; $7. L. C. Page.
Petrie, G. Tunis, Kairouan, and Carthage. *$4.80 net. Doubleday, P.

TUNNELS AND TUNNELING.
Prelini, C: Tunneling. $3 net. Van Nostrand.

Tunstall, A. C.
See Warwick, F. J.

Tunzelman, G. W. de.
Treatise on electrical theory and the problem of the universe. '10(O8) 8°, $4.50 net. Lippincott.

Tupman, W. F.
Grocery. '09(Ap28) D. (Pitman's traders' hdbks.) $1. Pitman.

Tupper, Mrs. Edith Sessions.
Stuff of dreams. '08(D5) c. il. D. $1.50. B. W. Dodge.

Turbervile, G:
Booke of Hunting, 1576. '09(Ja23) il. D. (Tudor and Stuart lib.) bds., $2.50. Oxford Univ.

TURBINES.
Collins, H. E. Steam turbines. $1. Hill Pub.
Garnett, W. H. S. Turbines. $1.60 net. Macmillan.
Harrison, H. H. Model steam turbines. 25 c. Spon.
Jude, A. Steam turbine. $6 net. Lippincott.
Leland, W. S. Steam turbines. $1.50. Am. Sch. Corr.
Moyer, J. A. Steam turbine. **$4 net. Wiley.
Neilson, R. M. Steam turbine. *$4.20 net. Longmans.
Sothern, J. W. Marine steam turbines. *$5 net. Van Nostrand.
Surplee, H: H. Gas turbine. **$3 net. Lippincott.
Swingle, C. F. Steam turbine engines. $1. Drake.
Thomas C. C. Steam turbines. $4. Wiley.
Walker, S. F. Steam boilers, engines and turbines. *$3.50 net. Van Nostrand.
Westinghouse, G:, *comp.* Broadening the field of the marine steam turbine. (Priv. pr.) G: Westinghouse.

Turk, Mrs. R. S.
See Turk, Willie Anne Cary.

Turk, Willie Anne Cary, [Mrs. R. S. Turk.]
Beatty-Asfordby: the ancestry of John Beatty and Susanna Asfordby, with some of their descendants. '09(N) c. 184 p. il. 12°, (Allaben genealogical ser.) $4. Allaben.

TURKESTAN, Asia.
Pumpelly, R., *ed.* Explorations in Turkestan expedition of 1904. 2 v. $10. Carnegie.
Wood, J: N: P. Travel and sport in Turkestan. *$3.50 special net. Appleton.

TURKEY.
Abbott, G: F: Turkey in transition. *$4.25 net. Longmans.
Barton, J. L. Daybreak in Turkey. *$1.50 net. Pilgrim Press.
Basmajian, K. H. Life in the Orient. $1 net. Am. Tr.
Brown, D. V. Haremlik; some pages from the life of Turkish women. **$1.25 net. Houghton M.
Buxton, C: R. Turkey in revolution. *$2.50 net. Scribner.
Cardashian, V. Ottoman empire of the twentieth century. $1. V. Cardashian.

TURKEY.—*Continued.*
De Bunsen, V. Soul of a Turk. *$3.50 net. Lane.
Eliot, *Sir* C: N. E. Turkey in Europe. $2.50. Longmans.
Garnett, L. M. J. Home life in Turkey. *$1.75 net. Macmillan.
Knight, E. F. Awakening of Turkey. *$3 net. Lippincott.
Ramsay, *Sir* W. M. Revolution in Constantinople and Turkey in 1909. $3.75 net. Doran.
Singleton, E., *comp.* Turkey and the Balkan States, as described by great writers. **$1.60 net. Dodd.
Smith, A. D. H. Fighting the Turk in the Balkans. **$1.75 net. Putnam.
Townshend, A. F. Military consul in Turkey. *$3.50 net. Lippincott.
Upward, A. East end of Europe. *$4 net. Dutton.
See also Albania;—Arabia;—Balkans;—Constantinople;—Mt. Athos;—Rhodes (*Island of*).

Turkey Hill ser. 8°. A. C. Bates.
—East Granby, Conn. Congregational church. Records. $3.50.

TURKEYS.
Nourse, H. A. Turkeys, ducks and geese. 50 c. Webb.
Turkeys, all varieties; their care and management; mating, rearing, exhibiting and judging turkeys; explanation of score-card judging, with complete instructions: collection of the experiences of best known successful turkey breeders, exhibitors and judges. '09(D) c. 93 p. il. 4°, 75 c. Reliable Poultry.

Turkish diplomatic life in Washington under the old regime, by the wife of a diplomat. '10(O15) pors. 16°, $1. Cochrane.

Turkish literature: comprising tables, belles-lettres, and sacred traditions; tr. into English for the first time: with introd. by Epiphanius Wilson. '08(Je27) c. il. $1.75; hf. mor., $3.50. Lamb Pub.

Turn of the tide. Porter, *Mrs.* E. H. †$1.25. Wilde.

Turn of the tide. Vachell, H. A. 75 c. Cupples & L.

Turneaure, F: Eug.
Hydraulic engineering. pt. 1, Hydraulics, by F: E. Turneaure; pt. 2, Water-power development, by Adolph Black. '09(F20) c. il. 8°, (American School of Correspondence pubs.) $1. Am. Sch. Corr.
Water supply: treatise on the sources, distribution, and consumption of water for commercial and domestic uses, and modern practice in the construction of water-works and purification plants. '08(Ap11) c. il. 8°, (American School of Correspondence pubs.) $1.50. Am. Sch. Corr.
See also Johnson, J: Butler.

—, and Maurer, E: Rose.
Principles of reinforced concrete construction. 2d ed., rev. and enl. '09(O16) c. il. 8°, $3.50. Wiley.

—, and Russell, Harry Luman.
Public water-supplies: requirements, resources, and the construction of works: with a chapter on pumping-machinery by D. W. Mead. 2d rev. and enl. ed. '08 (S12) c. il. 8°, $5. Wiley.

Turner, C: C.
Aerial navigation of to-day; popular account of the evolution of aeronautics. '09(D4) D. *$1.50 net. Lippincott.

Turner, Rev. C: H: Black, comp.
Some records of Sussex County, Del. '09, [1910.] (Ap) 387 p. pls. pors. 8°. $5 net. Allen, L. & S.

Turner, Claude Allen Porter.
Concrete steel construction. pt. 1, Buildings: pract. treatise for the constructor and those commercially engaged in the industry. '09(N20) c. 8°, $20. C. A. P. Turner.

Turner, Ed., pseud.
Standard guide for locomotive engineers and firemen, also railway machinists. '09 (N13) c. il. T. leath., 75 c. Laird.

Turner, Ethel, [Mrs. H. R. Curlewis.]
Family at Misrule. '09(Je5) il. D. (Girls' own lib.) †75 c. McKay.
Little Mother Meg. '09(Je5) il. D. (Girls' own lib.) †75 c. McKay.
Miss Bobbie. '08(N7) il. D. (Girls' own lib.) 75 c. McKay.
Seven little Australians. '08(N7) c. il. D. (Girls' own lib.) †75 c. McKay.
That girl. '10(Je4) D. (Girls' own lib.) 75 c. McKay.
Three little maids. '08(D5) il. D. (Girls' own lib.) 75 c. McKay.
The wonder-child. '08(Ag1) D. $1.50. Saalfield.

Turner, Fs. Marion.
Life of General John Sevier. '10(Ap2) c. por. D. $1.50 net. Neale.

Turner, F: Jackson.
The old West. '09(Ap17) map, O. pap., 35 c. State Hist., Wis.

Turner, G. C.
Graphics: applied to arithmetic, mensuration and statics. '08(F22) il. 12°, *$1.25 net. Macmillan.

Turner, G. Frederic.
Gloria. '10(Ap2) c. il. D. $1.50. Dodd.

Turner, Rev. H. Turner.
See Ratcliffe, Fs. Asbury.

Turner, Harry Baker.
Story of the island steamers; Nantucket freeze-ups; story of the "camels." '10 (Ag6) c. il. pors. 12°, 65 c. Inquirer

Turner, Herbert Hall.
Halley's comet: an evening discourse to the British Association. at their meeting at Dublin, on Friday, Sept. 4, 1908. '08 (N26) il. por. O. pap., 35 c. Oxford Univ.

Turner, J: Kenneth.
Barbarous Mexico. '10(D31) c. il. D. $1.50. Kerr.

TURNER, Joseph Mallord William.
Finberg, A. J. Turner's sketches and drawings. $4 net. Scribner.
Holme, C:, *ed.* Water colors of J. M. W. Turner. *$3 net. Lane.
Rawlinson, W. G. Engraved work of J. M. W. Turner. v. 1. *$6 net. Macmillan.

Turner, Luther Weston.
Basket maker. '09(S11) c. il. O. 75 c. Davis Press.

Turner, Percy M.
Millet. '10(S10) col. il. O. (Masterpieces in colour.) bds., 65 c. net; leath., $1.50 net. Stokes.
Van Dyck. '08(D19) il. O. (Masterpieces in colour.) bds., *65 c. net. Stokes.

—, and Baker, C. H. Collins, eds.
Stories of the French artists from Clouet to Delacroix. '09(D) il. 8°, (Art and letters lib.) *$3 net. Duffield.

Turner, Philip.
Aids to osteology. '08(My23) 12°, (Students' aids ser.) *$1.25 net. Wood.

Turner, T:
Metallurgy of iron: being one of a series of treatises on metallurgy; written by associates of the Royal School of Mines; ed. by Sir W. Roberts-Austen. 3d ed., rev. and enl. '08(Jl18) O. *$1.25 net. Lippincott.
Practical metallurgy. '08(O3) il. *$1.25 net. Lippincott.

Turner, W. V.
Brake operation and manipulation in general freight service, with review of some of the causes and conditions which produce shocks and break-in-twos; being paper presented before the Chicago Railway Club, Dec. 21, 1909. '10(Jl) 71 p. il. 8°, 50 c. Westinghouse.

Turner, W: Alden, M.D., and Stewart, T: Grainger, M.D.
Text-book of nervous diseases. '10(F) 17+607 p. il. 8°, *$6 net. Blakiston.

TURNING.
Colvin, F. H. Engine lathe work. $1. Hill Pub.
Crawshaw, F. D. Metal spinning. 25 c. Popular Mechanics.
Crawshaw, F. D. Problems in wood-turning. 80 c. Manual Arts.
Evans, J. H. Ornamental turning. $1. McKay.
Hartness, J. Hartness flat turret lathe manual. gratis.—Machine building for profit, and the Hartness flat turret lathe. (Add. pubs. for price.) Jones & Lamson.
Nicolson, J: T., *and* Smith, D. Lathe design for high- and low-speed steels. $6. Longmans.
Ross, G: A. Wood turning. $1. Ginn.
Simple lessons in wood turning. 25 c. Spon.
See also Woodwork.

Turning northward. Miller, J. R. **30 c. net. Crowell.
Turning points in teaching. Murphy, D. C. 60 c. Flanagan.

Turnour, Jules.
Autobiography of a clown; as told to I: F: Marcosson. '10(Mr26) c. il. D. **$1 net. Moffat.

Turnover books. D. 60 c. Reilly & B.
—Little Red Riding Hood and The three little bears.
—Moore. Night before Christmas and Cinderella.
—Potter *and* Bannerman. Story of Peter Rabbit.

Turpin, Edna Henry Lee.
English history stories. '09(Ap3) c. il. pors. 12°, (Graded supplementary reading ser.) *50 c. net. C: E. Merrill.
See also Soule, And. MacNairn.

Turquan, Joseph.
Love affairs of Napoleon; tr. from the French by J. Lewis May. '09(My22) pors. O. *$5 net. Lane.
Madame Royale, the last Dauphine; Marie-Therese-Charlotte de France, Duchesse d'Angouleme; ed. and tr. by Lady Theodora Davidson. '10(D3) il. 8°, $3.75 net. Brentano's.
Sisters of Napoleon: Elisa, Pauline and Caroline Bonaparte; after the testimony of their contemporaries; tr. and ed. by W. R. H. Trowbridge. '09(Mr13) il. pors. O. *$3.75 net. Scribner.

Turr'ble tales of Kaptin Kiddo. Hays, *Mrs.* M. P. G. 35 c. net. Stern.

Turrell, C: Alfr.
Spanish reader, for beginners in high schools and colleges. '08(S12) c. S. 80 c. Am. Bk.

Turrill, Sherman Marsh.
Elem. course in perspective. '10(F19) c. il. 12°, **$1.25 net. Van Nostrand.

TURTLES.
Hay, O. P. Fossil turtles of North America. $9. Carnegie.

Turton, W. H., comp.
Truth of Christianity; being an examination of the more important arguments for and against believing in that religion; comp. from various sources. 7th ed., rev. '09(O9) D. $1.25. Putnam.

Turton, Rev. Z. H.
See Alston, E. A.

TUSCANY, Italy.
Hutton, E: In unknown Tuscany. *$2.50 net. Dutton.
Hutton, E: Siena and Southern Tuscany. $2 net. Macmillan.
Lees, D. N. Tuscan feasts and Tuscan friends. *$1.75 net. Dodd.
Seymour, F: H. A. Up hill and down dale in ancient Etruria. $3 net. Appleton.
Vane, *Sir* F. P. F. Walks and people in Tuscany. $1.50 net. Lane.
See also Matilda, *Countess of Tuscany.*

Tuscany, and other poems. Mahany, R. B. (Add. pub. for price.) W: A. King.

TUSCARAWAS COUNTY, Ohio.
Rhodes, E. S., *comp.* First centennial history and atlas of Tuscarawas Co., Ohio. $10; $15. E. S. Rhodes.

Tusculan disputations. *See* Cicero, M. T.

Tutt, R. G.
Telephone accounting. '09(Ag21) c. figs. F. pap., $1. R. G. Tutt.

Tuttiett, Mary Gleed, ["Maxwell Gray."]
Suspicions of Mrs. Allonby. '08(O10) c. front. D. †$1.50. Appleton.

Tuttle, Alex. Harrison, D.D.
Nathan Bangs. '09(Ag21) c. por. nar. S. *25 c. net. Eaton & M.

Tuttle, C: R:
New idea; continuous course of study for self-life unfoldment. '08(O) c. 16°, $5. C: R: Tuttle.

Tuttle, E: W., ed.
See Camp, Edg. W.

Tuttle, Fk. W.
Atlas of Kansas City and vicinity. Ed. of 1907. '08(Je6) c. maps, f°, $60. Tuttle & P.

Tuttle, Mrs. G. F.
See Tuttle, Maria Jeannette Brookings, *comp. and ed.*

Tuttle, Hudson.
Arcana of nature; with an introd. giving an account of the phenomenon of its authorship, and the "superior condition" of Andrew Jackson Davis, Emanuel Swedenborg, and other psychics, by Emmet Densmore, M.D. '08(N7) c. pors. O. *$1.50 net. Stillman.

—, and Rood, Mrs. Emma.
Stories from beyond the Borderland. '10 (Mr5) c. por. D. $1.25. Tuttle Pub.

Tuttle, Maria Jeannette Brookings, [Mrs. G. F. Tuttle,] comp. and ed.
Three centuries in Champlain Valley; collection of historical facts and incidents. Tercentenary ed. '09, [1910.] (Jl) 485 p. il. pors. 8°, $1.50 net. D. A. R. Saranac Chap.

Tuttle, T: D.
Principles of public health. '10(S17) il. D. (New world text books.) 50 c. World Bk.

Tutton, Alfr. E: Howard.
Crystalline structure and chemical constitution. '10(F19) il. O. *$1.60 net. Macmillan.

TUXPAN, Mexico.
See Mexico.

Twain, Mark, pseud.
See Clemens, S: Langhorne.

TWEED RING.
See Drew, Daniel.

Tweedie, Mrs. Ethel B. Hartley, [Mrs. Alec. Tweedie.]
Hyde Park: its history and romance. '08 (O10) il. 8°, ¾ levant, *$7.50 net. Pott.

TWEEDMOUTH, *Lord* Edward Marjoribanks.
Aberdeen, I. M., *Countess* of. Edward Marjoribanks, Lord Tweedmouth. $2 net. Dutton.

Tweedy, E. Hastings, M.D., and Wrench, G. T., M.D.
Rotunda practical midwifery. '08(Ja18) il. tabs., O. (Oxford medical pubs.) $6. Oxford Univ.

Tweedy, J:
Hist. of the Republican National conventions from 1858 to 1908. '10(Jl) c. 408 p. pors. 8°, ¾ leath., $2. J: Tweedy.

Twelfth juror. Large, M. H. $1.50. C. M. Clark.

Twelve centuries of English poetry and prose. Newcomer, A. G. $1.75. Scott, F. & Co.

Twelve huntsmen. *See* Lang, Andrew, *ed.*

Twelve months with the 8th Massachusetts Infantry. Webber, H. E. $2. H. E. Webber.

Twelve months' work in the poultry yard. Wittman, W. T. 25 c. Item Pub.

Twelve outputs. Mason, E. L. $1.25. E. L. Mason.

Twelve steps to success. James, L. $1. A. Harriman.

Twelve thousand words often mispronounced. Phyfe, W: H: P. **$1.25 net. Putnam.

Twelve vitalized tissue remedies for private and domestic use. Littlefield, C: W. $2.50. C: W. Littlefield.

Twelve years in the saddle for law and order on the frontiers of Texas. Sullivan, W. J: L. $1.50. Von Boeckmann-J.

Twelvetrees, R. C.
Seven little women. '08(S5) c. il. obl. O. bds., 75 c. Stokes.

Twelvetrees, Wa. Noble.
Simplified methods of calculating reinforced concrete beams. '09(Jl3) figs. pap., 20 c. Macmillan.

Twentieth century American. Robinson, H. P. *$7.50 net. Putnam.

Twenieth century book of toasts. Lowe, P. E., *ed.* 50 c. McKay.

Twentieth century Christ. Hatch, D: P. $1 net. Fenno.

Twentieth century handbook for steam enneers and electricians. Swingle, C. F. $3. Drake.

20th century harmony text-book compend system. Schaaf, E: $1. Schirmer.

Twentieth century history of Erie County. Miller, J: $18. Lewis Pub.

Twentieth century history of Marshall Co., Ind. McDonald, D. 2 v. $18. Lewis Pub.

Twentieth century household lib.; complete **encyclop. of useful information; complete atlas of the U. S., in colors. [Rev. and enl. ed.] '10(F19) c. il. maps, f°, $3.50. Holman.**

Twentieth century poultry buildings. Banks, E. E. 50 c. E. E. Banks.

Twentieth century science ser. pls. D. 50 c. net. Stokes.
—Haddon. Races of man and their distribution.
—Hickling. Geology.
—McCabe. Evolution.—Prehistoric man.
—Podmore. Telepathic hallucinations.
—Wilson. Physiology.

Twentieth century Socialism. Kelly, E. $1.75 net. Longmans.

20th century tables. Fisher, J: I. $2.50. J: I. Fisher.

Twentieth century text-books; ed. by A. F. Nightingale. il. D. Appleton.
—Adams. Text-book of commercial geography. **$1.30 net.
—Burdick. Essentials of business law. **$1.10 net.
—Gilbert *and* Brigham. Introduction to physical geography. **$1.25 net.
—Goldsmith. The traveller and The deserted village. **30 c. net.
—Gorton. High school course in physics. $1.25.
—McLaughlin. History of the American nation. *$1.40 net.
—Washington *and* Webster. Farewell address. and First Bunker Hill oration. **25 c. net.
—Young *and* Jackson. Elementary algebra. **$1.12 net.
—Young *and* Jackson. **First course in elem. algebra.** 95 c. net.—Second course in elem. **algebra. 70 c. net.**

Twentieth century toasts. *See* Madison, Janet, *comp.* Toasts you ought to know.

Twenty beautiful stories. *See* Shakespeare, W:

Twenty English cathedrals. James, J. L. $1. M. C. James.

Twenty Father Goose melodies. Hyatt, N. I. 75 c. Ditson.

Twenty gymnastic lessons on the boom. Nissen, H. 30 c. Bassette.

Twenty lessons in free-arm movement writing. Harman, G. W. 25 c. Macmillan.

Twenty lessons in illustrating. Swisher, C: C. $5. Art Pub.

Twenty minute exercises. Warman, E: B. 10 c. Am. Sports.

Twenty talks to teachers. Sanders, T: E. 85 c. Teachers' Co-op.

Twenty thousand leagues under the sea. Verne, J. *35 c. net; *70 c. net. Dutton.

Twenty years a detective in the wickest city in the world. Wooldridge, C. R. $2; 75 c. C. R. Wooldridge.

Twenty years after. *See* Dumas, Alexandre.

Twenty years in hell with the beef trust. Shiel, R. R. 50 c. R. R. Shiel.

Twenty years in Hull House. *See* Addams, Jane.

Twenty years in Persia. Wishart, J: G. *$1.50 net. Revell.

Twenty years in public life. Fuller, T: O. $1.25. Nat. Bapt. Pub.

Twenty years in Siberia. De Packh, *Baroness* M. $1.25. Guarantee Pub.

Twenty years in the Himalaya. Bruce, C: G. $4.20 net. Longmans.

Twice around the world with Alexander. Davis, G: T. B. $1. Chr. Herald.

Twice-born men. Begbie, H. *$1.25 net. Revell.

Twig of thorn. Warren, M. J. W. H. Baker.

Twin of the tide. Gray, M. A. $1.25 Benziger.

Twin poems of the Revolution. Auringer, O. C. $1. O. C. Auringer.

Twin stars. Ellis, J: B. $1. Mayhew.

Twing, Catherine Struble, comp.
See Towne, *Mrs.* Eliz. Jones, *comp.*

Twining, Agatha G.
Childhood of our blessed Lord Jesus Christ; with a preface by the Lord Bishop of London. '09(Ap10) il. maps, bds., *60 c. net. Young Churchman.
Children's creed; with preface by the Lord Bishop of Kensington. '09(Ap10) il. bds., *60 c. net. Young Churchman.
Child's history of Westminster Abbey. '09 (Ap10) il. *$1.50 net. Young Churchman.

Twining, E. W.
Model aeroplanes; how to build and fly them; [five sheets of scaled drawings and booklet.] '09(D18) 50 c. Spon.
Model gliders, birds, butterflies and aeroplanes; how to make them fly; consisting of one large sheet cont. 12 butterflies and 2 birds, printed in colors; small cardboard aeroplane glider and descriptive booklet. '10(N5) 50 c., in folder. Spon.

Twining, Harry La Verne.
Wireless telegraphy and high frequency electricity; manual containing detailed information for the construction of transformers, wireless telegraph and high frequency apparatus, with chapters on their theory and operation; [with a chapter on Wireless telephony, by W: Dubilier.] '09(N) c. 202 p. il. tabs., 8°, $1.50. H. L. Twining.

Twins (The). Aldin, C. $2 net. Doran.

Twins in Ceylon. Woolf, B. S. 75 c. Estes.

Twins in twain. Loveridge, R. T. $1.50. R. T. Loveridge.

Twiss, G: Ransom.
See Mann, C: Riborg.

Twisted foot. Rideout, H: M. $1.20 net. Houghton M.

Twitchell, Ralph Emerson.
Hist. of the military occupation of the Territory of New Mexico from 1846 to 1851 by the government of the United States; together with biographical sketches of men prominent in the conduct of the government during that period. '09(S) c. 394 p. il. pors. maps, 8°. (Add. author for price.) R. E. Twitchell.

Two beautiful prayers from the lips of Jesus. Tobie, W. N. *50 c. net. Jennings.

Two boy gold miners. Webster, F. V. 35 c. Cupples & L.

Two boys in the tropics. Figyelmessy, *Mrs.* E. H. $1.35 net. Macmillan.

Two boys in war-time. Finnemore, J: $1.50. Macmillan.

Two Braids, *Scout.*
See Stringer, Thomas.

Two burglars. Hooker, W: B. 25 c. Dick.

Two centuries of costume in America, 1620-1820. Earle, *Mrs.* A. M. $2.50 net. Macmillan.

Two centuries of the Church of the Brethren. Church of the Brethren. $1.50; $2.50. Brethren Pub. Ho.

Two Christmas eves. *See* Atoned.

Two demands. Cartmell, F. S. Roycrofters.

Two Dianas in Alaska. Herbert, A. *$4 net. Lane.

Two dollars a day from poultry and eggs. Warren, E. 50 c. De Puy.

Two empires. Westcott, B. F. *$1.75 net. Macmillan.

Two ends of a house-boat. Eparde, T. $1.25. B'way Pub.

Two English queens and Philip. Hume, M. A. S. *$4.50 net. Putnam.

Two extensions of the use of graphs in elementary logic. Hocking, W: E. 15 c. Univ. of Cal.

Two family and twin houses; consisting of a variety of designs contributed by leading architects in all parts of the country; sel. and comp. by the editor of the *Architects' and Builders' Magazine.* '08(D26) c. il. Q. $2. W: T. Comstock.

Two gentlemen of Virginia. Eggleston, G: C. †$1.50. Lothrop, L. & S.

Two great questions. Hill, L. $2. L. Hill.

Two great rivals. Haggard, A. C: P. $4 special net. Appleton.

Two Hague conferences. Hull, W: I. $1.65. Ginn.
Two hundred recipes for making salads. Hulse, *Mrs.* O. M. $1. Hopewell Press.
Two hundred seating furniture. Baroggio, A. $12. A. Gerbel.
Two in Italy. Howe, M. **$1.50 net. Little, B. & Co.
Two kings. Schuh, L: H. 50 c. Lutheran Bk.
Two knights of the swan. Jaffray, R. $1.25 net. Putnam.
Two little Algonkin lads. Bayliss, *Mrs.* C. K. 50 c. Educ. Pub.
Two little Indians. Maguire, E. M. 30 c. Flanagan.
Two lovers. *See* Eliot, George, *pseud.*
Two Marys. Follett, *Mrs.* S. J. 75 c. Arts and Crafts.
Two of the most remarkable and interesting of the sonnets of Francis Bacon. Harwood, H: H. $1. H: H. Harwood.
Two Oxford physiologists. Gotch, F. 35 c. Oxford Univ.
Two runaways. Panting, J. H. †$1.25. Warne.
Two school-girls of Florence. Baldwin, M. $1.50. Dutton.
Two series of Lenten sermons. McGowan, F. X. 75 c. Pustet.
Two stowaways aboard the "Ellen Maria." Kaler, J. O. †75 c. Crowell.
Two travellers. Montenegro, C. $1.25. Badger.
Two years ago. *See* Kingsley, C:
Two years before the mast. *See* Dana, R: H:, *jr.*
Two years in a tent. Whitney, F. 50 c. net. Moffat.
Two years with poultry. '10(F) c. '09. 160 p. il. plans, 8°, 50 c. Poultry Trib.

Tyler, Alice Sarah, ed.
John W. Tyler, 1808-1888: memorial of the one hundredth anniversary of his birth, Sept. 27, 1908. '09(F) 69 p. por. (Priv. pr.) Torch Press.

Tyler, F: S.
Questions and answers on contracts; prepared with reference to Anson, Bishop, Clark, Lawson, Hammon, Smith, and selected cases on contracts. '09(Ja) c. 63 p. S. (J: Byrne Co.'s quiz books.) pap., 50 c. Byrne.
Questions and answers on real property; prepared with reference to Tiffany, Tiedeman, Hopkins, Blackstone, and other selected cases. '09(Ap) c. 57 p. S. (J: Byrne Co.'s quiz books.) pap., 50 c. Byrne.
See also District of Columbia. Corporation law.

Tyler, J: Mason.
Man in the light of evolution. '08(O17) c. D. **$1.25 net. Appleton

TYLER, John William.
Tyler, A. S., *ed.* John W. Tyler, 1808-1888: memorial of the one hundredth anniversary of his birth. (Priv. pr..) Torch Press.

Tyler, Lyon Gardiner.
Williamsburg, the old colonial capital. '08 (Ja11) il. pors. maps, facsims., plans, 8°, $2.50. L. G. Tyler.

Tyler, Royall.
Spain: study of her life and arts. '09(O23) c. 8°, *$3.50 net. M. Kennerley.

Tyler, W. F.
Dimensional idea as an aid to religion. '10 (Ja22) D. 50 c. Fenno.

Tynan, Katharine.
See Hinkson, *Mrs.* Katharine Tynan.

Tyndale, Wa.
Japan and the Japanese. '10(D10) col. il. O. $5 net. Macmillan.

Tyndall, C: H., D.D
Electricity and its similitudes: analogy of phenomena, natural and spiritual. New rev. ed. '08(Mr21) c. 12°, *$1 net. Revell.

Tyng, Eliz. McJimsey.
Latin prose exercises for second year work. '09(O30) c. D. 60 c. Longmans.

TYPE.
See Printers and printing.

Types from city streets. Hapgood, H. $1.50 net. Funk.
Types of California beauties. Henrich, H. C. $50. H. Heywood.
Types of English literature; ed. by W: Allan Neilson. D. **$1.50 net. Houghton M.
—Thorndike. Tragedy.
Types of tragic drama. Vaughan, C: E. *$1.60 net. Macmillan.
Typewriter bookkeeping. Brown, I. S. gratis. Underwood Typewriter.

TYPEWRITING.
Book, F: W: Psychology of skill with special reference to its acquisition in typewriting. $1. Univ. of Mont.
Cutler, I. M., *and* So Relle, R. P. Rational typewriting. $1. Gregg Pub.
La Tourette, C., *and* McDaniel, C: F. Commercial art typewriting. 65 c. C: F. McDaniel.
Lewis, W: W. Typewriting. $1. D. L. Musselman.
Osborn, A. S. Typewriting as evidence. (Add. pubs. for price.) Genesee.
Patton, I: W. New universal system of touch or sight typewriting. 60 c. Pitman.
Pugh, M. F., *ed.* Typewriting manual. $1.25. Peirce Sch.
Smith, C: E: Pract. course in touch typewriting. 50 c.; 75 c. Pitman.
Touch typewriting in a nutshell. '10(Ap) c. 20 p. 12°, 25. Park.
Worth, *Mrs.* M. T. Modern typewriting. $1. J. A. Lyons.
See also Commercial correspondence.

TYPHOID FEVER.
Lumsden, L. L. What the local health officer can do in the prevention of typhoid fever. U. S., Supt. of Docs.
Stiles, C. W. Soil pollution and its relation to hookworm disease and typhoid fever. (Add. Superintendent for price.) U. S., Supt. of Docs.
Tilden, J: H: Etiology of cholera infantum, typhoid fever and appendicitis. $5. Merchants' Pub.
Whipple, G: C. Typhoid fever. **$3 net. Wiley.
Typical general secretary. Warburton, G: A: 75 c. Y. M. C. A.

Typical Shakespearean stage. Albright, V. E. (Priv. pr.) Putnam.
TYPOGRAPHY.
See Printers and printing.
Tyranny of power. Clark, C: S. $1.50. C. M. Clark.
Tyrant (The). De la Pasture, E. B. *$1.25 net. Dutton.
Tyrant in white. Berman, H. $1.50. Lovell.
Tyrode, Maurice Vejux.
Pharmacology, the action and use of drugs. '08(D) c. 19+255 p. 8°, *$1.50 net. Blakiston.
TYROL, Austria-Hungary.
Baillie-Grohman, W: A. Tyrol. *$2 net. Macmillan.
Holland, C. Tyrol and its people. *$2.50 net. Pott.
Tyrrell, C: Alfr.
Royal road to health; or, the secret of health without drugs. 45th ed., completely rev., enl. '07, [1909.] (Mr) c. 223 p. il. por. 12°. (Not for sale.) Tyrrell's Hygienic Inst.
Tyrrell, Rev. G:
Christianity at the cross-roads. '09(N20) D. *$1.50 net. Longmans.
Medievalism: reply to Cardinal Mercier. '08(S12) D. *$1.25 net. Longmans.
Much-abused letter. '10(Je11) D. 90 c. net. Longmans.
See also Lodge, *Sir* Oliver Jos.
Tyrrell, H: Grattan.
Concrete bridges and culverts, for both railroads and highways. '10(F19) il. 16°, $3. M. C. Clark.
Tyrrell, Rob. Yelverton.
Essays on Greek literature. '09(D25) 12°, *$1.25 net. Macmillan.
Tyson, Ja.
Practice of medicine. 5th ed., rev. and enl. '09(N) c. 25+1438 p. il. (partly col.) 8°, $5.50. net; shp., *$6.50 net; hf. mor., *$7 net. Blakiston.
Tyson, Stuart Lawrence.
Teaching of Our Lord as to the indissolubility of marriage. '09(N) 12°, 50 c. Univ. Press (Sewanee.)
U. E. ser. D. $1. Hist. Pub.
—Dunlop. Recollections of the War of 1812.
UAP, Island of.
Furness, W: H:, *3d.* Island of stone money: Uap of the Carolines. $3.50 net. Lippincott.
Überwunden. Schmidt, O. E. 30 c. Holt.
Udden, Johan August.
Report on a geological survey of the lands belonging to the New York and Texas Land Company, Ltd., in the upper Rio Grande embayment in Texas. '07, [1908.] (My.) 51-103 p. il. diagrs., map, 4°. (Augustana Library pub.) pap., 50 c. Augustana.
See also Bartow, E:
UGANDA, Africa.
Purvis, J: B. Through Uganda to Mount Elgon. $1.50. Am. Tr.
Treves, *Sir* F: Uganda for a holiday. $3 net. Dutton.
Tucker, A. R. Eighteen years in Uganda and East Africa. *$8.50 net. Longmans.

Ugly duckling. Andersen, H. C. 25 c. Phonograph.
Uhde, Constantine.
Architectural forms of the classic ages, comprising the principal examples of the orders of columns and their entablatures, with descriptive text. 2d ed.; rev. by R. Phene Spiers. '10(Ap9) 75 col. pls. in portfolio, f°, $20. Hessling.
Uhde-Bernays, Hermann.
Rothenburg on the Tauber. '08(D5) 12°, *$1.50 net. Scribner.
Ullman, Berthold L:
Identification of the manuscripts of Catullus cited in Statius' edition of 1566. '09 (Ap3) O. pap., 75 c. B. L: Ullman.
Ulrich, Bartow Adolphus, comp.
Von Reisenkampff-Ulrich family history, (for use of family only.) '08(Mr14) c. il. pors. 8°, pap., 10 c. Co-operative Pr. Co.
Ulrich, J:
Democratic foundations. '07, [1908.] (My.) c. 93 p. 12°, pap., 10 c. Co-operative Pr.
ULRICH FAMILY.
See Genealogies.
Ultimo. Moser, G. v. 35 c. Holt.
ULTRAMICROSCOPY.
See Microscope.
Umé San in Japan. McDonald, *Mrs.* E. A. B. 60 c. Little, B. & Co.
Umphrey, G: Wallace.
Spanish prose composition. '08(Ja11) D. 75 c. Am. Bk.
Umpleby, Fenwick.
Textile design: working manual of approved practice in all details of the art of designing the various kinds of textile fabrics. '09(My8) c. il. diagrs., 8°, (American School of Correspondence pubs.) $3. Am. Sch. Corr.
Un-American character of race legislation. Kohler, M. J. 25 c. Am. Acad. Pol. Sci.
Un' idea di Ermes Torranza. *See* Fogazzaro, Antonio Pereat Rochus.
Un serviton y un liberalito ō tres almas de dios. Arrom de Ayala, C. F. J. B. von F. y L. 50 c. Heath.
Una donna. *See* Aleramo, Sibilla, *pseud.*
Unappropriated public lands of the United States. (Add. Superintendent for price.) U. S., Supt. of Docs.
UNBELIEF.
See Skepticism.
Unbidden guest. Cooke, F. $1.25. Benziger.
Unckless, Leslie.
How to find manufacturing costs and selling costs. '09(S) c. 4+90 p. 12°, $1.50. Modern Methods.
Unclaimed millions. Allen, W. A. $1. W. A. Allen.
Uncle Bob and Aunt Beckey's exciting trip. Williams, H. 75 c.; 25 c. Laird.
Uncle Carl. True, C. E. $1.50. Neale.
"Uncle Dudley," pseud.
See Postell, Jehu Glenn
Uncle Gregory. Sandeman, G: †$1.50. Putnam.
"Uncle Ned," pseud.
Little letters to boys grown tall. '08(Ja4) D. 80 c.; pap., 50 c. Abbey.
Uncle Polperro. Courlander, A. $1.35 net. Brentano's.

"Uncle Remus," pseud.
See Harris, Joel Chandler.
Uncle Remus and the Little Boy. Harris, J. C. $1.25. Small.
Uncle Remus, his songs and his sayings. Harris, J. C. $2. Appleton.
Uncle Sam. Matthews, A. (Not for sale.) Davis Press.
Uncle Sam's boys in the ranks. Hancock, H. I. $1. Altemus.
Uncle Sam's business. Marriott, C. $1.25. Harper.
Uncle Sim. Lake, F. P. $1.50. C. M. Clark.
Uncle Tom Andy Bill. Major, C: $1.50. Macmillan.
Uncle Tom's cabin. *See* Stowe, *Mrs.* Harriet Eliz. Beecher.
"Uncle Tom's cabin" in Germany. MacLean, G. E. $1.50. Univ. of Penn.
Uncle Walt. Mason, W. $1.25 net. G: M. Adams.
Uncle Wash. Moore, J: T. $1.50. Winston.
Uncle Wisdom's parlor tour. Lea, J: $1. Stokes.
Uncommercial traveller. *See* Dickens, C:
Uncounted cost. Gaunt, M. $1.20 net. Clode.
Uncrowned king. Wright, H. B. 75 c. net. Book Supply.
Under a fool's cap. Holmes, D. H: $1. T: B. Mosher.
Under Brazilian skies. Pool, B. F. $1. B. F. Pool.
Under five reigns. Neville, *Lady* D. F. W. $5 net. Lane.
Under groove. Stringer, A. J: A. †$1.50. McClure.
Under marching orders. Hubbard, E. D. *50 c. net. **Young People's Miss.**
Under Petraia with some saunterings; by the author of "In a Tuscan garden." '09(Ja23) 12°, *$1.50 net. Lane.
Under Scott in Mexico. Stratemeyer, E: †$1.25. Lothrop, L. & S.
Under the absolute Amir. Martin, F: A. *$2.25 net. Harper.
Under the ban. Home, C. M. pap., 60 c. Herder.
Under the crown, American history; selections from the *Youth's Companion.* '09 (N) 3-192 p. il. 12°, (Companion ser.) 50 c. Youth's Companion.
Under the deodars. *See* Kipling, Rudyard.
Under the flag of the cross. Ledbury, J. H. $1.50. C. M. Clark.
Under the grand old hills. Kettle, R. M. †$1.25 Estes.
Under the great bear. Munroe, K. †$1.25. Harper.
Under the greenwood tree. *See* Hardy, T:
Under the Maltese cross; Antietam to Appomattox; loyal uprising in western Pennsylvania, 1861-1865; campaigns 155th Pennsylvania Regiment, narrated by the rank and file. '10(Jl16) c. il. pors. O. $5. 155th Regimental Assoc.
Under the mulberry trees. Brown, T. $1.50. Badger.
Under the northern lights. Ward, *Mrs.* F. G. H. $1.50. Wessels.
Under the open sky. Schmucker, S: C. $1.50 net. Lippincott.
Under the red and gold. Cerezo, S. M. $1.25. Hudson.
Under the red patch. Hays, G. A., *comp.* $2. G. A. Hays.
Under the stars and bars. Jones, B: W. $1. B: W. Jones.
Under the thatch. Puddicombe, *Mrs.* B. $1.50. Dodd.
Under the window. Greenaway, K. $1.50 net. Warne.
Under world and its women. Hatch, D: P. 15 c. Roger Bros.
Underground water resources of Connecticut. Gregory, H. E. (Add. Superintendent for price.) U. S., Supt. of Docs.
Underground waters of southern Maine. Clapp, F: G. 55 c. U. S., Supt. of Docs.
Underhill, C: R.
See Massie, Wa. W.
Underhill, C: Reginald.
Solenoids, electromagnets and electromagnetic windings. '10(Jl30) il. 24°, $2 net. Van Nostrand.
See also Kemble, W: Fretz.
Underhill, Elsie Morris.
See Eaton, Wa. Prichard.
Underhill, Harry Clay.
Treatise on the law of criminal evidence, [etc.] 2d ed. '10(N) c. O. $7.50. Bobbs-M.
Treatise on the law of landlord and tenant, incl. leases, their execution, surrender, and renewal, the parties thereto, and their reciprocal rights and obligations, [etc.] In 2 v. '09(Je) c. O. $12. Flood.
Underhill, Ja.
Esperanto and its availability for scientific writings. '08(Ag1) 8°, pap., 50 c. Colo. Sci. Soc.
Mineral land surveying; technical treatise on the surveying and patenting of mineral land; designed for use of mineral surveyors and students of mining engineering. 2d ed., rev. '10(My14) c. il. 16°, $3. Mining Science.
Underhill, Mrs. Jennie E., comp.
Sunshine cook book; collection of valuable recipes and menus gathered from various sources. '10(Jl9) c. 8°, 50 c. J. E. Underhill.
Underneath are the Everlasting Arms. Lyman, A. J. 50 c. net. Pilgrim Press.
UNDERSTANDING.
See Brain;—Mind;—Psychology.
UNDERTAKERS.
See **Burial.**
Underwood, Clarence F.
Girls of to-day; with poems by various authors. '09(D25) c. por. Q. **$3 net, boxed. Stokes.
Underwood, Horace Grant, D.D.
Call of Korea: political, social, religious. '08(My23) c. il. 12°, *75 c. net; pap., *35 c. net. Revell.
Religions of eastern Asia. '10(F19) c. D. **$1.50 net. Macmillan.
Underwood, J: Curtis.
The iron muse. '10(Je11) c. D. $1.25 net. **Putnam.**

Underwood, Jos. Harding.
Distribution of ownership. '08(Ja25) 8°, (Columbia Univ. studies in hist., economics and public law.) *$2 net; pap., *$1.50 net. Lemcke.

Underwood, Mrs. Lillias Horton, M.D., [**Mrs. Horace G. Underwood.**]
Fifteen years among the top-knots; or, life in Korea: with introd. by Fk. F. Ellinwood. 2d ed., rev. and enl. '08(D5) c. il. pors. 8°, $1.50. Am. Tr.

Underwood, Loring.
Garden and its accessories. New popular ed. '10(O15) c. il. 12°, $1 net. Little, B. & Co.
Garden diary and country home guide. '08 (Ap11) c. Q. **$3.25 net. Stokes.

Underwood, P. H.
See Hopkins, J: W.

Underworld sewer. Washburn, J. $1.50. Washburn.

UNDERWRITING.
See Insurance.

Undesirable governess. Crawford, F. M. $1.50. Macmillan.

Undine. *See* La Motte Fouqué, Friedrich Heinrich Karl, *Freiherr* de.—Macgregor, Mary, *ed.*

Unemployed and trade unions. Jackson, C. 50 c. net. Longmans.

UNEMPLOYMENT.
See Capital and labor;—Labor and laboring classes.

Unexplored self. Montgomery, G: R. $1.25. Putnam.

Unfathomable sorrow. Opp-Dyke, O. $1 net. Revell.

Unfinished divorce. Gallatin, F. D. $1.50. Cochrane.

Unfinished melody. Hawkins, F. L. 50 c. Denrich.

Unfinished task of the Christian church. Barton, J. L. 50 c.; 35 c. Student Vol.

Unfolding life. Lamoreaux, *Mrs.* A. A. 75 c. Rel. Pub.

Unforeseen (The). Cutting, *Mrs.* M. S. D. $1.20, fixed. Doubleday, P.

Unforgotten (The). Gary, A. C. (Add. pubs. for price.) De Laurence, S.

Unfortunate prisoner. Pemberton, M. †$1.50. G: W. Dillingham.

Unfrequented France. Bentham-Edwards, M. $3 net. Stokes.

Ungava. Ballantyne, R. M. *35 c. net; *70 c. net. Dutton.

Ungebetene (Der) gast. Buchheim, E. S. 15 c. Oxford Univ.

Unicorn from the stars. Yeats, W: B. *$1.50 net. Macmillan.

Union army: a history of military affairs in the loyal states, 1861-65. 8 v. '08(Jl) c. pors. 8°, $48. Federal Pub. Co.

Union cause in St. Louis. Rombauer, R. J. $2. Nixon Jones.

UNION COUNTY, N. J.
See Sewage and sewerage.

Union of South Africa. Brand, R. H: $2. Oxford Univ.

UNION PACIFIC RAILWAY.
Dodge, G. M. How we built the Union Pacific Railway. Gov. Pr. Off.

Union prayer-meeting helper for 1909. '08 (N21) c. nar. T. 25 c.; 12 copies, $2.50; 25 copies, $4.75; 50 copies, $9; 100 copies, $15. Funk.

Union with God in thought and faith. Scull, D: **$1 net. Winston.

Unique message and the universal mission of Christianity. Love, J. F. $1.25 net. Revell.

Unison chant choir-book. Pollitt, A. W. $1. Oxford Univ.

UNITARIAN CHURCH.
Eliot, S: A. Heralds of a liberal faith. In 3 v. v. 1, The prophets; v. 2, The pioneers; v. 3, The preachers. ea., *$1 net; per set, *$2.50 net. Am. Unitarian.
Harvey, T. L. In antescript, two presidential nominees: [Unitarianism and Trinitarianism.] 25 c. T. L. Harvey.
Pierce, W. G. B. Religion of the spirit; five sermons. 25 c. Unitarian Club.
Secrist, H: T. Comparative studies in religion; introd. to Unitarianism. 45 c.; 35 c.; 65 c. Unitarian S. S.
See also Sunday-school.

UNITED BRETHREN.
See Plymouth Brethren.

United Brethren mission study course. il. 12°. Un. B. Pub.
—Mills, *and others.* Our foreign missionary enterprise. *50 c. net; *35 c. net. Un. B. Pub.

United Confederate Veterans; Arkansas Division. Confederate women of Arkansas in the Civil War, 1861-'65. '07, [1908.] (N.) 90 p. il. pors. $1. J. Kellogg.

United editors encyclopedia and dictionary: library of universal knowledge and an unabridged dictionary of the English language. '09(My22) c. 40 v., il. pors. maps, 8°, $96. Un. Editors.

UNITED KINGDOM.
See British Empire;—England;—Great Britain.

United Publishers' Association "blue book." '08(S12) c. Tt. leath., $30, (with service.) Un. Pub. Assoc.

U. S. documents all bear the imprint of the Government Printing Office, and copies should be ordered or missing prices asked from the Superintendent of Documents, Government Printing Office, Washington, D. C.

United States. *Adjutant-General's Office. Military Information Division.* Explorations in Alaska, 1899, for an all-American overland route from Cook Inlet, Pacific Ocean, to the Yukon; by First Lieut. Jos. S. Herron, March, 1901. '09(My) 77 p. il. map, 8°, pap. (Add. Superintendent for price.) U. S., Supt. of Docs.

United States. Biological Survey; bulletins, circulars and North American fauna of this bureau, Agriculture Department, U. S. A. '09(O2) 8°, gratis. U. S., Supt. of Docs.

United States. *Bureau of Education.* Bibliography of education for 1908-9. '10 (Mr5) 8°.

United States. *Bureau of Education.* List of publications of the United States Bureau of Education, 1867-1907. '08(O10); 1867-1910. '10(N) 8°, (U. S. Bureau of Education bull.) (Add. pub. for price.) **U. S., Supt. of Docs.**

United States. *Bureau of Education.* Statistics of public, society, and school libraries having 5,000 volumes and over in 1908. '09 (Ag14) 8°, (U. S., Bu. of Education, bull.) pap. (Add. Superintendent for price.) U. S., Supt. of Docs.

United States. *Bureau of Education.* Teachers' professional library; classified list of one hundred titles. '09(Ag14) 8°, (U. S., Bu. of Education, bull.) pap. (Add. Superintendent for price.) U. S., Supt. of Docs.

United States. *Bu. of Steam Engineering.* List of wireless telegraph stations of the world, incl. shore stations, merchant vessels revenue cutters, and vessels of the United States navy; corrected to October 1, 1910. '10(N) 114 p. 8°. Gov. Pr. Off.

United States. Circuit ct. for the Southern district of New York; rules, rev. by J: A. Shields, clerk. '09(N) c. 64 p. O. pap., 75 c. Baker, V. & Co.

United States. *Circuit cts. of appeals.* Repts., with anncts. v. 83. '08(F); v. 84 (Jl); v. 85 (N); v. 86 (D) ea., $3.35; v. 87. '08, [1909.] (Ap); v. 88 (Je); v. 89 (Jl); v. 90 (S); v. 91 (N); v. 92-95. '10(F); v. 96 (Ap); v. 97 (My); v. 98 (Jl); v. 99-100 (N); v. 101 (D) c. O. shp., ea., $2.85. Lawyers' Co-op.

United States. *Civil Service Commission.* Information for boards of examiners concerning applications, examinations, and appointments, June 1, 1909. '09(Ag21) 8°. (Add. Superintendent for price.) U. S., Supt. of Docs.

United States. *Coast and Geodetic Survey.* Results of observations made at the Coast and Geodetic Survey Magnetic Observatory at Baldwin, Kansas, 1905 and 1906, by Dan. L. Hazard. '10(O) 107 p. il. tabs., f°.

United States. *Coast and Geodetic Survey.* Results of observations made at the Coast and Geodetic Survey Magnetic Observatory at Vieques, Porto Rico, 1905 and 1906, by Dan. L. Hazard. '10(O) 110 p. il. f°.

United States. *Committee on Department Methods.* Message from the President of the United States, transmitting a report by the Committee on Department Methods on the documentary historical publications of the United States government; together with a draft of a proposed bill providing for the creation of a permanent commission on national historical publications. '09 (My) 45 p. 8°, pap. (Add. pubs. for price.) U. S., Supt. of Docs.

United States. Commissioners' manual of practice; by Barrett R. Wellington. '10(O) c. O. $2. W. H. Anderson.

United States. Comparative statement of the conference rates of duty with the rates in the Dingley tariff law, on all items in which changes have been made in H. R. 1438, to raise revenue, etc. '09(D4) 8°. (Add. Superintendent for price.) U. S., Supt. of Docs.

United States. Compilation of customs laws and digest of decisions thereunder rendered by the courts and Board of United States General Appraisers. '08(D12) 8°. (Add. Superintendent for price.) U. S., Supt. of Docs.

United States. Compilation of laws rel. to trust companies; compiled by B: Ja. Downer; supervised by Philip S. Babcock. '09(Ap) c. 7+516 p. O. (Add. pubs. for price.) Am. Bankers' Assoc.

United States. Compiled statutes. Supp. 1909; comp. by J: A. Mallory. '09, [1910.] (F) c. O. $7. West Pub.

United States. *Comptroller of the Currency.* Digest of national bank decisions. '08(My.) 647 p. 8°. (Treasury Dept. docs.) pap., $1. U. S., Supt. of Docs.

United States. *Congress. House. Committee on Industrial Arts and Expositions.* Alaska-Yukon-Pacific exposition, 1909; report of William A. Rodenberg. '08(Ag15) 8°, pap., gratis. U. S., Supt. of Docs.

United States. *Congress. House. Committee on the Judiciary.* Establishing boundary line between Colorado and New Mexico and Oklahoma: report. '08(Ag1) 8°, pap., 5 c. U. S., Supt. of Docs.

United States. *Congress. House. Committee on the Judiciary.* Hearing on woman suffrage, H. J. res. 112, [March 3, 1908.] '09(Mr6) 8°. (Add. Superintendent for price.) U. S., Supt. of Docs.

United States. *Congress. House. Committee on the Judiciary.* Power of federal government to acquire lands for national forest purposes; views of the members of the Judiciary Committee. '09(Mr6) 8°, pap. U. S., Supt. of Docs.

United States. *Congress. House. Committee on Public Lands.* To create the Calaveras bigtree national forest, and for other purposes: report. '08(Ag1) maps, pap., 5 c. U. S., Supt. of Docs.

United States. *Congress. House. Committee on Ways and Means.* Transportation of moneys by express. '08(Je13) 8°, pap., 25 c. U. S., Supt. of Docs.

United States. *Congress. Senate. Committee on Commerce.* Development of the American ocean mail service and American commerce. '08(Ag1) 8°, pap., 25 c. U. S., Supt. of Docs.

United States. *Congress. Senate. Committee on Commerce.* Ocean mail service between United States and foreign ports: report. '08(Ag1) 4°, pap., 10 c. U. S., Supt. of Docs.

United States. *Congress. Senate. Committee on Finance.* Statistics on banking and currency in the U. S. and other countries. '08(Je6) 4°, pap., 25 c. U. S., Supt. of Docs.

United States. *Congress. Senate. Committee on Patents.* Revision of copyright laws: hearings before the committees on patents of the Senate and House of Representatives on pending bills to amend and consolidate the acts respecting copyright, March 26, 27 and 28, 1908. '08(Ag1) 8°, pap., $1. U. S., Supt. of Docs.

United States. *Congress. Senate. Committee on the Philippines.* Catholic church claims in Philippine Islands: report. '08 (Ag1) il. 8°, pap., 15 c. U. S., Supt. of Docs.

United States. Constitution of the United States of America and Declaration of Independence. '09(O16) S. *25 c. net. G. A. Jackson.

United States. *Constitutional Convention, 1787.* Secret proceedings and debates of the convention assembled at Philadelphia, in the year 1787, for the purpose of forming the Constitution of the United States. '09(My) 208 p. 8°. (Add. Superintendent for price.) U. S., Supt. of Docs.

United States. Continental Congress. Journals, 1774-1789; ed. fr. the orig. records in the Library of Congress, by Worthington Chauncey Ford. In 14 v. v. 7, 8. '08 (Ja11); v. 9, 10 (My2); v. 11 (Je6); v. 12. '08(D); v. 13, 14. '09(Je12) Q. ea., $1. U. S., Supt. of Docs.

United States. *Courts.* Federal reporter, v. 156. Permanent ed. '08(Mr); v. 157 (My); v. 158 (Jl); v. 159 (Ag); v. 160 (S); v. 161 (O); v. 162 (N); v. 163. '08, [1909.] (F); v. 164 (Mr); v. 165, 166 (My); v. 167 (Jl); v. 168 (S); v. 169 (N); v. 170-173. '10(F); v. 174, 175 (Je); v. 176 (Jl); v. 177 (Ag); v. 178-179 (N); v. 180 (D) c. O. (National reporter system, U. S. ser.) shp., ea., $3.50.—Digest of decisions of the U. S. cts. rep. in v. 141-160 of the Federal reporter and in v. 27-28 of the Sup. ct. reporter. v. 7. '08, [1909.] (F) c. O. (National reporter system digests.) shp., $7.50. West Pub.

United States. Customs tariff act of Aug. 5, 1909; rev. to Mar. 1, 1910, with alphabetical schedule, [etc.] [1910.] (Jl) c. S. $2. Downing.

United States. *Dept. of Agriculture.* Agriculture: list of publications of the U. S. Agriculture Dept. additional to those entered in Price list 16; completed to October 7, 1908. '09(Mr6) 8°, gratis. U. S., Supt. of Docs.

United States. *Dept. of Agriculture.* Boys' and girls' agricultural clubs; by F: W: Howe; (farmers' bull.) '10(Ap) 23 p. il. 8°, pap.

United States. *Dept. of Agriculture. Bureau of Animal Industry.* Danger from products of tuberculous cattle. '08(D) 4 p. 8°. U. S., Supt. of Docs.

United States. *Dept. of Agriculture. Bureau of Animal Industry.* Danger from tubercle bacilli in environment of tuberculous cattle; by E. C. Schroeder and W. E. Cotton. '07, [1908.] 24 p. 8°, pap., 5 c. U. S., Supt. of Docs.

United States. *Dept. of Agriculture. Bureau of Animal Industry.* Relation of tuberculous lesions to mode of infection; by E. C. Schroeder and W. E. Cotton. '07, [1908.] (D) 19 p. 8°, pap., 5 c. U. S., Supt. of Docs.

United States. *Dept. of Agriculture. Bureau of Animal Industry.* Susceptibility of tubercle bacilli to modification; by J. R. Mohler and H: J. Washburn. '08(D) 4+113-163 p. il. pap., 15 c. U. S., Supt. of Docs.

United States. *Dept. of Agriculture. Bureau of Animal Industry.* Unsuspected but dangerously tuberculous cow; by E. C. Schroeder. '08(D) 19 p. il. pap., 5 c. U. S., Supt. of Docs.

United States. *Dept. of Agriculture. Bu. of Biological Survey.* Biological Survey; bulletins, circulars and North American fauna of this bureau, Agriculture Department, U. S. A., for sale by the Superintendent of Documents. [2d ed.] [1910.] (Jl) 9 p. 12°, pap., gratis.

United States. *Dept. of Agriculture. Bu. of Biological Survey.* List of publications of the Biological Survey. '09(Ag) 8 p. 8°, gratis. U. S., Supt. of Docs.

United States. *Dept. of Agriculture. Bu. of Chemistry.* Bulletins, circulars and food inspection decisions of the Chemistry Bureau for sale by the Supt. of Docs. '10 (Je) 18 p. D. pap., gratis.

United States. *Dept. of Agriculture. Bu. of Plant Industry.* Mistletoe pest in the Southwest; by W: L. Bray; (bulletin.) '10 (Ap) 39 p. il. 8°, pap.

United States. *Dept. of Agriculture. Bu. of Plant Industry.* New methods of plant breeding, by G: W. Oliver; (bulletin.) '10 (Ap) 39 p. il. 8°, pap.

United States. *Dept. of Agriculture. Bu. of Plant Industry.* Publications of the Bu. of Plant Industry. '09(S) 10 p. 8°, gratis. U. S., Supt. of Docs.

United States. *Dept. of Agriculture. Bu. of Plant Industry.* Traction plowing; by Lynn Webster Ellis; (bulletin.) '10(Ap) 45 p. map, 8°, pap.

United States. *Dept. of Agriculture. Bu. of Plant Industry.* Variegated alfalfa, by J: Minton Westgate; (bulletin.) '10(Ap) 63 p. il. 8°.

United States. *Dept. of Agriculture. Bu. of Soils.* List of soil surveys. '08, [1909.] (Ag) 8 p. 16°, pap., gratis. U. S., Supt. of Docs.

United States. *Dept. of Agriculture. Bu. of Soils.* Reference list on the electric fixation of atmospheric nitrogen and the use of calcium cyanamid and calcium nitrate on soils, by Stephen Conrad Stuntz; (bulletin.) '10(Ap) 89 p. 8°, pap.

United States. *Dept. of Agriculture. Bu. of Statistics.* Bulletins, circulars, foreign markets, separates from yearbook, and crop reporter, Agriculture Department, U. S. A.; for sale by the Superintendent of Documents, Washington. '10(Mr) 12 p. 8°, pap., gratis.

United States. *Dept. of Agriculture, Bureau of Statistics.* Exports of farm and forest products, 1906-1908, by countries to which consigned; division of production and distribution. '10(Mr12) tabs., O. (U. S., Dept. of Agriculture, Bu. of Statistics, bull.) pap., 10 c.

United States. *Dept. of Agriculture, Bureau of Statistics.* Exports of farm products from the U. S., 1851-1908; division of production and distribution. '10(Mr12) O. (U. S., Dept. of Agriculture, Bu. of Statistics, bull.) pap., 15 c.

United States. *Dept. of Agriculture, Bureau of Statistics.* Imports of farm products into the United States, 1851-1908; division of production and distribution. '10(Mr12) tabs., O. (U. S., Dept. of Agriculture, Bu. of Statistics, bull.) pap., 15 c.

United States. *Dept. of Agriculture. Bu. of Statistics.* Statistics Bureau: bulletins, circulars, foreign markets, separates from yearbook, and crop reporter, Agriculture Department, U. S. A.; for sale by the Superintendent of Documents. [2d ed.] [1910.] (Jl) 11 p. pap., gratis.

United States. *Dept. of Agriculture.* Federal legislation, regulations, and rulings affecting agricultural colleges and experiment stations. '09(Ag21) 8°, (U. S., Dept. of Agriculture; office of experiment stations, circular.) pap. (Add. Superintendent for price.) U. S., Supt. of Docs.

United States. *Dept. of Agriculture. Forest Service.* National forests of Arkansas. '10(Ja29) 8°.

United States. *Dept. of Agriculture.* How to destroy English sparrows; by Ned Dearborn; (farmers' bull.) '10(Ap) 11 p. il. 8°, pap.

United States. *Dept. of Agriculture.* Influence of sodium benzoate on the nutrition and health of man. '09(Ag) 784 p. il. tabs., 8°, pap., $1. U. S., Supt. of Docs.

United States. *Dept. of Agriculture.* Locoweed disease; by C: Dwight Marsh; (farmers' bull.) '09, [1910.] (Ap) 16 p. il. 8°, pap.

United States. *Dept. of Agriculture. Office of Experiment Stations.* Dietary studies in public institutions in Philadelphia, Pa., by Emma Smedley and R. D. Milner, and Dietary studies in public institutions in Baltimore, Md., by H. L. Knight, H. A. Pratt, and C. F. Langworthy; (bulletin.) '10 (Ap) 98 p. 8°, pap.

United States. *Dept. of Agriculture. Office of Experiment Stations.* Forestry in nature study. '10(Pa29) 8°, (U. S., Dept. of Agriculture; Office of Experiment Stations, special circular.)

United States. *Dept. of Agriculture. Office of Experiment Stations.* Irrigation in Texas, by Ja. C. Nagle; (bulletin.) '10 (Ap) 92 p. tabs., fold. map, 8°, pap.

United States. *Dept. of Agriculture. Office of Public Roads.* Publications of the Office of Public Roads; comp. by W: W. Sniffin. '09, [1910.] (F) 7 p. 12°, pap.

United States. *Dept. of Agriculture.* Organization, work, and publications of drainage investigations. '09(D) 6 p. 8°, (U. S., Dept. of Agriculture, Office of Experiment Stations, circular.) gratis. U. S., Supt. of Docs.

United States. *Dept. of Agriculture.* Organization, work, and publications of irrigation investigations. '09(D) 12 p. 8°, (U. S., Dept. of Agriculture, Office of Experiment Stations, circular.) pap., gratis. U. S., Supt. of Docs.

United States. *Dept. of Agriculture.* Public documents issued by the secretary's office, Agriculture Department: annual repts., farmers' bulletins, yearbook, etc.; for sale by the Superintendent of Documents. [3d ed.] [1910.] (Jl) 34 p. 8°, pap., gratis.

United States. *Dept. of Agriculture.* Publications of the United States Department of Agriculture and how they are distributed. '09(D) 3 p. 8°, (U. S., Dept. of Agriculture, Division of Publications, circular.) pap., gratis. U. S., Supt. of Docs.

United States. *Dept. of Agriculture. Weather Bu.* Bulletins, circulars, maps and Monthly Weather Review, Agriculture Department, U. S. A.; for sale by the Superintendent of Documents. [2d ed.] [1910.] (Jl) 9 p. 8°, pap., gratis.

United States. *Dept. of Agriculture. Weather Bu. Library.* Brief list of meteorological text-books and reference books; selection of works suitable for general, scientific and university libraries in the United States. 2d ed.; prep. by C. Fitzhugh Talman. '10(N) 18 p. 8°.

United States. *Dept. of Commerce and Labor. Bureau of the Census.* Census of manufacturers: 1905; earnings of wage-earners. '08, [1909.] (My) 179 p. il. f°, pap. (Add. Superintendent for price.) U. S., Supt. of Docs.

United States. *Dept. of Commerce and Labor. Bu. of the Census.* Century of population growth from the first census of the U. S. to the twelfth, 1790-1900. '09(S) 10+303 p. il. maps, f°. (Add. Superintendent for price.) U. S., Supt. of Docs.

United States. *Dept. of Commerce and Labor. Bu. of the Census.* Cotton production, 1908. '09(Ag7) il. charts, 8°. (Add. Superintendent for price.) U. S., Supt. of Docs.

United States. *Dept. of Commerce and Labor. Bu. of the Census.* Electrical industries of Porto Rico: 1907. '09(Ag) 29 p. f°, pap. U. S., Supt. of Docs.

United States. *Dept. of Commerce and Labor. Bureau of the Census.* Expenditures of the United States government, 1791-1907; general revenue; postal revenue; per capita expenditure. '09(Je5) 8°, pap. (Add. Superintendent for price.) U. S., Supt. of Docs.

United States. *Dept. of Commerce and Labor. Bureau of Census.* Heads of families at the first census, 1790; containing names of heads of families at the first census, in the states of Connecticut, Maine, Maryland, Massachusetts, New Hampshire, New York, North Carolina, Pennsylvania, Rhode Island, South Carolina, Vermont, and Virginia. In 13 v. '08(D) ea., $1. U. S., Supt. of Docs.

United States. *Dept. of Commerce and Labor. Bureau of the Census.* Instructions to special agents; census of the fish industry. '08, [1909.] (My) 58 p. 16°, pap. (Add. Superintendent for price. U. S., Supt. of Docs.

United States. *Dept. of Commerce and Labor. Bu. of the Census.* Marriage and divorce, 1867-1906. 2 v. '09(D4) Q. (Add. Superintendent for price.) U. S., Supt. of Docs.

United States. *Dept. of Commerce and Labor. Bureau of the Census.* Mortality statistics, 1908; general death rates, causes of death, occupational mortality, 2d decennial rev. of the International Classification of Causes of Death. '09(D) 133 p. tabs., f°, pap. (Add. Superintendent for price.) U. S., Supt. of Docs.

United States. *Dept. of Commerce and Labor. Bu. of the Census.* Supply and distribution of cotton for the year ending August 31, 1909. '09, [1910.] 32 p. il. f°, (Bulletin.)

United States. *Dept. of Commerce and Labor. Bu. of Fisheries.* Fur seals and the seal fisheries, by C: H. Townsend; address before the Fourth International Fishery Congress, held in Washington, Sept. 22 to 26, 1908. '10(Ap) 315-322 p. 4°, pap.

United States. *Dept. of Commerce and Labor. Bu. of Fisheries.* List of publications of the Bureau of Fisheries available for distribution. '09(D) 22 p.; '10(Jl) 17 p. 8°, gratis.

United States. *Dept. of Commerce and Labor. Bu. of Fisheries.* National aspects of angling and the protection of game fishes, by H. Wheeler Perce; address before the Fourth International Fishery Congress held at Washington Sept. 22 to 26, 1908. '10 (Ap) 193-198 p. 4°, pap.

United States. *Dept. of Commerce and Labor. Bureau of Immigration.* Treaty laws, and regulations governing the admission of Chinese; regulations approved Oct. 30, 1909. '10(Ja8) 8°, pap.

United States. *Dept. of Commerce and Labor. Bureau of Immigration and Naturalization.* Immigration laws and regulations, July 1, 1907. 3d ed. '07. 1908. (F) 8°, pap., 15 c.; 9th ed., Feb. 15, 1910, embodying amendments. '10(Ap) 87 p. 8°.

United States. *Dept. of Commerce and Labor. Bu. of Labor.* Increase in cost of food and other products; letter from the Secretary of Commerce and Labor, transmitting, in response to a Senate resolution of January 10, information rel. to the increase in prices of food and other products. '10(Ap23) tabs., 8°, gratis.

United States. *Dept. of Commerce and Labor. Bu. of Labor.* Investigation of telephone companies; letter from the Secretary of Commerce and Labor. '10(Je) 340 p. pls., tabs., diagrs., 8°.

United States. *Dept. of Commerce and Labor. Bureau of Labor.* Labor laws of the United States, with decisions of courts rel. thereto. '08, [1909.] (My) 1562 p. 8°, pap. (Add. Superintendent for price.) U. S., Supt. of Docs.

United States. *Dept. of Commerce and Labor. Bureau of Labor.* Mortality from consumption in dusty trades; [by F: L: Hoffman;] Charity relief and wage earnings, [by S. E. Forman.] '09(My22) O. (U. S., Dept. of Commerce and Labor; Bu. of Labor bull.) pap. (Add. Superintendent for price.) U. S., Supt. of Docs.

United States. *Dept. of Commerce and Labor. Bu. of Labor.* Retail prices of food in the U. S., 1900 to 1907; wholesale prices of commodities in the U. S., 1900 to 1908; wages and hours of labor in manufacturing industries in the U. S., 1900 to 1907. '10(Je) 34 p. 8°.

United States. *Dept. of Commerce and Labor. Bureau of Labor.* Wholesale prices, 1890-1908. '09(Jl3) O. (U. S., Dept. of Commerce and Labor, Bu. of Labor bull.) pap. U. S., Supt. of Docs.

United States. *Dept. of Commerce and Labor. Bureau of Labor.* Woman and child wage-earners in Great Britain. '09(Je12) O. (U. S., Dept. of Commerce and Labor, Bu. of Labor bull.) pap. (Add. Superintendent for price.) U. S., Supt. of Docs.

United States. *Dept. of Commerce and Labor. Bureau of Statistics.* Commercial America: showing commerce, production, transportation facilities, area, and population of each of the countries of North, South, and Central America, and the West Indies. '09 (O2) 4°. (Add. Superintendent for price.) U. S., Supt. of Docs.

United States. *Dept. of Commerce and Labor. Bureau of Statistics.* Foreign commerce and navigation of the United States for the year ending June 30, 1907. '08 (Je13) Q. $2.50; year ending June 30, 1908. '09(Je5); year ending June 30, 1909. '09, [1910.] (Je) U. S., Supt. of Docs.

United States. *Dept. of Commerce and Labor. Bu. of Statistics.* Statistical abstract of the United States, 1909. '10(Je) 793 p. O. pap.

United States. *Dept. of Commerce and Labor. Coast and Geodetic Survey.* Results of observations made at magnetic observatory at Sitka, Alaska, 1905-1906; by Dan. L. Hazard. '10(Je) 115 p. tabs., diagr., 8°.

United States. *Dept. of Commerce and Labor.* Flour and wheat trade in European countries and the Levant by Mack H. Davis, special agent, Department of Commerce and Labor; transmitted to Congress in compliance with the act of May 22, 1908, authorizing investigations of trade conditions abroad. '09(S18) 8°, pap. (Add. Superintendent for price.) U. S., Supt. of Docs.

United States. *Dept. of Commerce and Labor.* List of publications of the dept. available for distribution. 3d ed. '09(My); 4th ed. '09, [1910.] (Mr); 5th ed. '10(O) 8°, pap.

United States. *Dept. of Commerce and Labor.* Report on trade conditions in Colombia; by G. C: M. Pepper. '08(F) c. '07. 53 p. 8°, pap., 10 c. U. S., Supt. of Docs.

United States. *Dept. of the Interior. Bureau of Education.* Index to Reports of the Commissioner of Education, 1867-1907. '09 (O) 103 p. 8°. (Add. Superintendent for price.) U. S., Supt. of Docs.

United States. *Dept. of the Interior.* Coal lands in Oklahoma; message from the President transmitting repts. rendered. '10(Je) 374 p. fold. maps, 8°.

United States. *Dept. of the Interior. General Land Office.* Manual of instructions for the survey of the mineral lands of the U. S. '09(My) 94 p. il. 16°. (Add. Superintendent for price.) U. S., Supt. of Docs.

United States. *Dept. of the Interior. General Land Office.* Opening of Indian reservations. '09(D25) 8°. (Add. Superintendent for price.) U. S., Supt. of Docs.

United States. *Dept. of the Interior.* Reclamation projects; letter from the Secretary of the Interior, transmitting information in compliance with Senate resolution of Feb. 10, 1910, as to the amount of money required to finish reclamation projects now under consideration, and the amount of money expended upon each of the projects, etc. '10(Ap) 31 p. 8°.

United States. *Dept. of the Interior.* Unappropriated public lands of the United States by counties, land districts and states, on July 1, 1909. '09(D4) Q. (Add. Superintendent for price.)
U. S., Supt. of Docs.

United States. *Dept. of the Interior. U. S. Geolog. Survey.* Colloid matter of clay and its measurement, by Harrison Everett Ashley; (bulletin.) '09, [1910.] (Ap) 65 p. il. 8°, pap., 10 c.
"References" (4 p.).

United States. *Dept. of the Interior. U. S. Geolog. Survey.* Fire tax and waste of structural materials in the U. S., by Herbert Michael Wilson and J: L: Cochrane. '10(Ap) 30 p. tabs., O. pap.

United States. *Dept. of the Interior. U. S. Geolog. Survey.* Geology of the Lewistown coal field, Montana, by W: R. Calvert; (bulletin.) '09, [1910.] (Ap) 83 p. il. maps, 8°, pap., 35 c.

United States. *Dept. of the Interior. U. S. Geolog. Survey.* Innoko gold-placer district, Alaska, with accounts of the central Kuskokwim Valley and the Ruby Creek and Gold Hill placers, by Alfr. G. Maddren; (bulletin.) '10(Ap) 87 p. fold. maps, 8°, pap.

United States. *Dept. of the Interior. U. S. Geolog. Survey.* Iron ores, fuels, and fluxes of the Birmingham district, Alabama, by Ernest F. Burchard and C: Butts, with chapters on the origin of the ores, by Edn. C. Eckel: (bulletin.) '10(Ap) 204 p. il. maps, tab., 8°, pap.

United States. *Dept. of the Interior. U. S. Geological Survey.* Papers on the conservation of water resources. '09(O23) il. maps, 8°, (U. S. Geological Survey, Water-supply paper.) pap. (Add. Superintendent for price.) U. S., Supt. of Docs.

United States. *Dept. of the Interior. U. S. Geolog. Survey.* Pleistocene geology of the Leadville quadrangle, Colorado, by Stephen R. Capps, jr. '09, [1910.] (Ap) 99 p. il. fold. map in pocket, 8°, pap., 30 c.

United States. *Dept. of the Interior. U. S. Geolog. Survey.* Public utility of water powers and their governmental regulation, by René Tavernier and Marshall O. Leighton; (water-supply paper.) '10(Ap) 161 p. O. pap.

United States. *Dept. of the Interior. U. S. Geological Survey.* Publications; (not incl. topographic maps.) '09(My); '10(N) 8°, pap.

United States. *Dept. of the Interior; U. S. Geological survey.* Publications rel. to water resources. '09(Jl); '10(N) 8°, pap., gratis. U. S., Supt. of Docs.

United States. *Dept. of the Interior. U. S. Geolog. Survey.* Results of spirit leveling in Illinois, 1896 to 1908, inclusive; comp. by S: S. Gannett and D: H: Baldwin; in cooperation with the Illinois State Geological Survey, during 1905 to 1908, inclusive; (bulletin.) '10(Ap) 74 p. 8°, pap.

United States. *Dept. of the Interior, U. S. Geological Survey.* Technologic publications of the United States Geological Survey. '10(N) 3 p. 8°, pap., gratis.

United States. *Dept. of State.* **Affairs in the Kongo; message from the President of the** United States. '10(Ja29) 8°.

United States. *Dept. of State.* Correspondence rel. to wrongs done to American citizens by the government of Venezuela. '08 (Je13) 8°, pap., $1.50. U. S., Supt. of Docs.

United States. *Dept. of State.* Suppression of the white-slave traffic; message from the President of the United States, transmitting, with accompanying letters, in response to Senate resolution no. 86, of Dec. 7, 1909, information concerning the repression of the trade in white women. '10(Mr5) 8°.

United States. *Dept. of State.* Universal and International Exhibition, Brussels. Message from the President transmitting a report from the Secretary of State recommending an appropriation to enable the U. S. fittingly to participate in the Universal and International Exhibition to be held at Brussels, April to November, 1910. '09 (Mr6) 8°, gratis. U. S., Supt. of Docs.

United States. Description of azimuth instrument, models of 1900 and 1900Mi; with instructions for care and operation; rev. Dec. 1, 1905; rev. Dec. 31, 1906; rev. Aug. 26, 1909. '09(D4) il. 8°. (Add. Superintendent for price.) U. S., Supt. of Docs.

United States. *Engineer Dept.* Dredging; published by authority of the Secretary of War; Office of the Chief of Engineers. '10(D) 19 p. 8°.

United States. *Engineer School.* On the amelioration of rivers with unstable beds by the system Audouin; tr. from the French at the Engineer School, 1908. '08, [1909.] (Ap) 40 p. il. plans, 8°, (Occasional papers, Engineer School.) (Not for sale.)
Engineer Sch.

United States. Federal laws governing licensed dealers; by J: G. Capers. '10(Je) c. S. hf. roan, $3. Criterion.

United States. Federal penal code in force January 1, 1910; together with other statutes having penal provisions in force December 1, 1908; annotated by G: F. Tucker and C: W. Blood. '10(D) c. 52+507 p. 4°, $5. Little, B. & Co.

United States. Federal statutes, annot. Supp. 1909; comp. by W: M. McKinney. '09(N) c. 15+915 p. O. shp., $6. E: Thompson.

United States. Fire insurance laws, taxes and fees; rev. to Aug. 1, 1908; [incl. law of the U. S. and Canada.] '08(O) c. 387 p. O. shp. (Add. pubs. for price.) Spectator.

United States. *General Land Office.* Suggestions to homesteaders and persons desiring to make homestead entries; approved March 9, 1908. '08(Je13) 8°, pap., 10 c. U. S., Supt. of Docs.

United States. *Geological Survey.* List of publications of the United States Geological Survey rel. to water resources. '08(Ag1) 8°, pap., 10 c. U. S., Supt. of Docs.

United States. *Government Printing Office.* Monotype manual; book of arrangements and other useful information for the use of monotype keyboard operators in the Government Printing Office. 2d ed. '10 (Mr5) 8°.

United States. *Inspector-General's Office.* Brownsville affray: rept. of the inspector-general of the army; order of the President discharging enlisted men of companies B, C and D, Twenty-fifth infantry (colored); messages of the President to the Senate. '08(Je13) 8°, pap., 50 c. U. S., Supt. of Docs.

United States. *Interstate Commerce Commission.* Index-digest of the reports, rulings and decisions; by A. B. Van Buren. '10(Mr) c. O. $5. Edwards.

United States. *Interstate Commerce Commission.* Memorandum on lumber reparation cases; east of river yellow-pine lumber reparation cases assigned for hearing January 19, 1909, at Washington, D. C. '09 (Ag) 22 p. 8°. (Add. Superintendent for price.) U. S., Supt. of Docs.

United States. *Interstate Commerce Commission.* Regulations for the transportation of explosives, formulated and published Jan. 15, 1910; prescribed under act of Mar. 4, 1909. '10(Mr5) 8°.

United States. *Interstate Commerce Commission.* Regulations governing the construction and filing of tariffs and classifications of express companies. '08(D12) 8°. U. S., Supt. of Docs.

United States. *Interstate Commerce Commission.* Repts., v. 12. '08(Mr); v. 13 (O) c. O. shp., ea., $5. Lawyers' Co-op.

United States. Interstate commerce laws; full text of all the laws, including revisions to July 1, 1910. '10(Jl) c. O. pap., 50 c. Railway Age Gazette.

United States. Investigation relative to wages and prices of commodities: topical digest of evidence submitted in hearings held before the Select Committee of the Senate relative to wages and prices of commodities. '10(N) 95 p. 8°.

United States. Law of interstate commerce and federal regulation thereof, [etc.;] by Dewitt C. Moore. '10(D) c. 77+808 p. O. $7.50. M. Bender.

United States. *Library of Congress.* List of geographical atlases in the Library of Congress, with bibliographical notes; comp. under the direction of Philip Lee Phillips. 2 v. '09(D) 8°. (Add. Superintendent for price.) U. S., Supt. of Docs.

United States. *Library of Congress.* Preliminary list of subject subdivisions: (a) under names of countries or states; (b) under cities; (c) under general subjects; prep. by the chief of the Catalogue Division. '10(Jl) 30 p. 8°. Gov. Pr. Off.

United States. *Library of Congress.* Want list of American 18th century newspapers, 1909. '09(Je26) 8°, pap. (Add. Superintendent for price.) U. S., Supt. of Docs.

United States. *Library of Congress.* Want list of periodicals. New ed., 1909. '09 (O23) 8°, pap. (Add. Superintendent for price.) U. S., Supt. of Docs.

United States. *Library of Congress.* Want list of publications of societies. New ed., 1909. '09(Ag14) 8°, pap. (Add. Superintendent for price.) U. S., Supt. of Docs.

United States. *Marine Corps.* Instructions governing transportation for U. S. Marine Corps, 1909. '09(O) 24 p. 8°. (Add. Superintendent for price.) U. S., Supt. of Docs.

United States. *National Monetary Commission.* Interviews on the banking and currency systems of England, Scotland, France, Germany, Switzerland, and Italy. '10(Je) 541 p. fold. tabs., 8°.

United States. *National Monetary Commission.* List of conferences in London, Paris, and Berlin, held by representatives of the National Monetary Commission and of papers and statistics to be prepared for the Commission. '09(Ap) 22 p. 8°, pap. (Add. Superintendent for price.) U. S., Supt. of Docs.

United States. *National Monetary Commission.* Publications issued by and in preparation for the National Monetary Commission, Sept. 1, 1910. '10(O) 15 p. 8°.

United States. *National Monetary Commission.* Rept. to National Monetary Commission on the fiscal systems of the United States, England, France and Germany. '09 (My) 86 p. 8°, pap. (Add. Superintendent for price.) U. S., Supt. of Docs.

United States. Naval Academy. Notes on machine design prep. by the Dept. of Marine Engineering and Naval Construction. '08, [1909.] (My) 159 p. il. tabs., 8°, $2.50. U. S. Naval Inst.

United States. *Naval War College,* Newport, R. I. International law situations, with solutions and notes, 1908. '09(Je) 255 p. 8°, pap. (Add. Superintendent for price.) U. S., Supt. of Docs.

United States. *Navy Department.* Alleged structural defects in battle ships of United States navy: letters and papers. '08(Ag1) 8°, pap., 15 c. U. S., Supt. of Docs.

United States. *Navy Department.* Proposed removal of wreck of battle ship "Maine" in harbor of Habana, Cuba. '08(Ag1) 8°, pap., 15 c. U. S., Supt. of Docs.

United States. *Navy Dept.* Status of naval vessels on the Great Lakes; letter from the acting Secretary of the Navy. [1910.] (Jl) 6 p. 8°.

United States. New banking law; amendment to national banking law, act of May 30, 1908; by C: A. Conant. '08(D) c. 57 p. S. (Add. pub. for price.) Bankers' Pub.

United States. New railroad law; text of the act creating the new commerce court and the interstate commerce act as amended by the act of June 18, 1910; ed. by W: L. Snyder. '10(Ag) c. 6+70 p. O. pap., $1. Baker, V. & Co.

United States. New tariff bill full official text of the Payne tariff law; the new tariff and the old compared, showing the main changes. '09(N6) c. 4°, pap., 10 c. C. S. Hammond.

United States. *Office of Naval Intelligence.* Information concerning some of the principal navies of the world. '09(Je5) tabs., 8°, pap. (Add. Superintendent for price.) U. S., Supt. of Docs.

United States. Pierce's federal code, 1910; in force Mar. 4, 1907, with supp. to Jan. 1, 1910; comp. by Fk. Pierce. '10(Mr) c. O. $10.50. Nat. Law.

United States. Pocket ed. of the tariff act; comp. and ed. by W: W. Rich. '10(Mr) c. D. pap., 50 c. Vandegrift.

United States. *Post-Office Dept.* Domestic and foreign mail matter; classification; conditions; rates of postage; issued by direction of the postmaster-general. 5th ed. '08, [1909.] (Ap) 56 p. 24°. (Add. Superintendent for price.) U. S., Supt. of Docs.

United States. *Post-office Dept.* Investigations as to pneumatic-tube service for the mails; letter from the postmaster-general submitting the rept. of an investigation. '09 (My) 143 p. plans, 8°, pap. (Add. Superintendent for price.) U. S., Supt. of Docs.

United States. *Post-office Dept.* Navy mail service; instructions for the guidance of navy mail clerks and assistant navy mail clerks authorized by act of Congress, approved May 27, 1908. '08, [1909.] (My) 15 p. 8°, pap. (Add. Superintendent for price.) U. S., Supt. of Docs.

United States. *Post-Office Department.* Rural delivery service; instructions for the guidance of postmasters and carriers in the conduct of the rural delivery service in effect March 4, 1907. '08(Ag1) 8°, pap., 15 c. U. S., Supt. of Docs.

United States. *Post-office Dept.* Street directory of the principal cities of the United States, embracing letter-carrier offices established to Ap. 30, 1908. 5th ed. '08, [1909.] (My) 904 p. 4°, pap. (Add. Superintendent for price.) U. S., Supt. of Docs.

United States. *Post Office Dept.* Summary of the Department's reply to the Periodical Publishers' Association of America regarding second-class mail. '10(Ap23) 8°.

United States. *Printing Investigation Commission.* Rept.; letter from the chairman transmitting rept. recommending certain legislation rel. to the printing, binding and distribution of public documents. '09(My) 31 p. 8°, pap. (Add. Superintendent for price.) U. S., Supt. of Docs.

United States. Proceedings of Congress; being a complete list of the volumes of the Annals of Congress, Register of Debates in Congress, Congressional Globe, Congressional Record, now offered free to all organized public and school libraries. '09 (O2) 8°. (Add. Superintendent for price.) U. S., Supt. of Docs.

United States. *Public Health and Marine Hospital Service.* Publications of the United States Public Health and Marine Hospital Service, Jan., 1910. '10(Mr) 25 p. 8°, pap.

United States. *Signal Office.* Visual signaling, Signal Corps, United States Army, '10(O) 133 p. il. form, diagrs., 8°. Gov. Pr. Off.

United States. *Steamboat Inspection Service.* Findings in investigation of collision between steamer "Larchmont" and schooner "Harry Knowlton" on Feb. 11, 1907. '08 (F) 123 p. 8°, pap., 25 c. U. S., Supt. of Docs.

United States. *Steamboat-Inspection Service.* Pilot rules for the inland waters of the Atlantic and Pacific coasts and on the Gulf of Mexico, except rivers emptying into the Gulf of Mexico and their tributaries. '09(S) 26 p. il. 8°. (Add. Superintendent for price.) U. S., Supt. of Docs.

United States. *Superintendent of Documents.* Animal Industry Bureau; repts., bulletins, and circulars rel. to animal industry, Agricultural Department, U. S. A.; for sale by the Superintendent of Documents, Washington. '10(Mr) 53 p. 8°, pap., gratis.

United States. *Superintendent of Documents.* Chemistry Bureau; bulletins, circulars, food inspection decisions, etc., of the Chemistry Bureau, Agriculture Department, U. S. A. [2d ed.] '10(O) 19 p. 8°, pap., gratis.

United States. *Superintendent of Documents.* Education; list of government publications rel. to public schools, universities, technical and scientific education, etc., in United States and foreign countries. '10 (O) 74 p. 8°, pap., gratis.

United States. *Superintendent of Documents.* Engineering: mechanics; government documents which contribute to knowledge of these subjects are available for purchase through the office of the Superintendent of Documents, Washington, [3d ed.] '10(Je) 67 p.; [4th ed.] [1910.] (N) 75 p. 8°, ea., pap., gratis.

United States. *Superintendent of Documents.* Entomology Bureau; bulletins, circulars and technical series relating to insects; Agriculture Department, U. S. A.; for sale by the Superintendent of Documents, Washington. [2d ed.] [1910.] (D) 19 p. 8°, pap., gratis.

United States. *Superintendent of Documents.* Experiment Stations Office; bulletins, circulars, Experiment Station Record, and repts. of colonial experiment stations, Agricultural Department, U. S. A. [2d ed.] '10(O) 31 p. 8°, pap., gratis.

United States. *Superintendent of Documents.* Finance; public documents now available. [2d ed.] [1910.] (Je) 31 p. 8°, gratis.

United States. *Superintendent of Documents.* Food and diet; price list of public documents rel. to food and diet issued by scientific bureaus of United States government. 3d ed. '10(O) 48 p. 8°, pap., gratis.

United States. *Superintendent of Documents.* Forest Service; bulletins, circulars, silvical leaflets, etc., rel. to forests, Agricultural Department, U. S. A. [2d ed.] '10 (O) 22 p. 8°, pap., gratis.

United States. *Superintendent of Documents.* Indians; price list of public documents rel. to Indians principally of United States; for sale by the Superintendent of Documents, Washington, D. C. [1910.] (N) 81 p. 8°, pap., gratis.

United States. *Superintendent of Documents.* Laws of the United States for sale by the Superintendent of Documents. '09(Ag) 6 p. 8°, pap., gratis. U. S., Supt. of Docs.

United States. *Superintendent of Documents.* Library of Congress publications sold by the Superintendent of Documents at Washington. '09(My) 14 p. 12°, pap., gratis. U. S., Supt. of Docs.

United States. *Superintendent of Documents.* Periodicals issued by United States government, with foreign and domestic subscription prices; for sale by the Superintendent of Documents. [1910.] 8 p. 12°, pap., gratis.

United States. *Superintendent of Documents.* Plant Industry Bureau: bulletins, circulars, and misc. publications rel. to plants, Agriculture Department, U. S. A.; for sale by the Superintendent of Documents, Washington. '10(Mr) 31 p. 8°, pap., gratis.

United States. *Superintendent of Documents.* Plant Industry Bureau publications; Agriculture Dept., U. S. A. [2d ed.] '10(Je) 33 p. 8°, gratis.

United States. *Superintendent of Documents.* Proceedings of Congress: being a complete list of the volumes of the Annals of the Congress, Register of Debates in Congress, *Congressional Globe, Congressional Record,* reporting the debates and proceedings from 1789 to 1909; now offered for sale by the Superintendent of Documents. [2d ed.] '10(Mr5) 8°, gratis.

United States. *Superintendent of Documents.* Proceedings of Congress; being a complete list of the volumes of the annals of Congress, Register of Debates in Congress, Congressional Globe, Congressional Record, now offered free to all organized public and school libraries. '09(S) 15 p. 8°, gratis. U. S., Supt. of Docs.

United States. *Superintendent of Documents.* Public documents issued by the Secretary's Office, Agriculture Department: annual repts., Farmer's bulletins, Yearbooks, etc.; for sale by the Superintendent of Documents, Washington, D. C. [4th ed.] '10(N) 36 p. 8°, pap., gratis.

United States. *Superintendent of Documents.* Public Roads Office; bulletins and circulars relating to the improvement of roads; Agriculture Dept., U. S. A.; for sale by the Superintendent of Documents, Washington. [2d ed.] [1910.] (D) 7 p. 12°, pap., gratis.

United States. *Superintendent of Documents.* Sociology; public documents of the United States sold by the Superintendent of Documents. [2d ed.] '10(Mr5) 8°, gratis.

United States. *Superintendent of Documents.* Soils Bureau; bulletins, circulars, and field operations of the Soils Bureau, Agriculture Department, U. S. A.; for sale by the Superintendent of Documents, Washington, D. C. [3d ed.] [1910.] 8 p. 8°, pap., gratis.

United States. *Superintendent of Documents.* Tariff; list of United States public documents rel. to the various tariff laws enacted by Congress and tariff laws of foreign countries; for sale by the Superintendent of Documents, Washington. [2d ed.] [1910.] (D) 34 p. 8°, pap., gratis.

United States. *Supreme ct.* Cases argued and decided in the Oct. term, 1908. Bk. 52, 53. Lawyers' ed. '09(N) c. O. shp., ea., $5. Lawyers' Co-op.

United States. *Supreme ct.* Digest. v. 1-206. L. ed. books 1-51. v. 1-4. '08(O); v. 5-6. '08(D) c. O. shp., ea., $7.50. Lawyers' Co-op.

United States. *Supreme ct.* Encyclop. of repts.; being a complete encyclopedia of all the case law of the federal sup. ct. up to and incl. v. 206 U. S. sup. ct. repts. (book 51 lawyers' ed.); (T; Johnson Michie, *ed.*) v. 1. '08(N); v. 2. '09(F); v. 3 (Mr); v. 4 (Je); v. 5 (O); v. 6 (D); v. 7, 8. '10 (Ap); v. 9 (Je); v. 10 (S) c. O. shp., ea., $6. Michie.

United States. *Supreme ct.* Notes; supp. to Rose's notes on U. S. repts.; showing the present authority of each case as disclosed by the citations, [etc.;] by C: L. Thompson. Supp. 4. '09(Mr) c.—Supp. 5 (Ag) O. shp., ea., *$6.50 net. Bancroft-W.

United States. Supreme court reporter. v. 28. Permanent ed. '08(O) c. O. (National reporter system, U. S. ser.) $4; v. 29. '09 (N); v. 30. '10(O) c. O. ea., $5. West Pub.

United States. *Supreme ct.* Repts. v. 207-208; (C: H: Butler.) '08(Je); v. 209 (O); v. 210 (N); v. 211. '09(Ap); v. 212 (Jl); v. 213, 214 (O) ea., $2.30; v. 215. '10 (Ap); v. 216 (Jl) c. O. shp., ea., $2. Banks.

United States. Tariff act; Vandergrift's digest. Pocket ed.; comp. and ed. by W: W. Rich. '09(N) c. 172 p. D. pap., 50 c. Vandergrift.

United States. The tariff act of 1900: an act to provide revenue, equalize duties and encourage the industries of the United States, and for other purposes; with index; approved August 5, 1900. '09(S18) 8°, pap. U. S., Supt. of Docs.

United States. Tariff acts passed by the Congress of the United States from 1789 to 1909, including all acts, resolutions, and proclamations modifying or changing those acts. '09, [1910.] 1040 p. 8°.

United States. Tax on net income of corporations. '09(Ag21) 8°, pap. (Add. Superintendent for price.) U. S., Supt. of Docs.

United States. *Treasury Dept.* Balances of appropriations for river and harbor improvements; letter from the Secretary of the Treasury transmitting a reply to the inquiry of the House as to river and harbor expenditures. '09(Ag) 3 p. 8°, pap. (Add. Superintendent for price.) U. S., Supt. of Docs.

United States. *Treasury Dept.* Customs regulations of the United States. '08(D12) 8°. (Add. Superintendent for price.) U. S., Supt. of Docs.

United States. *Treasury Dept.* Eastern Cherokees against the United States; letter from the Secretary of the Treasury, transmitting papers and recommendations rel. to appropriations to satisfy the judgment in the case of the eastern Cherokees against the United States. '09(Ap) 11 p. 8°, pap. U. S., Supt. of Docs.

United States. *Treasury Dept.* Estates of American citizens dying abroad. '10(Je) 5 p. 8°.

United States. *Treasury Dept.* Information respecting United States bonds, paper currency, coin, production of precious metals, etc. '09(S18) 4°, pap. (Add. Superintendent for price.) U. S., Supt. of Docs.

United States. *Treasury Dept. Life-saving Service.* Directions for restoring the apparently drowned, for saving drowning persons by swimming to their relief and for the treatment of frostbites, as practiced in the United States Life-saving Service. '09 (D25) il. 8°. (Add. Superintendent for price.) U. S., Supt. of Docs.

United States. *Treasury Dept. Office of Internal Revenue.* Denatured alcohol at home and abroad; special and detailed rept. of the commissioner and the chief chemist of the Bureau to the Secretary of the Treasury reviewing observations in Europe regarding denatured alcohol, its manufacture and uses. '09(Ap) 39 p. 8°, pap. (Add. Superintendent for price.) U. S., Supt. of Docs.

United States. *Treasury Dept. Public Health and Marine Hospital Service.* The rat and its relation to the public health, by various authors. '10(My) 254 p. il. 8°.

United States. *Treasury Dept.* Rept. of Hon. Rob. J. Walker, Secretary of the Treasury, on the state of the finances, dated Dec. 3, 1845. '09(Je) 21 p. 8°, pap. (Add. Superintendent for price.) U. S., Supt. of Docs.

United States. *War Dept. Adjutant-General's Office.* Circular rel. to pay of officers and enlisted men of the army; comp. by Capt. Johnson Hagood. '08(Je6) il. tabs., 8°, pap., 25 c. U. S., Supt. of Docs.

United States. *War Dept.* Payment of certain claims in Panama; letter from the Secretary of War, transmitting corespondence rel. to the payment of certain claims in Panama. '09(Ap) 101 p. 8°, pap. (Add. Superintendent for price.) U. S., Supt. of Docs.

United States. *War Dept.* Roster of the organized militia of the United States, by divisions, brigades, regiments, companies, and other organizations, with their stations, Feb. 28, 1909. '09(My15) 8°. (Add. Superintendent for price.) U. S., Supt. of Docs.

United States. *War Dept. Surgeon-General's Office.* Index-catalogue of the library of the Surgeon-General's Office, United States Army. Authors and subjects. 2d ser. v. 13, Periodicity-Prussia. '08(N17) Q. $2. U. S., Supt. of Docs.

UNITED STATES.

Adams, C: K., *and* Trent, W: P. Hist. of the United States. $1.50. Allyn & B.

Allen, G. W. Our naval war with France. **$1.50 net. Houghton M.

American Academy of Political and Social Science. American business conditions. $1.50; $1. Am. Acad. Pol. Sci.

American civil government. 50 c. net; 60 c. net. Macmillan.

Ames, H. V. Outlines of lectures on American political and institutional hist. during the colonial and revolutionary periods. $1. Longmans.

Andrews, C: M., *and* Davenport, F. G. Guide to the manuscript materials for the history of the U. S. to 1783, in the British Museum, in minor London archives, and in the libraries of Oxford and Cambridge. $2. Carnegie.

Andrews, E: L. Napoleon and America. *$2 net. M. Kennerley.

Andrews, J. D. American law. 2 v. *$12 net. Callaghan.

Ashley, R: L. American government. $1 net. Macmillan.

Avery, E. M. Hist. of the U. S. and its people. In 15 v. v. 4-7. ea., *$6.25 net; per set, *$12.50 net; *$17.50 net. Burrows.

Baedeker, K. United States. *$4.50 net. Scribner.

Barnes, E. Short American history for intermediate grades. v. 1, 70 c.; v. 2, 75 c.; complete, $1. Heath.

Barrett, J: United States and Latin America. gratis. Int. Bu. Am. Republics.

Bartlett, W: H. Handy book of American government. 50 c. Crowell.

Beard, C: A. American government and politics. $2.10 net. Macmillan.

Beard, C: A., *comp.* Readings in American government and politics. **$1.90 net. Macmillan.

Beveridge, A. J. Americans of to-day and to-morrow. 50 c. Altemus.

UNITED STATES.—*Continued.*

Bigelow, F. H. Daily normal temperature and the daily normal precipitation of the United States. (Add. Superintendent for price.) U. S., Supt. of Docs.

Blake, G: H. United States paper money. $1. G: H. Blake.

Bosse, G: von. Deutsches Element in den Vereinigten Staaten. $3. Lemcke.

Bourne, J., *jr.* Popular versus delegated government. Gov. Pr. Off.

Bowden-Smith, A. G. An English student's wander-year in America. $1.50 net. Longmans.

Bradford, T: L., *comp.* Bibliographer's manual of American history. In 5 v. subs., per v., $3.50 net; per set, $17.50. Henkels.

Brooks, J: G. As others see us: study of progress in the United States. **$1.75 net. Macmillan.

Brooks, R. C. Corruption in American politics and life. $1.25 net. Dodd.

Brooks, Van W. Wine of the Puritans; study of the present day in America. *$1 net. M. Kennerley.

Brown, D: W. Commercial power of Congress. $2. Putnam.

Brown, F. R. Hist. of the Ninth U. S. Infantry, 1799-1909. $5.50. Ninth Infantry, Tex.

Bruce, H: A. B. Romance of American expansion. **$1.75 net. Moffat.

Bryce, J. American commonwealth. In 2 v. $4. Commonwealth Pub.; Macmillan.

Burke, E. Speeches and letters on American affairs. *35 c. net; *70 c. net. Dutton.

Burstall, S. A. Impressions of American education in 1908. *$1.25 net. Longmans.

Busbey, K. G. Home life in America. $2 net. Macmillan.

Butler, C: H: Review of the decisions of the federal and state courts in cases involving the relative effect of stipulations in treaties between the U. S. and foreign powers. (Add. pubs. for price.) Banks.

Butler, N: M. American as he is. **$1 net. Macmillan.

Byfield, S. Narrative of a light company soldier's service in the 41st regiment of foot (1807-1814). $2.75. Abbatt.

Caldwell, H. W. Outlines of American hist., 1785-1861. $1.25. Univ. Pub. Co.

Caldwell, H. W., *and* Clarke, E. P. Source history of the United States. *$1.25 net. Ainsworth.

Callahan, J. M. Evolution of Seward's Mexican policy. 75 c.—Introd. to American expansive policy. 50 c.—Russo-American relation during the American Civil War. 30 c. Univ. of W. Va.

Callender, G. S. Selections from the economic hist. of the United States. $2.75. Ginn.

Caracciolo, J. F., *comp.* Guida dell' operaio italiano in America. 50 c. Italian Am.

Carr, J: F. Guida degli Stati Uniti per l'immigrante italiano. 10 c. Doubleday, P.

UNITED STATES.—*Continued.*

Catholic church in the United States. In 6 v. v. 1, 2. subs., ea., $90; mor., $180. Cath. Editing.

Chadwick, F. E. Relations of the United States and Spain. **$4 net. Scribner.

Channing, E: Elements of U. S. hist. 90 c. net.—History of the United States. In 8 v. v. 2. *$2.50 net.—Short history of the United States. *$1 net. Macmillan.

Church, S: H. Religious progress in America. 25 c. R. P. Morris.

Clancy, J. American civics. $1. Democracy Pr.

Clayton, J. C. True constitution: suggestions towards its interpretation. *$3 net. Assoc. Pub.

Clemens, S: L. Travels at home. 50 c. Harper.

Cole, W: M. American hope. $1.50 net. Appleton.

Coleman, N. M. Constitution and its framers. $3; $5. Progress Co.

Collins, V. L. Continental Congress at Princeton [1783.] *$3 net. Princeton Univ.

Coman, K. Industrial hist. of the United States. $1.50 net. Macmillan.

Commons, J. K., *and others, eds.* Documentary history of American industrial society. In 10 v. *$50 net. A. H. Clark.

Convention between the U. S. and China; arbitration. '09(My) 4 p. 8°, pap. (Add. Superintendent for price.) U. S., Supt. of Docs.

Convention between the U. S. and Denmark. '09(My) 5 p. 8°, pap. (Add. Superintendent for price.) U. S., Supt. of Docs.

Conventions between the U. S. and the Netherlands; arbitration. '09(My) 5 p. 8°, pap. (Add. Superintendent for price.) U. S., Supt. of Docs.

Cooke, F: H. Commerce clause of the federal Constitution. $4.50. Baker, V. & Co.

Coolidge, A. C. United States as a world power. *$2 net. Macmillan.

Country to which you go. gratis. Y. M. C. A.

Croly, H. Promise of American life. **$2 net. Macmillan.

Cronau, R. Our wasteful nation. $1. M. Kennerley.

Crook, W: H: Through five administrations. $1.80 net. Harper.

Curry, F. E., *comp.* National flag; Magna Charta; Declaration of Independence, [etc.] gratis. Cal. Sec'y State.

Davis, A. C. Stories of the United States for youngest readers. 40 c.; 30 c. Educ. Pub.

Davis, J: Travels of four years and a half in the United States. *$2.50 net. Holt.

Davis, J: W., *ed.* Young America's manual. 25 c. Educ. Pub.

De Bary, R: Land of promise: account of the material and spiritual unity of America. *$1.50 net. Longmans.

UNITED STATES.—*Continued.*

Declaration of governors for conservation of natural resources. '08, [1909.] (My) 7 p. 8°, (U. S., Dept. of Agriculture; farmers' bull.) pap. (Add. Superintendent for price.) U. S., Supt. of Docs.

Devens, R: M., *and* Chase, C: W. Glory of our youth as portrayed in the events and movements that have chiefly distinguished the marvellous advance of the American nation from colony to world power. $3.75. C. A. Nichols.

Devlin, R. T: Treaty power under the Constitution of the United States. $6. Bancroft-W.

Dewey, D. R. Financial history of the United States. **$2 net. Longmans.

Dickens, C: American notes. *35 c. net; *70 c. net. Dutton.

Dutton, S: T., *and* Snedden, D: S: Administration of public education in the U. S. *$1.75 net. Macmillan.

Elliott, E: G. Biographical story of the constitution; study of the growth of the American union. **$2 net. Putnam.

Ellis, E: S. Guida per gl' immigranti italiani negli Stati Uniti d'America: [questions and answers in Italian relating to the government, etc., of the U. S., intended for immigrants.] gratis. C: M. Panunzio.

Ellis, E: S. Library of American hist. from the discovery of America to the present time. 9 v. $56. Jones Bros.

Ellis, E: S., *ed.* Hist. of our country from the discovery of America to the present time. 8 v. $48. Jones Bros.

Elson, H: W. Guide to American history. **$1.25 net. Baker & T.

Elson, H: W: History of the United States. 5 v. *$7.50 net. Macmillan.

Evans, C:, *and* Bunn, C. O. Study of civil government. 55 c. Bunn.

Evans, L. B. Essential facts of American hist. $1.—First lessons in American history. 70 c. B: H. Sanborn.

Everhart, E. Hdbk. of United States public documents. $2.50 net. H. W. Wilson.

Fanning, C. E., *comp.* Selected articles on the election of United States senators. $1. H. W. Wilson.

Federalist (The); interpreting the Constitution as agreed upon Sept. 17, 1787. $1.75; $3.50. Lamb Pub.

Fess, S. D. History of political theory and party organization in the U. S. $1.50. Ginn; World's Events.

Finley, J: H., *and* Sanderson, J: F. American executive, and executive methods. **$1.25 net. Century Co.

Fischer, H. Landeskunde der Vereinigten Staaten. 2 v. 40 c. Stechert.

Flack, H. E. Adoption of the fourteenth amendment. $2. Johns Hopkins.

Follett, M. P. Speaker of the House of Representatives. $1.75 net. Longmans.

Foote, A. E., *and* Skinner, A. W. Makers and defenders of America. 60 c. Am. Bk.

Ford, J. H. Cost of our national government. $1.60 net. Macmillan.

UNITED STATES.—*Continued.*

Ford, W. C. Campaign of 1844. 50 c. Davis Press.

Forman, S: E. Hist. of the United States for schools. $1 net. Century Co.

Foster, R. Treatise on federal practice, civil and criminal. $6.50. Callaghan.

Francis, A. Americans: an impression. *$1.50 net. Appleton.

Fritsch, W. A. Aus Amerika. 40 c. Lemcke.

Frothingham, R: Rise of the republic of the United States. $2. Little, B. & Co.

Fuller, H. B. Speakers of the House. **$2 net. Little, B. & Co.

Fuller, R. H. Government by the people: United States. **$1 net. Macmillan.

Galloway, G: W. Arkansas sharpshooter. 50 c. Smith.

Gauss, H: C. American government. $5. Hamersly.

Gerson, O. Our colonial hist. from the discovery of America to the close of the Revolution. 50 c. Hinds.

Gibbs' travellers' route and reference book of the United States and Canada. $3. Gibbs Bros. & M.

Gibson, J: W: Junior history of U. S. 60 c. Flanagan.

Gibson, R. A. College days essays. $1. Nixon-J.

Giesecke, A. A. American commercial legislation before 1789. $1.50. Appleton.

Gompers, S: Labor in Europe and America. $2 net. Harper.

Gordy, W. F. American leaders and heroes. Indian ed. 60 c.—Colonial days: historical reader. *50 c. net.—Elem. hist. of the U. S. 65 c. net. Scribner.

Goucher, J: F. Christianity and the United States. *50 c. net. Eaton & M.

Grady, B: F. Sectionalism and some of its fruits. 25 c. B: F. Grady.

Griffin, G. G., *comp.* Writings on American history, 1906; 1907; 1908: bibliography. *$2.50 net. Macmillan.

Gruber, C. L. Government of the United States. $1.50. C. L. Gruber.

Haines, C: G. Conflict over judicial powers in the United States to 1870. $1.50. Longmans.

Hall, J: M., *ed.* United States: account of past and contemporary conditions. $1.50. J: M. Hall.

Harding, S: B., *comp. and ed.* Select orations illustrating American political history. **$1.25 net. Macmillan.

Hart, A. B. Actual government as applied under American conditions. $2.25. —Epoch maps illustrating American hist. 60 c.—Formation of the Union, 1750-1829. $1.25. Longmans.

Hart, A. B. Manual of American history, diplomacy, and government. $2. Harvard Univ.

Hart, A. B., *ed.* American nation. In 27 v. v. 27. *$2 net. Harper.

Hasse, A. R. Materials for a bibliography of the public archives of the thirteen original states. (Add. Superintendent for price.) U. S., Supt. of Docs.

UNITED STATES.—*Continued.*

Hayford, J: F., *and* Pike, L. Hyperometry: precise leveling in the United States. 45 c. U. S., Supt. of Docs.

Hillquit, M. Hist. of socialism in the United States. **$1.50 net. Funk.

History making; story of a great nation. $2. Chapple Pub.

Hix, M. First year in United States history. Bks. 1 and 2. ea., 40 c. Hinds.

Hodgdon, J. R. First course in American history. 2 bks. ea., *65 c. net. Heath.

Howard, D. American history, government and institutions. 65 c. D. Howard.

Howard, G: E. Biography of American statesmanship; analyt. reference syllabus. 50 c. Univ. of Neb.

Howe, F. C. Privilege and democracy in America. **$1.50 net. Scribner.

Hrdlicka, A. Skeletal remains suggesting or attributed to early man in North America. 25 c. U. S., Supt. of Docs.

Hughes, H: C. Philosophy of the federal constitution. *$1.50 net. Neale.

Humphrey, L. H., *comp.* Poetic New-world. $1.50 net; $2.50 net. Holt.

Hurlbut, J. L. Story of our country. 75 c. Winston.

Hurlbut, J. L., *ed.* Lives of our presidents. 75 c. Winston.

Ingram, A. F. W. Early English colonies in America. *$2 net. Young Churchman.

James, J. A., *and* Sandford, A. H. American hist. **$1.40 net. Scribner.

Jenks, T. When America became a nation. $1.25. Crowell.

Johnson, E. R. Story of the Constitution of the United Statees. $1 net. Wessels & B.

Johnston, A. Hist. of American politics. 90 c. Holt.

Kent, O. B. Advisability of repealing the Fifteenth Amendment. gratis. Georgetown Univ.

Kohler, M. J. Un-American character of race legislation. 25 c. Am. Acad. Pol. Sci.

Krohn, J: A. Walk of colonial Jack. 25 c. J: A. Krohn.

Lea, H. Valor of ignorance. **$1.80 net. Harper.

League of American Municipalities. Book of American municipalities. $2. League Am. Municipalities.

Lodge, H: C. Short history of the English colonies in America. $3. Harper.

Low, A. M. America at home. *$1.75 net. Scribner.

Low, A. M. American people. **$2.25 net. Houghton M.

McConnel, G: M. Presidential campaigns. $1.25. Rand, McN. & Co.

MacDonald, W:, *ed.* Documentary source book of American history, 1606-1898. *$1.75 net. Macmillan.

Mace, W: H. Primary history. *65 c. net. Rand, McN. & Co.

McLaughlin, A. C. History of the American nation. *$1.40 net. Appleton.

McMaster, J: B. Brief hist. of the United States. Cal. Dept. Pub. Instruct.

UNITED STATES.—*Continued.*

McMaster, J: B. Hist. of the people of the United States, from the Revolution to the Civil War. In 8 v. v. 7. *$2.50 net. Appleton.

Madison, J., *comp.* Journal of the debates in the convention which framed the Constitution of the United States. 2 v. *$4.50 net. Putnam.

Mahan, *Capt.* A. T: Interest of America in international conditions. $1.50 net. Little, B. & Co.

Makers of America. 3 v. per set, $50. A. B. Caldwell.

Markoe, R. J. Startling statements; or, the downfall of the great republic. $1.50. R. J. Markoe.

Marriott, C. How Americans are governed in nation, state and city. $1.75.—Uncle Sam's business. $1.25. Harper.

Mathews, J: M. Legislative and judicial history of the Fifteenth Amendment. (Add. pubs. for price.) Johns Hopkins.

Matthews, A. Snake devices, 1754-1776, and the Constitutional courant, 1765. (Priv. pr.) A. Matthews.

Men of America: biographical dict. of contemporaries. $10. Hamersly.

Messages for new comers to the United States. 1st ser. pap., $23 per 100; 2d ser., $5 per 100. North Am. Civic.

Michaels, H. S. Principal automobile routes of the United States and Canada, 1910. $2. Henneberry.

Millard, T: F. F. America and the Far Eastern question. **$4 net. Moffat.

Mintz, F. S. New American citizen: reader for foreigners. **50 c. net. Macmillan.

Miyakawa, M. Powers of the American people. **$2.50 net. Baker & T.

Montgomery, D: H: Leading facts of American hist. $1. Ginn.

Moore, C: F. Hist. of the states, united and otherwise: [humorous.] *$1.50 net. Neale.

Morris, C: School history of the United States of America. **90 c. net. Lippincott.

Mowry, W: A: Elements of civil government. Illinois ed., Minnesota ed.; Vermont ed.; Michigan ed.; Mass. ed., ea., 72 c. Silver.

Murray-Aaron, E. Heart of our country: history, development and methods of the U. S. federal government. $11; $12.50; $15. G: F. Cram.

Music trade directory of U. S. and Canada. $5. Thompson.

Musick, J: R. Real America in romance: [fiction.] In 14 v. $43.50; $51.50; $62.50. W. H. Wise.

Myers, G. Hist. of the great American fortunes. In 3 v. ea., $1.50; per set, $3.50. Kerr.

National Business League of America. Schedule of inquiries concerning the lands, waters, forests, minerals and other resources of America. (Add. pubs. for price.) Nat. Business.

Neale, W. Sovereignty of the states. $1 net. Neale.

UNITED STATES.—*Continued.*

Newton, C: B., *and* Treat, E. B. Outline for review: American history. 25 c. Am. Bk.

Nichol, J: Tables of European history, literature, science and art; and of American history, literature and art. *$2.25 net. Macmillan.

Nott, C: C. Mystery of the Pinckney draught: [U. S. Constitution.] **$2 net. Century Co.

•Outline for the study of American civil government with special reference to training for citizenship. 50 c. net. Macmillan.

Patton, J. H., *and others.* Hist. of the American people. 4 v. $6.50. Walter.

Pecorini, A. Gli Americani nella vita moderna osservati da un Italiano. $1.25. F. Tocci.

Phelps, G: H. New Columbia; or the re-United States: [Utopian union of United States and Canada.] $1; 50 c. New Columbia.

Photo-auto maps: photographs of every turn and topographical outline of road with accurate distances between Chic. and N. Y., N. Y. and Chic., South Bend to Indianapolis, Indianapolis to South Bend, [etc.] $5. Rand, McN. & Co.

Pierce, F. Federal usurpation. **$1.50 net. Appleton.

Popular election of senators. gratis. Univ. of Wis.

Portraits of the presidents of U. S. and views of the Capitol and White House. $2. Lee & Co.

Putney, A. H. United States constitutional hist. and law. *$3.50 net. Illinois Bk.

Rader, P. S. Civil government of U. S. and the state of Oklahoma. 75 c. H. Stephens.

Rand, McNally & Co. Political atlas: presidential campaign of 1908. (Add. pubs. for price.) Rand, McN. & Co.

Redway, J. W. School hist. $1 net. Silver.

Reinsch, P. S:, *ed.* Readings on American federal government. $2.75. Ginn.

Remington, H. Treatise on the bankruptcy law of the United States. v. 1, 2. ea., *$6 net. Michie.

Riley, F. L., *and others.* Our republic; hist. of the U. S. for grammar grades. 65 c. Riley & C.

Roach, A. L. Graphic history: [United States.] $3. Dixon.

Robertson, J. A. List of documents in Spanish archives relating to the hist. of the United States. $2.25. Carnegie.

Robins, E: Romances of early America. $1.50. Jacobs.

Robinson, H. P. Twentieth century American. *$7.50 net. Putnam.

Royce, J. Race questions. **$1.25 net. Macmillan.

Rush, E. E. Constitution of the United States. 75 c. Hudson.

Russell, C: R., *Baron.* Diary of a visit to the United States of America in 1883. $3. Benziger.

UNITED STATES.—*Continued.*

Schouler, J. Ideals of the republic. **$1.50 net. Little, B. & Co.

Shadwell, A. Industrial efficiency: comparative study of England, Germany and America. *$2 net. Longmans.

Shaw, A. Political problems of American development. *$1.50 net. Columbia Univ.

Shepherd, W: R. Guide to the materials for the history of U. S. in Spanish archives. 50 c. Carnegie.

Slocum, C: E. Ohio country between the years 1783 and 1815. $2 net. Putnam.

Sonneck, O. G: T., *comp.* Rept. on "The star-spangled banner," "Hail Columbia," "America," "Yankee Doodle." (Add. Superintendent for price.) U. S., Supt. of Docs.

Sorley, L. S. Hist. of the Fourteenth U. S. Infantry, from Jan., 1890, to Dec., 1908. (Priv. pr.) L. S. Sorley.

Spencer, C: W. Industrial and financial development of the United States. 6 pts. ea., 15 c.; per set, 90 c. La Salle Extension.

Spencer, J. A. Hist. of the United States of America. 6 v. $10. Am. Educ. Alliance.

Stephen, F. F. Transitional period, 1788-1789, in the government of the United States. $1. Univ. of Mo.

Stimson, F. J. American constitution: national powers, the rights of the states, the liberties of the people. **$1.25 net. Scribner.

Stimson, F. J. Law of the federal and state constitutions of the U. S. *$3.50 net. Boston Bk.

Street, T: A. Federal equity practice. In 3 v. per set, $19.50. E: Thompson.

Supplementary commercial agreement bet. the U. S. and Italy. '09(Je) 5 p. 8°, pap. U. S., Supt. of Docs.

Sutherland, G: Powers of the national government. U. S. Supt. of Docs.

Taft, W: H. Delays and defects in the enforcement of law in this country. pap., 10 c. Civic Forum.

Taft, W: H. Political issues and outlooks. **$1.25 net. Doubleday, P.

Tappan, E. M. American hero stories. $1.50. Houghton M.

Thompson, W. Primary hist. of the United States. 60 c. Heath.

Thwaites, R. G. The colonies, 1492-1750. $1.25. Longmans.

Townes, J: C: Civil government in the United States and in the state of Oklahoma. (Add. pubs. for price.) Austin Pr.

Turner, F: J. The old West. 35 c. State Hist. Wis.

Under the crown; American history. 50 c. Youth's Companion.

United States. Commission on National Historical Publications; rept. [1910.] (Jl) 4 p. 8°.

United States. *Geological Survey.* Topographic and geologic atlas of the United States. '09, [1910.] (Ag) 16 p. diagrs., 8°. Gov. Pr. Off.

UNITED STATES.—*Continued.*

United States. *Superintendent of Documents.* Proceedings of Congress. gratis.

Van Dyke, H: J. Spirit of America. **$1.50 net. Macmillan.

Van Tyne, C. H., *and* Leland, W. G. Guide to the archives of U. S. in Washington. $1.25. Carnegie.

Vay de Vaya and Luskod, *Count.* Inner life of the United States. *$4 net. Dutton.

Vlasto, S. J., *and* Gortzis, N. Istoria ton enomenon politeion tes Amerikes; [in Greek.] $2. Atlantis Pub.

Want list of American historical serials. 2d ed. '09(My) 37 p. 8°, pap. (Add. Superintendent for price.) U. S., Supt. of Docs.

Waterton, C: Wanderings in South America, the northwest United States and the Antilles, in the years 1812, 1816, 1820 and 1824. $1.50. Macmillan.

Waterton, C: Wanderings in South America, the northwest of the U S., and the Antilles, in the years 1812, 1816, 1820 and 1824. *$2.50 net. Sturgis & W.

Watson, D: K. Constitution of the U. S. 2 v. $12. Callaghan.

White, W: A. Old order changeth; view of American democracy. $1.25. Macmillan.

White House conference on the conservation of natural resources, May 15, 1908; declaration of the governors as adopted May 15, 1908; The value of natural scenery, address del. before the Conference May 14, 1908, by J: Horace McFarland. '08, [1909.] (My) 16 p. 8°, (American Civic Association pubs.) pap. Am. Civic League.

Who's who in America. *$4 net. Marquis.

Willhauck, G: P. Our national government. 35 c. Monarch Pr.

Williams, M. A. Report on the teaching of English in the United States. $1. Bardeen.

Willson, R. W. Times of sunrise and sunset in the U. S. *$1 net. Harvard Co-op.

Wilson, W. Constitutional government in the United States. **$1.50 net. Macmillan.

Wilson, W. Division and reunion, 1829-1909. $1.25. Longmans.

Woerner, W: F. Evolution of the state universal from an American standpoint. gratis. W: F. Woerner.

Woodburn, J. A., *and* Moran, T: F. Elem. American hist. and government. $1 net. Longmans.

Wyer, J. I. United States government documents in small libraries. 15 c. A. L. A.

Yung Wing. My life in China and America. **$2 net. Holt.

See also Admiralty;—American Revolution;—Authors;—Banks and banking;—Battles;—Biography; — Boy scouts; — Buccaneers; — Catholic church;—Census;—Ceramics; — Chinese in the U. S.; — Citizenship; — Civil service; — Civil War;—Cliff dwellers;—Colleges and universities;—Colonial government;—Commerce;—Constitutional law;—Consuls;—Copyright;—Corporations;—Costume;—Country life;—Declaration of Independence;—Diplomacy;—Dutch in the U. S.;—Education; — Explorers; — Finance;—Firearms;—Fisheries; — Flags; — Fortification;—French and Indian War;—Germans in the U. S.;—Gettysburg;—Great Lakes;—Greenville (Treaty of);—Heraldry;—Hunting;—Hygiene;—Immigration;—Indexes; — Indians; — Insurance;—Irrigation;—Japanese in the U. S.;—King George's War;—Land;—Louisburg Siege;—Marriage; — Massachusetts Bay; — Mexican War;—Middle States;—Mines and Mining;—Mississippi river; — Missouri compromise; — Money;—Monroe doctrine;—Municipal government;—Natural history;—Natural resources; — Naturalization;—Naval art and science;—Negligence;—Negroes;—New England; — Newspapers;—Norwegians in the U. S.;—Orders of Knighthood and Chivalry; — Pacific coast; — Parks;—Parties (*political*);—Patents; — Peace;—Periodicals;—Philippine Islands; — Pilgrims;—Political science;—Postage stamps;—Prostitution;—Psychology;—Quarantine; — Railroads;—Roads;—Rocky mountains;—Salaries;—Santa Fé trail;—Schools;—Slavery; — Socialism;—South;—Spanish-American War; — Statistics;—Suffrage; — Sullivan's Indian campaign; — Swedes in the U. S.;—Tariff;—Taxation;—Telegraphy;—Temperature; — Tippecanoe (Battle of);—Trade-unions; — United States Navy; — Voyages and travels;—War of 1812;—Water-supply;—West; — West Point; — Wool; — *also* Webster, P.;—Wilson, James;—*also* names of states.

UNITED STATES ARMY.

Cook, F. A. Subsistence guide for the national guard. $1. U. S. Military Pub.

Mason, C: F. Complete hdbk. for the hospital corps of the U. S. army and navy and state military forces. *$4 net. Wood.

Stewart, M. B., *and* Davis, R. C. Notes and suggestions on the new infantry drill regulations. 50 c.; 75 c. Hudson.

United States. *Adjutant-General's Office.* Circular showing the distribution of troops of the line of the United States army, Jan. 1. 1866, to June 30, 1909. '09 (O) 69 p. 8°. (Add. Superintendent for price.) U. S., Supt. of Docs.

United States. *Inspector-General's Office.* Brownsville affray: rept. of inspector-general of the army. 50 c. U. S., Supt. of Docs.

United States. *War Dept.* Roster of the organized militia of the United States, Feb., 1909. (Add. Superintendent for price.) U. S., Supt. of Docs.

Youngberg, G. A. Hist. of engineer troops in the U. S. Army, 1775-1901. (Not for sale.) Engineer Sch.

See also Artillery;—Military art and science;—Soldiers.

United States Bureau of Education bulletin. O. pap. U. S., Supt. of Docs.

—Bailey. On the training of persons to teach agriculture in the public schools. 15 c.

—Eaton. Education for efficiency in railroad service.

—Fryer. Admission of Chinese students to American colleges. (Add. Superintendent for price.)

—Hunt. Daily meals of children. (Add. Superintendent for price.)

—Show. Movement for reform in the teaching of religion in the public schools of Saxony.

—Wyer *and* Phelps. Bibliography of education for 1907. (Add. Superintendent for price.)

United States Catholic Historical Society monograph ser. il. O. U. S. Cath.
—Waldseemüller. Cosmographiae introductio. $5.

UNITED STATES COLONIAL POSSESSIONS.
America across the seas. C. S. Hammond.
Browne, G: W., *and* Dole, N. H. New America and the Far East. $36.25; $49.75. M. Jones.
United States. *Dept. of Commerce and Labor. Bu. of Statistics.* Commerce of the non-contiguous territory of the United States with the United States and with foreign countries during the year ending June 30, 1908. '09(Ag) 1135-1203 p. tabs., 4°. (Add. Superintendent for price.) U. S., Supt. of Docs.
United States public documents rel. to non-contiguous territory and to Cuba; for sale by the Superintendent of Documents. [1910.] (Jl) 102 p. 8°, pap., gratis.
United States. *War Dept. Bureau of Insular Affairs.* Acts of Congress, treaties, proclamations, decisions of the Supreme Court of the United States, and opinions of the attorney-general rel, to noncontiguous territory. Cuba and Santo Domingo and to military affairs. 59th Congress—Mar. 4, 1905, to Mar. 3, 1907; Supreme Court cases—Jan. 1, 1907, to Je. 1, 1909; opinions of attorney-general—Jan. 1, 1898, to Je. 17, 1908; relations with Santo Domingo—Jan. 1, 1898, to July 25, 1907; list of officials—Dec. 1, 1908. '09 (N) 32+442 p. 8°. (Add. Superintendent for price.) U. S., Supt. of Docs.
See also Alaska;—Hawaiian Islands;—Philippine Islands;—Porto Rico.

United States commissioner's record of proceedings in criminal cases. '09, [1910.] (F) 21+230 p. forms, f°, $3.75. W. H. Anderson.

United States currency association law. '08 (Jl) 61 p. D. pap., gratis. Nat. City Bank.

UNITED STATES DEPT. OF AGRICULTURE.
Greathouse, C: H., *comp.* Hist. sketch of the U. S. Dept. of Agriculture. 25 c. U. S., Supt. of Docs.

United States, Dept. of Agriculture, Biological Survey bull. il. 8°.
—Cooke. Distribution and migration of American shore birds.

United States, Dept. of Agriculture, Bu. of Animal Industry bull. tab., 8°.
—Armsby. Feeding for meat production. 10 c.
—Armsby *and* Fries. Available energy of red clover hay. 10 c.
—Campbell. Leucocytes in milk.
—Crawley. Studies on blood and blood parasites.
—Fries. Methods and standards in bomb calorimetry.
—Lane. Medical milk commissions. 15 c.
—Marsh. Loco weed disease. 35 c.
—Mohler *and* Eichhorn. Need of controlling and standardizing the manufacture of veterinary tetanus antitoxin.
—Mohler *and* Rosenau. Origin of outbreak of foot-and-mouth disease.

United States, Dept. of Agriculture, Bu of Animal Industry, bull.—Continued.
—Pearl *and* Surface. Biometrical study of egg production. 15 c.
—Rogers *and* Gray. Influence of acidity of cream on the flavor of butter. 10 c.
—Rommel. Regeneration of the Morgan horse.
—Schroeder *and* Cotton. Tests concerning tubercle bacilli in the circulating blood.
—Shaw *and* Eckles. Chemical and physical study of large and small fat globules in cow's milk.
—Thom. Camembert cheese problems.

United States. Dept. of Agriculture. Bu. of Animal Industry circular. 8°.
—Dissemination of disease by dairy products.
—Farrington. Need of state and municipal meat inspection to supplement federal inspection.
—Hart. Rabies and its increasing prevalence. 15 c.
—Hastings. Cold storage evaporimeter.
—Hunter *and* Mitchell. Pract. demonstration of method for controlling cattle tick.
—Lane *and* Parks. Improved methods for the production of market milk.
—Lane *and* Weld. Competitive exhibitions of milk and cream.
—Mohler. Infectious anemia. 5 c.
—Murray. Diseases of the stomach and bowels of cattle.
—Schroeder. Milk and its products as carriers of tuberculosis. 5 c.—Tubercle bacilli in butter. 15 c.
—True *and* Sievers. Some factors affecting keeping qualities of American lemons.

United States, Dept. of Agriculture, Bu. of Biological Survey, cir. 8°. Gov. Pr. Off.
—Bailey. Key to animals on which wolf and coyote bounties are often paid.
—Lantz. Brown rat in the U. S.
—National bird and mammal reservations in Alaska.
—Palmer. Private game preserves and their future in the United States.

United States. Dept. of Agriculture. Bu. of Biological Survey. North American fauna. 8°. U. S., Dept. of Docs.
—Nelson. Rabbits of North America.
—Osgood. Biological investigations in Alaska and Yukon territory.

United States. Dept. of Agriculture. Bu. of Chemistry bull. 8°.
—Alwood. Enological studies.—Fermenting power of pure yeasts. 15 c.
—Bigelow. Food legislation during the year ended June 30, 1907. (Add. Supt. for price.)
—Bigelow *and* Cook. Meat extracts. 10 c.
—Bitting. Canning of peas. 10 c.
—Bryan. Methods for the analysis of maple products. 5 c.
—Chamberlain. Feeding value of cereals.
—Howard. Economic loss to people of the U. S. through insects.
—Haywood. Injury to vegetation and animal life by smelter wastes.
—Haywood *and* Warner. Commercial feeding stuffs. 25 c.
—Kebler. Drug legislation in U. S. 35 c.

United States, Dept. of Agriculture, Bu. of Chemistry, bull.—Continued.
—LeClerc *and* Wahl. Chemical studies of American barleys and malts.
—Straughn *and Church.* Influence of environment on composition of sweet corn.
—Walker. Some technical methods of testing misc. supplies.
—Wiley. Manuf. of denatured alcohol.
—Wiley, *and others.* Preliminary study of the effects of cold storage on eggs, quail and chickens.

United States. Dept. of Agriculture. Bu. of Chemistry circular. 8°.
—Cook. Comparison of beef and yeast extracts of known origin.
—Gore. Apparatus for use in determination of volatile acids in wines and vinegars.
—Ross. Suggested modification of the Winton lead number.

United States, Dept. of Agriculture, Bureau of Entomology bull. il. 8°.
—Banks. List of works on North American entomology.
—Gates. Misc. papers on agriculture.
—Jenne. Papers on deciduous fruit insects and insectides.
—Pierce. Studies of parasites of the [Mexican] cotton boll weevil. 25 c.
—Quaintance. Fumigation of apples for San Jose scale.
—Some insects injurious to truck crops.
—Woglum. Fumigation investigations in California.

United States, Dept. of Agriculture, Bu. of Entomology circular. 8°.
—Burgess. Requirements to be complied with by nurserymen.
—Chittenden. Control of the Mediterranean flour moth.
—Colcord, *comp.* List of publications of the Bu. of Entomology.
—Hopkins. Insect injuries to the wood of living trees.

United States, Dept. of Agriculture, Bu. of Plant Industry bull. il. 8°.
—Aaronstrohm. Agricultural and botanical explorations in Palestine.
—Brand *and* Waldron. Cold resistance of alfalfa and some factors influencing it.
—Briggs *and* Belz. Dry farming in relation to rainfall and evaporation.
—Burritt. Agricultural conditions in southern New York.
—Chilcott. Study of cultivation methods and crop rotations for the Great Plains area.
—Collins. New type of Indian corn.
—Cook. Local adjustment of cotton varieties.—Vegetation affected by agriculture in Central America.
—Farrell. Dry-land grains in the Great Basin.
—Gilbert. Root-rot of tobacco.
—Griffiths. Protected stock range in Arizona.
—Hansen. Wild alfalfas and clovers.
—Henkels. American medicinal barks.
—Jensen. Seasonal nitrification as influenced by crops and tillage.

United States, Dept. of Agriculture, Bu. of Plant Industry, bull.—Continued.
—Kellerman *and* Whittaker. Farm water supplies of Minn.
—Metcalf. Immunity of the Japanese chestnut to the bark disease. 5 c.
—Oliver. Production of Easter lily bulbs in the United States. 15 c.
—Patterson, *and others.* Some fungeous diseases.
—Powell *and* Chace. Italian lemons.
—Powell, *and others.* Decay of oranges. 15 c.
—Robinson. Seed sterilization and its effect upon seed inoculation.
—Rogers. Directions for home pasteurization of milk.
—Scofield *and* Rogers. Truckee-Carson experiment farm.
—Spillman. Application of some principles of heredity to plant breeding.
—Tracy. Production of vegetable seeds.

United States. Dept. of Agriculture. Bu. of Plant Industry circular. 8°.
—Ball. Three much-misrepresented sorghums.
—Brand. Alfalfa in cultivated rows.
—Carleton. Barley culture in the northern great plains. 15 c.
—Cook. Origin of Hindi cotton.—Mutative reversions in cotton.
—Cotton. Improvement of pastures.
—Ellis. Minor articles of farm equipment.
—Fitz. Handling wheat from field to mill.
—Gould. Fruit growing.
—Hunter. Clover seed production.
—Hunter *and* Jayne. Suggestions to settlers on the sandy soils of the Columbia River Valley.
—Spaulding. European currant rust on white pine in America.—Present status of white-pine blights.
—Stockberger. Necessity for new standards of hop valuation.
—Thompson. Cost of clearing logged-off land.
—Tracy *and* Reed. Comparative tests of sugar-beet varieties.
—Warburton. Improvement of the oat crop.
—Warren. Notes on the number and distribution of native legumes in Nebraska and Kansas.

United States, Dept. of Agriculture, Bureau of Soils bull. 8°.
—Carr. Preliminary rept. on the Volusia soils.
—Gardner. Fertility of soils as affected by manures. 15 c.
—Patten. Heat transference in soils.
—Schreiner. Isolation of harmful organic substances from soils.
—Schreiner *and* Skinner. Some effects of a harmful organic soil constituent.
—Whitney. Composition of commercial fertilizer.—Fertilizers for cotton soils.—Fertilizers for wheat soils.—Study of crop yields.

United States. Dept. of Agriculture. Bu. of Statistics bull. 8°.
—Clark, *comp.* Barley crops.—Buckwheat crops.—Corn crops.—Oat crops.—Potato crops.—Rye crops.—Wheat crops. ea., 5 c. —Hay crops of the U. S. 15 c.

United States, Dept. of Agriculture, Bu. of Statistics, bull.—Continued.
—Foreign trade of the U. S. in forest products.
—Rubinow. Russia's wheat trade. 15 c.
—Smith. Agricultural graphics.
United States. Dept. of Agriculture. Bu. of Statistics circular. 8°.
—Killebrew. Tobacco districts and types.
United States Dept. of Agriculture, circular. 8°, pap. U. S., Supt. of Docs.
—Adulteration and misbranding of the seeds of alfalfa.
—Knapp. Cotton.
United States. Dept. of Agriculture; farmers' bull. il. 8°.
—Abel. Care of food in the home.
—Atwater. Bread and bread making.
—Ball *and* Leidig. Milo as a dry-land grain crop. 5 c.
—Beattie. Onion culture.—Peanuts.—Sweet potatoes. ea., 5 c.
—Beavers. Farm practice in the use of commercial fertilizers in the south Atlantic states.
—Breazeale. Canning of vegetables.
—Brown. Drainage of irrigated land.
—Construction of concrete fence posts.
—Cox. Eradication of bindweed.
—Crosby. School exercises in plant production.
—Declaration of governors for conservation of national resources.
—Dodge. Farm management in northern potato-growing sections.
—Dorset. Hog cholera.
—Fortier. Irrigation in alfalfa.—Irrigation of orchards.
—Fuller. Use of windmills in irrigation in the semiarid west.
—Goodrich. Profitable cotton farm.
—Henry. Lightning and lightning conductors.
—Jaffa. Nuts and their uses as food.
—Kebler. Habit forming agents.
—Kebler, *and others.* Harmfulness of headache mixtures. 10 c.
—Knapp. Demonstration work on southern farms.
—Langworthy *and* Hunt. Economical use of meat in the home.
—Lantz. How to destroy rats.
—McClure. Conditions affecting the value of market hay.
—McLaughlin. Irrigation of grain.
—Milner. Use of milk as food. 5 c.
—Mohler. Tuberculin test of cattle.
—Oakley. Canada bluegrass.
—Oldys. Pheasant raising in the U. S.
—Pearl. Methods of poultry management.
—Pinchot. Conservation of natural resources. 10 c.
—Roeding. Irrigation of sugar beets.
—Rogers. Bacteria in milk. 5 c.
—Smith *and* Froley. Replanning a farm for profit.
—Spillman. Successful poultry and dairy farm.
—Thompson. Angora goat. 5 c.

United States, Dept. of Agriculture; farmers' bull.—Continued.
—Wente *and* Tolman. Potato culls as a source of industrial alcohol.
—Westgate. Alfalfa. 5 c.
—Whitaker, *and others.* Care of milk and its use in the home.
—Willis. Preservative treatment of farm timbers.
United States, Dept. of Agriculture; Farmers' Inst. lecture. 8°.
—Dryden. Syllabus of illustrated lecture on production and marketing of eggs. 5 c.
United States, Dept. of Agriculture, Forest Service, bull. il. 8°.
—Graves. Protection of forests from fire.
—Kellogg. Forests of Alaska.
United States. Dept. of Agriculture. Forest Service circular. 8°.
—Ayres. Commercial importance of the White mts. forest.
—Betts. Properties and uses of the southern pines.
—Carter. Methods of increasing forest productivity.
—Cleveland. Status of forestry in the U. S.
—Eastman. Experiments with railway crossties. 15 c.
—Fetherolf. Forest planting on the northern prairies. 15 c.
—Hall *and* Maxwell. Surface conditions and stream flow.
—Jardine. Coyote-proof pasture experiment, 1908.
—Kellogg. Forest planting in Illinois.—Timber supply of the U. S.
—Lumber saved by using odd lengths.
—Pearson. Reproduction of western yellow pine.
—Pierson. Consumption of firewood in the United States.
—Pract. assistance to the owners of forest land.
—Price. Forests of the U. S.
—Sampson. Natural revegetation of depleted mountain grazing land.
—Sherfesse. Seasoning and preservative treatment of hemlock and tamarack crossties. 15 c.—Primer of wood preservation. 5 c.—Wood preservation in the U. S.
—Weiss. Progress in chestnut pole preservation. 10 c.
United States, Dept. of Agriculture, Forest Service, forest planting leaflet. 8°.
—Basswood.
—Black walnut.
—Boxelder.
—European larch.
—Red oak.
United States, Dept. of Agriculture, Forest Service, silvical leaflet. 8°.
—Big shellbark.
—Paper birch.
—Pinon pine.
United States, Dept. of Agriculture, Office of Experiment Stations, bull. il. map, 8°.
—Atkinson. Irrigation in North Dakota.
—Bark. Irrigation in Kansas.
—Beach. Irrigation in Colorado.
—Benedict. Influence of muscular and mental work on metabolism. 15 c.

United States, Dept. of Agriculture, Office of Experiment Stations, bull.—Continued.
—Fortier *and* Cone. Drainage of irrigated lands in San Joaquin Valley, Cal.
—Fortier, *and others.* Irrigation in Sacramento Valley, Cal.
—Hatch. Simple exercises illustrating some applications of chemistry to agriculture. 15 c.
—Hills *and others.* Dietary studies.
—Knorr. Consolidated rural schools.
—Lea. Irrigation in South Dakota.
—Lewis *and* Cupper. Irrigation in Oregon.
—Morgan Preliminary rept. on the St. Francis Valley drainage project.
—Sherman, *and others.* Calcium, magnesium, and phosphorus in food and nutrition.
—Stephenson. Irrigation in Idaho.
—Sullivan. Irrigation in New Mexico.
—Wait. Studies on the digestibility and nutritive value of legumes. 25 c.
—Waller. Irrigation in the state of Washington.
United States. Dept. of Agriculture; Office of Experiment Stations circular. il. 8°. Gov. Pr. Off.
—Abbey. Normal school instruction in agriculture.
—Bryant. Progress rept. on experiments in supp. irrigation.
—Food and nutrition investigations of the Office of Experiment Stations.
—Forest in nature study.
—Gordon. Experiments in supplemental irrigation with small water supplies at Cheyenne, Wyo.
—Gregory. Selection and installation of machinery for small pumping plants.
—Hamilton. Farmers' institutes for women.
—Hamilton. Progress in agricultural education extension.
—Hamilton *and* Stedman. Farmers' institute for young people.
—Hays. Education for country life.
—Institutions in the U. S. giving instruction in agriculture.
—Organization, work and pubs. of food and nutrition investigations.
—Organization, work and publications of the Agricultural Education service.
—True. Secondary education in agriculture.
—True *and* Crosby. American system of agricultural education.
United States, Dept. of Agriculture, Office of Experiment Stations; Farmers' Inst. lecture. 8°.
—Dryden. Syllabus of illustrated lecture on production and marketing of eggs. 5 c.
United States, Dept. of Agriculture, Office of Public Roads, bull. 8°.
—Cushman. Preservation of iron and steel. 10 c.
United States. Dept. of Agriculture. Office of Public Roads circular. il. 8°.
—Progress repts. of experiments in dust prevention and road preservation.
—Spoon. Sand-clay and earth roads in the middle west.
United States, Dept. of Agriculture, Office of the Secretary, circular. 8°.
—Knapp. Hog raising in the South.
United States, Dept. of Agriculture, Weather Bu., bull. 8°. U. S., Supt. of Docs.
—Bigelow. Daily normal temperature. $1.75.
—Rept. on temperature and vapor tensions of U. S. $1.15; 75 c.
United States, Dept. of Agriculture, Weather Bu., Instrument Division, circular. 8°. U. S., Supt. of Docs.
—Marvin. Barometers.
United States. Dept. of Commerce and Labor. Bu. of Fisheries bull.
—Dennis. Some reasons for failure of fish protective legislation.
—Fryer. International regulations of the fisheries of the high seas.
—Jordan. Work of International Fisheries Commission of Gt. Britain.
—Olsen. International regulations of the fisheries on the high seas.
—Stevenson. International regulations of the fisheries on the high seas.
United States. Dept. of Commerce and Labor. Bureau of Manufactures; tariff ser. 8°. U. S., Supt. of Docs.
—Stone. Foreign tariffs on petroleum and petroleum products. (Add. Superintendent for price.)
—Stone, *comp.* Export tariffs of foreign countries. (Add. Superintendent for price.)
United States. Dept. of the Interior. Bureau of Education bull. 8°, pap. U. S., Supt. of Docs.
—Jewell. Agricultural education. (Add. Superintendent for price.)
—Thorndike. Teaching staff of secondary schools in the United States. (Add. Superintendent for price.)
United States, Dept. of the Interior, Bu. of Mines, bull. il. tabs., diagrs..
—Porter *and* Ovitz. Volatile matter or coal.
United States, Dept. of the Interior, U. S. Geol. Survey bull. 8°, pap. U. S., Supt. of Docs.
—Arnold *and* Anderson. Preliminary report on the Coalinga oil district.
—Ashley *and* Fisher. Valuation of public coal lands.
—Becker. Relations between local magnetic disturbances and the genesis of petroleum.
—Branner. Clays of Arkansas. (Add. Superintendent for price.)
—Brooks, *and others.* Mineral resources of Alaska.
—Burrows. Mine sampling and chemical analysis of coals. 5 c.
—Clapp. Underground waters of southern Maine. 55 c. (Water-supply paper.)
—Clarke. Analyses of rocks and minerals from the lab'y of the U. S. Geol. Survey.
—Covert *and* Ellsworth Water-supply investigation in the Yukon-Tanana region. (Water-supply paper.)
—Dale. Chief commercial granites of Massachusetts.
—Dall. Contributions to the Tertiary paleontology of the Pacific coast; 1, Miocene of Astoria and Coos Bay, Ore. (Professional papers.)
—Darton. Geology and underground waters of South Dakota.
—Diller. Geology of the Taylorsville region, California.

United States, Dept. of the Interior, U. S. Geol. Survey, bull.—Continued.
—Dole. Quality of surface waters in the U. S. pt. 1.
—Emmons. Reconnaissance of some mining camps. Some ore deposits in Maine.
—Fernald. Recent development of the producer-gas power plant in the United States.
—Fernald, *and others.* Incidental problems in gas-producer tests. (U. S. Geological Survey.)
—Fisher. Geology of the Great Falls coal field, Mont.
—Gilpin *and* Cram. Fractionation of crude petroleum by capillary diffusion.
—Girty. Fauna of the Caney shale of Oklahoma. 25 c.—Guadalupian fauna.
—Goss. Comparative tests of run-of-mine and briquetted coal on locomotives.—Utilization of fuel in locomotive practice. (U. S. Geological Survey.)
—Gregory *and* Ellis. Underground water resources of Connecticut. (Water supply paper.)
—Harder. Manganese deposits of the United States.
—Harris. Oil and gas in Louisiana.
—Hayes *and* Lindgren. Contributions to economic geology.
—Hess. Magnesite deposits of California.
—Hillebrand. Analysis of silicate and carbonate rocks.
—Hillebrand *and* Schaller. Mercury minerals from Terlingua.
—Howe. Landslides in the San Juan Mountains, Colo. (U. S. Geological Survey.)
—Humphrey. Fire-resistive properties of various building materials.—Strength of concrete beams. (Add. Superintendent for price.)
—Kindle. Devonian fauna of the Ouray limestone.
—Knopf. Geology of the Seward Peninsula tin deposits, Alaska.
—Leighton, *ed.* Surface water supply of the U. S., 1907-8. pts. 1-12. (Water supply pap.)
—Lindgren, *and others.* Ore deposits of New Mexico. (Professional paper.)
—Matson. Water resources of the Blue Grass region. (Water supply paper.)
—Mendenhall. Ground waters and irrigation enterprises in the foohill belt, southern California.—Ground waters of the Indo region, Cal.—Preliminary report on the ground waters of San Joaquin Valley, Cal.—Some desert watering places. (Water-supply paper.) 20 c.
—Moffit *and* Maddren. Mineral resources of the Kotsina-Chitina region.
—Moffit, *and others.* Mineral resources of the Nabesna-White River district, Alaska.
—Munroe *and* Hall. Primer on explosives for coal miners.
—Nickles. Bibliography of North American geology for 1908.
—Papers on the conservation of water resources. (Water supply paper.)
—Phalen. Economic geology of the Kenova quadrangle.

United States, Dept. of the Interior, U. S. Geol. Survey, bull.—Continued.
—Phelps. Disinfection of sewage.—Pollution of streams by sulphite pulp waste. 10 c. (Water-supply paper.)
—Prindle. Forty-mile quadrangle, Yukon-Tanana region.
—Randall. Purchase of coal under government and commercial supervision. 15 c.—Tests of coal and briquets as fuel for house-heating boilers. 10 c.
—Randall *and* Weeks. Smokeless combustion of coal in boiler plants.
—Ransome. Geology and ore deposits of Goldfield, Nevada. (Professional papers.) —Notes on some mining districts in Humboldt County, Nevada.
—Ray *and* Kreisinger. Comparative tests of run-of-mine and briquetted coal.
—Rice. Explosibility of coal dust.
—Schlundt. Radioactivity of the thermal waters of Yellowstone National Park.
—Spencer. Magnetite deposits of the Cornwall type in Pennsylvania.
—Stabler *and* Pratt. Purification of some textile and other factory wastes. (Water supply paper.)
—Stevens. Surface water supply of Nebraska. (Water-supply paper.)
—Strong. Commercial deductions from comparisons of gasoline and alcohol tests on internal-combustion engines.
—Tarr *and* Butler. Yakutat Bay region. (Professional papers.)
—Van Hise *and* Leith. Pre-Cambrian geology of North America.
—Van Winkle *and* Eaton. Quality of surface waters of California. (Water-supply paper.)
—Waring. Geology and water resources of the Harney Basin region.
—Watteyne, *and others.* Prevention of mine explosions. (Add. Superintendent for price.)
—Weeks. Bibliography of North American geology.
—White, D: Effect of oxygen in coal.
—Wright. Briquetting tests. 10 c.
United States General Staff pub. 12°, pap. U. S., Supt. of Docs.
—Steele. American campaigns. (Add. Superintendent for price.)
U. S. government's shame. Madden, E. C: 50 c. Nat. Bk. Co.
United States. Hydrographic Office pub. 8°, pap. U. S., Supt. of Docs.
—United States. *Hydrographic Office.* Navigation of the Gulf of Mexico and the Caribbean Sea. (Add. Superintendent for price.)
United States Inter-Collegiate Lacrosse League. Constitution, by-laws and playing rules, 1909. '09(Je); 1910. '10(Je11) c. pors. S. (Spalding's athletic lib.) pap., ea., 10 c. Am. Sports.
United States midshipman afloat. Stirling, Y., *jr.* †$1.25. Penn Pub. Co.
United States midshipman in China. Stirling, Y., *jr.* †$1.25. Penn Pub. Co.
United States midshipman in the Philippines. Stirling, Y., *jr.* $1.25. Penn Pub. Co.

UNITED STATES MILITARY ACADEMY, West Point.
See West Point.

UNITED STATES NATIONAL MUSEUM, Washington, D. C.
Casanowicz, I. M. Collection of rosaries in the United States National Museum. (Add. Superintendent for price.) U. S., Supt. of Docs.

UNITED STATES NAVY.
Abbot, W. J: Story of our navy for young Americans. $2. Dodd.
Beyer, T: American battleship and life in the navy. $1.25.—Life in the navy, (the American battleship;) also humorous yarns as told by a bluejacket. 25 c. Laird.
Burrows, J. C. Marine corps: history. U. S., Supt. of Docs.
Clark, G: R., *and others.* The navy, 1775 to 1909. v. 1. $3. Midshipmen's Storekeeper.
Evans, H. A. Trade follows the flag. 15 c. U. S., Supt. of Docs.
Evans, R. D. Admiral's log. **$2 net. Appleton.
Fanning, C. E., *comp.* Selected articles on the enlargement of the U. S. Navy. $1. H. W. Wilson.
Hill, F. S. Romance of the American navy as embodied in the stories of certain of our public and private armed ships from 1775 to 1909. **$2.50 net. Putnam.
Hoff, A. B. Battleship's order book. $1. U. S. Naval Inst.
Jones, R. D., *comp. and ed.* With the American fleet from the Atlantic to Pacific. $3; $4; $5. Harrison Pub.
List of government vessels; with tables giving number of men with comparative cost of those performing similar duties to enlisted men of the navy. '08, [1909.] (My) 45 p. 8°, pap. (Add. Superintendent for price.) U. S., Supt. of Docs.
Log of the voyage of the Atlantic fleet. 25 c. Navy Pub.
McLean, R. Bluejacket's manual. $1.25. U. S. Naval Inst.
Matthews, A. F. With the battle fleet. $1.50. B: W. Huebsch.
Matthews, F. Back to Hampton Roads; cruise of the U. S. Atlantic fleet from San Francisco to Hampton Roads. $1.50. B: W. Huebsch.
Military Historical Society of Massachusetts. v. 12, Naval actions and history, 1799-1898. (Add. pubs. for price.) Military Hist. Soc.
Miller, R. J: Around the world with the battleships. $1.25.—Pictorial log of the battle fleet cruise around the world. *$3 net. McClurg.
Neeser, R. W. Statistical and chronological history of the United States Navy. 2 v. **$12 net. Macmillan.
Olsson, A. Motor control as used in connection with turret turning and gun elevating. (Ward Leonard system.) 50 c. Van Nostrand.
On the Pacific with our navy. 25 c.; Atlantic coast, 10 c. L. H. Nelson.

UNITED STATES NAVY.—*Continued.*
Pate, M. Hdbk. of general information for men under instruction in the Artificer School. Dept. of C. & R. Navy Yard, Norfolk, Va. $1. U. S. Naval Inst.
Personnel of the navy; message from the president giving reasons why the ages of our senior officers should be materially reduced and opportunity given thereby for experience and training for battle ship and fleet commands. '10(Ap) 5 p. 8°. Gov. Pr. Off.
Raff, L. E. Landsman [drill manual]. 50 c. Rudder.
Regulations for the government of the navy of the U. S., 1909. '09(My) 754 p. 8°. U. S., Supt. of Docs.
Roberts, T: G. Merchant marine and the navy. Gov. Pr. Off.
Round the world with our navy. 25 c. L. H. Nelson.
Souvenir of the visit of the American fleet to Australia and New Zealand. 25 c. Am. News.
Spears, J: R. History of the United States navy. **$1.50 net. Scribner.
T., L. G. Three years behind the guns. **$1.50 net. Century Co.
United States. *Navy Dept.* Information relative to the voyage of the United States Atlantic fleet around the world, December 16, 1907, to February 22, 1909. '10(Ap) 25 p. tabs., 8°, pap.
United States. *Navy Dept.* Rules and regulations for the government of United States naval prisons and prison ships. '10(Mr) 13 p. 16°, pap.
Walling, B. T., *and* Martin, J. Electrical installations of the United States navy. $6; $6.85. U. S. Naval Inst.
See also Finger prints.

United States Navy, illustrated: a new series of over 60 reproductions from original photographs. '08(Ag29) c. il. Q. pap., 25 c. C. S. Hammond.

United States Navy electrical ser. il. 12°. Van Nostrand.
—Olsson. Motor control as used in connection with turret turning and gun elevating. 50 c.

United States Navy ser. *See* Stirling, Yates.

United States of America; pictorial history; editorial staff: W: T. Harris, E: Everett Hale, Nelson A. Miles, O. P. Austin. G: Cary Eggleston. '10(Ag6) 5 v., il. pors. 4°, $20. Imperial Pub.

United States service ser. il. D. Lothrop, L. & S.
—Rolt-Wheeler. Boy with the U. S. Foresters.—Boy with the U. S. Survey. ea., $1.50.

United States statute citer-digest; comp. and ed. by H: C. Ruen and E: L. Dwight. [1910.] (D) c. 467 p. O. flex. leath., $12. Citer-Digest.

UNITED STATES STEEL CORPORATION.
Taintor, C: W. Brief analysis of the United States Steel Corporation. $3. C: W. Taintor.

UNITED STATES SUPREME COURT.

Hermann, H: B. M., *comp.* Library of Congress list of works rel. to the Sup. Ct. of the United States. 20 c. U. S., Supt. of Docs.

Meyer, H. H: B., *comp.* Library of Congress list of works rel. to the Sup. Ct. of the U. S. (Add. Superintendent for price.) U. S., Supt. of Docs.

United States. Treasury Dept. Public Health and Marine-Hospital Service; Hygienic Lab'y bull. 8°.

—United States. Milk and its relation to the public health.

United States, Treasury Dept., Public Health and Marine Hospital Service; public health bull. 8°. Gov. Pr. Off.

—Smith. Relation of climate to the treatment of pulmonary tuberculosis.

United States vacant lands, located by states, territories, districts and counties, with brief description by counties: how to secure lands by homestead entry and purchase. Rev. to 1908. '08(Mr14) c. 24°, pap., 25 c. Webb.

United study of missions. D. Macmillan.

—Montgomery. Western women in eastern lands. $1.50 net.

—Zwemer *and* Brown. Nearer and farther East. 50 c. net.

Unity of good. Eddy, *Mrs.* M. M. B. G. (Add. pubs. for price.) A. V. Stewart.

Unity of religions. Randall, J: H., *ed.* $2 net. Crowell.

Unity of the spirit. National Federation of Religious Liberals. 75 c. Nat. Fed. Rel. Liberals.

Unity of the university. Dabney, C: W: (Not for sale.) Univ. of Cin.

UNIVERSAL AND INTERNATIONAL EXHIBITION.
See Brussels.

Universal and organ remedies. Rademacher, J. G. W. $1. Boericke & T.

Universal Bible. Hunt, M. A. $1.50. M. A. Hunt.

Universal brotherhood. Rogers, L. W. 10 c. Theosophical Bk.

Universal cook book. Phillips, *Mrs.* F. F., *comp.* $1; 50 c. F. F. Phillips.

UNIVERSAL FOOT BALL.
See Football.

Universal guide of standard routes and itineraries of tourist travel. Thorpe, D. $1.25. D. Thorpe.

Universal kinship. Moore, J: H. $1. Kerr.

UNIVERSAL LANGUAGE.
See Esperanto.

Universal neurasthenia. Gardiner, M. D. *$1 net. F. F. Sherman.

Universal peace. Duras, V. H. $2. B'way Pub.

Universal school reader. *See* Tucker, Louise Emery.

Universal self-pronouncing dictionary of the English language; under one alphabetical arrangement; thoroughly modernized by C: Morris; with an appendix cont. foreign words and phrases, Christian names of men and women, names of persons and places, etc. '08(O3) c. maps, D. leath., $1.75. Winston.

See also Webster, Noah.

UNIVERSAL HISTORY.
See History.

UNIVERSE.

Arrhenius, S. A. Life of the universe. 2 v. 75 c. net.—Worlds in the making: evolution of the universe. **$1.60 net. Harper.

Bray, H: T. Living universe. $3.50. Truro.

Hartford, I: J. Original treatise on electro-vital force: giving the source of vital force and its action. $2. I: J. Hartford.

Leland, S: P. World making: scientific explanation of the birth, growth and death of worlds. 75 c. S: P. Leland.

Meagher, J. L. Wonders of the universe. $1. Chr. Press.

Rolt-Wheeler, F., *ed.* Science-history of the universe. 10 v. $6. Current Lit.

Snider, D. J. Cosmos and dia-cosmos. $1.50. Sigma.

Sweet, M. P. Theory of the universe. $1. M. P. Sweet.

Tunzelman, G. W. de. Treatise on electrical theory and the problem of the universe. $4.50 net. Lippincott.

Warren, W: F. Earliest cosmologies. *$1.50 net. Eaton & M.

See also Astronomy;—Creation;—Earth; — Evolution;—Geology.

UNIVERSITIES.
See Colleges and universities.

University addresses. Folwell, W: W. *$1 net. H. W. Wilson.

University and the study of war. Wilkinson, S. 35 c. Oxford Univ.

UNIVERSITY OF ARKANSAS.

Reynolds, J: H., *and* Thomas, D: Y. Hist. of the University of Arkansas. $2. Univ. of Ark.

University of California, Berkeley, Cal. Publications, April, 1909. '09(N20) 12°, (Univ. of California bull.) (Add. University for price.) Univ. of Cal.

University of California Agricultural Experiment Station, circular. il. O. Univ. of Cal.

—Babcock. Suggestions for garden work in California schools.

University of California Library bull. O. Univ. of Cal.

—Mead, *comp.* Bibliography of George Berkeley.

University of California memoirs. il. F. Univ. of Cal.

—Merriam. Triassic *ichthyosauria.* $3.

University of California pubs. il. Q. Univ. of Cal.

—Adams. Mystical element in Hegel's early theological writings. (Philosophy.) 35 c.

—Alexander. Some textual criticism on the eighth book of the De vita Cæsarum of Suetonius. (Classical philology.) 30 c.

University of California pubs.—Continued.
—Barrett. Ethno-geography of the Pomo and neighboring Indians. (Am. archæology and ethnology.) $3.25.—Material culture of Klamath Lake and Modoc Indians. (Archæology and ethnology.) 75 c.—Pomo Indian basketry. (Am. archæology and ethnology.)

—Barrett *and* Kroeber. Geography and dialects of the Miwok Indians. (Am. archæology and ethnology.) 50 c.

—Birds and mammals of the 1907 Alexander expedition of Southeastern Alaska. (Zoology.) 75 c.

—Brandegee. Plantæ Mexicanæ Purpusianæ. (Botany.) 15 c.—II. 10 c.

—Brown. Judgment of difference, with special reference, to the doctrine of the threshold, in the case of lifted weights. (Psychology.) 50 c.

—Burnett. On the rise of temperature in rabbits. (Physiology.)

—Densmore. Origin, structure and functions of the polar caps in *similacina amplexicaulis,* Nutt. (Botany.) 35 c.

—Derleth. Moment diagrams and typical live loads. (Engineering.) 10 c.

—Dixon. Chimariko Indians and language. (American archæology and ethnology.) $1.—New harvest mouse from Petaluma, California. (Zoology.) 5 c.

—Du Bois. Religion of the Luiseño Indians. (Am. archæology and ethnology.) $1.25.

—Eakle. Notes on some California minerals. (Geology.) 15 c.

—Eaves. History of California labor legislation. (Economics.) $4.

—Gardner. Leuvenia. (Botany.) 10 c.—New *chlorophyceae* from California. (Botany.) 10 c.—Variations in nuclear extrusion among the Fucaceæ. (Botany.) 15 c.

—Gidley. Notes on a collection of fossil mammals from Virgin Valley, Nevada. (Geology.) 10 c.

—Gilbert. Evesthes Jordani. (Geology.) 15 c.

—Goddard. Kato texts. (Am. archæology and ethnology.) 50 c.

—Grinnell. *Biota* of the San Bernardino Mountains. (Zoology.) $2.—New cowbird. (Zoology.) 5 c.—Quaternary myriopods and insects of California. (Geology.) 10 c.—Three new song sparrows from California. (Zoology.) 5 c.—Two heretofore unnamed wrens of the genus *Thryamones.* (Zoology.) 15 c.

—Hagedoorn. Inheritance of yellow color in rodents. (Physiology.) 5 c.—Origin of two new retrogressive varieties by one mutation in mice. (Physiology.) (Add. University for price.)

—Hall. Compositæ of southern California. (Botany.) $3.—Studies in ornamental trees and shrubs. (Botany.) 75 c.

—Heller *and* Grinnell. Mammals of the 1908 Alexander Alaska expedition. (Zoology.) $1

—Hindle. Life history of *trypanosoma dimorphon,* Dutton & Todd. (Zoology.) 50 c.

University of California pubs.—Continued.
—Hocking. On the law of history. (Philosophy.) 20 c.—Two extensions of the use of graphs in elementary logic. (Philosophy.) 15 c.

—Jepson. Synopsis of the North American godetias. (Botany.) 40 c.

—Johnson. Quanitative study of salpa chain. (Zoology.) 35 c.

—Kellogg. Rodent fauna. (Geology.) 15 c.

—Knopf. Probable tertiary connection bet. Asia and No. America. (Geology.) 10 c.

—Kofoid. Revision of the genus ceratocorys based on skeletal morphology. (Zoology.) 10 c.

—Kroeber. Ethnography of Cahuilla Indians. (Am. archæology and ethnology.) 75 c.—Mission record of the California Indians. (Am. archæology and ethnology.) 25 c—Notes on Shoshonean dialects of southern California. (Am. archæology and ethnology.) 35 c.

—Kurtz. Studies in the marvellous. (Modern philology.) $2.

—Linforth. Epaphos and Egyptian apis. (Classical philology.) 10 c.

—McClendon. *Ophiurans* of the San Diego region. (Zoology; Contribs. from the laboratory of the Marine Biological Assoc. of San Diego.) 30 c.

—McEwen. Preliminary rept. on the hydrographic work carried on by the Barine Biological Station of San Diego. (Zoology.) 15 c.

—Maxwell. Experiments on the functions of the internal ear. (Physiology.)

—Merriam. New mammalia. (Geology.) 5 c.—Notes on the osteology of the *thalattosaurian* genus *nectosaurus.* (Geology.) 10 c.—Occurrences of strepsicerine antelopes in the tertiary of northwestern Nevada. (Geology.) 10 c.—Skull and dentition of a primitive ichthysaurian. (Geology.) 10 c.—Skull and dentition of an extinct cat. (Geology.) 15 c.—Tertiary mammal beds of Virgin Valley and Thousand Creek. (Geology.) 50 c.

—Merrill. Cicero's knowledge of Lucretius's poem. (Classical philology.) 10 c.—On the contracted genetive in I in Latin. (Classical philology.) 25 c.

—Miller. Condor-like vultures of Rancho La Brea. (Geology.) 15 c.—Pavo Californicus: a fossil peacock. (Geology.) 5 c.—Teratornis. (Geology.) 10 c.—Wading birds from the quaternary asphalt beds of Rancho La Brea. (Geology.) 10 c.

—Mission record of the California Indians. (Am. archæology and ethnology.) (Add. University for price.)

—Mitchell. Gold, prices, and wages under the greenback standard. (Economics.) $5.

—Moore, A. R. Biochemical conception of dominance. (Physiology)

—Moore, T. V. Process of abstraction. (Psychology.) $1.

—Nelson. Ellis Landing shellmounds. (Am. archæology and ethnology.) 75 c.—Shellmounds of the San Francisco Bay region. (Archæology and ethnology.) 50 c.

University of California pubs.—Continued.
—Nichols. Contributions to the knowledge of the California species of *crustaceous corallines.* (Botany.) 10 c.—II. (Botany.) 15 c.
—Nutting. Conspiracy at Rome in 66-65 B.C. (Classical philology.) 10 c.
—Osterhout. Value of sodium to plants. (Botany.) 10 c.
—Overstreet. Dialectic of Plotinus. 25 c.
—Pack. Notes on echinoids from the tertiary of California. 10 c. (Geology.)
—Pinger. Der junge Goethe und das publikum. (Modern philology.) 50 c.
—Ritter. Halocynthia Johnsoni n. sp. (Zoology; contribs. from lab'y of Marine Biolog. Assoc.) 50 c.
—Robertson. Proteins. (Physiology.) $1.
—Sapir *and* Dixon. Yana texts. (Achæology and ethnology.) $2.50.
—Schmidt. Tables of H + and OH-concentrations corresponding to electromotive forces determined in gas-chain measurements. (Physiology.) 10 c.
—Setchell. Genus sphaerosoma. (Botany.) 15 c.
—Shinn. Notes on the development of a child. (Education.) $2.50.
—Sinclair. Recent investigations bearing on the question of the occurrence of neocene man in the auriferous gravels of the Sierra Nevada. (Am. archæology and ethnology.) 35 c.
—Smithson. Old English Christian epic. (Modern philology.) $1.
—Sparkman. Culture of the Luiseño Indians. (Am. archæology and ethnology.) 50 c.
—Swarth. Two new owls from Arizona. (Zoology.) 10 c.
—Taylor *and* Dixon. Two new rodents from Nevada. (Zoology.) 20 c.
—Torrey. *Leptomedusae* of the San Diego region. (Zoology.) 20 c.
—Torrey *and* Kluberger. Three specimens of cerianthus from Southern California. (Zoology.) 10 c.
—Waterman. Religious practices of the Diegneño Indians. (Archæology and ethnology.) 80 c.
—Weaver. New *echinoids* from the Tertiary of California. (Geology.) 5 c.—Stratigraphy and palæontology of the San Pablo formation in middle California. (Geology.) 25 c.
—Weiss. Introd. to the philosophy of art. (Modern philology.) 50 c.
—Wilson. Gracilariophilor; new parasite. (Botany.) 10 c.
—Winther. Wilhelm Busch. (Modern philology.) 75 c.
—Yusuf Ibn Taghri Birdi. Annals entitled An-nujum az-zahira fi mulûk misr walkâhira. 2 v. (Semitic philology.) ea., $1.50.

University of California pubs., Library bull. O. pap. Univ. of Cal.
—Bradley. Notes on two amphipods. (Zoology.) 30 c.
—Kofoid. Exuviation, autotomy and regeneration in ceratium. (Zoology.) 50 c.

University of California pubs., Library bull.—Continued.
—Ritter *and* Bailey. On the weight of developing eggs. (Zoology.) 10 c.
—Robertson. Incrusting *chelostomatous bryozoa* of west coast of North America. (Zoology.) $1.—On the synthesis of paranuclein through the agency of pepsin. (Physiology.)
—Weinhold. List of first editions and other rare books in the Weinhold library. (Add. pub. for price.)

University of Chicago constructive Bible studies; ed. by W: Rainey Harper and Ernest De Witt Burton. O. Univ. of Chic.
—Atkinson. Story of Paul of Tartus, a home work book. *25 c. net.—Story of Paul of Tarsus, a manual for teachers. *$1 net.

University of Chicago Constructive Bible studies, Advanced and supplementary ser.; ed. by Ernest de Witt Burton. D. Univ. of Chic.
—Henderson. Social duties from the Christian point of view. $1.25.

University of Chicago, Constructive Bible studies, Elementary ser.; ed. by Rainey Harper and Ernest De Witt Burton. il. O. Univ. of Chic.
—Bible. O. T. Heroes of Israel.—Teacher's manual. ea., $1.
—Chamberlin *and* Kern. Child religion in song and story. [v. 2,] Walks with Jesus in His home country. $1.38.
—Ferris. Sunday kindergarten. *$1.25 net.

University of Chicago Constructive Bible studies; secondary ser.; ed. by Rainey Harpar and Ernest Dewitt Burton. D and O. Univ. of Chic.
—Burgess. Life of Christ. $1.
—Burton *and* Mathews. Life of Christ. $1.
—Walker. Greatest men of the Christian church. $1.50.
—Willett. Studies in the first book of Samuel. $1.50.

University of Chicago decennial pubs. O. pap. Univ. of Chic.
—Hale. Study of the stellar evolution. *$4 net.

University of Chicago historical and linguistic studies in literature related to the New Testament. 8°, pap. Univ. of Chic.
—Thomson. *Metanoeo* and *metamelei* in Greek literature. *25 c. net.

University of Chicago historical and linguistic studies in literature related to the New Testament. 2d ser. 8°. Univ. of Chic.
—Granbery. Outline of New Testament Christology. 50 c.

University of Chicago Mathematical ser.; ed. by Eliakim Hastings Moore. D. Univ. of Chic.
—Myers, *and others.* Second-year mathematics for secondary schools. $1.50 net.

University of Chicago studies in political science. D. pap. Univ. of Chic.
—Harper. New electoral law for the Russian Duma. *25 c. net.

University of Cincinnati, observatory pubs. 4°. Univ. of Cin.
—Porter. Variations of latitude, 1899 to 1906. $1.
University of Cincinnati studies. il. O. pap. Univ. of Cin.
—Belote. Scioto speculation and the French settlement at Gallipolis. 75 c.
—Brooks. Odd prices and bargains in retail trade. (Add. University for price.)
—Guyer. Deficiencies of the chromosome theory of heredity.
—Harry. Problems in the Prometheus. 50 c. —Question of divination. (Add. Univ. for price.)
—Krapp. Authority of law in language.
—Lurie. Effect of a constant stimulus upon touch localization. (Add. Univ. for price.)
—Tawney. Mills' theory of inductive logic. $1.
UNIVERSITY OF COLORADO, Boulder, Colo.
University of Colorado views, January, 1909. [1910.] (Ap) 36 p. il. 24°. (Add. pubs. for price.) Univ. of Col.
University of Colorado bulletins. 12°. Univ. of Col.
—Baker. Educational aims and civic needs. (Add. pubs. for price.) Univ. of Col.
University of Georgia bull. 8°. J. S. Stewart.
—Stewart, *ed.* Hdbk. for the secondary schools of Georgia. gratis.
University of Illinois. Studies from the psychological laboratory of the University of Illinois. v. 1. '10(Ap23) 4°, (Psychological monographs ser.) $1.75. Psychological Review.
University of Illinois bulletins. il. O and Q. pap. Univ. of Ill.
—Amrine. Comparative tests of carbon. (Engineering experiment station.) (Add. University for price.)—Lighting country homes by private electric plants. (Engineering Experiment Station.) gratis.
—Amrine *and* Guell. Tests of tungsten lamps. (Engineering Experiment Station.) gratis.
—Baker. Voids, settlement and weight of crushed stone. gratis. (Experiment station.) gratis.
—Bartow. Chemical and biological survey of the waters of Illinois. (Water survey ser.) gratis.—Municipal water supplies of Illinois. (Water survey.) (Add. University for price.)
—Breckenridge *and* Diserens. Full tests with Illinois coal. (Engineering Experiment Station.)
—Chemical and biological survey of Illinois. gratis. (Water survey ser.)
—Clement. On the rate of formation of carbon monoxide in gas producers. (Engineering experiment station.) (Add. Univ. for price.)
—Clement *and* Egy. Thermal conductivity of fire-clay. (Engineering Experiment Station.) gratis.
—Clement *and* Garland. Study in heat transmission. (Engineering Experiment Station.)

University of Illinois bulletins.—Continued.
—Goodenough *and* Moore. Strength of chain links. (Engineering experiment station.) (Add. University for price.)
—Hudson *and* Garland. Tests of a liquid air plant. gratis.
—Moore. History of cumulative voting and majority representation in Illinois. 50 c. (University studies.)
—Parr *and* Barker. Occluded gases in coal. (Engineering Experiment Station.) gratis.
—Parr *and* Francis. Modification of Illinois coal. (Experiment station.) gratis.
—Parr *and* Wheeler. Unit coal and the composition of coal ash.—Weathering of coal. (Engineering Experiment Station.) gratis.
—Ricker. Study of base and bearing plates for columns and beams.—Study of roof trusses. (Experiment station.) gratis.
—Sharp. Illinois libraries. pts. 3, 4, 5. ea., $1.
—Snodgrass. Fuel tests with house-heating boilers. gratis.—Tests of two types of tile-roof furnaces. (Engineering Experiment Station.) gratis.
—Stebbins. Photometric observations of double stars. (Water survey ser.) 75 c.
—Talbot. Tests of cast-iron and reinforced concrete culvert pipe. (Experiment station.) gratis.—Tests of reinforced concrete beams, ser. 1907-08. gratis. (Engineering Experiment Station.)—Tests of three large reinforced concrete beams. gratis. (Experiment Station.)
—Talbot *and* Abrams. Tests of brick columns. gratis. (Engineering Experiment Station.)
University of Illinois bull.; University studies. il. O. and Q. Univ. of Ill.
—Carnahan. Jean d' Abundance. $1.
—Ewing. Systemic and biological study of *acarina.* $1.
—Layton. Nibelungen of Wagner. 75 c.
—Paetow. Arts course at medieval universities. $1.
—Rietz *and* Shade. Correlation of efficiency in mathematics and efficiency in other subjects. 35 c.
—Studies from the geological department. 75 c.
University of Illinois; School of Education bull. O. Univ. of Ill.
—Colvin. Some facts in partial justification of the so-called dogma of discipline. gratis.
—Hollister. Public school buildings and their equipment. gratis.
University of Iowa bulletin; new ser. 8°. Univ. of Ia.
—Iowa University, College of Medicine. Contributions from the Dept. of Pathology and Bacteriology. v. 1. 25 c.
University of Iowa bulletin; studies in language and literature. 8°. Univ. of Ia.
—Bale. Syntax of the genitive case in the Lindisfarne Gospels. 50 c.
University of Kansas bull.; Debating ser. D. pap. Univ. of Kan.
—Davis. Training for debate.

University of Kansas bull.; Social betterment ser. 12°. Univ. of Kan.
—Blackman. Playgrounds and parks. gratis.
University of Kansas. Dept. of Entomology contributions. il. 8°. S: J: Hunter.
—Hunter *and* Glenn. Green bug and its enemies. gratis.
UNIVERSITY OF LEIPZIG, Leipzig, Germany.
Transactions. v. 15, July, 1900. To the University of Leipzig on the occasion of the 500th anniversary of its foundation, from Yale University and the Connecticut Academy of Arts and Sciences. $3.50. Yale Univ.
University of Michigan. Lab'y directions for general biology; the frog; zoological half; (second semester.) '10(Ap) 42 p. O. pap., 25 c. Wahr.
UNIVERSITY OF MICHIGAN, Ann Arbor, Mich.
Koch, T. W. Hdbk. of the libraries of the University of Michigan. 10 c. Wahr.
University of Michigan studies; Humanistic ser. 8°, pap. Macmillan.
—Armstrong. Autobiographic elements in Latin inscription. 40 c.
—Bible. O. T. Deuteronomy and Joshua (Washington manuscript). $1.
--Butler. Studies in the life of Heliogabalus. $1.25.
—Evans. Roman law studies in Livy. 40 c. net.
—Fairbanks. Athenian lekythoi. $4.
—Meader. Usage of idem, ipse and words of related meaning. 50 c. net.
—Sanders, *ed.* Roman hist. and mythology. $2.25.
—Stewart. Latin abstract substances.. 40 c.
—Swan. Use of adjective as a substantive in the De rerum natura.
—Winter. Myth of Hercules at Rome. 50 c. net.
—Woodruff. Reminiscences of Ennius in Silius Italicus. 40 c. net.
UNIVERSITY OF MINNESOTA.
Johnson, E. B. Dict. of University of Minnesota. 50 c. E. B. Johnson.
University of Missouri; contribs. from the Dept. of Botany. 8°. G: M. Reed.
—Reed. Mildews of the cereals. (Not for sale.)
University of Missouri, Engineering Experiment Station, bull. il. 8°. Univ. of Mo.
—Bowles. Acetylene for lighting country homes.
University of Missouri studies; ed. by W. G. Brown. Q. pap. Univ. of Mo.
—Elwang. Social function of religion. (Social science ser.) $1.
—Meyer. Introduction to the mechanics of the inner ear. (Science ser.) *$1 net.
—Stephens. Transitional period, 1788-1789. $1. (Social science ser.)
—Stewart. Origin of the werewolf superstition. 50 c. (Social science ser.)
—Vaughn. Origin and early development of the English universities. (Social sci. ser.) $1.
University of Missouri studies; Literary and linguistic ser.; ed. by W. G. Brown. il. F. Univ. of Mo.
—Chevalerie Vivien; facsimile phototypes of the Sancti Bertini manuscript. $1.25.

University of Montana pubs. il. O. pap. Univ. of Mont.
—Book. Psychology of skill. $1. (Psychology.)
—Rowe. Some economic geology of Montana. (Add. University for price.) (Geological ser.)
University of Nebraska studies. il. 8°, pap. Univ. of Neb.
—Christophelsmeier. First revolutionary step [in France.] $1.
—Le Rossignol *and* Stewart. Taxation in New Zealand. 75 c.
—Pierce. On the biologies of the *rhynchophora.* (Zoological laboratory.) (Not for sale.)
—Powers. Morphological variation and its causes in *amblystoma tigrinum.* $1.
—Taylor. Financial legislation. $1.
—Ward. Iconographia parasitorum hominis. (Zoological laboratory.) 50 c.
University of Nevada studies. 8°. Univ. of Nev.
—Hill. Sidney's Arcadia and the Elizabethan drama. (Add. University for price.)
University of North Carolina pubs. 8°. Univ. of N. C.
—Whitaker. Provincial council and committees of safety in North Carolina. (James Sprunt historical monographs.) (Add. Univ. for price.)
University of Ohio pubs. il. 4°, pap. Univ. of O.
—Hambleton. Genus *corizus.* 25 c. (Contribs. from Dept. of Zoology and Entomology.)
University of Oregon bull., new ser. 8°, pap. Univ. of Ore.
—Schafer. Acquisition of Oregon. pt. 1. gratis.
University of Penn.; anthropological pubs. of the University Museum. il. 4°. Univ. of Penn.
—Sapir. Takelma texts. $2.50.
—Seager. Excavations on the Island of Pseira. $5.
—Speck. Ethnology of the Yuchi Indians. $2.50.
University of Pennsylvania, Babylonian expedition, Ser. A., Cuneiform texts; ed. by H. V. Hilprecht. f°. Univ. of Penn.
—Clay. Legal and commercial transactions dated in the Assyrian, Neo-Babylonian and Persian periods. $6.
—Poebel. Babylonian legal and business documents. $6.
—Radau. Letters to Cassite kings. $6.
University of Penn., Babylonian expedition, Ser. D, Cuneiform texts; ed. by H. V. Hilprecht. f°. Holman.
—Hilprecht. Earliest version of Babylonian deluge story. 75 c. net.
University of Pennsylvania pubs. 4°. Univ. of Penn.; [Appleton.]
—Pennsylvania University Library. Calendar of the papers of Benjamin Franklin. (History.) $1.50.

University of Pennsylvania pubs., Astronomical ser. F. pap.
Univ. of Penn.; [Appleton.]
—Doolittle. Catalogue and remeasurement of the 648 double stars discovered by Professor G. W. Hough. (Add. pubs. for price.)
University of Pennsylvania pubs., ser. in philology and literature. 8°.
Univ. of Penn.; [Appleton.]
—Mendelsohn. Studies in the word-play of Plautus. $1.25.
University of Penn. ser. in political economy and public law. Q.
Univ. of Penn.; [Appleton.]
—Giesecke. American commercial legislation before 1789. $1.50.
—Vogt. Sugar refining industry. $1.50.
University of Texas. List of the publications of the University of Texas (April, 1901-December, 1909.) [1910.] (Ag) 13 p. 8°, (Univ. of Texas bull.) gratis.
Univ. of Tex.
University of Texas bull. 8°. Univ. of Tex.
—Bedichek *and* Baskett. Consolidation of rural schools. 25 c.
—Callaway. Incidental teaching of English. 15 c.
—Clark. Beginnings of Texas. (Humanistic ser.) 75 c.
—List of publications of the University of Texas. gratis.
—Potts. Crime and the treatment of the criminal. gratis.—Railroad transportation in Texas. (Humanistic ser.) (Add. Univ. for price.)
—Ries. Clays of Texas. (Scientific ser.) $2.
—York. Anatomy and some of the biological aspects of the "American mistletoe" 50 c.
University of Toronto studies. Q.
Morang; Univ. of Toronto.
—Wrong *and* Langton, *eds.* Review of historical publications relating to Canada. v. 12, 13, 14. ea., $1.50; $1.
University of Toronto studies, Biological ser. 4°. Univ. of Toronto.
—White. On polystely in roots of *orchidaceae.* 50 c.
University of Toronto studies, Philological ser. Q. Univ. of Toronto
—Clawson. Gest of Robin Hood. $1.
UNIVERSITY OF VIRGINIA, Charlottesville, Va.
Culbreth, D: M. R. University of Virginia. *$5 net. Neale.
Wilde, A. G. In and about the University of Virginia. 75 c. A. G. Wilde.
University of Virginia; Barbour-Page foundation. D. Holt.
—Gildersleeve. Hellas and Hesperia. *$1 net.
University of Virginia, School of Latin, bull. 8°. Anderson.
—Fitzhugh. Sacred tripudium. 75 c.
University of Washington bull. 8°, pap.
Univ. of Wash.
—Padelford *and* Benham, *eds.* Songs of Rawlinson ms. C813. (Add. University for price.) (University studies.)
—Sisson. High school's cure of souls. (Add. Univ. for price.)
—Smith. Contribution toward a bibliography of Marcus Whitman. (Add. University for price.)

University of West Virginia studies in American history. D. pap. Univ. of W. Va.
—Callahan. Alaska purchase. (Diplomacy.) 50 c.—Evolution of Seward's Mexican policy. 75 c. (Ser. 1, diplomatic history.)—Russo-American relations during the American Civil War. 30 c.
University of West Virginia studies in American history. O. pap. Univ. of W. Va.
—Callahan. Evolution of Seward's Mexican policy. 75 c. (Ser. 1, diplomatic history.)
University of West Virginia studies in West Virginia history; ed. by J. M. Callahan. O. pap. Univ. of W. Va.
—Callahan. Evolution of the constitution of West Virginia. 50 c. (Constitutional history.)
University of Wisconsin. Germanistische Gesellschaft. Deutsches liederbuch für amerikanische studenten. '08(F8) c. 8°, 75 c.
Heath.
University of Wisconsin bull. il. 8°.
Univ. of Wis.
—Ashmun. Composition in the high school. 10 c.
—Barnett. Indirect central administration of Wisconsin. 25 c.
—Bartlett. Frosts in Wisconsin. 25 c. (University extension ser.)
—Becker. Hist. of political parties in the province of New York, 1760-1776. (History ser.) 75 c.
—Boyle, Financial history of Kansas. (Economics and political science ser.) 50 c.
—Carlton. Economic influences upon educational progress in the U. S., 1820-1850. (Economics and pol. sci. ser.) 50 c.
—Evans, M. B. High school course in German. (Add. Univ. for price.) (High school ser.)
—Goodnight. German literature in American magazines. (Philology and literature ser.) 50 c.
—Haertel. German literature in American magazines. (Philology and literature ser.) 50 c.
—Haney. Congressional history of railways in the U. S. to 1850.—1850-1887. (Economics and pol. sci. ser.) ea., 50 c.
—Harper. Organization of certain *coenobic* plants. (Science ser.) 40 c.
—Harza. Investigation of the hydraulic ram. (Engineering ser.) 25 c.
—Helmholtz. Indebtedness of Samuel Taylor Coleridge to August Wilhelm von Schlegel. (Philology and literature ser.) 40 c.
—Hobbs *and* Leith. Pre-Cambrian volcanic and intrusive rocks of the Fox river valley. (Science ser.) 25 c.
—Huels. Comparison of the effects of frequency on the light of incandescent and Nernst lamps. (Engineering ser.) 25 c.
—Huntington. Fireless cooker. (University extension ser.) 25 c.
—Immigration. gratis.
—Larson. Financial and administrative hist. of Wisconsin. 50 c.
—Lyman. Principles of effective debating. 15 c.

University of Wisconsin bull.—Continued.
—McCullough. Tests on the permeability of concrete. (Engineering ser.) 25 c.
—Mangold. Labor argument in the American protective tariff discussion (Economics and pol. sci. ser.) 35 c.
—Phelan. The financial history of Wisconsin. (Economic and pol. sci. ser.) 50 c.
—Pooley. Settlement of Illinois. (History ser.) 75 c.
—Popular election of senators. gratis.
—Postal savings bank. gratis.
—Rastall. Labor history of the Cripple Creek districtt (Economic and pol. sci. ser.) 50 c.
—Reed. Infection experiments with *erysiphe cichoracearum.* (Science ser.) 35 c.
—Restriction of immigration.
—Schaffner. Labor contract. (Economic and pol. sci. ser.) 50 c.
—Sellery. Lincoln's suspension of habeas corpus. (History ser.) 35 c.
—Sharp. Study of the influence of custom on the moral judgment. 30 c.—Success. (High School ser.)
—Stewart. Investigations of centrifugal pumps. pt. 1. (Engineering ser.) 50 c.—Investigations of flow through large submerged orifices and tubes, pt. 1. (Engineering ser. Researches in hydraulics.) 25 c.
—Tariff on trust-made steel articles. gratis.
—Tibbals. Study of tellurides. (Science ser.) 25 c.
—Trooien. Current practice in steam engine design. (Engineering ser.) 25 c.
—Withey. Tests on bond between concrete and steel in reinforced concrete beams.—Tests on plain and reinforced concrete, ser. 1906, 1907. (Engineering ser.) ea., 25 c.
—Wolesensky. Study of the metallic tellurites. (Science ser.) 25 c.
—Woman suffrage. gratis.

University reprints; ed. by N. W: Walker and M. C. S. Noble. 8°. Univ. of N. C.
—Pattillo. Geographical catechism. 75 c.

University sermons. 8°, *$1.25 net. Revell.
—Black. Gift of influence.

University teaching. Newman, J: H: *75 c. net. Longmans.

Unknown quantity. Hall, G. †$1.50. Holt.

Unlived life of little Mary Ellen. Stuart, *Mrs.* R. E. $1. Bobbs-M.

Unlucky family. De la Pasture, *Mrs.* E. B. †$1.50. Dutton.

Unlucky Tib. Ellis, E: S. †$1.25. Estes.

Unmasked at last. Grainger, F. E: *$1 net. Fenno.

Unmasking of Robert Houdini. *See* Houdini, H.

Unmusical New York. Klein, H. $1.50 net. Lane.

Unofficial letters of an official's wife. Moses, E. B. **$1.50 net. Appleton.

Unofficial love story. Hickman. A. †$1. Century Co.

Unpublished orations. Fiske, J: (Priv. pr.) Bibliophile.

Unreached millions. American Association of Foreign-Language Newspapers. (Add. pubs. for price.) L: N. Hammersling.

Unseen dangers behind humanity. Shatzke, J. S. $2.50. New Humanity.

Unseen thing. Dyllington, A. $1.20 net. J: W. Luce.

Unstead, J. F.
Practical geography. pt. 1. '08(D19); pt. 2. '09(Ag14) maps, il. D. (Oxford geogphies.) ea., 40 c.; pts. 1 and 2, bound together, 60 c. Oxford Univ.

Unstrung bow. Batchelor, D: O. $1.20 net. Sherman, F.

Untangling Tony. Bagg, H. F. 25 c. Penn Pub. Co.

Untechnical addresses on technical subjects. Douglas, J. $1. Wiley.

Unter der mitternachtssonne. Gorbach, A. B. (Add. author for price.) A. B. Gorbach.

Until Shiloh come. Whish, E. 50 c. net. Longmans.

Until the evening. Benson, A. C. **30 c. net. Crowell.

Unto this last. *See* Ruskin, J:

Untraut, Hermann Jos.
Die krankenseelsorge; ein handbüchlein für die seelsorger, hrsg. nach den römischen rituale und bewährten autoren. [1910.] (N) c. 12+239 p. 16°, 60 c. Wiltzius.

Untrodden English ways. Shelley, H: C: $1.50 net; $3 net. Little, B. & Co.

Unveiling tributes. Butler, L. C. $1. La. Distrib. Co.

Unwin, G:
Gilds and companies of London. '09(D11) il. O. (Antiquary's bks.) *$2 net. Scribner.

Unwin, Raymond.
Town planning in practice; introd. to the art of designing cities and suburbs. '10 (Je4) il. 4°, $6 net. Scribner.

Unwin, W: Cawthorne.
The elements of machine design. pt. 1, General principles; strength of materials, rivets, bolts, and other fastenings; journals and shafting; couplings; pedestals; transmission of power by gearing. belting, ropes and chains. New ed., rev. and enl. '09(S18) figs. tabs., O. $2.50. Longmans.
Testing of materials for construction; textbook for the engineering lab'y and a collection of the results of experiment. 3d ed. '10(Jl30) O. $5 net. Longmans.

Unwritten history of old St. Augustine. Brooks, A. M., *comp.* 75 c. Record Co.

Up and down the sands of gold. Devereaux, M. †75 c. Little, B. & Co.

Up grade. Goodwin, W. †$1.50. Little, B. & Co.

Up hill and down dale in ancient Etruria. Seymour, F: H. A. $3 net. Appleton.

Up the grade. Edwards, D: W: $1.50. C. M. Clark.

Up the Orinoco. Mozans, H. J., *pseud.* $3 net. Appleton.

"Up to Calvin's." Richards, *Mrs.* L. E. H. $1.25. Estes.

Up-to-date courtship. Wright, *Mrs.* C. P. $1. Cochrane.

Up-to-date method of designing. Ratner, H: W. (Add. author for price.) H: W. Ratner.

Up-to-date sandwich book. Fuller, E. G., *comp.* *$1 net. McClurg.

UPANISHADS.
Brahma knowledge: outline of the philosophy of the Vedanta, as set forth by the Upanishads. *60 c. net. Dutton.
See also Vedas.

Upbuilders. Steffens, J. L. **$1.20 net. Doubleday, P.

Updegraff, Harlan.
Origin of the moving school in Massachusetts. '08(S5) c. 8°, (Columbia Univ., Teachers' Coll., contribs. to education.) pap., $1.50. Teachers' Coll.

Upham, Alfr. Horatio.
French influence in English literature; from the accession of Elizabeth to the Restoration. '08(Ag22) 12°, (Columbia Univ. studies in comparative lit.) *$2 net. Lemcke.
Old Miami: the Yale of the early West. '09(Jl31) c. il. D. $1. Rep. Pub.

Upham, Arth. Aquila.
Introd. to agriculture. '10(Ap23) c. il. D. 75 c. Appleton

Upham, Fs. Bourne.
Simon Peter, shepherd. '10(Mr26) c. D. *75 c. net. Eaton & M.
Thomas Coke. '10(Mr26) c. por. nar. S. (Makers of Methodism.) *25 c. net. Eaton & M.

UPHOLSTERY.
Pract. upholstery. 25 c. Spon.
Stephenson, J: W., *comp.* Upholsterer vest pocket compendium of drapery styles. 50 c. Clifford & L.

Upper Engadine. Musson, S. C. *$2.50 net. Macmillan.

Upper tenor notes. Schilling, W: P. $1. W: P. Schilling.

Upper Yukon native customs and folk-lore. Schmitter, F: 12 c. Smith. Inst.

UPPINGHAM (School), Eng.
Patterson, W: S Sixty years of Uppingham cricket. *$2 net. Longmans.

Ups and downs of a mail order aspirant. Berkwitz, W: L. $1. Mail Order.

Ups and downs of a wandering life. Seymour, W. $3 special net. Appleton.

Upshur, Rear-Admiral J. H.
See Adventures of pirates.

Upside down. Ellis, E: S. 75 c. Winston.

Upson, Arth. Wheelock.
Collected poems. 2 v.; ed. with an introd. by R: Burton. '09(Ag) por. 8°, subs., *$5 net. Upson Memorial.
Tides of spring, and other poems. '08 (F22) c. 12°, $1. Small.

UPSON, Arthur Wheelock.
Burton, R: Midsummer memory; elegy on the death of Arth. Upson. $1.25. E. D. Brooks.

Upson, H: Swift, M.D.
Insomnia and nerve strain. '08(Ag29) c. il. D. **$1.50 net. Putnam.

Upton, Bertha.
Golliwogg books. 12 v. '10(O15) il. in col. obl. O. bds., price reduced from ea., $1.50 net and $2 net to ea., $1 net. Longmans.
Contents: Adventures of two Dutch dolls and a golliwogg; Golliwogg's air-ship; Golliwogg's auto go-cart; Golliwogg's bicycle club; Golliwogg's Christmas; Golliwogg's circus; Golliwogg's desert island; Golliwogg's fox hunt; Golliwogg in Holland; Golliwogg in war; Golliwogg at the seaside; Golliwogg in the African jungle.
Vege-men's revenge. '10(O15) col. il. obl. O. bds., price reduced from $2 net to $1 net. Longmans.

Upton, C: Elmer.
Down Wild Goose Canyon. '10(D31) c. il. 12°, 75 c. C: E. Upton.

Upton, Florence K.
Adventures of Borbee and the Wisp. '08 (N14) il. obl. O. *$1.50 net. Longmans.

Upton, G: Putnam.
Musical memories: my recollections of celebrities of the half century 1850-1900. '08(O3) c. il. O. *$2.75 net. McClurg.
Standard concert guide: hdbk. of the standard symphonies, oratorios, cantatas, and symphonic poems for the concert goer. '08(Ag29) c. il. S. $1.75. McClurg.
Standard concert repertory and other concert pieces; a hdbk. of the standard overtures, suites, symphonic poems, rhapsodies, fantasies, etc., in the modern concert repertory, for the use of concert goers. '09(S4) c. pors. D. $1.75. McClurg.
Standard musical biographies; hdbk. setting forth the lives, works, and characteristics of representative composers. '10 (N5) c. il. pors. facsims., D. $1.75. McClurg.

—, ed. *See* Life stories for young people.

Upton, Mrs. Harriet Taylor.
Twentieth century hist. of Trumbull County, Ohio; narrative acct. of its historical progress, its people, and its principal interests. 2 v. '09, [1910.] (Je) il. pors. 4°, $12 net. Lewis Pub.

—, and others.
Hist. of the Western Reserve. In 3 v. '10(D10) c. il. pors. 4°, $21. Lewis Pub.

Upward, Allen.
East end of Europe: report of an unofficial mission to the European provinces of Turkey on the eve of the revolution; with preface by Major Sir E: FitzGerald Law. '09(Ap17) il. 8°, *$4 net. Dutton.
Lord Alistair's rebellion. '10(D3) 12°, $1.50. M. Kennerley.
New word; open letter addressed to the Swedish Academy in Stockholm on the meaning of the word idealist. '10(Je4) c. 12°, $1.50. M. Kennerley.
Secrets of the past. '10(Je4) 12°, $1.50. Brentano's.

Upward and onward ser. S. bds., *75 c. net; ooze cf., *$1.25 net, boxed; limp cf., *$1 net. McClurg.
—Catchwords of worldly wisdom.

Upward path. Helm, M. 50 c.; 35 c. Young People's Miss.

Ur-Engur, a bronze of the fourth millenium. Johns, C. H. W. (Priv. pr.) F. F. Sherman.

URANN FAMILY.
See Genealogies: Whittier, C: C.

Urban, Rev. A.
Easy catechetics for the first school year; primary instruction in the chief truths of religion. '10(D3) c. 8°, 60 c. Wagner.
Sunday-school teacher's explanation of the Baltimore catechism. '08, [1909.] (Mr) c. 437 p. 8°, $1. Wagner.

Urban, F. M.
Application of statistical methods to the problems of psychophysics. '08(Ap18) tabs., 8°, (Psychological monographs.) pap., $2.50. Psychological Clinic.

Urban, Wilbur Marshall.
Valuation: its nature and laws; being an introduction to the general theory of values. 09(My8) O. (Library of philosophy.) *$2.75 net. Macmillan.

URBANA UNIVERSITY, Urbana, O.
See Swedenborg, Emanuel.

URBINO, Italy.
Dennistoun, J. Memoirs of the Dukes of Urbino. 3 v. *$12 net. Lane.

Urgent surgery. Lejars, F. 2 v. per set, *$14 net; *$16 net. Wood.

Urheberrecht und nachdruck in Nord-Amerika. Steiger, E. gratis. Steiger.

URIC ACID.
Haig, A. Uric acid in the causation of disease. *$4 net. Blakiston.

Uriel Acosta. Gutzkow, K. F. 35 c. Holt.

URINE AND URINARY ORGANS.
Ciechanowski, S. Prostate hypertrophy. *$2 net. W: R. Jenkins.
Freyer, P. J. Clinical lectures on the surgical diseases of the urinary organs. *$4 net. Wood.
Holland, J. W: Urine and clinical chemistry of the gastric contents. *$1 net. Blakiston.
Kidd, F. Urinary surgery. $2.60 net. Longmans.
Kreiss, F. Urogenital therapeutics. $5. Cleveland Press.
Mann, J. D. Physiology and pathology of the urine. *$3.25 net. Lippincott.
Memminger, A. Diagnosis by the urine. *$1 net. Blakiston.
Ogden, J. B. Clinical examination of the urine. $3. Saunders.
Richardson, D. D. Treatise on diseases of the rectum, prostate and associate organs. (Add. pubs. for price.) Campbell Co.
Rohrer, C. W. G. Contributions to the comparative anatomy of the prostate gland. gratis. C. W. G. Rohrer.
Saxe, G. A. D. S. Examination of the urine. $1.75. Saunders.
Walker, J. W. T. Estimation of the renal function in urinary surgery. *$3 net. Cassell.

Urner, Mabel Herbert.
Journal of a neglected wife. '09(Mr6) c. D. *$1.10 net. B. W. Dodge.

Urquhart, Fk. J.
Short hist. of Newark, [N. J.] '08, [1909.] (F) c. 13+158 p. il. 12°, *75 c. net. Baker Pr.

Urquhart, W. W.
Reminiscences; merchant marine ocean travel in the sixties and now. '10(Je25) 75 c. W. W. Urquhart.

Urrea, Pedro Manuel de.
Penitencia de amor. '02, [1909.] (N) 70 p. 8°, (Bibliotheca hispanica.) $1. Hispanic Soc.

Ursenbach, Octave F.
Why I am a "Mormon." '10(Jl) c. 4+212 p. 16°, $1. O. F. Ursenbach.

URUGUAY, South America.
International Bureau of American Republics. Uruguay. (Add. pubs. for price.) Int. Bu. Am. Republics.

Urussov, Prince Serge Dmitriyevich.
Memoirs of a Russian governor; tr. from the Russian and ed. by Herman Rosenthal. Authorized ed. '08(F1) c. por. O. **$1.50 net. Harper.

Us. *See* Molesworth, *Mrs.* Mary Louise Stewart.

Us two cook book. Williams, J. C. $1. Barse & H.

Usage of idem, ipse and words of related meaning. Meader, C. L. 50 c. net. Macmillan.

Use and abuse of hypnotism. Lathrop, L. C. 50 c. L. C. Lathrop.

Use and need of the life of Carrie A. Nation. Nation, C. A. $1. F. H. Breyfogle.

Use of formulas in mechanics. '08(Ag1) diagrs., 8°, (Machinery's reference ser.) pap., 25 c. Indust. Press.

Use of logarithms and logarithmic tables. '10(My21) c. 8°, (Machinery's reference ser.) pap., 25 c. Indust. Press.

Use of milk as food. Milner, R. D. 5 c. U. S., Supt. of Docs.

Use of vestments in the English church. Simpson, W: J: S. *20 c. net. Longmans.

USEFUL ARTS.
Adams, J. H: Harper's indoor book for boys. $1.75. Harper.
Allen, N. B. Industrial studies. 65 c. Ginn.
Ashley, W: J., *ed.* British industries. *$1.80 net. Longmans.
Beard, D. C. Boy pioneers; [description of way to make things.] **$2 net. Scribner.
Bond, A. R. Scientific American boy at school. $2. Munn.
Bushnell, J. P., *comp.* What to do and how to do it. $2. Home Manual.
Carpenter, F. G: How the world is clothed. 60 c. Am. Bk.
Cunningham, W. English industry and commerce in modern times. In 2 pts. *$5.25 net. Putnam.
Domestic Engineering directory of jobbers and manufacturers of plumbing, heating, lighting, engine, mining and mill supplies. In 2 pts. $5. Domestic Engineering.
Douglas, J. Untechnical addresses on technical subjects. $1. Wiley.
Gephart, W: F. Transportation and industrial development in the Middle West. $2. Longmans.

USEFUL ARTS.—*Continued.*

Hasluck, P. N., *ed.* Handy man's enquire within. *$2.50 net. Cassell.

Hiscox, G. D., *ed.* Henley's twentieth century book of receipts, formulas, and processes. $3; $4. Henley.

Hobson, J: A. Industrial system; inquiry into earned and unearned income. $2.50 net. Longmans.

International Congress of Arts and science. International University lectures. In 12 v. per set, $49.50. New Alliance.

Louisville, Ky. Free Public Library. List of practical books in the Library on electricity, machine shop practice, foundry practice, plumbing and woodworking. Louisville Pub. Lib.

Lowe, C. M. Little workers; [book of rhymes and illustrations about trades and industries.] $1. Dutton.

Masters, E. T. One hundred useful things. *75 c. net. Cassell.

Monteverde, R. D. Commercial and technical terms in the English and Spanish languages. *70 c. net. Macmillan.

Paret, A. P., *ed.* Harper's handy book for girls. $1.75. Harper.

Perry, G: P.. Wealth from waste: [use of by-products.] *50 c. net. Revell.

Shadwell, A. Industrial efficiency: comparative study in England, Germany and America. *$2 net. Longmans.

Sower, J: W: Compendium of facts, figures and formulas, for the home, office, farm and shop. $1. J. W. Sower.

Spon's workshop receipts for manufacturers and scientific amateurs. v. 1. *$1.50 net. Spon.

Standage, H. C., *ed.* Decoration of metal, wood, glass, etc. $2 . Wiley.

Three hundred things a bright boy can do. $2 net. Lippincott.

Tolhausen, A., *ed.* Technological dictionary in French, English and German. In 3 v. ea., *$2.75 net. Macmillan.

Trades for London boys. *25 c. net. Longmans.

Trades for London girls. *25 c. net. Longmans

Who's who among American manufacturers gratis. Munn.

Williams, A. How it is made: describing how machines and articles are manufactured. $1.25. Nelson.

Workshop receipts for manufacturers and scientific amateurs. v. 1, Acetylene lighting-drying. *$1.50 net. Spon.

See also Agriculture;—Architecture;—Assaying;—Automobiles; — Basketry;—Bicycles;—Blacksmithing; — Bookbinders and bookbinding; — Brewing;—Bridges; — Building (*construction*); —Business;—Carpentry; —Carpets;—Celluloid; —Cement; — Ceramics; — Clay;—Cleaning;— Commerce; — Concrete; — Cookery; — Copper; —Cost;—Cotton;—Dairy;—Domestic economy; —Dressmaking;—Dyeing;—Electrical engineering;—Electricity; — Electro-metallurgy;—Electro-plating;—Engineering; — Explosives;—Factories; — Firearms; — Forge; — Foundries; — Furnace;—Gardens and gardening;—Glass;— Hardware; — Horseshoeing; — India rubber; — Inventions;—Iron;—Labor and laboring classes; —Leather; — Machinery; — Manual training;— Mechanics;—Metal work;—Metals and metallurgy;—Millinery;—Mines and mining;—Paint;— Painting (*mechanical*); — Paper; — Patents;— Pattern-making; — Photography;—Plastering;— Plumbing;—Printers and printing;—Repairing; —Ropes;—Ships and shipbuilding;—Sign painting;—Soap;—Soldering;—Stained glass;—Stair-building;—Steel;—Sugar; — Surveying;—Tailoring; — Tapestry; — Tariff;—Technical education; — Textile fabrics; — Tobacco; — Tools;— Toys;—Trade-marks; —Turning;—Typewriting; —Upholstering;—Weaving; —Woman;—Wood; —Woodcarving; — Woodwork; — Woolen spinning;—Worsted.

Usher, E: Preston.
Greek gospel; an interpretation of the coming faith. '09(Ag28) 12°, $1. E: P. Usher.

Usher, Roland Greene.
Reconstruction of the English church. 2 v. '10(Je25) c. O. $6 net, boxed. Appleton.

Usher, Susannah.
See Bevier, Isabel.

USURY.
Wassam, C. W. Salary loan business in New York City. 75 c. Charities Pub.
See also Interest.

Ut pictura poesis. Howard, W: G. $1. Grandgent.

Utah. Compiled laws of the state, 1907; comp., annot. and pub. by Ja. T. Hammond and Grant H. Smith. '08(My.) c. 24+1697 p. O. shp. (Add. pubs. for price.) Skelton.

Utah. *Supreme ct.* Repts.; (A. B. Edler and Alonzo B. Irvine.) v. 31. '08(Mr); v. 32-33 (O); v. 34. '09(Je); v. 35. '10 (D) c. O. shp., ea., $6. Callaghan.

UTAH.
Colborn, E: F. Glimpse of Utah. gratis. Denver & Rio Grande.
Whitney, O. F. Making of a state: a school history of Utah. $1. Deseret News.
Widtsoe, J: A., *and* Peterson, W: Dodge's Geography of Utah. *35 c. net. Rand, McN. & Co.
See also Great Salt Lake;—Mormonism;—Salt Lake City;—West.

UTERUS.
See Gynecology;—Midwifery.

Utica, N. Y. Public Library. Selected list of historical fiction. '09(Ag7) 12°, pap., gratis. Utica Lib.

Utica, N. Y. Public Library, 1893-1908. '09 (N) 20 p. il. 12°. (Add. Library for price.) Utica Lib.

Utilitarianism, liberty, representative government. *See* Mill, J: Stuart.

Utility of all kinds of higher schooling. Crane, R: T. $1. R: T. Crane.

Utility speller. Lewis, M. H. 30 c. Educ. Pub.

Utilization of wood waste by distillation. Harper, W. B: $3. St. L. Lumberman.

Utopia. *See* Moore, *Sir* T:

UTOPIAS.
See Political science.

Utrillo, Don Miguel, Alexandre, Arsène, Mourey, Gabriel, and others.
Five essays on the art of Ignacio Zuloaga; repr. on the occasion of the exhibition of the paintings by Ignacio Zuloaga, March 21 to April 11, 1909. '09(N20) 12°, 50 c. Hispanic Soc.

Uttermost farthing. Belloc-Lowndes, *Mrs.* M. A. $1.25. M. Kennerley.

Uyehara, George Etsujiro.
Political development of Japan, 1867-1909. '10(D10) 8°, $3 net. Dutton.

Uzanne, L: Octave.
Drawings of Watteau. '09(F13) il. Q. (Drawings of the great masters.) *$2.50 net. Scribner.

Vacandard, Elphege.
The Inquisition: a critical and historical study of the coercive power of the church; tr. from the 2d ed. by Bertrand L. Conway. '08(Mr14) c. D. *$1.50 net. Longmans.

Vacaresco, Hélène.
Royal lovers; the adventures of two empresses. '10(My7) D. $1.50. Lane.

Vacation days in Hawaii and Japan. Taylor, C: M. *$1.25 net. Jacobs.

VACCINATION.
Allen, R: W. Vaccine therapy and the opsonic method of treatment. *$2 net. Blakiston.
Bosanquet, W: C. Serums, vaccines and toxins. $2 net. Funk.
Matthewson, H: S. Prophylactic value of vaccination. (Add. Superintendent for price.) U. S., Supt. of Docs.
Vaccine therapy. $1.50 net. Longmans.
See also Serum;—Smallpox.

Vaccine and serum therapy. Schorer, E. H: $2. Mosby.

Vaccine therapy: its administration, value and limitations; discussion opened by Sir Almroth E. Wright. '10(D) 216+12 p. figs. Q. $1.50 net. Longmans.

Vachell, Horace Annesley.
Drama in sunshine. New ed. '09(Je12) D. *$1 net. Fenno.
The other side; being certain passages in the life of a genius. '10(S24) D. $1.20 net. Doran.
The paladin, as beheld by a woman of temperament. '09(O9) c. D. †$1.50. Dodd.
Turn of the tide. '08(O3) il. 12°, (New price fiction ser.) 75 c. Cupples & L.

Vade mecum du professeur de français. Tricoche, G. N. $1.50. G. N. Tricoche.

Vademecum of treatment. Seufert, E: $2.50. Chic. Med. Bk.

Vagabond in the Caucasus. Graham, S. $4 net. Lane.

Vagabond journey around the world. Franck, H. A. **$3.50 net. Century Co.

Vagabond Victor. Page, E. F. 50 c. Pub. Ho. of M. E. Ch., So.

Vagabonds (The). Trowbridge, J: T. 75 c.; 35 c. Hurst.

Vagrant, A., pseud.
See Osborne, Maitland Le Roy.

Vail, Barry.
Little book of too familiar family verse, to which are added a few philuppics. '10 (Ag) c. 3-25 p. 12°, $2. J: B. Ryan.

Vail, Rev. C: H.
Ancient mysteries and modern masonry. '10(F19) c. por. D. $1. Macoy Pub.

Vail, Morrison Huggins.
Church plans and designs. 4th ed. 09 (My) c. 40 p. il. plans, 8°. (Add. author for price. M. H. Vail.

Vail, W: H:, M.D.
Div-a-let, division by letters; pastime or mental diversion. [2d ed.] '10(Jl30) c. D. pap., 25 c W. H. Vail.

Vaile, Mrs. Charlotte M.
Orcutt girls; or, one term at the academy. '09(O9) c. il. D. †$1.50. Wilde.
Sue Orcutt; sequel to The Orcutt girls. '09(O9) c. il. D. $1.50. Wilde.

Vaile, P. A.
Modern golf. '09(Je12) il. D. *$2.25 net. Macmillan.
New Zealand. '09(Ag14) il. maps, 12°, (Peeps at many lands ser.) *75 c. net. Macmillan.
Strokes and science of lawn tennis. '10 (S3) c. il. 12°, (Spalding's athletic lib.) pap., 10 c. Am. Sports.

Vaill, Dudley Landon.
County regiment: sketch of 2d regiment of Connecticut Vol. heavy artillery. '08(Jl) c. 12+108 p. il. pors. 8°, $1.50. F. E. Partridge.

Vaiti of the Islands. Grimshaw, B. E. †$1.50. Wessels.

Vaizey, Jessie Bell, [Mrs. G. De Horne Vaizey.]
Fortunes of the Farrells. '08(Ag8) c. il. D. †$1.50. Jacobs.

Vale, Fk. Palmer.
Has surgical treatment lessened the mortality from appendicitis? '08, [1909.] (F) 165 p. tabs., 8°, (Fiske Fund prize dissertation.) 50 c. Snow & F.

Vale, Ruby R. and T: E., eds.
See Pennsylvania. **Digest of the decisions of the courts of the commonwealth.**

Vale of shadows. Erixon, A. $1.50. B'way Pub.

VALENCY.
See Chemistry.

Valentine, Carrie Syron.
How to keep hens for profit. '10(Ap30) c. il. D. $1.50 net. Macmillan.

Valera y Alcalá Galiano, Juan.
Pepita Jimenez; with notes and vocab. by C. V. Cushachs. '10(Mr5) c. S. 90 c. Am. Bk.
Pepita Jiménez; ed., with notes and vocab., by G. L. Lincoln. '08(S19) c. por. D. (Modern lang. ser.) 90 c. Heath.

Valgimigli, A.
Tourists' vade mecum of Italian colloquial conversation; with vocabs., tables, etc., and general rules on pronunciation. '10 (Mr26) S. (Pitman's tourists' vade mecum.) 40 c. Pitman.

Valid Christianity for to-day. Williams, C: D: **$1.50 net. Macmillan.

Valid religion for the times. Womer, P. P. $1. B'way Pub.

Valkyrie. *See* Wagner, Wilhelm Richard.

VALLADOLID, Spain.
See Spain.

Vallance, Aymer, and Salaman, Malcolm C:
Art in England during the Elizabethan and Stuart periods; with a note on The first century in English engraving by Malcolm C: Salaman; special spring number of *The Studio*, 1908. '08(Ag8) Q. *$3 net; pap., *$2.50 net. Lane.

Vallentine, E. J.
See Hatch, F. H.

Vallette, J. C.
Financial gatling gun: [currency question.] '07, [1909.] (Mr) c. 127 p. por. 8°, 50 c. J. C. Vallette.

VALLEY FORGE, Pa.
Burk, W: H. Historical and topographical guide to Valley Forge. 50 c. W: H. Burk.
Sons of the Am. Revolution. Maine Society. Maine at Valley Forge. (Not for sale.) S. A. R. Me. Soc.

Valley of Aosta. Ferrero, F. $2 net. Putnam.

Valley of love. Popham, W: L. 50 c. W: L. Popham.

Valley of shadows. Grierson, F. **$2 net. Houghton M.

Valley towns in Connecticut. Genthe, M. K. 50 c. Am. Geog. Soc.

VALLEY VIEW FARM, New Boston, N. H.
See Farms and farming.

VALOIS, Marguerite de.
Haggard, A. C: P. Amours of Henri de Navarre and of Marguerite de Valois. $4.50 net. Brentano's.

Valor of ignorance. Lea, H. **$1.80 net. Harper.

Valuation. Urban, W. M. *$2.75 net. Macmillan.

VALUE.
See Money;—Political economy;—Prices.

Value of Byzantine and modern Greek in Hellenic studies. Menardos, S. 35 c. Oxford Univ.

Value of happiness. *See* Barrows, Mary Minerva.

Value of humanistic, particularly classical, studies as a preparation for the study of theology. Classical Conference, Ann Arbor, Mich. Univ. of Mich.

Value of science. Poincaré, J. H. *$1.25 net. Science Pr., (N. Y.)

Value of sodium to plants by reason of its protective action. Osterhout, W. J. V. 10 c. Univ. of Cal.

Value of time. Lubbock, *Sir* J: 40 c.; 75 c. Caldwell.

Value, price and profit. Marx, K. 50 c. Kerr.

Value ser. O. $1.50-$5. Caldwell.
—Barrows, *ed.* Value of happiness.

VALVES.
Collins, H. E. Valve setting. $2. Hill Pub.
Colvin, F. H. Link motions, valves and valve setting. 50 c. Henley.
Kelley, H: H. Practical directions for marking and adjusting the Corliss valve gear. Included with subs. to *Southern Engineer,* $1. Southern Engineer.
Kennedy, J. M. Valve-setters' guide. 50 c. A. Sinclair.
Swingle, C. F. Walschaert valve gear. $1. Drake.
Wakeman, W: H: Air valves for steam heating systems. 25 c. Domestic Engineering.
Wood, W: W. Walschaert locomotive valve gear. $1.50. Henley.
See also Engines;—Gages.

"Vamba," pseud.
See Bertelli, Luigi.

Van Alstyne, Lawrence.
Diary of an enlisted man. '10(D17) c. por. 12°, $2. Tuttle, M. & T.

Van Benschoten, W: H:
Concerning the Van Bunschoten or Van Benschoten family in America. '07, [1908.] (Mr.) c. 40+813 p. il. pors. 4°, $4. Haight.

VAN BENSCHOTEN FAMILY.
See Genealogies.

Van Broekhoven, J.
True method of tone production: a new and complete course of voice training. '08 (Ap4) 4°, $1.50. H. W. Gray Co.

Van Buren, Arth. B:
Supp. no. 1 to index-digest of the repts., rulings and decisions of the Interstate Commerce Commission. '10(Ag) c. 63 p. O. pap., 35 c. Edwards.
—, rep. *See* United States. Interstate commerce commission.

Van Buren, Bp. Ja. Heartt, D.D.
Sermons that have helped. '08(N21) 12°, *$1.25 net. Dutton.

Van Buren, Sara.
Good-living: practical cookery-book for town and country. 3d ed., with additional material. '09(F27) c. 8°, $2.50. Putnam.

Vance, Rev. Ja. I:
Tendency; the effect of trend and drift in the development of life. '10(My14) c. 12°, $1.25 net. Revell.

Vance, L: Jos.
Black bag. '08(F8) c. il. D. †$1.50. Bobbs-M.
Bronze bell. '10(D) 75 c. Burt.
Bronze bell. '09(Mr27) c. il. D. †$1.50. Dodd.
Fortune-hunter. '10(F19) c. il. D. †$1.50. Dodd.
No Man's Land; romance. '10(O22) c. il. D. $1.50. Dodd.
Pool of flame. '09(D4) c. il. D. †$1.50. Dodd.

Vance, Wilson J.
Big John Baldwin. '09(O9) c. D. †$1.50. Holt.

VAN CLEEF FAMILY.
See Genealogies: Poole, M. E:

Vandal (The). Luby, W: J. $1.25. Hyland.

Van de Carr, Sara C.
See Dana, J: Cotton.

Van Deman, Esther Boise.
The Atrium Vestæ. '09(D4) il. fold. map, Q. (Carnegie Institution of Washington pubs.) pap., $1.50. Carnegie.

Van Demark, Harry.
Texas in a nutshell; dictionary of information concerning the greatest state in the American Union. '10(N) 40 p. 12°, 25 c. Nutshell.

Vanderbilt, Gertrude Lefferts.
Social history of Flatbush, and manners and customs of the Dutch settlers in Kings County. '09(Jl3) c. il. pors. fold. map, D. $1.50. F: Loeser.

Vanderbilt oriental ser.; ed. by Herbert Cushing Tolman and Ja. H: Stevenson. il. O. Am. Bk.
—Tolman. Ancient Persian lexicon.—Cuneiform supplement (autographed) to the author's ancient Persian lexicon and texts. ea., $1.25.
Vanderbilt University studies. O. pap. Lemcke.
—Darius I. Behistan inscription. 50 c.
Vanderburgh, F: A:, ed. and tr.
See Sumerian hymns.
Vanderlint, Jacob.
Money answers all things; or, an essay to make money sufficiently plentiful amongst all ranks of people, and increase our foreign and domestick trade; London, 1734. '08(F22) 8°, (Reprints of economic tracts.) subs., per set of 4 tracts, pap., *$2 net. Johns Hopkins.
Van der Smisson, W: H:
See Fraser, W: H:
Van Der Velpen, Jean Baptiste Henry.
Harmony and thorough bass. In 2 v. v. I, Harmony and thorough bass complete. '10(F19) c. 4°, $2. C. F. Summy Co.
Van der Weyden, Roger.
Masterpieces. '08(D12) T. (Dutch painters.) leath., *75 c. net; pap., *25 c. net. Stokes.
Van Deventer, E. M., ["Lawrence L. Lynch."]
Man and master. '08(Mr28) c. il. D. $1; pap., 25 c. Laird.
Sealed verdict; or, by whose hand? '09 (Ap3) c. il. D. $1; pap., 25 c. Laird.
Van Deventer, H. R.
Telephonology; description of modern telephone appliances. '10(Je4) c. il. 4°, $4. McGraw-H.
—, **comp.** Telephone hdbk. on the promotion, organization and construction of telephone lines and systems and the maintenance of telephone apparatus. '10(S) c. 127 p. il. 12°, 50 c. H. R. Van Deventer.
Vandewalker, Nina Catharine.
Kindergarten in American education. '08 (Mr28) por. D. **$1.25 net. Macmillan.
Van de Water, Mrs. Virginia Terhune.
From kitchen to garret. '10(Jl16) c. il. D. (Young farmer's pract. lib.) 75 c. net. Sturgis & W.
Van Dine, J: R:
Wonders of the golden west. '09(D) 160 p. il. 12°, $1. J. S. Ogilvie.
VAN DOORN FAMILY.
See Genealogies: Honeyman, A. V. D.
Van Dresser, Mrs. Jasmine Stone.
Little brown hen hears the song of the nightingale; and The golden harvest; with an introd. by Marg. Beecher White. '08(O24) c. il. S. bds., **75 c. net. Elder.
VAN DYCK, *Sir* Anthony.
Turner, P. M. Van Dyck. *65 c. net. Stokes.
Van Dyke, H: Jackson, D.D.
Counsels by the way. '08(O3) c. D. **$1 net. Crowell.
House of Rimmon: a drama. '08(O10) c. D. **$1 net. Scribner.
Music lover. [New ed.] '09(S4) c. front. D. bds., *50 c. net. Moffat.

Van Dyke, H: Jackson, D.D.—*Continued.*
Out of doors in the Holy Land. '08(O24) c. il. **$1.50 net. Scribner.
Spirit of America. '10(Mr5) c. D. **$1.50 net. Macmillan.
White bees. and other poems. '09(N20) c. D. **$1.25 net. Scribner.
—, **comp.** Poetry of nature. '09(O30) il. O. *$2 net. Doubleday, P.
Van Dyke, J: C:
Money god: chapters of heresy and dissent concerning business methods and mercenary ideals in American life. '08(My9) c. D. **$1 net. Scribner.
New New York: a commentary on the place and the people. '09(S11) c. il. O. **$3.50 net, boxed. Macmillan.
What is art?; studies in the technique and criticism of painting. '10(N12) c. front. D. $1 net. Scribner.
Van Dyke, Rev. Jos. Smith.
"Be of good cheer." '10(O) c. 5-60 p. 16°, $1. J. S. Van Dyke.
Van Dyne, Mrs. Edith.
Aunt Jane's nieces at Millville. '08(N7) c. front. D. 60 c. Reilly & B.
Aunt Jane's nieces at work. '09(D18) c. front. 12°, 60 c. Reilly & B.
Aunt Jane's nieces in society. '10(D3) c. 12°, 60 c. Reilly & B.
Van Dyne, F:
Our foreign service: "A B C" of American diplomacy. '09(Mr27) c. il. O. $2.50. Lawyers' Co-op.
Vane, Sir Fs. Patrick Fletcher.
Walks and people in Tuscany. '10(Ap30) il. D. $1.50 net. **Lane.**
VANE, *Sir* Henry, *jr.*
King, H. M. Sir Henry Vane, Jr., Governor of Massachusetts. $1.25. Preston.
Vane, Victor.
Bankruptcy of Bryan Kane. '10(Ag) 30 p. D. $1.20. Bates.
Van Epps, Howard.
Georgia form book; coll. of legal forms, based on the sections of the code of 1895, and amendments thereto, and the statutes passed since 1895, [etc.] Adapt. especially for the use of judges, justices of the peace, officers of court, lawyers and business men generally. '08(F) c. 1025 p. O. shp., $6. Harrison Co.
VAN EYCK, Hubert *and* Jan.
Konody, P. G. Brothers Van Eyck. 50 c.; $1. Macmillan.
Van Galder, Fk. O., comp.
Mother's day poems, contributed in Modern Woodman contest for the best original poem on mother. '10(My) c. 8+95 p. por. 8°, 30 c. Modern Woodmen.
Van Hise, C: R:
Conservation of natural resources in the United States. '10(O8) c. il. O. $2 net. Macmillan.
—, **and Leith, C: Kenneth.**
Pre-Cambrian geology of North America. '09(N) 939 p. fold. map, O. (U. S., Dept. of the Interior; Geolog. Survey bull.) pap. (Add. Superintendent for price.) U. S., Supt. of Docs.
Vanished Arizona. Summerhayes, *Mrs.* M. $1.60. M. Summerhayes.

Vanished ruin era. Stellman, L: J. $2.50. P. Elder.

Vanishing fleets. Norton, R. †$1.50. Appleton.

Vanishing smuggler. Chalmers, S. $1.50. Clode.

Vanitas. Lee, V., *pseud.* $1.50 net. Lane.

Vanity fair. Thackeray, W: M. *35 c.; *70 c. net. Dutton.

Van Kirk, Ja. W:
Brotherhood: the call of the century. '08 (N7) c. por. D. $1. J. W: Van Kirk.

Van Loan, Ida A.
Tour through the West with the Jersey City Elks, no. 211. '10(Jl16) c. il. por. 12° $1. I. A. Van Loan.

Van Meter, Anna R.
See Bevier, Isabel.

Van Meter, Harriet F., comp. and ed.
First quarter century of the Woman's Christian Temperance Union, Salem, N. J. '09, [1910.] (F) c. 7-129 p. 8°, gratis. H. F. Van Meter.

VAN METRE FAMILY.
See **Genealogies: Smyth, S: G.**

Van Ness, I: J., ed.
Training in church membership. '08(O24) c. 16°, 50 c.; pap., 30 c. S. S. Bd. So. Bapt.

Van Ness, T:
Search for God traced in Hebrew and Christian sources. '10(Ap9) c. 8°, 30 c. Un. S. S. Soc.

Van Norman, Hubert Everett.
First lessons in dairying. '08(Mr7) c. il. 12°, *50 c. net. Judd.

Van Nostrand's chemical annual; ed. by J. C. Olsen. 2d ed., rev. and enl., 1909. '09, [1910.] (F) 592 p. 12°, *$2.50 net. Van Nostrand.

Van Nostrand science ser. il. 16°, bds., 50 c. Van Nostrand.
—Bowles. Tables for the determination of common rocks.
—Cain. Pract. designing of retaining walls. —Theory of solid and braced elastic arches.
—Chatley. How to design an aeroplane.
—Hirschfeld. Engineering thermo-dynamics.
—Plympton. Aneroid barometer.
—Searle. "Sumner's method" for finding a ship's position.
—Wisser. Explosive materials.

Van Ogle, A.
Nobody's cousin. '10(Je) c. 108 p. 12°, 50 c. Cochrane.

Van Ormer, Abraham Brower Bunn.
Studies in religious nurture. '08(Je6) c. 12°, $1. Lutheran Pub.

Van Orsdale, Lynn F:
How to build up a heavy laying strain; thorough and exhaustive treatise on egg production and the conditions which govern the development of a heavy and persistent laying strain of fowls; comp. by Dan. Monroe Green. '09(Mr 6) c. il. 8°, 50 c. Poultry Monthly.

Van Orstrand, C. E., comp.
See Becker, G: F.

Van Peyma, P. W., M.D.
The why of the will: the unity of the universe. '10(S17) c. D. 80 c. net. Sherman, F.

VAN RENSSELAER, Henry.
Spillane, E: P: Life and letters of Henry Van Rensselaer, priest of the Society of Jesus. $1.25. Fordham Univ.

Van Rensselaer, Mrs. J: King.
Nonsuch euchre and kindred games. '08 (F29) c. Tt. pap., $2. Bond.

Van Rensselaer, Kiliaen.
Van Rensselaer Bowier manuscripts: being the letters of Kiliaen Van Rensselaer, 1630-1643, and other documents rel. to the colony of Rensselaerswyck; tr. and ed. by A. J. F. van Laer; with an introd. essay by Nicolas De Roever tr. by Mrs. Alan H. Strong. '08(S19) facsims., maps, 8°, $1.25. N. Y. State Educ.

Van Rensselaer, Mariana Griswold, [Mrs. Schuyler Van Rensselaer.]
History of the city of New York in the seventeenth century. [In 2 v.] '09 (Je12) c. O. **$5 net, boxed. Macmillan.
Poems. '10(O29) c. D. $1.25 net. Macmillan.

Van Rensselaer, Mrs. Schuyler.
See Van Rensselaer, Mariana Griswold.

Van Sant, Eliz., ed.
Munson shorthand dict. written in accordance with Manual of Munson shorthand. '10(Ap9) c. 16°, $1. J. A. Lyons.

Vansant, W: R.
Weaning the nation from strong drink: the crisis and the remedy; legal addenda (chaps. 39, 40, 41 and 42) by L. F. Cummings. '10(Mr) c. 16+9-416 p. col. il. 8°, $1.50. Vansant.

Van Schaack, D:, ed.
Safeguards for the prevention of industrial accidents. '10(My21) c. il. O. pap., 50 c. Ætna Life.

VAN SCHURMAN, Anna Maria.
Birch, U. Anna Van Schurman. *$2 net. Longmans.

Van Slyke, Lucius Lincoln, and Publow, C: Albert.
Science and practice of cheese-making. '08 (Mr27) c. il. tabs., 12°, *$1.75 net. Judd.

Van Speybrouck, Edouard.
Very Rev. Father Paul of Moll; Flemish Benedictine and wonder-worker of the nineteenth century, 1824-1896; tr. from the 2d French ed. by a member of the Order of St. Benedict. '10(Jl) c. 13+17-383 p. il. por. 8°, $1.25. Benedictine.

Van Steinburg, Dora F.
Aunt Tirzah. '10(D31) c. D. B'way Pub.

Van Tuyl, C: H.
See Scott, H. F.

Van Tyne, Claude Halstead.
See Hart, Albert Bushnell.

—, and Leland, Waldo Gifford.
Guide to the archives of the government of U. S. in Washington. 2d ed., rev. and enl. by W. G. Leland. '08(Mr21) Q. (Carnegie Institution of Washington pub.) pap., $1.25. Carnegie.

Van Velzer, Allan Clifford.
Fig culture; being a statement of the hist., varieties and botany of the fig, in Asia, Africa and America, and a special treatise on its propagation, cultivation and curing in North America. '09(D) c. 218 p. il. 16°, $1.50. Dealy.

Van Voorhis, J: S.
Pocket digest of criminal law and procedure. 2d ed. '09(D) c. 80 p. T. pap., 30 c. J: S. Van Voorhis.

Van Vorst, Mrs. J:, [Bessie Van Vorst.]
Cry of the children: study of child-labor; with an introd. by Hon. Albert J. Beveridge. '08(F15) c. D. **$1.25 net. Moffat.

Van Vorst, Marie.
First love. '10(O15) c. il. D. $1.50. Bobbs-M.
Girl from his town. '10(Mr26) c. il. D. †$1.50. Bobbs-M.
In ambush. '09(N13) c. D. †$1.50. Lippincott.
Sentimental adventures of Jimmy Bulstrode. '08(Mr28) c. il. D. †$1.50. Scribner.

Van Wagenen, Anthony.
Government ownership of railways considered as the next great step in American progress. '10(O1) c. D. $1.25. Putnam.

Van Wagenen, Kate.
Dictation day by day; 2d year, 3d year, 4th year, 5th year. 09(My1) 12°, 2d, 3d yrs., ea., *18 c. net; 4th, 5th yrs., ea., *20 c. net. Macmillan.

Van Winkle, Walton, and Eaton, F: M.
Quality of surface waters of California, by Walton Van Winkle and F: M. Eaton, in cooperation with the California Department of Engineering. '10(S) 142 p. fold. map (in pocket) 8°, (U. S., Dept. of the Interior, U. S. Geolog. Survey; water-supply paper.) Gov. Pr. Off.

VAPOR.
See Air;—Electricity.

VAPOR PROCESS.
See Lumber.

VAPORIZERS.
See Engines.

Variation and correlations of certain taxonomic characters of *grylius*. Lutz, F. E. 40 c. Carnegie.

VARIATION OF SPECIES.
Lock, R: H. Recent progress in the study of variation, heredity and evolution. $2 net. Dutton.
See also Mice.

Variations of latitude, 1899 to 1906. Porter, J. G. $1. Univ. of Cin.

Variations on an old theme. Pirscher, J. $1. Badger.

Varieties of the United States cents of 1796. Gilbert, E: H. $1. T: L. Elder.

Various verses. Bell, W: T. $1. Cochrane.

Varley, Rev. Telford.
Hampshire. '09(Je12) il. map, 8°, *$6 net. Macmillan.
Winchester. '10(Ag13) il. 8°, (Color books ser. of travel and description.) $3 net. Macmillan.

Varmint (The). Johnson, O. M. $1.50. Baker & T.

Varney, G: Leon, ed.
Favorite poems of famous people. '10(Jl2) c. por. 12°, $1.50. Vaughan Pub.

Varney, G: Reuben.
Out of the depths. '09(Je19) c. front. O. *$1.25 net. Am. Bapt.

VASCULAR PLANTS.
See Botany.

VASCULAR SYSTEM.
See Blood.

VASES.
See Ceramics.

VASILIKI, Crete.
See Crete (*Island of*).

Vassalage. Bell, A. F. $1.50. C. M. Clark.

VASSAR COLLEGE, Poughkeepsie, N. Y.
Wood, F. A. Earliest years at Vassar. 50 c. F. A. Wood.

VATICAN (The), Rome.
Sladen, D. B. W. Secrets of the Vatican. $2.50 net. Lippincott.

Vaubert, T. F.
How to walk before God; or, the holy exercise of the presence of God. In 3 pts; tr. from the French. Rev. ed. '10 (F) 149 p. 24°, 40 c. Herder.

VAUDEVILLE.
See Actors and actresses.

Vaudry, Telesphor, Smith-.
See Smyth-Vaudry, Telesphor.

Vaughan, Carrie Bourne.
Out of the depths: [poems.] '08(F8) c. D. bds., $1.25. Badger.

Vaughan, C: Edwyn.
Types of tragic drama. '08(Mr21) 8°, *$1.60 net. Macmillan.

Vaughan, D: Davies.
Lessons for Methodists. '10(My14) c. il. pors. 12°, $1. Jennings.

Vaughan, Earnest Vancourt.
Origin and early development of the English universities to the close of the XIII. century. '08(D5) c. Q. (Univ. of Mo. studies; social science ser.) (Add. Univ. for price.) Univ. of Mo.

Vaughan, Lawrence Ja.
Life and works of Father Vaughan; pt. 1, embracing sermons, lectures, poems and dissertations; pt. 2, embracing "A woman of the west" and other subject matter. In 2 v. '10(F5) c. il. 8°, $9; hf. mor., $12; mor., $15. Vaughan Pub.

VAUGHAN, Herbert, *Cardinal*, 1832-1903.
Snead-Cox, F. G. Life of Cardinal Vaughan. 2 v. $7 net. Herder.

Vaughan, Herbert Millingchamp, 1870-.
Medici popes, (Leo X. and Clement VII.) '08(O17) il. O. *$4 net. Putnam.

Vaughan, Rev. J: S.
Dangers of the day; with an introd. by Mgr. Canon Moyes. '09(Mr13) c. D. $1. Ave Maria.
Sermons from Shakespeare. '09(Ap) c. 124 p. por. 12°, $1. Bartlett.

Vaughan, Owen, ["Owen Rhoscomyl."]
A scout's story. '10(S17) front. D. $1.25. Estes.
Vronina. '08(O3) c. D. †$1.50. Dodd.

Vaughan's practical review for law students. Flanigan, D: W., *comp.* $5. D: W. Flanigan.

Vaughn, Mrs. W. W.
See Symonds, Marg.

Vauvenargues, Luc de Clapier, Marquis de.
See Pascal, B. L. R., *Duc* de, *Prince* de Marsillas.

Vay de Vaya and Luskod, Count.
Inner life of the United States. '08(N21) 8°, watered silk, *$4 net. Dutton.
Vayenne. Brebner, P. J. $1.50. J. McBride.
Veach, Rob. Wells.
King and his kingdom. '08(Je27) c. 12°, *60 c. net; pap., *35 c. net. Revell.
Veatch, Byron Elbert.
Men who dared. '09(Ap3) D. $1.50. Harisun.
Veatch, Otto.
Second rept. on the clay deposits of Georgia. '09(Je) 453 p. il. maps. 4°, (Georgia Geological Survey bull.) pap., gratis. S: W. McCallie.
Vecki, Victor G.
Prevention of sexual diseases; with introd. by W: J. Robinson. '10(S) c. 132 p. O. $1.50 net. J: J. Newbegin.
VECTOR ANALYSIS.
See Mathematics.
Vectors and vector diagrams. Cramp, W: *$2.50 net. **Longmans.**
VEDANTA PHILOSOPHY.
See Hinduism;—Vedas.
VEDAS.
Bloomfield, M. Religion of the Veda. **$1.50 net. Putnam.
Vedder, Elihu.
Digressions of V. '10(N19) c. il. O. $6 net. Houghton M.
Vedder, H: Clay, D.D.
American writers of to-day. [New ed., rev.] '10(D17) c. D. $1.50. Silver.
Christian epoch-makers: story of the great missionary eras in the history of Christianity. '08(Ag1) c. D. **$1.20 net. Am. Bapt.
Church history handbooks. Bk. 1, The early period. '09(Ap10); Bk. 2, The period of the Reformation. (Ap17); Bk. 3, Modern church history, from the Reformation to the close of the nineteenth century. (My15); bk. 4, Baptist hist. (O9) c. D. ea., **40 c. net. Am. Bapt.
Our New Testament; how did we get it? '08(D19) c. O. **$1 net. Am. Bapt.
"Vedette," pseud.
See Fitchett, *Rev.* W: H:
"Vedra, Yarmo," pseud.
See Merton, Holmes Whittier.
VEERE, Scotland.
See Scotland.
Vega, Garcilasso de la.
Obras; principe de los poetas castellanos. [facsim.] '03, [1909.] (N) 8°, $5. (200 copies.) Hispanic Soc.
VEGA, Lope de.
See Theatre.
Vega Carpio, Lope Félix de.
Rimas; aora de nvevo añadidas con el nvevoavte de hazer Comedias defte tiempo. 2 v. [facsim.] '03, [1909.] (N) 8°, ea., $4.50. (200 copies.) Hispanic Soc.
Romancero espiritval. para recrearse el alma con Dios. [facsim.] '03, [1909.] (N) 136 p. 8°, $6. (200 copies.) Hispanic Soc.
Vege-men's revenge. Upton, B. $1 net. Longmans.
VEGETABLE GARDENING.
See Gardens and gardening.

Vegetable proteins. Osborne, T: B. *$1.20 net. Longmans.
VEGETABLES.
Wickson, E: J. California vegetables in garden and field. $2. Pacific Rural.
See also Asparagus;—Beans;—Cabbage;—Cookery;—Farms and farming;—Gardens and gardening;—Legumes; — Onions; — Potato;—Preserving;—Seeds;—Sweet potato.
VEGETARIANISM.
Buttner, J. L. Fleshless diet. $1.35 net. Stokes.
Christian, E. Suncooked food. $1. Christians' Sch.
Colcord, *Mrs.* A. L. Friend in the kitchen: [vegetarian recipes.] 50 c.; 25 c. Review and Herald Pub.
Fulton, E. G. Vegetarian cook-book. $1. Pacific Press.
George, F. A. Vegetarian cookery. $1.25. Longmans.
Hanish, O. Z.-A. Mazdaznan encyclop. of dietetics and home cook book. $1.25. Mazdaznan.
Hazeldine, N. F. W. Therapeutic dietetics; or, the science of health food and their medicinal values. $1. N. F. W. Hazeldine.
Just, A. Jungborn dietary: vegetarian cookery book. 75 c. net. Dutton.
Rorer, *Mrs.* S. T. H. Vegetable cookery and meat substitutes. **$1.50 net. Arnold.
Sharpe, *Mrs.* M. R. L. Golden rule cook book; 600 recipes for meatless dishes. $2 net. Little, B. & Co.
Tanner, H: S: Human body a volume of divine revelations: [vegetarianism.] 35 c. H: S: Tanner.
See also Cookery.
Vegetation affected by agriculture in Central America. Cook, O. F. (Add. Superintendent for price. U. S., Supt. of Docs.
Vehicles of the air. Lougheed, V. *$2.50 net. Reilly & B.
Vehling, Paul.
Die moral des hotels. '10(Jl30) c. D. $1. Didion.
Veihmeyer, Fk.
See Patterson, *Mrs.* Flora Wambaugh
Veil (The). Norris, M. H. $1.50. Badger.
Veil (The). Stevens, E. S. †$1.50. Stokes.
Veiller, Lawrence.
Housing reform; hdbk. for pract. use in American cities. '10(Ap2) c. O. (Russell Sage Foundation pubs.) $1.25. Charities Pub.
Model tenement house law. '10(Je4) c. 8°, (Russell Sage Foundation, pub.) $1.25. Charities Pub.
Veitch, F. P.
See Wiley, Harvey Washington.
Veitch, H: Newton.
Sheffield plate: its history, manufacture and art; with makers' names and marks. '08 (D12) il. 4°, *$8 net. Macmillan.
VELASQUEZ, Diego Rodriquez de Silva.
Calvert, A. F:, *and* Hartley, C. G. Velasquez. *$1.25 net. Lane.
Veldt, the lion hunter. Reilly, J. M. $1.25. B'way Pub.
Velour series. In 12 v. '09(D25) Tt. per set of 6 v., $1.50, boxed. Stokes.

Venable, Emerson, ed.
Poets of Ohio; with biographical sketches and notes. '09(O30) c. front. O. **$1.50 net. Clarke.

Venable, W: H:
Floridian sonnets. '10(F19) por. D. $1. Badger.

Venable, W: Mayo.
Methods and devices for bacterial treatment of sewage. '08(Mr21) figs. 8°, $3. Wiley.

VENEREAL DISEASES.
Baum, W: L., *and* Moyer, H. N:, *eds.* Skin and venereal diseases. $1.25. Year Bk.
Baumann, F: Gonorrhea, its diagnosis and treatment. **$1.50 net. Appleton.
Cordiero, F. J. B. Gonorrhea. *25 c. net. W: R. Jenkins.
Dock, L. L. Hygiene and morality. $1.25. Putnam.
Findley, P. Gonorrhea in women. $2. Mosby.
Herb, F. Gonorrhea and sexual debility in men. $2.50. , R. & S. Pub.
Holt, W: L., *and* Robinson, W: J. Venereal peril; popular treatise on venereal diseases. 50 c. Altrurians.
Leedham-Green, C: Treatment of gonorrhea in the male. 2d ed. *$2 net. Wood.
Rupp, F: A. Purity and truth; letters of a physician to his daughters on the great black plague. 50 c. Vir
Vecki, V. G. Prevention of sexual diseases. $1.50 net. J: J. Newbegin.
White, J. W:, *and* Martin, E: Genito-urinary surgery and venereal diseases. $6. Lippincott.
Wilcox, S. S. Essentials of genito-urinary and venereal diseases. $1. Saunders.
See also Syphilis.

Venetia and northern Italy Headlam, C. *$2.50 net. Macmillan.
Venetian ser. 16°, pap., 50 c. net; cel., $1 net. T: B. Mosher.
—Browning. Italy, my Italy.
—Rossetti. Dante at Verona.
—Swinburne. Siena.

VENEZUELA, South America.
Ambard, E. M. Tourist guide to the West Indies, Venezuela and Isthmus of Panama. (gratis to passengers.) Hamburg-American Line.
Beebe, *Mrs.* M. B. R. *and* C: W: Our search for a wilderness. $2.75 net. Holt.
Bingham, H. Journal of an expedition across Venezuela and Colombia, 1906-'07. *$2.25 net. Yale Pub.
Corlett, W: T: American tropics: [West Indies, Central America, Venezuela.] $1.50. Burrows.
International Bureau of American Republics. Venezuela. (Add. pubs. for price.) Int. Bu. Am. Republics.
Moore, J. H. With Speaker Cannon through the Tropics: voyage to the West Indies, Venezuela and Panama. $2. Book Pr.
Thurber, O. E. Venezuelan question; Castro and the asphalt trust from official records. (Add. author for price.) O. E. Thurber.

VENEZUELA.—*Continued.*
United States. *Dept. of State.* Correspondence rel. to wrongs done to American citizens by the government of Venezuela. $1.50. U. S., Supt. of Docs.

VENICE, Italy.
Bacher, O. H: With Whistler in Venice. **$4 net. Century Co.
Crawford, F. M. Venice, the place and the people. 2 v. *$5 net. Macmillan.
Douglas, H. A. Venice and her treasures. *$1.50 net. Scribner.
G., A. E. Modern art at Venice. $2 net. Bowles.
Hare, A: J: C. Florence; [also] Venice. $2. Macmillan.
Molmenti, P. G. Venice; from the earliest beginnings to the time of the republic. In 3 pts. of 2 v. ea. pt. 3 in 2 v., The decadence. *$5 net; *$10 net. (Sold only in 2 v. sections.) McClurg.
Monnier, P. Venice in the eighteenth century. $3 net. Badger.
Okey, T: Venice and its story. $4 net. Dutton.
Ruskin, J: Stones of Venice. 3 v. ea., *$1 net. Dutton.
Staley, E. The dogaressas of Venice. $3.50 net. Scribner.
Thayer, W: R. Short history of Venice. *$1.50 net. Houghton M.
Weil, A. Navy of Venice. $5 net. Dutton.
See also Italy.

Venice preserved. *See* Otway, T: The orphan.
Venomous snakes. Fayre, C:, *ed.* *75 c. net. Macmillan.

VENOMS.
See Poisons.

VENTILATION.
American School of Correspondence. Heating and ventilation. pt. 1. $1.50. Am. Sch. Corr.
Baldwin, W: J. S. Ventilation of our court rooms and halls of justice. gratis. W: J. S. Baldwin.
Hoffman, J. D., *and* Raber, B: F: Hdbk. for heating and ventilating engineers. $3.50. J. D: Hoffman.
Hubbard, C: L. Fans, ventilation and heating. 25 c. Indust. Press.
Hubbard, C: L. Heating and ventilation. $1.50. Am. Sch. Corr.
Hubbard, C: L. Power, heating and ventilation. 3 v. $5 net. Technical Press.
King, A. G. Practical steam and hot water heating and ventilation. $3. Henley.
King, F. H. Ventilation for dwellings, rural schools and stables. 75 c. F. H. King.
Sloper, G: A. Air and ventilation of subways. $2.50. Wiley.
Wilson, G: B. Air-conditioning: treatise on humidification, ventilation, cooling, and the hygiene of textile factories. $1.50. Wiley.
Young, G: J. Ventilating-system at the Comstock mines. gratis. Univ. of Nev.
See also Fans;—Greenhouses;—Heating.

Venture in 1777. Mitchell, S. W. †$1.25. Jacobs.

Venture of rational faith. Benson, M. *$2 net. Macmillan.

VENUS Transit of.
See Astronomy.

VERA CRUZ, Mexico.
See Mexico.

Vera of the strong heart. Mole, M. $1.25. Putnam.

Vera scienza e vera religione. Miraglia-Gullotti, P. V. 30 c. P. V. Miraglia-Gullotti.

Vera, the medium. Davis, R: H. †$1.50. Scribner.

Vera's charge. Tiernan, *Mrs.* F. C. F. $1.50. Ave Maria.

Verbal notes and sketches for marine engineers. Sothern, J. W. *$2.60 net. Macmillan.

Verbeck, G.
Terrors of the Tiny Tads. '09(D18) il. bds., 60 c. Cupples & L.

Ver Beck, Mrs. Hanna Rion.
Garden in the wilderness, by a hermit. '09 (N6) il. D. **$1.50 net. Baker & T.
Smiling road. '10(N12) c. il. D. $1 net. Clode.

Verdy du Vernois, Julius von.
Studies in the leading of troops; tr. from the German by W: Gerlach. '07, [1909.] (N) $1.50. Hudson.

Verhoeff, Carolyn.
Four little Fosters. '08, [1909.] (F) c. 16+295 p. il. 12°, $1.15. A. H. Crist.

VERLAINE, Paul.
Lepelletier, E. A. de B. Life of Paul Verlaine. **$3.50 net. Duffield.

Verland, Frenharte.
Affinities who never meet. '10(O15) c. D. pap., 25 c. Homingwood.

Vermeer, Johannes.
Masterpieces of Johannes Vermeer (of Delft). '10(S10) il. T. (Dutch painters' ser.) leath., 75 c. net; pap., 25 c. net. Stokes.

VERMIFORM APPENDIX.
See Appendicitis.

Vermilion pencil. Lea, H. †$1.50. McClure.

Vermin in the dark. Markham, E. *See* Langdon, W: H.

Vermix (La): the harvest. Cole, S. $1.50. Connoisseurs' Press.

Vermont. *Geological survey.* Rept. of the state geologist on the mineral industries and geology of certain areas of Vermont, 1907-1908. '08, [1909] (Mr) 11+302 p. il. diagrs., 8°. (Add. pub. for price.) G: H. Perkins

Vermont. Public statutes of 1906; incl. the public acts of 1906 with the Declaration of Independence, the Articles of Confederation and the Constitutions of the U. S. and the state of Vt. '07, [1908.] (My.) c. 20+1302+380 p. Q. shp. (Add. pub. for price.) Vermont Lib.

Vermont. *Supreme ct.* Repts.; (J: W. Redmond.) v. 80. '08(Je); v. 81. '09(S) ea., $4; v. 82. '10(Mr) c. O. shp., $2.75. Free Press.

VERMONT.
Cram, J. Journal of a missionary tour through the new settlements of northern New Hampshire and Vermont. $1.50. G: P. Humphrey.
Dale, T: N. Granites of Vermont. U. S., Supt. of Docs.
Greene, F. L. Vermont, the Green Mountain state. gratis. C: S. Forbes.
See also Forests and forestry;—*also* Lake Champlain;—Rockingham;—Waitsfield.

Vermont digest, 1789-1905; by Rob. Roberts. '10(Jl) c. O. shp., $10. Free Press.

Vermont Forest Service pubs. 8°. A. F. Hawes.
—Hawes. Forest fires in Vermont. gratis.

Verne, Jules.
Abandoned. '09(Ap3) il. 16°, (Everyman's lib.) *35 c. net; leath., *70 c. Dutton.
Čarov posol; alebo; Strašné útrapy a dobrodruzstvá Michala Strogova; Román dl'a spisu Juliusa Verne. Poslovencil: "Slovák v Amerike." '10(Ag) 282 p. pls. 8°, $1. Slovak Press.
Dropped from the clouds. '09(Ap3) il. 16°, (Everyman's lib.) *35 c. net; leath., *70 c. net. Dutton.
From the earth to the moon. '08(Jl4) 12°, (Young America lib.) 50 c. Hurst.
Secret of the island. '09(Ap3) il. 16°, (Everyman's lib.) *35 c. net; leath., *70 c. net. Dutton.
Twenty thousand leagues under the sea. '08(S19) 16°, (Everyman's lib.) *35 c. net; leath., *70 c. net. Dutton.

Vernon, A.
Estate fences. '09(D18) price reduced from $6 to $3.50. Spon.

Vernon, Ambrose White.
See Morse, C: H.
—, ed. *See* Coffin, H: Sloan, *ed.*

Vernon, H. M. and Mrs. K. Dorothea Ewart.
Hist. of the Oxford Museum. '10(F19) il. S. 50 c. Oxford Univ.

Vernon, Mrs. H. M.
See Vernon, *Mrs.* K. Dorothea Ewart.

Vernon, Jos. Stanton.
Along the Old Trail; history of the old and a story of the new Santa Fe trail. [1910.] (N) c. 160 p. il. 8°, $1. Tucker-V.

Vernon, Mrs. K. Dorothea Ewart, [Mrs. H. M. Vernon.]
Italy from 1494 to 1790. '09(Mr) 8+516 p. 8°, (Cambridge historical ser.) *$1.75 net. Putnam.
See also Vernon, H. M.

Vernon, Max, pseud.
See Kellogg, Vernon Lyman.

Vernon, W: Warren.
Readings on Purgatorio of Dante; chiefly based on the Commentary of Benvenuto da Imola; text and literal translation by W: W. Vernon; introd. by the late Dean Church. In 2 v. 3d ed., rev. '08(Ja11) 12°, *$4 net. Macmillan.
Readings on the Paradiso of Dante; chiefly based on the commentary of Benvenuto da Imola; with an introd. by the Bishop of Ripon. 2d ed., rev. '09(F20) 2 v., plans, D. *$4 net. Macmillan.

VERNON, Ct.
Vital records of Bolton to 1854 and Vernon to 1852. $3. Conn. Hist.

VERONA, Italy.
Allen, A. M. Hist. of Verona. $3.50. Putnam.

Veronese, Paul, [Paolo Cagliari.]
Masterpieces of Veronese; sixty reproductions of photographs from the orig. paintings. '08(Ag8) T. (Painters' ser.) pap., *25 c. net; leath., *75 c. net, boxed. Stokes.

Veronica Playfair. Goodwin, *Mrs.* M. W. $1.50. Little, B. & Co.

Verplanck, Virginia Eliza Everett, [Mrs. W. E. Verplanck.]
Year in my garden; manual on the culture of flowers, vegetables and fruits. '10 (F12) O. $1. W: E. Verplanck.

Verplanck, Mrs. W. E.
See Verplanck, Virginia Eliza Everett.

Verplanck, W: E:, and Collyer, Moses Wakeman.
Sloops of the Hudson: sketch of the packet and market sloops of the last century. '08 (D26) c. il. D. **$1.50 net. Putnam.

Verrall, Anthony.
New commandment. '09(S18) c. D. *$1 net. Clode.

Verrill, Harry Mighels, and Booth, C: Dunbar.
Maine civil officer: guide and hdbk. for attorneys, trial justices, justices of the peace; with practical forms, rev. and enl. 7th ed. '08(O) c. 8+1110 p. 8°, $6. Loring, S. & H.

VERSAILLES, France.
See Petit Trianon.

Verschoyle, W. Denham.
Electricity: what is it? '08(Je6) il. 12°, *$1 net. Macmillan.

Verse and toast. Rowe, W: H., *jr.* 2 v. $1. W: H. Rowe.

Verse satire in England before the Renaissance. Tucker, S: M. *$1 net. Lemcke.

Verses. Peffley, D. F. (Not for sale.) D. F. Peffley.

Verses. Wells, *Mrs.* G. S. (Priv. pr.) Donnelley.

VERSIFICATION.
Bennett, P. P. Compact rhyming dict. 50 c. Dutton.
Bright, J. W., *and* Miller, R. D. Elements of English versification. Ginn.
Brown, W. Time in English verse rhythm: empirical study of typical verses by the graphic method. 70 c. Science Pr., (N. Y.)
Schipper, J. Hist. of English versification. $2. Oxford Univ.
See also Poetry;—Prosody.

VERTEBRATES.
Eigenmann, C. H. Cave vertebrates of America: study in degenerate evolution. $5. Carnegie
Gaskell, W. H. Origin of vertebrates. *$6 net. Longmans.
See also Amphibia;—Animals;—Birds; — Fish; — Marine zoology;—Reptiles;—Snakes;—Zoology.

Very first book. Donovan, M. 20 c.; 10 c. Hinds.

Very first series. v. 1-8. '09(D); v. 9, 10. '10(D) col. il. 12°, ea., 25 c. Doran.
Contents: My very first little book of letters; My very first little spelling book; My very first little arithmetic book; My very first little reading book; My very first little poetry book; My very first little history book; My very first little French book; My very first little book of countries; My very first book of animals; My very first Bible book.

VESALIUS, Andreas.
Ball, J. M. Andreas Vesalius. $5. Medical Science.

VESPUCCI, Amerigo.
See Waldseemüller, Martin.

Vest-pocket diary and memorandum book for the soldier. '09(Ag) 35 c. Hudson.

Vest-pocket handbook of mathematics for engineers. Waterbury, L. A. **$1.50 net. Wiley.

Vest pocket limericks. '09(Je19) c. Tt. bds., *50 c. net. Ball Pub. Co.

Vest-pocket memory-test Latin word-list. Browne, G: H: 75 c.; also, A memory-test note-book. 15 c. Ginn.

Vest pocket reference book ser. Ogilvie's (formerly Hill's). 30 v. ea., 25 c.; leath., 50 c. McKay.
—Conklin's Argument settler; Civil and business law; Don'ts for speakers and writers; 50,000 word speller and letter writer's manual; 500 ways to make money; Familiar quotations; Rapid commercial calculator; Proverbs and epigrams; Synonyms and antonyms; Shakespearean manual; Who wrote that—prose selections; Who wrote that—poetic selections; Who said that?; Writing desk book; Way to think and how to remember.
—Hill's Bridge whist; Hoyle's games; Rules of order.
—Hill's dictionaries: French-English, English-French; German-English, English-German; Italian-English, English-Italian; Latin-English, English-Latin; Spanish-English, English-Spanish; Swedish-English, English-Swedish.
—Jefferson Bible.
—Ogilvie's Concise atlas and gazetteer.
—Russell's Faulty diction.
—Thimm's French self taught; German self taught.
—Webster's Vest pocket dictionary (Hill's).

Vest pocket ser. See Mosher's.

Vest pocket toast book. '09(N6) c. T. 25 c.; leath., 50 c. Saalfield.

VESTMENTS.
See Catholic church;—Church of England.

VESTS.
See Tailoring.

VETERINARY MEDICINE AND SURGERY.
Baker, A. H. Theory and practice of veterinary medicine. $3.50. A. Eger.
Barton, F. T. Vet. book. *$1 net. Lane.
Brumley, O. V. Book of veterinary posology and prescriptions. $1.25. O. V. Brumley.
Burkett, C: W: Farmer's veterinarian. *$1.50 net. Judd.
Burnett, S: H. Clinical pathology of the blood of domesticated animals. *$2.50 net. Taylor & C.
Fair, W: C. People's home stock book. $3. R. C. Barnum.

VETERINARY MEDICINE AND SURGERY.—*Cont.*
Friedberger, F., *and* Fröhner, E. Veterinary pathology. 2 v. *$8 net. Chic. Med. Bk.
Kaupp, B: F. Animal parasites and parasitic diseases. $2.25. A. Eger.
Kinsley, A. T. Textbk. of veterinary pathology. $4; $4.50. A. Eger.
Malkmus, B. Outlines of clinical diagnostics of the internal diseases of domestic animals. $3. A. Eger.
Meinert, F. Biochemical treatment of domestic animals. $2. J: H. Meinert.
Mohler, J: R., *and* Rosenau, M. J. Origin of the recent outbreak of foot-and-mouth disease in the U. S. (Add. Superintendent for price.) U. S., Supt. of Docs.
Moore, V. A. Pathology and differential diagnosis of infectious diseases of animals. *$4 net. Taylor & C.
People's home library; people's home medical book, people's home recipe book, people's home stock book. $4.50. R. C. Barnum.
Rosenberg, A. v. Pocketbook of veterinary medical practice. 75 c. Boericke & T.
Rutherford, F. E. Private lessons on diseases of the horse and cow. $5. F. E. Rutherford.
Sisson, S. Text-book of veterinary anatomy. $7. Saunders.
White, G: R. Restraint of domestic animals. $3.75. G: R. White.
Williams, W. L. Veterinary obstetrics; incl. the diseases of breeding animals and of the new-born. $8. W. L. Long.
Winslow, K. Prevention and treatment of diseases of the domestic animals, including etiology and symptoms. $3.50.—Veterinary materia medica and therapeutics. $6. W: R. Jenkins.
See also Anatomy;—Bacteria;—Cat; — Cattle; — Dog;—Hog;—Horse; — Loco plant; — Poultry; —Serum;—Tetanus;—Tuberculosis.

Veth, Rev. Martin.
Medal or cross of St. Benedict. Rev. ed. '08(Ja25) il. 24°, pap., 5 c. Abbey Student.

Veto power in the several states; comp. and annot. by Arth. Crawford Wyman and Grace Mabel Sherwood. '07, '08(Je) 57 p. O. (Rhode Island State Lib., Legislative reference bull.) pap. (Add. pub. for price.) R. I. State Lib.

Viaud, Louis Marie Julien, ["Pierre Loti."]
Egypt (La mort de Philae); tr. from the French by W. P. Baines. '10(Ja29) c. col. il. O. **$2.50 net. Duffield.

Viavi hygiene. Law, H. $1. Viavi.

VIBRATION.
Atkinson, W: W. Practical mental influence: mental vibrations, [etc.] 50 c. Lycet Bk.
Woodruff, W: L. Therapeutics of light vibration. *$1.50 net. J. F. Elwell.
See also Personality.

Vibration ser. *See* Woodruff, W: Lawrence.

Vibrations of systems having one degree of freedom. Hopkinson, B. 75 c. net. Putnam.

Vicar of Sesenheim. Goethe, J. W. v. 35 c. **Holt.**

Vicar of the marches. Scollard, C. $1.20 net. Sherman, F.

Vicar of Wakefield. *See* Goldsmith, Oliver.

Vicar of Wakefield: [play.] Merington, M. $1.25. Duffield.

Vicious virtuoso. Lombard, L: 75 c. Estes.

Vicissitudes of Evangeline. Glyn, *Mrs.* E. S. †$1.50. Duffield.

VICKSBURG CAMPAIGN.
Hobart, E. L. Story of Vicksburg and Jackson. 25 c. E. L. Hobart.
Illinois. Illinois at Vicksburg. $4; $5. Blakely.
Vilas, W: F. View of the Vicksburg campaign. $1. Wisconsin Hist.

Victor, Ralph.
Comrades at school. '09(Ag14) il. 12°. (Comrades ser. for boys.) 60 c. Chatterton-P.
Comrades at Winton Hall; or, cadet pranks and winter sports. '09(Ag14) c. il. 12°, (Comrades ser. for boys.) 60 c. Chatterton-P.
Comrades in New York. '08(Je20) c. il. D. (Comrades ser. for boys.) 60 c. Chatterton-P.
Comrades on river and lake. '10(Jl2) c. il. D. 60 c. Chatterton.
Comrades on the farm. '08(My23) c. il. D. (Comrades ser. for boys.) 60 c. Chatterton-P.
Comrades on the great divide; or, the Aztec search. '09(Ag14) c. il. 12°, (Comrades ser. for boys.) 60 c. Chatterton-P.
Comrades on Winton Oval; or, the fight for the silver pennant. '09(Ag14) c. il. 12°, (Comrades ser. for boys.) 60 c. Chatterton-P.

Victor (The). Holmes, R: S. $1.50. Revell.

VICTORIA, *Queen of England.*
Argyll, J: D. S., *Duke* of. Life of Queen Victoria. *$1 net. Macmillan.
Hird, F. Victoria, the woman. **$2.50 net. Appleton.
Molloy, J. F. Victoria Regina. *$6 net. Dodd.

Victoria history of the counties of England; ed. by W: Page. In 174 v. '08(Ap18) 8°. (Add. pubs. for price.) Dutton.

VICTORIAN AGE.
See England.

Victorian chancellors. Atlay, J. B. In 2 v. v. 2. *$4 net. Little, B. & Co.

Victorious life. Halsted, L. B. $1.50. Metropolitan Press, (N. Y.)

Victorious manhood. Johnston, H. A. *75 c. net. Revell.

Victory (The). Gabriel, C: H., *ed.* 20 c. Jennings.

Victory (The). Watson, *Mrs.* A. W. R. $1.50. A. W. R. Watson.

Victory of Allan Rutledge. Corkey, A. $1.50. H. K. Fly.

Vidal, Emmanuel.
History and methods of the Paris Bourse. '10(N) 276 p. facsims., 8°. Gov. Pr. Off.

Viebig, Clara.
Absolution; tr. by H. Raahauge. '08(Je6) D. †$1.50. Lane.
Our daily bread; tr. by Marg. L. Clarke. '08(D5) D. $1.50. Lane.

Vielé, Herman Knickerbocker.
Heartbreak Hill. '08(O10) c. il. 12°, †$1.50. Duffield.
Inn of the Silver Moon. '08(D5) 12°, $1.25. Duffield.
Myra of the Pines. '09(Je5) 12°, †$1.50. Duffield.
On the lightship; with an introd. by T: Janvier. '09(O16) 8°, *$1.50 net. Duffield

VIENNA.
Society recollections in Paris and Vienna, 1879-1904. $3. Appleton.

Viereck, G: Sylvester.
Confessions of a barbarian. '10(Ap30) c. D. $1.25 net. Moffat.

—, Oppenheim, Ja., Kauffman, Reginald Wright, and others.
"The younger choir"; book of poems from the younger writers of poetry in America; with an introd. by Edn. Markham. '10(Ap23) 12°, Japan vellum, $1 net; autographed copies, $2.50 net. Moods.

View of the Vicksburg campaign. Vilas, W. F. $1. Wisconsin Hist.

Views and reviews. James, H: *$1.50 net; *$2.50 net. Ball Pub. Co.

Views of the Mission Mountains, Flathead Lake and Valley, Montana; with pictures fr. the Flathead Indian reservation. '08 (Ag22) obl. D. parchment, $1. M. J. Elrod.

Views on occupations in their relation to the tariff. Atkinson, E. (Add. Superintendent for price.) U. S., Supt. of Docs.

Vigilante girl. Hart, J. A. $1.50. McClurg.

VIGNAY, Jehan de.
Snavely, G. E. Æsopic fables in the Mireoir Historical of Jehan de Vignay. gratis. Johns Hopkins.

Vignier, R. M. de.
Model steam engine design. '08(F8) c. il. 8°, pap., 25 c. Spon.

Vigny, Alfred Victor, Comte de.
Chatterton; ed. by E. Lauvrière. '09(Ap3) S. (Oxford higher French ser.) $1. Oxford Univ.
Servitude et grandeur militaires; ed. by C. L. Freeman. '08(Ja18) D. (Oxford mod. French ser.) 60 c. Oxford Univ.

Vigorous Daunt: billionaire. Pratt, A. *$1 net. Fenno.

Vigouroux, G: E., ed.
Diary of a mining investor, graphically describing all of the incidents and experiences of an individual who for a period of twelve years has followed mining stocks. '10(N5) c. facsims., 8°, $1. Quick News.

Viking's skull. Carling, J: R. †75 c. Little, B. & Co.

Vilas, W: Freeman.
View of the Vicksburg campaign: paper read before the Madison Literary Club, Oct. 14, 1907. '08(D5) por. map, O. (Wisconsin History Commission; original papers.) bds., $1. Wisconsin Hist.

Villa Claudia. Mitchell, J: A. 50 c. Life Pub. Co.

Villa Rubein. Galsworthy, J: †$1.50. Putnam.

Village (The) beautiful. '10(N5) c. il. $3. Fellowcraft Shop.

Village by the sea. Popham, W: L. 50 c. W: L. Popham.

Village mystery. Mason, B: F. B'way Pub.

Village of vagabonds. Smith, F. B. $1.50 fixed. Doubleday, P.

Village sermons for Lent. Williams, J. H. *80 c. net. Whittaker.

VILLAGES.
New York [State.] Bender's village laws of the state. $5. M. Bender.
New York [State.] Village law. $3. Banks & Co.
See also Towns:—*also* names of states.

Villard, Oswald Garrison.
John Brown, 1800-1859; biography fifty years after. '10(O1) il. pors. O. $5 net. Houghton M.

Villari, Pasquale.
Mediæval Italy; from Charlemagne to Henry VII. '10(N19) 8°, $3.75. Scribner.

Ville, Georges.
Artificial manures; their chemical selection and scientific application to agriculture; tr. and ed. by Sir W: Crookes. New ed., rev. by Sir W: Crookes and J: Percival. '09(Jl17) il. foid tab., O. *$3 net. Longmans.

Villehardouin, Geoffroi de, and Joinville, Jean de.
Chronicles of the crusades. '08(S19) 16°, (Everyman's lib.) *35 c. net; leath., *70 c. net. Dutton.

Villette. *See* Brontë, Charlotte.

Villiers, Arnold.
Complete letter-writer for ladies and gentlemen. New ed., rewritten. '10(Jl30) 8°, 50 c. net. Dutton.
Dict. of foreign and American literature. '10(F19) 32°, (Miniature reference lib.) im. mor., 50 c. Dutton.

—, ed. Routledge's everyman's cyclop. of biography, history, geography, general information, law, spelling, abbreviations, synonyms, pseudonyms, etc. '10(Ap16) O. $1.50 net. Dutton.

Villiers, G:, Duke of Buckingham.
See Dryden, J:

VILLIERS, George, *Duke of Buckingham.*
Gibbs, P. H. Romance of George Villiers. *$3.50 net. Putnam.

Villiers, Rev. H: Montagu.
Perfect through suffering; being thoughts on the Book of Job; taken from addresses given at St. Paul's, Kingsbridge; with a prefatory memoir by Rev. W. E. Newbolt. '09(N13) por. D. *$1.50 net. Longmans.

Villiers-Stuart, Gerald.
See Stuart, Gerald Villiers-

Villiers-Wardell, Janie, [Mrs. Louie Villiers-Wardell.]
Spain of the Spanish. '09(D11) il. pors. D. *$1.50 net. Scribner.

Villuga, Pedro Juan.
Reportorio de todos los caminos de España; hasta agora nunca visto enel ql aliara qlquier viaje q quiera andar muy p uechoso pa todos los caminantes. [facsim.] '02, [1909.] (N) no paging, 8°, $5. Hispanic Soc.

Vincens, Cécile, [Mme. Charles Vincens, "Arvede Barine."]
Madame, mother of the Regent, 1652-1722; tr. by Jeanne Mairet, (Madame Charles Bigot.) '09(O23) c. il. O. **$3 net, boxed. Putnam.

Vincens, Mme. Charles.
See Vincens, Cécile.

Vincent, Sir Edg., and Dickson, J. G.
Hdbk. of modern Greek. '10(Ja) *$1.90 net; formerly *$1.60 net. Macmillan.

Vincent, Edg. La Verne.
Hot coals; story of to-day. '10(D3) il. 12°, $1.50. C. M. Clark.
Story of Garfield, [President of U. S.] '08 (My16) c. il. pors. 8°, pap., 15 c. L. H. Nelson.

Vincent, J: Heyl.
Calendar for 1909; arr. and ed. by Fred Winslow Adams. '08(O24); for 1910. '10(Ja1); for 1911 (D10) c. S. por. pap., ea., *10 c. net. Eaton & M.

Vincent, J: M.
History of the textual criticism of the New Testament. '09(Ap3) 12°, (New Testament handbooks.) Price raised from *75 c. net to *$1 net. Macmillan.

VINCENT, Strong.
See Gettysburg (Battle of).

VINCENT DE PAUL, *St.*
Dougaud, L: V. E. History of St. Vincent de Paul, founder of the Vincentians and of the Sisters of Charity. 2 v. in 1. *$1.50 net. Longmans.

VINCENZA, Italy.
Agnetti, M. P. Vincenza: the home of "The saint." $3.50 net. Doran.

VINCI, Leonardo da.
Brockwell, M. W. Leonardo da Vinci. *65 c. net; *$1.50 net. Stokes.
Cust, R. H. H. Leonardo Da Vinci. 50 c.; $1. Macmillan.
Hind, C: L. Drawings of Leonardo da Vinci. *$2.50 net. Scribner.

Vindication of Anglican orders. Lowndes, A. 2 v. *$3.50 net. Gorham.

Vindication of Warren Hastings. Hastings, G. W. $2. Oxford Univ.

VINEGAR.
See Chemistry.

Vinegar buyer. Kendall, E. F. 50 c. Cleveland News.

Vinogradoff, Pavel Gavrilovich.
English society in the eleventh century: essays in English mediæval history. '08 (My23) O. $5.25. Oxford Univ.
Roman law in mediæval Europe. '10(F19) 16°, (Harper's lib. of living thought.) *75 c. net. Harper.
—, **ed.** Oxford studies in social and legal hist. v. 1, English monasteries on the eve of the dissolution by Alex. Savine; Patronage in the later empire, by F. De Zulueta. '10(Ja1) 8°, $4.15. Oxford Univ.

Vintage of Spain. Smart, J. S. $1.50. C. M. Clark.

VIOLA.
See Pansy.

Violet book. Allen, W. B., *comp.* **$1.80 net. Jacobs.

VIOLETS.
Crane, H. H. Book of the pansy, viola and violet. *$1 net. Lane.
Cuthbertson, W: Pansies, violas and violets. 65 c. net. Stokes.

VIOLIN.
Broadley, A. Adjusting and repairing violins, 'cellos, etc. 40 c. Scribner.
Green, J: A. Tone and technique of the violin. $1. J: A. Green.
St. George, H: Fiddles. $1. Scribner.
Winn, E. L. Child violinist. $1.25.—How to prepare for Kreutzer. $1.—How to study Kreutzer. 75 c.—How to study Fiorillo. 75 c. Fischer.
Winram, J: Violin playing and violin adjustment. *$2 net. Scribner.
See also Violoncello;—*also* Stradivari, Antonio.

Violin making and adjusting; construction and adjustment of 'cellos fully described. '10(Je4) il. 12°, (Woodworker ser.) pap., 25 c. Spon.

VIOLONCELLO.
Broadley, A. Adjusting and repairing violins, 'cellos, etc. 40 c. Scribner.
Racster, O. Chats on violoncellos. *$1.25 net. Lippincott.

Virgil, D.
See Boyles, Kate.

Virgil [Lat. Virgilius] Maro, Publius.
Æneid. bks. 7-12; tr. by Harlan Hoge Ballard. '08(Mr14) c. D. **$1.50 net. Houghton M.
Æneid; tr. into Eng. verse by Thdr. C. Williams. '08(D26) c. O. **$1.50 net. Houghton M.
Æneid; tr. into English verse by Thdr. C. Williams. '10(Je4) c. il. fold. map, 12°, (Riverside literature ser.) 75 c. Houghton M.
Æneid, books I.-VI.; with introd., notes and vocabulary by H. R. Fairclough and Seldon L. Brown. '08(Jl4) c. il. D. (Students' ser. of Latin classics.) $1.40. B: H. Sanborn.
Æneid of Virgil; tr. into English verse by J: Conington. Cheaper reissue. '08 (Ap11) D. $1.25. Longmans.
Æneid of Virgil; tr. into English prose by J: Conington; ed., with introd. and notes, by Edg. S. Shumway. '10(Ap9) c. T. (Pocket Am. and Eng. classics.) 25 c. Macmillan.
Dryden's Æneid of Virgil; with introd. by Alfr. J. Church. '10(D) il. 16°, 75 c.; leath., $1.25. Cassell.
The ecologues (in English in hexameter verse); tr. by I. Perley Smith. '08(D5) c. D. *$1 net. W: B. Clarke.
Two dramatizations from Vergil: 1, Dido, the Phœnician queen; 2, The fall of Troy; arr. and tr. into English verse by Fk. Justus Miller; the stage directions and music for the Dido are contributed by J. Raleigh Nelson. '08(O24) c. plans, D. *$1 net. Univ. of Chic.

Virgil [Lat. Virgilius] Maro, Publius.—*Cont.*
Virgil; tr. by J. Jackson. '08(N21) D. $1. Oxford Univ.
See also Theocritus.

VIRGIL [Lat. Virgilius] Maro, Publius.
Church, A. J: Æneid for boys and girls. †$1.50. Macmillan.
Comparetti, D. Vergil in the Middle Ages. *$1.75 net. Macmillan.
DeWitt, N. W. Dido episode in the Æneid. $1. W: Briggs.
Ellis, R. Lecture on Prof. Birt's ed. of the Vergilian catalepton. 40 c. net. Oxford Univ.
Havell, H. L., *comp.* Stories from the Æneid. $1.50. Dodge.

Virgil (The). Begbie, H. †$1.50. Dodd.

Virgin birth. Grützmacher, R: H. *40 c. net. Eaton & M.

Virgin birth of our Lord. Briggs, C: A: *25 c. net. Whittaker.

Virgin in judgment. Phillpotts, E. †$1.50. Moffat.

VIRGIN VALLEY, Nevada.
Gidley, J. W. Notes on a collection of fossil mammals from Virgin Valley, Nevada. 10 c. Univ. of Cal.

Virgin widow. Charlton, R. †$1.50. G: W. Dillingham.

Virginia. *Board of Education.* List of books for rural school libraries in the state of Virginia, issued by the Department of Public Instruction, 1909; every library purchased with state aid must be selected from this list. '09(My8) 8°, pap., gratis. W: E. Jones.

Virginia. Business man's code of laws; cont. a compilation of such statutes as every business man needs and should have access to; and excl. the statutes rel. to crimes, governmental functions, matters of jurisprudence, and other matters not rel. to business, [etc.;] comp. and ed. by Christopher B. Garnett and Rob. N. Pollard. '07, [1908.] (Mr.) c. O. hf. im. mor., $5. B. D. Smith.

Virginia. Corporation laws; (being an act concerning corporations, which became a law May 21, 1903, with amendments, etc.;) Ashby Williams. '09(N) c. 22+282 p. O. $3. Stone Pr.

Virginia. Law of instructions to juries; with a collection of forms in civil and criminal cases, approved by the supreme court of appeals, by L: C: Phillips. '08(D) 55+708 p. O. (Add. pubs. for price.) Lyon.

Virginia. Pollard's supp. to the code, [etc.;] ed. by J: Garland Pollard. '10(D) c. O. shp., $7.50. Waddey.

VIRGINIA.
Ambler, C: H: Sectionalism in Virginia. $1.50 net. Univ. of Chic.
Bagby, G: W: Old Virginia gentleman. $1.50 net. Scribner.
Bassler, R. S. Cement resources of Virginia. Univ. of Va.
Bruce, P. A. Institutional hist. of Virginia in the seventeenth century. $6 net. Putnam.
Burt, I. L. Hist. of African methodism in Virginia. $.1. I. L. Burt.

VIRGINIA.—*Continued.*
Clark, W: M., *ed.* Colonial churches. $1.25. Southern Churchman.
Crozier, W: A., *ed.* Virginia heraldica: registry of Virginia gentry entitled to coat of arms. $3. Genealog. Assoc.
Duggar, J: F: Virginia supplement to Agriculture for southern schools. *12 c. net. Macmillan.
Hogg, C: E. Pleading and forms, now in use in Virginia. $6. Clarke.
Illinois State Historical Lib. Collections. v. 2. Virginia ser. v. 1, Cahokia records, 1778-1790. (Not for sale.) Ill. State Hist. Lib.
James, C: F. Struggle for religious liberty in Virginia. $1.25. Review and Herald Pub.
Lingley, C: R. Transition in Virginia from colony to commonwealth. $1.50 net. Longmans.
Long, C: M. Virginia county names: two hundred and seventy years of Virginia history. *$1.50 net. Neale.
McAllister, J. T. Hist. sketch of Virginia Hot Springs, Warm Sulphur Springs and Bath County, Va. (Add. author for price.) J. T. McAllister.
McBain, H. L. How we are governed in Virginia and the nation. 55 c. H. L. McBain.
McDonald, J. J. Life in old Virginia. $1.50. Old Virginia.
McDonald, W: N. Hist. of the Laurel brigade, originally Ashby cavalry of the Army of No. Va. and Chew's battery. $3. K. S. McDonald.
Miller, E. I. Legislature of the province of Virginia. *$2 net; *$1.50 net. Lemcke.
Munford, B. B. Virginia's attitude toward slavery and secession. $2 net. Longmans.
Page, T: N. The Old Dominion: her making and manners. **$1.50 net. Scribner.
Payment of certain moneys advanced by Maryland and Virginia; adverse report. U. S., Supt. of Docs.
Sale, E. T. Manors of Virginia in Colonial times. **$5 net. Lippincott.
Virginia State Library. Separation of church and state in Virginia. $1. Virginia State Lib.
Watson, T: L. Mineral resources of Virginia. gratis. C. A. Swanson.
Wertenbaker, T: J. Patrician and plebeian in Virginia. $1.50. Wertenbaker.
Wise, K. E., *ed.* Guide to historic places in Virginia. 25 c. Wise Pub.
Zigler, D. H. History of the Brethren in Virginia. $1.50. Brethren Pub. Ho.
See also Albemarle Co.;—Ashby Cavalry;—Bruton Parish Church;—Civil War;—Cookery;—Fredericksburg; — Gambling: — Indexes; — James river; — Loudoun Co.; — Madison Co.; —Mosby's Rangers;—Mt. Vernon;—Newport News;—Potomac river;—Richmond;—Roanoke; —Shenandoah Valley;—Truro parish;—University of Virginia;—Williamsburgh;—*also* Gordon, William Fitzhugh;—Lee, *General* Robert Edward.

Virginia. Gilmore, M. F. $1. Morton.

Virginia and West Virginia. Encyclop. digest; by T: Johnson Michie. v. 1-14. '09, [1910.] (F) c. O. shp., $7.50. Michie.

Virginia (Colony) General Assembly. House of Burgesses. Journals of the House of Burgesses of Virginia. In 10 v. v. 1, 2, 3, 4, ed. by J: Pendleton Kennedy; v. 5, 6, ed. by H: Read McIlwaine. '09(Ap) f°, ea., $10. H: R. McIlwaine.

Virginia Colony. *General ct.* Virginia colonial decisions; repts. by Sir J: Randolph and by E: Barradall of decisions of the General court of Virginia, 1728-1741; ed., with historical introd., by R. T. Barton. 2 v. '10(F5) c. por. 8°, $7. Boston Bk.

Virginia county record ser. 8°. Genealog. Assoc.
—Crozier. Virginia heraldica. $3.

Virginia Dare. Latimer, H: R. (Add. pubs. for price.) Lord Balto Pr.

Virginia feud. Lee, G: T. $1.50. Neale.

VIRGINIA HOT SPRINGS, Va.
See Virginia.

Virginia of the air lanes. Quick, J: H. †$1.50. Bobbs-M.

Virginia Russell. Schulder, *Mrs.* I. D. $1.25. Cochrane.

Virginia State Library, Richmond. Separation of church and state in Virginia; study in the development of the Revolution. '10 (My14) Q. 1. Virginia State Lib.

Virginia State Library, Richmond. Trial bibliography of colonial Virginia; special rept. of the Department of Bibliography, W: Clayton Torrence, bibliography. '08, [1909.] (N) 154 p. facsim., 8°, $1. Virginia State Lib.

Virginian holiday. Johnson, A. $1. Am. Tr.

Virginie. Oldmeadow, E. †$1.50. McClure.

Virtues of Christ ser. 16°. P: Reilly.
—Schuyler. Charity of Christ.—Courage of Christ. ea., 50 c. net.

Visceral surgery in abstract. Stewart, A. $1. Medical Abstract.

Vischer, Hanns.
Across the Sahara from Tripoli to Bornu. '10(Ap16) il. fold. map, O. $3.50 net. Longmans.

VISIGOTHIC CODE.
Scott, S. R., *tr. and ed.* Visigothic code. $5. Boston Bk.

VISION.
See Eye.

Vision from the wild. Webster, J: W. *$1 net. Cochrane.

Vision of Giorgione. Bottomley, G. $1.50. T: B. Mosher.

Vision of life. Figgis, D. *$1.25 net. Lane.

Vision of love revealed in sleep. Solomon, S. *$3 net. T: B. Mosher.

Vision of new Clairvaux. Pressey, E. P. *$1.25 net. Sherman, F.

Vision of Sir Launfal. *See* Lowell, Ja. Russell.

Vision of the Father, Son and three judges. Lowrie, A. W: $1.50. A. W: Lowrie.

Vision of unity. Robinson, J. A. 50 c.; 25 c. Longmans.

Visions. Landels, T: D. $1 net. Sherman, F.

Visions of heaven and hell. Gottschall, A. H. 75 c. A. H. Gottschall.

Visit of Humpty. Herbert, F. 30 c. Jacobs.

Visit (A) to the homeland of Washington's ancestors. [1910.] (Je) c. 3-19 p. il. 12°, gratis. P: Henderson.

VISITING NURSES.
See Nurses and nursing.

Visitor's guide and history of San Antonio, Tex. Taylor, H: R. 25 c. N. Tengg.

Visitor's guide to Westminster Abbey. Bond, F. 40 c. Oxford Univ.

Visscher, W: Lightfoot.
Fetch over the canoe: story of a song. '08, [1909.] c. 13-114 p. il. 16°. (Not for sale.) W: L. Visscher.
Ten wise men, and some more. '09(Je) 11+14-231 p. il. pors. 12°. (Not for sale.) W: L. Visscher.
Thrilling and truthful history of the pony express. '08(Je20) c. il. pors. 8°, 75 c. Rand, McN. & Co.

Visual signaling. United States. *Signal Office.* Gov. Pr. Off.

Vitæ sanctorum Hiberniæ. Plummer, C: 2 v. $9.75. Oxford Univ.

Vital American problems. Montgomery, H. E. **$1.50 net. Putnam.

Vital economy. Clarke, J: H. 50 c.; 30 c. Wessels.

VITAL FORCE.
Swing, P: F. What is life. (Not for sale.) P: F. Swing.
Thomson, W: H. What is physical life. **$1.20 net. Dodd.
See also Pathology.

Vital problems in social evolution. Lewis, A. M. 50 c. Kerr.

Vital records of Ashburnham, Mass., to the end of the year 1849. '09(Ap17) 8°, (Systematic history fund publications.) $2.70. F. P. Rice.

Vital records of Athol, Massachusetts, to the end of the year 1849. '10(My) c. 230 p. 8°, (Systematic history fund pubs.) $3. F. P. Rice.

Vital records of Bolton, Massachusetts, to the end of the year 1849. '10(My) 232 p. 8°, (Systematic history fund pubs.) $3. F. P. Rice.

Vital records of Bolton [Conn.] to 1854 and Vernon to 1852. '09, [1910.] (My) c. 22+291 p. 8°, (Vital records of Conn. ser.) $3. Conn. Hist.

Vital records of Brookfield, Mass., to the end of the year 1849. '09(S) 549 p. 8°, (Systematic history fund pubs.) (Add. pub. for price.) F. P. Rice.

Vital records of Danvers, Mass., to the end of the year 1849. v. 1. '09(Ap17) 8°, (Vital records of the towns of Massachusetts.) *$4.45 net. Essex Inst.

Vital records of Dover, Mass., to the year 1850. '08(My) 107 p. 8°, $1.50. N. E. Hist.

Vital records of Dudley, Mass., to the end of the year 1849. '08(Je) 288 p. 8°, (Systematic history fund pubs.) cl. (Add. pub. for price.) F. P. Rice.

Vital records of Essex, Mass., to the end of the year 1849. '08(Je) 86 p. 8°, (Vital records of the towns of Massachusetts.) cl. (Add. pubs. for price.) Essex Inst.

Vital records of Farmingdale, Maine, to the year 1892; ed. by H: Sewall Webster; pub. under authority of the Maine Historical Society. '09(N) 96 p. 8°, $1. H. S. Webster.

Vital records of Hamilton, Mass., to the end of the year 1849. '08(Je) 112 p. 8°, (Vital rceords of the towns of Massachusetts.) cl. (Add. pubs. for price.) Essex Inst.

Vital records of Haverhill, Mass., to the end of the year 1849. '10(N) 8°. Topsfield Hist. Soc.

Vital records of Holliston, Mass., to the year 1850. Holliston, Mass. $4.50. N. E. Hist.

Vital records of Lincoln, Mass., to the year 1850. '08(My) 179 p. 8°, $2.25. N. E. Hist.

Vital records of Lynnfield, Mass. to the end of the year 1849. '07, [1908.] Je.) 92 p. 8°, (Vital records of the towns of Massachusetts.) cl., $1.05 net. Essex Inst.

Vital records of Marlborough, Mass. to the end of the year 1849. '08(Je) 404 p. 8°, (Systematic history fund pubs.) cl. (Add. pub. for price. F. P. Rice.

Vital records of Methuen, Mass., to the end of the year 1849. '09(Ap24) (Vital records of the towns of Massachusetts.) *$3.65 net. Topsfield Hist. Soc.

Vital records of Natick, Massachusetts, to the year 1850; comp. by T: W. Baldwin. '10(My) c. 249 p. 8°, $2.75. T: W. Baldwin.

Vital records of Randolph, Maine, to the year 1892; ed. by H: Sewall Webster; committee on publication, Asbury Coke Stilphen; pub. under authority of the Maine Historical Society. '10(Jl16) 8°, $1.25. Reporter-Journal.

Vital records of Rockingham, Vt., from the beginning of the records to January 1, 1845. '08(F) c. 225 p. 8°, $3.50. Littlefield.

Vital records of Saugus, Mass., to the end of the year 1849. '07, [1908.] (Je.) 81 p. 8°, cl., *88 c. net. Essex Inst.

Vital records of Scituate, Mass., to the year 1850. 2 v. '09(Ap17) 8°, (Vital records of the towns of Massachusetts.) $11. N. E. Hist.

Vital records of Sharon, Mass., to the year 1850; comp. by T: W. Baldwin. '09(Ap24) 8°, $2.25. T: W. Baldwin.

Vital records of Spencer, Massachusetts, to the end of the year 1849. '09(N) 276 p. 8°, (Systematic history fund pubs.) (Add. pubs. for price.) F. P. Rice.

Vital records of Tisbury, Massachusetts, to the year 1850. '10(My) 244 p. 8°, (New England Historic Genealogical Society, vital records of the towns of Massachusetts.) $3.25. N. E. Hist.

Vital records of Warren (formerly Western), Massachusetts, to the end of the year 1849. '10(My) 196 p. 8°, (Systematic history fund pubs.) $2.40. F. P. Rice.

Vital records of Wayland, Massachusetts, to the year 1850. '10(My) 160 p. 8°, (New England Historic Genealogical Society, vital records of the towns of Massachusetts.) $2.25. N. E. Hist.

Vital records of Westminster, Mass., to the end of the year 1849. '08(Je) 258 p. 8°, (Systematic history fund pubs.) cl. (Add. pub. for price.) F. P. Rice.

Vital records of Weymouth, Massachusetts, to the year 1850. 2 v. '10(My) 8°, (New England Historic Genealogical Society, vital records of the towns of Massachusetts.) $9.25. N. E. Hist.

Vital records of Winchendon, Mass., to the end of the year 1849. '09(Ap17) 8°, (Systematic history fund publications.) $2.80. F. P. Rice.

VITAL STATISTICS.
See Statistics;—*also* under names of places.

Vital study of literature. Guthrie, W: N. $1.50. Sergel.

VITALITY.
See Hygiene.

Vitality, fasting and nutrition. Carrington, H. $5. Rebman.

"Viter Strikeshoulder," pseud.
See Spaulding, *Rev.* Wayland.

VITICULTURE.
See Grapes.

Vitrified paving brick. Wheeler, H. A. $2. T. A. Randall.

Vittoria. *See* Meredith, G:

Vittum, Willis Hall.
Orpheus and other poems. '10(D31) c. D. bds., $1.50 net. Badger.

Viva Mexico. Flandrau, C: M. **$1.25 net. Appleton.

VIVEKÂNANDA, *Swâmi.*
Noble, M. E. The master as I saw him. $1.50 net. Longmans.

Vivian, Alfr.
First principles of soil fertility. '08(F22) c. il. tabs., 12°, *$1 net. Judd.

Vivian, Evelyn C. H.
Shadow of Christine. '10(Ap9) c. D. $1.50. Fenno.

Vivian, Percival.
Dictionary of literary terms. '08(D19) 32°, (Miniature reference lib.) leath., 50 c. Dutton.

VIVISECTION.
Greene, J. M. Experiments on the subhuman: are they justifiable? (Add. pubs. for price.) N. Y. Anti-Vivisection.
Johnson, *Mrs.* M. K. Moloch: [argument against vivisection.] *50 c. net. W: B. Clarke.
Leffingwell, A. Vivisection question. o. p. S. R. Taber.
Myers, C: S. Vivisection problem. (Add. pubs. for price.) S. R. Taber.
Warbasse, J. P: Conquest of disease through animal experimentation. $1 net. Appleton.
Weaver, G. R. Priests of progress: [fiction.] $1.50. B. W. Dodge.

Vlasto, Solon J., and Gortzis, Nicholas.
Istoria ton enimenon politeion tes Amerikes; [in Greek.] '09(F6) il. pors. $2. Atlantis Pub.

Vocabulary for young fathers. E., Q. N., *pseud.* 75 c. Dodge.

Vocabulary of checkers. Call, W: T. $2. C. M. Potterdon.

Vocabulary of French words and idioms. Lewis, L. R. 35 c. Tuft's Press.

VOCAL ART.
See Singing.

Vocation of man. Fichte, J. G. 30 c. Open Court.

VOCATIONAL EDUCATION.
Gillette, J: M. Vocational education. $1. Am. Bk.
Haney, J. P. Vocational training and trade teaching in the public schools. 15 c. Am. Acad. Pol. Sci.
Snedden, D: S. Problem of vocational education. 35 c. Houghton M.
United States. Vocational education; hearings before the Committee on Agriculture and Forestry, United States Senate, April 12 and 13, 1910. '10(Jl) 82 p. 8°. Gov. Pr. Off.
Vocational education. '10(Ag) 26 p. 8°, gratis. N. Y. State Educ.
Warriner, E. C. Industrial and vocational training in the public schools. Mich. Supt. Pub. Instruction.

VOCATIONS.
Choosing a career: circular of information for boys; for girls. ea., 10 c. High School Teachers.
McKeever, W: A. Assisting the boy in a choice of a vocation. gratis. W: A. McKeever.
Parsons, F. Choosing a vocation. **$1 net. Houghton M.
Perkins, A. F., *ed.* Vocations for the trained woman. 60 c. Women's Educ.

Vogl, Virginia Douglas Hyde-.
See Hyde-Vogl, V. D.

Vogt, Paul L.
Sugar refining industry in the United States. '08(My23) 8°, (Pub. of the Univ. of Penn., Ser. in polit. economy and public law.) $1.50. Univ. of Penn.; [Appleton.]

VOICE.
Adams, H. T. Physical development in relation to perfect voice production. *75 c. net. Scribner.
Aikin, W. A. The voice. $2.25 net. Longmans.
Cone, R: W. Speaking voice; its scientific basis in music. $1. Evans Music.
Curtis, H: H. Voice building and tone placing. $2. Appleton.
Everts, K. J. Speaking voice. **$1 net. Harper.
Jones, D. D. Technique of speech. **$1.25 net. Harper.
Manchester, A. L. Twelve lessons in the fundamentals of voice production. $1. Ditson.
Miller, F. E. The voice; its production, care and preservation. *$1.25 net. Schirmer.
Mills, C: F. H: Voice and vocal exercises. $1. Univ. of Neb.
Morhart, C: C. Voice training for speakers. $1.50. Am. Luth.
Mott, F: W. Brain and voice in speech and song. 75 c. net. Harper.
Moure, J. G. E., *and* Bouyer, A., *jr.* Abuse of the singing and speaking voice. $1 net. Scribner.
Preetorius, C. Tone placed and developed. $1.50. C. Preetorius.

VOICE.—*Continued.*
Rix, F. R. Voice training for school children. 50 c. net. Barnes.
Southwick, *Mrs.* J. E. Expressive voice culture. 60 c. J. E. Southwick.
Witkowski's atlas of the mechanism of voice, speech and taste. *$2 net. W: R. Jenkins.
See also Breathing;—Elocution;—Singing;—Stammering and stuttering.

Voice and vocalism. Mills, C: F. H: $1.50. Hawk-Eye.

Voice from the Congo. Ward, H. $2.50 net. Scribner.

Voice from the West. Martin, I. T. $1. Becktold.

Voice in the rice. Morris, G. $1.25. Dodd.

Voice of the city. Henry, O. †$1. McClure.

Voices and visions. Scollard, C. *$1 net. Sherman, F.

Voices from Erin. McCarthy, D. A. $1 net. Little, B. & Co.

Voices of faith and love. Barnes, S. G. $1. Caledonian Press.

Voices of nature. Baker, E. A. *$1 net. Dutton.

Voices of prayer; or, thoughts on Psalm eighty-six, by the author of "Some aspects of meditation"; with commendation by the Rt. Rev. W: T. Gaul, D.D. '10(Mr5) S. $1. Longmans.

Voices of the city. Stow, M. C. $1. M. C. Stow.

Voices of the past, present and future. Bushnell, J. 50 c. J. Bushnell.

Voices of the West. Cole, L. E. 50 c. L. E. Cole.

VOLATILE ACID.
See Chemistry.

Volatile matter of coal. Porter, H. C. Gov. Pr. Off.

VOLCANOES.
Brooklyn Public Library. Earthquakes and volcanoes: list of books with reference to periodicals in the Library. gratis. Brooklyn Lib.
Wilson, J. F. Earthquakes and volcanoes—hot springs. $1.25. J. F. Wilson.
See also Earthquakes;—Hawaiian Islands;—Kilauea;—Mauna Loa;—Messina disaster;—Mt. Pelee.

Volkmann-Leander, Richard von.
Träumerein an französischen kaminen: märchen; sel. and ed., with introd., notes, exercises and vocab., by J. B. E. Jonas and Anne T. Weeden. '08(O31) c. por. S. (Internat. modern lang. ser.) 40 c. Ginn.

Vollmer, Rev. Philip.
John Calvin, theologian, preacher, educator, statesman, presented to the Reformed churches holding the Presbyterian system on the 400th anniversary of the reformer's birth; with contributions from Rev. Ja. I: Good, D.D., and Rev. W: H. Robers, D.D. '09(My22) c. il. por. 12°, 75 c. Heidelberg.

Volta Bureau, reprints of useful knowledge. 8°. Volta.
—Kunz. Physiology of the blind. 50 c.

Voltaire, François Marie Arouet de.
Works. '08(Je6) 43 v., il. 8°, per set, $60. St. Hubert Guild.
Life of Charles XII.; specially tr. by Miss Todhunter; introd. by J. Burns. '08(F22) 16°, (Everyman's lib.) *35 c. net; leath., *70 c. net. Dutton.
Zaïre; tragedy in verse in five acts; ed., with introd. and notes, by C: Cabeen. '10(My21) c. por. S. (Heath's modern language ser.) 30 c. Heath.
See also Froissart, *Sir* J: Chronicles of England.
VOLTAIRE, François Marie Arouet de.
Tallentyre, S. G.. *pseud.* Life of Voltaire. $3.50 net. Putnam.
VOLUMETRIC ANALYSIS.
See Chemistry.
VOLUNTARYISM.
Herbert, A. Voluntaryist creed, and A plea for voluntaryism.—Voluntaryist creed. ea., 80 c. Oxford Univ.
Volunteer with Pike. Bennet, R. A. $1.50. McClurg.
VOLUSIA SOILS.
See Soils.
Vom ersten bis zum letzten schuss. Wachenhusen, H. 35 c. net. Macmillan.
Vom kiel zum flaggenknopf. Paasch, H. *$10 net. Lemcke.
Von Boehm, Max.
See Fischel, Oscar.
Von Culin, C.
How to run and install gasoline engines. '08(D) 25 c. Van Nostrand.
Von Dobschutz.
Apostolic age; tr. by F. L. Pogson. '10 (N19) 12°, $1. Am. Unitarian.
VON GRAVENITZ, Wilhelmine, *Landhofmeisterin of Würtemberg.*
Hay, M. A. German Pompadour; being the true hist. of Wilhelmine von Gravenitz, Landhofmeisterin of Würtemberg. $1.50. Scribner.
Von Hase, Karl.
New Testament parallels in Buddhistic literature. '08(Ja4) S. (Foreign religious ser.) *40 c. net. Eaton & M.
Von Oettingen, Burchand.
Horse breeding in theory and practice. '10 (Jl16) 8°, $15 net. Little, B. & Co.
VON REISENKAMPFF FAMILY.
See Genealogies: Ulrich, B. A., *comp.*
Von Ruville, Alb.
Back to Holy Church; experiences and knowledge acquired by a convert; tr. by G. Schoetensack; ed., with a preface, by the Rev. Rob. Hugh Benson. '10(N19) por. D. $1.20 net. Longmans.
Voorhees, E: Burnett.
Fertilizers: the source, character and composition of natural, home-made and manufactured fertilizers. 10th ed. '08(F1) c. 12°, **$1.25 net. Macmillan.
Voorhees, Gardner T.
Indicating the refrigerating machine: application of the indicator to the ammonia compressor and steam engine. '08(N21) $1; flexible mor., $1.50. Nickerson & C.
Voorhees, Ja. Paxton.
Caverns of dawn. '10(Jl) c. 8+9-519 p. 8°, $1.25. Raidabaugh-V.

Vorbeck, Jos. Chester.
First aid to the sick by the use of domestic remedies. '09(D) c. 152 p. 8°, $1. J. C. Vorbeck.
Vorse, Mrs. Mary Marvin Heaton.
Breaking in of a yachtsman's wife '08 (My16) c. D. †$1.50. Houghton M.
Votaw, Clarence E.
Jasper Hunnicutt of Jimpsonhurst: [railway mail service.] 2d ed., *de luxe.* '09 (Ja23) c. il. pors. hf. leath., $1.50. Union Bk.
Votaw, Clyde Weber, comp.
See McFadyen, J: Edg.
Votes for Catharine and me. Ainslee, K. 25 c. Stokes.
VOTING.
See Elections;—Suffrage.
Voucher system accounting charts. Griffith, J. B. 50 c. Am. Sch. Corr.
Vox, Carol, [pseud. for W: Houghton Sprague Pearce.
Sphinx and the mummy: book of limericks. '09(Je19) c. il. S. 50 c. Caldwell.
Vox musarum. Smith, O. C. $1. O. C. Smith.
Voyage aux Pyrénées. *See* Taine, Hippolyte Adolphe.
Voyage (Le) des Mousquetaires. *See* Dumas, Alexandre.
Voyage du novice. Lamy, G. 35 c. net. Macmillan.
Voyage en Amerique. *See* Tocqueville, Alexis Charles Henri Clérel de.
Voyage en Espagne. *See* Gautier, Théophile.
Voyage of "The Two Sisters." Smith, E. B. $1.50. E. B. Smith.
Voyage of the "Wenonah." Langford, A. $1.50. C. M. Clark.
VOYAGES AND TRAVELS.
Bacon, E. M. Boy's Hakluyt.—English voyages of adventure. ea., $1.50. Scribner.
Bidwell, D. D. As far as the east is from the west. $1.50; $2.25. Scranton.
Bigger, L. A. Around the world with a business man. 4 v. $12. Winston.
Blatter, G: J: O'er oceans and continents. 3d ser. $1.29; per set of 4 v., $5.16. G: J: Blatter.
Burn-Murdoch, W. G. From Edinburgh to India and Burmah. *$3.50 net. Dutton.
Butler, *Lady* E. From sketch book and diary. *$2.50 net. Macmillan.
Carlisle, G: L. Around the world in a year. **$2 net. Baker & T.
Coffin, G: Pioneer voyage to California and round the world. $1.50. G. B. Coffin.
Cross, R. Voyage of the "Oregon" from San Francisco to Santioga in 1898. (Priv. pr.] Merrymount.
Curiosity land for young people: pictures and descriptions of animals, buildings, people, etc. 75 c.; $1. Cassell.
Davis, G: T. B. Twice around the world with Alexander. $1. Chr. Herald.
Dufferin, F: T. B., *Lord.* Letters from high latitudes. 35 c. net; 70 c. net. Dutton.
Foster, A. G. By the way. $1.50 net. P. Elder.

VOYAGES AND TRAVELS.—*Continued.*

Franck, H. A. Vagabond journey around the world. **$3.50 net. Century Co.

Frizell, W: G. Out of the way places. *$1.20 net. Un. B. Pub.

Grosvenor, G. H., *ed.* Scenes from every land. $1; $2; $2.50. Nat. Geographical Soc.

Hakluyt, R: Voyages. In 8 v. ea., *35 c. net; *70 c. net. Dutton.

Hakluyt, R: Voyages of Drake and Gilbert. 60 c. Oxford Univ.

Hogarth, D: G: Accidents of an antiquary's life. $2.50 net. Macmillan.

Hopkins, A. A., *comp. and ed. Scientific American* hdbk. of travel. $2 net; $2.50 net. Munn.

Huschart, F. M. Doing over: tour eastward around the world. $1.50. Clarke.

Jager, A. The emigrant: experience of [an] emigrant to South America, Australia, California. (Add. pubs. for price.) Southern California Pr.

Kipling, R. From sea to sea. **$1.50 net. Doubleday, P.

Lowe, F. J. Around Africa and across the Andes. International Press.

Miller, C. J. Newest way round the world. *$2.50 net. C. J. Miller.

Moncrieff, A. R. H. The world. *$1.50 net. Macmillan.

Morrison, S. G. From lotos to cherry blossom. $1.50. Cochrane.

Murray, J: Hdbk. of travel talk. $1.25 net. Scribner.

Nicoll, M. J. Three voyages of a naturalist. *$2.50 net. Scribner.

Niedieck, P. With rifle in five continents. *$5 net. Scribner.

Peck, H. T. New Baedeker. $1.50 net. Dodd.

Peebles, J M. Five journeys around the world. $1.75. Peebles.

Pendergast, *Mrs.* E. W. Over the sea; travel letters. $1. E. W. Pendergast.

Perkins, C. B. Travels from the grandeurs of the West to the mysteries of the East. $3. C. B. Perkins.

Polo, M. Travels. *35 c. net; *70 c. net. Dutton.

Presbrey, F. Information guide for transatlantic travelers. 25 c.; $1. Presbrey.

Raleigh, W. A. English voyages of the sixteenth century. $1.25 net. Macmillan.

Reed, M. A-roving he would go. *$1.25 net. Sherman, F.

Scarfoglio, A. Round the world in a motor car. *$5 net. M. Kennerley.

Seymour, W. Ups and downs of a wandering life. $3 special net. Appleton.

Smith, E. B. Voyage of "The Two Sisters" [to China and Japan.] $1.50. E. B. Smith.

Smith, J: True travels, adventures and observations. *40 c. net. Putnam.

Stay at home travels. $2. Nelson.

Stein, G. M. Glimpses around the world through the eyes of a young American. $2 net. Winston.

Stephens, E. W: Around the world. $5. Stephens.

Taylor, C: M. Odd bits of travel with brush and camera. *$1.25 net. Jacobs.

Taylor, H. A. Tales of travel. $1.50. Neale.

Thorpe, D. Universal guide of standard routes and itineraries of tourist travel all over the world. $1.25. D. Thorpe.

Warren, H: M. To and fro: [notes of travel.] $1.50. Fell.

Wilder, M. P. Smiling 'round the world. $1.50. Funk.

Wright, E: S. Westward round the world. $1.25. Dutton.

Wyman, W. Cruise on the U. S. practice ship "S. P. Chase," being the first impression of a surgeon at sea. $2 net. Grafton Press.

See also Antarctic regions;—Arctic regions;—Deserts;—Explorers;—Far East; — Geography; — Hunting; — Orient; — Rivers; — Yachts and yachting;—*also* names of voyagers and various parts of the world.

Voynich, Mrs. Ethel Lilian Boole.

Interrupted friendship. '10(Mr5) c. D. $1.50. Macmillan.

Voysey, C. F. A.

See Schultz, Rob. W.

Vreeland, N: Garretson, ed.

Hist. and genealogy of the Vreeland family. '09, [1910.] (Ja) c. 320 p. il. pors. fold. map, 8°, $5. Hist. Pub. Co., (N. J.)

Vreeland, Williamson Updike, and Michaud, Régis, comps.

Anthology of French prose and poetry. '10 (N19) c. D. $1.40. Ginn.

VREELAND FAMILY.

See Genealogies.

Vries, D. de.

See De Vries, D.

Vries, Hugo de.

See De Vries, Hugo.

Vronina. Vaughan, O. †$1.50. Dodd.

Vrooman, Carl Schurz.

American railway problems in the light of European experience; or, government regulation vs. government operation of railways. '10(D3) D. $2. Oxford Univ.

Vrooman, Fk. Buffington.

Theodore Roosevelt, dynamic geographer; based on a lecture delivered to the School of Geography, Oxford University, March 8, 1900. '09(Ag7) O. $1; pap., 75 c. Oxford Univ.

Vrooman, Rev. Hiram.

Religion rationalized. v. 1. '10(Mr5) c. D. 75 c. Nunc Licet.

Vulgate version of the Arthurian romances. *See* Sommer, H. Oskar, *ed.*

Vulté, Hermann Thdr., and Goodell, G: Arth.

Lab'y notes in household chemistry; for use of students in domestic science. 2d ed. '10(My14) c. 12°, $1.25. Chemical.

VULTURES.

Miller, L. H. Condor-like vultures of Rancho La Brea. 15 c. Univ. of Cal.

Vyner, Rob.

Notitia venatica; treatise on fox hunting, embracing the general management of dogs. New ed., rev., corrected and enl. by W: C. A. Blew; again rev. and brought to date by Cuthbert Bradley. 2 v. '10(D10) col. il. 4°, $10 net. Dutton.

W., A. H., (Canada.)
He restoreth my soul. '10('08) c. 8°, $1.50 net. Putnam.

Wachenhusen, Hans.
Vom ersten bis zum letzten schuss; Kriegserinnerungen, 1870-71. '10(D24) 16°, (Macmillan's new ser. of German texts.) 35 c. net. Macmillan.

Waddell, Mrs. C: Carey, ["Louise Forsslund," "C: Carey."]
Old lady number 31. '09(Ap3) c. D. $1. Century Co.

Waddell, C: Wesley.
Race problem; or, America's second emancipation. '08(Je) c. 78 p. D. pap., 25 c. C: W. Waddell.

Waddell, J: Alex. Low, and Wait, J: Cassan.
Specifications and contracts: examples for practice in specification and contract writing, together with Notes on the law of contracts. '08(F8) c. 8°, *$1 net. Engineering News.

Waddell, W:
Red-man; or, the destruction of a race. '09(Ag21) c. 12°, 85 c. W: Waddell.

Waddington, Mrs. Mary Alsop King, [Mrs. W: H: Waddington.]
Chateau and country life in France. '08 (O10) c. il. O. **$2.50 net. Scribner.

Wade, Jos. H., and Sylvester, Emma.
Fifth reader. '08(N14) c. il. O. (Language readers.) 65 c. Ginn.

Wade, Martin J.
Selection of cases on malpractice of physicians, surgeons and dentists. '09(Je) c. 12+896 p. O. (Add. pubs. for price.) Medico-Legal Pub.

Wade, Mrs. Mary Hazleton Blanchard.
Little folks of North America; stories about children living in the different parts of North America. '09(O9) c. il. D. †$1. Wilde.
New little Americans: stories about the children living in our new possessions. '08(O17) c. il. D. †$1. Wilde.

Wade, Reuben Alex. Slaven.
California songs. [1910] (My) c. 70 p. 12°, 75 c. B'way Pub.
Parchment, and other poems. '08(D12) 12°, $1. Cochrane.

Wadhams, F: E., ed.
See New York [State.] Consolidated laws.

Wadleigh, H: Rawle.
Munich: history, monuments and art. '10 (S10) il. fold. map, O. $2 net. Stokes.

Wadsworth, Ja. Wolcott, jr.
Forest preservation and conservation of water supply. '09(Ap3) O. pap., gratis. J. W. Wadsworth.

Wadsworth, Marshman E:
Crystallography; elem. manual for the lab'y. '10(F12) c. O. *$3 net. McVey.

Wagar, Vernon Wade.
Pocket tokens, and other poems. '08(F1) c. D. $1. Badger.

Wage-earning women. MacLean, A. M. $1.25 net. Macmillan.

Wager-Smith, A. Eliz.
Skat: principles and illustrative games. '10 (My21) c. S. $1.25 net. Lippincott.

WAGES.
American Academy of Political and Social Science. Labor and wages. $1. Am. Acad. Pol. Sci.
Chapman, S. J: Work and wages. pt. 2. $4. Longmans.
Rawie, H: Wages and the price of land. 25 c. H: Rawie.
Studniczka, H: Labor conditions and cost of living. Gov. Pr. Off.
United States. *Dept. of Commerce and Labor. Bureau of the census.* Census of manufactures, 1905; earnings of wage earners. (Add. Superintendent for price.) U. S., Supt. of Docs.
United States. *Dept. of Commerce and Labor. Bu. of Labor.* Retail prices of food in the U. S., 1900 to 1907; wages and hours of labor in manufacturing industries in U. S., 1900 to 1907.
United States. *Dept. of State.* Wages in Germany; message from the President.
United States. *Dept. of State.* Wages paid in Germany; summary of the contents of various memorials of German chambers of commerce and industrial establishments referred to Senate Committee on Finance by the State Dept. '09(Jl) 24 p. 8°. (Add. Superintendent for price.)
See also Business;—Capital and labor;—Cost of living;—Labor and laboring classes;—Prices;—Trade-unions.

Waggaman, Mrs. Mary Teresa.
Captain Ted. '10(Mr12) c. front. D. 60 c. Benziger.
Eric; or, the black finger; repr. from *The Messenger.* [1910.] (D) 183 p. il. 16°, 75 c. Kilner.
See also Nixon-Roulet, Mary F.

Waggett, Rev. P. N.
Holy eucharist. '08(Je13) *$1.25 net. Young Churchman.

Wagnalls, Mabel.
Palace of danger. '08(O10) c. il. D. †$1.50. Funk.

Wagner, Arth. Lockwood.
Catechism of outpost duty, including reconnaissance, independent cavalry, advance guards, rear guards, outposts, etc.: an abridgment, in the form of questions and answers, of "The service of security and information"; rev. by 1st Lieut., Leslie A. I. Chapman. 17th ed. Rev. 1907. '08(Mr14) c. il. 16°, 50 c. Hudson.

Wagner, Rev. C:
Home of the Soul; tr. from the French by Laura Sanford Hoffman; with an introd. by Lyman Abbott. D.D. '09(Jl3) c. por. D. **$1.20 net. Funk.

Wagner, C: Philip.
Spanish grammar. Rev. ed. '10(S17) 12°, $1.25. C: P. Wagner.

Wagner, Eduard.
Recipes for the preserving of fruit, vegetables and meat; tr. by C: Salter. '08 (Ag1) 16°, *$2.50 net. Van Nostrand.

Wagner, Ellasue Canter.
Kim Su Bang, and other stories of Korea. '09(D11) c. il. 12°, 50 c. Pub. Ho. M. E. Ch., So.

Wagner, Jos. Bernard.
Cooperage; treatise on modern shop practice and methods; from the tree to the finished article. '10(Ap) 17+396 p. il. 8°, $5. J. B. Wagner.

Wagner, Mary E.
See Faustine, Madeline.

Wagner, Philip Matthew.
After sunrise; or, second attempts at poetry. '09(D) c. 7-155 p. il. pors. 12°, $1. P. M. Wagner.

Wagner, Wilhelm Richard.
Judaism in music (Das Judenthum in der musik); being the original essay; together with the later supp.; tr. from the German and furnished with explanatory notes and introd., by Edn. Evans. '10 (Je4) 12°, $1.25 net. Scribner.
Richard to Minna Wagner: letters to his first wife; tr. by W: Ashton Ellis. 2 v. '09(My22) 8°, $7. Scribner.
Siegfried; dramatic poem, freely tr. in poetic narrative form by Oliver Huckel. '10(S10) c. il. D. 75 c. net. Crowell.
Song of the Niebelungen; Rheingold and Valkyrie; with a new tr. of the text; il. in color and black and white by Arth. Rackham; tr. by Marg. Armour. '10 (D17) 4°, $5 net; ed. de luxe, $15 net. (150 copies.) Doubleday, P.
Tristan and Isolde; tr. into English verse by R: Le Gallienne; with a critique by E: Ziegler. '09(N20) c. col. il. Q. $6, boxed. Stokes.
The Valkyrie (Die Walküre): a dramatic poem; freely tr. in poetic narrative form by Oliver Huckel. '09(S11) c. front. D. **$1.50 net. Crowell.

WAGNER, Wilhelm Richard.
Hadden, J. C., *comp.* Flying Dutchman; [from Wagner's opera.]—Meistersingers; [from Wagner's opera.]—Ring of the Nibelung; [from Wagner's opera.]—Tristran and Isolde; [from Wagner's opera.] ea., 50 c.; $1.—Operas of Wagner. $2.25. Stokes.
Maud, C. Tales of Wagner's heroes. 50 c. McLoughlin.
Neumann, A. Personal recollections of Wagner. **$2.50 net. Holt.
Smith, C. E. Stories from Wagner. 50 c. Dutton.
Wheelock, *Mrs.* E. M. Stories of Wagner operas for children. $1.25. Bobbs-M.
See also Nibelungen ring.

Wagner, W: H:
Wagner phonography; orig. and natural method of expressing sounds of speech; a connected-vowel, light-line, one-position system, very simple, legible and rapid; especially designed for high school, general class work and for the student without a teacher, developed and taught in the Los Angeles Polytechnic High School. '09, [1910.] (F) c. 80 p. 12°, $1. W: H: Wagner.

Wags. Shepard, M. 50 c. Wessels.

Wagstaff, Mrs. Blanche Shoemaker.
Atys, a Grecian idyl, and other poems. '09 (N13) c. O. $1.25. M. Kennerley.

Wahl, Rob.
See Le Clerc, J. Arth.

—, and Henius, Max.
American handy book of the brewing, malting and auxiliary trades. 2 v. 3d ed. '09(Mr6) c. il. 16°, $12. Wahl-Henius.
Brauereibetrieb in den Vereinigten Staaten von Nord Amerika, nebst gertenbewertung, malzbereitung und einleitenden kapitel über diastase, peptase, hefe. '10(O) 5-8+274 p. 8°, $3. Wahl-Henius.

Wahlert, Edna.
Completion of Coleridge's Christabel; story of destiny and peace. '10(Je18) c. 12°, 50 c. Cochrane.

Waineman, Paul.
Summer tour in Finland. '08(N21) il. 8°, *$2.50 net; ¾ levant, *$5 net. Pott.

WAISTCOATS.
See Tailoring.

Wait, C: Edm.
Studies on the digestibility and nutritive value of legumes at the University of Tennessee, 1901-1905. '08(Ja11) tabs., O. (U. S. Dept. of Agriculture, Office of Experiment Stations, bulletin.) pap., 25 c. U. S., Supt. of Docs.
See also Hills, Jos. Lawrence.

Wait, J: Cassan.
See Waddell, J: Alex. Low.

Wait and win. Alger, H., *jr.* †$1. Burt.

Waite, C: H. Burlingame.
History of the Christian religion to the year 200. 6th ed. '08(D5) $2.50. Waite.

Waite, Joslyn R., comp.
See Illinois. Personal injury cases.

Waite, R: Alfr., jr.
Gospel in athletic phrases. '08(F1) c. D. 40 c.; pap., 25 c. Y. M. C. A.

WAITERS.
See Hotels.

WAITSFIELD, Vt.
Jones, M. B. History of the town of Waitsfield, Vt., 1782-1908. $5. Littlefield.

Wakefield, J: Allen.
Hist. of the Black Hawk War; a reprint of the 1st ed. by J: A. Wakefield, Esq., from the press of Calvin Goudy, Jacksonville, Ill., 1834; with preface and notes by Fk. Everett Stevens. '08, [1909.] (S) 7-224 p. il. por. 8°. (Add. pubs. for price.) Caxton Club.

Wakeford, Rev. J:
Little sermons on the Sunday Gospels; the rainbow round the throne. '10 (My21) D. $1.50 net. Longmans.

Wakeham, Rob.
Simplified applications of the steel square. '08(D) c. 81 p. diagrs., 8°, $1.50. R. Wakeman.

Wakeman, W: H:
Air valves for steam heating systems: how used, why used, where used. '08(Ap4) c. il. 12°, 25 c. Domestic Engineering.
Manual of steam engineering; comprising suggestions, instructions and illustrations for progressive steam engineers, concerning the application to modern daily practice of the approved theory of steam engineering. '09, [1910.] (F) 411 p. il. tabs., 24°, gratis. N. Y. Belting & Packing.

Walcott, C: Doolittle.
Cambrian geology and paleontology. No. 1, Nomenclature of some Cambrian Cordilleran formations. '08(My2) 5 c.—No. 2, Cambrian trilobites. pap., 25 c.—No. 3, Cambrian brachiopoda: descriptions of new genera of species. 25 c.—No. 4, Classification and terminology of the Cambrian brachiopoda. '08(N) 10 c.—No. 5, Cambrian sections of the Cordilleran area. '08(D) 25 c.—No. 6, Olenellus and other genus Mesonacidæ. 70 c.—No. 7, Pre-Cambrian rocks of the Bow River Valley, Alberta, Canada. '10 (O) 10 c. il. fold. maps, O. (Smithsonian miscellaneous collections.) Smith. Inst.

Walden, C: O., and Mowry, Don Ensminger.
Revenue law informer; hdbk. for ready reference for dealers operating under the revenue laws of the United States: wholesale and retail liquor dealers, brewers, cigar dealers, druggists; other miscellaneous information. Dealers' ed. '08, [1909.] (Mr) c. 17-152 p. 12°, $1. Walden & M.

Walden, J: W: H:
Universities of ancient Greece. '09(N6) c. D. **$1.50 net. Scribner.

Walden. *See* Thoreau, H: D:

Waldin, Wa.
Truck farming in the Everglades. '10 (D3) c. il. 8°, $1. W. Waldin.

Waldo Trench and others. Fuller, H: B. †$1.50. Scribner.

Waldron, Lawrence Root.
See Brand, C: J:

Waldseemüller, Martin, [Hylacomylus.]
Cosmographiae introductio of Martin Waldseemüller in facsimile; followed by The four voyages of Amerigo Vespucci; with their tr. into Eng.; to which are added Waldseemüller's two world maps of 1507; with an introd. by Jos. Fischer and Franz Von Wieser; ed. by C: G: Herbermann. '08(D5) c. map, plan, O. (U. S. Catholic Historical Soc. monograph.) $5. U. S. Cath.

Waldstein, C:, and Shoobridge, Leonard.
Herculaneum; past, present and future. '08 (O17) il. maps, 4°, *$5 net. Macmillan.

Wales, F. H., ed.
See Bible. O. T.: **Psalms.**

Wales, Hubert, pseud.
Cynthia in the wilderness. '08(Je) 12°, $1.50. Stuyvesant Press.
Hilary Thornton. '09(Mr) c. 316 p. D. †$1.50. Estes
Mr. and Mrs. Villiers. '08(Je) c. 4+300 p. 12°, $1.50. Stuyvesant Press.
Old allegiance. '08(Je) c. 316 p. 8°, $1.50. M. Kennerley.
Wife of Colonel Hughes. '10(S) c. 308 p. 12°, $1.50. Stuyvesant Press.
The yoke. '08(F) 12°, $1.50. Stuyvesant Press.

WALES.
Cathedrals of England and Wales. 2 v. ea., *25 c. net. Stokes.
Edwards, O. M. Short history of Wales. *75 c. net. Univ. of Chic.

WALES.—*Continued.*
Giraldus Cambrensis. Itinerary and description of Wales. *35 c. net; *70 c. net. Dutton.
Happenings of future years foretold in the Welsh almanacs. 25 c. H: Blackwell.
Hissey, J. J: Charm of the road. $3 net. Macmillan.
Howel Dda, *the Good.* Welsh medieval law. $2.90. Oxford Univ.
Powell, E. T: Essentials of self-government (England and Wales). *$1.50 net. Longmans.
Stawell, *Mrs.* R. Motor tours in Wales and the border counties. $2.50. L. C. Page.
Yale, R. H. Yale genealogy and history of Wales. $5. R. H. Yale.
See also Education;—*also* Kenfig.

WALES FAMILY.
See Genealogies, Carter, *Mrs.* C. M. R.

Walford, Mrs. Lucy Bethia Colquhoun.
Baby's grandmother. '08(Je13) 12°, (Home ser.) 50 c. Hurst.
Leonore Stubbs: [novel.] '08(N21) D. $1.50. Longmans.
Recollections of a Scottish novelist. '10 (D17) pors. O. $3 net. Longmans.

Walgren, J: Arvède.
New health science: art of positivism and psychic laws of healing. '09(My1) c. nar. D. $1. Rand, McN. & Co.

Walk, C: Edmonds.
Paternoster ruby. '10(N12) c. il. O. $1.35 net. McClurg.
Silver blade. '08(Mr21) c. il. O. $1.50. McClurg.
Yellow circle. '09(O2) c. il. O. $1.50. McClurg.

Walk of colonial Jack. Krohn, J: A. 25 c. J: A. Krohn.

Walker, Albert E., comp. and ed.
The *Free Lance-Star* historical and industrial number, portraying the glorious past and future possibilities of Fredericksburg, Va. '07, [1908.] (Mr.) c. 40 p. il. f°, pap., 20 c. Free Lance-Star.

Walker, Alb. H:
Black elephant of Reading; being a study in coal and finance. [1910.] (Je) 15 p. O. pap., gratis. A. H: Walker.
Blackest Reading; being an investigation; [study of coal trade with special reference to the Reading Co.] '10(Je) 15 p. O. pap., gratis. A. H: Walker.

Walker, Annie Kendrick.
Memoirs of the Graham family. '08, [1909.] (Mr) 35 p. il. pors. 12°, $2. T. A. Wright.

Walker, C:, ed.
Ritual "reason why"; rev. with corrections by the Very Rev. T. I. Ball. '09 (Je12) S. *$1 net; pap., *50 c. net. Young Churchman.

Walker, C: E:
Hereditary characters and their modes of transmission. '10(N5) il. O. $2.40 net. Longmans.

Walker, Edn. C.
Sketch and an appreciation of Moncure Daniel Conway, freethinker and humanitarian; an address at the Paine-Conway memorial meeting of the Manhattan Liberal Club. '08(D19) 12°, pap., 15 c. E. C. Walker.

Walker, Emma Eliz., M.D.
Pretty girl papers. '10(O22) c. D. $1.25 net. Little, B. & Co.

Walker, F. D.
Log of the Kaalokai; being a description of the small islands, shoals and reefs lying w. n. w. of the Hawaiian group proper, together with a recount of the experiences of the voyage in a 47-ton schooner; and stories for the entertainment of sea folk, and others. '09(D) c. 64 p. il. por. map, 8°, $1. Hawaiian Gazette.

Walker, Frances M. Cotton-.
See Cotton-Walker, Frances M.

Walker, H. D., comp.
Manual of California securities and directory of directors. 2d annual number. '10(N19) c. O. $3. H. D. Walker.

Walker, H. Wilfrid.
Wanderings among South Sea savages and in Borneo and the Philippines. '10(Je4) il. 8°, $2.50 net. Scribner.

Walker, H: Cragin, pseud.
How to get a better situation. '08(Mr14) c. O. $2. Opportunity.

Walker, Hugh.
Literature of the Victorian era. '10 (Ap23) 12°, $3.50 net. Putnam.

Walker, J. W. Thomson.
Estimation of the renal function in urinary surgery. '08, [1909.] (Je) 16+275 p. il. figs. charts, O. *$4 net. Cassell.

Walker, Jacob Garrett, D.D., ed.
See American Baptist year-book.

Walker, Rev. Ja. Garfield.
Presbyterianism and the negro. '08, [1909.] 102 p. front. pap., 50 c. J. G. Walker.

Walker, J: Read, comp.
General lumber tariff. '08(Ag) c. 253 p. 8°, $5. Lumbermen's Pub.

Walker, Jos., comp.
Handy book of proverbs; arr. alphabetically for ready reference by writers and speakers. '10(Je4) c. T. (Handy information ser.) 50 c. Crowell.

Walker, Leslie J.
Theories of knowledge, absolutism, pragmatism, realism. '10(My21) D. (Stonyhurst philosophical ser.) $2.75. Longmans.

Walker, Marg. Coulson.
Bird legend and life. '08(D5) c. il. O. **$1.25 net. Baker & T.
Tales come true, and tales made new. '10(D31) il. 8°, $1.25 net. Baker & T.

Walker, Milton Barratt.
Treatise on the law of fidelity bonds with special reference to corporate fidelity bonds. '09, [1910.] (F) c. O. $3. King Bros.

Walker, Norman, M.D.
Introd. to dermatology. 4th ed. '08(Ag22) c. il. 8°, *$3 net. Wood.

Walker, Percy H.
Some technical methods of testing miscellaneous supplies, incl. paints and paint materials, inks, lubricating oils, soaps, etc. '10(My) 68 p. 8°, (U. S., Dept. of Agriculture, Bu. of Chemistry, bull.)

Walker, R. J.
Anti mias; essay in isometry. In 2 v. '10 (Ap9) O. $6.50 net. Macmillan.

Walker, Rollin Hough, and Miller, Russell B:
Studies in the prophets of Israel; normal course for Bible class teachers. '09(D18) c. il. 12°, 25 c. Eaton & M.

Walker, Rev. S. G.
Household catechism on the Decalogue. '09 (Je12) S. pap., 25 c.; cl., 40 c. S. G. Walker.

Walker, Sydney Ferris.
Electricity in mining. '08(Je20) il. 12°, $3.50. Van Nostrand.
Pocket book of electric lighting and heating. '08(S12) il. 12°, leath., $3. Henley.
Steam boilers, engines and turbines. '09 (My15) il. tabs., 8°, *$3.50 net. Van Nostrand.

Walker, T: Alfr.
Manual of public international law. '08 (F8) 8°, *$2.50 net. Macmillan.

Walker, T: Barlow.
Descriptive catalogue with reproductions of life-size bust portraits of famous Indian chiefs, great medicine men, notable Indian warriors and renowned explorers, scouts and guides; with authentic biograph. sketch of each subject and a brief hist. of the Indian tribes which they represent. '10(My14) 12°. (Not for sale.) Hahn.

Walker, T: Hamilton B.
Bebbly; or, the victorious preacher. [1910.] (Mr) c. 221 p. il. por. 12°, 60 c. Pepper Pub.

WALKER, *General* William.
Jamison, J. C. With Walker in Nicaragua. $1.50. J. C. Jamison.

Walker, Rev. W: Lowe.
Gospel of reconciliation or at-one-ment. '09(D11) O. *$2 net. Scribner.
Teaching of Christ: in its present appeal. New and revised ed. '08(Je20) D. *$1 net. Scribner.
See also Greenhough, J. G.

Walker, W: Slee.
American law of real estate agency, [etc.] '10(Ag) c. O. $6. W. H. Anderson.

Walker, Williston.
Greatest men of the Christian church. '08 (D19) c. D. (Constructive Bible studies, advanced and supplementary ser.) $1.50. Univ. of Chic.

Walking for health and competition; with special articles by E: Payson Weston, Sam Liebgold, America's champion amateur walker, and other prominent authorities. [1910.] (N) c. 69 p. il. pors. 16°, (Spalding's athletic lib.) pap., 10 c. Am. Sports.

Walking gentleman. Prior, J. †$1.50. Dutton.

Walkley, Arth. Bingham.
Drama and life. '08(Ag15) D. *$1.75 net. Brentano's.

Walks and people in Tuscany. Vane, *Sir* F. P. F. $1.50 net. Lane.

Walks and words of Jesus. *See* Bible, N. T.: Gospels.
Walks in Paris, Cain, G. $2. Macmillan.

Wall, Mrs. D. H.
See Wall, Ida Blanche Ford.

Wall, E. J., ed.
Photographic annual, 1910-11, incorporating the figures, facts and formulæ of photography. 6th ed., extended, largely rewritten and rev. '10(S3) figs. D. $1 net; pap., 50 c. net. Tennant.

Wall, Ida Blanche Ford, [Mrs. D. H. Wall.]
Comedy of petty conflicts. '08(Ag8) c. 12°, $1.50. B'way Pub.

Wall, J: Patrick.
New Brunswick [N. J.] in the critical period of the Revolution. '08, [1909.] (Mr) 8 p. 8°. (Priv. pr.) J: P. Wall.

Wall, Mary Virginia.
Daughter of Virginia Dare. '08(Je6) c. D. $1.50. Neale.

Wall, Oscar Garrett.
Recollections of the Sioux massacre; authentic hist. of the Yellow Medicine incident, of the fate of Marsh and his men, of the siege and battles of Fort Ridgely, and of other important battles and experiences; together with a historical sketch of the Sibley expedition of 1863. '09, [1910.] (Ap) 9-282 p. il. pors. front. 12°, $1.50. M. C. Russell.

Wall, W. C.
A mock trial, for amateurs; Miss Delicia Fewclothes vs. Mr. Charles Stringbeans; adapted to suit the requirements of fraternal societies. '09(S) c. 22 p. 8°, $1. W. C. Wall.

Wall, W: Edm.
Oldest paint shops in Massachusetts; paper read at the 19th annual convention of the Society of Master House Painters and Decorators of Massachusetts, held in the American house, Boston, Jan. 13, 1910. [1910.] (Mr) c. 74 p. 8°, 25 c. W: E. Wall.

WALL DECORATION.
Ganz, H: F. W. Practical hints on modelling, design and mural decoration. *$1 net. Lippincott.
Sanborn, K. Old time wall papers. *$5 net. Dutton.
Ward, J. Fresco painting. *$4.20 net. Scribner.
See also Plastering.

WALL STREET, New York City.
Clews, H: Fifty years in Wall Street. *$3 net. H: Clews.
Hill, F: T. Story of a street [Wall St.]. **$1.60 net. Harper.
See also Drew, Daniel.

Wallace, Alfr. Russel.
Is Mars habitable?: critical exam. of Prof. Percival Lowell's book, "Mars and its canals," with alternate explanation. '08 (Ja25) front. 12°, *60 c. net. Macmillan.

Wallace, Arth. Fuller.
Land cruising and prospecting: information for hunters, trappers, land cruisers, prospectors and men of the trail. '08(S12) c. il. por. S. 60 c. A. R. Harding.
Sorting, grading and curing furs. [1910.] (D) c. 93 p. il. 16°, $1. A. F. Wallace.

Wallace, Cathryn.
One Christmas eve at Roxbury Crossing, and other Christmas tales. '10(S10) c. S. 75 c. Pustet.

Wallace, C: W:
Children of the chapel at Blackfriars, 1597-1603. '08, [1909.] (Mr) c. 16+207 p. 4°, *$2.50 net. C: W: Wallace.

Wallace, D:
Simple mine accounting. '08(Mr7) 8°, $1. Hill Pub.

Wallace, Dillon.
Beyond the Mexican Sierras. '10(Ap30) c. il. O. $2 net. McClurg.

Wallace, Edg.
Angel Esquire. '08(S12) c. D. †$1.50. Holt.

Wallace, G:
The disinherited: observations in travel: conditions of old world people observed and depicted, with incidental study of the cause of the poverty which afflicts so many. '08(My2) c. D. $1. J. S. Ogilvie.

Wallace, Harold Fk.
Stalks abroad: account of the sport obtained during a two years' tour of the world. '09(Ja9) il. O. *$3.50 net. Longmans.

Wallace, Helen.
Blind hopes. '10(Ap9) front. D. $1.50. Cassell.
Life's chequer-board. '08(D12) D. $1.50. Cassell.

Wallace, Isabel.
Life and letters of General W. H. L. Wallace. '10(Ap23) il. 8°, $1.50 net. Donnelley.

Wallace, J.
Logarithmic land measurement; set of tables for the use of those engaged in measuring land. '10(N19) 8°, $2. Spon.

Wallace, Ja. Philip.
Study of ore deposits for the practical miner. '08(D5) il. *$3 net. Hill Pub.

Wallace, Lew.
Boyhood of Christ. [New ed.] '09(O2) c. il. O. $1.50. Harper.
Chariot race from "Ben-Hur." '08(O24) c. il. O. †$1.25. Harper.

Wallace, Wilfrid.
Sermons for the Christian year; with preface by Dom Bede Camm. 3 v. '10 (Jl2) c. 12°, $4. Herder.

Wallace, W:
Threshold of music: an inquiry into the development of the musical sense. '08 (Ap11) 8°, reduced from *$2.25 net to *$1.50 net. Macmillan.

WALLACE, William Harvey Lamb.
Wallace, I. Life and letters of General W. H. L. Wallace. $1.50 net. Donnelley.

Wallace collection, [London, Eng.] '09(N20) il. T. (Great art galleries.) bds., 35 c. H. M. Caldwell.

WALLACE FAMILY.
See Genealogies: Miller, W: H.

Wallace Rhodes. Davis, N. †$1.50. Harper.

Wallach, Mrs. Isabel Richman.
Second book in English for foreigners. '10 (F19) c. il. D. 50 c. Silver.
See also Richman, Julia.

Wallachian embroidery. Priscilla Pub. Co. 15 c. Priscilla.

Wallas, Graham.
Human nature in politics. '09(Ap24) O. *$1.50 net. Houghton M.
Life of Francis Place, 1771-1854. '09(F20) pors. O. *$1 net. Longmans.

Wallentin, Ignaz Gustav.
Introd. to scientific German; being the first six chapters of Grundzüze der naturlehre; ed., with notes and vocab., by P. M. Palmer. '09(N) 267 p. il. 12°, $1. Times Pub. Co., (Pa.)

Waller, Alfr. Rayney, ed.
See Ward, Adolphus W:, *ed.*

Waller, Effie.
Rhymes from the Cumberland. '09(N20) c. il. por. 8°, 75 c. B'way Pub.

Waller, Elbert.
Brief history of Illinois. '09(My8) c. il. pors. maps, S. 35 c. E. Waller.
Brief hist. of Illinois. 2d ed. '10(Mr26) c. il. por. 12°, 40 c. Wagoner.

Waller, Mary Ella.
Flamsted Quarries. '10(S17) c. il. D. $1.50. Little, B. & Co.
Our Benny: [narrative poem in memory of Lincoln.] '09(F13) c. D. **$1 net. Little, B. & Co.
Through the gates of the Netherlands. New ed. '08(D12) c. il. pors. plan, 8°, **$1.50 net. Little, B. & Co.
Year out of life. '09(Ap17) D. †$1.50. Appleton.

Waller, Osmar Lysander.
Irrigation in the state of Washington. '09 (Ag) 64 p. fold. map, 8°, (U. S., Dept. of Agriculture; Office of Experiment Stations bull.) pap. (Add. Superintendent for price.) U. S., Supt. of Docs.

Walling, Burns Tracy, and Martin, Julius.
Electrical installations of the United States navy. '08(S12) il. tab., 8°, $6; hf. mor., $6.85. U. S. Naval Inst.

Walling, Rob. Alfr. J:
George Borrow. '09(Ja23) por. O. *$1.75 net. Cassell.

Walling, W: English.
Russia's message: true world import of the revolution. '08(Je20) c. il. pors. map, O. **$3 net. Doubleday, P.

Walling, W: H., ed.
Sexology. Family medical ed. '09(S) c. 231 p. il. por. 12°, $2. Puritan Pub.

Wallington, W.
Chats on photography. '10(D3) il. 12°, $1.25 net. Lippincott.

Wallis, F.
See Hawkins, C: Cæsar.

Wallis, Fk. Edn.
How to know architecture; human elements in the evolution of styles. '10 (D3) c. il. O. $2 net. Harper.

Wallis-Chapman, Annie Beatrice and Mary.
Status of woman under English law; arranged as a continuous narrative, with references to authorities and acts of Parliament. '09(My22) 16°, limp mor., *75 c. net. Dutton.

Wallis-Chapman, M.
See Wallis-Chapman, A. B.

Wallis-Tayler, A. J.
See Tayler, A. J. Wallis-.

WALLS.
See Building materials;—Concrete.

Walls of Constantinople. Baker, B. G. $4 net. Pott.

WALNUT TREES.
See Trees.

Walpole, A. S., ed.
See Bible. N. T. Luke.

Walpole, Rev. G: H: S.
Kingdom of heaven; what it is and how we enter it. '09, [1910.] (F) 14+188 p. 12°, *$1 net. Dutton.

Walpole, Horace, [4th Earl of Orford.]
Earlier letters; sel. by A. T. Quiller-Couch. '08(D19) S. (Select English classics.) 10 c. Oxford Univ.
Last journals of Horace Walpole; during the reign of George III., from 1771-1783; with notes by Dr. Doran; ed., with an introd., by A. Fs. Steuart. In 2 v. '09 (N6) pors. O. *$7.50 net. Lane.

Walpole, Sir Spencer.
Essays: political and biographical; ed. by Fs. Holland. '08(Ag1) 8°, *$3 net. Dutton.
History of twenty-five years, 1856-1880. In 4 v. v. 3, 1870-1875; v. 4, 1876-1880. '08 (My23) O. $8. Longmans.

WALSCHAERT VALVE.
See Valves.

Walser, G: H:
Life and teachings of Jesus. '09(My1) c. 12°, *$1.35 net. Sherman, F.

Walsh, C: Harper, comp.
See Severance, H: Ormal, *comp.*

Walsh, Clara, tr.
See Masterpieces of Japan.

Walsh, D:, M.D.
Hair and its diseases. 2d ed. '08(Mr28) il. 12°, *$1 net. Chic. Med. Bk.

Walsh, Ja. Jos.
Chirpings of Dusty Mike, by Bill Tansy, the honorary member. '07, [1908.] (Mr) c. 69 p. il. por. 12°. (Add. pubs. for price.) Dietz Pr.

Walsh, Ja. Jos., M.D.
Catholic churchmen in science; second ser. '09(My22) 12°, $1. Dolphin.
Education, how old the new. '10(D3) c. 8°, $2. Fordham Univ.
Popes and science. '08(Je6) c. 8°, $2. Fordham Univ.
Thirteenth, greatest of centuries. 2d ed., with emendations and appendix. '09 (Ag7) c. il. O. $2.50. Cath. Summer Sch.
See also O'Reilly, Michael Fs.

Walsh, Rev. J:
Mass and vestments of the Catholic church, liturgical, doctrinal, historical and archæological. '09(N) c. 539 p. il. 8°, *$2 net. J: Walsh.

Walsh, J: H:
Arithmetic for upper grades. '08, [1909.] (F) c. 6+336 p. diagrs., 12°, 50 c.; with appendix, 55 c. Heath.
Graded mental arithmetic. '09(My) c. 6+284 p. il. 12°, *50 c. net. Heath.

Walsh, J: W.
Hepburn rate law. '10(Mr) c. 28 p. O. pap., 25 c. La Salle Extension.

Walsh, Ralph, M.D.
Desk book of facts for physicians and pharmacists. '09(My) c. 202 p. 8°, $1.50. R. Walsh.

Walsh, T:
Prison ships, and other poems. '09(N20) c. D. *$1 net. Sherman, F.

Walsh, Rev. Wa.
Moral damage of war. '09(Ja23) 12°, (International lib.) *90 c. net. Ginn.

Walsh, W: Shepard, ["W: Shepard."]
Abraham Lincoln and the London *Punch:* cartoons, comments and poems published in *The London Charivari,* during the American Civil War, (1861-1865.) '09 (Ap3) c. il. O. **$1 net. Moffat.
Story of Santa Klaus; told for children of all ages from six to sixty. '09(D11) c. il. D. **$1.50 net. Moffat.
—, comp. International encyclopedia of prose and poetical quotations from the literature of the world; under one alphabetical arrangement; with a complete concordance to the quotations, indexes of the authors quoted and topical indeves to subjects, with cross references. '08(O3) c. D. limp leath., **$5 net. Winston.

Walsh, W: T:
Mirage of the many. '10(S10) c. D. $1.50. Holt.

Walster, Harlow Leslie.
See Whitson, Andrew Robinson.

Walter, A.
Emperor William First; the great war and peace hero; tr. by G: P. Upton. '09 (S11) c. il. por. S. (Life stories for young people.) *60 c. net. McClurg.

Walter, Alice Hall.
Sec Walter, Herbert Eug.

Walter, Eug.
Great issue; or, the undertow. '08(Ap11) D. $1.50. Doscher.
See also Harding, J: W:—Sommerville, C:

Walter, F: pseud.
See Schultz, F: Wa.

Walter, Herbert Eug. and Alice Hall.
Wild birds in city parks; being hints on identifying 200 birds; prep. primarily for the spring migration in Lincoln Park, Chicago, but adapted to other localities. 4th enl. rev., with chart and key. Authors' ed. '10(Je4) c. fold. chart, 12°, 35 c. St. Johnsbury Repub.

Walter, L. Edna.
Russia. '10(N19) col. il. map, 12°, (Peeps at many lands ser.) 75 c. net. Macmillan.

Walter, Paul A. F., rep.
See New Mexico Territory. *Sup. ct.* Repts.

Walter W: Wilfred.
Doctor's daughter: sequel to "The pastor's son." '08(D) c. 253 p. 12°, $1.25. W: W. Walter.

Walter and Lillian. *See* Basel, Edm. Songs and ballads.

Walters, Clarence Lambert.
Presentation of Graham-Pitman phonographic shorthand, arranged in nine lessons. '07, [1908.] (Mr.) c. 25 p. D. 80 c. C. L. Walters.

Walters, F. Rufenacht, M.D.
Open-air or sanatorium treatment of pulmonary tuberculosis. '09(N) 338 p. 8°, *$2.25 net. Wood.

Walters, Fs. Marion.
Physiology and hygiene for secondary schools. '09(Je) c. 8+424 p. il. 12°, $1.20. Heath.

Walton, Alb. J.
Fractures and separated epiphyses. '10(S) 7+288 p. il. O. $3 net. Longmans.

Walton, Calvin L.
See Everly, Lu Lester.

Walton, Dudley W.
Pitmanic guide for students and teachers of Isaac Pitman shorthand, with especial regard to the Benn Pitman, Graham and Munson modifications. 2d ed. '10(Ap30) D. pap., 20 c. Pitman.

Walton, Esmeé.
Aurora of Poverty Hill. '09(Ja2) 12°, 50 c. B'way Pub.

Walton, G: A:, and Holmes, Stanley Harry.
Arithmetics. 2d bk. '08(Ja11) il. D. 40 c.; 3d bk. '08(S19) 45 c.; 4th bk. '09(S11) c. 50 c. Am. Bk.

Walton, G: Lincoln, M.D.
Practical guide to the wild flowers and fruits. '09(My1) c. il. por. figs. O. **$1.50 net. Lippincott.
Those nerves. '09(N13) front. D. **$1 net. Lippincott.
Why worry? '08(Je6) c. D. *$1 net. Lippincott.

Walton, Izaak.
Compleat angler. Riverside Press ed. '09 (Ap10) il. 16°, *$5 net. Houghton M.
—, and Cotton, C:
Complete angler; ed. by R: Le Gallienne. '10(Ja8) il. pors. 4°, *$6 net; Crown lib. ed., 12°, *$1.50 net. Lane.

WALTON, Izaak.
Marston, E: Thomas Ken and Izaak Walton. *$2 net. Longmans.

Walton, Ja. Henri, jr.
See Lincoln, Azariah T:

Walton, Mary Alice.
Hard times edition, by the bard of Camill; ["A collection of poetry and prose from my old scrap book, by the bard of Camill."] [1910.] (O) c. 57 p. il. 8°, 25 c. S. Walton.

Walton, Mrs. Octavius Frank.
Entre bastidores o' hasta hallarla. '10(N5) c. 12°, 50 c. Am. Tr.
Lost clue. '08(My16) D. $1.25. Am. S. S.

Walton, Stokes.
Poems. '10(O15) c. D. pap., 50 c. Eichelberger.

Walz, Max Fs.
Precious blood the price of our redemption; a manual for the members of the Archconfraternity of the precious blood. '09 (S) c. 147 p. il. 24°, 25 c.; pap., 15 c. St. Joseph's Pr.

WAMPANOG INDIANS.
See Indians.

Wanamaker primer on Abraham Lincoln, strength, mind, heart, will, the full-rounded man, the typical American example of the Rule of four; Wanamaker—originator. '10(Ap16) il. pors. 12°, gratis. Wanamaker.

Wander songs. McGroarty, J: S. $2. Grafton Pub.
Wander years. Yoxall, J. H: *$2 net. Dutton.
Wanderer in Holland. Lucas, E: V. $2.50 net. Macmillan.
Wanderer in London. Lucas, E: V. $2.50 net. Macmillan.
Wanderer in Paris. Lucas, E: V. $1.75 net; $2.50 net. Macmillan.
Wanderers. *See* Bruce, Wallace.
Wandering Jew. *See* Sue, Marie Joseph Eugène.
Wandering joy. Baker, J. W. $1. B'way Pub.
Wandering student in the Far East. Ronaldshay, L. J: L. D., *Earl of.* *$8.50 net. Scribner.
Wanderings. Boyd, M. A. 75 c. Times-News.
Wanderings among South Sea savages. Walker, H. W. $2.50 net. Scribner.
Wanderings in Arabia. Doughty, C: M. 2 v. $4.50. Scribner.
Wanderings in Ireland. Shoemaker, M. M. **$2.50 net. Putnam.
Wanderings in London. Chancellor, E. B. *75 c. net. Pott.
Wanderings in South America. *See* Waterton, C:
Wanderings in the Roman Campagna. Lanciani, R. A. *$5 net. Houghton M.
Wanderings of a literary pilgrim. Smith, L: P. 25 c. L: P. Smith.
Wanderings of Israel. Mord, W. 35 c. Stokes.
Wanderings of Jesus. Segal, J. $2.50. J. Segal.

Wang, Chung Yu.
Antimony: its history, chemistry, mineralogy, geology, metallurgy, uses, preparations, analysis, production, and valuation; with complete bibliographies, for students, manufacturers, and users of antimony. '09(Je5) figs. fold tab., O. *$4 net. Lippincott.

Wanhill, C. F., and Beveridge, Wilfred W: Ogilvy.
Sanitary officer's handbook of practical hygiene. '09(Je5) tabs., *$1.40 net. Longmans.

Wanted—a theology. Carter, S: T. **75 c. net. Funk.
Wanted by the police. Harper, O. 25 c. J. S. Ogilvie.
Wants. Dwiggins, C. V. $1; $1.50. Winston.

War.
Bloch, J. de. Future of war. 50 c. net. Ginn.
Bordwell, W. P. Law of war between belligerents. $3.50. Callaghan.
Bridgman, R. L. World organization. 50 c. net. Ginn.
Childers, E. War and the arme blanche. $2.10 net. Longmans.
Dodge, D: L. War inconsistent with the religion of Jesus Christ. 50 c. net. Ginn.
Erasmus, D. Treatise on war. *$6 net. Merrymount.

War.—*Continued.*
Foster, J: W. War not inevitable. per 100, $3. Int. Sch. of Peace.
Hearne, R. P. Aerial warfare. *$2.50 net. Lane.
Holland, T: E. Laws of war on land. $1.50. Oxford Univ.
Holland, T: E. Letters to *The Times* upon war and neutrality. *$1.75 net. Longmans.
Kirkpatrick, G: R. War—what for? $1.20. G: R. Kirkpatrick.
Latifi, A. Effect of war on property. *$1.50 net. Macmillan.
Ralston, J. H. Some supposed just causes of war. per 100, $3. Int. Sch. of Peace.
Sumner, C: Addresses on war. 50 c. net. Ginn.
Walsh, W. Moral damage of war. *90 c. net. Ginn.
Warner, H. E. Ethics of force. 50 c. net. Ginn.
Waste of militarism. per 100, $3. Int. Sch. of Peace.
Wilkinson, S. University and the study of war. 35 c. Oxford Univ.
See also Arbitration;—Aerial navigation;—Battles;—Cavalry;—Infantry;—International law;—Military art and science;—Naval art and science;—Peace;—Rifle;—Soldiers;—Submarine warfare;—*also* names of wars.

War children. Wheelwright, J. T. †$1.50. Dodd.
War dance and the fire-fly dance. *See* Seton, Ernest Thompson.
War for the Union ser. il. D. †$1.50. Lothrop, L. & S.
—Tomlinson. For the stars and stripes.—Young blockaders.

War games.
See Military art and science.

War in the air. Wells, H. G: †$1.50. Macmillan.
War in Wexford. Wheeler, H. F. B. $4 net. Lane.

War of 1812.
Dunlop, W: Recollections of the War of 1812. $1. Historical Pub.
Hampton, C. E. Twenty-first's trophy of Niagara. [Battle of Lundy's Lane, 1814.] $1. C. E. Hampton.
Leech, S: Thirty years from home; or, a voice from the main deck. $3.25. Abbatt.
See also Brock, Isaac.

War of the Secession.
See Civil War (United States).

War of words. Bonum Meritum, *pseud.* $1; 25 c. Donohue.
War on the sea. Darrieus, P. J. G. G. $2. U.S.Naval Inst.
War on the white plague. Tscholl, J: 60 c. net. Wiltzius.
War on the white slave trade. Bell, E. A., *ed.* $1.50. C: C. Thompson.

War-ships.
See Naval art and science;—Ships and shipbuilding.

War songs. Stone, C., *ed.* 90 c. Oxford Univ.
War-time journal of a Georgia girl. Andrews, E. F. **$2.50 net. Appleton.

Warbasse, Ja. P:
Conquest of disease through animal experimentation. '10(Ap) c. 13+175 p. por. 8°, $1 net. Appleton.
Medical sociology: a series of observations touching upon the sociology of health and the relations of medicine to society. '09(Ag) c. 355 p. $2. Appleton.

Warburton, Clyde W.
Improvement of the oat crop. '09(Ag) 10 p. il. 8°, (U. S., Dept. of Agriculture; Bu. of Plant Industry circular.) pap., 5 c. U. S., Supt. of Docs.

Warburton, G: A:
Typical general secretary; life of Edwin F. See. '09(Ja23) c. il. pors. 12°, 75 c. Y. M. C. A.

Ward, A. B., pseud.
See Bailey, *Mrs.* Alice Ward.

Ward, Adolphus W:
Electress Sophia and the Hanoverian succession. 2d ed., rev. and enl. '09(N13) D. *$2.75 net. Longmans.
See also Meredith, G:

—, ed. *See* Acton, J: E. E: D.-A., *Lord.*

—, and Waller, Alfr. Rayney, eds.
Cambridge history of English literature. In 14 v. v. 2, The end of the middle ages. '08(Je6); v. 3, Renascence and Reformation. '08(D12); v. 4, Sir T. North to Michael Drayton. '10(F12); v. 5, The drama to 1642, pt. 1; v. 6, The drama to 1642, pt. 2. (D3) c. O. ea., **$2.50 net; subs., per set, **$31.50 net. Putnam.

Ward, Agnes Snow.
Lessons in surgical technique. '08, [1909.] (Mr) c. 56 p. 8°. (Not for sale.) A. S. Ward.

Ward, Anna L., comp.
Dictionary of quotations from English and American poets based upon Bohn's edition: rev., corrected and enl., with 1200 quotations from American authors. '09 (O2) c. D. (Crowell's thin paper poets.) limp leath., $1.25, boxed; ooze, $1.75, boxed. Crowell.
Poetical and prose quotations. 2 v. '10 (D) il. $2.50, boxed. Crowell.

Ward, Archibald Robinson, and Jaffa, Myer E:
Pure milk and the public health. '09(My1) c. il. figs. O. *$2 net. Taylor & C.

Ward, Bernard.
Dawn of the Catholic revival in England, 1781-1803. '09(Ap10) 2 v., il. pors. O. *$7 net. Longmans.

Ward, Duren Ja. Henderson.
Classifications of religions. '09(O23) bds., 75 c. Open Court.

Ward, Mrs. Eliz. Stuart Phelps, [Mrs. Herbert Dickinson Ward.]
Gypsy Breynton. '09(My8) front. D. (Familiar friends ser.) $1. Sturgis & W.
Jonathan and David. '09(Ag28) c. il. D. **50 c. net. Harper.
Oath of allegiance, and other stories. '09 (S25) c. il. D. **$1.25 net. Houghton M.
Though life us do part. '08(O17) c. front. D. †$1.50. Houghton M.

Ward, Ernest F. and Mrs. Phebe E.
Echoes from Bharatkhand. '08 (Ag) c. 3-174 p. il. map, 12°, 75 c. Free Meth.

Ward, Florence Gannon Hanfeld, [Mrs. J. Carlton Ward.]
Under the northern lights. '09(S18) c. front. D. $1.50. Wessels.

Ward, Franklin Wilmer.
See Hines, Fk. T:

Ward, G: Kemp, comp.
Andrew Warde and his descendants, 1597-1910; being a compilation of facts relating to one of the oldest New England families and embracing many families of other names, descended from a worthy ancestor even unto the tenth and eleventh generations; comp. under the direction of the Association of Descendants of Andrew Ward. '10(N) 604 p. il. pors. facsims., 4°, $10. De La Mare.

Ward, H. Marshall.
Trees: hdbk. of forest botany. vs. 4, 5. '09 (My22) il. 8°, (Cambridge biological ser.) ea., *$1.50 net. Putnam.

Ward, Harry F.
Social ministry; introd. to the study and practice of social service; ed. for the Methodist Federation for Social Service. '10(O8) c. D. $1 net. Eaton & M.

Ward, H: Baldwin.
Iconographia parasitorum hominis: collation of figures with brief explanatory text, to aid in the study and diagnosis of the less common parasites of man. '07, [1909.] (F) 43 p. 8°, (Univ. of Neb. studies, Zoological laboratory.) 50 c. Univ. of Neb.

Ward, H: Snowden, ed.
Photographic annual. 4th ed., extended, largely rewritten, and rev. to March, 1908. '08(Ag8); 5th ed., extended, largely rewritten and rev. to June, 1909. '09 (Ag21) il. tabs., D. ea., $1; pap., 50 c. Tennant.

—, and Weed, Catherine.
Shakespeare's town and times. 3d ed., enl. '09(O9) il. 8°, *$1.50, boxed. Lippincott.

Ward, Herbert.
Voice from the Congo; comprising stories, anecdotes and descriptive notes. '10 (O15) c. il. O. $2.50 net. Scribner.

Ward, Mrs. Herbert Dickinson.
See Ward, *Mrs.* Eliz. Stuart Phelps.

Ward, Hilda.
Girl and the motor. '08(D26) c. S. $1. Gas Engine.

Ward, Mrs. Humphry.
See Ward, *Mrs.* Mary Augusta Arnold.

Ward, Mrs. J. Carlton.
See Ward, Florence Gannon Hanfeld.

Ward, Ja.
Fresco painting: its art and technique. '09 (Je26) il. O. *$4.20 net. Scribner.

Ward, Ja. W:, M.D.
Agnostic in medicine; presidential address del. at the 66th annual session of the American Institute of Homœopathy held at Pasadena, Cal., July 11, 1910. '10(D) 21 p. 8°. (Priv. pr.) Murdock Press.

Ward, Jane Olive Patricia.
The herd. '08(O3) c. por. D. $1.50. Cochrane.

WARD, John Adner.
Anderson, G: S. Adner Ward. 25 c. G: S. Anderson.

Ward, J: J.
Life histories of familiar plants. '08(D5) il. *$1.75 net. Cassell.

Ward, Mrs. Josephine Mary Hope-Scott, [Mrs. Wilfrid Philip Ward.]
Great possessions. '09(N6) c. D. **$1.35 net. Putnam.

Ward, Mrs. Mary Augusta Arnold, [Mrs. Humphry Ward.]
Lady Merton, colonist. '10(Ap23) c. front. D. $1.50. Doubleday, P.
Marriage à la mode. '09(Je5) c. il. D. †$1.20, boxed. Doubleday, P.
Testing of Diana Mallory. '08(S19) c. il. D. †$1.50. Harper.

Ward, P. R.
See Elliott, Berton E.

Ward, Mrs. Phebe E.
See Ward, Ernest F.

Ward, Rob.
Fucus histriomastix; comedy, probably written by Rob. Ward and acted at Queen's College, Cambridge, in Lent, 1623. '10(Je4) 12°, $1.10 net. Putnam.

Ward, Rob. De Courcy.
Climate considered especially in relation to man. '08(Ap18) c. O. (Science ser.) **$2 net. Putnam.

Ward, Wilfrid Philip.
Ten personal studies: A. J. Balfour, J. T. Delane, R. H. Hutton, Sir J. Knowles, Henry Sidgwick, Lord Lytton, Father I. Ryder, Sir M. E. Grant Duff, Leo XIII., Cardinal Wiseman, John Henry Newman, Cardinals Newman and Manning. '08 (D19) pors. O. *$3 net. Longmans.

Ward, Mrs. Wilfrid Philip.
See Ward, *Mrs.* Josephine Mary Hope-Scott.

Ward, W: Hayes.
Seal cylinders of western Asia. '10(Ap2) il. Q. pap., $7.50. Carnegie.

WARD FAMILY.
See Genealogies.

Ward Hill—the teacher. Tomlinson, E. T. †$1.25. Griffith.

Warde, Marg., [pseud. for Edith Kellogg Dunton.]
Betty Wales, B.A. '08(O3) c. il. D. (Betty Wales books.) †$1.25. Penn Pub. Co.
Betty Wales & Co.; story for girls. '09 (N13) c. il. D. $1.25. Penn Pub. Co.
Betty Wales on the campus; story for girls. '10(D3) c. il. D. $1.25. Penn Pub. Co.

Wardell, Mrs. L. Villiers-.
See Villiers-Wardell, *Mrs.* L.

Wardell, R. J.
First lessons in philosophy. '10(D31) D. $1.25 net. Eaton & M.

Warden, Florence, pseud.
See James, *Mrs.* Florence Alice Price.

Warden (The). *See* Trollope, Anthony.

Ware, Allison.
Course of study and teachers' handbook in the common literature of life. '09, [1910.] (Ap) c. 207 p. 4°, (San Francisco State Normal School; bull.; new ser.) 40 c. San F. St. Normal.
Course of study and teachers' manual in map geography. '08, [1909.] (Mr) c. 52 p. 4°, (San Francisco State Normal School bulls., new ser.) pap., 30 c. San F. St. Normal.
Course of study in literature for the grammar grades. '09(Mr) 4°, (San Francisco State Normal School bulls., new ser.) pap., 30 c. San F. St. Normal.
Plan of literature study for grammar grades. '09(O) 4°, (San Francisco State Normal School bull.; new ser.) pap., 30 c. San F. St. Normal.

Ware, Bruce Richardson, jr.
Handy book for the aid and instruction of the enlisted men in the Engineer Depart., United States Navy. '09(Ag) c. 88 p. il. 16°. (Add. Institution for price.) U. S. Naval Inst.

Ware, Eug. Fitch, ["Ironquill."]
Autobiography of Ithuriel [chapter in psychology.] '09, [1910.] 94 p. 12°. (Not for sale.) E. F. Ware.
Lyon campaign in Missouri: being a hist. of the First Iowa Infantry, together with a birdseye view of the conditions in Iowa preceding the great Civil War of 1861. '07, [1908.] (My.) 11+377 p. pors. maps, facsims., 12°, $1. Crane.

Ware, Horace Everett.
Forgotten prime meridian; repr. from the Publications of the Colonial Society of Massachusetts. '10(D) 383-398 p. diagr., 8°. (Priv. pr.) H. E. Ware.

Ware, J. Redding.
Passing English of the Victorian era: dictionary of heterodox English, slang and phrase. '09(Mr13) 8°, hf. mor., *$3 net. Dutton.

Ware, R: Darwin.
In the woods and on the shore. '08(Je20) c. il. maps, O. $2. L. C. Page.

Ware, Sedley Lynch.
Elizabethan parish in its ecclesiastical and financial aspects. '08(Je27) c. O. (Johns Hopkins Univ. studies in hist. and pol. science.) pap., 50 c. Johns Hopkins.

Ware, T: A.
Story of the centuries; or, the rise of the common people. '08(Je20) c. por. D. $1. Cochrane.

Ware collection of Blaschka glass flower models. Kent, G: H: 35 c. G: H. Kent.

WAREHOUSES.
Thompson, W: B. Central warehouse plan. W: B. Thompson.

Wares of Edgefield. White, E. O. **$1.25 net. Houghton M.

Warfare against tuberculosis. California Association for the Study and Prevention of Tuberculosis. (Add. pubs. for price.) Cal. Assoc. Tuberculosis.

Warfare of the soul. Hughson, S. C. **$1.20 net. Longmans.

Warfield, Ethelbert Dudley.
Abraham Lincoln: a memorial address del. before the American Society for the Extension of University Teaching. '09(S) 37 p. por. 8°, 25 c. E. D. Warfield.

Warfield, L. M., M.D.
Arterio-sclerosis, etiology, diagnosis, prognosis, prophylaxis and treatment; with an introd. by H. S. Thayer. '08, [1910.] (O) 200 p. il. $2. Mosby.

Waring, Eleanor Howard.
White path. '08(Ja4) il. D. $1.50. Neale.

Waring, Gerald A.
Geology and water resources of the Harney Basin region, Oregon. '09(Jl) 93 p. maps, 8°, (U. S., Geol. Survey; Water-supply paper.) (Add. Superintendent for price.) U. S., Supt. of Docs.

Waring, Rev. Luther Hess.
Hist. of the Evangelical Lutheran Church of Georgetown, D. C., Washington, District of Columbia, 1769-1909; prep. for the 140th anniversary, by the pastor, Oct. 31, 1909. [1910.] (F) 28 p. il. pors. 8°, 35 c. L. H. Waring.
Political theories of Martin Luther. '10 (O1) c. D. $1.50. Putnam.

Waring, Rob. Lewis.
As we see it. '10(Ap9) front. O. $1.50. R. L. Waring.

Warlick, Rev. C. W.
Christian ministry; or, the problem of the church. '09, [1910.] c. (Ja) 8+9-311 p. 12°, $1. C. W. Warlick.

WARM SPRINGS, Va.
See Virginia.

Warman, Cy.
Weiga of Temagami, and other Indian tales. '08(N7) c. il. por. O. $1.50; ooze leath., $2.50, boxed. Caldwell.

Warman, E: Barrett.
Health influenced by underwear; influenced by insulation; influenced by color; exercise, who needs it? '10(S) c. 34 p. por. 16°, (Spalding's athletic lib.) pap., 10 c. Am. Sports.
Indian club exercises. '10(Jl2) c. il. por. 12°, (Spalding's athletic lib.) pap., 10 c. Am. Sports.
Psychic science series. v. 1-4. v. 1, Psychology; v. 2, Personal magnetism; v. 3, Telepathy; v. 4, Hypnotism. '10(My21); v. 5-8. v. 5, Suggestion; v. 6, Spiritism; v. 7, Clairoyance and clair-audience, premonition and impressions; v. 8, Hindu philosophy in a nutshell. (N19) c. pors. D. bds., ea., 50 c. net, boxed. McClurg.
Twenty-minute exercises, with supplement "How to avoid growing old" and "Fasting: its object and benefits." '09(O23) c. il. 16°. (Spalding's athletic lib.) pap., 10 c. Am. Sports.

Warman, Rev. F. S. Guy.
New Testament theology. '10(D10) (Anglican Church hdbk.) 40 c. net. Longmans.

Warming, Johannes Eug.
Oecology of plants; introd. to the study of plant-communities, by Eug. Warming, assisted by Martin Vahl; prepared for publication in English by Percy Groom and T: Bayley Balfour. '09(Je19) O. $2.90. Oxford Univ.

Warnack, H: Christeen.
Life's new psalms. '10(D24) S. leath., $1; pap., 30 c. Roger Bros.

Warneck, Johannes L.
Living Christ and dying heathenism; tr. by Rev. Neil Buchanan. '09(O23) 8°, *$1.75 net. Revell.

Warner, Adam Dixon.
Folcarinia: political love story. '08, [1909.] (F) c. 279 p. 12°. (Add. pubs. for price.) Smith-B.
Modern city; cont. the author's answer to Hon. David S. Rose; del. at Salt Lake City, Dec. 5th, 1909. '10(Ap9) c. por. 8°, 25 c. Baumgardt.

Warner, Amos Griswold.
American charities; rev. and enlarged by Mary Roberts Coolidge; with a biographical preface by G: Elliott Howard. '08 (N21) c. D. **$2 net. Crowell.

Warner, Anna Bartlett.
Susan Warner, ("Elizabeth Wetherell.") '09(D4) c. il. pors. O. **$2.50 net. Putnam.

Warner, Anne, [Mrs. C: Ellis French.]
In a mysterious way. '09(My8) c. il. D. †$1.50. Little, B. & Co.
Just between themselves; book about Dichtenberg. '10(Ap30) c. front. D. $1.50. Little, B. & Co.
Original gentleman. '08(O3) front. c. D. †$1.50. Little, B. & Co.
The panther: tale of temptation. '08(O24) c. il. O. †$1.25. Small
Seeing England with Uncle John. '08 (Mr21) il. D. †$1.50. Century Co.
Susan Clegg; her friend and her neghbors; [two former Susan Clegg books combined.] '10(S10) c. D. $1.50. Little, B. & Co.
Your child and mine. '09(O9) c. il. D. †$1.50. Little, B. & Co.

Warner, Rev. D. S.
See Olmstead, *Rev.* W: B.

Warner, Mrs. Ellen E. Kenyon-.
See Kenyon-Warner, *Mrs.* Ellen E.

Warner, Mrs. Frances Lorimer.
Our invisible supply: how to obtain [pt. 1]; ser. of personal letters to students detailing methods of demonstrating health, wealth and every form of attainment. '07, [1908.] (Mr); pt. 2, Being an advanced series of instructions detailing methods and giving examples of demonstration of health, wealth and harmony. '09(O23) c. por. D. ea., *$1 net. Roger Bros.

Warner, H. E.
Ethics of force. [1910] (My) 12°, (International lib.) 50 c. net. Ginn.

Warner, H. J.
See Haywood, J: Kerfoot.

"Warner, Hannah," pseud.
See Jewett, J: Howard.

Warner, Harry Sheldon.
Social welfare and the liquor problem. '10(Mr26) c. D. $1: pap., 35 c. Intercollegiate Prohibition.

Warner, Susan, ["Eliz. Wetherell."]
Wide, wide world. '08(O10) il. D. (Bowman's illustrated lib. of world-favorite books.) $1. Bowman.

Wide, wide world. '10(O) il. 8°, $1.50. Fenno.

WARNER, Susan.
Warner, A. B. Susan Warner. **$2.50 net. Putnam.

Warrack, Rev. Alex.
Scots' dialect dict. '10(D10) 8°, $3 net. Lippincott.

Warre, Rev. Edm.
On the grammar of rowing; three lectures. '09(Je19) il. O. 85 c. Oxford Univ.

Warren, Carro Frances.
Little Danny Dandelion. '10(D3) il. 12°, (Garden ser. for children.) 75 c. C. M. Clark.

Little Goldie Goldenrod and her friends. '09(D4) c. il. D. (Garden ser.) 75 c. C. M. Clark.

Little Polly Primrose and her friends. '08 (D12) il. 12°, (Garden ser.) 75 c. C. M. Clark.

Warren, C:
Hist. of the Harvard Law School and of early legal conditions in America. 3 v. '08, [1909.] (My) il. pors. facsims., 8°, $25. Lewis Pub.

Warren, C: E.
Musket boys of old Boston; or, the first blow for liberty. '09(D18) c. il. 12°, (Revolutionary ser.) $1. Cupples & L.

Musket boys under Washington; or, the Tories of old New York. '09(D18) c. il. 12°, (Revolutionary ser.) $1. Cupples & L.

Warren, Edg.
Two dollars a day for poultry and eggs: book for beginners: how to start a poultry plant and make it pay. [2d ed.] '09(Jl) c. 94 p. il. 8°, 50 c. De Puy.

Warren, E: H:, ed.
Select cases and other authorities on the law of private corporations. '09(Ag) 10+703 p. 8°, $5. E: H: Warren.

—, and Hildebrand, Ira P.
Select cases and other authorities on the law of private corporations. Texas supp. '09, [1910.] (Mr) c. O. $4. E: H: Warren.

Warren, E: Royal.
Mammals of Colorado; acct. of the several species found within the boundaries of the state, together with a record of their habits and of their distribution. '10(Jl30) il. maps, 8°, $3.50 net. Putnam.

Warren, Fred D.
Warren's defiance to the federal courts; full text of speeches before the federal courts at Fort Scott and St. Paul. '10 (Jl16) S. pap., 10 c. Kerr.

Warren, G: A.
Musket boys on the Delaware. '10(D) il. 12°, (Revolutionary ser.) $1. Cupples & L.

Warren, G: F:
Elements of agriculture. '09(S4) il. D. **$1.10 net. Macmillan.

Teacher's manual to accompany The elements of agriculture. '09(N6) 12°, *12 c. net. Macmillan.

—, and Livermore, Kenneth Carter.
Lab'y exercises in farm management. '10 (Ag13) 12°, 80 c. net. Macmillan.

Warren, H: Mather.
To and fro: [travel in different parts of the world.] '09(F13) c. 8°, $1.50. Fell.

Warren, Bp. H: White, comp.
Fifty-two memory hymns. '08(Ja4) O. *50 c. net. Jennings.

Warren, Ina Russell, comp.
Book of friendship: collection of verse and prose. '10(S10) c. front. O. $1.50 net, boxed. Jacobs.

Warren, J:
Spanish grammar; simple and pract. '10 (D3) D. (Longmans' commercial ser.) $1. Longmans.

Warren, Jos. Allen.
Notes on the number and distribution of native legumes in Nebraska and Kansas. '09(Ag) 9 p. 8°, (U. S., Dept. of Agriculture; Bu. of Plant Industry circular.) pap. (Add. Superintendent for price.) U. S., Supt. of Docs.

Warren, Kate M., comp. and ed.
Treasury of English literature; from the beginning to the eighteenth century. '09 (Ag21) 8°, $2. Dodge.

Warren, Marie Josephine.
Twig of thorn; Irish fairy play in two in two acts. '10(D10) c. D. 50 c. net. W. H. Baker.

Warren, Maude Lavinia Radford.
Peter-Peter: romance out of town. '09 (Je5) c. il. D. †$1.50. Harper.

Warren, Maude Radford.
Land of the living. '08(Ag8) c. il. D. †$1.50. Harper.

Warren, T: Herbert.
Centenary of Tennyson, 1809-1909; lecture given to the university extension students in the Sheldonian Theatre on August 6, 1909. '09(N13) O. pap., 35 c. Oxford Univ.

Essays of poets and poetry ancient and modern. '09(Ag21) 8°, $3. Dutton.

Warren, W. R.
Program of the international centennial celebration and conventions of the Disciples of Christ (Christian churches). '09, [1910.] (Ja) c. 207 p. il. fold. map, 12°, $1. Am. Chr. Miss.

Warren, Waldo Pondray.
Thoughts on business, second series. '08 (N7) c. D. $1.25. Forbes.

Warren, W: Fairfield.
Earliest cosmologies: the universe as pictured in thought by the ancient Hebrews, Babylonians, Egyptians, Greeks, Iranians, and Indo-Aryans: a guidebook for beginners in the study of ancient literatures and religions. '09(S18) c. il. O. *$1.50 net. Eaton & M.

Warren, W: H:
Engineering construction in steel and timber. 2d ed. '10(Ap2) il. O. (Civil engineering ser.) $5 net. Longmans.

Warren, Winslow.
See Thayer, W: Roscoe.

Warren cook book; comp. and arr. by the Second Auxiliary Missionary Society of the Presbyterian Church, Warren, Pa. 3d ed. '08, [1909.] (Ja) 6-267 p, 8°, $1. J. W. Kitchen.

WARREN, Mass.
Vital records of Warren (formerly Western). $2.40. F. P. Rice.

Warrens of Virginia. Eggleston, G: C. †$1.50. G: W. Dillingham.

Warrior the untamed. Irwin, W: H: †50 c. Doubleday, P.

Warriors brave. Jamieson, M. M., *jr.* 50 c. Dutton.

Warriors of old Japan. Ozaki, U. T. **$1.25 net. Houghton M

Warriner, Eug. Clarence.
Industrial and vocational training in the public schools; prepared by Supt. E. C. Warriner, Saginaw, E. S., and published by the State Superintendent of Public Instruction. '09, [1910.] (Ap) 10 p. 8°, (Michigan, Dept. of Public Instruction; bull.) (Add. pubs. for price.) Mich. Supt. Pub. Instruction.

Wars of religion in France. Thompson, J. W. *$4.50 net. Univ. of Chic.

WARSHIPS.
See Naval art and science.

Warvelle, G: W:
Practical treatise on abstracts and examinations of title to real property. 3d ed. '09(O) *$4 net. Callaghan.
Principles of the American law of real property for the use of students. 3d ed. '09(O) c. O. $4. Callaghan

Warwick, C: Franklin.
Danton and the French Revolution. '08 (My9) c. pors. O. **$2.50 net. Jacobs.
Napoleon and the end of the French Revolution. '10(N12) c. pors. O. $2.50 net. Jacobs.
Robespierre and the French Revolution. '09(Je5) c pors. facsim. O. **$2.50 net. Jacobs.

Warwick, F. J., and Tunstall, A. C., M.D.
First aid to the injured and sick. '10(D) 16+226 p. 16°, leath., $1 net. W: R. Jenkins.
Formerly published by Saunders.

Warwick, Sidney.
House of lies. '10(Mr5) front. D. $1.50. Cassell.

Was Abraham Lincoln an infidel? Wettstein, C. T. $1.25. C. M. Clark.

Was der grosmutter lehre bewirkt. Spyri, *Mrs.* J. H. 25 c. Heath.

Was it Andros? Davis, A. McF. (Priv. pr.) A. McF. Davis.

Was William Shakespere a gentleman? Tannenbaum, S: A. 50 c. Tenny.

Washburn, Claude C.
Pages from the book of Paris. '10(O22) c. il. O. $3 net. Houghton M.

Washburn, Eva Jane.
"Eureka." '10(Je) 106 p. il. por. 16°, $1. Sun.

Washburn, G:, D.D.
Fifty years in Constantinople; and recollections of Robert College. '09(O30) c. il. pors. O. **$3 net. Houghton M.

Washburn, Howard E.
American pearls. '08(N) 48 p. il. 4°, pap., 50 c. H. E. Washburn.

Washburn, Josie.
Underworld sewer. '09, [1910.] (Ja) c. 7-342 p. por. il. 12°, $1.50. Washburn.

Washburn, Lucy Adelia.
Richard Webber family; genealogy from the first settlement in America. '09(N) 21 p. 8°. (Priv. pr.) A. I. Root.

Washburn, Mabel Thacher Rosemary.
Ancestry of William Howard Taft. '08 (N21) c. il. por. 8°, (Genealogical miniatures.) pap., $1. Allaben.

Washburn, Marg. Floy.
Animal mind: text-book of comparative psychology. '08(Mr7) il. 12°. (Animal behavior ser.) *$1.60 net. Macmillan.

Washburne, Mrs. Marion Foster.
House on the north shore. '09(O9) c. il. D. $1.25. McClurg.
Mother's year-book: pract. application of the results of scientific child-study to the problems of the first year of childhood. '08(My23) c. il. D. **$1.25 net. Macmillan.
Old fashioned fairy tales; retold from the poetic version of Tom Hood. '09(O23) c. col. il. O. †$1.25. Rand, McN. & Co.

Washed by four seas. Woods, H. C. *$2.50 net. Wessels.

Washington, Booker Taliaferro.
Story of the negro; the rise of the race from slavery. In 2 v. '09(D11) c. por. O. **$3 net. Doubleday, P.

Washington, G:
Washington year book: maxims and morals of "the Father of his country"; comp. by Wallace de Grott Cecil Rice. '08(O10) c. il. O. bds., *$1 net, boxed. McClurg.
Writings; ed., with introd. and notes, by Lawrence Evans. '08(D12) c. O. (Writings of American statesmen.) **$2.50 net. Putnam.

—, and Webster, Dan.
Washington's farewell address, and Webster's first Bunker Hill oration; ed., with introd. and notes, by Ja. Sullivan. '08 (D5) c. pors. 12°, (Twentieth century text-books.) **25 c. net. Appleton.
Washington's farewell address to the people of the United States; and Webster's first Bunker Hill oration; ed., with introd. and notes, by W: Trufant Foster. '09(N6) c. il. D. (Riverside literature ser.) **25 c. net. Houghton M.
Washington's farewell address; Webster's Bunker Hill oration; ed., with introd. and notes, by T. Arkle Clark. '08(Je20) c. il. por. facsim., S. (Scribner English classics.) **25 c. net. Scribner.

—, Webster, Dan., and Lincoln, Abraham.
Washington, Webster and Lincoln; selections for the college entrance English requirements; ed. by Jos. Villiers Denney. '10(Je11) c. S. (Lake English classics.) 25 c. Scott, F. & Co.

WASHINGTON, George.
Alloway, C: R. Ode to memory of our country's father. 50 c.; 15 c. C: R. Alloway.
Callahan, C: H. Memorial to Washington the Mason, to be erected at Alexandria, Virginia. $1. Alexandria-Washington.
Ford, W. C. George Washington. 50 c. net. Small.
Hill, F: T. On the trail of Washington. **$1.50 net. Appleton.
Hodges, G: **Apprenticeship of Washington.** **$1.25 net. **Moffat.**
Irving, W. Life of Washington. 2 v. $2.50. Crowell.
Knox, D. H. Heart of Washington: [fiction.] $1.50. Neale.
Mangasarian, M. M. **Religion of Washington, Jefferson and Franklin.** 10 c. **Independent Religious.**
Munn, C: A. Three types of Washington portraits: John Trumbull, C: Willson Peale, Gilbert Stuart. (Priv. pr.) **Gilliss Press.**
Parkinson, R: George Washington. 50 c. Lord Balto. Pr.
Schauffler, R. H., *ed.* **Washington's birthday.** **$1 net. **Moffat.**
Visit to the homeland of Washington's ancestors. gratis. P: Henderson.
See also Morris Mansion;—Mt. Vernon, Va.

Washington, H: Stephens.
Manual of the chemical analysis of rocks. 2d ed., rev. and enl. '10(My14) c. 8°, $2. Wiley.

Washington, W: D'Hertburn.
Answer to the charge of railroad robbery, an analysis of the profits of a railroad; extract from Progress and prosperity. '10(Ap) 16 p. 8°. (Priv. pr.) W. D. Washington.

Washington [State.] Adams' briefs on the negligence law, covering all cases reported prior to Jan. 1, 1910; by E. J. Adams. '10 (My) O. $7.50. E. L. Boardman.

Washington [State.] Code of public instruction of the state of Washington, together with official rulings and blank forms. '08(Je13) 8°, pap., 50 c. C. W. Gorham.

Washington [State.] *Dept. of Education.* A.-Y.-P. exposition as an educator; by R. D. Bailey, superintendent of educational exhibit. '09(D) 10 p. il. plan, 8°, gratis. Wash. Supt. Sch.

Washington [State.] *Dept. of Education.* Hist. of education in Washington; preliminary ed. issued for distribution at the A.-Y.-P. exposition; comp. and issued by H: B. Dewey. '09(N) 68 p. il. 8°. (Add. Superintendent for price.) Wash. Supt. Sch.

Washington [State.] Index to Remington & Ballinger's annotated codes and statutes, two volumes; by Eug. G. Kreider; consolidated by L: Horwitz. '10(Jl) c. O. shp., $2. Bancroft-W.

Washington [State] laws; comp. and abr. for popular use; by Ernest M. Card and O. H. Skotheim. [1910.] (D) c. 110 p. O. 25 c. Pacific Coast.

Washington [State] Railroad Commission. Findings of facts by the Railroad Commission of Washington relative to the value of railroads in the state of Washington. '09 (S) 354 p. 8°. gratis. Wash. R. R. Com.

Washington [State.] Realty law for owners, agents and tenants; by G: D. Yound. '10(D) c. O. $5. Vancouver.

Washington [State.] Remington & Ballinger's annot. codes and statutes; by R: A. Ballinger and Arth. Remington. In 2 v. v. 1. '10(Ap); v. 2 (My) c. O. shp., per set, $19.50. Bancroft-W.

Washington [State.] *Supreme ct.* Digest of the decisions covering all cases in the 3 Washington territorial repts., and v. 1 to 43 of the Washington repts., [etc.] In 3 v. v. 1. '08(Ja11); v. 2. '08(F); v. 3. '08 (My) c. O. buckram, per v., *$10 net; per set 3 v., *$27.50 net. Bancroft-W.

Washington [State.] *Supreme ct.* Repts. v. 44; (Arth. Remington.) '07, [1908.] (Mr); v. 45-48 (D) ea., $3; v. 49, 50. '09(Je) ea., $3.25; v. 51 (O); v. 52. '10(F); v. 53 (Jl) O. shp., ea., $4 net. Bancroft-W.

WASHINGTON (*State*).
Chandler, G: Textbook of civics for the state of Washington. $1. Am. Bk.
Dawson, W: L., *and* Bowles, J: H. Birds of Washington. 2 v. $12; $15; $20; $25. Occidental Pub.
Denny, E. I. **Blazing the way.** $2.50. **Rainier Pr.**
General laws and constitutional provisions of the state of Washington rel. to railroads; pub. by authority of the Railroad Commission. '08(F) 104 p. 8°, 75 c. C. W. Gorham.
Meany, E. S., *comp.* Hist. of the state of Washington. $1.25 net. Macmillan.
Meany, E. S., *comp.* **Indian geographical names of Washington.** 25 c. Hyatt-F.
Snowden, C. A. Hist. of Washington. 4 v. $25. Century Hist.
Waller, O. L. Irrigation in the state of Washington. (Add. Superintendent for price.) U. S., Supt. of Docs.
See also Mt. Ranier;—Puget Sound;—Seattle;—Spokane;—Tacoma.

Washington, D. C. Public Library. Work of the Public Library with the children of Washington. '10(D) 12 p. 16°, gratis. Washington Pub. Lib.

WASHINGTON, D. C.
Davis, M. **Old cannon foundry above Georgetown, D. C. (Washington, D. C.) (Add. pubs. for price.) New Era Print.**
Linsay, C: H. A. F. Washington, the city and seat of government. $3; $7. Winston.
Logan, M. S. C., *ed.* Our national government: life and scenes in our national capital. $3.25; $3.75; $4.25. Baldwin.
Monroe, *Mrs.* H. E. Washington: its sights and insights. **$1 net. Funk.
Van Tyne, C. H., *and* Leland, W. G. Guide to the archives of the government of U. S. in Washington. $1.25. Carnegie.

WASHINGTON, D. C.—*Continued.*
Weller, C: F: Neglected neighbors: [Washington poor.] **$1.50 net. Charities Pub.; Winston.
See also Cabin John Bridge;—District of Columbia;—Library of Congress;—National Gallery of Art;—Smithsonian Institute;—Soldiers' Home;—United States National Museum;—White House.

WASHINGTON (D. C.) CATHEDRAL.
De Vries, W: L. Foundation stone book, Washington Cathedral, A.D. 1907. $1.50. Cathedral.

WASHINGTON COUNTY, Mo.
See Genealogies: Wyand, E. C.;—*also* Missouri.

Washington party. Schenck, F. J. $1. F. J. Schenck.

WASHINGTON'S BIRTHDAY.
Sindelar, J. C:, *ed.* Washington day entertainments. 30 c. Flanagan.

Washington's headquarters. Patrick, L. S. 10 c. Quaker Hill.

Washington's home. Hudson, *Mrs.* S. E. J. (Add. pubs. for price.) Hanzsche.

WASHOE CO., Nev.
Commercial guide of Washoe County, Nev. '10(N) c. 4°, $10. H. M. Gulling.
"Showing assessed valuation in the different districts of Washoe County and giving names and residence of property owners."—*Introductory.*

Wasmann, Erich.
Berlin discussion of the problem of evolution; full rept. of the lectures given in Feb., 1907, and of the evening discussion. '09(Ag7) 8°, *$1.60 net. Herder.

Wason, Rob. Alex.
Happy Hawkins. '09(Ag28) c. D. †$1.50. Small.
Steering wheel. '10(O8) il. D. $1.50. Bobbs-M.
See also Nye, E:

Wassall, A.
See Siddons, A. W.

Wassam, Clarence W.
Salary loan business in New York City; rept. prepared under the direction of the Bureau of Social Research, New York School of Philanthropy; with extracts from an unpublished report by Fk. Julian Warne. '09(Ja16) c. tabs., forms, tab., facsim., 8°, (Russell Sage foundation.) 75 c. Charities Pub.

Wasson, G: Savary.
Home from sea: [short stories.] '08(Ap18) c. il. D. †$1.50. Houghton M.

WASTE.
See Factories;—Refuse and refuse disposal;—Useful arts.

Waste merchants standard code. Green, H. L. $5. H. L. Green.

Waste of militarism; from rept. of the Massachusetts Commission on the Cost of Living, 1910. '10(D) 15 p. O. (International School of Peace pamphlets.) pap., per 100, $3. Int. Sch. of Peace.

Watanna, Onoto, [Mrs. Winnifred Eaton Babcock.]
Tama. '10(O22) c. col. il. O. $1.60 net, boxed. Harper.

Watchers of the plains. Cullum, R. †$1.50. Jacobs.

Watchwords. *See* Brownson, Orestes Augustin.

WATER.
Bartow, E:, *and others.* Mineral content of Illinois waters. gratis. Univ. of Ill.
Coles-Finch, W: Water: its origin and use. *$5 net. Van Nostrand.
Collet, H. Water softening and purification of hard and dirty waters. $2. Spon.
Dole, R: B. Quality of surface waters in the United States. pt. 1. Gov. Pr. Off.
Greth, J: C: W: Water purification facts for steam users. gratis. Scaife.
Harrison Safety Boiler Works, Philadelphia. Purification of water for boiler feeding. (Priv. pr.) Harrison.
Lane, A. C. Mine waters. (Not for sale.) A. J. Yungbluth.
Leffmann, H: Examination of water for sanitary and technic purposes by chemical and bacteriological methods. $1.25. Blakiston.
Mason, W: P. Examination of water. $1.25. Wiley.
Prescott, S: C., *and* Winslow, C: E: A. Elements of water bacteriology. $1.50. Wiley.
Richards, *Mrs.* E. H. S. Laboratory notes on industrial water analysis. **50 c. net. Wiley.
Richards, *Mrs.* E. H. S., and Woodman, A. G. Air, water, and food from a sanitary standpoint. $2. Wiley.
United States. *Superintendent of Documents.* Water pollution; water purification: priced list of public documents rel. to the pollution and purification of water which have been issued by scientific bureaus of the government and are now submitted by the Superintendent of Documents. [3d ed.] '09(Je) 7 p. 8°, pap.
See also Boilers;—Distillation;—Edema;—Glaciers;—Hydraulic engineering;—Hydraulics;—Ice;—Meteorology;—Ocean;—Physical geography;—Rivers;—Steam;—Tides;—Water-supply;—*also* California;—San Joaquin Valley;—*also* names of states.

Water babies. *See* Kingsley, *Rev.* C:

WATER-COLOR PAINTING.
Frederick, F: F. Wash method of handling water color. 50 c. Manual Arts.
Redgrave, G. R. Water-color painting in England. $1.25. Gorham.
Wyllie, W: L. Sketch book. $1.50. Cassell.

WATER CURE.
Abbott, G: K., *comp.* Technique of hydrotherapy and Swedish massage. 25 c. Loma Linda Coll.
Baruch, S. Principles and practice of hydrotherapy: application of water in disease. *$4 net. Wood.
Dieffenbach, W: H. Hydrotherapy. $3 Rebman.
Hinsdale, G. Hydrotherapy. $3.50. Saunders.
Kellogg, J: H. Rational hydrotherapy. $6 net; $7.50 net. Davis.
Pope, C. Pract. hydro-therapy. $6. Cin. Medical.
Secor, W: L. Hdbk. of the principles and practice of modern hydrotherapy. $1.50. Chic. Med. Bk.

WATER GARDENS.
See **Gardens and gardening.**

Water goats. Butler, E. P. 50 c. Doubleday, P.

Water hammer in hydraulic pipe lines. Gibson, A. H. *$2 net. Van Nostrand.

WATER-MARKS.
See Paper trade.

Water pipe and sewer discharge. Ekin, T. C. *$3 net. Van Nostrand.

WATER POLO.
Handley, L. de B. How to play water polo. 10 c. Am. Sports.

WATER POWER.
See Electrical engineering;—Hydraulic engineering.

WATER-RIGHTS.
Nelson, K. Brief and memorandum rel. to riparian and water rights of the federal government of the various states. U. S. Supt. of Docs.
Weil, S: C. Water rights in the western states. $7.50. Bancroft-W.

WATER STREET MISSION, New York City.
McAuley, J. Jerry McAuley: apostle to the lost. *$1 net. Am. Tr.

WATER-SUPPLY.
Bartow, E: Chemical and biological survey of the waters of Illinois. gratis.—Municipal water supplies of Illinois. Univ. of Ill.
Bowman, I., *and* Reeds, C. A. Water resources of East St. Louis district. (Add. pub. for price.) Univ. of Ill.
Bridge, J. H. Purification of public water supplies. (Add pubs. for price.) Aldine Bk.
Chittenden, H. M. Forests and reservoirs in their relation to stream flow. $1.50. Am. Soc. of Civil Engineers.
Gregory, H. E., *and* Ellis, E. E. Underground water resources of Connecticut; with a study of the occurrence of water in crystalline rock. (Add. Superintendent for price.) U. S., Supt. of Docs.
Hazlehurst, J. N. Towers and tanks for water-works. $2.50. Wiley.
Jones, E: R: Notes on drainage. $1.25. E: R: Jones.
Leighton, M. O., *ed.* Surface water supply of the United States, 1907-8. pts. 1, 3, 4, 5, 6, 8, 9, 11, 12. pt. 1, 5 c.; pt. 3, 20 c.; pt. 12, 35 c. Gov. Pr. Off.
McPherson, J: A. Waterworks distribution: guide to the laying out of systems of distributing mains for supply of water to cities. *$2.50 net. Van Nostrand.
Martin, J: Public benefits derived from water power developments in California. gratis. J: Martin.
Mathews, J: L. Conservation of water. $2 net. Small.
Ohio. *State Bd. of Health.* Rept. of an investigation of water and sewage purification plants in Ohio. (Add. pubs. for price.) Heer.
Papers on the conservation of water resources. '09(N) 96 p. tabs., fold. map, O. (U. S., Dept. of the Interior; U. S. Geolog. Survey; Water supply paper.) pap. (Add. Superintendent for price.) U. S., Supt. of Docs.

WATER-SUPPLY.—*Continued.*
Phelps, E. B. Pollution of streams by sulphite pulp waste. 10 c. U. S., Supt. of Docs.
Turneaure, F: E. Water-supply. $1.50. Am. Sch. Corr.
Turneaure, F: E., *and* Russell, H. L. Public water-supply. $5. Wiley.
United States. *Dept. of the Interior. U. S. Geological Survey.* Publications rel. to water resources. gratis. U. S., Supt. of Docs.
United States. *Geological Survey.* List of publications of the U. S. Geol. Survey rel. to water resources. 10 c. U. S., Supt. of Docs.
United States. *Geological Survey.* Papers on the conservation of water resources. U. S., Supt. of Docs.
Wadsworth, J. W., *jr.* Forest preservation and conservation of water supply. gratis. J. W. Wadsworth.
Woodward, H. B. Geology of water-supply. $2.50. Longmans.
See also Hydraulic engineering;—Irrigation;—Plumbing;—Pumping;—Reservoirs;—Sanitary engineering;—Water;—Windmills;—*also* names of states.

Water wagon, and other poems. Grimes, W. B. 15 c. W. B. Grimes.

WATER-WHEELS.
See Hydraulic engineering.

Waterbury, Leslie Abraham.
Cement laboratory manual. '08(O3) figs. 12°, $1. Wiley.
Vest-pocket handbook of mathematics for engineers. '08(Je6) **$1 net; [New ed., with tabs.] '09(N) c. il. 24°, mor., **$1.50 net. Wiley.

Waterfield, *Mrs.* Aubrey. *See* Gordon, Lina Duff.

WATERLOO (Battle of).
Watson, T: E: Waterloo. $1.50. Neale.

Waterloo: [novel.] *See* Erckmann, Emile. The conscript.

WATERLOW, *Sir* Sidney Hedley.
Smalley, G: Life of Sir Sidney H. Waterlow. *$3 net. Longmans.

Waterman, Nixon.
The girl wanted; book of friendly thoughts. '10(My14) c. pors. O. $1.25. Forbes.

Waterman, S. D.
Practical aids to the teaching of civics. '09 (O16) c. 12°, 60 c. Whitaker & R.

Waterman, T: Talbot.
Religious practices of the Diegeño Indians. '10(Ap16) Q. (Univ. of Cal. pubs.; American archæology and ethnology.) pap., 80 c. Univ. of Cal.

Waterproofing: an engineering problem. Lewis, M. H. 50 c. Engineering News.

Waterproofing of structures, with special reference to sublevel construction, the envelope method and the application of "Tunaloid." [1910] (My) c. 43 p. il. O. pap. Bird.

Waters, H: Fitz-Gilbert.
Genealogical gleanings in England; ed., arr., completed and cross-referenced by Lothrop Withington. '08(F) 2 v., 8°, $10. N. E. Hist.

Waters, Marg., comp.
Toasts. '09(Je19) 16°, 50 c.; ooze, $1. Barse & H.

Waters, Rob.
Culture by self-help, in a literary, an academic or an oratorical career. '09(Mr27) c. D. **$1.20 net. Dodd.

Waters, Russell Judson.
El estranjero (the stranger); story of southern California. '10(N12) c. il. O. $1.50 net. Rand, McN. & Co.

Waters, Rev. T: Franklin.
Candlewood, an ancient neighborhood in Ipswich; [with genealogies of John Brown, William Fellows, Robert Kinsman.] '10(Ap30) map, 8°, $1.50. Salem Press.
Old Bay road from Saltonstall's Brook and Samuel Appleton's farm; [also] A genealogy of the Ipswich descendants of Samuel Appleton. '07, [1908.] (My.) 2+62 p. il. map, 8°, (Ipswich Historical Soc. pubs.) 25 c. Ipswich Hist.

Waters, Yssabella.
Visiting nursing in the United States; cont. directory of the organizations employing trained visiting nurses, with chapters on the principles, organization and methods of administration of such work. '09 (D18) c. map, tabs., O. $1.25. Charities Pub.

Waters from an Ozark spring. Terry, H. L. $1. Badger.

WATERS-PIERCE CASE.
Adams, F: U., *comp.* Water-Pierce case in Texas. 25 c. Skinner & K.

Waters' pocket flag manual, containing flags of American and Canadian yacht and power boat clubs and associations; also, flags of principal maritime countries, flags used on yachts, storm and weather signals and the international code of signals. '08, [1909.] (F) c. il. 8°. (Add. pubs. for price.) J. K. Waters Co.

WATERSPOUTS.
See Meteorology.

Waterston, David.
See Cunningham, Dan. J:

Waterton, C:
Wanderings in South America, the northwest of the United States and the Antilles, in the years 1812, 1816, 1820 and 1824. New ed., ed. with biog., introd. and explanatory index by Rev. J. G. Wood. '09(Je12) il. 12°, $1.50. Macmillan.
Wanderings in South America, the northwest of the United States and the Antilles in the years 1812, 1816, 1820 and 1824; with original instructions for the perfect preservation of birds, etc., for cabinets of natural history; incl. a memoir of the author by Norman Moore, M.D.; with brief introd. by C: Livingston Bull. '09(Je19) c. O. *$2.50 net. Sturgis & W.

Watertown, Mass. Watertown's military history. '07, [1908.] (Ag) 17+281 p. il. pors. plan facsims., 8°, $2.50. F. E. Critchett.

WATERVILLE, Maine.
Giveen, C. M. Chronology of municipal history and election statistics, Waterville, Maine. $1.50. Maine Farmer.

WATERWAYS.
See Inland navigation.

Waterworks distribution. McPherson, J: A. *$2.50 net. Van Nostrand.

Watkeys, F: W:
Old Edinburgh. '08(D5) c. 2 v., il. D. (Travel lovers' lib.) $3. L. C. Page.

Watkins, Amelia Warfield.
See Graves, Etta Merrick.

Watkins, Mrs. Cora Lowe.
Young life of famous folk. '09(D18) c. pors. D. 75 c. Pub. Ho. M. E. Ch., So.

Watkins, Edg.
Shippers and carriers of interstate freight. '09, [1910.] (F) c. 578 p. O. $6. Flood.

Watkins, E:
Secret of successful tailoring. [1910.] (Je) c. 103 p. il. 12°, $1. L'Art de la Mode.

Watkins, G: Pendleton.
Growth of large fortunes. '08(Ja4) O. (Pub. of the Am. Economic Assoc.) pap., $1. Macmillan.

Watkins, Ja. Lawrence.
King Cotton: historical and statistical review 1790 to 1908. '09(Ap3) c. il. tabs., 8°, $1.50. J. L. Watkins.

Watkins, Lucian Bottow.
Natural life in the human world. '10(Jl) c. 8 p. 8°, pap., 10 c. L. B. Watkins.
Old log cabin. '10(Jl) no paging, T. pap., 15 c. L. B. Watkins.
Soldiers' home. '10(Jl) c. no paging, T. pap., 15 c. L. B. Watkins.

Watkins, Rob. Lincoln.
Catechism of hæmatology: [examination of the blood.['08, [1909.] (F) c. 31 p. 12°. (Add. author for price.) R. L. Watkins.

Watkinson, W: L., D.D.
Fatal barter, and other sermons. '10(F12) c. 12°, *$1 net. Revell.
Frugality in the spriritual life. '08(Ap18) c. 12°, *$1 net. Revell.
Lessons of prosperity, and other addresses on personal conduct. '08(Ag1) 12°, *50 c. net. Revell.
Mistaken signs, and other addresses on Christian experience. '08(Ag1) 12°, *50 c. net. Revell.
Noon day addresses: on themes affecting life. '08(Ag1) 12°, *50 c. net. Revell.

Watseka wonder. Stevens, E. W. 60 c.; 35 c. Austin.

Watson, Mrs. Annah Walker Robinson.
"Of sceptred race." '10(Jl) c. 379 p. il. pors. 4°, $10. Early.
"Authorities" (1 p.).
The victory. '09(My15) c. il. sq. O. pap., $1.50. A. W. R. Watson.

Watson, Arth. Eug.
Storage batteries. '08(O17) c. il. 12°, $1.50. Bubier.

Watson, Bruce Mervellon, and White, C: E.
Grammar school arithmetic. '08, [1909.] (F) c. 6+415 p. il. 12°, 60 c. Heath.

Watson, Chandler Bruer.
Prehistoric Siskiyou Island and marble halls of Oregon. '09(Jl31) c. por. D. (Priv. pr.) C. B. Watson.

Watson, Sir C: Moore.
Life of Sir Charles Wilson, R.E., K.C.B. '09(Jl17) il. 12°, *$5 net. Dutton.

Watson, C: R.
In the valley of the Nile: survey of the missionary movement in Egypt. '08 (Je13) c. 12°, *$1 net. Revell.
See also Anderson, W: B.

Watson, D: Kemper.
Constitution of the U. S.; its hist., application and construction. 2 v. '10(S) c. O. $12. Callaghan.

Watson, Donald.
Poetical works; with memoir. [1910.] (F) c. '09. 211 p. il. pors. 16°, $1. D. Watson.

Watson, Ebbie Julian.
Addresses on immigration, [at the] annual convention American Manufacturers' Association, Philadelphia, May 15, 1907. '07, [1908.] (Mr.) 18 p. 8°, gratis. State Co.
See also South Carolina. Trucking industry.

Watson, Foster.
English grammar schools to 1660: their curriculum and practice. '08(D19) 8°, *$2 net. Putnam.

Watson, Fs. Sedgwick, M.D., and Cunningham, J: H:, jr., M.D.
Diseases and suigery of the genito-urinary system. 2 v. '08(O31) il. 8°, *$12 net; hf. mor. *de luxe*, *$17 net. Lea.

Watson, Fk. D.
See Nearing, Scott.

Watson, Rev. F:
Christian life here and hereafter. '08(Jl) 319 p. 12°, *$2 net. Whittaker.
Seven words from the cross. '08(Jl) 111 p. 12°, 81 c. Whittaker.

Watson, G: C.
Farm poultry. 6th ed. '08(Ja25) il. 12°, (Rural science ser.) **$1.25 net. Macmillan.

Watson, Gilbert.
Forbidden ground. '10(Ag27) c. D. $1.35. Lane.

Watson, H: Brereton Marriott.
Castle by the sea. '09(S25) c. il. D. †$1.50. Little, B. & Co.
Devil's pupit: [a story.] '08(N14) c. front. D. †$1.50. Dodd.

Watson, Ja.
Dog book. 2 v. in 1. '10(D) il. 4°, $5 net. Doubleday, P.

Watson, Ja. McLean.
Aristotle's criticisms of Plato. '09(My15) O. pap., $1. Oxford Univ.

Watson, J:, 1847-.
Outline of philosophy; with notes historical and critical. 4th ed. '08(Je6) 12°, *$2.25 net. Macmillan.
Philosophical basis of religion. '08(Ja11) 8°, *$3 net. Macmillan.
Philosophy of Kant explained. '08(O24) 8°, *$3.75 net. Macmillan.

Watson, J:, D.D., ["Ian Maclaren,"] 1850-1907.
Respectable sins. '10(O29) O. $1.25 net. Doran.

WATSON, *Rev.* John.
Nicoll, W: R. "Ian Maclaren": the life of Rev. John Watson. **$2 net. Dodd.

Watson, J: Broadus.
Kinaesthetic and organic sensations: their role in the reactions of the white rat to the maze. '07, [1908.] (D) 6+100 p. il. 4°. (Add. pubs. for price.) Psychological Review.

Watson, Kate Heintz.
Textiles and clothing. [Text book ed.] '10(D3) c. il. 12°, $1.25. Am. Sch. Home Economics.

Watson, Mary L., comp.
Our breakfast book; wholesome thoughts for every day. '10(My14) c. D. bds., $1, boxed. Volland.

Watson, Maryland.
Destiny and desire: poems passionate and perverse. '08(D) 63 p. D. (Add. pubs. for price.) Casino.

Watson, Rob. Alex.
The wolves: a fable with a purpose. '08 (O) c. 31 p. il. 12°, 10 c. Kerr.

"Watson, Rosanna," pseud.
See Whiteley, Lillian C.

Watson, T: E:
Foreign missions exposed. '09, [1910.] (Ja) c. 3-97 p. il. 8°, 25 c.; 2d ed. '10(Je) c. 141 p. il. 8°, 25 c. T: E: Watson.
Life and speeches. '08(Ag) $1.50. T: E: Watson.
Political and economic handbook. '08 (Ag9) c. 5-358 p. front. 8°, $1. T: E: Watson.
Sketches from Roman history. '08(O) c. 98 p. 8°, 50 c. T: E: Watson.
Waterloo. '08(O17); 2d ed. '10(O22) c. '08-'10. D. ea., $1.50. Neale.

Watson, T: Leonard.
Mineral resources of Virginia. '07, [1909.] (Mr) il. maps, fold tabs., 4°, gratis. C. A. Swanson.
Preliminary report on the manganese deposits of Georgia. '08(Ag1) il. maps, 4°, (Georgia Geological Survey bull.) pap., 12 c. S: W. McCallie.

Watson, Wilbur Jay.
General specifications for concrete bridges. '08(Ap18) c. tabs., 8°, $1. Vinson.
General specifications for concrete work as applied to building construction. '08 (Mr21) c. 8°, 50 c. W. J. Watson

Watson, W:
New poems. '09(N13) c. O. **$1.50 net. Lane.
Sable and purple; [poems.] '10(Ag6) c. D. $1.25 net. Lane.

WATSON FAMILY.
See **Genealogies.**

Watt, Alex.
Art of paper-making: hdbk. of the manufacture of paper from rags, esparto, straw, and other fibrous materials, incl. the manufacture of pulp from wood fibre. 3d ed. '08(Jl18) il. tabs., 8°, $3. Van Nostrand.

Watt, Sir G:
Commercial products of India: being an abridgment of the "Dictionary of the economic products of India." '08(D) 8+1190 p. 8°, *$5 net. Dutton.

Watt, Hansard.
Myths about monarchs: [nonsense verses.] '08(Ap11) D. **$1 net. Dodd.

Watt, H: J.
Economy and training of memory. '09 (My8) S. 50 c. Longmans.

Watt, Rev. Lauchlan MacLean.
Attic and Elizabethan tragedy. '08(O24) 8°, *$2 net. Dutton.

WATT-HOUR METER.
See **Electric meters.**

WATTEAU, George Frederick.
Hind, C: L. Watteau. 65 c. net; $1.50 net. Stokes.

Watteau, Jean Antoine.
Masterpieces. '08(D12) T. (Painters' ser.) leath., *75 c. net; pap., *25 c. net. Stokes.

WATTEAU, Jean Antoine.
Uzanne, L: O. Drawings of Watteau. *$2.50 net. Scribner.

Watters, H: Eug.
Bible of superhuman origin, a safe guide for man; containing arguments on the existence of God, the divinity of Christ, the immortality of the soul, and the reasonableness of eternal punishment. '08(Ag1) c. por. D. 50 c.; pap., 25 c. H: E. Waters.

Watters, Philip M.
Peter Cartwright. '10(Mr26) c. por. nar. S. (Makers of Methodism.) *25 c. net. Eaton & M.

Watteyne, Victor, Meissner, Carl, and Desborough, Arth.
Prevention of mine explosions; rept. and recommendations; with letter of transmittal by Ja. Rudolph Garfield. '08, [1909.] (F) 11 p. O. (U. S. Dept. of the Interior; Geolog. Survey bull.) pap.

Wattles, Wallace Delos.
Hell-fire Harrison. '10(D3) c. il. D. $1. L. C. Page.
New science of living and healing; with commentary by Elizabeth Towne. '08 (Ja11) D. pap., 50 c. E. J. Towne.
Science of being well. '10(S10) c. por. D. $1. E. J. Towne.
Science of getting rich. '10(Ap16) c. por. D. $1. E. J. Towne.

Watts, Ernest.
See Pennsylvania. Digest.

WATTS, George Frederick.
Hare, W. L. Watts. 65 c. net. Stokes.

Watts, I:, D.D.
Divine and moral songs for children. '08 (N7) il. D. $1. L. C. Page.

Watts, Ja. L., comp.
See Tennessee. Corporation laws.

Watts, Mrs. Mary Stanbery.
Nathan Burke. '10(Ap30) c. D. $1.50. Macmillan.
The tenants. '08(Ap4) c. D. †$1.50. McClure.

Watts, T: T.
Thoughts on education: a protest against our present system. '08(Ag15) 16°. [priv. pr.] T: T. Watts.

Watts, W. Benedict.
Engineers' quiz book. '08(Jl4) c. S. pap., $1. Democracy and Civil Service.

Watts-Mumford, Ethel.
See Mumford, Ethel Watts-.

Wauchope, G: Armstrong, comp.
Writers of South Carolina; with critical introd., biograph. sketches, and selections in prose and verse. '10(Mr5) c. 8°, $2. State Co.

Waugh, Fk. Albert.
American apple orchard. '08, [1909.] (Ja16) c. il. 12°, $1. Judd.
Landscape beautiful; study of the utility of the natural landscape, its relation to human life and happiness, with the application of these principles in landscape gardening, and in art in general. '10 (Mr26) c. il. 8°, $2. Judd.

Waugh, Ida.
See Blanchard, Amy Ella.

Wave of life. Fitch, W: C. $1.50. M. Kennerley.
Waverley. *See* Scott, *Sir* Wa.
Waverley synopses. McSpadden, J. W., *ed.* 50 c. Crowell.

WAXES.
See **Oils and fats.**

Way, Arth. S.
See Sophocles.

Way, L. N.
Call of the heart. '09(D25) c. front. 12°, $1.50. G: W. Dillingham.

Way, Norman.
Mary Jane's pa. '10(D) 75 c. Grosset.
Mary Jane's pa; from the play of the same name by Edith Ellis. '09(N20) c. il. D. $1.50. H. K. Fly.

Way (The). Pepper, G: W. *40 c. net; $1. Longmans.
Way down east. Grismer, J. R. 75 c. J. S. Ogilvie.
Way made plain. Long, S. P: $1. S. P: Long.
Way of all flesh. Butler, S: $1.50 net. Dutton.
Way of fellowship. Drake, F. W. $1 net. Longmans.
Way of initiation. Steiner, R. $1; 75 c. Macoy Pub.
Way of life. McCormick, J: N. 35 c. J: N. McCormick.
Way of perfect love. King, G. G. $1.25. Macmillan.
Way of prayer. McFadyen, J: E. 50 c. net. Pilgrim Press.
Way of the cross. 08(Mr14) 4 v., il. T. pap., ea., 15 c. Benziger.
Way of the woods. Breck, E: **$1.75 net. Putnam.
Way that He willeth for me. Emery, C. 25 c. Reid Pub.
Way things happen (The). De Sélincourt, H. $1.50. Lane.
Way to happiness. Slicer, T: R. *$1 net. Sturgis & W.
Way to peace. Deland, Mrs. M. W. C. $1.50. Harper.
Way to perfect healing. Towne, W: E. 50 c. W: E. Towne.
Way to the kingdom of heaven. Searcy, W: E. H. $1. Searcy.
Way to win. Ferguson, J: W. $1.50. Neale.
Way to win. Graham, D: W. $1.10. B'way Pub.
Way to win her. Didier, E. L. 10 c. Am. Press.

Way up. Willcocks, M. P. $1.50. Lane.
Wayfarer in New York; introd. by E: S Martin. '09(O16) c. S. **$1.25 net. Macmillan.
Wayfarers (The). Cutting, *Mrs.* M. S. D. †$1.50. McClure.
Wayfaring books. 16°. Dutton.
—Baker. Voices of nature. $1 net.
—Baker, *ed.* Praise of a simple life. *$1 net.
—Carlyle. Pocket Carlyle. *$1 net.
—Emerson. Pocket Emerson. *$1.25 net.
—Hyatt, *ed.* Winds of heaven. *$1 net.
Wayfaring ser. New ed. 11 v. '10(Mr) 12°, ea., leath., *$1.25 net. Dutton.
Waylaid by wireless. Balmer, E. †$1.50. Small.

Wayland, J: Wa.
Complete index to "The German element of the Shenandoah Valley of Virginia." '08(D5) 30 c. J: W. Wayland.
Wayland-Smith, Fs.
Materialism and Christianity. '09(N) c. 36 p. 8°, pap., 25 c. Wayland-Smith.
WAYLAND, Mass.
Vital records of Wayland. $2.25. N. E. Hist.
WAYNE, Anthony.
Pennypacker, S: W. Anthony Wayne: [an address.] (Not for sale.) S: W. Pennypacker.
Wayne, Kenneth H.
Building your boy; how to do it: how not to do it. '10(O1) c. S. bds., 50 c. net. McClurg.
WAYNE'S CAMPAIGN.
See Greenville (Treaty of).
Ways and days out of London. De Milt, A. R. $2.50 net. Baker & T.
Ways of a girl. Hutchinson, M. F. 75 c. McKay.
Ways of an aristocrat. Hill, J. S. (Add. author for price.) J. S. Hill.
Ways of Eleanor. Clark, J. G. (Priv. pr.) Case.
Ways of rebellion. Farrer, R. J. †$1.50. Longmans.
Ways of Yale in the consulship of Plancus. Beers, H: A. $1.20 net. Holt.
Wayside and woodland ser. 16°. Warne.
—South. Moths of the British Isles. *$3 net.
—Step. Wayside and woodland ferns. *$2.25 net.—Wayside and woodland trees. *$1.75 net.
Wayside jottings. Cook, H. M. $1.50. H. M. Cook.
Wayside lib. 12°, limp leath., $1. Brentano's.
—Balzac. Tales.
—De Musset. Tales.
—Gautier. Tales.
—Gorky, *pseud.* Tales from Gorky.
—Kipling. Wayside tales.
—Maupassant. Pierre and Jean.
—Omar Khayyam. Rubaiyat.
—Wilde. Happy prince.
Wayside lute. Reese, L. W. *$1.50 net; *$3 net. T: B. Mosher.
Wayside wisdom. Martin, E. M. *$1.50 net. Longmans.
Wayt, Hugh.
True source of a happy life. '10(Mr5) c. 12°, 50 c. Chr. Pub. Co.

Wayward Anne. Yorke, C., *pseud.* $1.50. Estes.
We and the world. *See* Ewing, *Mrs.* J. H. G.
We four and two more. Clark, I. †$1.25. Crowell.
We have with us to-nigh: Blythe, S: G: 50 c. Altemus.
We must stop forest fires. Rane, F. W: (Add. author for price.) F. W: Rane.
We preach Christ crucified. Herbert, L. *$1 net. Herder.
We three. Cotton, H. P. $1.50. C. M. Clark.
We two in West Africa. Guggisberg, *Mrs.* L. D. M. *$3.50 net. Scribner.
Wead, C: Kasson.
Music and science; address of the retiring president, read before the Philosophical Society of Washington, January 15, 1910. '10(Je) 169-187 p. 8°, (Philosophical Society of Washington bull.) pap., 10 c. Philosophical Soc.
Weak church and the strong man. Bosworth, E: I. 5 c. Y. M. C. A.
Weale, B. L. Putnam, [pseud. for Bertram Lenox Simpson.]
Coming struggle in eastern Asia. '08 (Mr7); 2d ed. '09(Ap3) il. maps, 8°, ea., *$3.50 net. Macmillan.
Conflict of colour: threatened upheaval throughout the world. '10(N19) c. O. $2 net. Macmillan.
Forbidden boundary, and other stories. '08 (N14) 12°, $1.50. Macmillan.
Human cobweb; romance of Peking. '10 (F19) c. D. †$1.50. Dodd.
Weale, J. C.
See Weale, W. H. Ja.
Weale, W. H. Ja. and J. C.
Memlinc. '09(O30) il. D. (Masterpieces in colour.) bds., *65 c. net; leath., *$1.50 net. Stokes.
WEALTH.
Davis, W: S. Influence of wealth in imperial Rome. $2 net. Macmillan.
Edwards, R: H:, *ed.* Concentrated wealth. 10 c. R: H: Edwards.
Jennings, E. B. People and their property. $1. B'way Pub.
Lee, G. S. Inspired millionaires. $1.25. Mt. Tom Press.
McCasland, C: O. Right and riches. *$1.50 net. Wilbur Pub.
Marshall, W: V. Curb to predatory wealth. $1. Fenno.
Mathews, B. C. Our irrational distribution of wealth. **$1.25 net. Putnam.
Myers, G. Hist. of great American fortunes. In 3 v. ea., $1.50. Kerr.
Russell, C: E: Lawless wealth: origin of some great American families. $1.50. B. W. Dodge.
Smith, A. Wealth of nations. 2 v. ea., 35 c. net; 70 c. net. Dutton.
Watkins, G: P. Growth of large fortunes. $1. Macmillan.
Wattles, W. D. Science of getting rich. $1. E. J. Towne.
Wood, H: A. W. Money hunger. **$1 net. Putnam.

WEALTH.—*Continued.*
Youngman, A. Economic causes of great fortunes. $1.50. Banker's Pub.
See also Capital and labor;—Finance;—Money;—Political economy.

Wealth from waste. Perry, G: P. *50 c. net. Revell.

Wealth of friendship. Rice, W. de G. C. $1.25; $2; $2.50. Barse & H.

Weaning the nation from strong drink. Vansant, W: R. $1.50. Vansant.

WEAPONS.
See Arms and armor.

WEASELS.
Barnum, E. M. Weasels, trapping, raising and preparing skins for market. 25 c. E. M. Barnum.

WEATHER.
See Climate;—Meteorology;—Temperature.

Weather and weather instruments. '08 (My23) c. il. map, D. *$1 net. Taylor Instrument.

Weather and weather instruments. '09(My) 175 p. il. $1.50; pap., 50 c. Van Nostrand.

Weather words of Polynesia. Churchill, W: 80 c. Am. Anthropological.

Weatherford, Willis Duke.
Negro life in the South; present conditions and needs; with special chapter on the economic condition of the negro, by G. W. Dyer. '10(N19) c. 12°, 75 c. Y. M. C. A.

Weathering of coal. Parr, S: W. gratis. Univ. of Ill.

Weathers, J:
Practical guide to school, cottage, and allotment gardening. '08(My2) il. tabs., D. $1. Longmans.

Weaver, Anderson.
Lesson book for Bible study; four-years' course for schools and colleges. '09, [1910.] (F) c. 265 p. 12°, $1. A. Weaver.

Weaver, Angus Bowman.
Abbreviated longhand; manual of short forms for longhand writers, adapted to all the popular uses of brief writing and for adoption in the public schools. '10 (Mr26) c. 12°, $2. Quikrite.

Weaver, C: E.
New *echinoids* from the Tertiary of California. '09(Ja23) Q. (Univ. of Cal. pubs.) pap., 5 c. Univ. of Cal.
Stratigraphy and palæontology of the San Pablo formation in middle California. '09(Mr6) tabs., Q. (Univ. of Cal. pubs.; Geology.) pap., 25 c. Univ. of Cal.

Weaver, Erasmus Morgan.
Notes on military explosives. 2d ed., rev. and enl. '10(My14) 8°, $3 net. Wiley.

Weaver, Gertrude Renton, [Mrs. Harold Baillie Weaver, "G. Colmore."]
Priests of progress: [arraignment of vivisection.] '09(F13) c. D. $1.50. B. W. Dodge.

Weaver, Gustine Courson.
House that a Jap built; pictures after paintings by the Japanese artist O. Ishikawa. '09(N6) c. D. bds., 75 c. Reilly & B.

Weaver, Mrs. Harold Baillie.
See Weaver, Gertrude Renton.

Weaver, Lawrence.
English leadwork, its art and hist. '10 (Ap2) il. Q. pap., $10 net. Scribner.

Weaver, Silas Matteson.
Iowa, its constitution and laws. '08, [1909.] (Mr) c. 141 p. 12°, *40 c. net. C: E. Merrill.

WEAVING.
Hooper, L. Hand-loom weaving. $2.25 net. Macmillan.
Nelson, H. W: Weaving. $3. Am. Sch. Corr.
Nelson, H. W:, *comp.* Jacquard machines. 50 c. Am. Sch. Corr.
Textile World Record. Kinks for boss weavers. 75 c. Lord & N.
White, J. Hand loom linen weavers of Ireland. (Add. pubs. for price.) Irish Hand-Woven.
See also Cotton;—Textile fabrics;—Woolen spinning.

Web of Indian life. Noble, M. E. *$1.75 net. Holt.

Web of life. Herrick, R. $1.50. Macmillan.

Web of the golden spider. Bartlett, F: O. †$1.50. Small.

Web of time. Knowles, R. E: $1.50. Revell.

Webb, B. R., rep.
See Texas. *Cts. of civil appeals.* Repts.

Webb, Mrs. Beatrice Potter.
See Webb, Sidney.

Webb, Clarence.
See Hensman, Howard.

Webb, Doris.
See Webb, Eliz. Carman.

Webb, Eliz. Carman and Doris.
Littlest fairy. '10(Ag20) c. col. il. Q. bds., $1.50. Dodge.

Webb, Eug. G:
Comparisons simplified; or, how to select the "best" life insurance company. '08 (O) c. 24+257 p. 8°, $2. E. G. Webb.
—, comp. Comparisons simplified: treatise dealing with the selection of life insurance companies. [6th ed.] '10(S) c. 8°, limp leath., $3. Bassette.
Comparisons simplified: treatise dealing with the selection of life insurance companies giving the most perfect protection at the lowest possible cost; comp. from the companies' 1909 rate books and policy contracts. [5th ed.] '09(My22) c. O. limp leath., $3. E. G. Webb.
Webb's comparisons simplified number 2, probable phase; a book of unique and comprehensive insurance statistics. '09 (S4) c. O. limp leath., $3. E. G: Webb.

Webb, Fk.
Switzerland of the Swiss. '10(Je4) il. 12°, $1.50 net. Scribner.

Webb, Ja. Morris.
Black man, the father of civilization; proven by Biblical history. [1910.] (Ag) 3-49 p. il. pors. 12°, 75 c. J. M. Webb.

Webb, Lucie T:
Grading simplified: a teacher's aid. '08 c. 21 p. a charts, 12°, 75 c. Hackney.

Webb, M. de P.
India and the empire: consideration of the tariff problem; with an introd. by Sir E: Fg. Low. '08(My2) tabs., D. *$1.20 net. Longmans.

Webb, Mabelle Philips.
Othello, an interpretation. '08(F15) c. 16°, leatherette, *50 c. net. M. P. Webb.

Webb, Sidney and Mrs. Beatrice Potter.
English local government from the Revolution to the Municipal Corporations Act. [v. 3 and 4,] The manor and the borough. '08(Ap11) 2 v., O. *$7 net. Longmans.
English poor law policies. '10(Mr12) O. *$2.50 net. Longmans.
The state and the doctor. '10(S10) O. $2 net.. Longmans.

—, eds. Minority Report of the Poor Law Commission, 1905-'09; ed. with introds. pt. 1, The break-up of the Poor law; pt. 2, The public organization of the labour market. '09(Mr20) O. pt. 1, *$2.50 net; pt. 2, *$1.75 net. Longmans.

Webb, Wa. Loring.
Railroad construction, theory and practice. 4th ed., rev. and enl. '08(N14) il. figs. 16°, mor., $5. Wiley.

—, and Gibson, W. Herbert.
Masonry and reinforced concrete. '09(F20) c. il. 8°, (American School of Correspondence pubs.) $3. Am. Sch. Corr.

Webb, Bp. W: Wa.
Cure of souls; manual for the clergy; based chiefly upon the English and Oriental authorities; with commendatory preface by J: Lea Nicholson, D.D. 2d ed. '10(Ap2) c. D. $1.50 net. Young Churchman.

Webber, Harry Endicott.
Twelve months with the 8th Massachusetts Infantry in the service of the United States: [Spanish-American war.] '08 (S) c. 392 p. il. por. 8°, $2. H. E. Webber.

Webber, Ja. Plaisted.
Elements of elocution for classes in declamation with selections for practice; for use in Phillips Exeter Academy. '07, [1908.] (Mr.) c. 40 p. 8°,. (privately pr.) J. P. Webber.

Webber, W: Hosgood Young.
Town gas and its uses; for the production of light, heat and motive power. '08 (Mr7) il. O. (Westminster ser.) *$2 net. Van Nostrand.

WEBBER FAMILY.
See Genealogies, Washburn, L. A.

Weber, Fred C:
Introductory bookkeeping arranged for use in the classes of high school commercial departments and private commercial schools. 2d ed. '09(N) c. 58 p. forms, 8°, 50 c. F. C. Weber.

Weber, N: Aloysius.
Hist. of simony in the Christian church. from the beginning to the death of Charlemagne (814). '09(Je) c. 11+254+17 p. 12, pap., *$1.50 net. Furst.

Webling, Wa. Hastings.
Fore!: the call of the links. '09(S4) c. il. por. D. bds., 75 c. Caldwell.

Webster, Alice Jean.
Much ado about Peter. '09(Mr27) c. il. D. †$1.50. Doubleday, P.

Webster, Dan.
See Washington, G: Farewell address.

Webster, Fk. V.
Bob the castaway; or, the wreck of the "Eagle." '09(Ag21) c. il. 12°, 35 c. Cupples & L.
Boy from the ranch; or, Roy Bradner's city experiences. '09(N6) c. il. 12°, 35 c. Cupples & L.
Boy pilot of the lakes; or, Nat Morton's perils. '09(D18) c. il. 12°, 35 c. Cupples & L.
Boys of Bellwood School; or, Frank Jordan's triumph. '10(D) il. 12°, 40 c. Cupples & L.
Comrades of the saddle; or, the young rough riders of the plains., '10(D) 200 p. il. 12°, 40 c. Cupples & L.
Jack the runaway; or, on the road with a circus. '09(N6) c. il. 12°, 35 c. Cupples & L.
Newsboy partners; or, who was Dick Box? '09(D18) c. il. 12°, 35 c. Cupples & L.
Only a farm boy; or, Dan Hardy's rise in life. '09(Ag14) c. il. 12°, 35 c. Cupples & L.
Tom the telephone boy; or, the mystery of a message. '09(N6) c. il. 12°, 35 c. Cupples & L.
Two boy gold miners; or, lost in the mountains. '09(Ag21) c. il. 12°, 35 c. Cupples & L.
Young firemen of Lakeville; or, Herbert Dare's pluck. '09(N6) c. il. 12°, 35 c. Cupples & L.
Young treasure hunter; or, Fred Stanley's trip to Alaska. '09(D18) c. il. 12°, 35 c. Cupples & L.

Webster, G. N., ed.
See New York State. Tax law.

Webster, Hanson Hart, ed.
American classics for seventh and eighth grade reading: with biog. sketches, portraits and suggestions for study. '09 (Jl31) pors. 12°, **80 c. net. Houghton M.

Webster, H: Kitchell.
King in khaki. '09(Ap17) c. il. D. †$1.50. Appleton.
The sky-man. '10(Ap16) c. il D. $1.20 net. Century Co
Whispering man. '08(O10) c. front. D. †$1.50. Appleton.

Webster, Hutton.
Primitive secret societies: study in early politics and religion. '08(F1) c. O. **$2 net. Macmillan.

Webster, Jean.
Four-Pools mystery. '08(Mr28) c. front. D. †$1.50. Century Co.

Webster, J:
Duchess of Malfi. '10(Ja1) 16°, (Swan dramatists.) 45 c. Sturgis & W.

WEBSTER, John.
Pierce, F: E. Collaboration of Webster and Dekker. $1. Holt.

Webster, J: Winfield, M.D.
Vision from the wild: [poem.] '09(Je26) *$1 net. Cochrane.

Webster, Lucia Washburn Hazen.
See Conn, Herbert W:

Webster, Noah.
Collegiate dictionary; thin paper ed. de luxe. '10(S17) c. il. por. 8°, $5. G. & C. Merriam.

Imperial dictionary of the English language and complete atlas of the world; with an exhaustive appendix, including Scripture proper names, and pronouncing vocabulary of Greek and Latin proper names prep. under the direction of Noah Porter; thoroughly rev. and greatly enl. and improved by over 100 educators, specialists, and other scholars, under the editorial supervision of T: H. Russell, Albert C. Bean and L. B. Vaughan. '08(F22) c. il. tabs., 4°, shp., $6; mor., $9; mor., $12. G: W. Ogilvie.

Imperial dictionary of the English language; thoroughly rev. and greatly enl. and improved by over 100 educators, specialists, and other scholars, under the ed. supervision of T: H. Russell, Albert C. Bean, and L. B. Vaughan. '08(O10) c. maps, 4°, shp., $6; hf. mor., $9; mor., $12. Saalfield.

Intercollegiate dict. of the English language; based on Webster's imperial and Webster's universal dictionaries and ed. by T: H. Russell. '10(My14) c. col. il. D. limp leath., $2.45, with *Success Magazine* for 1 yr. E. M. Dunbar.

Intercollegiate dict. of the English language, based on Webster's imperial and Webster's universal dictionaries, and ed. by T: H. Russell. '09(Je) c. 1074+148 p. il. 12°, $1.75; leath., $2.50. Saalfield.

Laird & Lee's Webster's new standard dictionary of the English language; comp. by E. T. Roe, [and others.] [High School and Collegiate ed.] '08(N) c. 830 p. il. map, 12°, hf. leath., $1.50. Laird.

Laird & Lee's Webster's new standard dictionary of the English language; adapted for all grammar and common school grades: comp. by E. T. Roe. '09(O2) c. il. por. map, D. 75 c. Laird.

New international dictionary of the English language, based on the International dictionary of 1890 and 1900: now completely rev. in all departments; incl. also a dictionary of geography and biography, being the latest authentic quarto edition of the Merriam ser.; W. T. Harris, ed.-in-chief, F. Sturges Allen, general ed. '09 (O23) c. il. F. (Merriam ser.) shp., marble edge, $12; hf. mor., marble edge, $14.50; hf. russia, marble edge. $14.50; full russia, marble edge, $17.50; full mor., vermilion edge, $18; full mor., gilt edge, $20; in 2 v., $12; shp., $14. G. & C. Merriam.

Practical dictionary; ed. under the supervision of Noah Porter, by Dorsey Gardner. '10(Ag6) c. il. 12°, 80 c. G. & C. Merriam.

School and office dict.; self pronouncing; thoroughly modernized by C: Morris. '10(D) 960 p. 12°, 50 c. Winston.

Unabridged dict. '10(D) $2.50. Reilly & B.

Webster, Noah.—*Continued.*
Universal dictionary of the English language and complete atlas of the world; under the editorial supervision of T: H. Russell, Albert C. Bean and L. B. Vaughan. '08(O17) c. il. 4°, shp., $10; Russia leath., $15. Saalfield.

Universal self-pronouncing dictionary of the English language. '08(D) c. 8+998 p. il. maps, 8°. (Add. pubs. for price.) Winston.

Vest pocket dictionary (Hill's). '08. (Vest pocket size.) 15 c.; 20 c.; indexed, 25 c.; leath., 50 c. McKay.

WEBSTER, Noah.
Allen, F. S. Noah Webster's place among English lexicographers. 25 c. G. & C. Merriam.

WEBSTER, Pelatiah.
Memorial to Pelatiah Webster; hearing before the Committee on the Library of the House of Representatives [May 5, 1908.] '08, [1909.] (Je) 11 p. 8°, pap. (Add Superintendent for price.) U. S., Supt. of Docs.

Taylor, H. To the Congress of the United States. Memorial in behalf of the architect of our federal Constitution, Pelatiah Webster. (Add. author for price.)

Webster, Ralph Waldo.
Diagnostic methods, chemical, bacteriological and microscopical. '09(N) c. 34+641 p. il. (partly col.) 8°, *$6 net; hf. mor., *$7.50 net. Blakiston.

Webster, W: Franklin, and Cooley, Mrs. Alice Woodworth.
Essentials of grammar and composition. '09(D) c. 6+260 p. il. 12°, **55 c. net. Houghton M.

—, and Heeter, Silvanus Laurabee.
Our present needs [by] W. F. Webster; the lagging half [by] S. L. Heeter. [1910] (My) 31 p. 8°. (Priv. pr.) W: F. Webster.

Weddings and wedding anniversaries. Clark, J. W., *ed.* 25 c. Butterick.

Wedekind, Fk.
Awakening of spring; a tragedy of childhood; tr. from the German by Fs. J. Ziegler. '09(S) 4+168 p. *$1.25 net. Brown Bros.

Wedel. Cornelius H.
Meditationen zu den fragen und antworten unseres katechismus. [1910.] (S) c. 322 p. 8°, $1.25 C. H. Wedel.

Wedgwood, A. F.
Shadow of a Titan. '10(S17) D. $1.50. Lane.

WEDGWOOD, Josiah.
Moore, *Mrs.* N. H. Wedgwood and his imitators. **$1 net. Stokes.

Wedgwood, Julia.
Nineteenth century teachers and other essays. '09(D) *$3 net. Doran.

"Wee tim'rous beasties." English, D. $1.50. Cassell.

Wee Willie Winkie: book of nursery rhymes. '08(S5) il. S. (Mother Goose's nursery rhymes.) bds., 50 c. Stokes.

Wee Winkles at the mountains. Jackson, *Mrs.* G. E. G. †$1.50. Harper.

Weed, Arth. J.
Pract. dynamo building for amateurs; or, how to construct a fifty-watt dynamo. '10 (My21) il. $1; pap., 50 c. Henley.
Weed, Catherine.
See Ward, H: Snowden.
Weed, Clarence Moores..
Farm friends and farm foes. '10(D31) c. il. D. 90 c. Heath.
Study of the evergreens in the public schools. '08, [1909.] (Ag) 30 p. il. 8°, pap., gratis. F. W. Rane.
Wild flower families: haunts, characters and family relationships of the herbaceous wild flowers. '08(My9) c. il. D. **$1 net. Lippincott.
See also Emerson, Arth. I.
—, and Emerson, Philip.
School garden book. '09(N20) c. il. 12°, $1.25. Scribner.
Weeden, L. L.
Fairy tales in Wonderland. '10(D) il. obl. 8°, $1.50. Dutton.
—, and others.
Model menageries. '10(D) il. 4°, bds., $2.50. Dutton.
Weeden, W: Babcock.
Early commercial Providence. '09, [1910.] (Je) 12 p. 8°, 50 c. Davis Press.
Early Rhode Island; social hist. of the people. '10(My14) c. il. D. (Grafton historical ser.) $2.50. Grafton Press.
WEEDS.
See Agriculture;—Botany.
Weeds and wild flowers. Bell, M. $1.25. Badger.
Week by week. Soulsby, L. H. M., *comp.* 30 c. Longmans.
Week-day prayers. Reisner, C. F. *35 c. net. Jennings.
Week in the White House with Theodore Roosevelt. Hale, W: B. **$1.25 net. Putnam.
Weekley, Bp. W: Marion, and Fout, H. H.
Our heroes; or, United Brethren home missionaries; introd. by J. P. Landis. '08 (S12) c. il. pors. 8°, (Denominational mission study course.) 50 c.; pap., 35 c. Un. B. Pub.
Weeks, Fk. Edg.
Pioneer hist. of Clarksfield. '08, [1909.] (S) 163+13 p. il. pors. 12°, pap., *$1 net. F. E. Weeks.
Weeks, Fred Boughton, and Nickles, J. M.
Bibliography of North American geology for 1906 and 1907; with subject index. '09(My8) O. pap. (Add. Superintendent for price.) U. S., Supt. of Docs.
Weeks, H. W.
See Randall, Dwight T.
Weeks, J: Elmer.
Treatise on diseases of the eye. '10(O) c. 9-944 p. il. 8°, $6. Lea.
Weeks, Lyman Horace, and Bacon, Edn. Munroe, comps. and eds.
Historical digest of the provincial press: collation of all items of personal and historic reference printed in the newpapers of the provincial period from the appearance of "The present state of the new-English affairs, 1689." "Publick occurrences," 1690, and the first issue of "The Boston News-Letter," 1704, ending with the close of the Revolution, 1783. '08 (F1) c. pors. map, facsim., O. (Massachusetts ser.) pap., subs., per set, $150; per v., $7.50. Soc. Americana.
Weepers in playtime. Sands, B. †$1.50. Lane.
Weeping cross. Stuart, H: L. **$1.40 net. Doubleday, P.
WEEVIL.
Pierce, W: D. Studies of parasites of the [Mexican] cotton boll weevil. 25 c. U. S., Supt. of Docs.
Weg (Der) zum glück. Bernhardt, W., *ed.* 40 c. Heath.
Wegelin, Oscar, comp.
Early American poetry, 1800-1820; with an appendix containing the titles of volumes and broadsides issued during the seventeenth and eighteenth centuries. '08(Ja11) O. bds., $3. O. Wegelin.
Wehs, Rev. J: Albert.
Ned Rieder; parochial school story. '10 (N12) c. front. D. 85 c. Benziger.
Weichmann, L: J.
Testimony of L: J. Weichmann given on examination in chief in the trial of John H. Surratt, indicted for the murder of Abraham Lincoln in the Criminal Court of the District of Columbia, 1867, in reporting style of phonography by Benn Pitman and Jerome B. Howard. '10(Je) 86 p. S. pap. Phonograph.
Weidel, Jos. Anton.
Instruction book for those using Weidel's combined tailor square and curves; complete treatise on drafting ladies' and children's garments by the square and curves combined. '10(Ap) c. 72 p. il. 4°, $5. Weidel.
Weiderseim, Grace G.
Bobby Blake. '09(D25) c. il. F. shaped bds., 50 c. Stokes.
Dolly Drake. '09(D25) c. il. F. shaped bds., 50 c. Stokes.
Tiny tots: their adventures. '09(D25) c. il. (partly col.) Q. bds., 70 c. Stokes.
Weiga of Temagami. Warman, C. $1.50; $2.50. Caldwell.
Weigall, Arth. E: Pearse.
Guide to the antiquities of upper Egypt, from Abydos to the Sudan frontier. '10 (Je18) maps, plans, 12°, $2.50 net. Macmillan.
Weight of the name. Bourget, P. C. J. †$1.50. Little, B. & Co.
Weight throwing. Mitchel, J. S. 10 c. Am. Sports.
WEIGHTS AND MEASURES.
Clarke, F. W. Recalculation of atomic weights. Smith. Inst.
Gurley's handbook for the use of sealers of weights and measures. 50 c. W. & L. E. Gurley.
Hatch, F: H:, *and* Vallentine, E. J. Weights and measures of international commerce. *80 c. net. Macmillan.
Measuring tools. 25 c. Indust. Press.
Siddons, A. W., *and* Wassall, A. Pract. measurements. 45 c. net. Putnam.
See also Arithmetic;—Electrical measurements;—Mensuration;—Metric system.

Weikel, Anna Hamlin.
Betty Baird's golden year. '09(O9) c. il. D. (Betty Baird ser.) †$1.50. Little, Brown & Co.

Weil, Alethea.
Navy of Venice. '10(Jl30) il. 8°, $5 net. Dutton.

Weil, Melanie Alice.
Book of my heart. '09(F) 12°, $1. Lib. Shelf.

Weill, Felix, ed.
Historical French reader; with notes, exercises and vocab. '10(O22) c. il. map, S. 40 c. Am. Bk.

Weiman, Rita.
Playing the game; story of a society girl. '10(S24) c. il. D. $1.50. Cupples & L.

WEIMAR, Germany.
Moore, R. W. Weimar, the Athens of Germany. *75 c. net. Stechert.

Weimer, Albert B., rep.
See Pennsylvania. *Superior ct.* Repts.

Weimer, Theresa.
See Buffington, Bertha Elinor.

Weindel, Henri de.
Real Francis-Joseph; private life of the Emperor of Austria. '10(Mr26) il. pors. O. *$4 special net. Appleton.

Weingreen, J.
Electric power plant engineering. '10 (My7) c. il. tabs., 8°, $5. McGraw-H.

Weinhold, Karl.
List of first editions and other rare books in the Weinhold library. '07, [1908.] (Jl) 144 p. 8°, (Univ. of Cal. pub., Library bull.) pap. (Add. pub. for price.) Univ. of Cal.

Weinmann, Karl.
Karl Proske, der restaurator der klassischen kirchenmusik, vom herausgeber. '09, [1910.] (F) 133 p. por. fold. facsim., 16°, (Sammlung "Kirchenmusik" hrsg. von dr. Karl Weinmann.) 30 c. Pustet.

Weir, Harrison W:
Poultry book; under the editorship of W. G. Johnson and G: O. Brown. 3 v. in 1. '10(D) il. 4°, $5 net. Doubleday, P.

Weir. Hugh C.
Conquest of the Isthmus; the men who are building the Panama Canal—their daily lives, perils, and adventures. '09 (S25) c. il. fold. map, O. **$2 net. Putnam.

With the flag in Panama: story of the construction of the Panama canal. '10(D) il. 12°, $1.50. Wilde.

Weir, T. H.
Arabic prose composition. '10(Ap30) 12°, $2 net. Putnam.

Weisbach, Julius, and Herrmann, Gustav.
Mechanics of pumping machinery; tr. by Karl P. Dahlstrom. '08(My16) il. 8°, price raised from *$3.75 net to *$4 net. Macmillan.

Weiss, Arth.
Introd to the philosophy of art. '10(F) 245-302 p. O. (Univ. of Cal. pubs.; Modern philology.) pap., 50 c. Univ. of Cal.
Bibliography (2 p.).

Weiss, Howard F.
Progress in chestnut pole preservation. '08 (Ag1) diagrs., 8°, (U. S., Dept. of Agriculture, Forest Service, circular.) pap., 10 c. U. S., Supt. of Docs.

Weiss, Johannes.
Paul and Jesus. '10(Ja29) 12°, (Harper's lib. of living thought.) *75 c. net. Harper.

Weitenkampf, Fk.
How to appreciate prints. '08(D26) c. il. pors. O. **$1.50 net. Moffat.

Weitzel, Fred W:
Law of deposits. '10(Ap) c. D. $1. Milans.

Weitzel, Louise A.
Quiver of arrows: [poems.] '08(N) c. 244 p. il. 8°, $1. L. A. Weitzel.

Welborn, W. C.
Elements of agriculture, southern and western. '08(F8) c. il. 12°, *75 c. net. Macmillan.

Welch, Catharine.
Little Dauphin: [story of the son of Louis XVI. and Marie Antoinette.] '08(D12) D. *$1.50 net. Scribner.

Welch, C: Howard.
Book of poems. '10(Mr5) il. pors. 12°, $1.50. C: H. Welch.

Welch, J. S.
Literature in the school; aims, methods and interpretations. '10(D24) c. O. $1.25. Silver.

Welch, Ninian Hetrick.
Cases on criminal law. '10(N) c. O. $1.50. Thompson & Co.

Welcome spring! Riley, A. C. D. 25 c. C. F. Summy Co.

Weld, Ivan C.
See Lane, Clarence Bronson.

Weld, L: Dwight Harvell.
Private freight cars and American railways. '08(Je6) c. O. (Columbia Univ. studies in hist., economics and public law.) pap., *$1.50 net. Longmans.

WELDING.
See Metals and metallurgy.

Welfare of the church [fiction.] Cooley, J. H. 75 c. J. H. Cooley.

Well in the desert. Knapp, A. †$1.50. Century Co.

Well-known piano solos. Wilkinson, C: W. *40 c. net. Scribner.

Well of Saint Clare. *See* France, Anatole, *pseud.*

Well spent quarters: fifteen-minute meditations adapted to the young; to which is added a three days' retreat; by a Sister of Mercy. '08(Mr) 12°, 85 c. Chr. Press.

Wellcome's photographic exposure record and diary, 1909. U. S. ed. '08(D26); 1910. '10(D10) il. O. ea., 50 c. Burroughs, W.

Welldon, S: A., comp.
Digest of state banking statutes. '10(My) 746 p. fold. tabs., 8°. U. S., Supt. of Docs.

Weller, C: F:
Neglected neighbors: stories of life in the alleys, tenements and shanties of the national capital; with one chapter by Eugenia Winston Weller. '09(Ja16); (Ap24) c. il. plans, O. **$1.50 net. Charities Pub.; Winston.

WELLINGTON, Arthur Wellesley, *Duke of.*
Gleig, G: R. Life of Wellington. *35 c. net; *75 c. net. Dutton.

Wellington, Barrett Rich.
See United States. Commissioner's manual.

Wellman, Fs. Lewis.
Day in court; or, the subtle arts of great advocates. '10(F19) c. O. **$2 net. Macmillan.

Wellman, Harry Richmond, comp.
See Grover, Edn. Osgood.

Wells, A. Wade.
See Bradford, Morgan, *jr.*

Wells, Amos Russel.
Bible miniatures; character sketches of one hundred and fifty heroes and heroines of Holy Writ. [2d ed.] '09(D18) c. 12°, *$1.25 net. Revell.
Caleb Cobweb's comparison: book of modern parables. '08, [1909.] (Mr) c. 157 p. 16°, 50 c. McNair.
Everyday poems. '10(S17) c. 12°, $1.25 net. Revell.
Introd. to Bible study; specially adapted for the members of adult Bible classes, and for all Bible students. '09, [1910.] (F) c. 36 p. 12°, 30 c. Presb. Bd.
Living Bible: course of Bible-reading, covering the entire Bible, a chapter a day. '08(Je13) c. 16°, 75 c. Un. Soc. C. E.
Why we believe the Bible; outlines of Christian evidences in question-and-answer form. '10(S17) c. 12°, $1. Un. Soc. C. E.
See also Peloubet, Fs. Nathan.

Wells, B: Willis.
Modern French literature. '09(D25) c. 12°, **$1 net. Little, B. & Co.

Wells, Carolyn.
Betty's happy days. '10(O1) c. il. D. $1.50. Century Co.
The clue. '09(O23) c. col. front. D. †$1.50. Lippincott.
Dick and Dolly. '09(O23) c. il. D. †$1.25. Dodd.
Dick and Dolly's adventures. '10(O15) c. D. $1.25. Dodd.
Happy chaps. '08(D5) c. il. O. $1.50. Century Co.
Marjorie in command. '10(S24) c. il. D. $1.25. Dodd.
Marjorie's busy days. '08(O10) c. il. D. †$1.25. Dodd.
Marjorie's new friend. '09(O9) c. il. D. †$1.25. Dodd.
Patty's friends. '08(S26) c. il. D. (Patty books.) †$1.25. Dodd.
Patty's pleasure trip. '09(S18) c. il. D. †$1.25. Dodd.
Patty's success. '10(S24) c. il. D. $1.25. Dodd.
Pleasant day diversions. '09(O2) c. D. **$1 net. Moffat.
Rubaiyat of bridge: [humorous rhymes.] '09(Ap17) c. il. D. $1. Harper.
Seven ages of childhood. '09(N6) c. col. il. O. **$2 net. Moffat.
Year book of old favorites and new fancies for 1909. '08(N14) c. il. D. $1.25, boxed. Holt.

Wells, C: Jeremiah, ["H. L. Howard."]
Joseph and his brethren: dramatic poem; with an introd. by Algernon C: Swinburne, and a note by Thdr. Watts-Dunton. '09(My15) S. (World's classics.) 35 c. Oxford Univ.

Wells, Dan. White and Reuben Field.
Hist. of Hatfield, Mass., 1660-1910. '10 (Jl9) c. il. O. $5 net. F. C. H. Gibbons.

Wells, Ebenezer Miller.
Guide to legal labels, in compliance with the Food and Drugs Act, June 30, 1906. '09, [1910.] (My) c. 228 p. O. $3. E. M. Wells.

Wells, Eliab Horatio, M.D.
Beneath the Star of Bethlehem: [poems.] '08(Ja18) D. $1. Neale.

Wells, Frederic Lyman.
Statistical study of literary merit, with remarks on some new phases of the method. '08(F1) diagrs., 8°, (Archives of psychology.) pap., 30 c. Science Pr., (N. Y.)

Wells, F: Howard, comp.
William Wells and his descendants, 1755-1909. '09(D4) c. il. O. $3.25. F. H. Wells.

Wells, Mrs. Grace Sherman.
Verses. '09(Je) c. 126 p. 12°. (Priv. pr.) Donnelley.

Wells, Herbert G:
Ann Veronica: modern love story. '09 (O16) c. col. front. D. †$1.50. Harper.
First and last things: confession of faith and a rule of life. '08(O17) c. O. **$1.50 net. Putnam.
History of Mr. Polly. '10(Ap2) c. D. $1.50. Duffield.
New worlds for old. '08(Mr14) c. D. **$1.50 net. Macmillan.
Socialism and the family. '08(D19) D. *50 c. net. Ball Pub.
This misery of boots: [socialistic treatise.] '08(D19) D. *50 c. net. Ball Pub.
Tono-Bungay: [novel.] '09(Ja23) 12°, $1.50. Duffield.
War in the air, and particularly how Mr. Bert Smallways fared while it lasted. '08 (N14) c. il. D. †$1.50. Macmillan.
See also Meek, G:

Wells, Ja., D.D.
Stewart of Lovedale: life of James Stewart, D.D., M.D. '09(Je26) 8°, *$1.50 net. Revell.

Wells, Ja. Monroe.
"With touch of elbow"; or, death before dishonor. '09(Jl3) c. il. pors. facsims., D. **$1.25 net. Winston.

Wells, J: D.
Swazy folks and others: [poems.] '09 (Ja23) il. 12°, $1.25. Ulbrich.

Wells, Mrs. Kate Gannett.
Little Dick's son. '08(S19) c. front. D. (Bimbi ser.) bds., **40 c. net. Crowell.

Wells, Percy A., and Hooper, J:
Modern cabinet work, furniture and fitments; acct. of the theory and practice in the production of all kinds of cabinet work and furniture, with chapters on the growth and progress of design and construction. '10(Ap9) il. Q. $5 net. Lane.

Wells, Reuben Field.
See Wells, Dan. White.

Wells, Rex W., comp.
"The Old South leaflets" classified by Rex W. Wells [repr. from the *History Teacher's Magazine* for Jan., 1910.] '10(Je) 8 p. 12°, pap., 5 c. McKinley Pub.

Wells, Webster.
First course in algebra. '08, [1909.] (F) c. 14+232 p. il. 12°, $1. Heath.
Key to First course in algebra; solutions by Rob. L: Short. '09(My15) c. 12°, $2. Heath.
New plane and solid geometry. '08(Je6) c. 12°, $1.25. Heath.
Second course in algebra. '09, [1910.] (O) c. 6+283 p. 12°, $1. Heath

WELLS, England.
Holmes, T: S. Wells and Glastonbury. *$1.75 net. Dutton.

Wells and palm trees. Aked. C: F. $1; $2. Dodge.

WELLS FAMILY.
See Genealogies.

Welsford, Jos. W: Wilson.
Strength of England; politico-economic hist. of England from Saxon times to the reign of Charles the First; with a preface by W. Cunningham, D.D. '10(F19) D. *$1.75 net. Longmans.

Welsh, C:, ["Ivor Ben McIvor," "Na Gael Shane."]
Chauffeur chaff: anecdotes, stories and bon-mots. '09(Je19) c. S. 50 c. Caldwell.
Irish toasts. '08(S19) c. T. bds., 50 c. Caldwell.
Scottish toasts. '08(S19) c. T. bds., 50 c. Caldwell.
See also Longfellow, H: Wadsworth.

—, comp. and ed. Fairy tales children love; collection of fairy tales arr. for children of various ages. '10(D17) c. 12°, $1.25. Dodge.

—, ed. Stories children love. '09(Ag28) il. 12°, $1.25; ooze, $2. Dodge.

Welsh, G: Austin.
See Philadelphia. Supp. to digest.

Welsh, Jane.
See Carlyle, *Mrs.* Jane Welsh.

Welsh, Lilian, M.D.
Outlines of lecture notes. '09(Ap) *$1.75 net. L. Welsh.

Welsh fairy-book. Thomas, W. J. $1.50. Stokes.

Welshimer, Pearl Howard.
Bible-school vision, for use in teacher-training classes, superintendents' training-classes, Sunday-school libraries, workers' libraries, conventions, Chautauquas, etc., and for general meetings. '09(Jl) c. 123 p. 16°, (Training for service ser.) 50 c.; pap., 30 c. Standard Pub.

Welt (Die) als arbeit. Nagel, O. 80 c. O. Nagel.

Weltmer, Ernest.
Realization; story of a climber. [Special ed.] '09, [1910.] (Mr) c. 199 p. 12°, $1. Weltmer.

Welton, Thurston S., M.D.
See Crawford, Mary Merritt, *M.D.*

Welty, Cora Gottschalk.
Masquerading of Margaret. '09(Ap3) c. il. D. $1.50. C. M. Clark.

Wemyss, Mrs. Mary C. E. Lutyens.
Professional aunt. '10(Mr19) c. D. **$1 net. Houghton M.

WENCKEBACH, Carla.
Müller, M. Carla Wenckebach, pioneer. **$1.25 net. Ginn.

Wendel, J: Adolph, M.D.
Mineral-fertilizer: treatise for farmers, wine-, fruit-, vegetable growers, and gardeners. '08(Mr28) c. O. pap., 25 c. J: A. Wendel.

Wendell, Barrett.
Mystery of education and other academic performances. '09(O16) c. D. **$1.25 net. Scribner.
Privileged classes. '08(O17) c. D. **$1.25 net. Scribner.

Wendell, Oliver Clinton.
Photometric observations made within the fifteen inch east equatorial during the years 1892 to 1902, by Oliver C. Wendell; printed from funds resulting from the will of Josiah Quincy, jr. '09, [1910.] (D) 97 p. tabs., diagrs., 4°, (Annals of the Astronomical Observatory of Harvard College.) $1. Harvard Univ.

Wendling, G: Reuben.
Man of Galilee. [Maplehurst ed.] '08 (Ja4) O. (Modern doubt.) *$3 net; library ed., *$1 net. Olcott.

Wenley, Rob. Mark.
Modern thought and the crisis in belief; the Baldwin lectures, 1909. '09(Ap17) c. D. **$1.50 net. Macmillan.

Wenner, Blanche Howard.
Hawaiian memories: [poems.] '10(Je) c. 30 p. 12°, 50 c. Cochrane.

Wenner, Fk.
Theoretical and experimental study of the vibration galvanometer. '10(Je) 347-378 p. 8°. U. S., Supt. of Docs.

Wente, Adam Oscar, and Tolman, Lucius Moody.
Potato culls as a source of industrial alcohol; with a general discussion of the availability of other wastes. '10(D) 40 p. il. 8°, (U. S., Dept. of Agriculture, farmers' bull.)

Wentworth, Franklin Harcourt.
Woman's portion; address del. in Carnegie Hall, New York City, Sunday afternoon, Feb. 27, 1910, under the auspices of the women of the Socialist Party. '10(Ap9) D. pap., 10 c. Socialist Lit.

Wentworth, G: Albert.
New elementary arithmetic. '09(Jl17) c. D. (Wentworth-Smith mathematical ser.) 35 c. Ginn.
Plane geometry; rev. by G: Wentworth and D: Eug. Smith. '10(S10) c. D. 80 c. Ginn.

—, and Smith, D: Eug.
Complete arithmetic. '09(Je5) c. D. (Wentworth-Smith mathematical ser.) 60 c. Ginn.
Oral arithmetic. '10(Je11) c. D. (Wentworth-Smith mathematical ser.) 35 c. Ginn.

Wentworth, Patricia.
Marriage under the terror. '10(My7) c. D. $1.35 net. Putnam.

Wentworth-James, Gertie de S.
Wild widow. '08(N) c. 319 p. D. $1.50. Empire Bk.

Wentworth-Smith Mathematical ser. See Wentworth, G:

Wenzell, H: Burleigh, rep.
See Minnesota. *Sup. ct.* Repts.

Wenzlaff, Gustav Gottlieb.
Mental man: outline of the fundamentals of psychology. '09(Jl10) c. D. $1.10. C: E. Merrill.

Wenzlick, W:, M.D.
Greatest good of mankind: physical or spiritual life. '09(S4) D. *$1.50 net. W: Wenzlick.

Wer ist's? zeitgenossenlexikon enthaltend biographien nebst bibliographien; zusammengestellt und herausgegeben von Herrmann A. L. Degener. 3 ausgabe, 1908. '08 (Ja18); 4 ausgabe, 1909, vollkommen neu bearbeitet und wesentlich erweitert. '08 (N14) O. ea., *$3.50 net. Stechert.

Wernaer, Rob. Maximilian.
Romanticism and the romantic school in Germany. '10(Ja8) O. **$2 net. Appleton.

Werner, Carl.
Textbook on tobacco. [1910.] (F) c. '09. 136 p. il. 12°, $1. Tobacco Leaf.

Werner-Spanhoofd, Arnold.
Erstes lesebuch: German reader for beginners in high school or academy. '09 (My15) c. D. (Modern lang. ser.) 75 c. Heath.

Werner educational ser. il. 12°. Am. Bk.
—Dunglison. New school physiology and hygiene. *$1 net.

Werner encyclopædia: standard work of reference; with new supplemental matter added to each volume, covering the very latest information on all important subjects. '09(Je5) c. 25 v., il. pors. maps, plans, 4°, $65; hf. leath., $85. Werner Co.

Werner's readings and recitations. 12°. Werner.
—Schell. Platform and all-around.
—Schell, *comp.* Werner's book of pantomines. 60 c.; 35 c.
—West, *comp.* All-round recitations.—Famous modern orations.—Old-time favorites. ea., 35 c.

Wernse, W: F., ed.
See American law digest.

Wertenbaker, C: P.
Colored antituberculosis league: proposed plan of organization. '09(S) 9 p. 8°. U. S., Supt. of Docs.
Plan of organization for suppression of smallpox in communities not provided with an organized board of health. '09 (My15) 8°. (Add. Superintendent for price.) U. S., Supt. of Docs.

Wertenbaker, T: Jefferson.
Patrician and plebeian in Virginia; or, the origin and development of social classes of the Old Dominion. '10(My7) c. 12°, $1.50. Wertenbaker.

Wertz, Adda P.
Outlines in picture study to harmonize with the Illinois state course of study. '08 (O17) c. 12°, pap., 30 c. Flanagan.

Wescott, Morgan Ebenezer.
Civil War letters, 1861 to 1865, written by a boy in blue to his mother. '09(N) c. 32 p. 12°, 25 c. M. E. Westcott.

Wesley, Rev. J:
Journal of the Rev. John Wesley, A.M., sometime fellow of Lincoln College, Oxford; enl. from orig. manuscripts, with notes from unpublished diaries, annotations, maps and il.; ed. by Nehemiah Curnock, assisted by experts. Standard ed. In 6 v. v. 1. '10(Ap9) 8°, $18 net per set, in advance. Eaton & M.

WESLEY, *Rev.* John.
Eltzholtz, C. F. John Wesley's conversion and sanctification. *25 c. net. Jennings.

WESLEYAN UNIVERSITY.
See Shanklin, William Arnold.

Wesseley, J. E., and Allan, H. Warner.
Spanish-English dictionary. '08(Je20) 32°, (Pocket dictionary ser.) 50 c. Dutton.

—, and Gray, F. H. T.
English-Italian and Italian-English dictionary. '08(Je20) 48°, (Miniature reference lib.) leath., 50 c. Dutton.
English-Italian and Italian-English dictionary. '08(Je20) 32°, (Pocket dictionary ser.) 50 c. Dutton.
Spanish-English dictionary. '08(Je20) 48°, (Miniature reference lib.) leath., 50 c. Dutton.

Wesselhoeft, Mrs. Eliz. Foster Pope, [Lily F. Wesselhoeft.]
Rover the farm dog. '08(O3) c. D. †$1.50. Little, B. & Co.

Wessels, E: J.
Struggle everlasting. '09(Mr) c. 352 p. il. 8°, *$3 net. E: J. Wessels.

West, And. Cassius.
Pract. stationary engineering in form of questions and answers. '09, [1910.] (Ja) c. 260 p. il. 8°, $5. A. C. West.

WEST, Benjamin.
Hart, C: H: Benjamin West's family. (Add. author for price.) H: C. Hart.

West, C:, M.D.
How to nurse sick children; with a preface by G: F. Still. New ed. '08(D12) D. *40 c. net. Longmans.

West, C: Ernest, and Scott, Sydney R.
Operations of aural surgery; together with those for the relief of the intracranial complications of suppurative otitismedia. '09(Je) 8°, *$2 net. Blakiston.

"West, Emery," pseud.
See Pollock, M. I.

West, Emma Elise, comp.
All-round recitations. '09(F6) c. D. (Werner's readings and recitations.) pap., 35 c. Werner.
Famous modern orations. '09(Ja30) c. D. (Werner's readings and recitations.) pap., 35 c. Werner.
Old-time favorites. '09(F6) c. D. (Werner's readings and recitations.) pap., 35 c. Werner.

West, Max.
Inheritance tax. 2d ed., completely rev. and enl. '08(Ja25) 8°, (Columbia Univ. studies in hist., economics and public law.) *$2.50 net; pap., *$2 net. Longmans.

West, Paul.
See Johnston, Andrew W:

West, Simeon H:
Life and times of S. H. West. '08(Jl) c. 298 p. il. pors. 8°, $1.60. Read & W.

West, T: Dyson.
Metallurgy of cast iron. 12th and 13th eds. '07, [1908.] (S.) c. il. tabs. 12°, ea., $3. Gardner Pr.

West (The).
Brent, J: Empire of the West.—What every school boy and school girl should know (a compilation). Un. Pacific R. R.
Bronson, E. B. Reminiscences of a ranchman. $1.50. McClurg.
Chase, E. B. Transcontinental sketches. $1.50. Winston.
Chicago, Milwaukee & St. Paul Railway. North Pacific coast country. (Add. pubs. for price.) Chic., Milwaukee.
Enock, C. R. Farthest west. $4 special net. Appleton.
Gaines, *Mrs.* N. V. S., *comp.* Pathway to western literature. 75 c.. N. S. Gaines.
Gephart, W: F. Transportation and industrial development in the Middle West. $2. Longmans.
Hewett, E. L. Ancient ruins of the Southwest. Denver & Rio Grande.
Hill, J. J. Highways of progress. $1.50. Doubleday, P.
Hill, R. T. Public domain and democracy. $2. Longmans.
McCarty, D. G. Territorial governors of the Old Northwest. $2. State Hist., Ia.
Mathews, L. K. Expansion of New England; spread of New England settlement and institutions to the Mississippi River, 1620-1865. **$2.50 net. Houghton M.
Mieir, W: O. Possible method of reclamation for the arid West. 25 c. W: O. Mieir.
Overland Route to the road of a thousand wonders. 25 c. U. P. & S. P. R.R.
Paine, R. D. Greater America. *$1.50 net. McClurg.
Parkman, F. Oregon trail. 25 c. net. Longmans; Macmillan.
Parkman, F. Oregon trail. 40 c. Newson.
Paxon, F. L. Last American frontier. **$1.50 net. Macmillan.
Rand-McNally guide to the great Northwest. 50 c. Rand, McN. & Co.
Roe, *Mrs.* F. M. A. Army letters from an officer's wife, 1871-1888: [in the West.] **$2 net. Appleton.
Roosevelt, T. Stories of the great West. **60 c. net. Century Co.
Sanders, H. F. Trails through western woods. $2 net. A. Harriman.

West (The).—*Continued.*
Sketches of the inter-mountain states [Utah, Idaho and Nevada]; together with biographies of many prominent and progressive citizens who have helped in the development and history of the marvellous region. '09(N) c. 376 p. il.. pors. 4°. (Not for sale.) Salt Lake Trib.
Smith, C: W. Check-list of books and pamphlets rel. to the hist. of the Pacific northwest to be found in representative libraries of that region. (Add. Library for price.) Washington State Lib.
Smith, F. D. Book of a hundred bears: [travel in Yellowstone Park, Denver, Utah, etc.] 75 c. Rand, McN. & Co.
Tallman, M. C. Travelling trio. $1. M. C. Tallman.
Travellers' railway guide; western section. 25 c. Am. Railway Guide.
Van Dine, J: R. Wonders of the golden West. $1. J. S. Ogilvie.
Van Loan. Tour through the West with the Jersey City Elks, no. 211. $1. I. A. Van Loan.
Visscher, W: L. Thrilling and truthful history of the pony express. 75 c. Rand, McN. & Co.
Whiting, L. Land of enchantment; from Pike's Peak to the Pacific. **$1.50 net. Little, B. & Co.
Williams, R. H. With the border ruffians. *$4 net. Dutton.
Wilson, E. N: Among the Shoshones. $1.25. Skelton.
See also **Greenville (Treaty of);—Pacific coast;—Texas;—*also* names of western cities and states.**

West Africa.
See **Africa.**

West Indies.
Ambard, E. M. Tourist guide to the West Indies. (gratis to passengers.) Hamburg-American Line.
Boyce, *Sir* R. W. Health, progress and administration in the West Indies. $3.50 net. Dutton.
Corlett, W: T. American tropics: [West Indies, Central America, Venezuela.] $1.50. Burrows.
Esquemeling, J. Buccaneers of America; true account of the remarkable assaults committed of late years upon the coasts of the West Indies by the buccaneers of Jamaica and Tortuga. $4 net. Dutton.
Lang, J. Gibraltar and the West Indies. *$2 net. Stokes.
Moore, J. H. With Speaker Cannon through the tropics: voyage to the West Indies, Venezuela and Panama. $2. Book Pr.
Ober, F: A. Guide to the West Indies and Bermudas. **$2.25 net. Dodd.
Treves, *Sir* F: Cradle of the deep. account of a voyage to the West Indies. $2.50 net; $4 net. Dutton.
Waterton, C: Wanderings in South America, the northwest of the United States and the Antilles, in the years 1812, 1816, 1820 and 1824. $1.50. Macmillan.

WEST INDIES.—*Continued.*
Waterton, C: Wanderings in South America, the northwest of the U. S. and the Antilles, in the years 1812, 1816, 1820, and 1824. *$2.50 net. Sturgis & W.
Wilcox, *Mrs.* E. W. Sailing sunny seas. $1.50. Conkey.
See also Buccaneers;—Cuba;—Dominican Republic;—Haiti;—Jamaica;—Mt. Pelee;—Porto Rico.

WEST POINT, N. Y.
Carter, W: G. H. West Point in literature. *$2.50 net. Lord Balto. Pr.
Dickinson, J. M. Address to graduating class of U. S. Military Acad., West Point, June 11, 1909. West Point.
Hammond, H. West Point; its glamour and its grind. $1.25. Cupples & L.
Latta, J. W: Was secession taught at West Point? M. O. L. L., (Pa.)

West Point cadet. Malone, P. B. †$1.25. Penn Pub. Co.

West Virginia. Code; supp. 1907. '08(Ja11) *$3.50 net; 1909. '10(Mr) c. O. $5. West Pub.

West Virginia. *Supreme ct. of appeals.* Repts.; (W: G. Conley.) v. 62. '08(D); v. 63. '08, [1909.] (Ap) ea., $4.50; v. 64 (N); v. 65. '10(F); v. 66 (S) c. O. shp., ea., $2.50. Acme; Tribune Pr. Co. (W. Va.)

WEST VIRGINIA.
Alderson, J. C. Hdbk. of southern West Virginia: the Kanawha or middle measures of coal; the Coal River basin; Alderson Land and Development Company's survey. 25 c. J. C. Alderson.
Callahan, M. F. Evolution of the constitution of West Virginia. 50 c. Univ. of W. Va.
Hogg, C: E. Treatise and forms in justices' courts and upon appeals therefrom to the circuit ct.; adapted to the state of West Virginia. $7.50. W. H. Anderson.
Lee, A. S. Hist. of West Virginia. 20 c. A. S. Lee.
Lewis, V. A., *ed.* How West Virginia was made. (Priv. pr.) News-Mail Co.
Virginia and West Virginia. Encyclop. digest. v. 1-14. $7.50. Michie.
See also Harrison Co.;—Pendleton Co.;—Shepherdstown;—Summers Co.

Westall, Mrs. Laura May Hill.
Common-sense view of the mind-cure. '08 (O3) c. figs. D. **75 c. net. Funk.

WESTCHESTER COUNTY, N. Y.
Sherman, A. O. Westchester County and the town of Rye. 50 c. Westchester Press.

Westcott, Bp. Brooke Foss.
The two empires; the church and the world. '09(D11) D. *$1.75 net. Macmillan.

Westell, W: Percival.
Book of the animal kingdom (mammals). '10(D10) il. (partly col.) 8°, $4 net. Dutton.
Fifty-two nature rambles. '08(Je20) il. D. $1.50. Dodge.
Insect book. '08(Je27) il. 16°, *$1 net. Lane.
See also Cooper, C. S.

Westerman, Harry J.
See Ryder, Rob. O.

Westermann, L. A., Company.
Drawings made for commercial use. '08 (My.) c. il. f°, gratis. Westermann.

Westermarck, E:
Origin and development of the moral ideas. In 2 v. v. 2. '08(D12) 8°, *$3.50 net. Macmillan.

Westermayr, Arth. Jos.
Power of innocence. '09(N20) c. il. D. $1.50. Fenno.

WESTERN, Mass.
See Warren, Mass.

Western Asia in the days of Sargon. Olmstead, A. T. **$1.25 net. Holt.
Western poultry book. Basley, *Mrs.* A. $1. A. Basley.

WESTERN RESERVE.
See Ohio.

Western women in eastern lands. Montgomery, H. B. $1.50 net. Macmillan.

"Westerner," pseud.
See Donovan, J: P.

Westgate, J: Minton.
Alfalfa. '09(Mr6) il. 8°, (U. S. Dept. of Agriculture; farmers' bull.) pap., 5 c. U. S., Supt. of Docs.
See also Brand, C: J:

Westinghouse, G:, comp.
Broadening the field of the marine steam turbine: problem, and its solution, the Melville and Macalpine reduction-gear. '09, [1910.] (Mr) c. 53+77 p. il. pors. tabs., 8°. (Priv. pr.) G: Westinghouse.

WESTINGHOUSE AIR-BRAKE.
See Air-brake.

Westlake, J:
International law. pt. 2, War. '08(F1) 8°, *$3 net. Putnam.

WESTMINSTER, Mass.
Vital records of Westminster, Mass., to the end of the year 1849. (Add. pub. for price.) F. P. Rice.

WESTMINSTER ABBEY, London.
Bond, F. Visitor's guide to Westminster Abbey. 40 c.—Westminster Abbey. $4. Oxford Univ.
Notes and documents relating to Westminster Abbey. no. 1-2. *$1.60 net. Putnam.
Rackham, R. B. Nave of Westminster. $2. Oxford Univ.
Troutbeck, G. E. Children's story of Westminster Abbey. $1.35. Stokes.
Twining, A. G. Child's history of Westminster Abbey. *$1.50 net. Young Churchman.

Westminster course of supplemental lessons; ed. by Ja. Russell Miller, D.D. '09(Je12) il. maps, D. and O. pap. Presb. Bd.
Contents: Supplemental lessons for the primary department, pt. 1, by Marion Thomas, 25 c.; pt. 2, by M. Florence Brown, 25 c.; Suggestions for teaching supplemental graded lessons in the junior department: first year, by Josephine L. Baldwin, 25 c.; second year, by F: G. Taylor, 25 c.; Supplemental lessons for the upper grades of the Sunday-school, by Rev. E. Morris Fergusson, first, second, third, fourth years, ea., 15 c.

Westminster ideal class book. '08(D) no paging, D. bds. (Add. pubs. for price.) Westminster.

Westminster lib.; ed. by the Rt. Rev. Mgr Bernard Ward and the Rev. Herb. Thurston. D. $1.20 net. Longmans.
—Barry. Tradition of scripture.
—Benson. Non-Catholic denominations.
—Scannell. Priest's studies.

Westminster New Testament. 16°. *75 c. net. Revell.
—Andrews. Acts of the Apostles.
—Clark. Gospel of St. John.
—Green. Gospel of St. Mark.
—Mackintosh. Thessalonians and Corinthians.
—Ramsay. Revelation and the Johannine epistles.
—Smith. Gospel of St. Matthew.
—Strachan. Captivity and pastoral epistles.

Westminster ser. il. O. *$2 net. Van Nostrand.
—Ball. Law affecting engineers.—Natural sources of power.
—Baterden. Timber.
—Davenport. The book.
--Davies. Electric power and traction.
—Duthie. Decorative glass processes.—Ornamental window glass.
—Goodchild. Precious stones.
—Kershaw. Electro metallurgy.
—Lewes. Liquid and gaseous fuels.
—Monckton. Radio-telegraphy.
—Munby. Introd. to the chemistry and physics of building materials.
—Murray. Soils and manures.
—Pendred. Railway locomotive.
—Rose. Precious metals.
—Rosenhain. Glass manufacture.
—Sindall. Manufacture of paper.
—Solomon. Electric lamps.
—Stansbie. Iron and steel.
—Swan. Law and commercial usage of patents, designs and trade marks.
—Terry. India-rubber.
—Tonge. Coal.
—Webber. Town gas and its uses.

Westmoreland, Priscilla Anne Wellesley Pole Fane, Countess of.
Correspondence of Priscilla, Countess of Westmoreland, 1813-1870; ed. by her daughter, Lady Rose Weigall. '10(F19) pors. 8°, *$5 net. Dutton.

WESTMORLAND, Eng.
Marr, J: E: Westmorland. 45 c. Putnam.

Weston, Eustace M.
Rock drills; design, construction and use. '10(D17) il. 8°, $4. McGraw-H.

Weston, Fk. E.
Scheme for the detection of the more common classes of carbon compounds. New ed. '08(F15) O. bds., 90 c. Longmans.

Weston, W. H.
School hist. of Essex. '09(N13) il. D. 50 c. Oxford Univ.

Westover of Wanalah. Eggleston, G: C. $1.50. Lothrop, L. & S.

Westphal, Alexandre.
Law and the prophets; or, the revelation of Jehovah in Hebrew hist. from the earliest times to the capture of Jerusalem by Titus; being the work entitled "Jehovah"; tr. and adptd. by Clement Du Pontet; with a foreword by the Right Rev. the Lord Bishop of Winchester. '10 (Je4) 8°, $2.75 net. Macmillan.

Westrum, Adriaan Schade van.
The devil; founded on Ferenc Molnar's play, as produced by Harrison Grey Fiske at the Belasco Theatre, New York. '08(O10) c. il. D. †$1.50. G: W. Dillingham.

Westrup, Marg.
Greater mischief. '08(F22) c. D. †$1.50. Harper.

Westward ho! *See* Kingsley, C:

Westward 'round the world. Wright, E: S. $1.25. Dutton.

Wetham, Catherine Durning.
See Whetham, W: Cecil Dampier.

Wetherell, Eliz., pseud.
See Warner, Susan.

Wetherill, Catharine Hall.
See Hale, And., *pseud.*

Wetmore, Mrs. C. W.
See Bisland, Eliz.

Wettstein, Carl Theodor, comp. and ed.
Was Abraham Lincoln an infidel?; the religious character of Abraham Lincoln as it appears in the light of his spoken and written word. '10(My14) c. por. D. $1.25. C. M. Clark.

Wetzel, Rev. Fs. Xavier.
Guide for girls in the journey of life; from the German. 4th ed. '08(D5) 16°, 40 c. Herder.

Weule, J. K. Karl.
Native life in East Africa: results of an ethnological research expedition; tr. by Alice Werner. '09(D11) il. maps, *$4.50 special net. Appleton.

WEXFORD, Ireland.
Wheeler, H. F. B., *and* Broadley, A. M. War in Wexford. $4 net. Lane.

Weyburn, Cornelia Morton.
Baby's book. '10(S) 4°, $1.50; silk, $3; velvet ooze, $4. Barse & H.

Weyman, Stanley J:
Wild geese. '09(Mr6) c. il. D. †$1.50. Doubleday, P.

Weymer, Marguerite Josephine.
See George, *Mlle.*

WEYMOUTH, Mass.
Vital records of Weymouth. 2 v. $9.25. N. E. Hist.

Weysse, Arth. Wisswald.
Synoptic text-book of zoölogy. '09(My1) il. 8°, price reduced from *$4 net to *$2.25 net. Macmillan.

WHALES AND WHALING.
Peabody Academy of Science. Whaling industry. gratis. Salem Pub. Lib.
Spears, J: R. Story of New England whaling. $1.50. Macmillan.
Wheeler, J. C. There she blows!: [fiction.] **$1.20 net. Dutton.

Whallon, Rev. E: Payson.
Pastoral memories. '08(Ja11) 12°. (Add. pubs. for price.) Monfort.

Wharton, Mrs. Anne Hollingsworth.
English honeymoon. '08(D5) c. il. D. **$1.50 net. Lippincott.

Wharton, Mrs. Edith Newbold Jones.
Artemis to Actæon, and other verse. '09 (Ap24) c. D. **$1 net. Scribner.
Hermit and the wild woman, and other stories. '08(O3) c. D. †$1.50. Scribner.
Motor-flight through France. '08(O24) c. il. **$2 net. Scribner.
Tales of men and ghosts. '10(O29) c. D. $1.50. Scribner.

Wharton, H: Marvin, D.D.
Stories, short and sweet. '10(D31) c. D. $1 net. Neale.

Wharton, H: Redwood, M. D.
Minor and operative surgery, incl. bandaging. 7th ed., enl. and rev. '09(S) 674 p. il. 12°, *$3 net. Lea.

What a superintendent can do. Howard, P. E. (Add. pubs. for price.) Westminster.
What a woman of forty-five should know. Drake, *Mrs.* E. F. A. $1. Vir Pub.
What a young boy ought to know. Stall, S. $1. Vir Pub.
What a young girl ought to know. Wood-Allen, *Mrs.* M. $1. Vir Pub.
What a young wife ought to know. Drake, *Mrs.* E. F. A. *$1 net. Vir Pub.
What and how. Henderson, A. W. $2. M. Bradley.
What Burlingame did. Cleveland, R. (Add. author for price.) R. Cleveland.
What can and do school reports show? Falkner, R. P. 20 c. R P. Falkner.
What Christmas brought to Tom and Nell. Russell, *Mrs.* H. S. 50 c. Cochrane.
What do the Jews believe? Enelow, H. G. gratis. J. Morgenstern.
What does Christmas really mean? McCutcheon, J: T. 50 c. Forbes.
What dreams may come. Neville, F: 75 c. net. Sherman, F.
What eight million women want. Dorr, *Mrs.* R. C. $2 net. Small.
What esoterism is. Marsland, A. E. 35 c. Oriental Esoteric.
What every school boy and school girl should know. Brent, J: Un. Pacific R. R.
What every singer should know. Ryan, *Mrs.* M. $1. Franklin Pub., (Neb.)
What experience has taught me. Burton, T: W: $1.50. T: W: Burton.
What happened to the little chicks. Jewett, J: H. 75 c. Small.
What have the Greeks done for modern civilization? Mahaffy, J: P. **$2.50 net. Putnam.
What help can any workingman expect from Taft or Bryan? Benson, A. L: 5 c. Socialist.
What I do not know of farming. Mygatt, J: T. 75 c. Broadway.
What is a picture? '09(Ap10) sq. O. bds., *60 c. net. McClurg.
What is essential? Andrews, G: A. $1 net. Crowell.
What is life? Swing, P: F. (Not for sale.) P: F. Swing.
What is life? Windle, B. C. A. $1. Herder.
What is man? Burns, J. $2. Cochrane.
What is physical life. Thomson, W: H. **$1.20 net. Dodd.
What is pragmatism? Pratt, J. B. **$1.25 net. Macmillan.
What is socialism? Kauffman, R. W. **$1.25 net. Moffat.
What is spiritualism? Peebles, J. M. 75 c. Peebles.
What is success? Field, W. T. 25 c. net. Pilgrim Press.
What is to be done? Tchernychewsky, N. $1. Manhattan Bk.
What is worth while ser. 12°, leatherette, **30 c. net. Crowell.
—Abbott. What thy did with themselves.
—Barclay. Wheel of time.
—Benson. Until the evening.
—Dole. Hope of immortality.
—Drummond. Greatest thing in the world.
—Gordon. Sure and loving faith.
—Higley. Homespun religion.
—Jenness. Our rich inheritance.
—Marden. Why grow old?
—Marden *and* Connolly. Do it to a finish.
—Miller. Cure for care.—Master's friendships.—Turning northward.

What it is that heals. Cheney, *Mrs.* V. $1. R. G. Cooke.
What Jesus said. Bible. N. T. Selections. $1.25 net. Revell.
What life means to me. Grenfell, W. T. *35 c. net. Pilgrim Press.
What pictures to see in Europe in one summer. Bryant, *Mrs.* L. M. $1.50 net. Lane.
What Salem dames cooked; being choice collection of recipes. '10(Ag6) c. O. pap.. $1. Ester C. Mack Indust. Sch.
What shall I believe?: addresses by the faculty of the Auburn Theological Seminary. '08(Je20) c. D. **$1 net. Presb. Bd.
What Sheila did. Baker, C. S. 50 c. Stokes.
What should New York's next comptroller do? New York City Bureau of Municipal Research. 5 c. Bu. Municipal.
What should New York's next mayor do? New York City Bureau of Municipal Research. 10 c. Bu. Municipal.
What the Dutch have done in the west of the United States. Hiuzinga, G: F. (Priv. pr.) E: Bok.
What the public wants. Bennett, E. A. $1 net. Doran.
What the white race may learn from the Indian. James, G: W. *$1.50 net. Forbes.
What they did with themselves. Abbott, E. H. **30 c. net. Crowell.
What think you of Christ? Otten, B. J. 25 c. Herder.
What times! Semple, H: C. 35 c. Benziger.
What to do and how to do it. Bushnell, J. P., *comp.* $2. Home Manual.
What to do at recess. Johnson, G: E. 25 c. Ginn.
What to do for the stomach. Dienst, G: E. $1. Boericke & T.
What to see in England. Home, G. C. *$1 net. Macmillan.
What was nominated on the bond? Hurlbut, E. (Add. pubs. for price.) Baur.
What was the religion of Shakespeare? Mangasarian, M. M. 10 c. Independent Religious.
What we are and what we will be. McDonald, D. W: $1.50. D. W: McDonald.

What we know about Jesus. Dole, C: F. *75 c. net. Open Court.

What you ought to know about your baby. Hirschberg, L. K., *ed.* 25 c. Butterick.

What's wrong with the world. Chesterton, G. K. $1.50. Dodd.

Wheat, Mrs. Lu.
Ah Moy: story of a Chinese girl. '08(S5) c. il. 12°, **$1.50 net. Grafton Press.
Helen: a story of things to be. '08(O10) por. 12°, †$1.50. Grafton Press.

WHEAT.
Clarke, C: C., *comp.* Wheat crops of the United States, 1866-1906. 5 c. U. S., Supt. of Docs.
Davis, A. McF. Barbery bushes and wheat: [pests.] (Not for sale.) A. McF. Davis.
Dondlinger, P: T. Book of wheat. *$2 net. Judd.
Fitz, L. A. Handling wheat from field to mill. Gov. Pr. Off.
Rubinow, I: M. Russia's wheat trade. 15 c. U. S., Supt. of Docs.
Smith, R. E. Wheat fields and markets of the world. $2.15. Modern Miller.
United States. *Dept. of Commerce and Labor.* Flour and wheat trade in European countries and the Levant. Davis, M. H. (Add. Superintendent for price.) U. S., Supt. of Docs.
Whitney, M. Fertilizers for wheat soils. Gov. Pr. Off.
See also Cereals.

Wheat among the tares. Lloyd, A. *$1.10 net. Macmillan.

WHEATLAND, N. Y.
Slocum, G: E. Wheatland, Monroe County, New York: brief sketch of its history. $1. G: E. Slocum.

Wheatley, H: B:
Hogarth's London: pictures of the manners of the XVIII century; il. with 52 plates from Hogarth's works. '09(D) 20+468 p. 8°, *$4.80 net. Dutton.

Wheel magic. Allen, J. W. *$1.25 net. Lane.

Wheel o' fortune. Tracy, L: $1.50. Clode.

Wheel of progress ser. 12°. Tower.
—Staley. Oram of the forest. $1.

Wheeler, Alex., and Jack, W: R., M.D.
Hdbk. of medicine and therapeutics. 3d ed. '08(Je20) 12°, *$3 net. Wood.

Wheeler, Carl Foster and Joel Rob.
Life of Scout Two Braids (Thomas Stringfield); also contains a sketch history of Chief Geronimo and the Apaches, and an exposition of Indian religion, Indian marriages, and other topics on Indian life. '09(Je5) c. por. 8°, 25 c. Wood-B.

Wheeler, Ethel Rolt.
Famous blue-stockings. '10(My14) il. O. $4 net. Lane.

Wheeler, F. G.
Billy Whiskers at the circus. '08(O24) c. il. O. bds., $1. Saalfield.
Billy Whiskers at the fair. '09(O30) c. il. O. bds., †$1. Saalfield.

Wheeler, Fs. Rolt-.
See Rolt-Wheeler, Fs.

Wheeler, G. Owen.
Old English furniture of the 17th and 18th centuries. '08(Mr28) 12°, $3. Scribner.

Wheeler, Giles, comp.
Genealogy of a branch of the Wheelers. '08 (Jl) 61 p. por. 12°, $1. G. Wheeler.

Wheeler, Harold Felix Baker.
Boys' Napoleon. '10(S24) por. D. $1.50. Crowell.

—, and Broadley, Alex. Meyrick.
War in Wexford; acct. of the rebellion in the south of Ireland in 1798 told from the orig. documents. '10(Ap30) il. pors. fold. map, O. $4 net. Lane.

Wheeler, Harriet.
See Gale, Oliver Marble.

Wheeler, H:, D.D.
History and exposition of the twenty-five Articles of religion of the Methodist Episcopal church. '08(F1) c. O. *$2 net. Eaton & M.
One thousand questions and answers concerning the Methodist Episcopal church; its hist., government, doctrines, and usages, including the origin, polity, and progress of all other Methodist bodies; with introd. by H: A. Buttz. Rev. ed. [1910.] c. '09. 304 p. 12°, 75 c. Eaton & M.

Wheeler, Herb. Allen.
Vitrified paving brick; review of present practice in the manufacture, testing and uses of vitrified paving brick. [2d ed.] '10(S17) c. 8°, $2. T. A. Randall.

Wheeler, Ja. Cooper.
Captain Pete of Alaska. '10(O8) c. 12°, $1.50. Dutton.
Captain Pete of Cortesana. '09(O2) il. 12°, $1.50. Dutton.
Captain Pete of Puget Sound. '09(O2) il. 12°, $1.50. Dutton.
There she blows!: a whaling yarn. '09 (Ag7) c. il. D. **$1.20 net. Dutton.

Wheeler, Ja. Rignall.
Archæology: [a lecture.] '08(N21) c. 8°, pap. (Add. pubs. for price.) Columbia Univ.
See also Fowler, Harold North.

Wheeler, Jos. Trank.
Zonal-belt hypothesis: new explanation of the cause of the Ice ages. '08(D19) c. O. **$2.50 net. Lippincott.

Wheeler, Marcus Pratt.
Hash; chopped, seasoned and warmed up: [verses.] '08(Ap25) c. il. pors. O. 75 c.; pap., 50 c. M. P. Wheeler.

Wheeler, Marianna.
The baby: his care and training. Rev. ed. '09(S) 16°, *$1 net. Harper.

Wheeler, Mrs. Post.
See Rives, Hallie Erminie.

Wheeler, Wilfred Forrest.
See Parr, S: Wilson.

Wheeler, W: Morton.
Ants; the structure, development and behavior of ants. '10(Ap30) il. 8°, (Columbia Univ. biological ser.) $5. Lemcke.

Wheeler, W: Ogden, comp.
Ogden family in America: Elizabethtown branch, and their English ancestry: John Ogden, the Pilgrim, and his descendants, 1640-1906; their hist., biography and genealogy; ed. by Lawrence Van Alstyne and Rev. C: Burr Ogden. '07, [1908.] (Je.) c. 14+531 p. il. pls. pors. maps, facsims., 4°, cl. (priv. pr.) Lippincott.

Wheeler, W: Webb.
Glimpse of the isles of the Pacific. '08 (F) c. '07. 212 p. il. 8°. (Not for sale.) Hardman.

WHEELER FAMILY.
See Genealogies.

Wheelock, Edn. Miller.
Proteus, rhapsody on man; with a biographical note by C: Kassel. '10(S) c. 8+58 p. por. 16°, $1. Open Court.

Wheelock, Eleazar.
See Rochester reprints.

Wheelock, Mrs. Eliz. Marian.
Stories of Wagner operas for children. '08(Ap4); [New ed.] '10(O31) c. O. ea., $1.25. Bobbs-M.

Wheelock, Ida S., [Mrs. T. B. Wheelock.]
Salads. '10(Ap30) c. 12°, 50 c. I. S. Wheelock.

Wheelock, Mrs. T. B.
See Wheelock, Ida S.

WHEELS.
See Gears and gearing;—Machinery.

Wheels of time. Barclay, *Mrs.* F. L. C. 50 c. net; 30 c. net. Crowell.

Wheelwright, Edm. March.
Lampy's early days, by an old Lampooner. '09, [1910.] (Mr) c. 70 p. il. pors. 8°, $5. (500 copies.) Harvard Lampoon.

Wheelwright, J: Tyler.
War children. '08(O10) c. il. D. †$1.50. Dodd.

Whelan, N: Jos.
Ten days in Cuba. '08(Ag) c. 94 p. il. 8°, pap., 35 c. N. J. Whelan.

Whelen, Townsend.
Suggestions to military riflemen; rev. ed., 1909. '09(Jl) (Add. pubs. for price.) Hudson.

Wheless, Jos.
See Mexico. Compendium of the laws. 2 v.

Whelpley, B:
See Tennyson, Alfr., *Lord.*

When a man marries. Rinehart, *Mrs.* M. R. †$1.50. Bobbs-M.

When a woman woos. **Marriott, C: $1.50. Lane.**

When America became a nation. Jenks, T. $1.25. Crowell.

When America won liberty. Jenks, T. $1.25. Crowell.

When and where of famous men and women. Hensman, H., *and* Webb, C. 50 c. Dutton.

When cattle kingdom fell. Stafford, J: R: $1.25 net. B. W. Dodge.

When daddy was a boy. Parry, T: W. $1. Hudson.

When folks was folks. Blunt, E. L. $1.50. Cochrane.

When good fellows get together. Bennett, J. O., *ed.* $1. Reilly & B.

When I am rich. Mason, R. $1.50. G: W. Dillingham.

When I grow up. **Denslow, W: W. **$1 net. Century Co.**

When Lincoln died. Thomson, E: W: $1.25. Houghton M.

When little souls awake. Bailey, H: T. 25 c. net. Pilgrim Press.

When love calls men to arms. Chalmers, S. $1.50. Small.

When mother lets us cook. Johnson, C. **75 c. net. Moffat.

When mother lets us garden. Duncan, F. **75 c. net. Moffat.

When mother lets us help. Johnson, C. **75 c. net. Moffat.

When mother lets us sew. Ralston, *Mrs.* V. **75 c. net. Moffat.

When mother was a little girl. Blanchard, A. E. $2. Dutton.

When railroads were new. Carter, C: F. **$2 net. Holt.

When Roggie and Reggie were five. Smith, G. **$1.30 net. Harper.

When Sarah saved the day. Singmaster, E. †$1. Houghton M.

When Sarah went to school. Singmaster, E. $1. Dodd.

When she came home from college. Hurd, M. K. **$1.35 net. Houghton M.

When skies are gray. Heazlitt, C. W. $1. Neale.

When the bugle called. Tatum, E. $1.25. Neale.

When the gates lift up their heads. Erskine, P. †75 c. Little, B. & Co.

When the King came. Hodges, G:, *comp.* **$1.25 net. Houghton M.

When the lilacs bloom. De Long, A. P. $1.25. Benton.

When the tide turns. Young, A. B. F. †$1.50. Estes.

"When the wildwood was in flower." Stanton, G. S. *$1 net. J. S. Ogilvie.

When Theodore is king. Spaulding, W. 25 c. W. Spaulding.

When things were doing. Steere, C: A. $1. Kerr.

When Valmond came to Pontiac. Parker, *Sir* G. $1.25. Harper.

When we dead awaken. *See* Ibsen, Henrik.

When we're in love. Jennings, N. I., *comp.* 50 c. Lone Star.

When yesterday was young. Sweeney, M. I. M. $1.50. F. F. Sherman.

Where and how. Parker, J: L. $1; 50 c. Broun-G.

Where flows the Hood River. Cook, M. $1. Hicks-Chatten.

Where ghosts walk. Terhune, *Mrs.* M. V. H. $2.50 net. Putnam.

Where men have walked. Rhodes, *Mrs.* H. H. $1.50. C. M. Clark.

Where snow is sovereign. Stratz, R. $1.50. Dodd.

Where the fishers go. Browne, P. W: $1.75. Cochrane.

Where the laborers are few. Deland, M. W. C. †$1.50. Harper.

Where the light dwelleth. Collyer, R. *$1.25 net. Am. Unitarian.

Where the wind blows. Pyle, K. $2. Dutton.
Where to go in the Adirondacks. Hardie, G: R. 25 c. G: R. Hardie.
Where to look. *See* Pitman's.
Where's master?, by Cæsar. 6th ed. '10 (O1) D. bds., 50 c. net. Doran.
Whetham, W: Cecil Dampier and Catherine Durning.
Family and the nation; study in natural inheritance and social responsibility. '09 (N20) O. *$2.50 net. Longmans.
WHEY.
See Milk.
Which? beer privilege anarchy or liberty? Flanders, E. B. 10 c. E. B. Flanders.
Which college for the boy? Cobin, J: **$1.50 net. Houghton M.
Which one? Pleasants, M. M. $1. Earle.
Whidden, Captain J: D.
Ocean life in the old sailing ship days. New ed. '08(S19) c. il. cr. 8°, **$1.50 net. Little, B. & Co.
Whiffen, Edn. T:
Jephtha sacrificing, and Dinah: two dramatic poems. '08(S19) c. D. **$1 net. Grafton Press.
Whigham, Wallace Hugh, and Frederick, Oliver D.
Bookkeeping and business practice. '10 (Je4) c. 8°, $1. Heath.
Whims and visions. Maw, J. M. $1. J. M. Maw.
Whinery, S:
Specifications for street roadway pavements. '08(Ap4) c. 8°, pap., *50 c. net. Engineering News.
Whipple, G: Chandler.
Typhoid fever; introd. by W: T. Sedgwick. '08(Ap25) c. figs. 12°, **$3 net. Wiley.
Whipple, Guy Montrose.
Guide to high school observation. '09 (Ja23) Q. (Cornell study bulletins for teachers.) 40 c. Bardeen.
Manual of mental and physical tests: book of directions comp. with special reference to the experimental study of school children in the laboratory or classroom. '10(D31) c. 8°, $2.50 net. Warwick-Y.
Questions in general and educational psychology. '09(Ja23) Q. (Cornell study bulletins for teachers.) 75 c. Bardeen.
Questions in school hygiene. '10(Ja8) O. (Cornell study bulletins for teachers.) 60 c. Bardeen.
Whipple, Leander Edm.
Mental healing. 6th ed. '08(Ag8) por. c. O. $1.50. Metaphysical.
Whipple, Orville B.
See Paddock, Wendell.
Whipple, Wayne.
Heart of Abraham Lincoln. '09(Mr20) c. por. D. 50 c. Biddle Press.
Story-life of Lincoln. Memorial ed. issued to commemorate the 100th anniversary of Lincoln's birth. '08(N14) c. il. O. **$1.75 net. Winston.
Story of the White House. '10(Ag13) c. il. pors. 8°, 50 c. Altemus.
Whips of time. Kenealy, A. †$1.50. Little, B. & Co.
"Whipster," pseud.
See Bradley, Cuthbert.
Whirl (The). Davis, F. †$1.50. Dodd.
Whirligigs. Henry, O., *pseud.* $1.20, fixed. Doubleday, P.
Whirlpools. Sienkiewicz, H. $1.50. Little, B. & Co.
Whish, Evelyn.
Until Shiloh come; with introd. by Rev. Jesse Brett. '10(O22) S. 50 c. net. Longmans.
WHISKY.
United States. Pure food act; what is the meaning of the term "whisky" under the Pure Food Act, and the proper regulations for branding various kinds of whisky under the Internal Revenue Act?; decision by President Taft. '09, [1910.] (Mr) 9 p. 8°, pap.
Whisper of destiny. Harrison, V. B. $1.25. Dutton.
Whispering man. Webster, H: K. †$1.50. Appleton.
WHIST.
See Bridge.
Whistler, Ja. Abbott McNeill.
"Ten o'clock": [art lectures;] del. in London. [New issue.] '08(D12) c. S. pap., *$1 net. E. D. North.
WHISTLER, James Abbott McNeill.
Bacher, O. H: With Whistler in Venice. **$4 net. Century Co.
Hartmann, S. Whistler book. $2.50. L. C. Page.
Kennedy, E: G., *comp.* Etched work of Whistler. $100. Grolier Club.
Mansfield, H. Descriptive catalogue of the etchings and dry-points of James Abbott McNeill Whistler. (Add. pubs. for price.) Caxton Club.
Metropolitan Museum of Art, New York. Paintings in oil and pastel, by James A. McNeill Whistler. 25 c. net. Metropolitan Museum.
Pennell, *Mrs.* E. R. and J. Life of James McNeill Whistler. 2 v. *$10 net. Lippincott.
Seitz, D. C. Writings by and about James Abbott M'Neill Whistler. $3. E. D. North.
Sickert, B. Whistler. *75 c. net. *$1 net. Dutton.
Wood, T. M. Whistler. *65 c. net. Stokes.
Whitaker, Bessie Lewis.
Provincial council and committees of safety in North Carolina. '08, [1909.] (S) 6+49 p. il. 8°, (Univ. of North Carolina; James Sprunt historical monographs.) (Add. Univ. for price.) Univ. of N. C.
Whitaker, Evelyn.
Baby Bob. '08(N7) il. D. $1.50. Lippincott.
Whitaker, G: Mason.
See Rawl, Bernard H.
—, Rogers, Lore Alford, and Hunt, Caroline Louisa.
Care of milk and its use in the home. '10 (O) 20 p. 8°, (U. S., Dept. of Agriculture, Farmers' bull.)
Whitaker, Herman.
The planter. '09(Mr20) c. front. D. †$1.50. Harper.

Whitaker, Nathaniel.
See Rochester reprints.

Whitaker, Olivar Barr.
Dick Haley; thrilling story of poverty, heroism and suffering. '10(Je18) c. il. 16°, 80 c. Chr. Pub. Co.

Whitaker, Rob.
Gospel at work in modern life. '10(O15) D. 50 c. net. Griffith.

Whitaker's almanack, 1909. '09(Ja16); 1910. '10(Mr26) 8°, hf. roan, ea., *$1.25 net. Scribner.

Whitaker's Reference catalogue of current literature; cont. the full titles of books now in print and on sale, with the prices at which they may be obtained of all booksellers and an index containing nearly 185,-000 references. In 3 v. '10(O22) O. hf. leath., $6 net; before Nov. 1, $5. Pub. Weekly.

Whitcher, W: F:
Descendants of Chase Whitcher of Warren, N. H., fourth in descent from Thomas Whittier of Salisbury (Haverhill), Mass. '07, [1908.] (Mr.) 7+128 p. il. pors. 8°, cl., *$3.50 net. W: F: Whitcher.

WHITCHER FAMILY.
See Genealogies.

Whitcomb, Carrie Gates Niles.
Autobiography of Jeremy L., the actor dog; written by Carrie G. Whitcomb for Jeremy L., because he couldn't write it himself. '10(Ag20) c. il. D. 50 c. net. Bassette.

Whitcomb, Ida Prentice.
Young people's story of music. '08(D19) c. il. pors. O. $2. Dodd.

—, and Grosvenor, Sarah E.
Christ-child in legend and art. '10(O1) c. il. D. $1 net. Dodd.
Christ-child in story, legend, art and song. '10(Ja8) il. 12°, 75 c. B'way Pub.

Whitcomb, Russell, ["Russ Ruscom."]
Skimming the skies. '09(Je5) c. il. 12°, (Comrades courageous ser.) $1.25. Badger.

White, Albert Beebe.
Making of the English constitution, 449-1485. '08(O10) c. O. **$2 net. Putnam.

White, Alfr. F., comp.
Coins of the world (a numismatography). '10(Mr5) il. 4°, $1. Banking Law.

White, Mrs. Alma.
Demons and tongues. '10(Jl30) c. D. pap., 30 c. Pentecostal Union.
Gems of life; selections for children. '08 (My16) c. il. por. O. 60 c. Pillar of Fire.

White, Almira Larkin.
Genealogy of the ancestors and descendants of John White of Wenham and Lancaster, Mass., 1574-1909. In 4 v. '09(O23) il. pors. maps, fold. tabs., O. ea., $5; per set, $28. A. L. White

White, And. Dickson.
Seven great statesmen in the warfare of humanity with unreason. '10(S17) c. O. $2.50 net. Century Co.

White, Ansley DeForest, jr.
Transgressor (published anonymously) and other stories, showing the effects of liquor upon society. '09(Ag28) il. map, O. 50 c.; 75 c. Interstate Prohibition.

White, Bouck, ed.
Book of Daniel Drew; glimpse of the Fisk-Gould-Tweed régime from the inside. '10(Ap30) c. D. $1.50 net. Doubleday, P.

White, Buchanan.
Rural school-teacher; or, a double West Virginia love story. 09(Jl17) c. il. 12°, $1. B'way Pub.

White, C: E.
See Watson, Bruce Mervellon.

White, C: Fred.
Plea of the negro soldier, and a hundred other poems. '08(Jl18) c. por. D. $1.25. C: F. White.

White, D:
Effect of oxygen in coal. '09(N) 74 p. tabs., O. (U. S., Dept. of the Interior; Geolog. Survey bull.) pap. (Add. Superintendent for price.)

White, E:, ed.
150 years of unparalleled thrift; Pittsburgh sesquicentennial. '08(O) c. 59 p. il. por. 4°, 25 c. E: White.
Pittsburgh the powerful: interpretation of the commercial, financial and industrial strength of a great city, and celebrating its corporate union with the city of Allegheny; official publication of the Chamber of Commerce. '08(Mr14) c. il. f°, $1.12. Industry.

White, E: Alb.
Second rept. on the hymeniales of Connecticut. '10(Ag27) il. O. (Conn. State Geological and Natural History Survey bull.) pap., 35 c. Conn. Lib.

White, E: Jos.
Law of personal injuries on railroads. In 2 v. v. 1, Injuries to employees; v. 2. Injuries to passengers, licensees and trespassers. '09(Je) c. 163+550; 38+827+1739 p. O. $13. F. H. Thomas.

White, E: Lucas.
Narrative lyrics. '08(S26) c. O. **$1.25 net. Putnam.

White, E: M.
Indiana laws made plain; laws and legal forms prepared for the use of farmers, mechanics and business men. '09(S) 100 p. 8°, $1. Parkers' Law Pub.

White, Eliza Orne.
Brothers in fur. '10(O22) c. D. $1. Houghton M.
Wares of Edgefield. '09(O9) c. D. **$1.25 net. Houghton M.

White, Ellen G. Harmon, [Mrs. Ja. White.]
Ministry of healing. '10(Mr12) c. il. O. $3. Pacific Press.
Steps to Christ. '08(Je6) c. il. 12°, 60 c.; leath., $1.25. Pacific Press.

White, Ernest Cleveland, and Clark, Ellery H.
All-around athletics. '08(D19) c. il. 16°, (Spalding's athletic lib.) pap., 10 c. Am. Sports.

White, Ernest G.
Science and singing; consideration of the capabilities of the vocal cords and their work in the art of tone production. '09 (D18) c. il. 8°, $1.25. T: J. Donlan.

White, Eustace E.
Complete hockey player. '09, [1910.] (Ja) c. il. 8°, **$2 net. Jacobs.

White, Frances E., comp.
Animal lover's birthday book. '10(Ap9) 16°, 50 c. Macmillan.

White, Frances Hodges.
Captain Jinks: the autobiography of a Shetland pony. '09(Jl31) c. il. O. $1. L. C. Page.

White, Fk.
On corporations; cont. the laws as amended to Jan. 1, 1910. 7th ed. '09(D) c. O. $7. Baker, V. & Co.

White, Fred Merrick.
Crime on canvas. '09(Ap3) c. front. D. $1.50. Fenno.
Five knots. '08(My23) c. il. D. †$1.50. Little, B. & Co.
Hard pressed. '10(Ap16) D. $1.50. Fenno.
Mystery of the four fingers: [detective story.] '08(Je6) c. il. 12°, $1.50. W. J. Watt.
Scales of justice. '09(S4) front. D. $1.50. Kearney.
The sundial. '08(D12) c. il. D. $1.50. B. W. Dodge.
The yellow face. '08(Ja25) D. *$1 net. Fenno.

White, F:
Bill, a cheerful dog: verses. '08(D12) c. il. O. **$1 net. Moffat.

White, F: A:
Laws on marriage, divorce and property rights of married women of all states and Alaska, Hawaii, Ariz., N. M. and D. C., [etc.] '10(Je) c. O. $5. Baumgardt.

White, G. M.
See White, W. L.

White, G: Ransom.
Restraint of domestic animals; book for the use of students and practitioners. '09(Ap) c. 302 p. il. 8°, $3.75. G: R. White.

WHITE, *Sir* Gilbert.
Shelley, H: C: Gilbert White and Selborne. *$1.50 net. Scribner.

White, Gleeson.
Practical designing. New ed. '09(Mr27) il. 12°, *$1.25 net. Macmillan.
—, ed. Master-painters of Britain. '09(S11) il. O. pap., *$3 net. Lane.

White, Mrs. Grace Miller.
Tess of the storm country. '10(Mr19) c. il. D. $1.50. W. J. Watt.

White, H. Williams-.
See Williams-White, H.

White, Hamilton.
New theology, by a Methodist layman. '10 (D31) c. D. $1.25. B'way Pub.

White, H: Alex.
Stonewall Jackson. '09(Ja30) c. D. (American crisis biographies.) **$1.25 net. Jacobs.

White, H: Clay.
See Hills, Jos. Lawrence.

White, H: Kirke.
Poems, letters and prose fragments; ed., with an introd., by J: Drinkwater. '08 (F22) 12°, (New universal lib.) 50 c.; leath., 75 c. Dutton.

White, Hervey.
New songs for old. '10(D) c. 80 p. 24°, 50 c. H. White.

White, Horace.
Abraham Lincoln in 1854: address del. before the Illinois State Historical Society at its ninth annual meeting at Springfield, Ill., January 30, 1908. '08 (Ag8) c. 8°, pap., gratis. State Hist.
Money and banking, illustrated by American history; rev. and continued to the year 1908. 3d ed. '09(Ja23) c. tabs., front. 12°, *$1.80 net; school ed., *$1.50 net. Ginn.

White, Horace H:
Notarial guide and book of forms for the use of notaries, clerks of court and lawyers. 2d ed. '08(S) c. 568 p. O. shp., $10. Hansell.

White, Ja.
Hand loom linen weavers of Ireland and their work. '08(O10) c. il. 8°. (Add. pubs. for price.) Irish Hand-Woven.

White, Mrs. Ja.
See White, Ellen G. Harmon.

White, Ja. Edson.
Past, present, and future. '09(Mr27) c. il. 8°, $1.50; $2; leath., $3. Southern Pub.

White, Ja. Herb.
On polystely in roots of *orchidaceae.* '07 [1908.] (My) 20 p. il. 4°, (Univ. of Toronto studies, Biological ser.) pap., 50 c. Univ. of Toronto.

White, Ja. Terry.
Character lessons in American biography for public schools and home instruction; prep. in response to the general demand for a better moral instruction in the public schools for the Character Development League. '10(Mr5) c. pors. 4°, 50 c. Character Development.

White, Ja. W:, and Martin, E:
Genito-urinary surgery and venereal diseases. 9th ed. '10(O) c. 7-24+1092 p. il. 8°, $6. Lippincott.

White, J: Barber.
Genealogy of the descendants of Thomas Gleason of Watertown, Mass., 1607-1909; ed. by Lillian May Wilson. '09, [1910.] (F) c. 672 p. pors. 8°, $7.50. Nichols Print.

White, J: Claude.
Sikhim and Bhutan; twenty-one years on the north-east frontier, [India,] 1887-1908. '09(D11) il. map, Q. *$6 net. Longmans.

White, J: G., ed.
Twentieth century hist. of Mercer County, Pa.; narrative acct. of its historical progress, its people, and its principal interests. In 2 v. '10(Je4) il. pors. 4°, $18. Lewis Pub.

White, J: Kearnes.
White rose, and a medley of themes: [poems.] '10(F12) c. O. 75 c. Hunter & Co.

White, J: Turner, rep.
See Missouri. *St. Louis and Kansas City cts. of appeals.* Cases.—Repts.

White, J: Williams.
Thomas Day Seymour, 1848-1907; memorial address given at Yale Univ. on Feb. 12, 1908. '09(My) 20 p. 8°, gratis. B. Perrin.

White, J: Z.
Dartmouth College case decision; with introd. by W: Marion Reedy. '10(F) 20 p. S. pap., 5 c. Timby.
Direct legislation: the initiative and referendum; reprinted from the *Public.* '09 (Ap) pap., 5 c.; per doz., 40 c.; per 100, $2. Timby.

White, Josiah.
Josiah White's history, given by himself; [hist. of introduction of canal navigation and use of anthracite coal in Penn.] '09(N) 75 p. 4°. (Add. pubs. for price.) Lehigh Coal.

White, Kirke.
Poems, letters and prose fragments of Kirke White; ed., with an introd. by J: Drinkwater. '09, [1910.] (F) 51+266 p. 16°, 50 c. Dutton.

White, Lloyd S.
See Russell, C: Taze.

White, Marian.
Fuels of the household: their origin, composition and uses. '09(S4) c. D. *75 c. net. Whitcomb.

White, Mary Culler.
Days of June; life story of June Nicholson. '09(Ap10) c. 12°, *50 c. net. Revell.

White, Oscar A.
Childhood and ponyhood blended. '09(D18) c. il. Q. bds., 35 c. Dunlap Pony Co.

White, Percy.
Rescuer. '09(Ag28) D. †$1.50. G: W. Dillingham.

WHITE, Peter.
Barbara, L. L. Peter White as man and citizen. (Add. Univ. for price.) Univ. of Mich.

White, R: Grant.
Every-day English: a sequel to "Words and their uses." '08(D) c. 31+512 p. 12°, $2. Houghton M.

White, Rosamond Jane, and Smith, Adelaide.
Little journey to South Africa and up the east coast. '08(D5) c. il. D. (Library of travel.) 50 c. Flanagan.

White, Stewart E:
Camp and trail. '09(D4) c. il. O. *$1.25 net. Doubleday, P.
Conjuror's house. '10(F) 75 c. Grosset.
The pass. '09(D4) c. il. map, O. **$1.25 net Doubleday, P.
The riverman. '08(Ag29) c. D. †$1.50. McClure.
Rules of the game. '10(N19) c. il. D. $1.40, fixed. Doubleday, P.

White, T. Hyler.
Petrol motors and motor cars; hdbk. for engineers, designers and draughtsmen. 4th ed. '10(Ap30) il. fold. tabs., D. $1.40 net. Longmans.

White, True W.
Grammar for thinkers. '10(F12) 20 c. Tufts Coll.

White, W. Holt-.
See Holt-White, W.

White, W. L. and G. M.
Heating engineers quantities; simplex system of taking out heating engineers quantities and measurements, obtaining a more equal basis of tendering and for checking deviations as the work proceeds. '10(D17) il. f°, $4.25. Spon.

White, W: Alanson.
Hospitals and asylums of Europe. '08 (Je6) 8°, (George Washington Univ. pubs., Medical science ser.) pap. (Not for sale.) George Washington Univ.
Outlines of psychiatry. '07, [1908.] (Mr.) c. 232 p. il. 8°, (Nervous and mental disease monograph ser.) $2. Journal Nervous Disease.

White, W: Alfr.
Harmony and ear-training. '08(Mr7) c. O. $1.50. Silver.

White, W: Allen.
Certain rich man. '09(Ag7) c. D. †$1.50; Kansas ed., †$2. Macmillan.
Court of boyville. Holiday ed. '10(Ja29) il. 12°, $2. Macmillan.
In our town. '10(Ja29) il. 12°, $1.50. Macmillan.
Old order changeth; view of American democracy. '10(My14) c. D. $1.25 net. Macmillan.
Real issue; book of Kansas stories. '09 (D25) c. S. **$1.25 net. Macmillan.
Stratagems and spoils; stories of love and politics. '09(D25) c. il. D. **$1.25 net. Macmillan.

White, W: Braid.
Regulation and repair of piano and player mechanism, together with tuning as science and art. '10(Mr12) c. il. 12°, $1.50. E. L. Bill.
Technical treatise on piano player mechanism. '08(Ag) c. 165 p. il. 12°, $1.50. E: L. Bill.

White, W: E: Bradden Holt-.
See Holt-White, W: E: Bradden.

White, W: Fk.
Scrap-book of elementary mathematics: notes, recreations, essays. '08(Mr7) c. il. D. $1. Open Court.

White, W: Hale, M.D.
Common affections of the liver. '08(O24) 12°, *$2 net. Wood.

White, W: Hale, ["Mark Rutherford."]
More pages from a journal, with other papers. '10(D31) S. $1.50. Oxford Univ.
Pages from a journal, with other papers. 2d ed. '10(D31) S. $1.50. Oxford Univ.

White aprons. Goodwin, *Mrs.* M. W. †75 c. Little, B. & Co.

White bees. Van Dyke, H: J. **$1.25. Scribner.

White cow and other tales. Morton, J. S. (Priv. pr.) P. Morton.

WHITE FAMILY.
See Genealogies: White, A. L.;—Williams, C. S.

White flame. North, L. $1. Golden Press.

White flame of sculpture. Pope, P. S. 65 c. Torch Press.

WHITE HOUSE, Washington, D. C.
Sage, A. C. Boys and girls of the White. $1.50. Stokes.
Whipple, W. Story of the White House. 50 c. Altemus.
Willets, G. Inside history of the White House. $1. Chr. Herald.
White kitten book. Aldin, C. 75 c. Doran.
White life. Biederwolf, W: E: 10 c. net. Revell.
White magic. Phillips, D: G. $1.50. Appleton.
White man's burden. Riley, B: F. $1.25. B: F. Riley.
White man's foot in Kansas. Dunbar, J: B. gratis. State Hist., Kan.
White mice. Davis, R: H. †$1.50. Scribner.
WHITE MOUNTAINS, N. H.
Ayres, P. W. Commercial importance of the White Mountain forests. (Add. Superintendent for price.) U. S., Supt. of Docs.
WHITE OAK.
Lillibridge, W: O. Quercus Alba, the veteran of the Ozarks. 50 c. McClurg.
White-paper garden. Shafer, *Mrs.* S. A. $2.50 net. McClurg.
White path. Waring, E. H. $1.50. Neale.
White peril. Andrews, L: R. $1. White Peril.
WHITE-PINE.
See **Pine trees.**
White prophet. Caine, T: H: H. †$1.50. Appleton.
White puppy book. Aldin, C. C. W. 75 c. Doran.
WHITE RATS OF AMERICA.
See **Actors and actresses.**
White River raft. Miller, L. B. $1.50. Estes.
White rose. White, J: K. 75 c. Hunter & Co.
White rose of weary leaf. Hunt, V. B. †$1.50. Brentano's.
White roses. Brown, K. H. $1.20 net. Duffield.
White sister. Crawford, F. M. †$1.50. Macmillan.
White slavery. Britton, W. $1.50. Werner Co.
WHITE SLAVE TRADE.
See **Prostitution.**
White stone. *See* France, Anatole, *pesud.*
White trail. MacDonald, A. $1.25. Caldwell.
Whitefield, C: T.
Plain American in England. '10(Je4) c. S. 50 c. Doubleday.
Whitehead, J. B.
Electric operation of steam railways; [repr. from *Popular Science Monthly,* Mar., 1909.] '09(N) pap. (Add. author for price.) J. B. Whitehead.
Whitehead, J:
Illusions of Christian science; with an appendix on Swedenborg and the mental healers. '08(Ja11) D. $1. Garden Press.
Study of Swedenborg's psychical states and experiences. '10(F19) O. pap., gratis. Mass. New-Ch. Un.

Whiteing, R:
Little people. '09(F27) por. O. *$1.50 net. Cassell.
Whitelegge, B: Arth., M.D., and Newman, G:, M.D.
Hygiene and public health. New ed., rev. [1910.] (My) 636 p. il. 16°, $1.75 net. Funk.
Whiteley, Lillian C., ["Rosanna Watson."]
Dana kids. '10(Mr5) c. front. 12°, 50 c. L. C. Whiteley.
WHITEMARSH, Pa.
Jones, C: H: Whitemarsh; an address. (Add. author for price.) C: H: Jones.
Whiteside, Guy Kenneth, ["J: Ferris St. John."]
Her wedding night. '10(Ja22) c. D. 50 c. G. K. Whiteside.
Whiteside, Mary Brent.
Bill Possum: his book. '09(Ap10) c. il. O. $1. Byrd.
Whitford, Caleb Bailey.
Training the bird dog. '08(Ag1) c. il. D. *$1.25 net. Outing.
Whitham, G. I.
Basil the page. '09(O23) D. †$1.25. Dodge.
Whither thou goest. Bell, J: J. *$1.20 net. Revell.
Whitin, Ernest Stagg.
Factory legislation in Maine. '08(Jl18) c. O. (Columbia Univ. studies in hist., economics and public law.) pap., $1. Longmans.
Whiting, C: E., comp.
See Chapman, F: E., *comp.*
Whiting, Lilian.
Italy, the magic land. [New popular ed.] '10(S10) c. O. $1.50 net, boxed. Little, B. & Co.
Land of enchantment; from Pike's Peak to the Pacific. [New popular ed.] '09(S18) c. il. O. **$1.50 net, boxed. Little, B. & Co.
Life transfigured. '10(N5) c. D. $1.25 net. Little, B. & Co.
Lilies of etenral peace: [Easter booklet.] '08(Ap18) c. D. bds., **75 c. net; leath., **$1.50 net. Crowell.
Louise Chandler Moulton; poet and friend. '10(O1) il. O. $1.50 net. Little, B. & Co.
Paris the beautiful. '08(D5) c. il. O. **$2 net. Little, B. & Co.
WHITING, *Abbot* Richard.
Gasquet, F. A. Last abbot of Gladstonbury. *$2 net. Macmillan.
Whiting, Rob. Rudd, comp.
Four hundred good stories. '10(O8) c. D. $1. Baker & T.
Whitlatch, Marshall.
Golf, for beginners and others. '10(My14) c. il. O. $2 net. Outing.
Whitley, W. T.
Missionary achievement: Gay lectures, 1907. '08(O24) 12°, *$1 net. Revell.
Whitlock, Brand.
Abraham Lincoln. '09(F6) c. por. T. (Beacon biographies of eminent Americans.) **50 c. net. Small.
Gold brick. '10(O22) c. D. $1.50. Bobbs-M.

WHITMAN, Marcus.
Eells, M. Marcus Whitman: pathfinder and patriot. *$2.50 net. A. Harriman.
Smith, C: W. Contribution toward a bibliography of Marcus Whitman. (Add. University for price.) Univ. of Wash.

Whitman, Roger Bradbury.
Motor-car principles: the gasolene automobile. '08(Ap25) **$1.25 net; New and enl. ed. '09(D11) il. fold. chart, 12°, ea., **$1.50 net. Appleton.

Whitman, Royal, M.D.
Treatise on orthopedic surgery. 4th ed., rev. and enl. '10(N) 12+17-908 p. il. 8°, $5.50 net. Lea.

Whitman, Stephen French.
Predestined; novel of New York life. '10 (Mr5) c. D. †$1.50. Scribner.
Shorty and Patrick, U. S. S. Oklahoma. '10(D3) c. il. D. $1. Collier.

Whitman, Walt.
Complete prose works; Specimen days and Collect, November boughs and Good-bye my fancy. '09(Je26) c. por. D. **$1.25 net; de luxe ed., **$2 net. Appleton.
Leaves of grass; incl. Sands of seventy, Good-bye my fancy, Old age echoes, and A backward glance o'er travel'd roads. '09(Jl3) c. por. D. **$1.25 net; ed. de luxe, **$2 net. Appleton.
Wisdom of Walt Whitman; sel. and ed., with introd. by Laurens Maynard. '08 (D5) c. Tt. (Wisdom ser.) leath., **$1 net. Brentano's.

WHITMAN, Walt.
Carpenter, G: R. Walt Whitman. **75 c. net. Macmillan.
Noyes, C. E. An approach to Walt Whitman. $1.25. Houghton M.
Perry, B. Walt Whitman. **$1.50 net. Houghton M.
Traubel, H. With Walt Whitman in Camden. v. 1, 2. **$3 net. Appleton.

WHITMAN, William, & Co.
See **Textile fabrics.**

Whitmer, T: Carl.
Considerations on music. '08(My23) c. Q. pap., 50 c. Stephens Coll.
Symbolisms. '10(Mr5) c. D. bds., $1. Badger.

Whitmore, Clara Helen.
Woman's work in English fiction, from the Restoration to the mid-Victorian period. '10(Je4) c. 12°, $1.25 net. Putnam.

Whitney, Mrs. Adeline Dutton Train.
Gayworthys. '08(Je13) 12°, (Home ser.) 50 c. Hurst.

Whitney, Alfr. Carpenter.
Pontiac; drama of old Detroit, 1763. '10 (Mr26) c. front. D. $1.50. Badger.

Whitney, Faith.
Two years in a tent; with preface by Rev. S: McComb. '10(S3) c. D. 50 c. net. Moffat.

Whitney, Fred.
Heart of the singer: [poems.] '08(Jl4) c. 12°, $1.25. F. Whitney.

Whitney, Mrs. Gertrude Capen.
I choose. '10(Je4) c. 8°, $1 net. Sherman.
Yet speaketh he. '10(Je4) c. 8°, 80 c. net. Sherman.

Whitney, Harry.
Hunting with the Eskimos; unique record of a sportsman's year among the northernmost tribe: the big game hunting, the native life, and the battle for existence through the long Arctic night. '10(O15) c. il. O. $3.50 net. Century Co.

Whitney, Mrs. Helen Hay.
Herbs and apples: [poems.] '10(O29) c. il. D. bds., $1.25 net. Lane.

Whitney, H: Clay.
Life of Lincoln; ed. by Marion Mills Miller. In 2 v. '08(D19) c. pors. D. **$2.50 net. Baker & T.

WHITNEY, Josiah Dwight.
Brewster, E. T. Life and letters of Josiah Dwight Whitney. **$2 net. Houghton M.

Whitney, Loren Harper.
Question of miracles; parallels in the lives of Buddha and Jesus. '08(D) c. 378 p. por. 12°, $1. Lib. Shelf.

Whitney, Marian P., and Stroebe, Lilian Luise.
Exercises in German syntax and composition for advanced students. '10(Mr26) c. D. 90 c. Holt.

Whitney, Milton.
Composition of commercial fertilizers. '10 (Jl) 39 p. tabs., 8°, (U. S. Dept. of Agriculture; Bu. of Soils; bull.)
Fertilizers for cotton soils. '09(D) 24 p. il. tabs., 8°, (U. S., Dept. of Agriculture, Bu. of Soils, bull.) pap. (Add. Superintendent for price.)
Fertilizers for wheat soils. '10(Jl) 48 p. tabs., il. 8°, (U. S. Dept. of Agriculture; Bu. of Soils; bull.)
Study of crop yields and soil composition in relation to soil productivity. '09(D) 127 p. il. tabs., 8°, (U. S., Dept. of Agriculture, Bu. of Soils, bull.) pap. (Add. Superintendent for price.)

Whitney, Orson Ferguson.
Making of a state: school hist. of Utah. '08(O) c. 4+327 p. il. 12°, $1. Deseret News.

Whitney, Wilson.
Epochs and phases of Christian experience; being the author's personal testimony of the dealings of God with the believer. [1910.] (Ja) c. '09. 96 p. 12°, $1. Observer.

Whiton, Rev. Ja. Morrie.
Interludes, ethical, social and theological. '10(Ja8) 12°, *$1.40 net. Whittaker.

Whitson, Andrew Robinson, and Walster, Harlow Leslie.
Notes on soils; outline for an elem. course in soils. '10(Mr5) c. il. tabs., 12°, 90 c. A. R. Whitson.

Whitson, J: Harvey.
Barbara, a woman of the west. '08(My.) c. 12°, (Popular ed. of recent fiction.) †75 c. Little, B. & Co.

Whittaker, Edm. Taylor.
Hist. of the theories of æther and electricity, from the age of Descartes to the close of the 19th century. '10(D24) O. (Dublin Univ. Press ser.) $4.50 net. Longmans.
Theory of optical instruments. '08(F29) 8°, pap., *25 c. net. Putnam.

Whittaker, T: W.
Comte and Mill. '09(Jl31) 12°, (Philosophers ancient and modern from Pythagoras to Spencer.) *50 c. net. Dodge.

Whittaker, W: H:
See Ohio. Annot. probate code.

Whittaker's arithmetic of electrical engineering. '08(F22) 12°, 50 c. Macmillan.

Whittaker's churchman's annual. *See* Living Church annual.

Whittaker's lib. of arts, sciences and industries. 12°. Macmillan.
—Bjorling. Pipes and tubes. *$1.25 net.

Whittaker's pract. hdbks. il. 12°. Macmillan.
—Oulton *and* Wilson. Pract. testing of electrical machines. *$1.40 net.

Whitteker, J: Edn.
Separated life: Biblical defence of the divinity of Christ; with an introd. by Thdr. E. Schmauk. '09(Jl) c. 204 p. 12°, $1. Gen. Council.

Whittemore, Mrs. Frances Dean Davis.
See Lovewell, *Mrs.* Caroline Forbes Barnes.

Whittemore, H: Weston.
Blueberry pasture, and other outdoor sketches made in New Hampshire. '10 (Ap30) c. il. 16°, 75 c. Tufts Coll.

Whittemore, Luther Denny.
Latin reading book, with grammar and composition for beginners. '09(My) c. 13+305 p. il. 12°, 75 c. O. P. Barnes.

Whittier, C: Collyer.
Urann family of New England, including the descendants of Margaret (Urann) Gammell. '10(S) 59 p. 8°, 75 c. C. C. Whittier.

Whittier, J: Greenleaf.
Complete poetical works. '08(D19) 12°, (Crowell's thin paper poets.) ooze leath., $1.75, boxed. Crowell.
From day to day with Whittier: sel. and arr. by Olive Van Buren. '10(Ag27) c. front. 12°, 75 c. Barse & H.
Poems. '10(D) 12°, (Autograph poets.) $1; hf. leath., $1.50. Houghton M.
Snow-bound; winter idyl; with introd. by Wa. Taylor Field. '10(D10) c. S. (Abbey classics.) pap., 25 c., boxed; bds., 50 c., boxed; limp leath., $1, boxed. Abbey Co.
Snow-bound; Songs of labor, and other poems; with an introd. and notes by E. Isabel Revell. '09(Jl10) c. S. (Classic lib.) pap., 15 c. Educ. Pub.
Snow-bound, and other early poems; ed., with an introd. and notes, by Archibald L. Bouton. '08(S19) 24°, (Pocket Am. and Eng. classics.) *25 c. net. Macmillan.
Snow-bound. '09(N6) c. il. 12°, (Neill gift book ser.) $1.25, boxed. Reilly & B.
Whittier day by day; ed. by Annie Russell Marble. '10(O8) c. por. D. (Day by day ser.) 60 c., boxed; leath., $1, boxed. Crowell.
Whittier in the schools; study of Snow-bound, The barefoot boy, Among the hills, The huskers and The corn song, by Arth. L. Hamilton. '10(O22) c. front. map, 12°, (Pract. aids to literature.) 25 c. Whitaker & R.
See also Poe, Edg. Allan.
—, **ed.** Child-life in prose. New ed. '09, [1910.] (F) il. sq. 8°, $1.50. Houghton M.

WHITTIER, John Greenleaf.
Faris, L. Study of the Quaker poet, [Whittier.] 25 c. Athens Pr.
Hayes, J: R. In memory of Whittier: [poems.] 50 c. Biddle Press.
Woodman, *Mrs.* A. J. Reminiscences of John Greenleaf Whittier. *$1 net. Essex Inst.
See also Sandwich, N. H.

Whittle, W: C.
Cruises of the Confederate States steamers "Shenandoah" and "Nashville." '10 (Je4) c. 8°, 50 c. W: C. Whittle.

Whittuck, E: Arth., ed.
See International documents.

Whitworth, Rev. W: Allen.
Sanctuary of God, and other sermons. '08 (F8) 12°, *$1.50 net. Macmillan.

Who answers prayer? Huntley, *Mrs.* F. C., *ed.* 50 c. Indo-Am. Bk.

Who builds? Mason, E. L. $2. E. L. Mason.

Who goes there? Benson, B. K. $1.50. Macmillan.

Who is who in insurance: international biographical dictionary and year book. '08 (My9) c. pors. tabs., O. $5; leath., $7. Singer.

Who makes what; book of reference for buyers; directory of manufacturers. directory of products, directory of foreign merchants, directory of wholesale hardware merchants, jobbers and exporting houses. '09, [1910.] (Ap) 368 p. 4°, $1. Mallett.

Who shall judge? Hocking, S. K. $1.50. Cassell.

Who was Paul Grayson? Habberton, J: 60 c. Harper.

Whole family: novel by twelve authors;—W: Dean Howells, Mary E. Wilkins Freeman, Mary Heaton Vorse, Mary Stewart Cutting, Eliz. Jordan, J: Kendrick Bangs, H: James, Eliz. Stuart Phelps, Edith Wyatt, Mary R. Shipman Andrews, Alice Brown, H: Van Dyke. '08(O24) c. il. D. †$1.50. Harper.

Whole hog book. Bengough, J: W. 25 c. Am. Free Trade.

Wholesale accounting. Goodyear, S: H. 30 c. Goodyear-M.

Wholesale, commission and storage accounts. Griffith, J. B. 50 c. Am. Sch. Corr.

Wholesale prices, 1890-1908. United States. *Dept. of Commerce and Labor. Bureau of Labor.* (Add. Superintendent for price.) U. S., Supt. of Docs.

Who's who along the north shore of Massachusetts. '09(Ag14) 12°. $2.50. Salem Press.

Who's who among American manufacturers: *Scientific American* index of manufacturers. '08(Je20) c. O. pap., gratis. Munn.

Who's who among the ferns. Beecroft, W. I., *comp.* *$1 net. Moffat.

Who's who among the wild flowers. Beecroft, W. I., *comp.* **$1.20 net. Moffat.

Who's who and what's what in base ball. '10(Jl16) c. il. 8°, 25 c. Klump.

Who's who in America; ed. by Albert Nelson Marquis. Rev. and issued biennially. '08 (Mr21) *$4 net; '10(Jl9) c. D. $5 net. Marquis.

Who's who in Denver society. '08(Jl) c. por. 8°, $1. Kistler.

Who's who in New England. '09(Ap17) c D. $5. Marquis.

Who's who in New York City and state; ed. by J: W. Leonard. 4th biennial ed., 1909. '09(Ja16) c. O. $5. Hamersly.

Who's who in Pennsylvania; ed. by J: W: Leonard. 2d ed. '08(Je13) c. 4°, $5. Hamersly.

Who's who in the General Convention of 1910 held at Cincinnati. '10(O) c. 122 p. il. pors. fold. plan, 16°, 50 c. Young Churchman.

Who's who, 1909. 61st year. '09(Ja9); 1910. 62d year. '10(Ja8); 1911. 63d year. '10 (D31) 12°, ea., $2.50 net. Macmillan.

Who's who on the stage, 1908; ed. by Wa. Browne and E. DeRoy Koch. '08(Ap4) c. pors. O. *$3.50 net. B. W. Dodge.

Who's who year-book for 1908. '08(F15) 12°, *35 c. net. Macmillan.

Whose son is Christ? Delitzsch, F. *80 c. net. Am. Unitarian.

Why. Rae, J: $1.25. Dodd.

Why American marriages fail. Rogers, *Mrs.* A. A. $1.25. Houghton M.

Why and how of foreign missions. *See* Brown, Arth. Judson.

Why and wherefore. Wilson, H. 25 c. Young Churchman.

Why did he do it? Capes, B. $1.50. Brentano's.

Why do we need a public library? Hadley, C. R. 5 c. A. L. A.

Why Doctor Dobson became a quack. Noyes, P. J. $1.50. Cochrane.

Why freight is lost or damaged. Kenly, A. C. 10 c. Baughman Sta. Co.

Why Friends (Quakers) do not baptize with water. Moon, J. H. 25 c. J. H. Moon.

Why grow old? Marden, O. S. **30 c. net. Crowell.

Why he is an elk. Ketler, W: H. 5 c. H. B. Ketler.

Why I am a Socialist. Russell, C: E: $1.50 net. Doran.

Why I am not a Roman Catholic. Battle, J. M. $1.50. J. M. Battle.

Why not now? Davis, C: G. $1. Badger.

Why of the will. Van Peyma, P. W. 80 c. net. Sherman, F.

Why pay tribute? Batdorf, J: W. 25 c. Volunteer.

Why should boys be taught to shoot? Wingate, G: W. (Add. pubs. for price.) Sub-Target.

Why the chimes rang. Alden, R. M. 50 c.; †$1.25. Bobbs-M.

Why the secrets of Freemasonry are withheld from members. Pierce, J: A. 10 c. J: A. Pierce.

Why we believe the Bible. Wells, A. R. $1. Un. Soc. C. E.

Why we love Lincoln. Creelman, J. *$1.25 net. Outing.

Why worry? Walton, G: L. **$1 net. Lippincott.

Whys and wherefores of the modern motor car. Longest, W: B. 50 c. W: B. Longest.

Wichelman, F: A:
Dangerous currency system of the United States. '09, [1910.] (Ag) 32 p. S. pap., 10 c. F: A: Wichelman.

Wickenden, W: Elgin.
Illumination and photometry. '10(F19) c. figs. O. *$2 net. McGraw-H.

Wickersham, Ja.
See Alaska repts. v. 3.

Wickham, Louis, and Degrais, —.
Radiumtherapy; tr. from the French by S. Ernest Dore, M.D.; with introd. by Sir Malcolm Morris. [1910.] (My) 300 p. 8°, $5 net. Funk.

Wickliffe, Eliz. Lockhart.
Flights and fancies. '09(Ag) 11-143 p. 12°, $2. E. L. Wickliffe.

Wicks, Mark.
Mars via the moon; astronomical story. '10(D31) il. 8°, $1.50. Lippincott.

Wickson, E: Ja.
California fruits and how to grow them. 4th ed., rev. and extended. '09(F13); 5th ed., rev. and extended. '10(My7) c. il. 8°, ea., $3. Pacific Rural.

California vegetables in garden and field. 2d ed., rev. and extended. '10(N19) c. il. 8°, $2. Pacific Rural.

Wicksteed, Rev. Philip H:
Common sense of political economy; incl. study of the human basis of economic law. '10(Ap16) O. $4.25 net. Macmillan.

WICKWARE FAMILY.
See Genealogies, Wickwire, A. M.

Wickwire, Arth. Manley.
Genealogy of the Wickware family; cont. an account of the origin and early hist. of the name and family in England, and the record of John Wickware, who emigrated to New London, Ct., in 1675, and of his descendants in America. '09(D) c. 13-283 p. il. pors. maps, facsims., 8°, $6. A. M. Wickwire.

Wide, Anders, M.D.
Home gymnastics according to the Ling system. 2d rev. ed. of the author. Eng. tr. '08(Ap25) il. D. *50 c. net. Funk.

Wide awake girls ser. *See* Ellis, Katharine Ruth.

Wide awake second reader. Murray, C. *35 c. net. Little, B. & Co.

Wide, wide world. *See* Warner, Susan.

Wider life. Miller, J. R. **65 c. net; **85 c. net. Crowell.

Wider use of the school plant. Perry, C. A. $1.25. Charities Pub.

Widnev, Rob. M.
National currency and banks. '07, [1908.] (Ag.) 12 p. 8°, pap. (Add. author for price.) R. M. Widney.

Widow (The). Rowland, H. $1. Dodge.

Widow's wiles. Callaway, E. H. 25 c. Dick.

Widow's wisdom. Fleckenstein, N. T. 75 c. Caldwell.

Widows. *See* Irving, Washington.

Widtsoe, J: Andreas, and Peterson, W:
Dodge's geography of Utah. '09(Mr27) c. il. 8°, (Dodge's geographical ser.) *35 c. net. Rand, McN. & Co.

Wie man sich bildet. Schmidt, E. 15 c. Oxford Univ.

Wiebalk, Anna.
Course of study in composition. '09(O) 4°, (San Francisco State Normal School bulls.; new ser.) pap., 30 c. San F. St. Normal.

Wiebé, E:
Golden jubilee edition of The paradise of childhood; pract. guide to kindergartners; ed. by Milton Bradley; rev. by Jenny B. Merrill; incl. a life of Friedrich Froebel by H: W. Blake. '10(Jl30) c. il. pors. 8°, $2. M. Bradley.

Wiederseim, Mrs. Grace Gebbie.
Baby's day. '10(D17) c. il. [in col.] F. bds., 60 c. Stokes.
Fido. '10(S10) F. shaped bds., 50 c. Stokes.
Kitty-puss. '10(S10) F. shaped bds., 50 c. Stokes.

Wiedersheim, Rob.
Comparative anatomy of vertebrates; adpt. from the German by W. N. Parker. 3d ed., (founded on 6th German ed.) '08 (Ja11) il. 8°, *$3.75 net. Macmillan.

Wiel, S: C.
Water rights in the western states. 2d ed., rev.; with forms. '08(O) c. 67+974 p. O. shp., $7.50. Bancroft-W.

WIELAND, Christopher Martin.
See Weimar.

Wienand, Paul.
Musenblüten: gedichte. '08, [1909.] (Je) 12+269 p. il. por. 12°, $1. Central.

Wiener, Harold Marcus.
Essays in Pentateuchal criticism. '10 (Mr26) c. O. $1.50. Bibliotheca Sacra.
Origin of the Pentateuch. '10(D17) c. O. pap., 35 c. Bibliotheca Sacra.

Wiers, C: Rob.
How to write a business letter; for use in offices, schools, and as a general reference book. '09(D4) D. $1. C: R. Wiers.

Wife as the family physician. Fischer-Dueckelmann, A. $5. Inst. Medical.

Wife (The): her book. Brown, H. **$1 net. Jacobs.

Wife of Altamont. Hunt, V. B. $1.50. Brentano's.

Wife of Colonel Hughes. Wales, H., *pseud.* $1.50. Stuyvesant Press.

Wife of Narcissus. Andrews, A. †$1.25. Moffat.

Wiggers, Carl J:, M.D.
Brief text of physiology for dental, premedical and college-students. '10(D3) c. il. O. $1.50. Wahr.

Wiggin, Kate Douglas Smith, [**now Mrs. G: Riggs.**]
Rebecca of Sunnybrook Farm. Il. holiday ed. '10(O22) c. '03. D. $1.50. Houghton M.
Susanna and Sue. '09(O9) c. il. O. **$1.50 net. Houghton M.

—, **ed.** *See* Arabian nights.

—, **and Smith, Nora Archibald, eds.**
The fairy ring. '10(O15) c. il. D. $1.25 net. Doubleday, P.
Tales of laughter: a third fairy book. '08 (N14) c. D. (Library of children's classics.) †$1.50. McClure.
Tales of wonder; fourth fairy book. '09 (O16) D. (Children's crimson classics.) †$1.50. Doubleday, P.

WIGGINS, *Captain* Joseph.
Johnson, H: Life and voyages of Joseph Wiggins, F.R.G.S. *$5 net. Dutton.

Wiggins, Mrs. Lida Keck.
Know thy neighbor; or, character reading; being a compilation of invaluable information upon character reading by physiognomy, temperament, palmistry, astrology, graphology, thumb impressions; designed by E. E. Miller. '09(Jl) c. 405 p. il. pors. 12°, $1.25. J. L. Nichols.

Wight, Rev. C: Albert.
Hatfield book. '08(D) c. 59 p. pors. 8°, $1.25. C: A. Wight.

Wightman, Lucius Irving, comp.
Compressed air; instruction paper. '09 (N) c. 2 v., il. 8°, (American School of Correspondence pubs.) $1. Am. Sch. Corr.

Wightman, W: W., comp.
Student's guide to the principles of bookkeeping. '09(N) c. 6+116 p. figs. 4°, $1. Ellis Pub.
Student's guide to the principles of bookkeeping in chart-form. 2d ed. '09(N) c. 6+38 p. figs. 4°, 50 c. Ellis Pub.

Wigmore, J: H:
List of legal novels. '09(My1) 4°, 40 c. Ill. Law Review.
Pocket code of the rules of evidence in trials at law. '10(F) c. S. flex. skiver, **$4 net. Little, B. & Co.
Preliminary bibliography of modern criminal law and criminology. 09(Ag7) 8°, (Gary lib. of law, Northwestern Univ. Law School, bull.) 65 c. Northwestern Univ.

Wigram, W: Ainger.
Hist. of the Assyrian Church, or the church of the Lassaina Persian Empire, 100-640 A.D. '10(D) $2 net. Gorham.

Wigwam evenings. Eastman, C: A. †$1.25. Little, B. & Co.

Wilamowitz-Moellendorff, Emmo Friedrich Wichard Ulrich v.
Greek historical writing and Apollo; two lectures del. before the University of Oxford; tr. by Gilbert Murray. '08(O24) O. pap., 70 c. Oxford Univ.

Wilberforce, Bp. S:
Agathos, The rocky island, and other Sunday stories and parables. '08(Je6) T. *45 c. net. Putnam.

Wilbert, Martin I.
See Hatcher, Rob. Anthony.

Wilbur, Mary Aronetta.
Every-day business for women; manual for the uninitiated. '10(My21) c. D. $1.25 net. Houghton M.

Wilbur, Sibyl.
Life of Mary Baker Eddy. '08(N21) il. pors. 12°, $3. Concord Pub.

Wilbur, W: Allen.
Exposition in English rhetoric. '10(Je) 32 p. O. pap., 50 c. Collins, H. & Co.
The syllable in English rhetoric. '10(Je) 28 p. O. pap., 50 c. Collins, H. & Co.
Bibliography (½ p.).

Wilcox, Delos Franklin.
Great cities in America; their problems and their government. '10(O1) c. D. (Citizens' lib. of economics, politics and sociology.) hf. leath., $1.25 net. Macmillan.
Municipal franchises; description of the terms and conditions upon which private corporations enjoy special privileges in the streets of American cities. In 2 v. '10(Ja22) 8°, ea., $5.
Gervaise Press; [Engineering News.]

Wilcox, Earley Vernon, and Smith, Clarence Beaman.
Farmer's cyclopedia of live stock. '08 (Je20) c. il. 8°, $4.50; hf. mor., $5.50. Judd.

Wilcox, Mrs. Ella Wheeler.
New thought common sense and what life means to me. '08(D) c. 292 p. por. 12°, $1.25. Conkey.
Poems of progress, and New Thought pastels. '09(My1) c. por. D. $1.25. Conkey.
Sailing sunny seas; story of travel in Jamaica, Haiti, Porto Rico, Dominica, Honolulu, Santo Domingo, St. Thomas, Martinique, Trinidad and the West Indies. '10(Ja8) c. il. D. $1.50. Conkey.

Wilcox, H: S.
Joys of earth: [poems.] '09(My22) c. front. O. $1. Wilcox Bks.

Wilcox, Reynold Webb, M.D.
Manual of fever nursing. 2d ed., rev. '08 (My23) c. il. 12°, $1. Blakiston.
Treatment of disease: manual of pract. medicine. 3d ed., carefully rev. and enl. '10(D) 25+1023 p. 8°, $6; hf. mor., $7.50. (Sold by subscription.) Blakiston.

Wilcox, Sidney Freeman.
Surgery of childhood. '09, [1910.] (Ja) c. 10+395 p. il. 8°, $3.50. Boericke & R.

Wilcox, Starling Sullivant.
Essentials of genito-urinary and venereal diseases, arranged in the form of questions and answers; prep. especially for students of medicine. '09(N) c. 11-321 p. il. 12°, (Saunders' questions compends.) $1. Saunders.

Wilcox, Wa. Dwight.
Guide-book to the Lake Louise region, incl. Paradise Valley, Valley of the Ten Peaks, and neighborhood of Lake O'Hara. '09(Ag) c. 54 p. il. 8°, $1. Judd & D.
Rockies of Canada. Rev. and enl. ed. of "Camping in the Canadian Rockies." '08 (D12) **$3.50 net; 3d ed. '09(Ap10) c. il. maps, O. **$5 net, boxed. Putnam.

WILCOX FAMILY.
See Genealogies, Merrill, S: P.

Wilcoxon, Mitchell Haney.
Roosevelt steam rolled by the Bible. '10 (Ap) c. 272 p. 8°, $1. M. H. Wilcoxon.

Wilczynski, Ernest Julius.
See Moore, Eliakim Hastings.

Wild, Helen Tilden.
Old Royall house. [1910.] (Ja) 8 p. 4°, pap., 50 c. Salem Press.

Wild animals of North America. Knobel, E: $2.50. Lovell.
Wild beasts of the world. Finn, F. In 2 v. $8 net. Dodge.
Wild birds in city parks. Walter, H. E. 35 c. St. Johnsbury Rep.
Wild duck. *See* Ibsen, Henrik. Doll's house.
Wild flower families. Weed, C. M. **$1 net. Lippincott.
Wild flower poems. Des Jardins, B: M. 50 c.; 75 c.; 25 c. Chapin News.
WILD FLOWERS.
See Flowers.
Wild-fowlers (The). Bradford, C: *$1 net. Nassau Press.
Wild fruit. Phillpotts, E. $1.50 net. Lane.
Wild geese. Weyman, S. J: †$1.50. Doubleday, P.
Wild ginger. Hoover, M. H: $1.50. B'way Pub.
Wild honey from various thyme. Bradley, C. *$1.65 net. Wessels.
Wild Irish girl. Smith, *Mrs.* E. T. $1. Hurst.
Wild life on the Rockies. Mills, E. A. **$1.75 net. Houghton M.
Wild oats. Oppenheim, J. $1.20 net. B: W. Huebsch.
Wild olive (The). King, B. $1.50. Harper.
Wild pastures. Packard, W. **$1.20 net. Small.
Wild rose. Raile, A. L. $1.50. Pub. Pr. Co.
Wild widow. Wentworth-James, G. de S. $1.50. Empire Bk.

Wilde, Adna Godfrey.
In and about the University of Virginia. '10(O) c. 35 p. il. 12°, 75 c. A. G. Wilde.

Wilde, Oscar.
[Works.] In 15 v. '08(D) Autograph ed., per v., $100; Collector's ed., per v., $50; ed. de grand luxe, per v., $30; Oxford ed., per v., $10; University ed., per v., $7.50; $3.50. Anglo-Am. Authors.
Complete works; auth. ed. by Rob. Ross. In 14 v. '10(Je4) 8°, $28 net. J: W. Luce.
Poetical works; with notes, bibliographical introd., index and facsimiles of title-pages. '08(N21) c. por. facsims., 12°, bds., *$4 net; Japan vellum, *$8 net. T: B. Mosher.
Ballad of Reading Gaol. '10(O15) c. D. (Rubric ser.) bds., 60 c. Duffield.
Ballad of Reading Gaol. '08(D19) nar. 16°, shp., *75 c. net. Jacobs.
De profundis; ed., with a prefatory dedication by Rob. Ross. 2d ed., with additional matter. '09(N20) por. 12°, **$1.25 net. Putnam.

Wilde, Oscar.—*Continued.*
Florentine tragedy: a play. '08(D5) D. *$1.25 net. J: W. Luce.
Happy prince, and other fairy tales. '09 (Je) 12°, (Wayside lib.) limp leath., $1. Brentano's.
Happy prince, and other stories. '09(Ap10) front. 32°, (Ariel booklets.) leath., 75 c., boxed. Putnam.
Pan, a double villanelle, and Desespoir, a sonnet; hitherto unpublished poems. '09 (D25) c. 8°, $1. (30 copies.) J: W. Luce.
Poems; ed., with biog. introd., by Temple Scott. '10(D10) 12°, $1.50 net; leath., $2.50 net, boxed. Brentano's.
Poems; ed. by Rob. Ross. '09(O23) $1.50. J: W. Luce.
Salomé: tragedy in one act. '10(D) 4°, bds., $1 net (925 copies); Japan vel., $2.50 net. (50 copies). T: B. Mosher.
Soul of man under socialism. Auth. ed. '10(Ap30) O. 60 c. net. J: W. Luce.
The sphinx. '10(O1) S. bds., $1 net. Lane.
Wisdom of Oscar Wilde. '09(Je) c. 32°, leath., **$1 net. Brentano's.

WILDE, Oscar.
Ingleby, L. C. Oscar Wilde. *$3.50 special net. Appleton.

Wilde, W.
Celestial ejectamenta; first Halley lecture del. May 10, 1910. '10(Ag27) c. O. $10. Oxford Univ.

Wildenbruch, Ernst von.
Neid; ed., with introd., notes and vocab., by C. W: Prettyman. '08(O10) c. S. (Modern lang. ser.) 35 c. Heath.
See also Eckstein, Ernst;—Szczepanski, Paul von.

Wilder, Eliz., and Taylor, Edith Mendall.
Self help and self cure; primer of psychotherapy. '1910(Je11) c. 12°, 75 c. net. Small.

Wilder, Harris Hawthorne.
Hist. of the human body. '09(D18) c. il. O. $3. Holt.

Wilder, Marshall Pinckney.
Smiling 'round the world. '08(My23) c. il. D. $1.50. Funk.
—, ed. Ten books of the merrymakers. 10 v. '09(My) pors. 8°, $6. Circle.

Wilder, Victor.
Mozart: story of his life as man and artist. '08(Je20) 2 v., D. *$3.50 net. Scribner.

WILDERNESS, Battle of the.
Schaff, M. Battle of the Wilderness. $2 net. Houghton M.

WILDERNESS CAMPAIGN.
See Civil War.

Wilderness dog. Hawkes, C $1.50. Jacobs.
Wilderness homes. Kemp, O. *$1.25 net. Outing.
Wilderness pets. Breck, E: $1.50 net. Houghton M.

Wildman, J: Raymond.
Cost accounting problems. '10(D10) 8°, $3. Accountancy.

Wildwood ways. Packard, W. **$1.20 net. Small.

Wile, Ira Solomon.
Blood examination in surgical diagnosis; practical study of its scope and technic. '08, [1909.] (F) c. 161 p. il. 8°, $2. Surgery.

Wiles of Sexton Maginnis. Egan, M. F. †$1.50. Century Co.

Wiley, Belle.
Mother Goose primer. '10(Je18) c. col. il. sq. 12°, 32 c. C: E. Merrill Co.

Wiley, Harvey Washington, M.D.
Principles and practice of agricultural analysis; manual for the study of soils, fertilizers and agricultural products. 2d ed., rev. and enl. v. 2, Fertilizers and insecticides. [1910.] (Je) il. 8°, $4.50. Chemical.
—, **Merriam, Clinton Hart, and Veitch, F. P.**
Durability and economy in papers for permanent records. '09(My8) O. pap. (Add. Superintendent for price.) U. S., Supt. of Docs.
—, **and others.**
Manufacture of denatured alcohol; based on the operations of an experimental still at Washington, D. C., and a course of lectures del. in connection therewith; by H. W. Wiley; with the collaboration of H. E. Sawyer, L. M. Tolman, A. H. Bryan, A. Given, and H. W. Berger. '10 (Mr) 166 p. il. 8°, (U. S., Dept. of Agriculture, Bu. of Chemistry, bull.) pap.
Preliminary study of the effects of cold storage on eggs, quail, and chickens. '08, [1909.] (My) 117 p. il. 8°, (U. S., Dept. of Agriculture, Bu. of Chemistry bull.) pap. (Add. Superintendent for price.)

Wiley, Kate.
Pet Marjorie and Sir Walter Scott. '09 (Je26) c. il. por. D. *$1 net; pap., *75 c. net. Cochrane.

Wiley, R: Taylor.
Elizabeth Methodist Episcopal Church; historical sketch prep. and read, May 15, 1910, in connection with the celebration of the 25th anniversary of the dedication of the second church building. '10(N) 34 p. il. 8°, 50 c. R: T. Wiley.

Wilgus, Horace La Fayette.
Legal education in the United States. '08 (S) 32 p. 8°, pap. (Not for sale.) Mich. Law Rev.

Wilgus, W: J:
Proposed new railway system for the transportation and distribution of freight by improved methods in the city and port of New York. '08(D26) il. map, tabs., plans, F. pap. (Add. author for price.) W: J: Wilgus.

Wilhelm, Donald.
Theodore Roosevelt as an undergraduate. '10(Jl30) c. D. 75 c. net. J: W. Luce.

WILKESBARRE, Pa.
Harvey, O. J. Hist. of Wilkes-Barré, Luzerne Co., Pa. 3 v. ea., $5. O. J. Harvey.

Wilkins, H. J., D.D.
Hist. of divorce and re-marriage for English churchmen; comp. from the Holy Scripture, church councils and authoritative writers. '10(D17) D. $1.25 net. Longmans.

Wilkins, Timothy.
Poems of life. '08(D) 239 p. il. pors. 12°, $1; gilt, $1.50. T. Wilkins.

Wilkins, W: H:
Mrs. Fitzherbert and George IV. New ed. '09(N13) il. pors. facsim., O. $5. Longmans.

Wilkinson, A. E., rep.
See Texas. *Cts. of civil appeals.* Repts.—*Sup. ct.* Repts.

Wilkinson, C: W.
Well-known piano solos: how to play them with understanding, expression and effect. '09(N) 64 p. 12°, *40 c. net. Scribner.

Wilkinson, E.
See Daniels, C: Wilberforce.

Wilkinson, Eliz. Hays.
The lane to Sleepy Town and other verses. '10(D31) c. il.. T. limp leath., $1.25. E. H. Wilkinson.

Wilkinson, Bp. G: Howard.
Invisible glory: selected sermons; with preface by the Bishop of London. 2d ed. '09(Ap10) *$2 net. Young Churchman.

WILKINSON, *Bp.* George Howard.
Mason, A. J. Memoir of George Howard Wilkinson: Bishop of St. Andrews. $2 net; 2 v. *$8 net. Longmans.

Wilkinson, H. D.
Submarine cable-laying, repairing and testing. New ed. '09(My1) il. 8°, *$6 net. Van Nostrand.

Wilkinson, H: Spenser.
Britain at bay. '10(F12) O. *$1.50 net. Putnam.

Wilkinson, Herbert Swann.
Alabaster box, and other sermons. '08(O) c. 78 p. 12°, 50 c. H. S. Wilkinson.

Wilkinson, J: Dallas.
Personal injuries and somewhat of the relation of master and servant, [etc.] '09 (D) c. O. shp., $7. Hansell.

Wilkinson, J: Wa.
Institute hdbk. on agriculture and domestic science for teachers. '09(N) 47 p. il. O. pap., 30 c. Oklahoma Bk.

Pract. agriculture: brief treatise on agriculture, horticulture, forestry, stock feeding, animal husbandry and road building. '09(N20) c. il. 8°, $1. Am. Bk.

Wilkinson, Mrs. Mary E. McNamara.
Cook book for the poor, the rich, the sick, the well; reform from the old wasteful methods to the saving, scientific and nourishing ones. '10(S3) c. il. 12°, $1. Conkey.

Wilkinson, Maurice.
The last phase of the League in Provence, 1588-1598. '09(D4) O. *$1.50 net. Longmans.

Wilkinson, Spenser.
University and the study of war; lecture. '10(Ja22) O. pap., 35 c. Oxford Univ.

Wilkinson, W. Camac.
Treatment of consumption. '08(O31) 8°, hf. leath., *$3 net. Macmillan.

Wilkinson, W: Cleaver.
Good of life and other little essays; de omnibus rebus et quibusdam aliis. '10 (Je18) c. D. $1.25 net. Funk.

Poetical works. In 5 v. v. 1, The epic of Saul; v. 2, The epic of Paul; v. 3, The epic of Moses; the exodus; v. 4, The epic of Moses; the wilderness; v. 5, Poems. '09(Ap10) il. 8°, ¾ leath., ea., $3. Funk.

Some new literary valuations. '09(Ja16) c. D. **$1.30 net. Funk.

Will, Arth. P., ed.
See Gould, Ja.

Will, W: R.
See Sadler, Warren H.

WILL.
Atkinson, W. W. The will. $1. Progress Co.
Haddock, F. C. Power of will. $3. Power-Bk.
Knowlson, T: S. Education of the will. *$1.50 net. Lippincott.
Leland, C: G. Mystic will. 50 c. Progress Co.
Payot, J. Education of the will. **$1.50 net. Funk.
Van Peyma, P. W. Why of the will. 80 c. net. Sherman, F.
Wodehouse, H. Logic of will. *$1.10 net. Macmillan.

Will of Allah. Rhodes, K. †$1.50. Estes.

Will of God and a man's lifework. Wright, H: B. 90 c. Y. M. C. A.

Will to believe. Stettheimer, E. $1. Science Pr., (N. Y.)

Will to doubt. Lloyd, A. H: *$1.25 net. Macmillan

WILLAMETTE VALLEY, Ore.
See Oregon.

Willard, De Forest.
Surgery of childhood, incl. orthopædic surgery. '10(O) c. 31+800 p. il. 4°, $7. Lippincott.
Bibliographical appendix (4 p.) and footnotes.

Willard, Ellen Melville.
Yuletide entertainments: Christmas recitations, monologues, drills, tableaux, motion songs, exercises, dialogues and plays, suitable for all ages. '10(D3) c. il. 12°, 25 c. T: S. Denison.

Willard, G. H., and Crawshay, Fred Duane.
Pattern-making, by G. H. Willard, to which are added chapters on core-making and molding, by F. D. Crawshaw. '10(Ap16) c. il. 8°, $1. Popular Mechanics.

Willard, Hobart Hurd.
See Richards, Thdr. W:

Willard, Josiah.
Census of Newington, Ct.; taken according to households in 1776, together with some documents rel. to the early hist. of the parish; ed. by Edn. Stanley Welles. '09, [1910.] (F) 41 p. 4°, *$1.75 net. Hartranft.

Willard, Josiah Flynt.
See Flynt, Josiah, *pseud.*

Willard, Wa. C.
Why the gas engine goes: practical talk in plain English on gas engines, especially as applied to marine uses. '09(D25) c. il. 12°, 75 c. Penton.

Willard, W: F.
Pract. course in mechanical drawing for individual study and shop classes, trade and high schools. '10(D3) c. il. 16°, 50 c. Popular Mechanics.

Willaumez, Comte Louis Edouard Bouët-.
See Bouët-Willaumez, *Comte* Louis Edouard.

Willcocks, Mary Patricia.
Man of genius. '08(Je13) c. D. †$1.50. Lane.
The way up. '10(Jl2) c. D. $1.50. Lane.

Willcox, Cornélis DeWitt.
French-English military technical dict. '10 (Mr26) 8°. U. S., Supt. of Docs.

Willcox, Mrs. Louise Collier.
Human way. '09(O2) c. O. **$1.25 net. **Harper.**
—, comp. Manual of spiritual fortification; being a choice of meditative and mystic poems. '10(N5) c. D. $1.25 net. Harper.

Willers, Diedrich.
New York State Agricultural College at Ovid, and higher agricultural education; an historical paper read at a meeting of the Seneca County Historical Society, held at Romulus, Sept. 5, 1906. '08(O) 27 p. front. 8°, gratis. M. A. Willers.

Willets, Gilson.
Double cross; romance of mystery and adventure in Mexico of to-day. '10(O8) c. D. $1.50. G: W: Dillingham.
Inside history of the White House; complete history of the domestic and official life in Washington of the nation's presidents and their families. '08(D) c. 492 p. il. pors. 8°, $1. Chr. Herald.

Willett, Herbert Lockwood.
Studies in the first book of Samuel. '09 (Mr13) c. D. (Constructive Bible studies; secondary ser.) $1.50. Univ. of Chic.

Willey, J: Heston.
Midsummer nights with the great dreamer [John Bunyan]: a pilgrim's progress in the twentieth century. '08(D12) c. O. *$1 net. Eaton & M.

Willhauck, G: Paul.
Our national government; brief catechism and reader on the Constitution of the United States, for elementary schools, academies and colleges. '09(N) c. 76+4 p. 12°, 35 c. Monarch Pr.

WILLIAM I., *Emperor of Germany.*
Walter, G. Emperor William First. *60 c. net. McClurg.

WILLIAM II., *Emperor of Germany.*
Burgess, J: W: German Emperor and the German government. (Add. University for price.) Columbia Univ.
Fischer, H: W: H. Private lives of Kaiser William II. and his consort. 3 v. $12. W. C. Adams.

WILLIAM *the Conqueror.*
Stenton, F. M. William the Conqueror and the rule of the Normans. **$1.35 net. Putnam.

WILLIAM *the Silent, Prince of Orange.*
Macgregor, M. The Netherlands. $2. Stokes.

William Belden Noble lectures. *See* Noble, (William Belden,) lectures.

William Jordan, Junior. Snaith, J: C. †$1.50. Moffat.

William Tell. Rees, A. D. (Priv. pr.) Lippincott.

William Updick: his philosophy. Smith, W. L. $1. Neale.

Williams, Anna W.
See Park, W: Hallock.

Williams, Archibald.
How it is done; or, victories of the engineer. '08(N21) c. il. figs. D. $1.25. Nelson.
How it is made: describing how various machines and many articles in common use are manufactured. '08(Mr21) il. D. $1.25. Nelson.
Motor-car Peter. '07, [1909.] (Jl) il. 4°, bds., $1.25. Jacobs.
Wonders of Asiatic exploration. '10(Ja1) il. 12°, 75 c. Lippincott.
Wonders of mechanical ingenuity. '10(Ja1) il. 12°, 75 c. Lippincott.
Wonders of the modern railway. '10(D31) il. 12°, (Wonder lib.) 75 c. Lippincott.

Williams, Ashby.
See Virginia. Corporation laws.

Williams, B. E.
See Hawes, *Mrs.* Harriet Boyd.

Williams, Bransby.
An actor's story. '09(S4) il. pors. D. *$2 net. Scribner.

Williams, Byron.
Barefoot days: [poems.] '09(Ja) $1.50. Conkey.

Williams, C. F.
See Lavinder, Claude H.

Williams, C. S.
Descendants of Thomas White of Weymouth, Mass., 1630-1907. '07, [1908.] (Je.) 88 p. pors. pls. 8°. (Not for sale.) C. S. Williams.

Williams, C: Bray.
Participle in the book of Acts: doctor's dissertation. '09(Ap10) c. 8°, pap., *50 c. net. Univ. of Chic.

Williams, Bp. C: D:
Valid Christianity for to-day. '09(Ap24) c. D. **$1.50 net. Macmillan.

Williams, C: Fs. Abdy.
Rhythm of modern music. '10(Ja15) 8°, *$1.50 net. Macmillan.

Williams, Clara Andrews.
Ark that glue built: [cut-out book.] '08 (O3) c. il. obl. Q. (Glue ser.) bds., $1. Stokes.
Children's stores. '10(O29) c. col. il. obl. Q. (Glue ser.) bds., 75 c. Stokes.
Children's theatre; Rip Van Winkle as played by scissors and glue. '09(D25) c. il. obl. Q. (Glue ser.) bds., $1. Stokes.
Doll's house that glue built. '10(D17) c. obl. Q. (Glue ser.) bds., $1. Stokes.
Farm that glue made. '09(D25) c. il. obl. Q. (Glue ser.) bds., $1. Stokes.
Games that glue played. '09(D25) il. obl. Q. (Glue ser.) bds., $1. Stokes.
Pin-wheel book to cut and glue. '10(O29) col. il. obl. Q. (Glue ser.) bds., 75 c. Stokes.
Puzzle pictures of animals to cut up and glue. '09(D25) c. il. obl. Q. (Glue ser.) bds., $1. Stokes.

Williams, Clara Andrews.—*Continued.*
Puzzle pictures of farmyard friends. '10 (D17) c. il obl. Q. (Glue ser.) bds.., $1. Stokes.
Railway that glue built: [cut-out book.] '08(O3) c. il. obl. Q. (Glue ser.) bds., $1. Stokes.
Ships that glue sailed. '10(O29) c. col. il. obl. Q. (Glue ser.) bds., 75 c. Stokes.
Tracing and coloring book of animals. '09 (D25) c. il. obl. Q. (Glue ser.) bds., $1. Stokes.

Williams, Mrs. Cora Gannaway.
The morning-glory; [life story of Mae McKenzie.] '10(My14) c. D. 75 c. net. Pub. Ho. M. E. Ch., So.

Williams, E. Baumer.
England's story, for children. '09(O2) il. D. $1.50. Stokes.

Williams, Fs. Howard.
Burden bearer: an epic of Lincoln. '09 (Ja2) c. 8°, hf. vel., **$2.50 net. Jacobs.

Williams, Gardner Stewart, and Hazen, Allen.
Hydraulic tables; elements of gagings and the friction of water flowing in pipes, aqueducts, sewers, etc. 2d ed., rev. and enl. '09(Ja30) 8°, $1.50. Wiley.

Williams, Bp. Gershom Mott.
Church of Sweden, and the Anglican communion. '10(My21) D. bds., 50 c. Young Churchman.

Williams, Rev. H: Fs.
In four continents; sketch of the foreign missions of the Presbyterian Church, U. S. '10(N19) c. il. 12°, 50 c. Presb. Pub.

Williams, H: Roger.
Blighted life of Methuselah. '08(O) c. 114 p. por. 12°, $1. Nat. Bapt. Pub.

Williams, H: Smith, M.D.
Alcohol; how it affects the individual, the community, and the race. '09(Jl3) c. D. bds., **50 c. net. Century Co.
Science of happiness. '10(Je11) c. O. $2 net. Harper.

Williams, H: W., ed.
See Maryland. Corporation law.

Williams, Herbert Upham.
Manual of bacteriology; rev. by B. Meade Bolton. 5th ed., rev. and enl. '08(D) c. 13+466 p. il. diagrs., 8°, *$2 net. Blakiston.

Williams, Herschel.
Fairy tales from folk lore. '08(Ag29) c. il. D. **$1 net. Moffat.
Making faces; study of facial expression. [Autograph album.] '10(O15) c. S. bds., 50 c. net. McClurg.
My advice book. '10(O15) c. front. S. bds., 50 c. net. McClurg.
My chums in caricature. '09(O16) c. S. bds., *50 c. net. McClurg.
Uncle Bob and Aunt Becky's exciting trip and the strange romance of Tom and Ruth. '09(Je5) c. il. D. 75 c.; pap., 25 c. Laird.

Williams, Hugh Noël.
Fascinating Duc de Richelieu, Louis Francois, Armand Du Plessis (1696-1788). '10(Jl30) il. 8°, $4 net. Scribner.
Madame de Montespan and Louis XIV. '10 (N19) por. 8°, $2. Scribner.

Williams, Hugh Noël.—*Continued.*
Madame de Pompadour. '08(D12) por. O. *$2 net. Scribner.
Madame du Barry. '09(D11) por. O. *$3.50 net. Scribner.
Princess of intrigue, Anne Geneviève de Bourbon, Duchesse de Longueville, and her times. '08(F1) 2 v., il. pors. O. *$6.50 net. Putnam.
Rose of Savoy. Marie Adélaïde of Savoy, Duchesse de Bourgogne, mother of Louis XV. '09(D11) il. O. *$3.50 net. Scribner.
Women Bonapartes: the mother and three sisters of Napoleon I. '08(D12) 2 v., pors. O. $6. Scribner.

Williams, Mrs. Isabella Burgess Riggs.
By the Great Wall: (letters from China.) '09(Je26) 12°, *$1.50 net. Revell.

Williams, Isabella Cecilia.
Alchemist's secret. '10(Je11) c. 12°, 85 c. Kenedy.
In the crucible; tales from real life. '09 (Jl) c. 177 p. 12°, 85 c. Kenedy.

Williams, J. B.
History of English journalism to the foundation of the *Gazette*. '08(D12) por. facsims., O. *$3 net. Longmans.

Williams, Rev. J. H.
Village sermons for Lent. '10(Mr5) 12°, *80 c. net. Whittaker.

Williams, Ja. R.
See Livermore, Virgil B:

Williams, Jennie C.
Us two cook book; cont. tested recipes for two persons. '09(D18) c. il. 12°, $1. Barse & H.

Williams, Jesse Lynch.
Girl and the game, and other college stories. '08(Je6) c. il. D. †$1.50. Scribner.
Married life of the Frederick Carrolls. '10 (D10) c. il.. D. $1.50. Scribner.
Mr. Cleveland: a personal impression. '09 c. front. D. **50 c. net Dodd.
My lost duchess. '08(Ap18) c. il. D. †$1.50. Century Co.
See also On the gridiron.

Williams, Rev. J:
Redeemed captive: returning to Zion; or, the captivity and deliverance of Rev. John Williams of Deerfield; repr. from the 6th ed. '08(Ag22) facsim., S. (Indian captivities ser.) bds., $2.50; large pap. ed., $5. Huntting.

Williams, J: Harvey.
Mountain that was "God"; being a little book about the great peak which the Indians called "Tacoma," but which is officially named "Rainier." '10(O8) il. maps, Q. bds., $1 net; pap., 50 c. net. J: H. Williams.

Williams, Rev. J: L.
Our brother in red: synopsis of the Indian life, characteristics and customs. '08 (Mr28) D. pap., 25 c. Pub. Ho. of M. E. Ch., So.

Williams, J: Whitridge, M.D.
Obstetrics; text-book for the use of students and practitioners. 2d rev. and enl. ed. '09(Mr) c. 28+950 p. il. 8°, $6. Appleton.

Williams, Leonard, M.D.
Arts and crafts of older Spain. '08(O17) 3 v., il. D. (World of art ser.) bds., *$4.50 net, boxed. McClurg.
Minor maladies and their treatment. 2d rev. and enl. ed. '08(Ap18) il. charts, 8°, *$3.50 net. Wood.
Vest-pocket guide to Paris. '09(F27) maps, plans, Ff. leath., *50 c. net. Doubleday, P.
Williams, Mrs. Leslie.
The cat: its care and management. '08 (Je27) c. il. D. (Altemus' handbooks for animal owners.) $1. Altemus.
Manual of toy dogs. 3d ed. '10(O15) il. D. 60 c. net. Longmans.
Williams, Lewis Milton.
Jacob the heel-grasper: [sermons.] '08 (Ap18) c. por. D. $1. L. M. Williams.
Williams, Linsly R.
See Soper, G: Alb.
Williams, Lloyd T., comp.
See Kinkead, Edg. B., *comp.*
Williams, L: L., and Rogers, Fernando E.
Supplementary exercises in bookkeeping. '08(Ap25) O. (Williams & Rogers ser.) pap.. 20 c. Am. Bk.
Williams, M. Atkinson.
Report on the teaching of English in the United States. '09(Ja23) D. $1. Bardeen.
Williams, Marie V.
Six essays on the Platonic theory of knowledge as expounded in the late dialogues and reviewed by Aristotle. '08(Ap11) 8°, *$1 net. Putnam.
Williams, Marjorie.
Paris. '10(D24) col. il. 12°, (Peeps at great cities ser.) 75 c. net. Macmillan.
Williams, Martha McCulloch.
Land-lover and his land. '09, [1910.] (Ap) 31 p. pls. O. pap. (Priv. pr.) E. W. Sells.
Williams, Michael.
See Sinclair, Upton Beall, *jr.*
Williams, Mrs. Milan Bertrand.
Among many witnesses: book for Bible students. 10th ed. (rev. and rewritten). [1910.] (D) c. 221 p. 12°, 80 c. Revell.
Sex problems. New and rev. ed. '10 (Ap9) c. $1 net. Revell.
Williams, Patrick Watson.
Rhinology; book of diseases of the nose and the nasal accessory sinuses. '10 (Mr) 16+273 p. il. O. cl., *$4.20 net. Longmans.
Williams, R. H.
With the border ruffians: memories of the Far West, 1852-1868; ed. by E. W. Williams. '08(F8) pors. 8°, *$4 net. Dutton.
Williams, R. L., rep.
See Oklahoma. *Sup. ct.* Repts.
Williams, Rob. Statham.
Mosses from tropical America. '08, [1909.] (Mr) 569-574 p. 8°, (Contributions from the New York Botanical Garden.) 25 c. N. Y. Botanical.
WILLIAMS, Roger.
Carpenter, E. J. Roger Williams. **$2 net. Grafton Press.
Eaton, A. M., *and* Craig, C. E. Roger Williams: the founder of Providence. gratis. R. I. Dept. Educ.
Williams, Roger D.
Horse and hound. '10(D24) il. 12°, $2.50 net. Outing.
Williams, Rufus Phillips.
Essentials of chemistry; experimental, descriptive, theoretical. '10(Ag27) c. il. pors. D. $1.25. Ginn.
Williams, S: W.
Pictures of early Methodism in Ohio. '09 (N) 319 p. por. 12°, $1. Jennings.
Williams, Sydney C:
Economics of railway transport. '10(F12) c. D. *$1.25 net. Macmillan.
Williams, Rev. T. Rhondda.
Shall we understand the Bible? Rev. and enl. ed. '09(D25) 12°, pap., *40 c. net. Macmillan.
Williams, Thdr. Chickering.
Poems of belief. '10(Ap16) c. front. D. $1 net. Houghton M.
Williams, T: J: Chew, comp.
State of Maryland; description of its lands, products and industries. [2d ed.] '10 (Jl16) D. pap., gratis. Sun Pr.
Williams, Tom A.
Psychoprophylaxis in childhood. [1910.] (Je) 9 p. 8°. T. A. Williams.
"References" (1 p.).
Williams, W. R.
Science of skirt drafting. 2d ed.; from actual measurements by the infallible skirt cutting device known to the trade as the infallible skirt rule. '08, [1909.] (F) c. 56 p. diagrs., 4°, $10. Gazette Co.
Williams, W. Roger.
Natural history of cancer. '08(Ag1) il. 8°, *$5 net. Wood.
Williams, Wa. Long.
Veterinary obstetrics, incl. the diseases of breeding animals and of the new-born. '09(Ag) 10+1127 p. il. 8°, $8. W. L. Long.
Williams, W: Carlos.
Poems. '09(Je5) c. D. pap., 25 c. W: C. Williams.
Williams, W: K.
Indiana farm laws with business forms and model business letters. '10(F) c. D. $1.50. Rural Pub.
Williams-White, H., and Robichez, E.
French vocabularies; arr. for repetition on a new plan. '10(S10) S. 50 c. Longmans.
Williams & Rogers ser. O. Am. Bk.
—Fitch. New commercial law. $1.05.
—Neal *and* Craigin. Modern illustrative bookkeeping. $1.
—Williams *and* Rogers. Supplementary exercises in bookkeeping. 20 c.
Williams College, Williamstown, Mass. Williams College: induction of Harry Augustus Garfield, LL.D., into the office of president, Oct. 7, 1908. '09(Jl) 127 p. por. 8°, $1. L. W. Spring.
Williams of West Point. Johnson, H. S. †$1.50. Appleton.
Williams on service. Johnson, H. S: $1.50. Appleton.
WILLIAMSBURG, Va.
Tyler, L. G. Williamsburg, the old colonial capital. $2.50. L. G. Tyler.
See also **Bruton Parish Church.**

Williamson, Mrs. Alice Muriel Livingston.
Adventures of Princess Sylvia. '09, [1910.] (N) 251 p. col. front. 12°. Metropolitan Press, (N. Y.)
Castle of the shadows. '09, [1910.] (F) il 12°, $1.50. Hudson Press.
House by the lock. '08(Ap11) c. 12°, (Popular priced copyrights.) 50 c. B. W. Dodge.
Silent battle. '09(D) 12°, 75 c. Doscher.
See also Williamson, C: Norris.

Williamson, C: Norris and Mrs. Alice Muriel Livingston.
Chauffeur and the chaperon. '08(My16) c. D. †$1.50. McClure.
Lord Loveland discovers America. '10 (Ja15) c. il. $1.20, fixed. Doubleday, P.
Motor maid. '10(Ag20) c. col. il. D. $1.20 fixed. Doubleday, P.
Set in silver. '09(My15) c. D. †$1.50. Doubleday, P.

Williamson, E: J:
Grillparzer's attitude toward Romanticism; dissertation. '10(My) 76 p. O. pap., 50 c. net. Univ. of Chic.

Williamson, G: C:
See Holme, C:, *ed.*

Williamson, H.
Metric tables for setting out curves in metres. '08(Ag1) 32°, 80 c. Spon.

Williamson, Ja. J.
Mosby's Rangers: record of the operations of the forty-third battalion of Virginia cavalry from its organization to the surrender. 2d ed., rev. and enl. '09(Ag14) c. pors. O. *$2.50 net. Sturgis & W.

Williamson, Marg.
John and Betty's history visit. '10(Ap30) c. il. D. $1.25. Lothrop, L. & S.

WILLIAMSPORT, Pa.
Bey, T. Williamsport illustrated. $1.50. T. Bey.
See also Christ Church.

Willis, Bailey.
Research in China, in 3 v. and atlas. v. 2, Systematic geology. '08(Ja25) maps, Q. (Carnegie Institution of Washington pub.) pap., $2. Carnegie.

Willis, Clarence P.
Preservative treatment of farm timbers. '10(Je) 19 p. il. 8°, (U. S., Dept. of Agriculture; farmers' bull.)

Willis, Hugh Evander.
Principles of the law of contracts. '09(N) c. O. $3. Keefe-D.
Principles of the law of damages. '10(Mr) c. O. $3. Keefe-D.

Willis, J: Christopher.
Agriculture in the tropics; elem. treatise. '09, [1910.] (F) 18+222 p. il. 8°, (Cambridge biological ser.) $2.75. Putnam.
Manual and dict. of the flowering plants and ferns. 3d ed. '08(Je6) map, D. (Cambridge biological ser.) *$2.75 net. Putnam.

Williston, S:
Law covering sales of goods at common law and under the uniform sales act. '09 (Ap) c. 109+1304 p. O. $7.50. Baker, V. & Co.

Williston, S: Wendell.
Manual of North American *diptera* [flies]. 3d ed. '08(O17) c. il. O. $4. J. T. Hathaway.

Willits, I. Pearson, M.D.
Early physicians of Germantown; address del. before the Site and Relic Society of Germantown, Mar. 12th, 1909. '09, [1910.] (Mr) 135-150 p. 4°, (Site and Relic Society of Germantown; historical addresses.) (Not for sale.) Site and Relic.

Willman, Reinold, M.D.
Errors of mind healing compared with the miracles of Christ and His disciples in the healing of the afflicted. '09(Jl31) c. D. $1. Advocate Pub.

Willmott, E. C. Morgan.
See Dan, Horace.

Willoughby, Jennie Evelyn.
Written exercises on direct and indirect quotations. '09(D11) c. il. D. 35 c. Am. Sch. Deaf.

Willoughby, Lois, ed.
Love in all ages; songs and fragments of days old and new. '10(Mr5) c. 16°, 50 c. Volland.

Willoughby, Westel Woodbury.
Constitutional law of the United States. v. 1, 2. '10(N) c. O. $12. Baker, V. & Co.

WILLOWS.
Mell, C. D. Basket willow culture. 25 c. C. D. Mell.

Wills, Anthon E.
Matinée idol: [a play.] '09(F20) c. 12°, pap., 15 c. Dick.

WILLS.
Church, W. S. New probate law and practice with annots. and forms for use in Alaska, Ariz., Cal., Colo., Id., Kan., Mont., Nev., N. M., N. D., Okla., Ore, S. D., Utah, Wash., and Wyo. In 2 v. per set, $12. Bender-M.
Costigan, G: P., *jr.* Cases on wills, descent and administration sel. from decisions of Eng. and Amer. courts. $4.50. West Pub.
Gest, J: M. Pract. suggestions for drawing wills and the settlement of estates in Pennsylvania. *$2 net. T. & J. W. Johnson.
Goodmann, G. Probate proceedings and administration of estates. 25 c. G. Goodmann.
Long, J. R. Notes of lectures on the law of wills and administration. $1. Michie.
Nebraska. Supp. to the law of probate and administration. $2. Keefe-D.
New Jersey. Law and the practice from the earliest times concerning the probate of wills. $1.50. Paterson Hist.
New York [State.] Notes on the law of wills. 75 c. Baker, V. & Co.
Price, B: L., *and* Stow, A. W: Wills and how to make them. (Add. author for price.) B: L. Price.
Remsen, D. S. On the preparation and contest of wills. *$6 net. Baker, V. & Co.

WILLS.—*Continued.*
Ross, P: V. Probate law and practice. 2 v. $13.—Supp. to Ross on probate law and practice. Bancroft-W.
Schouler, J. Law of wills and administration. $6. Boston Bk.
See also **Executors and administrators;—*also* names of states.**

Willson, H: Beckles.
Canada. '08(S5) il. O. (Romance of empire ser.) *$2 net. Stokes.
George III., as man, monarch and statesman. '08(Ag15) O. *$3 net. Jacobs.
Life and letters of James Wolfe. '10(D10) il. 8°, $4 net. Dodd.
Story of rapid transit. '10(F12) c. il. 12°, (Lib. of valuable knowledge.) 92 c. S. S. McClure.

Willson, Mrs. Minnie Moore-.
Seminoles of Florida. '10(Ja22) c. il. O. **$1.25 net. Moffat.

Willson, Rob. Newton, M.D.
Nobility of boyhood. '10(D) 16°, 50 c. Winston.

Willson, Rob. Wheeler, M.D.
Medical men in the time of Christ. '10 (Je18) c. il. D. 60 c. net. S. S. Times.
Times of sunrise and sunset in the United States. '09(Ja16) c. charts, O. pap., *$1 net. Harvard Co-op.

Willson, Rev. T: B.
Norway at home. '08(D5) il. 8°, *$1.75 net. Scribner.

Wilmot, Sainthill Eardley-.
See Eardley-Wilmot, Sainthill.

Wilmot-Buxton, Ethel M.
Stories from old French romance. '10 (Jl30) D. 75 c. net. Stokes.
Stories of Norse heroes told by the Northmen. '09(Ag7) il. D. $1.50. Crowell.
Stories of Persian heroes. '08(O3) c. il. †$1.50. Crowell.

Wilmot-Buxton, Rev. Harry J:
See Buxton, *Rev.* Harry J: Wilmot-.

Wilmshurst, W. L.
Christianity and science. '09(S) 92 p. 12°, (Psychic lib.) *$1 net. Badger.

Wilson, Mrs. A. J., [Augusta Jane Evans.]
St. Elmo. '10(F19) c. il. por. 12°, 50 c. Hurst.
St. Elmo. '10(Ap9) 12°, pap., 25 c. J. S. Ogilvie.

Wilson, Andrew, M.D.
Physiology; popular acct. of the functions of the human body. '10(Mr26) D. (Twentieth centnry science ser.) 50 c. net. Stokes.

Wilson, Anne.
Boggy solitudes of Nantucket. '08(Ag22) c. D. $1.25. Neale.

Wilson, Augusta Manie.
Principle of the ego in philosophy with special reference to its influence upon Schlegel's doctrine of "Ironie"; thesis presented to New York University. '09 (Jl3) O. pap., *50 c. net. Stechert.

Wilson, Calvin Dill.
Making the most of ourselves: talks to young people; second series. '09(Ap3) c. D. *$1 net. McClurg.

WILSON, *Sir* Charles.
Watson, *Sir* C: M. Life of Sir Charles Wilson. *$5 net. Dutton.

Wilson, C: Newton.
Through the buhrs. '10(D3) il. 12°, $1.50. C. M. Clark.

Wilson, Dan. Munro.
John Quincy, master of Mount Wollaston; provincial statesman; colonel of the Suffolk regiment; speaker of the Massachusetts House of Representatives; member of His Majesty's Council; address del. Sunday, Feb. 23, 1908, under the auspices of the Quincy Historical Society; prep. in collaboration with C: Fs. Adams. '09 (N) 84 p. il. pors. facsim., 8°. (Priv. pr.) C: F. Adams, jr.

Wilson, E. P.
Local and state government in Nebraska. '09(D) c. 90 p. 16°, 20 c. Univ. Pub.

Wilson, Edm. Beecher.
Biology: [a lecture.] '08(N21) c. 8°, pap. (Add. pubs. for price.) Columbia Univ.

Wilson, E: Stansbury.
Poetry of eating; collection of occasional editorials printed in the *Ohio State Journal.* '09(Ap3) c. 24°, 50 c. E: S. Wilson.

Wilson, Elijah N:, ["Uncle Nick."]
Among the Shoshones. '10(Mr5) c. il. por. 8°, $1.25. Skelton.

Wilson, Eliz. Lyless, [Mrs. W. H. Wilson,] and Huggins, Mollie.
Good things to eat; everybody's favorite. '09(N20) c. 8°, $3. Pub. Ho. of M. E. Ch., So.

Wilson, Emmet H.
See Los Angeles. Penal ordinances.

Wilson, Eug. B:
Cyanide processes. 4th ed., rev. and enl. '08(Ag29) il. 12°, $1.50. Wiley.

Wilson, Floyd Baker.
Discovery of the soul: out of mysticism, light and progress. '08(F29) c. D. $1. Fenno.

Wilson, Frazer Ells.
Peace of Mad Anthony; acct. of the subjugation of the north-western Indian tribes and the treaty of Greenville by which the territory beyond the Ohio was opened for Anglo-Saxon settlement. '09, [1910.] (Ja) c. 12 p. map, plan, facsims., il. pors. 8°, $1.25. F. E. Wilson.

Wilson, G: Buckland.
Air-conditioning: treatise on the humidification, ventilation, cooling, and the hygiene of textile factories. '08(Mr7) il. 12°, $1.50. Wiley.

Wilson, G: Grafton.
Hdbk. of international law. '10(S) c. 623 p. O. $3.75. West Pub.
—, and Tucker, J: Fox.
International law. 5th ed. [1910] (F) c. '09. 19+505 p. 8°, $2.50. Silver.

Wilson, G: Rob.
Hist. of Dubois County from its primitive days to 1910; incl. biographies of Capt. Toussaint Dubois and the Very Rev. Joseph Kundeck. '10(Ap) c. 412 p. il. pors. fold. maps, 8°, $4. G: R. Wilson.

Wilson, Gilbert Livingstone.
See Pepper, G: Hubbard.

Wilson, Rev. H.
Why and wherefore: [simple explanations of the ornaments, vestments and ritual of the church.] '09(Je) 16°, 25 c. Young Churchman.

Wilson, H. C., and Casey, Kellogg Kennon Venable, comps.
Rifle range construction; text-book to be used in the construction of rifle ranges, with details of all parts of the work; ed. by Colonel J. G. Ewing. '09(D) c. 149 p. il. fold. plan, 8°, $1. Du Pont de Nemours.

Wilson, Harold W., and Howell, C. M. Hinds.
Movable kidney: its pathology, symptoms, and treatment. '08(Jl11) il. O. *$1.25 net. Longmans.

Wilson, Harry Leon.
See Tarkington, Newton Booth.

Wilson, Mrs. Harry Leon.
See O'Neill, Rose Cecil.

Wilson, Mrs Harriet Louisa.
Gracilariophila, new parasite on *gracilaria confervoides.* '10(Je) 75-84 p. il. Q. (Univ. of Cal. pubs.; Botany.) pap., 10 c. Univ. of Cal.

Wilson, Harriette Dubouchet.
Memoirs of Harriette Wilson; written by herself. In 2 v. '10(F19) pors. O. *$8 net. Lane.

WILSON, Henry.
Wilson, M., *and* Simpson, A. B. Henry Wilson, one of God's best. $1. Alliance Press.

Wilson, H: E.
See Jenner, W: A.

Wilson, H: Lawrence.
Bungalow book. 3d ed. '08(D); 4th ed., thoroughly rev. and much enl. '08, [1909.] (Mr) c. il. plans, 4°, ea., $1. H: L. Wilson.

Wilson, Herbert Michael.
Irrigation engineering. 6th ed., rev. and enl. '09(Ag21) il. figs. 8°, $4. Wiley.

Topographic surveying: incl. geographic exploratory, and military mapping, with hints on camping, emergency surgery, and photography. 3d ed., rev. '08(Ag1) c. il. tabs., maps, chart, 8°, $3.50. Wiley.

Wilson, J. F.
Earthquakes and volcanoes, hot springs. '08(Ja4) il. O. $1.25; bds., $1. S. B. Newman.

Earthquakes and volcanoes—hot springs; incl. the theory of gravitation. 2d ed. '10(My14) c. il. 8°, $1.25. J. F. Wilson.

Wilson, J. Hunt.
See Richards, Thdr. W:

Wilson, Jacob.
New views on old subjects; social, scientific and political. '10(D3) 8°, $1.50. Lemcke.

WILSON, James.
Alexander, L. H., *ed.* James Wilson, (1742-1798,) signer of the Declaration of Independence. (Add. Society for price.) St. Andrew's Soc.

Konkle, B. A. James Wilson and the Constitution. gratis. Law Acad.

Wilson, Ja. Cornelius.
Fever-nursing; designed for the use of professional and other nurses, and especially as a text-book for nurses in training. 6th ed., rev. and enl. [1910.] (D) c. 259 p. il. diagrs., 12°, (Pract. lessons in nursing.) $1 net. Lippincott.

Hdbk. of medical diagnosis for the use of practitioners and students. '09(D); [2d ed.] '10(Je) c. il. 8°, ea., *$6 net. Lippincott.

—, ed. Infectious diseases; auth. tr. from "Die deutsche klinik" under the general editorial supervision of Julius L. Salinger, M.D. '10(Ap) c. 15+979 p. il. 8°, (Modern clinical medicine.) $6. Appleton.

Wilson, Ja. Grant.
Thackeray in the United States. New and cheaper ed. '09(D) il. 8°, *$3.50 net. Dodd.

Wilson, Ja. Harrison.
Free trade with Cuba; letter and speech advocating the establishment of a commercial union, under which free trade should exist bet. Cuba and the United States in natural and manufactured products, subject to an agreed tariff as between them and other foreign nations. '09(Je) 19 p. 8°, pap. (Add. Superintendent for price.) U. S., Supt. of Docs.

Wilson, Jean Bingham.
See Hurd, Marion Kent.

Wilson, J:
How God has spoken. '09(Ag21) 12°, *$2 net. Scribner.
See also Arnott, Ja. A.

Wilson, J: Mills.
Bible as literature. '09(N) c. 162 p. 8°, (Beacon ser.) 45 c.; pap., 35 c. Unitarian S. S.

Wilson, Jos. Rob.
Chapel in every home. '09(N) 48 p. facsims., f°. (Priv. pr.) J. R. Wilson.

Wilson, Lillian May, ed.
Barber genealogy (in two sections); section 1, descendants of Thomas Barber of Windsor, Conn., 1614-1909; section 2, descendants of John Barber of Worcester, Mass., 1714-1909. '09, [1910.] (Je) c. 659+164 p. il. pors., facsim. 8°, $10. J: B. White.

Wilson, L: N., comp.
Bibliography of child study for the year 1907. '08, [1909.] (F) 8°, (Pub. of the Clark Univ. Lib.) pap., *25 c. net. Clark Univ.

Wilson, Mrs. Lucy L. W., ed.
Picture study in elementary schools. 2 v. in 1. '09(Je19) il. 12°, *$1.25 net. Macmillan.

Wilson, Madèle, and Simpson, Albert B.
Henry Wilson, one of God's best. '08, [1909.] (F) c. 195 p. il. pors. 12°, $1. Alliance Press.

Wilson, Mary L. Q. Petrie Carus-.
See Carus- Wilson, Mary L. G. Petrie.

Wilson, Norman J.
See Oulton, Leonard.

Wilson, Rev. P.
Great salvation: a gospel for the day. '08 (Ap11) D. *$1.25 net. Jennings.

Wilson, Patten.
Nature round the house: [animals.] '08 (Ap4) il. 12°, $1. Longmans.

WILSON, Richard.
Fletcher, B. Richard Wilson, R.A. *$1.25 net. Scribner.

Wilson, Rufus Rockwell.
Noble company of adventurers. '08(D19) c. il. D. $1. B. W. Dodge.

Wilson, Lady Sarah Isabella Augusta Churchill.
South African memories, social, warlike and sporting, from diaries written at the time. '09(D4) il. pors. O. *$4.20 net. Longmans.

Wilson, Sir T:
Arte of rhetorique, 1560; ed. by G. H. Mair. '09(My15) D. (Tudor and Stuart lib.) limp bds., $1.75. Oxford Univ.

Wilson, T: W.
Knight Templar's pilgrimage to the Holy Land. '09(Ja9) c. il. por. D. $1.50; leatherette, $2. T: W. Wilson.

Wilson, Victor Tyson.
Descriptive geometry. '09(Jl31) c. figs. 8°, **$1.50 net. Wiley.

—, and McMaster, Carlos Lenox.
Notes on pract. mechanical drawing; written for the use of students in engineering courses. '08(Mr28); 2d ed. '08(D5); 3d ed., rev. and enl. '09(N20) c. il. 8°, ea., $1.50. Wilson & M.

Wilson, Mrs. W. H.
See Wilson, Eliz. Lyless.

Wilson, W. Lawler.
Menace of socialism. '10(F) 8°, **$1.50 net. Jacobs.

Wilson, Rev. Warren Hugh.
Quaker Hill in the nineteenth century. 2d ed. '07, [1908.] (Mr.) c. 36 p. map, D. (Quaker Hill local history ser.) pap., 10 c. Quaker Hill.

Wilson, W: Rob. Anthony, M.D.
Journeys of the Kit-Kat Club, England. '08 (O10) c. il. O. bds., **$2 net. Appleton.
A rose of Normandy. '08(My.) c. 12°, (Popular ed. of recent fiction.) †75 c. Little, B. & Co.

Wilson, W: T:
For the love of Lady Margaret: romance of the lost colony. '08, [1909.] (Mr.) 305 p. il. 12°, $1.50. Stone & B.

Wilson, Winifred H.
Leather work. '09(My8) c. il. 4°, $1. M. B. Willcox.

Wilson, Winter Lincoln.
Elements of railroad track and construction. '08(O3) c. figs. 12°, $2. Wiley.

Wilson, Wood Levette.
End of dreams. [1910.] (My) c. '09 348 p. il. 8°, $1.50. M. Kennerley.

Wilson, Woodrow.
Civic problems; address del. March 9, 1909, at the annual meeting of the Civic League of St. Louis. '09(Jl31) O. pap. (Add. pubs. for price.) Civic League.
Constitutional government in the United States. '08(Je13) c. O. (Columbia Univ. lectures, George Blumenthal foundation, 1907.) **$1.50 net. Lemcke.
Division and reunion, 1829-1909. [New ed., enl.] '09(O30) c. maps, S. (Epochs of American history.) $1.25. Longmans.
Free life: a baccaleureate address. '08 (O3) c. D. bds., **75 c. net. Crowell.
Minister and the community. '09(Mr) c. 17 p. 12°, (Claims and opportunities of the Christian ministry.) 10 c.; per 100, $8. Y. M. C. A.

Wilson-Carmichael, Amy.
Lotus buds. '09(D11) c. il. Q. *$5 net. Armstrong.

Wilson-Green, Arth.
Exercises on Erckmann-Chatrian's Waterloo. '10(Ja22) 16°, pap., *30 c. net. Putnam.

WILSON'S CAVALRY RAID.
See Civil War (United States).

Wilstach, Paul.
Richard Mansfield: the man and the actor. '08(N14) il. pors. O. **$3.50 net. Scribner.

Wilt, Abram Darst.
Banking and the currency problem; read before the Saturday Club, April, 1907. '08(Mr7) pap. (Add. author for price.) A. D. Wilt.

Wilt, Dorah W.
Man's influence with God. '10(Je11) c. por. 12°, 75 c. D. W. Wilt.

Wiltse, May Barnard.
Theorem or teleology of spiritualism. '09 (Je) c. 91 p. 12°, 75 c. Eddy County Provost.

WILTSHIRE, Eng.
Bradley, A. G. Wiltshire. 45 c. Putnam.
Hudson, W. H. Shepherd's impressions of the South Wiltshire Downs. $2.50 net. Dutton.

WIMAR, Charles Ferdinand.
Hodges, W: Romaine. Carl Wimar. $1.25; $1.50. C: Reymarshoffer.

Wimperis, Harry Egerton.
Internal combustion engine. '09(My1) il. 8°, *$3 net. Van Nostrand.

Wimple ser. *See* Lea, J: Stokes.

Wimshurst machine. Marshall, A. W. 25 c. Spon.

Winans, Wa.
Hints on revolver shooting. '08(D19) c. S. **50 c. net. Putnam.
Sporting rifle: the shooting of big and little game together with a description of the principal classes of sporting weapons. '08 (Ag8) c. il. por. Q. **$5 net, boxed. Putnam.

Winbigler, C: Fremont.
Suggestion, its law and application; or, the principle and practice of psycho-therapeutics. '09(O16) c. il. por. 12°, $2.50. S. A. Lewis.

Winchell, Alex. Newton.
See Winchell, Newton Horace.

Winchell, Newton Horace and Alex. Newton.
Elements of optical mineralogy; introd. to microscopic petrography. '09(Je26) c. il. tabs., 8°, *$3.50 net. Van Nostrand.

Winchell, S: Robertson.
Orthography, etymology and punctuation, embodying the essential facts of the English language, with concise rules for spelling, punctuation, the use of capital letters, etc. '09(Mr) c. 4+189 p. 12°, 60 c. Flanagan.
—, **comp. and ed.** Civic manual for Chicago, Cook County and Illinois; designed for use in schools as a text-book or supp. reader, and for reference by citizens generally. '10 (Mr26) c. D. bds., 50 c. Flanagan.
WINCHENDON, Mass.
Vital records of Winchendon, Mass., to the end of the year 1849. $2.80. F. P. Rice.
Winchester, Caleb T:
Group of English essayists of the early nineteenth century. '10(Ja29) c. D. **$1.50 net. Macmillan.
WINCHESTER, Eng.
Varley, T. Winchester. $3 net. Macmillan.
Winchevsky, Morris.
Stories of the struggle. '08(My23) c. S. 50 c. Kerr.
WIND.
Chatley, H. Force of the wind [in aeronautics.] *$1.25 net. Lippincott.
Wind along the waste. Annesley, *Mrs.* M. $1.50. Lane.
Wind in the willows. Grahame, K. †$1.50. Scribner.
Wind mill. *See* Longfellow, H: Wadsworth.
Windham, T: Wyndham-Quin.
See Dunraven, *Earl of.*
Winding waters. Parker. F. $1.50. C. M. Clark.
Windle, Bertram Coghill Alan.
What is life?: a study of vitalism and neo-vitalism. '08(Ag8) c. 8°, (Expository essays in Christian philosophy.) $1. Herder.
WINDMILLS.
Ball, R. S. Natural sources of power. $2 net. Van Nostrand.
Fuller, P. E. Use of windmills in irrigation in the semi-arid west. Gov. Pr. Off.
Windolph, Fs. Lyman.
To-day, and other poems. '08(Je27) c. Q. pap., *$1 net. W: U. Hensel.
Window at the White Cat. Rinehart, *Mrs.* M. R. $1.50. Bobbs-M.
WINDOW DRESSING.
Bird, T: A., *comp. and ed.* Hardware window dressing. $2.50. Merchants Record.
Mason, H. B., *ed.* Window displays for druggists. $1. E. G. Swift.
Tracy, C: A., *comp.* Art of decorating show windows and interiors. $3.50. Merchants Record.
WINDOW GARDENING.
Dorner, H. B. Window gardening. **$1 net. Bobbs-M.
See also Indoor gardening.
Window making for carpenters and joiners. '10(Je11) il. 12°, (Woodworker ser.) pap., 25c. Spon.
Windows. Day, L. F. *$7.50 net. Scribner.
Winds of heaven. Hyatt, A. H., *ed.* *$1 net. Dutton.

Windsor, H. H., ed.
Mission furniture, how to make it. pt. 1. '09(Jl17); pt. 2. '10(Jl2) c. il. 16°, (Popular Mechanics twenty-five cent hdbk. ser.) pap., ea., 25 c. Popular Mechanics.
WINDSOR, England.
Holmes, *Sir* R: R. Windsor. *$2.50 net. Macmillan.
WINDSOR CASTLE, Windsor, Eng.
Thomas, E: Windsor Castle. $1.25. Estes.
Windust, Florance Hufton-.
See Hufton-Windust, Florance.
"Windy Bill," pseud.
Going some, [joke book.] '09(Je5) il. 12°, pap., 10 c. J. S. Ogilvie.
WINE.
Alwood, W: B. Enological studies; 1, Experiments in cider making applicable to farm conditions; 2, Notes on the use of pure yeast in wine making. Gov. Pr. Off.
See also Chemistry;—Liquors.
Wine of the Puritans. Brooks, Van W. *$1 net. M. Kennerley.
Wine of wizardry. Sterling, G: *$1.25 net. A. M. Robertson.
Wines, F: Howard.
Punishment and reformation: study of the penitentiary system. New enl. ed. '10 (Ja22) c. D. (Lib. of economics and politics.) *$1.75 net. Crowell.
"Winfield, Arth. M.," pseud.
See Stratemeyer, E:
Wing, Jos. Elwyn.
Alfalfa farming in America. '09. [1910.] (Ap) 3-480 p. il. por. 8°, $2. Saunders Pub.
Wingate, General G: Wood.
Why should boys be taught to shoot? '08 (F1) c. T. pap. (Add. pubs. for price.) Sub-Target.
Wingfield, H. E., M.D.
Introd. to the study of hypnotism; experimental and therapeutic. '10(Jl) 12°, $2 net. Wood.
Wings of the morning. *See* Morrison, G. H. Addresses from a Glasgow pulpit.
Winjum, Atle Ragnwald Tarum.
Manual of physical exercises. '09(Je5) c. por. figs. D. $1.75. Modern Medicine.
WINKELRIED, Arnold von.
Höcker, G. Arnold of Winkelried. *60 c. net. McClurg.
WINKWORTH, Catherine *and* Susanna.
Shaen, M. J., *ed.* Memorials of two sisters. *$3.50 net. Longmans.
Winn, Edith Lynwood.
Child violinist. '09(F13) c. il. pors. 8°. $1.25. Fischer.
Etudes of life. '08, [1909.] c. 105 p. 8°, leath., $2.50. Fischer.
How to prepare for Kreutzer: book for teachers in private schools and academies, as well as the profession in general, giving thorough analysis of suitable material for the first four grades incl. explanation of the most important principles of bowing technic and tone production. '10 (Ag27) c. 12°, $1. Fischer.
How to study Fiorillo; detailed descriptive analysis of how to practice these studies. '10(Ag27) il. por. D. 75 c. Fischer.

Winn, Edith Lynwood.—*Continued.*
How to study Kreutzer: detailed, descriptive analysis of how to practice these studies, based upon the best teachings of representative, modern violin playing. '10 (Ag27) c. pors. 12°, 75 c. Fischer.

Winners of the world. Gardner, M. T. 35 c. Old Corner.

Winners of the world during twenty centuries. Gardner, M. T. 60 c. net; 30 c. net. Revell.

Winnie Wimple and ragged robin. Lea, J: 35 c. Stokes.

Winning chance. Dejeans, E. †$1.50. Lippincott.

Winning fight. Kaufman, H. $1.50. H. Kaufman.

Winning game. Macbeth, M. $1.50. B'way Pub.

Winning his shoulder straps. Brainerd, N. †$1.25. Lothrop, L. & S.

Winning his way. Coffin, C: C. 50 c. Hurst.

Winning his "Y." Barbour, R. H: $1.50. Appleton.

Winning lady. Freeman, *Mrs.* M. E. W. †$1.25. Harper.

Winning men one by one. Wood, H. W. *50 c. net. S. S. Times.

Winning of Fuji. Gray, E. T. 25 c. Dramatic.

Winning of immortality. Palmer, F. $1 net. Crowell.

Winning orations. Prather, C: E., *comp. and ed.* 2 v. v. 1, $1.25; v. 2, $1.75. Crane.

Winning orations in the national contests of the Intercollegiate Prohibition Association, produced and del. by college and university men and women. [1910 rev. ed.]; ed. for the Association by Harry S. Warner, gen'l secretary. '10(N) 89 p. pors. 12°, 25 c. Intercollegiate Prohibition.

Winning speeches. Trueblood, T: C., *ed.* $1. Am. Bk.

Winning ten. Woolley, E: M. $1.50. Appleton.

Winning the boy. Merrill, L. *75 c. net. Revell.

Winning the Eagle prize. Brainerd, N., *pseud.* $1.25. Lothrop, L. & S.

Winning the front place. Maclean, J: 75 c. Am. S. S.

Winning their way Faris, J: T. $1.50. Stokes.

Winnowing (A). Benson, *Father* R. H. $1.50. Herder.

Winram, J:
Violin playing and violin adjustment. '09 (Mr13) il. por. sq. O. *$2 net. Scribner.

Winsett, Rob. Emmet.
Standard rudiments; self instructor; complete course in all departments of the rudiments of music, melodies, rhythmics, dynamics and voice culture. '08, [1909.] (F) c. 25+7 p. 8°, pap., 15 c. R. E. Winsett.

Winship, G: Parker.
Early South American newspapers. '08, [1909.] (S) 14 p. il. 12°, $1. Am. Antiquarian.

Winship, Mary Gray.
Autumn leaves and other poems. '10(F26) c. S. pap., 50 c. M. G. Winship.

Winslow, Rev. Anna J. Frazer.
Jewels from my casket. '10(D31) c. il. pors. 12°, $1.25. A. J. Winslow.

Winslow, Mrs. Anne Rogers.
See Winslow, C: E: Amory.

Winslow, C: E: Amory.
See Kinnicutt, Leonard Parker;—Prescott, S: Cate.

—, and Mrs. Anne Rogers.
Systematic relationship of the *coccaceæ;* with a discussion of the principles of bacterial classification. '08(D19) c. 12°, $2.50. Wiley.

Winslow, Eben Evelethe.
Lectures on seacoast defense. '09, [1910.] (F) 213 p. 8°, (Engineer School, U. S. Army; occasional papers.). (Not for sale.) Engineer Sch.

Winslow, Erving.
Conditions and future of the Philippines article from the *North American Review.* '09(Jl) 8 p. 8°. (Add. Superintendent for price.) U. S., Supt. of Docs.

Winslow, Helen Maria.
Spinster farm. '08(My23) c. il. D. $2. L. C. Page.
Woman for mayor. '09(Jl3) c. front. D. $1.50. Reilly & B.

Winslow, Horatio.
Some wander sangs and other verse. '08 (D) c. 32 p. 16°, pap. (Add. pub. for price.) H. Winslow.

Winslow, I: Oscar.
Geography readers. 5 v. '10(D3) il. ea., 50 c. net. Heath.

Winslow, Kenelm, M.D.
Prevention and treatment of diseases of the domestic animals, incl. etiology and symptoms. '10(O) c. 303 p. 8°, $3.50. W: R. Jenkins.
Veterinary materia medica and therapeutics. 6th ed., rev. and enl. '08(O17) c. 8°, $6. W: R. Jenkins.

—, and Hill, H. W., M.D.
Production and handling of clean milk; incl. Practical milk inspection, by Kenelm Winslow, and Essentials of milk bacteriology, by H. W. Hill. [2d ed.] '09 (O16) il. tabs., O. $3.25. W: R. Jenkins.

Winsor, T:
Standard intrinsic unit. '08(Ag8) c. nar. D. $1. Winsor.

Winstanley, Denys Arth.
Personal and party government; chapter in the political history of the reign of George III., 1760-1766. '10(My7) c. $1.50 net. Putnam.

Winstanley, E: W:
Spirit in the New Testament; enquiry into the word πνευμα in all passages, and a survey of the evidence concerning the Holy Spirit. '08(Mr21) 8°, *$1.10 net. Putnam.

Winston's encyclopedia; compendium of information and instruction on all subjects for home, school and office; ed. by Charles Morris, A. R. Spofford, and other specialists. 8 v. '09(O16) c. il. pors. maps, facsims., 12°, $6. Winston.

Winchell, S: Robertson.
Orthography, etymology and punctuation, embodying the essential facts of the English language, with concise rules for spelling, punctuation, the use of capital letters, etc. '09(Mr) c. 4+189 p. 12°, 60 c. Flanagan.
—, **comp. and ed.** Civic manual for Chicago, Cook County and Illinois; designed for use in schools as a text-book or supp. reader, and for reference by citizens generally. '10 (Mr26) c. D. bds., 50 c. Flanagan.

WINCHENDON, Mass.
Vital records of Winchendon, Mass., to the end of the year 1849. $2.80. F. P. Rice.

Winchester, Caleb T:
Group of English essayists of the early nineteenth century. '10(Ja29) c. D. **$1.50 net. Macmillan.

WINCHESTER, Eng.
Varley, T. Winchester. $3 net. Macmillan.

Winchevsky, Morris.
Stories of the struggle. '08(My23) c. S. 50 c. Kerr.

WIND.
Chatley, H. Force of the wind [in aeronautics.] *$1.25 net. Lippincott.

Wind along the waste. Annesley, *Mrs.* M. $1.50. Lane.
Wind in the willows. Grahame, K. †$1.50. Scribner.
Wind mill. *See* Longfellow, H: Wadsworth.

Windham, T: Wyndham-Quin.
See Dunraven, *Earl of.*

Winding waters. Parker. F. $1.50. C. M. Clark.

Windle, Bertram Coghill Alan.
What is life?: a study of vitalism and neo-vitalism. '08(Ag8) c. 8°, (Expository essays in Christian philosophy.) $1. Herder.

WINDMILLS.
Ball, R. S. Natural sources of power. $2 net. Van Nostrand.
Fuller, P. E. Use of windmills in irrigation in the semi-arid west. Gov. Pr. Off.

Windolph, Fs. Lyman.
To-day, and other poems. '08(Je27) c. Q. pap., *$1 net. W: U. Hensel.

Window at the White Cat. Rinehart, *Mrs.* M. R. $1.50. Bobbs-M.

WINDOW DRESSING.
Bird, T: A., *comp. and ed.* Hardware window dressing. $2.50. Merchants Record.
Mason, H. B., *ed.* Window displays for druggists. $1. E. G. Swift.
Tracy, C: A., *comp.* Art of decorating show windows and interiors. $3.50. Merchants Record.

WINDOW GARDENING.
Dörner, H. B. Window gardening. **$1 net. Bobbs-M.
See also Indoor gardening.

Window making for carpenters and joiners. '10(Je11) il. 12°, (Woodworker ser.) pap., 25c. Spon.
Windows. Day, L. F. *$7.50 net. Scribner.
Winds of heaven. Hyatt, A. H., *ed.* *$1 net. Dutton.

Windsor, H. H., ed.
Mission furniture, how to make it. pt. 1. '09(Jl17); pt. 2. '10(Jl2) c. il. 16°, (Popular Mechanics twenty-five cent hdbk. ser.) pap., ea., 25 c. Popular Mechanics.

WINDSOR, England.
Holmes, *Sir* R: R. Windsor. *$2.50 net. Macmillan.

WINDSOR CASTLE, Windsor, Eng.
Thomas, E: Windsor Castle. $1.25. Estes.

Windust, Florance Hufton-.
See Hufton-Windust, Florance.

"Windy Bill," pseud.
Going some, [joke book.] '09(Je5) il. 12°, pap., 10 c. J. S. Ogilvie.

WINE.
Alwood, W: B. Enological studies; 1, Experiments in cider making applicable to farm conditions; 2, Notes on the use of pure yeast in wine making. Gov. Pr. Off.
See also Chemistry;—Liquors.

Wine of the Puritans. Brooks, Van W. *$1 net. M. Kennerley.
Wine of wizardry. Sterling, G: *$1.25 net. A. M. Robertson.

Wines, F: Howard.
Punishment and reformation: study of the penitentiary system. New enl. ed. '10 (Ja22) c. D. (Lib. of economics and politics.) *$1.75 net. Crowell.

"Winfield, Arth. M.," pseud.
See Stratemeyer, E:

Wing, Jos. Elwyn.
Alfalfa farming in America. '09. [1910.] (Ap) 3-480 p. il. por. 8°, $2. Saunders Pub.

Wingate, General G: Wood.
Why should boys be taught to shoot? '08 (F1) c. T. pap. (Add. pubs. for price.) Sub-Target.

Wingfield, H. E., M.D.
Introd. to the study of hypnotism; experimental and therapeutic. '10(Jl) 12°, $2 net. Wood.

Wings of the morning. *See* Morrison, G. H. Addresses from a Glasgow pulpit.

Winjum, Atle Ragnwald Tarum.
Manual of physical exercises. '09(Je5) c. por. figs. D. $1.75. Modern Medicine.

WINKELRIED, Arnold von.
Höcker, G. Arnold of Winkelried. *60 c. net. McClurg.

WINKWORTH, Catherine *and* Susanna.
Shaen, M. J., *ed.* Memorials of two sisters. *$3.50 net. Longmans.

Winn, Edith Lynwood.
Child violinist. '09(F13) c. il. pors. 8°. $1.25. Fischer.
Etudes of life. '08, [1909.] c. 105 p. 8°, leath., $2.50. Fischer.
How to prepare for Kreutzer: book for teachers in private schools and academies, as well as the profession in general, giving thorough analysis of suitable material for the first four grades incl. explanation of the most important principles of bowing technic and tone production. '10 (Ag27) c. 12°, $1. Fischer.
How to study Fiorillo; detailed descriptive analysis of how to practice these studies. '10(Ag27) il. por. D. 75 c. Fischer.

Winn, Edith Lynwood.—*Continued.*
How to study Kreutzer: detailed, descriptive analysis of how to practice these studies, based upon the best teachings of representative, modern violin playing. '10 (Ag27) c. pors. 12°, 75 c. Fischer.
Winners of the world. Gardner, M. T. 35 c. Old Corner.
Winners of the world during twenty centuries. Gardner, M. T. 60 c. net; 30 c. net. Revell.
Winnie Wimple and ragged robin. Lea, J: 35 c. Stokes.
Winning chance. Dejeans, E. †$1.50. Lippincott.
Winning fight. Kaufman, H. $1.50. H. Kaufman.
Winning game. Macbeth, M. $1.50. B'way Pub.
Winning his shoulder straps. Brainerd, N. †$1.25. Lothrop, L. & S.
Winning his way. Coffin, C: C. 50 c. Hurst.
Winning his "Y." Barbour, R. H: $1.50. Appleton.
Winning lady. Freeman, *Mrs.* M. E. W. †$1.25. Harper.
Winning men one by one. Wood, H. W. *50 c. net. S. S. Times.
Winning of Fuji. Gray, E. T. 25 c. Dramatic.
Winning of immortality. Palmer, F. $1 net. Crowell.
Winning orations. Prather, C: E., *comp. and ed.* 2 v. v. 1, $1.25; v. 2, $1.75. Crane.
Winning orations in the national contests of the Intercollegiate Prohibition Association, produced and del. by college and university men and women. [1910 rev. ed.]; ed. for the Association by Harry S. Warner, gen'l secretary. '10(N) 89 p. pors. 12°, 25 c. Intercollegiate Prohibition.
Winning speeches. Trueblood, T: C., *ed.* $1. Am. Bk.
Winning ten. Woolley, E: M. $1.50. Appleton.
Winning the boy. Merrill, L. *75 c. net. Revell.
Winning the Eagle prize. Brainerd, N., *pseud.* $1.25. Lothrop, L. & S.
Winning the front place. Maclean, J: 75 c. Am. S. S.
Winning their way Faris, J: T. $1.50. Stokes.
Winnowing (A). Benson, *Father* R. H. $1.50. Herder.
Winram, J:
Violin playing and violin adjustment. '09 (Mr13) il. por. sq. O. *$2 net. Scribner.
Winsett, Rob. Emmet.
Standard rudiments; self instructor; complete course in all departments of the rudiments of music, melodies, rhythmics, dynamics and voice culture. '08, [1909.] (F) c. 25+7 p. 8°, pap., 15 c. R. E. Winsett.
Winship, G: Parker.
Early South American newspapers. '08, [1909.] (S) 14 p. il. 12°, $1. Am. Antiquarian.
Winship, Mary Gray.
Autumn leaves and other poems. '10(F26) c. S. pap., 50 c. M. G. Winship.
Winslow, Rev. Anna J. Frazer.
Jewels from my casket. '10(D31) c. il. pors. 12°, $1.25. A. J. Winslow.
Winslow, Mrs. Anne Rogers.
See Winslow, C: E: Amory.
Winslow, C: E: Amory.
See Kinnicutt, Leonard Parker;—Prescott, S: Cate.
—, and Mrs. Anne Rogers.
Systematic relationship of the *coccaceæ;* with a discussion of the principles of bacterial classification. '08(D19) c. 12°, $2.50. Wiley.
Winslow, Eben Evelethe.
Lectures on seacoast defense. '09, [1910.] (F) 213 p. 8°, (Engineer School, U. S. Army; occasional papers.). (Not for sale.) Engineer Sch.
Winslow, Erving.
Conditions and future of the Philippines article from the *North American Review.* '09(Jl) 8 p. 8°. (Add. Superintendent for price.) U. S., Supt. of Docs.
Winslow, Helen Maria.
Spinster farm. '08(My23) c. il. D. $2. L. C. Page.
Woman for mayor. '09(Jl3) c. front. D. $1.50. Reilly & B.
Winslow, Horatio.
Some wander sangs and other verse. '08 (D) c. 32 p. 16°, pap. (Add. pub. for price.) H. Winslow.
Winslow, I: Oscar.
Geography readers. 5 v. '10(D3) il. ea., 50 c. net. Heath.
Winslow, Kenelm, M.D.
Prevention and treatment of diseases of the domestic animals, incl. etiology and symptoms. '10(O) c. 303 p. 8°, $3.50. W: R. Jenkins.
Veterinary materia medica and therapeutics. 6th ed., rev. and enl. '08(O17) c. 8°, $6. W: R. Jenkins.
—, and Hill, H. W., M.D.
Production and handling of clean milk; incl. Practical milk inspection, by Kenelm Winslow, and Essentials of milk bacteriology, by H. W. Hill. [2d ed.] '09 (O16) il. tabs., O. $3.25. W: R. Jenkins.
Winsor, T:
Standard intrinsic unit. '08(Ag8) c. nar. D. $1. Winsor.
Winstanley, Denys Arth.
Personal and party government; chapter in the political history of the reign of George III., 1760-1766. '10(My7) c. $1.50 net. Putnam.
Winstanley, E: W:
Spirit in the New Testament; enquiry into the word πνευμα in all passages, and a survey of the evidence concerning the Holy Spirit. '08(Mr21) 8°, *$1.10 net. Putnam.
Winston's encyclopedia; compendium of information and instruction on all subjects for home, school and office; ed. by Charles Morris, A. R. Spofford, and other specialists. 8 v. '09(O16) c. il. pors. maps, facsims., 12°, $6. Winston.

Winston's every child's lib. il. D. †75 c. Winston.
—Bunyan. Pilgrim's progress.
—Cooper. Leatherstocking tales.
—Dickens. Stories about children.
—Hurlbut. Lives of our Presidents.—Stories of great Americans.—Stories about children of all nations.—Stories of our naval heroes. —Story of Jesus and the early church.—Story of our country.
Winston's ideal classics. il. S. flex. leath., per v., $1.25, boxed. Winston.
—Blackmore. Lorna Doone. 2 v.
—Carlyle. French Revolution. 3 v.
—Eliot. Romola. 2 v.
—Hugo. Les misérables. 3 v.
—Plutarch. Lives of illustrious men. 4 v.
Winston's illustrated photogravure books. il. O. $3, boxed; mor., $7. Winston.
—Lindsay. Washington.

Winter, Georg, and Ruge, Carl.
Text-book of gynecological diagnosis, after the 3d rev. German ed. '09(Mr) c. 21+670 p. il. 4°, $6. Lippincott.

Winter, J: Garrett.
Myth of Hercules at Rome. '10(My7) 8°, (Univ. of Mich. studies; Humanistic ser.) pap., 50 c. net. Macmillan.

Winter, Mrs. Maria Beadnell.
See Dickens, C:

Winter, Nevin Otto.
Brazil and her people of to-day. '10(O15) c. il. fold. map, O. $3, boxed. L. C. Page.
Guatemala and her people of to-day. '09 (Ag14) c. D. (Travel lovers' ser.) $3, boxed. L. C. Page.

Winter, W:
Life and art of Richard Mansfield; with selections from his letters. In 2 v. '10 (F12) c. por. O. **$6 net. Moffat.
Old friends; being literary recollections of other days. '09(Je26) c. pors. O. **$3 net. Moffat.
Other days: being chronicles and memories of the stage. '08(O31) c. pors. O. **$3 net. Moffat.
Poems. Author's ed. '09(S25) c. por. O. **$2 net. Moffat.
Poems. Large paper ed. '09(Mr27) por. 8°. bds., *$15 net. Moffat.
Shakespeare's England. [New ed.] '10 (O1) c. O. $3 net, boxed. Moffat.

Winter pilgrimage. Haggard, H: R. $1.50. Longmans.
Winter queen. Hay, M. $4 net. Houghton M.
Winterfeast (The). Kennedy, C: R. $1.25. Harper.

Winternitz, Moriz.
Index to the names and subject matter of the sacred books of the East. '10(Ag27) c. O. (Sacred books of the East.) $5.75. Oxford Univ.

Winter's comedy. Sutcliffe, H. $1.50. Lane.
Winter's tale. *See* Greene, Rob.—Shakespeare, W:

Winther, Fritz.
Wilhelm Busch als dichter künstler, psychologe und philosoph. '10(O) 79 p. O. (Univ. of Cal. pubs.; Modern philology.) pap., 75 c. Univ. of Cal.

Winthrop, J:
Journal, "History of New England," 1630-1649; ed. by Ja. Kendall Hosmer. '08 (D5) c. 2 v., map, facsims., 8°, (Original narratives of early American history.) **$6 net. Scribner.

WIRE ROPE TRANSPORTATION.
Hewitt, W: Bleichert system of aerial tramways. gratis. Trenton Iron Co.

Wireless messages. Broadhurst, C. N. $1 net. Revell.
Wireless station at Silver Fox Farm. Kaler, J. O. $1.50. Crowell.

WIRELESS TELEGRAPHY.
Collins, A. F: Manual of wireless telegraphy and telephony. **$1.50 net. Wiley.
Fleming, J: A. Elem. manual of radiotelegraphy and radiotelephony for students and operators. *$2 net. Longmans.
Harrison, N. Making wireless outfits. 50 c.; 25 c. Spon.
How to make wireless instruments. 25 c. H. Gernsback.
Kennelly, A. E. Wireless telegraphy and wireless telephony. **$1 net. Moffat.
Laughter, V. H. Operator's wireless telegraph and telephone hand-book. $1. Drake.
Laughter, V. H., *and* Morgan, A. P. Wireless telegraphy made simple. 25 c. Popular Electricity.
Massie, W. W., *and* Underhill, C: R. Wireless telegraphy and telephony popularly explained. **$1 net. Van Nostrand.
Maver, W: Wireless telegraphy and telephony. $3. Maver Pub.
Monckton, C. C. F. Radio-telegraphy. *$2 net. Van Nostrand.
Morgan, A. P. Wireless telegraph construction for amateurs. $1.50. Van Nostrand.
Pierce, G: W. Principles of wireless telegraphy. $3. McGraw-H.
Radio communication; rept. 5 c. Gov. Pr. Off.
Radio-telegraphic installations and radiotelegraphers on certain ocean steamers. '09(My) 67 p. 8°, pap. (Add. Superintendent for price.) U. S., Supt. of Docs.
Russel, E. Wireless telegraphy. (Priv. pr.) E. Russel.
Twining, H. Le V. Wireless telegraphy. $1.50. H. L. Twining.
United States. *Bu. of Steam Engineering.* List of wireless telegraph stations of the world.
United States. *Navy Dept. Bu. of Equipment.* List of wireless telegraph stations of the world, including shore stations, merchant vessels, revenue cutters, and vessels of the United States Navy; corrected to Sept. 1, 1909. '09(D) 102 p. 8°.
United States. *Navy Dept. Bu. of Equipment.* Manual of wireless telegraphy for use of naval electricians, by S: S. Robison; with revisions and the addition of chapters III, IV and V by L: W. Austin. '09, [1910.] (Mr) 129 p. il. 8°.
United States. Wireless telegraphy and wireless telephony; rept. [1910.] (Jl) 9 p. 8°.

WIRELESS TELEPHONY.
See Telephone.

Wirgman, A. Thdr., D.D.
Life of James Green, Doctor of Divinity, Rector and Dean of Maritzburg, Natal, from Feb., 1840, to Jan., 1906. In 2 v. '09(N20) il. O. *$6 net. Longmans.

Wiring a house. Pratt, H. 25 c. Henley.

Wirtshaus (Das) zu Cransac. *See* Zschokke. Johann Heinrich Daniel. Der zerbrochene krug.

WIRZ, *Major* Henry.
Page, J. M., *and* Haley, M. J. True story of Andersonville prison: defense of Major Henry Wirz. $2. Neale.

Wisconsin. *Dept. of Education.* List of books for free high school libraries in the state of Wisconsin, with instructions for cataloging. '09, [1910.] 187 p. 8°, pap., gratis. C: P. Cary.

Wisconsin. Insurance laws in effect Jan. 1, 1908; (G: L. Ekern.) '07, [1908.] (Je.) 372 p. O. (Add. pub. for price.) Democrat Pr. Co., (Wis.)

Wisconsin. Shepard's Wisconsin citations. 3d ed. '07, [1908.] (My.) c. 227 p. 8°, $7.50. F. Shepard.

Wisconsin. State Historical Society. Checklist of publications of the society, 1850-1908; comp. by I: S: Bradley. '09(N) 46 p. 8°, (State Historical Society of Wisconsin; bull.) pap., 15 c. State Hist., Wis.

Wisconsin. *Supreme ct.* Digest of the decisions; new, rev. and complete. In 3 v.; by J: B. Simmons. v. 1. '09(N); v. 2. '09, [1910.] (Ja); v. 3 (Ap) c. O. ea., $10. Callaghan.

Wisconsin. *Supreme ct.* Repts., 131; (F: K. Conover. '08(Mr); v. 132 (Ag); v. 133 (N); v. 134; (C: F. Lamb and F: K. Conover.) '08, [1909.] (Ja); v. 135; (Eugene A. Gilmore and F: K. Conover.) '09(Mr): v. 136 (Jl); v. 137 (S) ea., $2.75; v. 138 (D) $2.50; (C: F. Lamb [for] F: K. Conover.) v. 139. '09, [1910.] (Mr); v. 140 (Je); v. 141 (S) c. O. shp., ea., $1.30. Callaghan.

Wisconsin. *Supreme ct.* Supp. to the law of negligence; summary and digest of negligence decisions in the Wis. reports, vs. 102 to 130, incl., with citations to the northwestern reporter and other pubs.; prep. and arr. by C: H. Hamilton. '08(Mr.) 34+568 p. O. shp., $5.50. G: I. Jones.

WISCONSIN.
Automobile blue book of Wisconsin. *$2 net. Caspar.
Barnett, J. D. Indirect central administration of Wisconsin. 25 c. Univ. of Wis.
Bartlett, J. L. Frosts in Wisconsin. 25 c. Univ. of Wis.
Bryant, E. E. Treatise on the civil and criminal jurisdiction of justices of the peace, and the powers and duties of constables in executing process in the state of Wis. *$6.50 net. Callaghan.
Cary, C: P., *ed.* List of books for free high school libraries in the state of Wisconsin. gratis. C: P. Cary.
Caspar's automobile road maps of Wisconsin. $1.25. Caspar.

WISCONSIN.—*Continued.*
Cheek, P. Hist. of Sauk Co. Riflemen, known as Company "A," Sixth Wis. Veteran Volunteer Infantry, 1861-1865. $1.50. P. Cheek.
Cory, C: B. Birds of Illinois and Wisconsin. $4. Field Museum.
Cronk, V. D. **Selection of business forms,** incl. local precedents and official forms under the laws of Wisconsin and Minnesota. (Add. pubs. for price.) Flood.
Fish, C. R. Some phases of the economic history of Wisconsin, 1860-70. 35 c. State Hist., Wis.
Foote, A. R. Speech del. before Wis. legislature: [public utilities bills of Wis. and N. Y.] A. R. Foote.
Joyce, J. A. Treatise on franchises, especially those of public service, corporations, cont. also in an appendix the public service commissions law of New York, and the public utility law of Wisconsin. $6.50. Banks.
Kellogg, L. P. Organization boundaries, and names of Wisconsin counties. 35 c. State Hist., Wis.
Kuehl, G: W. **Automobile blue book of Wisconsin.** *$2 net. G: W. Kuehl.
Nolen, J: State parks for Wisconsin. $1 net. J: Nolen.
Phelan, R. V. Financial history of Wisconsin. 50 c. Univ. of Wis.
Philipp, E. L. Political reform in Wisconsin. 50 c. net. Caspar.
Smith, C. J. Making of Wisconsin. 60 c. Flanagan.
Three chapters in Wisconsin local history. 25 c. State Hist., Wis.
Thwaites, R. G. Wisconsin; the Americanization of a French settlement. **$1.25 net. Houghton M.
See also Biography;—Burlington;—Ferns;—Fox River Valley;—Memorial Day;—Milwaukee;—Paper;—Portage County;—Rock River Valley;—Sewage and sewerage;—Superior.

Wisconsin Dept. of Education bull. 8°, pap. Wis. Dept. Pub. Instruction.
—Youker, *comp.* Training of rural school teachers. (Not for sale.)

Wisconsin Free Lib. Commission. American social questions. 12°. Wis. Free Lib.
—Ray. Immigration problem. 25 c.
—Sieg. Negro problem: a bibliography. 25 c.
—True. Labor problem. 25 c.

Wisconsin Free Library Commission, Comparative legislation bulletin. D. pap., 5 c. Wis. Free Lib.
—Campbell. Mortgage taxation.
—Curtis. Proportional representation.
—Hornbeck. Juvenile courts.
—Macgregor. Tenement house legislation.
—McKittrick. Accident insurance for workingmen.
—Schaffner. Initiative and referendum.—Municipal home rule charters.—Primary elections.—The recall.
—Scott. Telephones.

Wisconsin Free Public Library Commission. Study outlines for the use of clubs and reading associations. 22 nos. '08(Ag22) gratis. Wis. Free Lib.

Wisconsin History Commission; original papers. 8°. Wis. Hist.
—Haight. Three Wisconsin Cushings. $1.
—Kellogg. Capture and escape. $1.
—Vilas. View of the Vicksburg campaign. $1.
Wisconsin History Commission reprints. O. Wis. Hist.
—Haskell Battle of Gettysburg. $1.
Wisconsin State Historical Society bull. 8°. State Hist. Wis.
—Martin. Local history story hour. 10 c.
Wisdom for the foolish. Crittenton, C. D. 75 c. Badger.
Wisdom of Abraham Lincoln. Lincoln, A. **50 c. net. Wessels.
Wisdom of Dickens. Dickens, C: *$1 net. M. Kennerley.
Wisdom of Israel: extracts from the Babylonian Talmund and the Midrash Rabboth; tr. by Edwin Collins. '08(Je6) 16°, (Wisdom of the East.) *40 c. net. Dutton.
Wisdom of the ancients. *See* **Bacon, Fs.,** *Lord.*
Wisdom of the ancients lib. il. 12°. Monsalvat.
—Cebes. Greek Pilgrim's progress. $1.
Wisdom of the Apocrypha; with introd. by C. F. Lawrence. '10(Jl9) 16°, (Wisdom of the East ser.) 60 c. net. Dutton.
Wisdom of the East ser.; ed. by L. Cranmer-Byng and S. A. Kapadia. 16°. Dutton.
—Al Ghazzali. Alchemy of happiness. 60 c. net.—Confessions of Al Ghazzali. *40 c. net.
—Arabian wisdom. *40 c. net.
—Awakening of the soul. *40 c. net.
—Bachye. Duties of the heart. *40 c. net.
—Baerlein. Singing caravan. 60 c. net.
—Barnett. Heart of India. *60 c. net.
—Brahma knowledge. *60 c. net.
—Buddha: way of the Buddha. *60 c. net.
—Chuang Tzu. Musings of a Chinese mystic. *60 c. net.
—Confucius. Classics of Confucius: Book of history.—Books of odes.—Conduct of life ea., *40 c. net.—Sayings of Confucius. *60 c. net.
—Cranmer-Byng, *comp.* Lute of Jade. *60 c. net.
—Dennis. Burden of Isis. 60 c. net.
—Diwan of Abu'l-ala. *40 c. net.
—Hafiz. Rubâiyât. 60 c. net.
—Hammond, *comp.* Splendor of God. *60 c. net.
—Hsaio Ching. Book of filial duty. *40 c. net.
—Instruction of Ptah Hotep. *40 c. net.
—Kaibara. Women and wisdom of Japan. *40 c. net.
—Lâo-Tsze. Sayings of Lâo-Tzu. *40 c. net.
—Master singers of Japan. 60 c. net.
—Path of light. *60 c. net.
—Persian mystics: Jami. *60 c. net.
—Sadi. Rose-garden of Sadi.—Sa'di's scroll of wisdom. ea., *40 c. net.
—Wisdom of Israel. *40 c. net.
—Wisdom of the Apocrypha. 60 c. net.
—Wollaston. Religion of the Koran. *40 c. net.
—Zoroaster. Teachings of Zoroaster. *40 c. net.

Wisdom ser. Tt. leath., **$1 net. Brentano's.
—Carlyle. Wisdom of Carlyle.
—Emerson. Wisdom of Emerson.
—Franklin. Wisdom of Franklin.
—Lamb. Wisdom of Charles Lamb.
—Lincoln. Wisdom of Abraham Lincoln.
—Shakespeare. Wisdom of Shakespeare.
—Stevenson. Wisdom of Stevenson.
—Thackeray. Wisdom of Thackeray.
—Whitman. Wisdom of Walt Whitman.
—Wilde. Wisdom of Oscar Wilde.
Wise, B. R.
Commonwealth of Australia. '09(O2) il. fold. map, O. *$3 net. Little, B. & Co.
Wise, Jennings Cropper, comp.
Digested index and genealogical guide to Bishop Meade's "Old churches, ministers and families of Virginia"; embracing 6,900 proper names. '10(My21) c. O. pap., $2 net. Bell Bk.
Wise, Kate Ellis, ed.
Guide to historic places in Virginia, 1607-1907. 2d ed. '08(N) 168 p. il. fold. map, D. pap., 25 c. Wise Pub.
Wise, T: A., and Rhodes, Harrison Garfield.
Gentleman from Mississippi: novel founded on the popular play. '09(My15) il. D. *50 c. net. J. S. Ogilvie.
WISE COUNTY, Texas.
Cates, C. D. Pioneer hist. of Wise Co. $2. C. D. Cates.
Wise-Knut. *See* Björnson, Björnstjerne.
Wise sayings and favorite passages. *See* Fielding, H:
Wishard, J: G., M.D.
Twenty years in Persia: a narrative of life under the last three shahs. '08(N14) c. 12°. *$1.50 net. Revell.
Wishard, S: Ellis, D.D.
"Old, old story." '08, [1909.] (Mr) 252 p. 12°, 50 c. Montfort.
Testimony of the Bible concerning the assumptions of destructive criticism. '09 (S) c. 127 p. 12°, 60 c. S. E. Wishard.
Wishart, Alfr. Wesley.
Social mission of the church; pub. for the Social Service Commission of the Northern Baptist Convention. '10(Je4) c. 8°, (Social service ser.) 20 c. Am. Bapt.
Wishing books. 3 v. '10(D) ea., 25 c. Wilde.
Contents: Friend: some definitions of you; Little book of birthday wishes; Little book of friendly wishes.
Wislicenus, Paul.
Shakespeare's totenmaske. '10(N12) pors. bds., $1.50. Lemcke.
WISSAHICKON RIVER, Pa.
Bicknell, J. D. The Wissahickon. $1. (Sold to members only.) City Hist., Phil.
Wisser, J: Philip.
Explosive materials. 2d ed., rev. and enl. '08(My2) c. 24°, (Van Nostrand science ser.) 50 c. Van Nostrand.
Wistful years. Gilson, R. R. †$1.50. Baker & T.
WIT AND HUMOR.
Alford, F., *comp.* Wit of Lincoln. wisdom of Franklin. 25 c. Scott-M.
Allen, L. Airship almanac. 75 c. J: W. Luce.
Bangs, J: K. Autobiography of Methuselah. $1. B. W. Dodge.

WIT AND HUMOR.—*Continued.*

Bangs, J: K. Genial idiot. †$1.25. Harper.
Bardeen, C: W:, *comp.* Fifty fables for teachers. $1. Bardeen.
Blythe, S: G: We have with us to-night. 50 c. Altemus.
Browne, L. A. Cook-ed up Peary-oddical dict. and who's hoot in the best Arctic circles. *60 c. net. J: W. Luce.
Burtscher, W: J: Yellow Creek humor. $1. W: J: Burtscher.
Butler, E. P. Mike Flannery on duty and off. 50 c. Doubleday, P.
Caricature; wit and humor of a nation in picture, song and story. $3. Leslie-Judge.
Carrick, H. Muse in motley. *$1.10 net. Macmillan.
Carse, R. Monarchs of Merry England: humorous rhymes. $1.50. Stokes.
"Clivette, the Man in Black," *pseud.* Café cackle from dumps to Delmonico's. 50 c. Laird.
Coggins, H. L., *comp.* Stories worth telling. 50 c. Penn Pub. Co.
Crittenton, C. L. Wisdom for the foolish. 75 c. Badger.
Crowninshield, F. W. Manners for the metropolis. **$1 net. Appleton.
Dale, A., *pseud.* Great wet way. **$1.50 net. Dodd.
Dunne, F. P: Mr. Dooley says. $1 net. Scribner.
Dwiggins, C. V. Wants. $1; $1.50. Winston.
E., O. N., *pseud.* Vocabulary for your fathers. 75 c. Dodge.
Emanuel, W., *pseud.* Dog World and Anti-Cat Review. **25 c. net. Stokes.
Fitch, G: Big strike at Siwash. †50 c. Doubleday, P.
Flagg, J: M. All in the same boat. 75 c. Life Pub. Co.
Forsdick, M. A. Pertinent, penetrating pen points and peculiar parodies. $1. Neuner.
Freese, N. I. Without credentials. 35 c. N. I. Freese.
Gillilan, S. W. Including Finnigin: book if Gillilan verse. $1. Pearson Bros.
Goldberg, R. L. Foolish questions. **50 c. net. Small.
Graham, H. Bolster book. $1.50 net.—Deportmental ditties; [burlesque rules of etiquette.] $1. Duffield.
Healy, C. Escapades of Condy Corrigan. 50 c. Soc. Divine Word.
Herford, O. Simple jography. $1. J: W. Luce.
Herford, O., *and* Clay, J: C., *comps.* Cupid's almanac and guide to hearticulture. **90 c. net. Houghton M.
Herford, O., *and* Clay, J: C., *comps.* Cupid's cyclopedia. $1 net. Scribner.
Herford, O., Mumford, E. W., *and* Mizner, A. The complete cynic. 75 c. Elder.
Hitchcock, M. E. Tales out of school about naval officers. $1. Gotham Press.
Hobart, G: V. Dinkelspiel's letters to Looey.—Go to it. ea., 75 c. G: W. Dillingham.

WIT AND HUMOR.—*Continued.*

How, F: D. Clerical humour of olden time. $2. Pitman.
Humorous masterpieces; pictured by Phil May. *25 c. net. Stokes.
Irish wit and humor. 50 c. Pustet.
Irwin, W. A. Love sonnets of a car conductor. **50 c. net. P. Elder.
Irwin, W. A. The Teddysee. 75 c. net. B: W. Huebsch.
Irwin, W: H: Warrior the untamed: [fiction.] †50 c. Doubleday, P.
Jerome, J. K. Passing of the third floor back. †$1. Dodd.
Johnson, C. *and* B., *eds.* Year book of humor. 60 c.; $1. Crowell.
Jokes that we meet. 65 c. South-West Pub.
Jones, J., *pseud.* Book of nature. *25 c. net; *50 c. net. P. Elder.
Kempson, F. C. "Green Finch" cruise. $1.75. Longmans.
Kendall, E. F. Top Soil, rich in wit and humor, relating the happenings to one "Sandy Loam." 50 c. Cleveland News.
Kieffer, H: M. Funny bone. 75 c.; $1. Dodge.
Kinder, T: S: Rube's twenty years' adventures. 50 c.; 25 c. Laird.
Kleiser, G. Humorous hits, and How to hold an audience. **$1 net. Funk.
Kuhn, W. Little bird told me! 75 c. Life Pub. Co.
Kummer, C. B. Bible rhymes for the not too young. 75 c. net. Dodge.
Lampton, W: J. Jedge Waxem's pocket-book of politics. 50 c. G: W. Dillingham.
Lewis, E. C., *comp.* Smile, don't worry. 50 c. Mutual Bk.
Little, M. W. B. Rubaiyat of a huffy husband. $1. Badger.
Lloyd, J. A. Home made hash. $1.25. J. A. Lloyd.
Loomis, C: B. Just Irish: [humorous account of travels in Ireland.] $1. Badger.
Loomis, C: B. Little Maude and her mamma. †50 c. Doubleday, P.
Masson, T: T. New Plato. **75 c. net. Moffat.
Meader, H. L. Cupid the surgeon. †$1. Altemus.
Men, women and mirth. $2. Life Pub. Co.
Metcalfe, J. S. Diary of a district messenger. 25 c. Life Pub. Co.
Moore, C: F. Hist. of the states, united and otherwise. *$1.50 net. Neale.
Newell, P: The hole book: [verse.] $1.25. Harper.
Patten, W:, *comp.* Among the humorists and after dinner speakers. $2.25. Collier.
Pearson, P. M., *comp.* Humorous speaker. $1.25. Hinds.
Pemberton, M. H. Reuben, his book. $1.15. B'way Pub.
Pendleton, A. L., *jr.* Silly syclopedia. 50 c. C: G. Feldmeyer.
Phelps, W: L. Dash at the pole. 75 c. Ball Pub. Co.

WIT AND HUMOR.—*Continued.*

Ransom, F. C: My policies in Jungleland. $1. Barse & H.

Reddall, H: F. Wit and humor of business. **50 c. net; **80 c. net. Jacobs.

Reflections of a bachelor. $1. Dodge.

Rice, W. de G. C., *comp.* For the gaiety of nations; fun and philosophy from the American newspaper humorists. *50 c. net. Dodge.

Schaefer, F. W. Diana's diary.—Osgar und Adolf. ea., 50 c.; 25 c. Laird.

Schofield, R. J. Drummer's yarns and funny jokes. 25 c. Excelsior.

Seaman, O. Salvage: [contributions to *Punch.*] *$1.25 net. Holt.

Shepard, M. Wags; philosophy of a peaceful pup. 50 c. Wessels.

Simpson, H. Seven stages of golf: [pictures and verse.] *75 c. net. Lippincott.

Smith, B. 100 stories in black. 25 c. J. S. Ogilvie.

Smith, E. B. Chicken world. $2. Putnam.

Steppes, J: P. John Ritsch, Esq.: auslese aus den humoristischen briefen. $1. J: P. Steppes.

Stories of humor by Oliver Wendell Holmes, Bill Nye, Mark Twain, [etc.] †75 c. Doubleday, P.

Sweny, H. R. Big Stick and the Golf Stick: [verses about Roosevelt and Taft.] 50 c. Lyon.

Watt, H. Myths about monarchs. **$1 net. Dodd.

Wells, C. Rubaiyat of bridge. $1. Harper.

Welsh, C:, *ed.* Chauffeur chaff. 50 c. Caldwell.

Wheeler, M. P. Hash: [rhymes and limericks.] 75 c.; 50 c. M. P. Wheeler.

Whitefield, C: T. Plain American in England. 50 c. Doubleday, P.

Whiting, R. R., *comp.* Four hundred good stories. $1. Baker & T.

Wilder, M. P. Smiling 'round the world. $1.50. Funk.

Wilder, M. P., *ed.* Ten books of the merrymakers. 10 v. $6. Circle.

Williams, H. Uncle Bob and Aunt Becky's exciting trip: [fiction.] 75 c.; 25 c. Laird.

"Windy Bill," *pseud.* Going some: [joke book.] 10 c. J. S. Ogilvie.

Wood, H. E. Intellectual pup; extracts from his diary. 50 c. H. Wood.

Wood, R. W. Animal analogues. **50 c. net. P. Elder.

See also Authors;—Caricature;—Cartoons;—Children;—Epigrams;—Golf; — Parody; — Satire; —Toasts;—*also* Ireland.

Wit and humor of the stage; [comp. by H: Frederic Reddall.] '09(Ag7) c. por. S. (Wit and humor ser.) **50 c. net; leath., **80 c. net. Jacobs.

Wit and humor ser. S. **50 c. net; leath., **80 c. net. Jacobs.
—Reddall. Wit and humor of business.
—Wit and humor of the stage.

Wit of Lincoln. Alford, F., *comp.* 25 c. Scott-M.

WITCHCRAFT.

Gummere, A. M. Witchcraft and Quakerism. $1. Biddle Press.

Hueffer, O. M. Book of witches. *$2.50 net. J: McBride.

Taylor, J: M. Witchcraft delusion in colonial Connecticut. **$1.50 net. Grafton Press.

Witching hour. Thomas, A: †$1.50. Harper.

With a saucepan over the sea. Keen, A., *comp.* $1.50 net. Little, B. & Co.

With Dante on the mountains. Henderson, H: F. 75 c. Jennings.

With Evans to the Pacific. Codd, M. J. 60 c. Flanagan.

With fire and sword. Sienkiewicz, H. †75 c. Little, B. & Co.

With Grant at Vicksburg. Kaler, J. O. $1. Burt.

With gun and guide. Martindale, T: **$2 net. Jacobs.

With King James' Bible as exclusive authority can the Protestant Christian question the eucharist? Foley, J: T. $1.50. Pilot Co.

With Kit Carson in the Rockies. McNeil, E. $1.50. Dutton.

With Lyon in Missouri. Dunn, B. A. $1.25. McClurg.

With Mulai Hafid at Fez. Harris, L. $3 net. Badger.

With Osceola in Florida. Ober, F: A. †$1. Burt.

With other photographers. Phillips, R. W. $2.50. Eastman Kodak.

With pickpole and peavy. Burleigh, C. B. †$1.50. Lothrop, L. & S.

With Porter in north Missouri. Mudd, J. A. $2.50. J. A. Mudd.

With rifle in five continents. Niedieck, P. *$5 net. Scribner.

With Speaker Cannon through the Tropics. Moore, J. H. $2. Book Pr.

With Stevenson in Samoa. Moors, H. J. $1.50 net. Small.

With Sully into the Sioux land. Hanson, J. M. $1.50. McClurg.

With Taylor on the Rio Grande. Stratemeyer, E: †$1.25. Lothrop, L. & S.

With the American fleet from the Atlantic to the Pacific. Jones, R. D., *comp. and ed.* $3; $4; $5. Harrison Pub.

With the battle fleet. Matthews, A. F. $1.50 B: W. Huebsch.

With the beloved. M., G. *60 c. net. Young Churchman.

With the border ruffians. Williams, R. H. *$4 net. Dutton.

With the flag in Panama. Weir, H. C. $1.50. Wilde.

With the night mail. Kipling, R. †$1. Doubleday, P.

With the professor. Showerman, G. **$1.50 net. Holt.

With those that were. Grattan, F. W: $1.50. B'way Pub.

"With touch of elbow." Wells, J. M. **$1.25 net. Winston.

With Walt Whitman in Camden. Traubel, H. v. 1, 2. **$3 net. Appleton.

With Whistler in Venice. Bacher, O. H. **$4 net. Century Co.

Witham, Rose Adelaide, comp.
English and Scottish popular ballads; sel. and ed. for study under the supervision of W: Allan Neilson. '09(Ap10) c. D. (Riverside literature ser.) 40 c. Houghton M.

Withers, Hartley.
Meaning of money. '09(Je9) $2 net; 3d ed. '10(Jl30) O. $1.50 net. Dutton.
Stocks and shares. '10(D10) 12°, $2 net. Dutton.

—, and others.
English banking system. '10(N) 294 p. fold. tabs., 8°. Gov. Pr. Off.

Withers, Percy.
Egypt of yesterday and to-day. '10(S10) il. D. $1.75 net. Stokes.

Withers, Zachary.
Our inheritance: [argument for rights of negro people.] '09(O) c. 104 p. por. 12°, 50 c. Z. Withers.

Witherspoon, Mrs. Pattie French.
Elizabeth of Boonesborough, and other poems. '09(S) c. 122 p. 12°, $1.50. Badger.

Witherspoon Memorial Association. Witherspoon memorial; sketch of the association and unveiling of the statute. '09(Ag) 36 p. il. 8°. (Priv. pr.) B. S. Adams.

Withey, Morton Owen.
Tests on bond between concrete and steel in reinforced concrete beams. '09, [1910.] (O) 63 p. il. tabs., diagrs., 8°, (Univ. of Wis. bull.; Engineering ser.) 25 c. Univ. of Wis.
Tests on plain and reinforced concrete, series of 1906. '08(F1); ser. of 1907. '08. (Je6); ser. of 1908. '09, [1910.] (O) il. tabs., diagrs., O. (Univ. of Wis. bull., Engineering ser.) pap., ea., 25 c. Univ. of Wis.

Withington, Eliz., comp.
Lullabies of many lands. '08(N7) c. il. O. 50 c. Caldwell.

Without credentials. Freese, N. I. 35 c. N. I. Freese.

Without dogma. Sienkiewicz, H. †75 c. Little, B. & Co.

Witkowski, Georg.
German drama of the nineteenth century; author. tr. from the 2d German ed. by L. E. Horning. '09(Je26) c. D. $1. Holt.

Witkowski's atlas of female reproductive organs. [1910.] (Mr) *$3 net. W: R. Jenkins.
Formerly published by E. R. Pelton.

Witkowski's atlas of gestation. [1910.] (Mr) *$3 net. W: R. Jenkins.
Formerly published by E. R. Pelton.

Witkowski's atlas of male reproductive organs. [1910.] (Mr) *$3 net. W: R. Jenkins.
Formerly published by E. R. Pelton.

Witkowski's atlas of the bones of the foot. [1910.] (Mr) *$3 net. W: R. Jenkins.
Formerly published by E. R. Pelton.

Witkowski's atlas of the bones of the hand. [1910.] (Mr) *$2 net. W: R. Jenkins.
Formerly published by E. R. Pelton.

Witkowski's atlas of the brain. [1910.] (Mr) *$2 net. W: R. Jenkins.
Formerly published by E. R. Pelton.

Witkowski's atlas of the human body. [1910.] (Mr) *$2 net. W: R. Jenkins.
Formerly published by E. R. Pelton.

Witkowski's atlas of the mechanism of hearing. [1910.] (Mr) *$2 net. W: R. Jenkins.
Formerly published by E. R. Pelton.

Witkowski's atlas of the mechanism of vision. [1910.] (Mr) *$2 net. W: R. Jenkins.
Formerly published by E. R. Pelton.

Witkowski's atlas of the mechanism of voice, speech and taste. [1910.] (Mr) *$2 net. W: R. Jenkins.
Formerly published by E. R. Pelton.

Witmer, Lightner.
Mental healing and the Emmanuel Movement. '09(Ap10) 25 c. Psychological Clinic.

Witness for Jesus Christ. Scofield, W: J. 25 c. W: J. Scofield.

Witness of the heart. Stone, H: M. **$1.25 net. Longmans.

Witness of the spirit. Stone, D. 20 c. net. Longmans.

Witness of the Vulgate Peshitta and Septuagint to the Text of Zephaniah, (no. 4.) Zandstra, S. *$1 net. Macmillan.

Witness of the wilderness. **Lees, G: R. $1.25. Longmans.**

Wit's End. Blanchard, A. E. †$1.50. Estes.

Wits, beaux and beauties of the Georgian era. Fyvie, J: *$4 net. Lane.

Witte, G: Rudolph.
Cardiphonia; selection of poems. '09(Jl) c. 126 p. 12°, 75 c. Bookstore.

Witter, C: A.
Business and accounts, for public schools and home use. 6th ed., rev. and enl. '10 (Mr5) c. 12°, 75 c. C. A. Witter.

Witter Whitehead's own story about a lucky splash of whitewash. Hunting, H: G. †$1.25. Holt.

Witthaus, Rudolph August, M.D., and Becker, Tracy Chatfield, M.D.
Medical jurisprudence, forensic medicine and toxicology. 2d rev. ed. In 4 v. v. 3. '09(Ag) 1036 p. il. 8°, subs., per v., *$6 net; shp., *$7 net. Wood.

Wittman, W. Theodore.
Twelve months' work in the poultry yard. '10(Ja29) c. por. S. pap., 25 c. Item Pub.

Witwer, Ananias Clime, comp.
See Witwer, G:, *comp.*

Witwer, G: and Ananias Clime, comps.
Witwer genealogy of America. '09, [1910.] (Ja) 256 p. il. pors. 8°, $2.25. L. P. Hardy.

WITWER FAMILY.
See Genealogies.

Wives. *See* Irving, Washington.

Wiving of Lance Cleaverage. MacGowan, A. **$1.35 net. Putnam.

Wizard of Damavant. Parke, J. R. $1.20 net. Professional.

Wodehouse, Helen.
Logic of will: study in analogy. '08(Ag1) 12°, *$1.10 net. Macmillan.
Presentation of reality. '10(D24) D. $1 net. Putnam.

Wodehouse, Pelham Grenville.
Intrusion of Jimmy. '10(Je11) c. D. $1.50. W. J. Watt.
Love among the chickens. '09(Je12) c. il. D. $1.50. Circle Pub.
Mike; [public school story.] '10(Je11) il. 12°, $1.50. Macmillan.
Psmith in the city. '10(D17) il. 12°, $1.50 net. Macmillan.

Wodiska, Julius.
Book of precious stones; the identification of gems and gem minerals, and an account of their scientific, commercial, artistic and historical aspects. '09(D4) c. O. **$2.50 net. Putnam.

Woerner, W: F.
Evolution of the state universal from an American standpoint; address to a joint meeting of the Missouri Historical Society and the St. Louis Society of Psychology. [1910.] (S) 22 p. 8°, pap., gratis. W: F. Woerner.

Woglum, Russell Sage.
Fumigation investigations in California. '09 (Ag) 73 p. il. 8°, (U. S., Dept. of Agriculture, Bu. of Entomology.) pap. (Add. Superintendent for price.) U. S., Supt. of Docs.

Wohlfarth, Julia Helen, and Rogers, Lillian Emily.
New-world speller. '08(Ag8) c. il. D. 35 c. World Bk.

Wolcott, A. B.
Notes on some cleridæ of Middle and North America; with description of a new species. '10(Ag) 64 p. il. (Field Museum of Natural History pubs.; Zoological ser.) pap., 50 c. Field Museum.

Wolcott, Earle Ashley.
The open door; romance of mystery; time 1905. '10(S24) c. il. D. $1.25 net. Dodd.

Wolcott, Edn. Fs., comp.
Army horses: remount systems abroad, improvements suggested at home; some remarks about the proposed plant on the Crow Indian reservation, in Montana, for the breeding of cavalry horses by the Indians of that reservation. '08(My23) 8°, pap., $1. U. S., Supt. of Docs.

Wolesensky, E:
Study of the metallic tellurites. '09, [1910.] (O) 33 p. tabs., diagrs., 8°, (Univ. of Wis. bull.; Science ser.) 25 c. Univ. of Wis.
Bibliography (1 p.).

Wolf, Blair.
Patriotic and promiscuous poems. '10 (Ag27) c. 12°, pap., 40 c. net. B. Wolf.

Wolf, Herman Thdr.
Goldfish breeds and other aquarium fishes: their care and propagation. '08(Ag22) c. il. 12°, $3. Innes.

Wolf, Hugo.
Fifty songs; for high voice; ed. by Ernest Newman. '10(F12) c. F. (Musician's lib.) $2.50; pap., $1.50. Ditson.

Wolf, Hugo.
Newman, E: Hugo Wolf. *$2.50 net. Lane.

Wolf, Solomon.
See Louisiana. Code of practice.

Wolf-Eisner, Alfr., M.D.
Ophthalmic and cutaneous diagnosis of tuberculosis; together with a discussion of the clinical methods for the early diagnosis of pulmonary tuberculosis; a preface by Prof. H. Sevator and an introd. note to the English reader by C. Thdr. Williams; tr. from the German by Bernard I. Robert. '08(O17) il. charts, 8°, *$2.75 net. Wood.

Wolf.
Harding, A. R. Wolf and coyote trapping; up-to-date wolf hunter's guide. 60 c. A. R. Harding.
Hawkes, C. Wilderness dog. $1.50. Jacobs.

Wolf. McCord, P: B. $1. Dodge.

Wolf (The). Somerville, C: †$1.50. G: W. Dillingham.

Wolf hunters. Curwood, J. O. †$1.50. Bobbs-M.

Wolf patrol. Finnemore, J: $1.50. Macmillan.

Wolf, the storm leader. Caldwell, F. W. $1.60 net. Dodd.

Wolfard, Nathan Dordwin.
Popular manual of theology. '08. c. 181 p. por. 12°, pap., 65 c.; cl., $1; hf. leath., $1.25. I. M. Beaver.

Wolfarth, Julia Helen, and Rogers, Lillian Emily.
New world speller; grades 1 and 2. '10 (S17) (New-world text books.) 25 c. World Bk.

Wolfe, Arch. J:
Aspects of recent Russian literature. 2 pts. '08(Ag) 21 p. 8°, pap. (Not for sale.) A. J. Wolfe.

Wolfe, *General* James.
—Willson, H: B. Life and letters of James Wolfe. $4 net. Dodd.

Wolfe, S. Herbert.
Examination of insurance companies. '10 (D) c. 248 p. O. $3. Insurance Press.

Wolfe, T: Jefferson, ed.
Hist. of Sullivan County, Ind.; closing of the first century's hist. of the county, and showing the growth of its people, institutions and wealth. 2 v. '09, [1910.] (N) il. pors. 4°. Lewis Pub.

Wolfe & McKenzie.
Book of designs; cont. 98 house plans with figured measurements. '08(Mr21) c. il. plans, obl. O. pap., $2. Wolfe & M.

Wolferstan, Rev. Bertram.
Catholic Church in China from 1860 to 1907. '09, [1910.] (O) 37+470 p. tabs., fold. map, 8°, $1.30 net. Herder.
Bibliography (8 p.).

Wolff, Arth.
Practical accounting. '08(Jl) c. 7-167 p. tabs., 8°. (Not for sale.) Universal Business.

Wolff, Sir H: Drummond.
Rambling recollections. '08(F22) 2 v., il. pors. 8°, *$7.50 net. Macmillan.

Wolff, Julius.
Tannhäuser, minnesinger and knight templar; metrical romance of the third and fourth Crusades; tr. by C: G. Kendall from the German. [New ed. in 1 v.] '10 (D31) c. front. D. $2 net. Badger.

Wolff, Lawrence.
Essentials of medical chemistry, organic and inorganic; cont. also questions of medical physics, chemical philosophy, analytical processes, toxicology, etc., prepared especially for students of medicine. 7th ed., rev. by A. Ferree Witmer. '08, [1909.] (Je) 9-225 p. 12°, (Saunders' question-compend ser.) $1. Saunders.

Wolff, Solomon, comp.
See Louisiana. Constitution.

Wolfville folks. Lewis, A. H. †$1.50. Appleton.

Woll, Fritz Wilhelm.
See Farrington, E: Holyoke.

—, and others.
Handbook for farmers and dairymen. 5th ed., rev. '08(O3) c. il. 16°, $1.50. Wiley.

Wollaston, A. F. R.
From Ruwenzori to the Congo. '08(D12) il. maps, 8°, *$5 net. Dutton.

Wollaston, Sir Arth. Naylor.
Religion of the Koran. '08(Je6) 16°, (Wisdom of the East.) *40 c. net. Dutton.

—, comp. Tales within tales; adapt. from the Fables of Pilpai. '09((Ap17) 8°, (Romance of the East ser.) *$1 net. Dutton.

Wollaston, G: Hyde, comp.
Englishman in Italy; being a collection of verses written by some of those who have loved Italy. '09(Ag14) 8°, *$1.75 net. Oxford Univ.

Wollopors (The). Hare, A. 50 c. Saalfield.

Wollstonecraft, Mary.
See Godwin, *Mrs.* Mary Wollstonecraft.

Wolseley, Hon. Frances Garnet.
Gardening for women. '08(My16) O. *$1.75 net. Cassell.

Wolverine (The). Lawrence, A. L. †75 c. Little, B. & Co.

Wolves (The). Watson, R. A. 10 c. Kerr.

WOMAN.
Abbott, E. Women in industry. **$2 net. Appleton.
Abbott, L. Home builder. **75 c. net. Houghton M.
Blake, E. C. Great moments in a woman's life. 75 c. Forbes.
Blandin, *Mrs.* I. M. E. J. Hist. of the higher education of women in the South prior to 1860. *$3 net. Neale.
Bleackley, H. W: Ladies fair and frail. *$5 net. Lane.
Blei, F. Powder puff; ladies' breviary. *$1.25 net. Duffield.
Boulting, T: Woman in Italy. $4 net. Brentano's.
Brandeis, L: D., *and* Goldmark, J. Women in industry: decision of U. S. Sup. ct. in Curt Muller vs. State of Oregon, upholding constitutionality of ten hour law for women. gratis. L: D. Brandeis.
Brown, H. The wife: her book. **$1 net. Jacobs.
Burrage, W. L. Gynecological diagnosis. $6. Appleton.
Butler, E. B. Women and the trades. *$1.50 net. Charities Pub.
Creighton, *Mrs.* L. Some famous women. 50 c. Longmans.

WOMAN.—*Continued.*
Cromwell, J: H. American business woman. $2 net. Putnam.
Daffan, K. Woman in history. *$2 net. Neale.
Davies, E. Thoughts on some questions rel. to women, 1860-1908. $1.25 net. Macmillan.
Del Lungo, I. Women of Florence. *$2.25 net. Doubleday, P.
Didier, E. L. Way to win her. 10 c. Am. Press.
Dole, C: F. Noble womanhood. $1. Caldwell.
Dorr, *Mrs.* R. C. What eight million women want. $2 net. Small.
Downes, L. New democracy. $2. Sherman, F.
Drake, *Mrs.* E. F. A. What a woman of forty-five should know—What a young wife ought to know. ea., *$1 net. Vir Pub.
Folk, M. F. Heart thoughts: papers to be read at women's meetings. **75 c. net. Am. Bapt.
Gallichan, W. M. Modern woman and how to manage her. $1.50 net. Lane.
Graham, H. Group of Scottish women. *$3.50 net. Duffield.
Hale, P. L. Great portraits: women. $1.50. Bates & G.
Hamel, F. Fair women at Fontainbleau. *$3.50 net. Brentano's.
Hart, G. Woman and the race. $1. Ariel.
Harvey, G: B. M. Women, etc. **$1 net. Harper.
Hegyessy, J. Must women suffer everlastingly? $2.50. J. Hegyessy.
Holtzclaw, W: J. Women of to-day. *75 c. net. Bapt. Bk.
Hubbard, *Mrs.* A. M. Woman's work. $5-$25. Roycrofters.
Hubbard, E. Little journeys to the homes of famous women. (Add. pubs. for price.) Roycrofters.
Hume-Griffith, *Mrs.* M. E. *and* A. Behind the veil in Persia and Turkish Arabia. *$3.50 net. Lippincott.
Illinois. Legal rights of married women. F: R. Young.
Jackson, *Mrs.* G. E. S. Dawn of womanhood. *$1.25 net. Revell.
Johnston, R. E. Mission of woman. 40 c. Longmans.
Keith, M. C. How to take care of a wife. 50 c. Keith & G.
Kisch, E. H. Sexual life of woman in its physiological, pathological and hygienic aspects. $5. Rebman.
Latimer, C. W. Girl and woman. **$2 net. Appleton.
Lovely woman; pictured by famous American artists. $2.50. Bobbs-M.
Lucas, E. V., *ed.* Ladies pageant: [selections in verse and prose.] **$1.25 net. Macmillan.
MacLean, A. M. Wage-earning women. $1.25 net. Macmillan.
Mayne, E. C. Enchanters of men; 24 studies of fascinating women. *$3.50 net. Jacobs.

WOMAN.—*Continued.*

Mitchell, J: K. Self help for nervous women. **$1 net. Lippincott.

Mulliner, G. S. New York laws of interest to women. 25 c. G. S. Mulliner.

Olin, *Mrs.* H. M. R. Women of a state university. **$1.50 net. Putnam.

Overman, D: R. Womanhood; or, the physical life of maiden, wife and mother. $2. N. D. Thompson.

Penrose, C: B. Text-book of diseases of women. *$3.75 net. Saunders.

Putnam, *Mrs.* E. J. S. The lady. $2.50 net. Sturgis & W.

Reich, E. Woman through the ages. *$7 net. Dutton.

Richardson, A. S. Girl who earns her own living. *$1 net. B. W. Dodge.

Richardson, B. J. Woman who spends. *$1 net. Whitcomb.

Smith, F. E. Woman, the eternal question. 35 c. Chr. Witness.

Staley, E. Famous women of Florence. $3.50. Scribner.

Talbot, M. Education of women. $1.25 net. Univ. of Chic.

Talmey, B. S. Woman; treatise on the normal and pathological emotions of feminine love. $3. Practitioners' Pub.

Trowbridge, W. R. H. Seven splendid sinners. *$4.50 net. Brentano's.

United Confederate Veterans, Arkansas Division. Confederate women of Arkansas in the Civil War. $1. J. Kellogg.

United States. *Dept. of Commerce and Labor. Bureau of Labor.* Woman and child wage-earners in Great Britain.

Wallis-Chapman, A. B. *and* M. Status of woman under English law. *75 c. net. Dutton.

Wentworth, F. H. Woman's portion. 10 c. Socialist Lit. Co.

Wheeler, E. R. Famous blue-stockings. $4 net. Lane.

Woman's dict. and encyclop. $3. Anderson Pub. Co.

Woman's Educational and Industrial Union, Boston. *Dept. of Research.* Studies in economic relations of women. $1.20 net; pap., 60 c. net. Longmans.

Wyzewa, T. de. Some women, loving or luckless. *$2.50 net. Lane.

See also Abortion;—Actors and actresses;—Athletics;—Authors;—Beauty (*personal*);—Biography;—Business;—Celibacy; — Children;— Costume;—Divorce; — Domestic economy; — Domestic relations; — Etiquette; — Eugenics; — Family;—Generative organs; — Girls; — Gynecology;—Hygiene; — Hysteria; — International Council of Women;—Marriage;—Midwifery;—Missions and missionaries; — Mormonism; — Mothers;—Needlework;—Nunneries; — Nurses and nursing;—Painters and paintings;—Pregnancy;—Prostitution; — Saints; — Sex;—Suffrage;—Tailoring; — Vocations; — Young people.

Woman and the car. Levitt, D. *$1 net. Lane.

Woman and the sword. Lorraine, R. 75 c. McClurg.

Woman at bay. Aleramo, S., *pseud.* †$1.50. Putnam.

Woman for mayor. Winslow, H. M. $1.50. Reilly & B.

Woman herself. '09(Je) c. 261 p. D. $1.50. Stuyvesant Press.

Woman (A) in Canada. Cran, *Mrs.* G: $3 net. Lippincott.

Woman in question. Scott, J: R. †$1.50. Lippincott.

Woman in white. *See* Collins, Wilkie.

Woman of Corinth. Hagedorn, H. **$1 net. Houghton M.

Woman of uncertain age. Berry, M. A. $1.50. Stuyvesant Press.

Woman of war. Agnus, F. (Add. author for price.) F. Agnus.

Woman pays. Ladd, F. P. $1.50. M. Kennerley.

Woman suffrage. '09(Je12) D. (Univ. of Wis. bull.) pap., gratis. Univ. of Wis.

Woman (The), the man and the monster. Dawe, W. C. $1.50. Stuyvesant Press.

Woman who never did wrong. Conway, K. E. 75 c. T: J. Flynn.

WOMANHOOD.
See Woman.

Woman's answer to Roosevelt. Lusk, *Mrs.* A. F. 75 c. Commercial Pr. Ho.

Woman's cause. Norton, C. 50 c.; $1. Caldwell.

Woman's cause. Norton, C. **75 c. net. Estes.

WOMAN'S CHRISTIAN TEMPERANCE UNION, Salem, N. J.

Van Meter, H. F., *comp. and ed.* First quarter century of the Woman's Christian Temperance Union, Salem, N. J. gratis. H. F. Van Meter.

Woman's dict. and encyclop.; written, comp. and ed. by eminent authorities; contributors: Mrs. S. T. Rorer, Fannie Merritt Farmer, [and others.] '10(F19) c. il. 8°, $3. Anderson Pub. Co.

Woman's Educational and Industrial Union, Boston. *Dept. of Research.* Studies in economic relations of women. v. 1, Vocations for the trained woman; ed. by Agnes F. Perkins. '10(Je18) c. O. $1.20 net; pap., 60 c. net. Longmans.

Woman's guide to Paris. Ivimy, A. M. $1.25 net. Brentano's.

Woman's impressions of the Philippines. Fee, M. H. $1.50 net. McClurg.

"Woman's kingdom." Soulsby, L. H. M. 5 c. net. Longmans.

WOMAN'S SUFFRAGE.
See Suffrage.

Woman's way. *See* Somerville, C.

Woman's way through Labrador. Hubbard, L. B. **$1.50 net. McClure.

Woman's work in English fiction. Whitmore, C. H. $1.25 net. Putnam.

Woman's world cook book. Howland, M. R. 10 c. Currier Pub.

Women and other women. Hawthorne, H. $1.20. Duffield.

Women and wisdom of Japan. Kaibara, E. 40 c. Dutton.

Women as letter-writers. Ingpen, A. M., *comp. and ed.* $1.25 net. Baker & T.

Women Napoleon loved. Hopkins, T. $4.50 net. Little, B. & Co.

Women of all nations. Joyce, T. A., *ed.* In 24 pts. ea., 25 c. Cassell.

Women of the southern confederacy during the war 1861-5; original historic incidents of their heroism, suffering and devotion; published in "Our women in the war" supplements to leading newspapers. In 2 v. '08(D5) il. 4°, ea., $25. C. I. Walker.
Women stenographers. Chase, F. N. 40 c. F. N. Chase.
Women's eyes. Ryder, A. W: $1 net. A. M. Robertson.
Womer, Rev. Parley Paul.
Relation of healing to law; with answers to questions by C. Eug. Riggs and A. W. Dunning, M.D., and a chapter on psychotherapy by Isador H. Coriat, M.D. '09 (Jl3) c. D. $1.25. Magnum Bonum.
Valid religion for the times; study of the central truths of spiritual religion; with foreword by Washington Gladden. '10 (O8) 12°, $1. B'way Pub.
Won in the ninth. Mathewson, C. $1. Bodmer.
"Wonder, William," pseud.
See Kirwan, T:
WONDER.
See **Psychology.**
Wonder book. *See* Hawthorne, Nathaniel.
Wonder book. *See* Stokes wonder book.
Wonder book of birds and beasts. Darton, F. J. H. $1.50. Stokes.
Wonder book of light. Houston, E. J. **$1.50 net. Stokes.
Wonder book of magnetism. Houston, E. J. **$1.50 net. Stokes.
Wonder book of the atmosphere. Houston, E. J. **$1.50 net. Stokes.
Wonder books of science. *See* Houston, Edn. Ja.
Wonder-child. Turner, E. $1.50. Saalfield.
Wonder lib. il. 12°. Lippincott.
—Williams. Wonders of the modern railway. 75 c.
Wonder of his gracious works. Park, J: E. *$1 net. Pilgrim Press.
Wonder stories from the Mabinogions. Brooks, E: †$1.25. Penn Pub. Co.
Wonder-working providence. Johnson, E: $3 net. Scribner.
Wonderful Christmas in Pumpkin Delight Lane. Prichard, S. J. $1.25. Tuttle, M. & T.
Wonderful house that Jack has. Millard, C. N. *50 c. net. Macmillan.
Wonderful isles. Hamer, S. H. $1.25. Estes.
Wonderful little lives. Schwartz, J. A. $1.50. Little, B. & Co.
Wonderful story of life and death. Boyer, M. G. $1.50. Lutheran Pub.
Wonderland of stamps. Burroughs, W: D. $1.50. Stokes.
Wonders of animal ingenuity. Coupin, H. E. V. 75 c. Lippincott.
Wonders of Asiatic exploration. Williams, A. 75 c. Lippincott.
Wonders of life. Lyon, I. L. R. $1. Fenno.
Wonders of mechanical ingenuity. Williams, A. 75 c. Lippincott.
Wonders of physical science. Albe, E. E. F. d'. 50 c. net. Macmillan.
Wonders of the golden West. Van Dine, E. D. $1. J. S. Ogilvie.
Wonders of the insect world. Selous, E. 75 c. Lippincott.
Wonders of the modern railway. Williams, A. 75 c. Lippincott.
Wonders of the plant world. Elliott, G: F. S. 75 c. Lippincott.
Wonders of the universe. Meagher, J. L. $1. Chr. Press.
Wonders of the zoo. Gask, L. $1.25. Dodge.
Wood, Alice Ida Perry.
Stage hist. of Shakespeare's King Richard the Third. '09(O16) 8°, (Columbia Univ. studies in English.) *$1.25 net. Lemcke.
Wood, Mrs. Annie E.
Revival of the gifts of healing by a churchwoman. '10(D31) c. 8°, $1.25. Judd & D.
Wood, Arth. A., comp.
Luther Sisson of Easton, Mass.; his ancestry and descendants. '09, [1910.] (Ag) 13 p. 12°, 50 c. A. A. Wood.
Wood, A: Trew and Bertram Roy.
Ribbon roads; motor tour abroad. '10 (N12) c. il. map, O. $2.50 net. Putnam.
Wood, Bertram Roy.
See Wood, A: Trew.
Wood, Casey Albert.
System of ophthalmic therapeutics; being a complete work on the non-operative treatment, incl. the prophylaxis, of diseases of the eye. '09(My) c. 926 p. il. 8°, subs., $7. Cleveland Press.
—, **and Woodruff, T: Adams.**
Commoner diseases of the eye, how to detect and treat them. 3d ed., enl. and improved, with index. '08(Ja11) il. 8°, *$2.50 net. Chic. Med. Bk.
—, **Andrews, Alb. H:, and Head, Gustavus P., eds.**
Eye, ear, nose and throat. '10(Jl) 367 p. il. 12°, (Pract. medicine ser.; ser. 1910.) $1.50. Year Bk.
Wood, Mrs. Edith Elmer.
Oberland châlet. '10(D17) c. il. O. $2 net, boxed. Wessels & B.
Wood, Eric.
Famous voyages of the great discoverers. '10(S17) il. O. $1.50. Crowell.
Wood, Eug.
Folks back home. '08(Mr14) c. D. †$1.50. McClure.
Wood, Ezra Morgan, D.D.
Peerless orator, the Rev. Matthew Simpson, D.D., bishop of the Methodist Episcopal Church. '09(Jl31) c. il. pors. D. $1.50. Pittsburgh.
Wood, Frances Ann.
Earliest years at Vassar; personal recollections. '09(Je19) il. pors. D. 50 c. F. A. Wood.
Wood, Fs. Carter.
Chemical and microscopical diagnosis. 2d ed. '09(O) 24+767 p. il. 8°, $5. Appleton.
Wood, Harry Earl.
Intellectual pup: extracts from his diary. '09(F6) c. il. D. bds., 50 c. H. Wood.
Wood, Harry Wellington.
Winning men one by one. '08(Mr21) c. D. *50 c. net. S. S. Times.
—, **comp.** Golden words fitly spoken. '10 (D10) c. por. D. $1.50 net. Lippincott.

Wood, H:
New old healing. '08(Je20) c. D. **$1.20 net. Lothrop, L. & S.

Wood, H: Alex. Wise.
Money hunger: brief study of commercial immorality in the United States. '08 (Ja18) D. bds., **$1 net. Putnam.

Wood, H: Cleveland.
Night riders. '08(Ap18) c. il. D. 75 c.; pap., 25 c. Laird.

Wood, Rev. Hermon Gaylord.
Ideal metrology in nature, art, religion and history. '09(Jl3) c. il. O. $1.50. H. G. Wood.

Wood, Horatio Curtis.
Therapeutics: its principles and practice; thoroughly rev. and rewritten by Horatio C. Wood, jr. 14th ed. '08(D19) c. il. 8°, *$5 net; shp., *$6 net. Lippincott.

Wood, Howard Athons.
Burlington, [Wis.,] its early hist., growth and progress; manufacturing center. '08, [1909.] (Mr) c. 44-64 p. il. 8°, 35 c. H. A. Wood.

Wood, Ja.
Woods' Iowa Justice's form book and constable's guide. 5th ed., rev. and enl. by A. G. Bush. '09(O) c. O. shp. (Add. pubs. for price.) Fidlar & Co.

Wood, J: N: Price.
Travel and sport in Turkestan. '10(Mr26) il. map, O. *$3.50 special net. Appleton.

Wood, Joshua Gibson.
Fallacies of Christian science. '08(Ag29) c. 8°, pap., $1. J. G. Wood.

Wood, Katharine Hill.
See Laney, Fs. Baker.

WOOD, Lawson.
Johnson, A. E. Lawson Wood. $1.75 net. Macmillan.

Wood, Lenna.
Lennawood's monologues. '09(Ag21) D. bds., $1. Holliswood.

Wood, Mrs. Martha Buckingham.
Trip to the Land of the Midnight Sun; narrative of personal experiences. '10 (N5) c. il. pors. O. $2 net. Brandu's.

Wood, Mary Buell.
Just boys; jangles from the choir room. '09(S11) c. il. D. **75 c. net. Revell.

Wood, Rob. Williams.
Animal analogues: verses. '08(O17) c. il. D. **50 c. net. P. Elder.

Wood, Rev. Sumner Gilbert.
Taverns and turnpikes of Blandford, 1733-1833. '08(D26) c. il. map, O. *$2 net. S. G. Wood.

Wood, T. Martin.
Sargent. '10(Jl2) col. il. 8°, (Masterpieces in colour.) bds., 65 c. net; leath., $1.50 net. Stokes.
Whistler. '09(Ap17) il. O. (Masterpieces in colour.) bds., *65 c. net. Stokes.

Wood, T:
Pract. grammar and composition. '10(D10) c. 12°, 70 c. Appleton.

Wood, Wa.
Corner in Spain; introd. by Martin Hume. '10(N19) il. (partly col.) map, 12°, $2 net. Pott.
Revenge of Gilbert Strange. '08(D12) front. D. $1.50. Cassell.
Secret paper. '09, [1910.] (Ja) il. 12°, $1.50. Cassell.

Wood, Warren.
Tragedy of the deserted isle: chronicle of the Burr and Blennerhassett conspiracy. '09(Je12) c. il. pors. 12°, $1.50. C. M. Clark.

Wood, W: Wallace.
Walschaert locomotive valve gear. '09(D) c. 200 p. 12°, $1.50. Henley.
—, **and Westinghouse, E. T.**
An air brake instruction pocket book, nos. 5 and 6. '09(D) c. il. 12°, $2. Henley.
See also Fowler, G: Little.

Wood-Allen, Mrs. Mary, M.D.
What a young girl ought to know. '10 (Je11) 16°, (Self and sex ser.) $1. Vir Pub.
Making the best of our children. 1st ser.; 2d ser. '09(N6) c. D. ea., $1 net. McClurg.

Wood-Seys, Roland Alex.
Sappho in Boston. '08(N14) c. front. D. †$1.50. Moffat.

WOOD.
Baterden, J. R. Timber. *$2 net. Van Nostrand.
Boulger, G: S. Wood: manual of the natural and industrial applications of the timbers of commerce. $4.20. Longmans.
Kellogg, R. S. Timber supply of the U. S. U. S., Supt. of Docs.
Maxwell, H. Study of the Mass. wood-using industries. F. W. Rane.
Pierson, A. H. Consumption of firewood in the United States. Gov. Pr. Off.
Rowe, S: M. Hdbk. of timber preservation. $5. S: M. Rowe.
Sherfesse, W: F. Primer of wood preservation. 5 c.—Wood preservation in the United States. Gov. Pr. Off.
Snow, C: H: Principal species of wood. $3.50. Wiley.
Warren, W: H: Engineering construction in steel and timber. $5 net. Longmans.
Willis, C. P. Preservative treatment of farm timbers. U. S., Supt. of Docs.
See also Floors;—Fungi.

Wood and garden. Jekyell, G. $2 net. Longmans.

WOOD-CARVING.
Bond, F. Wood carvings in English churches. v. 1. $2.50. Oxford Univ.
Hasluck, P. N., *ed.* Wood carving. $3. McKay.
See also Decoration and ornament;—Furniture;—Sloyd;—Woodwork.

WOOD DISTILLING.
Harper, W. B: Utilization of wood waste by distillation. $3. St. L. Lumberman.

Wood finishing and cabinet work. Brace, G: M. 50 c. G: M. Brace.
Wood turning. Ross, G: A. $1. Ginn.
Wood wanderings. Packard, W. $1.20 net. Small.

WOOD WASTE.
See Wood distilling.

Wood worker ser. il. 12°, 25 c. Spon.
—Pract. upholstery.
—Simple lessons in wood turning.
—Violin making and adjusting.
—Window making for carpenters and joiners.

Woodberry, G: E:
Inspiration of poetry. '10(Mr5) c. D. *$1.25 net. Macmillan.
Life of Edgar Allan Poe; incl. his correspondence with men of letters. 2 v. [New ed., rewritten.] '09(Ap3) il. pors. facsims., 4°, **$5 net; bds., **$7 net. Houghton M.

Woodbine, G: E.
Four thirteenth century law tracts; thesis presented to the faculty of the Graduate School of Yale University in candidacy for the degree of doctor of philosophy. '10(Je25) c. O. $1.20 net. Yale Univ.

Woodbridge, F: Ja. Eug.
Metaphysics: [a lecture.] '08(N21) c. 8°, pap. (Add. pubs. for price.) Columbia Univ.
See also Dewey, J:

Woodbridge, S: Homer.
Air and the hospital. '09(O2) 8°, 20 c. A. D. Maclachlan.
Pure air as an investment. [1910.] (N) 23 p. il. 8°, 15 c. A. D. Maclachlan.

Woodburn, Ja. Alb., and Moran, T: Fs.
Elementary American hist. and government. '10(Jl9) c. il. por. maps, O. $1 net. Longmans.

Woodbury, Mrs. C. J.
See Woodbury, Lucia Prudence Hall.

Woodbury, Lucia Prudence Hall, ["Mrs. C. J. Woodbury."]
Potato child and others. '10(Ag13) c. front. 12°, 25 c. P. Elder.

Woodbury, Mary Hale.
Pract. business hints. '10(N5) c. 8°, $1.50. Newcomb.

Woodbury, Sarah Eliza.
Dramatization in the grammar grades. '09 (Jl) c. 49 p. il. 12°, 30 c. S. E. Woodbury.

WOODCOCK.
Davis, E. W. Woodcock shooting. (Priv. pr.) De Vinne.

Woodford, A. Louise.
Practical system in folding, cutting and modeling, etc. '08, [1909.] (My) 21 p. il. 12°, 75 c. B'way Pub.

WOODFORD COUNTY, Ill.
Moore, R. L. Hist. of Woodford County. $1. R. L. Moore.

Woodhouse, F: W.
Churches of Coventry. '09(D4) il. 12°, (Bell's cathedral ser.) *60 c. net. Macmillan.

Woodhouse, S. C.
Dictionary of classical mythology. '08(F22) 32°, (Miniature reference lib.) leath., 50 c. Dutton.

Woodhull, Alfr. Alex., M.D.
Military hygiene for officers of the line. 4th ed., rewritten and greatly enl. '09 (O30) c. O. **$1.50 net. Wiley.

Woodhull, J: Fs.
How the public will solve our problems of science teaching; paper read before the Wis. State Teachers' Association, Nov. 12, 1908. '09(My22) il. O. pap., gratis. C: P. Cary.

Woodman, Mrs. Abby Johnson.
Reminiscences of John Greenleaf Whittier's life at Oak Knoll, Danvers, Mass.; read before the Essex Institute on the 100th anniversary of the birth of John Greenleaf Whittier, with a list of the first editions, portraits, engravings, manuscripts, and personal relics of John Greenleaf Whittier, exhibited at the Essex Institute December 17, 1907, to January 31, 1908. '08(Ap18) c. 8°, bds., *$1 net. Essex Inst.

Woodman, Albert Stanton.
Treatise on the law of trustees in bankruptcy; with the national bankruptcy act of 1898 as amended, the general orders and the official forms. '09(My) c. 91+1103 p. O. $6.50. Little, B. & Co.

Woodman, Alpheus G.
See Richards, Ellen Henrietta Swallow.

Woodman, Hannah Rea.
Open road; book of outcast verse. '10 (D10) c. 12°, $1.25 net. H. R. Woodman.
Tumbleweed: [poems.] '09(Je19) c. D. $1. H. R. Woodman.

Woodman, R. Huntington, ed.
See Ives, C: Taylor, *ed.*

WOODMEN OF THE WORLD.
Butler, L. C. Unveiling tributes. $1. La. Distrib. Co.

Woodrow, Herbert.
Quantitative study of rhythm: the effect of variations in intensity, rate and duration. '09(Ag7) tabs., O. (Archives of psychology.) pap., 60 c. Science Pr., (N. Y.)

Woodrow, Nancy Mann Waddel, [Mrs. Wilson Woodrow.]
The beauty. '10(Mr26) c. il. D. †$1.50. Bobbs-M.
Silver butterfly. '08(O17) c. il. D. †$1.50. Bobbs-M.

Woodruff, C: E:
Expansion of races. '09(N) c. 11+495 p. tabs., 8°, $4. Rebman.

Woodruff, Clinton Rogers.
The city: as it is and is to be; published for the Social Service Commission of the Northern Baptist Convention. '10 (Je11) c. 8°, (Social service ser.) 20 c. Am. Bapt.
—, ed. Billboard nuisance. '08, [1909.] (Je) 48 p. 12°, (American Civic Association; Dept. of Nuisances pubs.) pap., gratis. Am. Civic League.

Woodruff, Fs. Eben.
Woodruffs of New Jersey who came from Fordwich, Kent, England, by way of Lynn, Massachusetts, and Southampton, Long Island; revised and enlarged from "A branch of the Woodruff stock." '09 (Je19) c. il. pors. maps, 8°, **$5 net. Grafton Press.

Woodruff, Ja. Albert.
Applied principles of field fortification for line officers. '09(My1) c. fold. plan, O. $1. Staff Coll.

Woodruff, Loura Bayne.
Reminiscences of Ennius in Silius Italicus. '10(Ag13) 8°, (Univ. of Mich. studies; Humanistic ser.) pap., 40 c. net. Macmillan.

Woodruff, T: Adams.
See Wood, Casey Albert.

Woodruff, W. E., ed.
See Pennsylvania. Luzerne [Co.] legal register repts.

WOODRUFF, Wilford.
Cowley, M. F., *ed.* Wilford Woodruff. $3.50. Deseret News.

Woodruff, W: Lawrence, M.D.
Therapeutics of light vibration. '08(Ag29) c. 16°, (Vibration ser., v. 2.) *$1.50 net. J. F. Elwell.

WOODRUFF FAMILY.
See Genealogies.

Woods, C. A.
"Intelligent labor"; address at the Industrial Conference of the Pee Dee country held at Florence, S. C., Nov. 7 and 8, 1909. '09, [1910.] (Ap) 18 p. 8°. (Add. pubs. for price.) State Co.

Woods, Clinton Edg.
Industrial organization, systematization and accounting. '09(Jl) c. 3 v., charts, forms, f°, $24. Woods.
Practical cost accounting. 2 v. '08(N) $2.50. Universal Business.
Reports on industrial organization, systematization and accounting. In 12 pts. pts. 1 and 2. '08(Ag1) c. charts, F. pap., per set, $15. C. E. Woods.

Woods, Rev. Edg.
History of Albemarle County, Virginia. '09(F13) $2. E. Woods.

Woods, H. C.
Washed by four seas: an English officer's travels in the Near East; with an introd. by Sir Martin Conway. '09(Ag21) il. 8°, *$2.50 net. Wessels.

Woods, H: Ernest.
Woods family of Groton, Mass.; record of 6 generations priv. repr. from v. 64 New England Historical and Genealogical Register. '10(Jl) 39 p. O. pap. (Priv. pr.) H: E. Woods.

Woods, Prince T.
Facts about white diarrhœa; practical methods of prevention and treatment; how to stop losses and reduce the mortality in small chicks; simple, safe and sure plan of successful chick rearing. '08, [1909.] (F) c. 28 p. 8°, pap., $1. P. T. Woods.
Poultryman's formulary; reliable, successful, tested recipes for ready-mixed grain foods; how to prepare balanced rations for poultry young and old. '08, [1909.] (F) c. 48 p. 8°, pap., $1. P. T. Woods.

Woods, R. J.
Strength and elasticity of structural members. 2d ed. '08(N14) figs. O. *$3.50 net. Longmans.
Theory of structures. '09(S11) figs. O. *$3 net. Longmans.

Woods, S: D.
Lights and shadows of life on the Pacific coast. '10(D24) c. por. O. $1.20 net. Funk.

WOODS FAMILY.
See Genealogies: Miller, W. H.;—Woods, H: E.

Woodsmen of the west. Grainger, M. A. $2.50. Longmans.

Woodstock. *See* Scott, *Sir* Wa.

Woodward, C. J.
A B C of five-figure logarithms for general use. 2d ed. '09(D18) 12°, $1.25. Spon.

Woodward, Horace Bolingbroke.
Geology of water-supply. '10(O22) D. (Arnold's geological ser.) $2.50. Longmans.
History of the Geological Society of London. '08(Je13) il. pors. O. *$2.60 net. Longmans.

Woodward, Jos. T.
Historic record and complete biographic roster, 21st Maine Volunteers. '08 (My16) pors. map, 8°, $2; hf. shp., $2.50. J. T. Woodward.

Woodward, Marcus.
See Jones, Owen.

WOODWORK.
Allen, E. G. Manual training for common schools; organized course in wood-working. $1. Scribner.
Baily, J. T:, *and* Pollitt, S. Woodwork for schools. 75 c. Manual Arts.
Binns, C: L., *and* Marsden, R. E. Principles of educational woodwork. $1.50 net. Dutton.
Burns, C. L., *and* Marsden, R. E. Principles of educational woodwork. *$1.50 net. Dutton.
Griffith, I. S: Essentials of woodworking. $1; $1.25. Manual Arts.
Johnson, B. W. Coping saw work. pap., 20 c. Manual Arts.
Noyes, W: Handwork in wood. $2. Manual Arts.
Park, J. C. Educational woodworking for home and school. *$1 net. Macmillan.
Seaton, G: A. Selected shop problems. 20 c. Manual Arts.
Stanley universal plane, for moulding, matching, ploughing, etc. 25 c. Spon.
See also Carpentry;—Manual training;—Pattern-making;—Sloyd;—Tools; — Turning; — Wood-carving.

Woodworth, Jos. Vincent.
Drop forging, die sinking, and machine forming of steel. '10(D17) il. $2.50. Henley.
Gages and gaging systems: design, construction and use of tools, methods and processes involved. '08(My9) c. il. diagrs., 8°, $2. Hill Pub.

Woodworth, Rob. Sessions.
Psychology: [a lecture.] '08(N21) c. 8°, pap., 25 c. net. Columbia Univ.

Wooing of Calvin Parks. Richards, *Mrs.* L. E. H. †1.25. Estes.

Wooings in rusticity. Adcock, J. P. $1.50. Adcock.

WOOL.
Bowman, F. H. Structure of the wool fibre. *$2.60 net. Macmillan.
Justice, T. Tariff: wool and wool goods. U. S., Supt. of Docs.
Shaw, J. T. Wool trade of the U. S. U. S., Supt. of Docs.

WOOL.—*Continued.*
United States. Wool and manufacture of wool; extract from the special rept. no. 13, made in May, 1866, of the United States Revenue Commission, on wool and manufactures of wool. '10(Jl) 156 p. 8°. Gov. Pr. Off.

Wright, C. W. Wool-growing and the tariff. $2 net. Houghton M.

See also Woolen spinning.

Woolard, S: Fs., comp.
Dear old father. [1910.] (Jl) c. 8°, 50 c. Goldsmith-W.

Glorious mother. '09(O9) c. nar. O. pap., *50 c. net; limp leath., *$1.25 net, boxed. Goldsmith-W.

Good fellowship. '09(O9) c. T. pap., *50 c. net; limp leath., *$1 net, boxed. Goldsmith-W.

Pictures of memory; compilation. '09(O) c. 61 p. il. 8°, *50 c. net; leath., *$1.25 net. Goldsmith-W.

—, ed. Beauties of friendship. '09(O9) c. il. nar. O. pap., *50 c. net; limp leath., *$1.25 net, boxed. Goldsmith-W.

Wooldridge, Clifton Rodman.
Twenty years a detective in the wickedest city in the world: [Chicago.] '08(D) c. 11+27-608 p. il. por. f°, $2; pap., 75 c. C. R. Wooldridge.

WOOLEN SPINNING.
Collins, M. Woolen and worsted spinning. $3. Am. Sch. Corr.

Priestman, H. Principles of woollen spinning. $2.50. Longmans.

Textile World Record. Kinks for wool and worsted finishers.—Kinks for wool and worsted superintendents. ea., 75 c. Lord & N.

Timmermann, J: F. Woolen and worsted finishing. $3. Am. Sch. Corr.

See also Textile fabrics.

Woolf, Bella Sidney.
Twins in Ceylon. '10(S17) il. D. 75 c. Estes.

Woollatt, G: H:
Laboratory arts: hdbk. dealing with materials and tools used in the construction, adjustment, and repair of scientific instruments. '08(S5) il. D. *$1 net. Longmans.

Woollen, W: Watson, and Thornton, W: Wheeler.
Intoxicating liquors; the law rel. to the traffic in intoxicating liquors and drunkenness. v. 1, 2. '10(Jl) c. O. $13.50. W. H. Anderson.

Woolley, E: Mott.
Winning ten. '10(N5) c. D. $1.50. Appleton.

Woolley, Edn. Campbell.
Mechanics of writing; compendium of rules regarding manuscript-arrangement, spelling, the compounding of words, abbreviations, the representation of numbers, syllabication, the use of capitals, the use of italics, punctuation, and paragraphing. '09(D18) c. facsim., 12°, $1. Heath.

Woolly horse. Bacon, A. S. $1. A. S. Bacon.

Woolman, J:
Journal, and other papers. '10(Ap30) 16°, (Everyman's lib.) 35 c. net; leath., 70 c. net. Dutton.

Journal; ed. and with introd. by J. G. Whittier. '09, [1910.] (F) 12°, $1. Houghton M.

Woolman, Mrs. Mary Schenck.
Making of a trade school. '10(Jl2) c. D. pap., 50 c. net. Whitcomb & B.

Sewing course. 4th ed., rev. '08(S) 136 p. il. 8°, *$1.50 net; interleaved, hf. leath., *$3.50 net. Fernald.

Trade schools and culture. '09(S) 181-187 p. 8°, pap., 5 c. Manhattan Trade.

Woolsey, C. M.
Hist. of the town of Marlborough, Ulster Co., N. Y., from its earliest discovery. '08(N) c. 471 p. il. pors. maps, facsims., 8°, $4. C. M. Woolsey.

Woolsey, G:, M.D.
Applied surgical anatomy regionally presented. 2d ed. '08(O31) c. il. 8°, *$4.50 net. Lea.

Woolsey, J: Martin.
Original Garden of Eden discovered and the final solution of the mystery of the woman, the tree and the serpent; being the lunar theory of mythology. '10(O15) c. O. $1.50. J: M. Woolsey.

Woolston, Howard Brown.
Study of the population of Manhattanville. '09(Jl17) c. O. (Columbia Univ. studies in history, economics and public law.) pap., $1.25. Longmans.

Woolwine, T: Lee.
In the valley of the shadows. '09(F20) c. D. †$1. Doubleday, P.

Wooten, W: Preston.
Provisional battalion of engineers in the Philippines. '10(N) 35 p. 8°, (Occasional papers, Engineer School, U. S. Army.) (Priv. pr.) Engineer Sch.

Wooton, Edn.
Toilet medicine. [1910.] (Mr) *$1 net. W: R. Jenkins.

Formerly published by E. R. Pelton.

Wootton, A. C.
Chronicles of pharmacy. In 2 v. '10 (N19) il. 8°, $6.50. Macmillan.

Worcester, Dean C.
Philippine Islands and their people. '09 (O2) il. 12°, map, *$2 net. Macmillan.

Worcester, Elwood, D.D.
Living word. '08(D26) c. D. **$1.50 net. Moffat.

—, and McComb, S:, D.D.
Christian religion as a healing power; defense and exposition of the Emmanuel Movement. '09(D18) c. D. **$1 net. Moffat.

—, McComb, S:, D.D., and Coriat, Isador H., M.D.
Religion and medicine: [Emanuel Church movement.] '08(Je27) c. D. **$1.50 net. Moffat.

Worcester, Jos. Emerson.
Academic dictionary; new etymological dictionary of the English language. Rev. ed. '09(F20) c. il. 8°, $1.50. Lippincott.

Worcester, Jos. Emerson.—*Continued.*
Lippincott's business and office dict.; new etymological dict. of the English language; prep. upon the basis of the latest ed. of the dict. of Jos. E. Worcester. Rev. ed. [1910.] (D) c. 692 p. il. 8°, $1.50. Lippincott.
Lippincott's correspondence dict.; condensed dict. of the English language; prep. upon the basis of the latest ed. of the dict. of Jos. E. Worcester. Rev. ed. [1910.] (D) c. 395 p. il. 12°, $1. Lippincott.
Lippincott's handy dict.; concise dict. of the English language; pronouncing and defining vocab. of the words in popular use, rewritten and enl. from the orig. ed. [1910.] (D) c. 354 p. il. 16°, 75 c. Lippincott.

Worcester, Rev. W: Loring.
On holy ground: [Palestine.] New ed. in 2 v. '08(D19) c. il. ea., **$1.50 net, boxed. Lippincott.

WORCESTER, England.
Green, S: S. Worcester, England and Worcester, Massachusetts. gratis. S: S. Green.

Worcester, Mass. *School Committee.* Course of study, elementary schools. '09, [1910.] (Ap) 91 p. 8°, gratis. Worcester Sch. Com.

WORCESTER, Mass.
Green, S: S. Worcester, England, and Worcester, Massachusetts. gratis. S: S. Green.
O'Flynn, T: F. Story of Worcester, Mass. $1.50 net. Little, B. & Co.
Worcester, the city of varied industries; an old New England municipality rendered pre-eminent by inventive genius; just a glimpse of its civic life and an epitome of its educational insurance and industrial eminence from 1658 to 1909. [1910.] (Je) 22 p. il. 8°, pap., gratis. Worcester Bd. Trade.

WORCESTER COUNTY, Mass.
Epler, P. H. Master minds at the commonwealth's heart. $2. F. S. Blanchard.
See also Botany.

WORCESTER FREE PUBLIC LIBRARY, Worcester, Mass.
See Green, Samuel Swett.

WORCESTERSHIRE, Eng.
Bradley, A. G. Worcestershire. *$3 net. Macmillan.

Word Hoosier. Dunn, J. P. *50 c. net. Bobbs-M.

Word lessons. Reed, A. 25 c. C: E. Merrill.

Word pictures. Tibbetts, F: $1. Gift Bk.

Word signs made easy. Hardcastle, *Mrs.* M. A. $1. Word Sign.

Worden, C. A.
See Gilbreth, Fk. Bunker.

WORDS.
Barrett, B. S. Book of homonyms. *75 c. net. Pitman.
Lang, A. Origin of terms in human relationship. 40 c. Oxford Univ.
Mead, W: L. How words grow: study of literary style, slang and provincialisms. 50 c. Crowell.

WORDS.—*Continued.*
Morris, J: Organic history of English words. pt. 1, Old English. $1.25. Stechert.
Taylor, I: Words and places. *$1.50 net. Dutton.
Taylor, J. S. Word study in the elem. school. $1. Educ. Pub.
Trendelenburg, A. Contribution to the hist. of the word person. 40 c. Open Court.
Winchell, S: R. Orthography, etymology and punctuation. 60 c. Flanagan.
See also Abbreviations;—Language;—Names (*personal*);—Pronunciation; — Rhetoric; —Spellers; —Spelling;—Zoology;—*also* names of languages.

Words and phrases calendar, 1909-10: definition for each day in the year. '10(F) Tt. (Not for sale.) West Pub.

Words and sentences. Hitchcock, A. M. 35 c. Holt.

Words of consolation. Jones, J: C. $2.75. J: C. Jones.

Words of help series. New ed. for 1909. 47 v. '09(O2) S. ea., hf. cl., 30 c.; full leath., 60 c. Caldwell.

Words of our Lord and Savior. Meissner, *Mme.* de. 25 c. Woodward & L.

Words spoken and written: a course in modern English. *See* Emerson, H: Pendexter.

Wordsworth, W:
Complete poetical works; with an introd. by J: Morley. '09(O2) c. D. (Crowell's thin paper poets.) limp leath., $1.25, boxed; ooze, $1.75, boxed. Crowell.
Intimations of immortality. '08(N21) c. 24°, pap., *40 c. net; bds., *60 c. net; Japan vellum, *$1 net. T: B. Mosher.
Longer poems; note by Ernest Rhys. '08 (Mr7) 16°, (Everyman's lib.) *35 c. net; leath., *70 c. net. Dutton.
Longer poems. '08(O17) 16°, (Best books ser.) leath., *$1 net. Dutton.
Lyrical poems; sel. and arr. by A. T. Quiller-Couch. '08(D19) S. (Select English classics.) 10 c. Oxford Univ.
LXXV sonnets. Riverside Press ed. '10 (D10) sq. 8°, $5 net. (400 copies.) Houghton M.
Shorter poems. '08(O17) 16°, (Best books ser.) leath., *$1 net. Dutton.
Wordsworth calendar; ed. by Albert E. Sims. '09(Ag28) c. por. D. (Chiswick ser.) 60 c.; ooze, $1, boxed. Crowell.
Wordsworth day by day; ed. by A. E. Sims. '10(D) 12°, (Day by day ser.) 60 c.; ooze, $1. Crowell.

—, Dorothy, and others.
Letters of the Wordsworth family from 1787 to 1855; collected and ed. by W: Knight. '08(Mr7) c. 3 v., por. D. *$7.50 net. Ginn.
See also Milton, J:

WORDSWORTH, William.
Gingerich, S. F. Wordsworth: a study in memory and mysticism. $1.20. Mennonite.

Work, Edg. Whitaker.
House of Chimham. '09(D25) c. il. D. 75 c., boxed. Am. Tr.

Work-accidents and the law. Eastman, C. $1.50. Charities' Pub.

Work and habit. Beveridge, A. J. 50 c.: $1. Altemus.

Work and wages. Chapman, S. J: pt. 2. $4. Longmans.
Work and win. Adams, W: T. 50 c. Hurst.
Work and win. Ellis, E: S. $1. Burt.
"Work" handbooks. il. S. 50 c. McKay.
—Hasluck, *ed.* Domestic jobbing.—Tinplate work.
Work of Christ. Forsythe, P: T. $1.50 net. Doran.
Work of the second Hague conference. Scott, J. B. gratis. Assoc. Int. Conciliation.
Work that is play. Gardner, M. 35 c. Flanagan.
Work, wages and profit. Gantt, H: L. $2. Engineering Mag.
Worker and his Bible. Eiselen, F: C. 55 c. Bd. S. S. M. E. Ch.
Worker and his work ser; correspondence course for Sunday school workers. il. 12°. Bd. S. S. M. E. Ch.
—Eiselen. Worker and his Bible. 55 c.
Worker and the state. Dean, A. D. $1.20 net. Century Co.
Workers in American history. Oneal, J. 25 c. J. Oneal.
WORKING CLASSES.
See Labor and laboring classes.
Working drawings and drafting-room kinks. '08(My23) c. il. 8°, (Machinery's reference ser.) pap., 25 c. Indust. Press.
Working faith of the social reformer. Jones, H: $2.40 net. Macmillan.
Working grammar of the English language. Fernald, J. C. **$1.50 net. Funk.
Working lad's clubs. Russell, C: E: B. *$1.50 net. Macmillan.
Working limits for suction gas producers. Flurscheim, A. *50 c. net. Spon.
Working manual of a successful Sunday-school. Laurence, M. *25 c. net. Revell.
WORKING MEN.
See Labor and laboring classes.
Working of the Boston Public Library. Benton, J. H: (Not for sale.) J. H: Benton.
Working people. Overlock, M. G: $2. M. G. Overlock.
Working theology. MacColl, A. **75 c. net. Scribner.
Working together. Bosworth, E: I. 40 c. Y. M. C. A.
WORKINGMAN'S INSURANCE.
See Insurance.
Workingman's view of the Bible. Donaldson, O. F. *$1.20 net. Sherman, F.
Workingman's wife. Harper, O. 25 c. J. S. Ogilvie.
WORKINGMEN.
See Labor and laboring classes.
Workingmen's insurance in Europe. Frankel, L. K. $2.50. Charities Pub.
Workman, Mrs. Fanny Bullock and W: Hunter.
Ice-bound heights of the Mustagh: pioneer exploration and high climbing in the Baltistan Himalaya. '08(My9) il. maps, 8°, *$5 net. Scribner.
Peaks and glaciers of Nun Kun; record of pioneer exploration and mountaineering in the Punjab Himalaya. '10(Mr26) il. map, O. *$4.50 net. Scribner.
Workman, H. B., ed.
See Townsend, W. J., *D.D.*

Workman, Mrs. Helen Chaffee, comp.
Recitations for children. '10(My) c. 96 p. 16°, 35 c. H. C. Workman.
Workman, Mary Christiana Sheedy, ["Mrs. Hanson Workman."]
American singer in Paris: a novel. '08 (D12) c. il. D. $1.20. F. Workman.
Workman, W: Hunter.
See Workman, *Mrs.* Fanny Bullock.
Works management lib. 12°. Engineering Mag.
—Carpenter. Profit making in shop and factory management. $2.
—Church. Production factors in cost accounting and works management. $2.—Proper distribution of expense burden. $1.
—Emerson. Efficiency as a basis for operation and wages. $2.
—Gantt. Work, wages, and profits. $2.
—Prindle. Patents as a factor in manufacturing. $1.
Works of Jesus. Little, E. S. $1.25; 75 c. P. Elder.
Workshop receipts for manufacturers and scientific amateurs. New rev. ed. v. 1, Acetylene lighting-drying. '09(Jl17) il. 12°, *$1.50 net. Spon.
Workshop wrinkles and recipes. Marshall, P. 50 c. Spon.
WORLD.
See Universe.
World a spiritual system. Snowden, J. H: $1.50 net. Macmillan.
World (The) almanac and encyclopedia, 1908. '08(Ja18); 1909. '09(Ja9); 1910. '10(Ja15) D. pap., ea., 25 c. Press Pub.
World an educational unit. Raub, A. D. 25 c. A. D. Raub.
World and Delia. Yorke, C., *pseud.* $1.50. Estes.
World and his wife. Nirdlinger, C: F. *$1 net. M. Kennerley.
World babies. Scantlebury, E. E. *35 c. net. Educ. Pub.
World book of temperance. Crafts, W. F. 75 c.; 35 c. Int. Ref. Bu.
World-call to men of to-day: addresses and proceedings of the Men's Missionary Convention, held in Philadelphia, February 11-13, 1908; ed. by D: McConaughy. '08 (Je20) c. front. O. $1. Presb. Bd.
World corporation. Gillette, K. C. $1. World Corporation.
World I live in. Keller, H. A. $1.20. Century Co.
World in picture ser. il. map, 8°. Macmillan.
—Barnard. British Isles in pictures. 75 c. net.
World in which we live. Meyer, R. J. *$1.50 net. Herder.
World (The) Missonary Conference: report of the Ecumenical Conference held in Edinburgh in 1910. In 9 v. v. 1, Carrying the Gospel; v. 2, The church in the mission field; v. 3, Christian education; v. 4, The missionary message; v. 5, Preparation of missionaries; v. 6, The home base; v. 7, Missions and governments; v. 8, Co-operation and unity; v. 9. History records and addresses. '10(D10) 12°, ea., 75 c. net; per set, $5 net. Revell.

World money. Stone, G: H. $1.25. G: H. Stone.

World of art ser. il. D. McClurg.
—Petrie. Arts and crafts of ancient Egypt. $1.75 net.
—Williams. Arts and crafts of older Spain. 3 v. *$4.50 net.

World of Homer. Lang, A. $2.25 net. Longmans.

World of suckers. Josaphare, L. $1. Danner.

World organization. Bridgman, R. L. 50 c. net. Ginn.

World we live in. Brackett, E: A. $1. Badger.

World-wide encyclopedia and gazetteer; comp. and rev. to date from the leading encyclopedias of the world; ed. by W. H. De Puy and a corps of eminent writers. 12 v. '09(My8) c. il. maps, 8°, $13.50. Chr. Herald.

World-wide Sunday-school work; the official report of the World's sixth Sunday-school convention, held in the City of Washington, U. S. A., May 19-24, 1910; ed. by W: N. Hartshorn, G: W. Penniman, associate ed. [1910.] (N) 8+32, 630 p. il. pors. 8°, $1. W. N. Hartshorn.

Worldly amusements. Hamilton, W: W. **10 c. net. Am. Bapt.

Worldly wisdom from Benjamin Franklin. Franklin, B: $1. Altemus.

Worldly wisdom ser. T. leath., $1, boxed. Altemus.
—Emerson. Worldly wisdom.
—Shakespeare. Worldly wisdom.

World's best books; suggestions for the selection of a home library [by Floyd Truesdell Short.] '10.(F19) c. D. bds., 50 c. Globe-W.

World's Bible auxiliary and beautiful teachings of the Bible; systematic course of Bible study, incl. chapters by Rev. Ja. M. Gray, D.D., an il. Bible commentary by J. W. Buel; also the Bible student's assistant; comp. popular and concise cyclop. of the Bible, self-pronouncing dictionary, concordance of subjects and complete index by Rev. J: Barr, Rev. J. L. Porter, and Rev. M. G. Easton. '10(O22) c. col. front. il. 4°, $8; hf. mor., $10; mor., $12. J. R. Gay.

World's childhood. Banks, L: A. $1.30 net. Funk.

***World's classics.* 16°. Oxford Univ.**
—Austen. Emma. 35 c.
—Brontë. Agnes Grey.—Tenant of Wildfell Hall. ea., 35 c.
—Brown. Horæ subsecivae. 35 c.
—Carlyle. Life of John Sterling. 35 c.—Past and present. 35 c.; 65 c.
—Cervantes. Don Quixote. 2 v. ea., 50 c.; 75 c.
—Coleridge. Poems. 40 c.; 75 c.
—Cowper. Letters. 50 c.; 75 c.
—Eliot. Scenes of clerical life. 40 c.; 75 c.
—Gaskell. North and south. 40 c.; 75 c.—Sylvia's lovers. 35 c. net; 65 c. net.
—Gibbon. Autobiography. 50 c.; 75 c.
—Irving. Chronicles of the Conquest of Granada. 35 c.
—Lesage. Adventures of Gil Blas. 40 c.

World's classics.—Continued.
—Marlowe. Dr. Faustus. 40 c.; 75 c.
—Peacock, *comp.* **Selected English essays. *40 c. net; *75 c. net.**
—Reynolds. Discourses. 35 c.
—Tennyson. Poems, 1830-1865. 35 c.; 65 c.
—Trollope. Three clerks. 35 c.; 75 c.
—Wells. Joseph and his brethren. 35 c.

World's epoch makers' ser. 12°. Scribner.
—Bussell. Marcus Aurelius, and the later stories. $1.25.
—Carrick. World's epoch-makers. *$1.25 net.
—Sarolea. Cardinal Newman. *$1 net.

World's gold. Launay, L. de. **$1.75 net. Putnam.

World's great character builder and practical thoughts for every day living. Doyle, J: 50 c. J: Doyle.

World's great events. Terhune, A. P. **$1.20 net. Dodd.

World's great pictures. '09(D18) Q. *$3.50 net. Cassell.

World's great sermons. Kleiser, G., *comp.* In 10 v. per set, $2.75. Westminster, (Chic.)

World's greatest disaster. Miller, J. M. $1.50. **Monarch.**

World's greatest sermons. Kleiser, G., *comp.* In 10 v. $7.50; $10. Funk.

World's orations. *See* Lee, G. C., *ed.*

World's peoples. Keane, A: H: *$2 net. Putnam.

World's sporting annual record book, 1908, 1909. Andrews, T: S., *comp.* ea., 10 c. T: S. Andrews.

World's story-teller's ser.; ed. by A. Ransome. 16°, *40 c. net. Dutton.
—Balzac. Stories.
—Cervantes. Stories.
—Chateaubriand. Stories.
—Flaubert. Stories.
—Hawthorne. Stories.
—Hoffman. Stories.
—Merimée. Stories.
—Poe. Stories.
—Stories by the essayists.

World's Sunday-School Convention. Sunday-schools the world around: official rept. of the World's fifth Sunday-school convention in Rome, May 18-23, 1907; ed. by Philip E. Howard. '08(F1) c. il. pors. facsims., O. *$1 net. S. S. Times.

World's triumph. Block, L: J. **$1.25 net. Lippincott.

Worlds in the making. Arrhenius, S. A. **$1.60 net. Harper.

Worley, G:
Priory church of St. Bartholomew-the-Great, Smithfield: short hist. of the foundation and a description of the fabric and also of the church of St. Bartholomew-the-Less. '08(Ag1) plans, 12°, (Bell's cathedral ser.) *60 c. net. Macmillan.

Worm gearing. '07(My23) c. il. 8°, (Machinery's reference ser.) pap., 25 c. Indust. Press.

WORMS.
See Teredinidæ.

Worrill, I. Gibson.
Narcoochee. '08(Ja4) il. D. $1. Neale.

WORRY.
Miller, Ja. R. Cure for care. **30 c. net. Crowell.
Walton, G: L. Why worry? **$1 net. Lippincott.

WORSHIP.
Atchley, E: G. C. F. **History of the use of incense in divine worship. *$17.50 net. Longmans.**
Burrell, D: J. Cloister book, for shut in worshippers and pastorless congregations. $1. Am. Tr.
Delany, S. P. Ideal of Christian worship. *50 c. net. Young Churchman.
Dimock, N. Ritual; its use and misuse. 75 c. net. Longmans.
Gottschall, A. H., *comp.* Abolished rites; or, spiritual not ceremonial worship. 75 c. A. H. Gottschall.
Helps for worship; for use in the Sunday school, the prayer meeting and the home. (Add. pubs. for price.) Presb. Bd.
Henke, F: G. Study of the psychology of ritualism. $1 net. Univ. of Chic.
Richard, J. W:, *and* Painter, F. V. N. Christian worship. $1.50. Lutheran Pub.
Robinson, C: H: **Studies in Christian worship. 25 c. Longmans.**
See also Bible;—Book of common prayer;—Catholic church;—Church music;—Cross;—Devotional exercises and meditations;—Evangelical Lutheran church;—Holy week;—Hymns;—Prayers;—Protestant Episcopal church;—Rites and ceremonies;—Sunday-school.

Worship of the golden calf. French, C: S. $1. C: S. French.

Worsley, F. W.
Fourth Gospel and the synoptists; being a contribution to the study of the Johannine problem. '09(D11) D. **$1.25 net. Scribner.

Worst boy in town. Habberton, J: $1. Jacobs.

WORSTED.
Collins, M. Woolen and worsted spinning. $3. Am. Sch. Corr.
Timmermann, J: F. Woolen and worsted finishing. $3. Am. Sch. Corr.
See also Textile fabrics;—Woolen spinning.

Worth, A. Stowell.
Mary's adventures on the moon. '09(N6) c. il. D. †$1. Badger.

Worth, H: Wa.
Ground tumbling. '10(S) c. 28 p. il. por. 16°, (Spalding's athletic lib.) pap., 10 c. Am. Sports.

Worth, Jonathan.
Correspondence; collected and ed. by J. G. de Roulhac Hamilton. 2 v. '10(F12) c. por. 8°, (North Carolina Historical Commission pubs.) gratis. Edwards.

Worth, Mrs. Mollie Tefft.
Modern typewriting. Remington ed. Rational presentation of the keyboard of the modern typewriting machine; manual which develops the touch method scientifically and contains all information necessary to the highest skill and efficiency in operation. '10(O) c. 79 p. il. 4°, $1. J. A. Lyons.

Worth, N:, pseud.
The southerner: novel; being the autobiography of Nicholas Worth. '09(O23) c. D. **$1.20, fixed. Doubleday, P.

Worth, Pauline Wilson.
Death Valley Slim, and other stories. '09 (Je) c. 48 p. il. 4°, 75 c. P. W. Worth.

WORTH.
See Ethics.

Worth of a man. McAfee, C. B. 30 c. **Northfield Press.**
Worth of a woman. Phillips, D: G: **$1.25 net. Appleton.
Worth of truth. Zellars, E. V. $1. Standard Pub.

Worthington, Arth. Mason.
Study of splashes. '08(Je20) il. O. *$2 net. Longmans.

Worthington, Lewis N:
Polyglot phrases. '09(Je19) 8°, *$1.10 net. Macmillan.

Worthington Society for the Study of Bird Life bull. il. O. pap., gratis. Worthington Soc.
—Miller. Experiment in colonization of the house martin.—Occurrence of the larvæ of a parasitic fly, *Protocalliphora chrysorrhoea* Meigen, in bird nests.

WOTTON, *Sir* Henry.
Smith, L. P. Life and letters of Sir Henry Wotton. 2 v. $7.75. Oxford Univ.

Wounded Eros. Gibson, C: *$2.50 net. C: Gibson.
Wounded word. Long, S. P: 35 c. S. P: Long.
Woven in the tapestry. Post, *Mrs.* E. P. **$1 net. Moffat.
Wraith of Knopf. James, H. $1. B'way Pub.

WRANGELL, Alaska.
See Alaska.

Wray, Angelina W.
Mother Tucker's seven. '09(S11) c. il. D. †$1.25. Lothrop, L. & S.

Wray, J. E:, ed.
How to play first base. '10(Je25) c. il. por. 12°, (Spalding's athletic lib.) pap., 10 c. Am. Sports.
How to play shortstop. '10(Jl2) c. il. por. 12°, (Spalding's athletic lib.) pap., 10 c. Am. Sports.
How to play third base. '10(Je25) il. por. 12°, (Spalding's athletic lib.) pap., 10 c. Am. Sports.

Wreath of song. Buckner, F. F. 75 c. Roberts Bros.
Wreathed dagger. Young, M. $1.50. Cassell.
Wreck of the "Grosvenor." *See* Russell, W: Clark.
Wreck of the nursery flyer. *See* Bird, Mary Herrick.
Wrecked on a coral island. Houston, E. J. †$1.25. Am. Bapt.
Wrecking the nation. Kinnear, P: (Add. pubs. for price.) Co-operative Pub. Co.
Wrecks and heroes. Adair, W. W. 10 c. Y. M. C. A.

Wrede, W:
Origin of the New Testament. '10(Ja29) 12°, (Harper's lib. of living thought.) *75 c. net. Harper.
Paul. '08(D19) 12°, *$1 net. Am. Unitarian.

WREN, *Sir* Christopher.
Milman, L. Sir Christopher Wren. *$2 net. Scribner.

Wrench, G. T., M.D.
See Tweedy, E. Hastings.

WRENS.
Grinnell, J. Two heretofore unnamed wrens of the genus *Thryamanes*. 15 c. Univ. of Cal.

WRENTHAM, Mass.
Baldwin, T: W., *comp.* Vital records of Wrentham, Mass., to the year 1850. 2 v. $5.50. Gilson.

WRESTLING.
Gotch, F. Wrestling and how to train. 10 c. R: K. Fox.
Hitchcock, E:, *and* Nelligan, R: F. Wrestling, catch-as-catch-can style. 10 c. Am. Sports.
Smith, E: W. Professional wrestling. 10 c. Am. Sports.
Toombs, F: R., *ed.* How to wrestle. 10 c. Am. Sports.

Wretches of Povertyville. Nascher, I. L. $1.50. J. J. Lanzit.

Wright, Allen Kendrick.
To the poles by airship; or, around the world endways. '09(N) c. 108 p. il. por. 12°, $1. Baumgardt.

Wright, Sir Almroth E:, M.D.
Studies on immunization and their application to the diagnosis and treatment of bacterial infections. '10(Mr) 506 p. charts, tabs., 8°, **$5 net. Wood.

Wright, Arius Luther.
Modernism according to the law of sensual impression and historical inspiration. '10 (Jl16) c. 8°, 75 c. J. McDonough.

Wright, Barton Lisle.
Treatment of tuberculosis by the administration of mercury; being a compilation of a preliminary rept. and a second paper on the subject. '08(D) 63 p. il. 8°, pap., 10 c. U. S., Supt. of Docs.

Wright, B: C.
Banking in California. '10(O15) il. 8°, $2. B: C. Wright.

Wright, Carroll Davidson.
Outlines of practical sociology, with special reference to American conditions. 7th ed., rev. '09(F20) diagrs., D. (American citizen ser.) $2. Longmans.
—, ed. New Century book of facts; hdbk. of ready reference. '10(Jl16) c. col. il. por. 4°, subs. only, $7.50. King-R.

Wright, C: L.
Briquetting tests at the United States fuel testing plant, Norfolk, Virginia, 1907-8. '09(Jl31) il. O. (U. S., Dept. of the Interior, Geol. Survey bull.) pap., 10 c.

Wright, C: Will.
Wright ancestry of Caroline, Dorchester, Somerset and Wicomico Counties, Md. '09, [1910.] (F) 218 p. 12°, *$2.25 net. C: W. Wright.
See also Wright, Fred. Eug.

Wright, Chester Whitney.
Wool-growing and the tariff; study in the economic history of the United States; awarded the David A. Wells prize for the year 1907-08, and published from the income of the David A. Wells fund. '10 (Jl2) c. O. (Harvard economic studies.) $2 net. Houghton M.

Wright, Mrs. Clara Parrish.
Up-to-date courtship. '10(F19) c. il. por. D. $1. Cochrane.

Wright, Edm. J.
Invariants of quadratic differential forms. '08(N14) 8°, (Cambridge tracts in mathematics and mathematical physics.) pap., *75 c. net. Putnam.

Wright, E: Stager.
Westward 'round the world. '09(Ja23) c. il. 12°, $1.25. Dutton.

Wright, Mrs. Eliz. Mary.
See Wright, Jos.

Wright, Mrs. Ella Frances Reed.
Reed-Read lineage; Captain John Reed of Providence, R. I., and Norwalk, Ct., and his descendants through his sons, John and Thomas, 1660-1909. [1910] (F) c. '09. 16+717+63 p. pls., pors. 8°, $10. Mattatuck Press.

Wright, Emily Dudley.
Child in our midst. '10(My21) 50 c. Cochrane.
Psychology of Christ. '09(S) c. 105 p. 12°, *$1 net. Cochrane.

Wright, Ernest Hunter.
Authorship of Timon of Athens. '10(Ag13) 8°, (Columbia Univ. studies in English.) $1.25 net. Lemcke.

Wright, Fannie J., ["Gretchen."]
Golden curves; or, glimpses into Paradise; simple thoughts of comfort for the bereaved and sorrowful. '10(Ag27) T. bds., 25 c. net. Hills & H.

Wright, Frederic B.
Inventions, how to protect, sell and buy them. '08(Ap11) c. front. 12°, 25 Spon.

Wright, Fred. Eug. and C: Will.
Ketchikan and Wrangell mining districts, Alaska. '08(D5) il. maps, O. (U. S. Geological Survey.) (Add. Superintendent for price.) U. S., Supt. of Docs.

Wright, G: E:
Crossing the Connecticut: an account of the various public crossings of the Connecticut River at Hartford. '07, [1908.] (D) c. 15+159 p. il. pors. 4°, $5. Smith-L.

Wright, Mrs. Hannah.
See Lovewell, *Mrs.* Caroline Forbes Barnes.

Wright, Harold Bell.
Calling of Dan Matthews. '09(Ag28) c. il. D. $1.50. Book Supply.
The uncrowned king. '10(O15) c. S. 75 c. net. Book Supply.

Wright, Helen S., comp.
Old time recipes for home made wines, cordials, and liqueurs from fruits, flowers, vegetables and shrubs. '09(N13) c. O. $1.50. Estes.

Wright, Mrs. Helen Saunders Smith.
Great White North; story of polar exploration, from the earliest times to the discovery of the pole. '10(N5) c. il. pors. D. $2.50 net. Macmillan.

Wright, H: Burt.
Life with a purpose: memorial of John Lawrence Thurston, [first missionary of the Yale Mission.] '08(My2) c. 12°, $1.50. Revell.
Recovery of a lost Roman tragedy: study in honor of Bernadotte Perrin, Ph.D., LL.D., professor in Yale University, 1893-1909. '10(Jl16) c. por. O. bds., $1.50. Yale Univ.
Will of God and a man's lifework. '09 (D25) c. 8°, 90 c. Y. M. C. A.

Wright, Herbert Edwards.
Handy book for brewers. 3d ed., rev. and enl. '09(Ja16) il. 8°, *$5 net. Van Nostrand.

Wright, Horace J.
Sweet peas. '10(S10) col. il. O. (Garden flowers in color.) bds., 65 c. net. Stokes.

—, and Wa. Page.
Beautiful flowers and how to grow them. In 2 v. '10(My14) il. in col. $8 net. Dodge.

Wright, Horace Winslow.
Birds of the Boston Public Garden: study in migration; with an introd. by Bradford Torrey. '09(My15) c. il. D. **$1 net. Houghton M.

Wright, Hugh.
Contractors' accounts; instruction paper. '09(D4) c. forms, 8°, (American School of Correspondence pubs.) 50 c. Am. Sch. Corr.

Wright, Irene Aloha.
Cuba. '10(D10) c. il. map, D. $2.50 net. Macmillan.

Wright, Ja. Homer.
See Mallory, Fk. Burr.

Wright, J:, D.D.
Some notable altars in the Church of England and the American Episcopal Church. '08(D12) il. 4°, *$6 net. Macmillan.

Wright, Archbishop J: C:
Thoughts on modern church life and work. '09(N20) D. *$1 net. Longmans.

Wright, J: Livingston.
Down the road with a tramp writer: [poems.] '09(Je26) c. D. $1. Black Lion.

Wright, J: Westley.
Text book of ophthalmology. 3d ed., thoroughly rev. '09(Ap) c. '08. 17+17-398 p. il. 8°. (Add. pubs. for price.) Blakiston.

Wright, Jos.
Grammar of the Gothic language, and the Gospel of St. Mark, selections from the Second Epistle to Timothy; with notes and glossary. '10(My21) D. $1.75. Oxford Univ.
Hist. German grammar. '08(F15) 8°, $2.40. Oxford Univ.

—, and Mrs. Eliz. Mary.
Old English grammar. '08(My23) O. (Students' ser. of historical and comparative grammars.) $2. Oxford Univ.

Wright, Lawrence.
Eighteen sermons on great themes; strong concise presentation of the great fundamental truths of the Gospel and of Christian living. '09(My) c. 8+9-274 p. por. 8°, $1. Chr. Un.

Wright, Mrs. Mabel Osgood, ["Barbara."]
The open window. '08(Je27) c. front. D. †$1.50. Macmillan.
Poppea of the post-office. '09(Jl17 c. front. D. †$1.50. Macmillan.
Princess Flower Hat; comedy from the perplexity book of Barbara, the commuter's wife. '10(N5) c. front. D. $1.50. Macmillan.

Wright, Marcus Jos., comp.
Tennessee in the war, 1861-1865: lists of military organizations and officers from Tennessee in both the Confederate and Union armies. '08(Mr14) c. 8°, $1.50. A. Lee.

Wright, Mrs. Marie Robinson.
Brazilian national exposition of 1908 in celebration of the centenary of the opening of Brazilian ports to the commerce of the world by the Prince Regent Dom Joãn VI. of Portugal, in 1808. '09(F6) c. il. pors. 8°, $2.50. Barrie.
New Brazil, its resources and attractions. 2d ed., rev. and enl. '08(Mr.) c. 494 p. il. por. f°, *$10 net. Barrie.
Old and the new Peru. '09(Ja16) c. il. por. map, f°, *$10 net. Barrie.

Wright, Lord Nathaniel.
See Bownocker, J: Adams.

Wright, P:
Three-foot stool. '09(S11) c. 8°, *$1.50 net. Dutton.

Wright, Rob. Catlin.
Indian masonry. '08(Ap18) c. il. por. D. bds., $1.50. Tyler Pub.

Wright, Sidney Harry, ["H. W. G. Hyrst."]
Adventures among the red Indians. '10 (D31) 12°, (Adventure ser.) $1.50 net. Lippincott.
Adventures among wild beasts. '08(N7) il. D. (Adventure ser.) *$1.50 net. Lippincott.
Adventures in the Arctic regions; romantic incidents and perils of travel, sport, and exploration around the poles. '09(O2) il. D. (Adventure ser.) *$1.50 net. Lippincott.

Wright, Tobias Alex., ed.
Records of the Dutch Reformed church of Port Richmond, S. I., baptisms from 1696 to 1772; United Brethren congregation, commonly called Moravian church, S. I., births and baptisms: 1749 to 1853, marriages: 1764 to 1863, deaths and burials; 1758 to 1828; St. Andrew's church, Richmond. S. I., births and baptisms from 1752 to 1795, marriages from 1754 to 1808. '09(N) 11+10-335 p. il. por. plan, 4°, (Collections of the New York Genealogical and Biographical Society.) $15. (100 copies.) T. A. Wright.

Wright, Wa. Page.
Cassell's A B C of gardening. '08(My16) D. *$1.25 net. Cassell.
Garden week by week throughout the year. '10(Ja22) O. *$2 net. Doubleday, P.

Wright, Wa. Page.—*Continued.*
Perfect garden: how to keep it beautiful and fruitful. '08(Ag1) il. O. *$2 net. Lippincott.
Popular garden flowers. '10(D24) col. il. $2 net. Clode.
See also Wright, Horace J.
—, ed. Cassell's dict of gardening. '10(O1) il. $10 net. Cassell.
Wright, W: H:
Black bear. '10(My7) c. il. O. $1 net. Scribner.
Grizzly bear; narrative of a hunter-naturalist. '09(O2) c. il. O. **$1.50 net. Scribner.
WRIGHT FAMILY.
See **Genealogies.**
Wrinkles. Bailey, S: W. 50 c. Bailey-T.
Wrinkles in practical navigation. Lecky, S. T. S. *$8 net. Van Nostrand.
Write it right. Bierce, A. *50 c. net. Neale.
Writer of books in his genesis. Snider, D. J. $1.50. Sigma; McClurg.
Writer's book. '10(D24) c. 12°, $2.50. Editor Co.
WRITERS.
See **Authors.**
WRITING.
See Abbreviations; — Authorship; — Cuneiform writing; — Hand-writing; — Letter-writing; — Lettering;—Penmanship; — Rhetoric; — Typewriting.
Writing and speaking. Baldwin, C: S. $1.20. Longmans.
Writing of English. Hartog, P. J. 60 c. Oxford Univ.
Writing on the clouds. Newman, A. 90 c. net. Sherman, F.
Writing on the wall. Marshall, E: †$1.50. G: W. Dillingham.
Writings of American statesmen. O. **$2.50 net. Putnam.
—Washington. Writings.
Writings on American history. *See* Griffin, Grace Gardner, *comp.*
Wrixon, Sir H: J:
Religion of the common man. '09(F13) D. *$1 net. Macmillan.
Wrong, G: McKinnon.
Canadian manor and its seigneurs: [Mount Murray Manor;] the story of a hundred years, 1761-1861. '08(D19) il. pors. maps, O. *$3 net. Macmillan.
—, and Langton, H. H., eds.
Review of historical publications relating to Canada. v. 12, 13. '09(Ap24) Q. (Univ. of Toronto studies.) ea., $1.50; pap., $1. Morang.
Review of historical publications rel. to Canada. v. 14. '10(My21) Q. (Univ. of Toronto studies.) pap., $1.50. Univ. of Toronto.
Wrong and peril of woman suffrage. Buckley, J. M. *75 c. net. Revell.
Wroth. Castle, *Mrs.* A. S. †$1.50. Macmillan.
WROUGHT IRON.
See Decoration and ornament.
Wrought-pipe drainage systems. Cosgrove, J: J. $2. Standard Sanitary Mfg.

Wu T'ing Fang.
Awakening of China: address del. before the Civic Forum. '08(D5) por. 12°, (Civic Forum addresses.) pap., 10 c. Civic Forum.
Wulf, Maurice M. C. J. de.
See De Wulf, Maurice M. C. J.
WULFSTAN.
Dodd, L. H. Glossary of Wulfstan's homilies. **$1 net. Holt.
Wullie McWattie's master. Bell, J: J. 60 c. net. Revell.
Wulwoth the wanderer. Inman, H. E. $1.50. McClurg.
Würdig, L.
Prince Eugene; the noble knight; tr. from the German by G: P. Upton. '10(O22) c. il. S. (Life stories for young people.) 50 c. net. McClurg.
Wurts, J:
See Minor, Raleigh Colston.
Wyand, E. Clayton.
Brief hist. of the Andrew Putman (Buttman Putnam), Christian Wyandt (Weyandt, Weygandt, Voint, Wyand), and Adam Snyder families (Schneider) of Washington County, Maryland. '10(Ap30) c. pors. O. $1. E. C. Wyand.
WYANDOTTES.
See Poultry.
WYANDT FAMILY.
See **Genealogies: Wyand, E. C.**
Wyatt, Fk., and Morris, W:
Mrs. Temple's telegram: farce in three acts. '08(D) c. 116 p. 12°. (Add. pubs. for price.) S. French.
Wyatt, F: Fuller.
Bible on instrumental music. '09(Jl31) c. por. 8°, 25 c. F: F. Wyatt.
Wyche, R: T:
Some great stories and how to tell them. '10(Ag13) c. D. $1. Newson.
Wyckoff, R: D., ["Rollo Tape."]
Studies in tape reading. '10(F19) c. il. S. limp leath., $3. Ticker Pub.
WYCLIFFE, John.
Carrick, J: C: Wycliffe and the Lollards. *$1.25 net. Scribner.
WYE RIVER, ENG.
Bradley, A. G. The Wye. $3 net. Macmillan.
Wyer, Ja. Ingersoll.
United States government documents in small libraries. 3d ed., rev. and enl. '10 (Ag27) 12°, (A. L. A. lib. hdbks.) 15 c. A. L. A.
—, and Phelps, Martha L., comps.
Bibliography of education for 1907. '08, [1909.] (Mr) 65 p. O. (U. S. Bureau of Education, bull.) (Add. Superintendent for price.) U. S., Supt. of Docs.
Wyeth, Adelaide H.
Pa's picnic: entertainment in two scenes. '09(N) 16°, pap., 25 c. Dramatic.
Wyeth, J: Allan.
History of La Grange Military Academy and the cadet corps, 1857-1862, La Grange College, 1830-1857. '07, [1908.] (My.) c. 202 p. pors. 12°, $2. M. S. Wyeth.
Surgery. '08(Jl4) c. il. 4°, $7. M. S. Wyeth.

Wyld, H: Cecil Kennedy.
Elem. lessons in English grammar. '09 (D4) D. 50 c. Oxford Univ.

Wylde, C. H.
How to collect continental china. '08 (Ja25) il. 8°, (How to ser.) $2. Macmillan.

Wylie, F. L.
Cecil Rhodes and his scholars as factors in international conciliation. '09, [1910.] (D) 14 p. D. (International conciliation.) pap., gratis. Am. Assoc. Int. Conciliation.

Wylie, Ida Alena Ross.
The native born. '10(S3) c. il. D. $1.50. Bobbs-M.

Wyllarde, Dolf, pseud.
Pathway of the pioneer: a novel. '08 (Je27) 12°, †$1.50. Lane.
Rose-white youth. '08(N14) c. D. †$1.50. Lane.
Tropical tales and others. '10(Je18) D. $1.50. Lane.

Wyllie, W: Lionel.
Sketch bock. '08(D12) il. obl. D. $1.50. Cassell.

Wylly, C: Spalding.
Seed that was sown in the Colony of Georgia, the harvest and the aftermath, 1740-1870. '10(Ap2) c. D. $1.25 net. Neale.

Wyman, Arth. Crawford, comp.
Automobile laws of the New England states, New York, New Jersey and Pennsylvania, published by the Legislative Reference Bureau of the Rhode Island state library. '08(O) 106 p. 8°, (Legislative reference bull., no. 2.) (Add. pubs. for price.) R. I. State Lib.
See also Veto power in the several states.

Wyman, Bruce.
Cases on public service companies, public carriers, public works, and other public utilities. 2d ed. '09(N) c. 4+607 p. 4°, hf. shp. (Add. pubs. for price.) Harvard Law.

Wyman, Mrs. Mary Eliz. Tisdel.
Genealogy of the descendants of Lawrence and Mary Antisell of Norwich and Willington, Conn., incl. some records of Christopher Antisell of Sraduff, Birr (Kings Co.), Ireland. '08(N) 355 p. pors. fold. facsim., 8°, $5. L. Wyman.

Wyman, Wa., M.D.
Cruise on the U. S. practice ship "S. P. Chase;" being the first impressions of a surgeon at sea; and experiences on a sailing vessel of the Revenue Cutter Service on a voyage to Spain and the Azores Islands. '10(O) 238 p. il. 8°, $2 net. Grafton Press.
Present organization and work for the protection of health in the United States. '10(D) 16 p. 8°. Gov. Pr. Off.

Wymper, C:
Egyptian birds, for the most part seen in the Nile Valley. '09(D11) col. il. O. (Color books, misc.) *$6 net. Macmillan.

Wyndham, Horace Cowley.
Call of the drum: [a story.] '08(My16) front. D. $1.50. Cassell.

Wyneken, L. Ernest.
Chronicles of Manuel Alanus. '09(F6) c. front. 8°, $2. Cochrane.

Wyngate, Ashmore.
Life of John Ruskin. '10(D24) 8°, (Great writers ser.) $1. Scribner.

Wynkoop, Ja.
Rebellion of hell: a poem. '08(Ap25) c. 12°, $1.25. B'way Pub.

Wynne, May.
For Charles the Rover. '10(D10) 12°, $1.50. Fenno.
Gipsy count. '09(Ap17) c. front. D. $1.50. J: McBride.
Henry of Navarre: a romance of August, 1572. '08(N14) c. front. D. †$1.50. Putnam.

Wynter, Wa. Essex.
Minor medicine; treatise on the nature and treatment of common ailments. '09, [1910.] (D) 10+275 p. 8°, $2. (Subs. only.) Appleton.

Wyoming. *Department of Immigration.* Some views of Wyoming. '08(O) 64 p. obl. S. pap. gratis. Wy. Dept. of Immigration.

Wyoming. Irrigation laws, codified from the Revised Statutes of 1899, and the session laws of 1901, 1903, 1905, and 1907. '07, [1908.] (Je.) 88 p. 8°. (Add. pub. for price.) C. T. Johnston.

Wyoming. *State Board of Immigration.* Agriculture in Wyoming. '08, [1909.] (My) 48 p. 8°. (Add. pubs. for price.) S. A. Bristol.

Wyoming. State of Wyoming; a book of reliable information published by authority of the legislature. '08(O) 141 p. il. 8°, pap. gratis. S. A. Bristol.

Wyoming. *Supreme ct.* Complete digest of all rept. cases to May 12, 1908; comp. and ed. by Sheridan Downey and V. J. Tidball, under the supervision of C: N. Potter, chief justice. '09(D) c. O. $10.50 Laramie Repub.

Wyoming. *Supreme ct.* Repts.; (C: N. Potter.) v. 15. '08(Je); v. 16. '09(Ja) ea., $5; v. 17 (N) c. O. shp., $3.50. Laramie Repub.

WYOMING.
Bryant, O. W. Progress rept. on experiments in supplemental irrigation with small water supplies at Cheyenne and Newcastle, Wyo., 1905-1909. Gov. Pr. Off.
Carrington, *Mrs.* F. C. My army life and the Fort Phil. Kearney massacre; with acct. of the celebration of Wyoming opened. $2 net. Lippincott.
Cooke, V. T. Dry farming in Wyoming. gratis. Wy. State Dry Farming.
Forms for use in the segregation and reclamation of arid lands in the state of Wyoming; comp. by Rob. P. Fuller. '09 (My) 41 p. 16°, pap. (Add. pubs. for price.) Wyoming Com. Public Lands.
See also Farms and farming;—Yellowstone National Park.

Wyoming: a story of the outdoor west. Raine, W: M. †$1.50. G: W. Dillingham.

Wysor, H:
Metallurgy. '08(O17) c. il. 8°, $3. Chemical.

Wyss, C. von.
Child's world in pictures. '10(Ap9) il. (partly col.) 8°, (Color books for boys and girls.) 75 c. net. Macmillan.

Wyss, Johann Rudolf, and Montolieu, J. I. P. de B., Baronne de.
Swiss family Robinson. '08(O10) il. D. (Bowman's illustrated lib. of world-favorite books.) $1. Bowman.
Swiss family Robinson. '10(Ap30) il. 16°, (Everyman's lib.) 35 c. net; 70 c. net. Dutton.
Swiss family Robinson; ed. by Wa. Jerrold. '10(D) il. 12°, (Children's classics.) $1.25. Dutton.
Swiss family Robinson; with il. by C: Folkard. '10(D10) col. il. 12°, $2.50. Dutton.
Swiss family Robinson; ed. by G. E. Mitton. '10(D10) il. 8°, $1.50. Lippincott.
Swiss family Robinson; or, the adventures of a shipwrecked family on an uninhabited isle near New Guinea; with an introd. by W: D. Howells. '09(N20) c. il. O. †$1.50. Harper.

Wyzewa, Teodor de.
Some women, loving or luckless; tr. from the French by C. H. Jeaffreson. '08(O24) pors. O. *$2.50 net. Lane.

X-RAYS.
See Roentgen rays.

Xanto, Madame.
Dream books; explains the meaning of any dream, and answers difficult questions. '08(O3) c. S. (Popular handbooks.) 50 c. Penn Pub. Co.
Fortune telling. '08(O3) c. il. S. (Popular handbooks.) 50 c. Penn Pub. Co.

Xenophon.
Anabasis. Bks. 1-4; ed., with introd., notes and vocab., by Maurice W. Mather and Jos. W: Hewitt. '10(D24) c. D. $1.50. Am. Bk.
Hellenica: selections; ed., with introd., notes and appendices, by Carleton L. Brownson. '08(Ag22) c. 12°, (Greek ser. for colleges and schools; ed. by Herbert Weir Smith.) $1.65. *Same.* Text ed. pap., 40 c. Am. Bk.
History; tr. from the Greek by Henry Graham Dakyns. Olympic ed. '10(Ja29) c. 5 v., il. 8°, (Historians of Greece.) $15. (1000 copies.) Tandy-T.
Xenophontis opera omnia; ed. by F. C. Marchant. 4 v. v. 1, Historia Graeca; v. 2, Libri Socratici; v. 3, Anabasis; v. 4, Institutio Cyri. '10(D24) 8°, (Oxford classical texts.) v. 1, 75 c.; v. 2, 90 c.; v. 3, 75 c.; v. 4, 90 c.; pap., 75 c. Oxford Univ.
See also Plato.

YACHTS AND YACHTING.
Barrie, R. *and* G:, *jr.* Cruises, mainly in the Bay of the Chesapeake. $2. Franklin Press, (Pa.)
Boardman, E. A: Small yacht. **$2 net. Little, B. & Co.

YACHTS AND YACHTING.—*Continued.*
Kempson, F. C. Misadventures of a crack cruiser. $1.75 net. Longmans.
See also Boats;—Flags;—Marine engineering;—Navigation.

Yacob Strauss. Adams, C: F. $1. Lothrop, L. & S.

YAKUTAT BAY, Alaska.
See Alaska.

Yale, Mrs. Elsie Duncan.
When mother lets us give a party; book that tells little folk how best to entertain and amuse their little friends. '09(N20) c. il. O. (When mother lets us ser.) **75 c. net. Moffat.

Yale, Rodney Horace.
Yale genealogy and history of Wales. '09 (My22) il. maps, pors. facsims., fold. geneal. tab., 12°, $5. R. H. Yale.

Yale cup. Dudley, A. T. †$1.25. Lothrop, L. & S.

YALE FAMILY.
See Genealogies.

Yale lectures on the responsibilities of citizenship. D. Yale Univ.
—Bryce. Hindrances to good citizenship.
—Hughes. Conditions of progress in democratic government. $1.15 net.

Yale readings in insurance. Zartman, L. W., *ed.* In 2 v. ea., *$2.25 net. Yale Univ.

Yale Review reprints. 8°. Yale Pub.
—Coulter. Organization among the farmers of the U. S. 10 c.

Yale studies in English; ed. by A. S. Cook. 8°, pap. Holt.
—Alain de Lille. Complaint of nature. 75 c.
—Beaumont *and* Fletcher. Knight of the burning pestle. $2.50; $2.
—Dodd. Glossary of Wulfstan's homilies. **$1 net.
—Hemingway. English nativity plays. $2.50; $2.
—Jonson. The New Inn. $2.50; pap., $2.
—Pierce. Collaboration of Webster and Dekker. $1.

Yale University. Directory of the living non-graduates of Yale University, 1910. '10(Je) 4+163 p. 8°, 50 c. Tuttle, M. & T.

YALE UNIVERSITY, New Haven, Ct.
Beers, H: A. Ways of Yale in the consulship of Plaucus. $1.20 net. Holt.
Burns, W: S., *comp.* Bibliog. of the writings of members of the class of 1887 in Yale College. Marigold-F.
Stokes, A. P., *ed.* Historical points of New Haven, Ct.; with special reference to Yale College and the Green. gratis. Tuttle, M. & T.
Yale University, Class of 1881. Hist. of the class of '81; covering 30 years from its admission into the Academic Dept.. 1877-1907. '09(N) 443 p. il. 8°. (Add. pubs. for price.) Yale Univ.
Yale University, Class of 1894. Quindecennial record; by E: Bliss Reed and F: Dwight, class secretaries. '09(D) 199 p. pors. 8°. (Priv. pr.) F: Dwight.
See also Gilman, Daniel Coit;—Kent, James.

YALE UNIVERSITY DRAMATIC ASSOCIATION.
Boucicault, D. London assurance; acting version of Yale Univ. Dramatic Assoc. 50 c. P. Roberts.

Yale University Library. Catalogue of an exhibition of manuscripts, first editions, early engravings and various literature rel. to Samuel Johnson, 1709-1784; arranged by Chauncey Brewster Tinker, assistant professor of English in Yale College, Yale University Library, November 1-6, 1909. [1910.] (Ja) 12 p. 12°, 25 c. Yale Univ. Lib.

Yale University Library. List of books and articles rel. to Samuel Johnson, 1709-1784; comp. on the occasion of the exhibition held at the Yale University Library, Nov. 1-6, 1909. [1910.] (Ja) 24 p. 12°, 25 c. Yale Univ. Lib.

Yale University pubs. O. pap. Yale Univ.
—Bishop. State works of Pennsylvania. $1.50.

Yale verse. Moses, R., *comp.* *$1.25 net. Yale Pub.

YAM.
See Sweet potato.

Yama Yama Land. Boylan, G. D. $1.50. Reilly & B.

Yama Yama ser. il. O. Reilly & B.
—Boylan. Yama Yama Land. $1.50.

YANA LANGUAGE.
See Indians.

YANGTZE RIVER.
See Yunnan, China.

Yankee Doodle book. Optimus, G. D. 75 c. J. B. Best.

Yankee Doodle detective. La Croix, A. 25 c. J. S. Ogilvie.

Yankee middy. *See* Adams, W: T.

Yankee ship and a Yankee crew. De Morgan, J: 75 c. McLoughlin.

YARA, Cuba.
See Cuba.

Yard and garden. Baker, T. **$2 net. Bobbs-M.

Yardley, Mrs. Maud H.
Nor all your tears. '08(My2) c. front. D. $1.50. Fenno.

Yardstick man. Goodrich, A. F. $1.50. Appleton.

Yates, Katherine Merritte.
By the wayside. '08(My9) c. D. 50 c. K. M. Yates.
Cheery and the chum. '08(O3) c. il. D. 60 c. K. M. Yates.
"Chet." '09(S25) c. il. D. $1.25. McClurg.

Yates, Rev. T:
Sculptors of life. '09(D11) D. *$1 net. Armstrong.

Ybarra, T: Russell.
Davy Jones's yarns and other salted songs. '08(N14) c. il. O. **$1.25 net. Holt.

Ye butcher, ye baker, ye candle-stick maker. Seaver, Rob. **50 c. net. Houghton M.

Ye Planry Building Company. Bungalows: a book published in the interests of economy and pleasing variety in the art of building and beautifying the home. '08(Jl4) il. plans, obl. S. pap., $1. Ye Planry.

Year book for primary grades. Graves, E. M. $1.25. M. Bradley.

Year Book of Photography and Amateurs' Guide. *See* Brown, G: E., *ed.* British Journal.

Year book of southern poets. Lynch, H. P., *comp.* $1.25. Dodge.

YEAR-BOOKS.
See Almanacs and manuals;—Calendars and year books;—*also* under special subjects.

Year in my garden. Verplanck, V. E. $1. W: E. Verplanck.

Year of beautiful thoughts. Greenough, *Mrs.* J. A. B., *comp.* $1. Crowell.

Year of Grace. Hodges, G: $1.25 net. Whittaker.

Year of ideals for every-day living. Porter, *Mrs.* D. L., *comp.* *75 c. net. Pilgrim Press.

Year of primary occupation work. Graves, E. M. 50 c. Educ. Pub.

Year out of life. Waller, M. E. †$1.50. Appleton.

Year's Bible readings. Soulsby, L. H. M., *comp.* 35 c. Longmans.

Year's work in an out-apiary. Doolittle, G. M. 50 c. A. I. Root.

YEAST.
See Fermentation.

Yeats, W: Butler.
Land of hearts' desire: [play.] '09(D) flex. vellum bds., *$1.50 net. T: B. Mosher.

—, and Gregory, Lady Augusta.
Unicorn from the stars, and other plays. '08(Je27) 12°, *$1.50 net. Macmillan.

Yeigh, Fk., comp.
5000 facts about Canada. 1908 ed., enl., improved, rev. '08(My16) D. pap., 25 c. Canadian Facts.

Yellow circle. Walk, C: E. $1.50. McClurg.

Yellow Creek humor. Burtscher, W: J: $1. W: J: Burtscher.

Yellow face. White, F. M. *$1 net. Fenno.

YELLOW FEVER.
Augustin, G: Hist. of yellow fever. $6. G: Augustin.

Yellow god. Haggard, H: R. 75 c. Cupples & L.

Yellow house. Oppenheim, E: P. 50 c. Doscher.

YELLOW PERIL.
Coleman, W: M. Pressure of Asia and the unification of the English speaking people. W: M. Coleman.
Gompers, S:, *and* Gutstadt, H. Meat vs. rice: American manhood against Asiatic coolieism. (Add. pubs. for price.) Asiatic Exclusion.

YELLOW PINE.
See Pine trees.

Yellow princess. Benson, I. E. 25 c. McLoughlin.

YELLOWSTONE NATIONAL PARK.
Haynes, J. E. Official guide, Yellowstone Nat. Park. 25 c. J. E. Haynes.
Raftery, J: H., *comp.* Historical and descriptive sketch of Yellowstone National Park. (Add. Superintendent for price.) U. S., Supt. of Docs.
Schlundt, H. Radioactivity of the thermal waters of Yellowstone National Park. U. S., Supt. of Docs.
Taylor, C: M. Touring Alaska and the Yellowstone. *$1.25 net. Jacobs.
See also Fish and fishing.

YELLOWSTONE RIVER VALLEY.
Illustrated history of the Yellowstone Valley. $4.50. Western Hist.

Yendes, Lucy A., and Brown, Wa. F. A., eds. Entertainments for every occasion; rev. and enl. '10(F19) c. 12°, $1.25. Hinds.

Yennycott folks. Cook, M. H. $1. J. S. Ogilvie.

Yeo, I. Burney, M.D.
Food in health and disease. 9th ed. [1910.] (My) 592 p. il. 12°, $2.50 net. Funk.
Therapeutics of mineral springs and climates. [1910.] (My) 760 p. 12° $3.50 net. Funk.

—, Crawford, Raymond, and Buzzard, E. Farquhar.
Manual of medical treatment; or, clinical therapeutics. 2 v. New ed. '09(Ap) 1652 p. 12°, *$6 net. Wood.

Yerf, Christopher.
Emily Bellefontaine. '08(Je6) c. il. D. $1.25. Conkey.

Yerkes, C: Tyson.
Catalogue de luxe of ancient and modern paintings belonging to the estate of the late Charles T. Yerkes (Louis S. Owsley, executor) to be sold at unrestricted public sale by C: C. Burlingham at Mendelssohn Hall, N. Y., April 5th-8th, 1910. '10(Ap30) c. il. pors. f°, $30. (250 copies) Am. Art Assoc.
Catalogue de luxe of the ancient rugs, sculptures, tapestries, costly furniture, and other objects belonging to the estate of the late Charles T. Yerkes (Louis S. Owsley, executor) to be sold at unrestricted public sale by C: C. Burlingham on [April 5th-April 13th, 1910;] the sale will be conducted by T: E. Kirby, of the American Art Association, managers. '10 (My) 274 p. il. F. $20. Am. Art. Assoc.

Yerushalmi fragments from the Genizah. v. 1; ed. by L: Ginzberg. '10(Ap30) 8°, (Texts and studies of the Jewish Theological Seminary of America.) pap. (Add. pubs. for price.) Jewish Theological.

Yesterday's children. Sowerby, G. $1.50. Duffield.

Yet again. Beerbohm, M. *$1.50 net. Lane.

Yet speaketh he. Whitney, *Mrs.* G. C. 80 c. net. Sherman, F.

Yetter, J: Milton.
Educational system of Pennsylvania. '09 (D) c. 115 p. 12°, $1. Cochrane.

YEW.
See Evergreens.

Yiddish sermons. Masliansky, H. $1. Turberg.

Yoakum, Clarence Stone.
Experimental study of fatigue. [910.] (Mr) 6+131 p. tabs., 4°, (Psychological monographs; Studies from the Psychological Laboratory of the University of Chicago.) $1.35. Psychological Review.
Bibliography (7 p.).

Yoder, J: Oscar.
Journeys of Jesus, with charts and harmony. '09(S) c. 8+9-156 p. maps, 12°, 90 c. Lutheran Pub.

Yoe, Shway.
The Burman; his life and notions. 3d ed. '10(My7) 8°. $3.25 net. Macmillan.

YOGI PHILOSOPHY.
See Mysticism;—Occultism.

"Yogi Ramacharaka," pseud.
See Atkinson, W: Walker.

Yoke (The). Wales, H. $1.50. Stuyvesant Press.

Yokefellow. Davisson, R. B. $1.50. **C. M. Clark.**

Yolanda of Cyprus. Rice, C. Y. **$1.25 net. McClure.

Yolland, Arth. H.
Dict. of the Hungarian and English languages. pt. 1, English-Hungarian. '08 (Ap18) 8°, *$4.50 net. Caspar.

Yonge, Charlotte Mary.
[Works.] New ed. '08(Je6) 13 v., 16°, ea., *50 c. net. Macmillan.
Book of golden deeds. '08(S19) 16°, (Everyman's lib.) *35 c. net; leath., *70 c. net. Dutton.
Dove in the eagle's nest. '08(S19) 16°, (Everyman's lib.) *35 c. net; leath., *70 c net. Dutton.
Dove in the eagle's nest. '08(Jl18) 12°, (Home ser.) 50 c. Hurst.
Heir of Redclyffe. '09(Ap3) 16°, (Everyman's lib.) *35 c. net; leath., *70 c. net. Dutton.
Little Duke, or Richard the Fearless. '10 (D10) il. 16°, (Everyman's lib.) 35 c. net; leath., 70 c. net. Dutton.

YONGE, Charlotte Mary.
Romanes, E. D. An appreciation: Charlotte Mary Yonge. $1.65. Young Churchman.

Yonge, Eug. I., M.D.
Hay fever and paroxysmal sneezing. '10 (D) 150 p. il. 8°, $2 net. Wood.

Yoreh-Malkosh U'Marveh. *See* Jews.

York, E: Plantagenet, Duke of.
Master of game; ed. by F. Baillie-Grohmann; with preface by Thdr. Roosevelt. '09(D18) il. *$4 net. Duffield.

York, Fs. Lodowick.
Text-book in simple strict counterpoint. '08 (Ja18) O. (Music students lib.) $1.25. Ditson.

York, Harlan Harvey.
Anatomy and some of the biological aspects of the "American mistletoe," *phoradendron flavescens (Pursh) Nutt.* '09 (Jl10) il. O. (Univ. of Tex. bull.) pap., 50 c. Univ. of Tex.

York, Wealthy Ann, pseud.
Some adventures of two vagabonds, by One of 'em. '08(Ap4) c. D. $1. B'way Pub.

York lib. See Macmillan's.

Yorke, Curtis, [pseud. for Mrs. Susan Richmond Lee.]
Girl and the man. '09(Ap10) D. $1.50. Estes.
Mollie Deverill. '09(My15) c. front. D. $1.50. Estes.
Only Betty. '09(Ap10) front. D. $1.50. Estes.
The other Sara. '08(N21) c. front. D. †$1.50. Estes.
Wayward Anne. '10(My21) c. D. $1.50. Estes.
World and Delia. '09(Ap10) D. $1.50. Estes.

YORKSHIRE, Eng.
Fletcher, J. S. Book about Yorkshire. *$2 net. Doubleday, P.
Home, G. C. Yorkshire vales and wolds. *$3 net. Macmillan.
Stawell, *Mrs.* R. Motor tours in Yorkshire. $1.75 net. Doran.
See also Gardens and gardening;—*also* Nunburnholme.

YORUBA, West Africa.
Dennett, R. E. Nigerian studies; religious and political system of Yoruba. $2.75 net. Macmillan.

YOSEMITE VALLEY, Cal.
Branson, I: R. Yosemite against corporation greed. gratis. I: R. Branson.
Clark, G. Indians of the Yosemite Valley and vicinity. $1; 50 c. G. Clark.
Clark, G. Yosemite Valley. $1; 50 c. Salter.

YOSHIWARA YUKWAKU.
See Prostitution.

You and some others. Foster, A. G. *$1.25 net. P. Elder.

You and your friends. McGill, M. R. $3. M. R. McGill.

Youker, H. S., comp.
Training of rural school teachers; paper read before the Wisconsin State Teachers' Association, Nov., 1907. '08, [1909.] (My) 19 p. 8°, (Wisconsin Dept. of Education bull.) pap. (Not for sale.) Wisconsin Dept. Pub. Instruction.

Yound, G: D.
See Washington [State.] Realty law.

Young, Alex. Bell Filson.
When the tide turns. '08(D5) c. D. †$1.50. Estes.

Young, Bennett Henderson.
Prehistoric men of Kentucky; hist. of what is known of their lives and habits, together with a description of their implements and other relics and of the tumuli which have earned for them the designation of Mound builders. '10(O1) c. il. plans, por. f°, (Filson Club pubs.) $4.50. Morton.
—, ed. Kentucky eloquence, past and present; library of orations, after dinner speeches, popular and classic lectures, addresses and poetry. '07, [1908.] (N) 7-471 p. pors. 4°, $5. B: La Bree.

Young, Bicknell.
Christian science: lecture del. in the Royal Albert Hall, London. '09(Ap3) c. 16°, pap., 6 c. Chr. Sci.

Young, C. F.
The Medici. 2 v. '09(D18) il. 8°, *$8 net. Dutton.

Young, Clarence.
Jack Ranger's gun club. '10(D) 320 p. il. 12°, (Jack Ranger ser.) $1. Cupples & L.
Jack Ranger's ocean cruise; or, the wreck of the "Polly Ann." '09(D18) c. il. 12°, (Jack Ranger ser.) $1. Cupples & L.
Motor boys in strange waters; or, lost in a floating forest. '09(D18) c. il. 12°, (Motor boys ser.) 60 c. Cupples & L.
Motor boys in the clouds; or, a trip for fame and fortune. '10(Jl30) c. il. 12°, (Motor boys ser.) 60 c. Cupples & L.

Young, Clarence.—*Continued.*
Motor boys on the Atlantic. '08(D12) c. il. 12°, (Motor boys ser.) 60 c. Cupples & L.
Motor boys on the Pacific; or, the young derelict hunters. '09(D18) c. il. 12°, (Motor boys ser.) 60 c. Cupples & L.

Young, Clyde, and Brooks, Standford M.
Spon's architects' and builders' pocket price-book, memoranda, tables and prices, (English.) 36th ed. '09(Je19) il. 18°, limp leath., $1.50. Spon.

Young, D. Hastings.
First aid to the child; guide to the feeding and treatment of infants in health and disease. '10(D10) 8°, $1.25. Dutton.
First aid to the sick; work of reference for the home. '10(Je11) 8°, $1.25 net. Dutton.

Young, Rev. Dinsdale T.
Gospel of the left hand: book of evangelical cheer. '09(D) 11+248 p. D. *$1.25 net. Doran.
Messages for home and life. '08(F29) D. *$1.25 net. Jennings.

Young, Duncan Fs.
Fiction writer's workshop; digest of modern fiction writing, embracing a dict. of the terms, tools, technique, plan and construction of fiction. '10(Mr5) c. 16°, 50 c. Editor Co.

YOUNG, Edward.
Kind, J: L: Edward Young in Germany: influence upon German literature. *$1.25 net. Lemcke.

Young, Ernest.
Corsica. '09(Ag14) il. map, 12°, (Peeps at many lands ser.) *75 c. net. Macmillan.
Siam. '08(Ag22) map, 12°, (Peeps at many lands ser.) *75 c. net. Macmillan.

Young, F. E. Mills.
Atonement. '10(S) 344 p. D. $1.50. Lane.
Chip. '09(My22) D. $1.50. Lane.
Mistaken marriage. '08(Ag1) D. †$1.50. Lane.

Young, Franklin Knowles.
Chess generalship. v. 1. '10(N19) c. 8°, $1.75 net. Int. Pub. Co.

Young, G: F:
Medici. In 2 v. '10(Ja22) il. pors. 8°, per set, *$8 net. Dutton.

Young, G: J.
Ventilating-system at the Comstock mines, Nevada. '09, [1910.] (N) 955-1009 p. plans, diagrs., 8°, (Univ. of Nev. bull.) gratis. Univ. of Nev.

Young, Gilbert Amos.
Elem. notes on thermodynamics. '09, [1910.] (Ja) 6+49 p. 8°, $1. G. A. Young.

Young, Jacob W: Albert, and Jackson, Lambert Lincoln.
Appleton arithmetics; primary book. '09 (F6) c. il. figs. D. 35 c. Appleton.
Appleton arithmetics; grammar-school book. '09(Ap3) c. il. figs. D. 55 c. Appleton.
Elementary algebra. '08(Jl11) c. il. D. (Twentieth century text-books.) **$1.12 net. Appleton.

Young, Jacob W: Albert, and Jackson, Lambert Lincoln.—*Continued.*
First course in elem. algebra. '10(My21) c. il. 12°, (Twentieth century text-books.) 95 c. net. Appleton.
Second course in elem. algebra. '10(My21) c. il. 12°, (Twentieth century text-books.) 70 c. net. Appleton.

Young, Ja.
See Stewart, Netta.

Young, Ja. Kelly.
Hdbk. of anatomy; being a complete compend of anatomy, including the anatomy of the viscera and numerous tables. 3d ed., rev. and enl. '09(N) c. 12+402 p. il. 8°, $1.75. Davis.

Young, Janet.
Subconscious mind and its illuminating light; an interpretation. '09(My) c. 3-54 p. 12°, *$1 net. Whitaker & R.

Young, Jesse Bowman, D.D.
Charms of the Bible; fresh appraisement. '10(Je11) c. D. $1 net. Eaton & M.
To-day: age of opportunity. '09(N6) c. D. *$1.25 net. Jennings.
—, **comp.** Helps for the quiet hour; prayers, collects, verses; collated from many sources; with prefatory essay on the culture of the devotional life. '10(My14) c. 12°, $1. Eaton & M.

Young, J: Cameron.
Children of Arabia. '10(N5) 12°, 60 c. net. Revell.

Young, Mrs. Julia Evelyn Ditto.
Barham Beach: poem. '08(Jl) c. 19-142 p. il. por. 8°, $1.50. Floyd-G.

Young, Karl, ed.
See Cunliffe, J: W:, *ed.*—Pyre, Ja. Fs. Augustine.

Young, Laurence Ditto.
Climbing doom. '09(Mr20) c. il. D. †$1.50. G: W. Dillingham.

Young, Marg.
Wreathed dagger. '09, [1910.] (Ja) il. 12°, $1.50. Cassell.

Young, Melvin.
Science and art of writing life insurance; standard course. '10(Je18) c. por. 8°, $2. N. Y. Insurance.

Young, Oscar E.
Little red mare: a farce. '08(Mr14) c. D. pap., 15 c. Dick.

Young, Sheila.
Letty Lane paper family: [paper dolls in portfolio.] '09(O30) c. $1. Jacobs.

Young, Sydney.
Stoichiometry; together with an Introduction to the study of physical chemistry, by Sir W: Ramsay. '08(F15) D. (Text-books of physical chem.) $2. Longmans.

Young, Rev. W. Montgomery.
Rushing waters and deep sea pearls: [poems.] 2d ed. '08(F) 32 p. por. D. pap., 10 c. Ulbrich Co.

Young, W: H:, 1863-.
Fundamental theorems of the differential calculus. '10(Ag6) c. 8°, (Cambridge tracts in mathematics.) pap., 75 c. net. Putnam.

Young, W: H:
How to preach with power. '09(N) c. 276 p. 12°, $1. How Pub.

Young Alaskans. Hough, E. †$1.25. Harper.
Young America lib. 12°, 50 c. Hurst.
—Adams. Brave old salt.—Fighting Joe.—Work and win.—Yankee middy.—Young lieutenant.
—Bullen. Cruise of "The Cachalot."
—Castlemon. Boy trappers.—Frank in the woods.—Frank on the prairie.
—Coffin. Following the flag.—My days and nights on the battlefield.—Winning his way.
—Cooper. Afloat and ashore.
—Marryat. Jacob Faithful.—Japhet in search of a father.—Masterman ready.—Mr. Midshipman Easy.—Rattlin, the reefer.
—Reid. Afloat in the forest.
—Trowbridge. Coupon bonds. — Father Brighthopes.—Lucy Arlyn.—Martin Merryvale, his X mark.
—Verne. From the earth to the moon.
Young America's manual. Davis, J: W., *ed.* 25 c. Educ. Pub.
Young American. Judson, H. P. *60 c. net. C: E. Merrill.
Young Americans in the British Isles. Tomlinson, E. T. $1.50. Houghton M.
Young blockaders. Tomlinson, E. T. $1.50. Lothrop, L. & S.
Young Buffalo in N. Y. Blaney, C: E: 25 c. J. S. Ogilvie.
Young captains of industry. *See* Godfrey, Hollis.
Young Christian and the early church. Conley, J: W. **50 c. net. Am. Bapt.
Young Christian teacher encouraged. Constantine, *Brother.* $1.25 net. Herder.
Young citizen's reader. Reinsch, P. S: 60 c. B: H. Sanborn.
Young continentals at Bunker Hill. McIntyre, J: T: $1.25. Penn Pub. Co.
Young continentals at Lexington. McIntyre, J: T: †$1.25. Penn Pub. Co.
Young converts. De Goesbriand, L: *75 c. net. Chr. Press.
Young (The) detectives, by Alb. Lee and others. '10(O29) c. il. D. (Harper's young people ser.) 60 c. Harper.
Young Dr. Hamilton. Fisher, M. A. 75 c. Cochrane.
Young duck-shooters in camp. Kellogg, F. E. $1.25. Stokes.
Young electrician. Hall, H. $1.50 net. Macmillan.
Young farmer's practical lib.; ed. by Ernest Ingersoll. il. D. Sturgis & W.
—Stern. Neighborhood entertainments. 75 c. net.
—Van de Water. From kitchen to garret 75 c. net.
Young fireman of Lakeville. Webster, F. V. 35 c. Cupples & L.
Young folks' cyclopædia of persons and places. Champlin, J: D. **$3 net. Holt.
Young folks' library. 49 v. '09(O2) il. S. ea., bds., 50 c. Caldwell.
Young folks' treasury. Mabie, H. W., *ed.* 12 v. Univ. Soc.
Young forester. Grey, Z. $1.25. Harper.
Young guide. Burleigh, C. B. $1.50. Lothrop, L. & S.
Young lady across the way. Ryder, R. O. *50 c. net. Young Lady Across the Way.

Young lieutenant. *See* Adams, W: T.

Young life of famous folk. Watkins, *Mrs.* C. L. 75 c. Pub. Ho. of M. E. Ch., So.

Young Lord Stranleigh. Barr, R. †$1.50. Appleton.

Young malefactor. Travis, T: **$1.50 net. Crowell.

Young man's affairs. Brown, C: R. **$1 net. Crowell.

Young man's guide. Lasance, F. X. 75 c.; $1; $1.25. Benziger.

YOUNG MEN.

Brown, C: R. Young man's affairs. **$1 net Crowell.

Dawson, W. J. Threshold of manhood. *$1.25 net. Revell.

Mackinnon, A. G. Truths of to-day: young man's creed. *75 c. net. Eaton & M.

Shepherd, A. Men in the making; addresses to young men. $1.25 net. Doran.

Swain, J: D. Father to his son; letter to an undergraduate upon his entering college. *50 c. net. Yale Pub.

Tucker, W: J. Personal power; counsels to college men. **$1.50 net. Houghton M.

See also Boys;—Business;—Colleges and universities;—Conduct of life;—Sex;—Success;—Vocations;—Young people.

Young Men's Christian Association. *Educational Dept.* Education and railroad men; hints, suggestions and outlines for conducting educational privileges in R. R. Y. M. C. A. '08(D) 25 c. Y. M. C. A.

Young Men's Christian Association. *Educational Dept.* Outlines of courses of study, (Revised prospectus.) G: B. Hodge, educational secretary. [6th ed.] '08(My9) c. 12°, 50 c.; pap., 35 c. Y. M. C. A.

Young Men's Christian Association. Gymnastic nomenclature of the Y. M. C. A. of North America. 4th ed., rev. and ed. '08, [1909.] (F) c. 9+157 p. il. 12°, $1. Y. M. C. A.

Young Men's Christian Association. Year book, 1908-9; ed. by H. S. Ninde. '09(S18) $1.25; pap., $1. Y. M. C. A.

YOUNG MEN'S CHRISTIAN ASSOCIATION.

Bosworth, E: I., *and* Hutchinson, R. Working together: the association and the church. 40 c. Y. M. C. A.

Murray, W: D. Principles and organization of the Young Men's Christian Association. 60 c. net. Y. M. C. A.

Safford, J: H. Practical service, by the Student Association. 15 c. Y. M. C. A.

Young miner. Alger, H., *jr.* 50 c. Hurst.

Young mineralogist ser. *See* Houston, Edn. Ja.

Young Missourian ser. *See* Dunn, Byron Archibald.

Young Nemesis. Bullen, F. T: $1.50. Dutton.

Young pearl hunters. Ely, W. M. †$1. Burt.

YOUNG PEOPLE.

Addams, J. Spirit of youth in our city streets. **$1.25 net. Macmillan.

Banks, L: A. Problems of youth. **$1.30 net. Funk.

Forbush, W: B. Broadening path: treasure book for boys and girls. 2 v. $5; $8. B. F. Bowen.

YOUNG PEOPLE.—*Continued.*

Jefferson, C: E: Talks on high themes for young Christians. *75 c. net. Pilgrim Press.

Peters, M. C. Strenuous career: [advice for young people.] $1.25. Laird.

See also Boys;—Children;—Education;—Girls:—Hygiene;—Success; — Vocations;—Woman;—Young men.

Young people ser. *See* Harper's.

Young people's lib. of choice literature. il. 16°. Educ. Dept.

—Reddall. Climbing the ladder of fame. 75 c.

Young People's Missionary Movement. Church and missionary education. '08(Jl) c. 11+320 p. il. pors. 8°, $1.25. Young People's Miss.

Young people's story of music. Whitcomb, I. P. $2. Dodd.

Young pioneers. Ellis, E: S. †$1. Burt.

Young plume hunters. Ely, W. M. $1. Burt.

Young privateersman. Stevens, W: O. $1.50. Appleton.

Young railroaders. Coombs, F. L. $1.50. Century Co.

Young reporter. Drysdale, W: †$1.50. Wilde.

Young supercargo. Drysdale, W: †$1.50. Wilde.

Young switch tender. Palmer, W. 50 c. McLoughlin.

Young train master. Stevenson, B. E. †$1.50. L. C. Page.

Young treasure hunter. Webster, F. V. 35 c. Cupples & L.

Young Wallingford. Chester, G: R. $1.50. Bobbs-M.

YOUNG WOMEN.

See Girls;—Women.

Youngberg, Gilbert Albin.

Hist. of engineer troops in the United States army, 1775-1901; prep. under the direction of Major Thomas H. Rees. '10 (Ap) 78 p. 8°, (Engineer School, U. S. Army; occasional papers.) (Not for sale.) Engineer Sch.

Younger, E. G.

Insanity in every-day practice. 2d ed. '10 (D) 124 p. 12°, $1.25 net. Chic. Med. Bk.

"Younger choir." Viereck, G: S., *and others.* $1 net; $2.50 net. Moods.

Younghusband, Sir Fs. E:

Kashmir. '09(O30) il. O. (Color books ser.) *$6 net. Macmillan.

Younghusband, G: J:

Story of the Guides: [English regiment.] '08(My2) il. 8°, *$2.25 net. Macmillan.

Youngman, Anna.

Economic causes of great fortunes. '10 (Ja15) c. 12°, $1.50. Bankers' Pub.

Youngs, Mrs. Clarence Herbert.

See Pratt, Florence Evelyn.

Your boy, his nature and nurture. Dickinson, G: A. *$1 net. Doran.

Your child and mine. Warner, A. †$1.50. Little, B. & Co.

Your hidden skeleton; novel autograph book which reveals the secret skeletons of your friends through their handwriting. '10 (Ja1) S. 30 c. Winston.

Your home and its decoration; series of pract. suggestions for the painting, decorating, and furnishing of the home; comp. by the Sherwin-Williams Co. '10 (Je11) c. col. il. 8°, $2. Sherwin-H.

Yours truly. Judge. $1.25. Judge.

Youth and spring. Clough-Leighter, H: *$1.25 net. Boston Music.

Youth of the great Elector. Schmidt, F. *60 c. net. McClurg.

Youthful man-o'-warsman. Maclay, E. S. $1.50. Navy Blue.

Yoxall, Ja. H:

A B C about collecting. '10(D10) il. 12°, $2 net. Jacobs.

Wander years; being some account of journeys into life, letters and art. '09(My22) 8°, *$2 net. Dutton.

Yozondè of the wilderness. Greene, H. I. $1 net. Fitzgerald.

Ysbrand. Eeden, F. W. v. 25 c.. Lawrence Journ.

YUCATAN, Mexico.

Arnold, C., *and* Frost, F: J. T. American Egypt; record of travel in Yucatan. *$3.80 net. Doubleday, P.

See also Mayas (The).

YUCHI INDIANS.

See Indians.

YUKON.

See Alaska.

Yukon Bill, pseud.

Derby day in the Yukon, and other poems of the "Northland." '10(O1) c. il. O. $1 net. Doran.

YUKON-TANANA REGION.

See Alaska.

Yuletide entertainments. Willard, E. M. 25 c. T: S. Denison.

Yuma and Yuma valley, Arizona; true pictorial story of the most promising city and the most richly endowed section of the great Southwest. '09(Je) no paging, il. sq. O. pap. (Add. pubs. for price.) Yuma County.

Yung Wing.

My life in China and America. '09(D25) c. por. O. **$2 net. Holt.

YUNNAN, China.

Davies, H: R. Yün-Nan; the link between India and the Yangtze. *$5 net. Putnam.

Yusuf Ibn Taghrî Birdî.

Annals, entitled An-Nujûm az-Zâhira fi Mulûk Misr wal-Kâhira; [chronicles of rulers of Egypt;] ed. by W: Popper; [v. 1,] '09(N) 128 p.; [v. 2.] '10(D) 129-297 p. Q. (Univ. of Cal. pubs.; Semetic philology.) ea., pap., $1.50. Univ. of Cal.

Yvan Gall, le pupille de la marine. Compayré, J. G. 35 c. Holt.

Yzdra. Ledoux, L: V. **$1.25 net. Putnam.

Zagel, Hermann H.

Jack Roostand. '09(D) c. 255 p. il. 8°, $1. Lange.

Zahn, Theodor.

Introd. to the New Testament; tr. from the 3d German ed. In 3 v. '09(D11) O. *$12 net. Scribner.

Zaïre. *Sec* Voltaire, F. M. A. de.

Zamacoïs, Miguel.

The jesters, [Les bouffons:] a simple story in four acts of verse adapt. from the French by J: N. Raphael. '08(Ap11) c. 12°, **$1 net. Brentano's.

ZAMORA, Spain.

See Spain.

Zandrie. Richards, M. E. †$1.50. Century Co.

Zandstra, Sidney.

Witness of the Vulgate, Peshitta and Septuagint to the Text of Zephaniah, (no. 4.) '09(Jl17) 8°, (Columbia Univ., contributions to Oriental history and philology.) pap., *$1 net. Lemcke.

Zangwill, Israel.

Italian fantasies. '10(D10) c. front. D. $2 net. Macmillan.

Melting-pot; drama in four acts. '09(S18) c. D. $1.25. Macmillan.

Zapf, Alfr. E., ed.

See Plant, J: C.

ZARAGOZA, Spain.

See Spain.

Zaring, Philip Aloin, M.D.

The cosmos; [poem.] '10(D31) c. D. bds., $1.50 net. Badger.

Zarlah, the Martian. Grisewood, R. N. $1. Fenno.

Zartman, Lester W:, ed.

Yale readings in insurance. In 2 v. v. 1, Life insurance; v. 2, Fire insurance. '09 (O9) c. O. ea., *$2.25 net. Yale Univ.

Zartman, Rev. Rufus Calvin.

Zartman family. '09, [1910.] (F) c. 16+431 p. il. pors. facsim. 8°, $1.50. Lyon & A.

ZARTMAN FAMILY.

See Genealogies.

Zastro, Karl.

Wilhelm der Siegreiche; ein keiser und heldenbild aus der neuzeit der Deutschen jungen gewidnicte. '10(D24) 16°, (Macmillan's new ser. of German texts.) 35 c. net. Macmillan.

Zayas Enriquez, Rafael de.

Porfirio Diaz [president of Mexico[; [tr. by T. Quincy Browne, *jr.*] '08(S26) c. pors. D. **$1.50 net. Appleton.

Zeagler, J: Wesley.

A trip through New Zealand; where I went and what I saw. '10(S) c. 68 p. il. por. 16°, 40 c. J: W. Zeagler.

Zeeman effect for titanium. King, A. S. (Add. Carnegie pubs. for price.) Carnegie.

Zeidler, J., and Lustgarten, J.

Electric arc lamps. '08(S12) il. 8°, *$2 net. Van Nostrand.

Zeigen, Frederic,

"Therold Archer Knowlton," poet; love story of Violet and violets. '10(D10) c. il. D. $2. Conkey.

Zeiner, E: J. A., comp.

High school song book. '08(My9) 8°. *85 c. net. Macmillan.

Zeisberger, D:

Hist. of northern American Indians; ed. by Archer Butler Hulbert and W: Nathaniel Schwarze. '10(S17) 8°, $2. Ohio Archeolog.

Zeisler, Alex.
Hungarian-English self pronouncing pocket interpreter. '08(My16) c. 16°. (Add. pub. for price.) Nyitray.

Zeitlen, Jacob.
Accusative with infinitive and some kindred constructions in English. '08(N21) 8°, (Columbia Univ. studies in English, 2d ser.) pap., **$1 net. Lemcke.

Zelie, J: Sheridan.
"Lead, kindly light"; intimations from Cardinal Newman's hymn. '09(D25) c. 12°, 75 c. Dodd.

Zell, F., and Genée, Franz Friedrich Richard.
Boccaccio; or, the prince of Palermo; comic opera in three acts; [music] by Franz von Suppé; with Eng. tr. and adaptation by Dexter Smith. '08(N21) c. 12°, $2. Ditson.

ZEND-AVESTA.
Mills, L. H. Avesta eschatology compared with the books of Daniel and Revelations. 50 c.; 75 c. Open Court.

Zenner, Philip.
Education in sexual physiology and hygiene: physician's message. '10(Jl) c. 8+126 p. 12°, $1. Clarke.

Zenos, Andrew Constantinides, D.D., ed.
See Jacobus, Melancthon **Williams.**

Zephaniah. *See* Bible.

Zepp, Rev. Arth. C.
Progress after entire sanctification. '09, [1910.] (Ja) 8+9-108 p. 12°, 50 c. Chr. Witness.

Zerbrochene (Der) krug. Zschokke, J. H. D. *50 c. net. Allyn & B.

Zerr, G:, and Mayer, C.
Tests of coal colors in aniline lakes. '10 (D31) $5.50 net. Lippincott.

Zerr, G:, and Rübencamp, R.
Treatise on colour manufacture: guide to the preparation, examination, and application of all the pigment colours in pract. use; author. Eng. ed. by Dr. C: Mayer. '08(N7) il. tabs., O. (Add. pubs. for price.) Lippincott.

Zicklen, Eliz. von, pseud.
See Jeffers, *Mrs.* Helen Eliz. Van Sickle.

Zieber, Eug.
Heraldry in America. 2d ed. '10(My21) il. O. $5. Bailey, B. & B.

Ziegler, Ernst.
General pathology; tr. from the 11th rev. German ed.; ed. and brought up to date by Aldred Scott Warthin. '08(N7) c. il. 8°, *$5.50 net; *$6.50 net. Wood.

Zielinski, Faddej Francevic.
Our debt to antiquity; tr. by Strong A. Hopkins and Stewart Hugh. '09(N) 16+240 p. 16°, (English lib.) *75 c. net. Dutton.

Zigler, D. H.
History of the Brethren in Virginia. '08 (Jl) c. 16+19-278 p. il. pors. facsims., map, 8°, $1.50. Brethren Pub. Ho.

Zigzag lightning shorthand. Miller, C. C. (Add. pubs. for price.) Zigzag.

"Zim," pseud.
See Zimmerman, Eug.

Zimmerer, H.
Medical language. '08(S5) Q. pap., *25 c. net. Stechert.

Zimmerling, C: B., comp.
Directory of members of Philadelphia bar, 1908. '08. Fe. gratis. Guarantee.

Zimmerman, Eug., ["Zim."]
Cartoons and caricatures; or, making the world laugh. '10(Ag20) c. il. D. hf. leath., $5. Corr. Inst.

Zimmerman, L. M., D.D.
Dot. '09(N20) c. il. por. O. $1. L. M. Zimmerman.
Pearls of comfort, from Tennyson's "In Memoriam." '10(F) 30 p. S. pap. (Add. author for price.) L. M. Zimmerman.

Zimmern, Alice.
Gods and heroes of the north. '08(Ap4) il. D. *60 c. net. Longmans.
Gods and heroes of the north. '08(Ap18) il. D. (Class-books of English literature.) *36 c. net. Longmans.

ZINC.
Ingalls, W. R. Lead and zinc in the United States. *$4 net. Hill Pub.
Ruhl, O. Rationale of investment in zinc mining. 25 c. Mining News.
United States. *Dept. of Commerce and Labor. Bu. of Manufactures.* Zinc industry in Mexico. '09(Jl) 14 p. 8°. (Add. Superintendent for price.) U. S., Supt. of Docs.

See also Paint.

Zinsser, Hans.
See Hiss, Philip Hanson, *jr.*

Zittel, Karl Alfr. v.
Text-book on palæontology. '10(Ja29) price changed from *$6 net to *$7.40 net. Macmillan.

Ziv, R. L.
Tree of modern life; treasure of thinking thoughts for thinking people in treatise, prose and verse. '10(O1) por. D. 75 c.; pap., 50 c. R. L. Ziv.

Zodiac birthday book. Ruyl, B. B. $1 net. Baker & T.

Zoëga, G. T.
Concise dictionary of old Icelandic; ed. by W. A. Criegie. '10(Ag20) O. $3.40. Oxford Univ.

Zogbaum, Rufus Fairchild.
Junior officer of the watch. '08(Mr21) c. il. D. †$1.50. Appleton.

Zollars, Ely Vaughan.
Hebrew prophecy. '08(O) c. 213 p. 12°, $1. Standard Pub.
Worth of truth. v. 1. '10(D10) c. 12°, $1. Standard Pub.

Zollenstein. Ferguson, W: B. M. †$1.50. Appleton.

Zollinger, Gulielma, [pseud. for W: Zachary Gladwin.]
Boy's ride. '09(O2) c. il. D. $1.50. McClurg.
Maggie McLanehan. New ed. '09(O9) il. D. $1.50. McClurg.
Rout of the foreigners. '10(N12) c. il. D. $1.50. McClurg.

Zonal belt hypothesis. Wheeler, J. T. **$2.50 net. Lippincott.

Zoo babies. Farrow, G: E: $1.25. Stokes.

ZOOLOGY.
Adams, C: C. Ecological survey of Isle Royale, Lake Superior. 85 c. Mich. Geol.

ZOOLOGY.—*Continued.*
Baker, F. S. Ecology of the Skokie Marsh area. 60 c. Ill. Lab'y Nat. Hist.
Budgett, J: S: Work of John Samuel Budgett: [zoological papers.] *$7 net. Putnam
Burnet, M. Laboratory manual of zoölogy. 50 c. Am. Bk.
Crampton, H: E: Zoology: [lecture.] 25 c. Lemcke.
Crary, L. E. Text book of field zoology. $1.25 net. Blakiston.
Edmondson, C: H. Lab'y guide in invertebrate zoology. 25 c. C. H. Edmondson.
Galloway, T: W. First course in zoology. *$2 net.—Text-book of elem. zoology. $1.25 net. Blakiston.
Gamble, F: W: Animal life. *$2 net. Dutton.
Girty, G: H. Guadalupian fauna, (New Mexico.) (Add. Superintendent for price.) U. S., Supt. of Docs.
Grinnell, J. *Biota* of the San Bernardino Mountains. $2. Univ. of Cal.
Hegner, R. W. Introd. to zoology. $1.90 net. Macmillan.
International Commission on Zoological Nomenclature. Opinions rendered by the International Commission on Zoological Nomenclature. 2 v. v. 1, Opinions 1-25. Smith. Inst.
Kofoid, C: A. Exuviation, autotomy, and regeneration in *Ceratium.* 50 c. Univ. of Chic
Lankester, *Sir* E. R., *ed.* Treatise on zoology. In 10 pts. pts. 1, 2, 3, 4, 5, 7, 9. pts. 1, 3, 4, 5, 7, ea., $5.25; pt. 2, $5.50; pt. 9, $6.50. Macmillan.
Meek, S. E. Zoölogy of lakes Amatitlan and Atitlan, Guatemala, with special reference to ichthyology. 50 c. Field Museum.
Osborn, H. Economic zoology. *$2 net. Macmillan.
Parker, T. J. Elem. course of practical zoology. *$2.60 net. Macmillan.
Schwartz, J. A. Wonderful little lives. $1.50. Little, B. & Co.
Sedgwick, A. Students' text-book of zoölogy. v. 3. *$5.50 net. Macmillan.
Sigerfoos, C: P: Lab'y directions in general zoology. 65 c. H. W. Wilson Co.
Standard library of natural history; living animals of the world and living races of mankind. 5 v. $16.50; $19.50. Univ. Soc.
Weysse, A. W. Synoptic text-book of zoölogy. *$2.25 net. Macmillan.
See also Alligator;—Amphibia;—Anatomy;—Animals;—Biology;—Birds; — Cattle; — Cells;—Crustaceans;—Domestic animals;—Embryology;—Evolution;—Fish; — Heredity; — Insects;—Jellyfish;—Mammalia; — Man;—Marine zoology;—Mollusks;—Natural history;—Nature; —Paleontology;—Parasites; — Physiology;—Protozoa;—Reptiles;—Snakes;—Vertebrates.

Zorn, Carl Manthey.
Dies und das aus dem leben eines ostindischen missionars. 2d ed. '08(F) c. 292 p. il. por. 8°, $1.25. Concordia Pub.
Grossvaters jugenderinnerungen; wie seinen kindern und enkeln erzählt. 2 v. '10 (O) fronts. il. pors. 12°, $2. Northwestern Pub.

Zorn, Carl Manthey.—*Continued.*
Hdbk. for the beginner's home study in the word of God; tr. by H. M. Zorn and J. A. Rimbach. '08(Ja18) 8°, hf. mor., $1.25. Concordia Pub.

ZOROASTER.
Dhalla, M. N. Nyaishes or Zoroastrian litanies. **$2 net. Lemcke.
Teachings of Zoroaster, and the philosophy of the Parsee religion; tr. by Dr. Shaporji Aspaniarji. '08(Je6) 16°, (Wisdom of the East.) *40 c. net.
See also Zend-Avesta.
Zoroaster. Crawford, F. M. †$1.50. Macmillan.

Zschokke, Johann Heinrich Daniel.
Der zerbrochene krug; Das wirtshaus zu Cransac; novellen; ed., with notes, questions, vocab. and composition exercises based upon the text by E: Manley. '09 (My) c. 9+160 p. 12°, (Allyn and Bacon's ser. of German texts.) *50 c. net. Allyn & B.

Zsigmondy, Richard Adolf.
Colloids and the ultra microscope: manual of colloid chemistry and ultramicroscopy; author. tr. by Jerome Alexander. '09 (My8) il. 8°, $3. Wiley.

Zuchtmann, Friedrich.
New American music reader, no. 2; introductory—4. '09(My1) 8°, no. 2, *45 c. net; introductory—4, *32 c. net; no. 3. Enl. ed. '09(Ap) 12°, *50 c. net. Macmillan.

Zueblin, C:
Democracy and the overman. '10(D10) c. D. $1 net. B: W. Huebsch.
Religion of a democrat: [relation of the church to the state.] '08(My9) c. D. bds., *$1 net. B: W. Huebsch.

ZULOAGA, Ignacio.
Hispanica Society of America. Catalog of paintings by Ignacio Zuloaga. 50 c. Hispanic Soc.
Utrillo, *Don* M., *and others.* Five essays on the art of Ignacio Zuloaga. 50 c. Hispanic Soc.

Zulueta, Rev. F. M. de.
Ministry of daily communion: a consideration for priests. '08(Ag8) 60 c. Herder.
Spouse of Christ and daily communion. '08(Ag8) 30 c. Herder.

Zuzman, Suares, Vincente de.
Rimes varias en alabança del Nacimiento del principe N. S. Don Balthazar Carlos Domingo. [facsim.] '02, [1909.] (N) 50 p. 8°, $6. (200 copies.) Hispanic Soc.

Zwemer, S: Marinus.
Islam: a challenge to faith. '08(Ja4) il. maps, tabs., 12°, $1; pap., 35 c. Student Vol.
—, **and Brown, Arth. Judson, D.D.**
Nearer and farther East: studies of Moslem lands and Siam, Burma, and Korea. '08(My16) c. maps, D. (United studies of missions.) **50 c. net. Macmillan.

Zwierlein, F: J.
Religion in New Netherland; dissertation presented to the University of Louvain. '10(N) 6+365 p. 8°, map, $2 net. Stechert.